INDEPEN[illegible] SCHOO[illegible] YEARBOOK

2001–2002

Boys' Schools, Girls' Schools, Co-educational Schools & Preparatory Schools

THE OFFICIAL BOOK OF REFERENCE OF

THE HEADMASTERS' AND HEADMISTRESSES' CONFERENCE
THE GIRLS' SCHOOLS ASSOCIATION
THE SOCIETY OF HEADMASTERS
AND HEADMISTRESSES OF INDEPENDENT SCHOOLS
THE INCORPORATED ASSOCIATION OF
PREPARATORY SCHOOLS
AND OF THE INDEPENDENT SCHOOLS ASSOCIATION

All are members of The Independent Schools Council

EDITED BY
GILLIAN E B HARRIES

A & C BLACK · LONDON

INDEPENDENT SCHOOLS YEARBOOK

This book contains details of 1,300 schools for pupils of 3–18 years. It is divided into eight parts.

PART I (pp. 1–460) ***THE HEADMASTERS' AND HEADMISTRESSES' CONFERENCE***

describes the two hundred and fifty schools for pupils from 11 to 18 whose Heads are members of HMC. They are boys schools, co-educational schools or boys schools taking girls in the sixth form.

PART II (pp. 461–766) ***THE GIRLS' SCHOOLS ASSOCIATION***

describes the two hundred and one schools for pupils from 11 to 18, whose Heads are members of GSA. They are mainly girls schools, but some take boys in the sixth form.

PART III (pp. 767–850) ***THE SOCIETY OF HEADMASTERS AND HEADMISTRESSES OF INDEPENDENT SCHOOLS***

describes the fifty-seven schools for pupils from 11 to 18 whose Heads are members of SHMIS. The majority are co-educational schools, but membership is open to boys and girls schools.

PART IV (pp. 851–852) ***THE CHOIR SCHOOLS' ASSOCIATION***

There are thirty-seven choir schools in membership. Limited information is given in this section, but each school is a member of either HMC, SHMIS or IAPS, where fuller details can be found.

PART V (pp. 853–1076) ***THE INCORPORATED ASSOCIATION OF PREPARATORY SCHOOLS***

describes the five hundred and fifty-six schools whose Heads are members of IAPS; thirty-four of these are overseas. Most of the schools are co-educational; some cater for boys only or girls only. The preparatory school age range is 7 to 13, but many schools have a pre-preparatory department, for children of 3 or 4 years upwards.

PART VI (pp. 1077–1165) ***THE INDEPENDENT SCHOOLS ASSOCIATION***

describes the two hundred and eighty-nine schools in membership of ISA. Schools in this association are not confined to one age range and pupils can range from 3 to 18 years.

PART VII (pp. 1167–1175) ***TUTORS/SIXTH FORM COLLEGES***

PART VIII (pp. 1177–1193) ***UNIVERSITIES AND COLLEGES OF EDUCATION***

In each section full details are given of each school's

- admission procedures
- entrance examinations
- fees
- scholarships and bursaries
- staff
- governing bodies
- provision for art, drama, music and sport

There is detailed information on the nature and character of each individual school.

Information about the Associations to which the schools belong is also included. See pages xviii–xxviii.

There are sections on universities and colleges and tutorial establishments.

A complete list of schools appears alphabetically on page 1194. In addition each of the school sections has its own alphabetical index and geographical index.

CONTENTS

GENERAL INDEX

INDEX TO ADVERTISERS

Schools and Colleges, Tutorial Colleges

Trade

Advisory Services etc

Career Opportunities

INDEPENDENT SCHOOLS COUNCIL (ISC)

Established as the Independent Schools Joint Council 1974
Reconstituted as the Independent Schools Council (ISC) 1998
Incorporated National ISIS (Independent Schools Information Service) 1986
National ISIS reconstituted as ISC information service (ISCis) 2001

The constituent associations of ISC are:
Girls' Schools Association (GSA)
Governing Bodies Association (GBA)
Governing Bodies of Girls' Schools Association (GBGSA)
Headmasters' and Headmistresses' Conference (HMC)
Incorporated Association of Preparatory Schools (IAPS)
Independent Schools Association (ISA)
Independent Schools' Bursars Association (ISBA)
Society of Headmasters and Headmistresses of Independent Schools (SHMIS)

Chairman
Mrs Jean Scott

Deputy Chairman
Roger Trafford

General Secretary
Dr Alistair B Cooke, OBE

Director of Information & Deputy General Secretary
David Woodhead

Joint Director of Information
Richard Davison

Administrative Director
Mrs Carolyn Parrish

Grosvenor Gardens House
35–37 Grosvenor Gardens
London SW1W 0BS
Tel: 020 7798 1590 (ISC)
Fax: 020 7798 1591 (ISC)
email: abc@isis.org.uk
Tel: 020 7798 1500 (ICSis)
Fax: 020 7798 1501 (ISCis)
e-mail: national@isis.org.uk
website: www.isis.org.uk

The Council provides a single, unified organisation that speaks and acts on behalf of the eight independent schools' associations (listed above), by which it was constituted. More than 80 per cent of children educated in the independent sector attend its 1,275 member schools, which have 492,000 pupils. ISC promotes the common interests of these schools at the political level by making vigorous representations to government ministers, politicians of all parties and civil servants. It also provides common services through bodies such as the Independent Schools Inspectorate (ISI, qv), the ISC Teacher Induction Panel, and the Westminster Centre for Education (Chairman: Margaret Rudland), which conducts research into longer-term issues relevant to ISC schools.

Through its media and public relations arm, the **Independent Schools Council information service (ISCis)**, it explains what the diverse range of independent schools can provide and publicises their academic achievements. ISCis offers comprehensive marketing and briefing services for parents, schools, the media and researchers, and an educational grants advice service; it publishes *The ISCis Guide to Accredited Independent Schools* (with CD-Rom) in October, an Annual Census in April, a magazine (three times a year) and a range of leaflets and booklets.

ISCis International helps parents living overseas to find suitable ISC schools in the UK for their children. It offers advisory and placement services for individual families and for multinational companies. For further details please write to the above address.

Within ISC, the *Friends of Independent Schools (FIS)* undertakes political action on behalf of those who wish to see a continuation of a flourishing private sector of education. For further details please write to the above address.

ICSis London & South-East England and ISCis Wales are part of ISC. ISIS Scotland is part of the Scottish Council of Independent Schools. These and the ISIS offices elsewhere in the UK also offer information and advice to parents about ISC schools in their regions and promote the case for independent education.

G B A

Governing Bodies Association
Founded 1941

THE OBJECTS OF THE ASSOCIATION ARE:

(1) To advance education in Independent Schools.
(2) To discuss matters concerning the governance of Independent Schools, and to encourage co-operation between their Governing Bodies.
(3) To consider the relationship of such Schools to the general educational interests of the community.
(4) To express the views of Governing Bodies on the foregoing matters, and to take such action as may be expedient

Membership. Membership is restricted to the Governing Bodies of independent schools for boys (and co-educational schools) in the United Kingdom which are constituted as educational charities. The Head must belong to HMC, SHMIS, ISA or IAPS and there are requirements concerning the nature of the governing body and the school's finances. There are 319 schools in membership. Overseas schools are considered for membership provided that they follow a similar pattern of education and that at least one-third of the pupils are of British nationality, most of whom anticipate proceeding to higher education in the UK.

Committee Members 2001/2002

Chairman: Michael Edwards
Deputy Chairmen: The Rt Hon. John MacGregor, Robin Reeve
Honorary Treasurer: Robert Alexander

Members Retiring 2002
Dennis Colgrove (King Edward's, Witley); Megan Waugh (Queen Elizabeth's GS, Wakefield); Robin Wilson (Brentwood)

Members Retiring 2003
Clyde Binfield (Silcoates); Derek Bunting (Abbeygate); Brian Wilson (King Edward's, Bath); Hugh Wright (Kingswood)

Members Retiring 2004
Sam Alder (King William's, IOM); Michael Button (Taunton); Peter Lapping (Christ's, Brecon); Charles Moseley (Arnold, Blackpool)

Co-opted Members
Michael Wakeford (Emanuel School); David Peck (Merchant Taylors)

Secretary
Mr F V Morgan, The Ancient Foresters, Bush End, Takeley, Bishops Stortford, Herts, CM22 6NN.
Tel/Fax: 01279 871865

GBGSA

Governing Bodies of Girls' Schools Association

Constituted 1942.
Objects of the Association:

(1) To discuss matters concerning the governance of Girls' Independent Schools, and to encourage co-operation between their Governing Bodies.
(2) To consider the relation of such Schools to the general educational interests of the community.
(3) To express the views of Governing Bodies on the foregoing matters and to take such action as may be expedient.

Membership. Membership is restricted to the Governing Bodies of independent schools for girls in the United Kingdom and which are constituted as educational charities. The Head must belong to GSA, SHMIS, ISA or IAPS and there are requirements concerning the nature of the governing body and the school's finances. There are 222 schools in membership. At the discretion of the Committee membership can be extended to overseas schools of a similar pattern to schools in the UK.

Executive Committee 2001/2002

Chairman: The Rt Hon. Dame Angela Rumbold, DBE

Deputy Chairman: Jennifer Carter, OBE

Honorary Treasurer: Susan Meikle

Members Retiring 2002
Margaret Bunford (North London Collegiate School)
Sr Christina Kenworthy-Browne (St Mary's School, Ascot)
Caroline Wales (Loughborough High School)

Members Retiring 2003
Margaret Banks (Leicester High School)
June Cull (Talbot Heath School, Bournemouth)
Sir Jeremy Elwes (Walthamstow Hall, Sevenoaks)
Judith Hillman (Cheltenham Ladies' College)
Harry Salmon (Beneden School)

Members Retiring 2004
Margaret Carter-Pegg (Croham Hurst, Croydon)
Elisabeth Elias (Shrewsbury High School)
Mary Milford (Westfield School)
Gillian Perrin (Wimbledon High School)
June Taylor (Godolphin & Latymer)

Reciprocal Delegate from GSA
Lynda Warrington (Bradford Girls' Grammar School)

Secretary
Mr F V Morgan, The Ancient Foresters, Bush End, Takeley, Bishop's Stortford, Herts, CM22 6NN.
Tel/Fax: 01279 871865

THE HEADMASTERS' AND HEADMISTRESSES' CONFERENCE

HMC dates from 1869, when the celebrated Edward Thring of Uppingham asked thirty-seven of his fellow headmasters to meet at his house to consider the formation of a "School Society and Annual Conference". Twelve headmasters accepted the invitation. From that date there have been annual meetings. Thring's intention was to provide an opportunity for discussion at regular intervals, both on practical issues in the life of a school and on general principles in education. He believed that his guests would discharge their practical business the more effectively at a residential meeting where they could also enjoy being in the company of like-minded men. Annual Meetings of HMC still combine formal debate on current educational questions with the second element of conversational exchanges in an agreeable environment. These gatherings, which up to 1939 were usually at individual Schools, now take place at a University. They are held early in the Autumn term. In addition to these annual conferences attended by all members, there are local meetings each term arranged by the seven branches or Divisions into which the country is divided.

Present membership of the HMC is a total of two hundred and forty two, apart from Associates and Overseas members. In considering applications for election to membership, the Committee has regard to the degree of independence enjoyed by the Headmaster and his school. Eligibility also depends on the academic standards obtaining in the school, as reflected by the proportion of pupils in the Sixth form pursuing a course of study beyond the General Certificate of Secondary Education and by the school's A' level results.

The Constitution provides that the membership shall consist mainly of headmasters of independent schools. At the same time, it is held to be a strength to the Conference to include headmasters of schools of other status. There is provision therefore for the election of a small number of headmasters of Voluntary and Maintained schools (Additional Membership).

In addition to the Ordinary membership, the Headmasters' Conference has a number of Overseas members, who are headmasters of noteworthy schools in the Commonwealth and other countries abroad. There are also a few Honorary Associates, who have been elected to life membership on ceasing to be Ordinary members.

HMC is closely associated with the Governing Bodies' Association, the Independent Schools Council, the Independent Schools Bursars' Association, the Medical Officers of Schools Association, the Incorporated Association of Preparatory Schools, the Independent Schools Careers Organisation and the Independent Schools Information Service.

The Secretariat of HMC, the Girls Schools Association and the Secondary Heads Association are accommodated in the same premises. This arrangement, apart from its practical convenience, serves as a symbolic recognition that in their interests and practice the organisations have much in common.

The registered office is at 130, Regent Road, Leicester LE1 7PG (Secretary G H Lucas, BA, MEd, PGCE). Tel: (01162 854810). The Membership Secretary (D E Prince MA) also at Leicester. Tel: (0116 2551567).

HMC Committee 2001

Chairman: Christopher Brown (Norwich School); *Vice-Chairman:* Tom D Wheare (Bryanston School); *Chairman Elect 2002:* Edward Gould (Marlborough College); *Hon Treasurer:* Tim Young (Royal Grammar School, Guildford); *Chairman – East Division:* Richard Youdale (King's School, Ely); *Secretary – East Division:* John Richardson (Culford School); *Chairman – Irish Division:* Michael Ridley (Royal Belfast Academical Institution); *Chairman – North East:* David Younger (King's, Tynemouth); *Secretary – North East:* Chris Hirst (Sedbergh School); *Chairman – North London:* Priscilla Chadwick; (Berkhamsted Collegiate School); *Secretary – North London:* Andrew Boggis (Forest School); *Chairman – North West:* David Hempsall (QEGS, Blackburn); *Secretary – North West:* Julian Wilde (King Edward VII & Queen Mary School); *Chairman – Scottish:* David Comins (The Glasgow Academy); *Secretary – Scottish:* John Light (The Edinburgh Academy); *Chairman – South Central:* Geoff Buttle (Churcher's College); *Secretary – South Central:* Ian Power (Lord Wandsworth College); *Chairman – South East:* David Haywood (City of London Freemen's School); *Secretary – South East:* Ian Walker (King's School, Rochester); *Chairman – South London:* Joseph Peake (St George's College, Weybridge); *Secretary – South London:* Rob Davey (Caterham School); *Chairman – South West:* Jonathan Leigh (Blundell's School); *Secretary – South West:* Neil Gamble (Exeter School); *Chairman – West:* Bernard Trafford (Wolverhampton Grammar School); *Secretary – West:* Howard Tomlinson (Hereford Cathedral School); *Co-opted members:* Graham G Able, *Chairman of Education and Academic Policy* (Dulwich College); Chris Tongue, *Chairman of Professional Development* (St John's School, Leatherhead); Stephen Borthwick, *HMC Representative on ISC Unity Committee* (Epsom College); Philip Evans, *Chairman of University Working Party* (Bedford School); Tony Little, *Chairman of Inspection Steering Group* (Oakham School)

HMC Sub-Committees 2001

Education & Academic Policy (with GSA) – I. Galbraith (96) (E); P Evans (98) (NL); A Grant (98) (NL); G Able (95) (98) (Chairman) (SL); C Jamison (98) (SE); Vacancy (Currently being filled); S Dawkins (00) (NW); J S Robertson (97) (SCOT).

Universities Working Party (with GSA) – J. Richardson (99) (E); I P Evans (00) (*Chairman*) (NL); P Chadwick (99) (NL); A Evans (94) (97) (SL); M Stephen (96) (99) (NW); B. Lockhart (00) (SCOT).

Professional Development – W Jones (00) (W); R Ullmann (98) (E); K Durham (00) (NL); I Davies (99) (SL); C Tongue (96) (*Chairman*) (01) (SE); M Cuthbertson (97) (SW); I Power (00) (SC); T Turvey (00) (NW); M Spens (99) (SCOT); R Collard (01) (NE).

Inspection Steering Group – S Nuttall (01) (W); R Youdale (00) (E); A Little (00) (*Chairman*) (E); S Baldock (98) (SL).

Membership – G E Jones (99) (W); R Peel (96) (E); S Westley (00) (NL); D Baxter (01) (SL); K Riley (00) (SW); T M S Young (99) (*Chairman*) (SC); D Welsh (98) (NE); I Mellor (00) (NW); I. Templeton (Aug 00) (SCOT); T Macey (00) (I).

Community Service Committee – R Ullman (95) (E); J Trotman (99) (NL); C Tarrant (01) (SL); Dr P Southern (00) (SE); G Best (96) (SW); P M de Voil (until June 01) (*Chairman*) (SC); A F Trotman (97) (NE); M Pyper (96) (SCOT).
Junior Schools Sub-Committee – J Stephen (00) (*Chairman*); A Boggis; J Croker/P Pallant/T Mulryne.
Finance Steering Group Conference & Common Room – Remit and Membership currently being determined.
Sports Committee – D Derbyshire (00) (W); J S Lee (98) (E); S Smith (97) (from 2001) (*Chairman*) (NL); D Jarrett (01) (SL); J Franklin (00) (SE); J Lever (00) (SC); D Younger (95) (NE); D Comins (98) (SCOT); S Haggett (00) (NW); N W Gamble (95) (SW).
Co-Education Group – B Trafford (98) (*Chairman*); I M Small (99) (*Secretary*).
Boarding – Dr S Winkley (98) (*Chairman*).
Small Schools Group – J. Leigh (99) (*Chairman*).
Working Group for Central & Eastern Europe – R Wicks *Administrator* (Tel 01223 234708); C Bradnock (98) (*Chairman 2000*).
The Chairman HMC, Secretary HMC and Membership Secretary HMC are ex officio members of all Sub-Committees.

REPRESENTATIVES ON OTHER BODIES

Independent Schools Council – The Chairman and Vice-Chairman of HMC and The Secretary of HMC.
Assisted Places Committee – C S Parker (96).
Europe Committee – J Whiteley (00).
Unity Committee – S Borthwick (97).
Finance Committee – Treasurer of HMC.
Policy Committee – E H Gould (00).
Inspection – A R M Little & S Baldock.
Joint Standing Committee of Independent School Heads' Associations – T Jones-Parry (00); G E Jones (94); J N D Gray (97); Membership Secretary HMC.
Independent Schools Examination Board – G E Jones (98); T Jones-Parry (00); S Cole (96); J N D Gray (97); T M S Young (99); A G Boggis (96); J D Lever (96).
Boarding Schools Associations Executive – A P Millard (96); S Winkley.
Cambridge University Admissions Examination Committee – Chair of AcPol & Chair of UWP.
CCPR – S Smith (00).
Conference and Common Room Editorial Board – Chairman of HMC; N Richardson (00).
Cricket, English Schools Association – D R Walsh (Tonbridge) (81).
Football Association Council – C J Saunders (82).
ISEB Publications – Treasurer HMC.
Joint Educational Trust – D W Jarrett (99).
Music Masters' and Mistresses' Association – Chairman of HMC; Secretary of HMC.
Oxford University Admissions Examination Committee – Chairman of HMC; Chairman of AcPol.
R.F.S.U. – P Johnson (97).
Representative to the Services – H C K Carson (97).
Science & Technology, Standing Conference on Schools – G G Able (97).
Universities Council for the Education of Teachers – Professional Development Sub-Committee.
UCAS Board – P Cheshire (98).

University Courts – University of Bath (HM Monkton Combe); University of Birmingham (HM RGS Worcester); University of Bradford (HM Bradford GS); University of Essex (Warden of Forest); University of Exeter (HM Plymouth); University of Hull (HM Hymers College); University of Imperial College (Master of Dulwich); University of Kent (HM King's Canterbury); University of Leeds (not known); University of Liverpool (HM Merchant Taylors' Crosby); University of Loughborough (HM Loughborough GS & HM Nottingham HS); University of Nottingham (HM's Nottingham & Repton); University of Salford (HM, Manchester GS); University of Southampton (HM Winchester); University of Surrey (HM RGS Guildford); University of Sussex (HM Hurstpierpoint); University of Warwick (HM Bablake); University of York (HM St Peter's, York).

THE GIRLS' SCHOOLS ASSOCIATION

The Girls' Schools Association (GSA) is the professional association of the Heads of 207 leading independent secondary schools for girls in the UK, educating over 110,000 girls. Schools in the Association offer a choice of day, boarding, weekly and flexi-boarding education; and range in type from large urban schools of 1,000 pupils to small rural schools of around 200. Many schools have junior and pre-prep departments, and can offer a complete education from four to eighteen. A significant proportion of schools also have religious affiliations. All the schools in the Girls' Day School Trust (GDST) are in membership of GSA.

GSA schools are widely recognised for their exceptional record of examination achievements. Education is, however, not only about success in exams. Girls' schools offer wider development opportunities, and are special for a number of reasons. They provide an environment in which girls can learn to grow in confidence and ability. In a girls' school, the needs and aspirations of girls are the main focus, and the staff are experts in the teaching of girls. Girls hold all the senior positions in the school, and are encouraged by positive role models in the schools' teaching staff and management. Expectations are high. In GSA schools, girls do not just have equal opportunities, they have *every* opportunity.

The Girls' Schools Association plays a vital role in advising and lobbying educational policy makers on issues relating to girls' schools and the education of girls. As the specialist organisation for the education of girls, the Association is regularly consulted by the Department for Education and Employment, the Office for Standards in Education, the Qualifications and Curriculum Authority and other bodies. However, GSA is not only a 'single-issue' organisation, and is a powerful and well respected voice within the educational establishment.

The GSA is one of the constituent bodies of the Independent Schools' Council. The ISC operates, on behalf of GSA, a strict accreditation scheme for schools wishing to join the Association. Once in membership, schools are required to undergo a regular cycle of inspections to ensure that these rigorous standards are being maintained. Schools must also belong to the Governing Bodies of Girls' Schools Association, and Heads must be in membership of the Secondary Heads Association.

A programme of professional development for members ensures that the Heads of all GSA schools are highly trained, and are fully up-to-date with all aspects of their profession. Courses are also regularly held for staff and opportunities are available for subject teachers to meet together on curriculum issues.

The Association's Secretariat is accommodated in Leicester in premises shared with the Headmasters' and Headmistresses' Conference and the Secondary Heads Association.

Council and Committees of the Girls' Schools Association for 2001/2002

President: Sue Singer (Guildford High School).
Vice President: Lynda Warrington (Bradford Girls' Grammar School).
Past Vice President: Vacant.
President Elect: Carole Evans (Birkenhead High School, GDST)
Treasurer: Helen Harvey (99,00,01) (St Swithun's School)
Committee Chairmen: Penelope Penney, *Inspections* (Haberdasher' Aske's School for Girls); Carol Daly, *Professional Development* (St Albans High School); Sue Pennington, *Boarding* (St Mary's School, Shaftesbury); Lorna Ogilvie, *Membership* (Croydon High School, GDST); Sarah Evans, *Education* (King Edward VI High School).
Regional Representatives: Debbie Forbes (01,02,03), *South Central* (Queen Anne's School); Cynthia Hall (99,00,01), *Midland* (School of St Helen & St Katherine); Helen Hamilton (99,00,01), *North East* (Polam Hall); Jane Panton (00,01,02), *North West* (Bolton School, Girl's Division); Juliett Austin (01,02,03), *Scotland* (Kilgraston School); Susan Ross (00,01,02), *London* (Sir William Perkins's School); Carolyn Shaw (99,00,01), *SW & Wales* (St Mary's School, Calne); Janet Mark (01,02,03), *Eastern* (Hethersett Old Hall School); Pat Wood (00,01,02), *South East* (Greenacre School for Girls).
Other Representatives: Anne Coutts (01,02,03), *Research Working Party* (Sutton High School, GDST); Angela Rees (01,02,03), *Day Schools* (Nottingham High School, GDST); Jackie Lang, *Co-opted* (Walthamstow Hall); Margaret Connell, *Co-opted* (Queen's College).
Secretariat: Sheila Cooper, *General Secretary*; Jane Carroll, *Deputy General Secretary*; Sue Massey, *Administrator.*

The Girls' Schools Association, 130 Regent Road, Leicester LE1 7PG. Tel: 0116 254 1619. Fax: 0116 255 3792.
E-mail: office@girls-schools.org.uk. Website: www.girls-schools.org.uk

THE SOCIETY OF HEADMASTERS AND HEADMISTRESSES OF INDEPENDENT SCHOOLS

The Society is an Association of Headmasters and Headmistresses of some 95 well-established independent schools. It was founded in 1961 at a time when the need arose from the vitality and growth of the independent sector in the 1950's and the wish of a group of Heads to share ideas and experience.

The Society continues to provide a forum for the exchange of ideas and consideration of the particular needs of the smaller independent school. These are frequently different from the problems and approach of the larger schools. All members value their independence, breadth in education and the pursuit of excellence, particularly in relation to academic standards.

The Society's policy is to maintain high standards in member schools, to ensure their genuine independence, to foster an association of schools which contributes to the whole independent sector by its distinctive character and flexibility, to provide an opportunity for the sharing of ideas and common concerns, to promote links with the wider sphere of higher education, to strengthen relations with the maintained sector and with local communities.

Within the membership there is a wide variety of educational experience. Some schools are young, some have evolved from older foundations, some have behind them a long tradition of pioneer and specialist education, the great majority are now co-educational but we also have boys' and girls' schools. Many of the member schools have a strong boarding element but some have become day schools. Some have specific religious foundations and some are non-denominational. All offer a stimulating Sixth Form experience and at the same time give a sound and balanced education to pupils of widely varying abilities and interests.

The Society is one of the constituent bodies of the Independent Schools Council and its Chairman and Chairman Designate are members of the ISC Governing Council. Every Full Member school has been accredited by ISC and is subject to a Review Visit by the Independent Schools Inspectorate every six years to ensure that standards are monitored and good practice and sound academic results are maintained. The Society is also represented on many other educational bodies.

All members are in membership of the Secondary Heads Association and Full Member schools belong to either the Governing Bodies Association or the Governing Bodies of Girls Schools Association.

There is also a category of Additional Membership to which are elected Heads whose schools do not fulfil all the criteria for Full Membership but whose personal contribution to the Society is judged to be invaluable. They are recorded separately at the end of the entries.

The Society meets together each term: in London; at a member school; and for a three-day residential conference at a hotel or conference centre.

Officers 2001–2002

Chairman: C C Robinson (Hipperholme GS, Tel: 01422 202256)

Vice-Chairman: S J W McArthur (Reading Blue Coat, Tel: 0118 944 1005)

Chairman Designate: Susan Freestone (Sibford, Tel: 01295 781200)

Hon Treasurer: Charlotte Rendle-Short (Church Schools Company, Tel: 01832 735105)

SHMIS Committee 2001–2002

R A Baker
Dr P Bodkin
Susan Freestone
W J Hughes-D'Aeth
M S James
S J W McArthur
E W Mitchell
J A Peake
Charlotte M Rendle-Short
C C Robinson
Dr A B Cooke (General Secretary, ISC) and/or D J Woodhead (Joint National Director, ISIS) in attendance).

Secretariat

General Secretary: I D Cleland, Celedston, Rhosesmor Road, Halkyn, Holywell CH8 8DL (Tel & Fax: 01352 781102)

PA to the General Secretary: Jane Brannigan

Members who are also members of the Headmasters' and Headmistresses' Conference:

N V Bevan (Shiplake College)
P C Bodkin (Tettenhall College)
I Brown (Rougemont School)
G W Buttle (Churcher's College)
D G Crawford (Colston's Collegiate School)
S Darlington (St Columba's College)
M J Dickinson (Ackworth School)
D M Dunn (Yarm School)
J H Dunston (Leighton Park School)
N J England (Ryde School)
K M Greig (Pangbourne College)
G Holden (Rendcomb College, Cirencester)
M S James (Rydal Penrhos)
D W Jarrett (Reed's School)
S J W McArthur (Reading Blue Coat School)
J A Peake (St George's College, Weybridge)
I G Power (Lord Wandsworth College)
R S Repper (Wisbech Grammar School)
A P Spillane (Silcoates School)
B Stacey (Kirkham Grammar School)
S D Tommis (Abbotsholme School)
N K D Ward (Royal Hospital School)
Alison Willcocks (Bedales School)

Members who are also members of the Girls' Schools Association:

Sarah H Evans (King Edward VI High School for Girls, Birmingham)
Ann Harris (Moira House Girls' School)

Associate Members

Professional:

R J Buley (Truro School, formerly Headmaster, Shebbear College)
W T Gillen (Arnold School, formerly Headmaster, King's Tynemouth)
Dr C Greenfield (Sherborne International Study Centre, formerly Headmaster, Sidcot School)
T Halliwell (Welbeck College, formerly Headmaster, Bentham Grammar School)
W M Harvey (Woodard Schools, formerly Headmaster, Bethany School)
D C Haywood (City of London Freemen's School)
H Heard (Yorkshire Residential School for the Deaf, formerly Headmaster, Lord Mayor Treloar School)

D S Hempsall (QEGS Blackburn, formerly Headmaster, Scarborough College)
A J Morsley (Plymouth College, formerly Headmaster, Rishworth School)
D E Prince (Membership Secretary HMC, formerly Headmaster, Reed's School)
Charlotte M Rendle-Short (Church Schools Company, formerly Head, Sunderland High School)
P Skelker (Headmaster Immanuel College, formerly Headmaster, Carmel College)
C H Tongue (St John's School, formerly Headmaster, Keil School)
F R Ullmann (Wellingborough School, formerly Headmaster, Ruthin School)

Emeritus:

J C Baggaley (formerly Headmaster, Silcoates School)
K J Bain (formerly Headmaster, The Purcell School)
R D Balaam (formerly Headmaster, Royal Russell School)
M Barratt (formerly Headmaster, Rannoch School)
D J Beeby (formerly Headmaster, Clayesmore School)
R J Belcher (formerly Headmaster, Bearwood College)
D I Brooks (formerly Headmaster, Churcher's College)
Rev A C Charters (formerly Headmaster, King's School, Gloucester)
I D Cleland (formerly Headmaster, Fulneck Boys' School)
E C Cooper (formerly Warden of Kingham Hill School)
A E R Dodds (formerly Headmaster, Ottershaw School)
M Downward (formerly Headmaster, West Buckland School)
D J Farrant (formerly Headmaster, Abbotsholme School)
R J Gould (formerly Headmaster, Stanbridge Earls School)
D M Green (formerly Headmaster, Warminster School)
R C Hannaford (formerly Headmaster, Seaford College)
D S Harris (formerly Headmaster, Ackworth School)
Rev M D A Hepworth (formerly Headmaster, Birkdale School)
A S Hill (formerly Headmaster, Ruthin School)
T D Holgate (formerly Headmaster, Warminster)
Rev P C Hunting (formerly Headmaster, St George's College)
Canon C E Johnson (formerly Headmaster, Seaford College)
M A B Kirk (formerly Headmaster, Royal Hospital)
J D Payne (formerly Headmaster, Pierrepont School)
M H Payne (formerly Headmaster, Kingham Hill School)
The Hon Martin Penney (formerly Headmaster, Bearwood College)
A O H Quick (formerly Headmaster, Rendcomb College)
Rev A C E Sanders (formerly Headmaster, Reading Blue Coat School)
G W Searle (formerly Headmaster, Colston's)
G R Sims (formerly Headmaster, Rougemont School)
T W Slack (formerly Headmaster, Bedales School)
M J Summerlee (formerly Headmaster, Kirkham Grammar School)
K N Symons, OBE (formerly Headmaster, Ryde School)
R N Tate (formerly Headmaster, Yarm School)
D J Taylor (formerly Headmaster, Adams' Grammar School)
Col G H Wilson (formerly Headmaster, Duke of York's Royal Military School)
G S Wilson (formerly Headmaster, Bedstone College)

THE INCORPORATED ASSOCIATION OF PREPARATORY SCHOOLS

Schools
IAPS schools include boys', girls' and co-educational; boarding, day and mixed; urban, suburban and rural schools. The size varies from over 800 to under 100 pupils, with the majority between 150 and 400. Most schools are charitable trusts, some are limited companies and a few are proprietary. There are also junior schools attached to senior schools, choir schools, schools with a particular religious affiliation, and schools that offer some specialist provision. The average pupil/teacher ratio throughout the Association is 1 to 11.

Curriculum
The targets of the National Curriculum are regarded as a basic foundation, which is greatly extended by the wider programmes of study typically available in IAPS prep schools. Specialist subject teaching is widely available from Year 3 onwards. More than thirty sports and games are played competitively and recreationally to very high standards.

Membership
At present there are over 500 member schools in the United Kingdom with a total of 129,000 pupils. In addition the Heads of some 40 schools overseas are in membership.

Qualification for membership
In order to be elected to membership a Head must be suitably qualified, and schools in England and Wales must be accredited by the Independent Schools Council. Accreditation is accorded only after a satisfactory inspection, based on the same criteria as those used by OFSTED. Schools outside England must be recognised as efficient by the appropiate authority.

Services
IAPS offers a wide variety of services in support of its members and of the schools of which they are the Heads. A comprehensive and up-to-date programme of continuing professional development is provided for Heads and staff, helping to maintain excellent teacher quality and high standards of school management. Further information about these services is obtainable from IAPS Headquarters.

History
IAPS was founded in 1892 and incorporated in 1923. Until 1980 membership was confined to Heads of boys' and co-educational schools.

In 1981 IAPS amalgamated with the Association of Headmistresses of Preparatory Schools, which had been founded in 1929 and which at that time had 120 schools in membership. The combined Association took the name IAPS.

Organization
IAPS is divided into twelve Districts which cover the whole of the United Kingdom. It is controlled by an elected Council which has 22 members (plus the President and Vice-Presidents) and meets three times a year. The Chairman is elected by Council.

The General Secretary and officials work from the IAPS Headquarters. Their names and addresses are given below.

The Council and Officers for 2001/2002

President:
A H Mould

Vice-Presidents:
J R Hawkins, Mrs C E M Prichard, G C Smith

Chairman: Mrs G M Lumsdon

Chairman Elect: H S Thackrah

Vice-Chairman: R Constantine

Members of Council:
I H Angus, J E A Barnes, M E Beale, A J L Boardman, E H Bradby, J A Brett, S Carder, Mrs L E G Cavanagh, Q G Edwards, W J Hilton, M J Hodgson, D N Hopkins, Mrs W H Holland, D G Kidd, Mrs A Lloyd, G Marsh, C T O'Donnell, A M Synge, D Whipp)

Officials:
General Secretary: J H Morris, MA, MBA, FRSA
Director of Education: D P Hanson, BA, MA, FRSA
Treasurer: D E Leafe, BA, FCA
Schools Administration Adviser: Mrs H A Kingham, BSc, FInstD
Association Administrator: Miss F A Hubbard

Address:
11 Waterloo Place, Leamington Spa CV32 5LA
Tel: 01926 887833
Fax: 01926 888014
email: hq@iaps.org.uk
website: www.iaps.org.uk

THE INDEPENDENT SCHOOLS ASSOCIATION

The Independent Schools Association, which celebrated its centenary in 1979, is one of the oldest of the various organisations of independent schools. It differs from most of the others in that it is not confined to any one type of school, but includes Public, Preparatory, Junior, Nursery, Co-Educational, Single-sex, Boarding, and Day schools. The only criterion is that the school should be good of its kind.

The Association began as the Association of Principals of Private Schools, and was the first attempt to encourage high standards in private schools and to foster friendliness and co-operation among Heads who had previously worked in isolation. In 1895 it was incorporated as The Private Schools Association. In 1927 the word 'private' was replaced by 'independent', since by then many of the schools were no longer 'private' in the sense of being owned by private individuals. At present, although a number of the smaller schools are still privately owned, most are controlled by Boards of Governors constituted as Educational Trusts or Companies.

Membership is limited to Heads of schools which are not under the control of the Department for Education or a Local Education Authority. Principals of such schools are eligible provided the Executive Council is satisfied as to their suitability and the efficiency of the school. In addition the school must fulfil the Accreditation requirements of the Independent Schools Council and undergo Review every ten years.

The Association exists:

to promote fellowship and co-operation among Members both nationally and within the ISA Areas through Area meetings and through inter-school and inter-Area competitions and festivals in Sport, Drama, Art and Music.

to help and support individual Members by providing information and advice from the ISA office and from Area Co-ordinators.

to foster high educational standards in the independent sector by providing training opportunities and conferences.

to co-operate with other bodies which stand for professional freedom in eduction by maintaining due recognition for independent schools by Government and the public.

Membership is vested in the individual Head or Principal, and not in the school as a corporate body. A Head appointed to succeed an existing member will normally be accepted provisionally for two or three terms. During that period it is hoped that he or she will apply for permanent membership, and arrange for a visit by representatives of the Association to confirm it.

As well as pursuing the professional and educational aims set out above, the Association has a lively programme of social, cultural, and sporting activities. The Annual Conference, enables members to exchange views, hear distinguished speakers, and enjoy various social occasions both formal and informal. There is one other short conference in the Autumn, and the eight Areas into which the Association is divided organise their own programmes of meetings.

The Association currently represents some 294 schools with a roll of 60,000 pupils.

The Council and Officers for 2001/2002

President: Dr A G Hearnden, OBE

Vice-Presidents:
The Rev P A F Calaminus, BA
Mrs M Grant, CertEd
B J Maybee, JP, MA
Mrs M J Milner-Williams, CertEd
J S Riley, BA, FRGS, DipEd
Mrs A D Stranack, BA, CertEd

Honorary Officers:
D E Wood, MA, CertEd, CertMus, ACP, FCollP, FGMS (*Chairman*)
J L Wade, BA, DASE (*Vice Chairman*)
J T Wilding, BSc (*Vice-Chairman*)

Elective Councillors:
P W Bate, BA, PGCE, DipMkt
Mrs J D Billing, GGSM, CertEd, FRSA
Mrs P Dangerfield, BA ATD
Mrs H P Laidler, MA, BA, CertEd
P S Larkman, LVO, MA, CertEd
F Loveder, MA, PGCE
P. Moss, CertEd
P J Owen, MA
S Robinson, BEd
C M Sanderson, BA, PGCE
J Sinclair, BSc, FCA
P F Smith, BA, CertEd
R P Spendlove, CertEd, ACP, FCollP
D G Vanstone, MA, PGCE

Representative Councillors:
C J Ashby, BSc, PGCE (*South West*)
D H Blackburn, BA, CertEd (*North West*)
Mr D Baldwin (*London North*)
A G Bray, CertEd (*London West*)
Mrs P Burton, CertEd (*North East*)
M J Hewett, BA, FCollP (*East Anglia*)
Mrs R L Lait, BA, CertEd, MBA (*London South*)
Mrs Z Røisli, CertEd (*Overseas*)
R S Willmott, MA, CertEd (*Midlands*)

Officials and Advisors

General Secretary: Timothy Ham, MA, DipEd
Membership Secretary: Mary Benwell
Treasurer: Michael Phizacklea, FCA

Boys' British School, East Street, Saffron Walden, Essex CB10 1LS. Tel: (01799) 523619. E-mail: isa@dial.pipex.com

Consultant Accountants and Auditors: Messrs Russell, New and Co, The Courtyard, Beeding Court, Steyning, West Sussex BN44 3TN. Tel: 01903 816699.

Insurance Advisers: HSBC Schools Division, 9–17 Perrymount Road, Haywards Heath, W Sussex RH16 1TA. Tel: Haywards Heath (01444) 458144.

Solicitors: Messrs Pothecary and Barratt, Talbot House, Gracechurch Street, London EC3V 0BS. Tel: 020-7623 7520.

THE INDEPENDENT SCHOOLS INSPECTORATE

INCORPORATING THE ISC CONSULTANCY SERVICE

The Independent Schools Inspectorate (ISI) superseded the ISC's Accreditation Review and Consultancy Service (ARCS) in September 1998. It amalgamated with the HMC inspection service in April 2000, and is responsible for all ISC inspections. ISI has been officially approved by the Government to carry out inspections in ISC schools. It brings major improvements to the system established by ARCS – including publicly available reports, more detailed assessments of standards and inspections on a six-year cycle.

All ISC schools undergo initial accreditation to establish whether general standards in a school are acceptable to the ISC. The ISI monitors standards by arranging Accreditation inspections of schools applying to join ISC associations, and Review inspections for those already in membership. The basic procedures for Accreditation and Review are well established, having been set up in 1980 following the withdrawal in 1978 by the (then) DES of the designation "Recognised as Efficient". The procedures have recently been revised and extended in consultation with Ofsted. Teams of practising or recently retired heads and deputies, led by former members of HM Inspectorate or Ofsted Reporting Inspectors, monitor standards and member associations provide support in bringing about improvements. Schools which meet Accreditation standards often describe themselves as "Accredited by the ISC" in their literature.

All ISI inspection reports are publicly available.

The ISC Consultancy Service, which ISI also runs, provides advice and help on particular subjects or topics, to schools and associations within ISC.

Chairman of the ISI Committee
Hugh Davies Jones (formerly Headmaster of St Andrew's School, Eastbourne)

Director
Tony Hubbard (a former HMI)

Administrative Secretary
Mrs Mary Gallagher, **ISI Office**, Northway House, 1379 High Road, Whetstone, London N20 9LP. Tel: 020 8445 6262, Fax: 020 8445 7272

BOARD OF MANAGEMENT FOR METHODIST INDEPENDENT SCHOOLS

Methodist Church House
25 Marylebone Road, London NW1 5JP Tel: 020 7935 3723

Chairman: The Rev Dr R G Jones, MA, BD

Secretary: Mr Graham Russell, MA

Schools for Boys and Girls
Culford School, Bury St Edmunds IP28 6TX Tel: 01284 728615
Edgehill College, Bideford, North Devon EX39 3LY Tel: 01237 471701
Kent College, Canterbury CT2 9DT Tel: 01227 763231
Queen's College, Taunton TA1 4QS Tel: 01823 272559
Shebbear College, Shebbear, North Devon EX21 5HJ Tel: 01409 281228
Truro School, Truro, Cornwall TR1 1TH Tel: 01872 272763
Woodhouse Grove School, Apperley Bridge, Yorks BD10 0NR Tel: 01132 502477

Schools for Girls
Farringtons and Stratford House, Chislehurst, Kent BR7 6LR Tel: 020 8467 0256
Kent College, Pembury, Nr Tunbridge Wells TN2 4AX Tel: 01892 822006

OTHER METHODIST INDEPENDENT SCHOOLS

Schools for Boys and Girls
Ashville College, Harrogate HG2 9JR Tel: 01423 566358
Kingswood School, Bath, Avon BA1 5RG Tel: 01225 734200
The Leys School, Cambridge CB2 2AD Tel: 01223 508900
Rydal Penrhos School, Colwyn Bay, North Wales LL29 7BT Tel: 01492 530155
Wesley College, Dublin Tel: Dublin 987066
Methodist College, Belfast 9 Tel: Belfast 669558

Schools for Girls
Queenswood School, Hatfield, Herts AL9 6NS Tel: 01707 652262

A School prospectus, together with particulars of fees, and other information may be obtained from the Headmaster or Headmistress.

In cases of need applications may be made to a Central Bursary Fund for financial help to enable Methodist children to attend these schools. This fund is available to day pupils as well as boarding pupils. Details are available from the Board of Management.

Information regarding other sources of assistance with fees may be obtained from ISIS, Grosvenor Garden House, 35–37 Grosvenor Gardens, London SW1W 0BS. Tel: 020 7798 1500.

THE BOARDING SCHOOLS' ASSOCIATION

Aims

The Association is committed to the view that boarding education, either for the whole or part of a child's school career, is of benefit to many children and is essential for some. The BSA aims are:

- To promote the qualities of boarding life provided by all types of boarding schools
- To provide information about boarding and boarding schools which are in membership of BSA
- To organise training programmes and professional development opportunities for all staff and governors of boarding schools
- To produce a range of material on boarding issues and good practice
- To conduct and authorise appropriate research
- To work with other bodies concerned with boarding education
- To maintain a regular dialogue with appropriate Government Ministers and their departments, Members of Parliament, and Local Government Officials

Membership

Membership is open to all schools with boarders which are accredited to the Independent Schools' Council (ISC), to schools in membership of the Scottish Council of Independent Schools (SCIS), and also to state maintained boarding schools (which may then also become members of the State Boarding Schools' Information Service - STABIS). Membership may also be offered to boarding schools overseas at the discretion of the Executive Committee. Current membership comprises 500 schools (fully boarding, weekly/flexi boarding, or day schools with boarding provision; co-educational or single-sex; preparatory or secondary).

Associate Membership is available to individuals, day schools and other bodies at the discretion of the Executive Committee. They will be entitled to receive all Association mailings and attend Conferences. Associate membership is open to former heads of member schools and anyone else interested in supporting the cause of boarding.

Support for Schools

The Training programme

In partnership with ***the University of Surrey Roehampton*** and the Department for Education and Employment (DfEE), the BSA has established a Training Programme for all staff working in boarding schools. These BSA courses lead to university validated Certificates of Professional Practice in Boarding Education. Other courses in Child Protection, Boarding Legislation and Good Practice are offered as well as individual courses tailored to the particular needs of a school or group of schools.

BSA training is available to all staff who work in boarding schools and to the Governors of boarding schools.

BSA Training Programmes are being developed to enable them to be offered to schools throughout the world.

The DfEE is making a significant contribution to the Training Programmes to enable them to be available to as many staff as possible and to lower the costs to member schools and staff.

Residential Conferences

Four conferences are held annually for:

Heads of Boarding Schools and representatives of their member associations (The BSA Annual Conference)
Deputy Heads
Housemasters and Housemistresses
Matrons and Sanatorium Staff

The latter two conferences incorporate part of the BSA/University of Surrey Roehampton Training Programme

Publications

These include

- ***Good Practice in Boarding Schools – A Resource Handbook for all those working in boarding***
  Edited by Timothy Holgate
- ***Running a School Boarding House – A Legal Guide for Housemasters and Housemistresses***
  By Robert Boyd
- ***Training Issues for Boarding Schools***
  By Brian FitzGerald
- ***The Guide to Accredited Independent Boarding Schools in the UK*** – The official Guide to the 600 Independent Boarding Schools accredited by the Independent Schools Council
- ***Choosing a Boarding School – a Guide for Parents***
  By Tim Holgate
- ***Boarding School*** – two editions of the BSA magazine each year
- ***Newsletter*** – published every two months
- ***Boarding Briefing Papers*** – are published at regular intervals on matters concerning boarding legislation and good practice

BSA publications are given financial support by the DfEE which also sponsors and publishes:–
Parents' Guide to Maintained Boarding Schools

National Boarding Standards

The Association is a member of the Committee establishing National Boarding Standards.

Promotion

The Association promotes the benefits of boarding education through a programme of initiatives involving member schools, the media and other educational organisations.

Liaison with National Bodies

The Association meets regularly with the Department for Education and Employment to discuss issues concerned with boarding.

It also liaises with Local Government, ISI (Independent Schools' Inspectorate), OFSTED (Office for Standards in Education), SCE (Service Children's Education) and all the national educational organisations.

Organisation.
At the Annual General Meeting, held at the Heads' Annual Conference, Officers of the Association are elected together with the Executive Committee, the composition of which reflects the categories of schools in membership. Co-opted members will include representatives National Bodies involved in boarding education. The Honorary Treasurer is usually a Bursar from a member school.

Offices
The Offices of the Association are located in London in the same building as the Independent Schools Council (ISC) and the Independent Schools Information Service (ISIS). The BSA enjoys Associate status with ISC and works in close partnership with ISC on educational issues of mutual interest.

National Director
Adrian Underwood BA(Hons), MA, FRSA, The Boarding Schools' Association, Grosvenor Gardens House, 35–37 Grosvenor Gardens, London SW1W 0BS. Tel: 0207 798 1580; Fax: 0207 798 1581; e-mail: bsa@isis.org.uk; website: http//www.boarding.org.uk

Director of Training
Tim Holgate BSc(Hons), MSc, BSA Director of Training, 4 Manor Farm Cottages, Etchilhampton, Devizes, Wilts SN10 3JR Phone & Fax: 01380 860953; e-mail: tim.holgate@btinternet.com

THE INDEPENDENT SCHOOLS' BURSARS ASSOCIATION

Membership. Full membership of the Association is open to Schools who are members of one of constituent associations in membership of the Independent Schools Council. Bursars or other officials of other independent schools may apply for Associate Membership provided that the school is recognised as an educational charity.

The Work of the Association. The Association exists in order to promote administrative efficiency in Independent Schools; to assist members in their work by the sharing of information on matters of common interest; and to undertake joint negotiation with Government Departments and other bodies where this is considered advisable. Close contact is maintained with the two Governing Bodies' Associations, the Headmasters' and Headmistresses' Conference, the Society of Headmasters and Headmistresses of Independent Schools, the Girls' Schools Association, the Incorporated Association of Preparatory Schools and the Independent Schools Association through a Joint Council on which sit representatives of each body.

Bulletins are circulated at intervals to all members containing notices about decisions of the Executive Committee, information received by the Secretary, and other matters of day to day interest, as well as contributions from members and digests of information collected by means of questionnaires. There is also an Annual Report.

Schools Represented. The first meeting of the Association was held in London in 1932, and was attended by representatives of 47 Schools. There are now over 780 Schools in membership.

Management. The Executive Committee consists of the Chairman of the Association, Mr W G F Organ, the Bursar of Winchester College and the Bursars of twelve other leading independent schools.

The Hon Treasurer is the Bursar of Radley College.

The General Secretary is Mr M J Sant whose address is 5 Chapel Close, Old Basing, Basingstoke, Hampshire RG24 7BZ Tel: 01256 330369.

THE CATHOLIC INDEPENDENT SCHOOLS' CONFERENCE

Objects

The CISC exists to:

- promote Catholic Independent Schools
- provide a forum for Catholic Independent heads to exchange views and discuss common issues
- promote good relations within the area of Catholic education
- provide assistance and support to heads when requested
- work with the trustees, governors and heads to ensure good government and the Catholicity of member schools.

Schools

There are 140 schools currently in membership of the CISC. The majority of members are also in membership of one or more of the eight independent school associations that constitute the Independent Schools Council. Schools in membership include day and boarding schools, single-sex and co-educational, senior and junior schools.

Membership

Full membership will be the head of a school that satisfies the following conditions:

- the school shall be recognised by the local Catholic bishop as being Catholic
- the school shall have been recognised as a charitable foundation by the Charity Commission
- the school shall be independent
- the school shall be in the United Kingdom
- the school will have been subjected to a nationally accredited inspection and found to be in good standing.

Associate membership is available to Catholic and other Christian heads that are in sympathy with the aims of the CISC.

Officers for 2001/2002

Chairman:
Dr R G G Mercer MA DPhil

Vice-President:
Mr Dermot Gogarty

Committee:
Mrs Wanda Nash BA MEd (*Vice-Chairman*)
Mr Philip Sweeney BA
Mrs Linda Hayes BA
Mrs Mary Breen MSc
The Rev Antony Sutch OSB MA

General Secretary:
Sr Frances Orchard IBVM BA

Address:
St Mary's College
Waldegrave Road
Twickenham TW1 4SX
Tel: 020 8891 2260
Fax: 020 8891 2146
email: francescisc@talk21.com
website: www.catholicindependentschools.org.uk

CHURCH SCHOOLS COMPANY

Church Schools House, Titchmarsh, Kettering, Northants NN14 3DA
Tel: (01832) 735105 Fax: (01832) 734760
email:admin@church-schools.com
website:www.church-schools.com

Church Schools Company's School

Ashford School, Kent (GSA, boarding and day)
Atherley School, Southampton (GSA, day)
Caterham School, Caterham (HMC, IAPS, boarding and day)
Guildford High School, Guildford (GSA, boarding and day)
Hull High School, Anlaby (Tranby Croft), Hull (GSA, day)
Lincoln Minster, Lincoln (SHMIS, IAPS, boarding and day)
Sunderland High School, Sunderland (SHMIS, IAPS, day)
Surbiton High School, Kingston (GSA, IAPS, day)

(Particulars of the schools will be found in the Book under the above titles).

The Company's objective for each pupil is that they:
become a balanced, articulate person with the intellectual freedom to be creative, the confidence to initiate, the resilience to cope with adversity, the compassion to serve others, and motivated to have a lifelong love of learning.

The Church Schools Company was founded as an educational charity in 1883 with the principal objective of creating schools that would offer pupils a good academic education based on Christian principles with particular reference to the Church of England. In 1992 the articles were widened to embrace other mainstream Christian Churches, which subsequently enabled Caterham School, with its United Reform Church foundation, to become a Company school. Although the schools have this Christian background, pupils and staff from other faiths are all welcomed.

The Company's Council has developed the concept of a group of individually strong schools each capable of offering a broad and challenging education. To achieve this it has invested in the provision of excellent buildings and facilities at each school in the belief that growth helps to enhance the academic and extra-curricular opportunities available to pupils in both the primary and secondary stages of education. The success of this policy is reflected in the growth in pupil numbers from 3,200 in 1990 to over 5,400 in 2000.

This ideal of strong schools embraces not just academic learning to high standards, but also the development of skills that will be essential throughout life both at work and socially. Teamwork, leadership, an enthusiastic response to challenge and an active concern for others are all attributes which are valued at Church Schools. These skills, increasingly identified by employers as the key to future success, are developed throughout each young person's time in school from the earliest years through to the Sixth Form.

Academic scholarships, exhibitions and bursaries are awarded at all schools. In addition the Church Schools Foundation Assisted Places are available at each school. The tuition fees vary according to age and school, from £3,464 to £7,632 a year (day) and £9,810 to £16,770 (boarding).

The Church Schools Company is a charity (Registered Charity Number: 1016538). It was a charity founded to further education based on Christian principles. Caterham School is a separate charity (Registered Charity Number: 1050847).

INDEPENDENT SCHOOLS EXAMINATIONS BOARD COMMON ENTRANCE EXAMINATIONS

Chairman: G E Jones, MA
General Secretary: Mrs J Williams, BA, Independent Schools Examinations Board, Jordan House, Christchurch Road, New Milton, Hampshire BH25 6QJ (Telephone 01425 621111; Fax: 01425 620044; e-mail: ce@iseb.co.uk; website: www.iseb.co.uk)

The Common Entrance Examinations are used for transfer to senior schools at the ages of 11+, 12+ and 13+. The syllabuses are devised and regularly monitored by the Independent Schools Examinations Board which comprises members of the Headmasters' and Headmistresses' Conference, the Girls' Schools Association and the Incorporated Association of Preparatory Schools.

The papers are set by examiners appointed by the Board, but the answers are marked by the senior school for which a candidate is entered. A list of schools using the examination is given below. Common Entrance is not a public examination as, for example, GCSE, and candidates may normally be entered only in one of the following circumstances:

(*a*) they have been offered a place at a senior school, subject to their passing the examination, or
(*b*) they are required to take the examination as a preliminary to sitting a scholarship examination, or
(*c*) they are entered for a 'trial run' in which case the papers are corrected by the junior school concerned.

Candidates normally take the examination in their own junior or preparatory schools, either in the UK or overseas.

Dates

The dates of the written examinations for 2002 are
11+ 28–29 January.
12+ 25–26 February.
13+ 25–28 February, 27–30 May.

The dates of listening and speaking examinations for 2002 are 28 January, 25–28 February, 8–11 May.

Entries

In cases where candidates are at schools in membership of the Incorporated Association of Preparatory Schools, it is usual for heads of these schools to make arrangements for entering candidates for the appropriate examination after consultation with parents and senior school heads.

In the case of candidates at schools which do not normally enter candidates, it is the responsibility of parents to arrange for candidates to be entered for the appropriate examination in accordance with the requirements of senior schools.

Conduct of the Examination

Regulations for the conduct of the examination are laid down by the Independent Schools Examinations Board.

Fees

The Independent Schools Examinations Board decides the fees to be charged for each candidate. Schools are notified annually in the spring term of fees payable for the following three terms. Parents seeking information about current fees should contact the ISEB office.

Syllabus and past papers

Copies of the syllabuses, past papers and other publications are available from CE Publications Limited at the same address.

Correspondence

Correspondence about academic matters relating to the Common Entrance examinations and requests for further information about the administration of the examinations should be addressed to the General Secretary, ISEB, Jordan House, Christchurch Road, New Milton, Hampshire BH25 6QJ (Telephone 01425 621111; Fax: 01425 620044; e-mail: ce@iseb.co.uk; website: www.iseb.co.uk).

APPENDIX

SENIOR SCHOOLS USING THE COMMON ENTRANCE EXAMINATIONS TO INDEPENDENT SCHOOL

MEMBERS OF THE HEADMASTERS' AND HEADMISTRESSES' CONFERENCE

Abbotsholme School
Abingdon School
Aldenham School
Ampleforth College
Ardingly College
Ashville School
Barnard Castle
Bedford School
Bedford Modern School
Berkhamsted Collegiate School
Birkenhead School
Bishop's Stortford College
Bloxham School
Blundell's School
Bootham School
Bradfield College
Brentwood School
Brighton College
Bromsgrove School
Bryanston School
Canford School
Caterham School
Charterhouse
Cheltenham College
Chigwell School
Christ College
Churcher's College
City of London Freemen's School
Clifton College
Cranleigh School
Culford School
Dauntsey's School
Dean Close School
Denstone College
Dover College
Downside School
Dulwich College
Durham School
Eastbourne College
Elizabeth College
Ellesmere College
Emanuel School
Epsom College
Eton College
Exeter School
Felsted School
Fettes College
Forest School
Framlingham College
Frensham Heights
Giggleswick School
Glenalmond College
Gordonstoun School
Gresham's School
Haberdashers' Aske's School
Haileybury
Hampton School
Harrow School
Highgate School
Hurstpierpoint College
Ipswich School
Kelly College
Kent College
Kimbolton School
King Edward's School (Witley)
King's College (Taunton)
King's College School (Wimbledon)
King's School (Bruton)
King's School (Canterbury)
King's School (Ely)
King's School (Gloucester)
King's School (Macclesfield)
King's School (Rochester)
King's School (Worcester)
Kingston Grammar School
Kingswood School
Lancing College
Latimer Upper School
Leicester Grammar School
Leighton Park School
The Leys School
Lord Wandsworth College
Loretto School
Loughborough Grammar School
Magdalen College School
Malvern College
Marlborough College
Merchant Taylors' School
Merchiston Castle School
Millfield School
Mill Hill School
Monkton Combe School
Monmouth School
Mount St Mary's College
Norwich School
Oakham School
Oratory School
Oundle School
Pangbourne College
Plymouth College
Pocklington School
Portsmouth Grammar School
Prior Park College
Queen Elizabeth Grammar School (Wakefield)
Queen's College
Radley College
Ratcliffe College
Reading Blue Coat School
Reed's School
Reigate Grammar School
Rendcomb College
Repton School
Royal Grammar School (Guildford)
Royal Grammar School (Newcastle upon Tyne)
Royal Grammar School (Worcester)
Rugby School
Rydal Penrhos School
Ryde School
St Albans School
St Benedict's School
St Columba's College (Dublin)
St Edmund's College
St Edmund's School
St Edward's School
St George's College
St John's School (Leatherhead)
St Lawrence College
St Paul's School
St Peter's School
Sedbergh School
Sevenoaks School
Sherborne School
Shrewsbury School
Stonyhurst College
Stowe School
Strathallan School

Sutton Valence School
Taunton School
Tettenhall College
Tonbridge School
Trent College
Trinity School
Truro School
University College School
Uppingham School
Victoria College
Wellingborough School
Wellington College
Wellington School
Wells Cathedral School
West Buckland School
Westminster School
Whitgift School
Woodbridge School
Worksop College
Worth School
Wrekin College
Wycliffe College

MEMBERS OF THE GIRLS' SCHOOLS ASSOCIATION

Ashford School
Badminton School
Bedgebury School
Benenden School
Casterton School
Cranford House School
Downe House
Godolphin School
Headington School
Heathfield School (Ascot)
Kent College (Tunbridge Wells)
Kilgraston School
The Ladies' College (Cheltenham)
Malvern Girls' College
Moira House School
Moreton Hall School
North Foreland Lodge
Princess Helena College
Queen Anne's School
Queen Ethelburga's
Queen Margaret's School
Queenswood School
Roedean School
Royal School (Hindhead)
Rye St Antony School
St Antony's-Leweston School
St George's School
St James's School
St Leonards School
St Leonard's-Mayfield School
St Mary's Hall
St Mary's School (Calne)
St Mary's School (Shaftesbury)
St Mary's School (Wantage)
St Swithun's School
Sherborne School for Girls
Stonar School
Tudor Hall School
Wentworth College
Westonbirt
Wispers School
Woldingham School
Wycombe Abbey School

MEMBERS OF THE SOCIETY OF HEADMASTERS AND HEADMISTRESSES OF INDEPENDENT SCHOOLS

The following schools use the Common Entrance for some candidates

Battle Abbey School
Bearwood College
Bedstone College
Bethany School
Birkdale School
Box Hill School
Claremont Fan Court School
Clayesmore School
Cokethorpe School
Embley Park
Ewell Castle School
Grenville College
Halliford School
Lincoln Minster School
Milton Abbey School
Rannoch School
Rougemont School
Royal Hospital School
Royal Russell School
St Bede's School
St David's College
Seaford College
Shiplake College
Warminster School

MEMBERS OF THE INDEPENDENT SCHOOLS ASSOCIATION

Claires Court School
Dixie Grammar School
d'Overbroeck's College
Heathfield School (Wolverley)
Licensed Victuallers' School
Newlands School
Northamptonshire Grammar School
Presentation College (Reading)
Rodney School
Rookwood School
Sackville School
St Columba's College (St Albans)
St James Independent School
Westbourne College

OTHER SCHOOLS

Academic International School (Kenya)
Ballard College
Chilton Cantelo School
Cranbrook School
Harrodian School
Hillcrest Secondary School (Nairobi)
Imani School (Kenya)
Laxton School
Nairobi Academy
Old Swinford Hospital School
Peponi Secondary School (Nairobi)
Queen Mary's School
St Andrew's School (Kenya)
St John's College
St Joseph's College (Ipswich)

INDEPENDENT SCHOOLS CAREERS ORGANISATION

President:
Vice Presidents: D A Emms, OBE, MA
B J Bowden, FCA
G W Searle, MA
Chairman: J D Andrewes, MA, FCA
Hon Treasurer: A J Popham, BA, FCA
National Director: J D Stuart, MA

COUNCIL 2000/2001

Governing Body Members:

* J D Andrewes (Reed's School)
Miss C Avent (South Hampstead High School)
* Mrs J D N Bates (King William's College)
W R Broadhead (Caterham School)
Miss C Holme (King's School, Gloucester)
Mrs G Hylson Smith (Stowe School)
P E Mee (Hampton School)
Dr C Milton (St Margaret's School for Girls)
*N G U Morris (Malvern College)
Mrs J Munro (Nottingham High School for Girls)

Member Heads:

Mrs L Croston (Westholme School)
Miss S R Cameron (North Foreland Lodge)
Mrs M Henderson (Westonbirt School)
* D W Jarrett (Reed's School)
* D J J McEwen (St Edmund's College)
Mrs E E A McKendrick (Downe House School)
S J W McArthur (Reading Blue Coat School)
Dr A Seldon (Brighton College)
Dr R M Reynolds (Newcastle-under-Lyme School)
Mrs P Watson (Leicester High School for Girls)

Co-opted Members:

* A A Bridgewater (CRAC/ECCTIS)
Mrs M Brooks (Cadence Designs Ltd)
Mrs B A Harrison (Girls Day School Trust)
Miss D Langley (King's College, London)
Ms K Howard (Construction Industry Training Board)
Mrs A Mulvie (Wellpark Consultancy & Chairman of Scottish Council)
* A J Popham (PricewaterhouseCoopers)
D Prince (HMC)
* Capt J Roberts, RN (White Ensign Association)
G Ward (University of Hertfordshire)
W Worsley (Hovingham Estates)

Observers:

Commander T I Hildesley, OBE, RN (ROI) (Asst Director (Officers), Directorate of Naval Recruiting)
Mrs C Parrish (ISIS)
Mrs D C Bisp (Stowe School)
Mrs A Hoverstadt (Cheadle Hulme School)
Mr A Hunwicks (The Royal School)

* Members of Finance Committee

CONTACTS

Who to ask for information and help

Information on careers, further and higher education and training courses – Kate Bennett. *Tel/Fax:* 020 7487 7417; *e-mail:* info@isco.org.uk

Advice on guidance on options ahead – If still at school: your Regional Director (see list of Directors); If you have left school: Judith Elkan (*ISCO London Director*). *Tel:* 020 7487 3660; *e-mail:* judith.elkan@isco.org.uk *or* Alison Ambler (*ISCO Edinburgh Office*). *Tel:* 0131 220 5885; *e-mail:* alison.ambler@isco.org.uk

Questions about ISCO Publications, Careers Experience Courses or Membership matters – ISCO Administration at Camberley. *Tel:* 01276 21188; *e-mail:* admin@isco.org.uk
Publication Sales: Sylvia Pool. *e-mail:* sylvie.pool@isco.org.uk *Career Experience Courses:* Pam Baker. *e-mail:* pam.baker@isco.org.uk *Administrative Director:* Keith Beale. *e-mail:* keith.beale@isco.org.uk *National Director:* John Stuart. *e-mail:* john.stuart@isco.org.uk

Enquiries and Suggestions concerning CareerScope – Anna Alston (*Editorial content*). *Tel:* 020 8883 9275; *e-mail:* anna.alston@isco.org.uk Emma Jackson (*Advertising*), *Tel:* 020 7005 2631; *e-mail:* e.jackson@independent.co.uk

For current matters concerning ISCO and its members: website: www.isco.org.uk

ISCO REGIONAL DIRECTORS

by area of operation and, where more than one, where they are based

Scotland – Joan Smith. *Tel:* 0131 441 9950; *e-mail:* joan.smith@isco.org.uk
North East & Central England – Sue Hargreaves. *Tel:* 01629 815203; *e-mail:* sue.hargreaves@isco.org.uk
North West England – Chris Marley. *Tel:* 0161 904 8676; *e-mail:* chris.marley@isco.org.uk
Midlands – Liz Barker. *Tel:* 01235 555294; *e-mail:* liz.barker@isco.org.uk
Wales & West Midlands – John Morris. *Tel:* 01432 379130; *e-mail:* john.morris@isco.org.uk
East Anglia – John Watson. *Tel:* 01572 823073; *e-mail:* john.watson@isco.org.uk
North London – Tony Darbyshire. *Tel:* 01494 766273; *e-mail:* tony.darbyshire@isco.org.uk
South London – Simon Clarke. *Tel:* 020 8946 4414; *e-mail:* simon.clarke@isco.org.uk
Sussex and Kent: Helen Davison. *Tel:* 01342 317537; *e-mail:* helen.davison@isco.org.uk

Surrey and Kent: Liz Berner. *Tel:* 020 8290 4959; *e-mail:* liz.berner@isco.org.uk
Berkshire: Katherine Skinner. *Tel:* 0118 926 5861; *e-mail:* katherine.skinner@isco.org.uk
Surrey & Berks (Camberley): Jane Reeves (also ISCO Training Manager). *Tel:* 01306 7101021; *e-mail:* jane.reeves@isco.org.uk Stuart Day (also ISCO IT Development Manager) *Tel:* 01276 21188; *e-mail:* stuart.day@isco.org.uk
Hampshire and Dorset: Sarah Webster. *Tel:* 01483 813733; *e-mail:* sarah.webster@isco.org.uk
Avon: Louise Davidson. *Tel:* 01373 831356; *e-mail:* louise.davidson@isco.org.uk
Monmouth: Janet Cuthbert-Smith. *Tel/Fax:* 01291 689662 *e-mail:* janet.cuthbert-smith@isco.org.uk
Devon: Sue Norman. *Tel:* 01392 824097; *e-mail:* sue.norman@isco.org.uk
Dorset: Liz Boddy. *Tel:* 01722 413870; *e-mail:* liz.boddy@isco.org.uk
Spain – George Dale. *Tel:* 0034 950 472805; *e-mail:* george.dale@isco.org.uk

PURPOSE AND AIMS OF ISCO

1. To advise and assist careers and other staff in member schools:

To enable them to establish a careers and higher education guidance service by supplying up-to-date information about entry to and conditions of service in careers of all kinds.

To further these aims by arranging conferences, courses and conventions.

2. To advise and assist employers:

By making opportunities for careers known to young persons in the upper forms of member schools, and to careers staff.

3. To advise and assist individual young persons and their parents:

To help them in their choice of careers and higher education.

To further these aims by arranging appropriate aptitude tests and questionnaires and by organising careers experience courses for young persons.

ISCO SERVICES TO SCHOOLS

Tests, Questionnaires and Computer Programs

: MORRISBY TESTS of personality, aptitudes and interests with an 18 page printed report and career suggestions.
: ISCOM computer program which suggests careers based on interests and academic performance.
: DISCOURSE computer program which suggests degree courses.
: DISCOVER computer database describing 350 occupations.
: ISCOPE – Combines ISCOM, DISCOURSE and DISCOVER.
: ECCTIS CD-ROM database of 100,000 post GCSE courses including degrees.
: ODYSSEY database of over 1000 careers.
: PATHFINDER – Careers interest questionnaire.
: EXODUS – Worldwide careers information database.
: HIGHER IDEAS Guide to Universities.
: CID Careers Database.
: WORLDWIDE VOLUNTEERING FOR YOUNG PEOPLE – Database search for GAP experience

Individual interviews at school, and after leaving school up to the age of 23.

Courses for boys and girls

: Over 120 career experience courses throughout the UK for sixthformers and Scottish 5th year. More than 2,200 attend these courses annually.
: Locally based career visits for sixth formers and Scottish 5th year during term time.

Courses and Seminars for Staff

: Residential training courses, including an Annual Conference and In-House courses at school (if required) for training staff to use the Morrisby Tests and reports, and to deal with careers and Higher Education issues.
: National and Regional day courses with business, industry and higher education.
: Workshops and training courses.

Publications

: The termly Careers Magazine "CareerScope".
: Information Sheets on 130 careers.
: 36 "Guidelines" on specific aspects of careers counselling such as "Employment at 18+", "Successful Interviews" etc.
: 'Sixthformer's Guide to visiting universities and colleges of higher education.'
: The termly newsletter to schools giving information on all careers and higher education issues.
: "Opportunities in the GAP Year".
: Careers Education Programmes for years 9, 10, 11, 12 and 13 (S2, 3, 4, 5 and 6) on CD Rom.
: Skills Training Programmes: "Study Skills CD Rom" – Classroom programmes for years 9, 10, 11 and 12 (S2, 3, 4 and 5).
: 'Art and Design Directory' Details of all higher education courses in the UK.
: Experience Erasmus: The UK Guide to Socrates – Erasmus Programmes.
: 'Awards' – A guide to scholarships and bursaries at UK universities.
: 'Independent Colleges' – Directory of Courses.
: 'Revision Courses' – A guide to revision courses and study days for students taking A-levels, Highers or GCSE's.

An Information Service answering enquiries on training courses, higher and further education establishments, qualifications needed, GAP Year possibilities etc.

Regional Directors who visit the school, meet pupils and staff and, where requested, attend parents' meetings and careers conventions.

Advice on lay-out, equipment required and the publications recommended for **Careers Rooms**.

Access to university and college vacancies in August and September through the Camberley or London Office which has the ECCTIS CD-ROM database.

Heads are asked to allow at least one member of the staff to attend a Morrisby Training Course. This training course will enable the careers adviser to interpret the ISCO/Morrisby Tests and to write a cogent report to parents. The report provides the basis for career exploration and can be invaluable both to parents and their children.
It is hoped too that Heads will be willing to send newly-appointed members of the careers staff to the training course at Cirencester in August. This course covers a wide range of issues to do with careers and higher education.

THE COST TO SCHOOLS:

* The annual subscription depends on the size of Year 11/S4 at the beginning of the autumn term according to this scale:

1–29 pupils	£470	
30–59 pupils	£535	
60–89 pupils	£660	inclusive of VAT
90–119 pupils	£765	
120 pupils and over—	£870	
One Year introductory Membership	**£235 Regardless of size of school**	

Heads who join ISCO are asked to circulate to parents, usually at the start of Year 11/S4, an ISCO pamphlet entitled the ISCO 'Student Scheme' for your son or daughter which gives details of the services offered and how to join. Alternatively, schools may choose the **'all-in' option**, which means that all pupils are 'enrolled' in the Scheme and parents are not asked to join individually. The fee for the 'all-in' option is £109.80 per pupil, (10% less than the full rate). Schools choosing the 'all-in' method can have 'new' sixth formers/S5 enrolled for £85. They also receive the ISCO computer programs, ISCOM, DISCOVER AND DISCOURSE free of charge.

THE COST TO PARENTS:

* Parents enrol their children in the Student Scheme by making a once-only payment of £122 usually in year 11/S4, which entitles their son or daughter to all the services outlined above including the Morrisby tests up to the age of 23. Parents who do not enrol in the Scheme may use the services on a *pro-rata* basis, as follows:

Interview after leaving schools	£63 – inclusive of VAT
Careers experience courses	Charges vary according to the degree of sponsorship. Priority is given to pupils enrolled in the Student Scheme who, where there is a charge, pay a lower rate.
Interview Preparation with Video	£58.75 – inclusive of VAT

* These fees are operative until 31 August 2002.

HOW TO JOIN:

Heads who wish to join ISCO should send a brief letter of application (or a request for further information) to the National Director, Independent Schools Careers Organisation, 12A Princess Way, Camberley, Surrey, GU15 3SP.

MEDICAL OFFICERS OF SCHOOLS ASSOCIATION

FOUNDED 1884

Objects
Mutual assistance of members in promoting school health, and the holding of meetings for consideration of all subjects connected with the special work of medical officers of schools.

Membership
Medical officers of schools and medical and dental practitioners especially concerned with the health of the schoolchild are eligible for membership, and members of the teaching profession for associate membership. The present membership currently stands at 415.

The work of the Association
The Council meets three times a year and is chaired by the current President Dr Ailsa Borthwick, currently MO to Charterhouse School in Surrey. The Hon Secretary sends out three newsletters a year and is available for advice to members and non-members. Clinical meetings are arranged each year together with an annual summer visit to a school. Research projects are carried out individually and collectively. The Association strongly recommends that all independent schools appoint medical officers to carry out preventative medicine duties which are undertaken in maintained schools by the School Health Service.

Publications
The 18th edition of the Handbook of School Health, published in May of 1998, deals in detail with the administrative, ethical, public health and clinical aspects of the school medical officer's work and is widely accepted as the definitive guide to current practice. A Proceedings and Report are published annually. The Association also publishes and updates appropriate guidelines for its clinical Medical Officers and these are updated regularly.

Further information about the Association and other related business should in the first instance be directed to the Hon Secretary Dr Neil D Arnott, Amherst Medical Practice, 21 St Botolph's Road, Sevenoaks, Kent TN13 3AQ. Tel: 01732 459255. Fax: 01732 450751. For administrative information and background please contact the Executive Secretary directly, Mrs Francesca Wade Tel/Fax: 01732 750586, MOSA Web Site www.mosa.org.uk

THE ASSOCIATION OF DEVELOPMENT DIRECTORS IN INDEPENDENT SCHOOLS

FOUNDED 1993

ADDIS Secretariat: The White House, 31 Connaught Way, Tunbridge Wells, Kent TN4 9QP (*temporary address*)
Tel/Fax: 07000 623347
e-mail: AddisSec@compuserve.com
website: www.addis.uk.com

Objectives:

- To promote and develop good marketing practice in independent education
- To help increase the effectiveness of the marketing representatives of Member Schools
- To encourage personal development within the schools' marketing profession

Achieved through:

- Termly seminars on a variety of marketing-led subjects (a list of recent seminars may be obtained from the Secretariat) held at locations thoughout the country
- Termly Newsletters with articles from Member Schools and invited contributors
- Help Line – manned during normal office hours
- Website
- Speakers profided for conferences, inset days and similar

Membership:

- Membership by subscription: Fees for 2000–2001 £125 senior school, £65 prep school
- Associate membership considered on application

The Association is directed by a Chairman, Vice Chairman and Treasurer together with an Executive Committee of 11 members. The Chairman, Vice Chairman and Treasurer together with members of the Executive Committee are selected (or re-elected) annually at the ADDIS AGM.

The ADDIS Secretary, Mrs V A Pratten, administers the Association from the ADDIS Secretariat.

THE ASSOCIATION OF REPRESENTATIVES OF OLD PUPILS' SOCIETIES (AROPS)

Origins and Membership

The Association of Representatives of Old Pupils' Societies was started by M E C Comer (Old Johnian Society) at an inaugural conference in December 1971. The objects are clearly defined: 'to provide a forum for the exchange of views and experiences between representatives of Old Pupils' Societies'. Within that ample framework the Association has steadily progressed both in membership and in breadth of discussion. Membership is available to girls, boys, co-educational and preparatory schools' old pupils societies 'or any other establishment approved by the executive committee'. Today in excess of 250 schools are represented. Representatives are nominated by their societies and report back to them, but they participate at meetings as individuals.

Meetings

Meetings are held in host schools and the net is cast widely throughout the country; over 40 schools having already been visited. Knowledge and interest concerning the work of AROPS are thus readily imparted to Staff and senior pupils taking part in the organisation of meetings.

Each Spring a whole day Saturday conference is held at which the opening address is given by the Head of the host school. Then follow sessions on educational policy and innovative ideas of concern for Old Pupils' societies, with appropriate speakers from industry, commerce, education and government. Ample time is allowed for questions and discussion. Each November the AGM is held in the Greater London area as an evening meeting, the brief formal business being followed by a Speaker talking on a topical matter of educational interest. Additional meetings may also be held to meet special circumstances.

The Association strongly supports close liaison with Heads on all matters in which Old Pupils can play their part within the school community. Heads are always welcome both as speakers and as participants.

Discussion Subjects

In line with its original objects, at least one session of the conference is devoted to administrative problems facing all societies: the effect of inflation; collection of subscriptions; printing costs; use of computers; collaboration with 'Friends of the School'; maintenance of interest some years after leaving school and effective ways of helping to promote their own schools. There is evidence that societies have benefited from, and have acted upon the successful experience of others. Reports of meetings are circulated to all Representatives.

The Support of Independent Education

AROPS supports the work of ISIS and the Independent Schools Council. AROPS is a non-political body but its interests have always been opposed to any political threat to Independent Education.

Fees

The current annual subscription is £18, with an affiliation fee of £5. Societies interested in membership should write to the Hon Registrar, AROPS, Mrs Rosemary Hamilton, Blacks Farm, Boston Road, Eastville, Boston, Lincs, PE22 8LJ.

THE ENGLISH-SPEAKING UNION OF THE COMMONWEALTH

The Secondary Exchange Scholarships to the United States and Canada

Chairman – Lady Appleyard

Executive Secretary: The Director of Education.

A number of North American Independent Schools generously offer free places for a year to British girls and boys, with the intention of furthering understanding between Britain and North America by giving young people an opportunity of living and working with their North American counterparts. Free board and tuition is offered, travel and incidental expenses being borne by parents.

The Committee interviews and selects boys and girls to be holders of these scholarships. Under reciprocal arrangements British schools offer free board and tuition to senior students from North America.

In addition, a number of American Schools offer places for two terms only, commencing at the beginning of January.

British applicants should have completed A levels and they should normally be over the age of 17. Details may be obtained from The Awards Manager, The English-Speaking Union, Dartmouth House, 37 Charles Street, London W1X 8AB.

PART I

Schools appearing in Part I are those whose Heads are members of the Headmasters' and Headmistresses' Conference

Abbotsholme School
Derbyshire

Rocester Uttoxeter ST14 5BS.
Tel: (01889) 590217
Fax: (01889) 591001

Abbotsholme School was founded in 1889 by Dr Cecil Reddie and was the first of a series of new schools which were to have considerable influence on European education. The aim was to give young people a wider and more balanced education than had been customary and this philosophy continues today. Abbotsholme is a small School of about 260. Girls were first admitted in 1969 and the school is now fully co-educational. It is inter-denominational and is governed by a Board of people prominent in education, industry and the professions. There is a vigorous Parents' Association with representation on the Governing Body.

Patron: His Grace The Duke of Devonshire, MC, JP

President: The Rt Revd Ian Harland, former Lord Bishop of Carlisle

Members of the School Governors:

N J Wilford, FRICS (*Chairman*)
J Ackerley, BA
Lt Col R M Bend, CEng, MIMechE, RE
Mrs L Burton, BA
H S Johnson, Hon DLitt
T H F Kirby, BSc
Mrs B A Parks
I M Small, BA, FRSA
R G L Waller, BA
R Wickson
A J Gill (*Solicitor and Secretary*)

***Headmaster:* Dr S D Tommis**, MA, DPhil, FRGS

Deputy Head: Mrs K Warde, BSc

Senior Master: S R Barber, BA, MA *Head of History; Round Square Representative*

Senior Mistress: Ms J M Richardson, BA *Head of English & Drama*

Director of Studies: Dr L J Whyte, BSc, PhD *Head of Science; Head of Chemistry*

Head of Sixth Form: Mrs D H Wainwright, BA, DipSpLD *Head of Dyslexia Unit, Geography*

Assistant Staff:

Agriculture:
B J Edward, BEd, CertHort (RHS) *Farm Manager, Agriculture and Junior Science*

Art:
J Rattigan, BA, DipArtHist *Head of Art; Media Studies*
Mrs S Dymock, BA *Art, Pottery*

* Head of Department	§ Part Time or Visiting
† Housemaster/Housemistress	¶ Old Pupil
‡ See below list of staff for meaning	

Business Studies:
T E Palmer, BA *Head of Business Studies; Head of Outdoor Education*

Dyslexia:
Mrs D H Wainwright, BA, DipSpLD *Head of Dyslexia Unit; Head of Sixth Form, Geography*
Mrs J Okell, BSc *Mathematics*
Mrs L Donnachie, BSc

English:
Ms J M Richardson, BA *Head of English & Drama*
Mrs S McCook, BEd
P A Fox, BA *Media Studies*

Equestrian:
Mrs S Pendleton, BHSAI/BHSISM *Equestrian Manager*

Geography:
Ms M Chadbourne, BA *Head of Geography*
Mrs D H Wainwright, BA, DipSpLD *Head of Dyslexia Unit; Head of Sixth Form; Geography*
A F Nutt, BA (*+History*)

History:
S R Barber, BA, MA, DipEd *Head of History*
A F Nutt, BA (*+Geography*)
Mrs N Knott, BA (*+RE/PSE*)

Information Technology:
H McCook, BSc, MSc, MRSC, GradBCS *Head of Information Technology*
A R Checkett, BSc, MA, CPhys, MInstP
S Langford, BSc

Junior School:
Mrs M M Shermer, CertEd *Head of Junior School; Housemistress of Orchard Girls' House*
Mrs S Wood, BEd
Miss L Coates, BEd

Library:
Mrs B J Griffin, BA, DipM, ALA *Housemistress of Clownholme Boarders*

Mathematics:
G C Selwyn, BEd *Head of Mathematics; Internal Examinations Officer*
S Langford, BSc *Resident House Tutor of Grafton House*
A L Griffiths, BEng

Modern Languages:
C J Sassi, BA, MA *Head of Modern Languages; Spanish Co-ordinator of Activities; Housemaster of Millholme Boys' House*
Miss M Y Spencer, BA, PDESL (*French*); *English as a Foreign Language*
Ms E A Mullan, BA (*French*); *Housemistress of Orchard Day Girls*
M Lund, BA (*German*)

Music:
T J Moon, BA, ARCO, ARCM *Director of Music*
Ms J M Henbest, MA, CTABRSM *Assistant Director of Music*
T Williams, BA

PE:
S D Kibler, BA *Head of Boys' PE*

Miss R E Jackson, BA *Residential House Tutor of Orchard House*
Mrs K Warde, BSc *Deputy Head*

Religious Studies/PSHE:
Mrs N Knott, BA *History; Girls' Games*

Science:
Dr L J Whyte, BSc, PhD *Head of Science; Head of Chemistry*
W G R Bain, BA, MA *Housemaster of Grafton Boys' House*
A R Checkett, BSc, MA, CPhys, MInstP *Head of Physics; External Examinations Officer*
J R W Heppell, BSc *Head of Biology; Housemaster of Grafton Day Boys*
Mrs L O Wheeldon *Laboratory Technician*

Technology:
E C Shermer, BA *Head of Technology*

Visting Music Staff:
Mrs B Boyden (*Singing*)
M H Chilton (*Brass*)
Miss S Freeman (*Saxophone*)
D Gore (*Guitar*)
Mrs S Hardie (*Piano*)
I Otley (*Woodwind*)
D Simpson (*Percussion*)
Mrs S Stewart (*Violin and Viola*)
Mrs J Young (*Flute*)

Administrative Staff:

Bursar: Mr A P Upton
Bursar's Secretary: Mrs I Clouston
Headmaster's Secretary: Mrs E Ferriday
Accounts Manager: Mr I Hitch
School Medical Officer: Dr A A Burlinson, MBBS, DRCOG
Health Centre Sister: Mrs E Linton, RGN, SCM
Assistant Health Centre Nurses: Mrs J P Chatfield/Mrs A Macbain
School Secretary: Miss S Brooks
School Receptionist: Miss S Somers
Residential Services Manager: Mr N Winn

Number in school. Co-educational, with 260 pupils.

Educational philosophy. It has always been our aim to educate the whole person in the true sense that education is about rounded opportunities and experiences. Activities and outdoor education therefore play an important part in the curriculum alongside the academic work.

Buildings and Estate. The school estate consists of 140 acres with 20 acres of playing fields circumscribed within a meander of the River Dove. The working farm occupies 80 acres and the balance is given over to a combination of the equestrian centre and school buildings. Many pupils are given considerable responsibility in livestock management and horse husbandry if that is their preference. In addition there are dedicated classroom areas for each subject, including five specialist Science laboratories, a technology centre, computer suites, a fully equipped sports hall, facilities for the creative arts and a purpose built studio theatre.

In the main building there is an attractive chapel that is also the venue for concerts, a large and recently refurbished dining hall, and a library which houses over 10,000 volumes. The school also possesses a swimming pool and a fully equipped Health Centre with a resident, qualified nurse who is available to all pupils.

There are four boarding houses, two each for boys and girls. Most accommodate all-age pupils (11-18 years) and each has a resident Houseparent and three have a resident house tutor. Each house is well equipped with bathrooms and showers, common rooms and kitchens in which pupils can prepare light snacks. There are no boarding pupils under the age of 11 years.

In the main building, there is an attractive Chapel/concert hall, the Dining Hall, and a Library which houses over 10,000 volumes. The School also possesses a swimming pool and a fully-equipped sanatorium with a resident nursing sister. A new theatre was completed in September 1999.

Structure. There are two major units to the school.

The Junior School (7-11 years) is housed in a building separate from the Senior School but within the estate so that pupils have easy access to all the facilities of the Senior School. Entry is normally at 7+ years but pupils are also taken up to 10 years.

The Senior School (11-18 years) occupies the greater proportion of the school estate and normally takes pupils at 11+, 13+ and 16+ but other points of entry are always considered. Class sizes do not exceed 20 pupils and the Sixth Form averages about 75 pupils each year.

Curriculum. It is a particular feature of the school that the curriculum embraces Outdoor Education and activities as a normal part of school life and integrates them into the weekly timetable. In the Junior School there is a developed system of literacy and numeracy and subjects such as History and Geography are taught via topics. Differentiation is a key feature of the teaching strategy. French is introduced at this level.

In the Senior School pupils are introduced to a broad range of subjects so they can make rational choices later. Spanish is currently made available in Year 8. In Year 9 pupils make choices for GCSE from a structure consisting of compulsory core subjects and several options. A normal diet would be 11 GCSE subjects. ICT is compulsory from the Fourth Form as an examinable subject, and at all levels Religion and PSE are taught. Breadth and balance are two important principles shaping the curriculum.

In the Sixth Form a comprehensive range of AS and A2 subjects are taught. Most pupils take four AS subjects in the LVI, reducing to three A2 subjects in the UVI. General Studies and Key Skills ICT (at level 3 and above) are taught to all. Virtually all proceed to university each year and there is a fine record of admissions to Oxford and Cambridge.

Tuition in a wide range of musical instruments is available to all pupils from 7 years upwards.

Out of class. Rugby, Hockey, Soccer, Cricket, Netball, Rounders, Tennis, Cross-Country and Athletics are the main games. Full use is made of the estate and countryside through an extensive programme of Outdoor Education. Pupils are introduced to camping, canoeing, rock-climbing and caving. Many are involved in the Duke of Edinburgh's Award Scheme, and all participate in two expeditions per year in mountain country. There is also a full riding programme with an exercise manège and pupils may stable their own horses at the school.

Many clubs and hobby activities flourish, including Photography, Clay-Pigeon Shooting, Pottery, Electronics, Fishing, Computing and Drama. Major play productions are staged regularly, either in the theatre or outside in the Summer term.

Responsibilities and Service. Everyone is entrusted with a definite responsibility in the community, so that a sense of community is widely spread. Prefects are elected by staff and VIth formers and they head a daily duty team on which all pupils from the Vth form and above have the opportunity to serve.

Throughout the year the School is responsible for various community service tasks and a number of pupils from the senior school undertake specific projects with elderly and young people, as well as the handicapped. Abbotsholme also belongs to Round Square, an international association of schools which place great emphasis on service to the community and overseas. Regular opportunities for pupil exchanges overseas are thus provided.

Careers and Higher Education. There is a team of staff, headed by the Head of Careers, available to give advice to all pupils in the school and particularly the Sixth Form. The Careers rooms are fully computerised and a wide stock of literature is available. ISCO is used in the Fifth Form and above.

Overseas Students. The school welcomes students from overseas, whether of foreign nationality or British expatriates. Entrance examination papers are sent to overseas schools whenever requested, and full assistance is provided with travel arrangements to and from airports.

Abbotsholme Arts Society. The school is host to an outstanding Arts Society, membership of which is open to the general public on a subscription basis. Usually about 12 recitals per year are given by musicians of international renown, and pupils may attend all concerts free of charge.

School fees. As of September 2000 the fees structure is:

Junior School: £1,896 per term for day pupils. Senior School: £2,336 to £3,237 per term for day pupils. £4,588 to £4,840 per term for boarding pupils.

Scholarships. (*see* Entrance Scholarship section) There are a number of scholarships for entry at 9+, 11+ and 13+ that are awarded by competitive examination at the end of January each year. Scholarships into the Sixth Form are available as a result of examinations held in mid March each year.

Bursaries. For those in financial hardship there is a number of bursaries available which are means-tested and reviewed each year by the Bursar and Headmaster.

Applications for Scholarships and Bursaries should be made to the Headmaster's Secretary.

The Abbotsholmians' Club. The Old Abbotsholmians have a meeting at the school every term, and regular social events elsewhere. Former pupils include H G Selfridge, Olaf Stapleton, Sir Stanley Unwin, Jeremy Kemp and Sir Peter Platt.

Charitable status. Abbotsholme School is a Registered Charity, number 528612. It believes strongly in the education of the whole man and woman. Its programmes of academic excellence, athletic skills, community service and outdoor education are fully committed to the achievement of this aim.

Abingdon School

Abingdon Oxfordshire OX14 1DE
Tel: (01235) 521563 (School); (01235) 849041/849078 (Admissions)
Fax: (01235) 849077 (Headmaster); (01235) 849029 (Bursary); (01235) 849079 (School); (01235) 849085 (Registry)
e-mail: hm.sec@abingdonschool.co.uk
e-mail: registrar@abingdon.org.uk
website: http://www.abingdon.org.uk

The foundation of the School appears to date from the twelfth century; the first clear documentary reference occurs in 1256. After the dissolution of Abingdon Abbey, the School was re-endowed in 1563 by John Roysse, of the Mercers' Company in London. It was rebuilt in 1870 on its present site, and further buildings have been added in recent years. Abingdon's Junior School, known as Josca's (see IAPS section), is situated at Frilford, near Abingdon. The total establishment numbers nearly 100 boys.

Stewards:
J W Greening
Mr and Mrs Q M E Hoodless
Mrs T Hendley

Governing Body:
The Rt Hon F A A Maude, MP (*Chairman*)
C R Dick (*Vice-Chairman*)
J N Driver (*Vice-Chairman*)
The Mayor of Abingdon
The Master of Christ's Hospital, Abingdon
R W Ainsworth, DPhil
C Belson
H A F Buxton
D Christie
Miss J E Cranston
O Darbishire
E Ferguson
Sir Andrew Hugh Smith
Mrs V Kelly
D P Lillycrop
T A Marsh
M W Matthews
C J W Owen
G M M Wakeford, OBE
P R Williams, CBE, PhD, DL

Clerk to the Governors: T J Pegram, MA

***Headmaster:* M St John Parker**, MA

Headmaster-elect: M Turner, MA (*from January 2002*)

Second Master: T R Ayling, MA
Second Deputy Head: T J King, MA, DPhil, FIBiol, FLS, FRGS
Director of Studies: D J Dawswell, BSc
Chaplain: The Revd T P Lewis, MA
Upper Master: A D Watkins, BEd, MPhil, MEd
Middle Master: M D Martin, BA
Master of Scholars: R S Elliott, MA, LGSM

Housemasters:

Boarders:
School House: B A H Figgis, BA
Waste Court: W T Phelps, BA
Crescent House: S P Davies, MA

Dayboys:
J D E Drummond-Hay, BEd
P J Wilmore, BSc, PhD
R S K Mearns, MA, MLitt, LLB
J Townsend, MA
I C Fishpool, BSc, FRGS
T J C Garnier, BSc

Lower School:
A M Broadbent, BEd
R S Slatford, BSc, BA

Assistant Masters:
N A F Pritchard, MA
R C B Coleman, MA
D J Haynes, MA
G G Barrett, MA
C J Biggs, BA
P Willerton, MA
W H Zawadzki, MA, DPhil, FRHistS
I A Macdonald, BA
G C Rolfe, BA, DPhil
N J Brown, MA
K D Bingham, BA, DPhil
R P Finch, BA
The Revd C M Manship, BMus, FRCO, GRSM, ARCM, CertTheol
N M Revill, BA
A J Mansfield, BSc
Mrs A M Soper, MA
R G Hofton, MA
M A Stinton, MA, ARCM, LRAM
J F Henderson, BA
Mrs J E Fishpool, MA
R J Strawson, MA, BSc
D J Pope, MA
S A Evans, BA
P K H Raffell, MSc
S C White, MA, BSc
R S Hamilton, BEd
P E Richardson, BSc, MSc
D Evans, BA
S Hullis, MA
Mrs S Wigmore, BEd
T C Gunn, BA, PhD
J H Taylor, BA
Mrs M M Hankey, BA
S P Ocock, BA
K J Spencer, BSc
A P Swarbrick, BA, MPhil

D G Aitken, BA
A J P English, BA, MLitt
J P G Brooks, BSc
N J Hele, BA
A J Jenkins, MA
J F Bromley, BA
S P G Spratling, BA
D J T Franklin, MA
S R Whalley, MA
J P Nairne, BFA
D Forster, MA
M R Webb, BSc
M Schofield, BSc
P R Williams, BA

Librarian: Mrs G J Cooper, BSc

Part-time:
Mrs M Pringle, MMus, FTCL, LRAM
Mrs S E Finnimore, MA
Dr C J May, BA, PhD
Mrs J P Jelley, BSocSc
Miss F Parker, LLCM
P A Kilby

Bursar: Commander R F M Jackson, FCIS, RN

Estates Bursar: D J M Carson

Domestic Bursar: J Casselden

Registrar: Mrs F M Rutland, MA

Foundation Development Director: Mrs E H W Curran

Medical Officer: D R May, MA, BM, BCh, DRCOG, MRCGR

There are some 800 boys in the Senior School, of whom about a fifth are boarders.

Boarding. The boarding side is organised in three houses, School House (Mr B A H Figgis), Waste Court (Mr W T Phelps), Crescent House (Mr S P Davies). The School values its boarding element very highly, and has recently completed a major programme of reconstruction and reorganisation of the boarding side, involving the conversion of existing accommodation and the development of new facilities. Weekly boarding features positively as part of a policy aimed at asserting a distinctive regional identity for the School.

Pastoral Care. The Lower School has a self-contained system of pastoral care, led by two housemasters. All boys join a senior house on entering the Middle School. Within the house system there are distinct tutoring arrangements for Middle School and Upper School boys, which are co-ordinated by the Middle Master and Upper Master respectively. Special stress is placed on the value of parental involvement, and also on the provision of careers guidance at appropriate points in a boy's development. Great importance is attached to pastoral care and the School's teaching philosophy is based on a tutorial approach.

Land and Buildings. The School is surrounded by 35 acres of its own grounds, yet is within a few hundred yards of the historic centre of Abingdon, which lies 6 miles down the Thames from Oxford. A further 30 acres of playing fields are located at Frilford, three miles from Abingdon.

The last quarter century has seen a considerable expansion in the School's stock of buildings. A recent major development is Mercers' Court, which celebrates the School's historical link with the Mercers' Company of London. Planning is well advanced for major extensions to the existing Arts Centre, to provide additional space for music, art and drama.

Courses of Study. The School is essentially academic in character and intention, and levels of both expectation and achievement are high. Subjects taught include English, history, French, Russian, German, Latin, Greek, ancient history, economics, geography, mathematics, physics, chemistry, biology, art, religious studies, music and theatre studies. Design and technology, and information and communications technology play significant roles in the curriculum. The economics department teaches economics and business studies to A level, and is developing close ties with local industry and commerce. The School is well equipped with computing facilities and audio-visual teaching aids.

All boys spend three years in the Middle School (13 to 16 year-olds), in which many different subject combinations are possible, and there is no specialisation before A level. In the VIth form many boys combine courses in arts and sciences; four subjects are normally taken at AS in the Lower Sixth, followed by four at A2 in the Upper Sixth. Classroom teaching at all levels is supplemented by a programme of specialist lectures and outside visits. In general terms, the curriculum aims to combine academic discipline and excellence with the fullest encouragement of a wide range of interests and pursuits.

Games and Activities. The School enjoys some 60 acres of playing fields, and has its own sports hall, swimming pool, and boathouse on the River Thames. The major sports are rowing, rugby, cricket, hockey, tennis, athletics and cross-country. Special success has been achieved recently in badminton and shooting. Other minor sports include sailing, golf, fencing and fives.

Importance is attached to the development of a sense of social responsibility, through voluntary membership of Community Service and the Duke of Edinburgh's Award Schemes. There is a contingent of the Combined Cadet Force based on voluntary recruitment.

There are numerous societies catering for all kinds of interests and enthusiasms. Music is particularly strong, with over half the boys taking instrumental or vocal lessons in the School. In addition to the Chapel Choir, Choral Society and three orchestras, there are excellent opportunities for ensemble playing, including jazz.

Religion. The School is Anglican by tradition, but boys of other denominations are welcome, and normally attend the short non-denominational service with which the working day begins.

Health. The School has its own doctor and there is a well-equipped sanatorium in the School grounds. In cases of emergency boys are admitted to the John Radcliffe Hospital, Oxford.

Admission. The normal ages of entry to the Senior School are 11, 13 and 16; there are from time to time chance vacancies at other ages. Registration at age 9 or 10 is recommended. The Junior School (Josca's) has its own entrance arrangements - see entry under the IAPS section, Part V of this Book.

Details of the entrance examination procedures for 11- and 13-year-old candidates are available from the Registry. Entry to the Sixth Form at 16 generally depends on a successful showing at GCSE level as well as on an interview and a report from the previous school.

Term of Entry. Boys may be accepted in any of the three terms if vacancies are available in their age group; however, September is the usual date of entry, and is preferred by the School.

Fees. The tuition fee, for dayboys, is £7,779 a year. This includes the cost of lunches and textbooks.

For boarders, the total fee (including tuition and all extras except for instrumental music lessons and some disbursements directly incurred by individual boys) is £14,208.

Scholarships. (*see* Entrance Scholarship section) The School offers a number of means-tested Scholarships at ages 13 and 16; full details are published in the spring of each year, and are available, on application, from the Registry.

The School also offers a small number of Foundation Places for the two years of the Lower School.

Honours. Oxford and Cambridge 2000: 22 offers.

Old Abingdonian Club. Membership Secretary: Mr H T Randolph; Administrator: Mrs E H W Curran, both c/o Abingdon School.

Charitable status. Abingdon School Limited is a Registered Charity, number 1071298. It exists to provide educational opportunities which are open to talented boys without regard to their families' economic standing. Its curriculum is designed to promote intellectual rigorousness, personal versatility and social responsibility.

Ackworth School

Ackworth Pontefract West Yorkshire WF7 7LT
Tel: (01977) 611401
Fax: (01977) 616225
e-mail: ackworthq@aol.com
website: http://www.ackworthw-yorks.sch.uk

This co-educational boarding and day school was founded in 1779 and occupies a large rural estate which surrounds the gracious Georgian buildings and spacious gardens and playing fields that form the School Campus. It is one of the seven Quaker Schools in England.

Governing Body: Members appointed by The Religious Society of Friends

Clerk: Grace Hunter

Secretary and Bursar: Christopher Jones, ACIB

Full time Teaching Staff:

Head: **Martin J Dickinson**, MA, PGCE

Deputy Head: Lorna Anthony, BSc, PGCE

Director of Studies: John Wooffindin, BA, DipEd

Heads of Subject Departments and Heads of Boarding Houses:

Anthony Stroker, BA, MA, PhD (*English and Drama*)
Robert Hall, BSc (*Mathematics*)
Andrew Ward, BSc, PGCE (*Biology*)
Taras Anthony, BA (*Chemistry*)
Francis Hickenbottom, BSc, PGCE (*Physics*)
Colin Williams, BA, PGCE (*Modern Languages*)
Lionel Hill, CertEd (*Technology*)
David Palmer, BSc, PGCE (*Information Technology*)
Diana Rothwell, DipAD, ATC (*Art*)
Richard Ellis, BA, DipEd (*Music*)
Neville West, CertEd (*Religious Education*)
Thomas Plant, BA, PGCE (*History*)
Stephen Minihan, BA, PGCE (*Geography*)
Marion Mitchell, BA (*Business Studies*)
Martin Gosney, CertEd (*Physical Education*)
Julie Hoar, BEd (*Physical Education*)

Anne Wise (*Housemistress*)
Thomas Bootyman, BSc, PGCE (*Housemaster*)

Coram House (*Junior School*):
Lynda Sharpe, CertEd (*Head*)

§Librarian: Sally Brooks, BA, ALA
Sanatorium Sister: Janet Duffy, SRN
Medical Officer: Ivan P G Hanney, MB, BCh, BAO, DRCOG, DCH, MRCGP

There are 460 boys and girls from 4-18 years, 360 of whom are day pupils. About one tenth of the pupils are from Quaker homes and the School has long been open to boys and girls unconnected with the Society and they are now in the majority. The pattern of school life has as its basis the belief of Quakers that religion and life are one: that this spiritual conviction directly affects the way in which people behave toward each other and determines their attitude to life in general. While the life of the School is, therefore, based on Quakers' interpretation of Christianity, the approach is broad based and open minded, for the life of the community is enriched by contributions made by those of other denominations and faiths, and they are always welcomed into the School. Although all pupils attend school assemblies and Meetings for Worship, arrangements can generally be made for pupils to worship in their own churches and boys and girls can be prepared for confirmation.

Houses. Boys and girls live separately in two houses with resident house staff and matrons responsible for their welfare.

Curriculum. The School provides for those with the ability to study courses leading to the GCSE and Advanced level. There is a wide range of subjects taken below the Sixth form. French and German are the main foreign languages taught. A 25 station Computer Room is in operation and there are six recently modernised Science laboratories. There is a strong Music department and group instrumental tuition is part of the first year course, Design & Technology and Art are well provided for and all these are an integral part of the common core curriculum. The heated swimming bath is used throughout the year, there is a modern Sports Centre and spacious playing fields. A large academic Sixth form prepares students for entry to Universities and life is enriched by students from other countries taking advantage of what is offered.

Leisure Time. There are many clubs and societies which cater for most tastes and age groups and the facilities for Crafts, Art and Music are freely available outside the teaching day. Team and individual sports are widely available to all. There is a very full programme of weekend activities and visits.

Buildings. A policy of expansion and upgrading has been maintained over the years. Within the last decade, study accommodation for Sixth formers has been enlarged and modernised and boarding facilities have been upgraded to meet current demands. Advanced Science laboratories have been re-equipped, Art and Craft provision is well established with a new Design & Technology Centre opened in 1996, and the spacious, well appointed study, reference and careers library caters for all age groups. A superb modern Sports Centre and a fully resourced Information Technology Centre are in constant use. A new Music Centre was opened in early 1994 and provides spacious facilities for our musicians. The school has recently refurbished its theatre.

Scholarships and Bursaries (*see* Entrance Scholarship section). A number of awards are made each year to selected boys and girls entering the School. These are awarded to those with high academic ability and to those who show exceptional talent in Art or Music. These vary in value up to 50% of the School day fees. Bursaries are available to members of the Society of Friends and others according to need. There are Travel Scholarships for those completing their first year in the Sixth.

Admission. Interested parents will be sent a prospectus upon application to the Head and a visit can always be arranged promptly. There are also three Open Mornings and one Open Afternoon in the year at which parents and families are welcome for a tour and opportunity to talk to staff and pupils. Pupils for entry at age 7 and above take the School's entrance test. Entry at 4 is based on interview. The majority of senior school children enter at the age of 11+ but there is also a sizeable entrance at 12, 13, 14 and 16+. Entry is always possible at other ages if places are available, and there is a direct entry into the Sixth Form for pupils who are able to take the full two year A-level course.

Junior School. For day boys and girls aged 4 to 11, the majority of whom move on into the Senior School.

Fees per term. Junior School (Day) £1,228; Senior School (Boarding) £4,011; Senior School (Day) £2,281. The day pupil fees include lunch (and other meals if required).

The Ackworth Old Scholars' Association. This is a

flourishing Association with a membership of over two thousand. Annual gatherings are held at Ackworth at Easter and there are Guild Meetings held in the regions at other times in the year. General Secretary, John Banks, Carpendale, 42 Pinkneys Drive, Pinkneys Green, Maidenhead, Berks SL6 6QE.

Charitable status. Ackworth is a Registered Charity, number 529280. It was established for the purpose of providing independent education.

Aldenham School

Elstree Herts. WD6 3AJ.
Tel: (01923) 858122
Fax: (01923) 854410
website: www.aldenham.com
Station: Radlett (British Rail) 20 minutes from Kings Cross Midland.
Heathrow Airport: 35 minutes.

The School was founded in 1597 by Richard Platt, 'Cytyzen and Brewer of London.' The Founder originally endowed his Foundation with 'All those three Pastures of Ground lying nighe the Churche of St Pancrasse in the County of Mid'x. besides London . . . together with all and singular Woods, Underwoods, Hedgrowes, Trees and Ponds, Waters and Fishings in or upon the same P'emysses'.

Motto: *'In God is all our Trust'.*

Governing Body:

Chairman: J H Wells, DL, JP, MA

H W Whitbread, MBA, BA
Field Marshal The Lord Vincent, GBE, KCB, DSO (*OA*)
J S Lewis
D A Longbottom
M Hodgson
A Kilkerr
V Davies
R Munyard
P J Easby
S H Wingfield Digby
R C Nolan
B Watkins
Mrs A Butler
R H B Neame, CB, DL
¶J Woodrow, LLB
S J B Redman
D Ross

***Headmaster:* R S Harman**, MA

First Deputy Head: K Jones, MA

Second Deputy Head: N Roskilly, BA

Head of Sixth Form & Careers: H N Dymock, BA, MA

Heads of Department:
M D L Hancock, BA (*Art*)
C W Gray, BSc (*Biology*)
M J Field, CertEd (*Business Studies*)
S P Williams, MA (*Chemistry*)
S Morris, BA (*English*)
A P Stephenson, BA (*Games and Physical Education*)
Mrs N Touhey, BA (*Geography*)
T Lello, BA, MA (*History*)
M A Burley, BSc (*Maths*)
D Short, BA (*Modern Languages*)
R A C Pomeroy, BSc (*Physics*)
D S Watts, MA, CChem, MRSC (*Sciences*)
E A Cockerill, BEd (*Design Technology*)
The Revd A M Stead, BA (*Theology*)
E D Walker, BA (*Information Technology & Co-ordinator of Information Technology*)
A R Leigh, MA (*Special Needs*)
Mrs J Harris (*Principal of Pre-Prep and Nursery School*)

Chaplain: Revd A M Stead, BA

Director of Music: J R Wyatt, GRSM, LRAM, ARCO

Librarian: Mrs S A Price, BA, ALA

Bursar: A W C Fraser, FCIS

Number in School. 415, of which 114 are boarders, 10 dayboarders and 291 day pupils. (There are 15 girls in the 6th form).

Boarding Houses. *McGill's* (Mr W R J Waite); *Beevor's* (Mr D B G Boothby); *Kennedy's* (Mr J Coates); *Paull's* (Mr N D Pulman).

Day Houses. *Paull's* (Mr N D Pulman), *Leeman's* (Mr P W Bounsall), *Riding's* (Mr D S Watts).

Junior House (Day). *Martineau's* (Mr M J Langston).

Aldenham is situated in its own beautiful 135 acre site in the Hertfordshire green belt, with excellent access to London (ThamesLink/Jubilee Line) and close to the M1 and M25. Aldenham's particular reputation as a close knit, small and supportive community with a strong boarding ethos makes it the very best environment for a high quality all-round education encouraging children to enterprise. The achievement of every child's academic potential remains central but the building of confidence comes too from sports, music and drama, and by living and working together within the disciplined and vigorous community that is Aldenham today.

Admission. The first step towards gaining a place is to visit the School. The feel of the School is only properly captured by seeing and talking to pupils at work and meeting with those who will be responsible for your son's and daughter's education. In September 2000 Aldenham opened a Pre-Preparatory department up to 7 years as an extension of the long established nursery facility.

At 11, entry is by tests and interview, at 13 by Common Entrance or the School's Special Test, and at 16 by Entry Test, interview and GCSE results. Girls are admitted into the Sixth Form. Scholarships and Bursaries are available at each point of entry. Every effort is made to meet parents' wishes as regards which House is chosen for their son or daughter. Applications for admissions and all correspondence concerning entries should be addressed to Janet Scott, Headmaster's Secretary.

Fees. Registration fee £50; Deposit £900. Boarders £4,830 per term; Day boarders, £4,000 per term; Day Pupils £3,405; Junior House, £2,275; Junior Boarders £3,425. These fees include most compulsory extras.

Scholarships and other awards. (*see* Entrance Scholarship section) Scholarships and Exhibitions are awarded to pupils who have shown outstanding achievement and who have the potential to make a special contribution to Aldenham. These fields of excellence include art, music, technology and sport, as well as the traditional range of academic subjects.

Bursaries are available to help pupils who will benefit from an education at Aldenham but whose parents would not otherwise be able to afford to pay the full fees. They are also used to help in cases where parents' financial circumstances have changed during their son's or daughter's time at the School. These Bursaries include the Lloyd's Cuthbert Heath awards, generous awards made available by the Brewers' Company and awards made by the OA War Memorial Fund. Awards vary from approximately one sixth to two thirds of the fees. Additional Bursaries are available at Sixth Form level, including 4 Millennium Scholarships.

Curriculum. From 11 to 16 the timetable closely reflects the National Curriculum. Boys are prepared for GCSEs across a range of subjects including Maths, English, French, Science and a number of other Arts and language options. Care is taken that all boys include Art, Music, Technology and Computing in their programme and there is a progressive course of Theology throughout the School with GCSE taken in the 5th form. The aim is to ensure that subject choices affecting AS/A2 levels are made as late as possible and the ISCO programme of Tests and interview are used as a basis for career planning and AS/A2 level choice in the 5th form year.

Those in the Lower Sixth Form normally take 4 AS levels from a range of 16 subjects, which narrows to three choices at A2 in the Upper Sixth Year. These will be supplemented with general studies and a key skills programme, which will support learning in all subject areas. In combination with the extensive extra-curricular programme, work experience and UCAS advice, the curriculum in the Sixth Form continues to give pupils their best opportunities for university entry. The majority go on to degree courses at universities. There are regular successes at Oxford and Cambridge. All those in the Sixth Form attend an Introduction to Industry Conference, and Aldenham runs a European wide Work Experience Scheme.

Games and Other Activities. Great value is placed on the participation of every pupil in Games and Activities. A programme integrated into the working week offers enormous variety across all ages. The School has a fine record in traditional team games, and a floodlit Artificial Turf Pitch was opened by HRH The Princess Royal in November 1998. Soccer, Hockey, Cricket and Athletics are the major sports for boys, whilst girls benefit from a breadth of in and out of school activities including Tennis, Badminton, Squash, Trampolining, Aerobics and Sailing. In addition there is a full programme of House and School competition in Squash, Eton Fives, Basketball, Tennis, Sailing, Fencing, Badminton, Table Tennis, Shooting, Swimming, Cross-country. Volleyball, Climbing, Judo and Golf are also available. The Sports Hall provides excellent facilities for expert and novice alike and incorporates a full size indoor hockey pitch and a rifle range. Time is set apart for activities and societies; these include Adventure activities, the Duke of Edinburgh Award Scheme, Community Service, Electronics, Chess, Computing, Motor Club, Photography and Model Railway. The Debating and Philosophy societies meet regularly through the winter.

Music and Drama. Music flourishes in the School. A third of the School take individual instrumental tuition. There is a Chapel Choir, School Orchestra and wind and brass groups. A spring concert is performed annually, recently taking place in the Barbican concert hall to celebrate the School's Quatercentenary, and in The Coliseum, Watford in 2000. A number of boys and girls learn to play on the fine, modern, 3-manual pipe organ in the Chapel. A new music school with practice and performance facilities opened in September 2000.

As well as an annual School Play there are Senior and Junior House Play competitions and boys and girls are encouraged to produce and design as well as to perform in the various productions. The School's proximity to London makes possible frequent visits to theatres and concerts. Theatre Studies is offered as a full A level subject.

Organisation. Whilst the framework of the School is contemporary, it takes as its basis the long established 'House' system. Each House creates an extended family and provides the formal and social focus of the School. There are three boarding and three day Houses together with a distinct yet fully integrated Junior House for 11–13 year olds. Each has a Housemaster and a team of tutors so every pupil has a personal tutor. In the Boarding Houses the Housemaster, his family, Matron and tutors live at the centre of the community ensuring the well-being of each child.

Boarding. Aldenham recognises that each option in education is right for different children and therefore offers a number of opportunities for families within a traditional framework of Day and Boarding. Aldenham's unique array of day and boarding options enables it to provide the educational benefits of a boarding school to Day and Day Boarding pupils and to offer real flexibility with its arrangements for boarders, 95% of whom live within 20 miles of the School. Boys may board from entry at 11+.

Religion. Aldenham is a Church of England foundation and seeks to maintain a strong Christian ethos to which those of other faiths are warmly welcomed.

A fully illustrated prospectus is available on request from the Headmaster's Secretary, and prospective parents are encouraged to visit the School with their sons and daughters, either individually or at one of the school's 2 open days in June and September.

Old Aldenhamian Society. There is a thriving Old Aldenhamian Society. Further details from the Secretary at the School from whom the 12th edition of the Aldenham School Register is available.

Charitable status. The Aldenham School Company is a Registered Charity, number 298140. It exists to provide high quality education and pastoral care to enable children to achieve their full potential in later life.

Alleyn's School

Dulwich London SE22 8SU
Tel: Headmaster: 020 8557 1500
Bursar: (Mr T Mawhinney) 020 8557 1450
Common Room: 020 8557 1454
Fax: 020 8557 1462
e-mail: alleyns@rmplc.co.uk
website: www.alleyns.org.uk

The School is part of the foundation known as 'Alleyn's College of God's Gift' which was founded by Edward Alleyn, the Elizabethan actor in 1619.

Motto: *Detur gloria soli Deo.*

The Governing Body:

Chairman: R G Gray, MA

Miss J E L Baird, OBE, MA, FEIS
Admiral Sir Michael C Boyce, GCB, OBE
Mrs M C H Campbell, BVetMed, MA, MRCVS
R J R Cousins, BSc(Eng), FICE, FRSA
T Franey, FIMI
C Holloway, MA
Miss A M Horne, LLB
A K Kakkar, BSc, PhD, FRCS
R Ling, FCA, FCMA, FIOD
Prof M Meredith Smith, PhD, DSc, FLS
J F Pretlove
H J C Pulley, MA, FCII

***Headmaster:* C H R Niven**, MA (Cantab), DipEd (Oxon), L-ès-L (Nancy), Dr de l'Univ (Lille), FRSA

Deputy Headmaster: P C Thompson, MA

Assistants:
Ms A K S Ackerman, MA (*Religious Studies*)
Miss C L Alexander, MA (*English*)
R J Alldrick, BA (*Co-ordinator of Duke of Edinburgh Award Scheme & Field Centre*)
§C J Arch, BSc (*Chemistry*)

§Mrs S E Arthur, BSc (*Chemistry*)
*P J Barlow, MA, CertCouns (*Head of Classics*)
K C Beckley, MSc (*Biology*)
Miss A L Boltsa, BA (*Art*)
Mrs J K Bowen-Jones, BSc (*Deputy Head of Middle School, Biology, Head of Health Education*)
*Miss C L Bracken, BSc, MSc (*Head of Mathematics*)
A M Bruni, BSc, BEd (*Mathematics*)
*Mrs G Burtenshaw (*Deputy Head of Lower School, Head of Food Studies*)
§Mrs J Cary Elwes, BA (*English*)
†Miss S P Chandler, BSc (*Housemistress of Dutton's, PE*)
*F H L Chow, BSc, DPhil (*Head of Biology*)
Miss S G Clark, BA (*English, Drama*)
Mrs H Clarke, BSc, PhD (*Physics*)
§Miss J Clarke, BA (*Art*)
P M Cochrane, BSc (*Chemistry*)
*Miss W L Collins, BSc (*Head of Chemistry*)
Ms S B Connolly, BA (*Music*)
Revd S C Dalwood, BA (*Mathematics*)
D M Davies, BSc (*Physics*)
Miss A Day, BSc (*Physics*)
Miss J M Debenham, BA (*Modern Languages*)
†M Fosten, BA (*Housemaster of Roper's, Economics, Business Studies*))
P L Friedlander, DipAD (*Art*)
*Miss L J Gabitass, BA (*Head of English*)
Ms L Gardner, GRSM, LRAM (*Music*)
R L Geldeard, BA (*Classics*)
Miss S Goodenough, BA (*Modern Languages*)
M S Grant, MA (*English*)
Mrs E T Hall, BSc (*Examination Officer*)
Mrs P Hall, BA (*Spanish*)
†R G Halladay, BA (*Housemaster of Cribb's, English*)
§Miss A Hamburger, BA (*Art*)
Mrs J M Helm, BSc (*Deputy Head Upper School, Geography*)
*J Hodgkinson, MA (*English, Drama, Head of General Studies*)
Miss A M Hughes, MSc (*Information Technology*)
†E M D Jones, MA, BEd (*Housemaster of Spurgeon's, Geography, OC CCF*)
Revd J H Jones, MA (*Chaplain, Biology*)
A T Kermode, MA (*Director of Music*)
N R Kinnear, MA (*Mathematics*)
Miss M D Knowles, ALA (*Librarian*)
†Miss S A Lane, DipPE (*Housemistress of Brown's, PE*)
Miss A M Legg, BA (*English*)
Ms J Liddle, BA (*Design Technology*)
*C L Liffen, MA, MSc (*Deputy Head Resources, Head of Science*)
J G Lilly, BA (*History*)
*C P Long, BA (*Head of Geography*)
*Mrs N Long, BA (*Head of History*)
*P A Mackie, MA (*Head of Modern Languages*)
E D Mann, BA (*Mathematics*)
*M McCaffrey, BA (*Head of French*)
D R McGill, MA (*History*)
T G McNeal, BA, PGDipRNCM (*Music*)
*R N Ody, BEd (*Head of Boys' PE*)
Miss K J Owens, BEd (*Design Technology*)
Mrs S Patterson, MA (*History*)
Miss A Poole, BSc (*Mathematics*)
Mrs B Portwin, BA, MSc (*History, Politics*)
Miss C M L Preston, BA (*Modern Languages*)
Miss C Purvis, BSc (*Mathematics*)
§Mrs S Reeve (*Food Studies*)
*G Reid, MA (*Head of Religious Education, Head of PSHE*)
*Z A Rogalski, BA (*Head of Design Technology*)
Miss J C Savage, MA (*Geography*)
†P R Sherlock, DipPE (*Housemaster of Tulley's, PE*)
R J S Skelly, MA, DipSL (*English*)
J R Skidmore, BSc (*Chemistry*)
P A Smith, BMus, LRAM, ARCM (*Head of Instrumental Studies*)
P F Smith, BA (*Chemistry*)
Miss R M Smith, BA (*Modern Languages*)
†S E Smith, BA (*Headmaster of Lower School, Classics*)
A Sood-Smith, CertEd (*IT*)
*D P Stretton, BA, MSc (*Head of Economics and Business Studies*)
*R J D Sutton, MA (*Head of Art*)
*Miss C H Symes, BSc (*Head of IT*)
Mrs I Termanis, MA, DipLib (*Deputy Head Personnel, Modern Languages*)
†Mrs R A Thomson, BA (*Tyson's House, Religious Studies*)
T M Thomson, BEd (*Information Technology*)
†D J Tickner, BA (*Brading's House; English*)
*G J Tonkin, BA (*Head of Drama, English*)
§Mrs F E Twinn, BSc (*Geography*)
P J Venier, BEd (*Sports Hall Manager, PE*)
Miss M J Walker, BA (*Director of Sports*)
D E Wallis, MA, DPhil, CMath, MIMA (*Head of Upper School, Mathematics*)
T J R Walsh, BA, MPhil (*Classics*)
*J N C Walton, MSc (*Head of Physics*)
Miss S L Ward, BSc (*Biology, Psychology*)
Mrs C L Wells, BSc (*Mathematics*)
D P Williams, BA (*Art*)
*Mrs E M Wright, BA (*Head of German*)
A York, BSc, ARCS (*Head of Middle School, Physics*)

The School. Alleyn's is a day co-educational school for pupils aged 11 to 19 years, some 920 strong, of whom approximately 250 are in the Sixth Form. Alleyn's Junior School, for ages 4 to 10 years, opened in September 1992. The Headmaster is a member of the Headmasters' and Headmistresses' Conference.

It is, with Dulwich College, the lineal descendant of the School for 12 poor scholars endowed by Edward Alleyn, the Elizabethan actor manager, under a Royal Charter of 1619.

It was a Direct Grant school from 1958 until the abolition of this status in 1975; the Governors then opted for Independence and at the same time opened the entry to girl pupils. The school is now fully co-educational, with approximately equal numbers of boys and girls.

Entrance. A registration fee of £40 is charged for all applications.

(1) Admission to the School is by competitive examination open to both boys and girls at age 11, the normal age for transfer from primary to secondary school; entrance is decided on the basis of the examination held in January for entry the following September, report from the Head of previous school, and interview. Fee paying pupils enter by this means, and scholarships are given on the results of the entrance examination. The examination consists of a Reasoning paper, English Essay and Comprehension papers and a Mathematics paper. Candidates should be entered at the School before the New Year, for admission the next September.

(2) There is a smaller entry by examination open to both boys and girls at age 13. The procedure is similar to that for the 11 Year old entry, with the addition of papers in Languages and Science and the omission of Reasoning papers.

(3) Both girls and boys may enter the Sixth Form directly; entry is granted on satisfactory results at GCSE, recommendation by the candidate's previous Headteacher, and interview. An Upper School scholarship and a limited number of Upper School bursaries are now available.

(4) Opportunities for entry at other ages occur from time to time. Subject to the agreement of their Headteachers,

overseas candidates may take the entrance paper at their own schools by arrangement.

(5) At 4 and 7 Junior School places are awarded on the basis of interview, report and practical assessment during the Lent Term.

Fees. In September 2000, fees were £2,475 per term (£7,425 pa).

Scholarships. (*see* Entrance Scholarship section) Awards available for 2001 will include up to twelve major scholarships of half of the full fees. At least one scholarship will be awarded to a candidate showing particular talent in Music, Art and Sport and at least one on the results of the 13 year old examination.

Bursaries. The financial equivalent of up to 10 half-fee bursaries are awarded annually, normally at 11+, 13+ and 16+, for very able children.

Curriculum. A general education is given to all pupils in the first 3 years from age 11; this includes English, French, Latin, German/Spanish, History, Geography, Mathematics, Physics, Chemistry, Biology, Art, Music, Design Technology, Religious Education, Physical Education and Information Technology. In Years 10 and 11 leading to GCSE, all pupils will take English, English Literature, Mathematics, a Modern Foreign Language, History or Geography, and Science (Dual or Triple Award); in addition to these subjects a further two subjects are to be chosen from the total (17) available.

In the Upper School 4 main subjects are followed to AS level; in addition to those listed above, Business Studies, Economics, Classical Civilization, Computer Science and Theatre Studies are available. These also include Politics, Psychology, Media Studies, Philosophy and Sports Studies. In the Upper Sixth 3 or 4 A levels are taken. Most pupils also take General Studies at A level in Year 12. On the results obtained pupils are admitted to universities, medical and dental schools, Art Colleges, the Services' Colleges, industry and the professions. Some 95% enter Higher Education each year.

Selected pupils are prepared and entered for Colleges at Oxford and Cambridge, where a good record of places is maintained each year.

Organisation. The Lower School (Year 7 and Year 8) has its own separate building and its own Head. Pupils in the Upper and Middle Schools belong to one of eight Houses; Housemasters are responsible, not only for organised games, but also for the welfare of each of their pupils throughout their time in the school. This care is supplemented by a system of form tutors for supervision of academic progress and the giving of appropriate advice. Parents are invited to Open Evenings during the year, at which pupils' work and progress are discussed with the teaching staff. The Headmaster and all members of the teaching staff are available for private meetings by appointment.

Games. The School stands in its own grounds of 26 acres, affording adequate room for a wide variety of organised games; these include: Soccer, Hockey, Cricket, Swimming, Athletics, Netball, Cross-country running, Rugby Fives, Water Polo, Badminton, Fencing, Judo and Golf.

Religious Education. The Foundation belongs to the Church of England. Religious Education of a non-denominational nature is given throughout the school, and pupils also attend worship daily in Assembly and termly at Services in the Foundation Chapel. The School Chaplain holds a voluntary weekly Service of Holy Communion. They may be excused from religious education if parents request.

Buildings. The main school building dates from 1887. Extensive development since the 1960s provided a new Lower School Building, Dining Hall, Science Laboratories, an indoor heated swimming pool, Technology Centre, Sports Hall and Music School. In 1996 a new Mathematics suite and Sixth Form Centre were opened, followed by a new IT Suite. A new astro-turf has been added and a new pavilion has been built. An extended Literary and IT Resource Centre will open in 2001. The School has its own Field Centre near Buxton.

Libraries. The main Library is well stocked and is available to all pupils for private study.

Special Features. Particular attention is paid to the individual needs of pupils, including those with slight physical handicaps which do not detract from their ability to profit from an academic education. Psychological guidance and help is sought, whenever it appears necessary, from qualified educational psychologists.

Music, Drama and Art feature very strongly in the life of the school. There are five major concerts each year; the school runs five orchestras and has over 30 Chamber groups, chosen by ability rather than age. Six dramatic productions are staged each year, one by the Bear Pit, a drama society directed entirely by the pupils themselves. All pupils are taught to work in different media (Painting, Drawing, Sculpture and Ceramics) and Photography is often available as part of the GCSE course.

There are many clubs and societies in the school; these include, in addition to Drama groups, Debating, Photography, Chess, Bridge, Natural History, Electronics, and the Christian Union.

The Combined Cadet Force has long been one of the most flourishing in the country, containing Army, Navy and RAF sections, and providing opportunities for such other activities as Skiing, Sub-aqua Diving, and Orienteering. Pupils are encouraged to join at age 14 and serve for a minimum of 2 years. Pupils who do not join the CCF will be expected to join either the Duke of Edinburgh scheme or to give some service to the community in the flourishing Community Service Group.

Career Guidance is given by staff with the time and facilities for this important work. In Year 11 systematic aptitude testing is followed up by talks by parents themselves who give freely of their time to talk about their own careers and who give help with offers of work experience to pupils.

University lecturers help pupils to develop their skills on Upper School "Interview Day" and experts from leading firms offer their advice on "Interface Day".

A School Council, with members of all ages from Year 9 to the Upper School, advises the Headmaster on many school matters.

Relations with Parents. Close touch is maintained with parents throughout the school career of pupils. The Alleyn's Association deals with all matters of interest to parents and the Social Sub-Committee raises considerable funds for School purposes. A Sports Club enables parents to enjoy the facilities of the Sports Hall and gymnasium.

The Edward Alleyn Club can be joined by pupils on leaving School; this enables pupils to keep in touch with the school and their contemporaries, and also to take part in sporting activities if they wish. The Club is open to both boys and girls. Communications should be sent to the Secretary, Mr Peter Rodway, c/o Alleyn's School.

Charitable status. Alleyn's College of God's Gift is a Registered Charity. Its purpose is to provide Independent Education for boys and girls from age 4 to 18.

* Head of Department	§ Part Time or Visiting
† Housemaster/Housemistress	¶ Old Pupil
‡ See below list of staff for meaning	

Ampleforth College

York YO62 4ER.
Tel: (01439) 766000
Fax: (01439) 788330

Ampleforth Abbey is an English Benedictine Foundation which was founded in 1607 at Dieulouard in Lorraine by English monks who had strong links with the mediaeval Benedictines of Westminster Abbey. After the French Revolution the monastic community was resettled at Ampleforth in 1802 and the present School was started there soon after.

The Community is dedicated, first to prayer, and then to religious and charitable works. Ampleforth College and Ampleforth College Junior School are the works of St Laurence Educational Trust. The other works of the Community include parishes in Yorkshire, Lancashire and Cumbria, St Benet's Hall in Oxford and pastoral involvement both at Ampleforth and elsewhere.

Motto:*'Dieu le Ward'*.

The Governing Body:

The Abbot of Ampleforth Abbey, who is elected by the Community for 8 years at a time and presides over the Community and its works, is the Chairman of Governors. He acts with the Council and Chapter of Ampleforth Abbey and with the assistance of a lay Advisory Body.

Headmaster: **Rev G F L Chamberlain**, OSB, MA

Second Master: K R Elliot, BSc

Third Masters:
Rev J C Madden, OSB, MB, BS, MRCP
Rev C G Everitt, OSB, MA, DPhil

Director of Studies: I F Lovat, BSc, MInstP

Director of Professional Development: Mrs R M A Fletcher, MA

Director of Admissions: H C Codrington, BEd

Director of Arts: C J N Wilding, BA

Head of Sixth Form: to be announced

Guestmaster: Rev P A Convery, OSB, MA

Assistant Masters:

Christian Theology:
*Rev C G Everitt, OSB, MA, DPhil (*Housemaster, St Oswald's*)
J K Bindloss, BA
Rev C Boulton, OSB, BA
Rev O McBride, OSB, BSc
Rev K Monahan, OSB, BTh
Rev A McCabe, OSB, MA
Rev D Humphries, OSB, BD
Rev S Jobbins, OSB, BA
Rev L McTaggart, OSB, MA
Rev E R ffield, OSB, BSc, ACGI, AMIMechE
Rev M J Callaghan, OSB, MA
Miss P Dixon, BA (*Housemistress, St Aidan's*)

Classics:
*W F Lofthouse, MA
Rev P S Trafford, OSB, MA
J Layden, BA
E V Thomas, BA, DPhil
Miss J Sutcliffe, BA

History:
*to be announced
Rev G F L Chamberlain, OSB, MA
Rev M E Corbould, OSB, MA (*Housemaster, St Edward's*)
H C Codrington, BEd
P T Connor, MA (*Careers Master*)
R D Eagles, MA, DPhil

English:
*A C Carter, MA
Mrs R M A Fletcher, MA (*Head of Professional Development*)
D R Lloyd, MA (*Special Needs*)
Miss A M Beary, MA, MPhil

Modern Languages:
*J P Ridge, MA
C J N Wilding, BA
Rev M J Callaghan, OSB, MA (*Housemaster, St Wilfrid's*)
J D Cragg-James, BA, DipGenLing
K J Dunne, BA
M J McPartlan, BA
Mrs R E Wilding, BA
M Torrens-Burton, BA (*EFL*)
*Ms S M Mulligan, BA (*EFL*)
Rev A McCabe, OSB, MA
Miss P Dixon, BA (*Housemistress, St Aidan's*)

Geography:
*P M Brennan, BSc, FRMetSoc
R Sugden, BA
Mrs N M Thorpe, BSc

Modern Studies:
*P T McAleenan, BA, AcDipEd (*Housemaster, St Cuthbert's*)
Rev T F Dobson, OSB, DipSocStudies, FCA
G W G Guthrie, MA (*Housemaster, St Dunstan's*)
J G Yates, BA

Mathematics:
*C G H Belsom, BA, MPhil, CMath, FIMA
Mrs P J Melling, BSc, BA (*Head of Activities*)
G Simpson, BSc
R Warren, BSc, PhD
D Willis, BEd, MEd
Rev P W Wright, OSB, BSc (*Housemaster, St Bede's*)

Physics:
*Mrs M F S Wheeler, Licenciatura em fislica, PhD
I F Lovat, BSc, MInstP
K R Elliot, BSc
Rev E R ffield, OSB, BSc, ACGI, AMIMechE (*Housemaster, St Thomas's*)
A B Garnish, BSc

Chemistry:
*A S Thorpe, BSc, CChem, MRSC (*Head of Science and Technology*)
D F Billett, MSc, PhD, CChem, FRSC
D L Allen, MA, DPhil, CChem, MRSC
S J Howard, BSc

Biology:
*S Smith, BSc
Rev P C Shore, OSB, BSc, AKC (*Housemaster, St Hugh's*)
A J Hurst, BSc
Rev J C Madden, OSB, MB, BS, MRCP
Rev O McBride, OSB, BSc

Music:
*I D Little, MA, MusB, FRCO, ARCM, LRAM
W J Dore, MA, FRCO
D S Bowman, MusB, FRCO, ARMCM
W Leary
S R Wright, FRCO, ARMCM
M A S Weare, MA, GRSM, ARCM, LRAM
Miss S Keeling, BA

Craft, Design and Technology:
*B W Gillespie, BEd
B Anglim, BEng

ICT:
*M A Barras, BSc

Art:
*S G Bird, BA, ATC, DipAD
L Quigley, MA, ATC

Theatre Director:
E Max, MA

PE and Games:
*G D Thurman, BEd (*Games Master*)
R Carter, MBE
Miss K Fraser, BA

Houses and Housemasters/Housemistresses:
St Aidan's: Miss P Dixon, BA
St Bede's: Fr William Wright, OSB, BSc
St Cuthbert's: P T McAleenan, BA, AcDipEd
St Dunstan's: G W G Guthrie, MA
St Edward's: Fr Edward Corbould, OSB, MA
St Hugh's: Fr Christian Shore, OSB, BSc, AKC
St John's: Fr Cuthbert Madden, OSB, MB, BS, MRCP
St Oswald's: Fr Gabriel Everitt, OSB, MA, DPhil
St Thomas's: Fr Richard ffield, OSB, BSc, ACGI, AMIMechE
St Wilfrid's: Fr James Callaghan, OSB, MA

Counsellor: J G J Allisstone, BA

Procurator: P N Bryan, BA, ACA

Medical Officer: to be announced

Headmaster's Secretary: Mrs L M Featherstone

Number in School. There are 507 pupils, 458 are Boarders, 41 are Day Boys and 8 Day Girls.

Our aims are:

- to share with parents in the spiritual, moral and intellectual formation of their children, in a Christian community with which families may be joined in friendship and prayer for the rest of their lives.
- to educate the young in the tradition and sacramental life of the Church and to encourage each towards a joyful, free and self-disciplined life of faith and virtue, ready to listen to the Holy Spirit.
- to work for excellence in all our endeavours, academic, sporting and cultural. We ask students to give of his or her very best. We ask much of the gifted and we encourage the weak. Each is taught to appreciate the value of learning and the disinterested of truth.
- to help Ampleforth boys and girls grow up mature and honourable, inspired by high ideals and capable of leadership; so they may serve others generously, be strong in friendship and loyal and loving towards their families.

Organisation. St Martins, Ampleforth, an independent preparatory school at Gilling Castle, educates boys and girls from 3-13. The Upper School has 9 houses for boys aged 13 to 18 and one house for girls aged 16 to 18. In the boys House a Housemaster is responsible for about 50 boys. The girls' house is somewhat smaller and has a Housemistress. Each House includes a small number of day pupils. Each House has its own separate accommodation, but the work and games of the whole school are centrally organised. Five tutors are allotted to each House, to supervise children's work and provide the appropriate guidance at each stage in their school career. The Careers Master provides information and assistance and can arrange expert advice for pupils, parents, and tutors.

Curriculum. The first year's work (Year 9) provides a broad basis from which to make informed GCSE choices. In the second and third years a core of English, Mathematics, Science and Christian Theology is studied to GCSE together with a balanced selection from a wide range of subjects. In the first year Sixth Form (Year 12), up to five subjects may be studied to AS level. One of those subjects may be AS level Christian Theology but, if not, students follow a Christian Theology short course. Normally three subjects will be taken on to A level in the second year (Year 13). A comprehensive Health Education programme is provided in all years.

Games and Activities. There are opportunities to play a wide variety of representative sports at all levels with excellent indoor and outdoor facilities. Many activities take place during the week and weekends, including drama, debating, outdoor pursuits and creative arts. Music, which is a strong academic subject, plays a major part in the extra-curricular life of the school. The Schola Cantorum, our liturgical choir, sings for Mass in the Abbey and performs sacred music in Britain and abroad.

Admission. Applications may be made through the Admissions Office.

Fees and Charges. Registration £50. Board and Tuition £5,255 per term. The fees are inclusive, the only normal extras being for individual tuition in Music (£18 per lesson – £16 for a second instrument); TEFL (£425.00 per term); Extra English (£26.50 per class).

Entrance Scholarships. (*see* Entrance Scholarship section) Academic and Music Scholarships are awarded at 13+ and for entry to the Sixth Form.

Charitable status. St Laurence Educational Trust is a Registered Charity, number 1063808. Its aim is to advance Roman Catholic religion.

Ardingly College

Haywards Heath Sussex RH17 6SQ.
Tel: 01444 892577
Fax: 01444 892266

Ardingly is a co-educational School in the Woodard Family founded to teach the Christian Faith.

Our aim is to enable all boys and girls to develop their love of learning, academic potential and individual talents, in a caring community which fosters sensitivity, confidence, a sense of service and enthusiasm for life

Motto: *'Beati Mundo Corde'*.

School Council:

Chairman: Sir Robin McLaren, KCMG

The Rt Rev M Adie (*Provost*)
Mrs C Bennet
S M W Bishop, BA
Mrs G Cox
The Revd Canon L F P Gunner, MA
A Holmes, Esq (*Divisional Bursar*)
Mrs C Rich
S Rigby, Esq
A Stewart-Roberts, Esq
N P Smith, Esq
Prof M M McGowan, CBE, FBA
S Ward, Esq
M V C Williams, MA

***Headmaster:* John Franklin**, BA, MEd

Deputy Headmaster: M Eagers, MA, MEd

Chaplain: The Revd R Harrison, RKM

Head of the Junior School: Julie Robinson, BA, PGCE

Bursar: T Waitson

Medical Officer: Dr B Lambert

History and development of the College. Ardingly College, the third of Nathaniel Woodard's schools was founded in Shoreham in 1858 and moved to its present beautiful site in Mid Sussex, about halfway between Gatwick and Brighton in 1870. The College now consists of a Pre-Prep Day School and a boarding and day Junior School, for boys and girls between the ages of 2½ and 13, and of a boarding and day Senior School for boys and girls aged between 13 and 18.

In the Junior School, which has been co-educational since 1986, there are 170 pupils, of whom 99 are boys and 21 are girls, and 37 are boarders.

In the Senior School, which started to become fully co-educational in 1982, there are 394 pupils of whom 163 are in the VIth Form. There are 231 boys and 163 girls, and 252 are boarders, and there are now as many girls as boys in the Lower VIth.

Further details about the Junior School can be found in the IAPS section, Part V.

Academic. Ardingly has an extremely good academic record in both arts and science subjects achieved by boys and girls who come from a wide spectrum of ability. Consistently the 'A' level percentage pass rate has been around the 90's and in 1999 reached 96.3%. Every year about four Ardinians gain entry to Oxford or Cambridge and overall more than 80% of the Upper Sixth go on to Higher Education, about half to Universities and half to Polytechnics and Colleges of Higher Education. At GCSE the A B C pass rate is usually about 92% and most candidates take 9 subjects.

Curriculum. *First year:* A broad course in which all pupils do virtually everything: second Modern Language (German or Spanish), Classical Studies; Greek available outside the timetable; Expressive Arts, Design Technology and Information Technology for all.

GCSE (2nd and 3rd years): All take English and English Literature, Maths, Science and at least one Modern Language, and the usual wide range of options.

Sixth Form Curriculum: Standard choices in a highly flexible 5 block system. Unusual subjects are Archaeology, Craft, English Language and Theatre Studies.

All LVI pupils receive a refresher course in Information Technology.

Pastoral. There are 7 Middle School Houses, four for boys and three for girls which contain everyone from the first year to the Lower Sixth. In the Upper Sixth all boys and girls transfer to a separate, integrated coeducational House, "Woodard" (opened in 1988), in which they are able to concentrate more fully on their 'A' level studies and can be given greater responsibility for themselves and be better prepared for life at University or in the outside world. Each House has its own Housemaster or Housemistress, Assistant and House Tutors. In addition every boy and girl will have a Tutor (chosen after the first year by the pupil) who has responsibility for the work, progress, choices and many other aspects of the pupil's life. Tutorials are regular, one to one and usually weekly. Tutors work closely with careers staff which includes a professional adviser who comes in one day a week.

In the second year pupils study and discuss life topics in small mixed groups as part of a specially designed course called 'Learning for Living' and within the Religious Studies course in other years, and General course in the Lower Sixth.

There is an efficient compact Sanatorium in the centre of the school with a residential Sister in charge. The School Doctor takes three surgeries a week in the School and is always on call.

Expressive Arts. *Music:* Choir, Chamber Choir, Choral Society, Jazz Singers, Orchestras, Concert Band, Jazz Band, Chamber Music. Instrumental lessons taken by about half the boys and girls.

Art: Painting, drawing, printing, ceramics, sculpture, fashion & textiles, photography, etching.

Design Technology: Real design problems solved in a variety of materials and forms.

Drama: Many productions in the course of the year for all ages. Large flexible theatre and a small workshop theatre.

All four of these expressive arts are studied in modular form in the first year, are options for GCSE and 'A' level and offer scholarships for talented candidates, at both 13+ and for the Sixth Form.

Sport. Boys play Football, Hockey, Cricket, Tennis; Girls play Hockey, Netball, Tennis, Rounders. (Football and cricket are also available for girls).

Also (for both boys and girls) there is Squash, Cross Country, Swimming, Shooting, Golf, Lacrosse, Volleyball, Horseriding, Clay Pigeon Shooting, Basketball, Badminton (new Sports Hall opened in 1999), Fencing, Judo, Multi-gym, Croquet, Sailing, etc.

The indoor pool is open to both Junior and Senior Schools and pupils who cannot swim are taught to do so.

Activities. Combined Cadet Force (Army based), Outward Bound (compulsory modular programme in first year), Duke of Edinburgh, Cooking, Sewing, Stage work, Modern dance, Photography, Computers, etc.

English for Young Europeans. Ardingly offers places to children from the whole of Europe for periods of a term or more (occasionally less).

After Ardingly. 'A' level candidates are encouraged to consider taking a 'Gap' year between school and university, particularly in Third World placements with Schools Partnership Worldwide, Operation Raleigh or GAP.

Admissions. Admission to the Senior School normally takes place at 13+ or directly into the VIth Form at 16+. Admission is also possible at 14+ but is not advisable at the beginning of the years in which GCSE or A levels are taken unless there are very special reasons.

At 13+ qualification is either by Common Entrance or the School's own test papers (for those not attending Preparatory Schools) in English, Maths and usually French, together with IQ test, report and interview. The selection of candidates for direct entry to the VIth Form takes place at the end of November in the year prior to entry. All candidates are interviewed and take the school's standard IQ test. A report from their Head is also required. Places will then be offered subject to the candidate gaining a minimum of 6 grade C's or above at GCSE. Modifications of these procedures and of the timing for individuals at any stage are almost always possible. Ardingly also accepts 'second choice' candidates in the Common Entrance examination.

The Junior School has entry at 7+ and 11+, or at any other time between the ages of 7 and 11. Transfer into the Senior School is by Common Entrance.

Scholarships. (*see* Entrance Scholarship section) A number of Scholarships and Exhibitions are offered for annual competition. They include Academic, Art, CDT, Drama, Music and Sports Awards and Ashdown Awards for all-rounders for those entering at both 13+ and 16+. The Junior School offers Academic, Art, Music and Sports Awards at 11+ with Academic and Music Awards for the under 11s. Some Junior School awards are tenable in the Senior School and others are for the Junior School years only. Along with other HMC schools, the maximum value of a scholarship is 50% of the basic fees per annum but all may be supplemented by a means-tested bursary if need can be shown.

Ardingly is one of the selected schools for Barclays Bank Educational Awards.

A limited number of bursaries (value up to 50% of basic fees per annum) are available for the children of the Clergy.

Please address all enquiries about admissions, scholarships and bursaries to either Junior or Senior Schools to the Registrar (Tel: 01444 892577/fax: 01444 892266/e-mail: registrar@ardingly.com).

Term of Entry. Main 13+ and sixth form intake in September.

Intake at other ages and other times on an individual basis.

Music. Ardingly has a good tradition in all aspects and particularly in its Chapel Choir.

In the Music School, facilities are provided for instruction and practice in all branches of Music. All orchestral instruments, strings, wind, brass, percussion and singing are taught by fully-qualified teachers, and the Junior and Senior School Orchestras give concerts at the end of each term.

The Choral Society meets weekly and, generally with the School Orchestra, performs a major choral work each year. Most pupils, both in the Junior and Senior Schools, have musical tuition of some kind, either as part of the curriculum or as a voluntary out-of-school activity

Art. Art is taught as part of the normal curriculum in both Senior and Junior Schools. The Art School is open at other times for those who wish to pursue their studies further.

Technology. The Technology Centre occupies a range of former farm buildings, the original, initial conversion being carried out by boys in the sixties. Technology is taught as a class subject to junior pupils. Senior pupils undertake more ambitious projects in their spare time in addition to formal tuition for GCSE and A Level.

Leisure Activities. Official timetabled 'Afternoon Activities' and a plethora of voluntary clubs and societies foster and encourage the sensible use of time outside the classroom. These may cater for manual, craft, cultural or intellectual interests, and are an essential part of a child's school life.

Physical Training. There are regular classes in both Junior and Senior Schools.

Corps and Scouts. The Combined Cadet Force, though voluntary, has over 150 members (boys and girls) who attend weekly parades and regular field days. The Contingent has camps in the Easter and Summer holidays. There are Scout troops in both Junior and Senior School.

Registration. The School Prospectus may be obtained from the Registrar, and is generally sent whenever an enquiry about a vacancy is received. Registration (where a non-returnable fee of £50 is charged) can be made at any age subject to the availability of places. No separate registration is required for children transferring from the Junior to the Senior School.

Fees (Michaelmas 2000). The Junior School termly *inclusive* fee for boarders is (7–13) £3,275 and, for day pupils (7–9) £1,735/(10–13) £2,215 and the termly *inclusive* fee for the Senior School is £4,735 (boarders), £3,550 (day pupils). There is a surcharge of £150 per term for those entering at the Sixth Form stage.

Further Particulars. For further information, application should be made to the Registrar. A personal visit to the School is an easy matter from London: frequent fast trains run from Victoria to Haywards Heath – and a taxi can always be found outside the railway station.

Charitable status. The Ardingly College Charitable Trust is a Registered Charity, number 1076456. It exists to provide high quality education for boys and girls aged 2½ to 18.

* Head of Department	§ Part Time or Visiting
† Housemaster/Housemistress	¶ Old Pupil
‡ See below list of staff for meaning	

Arnold School
Blackpool

Blackpool FY4 1JG.
Tel: 01253 346391
Fax: 01253 405699
e-mail: arnold.principal@cableinet.uk
website: www.arnold.blackpool.sch.uk

The foundation dates from 1896 when Frank Truswell Pennington opened a school with 8 pupils in his rooms in Bright Street, South Shore, Blackpool. In 1903 he moved his school to the present site in Lytham Road and called it Arnold House after a school which had previously occupied the building.

In 1937 the School was reconstituted since when it has been administered by a Governing Council of 20 members, the majority of whom are Old Arnoldians. In 1938 the School – now called Arnold School – was placed on the Direct Grant list where it continued to flourish before reverting to independent status in 1976. Arnold has been fully co-educational since September 1980 and is now a 5-form entry day school for 800 boys and girls over 11 years with a Kindergarten and Junior School for 350 boys and girls.

The Governors are committed to an on-going capital development programme and the most recent additions to the campus include a new Sports Complex, Performing Arts Studio, Languages Centre, Design & Technology Centre and an all-weather playing surface.

Motto: *Honor Virtutis Praemium.*

Governing Council:
Chairman: ¶Sir Martin Holdgate, CB, MA, PhD
Deputy Chairman: ¶J C Armfield
Chairman of Executive Committee: K Cartmell, LLB
Chairman of Finance Committee: M Muschamp, FCA
Chairman of Buildings Committee: ¶R Dunn, FCA
Chairman of Development Committee: ¶M S Brennand

A E D Baines, BA, RIBA
W Beaumont, OBE
Mrs G M Connolly, BSc, MA
Air Commodore C R Fowler, ADC, RAF
Revd J M Holmes, MA, PhD, VetMB, MRCVS
Mrs A Jack, CertEd
¶Professor P J Lea, BSc, PhD, DSc
Dr A Lucking, MB, BS
Dr C W R D Moseley, MA, PhD
P M Owen, ACIB
¶J R Taylor, LLB
¶S R Walker, MRPS
Mrs P Wilcock
J M Wooding, BSc, CEng, FRAeS
M J Youd

Bursar to the Council: ¶A Chadwick, ACMA

Clerk to the Council: Mrs S L Fenton

Tutorial Staff:

Principal: **W T Gillen**, MA (Queen's University, Belfast and St Catharine's College, Cambridge)

Vice Principal (Pastoral, Discipline & Staff Development): G N Hogg, BA
Vice Principal (Administration): P McCarthy, RN
Deputy Principal & Head of Junior School: C F D White, BEd
Deputy Principal & Director of Studies: J P Maddox, MA
Senior Teacher (Higher Education, Careers & Admission): Mrs M A Thornton, BSc
Head of Sixth Form: M M Hall, BA

Head of the Middle School: M B Kirkham, BSc, MRSC, CChem
Head of the Lower School: J A Nicholls, CertEd

Heads of House:
School: R Bedford, BSc
Howarth: P R Oliver, DPLM
Pennington: P McMahon, BA, MSc
Liston: Mrs M M Ingham, BEd

Biology:
*Mrs E L Moorhouse, BA, BSc
I Mehta, BSc
Mrs H Holt, BSc
A J Treharne, BSc, PhD (*Examinations Officer*)
A J McKeown, BSc

Business Studies:
*R Bedford, BSc

Chemistry:
*J Young, BSc, DPhil (*Head of Science*)
Mrs M Thornton, BSc
M B Kirkham, BSc, CChem, MRSC
C W Woodruff, CChem, MRSC, DPSE (*Comp*)

Classics:
*I J Morton, MA
Mrs V Kellett, BA, BSc

Design Centre:
*M J Salmon, BSc
D G Summerville, BEd (*Ceramics/Photography*)
Mrs J Fawcett, CertEd (*Food Technology*)
E R Lawson, BEng, CEng, MIMechE (*Technology*)
Miss H A Fitzgerald, BA (*Art*)
A J G Bell, BA (*Photography*)
P R Oliver, DPLM (*Design*)
C C Woodruff, CChem, MRSC, PPSE

Drama and Theatre Studies:
*C G Snell, BA

Economics:
*M M Hall, BA
*†R Bedford, BSc

English:
*S J Everson, MA
D E Smyth, BEd
G N Hogg, BA
Mrs P Massey, BA
P E Hayden, BA
Miss D Lowe, BA
Miss S Currie, BA

Geography/Geology:
*K H Lee, BSc
J B Ashcroft, BA
I R Winterflood, BSc
T Brown, BSc

History:
*J R Davey, BA
Mrs J A Nicholls, CertEd
G R P Ford, BA
R E Golding, BA

IT:
*J Maddox, MA
Miss C Burke (*Senior Technician*)

ICT Co-ordinator: to be appointed

Law:
Miss K M Hollinworth, BA, LLB

Library:
Mrs J E Darkins

Mathematics:
*C R Streule, BSc
†P McMahon, BA, MSc
†A J G Bell, BA
†K M Kneale, BSc
Mrs D Nield, BSc
Mrs P J Taylor, BSc
J Maddox, MA
K W Ward, BSc
P D Sudlow, BSc
Miss R Matheson, BSc

Modern Languages:
*C W Jenkinson, MA
Mrs K M Eccles, BA
C D Eccles, BA
Mrs D J Pailing, BA
G R Moffat, BA
Miss S A Illidge, BA
G R P Ford, MA
Miss C S Bacon, BA
Mrs D A Jenkinson, BA

Music:
*K S Shenton, GRSM, LLCM, ARCO
P R Oliver, DPLM
Mrs L Cooper, CertEd, LRAM, LTCL

Instrumental Staff:
Mrs J S Wade, LRAM, ATCL
A Lingings, ARCM
Mrs S Swainson, Dip (Prague)
L Weddell
Miss P Holt, BA

Physics:
*Ms G Chilver, BSc
P D Sudlow, BSc, MSc
Miss R Matheson, BSc
R Salisbury, BSc
K W Ward, BSc, BA

Physical Education:
*R L Jones, BEd (*Director of PE and Games and i/c Rugby*)
Miss A De Miranda, BEd (*i/c Girls' PE and Games*)
C J Marshall, BPhEd (*i/c Boys' Swimming and Cricket*)
†Mrs M M Ingham, BEd (*i/c Girls' Swimming and Tennis*)
Miss G Raby, TCert
Ms K E Preston, RAD, BTDA (*Dance*)
G R P Ford, BA (*i/c Boys' Tennis*)
Ms G Chilver (*i/c Badminton*)
P R Oliver (*i/c Cross Country and Golf*)
I J Morton, MA (*i/c Girls Cricket*)
Mrs M Whorlton-Jones, BEd
Mrs J M Malin, BEd

Religious Education:
*M A Harding, BEd
Mrs J A Nicholls, CertEd

Careers and Higher Education:
*Mrs M A Thornton, BSc
Miss G Raby, TCert

P Hayden, BA

Combined Cadet Force:
Lt Col J B Ashcroft (*Commanding Officer*)
Sqn Ldr C R Streule, VR(T) (*Corps 2IC*)
WO1 T F Beck, MISM (*School Staff Instructor*)

Royal Navy Section:
Lt Commander E R Lawson, RNR (*Officer Commanding*)
Lt K Cartmell
Sub Lt A Jethwa
Sub Lt T Brown

Army Section:
Capt B Carroll
Lt L Pritchard
2nd Lt A Treharne
2nd Lt A Crowther

Royal Airforce Section:
Sqn Ldr J Maddox
Flt Lt P R Oliver (*Training Officer*)
Pilot Officer J R Davey

Junior School (including Infants and Kindergarten):
Head of Junior School & Deputy Principal Arnold: C F D White, BEd
Deputy Head of Junior School: C H Johnson, CertEd
Head of Infants & Early Years: Mrs F A Lawson, CertEd, DipEd

Miss J Allen, BA(Ed)
Mrs L Buck, BSc
Mrs L Cole, BEd
A Coyne, BEd
A Crowther, BEd
Miss A Cunningham, BSc
Mrs A Dickson, BA, MEd, MCollP, PGCE
G Dresser, CertEd
R A Fielder, BEd
Mrs L Fielder, BEd
Mrs E Foster, BEd
Mrs M Hecht, CertEd, DipSpOd
A Hodgkinson, BSc, PGCE
Mrs W Parkinson, CertEd
J Storey, CertEd
Mrs B Taylor, CertEd
Mrs S Taylor, CertEd
Mrs G Ward, BEd
Mrs J Woodhead, CertEd

Mrs S Cartmell, NNEB
Miss J Davies, NNEB
Mrs J Laing, PPACert
Miss K Norton, NNEB
Mrs S Rigby, BTecCert
Miss E Stoneman, NVQ2

Site and Buildings. The School lies on the south side of Blackpool, half a mile from the sea. The facilities include the normal classrooms and specialist rooms, modern well-equipped laboratories, an ICT Centre, a Sixth Form Centre and the Memorial Hall. Recent additions include a new Sports Complex, Performing Arts Studio and Languages Centre, Design and Technology Centre and an all-weather pitch which is adjacent to our playing fields. The School also possesses an Outdoor Pursuits Centre at Glenridding in Cumbria.

The Junior School (3–11 years) is situated on the same site as the Senior School and is therefore able to benefit from its facilities.

Curriculum. The School aims to give its boys and girls a broad education in general, and in particular to prepare them for public examinations and for entry to Universities (including Oxford and Cambridge) and other places of Further Education. The curriculum is broadly based up to GCSE level and includes Design/Technology, Computing, Drama, Latin, German and Spanish. The Advanced Level specialisations include Computer Science, Law, Economics, Business Studies, Theatre Studies, Geology and Psychology in addition to the more traditional options. There are over 200 students in our Sixth Form, the vast majority of whom proceed to degree courses.

A period of work experience is arranged for all Fifth Year pupils immediately after the GCSE examinations. The School has excellent links with Industry. Careers education is provided from the Third Year onwards.

Clubs and Activities. There is a very wide range of co-curricular activities: Brass Band, Choir, Orchestra, Dance, Drama, Art, Fencing, Christian Fellowship, Chess, Philately, Debating, Photography, Creative Writing, Orienteering, Community Service, Outdoor Pursuits and the Duke of Edinburgh's Award Scheme.

Games. Organised games and Physical Education periods play an important part in the School life and every pupil is expected to participate unless excused on medical grounds. Playing fields of 13 acres adjoin the School for Rugby Football and Hockey in the Winter terms and for Cricket, Tennis and Athletics in the Summer. Swimming and Life Saving are taught all the year round and other Sports include Golf, Squash, Basketball, Badminton, Netball and Fencing. There are dance classes in both ballet and modern dancing for the girls.

Combined Cadet Force. Membership is open to all pupils from the Third Year, and pupils may join the RAF, Naval or the Army Section. The Contingent has a successful record and emphasis is placed upon Adventure Training and preparation for the Duke of Edinburgh's Award Scheme. The Naval Section has an excellent base on Coniston Water and there is a fleet of various dinghies and other craft.

Junior School. Since September 1970 girls have been admitted as well as boys. All Junior School pupils occupy buildings that have been built since 1970. Admission is at 3+, 4+ or 7+. Entry at other ages depends upon vacancies occurring. Pupils transfer to the Senior School at 11 years but are required to sit an examination. The Junior School has its own separate buildings (including an ICT Centre) and a distinct corporate life, though it is situated alongside the Senior School whose facilities it also uses. The games played are Association Football, Rugby, Hockey and Cricket. Athletics and Swimming sports are held annually. Music is encouraged and there is a flourishing Choir. There is a full range of girls' activities, including Games and Dancing.

Admission. Prospectus and Admissions forms can be obtained from the School Registrar.

All entries to the Senior School are made through the Principal. Pupils are admitted to the Senior School on the basis of the School's examinations in English and Mathematics and an interview with the Principal. The main intake to the Senior School is at 11 and 13 years at the beginning of the Autumn term, though entry at other times is possible depending on availability of places.

For entry at Sixth Form level respectable GCSE grades in at least five subjects are normally expected in addition to a satisfactory report from a pupil's current Head. Sixth Form scholarships are available.

Entry into the Junior School (3–11 years) is at the age of 3, 4 and 7. Enquiries should be made to the Junior School Secretary.

Fees (at September 2000). Senior School Tuition £4,950 pa, Junior School, Infants and Kindergarten Tuition £3,810 pa, including books and stationery. Extras are minimal. Lunch is provided at cost.

Entrance Scholarships and Bursaries. (*see* Entrance Scholarship section) There are several scholarships (including those for Music, Art & Design, and Sport) for entry both at 11 years and to the Sixth Form. Bursaries are also available.

Registration. Pupils may be registered at any time although this should be as early as possible if entry is requested at ages other than 3, 4, 7 or 11 years. Candidates will be called for examination and interview in the year of entry although those who live at a distance may have the papers sent to their Schools.

Charitable status. Arnold School is a Registered Charity, number 331031. It exists to provide education for boys and girls.

Ashville College

Harrogate Yorkshire HG2 9JP
Tel: (01423) 566358
Fax: (01423) 505142
e-mail: ashville@ashville.co.uk
website: ashville.co.uk

Ashville was founded in 1877 by the United Methodist Free Church, but has been strengthened by taking under its wing at different times two older non-conformist schools: Elmfield College, founded by the Primitive Methodists in 1864, which amalgamated with Ashville in 1932; and New College, which began in 1850 with strong Baptist connections and merged with Ashville in 1930.

Motto: *'Esse quam videri'*

Visitor: The President of the Methodist Conference

Governing Body
Chairman: R W Search

Ex-officio:
The General Secretary of the Methodist Division of Education and Youth.
The President of the Ashvillian Society.

J A Beaumont
M Bethel, QC, MA, LLM
Revd D Deeks
J Hardwick, MA
G M L Hirst
Mrs J Jackson, MA
R Manby
Mrs A Portlock
D Robson, MA
G Russell, MA
Revd M Townsend, MA
M Verity, FRICS
D A Whitehead
Mrs A Willey, BA (*Deputy Chairman*)

***Headmaster:* M H Crosby**, JP, MA

Deputy Heads:
A T Johnson, BA
Mrs V Davies, MA

Chaplain: Rev Dr Paul Glass, BA, PhD

Assistants:
R W Upton, BSc
R M Pygott, BA
D M Manning, BA, BEd
P D Forster, BSc
R Horsley, BA
L G Smith, MA, CChem, MRSC
G T Wise, BSc
M J Davis, BSc
K A Bolton, MA
J Mullin, MA DAD
T M Cundy, MA
A J Barker, MA (*Housemaster*)
C Pearce, BEd
Mrs M J Petts, CertEd
G R Fletcher, BSc
Mrs P Cousen, CertEd
I Gould, BA
N P Cornforth, BSc
Mrs B Bromley, MA
Mrs F Adamson
P R Williams, BSc
P Hampson, BEd, BA (*Senior Housemaster*)
I Walker, BEd
D A C Archer, CertEd
S Taylor, MA
G Warren, BA
D Webster, BA
Mrs S Ellis, BA (*Housemistress*)
P Gilmore, MA
I Popely, BSc
Mrs N Donoghue
Mrs B Tullie
Miss J Spencer
C Davis
Miss J Ellis
Miss E Sneddon
Dr C Taylor, DPhil
Mrs E Marsh, BSc
Mrs C Guy, BA
J Riches
Mrs G Cuttress

M Howell
J Stewart
H Jarrold
D Normanshire

Junior School:
C J Britt-Compton (*Head*)
J Thompson (*Deputy Head*)
I Dimmick, BEd
Mrs L Gray
Mrs M Russell, CertEd
Mrs M E Richardson
Miss H J Dexter
Mrs J Bourgeois
Miss H Dexter
Miss R Collinson, BSc
Mrs A Taylor, BA

Miss C Pearson

Pre-Prep:
Mrs L Dimmick, BA
Mrs L Nicholson
Mrs R Warren
Miss A Fothergill, BA
Mrs J Hopkins, BA
Mrs D Adams
Mrs S Carroll
Mrs P Dyke

Director of Music: J Dunford, ARCO, GTCL, ALCM, AMusTCL, LTCL
Assistant: Mr J Davies

Medical Officer: S Foley, MB
Bursar: Mr M Gear
Headmaster's Secretary: Mrs C M Haxton

Although a Methodist foundation a large proportion of its pupils come from non-Methodist homes, and the school welcomes pupils from overseas. Until 1976 Ashville was a Direct Grant school. When the Government decided to bring Direct Grant to an end, it was unanimously resolved that Ashville should revert to fully Independent status. In 1982 the school became co-educational.

Numbers. Ashville is a co-educational boarding and day school. There are 585 boys and girls in the senior school, 180 in the junior school (aged 7–11), and 60 in the Pre-Prep.

Site and Buildings. The Ashville estate consists of 45 acres of land on the south side of Harrogate.

The original house has been considerably extended to provide all the administrative accommodation, and also houses the library and several of the arts faculties.

A programme of continuous building and improvement has taken place over the last 20 years. This includes the Design Centre (1977), Sports Hall (1983). The girls' boarding house was built in 1985 and extended in 1988. At the same time improvements were made to boys' boarding to provide more comfort and greater privacy. A successful appeal in 1989 provided a new Music and Drama Centre. In 1994 a magnificent Sixth Form Centre was opened, and at the same time, the Design Technology workshop was extended, a pottery was created for the Art Department and an additional Biology Laboratory was built. A Pre-Prep was opened in 1995, and moved into its own purpose built accommodation in September 2000.

Curriculum. The Pre-prep and Junior Schools aim to give a firm grounding in National Curriculum core and foundation subjects. French is introduced at 9+. All pupils are prepared for the General Certificate of Secondary Education at 16, and the Advanced Level GCE examinations two years later. From the age of 11 pupils spend five years on the GCSE course, which includes the study of English Language and Literature, History, Geography, Music, Art, Religious Education, French, German, Latin, Mathematics, Physics, Chemistry, Biology, Design Technology, Home Economics and Computer Studies. At Advanced Level Economics and Business Studies are also available. Guidance is given by the Careers Staff in the choice of Sixth Form studies and decisions are made after consultation with parents. Most pupils who complete the Advanced Level course go on to study at university or other institution of higher education. In addition to their specialist subjects all pupils continue their general education and most offer General Studies as a subject at GCE 'A' level.

In addition to A level courses we offer a GNVQ in Business (level 3) which has proved extremely popular. The course runs in parallel to A level, and the students following it have every opportunity to play a full part in the life of the school.

Physical Education. Physical Education is a part of the curriculum for all pupils, and there are games afternoons for all during the week.

The main school games are Rugby and Cricket for the boys, Netball and Rounders for the girls but there are school fixtures also in Hockey, Cross-Country, Swimming, Athletics, Lawn Tennis, Squash and Badminton.

Careers. Careers guidance is regarded as a very important part of the service provided by the school. Ashville is in membership of the Independent Schools Careers Organisation, and parents are encouraged to share with the careers staff the responsibility for giving appropriate guidance at the Fifth and Sixth Form stage. Pupils are helped in their choice of university and degree course, and arrangements are made for them to visit universities and go on careers courses.

Religious Life. All pupils attend Morning Prayers every weekday, and there is a school service for boarders on Sunday evening. Confirmation classes are held in the Spring Term each year, and boys and girls are prepared for Joint Confirmation in the Church of England and the Methodist Church. The School Chaplain is always glad to meet parents by appointment.

Leisure Activities. There are school societies which cater for a wide range of interests, and pupils are guided in the use of their free time in the early years. The school has no cadet corps, but boys and girls are enabled to take part in the Duke of Edinburgh award scheme. Drama has a strong following and the school play is a highlight of the year's programme.

Music is well provided for, and pupils are encouraged to take up the study of piano, organ or an orchestral instrument. The School Choir has acquired a high reputation by its contributions at the Harrogate and Wharfedale Festivals.

Fees per annum. Senior School: Boarders £11,781, Day Pupils £6,330. Junior School: Boarders £10,776, Day Pupils £5,328. Pre-prep: £3,513.

Admission. (*see* Entrance Scholarship section) The school is prepared to admit pupils at any convenient time. Entry to the Junior School is by means of an interview and test papers in English and Arithmetic.

Candidates for entry at the age of 11 are required to take the Ashville Entrance Examination in the February preceding the September of entry. The examination consists of papers in English, Mathematics and Reasoning. Up to eight Scholarships worth up to half the tuition fee are awarded on the results of the Entrance Examination.

Candidates at Preparatory Schools seeking entry at the age of 13 are required to sit the Common Entrance Examination.

Candidates for entry at other ages and into the Sixth Form are considered on the evidence of a headmaster's report and interview.

Registration forms and prospectus are obtainable from the Headmaster's Secretary. There is a registration fee of £15.

Charitable status. Ashville College is a Registered Charity, number 529577. It aims to provide a boarding and day education for boys and girls.

* Head of Department	§ Part Time or Visiting
† Housemaster/Housemistress	¶ Old Pupil
‡ See below list of staff for meaning	

Bablake School

Coundon Road Coventry CV1 4AU
Tel: 024 7622 8388
Fax: 024 7627 1292
e-mail: bablake@rmplc.co.uk

Bablake School was originally part of the College of the same name founded by Queen Isabella in 1344. After the dissolution of the monasteries it was refounded in 1560 by the city; but it is chiefly associated with the name of Thomas Wheatley, whose indentures of 1563 put its finances on a firm foundation.

The Governing Body is Coventry School Foundation, on which are represented Sir Thomas White's Charity, the Coventry Church Charities, Coventry General Charities, Oxford and Warwick Universities and the University of Coventry. There are also several co-opted governors.

Since Septermber 1977, the schools of Bablake and King Henry VIII, which had led separate existences for hundreds of years in the City of Coventry have been administered by a joint Governing Body, though the activities at each site remain autonomous and complete and pupils are not required to move from one site to the other for any part of their studies. There is a common policy for entry and a common fee structure.

Chairman of Governors: C Leonard, MSc, MIBiol

***Headmaster:* Dr S Nuttall**, BSc, PhD, FRSA

Deputy Heads:
R E Jones, BA, JP
Mrs G F Thomas, BA

Assistant staff:
*W I Appleby, BA, MA
Dr P B M Archer
Mrs K Baker, BA
*S R Beer, BSc, MSc
Mrs D R Booth, BSc
*A C Brown, CertEd
Mrs F S Bunney, BSc
P F Burden, MA
G L Burgess, BSc
J G Burns, MA (*Head of Sixth Form*)
Mrs F M Chapman, MA
A D Chowne, BSc
Mrs J Collins, BSc
R J Dougall, MA
P J Dowsett, BA
J M Drury, BSc
M Duerdin, BSc
*D L Faulkner, BSc
Mrs M Field, L-ès-L
*Mrs C Friebe, CertEd (*Learning Support*)
L W Gamble, BSc
Mrs P Goodwin (*Art*)
*Mrs P Goodyer, BA
*Mrs K M Hall, MA
P R H Hancock, CertEd
Miss M J Harding
Mrs A S Heath, BEd, CertEd
Mrs S E Hill, BA
J C Hobday, BSc
T Hyde, BSc (*Head of Lower School*)
Mrs L J Jackson, BA
*S W Jackson, BSc
*E Jenkins, MA
Dr S A Johnson, BSc, PhD
Mrs A J Jones, BSc
R Jones, DipPE
Dr P J Knight, BSc, PhD, MPhil
Miss S V Ledbrook, BA (*Head of Shells; First Year*)
Mrs P A Lloyd, BA
Mrs P Marchant, CertEd
Mrs M E Mason, BEd
*M J Masters, BSc
*C Mellers, CertEd
N P Meynell, BA
*A J McConaghy, BA (*Director of Studies*)
T W Patchett, BA
Mrs S A Peters, BA, ALP
D F Prescott, BA (*Director of Drama*)
*Mrs J J Price (*Textiles*)
T R Proctor, BSc
Mrs M R Prowse, BSc
Mrs A J Reed
D M Rhodes, BSc
Mrs C L Scott, CertEd
Mrs J Shaw, BA
Mrs S M Smith
Mrs A M Steen, BSc
Mrs E D Surgey, CertEd
*B J Sutton, MusB, GRSM, ARMCM
*J D Swales, MA
Mrs P A Tatum, LRAM (*Head of Middle School*)
*Mrs D A Thomas, BEd
*Mrs G A Timothy, BA
S C R Timothy, BSc, MSc
Mrs A J Tumber, BA
*R L Warmington, BEd
*M Warner, BA
C R West, BEd
B G Wilson, BEd
P C R Wood, MA
M G A Woodward, BA (*Head of Careers*)
Mrs L A Yates, BA, MPhil

Junior School:
Headmaster: J S Dover, ACP

Assistant staff:
C Baker, BA
A Bogyor, CertEd, NCollP (*Deputy Head*)
J Collier, BA
Mrs J Crisford, CertEd
Mrs K Francis, BEd
G Locock, BSc
Mrs J Locock, BA (*Deputy Head*)
Mrs L M Noble
Mrs A Reed, CertEd (*Learning Support*)
Mrs J Shilton

Number in School. There are about 840 pupils (including 400 girls) and 200 in the Junior School.

Buildings. In the Home Field of 11 acres stand the main buildings which have been considerably extended to include a purpose-built Sports Hall, squash courts and heated indoor swimming pool and a purpose built Modern Language block. A purpose-built English, Music and Drama block was completed in July 2000. In 1993 Bablake Junior School was opened on the Home Field site for pupils aged 7–11. The school has its own nationally recognised weather station. At Hollyfast Road there are 27 acres of playing fields, a large pavilion and two all-weather hockey pitches. The school has a study centre in Fougeres in the Normandy region of France and each pupil spends one week there in the first three years at the School.

£2m new English, Music and Drama Block. In 1997, the Governors of the Coventry School Foundation, which manages Bablake School, took the decision to improve the facilities of the school by building accommodation for the English, Music and Drama Departments. After an initial planning stage, the Architects, John Viner and Richard Baily, along with Harrabin Construction Company were chosen to spearhead the project. Work started in March 1999 and the Foundation Stone was laid by one of the School's eminent former pupils, Sir John Egan (ex Managing Director of Jaguar Cars). The £2m building was finished in July of last year and is now being used by all the pupils.

All three departments are exceptionally well catered for. English has eight teaching rooms plus a small study area and computer suite of 26 computers. There is a large Drama Studio which can seat up to 240 people and boasts state of the art lighting and sound systems. Visitors from other theatre groups have been very impressed with the facilities. The Music Department has three teaching rooms, all equipped to the highest standard with computers and music equipment. In addition, there is a Music Library, six practice rooms to accommodate the large number of visiting music teachers who give pupils individual tuition in most instruments. Larger groups of musicians, choirs and orchestras have not been neglected and there is a large music rehearsal room. This can be used for small concerts seating up to 80 people. As with the Drama Studio great attention has been paid to the acoustics of the rooms.

Everyone in the school is delighted with the new facilities. Pupils have been very impressed with the building which will certainly enhance their learning and education in the three subjects.

Bablake has long had a local and increasingly national reputation for the quality of its Music and Drama. Several of its former pupils have gone on to gain recognition professionally, including Lyndi Smith (soon to appear at the Belgrade) and Darren Carnall (currently appearing in the West End production 'Fosse'). The Dramatic Society has recently performed 'Habeas Corpus' to audiences in Edinburgh and Coombe Abbey.

Dr Stuart Nuttall, the Headmaster, said "It really is a magnificent building and the number of superlatives used to describe it and the facilities it has are testimony to the work of the Architects and Contractors as well as the vision of the Governors. We now have a facility which matches the excellent quality of our Music and Drama and the fine work and teaching of the English department".

Dr Nuttall hopes that, in addition to benefiting generations of Bablake pupils it will be used by the local community and City theatre and music groups. He firmly believes that the excellent facilities will not only be an asset to the school but to the community as well. Anyone who might be interested in using the building should contact him on 024 7622 8388.

Curriculum. The Junior School is for children aged 7 to 11. The curriculum comprises English, Mathematics, History, Geography, Religious Studies, Science, PSE, ICT, French, Music, Art, and Design Technology.

Pupils take and must pass the Governors' Examination for entry to the Main School at either Bablake or King Henry VIII. The Main School provides courses leading to the GCSE examinations and GCSE 'A' levels. Subjects available include, English, History, Geography, German, Spanish, Religious Studies, Latin, Classical Civilisation, French, Physics, Chemistry, Biology, Music, Art, Mathematics, Home Economics, Design and Technology, Information Technology and Textiles. Design Technology and Home Economics courses are followed by both boys and girls. The separate sciences are taught up to GCSE. All pupils take a short GCSE course in ICT.

All pupils study 9 subjects at GCSE, the majority progressing into the Sixth Form where 4 subjects and sometimes 5 are taken at 'AS' level. At A2 level all students take a minimum of three subjects. Most of the subjects named are available up to 'AS' level and A2 level. In addition several new subjects are available ranging from Business Studies, Economics, Electronics, Geosciences, Psychology, to Sports Studies and Theatre Studies. All pupils cover Key Skills. There is a wide range of General Studies options including Art, Computing, Design and Music. All pupils follow a structured programme of PE and Games.

Games and Activities. Rugby Football, Hockey, Netball, Basketball, Cross-Country Running, Athletics, Rounders, Tennis, Cricket, Squash and Swimming. In addition, Soccer and Rounders are played in the Junior School. In 1986 the school took into use the largest artificial turf games area in the United Kingdom, used mainly for hockey, but providing in the summer an additional 24 tennis courts. A wide range of extra-curricular activities are offered ranging from Music to Water-polo. There are approximately 25 societies and clubs. All pupils are involved in the charity work of the school and there is a large Community Service programme for the Senior pupils in the fifth and sixth forms.

Scholarships. The Governors award annually a number (not fixed) of Entrance bursaries and full scholarships each year. These are dependent on academic ability and on parental means.

Academic and Music Scholarships are available in the Sixth Form.

Fees. (September 2000): Junior School £1,188 per term, Main School £1,728 per term.

Admission. Entry is via the School's own Entrance Examination held annually in January for entrance the following September. The normal age of entry is 11 but there are smaller intakes at 12 and 13. Entry to the Sixth Form is based on gaining 5 GCSE passes at level B and an interview with the Headmaster and Head of Sixth Form. Enquiries about admissions should be addressed to the Headmaster. The School is entirely a day school and is fully co-educational.

Charitable status. Bablake School is a Registered Charity, number 528961. It exists to provide quality education for boys and girls.

Bancroft's School

Woodford Green Essex IG8 0RF.
Tel: 020 8505 4821.

By the will of Francis Bancroft (1727) all his personal estate was bequeathed on trust to the Worshipful Company of Drapers of the City of London to build and endow almshouses for 24 old men, with a chapel and schoolroom for 100 poor boys and 2 dwelling-houses for masters. The Foundation was originally situated at Mile End, but by a scheme established by the Charity Commissioners in 1884 the almshouses were abolished and the School transferred to Woodford Green, Essex. In 1976 the School reverted to independence, and became a fully co-educational day school, with a Preparatory School being added in 1990.

Motto: *'Unto God only be honour and glory'*

Trustees: The Worshipful Company of Drapers

Visitor: The Master of the Drapers' Company

Governors:
Appointed by the Drapers' Company:
R W P Beharrell (*Chairman*)
G F Crome
J R Rathbone
D J Bettinson
R A Shervington

Co-opted:

Appointed by the London Borough of Redbridge:
R I Barden
B W Tarring

Appointed by the Essex C.C.:
R Wallace

Co-opted:
Mrs R Abbott
Mrs A Coutts

Clerk to the Governors: Miss J Place, Drapers' Hall, London EC2N 2DQ

***Head Master:* P R Scott**, MA DPhil

Deputy Heads:
J G Bromfield, BA
Mrs C Russell, BSc

Headmaster, Preparatory School: D A Horn, MA, ARCM, LLCM

Assistant Staff:

D Copsey, BA
R B Baker, Ac DipEd
J D Pearce, MA
A M Pourgourides, MSc
T R C Jones, MA (*Housemaster*)
C H Pearson, BA
Mrs A H Taylor, BA (*Senior Mistress*)
G E Watkins, BSc
N R Poore, BSc, MPhil
T Smith, BSc
R F Tatam, MA
N Gleeson, MA
Mrs P Kyrou, BSc
C J Bates, PhD
A P Macleod, BEd
Mrs R Howgrave-Graham, BA (*Housemistress*)
A H J Krzyz, MSc
C N Taylor, BA
Mrs J J Davies, BA
L M Gibbon, MA MPhil
Mrs V Smeaton, BA (*Housemistress*)
Miss P Telford, BEd

M Heald, BA
Mrs S A Huk, BA, BSc
J K Lever, Essex CCC and England
D G Morgan, MA
Mrs A M Scurfield, BSc
Mrs S P Thompson, BSc
S P Woolley, BSc
Mrs P R Tindall, BA
Miss J K Robbins, BA
Ms H M Andrews, BSc
Mrs B Noble, CertEd
Miss M Aylett, CertEd
Mrs S Worthington, MA, BA
Mrs R Philip, BEd
Mrs S Goshawk, MA
Mrs C Smith, BSc
Mrs C Lavender, BA
Mrs P Morley
N A Jaques, BA
Mrs C A Rampton, BA
R M Bluff, MA, FRCO
Miss J H Bufton, BA
G P Woods, BA
Mrs R Porter, BA
Mrs J Colman, CertEd
T J Hietzker, BSc
G F Welstead, BA
Mrs M P Richardson, BCom
R C de Renzy Channer, BA
J C Pollard, BEd
A G Taylor, BSc
Miss H J Prescott-Martin, BSc
Mrs S B O'Leary, BSc (*Housemistress*)
Mrs A M Shaer, BEd
S Burton, BA
Miss J M Green, BA
S D Lott, BEd
M E Smeaton, BA
Miss R E Thomas, BA
S A Hunn, BA, DPhil
J A H Williams, BA
J P Weller, BMus
Mrs L E M Lovett, BA
D J Cupit, BEd
N Goalby, MEng
I Moore, MA, MTh
S H Gibbs, BA
Mrs N Doctors, BA
Miss C G Edwards, BA
Mrs E F de Renzy Channer, BA
Miss A M H Wainwright, BA
Miss V Cawthorn, BA
Miss R A Barnes, BA
P A Caira, BSc
Miss G R Abrams, MSc

Bursar: J R Partridge, MA

Matron: Mrs L A Summers, SRN, OHNC

Bancroft's School is a co-educational day school of about 990 pupils. It stands in its own grounds with about five acres of playing fields and it has a further 16 acres of playing fields near Woodford Station, including an all-weather hockey pitch. Its buildings have successfully combined the spacious style of the original architecture with the constant additions demanded by developing needs. These include a Gymnasium, Swimming Pool, Sports' Centre, a Creative Arts Centre and improved premises for the Library and Computer Rooms.

Meals are taken in a well-equipped central dining room, and there is a good variety of menu with self-service on the cafeteria principle.

Pupils are grouped in four Houses – North, East, West and School Each of the Houses has its own Housemaster or Housemistress and a tutorial system.

The School offers a wide range of subjects at GCSE and A Level and has a strong record of academic success. Virtually all Bancroftians go on to university, with about 20 each year to Oxford or Cambridge.

The major sports for girls are Hockey, Netball, Tennis and Athletics. Rugby Football, Hockey and Cricket are the main games for boys. Swimming, Squash, and Basketball are also provided. The Physical Education programme includes gymnastics, trampolining, dance and badminton.

The School has a Contingent of the CCF, a Sea Scout Group, a Branch of the Duke of Edinburgh's Award Scheme, and a Social Service Group, each of which caters both for girls and boys. The School has enjoyed considerable success in the Engineering Education and Young Enterprise Schemes. The programme of concerts and plays through the school year offers opportunities for pupils of all age groups.

Preparatory School. The School opened in September 1990 occupying purpose built accommodation on a separate site within the school grounds. There are 8 classrooms, a hall, a library and specialist rooms for Art and CDT, computing, and languages. Extensive use is made of the sports, music and drama facilities of the main School. There are 11 specialist teachers and some sharing of staff with the main School.

Admission. 50 places are available each year for boys and girls wishing to enter the Preparatory Department at 7+; entry tests take place in the January. Transfer to the Senior School is automatic. At 11+ there are another 60 places available for children entering Bancroft's who take an examination in mid-January. A few places are available for candidates at 13+; for candidates of other ages individual arrangements are made. Applications must be made before 1 January in the year of entry. There is a direct entry for boys and girls into the Sixth Form.

Drapers' Scholarships. (*see* Entrance Scholarship section) Each year up to 12 Drapers' Scholarships, worth up to 50% of the full fees, are awarded to candidates at 11+. Two will generally be awarded as music scholarships. Five Scholarships, worth up to 50% of the full fees, are available each year to external candidates entering the Sixth Form; a further three awards are available to internal candidates. A further Scholarship is available every other year for a boy or girl resident in the London Borough of Newham joining the Sixth Form.

Bancroft's Assisted Places. Five Bancroft's Assisted Places are available at age 11; support is similar to that previously offered by the Government Scheme, and can cover the full fees.

Fees. As at September 2000, including lunch and books: Senior School £7,398 pa, Prep School £5,607 pa.

Leaving Awards. The Drapers' Company makes six Leaving Awards of £200 each year. The Littlewood Scholarship of £100 pa for three years for Science subjects is awarded annually.

Old Bancroftians' Association. Hon. Secretary: Miss H M Rogers, Minton Cottage, 22a Smarts Lane, Loughton, Essex IG10 4BU.

There is a strong Old Bancroftians' Association with a number of affiliated Clubs. The OBA also helps to organise work experience for members of the school.

Charitable status. Bancroft's School is a Registered Charity, number 1068532. It exists to provide an academic education to able children.

Bangor Grammar School

Bangor Co. Down BT20 5HJ Northern Ireland.
Tel: *School:* 02891 473734
Sports Pavilion: 02891 465085
Fax: 02891 273245
e-mail: office@bgs.bangor.ni.sch.uk

Bangor Endowed School was founded in 1856 as a result of a bequest by the Rt Hon Robert Ward. The School is now known as Bangor Grammar School. Its Governing Body is composed of 10 representative Governors elected by Subscribers, 4 Governors nominated by the Department of Education, 2 Parent Governors and 2 Teacher Governors.

Motto: *'Justitiae Tenax'*.

Governors:

Chairman: D B Thompson, BSc(Econ), FCA, MIMC

D G Gray, BSc(Econ), LGSM, FCA
W R T Dowdall
Mrs L Braid
R J Clegg, DipEd
W A Cree, BA, MEd
J Gillvray, BSc, CEng, FICE, FIHT
I G Henderson, OBE, MSc(Econ)
Lady S Herman

M C Johnston, LLB (*Vice-Chairman*)
S B E Johnston, BSc, CEng, MIMechE (*Hon Treasurer*)
R A Milliken, BA, FCA (*Vice-Chairman*)
Mrs E Roche, MA, SRN, SCM, RNT
S Smyth
W R Stevenson, BA

Bursar and Secretary to the Governors:
D J Hunter, LLB, FCA

Headmaster: **N D Argent**, BA, PhD

Senior Vice-Principal: P L Moore, BSc, PhD

Vice Principal: T C Magee, BEd, MA

Senior Teachers:
C C J Harte, BA
D Cairnduff, BA (*English*)
A J Mackie, BA
A J Macpherson, BA

Assistant Staff:
*G H Aiken (*Physical Education*)
M R J Anderson, BSc
*J M Andrews, MA (*English*)
J Atkins, BSc
Mrs P H Bates, BA
*A S Beggs, BSc (*Geography*)
†S E F Blake-Knox, BA (*School*)
Miss S Bromett, BSc
Mrs R Browne, BSc
†A Cardwell, BSc, BAgr (*Dufferin*)
†B S M Christy, BSc (*Dufferin*)
W A Cree, BA, MEd
J W Culbert, BSc
Mrs M Faulkner, BSc, PhD
Miss E I Foster, BSc
A Gray, BA
Mrs L Henry, BA
Mrs C E Hewitt, BA
*I A F Hunter, BA, LTCL, LGSM (*Music*)
*R Jones, BA (*History*)
Mrs C Kerr, BA
C M McDonald, BSc
R McLoughlin, BSc
G C McSorley, BA
R H Mairs, BSc
P Moore, BA
D J Napier, CertEd
M S Nesbitt, BD
N Nourtarshi, BSc, HRes
Mrs J K Payne, BSc, ATD
*Mrs J E Peden, BA (*Art*)
A S Ragg, BSc
*D H Rea, MSc (*Science*)
†J Rea, BA (*School*)
*N Riddell, BSc, PhD (*Mathematics*)
Mrs R Shaw, BA
N J Shields, BA
S Sinclair, MA
C D Steele, BA
†S W Stevenson, BA, PhD (*Crosby*)
W R Stevenson, BA
*J T Titterington, BEng (*Design Technology*)
S Waddell, BA
*Mrs I S Weir, BA
†J B Wilson, BA (*Ward*)
Mrs V J Woods, BSc, PhD

Headmaster's Secretary: Miss M Hamilton

Preparatory Department:
J L Ekin, BA (*Head of Connor House*)
Mrs S Williams, CT (*Deputy Head*)
Mrs M Baker, BEd BEd
Mrs P McDowell
Mrs Kitchen
Mrs J Alexander, BEd Hons
Miss C H Montgomery
Mrs A Ormsby
Miss C E Patterson, BEd
Miss J Pinkerton, BA, MSc
Mrs A Ruding, BSc

There are 2 departments in the School: the Preparatory, with 130 boys and girls, and the Senior with 900 boys. *The Preparatory Department.* Connor House is a self-contained unit with its own building adjoining the main campus. A full range of subjects is taught, including French. Sport is well catered for and mini-rugby, hockey, football and cricket are played against other schools.

There is a Pre-Prep in operation each morning in term-time for boys and girls of 3 and 4 years of age.

School Buildings. In the last decade there has been major development of new buildings and equipment. A new, full-sized Sports Hall and a new, three-storey Design Centre have been built. In addition, a new Sixth Form Centre, Library and Music Suite have been provided and 2 new fully-fitted Computer Laboratories were opened in December 1998. Six new classrooms have been added. Work on a new Science and Technology Block will be completed late in 2001. The School is now very well accommodated and equipped to cope with all the demands of the new National Curriculum.

Admission and Curriculum. Boys are admitted to the Senior School after the age of 11 as a result of their performance in the Department of Education transfer procedure. All boys follow a common curriculum for the first three years. The choice of subjects for the IV and V Forms is kept as wide as possible to enable boys to keep their future options open right up to the GCSE examinations. The School's policy is to encourage boys to undertake a wide range of studies. There is a very strong Music Department and high standards of choral and instrumental work are set and achieved.

A Sixth Form of 200 plus makes possible a wide range of subjects from which boys normally take three or four A level subjects.

Activities. School games include rugby football, cricket, sailing, tennis, squash, badminton, golf, hockey, swimming, athletics and cross country running. There are numerous societies and clubs. Adventure training is catered for by a flourishing contingent of the Combined Cadet Force (with Army and Naval Sections) and the Duke of Edinburgh Award Scheme. Boys are encouraged to gain an experience of social work through the active Community Service Group. Frequent continental visits are arranged.

The School has very high standards in sport. The rugby first XV dominated the Ulster Schools Rugby Cup in the Eighties, with seven appearances in the final, including four victories. Other teams have been successful in the Ulster Schools Golf Championship, the major Ulster Hockey cups, the Ulster and Irish Squash Championships and in the major Ulster Cricket cups and the Ulster Badminton Championships. Recent foreign tours have included Zimbabwe (Rugby) and Australia (Cricket).

Careers. Extensive and continuous help is available to boys in connection with careers. There are five careers staff under the leadership of the Head of Careers. Careers courses, lectures, visits, interviews, work experience, work shadowing and a Challenge of Industry Conference are part of the regular careers structure for boys in Form III and above.

Honours. Boys from the School enter all the major universities in the British Isles. Open scholarships have been won regularly at Oxford, Cambridge and other universities.

Bangor Grammarians Association. *Hon Sec:* Barry McAllister, 22 Glenganagh Park, Groomsport Co Down, Northern Ireland.

Barnard Castle School

Barnard Castle Co Durham DL12 8UN
Tel: (01833) 690222
Fax: (01833) 638985
e-mail: secretary@barneyschool.org.uk

The St John's Hospital in Barnard Castle was founded in the 13th century by John Baliol, whose widow founded the Oxford College. By a Scheme of the Charity Commissioners, bequests under the will of Benjamin Flounders of Yarm were combined with the funds of the St John's Hospital and public subscriptions to build and endow the present foundation in 1883. Originally known as the North Eastern County School, the name was changed to Barnard Castle School in 1924.

Motto: *'Parvis imbutus tentabis grandia tutus'.*

The school is ex Direct Grant.

The Governing Body:
Chairman: J C Macfarlane, CBE

Vice-Chairmen:
W R Atkinson, CB
F Turnbull, MBE

I Forster
J R Hinchcliffe
Mrs A McBain
Mrs S Pollard
D F Starr
R Sale
D N Williams
R G Booth
Dr W J B Cherry
G A Camozzi
C Dennis
Miss C Elgey

Clerk to the Governors: M White

***Headmaster:* M D Featherstone**, MA

Second Master: D H Ewart BA, MA, DMS (*Geography*)

Senior Mistress: Mrs H M McGill, BA (*English*)

Chaplain and Director of Studies: The Revd S J Ridley, MA

Assistant Staff:
A Chadwick, MA (*Chemistry*)
*R D Sellick, BSc, MPhil (*Biology*)
J G Worsnop, BA (*English*)
*P G Wise, BSc (*Science*)
†*G Bishop, BA (*Economics & Business Studies*)
*C P Johnson, BA (*Modern Languages*)
*A R Farrar, BA (*Classics*)
G H Charlesworth, BSc (*Chemistry*)
Mrs S M Stewart, BA (*Modern Languages*)
S Kean, BSc (*Mathematics*)
†P McHarry, BSc (*Physics*)
Mrs E G Niven, MA (*Modern Languages*)
*G C Parkin, BSc (*Technology*)
†*D C S Everall, BEd (*PE and Maths*)
*D M P Blakely, MA (*Maths*)
*R M Anderson, MSc (*Information Technology*)
*A M Waddington, BA (*English*)
Mrs S R Cuthbertson, BA, ATC (*Art*)
R Child, BSc, PhD (*Biology*)
M N R Fuller, BEd (*Biology and Careers*)
*G S Herbert, BSc, PhD (*Chemistry*)
A P Moorhouse, BA (*English*)
†A J Parkinson, BA (*Maths*)
†J D N Gedye, BA (*Classics*)
Mrs B Ellison, BA (*Modern Languages*)
*P Harrison, GLCM, LTCL, MA (*Director of Music*)
*§Mrs C Le Duc, CertEd (*PSHE & Religious Studies*)
†M H Nicholson, BSc, BA (*Maths*)
Miss F Cover, BEd (*PE and Geography*))
Mrs C Shovlin, BA, ALA (*Librarian*)
Mrs A Armstrong, BEd (*PE*)
*D W Dalton, BA (*Geography*)
§Mrs S R Pender, CertEd, CertFPS (*EFL*)
M Donnelly (*Music*)
*D S Gorman, BA (*History & Politics*)
R A Hall, BA, ARCO (*Music*)
B C Usher, BSc (*Mathematics*)
§†Mrs D M L Everall, BA (*EFL*)
C H Alderson, BSc (*Geography and History*)
*Mrs I V Ewart, BEd, DipSpLD, AMBDA (*Learning Support*)
M P Ince, BA (*History and Politics*)
M M Hudson, BSc (*Physics*)
M T Pepper, BA (*PE*)
N Toyne, BSc (*Maths*)
§M Bright, CertEd (*Business Studies*)
§Miss L Konstacka, Mgr (*EFL*)
A M Beaty, BSc (*Technology*)
Miss T C Broadbent, BA (*PE*)
Mrs A M Gorman, BA (*English*)
N Gregory, BA (*Modern Languages*)
Miss M E Mitchell, BA, BSc (*Art*)

Combined Cadet Force:
Com Officer: Major S Kean
M G Lewis, WO1, SSI

Preparatory School:
E J Haslam, ACP, Dip Ed (*Headmaster*)
N I Seddon, BEd (*Second Master*)
Miss C E Lane, CertEd (*Director of Studies*)
§A Dougherty, BEd, MEd, FRGS
Mrs S M Seddon, BEd
Mrs J C A Tulip, BEd
Mrs H Brown, BEd
Mrs L Rowlandson, BA
†M B Wilson, BEd

Bursar: A J White, BA, DMS

Medical Officer: Dr J J White, MBBS, DRCOG, MRCGP

Medical Centre: Mrs H Nevin, RGN

Headmaster's Secretary: Mrs J Hazell

Barnard Castle is a day and boarding school for boys and girls between the ages of 4 and 18.

Organisation and Numbers. There are 500 pupils aged 11-18 in the Senior School, of whom 155 are boarders. The Preparatory School comprises a Pre-Prep Department of 30 pupils between the ages of 4 and 7, and 120 pupils between the ages of 7 and 11, of whom 30 are boarders. The Senior and Preparatory Schools are located on adjacent sites and operate separately on a day-to-day basis whilst enjoying the mutual benefits of being able to share a number of resources and facilities. Girls were first admitted in 1981 and the School has been fully co-educational since 1993.

Location. The School is situated in its own extensive grounds on the outskirts of an historic market town in an area of outstanding natural beauty. The area is well served by Teesside and Newcastle airports and by Darlington railway station. The School also operates its own bus service for pupils from a wide area.

Curriculum. This is designed to provide a broad, balanced and flexible programme, avoiding undue specialisation at too early a stage. In the Prep School emphasis is given to literacy and numeracy skills, as well as Science, History, Geography, French (from age 8), Religious Education, Technology, Art, Music, Information Technology, Physical Education (including swimming) and Games. These subjects are developed further in the Senior School, with the addition of Latin or Classical Civilisation, Personal, Social and Health Education, and three separate sciences. German or Spanish is added at age 14, whilst Business Studies increases the list of GCSE options at age 15. There are some twenty A or AS level subjects to choose from in the Sixth Form, where a large number of combinations are possible. Almost all Sixth Form leavers go on to University or College courses. A Learning Support Department provides specialist help for those who need it in both the Preparatory and Senior Schools, and tuition is offered in English as a Second Language.

Religious Education. The School is a Christian foundation and the Chapel stands at the heart of the School in more than just a geographical sense. The School Chaplain, who plays an important role in the pastoral structure of the School as well as being responsible for religious education and Chapel worship, is an ordained member of the Church of England, but the School is a multi-denominational one which welcomes and supports pupils of all faiths. Pupils attend weekday morning assemblies in Chapel, and there is a Sunday service for boarders.

Boarding and Day Houses. There are seven single-sex Houses within the Senior School - three boarding and four day - each small enough for pupils to know each other well, but large enough to allow a mixture of interests, backgrounds and abilities, as well as opportunities for leadership. Housemasters and Housemistresses, each supported by a team of Tutors and Assistants, are responsible for the welfare and progress of each pupil in their charge.

Junior Boarders (boys and girls aged 7-11) and Senior Girl Boarders live in their own modern Houses in the School grounds, alongside their Houseparents and Boarding Tutors. The two Senior boys' Houses have recently undergone a major programme of restructuring and refurbishment, and offer comfortable accommodation within the main building of the School. The resident Housemasters are supported by resident boarding tutors and matron, and by the School Sister in the School's new Medical Centre. The School Doctor visits daily.

Cultural and other activities. The School has a flourishing music department in which the Chapel Choir, Orchestras, Wind and Jazz Bands and smaller ensembles perform regularly.

Drama is also prominent, with a regular programme of productions taking place throughout the year. There is a strong tradition of after-school activities, which enables both day and boarding pupils to take part in a wide range of clubs and societies.

Games. Rugby, Hockey, Netball, Cricket, Athletics, Squash, Cross-Country Running, Tennis and Swimming are the main sports, and other options such as soccer, badminton, lacrosse, basketball, fencing and golf are available. The School has extensive playing fields, a modern Sports Hall, squash and tennis courts, and a heated indoor swimming pool. Regular inter-school matches are arranged at all levels.

Outdoor Activities. There is a strong emphasis on providing instruction, opportunity and challenge in a wide range of outdoor activities. Much of this takes place under the auspices of a flourishing Cadet Force (Army and RAF sections) or the Duke of Edinburgh Gold and Silver Award Schemes.

Careers. The School is a member of the Independent Schools' Careers Organisation and receives support from the Durham County Careers Service. There is a well-equipped Careers Room, and a team of careers staff work together with the Higher Education Co-ordinator to provide pupils at all stages of the School with expert advice and help in decision-making and application procedures.

Admission. Pupils are admitted at all stages either via the School's own Entrance Examination or via the Common Entrance Examination. There is also direct entry into the Sixth Form subject to satisfactory performance at GCSE level. Details of the application procedure are obtainable from the Headmaster's Secretary.

Scholarships and assisted places (*see* Entrance Scholarship section). The School makes Entrance Awards on entry to the Senior School (including at Sixth Form level). In addition to academic awards, these may include awards for musical, artistic and sporting ability and potential. The School is also able to offer a small number of its own means-tested assisted places for able children whose parents would not otherwise be able to send them. Details are available from the Headmaster's Secretary.

Fees per term. Fees are inclusive and subject to annual review. Senior Boarders: £3,727. Senior Day Pupils: £2,206. Prep Boarders: £2,856. Prep Day Pupils: £1,535. Pre-Prep: £964.

The Old Barnardians' Club. The Club organises a number of functions each year, including a Summer Gathering at the School, and Dinners both in London and the North East.

Charitable status. Barnard Castle School is a Registered Charity, number 527383, whose aim is the education of boys and girls.

Batley Grammar School

Batley W Yorks WF17 0AD
Tel: (01924) 474980 (Head's Office); (01924) 470020 (Bursar)
Fax: (01924) 471960; 420513 (Bursar)
e-mail: info@batleygrammar.leeds.sch.uk
website: http://www.batleygrammar.leeds.sch.uk

Batley Grammar School was founded in 1612 by the Reverend William Lee "..... to make such as be capable fit for the University". For some years the school was Voluntary Aided, but since 1978 it has been fully independent and is now represented on both the Headmasters' Conference and the Governing Bodies Association. There are 460 pupils in the school. Girls have been entering the Sixth Form since 1988, and in September 1996 the school welcomed its first co-educational intake at 11+. The Junior Department (4-11 years) opened in September 2000.

Motto: *'Forte non Ignave'*.

Governors:

Chairman: Dr M C J Barker, BSc, PhD, MInstP, CPhys

Vice-Chairman: A W Barraclough, BSc

J M Beaumont, JP
D Brereton
Mrs S J Clay, JP
Dr S Collins, PhD, MSc
Professor J A Double, BTech, PhD, DSc
D Forrest, FCA
S B Oakes, LLB
A L Palfreeman, JP, BSc
J S W Sheard, DMS, DipM, GInstM, FIMgt
E Suleman, ACA
The Reverend K Williams

Bursar and Clerk to the Governors: Mr C M Bremer, BA, MBA

Teaching Staff:

Headmaster: **¶B Battye**, MA

Deputy Head: M I Cook, BSc, MSc, CPhys, MInstP

Director of Studies: *P H Gott, MA

*R Bunford, BSc	*J A Hartley, BA
*B Ellis, DLC	*Mrs A J Thomas, BEd
*P H Gott, MA	*Mrs J E Wilson, BA
†J D Carter, BSc	*S Haigh, BEd
*C G Marsden, BTech, PhD, ARIC	Mrs E Jenkins, BSc
D N Scriven, MA	P Wrigley, BSc (*Econ*), MSc
A Turnbull, BSc	¶A J Brooke, BA
P D Wilby, BA	D A Barker, BSc, PhD
B Cooper, BSc	Mrs N Rollinson, BEd
*G Bellamy, MA, DipRE	Dr P L West, MA, BD, PhD
J C Sanderson, BEd	G Williams, MA
†*¶S M Emsley, BA	H J Lorriman, FTCL, LTCL
G Dawson, BA	C J Bowman, BSc
J L O'Dwyer, BA	Ms E L Bond, BA
H P Bowden, MA	R S Bocking, BSc, MSc
*P N Renold, BA, CNAA	Miss C J Gammons, BA
B G Woodley, MA	Mrs J Haycock, BEd
¶J E Hargreaves, BA	

Priestley House Junior School

Headmaster: G Bellamy, MA, DipRE

Mrs K Barker, BSc
Mrs H Hawkes, BEd
Ms F Steinitz, BA, LLCM

Facilities: The school has occupied its present site for over a hundred years with considerable expansion taking place during this period.

In 1980, shortly after Independence, the Science Block was built with six spacious and well-equipped laboratories and ancillary rooms, whilst in the main school adaptations included: the remodelled and refurbished Art Rooms, two new classrooms, a Computer and Maths room, a Careers room, and a Sixth Form Common Room.

In 1989 the new Sports Hall was finished, and extensions made to changing facilities, and in 1999 a Sports Studies laboratory was added.

In 1991 the Priestley Language Centre was added with 30 audio booths and satellite television. The Priestley Design and Technology Centre is equipped with several PC computers which are linked to the school's main computer network fileserver.

The Information Technology department has two dedicated work centres. In 1999 both rooms were refitted with PCs served by the school network and Internet.

From September 2000 the school had a new Careers Room, equipped with computer and CD-ROM facilities. A regular link has been opened with the local careers advisory service. A new resource centre and library was added in September 2000, and Sixth Form facilities were refurbished.

During 1999 the former Headmaster's House was converted into a Junior Department which opened in September 2000. The age range has now expanded to 4-11.

Admissions. All candidates for admission must be registered and registration forms can be obtained from the General Secretary's Office. The main point of co-educational entry is at 4, 7 or 11, but there are also small annual entries at other ages. Entrance examinations for 7+, 11+, 12+ and 13+ take place in January for admission the following September. Admission is offered to the Sixth Form on the results of GCSE examinations and interview.

Awards. The Governors award a number of Scholarships and Bursaries each year, mainly at 11+.

Fees. The present fees are £5,205 per annum.

Curriculum. Normally entry to the senior school is at the age of eleven and in the first three years pupils are given a broadly-based curriculum. Almost all academic subjects are studied with the three sciences being covered separately as well as Information Technology and Design Technology.

At the end of the third year the pupils, in consultation with parents and staff, choose from a number of option blocks. All pupils follow a core curriculum supported by other options so that at the end of year eleven each sits a full range of nine or ten GCSE examinations.

In the Sixth Form the individual requirements of each student are catered for as much as possible with the vast majority taking four AS levels, including General Studies, followed by three A2.

Physical Education and Games. Physical Education is regarded as an essential part of the school curriculum. All pupils are expected to spend some time on general aspects of the subject each week, whilst each year group is allocated a separate session for Games within the timetable. In the Winter these games are Association Football, Hockey, Netball, Basketball and Cross Country, whilst in the Summer Term, Cricket, Athletics, Tennis and Rounders are the main alternatives.

The Sports Centre consists of a large multi-function sports hall with additional circuit-training and table tennis area linked to a weight-training area, changing rooms and showers. The four soccer/hockey pitches, two cricket squares, a new hard-surface area with tennis and netball courts, and the tartan track and jumping/sprinting areas are adjacent to the school.

The school is divided into four Houses; Akroyd, Benstead, Lee and Talbot. Inter-House competitions are organised in a variety of sports. In addition the school has regular fixtures in Association Football, Cricket, Athletics, Cross Country, Hockey and Netball in all relevant age-groups.

Clubs and Activities. The school has a very full range of societies, clubs and extra curricular activities, ranging from Drama to Textiles and from Ski-ing to Chess. These encourage the pupils to develop their own interests and skills, widen horizons and experiences, and give service to the community. Parties of all ages regularly go to European countries and exchanges with French and German schools are arranged.

Each year the School Community Service Group gives generous support to local charities, the bulk of the funds being raised by a strenuous ten-mile sponsored run.

The CCF comprises RN, Army and RAF Sections and is run on a purely voluntary basis. Recruits are admitted towards the end of the third year of the school. In addition to the specialist and adventure training in the programme Cadets may also prepare for the Duke of Edinburgh Silver and Gold Awards.

Music plays an important part in the life of the school. The full-time members of the Music Department are assisted by six visiting instrumental teachers and other members of the school staff. The school has a Choir, a Concert Band, an Orchestra, a Brass Ensemble, a Junior Band and Recorder Groups. Bands regularly compete in regional competitions: in 1991 the Brass Band was the first school band ever invited to play at Wembley Stadium.

Leaving Scholarships and Exhibitions. Non-recurring grants are awarded by the Trustees each year to sixth formers proceeding to higher education/training. Most leavers go on to Further Education and 80-90% each year go to university.

Junior School Curriculum. The Curriculum in Priestley House is very close to the National Curriculum. Work in English, Mathematics and Science is aimed toward SATs tests. There are also lessons in History, Geography, DT, Music, PE, Computing, RE and Art. French is taught to years 5 and 6.

Old Batelians Association. *Membership Secretary:* B Battye, Esq, 72 Greenacres Drive, Birstall, Batley. (Telephone: 01924 470018)

Charitable status. The Batley Grammar School Foundation is a Registered Charity, number 529335. Its aims and objectives are to provide a first class education for pupils above the age of 11.

Bedales School
(Coeducational)

Petersfield Hampshire GU32 2DG.
Tel: (01730) 300100. Registrar: (01730) 304274.
Fax: (01730) 300500

Governors:
M Blakstad, MA, MSc (*Chairman*)
N M Allen, BA
R P Baker-Bates, MA, FICA, AIMC
Mrs L V Brett, BSc(Soc)
Prof K Crouan, BA, FRSA
Ms C R Donoughue, MA
D T Handley, CMG, BA
Mrs R Hollingsworth, BA (Hons), DipSocSci
Prof R G Scurlock, MA, DPhil, CEng, FIMechE
J M G Taylor, BA (Hons)
J Wilkinson, MA, AdvDipEd

Clerk to the Governors and Bursar:
R B A Moore, MBE

***Head:* K J Budge**, MA (University College, Oxford)

Deputy Head: J F J Taylor, BA, MEd

Assistant Staff:
K J Adlam, BSc
Mrs O Allen (*Diplôme Universitaire*)
Mrs A W Archer, BSc, MSc (*Librarian*)
D F Archer, MA
G T H Banks, BA
Ms C L A Black, BA
M W Box, BA
Mrs R E Carpenter-Jones, BA
P W Coates, BEd
Miss L Collison, BSc
A T Davis, BEd
T Drot, MA
S Elia, AGSM
J C Fothergill, BSc
N E Gleed, MA (*Director of Music*)
C Hamilton, BA, AKC, MPhil, PhD
Mrs A F Hardie, BEd (*Registrar*)
T A Hardy, BSc
G J Hatton, BA
C J Howarth, BA
P Jones, BSc
A J Monk, BSc
A Muir, BA
G H Noble, BA
Ms S Oliver, BA (*Housemistress*)
P C Parsons, BA (*Housemaster*)
E Patterson, BA
H Pearson, BSc, PhD (*Housemaster*)
J C Pearson, MA
C W Prowse, BSc, PhD
Ms A Reid, MA, BA
P J Robinson, BSc
K A C Rowe, ARCM, LRAM (*Housemaster*)
Mrs C L Sankey, BA (*Housemistress*)
W Saunders, BA
J A Scullion, MA, BA (*Housemaster*)
R A Sinclair, BA
G J Skinner, BA, PhD
Mrs S Stephenson, BSc
Mrs J Sueref, BA
Miss N S C Woodroffe, BSc
Mrs M C Woolley, BA
A P Young, MA, MusB (*Director of Studies*)

Dunhurst (*Junior School*)
Head: M R Piercy, BA

C Baty, BEd, DipTeaching (*House Tutor*)
Mrs F Box, DipDysInst, AMBDA
D R Cochrane, BPhil
J R Culley, BA (*Director of Studies*)
S Ekins, BSc
Ms Z Flack, BA(Ed) (Hons)
Miss A Foley, BA, DipEd
Mrs M R Fuller, ARCM
R Hancock, AdDipEd, PGCE (*Deputy Head, Housemaster*)
Mrs E Hewitt, BA
Ms W Houston, BA
S Kingsley-Pallant, BA (Hons)
Ms M Lovell, BA, PGCE (*House Tutor*)
Mrs D Mills, BA, QTS (Hons)
Miss L S Palmer, BSc
Mrs J Samuelson, BSc
A Smee, BEd
A Suart, BSc
R Warboys, BA
Mrs P Weston, BSc (*Housemistress*)

Dunannie (*Pre-Prep School*)
Headmistress: Miss D S Webster, MA, BEd

Mrs J A Brown, BEd
Miss C Rodgers, BA, MSc
Mrs S A Sackfield, CertEd
Mrs G Wicksteed, CertEd

School Physicians:
Dr A J H Holden, MB, BS, DRCOG, DFFP
Dr C Christie, BMedSc, BM, BS, MRCP, DRCOG, DFFP, FRCGP

Number in School. 400 in Senior School. Equal numbers of boys and girls. 25% day students.

Bedales stands in an estate of 120 acres in the heart of the Hampshire countryside, overlooking the South Downs. Although only one hour from London by train, this is one of the most beautiful corners of rural England. Founded in 1893, Bedales is one of the oldest co-educational schools. The community is a stimulating and happy one, in which tolerance and supportive relationships thrive at all levels.

The School has strong traditions in both humanities and the sciences, in Art, Design, Drama and Music.

Admission. Entry to the School is from 3+ (see Dunannie), 8+, 9+, 10+, 11+ (see Dunhurst), 13+ and 16+ (Bedales). Once in the School pupils can proceed to the next stage, if they so wish, provided they perform satisfactorily.

Entry Tests. Entry for newcomers at 8+, 11+ and 13+ takes the form of residential tests in the January preceding the September entry. Entry at 16+ is by a series of interviews spread over a single day. Write in the first instance to the Registrar.

Senior School (13 to 18): 80 in each year. In the first year, all follow a broad-based curriculum, then there follows a two-year course leading to GCSE. All pupils study Art, Design, Music and Drama in the first year and are required to take at least one of these subjects to GCSE. The usual range of subjects is offered. At AS and A2 level, pupils can do Mathematics, Further Mathematics, Design, Economics, Chemistry, Physics, Biology, English, Philosophy, Psychology, French, German, Spanish, Latin, History, Geography, Music, Art and Theatre Studies. There are field courses in Geography and Biology, and there are camping expeditions with adventure training. In the Sixth Form a broad and interesting programme is followed including Current Affairs. IT facilities are continually updated, each child having an e-mail address and monitored access to the internet. (There is also a laptop scheme available to all pupils). There are excellent recreational facilities, including extensive playing fields, gymnasium, sports hall, covered heated swimming pool and a floodlit astro-turf pitch. A programme of Outdoor Work is offered on the School estate as an option in the Games programme. The pupils have reconstructed two 18th century barns in the grounds and these form the centre piece for the Outdoor Work conservation project.

There are no prefects but pupil-chaired committees which take responsibility for a wide variety of aspects of school life. There is a School Council which represents all levels of the school. Until the final year, the children sleep in small mixed aged dormitories and in the final year (6.2) the students move to a co-ed House with exceptional facilities. This arrangement fosters very good relationships across the age range. The School is non-denominational in character.

Dunhurst (8 to 13): (See IAPS section, Part V).

Dunannie (3 to 8): Entrance at 3+ is by date of registration, after this acceptances are made following informal assessments should vacancies arise. 90 pupils. Dunannie has five classes including a nursery. It is in a purpose-built building sharing facilities, extensive grounds and specialist teachers with the other two schools. Dunannie offers a lively, stimulating educational environment where there is emphasis on the individual development of the child. A thorough grounding is given within a broad, balanced curriculum.

Bursaries and Scholarships. (*see* Entrance Scholarship section) Music scholarships are available at 8-12, 13+ and 16+. Other scholarships are available at 13+ and 16+. Boarding scholarships at 8+. For full details of scholarships see separate announcement or contact the School.

Fees 2000/2001. Boarders £5,529 per term. Day £4,227 per term. Dunhurst Boarders £3,800 per term, Day £2,760 per term. Dunannie £721–£1,559 per term.

Charitable status. Bedales School is a Registered Charity, number 307332-A2-A. Its aims and objectives are to educate children as broadly as possible in a creative and caring environment.

Bedford Modern School

Manton Lane Bedford MK41 7NT.
Tel: (01234) 332500
Fax: (01234) 332550
e-mail: info@bedmod.co.uk
website: www.bedmod.co.uk

Bedford Modern School is one of the Harpur Trust Schools of Bedford, sharing equally in the educational endowment bequeathed for the establishment of a school in Bedford by Sir William Harpur in 1566.

Chairman of the School Committee: D K Brownridge, LLB, CPFA

***Headmaster:* S Smith**, MA

Second Master: C R Barcock, BA

Deputy Head (*Academic*): J D Davies, MA, DPhil
Deputy Head (*Pastoral*): G M Lavery, BA, BMus
Director of Studies: T J Wilkes, MA, DPhil
Director of Information Systems: D Walsh, BEd, MSc
Head of Sport: N J Chinneck, BEd
Co-ordinator Co-curricular Activities: R M Chadwick, DLC, BA, BISC

Head of the Junior School: N R Yelland, BEd

Art:
R W Cox, DipAD, ATD
Mrs P Edwards
A Matheson (*Artist in Residence*)

Classics:
D G Hope, BA
Miss J Newton, MA

Computing:
Mrs S Harris, MSc, MA
Mrs K Taneja, MA, BEd

Design & Technology:
A J Brien, MSc, BEd
P Kennington
I C Grainger
J P White, BEd

English/Drama:
Mrs M D Hetherington, MA
Miss G Arger, BEd, TEFL
J P Barnes, MA, PhD
Mrs R Beggs, BA
S D Bywater, BA
E H Carwithen, MA
P F Habershon, BEd
Mrs H Rees-Bidder, BEd
Mrs C A Rogers, AD, BEd
Miss A Bryan (*Theatre Technician*)

Economics:
J D W Richards, BA, MA, PhD
J R Ryan, BA
to be announced

Geography:
N C Robinson, BSc, MA
R M Chadwick, DLC, BA, BISC
Miss A Moody, BA
I R D White, MA

History:
M J Muncaster, MA, PhD
J D Davies, MA, DPhil
C Wilson, BEd, MA, DipCareers Education and Guidance (Herts)
Mrs S E Wright, MA

Information Systems:
D Walsh, BEd, MSc

Mathematics:
P J Birch, BSc
S A Brocklehurst, BA
M G Gant, MA
D M King, BSc
Mrs J Monk, MA
A Rome, BSc, CertRS
Mrs P J Russell, BSc, MSc
M J Stellman, BEd

Modern Languages:
J R Chatburn, MA
G A Watkins, BA
Mlle G Amoros, L-ès-L
M J Cooper, BEd
C De Vido, BA
M Harrington, BA, BEd
Miss L Hendry, BA
R J Killen, BA
Mrs S Mitchell, MIL
Mlle P Ozkan, L-ès-L

Junior School Staff:
N R Yelland, BEd (*Head*)
Mrs E P Sheldon, BA (*Deputy Head*)
Mrs H Avery, BEd
Mrs G M Colling, CertEd
Mrs S E Cox, CertEd
Mrs R A Marek, BEd, Dip Management Studies(Educ)
S D W Orton, BEd
Mrs J C Rex, BA
C W H Rees-Bidder, BA, MEd
Mrs J Robinson, BA
J R Robinson, CertEd
Mrs J Smith, CertEd
R W Wall, CertEd, ACP
M Whitford, BSc, MPhil

Boarding House Staff:
Mr and Mrs G M Lavery (*Houseparents*)
Mr and Mrs C Francis (*Tutors*)
S Starr (*GAP student*)
D Hankin (*GAP student*)

Religious Education:
D Kendall, BA, MA
A J Rowley, MA, PhD

Music:
Mrs M Francis, BMus, LRAM, ARCM
Miss K Bywater (*Head of Wind & Brass*)
J Mower, GRSM, ARCO, ARCM, DipRAM
S Cartledge, LTCL (*Head of Strings*)

PE:
N J Chinneck, BEd
R J Follett, BA
A Higgins, BSc
B J R Morrison, BEd
T E Rex, BEd
P J Smith, BSc
M Swarfield, BA
A Tapper, BSc, MSt
N T Whitwham, BA

Science:

Biology:
J M Shipway, BSc
R J Brand, BSc
D A Jenkins, BSc, MSc, DipEdTech
B H Stratton, BSc

Chemistry:
N R Else, MA, BEd
S Burridge, BSc
Dr G R Hobbs, BSc, PhD
M J Maisey, BEd
P R Temple, BSc

Physics:
R J Turner, BSc, BA
M English, BSc, MSc
S S Harvey, BSc
T P Mullan, BSc
T J Wilkes, MA, DPhil

Careers:
Mrs M S Brown
Mrs S Mitchell
Miss A Moody
Mr D Jenkins (Forces)
Mrs P Russell

Bursar: A T Smyth

School Librarian: Mrs M S Brown, BSc, ALA

SSI: RSM B Simpson, MISM

Medical Officer: Dr S Lowe, MB, ChB, MRCGP, DRCOG, FpCert

Bedford Modern School was a Direct Grant Grammar School which became independent in 1976. There are 228 boys in the Junior School (aged 7–10) and 882 boys in the Senior School (aged 11–19).

In April 1974 the school moved from its town site to entirely new buildings on a wooded hill site overlooking the school playing fields on the northern outskirts of Bedford. Since then, substantial further building work has included a Sports Hall of 7,000 sq ft and also a specialist Gym (1982), a Design Technology Centre (1989), enlargements to the Music Centre (1992), a Practical Skills Centre for the Junior School (1994), a Sixth Form Centre (the Robert Luff Centre) (1996) and a Junior School Library (1998). A major Junior School development is planned for September 2002.

Admission. Day boys are admitted between the ages of 7 and 16. The school conducts its own Entrance Assessments which are held in February and March.

Fees. Registration fee is £50.

Tuition: Junior School £4,860 pa; Senior School £6,537 pa.

Assistance with Fees. There is a variety of bursaries, scholarships and exhibitions available. Details may be obtained from the school.

Organisation and Curriculum. The Junior School (ages 7–10) curriculum covers Mathematics, English, Science, Technology, French, German, RE, History and Geography. It is significantly enriched by the provision of specialist teaching from the Senior School for the 9 and 10 year old classes. Boys benefit both from a purpose-built Practical Skills Centre (Art, Computing, Technology, Science), and from the Senior School Music, PE and Games facilities.

In the Senior School, the curriculum includes all the core subjects, as well as Technology, IT, RE, Music, Art and Drama. All boys begin Latin at 12+. From 13+ many continue with three languages and all take separate subject sciences for this stage. Students opt for between nine and ten GCSE subjects depending on their ability and the guidance offered by the school's Careers Team. For the Sixth Form, students select from a wide range. In addition to all the traditional options, the choice of subjects also includes ICT, Government and Politics, Economics, Business Studies, Religious Studies, Philosophy, Elec tronics, Classical Civilisation and Theatre Studies. Most subjects can be taken both to A2 and AS level. There is a challenging General Studies programme.

Computing facilities. The School has a fully integrated PC Network for both administrative and academic use, with internet access. The school has its own website: www.bedmod.co.uk.

Religious and Moral Education. The School is multifaith and multicultural, and religious and moral education is given throughout. All major world religions are covered and it is hoped that students can learn to be tolerant whilst accepting the place for firmly held beliefs. Personal and Social Education is a fundamental and well-established part of the timetable.

Drama. There are several productions every year in the Howard Hall, the well-equipped theatre. There are also separate Drama Studios. Theatre Studies is offered to A2 level.

Music. Boys can learn all the orchestral and band instruments as well as piano, keyboard, guitar and synthesizer. The school has a large variety of choirs, orchestra, bands and ensembles. Boys can follow courses for GCSE and A level music as well as A level Music Technology.

Activities. There are many school societies and clubs catering for a variety of tastes and interests. The voluntary Combined Cadet Force, joint with Bedford High School, is 180 strong with Army, Navy, RAF and Marine sections. Boys may learn flying, sailing and paragliding. Community Service and the Duke of Edinburgh's Award Scheme are very popular.

Games. There are 30 acres of playing fields, tennis courts, squash courts and an indoor heated swimming pool. Physical Education is taught to all boys below the Sixth Form. In the Autumn Term, Rugby Football is played. Association Football, Hockey, Rowing, Swimming and Cross Country occupy the Spring Term, and Cricket, Athletics, Rowing and Swimming take place during the Summer Term. Badminton, Table-tennis, Shooting and Water Polo are also offered.

Houses. There is a flourishing House system.
Bell House (Mrs S Mitchell)
Farrer House (Mr S Harvey)
Mobbs House (Mr A Tapper)
Oatley House (Mr P Temple)
Rose House (Dr P Barnes)
Tilden House (Mr D J Kendall)

Higher Education. There were over 100 entrants to degree courses in 2000.

Old Bedford Modernians' Club. Secretary: R H Wildman, Esq., Bedford Modern School, Manton Lane, Bedford MK41 7NT.

Charitable status. The Bedford Charity (The Harpur Trust) is a Registered Charity, number 204817. It includes in its aims the provision of high quality education for boys.

Bedford School

De Parys Avenue Bedford MK40 2TU
Tel: (01234) 362200
Fax: (01234) 362283
e-mail: registrar@bedfordschool.org.uk

Bedford School is first mentioned in a document of Henry II's reign. At the monastic dissolutions of 1540, the School was handed over to the "Mayor, Bailiffs and Commonalty of Bedford", and in 1552 received a licence by Letters Patent from Edward VI for the "education and instruction of boys and youths in grammatical learning and good manners". In 1556 it was endowed by Sir William Harper, a citizen of Bedford, who became Lord Mayor of London. The School House, erected by Sir William Harper and reconstructed in the 18th century, became the Town Hall in 1891, when the present School buildings were opened on an extensive estate to the north of the town centre. Recent investment has provided a Recreation Centre, Theatre, Indoor Swimming Pool, Technology Centre, Information Technology Suite, an observatory and two all-weather surfaces (one floodlit). The School also has two notable Concert Halls.

Motto: *"Floreat Schola Bedfordiensis"*.

School Governors:

Chairman: The Rt Hon The Lord Naseby, PC, MA
Vice-Chairman: R P F Shorten, Esq
Chairman of the Harpur Trust: Prof C J Constable, MA, BSc, DBA

Dr M A H Cook, BSc
Cllr C M Ellis
Mrs S Peck

T Snow, Esq, MA
Mrs A R Watson, JP

Co-opted Governors:
S A G Abrahams, Esq, TD
R S Dawes, Esq
R E Gordon, Esq, CA
B E Howard, Esq, MA

***Head Master:* I P Evans**, OBE, MA, PhD, CChem, FRSC, Churchill College, Cambridge

Vice Master: A M Thorp, MA, Selwyn College, Cambridge

Director of Studies: R G Miller, MA, Trinity College, Cambridge

Registrar: T A Riseborough, MA, Keble College, Oxford

Senior Housemaster: B G Law, BA Hons, Port Elizabeth, HDE, Cape Town

Director of Sports and Activities: T J Machin, MA, St Edmund Hall, Oxford

Assistant staff:

Art:
R H Campbell, BA
C N Ferry, BA, DPSE (DR Tech)
D S Odom, DFA(Lond)

Biology:
M A Beale, BSc, CAPSE, MEd
Ms F D Bell, BSc
P B Churcher, BEd, MSc
L J Guise, MA
M J Gunn, BSc, MIBiol, CBiol

Chemistry:
C Baker, BSc, CChem, MRSC
A J Crowe, BSc, PhD
C W Duckworth, BSc
A P Millar, BSc, PhD
G W Mines, BSc, PhD (*also Head of Science*)
P A Young, BSc

Classics:
Miss C M Wilson, MA
Miss E Dale, MA

Design Technology:
D W Jacobs, BEd, CNAA, MEd, HNC (ProdEng)
K Spencer, BEd, HNCMechEng, MIMI
Miss I C Bowis, BA
C H Smith, BEd, CNAA

Economics:
J E Keefe, BA
M H Cassell, BSc
M R Hordley, BCom
A M Thorp, MA

English:
R H Palmer, MA, PhD
Mrs J P Crizzle, BA
D M Cundall, MA
A W Grimshaw, BA
B G Law, BA Hons, HDE
R J B MacDowell, MA
A J Speedy, BA

Geography:
R J Walker, BA
S T Burt, BSc
H A Collison, BSc, MPhil
Miss E M Ellwood, BA
D E Pounds, BSc

History:
P S Wiser, BA
J J Farrell, MA
J N W Fleming, MA
T J Machin, MA
R G Miller, MA

Information Technology:
Revd A P Manning, MA, CTMin
D C Bach, MA
R A Eadie, MA (*Computer Manager*)

Mathematics:
C G Jeavons, MSc
P J Coggins, BSc, MPhil
N J Cox, MA
T V Jennings, BSc, MA, MPhil, PhD, CMath, FIMA
M J F Rea, BA
Mrs S Staincliffe, BSc
G C Taylor, BSc
J B Watson, MA
Miss K L Welch, BSc(Ed)

Modern Languages:
C L Marsh, MA, MLitt
A J R Huxford, MA
F J G Inglis, BA, MLitt
J E J O'Neill, BA, MIL
J C Osman, BA
Mlle G C J Prual, Licence d'anglais
Mrs M P Wood, MA, MIL

Music:
A W Morris, MA, BMus, GRSM, FTCL, ARAM, ARCO(CHM), LRAM, ARCM
G V Bennett, GGSM
M C Green, GRSM, LRAM, ARCM, DipRAM
B C W Grindlay, MA, MusB, FRCO(CHM), FCSM
R Heyes, MA, BMus, GRSM, LRAM, ARCO
N J Keatley, ARCM, ABSM

Physical Education:
G M K Fletcher, BEd, DipPhysEd
B J Burgess, BA(Ed)
R J Midgley, BA(Ed)

Physics:
A M Dixon, MSc, MInstP, CPhys
P N Brough, BSc
M P Linahan, BSc
P R Waghorn, BEng
D J Waugh, BSc
R T Williams, BSc, DipEd

Politics:
T J Machin, MA

Religious Education:
S W Morris, BA, MEd
A D Finch, MA, MA
The Revd Fr D L Lawrence-March, BA (*Chaplain*)

Theatre Studies:
Mrs S Swidenbank, MA(Ed)

Academic Support:

EFL:
Mrs J Arthur, CertEd, RSA, CELTA
Mrs L Grindlay, MA, CELTA
Mrs M Hanlon, BEd, MA, DipTESOL
Mrs F McEwan-Cox, BA, RSA, DipTEFL
M R Vogel, MA, CertTEFLA
K Wilford, BA, PGCE TEFL, MA(Ed) TESOL

AS:
Mrs H Campbell, DTC
Mrs G Sutton, BEd

Houses and Housemasters:

Boarding Houses:
Sandersons: J E Keefe
Burnaby: R T Williams
Pemberley: G V Bennett
Redburn: B G Law
Phillpotts: R H Campbell
Talbots: B C W Grindlay

Day Houses:
Ashburnham: A J R Huxford
Bromham: Mrs S Staincliffe
Crescent: Dr A J Crowe
Paulo Pontine: P N Brough
St Cuthberts: M C Green

Chaplain: The Revd Fr D L Lawrence-March, BA

Librarian: Mrs J R Baxter, BSc(Econ) Hons

Bursar and Clerk to the Governors: Lt Col H A Culley, FFA, FIMgt, MIPD

Medical Officer: Dr A P Gray, MB, BS

Number in School. There are some 650 boys in the Upper School of whom some 212 are boarders and 438 day boys.

The Curriculum. Boys enter the Preparatory School from 7 and the Upper School at 13 years of age. The Preparatory School has its own Headmaster and specialist staff. A co-ordinated curriculum takes boys through the two Schools. The emphasis is on breadth of experience: as few doors as possible are closed at option stages. Boys are prepared for GCSE and for the new broader portfolio of AS and A Levels, and for Key Skills and General Studies. Notably strong are Languages, Mathematics and the Sciences, and there has recently been heavy investment in Technology and Information Technology.

Boys are encouraged to make good use of non-teaching time. There are extensive departmental and central library facilities, and strong emphasis is placed upon Music, Art, Drama and IT. Clubs and Societies abound for both boarders and day boys. Concerts, plays, lectures and film performances are given in the Great Hall, the Erskine May Hall and the Theatre.

Classes: In the Preparatory School pupils are taught in

forms until age 11, and are setted for most subjects. For all post-GCSE work, a generous block system is used which enables boys to study a variety of subjects at AS and A Level, combining, if desired, Arts and Science subjects. In addition a full range of subsidiary teaching is provided in Key Skills and General Studies.

Information Technology. A timetabled IT course is run for pupils in the 13+ age-group. During the remaining GCSE years IT is regarded as a cross-curricular subject, not appearing in the timetable but promoted within the teaching of other subjects. AS and A Level Computing and a number of non-examination Sixth Form courses are offered covering Key Skills. Resources, using an extensive School network of some 200 computers, include five IT laboratories and computing facilities in almost all subject areas. The computers include Acorns, PCs and Network computers, all of which can run the latest Microsoft packages. Activities include word-processing, art and graphics, desktop publishing, music composition, the Internet and E-mail.

Careers and Higher Education. The School is a member of the Independent Schools Careers Organisation. There is a team of Careers Staff who maintain close contact with the Services and professional bodies, and commercial and industrial undertakings. There are regular contacts with local industry and Institutes of Technology and Higher Education. Annual Careers Conventions are held in Bedford.

Annually almost all of the Upper Sixth enters Higher Education, with about 10% entering Oxford and Cambridge Universities (13% in 1999).

Games. A very great variety of sporting activities is offered, and senior boys in particular have a wide choice. The major sports are Cricket, Rugby Football, Rowing, Hockey; and there is ample opportunity also for Athletics, Swimming, Tennis, Association Football, Rugby Fives, Squash, Badminton, Fencing, Basketball, etc. In addition, there are regular PE classes. The Recreation Centre facilities include a large sports hall, squash courts and heated indoor swimming pool.

Services and Activities. Combined Cadet Force: There are RN, Army and RAF Sections. Membership of the CCF is voluntary. The Duke of Edinburgh Award Scheme is followed by a large number of boys to Gold Level. The Community Service Unit offers notable opportunities in the town for service to the elderly and very young, the disabled and disadvantaged. A committee of staff and boys arranges fund-raising events in support of local and national charities. Further opportunities exist to pursue a wide range of activities, projects and courses within and outside the School.

Music. As well as the two Senior Symphony Orchestras, a Chamber Orchestra, a Concert Band and a large Choral Society, there are a Chapel Choir trained in the English Cathedral tradition, two Junior Orchestras, a Dance Band, Jazz Band, a large number of chamber music groups, and a Music Club. There is a well established Music School in its own buildings.

Drama. A range of formal and informal dramatic productions is performed annually by all age groups. The well-equipped and recently refurbished School Theatre provides a venue for visiting touring companies, performing for the benefit of pupils and the general public. House Plays are also produced on a regular basis.

Association with The Harpur Trust Girls' Schools. A large variety of co-educational activities is organised in association with the girls at our sister schools. In particular, the School has a "memorandum of understanding" with Bedford High School (see GSA section of this Book) which details all aspects of the extensive co-operation between the two schools. These include academic co-operation in minority subjects, joint seminars in major subjects, and involvement in concerts, debates, conferences and a wide range of more informal social events.

Pastoral Supervision. We have a highly developed Pastoral system. Upper School pupils are under the supervision of a Tutor within small Tutor Groups; these "family" groups are organised on a vertical structure in terms of age.

Day Boys and Boarders. In the Upper School a careful balance of Boarders and Day Boys is maintained. The organisation and tradition of the School is such as to promote mixing and to avoid any discrimination between the two groups. They are combined in work, games and all other School activities, and are equally eligible for positions of responsibility whether in House or School. There are six Senior Boarding Houses, each containing up to 45 boys; and one Junior boarding House of up to 35. There is also an international Sixth Form boarding house.

Visits and Exchanges. Well-established language-exchanges occur annually between Bedford and schools in France, Spain and Germany. There are also plentiful opportunities for educational travel including outward-bound and adventure camps and expeditions, annual skiing holidays, cultural visits to a range of countries, and inter-continental sports tours.

Admission to the Upper School. Applications should be made to the Registrar. Applicants for the Upper School from Preparatory Schools are expected to take the Common Entrance Examination. All applicants must furnish evidence of good character from their previous school. Applicants from Maintained Schools are examined in English, Mathematics, Science and French. They also sit a Verbal Reasoning test.

Fees. (*see* Entrance Scholarship section) The Registration fee is £50. For Day Boys the fees are £3,040 per term. For full boarders the total necessary fees per term (boarding and tuition) are £4,820, and for weekly boarders £4,690. Fees are payable to The Clerk, Harpur Trust Office, Pilgrim Centre, Brickhill Drive, Bedford MK41 7PZ.

Old Bedfordians Club. *Secretary:* J Sylvester, 7 Glebe Road, Bedford MK40 2PL. Tel: 01234 362200.

Charitable status. The Bedford Charity (The Harpur Trust) is a Registered Charity, number 204817. It exists for the relief of poverty and the promotion of education in the Borough of Bedfordshire.

Belfast Royal Academy

Belfast N Ireland BT14 6JL
Tel: (02890) 740423.

Board of Governors:
K A Knox, MSc (*Warden*)
N W Beggs, Esq (*Vice-Warden*)
P S Sefton, LLB (*Vice-Warden*)
Mrs J Love, MB, BCh, BAO, DCH (*Hon Secretary*)
W J Andrews, MD, FRCP (Lond), FRCPI, FRCP(Ed), DCH, JP
Miss K M Bill, MB, ChB, FFARCSI
A L Boyd, FCA
G D Bustard, FCA
J A R Cameron, BA
Mrs A Clements, BA
A R Creighton, BEd
J Cross, BA, LLB
J A Hill, BSc, CEng, FICE, FIStructE, FIHT, MConsE
C F Kennedy, ARIBA
R H Lilley, Esq, OBE
J W Martin, FRICS
B W McCormack, BSc(Econ), FCA
S McDowell, BSc(Econ), FCIS
Professor J G McGimpsey, BSc, BDS, MDS, FDS, RCPS, FFD, RCSI

S R Potts, MB, BCh, BAO, FRCSI
D R S Rankin, BA
T C Reid, FIB
Mrs C Scoffield, CertEd, DipEd
D Sharp, Esq
G Simon, FRICS
Professor J A C Stewart, PhD, CEng, FIEE, MIEEE, MRIA
Mrs J Weir, BSc, CMath, MIMA
W S F Young, MA

***Headmaster:* W S F Young**, MA
Deputy Head: Mrs Y A Hollinger, BSc

Vice-Principals:
J M G Dickson, MA
N A McLeod, BSc, FSS

Senior Mistresses:
Miss M E A Armstrong, BA
Miss R Bourns, BSc

Senior Masters:
L H Campbell, BSc, PhD
S D Connolly, MA

Senior House Master: D A McBride, BSc, PhD

Deputy Senior Masters:
A R Creighton, BEd
M McCoy, MA

Heads of Departments and Senior Subject Teachers:
Mrs R McWhirter, DipAD, ATD (*Art*)
Mrs E McMorran, BSc (*Biology*)
D R S Rankin, BA (*Careers*)
L H Campbell, BSc, PhD (*Chemistry*)
J D L Reilly, MBE, BA (*Classics*)
Miss A E Campbell, BEd, DDomSci (*Home Economics*)
S D Connolly, MA (*English*)
R S H J Magowan, MSc (*Geography*)
E G A McCamley, MA (*History*)
N A McLeod, BSc, FSS (*Information Technology*)
Ms C N Scully, BSc, PhD (*Mathematics*)
J A R Cameron, BA (*Modern Languages*)
N P Finlay, MA, GRSM, FRCO (*Music*)
R G Moffett, BA, DipPE (*Physical Education and Games*)
D A McBride, BSc, PhD (*Physics*)
A R Creighton, BEd (*Religious Studies*)
N E Moore, BSc (*Technology*)
W G F Blair, MBE, BSc, PhD, CPhys, MInstP (*Physics*)
P Cupples, BSc (*Computer Studies*)
M McCoy, MA (*Deputy Examinations Officer*)
Miss R McCay, MA (*German*) (*acting*)
Miss S Stewart, DipPE (*Girls PE and Games*)
Miss M P McCullough, BA (*Special Needs*)
Mrs B Lomas, BA, MEd, PhD (*Political Studies*)
Ms B Maguire, BA (*Spanish*)
Mrs G McQuiston, BEd (*Business Studies*)

Form Masters:
R D C Evans, BA
J Carolan, MA
D Gray, BSc
C A Stewart, BSc
T M A Baldwin, BSc, MIBiol, CBiol
D R S Nash, BSc, DASE, MEd
R J Jamison, BSc

Form Mistresses:
Mrs J M Clelland, BSc
Mrs M Gray, BSc
Miss J Gallagher, BSc
Miss H E M McKeown, BA
Miss M E A Armstrong, BA
Miss S B Park, BA
Mrs K A Black, BA

Assistant Staff:
Miss J R Adams, BEd
Miss A Adrain, BA
T M A Baldwin, BSc, MIBiol, CBiol
I P B Bamford, BA, PhD, MEd, DASE
Mrs J C Bell, BSc
Mrs K A Black, BA
S Bogle, BSc
G J N Brown, BA, PhD
S P Cairns, BMus
Mrs I A Cameron, BA
J Carolan, MA
R Carroll, BEd
Miss V Carson, MA
Mrs J M Clelland, BSc
Mrs J A Connolly, BA
Mrs C E Currie, BA
R D C Evans, BA
A Fawcett, BEd, MA, MSc, DASE
Mrs C L Frazer, BSc
Miss J Gallagher, BSc
D Gray, BSc
Mrs M Gray, BSc
K L Hawtin, BA
Mrs V Heaslip, BEd
Mrs N Henry, BSc
N Irwin, BEd
R J Jamison, BSc
Ms D Keenan, BA, MSc
Mrs P Kerr, BA, ATD
Mrs E Keys, BA
Miss J D Law, BSc
Mrs C Leyden, BA
M N Long, BA
Mrs I Lyttle, BA
J E Malcolmson, BA
Miss L I Marsh, BSc
P J Martin, BEd
Mrs G McCadden, DipAD, ATD
Mrs S A McGonigle, MA
W I McGonigle, BEd
N D McKee, MBE, MSc
B C McKenna, BSc
Mrs I R M McKenna, BSc
Miss H E M McKeown, BA
B T McMurray, BSc, PhD
Mrs H Millar, BA
A K Moles, BSc
Miss R Monteith, BSc
D R S Nash, BSc, DASE, MEd
M J Neill, BSc
Mrs D M Nicholl, BA
Mrs N S Nicholl, BA
J R N Nicholson, MA, FSS, CMath, FIMA
Mrs R O'Donnell, BA
Miss S B Park, BA
J M Patterson, BSc(Econ)
Mrs A Reynolds, BSc
Miss D Scott, BA
C A Stewart, BSc
Mrs K H Tate, BA
Mrs A P Terek, BSc
Miss M N West, BA

Careers Advisers:
Mrs V Heaslip, BEd
Mrs C Leyden, BA
W G F Blair, MBE, BSc, PhD, CPhys, MInstP
A K Moles, BSc
A Fawcett, BEd, MA, MSc, DASE
J M Patterson, BSc(Econ)

Preparatory Department:

Principal: Mrs V M McCaig, BEd, DASE
Deputy Principal: W T Wilson, BEd, LTCL

Mrs G P Crothers, TC
Mrs S Haslett, DipPE
P J Ingram, BEd
Mrs P Lennon, BEd
Miss S E Mairs, BA
Mrs B Marshall, CertEd
Mrs P McDade, BSc
Mrs S Sherrard, CertEd
G Warner, BA, CertEd
Mrs A Whitten, BA, AdvDipEd
Mrs E N E Wilson, BEd

Administration:

Bursar: J Miskelly, MBE, ACIS
Assistant Bursar: D W Ritchie, BSc (Econ)
Supervisor of Grounds: T D Robinson
Headmaster's Secretary: Mrs D McGrath

Belfast Royal Academy, founded in 1785, is the oldest school in the city. It moved to its present site, on the Cliftonville Road in North Belfast, in 1880, and the Gothic building erected at that time has been extensively modernised and refurbished. Inside the past thirty years a number of new Teaching Blocks have been built. The fourteen Science Laboratories were opened in 1971, a 25-

metre indoor heated Swimming Pool was completed in 1974, a new building for Art and Craft came into full use in 1982, and a Sports Hall was opened to mark the Bi-Centenary year. In 1989 a new Sixth Form Centre and Careers Suite were opened and a purpose-built four room Technology Suite was completed in September 1991. There is extensive provision throughout the school for computing and information technology. An additional classroom block for English and Drama was opened in September 1994, and a new building to house the Mathematics department came into use in 1998.

The Academy is a co-educational day grammar school and there is also a preparatory and kindergarten department. The grammar school has some 1,400 boys and girls, between the ages of 11 and 19. The kindergarten and preparatory department, known as Ben Madigan, has some 220 children, aged from 4 to 11; it is situated at 690 Antrim Road.

The curriculum has a strong academic bias and former pupils of the school are among the members of almost every university in the United Kingdom.

The work of the junior and middle Forms is directed mainly towards the GCSE examinations of the Northern Ireland Council for the Curriculum Examinations and Assessment, the Assessment and Qualifications Alliance, Edexcel or OCR, with a minimum of specialisation, all the usual subjects being provided and careful attention being given to the requirements of the universities and the professions. Religious studies are on an undenominational basis.

There are more than 350 pupils in the Sixth Forms, where GCE Advanced Level courses are available in English Literature, French, German, Spanish, Latin, Greek, Pure Mathematics with Mechanics; Pure Mathematics with Statistics, Mathematics and Further Mathematics, Physics, Chemistry, Biology, Geography, History, Classical History and Civilsation, Economics, Politics, Art, Music, Home Economics, Business Studies, Computing and Religious Education. A/S levels are available in all the above subjects and also in Sociology and Technology. Some Sixth Formers take a course in Russian: many take an additional Certificate of Competence in Information Technology, or a qualification in keyboard skills. Pupils are prepared for entry to Oxford or Cambridge in all the main subjects.

Much attention is given to careers guidance by the Careers Masters, the Careers Mistresses, other senior members of Staff, and the Form Masters and Form Mistresses.

The normal school day is from 8.50 am to 3.30 pm. There is no Saturday school but matches are played in the major sports on Saturdays. The school year runs from the beginning of September to the end of June, with holidays of about a fortnight at Christmas and at Easter.

There are some sixty different activities in the extra-curricular programme.

The principal games are, for boys, Rugby, Cricket, Cross-Country running, Hockey, Swimming and Athletics; for girls, Hockey, Tennis, Swimming, Cross-Country running and Athletics. Sailing, Orienteering, Skiing and Racquet sports are also available.

There is an orchestra, senior and junior choirs, a wind band, Jazz band, Junior string ensembles and an Irish traditional group. Individual tuition in orchestral instruments is also provided. School organisations include Societies for Music, Drama, Chess, Bridge, Photography and Debating, an Air Training Corps, an Amateur Radio Club, Community Service and Christian Union groups and the Duke of Edinburgh's Award Scheme.

Parents pay a capital fee of £80 each year and a voluntary contingency charge of £50 per term.

In Ben Madigan the annual fee is £2,025.

Hon Secretary BRA Old Boys' Association: Mr G Calwell, 101A Shore Road, Carrickfergus BT38 8TZ.

Hon Secretary BRA Old Girls' Association: Mrs S Swanton, BA, 139 Ballymena Road, Doagh, Ballyclare, Co Antrim, BT39 0TN.

Berkhamsted Collegiate School

Castle Street Berkhamsted Hertfordshire HP4 2BB
Tel: 01442 358000
Fax: 01442 358040

Motto: *'Virtus laudata crescit'.*

Patron: Her Majesty The Queen.

The Governors:

¶Mr P J Williamson (*Chairman*)
¶Mrs A F Moore-Gwyn (*Vice-Chairman*)
¶Mrs F M Altman
Dr V J L Best
Mr C J Butcher, Fellow of All Souls, Oxford
Mr R de C Chapman
Mrs J Dunbavand
¶Mr D G Flatt
Mr C N Garrett
Mr R G Groom
Mr J N P B Horden, Fellow of All Souls, Oxford
Mr M P Horton
Mr J D Lythgoe
Mr K J Merrifield
Mr A H Noel
Mrs R Randle
Mrs H Rost
Mrs J Sewell
Miss S E Wolstenholme

Clerk to the Governors & Business Director: Mr P Maynard, RD, FCIS

Principal: **Dr P Chadwick**, MA, PhD, FRSA

Deputy Principals:
Dr P G Neeson, BSc, PhD
Dr H Brooke, BSc, PhD

Head of Sixth Form: Dr J S Hughes, BSc, MSc, PhD

Director of Studies: Mr W R C Gunary, BSc

Senior Master: †Mr C Nicholls, CertEd

Teaching staff:

Mrs L J Allen, MA, DipEd
Mrs H R Andrews, BA
Dr J W R Baird, BA, PhD
Mrs E A Baker, BA
†Mr M E Batchelder, CertEd, DipEd, MA
Mr R Batstone, MA
*Mr T H Bendall, MEd
Mrs K Bly, BA
Mrs J A Brannock Jones, BA
Mrs L C Briand, BA, DipTESOL
*Mr J R Browne, BA, FRCO, FRSA
†Mr G R Burchnall, BEd
Mr F Charnock, CertEd
*Dr E J Chevill, BA, BPhil, PhD, AKC, MMus
Mrs S A E Clay, Dip Central School of Speech & Drama, CertEd
Miss F Colyer, Teacher's Diploma, LGSM
†Mr D J Coulson, BEng, MEng, CEngIChemE
Mr P C Cowie, MA
†Mrs M A Crichton, MA
†Mr S J Dight, BA, DipEd
Mr P E Dobson, BSc, LChem, MRSC
Mrs A M Doggett, BSc
*†Mr C H Eaton, BSc
Mr A J Esland, MA, MMus, PGCE
*Mrs B Evans, MA
Mr B P Evers, BA
Miss J F Freeman, BA, MA
Mrs D Galloway, MA
Ms F M Garratt, BSc
Miss L Gent, BA, MA
Miss A Gold, BA
Revd S Golding, BA, CertEd, DipPastStuds
Mr T A Grant, MA
Mr M J Green, BSc, HDE
*†Mrs J A Hallett, MA
Mr M Hamilton, BSc, DipEd
Mr J C Harber, BA (Hons), PGCE
*Miss J Hart, BA
Miss M Hatley, BSc (Hons)
Mrs A Hatton, BA
Mr C J Hayward, BA
†Mrs E M Hines, BA
†Mrs S L Horsnell, BSc
Mrs H I S Howgate, BEd

Mrs J I Jenkins, BA
†Mr P C Jennings, BA
Mrs T K Kelly, BEd
Miss E Kennedy, BSc
Mrs P Kent, CertEd
*Mrs W L Keppel, BSc
*Miss S B Kirton, BA, MA
Miss L Lewin, BEd
Mr J A Leyland, BA
Mrs E M Lindop, BA
*Mr T D Lines, BA, MA, MEd
Mr P R Luckraft, BA
Mrs B S Macgregor, CertEd
Mr A Mackay, BSc, MA
Mr R J McIlwaine, CertEd
†Mr T J McTernan, BA, MA
Mr R H Mardo, BSc
Mr M S Metcalfe, BSc, MInstP, CPhys
*Mrs R E Miles, BSc
†Mr R K Mowbray, MA
Mrs A Mulcahy, DipEd, MIL
†Mr R F Newport, BA
Mrs B J Newton, MA
Mrs S Nicholls
Mrs V A Ostle, CertEd
Mr M A Pearce, BA
Mr M S Pett, BA
*Mrs A M Pike, CertEd, RSADipSLD
Mr A Powles, BSc
Mr S J E Rees, BA
*Mr D G Richardson, BSc
Mrs E A Richardson, BA
*Mr P T Riddick, MA, MSc
Miss C L Ringrose, MChem
*Mrs A R Roberts, BA
*Mr D K Roberts, BSc
†Mrs E A Roberts, BA
Miss P J Rowan, BA
†Mrs C G Ryder, BSc
Mrs S C Sansome, BSc
†Mr D H Simpson, CertEd, AdvDipDesTech
*Miss A E Smith, BEd
Mrs S Sneddon, BEd
Miss D H Spain, BA
Mr M Sparrow, BA
†Mr N Stevens, BA
*†Mr I R Stewart, BA, MA
Mr R Thompson, BA
Mr M J Thum, MA
†Mr W A Webb, BA, BEd, MEd
†Mrs L Wheater, BSc
Mrs J M Wild, GLCM, ALCM, LLCM(TD)
Mr D J Wiles, BSc
Mrs P Williams, CertEd
Miss T J Woolley, BA (Hons), Grad IPD

Additional Staff:

Music: There are 30 visiting music staff and the following musical instruments are offered in the school: acoustic guitar, bagpipes, bassoon, cello, clarinet, double bass, electric guitar, euphonium, flute, French horn, harpsichord, jazz piano, oboe, organ, percussion (*including kit drumming*), piano, recorder, saxophone, trombone, trumpet, tuba, viola and violin.

Swimming Manager and PE Coach: Mr K W Ayers
Librarian: Mrs S Bartlett, BA, ALA
Chaplain: The Revd S Golding, BA
Medical Officer: Dr N Ormiston, MBBS, MRCP, DRCOG

Principal's Secretary: Mrs N M Golder (*Tel:* 01442 358002; Fax: 01442 358003)
Deputy Principal's Secretary: Mrs F J Stephens (*Tel:* 01442 358031; Fax:01422 358032)

History. In 1541 John Incent, Dean of St Paul's, was granted a Licence by Henry VIII to found a school in Berkhamsted, Incent's home town. Until the end of the 19th Century Berkhamsted School served as a grammar school for a small number of boys from the town but over the last century it has developed into a school of significance. In 1888 the foundation was extended by the establishment of Berkhamsted School for Girls. In 1996, these two schools formalised their partnership to become Berkhamsted Collegiate School, offering the highest quality education to pupils from ages 3 to 19.

There are 300 pupils in the flourishing co-educational Sixth Form; between the ages of eleven and sixteen 350 boys on Castle Campus and 250 girls on Kings Campus are taught in single-sex groups; and 400 pupils from ages three to eleven attend the Preparatory School. The Principal is a member of both HMC and GSA.

Aims. The School seeks to enable pupils to achieve their full potential. In addition to the development of the intellect, social, sporting and cultural activities have an important part to play within the framework of a disciplined and creative community based on humane Christian values. It is important that pupils come to value both the Individual and the Community through School life. The School seeks to encourage spiritual and moral values and a sense of responsibility as an essential part of the pursuit of excellence.

Organisation. The School stands in the heart of Berkhamsted, an historic and thriving town only thirty miles from London. It enjoys excellent communications to London, the airports, to the Midlands and the communities of south Buckinghamshire, Bedfordshire and Hertfordshire.

The original site has at its heart a magnificent Tudor Hall used as a Schoolroom for over 300 years, which is still in use. The complex of other buildings are from late Victorian to modern periods and of architectural interest (especially the Chapel which is modelled on the Church of St Maria dei Miracoli in Venice). There are new Science laboratories, Library and Learning Resourses Centres, Information Technology suites, Sixth Form centres, Careers library, Dining hall, Medical centre, House rooms, Deans' Hall (an Assembly/Concert Hall and Theatre) and Centenary Hall (a very modern 500 seat Lecture Hall also used for concerts and theatre productions). Recreational and sports facilities include extensive playing fields, a listed indoor swimming pool, an open-air heated swimming pool, Fives courts, Squash courts, Tennis courts, two Gymnasia, Drama studio, Music school and Art studios.

The Berkhamsted Collegiate Preparatory School is housed in separate buildings nearby, including a nursery. The school is fully co-educational from Y1 to Y6.

For further information, please see entry under IAPS, Part V of this Book.

At age 11, boys and girls transfer into **single-sex senior schools** on adjacent sites, where they are taught separately up to GCSE. Pupils are supported by a coordinated pastoral system and extra-curricular activities take place across the campuses.

At age 16, pupils join the **fully co-educational Sixth Form,** which offers an extensive range of 'A' level subject choices with highly experienced staff and impressive teaching facilities. Clubs, societies, sports, work experience and community service all complement a stimulating programme of activities, which provide students with valuable opportunities for responsibility and enhance their university applications. Careers guidance and personal tutoring are offered throughout the Sixth Form.

Day and Boarding. Pupils may be full boarders, weekly/flexible boarders or day pupils. The two Boarding houses, accommodating boys and girls separately, are well equipped and within a few minutes walk of the main campus. There are 100 boarding places. Day pupils come from both Berkhamsted and the surrounding area of Hertfordshire, Buckinghamshire and Bedfordshire.

Pastoral Care and Discipline. The main social and pastoral unit is the House; the Head of House and House Tutors provide continuity of support and advice and monitor each individual pupil's progress.

The aim is to encourage self-discipline so that pupils may work with a sense of responsibility and trust. Those rules which are laid down cannot cover every contingency but, generally, pupils are expected to be considerate, courteous, honest and industrious. Any breach of good manners or of common sense is a breach of the School Rules as is any action which may lower the School's good name. Bullying is regarded as a most serious offence. Alcohol, proscribed drugs and smoking are banned. Every member of the School is expected to take a pride in his or her appearance and to wear smart school uniform.

There is a Medical Centre with qualified staff. The School Medical Officer has special responsibility for boarders. A qualified Counsellor is available to all pupils for confidential counselling. The school also has a full-time Chaplain.

Curriculum. The curriculum includes: English, English Literature, Mathematics, Physics, Biology, Chemistry, History, Geography, Religious Studies, French, Latin/Classics, German/Spanish, Music, Art, Design and Technology. Up to eleven subjects may be taken for GCSE. In the Sixth Form, 'A' levels are offered in around 27 subjects, complemented by AS General Studies. Pupils are prepared for university entrance, including Oxbridge. All pupils are taught computer skills and have access to Information Technology centres.

Sport and Leisure Activities. A number of different sports are pursued including Athletics, Badminton, Cricket, Cross Country, Eton Fives, Fencing, Golf, Hockey, Judo, Lacrosse, Netball, Rowing, Rugby, Shooting, Soccer, Squash, Swimming and Tennis. The School also has use of the local Sports Centre. Team games are encouraged and pupils selected for regional and national squads.

There is a flourishing Duke of Edinburgh Award scheme at all levels. The CCF, community service, work experience and 'Young Enterprise' are offered, along with clubs for gymnastics, drama, computing and technology. Regular school theatre productions, orchestral and choral concerts achieve high standards of performance.

Careers. A team of advisors, internal and external, is directed by the Head of Careers. Heads of House supervise applications for higher education. Parents and pupils are encouraged to consult them and the Careers advisors. The great majority of leavers proceeds to university and higher education.

Entry. Entry to the Preparatory School from the age of 3 onwards and pupils transfer to the Senior School at age 11. Entry to the Senior School is from 11. The School's Entrance Assessments and an interview are required. Those working towards the Common Entrance Examination sit this examination in addition to the School's Assessment. Sixth Form entry normally requires at least 3B and 2C grades at GCSE. Entry is normally in September but a few places may be available for the Spring or Summer Terms.

Scholarships and Bursaries. Details of the range of awards (eg music, art, academic) can be obtained from the School.

Fees. Day Pupils: Nursery, £1,381, Preparatory, £1,662–£2,219 per term; Senior, £2,655–£3,122 per term.

Boarding Pupils: £4,499–£4,966 per term.

Old Berkhamstedians. Hon Secretary: Mr J R Bale, The Spinney, 128 Horsham Road, Cranleigh, Surrey GU6 8DY. Tel: 01442 864719.

Charitable status. Berkhamsted Collegiate School is a Registered Charity, number 311056. It is a leading Charitable School in the field of Junior and Secondary Education.

D F Booker, BA, FCA
M H Crosby, MA
R McN Fearnehough, BSc
N J A Hutton, MBE
Professor A G Johnson, MA, MChir, FRCS
Mrs C M MacKinnon, MMedSci, RGN
District Judge J F W Peters, LLB, AKC
Mrs A M Rees, MA, BEd
The Revd C P Williams, MA, BD, MLitt, PhD

Bursar and Clerk to the Governors: D H Taylor, BSc

***Head Master:* R J Court**, MA (Clare College, Cambridge)

Deputy Head: R S Dillow, BA

Director of Studies: E Stevens, BSc

Senior Tutors:
K D Brook, BA
D E Franklin, MA
S H Kenyon, MA
Mrs H A Parsons, MA

Assistant Staff:

*J D Allen, BSc	E K Noble, PGCE
P G Allen, BSc	J R Nolan, BEng
*K Balkow, BA, DPhil	B J Ogilvie, BA, BSc
*M S Clarke, MA	*Mrs A M Oliver, BA
C J Cook, BSc	H Parker, BSc
*R J Cottom, BEd	M A Potter, BEd
D Craddock, BEng	Dr P Rangecroft, MA, BSc
Mrs R L Crapper, BA	Mrs M B Reynolds, BEd
*R W Currins, BA, MPhil	S T Reynolds, BSc
Mrs M A Daly, MA	C F Rodgers, BSc
* C D Dean, BA	*M H Rose, BA
*S R Gordon, MA	*Mrs K Rose, MA
P C Harris, BSc	Mrs F Rusling, BA
*R D Heaton, BEd	*A M Sanderson, BA
Miss R J Hicks, MA	Mrs J A Savage, BA
*Mrs K M Higham, BA, MEd	Mrs H V Sherborne, BA
J C Hudson, MA	Miss I M Sherwood-Jones, LRAM
Mrs J E Ireland, BSc	D S Smith, BMus
Miss S J Lawless, BA	P C Snell, BSc
K Lowes, BA	Mrs F M Stevens, BA
*E R Mather, BSc, DipTheol	Mrs C R Swainsbury, BA
*Dr C Merrall, BA, DPhil	*Mrs W Taylor, BEd
Miss S D Miles, BA	Mrs H Thaw, BA
*G Moody, MA	R N Willatt, BSc
*A R Nickless, BA	*A P Wilson, BSc
	A J Woodley, BEd

Librarian: Mrs J Shapland, ALA

Preparatory School:

Head of Prep School: A D Jones, MA, BA

Assistant Staff:

K F Allchin, BEd (*Deputy Head*)	F G Kirkham, TD, BEd
A J Oakey, BA (*Director of Studies*)	Miss R M Kitt, BEd
Mrs A B Camm, BEd (*Senior Mistress*)	J Lockwood, LLB, BA
R J Anderson, BA	Mrs F G Noble, BEd
Mrs E J Arcari, BA	Mrs H J Oakey, BEd
Mrs E A Barratt, BA	Miss L Peacock, BA
Miss J V Black, BEd	Mrs A H B Peel, BEd
Mrs P Bradwell, CertEd	Mrs D J Robinson, BMus
Mrs C Doran, BEd	Mrs K J Silver, BSc
Mrs S E Dunstan, DipEd	M S Stones, CertEd
Mrs N Hall, CertEd	Mrs J E Taylor, CertEd
Mrs A Hunter, CertEd	Mrs G Vallance, CertEd, CertSLD
D P Jones, GGSM	Mrs F L M Walton, MA
	Mrs M S Whitt, BA

Birkdale School

Oakholme Road Sheffield S10 3DH
Tel: (0114) 266 8408
Fax: (0114) 267 1947

Birkdale School is a day school for 830 pupils, boys from 4 to 18 with a co-educational Sixth Form. The 4–11 Preparatory School is on a separate campus nearby. The Sixth Form was launched in 1988 and now has 160 pupils, 95% of whom in recent years have entered university. The Governing Body is in membership of the Governing Bodies Association.

Motto:*Res non verba*

Chairman of Governors: S A P Hunter, JP, MA

Visiting Music Staff:

Ms F Bayles, MA (*Oboe*)
Miss K Burland, BMus (*Clarinet/Sax*)
T Canneli (*Percussion*)
R Dawson, GGSM, DipOrch (*Violin/Viola*)
Miss K Holtham, ATCL (*Flute*)
M Leeson, BMus, LRSM, ALCM (*Brass*)
Mrs V Leppard, BMus, LRAM (*Flute/Piano*)
Miss R Moore, BA (*Cello*)
Miss C L Osborne, BMus, MMus, LRAM (*Singing/Piano*)
P Scott (*Oboe*)
R Sayle, GCLCM (*Guitar*)
Mrs H R Williams, MA (*Piano/Clarinet*)

Head Master's Secretary: Miss S van der Merwe, BSc

Registrar: Mrs C M Brown, BA

Set in a pleasant residential area near the University 1.5 miles from the city centre, and 5 miles from the Peak District National Park, the school has expanded in recent years to provide for Sheffield and South Yorkshire the only independent secondary school for boys, with a co-educational Sixth Form. Birkdale Preparatory School for 300 boys is on a separate campus half a mile from the Senior School. School coaches bring pupils from Worksop, North Derbyshire, Rotherham and Barnsley.

Birkdale is a Christian school, reflecting its foundation in the evangelical tradition. There is nothing exclusive about this: entrance is open to all, and there is no denominational emphasis. We seek to develop the full potential of each individual: body, mind and spirit. Within a framework of high academic standards, pastoral care is given a high priority, balanced by an emphasis on sport and outdoor pursuits, music and drama with a range of extra-curricular activities available.

At 18, over 95% of pupils go on to university, with a good proportion each year gaining places at Oxford and Cambridge.

Admission. The main ages of admission are at 4, 7, 11 and 16, although it is possible to admit pupils at other ages if a place is available. Entrance examinations for candidates at 11 are held annually in February. Entrance to the co-educational Sixth Form is subject to interview and a satisfactory performance in GCSE examinations.

Academic Curriculum. Over 20 subjects are offered at AS and A level. A full range of academic subjects are offered to GCSE. All pupils study English Language and Literature, Mathematics, Double Award Science, at least one Modern Foreign Language (French, German, Spanish) and at least one of the Humanities subjects (Classical Studies, Geography, History, RE). Optional subjects include Art, DT: Electronic Products, DT: Resistant Materials, Latin and Music. The wider curriculum includes ICT, Religious Education, Health Education, Careers and Economic Awareness. Latin, German and Spanish are compulsory subjects in the Lower School (11-13) in addition to the usual range of National Curriculum subjects.

Games and Outdoor Pursuits. The major games are Rugby, Soccer, Cricket and Athletics, with Cross Country, Hockey, Netball, Tennis, Squash, Basketball, Volleyball, Swimming and Golf also available. The playing fields are a short bus ride away from the school, and all members of the school play games weekly. Additional team practices take place on Saturdays or at other times, and there is a full fixture list in the major sports. The school enjoys regular use of the university swimming pool nearby. The Sports Hall is at the centre of the Senior School campus.

Outdoor Pursuits play an important part in the overall leadership training programme. All members of the school participate in regular training sessions leading in each age group to a major expedition. This programme culminates in the 4th Form camp held annually in Snowdonia: this includes a trek involving all participants in leadership training. Virtually all members of the Third Form take the Bronze Award of the Duke of Edinburgh Award Scheme, and an increasing number progress to Silver and Gold awards.

Music and the Arts. Music, Art and Drama flourish both within and outside the formal curriculum. The Art School is located in a newly refurbished building, and a full annual programme of dramatic and musical productions is arranged. Over 120 pupils receive weekly instrumental music lessons at school, and a wide range of orchestras and choirs provide opportunities for pupils to experience group musical activities at an appropriate level.

Extra curricular activities. There is a broad range of over fifty clubs and societies which meet outside the formal school day, providing opportunities for members of the school to explore and excel in activities such as Chess, Debating, Design and Drama, as well as in the usual activities such as sport, outdoor pursuits, art and music.

Careers. The school is a member of the Independent Schools' Careers Organisation, and there is a well equipped Careers Centre in the Grayson Building. A biennial Careers Convention is held in the school and regular visits are made by services liaison officers and others to give advice and help to individual members of the school under the guidance of the school's careers staff.

All members of the Lower Sixth participate in a Work Experience scheme for a week each January, placed in a work environment in line with their possible choice of career.

The school runs Young Enterprise companies each year which introduce Sixth Formers to the world of business and management, and awards are often won in local competition.

Information and Communications Technology. In addition to the main ICT Centre, the computer network extends throughout the Campuses of both the Senior and Preparatory schools. Each member of the school is able to access the system in every part of the school using a personal identity code, and CD Rom facilities are amongst features which are constantly being added to the network, as is supervised access to the Internet.

Learning Support Unit. Both the Senior and Preparatory school have their own Learning Support Centres. Pupils with dyslexic difficulties are given expert help within the school context and in full consultation with subject staff and are encouraged to achieve their full potential in public examinations.

Fees and Scholarships. Current fees range from £1,352 to £1,922 per term, and include lunches, books and stationery.

The following Scholarships are available:
Academic Scholarships at 11 and 16.
Music Scholarships at 11 and 16.
Arkwright Scholarship to read A level Design and Technology at 16.

Most scholarships are worth up to 25% of fees, with Bursaries available up to 100% of fees in case of need.

Charitable status. Birkdale School is a Registered Charity, number 1018973. It exists to develop the full potential of its members within a Christian community.

* Head of Department	§ Part Time or Visiting
† Housemaster/Housemistress	¶ Old Pupil
‡ See below list of staff for meaning	

Birkenhead School

Wirral Merseyside CH43 2JD
Tel: 0151 652 4014.
Fax: 0151 651 3091
e-mail: enquire@birkenheadschool.co.uk
website: www.birkenheadschool.co.uk

Birkenhead School was opened in 1860, with the object of providing a public-school education, both Classical and Modern.

Motto: *'Beati mundo corde'*

Visitor: The Rt Revd The Lord Bishop of Chester, DD

President: The Rt Hon Lord Nicholls of Birkenhead

Vice-Presidents:
Air Chief Marshal Sir John Aiken, KCB
J A Gwilliam
A G Hurton
A Whittam Smith
Lord Wade of Chorlton
W T C Rankin
K J Speakman-Brown
H W McCready
G De Ritter
D A Fletcher

Governors:
Chairman: A L B Thomson, FRICS
I G Boumphrey
Mrs L Dodd, BA, FSI
C C Johnson, FRICS, FSVA
A T R Macfarlane, BA, FCA
Dr A G Mathie, MB, BSc, FRCGP
Professor M C L Orme, MA, MD, FRCP
M B Owen, BA
R J Phillips, LLB
Mrs L A Rennie
W D C Rushworth, BA
D R Swaffield, MA
Mrs E Taylor, LLB
J Taylor

***Headmaster:* S J Haggett**, MA, Downing College, Cambridge

Deputy Headmaster: D J Clark, MA

Head of Junior School: M Roden, BA

Head of Middle School: D S Coventry, MA

Head of Sixth Form: D R Edmunds, BSc

Director of Studies: R E Collier, MA

School Chaplain: The Revd H L Kirk, MA

Bursar and Clerk to the Governors: C F Button, BSc, MInstDir

Assistant Teachers:
W I H Allister, MA
Miss N Benzerfa, BA
A J Blain, BEd (*Head of Art*)
M H Bowyer, TCert
Mrs M H Bratherton, BSc
K M Britton, MA, MSc (*Head of Biology*)
D J F Cameron, MA (*Data Co-ordinator*)
S Charters, BEng, BEd
N D A Clark, BSc
A S Davies, MA (*Head of ICT*)
W M Davies, MA
A M Durling, BA
G J Ellis, BEd (*Director of Music*)
J L Fox, MA
N J Frowe, BA
S M Gill, MA (*Head of Geography*)
N P Gorman, BSc
J B Green, BA
M J Hayward, BSc (*Head of Science*)
D W Highcock, BSc (*Head of Physics*)
G Hopkins, MA
M J Hudson, MA (*Head of Classics*)
W A Hughes, MA, PhD
C B Hunt, BSc, PhD (*Head of General Studies*)
R Keyse, BSc, DPhil
R E Lytollis, BSc (*Head of Physical Education*)
J McGrath, MA (*Head of Careers*)
B P McGuirk, MA, MSc (*Head of Mathematics*)
I D McKay, BSc
E McKevitt, CertEd
J G Melville, MSc
M C Metcalfe, BSc (*Head of PSE*)
R J Millington, MA
G Prescott, MA (*Head of Chemistry*)
D K Rule, BA (*Head of Economics*)
C L Smale, MA (*Head of English*)
Miss L Smeaton, BA
Mrs K Starling, BSc
Miss R Volkert, BA
Mrs M L Voronoy, BA
P G Walton, MA (*Head of Modern Languages*)
Miss E Wilday, BA
Mrs E O Williams, BSc
R G Wiltshire, BSc (*Head of Design Technology*)
J P Young, BA

Librarian: Mrs J Laxton, BA, ALA
Assistant Librarian: Mrs M Butterworth, BA
SSI: Sergeant Major T Rowley
Careers Liaison Officer: Mr S Jackson
Nurse: Mrs R Morton, RGN

Preparatory Department:

Headmistress: Mrs J A Skelly, BEd

Deputy Headmistress: Mrs D M Hodgkinson, TCert

Assistant Staff:

Mrs V Belchier, TCert
Mrs S M Berry, TCert
Mrs J A Chamberlain, BEd
N J Corran, BEng
Mrs L J Dale-Jones, BEd
M J Goosey, BEd
Dr J M de Groot, BSc, PhD
Mrs E B Hall, JP, TCert
D A Hendry, BEd
Mrs A J Hipps, BEd
Dr S M Jarvis, BSc, PhD
Mrs S J Martindale, BA
Mrs P J McDonald, TCert
A V McGibbon, BEd
Mrs S G Mills, BEd
Miss A Noble, BA
Mrs S Porter, TCert
Mrs S Sharman, TCert
Mrs I Smith, TCert
M G Stockdale, BA
Miss E Talbot, BSc
Mrs N J G Williams, BA
Mrs C E Winn, BEd

The School consists of a separate Preparatory Department of 350 boys aged 3–11; a Junior School of 150 boys aged 10–13; and a Senior School of 440 pupils aged 13–19, of whom 160 are in the Sixth Form, which became co-educational in September 2000. The Heads of Junior

School, Middle School and Sixth Form have direct responsibility for the pastoral welfare of pupils in their section of the School and each oversees and co-ordinates the work of a team of Form Tutors.

Pupils come from all areas of Wirral, North Cheshire and North Wales. Public transport is good and there is an extensive network of School buses.

The School buildings are grouped around a spacious campus in the residential area of Oxton, and a development programme in recent years has added very considerably to the School's already extensive facilities. The Preparatory Department now occupies the whole of the Shrewsbury Road site and a purpose-built Infant Department was completed in 1992. The former Preparatory building in Beresford Road has been converted to provide an extensive Music School. Developments in the Senior School include a new Science Block, a new Sports Hall, and most recently a new Art Department, a new IT Suite within the Middle School building and a substantial extension to facilities for Technology and Electronics. Separate recreational facilities for Sixth and Fifth Forms have also been developed.

Curriculum. All pupils follow a common curriculum in the Junior School (Forms 1 and 2) and this pattern continues into the Third Form with the addition of a second language option (German, Greek or Spanish) and the introduction of a cross-curricular IT programme. This wide spectrum of subjects means that pupils are then ideally placed to make GCSE option choices at the end of the Third Form. As well as the compulsory subjects – Mathematics, English Language, English Literature and French – pupils choose five more subjects from Art, Design Technology, Biology, Chemistry, Geography, German, Greek, Spanish, Religious Studies, History, Latin, Music and Physics. Almost all combinations are possible, but attention is given to ensuring at this stage that pupils choose appropriate subjects which will not restrict their future career choices. The School has remained committed to the teaching of Biology, Chemistry and Physics as separate subjects. A programme of Personal and Social Education is provided for all pupils from First to Fifth Form in the form of a series of Focus Days, drawing on external agencies, as well as the School's own expertise.

The vast majority of pupils move into an academic Sixth Form environment where their AS and A Level preparation is geared towards post-18 university openings. All Lower Sixth pupils choose four 'AS' Levels from Ancient History, Art, Biology, Chemistry, Computing, Design and Technology, Economics, Electronics, English Language, English Literature, French, Further Mathematics, Geography, German, Greek, History, Latin, Mathematics, Music, Philosophy, Physics, Spanish and Theatre Studies. Upper Sixth students will continue four subjects, or three subjects plus General Studies, to A2 level. An important part of the General Studies programme for all Sixth Form pupils is the Friday Lecture given by guest speakers from a wide range of backgrounds. The Careers Department provides classes and individual preparation for university applications; for most pupils the careers staff will have been involved in their decision-making from as early as the Third Form. Advice on direct employment is also offered, although in practice over 95% of leavers move into Higher Education.

Houses and Housemasters. Bushell's House (Mr I D McKay); Davis's House (Mr R E Lytollis); Griffin's House (Mr B P McGuirk); Pearse's House (Mr D W Highcock); School House (Mr G Hopkins); Sloman's House (Mr K M Britton).

School Chapel. The School has its own Chapel and, although there are no longer boarders, has retained the position of a permanent Chaplain. As well as being responsible for daily worship and Religious Education, the Chaplain also has an important pastoral role in the wider School community. There is an outstanding Chapel Choir which sings daily services and at the regular Sunday Evensong. Each summer the Chapel Choir performs in cathedrals and churches both in Britain and abroad.

Parents' Association. There is an extremely active Parents' Association which provides opportunities for parents to meet informally and organises social events, as well as being involved on a day-to-day basis in the life of the School.

Societies. Involvement in extra-curricular activities is strongly encouraged and there is a wide range of clubs from which to choose, including scientific, cultural and recreational. There is a strong tradition of drama, with regular productions, some in co-operation with Birkenhead High School, and an annual House Drama competition. The School has two Orchestras, a Concert Band and Brass Ensemble. The School has a fine reputation for choral music and for a number of years the Choral Society, consisting of pupils, parents and friends of the School, and girls from Birkenhead High School, has performed a major choral work annually at the Philharmonic Hall in Liverpool.

Games. Competitive sports are rugby, hockey and cross-country during the winter terms and cricket, athletics, tennis and golf during the summer. There are representative teams at all levels and the playing fields cover about 40 acres on three different sites. At McAllester Field a floodlit astroturf surface for hockey and tennis has been built and is shared with Oxton Cricket Club. A large sports complex, including squash courts, provides a focus for the School's comprehensive 'Sport for All' programme.

CCF and Outdoor Pursuits. The School has flourishing Army, Navy and RAF sections. From the Fourth Form onwards pupils may opt either to join one of these sections or to take part in the School's Community Service programme. The School runs its own Duke of Edinburgh's Award Scheme at all levels. Outdoor Pursuits also form part of the regular games programme.

Admission is by the School's own Entrance Examination held on a Saturday at the end of January for boys over ten but not over twelve on 1st September. Entrance at thirteen is through the Common Entrance Examination or our own Supplementary Examination. Sixth Form entrants, both boys and girls, are also welcome and this selection is based on GCSE grades and interview. Prospective parents are always welcome to visit the School and the Headmaster is happy to meet parents and assist with queries over dates and methods of entry.

Fees. Senior School – £5,526. Preparatory Department – £4,311. The Birkenhead School Foundation Trust was established in 1998 to provide Scholarships and Funded Places. Particulars may be obtained from the Headmaster.

The Old Birkonian Society. Hon Secretary: Ian W Bakewell, Rolleston, Oldfield Drive, Heswall CH60 6SS.

Charitable status. Birkenhead School Limited is a Registered Charity, number 525933. Our charitable status means the School not only accepts fee paying pupils but can offer places to able children from less advantaged backgrounds.

Bishop's Stortford College

Bishop's Stortford Herts. CM23 2PJ.
Tel: (01279) 838575
Fax: (01279) 836570

Bishop's Stortford College is a busy and thriving day and boarding school which achieves high standards, particularly academically and in sport, but also increasingly in Music and Drama. The atmosphere is friendly, discipline good, and considerable emphasis is placed upon pastoral care. Pupils are encouraged to develop their individual talents, to fulfil their academic potential and to grow in confidence, self-reliance, and social awareness. A flourishing Junior School and a Pre-Prep Department, sharing many facilities with the Senior School, give all the advantages of educational continuity.

When founded in 1868, it was intended that the College should provide "a liberal and religious education" acceptable to Nonconformist families in the Eastern Counties. In practice, "Stortford" welcomes boys and girls of all denominations, and, while the majority of present pupils' homes are in the Home Counties and East Anglia, a substantial number of parents work and live overseas.

Motto: *'Soli Deo Gloria'*.

Governing Council:
J R Tee, MA (*Chairman*)
P E Radley, BA, PhD (*Vice-Chairman*)
Sir Brian Corby, MA, FIA
The Revd G Corderoy
R B Norden, FRICS, FSVA
D M Turner, MA, PhD
H P Joscelyne, JP
D P Bateman, FCA
C I M Jones, MA
Dr J Swainsbury
Mrs J Beynon, BEd
The Revd N Rogers

***Headmaster:* J G Trotman**, MA (St Edmund Hall, Oxford)

Assistant staff:
N P Alexander, MSc (*Mathematics*)
Mrs K Adkins, CertEd
S Bacon, BSc
Mrs H G Bailey, BA
A H Baker, BSc
C S Bannister, MA (*Chemistry*)
J N Birchall, MA (*Business Studies/Economics*)
†D M Borthwick, BSc
T G S Borton, BA (*Head of Sixth Form*)
P L J Branford, CertEd
R D B Butt, BA
R Carter, MA, BSc
Mrs V G Charters, MA
Mrs A J Clough, BA
Mrs L G Dickinson, BA
Miss J C Duncalf, MA
S J Fairclough, BSc, MSc
M G Gibson, BA (*Media Studies*)
Mrs S L Gibson (*Theatre Studies*)
Miss K Gill, BA
P M Griffin, BSc
Mrs K Griffiths (*Marketing Co-ordinator*)
Revd S E Hall (*Chaplain*)
Dr R Heidbreder (*Psychology*)
T A Herbert, MA (*Examinations*)
†Dr A B Hill, PhD, BSc
D A Hopper, BA (*History*)
†R M Honey, MA (*Art*)
T G Hudson, MA (*Modern Languages*)
K Irvine, BA (*Geography*)
M S Johnson, BSc
J Kirton, BSc
R D Kisby, BA, DPE (*PE*)
F Q Livingstone, MA (*English*)
G J Morris, BSc, CEng, MIChemE
†Mrs P Mullender, MA (*German*)
P W O'Connor, PhD
Mrs J Oldfield, BSc
M S Roper, BA, LTCL, ALCM, ARCO (*Music*)
D H Shoukry, BA (Oxon)
†Mrs A N Sloman, CertEd
H Sykes, BSc (*Biology*)
I D Taylor, MA (*Physics, Science, IT*)
Miss M Tappenden, CM
†M A Tomkys, BA
J H Trant, BA (*Design & Technology*)
C H Williams, BSc (*Director of Studies*)
Mrs S J Wilson, BA
C J Woodhouse, BSc (*Deputy Head*)
Mrs T Wright, BA
Mrs V Jones (*Careers Manager*)
Mrs M Hilton (*Librarian*)
Mrs F M H Williams, BA (*Librarian; English as Second Language*)

Junior School:
Head of Junior School: J A Greathead, MEd

G J Burnell, BA (*Deputy Head*)
Miss N Arkle, BA
S Bailey, CertEd
A J R Barnard
Miss J E L Barlow, BSc
Miss A Brain, BA
A M Bruce, BA
†R J Clough, BA
N B Courtman, BA
Mrs E J Duncan, BEd
D Edwards, BA
C W Fisher, BA
Mrs V J Foulkes-Arnold, BEd (*Senior Mistress*)
Miss S Goldsmith, BEd
T Handford, BSc
Mrs N P Hatchett, BEd
A J Hathaway, BEd
D A Herd, BSc
J J Herd, BSc
Miss S Johnson, BA
A R Lamb, BEd
Mrs R Lamb, BA
Miss N McLean, LLB
G Millard, BA
C I Murchie, BA
D F R O'Kane, BA
Miss E Piachaud, BA
Mrs R A Pike, BA
R S Quinton-Jones, BA (*Senior Master*)
Miss R Smith, BA
R J H Thomas, BEd

Pre-Preparatory Department:
Head: Mrs A M Cullum, BA

Mrs B J Birley, CertEd
Mrs B Cormack
Mrs M E Davison, CertEd
Mrs J M Forgham, BEd
Mrs A D Foy
Mrs H M MacHardy
Mrs C Martin, MA
Mrs R Padman
Mrs J Perkins, MEd
Mrs G Quinton-Jones
Mrs J B Raymont
Mrs S J Shepherd
Mrs S B Somerset

Bursar: I J McCulloch

Medical Officer: M A Jenns, MB, BS

There are 370 boys and girls in the Senior School (boarders and day), 350 boys and girls in the Junior School and 112 in the Pre-Prep Department.

Site and Grounds. Bishop's Stortford is almost midway between London and Cambridge and is quickly reached from Liverpool Street or via the M11 motorway. Stansted Airport is less than ten minutes away by car. The College is situated on the edge of the town adjacent to open countryside. The gardens and grounds cover over 100 acres.

In addition to the various classroom blocks, there are modern Science Laboratories, a Language Laboratory and two Computer Centres; there are well-equipped centres for Art, Design and Technology and Music/Drama. A purpose-built Centre for Physics, Technology and Information Technology is popular. The main school Library, which is administered by full-time Librarians, is a notable feature.

At the centre of the School stands the Memorial Hall, used daily for Assembly, which was erected in 1921 as a memorial to Old Boys who served and fell in the 1914–18 war.

Boys' Boarding Houses are: Robert Pearce House (Mr S J Fairclough); School House (Mr A Keir). **The Day Boy Houses are:** Hayward House (Mr M A Tomkys); Sutton House (Dr A B Hill); Collett House (Mr R Honey). **Girls' Houses are:** Young House (Mrs A N Sloman) and Benson House (Mrs P Mullender).

Junior School. Grimwade House for Boarders (Mr and Mrs R Clough); Monk-Jones House, Westfield House and Newbury House for Day Pupils.

Academic Organisation. The Curriculum is designed to give as broad a course of study as possible up to the inevitable specialisation at 'A' and 'A/S' Level and Oxbridge entry.

In addition to the three Sciences, French, English, Maths, Geography and History, all new pupils joining the 4th Form (Year Nine) take Design and Technology, ICT, Art and Music as well as one period each of RE and PE. Most also begin German and a number continue with Latin.

In the Lower and Upper Fifth Forms (Years 10 and 11),

the 'core' subjects, taken by all, are English, English Literature, French, Maths and generally all three Sciences. Three others are chosen from History, Geography, Design and Technology, Latin, German, Art and Music. Pupils also have one period each of RE and PE.

At all stages, progress is carefully monitored by Housemasters, Housemistresses and Tutors, and in Staff Meetings. The maximum class size in the Fourth and Fifth Forms is 24 and averages 10 in the Sixth Form.

The Sixth Form. Pupils will choose between three and five subjects at AS level in the Lower Sixth, before specialising in three or four in the Upper Sixth at A2 level. Some may take an extra AS level in the Upper Sixth, while others will top up their Key Skills components or take one of a variety of extension subjects such as Japanese, Spanish or ICT. Sixth Formers will select from the following subjects: Art, Biology, Business Studies, Chemistry, Design & Technology, Economics, English Literature, French, Geography, German, History, Maths, Further Maths, Latin, Media Studies, Music, Music Technology, Physical Education, Physics, Psychology, Theatre Studies

An extensive PSE programme operates throughout the school and there is a weekly Sixth Form lecture.

Each Department organises visits and invites guest speakers to meetings of Societies, which are held in lunch hours or evenings. These, together with small group teaching, seminars and often the vocational nature of Sixth Form courses, help to encourage students to develop their self-reliance, their analytical skills and their spirit of academic enquiry to equip them for the Higher Education courses to which almost all will move on when they leave.

As in the Junior Forms, the progress of Sixth Formers is constantly assessed by House Masters, and Mistresses and Academic Tutors, and in Staff Meetings under the overall supervision of the Head of Sixth Form. Parents are closely involved and regular Parents' Meetings are held.

Throughout the Senior School, grades for Effort and Attainment are given twice termly, and at the end of each term full reports are sent home.

Careers. A purpose built Careers Centre is open daily and managed by a full-time Careers Co-ordinator with advice provided by a team of Staff and Tutors. The College has close ties with ISCO, local commerce and industry and the Hertfordshire Careers Service. Links with local business are strong and there is an extensive programme of Work Shadowing/Experience organised for pupils in the Upper Fifth and Lower Sixth Forms.

The **Religious Instruction** and Sunday Worship are inter-denominational. Pupils are prepared for membership of their own Churches and a Confirmation Service is held each year.

Activities. In addition to the meetings of Clubs and Societies, Wednesday and Friday sessions are set aside within the timetable for Activities. We thus encourage pupils to pursue their own interests and introduce them to others, so that they will wish to carry these on into their spare time and beyond the confines of the School. Activities currently on offer include: Astronomy, Cookery, Ecology, Fencing, Experimental Science Club, Junior Sports Leadership, Art, Basketball, Bridge, Chess, Choir, Community Service, Computing, Debating, Design & ICT, Drama, Engineering, Golf, introduction to Guitar, Judo, Karate, Language Laboratory, Lifesaving, Local History, Radio, Spanish Club, Orchestra, Photography, Pottery, Squash. The Friday Activity Programme offers opportunities to pursue the Duke of Edinburgh Award Scheme and regular expeditions are organised. A range of Community Service projects also undertaken.

Music and Drama. A general interest in and appreciation of all kinds of music is encouraged throughout the school. In their 1st and 2nd forms, all pupils in the Junior School are taught an instrument in class, and those who show promise are encouraged to continue individually in the Senior School.

There is an Orchestra, Wind Band, Dance Band and other Ensembles, a Choral Society, a Chapel Choir and a Secular Choir, and pupils are encouraged to make music in small groups from the earliest stages. There is a fully equipped Recording Studio. The Music Staff includes visiting teachers of all the main instruments and of singing, together with the Directors of Music and their Assistant. The House Music Competition is a major event in the school year, including all pupils. Pupils have regular opportunities to perform in public at Pupils' Concerts and in School Assemblies.

Drama has enjoyed great popularity in recent years, and the College is developing this deliberately. As well as main College productions before Christmas and during the Summer Arts Week, there is each year a Fourth Form Play, House Plays, a Sixth Form Play and Drama Festival. Pupil initiatives are encouraged.

Sport. Physical Education is taught in the Fourth and Fifth forms and facilities include a Sports Hall, indoor and outdoor pools, a new floodlit all-weather Surface hockey pitch, hard tennis courts and 100 acres of playing fields.

The major games for boys are Rugby Football in the Winter Term, Hockey, Swimming and Water Polo in the Spring Term and Cricket in the Summer Term. Girls play Netball, Hockey, Tennis, Rounders, Swimming and Water Polo as their main sports. Athletics, Badminton, Basketball, Judo, Volleyball, Aerobics, Fencing, Cross-Country Running, Tennis, Squash and Weight-training are other choices. Those who wish may do extra Music, Drama, Cookery, ICT or Community Service, Motorcycle Maintenance, Amateur Radio instead of some games sessions. Swimming is taught to all pupils and the College teams have a long tradition of outstanding results.

Health. The Sanatorium is staffed by a resident Sister and her SEN Assistant. Regular Surgeries are held by the School's Medical Officer.

Varied and wholesome meals are provided in the College central Dining Hall, with plenty of choice. All day pupils take lunch at School and the cost is included in the fees.

Junior School. The organisation of the Junior School (for pupils up to age 13+) is largely separate from that of the Senior School, but the curricula of the two Schools are carefully integrated. The School has its own playing fields and pupils are able to share Senior School resources in Sport, Design and Technology and Music.

A new networked computer facility was installed in 1998. Extensive additional facilities, including a new library, art room and extra classrooms were completed in 1999.

Pre-Prep. This purpose-built Department with 6 classrooms, a Library and a Music Room was opened in 1995. A new play area was opened in 1999.

Admission. Testing for Junior School entry (7–13) takes place in January. Entry to the Senior School at 13+ is generally through the Common Entrance Examinations in June or through alternative testing where appropriate by arrangement with the Headmaster.

Sixth Form Entry Interviews and Examinations are held in the November before year of entry.

Scholarships. (*see* Entrance Scholarship section) Academic Scholarships and Exhibitions as well as Art and Music Awards, up to the value of 50% fees, are made at three levels: (1) Sixth Form; (2) at 13+ for Senior School Entry; (3) at 10+ or 11+ for pupils entering the Junior School. All awards may be supplemented by Bursaries according to need. A number of additional bursaries, including Lloyds' Cuthbert Heath Centenary Bursaries, are granted annually to deserving cases.

Fees. The fees per term for the Calendar Year 2001, inclusive except for individual music tuition, are: Senior

School: Boarders £4,416: Day £3,144. In the Junior School: Boarders £3,355; Day £2,545 (10–13), 'Shell' Boarders £3,080, 'Shell' Day £2,231. Pre-Prep Day £1,483.

Charitable status. The Incorporated Bishop's Stortford College Association is a Registered Charity, number 311057. Its aims and objectives are to provide Independent Boarding and Day education for boys and girls from age 4 to 18.

Bloxham School

Nr Banbury Oxon OX15 4PE.
Tel: (01295) 720222
Headmaster: (01295) 720206
Fax: (01295) 721714 (School) 721897 (Headmaster) 721473 (Common Room)
e-mail: registrar@bloxhamschool.co.uk
website: www.bloxhamschool.com

The School was founded in 1860 by the Rev P R Egerton. Since 1896 it has been a member of the Woodard Corporation.

Motto: *'Justorum Semita Lux Splendens'.*

Provost: The Revd Canon John W Rating, MA

Chairman: B Hurst, Esq, BSc, CEng, FIEE

Members:

Tony Baldry, Esq, MP, BA, LLB
The Revd Canon Geoffrey Brown, MA
A D Pickering, Esq, MA
Professor R P Johnson, MA, FICE, FIStructE
P J P Barwell, MBE
M R Deeley, Esq
D J B Long, Esq, BA
Mrs J Findlay, LLB (Hons)
C P Jackson, Esq
Mrs A F Beer
R Towner, Esq

Divisional Bursar: A A Holmes, Esq, SCA

***Headmaster:* D K Exham**, MA

Deputy Headmaster: L G Harrop, BA

Director of Studies: P C Perkins, MSc

Chaplain: The Revd M G Price, MA, MPhil

Assistant Masters:

M J Tideswell, DipPE
N C W Furley, BA
C D Stewart, BA
E G Wilkowski, BSc
T I Hatton, BA (*Director of Sixth Form Studies*)
C Newbould, BSc
C M Fletcher-Campbell, MA, ARCO, LRAM, ARCM (*Director of Music*) (*Officer Commanding CCF*)
T M Skevington, BEd
S J Batten, MA
G P Cruden, BA
J L Ekers, BSc
Mrs J M Summers, MSc
C N Boyns, BSc
Mrs C E Brooks, BA,
A G Whiffin, MA
C V Atkinson, BA
J P Horton Cert Ed (*Director of PE*)
R M Joiner, BSc, BA
M Pye, DipFA (*Director of Art*)
Mrs H M Smith, BA (*Head of Lower School*)
A C Benn, MA
N StJ D Pigott, BA
G A Stindt, BSc (*Head of Science*)
Mrs F Waddy, BA
J F Berry, BSc
H J Alexander, MA
D F McLellan, BA
R S Thompson, BA
Mrs E C Jeffrey, BA
Miss M M Smith, BA
D B Machin, BA
Mrs E N Shergold, BA
Mrs J H White, BEd
C B Arblaster, BSc
M J M Moir, BSc
Mrs B M Whithead, BA
N E Evans, BSc
Miss F Aslam, BSc
D R Best, BA

There are a number of visiting Instrumental teachers.

Headmaster's Secretary and Registrar: Mrs H M Hill

Medical Officer: S A Haynes, MBBS, MRCGP, DFFP

State Registered Nurses: Miss S Ashton, RGN, Mrs J Wilkowski, BA, RGN, SCM

School Bursar: N A Halfpenny, BSc, MSc, MBIM

Director of Marketing: A N Irvine, CertEd

Organisation. There are approximately 206 boarders and 154 day boarders. Day-boarders are full members of their Boarding Houses and are allocated House Rooms, Studies, etc. according to seniority in the same way as full boarders. They have all meals except breakfast at the School, and stay for preparation.

Lower School: for day or weekly boarding pupils 11-13, is an integral part of the school. We admit around 30 each year. Entry is through our own examination.

Houses. There are 4 Boys Houses: *Crake*, Mr C D Stewart; *Egerton*, Mr J L Ekers; *Seymour,* Mr C N Boyns; *Wilson*, Mr S J Batten. There are 3 Girls Houses: *Raymond* Mrs E C Jeffrey; *Wilberforce*, Mrs F Waddy; *Park Close (6th Form House),* Mrs J M Summers. *Stonehill (Lower School Boarding), Mr & Mrs A N Irvine.*

School Buildings and Grounds. The School is situated in a village on the edge of the Cotswolds. It is 3 miles to the south of Banbury and close to the M40 London-Birmingham motorway. It is within easy reach of Heathrow and Birmingham International Airports. The original buildings were designed by Street and most of the School is of local stone. The Dining Hall and Kitchen, which have been substantially expanded and refurbished, lie within these early buildings, as do the Chapel, one IT Room and two boarding houses. Other new buildings and major conversions completed within recent years include the Science Building (13 Laboratories and Lecture Rooms, Workshop, Science Library and Careers Room), the Sam Kahn Music School, the White Lion building housing the Lower School, and The Wesley Theatre. Other buildings of importance are the Arts Teaching Block with Great Hall, stage and green rooms, the Art School, the Theatre Workshop, the covered Fives and Squash Courts, the Armoury with Indoor Shooting Range, the Library, the combined Pavilion and Sixth Form Common Room, and the new Raymond Technology Centre which opened in 1997. The boarding modernisation programme has provided study bedrooms for all those in the Fifth and Sixth Forms. There are playing fields of about 37 acres, including Sports Hall, Tennis Courts, indoor heated swimming pool and an all-weather pitch used for hockey and tennis.

Admissions. At 11 (for day pupils or weekly boarding pupils) by entrance examination set by the school.

At 13 (boarding and day). Those from prep schools are required to pass the Common Entrance Examination, while candidates from state schools are given an alternative examination specially designed to suit their courses of instruction.

At 16 (boarding and day). Those who wish to start a two year 'A' level course are admitted to the Sixth Form on the basis of interview and school report.

There is a Dyslexia Unit which takes up to six pupils each year, at age thirteen, with full scale IQ's of 120+.

Applications should be made to the Headmaster.

Scholarships and Exhibitions are awarded at 11+, 13+ and for entry to the Sixth Form. Academic awards are made on the basis of a competitive examination. Awards for Art, Design Technology, Music (with free instrumental tuition) and Sport (not at 11+) are also made.

All the above awards may be up to 50% of fees according to merit, but they may be augmented up to 100% of fees, either boarding or day, according to the financial needs of parents.

Chapel Centenary Awards of up to £3,000 per year may

be awarded to good candidates of less than Exhibition standard on the basis of ability in the above areas, or of all-round merit and promise.

Sir Lawrence Robson Scholarships and Exhibitions are awarded each year to Sixth Form entrants. The value of these will be up to 50% of fees (up to 100% in cases of financial need).

Age limits for candidates on 1 September: 11+, under 12, 13+, under 14, Sixth Form and under 17.

Further details may be obtained from the Registrar.

Fees. (*see* Entrance Scholarship section) Boarders, £15,930 pa; Day £12,430 pa; both inclusive (and covering all meals, lunch, tea and supper, taken at School by day pupils.) Lower School: Day £8,285 pa; Weekly Boarding £10,305.

Information on the payment of fees by Insurance Schemes, and a School Fees Remission Scheme in case of absence, are obtainable from the Bursar.

Optional Extras. Private tuition in a particular subject, £23, £18, £14 and £12, according to the number of pupils in a group. Instrumental Music £130 per term.

Curriculum. For the first three years pupils have a broad based curriculum which leads to nine or ten GCSE's. No choices need to be made in the Third Form and the full range of subjects is studied. In the Fourth and Fifth forms all pupils continue to study for GCSE's in English Language, English Literature, Mathematics, French, Physics, Chemistry, Biology, Religious Studies (short course), and in addition choose three other subjects from a range of options including History, Geography, Latin, Spanish, German, Art, Music, Design Realisation, Electronics and Business Studies. In the Sixth Form A level Courses are available in Art, Biology, Business Studies, Chemistry, Design Technology, Economics, English, French, Further Mathematics, Geography, German, History, Mathematics, Music, Physics, Politics, Spanish, Theatre Studies and Physical Education. A wide choice of combination is again offered. All pupils follow a comprehensive General Studies programme throughout the Sixth Form and the majority take General Studies 'A' Level. Boys and girls are prepared for entrance to Oxford and Cambridge.

Tutorial System. In addition to the Housemaster or Housemistress, pupils have a House Tutor. Every Tutor looks after about 12 pupils and is thus able to give close personal attention to the development of each, both in and out of School. At regular intervals of three weeks the tutor reviews each pupil's Form Assessment which gives details of standard and approach to work in all subjects as well as information on extra mural activities.

Music. There is a wide range of instrumental and choral opportunities ranging from the School Orchestra and Concert Band to chamber ensembles and close harmony groups.

Games and Outdoor Activities. Boys and girls play the traditional major sports, rugby, athletics, hockey, cricket and netball according to season and in addition there are good facilities for badminton, basketball, squash, fives, sailing, shooting, swimming, canoeing, cross-country, fencing and tennis. Boys and Girls are strongly encouraged to develop their own particular talents. In the Third Form and below, pupils are expected to participate in major sports, but they have an increasing range of choices as they progress up the school. Boys and girls are also given the opportunity of participating in a flourishing Community Service Organisation.

CCF. All those in the Third Form enter the "Forty", where they undertake Duke of Edinburgh Award Scheme type training. In their second year many join the CCF, to which there are various challenging alternatives. Adventure Training Camps are held annually at Easter as well as the usual CCF Summer Camps.

Societies. There is a large number of societies, academic and practical. All pupils are expected to participate in some of these activities according to their interest.

Old Bloxhamist Society, *Resident Secretary:* R L Stein. *Chairman:* T J Petersen

Charitable status. Bloxham School is part of the Woodard Corporation and is a Registered Charity, number 269673. Its aim is to provide high quality academic education in a Christian environment.

Blundell's School

Tiverton Devon EX16 4DN.
Tel: (01884) 252543
Fax: (01884) 243232
e-mail: registrars@blundells.org
website: www.blundells.org

The School, with its attendant Scholarships at Balliol and Sidney Sussex Colleges, was built and endowed in 1604 at the sole charge of the estate of Mr Peter Blundell, Clothier, of Tiverton, by his executor the Lord Chief Justice, Sir John Popham. In 1882 the School was moved to its present 100-acre site on the outskirts of Tiverton.

Governors:
E D Fursdon, MA, FRICS, FAAV (*Chairman*)
Sir Ian Heathcoat Amory, Bt, DL, FCA (*Representative of the Lord Lieutenant of Devon*)
R R A Breare
M I R Bull, LLB
B M Currie, MA, FCA, FIMC
The Revd A R Gibson
C W M Grose
Dr J H Jones, MA, DPhil, CChem, FRSC, FRHistS (*Representative of Balliol College, Oxford*)
P J Lough, MA
Mrs A C Mayes, MBC, BSc
Mrs S Robinson
R N Swarbrick, MA
His Hon Judge W E B Taylor
Cllr N Thom
B W Wills-Pope, FInstD
P C Ondaatje (*Governor Emeritus*)

Clerk to the Governors and Director of Finance and Administration: P Armstrong, BSc

***Head Master:* J Leigh**, MA, Corpus Christi College, Cambridge, FRSA

Second Master: R W Thane, BA, FRGS

Director of Studies: P F Rivett, MA

Chaplain: The Revd T C Hunt, MTh, BD, ARICS

Assistant Masters:
T H C Noon, MA
G Clarke, BA, MSc, FRGS
B Wood, BSc
D H Brabban, PhD, BSc
A J Deighton-Gibson, BSc
T D Dyke, MA
A H Barlow, MPhil, MA
J G Pilbeam, BEd
S J Goodwin, BA
R S Tranchant, BA
*N J Ridgway, BSc
J S Shrimpton, BA
*N A Folland, BSc
*Mrs H M Barlow, BEd
Mrs D B Kite, CertEd, CTEFLA
*P H Gordon, BA, BEd
*J W Brigden, BEd
Mrs D Brigden, BEd
R N Giles, MA
M P Dyer, MSc
Mrs D K Assinder, BA
*A J R Berrow, MA
I Homer, BSc
*Mrs N J Klinkenberg, BSc
*Mrs S J Rumble, BA
A J Morley, BA
J T Balsdon, PhD, BSc
Miss J Clark, BA
Miss S L Taylor, BA
H G Thomas, BSc
G F W Case, BSc

Miss E J Gillan, BA
Miss D J Hosking, BEd
Miss L E Pike, BSc
Miss C M B Planques, BA
J L Ross, BMus
Miss I G Scott, MA
Mrs K J Wright, BA
S Berger, BA, MSc
C L L Gabbitass, BEd
I C Henwood, BSc
R D J Matthew, BA
Mrs A M Menheneott, BEd
Miss S A Norman, BSc (*Careers*)
Mrs G J Charlesworth, BA
A J Coull, BA
L Menheneott, BEd, MBA
Mrs G M L Batting, BEng
C M Hamilton, BA
Miss R E Symonds, MA
Miss T J Warne, BSc

Head Master's Secretary: Miss J J Rowlandson

Registrars:
P J Klinkenberg, BEd
Mrs E Thane

Medical Officer: Dr G K Peters, MB, ChB, MRCP, MRCGP, DRCOG

Admission. Entry is at 11 or 13 for most pupils. This is via the Blundell's Entrance Test or the Common Entrance Examination. Most join the School in September, though a January entry is welcome.

Numbers. There are 515 pupils of whom 190 are girls. Two thirds board or flexi-board. Three Houses are for girls whilst there are four senior boys' Houses and also a Junior Department (11-13) who share facilities but are taught and housed separately.

Fees. From £3,335 to £5,020 per term (boarding) or from £1,770–£3,060 per term (day). Flexi-Boarding exists for a supplement of £300 per term. A basic tuition fee is charged for those living within ten miles of Blundell's (over the age of 13).

Scholarships. (*see* Entrance Scholarship section) - Blundell's offers a wide range of generous fee remissions at the age of 13, primarily for academic merit. Each February awards are made of up to 50% of the basic tuition fee on the basis of set examinations. Music, Art and all-round awards are also examined at the School in February. Sporting aptitude is also taken into account and may be acknowledged with its own award. Two Military Bursaries are awarded each year to the sons or daughters of serving officers. There are also four Foundation Awards for candidates from the Ancient Borough of Tiverton or those who reside in Devon. These can be awarded at the age of 11. All awards may be supplemented in cases of financial need. Full details of all scholarships and bursaries are available from the Registrars.

School Work. There are four forms at age 11 through to GCSE. For three years Divinity, English, History, Geography, French, Maths, Physics, Chemistry, Art, Technology, Class Music, Biology, Drama, Information Technology, Physical Education, Personal and Social Development and Health Education are common to all. Latin is available and so are German, Spanish and Greek.

During the GCSE years the range of subjects remains broad. Extensive advice is provided by the School to assist both GCSE and A Level choices and an Academic Fair is staged in the Spring Term. Parents are encouraged to put their children in for the Independent Schools' Careers Organisation tests.

Sixth Form options enable a wide combination of subjects to be taken. Four of the following are taken to AS Level and three to A Level: English, Modern History, Geography, Latin, French, German, Spanish, Religious Studies (Ethics), Business Studies, Mathematics, Further Mathematics, Biology, Chemistry, Physics, Physical Education, Music, Art, Design Technology, Drama.

Mark Orders, Tutorial System and Reports. Frequent Mark Orders and Staff Meetings are held to monitor each pupil's work. The Blundell's "curriculum vitae" enables pupils to record their achievements and self-assessment is conducted once a term. All pupils have academic tutors. Parents receive three sets of formal reports each year. There are regular parents' meetings.

Societies and Activities. Blundell's has a wide range of extra-curricular activities; one afternoon each week is devoted to a choice of essentially non-sporting "activities".

Music and Drama. Blundell's music is excellent. Based on our own music school there are several choirs, an orchestra and varying musical ensembles. These range from a jazz band through a chamber choir to brass, woodwind and string groups. The Department has a good electronic section and in addition to School concerts there are visits from professional musicians. The Choir undertakes a European tour at Christmas, the most recent being to Aachen, the Czech Republic, Chinon and Hungary.

Similarly, Drama plays a key role in the School. There is an inter-House Drama competition, three major School Plays each year and an annual Prep Schools' Drama Festival. The magnificent, purpose-built Ondaatje Hall offers the combined facilities of a theatre, a concert hall and an art studio. Frequent visits are made by theatre companies and Blundell's is a cultural core for Mid-Devon.

Games and Physical Training. Boys play Rugby football in the Autumn Term whilst girls play hockey. Lent Term sports include cross-country, squash, rugby fives, hockey, soccer, fencing, basketball, netball and rugby sevens. In the Summer Term cricket, tennis, swimming, athletics and sailing take place. Golf, clay pigeon shooting, canoeing and miniature range shooting are also available, whilst the Sports Hall gives further scope to the range of sport.

Computing and Technology. All Blundellians have the opportunity to learn to use the School's computers and there is a resources centre adjacent to the Library.

Recent New Facilities. An all-weather playing surface opened in 1995 as did a new Sixth Form Centre. 1999 saw the upgrade of the Physics and Biology Departments. Provision of advanced technological and careers arrangements as part of the resources included in the handsomely redesigned Library was completed in 1998. September 2000 saw the relocation of St Aubyn's Preparatory School at Blundell's. The Blundell's Foundation has been set up to advance plans for the future and plans now include the building of the Colin Beale Centre (2001).

Community Service. The School is involved in a wide variety of activities, both local and national. Every third year the School hosts the Inner Cities Schools' Project.

Adventure Training. Blundell's is well placed to make full use of Dartmoor and Exmoor, the coast and rivers of the area, for academic fieldwork or adventure training. For many years the School has entered teams for the Ten Tors Expeditions on Dartmoor and canoes the Devizes-Westminster race.

CCF. Everyone in Years 9 and 10 serves for a year in the CCF. Thereafter it is manned by a body of volunteers who provide the NCO Instructors. There are close links with the affiliated Devonshire and Dorset Regiment and HMS Gloucester.

Religion. The School maintains a Christian tradition, while welcoming members of other faiths. All pupils are expected to attend weekday morning Chapel and the School Service on Sundays. The Chaplain prepares boys and girls who offer themselves for Confirmation, which takes place annually in the Spring Term.

Accessibility. Blundell's is close to the M5, and is served by Tiverton Parkway Station, two hours from Paddington, London. Airports at Bristol and Exeter are close at hand.

Prospectus. Fuller details of School life are given in the prospectus, available from the Registrars. Prospective parents are invited to visit the School, when they will meet the Head Master, and a Housemaster or Housemistress and have a full tour of the School with a current pupil. The

Blundell's website (www.blundells.org) is regularly updated throughout the academic year and as well as giving details of the school and academic departments, lists the main sporting, musical and dramatic events of each term and some match results.

Preparatory School. September 2000 saw the relocation of St Aubyn's School (age range 3 months to 11 years), onto a ten-acre site at Blundell's. For further information apply to Mr B J McDowell, the Headmaster of St Aubyn's School (see Part V).

Charitable status. Blundell's School is a Company limited by guarantee, registered in England, number 4016403 (Registered Office: Blundell's School, Tiverton, Devon EX16 4DT), registered charity number 1081249. It exists to provide education for children.

Bolton School

Chorley New Road Bolton BL1 4PA.
Tel: (01204) 840201
Fax: (01204) 849477

The School, founded in the early 16th century, was rebuilt and endowed by Robert Lever in 1641. In 1913 a new and large endowment was settled upon the School by Sir W H Lever, Bart. (later Viscount Leverhulme), and plans were drawn up for the construction of a new School building. This was completed in 1965.

Motto: *'Mutare vel timere sperno'*.

The Governing Body:

Chairman: Sir Alan Cockshaw

G Banister, LDS, VU (Manc)
Mrs S E Fisher, MSc, FRCS
M T Griffiths, BA, FCA
Judge J M Lever, QC
Mrs G E Sidebottom
R J Duggan, BSc
Mrs W P Morris, OBE
P Jarvis, CBE, MA
B H Leigh Bramwell
R J Byrom, JP, BA (Arch)
Mrs L A Hopkinson
Mrs C Boscoe
Mrs S R Tonge
Ms S K Hodgkiss
Hon Mrs M J Heber-Percy
Mrs M Kenyon

Clerk & Treasurer:
R T Senior, BA

***Headmaster:* A W Wright**, BSc

Deputy Headmaster: D E Shaw, BSc

Second Master: R D Wardle, BA

Teaching Staff:
Mrs H M Baker, BA
J Bleasdale, BA, LLCM
K Brace, BA
Miss R P Brandrick, BA
R Britton, MA, PhD
Miss S V Burgess, BA
A P Burrows, BSc, PhD
G Butchart, BEd
T Cairns, BSc
R A Catterall, BA
A C R Compton, BA
N Cropper, BA
E J Dawber, BSc
R Eastham, ABSM
Miss H L Eckhardt, BA
C G Edmundson, MA, FRCO(*CHM*), ADCM
D A Field, DPE
R A Freem, BA
D L Frost, MA
R D Frost, BEd
Mrs A Green, BA
R Griffiths, BA
R R Hannah, BA
R M Harrison, BSc
P A Hassall, BSc
K M Hiepko, MA
S W Holland, BA, PhD
P J Humphrey, BSc
C Hunter, BSc
A E Jackson, BA
D J Jones BSc
S P Jones, BSc
C C Joseph, MA
K Knibbs, BA
S J Martin, BMus
A I McNeil, MA
F H Mullins, BSc, PhD
T P Pledger, BA
C A J Pownall, BA
A M Prince, BSc, ARC, ATS
A J Raitt, BA
D R A Rees, BA
J W Rich, BA
C J Rigby, BA
I J Robertson, BSc, CBiol, MIBiol
Miss J C Robertson, BSc, PhD
A C Robson, BA
D Rogers BSc, DPhil
Mrs M A Ryder, BA
H H Schenk, BSc
Mrs M V Senior, BA
M Shewan, BEd, MA
Mrs C A Southworth, Inter NDD
D L Stevens, BSc
Miss J F Taylor, BSc
J L Taylor, BA
Mrs J M Thatcher, BSc, PhD
D S Thompson, BSc
M Townson, BA
Miss H Tunstall, MSc
M P Wadsworth, BA
C J Walker, BA
D G Watson, BSc, PhD
M Whitmarsh, BEd
R C J Whitten, MA
M Yates, BSc, PhD

Part-time:
J C Bernardin, BA
I C Dawkins
P Fowles, BA, LLCM, AMusTCL
Mrs C E Fox, BA
Mrs E M Greenhalgh, BSc
Mrs A J Hampson, BMus
Mrs S Neal G Mus, RNCM
M Pain, MA, FRCO, LRAM, ARCM
Mrs J Pearse, LTCL, LRAM, LGSM, AMusTCL
Mrs J V Pledger, MSc
J Powell, MA, CertEd, ARCM
Mrs P Pownall, BA
R Safhill, BA, RNCM
Mrs V Tymczyszyn
Mrs M Webb, LRAM, GRSM
M Wildgust, GMus, ARCM, LTCL
Mrs P Wilson, BA, ATD
Mrs V J Wright, BSc

Junior Department:
Mrs T Clarke, DipEd
T Dickinson, BEd
A B Harrison, DipEd
Mrs A L Hough, BSc, DPS
C D Hough, BSc
Mrs P J Lockett, BEd
Mrs S J Neal, BA
M Percik, BA, Master in Charge
S C Rashleigh, BA

Headmaster's Secretaries:
Mrs M P Jones
Mrs S Yates

Situated in imposing sandstone buildings on a thirty-four acre site two miles north of the town centre, Bolton School at present contains 1,000 boys, all day-pupils. Of these 150 are members of the Junior School which is housed in an adjacent separate building close to the main site providing education for boys for three years from the age of 8. In the Senior School of the 850 boys 200 are in the Sixth Form.

Curriculum. In the senior school a five year course to GCSE in which ten or eleven subjects are offered is followed. All boys include two languages (drawn from Latin, Greek, French, German and Russian) in their GCSE programme and also take all three sciences (Biology, Chemistry and Physics) as separate subjects. The wide middle school curriculum ensures a minimum of early specialisation thus ensuring that all options for Sixth Form study are preserved. At 'A' level 22 different subjects are currently on offer. Boys study three subjects to GCE Advanced and, in addition, also take a fourth or fifth subject to AS standard. While many boys elect to take standard combinations of either Arts or Science subjects in the Sixth Form, a high degree of flexibility is maintained thus ensuring that any desired combination of subjects can be offered. There is an additional and extensive programme of supportive academic work in other fields than the direct GCE Advanced curriculum throughout both of the two years of the Sixth Form.

Facilities and organisation. The Boys' and Girls' Divisions of Bolton School are housed in separate buildings on the same site and, though the organisation of the two Divisions provides basically single-sex schools, there are many opportunities for boys and girls to meet and to co-operate in the life of the school community. In some subjects co-educational arrangements are in operation. The buildings of the Boys' Division include the Great Hall, two libraries, gymnasium, sports hall, laboratories, art rooms, sixth form common room and ICT learning centre, design technology centre, performing arts centre, classrooms and dining hall. The Junior School building contains eight form rooms and specialist rooms for ICT, art & design and science & technology together with a gymnasium and library. Use of the sports hall and the adjacent 25-metre swimming pool and the new arts centre is shared by all sections of the school.

Games and PE. The extensive playing fields which adjoin the School contain thirteen pitches. Principal games are football and cricket. Rugby, tennis, hockey, swimming, water-polo, badminton, athletics and cross-country running are also all played at representative school level. Games and physical education feature in the timetable of all boys. The School is divided into four Houses for the purpose of internal sporting competitions.

Art, Drama, Design, Music. In addition to timetabled sessions in each discipline there are many opportunities for extra-curricular activities in all these pursuits. Facilities in the art department include a pottery room with kiln; within the very active musical life of the School there are choral groups, orchestras and ensembles catering for all ages and abilities. In addition arrangements can be made for individual lessons on all orchestral instruments, piano, organ and in singing. Drama is an important part of the work of the English department and boys are encouraged to develop their talents in the arts centre. The annual major school play, musical or opera is produced in co-operation with the Girls' Division. Design and technology features strongly in the curriculum in both Junior and Senior Schools with considerable success each year in the 'A' level technology courses, many boys gaining industrial sponsorships as a result. In addition, a wide variety of extra-curricular opportunities exists in both the design technology base and the computer rooms.

Outdoor Pursuits. All junior school pupils and all students up to and including Year 12 in the senior school undertake an annual period of outdoor education within curriculum time. In addition many boys go on camps or treks at home or abroad during holiday periods. The School has its own 60 bed Outdoor Pursuits Centre, Patterdale Hall in Cumbria, used by parties of boys regularly for curriculum, week-end, holiday and fieldwork expeditions. There is a large and active Scout Group with its own newly-built headquarters in school premises.

Religion. The School is non-denominational; all boys have periods devoted to religious education. In assemblies the basic approach is Christian although a great variety of readings and methods of presentation are adopted. Religious education is taught in a broad undogmatic style which encourages free discussion on many issues.

Careers and Higher Education. The Careers Master arranges personal interviews for all boys in Years 10 and 11 to help with choice of AS & A2 subjects and boys take career aptitude tests coupled with a computerised careers programme. A fully-stocked careers information room, in which a careers assistant is always on hand to give help and advice, is open at all times to all boys. Work experience is arranged for Year 11 and Year 12 pupils.

Transport. The School organises an extensive coach and bus transport service to provide easy access for pupils from a wide surrounding catchment area. Currently twenty-two routes are being operated by either the School's own fleet of coaches or by contract hire arrangements.

Admission. An entrance examination is held in January annually for boys over 8 and under 9 on August 31st of the year of admission and also for those over 9 and under 10 on the same date. Fifty places are available at 8+ and a few additional places at 9+. Admission to the first year of the Senior School (120 places) is by entrance examination held annually on the third Thursday in January. Boys who are over 10 and under 12 on August 31st of the year of entry are eligible. Entry to the Sixth Form is available to boys who have taken GCSE examinations elsewhere on the basis of interview and agreed levels of performance in these public examinations. Boys are also admitted at other ages when vacancies occur; in these cases admission is gained through satisfactory interview and test performances. There is a co-educational pre-preparatory section of the Girls' Division (Beech House) where admission is from the age of 5 and for which enquiries should be made to the Headmistress of the Girls' Division. There is also a new nursery unit providing facilities for children from 3 months to 4 years old.

Fee and Fee Assistance. School fees for 2001/2002 are £6,090 p.a. for the Senior School and £4,597 for the Junior School. In both cases the fees are inclusive of the school midday meal which is attended by all boys. Foundation Grants are available to provide assistance with fees.

Prospectus and Open Day. The School holds an annual Open Morning for the benefit of prospective candidates and their parents. This is normally on the fourth Saturday in November. Further information concerning all aspects of the School is contained in the School Prospectus, copies of which may be obtained by writing to the Headmaster at the School, or telephoning the Headmaster's Secretary. Enquiries concerning admission are welcome at any time of the School Year although formal application for the two entrance examinations need to have been received at the School by the end of December of the year prior to entry.

Charitable status. The Bolton School is a Registered Charity, number 526618. Its aims and objectives are to maintain in or near the County Borough of Bolton a public secondary school for boys and girls as a day school. Under the terms of the Charity it is to be administered as two separate Divisions providing for boys and girls under a separate Headmaster and Headmistress and it exists in this form until the present day.

Bootham School

York YO30 7BU.
Tel: School: (01904) 623261
Headmaster: (01904) 623636
Fax: (01904) 652106
website: http://www.bootham.york.sch.uk

Bootham offers Full and Weekly Boarding and Day Education to both boys and girls from 11–18. There are now over 400 pupils in the school, nearly one-third of whom are boarders. There are approximately 160 girls and 250 boys.

The School was founded in 1823 by Quakers, but pupils of all denominations or none are welcomed. All pupils attend Meetings for Worship and arrangements are made for pupils to be prepared for confirmation or membership of their own churches.

Headmaster: **Ian M Small**, BA (Sussex), FRSA

Deputy Headmaster: Graham J Ralph, BA, MA

Assistant Staff:
*Sarah Allen, BD, BEd
§Rachel Antill, BA
Mathew D Aston, BEd
†*Jennifer L Bailey, BA (*Housemistress, Rowntree House*)
Michael Bardsley, BSc
§Susan Barlow, MA
*Richard M Barnes, BA, MA
§Margaret Bland, BSc
Richard N Burton, BA
*Paul K Burton, BTech, MInstP, CPhys
Carol L Campbell, BA
Marie-Josephe Cockcroft, L-ès-L
§Joan Daniels, CertEd
Christopher Dobson, BSc
§Joanna Dowson, CertEd
§Fiona Dunlop, BA, MA
§Susanne Gair, MA
Emma Glover, BA
§Margaret Glover, BSc
Robert E Graham, BEd
Suzanne Hall, BA, PhD
Elisabeth Hooley, BA
†*A Max A Hull, BA, MA (*Housemaster, Penn House*)
§Harriet Humfrey, BSc
§Leslie Jackson, BA, MSc
*Alasdair D Jamieson, MA, MLitt, CertEd, ARCO (*Director of Music*)
§Anna Kempster, MA
§Sheil Khanna, MEd, MInstP, CPhys
*William R Lewis, MA
§Clive Marshall, MA
Pauline Marshall, BA
Elizabeth McCulloch, MA
*Eamonn Molloy, BEd
Anne Parry, BEd
*Robin L Peach, MA
*Colin Raper, CertEd
*John M Reed, BSc, MIBiol, CBiol
†David M Robinson, BSc, CPhys, MInstP (*Senior Housemaster, College House*)
*Mark Robinson, BA, MA
Hilary Rossington, BA
Jennifer Royle, MA (*Director of Studies*)
†Michael Shaw, BSc (*Housemaster, School House*)
Ruth Sillar, MA
*Richard Taylor, BA, MA
*Peter R Warn, BSc, MEd, FRGS
Paul Woodward, BA

Bursar: Nicholas J Marten, MIMgt

Curriculum. In the Lower School all pupils pursue a course of study which includes English (including Drama), History, Religious and General Studies, Careers, Geography, Latin, French, German, Mathematics, the three separate Sciences, Music, Art and Craft, Physical Education, Design & Technology and Computer Studies.

Every effort is made to enable a pupil in the Middle School to follow a curriculum suited to his or her particular abilities and future needs, leading to GCSE.

The College Classes (VIth Forms) are preparatory to university entrance. The majority of pupils remain at school until the age of 18 and each year there is a strong entry for the Advanced and Special levels. A wide choice of subjects is offered. It is usual to study 4 or 5 examination subjects, and to study subjects of wider interest.

The following subjects may be taken, in many combinations, to the A/S & A2 and University Entrance levels: Mathematics, Further Mathematics, Physics, Chemistry, Biology, English, French, German, Modern History, Classical Studies, Geography, Economics and Business Studies, Music, Art, Design Technology, Information Techology and Religious Education. Additional AS level subjects include Art History (depending on demand), Drama and Theatre Studies, English Language, Government and Politics, Latin (by arrangement), Psycology and Sports Studies. To counter-balance the effects of specialisation, pupils in the College classes are required to follow courses in Religious, Physical and General Education. In General Studies pupils follow a joint course with pupils from The Mount in a wide range of topics such as English Literature, Political History, Music Appreciation and International Affairs, given by members of the staff and, from time to time, by specialists who visit the School for this purpose. Particular emphasis is placed on the study of personal relations and the structures of communities.

Site and Buildings. The School is situated close to York Minster. From the road it appears as an impressive line of Georgian houses but behind this is the spacious main school built in 1902, which includes the John Bright Library. There is a steady programme of development, and the buildings now include 7 well-equipped Laboratories, a Music School, 3 Workshops, an Astronomical Observatory, an up-to-date Physical Education Department with new Sports Hall (opened 1998), Indoor Swimming Pool and Squash Courts, and a modern Assembly Hall, which received a national RIBA award. There are many facilities for leisure time pursuits which are an important feature of the lives of pupils at the School. The buildings are complemented by formal gardens and a beautiful Cricket Field, overlooked by the Minster. Another large Playing Field is situated nearby, in Clifton.

Pastoral Care. As a Quaker School, Bootham places great emphasis on caring relationships within a friendly community. There are four boarding houses, under the special care of House staff. Each House has its own recreational facilities. Throughout the Lower and Middle School, both boarding and day pupils are supervised and guided by form tutors. In College, pupils have Personal Tutors who are responsible for both academic and pastoral matters, and guidance towards Higher Education.

Admission. Pupils from Preparatory Schools usually enter Bootham at the age of 13, having taken Common Entrance in June. Pupils from LEA Schools are admitted at 11, 12 or 13; for these pupils an entrance examination is held annually in the Spring Term. In special circumstances late entrants can be considered.

Applications for entry to Year 10 can be considered if places are available.

Bootham admits several entrants to the sixth form each year to study Advanced level courses. Sixth form Entry Scholarships can be awarded to suitable applicants.

Leisure Time Activities. The School has long been recognised as a pioneer in the right use of leisure. There is a tradition of liberal provision for Natural History, Archaeology, Astronomy, Photography, Electronics, and crafts such as pottery. The Natural History Society, founded in 1832, claims to be the oldest society of its kind with an unbroken history in this country. Pupils become involved in, for example, regional surveys, meteorological observations, and the examination of Roman and prehistoric sites which abound in the city and district. Other clubs and societies include Debates, Drama, Bridge, Chess, Printing (using the school's own printing centre), Cookery and Jazz. There are around 100 activities offered each week. Pupils follow the Duke of Edinburgh's award scheme and are involved in Community Services.

Music. A full-time Musical Director and his assistant are supported by 14 visiting teachers. Tuition is arranged in a wide variety of instruments and a strong tradition of music in the School is maintained.

Games. Association Football, Hockey, Tennis, Fencing, Cricket, Swimming, Athletics, Netball, Badminton, Squash, Rowing, Rounders. There is no cadet force.

Fees. The fees are announced in the Summer term. Fees for instrumental music lessons are extra. Enquiries for up to date information are welcome.

Scholarships. (*see* Entrance Scholarship section) Up to four John Bright Memorial Boarding Scholarships of up to 50% of full fees are awarded at 11+ and 13+. Other Major and Minor Scholarships of up to 50% of full fees are also awarded to both boarding and day pupils at 11+, 13+ and 16+. Some Bursary help is also available to supplement scholarships; this assistance is means-tested.

Several Music and Art Scholarships are available

Bootham Old Scholars' Association. There is an annual Reunion in York during the second weekend in May at the same time as the Reunion of Mount School Old Scholars. The Bootham Old Scholars Association has branches in all parts of the country and Eire. The Secretary may be contacted through the School.

Charitable status. Bootham School is a Registered Charity, number 513645. Its objects are to conduct Bootham School in accordance with the principles of the Religious Society of Friends for the education of the children of members of the Society of Friends and others.

Bradfield College

Bradfield Berkshire RG7 6AR
Tel: General Enquiries: 0118 9644500
Head Master: 9644510
Bursar: 9644530
Fax: 0118 9644511
website: www.bradfieldcollege.org.uk

St Andrew's College, Bradfield, was founded in 1850 by Thomas Stevens, Rector and Lord of the Manor of Bradfield.

Motto: *'Benedict us es, O Domine: Doce me Statuta Tua'.*

Visitor: The Right Rev The Lord Bishop of Oxford

Council:

The Lord Iliffe (*Warden*)	T N Clark
J M Tyrrell	Mrs P Thomson
P H C Brader	The Lady Ryder
Professor M P Furmston	J M Latham
The Hon Peter Dixon	A J Kerevan
Sir John Lucas-Tooth	M D'Arcy-Irvine
M J C Stone	P G F Lowndes
C R Lucas	M H Young

Clerk of the Council: T M Sills

***Head Master:* P B Smith**, MA, FRSA

Deputy Head: N A Marshall, MA

Bursar: Brigadier M T A Lord, BSc, CEng, FIMechE

Houses and Housemasters:

A – Loyd (*D T Palmer*)

B – College (*R Keeley*)

C – Army (*T J Kidson*)

D – House on the Hill (*R J Wall*)

E – Field (*S P Williams*)

F – Hillside (*R P Backhouse*)

G – House on the Hill (*T H Chaloner*)

H – The Close (*E W Balfour*)

I – Palmer House (*Girls*) (*Mr & Mrs C Bond*)

J – Armstrong House (*Girls*) (*Mr & Mrs K L Smallwood*)

K – Stevens House (*Girls*) (*Mr & Mrs D F Moss-Gibbons*)

Faulkner's (*Year 9*) (*R J Clapp*)

Day pupils are attached to boarding houses. The Housemaster is assisted by House Tutors and a Matron

Academic Staff. There are 72 members of the Academic Staff, who cover all the main subjects. These are almost entirely graduates recruited from British universities, although there are also native speakers of German, French and Spanish in the Modern Languages department. A full list of staff, together with their subjects and qualifications, is available from the Head Master's Secretary.

Position. Bradfield College occupies the village of Bradfield, 8 miles west of Reading and 9 miles east of Newbury. It is 2 miles from Junction 12 of the M4 (the Theale access point). There are good road and rail communications with Reading, London and Heathrow.

General Arrangements. There are 580 pupils in the School, of whom about 70 are day pupils. 60 girls are admitted to the Sixth Form each year. The School is divided into 11 houses, each with its own sleeping, studying and recreational facilities. All meals are served in the central Dining Hall on a cafeteria system. Boys in their first year are accommodated in Faulkner's, a separate, purpose-built unit, which provides appropriate facilities for the induction year.

Admission to the School. Boys are admitted between the ages of 13 and 14 and qualify by taking either the Common Entrance Examination or the Bradfield College Scholarship Examination. Boys may be admitted at a later age through interview and school reports. Girls are admitted to the Sixth Form by interview, tests and a school report. A school prospectus and details of the entry procedure may be obtained from the Head Master.

Term of Entry. Boys are admitted at 13+ only in September. Older pupils will be accepted normally in September, but it may be possible to arrange for admission at other points in the school year.

Fees. A fee of £25 is payable on registration. About two years before the date of entry a Guaranteed Place fee of £500, which is later credited against the final account, is payable. The termly fee is £5,375 for boarders and £4,031 for day pupils.

Entrance Scholarships (*see* Entrance Scholarship section). Academic Scholarships and Exhibitions are awarded annually after a competitive examination in the Lent term. Their value varies between 50% and 10% of the fees, but the value of an award may be increased where need is shown. Music Scholarships up to 50% of the full fees are offered annually, and Art/Design and Technology Scholarships up to 50%. Full details may be obtained from the Head Master.

Academic Organisation. Boys enter the School in September and will follow a three year course to GCSE examinations, and then a two year course to 'A' level.

In the first three years all the normal school subjects are taught in a core curriculum, but there is also opportunity to emphasise the linguistic or the aesthetic or the practical elements through a system of options.

In the VIth form GCE AS and A2 level courses are offered in all subjects studied for GCSE with the addition of Economics and Politics, History of Art, Theatre Studies, Information Technology and Physical Education.

Careers. Advice and assistance is available to all pupils on a wide range of career possibilities through the Careers Department. All boys receive a careers report based on interviews and tests in the third year, and thereafter there are opportunities to find out about the professions, industry and the Services through talks, visits, conventions and courses. Specialist advice is also available on University and Polytechnic entrance.

Games. The main games are association football in the Michaelmas term, hockey in the Lent term and cricket and tennis in the Summer term. In addition teams represent the School at squash, fives, cross-country, rugby, fencing, athletics, lacrosse, golf, sailing, swimming, shooting and basketball. There are also facilities for badminton, judo and gymnastics.

There is an all-weather artificial grass pitch used for hockey, football and tennis, a 3 court indoor tennis centre, 6 other hard tennis courts, 4 fives courts, 4 squash courts and a very large and modern sports complex, including an indoor swimming pool. The school grounds extend to nearly 200 acres and include fine playing fields, a nine-hole golf course and fly fishing in the river Pang.

Recreation, Drama and Music. Every encouragement is given to pupils to develop their interests and talents in a wide variety of creative activities. There is a modern and well-equipped studio for art and pottery, an Information Technology Centre, a purpose-built and very extensive Design and Technology Centre and a Music School with a Concert Hall and practice rooms. The Greek Theatre is the venue of a classical Greek Play produced every three years, and of Shakespearean plays in the intervening years. There are also facilities for indoor productions. In addition, there are about 30 Societies covering a wide range of other interests.

Religion. Chapel services are those of the Church of England, and Religious Education is part of the core curriculum. A Confirmation Service is held each year.

Combined Cadet Force. The School maintains a contingent of the Combined Cadet Force, which all pupils have the opportunity of joining. There is a full range of alternative activity, including Community Service and Duke of Edinburgh's Award. All pupils take part in a programme of Adventure Training.

Old Bradfieldian Society. The School values its links with its former pupils and a series of social and sporting occasions is held each year to enable friendships to be maintained and renewed. The Secretary of the Old Bradfieldian Society is E B Williams, Bradfield College, Reading, Berkshire RG7 6AR.

Charitable status. St Andrew's College Bradfield is a Registered Charity, number 309089. Its aims and objectives are to provide an education which, following the broad tradition of an English liberal education, enables pupils to find out about their real interests and talents, and enables the College to develop those interests and talents to the maximum extent.

Bradford Grammar School

Keighley Road Bradford BD9 4JP.
Tel: (01274) 542492.
Headmaster: (01274) 553701.
Fax: (01274) 548129
e-mail: hmsec@bgs.bradford.sch.uk
website: www.bgs.bradford.sch.uk

Bradford Grammar School is known to have existed in 1548 and received a title of Incorporation as 'The Free Grammar School of King Charles II at Bradford', in 1662. It was reorganised in 1871, and the Scheme was revised in 1909, and again in 1973.

Motto: *'Hoc Age'*

Governors:
Chairman: A H Jerome, MA

Vice-Chairman: J E Barker, MA

The Vicar of Bradford
P J M Bell, JP, FCIS, CText, FTI, FRSA
D I Bower, MA, DPhil, CPhys, MInstP
W Bowser, ACIB
Professor A W Boylston, BA, MD, FRCPath
Mrs A C Craig, DCR
I Crawford, FCA
Mrs J D Fenton, MCSP, SRP
Mrs C Hamilton-Stewart
His Honour Judge K M P Macgill, LLB
Professor C Mellors, BA, MA, PhD
A D Pollard, MBE, LLB
T H Ratcliffe, LLB
C E Schofield, MA
C M Wontner-Smith, BA, FCA

Bursar and Clerk to the Governors: R G Hancock, MA, FCIS, MIMgt

***Head Master:* S R Davidson**, BSc

Second Master: The Revd L J Slow, BSc, MSc

Director of Studies: R I Page, BA, MSc

Art:
*R I Walker, BA
Mrs L A Hepworth-Wood, BA
A P Leedham, BA

Biology:
*D M McArthur, BSc, PhD
Mrs M Bibby, BSc
Mrs L C Goodwin-Presley, BSc
S R Hoath, BSc
M J Sharpe, BSc, PhD (*Head of Sixth Form*)

Chemistry:
*B B Parker, PhD, CChem, MRSC
S P D Burnett, BSc
Miss J E Hamilton, BSc, PhD
P J Palmer, BA, PhD

Classics:
*R A West, MA
T C Bateson, MA
B I Bentley, MA
Mrs M J Chapman, BA

Design and Technology:
*M D McKay, BA
D Leake, BEd
S G Taylor, BSc
N J Walker, BEd

Economics and Business Studies:
*P Kewley, BA, MA
A G Hartley, BA, MBA
Mrs D M Hicks, BSc
P S Bachra, BA

English and Drama:
*S N C Durrant, BA, MA
Mrs S Brear, BA
A M Hopkins, BA
A P Johnson, BA
P M Lawrence, BA
R W J Sisson, BA, PhD
D W Stokes, BA, MPhil (*Head of Drama*)

Geography:
*M D Raw, BA, MPhil
D C Elstub, BA
Miss J K Knight, BSc, PhD
A G Smith, BSc
N R Smith, BSc, MEd (*Head of Middle School*)

History:
*N A Hooper, MA, FRHistS
J D Devlin, BA, DPhil
J Reed-Purvis, BA, MA
Miss K E Roper, BA

Information Technology:
*D S Conroy, BSc
Miss N C Haggerty, BSc

Mathematics:
*A K Jobbings, BSc, PhD
A Crabtree, BSc
A Durant, JP, BTech, MPhil, FSS
D W Fishwick, BSc, PhD
P Merckx, BSc
L Nelson, BSc, PhD
N A Shepherd, BSc
M A Thompson, BSc

Modern Languages:
*M A Lumb, BA
G D Butler, MA
B Ching, BA
S B Davis, MA, LTCL (*Head of Russian*)
A J Kingham, BA
Mrs E J Kingsley, BA, MSc
Ms K Murach, MA
P A Murphy, BEd
R A Salter, MA
Mrs H C Shovlar, BA
M Skelton, BA (*Head of French*)
Mrs S Woodhead

Music:
*B Lancaster, MA, ARCO, LTCL
C J Brook

Physics and Electronics:
*H S Fricker, BA, PhD, CPhys, MInstP
J D Boardman, BSc (*Head of First Year*)
T W Carman, BSc, PhD, ARCS
P Ratcliffe, BSc
P Shepherd, BEng, PhD (*Head of Electronics*)
I M Stoney, TD, BSc, LRPS, CPhys, MInstP

PE and Games:
*C W Lines, BA
S Darnbrough
A J Galley, BA
Miss J L Kellington, BEd (*Head of Girls' Games*)
C E Linfield, BA
J D Veall, BA
M A Wilde, BA

Politics:
*M P J Simpson, MA
M McCartney, BSc

Religious Studies:
*S R Valentine, LLB, BD, MA, PhD, FEHS
K Ravenscroft, BA, MEd

The Clock House:
G Lee-Gallon, BTech (*Head of Clock House*)
Mrs M M Ashton, CertEd
P H Foster, BEd
N H Gabriel, BA, RIBA
Mrs A C Hood, BEd
Mrs L Morris, BEd
D Reddish, BEng
Mrs P Reddish, BSc
P Smales, BEd
G P Smith, BEd
N E Sykes, GLCM, ARCM
Mrs A Y Woodward, CertEd

Visiting Music Staff:
J Griffett, ARCM (*Singing*)
Mrs J Harrison, GRNCM (*Singing*)
Mrs P Jordan, ARCM (*Lower Strings and Piano*)
Mrs P R Lancaster, GRNCM (*Woodwind*)
Mrs G M Lindsay, GTCL (*Guitar*)
C M Marks, LLCM (*Electric Guitar*)
Mrs J E Osborne, ARCM, DipRCM (*Cello*)
B Price, BA (*Percussion*)
D Roberts, LRAM, LGSM (*Brass*)
P Seeley, BA, BMus, FLCM, LTCL (*Piano*)
Mrs C Shulman, BA (*Upper Strings*)
N Turner, BA (*Woodwind*)

Bradford Grammar School aims to provide a stimulating and supportive environment in which bright boys and girls can work together to achieve their individual potential. There are currently 935 boys and 119 girls aged 7-18.

Situation and Buildings. The school stands in fine buildings and extensive grounds about one mile from the centre of Bradford. There are excellent road and rail links with Wharfedale, Airedale, Calderdale and Huddersfield. The Junior School occupies Clock House, a seventeenth-century Manor House within the school grounds, where it enjoys its own assembly hall and teaching accommodation. Facilities available to both Senior and Junior Schools include the Hockney Theatre, the Library and Information Technology Centre, the school debating chamber, the Design and Technology Centre, Sports Hall and Swimming Pool. The Price Hall is the centrepiece of the main school building and provides a magnificent setting for assemblies, concerts and other major events.

Clock House Curriculum. All pupils study English, Mathematics, Geography, History, Science, Music, Art, IT, Design and Technology, Physical Education, Games, Religious Studies and French (Fourth Form only).

Senior School Curriculum. In the First Year all pupils study English, Mathematics, French, Latin, Science, Geography, History, Art, Music, Design and Technology, Information Technology, Religious Studies, Physical Education and Games. In the Second Year German is introduced. In the Third Year, pupils follow a common core of English, Mathematics, Geography, History, Physics, Chemistry, Biology, Religious Studies, Physical Education and Games, a choice of French or German and two subjects from German, Russian, Latin, Greek, Art, Music and Design and Technology. In the Fourth and Fifth Year, all pupils take English, Mathematics, French or German, Biology, Chemistry, Physics, RS, PE and Games and two or three subjects from: Geography, History, German, Russian, Latin, Spanish, Greek, Art, Music, Design and Technology and Information Technology. Pupils are divided into two parallel groups of forms both of which are entered for nine GCSEs including both English and English Literature. Pupils who choose GCSE Dual Award Science have one more subject option than those aiming at GCSE in the three separate sciences.

Sixth Form Curriculum. Pupils choose four Advanced Subsidiary Level subjects from Accountancy, Art, Biology, Business Studies, Chemistry, French, German, Greek, Design and Technology, Drama, Economics, Electronics, English Language, English Literature, English Language & Literature, Geography, Geology, History, Information Technology, Japanese, Latin, Mathematics and Further Mathematics, Music, Music Technology, Philosophy, Psychology, Physical Education Physics, Politics, Russian, Religious Studies and Spanish. Pupils taking GCSE Drama in the Lower Sixth have the option to take A Level Theatre Studies in the Upper Sixth. There is also a General Studies programme. In the Upper Sixth pupils take four or three A Level subjects. The school has a strong record of success at public examinations and university admissions; over the last six years 100 pupils have gained places at Oxford or Cambridge. A comprehensive Career Service operates throughout the school.

Extra-Curricular Activities. There is a thriving culture of extra-curricular activities. Music and Drama are an important part of school life; Debating flourishes and there are active CCF units and Community Service groups. Most academic subjects have societies run by pupils, and religious interests are represented in the Christian Fellowship and Islamic Society. A wide variety of sporting activities is offered, including Athletics, Badminton, Basketball, Cricket, Cross Country Running, Hockey, Netball, Rugby, Rowing, Table Tennis and Tennis. Recent additions to the extra-curricular programme include Sailing and Canoeing, Climbing, and Mountain Biking.

Pastoral Care. A team of Year Heads and Form Teachers works closely with pupils and parents to ensure that support is available in school and at home. An extensive Peer Support scheme and a growing system of Year Group Councils are just two ways in which pupils are encouraged to take responsibility for each other and themselves in school.

Admission. Boys and girls can join the school at the ages of 7, 8, 9, 10 in the Junior School or 11, 12, 13 in the Senior School. Pupils are admitted into the Sixth Form on the basis of interview and GCSE results. Candidates for entry at 7+ and 8+ are invited to spend an informal day in Clock House. Admission for all other ages is by examination in Mathematics and English in January each year.

Bursaries. Bursaries are available each year on a means-tested basis for entrants at 11+ and possibly 13+ to support the education of the successful candidates throughout their time at the school. Family circumstances will be reviewed annually and the value of any bursary adjusted accordingly.

Fees (for Spring term 2001). Current fees are £1,900 per term for pupils in the Senior School and £1,575 per term for pupils in the Junior School.

Old Bradfordians' Association. President: Mr R Bowers, c/o The Grammar School.

BGS Society (previously The Parents' Association). Chairman: Mr C Webster, c/o The Grammar School.

Charitable status. The Free Grammar School of King Charles II at Bradford is a Registered Charity, number 529113. It exists to provide education for children.

Brentwood School

Ingrave Road Brentwood Essex CM15 8AS
Tel: (01277) 243243.
Fax: (01277) 243299
e-mail: headmaster@brentwood.essex.sch.uk

Brentwood School was founded in 1557 and received its charter as the Grammar School of Antony Browne, serjeant-at-law, on 5th July, 1558. The Founder became Chief Justice of Common Pleas shortly before the death of Queen Mary, and was knighted a few months before his death in 1567. The Foundation Stone over the door of Old Big School was laid on 10th April, 1568, by Edmund Huddlestone and his wife Dorothy, who was the step-daughter of the Founder. The Elizabethan silver seal of the School Corporation is still in the possession of the Governors. In 1622 Statutes were drawn up for the School by Sir Antony Browne, kinsman of the Founder, George Monteigne, Bishop of London, and John Donne, Dean of St Paul's. They require that all boys shall be instructed in Virtue, Learning and Manners.

Motto: *'Virtue, Learning and Manners'.*

Governors:
C J Finch, FRICS (*Chairman*)
R E Ramsey, LLB (*Vice-Chairman*)
P R Baker, MA
G Bender
K Brown
B P Davies, MA
H E Flight, MA, MBA, MP
Professor R Floud, MA, DPhil
Lord Hanningfield
H Human, MA
H Kempe
Mrs S M F McAllister, BSc
Mrs W E McIntyre
J M May, MA, LLB
J H M Norris, CBE, DL
Dr P E Reynolds, MA, PhD
M J Snyder, FCA
R W Wilson, MA

Bursar and Clerk to the Governors: Col J A Cook, FCCA, FCMA, FCIS

***Headmaster:* J A B Kelsall**, MA, Emmanuel College, Cambridge

Second Master: D M Taylor, GRSM

Deputy Headmistress: Mrs J Goyer, MA

Senior Master: N J Carr, MA

Head of Sixth Form: J C Fowler, BA, PGCE

Head of Middle School: J R Brown, BA

Head of the Junior School: Mrs S M Edwards, BA, DipPC

Head of 1st Year Boys: L P Bishun, MSc, MIS

Head of Girls' Section: Mrs G Hallgate, BEd

Assistant Staff:
Mrs O Addison, BSc
Miss J L Ainsworth, BA, PGCE
Mrs A R Bailey, BSc
Mrs M Belshamy, BSc
Miss R Biggs, BSc
G A Bond, BA
*† C P Bouckley, BEd (*Head of PE; South Headmaster*)
M G Bowles, BA
Miss K Bradley, BA
*M S Chambers, BSc, MIBio (*Head of Biology*)
*S Chambers, MA (*Head of Classics*)
A Chappell, BSc, PGCE
Mrs J Collins, BEd, BSc
C C Cole, BSc
K J Cooper, BSc, PhD
S Coppell, BSc
Mrs J J Coppin, BSc
†N Copplestone, BSc (*Hough Housemaster*)
†Mrs L Coyne, BA (*Weald Housemistress*)
Miss K Crane, BA
Miss E J Creber, BSc
†N S Crosby, BA (*Head of Geography*) (*North Housemaster*)
*A J Drake, MA (*Head of Mathematics*)
*D S R Dunn, MA (*Head of English*)
H Ebden, BA, PGCE
S D Evans, BA PhD
Miss R Fairfull, BA
†G J Fisher, MA, PhD (*West Housemaster*)
Mrs A Godfrey, BA
*W M Gray, MA (*Head of Physics*)
B Hardie (*Cricket Professional*)
Mrs S Heyn, BA
Miss C Holding, BEd (*Deputy Head, Girls' Section*)
R Holt, ACP, DipEd
Mrs R Hoyle, BEd
Miss M Hunter, BA
Mrs A Jackson, BSc
R Jacques, BA
D Johnston, BA, PhD
*D H Jones, BA (*Head of Art*)
L Jones, BA
Miss W L Juniper, BEd
G M Kiff, BA (*Director, Design Centre*)
†J L Killilea, BEd, AIST (*East Housemaster*)
D Klempner, BA
Miss R Lapish, BEd
*M P Lee, BA, MA, PGCE (*Head of Religious Studies & PSE*)
B Lockyer, BA
C Long, BA
M C McClean, BSc, PGCE
G J McSkimming, BSc
D J Mechan, BSc, MSc, PhD
Miss A Mitchell, BA
Dr C Moloney, BA, PhD
B J D Morgan, BSc, DMS, MITD, MIMgt
†D C Morgan, BSc(*Eng*), MSc (*Mill Hill, Housemaster*)
S L Moss, BSc
J Moston, BA
*Mrs L J Oliver, BEd (*Head of Games, Head of Girls' PE*)
*G Orr, BA, PGCE (*Head of History*)
Mrs T Paules Sanagustin, BSc
*Mrs E A Penfold, BA, PGCE (*Head of Spanish*)
*D J H Pickthall, MA, FRCO (*Director of Music*)
*Mrs R E Prior, MA (*Head of Drama*)
R Pritchard, BA
A Rees, BSc
*P Rees, BA (*Head of Economics/Business Studies*)
Mrs S Roast, BEd
*A C Robinson, BSc, MSc(*Eng*), MEd, MInstP (*Head of Applied Science*)
P I Rollitt, BSc
S R Rumsey, BA
B L Ryan, BA
D E G Saunders, BA
Mrs E A Shotton, BA (*Deputy Head of Sixth Form*)
Miss M Sorohan, BA (*Deputy Head of Sixth Form*)
Miss P Spilsbury, BSc
J J Stevens, MA
*Dr R M Storey, BA, PhD (*Head of Modern Languages*)
M Sullivan, BA, DPhil
C Taylor, BA, PGCE
*D S Taylor, BSc, PhD (*Head of Science*)
Mrs G Taylor, BSc
Mrs M Taylor, BA
F J Taylore, BA
A J P Towner, BSc
I Walton, BA
Miss R Wardence, MA, PGCE
R G Whitehall, BSc
Mrs H F Williams, BEd
J Williams, BSc
Mr K Williams, BSc, MSc
Miss J Williamson, BA
M V Willis, BA
Miss S Winter, BA
Mrs F Wood, BA
Miss G Woollard, BA

Chaplain: The Revd David Gilchrist, MA

Medical Officers:
V D Bradbury, MRCS, LRCP
R Gupta, MB, CRB
S J Watts, BSc, MB, BS
M A Hamilton, MB, BS
A Naeem, MB, BS

Brentwood School is a co-educational school with a total of 1,442 pupils including 140 in the Pre-Preparatory School and 232 in the Preparatory School. The Pre-Preparatory

School and Preparatory School are fully co-educational as is the Sixth Form but boys and girls are taught separately between the ages of 11 and 16. Boarding is available for boys and girls from 11.

Buildings and Grounds. The School occupies a 70 acre site on high ground at the northern end of the town some 20 miles north-east of London. Old Big School, the original school room, is still in regular use thus maintaining a direct link with the school's founder. Over recent years a major building programme has seen extensions to the Science building and Dining Hall; refurbishment of the Junior School, Preparatory School, Middle School, Boarding Houses and Sixth Form accommodation; the building of the magnificent Courage Hall Sports Complex; a Performing Arts Centre, an all-weather pitch, an Art and Design Centre. Further plans see the building of an indoor heated swimming pool this year.

Organisation. The school is one community within which, for good educational reasons, girls and boys are taught separately from age 11 to 16. They are encouraged to participate together in all non-academic activities such as music, drama, exchanges etc. For administrative convenience the Senior School is divided into four sections; Sixth Form, Girls 11–16, Middle School Boys and Junior Boys. The vast majority of pupils join the school at 11 after successfully completing our Entrance Examination. A broad curriculum is followed through the 1st three years and this continues through careful choice of GCSE subjects to the end of the 5th year. Entry to the Sixth Form is conditional upon success in the GCSE examinations. Virtually all Sixth Formers will take 4 AS level subjects under the new arrangements, and the great majority go on to University. Pass rates at Advanced Level reach 98% and some 10–15 pupils gain places at Oxford and Cambridge each year.

Religion. The School is an Anglican Foundation. There is a resident Chaplain and all pupils attend Chapel weekly. Regular Communion Services are held. Members of other faiths are welcomed and their views respected.

Boarding. There are two Boarding Houses, both of which have been thoroughly modernised. The boys reside in Hough House which can accommodate up to 48 students; the girls reside in Mill House where 27 can be accommodated. Units are small, public rooms spacious and both Houses generously staffed. Full and weekly boarding are available. A resident, qualified Matron runs an efficient Sanatorium.

Pastoral Care. Brentwood School takes very seriously its pastoral responsibilities and provides two supportive systems. Responsibility for pastoral care is vested in the Form Tutors under the guidance of the Section heads and the Deputy Head, Pastoral. This system is complemented by a strong House system with Housemasters/Mistresses and House Tutors. Partnership with parents is regarded as essential and they are encouraged to join in activities and to visit regularly.

Music, Drama, Art. Music plays an important part in the life of the School, as do drama and art. There are 4 orchestras and several ensembles and jazz groups. The Big Band is internationally acclaimed. There are at least three dramatic productions each year, together with regular Art Exhibitions.

Design, Technology. The school believes that all pupils, boys and girls, should have the opportunity to experience work in this important area. The building of a new centre, opened in 1999, underlines our commitment. The School has a long record of success in this field.

Careers. There is an excellent Careers Department where students receive advice and can obtain information about courses and/or careers. Aptitude Tests; Work Experience; visits to colleges, universities and places of work; visiting speakers are all part of the provision. A careers convention is held every two years.

CCF and CSU. All pupils either join the Combined Cadet Force for at least two years or, through the Community Service Unit, engage in a wide-ranging series of activities which bring them into contact with the Community. The Duke of Edinburgh's Award Scheme may be followed in either organisation.

School Societies. There are many flourishing societies covering a wide range of interests, catering for all ages.

Games and Physical Education. The playing fields are part of the School complex and provide ample space for soccer, cricket, hockey and tennis. There is a cinder athletic track. The Courage Sports Hall Complex includes an indoor soccer/hockey pitch, six badminton courts, indoor cricket nets, basketball courts and a Fencing Salle, as well as squash courts and a multi-gym. There is a heated outdoor swimming pool and an all-weather pitch. Provision is made for golf, sailing and table-tennis. Physical Education is included in the curriculum and instruction in swimming forms part of all pupils' training.

Preparatory and Pre-Preparatory Schools. See Part V of this Book for details.

Entry. Entrance Examinations for both boys and girls aged 11 are held at the School in January each year. Entries are also accepted at 13 plus, following the Common Entrance Examination, vacancies permitting. Transfers at other ages are also possible. VIth Form entry is through GCSE success, and interview.

Scholarships. (*see* Entrance Scholarship section) Scholarships for academic performance and music are awarded to successful candidates at 11+ entry in January; Art Scholarships are awarded to Lower Sixth Formers in March of the year preceding entry. The School has its own Bursary Scheme.

Fees. Main School: Tuition £7,785 pa; Boarding £13,515 pa; Music Lessons £140 per term.

Old Brentwoods' Society: There is a flourishing Society. The Secretary is Ian West, 37 Regent Square, London E3 3HQ

Charitable status. Brentwood School is a Registered Charity, number L5310864/A3. It is a Charitable Trust for the purpose of educating children.

Brighton College

Brighton BN2 2AL.
Tel: Head Master: (01273) 704200;
Bursar: (01273) 704247;
Junior School: (01273) 704210.

Brighton College was founded in 1845 by a few prominent residents in the town, with the object of providing 'a thoroughly liberal and practical education in conformity with the principles of the Established Church'.

The College admitted girls to the VI Form in 1973 and became fully co-educational in 1988.

There are 573 pupils in the College of whom 398 are boys and 175 are girls. Of these 62 boys and 36 girls are boarders.

Motto: *TO Δ 'EY NIKAT Ω*

Patron and Visitor: The Right Rev the Lord Bishop of Chichester, DD

Council
President: ¶The Lord Alexander of Weedon, QC

Vice-Presidents:
Mrs J Lovegrove, MA
I J White, FRICS
I W Dodd
S J Cockburn, BA

P D C Points, MA
Lady H Trafford, DSc, SRN
Dr J Wade, JP, MB, BChir

Chairman: R J Seabrook, QC

Vice-Chairman: S J Cockburn, BA

Governors:
Mrs V Gebbie, BA Hons, MIPM
R F Jones, DipMS, IPFA
G R Miller, FCIB
D A Nelson-Smith, MA
P D C Points, MA
Prof Lord R Skidelsky, FBA
Mrs J A Smith, JP, BA Hons
P J Squire, MA, FRSA
A J Symonds, MICOS, FRICS
I J White, FRICS

***Head Master:* A F Seldon**, MA, PhD, MBA, FRHistSoc, FRSA

Deputy Heads:
Mrs M A Collins, BEng
S G R Smith, BA

Director of Studies: P V Robinson, MA

Bursar: Mr John Bone
Medical Officer: Dr S L Lipscombe, MB, ChB, MRCP, FPCert

Academic Staff:
M B Abington, BSc (*Housemaster, Aldrich House*)
C I Bainbridge, BA (*Head of Business Studies*)
L C Bambridge, BA (*Head of Spanish*)
C W Bowles, MPhys
M B M Brown, MA (*Head of Classics*)
S A Burns, MA (*Housemaster, School House; Head of French*)
The Revd A K Burtt, MA, LTh (*Senior Chaplain*)
Miss C E Coates, BA (*EFL*)
Miss E T M J Cody, BA (*Housemistress, Chichester House*)
Miss C J Connor, BA
D A Crichton, BA (*Housemaster, Ryle House*)
J E L Dahl, BA
N L Dawson, BSc (*Head of Mathematics*)
Ms I J M Dowds, MA (*Head of Psychology*)
M J Edmunds, CertTEFL
W Glover, BA
G M Green, BA, BEd (*SENCO*)
K A Grocott, MA (*Senior Master i/c Boarding, Head of Geography*)
R Halsall, BSc (*Head of Academic PE*)
Miss C J Herd, BA
D Kerr, BA (*Head of Drama*)
B L Lambe, BSc (*Head of Information Technology*)
Miss M P M Langan, BA
D M Lowe, BA
R D Mace, BA
Miss R Merrett, BA (*PSHE*)
Miss H C Naylor, BA
D C Ollosson, BA (*Director of Dyslexic Support Centre*)
Mrs J M Osborne, BSc (*Internal Exams Officer*)
Mrs K H Payne, BA (*Head of Modern Languages*)
Dr D M Pearson, BSc, PhD (*Head of Biology*)
Dr J H Penny, BSc, PhD (*Head of Science*)
J S Pope, Dip Ed
J C Prideaux, MA, MRSC (*Head of Chemistry*)
S Radojcic, BSc (*Housemaster, Hampden House*)
Miss H Rifkin, BSc
D Roberts, BA, LSDC (*Head of Design & Technology*)
T M J Sagar, BA
C G Sandercock, GRSM, LRAM (*Music; External Exams Officer*)
Ms S B M Saunders-Watson, BA
Dr J Seldon, MA, DPhil
P J Smales, BEng
O M Smyth, MA (*Careers Adviser*)
J Spencer, MA
Mrs M C Startin, BA
P M Thomas, BSc (*Head of Economics and Politics*)
Miss J D Thornhill, BA (*Housemistress, Leconfield House*)
Mrs G Tissier, BSc (*Head of Physics*)
Mrs H E Tomlin, CertEd (*Housemistress, Williams House, Senior Mistress, Head of Food Technology*)
D U Turnbull, BSc (*Housemaster, Durnford House*)
E F Twohig, MA, NDipAD (*Director of Art*)
Ms J A Warn, BA (*Head of History*)
J R Weeks, BA
A E N Whitestone, MA (*Senior Tutor, President of the Common Room*)
J A St J Withers, BEd (*Housemaster, Fenwick House*)
Mrs A Withers, SEN (*Housemistress, Fenwick House*)
Miss M H Yates, BA

There are twenty Part-time Academic Staff and fifteen Visiting Music Staff.

Headmaster's Secretary: Mrs A M Moore
Registrar: Mrs M A E Brightwell

The College is situated on high ground in the Kemp Town district of Brighton. The main block of buildings, designed by Sir Gilbert Scott, RA, was built between 1848 and 1866. Additions were made to the design of Sir T G Jackson, RA, an Old Brightonian, in 1885, and the accommodation and amenities have been considerably increased in recent years. The College became fully co-educational in 1988. There are now 544 pupils in the College (134 girls and 324 boys) of whom 86 are boarders (divided into 2 Houses), and 458 are day pupils (divided into 7 Houses).

Buildings. These include the Chapel (originally built in 1858 and extended in 1923 as a memorial to the Old Brightonians who gave their lives in the First World War), Assembly Hall, Classrooms, Music Rooms, Swimming Bath, Armoury and covered Miniature Range, Squash Courts, and a modern Central Kitchen. The Science Building has first class provision for Physics, Chemistry and Biology. New Workshops for Technical Studies, Engineering and Carpentry and two additional day boy Houses were occupied in September 1959, when the Library was also re-designed and moved into the Main Building.

A Classroom Block, complete with Lecture Room, was completed in 1972, and the Sports Hall in 1973. A further Classroom Block and the Pavilion were opened in 1980. A Computing, Electronics and Mathematics Centre was built in 1986, and a new Day Girls' House was opened in 1990. The Hordern Room, a small theatre and concert hall was opened by Sir Michael Hordern, an Old Boy, in January 1995 as part of the College's 150th Anniversary Celebrations.

An extensive programme of development is currently taking place, with a new 3 storey Performing Arts Centre, incorporating a Dance Studio, Café de Paris and Music practice classrooms, opened in Summer 2000. Further development includes a new Art Centre, Lecture Theatre, Multi-Gym, enhanced Library facilities.

Admission. Pupils are admitted to the Fourth Form between the ages of 13 and 14 via the Common Entrance examination, the Scholarship Examination, or by special Assessment and interview, and into the Sixth Form for a two-year A2 course, between the ages of 16 and 17, subject to a minimum of 12 points at GCSE (based on three points for an A grade, two points for a B grade and one point for a C grade) and ideally an A grade in the subjects to be studied at A level. In both cases pupils must also produce evidence of good character and conduct from their previous school.

The College Prospectus and registration form can be obtained from the Registrar.

Hampden, Leconfield, Aldrich, Durnford, Ryle, Chichester and Williams are day Houses. Day pupils are an essential part of the School and are given every opportunity to enter into the full community life of the College. School and Fenwick are Boarding Houses.

Entry for new Fourth form and Sixth form pupils is at the beginning of the Michaelmas term.

The Hawkhurst Court Dyslexic Centre enables children who are assessed as Dyslexic, but with high intelligence, to take a suitably adjusted GCSE course within the normal College curriculum with the opportunity to proceed to A levels in the Sixth Form.

Health. There is a Central Health Centre with a qualified Matron, and the Medical Officers visit regularly.

Catering. There is self-service dining room, managed by a qualified Catering Manager.

Holidays. The usual School holidays are about 4 weeks each at Christmas and Easter, and 9 weeks in the Summer. There is a half-term holiday in all three terms.

Boarding. There are many weekly boarders (5.10 pm Friday–9.30 pm Sunday), while full boarders may have exeats, if they desire it, most weekends. A proportion of boarders remains at school, however, every weekend. All pupils in the Sixth Form have study bedrooms.

Religion. Religious Studies are taught in all Forms once a week. A short morning service is held in Chapel on weekdays, and there are services for all pupils on some Sundays. Parents and visitors are welcome at these services. Candidates are prepared by the Chaplain for Confirmation.

Curriculum. The School is divided into 5 Forms – IVth, Lower Vth, Upper Vth, Lower VIth and Upper VIth. In the IVth form the curriculum is as wide as possible including Latin, Spanish and German for those with ability at languages. Pupils select their GCSE subjects (9/10) in the Lower Vth and take the GCSE examination in the Upper Vth. Specialisation begins in the Lower VIth and is continued in the Upper VIth where boys and girls take the GCE at 'A' level and STEP, and are prepared for Higher education at Universities and the Medical Schools, the Service Colleges, the Civil Service and for careers in Commerce and Industry. Different 'A' levels and AS levels are offered and a wide variety of combinations is possible. A combination of Arts and Sciences is available for individuals whose interests are best served by this rather than the traditionally allied courses.

Games. The College enjoys a strong record of excellence at most sports. The main playing-field adjoins the College buildings and there is another ground about 1½ miles away. Unless excused by a Medical Certificate, all pupils must take part in the School Games and Physical Education. The main games are Rugby Football, Soccer, Hockey, Cricket, Squash, Netball, and Tennis, while options are also available in Athletics, Fencing, Basketball, Badminton, Squash, Swimming, Judo, Association Football and Cross-Country. There is a flourishing Sailing Club attached to the Sussex Yacht Club at Shoreham. The College has its own indoor heated Swimming Pool, open the whole year round. Golf is available at a nearby course.

Combined Cadet Force. Recruits may join one of the 3 Service sections or the Duke of Edinburgh Award Scheme, and the aim of the training is to give pupils opportunities for leadership and initiative as soon as possible. Annual camps in the Easter and Summer holidays provide Adventure Training.

Music. One in five pupils learns at least one musical instrument. There is a strong musical tradition and pupils reach a very high level of performance. The Choir, Orchestra and Concert Band perform both inside and outside the College. There are several Chamber groups, and the Choral Society and Orchestra usually perform major works in the annual Brighton Festival.

Drama. A school play or musical is performed in the Lent Term, Lower School play in the Michaelmas term, and a Lower VIth play in the Summer term. There is a junior Drama Club for aspiring actors.

Activities. Creative activities are encouraged both in and out of school time, and the College has its own Art School and Gallery where exhibitions by leading Artists are regularly staged. There is also a well established Sixth Form Voluntary Service Unit.

Brighton itself gives opportunities for Theatre, Art and Concert visits, both locally and in London.

Careers. Mr O M Smyth heads a team of tutors who advise pupils on careers. The College is a member of the Independent Schools Careers Organisation.

Entrance Scholarships. (*see* Entrance Scholarship section)

Fees. The fees are from £5,437 per term for full boarders; £4,776 for weekly boarders and £3,507 for day pupils. The Registration Fee is £75.

Old Brightonian Association. The Old Brightonian Association has annual Dinners and a number of flourishing sports clubs.

Preparatory School. The College has its own fully coeducational Junior School with a pre-preparatory department (see under Preparatory Schools for details).

Brighton College Family Society. The society organises talks, outings and other social events and is open to all parents, Old Brightonians and other well-wishers.

Charitable status. Brighton College is a Registered Charity, number 307061. It exists for the purpose of educating boys and girls.

Bristol Cathedral School

College Square Bristol BS1 5TS
Tel: 0117 929 1872
Headmaster: 0117 925 4545
Staff Room: 0117 926 4532
Music Dept: 0117 925 3448
Bursar: 0117 926 5534

Fax: 0117 930 4219
e-mail: HeadMaster@Bristol-Cathedral.fsbusiness.co.uk
website: http://www.cathedral.demon.co.uk

The origins of the School are in the Grammar School of St Augustine's Abbey, founded in 1140. The School was refounded by King Henry VIII in 1542 as "The King's School" or "The Royal Grammar School" and is Bristol's only Royal educational foundation. Throughout its history it has been closely linked with the Abbey and the Cathedral and its aims are to provide a first class education, to encourage a Christian outlook and a respect for persons as individuals.

Governors:

R Tovey, Esq, CertEd
A S Waycott, Esq, CertAg, AIAT
Lady White, MA, FRSA
G Wood, Esq, FCA, FTII

Clerk to the Governors: Mr A L Stevenson, FCA

***Headmaster:* K J Riley,** BA, MEd

Deputy Head: N G Folland, BA, MSc

Director of Studies: J A Pearson, MA

Head of Sixth Form: S G I'Anson, BSc

Assistant Staff:

J R Allin, BA
P G Atkins, BSc
Mrs A J Ballance, BSc
I Barraclough, BA
P G Bond, MA
C R Bretherton, BSc
Mrs V Britner, BA
D M Crabtree, BEd
P Cummings, BA
J P Dabbs, MA
P E Davies, BA
J Dowty, BA
C J Fance, MA
J S Frost, BEd
Mrs N Gething, BSc
M J Gunn, BA
Miss R Honeywill, BA
N P Hoskin, MA
Mrs J Jephcote, BEd
Mrs M E John, MA
Miss K L Johnston, BA
Mrs K T McGregor, BA
C J Miller, BEd
J Moyle, BSc
B D Murphy, MA
Dr S Pearce, BSc, PhD
D F Perry, BEd
B J Salisbury, BA
Mrs D Slater, L-ès-L
P J Smith, BSc
R J Stride, BA
Miss H R K Thomson, MA
Miss K C Welham, BA
R R B Willoughby, BEng
J Young, BA (*Director of Music*)

Librarian: Mrs L Price, BLib

Language Assistants: to be appointed

Instrumental teachers:

Mrs V Britner (*Saxophone/Clarinet*)
J E Griffin (*Head of Brass*)
R Huckle (*Violin*)
Miss C A Johnstone (*Cello*)
D Kenna (*Piano*)
Miss E Palmer (*Bassoon/Oboe*)
Mrs P Rudge (*Singing*)
Dr P Sawbridge (*French Horn*)
C Smith (*Jazz Piano*)

Finance Bursar: M Collett

Estates Bursar: Mrs L Cole

Head Master's Secretary: Mrs J V Richardson

School Secretary: Mrs M A Sebright

Groundsman: M Milsom

Admission. The School was a Direct Grant School which reverted to full independent status in September 1976. There are 430 pupils of whom 110 are in the Sixth Form, where there are 20 girls. Admission is decided on the results of a Joint Entrance Examination held in January in conjunction with Bristol Grammar School and Queen Elizabeth's Hospital for 11+ entrants. There is also a small selective entry at 13+. Boys and girls are admitted to the Sixth Form on the basis of their GCSE results. Cathedral Choristers enter the School at the age of 10 and are awarded Choral Scholarships. Academic and Music Scholarships are awarded at 11+, 13+ and 16+ and the School provides a number of Bursaries.

Buildings. The School stands in the Cathedral precinct and occupies the monastic buildings of the Augustinian Abbey. The teaching accommodation is well equipped and the School's facilities are good. Specialist rooms are available for all subjects and the site is well maintained. The Cathedral School Studios were opened in May 1999, comprising 2 Art Rooms, a Design Technology Laboratory and the Fortune Theatre. A new Lower School building has received planning permission.

Curriculum. A broad-based curriculum is adopted in Years 1, 2 and 3 (Years 7, 8 and 9) including English, Mathematics, Combined Science, Latin, French, German, Geography, History, Art, Music, Drama, Information Technology, Design Technology and Religious Studies. At the end of Year 2 (Year 8) boys choose two subjects from French, German, Latin and Classical Studies. There is also the opportunity to study Greek.

At GCSE, boys study for 9 or 10 subjects. Core subjects are English, Mathematics, Science (Single Sciences or Dual Award) and either French or German. Three further subjects are chosen from a wide range of options.

In the Sixth Form, there is a very wide range of AS, A2 and other post-16 GCSE courses from which to choose.

Religious life. Most pupils belong to the Church of England but the religious life of the school is truly interdenominational in spirit and practice. The Cathedral is the School's Chapel.

Sport. The School offers a wide ranage of sporting activities and fields teams in Rugby football, Association football, Cricket, Hockey, Tennis, Badminton and Golf. There are a wide range of other activities and outdoor pursuits are organised for the first three years in the School.

Expressive Arts. The School enjoys a first-class reputation for the quality of music, art and drama. The School has three orchestras and many other ensembles and the School's musicians perform regularly at a wide variety of venues. Two Art Exhibitions are held a year and there are four Dramatic productions.

Fees. The fees, which include stationery and text-books, are £1,696 per term from September 2000.

Charitable status. Bristol Cathedral School is a Registered Charity, number 311730. It exists to provide education for its pupils.

Bristol Grammar School

University Road Bristol BS8 1SR
Tel: 01179 736006.
Fax: 01179 467485

'The Grammar School in Bristowe' existed under a lay master in 1532, in which year, under a charter of Henry VIII, it was endowed with the estates of St Bartholomew's Hospital by the merchant and geographer Robert Thorne and others, and the trust was placed in the care of the Corporation of Bristol. In 1836, the Corporation was replaced under the Municipal Reform Act by the Trustees of the Bristol Municipal Charities, in whom the property is now vested. The School is now governed under a scheme framed by the Charity Commissioners in 1978.

Motto: *'Ex Spinis Uvas'.*

Governors:

D L J Watts, MA, FRICS, JP (*Chairman*)

J B Ackland, OBE
Mrs A I Brooking, JP, MA
K I Crawford, LLB
K Dawson, MA
B R England, ACIB
D K Golledge, FCA
J C Higson
P F Hoare, BA
Mrs N A Kalfayan, MA, MB, BChir, MD, MRCOG
Lady Kingman, BA, MA
M P MacInnes, MA

Mrs C R Monk
R Neale, OBE, MA, FIA
L Perrin
Professor K G Robbins
Air Commodore B T Sills, MIMgt
Mrs C Slater, MA, DPhil
E A Warren, MA

***Head Master:* D J Mascord**, BA, PhD

Deputy Head: Miss J E Barker, BSc

Assistant Head: P R Roberts, BSc, MSc

Miss N Alexander, BA
Mrs P J Arnold, MA
Mrs R Atkins, BSc
N G Attwood, BA
C Bainbridge, BA
A K Barker, BSc
Mrs R Barker, BSc
T J Bell, BA
K R Blackburn, BSc
H B Briggs, BA
Miss J A Bryant, BSc
Miss L J Burfoot, BSc
J A F Burns, MA
R P Clare, MA
G S Clark, BSc
Mrs M F Colborn, BSc, BA
R A D Cox, BSc
Miss L M Cummings, BSc
C S Dammers, BA
Mrs S Davies-Walters, BEd
B Davis, MEd
Mrs N A Diamond, BSc
A Dimberline, BSc, PhD
Mrs R Dods, BSc
O Edwards, BA
Mrs N M Elliott, BSc
Mrs D E S Ellis-Gray, MA
G D Fellows, BA
Mrs J L Foster, BSc
Mrs L J Fowler, BSc
N S Fuller, BSc, MSc
Miss C Gillam, MA
D W Goodhew, MA
Mrs M L Guy, CertEd
Mrs D C Haas-Evans, BSc
S R Holman, MA
D R Homer, MSc, PhD
R J Houchin, BA
P R Huckle, BA, MEd
G R Iwi, MSc
P Z Jakobek, BEd
R S Jones, BSc
Mrs S M C Kaye, BA, MA
Mrs J M Kearey, MA
A J Keen, BA
Mrs V M Kendall, BA
Mrs J D Knox, BSc, PhD
Miss M Kouroumalis, BA
Mrs J B Lewis, CertEd
Mrs C V Maddock, BA, MEd
G L Martin, BA, MA
R A Massey, BA, PhD
W McCormack, BSc, BA
Mrs P McGee, BSc
Mrs H B Millett, DipAD, ATD
R G W Morris, BSc, CBiol, MIBiol
D M Nott, BSc
R T Osmond, MA
Mrs E V Page, BA
D Panchaud, BEd
Mrs M E Paul, BA
A E Pearson, BSc, MSc, PhD, FRSC
Miss S M Poole, BSc
Mrs H Powell, BA
S Powell, BA
M G Ransome, BA, PhD
Mrs E Reid, BA
Miss F A Ripley, BSc
I H Rolling, CertEd
Mrs C A Rosser, BSc, PhD
Miss R Saunders, BA
Miss J M Scullion, BSc
R M Sellers, BSc
D M Selwyn, BA, MMus
M J M Shipway, Cert Ed
Mrs C A Smith, BA
C G Snook, BCom, DipEd
M A Speake, BSc
Mrs B M Stacey, GBSM, ABSM, LRAM
P V Starling, MA
Miss J Subra, BA, MA
Mrs D M G Swain, BA
C H Taylor, BA
Mrs C J Taylor, BA, M-ès-L
P Thomas, BA
Mrs J Thomson, MBA
Mrs E M Thorne, BA
M Tong, MEng
C P Wadey, MA
Miss J Wall, BSc
C Watson, BSc
P M Whitehouse, BSc

Music:
R T Osmond, MA, ARCO
Miss B M Stacey, GBSM, ABSM, LRAM

Physical Education:
R M Sellers, BSc,
K R Blackburn, BSc
Miss J A Bryant, BSc
P Z Jakobek, BEd
Miss F A Ripley, BSc
Miss J M Scullion, BSc
Miss R Saunders, BA

Careers Adviser: Mrs M L Guy, CertEd

School Librarian: Mrs M Lane, BA, ALA

Clerk to the Governors and Bursar: D F M Collyer

The School is a co-educational day school with c 1,050 pupils from age 11 to age 18, the different age groups being housed in separate, self-contained buildings. Entry to the School is normally in September at age 11+, following a satisfactory performance in the entrance examination held in the previous spring and a creditable school report but an additional 20-25 places become available each year at ages 13+ and 16+. The School's Assisted Places Scheme is able to offer substantial financial assistance towards the fees of able pupils whose parents have limited means. The scheme is kept under regular review by the Governors who are looking all the time for ways to extend it. The School became a member of the Ogden Bursary Scheme in 2000.

The site of the School at Tyndall's Park is adjacent to the University of Bristol. The buildings, which owe much to the considerable generosity of benefactors with Bristol associations, include The Great Hall (with an organ to which pupils may have access), sixth form centre, library, 14 science laboratories, and The Princess Anne building, which houses the pupils in the first two years, which was opened in 1983. The existing laboratories were completely refurbished and additional new laboratories were built in 1985. A music school was opened in 1987, as were a theatre and language centre in 1990, a sports hall in 1991, an art school in 1992, a technology centre in 1994, and a geography and classics centre in 1999. The School IT network has over 350 computers, 5 dedicated rooms, and provides universal e-mail and Internet access.

Organisation and Curriculum. The school provides the National Curriculum +. Setting is used in some subjects. There is no streaming. In the first two years all pupils follow a curriculum which includes English, Mathematics, Science, French, History, Geography, Technology, IT, Latin, Religious Studies, Art, Music and Physical Education. Further up the School other subjects become available such as Russian, German, Greek and Economics and at the end of Year 11 all pupils take 10 GCSEs drawn from the core subjects of English, Mathematics, Science and French, together with a selection of other subjects, chosen from a carefully balanced range of options. The sixth form provides a flexible range of A Level options chosen from English, Mathematics, the Sciences, Technology, Modern Languages, Classics, History, Geography, Economics, Business Studies, Computing, IT, Psychology, Theatre Studies, Sports Studies, Art and Music. In addition all pupils follow enrichment and key skills courses and attend a richly diverse programme of weekly lectures by visiting speakers. Students from the Sixth Form proceed to a wide range of faculties at universities around the country.

There are frequent opportunities for parents to consult form tutors, heads of houses and year heads and, in addition, regular meetings are held at which parents meet the teaching staff. All parents join the Friends of Bristol Grammar School, an association whose aim is to promote the well-being of the School.

The Houses. The School is divided into six houses, each organised by a head of house, with the assistance of house tutors. The house system is regarded as being of great importance at all levels of the School, providing continuity of pastoral care and enhancing school/family links.

Games. The games options, which vary with different age groups, include Rugby, Hockey, Cross-Country, Cricket, Athletics, Swimming, Golf, Tennis, Soccer, Rounders and Netball. Facilities for Orienteering, Aerobics, Dance, Judo, Fencing, Badminton and Squash are available. There are extensive playing fields at Failand, which include an all-weather Hockey/Tennis area, and in Summer 1999 a new astroturf hockey pitch was added. Below the Sixth

Form, all pupils, unless excused for medical reasons, are required to participate in School games; the full range of sports is available to the Sixth Form on a voluntary basis.

Activities and Societies. All pupils take part in a wide ranging programme of extra-curricular activities one afternoon a week. There are flourishing choirs and orchestras; tuition can be arranged in a large number of instruments. Drama productions are regularly staged by different age levels of the School and by the houses. Ski trips are offered each year. Regular excursions are made abroad, as well as exchange visits, both on an individual and on a school basis. Pupils may join the Duke of Edinburgh Award Scheme in Year 10 and there is a flourishing Community Service Unit. World Challenge expeditions take place every two years and have visited Borneo, Bolivia and the Himalayas.

Scholarships. (*see* Entrance Scholarship section) In addition to, but quite separate from, the assisted places outlined above, the School offers 8 academic scholarships to entrants at 11+. These scholarships are currently valued at £100 per term, subject to regular review. They are awarded on academic merit and are irrespective of parental means. Music Scholarships, which pay for instrumental tuition, are available at 11+, 13+ and 16+.

For students (internal and external) who will study Mathematics at A level there is the opportunity in the spring of Year 11 to sit a competitive examination paper in Mathematics for the award of the Pople Scholarship (in memory of the OB who recently won the Nobel prize for Physics) valued at £1,000 for each of the two years of the A level course.

Fees. The fees, which cover the cost of all textbooks and stationery, are £5,160 pa in 2000/2001.

Admission Procedure. Applications should be made to the Headmaster at the School. Parents of prospective entrants are welcome to visit the School, at any time by appointment or without appointment on Open Day.

School Entry. Pupils are accepted into the school during any term subject to the availability of places.

Bristol Grammar School Lower School: The Lower School admits pupils aged 7-11 and is housed in its own buildings on the same site as the Upper School. For further details see Part V under the Incorporated Association of Preparatory Schools.

Old Bristolians Society. Close contact is maintained with former pupils through the Old Bristolians Society whose honorary secretary can be contacted at the school.

Charitable status. Bristol Grammar School is a Registered Charity, number 311731. It has existed since 1532 to provide an education for Bristol children.

Bromsgrove School

Bromsgrove Worcestershire B61 7DU
Tel: (01527) 579679
Fax: (01527) 576177

The date of the School's Foundation is unknown but it was re-organised by Edward VI in 1553 and was granted a Royal Charter 6 years later. It was refounded in 1693 by Sir Thomas Cookes, Bt, at the same time as Worcester College, Oxford (formerly Gloucester Hall). The link between School and College has been maintained ever since.

Motto: *'Deo Regi Vicino'*.

President: Mr G R John, CBE

Visitor: The Right Reverend Dr Peter Selby, The Lord Bishop of Worcester

Vice President: Rear Admiral Sir D Haslam, KBE, CB

Governing Body:
N J Birch, MIMechE (*Chairman*)
T Denham-Cookes
D L Cariss, FRICS, IRRV
J M Baron, TD, MA
Prof K B Haley, BSc, PhD, FIMA, CMath, FIEE, CEng
J A Hall, FCA
Dr J D Lewins, DSc(*Eng*), CEng
Prof Sir Michael Drury, OBE, FRCP, FRCGP, FRACGP
R G Noake, FCA, FCCA
Dr L Newby, MA, PhD
V S Anthony, BSc
R G Smethurst, MA (*Provost of Worcester College, Oxford*)
R D Brookes, FRICS
G Strong
Mrs C Fitzpatrick, BSc, MSc
Mrs A Doyle
M Horton, BA
Miss J Longmuir
Prof J G Perry
Mrs S Wilmott
Mrs W Binham
Mrs L Wyatt

Clerk to the Governors: S Arrowsmith

***Headmaster:* T M Taylor**, MA (Oxon), DipEd

Director of Services: Group Captain J P Rogers

Deputy Headmaster: P St J Bowen, BA, PGCE

Second Deputy Head: P G Walsh Atkins, MA, DPhil (Oxon)

School Medical Officer: Dr B Bywater, MB, ChB, DRCOG, FRCGP

Staff:
J F Thomas, BA, PGCE (*Director of Sport and Extra-Curricular Education*)
B J Allen, BSc
Mrs G S Hayward, BEd, CNAA (*Senior Mistress*)
G F Carey, BSc
Mrs C P M Maund, BSc, PGCE (*Head of Sixth Form*)
D E M Morrell, BA, PGCE, ACE (*Head of Classics*)
D Langlands, BSc, CertEd
Mrs E Langlands, BSc, CertEd
A W Burton, MA (*Cantab*), PGCE
W K Hamflett BSc PGCE (*Senior Head of Department, Director of Planning and Head of Mathematics*)
M D Bowen-Jones, BSc, MEd, PGCE (*Head of Science and Senior Boarding House Parent*)
Mrs P T Kenward, BA, PGCE
J Stateczny, BA, PGCE
Mrs A Grunsell, BA, CertEd (*Co-ordinator of Staff and Pupil Development*)
C A Dowling MA (Cantab), PGCE (*Head of Chemistry and Joint Co-ordinator of Timetable*)
Mrs A M Bowen-Jones, CertEd, BPhil(Ed)
S J Lee, MA, PGCE (*Head of History*)
Dr D A Wilson, BSc, PhD, PGCE (*Head of Physics*)
Dr A S Woollhead, BSc, PhD, PGCE (*Head of Biology and Assessment Manager*)
S Challoner, BSc, PGCE (*Head of Business Studies and Head of Lower Sixth Form*)
Miss S A E Dixson, MA, BD, PGCE
Dr M R Werrett, GRSC, PhD, PGCE
N P Moore, BA, PGCE (*Head of Spanish*)
Mrs S G Perks, AENA
S P Rands, BA, PGCE (*Head of Design Technology*)
M A Stone, BEng, ACGI, PGCE
A P Jarvis, MA, PGCE (*Head of English*)
Mrs H S Barnett, BSc, PGCE
Ms C A Simpson, BA, DPSE (*Head of Art*)

S P Matthews, BA, PGCE (*Head of Upper Fourth Form*)
R E W Stephens, BA, PGCE, MMus, ARCO, ARCM (*Assistant Director of Music and OC Combined Cadet Force*)
Mrs J A Holden, MA, PGCE (*Head of General Studies*)
Mrs C Nightingale, BSc, PGCE
M C Perry, BEd (*Director of Drama & Performing Arts*)
Miss C J Ralph, BEd (*Head of Girls Physical Education*)
R Wallace, BA, MA, PGCE
J Wingfield, BA, PGCE (*Head of Fifth Form, Head of Economics*)
P S T Mullan, BA, PGCE (*Head of Boys' Physical Education*)
Miss K C Baldock, BA, MA, PGCE
M P Chappell, BA (*Head of Modern Languages*)
Miss S Dick, BSc, PGCE
S P Floyd, BEd (*Recreation Facilities Manager*)
Dr A R Johns, BSc, PhD, PGCE
Mrs K E Mackay, BA, PGCE
T D Smith, BA, PGCE
Miss R L Wartnaby, BA, PGCE
R A C Barr, BA, MA, PGCE (*Head of Geography, Head of Careers and Entrance to Higher Education*)
Mrs A Clee, BA, ALA (*Head Librarian*)
Ms S J Cronin, BA, DMS, PGCE (*Co-ordinator of GNVQ*)
Miss R M Scannell, BA, PGCE
Miss A L Wright, BSc, PGCE
Mrs F K Bateman, BSc, PGCE
Mrs C Bentham, BEd (*Co-ordinator of International Students and Head of English as an Additional Language*)
Miss S J Foster, BSc, PGCE
Miss H L Leathart, BSc (QTS)
Mr N M Linehan, BA, PGCE
Miss J Southcott, BCom, PGCE
A B Wild, BSc, PGCE
Mrs M B Kirk, CertEd, CTEFLA
Mrs A Kitson, CertEd
Mrs S Wood, BEd, CertEd
Mrs S Frend, MA, DCG
A E Bird, MA (Cantab), MA (Ebor), ARCM, PGCE (*Director of Music*)
Mrs N J Starkie, BA (Cantab), PGCE, ARCO
Revd E C Reed, BD
Miss M A Allsopp, BA, PGCE
Mr J W B Brogden, BA, PGCE
Mr A Bussey, BA, PGCE
Miss D A Edwards, BSc, PGCE
Mr J J Haggett, BA, PGCE
Miss K L Hansler, BSc, PGCE
Miss S E Harding, BSc, PGCE
Miss H K Hunter, MA, PGCE
Miss C E King, BA, PGCE
Mr K N Lindsay, BSc, QTS
Miss E M McLaughlin, BA, PGCE
Miss L C Osman, BA, MA
Miss K E Tansley, BA, MA, PGCE
Mr D G Wilkins, BA, SCITT

Music Staff:
A E Bird, MA (Cantab), MA (Ebor), ARCM, PGCE (*Director of Music*)
Mrs H N Holland, GRSM, ARCM, CertEd (*Head of Music, Lower School*)
Mrs T M Bird, BA, ARCM
R E W Stephens, MMus, BA, ARCO, ARCM, PGCE (*Assistant Director of Music*)
Mrs N J Starkie, BA (Cantab), PGCE, ARCO

Visiting Music Staff:
Mrs R J Polybank, ARCM, AGSM
J Dunlop, BA, GBSM, ABSM
Mrs J Hiles, GBSM, ABSM
Mrs J Ayres, ABSM
Mrs N Kristy, GBSM, ABSM
R Bull
D Harper
Miss C Beckett, BMus
Mrs S Timms, BA, LRAM
Miss J M Sealey, GBSM, ABSM, HonBC
Miss H Bool, GBSM, ABSM, BTechNat
Miss M Dodd, BA, ABSM
D J G Whitehouse, ABSM
Mrs E Mills, BA, LLCM, ALCM
N Perfect
D Scally, MA, BMus, LTCL, DipCSM
J M Burton, BMus
Mrs J A Wood

Lower School:

Acting Head & Deputy Head: A J Young, CertEd

Second Deputy Head: Mrs M Purdy, BSc, PGCE

Staff:
Director of Studies: W R Caldwell, BA, MA, MEd, PGCE
Senior Teacher: Mr S J P Loone, MEd, BA, BTheol, PGCE
Co-ordinator of Junior Unit: R J Newton, BEd

Mrs J Agnew, BA, PGCE
Mrs R Al-Nakeeb, BEd
Mrs S M Bourne, BSc, PGCE
Mrs M L Caldwell, CertEd (SENCO)
Mrs J Chappell, BA
G Clark, BEd
Miss J C Drinkall, BA, PGCE (*Head of Art; Head of Year 7*)
M Faulkner, BA, CertEd
Miss J Fisher, BA, PGCE (*Head of Girls' Games*)
C F Harris, DipPE, CertEd (*Director of PE & Games; Head of Year 8*)
M Hill, BA, CertEd (*Head of Mathematics*)
Mrs H Holland, GRSM, ARCM, CertEd (*Head of Music*)
H R Holt, BA, MA, DipEd (*Head of Classics*)
Mrs J Jones, BA, CertEd (*Head of Library*)
S J Kingston, BEd (*Head of Design Technology; President of the Common Room*)
Mrs C M Leather, BSc, PGCE
Mrs S Lewis, BA, PGCE (*Head of Year 6*)
J Marks, BEd (Hons) (*Head of English*)
Mrs H Newton, CertEd
Mrs J Ormerod, MEd, CertEd
Mrs M Parmee, BA, CertEd (*Head of Years 3 & 4*)
C Pickering, BEd, DipCompEd, AdvCertEd, CertEd (*Head of ICT*)
J Pollard, BSc, ARICS, PGCE (*Head of Geography*)
Mrs H Powell, CertEd
Mrs A Purver, BA, PGCE (*Head of History*)
Mrs C B Rhoden, BA, PGCE
Mrs R Sumner, BA, MLitt, MPhil(Ed)
R Thorp, BA, PGCE
Miss S Vanstone, BEd
Miss A White, BA, MA, PGCE
Mrs B J Young, CertEd (*Head of Year 5*)

Situation. This co-educational boarding and day school is situated some 13 miles north of the Cathedral City of Worcester and an equal distance south of Birmingham. Birmingham International Airport and Station are a 20 minute drive by motorway. The M5, M6, M42 and M40 motorways provide easy access to the School.

The School stands in 100 acres of grounds on the south side and within walking distance of the market town of Bromsgrove.

Over the last twenty years there has been a significant programme of modernisation involving the expenditure of sums well in excess of £11m. There is a modern Sports Hall and heated indoor Swimming Pool. In 1990 a building for

Art, Design Science, Technology and Computing was opened in the Lower School. A new classroom block was opened for the 10–13 age range in December 1994. A Sports Hall for the Lower School was opened in 1996. A flood-lit all-weather pitch for Hockey, Soccer and Tennis was completed in January 1991. In the Upper School a £2.5 million Library and Resources Centre was completed in June 1994 and a £750,000 extension to Mathematics and Modern Languages in 1997. In November 1999 a new £2.5 million Art, Design & Technology Centre was opened in the Upper School.

Numbers. There are 690 pupils in the Upper School, of whom 400 are boys. The adjacent Lower School has a further 420 pupils aged 7 to 13.

Admission. Entrance at 13 is by Common Entrance and/or English, Mathematics and Verbal Reasoning Tests. Boys and Girls may be admitted to the Lower School at any age from 7 to 12 inclusive. Entrance Tests take place in late January. Places are also available in the VIth Form to boys and girls who have had their GCSE education elsewhere.

Curriculum. In the Lower School and throughout the first year in the Upper School a broadly based curriculum is followed. In addition to the normal academic subjects time is given to Art, Music, ICT, Drama, Design, Technology and to a full programme of Physical Education. Languages on offer include French, German, Spanish and Latin.

As pupils move up the School other options become available and some narrowing of the curriculum is inevitable. 9 subjects is the norm at GCSE. 15 points is the minimum qualification for entry to the Sixth Form (A=3, B=2, C=1). From September 2000 most pupils will study 4 AS level subjects, the more able will study 5 subjects. Subjects are as follows: Art, Biology, Business Studies, Chemistry, Classical Civilisation, Drama, Economics, English, English Literature, French, Geography, German, History, Latin, Mathematics and Further Mathematics, Music, Physical Education, Physics, Politics and Economics, Business Studies, Spanish, Technology. VCE Courses in Business Studies, Science, Leisure & Recreation and Art & Design are also offered. About 80% stay on to do AS Levels. About 98% of A Level leavers go on to degree courses at Universities.

Religion. There is a daily service in the School Chapel or an Assembly which all pupils are required to attend. The services and religious teaching are in accordance with the forms and principles of the Church of England. Boys and girls have the opportunity of being prepared for adult membership of the Anglican Communion. Pupils of other denominations and faiths are welcome as members of the School.

Extra-Curricular Activities. A wide range of sports is offered including opportunities for Rugby, Hockey, Cricket, Athletics, Swimming, Shooting, Sailing, Tennis, Rowing, Squash, Badminton, Basketball, Netball, Archery and Fencing. The Expedition Club offers facilities for Rock-Climbing, Sub-Aqua and Canoeing: there is a strong emphasis placed on Community Service. There is a combined Cadet Force (Army and RAF) and a well-supported society for Social Service. Over 50 pupils are involved in the Scheme for the Duke of Edinburgh's Awards.

Entrance Scholarships. (*see* Entrance Scholarship section) The following awards are made on the results of open examinations held at the School in January: Scholarships and Exhibitions to the value of half the tuition and boarding fees awarded at 11+ and 13+; a significant number of bursaries for pupils of academic, athletic, musical or all-round ability awarded at 11+ and 13+; Music Scholarships (half tuition fees and free tuition in two musical instruments) and a number of Music Exhibitions up to the value of half tuition fees awarded at 13+. Sixth Form Scholarships, Bursaries and Exhibitions are also available up to the value of fifty per cent of the tuition and boarding fees.

Term of Entry. Although pupils are normally accepted into the School only at the start of the Michaelmas Term of the year in which they have reached their eleventh, thirteenth or sixteenth birthdays, the Headmaster considers sympathetically applications for admission at other ages and at other times of the academic year.

Fees. Boarders (eight to ten years old) £3,490. Day pupils (eight to ten years old) £1,955. Boarders (eleven to thirteen years old) £3,590. Day pupils (eleven to thirteen years old) £2,055. Boarders (13+) £4,670. Day Pupils (13+) £2,810.

Reports and Consultation. Reports are issued termly. Supervision is shared by Housemasters, Housemistresses and House Tutors, and parents may meet them informally by appointment. There are regular parent-teacher evenings. Parents may arrange appointments to meet members of the Careers Department.

Careers. A comprehensive careers counselling programme is pursued for pupils of all ages.

Charitable status. Bromsgrove School is a Registered Charity, number 527450. It exists to provide education for boys and girls.

Bryanston School

Blandford Dorset DT11 0PX
Tel: (01258) 452411
Fax: (01258) 484661
e-mail: headmaster@bryanston.co.uk

Founded in 1928, Bryanston School aims above all to develop the all-round talents and needs of individual pupils. A broad, flexible academic and extra-curricular programme together with an extensive network of adult support encourages pupils to maximise their particular talents as well as to adapt positively to the demands of the society of which they are part. Creativity, individuality and opportunity are the school's key notes, but a loving community is the school's most important quality. Happy children growing up in a secure environment, aware of beliefs and values and confident of their own worth, will be well balanced 18 year olds. That is what we seek to produce.

Motto: *'Et Nova et Vetera'.*

Headmaster: **T D Wheare**, MA, DipEd, FRSA
Second Master: P J Hardy, JP, MA, PGCE

Director of Studies: N S Boulton, MA, PGCE

Senior Mistress: Mrs H Daynes, CertEd

Staff:

C S Poole, BSc, CertEd, AFIMA
B G Stebbings, BA, CertEd
G Leadbetter, BA
F J Bristow, CertEd
R J D'Silva, MA
G Q Craddock, BSc, CertEd
M J Adams, PhD, MA
P B Searle-Barnes, MA, ARCM, FRCO
A M Taylor, BA, MSc
The Rev A Daynes, MA, CertEd
J D T Rose, BPhil, CertEd
Mrs T J Doble, BSc, PGCE
P A L Rioch, BMus, BA
†G R Markham, BSc, CertEd
S R L Long, CertEd
†D C Bourne, MA, PGCE, FRGS
D Boyle, BA, CertEd
Mrs S Stacpoole, BA
G S Elliott, BA, PGCE
B G Mills, BA, CertEd
†M N Pyrgos, BSc, PGCE
Mrs F K Pyrgos, BSc, PGCE
J R K Roe, BSc, PGCE
Miss B M Ludgate, MA, PGCE
†I R Haslam, CertEd
W G Davies, DipED
J N G Fisher, BEd, PGCE
J L Jones, MA, PGCE
†Mrs E M Long, CertEd
†D Fowler-Watt, MA
†P Simpson, MA
T J Hill, MA
I Lowes, BA, LTCL
†Mrs E M Barkham, BA, MSc, PGCE
S C Oxlade, MA, DipEd
Mrs R A Simpson, BA
Mrs E A Boddy, LlB, PGCE
Mrs J E Little, MA(Ed)
†A J Marriott, BA, PGCE
Mrs J S Le Hardy, BA, PGCE
Mrs G C Kohn, BA, PGCE
S J Richardson, MA, BEd, FRMetS
M T Kearney, MA, PhD
†Mrs D M Rose, AdCE, CertEd
Ms P Quarrell, BA, PGCE
†Mrs J A Price, BA, PGCE
C Burrows, BSc, PGCE
Miss J G S Stewart, BA, PGCE
G S Smith, BSc, PGCE
M J Owens, MA, PGCE
Mrs S M Haslam, CertEd
P Hart, HND, CertEd
S J Turrill, BSc, PGCE
Mrs K A Grugeon, BSc, PGCE, CChem
Miss S J Nicholas, BEd
N J Davies, BEd
J D Cooke, BEd, MSc
Miss C L Bowen, BA, BSc, PGCE
R S Miller, BSc, PGCE
L C Johnson, BA, LTP
Miss V A Patten, BA, PGCE
J Lynch, BA, PGCE
I Carr, BEng, PGCE
Miss J F Quan, MA
S R Bowler, BMus, ARCM
C T Holland, BA
D S H Jones, BSc, PGCE
P S Bachra, MA
Mrs J A Blan, BA, PGCE
Miss A Steadman, BA, PGCE
†Mrs L C Kearney, BEd
S Jones, BA, PGCE
S P Wood, BA, PGCE

Situation. Occupying a magnificent Norman Shaw Mansion, the School is located in beautiful Dorset countryside near the market town of Blandford. There are 400 acres of grounds, which include a stretch of river used for rowing and canoeing, playing fields, woodland and parkland.

Numbers. There are approximately 375 boys and 275 girls in the School.

Admission. Boys and girls are normally admitted between 13 and 14 years of age on the results of Common Entrance or Special Papers. VIth Form entrants are admitted after interview, conditional upon securing at least 6 GCSEs at A, B and C grade.

Scholarships. Eight Academic, one Art, one Technology, four Music and up to four Sports Scholarships are available annually for entry at 13+. In addition there are Richard Hunter All-rounder awards open to competition for the same range of pupils. Supplementary grants beyond a ceiling of 50% fee remission will only be made at discretion after means-testing.

Two Academic and two Music Scholarships are offered to boys and girls entering the VIth Form as well as (usually) two Udall Awards for Sport.

Organisation. The School is organised on a House basis with 5 senior boys' houses, 5 girls' houses, and 2 junior boys' houses. All pupils have a tutor throughout their time in the School. No tutor has more than 15 pupils. Feeding and medical care are organised centrally. All VIth Form pupils in their final year have individual study-bedrooms. Lower VIth Formers usually share study-bedrooms.

Religion. Religious instruction is widely based and is carried on throughout the School. There are two assemblies each week for the whole school. Pupils attend either assemblies or services on most Sundays during the term. Holy Communion is celebrated every Sunday and on some week days. A Chaplain is responsible for pastoral work and preparation for Confirmation.

School Work. The School aims at leading pupils, over a period of 5 years, from the comparative dependence on class teaching in which they join the school, to a state in which they are capable of working on their own, for a University degree or professional qualification, or in business. In addition to traditional class teaching, there is, therefore, increasing time given to private work as a pupil moves up the School. This is in the form of assignments to be completed within a week or a fortnight. Teachers are available to give individual help when required, and Tutors supervise pupils' work and activities in general.

Every pupil is encouraged to explore a range of opportunities. All pupils follow the same broad curriculum in Group D (the first year), if at all possible. This curriculum includes Latin and German as well as French, three separate sciences, creative arts, technology and music. GCSE is taken after 3 years when a pupil is in Group B. There is a highly flexible choice of subjects at this level and subjects are setted independently. In the Sixth Form (Group A) pupils are expected to study up to five subjects at AS Level in the first year and to continue with three or four subjects to Advanced (A2) Level in the second year. 24 subjects are offered at AS Level and 23 at A2 Level and there are few restrictions on combinations. All Lower VIth formers follow a compulsory Personal and Social Education course and the Humanities programme provides supplementary courses to develop key skills and thinking techniques.

Music. Music plays a very important part in the life of the School. There are 2 Orchestras, a Concert Band, a String Chamber Orchestra, five Choirs, a Choral Society and many informal ensembles: numerous professional and amateur concerts take place throughout the year. Lessons are given in all orchestral instruments and in piano, organ, guitar and singing. All pupils must learn an instrument for their first term in Group D and this tuition is provided free of charge. Well over half the pupils have regular instrumental lessons.

Drama. A well-equipped, modern theatre provides the venue for the many school productions which take place during the year and for touring professional companies. In addition to acting, pupils are involved in Stage Management, Stage Lighting and Sound, and front-of-house work. There is also a large Greek Theatre in the grounds.

Sport and Leisure. A wide variety of sports is on offer at the school, including Athletics, Archery, Badminton, Canoeing, Cricket, Cross-Country, Fencing, Fives, Hockey, Lacrosse, Netball, Riding, Rowing, Rugby, Sailing, Shooting, Squash, Swimming and Tennis. Extensive playing fields between the School and the River Stour provide 46 tennis courts, 2 astro-turf pitches, 9 netball courts, an athletics track and grass pitches for all major sports, an all-weather riding manège and cross-country course. A Sports Complex provides an indoor heated 25m Swimming Pool, Gymnasium, large Sports Hall, Squash courts and Fitness

Centre. Sailing takes place at Poole Harbour where the School has 6 dinghies at its own base. In addition to sport, a number of clubs and societies, catering for a wide range of interests, meet in the evenings and at weekends.

Additional Activities. To encourage a sense of responsibility towards the community, a growing self-reliance and a practical training in the positive use of leisure, all pupils take part in all or some of the following:

1. *Community and Social Service.*
2. *Extra-curricular activities chosen from a wide range of options.*
3. *The Duke of Edinburgh's Award Scheme.*
4. *Adventure Training.*

Bryanston Arts Centre. This organisation brings about 20 professional performances of Concerts, Plays and Opera to the Coade Hall during the course of the year. Pupils are encouraged to attend.

Dress. There is no school uniform but there are certain restrictions.

Careers. There is a well-resourced Careers Room and the school maintains close links with ISCO. A full time member of staff runs a careers programme which covers the pupils' five years in the school. All pupils undertake Work Experience after their GCSEs and specific advice is given to help with A Level and University degree choices. In the Sixth Form, a mock interview course and the teaching of presentation skills ensures that pupils are well-prepared for the future.

Further Education. The vast majority of pupils in the VIth Form gain admission to Universities or other academies of further education.

Fees. (*see* Entrance Scholarship section) Boarders £16,755 pa.

Charitable status. Bryanston School Incorporated is a Registered Charity, number 306210. It is a charitable trust for the purpose of educating children.

Bury Grammar School

Bury Lancs BL9 0HN
Tel: 0161-797 2700
Fax: 0161-763 4655

The School, formerly held in the precincts of the Parish Church of St Mary the Virgin, was first endowed by Henry Bury in 1634, but there is evidence that it existed before that date. It was re-endowed in 1726 by the Rev Roger Kay and was removed to the present buildings in 1966.

Motto: '*Sanctas clavis fores aperit*'.

Governing Body:
3 representatives of the Estate Governors
3 of the Hulme Trustees
2 of the Bury Metropolitan Borough
2 of Manchester University
1 of Salford University
1 of the Bury Parish Church Parochial Church Council
8 co-opted members

Chairman of Governors: J A Rigby, LlB
Bursar and Clerk to the Governors: D A Harrison, BSc, FCA

***Headmaster:* K Richards**, MA (Sidney Sussex College, Cambridge)
Second Master: D E Armsbey, BA
Senior Masters:
D A Wilson, BA
A C J Young, BSc, MSc

Assistant Masters:
M Clarke, DipPE
J Sephton, BSc, MSc, PhD
J M Skinner, BA
J Bishop, BSc
M J Curtis, BA
S Brady, BSc
P M Skinner, BEd, MCCEd
I R Edmondson, BSc, PhD
J Kendall, MA
K S Whittaker, BA
C J Horsfield, BA
A Harrison, BA
T A Burns, BA
Mrs S Golightly, BA
D S Benger, MA
D R Lee, BA
P Koziura, BEd
A A Phillips, BA
L W Robinson, BA
M J Sherlock, BSc
D A Bishop, BSc
K M Cryer, BA
M J Hone, MA
C R Johnson, BSc
Mrs C A Brooks, BSc
D Hailwood, BEd
Mrs C Stirzaker, BA
K Reavey, BSc
Mrs S Glancy, BEd
P F Curry, BSc
M Aston, BSc
M E Bradley, BSc
B Hardman, BSc, MA
Mrs R L Bradley, BA
Mrs T J Taylor, MA
G D Feely, MA
G Halpin, BEd
H D McWilliam, BA
A L Stacey, BEd
Mrs V A Fletcher, CertEd, BSc
P Meakin, BSc
B Alldred, BSc
D F Lawson, BA
Miss J M Byrne, BA, PhD
A C Eadie, BSc
A Ellison, BA
Miss L Love, BA, MA
M J B Pye, BA
M D Richmond, BSc
Mrs C S Schofield, Maîtrise
Mrs J Yates, BSc, PhD
W L M Atkins, BSc
D P Cassidy, BSc
A E Dennis, BSc
J Lever, BSc, MSc
Mrs J Smith, BA
Miss H L Smith, BA
G P Cox, BSc

Junior School:
D J Crouch, CertEd (*Head of Junior School*)
M Byrne, BEd (*Deputy Head*)
P G Newton, MA
Mrs I E Pope, BSc
Mrs S L Courtney, BEd
Mrs J M Harrison, BEd
D J Scourfield, BEd
N G Robson, BA
Miss C E Berry, BA
Mrs H R Scourfield, BEd

Number of boys in the School: 835 Day Boys.

The School accommodation has been completely rebuilt over the last 35 years and this ancient grammar school now possesses a full range of modern facilities. The CDT facilities have been much improved. The CCF has its own Armoury and modern Rifle Range. A sport turf pitch beside the sports hall has been laid; the baths and changing rooms have been significantly improved and extended, and an additional Biology laboratory completed. Six new classrooms were built in 1995, since when a second Computing Room has been installed and the Assembly Hall and Stage completely refurbished.

Admission. Admission to the Senior School is by examination, held each year at the end of January. Candidates for admission must be between the ages of 10 and 12 on the 31st August in the year in which they are admitted.

There are currently 186 boys in the Junior School. From September 1993 the Junior School has occupied a separate building close to the Senior School, and since then boys have been admitted at the age of 7 rather than 8. Some places will continue to be available also at 8+, 9+ and 10+.

Scholarships, etc. One Kay Scholarship and a small number of Governors' means-tested bursaries based on academic performance and financial need are awarded each year at 11+.

Curriculum. The Junior School curriculum is consistent with that found in Primary Schools but extended to take advantage of the facilities available.

In the Senior School all boys follow for 3 years a common curriculum of English, Maths, French, Science, History, Geography, German, Classics, Religious Studies, Computing, Music, Art, PE, Games and Swimming. The core subjects to GCSE are English, Maths, French and Sciences; the range of additional optional subjects has recently been increased.

The curriculum is such that right up to the time that they enter the VIth form boys are free and able to choose a wide variety of subjects on either the Science or Arts side - or indeed straddling the two.

Boys entering the Sixth Form study 4 AS subjects (excluding General Studies) at least 3 of which they must then pursue to A2.

Fees. Senior School (Autumn Term 2000) £4,770 pa. Junior School £3,402 pa.

Term of Entry. Boys normally enter the school in the autumn term. Occasional vacancies may be filled in the spring and summer terms.

Leaving Scholarships. These are for boys entering university – John Openshaw Scholarship, Thomas Haworth Scholarship, Mellor Scholarship, Kay Exhibitions.

Games. Association Football, Athletics, Badminton, Basketball, Cricket, Cross-Country, Hockey, Rugby Football, Swimming and Tennis.

CCF. There is a voluntary but strong contingent of over 130 cadets. Its post-proficiency syllabus is designed to give the older members a wide variety of experience and training which is by no means exclusively military.

Bury GS, Old Boys' Association, *Secretary:* S J Crompton, 84 Ramsbottom Road, Hawkshaw, Bury BL8 4JS. Tel: 01204 852961.

Charitable status. The Governors of Bury Grammar Schools is a Registered Charity, number 526622. The aim of the Schools is to promote educational opportunities for boys and girls living in or near Bury.

Campbell College

Belmont Road Belfast BT4 2ND.
Tel: 028 9076 3076
Fax: 028 9076 1894
e-mail: hmoffice@campbellcollege.co.uk
website: www.campbellcollege.co.uk

Campbell College, which was opened in 1894, was founded and endowed in accordance with the will of Henry James Campbell, Esq., of Craigavad, Co. Down, its object being to provide in Ireland a Public School conducted on the same lines as the great Public Schools of England and Scotland.

Motto: *'Ne Obliviscaris'.*

Governors:
A J Boyd, BSc(Econ), FCA (*Chairman*)
Sir John Semple, CB (*Vice-Chairman*)
Professor K L Bell, MA, BSc, PhD, CPhys, FInstP, FAPS
P D Black, FCA
T J B Fletcher
T M Horner, QC
W J McKee, BSc, DipEd
M A D Moreland, LLB, FCA
J Nicholson
B Rebbeck, MA, FCA
N W Shaw, CBE, BSc
J I Taggart, ARICS
W B W Turtle, LLB

***Headmaster:* R J I Pollock**, BSc, PhD, CertEd, MEd, CChem, MRSC

Vice-Master: B W Funston, MEd, BSc, DipEd, DASE, DMMA

Senior Teachers:
D L Fullerton, MSc
M J Caves, BSc, DLC, CertEd
J N Morton, BA, BSSc, DASE
A R Cluff, BSc, PGCE

Assistant Teachers:
J M R Knox, BA, DipEd
Mrs D McGuffin, BA
†J W D Semple, MA
D S Oldfield, MA, DipEd, PGCEM
†P J Mitchell, BA
D C Driscoll, MA, CertEd
The Rev J J Nelson, MA (*Th*), BA, DipSocS
Mrs E J McLeod, BSc, CertEd
†H J McKinney, BSc, CertEd
P J Monahan, BA, CertEd, DASYC, MEd
†S D Quigg, BSc
†R J S Taylor, BSc, PGCE
†W J McKee, BSc, DipEd
W J Hamilton, MSc, MBA, DipEd
D W D McDowell, BSc, PGCE
†I B Armstrong, BA, PGCE
†D M McKee, BA, PGCE, DipModLit
H H Cathcart, BSc, CertCompEd
†C G Oswald, BSc, PGCE
†A D Stevens, BA, PGCE
†Miss K E Thompson, BSc, PGCE
†Mrs W Keys, BA, CertEd
†M W Millar, MSc, PGCE
†S J Johnston, BSc, PGCE
B R Robinson, BA, PGCE, MSc
A W Templeton, BSc, PGCE
Miss E P Bryans, BEd
N R Ashfield, BSc, PGCE
M T J Page, BSc, PGCE
Miss L Stewart, BSc, PGCE
Miss R M Dunlop, MA, PGCE
J M McCabe, MSc, PGCE
G Fry, BA, PGCE
D Walker, BEd
P L Laird, BSc, PGCE
Miss E A Woodhouse, BA, PGCE
Mrs E P Hogg, BA, PGCE
Mrs C Caldwell, BA, DipEd, PGDFS, MA
Mrs E Ramsay, BA, GradCertEd
J T C King, MA, PGCE, PhD
Miss C E Scott, BSc, PGCE
Miss K Livingston, BSC, PGCE

Art:
Mrs K P Crooks, BA, ATD
J Marks, BA, PGCE
Mrs M G Kearney, BA, ATD

Design and Technology:
†A D Boyd, BEd, DipEd, TEng, AIWM
P T Dermott, BEng, PGCE

Music:
D Catherwood, BMus (*Director*)
Miss S L Tutton, BMus, PGCE
P Young
P Schumann
Mrs H Neale
J Lawrence
R Kendall
Mrs G Pickett
Mrs L Molyneaux
Mrs H Gamble
B Overton
G Hopkins
R Douglas
Mrs J Leslie
M Wilson

Bursar: J M Monteith, FCA

Headmaster's Secretary: Mrs Y J Mallon

Medical Officer: J M Bell, MB, BCh, DRCOG, MRCGP

Matron: Mrs J Moore, SRCN

Preparatory School:
Headmaster: N I Kendrick, MA, BEd (Hons)
Vice-Master: J Walker, BEd(Hons), AdvCertEd

J W Paton, MSSc, BA, CertEd
P S Marshall, MA, DipEd
Mrs E M Gwynne, BEd (Hons)
C G A Farr, BA(Hons), MEd, DASE, AdvCertEd
Miss D H Shields, MA, MSc, PGCE
Mrs D Morrow, CertEd, DASE

Mrs A E Carroll, BA, PGCE
Miss B Coughlin, BEd
M W Wood, BEd(Hons), CertEd, DipRSA
A P Jemphrey, BEd, DASE
Mrs G E Wilson, BMus(Hons), MTD (*Director of Music*)
D Styles, BA(Hons), PGCE
Mrs H Rowan, BA, GradCert
R B Boyd, BA (Hons), PGCE
S P Collier, BA (Hons), PGCE
J T C King, MA (Hons), PGCE
Miss A Burns, BEd (Hons)

Pre-Preparatory Department:
Head of Department: Mrs E J Michael, CertEd
Mrs A Rintoul, CertEd
Mrs V A Vance, BEd
Mrs E N Caves, CertEd (*Kindergarten Class*)

There are 680 boys in the College and 302 in the Preparatory School. The College stands on the edge of Belfast, 5 miles from the city centre and is set in the beautiful grounds of the Belmont estate which totals some 110 acres.

Though the majority of its pupils are now day boys, the College still runs on traditional boarding-school lines. It is divided into Houses, each in charge of a Housemaster; School House (Mr McKinney); Allison's (Mr Mitchell); Armour's (Mr Quigg); Bowen's (Mr Johnston); Chase's (Mr Oswald); Davis's (Mr Taylor); Dobbin's (Mr Stevens); Lyttle's (Mr Millar); Price's (Mr D M McKee); Yates's (Mr W J McKee); Netherleigh (Mr Armstrong) and Ormiston (Mr Semple). There are House competitions in Rugby, Hockey, Cricket, Swimming, Athletics, Drama, Music and Chess.

Education. The College provides a broad and balanced curriculum leading to GCSE, AS and A2 levels. Under Article 5 of The Education Reform (Northern Ireland) Order 1989 the College organises its curriculum to cover the areas of study and compulsory subjects currently defined therein.

In **Years 8 and 9** all boys take the following subjects: English, Mathematics, Science, French, History, Geography, Latin, Religious Studies, Art, Music, Design and Technology, Information Technology and Physical Education. In Year 9 boys take up German or Spanish.

In **Years 10-12** the College maintains, as far as possible, a balanced and coherent curriculum.

In **Year 10** (the last year of Key Stage 3) boys are setted (six sets) by ability across the full range of subjects as evidenced by performance in the first two years of secondary education. All of the above subjects are developed but only the top two sets continue with Latin and only the top four sets continue with a second foreign language. At this stage Science is studied as the three separate disciplines of Biology, Chemistry and Physics.

At the end of **Year 10** pupils must select their courses of study for GCSE. Parents and pupils are encouraged to consult with subject teachers and Housemasters before any final decisions are made.

In Year 11 boys are divided into subject sets according to their ability in the individual subjects.

In **Years 11 and 12** (Key Stage 4) a varied programme of GCSE subjects is offered within the requirements of the statutory Northern Ireland Curriculum. The compulsory subjects within this Curriculum are English, Mathematics, Science (offered as either Double Award Science or the three separate Sciences), History or Geography or Business Studies, French and Physical Education to which are added up to three optional subjects of the pupil's choice. The options cover all the subjects offered in Key Stage 3 with the inclusion of Additional Mathematics. Religious Studies is available either in the GCSE subject options or as a non-examination course.

Pupils in Lower Sixth (Year 13) take three or four AS subjects chosen from a wide range which includes all the previously mentioned subjects plus Economics, Further Mathematics, Political Studies and Sociology. At Upper Sixth (Year 14) all of the above subjects may be taken to A2 level, with the exception of Sociology. There is ample opportunity for discussion between parents, teachers, Housemasters and careers advisers before the final package is decided.

The School has an Art Centre, with facilities for painting, sculpture, pottery, photography, etc and a well-equipped Technology Centre. It has four Physics, four Chemistry and four Biology laboratories, an audio-visual room, lecture theatre, two computer rooms, Assembly Hall, Sixth Form Centre, Junior Common Room and a Library.

Religious Education. All pupils are expected to adhere to the routines of a Christian community. During the week Religious Studies form part of the ordinary school curriculum and daily services are held in Chapel. On Sundays boarders either attend the parish churches or the Family Service which is held in the School Chapel once a month.

Physical Education. PE is part of the school curriculum for all boys. The College's sporting facilities are excellent. As well as extensive playing fields, it is equipped with a large Sports Hall, heated Swimming Pool, Tennis and Squash Courts. There is an all-weather area capable of providing three Hockey pitches or a 400m Athletics track. The traditional team games of rugby, hockey and cricket are still popular, and there are opportunities open to boys to compete in athletics, tennis, golf, sailing, orienteering, squash, triathlon, cross-country, shooting, basketball, badminton, archery and volleyball. Standards are high and many of our pupils attain representative honours at national and international level.

The Arts. The College has strong traditions in both Music and Drama. There are several concerts throughout the year featuring the Orchestra, Choir and Jazz Band and boys are encouraged to take advantage of tuition on the wide variety of instruments available. The Dramatic Society is also very active and productions often involve local girls' schools and members of staff. The House Drama competition is fiercely contested each year.

Combined Cadet Force. There is a large contingent of the Combined Cadet Force at Campbell. Attendance at a Camp in the Easter or Summer holidays is compulsory for all members not excused on account of age or for medical reasons. As well as the Army, Navy and Air Force sections, there are a REME section, an Arduous Training section and, for junior boys, the Pioneers. The Pipe Band plays at events in Northern Ireland, England and Europe.

Hobbies, Interests, etc. Societies wax and wane according to current enthusiasms, but in addition to the Sporting Clubs there are societies to encourage interest in chess, computers, Scripture Union, Jazz, Life-saving, mountaineering and Young Enterprise.

Careers. There is a well equipped Careers Suite. The Careers Master and his assistants provide a developing service to all boys and are regularly available for consultation. A computer assisted careers advice system is used to support the work of the careers staff.

The Holidays are 3 annually: 2 weeks at Christmas and Easter and about 8 in the summer. In the long Christmas Term there is a Half-Term break of about a week, during which parents are required to make provision for their sons to be away from the School.

Entry is by application to the Headmaster and is normally at 11+, 13+, or at 16+ for AS/A2 level studies.

Term of Entry. Pupils are accepted for entry in any term but September is preferred.

Fees Annual fees are charged on a termly basis. Boarding is available from the age of 13 years. Dayboy fees range from £1,260 to £1,464 per annum. Boarding fees are an additional £5,691 per annum. Students from non-EC countries will pay a tuition fee, details of which may be obtained from the Bursar's Office.

Additional charges will be made in respect of clothing and equipment supplied, private tuition, Combined Cadet Force and school trips together with, in the case of dayboys, the cost of meals.

Reductions are made in respect of 2 or more brothers boarding and 3 or more brothers attending the College as dayboys. Allowances are also made for the sons of clergymen and boarding fees in respect of sons of servicemen. Full details are available from the Bursar's Office.

Scholarships. (*see* Entrance Scholarship section) Annual Scholarships and Exhibitions are offered from Year 10 as follows:

Open Scholarship for boarders of £1,000; 2 Open Academic Scholarships of £300; Open Scholarship for Music of £300 plus free tuition; Open Scholarship for Art of £300; Academic Exhibition of £100; Music Exhibition of £100 plus free tuition.

Leaving Scholarships to the total value of £500 per annum may be awarded by the Governors to deserving pupils proceeding to university.

Prospectus. Further information is included in the prospectus which can be obtained from the Headmaster's Secretary.

The Preparatory School. This is located separately on the College estate and is self-sufficient in terms of teaching, sports and boarding (age 8-13). Boys may enter the Preparatory School at 4 years of age and leave at 13. Pupils in the secondary department will follow the same curriculum as the Senior school. Whilst Cabin Hill is subject to the general jurisdiction and control of the Headmaster of Campbell College, the day to day running of the Preparatory School is the responsibility of its Headmaster, Mr N I Kendrick.

Fees are as follows: Pre-preparatory £2,226, Preparatory £3,240, Secondary £1,260. Boarding fees (in addition): Preparatory £4,188, Secondary £4,998.

Old Campbellian Society. *Register, 1894–2000,* Sixth Edition, 2000.

Charitable status. Campbell College is registered with the Inland Revenue as a charity, number XN45154/1. It exists to provide education for boys.

Canford School

Wimborne Dorset BH21 3AD.
Tel: 01202 841254 Headmaster, Registrar, Bursar and Staff
Fax: 01202 881009
e-mail: canford.admissions@dial.pipex.com

Canford School was founded in 1923.
Motto: *'Nisi Dominus Frustra'.*

Governors:
Chairman: Dr J W Soper, MA, MB, BChir, DA, DRCOG

R W Daubeney, BA
Sir Timothy Hoare, Bt, OBE, MA
General Sir Brian Kenny, GCB, CBE
The Rt Rev John Kirkham, Bishop of Sherborne
C N Lainé, FCA
D Levin, BEcon, MA, FRSA
Sir Roger Palin, KCB, OBE, MA
C B Patrick
Mrs R A Prior, MA
A H Smith, BSc, FCA
Dr K J Torlot, MB, BS, FRCAnaes
M E Wates, CBE
Mrs E T Watson, BA
Vice Admiral Sir John Webster, KCB
Professor J M A Whitehouse, MA, MD, FRCP, FRCP(Ed), FRCR

Secretary to the Governing Body: N A E Coulson, MA, MBA

***Headmaster:* J D Lever**, MA, PGCE

Second Master: R J Knott, MA, ARCM

Director of Studies: F T Ahern, MA, PGCE

Registrar: P R Cadogan, MA, CertEd

Senior Mistress: Mrs E Byde, BSc, PGCE

Assistant Staff:
M D Harms, BSc, PhD
P R Cadogan, MA, CertEd
B M E MacFarlane, MA, CertEd
K D R Hay, BA, CertEd
M H C Symonds, MA, DipEd
R S Raumann, BA, CertEd (*Geography*)
J R Orme, MA, PGCE
D V Collison, BEd
†A W Browning, MA, PGCE, CChem, MRSC
†D A Dodwell, BA
C L Fenwick, BSc (*Physics*)
†M A Owen, BA
J D R Parsonage, BA (*Modern Languages*)
†P D A Rossiter, MA, PGCE
†Revd C Jervis, BEd
C M S Rathbone, MA, PGCE (*History*)
M A Bartlett, BSc, PGCE
A F U Powell, MA, PGCE (*Biology*)
†A R Hobbs, MA, PGCE (*Classics*)
J N James, BA, PGCE (*English*)
A C Fearnley, BA, MLitt
R H J Hooker, BSc
J G Lyons, MA (*Economics & Business Studies*)
Mrs C D Byng, BA
†D P Culley, MA
T J Street, BSc, PGCE
A Copp, BSc, PGCE
S K Wilkinson, MSc, DPhil (*Mathematics*)
P P Burgess, MA, CertEd
S H Davies, MA
P A Fryer, BA, PGCE
†Mrs P J Batch, BEd
Miss H K Wicks, BA, PGCE (*Spanish*)
Mrs M Marns, Maitrise d'Anglais, PGCE
S J Hattersley, DipEd Drama, LAMDA (*Drama*)
Miss H L Chartres, BSc, PGCE
L M Corbould, BSc, PGCE
J C Miller, BA, PGCE
C H Jeffery, BA, MEng
Mrs S A McCarroll, BSc, PGCE
D Neill, BSc, PhD, PGCE (*Chemistry*)
J D Gilhooly, BSc, PGCE (*ICT*)
Miss E Gutulan, MA
†Mrs J Smith, MA, PGCE
Miss E def Amo-Rodriguez, BA, PGCE
W J Ainsworth, MA, DipEd
D L Pattison, BA, DipEd
C P H Dawkins, MA
C Pedder, MA
D E Kirk, BEng, CertEd
Mrs H O Jarvis, BA
Mrs C E Kilpatrick, BSc
Miss H J Fuller, MA, PGCE
Mrs R S Parker, MA, PGCE (*German*)

Chaplain: Revd K K Sugden, BSc, MA, PGCE
Careers Master: K D R Hay, BA, CertEd
Further Education: W J Ainsworth, MA, DipEd

Music:
D A Warwick, MA, FRCO, ARCM (*Director*)
A F Barnes, LTCL (*Woodwind*)
Mrs E J F Hattersley, BA
C C Sparkhall, BA, ARCO, PGCE
Miss N R Phipps, GMus, PGCE (*Strings*)

Art:
D F Lloyd, BA, PGCE (*Art*)
Miss K H Parker, BA, PGCE
Miss A L Shipsey, MA, PGCE

Design:
N Watkins, BEd (*Design*)

P A Effick, BSc, BEd
O J V Martin, BEng, MSc, PGCE

Director of Physical Education & Sports Centre Manager:
N R Baugniet, BA

Medical Officers:
D C Pope, MB, BS, FRCS
B L Lear, MB, BS, MRCGP
P J N Dickens, MA, MB, BS, DCH, DRCOG, MRCGP

Bursar: Colonel D S B Phipps, BA

Since September 1995 the School has been co-educational. There are 373 boys and 204 girls; 389 boarders and 188 day pupils.

The School stands in an enclosed Park of 300 acres. It is 2 miles from Wimborne Minster. The Park contains many beautiful trees and is rich in bird life. The River Stour, which forms the northern boundary, is convenient for rowing, canoeing and fishing.

Buildings. The oldest part of the main building is the fine Hall known as John of Gaunt's Kitchen, which is all that remains of the mediaeval Canford Manor. To this was added the present house, designed by Blore in 1825 and remodelled by Sir Charles Barry in 1846. Since the foundation of the School in 1923 there have been many additions.

Houses. School House, Mr P D A Rossiter; Franklin House, Mr A R Hobbs; Court House, Mr M A Owen; Monteacute House, Mr D A Dodwell; Marriotts, Mrs P J Batch; Beaufort, Mrs J Smith. The mixed day houses are Salisbury, Revd C Jervis; Lancaster, Mr D P Culley; Wimborne, Mr A W Browning.

The Curriculum. There is considerable breadth in the Lower School. In their Shell year pupils study the core subjects of English, French, Mathematics, Physics, Chemistry and Biology, all of which are followed through to GCSE. In addition they study German or Spanish, Latin or Classical Civilisation or Extra English, Music, Art and Design Technology, History and Geography. In the fourth form Economics and Theatre Studies are added to these non-core subjects, from which pupils are asked to choose three to study for GCSE. At least two Sciences must be taken to GCSE. The short course RE syllabus is followed.

A level subjects offered are Latin, English, History, Theology, Political Studies, Geography, Economics, Business Studies, Modern Languages, Mathematics, Physics, Chemistry, Biology, Music, Art, Design Technology, Theatre Studies and Sports Studies. Combinations of subjects are as flexible as possible. All lower sixth pupils follow a General Studies course. Personal and Social Education is provided at junior and senior level.

Further Education. 95% of pupils proceed to Higher Education, the most popular universities being Oxford, Bristol, London, Southampton and Cardiff. About a dozen places are gained at Oxford and Cambridge annually.

Tutorial System. In addition to their Housemaster/mistress and House Tutor the pupils in the Sixth Form each have an Academic Tutor who is responsible with the Housemaster/mistress for academic progress, University entry, and careers guidance. There are monthly academic assessments throughout the school which are monitored by the tutorial staff.

Religion. Religious Education is taught in the Sixth Form and Lower School. Some services are held in the Norman church of Canford Magna which stands in the school grounds. Arrangements can be made for those of different faiths and denominations to worship independently.

Music. There is a school orchestra, a string chamber orchestra, several string quartets, a concert band, jazz band, chapel choirs and choral society. Regular subscription concerts are given by visiting musicians.

Drama. There is opportunity for a variety of dramatic activity in a range of venues in and out of doors. A musical and other productions are staged annually. Theatre Studies is offered at GCSE and A level.

Art and Design Technology Art and Design Technology are compulsory for all pupils in their first year during which they are introduced to drawing, painting, printing, photography, metalwork, woodwork, pottery, plastics and textiles. They may also pursue these interests in their daily activities time and at weekends. Pupils may take GCSE and A Level.

Information Technology. The well equipped Information Technology Centre provides cross-curricular induction courses to all, aiming to establish IT as a natural tool for learning and life, and enabling pupils to apply it to a range of academic and other work, from preps to projects, personal correspondence to school publications. Each department has a teacher assigned to the development of IT within its subject curriculum. There is open access to the centre for all pupils and staff throughout the day and in addition all houses are equipped with computers as is the library.

Games. All the pupils play games. The principal games are: in the Winter Term rugby for boys and hockey for girls; in the Spring Term hockey and rowing for boys, and netball and rowing for girls; in the Summer Term cricket for boys, and rowing, tennis and athletics for girls and boys. The school also has representative teams in cross-country, sailing, swimming, golf, squash and royal tennis. There are other sports available. The school facilities include: a new sports centre, astro surface; two hard court areas suitable for tennis and netball; four squash courts; a royal tennis court; a nine hole golf course. The school employs professional cricket, squash, royal tennis, rowing, hockey, rugby and netball coaches.

Societies, Hobbies and Activities. Various societies meet on a regular basis including Debating, Literary, Science and Art. Space is reserved for Hobbies and Activities.

Community Service. About 100 pupils work in the local community each week, teaching in schools, helping the elderly, visiting patients in hospices and respite care centres. They also help to give lessons in swimming and science. Each year at Easter a party of Canfordians helps in an orphanage in Southern India.

Combined Cadet Force. Army, Navy and Marines sections make up a 200 strong cadet force staffed by 10 officers. About 90% of pupils join in their second year on a voluntary basis and remain in the CCF for two years. A number stay on until the end of their sixth form as NCOs. There are numerous opportunities for training exercises in the UK and abroad.

Careers. The careers programme at Canford starts in the 5th Form. The whole year group undergoes testing for career directions and A level choices. The lower sixth year starts the advice procedure for higher education applications with talks, lectures (Brian Heap) and one to one consultations. The upper sixth year completes these processes. A well appointed careers room is always available and parental participation at all stages of the programme is supported by regular visits by the ISCO Regional Secretary.

Medical. The newly built School Sanatorium is staffed by two qualified Nursing Sisters. A Medical Officer visits the Sanatorium daily during the week.

Admission. Boys and girls may be registered at any time. Application should be made to the Admissions Office. The examination normally used for entry is the Common Entrance Examination, but the School uses its own entry tests for those who are not at preparatory schools. Pupils are admitted between their 13th and 14th birthdays.

Scholarships. (*see* Entrance Scholarship section) It is Canford's policy to encourage excellence and to enable pupils to come to the school who, without the assistance of a scholarship, would not be able to do so. In accordance with the agreement of the majority of HMC schools, Canford limits the value of any one scholarship to 50% of fees. All Canford's scholarships are indexed as a percentage of the fees so that their relative value remains constant throughout the scholar's school career.

Scholarships at 13+. Scholarship examinations are held in February and March for the following awards: Academic and Music Scholarships worth from 10% to 50% of the fees; Assyrian Scholarships worth from 10% to 40% of the fees for an extra-curricular contribution of excellent quality to school life; an academic Royal Naval Scholarship worth 20% of the fees to the son/daughter of a serving Naval Officer; one or two Art Scholarships worth in total 20% of the fees. Candidates must be under 14 on 1 September in the year of their examination. All scholarships are tenable with effect from the September of the year in which they are awarded. Candidates may enter for any combination of scholarships.

Entrance Scholarships at 16+. Entrants to the school at Sixth Form level may apply for any combination of the following scholarships: Academic, Music, Assyrian. The examinations are held in the November prior to entry. Assyrian awards are offered for an extra-curricular contribution of excellent quality to school life and are worth from 10% to 40% of the fees; Academic and Music Scholarships are worth from 10% to 50% of the fees.

Bursaries. Bursaries for the sons/daughters of clergymen of the Church of England are also available; these are awarded on interview and record, and candidates must pass the June Common Entrance Examination. Bursaries are sometimes available from the School where the financial need of the parents has been established.

Further details about any awards can be obtained from the Registrar.

Canford Assisted Places. The school offers a small number of places at 13+ (candidates must be under 14 on 1st September) and 16+ each year. These places are open only to applicants from state schools.

School Fees. A prospectus and information about current fees may be obtained from the Registrar.

Composition Fee. At any time in advance a composition fee at special rates may be paid to cover the cost of a pupil's education for his/her career at the School. Details are in the Prospectus.

Insurance. There is a fees insurance scheme also covering medical and operation expenses, at the option of the parents.

The Old Canfordian Society. *Secretary:* Mrs E J F Hattersley, Canford School.

Charitable status. Canford School Limited is a Registered Charity, number 306315. It exists to provide education for children.

Caterham School

Harestone Valley Caterham Surrey CR3 6YA.
Tel: (01883) 343028.
Fax: (01883) 347795/344248

Motto: *Veritas Sine Timore.*

Founded in 1811 in London as a school for the education of the sons of Congregational Ministers, the School is now open to boys and girls irrespective of denomination or creed.

In 1995 the School became an associate member of the Church Schools Company and benefits from the strength provided by this partnership.

Board of Governors:
Chairman: to be appointed

Vice-Chairman: M C Newlan

Cllr D G Bailey, FIML
W R Broadhead
A Chapman
D P Charlesworth, MBIM, MIIM
Rev D L Helyar, MA
Mrs M Hide
J Joiner
A Mack
Miss A M Mark
J R Mathias
P F Watkinson, MA
Mrs S Whittle
Mrs B M Winterbotham

Bursar and Clerk to the Governors: J A Ross, FHCIMA

The School Staff:

***Headmaster:* R A E Davey**, MA (Dublin)

Deputy Headmaster: M J Bishop, MA

Assistant Deputy Headmaster: Mrs Z M Braganza, BSc, MSc

Senior Master: J P Seymour, BSc

Director of Studies: T J Murphy, MA

Assistant Staff:

Art:
*Mrs M Kyle, MEd
G Ratcliff, BA
Mrs K Rogers, BA
M Sherrington, BA

Biology:
*J P Seymour, BSc *Head of Science*
S F Hayes, BSc (*Housemaster of Harestone*)
A P Taylor, BSc
D Quinton, MA
Mrs Z Braganza, MSc

Chemistry:
R S Cowan, BA
J W Jones, BA (*Head of Upper School; Assistant Director of Studies*)
D J Evans, BSc
R Dexter, BSc Hons

Classics:
*Mrs S Herbert, BA

Information Technology:
*P R Hoad, BA (*Director of ICT Development*)
J Baldwin
P Du Toit, BCom

Design and Technology:
I V Sheffield, BEd (*Head of Aldercombe*)
A G Simon, CertEd (*Head of DT*)

Drama:
Mrs C Hudson, BEd (*Head of Drama*)
Miss S Zand, BA

Economics and Business Studies:
*P Markham, BA (*Head of Economics & Business Studies*)
Mrs R Stowell, MA
C Leeder

English:
*G C Killingworth, MA
Mrs K Abrams, BA, HDE (*Librarian*)
Miss L MacKenzie
Miss Y Howard, BA
C G Nicholls, BA
Miss A Cox
Miss S Zand, BA
Mrs L Tapley, BA (*Head of Lower School*)

Geography:
*M G Bailey, BA Hons, BEd

Mrs L Redding, BSc (*Head of Beech-Hanger*)
Mrs P Stumbles, BSc Hons
C Carolan, BEd

History:
R Salem, BA
*C W Jones, MA (*Head of Underwood House*)
Miss T Acheson, BA
P Keenleyside, MA (*Head of Curriculum Support*)
T Murphy, MA (*Director of Studies*)

Home Economics:
Mrs P Pulling-Smith

Mathematics:
*D J Rogers, BA
J P Armitage, BSc
P Du Toit, BCom, HTD
D T Evans, BA
J Moulton, MA (*Head of 5th Year*)
M Wallace, BA
J Smith, BA
Miss N Dawrant, MA
Mrs R Stowell, MA
Mrs L Boubée-Hill, BA, MEd

Modern Languages:
*S P F Talleux, BA
Ms J Cook, BA
Mrs J Laverick, BEd
Mrs L Tapley, BA (*Head of Lower School*)
Mrs C M Turner, BA
Mrs M Weiner, BA
B Doherty, BA
Miss D Williams, BA

Music:
*A C Goss, BMus, GRSM, LRAM, ARCO (*Director of Music*)
M G Dow, BA

Physical Education:
*P H D Lavery, CertEd (*Director of Sport*)
*Miss A P Collins, BEd (*Head of Girls' PE*)
Miss T K Acheson, BA (*PE*)
R Smith, CertEd (*Head of Rudd and Townsend*)
J M Wallace, BA (*Housemaster of Viney*)

Physics:
J P Armitage, BSc
Miss J A Fraser, BSc
*K G Simpson, BSc, BA
R East, MPhys

Politics:
O Clark, BA
T Murphy, MA
R Salem, BA

Religious Education:
*Revd Dr R Mearkle, BA, MDiv, DMin
Miss H Trehane, BA

Special Needs:
P Keenleyside, MA
C Carolan, BEd

Careers:
Mrs C Brown

Preparatory School
Headmistress: Mrs S Owen-Hughes, BSc, BEd, MBA
Deputy Headmistress: M Taylor, BA, PGCE
Head of Pre-Prep: Mrs F Porter, MA, PGCE

Assistant Staff:
R Andersen, BA, DipEd Hons
Mrs P Dand, CertEd
Mrs E L Harbott, BA(Ed) Hons
R P Harrison, LGSM, CertEd
Mrs E Hewlett, CertEd
Mrs N Hickey, LRAM, ARCM
Mrs V A Hoad, BEd
Mrs M Hudson, BSc, PGCE
Mrs M Lidbury, CertEd
Mrs J Lister, BEd
Mrs J M Moy, BPhilEd Hons, CertEd, DipSpLD
Mrs C A Raina, CertEd
W Raja, MA, PGCE
Mrs M Routledge, BA(Ed) Hons
Mrs V Sergeant, BEd
Mrs P Sparrow, CertEd
T Sparrow, CertEd, BA
Mrs L Woodhouse, BA
Mrs G Woods, CertEd, DipEd

For further information see Preparatory School Section.

Number in School. In the Senior School there are 730 pupils, of whom 134 are boarders. In the Preparatory School there are 265 pupils.

Aims. The School admits both boarders and day pupils of all denominations. Strong links remain, however, with the United Reformed Church which is represented on the Board of Governors. From a pupil's earliest years in the School, the aim is to provide a broad education based on Christian principles and practice. Pupils learn the disciplines of work in an environment which is both friendly and firm, and they are able to develop character and talents whether they be academic, artistic or sporting.

Situation. The School's 80 acre site is situated in a beautiful wooded valley. This rural setting belies its good accessibility: Caterham Station is one mile away and the frequent trains to London take 35 minutes. Gatwick and Heathrow airports are in easy reach.

Every pupil is allocated to a House-based Tutor Group. The Tutor monitors academic progress and provides a regular point of pastoral contact for pupils and parents. In this way every pupil is known well and encouraged to develop their talents to the full. There are separate boarding houses for boys and girls. Common Rooms, dormitories (for younger pupils) and study bedrooms are comfortably furnished, many with en-suite facilities.

In recent years there has been a substantial building and development programme. A new 24 room teaching block, a new sports centre, a new theatre/assembly hall, language laboratories have been built and very extensive investment in ICT.

The Preparatory School. This consists of 2 large houses in the school grounds. Mottrams contains the Pre-Prep department and the kitchen and dining rooms and a house for the Headmaster of the Preparatory School. Shirley Goss contains classrooms, assembly hall, a library, an IT room, separate art and craft rooms, and changing accommodation for the Prep department.

Continuity of education is provided as boys and girls move from the Preparatory School to the Senior School at the age of eleven.

Admission. Details concerning the admission of pupils to the Pre-Preparatory and Preparatory School are published separately (see IAPS section, Part V of this Book).

Admission to the Senior School is through an entrance examination at 11+ in January, Common Entrance at 13, and is conditional upon good GCSE grades at 16. Further details are available from the School.

Term of Entry. Pupils are normally accepted for entry in September each year, but vacancies may be filled at other times.

Scholarships and Bursaries. (*see* Entrance Scholarship section) Academic Scholarships are awarded at 10+, 11+, 13+ and 16+. In addition to these, pupils joining the school at 13+, via Common Entrance, may apply for All-Rounder

Scholarships and Art Exhibitions, and pupils entering the Sixth Form may apply for Sixth Form Science Scholarships.

Music Scholarships are available to pupils joining the school at 11+ and 13+.

Bursaries for the sons and daughters of clergy, Old Caterhamians, Forces and Service Personnel are available. There are also a number of Caterham Assisted Places for those joining the School at the age of 11.

Caterham School Assisted Places are available at 11, 12, 13 and 16 years.

Fees. Boarding Fees range from £5,061 to £5,334 per term. Day Fees range from £2,730 per term to £2,860 per term.

The Curriculum. Preparatory School: A wide range of subjects is provided following National Curriculum guidelines. For further details see Preparatory School section.

Senior School: National Curriculum core subjects are taken by all pupils with a wide range of options in the GCSE years, including Latin, Greek, German, Spanish, IT, Sports Studies, Drama, Religious Studies, Design Technology, History and Geography. All pupils learn two modern languages up to the age of 14 and can pursue both to GCSE. Pupils may take a varied combination of subjects in the Sixth Form selecting from English, French, Spanish, German, Geography, History, Latin, Greek, Politics, PE, IT, Theatre Studies, Religious Studies, Art, Music, Economics, Business Studies and Design Technology.

Music, Drama and Creative Arts. Music is an important feature of the life of the School. Individual lessons are given on the piano, in string, brass and wind instruments, and the organ. The Choral Society performs at least one major choral work each year. Each term there is a School concert and a programme of recitals is arranged. In addition there are Summer and Winter residential music courses. Drama is also well-supported. Each year there are two major productions which involve a large number of pupils both on and off stage. The Art and DT Departments encourage pupils to pursue their interests in creative work, such as ceramics, modelling, metal work, wood-carving and graphic design. Robotics, Information Technology and desk-top publishing, textiles and cookery courses are also provided.

Societies and Hobbies. All pupils are encouraged to pursue a hobby or constructive outside interest, and there are a large number of active School Societies, including: CCF, Choir, Chess, Christian Fellowship, Community Service, Computer Club, Copec (VIth Form discussion), Orchestra, Debating, Duke of Edinburgh's Award, Technology, Moncrieff (VIth Form Science), Music, Meteorology, Young Enterprise, Photographic.

Games. Most of the playing fields adjoin the School including an 'all weather' synthetic grass pitch for Lacrosse, Hockey and Tennis. There is a wide range of sports available, but in each term at least one major game is played. For boys in the Autumn Term this is Rugby; (Association Football for Under 11s); in the Spring Term it is Hockey; and in the Summer both Cricket and Athletics. Other options include Tennis, Squash, Badminton, Cross-Country, Golf, Swimming. The girls play Hockey, Lacrosse, Netball, Tennis, Athletics and Swimming.

Health. There is a well equipped Sanatorium with SRN Sister. The School Doctor attends regularly.

Careers. The Careers staff are available to give advice. The School has membership of the Independent Schools Careers Organisation and parents are encouraged to enter their sons or daughters for the ISCO Aptitude Test in the Vth Form year. The School arranges Careers and Higher Education Forums and the Headmaster and Careers staff are available to discuss careers with parents.

Old Caterhamians' and Parents' Associations. The School has a flourishing Old Caterhamians' and Parents' Associations. Information about these may be obtained from the School.

Charitable status. Caterham School Trustees Registered is a Registered Charity, number 1050847. Its aim is to develop the academic and personal potential of each pupil in a Christian context.

Charterhouse

Godalming Surrey GU7 2DN.

Tel: Admissions: (01483) 291501; Headmaster: (01483) 291600;
Bursary and Enquiries: (01483) 291500
Fax: Admissions: (01483) 291507; Headmaster: (01483) 291647
e-mail: admissions@charterhouse.org.uk

Charterhouse was founded in 1611 as part of Thomas Sutton's dual foundation in London, and was moved to its present beautiful setting in Surrey in 1872. The original Medieval, Tudor and Jacobean buildings still survive behind St Bartholomew's Hospital, providing a meeting place for the Governing Body and for gatherings of Old Carthusians.

The School offers outstanding facilities on its 200 acre estate near Godalming. The boarding accommodation is divided into 11 houses. Charterhouse is essentially a boys' boarding school. There are nearly 700 pupils including 90 girls in the Sixth Form. The School prides itself on the excellence of its all-round education, based on a long tradition of distinguished teaching and academic success.

Motto: *'Deo Dante Dedi'*.

Governing Body:
Chairman: M H Boyd-carpenter, CVO, MA

The Archbishop of Canterbury
C A K Fenn-Smith, MA
M J Collins, MA, DPhil
The Rt Hon The Lord Wakeham, PC, JP, DL, FCA
G R Bristowe
T C Frankland, FCA
G A Reid, PhD
J G Parker, CBE, MA
Prof G A Parker, BSc, PhD, EurIng, CEng, FIMechE, MemASME
J R Davidson, BA
C W Jonas, CBE, FRICS
The Hon Mrs Sealy, MA
Lady Toulson, CBE, LLB
D C R Lincoln, BSc, PhD
J L Walker-Haworth, BA

Clerk to the Governing Body and Bursar: N Durkin, MA

Headmaster: **The Revd J S Witheridge**, MA, FRSA

Second Master and Registrar: R M C Gilliat, MA

Under Master: A J Bennett, BEd, MA, PhD

Director of Studies: D R Smith, MA

Assistant Staff:
S P M Allen, MA
P G Allison
Mrs A B Bailey, MA
M J Bailey, MA
M L J Blatchly, MA, FRCO
R A Bogdan, MA
Miss J Bratten, BA, MLitt
S F C Brennan, BA
Mrs C F Clive, DipTEFL
N T Cooper, MBA
R A Crowsley
M Daniel, BA
P J Deakin, BSc
P A Duncan, BA
C J Ellis, BSc, PhD, MIBiol
M K Elston, BSc

S P Fielder
Miss E J Fox, BA
J P Freeman, MA
H D Gammell, MA
N S Georgiakakis, MSc
G H M Gergaud, L-ès-L
C T B Gilbart-Smith, MA
Miss A L Gilbert, BSc
Miss L Goodwin, BA
N Hadfield, MA
J S Hazeldine, BSc
S T Hearn, MSc, MInstP
C N Hill, MA
I A Hoffmann de Visme, BSc
D S Holloway, MA, PhD
Mrs E H H Holloway, BSc, PhD
P Hoskin, BSc, PhD
G S Howlett, MA
R A Ingram, MA
A G Johnson, MSc
D R H Johnson, BSc, DPhil
R M C Kitt, MA
W J Lane, MA
B K Larrigan, BSc, MBA
M F D Lloyd, BA, DITE
M Loughlin, MA, PhD
Mrs J S Mathews, MA, BLitt
Mrs E P Nelson, BSc, MSc
Mrs F C Noble, BEd
R P Noble, BA
Mrs M H Norris, BA
Rev C J B O'Neill, MA, CertTheol, ALAM, LGSM
C J Oakes-Monger, BSc
J Opland, BSc, MA, PhD (*Master of the Scholars*)
The Revd J J Page, MA, BD
J N Parsons, BA, LRAM
I W Payne, BSc
N S Pelling, MA
A L R Peterken, BA
J Peters, BA
Miss H E Pinkney, BA
P A Reeves, BA
J M Richardson, BA
B J Robinson, BA
S A Rowse, MA
Miss E Ryder, BSc, PhD
S J Shuttleworth, MA
R W Smeeton, ARCM
B R Souter, BA, ATC (*Director of Art*)
J H Sparks, BSc
J A Spencer, MA
P R Stapleton, BSc
J I Stenhouse, MA
Mrs M H Swift, BDS
Mrs N D C Tee, MA
A J Turner, BA, LLM
R J A Wells, FRCO, GRSM, ARCM (*Director of Music*)
C K Wheeler, BA
Mrs E L Williams, BA
A R Wilson, MA, BLitt
F Wiseman, MA
D G Wright, LTCL
R A Wright, BSc, PhD
E H Zillekens, BA, DPhil

Senior Chaplain: The Revd S J Harker, MA

Librarian: Mrs A C Wheeler, BA

Curator of Museum: D S Holloway, MA, PhD

Composer in Residence: R Millard, BA, MPhil

Cricket Professional: R V Lewis

Rackets Professional: M J Crosby

Estate Bursar: A M Kingston, BSc, CEng, MICE

Deputy Bursar: M G Bates

School Accountant: P G Hay

Medical Officer: Dr A Borthwick, MA, MB, BChir

School Counsellor: Mrs V Gordon-Graham, MA

Admissions Secretary: Mrs S Stevens

Houses and Housemasters
Saunderites: R A Ingram (*Senior Housemaster*)
Verites: N Hadfield
Gownboys: J P Freeman
Girdlestoneites: M J Bailey
Lockites: S F C Brennan
Weekites: M Loughlin
Hodgsonites: I A Hoffman de Visme
Daviesites: G H M Gergaud
Bodeites: I W Payne
Pageites: N T Cooper
Robinites: H D Gammell

Admission. Parents wishing to enter their sons for the School should write to the Registrar, Charterhouse, Godalming, Surrey GU7 2DX. Boys normally join the School in September when they are between thirteen and fourteen years of age. At some time between the boy's 10th and 11th birthday a report from his current Headmaster will be sought concerning his suitability for Charterhouse. Parents can then be offered a guaranteed school place (subject to success in the Common Entrance Examination).

Parents wishing their sons or daughters to enter Charterhouse after GCSE to study A levels in the Sixth Form should write to the Registrar at the beginning of the summer term in the year before the September entry.

At least one term's notice is required before the removal of a pupil from the School.

Date of admission. Boys and girls are accepted for September entry only.

Fees. From September 2000 the inclusive fees have been £5,482 per term for Boarders, £4,530 per term for Day pupils. The Governing Body reserves the right to alter the School Fee at its discretion.

Scholarships, Bursaries and Exhibitions. (*see* Entrance Scholarship section) *For entry at 13+:* 12 Foundation Scholarships (not less than 6 of these are Major Awards), 5 Exhibitions, a Benn Scholarship for Classics, a number of major Music Scholarships and 2 Art Scholarships are offered annually. In addition 4 Peter Attenborough Awards are given annually to candidates who demonstrate all-round distinction. The Blackstone Award, for the sons of lawyers, is made two years before the winner joins the School.

For entry into the Sixth Form: 6 Sir Robert Birley Academic Scholarships, 12 Academic Exhibitions, 3 Music Scholarships and 2 Art Scholarships are offered.

All Scholarships may be increased to the value of the full school fee in cases of proven financial need.

Music. Over 400 lessons are given each week and the music at Charterhouse enjoys a very high reputation. A Composer-in-Residence works in the School to encourage composition. The Ralph Vaughan Williams Music Centre was opened in October 1984.

Art. Instruction is given in drawing, painting, printmaking, graphic design, photography, theatre design and pottery, as well as the history of painting, sculpture and architecture.

Design. The John Derry Technology Centre provides facilities for the teaching of GCSE and A level Design and Technology. The Centre offers boys and girls the opportunity to work in a wide range of materials.

Drama. The School has its own modern Theatre which is used extensively by pupils in term time, as well as by the public in school holidays.

Golf. A 9-hole golf course was given to the school in July 1988 by the Old Carthusian Golfing Society.

Sports Centre. A £3.8 million Sports Centre was opened by The Queen in February 1997. It includes a 25m x 6 lane Swimming Pool, a multi-purpose Sports Hall, Fitness Suite, an Activities Room and an internal Climbing Tower.

Athletics Track. An all-weather Athletics Track was opened during the autumn of 1996.

Old Carthusian Club. All enquiries should be made to Mrs M F Mardall, The Recorder, Charterhouse.

Prospective parents and their children are warmly invited to visit Charterhouse where they normally meet the Headmaster or Second Master, other staff and members of the School.

Charitable status. Charterhouse School is a Registered Charity, number 312054. Its aims and objectives are the provision of education through the medium of a secondary boarding school for boys, and girls in the Sixth Form.

* Head of Department	§ Part Time or Visiting
† Housemaster/Housemistress	¶ Old Pupil
‡ See below list of staff for meaning	

Cheadle Hulme School

Claremont Road Cheadle Hulme Cheadle Cheshire SK8 6EF.
Tel: 0161-488 3330.

Founded in 1855 as the Manchester Warehousemen & Clerks' Orphan Schools, the school moved to its present site in 1869. Co-educational since its founding, there are now about 1,409 pupils of whom 261 are in the Junior School and 279 in the VIth Form.

Motto: *'In loco parentis'*.

President of the Foundation: Professor H C A Hankins, CBE, BSc(Tech), PhD, DSc, DEng, DUniv, FIEE, FEng

Governing Body:
S L Jones (*Chairman*)
J M Anderson
Prof H C A Hankins
P R Johnson
Dr J Langrish
Mrs C Leigh
R Meadowcroft
Dr T O'Brien
D C Shipley
P Sidwell
Mrs J M Squire
R Storey
Dr E Teasdale

>*Bursar and Clerk to the Governors:* A Godfrey

***Headmaster:* P Dixon**, MA, MIBiol, CBiol

Deputy Headmaster: A H Chicken, BA

Director of Studies: L H Carr, BSc

Co-ordinator of Pastoral System: P C Allen, BEd

Assistant Masters and Mistresses:
Mrs A C Ashton, BSc
Mrs A K Badger, BA (*Head of Middle School*)
D J Ball, BSc (*Head of Physics*)
Mrs P M Ball, CertEd (*Head of Home Economics*)
Mrs J Beech, MA
Miss S L Beetlestone, BA
M Blaylock, BA (*Head of Mathematics*)
M J Boden, MA (*Head of German*)
J M Bowen, CertEd, (*Head of DT*)
Dr P M Bowyer, BSc
S H Buckley, MA (*Head of Modern Languages*)
P D Bullock, MA (*Deputy Head of Careers*)
S Burnage, BEd (*Head Boys' PE*)
Ms U Butt, BA
Mrs E Carter, MA
Dr A Carlin, MSc
Ms R A Chakrabarti, BEd
Mrs Y C Cheung, BSc
I Chippendale, BA (*Head of Chemistry*)
A R Clarke, BSc
Ms L Cleary, BA
Mrs S Cocksedge, MA (*Deputy Director of Music*)
Mrs S K Davies, BEd
R S Davis, BA (*Head of Year 10*)
P Dewhurst, BA (*Director of Music*)
Mrs H J Ellison, MA
Mrs M P Evans, BSc
Mrs S Evans, BMus
Mrs A Foster, BA, MEd
K Foster, BEd
Mrs L Fowler, BEd
Mrs J Fullford, CertEd
Mrs A Gardener, BA
Miss R E Garrett, CertEd
Mrs G Gee, CertEd
Ms C Harms, BA
Mrs E Harper, DipEd
Miss F L Harris, BA
Mrs V J Heath, BEd
Miss D A Hodgkinson, BEd
Mrs A Hoverstadt, MSc (*Head of Careers and PSE*)
A C Hunter, MSc, PhD
N J Hurst, BA (*Hd Classics*)
D A Jackson, BSc
S C James, BA
Mrs A M Johnson, BA (*Head of Year 9*)
Mrs J Jones, BA
Miss H Kahn, BSc (*Head of Junior School*)
Miss M Kennedy, BSc
Miss H C Knight, BA (*Deputy Head of Junior School*)
Miss R Lago Costa, BA
Miss N Lees, BSc
Mrs L A Leverton, BA
Mrs H A Livingston, BSc
Mrs A M Losse, MA
Mrs F Lucas, BA (*Head of Spanish*)
Mrs J C Maher, BA (*Head of History*)
Mrs V Marks, BSc (*Head of Year 7*)
G Mason, BEd
Mrs S M Matthews, BSc
Mrs Y T Menzies, BA (*Head of French*)
Mrs M Miller, BEdBA
I G Moores, BSc (*Director of Science and ICT*)
Mrs G M Mutch, BA
Mrs B A Myers, BA
P G Neal, BA
Mrs I Nichols, BA
D Parkes, BA
Mrs L Parkin, CertEd
K Pearson, BSc
G C Peat, BSc (*Head of Biology*)
Mrs S E Petrie, BA (*Head of Upper School*)
Mrs B Rawling, BSc
I G Ray, MA (*Head of Geology*)
A P Reeve, BA
Miss L J Reid, BSc (*Director of PE and Games*)
L Richardson, BA
Miss E Rowley, BSocSc (*Head of Business Studies & Economics*)
Mrs J D Shand, MA
Mrs S Sharples, BSc
Mrs V A Shelley, BA (*Head of Year 11*)
P Shipston, MA
Mrs T M Slack, BA
Mrs A Smith, BSc
N D Smith, BA (*Head of Politics and Deputy Head of Sixth Form*)
A Snowden, BSc (*Co-ordinator of IT*)
M P Sparrow, BSocSc
Mrs S Standing, BA (*Head of Psychology*)
Mrs E J Sweeting, BSc
Mrs J Sym, BEd
S Treadway, BEd
Mrs K M Turner, BA (*Deputy Head of Sixth Form*)
P Upton, BEd
Mrs A J Vernon, BEd
Miss S Vines, BA
Mrs L Ward, CertEd
Miss M J Webster, BA
P G J Welch, BSc
N O Westbrook, BA (*Librarian*)
K W Whittaker, MA (*Head of RE*)
V Wilcock, BSc
Mrs B J Williams, BSc (*Head of Year 8*)
J Wilson, BA
J C Winter, BA (*Head of Sixth Form*)
Miss R J Woodley, BA (*Head of Geography*)
Mrs N Woollard, BA
A Wrathell, BSc
K Yearsley, BA (*Head of Art*)

There are visiting Coaches for:
Physical Activities
French Assistante
and visiting staff for individual tuition in Piano, Violin, Clarinet, Oboe, Brass etc.

Number in School. 1,409 boys and girls of whom 261 are in the Junior School and 279 in the VIth Form.

General. The School which is about 10 miles south of Manchester, 3 miles from the Airport and 10 miles from the Derbyshire Hills consists of the original and many new buildings in its own 80 acres of open land.

Pupils are admitted, as a result of examination, at 4, 7, 8, 9 and 11; to the VIth Form for 'A' level work with 7 GCSE passes, or at other ages when chance vacancies occur.

The entrance test, which is competitive, because many more children apply than places exist, is designed to determine that the child can profit from the type of education and life provided.

Organisation and Curriculum. For pastoral care and administrative purposes the School is divided into Sixth Form; Upper (Years 10 & 11); Middle (Years 7, 8 & 9), Juniors and Infants. The curriculum is kept as broad as possible to the end of Year 11 and no vital choice has to be made between Arts and Sciences until this point. In the VIth Form pupils choose their AS and A2 levels from a wide range of subjects. Provision is made for those who wish to enter Oxford or Cambridge Entrance Examinations.

Clubs and Societies. There are many extra-curricular activities. There are 3 Orchestras, 3 Choirs, and annual Dramatic and Musical Productions. Among the Societies are those catering for the interested in Art, Pottery, Chess, History, Hiking, Photography, Science, Equine, Music, Debating and Social Service. No combined Cadet Force.

Games and Physical Activities. There is a full range of usual Field and Team Games, and, additionally, in the Vth and VIth, Archery, Fencing, Judo, Yoga, Badminton, Volleyball and Basketball. Swimming is for all in the School's heated Indoor Pool.

Fees. (*see* Entrance Scholarship section) As at September 2000 (Subject to termly review). Junior School £1,427 per term. Senior School £1,805 per term.

On Leaving most pupils go to further education; some 90% per annum to Universities.

Charitable status. The Manchester Warehousemen and Clerks' Orphans School is a Registered Charity, number 1077017. The original aim of the Charity was to provide education for the orphans of "necessitous warehousemen and clerks"; the Foundation Scheme now ensures that any current pupil who suffers the loss through death or disability of the major earner in his or her family can remain in the school.

Cheltenham College

Bath Road Cheltenham GL53 7LD.
Tel: Headmaster (01242) 513540; Bursar (01242) 513540; Registrar (01242) 265662
Fax: (01242) 265685 (Headmaster); (01242) 265687 (Bursar); (01242) 265630 (College)

Cheltenham College was founded in 1841. It was incorporated by Act of Parliament in 1894.

Motto: *'Labor Omnia Vincit'.*

Visitor: The Rt Revd The Lord Bishop of Gloucester

The Council:
President: P D Brettell, BSc, CEng, MICE

Deputy President: Lady Mynors, BA, CertEd

Dr Linda Baggott La Velle, BEd, MSc, PhD
Mrs P K Cadbury, BA, FCA
Dame Fiona Caldicott, MA, BM, BCh, HonMD, HonDSc, FRCTsych, FRCP, FRCPI, FRCGP, FAMS
G A G Dodd, MA
T B Fortune, CEng, MIMechE, MMI
J C Horan
Mrs H Hyde, BA
A J Priddle, BA, BSc, FFB, RIBA
C C B Rogers, BA, ACA
General Sir Michael Rose, KCB, CBE, DSO, QGM, MA
D L Setchell, MA, FCA
Dr D G Stevens, BSc, MBBS, MRCGP, MRCPsych
N J Street, LLB
R S Trafford, MA
G E Tuppen, MBA, FCA
Dr J C Wilson, MA, PhD, FRSA

***Headmaster:* P A Chamberlain,** BSc

Bursar: D N Smith

Second Master: Dr M Sloan, BSc, PhD

Director of Studies: Dr C A J Runacres

Chaplain: Revd Dr R de la Bat Smit

Assistant Masters and Mistresses:

Miss M Abbott, DipAD, DipTEFLA
T R C Adams, MA
Miss H T Allen, BA
Mrs G M A Bolton, MEd, AMBDA
M C Brunt, BEd
S F Bullock, BA
R V Burnside, BA
I S Carter, BSc
Dr P D Chipman, PhD
S G Clark, MBE
R I Clarke, BA
Miss S J Clarke, BEd
S E Conner, BSc
K A Cook, BA, PRA
S H Cox, MA, FSS
A M Durston, BSc
M A Egan, BSc
A Endicott, BA
B E Enright, BSc, PhD
D R Faulkner, BSc
Mrs M J Frampton-Stoate, BSc
J K G Fyleman, BA
A J Gasson, MA
R S Gilbert, MA, MFA
T R Grew, MA
J B Harris, BA
Mrs C E Harrison, BSc
D J Harvey, BSc
Mrs J Heckstall-Smith, CertTEFL
Mrs S E Hillier-Richardson, BSc, MA
A G House, BA
Dr T R Johnson, BSc, PhD
J L Jones, MSc
Dr M D Jones, MA, PhD
B J Lambert, BSc
Mrs H L Lawrence, BSc
The Revd N G Lowton, MA, FRSA
A J W Lyons, BA
A J McGrath, BA
Miss S L Millyard, BA
N Nelson, BA
Miss L L Orr, BA
Mrs I T M Pemberton, BA
Miss Z L Powell, BA
M J Price, MA
Mrs C I Pynn, BSc
Mrs J C Quickfall, BA, MPhil
Mrs S Ramsay, HDE, FDE
A J D Rees, MA
C L Reid, MA
N A Rollings, BA, MEd
C Rouan, BSc
Dr C A J Runacres, MA, PhD
Mrs B Saluveer, BSc
Dr G Silcock, MSc, PhD
G E Simmons, BSc
G L Smith, BA
Mrs G M Stopford, BSc
M W Stovold, CertEd
P R Summers, MA
Mrs M E Swingler, MA
Mrs E C Taylor, BA
Mrs R M Vazquez-Gonzalez, BA
M H Ward, CertEd
P Weir, BA
Mrs F J Weldin, MA
J B Wild, MA
R D A Woodberry, MA, MLitt
Dr S J Wormleighton, BEd, PhD
C C Wright, MA

Director of Music and Organist: G S Busbridge, BA, MMus, FRCO(CHM), ADCM, LRAM, ARCM
Assistant Director of Music: A J McNaught, GRSM, LRAM, ARCM
N S Grigsby, BMus

Head of Junior School: N I Archdale, BEd, MEd
Medical Officers:
Dr M F S Ellis, MB, BS, DA (*Chairman*)
Dr R Dalton, MB, ChB, DObst, RCOG, DCH
Dr J G Pearson, MB, BS, MRCS, LRCP
Dr R J Williams

Cheltenham College, the first of the great Victorian schools, was founded over 150 years ago. Fine buildings and first-class playing fields provide a magnificent setting near the centre of Regency Cheltenham. Situated in the heart of the beautiful Cotswolds with excellent road and rail connections with London and the major airports, the College offers all the advantages of life in a thriving town community, whilst maintaining a separate campus life.

Boarding Houses. Boys: Boyne House, Dr S J Wormleighton; Christowe, Mr A M Durston; Hazelwell, Revd N G Lowton; Leconfield, Mr K A Cook; Newick House, Mr M W Stovold. Girls: Ashmead House, Dr T R Johnson; Chandos, Mrs F J Weldin.

Day Boy House. Southwood: Mr B J Lambert

Numbers. Boys: 224 boarders; 141 day boys. Girls: 118 boarders; 27 day girls.

Entry to the School. Entry is at 13, subject to passing the Common Entrance Examination and to a favourable report from the preparatory school. Pupils may also be admitted at age 14, into the Fourth Form, and a large number of able pupils enter directly into the Sixth Form. The College has been fully co-educational since September 1998.

Scholarships. (*see* Entrance Scholarship section) Awards are available for entry at 13+ and for those joining the College at Sixth Form level. In addition to academic scholarships and exhibitions, awards are also made for Music, Art, Sport, Electronics and Design Technology, and to candidates who display all-round ability.

Chapel. There is a ten-minute service in the Chapel each weekday morning and a main service each Sunday. There is a Confirmation service every year.

Recent Developments. All areas of College life have benefited from recent building or extensive conversion. The boarding houses provide individual study bedrooms for all Sixth formers and many Fifth formers have their own room. A new boarding house for girls was opened in September 2000. The College is also engaged in a major programme of refurbishment for all the boys' houses: the first has already been completed. The resulting accommodation will be outstanding for both boys and girls.

Curriculum. On entry at thirteen, pupils follow a broad course for one year, before embarking upon GCSE in the Fourth Form. The core of the curriculum at GCSE comprises: English, Mathematics, all three Sciences plus PE and PSE. All then choose at least four options from: Art, Design Technology, Electronics, French, German, Geography, Greek, History, Latin, Music and Spanish. Most pupils take the opportunity to choose five rather than four subjects. In the Sixth Form, twenty-four AS and full A Level subjects are offered. Boys and girls are given extensive preparation for entrance to Oxford, Cambridge and other universities. Over 95% of leavers go on to university.

Cultural Activities. The Arts are central to the life of the College. At least nine plays are staged each year, in Big Classical – the main theatre – in the Jack Ralphs Studio Theatre, or in other locations around the College. Art is housed in Thirlestaine House, a beautifully elegant early nineteenth century mansion, with a Gallery which houses an exhibition of current Art and which also serves as an excellent chamber music concert hall. The Chapel Choir, the orchestras and smaller musical ensembles have a repertoire of nearly one thousand works a year, performing in the Town Hall as well as in the Chapel and other venues. There are joint musical activities with The Cheltenham Ladies' College. The College Orchestra, Choir and Choral Society offer many opportunities to players and listeners. Music plays a vital part in the life of the College. Boys and girls are encouraged to attend concerts, plays, films and lectures in Cheltenham, London, Oxford, Stratford, Bristol and elsewhere. Electronics is an area in which College has built an enviable reputation. Boys and girls are encouraged to take part in national competitions, and have won many accolades in the Year of Invention and Electronics Designer awards.

Games. The main boys' games are: rugby, hockey, cricket and rowing, while for girls they are hockey, netball, tennis and rowing. In addition to the two astroturf pitches, the Sports Hall and swimming pool, there are excellent facilities for other sports, which include rackets, squash, tennis, badminton, basketball, polo, sailing and fencing.

Service. There is a strong Community Service scheme which serves the town, and an Industrial Link scheme enables all College Sixth-formers to experience the world of work. The College's Romanian Orphanages Support Group raises funds for building and refurbishment work in a number of orphanages and the members of the group regularly visit Romania to provide practical assistance. Wherever possible, all College facilities are made available to the town and other schools. The CCF is compulsory in the Fourth year, except in cases of religious or conscientious objection, after which the pupils may choose the community service scheme or other service activities.

University entry and Careers. There is a full-time teacher in charge of Careers, and another responsible for University and Higher Education advice. In addition, every Sixth-former has a tutor who is charged with ensuring that he or she is fully aware of the opportunities and challenges available.

Honours. 12 offers and places at Oxford and Cambridge.

Fees. Boarders – £5,300 per term. Day pupils – £3,985 per term.

Admission. Prospectuses and application forms may be obtained from the Registrar, who will always be glad to welcome parents who wish to see the College. There is a registration fee of £75, and a final acceptance fee of £500 (for pupils aged 13-16) or £1,000 (for Sixth Form entrants) which is deducted from the final term's account.

Co-education. The College became fully coeducational in September 1998, with the admission of the first girls at the age of thirteen. This completed the transition to full coeducation begun in the early 1980s when the first Sixth Form girls were admitted. The College continues to welcome boys and girls to join the school after GCSE and a substantial number of places are available for such candidates.

Sixth Form entrance requirements. Scholarship and entry tests in November or March, good GCSE results and testimonial from previous school, plus interview.

Cheltonian Society, *Secretary:* T S Pearce, The College, Cheltenham. Tel: 01242-265664.

Cheltenham College Junior School. For details, see Part V.

Charitable status. Cheltenham College Charity Trust is a Registered Charity, number 311720. As a charity it is established for the purpose of providing an efficient course of education for boys and girls.

* Head of Department	§ Part Time or Visiting
† Housemaster/Housemistress	¶ Old Pupil
‡ See below list of staff for meaning	

Chetham's School of Music

Long Millgate Manchester M3 1SB
Tel: 0161 834 9644
Fax: 0161 839 3609

Chetham's is a co-educational school for boarding and day pupils aged eight to eighteen. The School teaches a broad curriculum set within a framework of music. At the centre of every child's course is a 'musical core' of experiences rooted in a determination to educate the whole person. Originally founded in 1653, through the Will of Humphrey Chetham, as a Bluecoat orphanage, the School was re-constituted in 1969 as a specialist music school.

Governors:
P A Lee, MA, LLB (*Chairman*)
Mrs A V Burslem
Prof E Gregson, BMus, GRSM, LRAM, FRAM
G D Henderson
A Jones
C G Kenyon, MA
Sir John Manduell, CBE, Chevalier des Arts et Lettres, HonDMus, FRAM, FRCM, FRNCM, FRSAMD, FWCMD, HonFTCL, HonGSMD, FMP, FRSA, FBSM
M Masters
Mrs G Morrison
Mrs R Pike, JP
P Ramsbottom, MusB, FCA
The Very Revd K Riley, BA, MA
Councillor W T Risby
W J Smith, JP, DL
A F Spencer
Mrs J E Stephen, BSc, JP

Staff:

***Head:* Mrs Claire Moreland**, MA

Director of Music: S Threlfall, GRNCM (Hons)

Deputy Head, Academic Administration: G R Jones, BSc, AFIMA

Deputy Head, Curriculum: Mrs D J Peak, MA

Music:

Consultants:
Lady Barbirolli (*Oboe*)
Rodney Slatford (*Strings*)
Philip Jones (*Brass*)
Gordon Crosse (*Composition*)
Christopher Rowland (*Chamber Music*)
Michael Brewer, OBE (*Voice and Choral*)

Visiting Professors:
William Boykens (*Clarinet*)
Steven Doane (*Cello*)
Lorand Fenyves (*Violin*)
Paul Galbraith (*Guitar*)
Brian Hawkins (*Viola*)
Ifor James (*Horn*)
Lewis Kaplan (*Violin*)
Howard Klug (*Clarinet*)
Peter Lloyd (*Flute*)
John Miller (*Trumpet*)
Gustavo Nunez (*Bassoon*)
Ronan O'Hora (*Piano*)
Eric Ruske (*Horn*)
Eric Sammut (*Percussion*)
Patrick Sheridan (*Tuba*)
David Strange (*'Cello*)
Michael Vaiman (*Violin*)
Zvi Zeitlin (*Violin*)

Full-time Tutorial Staff:
Miss S M Bettaney
Ms B Blewett, MA, ARCM
S Bottomley, GRNCM
M Bussey, MA (*Head of Academic & Choral Music*)
D Chatterton, MusB, GRNCM
Ms E Cunliffe, BMus, ATCL
J Dickinson (*Head of Wind, Brass and Percussion*)
P N Hatfield, LRAM, ARCO, GRSM
N Jones, ARCM (*Head of Strings*)
S King, BA, MA, MPhil
P G Lawson, GRSM, ARMCM
R Lomas, GRSM, ARMCM (*Head of Accompaniment*)
D Mason, BA
M McLachlan, BA, MA, LRAM (*Head of Keyboard*)
N Oliver, GRSM, LRAM, PGRNCM
Mrs C Perkins, GRNCM
J Pike, MA, LRAM (*Head of Composition & Electronic Music*)
J M Ritchie, ARMCM, GRSM
C Stokes (*Head of Organ*)

Music Manager: Miss C Dickinson, BA
Concert Administrator: D Curtis, BSc

Visiting instrumental tutors in association with the Royal Northern College of Music, the Halle and BBC Philharmonic Orchestras.

Academic Music:
M Bussey, MA
Ms E Cunliffe, BMus, ATCL
M Dow, BA
P N Hatfield, LRAM, ARCO, GRSM
S King, BA, MA, MPhil
B Madden, BA
D Mason, BA

Languages:
Miss S Davidson, MA
Mrs D J Peak, MA
P Brun, BA
P Chillingworth, BA
Mrs K M Dibbs, BA

English:
Miss G Simpson, MA
I Little, BA
M Roughley, MSc

Drama & Theatre Studies:
Miss K Brindle, BA

Special Needs/Compensatory Education:
Mrs B L Owen, BEd, RSA, DipSLD
Miss C Lynch, BA

Sciences:
A Thompson, BTech
K Champion, BSc
Mrs A Dack, BSc
Mrs K Armstrong, BSc

Mathematics & Computer Studies:
Mrs E James, BA, LRAM, ARCM, ARCO
G R Jones, BSc, AFIMA
M Kurutac, PhD
N Dixon, BSc
Mrs J Maric, BSc

History:
C Newman, MA

Geography:
A Kyle, BA

Art/Craft:
Miss A Boothroyd, BA

Recreation:
Miss J K Riding, BEd
A Bell, BA

PSE & RE:
Revd Canon P Denby
Miss H Woods, BA

Primary:
Miss R Reeves, BEd
Mrs H Jackson, BA

Librarian: Miss C Bowden, BA

Careers:
P G Lawson, GRSM, ARMCM (*Music Colleges*)
C Newman, MA (*Universities*)

Houses:
Mr & Mrs N Dixon (*Boys' House*)
Mr & Mrs P Brun (*Girls' House*)
Mrs J Maric (*Sixth Form Girls' House*)
Mr & Mrs K Champion (*Victoria House*)

Bursar: C D Barratt, CIMA
School Doctor: Dr J Tankel
Nurse: Mrs L Catterall, RGN
Head's Secretary: Mrs P J McGrath

The School numbers 284 pupils, of whom 144 are girls. There are 213 boarders. Admission is solely by musical audition, and any orchestral instrument, keyboard, guitar, voice or composition, may be studied. Each pupil studies two instruments, or voice and one instrument, as well as following academic courses which lead to GCSE and A Levels and to university entrance. The School stands on the site of Manchester's original 12th century Manor House adjacent to the Cathedral, and is housed partly in the fine 15th century College Building, around which are grouped Palatine Building (1846), Millgate Building (1870, formerly The Manchester Grammar School), the 'Chapel' (1878) and the classroom and laboratory block (1954). A new boarding house has recently been built and academic classrooms have been completely renovated.

Music. Instrumental tuition is guided and monitored by the advisers in each specialism, who visit regularly to survey pupils' work, conduct internal examinations and give Master Classes. Internationally renowned musicians hold residences at the School for string, wind, brass, percussion and keyboard players. The Director of Music has responsibility for the full-time Music Staff and also for about 90 visiting tutors. All pupils receive three sessions of individual instrumental tuition each week. Practice is rigorously set and supervised. Music is normally studied at A Level.

Boarding. There are boarding houses for Sixth Form Girls, for girls aged 13 to 16, for boys aged 13 to 18 and for Juniors aged 8 to 13. Each House is run by a married couple in residence, with resident assistants. All members of staff act as Tutors and are involved with pastoral care. In addition, when necessary, pupils have open access to the School Counsellor.

Recreation. Serious attention is paid to recreation, PE and games and the pupils' physical well-being. On-site facilities include an indoor swimming pool, gym, multi-gym and a squash court.

Applications, Visits. The Prospectus and application forms are sent on request. Preliminary assessment auditions are held throughout the year, with final auditions in the Christmas and Spring terms. Parents and prospective pupils are welcome to visit the School, by arrangement with the Registrar.

Fees, Grants. All entrants from the United Kingdom are eligible for grants from Central Government. Parental contribution to cost is calculated according to circumstances under DfEE Scheme.

Choristers. The School is a member of the Choir Schools' Association and Choristerships at Manchester Cathedral for day boys and girls are available under a separate scheme. Choristers' Fee: £5,907 pa (subject to 50% Cathedral Bursary: Net charge to parents £2,953.50 pa).

Chigwell School

Chigwell Essex IG7 6QF.
Tel: 020 8501 5700 (School Secretary); 020 8501 5702 (School Registrar)
Fax: 020 8500 6232
e-mail: hm@chigwell-school.org
website: http://www.chigwell-school.org

The School was founded in 1629 by Samuel Harsnett, Archbishop of York, "to supply a liberal and practical education, and to afford instruction in the Christian religion, according to the doctrine and principles of the Church of England".

Motto: *'Aut viam inveniam aut faciam', 'Find a Way or Make a Way'.*

Governing Body:
Chairman: C P de Boer, Esq
Vice-Chairman: R L Thomas, Esq, MA, FIA

A B Brooker, Esq, JP, DL, FCA
L G Bridgeman, Esq, JP
D G Burton, Esq, FCA
A O Dean, Esq, MA
Mrs M Foster Taylor, JP
R Howard, Esq, BA
Mrs E Laing, MP
D Morriss, Esq, BSc, CEng, FIEE, FBCS
H E Savill, Esq, BA, FRICS
Mrs M Shaw, JP
The Venerable P F Taylor, MA, BD, LCD
The Revd P J Trendall
The Revd Canon G K Welch, AKC
C G Wilcockson, Esq, MA

Clerk to the Governors: Group Captain G M Maloney, FIMgt, RAF

***Headmaster:* D F Gibbs**, BA

Deputy Head: J B Hawkins, MA

Master of the Junior School: P R Bowden, MA

Deputy Head of the Junior School: Mrs J Gwinn, BSc

Assistant Staff:
Miss V Barnes, BEd
M L Bradley, BA, MMus, MLitt
P F Burd, PhD, BSc, MIBiol (*Director of Studies*)
Miss K S Callaghan, BSc
Mrs A Carroll, MA (*Senior Mistress*)
B P H Charles, BA
Mrs J Charlesworth, MA
S M Chaudhary, MA
P G Clayton, PhD, BSc, DIC, ARCS
J Cleaver, MA
P I Cocks, BSc
Revd C P Collingwood, MA, BMus (*Chaplain*)
I E Dalgleish, MA
Mrs D E Dimoline, BA
W P Eardley, BSc
K Farrant, BEd
P R Fletcher, MA
D K Goodwin, MA
D J Gower, BSc
D Harryman, BSc
D J L Harston, MA
D W Hartland, MA
M M Henderson, MA
C J Hill, MA
Miss A C Hynd, BEd
G S Inch, BA
Miss C S James, BA
Miss S E Jones, BEd, DipIT
A Jukes, MA
J Knapman, BSc

Miss F M Leach, BMus
C J Lord, MA
H J Lukesch
R J Maloney, MTheol
P W Marchant, BA
A McKenzie, MA
A R Mantiziba, BSc
Dr T Martin, PhD
Miss J Mitchell, BEd
Miss E R Moore, BA
J P Morris, BSc
D N Morrison, MA
Mrs K L Nash, MA
Mrs A M O'Sullivan, MA
Miss N J Pestell, BA
Mrs P Pewsey, BSEd, TEFL
R L Punter, BA
P A Rand, BEd
Mrs V R Richardson, BSc
Miss K E Robb, MA
N M Saunders, BSc
R Sliwa, CertEd, DipSEA
A Stubbs, BA
Mrs C E Tilbrook, BEd, DipSEA
J C Wilson, BA
S C Wilson, BSc
T R Wood, BA
H B D Wilkins, BA (*Designer in Residence*)

Bursar: Commander R C Seaward, OBE, RN

Medical Officer: Dr A Dhanji, BSc, MBBS, DRCOG, DFFP, MRCGP

Grounds. Chigwell School stands in a superb green belt location in 70 acres of playing fields and woodlands, midway between Epping and Hainault Forests and enjoys excellent communications. It is easily accessible from London (by Central Line Undergound network). Both the M25 and M11 motorways are close by, while Heathrow, Gatwick, Stansted and Luton Airports are all reachable from the School within the hour.

The School and the Buildings. The School was founded in 1629 and William Penn, founder of Pennsylvania, is the most famous Old Chigwellian. Currently there are just over 700 pupils, including over 50 Full and Weekly Boarders. The School became co-educational in September 1997.

The original building is still in use and houses the Senior School Swallow Library. There has been a considerable amount of building in the past 10 years and all the older buildings have been modernised while retaining their character. New buildings include the Junior School Classroom and Office Extension, the Junior School Library, the Sports Hall, the Art, Design and Technology Centre, the Information Technology and Economics Centres, the Browning Building for Maths and Modern Languages, the expanded and refurbished Science School, the Roding Lane Humanities Centre and the new Music School Extension.

Organisation. The School is divided into the Senior and Junior Schools but is administered as a single unit with a common teaching staff.

The Master of the Junior School is responsible for all pupils between the ages of 7 and 13. The Junior School is on the same site as the Senior School and all facilities and grounds are used by Junior pupils. Assembly, Games and Lunch are all arranged separately from the Senior School.

In the Senior School, all the day pupils and boarders are divided into four Day Houses: Penn's (Mr J K Knapman) Swallow's (Mrs A Carroll), Caswalls' (Mrs W P Eardley), Lambourne (Mr D J Gower). Each House has a large House room, a small kitchen, a quiet room, studies for Senior pupils and a Housemaster's or Housemistress' study.

Curriculum. Pupils follow a broad based course leading to GCSE. Maths, English, Science and one modern language form the common core of subjects. Science is taken either as three separate subjects, (Physics, Biology, Chemistry) or as Co-ordinated Science. In addition, a wide range of options is taken at GCSE including Art and Design, Graphic Design, Design Technology, Electronics, French, German, Spanish, Latin, Greek, Geography, History, Religious Studies, Drama and Music.

Sixth Form. The Head of VIth Form is Mr N M Saunders. Almost all boys and girls take 5 AS level subjects in the first year including General Studies and 3 A2 level subjects in the second year. Subjects taken include, Latin, Greek, Classical Civilisation, French, German, English, Economics, History, Geography, Maths, Further Maths, Physics, Chemistry, Biology, Music, Art, Design and Technology, Religious Studies and Theatre Studies. Many of these subjects are available at A/S level.

Games and Activities. Cricket, Association Football, Rugby, Netball, Hockey (Boys and Girls), Athletics, Cross-Country Running, Swimming, Squash, Tennis, Golf, Basketball and Badminton. There are numerous School Societies and a large Venture Scout Troop. Many pupils join the Duke of Edinburgh Award Scheme. There is a swimming pool, two Sports Halls and extensive playing fields on site, including 18 sports pitches.

Art & Design, Ceramics & CDT. Art is taught throughout the School and there is excellent provision for Ceramics and CDT which form part of the curriculum for all pupils between the ages of 10 and 14.

Music. There are 2 Orchestras, Wind and Jazz Bands, 4 Choirs (Boys and Girls Choir, Chapel Choir, and a Chamber Choir) and a Choral Society. Pupils may learn any instrument (including the Organ). Several Concerts are given each year in addition to pupils' Concerts and Concerts given by visiting performers.

Boarding. Boy Boarders are accommodated in Grange Court, a fine Georgian mansion, led by Mr D N Morrison, the Senior Boarding House Master. Boys in the VIth Form are provided with shared study bedrooms.

Sandon Lodge, set in the middle of the beautiful School Grounds, accommodates Sixth Form Girl Boarders under the care of Mrs A M Lord.

Hainault House, under the supervision of Mrs S McKenzie, lies adjacent to the Junior School and is for girls 11-16.

Each House has a small sanatorium under the overall supervision of a qualified State Registered Nurse.

Fees. The fees are inclusive of all extra charges except some books and Instrumental Music. Fees vary depending upon age. Weekly boarding from £3,646 to £3,870 per term. Full boarding from £4,088 per term. Day pupils from £1,749 to £2,689 per term. Plus Lunch/Tea charge (day pupils only) £198 per term.

Entrance Scholarships and Bursaries. (*see* Entrance Scholarship section) Sixth Form entrance interviews are held throughout the year, principally in November and January and there are generous Academic, Art and Music Scholarships available. Music Scholarships are also offered from 11 years of age. A competitive examination for Academic Scholarships is held each year during the Lent Term for pupils of 7, 11 and 13. Up to 3 Scholarships are offered at 7 years of age, up to 12 Scholarships are offered at 11 years of age and 2 Scholarships at 13 years of age. Further details may be obtained from the Headmaster.

Chigwell Bursaries may be available for able pupils who could not otherwise afford the opportunity to attend Chigwell.

Term of Entry. Pupils normally enter the School in September of each year, but exceptions may be made according to individual circumstances.

The Old Chigwellians' Club. *Secretary:* The Old Chigwellians' Club, Roding Lane, Chigwell, Essex.

Charitable status. Chigwell School is a Registered Charity, number 310866. It exists to provide a rounded education of the highest quality for its pupils.

* Head of Department	§ Part Time or Visiting
† Housemaster/Housemistress	¶ Old Pupil
‡ See below list of staff for meaning	

Christ College, Brecon

Brecon Powys LD3 8AG.
Tel: Headmaster: (01874) 623359. Bursar: (01874) 622786.
Fax: (01874) 611478
e-mail: christcolbrecon@clara.net

Founded by Henry VIII, 1541. Reconstituted by Act of Parliament, 1853.
Motto: *'Possunt quia posse videntur'*.

Visitor: Her Majesty The Queen

Governing Body:
His Honour T Michael Evans, QC (*Chairman*)
The Rt Revd The Lord Bishop of Swansea and Brecon
The Venerable The Archdeacon of Brecon
Dr A J M Cavenagh, BA, DObst, FRCGP
W R M Chadwick
Maj Gen P I Chiswell, CB, CBE, DL
C L D Clarke, LLB, FRICS
D G Clarke, BA
Mrs J Daly
Rev Prof D P Davies, MA, BD
Prof M C R Davies, BSc(Eng), AKC, MPhil, PhD, CEng, MICE, FGS
M Gittins
R J Harbottle, BA
R Jones, OBE, BPharm, MSc
P H Lapping, MA
Sir Andrew Large
The Hon Mrs E S J Legge-Bourke, LVO, Lord Lieutenant of Powys
Sir R Mason, KCB, FRS, DSc
R Morris
A L Price, CBE, QC, MA
Mrs M R Rowlands, FCCA
C R Whiting, MBA, DipM, MCIM, MIMgt
Mrs J S Williams

Registrar: T J P Davenport, LLB

***Headmaster:* D P Jones**, MA, Fitzwilliam College, Cambridge

Second Master: C G S Widdows, MA (*History*)

Third Master: S A Spencer, BA (*English*)

Senior Mistress: †Mrs L Webber, CertEd, DipPsych, MEd(Psych) (*PE*)

Director of Studies: *J D Bush, MA (*English*)

Assistant Staff:
*The Revd S A Baker, BEd (*Chaplain*)
G B Bayley, BA (*IT*)
*N C Blackburn, BSc (*Mathematics*)
*†P Chandler, BA (*Classics*)
J-M Collin, LIC, LCE (*French*)
*Miss C L Collins, BA (*Modern Languages*)
*J T Cooper, BA, ARCO (*Director of Music*)
R J Crockett, BSc (*OC, CCF and Head of Careers*) (*Mathematics*)
N J Davies, BA (*Art*)
*Mrs A Duggan, BA (*Art*)
†M Dyer, MA, ARCM (*Music*)
†Mrs S M Edwards, BSc, DipTEFL (*EAL*)
*Mrs S Elliott, BA (*History*)
P K Edgley, ARPS (*Photography*)
Mrs A V Frazer, BEd (*English and Drama*)
D R Grant, BSc (*Chemistry*)
K W N Jess, BSc, MSc (*Geography*)
*A B Keeble, BA, MSc (*Geography*)
*Mrs F Kilpatrick, BA, RSADipSpLD, AMBDA (*Librarian, Dyslexia*)
*†R McGovern, MA(Ed Man), CertEd (*Design & Technology*)
D J McMahon, MA(Ed, BSc (*Biology*)
D P Marshman, BSc (*Mathematics*)
D R Morgan, BA (*Classics*)
*A Reeves, BSc (*Physics*)
T W Reynolds, BMus, MA, PhD, ALCM, LTCL, ARCO (*Music*)
Dr Joanna K Ripley, BSc, PhD (*Biology*)
R G Rogers, BA (*Design & Technology*)
*M P Sims, BSc (*Biology*)
R C Slaney, BA (*Modern Languages, EAL*)
*P W Smith, BSc, PhD, MRSC, ChChem (*Chemistry*)
Mrs H A Thomas, CertEd, BEd, CertTESOL (*EAL, Dyslexia*)
*C J Webber, BEd (*PE*)
†J R Williams, BSc (*Economics*)
*G M Wolstenholme, BA (*Business Studies*)

Visiting Music Staff:
M E Bennett, GTCL, LTCL
R Clift
Mrs H Gedge, GRSM, LRAM, ARCM, ARAM, AWACM
Miss C Greenwood, BA, AdvDip
Mrs C Handley, LRAM, GRSM, DipRAM
J C Herbert
Mrs C Morgan, MA
Mrs E Priday, LRAM
G F Rees, LWCMD
Mrs C E Walker, BA, ARCM

Medical Officer: Dr M B J Heneghan, BSc, MB, BCh, MRCP, DRCOG

Bursar: H Pattison-Appleton, ARICS, MBIFM
Admissions Registrar: Mrs M L Stephens
SSI: W J Dowling
OBA Secretary: J D Payne, MA
Foundation Director: Major General The Revd R M Llewellyn, CB, OBE, FIMgt

Christ College Brecon lies in a setting of outstanding natural beauty at the foot of the Brecon Beacons. The River Usk flows alongside the playing fields and provides good facilities for canoeing and fishing: the nearby Llangorse Lake is available for sailing and windsurfing. The small market town of Brecon is just 3 minutes walk away on the opposite side of the river.

The College was founded by King Henry VIII in 1541 when he dissolved the Dominican Friary of St Nicholas. In recent years the Governors have completed a series of major developments, the most recent of which have been two completely refurbished boarding houses, one for girls and one for boys; an extension to the Music School, the large-scale conversion of a former inn which is now dedicated to Art, Ceramics and Photography, and a new Sixth Form Centre. Every pupil in at least the last year in the school enjoys the privacy of his or her own study bedroom.

Organisation. Until 1987 Christ College was a school for boys only. In that year girls were admitted to the 6th Form, and in 1995 the school became fully coeducational. There are 304 pupils in the school, of whom 207 are boys, 97 girls. 230 are boarders, 74 day pupils. There are three senior boys' houses (School House, Orchard and St David's), two senior girls' houses (de Winton and Donaldson's), and a junior house (Alway) for 11–13 year old boys and girls. The School feeds centrally on a cafeteria basis in the Dining Halls served by modern kitchens.

Chapel. The Chapel Services are conducted in accordance with the liturgy of the Anglican Church, but entrance to Christ College is open to boys and girls of all faiths.

Pupils are prepared for Confirmation by the School's Chaplain.

Curriculum. Up to the 5th Form pupils follow a balanced curriculum leading to the GCSE. All pupils study English Language, English Literature, Mathematics, French or Spanish, Physics, Chemistry, Biology, *two* from Latin, History, Geography, German and Religious Studies and *one* from Art, Music, Design Technology and PE. Greek is sometimes available as an extra subject outside the timetable. The number of subject options is the minimum possible, so that pupils do not have to make decisions which will affect their future careers until the end of their GCSE course.

In the 6th Form subjects to be taken at AS and A2 level are chosen from a wide range: English, Mathematics, Further Mathematics, French, German, Spanish, Latin, Greek, History, Economics, Business Studies, Geography, Physics, Chemistry, Biology, Scripture, Music, Design & Technology, Art, PE, Computing, Photography.

In addition to the subjects which are taken for external examinations, pupils in the Lower School have lessons in Religious Studies, Music, Art, D&T, Drama, PE and General Studies: 6th Formers follow a full programme of careers lessons and General Studies in addition to their A levels.

In the 2 years leading to GCSE the size of the classes rarely exceeds 20, while many of the 'A' level sets number fewer than 10.

Games. The main school games are Rugby Football, Cricket, Hockey, Soccer, Netball, Cross Country and Athletics. Tennis, Badminton, Squash, Volleyball, Basketball, Golf, Angling, Swimming, Shooting, Mountain Biking, Canoeing, Fencing, Indoor Cricket, Hill Walking, Climbing, Triathlon and Aerobics are also available. The playing fields are extensive and lie within the School grounds.

Thursday Afternoons. On Thursday afternoons when the CCF Contingent meets, there is a choice between Royal Navy, Army and Royal Air Force Sections: the CCF has its own Headquarters, Armoury and covered 30m Range in the School Grounds. Most pupils pass their Proficiency Certificate after 2 years: they may then choose to continue as signals operators or instructors in the Service Sections, undergo training for the Duke of Edinburgh Award or leave the CCF and become involved in Community Service. Pupils in the Community Service Section spend their time visiting older people in Brecon or helping with mentally handicapped children from the local centre.

Music. The Chapel Choir enjoys a high reputation with several radio and television broadcasts to its credit; and most pupils receive instruction in musical appreciation and singing. The various orchestras rehearse regularly and individual tuition is available on all orchestral instruments. Both orchestral and choral concerts are given.

Societies. Each day time is set aside for meetings of School Societies, and all pupils are encouraged to take part in these. Societies exist for those interested in Drama, Stage Management, Choral Singing, Jazz Band, Ballet and Tap, Crusaders, Photography, Pottery, Railway Modelling, Ornithology, Debating and Public Speaking, Computing, Amnesty International, Welsh, Technology Workshop, Business Enterprise and Weightlifting.

The Duke of Edinburgh's Award Scheme has been popular for many years. Many pupils have gained Bronze, Silver or Gold Awards after successfully completing the four parts of the Scheme: an expedition, some public service, the development of a hobby or interest and improvement in a sport.

Journeys Abroad. A number of study tours, team tours and holidays abroad are arranged each year.

Careers. There are 2 Careers staff and a well-equipped Careers Library, with two computers and CD-ROM. All the services of the Independent Schools Careers Organisation are used and guidance is given on Higher Education, with video interview practice.

Entrance. Boys and girls are admitted at the age of 11 years and for these pupils Christ College has its own Entrance Examination which is held each February. As almost all Junior Entrants come from State Primary Schools, the examination is geared to the teaching of such schools. Boys and girls entering Christ College at 13 are required to take the Common Entrance Examination if they are at a Preparatory School or a suitable Entrance Examination if they are at a State Secondary School. Boys and girls are admitted direct to the 6th Form on the basis of GCSE grade estimates, a verbal reasoning test and an interview.

Terms of Entry. Pupils are accepted in the Michaelmas, Lent and Summer terms.

Scholarships. (*see* Entrance Scholarship section) Up to 10 academic scholarships, to a maximum value of half fees, are offered annually: and music scholarships of similar value are also available. There are four additional awards: one or more W G Fryer all-rounder scholarships and one Art scholarship, for competition at 13+, and two sports awards for those entering the Sixth Form. All these awards are subject to upward adjustment whenever the School's basic fees are increased and all may be augmented in cases of financial need. Bursaries worth 10% of the fees are available annually for children of service personnel, and there is a 25% remission for sons and daughters of the Clergy.

Scholarship Examinations are held at Christ College each February and March for Juniors and Seniors (under 12 and under 14 respectively on 1 September in the year of examination).

Fees per term. 1st and 2nd Forms (Years 7 and 8): Day £2,500; Boarders £3,333. 3rd Form (Year 9) upwards: Day £3,306; Boarders £4,266.

Charitable status. Christ College, Brecon is a Registered Charity, number 525744. Its aims and objectives are to provide a fully rounded education for boys and girls between the ages of 11 and 18.

Christ's Hospital

Horsham Sussex RH13 7LS
Tel: (01403) 211293
Fax: (01403) 211580

***Head Master:* P C D Southern,** MA, PhD

Deputy Heads:
Dr S Connors, MA, PhD
Mrs M Ireland, BSc

Chaplain: The Revd A Mitra, MA

Assistant Staff:
*A J Adlam, MA
J Anderson, BA
W J Avenell, BA, DipPE
*R S Baker, BEd
†Mrs J Barwise, BSc, MA
Miss K E Biggs, BA
*Miss C Brownhall, BEd
C Brierley
Miss C E Brotchie, BSc
†Mrs V E Buckman, BSc
T J Callaghan, BMus, LRAM
J B Callas, BSc
R M Castro, BSc
†G N Chandler, BA
S A Cowley, BA
†Mrs J Davey
*S Davey, BSc, MA
R del Pino
†The Revd G W Dobbie, MA, BD, FSA(Scot)
P R Drummond, BA
Miss A T Dyke, BA
S T Eason, BA, MIL
†P N Edwards, BSc
*Mrs M A Fleming, BA
*†N M Fleming, BA, DipArch, LRPS
J Forster
P Gamble, MA

M J Gladding, BSc
B C W Grindlay, MA
R Q Hackett, MA, DPhil, CPhys, MInstP (*Director of Studies*)
†Miss L Helyar, BA
*Mrs S M Higgins, BA
†I C Hobson, BSc, PhD
H P Holdsworth, BA, CertEd
P D Holland, BA
†I B Howard, MA
Mrs J B Jeffers, ALA
*T J Jeffers, MA, LGSM
C H Kemp, BA
D M L Kirby, BA
Miss S Larrivé, MA
*K S Leadbeater, HD/Design
A R Lewis, BSc
K McArtney, BA
†Mrs D McCulloch, MSc
†F McKenna, BTech
*P S Maddren, BSc, PhD
†O K Marlow, MA
Miss J B Marsh, MA, FRCO
*S Mason, BSc
A Mayhew, BSc
*J Mayhew, BA, MA
Revd N J Mitra, MA
Mrs K L Newson, BA
†S J O'Boyle, BSc, ARCS
*M A O'Connor, MA
Mrs J S O'Connor, CertEd
D J O'Meara, MA
*M J Overend, MA
N J Parrans-Smith, DipTCL
*F R Pattison, MA
Miss S J Pilling, BA, MA
*M J Potter, MBE, BEd
†S H C Reid, BA
I Richards
*J C Roberts, MA, MPhil, DPhil
†*Mrs E A Robinson, BA
Mrs A J Röhrs, BSc
Mrs H Rowland-Jones
Miss D R Sellers, BA
J D Shippen, MA, FRGS
*Miss J M Simmonds, BSc
Mrs V Simms, BA, AMBDA
*A L Smith, BSc
†Mrs D J Stamp, BEd
*I N Stannard, BA
†R W Stuart, MA, PhD
†Miss L E A Thornton, MA
Miss E Toland
I H Torkington, MA
†S W Walsh, MA
P T Ward, BA, LRAM, ADB
K Wells, BSc
T W Whittingham, BA, LTCL (*Bandmaster*)
†A M Williams, BSc
*Mrs J A Williams, BSc
*A R Wines, MA, PhD
*Mrs L Wyld, MA
W J M Yates, BSc

Clerk: M L Simpkin, OBE, FIPD

Admissions Officer: Mrs P Gilbert

Finance Officer: G Wheeler, FCA

Head Master's Assistant: Miss S La Plain

CHRIST'S HOSPITAL was founded in the City of London by King Edward VI in 1552. In 1902 the boys moved to Horsham, where they were joined by the girls from their Hertford school in 1985.

Christ's Hospital is now a fully co-educational 11-18 boarding school for 800 pupils set in over 1000 acres of magnificent Sussex countryside. Its very substantial Foundation allows it to maintain the charitable purposes of its Founder so that currently 99% of pupils are subsidised in some degree and 42% are educated free of charge. Parental contributions are means-tested annually and range between nil and £13,856. Substantial reductions are available for siblings.

The normal age of entry is at 11, although occasionally those who have finished Year 6 may be considered early. Candidates for admission spend two days at the School in the January before the academic year of entry, taking a number of tests and experiencing the atmosphere of a full boarding school. All candidates have to show they can respond positively to the academic challenges of a school which in due course will expect them successfully to take 9 GCSEs, followed by 4 AS Levels and 3 A2s. About 40% of entrants each year who have gained 'Presentations' are automatically offered places if they qualify academically. The remaining places are awarded competitively but, in the allocation of all places, the need of the candidate for an assisted place at a boarding school is an important factor. Details on admissions and the presentation system can be obtained from the Admissions Officer.

Christ's Hospital has remarkable facilities for all aspects of its life. Two new Boarding Houses have been completed for occupation by Grecians (Year 13) and all the other sixteen Houses, for boys or girls between 11 and 17, are being refurbished over the next five years as part of a #60 million development programme. Two new classroom blocks will soon be started and other buildings are planned for completion over the next ten years. These facilities join an already well-provided school, with an exceptional theatre, an extensive sports centre with swimming pool, gym, sports hall, squash and fives courts. The original 1902 buildings include a noble chapel and imposing Dining Hall and Big School, each of which can contain the whole school together.

The school has a distinguished academic record, numbering four current heads of Oxford colleges among its former pupils. Other Old Blues include S T Coleridge, Charles Lamb, Edmund Blunden, Constant Lambert, Barnes Wallis, Sir Colin Davis and Bernard Levin. Notable aspects of the school's life include its music, art, sport, drama and community service.

The academic programme is compatible with the National Curriculum but not constrained by it. Emphasis is placed on encouraging each pupil to become a confident and independent learner, assisted by an extensive ICT network and an excellent library. The normal day is a busy blend of lessons, activities, games, meals, rehearsals, tutorials, private study and social time. Pupils become responsible in the allocation and use of their time. In addition to the support of House staff, the three Chaplains, the confidential counsellor and an active peer-support group, each pupil in Year 9 and above has an individual tutor to assist with academic advice, learning and life skills. The Chapel provides a blend of corporate and voluntary services during the week which form an important aspect of the life of the school community. An energetic programme of hobbies and adventurous activities, including Scouts, Duke of Edinburgh's Award and Cadet Force, which gives pupils extensive opportunities for involvement in holidays too, is seen as an integral part of the educational provision of the School. Pupils receive extensive career guidance and nearly all leavers go on to university.

Their Boarding House is a major focal point for pupils, who have generous study, recreational and private space, kitchens and social areas. The youngest are in groups of four in House and the top three years have individual study bedrooms. Each House has three resident members of staff, including a matron. The Infirmary is served by three qualified nurses and the school doctors visit daily. Every third weekend pupils are encouraged to visit parents or friends, but arrangements are made to look after those who choose to stay in School.

Charitable status. Christ's Hospital is a Registered Charity, number 306975. It aims to provide outstanding education and care for children from all walks of life. Parents contribute according to their means.

Churcher's College

Petersfield Hampshire GU31 4AS.
Tel: (01730) 263033
Fax: (01730) 231437

The School was founded in 1722 by Richard Churcher for boys to be taught English, Mathematics and Navigation in preparation for apprenticeships with the East India Company; the terms of his will were modified by Act of Parliament in 1744. The school moved to its present site in 1881. There are approximately 700 pupils. The Sixth Form totals 120 and the Junior Department (ages 4 to 11 years) totals 140.

The school is fully co-educational.
Motto: *Credita Cœlo*

Governing Body:

J N F Fairey, Esq, NDA, MBIM (*Chairman*)
M J Gallagher, Esq, DipArch(Hons), RIBA, MIOD, FIMgmt (*Vice-Chairman*)
R Copsey, Esq
Mrs D Cornish, BA, MLitt
Dr D Jones, BA, PhD
I S V Judd, Esq, FRICS, FAAV
Mrs D J Luff
P M N Luscombe, MA, Esq
Dr D J Martin, MB, BS, DObst, RCOG
F W Parvin, Esq, ACIB
A P Phillips, Esq, BDS
C J Saunders, Esq, MA
Ms A J Spirit, BA

Staff:

***Headmaster:* G W Buttle**, BA, MA, PGCE, FRSA

Deputy Heads:
P W Sutton, MA, PGCE
Mrs G Clarke, BA

Teaching staff:
M J B Adams, BEd
Mrs E Barkworth, CertEd
R M Barron, BSc
Dr R E Bowden, BSc, MSc (*Econ*), MRES, PhD, PGCE
A E G Butterfield, CertEd, HNC, BSc
Mrs J M Buttle, BA
Dr D P Cave, PhD, BSc, MSc, PGCE
C J Condrup, MSc, CertEd
Mrs S E Counter, GTCL, LTCL, PGCE
Dr T J K Dilks, BSc, DPhil, MIBiol
Mrs S M J Dixon, BSc, PGCE
K F Donovan, CertEd
M A Eaton, BEd
Mrs C Eaton, CertEd
Mrs H Farmer, BA
I G Ferguson, BA
Mrs D Flack, CertEd
Mrs V A Godeseth, MA, PGCE
Mrs P E Green, BSc, ASTA, PGCE
A R Greenaway, BEd
Mrs J R Grill, BA, MA, DMS, PGCE
D H Groves, BA, FTCL, FRCO
Mrs H B G Groves, BA
Miss J E Hart, BEd
Mrs J Harvey, BA, PGCE
Mrs J Helyer, TCert, RSA
H P Hewlett, BSc, PGCE
Miss K M Humphreys, BEd
Mrs A E Jones, BA, PGCE
T J H Lloyd, BSc, PGCE
R J Lynn, BA, PGCE
Mrs P Marshall, BSc, PGCE
Miss K M Martindill, BA, PGCE
Dr C J Matthews, BSc, PhD, FRSC, PGCE
Miss S McAllister, BA, PGCE
Mrs J B Millard, BSc, ARCS, PGCE
Mrs S J Moore, ARCM, GRSM, PGCE
M Parrish, BSc, PGCE, DipArch
Mrs D Pont, BA, DMS
D J Pook, BA, PGCE
J G Power, BSc, DipEd
Dr S G Pumphrey, BSc, PhD, PGCE
Mrs H J Purchase, BA, LTCL, PGCE
P J Randall, BA, PGCE
Mrs S M Rivett, CertEd, DipDrama
Mrs J Ross, CertEd
A Saralis, BA, ATCert
K J Scott, BA, PGCE
Mrs K A Shaw, BA, PGCE
Mrs G B Silvester, BSc, PGCE
M L K Singodia, BA, MA, PGCE
Mrs R P Smith, BA, PGCE
Miss S J Sowden, BSc, PGCE
Mrs S M Weiss, DipSocAdmin, BA, PGCE
Mrs P Wettone, CertEd
Mrs C M Wheeler, CertEd
C J Wolsey, BA, MA, PGCE
Mrs P Yugin Shaw, BSc, QTS

Librarian: A P T Simpson, BA, MA, PGCE
Assistant Librarian: Mrs L M Robbins, BSc, MIEH

Bursar: D T Robbins, BSc, FCCA

Chaplain: The Revd S J Chapman, DipCOT, GME

Admission. The normal age of admission to the Senior School is 11+ (after examination in the Spring Term) and 13+ (having passed the Common Entrance Examination). However, if vacancies exist, pupils are considered for admission at other ages (Autumn Term preferred).

Disabled pupils are considered.

A prospectus and application form, with details of fees are available from the Headmaster.

The Sixth Form. Students are prepared for GCE, 'A' and 'A/S' levels.

A wide combination of choices is offered from English, History, Geography, Economics, French, German, Spanish, Art & Design, Music, Drama, Philosophy & Ethics, Business Studies, Mathematics, Further Mathematics, Physics, Chemistry, Biology, Human Biology, Design & Technology, Sport and Physical Education and ICT. At this level students follow a course in General Studies, which includes careers education, to which outside speakers are regularly invited.

Years 1–5. From the 11+ entry all pupils follow a common academic programme comprising Mathematics, English, French, Physics, Chemistry, Biology, Latin, History, Geography, Religion and Philosophy, Music, Art, Design & Technology, ICT, Drama and PE. In Year 2 an additional Modern European language (German or Spanish) is added to the programme. All pupils follow GCSE courses in Mathematics, English, Science, a Modern Language, Humanity and 2 additional optional subjects, although no pupil will take more than 10 subjects to examination level.

Pupils are tested and examined regularly with formal assessment procedures each half term and each end of term.

Buildings. The main buildings were erected in 1881 and there have been substantial later additions. A Music and Art Centre was completed in 1980. There are specialist classrooms for Computer Studies, Economics and Religious Studies. A new classroom block was completed in June 1990 which comprises suites of rooms for Mathematics, Modern Languages and Humanities. A new Sports Hall was opened in January 1992 and a Drama Studio in 1995. The new Library, Science facilities, Lecture Theatre and Careers Suite were completed in March 2000. A major refurbishment programme took place in the Summer of 2000, providing a new ICT Centre, Arts Centre and Music School.

Games and Other Activities. The major sports played are Rugby, Hockey, Netball and Cricket. There are also facilities for Badminton, Basketball, Volleyball, Tennis, Athletics, Aerobics and Cross-country, to name but a few. All pupils swim in a heated open-air pool, which was recently modernised. The School has a strong CCF unit with Army, Air Force and Naval Sections. Pupils may enter for the Duke of Edinburgh's Award. Other activities include Mountain Biking, Canoeing and Gliding and, in the holidays, Mountain Climbing and Adventurous Training in North Wales.

School and House plays are produced annually and there is a wide range of out-of-school activities. The school also has an orchestra, wind band and choir.

Careers. The College has a full time Careers adviser on the staff and regular visits are made by other professional Career Advisers. Talks are given to pupils in the Third Form and above, and individual interviews are arranged.

A Parents' Association was formed in 1967 and meetings are held each term.

Charitable status. Churcher's College, Petersfield, Hampshire is a Registered Charity, number 307320. Its aims and objectives are to provide a school for boys and girls between the ages of 4 and 18 in the Parish of Petersfield.

City of London Freemen's School

Ashtead Park Surrey KT21 1ET.
Tel: (01372) 277933
Fax: (01372) 276165

The City of London Freemen's School was founded at Brixton by Warren Stormes Hale in 1854. It is one of 3 schools governed and maintained by the Corporation of London. It removed to Ashtead Park in 1926.

Motto: *Domine dirige nos.*

The Board of Governors:

Chairman: M Henderson-Begg

Deputy Chairman: D J L Mobsby, Deputy

Aldermen:
Sir Richard Nichols
Sir Christopher Walford

Members:
W W Archibald, Deputy
F M Bramwell
J W Brewster, OBE
W I B Brooks
J C F B Byllam-Barnes
R A Eve
K M Everett
Mrs P Halliday
Mrs W Mead
Mrs B P Newman, CBE
Mrs J Owen
D G Warner
P J Willoughby, JP, Deputy
Mrs M W Kellett, JP
Dr A C Parmley, PhD, MMus
P C K O'Ferrall, OBE (*co-opted*)
R Fox (*co-opted*)

Clerk to the Governors: Mrs D Stride

***Headmaster:* D C Haywood Esq**, MA (Jesus College, Cambridge)

Deputies:
Mrs D M Hughes, BSc, MSc
I E Long, MA

Head of Junior School: J F Whybrow, BEd

Head of Upper School: Mrs M A Lawson, BSc

Head of Sixth Form: M G Hearne, MA

Assistant Staff:
J N Williams, BA
T R Cox, BSc
R B Steptoe, BA, MA
Mrs E J Deighton, CertEd
F U Batchelor, BA, MA
W T Deighton, BEd
M Carslaw, BSc, MBA
P M Dodds, BA
Mrs S D Rodgers, BA
Mrs H M Williams, BA
M J Bird, GNSM, MTC
Mrs M M Boland, BA, MA
B T Carson, BEd
Mrs P M C Darke, CertEd
Mrs S E Povey, BEd
Mrs S J Mitchell, BSc, MSc
Mrs J A Hawkes, BSc
J N Arthur, BA
Mrs B A Wood, BA
Miss R Gregory, BA
Mrs V C Symonds, BSc
Mrs L J Jowitt, BA
Mrs R M Hobbs, BSc, MEd
Mrs H M Irwin, BEd
Ms L K Burningham, BA
O F Anderson, BA, MA
D I Crooks, BEd, RSA, DipIT
I Bentley, MA
Mrs A C Grachvogel, BSc, MA
J D Hallam, BSc
M S Coote, BA, MA
Mrs S J Banks, BA
Mrs N C David, BEd
J G Moore, BA
Miss L R Vickers, MA
R A Metcalfe, BA
Miss A J Tomlinson, BSc
Dr S L Lawson, BSc, PhD
M L Blake, BSc
Mrs E J Webster, BA
Mrs F I Moncur, BEd
Mrs K S Purves, BA
K D Stone, BA
Mrs S Sambrook, BSc
R R Taylor-West, BA
T C Thomas, BSc
N S Platt, BA
B J Lewis, BA
Mrs M J Willis-Jones, Licendiado en Filosofia y Letras
P M Tong, MA
Miss A N Humphrey, BA
Miss M S Simmons, BEd
Miss V A Duncombe, BEd
Miss L J Simmons, BEd
M P Valkenburg, HDE
Miss L J Crouch, BA
J A Webb, MA
M J Collier, BEd
Mrs L M Winter, BA
Miss R J Harris, BEd
A F Harmer, BSc, PhD
Miss A C Hemment, BSc
Mrs K L Connor, BSc
Mrs E E Guest, BA
R A Macduff, BSc
Mrs S E Marshall, BA
Mrs R Houseman, BA

Part-time Staff:
Mrs L M Wells, BSc
Mrs C M Howell, CertEd
Mrs D McDonagh, BSc
D S Goldhawk, BSc
Mrs A E Gillott, CertEd
Mrs J E Cooper, BEd
B D Flecknoe, CertEd
Mrs P G Whiteley, BSc
Mrs M A Cast, BSc
Mrs L Harrow, BA, MA
Mrs L K Smith, BSc
Mrs N Williams, BDram

Chaplain: Revd D F Rutherford, BA

Visiting Instrumental Staff:
A Jermey, DipMus (*Instrumental Studies Co-ordinator*)
A O Hartwell, LTCL, ARCM
Miss R Chappell, AGSM
G Russell, Hon FLCM, GRSM, LRAM, ARCM
N Perona-Wright, LRAM, LTCL, LLCM (*TD*)
Miss S Bixley, ARAM
D Ward, AGSM
Mrs H Pratt, BA, LTCL
Miss E Cook, BSc ARCM
C Hurn, BA, MusEd, LGSM
Miss G Cook, LRAM, GRSM
Mrs D Rogers, DipRCM
Mrs J Searle, BMus
Miss B John, BMus, LGSM, TCM
M Packman, BMus
P Søgaard, DipClasseSuperieure de la Guitare
P Price, ALCM, LTCL, LRAM
R Deering, FTCE, GTCL, LRAM, ARCM
Mrs B North, BMus
Miss C Webster, BMus, LRAM

Cricket Professional: N M Stewart

Cricket Consultant: M J Stewart

Administrative Staff:
Bursar: M D Fowle, FBIFM
Assistant Bursar: Mrs A Wills
Catering and Domestic Services General Manager: P Davidson
Housemistress Girls' Boarding House: Miss R Gregory, BA
Housemaster Boys' Boarding House: B J Lewis, BA
Assistant Housemistress (Girls): Miss A N Humphrey
House Parent (Boys): Mrs P Lewis
Headmaster's Secretary: Mrs E Osborne
Deputy Heads' Secretary: Mrs G Batten, BSc
Junior School Secretary: Miss S Heckscher
Admissions Secretary: Mrs H Langner, BEd
Bursar's Secretary: Mrs S Broughton
Reprographics Officer: Mrs C Cox
Assistant Secretaries: Mrs G Anklesaria, Mrs C Ward

Finance Secretaries: Mrs A Thomas, Mrs S Buckland
School Doctor: Dr J Lowes, MA, MB, BChir
School Sister: Mrs P Goulstone, SRN
Senior Librarian: Mrs T Siddiqi, BA
Assistant Librarian: Mrs C Solomon, LLB

The School numbers 785 – approximately equal numbers of boys and girls – including up to 25 girl and 25 boy boarders. There are 425 pupils over the age of 13, including a VIth Form of 165. The School stands in 57 acres of playing fields and parkland between Epsom and Leatherhead with easy access to Heathrow and Gatwick via the M25. Buildings include a central Georgian mansion containing the Girls' Boarding House, Dining Hall and Music Department. Other facilities include a modern Assembly Hall and heated 6 lane swimming pool, a floodlit all-weather pitch and a Sports Hall complex completed in 1995. The School Medical Centre is attached to the Boys' Boarding House. The current multi-million pound building programme includes the new Sixth Form Centre (opened 1997), a new Art and Design Centre (September 1998) and a new Science and Technology Centre (January 1999). New teaching facilities for all subject Departments were completed with the opening of The Haywood Centre in September 2000. This provides classrooms, a new Library/ Resource Centre and multi-media facilities, as well as two Senior Computer Laboratories and the Careers Department. Currently a new Theatre is under construction for completion in September 2001, providing an auditorium for all productions, recitals, concerts and lecture facilities.

Junior School. From September 1988 the Junior School, ages 7–13, has been accommodated in a new complex in Ashtead Park. This provides 18 classrooms with 3 classes of 20 pupils in each year group and therefore up to 360 pupils in total. The Junior School is fully integrated within the framework and policies of the whole school and other facilities include specialist rooms for Art and Design, Science, Music and an integrated Technology Centre as well as a large Assembly Hall and Library.

Organisation and Entry. The School is divided into 2 sections but is administered as a single unit. The Junior Department has its own specially trained staff and its own self-contained building, but otherwise all staff teach throughout the School.

Junior entry is by the School's own competitive examination at 7+ (normally in late January).

Senior School entry is by passing the Common Entrance examination, normally at the age of 13+, or by the School's own 13+ examination. Junior School pupils may expect to transfer satisfactorily to the Senior School at 13+ without sitting a special examination.

Sixth Form entry is by obtaining good GCSE grades with a minimum of 35 points (from nine subjects), at least 5 passes of grade C or better and at least grade B in the subjects for Advanced Level.

Foundation entry is open to orphan children of Freemen at any age from 7+ to 16+, subject to satisfactory academic potential.

(Except for Foundationers, it is not necessary for applicants to be children of Freemen of the City.)

Curriculum. The first four years (7+ to 10+ in Years 3 to 6) are largely taught by class teachers up to Key Stage 2 following the broad outlines of the National Curriculum. Up to the age of about 14 all pupils have substantially the same curriculum which comprises English, French/German, Mathematics, Physics, Chemistry, Biology, History, Geography, Religious Education, Design Technology, Art and Music. Thereafter, apart from a common core of English, French or German, Mathematics and the 3 Sciences, selection is made, depending on choice and ability, for the course to GCSE from 15 other subjects including Spanish, Computer Studies, Drama, Electronics, Latin, Social Science and Graphic Products so that the average pupil will offer 10 subjects. The principles of the National Curriculum are followed at all levels.

Sixth Form courses may include the following main AS and A level subjects: Mathematics, Further Mathematics, Physics, Chemistry, Biology, Electronics, English, History, Geography, Politics, French, German, Spanish, Business Studies, Computing, Drama, Art, Music, Physical Education and Design. History of Art, Classical Civilisation and Home Economics can be added if there is sufficient demand. All pupils are required to include some Physical Education and General Studies in their programme. Key skills are delivered in the latter.

The School has an excellent academic record. Recent GCSE and A level pass rates have exceeded 98% and nearly all leavers go on to degree courses at Universities or other higher education institutes.

Equipment and methods include modern aids and techniques. Computer Studies is well equipped and established, with specialist rooms in each of the Junior and Senior Schools, as well as substantial departmental resources as appropriate.

Each pupil is allocated to a House comprising a cross-section of boys and girls, both day and boarding, throughout the School. House teams compete in all forms of sport as well as Music and Drama.

Scholarships and Exhibitions. (*see* Entrance Scholarship section) The Corporation of London provides a comprehensive scholarship policy.

There are currently up to four awards at 8+, valued at one-third of the tuition fees, and at least eight awards at 13+ valued at up to half of tuition fees.

Additionally there are at least 15 awards for Sixth Form entry valued at up to half of tuition fees – or more awards of lesser value pro rata.

Music awards at 13+ include a Scholarship valued at one half tuition fees and an Exhibition for one-third tuition fees as well as various minor awards covering instrumental tuition at all age groups.

There are a large number of Sixth Form Bursaries sponsored by the Livery Companies.

Games. *For Boys:* Principally Rugby, Cricket, Athletics and Swimming. Badminton, Basketball, Hockey, Squash, Tennis are also available.

For Girls: Principally Hockey, Tennis, Athletics and Swimming. Badminton, Netball and Squash are also available.

There is a very wide choice of extra curricular activities throughout the School. The Duke of Edinburgh's Award Scheme is a very popular option in the Senior School.

City of London School

Queen Victoria Street London EC4V 3AL.
Tel: 020 7489 0291
Fax: 020 7329 6887
website: www.clsb.org.uk

The City of London School occupies a unique Thameside location in the heart of the capital and has 880 day boys between the ages of 10 and 18 from all social and ethnic groups and from all parts of the capital. It traces its origin to bequests left for the education of poor boys in 1442 by John Carpenter, Town Clerk of the City. The Corporation of London was authorised by Act of Parliament in 1834 to use this and other endowments to establish and maintain a School for boys. This opened in 1837 in Milk Street, Cheapside, and moved to the Victoria Embankment in 1883. In 1986 the School moved again, to excellent purpose-built premises provided by the Corporation on a fine riverside site in the City, to which a new Design Technology building was added in 1990. The school lies on the riverside with St Paul's Cathedral to the north and the Globe Theatre and Bankside Tate Gallery of Modern Art across the Thames to the south. The School's Board of Governors is a committee of the Court of Common Council, the Corporation of London's governing body.

***Headmaster:* D Levin**, BSc(Econ), MA

Second Master: IA J Tolhurst, BSc, MSc

Assistant Headmaster: G S Griffin, BA

Assistant Masters:

P Abrahams, BA
J D Allan, BSc, PhD
J F Allman, MA
P A Allwright, MA
M E C Anderson, BA, MEd
N J Baglin, BSc
J E Bertram, BA
R S Blanch, MA
C H Branch, BSc, MSc
D J Chamberlain, BSc, MSc
K H Churchman, BSc
F J Chute, MA, MSc
M P Clements, BA
J B Cook, BSc
N F Cornwell, BEd
G R Cort, BSc
S P Cotton, MA
P A Cox, BA
S R Crook, BA, PhD
R P Cruz, MA
M R Dakin, MA(RCA)
S Dakin, BEd
R F Davey, BSc, MSc
E T Day, ARCA
G J Dowler, MA
T E Duley, MA, MSc
D W Dyke, BA
J Easingwood, CertEd, BA
R J Edmundson, BA
R J A Edwards, MVO, FTCL, GTCL
W Ellis-Rees, MA
R J Evans, BSc
G P L Farrelly, BA
M R Flecker, BA
A J Heaf, MA
C B Heath, BSc
D R Heminway, BD
R A Hemingway, BA
R P Hubbard, BSc
C A Hudson, BSc
K Ireland, BA
B L Jones, BA
E R Jones, BSc
H R S Jones, BSc
L Kane, BSc
J B Keates, MA, FRSL
P Kilbride, BA, MA
L A Knight, MA
A T Laidlaw, MA
D O Lee, BSc, PhD
P R Letters, BSc
J Levinson, BSc, BA
B D Lowe, BA
N O Mackinnon, BSc, PhD
V P Marsland, BEd
D R Martin, MA
R J Maynard, MA, MDes
P C McCarthy, BSc
S M McConnell, BA, BMus, MMus, LTCL
N P McMillan, BEd
N H Murphy, BA
R P Nagy, BSc, MEng
P J Naylor, BSc
A J Nelson, BSc, DipAD, DipEd
J M Nutt, MA
A I O'Sullivan, MA
C Pearce, BA, PhD
G Phillipson, MA
D C Pike, BSc
H L Pike, MA, MA
R G Pomeroy, BA
S L Ralph, BA
T R A Reader, MA
R J Reardon, BA, MPhil
L M Redit, BSc
C L Rose, BA
H Rosenberg, BSc, MSc
G Sanderson, MA
M Smedley, BMus, ARCM
C J Smith, BEd Hons
G Waller, BA
M J Winter, MA

Bursar: E M Hatley, MInstAM

Admissions. Pupils are admitted aged 10, 11, 13 and 16 (as on 1st September of year of entry), on the results of the School's own entrance examination held once a year in January. Those admitted into the Sixth Form are selected by interview only in February. Application forms for admission may be obtained from the Admissions Secretary at the School.

Fees. £2,557 per term.

Entrance Scholarships. (*see* Entrance Scholarship section) At least 30 Scholarships, a Music Scholarship, with a value of up to half of the school fee, and a number of minor awards, are awarded annually to candidates at all ages of entry. Candidates for entry to the School may also apply for Choristerships at the Temple Church or the Chapel Royal, St. James's (the choristers of both choirs are all pupils at the school): choristers receive Choral Bursaries whose value is two-thirds of the school fee. Potential choristers may also take auditions and academic tests at the age of 8 or 9: successful applicants will be offered an unconditional place in the school for the year after their 10th birthday.

Academic Bursaries. Following the withdrawal of the Government Assisted Places Scheme, the School still wishes to offer financial assistance for boys who achieve a very high mark (scholarship or near scholarship standard) in the 11+ entrance examination and whose parents cannot afford full fees. Interested parents, whose gross income does not exceed £30,000, should write to the Bursar for further details.

Curriculum. All boys follow the same broad curriculum up to and including the Third Form. The First Form curriculum includes an introduction to the use of computers: and in the Third Form boys spend some eight afternoons throughout the year on educational visits to institutions and places of interest in and around the City. Latin and French are started by all in the First Form and Greek, German and Spanish may be added as options in the Third Forms. Fourth and Fifth Form boys take a core of English, Mathematics, three Sciences, and at least one modern foreign language (which can include Russian) and choose three other subjects from a wide range of subjects available for study to GCSE. In the Sixth Form boys take a combination of A or AS level subjects together with other general courses. Virtually all boys leaving the Sixth Form proceed to University or Medical School.

Games. The school's playing fields, at Grove Park in South London, offer excellent facilities for soccer, cricket, athletics, and tennis. Sporting facilities on the School site include a sports hall, a gymnasium with conditioning room, three squash courts, a fencing salle, and a 25-metre swimming pool. Of the on-site sports, particular success has been achieved in water-polo, fencing, table tennis, basketball and badminton.

School Societies. There is a large number of School Societies, catering for a very wide range of interests. Every encouragement is given to benefit from the School's central position by participation in the cultural and educational life of London and of the City in particular. The School has a strong musical tradition; tuition is available in any instrument, and membership of the School choirs and orchestras is encouraged. Choristers of the Temple Church and of the Chapel Royal are educated at the School as bursaried scholars provided that they satisfy the entrance requirements. There is much interest in Drama, and the staff includes a full-time Director of Drama: the School has a fully-equipped Theatre and also a Drama Studio. There is a CCF Contingent which boys may join from the age of 14 until 17, with Army, Naval and RAF Sections, those not doing so engage in community service work.

The Old Boys' Society is known as the John Carpenter Club. Letters to the Secretary can be addressed to the School.

Clifton College

Bristol BS8 3JH
Tel: (0117) 3157 000
Preparatory School Headmaster (0117) 3157 502
Fax: (0117) 3157 101

Clifton College was founded in 1862, and is a Corporation by Royal Charter granted 16 March 1877.

Motto: *'Spiritus intus alit'*.

Council:
President: Professor J P Barron, MA, DPhil, FSA
Chairman: A R Thornhill, QC
Vice-Chairman: Dr A Robinson, MA
Treasurer: J Cottrell, PhD, MA, FCA

J Bretten, MA
N J B Cooper, MA, LLB
H Davies Jones, MA
The Rt Revd P J Firth, MA
Dr M Holdcroft, MBBS
Dr S R Lang, BSc, PhD
Miss C Mercer, BA
R M Morgan, MA
T S Ross
P L M Sherwood, MA, MBA
C R Streat, MA
D N Tarsh, BA
B Worthington, MA

Secretary and Bursar: O D L Delany, OBE, BA

***Headmaster:* M S Spurr**, DPhil

Deputy Heads:
Mrs F J W Hallworth, MA
Dr C V J Ferrario

Senior Master: D C Henderson, BA
Director of Studies: T A Meunier, MA
Senior Housemaster: S J M Reece, MA
Director of Admissions: P C Hallworth, MA, MEd

Heads of Department:

O J G Cullen, BA *Head of Classics*
D R B Barrett, BSc, CBiol, MIBiol *Head of Biology*
D C Henderson, BA *Director of Drama*
P A Lee-Browne, MA *Head of English*
P L Bright, BA *Head of PSE*
D G Spence, BA *Head of Modern Languages*
C R P Kinsey, BSc *Head of Chemistry*
M J West, BA *Head of Mathematics*
G H Sutton, MA, MLitt *Head of French*
A J Brown, BA, FCA *Director of Activities*
C D Gardiner, MSc *Head of Careers*
N R Ingram, MSc, PhD *Head of Science*
I L Williams, BEd *Director of PE*
P G Lidington, BA *Head of History*
J Talbot, BA *Head of Geography*
M I Dixon, BSc *Head of Physics*
I R Lowles, BA *Head of Design & Technology*
R T Jones, BA *Head of Economics*
Mrs C Duke, BA *Head of Spanish*
J C Heritage, MMus, CGSM *Director of Music*
C Lewis, BSc *Head of Information Technology*
Mrs J J Renfrew, MA *Director of Art*

Clifton College was founded in 1862, and incorporated by Royal Charter in 1877. It is situated in the City of Bristol, on the edge of Clifton Down and not far from open country. The School is well placed to take advantage of the many cultural and educational activities of the City, and to gain much else of value from its civic and industrial life. There are friendly links with the University and with other schools of various types.

Admission. Boy and girl boarders are normally admitted in **September** between the ages of 13 and 14, and most are required to pass the Common Entrance examination, which can be taken at their Preparatory Schools. Credentials of good character and conduct are required. Registration Forms can be obtained from the Director of Admissions, 32 College Road, Clifton, Bristol BS8 3JH. It is usual for a pupil to be entered for a particular House, but where parents have no preference or where no vacancy exists in the House chosen, the Headmaster will make the necessary arrangements.

The names of the Housemasters/Housemistresses are as follows:
School House: S J M Reece
Moberly's: C M E Colquhoun
Oakeley's: Mrs S A Meunier
Wiseman's: A C Sibley
Watson's: G B E Coulson
Polack's (for Jewish boys): J H Greenbury
North Town: J S Tait
South Town: A J O'Sullivan
East Town: J H Thomson-Glover
Worcester House: Mrs L J Hill
West Town: Miss A C Tebay

Day Boys and Day-boarders. Day Boys are divided into Houses, 'North Town', 'South Town' and 'East Town'. Day Girls enter West Town. The Town Houses have the same status as Boarding Houses and Day pupils are encouraged to take a full part in the various activities of the School. A small number of day-boarder places are available for boys and girls.

Catering. The feeding arrangements are managed by experienced contract caterers and boarders take all meals in the School Dining Hall. Day pupils and day-boarders are required to have their midday meal at School, and arrangements are made for their tea and supper at the School when necessary.

Fees. Boarders: £5,525 a term. Jewish boys are received at special rates in Polack's House. Day Boarders: £3,575 a term, Day pupils: £3,580 a term. Jewish girls are received in Oakeley's House, Worcester House and West Town but share in the religious life of Polack's House.

Scholarships. (*see* Entrance Scholarship section) In accordance with HMC policy, all awards are limited to 50% of the fees, and some may be augmented by bursaries. The following Entrance Scholarships and Exhibitions are offered each year. Candidates must be under 14 years of age on the 1st of September. Boys and girls under 14 already in the School may compete:

(a) Up to 20 Academic awards up to the value of half fees. (b) Awards for Music, of the value of up to half fees with free tuition in Music. (c) One Art Scholarship of half fees and other awards of lesser value. (d) A Birdwood Scholarship for sons or daughters of serving members of HM Forces. (e) A number of all-rounder awards for entry at 13 or 14. (f) Six scholarships a year for entrants at sixth-form level.

Scholars and Exhibitioners are assured of places in the School. The Headmaster distributes them to Houses, if possible in accordance with parents' wishes.

Academic structure. Boys and girls enter the School in the Third Form, following a general course for their first year. Most GCSEs are taken at the end of the Fifth Form.

Thereafter boys and girls enter Block I (Sixth forms) and take an advanced course consisting of 4 subjects at AS level, then 3 at 'A' level, including a Key Skills course in ICT. A great many combinations of subjects are possible. Boys and girls are prepared for entrance to Oxford and Cambridge.

Service. All pupils are given a course in outdoor pursuits and other skills in the Third form. In the Fourth form they are given more advanced training, which may include involvement in the Duke of Edinburgh Award Scheme, and at the end of the year they decide whether to join the Army, Navy or Air Force sections of the CCF or to take part in Community Service. There is regular use of a property owned by the school in the Brecon Beacons for all these activities.

Societies. Voluntary membership of Scientific, Historical, Literary, Dramatic, Geographical, Debating and many other Societies is encouraged.

Music and Art. The Musical activities of the School

are wide and varied, and are designed for musicians of all standards. They include the Chapel Choir, Choral Society and Chamber Choir, a full orchestra, 2 string orchestras, 2 wind bands, a jazz band, as well as numerous chamber music activities. Visiting concert artists regularly run masterclasses, and there are wide opportunities for performance. Teaching is available on virtually all instruments and in all styles. Instrumental and vocal competitions are held at House level and individually annually. The well-equipped Music Schools include practice facilities, computers, an extensive sheet music library and a large record/compact disc library.

Drawing, Painting, Sculpture, Pottery, Textiles and various Crafts are taught under the supervision of the Director of Art in the Art School. There is an annual House Art Competition and various exhibitions throughout the year.

Theatre. Drama plays an important part in the life of the School. The Theatre, opened in December 1966, is used for School Plays, the House Drama Festival, and for other Plays that may be put on (eg by individual houses, the staff or the Modern Language Society). Each House produces a play each year. It is also used for teaching purposes, and in addition for Concerts, Lectures and Meetings. A Level Theatre Studies was introduced in 1994.

Information and Communication Technology. A new ICT Centre at the heart of the school houses the most advanced Internet Facility of any school in the west.

Physical Education. Physical Education is part of the regular School curriculum and games are played at least twice per week by all age groups.

Careers. Careers advice is the shared responsibility of the Headmaster, Housemasters, Housemistresses, Heads of Departments and Careers Staff. The School is a subscribing member of the Independent Schools Careers Organisation and of the Careers Research and Advisory Centre at Cambridge. The proximity of the City of Bristol enables the Careers Department and other members of the staff to keep in close touch with Universities, business firms and professional bodies about all matters affecting boys' and girls' careers.

Games. In the Michaelmas Term, boys play Rugby Football and girls play Hockey. There is a multi-sport option for seniors who are not in team squads. In the Lent Term, Hockey and Soccer are the main options for the boys whilst the girls mostly play Netball. Rowing, Running, Squash, Swimming, Shooting, Tetrathlon and Fives are among the alternative options for senior boys and girls. In the Summer Term, Cricket is the main sport for the boys and Tennis for the girls, with Tennis, Athletics, Rowing, Swimming and Shooting as alternatives for seniors. The Beggar Bush Lane playing fields includes two floodlit all-weather hockey and football pitches, six floodlit tennis courts, and a Real Tennis court.

Clifton College Preparatory School. *Headmaster:* R J Acheson, MA, PhD

The Preparatory School has separate buildings (including its own Science laboratories, Arts Centre, ICT Centre and Music School) and is kept distinct from the Upper School. The two Schools nevertheless work closely together and share some of the facilities, including the Chapel, Theatre, Sports complex, all-weather playing surfaces and swimming pool. Most boys and girls proceed from the Preparatory School to the Upper School. Pupils are also prepared for schools other than Clifton. There is a Pre-Prep (Butcombe) for day pupils aged between 3 and 7, and older pupils are divided into nine houses, some boarding, some day and some mixed. Boys and girls are accepted at all ages and Scholarships are available at ages 8 and 11.

For details see Part V of this Book.

Old Cliftonian Society. *Secretary:* T C W Gover, MA, 32 College Road, Clifton BS8 3JH (Tel: 0117 3157 156). Clifton College Register Vol 4 1962–1978 (1979).

Charitable status. Clifton College is a Registered Charity, number 311735. It is a charitable trust providing boarding and day education for boys and girls aged 3–18.

Clongowes Wood College

Naas Co Kildare Ireland
Tel: 353-45-868202
Fax: 353-45-861042
e-mail: reception@clongowes.net
website: http://www.clongowes.com

Motto: *Aeterna non Caduca*

Clongowes Wood College was founded in 1814 in a rebuilt Pale castle - Castle Brown in North Kildare, about 25 miles from Dublin. A boarding school for boys from 12-18, the school has developed steadily ever since and now has 440 pupils on the rolls, all of whom are boarders.

Trustee of the School: Fr Gerry O'Hanlon, SJ, Provincial of the Society of Jesus in Ireland

Chairman of the Board of Governors: Jim O'Connor, BA (NUI)

***Headmaster:* Fr Dermot Murray,**SJ, BSc, HDipEd, MA in Education (London)

Assistant Headmaster: Mr Martin Nugent, MA, HDipEd, HDip in Educational Management

Deputy Assistant Headmaster: Fr Michael Sheil, SJ, BA, HDipEd

The College is situated on 150 acres of land, mostly comprising sports fields and a 9-hole golf course. It is surrounded by about 300 acres of farmland. Clongowes is listed as a historic building.

Admission. Application for admission should be made to the Headmaster. There is a registration fee of £30. An assessment day is held in early October prior to the year of entry and entry is determined by a variety of factors including family association, geographical spread including Northern Ireland and abroad, date of registration, and an understanding of the values that animate the College. Normal entry is at the age of 12; entry in later years is possible in exceptional circumstances if a place becomes available.

Curriculum. A wide choice of subjects is available throughout the school and pupils are prepared for the Irish Junior Certificate and the Irish Leaving Certificate. This latter is the qualifying examination for entry to Irish Universities and other third-level institutions. It is acceptable for entry to almost all Universities in the United Kingdom, provided the requisite grades are obtained. All pupils take a Transition Year programme following the Junior Certificate. This programme is recommended by the Department of Education in Ireland. Work experience modules, social outreach programmes, exchanges with other countries and opportunities to explore different areas of study are all included in this programme.

Religious Teaching. Clongowes is a Jesuit school in the Roman Catholic tradition and there are regular formal and informal liturgies. Boys are given a good grounding in Catholic theology and are encouraged to participate in retreats, prayer groups and pilgrimages (Taize, Lourdes). Social Outreach is part of the curriculum in Transition Year and is encouraged throughout the school. A small number of boys of other faiths are pupils in the school.

Sport. All boys play rugby in their first year in school. They then have the choice to continue in that game or to play other games. Rugby pitches, a golf course, tennis courts, soccer pitches, squash courts, a cross-country track, an athletics and cricket oval, a gymnasium and a swimming pool provide plenty of opportunity for a variety of activities. Athletics, Gaelic football and cricket are popular activities in the third term. Clongowes has a strong rugby tradition and has won the Leinster Championship three times in the last decade.

Other activities. Following the Jesuit tradition, the school has a fine reputation for debating and has won competitions in three different languages (English, Irish, French) in the last decade. A large school orchestra and school choir gives a formal concert at Christmas and another before the summer holidays. Drama productions take place at every level within the school. A large-scale summer project for charity has been undertaken each year. A residential holiday project for children with disabilities takes place in the school each summer and is animated by teachers and pupils. The College has recently created link programmes with schools in Hungary and Romania.

Pastoral Care. The school is organised horizontally into Lines. Two 'prefects', or housemasters look after each Line, composed of two years. In addition, an Academic Year Head oversees the academic work of each of the 70 pupils within each year. A Spiritual Father or Chaplain is attached to each line. There is a strong and positive relationship with parents and a good community spirit throughout the school. The school seeks to foster competence, conscience and compassionate commitment in each of the boys in its care.

Fees. Fees for the school year 2000-2001 are £5,870. Parents are also asked to support the continuing development of the College through various fund-raising activities.

Clongowes Union. This association of past pupils of the school can be contacted through *The Secretary, The Clongowes Union, Clongowes Wood College, Naas, Co. Kildare.*

Coleraine Academical Institution

Castlerock Road Coleraine N Ireland BT51 3LA.
Tel: 028 7034 4331
Fax: 028 7035 2632

Coleraine Academical Institution was opened on 1 May 1860, the foundation stone having been laid on the 4th June, 1857. The School owes its origin to the enterprise and generosity of a group of Coleraine merchants and gentry. It has been generously endowed by The Honourable The Irish Society and the Worshipful Company of Clothworkers of London.

Governing Body:
Chairman: K H Cheevers, BSc, CEng, MICE, FIHT

J I Smyth, BSc, CEng (*Vice-Chairman*)
M C Black
Miss M C Boyce
E Boyd
H R Cameron, BSc, AMICE, MInstHE
N Cully
W S Dale
Rev T Donnelly
J K L Ford
T N Hamilton
D A Harkness
D A Irwin
A J M Knox
W A Linnegan
T L MacFarlane
M F G McIntosh, LLB
Rev W D F Marshall, MA
D McClarty
W G McCollum
Mrs H R A Millar, LLB
F J Mullan
L J Morrell, BAgr, JP
W Oliver
J C Stevenson, FRICS, FIQS
R J White, OBE, JP, MPS

***Headmaster:* R S Forsythe**, BSc, DASE

Deputy Headmasters:
L F Quigg, BA
J M Gordon, BA

Senior Masters:
*J J Flanagan, BA, DipEd
S L Turtle, BA, DipEd (*Careers*)

Assistant Masters:
T W A Blair, BA, DipEd
*B Drummond, MA, FRCO, ARCM
J K L Ford, BSc
Mrs H Drummond, ARCM, LLCM, GLCM, LGSM, LRAM
J A Cassels, BA, ACTL, DipEd
R A V Gilmour, BA, DipEd
*R Blair, BSc
*J W Martin, BA, DipEd
S L Turtle, BA, DipEd
J S Patterson, BSc (*Econ*), PGCE
*D A Harkness, BSc, DipEd
A Lee, BA
M McNay, BA, DipEd
L Robinson, BA, DipEd
*J Brown, BA, CertEd
R T Adams, BSc, PGCE
P Blayney, BSc, CEd
J V Boyd, BA, DipEd
R J Simpson, BA, DipEd
W G McCluskey, BSc, DipEd
S Graham, BEd
A J Breen, BSc
G S Buick, MSc
W S A Mitchell, BSc, DipEd
N Cully, BSc, DPhil
Miss A McCausland, LLCM, ARCM
R I Crown, BSc, PGCE
M Reavey, BEd
R Kane, BSc, PGCE
P Livingstone, BSc, PGCE
J McCully, BA, PGCE
M Irwin, BEd
K Davis, BSc, PGCE
G Knox, BA, PGCE
Miss L Montgomery, BA, PGCE
R Beggs, BA, PGCE
Mrs T Reid, BSc, PGCE
T Smith, BA, PGCE
D Stewart, BSc, PGCE
*Mrs A Blackwell, BA, PGCE
Miss J Davis, BA, PGCE
Miss K Poots, BA, PGCE
R McGregor, BSc, PGCE
Mrs H Giffin, BA, PGCE
Miss T A L Hunter, BSc, PGCE
*Mr G J Spence, BA, PGCE

Bursar and Secretary to Governors: C Beck

Number of Pupils. Approximately 800 boys now attend.

Age of Entry. No boy under the age of 11 years is admitted, unless there are special circumstances.

Estate. The School stands on the outskirts of the Borough of Coleraine and commands a wide view over a beautiful landscape with the lower reaches of the River Bann in the middle distance and seventy acres of Playing Fields reaching from the School by terraces down to the river side. These comprise 10 rugby pitches, with 5 cricket wickets, 4 hard tennis courts, basketball facilities and a hard surfaced athletics complex.

Beside the river is a boathouse fitted with an indoor rowing tank for coaching purposes. This boathouse is the headquarters of a thriving Boat Club for rowing, canoeing and sailing on the Bann estuary. There is also a large Sports Hall.

Teaching Accommodation. The School has a fine suite of the most up-to-date classrooms. The Science Block contains 12 highly equipped laboratories, with stores and preparation rooms, as well as 2 lecture theatres, for instruction in Physics, Chemistry and Biology up to 'A' level and Open Scholarship standards. Our most recent addition has been a Technology Centre.

Library and VIth Form Study Centre. In 1968 the existing Assembly Hall was converted into a spacious Library with fiction and reference sections. It has a balcony along 2 sides, partitioned off to provide small group study rooms for VIth formers. There is also a large reading room supplied with daily papers and current magazines. An area of 1,600 sq ft adjoining the Library is fitted out with individual carrels plus reading spaces to form a VIth Form Study Centre.

Assembly Halls. A large Assembly Hall capable of seating the whole School is supplemented by an auditorium designed to accommodate 300. Underneath this auditorium is a suite of music class and practice-rooms.

Physical Education. There is a large Sports Hall where basketball, volleyball, badminton and weight lifting are co-curricular activities. In a 25 metre heated pool, swimming coaching is part of the curriculum. This pool is also used for supervised casual swimming in the afternoons and evenings and is the headquarters of the life saving, personal survival and sub-aqua clubs, as well as being used for teaching canoe techniques and water safety precautions.

Education. The School aims at providing a full and thorough instruction in all branches of a liberal education. Boys in the lower school (Forms I – III) are given the foundations of a general education in a wide range of subjects. In the upper school a moderate amount of specialisation is allowed so that boys may give more time to 'Career Subjects'. The choice of subjects is a wide one, and normally a minimum of 8 is chosen for GCSE to be taken in the Vth Form. Special arrangements are made in the VIth Form to enable boys to study subjects of their choice to 'A' and Scholarship levels, and they are encouraged to compete for University Scholarships and Exhibitions. The VIth Form timetable allows for a number of periods per week for General Studies, with additional allocations for private study.

Careers. A section of the Library is fitted out as a Careers' Department, which is supervised by Senior Masters, from whom parents and boys can obtain information and advice about possible careers.

Games. Rugby, football, cricket, rowing, tennis, badminton, golf, cross-country running, athletics, swimming, canoeing and sailing are the chief sports and games for which excellent facilities are available. Coaching in Golf is available to boys of the VIth Form under the Golf Foundation.

Societies and Clubs. These include: Bridge, Junior and Senior Dramatic, Junior and Senior Debating, Junior and Senior Badminton, Junior and Senior Chess, Musical, English Literature, Senior Scientific Society, Geographical, Swimming, Canoeing, Sailing, Angling, Circuit Training and Weight Lifting, Computer programming, Modelling, Electronic, Table Tennis, Junior and Senior Scripture Unions, Choir, Orchestra and Social Services Group.

Scholarships. No Entrance Scholarships are offered but a number of bursaries and prizes are annually awarded within the School.

Fees. Day boys pay only £75 per annum, provided their parents are EC Nationals and resident in Northern Ireland.

* Head of Department	§ Part Time or Visiting
† Housemaster/Housemistress	¶ Old Pupil
‡ See below list of staff for meaning	

Colfe's School

Horn Park Lane London SE12 8AW
Tel: 020 8852 2283/4
Fax: 020 8297 1216

In 1652 the Rev Abraham Colfe, Vicar of Lewisham, refounded a grammar school, whose origins are in a Chantry School founded at Lewisham Parish Church in the late 15th century. In 1574 the Rev John Glyn secured from Elizabeth I a charter for "the free Grammar School of Queen Elizabeth in Lewisham". In his will Colfe instructed the governors how children of the 'hundred of Blackheath' should be chosen and educated. He also nominated the Worshipful Company of Leathersellers to be the Trustee to his will and they have governed the school from that time.

Mottos: *Soli Deo honor et gloria* (Leathersellers) *Ad Astra per Aspera* (Colfe)

Visitor: HRH Prince Michael of Kent

Board of Governors:
Ex-officio:
The Master of the Leathersellers' Company
The Vicar of Lewisham

Leathersellers:
D R Curtis, MA (*Chairman*)
M Biscoe
S W Polito
D R G Scriven
P R Shand
R M Templeman
A C L Thornton

University of Oxford:
Dr H Mardon, BSc

University of Cambridge:
Dr B Landy, Fitzwilliam College, Cambridge

Co-optative Governors:
J A E Evans, MA, FRSA
Dr M Spurr, OBE

Clerk to the Governors: F B Rossiter, MA

***Headmaster:* A H Chicken**, BA

Deputy Headmaster: G E Bull, BA
Director of Studies: E D A Barnes, BA
Senior Master: M L Taylor, BA
Head of Sixth Form: R D Paine, BA
Head of Preparatory School: N L Helliwell, BEd, MA
Head of Pre-Preparatory School: to be appointed

Staff:
*Miss K J Allison, BSc
Miss J M Arnold, BSc
J W F Arnold, MA, BA
*C R Bagnold, BA
A R Bee, BSc
Mrs P Booth, BA
*A J Brooker, DLC, MIDPE
G D Bruce, BA
Mrs J Burnett, CertEd
Mrs J Burton, BA
Mrs A C Chapman, BA
*A G B Chapman, CertEd, DipPhys
C J Cherry, BSc
*Rev A C Collier, MA, DipTheol (*Chaplain*)
*P C Cummins, BSc
R H Dickson, BEd
S Drury, BA, MA
*J Gallagher, BA
*D E Gardner, DLC
Mrs J C German, BA
*P R Gibbs, BA
Miss R A Hargrave, BEd
*P J Hopkins, BA, BMus, FRCO, ARCM
*D G Jackson, BA
Mrs E Karavidas, BA, MA
Miss C A Keily, BA
*J G King, BSc, MA
Ms C A Kirsop, MA
*Mrs H E Lascelles, BSc
J M Lascelles, BA
C D Lloyd, BSc
Mrs A McAuliffe, BA
Ms U M McDevitt, BA
*P J Marson, MA

N W E Miller, BSc
*K W Moody, BA
Ms L A Murphy, BEd
*A C Newell, BSc
J A Nield, BSc
E O'Sullivan, BSc
*Mrs C M Parker, MA
B D Pavey, BSc
M C Percival, BSc, BA
A R Rickus, BSc, MSc, CPhys, MInstP
Miss R C Rolls, BA
C E Rowe, BEd
A T Rowley, BSc, DPhil
A Seddon, BA
*D E Shelbrooke, BEd, (*Careers*)
*C P Smith, BSc, CPhys, MInstP
*D S Smith, BEd, MA
J Smith, BA
Miss J C Thomas, BSc
R P Thompson, BMus, MMus, LGSM, PhD
Mrs N J Tod, BA
*Mrs P K Turrent, BA
Mrs J Vander Gucht, BA
*S P Varley, BA, CertEd, MA
J D Walker, BSc
*A W Ward, BSc, DipEd
*M S West, BSc, MRSC, CChem
D J Wiseman, BEd
*S Wolfson, BA
S R Zivanovic, BA

Preparatory School Staff:
Mrs A Curry, BTech
G J Iles, BEd
J Lancashire, BSc
Miss D A Lempriere, BA
Miss A D Manning, BA
Miss J M McCleery, BEd
C Murray, Teaching Diploma
M Potter, BA
Miss H R Richards, BSc
Miss C B Rowling, BA, CertEd, ARCM
V Spencer, BMus, ALCM
C Stringfellow, CertEd
Miss M Webb, BA

Nursery and Pre-Preparatory School Staff:
Mrs J M Broughton, NNEB
Mrs L Brown, NNEB, CertEd
Mrs S W Brown, NNEB
Mrs M R Cooper, NNEB
Miss A A Crawford, NNEB
Mrs J Dunmore, BA
Mrs E R Frost, BEd
Mrs S Gaunt, BEd
Ms E Gibbs, BA
Ms S J Grover, NNEB
Mrs K Johnson, BSc
Miss C Linton, BEd
Miss H E Otley, NNEB
Mrs E Wright, BA

Bursar: F B Rossiter, MA

Registration Secretary: Mrs R Dyer

Librarian: Mrs J A Cardnell, BA, DipLib, ALA

Admissions. There are 700 pupils in the Senior School including 200 in the VIth Form. The Preparatory School (7–11) has 190 pupils. Girls are currently admitted to the VIth Form, at 7+, 8+ and 9+ in the Prep and at 11+, 12+ and 13+, and the intention is to extend co-education in the coming years. A co-educational nursery and pre-preparatory school was opened in September 1992 and there are 150 pupils (3–6). Admission to the Senior School is by examination, interview and school report for 11+, 13+ and VIth Form candidates. Admission to the Preparatory School at 7+ is by interview and report; candidates at other ages are examined. Admissions to the Nursery and Pre-Prep are made in the order of application with special arrangements for siblings.

Buildings. The School moved from its original site below Blackheath to a new building on the games fields in Lee in 1964. This building houses specialist laboratories for all the sciences, groups of classrooms for Mathematics, Geography, History, Politics and Religious Studies, and suites of rooms for Art, Design Technology and Information Technology. The Beardwood Centre, which was opened by HRH Prince Michael of Kent in 1984, provides a splendidly equipped theatre and concert hall, music practice rooms and classrooms for the teaching of English, Drama, Media Studies and Music. The Newton Sports Centre, comprising sports hall, swimming pool and fitness room was opened in November, 1991. A new Library with extensive private study facilities opened in April 1992, and a new classroom block for Economics, Business Studies and Languages was completed in October 1996. A new Sixth Form Centre was opened in September 1999. A new centre for the Performing Arts is planned for 2002.

Curriculum. The Curriculum is in the spirit of the National Curriculum, but is not limited to it: in particular, emphasis is placed on Humanities, Religious Studies and Personal and Social Education at KS3; pupils may study three languages; they study all three sciences as separate subjects within the Dual Award system. Physical Education, Games, Art, Design Technology, Music and Drama also have an important place in the curriculum. The School has good provision for ICT, with two dedicated suites of computers and mini-networks in most departments. There is an on-going programme of adding subject areas to the networks.

In the Lower School a firm basis is laid for all of the core and foundation subjects which are available for study in the Middle School. Pupils are not setted initially, although banding is introduced in Year 8. Throughout Key Stage 3 all pupils study the following subjects which are available at GCSE: Mathematics, English, Languages (they all take French in Y7 and may take Latin; thereafter they study two of French, Latin and German), Science (Combined Science gives way to the separate study of Biology, Chemistry and Physics), Geography, History, Religious Studies and PE. In Years 7 & 8 they also study Design & Technology (including Information Technology), Art, Music and Drama, and in Year 9 they continue with 3 of these 4 subjects, all of which may also be taken on to GCSE. In addition, pupils have courses in Active Citizenship. ICT is taught in Y7 as a separate subject and across the curriculum thereafter.

In the Middle School all those subjects listed above, as well as Spanish and Business Studies, are available for GCSE. The exact combinations available vary from year to year, but normally all pupils take English and English Literature or Drama or Media Studies, Mathematics, one Modern foreign language, Biology, Chemistry, Physics (leading to the Dual Award certificate at GCSE). They then choose up to four more subjects which must include History or Geography and they are encouraged to take a creative subject. Most pupils take nine or ten GCSEs and some take 11 subjects. Pupils continue to take courses in Physical Education and Active Citizenship (including Information Technology).

In the Sixth Form all students take four mainstream subjects to AS level in the Lower Sixth, as well as AS level General Studies. Key skills are acquired through both mainstream subjects and General Studies. In the Upper Sixth students may continue with 3 or 4 A2 courses or continue with 3 A2 courses and begin a new AS course. A2 General Studies may be taken so that a full A level can be awarded. All the subjects on offer at GCSE can be studied in the Sixth Form, as well as Economics, Politics, Computer Studies. Sixth formers also take Games options and, as part of their General Studies, attend weekly lectures to stimulate discussion and have sessions on Careers guidance, Cultural History, Moral and Political Education, Personal and Social Education, etc. In the Lower Sixth most private study is under supervision from subject specialists, but thereafter it may be undertaken in the study room in the Sixth Form Centre or in the Library.

Physical Education and Games. Boys and girls follow a full games programme. In the Autumn Term, Rugby football is the major game for boys, and hockey and netball for girls. In the Lent Term, girls continue with these two sports, whilst the boys play Association Football except for Years 7 & 8 who continue with Rugby. In the Summer Term, cricket is the major boys' sport, whilst the girls participate in tennis and athletics. Other sports are pursued with enthusiasm and success, including badminton, basketball, cross-country, squash, swimming, tennis and water-polo. There is a full programme of fixtures at the weekend including matches at B & C levels, giving many pupils the opportunity to represent the school. The PE programme is now supported with the addition of GCSE and A level PE. The Sports Centre comprises a covered 25 metre pool, 2 multi-gyms, a large hall, equipped with cricket nets and six badminton courts. A recent addition has been three new all-weather tennis/netball courts. In close proximity is the Leathersellers playing field, owned by the school and offering 4 games pitches, a cricket square and pavilion. The Old Colfeians Sports Ground and clubhouse is also nearby and offers additional sporting facilities, including 2 squash courts used by the school.

More than half the School are involved in musical activities. The Orchestra, Second Orchestra, Chamber Orchestra, Band, Wind Ensemble, Brass Group, Recorder Groups and Chamber Groups provide the opportunities for the instrumentalists taught by visiting teachers for all orchestral and key board instruments. The School Choir is augmented by parents, staff and OCs and combines with other schools, some on exchange from overseas, for performances at the Royal Albert Hall and other major concert halls. Recently music tours have been undertaken to South Africa, USA, Germany & France. Services are sung at Cathedrals during vacations. The Male Voice Group and other groups compete in Music festivals. Musicals are performed in cooperation with the Drama department. In the Autumn, the Main School play alternates annually with a musical production; in the Spring, House drama competition is held; and in the Summer, a Junior Players' Production. Drama and Music are an important part of the curriculum.

The Art Department organises an annual exhibition of work of pupils and local artists. Along with Design Technology it provides facilities for a wide range of practical activities. Societies cater for most of the interests of Colfeians and the CCF is particularly active in its new headquarters.

The Careers staff arrange conventions, interviews and visits. They have a good library and interview rooms, and teach in the general studies programme.

A School Chaplain coordinates the school's religious activities including daily assemblies and visiting preachers. There is a lively Christian Union.

Scholarships. The Leathersellers' Company, the Colfe Foundation, the Colfe Charitable Trust and other benefactors provide scholarships, bursaries and exhibitions. 5 Leaving Exhibitions are awarded by Leathersellers to students going on to university.

Fees. The Senior School Fee is £2,554. The Preparatory School Fee is £1,968

Preparatory School. The Preparatory School building, with splendid facilities, was opened by HRH Prince Michael of Kent in 1988. Specialist rooms of the Senior School are also used. While the curricular emphasis is on high standards in basic Mathematics and English, a wide range of other subjects is taught, including Science and French. There is also a range of activities similar to those enjoyed by the Senior School and all pupils are expected to participate. All pupils proceed to the Senior School if they achieve the qualifying standard.

A co-educational nursery and pre-preparatory school for pupils aged 3 to 7 opened in custom-built accommodation in September 1992.

Old Colfeians Association. Enquiries to the Hon Secretary, Eltham Road, London SE12 8UE. Tel. 01-852 1181.

Charitable status. Colfe's School is a Registered Charity, number 274527. It exists to provide education for boys and girls.

Colston's Collegiate School

Stapleton Bristol BS16 1BJ.
Tel: (0117) 965 5207
Fax: (0117) 958 5652
e-mail: headmaster@colstons.bristol.sch.uk

Colston's School was founded in 1710 by Edward Colston. In September 1991 the School merged with The Collegiate School, Winterbourne, to form Colston's Collegiate School, a co-educational day and boarding school for pupils aged 3 to 18 (boarders from 11). The Estates Governors of the School are The Society of Merchant Venturers, Merchants' Hall, Bristol BS8 3NH.

Motto: *Go, and do thou likewise.*

Governors:

Brigadier H W K Pye (*Chairman*)
Mrs S Avery
J M M Baker
The Rt Rev the Lord Bishop of Bristol
Mrs J Clarke
Mrs F C C Densham
J A Heaford, FCA
J R Hunt
Mrs C Jenkins
R T Johnson, BA, UB
D J Medlock
P J Mitchell
K T Pearce
M C Pitman
R W Smedley, MBE
J M Woolley, BSc
J P Wroughton, MA, PhD, FRHistS

***Headmaster:* D G Crawford**, BA, DLC

Deputy Headmaster: A J Martinovic, BA

Director of Studies: M J Graham, BSc, MSc, MEd

Assistant staff:
Mrs H J Baguley, BA
L R Baguley, BA
W J Barnes, BSc
D J Betterton, BSc
P R Borg, BA
G G Boyce, BA
Mrs J Brighton, BSc
J M Bunce, MA
Miss J L Butters, BA
Mrs A J Chisnell, BA
Mrs D Currie, BA
K Dawson, BA, PhD
N J Drew, BA
Miss C E Elliott-Hunt, BEd
M W E Eyles, BSc
Mrs J Fisher, CertEd
Mrs S Foley, BSc
H Griffiths, CertEd
D A Grove, BA
Mrs G Henderson, BA
I R Holmes, BA, ARCM
P A Jones, BSc
Ms E A M Lane, BMus
Ms A Lester, MA
R D Mardle, BSc
Mrs A A C Marshall, BA
A D E Martin, BSc, PhD
D L Mason, BSc
Mrs J L Poppy, BA
S Pritchard, MA
G S Ricketts, MA
Miss R Shankar, BA
M P B Tayler, CertEd
P T Thornley, BEd
Dr J A Tovey, BA, PhD
Miss A J Troath, BA
S Truscott, BA, DipTh
C R Warren, CertEd
S W A Waters, BA
Miss L J Wight, BEd
Miss C L Wilkinson, BA
N C J Yaxley, BEd

Lower School:
G N Phillips, BEd (*Headmaster of Lower School*)
K Watts, BEd
Miss J Tailby, BEd
Mrs E M Coatsworth, BEd
Mrs A S Phillips, BA, CertEd
Mrs R Powell, LGSM, LLAM

Mrs C E Ricketts, MA	E J Wilson-Smith, BSc
Miss C Bowden, BA	W Barber, BSc
J G Digby, BEd	Mrs N Davies, BEd
C E G Stock, BA	Miss J Swan, BA
Mrs T A Warr, CertEd	Miss F Gillette, BEd
Mrs P M Webley, BA, CertEd	Mrc V C Jones, NNEB
	Mrs C F Bastin, NNEB
Mrs N Whitaker, BA Hons, PGCE	Mrs M Drake
	Mrs J Lloyd, NNEB

Headmaster's Secretary: Miss A M Meade

Lower School Headmaster's Secretary: Mrs R Nowak

School Medical Officer: Dr J Mandeville, MB, BS

Organisation There are approximately 810 pupils in the School, one third of whom are girls. The Lower School, catering for the 3-11 age range, is located on a site adjacent to the main site which accommodates the Middle School (11-13) and the Upper School (13-18). Pastoral care is exercised through a form system up to the age of 13, thereafter through a house system. The Sixth Form of some 140 boys and girls is administered separately.

For details of the Lower School, see the Preparatory School section, Part V of this Book.

Admission. Pupils are admitted to the School at the age of 11+ through the school's own examination or at 13+ through the Common Entrance Examination or the School's own examination. Admission direct into the VIth Form is also quite normal. Scholarships and bursaries are available, including Music Scholarships and Sports Scholarships.

Work. The curriculum is broadly based, avoiding premature specialisation, and is in line with the provisions of the National Curriculum. German, Spanish, Religious Knowledge, Art, Music, Technology and Design Technology are optional subjects. There is a wide choice of A level subjects available in the Sixth Form.

Chapel. Colston's is a Church of England Foundation, and the School Chaplain prepares candidates for Confirmation. Boys and girls of other denominations are also welcomed.

Games and activities. There are over 32 acres of playing fields adjoining the School, which include a Sports Hall, Squash Courts, All-weather pitch and Swimming Pool. Rugby, Cross Country, Cricket, Squash, Hockey, Tennis, Netball and Rounders are the principal games, and the regular adventure activities such as canoeing, camping, sailing and flying are provided by the CCF. Part of one afternoon is devoted to a range of other activities and a scheme which gives opportunities for social service in the neighbourhood and other parts of Bristol.

Music and Drama. Music and Drama play an important part in the life of the School. Plays are produced each term and all pupils have the opportunity to act, produce and to help with staging and lighting. Regular theatre visits are arranged. About one-half learn musical instruments and there is an Orchestra, Dance Band, Brass Band and a variety of Choirs. A Choral Society meets weekly.

Careers. There is ample opportunity for boys and girls to obtain skilled advice on the choice of a career. The School is a member of the Independent Schools Careers Organisation, whose services are available, and the Head of Careers also arranges appointments with the local Youth Employment Officers. Careers Conventions are held and visits arranged to Universities and employers.

Fees. Full Boarders £11,670 pa. Day boys and girls £5,430 pa (excluding lunches).

Modernisation. An extensive building programme has been carried out over the last few years. A new performance hall has been completed and, with the help of lottery funding, a new Swimming Pool is proposed.

Situation. Colston's is ideally situated within the city of Bristol and yet with all its playing fields and facilities on site. Bristol itself offers extensive opportunities in the field of cultural and sporting activities of which the School makes full use, particularly with theatre and concert visits. Road and rail communications are excellent with other parts of the United Kingdom particularly since the School is one mile from junction 2 of the M32. Heathrow can be reached in one and a half hours by road or rail.

The School is large enough to sustain a wide range of activities at a high level and yet small enough for each boy or girl to contribute actively. Every effort is made to provide for, and develop each individual's abilities in academic, cultural and other leisure-time activities.

Charitable status. Colston Hospital Trust is a Registered Charity, number 1079552. Its aims and objectives are the provision of education.

Cranleigh School

Cranleigh Surrey GU6 8QQ.
Tel: (01483) 273666; (01483) 276377 (Headmaster)
Fax: (01483) 267398; (01483) 272696 (Headmaster)

Cranleigh School was founded in 1865.
Motto: *'Ex cultu robur'*.

Visitor: The Rt Revd The Lord Bishop of Winchester

Governing Body:
Chairman: D W M Couper, MA

Dr R Chesser, MA, MB, BChir, MRCP
D G Fowler-Watt, MA, JP
Mrs D G Fowler-Watt
A J Lajtha, MA
M J Meyer, Esq
Dr J M Moore, MA, FRSA, JP
M A McLeod, FRICS
D H Powell, Esq
A Ramsay, AADipl, RIBA
Dr T J Seller, BSc, PhD
His Honour Judge Sleeman
Mrs E Stanton, BSc, ACA
Dr J Stevenson, BA, DPhil
J A V Townsend, MA
Mrs T C van Hasselt, JP
Major General C G C Vyvyan, CB, CBE
D G Westcott, BA, BCL
Dr J C Wilson, MA, PhD

Bursar and Clerk to the Governors: Brigadier M S Rutter-Jerome

Headmaster: **Guy Waller**, MA, MSc, FRSA (Worcester College, Oxford)

Deputy Headmaster: C D Ramsey, MA

Senior Master: C J Allen, MSc, BEd

Headmaster's PA: Mrs J Harradine

Members of Common Room:

M J Abbott, BSc	Mrs J A Childs, BA
I M Allison, MA (*Director of Studies*)	R A Clarke, BA, BPhil
	J R Coleman, MA
Mrs C Allison, BEd	R J Collin, PhD, BSc, CChem, MRCS
R M Allon-Smith, MA (*Careers*)	
	J M Cooke, MA, DipComp
W N Bennett, DipEd	Mrs S D Cooke, BSc
C H D Boddington, BA	D J Cottrell, BA
D R Boggitt, BEng	P J Crosfield, BA
S G Briggs	A D Cunningham, MA, PhD
Miss C A Cameron, BA	

R M Dunnett, MA
T R Fearn, BSc
The Revd J P Frith, BA, DipTheol (*Chaplain*)
Mrs R A Frith, BA
Miss R S Gibson, BTh
Miss S L Greenwood, BA
A J Griffiths, BSc, MSc, DIC, CGeol, FGS (*Housemaster, Cubitt*)
N J R Haddock, MA (*Housemaster, 1 North*)
K D James, LLB
R C E K Kefford, BSc
P J Kemp, BA
R Lailey, MA
P Leggitt, MA
P J Longshaw, MA
T I McConnell-Word, BSc (*Housemaster, 2 North*)
Miss A J McIlwaine, MA (*Director of Drama*)
P A McNiven, DipAD (*Director of Art*)
J C E Mann, BSc, PhD, CBiol, MIBiol (*Head of Science*)
Mrs C E Mayo, MA
R G Mayo, MA, MusB, FRCO (*Director of Music*)
Miss H Meers, BA
R A Morris, BA
D J Morrison-Smith, BSc, PhD
Miss O Mullins, BA
Miss C E Nicholls, MA
S Owen
T C Owen, MA (*Housemaster, 2 & 3 and 1 & 4 South*)
D W S Roques, BA
Mrs P A Selwood, BA
A J Smith, MA (*Master of the Scholars*)
Miss N R Smith, BFA
Miss S M Spencer, BA
C N Staley, BA
J F G Thompson, MA (*Director of Admissions*)
Mrs N Y White, M-ès-L
M P Whitehead, BSc (*Director of IT*)
D C Williams, BSc
A Wilson, BSc
F J Wilson, BSc
M T Wilson, BSc (*Housemaster, Loveday*)
S A H Young, BSc, MSc, PhD

Medical Officer: M J Bundy, MB, BS, DCH, DRCOG, MRCGP

Preparatory School:

Master: M W Roulston, CertEd, BPhil, MEd (University of Ulster)

Assistant Masters:
J D R Adcock, BA, PGCE
T P C Avery, TCert
H R Clesham, MA
R C Gainher, BSc
Mrs S D Gravill, BA, PGCE
M J Halstead, BSc, PGCE
C D Henderson, BA, PGCE
M S F Howard, BA, CertEd
Mrs J S Ironmonger, BA, PGCE
Mrs S Lock, CertEd
P J B Millburn-Fryer, BEd
D A I Murphy, BA
C P St J Perry, BA, PGCE
S A Rigby, BA, PGCE
Mrs J C Robertson, PhD, MMus, BA
J A D Slater, BA, PGCE

Master's Secretary: Mrs G V North

Set in two hundred acres of Surrey farmland, eight miles from Guildford and near to a thriving small town, Cranleigh enjoys a country environment within an hour of London, Heathrow and Gatwick. Founded in 1865 originally as a boys' boarding school, it now has just over 500 pupils, and is fully co-educational, with 120 girls already. The first group of 13 and 14 year-old girls arrived in September 1999 and a new boarding house will open in September 2001, to accommodate increased numbers.

Style. Cranleighans are encouraged to make the most of their varied potential, to relish challenge, to feel they are known as individuals, and to become talented and wise adults, well able to adapt to a fast-changing world. The School aims at least for excellence in academic achievement: its standards are high, but it is not elitist. Most students take three A levels, and over the last five years more than 95% have gone on to University, including one in ten to Oxford or Cambridge. Indeed, in 2000 Cranleigh achieved its best-ever A Level results, and in 1999, its second-best A Level results. In 1999, the School achieved its best-ever GCSE results.

Cranleigh flourishes as a strong boarding community but also welcomes day pupils, who are fully integrated into the Cranleigh community, playing their part in the activities of the Houses and benefiting from the advantages offered. Although the School endeavours to be flexible in order to meet the needs of its day pupils, allowing a choice of leaving times and flexible transport arrangements, day pupils are encouraged to stay for supper and for supervised prep. Day Pupils are cared for by a Day Warden within one of the Houses; the Day Warden of each House works closely with the Housemaster/mistress.

Part of the School's style is a close relationship and mutual respect between Common Room and members of the School (there is a pupil:teacher ratio of 1:8). Members of Common Room live on or near the School campus to remain close to the pupils. Parents are also encouraged to visit the School as often as they can.

House Structure. The House structure provides a strong focus on pastoral care and personal development, and most members of Common Room are attached to Houses. Each House has a resident Housemaster or Housemistress and also a resident Deputy. An individual tutoring system operates to enable each pupil's potential to be realised. Sixth Formers choose their own Tutor.

Developments. Recent projects have included a totally refurbished Music School, a large teaching block for Mathematics; an indoor, heated swimming pool, adjoining the open-air heated one; a new theatre (named after an Old Cranleighan, Vivian Cox); major refurbishments to all boarding houses; a second Astroturf playing field (floodlit); a complete update of the Computing facilities, situated in the heart of the main school building to encourage easy access and use of IT for any subject; new boarding wings for two boarding houses. Advanced plans for 2001 include a Design School, an impressive Sports Hall complex and a new Girls' boarding house.

Religion. The Chapel was built as a central point of the School and Cranleigh maintains its concern to present Christian values as a way of life. Although the School is a Church of England foundation, Chapel services are varied, attracting preachers from all denominations.

Planning for the Future. Cranleigh takes the future of its pupils very seriously. The Old Cranleighan Society enables the current and past boys and girls to maintain lasting links with each other. Cranleigh also aims to retain good contact with the Professions, Industry and Commerce, through links developed as part of the careers advice structure. All pupils are personally assessed at least twice during their time at the School, and this process includes a period of Work Experience at the end of the Upper Fifth year.

Academic Pattern. Our aim is to act within the spirit of the National Curriculum, but to offer more, taking full advantage of our independence and the extra time available to a boarding school. We therefore retain a very broad curriculum in the Fourth Form, and have an options system in the Lower and Upper Fifth Forms which enables a pupil to take between nine and ten GCSE subjects before moving on to A/S Levels in the Sixth Form. We offer three separate Sciences, Double Award Science, and a broadly-based Technology course, as well as giving good linguists the chance to take two foreign languages (with Latin if they wish). In the Sixth Form pupils have a wide choice from about twenty A/S Level subjects. There is no Arts or Science bias.

Work on languages with an emphasis on commercial and colloquial fluency is encouraged for non-specialist linguists, and much use is made of the Language Laboratory. Exchanges take place with pupils in schools in France, Spain and Germany.

We have excellent facilities for Science with an emphasis on experimental work. Technology is catered for by the Electronics, Woodwork (we have our own

Designer-in-Residence) and Engineering Workshops, which also provide extra-curricular hobby and recreational facilities. Information Technology is incorporated into the teaching of **all** other subjects, each academic department having its own IT policy, with overall co-ordination by the Director of IT. There are three teaching rooms of networked PCs and every House and academic department have PCs available for use, all linked to the School's network and the Internet.

All members of the Sixth Form participate in a "Societies" (General Studies) programme and attend a regular lecture series to help broaden their education. The proximity of Cranleigh to London allows frequent attendance at professional theatre, music and opera productions.

Arts and Recreation. Cranleigh has for many years maintained a high reputation for Music: a large staff and generous Scholarships have ensured good results in public examinations and high standards in public concerts including world-famous performers like Evelyn Glennie. We send Choral and Organ Scholars to Oxford, Cambridge and major Music Departments and Colleges elsewhere; and boys and girls successfully take part in national competitions. Over a third of the School learns a musical instrument. Keyboard players have access to a fine Grant Degens and Bradbeer tracker-action organ and to a Steinway concert grand piano.

There is also a strong theatre tradition with about ten productions a year including House plays and foreign language plays. Many of these productions are directed by pupils. Large-scale productions take place in the newly-refurbished Speech Hall, to which is linked the new Vivian Cox Theatre.

The Art School offers a wide range of disciplines in drawing and painting, sculpture, printmaking and ceramics; the studios are open every day and the Sixth Form have their own studio. Frequent use is made of slides, and art history visits are made to London and abroad. There is a variety of exhibitions throughout the academic year, culminating in the Upper Sixth Exhibition. The Department is staffed by practising artists.

Games are played seriously but not obsessively, and high standards have been maintained, despite the diversification by which we seek to offer real choice to pupils. The main school games are Rugby in the Michaelmas Term, Hockey in the Lent Term and Cricket, Tennis, Athletics and Swimming in the Summer Term. Many also play Squash, Fives, Golf and other sports include Soccer, Badminton, Cross-country, Fencing, Shooting, Clay Pigeon Shooting, Polo, Fly-fishing and Karate. The School has its own riding stables and there is also a nine-hole Golf course within the estate. The more serious golfers have access to a high-quality 18-hole course within five minutes of the school. We have two artificial grass surfaces (one floodlit) to provide Hockey pitches and twelve match-quality Tennis courts. There is a wide-ranging games programme for girls including Hockey, Netball and Lacrosse. In recent years a girls' Hockey team has toured Australia, our Rugby players have been to Canada and our highly successful cricket team toured South Africa; most recently our Junior Colts Hockey side toured Holland. In 2001, a rugby tour to South America, and a girls' netball and hockey tour to South Africa, will take place. Several of our current pupils are internationals, or national champions, in their age-groups: including current England School Rugby and Hockey Internationals. We also have an Athletics National Champion.

One afternoon each week is kept free for 'service' activities. Boys and girls may join the CCF and learn shooting, adventure training techniques and go on expeditions and visits to military units. Regular weekend adventure training trips take place; and there is also a Fire Brigade Section, fully-trained and equipped with its own fire engine. Other options are offered, including Community Service or Ecology, but all are designed to focus pupils' thoughts on others beyond the school.

Cranleigh is indeed well situated to serve the local community and the world outside School. The best example of this is the PHAB (physically-handicapped and able-bodied) course, a residential event held at the School. Cranleighans help old people in their homes and also have links with local schools for children with learning difficulties and with a home for mentally retarded adults. Many Houses raise money to subsidise the education of children in the Third World. We also sponsor five leavers each year to teach in the developing world as part of the Schools Partnership Worldwide Scheme.

Admission and Registration. Parents wishing to enquire about places at the School should write to the Headmaster's PA for the detailed Prospectus. If you wish to visit the School, the Headmaster would be delighted to welcome you, and you should make an appointment by telephoning 01483 273666. Pupils are admitted in September between the ages of 13 and 14 via the Common Entrance or the Scholarship examination. There may be vacancies at other levels and there is a regular intake at Sixth Form level. Entrance at Sixth Form level is by interview and/or the Sixth Form Scholarship examination.

Scholarships (*see* Entrance Scholarship section) **and Allowances.** The Master of the Scholars has responsibility for all Scholars, who are members of their Houses and attend normal lessons. Scholars have an additional programme throughout their time at the school which covers a wide variety of cultural, academic, social and commercial areas beyond the syllabus. All Scholarships and Exhibitions awarded will be fees linked. The following Scholarships for entrance at age thirteen are offered for competition annually: four of half fees and nine other awards of up to one-quarter fees (one may be reserved as an Art Scholarship if a suitable candidate comes forward; one will be reserved for a candidate of high ability who can contribute significantly to the life of the School) – in certain circumstances, special consideration may be given to children of public servants, members of the armed forces and the clergy of the Church of England; one or two Music awards of half-fees and two Music awards of up to one-quarter fees depending on the merit of candidates (Music awards include free musical tuition). In addition, the School offers up to six Academic, one Drama and two Music Scholarships of one-quarter fees to boys and girls entering at LVI level. Within the School, further Scholarships can be awarded to boys and girls not already in possession of an award if their progress merits it. Full details of the Scholarships can be obtained by telephoning 01483 273666.

Fees. £5,500 per term inclusive (as at September 2000); text books are supplied until the Sixth Form where pupils are encouraged to buy their own, so that they may take them on to University. It is the policy of the School to keep extras down to an absolute minimum and limited to such charges as individual music tuition. The fee for day boys is £4,200 per term. A scheme is available for the payment of fees in advance.

Preparatory School. The School has its own Preparatory School and boys and girls are normally admitted at seven or eight, but also at other ages. For further information apply to the Master of the Preparatory School (see Part V).

Charitable status. Cranleigh School is a Registered Charity, number 1070856. It exists to provide education for children aged 13–18 and the Preparatory School for those aged 7–13.

Culford School

Bury St Edmunds Suffolk IP28 6TX.
Tel: 01284 728615.
Fax: 01284 728631.
e-mail: culfordschool@culford.co.uk
website: www.culford.co.uk

Motto: *Viriliter Agite Estote Fortes*

Visitor: The President of the Methodist Conference

Governors:
Sir David Plastow (*Chairman*)
R A Jacklin, MA
Dame M E Kellett-Bowman, DBE, MEP
Lady E Ralphs, CBE, BA, JP
R J Black
Revd M Braddy, MA
S R K Taylor, MA
T J M Keall, MA
R J B Beaney, FRICS, FAAV
C J Hilder
R R McLone, MA, PhD, FIMA
L Bolton
Mrs R J Black
Mrs S E Kohl
G Russell, MA
Professor R Swanston
Revd D Deeks, MA
Revd Dr P Luscombe, MA

***Headmaster:* J S Richardson**, MA (Cantab)

Chaplain: Revd S W Roebuck, BD, FCII

Assistant staff:
A H Morgan, MA (*Deputy Headmaster*)
J W Beatty, MSc, CBiol, MIBiol
Miss J Benfield, BA (*Deputy Head, Curriculum*)
Miss K Bleazard, CertEd (*Housemistress*)
D Bosworth, BSc, PhD
G M Brooks, CertEd
Mrs C Byrne, BA
J M Byrne, MA, PhD
Miss H Coote, MA
Miss A Cope (*Director of Sport*)
Miss D A Copping
Miss J Cossey, BA
R N Cox, BA
Revd P Dainty, BA, BD
R J Davie, BA, BSc, MEd
B Davies, BA
C J Davies, BSc
Mrs K Dearling, CertEd, PE
I C Devlin, BEd
A Dures, BA
Miss M Egan-Smith, BSc
P Eiles, BD
S Eldridge, BSc
Mrs J Fison, BEd
Mrs A G Grinham, BA, LGSM
D P Haselhurst, MA
I E Hobley, BSc (*Senior Master*)
L H Hoggar, BA
Mrs D Hollins, BA
J A Humphries, BA (*Registrar*)
Mrs V O Humphries, BA
Mrs B Hunt, BA
Miss L Leech, BA
R Lovelock, BA
A H Marsh, CertEd
M J Marsh, CertEd (*ICT Technician*)
Mrs L Martin, MA, DipLib (*Librarian*)
Mrs C C Meadows-Smith, BEd
S Nicholson, MA, MBA (*Housemaster*)
Mrs A Parsons, BSc
Miss J R Poole, CertEd
J D Recknell, MA, FRCO (*Director of Music*)
Mrs B Recknell, BA, MA
Mrs L Robinson (*Assistant Librarian/Archivist*)
Mrs M Rolton, CertEd
P S B Salmon, BSc, PhD
M Schofield, BEd (*Housemaster*)
R P Shepperson, CertEd
D C Swann, BSc
Revd P Taylor, CertEd (*Assistant Chaplain*)
N J Tully, BSc
Mrs K Turner, BA
D A Waller, BA, MA (*Dramatist-in-Residence*)
S J Walsh, BEd
I Webber, BSc
Miss H S Wing, BSc

Preparatory School:
D G Kidd, CertEd, FCP (*Headmaster*)
R P Hopper, BA (*Deputy Head*)
Mrs E Rowlands, CertEd (*Senior Mistress*)
Miss J Hatton, BEd (*Director of Studies*)
Mrs P Burton-Hopkins, CertEd
Mrs S B Clark, MA
Mrs D A Copping, CertEd (*Special Needs*)
Miss J Foster (*Girls' Games*)
A P Lawn, CertEd
Mrs M-A Mackenzie, BEd (*Special Needs*)
Mrs A MacMullen, BA (*English Co-ordinator*)
Mrs C Orton, BEd, CertEd (*Housemistress*)
Miss J Scott, CertEd
S G Turton, GRSM, ARMCM, ARCM (*Director of Music*)
Mrs V Wallis Miller, CertEd
J A White, BSc
Miss L Wilson, BSc

Fieldgate House: Pre-Preparatory Department:
Mrs L Blacker, BEd (*Head of Department*)
Mrs K Hopper, CertEd
Mrs J E M Stocker, CertEd
Mrs E Bonnett, CertEd
J Wilford, BA
Mrs J Palmer, BSc (*French*)
Miss H Livermore, BEd (*Nursery Supervisor*)

Peripatetic Music Staff
D Bolton (*Brass*)
Mrs M Carlson (*Violin*)
N Carlson, LRAM, ARCM (*Oboe and Bassoon*)
Mrs C Cass, GTCL, LTCL (*Singing*)
M Cass (*Guitar*)
Mrs K Evans (*Piano*)
Mrs B A Filby, ARCM, LGSM (*Clarinet*) (*Head of Woodwind*)
Mrs S Francis (*'Cello*)
Mrs K Livermore, LRAM (*Violin*) (*Head of Strings*)
B Metcalfe, GNSM (*Double Bass*)
M Pope (*Guitar*)
M Porter, ARCM (*Wind*)
P Robson (*Woodwind*)
Mrs K Thomas
M Westlake (*Percussion*)
Miss J Wright, LTCL, GTCL (*Piano*)

Medical Officer: R Soper, MRCS, LRCP

Bursar: Lt Col M B Woolley, RM

Headmaster's Secretary: Mrs S C Tilly

Number in School. Senior School: 360. Boys 218, Girls 142; Boarders 155, Day pupils 205. Preparatory School: 214. Boys 125, Girls 89; Boarders 52, Day pupils 162. Pre-Prep: 70 boys and girls.

Culford School is situated in a 480-acre landscaped park on the edge of the Breckland, four miles north of Bury St Edmunds and close to the university town of Cambridge.

Founded in 1881 in Bury St Edmunds, the School moved to its present site in 1935. The School is under the overall control of the Board of Management for Methodist Residential Schools, but is administered by a Board of Governors, of whom at least half are members of the Methodist Church.

Culford is a fully coeducational boarding and day school of about 640 pupils within the top 55% of the ability range. There is a clear commitment to excellence in all areas of school life, and hard work in the classroom is complemented by full sporting and extra curricular programmes. Integrity and respect for the individual are encouraged along with a sense of responsibility towards the wider community. Pupils are also given every opportunity to learn to take responsibility both for themselves and others. Well-founded House and tutorial systems ensure that the pastoral care is close and effective and this is made possible by a pupil/staff ratio of approximately 9:1. The School respects its Christian foundation and continues to witness to it, not aggressively but pervasively and distinctly.

The Buildings. The Main building is Culford Hall, an 18th century mansion formerly the seat of Marquis Cornwallis and Earl Cadogan. This building with a blend of Robert Adam and *Louis Seize* interior design, houses the Main Library and Computer Centre, the Workman Library, the Old Assembly Hall, the Music School, the Language Laboratory and administrative offices. Extensive renovation of the upper floors has enhanced the facilities available to several Humanities departments. In addition, the Hartley suite of lecture rooms with new audio-visual facilities and a well-equipped careers library and office have been created.

Set within Culford Hall is the Centenary Hall, opened by the Duke of Gloucester in 1981. This multi-purpose Hall can seat the whole school in comfort, and is extensively used for lectures, concerts, as an examination hall, and for dramatic productions.

Set in close proximity to Culford Hall and the Boarding Houses are the Hastings Building (Mathematics, English) and the Skinner Building (Modern Languages). The Bristol-Myers Biology Building was opened in 1988 and the William R Miller Science Centre in September 2001. Extensive alterations to the Art Block have enabled Food and Nutrition and Textiles to move into new and fully up-to-date rooms, and there is a very good suite of rooms for Art and Pottery. The School also has excellent Design and Technology facilities in the Pringle Centre which was opened in 1990.

In 1985 Fieldgate House was opened. A combination of new and entirely refurbished buildings, it provides pre-preparatory teaching for 70 boys and girls in a delightful setting within the grounds. In 1994 Fieldgate House was extended to incorporate a Nursery.

New boarding houses for middle and senior school pupils were opened in 1973 and 1975; these comprise Robson House for middle school boys, Jocelyn House for middle school girls, and Storey House for sixth form boys and girls. These Houses are set around a landscaped Court, which also includes the Ashby Room, the main Dining Hall and the Kitchens. All the study bedrooms in these Houses are well appointed, including washbasins in each room, and there are good Common Room and recreation facilities. No middle school boarder shares with more than four pupils, and many have twin-bedded rooms. Storey House accommodation is in either twin or single rooms and a Sixth Form Study Centre is an integral part of the House. Cadogan House for junior boys and girls also offers very good facilities, especially for activities and recreation. Each House is run by a Housemaster or Housemistress, assisted by resident and non-resident staff and a Matron.

A fully-equipped Medical Centre, supervised by a resident SRN, was opened in 1985. The School also has a Tuck Shop and a Nearly-New Uniform Shop.

A new Sports Centre, comprising a 25-metre pool, three Squash Courts, Sports Hall and changing facilities, was opened in Summer 1991.

Games. The School is set in a 480-acre park of great beauty landscaped by Humphry Repton, and there are ample facilities for physical recreation. The grass Hockey pitches are among the finest in the region, and the 1st XI Cricket pitch has been described as one of the most beautifully sited in the country. The main games are Rugby, Hockey and Cricket for the boys, Hockey, Netball, Tennis and Rounders for the girls. However, many options are available to older pupils including Athletics, Swimming, Canoeing, Squash, Sailing and Golf (at Flempton Golf Club). Riding is popular with junior and middle school girls, and transport is provided to a local riding school. Fishing in the well-stocked lake is a popular weekend pastime.

Curriculum and Organisation. From 8 to 11 most of the teaching is done by form teachers in the Preparatory School, which is set in a Court of classrooms next to Cadogan House, and is administered by its own Headmaster, a member of IAPS. From 11 to 13 a transition to specialist teaching is made. From 13 to 16 there is specialist teaching in all subjects, and pupils choose what they will study to GCSE level from a range of options. Their choice is guided by their House Tutor who, with the Housemaster or Housemistress, has responsibility for their academic and social progress. The Activities House structure involves day and boarding pupils from upper fourth to second year sixth in a full range of academic, sporting and recreational activities.

The aim of the School is to provide a broad and balanced education in line with the National Curriculum, thus ensuring it makes the best of a pupil's academic potential. The Sixth form offers a very wide choice of subjects at A and AS Levels together with one-year courses. All Sixth form students follow a two-year course of General Studies leading to an external examination (several take an 'A' level in General Studies) in addition to specialist work for 'A' level. Oxbridge candidates have special arrangements in the second year sixth. All pupils in the Middle School receive a full and balanced course in Personal and Social Education. The teaching of Information Technology is an integral part of the curriculum and many pupils also make use of the facilities informally.

There is a Parents' Meeting for each year group at least once during the year.

Religion. The School is a Methodist foundation and the resident Chaplain is a Methodist minister, but children of all backgrounds are welcomed. All pupils attend Christian assemblies and all boarders attend a service on Sunday mornings. Pupils are prepared for confirmation into both the Anglican and Methodist Churches in accordance with their parents' wishes. There is also a voluntary Christian discussion group.

Careers. There is a Careers suite including a well-stocked Careers Library, and the School makes use of independent careers advice, including aptitude and diagnostic tests, which are followed by in-depth interviews and counselling by experienced staff.

Music. Music plays an important part in the life of the School. There are many choirs, orchestras and chamber ensembles. Regular concerts are held in order to give pupils of all ages opportunities to perform in public. Individual music tuition is offered in piano, organ and all orchestral instruments.

School Activities. There is an extensive range of clubs and societies including the academic (eg Science and History) the creative (eg Art and Dance) the general (eg Computing and Debating) the practical (all aspects of Design/Technology) and the sporting and outdoor (eg Duke of Edinburgh and minor sports). The School also has an expanding audio visual facility. Drama is very strong, including House plays as well as major productions: these include regular musicals and plays for different sections of the school. The School arranges a varied programme of lectures and recitals of general interest. Many pupils participate in the Duke of Edinburgh's Award Scheme and in the School's own Culford Award Scheme.

The four Activities Houses (Floyd, Honess, Leigh and Newman) are each led by a member of staff and sixth-form House Captains; over 30 varied events contribute to the awarding of the David Anderson Shield each year.

Pupils in the upper fourth (Year 9) and above are encouraged to take part in Community Service Activities, which cover a wide range of services to the School and the local community. In addition there are sponsored activities in support of local and national charities.

Members of staff regularly take pupils on visits and expeditions. All departments take pupils on shorter visits, go to day conferences and theatre visits or invite visiting speakers. Recent expeditions include Russia, Borneo and the Himalayas, winter skiing in France, Switzerland and the USA (separate parties for junior and senior pupils), and sports tours in the United Kingdom, Europe and Australia.

Entrance. (*see* Entrance Scholarship section) The School holds its own entrance examinations between January and March. Pupils from Preparatory Schools may take the Common Entrance Examination. Scholarship examinations for entry at 8+, 11+, 13+ and 16+ are held in February and March. The Culford Assisted Places' Scheme (CAPS) has been instituted. Details may be obtained from the Admissions Office.

Fees. On application to the Headmaster's Secretary.

Forms. *VIth Form.*

Middle School. Upper IV, Lower V, Upper V.

Preparatory School. I, Lower II, Upper II, III and Lower IV.

Pre-Preparatory (4 classes plus Nursery class).

Old Culfordians' Association. Chairman of OCA, c/o Culford School.

Charitable status. Culford School is a Registered Charity, number 310486. It exists to provide education for boys and girls.

Dame Allan's Boys' School

Fenham Newcastle upon Tyne NE4 9YJ.
Tel: (0191) 2750608. Bursar: (0191) 2745910
Fax: School: (0191) 2745428; Bursar: (0191) 2747684
website: www.dameallans.newcastle.sch.uk

The School was founded in 1705 by Dame Eleanor Allan and in 1935 was moved to Fenham on a site of 13 acres.

Governors:
Chairman: Mrs D J Salmon
Vice-Chairman: Mr G S Brown

Ex-Officio:
The Lord Mayor of Newcastle upon Tyne
The Provost of Newcastle upon Tyne
The Vicar of the Parish of St John

Miss M Foster, BA, FRGS
Mr C J Hilton, MA
Dr J A Hellen, MA, DPhil
Mr M Bird
Mrs M E Slater
Prof P D Manning
Mr W Miles, MA, LLM
Mr L Cassie, MA, MEng
Mr T St A Warde-Aldam
Mrs M Kindred
Mr G Smith
Mr E Ward

Clerk to the Governors and Bursar: J Fleck, ACMA

***Principal:* Mr D W Welsh**, MA

Vice Principal: Mr W J Lomas, MA
Director of Admissions: Mr S N Hamilton, MA (*Pupil Administration*)
Head of Sixth Form: Mrs E J Hilton, BSc, AHA, MEd
Assistant Head of Sixth Form: Mr D C Henry, BSc
In addition there are 35 full-time members of staff

There are approximately 500 boys in the School, which has a three form entry of some 60 boys at 11+. With the Girls' School, which is in the same building, it shares a mixed Sixth Form and a mixed Junior Department (8+–10+).

The Main School follows the normal range of subjects, leading to examination at GCSE. German is introduced in Year 8.

Most boys stay on into the Sixth Form and from there normally go on to Higher Education.

Buildings. In the last 6 years developments have included a Sports Hall, new Science Laboratories, additional classrooms, Computer Resource Centre, Sixth Form Centre, Technology Centre.

School Societies. The current list includes: outdoor pursuits (including Duke of Edinburgh scheme and orienteering), choirs, orchestra, drama, computing, art, chess, Christian Fellowship, Amnesty International, history, science, electronics, mathematics, dance, public speaking, debating and desktop publishing.

Pastoral. Each boy is placed in the care of a Form Teacher who oversees his progress and development. In the Sixth Form he has a Tutor who is responsible for both academic and pastoral care.

Careers. There is a structured programme, beginning in Year 10.

Sixth Form. In 1989 the Sixth Form was merged with that of our Sister school, giving both Schools the rare constitution of single-sex education (11-16) with a co-educational Sixth Form. The Head of Sixth Form is Mrs E J Hilton who will welcome inquiries concerning admission.

Games. The principal games are Rugby Football and Cricket. The School playing field adjoins the premises, and the School has the use of additional fields, all-weather surfaces and tennis courts nearby. Cross-Country, Swimming and Athletics are also available. Hockey and Tennis are introduced as options from Year 9 and older boys may also participate in a range of other sporting activities.

Admission. Governors' Entrance Scholarships are awarded on the results of the Entrance Examinations held annually in the Spring Term at all ages from 8+ to 13+. Bursaries are available to pupils aged 11+ and over on entry.

Fees. Full fee: £5,022 per annum; Junior Department: £3,954 per annum.

Dame Allan's Old Boys' Association. Hon Secretary: Mr W Armstrong, 17 Bamburgh Grove, Jarrow, Tyne & Wear NE32 5QQ.

Charitable status. Dame Allan's Schools is a Registered Charity, number 1084965. It exists to provide education for children.

Daniel Stewart's and Melville College

Queensferry Road Edinburgh EH4 3EZ.
Tel: 0131-332 7925.
Fax: 0131-343 2432
e-mail: schoolsecretary@stewarts-melville.edin.sch.uk

'Daniel Stewart's Hospital' was founded (1855) by Daniel Stewart and has been administered since its inception by the Company of Merchants of the City of Edinburgh. It was transformed into a day school in 1870.

Melville College, formerly The Edinburgh Institution, was founded in 1832 by the Reverend Robert Cunningham.

The two schools combined in 1972 to form Daniel Stewart's and Melville College. Since 1989 management of the School has been delegated by the Merchant Company Education Board to the Erskine Stewart's Melville Governing Council. In a unique arrangement this Governing Council also administers The Mary Erskine School, as well as the combined Mary Erskine and Stewart's Melville Junior School.

The Principal is directly responsible for both senior schools. This facilitates a common academic policy and much extra-curricular collaboration between the two schools. There is a fully co-educational Sixth Form with facilities at both senior schools. All girls and boys are members of a 'twinned' House structure and girls are jointly involved in choirs, orchestras and dramatic productions. The combined Form III enjoys an eight-day programmme of outdoor education based on Carbisdale Castle, Sutherland and over 100 girls participate in the Stewart's Melville Combined Cadet Force.

Governing Council:

Chairman: Iain Gotts

Members:
The Revd Dr Russell Barr
Mrs Monica Cameron
Andrew Dobson
Mrs Fiona McLaren
Graeme Millar
Ms Elizabeth Milligan
Steven Paterson
Alan Robertson
Mrs Judy Wagner
Mrs Janice Webster

Clerk to the Governors: John N Kerr

***Principal:* J N D Gray**, BA

Bursar: F C H McLeod, CA

Operations Director: G R S Wilson, MA

Senior School:

Deputy Headmaster: N G Clark, MA

Director of Studies: D W A McDiarmid, BSc, DipEd

Head of Forms II-V: D G Girdwood, BSc, MEd

Assistant Head Teacher, Guidance: G J Brown, BEd

†J C Allan, BA
R G Allan, BEd
Ms P J Ambrose, BSc
*R M Askew, BA, BMus
*C R Bagnall, MA
S Basu, BA, MA
L C Benzies, BSc
D A Brett, BSc
*Mrs M Brown, MA, DipEdPsyc
M R Burgess, BA(Ed)
Mrs C Burns, BA
*M J Carrington, BSc
Dr E L Clement, BA, BMus
*A S Cochrane, BSc, MSc
M Constable, BA
*I Crosbie, MA
Dr M G Davies, BA (Hons), PhD
*Mrs M Douglas, DA
B W J Dunlop, BSc
A J T Dunsmore, BEng, MSc
Mrs E P Elder, MA, MLitt
D G Ellis, BEd
Mrs M M Elswood, BA, Dip TESL
Z Fazlic, BA
†M T Garden, BA
*M Z Hamid, MA
S Hart, MA
Mrs V Higson, BSc, DipSpld, AMBDA
A J Hyslop, MA
P Johnson, BSc
G Johnston, MPhys
Ms B M Jones, MA, PhD
†M Kane, MA
Mrs L A Lim, BSc
B G Lockie, BEd
M Longmuir, BA, CAM
Miss J Macdonald, BSc
I Maciver, BA, NDD
Miss J D McIntosh, MA
Mrs R E McKee, MA
G A McKenzie, BEd
H I McKerrow, BSc
M J McLaughlin, BA, MA
*A K J Macnaughton, MA
Mrs A Mallon, MA
*R E Mannifield, MA, MEd
J F Marsh, BA
Mrs C G C Maxwell, BA
*G Millar, BSc, MInstP, CPhys
*R D Miller, BSc, CBiol, MIBiol
G W Mitchell, BSc
C A Nasmyth, BA
Miss C Norman, BSc(Hons)
†D A Orem, MA, MPhil, Certificate in Media Education
G F W Park, BD
Miss C-L Paterson, BA
T Paxton
Mrs J Pollock, MA
†S W Primrose, BSc
†J J Robertson, BSc
D A Roxburgh, BEd
A J Samson, Dip RSAMD
A Scott, BEng (Hons)
P M Shaw, BSc, MPhil
S W Shepherd, BA, DipEd
Mrs C R Siljehag, MA
*C S Spence, BEd
J D Stephenson, MA
*C I Tait, MA
Miss S Thompson, MA
A Thomson, BA
P G M Waine, CertEd, BEd
A A Walkey, BSc, MSc
Miss A Wallace, MA
J A Weatherby, BCom, BEd
A D Weir, BSc
E J Wilkins, BSc, MSc, PhD, MRSC, CChem
Ms J Williams, BA, UED
*R W Willis, DTE, HNC
*D J Wood, MA, MEd

The Mary Erskine and Stewart's Melville Junior School:

Head Master: Mr B D Lewis, MA

Deputy Head (Primary 4-7): Mrs L Greer, MA, PGCE

Deputy Head (Early Education): Mrs M Rycroft, DPE

Mrs W Ainge, MA, PGCE
R Allison, BA, PGCE
Mrs A Armstrong, BA, PGCE
Mrs S Bownes, BSc, PGCE
Mrs A Bruff, DCE
Mrs S Brown, DPE
Miss K Buchanan, BA, PGCE
Miss P Campbell, BA, PGCE
Mrs M H Cochrane, DCE
Mrs G Cursiter, DCE
Miss E Day, BSc, PGCE
P Dorman, DPE, DCE
Mrs F Drew, MA, PGCE
Miss H Drummond, DipPrimEd
Mrs J Duffy, BEd
Miss L Gallagher, MA, PGCE
Miss J Graham, BEd
Mrs C Gray, DPE, DipRSA
Miss C Hartley, DipEd
Mrs T Hopkins-Brown, BA, PGCE
R J Howden, BA DCE
C Johnston, LLB(Hons), PGCE
Mrs F Johnston, BEd
Mrs E Karolyi, MA, PGCE
Mrs E M Kelly, MA, PGCE
Mrs L Kibble, BEd
Mrs V Lewis, MA, PGCE
Mrs A Lydon, BA(Ed), MA(Ed)
Mrs G Lyon, DipEd
Miss S M Mackay, MA, PGCE
Mrs K MacArthur, MA, PGCE
P R MacKenzie, BA (*Hons*), MPhil, PGCE
Miss A McCabe, BEd
Mrs S McCarter, DipEd
Mrs E G McLauchlan, DCE
D J McLeish, DCE
Mrs G MacRae, MA, PGCE
Miss A R McVey, DCE
Mrs C Melville, CertEd
Mrs J Melvin, CertEd
Mrs M A B Milne, DCE
Mrs C Morrison, BA, PGCE
S Morrison, BSc, PGCE
Mrs H Pennycook, SNNEB
Mrs S Phillips, MA, BEd
Mrs M Rodgers, DCE
Mrs S Ross, LLB, DLP, PGCE
Mrs M Rycroft, DPE
Mrs S Semple, NNEB
Mrs C Sharp, BEd
Miss A Sim, BMus, PGCE
Mrs S Spiers, BEd, PGCE
Miss K Standley, BA, PGCE
Miss J Sweeney, BA, PGCE
P J Syme, DCE
Mrs E B Tait, DCE
Mrs C Timons, SNNEB
A R Tinniswood, DCE
Miss G Torrie, BEd
Mrs P M Tulloch, ALAM
Miss R Warrender, BEd
Mrs I Williams, TEFL
Miss J Wilson, BEd
Miss M Wilson, BEd
A Witherspoon, BEd
Mrs C Witherspoon, DCE

The Mary Erskine & Stewart's Melville Junior School (1152 pupils). Girls and boys are educated together from 3-12. Children in Primary Start (formerly the Nursery) and in Primary 1-3 are based on the Mary Erskine School site at Ravelston, while boys and girls from Primary 4 to 7 are taught on the Stewart's Melville site. Normal entry points are Nursery, Primary 1, Primary 4, Primary 6 and Primary 7 but there are always a few places available for each year-group at the start of the session. The school is remarkable for the breadth of its educational programme and the quality of its cultural activities.

The Senior School (785 boys). Forms I and II follow a broad curriculum, whereby boys are equipped to pursue all routes to Standard Grade. In Form III boys commence eight Standard Grade courses, including English, mathematics, at least one modern language, at least one science, and a "humanities" subject. In Form V boys are expected to take 5 subjects at Higher level. A majority will continue their studies for a Sixth Year, usually three Advanced Highers to provide a firm foundation for degree courses in Scotland and England. Most boys proceed to such courses.

The School enjoys a commanding position on the Queensferry Road, a mile from the West End of Princes Street. The original College building is occupied mainly by the Senior School while the Junior School is in a modern building. There is a well-equipped Science block and recent additions include a Games Hall, and Dining Accommodation. In 1991 a state-of-the-art Technology Centre was opened by HRH Prince Philip, The Duke of Edinburgh and a new swimming pool and Sixth Form Centre have recently been completed.

The School has a sophisticated system of guidance. Boys in the first year are with a Form Tutor, under the overall direction of an Assistant Head Teacher. The next four years in the Upper School are spent in Houses of approximately 90 boys, each with its own Head of House and House Tutors. Form VI is a co-educational year, as the girls from The Mary Erskine School join with the boys of Stewart's Melville College in a completely 'twinned' Sixth Year. There is a well-established Careers department. The Learning Resource Co-ordinator helps boys with specific learning difficulties.

Games. Rugby and Cricket are played on the school playing fields at Inverleith, while Hockey and Tennis are played at Ravelston. There are also opportunities for Athletics, Curling, Golf, Swimming, Squash, Sailing and Shooting as well as the many sports played in the Games Hall. Boys from the school are frequently selected for national teams in many sports.

Music is much-valued and flourishes within the school. Approximately 500 instrumental lessons are given each week by an enthusiastic staff of 25 visiting teachers. Most orchestral activity is combined with The Mary Erskine School, including a junior orchestra of 100, middle and senior orchestras of 50 each, two concert bands, a jazz band and numerous chamber groups. Choral singing is also very strong, from large junior choirs to more specialised groups for madrigals and close harmony. A full programme of public performances includes two major musicals every year and large choral and orchestral concerts in which our musicians combine with an active parents' choir. Notable recent ventures include the staging of Noye's Fludde with over 600 performers drawn from the senior and junior schools. The Concert Band was involved in an exchange visit to Prague in March 1998 and toured Spain in 2000.

Activities. The Combined Cadet Force comprises both Army and RAF sections. The School Shooting VIII competes annually at Bisley and the Pipe Band enjoys an international reputation. Instruction in piping and drumming is provided for members of the CCF and for younger boys. The School encourages boys to take part in the Duke of Edinburgh's Award Scheme, in hill walking and in other outdoor activities.

Each week the School offers a very wide variety of clubs and societies to suit the appetites of all boys. Debating is particularly popular with senior teams reaching the finals of four UK competitions in 2000. In sport the school has particular strengths in rugby, swimming, basketball, hockey, athletics and skiing with representation at district or national level.

Fees. Termly tuition fees range from £929 (Nursery) to £1,818 (Senior). A full school lunch is provided for all boys who opt for it, in which case an adjusted composite fee is charged to parents. Funds for means-tested bursaries are available, particulars of which may be obtained from The Bursar.

Boarding. Dean Park House, adjoining the school grounds, serves as the boarding house for approximately 35 boys. They share dining and recreational facilities with The Mary Erskine boarders next door in Erskine House. The senior school boarding-and-tuition fee is £3,808 per term.

Entrance Scholarships. There are two Merchant Company Appeal Scholarships of up to 50% of fees and, typically, four Merchant Company Schools Appeal Bursaries of a maximum value of 30% of fees. Music Scholarships and Awards are also available to talented musicians.

Means-tested Bursaries. The school offers means-tested Bursaries to pupils who would otherwise not be able to attend. These are funded by the Melville College Trust.

Daniel Stewart's & Melville College Former Pupils' Club. *Hon Sec:* Dr E J Wilkins, c/o Stewart's Melville College, Queensferry Road, Edinburgh, EH4 3EZ

Charitable status. The Merchant Company Education Board is a Registered Charity, number Ed CR4 551A. It is a leading charitable School in the field of Junior and Secondary education.

Dauntsey's School

West Lavington Nr Devizes Wiltshire SN10 4HE.
Tel: (01380) 814500
Fax: (01380) 814501
e-mail: information@dauntseys.wilts.sch.uk
website: www.dauntseys.wilts.sch.uk

Founded in 1542 by Alderman William Dauntesey of the Mercers' Company. New School buildings erected in 1895 and extended regularly from 1919 to the present.

Governors:
Chairman: R E J Bernays, Esq, DL
Lady J Benson, OBE, JP (*Vice-Chairman*)
J P G Wathen, Esq
Lt General Sir Maurice Johnston, KCB, OBE, LL
Prof L M Harwood, MA, BSc, MSc, PhD, CChem, FRSC
D C Watney, Esq
Mrs D J Main
H E Harris, MA, PhD, (University of Cambridge)
The Hon T J Palmer
Air Chief Marshal Sir Joseph Gilbert, KCB, CBE, BA, LLD, RAF (retd)
Mrs M Clough
M J H Liversidge, Esq, BA, FSA, FASA
Mrs C Samuel, CBE
Major R P Matters
J A Rendell, Esq, BSc, FCA
A S Macpherson, Esq, BA (Hons), ACA, JP
The Rt Revd P F Hullah
The Hon Mrs H W Palmer

Clerk to the Governors: P F Wyles, MA

***Head Master:* Stewart Roberts**, MA

Staff:
B M Hughes, BSc (*Second Master*)
Mrs J F E Upton, BSc (*Deputy Head*)
J P Rushworth, BA
A S Whitney, BA, JP (*Registrar*)
R D M Dunn, BA
M B Ritchley, BSc
R G D Price, MA
P F B Barnard, BSc, PhD
M A C Neve, BSc (*Director of Studies*)
A J Hatcher, BSc
M K F Johnson, MA
W J Corke, BSc, CBiol, MIBiol
M K Dolan, MA
R H Priest, MA, MEd, CChem, MRSC
I L Hanson, CertEd
S J Hardman, BEd
Mrs S M Nethercott, MSc
Mrs S J Corke, BSc
Mrs H M Rushworth, BSc
Mrs W M Smith, ATD

A M Lees, MA
Mrs A K Smith, MA
A C C Cooper, MA
T S L Gardiner, BA
G R Parry, BSc
Mrs C V Wakefield, BA
Mrs S Woods, BSc, CBiol, MIBiol
P F Charters, BA, BPhil
Mrs M E Charters, BA
Miss E S Conidaris, HDipEd (PE)
Mrs N-J Wingham, MA, RCA
Mrs K M Phipps, BA
Mrs L Lloyd-Jukes, BA
Mrs E C Gardiner, BA
P K Wheatley, MA
T R Marris (*Sailing Master*)
Mrs J D Thomas, BEd
N Yates, BSc, MSc
Mrs E K Wiesenmüller, MA
B A M Vessey, BA
Miss J E Dalton, BA
Miss S Cooke, BA
J P Plews, BA
Miss M Akakios, BA
Mrs E A Urquhart, CertEd, DipRSA, AMBDA
Mrs P Morrison, BEd
A J Palmer, BSc
T J Price, MA, DPhil
Revd O J D Bayley, MA
Miss L Scrace, BA (PE), HDE
Miss E Davies, BA
L Hedges, BA
J F O'Hanlon, BSc
Mrs C Coupe, BEd
Mrs L Cook, BA, LGSM
Miss K J Evans, BA
T Fitzsimmons, BEd
J R Hunt, BA
The Revd A P Jeans, BTh, MIBC
Miss S Pullen, BA
Miss C Swinbank
R A Allfree-Reid, BA
D James, PhD
Mrs R M Keen, BSc
A J Lewis, BSc
A Pickford, BA
Mrs A Abbatt, BA
K Brewer, BA, QTS
R C F Campbell, MSc
M A T Harrison, BSc
J J Hutchinson, BSc
Lady M Milverton, BD
M Olsen, BA
Mrs M C Siggers
Mrs J Priestley, BSc
Mrs C E Maggs, BA
M R Dyson, BEd
D Morton, BA
Miss K M Watts, BA
Miss A M Dunn, BSc
Mrs S Somerville, BSc

Music
C B Thompson, GMus (*Director*)
N J Hale, MA (*Assistant Director*)
Mrs D Thompson, GMus (*Double Bass*)
Mrs C Brown, CertEd, LRAM, BPdeCh (*Singing*)
Mrs G Alford, BA (*Oboe*)
Sqn Ldr G J A Kerr, AFC, ALCM, CertEd (*Guitar*)
Mrs L A Hatcher, (*Flute*)
P Skelton, BA, LRAM (*Piano*)
Miss R Jardine, BA, MTC, ALCM (*Brass*)
Mrs K Alder, BSc, LRSM (*Piano*)
Mrs M J Skelton, BA, LRAM, LTCL (*Piano*)
A D Stockley, LGSM (*Percussion*)
T C Richards, ARCM (*Violin and Viola*)
S Cippola, ERNCM, PPRNCM (*Clarinet and Saxophone*)
Mrs P M Jones, BA, CertEd, LRAM (*Piano*)
S J Kerr (*Electric Guitar*)
D R Kniveton, BA, LTCL (*Flute*)
Miss J A Britton, LWCMD, LTCL (*Clarinet and Saxophone*)
Miss J J Broome, MA (*Harp*)

Houses and Housemasters/Housemistresses:

Upper School:
Evans: Mr & Mrs N Yates
Farmer: Mr J F O'Hanlon
Fitzmaurice: Mr & Mrs A J Hatcher
Hemens: Mr R G D Price
Jeanne: Mr & Mrs R D M Dunn
King-Reynolds: Mrs S M Nethercott
Lambert: Mrs K M Phipps
Mercers: Mr & Mrs S J Hardman

Lower School:
Manor: Mr & Mrs B A M Vessey
Forbes: Mr J P Plews
Rendell: Mrs A K Smith
Scott: Mrs S J Corke

Medical Officers: D A N Twiner, MB, BS (*Lond*), MRCS (*Eng*), LRCP (*Lond*)
B J Jones, MA, FRCS, DRCDG

Bursar: Group Captain H K W Middleton, BA, RAF(Ret'd)

Assistant Bursar: P W Hagelthorn, Esq

Head Master's Secretary: Mrs S Walters

Sanatorium Sister: Sister I A Richardson

Number. 675 Pupils aged between 11–18 years: 211 day boys, 155 boarding boys; 197 day girls, 112 boarding girls.

Residence. On entering the School at 11 or 13 pupils are in the Lower School where they stay until they reach the end of Year 9. They then move into the Senior School Houses. Half the Houses are for boarders and the other half for day pupils.

Situation. The School is pleasantly situated in its own grounds, of over 100 acres. The Manor House, a mansion in its own park, woodland and playing fields, is the Junior boarding house for pupils in Years 7–9.

Recent Developments. Generous benefactions by the Mercers' Company and the Farmer Trust, and the generosity of parents and Old Dauntseians, have made possible the following additions: Memorial Hall which includes the Chapel; Music School; new Biology Laboratories. A block of Physics and Chemistry laboratories was built with the help of the Industrial Fund for the Advancement of the Teaching of Science and significantly extended in 1989. A Senior Girls' Boarding House opened in 1977 and was completely extended in 1988. The Tedder Building came into use in September 1979, providing language rooms, computer rooms and lecture theatre. The Awdry Sports Hall was built in 1980 and next to it a 25-metre Indoor Heated Swimming Pool was opened in 1985. The Design and Technology Centre was opened in 1987 and in 1989 the Mathematics, Biology and Physics Departments were extended with new buildings with the assistance of a major grant from the Wolfson Foundation. A new Senior Boys' Boarding House opened in September 1991. An all-weather floodlit playing surface was completed during 1992, and another Senior Boys' Boarding House was extended in 1993 to accommodate additional demand for boarding places. In 1995 there were major extensions to the Music and Dining facilities, and in 1996 a second senior girls' boarding house was opened. During 1999 a 5-Studio Art Centre opened, and in the summer of 2000 a new Library and Study Centre (including IT stations) opened.

Curriculum. The School is modern in its outlook and affords wide facilities. Briefly the curriculum (i) provides a good general education which includes Religious Education, English, History, Geography, Economics, French, German, Latin, Greek, Russian, Pure and Applied Mathematics, Physics, Chemistry, Biology, Information Technology, Music, Art, Craft, Design, Technology; (ii) prepares for the General Certificate of Secondary Education, Advanced Subsidiary and Advanced Levels and University Entrance.

Games. The major sports are Rugby Football, Hockey, Cricket and Netball. Other games played include Tennis, Squash, Athletics, Swimming, Water Polo, Fencing and Badminton. Special attention is given to Physical Education.

Societies and other Activities. The following Societies have regular meetings: Science, History, Literature, Dramatic, Music, Dance, Art, Natural History, Debating, Information Technology, Electronics, Juggling, Bee Keepers and Adventure Club.

The Sailing Club provides ocean sailing and racing in the famous yacht 'Jolie Brise'. (Winner of trans-Atlantic Tall Ships 2000).

All pupils in Year 9 are members of the 'Moonrakers',

an outward-bound organisation providing specific courses and activities.

Fees. Boarders £14,025 pa; Day Pupils £8,490 pa. There are no compulsory extras.

Admission. Boys and girls are admitted at 11 on the result of a competitive examination and at 13 on the results of Scholarship and Common Entrance examinations. Entry to Year 12 is dependent upon academic record and reports.

Scholarships and Exhibitions. (*see* Entrance Scholarship section) Scholarships open to boys and girls are awarded on examinations held early in each year. Awards for Music and Art are available.

Full particulars from the Registrar.

Charitable status. The Dauntsey School Foundation is a Registered Charity, number 309480. It is dedicated to the education of boys and girls.

Dean Close School

Cheltenham GL51 6HE.
Tel: 01242-522640.
Fax: 01242 258003

The School was opened in 1886, in memory of Francis Close, DD, Rector of Cheltenham 1826–56 and later Dean of Carlisle. It is administered under a Deed of Trust by a Committee of Governors. It was the intention of the founders to combine the ideal of Christian Service with sound learning, and this has continued to the present day. The Preparatory School is independent.

Motto: *'Verbum Dei Lucerna'.*

Visitor: The Rt Revd D Bentley, The Lord Bishop of Gloucester

President: Baroness Cox of Queensbury

Vice-Presidents:
[1]Mrs L S M Hardy, OBE, JP
[1]S BonBernard
¶[1]C P Lynam, Esq, MA
¶[1]C J Buckett, Esq, FCA
¶The Rt Revd J D Wakeling, MC, MA, DD
[1]E A W Jones, Esq

Governors:
[1]The Rt Revd P St G Vaughan
The Revd Canon D R MacInnes, MA
[1]The Revd N J W Barker, MA, BTh
[1]Mrs B Abbatt, SRN
[1]Sir John Adye, KCMG, MA
[1]C G C Cocks, Esq, OBE, MA (*Chairman, Executive Committee*)
[1]C R Evans, Esq, MA
¶R J W Evans, Esq, MA, DPhil, FRA
[1]Miss C A Griffith, MA
[1]M W Kingston, QC
B W Knight, Esq, JP
[1]Mrs C Lainé, BA, JP
¶Dr J M Latham, MA, BM, BCh, D(Obst), RCOG
[1]¶I W Marsh, Esq, BSc (*Treasurer*)
[1]Mrs P G Napier
[1]C R H Rank, Esq
[1]The Revd T P Watson
[1]The Rt Revd J S Went, MA
¶[1]H F Wickham, Esq
[1]¶The Revd P C Youde, LLB

[1] Executive Member of Committee

***Headmaster:* The Revd T M Hastie-Smith**, MA, CertTheol (Magdalene College, Cambridge)

Old Decanian Registrar: R C Padfield, MA, DipEd, CFPS

Houses:
Brook/Court: J P Watson (*1998*)
Dale: R I Kirby (*2000*)
Fawley: Mrs V E Burroughs (*1997*)
Field: C J Townsend (*2000*)
Gate: D J R Pellereau (*1995*)
Mead: Mrs P Watson (*2001*)
Shelburne: Mrs J D Kent (*2001*)
Tower: G T Williams (*2000*)

Senior School Assistant Staff:
Senior Mistress: Mrs R C Padfield, BA, DipEd
Second Master: R F Taylor, MA, CertEd
Director of Studies: A R Marchand, BSc, PGCE

K R Davis, CertEd (*Head of Art*)
P M Cairns, MA, DipEd (*Head of English*)
M R Bowden, BA, PGCE (*Head of Economics*)
S J Gane, CertEd (*Head of Design Technology*)
R F Akenhead, CertEd
Mrs K R Aris, MBE, BSc, MSc (*Head of Careers*)
J R J Burrows, BA, DipEd, FRGS, MACE (*Head of Geography*)
A C Forbes, CertEd (*Director of Physical Education*)
J S Brock, BSc, MSc, PGCE (*Head of Biology*)
R F Taylor, MA, CertEd
Miss S F Villiers, BA, PGCE
L S Allington, BA
Mrs H L Porter, BA, LRAM, PGCE
Mrs V E Burroughs, CertEd
D J R Pellereau, MA, PGCE (*Head of Physics*)
C J Leigh, BSc, DipTheol, PGCE (*Head of Computing*)
P S Montgomery, BA, PGCE
Mrs F M Harris, BA, PGCE
Mrs C Allen, BMus, ALCM, LGSM, PGCE
Miss A E Ash, BDes, PGCE
J R B Stott, BSc, PGCE
P J P Anstis, MA, MEd, PhD (*Examination Co-ordinator and Head of Chemistry*)
K F Downes, BSc
J M Allen, MA, PGCE (*Head of Classics*)
D M Fullerton, MA (*Head of Modern Languages*)
Miss P M Smart, MA, PGCE
C J Townsend, BA
N P Stokes, BSc, PGCE
Miss R F Lea, BSc, PGCE
Miss I M Carames-Castelo, BA, PGCE
J G Brown, MA, LTCL
Mrs J D Kent, GDLM
N P Moor, GRSM, ARCM
J P Watson, BA, CertEd
B J Ricketts, CertEd
A J George, MA, PGCE (*Head of Mathematics*)
T A Dobbs, BA
R I Kirby, BA, PGCE
Miss E C Phillips, BSc, PGCE
Mrs S P Robbins, MA, MPhil, PGCE
Miss P Atkinson, BSc
R C Boyle, BSc
Miss E L Davies, BSc, PGCE
Mrs S Thomas, BEd, MPhil, PhD
The Revd L Browne, MA (*Chaplain*)
Mrs S L Low, BEd
G T Williams, BA, PGCE (*Head of History*)
Miss L Chandler, BSc, FAETC
Mrs C A McClure, BA
R Evans, BSc, PGCE
C Haslam, MA,PGCE
Mrs E L C Taylor, BA, PGCE
A M Cleary, BA (*Head of Music*)

Medical Officers: (*Both Schools*) I D Ramsay, MB, ChB, DObst, RCOG; C C Burgess, MB, ChB

SSI, CCF: RSM M M Hart

Preparatory School (*see Part V of this Book*)
Headmaster: S W Baird, BA, PGCE
C E Whitney, BA, ACP, PGTC (*Deputy Head*)
Mrs A F Primrose, MA, MEd, PGCE (*Deputy Head (Academic)*)

P V Coleman, BEd
A J Judge, MA (*Senior Master*)
Mrs M F Judge, CertEd
Mrs J M Dunlop, BA, PGCE
J L Phillips, BA
Mrs C M Padley, CertEd
S Cahill, BEd
P E Auster, BA, MTC (*Director of Music*)
Mrs R G Phillips, CertEd
Mrs C J Huckvale, MA, PGCE
Mrs J L Oke, CertEd
Miss C M Huxtable, MA, BEd, DMS
Mrs S E Bennett, CertEd (*Head of Pre-Prep*)
M J Dobbs, BA, PGCE
J E B Harris, BA, PGCE
D S Cormack, BA, DipCS, MTh
R S E Brown, BEng, PGCE
J D M Ward, BSc, PGCE
Mrs C Dobbs, BA(Ed)
M Dawson, BA, PGCE
M D Ede, BSc, PGCE
Mrs S J Holyfield, NNEB
Mrs M E Hunter, CertEd
Mrs G E McHardie-Jones, CertEd
Miss C M Parker, NNEB
Mrs J Vicarage, BEd
Mrs A Reynolds
Miss R Shouksmith, BMus, PGCE
Miss I L Short, BSc
T G Goodwright, BA
Mrs L Minchin
Mrs S A Davies, BA, PGCE
Mrs S A Paget, MEd, RgNI
Miss E Krick, BSc, PGCE
Mrs C McClure, BA, PGCE
M Hill
Miss K Arnold, BEd
Mrs A Meredith, BSc, PGCE
Bursar: Mr J M Lancashire, BA

Financial Controller: Mrs N A Mosley, BA, ACA
Registrar (*DCS*): Mrs S F Humphreys, BSc
Registrar (*DCPS*): Mrs E J Baird, BEd

Head of Communications: Mrs T C Colbert-Smith, BA

Admission and Withdrawal. The normal entry into this co-educational School is between the ages of 12½ and 14. In such circumstances boys and girls are expected to pass the Common Entrance Examination. Special papers are set for those entering the School from the maintained system. A limited number of pupils may enter at VIth Form level. In all cases of entry a report will be required from the pupil's present school. All enquiries about entry should be addressed to the Headmaster. Names may be registered at any time, but a few years' notice is advisable. There is a non-returnable registration fee of £100 and a returnable deposit of £500 payable one year before entry. One term's notice is required before the pupil is withdrawn from the School.

Inclusive Fees. Senior School Boarders, £5,310 per term, Senior Day Pupils, £3,710 per term, Prep School Boarders, £3,880 per term, Prep Day Pupils £2,650 per term. The Governors normally set the fees in September and do not vary them during the year.

Term of Entry. We prefer to accept pupils in September but will make exceptions at any time of year, even in the middle of a term, if a good reason exists.

Scholarships. (*see* Entrance Scholarship section) The School offers the following Entrance Scholarships:

(1) Governors' Open Scholarships.

(2) Fergus McNeile Scholarships for children of Clergy and Missionaries.

(3) W A M Edwards Science Scholarships for VIth Formers to read Science.

(4) Daisy Cross Arts Scholarships for VIth Formers to read Arts Subjects.

(5) Scholarships and Bursaries for the children of Schoolmasters and those serving in HM Forces.

(6) Major Scholarships in Music (including Organ), Art and Sport

The sizes of all awards are the subject of negotiation and a descriptive leaflet is available.

Number and Organisation. There are 450 in the Senior School (13–18). The VIth Form comprises approximately 40% of the School. There are eight Houses (three for boarding boys, two for day boys, two for girl boarders and one for day girls). All pupils entering the school go straight into their Senior Houses. Housemasters take immediate responsibility for pupils' work, careers, applications for Universities and further education. There is a Careers centre run by eight members of staff and a colleague who advises on University Entrance. The Prep School (2½–13) has approximately 299 pupils of whom 131 are girls. There are scholarships available for entry into the Prep School from the maintained sector.

Work. Pupils do not have to choose between science and arts until after GCSE and even then the choice of subjects for 'A' level is wide enough to allow a mixed course if desired. In the lower part of the school pupils are setted rather than streamed. Included in the Lower School timetable are Design Technology, Physical Education, Ceramics, Cooking, Computer Studies and Art, as well as a normal academic curriculum. Modern Languages are taught with the aid of audio-active equipment. The language centre, high technology seminar room, music school, art school, modern laboratories, computer, electronics, photographic and creative workshops combine excellent teaching and leisure facilities which are available both in timetabled and extra-curricular time. Much of the accommodation has been built in the last twenty years and is modern and purpose-built. There is a fine theatre and much drama is performed in it. There is also an open-air theatre. As well as several Orchestras, Wind Band, many ensembles and the Chapel Choir, the School has a Choral Society which performs a major work at least once a year. Tuition in any number of musical instruments is available as an extra. Free tuition is provided for music award holders and high-grade musicians. The theatre also affords first-class concert facilities.

Religious Education. The teaching and Chapel Services are in accordance with the Church of England and the School's strong Evangelical tradition is maintained. The Chaplain prepares members of the School for Confirmation each year. Most services are in the School Chapel. There is a fine pipe organ. There is a thriving Christian Union and each House has a Bible Study.

Games. The School has a 25m indoor Swimming Pool and Sports Centre, both used all the year round. There are two astroturf pitches and more than twenty hard Tennis courts. Hockey, Rugby, Cricket, Sailing, Basket-Ball, Netball, Rounders, Badminton, Athletics, Squash and Cross-Country Running are the main sports.

Health. The School has three qualified Sisters with Assistants and visiting Doctors. There is a Surgery and a sanatorium. The School uses the Nuffield Nursing Home adjacent to the School's playing fields.

The School pays careful heed to good dietary practice and the Dining Hall and Kitchens are first-class.

Outside Activities. All pupils during the first year at the School work for the Duke of Edinburgh's Bronze

Award and for lifesaving and first aid awards, as part of pre-CCF training. They can then opt for CCF or further Duke of Edinburgh work or take part in Estate Management. Later they can select leadership roles or Social Service.

General. The School is a family school with an emphasis on small groupings. All pupils are encouraged to develop a wide range of skills and interests not just the conventional work and games. It is an important aim for all House Colleagues to initiate an instinct for responsibility and leadership.

Forms VIths: Upper & Lower 'A' level. Vths: GCSE Removes: IVths:

Charitable status. Dean Close School is a Registered Charity, number 311721. This is a Christian School offering all-round education for both day and boarding scholars.

Denstone College

Uttoxeter Staffs ST14 5HN.
Tel: (01889) 590484.
Fax: (01889) 591295

Denstone College was founded in 1868. It lies in attractive countryside between Ashbourne and Uttoxeter. All school buildings, playing fields and the golf course are located within its grounds. It is one of a group of Church of England Public Schools founded by Canon Nathaniel Woodard in the nineteenth century. The College seeks to prepare young men and women for the demands of the early twenty first century, while upholding its Christian tradition.

Motto: *'Lignum Crucis Arbor Scientiae'*.

Visitor: The Bishop of Lichfield

School Council:
The Revd Preb J D Makepeace, MA (*Custos*)
The Revd Canon W M Weaver, BA, BD (*Provost*)
R Bokros
M Coyne
Mrs P Gee
Dr J A Moulton, MB, ChB, MFCH
R E Nadin, FCA
His Honour Judge R T N Orme, LLB
G E Paskett
A D Roper
E S Roper
G H Stow, FIPD
T N Tookey, MA

***Headmaster:* D M Derbyshire**, BA, MSc

Second Masters:
K C Ryder, BA, MPhil
B J Gillions, BEd

Chaplain: The Revd R M D Oram, BA

Masters and Mistresses:
D M Pritchard, BTech, MSc, MRSC
D J Dexter, MA
J S Jilbert, BA, FRGS
N M Green, BTech
†A N James, BA (*Shrewsbury*)
D A Barker, BSc
†Miss J R Morris, GMus (*Meynell*)
T P S O'Brien, DA
M R Jones, BSc
R C Menneer, BSc, CNAA
R Farrington, MA (*Head of Senior School*)
S J Dean, BEd (*Head of Middle School*)
†M P Raisbeck, BA, CNAA (*Selwyn*)
E G C Ashbee, BSc, MPhil, PhD
J Hartley, BA (*Head of Junior School*) (*Registrar*)
D G M Edwards, BSc
Mrs S A Leak, BEd
Mrs J A Buttery, BA (*Senior Mistress*)
†S J Phennah, BEd (*Head of Moss Moor*)
†Mrs L Phennah (*Head of Moss Moor - Girls' Boarding*)
†Miss J H Plewes, BA (*Woodard*)
†G A Jones, MSc (*Philips*)
†C McDade, BA (*Heywood*) (*Director of Music*)
W Odell, MA
R Luker, BA, MA, PhD (*Director of Studies*)
Miss D Whitmill, BSc
A Wray, BA
M J Bennett, BSc
Mrs R L Smith, BSc
J Tomlinson, BSc
Mrs V Derbyshire, BA
Mrs Y J Luker, BEd
Mrs A E Jones, BSc
Mrs P Jilbert, BA
Mrs K L Farrington, BEd, DipTEFL
Mrs P A Provan

Visiting Music Staff:
Mrs A O'Brien, DRSAMD, PGDip (RSAMD), ARCM *Piano, Singing, Recorder*
Mrs R Clarke, GRSM, LRAM, ALCM *Woodwind, Singing*
D Gore *Guitar*
R Banks, FTCL, ARAM, ARCM, LGSM *Brass*
D Simpson, FLCM, LGSM *Percussion*
Miss D Wright, BMus *Flute*
C Gill, BMus, PGDip (BSM) *Violin*

Chapel Organist: M M Davey, MA, FRCO, ARCM, LRAM

College Bursar and Clerk to the School Council: D M Martin, ACIB

Headmaster's Secretary : Mrs T F Wedgwood, BA

Admissions Secretary: Mrs V J Carman

Preparatory School: **Smallwood Manor**

Headmaster: The Revd C Cann

(*For further details about the Prep School, see Part V of this Book*)

The College is situated 6 miles north of Uttoxeter in 100 acres of grounds. The College is divided into units designated to Senior (16–18) 128 pupils, Middle (14–16) 128 pupils, and Junior School (11–14) 144 pupils, as well as separate girls' accommodation. Side by side with this all pupils are in one of the six houses, each numbering 65 to 70 members, with a total roll of 400. Weekly boarding is a popular option. Just under half of our pupils board, and one third are girls. One point six million pounds has been spent on improving our buildings and on building new facilities in the last three years.

The main building is on the Woodard pattern housing Classrooms, Dormitories, Common Rooms, Studies, Dining Hall, Chapel, Assembly Hall and resident staff accommodation. A great deal of school life is thus centred in this main block, including new facilities for IT and a Language Laboratory, with a consequent strong sense of community.

Laboratories, other classrooms, Indoor Pool, Art Centre, Design and Technology Centre, Music School and other buildings, such as the Sanatorium and School Shop, are elsewhere in the grounds.

Smallwood Manor, also a Woodard School, is 9 miles away. Age range 3–11.

Recent, Future Developments. As well as the recent installation of modern language and two information technology centres, and the creation of more teaching rooms, all the boys' boarding accommodation has been radically altered and updated (costing £1 million). The College has launched a major fund-raising campaign which to date has enabled the completion of a £615,000 Sports Hall in Summer 2000.

Curriculum. In the Junior School (11–14), that is Years 7, 8, 9, all follow roughly the same spread of subjects: English, French, German, Mathematics, Physics, Chemistry, Biology, History, Geography, Art, DT, Music, Religious Studies, Information Technology, and Drama, with some Latin.

Pupils enter the Middle School, from the beginning of the fourth form, (Year 10). Subjects are studied in an option system. Mathematics, English Language and Literature, a Modern Language and Science are the core subjects, and three others are chosen from those listed above (including Latin and German), together with Physical Education. There is a compulsory programme of Health Education.

A pupil then specialises in AS and A2 levels, chosen in an option system appropriate to the current discussions regarding Sixth Form Curriculum nationally. Four AS levels will normally be taken in the Lower Sixth. Subjects offered are Mathematics, Physics, Chemistry, Biology, English Language, English Literature, French, German, Latin, History, Geography, Economics, Politics, Art, Theatre Studies, Physical Education, DT and Business Vocational A level. There will also be a minority who will study, in varying numbers from year to year, Latin, Music and Religious Knowledge. An extremely flexible timetable is possible and most combinations of subjects can be offered.

The majority of pupils take 'A' levels, and over 95% go on to University, Art College, or some other Higher Education establishment.

Each year candidates are prepared for Oxford or Cambridge entrance.

The School is well-equipped with Laboratories, Modern Language equipment, films and video recordings and new computer rooms. Each department remains up-to-date with subject development and members of staff regularly attend courses and conferences.

Class sizes are small. Up to Year 11, 20 is the normal class size, and in the Sixth Form sets vary from 6 to 14.

In addition to having a Head of School and Head of House each pupil has a Tutor to whom he or she goes regularly to discuss work and career matters, and reports appear every five or six weeks

In order to encourage private, unsupervised work, each pupil has a work-station. By their GCSE year all pupils have moved to a study, and in fact all boarding members of Fifth Form, Lower Sixth and Sixth Form occupy bedsitters.

Out of Class Activities. The aim is to provide as wide a variety of opportunities for pupils of differing aptitudes and inclinations as possible.

Games The College has a full-size, floodlit, all-weather hockey pitch which also provides 9 tennis courts. A nine-hole handicap-standard golf course has been laid out to the west of the College. There is an indoor swimming pool, and the new sports hall accommodates all the major indoor sports as well as a fully equipped fitness room.

The main sports in the Michaelmas Term are rugby for the boys and hockey for the girls, with plenty of opportunities for other games. In the Lent Term these are replaced by hockey and football, and netball, side by side with the wide range of other school sports that one would imagine. In the summer there is a degree of choice between cricket, athletics, swimming, golf, tennis and rounders.

In the course of the year in fact there are opportunities for all the above plus cross country, clay pigeon shooting, squash, badminton, table-tennis, dance, basketball, volleyball and a reasonable cross section of what one might imagine would interest the average pupil.

CCF and Pioneers. There is also a Combined Cadet Force with Army and Royal Air Force sections, and an alternative outward bound group which undertakes climbing, canoeing and The Duke of Edinburgh Scheme. Over the last decade over 25% of sixth formers have gained the Gold Award. There is also a community service group.

The Arts. There are set times each week when priority is given to non-sporting clubs and activities, giving pupils opportunities in a wide range of experiences. Music plays a central role in College life. The Chapel choir sings at the main service each Friday. There are also other specialist choirs and small instrumental groups in addition to the main orchestra. Music is included in the curriculum of forms 1–3 and in addition tuition in most instruments from both resident and visiting staff is available. A number of musical events takes place annually, from Concerts and the House Music Competition to recitals by visiting artists.

Traditionally there is a major play or musical at the end of the Michaelmas term. The College has a proud record of 103 Shakespearean productions. In 2000/2001 there were three major productions and a Junior Drama festival (involving all six houses) in the Summer Term. The 2000 School Play was "Guys and Dolls".

There is a new DT centre, as well as fully equipped Art and Pottery centres. These facilities are housed in the Centenary Building and allow pupils to fulfil abilities in design, woodwork, metalwork, painting, drawing, ceramics, printing and photography.

Entrance. Many pupils enter in the September following their 13th birthday after passing the Common Entrance Examination to Senior Independent Schools which they sit in June.

A growing number of pupils sits an examination in January or February at the College. Most will be between 11 and 13, and a few older candidates. There is a good entry into the Sixth Form.

Occasionally pupils enter at other ages and times. They need to show that they have attained the necessary academic standard either by public examination results or by sitting papers set by the College.

Scholarships (*see* Entrance Scholarship section). Scholarships and Exhibitions are offered annually, of varying value up to 50%. They are competed for in three main age groups:

First, some are awarded to the best candidates in the January and February examinations referred to above; second, to candidates from Preparatory Schools (and internal College candidates) who are under 14 on 1 June of the year in which the examination is taken; and third for Sixth Form entry.

In all Scholarships, in addition to academic excellence, all-round ability and out-of-school activities and interests are taken into account.

Scholarships are offered annually for Music (instrumental and choral), Art, DT, Drama, Sport, Golf and 'All Round' ability.

A number of bursaries may be awarded to those in genuine financial need. Special consideration is given to the children of Clergy, Old Denstonians and Service Children.

Fees. The Registration Fee is £50 and the Entrance Fee £100. School Fees are Junior Boarding, £3,323 per term, Senior Boarding £3,695 per term, and include all items of board and education other than music lessons and extra tuition. Day fees are £1,672 per term for Junior School, £2,117 per term for Middle School and £2,451 per term for Senior School.

The Old Denstonian Club. *Secretary:* Mr M K Swales, Denstone College, Uttoxeter, Staffs. Regional Clubs based in London, Manchester and at the College.

Charitable status. The Woodard Schools (Midland Division) Limited is a Registered Charity, number 269671. It exists to provide Christian education for children.

* Head of Department	§ Part Time or Visiting
† Housemaster/Housemistress	¶ Old Pupil
‡ See below list of staff for meaning	

Dollar Academy

Dollar FK14 7DU.
Tel: (01259) 742511
Fax: (01259) 742867
e-mail: rector@dollaracademy.org.uk
website: www.dollaracademy.org.uk

The Academy, founded in 1818 and the oldest co-educational boarding and day school in Britain, is situated in forty acres of its own grounds on the southern slopes of the Ochil Hills, 30 miles from Edinburgh, 38 from Glasgow, 40 from St Andrews and 10 miles east of Stirling. The Academy is renowned for its academic reputation and for its range of extra-curricular activities of remarkable quality. In recent years, all five boarding houses have been extensively refurbished, and the quality of the facilities throughout the school campus is of the highest order.

Motto: *'Juventutis veho fortunas'*.

Governors:
Chairman: J B Cameron, CBE, FIAgricF, AIAgricE.

Vice-Chairman: R P S Harris, BCom, DipCom, CA

Members:
K Brown, MA
H N Buchan
Mrs D Buchanan, FHCIMA
Cllr A Campbell, CA
Mrs E Carnegie
D M Clark, MA, LLB, WS, NP
R R Cumming, BSc, MBIM
Dr D E Donaldson, MB, BS, DA, LRCP, MRCS
Mrs H Fraser, MA
E T I King, LVO, MBA, MRAeS
J G Logie, BSc, FICE, FIStructE, MConsE
A H McCutcheon
Professor J McEwen, MBChB, DIH, FFPHM, FFOM, FRCP
R E Morris, MA, DPhil
Sir Ian Morrow, CA, FCMA, JDipMA, FBIM, CompiEE, DUniv, HonDLitt
Rev J P S Purves, BSc, BD
Mrs E Sharpe, BDS
Professor S J Thomson, PhD, DSc, CChem, FRSC, FRSE
W F Faulds, BArch, DipTP, FRIBA, MTPI, AMI, Arb

Bursar and Clerk to Governors: Mr J Wilkes, MA
Assistant Bursar: Mr N Haworth, BA

***Rector:* J S Robertson**, MA

Deputy Rector: G P Daniel, MA

Assistant Rectors:
Mrs K Robertson, MA (*also Head of Preparatory & Junior School*)
J M Hendry, BSc, PhD, CPhys, MInstP
Mrs L H Hutchison, BA

Director of Communication: Mr R Vanstone, MA

Preparatory School:
Mrs J G Adamson, BA, AUPE (*Assistant Head*)
Mrs A W Alexander, DipCE
Miss K Barr, BEd
Mrs A Briggs, BA, DipCE, AUPE
Mrs E M M Dow, DipCE
Miss R E Foster, MA
Mrs L Hudson, BA
Miss N M Ingleby, BEd
Mrs E Lang, BEd
Miss J Macmillan, BEd
Mrs M Nesbitt, DipCE, SQIE
Mrs K Bunyan (*Prep Assistant*)
Mrs P Ramsay (*Prep Assistant*)

Junior School:
Miss F Goudie, BEd (*Assistant Head*)
Mrs C M Bell, BA, DipCE
Mrs V Currie, DipCE
G E Davies, BEd, MEd
Mrs G A McFadyean, BA
A Mills, BEd
Miss L Webster, MA

Senior School:

Art:
†*A K MacLean, DA
Miss T Croft, BA
Miss C Fairbairn, BA
Mrs C MacLean, DA
†Mrs C McGirr, BA

Biology:
*A N Morton, BSc
C Ainge, BSc
J Fraser, BSc
Mrs F McDonald, BSc
Miss L A Payne, BSc, PhD
Mrs M A Smith, BSc

Business Education:
*W W McFarlane, BA
A S Blyth, BA
Mrs J M McFarlane, BA
Mrs A Marshall, DipCom
†Mrs M Waddell, DipCom

Chemistry:
*W Beveridge, BSc, PhD, CChem, MRSC
N Blezard, BSc
Miss C Doughty, BSc
D J Lumsden, BSc

Classics:
*S Peake, BA, PhD, FCU(CorpChr), MAMBS
Mrs C B Mason, MA
P R Murray, MA

Computing:
*R W Marchant, BSc
Ms R McGuinness, MSc

English:
*Mrs C Murray, MA, MPhil
Mrs S Miller, BA, MPhil
Ms E Poole, MA
Mrs M Robertson, MA
R Robinson, MA
P G Russell, BA

Geography:
*D A Carmichael, MA
Mrs F M McBride, MA
Mrs S A Scott, BSc
Mrs A M Thompson, MA, DipRSA

History:
*Miss M D Sharp, MA
Miss D Jamieson, MA
N J McFadyean, MA, MPhil

Librarian: Mrs C Gough, MA, ALA
Registrar/Secretary: Mrs C Beesley
Janitor: W Anderson
Groundsman: L Spendlove
Piping Instructor: C Stewart
Swimming Coach: A Harris

N J Seaton, MA

Home Economics:
Mrs J M Brown, DipDomSci
Mrs C Fleming, DipHome Economics

Learning Support:
*Mrs H Archibald, MA
Mrs S Morgan, DipCE

Mathematics:
*S P Johnson, MA
Miss F G Davidson, BSc
R W Durran, BA
Mrs L Jeffrey, BA
Miss K Lothian, BEng
D S Payne, BSc
Miss C M Welsh, BSc

Modern Languages:
*D Delaney, MA
J A Allan, MA
Miss H Prifti, MA
H I Soga, MA, BA, BMus, PhD, LTCL
Miss M McNeill, MA
Mrs A M Smith, MA
Mrs J Tait, MA, MIL

Assistants:
Mlle S Juillet (*French*)
Herr K D Potschka (*German*)
Snr A Garzón Capilla (*Spanish*)
Miss F Nakagawa (*Japanese*)

Music:
*J McGonigle, DipMus, RSAMD
S Gibb, MA
T S Irvine, DRSAM
Mrs S A Nelson, DipCE, LTCL

Physical Education:
*C MacKay, BEd
†J Foster, DipPE (*Head of Sport*)
Mrs E A Borrowman, DipPE
J G A Frost, BEd, MSc
Mrs C Galloway, BEd
Mrs G Robb, BEd

Physics:
*†J T A Fulton, BSc
D W Brown, MA
Miss S Fulton, BSc, PhD
A Johns, BSc, CPhys, MInstP

Technology:
*R Carter, BSc, DipTechEd
R L Beath, DipTechEd
S W Cochrane, BEdTech

Housemistresses:

Argyll: Mrs M Waddell, DipCom
Heyworth: Mrs C McGirr, BA
McNabb: Mrs J Foster
Playfair: Mrs C B Fulton, SRN, SCM, HV
Tait: Mrs C MacLean, DA

Organisation. The Academy is divided into the Senior School (ages 12–18, 762 pupils), the Junior School (ages 10–12, 175 pupils) and the Preparatory Department (ages 5–9, 205 pupils). It is fully co-educational throughout.

Pupils are prepared for the Scottish Certificate of Education at Standard Grade and Higher Grade and then afterwards for 'A' Levels or Advanced Highers. Over 90% then proceed to degree courses at a wide range of universities in Britain and overseas.

Careers. A senior member of staff coordinates Careers and others advise on University Entrance. All pupils are offered the services of Careers Central and JIGCAL testing is also used. The Academy has a flourishing Work Experience programme both locally and in mainland Europe for senior pupils.

Games and Activities. The playing-fields are immediately adjacent to the school, as are the Games Hall, Fitness Centre, Squash Courts, 25 metre indoor heated swimming-pool and the .22 Rifle Range.

Teams represent the school in rugby, cricket, hockey, tennis, badminton, fencing, athletics, swimming, shooting and golf.

The Combined Cadet Force has equal numbers of boys and girls, a Royal Signals Troop, an RAF Section, an RN section and a Pipe Band.

There is a wide variety of Clubs: Chess, Photography, Drama, Debating, Computing, Riding, etc . . . Sixth Formers have their own Club Room.

Music is taught as part of the curriculum and tuition is offered as an extra in most orchestral instruments. There are five choirs and three orchestras, housed in the spectacular Sir Alexander Gibson Building.

Boarding. Boarding pupils are accepted from the age of nine. There are three Boys' Houses and two Girls' Houses. Weekly boarding is offered for those who live near enough to Dollar to spend weekends at home, but who wish to have many of the advantages of boarding education.

Fees. The tuition fees range from £4,068–£5,400 per annum and the boarding fee is £6,588 per annum.

Admission. This is by interview and/or test with the Head of the Junior and Preparatory School, and by examination and interview for the Senior School. The biggest single intakes are at ten and eleven to the two years of the Junior School. There are intakes at Prep 1, Form 1 and post S Grade/GCSE, and in other years as vacancies occur.

Charitable status. The Governors of Dollar Academy Trust is a Registered Charity. It exists to provide education for boys and girls.

Downside School

Stratton-on-the-Fosse Bath BA3 4RJ
Tel: (01761) 235100. Head Master (01761) 235101.
Fax: (01761) 235105
e-mail: admin@downside.co.uk
website: http://www.downside.co.uk

This School, attached to the English Benedictine Community of St Gregory, was founded at Douai in 1606, to provide for English Catholics the opportunities of education which were closed to them in their own country. At the time of the French Revolution the School was transferred to Acton Burnell, near Shrewsbury, and in 1814 it was removed to Downside. There are 315 boys, over 85% of whom board.

The Abbot of Downside and Chairman of the Governors and the Trustees: Rt Rev Dom Richard Yeo, MA, JCD

Head Master: **Dom Antony Sutch**, MA

Deputy Heads:
M B Fisher, MA (*Senior Deputy*)
J W Moretti, BSc (*Director of Studies*)
Mrs C E Matthews, BSc, FRGS, MIBiol (*Senior Tutor*)

Bursar: Dom James Hood

House Master of Caverel: A Molloy, BA
Co-House Master of Caverel: Dom Boniface Hill
House Master of Barlow: P V Griffin, BA
House Master of Roberts: Dom Augustine Clark, BA, PhB, STL, DipRSA
House Master of Smythe: G G Pearce, MA
House Master of Powell: K J M Burke, MSc, BEd
House Master of St Oliver's: D J Ettinger, MA

School Chaplain: Dom David Foster, MA, STL

Games Director: A C Woodin
Careers Guidance: R L Gilmour, BSc
School Librarian: Dom Aidan Bellenger, MA, PhD, FRHistS

Heads of Department:

Religious Studies: D J Ettinger, MA
English: B J Fogarty, MA
History: P V Griffin, BA
Classics: M B Fisher, MA
Modern Languages: R C Rawlins, MA
Mathematics: N J Weatherhogg, BSc, DD
Physics: J G Curtis, BSc
Chemistry: P B N Gunasekera, BSc, CChem, MRSC
Biology: Mrs C E Matthews, BSc, FRGS, MIBiol
Geography: R L Gilmour, BSc
Economics & Business Studies: N J Bryars, MA
Music: C P Tambling, MA, FRCO
Design and Technology: N Barrett, BEd
Information and Communications Technology: M G Daniels, DipRSA
Special Needs: D Jones, BA
English as a Second Language: Miss D Pickard, MA

School Doctors:
Dr A A G Morrice, BSc, MB, BS, MD, MRCGP
Dr E J Widdowson, MB, BS, BSc, MRCGP, DCH, DRCOG

School Matron: Sister J Glide, RGN

Registrar: Mrs M Miland

St Oliver's. St Oliver's is the Junior House of Downside and accepts boys at 9+ and at 11+. The vibrant and homely boarding house, which is situated on the edge of the Downside campus, is run by a married layman with the help of an assistant house master, a house mother, an assistant house mother, a chaplain and various tutors. There are two fixed exeat weekends each term, which begin on a Friday afternoon with the boarders returning on Sunday evening. On other weekends various activities are organised but parents are welcome to take their sons and their friends out on Sunday afternoon.

In the first two years the boys are taught by Key Stage 2 class teachers for the majority of their curriculum, with some assistance from specialist staff in the Main School in areas such as Design, Music, ICT, Physical Education and Religious Studies. In the last two years they are taught by subject specialists from the Main School in each subject.

There is a qualfying entrance test held in March. Boys normally move into the Main School at 13+ provided they pass the school examinations at the end of their time in St Oliver's.

Main School. Boys usually enter the Main School at 13+. External applicants usually sit either the Common Entrance examinations in June or the Downside 13+ Scholarship examinations in May. Other assessment arrangements can be made for prospective pupils for whom neither of these modes of assessment is suitable. Entrance into the Fourth Form is usually on the basis of reports and interview. Sixth Form places are offered after interview and are dependent upon a satisfactory performance in the GCSE examinations.

In the Third Form (Year 9) all pupils are members of Powell House, whose house master is a married layman. This gives boys the opportunity to make lasting friendships with everyone in their year group before they move on to their respective senior houses to which they are attached for the remaining four years. All of the houses in the Main School are under one roof, in different areas of the School. The houses have their own individual identities but the social life of a boy is not confined exclusively to members of his own house. In the last three years each boarder has his own study/bedroom. Dayboys are successfully integrated into the life of each of the separate houses. There is a strong tutorial system, which is house based. Each boy in the Main School is assigned a tutor who is in regular contact with him and who monitors his academic progress, as well as taking an active interest in his general well being. There are no fixed exeat weekends in the Main School, though there are two weekends each term when the Schola Cantorum does not sing at the Sunday Mass: these weekends are popular times for exeats.

Curriculum. The curriculum in St Oliver's, and in the first year in the Main School, is broadly based. In the penultimate year in St Oliver's boys take up both Latin and French, whilst in the Third Form they start either a second modern language (chosen from German, Italian and Spanish) or Classical Greek.

In the Fourth and Fifth Forms (Years 10 and 11) all pupils follow courses in English Language (with a majority also being prepared for the GCSE in English Literature), Mathematics, Religious Studies and Science. Science is taught separately as Biology, Chemistry and Physics and pupils are ultimately entered for the Dual Award Coordinated Science GCSE examinations. In addition to the compulsory subjects, pupils will usually choose an additional four subjects from: Fine Art, Ceramics, Classical Greek, Design and Technology, Geography, German, History, Italian, Latin, Music and Spanish. The choice usually includes at least one modern foreign language and either Geography or History (or both). This curriculum leads to the majority of pupils gaining nine or ten GCSEs at the end of the Fifth Form.

In the Sixth Form pupils are currently encouraged to study four subjects to AS level in the first year and then to continue three or four subjects to full A level standard in the second year, though the option system does allow the brightest pupils to study five. In addition to the subjects available at GCSE, pupils may opt for Business Studies, Classical Civilisation, Economics and Physical Education. All members of the Sixth Form have one period of non-examined Religious Studies each week and the Lower Sixth also follow a Geneal Studies programme.

Music. Downside has a strong musical tradition and this is reflected in the number of different musical groups that exist ranging from Jazz through Chamber and Orchestral to Choral. A number of large scale and chamber recitals take place during the academic year, all of which are open to parents and visitors from outside the School who would like to attend. Students are actively encouraged to consider taking up tuition in an instrument and are prepared for the grade examinations of the Associated Board. Recent leavers have gained Oxbridge Choral and Organ Scholarships. The Schola Cantorum sings at Mass when it is attended by the School on Sundays and major Feast Days during term time.

Sport. In addition to the non-examined Physical Education programme for all boys in the Fifth Form and below, the majority of boys take part in a structured Games programme three afternoons a week. In the Michaelmas Term priority is given to Rugby; in the Lent Term to Hockey and Soccer; in the Summer Term to Cricket and Tennis. However, if their talents do not lie in these areas, boys are encouraged to get involved in a wide range of minor sports which include Athletics, Basketball, Cross Country, Fencing, Golf, Judo, Shooting, Squash, Swimming and Weight Training. Fixtures generally take place on Saturday afternoons and on occasional Wednesdays, and the support of parents at these is welcomed.

Extra-Curricular Activities. At Downside boys are actively encouraged to engage in extra-curricular activities. Where a club does not exist, boys are encouraged to form new societies.

Downside has a strong reputation in the sphere of debating as evidenced by the Sixth Form debating society (the Abingdon), participation of all year groups in Model United Nations (Bath and Belfast) and individual participation in the annual Oxford and Cambridge Union debating competitions. The School also enjoys considerable success in orienteering. Each year at least two teams are entered for the Ten Tors Competition on Dartmoor (a training camp takes place during the Easter vacation) and often boys take part in the annual Devizes to Westminster canoe race. Every member of the Third, Fourth and Fifth Forms is expected to either be a member of the CCF (Army or Navy Section), to participate in the Duke of Edinburgh Award Scheme or to be a member of the Community Service Group. In the Sixth Form boys have the opportunity to be prepared for the CCPR sports leadership award and to be trained as lifeguards.

Infirmary. The School Infirmary is staffed 24 hours a day throughout term time by qualified nursing sisters. A Docter's surgery is held three times each week.

Fees per term. Boarding £4,724 (St Oliver's £3,752); Day £2,420 (St Oliver's £2,176), payable in advance. The current registration fee for prospective pupils is £50.

Scholarships. (*see* Entrance Scholarship section) Academic, Music and Choral awards are available for entry into St Oliver's at 11+ and into the Main School at 13+ and 16+. Details can be obtained from the Registrar.

Old Boys Society. St Gregory's Society, Downside School, Bath. *Secretary:* Dom Daniel Rees. List of Old Boys at St Gregory's 1614–1972. *First Supplement* 1967–1982. *Second Supplement* 1976–1992.

Charitable status. Downside School is a Registered Charity, number 232548. Its purpose is to advance the cause of Catholic Education.

Dulwich College

London SE21 7LD.
Tel: 020 8693 3601.
Fax: 020 8693 6319.

Dulwich College was founded by Edward Alleyn, the famous Elizabethan actor-manager. On 21 June 1619, a licence was granted for his 'College of God's Gift' at Dulwich, a foundation consisting of a Master, a Warden, 4 Fellows, 12 poor scholars and 12 alms people. In 1857 Alleyn's College was reconstituted by a special Act of

Parliament. The upper part of the Foundation was henceforth known as Dulwich College, and in 1870 moved to its present site.
Motto: *'Detur gloria soli Deo'.*

The Governing Body:

Chairman: Lord Butler of Brockwell, GCB, CVO
¶R D Amlot, QC
¶The Very Revd Dr A W Carr, MA, PhD
¶E A J George, MA
Mrs J M Gooder, MA
J M B Gotch, MA, FCIT
Miss J A Gough, MA
¶J C Norton, MA, FCA
A Seth, MA, DBA, FRSA
Dr R C Smith, CBE
J A Strachan, BSc, FRICS
¶N A Tatman, MSI (Dip)
A G L Wright, FSVA

Clerk to the Governors: J H Jackson, MA, FCIS

***Master of the College:* G G Able,** MA, MA, FRSA

Deputy Masters:
S R Northcote-Green, BA (*Pastoral*)
B G Thompson, MA, PhD (*Academic*)

Third Master: J Charnley, MA

Head of Upper School: T J Cook, BA

Head of Middle School: R I Mainard, BA, MA(Theol), MA(Educ)

Head of Lower School: J P Devlin, BA, PhD

Head of Junior School: Mrs P A Horsman, CertEd

Registrar: T F Price, MA

Assistant Masters:
Miss J Akrill, BA
P A Allen, BA
S Arscott, BA
*M Ashcroft, GNSM, ARCO(*CHM*), LRAM (*Director of Music*)
†A Avshu, BSc, PhD (*Blew*)
H D Bain, MA
J A Bardell, BSc
Miss R Barnes, BA(Ed)
§T Barratt, ARAM, GRSM, LRAM, ARCM, LMusTCL, ATCL
A A Barrett-Greene, MA
§D J Beard, MCSD
A J Binns, BA
*N D Black, BA (*History*)
Mrs J Borek-Coxen, CertEd, RSA
Mrs A M Bradnock, BA, ALA, DipNZLS, MIInfSci
Miss J N A Brind, BEd
I R T Brinton, MA
N C Brown, BEd
J P Brownridge, BSc, ARCS
D P Burns, BSc(*Econ*)
S W Burton, MA
P Callender, CertEd
J Carnelley, BMus, MMus, ARCO
I Carter, BA, MIL
†D Cartwright, MA (*Ivyholme*)
J D Cartwright, MA
M Childs, BA
Mrs R M R Collier, BA
Mrs A H Collins, BA
D J Cooper, BSc (*Orchard*)
*†N D Cousins, BEd (*Physical Education*)
*¶N T Croally, MA, PhD (*Classics*)
Miss D Cronin, BA, DipRSA
Mrs S C J Crossley, BA, MTh
P J Cue, BSc, PhD
T Edge, BA
M J Edwards, BA, PhD
D M Emerson, BMus
M J Emson, BSc
K G Eyre, MA
S J Farrow, BA, MPhil, DPhil
R J Field, MA, CPhys, AIEE
Mrs S Gardener, BA
§Mrs J A Gillard, LRAM
C J Gold, MA, AKC (*French*)
Miss R E Grange, BA
M Grantham-Hill, BSc
Mrs J C Henderson, BA
R A Henderson, BSc
M J P Higgins, BSc, PhD
Miss J M Hounsell, BA
*S G Hoyle, BA, PhD (*Master in charge of Games*)
§Mrs J A James, BEd
N F Jamieson, MA
Miss M A Jarman, MA
Mrs G M Jenkins, BA
Miss H T Johnson, BSc
*J N Johnston, BSc (*Physics*)
¶P V Jolly, BA, DipRSA (*Director of Drama*)
*R O Jones, MA, MSc, PhD (*Chemistry*)
D Kent, BA
*T D Kent, HTC (*Technical Studies*)
M B Kochanowski, BA
D A Kuehn, BA, MA, PhD
Mrs B Lake, GRSM, LTCL
Miss L Larkum, BMus, MMus, DipRCM, ASCM
*J H Lever, HDFA (*Director of Art*)
¶*T Llewellyn, MA (*Geography*)
*J Lord, BSc, AFIMA (*Mathematics*)
§D Ludford Thomas, BA
W R McDowell, BA (*German*)
*N Mair, BA (*Modern Languages*)
§Mrs B Martin, AA
I R Martin, BEd, BA
H Maxfield, BSc (*PSHE*)
§K J Maycock, MA
S B Medland, BA
S C J Middleton, BEd
Miss K J Millburn, MA
§R J Mills, MA
B O Moses, BEng, PhD
G R Nicholls, MSc, HTC
Miss R Norman-Bailey, BA(Ed)
J M O'Neill, BSc, MSc, PhD
C J Ottewill, BA, MPhil
R Oubridge, BEd
J R Piggott, MA, PhD (*Archivist*)
G E Powell, BSc, PhD
Mrs T J Price, BSc, MSc
S Pugh, DipAD, FCSD, FRSA
C S B Pyke, MA
*E J Rand, BSc, CChem, FRSC (*Head of Science*)
Mrs J M Rand, BSc, CPhys, MInstP
Miss M J Raybould, BSc, MSc, DIC
*E J F Reddaway, BSc, CBiol, MIBiol (*Biology*)
E J Rees, BA(Ed)
G W Roberts, BSc, PhD
Miss S A Roberts, BSc, DMS
A H Ronald, MA
D J G Rose, BA
J R Ruffo, BA
Ms M K Russell, MA
G E Rutter, BA, CertEd, HTC
A J D Salter, TD, BA, DLC
I L H Scarisbrick, BSc
I Senior, BA, MA, MSc, CBiol, MIBiol
A J Shortland, BSc, ARCS, PhD
Ms E Sioufi, MA
A I Slabczynski, MA (*Spanish*)
D R Smith, BA
Mrs F Southern, BA
C G Spikesman, BEd, BA, DipMus
M J Sprague, BSc
K A Stinson, CertEd
*A C Storey, BA, MSc, PhD (*Information Technology*)
M J Storey, BA, PhD
*P J Storey, BA (*Economics and Business Studies*)
A J Threadgould, BSc
C Trussell, BA, MA
¶The Ven P R Turner, CB, AKC, BA, MTheol
S A H Wakely, MA
C M Wall, BSc
*J Ward, BA, PhD (*English*)
*R Weaver, BA, MA, FSA(*Scot*), FRSA (*Religious Studies*)
Mrs E Whale, BA
D Wickes, BA, MA
Mrs K A Williams, BA
Miss S Wood, BSc
N P Young, BSc
C Zekraoui, BA, MPhil

Bursar: A W Skinner, MA

Music:
§K C Abbott, DipRCM
§J C Allen, LRAM, ARCM
§Ms N J Baigent, BA
§J P Barber, GLCM, LTCL(TD), ALCM
§Mrs C Barnes, GRNCM, DipNCOS
E P Barry, DipMus, LTCL
§D Battersby, ALCM, LRAM, ARCM
§P Beer
§Miss G Brown, AGSM, LLCM
§Miss M Bruce-Mitford, LRAM, ARCM
J Cherry, DipRAM, LRAM
§Miss J Fitton, ARCM
§S Foley, LTCL
§Miss J Friend, ARCM
§Mrs J A Gillard, LRAM
§B D Graham, FTCL, LTCL, ARCM
Ms S Grint, GRSM, ARCM, LRAM
§Miss H Gritton, LRAM
§H Hambleton, ARAM
§J M Hargreaves, BA
§S C Hargreaves
§J Kirby, AGSM, GGSM
§Ms Z Lake, BMus, LRAM
§B J Lees, LRAM, ARCM
§G Molyneux, BMus, GGSM

§Miss G Morgan, MA, ARCM
§R M Nicholas, FTCL, LRAM, ARCM
§Mrs M Porter, GRSM, LRAM, ARCM
G Sanbrook-Davies, ARCM
M Simmonds
W J R Whitehead, BA, MMus, FRCM

SSI: P A Titmarsh, RA(*Retired*)

Medical Centre Charge Nurse: Miss J M Neary, RGN

Medical Officer:
M R Kiln, MB, BS, DRCOG

Master's Secretary: Mrs R Uddin

Organisation. The School is divided into 4 sections but is administered as a single unit. In both the Junior School (Y3-Y6) and the Lower School (Y7 and Y8) all forms at the same level follow a common curriculum. Between the ages of 13 and 16 boys are in the Middle School (Y9-Y11) following a broadly based, balanced programme leading to a minimum of nine subjects at GCSE. Boys in the Upper School, consisting of the Remove and the Sixth Form, study at Advanced Level. In the Remove, they select four subjects at Advanced Subsidiary (AS) Level from the following: Ancient History, Art, Biology, Business Studies, Chemistry, Computing, Design and Technology, Economics, English, French, Geography, Geology, German, Greek, History, History of Art, ICT, Italian, Latin, Mathematics, Music, Physical Education, Physics, Religious Studies, Spanish and Theatre Studies. In addition, boys take a course in General Studies which is examined, along with their four other AS levels, at the end of the Remove year. In the Sixth Form, boys continue at A2 Level with three or four of their chosen subjects, as appropriate, to complete their Advanced Level courses. Boys in the Sixth Form are prepared for university entrance. Oxford and Cambridge feature prominently among the many places gained, while increasing numbers also succeed in their application for university places in the United States.

Entry. Boys are admitted to the College as day boys, boarders or weekly boarders. The School year runs from 1 September and ages for entry are reckoned at that date. Vacancies occur at 7, 10, 11 and 13. Casual vacancies occur from time to time at ages 8, 9 and 12. At 7 places are awarded on the basis of interview, report and practical assessment during the Lent Term. At 10 and 11 places are awarded on the results of the Combined Entrance and Scholarship Examination held in the Lent Term. Candidates take papers in English and Mathematics and also a Verbal Reasoning test. At 13 boys may take either the College's own Combined Entrance and Scholarship Examination held in the Lent Term or the Common Entrance Examination in June. All candidates from abroad must pass the Entrance Examination. Subject to the consent of their preparatory school Headteachers, boys may take the papers at their own schools by arrangement. Boys are also admitted to do Sixth Form work. Admission is normally dependent on GCSE results and a recommendation from the boy's previous school. Application should be made as early as possible.

Term of Entry. Boys normally enter the school at the beginning of the Michaelmas term. Only in exceptional circumstances are they accepted at other times of the year.

Scholarships and Bursaries. (*see* Entrance Scholarship section) A number of scholarships are awarded each year to the value of one half, one third or one quarter of the tuition fee, with a few of lesser value, although these amounts can be increased in cases of genuine financial need. There are two scholarships for Music, one for Art and one for Design and Technology. One boarding bursary for half the boarding fee is offered to a successful scholarship candidate. The College has a Bursary Fund from which a number of means-tested awards are made annually.

These scholarships and bursaries are available for competition for all new boys entering the College between the ages of 10 and 14 years on 1 September in the year of entry, and are awarded on the results of the College's Combined Scholarship and Entrance Examination held in the Lent Term.

Other awards are available for boys entering the Sixth Form.

Each year the Governors award some scholarships to boys already in the school upon entering the First Forms (Y7) at age 11 and the Third Forms (Y9) at age 13.

Fees and Expenses. The consolidated day fee of £8,730 pa covers tuition, use of class, text and library books, school stationery, scientific materials, games and School Magazine subscriptions. It does not cover fees for external examinations.

Boarding Houses. There are three Boarding Houses, Blew House (Mr A Avshu), Ivyholme (Mr D Cartwright) and Orchard House (Mr N D Cousins). The consolidated boarding fee of £8,340 pa exclusive of tuition fee includes laundry and Sanatorium charges. Provision can be made for boys whose parents live near the College to board on a weekly basis. The fee for weekly boarders is £7,665 pa.

Dulwich Picture Gallery. The College is very fortunate that it retains close links with the magnificent picture gallery designed by Sir John Soane which contains paintings by Canaletto, Gainsborough, Hobbema, Hogarth, Murillo, Poussin, Rembrandt, Reynolds, Rubens, Van Dyck and Watteau even though ownership has now passed to an independent charity.

The Alleyn Club. The Alleyn Club is the overall organisation for sporting clubs, dinners, and other gatherings of old boys, both at home and abroad. The Secretary is Mr T J Walsh, who has an office at the College. There is a handsome clubhouse and grounds on Dulwich Common. Renunions of year-groups are held regularly at the College.

Charitable status. Alleyn's College of God's Gift; Dulwich College is a Registered Charity, number 312755. It exists for the education of children.

The High School of Dundee

Euclid Crescent Dundee DD1 1HU
Tel: (01382) 202921.
Fax: (01382) 229822

The present School traces its origins directly back to a 13th century foundation by the Abbot and Monks of Lindores. It received a Royal Charter in 1859. Various Acts of Parliament in the 19th Century were finally consolidated in an Order in Council constituting the High School of Dundee Scheme 1965, which was revised in 1987.

The School is now an independent foundation.

Motto: *'Prestante Domino'.*

Board of Directors.

The Board comprises, Chairman, 2 Ex Officiis Directors, viz, The Lord Dean of Guild and The Parish Minister of Dundee. Three Directors are elected by the Dundee and Tayside Chamber of Commerce and Industry and one each by the Guildry of Dundee, the Nine Trades of Dundee, the Old Boys' Club and the Old Girls' Club and the Parents' Association respectively. Six Directors are elected by The Patrons' Association and 6 co-opted by the Board.

School Staff:

***Rector:* A M Duncan**, MA (St Andrews), BPhil, DipEd

Deputy Rector: P M Leckie, MA (Glasgow)

Bursar: C M Sharp, FCCA

Assistant Rector: Mrs A F McDonald, MA, DipEd
Assistant Rector: C J G Allison, MA, DipEd
Assistant Rector: D C Holmes, BA
Assistant Rector: R M Parlour, BSc, BA, FIAP

JUNIOR SCHOOL:

Head of Junior School: Mrs M Woodman, DipCE, LCP

Assistant Principal Teachers:

Mrs S N Leadbitter, DipCE
Mrs K J I McIntosh, DipCE
Mrs P L Hourd, BSc

Staff:
Miss E M Halliday, BSc
Mrs L J Mooney, DipCE
Mrs L Docherty, DipCE
Mrs E D Cargill, DipCE
Miss M A Keenan, BEd
Mrs M J Thurston, MA, PGCE
Miss M Cardno, MA, PGCE
Mrs L M Coupar, MA, PGCE
Mrs G M Wood, DipCE
Mrs L Smith, BEd
Mrs M A Ross, MA, PGCE
Miss C E Hulbert, MA, PGCE
Mrs A Davie, BEd
Mrs P J Halliwell, BEd
Mrs L Sutherland, BEd
Miss A L McCabe, BEd
Mrs I Goddard, BEd

Senior School:

English:
A T Chynoweth, MA (*Head Master*)
T F W Durrheim MA
Mrs E J Tosh, MA
Mrs D M Wilson, MA
M Stewart, MA, MPhil
Mrs M Massie, BA, MA
Miss J Fulton, MA

Drama and Media Studies:
R W Illsley MA (*Head Master*)
Miss J Fulton, MA

Modern Studies:
G J Rennet, MA (*Head Master*)

History:
I E R Wilson, MA (*Head Master*)
Mrs A F McDonald, MA
Mrs L A Hudson, MA
R M Toley, BA, MPhil
Miss T O'Reilly, BA

Geography:
Mrs V A Vannet, MA, DipEd (*Head Mistress*)
C R McAdam, MA
P M Leckie, MA
D C Holmes, BA
Mrs S B Williams, MA

Religious Studies:
Mrs F M Martin, MA (*Head Mistress*)
Ms B D Quigley, MTheol

Economics:
W S McCulloch, BA (*Head Master*)
Ms A L Ruxton, DipCom, DipEd
Mrs I Rattray

Classics:
J Meehan, MA (*Head Master*)
S A A McKellar, MA

Modern Languages:
P A B Mackenzie, MA (*Head of French*)
D O C Richterich, MA (*Head of German*)
Mrs L J Swankie, MA (*Head of Spanish*)
Mrs I M McGrath, MA (*Second Master, French*)
Mrs J L Seith, MA
Mrs I E Duncan, MA
Mrs F Cram, MA
Mrs G A Mackenzie, BA
C J G Allison, MA, DipEd

Mathematics:
G A Mordente, BSc (*Head Master*)
A G Blackburn, BSc
Miss S G Cannon, BSc
Mrs M A Oliver, BSc
A D Bell, BSc, BA
D J C Elgin, BSc, MSc
Mrs J McMeeken, BSc
R C Middleton, BSc

Chemistry:
R M B Macdonald, BSc (*Head Master*)
N P Forrest, BSc (*Second Master*)
C Foreman, LRSC
Mrs C A Sinclair, BSc

Biology:
Dr E Duncanson, BSc, PhD (*Head Master*)
Mrs R A Gibson, BSc
Mrs L A Woodley, BSc
G M S Rodger, BSc

Physics:
Mrs S H Fletcher, BSc, MSc (*Head Mistress*)
T Guild, BSc
R W Dollman, BSc
Dr G MacKay, BSc, MSc, PhD

Technology:
J Lewis, BSc (*Head Master*)
S S Blyth, DipTechEd

Computer Studies:
M Ryan, BSc, MSc, MEd (*Head Master*)
C P Stuart, BSc
A D Bell, BSc, BA
R M Parlour, BSc, BA, FIAP

Art and Craft:
G R Mackenzie, DipGrDes (*Headmaster*)
J T Cunningham, DA
Mrs I A Finnie, BA
Mrs A E Gouick, DA

Music:
Mrs J F Melville, DipMusEd (*Head Mistress*)
Mrs S J Magill, BMus
Mrs A Duffus, DipCE
D G Love, DipMusEd, DRSAMD
Mrs G Robertson, DipMus, ALCM
Mrs F M Crammond, DRSAM, ARCM, LTCL
S Armstrong, DRSAM

Learning Skills:
Mrs P A Maxwell, BEd (*Head of Department*)
A Wilson, BA

Physical Education:
A H Hutchison, DipPE (*Head Master*)
G W Spowart, BEd
Mrs J A Hutchison, DipPE
Mrs P Spowart, BEd
Miss J L Erskine, BA
P N Gallagher, BEd
W Nicol, SSI/Instructor in Outdoor Activities

Home Economics:
Mrs G A Madden, DipHome Econ (*Head Mistress*)
Miss L J Smith, MA

Guidance:

Principal Teachers:
Mrs L Hudson, MA
Mrs G A Madden, DipHomeEcon
C R McAdam, MA
G W Spowart, BEd

Assistant Principal Teachers:
Mrs F Cram, MA
Mrs I Finnie, BA
Mrs P Spowart, BEd
C Stuart, BSc

Careers Co-ordinators:
Miss L Smith, MA
R M Toley, BA, MPhil

Admission. The School comprises two sections:
The Junior School – 360 pupils (Primary 1 to Primary 7).
The Senior School – 725 pupils (Form 1 to Form 6).

The normal stages of entry are Primary 1 and Form 1. Entry to Primary 1 (age 4½ to 5½ years) is by interview held in January and to Form 1 (age 11 to 12 years) by an Entrance Examination held in February. Entrance is usually available at all other stages subject to satisfactory performance in an entrance test and interview.

Scholarships and Bursaries. A limited number of scholarships and bursaries are provided to pupils entering Form 1.

Fees per term. Junior School (Classes L1 to L5) £1,248; Junior School (Classes L6 and L7) £1,307; Senior School £1,775.

Buildings. The 3 main school buildings are in the centre of the city and form an architectural feature of the area. Two excellent playing fields – Dalnacraig and Mayfield – are situated some 1½ miles to the east of the school.

Curriculum. The Junior School follows the primary curriculum set down in the 5–14 Programme. Subject specialists are employed in Physical Education, Art, Home Economics, Music, French, Information Technology.

In the Senior School, after two years of a general curriculum, some specialisation takes place with pupils prepared for the Scottish Qualifications Authority Examinations at Standard Grade, Higher and Advanced Higher which lead directly to university entrance.

Extra-Curricular Activities. A wide range of activities is offered. There is a flourishing contingent of the Combined Cadet Force (Army and Navy Sections) including a pipe band; a company of Guides, Brownies and Rainbows. Drama, Public Speaking and Debating, Chess and Duke of Edinburgh Award Scheme are examples of the wide variety of activities available.

Music plays an important part in the life of the school. Special tuition is provided in a wide variety of instruments.

Former Pupils Clubs. Old Boys' Club: *Secretary:* N Barclay, Thorntons W S, Solicitors, 50 Castle Street, Dundee, DD1 3RU.

Old Girls' Club: *Secretary:* Mrs Lynda Boyle, 18 Glamis Road, Dundee, DD2 1ND.

Charitable status. The Corporation of the High School of Dundee is a Registered Charity, number SCO 11522. The school is a charity to provide quality education for boys and girls.

Durham School

Durham City DH1 4SZ.
Tel: (0191) 386 4783; Headmaster: (0191) 384 7977.
Fax: (0191) 383 1025; Headmaster: (0191) 386 9400
e-mail: headmaster@durhamschool.freeserve.co.uk
website: www.durhamschool.co.uk

Durham School is one of the oldest in England. It probably has a continuous history from Saxon times and has always been closely associated with the Diocese of Durham. As the Bishop's School it was re-organised and endowed by Cardinal Langley in 1414 and was re-founded in 1541 by Henry VIII as a Lay Foundation under the control of the Dean and Chapter of Durham. In 1995 it left the Cathedral Foundation to become a separate body and is now an associate school of the Woodard Foundation. The school became fully co-educational in September 1999.

Governing Body:
The Venerable J D Hodgson (*Chairman*)
Dr R G Baxter, BSc, PhD, FRAS
Mr P S Bell
Miss J L Hobbs
Revd Canon M Kitchen
Mr R A Langdon
Dr J W Marshall, BSc, PhD, FRAS
Mr F Nicholson
Dr S Oliver
Mr C M Watts, FCA, OD
The Rt Revd F Weston
Mrs H G Weston

Company Secretary and Clerk to the Governors: Mrs A M McWilliams, BA, ACIS

***Headmaster:* N G Kern**, MA, MSc

Deputy Headmaster: D R Best, BA

Chaplain: The Revd T J E Fernyhough, BD

Bursar: Mrs A M McWilliams, BA, ACIS

School Medical Officer: Dr B Docherty, MBChB, OBE

Assistant Staff:
A H Adams, MA
Miss P M Alpine, BA
J E Bell, BSc
J A Burgess, MA, BSc
M J Bushnell, BSc (*Housemaster*)
D M Crook, BA
J Curry, MA, BSc
H S Dias, BA (*Housemaster*)
Mrs K E Dougall, BA
Mrs J Duffitt, BSc
G J Earnshaw, BSc
J D Everatt, MA (*Director of Studies*)
Mrs D Evans, MA
M Farmborough, MA (*Housemaster*)
G R Froud, BA
P C Gerrard, BEd
R Gibbon, BSc
G Hallam, BSc (*Housemaster*)
Mrs E L P Hewitt, MA (*Housemistress*)
R N Hewitt, BEd
K S Jones, BSc
S Kime, BA
A M Mawhinney, BA
R A Muttitt, BMus
Mrs M F Proud, MA
J C Renshaw, BA
C N Riches, BA, MPhil
M O Stephens, BA
R Thomas, MA (*Senior Master - Marketing*)
A Wallace, BSc
Miss K L Wells, BA

The School is magnificently situated above the steep banks of the River Wear, overlooked by the West Towers of Durham Cathedral on the opposite bank, and has occupied its present site since 1844. A considerable sum of money has been spent during the last 15 years to provide first-class modern facilities for a wide variety of activities. A 47-terminal state-of-the-art ICT centre was opened in September 1999. While pursuing the highest academic standards, the School has an intellectual range which includes both prospective Oxford or Cambridge entrants and pupils who will succeed at 'A' level only with the careful teaching and support the School provides. The School's main objective is to bring out the best in every pupil. Everyone is expected to contribute fully to the life of the School and thus to develop their talents. The School provides the care, the teaching and the facilities to do this in happy and attractive surroundings. The School is closely connected to the Cathedral and all pupils attend Chapel on a regular basis.

Numbers are small (around 330), there is an excellent staffing ratio and the School is physically compact (all the buildings are within 2 minutes' walk of each other; the playing fields and the river are adjacent).

There are 5 Houses: 4 Senior and 1 Junior. Day pupils are fully integrated with the boarders and may leave School at 6, 7 or 9 pm each evening. School House, The Caffinites and Poole House are the senior houses for boys and Pimlico is the house for all girls with Ferens House being for Junior boys. The School thereby provides single sex Houses within a co-educational environment.

Admission. Up to a third of the intake enter Ferens House (boys) or Pimlico House (girls) at age 11, having taken the Durham School 11+ Entrance Examination in the previous February. Two-thirds of the School's pupils enter at age 13, having taken either the King's Scholarship Examination or the Common Entrance Examination. A number of pupils with good GCSE qualifications enter directly into the Sixth Form, including a significant number of girls. Such admission is by interview, testimonial and GCSE results. A prospectus with full details can be obtained on application to the Headmaster.

Academic. Academic courses are followed to GCSE, AS and A2 Levels. A broad programme is pursued during the years up to GCSE and there is a wide choice and flexible programme for the Sixth Form, which numbers about 120. There is a fully developed Careers Advisory Service.

Extra-Curricular Activities. A wide variety of Musical, Artistic, Dramatic, Sporting and other activities is available and new facilities have recently been provided for all of these. Various types of Adventure Training are pursued through the CCF, which includes the usual three Sections.

There is a strong tradition of excellence, particularly on the games field. Rugby is the main boys game in the Winter Term, Cricket, Athletics, Tennis, Swimming and Rowing in the Summer Term, while in the Easter Term pupils have a choice of ten different sports. Hockey, Netball, Rowing and Tennis are the main sports played by the girls, but, as for the boys, a wide range of other options is available.

Scholarships. (*see* Entrance Scholarship section) A generous range of Academic, Music, Design & Technology and Art Scholarships, together with All-Rounder and Sporting Awards, is available. King's Scholarships are awarded to pupils aged 13 to a possible maximum value of 50% fees for a boarder or a day pupil, while the Burkitt Scholarships are available for those seeking entry to the Sixth Form. Exhibitions are available to pupils aged 11. Clerical Bursaries are available for the sons of Clergy, and three Foundation Bursaries have been created at 11+ to fill the gap left by the Assisted Places Scheme.

Fees. Senior Boarder £4,538 per term; Senior Day £2,970 per term; Junior Boarders £3,863 per term; Junior Day £2,052 per term. Extras are kept to the minimum; there is a 10% sibling allowance for the younger brother or sister and a 5% discount for the children of Armed Services or Clergy families.

Bow School (the Durham School Preparatory School) became part of the Foundation in 1976. It has its own Headmaster and is run as a separate School, though it makes use of some of the Durham School facilities. Further details may be found in Part V.

The Old Dunelmian Society: *Secretary:* N G E Gedye, MA, Durham School, Durham DH1 4SZ

Charitable status. Durham School is a Registered Charity, number 1023407. It exists to provide a high quality education for boys and girls.

* Head of Department § Part Time or Visiting
† Housemaster/Housemistress ¶ Old Pupil
‡ See below list of staff for meaning

Eastbourne College

Eastbourne Sussex BN21 4JX.
Tel: Headmaster, (01323) 452320; Bursar, (01323) 452300
Fax: Headmaster, (01323) 452327; Bursar, (01323) 452307
e-mail: hmsec@eastbourne-college.co.uk
website: www.eastbourne-college.co.uk

Founded 1867; Incorporated 1911

Governing Body:
President: His Grace The Duke of Devonshire

Vice-Presidents:
The Marquess of Hartington, CBE
The Bishop of London

Council:
¶Sir Christopher Leaver, GBE, JP (*Chairman*)
¶P F Jeffery, FCA (*Vice-Chairman*)
Mrs L A Agutter
Mrs J E Atkinson
Dame Anne Barker, DBE (*The Hon Mrs Justice Rafferty, LLB*)
P A J Broadley, MA (Oxon), FCA
J Crawshaw
H Davies Jones, MA
C H D Everett, CBE, MA
A O MacKay, FRICS
Sir Charles Masefield, MA, CEng, FRAeS, FIMechE
The Rt Hon The Baroness Noakes, DBE
Dr M L Price, MA, FRCP
¶E G S Roose
¶Dr D L Smith, MA, PhD, PGCE, FRHistS
R J Wainwright, FRICS
¶D Winn, OBE, MInstM
¶S J D Yorke, MA

In attendance:
C M P Bush, MA
Sir Michael Richardson
F W Roache, MA, MBA, FRSA

Clerk to the Council and Bursar: M R H Lower, MBA, MSc, CEng, FIMechE

***Headmaster:* C M P Bush**, MA

Second Master: D A Stewart

Director of Studies: S A White, MA

Registrar: Mrs P M Duffill, CertEd

Chaplain: The Revd C K Macdonald, BA

Assistant Chaplain: The Revd C J Comyns, MA, BD

Art:
*N P Moseley, BA
§J Gray, BA
Mrs J L A Harriott, BA
§Miss V J Morris, BA
§B L Kent, CertEd, HNC(Tech)

Drama:
*T W Marriott, BA
§K W Lawrence, BEd

Classics:
*S J Beal, BA
§Miss S Norman, BA
J S Radcliffe, BA
§Mrs S J R Wooldridge, MA

Economics & Business Studies:
*R E Heale, BSc
Mrs J White, MA

Design Technology:
*W L Trinder, BEd
E Firkins, BSc
Miss L E Le Lievre, BA

EFL:
§Mrs A E B Williams, BA, MA
§Mrs A V Sweet, CertTESOL

English:
*C B K Polden, MA
Mrs P M Duffill, CertEd
S G Hamill, BA
†P H Lowden, MA
N J Russell, MA
D A Stewart
§N L Wheeler, JP, BA

General Studies:
*J Thornley, BA

Geography:
*A T Lamb, BA
†G J L Kene, BSc
Miss F E King, BA, MA

History:
*A K Boxer, MA
R H Bunce, BA
¶D N West, BA

Information Technology:
*R A Wilson, CertEd

Learning Resources:
Ms K F Ecclestone, BA, MLib

Mathematics:
*N G Pendry, BSc, BA
C H Allison, BA
I R Shakespeare, BSc
J C Stevens, BEng
†J A Sykes, BSc
†J R Wooldridge, MA

Modern Languages:
*D J Ruskin, BA
†Miss F E Donaldson, MA
†J H Newton, MA, MCollP, DipMS(Ed), PhD
R A Penn, BA
J Thornley, BA
§Mrs L Topham, BA
C D Waller, MA, PhD, FIL

Music:
*G L Jones, BA
D R S Force, BA
S J Vegh

Physical Education:
*A P Wynn, BA
Miss A L Keelan, BA
Miss J M Lawes, BA

Science:

Biology:
*C C Corfield, BSc
†D J Beer, BSc
†C S Bostock, BA, MSc
§Mrs S E Morison, BSc
Mrs D Tomanoczyora, MA
¶A S Wood, BSc

Chemistry:
*R C Edmondson, BScTech, MSc, PhD
¶†D C Miller, BSc
D A Parker, BSc, PhD, FRSC
O L Richards, BA

Physics:
*G L Jones, MA, PhD
D J Hodkinson, BSc
J E Little, BA, MSc
S A White, MA

Part-time Musicians:
Mrs B Ashby, GRSM, CertEd (*Oboe*)
Miss S Carter, GMus (*Flute*)
Miss C Clipsham, BMus (*Piano*)
Miss R Dines, LRAM, ARCM, BMus, MMus (*Piano*)
P Edwards, GRSM (*Head of Woodwind*)
M Elliott, MA (*Singing*)
Miss C Emery (*Double Bass*)
K Goddard (*Guitar and Bass Guitar*)
C Horton (*French Horn*)
H Jones, AGSM (*Percussion and Bassoon*)
Mrs J Mansergh, FTCL, LTCL, ARCO (*Head of Keyboard*)
Ms S Scriven, GGSM (*Trumpet and Trombone*)
Miss S Stuart-Pennink, ARCM (*Cello*)

Boarding. There are 3 Boys' Boarding Houses (Wargrave, Gonville and Pennell) and 2 Girls' Boarding Houses (Nugent and School House).

Day. There are 3 Day Boy Houses (Powell, Reeves and Craig) and one Day Girl House (Blackwater). They are run on similar lines to the Boarding Houses and day pupils eat supper at school and do their prep in their Houses before returning home.

Co-education. The College has taken girls into the Sixth Form since 1969 and went fully co-educational in September 1995.

Situation. The College is situated in the prime residential part of the town adjacent to Devonshire Park and close to the Congress Theatre which gives access to a wide range of cultural opportunities. Access to the train to Gatwick and London at Eastbourne Station is a 10 minute walk. The College plays a full part helping people in need in the local community through its SAS (Service and Skills) and PIPS (Pupils in Primary Schools) programmes.

Work. All pupils study a wide range of subjects in their first year which includes an opportunity to study Classics as well as a second Modern Language. At GCSE pupils take Maths, English, French, Science, a humanity and choice of options. At AS Level, pupils select four subjects from a total of 25 offered.

Religion. Eastbourne College is a Christian school and all boys and girls are given instruction in the Christian faith and experience of Christian worship in the College Chapel.

Sport. A wide variety of sports is offered: Rugby and Cricket for boys; Netball for girls. Hockey, Rowing, Athletics, Tennis, Squash, Fives, Cross-Country Running, Sailing, Fencing, Swimming, Golf, etc. for boys and girls. All games pitches are within a short walking distance. There is an artificial hockey pitch, which also forms 12 tennis courts and a second all-weather surface.

Numbers. In 2000/2001 there were 530 pupils, of which just over half were boarders. Girls made up nearly one third of the school.

Fees. Boarding, Boys/Girls £15,465, Day Boys/Girls £9,990. These figures include meals and almost all extras.

Scholarships and Bursaries. (*see* Entrance Scholarship section) Junior Academic, Music and Art Scholarships and Exhibitions are offered up to 50% to candidates of sufficient merit who present themselves. They must be under 14 on 1 September in the year they are due to enter the College. 1998 saw the introduction of 4 new all-rounder awards annually, the Forbes Wastie Awards, worth 25% of the fees. The same age restriction applies. Senior Academic (including Art) and Music Scholarships and Exhibitions are offered to pupils who join the school after GCSEs in Year 12.

Admission. Boys and girls are generally admitted between the ages of 13 and 14 years in Year 9 or for the Sixth Form Year 12 after GCSE examinations. A prospectus and application form may be obtained from the Registrar who is always glad to welcome parents who would like to visit the school. A £30 Registration Fee is charged and a guaranteed acceptance of a place is confirmed on payment of £300 fee a year before a pupil is due to come to the College. £250 of this fee is held as a deposit against extras and is returned on the final account. Sixth Form pupil registration takes place after the interviews in November or March when £300 is payable to confirm a place with £250 refunded on the final account.

Term of Entry. All pupils start in September. Exceptional cases are considered at other times.

Development Plan. All boarding and day houses have been rebuilt or totally refurbished recently. The conversion of the Cavendish Library into a modern Learning Resources Centre was completed in October 1998. Plans are in place for a whole site review and further building is imminent. Science and Design Technology will be the major priority.

Activities. No special emphasis is placed upon any particular activity and so excellence exists in many areas. A pupil may be a valued member of the community without being an athlete or a scholar, but all pupils are encouraged to do something well. A variety of clubs and societies flourish, standards in drama and art are excellent and music thrives with a strong choral tradition. The CCF offers a huge range of activities and leadership opportunities, including the Duke of Edinburgh Award Scheme. College expeditions have visited Bolivia, Borneo, the Himalayas and Sulawesi in the last four years. ICT is central to the learning experience and the College is now networked with its own Intranet. Coursework in the History, Geography and Biology Departments benefits from a location close to the Sussex countryside and the coast.

Old Eastbournian Association. A thriving OEA, which celebrated its century in 1995, maintains a strong link with past pupils and publishes a Careers' Directory to link OEs and offer assistance to current pupils. *Secretary:* R

B Harrison Esq, Marlborough House, Old Wish Road, Eastbourne, E Sussex BN21 4JY.

Preparatory School. The College has close links with St Andrew's School, Meads, Eastbourne. These were forged following a merger with the College Preparatory School in 1977. St Andrew's is an Independent Preparatory School preparing boys and girls for a variety of schools but with a significant number of pupils coming on to the College, many on scholarships.

Charitable status. Eastbourne College Incorporated is a Registered Charity, number 307071. It exists for the purpose of educating children.

The Edinburgh Academy

42 Henderson Row Edinburgh EH3 5BL.
Tel: 0131-556 4603
Fax: 0131 556 9353

Lord Cockburn, Leonard Horner and John Russell, WS, were chiefly responsible for the foundation of The Edinburgh Academy, which was incorporated by Royal Charter 5th Geo. IV. Sir Walter Scott, one of the original Directors, presided at the opening ceremony in 1824. The Academy is an independent School governed by a Court of Directors, usually composed of Academicals.

Court of Directors:

Chairman: J H W Fairweather, MA, DBA

Co-opted Members:
The Rector
The Headmaster of Junior School

Extraordinary Directors:
Major General D C Alexander, CB
The Hon Lord Cameron of Lochbroom, PC, FRSE
Dr A G Donald, CBE, MA, MB, ChB, DPH, FRCGP, FRCPEd
V Lall, BA, CA (*FGPC Committee*)
J B Leggat, LLB, NP, WS (*PPC Chairman*)

Elected Directors:
G A Allan, MA (*PPC*)
Mrs R Bell, BA (*PPC*)
A D Burnett, LLB
Mrs A Campbell (*PPC*)
M W Gregson, BSc, MBA (*FGPC; EA Sports Ltd*)
A M Hathorn, CA, CPSA (*FGPC*)
W R M Henderson, MA, FRICS (*PPC; Chairman EA Sports Ltd*)
Dr I A Laing, MD, FRCPE, FRCPCH (*PPC*)
Ms R Marshall, BSc, FCCA
Sir Bruce Pattullo, CBE
P D Stevenson, BA (*PPC*)
M T Thyne, MA, FRSE
A M R Tod, MA, FSI (*FGPC*)
J D B Workman, MA, FCIBS

Representative Director (*appointed by the Edinburgh Academical Club Council*):
R A Lutton

FGPC = Finance & General Purposes Committee
PPC = Planning & Policy Committee

Secretary and Bursar: Colonel A W Blackett, OBE

***Rector:* J V Light**, MA (Clare College, Cambridge)

Deputy Rector: D M Standley, MA (Oxon), CPhys, MInstP

Senior School Staff:
R T Wightman, BSc (Edinburgh), PhD (OU)
J J C Fenton, MA (Cantab)
G H Harris, MA (Cantab)
T Blackmore, BSc, PhD (Bristol)
H E Marsh, BA (Strathclyde)
A Cook, BSc, CBiol, MIBiol (Aberdeen)
J M Ellis, RA Schools (London)
D M Bonnyman, MA, BPhil (St Andrews)
*D F Buckley, BA (Oxon), AIA
*J H Clearie, MA, MSc, MIL (Edinburgh)
T Blackmore, BSc, PhD (Bristol)
*P B Hall, MA (Oxon)
Mrs V A Bland, BSc, MIBiol (Nottingham)
J D Hudson, BSc (Belfast) (*Geits Year Head*)
G M Trotter, MTheol (St Andrews)
Miss G Arbuthnott, BSc (St Andrews)
Mrs D Hope, DA, (Edinburgh) (*Art*)
J R Meadows, BA (Dunelm)
J E Miller, BA (Oxon)
M A L Shipley, BSc (Heriot Watt)
Miss S M Hennessy, BA (Cardiff)
Mrs J M Marsh, MA (Dundee)
H A Hashmi, MA (Aberdeen)
R W Tiplady, DPE (Otago)
P Davidson, BEng (Edinburgh), BA(OU)
E K G Saunders, BA (Leeds Metropolitan)
Miss S G S Lamb, MA (Glasgow)
A K Tart, MA (Cantab)
C A Brookman, BSc, PhD (Edinburgh), GRSC, MInstP
M Bryce, BSc (Stirling)
Mrs Y D Harley, LL (Sorbonne)
Mrs E Murby, BA (Edinburgh)
C E Cooke, BSc (Napier)
N Armstrong, MA, CPhys, MInstP
G Glen, BSc
Dr J R Coutts, BSc
S Matthews, MA (Dundee)
D P Tidswell
Mrs E Stark, MA (St Andrews)
S A Mair
Mrs C A Trotter

Music
*P N Coad, MA, PhD (Cantab), FRCO (*Director*)
P E Backhouse, BMus, FRCO, ARCM
L Morrison, DRSAM
Mrs M A Ferguson, DRSAM

Chaplain: Canon P J D Allen, MA (Cantab), PGC

Librarian: Mrs E Mackay

CO, CCF: Major R G Turner, QOHldrs

CCF Staff Instructor: R Munro, QOHldrs

Junior School Staff:

Headmaster: C R F Paterson, MA (Aberdeen)
Deputy Head: A R Dyer, MA (St Andrews)
Head of Early Years: Mrs L A Becher, DCE (Dundee), INSC
Director of Studies: A Dickenson, MA (St Andrews)

Mrs J T Cairns, DCE (Moray House)
Mrs L A Cormack, DCE (Moray House)
R A J Gray, DCE (Moray House)
W D Wilson, DipEd (Auckland)
Mrs E F Black, BEd (Stirling), DCE (Moray House)
Mrs J F Murray, CertEd (Edgehill)
Miss M P Murray, DCE (Call Park)
Mrs B Robertson, BEd (Dundee)
Mrs E Watt, CertEd (Moray House)
R Clarke, BSc (Aberdeen)
A Morrison, BA (Durham)
Miss A Thomson, BSc (Napier), PGCE (Paisley)
Mrs C Petrie, BEd, HDNS (Northern College)
Miss K L Davidson, BEd (Northern College)
Mrs L Matthews
S G McRae
Mrs E B Mackie
J R Gavel

Head of Nursery: Mrs E Denholm, DipEd (Moray House)

Denham Green Nursery:
Mrs A Addison, NNEB
Mrs K Thomson, PCNN

Scott House Nursery:
Mrs M Noakes, DCE, INSC
Mrs K Jones, NNEB
Mrs M McEwan, NNEB
Miss T Hope

Art: Ms V Leckie, BA Hons, Fine Art (Nottingham)
Head of Physical Education & Games: Mrs A M Connor, BEd (Dunfermline), MEd (Edinburgh)
Learning Support: Mrs P M Moubray, MA, MEd (Edinburgh)
Music:
Miss S C Graham, DRSAM
Mrs M M Donaldson, BMus (Edinburgh), LRAM

The Edinburgh Academy consists of a Senior School, containing about 500 boys (ages 10½ to 18), over 30 girls (in the VIth Form), and a Junior School containing about 300 boys (ages 4½ to 10½). A Nursery Department was opened in January 1984.

Site and Buildings. The Senior School occupies a site in Henderson Row, less than a mile from Princes Street and at the northern limits of the Georgian 'New Town', of which it was designed to be a part. The buildings there include a School Hall, Library, a Music School built in 1990, a Seventh Form Centre, extensive Laboratories, Dining Hall, Gymnasium, Miniature Rifle Range, Fives Courts, etc. In the Spring of 1977 an adjacent school in its own grounds was acquired thereby doubling the area of the existing site and allowing for a programme of immediate development aimed at major improvements to the general facilities of the Senior School. The Playing-fields are about half a mile from the main buildings – Raeburn Place (8½ acres) (shared with the Old Boys), New Field in Inverleith Place (20 acres), and a further 5 acres, also at Inverleith, with a Running Track. There are Squash Rackets courts both at Raeburn Place and at Inverleith and all-weather Tennis Courts at New Field. The Academy possesses its own Field Centre in the Highlands (Glen Doll, Angus).

Forms. (Senior School only). VIIth and VIth Classes: by tutor groups studying either GCE 'A 'levels or Highers. Vths: 4 Classes in sets for subjects. IVths: 4 Classes in sets for subjects. IIIrds: 3 Classes in sets for subjects. IInds: 3 Classes in sets for subjects. Ists: 3 Classes. No teaching group consists of more than 24 boys, and many are substantially smaller.

VIth Form Girls. A number of girls, day and boarding, are admitted each year to take an 'A' level or Highers course.

Scheme of Work. In the Junior classes of the Upper School all boys do English, History, Geography, Latin, French, Mathematics, Science, Art and DT, Electronics, Computing, Drama and Music. German may be started in the IIIrds, Business Studies, Technology, CDT, Electronics, Art and Music may be studied as full subjects in the IVths. GCSE is taken in the Vths. In the VIth a number of boys take SCE Highers (whereby many achieve Scottish university entrance qualifications) and others do first year work in preparation for GCE 'A' level. A wide choice of subjects is possible. GCE 'A' level and STEP are taken in the VIIths in Classics, History, English, Modern Languages, Mathematics, Physics, Chemistry, Biology, Geography, Business Studies, Economics, Art, Music, and pupils are prepared for University entrance. Options in Philosophy and Computer Studies are also available. Places at Oxford and Cambridge have been regularly won in all departments. In 2000 over 80% of our pupils went on to study degree courses.

Divinity. An assembly for Prayers is held at 8.50 am each morning, and is attended by the whole school. In every class one period a week is devoted to Religious Education. On Sundays the boys in the Boarding Houses attend one or other of the nearby churches (according to denomination). School Services for the whole School are held on several occasions during each term.

Physical Education and Games. All pupils take Physical Education and Games (which are regarded as an integral part of the curriculum) unless they are specially exempted on medical grounds. Rugby Football is played in the Autumn Term and during half of the Spring Term as are Hockey and Association Football. Cross-Country Running and other games occupy the first part of this Term. Cricket is the principal game in the Summer Term, with Athletics, Hockey, Sailing, Shooting, Swimming and Tennis as alternatives for senior boys. Golf, Rugby Fives, Squash Rackets and Badminton are also played, and instruction in Fencing and Judo is available.

Combined Cadet Force. All boys over 14½ join the CCF unless specially exempted and they may enter directly into either the RN, Army or RAF Sections. All members of the CCF are required to attend at least the Annual Camp in their first year and in 1 other year at their choice. After 6 terms of service a boy is free to leave the CCF. The Academy has a Pipe Band. Piping and Drumming classes are held for boys in the Junior classes of the Upper School as well as for members of the CCF.

Duke of Edinburgh's Award and Outdoor Activities. Considerable importance is attached to the preparation and training of boys to take the various stages of the Award. A large number of boys participate and there are regular weekly meetings for practice and instruction as well as week-end expeditions from time to time. Apart from the Award, boys are encouraged to take part in outdoor ('Adventure') activities. The Academy's Field Centre in Glen Doll, Angus, is ideally situated as a centre for Hill-Walking, Climbing, Skiing, Fishing, and for Geographical and Biological Field Studies.

Music, Drama, Art. A purpose-built Music School was opened in 1992. In addition to the full-time Music Staff, there are a number of visiting teachers for various instruments. Musical appreciation and Singing form part of the curriculum of the Junior Classes. Throughout the rest of the Senior School there are regular periods of Music Appreciation. Boys are encouraged to learn a Musical Instrument and over 300 do. There is a Choral Society, a Choir, and a special 'Small Choir', a School Orchestra, Junior Orchestra, and a Wind Band. Inter-Division Music Competitions, both Choral and Instrumental, are held annually. Also important are the Pipe Band and the Dance Band and Jazz Band.

There are several Senior and Junior Dramatic productions each year, including a major Play, Opera or Musical, and there is a Drama Competition involving all pupils in the IVth classes. A major Choral work is performed each year, and a number of informal Saturday evening Concerts are given through the year.

Art and CDT are included in the curriculum from the Junior Classes and there are regular lessons in Art Appreciation throughout the School. With a new Art Centre recently opened, facilities are good and standards high. Pupils are regularly prepared for GCSE and 'A' level or for SCE 'Higher' in Music and Art.

Other Activities. There are Arts, Debating, History, Modern Languages, Photographic, Fly Fishing, Jazz, Motor, Mountaineering, Opera, Politics, Computer and Electronic, Scientific and Mathematical Societies; Scripture Union and Video Club, Bridge, Chess, Fencing Clubs, and Classes for the further study of Art and for Scottish Country Dancing. All boys have an opportunity each week to devote some time to some creative art or craft, Music, Painting, Pottery, etc. for which good facilities are available.

Junior School. The Senior Department of the Junior School (ages 6½ to 10½) is in a building opened in 1960, close to New Field and the Boarding Houses. The Early Years Department (ages 4½ to 6½) is in Denham Green House, built in 1987 on the same site. The Nursery (boys and girls aged 3+) is also housed at Denham Green and shares its facilities, with a qualified Mistress in charge. The work of the Junior School is arranged so as to ensure a smooth transition to the Senior School. All boys in the Junior School have Physical Education. Boys in the Senior Department play Rugby and Association Football and Cricket. For Music, there are 2 full-time teachers and a number of visiting teachers for various instruments. Musical Appreciation and singing form part of the curriculum and every encouragement is given to boys to learn a Musical Instrument and to take part in the wide range of Musical Activities offered by various Choirs and Instrumental Groups.

Boarding. Jeffrey House is attractively situated in Kinnear Road in Inverleith, a particularly pleasant part of the city. It is adjacent to the Junior School.

Boarding is recommended for boys from Primary 5 to Senior 7 and girls in Senior 6 and 7.

It is a particular advantage that, in and out of school, boarders mix easily with day pupils. They can benefit from the participation of families in the life of the school, and take a full part in the rich cultural life of Edinburgh. This includes theatres, cinemas, concerts, exhibitions and the Festival Theatre.

Leave to visit relatives or friends can be arranged to suit individual requirements.

The Housemaster is assisted by his wife, the Matron and the Assistant Matron. Boarders normally register with the local group practice under the National Health Service, and a doctor holds a surgery weekly in Jeffrey House.

Residence. No day boy may attend the Academy who does not live under the charge of his parents or legal guardian. Exemptions from this rule are rarely made by the Directors, and only in very exceptional cases.

Fees. The fees per term from 1 April 2001 are: Henderson Row (11–18) Class 1 £1,729, Classes 2-7 £2,105; (9–11) (Primaries 5 and 6) £1,477; (7–9) (Primaries 3 and 4) £1,394. Denham Green (6–7) (Primary 2) £1,098; (5–6) (Primary 1) £1,031. Boarding Fee £2,383; Weekly Boarding and Flexi-boarding are also provided.

When 3 or more brothers or sisters are in attendance at the School at the same time, a reduction of one-third of the tuition fees is made for each brother or sister after the first two. Comparable discounts are given where families have three or more children at the Academy and at St George's School at the same time – details on application to the Secretary and Bursar.

Scholarships. (*see* Entrance Scholarship section) A number of Entrance Scholarships or Exhibitions are offered for competition each year, including awards recently introduced for Sixth Form entrants. Other candidates must be under 14 on 1 March. Boys already at the Academy are not eligible to compete. The Examination takes place in mid February. Further details are available from the Registrar. There are a number of Exhibitions available during a boy's career in the Upper School, and Bursaries for award in cases of need which may arise. A number of awards are available to former Academy pupils attending Universities, including a closed Scholarship to University College, Oxford.

Admission. The majority of new boys are admitted at the beginning of the Autumn Term in September, though they can be accepted at any time. Places can always be found at P5 (8½–9½), and there are places each year at VIth Form level in the Upper School, and also in the Ist and IInd Classes (10½–12½), where special provision is made for boys who have previously done no languages; and there are often casual vacancies at other levels.

All candidates for admission to the Academy must first be assessed by the School. For admission in September, candidates for the Junior Department of the Junior School are assessed in January; those for the Senior Department, and for the Upper School in February. Boys who have been prepared for Common Entrance may take it in February or June.

Boys should be registered as candidates for entry as early as possible. Application forms are obtainable from the Admissions Secretary. There is a registration fee of £20.

There is a strong Academical Club, whose headquarters are at Raeburn Place, Edinburgh 4 (Tel: 0131-332 1070). *Secretary:* J J Burnet Esq., The Edinburgh Academy, 42 Henderson Row, Edinburgh EH3 5BL. (Tel: 0131-556 4603).

Charitable status. The Edinburgh Academy is a Registered Charity, number 32356. It exists to provide good quality education.

Elizabeth College

Guernsey Channel Islands.
Tel: 01481 726544.
Fax: 01481 714176

Elizabeth College was founded in 1563 by Queen Elizabeth I in order to provide education for boys seeking ordination in the Church of England. It is one of the original members of the Headmasters' Conference and has Direct Grant status. It provides a broad education while maintaining the Christian aspirations of its Foundress. There are approximately 700 boys in the College, of whom about 130 are in the Lower School. Girls are accepted into the Sixth Form.

Motto: *'Semper Eadem'*.

Visitor: The Bishop of Winchester

Directors:
The Very Rev The Dean of Guernsey (*Chairman*)
Jurat D C Lowe
Mrs S Beaton
Jurat M J Wilson
Mrs L C Morgan
Deputy J Kitts
Conseiller M W Torode
Advocate J N van Leuven
Mr R Pittman

***Principal:* D E Toze**, MBE, EdM (Harvard)

Vice-Principal: S G D Morris, BSc

Director of Studies: A R Cross, MA

Members of Teaching Staff:

J R Pedlar, BSc
I J Rawlins-Duquemin, CertEd
M P Higgins, BSc
R H Surcombe, BA, LTCL
P L Le Cocq, CertEd
S Rahman, MA
T H Bell, MA
B W Allen, CertEd
G Guilbert, BSc, MIBiol
J R Hooker, BA
R J W James, BA
C R W Cottam, MA
Dr D F Raines, BSc, DPhil
M E Kinder, BEd
Dr C D van Vlymen, BSc, PhD
B E H Aplin, BSc
A M Jewell, BEd
Mrs E M Adams, DipID
J M Hunter, MA
C A Gillespie, BA
D R L Inderwick, BA
M S Webb, BEd
G S Cousens, BA
Mrs A Thibeault, MA
Mrs P E Maher, BA, ARCM
G ap Sion, BSc
Mrs M C Dudley, BA
K I Mathieson, MA
Miss P C Voûte, MA
L Hudson, BA (Hons), PGCE
D Vaughan, PGCE, BSc

A Hale, BSc, PGCE
P Brooks, BEd
M Garnett, BA, PGCE
Miss C D Hedges, BSc, PGCE
Miss C S Duncan, BA, PGCE
J C S F Smithies, BSc, BA, MBA, PGCE
Miss C Hélie, LLCE
Dr M E Ogier, BSc, PhD
J B Slingo, BSc, PGCE

Chaplain: The Revd S A Baker, BEd

Director of Music: P C Harris, GRSM, ARCM

Games and Physical Education: D Wray, BEd

Head of the Lower School: Mrs S Battey, CertEd

Mrs S J Holland, BEd
Mrs N J Stevens, BEd
Mrs J Hunter
N Rothwell, BA Hons, PGCE
Mrs K Robinson, BEd
Mrs D Parrott, CertEd
A Fooks, BA
Mrs L Eyton-Jones, BEd

Headmistress of Pre-Prep: Mrs B A Amy, BPhilEd

Mrs A Bodman, BSc
Miss C Matthews, BEd
Mrs Jurkiewicz
Mrs S Appleton, DipEd

Bursar and Clerk to the Directors: K V Austin, Esq

Buildings and Grounds. The Upper School (for boys over 11 years and VIth form girls) is situated in imposing buildings dating from 1826 which stand on a hill overlooking the town and harbour of St Peter Port. The classrooms and laboratories, all of which are equipped with appropriate modern teaching aids, the Hall, Sports Hall and Swimming Pool are accommodated on this site. Recent improvements have included a new Art School, improved Design and Technology and ICT facilities. There are two large games fields, where one of which includes an artificial pitch for hockey, soccer and tennis. The Lower School, Beechwood, has its own site some ten minutes walk away. It takes boys from 7 to 11 years old. The Pre-Prep School, Acorn House, accepts boys and girls from 4 to 7 years old and also has a nursery facility for younger children.

Academic Curriculum. In their first three years in the Upper School boys follow a broad curriculum which is common to all - covering arts, sciences, creative and practical subjects. Information Technology is timetabled in all three years to develop the skills needed for the demands of GCSE and A Level courses. Opportunity is also afforded to boys to sample both Latin and a second Modern Foreign Language in addition to French. PSHE, RE and PE and Games are timetabled throughout. In years Four and Five the aim is to produce a high level of satisfaction and achievement in GCSE subjects by offering flexibility wherever possible. Three separate sciences will, therefore, be taken by some, but the majority do Combined Science (Dual Award). At least one modern language must be taken, although two are available as an option. English Literature is studied within the English teaching groups, but is not compulsory for all. Other GCSE options combine the traditional with the contemporary. Art, Business Studies, Classics, Graphics, History, Information Technology, Latin, Music, PE and RS are currently offered. Alongside the GCSE courses PSHE and RE continue to be taught. The Sixth Form is run in partnership with The Ladies' College, with interchange of pupils between schools and shared teaching of many groups. From September 2000 the Sixth Form will offer a very broad array of choices. Students will be able to study varying combinations of AS and A2 Levels up to a maximum of four A2 Levels and one AS Level. Some AS Levels will be offered as 2 year courses, for example, Film Studies and Psychology. Key Skills will be delivered and monitored within the timetable and a programme of visiting speakers will be scheduled at regular intervals. Tutorial periods will be built in to enable vocational, careers and pastoral guidance to be available.

Music. There are two orchestras, a brass band, a wind band and a number of chamber music groups. The College choir makes regular visits to the French mainland to sing in Cathedrals and at concerts. Instruction is available in all the usual orchestral instruments in addition to the piano and organ. The Lower School has its own choir, orchestra and recorder group. Each summer holiday the College hosts a weeklong orchestral course when tuition is provided by eminent professionals to over one hundred and fifty boys and girls.

Games. The sports fields cover some 20 acres. The Lower School has its own small playing field, and also has access to the facilities of the Upper School. The major College games are Association Football, Hockey and Cricket. Athletics, Badminton, Basketball, Cross-country Running, Fencing, Golf, Rugby Football, Sailing, Shooting, Squash, Swimming, Tennis and Volleyball also flourish. Physical Education forms a regular part of the curriculum for all boys up to the end of the Fifth Form. Some seniors specialise in Outdoor Pursuits (principally canoeing and climbing) as their "sport". This is under the guidance of a fully qualified expert. Despite the size of the Island, plentiful opposition is available. The College competes against other Island schools, has a traditional rivalry with Victoria College in Jersey, makes regular tours to the mainland and hosts return visits from UK schools.

Combined Cadet Force. The Contingent includes all three arms: Royal Navy, Army and Royal Air Force sections. Parties go annually on Summer Camp and Adventurous Training. The College Shooting VIII forms a part of the Combined Cadet Force and has a long record of distinguished appearances at Bisley and elsewhere. The CCF is the only weapon-carrying force in the Island and, therefore, has an important role in providing guards of honour on many ceremonial occasions.

Duke of Edinburgh's Award. Boys are encouraged to participate in this scheme at all three levels. The expedition work necessarily takes place on the mainland during the Easter and Summer holidays.

Community Service Unit. This Unit draws boys from the Fourth year and above. It serves those in need and those who are handicapped throughout the Island community.

Scouts. There is an active Scout Group, whose headquarters is situated on the College Field. At the Lower School there is a Cub Scout Group.

Clubs and Societies. The College stresses the importance of extra-curricular activity. Among currently active clubs are those which foster Bridge, Canoeing, Chess, Debating, Drama, Fencing, Life Saving, Model Railways, Music, Sailing, Science, Shooting, Table Tennis, Tai-Chi, War Gaming and Windsurfing.

Pastoral Care. In the Upper School each year has a Head of Year assisted by four Tutors. The Lower School has its own Headmaster and the Pre-Prep has a Headmistress. All these staff provide pastoral care and academic guidance for their own sections of the College. They are supported by a full-time Chaplain who conducts services in all three schools as well as annually preparing boys for Confirmation.

Parental Involvement. Parents are strongly encouraged to take an active part in their son's education. There are regular assessments and reports to which they are invited to respond, either immediately or at annual parent's evenings. Masters responsible for pastoral matters are also available on the telephone during out of school hours for discussion about problems or progress.

Admission. The principal ages for admission into the school are 4, 7, 11, 13 and 16, but there are usually vacancies for entry at other ages. Entry is either by means of tests which are adapted to the age of the applicant or, at

13, by Common Entrance. There is a £75 non-refundable registration fee. Applications for entry should be addressed to the Principal.

Scholarships to the College. (*see* Entrance Scholarship section) The Gibson Fleming Fund provides Scholarships whose value depends to some extent upon the needs of the applicant's parents. The Trustees review their Scholars each year and take account of general personal qualities as well as academic performance. Entries should be made by the 31st March, although they may be accepted after that date.

Choral and Instrumental Scholarships are also available. Details of these may be obtained from the Principal.

Scholarships to the Universities. The College Exhibitions, Scholarships and Prizes include the Queen's Exhibition, the Lord de Sausmarez Exhibition; the Mainguy Scholarship; the Mansell Exhibition and the Mignot Fund. The Gibson Fleming Trust can also provide awards to its Scholars for their future education.

Travel. There are several flights each day from Southampton (half an hour), Gatwick (about three quarters of an hour) and Stansted (about one hour). There are also regular flights to the West Country and to Midlands and northern airports. There are frequent sailings to and from Poole and Weymouth, which offer vehicle transportation.

Old Boys. The Honorary Secretary of the Old Elizabethan Association is R C N Roussel, Esq, Cobo Farm, Castel, Guernsey. Telephone: (01481) 255862.

Annual School Fees. Day: £3,600. Pre-Prep: £3,255 (including lunches).

Ellesmere College

Ellesmere Shropshire SY12 9AB.
Tel: (01691) 622321
Fax: (01691) 623286

Ellesmere College is one of the Schools of the Society of SS. Mary and John of Lichfield, the Midland Division of the Woodard Corporation, and was opened on 8 September 1884.

Motto: *'Pro Patria Dimicans'.*

Founder: The Revd Nathaniel Woodard, DCL, then Dean of Manchester

Visitor: The Rt Revd The Lord Bishop of Lichfield

College Council:
The Revd W Weaver, BA, BD (*Provost*)
A J Vernon
Mrs P Woodward
P J McNair, MA
Mrs P C Griffith (*Custos*)
T F Neville, CA
The Rt Revd D Hallatt, Bishop of Shrewsbury
R F Taylor, MA
J R Bridgeland, MA (*ex officio*)

***Head Master:* B J Wignall**, MA, MIMgt

Senior Deputy Head: J M Marshall, BSc

Second Deputy Head: *A P Corish, BSc, BA

Senior Mistress: Mrs C S Newbold, BA

Head of Lower School: N A Price, BA

Director of Studies: M D T Sampson, BSc

Director of Activities: K J Shuttleworth, MA

Chaplain: The Revd T J Harvey, MA

Senior Tutor: *P A Wood, MA

Bursar: Lt Col T Lowry, FCIS, MIMgt

Assistant Teachers:
*T C Howitt-Dring
W C Newbold, BA
*S F W Purcell, BA
*P A Goodwin, BEd
*R A Yarrow, BA
†G Hutchinson, MA
†D W Reffell, BA
Mrs S Hooper, BA
†*C H Deakin, ARMCM
Mrs R C Ashley, BSc
†M P Clewlow, BSc
Mrs J E Purcell, BA
Mrs I M Peacock, PhD
*N M Blake, BSc
F S Williams, CertEd
P J Hayes, MA
†M R D Stone, BA
Mrs H Scarisbrick, BA
*Miss K A Savage, BA
*Mrs R A McCarthy, MA, DipBDA, AMBDA
*C D Richmond, BSc
*A D Ashworth-Jones, BSc
Mrs S E Morgan, BEd
Mrs A M Murray, CertEd
Mrs O Purslow, BA, MEd, AMBDA
Mrs S Murdoch, BA, AMBDA
Mrs A M Hendrikson, BA, AMBDA
C Moir, BSc
J A Brodie, BA
Miss D Joynson, BEd
*Miss T Turner, MA
Mrs A L Wignall, BA
†Mrs N L Stone, BEc
Mrs M V Pritchard, BSc, AMBDA
*A McClure, BA
Mrs S V Ashworth-Jones, BSc
C R Davies, BA
*H B Orr, BD
*M T Gareh, BSc, MSc, PhD
Mrs J C Mills, BSc
Mrs H V Cox, CertEd
*R P Boswell, BA
A J Baldery, BMus
Miss M Hennessey, BA
*L A Kent, BSc, CBiol, MIBiol
Mrs S Owen, BEd
Mrs J Cartner
Mrs G R Dutton, BEd

School Medical Officer: Dr E A M Greville, MB, ChB

Sanatorium Sisters: Ms M Thomas, Mrs K Hilton, Mrs H Caldecott

The College Building. The main school building contains all four boys' Boarding and Day Houses, bachelor and married accommodation for Housemasters and/or Assistant Housemasters, the Chapel, the Dining Hall and a refurbished Lower School. The Nankivell block of 60 individual study bedrooms for boys in their final year completes the main quadrangle. A 13-16 girls' Boarding and Day house has its own wing in the main building and was opened in response to demand in 1996. The girls' VI Form Boarding and Day house which accommodates 50 girls in a combination of shared and single study bedrooms was completed in 1986. The Sports Hall, Big School (Assembly Hall) which houses the Schulze Organ, and three subject Departments are also located in the main building.

Additional wings contain the Learning Support Department, Library and Sixth Form Centre. Other subjects are taught in their own Departmental blocks close to the main building, and include Science laboratories, a Modern Languages Department with a Language Laboratory, an Art School, a Design & Technology Centre, and a Business Studies department with its own computer lab.

The House System. There are four Houses for boys, two girls' houses, all catering for full boarding, weekly boarding and day pupils, and a Lower School for junior (aged 9-13) boys and girls. A new Lower School building, at a cost of £1m, was opened in September 1999. Each House has its own team of tutorial staff headed by a Housemaster or Housemistress and Assistant. Each of the Houses also has a non-resident Housekeeper to cater for the domestic needs of the pupils.

A major refurbishment programme has been completed which has converted all Boarding Houses to study bedroom accommodation. In addition to the study bedrooms, each

House is provided with recreation rooms, a TV room and a House Library.

School Work. Until GCSE all boys and girls are guided in their academic work by a Tutor, whom they see at least once a week to report progress. In the VI Form each pupil has an academic supervisor who is a teacher in the pupil's primary 'A' level subject.

In the first year in the Senior School a full range of fourteen subjects is studied, including Art, Design and Technology, Computing and Technical Drawing. This curriculum is designed to give all pupils a comprehensive introduction before reducing to a basic eight subjects for GCSE. At GCSE all pupils take English, Mathematics, and either Dual Award Science or the three Sciences studied separately. Other subjects depend on individual aptitude and choice.

In the Sixth Form some 26 different academic subjects are available for study to A level to prepare for University Entrance or entry to the Services and the Professions.

Music. The College has a very strong musical tradition. It possesses two of the finest organs in the country, including the internationally renowned St Mary Tyne Dock Schulze Organ. The Chapel Choir has a wide repertoire of Church Music. There is a Big Band, a Choral Society, a Jazz Group and other ensembles, all of which give regular concerts. There are House Music Competitions every year.

An annual programme of Celebrity Concerts brings distinguished musicians to the College.

The Music School is part of the College Arts Centre which provides first-class facilities, including 8 Practice Rooms, a Record Library, Teaching Rooms and a Studio Theatre designed for small Concerts and seating about 220 people.

The department has 2 full-time and 14 part-time teachers.

Arts Centre. This purpose-built complex was opened in 1976 for Drama, Dance, Film, Music and Art Exhibitions. A programme is organised in which international artists in all these fields visit the Centre, which shares its facilities with the local community.

Careers. At all levels pupils are encouraged to seek advice from the college careers masters and mistresses as well as and representatives from the Independent Schools Careers Organisation. The ISCO aptitude tests are available for all pupils in their GCSE level year. A Careers' Convention is held each year for pupils in the Fifth Form.

School Societies. There are a large number of flourishing societies which range from debating and play reading to bridge and chess, from architecture and electronics to philately and photography.

Games and Physical Education. All members of the School are required to participate in a regular programme of games, though particular inclinations and aptitudes are taken fully into consideration. Facilities include a sports hall, a flood-lit multi-sports area, a weight training room, squash courts, a heated outdoor swimming pool, a gymnasium, tennis courts, a golf course, rugby pitches, hockey pitches, cricket squares, and an athletics track.

Ellesmere is superbly placed for outdoor pursuits. Easily accessible lakes, rivers and hills provide opportunities to develop talents and interests.

Sailing takes place on Whitemere. The School owns six boats and pupils are allowed to bring their own craft. Canoeing takes place on the Ellesmere canal and on local rivers such as the Dee and the Severn.

At Cwm Penmachno, a village near Betws-y-Coed, the School has its own Centre for mountaineering expeditions. As well as being extremely useful for Biology and Geography Fieldwork, the Centre makes an excellent base from which to explore the Snowdonia National Park.

All pupils are expected to join one of the following: Outdoor Training Unit; CCF; Social Service.

The above organisations operate on one afternoon a week but in order to extend their activities a weekend is set aside each term when all members of the School participate in 48 hour expeditions.

Admission. Boys and girls are admitted at all points of entry into the school. Entrance examinations are held in February for Lower School, Senior School and Sixth For entry. Scholarships for Prep School candidates are held in May, while others take the Common Entrance Examination in June.

Scholarships and Exhibitions. (*see* Entrance Scholarship section) A wide range of Scholarships and Exhibitions recognising a range of talents are available. Bursaries are awarded to the sons of Clergy, and Foundation Awards to sons of parents who could not normally afford this type of education. All details may be obtained from the Headmaster. In cases of need these awards may be further supplemented.

Fees. The School fees are: Boarders, £4,300 per term; Day pupils, £2,847 per term; Lower School, £1,906 per term inclusive of general School charges. Music lessons are given at a charge of £126 for ten lessons and individual tuition for dyslexic pupils also incurs an extra cost. A scheme of insurance is in force under which the School Fees may be insured for a small termly premium for any number of years and which enables a pupil to remain at Ellesmere to complete his/her education free of all board and tuition fees, if a parent dies before the pupil's School career is ended. There is also a School Fees Remission Scheme for insurance of fees in cases of absence through illness and of surgical and medical expenses. Arrangement can be made for a single advance payment of fees.

'Old Boys and Girls'. Former pupils of the school normally become members of the Old Ellesmerian Club, which in turn enables them to take part in a number of societies and activities. For further information contact: Old Ellesmerian Club Secretary, Ellesmere College, Ellesmere, Shropshire, SY12 9AB.

Charitable status. Woodard Schools Midland Division is a Registered Charity, number 269671. It exists to provide Christian education for children.

Eltham College

Grove Park Road London SE9 4QF.
Tel: 020 8857 1455
e-mail: mail@eltham-college.org.uk
Internet: http://www.eltham-college.org.uk

Governors:

The Governing Body consists of a maximum of 11 elected Trust Governors, 1 Governor nominated by the Baptist Missionary Society, 1 by the Council for World Mission, 1 by the United Reformed Church, 2 parent nominated and 1 teacher nominated Governors, 1 Governor nominated by each of the London Boroughs of Bexley and Bromley.

Chairman of the Board: D J Norris, Esq, LLB

***Headmaster:* P J Henderson**, BA, FRSA

Deputy Head: P L S Condren, BA, PhD

Housemaster of Turberville House: J A C Yarnold, BA

Bursar: D Cooper, ACCA

Academic Staff:
P D Agate, BA (*Sculpture/Pottery*)
K L Barron, MA (*Senior Master/Director of Studies*)
A D Beattie, MA (*Geography*)
T Beaumont, MA (*History*)

A S Bligh, BSc, PhD (*Chemistry*)
V Broncz, BSc (*Mathematics*)
A Chadwick, BA (*Latin*)
P G Cheshire, MA (*Head of German*)
P L S Condren, BA, PhD (*Deputy Headmaster/History*)
D K Cotterill, BSc (*Head of Geography and Careers*)
A A Cousins, BSc, MSc (*IT and Computing*)
M Dent, BSc (*Economics and Business Studies*)
Mrs S M Donaldson, BSc (*Computer Science*)
The Revd R J Draycott, MA, MTh (*Chaplain and Head of RS*)
Ms S M Dunne, BA (*Spanish and French*)
A J Earl, MA, AIL, FRSA (*Head of Modern Languages*) (*Oxbridge entry*)
Mrs S B Fearn, BA, ALA (*Librarian*)
Mrs E M Galloway, MA (*Physics*)
D R Grinstead, BA (*Deputy Head of Sixth Form; Head of History*)
M F Harris, BSc (*Head of Economics & Business Studies*)
Mrs C A Head-Rapson, BSc (*Mathematics and Physics*)
A Hillary, BEd (*Design and Technology*)
J F Hind, BSc (*Mathematics*)
Mrs C M Hobbs, BSc (*Biology*)
T A Hotham, BA (*Head of Classics and PSE Co-ordinator*)
P A Howls, BA (*Modern Languages*)
T J Johnson, MA (*Director of Music*)
C Jones, MA, PhD (*Mathematics*)
I Latham, BSc (*Physical Education*)
N Levy, GGSM (*Music*)
Miss D C Lloyd, BA (*Mathematics*)
P C McCartney, BSc, MSc (*Head of Chemistry and Geology; Examinations Officer*)
S J McGrahan, MSc (*Senior Master* (*Curriculum*)/Head of Science)
G S Morgan, MA, PhD (*Science and Chemistry*)
R Morrow, BMS, MSc (*Biology and Chemistry*)
B Pollard, MA (*German and French*)
J P Pringle, BSc (*Head of Computer Science*)
P B Richards, CertEd (*Head of Art*)
Mrs J H Roberts, BSc, MIBiol (*Head of Biology*)
K G Roberts, TEng(*CEI*), DipEd (*Head of Design and Technology*)
K Shipton, MA (*English*)
R Sutton, BA (*Head of English*)
A Thomas, BEd (*Head of Physical Education*)
L Watts, BSc (*Senior Master* (*Sixth Form*)/Head of Mathematics)
Ms K Wilson, BA (*English*)
S J Wintle, BEd (*Physical Education*)
B M Withecombe, MSc (*Mathematics*)
J A C Yarnold, BA (*English and Head of Drama*)
P Zdarzil, LLB (*Director of Information Technology Services*)

Part-time:
Mrs O Ball (*German*)
Mrs P Corp, BA (*French*)
The Revd G Heskins, BD, MA, MTh (*Religious Studies*)
Mrs A Senior (*French*)
Ms A C E Streeter, BA (*Art and Design*)

Junior School:
K L John, BSc (*Master in charge*)
Mrs R Brown, BMus, CertEd
Mrs A Howes, BA
D Mouqué, BEd
M O'Dwyer, BEd
Mrs A Pain, BEd
Miss K Partridge, BMus, CertEd
J M G Poole, BA
K L Schaper, MA
Mrs T Sidney-Roberts, BA
P J Spencer, BA, DipLib, ALA
Mrs L Wrafter, CertEd

Eltham College was a Direct Grant School which reverted to independent status in 1976. It was founded in 1842 as the School for the Sons of Missionaries. In 1912 the School moved from Blackheath to its present site, and thereafter began to admit boarders and day boys in increasing numbers. The School has always contained a nucleus of boys who have come as scholars in accordance with the foundation scheme; but the majority of both boarders and day pupils now come from a wider range of backgrounds. The aim of the School is to provide a balanced and stimulating education based on Christian principles and practice. The buildings are surrounded by 32 acres of playing fields. There are about 550 boys and 40 girls in the Senior School, and there is a Junior School of 180 boys attached.

Main School Buildings. The main part of the School is built round a large country mansion, now extended and adapted to include a Library and VIth Form Reading Room, Dining Hall, Art and Sculpture Studios, and other teaching areas. An extensive teaching block including newly-equipped Laboratories is devoted mainly to Science, Computing, Technology and Mathematics. A building containing the headquarters of most of the Arts subjects, the Music School, and a Language Laboratory, was completed in 1963. There is also a magnificent Sports Centre, an indoor Swimming Pool, Tuck Shop, and Sixth Form Social Area. The School Chapel stands as a separate building. A fine Performing Arts Centre, for curricular drama, plays and concerts, has been in use since 1987. A new Technology centre has recently been built, and a new Library was opened in 1999.

Curriculum. In the Lower and Middle School the curriculum is broadly based. In the Middle School boys normally take 10 subjects, always including a range of both Arts and Science studies, for the GCSE examination, before entering the VIth Form, in which they specialise in courses leading to the 'AS' and 'A' level. Subjects available include Art, Biology, Business Studies, Chemistry, Computer Science, Design and Technology, Drama, Economics, English, French, Geography, Geology, German, History, Latin, Mathematics (Pure, Applied and Statistics), Music, Politics, Physics, Religious Studies and Spanish. Most VIth Formers then enter Higher Education, and during the last five years 70 pupils have been offered places at Oxford and Cambridge.

A proportion of the VIth Form timetable is given to Community Service, General Studies and Games.

Physical Education forms part of every pupil's timetable, and all are expected to take part in games. In the Autumn term Rugby Football is the major sport, whilst in the Spring term it is Hockey. Other sports offered are Association Football, Cross-Country, Badminton, Basketball and Net-ball; and in the Summer term Cricket, Athletics, and Tennis. Swimming and Water Polo is available all year round and there are opportunities for Table Tennis, Weight training and Aerobics. There are facilities for private music lessons; and in addition to a wide range of School Societies there are many hobby activities. It is the School's policy to arrange frequent expeditions abroad and adventure courses in the UK. There are links with schools in France, Germany, Russia, Estonia, Italy, Argentina, Nepal, Australia and South Africa, and foreign exchanges are actively encouraged.

Forms in the Lower and Middle School are composed of about 26 boys. There is some streaming in languages and science, and setting in Mathematics.

The Careers Master and other staff undertake to provide detailed and regular advice and information on Higher Education, GAP years and choice of career at the appropriate stages.

The role of parents in partnership with the School is regarded as extremely valuable, and there is a very strong and active Parent/Teacher Association.

Boarding, in a family atmosphere, is provided in a separate wing of the school for a small number of boys, who are in the charge of a resident master with support staff, including a married couple.

Admission. Day boys and boarders are admitted by entrance examination to the Main School at the age of 11 and a few places may be available at other ages. VIth Form places are available by examination for both boys and girls.

Scholarships. (*see* Entrance Scholarship section) Up to 10 entrance scholarships may be awarded on performance in the entrance examination. A number of Sixth Form Scholarships (usually 10), are offered annually to qualified boys or girls. 4 Music and Sports Scholarships are available at ages 11 and 16, and Art Scholarship at 16. Details on application.

Term of Entry. We normally accept pupils only for the beginning of the academic year in September but, if gaps in particular year groups occur, we are willing to interview and test at any point in the year with a view to immediate or subsequent entry.

Junior School. A large house on the School estate has been converted and extended to accommodate about 180 day boys in classes of not more than 24. A new laboratory was opened in 1991, and a computer suite in 1999. There is ample provision for Cricket, Rugby, Association Football, Swimming, Athletics, Basketball, Tennis and Judo. The teaching is in the charge of an experienced master responsible to the Headmaster. Admission is at the age of 7, though a small number of candidates are admitted at 8, and Junior School boys almost always qualify for admission to the Senior School at 11.

The School thus provides an opportunity for 11 years' uninterrupted education in healthy surroundings.

Applications should be made to the School Secretary.

Fees. (Subject to revision): Day – Senior School £2,466 per term. Junior School £2,128 per term. (Boarding Fees on application).

Honours. 130 pupils have gained entry to Oxford and Cambridge during the last ten years.

Charitable status. Eltham College is a Registered Charity, number 1058438. It exists to provide education for boys.

Emanuel School

Battersea Rise London SW11 1HS.
Tel: 020 8870 4171
Fax: 020 8877 1424
e-mail: enquiries@emanuel.org.uk

The School was founded in Westminster by Lady Anne Dacre in 1594, and moved to its present site on the north side of Wandsworth Common in 1883 as one of the three schools of the United Westminster Schools Foundation.

Motto: Pour bien désirer

Governing Body:
Chairman of the Governing Body: The Right Hon The Viscount Hampden, DL

Vice-Chairman: F R Abbott, BA

The Right Hon The Baroness Dacre
¶R G Dear
Miss M d'Mello, MSc
¶Professor P Goddard, MA, PhD, FInstP, FRS
T F Godfrey-Faussett, MA, FIPM
P M Kennerley, RD, FRICS
P A Lendrum
Mrs M Parsons, MA
J R D Scriven, MA
G M M Wakeford, MA, LLB
P C R Wates, FSVA

Clerk and Receiver: R W Blackwell, MA

***Headmistress:* Mrs A-M Sutcliffe**, MA

Deputy Head: J Hardy, MA

Director of Studies: W M Rogers, BSc

Head of the Lower School: Mrs S E Neale, BA

Head of Middle School: N M Mullen, MA

Head of Sixth Form: R R Marriott, MA

Teaching staff:
Miss S Aitken, BA
Miss A Beech, BSc
J F W Benn, BA, MBA
Mrs J E Bettesworth, Dip AD, ATC
S J Bettinson, MSc
*¶D S C Bratt, BA
Miss L M Brown, MA
R Candlish, TCert
K Cousineau, BSc
Miss P F Damji, BTech
*F P Danes, BA
¶G J Dibden
Mrs C E Dodson, BA
J M Driver, BD, AKC
D Eade, BA
S Fairlamb, BEd
Miss L Fitzgibbon, BSc
A P Friell, BEd
*Ms S J Grainger, BA
S J Gregory, MA, ARCO
S Halliwell, BA
M D Hand, MA
*The Rev E M Hill, BA (*Chaplain*)
*J Holmes, BMus, MA, FRCO, ARCM
Mrs S Holmes, MA, ARCO
*B P Howard, BSc, BA, CChem, MRSC
H Jackson, BA
Mrs F M Johnson, BA
A F S Keddie, MA, ACIB
C O Labinjo, BSc
Dr H Langelüddecke, DPhil
Dr B W Last, BA, MPhil, PhD
S M Latham, BA
J P Layng, BSc, MNCA
Miss A Legh, BA
Mrs R A Lewis, MA
†*C J Lynn, JP, MIET
A McCleave, MA
P McMahon, MA
Miss S E MacMillan, BA
Mrs C M Maher, BSc
Ms G Marmion, BSc
Ms P S Marmion, TCert
Miss K Marvell, BA
*N M Mullen, MA
*J Naylor, MA
¶J A Neale, TCert
A I Ogilvie, BA
A Patterson, BEng
Mrs K Patterson, MA
Miss J Pattmann, MA
T B Patu, BA
*W J Purkis, BSc
Dr B Reynolds, PhD
*Mrs J E Sanderson, BSc, ARCS
Miss E J Testa, BA
S J Thomson, MA
Mrs A M Thorne, BA
Miss H Ulferts, MA
N Veerasamy, BEng
A Zaratiegui, MA

Bursar: Mrs J E Kirkup

Headmistress's PA: Mrs A S Parrott

Visiting Music Teachers:
Mrs J Friend (*'cello*)
Miss J Watts (*violin*)
R Schunter (*guitar*)
Mrs E Mantzourani (*piano*)
J F Webb (*percussion*)
S Gregory (*Clarinet and Saxophone*)
Mrs S Beales (*Flute*)
A Kendall (*singing*)
M Crowther (*lower brass*)
Mrs T-F Liu (*piano*)
Ms S Jones (*oboe*)
Ms E Harding (*bassoon*)
A Meryon (*clarinet*)
Ms B Symons (*double bass*)
F Baird (*percussion*)

Emanuel is now a fully co-educational day school. We have about 750 pupils, with 160 in the Sixth Form. About a third of lower school pupils are girls.

Admission. Each September about 20 pupils are

admitted at age ten, 90 pupils at age eleven and about 20 at age thirteen. Entry at age ten and eleven is by competitive examination, held at the school each year in late January or early February. Applications to sit these examinations should be made before 1st December of the preceding year.

Entry at age thirteen is by means of the June sitting of the Common Entrance Examination or by an Emanuel examination in January. Entry to the Sixth form is by interview and subject to the quality of a candidate's GCSE record.

Fees. The fees from September 2001 are £2,581 per term for the Hill form, £2,691 for the main school, and cover tuition, stationery and books. The only extras charged are for a lunch at school, if required, and for individual instrumental tuition.

Site and buildings. Emanuel was founded in 1594. In 1873 it moved from Westminster to a new site in Wandsworth, then occupied by a redundant Crimean war orphanage. This building is the core of the school, with most of its classrooms and a fine dining hall and chapel. The first addition made was the new building of 1896, which now houses our concert hall and music rooms, and the science laboratories. These have been completely refurbished in the last few years to a very high standard.

Over the last century many further additions have been made, most recently a large Sixth Form Centre. The school's playing fields adjoin the school buildings and there is a full size swimming pool. Less usual facilities include fives courts.

Scholarships. Academic scholarships of up to half fees are awarded as a result of performance in the entrance examinations at 10+, 11+ and 16+. Sixth form academic scholarships are awarded on the basis of distinguished performance at GCSE. including Music and Art Scholarships.

Art and music scholarships are also offered at these stages.

Organisation. There is one form for pupils who join at age ten. Pupils joining at age eleven are streamed by ability in four forms, and primary responsibility for their care rests with the form teacher and the head of year, under the overall supervision of the head of the lower school, who deals with the Hill, first and second forms. Most pupils who join at age thirteen are placed in a specially created extra form for one year. As all pupils move from the third to fourth year there is a radical re-grouping along the lines of the subjects chosen for GCSE examinations. In the sixth form a tutor system operates.

Pupils are placed in houses when they join the school, and they stay in these houses throughout their school career. Although originally intended as a means of fostering competition in games, these houses have developed over many years a strong community spirit, often involving former pupils.

For fuller details please ask for the school prospectus.

Times. The normal school day runs from 8.45 am to 4 pm, and to 3.20 pm for the junior form, but many activities extend into the late afternoon beyond 4 o'clock.

There is no Saturday school. However, many school activities, especially games, take place on Saturday mornings.

Curriculum. Pupils are prepared for the GCSE. There is a wide range of options; most pupils take nine subjects.

Thereafter, in the sixth form, there is a further range of options from which pupils choose four A/S level subjects leading to examination at the end of the lower sixth. They can then choose to continue with all four or to take just 3 through to A level. Most sixth form leavers go on to university, art college, or other forms of higher education.

Religious Education. The chaplain and his assistant work in the school, whose general religious tenor is that of the Church of England. A daily service is held in the school chapel. A daily service is held in the school chapel. Pupils in the Hill, first, second and third forms receive one or two periods per week of religious education, which continues into the fourth, fifth and sixth forms as a GCSE or A-level option.

The Arts. Emanuel has a long-standing tradition of excellence in these areas and all pupils are encouraged to participate in one or more of these activities. The school has a chapel choir and a chamber choir, an orchestra and ensemble groups, and a major musical production is presented each year.

There is a specialist suite of art rooms with facilities for all kind of creative activity. A great deal of high quality work is displayed around the school and several pupils a year go on to foundation courses at art college.

Drama is taught throughout the school and there is a major school production every year, usually in the autumn term, and smaller scale events during the year.

We have an annual arts festival in June with an art exhibition, summer serenade, performances by pupils and visitors, and a series of talks by visiting speakers.

Games and Activities. At present cricket, rowing, rugby, athletics and soccer are the main school games for the boys. For the girls the main activities are netball, hockey, gymnastics, tennis, athletics and swimming. Many others become available as a pupil moves up the school. Each pupil will have one games afternoon each week, and other opportunities for physical education and swimming. The school has its own swimming pool and fives courts.

The Duke of Edinburgh award scheme is offered at all levels to pupils from the third form upwards. Community service is arranged for senior pupils and can involve hospital visiting, voluntary work in local primary schools or charity shops, or our local hospice. More formal work experience is offered as part of an extensive careers and further education advice programme from the third form upwards.

Careers. Careers and Further Education advice is readily available from an experienced team.

Old Emanuel Association. *Hon Secretary:* J B Seaward, 79 Knightwood Crescent, New Malden, Surrey.

Charitable status. Emanuel School (administered by the United Westminster Schools' Foundation) is a Registered Charity, number 309267. Its aims and objectives are for "the bringing up of children in virtue and good and laudable arts".

Epsom College (With Royal Medical Foundation)

Epsom Surrey KT17 4JQ
Tel: Headmaster: (01372) 821004
Registrar: (01372) 821234
Bursar: (01372) 821133
Fax: (01372) 821005

Epsom College was founded in 1853 by John Propert and established as a School in 1855. It lies about 15 miles south of London, close to much attractive countryside. The College occupies 80 acres of its own land on Epsom Downs, 300 feet above sea-level, and all the buildings and playing fields are within the grounds.

In the last twenty years the Boarding and Day Houses have been modernised and many new buildings have been erected. The Science Laboratories have been completely redeveloped and there is a new Department of Design Technology. Games facilities have also been greatly extended, including the construction of an Indoor Sports Centre with a Swimming Pool, two large Sports Halls, 10 Squash Courts, a Gymnasium, a Fitness Room and a

Climbing Wall. An Astroturf Hockey Pitch, giving further Tennis Courts, has recently been opened. In September 1996 a new Library with space for 50 study carrels was completed from the old gymnasium, and in September 1999 a new Classroom Block with 13 classrooms for the Economics, Geography and History Departments was completed. So far nearly eight million pounds have been spent in the period on the development of the College.

Motto: *'Deo non Fortuna'*.

Patron: Her Majesty The Queen

President: Sir Mark Richmond, ScD, FRCPath, FRS

Visitor: The Rt Revd The Lord Bishop of Guildford

Treasurer: P G Hakim, FCA

Council:
A Hagdrup, LLB (*Chairman*)
G B Pincus, MIPA (*Vice-Chairman*)
R P Barker, MA
Mrs E Berwick
Mrs C B Brigstocke
J M Clubb, MRCS, LRCP, FRCGP, JP
His Honour Judge Michael Cook, LLB
P M Dodd, TD
J M Dunlop, MB, DPH, FFCM
R P Hancock, ACII
J Hunt, MBE
Vice Admiral A L Revell, CB, QHS, FRCA
H D Sinnett, MB, MS, FRCS
Dr A J Vallance-Owen, MB, ChB, FRCS, MBA
Vice-Admiral Sir James Watt, KBE, MD, FRCP, FRCS
E J Wright, BA, MSc, MICE, FIHT, MBCS

Secretary to the Council: K Slatter, FCA

***Headmaster:* S R Borthwick**, MA

Deputy Head: D N Rice, BSc

Director of Studies: D J Young, BSc, PhD

Senior Master: N P M Laing, BA

Chaplains:
*Revd S L Green, BD, MTh
Revd Paul Thompson, BD

Registrar: R Worrall, MA

Assistant Teachers:
B J Ainge, MA
T Allen, BSc
C J Baverstock, BSc
C B Buchholdt, BA, AKC
Miss C Cens, BA
Miss K Chandley, BA
M C Conway, BA
F J Cooke, BA
Miss F C Corbett, BSc
Miss C L Creevey, BA
B J Curtis, MA
Mrs A Davies
*C J Davies, BSc
M Day, BA
Mrs J V Dibden, BSc
J M Drinkall, BSc
*R Ellison, MA
R Gill, MA
P J Green, BSc
Miss V J Guthrie, BSc
M Hampshire, BA, FRSA
Mrs R J B Harrop, BA
J R L Hartley, BSc
M D Hobbs, BSc
*C I Holiday, BEd
M J Horrocks-Taylor, BSc
E A Huxter, MA, MSc
*P J Irvine, MA
Miss E Jardine Young, BA
G A Lodge, BMus, MA, LTCL
A J McGrath, BA
C de L Mann, BSc
Miss K R Morris, BSc
Mrs T M Muller, MA
P J R Neild, BA
I D Newman, BA
J B Odell, MA, LRAM
M C Oliver, BSc
*S J Oliver, MA
D C G Ottridge, BSc
Mrs D A Parsons, BA
N S A Payne, BSc
M S Pollard, BA
*D R Poore, BSc
J R W Postle, BA
*G Poupart (*Art*)
*A G Scadding, BA
R A Sheehan, BA, MA
*P M Shephard
*G J A Simpson, BSc
*K Siviter, MA
Dr P L I Skelton, BA, PhD
D A Stout, BSc
*B M Summers, BSc, PhD, FRSC
Miss H E Thomas, BA
A P Thompson, BSc
A Vaughan, BSc, ARSM
S A Wade, BSc, PhD
M J Walker, MA
R I Whiteley, MA
S K Whitlock, MA
P J Williams, BSc
*A J Wilson, BSc, MSc
*A Wolstenholme, BEd

Bursar: Mrs S Meikle, BA

Headmaster's Secretary: Mrs J Stone

School Medical Officer: Dr T Richardson, MB, ChB

Numbers and Houses. From September 1996 the College became fully co-educational. There are about 677 students in the School, 335 boarders or weekly boarders and 330 day students, divided among 4 Boarding Houses and 5 Day Houses. There are 75 girls in the VIth Form either as boarders, weekly boarders or day girls. They are all members of the White House (Dr P L I Skelton). There are now 2 separate Houses for girls, Wilson House (Mrs D A Parsons) and a new Day House for girls from 13, Raven House (Miss E Jardine-Young).

The boys' Boarding Houses are: Fayrer (Mr P J Williams), Forest (Mr M D Hobbs), Granville (Mr M C Oliver), Holman (Mr R Gill). Propert (Mr J R L Hartley) is partly boarding and partly day.

All boarding Sixth and Fifth Formers and Upper Fourth Formers have study bedrooms in the modernised Houses. Each term full boarders have 2 exeats when they can spend a night at home in addition to a half-term holiday. Weekly boarders may go home each weekend.

The day boy Houses are: Carr (Mr M J Horrocks-Taylor), Crawfurd (Mr G A Lodge), Robinson (Mr M J Walker) and Rosebery (Mr M Hampshire). Day boys and girls are full members of the School community and have lunch and tea in College.

All members of the School, boarders and day, eat centrally in the Dining Hall which makes for efficiency and strengthens the sense of community.

Pupils who are ill are looked after in the School Sanatorium which has 8 beds with a resident sister and nurse who are both qualified. The School Doctor visits daily.

Work. Below the VIth Form the course is broad and involves little specialisation. All pupils take English, French, Mathematics, Physics, Chemistry, Biology and Religious Studies while substantial numbers do Drama Studies, Latin, Spanish or German, Geography, History, Art, Music, Information Technology and Design Technology. The normal programme is to enter the Middle Fourth at the age of thirteen and take the main block of GCSEs at the end of the third year. Almost everyone then enters the large VIth Form of over 300 pupils. A wide range of AS and A2 level subjects is offered, including French, German and Spanish as Modern Languages, Drama Studies, Business Studies, Politics and Classical Civilisation, and there are excellent facilities to work in one's own study, the main Library or one of the specialist Libraries. There is a fully equipped Information Technology Room adjoining the Design Technology Department, and all are introduced to Information Technology in their 1st year.

The College, always having had close links with the medical profession, is particularly strong on the Science side, and each Science subject has its own modernised Laboratories and lecture rooms. There is a fine Biology Museum. About a sixth of the pupils become doctors or dental surgeons, but the majority are not doctors' sons or daughters and they enter a great variety of professions and careers. Nearly all pupils go on to a University education each year.

Careers. There is a well-stocked Careers Room attached to the Library, and much care is taken to assess a pupil's potential and aptitude and to provide proper guidance on careers. All pupils belong to the ISCO Scheme and all Fifth Form pupils take careers aptitude tests. A Careers Convention is organised each year for the Lower VIth.

The **Religious Teaching** and the Chapel Services follow the doctrines of the Church of England, but there are always pupils of other denominations and faiths. There are two Resident Chaplains.

Games and other Activities. Games contribute much to the general physical development of boys and girls at Epsom and the College has a strong tradition of high standards in many sports. The very large number of teams means that almost all pupils are able to represent the School each year. The main games are Rugby, Hockey, Netball, Cricket, Tennis, Athletics and Swimming. Among the other sports available are Rowing, Squash (10 courts), Shooting (with a .22 range), Soccer, Cross-Country, Fencing, Gymnastics, Golf, Badminton, Rounders, Basketball, Judo and Sailing. The Indoor Sports Centre was opened in 1989 by the Patron of Epsom College, Her Majesty the Queen.

The CCF has Naval, Army and RAF Sections and pupils over the age of 14 are expected to join for 2 years when much time is spent on camping and expeditions. Older boys and girls may join instead the Duke of Edinburgh's Award Scheme, while others are involved with Social Service work in Epsom.

Each week time is set aside for leisure activities. The College Societies are numerous and include the XVI Club, the Mermaid Tavern (Dramatic Society), the Chess and Bridge Clubs, the Debating, Natural History, Medical, Modern Languages, History, Science and Photographic Societies. A VIth Form Social Club flourishes.

Music, Art and Drama. There are three full-time Music Masters and a large staff of visiting music teachers. Over one-third of the pupils learn Musical Instruments, and virtually any instrument can be taught. There are several Choirs, a School Orchestra and a Concert Band. Visits are arranged each term to concerts in London and elsewhere. The Music School has a Concert Hall and 18 practice rooms.

Art, which includes Pottery, Printing and Sculpture as well as Painting and Drawing, is housed in spacious quarters with 8 studios, a Library, an Exhibition Room and an Exhibition Hall. There are three full-time Art Masters and Art is studied up to GCSE and 'A' level. At the same time it is an important creative leisure activity for many pupils.

There is a School play each year on the well-equipped stage in Big School, a Junior School play and various plays produced by Houses or by pupils. These give boys and girls an opportunity to develop their talents and interests in drama.

Admission. Almost all pupils enter Epsom College in September. Most pupils come at the age of 13 after reaching a satisfactory standard in the Common Entrance or Scholarship Examination or the Epsom College examination set specially for those who are not at Preparatory Schools. Some come later than this and there is always a direct entry into the VIth Form, both for girls into White House and for boys. The Headmaster will be pleased to supply particulars.

A boy or girl may be registered at any age by sending in the registration form and fee.

Fees. Boarders: £5,141 per term. Weekly Boarders £5,072 per term. Day Pupils: £3,784 per term.

The fees are inclusive and cover the normal cost of a pupil's education. The main extras are for examination fees, private tuition and a pupil's personal expenses. Fees for day pupils include lunch and tea.

There is a College Store for the provision of uniform, clothing and other requirements.

Entrance Scholarships. (*see* Entrance Scholarship section) Candidates may compete for one or more of the following types of Award: Academic Scholarships, Music Scholarships, Art Scholarships, All-Rounder Scholarships or Sports Awards. There are generally about 30 Awards. Scholarships can be up to 50% of the initial fees. Some Awards are open only to the sons or daughters of Doctors. Candidates must be under 14 on 1st May or entering the Sixth Form.

Foundation Scholarships and Bursaries. Foundation Scholarships, up to full fees, are awarded to sons and daughters of doctors in cases of need.

Trust Fund Awards. Various other special Scholarships and Exhibitions are available for boys and girls in need of some assistance.

Full details of all Scholarships and Awards are available from the Headmaster.

Old Epsomians. There is a flourishing Old Epsomian Club with strong cricket, rugby, shooting, golf and Business sections. There are regular dinners at the College where the OE Secretary is also based.

All enquiries should be sent to the Headmaster from whom a prospectus may be obtained.

Charitable status. Epsom College is a Company limited by Guarantee registered in England, number 4009200. The aims of the College are educational and benevolent.

Eton College

Windsor Berkshire SL4 6DW.
Tel: 01753 671231 (Head Master)
01753 671000 (Bursar, Registrar, Eton List Secretary).

The King's College of our Lady of Eton beside Windsor was founded by Henry VI in 1440. The College Foundation comprises a Provost, 11 Fellows, Head Master, Lower Master, Bursar, Chaplain and 70 Scholars. There are some 1,200 Oppidans, or boys not on the Foundation.

Motto: *'Floreat Etona'*.

Visitor: The Rt Revd The Lord Bishop of Lincoln

Provost and Fellows (*Governing Body*):
Dr Eric Anderson, MA, BLitt, HonDLitt, FRSE (*Provost*)
James Cook, MA, BSc (*Vice-Provost*)
The Provost of King's College, Cambridge (*Senior Fellow*)
The Hon Mr Justice Cazalet, MA
Sir James Douglas Spooner, MA, FCA
Professor Sir Richard Southwood, MA, PhD, DSc, FRS
Sir Geoffrey Holland, KCB, MA
Nicholas Woodhouse, PhD, MA
Sir Dominic Cadbury
Baroness Hogg
Professor Peter Toyne, BA, HonDEd, FRSA, CIMgt, DL
Mr David Verey

Honorary Fellows:
John Butterwick, TD
Sir David Money-Coutts, KCVO

Steward of the Courts: The Rt Hon Lord Carrington, KG, CH, GCMG, MC, PC

Conduct: The Rev C W Mitchell-Innes, MA

Precentor and Director of Music: R Allwood, BA

Bursar: A G Wynn, LVO, MA

Assistant Bursars:
I C Mellor, ARICS
J G James, MBE, BA

College Librarian & Keeper of College Collections: M C Meredith, MA

Custodian:

Clerk to the Provost and Fellows: A G Wynn, LVO, MA

Registrar: R A Hutton

School Clerk: L N Cross

School Doctor:
J J C Holliday, MB, BS, MRCS, LRCP, MRCGP, DCH, DRCOG, FPCert

***Head Master:* J E Lewis**, MA

Lower Master: D S Lowther, MA

Assistant Masters:

Art:
*I Burke, MA
S Brown, MA
R A Catchpole, BA, Slade HDip
S Forsyth, MA
S I Tierney, MA

Classics:
M J Atkinson, MA, DPhil
†J A Claughton, MA
S D A Griffiths, BA
†I Harris, MA
T E W Hawkins, BA
P D Hills, BA, MPhil, PhD
E J Holloway, MA
J Macartney, BA
I McAuslan, MA
*A J Maynard, MA
W H Moseley, MA
R D Oliphant-Callum, BA
R E C Shorrock, BA, MPhil, PhD
C J Smart, BA
P B Smith, MA

Computing:
*C H Jones, MA, JP
G J Pierce, BEd

Design:
*G C Desborough, CertEd
Mrs S Campbell-Connolly, BA
K R N Ross, BSc
T Smith, BA
S G P Tilley, BA

Divinity:
Rev D Cooper, AKC (*Chaplain*)
†Rev C M Jones, MA (*Chaplain*)
Rev C W Mitchell-Innes, MA (*Senior Chaplain*)
Rev T D Mullins, BA (*Chaplain*)
*M L Wilcockson, MA

Economics:
†J R Clark, MA
S M Cullen, MA, DPhil
D J Fox, BA
G T Galletly, BA, MA
†D M Gregg, BSSc
R G G Pratt, MA
*G R Riley, BA
†P R Thackeray, BA

English:
M J L Bashaarat, MA
*J J Branch, MA, JP
†P Broad, MA
C J Davis, MA
S Dormandy, BA (*Director of Drama*)
J E Francis, BA
†A C D Graham-Campbell, MA
M A Grenier, BA
P Hopwood, BA
R J Martin, BA
M C Meredith, MA
†C W Milne, BA, MPhil
F D Newton, BA
†J M Noakes, MA
H-E Osborne, MA
†J A Piggot, MA
C A Stuart-Clark, MA
N R F Welsh, MA

Geography:
D E Anderson, PhD
C J O Cook, MA
T F X Eddis, BA
D S Lowther, BSc (*Lower Master*)
P I Macleod, BEd
M G H Mowbray, MA
*K P Stannard, MA, PhD
M A Town, MA

History:
*G J Savage, MA
T P Connor, MA, DPhil
D A Eltis, BA, DPhil
D A Evans, MA
†A L H Gailey, MA, PhD
C N Goodman, MA, BSc(Econ)
J D Harrison, MA
T E J Nolan, BA
H S J Proctor, MA
A S Robinson, MA, MLitt
J L Sillery, MA, DPhil
†J A F Spence, BA, PhD (*Master-in-College*)

Mathematics:
†T C Basey, BSc, PhD
I T Batty, BSc
J M Bradley, MSc
S J Dean, MA
R J Gazet, BA
T Gordon, BSc
L J Henderson, BA
B J Holdsworth, BA
†P J McKee, MA
W F Moore, BSc(Eng)
R G Prior, MA
*Revd J C Puddefoot, MA, BD
J C M Rose, BSc
M J Salter, MA
M Strutt, BSc
J E Thorne, BSc
S P Vivian, MA, MSc, CStat
A Warnes, BSc, PhD
C M B Williams, MA
P G Williams, MA
J M S Woodcock, BSc, MSc

Modern Languages:
J G Ball, MA
T E Beard, BA, PhD
M E Broncano Rodriguez, MA
D J J Colman, MA
†R A A Coward, MA
J-P Dubois, Agrégé
*G J D Evans, MA
†G M Evans-Jones, BA
N W Fassnidge, MA, MLitt
R D Haddon, MA
A D Halksworth, BA, MLitt
†J R King, MA
M T Phillips, MA
M J Polglase, MA
A Powles, BA
†W H Rees, MA
P Reznikov, BA
N J Roberts, MA
N C W Sellers, MA
K S Storie, MA

Music:
*R Allwood, BA
C S Ball, BMus
N D Goetzee
A H Sampson, BA
K R Smith, MA
I M Wallace, BA
J B Wortley

Oriental Languages:
D M Stanford-Harris, BA

Physical Education:
A P Halladay, BA
*P I Macleod, BEd
†P K Manley, BEd, MSc
W E Norton, BA
G J Pierce, BEd

Science:
F W S Benfield, BSc, DPhil
A T J Byfield, BSc, DPhil
M G Corry, MSc
R N Edmonds, BA, PhD
†M N Fielker, BSc
R Fisher, BSc
R P D Foster, MA
*K Frearson, MA
G D Fussey, BSc
P Gillam, MA
B G Grainger, BSc
F Grenfell, MA
*C F Harris, MA (*Director of Studies*)
*P R Harrison, MA, DPhil
†C H Hurst, MA, PhD
W M A Land, MA
†P K Manley, BEd, MSc
A M Miles, BSc
*S P Newman, BSc
J H Owen, BSc, PhD
G R Pooley, BSc, PhD
G H Rutter, MA, MSc
*J A Steadman, MA, PhD
†R M Stephenson, BSc, PhD
D C Townend, MA
†P S T Wright, MA

Roman Catholic Chaplain: Revd D W F Forrester, MA, DPhil, STL

The King's Scholars (*see* Entrance Scholarship section) (Collegers) normally number 70 and are boarded in College, each in his own room, under the care of the Master-in-College. About 14 Scholarships are awarded each year. Candidates need be registered only a few weeks before the examination. For information apply to *The Registrar, Eton College, Windsor, Berkshire SL4 6DB.*

The Scholarship Examination is held at Eton in May. Candidates must be under 14 (and over 12) on 1st September. Boys normally enter College between the ages of 12.9 and 13.11. All candidates take English, Mathematics A, General I (general questions requiring thought rather than knowledge) and Science. They must also offer three or more of the following: French (written, aural and oral), Latin, Greek, Mathematics B, History and Geography, General II (Literature, the Arts, moral and religious issues, etc). The examiners may take some account of age.

The value of the Scholarship varies according to the Scholar's financial need, but is never less than half of the full fee.

A Scholarship is normally tenable for five years.

Term of Entry. With the exception of some Music Scholars and a very few special cases, all boys enter in September.

Oppidans. There are some 1,200 Oppidans housed in 24 Boarding Houses, each under the care of a House Master, and every boy has his own room. A boy must normally be over 12 and under 14 on 1st September of the year of admission, and must pass the Common Entrance unless granted exemption on his performance in the Scholarship Examination. School Fee £5,496 per term, Entrance Fee £300.

Parents wishing to send their sons to Eton as Oppidans should apply to *The Eton List Secretary, Eton College, Windsor, Berkshire SL4 6DB,* as early as possible, for a copy of the Prospectus, which gives full details of the registration procedure. Boys may be registered at any time between birth and the age of ten and a half.

Music Scholarships. Up to eight Music Scholarships are awarded annually: four of 1/2 fees and four of 1/6 fees. All awards carry remission of instrumental lesson fees up to two hours tuition per week. Awards will be supplemented up to the value of the full fee in cases of need. In addition there are up to six Music Exhibitions, carrying remission of instrumental lesson fees up to two hours tuition per week. One also carries a place in the school, the other five only being open to boys who are already registered for Eton. Two Honorary Exhibitions may also be awarded, carrying no financial remission. Special consideration will be given to cathedral choristers who would still be able to sing treble in the College Chapel Choir. Further particulars and entry forms may be obtained from *The Registrar, Eton College, Windsor, Berkshire SL4 6DB.*

Bursaries. A number of Bursaries are available for boys who would be unable to receive education at Eton without financial assistance. All bursaries are awarded according to need and may be worth up to one half of the School fee. The sons of OE clergymen, university and school teachers and other professional parents are generally considered particularly sympathetically.

Junior Scholarships and Junior Music Scholarship. Up to 4 Junior Scholarships and 1 Junior Music Scholarship are awarded each year to candidates over 10 and under 11 on 1 September of the year of the examination who are attending state schools. An examination is held at Eton in January each year. Candidates need be registered only a few weeks before the examination. For information apply to *The Registrar, Eton College, Windsor, Berkshire SL4 6DB*

A Junior Scholarship/Junior Music Scholarship is tenable for 2 or 3 years at a Preparatory School (St George's, Windsor Castle in the case of Junior Music Scholarship) as a day-boy or a boarder, and, depending on the parental means, will cover the whole or part of the fees and other educational expenses at the Preparatory School and subsequently at Eton.

Sixth Form Scholarships. Up to 4 Sixth Form Scholarships are offered each year to enable boys taking GCSE at maintained schools to have two years of Sixth Form education at Eton. Each year in February, selected candidates are invited to attend interviews in those subjects which they intend to offer at A-level. All those attending the interviews will sit a written General Paper and an aptitude test. Candidates must register on, or before, a date specified in mid-December. The scholarships will cover the whole or part of the fees, and other educational expenses depending on the Scholar's financial need. For information apply to *The Registrar, Eton College, Windsor, Berkshire SL4 6DB.*

Charitable status. Eton College is an exempt Charity, tax reclaim reference number X6839. By Charter of Henry VI confirmed by Acts of Parliament.

* Head of Department
† Housemaster/Housemistress
‡ See below list of staff for meaning
§ Part Time or Visiting
¶ Old Pupil

Exeter School

Exeter Devon EX2 4NS.
Tel: 01392 273679.
Fax: 01392 498144
e-mail: admissions@exeterschool.org.uk
website: exeterschool.devon.sch.uk

Founded in 1633, Exeter School now occupies a 25 acre site, located within a mile of the city centre, having moved from its original location in the High Street in 1880. Many of its well designed buildings date from that time but many new buildings have been added over the past twenty years and the school now enjoys first rate facilities on a very attractive open site. The school is fully co-educational and offers education to boys and girls from 7 to 18. It has its own Junior School of over 115 pupils, nearly all of whom transfer to the Main School at the age of 11. The Main School has 700 pupils, including a Sixth Form of over 200.

Exeter School is a well run school with high all-round standards and very good academic results. It prides itself on strong cultural, sporting and extra curricular achievement. Its performance music is outstanding and there is a strong tradition of performance drawn from all age groups in the School. It offers a very wide range of sports and maintains consistently high standards especially in hockey, rugby and cricket. It is well placed for outdoor pursuits (eg Ten Tors on Dartmoor) and has its own very large voluntary CCF unit. The School is closely involved with the life of the City of Exeter and its university and it has a substantial commitment to support the local community.

Motto: XPYðOð APETHð OUK ANTAΞIOð

Governors:
Prof W E Yates, MA, PhD (*Chairman*)
The Lord Lieutenant of the County of Devon
The Lord Bishop of Exeter
The Rt Worshipful the Mayor of Exeter

J F Landers, ACII
¶W G Selley
M C Browning
Prof C Dobson, MA, DPhil, FRS
¶Dr C J Burgoyne, MA, PhD
¶G F Cornish
M H Gregory, BDS, LDS, RPS
Mrs U J Parkinson, JP
M G Golby MB, ChM, FRCS
¶T E Hawkins
¶D A Evennett, BDS
Mrs C Channon, MA
A K Dawson, MA, FRSA
A C W King
Mrs M Giles, LLB

***Headmaster:* N W Gamble**, BA(Econ), MEd

Deputy Headmaster: P M Sljivic, MA (Oxon)

Assistant Staff:
*T J Huxtable, BSc, ARCS
*J W Davidson, MA, MSc
J D Allen, BSc
R J Scarrott, BSc
*I G Wright, BA
*C M Finn, MA, PhD
R M Fryer, MA
†L C May, BEd (*Daw House*)
D Wybrow, BSc
*D H Mollart, MSc
*N Shiel, BA, MPhil, FRNS
M R W Pettifer, BSc
*R G Walker, BA
R A Frost, BEd
*†M S W Rodgers, BEd (*Collins House*)
*D W J Carne, BEd
†*R P P Browne, MSc (*Raleigh House*)
*S D Foxall, BMus, LGSM
†S J Harris, MA (*Buller House*)
§R C Duggan, BA DPhil
*B A Christley, BEd
D E Hughes, MA, DPhil
P Scott, BSc
R J Sutton, BA
†M C Wilcock, BEd (*Crossing House*)
†*M H R Porter, BA (*Drake House*)
*D A Seddon, DipGD
L P Hunt, BA
*R J Tayler, BA
*Mrs S Chrupek, BA
M K Chitnavis, BSc

†G R Willson, BSc (*Goff House*)
†*R C Dawson, MA (*Acland House*)
*I E Davis, BA
D Beckwith, BA, MSc
Miss M E Doyle, BA
§Mrs U Cloke, BA
Mrs V Stevens, BA
J D Poustie, BEd
Mrs J M Fenner, BA
§Mrs G Seale, BSc
*S N Leader, BA
Miss S L Stewart, BA
†G N Trelawny, BEd, MA (*Townsend House*)
M D B Johnson, BSc
R H S Donne, BA
*Dr A P Tyrer, MA, DPhil
§Ms C Gimber, BA
§Miss J Wynne, MA
§Mrs G Harris, BA
N A Moon, BSc
Miss J Pegg, BA
Ms P Knight, BSc
§Mrs B Shiel, BA
G Strugnell, BA, MLitt
N L Brown, BA
W A Hughes, BA
§D Bowen, BEd
§I H Chapman, BSc
Miss S L Commings, MA, MPhil
N P L Keyes, MA
§P Painter, DipMusEd
§Dr P M Smallwood, BSc, PhD
§Mrs E Williams, BA
§Mrs B Potts, LRAM
§A Gillett, ARCM

Junior School:

Head: Miss M T Taylor, BA

Assistant Staff:

R Bland, BEd
Mrs S Henton, BA
Mrs R A S Garnham, CertEd
Mrs P L Butler, BA
G E L Ashman, BA
Mrs P A Goldsworthy, BA, LTCL

School Doctor: N C A Bradley, MA, MB, BChir, MRCGP

Bursar and Clerk to The Governors: Brig G D Williams, BA, FIMgt

Buildings, Grounds and General Facilities. The Main School block includes a large multi-purpose assembly hall, a library, a private study area, dining hall and Sixth Form Centre as well as many well-appointed classrooms. There are separate buildings on the site housing the Chapel, the Music Centre, the Science Centre, Art Studios, Drama Studio, Craft Design Technology Centre and Exonian Centre. The Science Centre provides 14 laboratories and there are two fully equipped computer rooms. All departments have access to their own computers and the School has a wide, controlled access to the internet. There is a large modern well-equipped Sports Hall with its own squash courts and nearby access to floodlit all-weather sports arena, top-grade all-weather tennis/netball courts and a heated swimming pool. The playing fields, which are immediately adjacent to the School buildings are well kept and provide, in season, rugby, cricket, hockey, football, rounders and athletics areas. The Junior School, which was extended in 1997, has access to all the Main School facilities but is self-contained on the estate.

Admission. The majority of pupils enter the Junior School at 7 or 8 and the Main School at 11. Admission is also possible at 12 or 13 and a significant number of pupils join at the age of 16 for Sixth Form Studies.

Entrance to the Junior School is by assessment in January. This includes a report from the child's previous school, classroom sessions in the company of other prospective pupils, observation of reading and numeracy and a non-reading intelligence test.

Entrance examinations for the Main School are held in January. Most pupils take these tests at the age of 11 but examinations are also held for those aged 12 and 13. Pupils are also admitted at the age of 13 having taken the Independent Schools Common Entrance examination at their Prep School in the Summer Term.

Assessment for entry to the Sixth Form at 16 is by interview and the achievement of good grades at GCSE, normally a minimum of a B grade in the subjects chosen for study.

Fees. Registration Fee, £25. Junior School: £1,680 per term (includes text books). Main School: £1,985 per term (includes text books). Sibling discount of 10% for the second child and 20% for the third or subsequent child attending concurrently.

Scholarships and Financial Awards. (*see* Entrance Scholarship section) Up to two Scholarships a year may be awarded for entrance at the age of 11, up to two at 12 and one at 13. There are also several Exhibitions. Value 10% to 50% of the tuition fees according to income. Music Scholarships of up to 50% of tuition fees may be offered at 11, 12, 13 and 16. Sixth form Art and Drama Scholarships of up to 50% of tuition fees may be offered each year. There are also a number of special scholarships made possible by donations from local benefactors for able pupils whose parents require financial assistance.

The School offers a number of Governors' Awards, for parents who need financial assistance, at 7-8, 11-13 and in the Sixth Form. The value is up to 50% of tuition fees, according to income and academic potential.

Curriculum. In the first 3 years in the Main School all pupils take English, History, Geography, French, Mathematics, IT, Latin, Physics, Chemistry, Biology, Art, Design Technology, Drama, Music and Religious and Physical Education. In the 3rd year German is introduced. After this there is a wide choice of subjects to GCSE level, including English, French, Mathematics and 5 of the following: Latin, Greek, German, Physics, Biology, History, Geography, Music, Drama, Art, Chemistry, Design and Technology and Information Systems.

Students enter the VIth Form choosing from 27 different AS and A2 subjects and follow whatever curriculum is appropriate to their ability and objectives, being prepared for university scholarships, university entrance and admission to other forms of further education or vocational training. Over 95% go on annually to Degree Courses.

Houses. There are nine Pupil Houses. Each is under the personal supervision of a Head of House, with whom parents are invited to keep in touch on any matter affecting their child's general development and future career.

Religion. All pupils attend Religious Education classes, which include VIth Form discussion groups. Sunday services are held in the School Chapel two or three times each term. Pupils may be prepared for Confirmation which takes place in March.

Games. Rugby, Hockey, Cricket, Swimming, Athletics, Cross Country, Tennis, Badminton, Squash, Shooting, Basketball, Netball, Cycling and Golf. All pupils take part in some game, unless medically unfit. Alternative activities are available for the VIth Form.

Community and other Service. All pupils learn to serve the community. Many choose to take part in Social Service, helping old people and the handicapped young. There is a voluntary CCF Contingent with thriving RN, Army and RAF Sections. The CCF offers a large variety of Outdoor Activities, including Adventure Training Camps, Ten Tors Expedition Training as well as specialist courses. Unusually, the School possesses a thriving St John Ambulance Brigade Unit. Pupils are encouraged to participate in the Duke of Edinburgh's Award Scheme.

Music. Pupils are taught Singing and Musical appreciation and are encouraged to learn to play Musical Instruments. More than one third of all pupils have individual lessons on at least one instrument. There are 3 Orchestras, a Choral Society which annually performs a major work in Exeter Cathedral and 3 Choirs as well as numerous ensembles. There are over 30 visiting instrumental teachers. Over 20 public concerts are given each year. Different ensembles have performed regularly at the National Festival of Music for Youth at the Festival Hall, and the Schools Prom at the Royal Albert Hall.

Drama. Drama is developed both within and outside the curriculum. The School Hall with its large and well-equipped stage provides for the dual purpose of studio workshop and the regular production of plays, operas and musicals. The Drama Studio is used for smaller productions.

Art and Design. Art lessons are given to Junior and Senior Forms. Apart from the formal disciplines of GCSE and A level, which can be taken by those who choose, all pupils have opportunity for artistic expression in painting, print-making, photography, pottery, construction in many materials and carving wood and stone. All younger pupils learn to develop craft skills in wood, metal and plastic and to use them creatively in design work. Many then follow GCSE or A level courses in Design and Technology. There is an annual art exhibition in July.

Expeditions. Throughout the school a large number of residential field trips and expeditions take place each year including a 3rd form new pupils Dartmoor weekend, a 6th form Politics trip to Washington, and several foreign exchanges. Pupils are also encouraged to compete for external expeditions, and recently a record eleven places were offered in the same year to Exeter School pupils by the British Schools Exploring Society (BSES) for a variety of destinations.

Societies and Clubs. Pupils are encouraged to pursue their interests by joining one of the School Societies. Groups of enthusiasts can form new Societies or Clubs, but the following are at present available: Art, Badminton, Basketball, Canoeing, Chess, Choral Society, Christian Union, Computing, Cycling, Debating, Drama, Electronics, Music, Natural History, Photography, Politics, Sailing, Shooting, Soccer and Squash. Teams are also entered for equestrian events.

Social. Close contact is maintained with the City and the University. Association between members of the School and the wider society outside is fostered wherever opportunity offers.

The staff believe strongly in the value of association with parents, who are invited to meetings annually throughout their sons' or daughters' time at the School. The Friends of Exeter School, founded in 1994, exists to promote closer relations between the School, parents and those having close ties with the School.

Careers. Careers education begins with group work at the age of 13 and continues on a progressive programme until students leave the school. The Careers Officers of the Cornwall and Devon Careers Service Ltd regularly visit the School to interview pupils and there are frequent opportunities for pupils and their parents to consult representatives of the professions, industry and commerce.

In the last 10 years Medicine, Law and Engineering have been the most popular courses chosen for higher education.

Honours. 12 pupils secured places at Oxford & Cambridge in 1999-2000. Of 91 UVIth formers last year, 90 were accepted for Honours Degree Courses at University in 2000 or 2001.

Charitable status. Exeter School is a Registered Charity, number 306724. It exists to provide education for children.

Felsted School

Dunmow Essex CM6 3LL.
Tel: Headmaster: (01371) 820258.
Bursar: (01371) 820238.
Fax: (01371) 821179 (School) 01371 821232 (Headmaster)

Founded in 1564 by Richard, Lord Riche, Lord Chancellor of England.

Motto: *'Garde ta foy'*.

Governing Body:
¶K M R Foster (*Chairman*)
His Honour Judge Peter Beaumont, QC
¶C Bradley, CBE, MA
The Rt Hon The Lord Newton of Braintree, OBE
The Rt Hon Sir Alan Haselhurst, MP
R M Shaw
P G Lee, DL, FRICS
Mrs M R Chalmers
P J Cooper
S J Ahearne
J H Davies
Mrs J Simpson
C Daybell
Professor C Temple

Bursar & Clerk to the Governors: P D Watkinson, BSc, MBA

***Headmaster:* S C Roberts**, MA

Deputy Head: M E Allbrook, MA (*Classics*)
Director of Studies: R L Feldman, MSc (*Mathematics*)
Second Deputy (*Common Room*): *J M Shaw, BA, PhD (*History*)
Second Deputy (*Curriculum*): *Dr K Stephenson, BSc (*Science*)
Senior Master: *N S Hinde, MA (*Spanish*)

Assistant Teachers:
*R P Ballingall, BSc (*Physics*)
*D R Everett, BSc (*Chemistry*)
*C C H Dawkins, MA (*Computing*)
N L Osborne, MA (*History and History of Art*)
†A W S Thomson, BEd (*PE*) *Windsor's*
*A M Homer, MA (*English*)
A N Grierson Rickford, MA (*English*)
*C J Megahey, BA (*Maths*)
N J Spring, MA (*English*) *Head of Careers*
†M Surridge, BA (*History*) *Deacon's*
A D G Widdowson, BSc (*Maths*)
P G Statter, BSc (*Maths and IT Co-ordinator*)
†I W Gwyther, BA (*Geography*) *Elwyn's*
*J Oakshatt, BSc (*Biology*)
*†D J Smith, BA (*Art*) *Gepp's*
M E Surridge, BSc (*CDT*)
*L Siddons, MA (*French and Classics*)
J Clarke, MSc (*Maths*)
*J M Shaw, BA, PhD (*History*)
Mrs H Trollope, BA (*Librarian*)
*M J A Sugden, MA (*Modern Languages*)
A Dearns, BSc (*Physics*)
†Mrs J M Burrett, BA (*Modern Languages*) *Follyfield*
A G Chamberlain, BA (*Modern Languages*)
§Mrs D E Platts, BA (*English*)
*J L Thorogood, GRSM, LRAM (*Music*)
*C R S Lee, MA (*Drama and English*)
*G R Proto, BSc (*Geography*)
†Mrs K A Megahey, BSc (*Maths*) *Stock's*
†R A Campbell, MA (*Modern Languages*) *Montgomery's*
Mrs M Grierson Rickford, BA (*Modern Languages*)
Miss A L F Simpson, BSc (*Chemistry & Biology*)
Miss F J Gallantree, BSc (*Geography*)
†Mrs B J L Chamberlain, L-ès-L *Garnetts*
C D J Hamilton, BSc (*Physics*)
E R Hall, BSc (*Economics*)
Miss J T Mogridge, BSc (*Sports Studies*)
J D Lowry, BA, ALCM (*Music*)
B Coppel, BA (*Art*)
Mrs F M Marshall, BSc
The Revd J Hart, BA, BD (*Chaplain*)
*Ms H Konopacka, BSc (*SENCO*)
Miss R E Lees, BA (*Biology*)
*Mr N Stannard, BA (*Religious Studies*)
*Miss N A Wormell, MA (Oxon) (*Classics*)

*P J Golden, BSocSc, MBA (*Economics & Business Studies*)
§Mrs D K Tibbitts, CertEd (*Mathematics*)
§Mrs P L McGuinness, BSc (*Mathematics*)
§Ms R Ryan, BA (*Business Studies*)
*S Newton, BEng (*CDT*)

Headmaster of the Preparatory School: E J Newton, BA

Roman Catholic Chaplain to Felsted: Father G Godfrey

Medical Officers:
M C Slack, MB, BS
Dr S Raybould

Felsted is primarily a co-educational boarding school of around 400 pupils. Of this number 65% are boys, 35% are girls and 25% are day pupils. The School is situated in an attractive village in the unspoilt North Essex countryside, 35 miles from both Cambridge and London. Road and rail links are good and Stansted airport is nearby.

Curriculum. The two principles on which the curriculum is constructed are the minimum of specialisation and the maximum of choice within it.

Modern teaching techniques audio-visual aids, computers, and video are used in all academic departments, but not to the neglect of basic skills. A system of continuous assessment operates throughout the school.

In the Third form a broad curriculum is followed, including nine periods per week of Science, and two each of Art, Technology, Music and, for one term, Computing. German, Spanish and Greek may also be started. At the end of the Fifth form year most pupils take between eight and ten subjects in the GCSE examinations.

In the Sixth form specialisation has to begin, but the choice of three subjects for 'A' levels is a wide one, covering some two dozen subjects in a variety of permutations.

In addition to their 'A' level courses, all Sixth formers devote a significant portion of their time to General Studies, aimed at broadening knowledge and an understanding of the world, at providing a balance to main 'A' level subjects, and at developing basic practical skills, such as pottery, CAD and cookery.

The main *School Library,* housed in a handsome room, is a central academic resource. There is a full time Librarian and two assistants. The Library is fully catalogued with an up to date book stock. Considerable use is made of IT.

Boarding organisation. There are five boarding Houses for boys and three for girls. Each House contains boarders and day pupils. All are within a few minutes' walk of the main classroom blocks. Each House has a resident Housemaster/Housemistress, Assistant Housemaster/Housemistress and Matron. The Housemaster or Housemistress is responsible for a pupil's general welfare and, in consultation with parents, for taking the major decisions affecting a pupil's school life and career preparation.

Over two-thirds of the pupils in the school are in studies, single or shared. For the younger pupils there are House common rooms, in which each pupil has his or her own working place, bookshelves and cupboard, and well appointed, small dormitories.

Careers guidance. The school pays particular importance to careers advice, starting in the Third form and increasing in momentum as pupils move up the school. The Head of Careers and the University Liaison Master have specialist knowledge. The Careers Room contains an extensive collection of well-indexed material.

Religious life. Felsted is a Church of England foundation, but welcomes pupils from all Christian denominations and those with other religious traditions. All pupils normally attend the various services in Chapel, including a short service before school on three weekdays and one compulsory service on Sundays, alternately mornings and evenings.

Creative activities. As well as on academic excellence, great store is set on creative activities. All pupils produce a creative project during their first term in their own time. This may be in any sphere: music, art, drama, technical studies, computing or whatever, and it is hoped that this will stimulate a creative interest for the future which they will continue to develop.

Music at Felsted enjoys excellent facilities and covers many facets. The Music School contains a spacious hall for rehearsals and concerts as well as practice and teaching rooms. Three full-time members of the music staff, assisted by some 20 visiting staff, provide specialist teaching on piano, organ, and every orchestral instrument.

The Art School is in the picturesque building which first housed the school in 1564, close to the medieval church and Bury gardens. There are two painting studios, an art library, an etching and printing room and a small lecture room. Every pupil studies Art during their first year at the school, and pupils are also encouraged to paint in their spare time.

Drama. Annual House plays and two major school drama productions each year provide ample opportunities for pupil involvement on stage and back-stage. A studio theatre/workshop has been built in the Old Gym.

Technology. Felsted was one of the earliest schools in England to develop workshops and its superb technical facilities enable many different activities to be accommodated, such as boat, car and cycle maintenance, jewellery, pottery, cookery, electronics and CAD/CAM. All pupils in the Third Form learn basic skills for technology which combine intellectual discipline with many practical skills and the subject is established at GCSE and 'A' level.

The School was also one of the pioneers of computer studies as part of the syllabus and the school has contributed to the design of several commercial computer systems. The purpose-built Computer Block is well used both in and out of formal teaching time.

Games and sports. For outdoor games the school has, on its doorstep, 70 acres of playing fields, a floodlit, all-weather hockey pitch, eleven grass and six hard courts for tennis, a grass running track, two sets of pits and circles to cater for the full range of athletics field events, and facilities for golf practice. Indoors, in the Palmer Sports Hall, are facilities for cricket, tennis, hockey, basketball, volleyball, badminton, etc., three excellent squash courts linked to the Sports Hall, a multigym, two rugby fives courts, a modern heated swimming pool which is in use all the year, and a miniature shooting range.

Girls enjoy a full sporting programme, playing hockey as the main game in the Autumn Term, netball in the Spring Term with squash, aerobics, swimming, badminton also available and in the Summer athletics, swimming and tennis.

The main games for boys are rugby (Autumn Term), hockey (Spring Term), and cricket (Summer Term). Rugby is played competitively by ten School teams, but about 75% of the pupils represent either School or House on a regular basis. Hockey is Felsted's most famous game, and over the years the School has produced many 'blues' county players and internationals. Felsted's reputation for cricket is approaching that of its hockey.

Societies and other activities. The Bury is a large 15th century manor house, with later additions, which, with its beautiful pond and garden, acts as a focus for all kinds of spare-time activities and interests. It is a centre for society meetings and individual use in a relaxed atmosphere.

There are over 40 active societies in the school, most of which have been going strong for many years.

Two afternoons a week throughout the year are devoted to non-sporting activities. On these afternoons all pupils below the Lower Sixth are occupied with activities such as CCF and Duke of Edinburgh's Award.

Felsted School Scholarships. (*see* Entrance Scholarship section) Academic Entrance Scholarships are awarded annually varying in fixed value up to 50% of the fees. Music and Art Scholarships are awarded up to the value of 50% of the fees. Bursaries are available to increase the awards in case of need up to 100% of the fees in certain cases. Entrance Scholarship candidates must be under 14 on 1st September following the examination which is held in May. Scholarships are also awarded at 11+ at Felsted Preparatory School and these may be carried through to the Senior School. Academic Sixth Form Entrance Scholarships are available (one at 50% and two at 25%) as well as Art and Music Scholarships up to the value of 50%. The examinations for the Sixth Form Scholarships take place each November and February. Arkwright Foundation Scholarships are also available to talented students in Design at 16+.

All-rounder Scholarships and Foundation Awards which recognise all round ability or specific ability in one area are available on entry at 11, 13 and 16 years old.

Registration and entry. Boys' and Girls' names can be registered at any time. All those, who pass an examination at the Preparatory School at 11+, will enter the Senior School without a further need to qualify. Before admission to Felsted all pupils at other preparatory schools must pass the Common Entrance or Scholarship Examination. Entry from other schools is by Headmaster's Report and Verbal Reasoning Test, or, for VIth Form entry, 6 GCSEs and interview.

Fees. £5,240 per term for boarders, £4,130 for home boarders, £3,830 for day pupils. Registration Fee £50.

For the Preparatory School the termly fees are £3,910 for boarders, £3,030 for home boarders, £2,870 for day pupils. Pre-Preparatory Department £1,180 to £1,660 per term. Registration fee £30.

Felsted Preparatory School, which is in membership of the Incorporated Association of Preparatory Schools (IAPS) shares the same governing body as Felsted School but has its own spacious buildings and grounds on a neighbouring campus. It is fully co-educational with a Pre-Preparatory Department (age 4–7). (For further information, see Part V of this Book relating to Preparatory Schools).

Old Felstedian Society. There is a thriving Old Felstedian Society with both social and sporting activities. The *Secretary* is: M A Jones, 10 Parkhill Road, London E4 7ED. The Old Felstedian Liaison Master, Mr N S Hinde, would be pleased to answer queries about the Alumni.

Charitable status. Felsted School is a Registered Charity, number 310870. The charity is based upon the Foundation established by Richard Lord Riche in 1564 with the objective of teaching and instructing children across a broad curriculum as ordained from time to time by its Trustees.

Fettes College

Edinburgh EH4 1QX
Tel: 0131 332 2281
Fax: 0131 311 6714
e-mail: enquiries@fettes.com
website: www.fettes.co.uk

Fettes College was founded in 1870 under the will of Sir William Fettes, Bart, twice Lord Provost of Edinburgh. The administration of the endowment is now in the hands of the Governors of the Fettes Trust acting under the Fettes College Scheme. It is an independent co-educational boarding and day school for 580 pupils aged 8–18 which includes a Preparatory School for pupils aged 8–13.

Motto: *'Industria'*.

Governors:
The Hon Lord MacLean, QC (*Chairman*)
B O Lloyd
N J Crichton, WS
Professor P H Jones, FRSE, FRSA, FSA(Scot)
C M Campbell, QC
Sir John Blelloch, KCB
Councillor I Whyte
Professor J D Cash, CBE, PhD, FRCP
D B McMurray, MA (*Deputy Chairman*)
S W Morrison
A E H Salvesen
B Smellie
The Very Revd J Harkness, CB, OBE
A A McCreath
Mrs E Ross, CBE
Mrs E J S McClelland

Clerk to the Governors: A G Fox, WS

***Headmaster:* M C B Spens**, MA (Selwyn College, Cambridge)

Deputy Headmaster and Headmaster of the Preparatory School: A G S Davies, BSc

Deputy Head and Director of Studies: A F Reeves, MA

Deputy Head: Mrs J A Campbell, BA

Chaplain: The Revd B S McDowell, BA, BD

Assistant Staff:
D Kennedy, BSc
P F Coshan, BSc, PhD
M H Davies, MA, DPhil
D A R Barnett, DipTech
J K Foot, BA
D M Goude, BSc
A V M Murray, MA
M C G Peel, MA
A M Hall, MA, PhD
G A Blair, MA
Miss R MacVicar, BSc
R E Hughes, MA, MPhil
A Shackleton, MA
†Mrs M Goude, BSc
Mrs E Thomson, BA, MLitt
D F Mather, BSc
†B P Butler, BA
A S Alexander, MA
J J Morris, BA
†R H V Harrison, BA
Mrs C M Harrison, BA
C M Rose, BA
Mrs E H Young, BSc
Miss C J Cecil, BSc
J S M Wilkie, BA
Mrs M J Palfery, MA
D S Wideman, MA
J Darmody, BA
†Ms P R S Donald, MA, MPhil
Miss S A Lewis, BSc, PhD
Mrs S E McCullough, BSc
†J S McCullough, BA
Mrs H F Harrison, MA
Mrs C S Collins, MA
Mrs S M McKinnon, MA
†J W J Gillespie, MA
Mrs M I Mackenzie, MA
Mrs C A Elliot, MA
Miss C M Reed, BEng
†Mrs F J E Wideman, MA
P Kesterton, BSc
J P McKee, BA
M P Ford, BA
Miss F C White, BA
C S Thomson, BA
S French, BSc, PhD
I Batty, BEng
Miss L Stansbie, BA
H S Hunter, BA
P F Heuston, BSc
Miss M D Russell, MA
Miss A Hodgson, MA
A Aidonis, MA, PhD
Miss E R Davies, BA
Miss S A Richards, BSc
Miss G McCrum, BSc
Miss A A F Mair, MA
Miss C M Jainsh, BEd, BA
Miss F Macalister, MA
N Boyd, BA
B Welsh, BSc

Fettes College Preparatory School
Headmaster: A G S Davies, BSc

Music:
D A Goodenough, GGSM, FTCL, ARCO, ALCM (*Director*)
Mrs J D Armstrong, BA, MSc
Mrs S Jones, BMus
S J Nieminski, MA, FRCO

Bursar: M A Tolhurst, MA

Assistant Bursar: J V Oatts, BA, MSc

Accountant: A Malcolm

Master of Works: H Jessop, BSc

Medical Officers:
Dr G Craig, MB, ChB, DO, DRCOG, MRCP, MRCGP
Dr G Price, MB, ChB

Keeper of the Register: G D C Preston, MA

Headmaster's Secretary: Mrs F M Sprott

Situation and Buildings. Fettes stands in a park of 85 acres on a remarkable site between the centre of Edinburgh and the Firth of Forth. The College building is a magnificent landmark set within a wooded and attractive campus containing extensive playing fields. Full advantage is taken of the academic, historical and cultural facilities which Edinburgh affords, and at the same time the sea and the countryside are close by, offering excellent opportunities for water sports, ski-ing and mountaineering.

The main building contains the Chapel, Library, some classrooms including the language laboratory, Computer centre, the Sanatorium and two Boarding Houses. The other six Boarding Houses, the Dining Hall, the Music and Art Schools, the Concert Hall, the Science and Technology Centre, Gymnasium, Squash and Fives Courts and Indoor Swimming Pool are situated in the grounds

Communications by road, rail and air are excellent.

Organisation. There are approximately 580 pupils aged 8–18, and each member of the School is the responsibility of a Housemaster or Housemistress. There are four Houses for boys, three for girls and a Preparatory School; a major programme of refurbishment has now been completed which provides all senior pupils with excellent studies and study bedrooms. Almost 80% of the pupils are boarders, but boys and girls who live close to the School are accepted as day pupils. There is a strong tutorial system for the encouragement and guidance of each pupil.

Aims. The purpose of the School is to provide an education based on Christian principles which will enable each pupil to develop his or her individual talents to the full. Particular emphasis is placed on academic excellence, good personal relationships and strong pastoral care. Thriving artistic, dramatic and musical traditions exist alongside a wide range of sporting activities.

Curriculum. The curriculum provides GCSE courses in English, Latin, Greek, French, German, Spanish, Religious Studies, History, Geography, Mathematics, Physics, Chemistry, Biology, Business Studies, Technology, Drama, Art, Music and PE; option systems permit pupils to select the combination of subjects best suited to their abilities.

In the Sixth Form there is the attractive alternative of the specialisation offered by GCE A and AS levels or the breadth of education offered by the 'Higher' Grade examinations of the Scottish Certificate of Education. Through these two systems over 90% of pupils gain university entry qualifications, and a good number each year secure places at Oxford and Cambridge.

Careers. The School is a member of the Independent Schools Careers Organisation, and a team of Staff are responsible for providing specialist advice on careers and Higher Education and for developing links with industry and commerce. The Headmaster, Housemasters and Housemistresses are also involved in this work, and parents are invited to meet the Staff at termly receptions so that they can discuss pupils' progress, future options and career plans.

Chapel. The whole School attends short regular services in Chapel, and there are House Assemblies in the evening. The interdenominational nature of the School is reflected in the Holy Communion Services and in the Joint Annual Service of Confirmation for which candidates are prepared for membership of the Anglican Church and the Church of Scotland.

Games. Pupils take exercise on at least four afternoons a week. The major sports for boys are Rugby Football, Hockey, Cricket and Athletics. The girls play Hockey, Lacrosse and Netball during the winter, and the principal sports in the summer are Tennis and Athletics. A large number of other sports flourish; the School has its own Sports Centre, all-weather pitch, indoor Swimming Pool and courts for Fives, Squash and Badminton.

Other activities. There is a variety of societies and clubs, and each pupil is encouraged to develop cultural interests. On Saturday evenings, in addition to lectures, plays and concerts, there are regular dances and discos, and committees of pupils, with the assistance of members of Staff, are responsible for planning and organising social events for different age groups.

Music. The College possesses a strong musical tradition, and many pupils receive instrumental tuition. In addition to the orchestras there are ensembles, a wind band, Chapel Choir and Concert Choir.

Drama. Drama is lively and of a high standard. Each year the School Play, Lower Sixth Form Play, House Plays and drama festivals offer great opportunities for large numbers of boys and girls to act and to participate in Lighting and Stage Management.

Art. The Art School is flourishing, and the standards of pupil attainment are very high.

Combined Cadet Force, Duke of Edinburgh's Award Scheme, Outside Service. Pupils are members of the CCF for two years and may choose to extend their service while they are in the Sixth Form. There are Navy, Army and RAF Sections and a thriving Pipe Band. Training is offered in Shooting, Vehicle Engineering, Canoeing, Rock-Climbing, Ski-ing and Sub-Aqua.

In the Sixth Form many pupils pursue the Gold Standard of the Duke of Edinburgh's Award Scheme, and some 70 members of the School join the Outside Service Unit which provides help for others in difficult circumstances and raises funds for Charities.

Outdoor Activities. The School aims to make full use of its proximity to the sea, the Dry Ski-Slope and the mountains of Scotland. Outdoor activities are encouraged for the enjoyment that they give and the valuable personal qualities which they help to develop. A number of members of Staff are experts in mountaineering, ski-ing and water sports, and all pupils have opportunities for receiving instruction in camping, canoeing, hill-walking and snow and rock climbing. There are regular expeditions abroad.

Preparatory School. The Preparatory School for 160 boys and girls aged 8 to 13 is situated in the School grounds. Boarders stay in the modern purpose-built House. Pupils in the Prep School share the staff and facilities of the senior school and participate in the full range of activities enjoyed by the College as a whole.

Admission. (*see* Entrance Scholarship section) Scholarship and Entrance Examinations for the Junior House are held in February.

Boys and Girls from Preparatory Schools take the Scholarship Examination in February/March or the Common Entrance Examination. Candidates from Maintained Schools can take the School's own Entrance Examinations in English and Mathematics.

Candidates for the Sixth Form take the Sixth Form Scholarship and Entrance Examinations in November or can be considered on report and interview only.

The Headmaster is prepared to give individual consideration to other candidates.

Scholarships, Foundation Awards and Bursaries. Scholarships to maximum value of 50% fees are available for candidates aged 11 or 13 and also for entry to the Sixth Form; these awards can be supplemented by bursaries in case of financial need.

Foundation Awards and Bursaries are available to those candidates whose parents cannot meet the full fees. The value of these awards depends on parents' financial means, and they can cover the full boarding fees. These awards are made not only on the basis of academic standard but also on the ability and enthusiasm of the candidate to contribute strongly to the sporting and cultural activities of the School.

Music Scholarships of up to the value of 50% fees are available.

Art Scholarships up to the value of 50% of the fees are also available.

All-Rounder Awards offer up to the value of 50% of the fees.

Bursaries provide 12.5% reduction in fees for children of H.M. Forces.

Fees. Registration Fee £50; Boarding fees £3,639 to £5,309 per term. Day Fees £2,282 to £3,582 per term. The fees cover all extras except books and stationery, music lessons and subscriptions to voluntary clubs and activities.

Old Fettesian Association. *Liaison:* C P Cheetham, BPhil, MA, Fettes Foundation Office, Fettes College (Telephone 0131 311 6736).

Further Details from The Headmaster, Fettes College, Edinburgh EH4 1QX (Telephone 0131 332 2281).

Charitable status. "Governors of the Fettes Trust" is a Registered Charity, number SCO 17489. Fettes aims to provide a quality education at Junior and Senior level.

Forest School

Snaresbrook London E17 3PY.
Tel: 020 8520 1744.

Founded in 1834 as 'The Forest Proprietary School' to 'provide a course of Education for youth, comprising classical learning, mathematics and such modern languages and other branches of science and general literature as might from time to time be introduced; combined with religious and moral instruction in accordance with the doctrine of the Church of England.' Incorporated 1947.

Motto: *'In Pectore Robur'.*

Council:
Chairman of the Governors: C B Smith

Members of the Council:
Professor J E Banatvala, MA, MD, MRCP, FRCPath, DCH, DPH
Mrs S R Campion, MA
B M de L Cazenove, TD
G S Green, MA
G Hewitson, MA
The Revd W Hurdman
J A Little, MA, PhD
J Matthews, FCA
Mrs P Morton
Mrs S K Rankin, MA, PhD
G Smallbone, MA

***Warden:* A G Boggis**, MA

Deputy Warden and Head of the Boys' School: R F Russell, MA

Deputy Warden and Head of the Girls' School: Mrs P A Goodman, MA

Bursar: R W G Banks, MA

Boys' School Assistant Staff:

B A Hardcastle, MA (*Senior Master*)
*P M Francis, BEd (*Senior Housemaster*)
M C V Spencer Ellis, MA (*Director of Sixth Form*)
†J D Waller, BA
*C Barker, BSc, PhD
K Webster, MA
R J Cherry, LSIAD
†*P Henley-Smith, BSc, PhD
*R H Bishop, MA, BA
I R Honeysett, MA
†Mrs D Barker, BSc
†M S Watson, BA
S Turner, Essex CCC
*A R Dainton, BSc
P M Oliver, MA (*Director of Drama*)
S T Kew, BA
D W Moore, BSc
W J Hall, CertEd, ADPMCollP
*G Paynter, BA (*Marketing and press liaison*)
*C D Brant, MA
S C Jalowiecki, BSc
J C B Hawdon, MSc
†M Gray, BA
*Mrs B J Lane, BSc
M E Peel, BA
Mrs E M Pribul, BA
M J Smith, BSc
*Mrs A E G Casson, BA
A D Ford, BA
†O E Ling, BA
*Mrs S M Feldman, BSc
P H S Corbett, MA
†T C Hewitt, BA
Mrs H P R Miller, BA
R Pathak, BA
S L Thompson, BSc
Miss K Green, BA
†S A Heron, BEd
Ms A N Berges
*S Brown, MA
M Gemelli, BSc
P Botton, BSc
M S Christie, MA
J T S Haskey, BA
S J Reid, BA
S Barker, BSc
R J A Martin, BEd, MSc
Miss K Currie, BA
M Lennon, BA
Z H Nazir, BSc, DPhil
J Holt, BA

Girls' School Assistant Staff:

Mrs J Carr, BSc (*Senior Mistress*)
Mrs P Fine, BSc (*Senior Housemistress*)
Mrs J E Martin, BSc, MEd (*Assistant Director of Sixth Form & Careers Advisor*)
*J L Harrison, MSc, PhD
*Ms L E Murray, BA
Mrs P B Todd, CertEd
N V Gray, MA
A Royall, BSc, MSc, DIC
A J Eccles, MSc
*Mrs G Morrell, MA
Mrs H Jolly, BEd
†Mrs S M Harris, BA
Mrs R M Mechan, BA
†*Miss L King, BA
*Miss A R Chapman, MA
Mrs M Jones, BEd
J S Casson, MA
*A G van den Broek, MA, PhD
Mrs M R Russell, BSc
Miss P M Greig, BSc
*Mrs C Ambler, BA
A H Todd, BSc, PhD
†Mrs P A Smith, BEd
Mrs S C Keating, BEd
Miss T C Meadows, BA
†Miss M V T McKenzie, MA
Miss K Dubois, MA
†Mrs S Alliott, MA
Miss L C Cooper, BA
Mrs M A Wright, BA
Mrs A E Gould, MA
Miss C Reay, BSc

Junior School:
Head of the Junior School:
M J Lovett, BA

Assistant Staff:

Mrs S A Shen, CertEd
Mrs L F Porter, CertEd (*Mistress in charge of Girls*)
Mrs P H Gardner, BEd
Mrs M Healey, CertEd
Mrs C Bristow, BA
Mrs G A Tarling
J S Rodriques, CertEd
Mrs C P A Browne, BEd, MA (*Mistress in charge of Boys*)
Mrs K M Finnegan, BEd
E J Hickman, CertEd
Mrs C A Joyce, BA
Miss L C Morris, BA
Mrs R Farnfield, CertEd
Miss E Marshall, BSc

Chaplain: The Revd J G Gascoigne, MA, BPhilEd

Director of Music: M D Palmer, BMus, FRCO, LRAM

Computer Systems Manager: D H Posner, FCA, FCCA

Warden's Secretary: Miss D Bell, CertEd

There are currently 1,170 pupils in the School, (520 boys in the Boys' School, 440 girls in the Girls' School, 210 boys and girls in the Junior School). There is accommodation for 20 boy boarders.

The three Schools share the main School campus and facilities such as Chapel, Sports Hall, Theatre and Computer Centre, but each has its own separate teaching block. The Sixth Form is then organised on co-educational lines.

Buildings. The School is situated in an open part of Epping Forest. The original building is Georgian, converted to provide dormitories, libraries, recreation rooms and offices. 19th century expansion led to the building of the Chapel, Gymnasium, Dining Hall and Swimming Bath. Modern classrooms and changing rooms have been built and the main Laboratory Block substantially extended. Art and Craft departments, VIth Form studies, Dormitories, Kitchens, The Deaton Theatre seating 375, a Sports Hall, Music School, VI Form Centre and Computer Centre have been added in recent years. The Junior School is a modern block, rebuilt in 1950 and extended in 1970 and 1975. The Girls' School was founded in 1978 and its buildings opened and dedicated in 1981. Additional Art, Drama and Design facilities were opened in 2001. The surrounding playing fields cover nearly 27 acres.

Organisation. The School is divided into 3 clear sections under the overall direction of the Warden: Junior School (ages 4–11); Boys' School (ages 11–18): Girls' School (11–18). There are 8 Houses in the Boys' School and 6 in the Girls' School.

Curriculum. Courses are designed to give a broad education as far as GCSE, each pupil taking English, Mathematics, either separate Sciences or Balanced Science, one Modern Foreign Language and other subjects depending on the individual's ability. A high priority is given to ICT throughout the School. There is a wide variety of VIth Form courses designed to prepare pupils to enter University, Business, the Services or the Professions. The full range of AS and A2 levels are offered; all Sixth Formers take General Studies. Private tuition is available in Piano, Organ and Orchestral Instruments, and there are several Orchestras, Bands and Choirs.

Religion. Worship in the School Chapel is in accordance with the faith and practice of the Church of England. All pupils are required to attend the daily services in chapel. Religious Education is broadly based and is taught as an academic subject.

Societies. The School has a thriving Combined Cadet Force, a Voluntary Service Group and a branch of The Duke of Edinburgh Award Scheme. Other Societies include Chess, Choral, Debating, Film, Music, Natural History, Photography, and Science. There are Badminton, Fencing, Bridge, Squash and Shooting Clubs and a specialised TV studio.

Drama. There are frequent productions and drama competitions. Music, Plays, Concerts and Lectures take place in the Theatre.

Games. The main games are Cricket, Association Football, Hockey, Netball, Athletics, and Swimming. There are Tennis Courts and Squash Courts. All pupils are expected to take part in games.

Fees. Aged Over 11. Boarding Fee (including tuition) £11,826 pa. Day Pupils' Fee (including lunches) £7,545 pa.

Aged 8-10. Day Pupils, £5,835

Aged 7 years. Day Pupils, £5,160

Aged 4 years. Day Pupils, £4,770

Admission. Examinations for pupils at 7+ and 11+ take place in January for entry in the following September. Some places are available at 13+, at 16+ and at other ages.

Careers. Almost all pupils go on to Universities to take Degree Courses, including 10-12 each year to Oxford and Cambridge. Careers advice is given to all pupils.

Scholarships and Bursaries. (*see* Entrance Scholarship section) Academic Scholarships, Bursaries and Music Scholarships to cover up to full fees are offered annually to pupils at 11+ and 16+. There are also Boarding Scholarships and at 16+ Drama and Art Awards. Further fee reductions are available to children of the Clergy.

Further details may be obtained from the Warden.

Old Foresters Club. *Hon Secretary:* Mr R Smith, c/o Forest School.

Charitable status. Forest School, Essex is a Registered Charity, number 312677. The objective of the School is Education.

Framlingham College

Framlingham Woodbridge Suffolk IP13 9EY.
Tel: (01728) 723789.
Fax: (01728) 724546.
website: www.framlingham.suffolk.sch.uk

The School was founded in 1864 by public subscription as the Suffolk County Memorial to the Prince Consort and was incorporated by Royal Charter. Under the Charter, the School is administered by a Corporation of 25 members.

Motto: 'Studio Sapientia Crescit'.

President: The Rt Hon The Lord Belstead, PC

Vice-President: Maj Gen J B Dye, CBE, MC, DL

Governors:
J Clement, Esq (*Chairman of the Governors*)
The Rt Revd The Lord Bishop of St Edmundsbury and Ipswich
The Master of Pembroke College, Cambridge
J W Edwards, Esq
S C Pryor, Esq
J Kerr, Esq, MBE, JP, DL
R W R Smith, Esq, MA
R C Rous, Esq, DL
R J Blythe, Esq
J G Ruddock, Esq, FCA, FBIM
Mrs S E van den Arend
A W M Fane, Esq, MA, FCA
J G Thurlow, Esq
Mrs E Gurney
M M Orr, Esq, BA
Air Cdre J Ford, FRAeS
Mrs M A Makey, BA

***Head:* Mrs G M Randall, BA**

Second Master & Deputy Head Pastoral: A N Lawrence, BEd
Deputy Head, Academic: C A Norton, MA, PGCE
Senior Master and Registrar: R T Liddell, DLC, CertEd
Senior Academic Tutor: M D Robinson, MA, BEd

Assistant Staff:
M J Cooke, MA
B P Smallcombe, BEd, ACP
H F Robinson, BSc CertEd
P D Barker, MA, PGCE
D J Boatman, BA, PGCE
C R Thorpe, MA, PGCE
D J Morgan, CertEd
R W Skitch, BSc, PGCE
†M K Myers-Allen, BSc, PGCE
C R Suter, MA, CertEd
C P Lenton, MA
†Mrs F J Read, BSc, PGCE
Mrs C E Mallett, BA
S Reeve, BEd
Miss N K Rice, BSc, PGCE
Mrs G M Knights, BSc
Mrs H Myers-Allen, BSc
Mrs K M Evans, BSc, PGCE
Mrs J A Sanders, BA
Mrs E Walwanda, MSc, FSS, PGCE
R Rogers, BMus, LRAM
Dr S Barker, PhD
Mrs D H Jones, CertEd
Mrs S A Hoole, BA
Dr R J Hoole, MA, PhD
†Mrs J S Hobson, BA, PGCE
K R S Hoyle, BSc, PGCE
C Caiger, BA, MSc, PGCE
C E Hobson, BA, PGCE
J T Williams, BSoc
Dr D Higgins, MA, PhD, PGCE
†M Kendall, BA, PGCE
T Vignoles, MA, PGCE
I Abrahams, MSc
†H Clelland, MA
P Giannone, BA, MLitt
J Lawson, BSc
M Taylor, MA
M Brown, CertEd
Miss J Dalton, BA
R B Curtis, BEd
The Revd C Jefferson, MA
A Bennett, BA, PGCE
†Mrs S Wenn, BEd, PGCE
Miss S-J Page, BA, PGCE
M M T Adams, BSc
R W Goodrich, BA, LTCL, PGCE
Miss K L Tipton, BSc, PGCE
J D Cuff, BA

Junior School Staff

The Master: S J Player, MA

Second Master: R Sampson, BSc, PGCE
Senior Master: R G Williams, CertEd, ACP

M A Baic, CertEd, Dip L-ès-L Sorbonne
M G Vipond, BEd, ACP, CertEd
R J Daykin, BEd
P Baker, BEd
Miss S J Thomson, BEd
Mrs J Johnson, CertEd, BDADip
Mrs E Tydeman, CertEd (*Head of Pre-Prep*)
Mrs B S Hamilton, DipEd (*Pre-Prep*)
J A Clough, BA, PGCE
S W Cullum, BA
Mrs S J Dring, BLib, ALA
J McIlveen, BEd
Mrs C Anderson, BSc, PGCE
Mrs C Lawson, CertEd, DipRSA
Mrs S Stephenson, BEd
N Prowse, BEd
Mrs R Barnes, BEd
C R Reynell, BEd
Mrs J Norton, BEd
Miss A Reed, BA, PGCE

Bursar: A Budd, FCMA, FCCA

Head's Personal Assistant: Mrs M J Prebble

Framlingham College is a fully co-educational school that is proud of its traditions and past achievements yet has a forward-looking approach to the education of boys and girls in the new millennium. The school stands in a magnificent rural situation overlooking Framlingham Mere and Castle. It has its own Junior School at Brandeston Hall (IAPS see Part V).

At Framlingham, we believe that the academic potential of each individual is unlocked in an environment where opportunities abound and in which a firm sense of community prevails.

Organisation: The Senior School numbers some 450 pupils of whom two-thirds are boarders. There are currently 150 girls in the school. The flourishing Sixth Form is approximately 200 strong. There is a fully integrated House system for day and boarding pupils. We have 3 girls' Houses and 4 boys' Houses led by married House staff and committed teams of House Tutors, both resident and non-resident.

Facilities: An imaginative building programme over recent years has produced a superb range of facilities. Science, Technology, Art, Music and Drama enjoy purpose built accommodation, and recent redevelopment of the heart of the school has provided a fully integrated and resourced Humanities suite and a fine library equipped to access the Internet and other libraries. A new indoor swimming pool and fitness suite, completed in February 2000, enhances the superb ranage of sports facilities. There is a popular Sixth Form Centre and an attractive central concourse for informal gatherings.

Curriculum: The curriculum is framed to combine the best of academic tradition with emphasis on depth and rigour of learning; other courses and skills are designed to prepare pupils for the increasingly complex challenges of the modern world.

In Year 9, the first year for pupils aged 13+, the curriculum follows the National Curriculum, with everyone studying all the main subjects and having exposure to a range of practical and creative activities. German, Spanish and Latin are available as options, and all follow a course in personal, religious and social education.

In Years 10 and 11, there is a two year course to GCSE. Everyone studies English (2 GCSEs), Maths, a language and co-ordinated science (2 GCSEs). Other subjects are optional. Most subjects are setted so that each individual can proceed at the right pace.

In the Sixth Form there is an imaginative post-GCSE curriculum. Thanks to the popularity of our Sixth Form, we are able to offer a particularly wide range of A and A/S levels and most combinations are possible. The potential Oxbridge student is carefully nurtured and stretched, and similar care is taken with those who may experience academic difficulties.

All teaching staff act as Academic Tutors, so tutorial groups are small and supportive. The individual pupil is meticulously monitored, and House staff are kept fully informed about performance in the classroom and behaviour in school. Parents receive full written reports regularly and are invited to at least one formal parents' meeting a year. In addition, they receive copies of all mid-term grades for attainment and effort so that a cumulative picture of progress is achieved. Class sizes up to GCSE are usually below 20. The average number is currently 16.

Set sizes for A level are smaller, averaging 8 and rarely exceeding 10. The overall pupil:teacher ratio is better than 9:1.

Out of School Activities: Framlingham believes that every pupil has ability and potential outside the narrowly academic and that success in out of school activities produces a self-confidence that spills over into academic success.

Games. Framlingham College enjoys an enviable reputation for sport. We field a large number of teams to give as many pupils as possible the right sort of opportunity. Girls' games are taken as seriously as boys', and their facilities are equally good.

The major games are rugby, hockey, cricket, athletics and tennis for boys, and hockey, netball, tennis and athletics for girls. There is a wide range of other sporting opportunities, including squash, soccer, badminton, basketball, swimming, archery, riding, shooting, sailing, volleyball and table tennis. The immaculately tended grounds include an Astroturf, a golf course and one of the finest Cricket squares in Suffolk.

Music and Drama: For the talented musician and for the keen but less talented, musical opportunities are considerable. Framlingham has a very strong choral tradition, and there is a wide range of orchestras and instrumental ensembles. The College's dramatic productions have a very high reputation. The main productions each year include at least one musical, one major drama and one junior play.

CCF: Framlingham has an active CCF and, though membership is voluntary, more than half the school takes part. More than 200 are involved in the Duke of Edinburgh scheme, concentrating on outward bound and community service, particularly of an ecological nature.

Other activities: As part of our pursuit of breadth, we promote a very wide range of other activities from jewellery making to photography and from a Debating Society to the Philosophy Club. There are also various holiday and half-term visits including an annual skiing trip. Other recent trips have included expeditions to the Himalayas, Namibia and Bolivia.

Worship. The College Chapel exists to provide access to the spiritual side of life and to give a daily opportunity for quietness and reflection, for community life and to be a focus within the school. The Church foundation of the College is not interpreted in a narrowly denominational way. The Chaplain stands outside the disciplinary structure of the school, and he is the confidential listening ear to all members of our College community.

Admission: Standard entrance at 13+ is via Common Entrance, but special arrangements are made for applicants for whom this is inappropriate. There are also places available for both boys and girls in the Sixth Form. Applications should be made to the Head.

Boys and girls are admitted at 4 into the pre-prep department of the Junior School and from 7 upwards to the Junior School proper; applications should be made direct to the Master at Brandeston Hall. Transfer to the College or other schools is at 13.

Scholarships. (*see* Entrance Scholarship section) Academic, Art, Design and Technology, Music, Drama and all-rounder scholarships are available with values up to 50% of tuition fees. The Porter Science Scholarship is offered for outstanding Year 9 entrants. The Stapleton Scholarships cater for those with Oxbridge potential at 16+. Our foundation requires us to offer six full Pembroke scholarships to pupils resident in the parishes of Framlingham, Debenham and Coggershall in Essex. These may be awarded in any year group. Two Continuation Scholarships (taken by 10 and 11 year olds and covering the last two years of education at Prep School) are offered, each worth 25% of the Prep School's fees. Full details of all scholarships are available from the Head's Personal Assistant.

Fees. The College: Boarding – £12,960 pa; Day – £8,316 pa. Brandeston Hall: Boarding – £10,221 pa; Day – £6,342 pa. Pre-prep: Day – £3,630 pa. Fees are almost totally inclusive.

The Society of Old Framlinghamians: *Secretary:* N Bromage Esq, 51 Park Road, Aldeburgh, Suffolk IP15 5EN.

Charitable status. The Albert Memorial College (Framlingham College) is a Registered Charity, number 310 477 a/2. The object of the charity is to provide day and boarding education for boys and girls from the ages of 4 to 18 at Framlingham College and Brandeston Hall in the county of Suffolk.

Frensham Heights
(Coeducational)

Rowledge Farnham Surrey GU10 4EA.
Tel: Headmaster: (01252) 794813; Admissions: (01252) 792134
Fax: (01252) 794335
e-mail: Headmaster@frensham-heights.org.uk
website: http://www.demon.co.uk/frensham-heights

Board of Governors:

President: ¶T M Aldridge, QC, MA (*President of the Special Educational Needs Tribunal*)
Chairman: A I Macgregor, FCA (*Chartered Accountant*)
Vice-Chairman: ¶Mrs J Read, BA, MIPM (*Personnel Officer*)
Treasurer: P R Biddle (*Banker*)
Clerk to Governors: Bryan Jones, MBA, DMS
C R Butler (*Property Developer*)
¶Ms F Hitchcock (*Director*)
P S Morris (*Financial Director*)
Mrs S V Palfreyman (*Lecturer*)
¶Mrs R G Slingsby, BA (*Solicitor*)
S A Watson, MA (*ex-Headmaster, Hurstpierpoint College*)
C C B Wightwick, MA (*Education Consultant - former HMI*)
Mrs C A Wilson (*ex-Head Infant School*)

***Headmaster:* Peter M de Voil**, MA, DipEd, FRSA (*King's College, Cambridge :* New College, Oxford)

Senior Management Team:

Deputy Headmaster: Simon Pettegree, BSc
Senior Master: John Bayston, DLC, CertEd
Senior Housemaster: John Atkinson, BSc, PGCE, CertTheol (*Head of Department*)
Sixth Form Senior Tutor: Diana Lobban-Small, BSc, PGCE, CChem, MRSC
Bursar: Bryan Jones, MBA, DMS
Development Director: Rosellen Mates

Paul Baker, BSc, PGCE
*Patricia Bayston, MCollP, SROT (*Head of Lower School*)
§Hilary Blake, CertEd, BEd
Jeremy Bourne, BA PGCE
Deidre Butler, BSc, PGCE
Barry Carr, MA, PGCE
§Liz Clifford, BEd
§Wendy Coxell, BEd, CertEd, CertComput
Eileen Daw, BEd
*Lynne Elgy, BA
*¶Richard Evans, NDD, ATD
†Stephanie Evans, BSc (*Senior Housemistress*)
Sue Fenton, CertEd
Rosemary Giraudet, BEd, DipEd
Kim Goodwin, MA, PGCE
Shelagh Harris, GGSM, ARCM, PGCE
Caron Hawkes, BEd
Jenny Haynes, BA, PGCE
Oliver Holliday, BEd, PGCE
*Sheila John, MA, PGCE
*Geraldine Jones, BA, CertEd
*Jonathan Lambe, BA, PGCE
§Jude Latham, BA
§Anna Lowe, BSc, TESOL
*Stuart McFarlane, BA, DipEd
Rosemary McMillan, CertEd
§Carol Mallett, BEd, DipRSA
†Gregory Meakin, BSc, PGCE
Andrew Melbourne, BSc, PGCE
Susan Millerchip, BSc, PGCE
Fiona Morgan, BEd
§Marion Netley, MA
†Raphaelle Ranchin, MA, PGCE
*Edwin Rolles, BA, FTCL, ANSM, ARCM, CertEd (*Mus*) (*Director of Music*)
§Lorna Sanders, DipLCCD, BA, MA
Susan Slater, CertEd
§Suzanne Stephenson, CertEd
Jacquelin Stinton, DipDramArt, LLB
Ian Stoten, BSc, PGCE
*Peter Tanner, BA, CertEd (*Head of Middle School*)
†Mark Trollope, BEd
Raymond van den Brandt, BA, BEd
Jane Vickery, BEd
Julia Webster, BA, PGCE
*Peter Wicks, BSc, PGCE
§Geraldine Wilson, BSc, PGCE
Shirley Worsfold, BEd

Deputy Bursar: Wendy Hamilton, FCA

Admissions Registrar: Sue Pettegree, CertEd

Domestic Bursar: Ian Garland

Secretary to the Headmaster: Liz Bownass-Clark

School Nurse: Jan White, RSCN, SRN

School Counsellor: §Karen Rand, MA, DipEd

Librarian: Marion Crawford, MA, ALA, PGCE

Medical Officers: Dr J Elliott, Dr P Adams

Founded in 1925 as one of the Country's first coeducational boarding and day schools, Frensham Heights has always been characterised by a friendly, informal atmosphere in which the individual child feels secure and happy. As a coeducational community, the school believes in equality of the sexes; it opposes all forms of bigotry, racial, religious or social, and every effort is made to deepen understanding of human nature and behaviour and develop self-esteem.

Pupil numbers. 435 boys and girls aged 4 to 18 (plus Nursery). Average class size : 16.

Entry. Children entering the school at the age of 11–12 sit the Frensham Heights Entrance Examination, held in January. Children entering at the age of 13 sit the Frensham Heights Entrance Examination or the Independent Schools' Common Entrance Examination. A minimum of six GCSE passes at Grade C or above is required for entry to the Sixth Form. The school holds frequent Open

Days for prospective parents. Individual appointments to visit the school may also be made through the Admissions Registrar.

Curriculum. The school has harmonised its teaching programme with that of the National Curriculum. Up to the end of Key Stage 4 (GCSE) all pupils study English Language and Literature, Mathematics, Balanced Science, French, Geography or History, together with the possibility of a further humanity (Geography, Business Studies, History), a second modern language (German or Spanish) or PE. In addition, all pupils choose two creative and performing arts (Art, Ceramics, Design Technology, Drama, Dance, Music), a policy consistent with the School's regard for creative as well as academic intelligence. During Key Stage 3 (ages 11–14) the curriculum includes PE, RE and Information and Communication Technology (ICT). PSME is taught throughout the school. A-Level subjects include most of those taught to GCSE, with the addition of Psychology and Theatre Studies. The school has a long tradition of pupils going on to study Science at university.

Academic Results. Examination results are very good. There is a strong Sixth Form, most of whom go on to further education, including Oxford and Cambridge Universities. Public examination results: A-level 97%; GCSE grades A*-C 90%.

Sport. The school has excellent sporting facilities which include playing fields, a swimming pool, tennis courts and an indoor sports centre. Sports include basketball, soccer, netball, hockey, cross-country running, athletics, volleyball, badminton, rounders and cricket. Annual ski and snowboarding trips take place abroad in the holidays.

Outdoor Education. Outdoor education is part of the curriculum for all pupils. Training takes place in the school's extensive adventure training centre and leads to weekend and holiday expeditions in camping, climbing, caving, canoeing and trekking, which are open to all members of the school. World Challenge expeditions to Borneo and Kyrgysten.

Extracurricular Activities. All pupils are expected to take part in extra-curricular activities. An extensive and varied selection of approximately 60 activities includes sports of all sorts, art, music, dance, drama, hobbies and clubs, sailing, and the Duke of Edinburgh Award Scheme.

Facilities. 100 acres of parkland in beautiful countryside, £2m Performing Arts Centre opened November 2000, new Lower School classrooms finished September 2000, new Music School wing opened January 2000, two other wings, to complete rebuilding, will open in September 2001, modern science laboratories, art & design centre, new ICT centre, junior and senior library, sixth form centre, photographic studio. Completely refurbished First School (ages 3-8).

Music. Music is held in high esteem at the school and is regarded as an essential part of a person's education. It is studied by all pupils until the end of Year 9. The school has an impressive record for its choral and instrumental music. There are senior and junior choirs, two orchestras, a jazz group, a barbershop choir and a number of instrumental groups. Concerts are put on nationally and locally. An overseas concert tour takes place every year.

Boarding. Full and weekly boarders are housed in small and friendly boarding houses. Each has a resident housemaster or housemistress and house tutor. There is a programme of weekend activities for the boarders, but weekly boarders may leave after Friday afternoon, returning on Sunday evening. The School organises a coach to London at weekends.

Religion. There are no religious services. Pupils are free to attend local churches and several pupils sing in church choirs.

Dress. There is no uniform. There is a dress code.

Welfare and Discipline. The Housestaff are supported by a resident school nurse and a part-time counsellor. Every pupil has a personal tutor. The school's discipline is firmly based on good relationships between staff and pupils and reflects the values of the school, which promote a rational and caring approach. Senior pupils act as mentors to younger members of the school. A thriving School Council, consisting of elected representatives from all age groups, meets regularly to discuss matters of mutual interest and concern.

Learning Difficulties. The school is sympathetic to those with dyslexia and other specific learning difficulties and offers limited support.

Overseas Pupils. The school admits a few boarders from overseas each year and provides tuition in English as a Second Language as part of their curriculum.

Scholarships. (*see* Entrance Scholarship section) There are scholarships and exhibitions awarded each year for exceptional ability in academic work, music, art, drama and craft. The school is particularly interested in musically gifted pupils.

Frensham Heights Lower School is situated in its brand new purpose-built blocks of classrooms. **The First School,** for pupils aged 3-8 is in its own specially adapted building and has its own gardens within the main school grounds. Both schools provide firm foundations in English and Mathematics, supported by a well-balanced curriculum that includes Science, French, Information Technology and Music at a level appropriate to the year group. Pupils have access to all the main school's facilities.

Charitable status. Frensham Heights Educational Trust is a Registered Charity, number 312052. It exists to provide high quality education for boys and girls.

George Heriot's School

Lauriston Place Edinburgh EH3 9EQ.
Tel: 0131-229-7263.
Fax: 0131 229 6363.
e-mail: headmaster@george-heriots.com
prospectus: www.george-heriots.com

Motto: *'I distribute chearfullie'*.

Heriot's Hospital was founded in 1628 to care for the fatherless sons of Edinburgh burgesses. Today it is a fully co-educational day school, deeply rooted in the Scottish tradition.

The School is attractively situated in its own grounds close to the city centre and within easy walking distance of bus and rail terminals. A number of bus routes also service the School. Edinburgh Castle forms a magnificent backdrop, and Edinburgh's flourishing financial centre, the University of Edinburgh, the College of Art, the National Library and the Royal Scottish Museum are located close by.

The original building, described as a bijou of Scottish Renaissance Architecture, has been carefully preserved and, as a historic monument, is open at certain times to the public during school holidays. The Chapel, Council Room and Quadrangle are particularly notable.

Over the last century a succession of new buildings has provided the full complement of educational facilities. A new Lower Primary building was opened in 1983, a Nursery in 1992 and a further Junior School extension in 1996. Similarly, improvements and additions have been made over the years to provide excellent sports fields and facilities at Goldenacre. The School has sole use of an outdoor centre in the Scottish Highlands.

The School is administered under the terms of the

George Heriot's Trust Scheme 1992. The Governors of George Heriot's Trust is a charity recognised in Scotland by the Inland Revenue.

Governors of George Heriot's Trust:
Chairman: M J Gilbert, CA
Vice-Chairman: Rear Admiral D M Dow, DL
Finance Convener: J D M Hill, CA
Education Convener: H L Philip
Buildings Convener: J A G Fiddes, OBE, MA, DIPTP, FRICS, FSVA
Foundationers' Convener: D H Robertson, MA, PGCE, CCFD
Revd A F Anderson, MA, BD
Dr E C Benton, FRCP
R H Davis, BSc, PhD, CEng
F Henderson
Prof R N Ibbett
N M Irons, CBE, JP, DL
Mrs A Irvine
A Paton, MCIBS, FRSA
J Simpson
Councillor K Thomas
J N Wright, QC

Secretary and Treasurer to George Heriot's Trust: F M Simm, FCA

***Headmaster:* A G Hector**, MA

Depute: J S Barnes, DipPE

Assistant Headteachers:
Mrs E M R Henderson, MA
J S W Naismith, MA
G Sydserff, BSc
C D Wyllie, MA, DipEd

Chaplain: Mrs A G Maclean, BD, DCE

Headmaster's Secretary: Mrs E A Firoozi

Art:
*Mrs J Newman, DipArt
Mrs R Aitken, DipArt
Mrs C Gerrard, DipArt
T J Henry, BA
Miss C M Lonie, BA
Mrs A J E Thomson, BA

Biology:
*J C Wilkinson, BSc
A A N Ramage, BSc
Mrs G Lippok, DipEd
Ms K L McNish, BSc, MSc
Mrs B M Smyth, BSc
G J Stewart, BA, DipEd, DipCCP

Business Studies:
*Mrs M Lannon, BA
Miss K A Macnab, MA
J Payne, BA
Mrs J M Welton, DipBS

Chemistry:
*E R Allan, BSc, DipEd
F I McGonigal, BSc
J H Harris, BSc, DipEd, CChem, MRSC
Mrs J Blaikie, HND
J D Broadfoot, BSc, CChem, MRSC

Classics:
Mrs A M S Jennings, MA, DipEd

Computer Studies:
*B Lepper, BSc, MSc, DipComp
J C Davies, BSc
Mrs M E Mitchell, BSc
G Sydserff, BSc

English:
*R C Dickson, MA, DipEd
N H Grant, MA
Miss S M T Mort, BA, DipEd
A M M Chalmers, MA, MA, DipEd
Miss G K Drury, MA
Mrs T Halliday, BEd
Mrs E M R Henderson, MA
Mrs L M Nicol, MA
J J S Tait, MA
C D Wyllie, MA, DipEd

Geography:
*Mrs I P Robertson, MA
D Armstrong, BSc, DipEd
Miss S E A Brooks, MA
K J Ogilvie, MA

History:
*Ms A Connor, MA
M A McCabe, MA, MTh, PhD, BD
Mrs S M McGhee, MA
D R Moffat, MA, MEd
J S W Naismith, MA

Home Economics:
*Mrs J M Mitchell, DipHE
Mrs G C Jones, BA
Mrs N Gaffney, DipHE

Support for Learning:
*Mrs M N Williams, MA, DipRSA
Mrs B A Brodie, DipEd
Mrs A M H Hackland
Mrs S M McGhee, MA

Mathematics:
*C M Neil, BSc, DipEd
Miss F Findlay, BSc
J C Davies, BSc
G A Dickson, BSc
Mrs H R B Holton, BSc
D C Porteous, BSc, DipEd
Mrs R F Skinner, MA
P C Walker, BSc

Modern Languages:
*M G Grant, BA
Ms E M Brown, MA
J G Buchanan, MA, DipEd
Mrs J Sutherland, MA
Miss S S Gilbert, BA
Mrs C López, MA
Mrs C McDougall, BA
Mrs D M Mullen, BA
Mrs J M Semple, MA

Music:
*H A Duthie, MA, FRCO
Mrs J F L Anderson, BMus, LRAM
G C W Brownlee, BA, LLCM, ALCM
Mrs F Cantlay, BMus, LRAM, ARCM
Miss R S J Rowe, BMus

PE/Games:
*D J West, CertEd
Mrs D J Barnes, BEd
Miss G S Laidlaw, BEd
Mrs G J M McIntyre, DipPE
R Stevenson, BEd
K M Yuille, DipPE

Physics:
*R H C Neill, BSc, DipEd
Mrs M Hutton, BA
D Bryden-Reid, BSc
R M Bush, BSc
N R Short, BEd, MEd

Religious Education:
*Mrs A G Maclean, BD
Mrs J Stevenson, MA, BD

Technical:
*C N Cruickshank, DipTechEd, DipEdTech
J C Clyne
G A Laing, OND, HND, DipTechEd
D W Urquhart, HNDEng, DipTechEd, CertEdComp

Junior School:

D S Adams, BA (*Head of Junior School*)

Mrs C S Bashford, BA (*Depute Head of Junior School*)

Mrs L M Franklin, MA (*Assistant Headteacher - Upper Primary*)

D H Porteous, DipCert (*Assistant Headteacher - Upper Primary*)

Mrs M J Marquis, DipEd (*Assistant Headteacher - Lower Primary*)

Upper Primary:
Mrs R M Armet, MA, DipEd
Mrs V E J Clark, MA
Mrs M S Cluness, DipEd
Mrs E S B Couper, DipEd
J D Curt, MA
Mrs S Gilkison, MA
Mrs B I S Hunt, BEd
Mrs J S Maclean, BEd
Mrs R A Morris, DipEd
Mrs J A Mulholland, BSc
Mrs K S O'Hagan, BEd
Mrs J F Ponsford, MA
P Swierkot, BA
I J A S Woolley, DipEd

Lower Primary:
Mrs E S Clarke, DipEd, INSC
Miss L C Davis, BA
Mrs S Gilkison, MA
Mrs A C Garden, BEd
Miss K S E Henderson, BA
Mrs E McLeish, DipEd
Mrs P Pibworth, BEd
Mrs P M Roberts, DipEd
Miss S L Simpson, BSc
D Thain, BEd

Nursery:
Mrs E C Robertson
Mrs J E Montgomery

Our aim is to introduce all our pupils to the broadest possible spectrum of academic, spiritual, cultural and sporting interests and experiences, which will enable them as articulate, self-reliant adults to play a full part in an ever-changing society.

Heriot's has long enjoyed a reputation for academic excellence, and we strive to help pupils to attain the highest possible level of competence. In the same spirit, every pupil is encouraged to participate in an extensive array of extra-curricular activities. We value sporting achievement, particularly in team games, and we encourage activity in art, music and design. In addition, pupils are introduced to religious, moral and philosophical concepts in the search for the answers to the more abstract questions that life poses.

The Nursery (40 children). The Nursery accommodates children in their pre-school year in either a morning or full-day class. It is very closely linked to the Lower Primary Department. Admission to the Nursery is open to all.

The Junior School (617 pupils). The 5–14 Programme has largely been adopted: particular emphasis is given to core subjects to provide a sound basis for secondary education. Art, Modern Languages, Music and all areas of Physical Education are taught by specialists, and Junior School staff liaise closely with their secondary colleagues to provide curricular continuity throughout a pupil's time here.

A very active Junior School extra-curricular programme includes music, drama, adventure weeks and support for charities.

The Senior School (881 pupils). For the first two years a system of flexible streaming provides a broad curriculum for all. An extensive choice of subjects is available from S3 to S6 in preparation for Scottish Qualifications Agency examinations at every level. Most pupils stay on for a Sixth Year and proceed to university or other forms of tertiary education.

Our vast Senior School extra-curricular programme is designed to suit all interests and abilities, and it provides recreation, enjoyment and excellence. Pupils achieve national and international recognition in their chosen activities, and many Former Pupils have pursued their interests with similar success in adult life.

Music and drama are very strong. Performances are given annually in our two halls, our Chapel, in the adjoining Greyfriars Church, in the Usher Hall and in other venues in Scotland and Europe.

The CCF has active Army, Air Force and Naval sections and our Duke of Edinburgh's Award Scheme is one of the largest in Scotland. The main sports are cricket, cross-country running, hockey, rowing, rugby and tennis but most other sports are available in school or at Goldenacre.

Heriot's enjoys a reputation as a caring community. The greatest importance is given to pastoral care and a sophisticated careers advisory programme is in place. The Learning Support Department provides invaluable help to all Junior School and Senior School pupils, be it that they have a specific learning difficulty or are outstandingly gifted.

Admission. Admission (other than for Nursery) is by assessment or examination. Application for occasional places is welcome at any time, but for the main stages should normally be submitted by the end of November.

Fees. Nursery: mornings £740 per term; full day £1,126 per term; P1 to P3: £3,378 per session; P4 to P7: £4,140 per session; Senior School: £5,106 per session.

A limited number of Bursaries is available from P1 to S6 and there are Scholarships for entry at S1. Fatherless children may qualify for free education and other benefits through the Foundation. Full information is available from the Headmaster's Secretary on request.

The Heriot Club. *Secretary:* E Allan, 10 McLaren Road, Edinburgh EH9 2BH.

Charitable status. George Heriot's Trust is a Registered Charity, number CR3192A. It exists to provide education for children.

George Watson's College

Colinton Road Edinburgh EH10 5EG.
Tel: 0131-447 7931.
Fax: 0131-452 8594
e-mail: g.edwards@watsons.edin.sch.uk

The College was founded by George Watson, first accountant of the Bank of Scotland, who died in 1723, and opened in 1741. Transformed into a predominantly day school in 1870. Amalgamated with George Watson's Ladies College to form a co-educational school in 1974.

Motto: *'Ex corde caritas'.*

Governors:
The Education Board of the Company of Merchants of the City of Edinburgh has ultimate responsibility for the Governing of the School, but delegates responsibility to the School Governing Council.

Chairman: Professor N Lothian, OBE

Members:
N Murray (*Vice-Chairman*)
Mrs J Brown
Sir Kenneth Scott
J Clydesdale
Revd P Graham
N Ryden
A Hartley
G Wilson
Mrs D Sleigh
D Johnston
I A Murning

Bursar: R T Bellis, MA, CA

***Principal:* G H Edwards**, MA

Deputy Principals:
H Ouston, MA
Mrs H Wilson, BA

Director of Studies: Mrs D Meiklejohn, BSc

Director of Guidance: Mrs F Denyer, MA

Director of Careers: R Mallinson, BSc, PhD

Director of Resources: D B Hughes, MA

Examinations Co-ordinator: Miss E Rogers

Classics:
R M Looker, MA
I G McHaffie, MA
Mrs L O'Donnell, MA

Mathematics:
¶N Hopley, MA
H Gilchrist, BSc, PhD
R F Vander Steen, MA
Mrs H Rifkind, BSc
P J Stark, BSc
Mrs D Coventry, BEd
Mrs A Symington, BSc
¶Mrs M Pringle, BSc
Miss E C S Crawford, BSc
K J Thomson, BSc
Mrs T Johnson, BSc
D Johnson, BSc

Physics:
G K Black, BSc, MA
¶P Edington, BSc, PhD
R Mallinson, BSc, PhD
J Barrow, BSc, PhD
Mrs E A Wylie, BSc
Miss M Vass, BSc

Chemistry:
Mrs J Cheyne, BSc
D Livingston, BSc, PhD
Mrs S Floyd, BSc
Mrs D Meiklejohn, BSc
Mrs F Hewitt, BSc
J Coull, BSc
G McIntyre, BSc

Biology:
J A Braithwaite, BSc
Mrs I Pyper, BSc
D L Lloyd, BSc
J G Rennie, BSc
G Morgan, BA
Mrs F Graham, BSc
Miss K Lindsay, BSc

English:
H E Quinn, MA
Mrs L M MacKenney, BA, MA
I Jordan, BA

Miss J M Carter, MA
¶A L MacLaren, MA, DipEd
Miss G L Durham, BA
Miss G Mellor, BA
¶Mrs M Taylor, MA
Mrs P Duncan, MA
Mrs S Haywood, BA
Mrs A Giegerich, MA
Miss E Langley, MA
R Kettley, BA

Drama:
H Paterson, DipEd
Mrs A R Porteous, DipEd

Modern Languages (French, German, Spanish, Russian):
R M Slater, MA
¶A Skinner, MA
Mrs S Flannery, BA
Miss E Rogers, BA
Mrs S Arnott, MA
Mrs C Binnie, BA
Miss E White, BA
Mrs F Denyer, MA
I Geddes, MA
R A Crawford, BA
Mrs A Allan, MA
J V Rolandeau, MA
Mrs H Wilson, MA

History and Modern Studies:
M Longmore, MA
Mrs S A Delahunt, MA
L Howie, MA
G L Gibb, MA
Mrs J Hind, MA
H A Ouston, BA, MA
M Casey, BA

Geography:
D Pyper, MA
D B Hughes, MA
Mrs O Watters, MA
T Young, BA
Mrs E Sykes, MA
Mrs L Cooper, MA

Economics/Business Studies:
P Arlidge, BA
Miss T Wright, BA
M Bergin, BSc
R MacFarquhar

RE:
Mrs P E Boyd, BA, MEd
The Revd P F Marshall, BA, BA(*Div*)
The Revd C Barrington, MA, BD

Art:
W Robb, DA
I T G Coutts, DA
Mrs C W Robinson, DA
Mrs C Stevenson, DA
Miss A Orr, BA
D Prosser, BA

Information Technology:
L M Smith, BSc
Mrs L Anderson, MA
J D Ferguson, BSc
Mrs N Tait, BSc
G McCartney, BSc

Technical Subjects:
R J Grant, BSc
P Dean, BEd
K Tait, BSc, DipTechEd
C McGonigle, BEd

Home Economics: to be appointed

Music:
N J B Mitchell, LTCM
I C Macdougall, BMus, MA, PhD
Mrs M Leach, DipMusEd
H Scott, DRSAMD
S Griffin, BA

PE:
I N Brown, DPE, BEd
R Mack, DPE
¶Mrs A C Riddell, BEd
A M Bennett, BEd
A Donaldson, BEd
¶Mrs J Campbell, DipPE
A Ker, DipPE
Mrs H Dean, BEd
Mrs E S M Batchelor, BEd
M Gifford, BEd
M Leonard, BEd
M Craig, BEd
Miss K Joiner, BEd

Learning Support:
Dr C Weedon, BEd, MEd, PhD
Mrs A J Thornton, MA
G B Lyon, MA

Primary Department:
D M McGougan, BEd (*Headmaster*)

Deputies:
Miss A M Waddell, BEd
Mrs P Snell, BA, MEd

Assistant Heads:
Mrs L Fleming, MA
Mrs M McCreath, DipCE
A R Robertson, BEd

Upper Primary:
Miss D F Paton, MA
¶Mrs E E C Easton, DipCE
Mrs R E Dickerson, DipCE
Mrs V Barrie, DipCE
Mrs K A Grandison, MA
Mrs K Robertson, BEd
Mrs F A McCallum, MA
¶Mrs S Marshall, MA
Mrs P Walkinshaw
Mrs M Broadie, DipCE
Mrs M E Graham, BEd
Mrs E P Bell, MA
Mrs E A Mackie, DA
B Dean, BEd
Mrs S Dick, LLB, CertEd
Miss R McKerchar, DipMus
G Salmond, BEd
Mrs M Rogers, L-ès-L
I Smith, BSc
D Gould, BSc
A MacRae, MA
Miss R Hamilton, BA

Lower Primary:
Mrs K Wilson
Mrs N M Titterington, DipCE
Mrs M Rogers, L-ès-L
Mrs J M Dickie, DipCE
Mrs P M French, MA
Mrs G Quinn, CertEd
Miss S Carbarns, DipCE
Mrs P McNaught, DipCE
Mrs K A McIver, MA
Miss E Smith, DipCE
Mrs C Hood, DipEd
Miss L Robertson, BEd
Mrs A Reid, DipCE
Mrs L Kemp, DipEd
Mrs B Ferguson, DipCE
Mrs A Offer, BEd
Mrs E Thow, DipCE
Miss K Jones, BEd
Mrs K Holdgate
Mrs S Brown
Mrs C Gregory, BEd

The School is divided into the Secondary Department (ages 12–18, 680 boys, 570 girls), the Upper Primary Department (ages 8–12, 260 boys, 210 girls), the Lower Primary Department (ages 5–8, 150 boys, 130 girls) and the Nursery Unit (ages 3–5, 50 boys, 50 girls).

Since the present buildings were opened by HRH The Duke of Kent in 1932, extensive alterations have been carried out and additions made. Recent new building includes the Music School, special facilities for the VIth Form, a new Art School and Technology Centre, Lower Primary a new Nursery Unit and a Games Hall next to the indoor Swimming Pool. There are ample recreational facilities in the adjacent grounds: in addition to the traditional winter and summer games – Rugby, Hockey (boys as well as girls), Cricket, Netball, Tennis – an extensive range of other sports is offered, including Swimming, Athletics, Rowing, Badminton, Basketball, Golf, Squash, Volleyball, Skiing, Sailing and Fencing. There are opportunities to take part in Sailing, Hill-Walking and Field Work. There are School Scout and Guide Groups and a Community Service Group and a very active Duke of Edinburgh Award Scheme. Normal School hours are from 8.45 to 3.30, Monday to Friday. After School Club in Junior School.

Organisation. The first 2 years of the Secondary Dept. have a general curriculum; after that some specialisation is allowed for the 2 years to the Scottish Certificate of Education (Standard Grade), Scottish National Qualifications (Intermediate and Higher Grades), and in the final year fuller specialisation for University entry purposes (Advanced Highers). In Art, examinations are GCSE, AS and A level. Pupils proceed to the full range of British Universities.

Fees. Tuition fees, which are inclusive, range from £465 (Nursery) to £1,168 (P1+2) to £1,409 (P3–7) to £1,810 (Senior School) per term.

Admission. Pupils are normally admitted by interview or examination in Jan/Feb either at 3 for the Nursery Unit or at 5 for the Primary Dept. or at 12 for the Secondary Dept. Applications should be made by the preceding 30th November or as soon as possible thereafter; candidates will be considered for admission at stages other than Primary I or Secondary I if chance vacancies arise. Special consideration is given to pupils moving into the Edinburgh area from elsewhere. In the case of candidates for SII–VI, interviews are held in the first week of February by which time it is possible to gauge what vacancies, if any, will be available in the autumn. Applications for these interviews should normally be submitted by 31 January.

Foundations, Scholarships, etc. There are a number of awards, including up to 12 Entrance Scholarships to the Secondary Department, value £600–£2,750 each, and several Music Bursaries, value £300 to £2,750, are open to competition each year. The school provides assistance with fees on an Income sliding Scale to pupils aged 11 and over on 31st July. Awards for Service, Adventure, and Foreign Language projects are also available to pupils in the Upper School. There are up to 4 leaving Exhibitions, valued up to £200 each for 4 years.

Boarding. There is accommodation for approximately

25 boys and girls in the Boarding House. The additional fee for Boarding is £1,948 per term. Applications for vacancies should be made to the Principal, to whom enquiries about financial assistance should also be made.

Former Pupils' Club. "The Watsonian Club", open to men & women who have attended George Watson's College, exists to foster links between former pupils and the School. It has many branches throughout Britain and overseas and a great variety of active Sports sections in Edinburgh. There are excellent modern "Club" facilities in The Pavilion, Myreside Road, Edinburgh 10, within the School grounds. Enquiries should be addressed to The Secretary of The Watsonian Club at the School. Tel No: 0131-447 7931.

Charitable status. The Merchant Company Education Board (which administers George Watson's College) is a Registered Charity, number SCO 019747. George Watson's College is a charity devoted to educational excellence.

Giggleswick School

Giggleswick Settle North Yorkshire BD24 0DE.
Tel: Headmaster's Office: (01729) 893000
Bursar's Office: (01729) 893012.
Fax: (01729) 893150
e-mail: office@giggleswick.n-yorks.sch.uk

Giggleswick School, founded by 1499, was granted a charter by Edward VI on 26 May, 1553, at the instance of John Nowell, then Vicar of Giggleswick, and one of the King's Chaplains.

The Governing Body:
Chairman: ¶D A Stockdale, Esq, QC, MA
Vice-Chairman: P J S Thompson, Esq, LLB

E M Atkins, PhD
J C Baggaley, Esq, MA
Mrs C Cass
Professor P J Dobson, BSc, PhD, MInstP, CPhys, Member of ACS
Dr M Dörrzapf, DPhil
D L Gillibrand, Esq, BSc(Econ)
County Councillor Beth Graham, BSc
J A Hartley, Esq
Mrs W Jennings, MA
A Jervis, Esq, BSc (Hons), CChem, MRSC
Amanda Nevill, HonDLitt, HonFRPS, FRSA
The Very Reverend J S Richardson, BA
Lord Shuttleworth, FRICS
G Watson, Esq, MBE, MA, JP
¶J S Westhead, Esq, FCA, ATII
¶J R Whiteley, Esq, MA
The Honourable Mrs A H Widdows

***Headmaster:* G P Boult**, BA (Durham)

Deputy Head: J D B Christian, MA (Cantab)

Senior Master: *D P Fox, BA (London)

Assistant Staff:
*N J Mussett, MBE, BSc, MA, FIBiol, FLS
*M J J Day, MA
*D H Blackburne, BA
G Wigfield, CertEd
*M E Peek, BSc, PhD
†*N A Gemmell, BA
T M Harvey, BA, ARCO
*Mrs C Gemmell, BEd
P Thomas, BSc
*Miss S L Williamson, BA
*Mrs G E Taylor-Hall, BA
†*A J Scholey, BSc
†*J M Hall, BSc, CPhys, MInstP
*Miss A L Wood, MA
†Miss E J Wrenn, BA
*†C R Farmer, MA
†*J P Bellis, BA
*C D Knight, BA
Miss R C Gorner, MA, CT, ABRSM
R Barrand, BA
P C R Andrew, BEng, AMIEE
Mrs L M Kenchington
*Revd J J N Sykes, MA
Miss J Flynn, BA
*J M Gilbert, BSc
Miss S Thompson, BSc
*M C Lawson, BA, MSc
B P Fell, MA
Miss N Kinley, MA
S Ball, MA, PGRNCM
Miss L J Hogg, BEd
*M Mortimer, BA
Miss S E Lawrence, HND, GDip
J E Reeson, BA, MSt, PhD
P K Hucknall, BSc, PhD
*J Huxtable, BA
Miss E O'Mara, BA
*W S Robertson, BA
P Adams, MBA
Mrs A Shorrock, BSc, MEd
Miss S A Musa, BA
N M Walker, BSc, PhD
Mrs J E Farmer, BA
Miss M Magson
Mrs A Clements, MA
D Shackleton, BSc
Mrs S Woods, BA

Bursar and Clerk to the Governors: G R Bowring, Esq, MA

Headmaster's Secretary: Mrs D M Lambert

Catteral Hall
Headmaster: R D Hunter, MA (Cambridge)
Deputy Head & Director of Studies: R M Jones, MA (Cambridge)
Deputy Head: Mrs E M Bamford, CertEd

S Heap, BEd
F D G Ogilvie, BEd
Mrs K N Rose, BA
M J Caithness, BSc
Miss L M Neville, BA
Mrs C M Jones
Mrs S A Hunter, CertEd
S P Anderson, BA

Mill House
Head: Mrs S M M Luchetti, CertEd, BA

Miss J A Middleton, BA

Giggleswick provides continuous boarding education for about 500 boys and girls aged from 3–18. The School is situated in beautiful Yorkshire Dales' scenery, close to the borders of Cumbria and Lancashire and is an hour's drive from Leeds, Manchester and The Lakes. It can be reached from the M6 or M1 motorways or by rail via Settle or Giggleswick stations. Overseas students fly to Leeds/Bradford or Manchester Airports.

Senior School For thirteen year olds admission is usually based on reports, interviews and performance in the Common Entrance Examination. However, for boys and girls from maintained schools and schools abroad, some other appropriate academic assessment will be used.

Admission direct to the Sixth Form is on the basis of reports and interviews, and is conditional upon the applicant obtaining a minimum of five GCSE passes at Grade C or above. There are approximately 180 pupils in the Sixth Form. Generous Academic, Music, Art, Design & Technology, Drama, Sport and General Distinction Scholarships are available.

Boarding. Nearly 90% of Senior School pupils are boarders and the School's routine is entirely geared to boarding education. There are six Houses, four for boys and two for girls, with 50–60 pupils in each. The Housemaster or Housemistress is responsible for the well-being and progress of pupils in the House and is assisted by House Tutors.

An extensive refurbishment programme has recently been completed and provides all pupils with first class accommodation. Most Sixth Formers and Fifth Form pupils have their own Study Bedroom; other pupils share Study Bedrooms or small Study Dormitories.

Day Pupils Day pupils are fully integrated with boarders; they arrive before Morning Assembly, share studies and use all School facilities. They have lunch and tea at School and return home after prep.

Courses of Study. The Year 9 course comprises English, French, Mathematics, Sciences, History, Geography, Arts (including Drawing), Music, Drama and Pottery, Technology (including Home Economics, Graphics and Design), Religious Studies, Physical Education (Gymnastics and Swimming) and PSE. Latin, German, Russian and Spanish are also available.

In Years 10 and 11 a pupil chooses 10 subjects leading to the GCSE examinations.

In the Sixth Form, a pupil normally studies four subjects leading to GCE A or AS level examinations. The subjects available are Mathematics, Further Mathematics, Physics, Chemistry, Biology, Business Studies, English, French, German, Latin, Greek, Spanish, Russian, History, Geography, Art, Design, Music, Home Economics, Economics, Government & Politics, Religious Studies, Theatre Studies, PE and Information Technology. In addition, there is a broad based programme of topics leading to the General Studies A level examination and Key Skills.

Pupils are prepared for Oxford and Cambridge University Entrance.

Religion. The religious life of the School is supervised by a full-time resident Anglican Chaplain. At their own wish pupils may be prepared for Confirmation into the Church of England. Catholic pupils are excused certain Chapel services in order to attend Mass. The School respects and allows for other religious convictions.

Health. There is a surgery in the charge of a resident SRN with a Deputy who is also an SRN. The School Doctor visits regularly 4 or 5 days a week and is available in emergencies.

Games. In the Autumn Term the main games are rugby for boys and hockey for girls. In the Summer Term the main sports are cricket for boys and tennis for girls, but athletics, swimming, and tennis are available for boys and girls. In addition, there are excellent facilities for soccer, squash, fives, golf, badminton, basketball, netball, cross-country and fell running etc. There are regular overseas tours by the sports teams. In Summer 1999 Giggleswick undertook two major sports tours in the space of six weeks. The first went to eastern Canada with a Rugby XV and a Girls' 1st XI Hockey squad. In the last two weeks of the holiday the 1st XI Cricketers went to Zimbabwe. Future tours are planned with possible venues being Australia and South America.

Outdoor Education. This is an important part of the School's extra-curricular life. All pupils have introductory courses in map reading, orienteering and camp craft, and train for the Bronze Award of the Duke of Edinburgh's Scheme. Many go on to the Silver Award and some each year to the Gold. Trained and qualified members of staff lead these activities in addition to canoeing. There is a major expedition each summer climbing in the Pyrenees or canoeing around Switzerland. In the summer of 2001 a party will go on expedition in the Himalayas.

Music. Tuition, given by five full-time musicians and a number of visiting teachers, is available in all keyboard and orchestral instruments. The Music School has excellent recital, rehearsal, teaching and practice rooms. Concerts are given by the School Orchestra, the Concert Band, Ensembles and the Choral Society. The Chapel Choir sings regularly in York Minster and Liverpool Cathedral; in 1998 they sang evensong in St George's Chapel, Windsor. Three recordings have recently been released. Recent concert tours have been undertaken in the USA, Spain and Holland.

Drama. There are major productions each term. Drama is a timetabled subject for Year 9 and there is a Junior Drama Festival in October. Smaller drama-workshop productions are encouraged. The School has an extensive theatre wardrobe of its own. Drama tours are a regular feature of school life. In 1998 "The Dream Tour" performed A Midsummer Nights Dream in the USA. The School took a play to the Edinburgh Fringe Arts Festival in the summer of 1999.

Art. The Art Department is fine-art-based concentrating on drawing, painting, print-making and sculpture. It boasts excellent examination results. In 2000 the majority of A level candidates obtained an A grade whilst at GCSE 100% gained an A grade or above.

CCF. All pupils follow a structured course lasting six terms, divided equally into military and non-military skills. The contingent has Army, RAF and Royal Marine Sections. At the end of the two-year period, pupils may opt to leave or remain in the CCF. Advanced training is given in a variety of skills. The contingent fields strong teams for the District competitions and sends many cadets on further training at camp and on various courses.

Societies. There is a wide variety of societies. Sixth Formers have their own Social Centre.

Recent Developments. Nearly two million pounds have been spent on boarding accommodation for boys and girls, providing some of the finest facilities in the north of England. A new dining hall and Learning and Information centre have recently opened, and a floodlit synthetic hockey pitch opens in August 2001.

Careers Advice and Staff-Parent Conferences. An experienced Careers Master and his team of assistants supplement the advice of House Staff and Heads of Academic Departments in guiding academic choices and career decisions. The School is a member of ISCO and uses the ISLO/Morrisby Scheme of Careers Education and guidance. Regular Staff-Parent conferences are held at School to enable discussion of pupils' past, present and future progress and needs. Parents are always welcome at other times, especially at Chapel, sports fixtures, concerts, plays, etc.

Preparatory School. Catteral Hall stands in its own grounds on a site adjacent to the Senior School. It has its own staff but also has the advantage of specialist teachers and facilities of the Senior School. Recent improvements include new facilities for Science and Music; and dormitories have been refurbished. Generous Academic and Music Scholarships are available.

Admission is possible at any age between 7–12. At thirteen, pupils transfer in the Autumn Term to the Senior School, enjoying continuity of environment, curriculum and friendships. (Further information in Part V.)

Pre-Preparatory School. Mill House is a self-contained unit for day pupils aged 3–7. In a modern well equipped classroom the children are given an excellent start to their schooling.

Entrance. Most pupils enter in the September term, but a few are admitted in January and April.

Entrance Scholarships. (*see* Entrance Scholarship section) See Scholarship section.

Fees. Registration fee £100. The fees are fully inclusive and in 2000/2001 are: Senior School – Boarders £15,402 pa. Day Pupils, £10,221 pa. Catteral Hall – Boarders £12,573 pa (7–10 £11,700), Day Pupils £8,406 (7–10 £7,830).

Further details are available in the Prospectus which may be obtained from the Headmaster, to whom applications for entry should be made.

Charitable status. The School is a Registered Charity, number 532296. It exists to provide education for boys and girls.

* Head of Department	§ Part Time or Visiting
† Housemaster/Housemistress	¶ Old Pupil
‡ See below list of staff for meaning	

The Glasgow Academy

Colebrooke Street Glasgow G12 8HE.
Tel: 0141-334 8558.

The School was founded in May 1845, to meet in particular the needs of the western localities of the city. Since June 1920, it has been controlled by the Glasgow Academicals' War Memorial Trust, formed in that year in memory of the 327 Academicals who gave their lives in the war of 1914–18. In September 1991 it joined with the Westbourne School for Girls forming a co-educational school. In August 1999 Atholl Preparatory School in Milngavie joined The Academy. Parents now have a choice of location for their children in the Nursery to Prep 4 age group. At Prep 5 Atholl pupils transfer to The Academy site at Colebrooke Terrace. The affairs of the Trust are managed by a body of 14 Governors.

Motto: *'Serva Fidem'*.

Chairman: W M Mann, CA

Honorary Governors:
Prof Sir John Gunn, CBE, MA, FRSE
Prof Sir W Ferguson Anderson, OBE, KStJ, MD, FRCP
W Leggat Smith, CBE, MC, TD, JP, DL, BA, LLD
A D S Rolland, CA, FRCPS
Prof Norman Stone, MA
A L Howie, CBE
Sir Iain Vallance, BA, MSc
C W Turner, BSc, AKC
Prof Sir Malcolm Macnaughton, MD, FRCOG, FRCP, FFP, FRSE
Prof Sir David Mason, CBE, LLD, BDS, MD, FRCS, FDS, FRCPath
The Very Revd William J Morris, KCVO, PhD, LLD, DD
Sir Angus Grossart, CBE, LLD, FRSE, DL, DBA, MA, LLB, CA Advocate
Sir Matthew Goodwin, CBE, CA
C Miller Smith, MA, ACCA, LLD

Nominated and Elected Governors:
F A L Alstead, CBE, DL, MPhil
R de C Chapman
L M Crawford
D S Gee, FSVA
J W Gilchrist, BArch, RIBA, ARIAS
R A Graham
Mrs K Kelso, LLB, DipLPNP
C K MacLennan, CA
Mrs C S Mills
K Sandford, CA
Mrs M E Smith, BSc, CEng, MICE
Dr A G Wade
J M Watson, FIOP

***Rector:* D Comins**, MA

Deputy Rector: I M MacLeod, MA
Assistant Rector: Dr J Andrews, BSc, PhD
Assistant Rector: A P Jeffreys, MA

Assistant Staff:
P W Armit, BSc, PhD
Miss N L Bannerman, BEd
Miss A J Beaumont, MA
Mrs E W Clarke, MA
Mrs S M Crawford, DCE, DPE
Mrs M M Currie, DipIII
R A Davies, BSc
A de Villiers, BA
Mrs J A Dougall, MA
Mrs A A Drummond, BSc
Mrs M Duguid, MA
A L Evans, BSc
Miss P Fallone, BEdMus
K L Fraser, DTE
Ms J Fulton, BA Hons
V W Hadcroft, BA
Ms A Harvie, BA Hons
K Hussain, BSc, PhD
A Hutchinson, MA
C W Johnson, BSc
R C Latimer, BA
A G Lyall, BEd
Mrs F M Macdonald, BSc, MSc
S W McAslan, BEd
Mrs E F McCallum, MA
A J McCaskey, MA
Mrs C M McClure, BSc
Mrs O S McCrorie, DipMusEd, RSAMD
Miss J E McElroy, MA
M McGranaghan, BSc
Mrs S McKenzie, MA
Mrs H McMillan, BSc
J M McNaught, DA
M R McNaught, MA
T Menzies, BSc
Mrs M Muirhead, BA Hons
C A Oates, BEd
Mrs M E R Price, MA
W T Ritchie, DipMusEd, RSAM
D K Robertson, DA
Mrs S M Robertson, BSc
W Robertson, BA
A P N R Rowley
Mrs P M Ruddock, BSc
Dr S L Scheuerl, BSc, PhD
Mrs E B Semple, MA
I M Shirley, BSc, PhD
N T Spike, MA
C D Stewart, BSc
Dr F M Stewart, BSc, PhD
Mrs I C Stewart, BSc
Mrs M V Thomson, DipIII
Mrs E M Wallace, MA
Mrs A F Watters, MA
T A Whiteside, BSc

Preparatory School:
Mrs H M Fortune, BSc (*Head of the Preparatory School*)
Mrs J K Deane, TCert
G R M Anderson, DYS, DCE
Miss A N Campbell, BEd
Mrs M I Cram, DCE
Mrs E J David, DCE
Miss D J Elmslie, NNEB
Mrs E A Gilmour, DCE
Mrs F A Halliday, BEd
Mrs A F Ivins, BEd
Mrs P A King, BEd
Mrs P Laws, MA
Miss H J Logie, BEd
Mrs C J Lyall, BEd
Mrs J M Mabon, BEd, DCE
Mrs G E McGuire, DCE
Miss J A McMorran, DCE
Mrs L J R Melville, BA
Ms A C R Park, RGN, DCE
Miss L Riberzani, BA
Mrs W L Robertson, DCE
Miss P Solari, NNEB
Mrs L Thomson, TCert
Mrs L Trainer, BEd
R M I Williams, BA

Atholl:
Mrs J E Donaldson, ACE, NFF (*Head*)
Mrs A Alexander
Mrs A Clark, SNNEB
Mrs A Duff, BA
Mrs O Louden, DCE, ITQ
Mrs A McDonald, DCE
Mrs L McLellan, DCE
Mrs L Scott, DCE, ITQ
Mrs J Tait
Mrs F Tyrwhitt-Drake

Chaplain: The Very Revd William J Morris, KCVO, PhD, LLD, DD

CCF: Lt Col G R M Anderson

SSI: D Scott

Rector's Secretary: Miss M Campbell

Academy Secretary: Mrs S McKenzie

Organisation. The Preparatory School contains some 400 pupils (240 boys, 160 girls) between the ages of 4½ and 11 and prepares pupils from the earliest stages for the work of the Senior School. The Senior School contains about 600 pupils (400 boys, 200 girls). They are prepared in the first instance for the Scottish Certificate of Education at the end of Fifth or Sixth year. The VIth Form provides courses in most subjects leading to presentation at Advanced Higher. Pupils are prepared for entrance to Oxford and Cambridge. The Academy has a fine record both at Oxford and Cambridge and at the Scottish Universities.

Buildings. The magnificent main building comprises Class Rooms for the Senior School with the Preparatory School on the other side of the recently pedestrianised Terrace. Physics, Chemistry and Biology are housed in separate spacious buildings. As well as an Assembly Hall, Gymnasium and Sports Hall including miniature Rifle Range, new buildings for Music (1994) and Design (1998) considerably enhance the Academy's facilities. A comprehensive computer network (1998) linking all rooms throughout Prep and Senior Schools enables all pupils to access the Internet, send Email or access facilities from home. The Library is the centrepiece of the main building which also houses a well equipped Audio-Visual Lecture Theatre.

Music and Drama. Music tuition is offered in a wide range of instruments. There are Senior and Junior Choirs, a Wind Band, a String Ensemble and an Orchestra.

Societies. These range from Literary and Debating Societies to a Mountaineering Club. Large numbers of pupils undertake each section of the Duke of Edinburgh's Award and there is a thriving Young Enterprise group.

Games. All pupils, unless exempted by a medical certificate, take part in Physical Education and Games. Teams represent the School in Rugby, Hockey, Cricket, Swimming, Golf, Tennis, Athletics, Curling, Shooting and Squash. Cross-Country Running is also offered as an option.

Combined Cadet Force. The Academy has a strong contingent with RN, Army, Signals and RAF Sections. In addition there is a Pipe Band.

Entrance. Pupils may be registered at any age. The main entry points are (a) in the Preparatory School: age 4½, 6 and 9; (b) in the Senior School: age 11 or 12.

Fees. (2000/2001 figures) These range from £3,730 pa in the lowest class of the Preparatory School to £5,424 pa at the top of the Senior School.

Charitable status. The Glasgow Academy is a Registered Charity, number 11313. It exists to provide education for girls and boys.

Glenalmond College

Glenalmond Perth PH1 3RY.
Tel: 01738 842061
Admissions Office: 01738 842056
Fax: 01738 842063
e-mail: registrar@glenalmondcollege.co.uk
website: http//www.glenalmondcollege.co.uk

Glenalmond College, was founded by Mr W E Gladstone and others in 1841 and opened as a School in 1847.

Motto: *'Floreat Glenalmond'*

Chairman of Council: Lord Wilson of Tillyorn, Kt, GCMG

Committee of Council:
R L Wilson, CBE, BSc, FEng (*Chairman*)
I E Ivory, CA
A H Primrose, Esq
D J C MacRobert, LLB
I R Wilson, Esq, CBE
The Rt Revd M H G Henley, The Bishop of St Andrews, Dunkeld & Dunblane
Professor J Mavor, BSc, PhD, DSc, FRSE, FEng
A J P Mackie, Esq

***Warden:* I G Templeton**, MA, BA, CertEd

Sub-Warden: J R Chenevix-Trench, BSc, PhD, CertEd
Senior Housemaster: J D Wright, MA
Director of Studies: T Rowell, MSc, BSc
Registrar: J B M Poulter, MA, PGCE
Chaplain: The Revd P M Konig, DipTheol
Director of Development: Mrs J McKeown, BA
Matron: Miss V Underwood, RGC, SCM
Sister: Miss C Dolan, RGN
Bursar: Lt Col K H Montgomery, BSc (Hons), MBA, MIMgtRE
Secretary to the Council and Treasurer: I J A Moir, CA

Teaching Staff:

English:
*J D Byrom, MA
*J Reynolds, BEd (*Head of Drama*)
Mrs E McCarthy, BA (*Housemistress, Home*)
Mrs F Given, BA
Mrs J McKeown, BA
J W J Mitchell, MA
Mrs A M König, LGSM
Mrs A Haylock, BEd (*Housemistress, Lothian*)

Mathematics:
D Jeffers, BSc, CertEd
M Allnutt, BSc, CertEd (*Assistant Director of Studies*)
J Hunter, BSc, DipEd
*M A Hill, BEd, CertPhysEd (*Head of Games*)
Mrs M Trygger, BA (Hons), PGCE
*M T Jeffers, BSc, PGCE

Classics:
*J D Wright, MA (*Housemaster, Matheson's*)
D R Willington, MA, FSA
J W J Mitchell, MA (Hons)

Modern Languages:
*J N M Gillespie, BA, DipEd
P A R Shelley, BA, MPhil
J B M Poulter, MA, PGCE
Miss S Hengy, BA
J A Gardner, BA (Hons), PGCE
Mrs L North, BA (Hons), PGCE

Geography:
*T Rowell, BSc, MSc
J R Chenevix-Trench, BSc, PhD, CertEd (*Sub Warden*)
S Hill, BA, PGCE (*Housemaster, Patchell's*)
Mrs G Hamilton, BSc, MSc, PhD
Miss C J H Barker, BA
R Ackerman, BA (Hons), DipTeaching

History:
*R R Mundill, MA, PhD, PGCE
C T Shiffner, MA

Biology:
*C I K Lallyet, BSc, PhD
J R Chenevix-Trench, BSc, PhD, CertEd (*Sub Warden*)
F R Batstone, BSc, PGCE

Chemistry:
*J Owen, BSc, CertEd
J Stewart, BSc, PhD, CertEd
Miss A J Nesbit, BEd

Physics:
*Mrs M E Pitkin, BSc (Hons), CPhys, MInstP
H M Given, BSc, DipEd
R J Armstrong, BEng, PGCE

Economics:
*J C Robinson, BA, PGCE (*Housemaster, Goodacre's*)

c*Music:*
*R D Gower, MA, FRCO, LRAM, ARCM, FRSA (*Housemaster, Skrine's*)
N Smith, BA (RSAMD), DRSAM
Miss D Smith, LRAM, DipRAM
B J Elrick, LLB

Art:
*I H Smith, CertEd
Mrs E Smith, CertEd

Divinity:
*Revd P König, DipTheol

Library:
Mrs E Mundill, MA, DipLib, ALA

Technology:
*A A Purdie, BSc, BEd
*G M Feather, BSc (*Head of IT*)

Physical Education:
*M A Hill, BEd, CertPhysEd
Mrs J Gillespie, CertPhysEd
Miss A J Nesbit, BEd (*Head of Girls' Games*)

The College is built on the south bank of the Almond, from the north bank of which rise the Grampians. It is about 50 miles north of Edinburgh and 10 miles from both Perth and Crieff.

The College Buildings, grouped round a cloistered quadrangle, comprise the Chapel, Hall, Library, house-rooms and studies, study bedrooms, classrooms and laboratories. A separate block houses additional laboratories and a modern Theatre. A few yards away are the Art School and the Design and Technology Centre. Next to these are the Music practice rooms and a Concert Hall.

The nearby Sports Complex consists of squash courts, a gymnasium, an indoor sports hall and a heated indoor swimming pool, fitness suite and an indoor .22 range.

A brand new and state-of-the-art Science Block will be open for September 2001.

Boys' Houses. There are 5 Houses for boys, 4 in College and 1 out of College. The organisation of all the Houses is the same, each having married accommodation for resident Housemaster. Senior boys have study-bedrooms or studies of their own, and the College is currently refurbishing junior accommodation to create double and triple rooms.

Girls' Houses. A new purpose-built boarding house was completed in September 1990. Girls are admitted throughout the school. The second House was opened in September 1998, and a small extension will be completed for September 2001.

Religion. The College is an Episcopalian foundation and has a splendid Chapel. However all denominations are welcomed. Religious Education is given throughout the School.

Admission. Boys and girls may be registered for admission at any time after birth and enter the College between the ages of 13 and 14 provided they have qualified in the Common Entrance Examination or Entrance Scholarship papers. A junior entry at age 11 or 12 may qualify by tests and examinations for those not preparing for CEE. This entry is geared towards pupils leaving Primary Schools. Girls and boys may also qualify for entry into the Lower VIth, or at other points during their school career.

Curriculum. In the first 3 years this ensures that all pupils take a wide range of subjects up to the GCSE with English, History, Geography, French, Latin or General Classics, Mathematics and the 3 Sciences as basic subjects. Greek, Spanish, German, Statistics, Electronics, Art, Music and Design/Technology are optional subjects to GCSE and beyond. From the start of his or her career, each pupil is guided by a tutor and the curriculum avoids early specialisation which would limit a pupil's choice of VIth Form course or eventual career. All pupils take computer and microelectronics courses in their first year.

The VIth Form provides specialist courses in the Arts or Sciences (or a combination of the two) leading to GCE AS and A2 level. Scottish CE Higher grades may also be taken and offer a wider based alternative. Lectures from outside speakers on social, economic and cultural subjects of topical interest take place regularly.

Economics, Business Studies and Theatre Studies are now fully established in the Sixth Form.

Careers. Over 90% of pupils qualify for entry to university; some go direct to professional careers, industry, the Services, etc. Great emphasis is placed on careers guidance: careers talks, visits and advice along with a well-stocked careers room assist pupils in their choice and provide the necessary information. Most pupils take careers aptitude tests at age 16.

The new computer network with fibre optic cabling to all parts of the campus means that as well as ICT being available in libraries and for teaching purposes all pupils have access to e-mail and the internet within their Houses.

Art, Drama and Music. Music plays a central part in the life of the school: there is an Orchestra as well as smaller String, Woodwind and Brass Groups. A large Choir and Choral Society perform at the College, in Perth and in Edinburgh. The Concert Society arranges recitals and concerts at the College; frequent visits are made to concerts in Perth and elsewhere. There are currently two Pipe Bands.

The Drama and Art departments flourish, in conjunction with the well-established Design and Technology Centre. Both Art and Music as well as Design/Technology form part of the normal curriculum and can be taken at GCSE and 'A' level, or Scottish Higher. Theatre Studies is available at Higher.

Games and Recreations. Rugby Football (boys) and Hockey (girls) and Lacrosse are played in the Michaelmas Term, and there is a wide variety of activities to choose from in the Lent Term. Cricket, Athletics, Shooting, Sailing, Tennis and Golf are the chief activities in the Trinity Term. Shooting on the Miniature Ranges takes place during the 2 Winter Terms and on the open range in the Trinity Term. There is a large indoor heated Swimming Pool and pupils are trained in personal survival and Lifesaving. Instruction in Sub-aqua and Canoeing is given. There are also Squash Courts, Tennis Courts, a dry Ski Slope and a full length private Golf Course. There are two full-size all-weather pitches for hockey, netball and tennis.

During the Summer, pupils have the opportunity to explore the hills and the neighbouring countryside. There is also a Sailing and Windsurfing Club which uses a neighbouring loch. Weekend camping expeditions are arranged to encourage self-reliance and initiative.

In the Winter the slopes beside the College provide opportunities for Tobogganing and Ski-ing when there is snow. When conditions are suitable longer Ski-ing expeditions are organized.

Clubs and Societies. Voluntary membership of Societies such as the Dramatic, Historical, Debating and Public Speaking, Electronics, Engineering, Chess, Photographic and Film Societies is encouraged. There are Music, Opera, Computer, Mountaineering, Badminton, Clay Pigeon Shooting and Fishing Clubs.

Combined Cadet Force. There is a contingent of the Combined Cadet Force which still remains (unofficially) attached to the Black Watch. The ceremonial dress, as worn by the Pipe Band for example, is the Highland dress with the Murray of Atholl tartan. Girls may join the CCF.

There are Army and Air sections, with a Pre-Service section for Junior Pupils, which is organised on the basis of the Duke of Edinburgh's Award. Shooting and Adventure Training figure prominently; pupils may also be engaged on Conservation or Community Service Work. There is a Mountain Awareness Group.

School Fees. £5,100 per term. These fees include extras common to all pupils, such as membership of the CCF, Games, Subscriptions, journeys to matches, the use of the Golf Course, etc. Day pupils, for whom transport is arranged, pay £3,400 and the fee for the Juniors is £3,825 (Day £2,550).

Term of Entry. Entry is normally in September at the beginning of each academic year. Entry in January or April can be considered where special circumstances exist.

Entrance Awards. (*see* Entrance Scholarship section) Open Scholarships and Exhibitions range in value and Music Scholarships worth up to 50% of the fees are offered each year. Awards are also made for Art. All awards can be increased in case of need. The Examination for Scholarships is usually held in March for younger pupils and in November for entrants in the Sixth Form. Candidates may be considered for an 'All-Rounder Award'.

'Fil. Cler.' Bursaries. A number of Fil. Cler. Bursaries are available for sons and daughters of Clergy. The value of these is subject to a means test; they are awarded on the result of the Common Entrance or Scholarship Examination (or special qualifying tests) and an interview.

Services' Discount. There is an Award available to the sons and daughters of serving members of the Armed Forces.

Discretionary Awards. These are awarded at the discretion of the College. They are means-tested.

The Old Glenalmond Club. *Hon Secretary:* D Sibbald, 21 Ravelston Park, Edinburgh EH4 3DX.

Charitable status. Glenalmond College is a Registered Charity, number Ed CR 30884 (SC 006123). It exists for the all-round education of Boys and Girls in the tranquillity of a Highland setting.

Gordonstoun School

Elgin Morayshire IV30 5RF.
Tel: (01343) 837807 (Headmaster)
Fax: (01343) 837808

The philosophy of the school.

Gordonstoun aims to prepare young men and women for life in a challenging and changing world. Thus an education to ensure the best academic qualifications sees strong emphasis placed on the development of personal qualities through the encouragement of the cultural, physical, social and spiritual attributes of every boy and girl. To achieve this genuinely holistic objective, the School provides an environment of unparallelled opportunity with an expectation to participate and contribute; an all-embracing curriculum which operates seven days a week; a highly talented and fully committed staff; an ethos underpinned by challenge, responsibility, service and internationalism.

The School's motto 'Plus est en vous' is a living guide for every member of the community, for there is no limit which can be set on human potential.

Board of Governors:
Chairman: Vice Admiral Sir James L Weatherall, KBE
Deputy Chairman: Professor B Williams, MA, CQS

Mrs C J Caunt, BEd
J G D Ferguson, BA
Miss T J Gibbs
Mrs P M Gordon-Duff, BA, DipLE, ARICS
A Morgan, MBE
J R Nicholson
HRH The Princess Royal, KG, GCBO, QSO
Lady Strathnaver
Major General M J Strudwick, CBE
J Yeoman, MA, CA
Miss S Cameron, BA (Hons)

Bursar, Secretary to the Board: Sqdn Ldr J R Spencer, ACIS, RAF Retd

***Headmaster:* M C S-R Pyper**, BA

Senior Management Team:

Director Planning and Staffing: A R Gabb, BSc
Director of Curriculum: J A Hall, BA
Deputy Head, Director of Pupil Admissions & Welfare: C J Barton, BEd
Development Director: Ms A E Harkness

Assistant Teaching Staff:
J N Barclay, BA
J Barnett, BSc (*Careers*)
Mrs K J Barton, BSc
*D A Bell, BA, PhD (*Biology*)
Mrs M-T Bertin-Hughes, BA
K G Bews, DipMusEd, RSAMD (*Head of Lower School*)
†Mrs C M Broad, BA
†S L Brown, MA, BSc
†Dr E E Bull, BSc, PhD
R J Burt, BSc
*A J Cox, BEd (*Design & Technology*)
*S W DaBell, BSc, ARCS (*Chemistry*)
†R D Devey, BEd
*D M Evans, MA, DipAD (*Art*)
*Mrs M Evans, BA (*Learning Support*)
C R M Farmer
J R Forshaw, BA
A R Gabb, BSc
N R Gaston, BMus
A M Gordon-Rogers, BSc, CBiol, MIBiol
B C Goss, BEd
Miss S Grove, BSc
J Hamilton, MA
*C J Ince, BA (*Geography*)
*N K James, BA (*Business Studies*)
S A Kirkwood, MA, LLCM
†I A Lavender, MA
Dr A Lennard, BSc, PhD
I L Lerner, BA
J R Lythgoe, BA
Mrs K L Maltman, MA, DipEd
D J Monteith, BA
Mrs D L Monteith, MA
Miss L V Morrin, BA
*D J Morton, BEd (*PE*)
Mrs S L Morton, BEd, CELTA
D J Parker, BA
†Mrs J A Parker, BEd, MA
R Pearce, LCGI
*J S Pownall, BA (*Languages*)
M Reuss-Newland, BSc
N P Sanderson, BSc
*T J Schroder, BSc (*Information Technology*)
Dr A Seele, MA, PhD
P G Snyman, BSc
Mrs G H Souter, BA
*P R B Sutton, BD, MTh (*Religious Studies*)
*L Tattersall, BSc, MA (*Physics*)
A Thomas, BA
Mrs J E Thomas, BA, MLitt
J K Thomson, MSc, PhD, MInstP (*Physics*)
J E Trythall, MA, MSc
T J Watson
*Miss G A West, BA (*History*)
†J Whittaker, BSc
*N J Williams, BEd, MA (*Drama*)

Medical Officer: Dr J M Mobbs, MBChB, FRCOG, MRCGP, DCH

Size and Range. The School, set in an imposing estate in temperate Morayshire, is relatively small (410) and fully co-educational with 240 boys and 170 girls, almost all of whom are boarders. Most who enter the School at the Third Form level have taken the Common Entrance examination, but over 20 Scholarships are awarded annually at both junior and senior levels. There are about 40 Sixth Form entrants each year. Some boys and girls come into the School from the maintained sector (at both 13 and 16) by means of interview and report. A substantial number of parents are helped to a greater or lesser extent with the fees and the wide range of pupil backgrounds is an important aspect of School life. The School is international in both outlook and composition with one third of pupils coming from Scotland, one third from the remainder of the UK, and one third from the rest of the world.

Course of Studies. Each pupil has a tutor with whom work and progress are discussed every week; the attainment of each pupil is formally and frequently assessed. All departments and boarding houses are linked by the School's Information Technology network.

New pupils who join the Third Form study a full range of subjects in a broad foundation course including Religious Studies and Personal and Social Education which are taught throughout the Lower School. Support in the areas of English, Mathematics, English as a Second Language and Study Skills, can replace one of two languages. In the Fourth and Fifth Forms pupils are able to select some of their GCSE subjects from an extended list, although a core, similar to that of the National Curriculum, is followed by all. All pupils take English, Mathematics, Combined Science and almost all a Modern Language, usually French. Three optional subjects are then taken from History, Geography, Music, Art, Drama, Design, Information Technology, Physical Education, Latin, German, Spanish and Business Studies. A balanced diet is ensured. In 2000, the pass rate at GCSE was 90%, with pupils taking an average of 9 subjects.

For A-Level, Sixth Formers prepare four subjects to AS level and may choose from English Literature, History, French, German, Spanish, Geography, Classical Civilisation, Information Technology, History of Art, Art & Design, Mathematics, Music, Physical Education, Physics, Chemistry, Biology, Design Technology, Business Studies, Economics and Theatre Studies. Three subjects are then taken to A2 level. In 2000 the pass rate at A-Level was 86% and over 95% proceeded to Higher Education. There is an extensive programme of General Studies.

The Arts. The School combines inherent artistic traditions with an appreciation of the importance of creativity and contemporary initiatives. Thus Drama is firmly established in the academic curriculum and productions of every description are staged frequently, while much is achieved in impromptu workshop sessions. Groups perform outside the School, particularly at the Edinburgh Festival.

Music is also central to the life of the School. Over 200 pupils learn musical instruments. The Music Department caters for all the normal and several Celtic instruments as well as voice. Performances include a weekly lunch-time concert and a flourishing subscription Concert Society. Gordonstoun operas and musicals have earned a reputation which stretches well beyond the immediate neighbourhood. Frequent tours overseas are arranged for both the orchestra and smaller groups.

The School has an enviable record in Art, particularly in Ceramics and Design, both in terms of examination results and as a preparation for admission to Art Colleges. The Design and Technology Centre is the focus for project-based activity, underpinning the practical approach to life and development, and awards in national competitions are frequently won.

Games and Sport. Rugby, hockey, netball, soccer, cricket, athletics, cross-country running and tennis are the major sports. Regular fixtures against other schools and clubs also take place in squash, basketball, alpine skiing, swimming, golf and badminton. Canoeing, orienteering, dinghy sailing, tae-kwon-do, clay pigeon shooting, aerobics, dance and riding are popular weekend activities, and on Sundays in the Spring term, pupils can go skiing in the Cairngorms. There is a multi-purpose Sports Centre with a large indoor playing surface, heated swimming pool, multi-gym, climbing wall and squash courts. A floodlit Astroturf playing surface accommodates a full-size hockey pitch or twelve tennis courts.

Responsibility and Service. The school places considerable emphasis on personal development and, in particular, the appreciation of responsibility. In terms of their daily lives and many unique opportunities, pupils learn to organise their own lives while simultaneously understanding the importance of contributing towards the welfare of others. This finds structure in the School's service programme. In their second year, all pupils do a pre-service course which includes First Aid, Police Course, Motor Maintenance and Accident Prevention. They then join one of the Services. The Rescue Services are designed to meet the needs of the local and wider community and to help to integrate the School into local affairs. In addition to a Unit of the Grampian Fire Brigade, the Mountain Rescue Service, the Coastguards, the Inshore Rescue Service, the Special Boat Service, the Corps of Canoe Lifeguards, and the Nordic Ski Patrol, there is also a Squadron of the Air Training Corps as well as a Nature Conservation Service, and a large and thriving Community Service Group.

Challenge Through Outdoor Education. Expeditions play an important part in the curriculum involving all pupils throughout their time at Gordonstoun. Boys and girls are gradually introduced to camp craft and inter-personal skills in the unique setting of the Scottish Highlands. Safety is always regarded as paramount, with all the expeditions closely monitored by staff, although as pupils progress through the School they are given increasing responsibility for planning their own routes, and eventually undertake some expeditions unaccompanied. Those who develop a strong love of the hills are, in the senior part of the School, able to join the Mountain Rescue Service. Longer expeditions of various sorts are undertaken in the holidays, and some of these make use of the School sail training vessel. Seamanship forms part of the curriculum for all boys and girls. Pupils sail open boats in the Moray Firth and the purpose designed School sail training vessel, "Ocean Spirit of Moray", provides sail training for all pupils off the West Coast of Scotland in the Summer and in the early weeks of the Autumn term. Cruises also take place in the holidays and in recent years the School has competed in the Scottish Three Peaks Race, the Cutty Sark Tall Ships' Race and the Banff to Stavanger Race.

Internationalism. The School has close connections with schools in Germany, France, New Zealand, South Africa, India, Australia, Canada, Spain and the USA, and exchange visits are often arranged with little extra cost to parents. Gordonstoun is a founder member of "Round Square", a group of schools committed to education through service, adventure and international understanding. Through it, and on its own account, Gordonstoun is fully involved in international service projects and the overwhelming majority of pupils have one major international experience during their time in the school.

Careers. The member of staff responsible for careers guidance is a specialist in the field and is assisted by several others. The School is an all-in member of the Independent Schools Careers Organisation; it also receives advice and help from the National Advisory Centre on Careers for Women. Full advice and planning assistance is given with Higher Education planning through UCAS, and the School is an SAT testing centre for USA Colleges.

Aberlour House. Boys and girls are accepted at Aberlour House, Gordonstoun's affiliated Preparatory School, from the age of eight. Applications should be made to the Headmaster, Aberlour House, Aberlour, Banffshire AB38 9LJ. Most boys and girls move from there to Gordonstoun. Progress from Aberlour House to Gordonstoun is normally guaranteed for boys and girls attending Aberlour House from age eleven.

Fees. From September 2000 the termly boarding fee is £5,222-£5,555. There are very few extras and School books, stationery and most normal laundry are included in the fees.

Travel. There is easy access to the School by road, rail and air, with Aberdeen and Inverness airports close by and Elgin railway station 5 miles from the School. The School undertakes the responsibility to organise group travel at the beginning and end of terms and makes individual travel arrangements, both on planes and trains, and provides supervision on coaches and trains.

Scholarships. (*see* Entrance Scholarship section) The School offers a very large number of scholarships and bursaries at both 3rd year and 6th form levels for academic achievement and potential, all round qualities, music, art and at 6th form level in several other individual areas.

Former Pupils. There is a flourishing Association for ex-pupils which holds many annual functions at the School, elsewhere in Scotland and England and all over the world. The Association may be contacted through the school. Tel: (01343) 837923.

Charitable status. Gordonstoun Schools Limited is a Registered Charity, number 288105. It exists to promote the education of the whole person.

The Grange School

Bradburns Lane Hartford Cheshire CW8 1LU
Tel: (01606) 74007
Fax: (01606) 784581
e-mail: office@grange.org.uk
website: www.grange.org.uk

The Grange was founded in 1933 as a Preparatory School, the Senior School opening in 1978. The School is co-educational, with 1100 pupils from 4–18 years, and is situated in the village of Hartford, half an hour away from Chester and Manchester and eight miles from the M6 motorway.

Motto: *E Glande Robur*

Governing Body:

Chairman: R Fildes, MA

F H Appleby, FRICS
Mrs A Arthur
Dr W J Forsyth, MB, ChB, MRCGP, AFOM
G Halman, FRICS
Mrs J Hannah, LLB
C P Jackson, BSc, MIHT
T K Johnston, LLB
Mrs I J Ritchie, DipEd, CertEd, NFFC
R J Taylor, BSc, FCA

***Headmistress:* Mrs J E Stephen,** BSc

Deputy Head: A Testard, BA

Senior Mistress: *Mrs G A Bushill, DipDomSci, BA

Director of Studies: D Clapperton, BSc

Director of Sixth Form Studies: D Shaw, BSc, MSc

Assistant staff:

Mrs H Ashall, CertEd *Home Economics*
*E Ball, BA, CertEd *Information Technology*
Mrs C Barker, MA *English*
Miss K E Black, BSc, MSc *Geography*
M C Blair, BSc *PE; Geography*
*Mrs J Bloor, BA *Speech & Drama*
Mrs B A Broderick, BSc *Chemistry; Geography*
*P Buckley, BA *Classics*
Mrs V Buckley, BA *Religious Studies*
Mrs J Corrigan, CertEd *PE and Games*
*Mrs A B Doran, BA *Art*
Mrs J England, BSc *Mathematics*
Mrs L Finney, LLAM *Drama*
T H Giles, BA *PE and Games*
A Graham, BSc *Information Technology*
Mrs E Heyes, MA *German*
*R A Hibbert, BA *Modern Languages*
*R A Hough, BA *Religious Studies & Philosophy*
*C Howe, BSc *Chemistry*
Mrs C Hughes, GNSM, ARCM *Music*
Mrs H Kerr, BA *History & Politics*
I H Killey, BEng, BSc *Physics*
Mrs C Lawrence, Dip Northern School of Music *Drama*
Miss H R Lawson, BA *PE & Games*
B C Marsh, BA *Craft, Design, Technology*
Mrs A Mathias, ALAM *Drama*
*A J Millinchip, MA, FRCO(CHM) *Music*
*A Milne, BSc, MSc *Biology*
*W Morrison, BA *Economics & Business Studies*
*A Near, BSc *Mathematics*
Mrs J S Oakes, BSc *Biology*
Dr J R Oliver, BSc, PhD *Biology*
Mrs C J Osborne, BSc *Mathematics*
*M Pearson, BA *Geography*
Mrs S Pemberton, BSc *Mathematics*
Mrs S A Percy, BA *French*
R K Robson, BA *History*
D Shaw, BA *Classics*
*P Simpson, BA *History*
*J Slack, BSc *Physics*
*D L Stewart, BA *English*
Mrs A B Taunton, MA *Religious Studies & English*
M Thomas, MA *Economics & Business Studies*
Mrs S Thornes, BSc *Physics*
Mrs P Tideswell, BA *French*
*T W Tindale, BSc *PE; History*
Dr A O Ward, PhD *English*
Mrs S Warner, BA *English*
S Whitehouse, BSc *Mathematics*
Miss L Wilbraham, BA *Craft, Design, Technology*
R G Williams, MA *Chemistry; Mathematics*
Mrs C Wilson, BA, BEd *Spanish & French*

Preparatory and Kindergarten Department

Head of Junior School: D K Geddes, MA
Deputy Head of Junior School: Mrs K J Hill, BEd
Head of Pre-Prep: Mrs F Taylor, BA

Mrs F Alexander, BA
Mrs C Carson, CertEd
Mrs A Connolly, BEd
Mrs C Elliott, CertEd
Ms A Evans, BEd
A M Evans, BEd
Mrs D M Gresty (Tours)
Mrs S Hancock, CertEd
Mrs J Haynes, BEd
Mrs M J Howard, CertEd
Ms E Johnson, BEd
H Jones, BEd
J P Land, BEd
Mrs Z A Pidcock, BA
Miss A Pollen, CertEd
Mrs R E Preston, BA
Mrs G L Rosa, BA
Mrs M J Shaw, BEd
Mrs R Speed, CertEd
Mrs J Taylor, CertEd
Mrs E Walker, BEd

Peripatetic Staff:

Mrs J Bingham, GNSM, CertEd (*Violin, Viola*)
Mr D Browne, GRNCM (*Cello*)
Miss D Clementson, GRSM, ARMCM, FTCL (*Clarinet and Oboe*)
Ms A Duthie, CTABRSM (*Flute*)
Ms S Hadfield, GRNCM, BMus (*Oboe, Bassoon*)
Mrs B Hammond, BMus, PGCE (*Piano*)
Mrs S Hoffman, BMus (*Flute*)
Mrs C Hughes, GNSM, ARCM (*Piano*)
Miss L Hughes, BA (*Brass*)
Mrs J Panter, GRSM, LPCL (*Violin*)
Mrs A Rogers, LGSM (*Piano*)
Ms C Smiga, BA (RNCM) (*Singing*)
Mr P Smith, BMus, FTCL, FCSM, ARCM (*Singing*)
Ms A Thompson, BA (*Clarinet, Saxophone*)
Mr S WatkissCT, ABRSM (*Guitar*)
Miss S Wood, GMus, RNCM, PPRNCM (*Percussion*)

The Kindergarten and Junior School (450 pupils). 1996 saw the opening of a brand new, purpose-built Kindergarten and Preparatory School for children aged 4–11. This development has brought together all the children of this age group on to one attractively landscaped eleven acre site which is within walking distance of the Senior School.

The main teaching takes place in 21 large, self-contained classrooms on two floors with the younger children located on the ground floor separated from the older children. The School has its own extensive playing fields and generous play areas while two large halls provide facilities for dining, teaching, gymnastics and school productions. Rooms are provided for specialist teaching with music having a large room next to the hall and no fewer than five individual music practice rooms. As well as a broad curriculum junior pupils study ICT and a modern language, they have regular swimming lessons and compete in sport with other schools. Close attention is given to each child's progress with two parents' evenings each year. Children learn to use computers from a young age, there is a junior orchestra and opportunities for private music and drama lessons. Extra-curricular activities are held mainly at lunchtime.

The Senior School (650 pupils). The Senior School has modern buildings which include seven well-equipped laboratories, Design Technology and Information Technology suites, art block, library, new Sixth Form Common Rooms, multi-purpose sports hall and dining room. A new teaching block, opened in 1996, houses the English and Modern Languages Departments. This contains a Language Laboratory, satellite television and PCs with CD Rom and Internet facilities. The year 2001 will see the opening of a brand new Science and Information Technology Centre.

Curriculum. Years I, II and III follow a broad curriculum with all IInd years studying two modern languages. In the IIIrd year pupils continue to study English, Mathematics, Biology, Chemistry, Physics, History, Geography, Classical Civilisation or Latin, Religious Studies, Information Technology, PE/Games, two Modern Languages, and select two of five practical subjects. At the end of the IIIrd Year pupils opt for nine subjects which must include Mathematics, English, at least one science and at least one modern language. Personal and Social Education is taught in Years I to V.

From the IIIrd Year advice and assistance is available to all pupils on a wide range of career possibilities. The careers team arrange a biennial careers convention supplemented with regular visits and talks when advice is given by consultants from a variety of professions. There is a fully equipped careers room.

Pastoral Care. The School provides a disciplined, caring and secure environment in which pupils may work and play without being subjected to harm or distress, in which they may develop their personalities to the full and enjoy their time at school. The Form Teacher is the key figure in each pupil's academic and pastoral welfare and is the first point of contact with parents. The Form Teacher is supported by Heads of Year and regular meetings are held to ensure that the pastoral needs of all our pupils are met. The system is enhanced by a Peer Support scheme which allows trained senior students to listen to younger pupils' concerns.

House Activities. Each pupil is allocated to one of four Houses on entry to the school; siblings are allocated to the same House. A House Convener arranges meetings with Heads of House to discuss policy, procedure and House activities. These activities range from sporting competitions to an art and a literary competition. Each year the pupils produce their own play for the drama competition and their own repertoire for the music competition. The organisation of such activities is carried out by the pupils themselves with staff providing support and guidance. All pupils are actively encouraged to participate in the full range of activities in order to raise their self-esteem and to allow each to shine; they gain much from the experience. Junior, Intermediate and Senior House Assemblies are held on a weekly basis.

Sixth Form and Higher Education. Students take four or five subjects plus General Studies to AS Level in the Lower Sixth. They continue with three or four of those subjects plus General Studies to A2 Level in the Upper Sixth. The subjects are chosen from an extensive range with 27 presently available. All Sixth Formers participate in Games lessons, where a wide choice of activities is provided. Supplementary courses provided include Information Technology, Application of Number and Communication to facilitate the Key Skills qualification.

Careers guidance is given considerable emphasis in the Grange Sixth. Each student is attached to a member of the careers team and all students participate in the school work experience scheme, with linguists being given the opportunity to undertake their work experience abroad. Almost all the students progress to higher education, with around 15% going on each year to Oxford and Cambridge.

Sixth Formers are expected to play a leading role in school life with the School's prefect body being selected from their number. They also participate in the extensive programme of House activities as well as in the Duke of Edinburgh's Award Scheme and outward bound courses.

All students are required to participate in the execution of duties around school and there is a Sixth Form Council, run by the Head Girl and Head Boy, to co-ordinate the various aspects of Sixth Form life. Students have the use of their own common rooms.

Reporting to Parents. The School recognises that our pupils are best served when parents and the School work together and to this end we consider it important to report to parents fully and regularly. We encourage full discussion of the pupils' progress and well being. Each pupil receives at least two full reports per year. Each half term brings a progress report with academic grades and a profile of the pupil's extra-curricular involvement and pastoral welfare. There are two parents' evenings each year for Years I, IV and Lower Sixth and one for all other year groups. If parents have any concerns, they are encouraged to discuss these with the relevant staff at the earliest opportunity and the School will always contact parents and invite them to discuss issues should we feel it necessary.

Games. The School has 22 acres of sports fields. The principal games are hockey, netball, rugby, rowing, football, cricket, cross country, athletics and tennis. There are four all-weather tennis courts as well as three badminton courts.

Art, Design, Drama, Music. In addition to timetabled lessons for these subjects there are numerous opportunities to participate in extra-curricular activities. There is a pottery room, photographic studio, art club and life drawing classes are provided for Sixth Form students.

In the music department no less than 15 peripatetic teachers provide 420 private lessons a week. There are two orchestras, jazz, string, recorder and saxophone ensembles, senior choir and choral society. Cantores Roborienses, the School's senior singing group, and the Chamber Orchestra perform at the many informal concerts held during the year and at numerous public events.

Considerable emphasis is placed on Drama in the school with two part-time and two full-time members of staff and pupils participate in a number of drama festivals with a high degree of first and second placings. Over 80 private lessons take place each week. All pupils are entered for Guildhall examinations from Junior Preliminary to Grade 8. Regular school productions take place each year with frequent theatre trips.

Religion. The School is Christian based but pupils of all denominations are accepted as long as they are prepared to take a full part in the life of the School. Full School Assemblies take place twice a week.

Roburians. The Grange's Past Pupils' Association organises an annual ball as well as a Sports Day when they challenge the School in cricket, hockey, football and rowing.

Transport. Hartford is served by two main line stations, Manchester to Chester and Crewe to Liverpool. The majority of children travel to and from school by car or by one of the eight private buses.

Admission. Kindergarten by interview in March; Senior School by entrance examination on the first Saturday in February; Sixth Form by interview and good GCSE results.

Pupils are also admitted at other ages as vacancies occur. Admission is gained by interview and test performance. Enquiries for admission are welcome at any time of the year and a copy of the school prospectus may be obtained by contacting the Admissions Secretary.

Open Morning. The School holds an Open Morning on the first Saturday in November when prospective parents and pupils are welcome to see the facilities available and to talk to the pupils and staff. Appointments to view the school can be made at other times by contacting the Admissions Secretary.

Fees. With effect from January 2001 termly fees range from £1,250 for Kindergarten to £1,635 for Senior School.

Scholarships. Several scholarships are offered for entry to the Senior School for exceptional academic ability, sport, music and drama. A number of VIth Form Scholarships are awarded for outstanding academic potential after an examination held at the end of spring term preceding Sixth Form entry.

Charitable status. The Grange School is a Registered Charity, number 525918. It exists to provide high quality education for boys and girls.

Gresham's School

Holt Norfolk NR25 6EA.
Tel: Headmaster: (01263) 713271
Bursar (01263) 713179.

Founded 1555.
Motto: *'Al Worship Be To God Only'.*

Governors:
D T Young (*Chairman*)
The Earl of Erroll
M Drummond, OBE, JP, DL
Mrs A MacNicol
The Earl of Antrim
The Hon Sir M Lennox-Boyd, MP
A N G Duckworth-Chad (*Deputy Chairman*)
Mrs S M Lennane
G R C Shepard
Sir Thomas Stockdale, Bt
J P Gough
A H Scott
The Hon Andrew Cairns
The Rt Revd Tony Foottit, The Lord Bishop of Lynn
Mrs M J King
H C Cordeaux
The Hon Mrs J Soames
Dr I Waterson, FRCP
A Payne
Baroness Perry
J Woodhouse
A Martin Smith
Mrs I E Floering Blackman
Sir A Stirling
Sir M Farrer, GCVO
M Edwards

Estate Trustees: The Fishmongers' Company

Clerk to the Governors: K S Waters, Fishmongers' Hall, London Bridge, EC4R 9EL

***Headmaster:* J H Arkell**, MA (Cantab)

Deputy Head: Mrs S Smart, MA (Oxon)

Director of Studies: N Semple, HND, CertEd

Chaplain: The Revd B Roberts, BD

Assistant Masters:
Mrs C Alban, BA (Jt Hons) (*Business Studies*)
Dr C M A Badger, BA, DPhil (*Physics and Chemistry*)
†P Badger, BA (*Geography*) (*Howson's*)
N Ball, QM (*Mathematics*)
*M J Barrett, BA, MA, (*History and General Studies*)
*G Bartle, BSc (*Computing*)
D Beaney, BSc, PGCE, (*Mathematics*)
P H F Cooper, BA (*French and Careers*)
*T J Cross, BSc (*Physics*)
Mrs J Dovey, BA (Hons), PGCE (*Special Needs*)
*N G Dovey, BA (*Hons*), MSc (*Economics*)
†A A Edwards, BA (*Hons*) (*History*) (*Farfield*)
Miss J S Emeney, BA (*English*)
P Farmer-Wright, BSc (Hons), PGCE (*Maths*)
N C Flower, BA (*English*)
N J Fulford, BSc (*Physics*)
†Miss F Gathercole, BA (*Biology*) (*Oakeley*)
*Dr P S Gomm, MSc, PhD (*Chemistry*)
†D C Hamill, MTh (*History*) (*Woodlands*)
*P J Hands, BA (*Drama*)
D Hawke, DesRCA, NDD, LCADip (*Technical Studies*)
R G Heaney, BA (*Physics*)
*Miss S Hincks, BA (*Modern Languages*)
*D T Horsley, BSc, PhD (*Biology*)
N Humphrey, BA (Hons), PGCE (*Design Technology*)
*M H Jones, GRSM, FRCO, ARCM (*Music*)
N Jones, BA, MA, PGCE (*English and Drama*)
Mrs R Kimmins, LRAM, ARCM (*Music*)
Miss C Lain, BA (Hons), PGCE (*Art*)
A R Leech, MA, DPhil, PGCE (*Biology*)
Mrs B Leech, MA (*Geography*)
*S Moore, TeachCert (*Technical Studies*)
*R Myerscough, BD, PGCE (*RE*)
A P Osiatynski, BA, PGCE (*Music*)
†P A Paskell, BSc, BA (*Economics*) (*Tallis*)
Mrs P F Paskell, BA, PGCE (*German*)
*N Paterson, BA (Hons), PGCE (*Art*)
R H Peaver, TD, MA, MIL (*French*)
A M Ponder, BSc, DipEd (*Mathematics*)
Ms C Pooley, BA (Hons) (*Drama*)
†*Mrs S Radley, BEd (*Home Economics*) (*Edinburgh*)
J S Rayner, MA, CertEd (*English*)
F J V Retter, BA, PGCE (*Languages*)
*Mrs L Rose, BEd (*Special Needs*)
M J Runnalls, BA, PGCE (*Classics*)
J Seaman, BSc (Hons), MSc, GRSC, PGCE (*Chemistry*)
*J D Smart, BA (*Hons*), BLitt (*English*)
*G S Smithers, MA, MSc, AFIMA (*Mathematics*)
Miss C Spry, MPhil (*French*)
Mrs C A Thomas, BA, PGCE (*English*)
J Thomson, BEng, PGCE (*Mathematics*)
†Mrs S Thomson (*Home Economics*) (*Britten*)
*J N Walton, CertEd (*Geography*)
P Watson, PGCE
*Dr N G White, BSc, PhD (*Physics*) (*Assistant Director of Studies*)
G B Worrall, CertEd, DPE (*English*)

Preparatory School Headmaster:
A H Cuff, CertEd, DPE

Assistant Staff:
*R T N Brearley, CertEd (*Geography*)
*G A Britton, BSc, PGCE (*Mathematics & IT*)
Mrs H D Brotherton, BA (Hons), PGCE
*S J S Clarke, BA (Hons) (*Drama, English*)
*Mrs H Cuff (*Art*)
S Fields, BSc (*Physics*)
*Mrs L Gillick, BEd, CertEd (*Special Needs*)
†Mrs C Gutteridge, CertEd (*Crossways*) (*Design Technology*)
*P A J Hawes, CertEd (*Director of Studies, History*)
Miss C A Henry, BEd (*Science*)
Mrs C Hunt, BSc (*Science*)
*D G Jackson, CertEd (*Mathematics*)
*R J G Mansfield, MA (*Deputy Headmaster, English*)
Miss D Moore, BEd (*General Subjects*)
J M B Roberts, BA (*English*)
*N Thomas, BA (*French*)
Mrs D West, BA (*English*)
†S C Worrall BA Hons (*Kenwyn*) (*Mathematics*)

Bursar: Wg Cdr R C Betts, BA, RAF, (*Retd*)

Medical Officer: Dr H Crawley

SSI: C C Scoles, MBE

The School was founded in 1555 by Sir John Gresham, Kt., and the endowments were placed by him under the management of the Fishmongers' Company.

There are 520 pupils in the Senior School, 310 boys and 210 girls, of whom 200 are VIth Form, and 310 are boarders (186 weekly).

The School is situated some 4 miles from the sea near Sheringham and Blakeney, in one of the most beautiful and healthy parts of England. The School has a spacious setting in 150 acres including 50 acres of woodland. Numbered amongst its old boys are W H Auden, Benjamin Britten, Stephen Spender, Lord Reith on the Arts side; and Christopher Cockerell, inventor of the hovercraft, Ian Proctor, yacht designer, Leslie Everett Baynes, who first patented swing-wing variable aircraft geometry and James Dyson of more recent fame on the engineering side. It strives to remain a balanced school.

There are four boys' boarding houses and three girls' houses. After the first or second year all pupils move into study bedrooms.

There has been a substantial building programme in the last two decades: Sports Hall (1983), Edinburgh Girls House (1987), English department building (1988), Junior and Senior Social Centres (1989), two all weather pitches (1994)

As a result of a successful Appeal the Cairns Centre for Art and Design was opened in June 1990, providing modern facilities for technology and design education. The Auden Theatre was completed in March 1998. A third girls house (Britten House) opened in September 1996 for 65 boarding and day girls.

Curriculum. In their first year pupils cover all the traditional subjects including separate lessons in the three sciences. Pupils may study French, German, Spanish, Latin or Japanese. Some choices are made for the 2 year GCSE course and most pupils take between 8 and 11 subjects including English, Maths, one language and 2 or 3 Sciences. In the Sixth Form pupils normally take 4 AS level subjects and 3 A levels (A2). The School has a particular strength in Mathematics and of the Sixth Form currently over 60% take Mathematics at A level. Detailed careers advice is given and computerised aptitude tests, developed at Gresham's, are given to 5th and 6th formers. The School employs specialists to assist a small number of pupils suffering from dyslexia.

General. Gresham's is a Church of England foundation but all religious denominations are welcomed. The School has its own Counsellor who instructs new pupils and present pupils in life skills, and who is available to advise and help pupils throughout their time at Gresham's.

Recreation, Music and Drama. The School has abundant playing fields. The main games are rugby football, hockey and cricket for boys, and hockey, netball, rounders and tennis for girls. Shooting, sailing, swimming, squash, badminton, cross country running, athletics and golf are also very popular, and national and international success has been consistently achieved in shooting and sailing, and recently in hockey. A unique option also available is Forestry.

There is a flourishing CCF contingent and Duke of Edinburgh section and approximately 25 gold awards are achieved each year. The School has a very strong choir which makes an annual tour abroad and performs regularly in East Anglian churches. Five of its members have recently sung in the National Youth Choir. Art and drama are also strong, and Drama and Theatre Studies are offered at GCSE and A level.

Entry Scholarships. (*see* Entrance Scholarship section) Those entering at 13+ from Preparatory Schools take the Common Entrance Examination or scholarship. Tests in Maths, English and, where applicable French or German, are given to those entering from independent schools which do not prepare for Common Entrance, and from the maintained sector. Able foreign pupils are welcomed especially into the Sixth Form.

There are several academic scholarships available, some up to 100% in cases of need for pupils from preparatory and maintained schools, and 2 Sixth Form academic Scholarships. Several Scholarships in Music, Art and Drama are awarded for 13+ and Sixth Form entry. There is a Sports Scholarship for entry to the Sixth Form, two for entry at 13+. Three Continuation Scholarships are also available for pupils with 2 more years at Preparatory School. The Philip Newell Scholarships and other awards are available for GAP year activities. The Fishmongers' Company sponsor 3 places annually on Sail Training trips.

Boarding Fees. £15,555 pa for the Senior School, £11,340 pa for the Prep School. Weekly boarding £14,400 (Senior); £10,500 (Prep). These are inclusive fees; no extra charge is made for laundry, games, medical attention, etc.

Day pupils' fees. Senior £11,940 pa. Prep £8,610 pa. Day pupils' meal charges are: Senior £607 pa., Prep £471 pa. Necessary extras are very few.

Honours. In 2000 the A level pass rate was 97.3% with 56.83% A and B grades. 98% of the Upper Sixth went on to university. 9.0 passes at C grade or above was the average per pupil at GCSE in 2000.

The Old Greshamian Club. The Club is active on behalf of present and former members of the School and it can be contacted through its Coordinator, John Rayner at Gresham's School.

Gresham's Preparatory School is a flourishing boarding, weekly boarding and day co-educational preparatory school of 230 pupils within half a mile of the Senior School. Its Headmaster is a member of IAPS and further details can be found in Part V of this Book. There is also a Pre-Prep School of 80 pupils.

Charitable status. Gresham's School is a Registered Charity, number 311268. The School is a charitable trust for the purpose of educating children.

* Head of Department	§ Part Time or Visiting
† Housemaster/Housemistress	¶ Old Pupil
‡ See below list of staff for meaning	

The Haberdashers' Aske's School

Butterfly Lane Elstree Borehamwood Herts. WD6 3AF.
Tel: 020 8266 1700
Fax: 020 8266 1800
e-mail: office@habs.herts.sch.uk
website: http://www.habs.herts.sch.uk

Station: Elstree (Rail from Moorgate & Kings Cross Thameslink)

The School was founded in 1690, its income arising from an estate left in trust to the Haberdashers' Company by Robert Aske, Citizen of London and Liveryman of the Haberdashers' Company. In 1898 it was transferred from Hoxton to Hampstead and in 1961 to Aldenham Park, Elstree, Hertfordshire.

Motto: *Serve and Obey.*

Governing Body:
The Governing Body consists of representatives of the Worshipful Company of Haberdashers, the world of education, the catchment area of the school and former pupils.

***Headmaster:* P B Hamilton,** MA (*from April 2002*)

Acting Headmaster/Second Master: S Boyes, MA (*for first two terms*)

Senior Master: J A Corrall, MA

Head of the Sixth Form: F H Hanbidge, MA

Head of the Middle School: M J Cook, BEd

Head of the Junior School: S Wilson, MA

Head of the Preparatory School: Miss Y M Mercer, BEd

Bursar: M A Gilbertson, MBE, FIMgt

Assistant Staff:
D I Yeabsley, CertEd
R G Norton, BA
P Hayler, BSc
D J Griffith, BSc
G J McGrogan, BSc, CPhys, MInstP, MBCS, AMIEE, CEng
J Wigley, BA, PhD
F J Rose, BMus
M G Day, BA
D R Delpech, BSc, MSc, CBiol, MIBiol
A C Bagguley, BSc, CBiol, MIBiol
C P H Keenlyside, MA
M J Lexton, BSc, PhD,CChem, FRSC
M P Lemprière, BA
J A Alvarez, BSc, PhD, CPhys, MInstP
Rev D M Lindsay, MA, DipTheol
A K Keenleyside, BA
P A Barry, BSc, PhD
Miss L M Bird, BA
P J Stiff, BA, PhD
J K Tarpey, BSc
S N Todhunter, BA
N P Holmes, BEd
P H Parr, MA
Mrs J B Swallow, BA
J C Swallow, MA
R C Sloan, MA, PhD
M J Donaghey, BA
P E Morris, BA, MPhil
Mrs J Hayes, BA
A M Ward, BSc
P C Marx, BSc, MPhil
Mrs D Meehan, LRAM, ARCM
C J Netto, MA, PhL
R D Reid, MA, BSSc
M L Williams, BA
Mrs K R Wilson, BA
T B Hyde, BSc, ARCM
S D Charlwood, BSc
Mrs J Robson, BA
Mrs J Gleeson, BEd
Mrs B Wood, BA, DipEd
Mrs K A Hedges, BA
P I Dathan, BEd
T B W Hardman, BEd
A P A Simm, BA
Mrs D Williams, BA
C Glanville, BSc, BA
M L S Judd, BA
N P Saddington, BA
Mrs A Thakar, BSc
C R Bass, BA
Mrs C B Lyons, MA
Mrs D L Robertson, BSc
M C Morrish, BA
S A Kinder, BA
I B Jacques, DPhil
A F Metcalfe, BSc
Mrs J E Beeson, BSc
M J Davies, BA
A J Herzmark, BA
P M Amor, BA
J A Fenn, MA
D T Jones, PhD
R O Kerr, BSc
Mrs J Letts, BSc
C D Muhley, GRSM, ARCO, ARCM, LRAM, FRSA
T R Walker, MA
M I Yeabsley, BSc
A J Hardwicke, MA
Mrs M J C Jones, BEd
K Long, BEd
T J Norton, BA
Dr A D S Perera, PhD
Mrs A C C Baron, BSc
L Canny, BA
D J Payne-Cook, BEd
Mrs K Shah, BSc
R C Elliott, MA
R J West, BA
J A Barnes, BSc
S P H Clark, BA
Mrs J Courtney, BSc
Mrs E Gomez, BA
G F Hunter, BA
Miss L I Leyshon, BSc
Mrs D H Morris-Wolffe, BA
I StJohn, DPhil
R J West, BA
B J Evans, BSc
P I Roncarati, BA, MSc
R C Whiteman, MA

Librarians:
Mrs J B Mulchrone, BSc
Mrs J P Sutton, ALA
Mrs A M Williams

Language Assistants:
Mrs M C Griffiths, BA
Miss A Lecorps
Miss M Müller

Preparatory School:
Mrs K M Francis, CertEd
I T C Rice, CertEd
Mrs S A Fancy, BSc, ARCM
Mrs C M Griggs, DSD, CertEd
S Lowe, BEd
M G Brown, BSc (*Deputy Head*)
Mrs S M E Herbert, BEd
Miss H M R Johnston, BEd
Dr C A Lessons, PhD
Miss C A Grimes, BEd
D J Jewell, BA

Music:
H J Legge, LRAM
G T Hayburn, GRSM, ARCM
R E Tearle, LTCL
P L D Chandler, ARCM
Mrs D S Meehan, LRAM, ARCM
J W Beryl
Mrs E O Perrottet, AGSM
M Pritchard, DipRCM
Miss I C Mair, MMus, LRAM, ARCM
S D Munting, ARCM
S R Topping, ARCM
Miss M B Parrington, ARCM
R A Carter, FRCO, FTCL, ARCM, LRAM
S D Lyon, GRSM, MA
Miss C Maguire, LRAM
Mrs L M Rive, LRAM
L Gee, GBSM, ABSM, HonBC
Miss S D Duncan, MMus
J Saipe, BA
P Cox, BA, ABSM, LTCL
Miss P Worn, LRAM, ABSM, ALCM

Clerk to the Governors: J P R Mitchell, BA

Administrative Staff:

Bursar: M A Gilbertson, MBE, FIMgt

Bursar's Secretary: Miss E M Tomlin

Assistant Bursar: W W M Hardy

Accountant: Mrs E Bennett

Headmaster's Secretary: Miss C J Jennings

School Support Director: D I Yeabsley

School Nurses:
Mrs S C O'Donovan, RGN
Mrs J Kraft, RGN, SCM

Catering Manager: E Johnston
Buildings Manager: P J Newcombe, BA
Transport Manager: W W M Hardy
Head Groundsman: M D Stanhope
Shop Manager: Mrs I C Burt

The aim of the School is the fullest possible development of the varied talents of every boy within it, and to this end a broad curriculum is provided, together with extensive facilities for the development of each boy's cultural, physical, personal and intellectual gifts. The School sets out to achieve high academic standards and sets equally high standards in cultural and other fields. In matters of behaviour a large degree of self-discipline is expected, and of mutual tolerance between members of the School community.

The School, which is a day school, has 200 boys in the Preparatory School (ages 7–11), 300 in the Junior School (ages 11–13), 500 in the Middle School (ages 13–16) and over 300 in the VIth Form (over 16). There are 6 Houses.The School regards pastoral care as important; all the Housemasters and Heads of Section have a large responsibility in this field but so also do House Tutors, the Senior Master and the Chaplain, as well as other members of the staff.

The School and its sister Girls' School, the Haberdashers' Aske's School for Girls, enjoy the use of a campus of over 100 acres with extensive woodlands. The playing fields surround the buildings, which in the Boys' School include the following: Assembly Hall, Dining Hall, Library, Study Room, special accommodation for Classics, English (including a Drama Room), History, Geography, Mathematics, Information Technology, Modern Languages including 2 Languages Laboratories, Music School, Science Laboratories, a Design Centre for Art, Craft and Technology, Sports Centre, Gymnasium, Indoor Swimming Bath, Artificial Grass Pitch and Squash Courts. The Preparatory School is situated on the same campus in a new building of its own.

The Curriculum up to the age of 13 is common for all, with no streaming or setting. From the age of 11 in addition to the usual subjects it includes three Sciences and two foreign languages (French and one chosen from German, Spanish and Latin). From the age of 13, subjects are taught in sets, but there are no major choices of subjects until the age of 15 and all boys follow a full 5-year secondary course before they may enter the VIth Form on completion of the GCSE examination. In the VIth Form students study four subjects to AS in the Lower VIth, narrowing to three A2 subjects in the Upper VIth. The School takes seriously its commitment to General Studies; this non-examined part of the curriculum occupies 10% of the week in both Upper and Lower VIth. Boys are entered for the GCE examination at 'A' level at the age of 18 and are prepared for entry to degree courses at Universities. The wide scope of the School's curriculum gives ample opportunity for all its boys whether preparing for University, for a profession, for the services, or for commerce or industry. The Careers Department has its own modern facilities, and careers advice is readily available to parents and to boys.

Forms. In the Preparatory School there are 2 forms in each age-group, and in the Main School 6 forms in 1st and 2nd Years with approximately 25 boys in each form. There are 12 forms in the 3rd Form (Year 9) each with about 14 boys. 4th and 5th Form boys (Years 10 and 11) are divided amongst 18 forms each with 17-18 boys. The usual size of teaching groups in the VIth Form is about 10–15.

Religious Education. The School is by tradition a Church of England school, but there are no religious barriers to entry and no quotas. It is part of the ethos of the School that all its members respect the deeply-held beliefs and faith of other members. The School Chaplain is available to, and holds responsibility for, all boys in the School of whatever faith. He prepares for Confirmation those who wish it, and there are weekly celebrations of Holy Communion and an annual Carol Service in St Albans Abbey. The morning assembly and class teaching, however, are non-denominational in character.

Physical Education. A wide variety of sports is available, including Athletics, Badminton, Basketball, Cricket, Cross-country running, Fencing, Golf, Gymnastics, Hockey, Rugby Football, Sailing, Soccer, Squash, Shooting, Swimming, Tennis, Table Tennis and Water-polo. All boys are expected to take part in physical education unless exempt on medical grounds.

Out of School Activities. The extensive range includes a period of 1½ hours on Friday afternoon when boys can choose one of a large variety of activities of a service nature. This includes Community Service, both on the School campus and among those who need help in the surrounding district. It also includes the Combined Cadet Force which has Navy, Army and Air Force sections.

Music and Drama both have a prominent place in the School. The Music School has a Recital Hall and some 12 other rooms; 21 visiting instrumental teachers between them teach 500 instrumental pupils each week covering all the normal orchestral instruments together with Piano and Organ. There is a Choir of 250, and several orchestras. For Drama the facilities include a generously equipped stage and a separate Drama Room with its own lighting and stage equipment.

School Societies. School Societies and expeditionary activities in term time and holidays include Amnesty, Archery, Art, Badminton, Bridge, Canoeing, Chess, Choral, Classical, Crosstalk, Debating, Duke of Edinburgh's Award, Dramatics, English, Football, History, Jazz, Jewish Soc., Life-saving, Life Drawing, Model Railway, Modern Languages, Mountaineering, Philosophical, Photography, Politics, Puzzles and Games, Rifle, Sailing, Science, Squash, Stamp Club, Windsurfing.

The Old Haberdashers' Association (*Hon Sec:* Roger Lyle) provides a focal point for boys after they have left school.

Transport. A private bus service is provided from some 109 pick-up points, to enable boys to attend the School from a wide area, and to remain for after-School activities.

Admission. Boys are admitted only at the beginning of the school year in September, except on transfer from a school in another area. They may be admitted at the age of 7 and may remain in the School until the end of the academic year in which the age of 19 is attained, subject to satisfactory progress at each stage of the course and to compliance with the School Rules currently in force. Approximately 50 boys are admitted at age 7 each year, approximately 100 at age 11, approximately 25 at age 13 and small numbers at 16. There are competitive examinations including written and oral tests of intelligence, literacy and numeracy at the ages of 7 and 11, held in January for admission in the following September. Applicants aged 13 also take examinations at the beginning of January and are interviewed later in the month for entry in September. At 16 admission is by GCSE and interview. An Open Day for prospective parents is held each year early in October.

A small number of Scholarships are awarded annually to pupils entering the Main School. Music Scholarships are awarded each year to candidates showing special promise in music. Governors Bursaries are open to all pupils entering the Main School; they are based upon financial need.

Full details of all these awards are included in the prospectus available from the Headmaster's Secretary at the School who is glad to answer enqquiries.

Alternatively you can request a prospectus on-line from our website which is: http://www.habs.herts.sch.uk.

Fees. Registration Fee £50; Termly Fees: Tuition £2,550 (Preparatory Forms £2,350); Piano, Organ and Orchestral Instruments (optional) £128; Orchestral classes £82; Aural classes £36.

Honours. In 2000, 34 pupils gained places at Oxford and Cambridge, and approximately 115 gained places at other Universities.

Charitable status. The Haberdashers' Aske's School is a Registered Charity, number 313996. It exists to provide education for boys.

Haileybury

Hertford SG13 7NU.
Tel: Reception – (01992) 462507
The Master – (01992) 706222
The Bursar – (01992) 462507
The Registrar – (01992) 463353
Fax: (01992) 470663
Motto: *Fear God. Honour the King. Sursum Corda*

Visitor: The Most Revd and Rt Hon the Lord Archbishop of Canterbury

President of the Council: The Rt Revd the Lord Bishop of St Albans

Council:
R M Abel-Smith
Mrs D Adams
The Revd R W Bowen, MA
Dr C B Challacombe, MB, BS, MRCS, LRCP
The Revd J Cresswell
Mrs M Evans, MA
M J Freegard
R D Galpin
Sir Alan Hardcastle, FCA
The Revd Dr E Hebblethwaite
D F MacLeod
Sir Bruce MacPhail, MA, MBA, FCA
I H McCorquodale, MA
A Oliver, MA
G C Smith, MA
G W Staple, CB, QC
Mrs A Templeman, MA, DipTh
J D Thornton, BSc (Hons), MA, CEng, MICE, MCIOB
Major General T P Toyne Sewell, DL
The Rt Hon Lord Trefgarne, PC
S W Urry, LLB, FCA

Secretary and Bursar: J B Palmer, BSc, CEng, FIMechE

***Master:* S A Westley**, MA

Second Master: The Revd J S Pullen, MA, BSc

Senior Master: R L Turnbull, MA

Senior Mistress: Mrs T Macpherson-Smith, BHum

Staff:
L S Bookless, MA (*Classics*)
I R Williams, MA, DPhil
D P Wright, BA, CPhil
R R Campling, BA
P R Woodburn, BSc (*Head of Science*)
W H Flint Cahan, MA (*Modern Languages*)
B W Thomas, MSc, DPhil
P C T Monk, MA
N Athey, MA (*Director of Technology*)
N Jardine, MA (*English*)
R H Bishop, BSc, MA (*Economics*)
Mrs J Howard, BSc
I J Pinnington, BA
Mrs A R B Spavin, MSc
A S Bartholomew, BEd, MA, FRGS
M W G Goff, BA (*Religious Studies*)
Mrs F A Ronald, BEd
V P Strike, BEd (*Physical Education*)
D J Ross, MA (*Director of Drama*)
Mrs P J Ross, BA
D Pyle, BA, AKC (*Head of the Lower School*)
M D Grant, MA, PhD (*Universities Adviser*)
B W Williams Jones, BA (*Design & Technology*)
I K George, DipPE
P F Johns, BEd
D R A Harvey, MSc, DPhil (*Mathematics*)
C B Hurley, MA
Mrs E Harvey, BA (*Librarian*)
P J Greer, MA (*Geography*)
R W Brown, BA (*Careers*)
Mrs P Crook, BSc (*Physics*)
T Woffenden, MA (*Director of Studies*)
Mrs C J Gandon, BA
S J George, BSc, MPhil
Mrs N A Huggett, BA
Mrs F A Hughes, BSc, PhD
H H Robinson, BSc
A Box, MA
Miss K J Adam, BA
J A C Phillips, BEng
A M Goldsmith, BA
J Kean, BA
Mrs R E Keys, MA (*IB Co-ordinator*)
I E W Sanders, BSc
T P Newman, BSc
J R Standing, BA (*Psychology*)
N Adams, BSc
J F Alliott, BSc
Mrs N L M Plewes, BSc
C E Igolen-Robinson, BA
J R Jennings, BSc
C D Jones, MA (*History*)
R L Matcham, BEd
Ms S N Piegelin, Md'A
Miss C Johnson, BSc
J H Kazi, BA
J G Pearson-Phillips, BA (*Art*)
I A Sheldon, MChem
M A Perrins, BA (*Politics*)
Miss T S R Smith, BA
M S Elliot, MA, PhD
S J Dixon, BA (*Chemistry*)
Ms S Beales, BA
Mrs M J Brooking, BEd
Mrs C J Kean, BSc
J O Bell, BSc
Miss J N M Burge, BSc
Mrs H E George, BA
M P J Wright, BA
Revd C R Briggs, BD, AKC (*Senior Chaplain*)
E R L Bond, BA
Miss N C Powell, BSc
Mrs A J Grant, BA
Mrs C C Robinson

Music Teaching Staff:
P Davis, BA, ARCO (*Director of Music*)
D H Longman, BA, MMus, FRCO
W H Bowman, BA
Z W Dunbar, BA, MMus
and 15 Visiting Musicians

Instructors:
H R Angus, MBE, MA (*Rackets*)
WO 2 (*SSI*) H Slater, RA (*CCF*)
Cricket Professional: G Howarth, OBE

Houses and Housemasters/Housemistresses:
Albans: Mrs J Howard
Allenby: Mrs N A Huggett
Bartle Frere: Mr P F Johns
Batten: Mr I K George
Colvin: Dr F A Hughes
Edmonstone: Mr A S Bartholomew
Hailey: Mr I J Pinnington
Kipling: Mr R L Matcham
Lawrence: Mr H H Robinson
Melvill: Mrs A R B Spavin
Thomason: Mr I E W Sanders
Trevelyan: Mr P C T Monk

The Russell Dore Lower School: Mr D Pyle

Registrar: N J C Gandon, BA

Number in School: 657.

Location. Haileybury is situated 20 miles due north of central London and 2 miles east of Hertford. It is easily accessible by motorway and train to and from London and its airports. The school's 500 acre rural campus, with all its facilities and magnificent grounds on a single site, makes Haileybury unique.

History. Many of its buildings were designed by William Wilkins in the early 1800s for the East India Company's training college. The East India College was closed in 1858 after the Mutiny and re-opened as a school in 1862. During the Second World War the Imperial Service College at Windsor was amalgamated with Haileybury to become Haileybury and ISC, but to all intents and purposes our school is known simply as Haileybury. The old Imperial Service Junior School at Windsor served as Haileybury's junior school until 1997 prior to its amalgamation with Lambrook School in Bracknell.

Co-education. Since 1973 Haileybury has welcomed girls into its Sixth Form. In 1997 the Council took the decision to admit additionally girls aged 11 and 13 with effect from September 1998. By the year 2001 there will be girls in every year at Haileybury, making up 37% of the school roll.

Student Profile. Pupils can join at three levels: 11 year olds enter the Lower School, which has an annual intake of 48 and is a distinct unit within the main school. The majority of pupils join at 13, while a number of girls and boys arrive at 16 to study AS and A Levels and the IB diploma. Just over 60% of pupils are boarders. Approximately 17% are from overseas.

Campus Life. Pupils joining at 11 enjoy the benefits of self-contained teaching and recreational space on campus together with access to all the specialist facilities of the senior school. Newly refurbished, small dormitory style boarding accommodation exists exclusively for under 13 year olds.

All accommodation for 13 to 18 year olds is centred around the Quadrangle and Houses are either recently built, or are newly refurbished older buildings to provide high-quality living and working conditions. In the Fifth Form pupils can expect to share a room; in their final two Sixth Form years they usually enjoy a single room. room.

Three existing girls' houses will be supplemented by a fourth in 2001.

Day pupils join members of the boarding community to form houses that total roughly 50 in number. They are expected to remain in school until 6.30 pm each working day, although they are welcome to stay longer if they choose. By arrangement with their housemaster and housemistress they may stay overnight. This flexibility allows for an easy transition into boarding, an option that increasing numbers of day pupils choose.

Welfare. The provision of a stimulating, caring environment in which all pupils can thrive is at the heart of our school. This is primarily achieved through open communication with children and their parents, vigilance and common sense, underpinned by our responsibilities under The Children Act.

Children in the Lower School have the supervision, support and help of a team of tutors whose pastoral role at Haileybury is dedicated to them. Once they join a House at 13 a pupil's housemaster or housemistress undertakes prime responsibility for his or her care and should be regarded as the first point of contact for pupils and parents alike. Housemasters and housemistresses are supported by teams of tutors, each with an important pastoral role, from the teaching staff.

A full-time doctor is resident at school to attend to all medical and health education matters from the Sanatorium. Together with the Chaplains and a School Counsellor, he is available to listen and counsel pupils confidentially as they grow towards maturity.

Tuition and Curriculum. Our students are taught in small groups: 16 during years 7 and 8 in the Lower School, 20 or fewer from Years 9 to 11. 'A' Level and IB classes average about 10-12, and never exceed 15. Pupils' progress is formally monitored by means of three-weekly reports and regular tutorials. Furthermore, teachers are constantly in touch with tutors, housemasters and housemistresses to keep all involved up to date with every pupil's performance.

All pupils have ready access to computers and there is dedicated teaching in their use for younger pupils. A computer leasing scheme exists enabling families to spread costs if they are investing in their own equipment, whilst providing a range of options covering use of equipment at school and home.

In a school that is reasonably selective but not highly selective, the principles of stretching the most able and encouraging those in need of particular support apply. As such pupils are 'setted' and 'fast-tracked' on grounds according to ability, where this is deemed appropriate. Years 7 and 8 study English, Mathematics, Biology, Physics, Chemistry, Design Technology, Information Technology, History, Geography, French, Latin and Classical Civilisation, Art, Drama, Religious Studies and PE. Homework is set daily and the day pupils are able to complete it with supervision before going home.

Core elements of the Year 9 programme are Mathematics, the three Sciences, English, History, Geography, French, Art, Music, Religious Studies, Technology and Physical Education. Two options are chosen from: German or Spanish, Latin, Greek, Classical Civilisation, Drama, extra English or extra French. A programme of PHSE and Information Technology continues throughout the year. Weekly Religious Studies classes are part of the school curriculum.

GCSE courses begin in Year 10. Most pupils will study 10 subjects. The most able will be encouraged to take these examinations early, especially in Mathematics and Modern Languages.

In addition to the AS/A level courses, the IB (International Baccalaureate) Diploma is also offered at Sixth Form to a maximum of 40 pupils.

In the Sixth Form pupils usually choose four AS followed by 3 A Levels in the Upper Sixth from a range of 26 subjects arranged in five groups. Almost all Haileybury leavers proceed to university. A full university and careers advice is continually available and the school is a member of the Independent Schools Careers Organisation.

Out of Class Activities. The principles of a rounded education demand access to rich and varied opportunities. Haileybury provides these in many ways:

Games.

The girls play Lacrosse, Hockey and Netball in the two winter terms and choose between Tennis, Athletics and Swimming in the summer. Boys and girls have regular access to our new indoor swimming pool enabling swimming to be enjoyed both as a leisure activity and as a competitive sport. The main boys' game in the Christmas term is Rugby Football. In the winter months there is also provision for Rackets, Squash, Basketball, Cross Country, Fencing and Judo.

Soccer and Hockey are the main games in the Easter term, and Cricket in the Summer term. In the summer there is also the option of Athletics, Tennis, Swimming, Shooting, Sailing, Rowing and Golf.

The Sports Hall provides excellent facilities for all indoor games, including two indoor tennis courts and for all forms of personal training. The floodlit Astroturf pitch was added in 1990 to provide for Tennis (12 courts) in the summer and for Hockey in the winter.

Activities. School societies and activities flourish, either in the evenings after prep or during set activity times. The Design Technology Centre offers computing, electronics, metalwork, plastics and woodwork, with an emphasis on design and 'hands-on' skills.

Drama at Haileybury has always been strong and there are usually at least 12 productions during the year. There are two venues, the Ayckbourn Theatre providing fully equipped studio facilities, and the larger auditorium in Big School, with a computerised lighting system. The major production of the Easter term is taken on tour to Europe.

The School's musical life is exceptionally lively. The musicians, like our actors, perform outside Haileybury regularly. The Chapel Choir and Chamber Orchestra perform annually at St Martin-in-the-Fields and recent tours have included performances in Venice and Barcelona. The installation of our new Chapel organ has provided a magnificent focal point for music here.

The Art School is an exciting and creative department producing very high standards. In a separate purpose built area, it has extensive facilities for work in fine art, design and ceramics and it stages regular exhibitions including the annual Speech Day exhibition.

A popular but voluntary CCF exists for pupils who join initially for two years in order to take advantage of the specialist courses, shooting and adventure training. There is an indoor .22 rifle range. Alternatives to the CCF are the Duke of Edinburgh Award scheme and Community service programmes.

Expeditions have taken place recently to Nepal and Venezuela.

Admission. Pupils can join at 11, 13 and 16. Eleven year olds are asked to complete standardised tests in English, Mathematics and Reasoning to supplement assessments from their current school. Boys and girls joining at 13 are asked to sit Haileybury's own entrance examinations or Common Entrance. Children joining the school at 11 usually gain entry to the main school at 13 automatically.

Sixth Form entry for girls and boys is by test and interview. The selection procedure takes place at Haileybury in November and again in February.

All enquiries and applications for admission should be addressed to the Registrar who is happy to discuss any aspect of the admissions procedure, and from whom details regarding visits and of Open Days are available.

Entrance Scholarships. (*see* Entrance Scholarship section) Many generous Scholarships are available. Academic and All Rounder Awards are available for 11, 13 and 16 year old entrants. Music and Art awards are also available to 13 and 16 year olds. In addition, there are some specially founded Scholarships which are awarded as they fall vacant.

Scholarships may be awarded for outstanding work in a single subject or for a high general standard. They can be made up to the value of 50% of school fees and are tenable for the whole of the pupil's career at Haileybury.

Fees. The inclusive fee is £16,440 pa for boarders. The fee for day pupils is £11,895 pa. The fee for 11-13 year old day pupils is £7,785 pa and £10,530 for boarders. There is a registration fee of £40, a refundable deposit of £500 and an entrance fee of £45 for boarders, £30 for day pupils. Books and stationery are charged as extras and there are extra charges for music lessons, private tuition and for some of the summer sports.

Bursaries. There are Trust Funds from which Bursaries may be awarded to increase the value of any Scholarship in case of genuine financial need. Application for a Bursary entails confidential disclosure of capital and income of the parents, for which purpose a form may be obtained from the Registrar.

Charitable status. Haileybury is a Registered Charity, number 310013. It exists to provide education for boys and girls.

Hampton School

Hanworth Road Hampton Middlesex TW12 3HD.
Tel: 020 8979 5526
Fax: 020 8941 7368
website: http://www.hampton.richmond.sch.uk

Founded in 1556 by Robert Hammond, a Hampton merchant, and re-established in 1612. From 1910 the School was administered by the local authority, latterly as a voluntary aided school, but in 1975 reverted to independent status.

Motto: *Praestat opes sapientia.*

The Governing Body:

Chairman: Prof M J H Sterling, BEng, PhD, DEng, FEng, FIEE, FInstMC, FRSA

Vice-Chairmen:
L R Llewellyn, Esq, BSc, MBA, FCMA
A H Munday, Esq, LLB, QC

P Baker, Esq, BSc, FRSA
M Deere, Esq, BSc(Eng), ACGI, CEng, FIMechE, FRSA
Prof J S Higgins, MA, DPhil, CChEm, FRSC, FIM, CEng, FRS
Mrs E G Jessel
B H May, Esq, BSc
P E Mee, Esq, MBE, TD, BSc(Econ)
A H Munday, Esq, LLB, QC
D C Peters, Esq, MA, MBA
The Revd J E Platt, MA, MTh, DPhil
M F Savage, Esq, FCIS
The Revd D N Winterburn, BSc, MA, Vicar of Hampton
Cllr B Woodriff, BA (Hons), PGCE, MEd, MBA, LTCL, FRSA

Clerk to the Governors and Bursar: E H Barker, CBE, MA

***Headmaster:* B R Martin**, MA, MBA, FIMgt, FRSA

Deputy Headmasters:
A R Stranks, BSc
S Paraskos, MA

Senior Tutors:
N L Francis, BSc
Miss P Z M S Message, BSc
J P Orr, MA

M G Acher, BA
Miss C L Albion, BEd
*S R Alexander, BA, PhD
W Bailey, MISM
A J Bannister, BA
A Barnett, BSc
C J Barnett, MA
*B S Bett, BA, MA
R Bigwood, GRSM, ARCM, MMus
S Bird, BA
B G Blyth, BA
C M Bond, MA
Mrs H Booker, BA
R J Boulton, BA
Miss F A Boylan, BA
A B Brook, BA
M R Bryan, BA
Mrs A Burke, BA
D R Clarke, BHum
P A Coleman, BSc
*A J Cook, MA
T P Cooper, BSc
*J S Coulter, BSc
G D C Creagh, BA
R D Crew, BSc
M Cross, BA
*Mrs P A Croucher, BA, MA
*C G Cullen, MA
R J Davieson, BSc
*I C Donald, BA
*Miss K F Dore, BA, MSc
D J N Fendley, BEng
D Fisher, BSc
†C J Flood, MA
Miss C E Fowler, BA

*N L Francis, BSc
M Franzkowiak, BEd
A T W Frazer, BA, MA
G S Galloway, MA
R J Gill, MA
*M P Godfrey, BA, MEd
E Gordo Garcia, BA
Mrs A E Gray, BA
F A Hall, BSc
J D Hamm, BEng
R G R Harris, MSc, PhD
Mrs G Haskell, BSc, MSc
S T Hill, BA
S J Huxtable, MA
D P Hyde, BMus, ALCM
M Jelley, BA
E J Kendall, BA
D J Kenney, BSc
D Keyworth, BSc, MSc
Mrs W King, DipAD
D Knapman, BA, BSc
†Mrs P M Kyle, BSc
P H Langton, BSc, DipEnvSci
*T J Leary, BA, PhD
A McBay, BSc, MSc
*I L Maclean, MA
D Martucci, HNC
I McMechan, BA, MA
J Medcraft, BSc
C T Mills, BSc
Miss S C D Nicolle, BA
Mrs A M Novo-Abad
J G Owen, BSc
Mrs A M Payne, PhD
M Payne, BA, MA
J E G Pile, BA
Miss V E Preston, BSc
†K A Rice, BA
D J Ridings, BSc
J R Rugg, BA
*J Sadler, BSc
C D Salkield, BSc
*R J Sims, BA
J D Slater, BA
C R Smalman-Smith, BA
J A Spencer, BSc, PhD
*G A Stone, MA, MIL
P J Talbot, MA
Ms J C Taylor, BA
*S Timbs, BA
*M Tompsett, BA
P G Turner, BA
R T Vyvyan, MBA
†Mrs E T Watson, BA
E M Wesson, MA
S A Wilkinson, BA
Mrs K A Williams, BA
Miss K L Woolley, BA
R D Worrallo, MA
M D Xiberras, MA
*J W Zablocki, BSc

Librarian:
Mrs K M McCartney, PhilCand, DipLib, DipEd, ALA

Facilities Manager: M A King, BSc

Hampton is a day school of about 1,000 boys from 11 to 18 years old, including a VIth Form of about 300. The School offers an academic education, combining the traditional and modern, within a tolerant but ordered community; considerable importance is attached to participation in a wide range of voluntary extra-curricular activities during the mid-day break and after school hours.

Buildings and Grounds. The main School buildings include an Assembly Hall, a new Dining Hall, Sports Hall, classrooms, and a full set of laboratories for the separate sciences, technology, information technology, and languages.

The School is fortunate enough to stand in its own grounds of some 25 acres, which afford ample space for playing fields; at present there are three rugby pitches, five football pitches, four cricket squares and six hard tennis courts.

The Garrick Building, opened by Edward Heath MP in 1978, provides specialist music accommodation, a drama hall, and additional teaching rooms.

Opened in 1980 by Sir Hermann Bondi FRS, the Grundy Technology Centre includes provision for practical work in metal, plastics, wood and pneumatics, as well as a drawing-office, a large project space, a dark-room and an applied science laboratory for electronics and control technology.

The Mason Library was opened in 1984 by Lord Dacre (the historian Hugh Trevor-Roper); professionally staffed, it houses an ever-increasing stock of books and journals, supplemented by other information retrieval facilities such as CD ROM.

The Steedman Sports Hall, named after a former Chairman of Governors, was formally opened by Sir Roger Bannister in December 1987. Designed as a centre for the development of personal fitness as well as for sports training and recreation, it offers facilities for a wide range of physical activity.

The Alexander Centre was opened in 1994 and accommodates the Woolfson Department of History together with three common rooms and a quiet work room for the Sixth Form. The north side of the building houses pavilion and changing room facilities for cricket. The Shepherd lecture theatre, fully equipped and seating 150, adjoins the Centre. A new Computer Room (equipped with a network of 27 PCs) and a new Careers Department were established within the main building at the same time.

New Dining Rooms and kitchens were opened in September 1997. An extension to the main building, completed in December 1998, provides a language laboratory and a second networked computer room. A new boathouse, new laboratories and art studios will be completed by early 2001. Other projects for the future include extensions to the Sports Hall and additional provision for music and drama.

A massive new extension was completed in 2000 to provide additional laboratories, and to house art, geography, classics, economics and business studies.

Admission. About 100 boys a year are admitted at 11 by the School's own entrance examination. A further 50 enter at 13 through the Common Entrance Examination. Boys are also admitted into the VIth Form and to fill casual vacancies at other ages.

Term of Entry. Boys normally join the School in September.

Curriculum. Boys in the Lower School follow a wide syllabus including Technology, Physics, Chemistry, Biology, French and Latin. Greek, German, Russian and Spanish are optional subjects begun in the third year. In the fourth and fifth years all boys continue to study, in addition to PE, Games and RS, English Language, English Literature, French, Mathematics and the three sciences for GCSE and choose 3 other subjects from Art, Drama, Geography, German, Greek, History, Latin, Music, Religious Studies, Russian, Spanish and Technology. Most of these GCSEs are taken at the end of the fifth year.

The VIth Form offers virtually free choice of 3 'A' level subjects (in some cases 4) as well as a wide range of courses leading to 'A' level General Studies and a considerable choice of AS levels. Special teaching is provided for boys seeking entrance to Oxford or Cambridge.

Organisation. A boy's form tutor is responsible in the first instance for his welfare and progress, and the work of form tutors is co-ordinated by year heads under the Headmaster's general direction. Parents are always welcome to discuss their son's work with any of these tutors, and Parents' Evenings provide an opportunity to meet subject teachers. There is also a lively Parents' Association.

Careers. Each boy is individually interviewed by the Careers staff at least 3 times during his school life; in particular guidance is freely available to both boys and parents at those points where subject choices must be made. The School is also a member of ISCO. A Careers evening is held annually.

Games. Games and Physical Education are part of every boy's school week, though other activities are permissible alternatives in the VIth Form. Many boys also take part in voluntary sport on Saturdays when representative fixtures are arranged for each age group. Generally boys are able to choose freely which sport to follow. In winter, the major games are Rugby, Association Football and Rowing; in summer, Cricket, Athletics and Rowing. Other sports include Tennis, Real Tennis, Squash, Sailing and Swimming.

Societies. The voluntary CCF contingent, run jointly with The Lady Eleanor Holles School, comprises Army and RAF sections and has a programme which includes adventurous training, orienteering and gliding. Boys may also participate in the Duke of Edinburgh's Award scheme or the activities of the School's Adventure Society, which organises camps and expeditions both in the UK and overseas.

The Service Volunteers offer practical help and friendship to the disadvantaged, especially the handicapped and the elderly.

The Music Society fosters solo and ensemble performance as well as composition, and offers a platform to the School orchestras and bands; the Choral Society gives several concerts each year; there is at least one dramatic production each term, and occasionally an opera. In all these activities, as in the Service Volunteers' work, the School enjoys close co-operation with the neighbouring Lady Eleanor Holles Girls' School.

There is also a full range of subject and hobby societies, among which Chess, Debating and the Astronomy Society are particularly strong.

Scholarships and Exhibitions. (*see* Entrance Scholarship section) At present, at 11 the Governors offer 5 open academic scholarships and two Hammond Scholarships (geographically restricted). At 13 at least three academic Scholarships and two Exhibitions are offered through the School's Scholarship examinations. All rounder and sports awards may be available at 11 and 13.

Instrumental music Scholarships (including free instrumental tuition) are offered at both levels. The Chapel Royal Choral Scholarship is available for boys of 11 with treble voices who are, or will become, choristers of the Chapel Royal at Hampton Court. These Scholarships remit one-third of school fees.

The School has a Bursary Fund.

Fees. The tuition fees from September 1998 are £1,920 per term inclusive of books and stationery.

Old Hamptonian Association. Leavers are normally entitled to free life membership of this Association which has active sporting and dramatic sections. The OHA Office is located at the School

Charitable status. Hampton School is a Registered Charity, number 312667. It aims to provide a challenging and demanding education for boys of high academic promise from the widest possible variety of social backgrounds.

Harrow School

Harrow on the Hill Middlesex HA1 3HW
Telephone: 020 8872 8000
Head Master: 020 8872 8003
Fax: 020 8423 3112 (School) 020 8872 8012 (Headmaster)
e-mail: admin@harrowschool.org.uk

Harrow School was founded in 1572 by John Lyon, yeoman, of Preston, in the parish of Harrow, under a Royal Charter from Queen Elizabeth.

Motto: *Donorum Dei Dispensatio Fidelis.*

Visitors:
The Archbishop of Canterbury
The Bishop of London

Governors:

Sir Michael Connell, MA (*Chairman*)
P R Siddons, MA, FCA (*Deputy Chairman*)
J Hopkins, MA, LLB
Professor M M Edwards
P M Beckwith, MA
H V Reid
Professor D M P Mingos, BSc, DPhil, FRS
Mrs G M Baker, BEd
N W Stuart, CB, MA
F R F Singer
R C Compton
Mrs A R Longley, MA
Major General Sir Timothy Granville Chapman, CBE, KCB
D J L Fitzwilliams, MA
T H Walduck, MA
The Hon Mrs I Danilovich, BA
J A Strachan, BSc, FRICS
J F R Hayes, MA, FCA

Clerk to the Governors: A J F Stebbings, MA, 45 Pont Street, London SW1X 0BX

***Head Master:* B J Lenon**, MA

Second Master: J R Beckett, OBE, MA

Third Master: A S Lee, MA

Bursar: N A Shryane, MBE, BA, MPhil

Assistant Staff:

J A Smith, MA
M J Duncan, BSc (*Organisation Master*)
M Thain, BA, MSc
P A G Stilwell, BA
T G Hersey, BSc
F W Dalton, BSc, PhD
R G Collins, MA (*Registrar*)
M T Bruce-Lockhart, MA
A H M Thompson, MA
D R Elleray, BA (*Director of Boarding*)
I W Farrell, MA, DPhil (*Director of Studies*)
A Jaggs (*Head of Design Technology*)
J P M Baron, MA
C J Deacon, MA
R D Burden, BSc
J E Holland, BA, PhD, MLitt
M E Smith, MA
P G Dunbar, MA
W Snowden, BA
S J Halliday, BA
R M Uttley, OBE, MA, MEd (*Head of Games*)
M G Tyrrell, MA (*Head of Drama*)
A J F Alban, BEd
P J Bieneman, BSc
J A R Braham, BA (*Head of Art*)
W J McKinney, MA
P J Warfield, BA
S F MacPherson, MA
J L Ing, BEd
P D Hunter, MA
S P Berry, MA
M L Mrowiec, MA
A R McGregor, MA
C J Tyerman, MA, DPhil, FRHistS
D S Dawes, BSc, BA
C D Barry, BSc
M P Stead, MA
The Rev J E Power, BSc, BA
C J Farrar-Bell, MA
C V Davies, BSc
D A Luckett, BA, DPhil (*Head of History*)
R H Porter, MA, MBA
J P Turner, BSc
Mrs P G Davies, BSc, PhD (*Head of Mathematics*)
A D Todd, BA, MPhil
D Swift, MA (*Head of Modern Languages*)
M J Tremlett, BA
C A Baker, BSc
N J Marchant, BEng (*Head of ICT*)
J Medlicott, BSc
Mrs L A Moseley, BA
Miss J P Affleck, BA (*Head of Classics*)
N C Hulme, BA, MA (*Head of Spanish*)
M J M Ridgway, BSc (*Head of Biology*)
A J Howard, BSc
J M O'Brien, MA
M J Swift, BSc
Miss K M Fleming, BA
D N Burov
Revd Mrs V L Baron, MA, BSc
Mrs A M Cannon, BA, MA
Mrs C R Leder, MA
S N Page, BEd
G S Wilson, BSc
P J Weir, MA
T A C N Dawson, MA
G A Forrest, MA
T Wickson, BA, MEd, AMBDA
The Revd A R Wadsworth, MA, GTCL, LRAM (*Roman Catholic Chaplain*)
G D Cooke, BEd, MSc (*Director of Computing Services*)
I R Gray, BSc, PhD (*Head of Physics*)
I Hammond, BSc
O J Peers, BA
B J D Shaw, BA
D Atkins, MSc, BSc (*Head of Business Studies and Economics*)
E H B Sie, BSc, PhD (*Head of Chemistry*)
K M Wilding, BA (*Head of Geography*)
C J Lee, BA
N Page, BA
A K Metcalfe, BA
O J H Gooch, BA
C Openshaw, BA
R B Corthine, MA

M R Amherst Lock, BA, MA (*Head of English*)
Miss A L Wall, BA (*Head of Religious Studies*)
Miss H T Painter, BA
Miss J S L Salley, BA
E W Higgins, BSc
S M Griffiths, BA

Music Staff:
R H Walker, MA, FRCO (*Director of Music*)
P J Evans, BA (*Assistant Director of Music*)
D N Burov (*Head of Strings*)

and 27 visiting teachers

Librarian: Mrs M Knight, ALA, MIInsf.Sc

Careers Master: R H Porter

Officer Commanding CCF: Major J L Ing

School Medical Officer:

Houses:
Bradbys (*Mr P G Dunbar*)
The Grove (*Mr P J Bieneman*)
Rendalls (*Mr M L Mrowiec*)
The Park (*Mr P D Hunter*)
West Acre (*Mr M E Smith*)
The Knoll (*Mr A H M Thompson*)
Druries (*Mr D R Elleray*)
The Head Master's (*Mr J P M Baron*)
Elmfield (*Dr J E Holland*)
Moretons (*Mr S P Berry*)
Newlands (*Mr R D Burden*)

Boarding Houses. There are eleven boarding houses, and a major programme for their refurbishment is now complete. In all houses boys have their own bed sitting rooms, usually shared with one other pupil in the first and second years.

The School estates, on and around the Hill, extend to over 300 acres. They include cricket and football fields, athletics track and sports hall (with indoor swimming pool), golf course and farm. Apart from the Science Schools there is a Design Technology Centre which caters for GCSE and A level courses as well as extra-curricular work. The strong CCF contingent has RN, RM, Army and RAF sections.

Admission. Application for admission should be made to the Registrar. Boys are admitted between the age of 12 and 14, but preferably in the September before their fourteenth birthday. Most candidates take the Common Entrance Examination at their Preparatory Schools usually in the term preceding entrance to Harrow. There are also occasional vacancies for Sixth Form boys.

Registration. A Registration Fee of £75 is payable when a boy's name is entered for the school. An application form may be obtained from the Registrar.

Fees. The fee is £5,900 a term. A small number of optional charges are not covered by the consolidated fee (for private tuition in music, for example).

Entrance Scholarships. (*see* Entrance Scholarship section) 25 Scholarships range in value from £500 per annum to half fees and are awarded for excellence in academic work, or music, or art, or for some other talent. These Scholarships may be supplemented where financial need is shown although such supplementable Scholarships are awarded only to boys of high academic or musical ability. Full particulars may be obtained from the Registrar, 1 High Street, Harrow on the Hill, Middlesex HA1 3HW.

Curriculum. On entry all boys take English, French, Latin, History, Geography, Mathematics, Science, Religious Studies, Art, Design and Information Technology, Physical Education and Music. They may also take Greek, German or Spanish. In the next two years a wide-ranging options scheme is introduced leading to GCSE; English, French, Mathematics and at least one Science subject remain compulsory.

In the Upper School, varied programmes (leading to four or more A levels) are arranged to suit the requirements of the universities and of individual boys.

School Societies. These include the Art History Society; Choral Society; Classical Society; Bridge Club; Sailing Club; Geography Society; Scientific Society; '27 Club (for political discussion); Chess Club; Play Reading Society; Film Society; Fishing Club and many more. **The Harrovian** is published weekly in term-time.

A Shakespeare play, produced in the tradition of the Elizabethan stage, is acted every year in Speech Room by members of the School. The Ryan Theatre and drama studio cater for a full programme of dramatic activities.

Old Boys' Society: Harrow Association. *Director:* J D C Vargas, Harrow School, Harrow on the Hill, Middlesex HA1 3HW.

Charitable status. The Keepers and Governors of the Free Grammar School of John Lyon is a Registered Charity, number 310 033. The aims and objectives of the Charity are to provide education for the pupils at the two schools in the Foundation, Harrow School and John Lyon School.

Hereford Cathedral School

Old Deanery The Cathedral Close Hereford HR1 2NG.
Tel: (01432) 363522
Fax: (01432) 363525

Founded ante 1384

Governing Body:

Chairman: The Very Revd Robert Willis, BA, DipTh, FRSA, Dean of Hereford
Vice-Chairman: Mrs M E M Oliver, MA, MLitt

The Revd Canon Paul Iles, MA, FRCO
W S C Richards, Esq, MA
I D L Richardson, Esq, LLB, FCIS, FRSA
T J Gregory, Esq, BA (Econ), ACA, MCT
Dr J S Rowett, MA
G R John, Esq, CBE, BA
J H Chapman, Esq, MA, MSc
Dr L Seal, MB, ChB, DA, DObst, RCOG
Mrs J Warren, LLB
W T Morris (OH)
The Revd Canon J Tiller, MA, MLitt

Clerk to the Governors: F D Langstaff, FCMA, ACIS, MIMgt

***Headmaster:* Dr H C Tomlinson**, BA, FRHistS, FRSA
Deputy Headmaster: G C Rawlinson, MA, MEd

Heads of Department:

Art:
R G Talbot, BA (Fine Art), OUCFA

Biology:
J A Taylor, BSc

Chemistry:
J E Dunn, MA

Classics:
Mrs S G N de Souza, BA

Computing:
R J Toll, BSc

Drama:
Ms L D A Zammit, BEd

English:
C H Gray, MA

Geography:
Mrs L Miles, BSc

History & Economics:
Mrs M A Bigley, BA (*Professional Co-ordinator*)

Mathematics:
P S Thornley, BA

Modern Languages:
M T Jones, MA

Music:
J M Williams, MA, FTCL, ARCO (*Director of Music*)
J H Seymour, BA

Physics:
C J Spencer, MA

Religious Studies:
Revd A P Law, MA (*Chaplain*)

PE and Games:
D G Cummins, BA (*Director of PE/Games*)

Technology:
†R W Clarke, MA, AdvDipEd

Careers Adviser: J H Morris, DGC, MIPD, MICG

OC CCF: Lt Col A K Eames, RM

Bursar: F D Langstaff, FCMA, ACIS, MIMgt

Headmaster's Secretary: Miss E A J Cole

School Secretary: Mrs M R Powell

The Junior School

Headmaster: T R Lowe, CertEd, FCollP
Deputy Headmaster: R I Hall, BSc, CertEd *Science*
Director of Studies: R A Wintle, MSc, MA, MPhil, BEd
Head of Pre-Prep: Miss J A Bunker, BEd

Assistant Staff:
Mrs E A A Ashford, CertEd
Mrs L M Bandtock, BA *English*
Mr T Brown, BA *History, Geography*
Mrs A Dale, CertEd, DipRSASpLd *Special Needs*
Miss C Davies, BEd
Miss K A Davies, BEd
Mrs A F Davis, CertEd
Mrs P Gammage, DipEd
Mr D Grace, BEd, CertEd *Mathematics, Physical Education*
Mr T Hutchinson, BSc (*Information Technology*)
Miss N Jaynes, BEd
Mrs P Lewis, CertEd *French*
Miss L Loveless, BA *Art*
Miss K A Nation, BA
Mrs D J Parry, BA *PSE*
Mrs E A Rhodes, CertEd
Mrs H M Roberts, CertEd
Miss R M Shepherd, BA, MPhil *Music*
Miss A Sutton, BA
Mrs S V Talbot, CertEd
Dr H Tomlinson, BA, CertEd *RE*
Mrs B Walker, CertEd *Head of Nursery*
Mrs R Walker, BA (*Girls' Games*)
Mrs M J Wictome, CertEd

No record of the School's foundation survives, though its close association with the Cathedral is indicated by Bishop Gilbert's response to the long-standing right of the Chancellor to appoint the Headmaster in a letter of 1384, and it is probable that some educational institution was always associated with the Cathedral, which was founded in 676.

The School is a former Direct Grant School, and now offers Assisted Places, taking boy and girl boarders, and day-boys and day-girls, who may be admitted at the ages of 11, 13 or to the VIth Form. Of the School's 630 pupils, some 40 are boarders.

The School is situated in the lee of the Cathedral. It occupies many historic buildings and some later ones, all adapted for School use, as well as purpose-built facilities. On the main campus are, in addition to some of the main departments, eight science laboratories, a large music school an Art, Technology and Computer Centre (that gained Hereford's first RIBA award for architecture), the Gilbert Library, the Dining Hall and the half-timbered Buttery (Tuck Shop). The recent acquisition of the superseded BT Exchange (now the Zimmerman Building) provides 27,000 square feet of robust working space for Modern Languages (moved January 1997), examination/functions hall, Geography and Drama departments and indoor games/cricket school (all in 1997). A new play based on the musical history of the School was commissioned for the opening of the New Studio Theatre in December 1997. The displaced departments allow the continuing expansion of the Junior School, an increase in pastoral rooms and the development of a major library complex, which opened in 1998.

Sports facilities are situated on campus (gymnasium, squash court, indoor cricket nets), by the Cathedral (tennis and netball) and at Wyeside (all major games and HCS rowing club).

Curriculum. Pupils are divided on entry at 11 into 4 parallel forms, and setted from the IInd Forms in some subjects where appropriate. Below the VIth Form all pupils take a normal range of general subjects, including Religious Studies, English, Latin, French, German, Mathematics, Physics, Chemistry, Biology, Computer Studies & Technology, Classical Civilisation, History, Economics, Geography, Drama, Art and Music. Option choices are made at the end of the IIIrd year. In the VIth Form pupils are prepared for the GCE at 'A' and 'S' levels, for entry to Universities and Colleges, and to the Services and other professional or business careers. In the VIth two-thirds of a pupil's time is occupied on Advanced courses, for which there is a wide choice of subjects: Latin, Greek, Ancient History, English, French, German, Theology, Spanish, Economics, History, Geography, Mathematics, Further Mathematics, Biology, Physics, Chemistry, Computer Science, Technology, Art, History of Art, Music and Practical Music, Theatre Studies and Physical Education. AS levels are available in several of these subjects, as are GCSE/AO Electronics, Geology, and French/German for Business. Courses in a wide range of general cultural subjects are a compulsory part of the non-specialist curriculum.

The Religious Instruction throughout is in accordance with the doctrines of the Church of England. The School is privileged to have the daily use of the Cathedral for School Services.

Admission. Pupils are admitted from the age of 11 by sitting the Junior Entrance Examination at the School and at 13 by taking the Common Entrance Examination at their Preparatory Schools, or a Summer Entrance Examination for those not at Preparatory Schools. Suitably qualified boys and girls may be admitted at VIth Form level.

Sports/Activities include Rugby Football, Squash, Cricket, Badminton, Tennis, Hockey, Netball, Athletics and Rowing. There is a CCF and Scout Group and a wide range of societies active within the School. The School is an Operating Authority for the Duke of Edinburgh's Award Scheme. Drama flourishes, with several productions each year.

Music. The school is particularly strong in Music: over 330 pupils receive tuition in the full range of orchestral instruments, piano, organ and classical guitar. There are two orchestras, two concert wind bands, a choral society, chamber choir and two junior choirs, recorder ensembles, and many chamber music groups. There is at least one Musical each year and operas are produced from time to time. The musical tradition is strengthened by the presence of the cathedral choristers in the school.

Fees. Day-pupils: £6,027 pa.

Extras. Scouts £12 per term; CCF/DOE £12 per term; Instrumental Tuition £21.50 per hour.

Scholarships – Tenable at the School. (*see* Entrance Scholarship section)

(a) Cathedral choristers are members of the School from entry. They are accepted from the age of 8 as probationers following voice and educational tests held in November each year, and are educated initially at the Junior School. Choral scholarships are awarded jointly by the Governors and the Chapter annually. Details are available from the Headmaster's secretary.

(b) A number of entrance scholarships may be awarded on the result of the Junior Entrance or Common Entrance Examinations.

(c) Fees concessions are awarded to children of Anglican clergy working in the diocese.

(d) Up to four Music Exhibitions are awarded each year as a result of auditions held in the first half of the Spring Term. 11+, 13+ and Sixth Form Music Scholarships are also available. Details are available from the Director of Music.

Bursaries. A number of bursaries are available to able children from families of limited means.

Old Herefordian Club. *Membership Secretary:* Mike Moffatt. Tel: 01432 363539.

The Junior School. This is situated next door to the main school; for details, please see our separate entry under Preparatory Schools.

Charitable status. Hereford Cathedral School is a Registered Charity, number 518889. Its aims and objectives are to promote the advancement of education by acquiring, establishing, providing, conducting and carrying on residential and non-residential schools in which boys and girls of all sections of the community may receive a sound general education (including religious instruction in accordance with the doctrines of the Church of England).

Highgate School

North Road London N6 4AY
Tel: 020 8340 1524
Fax: 020 8340 7674
e-mail: office@highgateschool.org.uk
website: http://www.highgateschool.org.uk

Highgate School was founded in 1565 by Sir Roger Cholmeley, Knight, Lord Chief Justice, and confirmed by Letters Patent of Queen Elizabeth in the same year.

Motto: *Altiora in votis.*

Visitor: H M The Queen.

Governors:
J F Mills, MA, BLitt (*Treasurer and Chairman*)
Sir Malcolm Field (*Deputy Chairman*)
Mrs J M E MacGregor, JP
J M Rae, MA, PhD
Sir Jeremy Sullivan
B C Russell, MSc, FICE
J H Hill, CBE, MA
The Hon N P G Boardman, BA
R M Rothenberg, BA, FCA
Ms J Carr
The Ven M C Lawson, BA
Mrs C M Roueché, MA, FSA

Bursar and Secretary to the Foundation: J H McGeeney, MA

***Head Master:* R P Kennedy**, MA

Principal Deputy Head: M R Buchanan, BSc

Deputy Heads:
M D Hanley-Browne, MA (*Pastoral*)
Mrs C L Ricks, BA (*Academic*)

Admissions Registrar: T H W Barnikel, BSc

Assistant Staff:

Art:
Mrs H R Tweedale
*G H Tweedale
Miss A M Hastie, BA

Classics:
*D M Fotheringham, MA
†R W Halstead, MA
J E Hegan, BA
W J Lawrence, BA

Design Technology:
*P R Aston, BEd

Economics:
D Amatt, BSc
*S J Grills, BSc, MPhil
P M Lindström, BA

English:
S G Appleton, MA
*G J H Catherwood, BA
R G W Marsh, BA
Mrs C L Ricks, BA
G C Triger, BA

Geography:
*D J Ford, BSc, FRGS
†L A Francis, BA
†G J Hartley, MA, MSc
J R Lewis, BA, PhD, FRGS

History and Politics:
†G R Ferguson, BA
J G Howard, BA, PhD
*P C K Rowe, MA
D J Tabraham-Palmer, MA, MSc

Information Technology:
D H Whittaker, BSc

Mathematics:
K J Baker, BA
J D Jenkins, BSc, PhD
J T H Lo, MMath
J W Partridge, BA
R C Read, MA
S A Whyte, BSc, MSc
J L Williams, BSc, BA
*R C Wilne, MA

Modern Languages:
†S N Brunskill, BA
†Miss C S Jones, BA
†B C Matthews, MA
†Mrs J F Morelle, BA
P-X Pillet, BA, MA
*Miss M R Stiven, BA
Miss C E Walker, BA
T C J Wilding, BA

Music:
M L Bowden, ARCM, FRCO, GRSM, LRAM
*J Q March, BA, FRCO, FTCL (*Director of Music*)
J P Murphy, GRNCM

Physical Education:
S Evans, BA
*G L Williams, DLC

Religious Education:
*The Rev P J J Knight, AIB, DipTheol (*Chaplain*)

Science:
†W J Atkins, BA
T H W Barnikel, BSc
M R Buchanan, BSc
M D Hanley-Browne, MA
*P J Knowles, MA, DPhil
Miss L C MacMaster, BEng
†A W MacPherson, BSc, MSc, PhD
†K M Pullinger, BSc
S W Radford, BA, MSc, MA
†M J Short, BA
*D J Smith, BA, MSc
A Z Szydlo, MSc, PhD
*M R Weaver, MA

Highgate Junior School, Cholmeley House,
3 Bishopwood Road, London N6 4PL
Tel: 020 8340 9193; Fax: 020 8342 8225
e-mail: jsoffice@highgateschool.org.uk

Master of the Junior School: H S Evers, BA

Highgate Pre-Preparatory School
7 Bishopswood Road, London N6 4PH
Tel: 020 8340 9196; Fax: 020 8340 3442
e-mail: pre-prep@highgateschool.org.uk

Principal: Mrs J M Challender, BEd, MA

There are some 600 boys in the Senior School. The Junior School has 370 boys, aged 7 to 13, and prepares boys only for the Senior School. The Pre-Preparatory School has 125 boys and girls aged 3 to 7.

Situation and Grounds. The academic centre of the main School is in the heart of old Highgate, which has retained much of its village atmosphere. In addition to the Victorian buildings, such as the Chapel, Big School and central classrooms, the pupils have the benefit of modern facilities such as Dyne House, devoted mainly to the Arts and containing a 200 seat auditorium, the Garner Building for Mathematics and Information Technology, and the Library, created in 1985 from an early 19th Century Tabernacle.

Highgate underground station, on the Northern line, is a short walk away and there is easy access to the School by car or bus. It is four miles to central London (City or West End).

A few hundred yards along Hampstead Lane in Bishopswood Road lie more than twenty acres of playing-fields together with the Mallinson Sports Centre, indoor swimming pool and other extensive sporting facilities, the dining hall, the Junior School and the Pre-Preparatory School. Hampstead Heath and Kenwood, the largest expanse of open country in London, are adjacent.

Pastoral care. Throughout his time in the Senior School each boy is a member of a House. There are twelve Houses based on particular areas of North London. A boy will find in his House others whom he will see as he travels to school, or at weekends, or near whom he lives. A Housemaster, helped by three tutors, is responsible for monitoring the day-to-day progress and welfare of the fifty or so boys in his care and for liaising with their parents.

Academic Curriculum. Boys joining the Senior School at age 13+ enter the Third Form (Year 9). There are five or six forms of entry and the curriculum is broad. At present, in addition to the usual range of subjects, Art, Music and Technology are taken by all; most take Latin, and for all boys a second modern language is an option. During that year the effects of differing educational background will become less marked and boys will develop an appropriate pattern of work, both in the classroom and out of school. Homework is an integral part of each pupil's programme of study.

The two-year GCSE courses begin in the Fourth Form (Year 10). The core subjects, studied by all, are: English, English Literature, Mathematics, French and double subject Coordinated Sciences (taught by separate teachers of Physics, Chemistry and Biology). A further three subjects are then chosen from: Art, Classical Civilisation, Design Technology, Geography, German, Greek, History, Latin, Music, Spanish and Russian. In addition to their GCSE subjects, all boys take Religious Education and Physical Education. Many subjects require assessed coursework and most syllabuses lead to examinations at the end of the Fifth Form year (Year 11).

The teaching staff are experienced and well-qualified subject specialists and the teacher/pupil ratio is about 1:10. Class sizes are generally in the low twenties up to GCSE, although for some subjects they will be much smaller; in the Sixth Form classes of 6–16 are usual.

Educational resources include a fully equipped audio-visual centre, satellite receiving equipment, a networked computer centre and a large, modern lending library. The use of all these is guided by trained professionals and they complement the facilities available in the academic departments, which have their own specialist teaching rooms, equipment and, where appropriate, technicians, computers and libraries. Fieldwork and visits to galleries, museums, exhibitions and lectures are an integral part of the academic programme.

When they enter the Lower Sixth Form, boys choose four (sometimes three) subjects from the wide range of AS and A level courses on offer. Prospective Sixth-formers are assisted in selecting the best programme of study according to their known ability and future plans. A booklet listing the options available and containing details of the courses is published each year and given to Fifth Formers and their parents before those choices are made.

A feature of the General Studies programme is the weekly presentation by a distinguished visitor: leading men and women in politics, the arts and academic or public life come to Highgate and address the Sixth Form who are joined by the Sixth formers from Channing, the local girls' independent school.

Emphasis is placed on learning to work independently and to develop more advanced study skills. At this stage a boy will for the first time have a number of private reading periods. A Sixth Form Common Room acts as a social and recreational base for senior pupils.

Each Sixth former has a tutor who, in conjunction with the Housemaster, exercises supervision over his general academic progress and who advises on and monitors higher education applications. Highgate is a member of the Independent Schools Careers Organisation.

Religion. Highgate is a Christian foundation but pupils from all faiths and denominations are welcome. Boys attend Chapel once a week, by houses, and there are occasional voluntary celebrations of Holy Communion; Choral Evensong is sung on some Sundays, at which parents are welcome. Greek Orthodox and Roman Catholic services are also held each term and there are weekly meetings of the Jewish Circle and an assembly for boys of other faiths.

Music, Drama and Art. Highgate music has a long and distinguished tradition and many former pupils are now leading composers, conductors or performers. Boys are offered a wide range of musical activities designed both to encourage the beginner and to stimulate and further the skills of the talented musician.

The orchestra and concert choir are often joint ventures with Channing School, and there is also a training orchestra, a wind band and a chapel choir. There are many opportunities for playing chamber music and regular concerts are arranged, together with masterclasses, workshops and an annual house music competition.

Individual music lessons are available with specialist visiting teachers in all the main instruments and in singing. Orchestral instruments can be hired by beginners, who may be offered a free term's trial of lessons. Some of the leading pupils attend the Saturday junior departments at the London music colleges.

Every encouragement is given to boys to participate in drama, as actors, in stage management, or by assisting with sound and lighting. Major productions in recent years have included Cabaret, Amadeus, Guys and Dolls, The Merchant of Venice and Comedy of Errors. Small-scale plays are staged in most terms, some by younger pupils. A separate arts studio provides additional rehearsal and performance space. Regular visits to the professional theatre are also arranged.

The Art department has facilities for painting, printmaking, life drawing, sculpture, pottery, photography, video and computer graphics. Whether taking part in formal classes or working in their free time boys are encouraged to explore their own ways of expressing ideas visually. Boys' work is regularly exhibited, both in the department and elsewhere in the school.

Games. Highgate is exceptionally fortunate in its sport facilities. The extensive playing fields are complemented by the Mallinson Sports Centre and by courts for squash, tennis and Eton fives.

One afternoon each week is devoted to games, in which all boys who are physically fit take part. Teams are selected in each age-group, and also practise at other times. Matches are played on Saturdays as well as during the week. The main games played are association football, cricket, Eton fives, athletics, swimming and cross-country, but a very wide range of other sports is offered at both recreational and competitive level: they include badminton, basketball, canoeing, fencing, golf, gymnastics, hockey, karate, rugby football, sailing, shooting, squash, tennis, volleyball, water polo and weight-training. Countries visited on recent tours by school teams include Holland, Spain and Germany. Many of the magnificent facilities of the fully-staffed Mallinson Sports Centre are also available for family use in the evenings, at weekends and in the holidays.

Activities. We aim to provide as many opportunities as possible in which boys will develop qualities of self-reliance, endurance and leadership, in which they can serve the community and in which they can develop their own interests and enthusiasms. There are a large number of societies and clubs run by the boys, usually meeting in the lunch hour or after school. The School is an operating authority for the Duke of Edinburgh's Award scheme and each year many boys gain the bronze award and often go on to gain the silver and gold awards. There is also a Community Service scheme and an Urban Survival award scheme. One of Highgate's greatest assets is Cerrig Pryfaid, our field centre in Snowdonia with its own Warden, which is used as a base for outdoor activities and for fieldwork.

Admission. Normal entry to the Junior School is at the age of 7; there are some places in other years for older boys, including an entry from Primary Schools at 11. All candidates take an entrance examination in January for entry the following September. Application should be made in writing to the Master of the Junior School, 3 Bishopswood Road, London N6 4PL.

Enquiries about places at Highgate Pre-Preparatory School, for girls and boys aged 3 to 7, should be addressed to the Principal, 7 Bishopswood Road, London N6 4PH.

Half the boys in the Senior School are admitted from Preparatory Schools at the age of 13, following tests and interviews in January before the Common Entrance examination in June. The remainder enter from Highgate Junior School.

Boys from other schools are also admitted to the Sixth Form at Highgate, following interviews and conditional upon satisfactory GCSE results. Only occasionally are there vacancies at other levels of the School. All enquiries concerning admission to the Senior School should be addressed to the Admissions Registrar.

Scholarships, Bursaries and Fees. (*see* Entrance Scholarship section) Foundation Scholarships and Music Scholarships are offered each year to boys who will be under 14 on 1st September. The examinations are held at Highgate at the time of the entry tests in January. Music Scholarship candidates sit a short written examination and are auditioned and interviewed. Many will already be playing to a high standard but those with good potential should also apply. Enquiries to the Director of Music are welcomed. A number of Cholmeley Scholarships and Bursaries are available starting in the Junior School, at age 11, at 13 on entry to the Senior School and in the Sixth Form. Further Bursaries are available through the Friends of Highgate School Society. Details of the fees and of all awards are available from the Admissions Registrar.

Old Cholmeleian Society. Former pupils are known as Old Cholmeleians. Enquiries should be addressed to the Foundation Manager at the School.

Charitable status. The Wardens and Governors of the possessions revenues and goods of the free Grammar School of Sir Roger Cholmeley Knight in Highgate are a Registered Charity, number 312765. The aims and objectives of the charity are educational, namely the maintenance of a school.

The High School of Glasgow

637 Crow Road Glasgow G13 1PL
Tel: 0141-954 9628

The High School of Glasgow was founded as the Grammar School of Glasgow in the 12th century and was closely associated with Glasgow Cathedral. Despite its high standing and achievements the School was closed in 1976. The new, independent, co-educational High School of Glasgow came into being the same year following a merger involving the Former Pupil Club of the old High School and Drewsteignton School in Bearsden.

Motto: '*Sursum semper*'.

Governing Body:
Honorary President: Lord Macfarlane of Bearsden, KT
Chairman: G A Anderson, CBE, CA, FCMA
B C Adair, TD, LLB
G A F Arthur, CEng, FICE
Professor Sir Michael Bond, MD, PhD, FRCS, FRC Psych, FRCP, DPM
Mrs A M B Currie, LLB
Sheriff W Dunlop, LLB
W G Gardiner, CA
Mrs S C Harkness, DCE, NFF, NFTD
Mrs L Keith, MA, PGCE, ITQ
D J Maclay, BSc, CA
P Morrison, MA, BSc
Professor V A Muscatelli, MA, PhD, FRSA
T F O'Connell, CA, ATII
K A Scott
Dr A C E Short, MB, ChB, DRCOG, MRCGP
R M Williamson, MA, LLB

***Rector:* R G Easton**, OBE, MA (Cantab)

Deputy Rector: C D R Mair, MA

Assistant Rectors:
Mrs L A Douglas, BEd
M A M Brown, BEd

Staff:

English:
*Mrs R E Elstone, MA
Mrs M A Easton, BA
Mrs F M Feldman, BA
†Mrs G R Fergusson, MA
Mrs M I McGougan, BA
G A McNicol, BA
Mrs J Ogston, BA
†P A Toner, MA
Mrs M Weir, MA

Mathematics:
*P F Edmond, BSc
Mrs M Adams, BEd
Mrs L A Douglas, BEd
Miss C Knox, BSc
†J G MacCorquodale, BSc
P Moon, BSc
Mrs L S Moon, BSc
Mrs M C Reid, BSc

Computer Studies:
*D L McCorkindale, BEd
Mrs K M Farley, BSc
N R Clarke, BSc

Science:
*A E Baillie, BSc (*Physics*)
*Mrs G K Stobo, BSc (*Chemistry*)
*Dr D P Williams, BSc, PhD (*Biology*)
Mrs J E R Andrew, BSc
Mrs L McGuigan, BSc
I C Morrison, BSc
Dr L A A Nicholl, BSc, PhD
Mrs K S M O'Neil, BSc
G H Rowe, BSc, MSc
Miss M A Kelly, BSc

Modern Languages:
*M H Bennie, MA
†Miss J M Alexander, MA
A C Greig, MA
Miss M S I Ramsay, MA
Mrs F B Slavin, MA
Mrs L E Thompson, MA

Classics:
*Mrs K J V Thomson, MA, BPhil
Mrs M H S Campbell, MA
C D R Mair, MA

Economics and Business Studies:
*A J Jensen, BA
Mrs B C Caplan, DipComm

Geography and Modern Studies:
*I M M Currie, BA, MPhil
R Dunlop, BEd
K F FitzGerald, BSc
T P L King, MA (*Head of Outdoor Education*)

History:
*G K Sinclair, MA
Mrs G Allbutt, MA
Mrs M Barclay, MA
R J Broadbent, BA, MEd (*Head of Careers Dept*)

Art:
*P J Gilchrist, BA
Mrs J F MacKechnie, BA
Mrs K M Waters, BA, DipDesign

Home Economics:
*Mrs H M Burnet
Mrs C Cammidge, DipHE, MBA

Music:
*P S Douglas, DRSAM
M Duncan, DRSAM
D R Fleming, BMus
N G McFarlane, BA
R McKeown, DRSAM
Mrs J Tierney, BMus
Mrs M Scott, DipMusEd, LRAM

Religious Education:
*C F Price, MTheol
Mrs M H S Campbell, MA

Physical Education:
*D N Barrett, BEd
Miss M A G Macpherson, DPE (*Head of Girls' PE*)
M A M Brown, BEd
K F FitzGerald, BSc
Mrs R Owen, BEd
Mrs B A Bell, DPE
A Crawford, DPE
C S Forsyth, DPE
Mrs M Gillan, DPE
Mrs M Jefferies, DPE
Mrs C Mackay, DPE
Mrs M J McNeill, BEd

Junior School Staff:
Headmistress: Miss E N D Robertson, MA
Mrs J M Smart, BEd (*Deputy Head*)
Miss C Armour
Mrs C Brown
Mrs J Carr
Miss K Dougall, BEd
Mrs M A Easton, BA (*Drama*)
Mrs E Gibson, BEd
Mrs W Gray
Mrs K Harris, DPE (*PE*)
Mrs C M Jaberoo, BA
Mrs A Lamont
Mrs L Latimer
Mrs E McCormick
Miss S McDonald, BEd
Mrs S E MacDougall
Mrs I McNeill, DA (*Art*)
Mrs J Moir
Mrs M Moreland
Mrs J Ogston, BA (*Drama*)
Mrs J O'Neill
Mrs D Peck
Mrs M Scott, DipMusEd, RSAM, LRAM (*Music*)
Miss I Skinner, MSc (*Senior Teacher*)
Mrs F B Slavin, MA (*French*)
G J Walker, BSc
Mrs M Watt

Bursar: G Simonis

Rector's Secretary: Miss L M Cook

Buildings. The Senior School occupies modern purpose-built buildings at Anniesland on the western outskirts of the city immediately adjacent to twenty-three acres of playing fields. The Junior School is in the extended and modernised former Drewsteignton School buildings in Bearsden about three miles away. New facilities opened during the last few years include a new Art Department, additional Science and Computing Laboratories, a Sixth Form Common Room, a Junior School Hall and Classrooms, Music Rooms, a Kindergarten, an artificial grass hockey pitch, a Drama Studio, a Refectory, a Fitness Centre and a Grandstand.

Organisation. The School is a day school with about 1,040 boys and girls. The Junior School, which includes a pre-school Kindergarten, has some 380 pupils (ages 3–10). Primary 7 pupils are included in the Senior School which has about 660 pupils (ages 11–18). A general curriculum is followed until the 3rd Year of the Senior School when, with the Standard Grade examinations of the Scottish Certificate of Education in view, a measure of choice is introduced. In 5th Year Higher examinations are taken and in 6th Year courses for Advanced Highers or the Certificate of Sixth Year Studies are offered. Whilst the majority of pupils are aiming for the Scottish universities, places are regularly gained at Oxford, Cambridge and other English universities.

Throughout the School, time is allocated to Art, Music, Personal, Social and Health Education, Physical Education and Religious Education. All pupils will also take courses in Computing Studies, Drama and Home Economics at various stages in their school careers.

Games. The main sports are hockey, rugby, athletics, cricket, tennis and swimming. Pupils participate in a wide variety of other sports, including badminton, basketball, netball, volleyball, golf, cross-country running and skiing.

Activities. Pupils are encouraged to participate in extra-curricular activities. Clubs and societies include debating, zoological and historical societies, Scripture Union groups, and computer, table tennis, chess, art, bridge, chemistry, French, drama and orienteering clubs. Pupils take part in the Duke of Edinburgh's Award Scheme and the Young Enterprise Scheme, and parties regularly go on tour. There are choirs, orchestras and a jazz band and tuition in Instrumental Music is arranged as requested. Each year there are several concerts and dramatic productions.

Admission. Entrance tests and interviews are held in January. The principal points of entry are at Kindergarten (age 4), Transitus (age 11) and 1st Year (age 12) but pupils are taken in at other stages as vacancies occur.

Fees. Fees range from £1,782 per annum (Kindergarten) to £5,490 per annum.

Bursaries and Scholarships. The School operates a Bursary Fund to give assistance with fees in cases of need. Some Academic Scholarships are also offered at the Senior School.

Former Pupils' Club. The Glasgow High School Club Limited is the former pupils' association of the old and new High Schools. Former pupils all over the world maintain an interest in the life and work of the School. *Secretary:* N M Alexander, LLB.

Charitable status. The High School of Glasgow Limited is a Registered Charity, number 45882 (Edinburgh). It is a recognised educational charity.

The Hulme Grammar School

Oldham Lancs OL8 4BX.
Tel: 0161-624 4497
Fax: 0161-652 4107

The School was founded in 1611, was reconstituted in the 19th century under the Endowed Schools Act and was a Direct Grant School until 1976. It reverted to independence with the phasing-out of the Direct Grant. The main buildings were erected in 1895 by the Hulme Trust on a commanding south-west facing site overlooking the city of Manchester. Although it is Oldham's independent boys' school, it is within easy reach of Manchester, Rochdale, Stalybridge and Ashton-under-Lyne. Improving transport systems put the school within easy reach of almost all parts of Greater Manchester.

Motto: *Fide sed cui Vide.*

Patron: The Lord Clitheroe of Downham

The Governing Body:

Chairman: Mrs R Brierley, JP, BA

Vice-Chairman: Barrie Williams, LLB

Honorary Treasurer: Andrew Scholes, AMCST

J Ainley
Mrs Elizabeth M M Boon, MBE
Stuart M Brook, ACIB
G Malcolm George, QPM
David J Illingworth, BA, FCA
Mrs Barbara Jackson
Mrs Sylvia Jackson
Graham F Partington
Raymond J Whitehead, OBE
Graham Winterbottom

Clerk to the Governors and Bursar: H David Moore

***Headmaster:* K E Jones**, MA (Cantab)

Deputy Headmaster: P T Byrne, BSc

Third Masters:
J J Melican, MA (*Senior Tutor*)
Head of Sixth Form: J C Budding, BEd

Assistant Staff:
*S Baty, GRSM, ARMCM (*Director of Music*)
Mrs S E Beard, BSc (*Chemistry*)
P D Bolton, BSc (*Games/PE*)
N L Brown, BA (*French*)
Mrs M Castleton, DA, NDD (*Art, Ceramics*)
E R Collinge, BSc (*Chemistry, Physics*)
*I T Coulton, BSc (*Biology*) (*Officer Commanding CCF*)
A Coyle, BEng (*Physics, Technology*)
*C M B Crossley, BA (*English, Philosophy*)
D J Dalziel, BSc (*Biology*)
R A Davies, MA (*Art*)
M Davis, MA (*Mathematics*)
M Dowthwaite, BA (*History, Politics*)
P Galloway, BSc (*Physics*)
M J C Garnett, BA (*French, German*)
*G P Grime, CertEd (*Technology*)
*M J Harrington, BA, MSc (*Chemistry*)
I K Harris, BSc (*Physics*)
*M Harris, BA (*Modern Languages*)
*G Hepworth, BSc (*Mathematics*)
Mrs L Hewitt, CertEd (*Mathematics*)
*I G Holt, BSc (*Physics*)
G Hulme, ARCO, LTCL (*Music*)
*N G H James, MA (*General Studies, History, Politics*)
*R J Lapsley, MA (*History, Politics*)
M Lomas, BA (*Spanish, French*)
*S McRoyall, BA (*Art*)
C J D Mairs, MA (*English*)
A H Marshall, BSc (*Geography*)
P Matthews, MA, MEd, MPhil, LLB (*Classics*)
P M Miles, CertEd (*French, Spanish*)
H Milling, BA (*Games/PE, Religious Studies*)
P Newbold, BSc (*Geography*)
P J O'Donnell, BA (*Games/PE*)
C P Ogden, BSc, PhD (*Mathematics*)
Miss J E O'Neill, BSc (*German, French*)
A Peacocke, BA (*Geography*)
S D Pearce, BA (*ICT*)
Mrs M Reddish, BA (*English*)
*M W Reid, BA (*English*)
Mrs A Schofield, BSc (*Biology*)
*K Schofield, BA (*Classics*)
R V Sharples, BSc (*Chemistry*)
M A Sharrock, BA, MIEx (*Economics, Business Studies*)
*T E Sheer, BA (*Economics, Business Studies*)
D A Smith, MSc (*Mathematics*)
J P Spalding, BSc (*Mathematics*)
*P J Sutherland, BA, PhD (*Geography*)
C J Taylor, MA (*English*)
Mrs D Thornley, DPE, DASE (*IT*)
C S Wood, MSc (*Biology, PSHE*)
*P F Wood, CertEd (*Director of Physical Education*)

Hulme Court Preparatory School
Head: D Washington, BEd

Mrs J Coulton, ARMCM (*Music*)
Mrs B J Gibbon, CertEd
J A Keen, BSc
Mrs C Kershaw, BEd
Mrs J E D Selby, BEd

Werneth Preparatory School
Head: Mrs A S Richards, BSc

Visiting music teachers:

Miss K Brown, BA(Mus), GRNCM (*Clarinet, Saxophone*)
Miss R Clegg, GRNCM, PPRNCM (*Oboe, Viola*)
Miss C Constable, BMus, LTCL (*Violin*)
Mrs J Crisswell, GRSM (*Violin*)
Miss R Darby, BMus (*Saxophone*)
M Evans, BEd (*Brass*)
Miss J Hallett, GRNCM, PGDip (*'Cello*)
K Heggie, GRNCM (*Guitar*)
Miss L James, BMus, PPRNCM (*Clarinet, Saxophone*)
Mrs J Kent, CTABRSM (*Horn*)
Mrs J Lund, LRAM, ALCM (*Piano*)
J R Meaden, CertEd (*Brass*)
Miss M Rayner, GRNCM, PPRNCM (*Piano*)
Mrs A Reynolds, BMus, GRNCM (*Piano*)
Miss C Smith, BMus, PPRNCM (*Piano, Percussion*)

Medical Officer: M B Kostecky, MA, MB, ChB

School Nurse: Mrs A Baulk, RGN

Headmaster's Secretary: Mrs D Webb

Organisation and Accommodation. There are around 700 boys in the School, including 138 in Hulme Court (the Preparatory School) and 140 in the sixth form. Werneth Preparatory School, which has recently been acquired by the Hulme Grammar Schools, is co-educational and occupies a self-contained site a mile from the main school, housing around 130 children. The Main School buildings accommodate most of the School's departments and occupy two floors. The second floor was completed in 1992-3, along with new catering facilities and an additional hall. The ICT room has recently been refitted and equipped with an up to date PC network. The physics and chemistry departments are in a science wing which adjoins the main buildings. The art and technology departments occupy a separate building adjacent to the main site. Hulme Court is in a separate building a few minutes' walk from the main site. On the same site as Hulme Court are the sports hall (built in 1987), multi-gym and the indoor heated swimming pool.

Hulme Grammar School for Girls has separate accommodation on the Main School site and shares some of the facilities, including the new Centenary Library with its state-of-the-art ICT resources area.

Curriculum and results. In their first year in Main School (year 7) all boys follow a common curriculum comprising English, mathematics, French, history, geography, physics, chemistry, biology, RS, music, art, ICT, technology and PE. A second language is started in year 8. During years 7 to 9 boys are taught in mixed ability groups in most subjects. There is limited setting in mathematics and English. At GCSE all boys study English, English literature, mathematics, three separate science subjects or dual award science, and at least one foreign language (French, German, Latin or Spanish). All boys are encouraged to study a humanity, although narrower specialisation is not usually prevented. In the sixth form all boys are expected to take four specialist subjects at AS level and a minimum of three at A2, together with General Studies. A wide, though quite traditional, range of subjects is offered and the aim is to provide a timetable which will allow each boy to follow his first choice of subjects. The examination results at GCSE and A-level are consistently impressive with a pass rate of 90% or better the norm at A level and at GCSE. The vast majority of boys proceed to university with a number going to Oxford or Cambridge each year.

Games. The main school games are association football in the winter months and cricket in the summer. The school also provides opportunities for, and coaching in, athletics, badminton, basketball, cross-country, golf, hockey, rugby union, swimming and volleyball. Many of these are taught during timetabled PE although much coaching takes place in lunch hours and after school. Large numbers of boys have opportunities to represent the school, the town, their county and English independent schools in their chosen sport and over the years there have been many Hulme boys on national youth teams in various sports. The school has achieved the Sportsmark Award for the excellence of its PE and games provision.

Music. Music is strongly encouraged at Hulme and all boys study music on the curriculum in years 5 to 9. Tuition is provided in all the major orchestral instruments as well as on piano, organ, saxophone and percussion. Around 100 boys take such lessons each year and many enter for the examinations of the Associated Board of the Royal Schools of Music. Music at GCSE and A level flourishes and a significant number of boys go on to read music at university or music college. Much group music work is undertaken during lunch hours, after school and at other times and currently the following ensembles flourish: orchestra, choral society, chamber choir, brass ensemble, string ensemble, big band, jazz group and recorder consort. Junior orchestra and brass groups act as training grounds for pupils as young as 8 years.

Extra-curricular activities. Apart from musical and sporting activities much else takes place outside the timetable. This allows those who are not particularly musical or sporting to play a full part in the life of the school, although many boys are in a number of different activities. There is a flourishing CCF which is open to boys from year 10 upwards. The CCF has an army section and an RAF section and offers activities as varied as adventure training, camping, mountaineering, flying and gliding. The Duke of Edinburgh's Award scheme has been running successfully at Hulme for many years and operates with the help of many parents. Dozens of boys each year complete their bronze and silver awards and many go on to complete their gold award just before or just after leaving school. The award may include an element of service to the community. This links well with the school's own strong tradition of service through its community action group. Senior boys help in local primary schools and special schools, on hospital wards or in old peoples' homes. Money is also raised for many charities by events organised and run by the boys themselves. Senior boys organise and run clubs for juniors. There is a computing club, a junior debating society and a games workshop group. There is also an active senior debating society, a cinema club and a chemistry club, which attract a wide following. Regular plays and musicals are mounted, at least one a year, involving boys from all years of the school. All told there are over 30 different extra-curricular activities taking place and many of them are organised as joint activities with the Girls' School. A number of educational trips are undertaken by Hulme Court and during years 7 to 9 in main school, notably by the history and classics departments. In addition GCSE and A level courses may demand working visits to sites in subjects such as art, geography, biology, business studies and history and these are arranged to take place with minimum cost to parents and minimum disruption to lessons. There are regular theatre trips which take advantage of the splendid cultural opportunities that Manchester provides. There is an annual ski trip each February and an annual summer holiday trip to Austria. Staff give freely and generously of their time to make these activities possible.

Careers and higher education advice. The careers department is very experienced and the careers staff work closely with the Oldham Careers Service offering a very wide range of sound advice about careers and higher education. Aptitude testing is undertaken with all boys in year 10, and every boy has formal contact with the higher education advisors at least once during each of years 10 to 13. There are regular visits by the armed services liaison officers and we have strong links with local industry and commerce. The school runs its own work experience scheme and all boys in year 12 have the opportunity of two work experience sessions if they so wish. A higher education evening is held in school each year when many universities send representatives to meet and talk with the boys in small groups. Each sixth former is assigned to a senior member of staff who oversees his UCAS application, offering him guidance and advice, including trial interviews where needed.

Pastoral care, discipline and reward. Each boy is under the direct charge of a Form Tutor who deals with every day matters in this respect. The work of the Form Tutors is co-ordinated by Heads of Year who work as a team, meeting regularly with the Senior Tutor, and referring disciplinary matters to the Headmaster as necessary. There is a whole school system of rewards and merits, recognising good effort and achievement in all areas of school life: work, sport, music, service and general helpfulness and good behaviour. This is matched by a firm but fair system of sanctions, underpinning the school rules. Co-operation and tolerance are encouraged as are common sense, self respect and pride in one's appearance. Bullying and all forms of discrimination are taken very seriously and such matters are dealt with sensitively but firmly, and involve the education of the whole community.

Religion. The School is non-denominational and boys of many faiths take full part in all its activities. RS on the curriculum examines all faiths including Christianity and religious tolerance and understanding is promoted. There are regular morning assemblies which are often broadly Christian in character. In main school each form takes morning assemblies once a year and boys are encouraged to use this opportunity to explore their own beliefs and to present their own ideas on suitable themes.

Hulme Court Preparatory School. Hulme Court

occupies a separate site a short distance from the main school. The 138 boys are divided into five forms each under the direct care of a Form Teacher. The recent addition of two classrooms improved the accommodation and full use is made of the sports hall and swimming pool. PE is taught by the specialist staff from the main school and there is a growing use of its computing facilities. There is general adherence to the principles of the National Curriculum. In addition a wide range of extra-curricular activities is offered on a regular basis.

Werneth Preparatory School. Werneth Preparatory School is located about a mile from the main school on a self-contained site housing around 130 boys and girls. Entry is at Nursery level although places may from time to time become available in other years. There is a small junior department which is being phased out over the next few years. In time Werneth will operate as a nursery and infant school, preparing boys and girls for entry to Hulme Court and Estcourt (the preparatory school of the girl's school). All teaching of children between the ages of 3 and 7 takes place at Werneth, although full use is made of the facilities of the main school.

Admission. Admission to Werneth Preparatory School is at age 3. Entry to Hulme Court is at age 7 and to the main school at age 11. Entry is by examination in January of each year. Further details may be obtained from the School Office. Places may become available for entry at ages other than 3, 7, 11 and 16 and it is always worth enquiring from the School Office. The majority of boys in Hulme Court transfer to main school without further examination. Direct entry into the sixth form is encouraged and further details may be obtained from the Head of Sixth Form. Each year a number of assisted places and Oldham Hulme bursaries are available at age 11 with a further number of places for entrants to the sixth form. The Governors may also be able to assist with fees in other cases of need.

Fees. These are currently (2000-2001) £4,743 pa for the main school and £3,393 pa for Hulme Court. Fees at Werneth vary with the age of the child, but range from £3,006 to £3,066 pa. These fees include all essential stationery and textbooks. There are no compulsory extras.

Old Hulmeians. *Secretary:* E S Cresswell, Esq, Garden Cottage, Bamford Old Hall, Bury Old Road, Heywood, Lancs. Old Hulmeians website: http://www.ohgs.co.uk.

Charitable status. The Hulme Grammar Schools, Oldham is a Registered Charity, number 526636. Its purpose is the education of the young.

Hurstpierpoint College

Hassocks West Sussex BN6 9JS.
Tel: (01273) 833636
Fax: (01273) 835257
e-mail: info@hppc.co.uk
website: http://www.hppc.co.uk

Founded 1849 by Nathaniel Woodard, Canon of Manchester.

Motto: *Beati mundo corde*

Visitor:
The Rt Revd The Lord Bishop of Chichester.

Provost:
The Revd Canon J W Ratings, MA

School Council:

Chairman: S B Edell, Esq

Members:
The Provost
The Hon C W Byers
¶R J Ebdon, Esq
Mrs B J Hanson
Miss D Mason, OBE
I R McNeil, JP, FCA
Dr E M Moult, MRCS, MCRCGP
R W H Reed, Esq
¶B D Renn, Esq
D T Streeter, BSc, CBiol, FIBiol
The Revd Rebecca Swyer
A Synge, Esq

***Headmaster:* S D A Meek**, MA

Deputy Head: T Firth, BA

Chaplain: The Revd P A Hess, BA

Director of Studies: C Lambert, BSc, MSc

Bursar: R J Smith, MA, DipM

School Doctor: Dr P J Heeley, MB, BS, DCH

Staff:
T J Baxter, BSc, DPhil
Miss J Beaven, BSc
Miss C Bingham, BA
D C Clark, DLC (*Registrar*)
§R J S Cooke, BSc
Ms J Douglas-Laird, BA
N J Edey, BSc, MSc
Mrs A L Firth, BA
A C Forsey, BA
J Fox, BA
Mrs A-M Giffin, BA
§J A Gowans, MA
*K T Grant, MA (*History*)
†C W Gray, BEd (*Star House*)
†J P Green, BA (*St John's*)
*M P E Grubb, BA (*Art*)
Mrs J Harris, BEd, RSADipTEFL
*D M Higgins, BA (*Design & Technology*)
N Houghton, BA (*Director of Music*)
*R G Hurley, BSc (*Information Technology*)
Mrs L Johnson, BA
*R M Kift, BEd (*Director of Sport*)
†Mrs J Leeper (*Martlet House*)
*T F Q Leeper, BSc (*Biology*)
Mrs E Liebig, DipPed, BA
D P Lovering, BSc
S H K Maddock, BA
†M J May, BEd (*Eagle House*)
Mrs C Meek, BEd, DT, RSA, Dip SLD
*P J McKerchar, MA, CChem, MRSC (*Head of Science and Chemistry*)
Mrs E Morley-Arnold, BA
†¶N A M Morris, BA (*Red Cross House*)
†Miss J Parry, BSc, MPhil (*Shield House*)
I D Pattison, BSc
*M J Pulsford, BSc (*Head of Physics*)
K L Ralph, BSc, PhD
*J R Rowland, BA (*Head of Economics & Business Studies*)
†N G C Searls, GRSM, LRAM, ARAM (*Fleur de Lys House*)
*R Taylor-West, BA (*Head of English*)
V M Thomas, BA
*Mrs D Treyer-Evans, BA (*Modern Languages*)
Miss S J Waterhouse, BA
R G Winton, BSc

D J Semmence (*Cricket Coach*)
F J Simkins (*CCF*)
Mrs C Adams (*Netball Technical Adviser*)

There are 15 visiting Music Teachers

Preparatory School:

Head: S J Andrews, BA, L-ès-L

Deputy Head: R P K Barnes, BA

Director of Studies: A R Harvey, BEd

Staff:

Mrs R C Andrews, BA
J R Bettridge, TCert (*Senior Housemaster*)
R G Birch, BA
Miss E Brasher, BA
T A Cattaneo, BEd, CertEd
Mrs I Cheer, BA
C W Goldsmith, BA
Mrs J Grubb, BA
Mrs J Hallings-Pott
Mrs J McKerchar, BEd
R O'Grady, HDE
Mrs D K Stoneley, BEd
M J Temple, CertEd
J V Vick, BA
Mrs S H Wong, BA
M P Woods, BSc

Hurst House Nursery & Pre-prep School:

Head: Miss E Russell, BEd

Staff:
Mrs T Mayfield, BA, PGCE, BPhil
Miss V Atkinson, BEd
Miss C Gillett, NVQ Level 3 (*Classroom Assistant*)

Additional staff being appointed for the school which will open in September 2001.

Hurstpierpoint College was founded in 1849 by the Revd Canon Nathaniel Woodard. It is one foundation composed of three schools linked by common values, standards and goals, as well as by a common academic and administrative framework, to provide a complete education. The Senior School became fully co-educational in September 1997. There are currently 235 boys and 115 girls. 50% of the pupils are boarders. The Preparatory School has a further 184 pupils.

Site and Buildings. The school stands in 140 acres amid open countryside just to the north of the South Downs, 9 miles north of Brighton and 25 minutes from Gatwick Airport. The nearest railway station is Hassocks.

The main Senior School building of knapped flint consists of two quadrangles, the inner one containing the School Chapel, Dining Hall, Common Room and two day Houses. The outer quadrangle, open to the south, contains a boys' and a girls' boarding House, both recently renovated, a fully equipped ICT Centre plus administrative offices. The whole is joined by a fine enclosed cloister. A brand new Astroturf lies immediately to the south of the main Senior School building, providing the focus for hockey and tennis. To the east lie the School Library and a third boys' boarding house. Across the adjoining road are the Medical Centre and the second girls' House.

To the west lies a fourth boys' boarding house and St John's, a co-educational facility built in 1990 to house the Upper VI to enable them to be treated in a more adult manner prior to entry to university. In addition there are the academic facilities of the Lecture Theatre, Music School, Classrooms, Art School, Science Block and Design & Technology Centre plus the Theatre, Sports Hall and Indoor Swimming Pool. Further west is the Preparatory School which has recently undergone major redevelopment and shares several of the Senior School facilities.

Chapel. As a Woodard School, Hurstpierpoint is pledged to Church of England practice and teaching. Pupils receive religious instruction in class and attend three services during the week. The main Eucharist, which parents and friends are most welcome to attend, takes place mainly early on Friday evenings, although there are also occasional Sunday services in addition to voluntary celebrations of the Holy Communion. Pupils are prepared in small classes for the annual Confirmation taken by one of the Bishops of the diocese.

Curriculum. The weekly programme of 41 periods is structured to allow boys and girls to study a variety of subject options that can be adapted to suit their natural ability. The entry year (Shell) is designed to retain as much choice as possible involves the study of English, History, Geography, French, Latin or German or Spanish, Mathematics, Physics, Chemistry, Biology, Theology, Art, Drama, Design & Technology, Music, Physical Education, Professional Skills (IT) and Personal, Social & Religious Studies. In the second (Remove) year they make their GCSE choice of the core subjects plus three optional subjects from the list above.

Sixth formers are required to study four AS levels in the Lower Sixth. The choice is wide, with 20 AS subjects to choose from including Business Studies, Economics, Further Maths and various applied Art courses which are introduced to the subjects listed above. There is also a General Studies programme that ensures all the Key Skills are fully developed. The Upper Sixth can take a varied programme with the most able studying four full A levels, and the less able being allowed to build a valuable qualifications portfolio by studying a varying number of AS subjects along with at least two full A levels.

All pupils' work is overseen by academic and pastoral tutors and we take particular care to ensure that university applications are properly targeted to suit the students' aspirations and talents.

Professional Skills. While academic studies are given every priority, we recognise that other aspects are necessary to prepare students for university and careers. A programme has been devised, which lasts throughout the full five years of the Senior School. Starting with an introduction to keyboard and IT techniques, it goes on to develop public speaking and presentational skills. Lectures, Interest and Aptitude Tests, Seminars, to many of which parents are invited. Young Enterprise and Work Shadowing schemes are all designed to prepare pupils for the demands of their future lives.

Games. The School operates a "Sport for All" policy that seeks to place pupils in games most suited to their tastes and abilities. During the first two years they are expected to take part in at least some of the major sports but thereafter a greater element of choice occurs. The major sports are Rugby, Hockey, Cricket and Athletics for boys; Hockey, Netball and Rounders for girls. Overseas tours form an important part of a wider education. In addition there are teams in Basketball, Cross Country, Fencing, Football, Golf, Shooting, Squash, Swimming and Tennis. The Sports Hall and indoor Swimming Pool provide opportunities for many other pursuits such as Aerobics, Badminton, Weight Training and Water Polo, while the Outdoor Activities Group enables pupils to enjoy challenges such as Rock Climbing and Canoeing.

Service Afternoons. On Wednesdays pupils have a choice of activities. The Combined Cadet Force is one of the oldest in the country. Those who join the Army or RAF sections spend five terms working for the proficiency certificate after which they may remain as instructors and NCOs. As an alternative, pupils may join the Community Service Volunteers or the Conservation Group.

Music. There has alway been a strong musical tradition at Hurstpierpoint with an orchestra and several other more specialised ensembles. A large proportion of the pupils take individual instrumental lessons and give frequent recitals. The Chapel Choir plays a major part in regular worship and there are several other choral groups including the Barbershop and Madrigal Choirs. The Choral Society concert forms one of the focal points of the summer term.

Drama. The Shakespeare Society is the oldest such school society in the country and organises an annual production. Drama covers a wide range and varies from major musicals to more modest House plays and pupil directed productions. The 250 seat Bury Theatre also gives the more technically minded ample opportunity to develop stage management, lighting and sound skills.

Other Activities. Monday afternoons are reserved for general interest activities although they also take place at other times throughout the week. Activities vary from the literary through the practical to the energetic. The Hurst Johnian team are responsible for the production of the longest established school magazine in the country. Art, Bridge, Chess, First Aid, Japanese, Self Defence, Woodwork and the Duke of Edinburgh Award Scheme are among the many other opportunities available.

Hurst Johnian Club. In addition to providing facilities and events for Old Pupils, the Club also assists with many aspects of the Professional Skills course. The Secretary is Roger Moulton, c/o Hurstpierpoint College.

Fees at Senior School, 2000/2001. £4,865 a term inclusive for Full Boarders; £4,635 for Weekly Boarders; £3,765 a term for Day Pupils. Flexi-boarding is available.

Awards. (*see* Entrance Scholarship section) Scholarships and Exhibitions available at 13+: Academic, Art, Music, Sport (Downs) and IT in February.

Scholarships and Exhibitions available at 16+: Academic, Art, Design & Technology, Music, Sport (Downs) and All Rounder (Hurst) in November; DT (Arkwright) in February.

Bursaries are also available for the children of Clergy and the Services.

Preparatory School. Details about the Preparatory School can be found in Part V of this Book.

Further Details. Further details are available from the Registrar, Mr D C Clark

Charitable status. Hurstpierpoint College is a Registered Charity, number 1076498. It aims to provide a Christian education to boys and girls between the ages of three and eighteen in the three schools on the campus.

Hutchesons' Grammar School

21 Beaton Road Glasgow G41 4NW.
Tel: 0141 423 2933
Fax: 0141 424 0251
e-mail: rector@hutchesons.org
website: www.hutchesons.org

Founded and endowed by the brothers George and Thomas Hutcheson (Deed of Mortification 1641). The School is administered by the Hutchesons' Educational Trust.

Motto: *Veritas.*

Governors:
Not more than 17 in number – Representatives of the following Bodies: Glasgow Presbytery of the Church of Scotland (2), Senatus of Glasgow University (*1*), Merchants' House of Glasgow (*1*), Trades House of Glasgow (*1*), Patrons of Hutchesons' Hospital (2), Glasgow Educational Trust (*1*), Senate of the University of Strathclyde (*1*), FP Club (*1*), School Association (*1*) and not more than 6 persons co-opted by the Governors.

Chairman: D S Mason, CBE, JP, FRICS, FFB

***Rector:* The Revd J G Knowles**, MSc, FRSA

Bursar: Mr I B Tainsh, CA

Assistant Bursar: Mrs A Sloane, BA, CA

Deputy Rectors:
Dr S Macdonald, BA, PhD (*Senior School*)
A L Strang, MA, DipEd (*Senior School*)
Mrs L McIntosh, MA (*Senior School*)
Mrs L McKie, AGSM, DCE (*Junior School*)

Assistant Rectors (Senior School):
Dr S Cowling, BSc, PhD
D C Elstone, BA
G W A MacAllister, MA, DipEd
Miss C G Stevenson, BSc, DipEd

Assistant Rectors (Junior Schools):
Miss F Macphail, BA, MBA
N R Malvenan, DPE
Mrs C Hatfield, BEd

Heads of Departments:
D A Brunton, DA (*Art*)
Miss C G Stevenson, BSc, DipEd (*Biology*)
P H B Uprichard, BSc (*Chemistry*)
J S McKie, MA (*Classics*)
Ms R Housley, BSc, DipCompEd (*Computer Studies*)
Mrs V Alderson, DipSD (*Drama*)
Mrs F S Mitchell, DipCom (*Economics & Business Studies*)
A D Dunlop, BA, MEd, DipEd (*English*)
C C Clarke, BSc (*Geography*)
Dr R H Gaffney, MA, PhD (*History*)
Mrs E A McLean, DipHEcon (*Home Economics*)
Mrs M T Fyfe, BSc (*Mathematics*)
N J Fraser, MA (*Modern Languages*)
G F Broadhurst, MA (*Modern Studies*)
F Walker, BA (*Music*)
Dr J Hall, BA, MA, PhD (*Philosophy*)
Mrs W Justice, BEd (*Physical Education*)
A H J Reid, BSc (*Physics*)
S J Branford, MA (*Religious Studies*)
R W Furness, BEd (*Technology*)

Assistants:
Mrs A Alderton, BA (*English*)
Mrs S M Anderson, BSc, MSc (*Mathematics*)
Mrs M Anderson, BSc (*TEFL*)
T B Anderson, MA (*Modern Languages*)
Mrs C M Andrew, BSc, DipEd (*Chemistry*)
Mrs R Arnold, BA, MPhil (*English*)
Mrs C Arthur, DCE (*Primary*)
Mrs E Bain, BSc (*Biology*)
Miss A D Barrie, BEd (*Primary*)
Mrs C A Beattie, BSc, (*Physics*)
Mrs E M Beattie, DCE (*Primary*)
Miss L J Bell, BA (*History*)
P G Bell, MA (*History & Drama*)
Mrs S H Bell, BEd (*Primary*)
R A Benn, MA (*English*)
Mrs R Bishop, BSc, DipEd (*Chemistry*)
Mrs C Blair, MA (*English*)
Miss M Borland, BEd (*Primary*)
Mrs J Brankin, MA (*English*)
Miss J Brown, MA (*Primary*)
Mrs P A Brown (*Primary*)
S M Brunton, BSc (*Physics; Year Tutor*)
Mrs F M Buckle, BSc (*Biology & Chemistry*)
Mrs G Calder, DRSAM (*Music*)
S Cameron, MA, PhD (*Modern Studies*)
D G Campbell, MA (*English; Year Tutor*)
Mrs V M Carty, DCE (*Primary*)
Miss A J Chapman, DCE (*Primary*)
Miss K Chisholm, BSc (*Mathematics*)
Mrs I Colvil, MA (*Primary*)
P M Colvin, BSc (*Mathematics*)
F Cook, BSc, PGCE (*Technology*)
Mrs M C Crawford, BEd (*Primary*)
N Daldry, BEd, DCE (*Primary*)
Mrs I J Davis, MA (*Modern Languages*)
R Dewar, BEd (*PE*)

J Di Mambro, BSc, BA, MA, DipEd (*Biology*)
D A Donaldson, BSc (*Physics*)
M Dougall, MSc (*Biology*)
D D Drysdale, BEd (*Primary*)
G B Dunlop, BA (*Physical Education*)
S Easton, MA (*English*)
W Edmonds, BA, MFA (*Art*)
W J J Ferguson, BSc (*Chemistry*)
Mrs M Firth, MA, DipEd (*English and Year Tutor*)
Mrs M H Flannigan, BEd (*Modern Languages*)
Mrs V H Fraser, BA (*Mathematics and Computing*)
Miss H Gibson, BEd (*Primary*)
Mrs A S Gifford, DipMusEd (*Music*)
Mrs A J D Graham, DCE (*Primary*)
Miss L M Graham, DCE (*Primary*)
R C W Grant, BA (*Primary*)
Miss M R Harrison, MA (*Modern Languages*)
I J Harrow, BAcc (*Economics and Year Tutor*)
Miss R Hems, MA, MEd (*Primary*)
Mrs J Hill, MA (*Modern Languages*)
Dr P D Holmes, BSc, PhD (*Chemistry*)
Mrs J M Hunter, MA (*Modern Languages*)
Mrs A R Jack, MA (*Modern Languages and Year Tutor*)
D S K Jacobs, BSc, DipEd (*Physics*)
Mrs M J Jheeta, BSc, MSc (*Biology*)
Mrs E Johnston, DCE (*Primary*)
Mrs C Kennedy, DCE (*Primary*)
Mrs K A Kilday, BSc (*Mathematics*)
Mrs A R Laing, DipHEcon (*Home Economics*)
Mrs S Lang, BEd (*Physical Education*)
S Lang, BEd (*Physical Education*)
Mrs H E Lennox, DCE (*Primary*)
Miss R Leonard, BSc (*Biology*)
Mrs S I C Leslie, DipHEcon (*Home Economics*)
Miss A Lidwell, BA (*Geography*)
R J Livingston, BSc (*Mathematics*)
Miss D R Lovell, MA (*Art*)
Mrs C McAllister, DCE (*Primary*)
Mrs F McCash, BA (*Modern Languages*)
Mrs F McGregor, BA, CertTEFL (*TEFL*)
Mrs S M McIntyre, BSc (*Biology*)
Miss E M McKee, MA (*Modern Languages*)
Miss M B McLeod, BSc (*Mathematics*)
Mrs L A R McNeill, MA (*Modern Languages*)
Mrs N M I MacConnell, Licence d'Anglais (*Modern Languages*)
Mrs K MacSweet, BA (*Art*)
Mrs G I K Mackay, BEd (*Primary*)
Mrs R A A Maclean Ross, BEd, MPhil (*Primary*)
C D Macleod, BSc (*Computing*)
L Macleod, DRSAMD (*Music*)
Mrs M Madden, MA (*Classics and Year Tutor*)
Mrs J A Matthews, BSc (*Mathematics*)
Miss E Meek, MA (*Drama*)
Miss D G Milne, BA (*Primary*)
D J Mitchell, BSc, DipEd (*Physics*)
Mlle S Montane (*Primary*)
Mrs M Mungall, BSc (*Mathematics*)
Mrs I Munro, BEd (*Modern Languages & Year Tutor*)
Miss C-A Murray, BA (*Economics*)
Mrs F Organ, MA (*Geography*)
D N Paton, MA, BSc (*Computing*)
Mrs J Paul, MA (*Modern Languages and Year Tutor*)
Mrs C E Pendleton, MA, LLB (*Modern Languages*)
Mrs A T Pickering, BA (*Art*)
Mrs B Pycraft, BMus (*Music*)
Dr A G Ralston, MA, DPhil (*English and Year Tutor*)
A J Rannie, MA (*Modern Languages and Careers*)
Mrs C Ross, MA (*Primary*)
P G Russell, BEd (*Physical Education & Year Tutor*)
S Russell, BSc (*Mathematics*)
S K Sen, BSc (*Mathematics*)
Mrs K Shields, BA (*Mathematics*)
Miss R Simpson, BEd (*Physical Education*)
Mrs C A Singerman, MA, BA (*General Studies & History*)
Mrs M A Smart, DCE, BA (*Primary*)
Dr S Smith, BSc, PhD (*Chemistry*)
Mrs M E Smith, MA, DipEd (*Modern Languages*)
Mrs C M Stevenson, BA, DipEd (*Music*)
Mrs H Stewart, BSc (*Chemistry*)
Mrs L Stewart, BAcc (*Computing*)
M J Symington, MA (*English*)
Mrs P M Taylor, MA (*Modern Languages*)
D Tearney, BEd (*Physical Education*)
S Thomson, BSc (*Physics and Year Tutor*)
Miss C Townson, BA (*Economics*)
E W M Trotter, BMus (*Music*)
Mrs M Wainwright, MA (*English*)
Mrs L M Watt, BA (*Economics*)
Mrs M C Weatherill, DCE (*Primary*)
G R West, BEd (*Physical Education*)
Miss E J Williamson, DPE (*Physical Education*)
B A Williamson, BA, DipEd (*Geography*)
A W Wood, MA (*Classics and Year Tutor*)
S M Wood, MA (*History*)
Miss P Young, BEd (*PE*)

Laurel Park Staff:

D Bain, BMus, DipIA (*Music*)
Mrs H J Beall, BA Hons, PGCE (*Art*)
Mrs J Beattie, DipCom
Mrs C Bryce, MA (*English*)
Mrs J Campbell, DipEd, Dip Careers Guidance (*Careers*)
Mrs J Chambers, BSc Hons (*Chemistry*)
Mrs M Craig, BA Hons (*Modern Languages*)
Mrs S E Crichton, BEd Hons (*Physical Education*)
Mrs A W Dickinson, MA, LTCL (*Music*)
Mrs S Frame, MA (*Modern Studies*)
Mrs S Frisher, BSc (*Mathematics*)
C Fry, BA, PGCE (*Art*)
Mrs J Garvie, MA Hons (*Classics*)
Mrs H D Hamilton, BEd (*English*)
Mrs E Henderson, MA (*English*)
Mrs J Henderson, BA (*English*)
Miss M A Kennedy, MA Hons (*Modern Languages*)
Mrs E Laidlaw, BEd (*Biology*)
W Laidlaw, BSc Hons (*Physics*)
Mrs M Loughran, BSc (*Computing*)
P McGrath, BSc Hons (*Chemistry*)
Mrs M Moffat, MA Hons (*Modern Languages*)
Miss C Munn, BSc (*Mathematics*)
Mrs A Munro, BSc (*Biology*)
Mrs R Nicholson, DPE (*Physical Education*)
Mrs S Niven, MA (*Geography*)
Mrs S Nobbs, MA Hons (*History*)
Mrs S Steele, MA Hons (*Modern Languages*)
Mrs A M Thomson, BMus, LRAM, ARCM (*Music*)
P Tolland, DipCom (*Computing*)
Mrs F Warnock, BA Hons (*History*)
Mrs C Watt, BSc Hons (*Mathematics*)
Mrs J Weightman, BD Hons, DipEd (*Religious Education*)

Primary Department:
Mrs C Anderson, VEd Hons
Mrs J Brooks, DCE, ITQ
Miss M Hunter, BEd Hons
Miss M E Osler, MA
Mrs C R Richmond, MA
Miss S M Wallace, BEd

Nursery:
Mrs J Ferris, DipEd (*Senior Teacher*)
Miss S Cooper, NNEB
Miss J Edgar, NNEB

Computer Services:
Mr J Caddy, BSc, MPhil, MSc

Mr E Maurer, BSc
Mr G McEwan
Mr C Murdoch

Laboratory Assistants:
Mr H L G Tucker
Mrs M Lang
Mrs L Hawthorne
Mrs E Docherty
Mrs K Cooper

Librarian: Miss J Bulloch, BSc

Assistant Librarian: Miss K Sproat, BA, MSc

Rector's Secretary: Mrs M E Norman

Rector's Assistant Secretary: Mrs S Burrowes

School Secretary (Secondary): Mrs N M Brunton

School Secretary (Primary): Mrs A Kerbyson

Assistant School Secretaries:
Mrs E C Ross
Mrs M Jacobs
Mrs C McKinnon
Mrs C Borland

Music Administrator: Mrs E J Rae, MA, DipILS

Calendar & Events Administrator: Mrs G R Tooth, MA

Former Pupil Administrator:

School Matrons:
Mrs K Reid (*Secondary*)
Mrs J Johnstone (*Secondary*)
Mrs E Phillips (*Primary*)

Auxiliaries (Primary): Mrs I S McLaren, Mrs A Mitchell, Mrs A Carson, Mrs E Maguire

After School Club Co-ordinator: Mrs G S Gillman

The School currently consists of a Senior School of about 1,250 girls and boys from 12 to 18 years of age and a Junior School of some 700 girls and boys from 5 to 12 years of age. In the of 2001, Hutchesons' is merging with Laurel Park, a girls' school (Nursery to aged 18), situated in the West End of Glasgow. The plan is to develop this site into a second Hutchesons' co-educational primary school, running in parallel with the existing primary school in Kingarth Street. Pupils from both sites will move on to the Senior School in Beaton Road. (In 2001/2, there will still be senior girls on the Laurel Park site but they will all move to Beaton Road in August 2002).

For 118 years Hutchesons' Boys' Grammar School was situated in Crown Street, but in May 1960 moved to a new building on an open site at Crossmyloof. In 1976 the Boys' School combined with the Hutchesons' Girls' Grammar School, founded in 1876, to form one co-educational establishment housed on two sites a mile apart. The Boys' School in Beaton Road became the Senior School with the Girls' School in Kingarth Street evolving into the Junior School. The last decade has seen substantial development on both sites including a new Infant Block, Science Wing, Sports Hall, Library and several new classrooms. The School recently acquired the Church adjoining the Beaton Road site and this is being converted into a Music and ICT Centre. In addition to playing fields on site at Beaton Road, the Auldhouse sports ground has pitches for rugby, hockey and cricket. The Laurel Park site in the West End comprises a terrace of four houses together with a large former church, housing a large assembly hall and the dining room. The Laurel Park Sports Centre in Anniesland has been extensively developed within the last few years to provide an astroturf pitch, Sports Hall and squash courts.

Admission. Pupils are normally admitted on interview at 5 and by examination at 9 to the Junior Schools or at 12 to the Senior School.

Time of Entry. New Pupils normally start at the beginning of the Academic Year but intermediate entries are possible from time to time where circumstances dictate.

Fees per annum. Junior School Primary 1–4, £4,166; Primary 5–7, £4,477; Secondary 1–2 £5,024; Secondary3–6 £4,894. All fees from Primary 1 to Secondary 2 include books.

Financial Assistance. The School offers a limited number of scholarships each year for entry to the secondary school which are financially means tested.

The School is non-denominational but assembles each morning for a broadly Christian service. Religious Studies are taught in the first two years of the Senior School.

Curriculum. In the Junior School the pupils receive a thorough grounding in the usual subjects of an elementary curriculum and are taken for Art, Craft, French, Music and Physical Education by specialist teachers.

For the first two years of the Senior School all pupils take English, French, Latin – and German in Form 2 – History, Geography, Mathematics, Science, ICT, Art, Music, Physical Education and Religious Studies. They then follow more specialised courses leading to presentation for SQA Highers in Form 5. There is a strong 6th Form offering a wide range of courses, including both CSYS, Advanced Highers and 'A' level work.

In general pupils are prepared for the universities and Higher Education. They are given vocational guidance at various stages in their course.

Games. Rugby, Football, Hockey, Cricket, Rowing, Netball, Tennis, Golf, Badminton, Cross Country Running and Curling, with special attention to Swimming and Athletics.

Clubs and Societies include the Literary and Debating Society, the Photographic Society, the Chess Club, the Bridge Club, Dramatic Societies, the Art Club, the Stamp Club, the Computing Club, the Technology Club, the School Choir, Ensembles and the Orchestra and the Scripture Union. There is also a Community Service Group, a Duke of Edinburgh Award section and Young Enterprise Groups. A School magazine, 'The Hutchesonian' is published annually. Special tuition in musical instruments is available as an extra.

Charitable status. Hutchesons' Educational Trust is a Registered Charity, number 2660. It exists to provide education for boys and girls through Hutchesons' Grammar School

Hymers College

Hull Humberside HU3 1LW.
Tel: 01482 343555
Fax: 01482 472854

Hymers College was opened in 1893, through the generosity of the late Robert Hymers, of Stokesley, Yorkshire, and in accordance with the original intention of the late Rev John Hymers, DD, FRS, Fellow of St John's College, Cambridge.

The buildings consist of 35 classrooms, nine specialist laboratories, a 30-booth language laboratory, extensive IT facilities, audio-visual room, art rooms, theatre, Design/Technology Centre and a music centre containing teaching, practice and recital rooms, a gymnasium and very large sports hall. The Junior School, which is on the same site, has its own buildings but shares many facilities of the Senior School. The grounds, which extend for over 30 acres, include six tennis courts and two squash courts. Extensive additions to land and facilities are planned over the next 5 years. Additional science laboratories opened in January 2001.

Governors:

Chairman of Governors: S Martin, MA, FCA

R P Ashton
Professor J A Patmore, BLitt, MA, JP
J H Robinson, BSc, CEng, FIChemE
J E Townend, MP, FCA
E A Waddington

Co-optative:
Mrs D Fisher, LLB
N A C Hildyard, FCA
R Laucht, BA, ACMA
Cllr E A McCobb, BA, PhD
Mrs P M Wilkinson, BA, JP, SRN
A E Wood, BA

Nominative:
B K Appleyard, ACII
Cllr Mrs M Crampton, BA
J C Downing, MA
Mrs G Greendale
Capt J T Holmes
Professor H A Lloyd, DPhil, FRHistS
A Milner, DMS, DipCInst, MICM, FBIM
M deV Roberts, FCA
D Westwood, MA, PhD
Dr E B White, BSc, PhD
P J E Wildsmith, LLB

***Headmaster:* J C Morris**, MA

Deputy Headmaster: J Tinnion, BSc

Bursar and Clerk to the Governors: G D Noble, BA, CDipAF, FIMgt, FInstAM, MInstD

Senior Teachers:
J G Bell, MA (*Head of Science*)
P C Bryan, MEd (*Head of Junior School*)
Mrs M B Chorlton, BA (*Senior Mistress*)
N J King, BA (*Head of Sixth Form*)

Assistant Teachers:
*C Aldred, MA
Mrs S Atkinson, CertEd
Miss J Benwell, BA
S Brock, BSc
M Brooks, BSc
Mrs J M Brown, BA
Mrs D Bushby, LRAM
Mrs V A Chesters, MA
Mrs J Dex, CertEd
Mrs J I Duffield, BA
Mrs P Eastwood, BA
Mrs A Exley, BA
N Exley, BA
Miss H Ferguson, BA
*C J Fitzpatrick, BA(Ed)
I Franklin, BSc, PhD
C Gaynor-Smith, BA
T W Glenville, CertEd
*J Gravelle, BSc
*R H Grayson, BA
Mrs F M Green, BA
D Guy, BA
Mrs S Guy, BA
*D Hales, CertEd
D Harrison, MA
*J Harston, BEd
D Hickman, BSc
T D Hughes, BA
Mrs H Jackson, BSc
M Jones, BSc
Mrs J K Kelsey, MA, LRAM
P R Kelsey, BEd
G Lansdell, BEd
M Lynch, BEd
M McTeare, BA
Miss S May, BA
P Meadway, BSc
D A Merrick, BSc
Mrs C Mitchell, BA
I Nicholls, BA
*T P O'Byrne, BMus
J S Paice, BA
A Penny, GRNCM, ARNCM
Mrs A R P Powell, MA
*Mrs E L Powell, BA
L Price, CertEd
R Quick, ALCM, ARCM
A Raspin, BSc
*P J Roberts, MA
Mrs S E Sinkler, BPharm
*Ms F A Stanyon, BA
*I Stead, BSc
Mrs D Summer, BA
R J Summers, BSc
*A Sutton, BSc
J Swinney, BSc
Mrs J Tapley, BEd
N A Taylor, BA
D Thompson, BSc
*A J Tordoff, BA
J W Torne, BSc
Dr J Walker, MA, PhD
S J Walmsley, BA
A P Ward, BSc, PhD
*G J Wilson, BA, PhD
R K Wooldridge, BSc

The school became fully co-educational in September 1989.

The number of pupils is 960.

The Junior School numbers 220 pupils aged 8–11 and is staffed by specialist teachers. Admission is by competitive examination at ages eight and nine. Class sizes are kept low, and there is a full range of academic and sporting activities. Most pupils proceed at age eleven into the Senior School by a competitive examination taken also by pupils from other schools.

Pupils are prepared for the GCSE in a broad curriculum which includes music, business-related subjects, computer studies, technology and the crafts. Almost all pupils qualify for the VIth Form through GCSE results.

Girls and boys from other schools are admitted to the VIth Form on the basis of good GCSE results. There is a full range of courses leading to AS and Advanced Level examinations, and special preparation is given for Oxford and Cambridge entrance.

All pupils are strongly encouraged to participate in the very wide range of extra-curricular activities. The main school games are rugby, cricket, hockey, netball, tennis, rounders and athletics, and there are also school teams in basketball, badminton, swimming and fencing. The school regularly competes at national level in these sports and provides members of county and national teams. Many pupils take part in the Duke of Edinburgh Award Scheme and Young Enterprise. Other clubs include ACF, chess, modelling, debating, photography, community service and Christian Union. Drama is particularly strong, with several productions a year. Music is a major school activity; there are three full orchestras, a large choir, and several chamber and "academy" groups in each part of the school. Individual tuition is available in most instruments.

Fees (including text-books): Senior School £4,851 pa. Junior School £4,266 pa. Hymers Bursaries are awarded at ages 8, 9, 11 and 16.

The Old Hymerians Association: c/o Headmaster, Hymers College, Hull HU3 1LW.

Charitable status. Hymers College is a Registered Charity, number 529820-R. Its aims and objectives are education.

Ipswich School

Ipswich Suffolk IP1 3SG.
Tel: 01473 408300
Fax: 01473 400058
e-mail: registrar@ipswich.suffolk.sch.uk.
website: http://www.ipswich.suffolk.sch.uk.

The School was founded about 1390 by the Ipswich Merchant Guild of Corpus Christi. Its first Charter was granted by Henry VIII and this was confirmed by Queen Elizabeth I. In 1852 the School moved into new buildings, to which extensive additions and improvements have since been made.

Motto: *Semper Eadem.*

Visitor: Her Majesty The Queen

Chairman of Governors: D J Coe, JP

***Headmaster:* I G Galbraith,**MA

Deputy Head: D Ayling, MA

Head of Sixth Form: E R Cavendish, MA

Head of Middle School: J R C Cox, MA

Head of Lower School: D F Walsh, MA

Director of Studies: Miss J C Limrick, BSc

Chaplain: The Revd P M Hamlet, BA, MEd

Heads of Houses:

M J Bannan, BSc
A D Brown, MA
N D Cameron, BSc
Mrs N M Hardman, BA
Mrs K M Hoskins, MA
S J Tidball, MA

Heads of Department:

A J Burnett, BA (*English*)
R L Clayton, BEd (*Physical Education*)
S J Connelly, BA (*ICT*)
J R C Cox, MA (*Classics*)
S J Duncombe, BA (*Design Technology*)
Mrs M E Flude, BA (*Business Studies*)
S Godfrey, CertEd (*German*)
P M Godsell, BSc, PhD (*Biology*)
The Revd P M Hamlet, BA, MEd (*Religious Education*)
Mrs G S Holt, BA (*Russian*)
H R Holt, MA (*Modern Languages*)
R H Ingham, MA (*Careers*)
G D R Jones, BSc, PhD (*Chemistry*)
A D Leach, MA, BMus, ARCO, LRAM (*Music*)
M W A Scoging, BA, ATC (*Art and Design*)
J Sinclair, BSc, BA, MA (*Mathematics*)
S J Tidball, MA (*Economics*)
D J Warnes, MA (*History*)
R G Welbourne, BA, FRGS (*Geography*)
J Woolnough, BScEng (*Physics*)

Head of Preparatory School: Mrs J M Jones, BA

Head of Pre-Preparatory Department: Mrs M Poet, CertEd

Bursar: P V Boughton

Registrar: Mrs C J Robinson, BA

Headmaster's Secretary: Mrs S Dawson

Ipswich School occupies an attractive site adjacent to Christchurch Park. The cricket field lies within the perimeter of the school buildings and other playing fields of 30 acres are ten minutes' walk from the school.

There are 630 pupils in the Senior School (11–18), including 48 boarders. Of these, 175 boys and girls are in the sixth form. There are 290 pupils in the co-educational Preparatory School (3–11). The Senior School became co-educational in 1997.

The Boarding House stands in its own grounds a short distance from the school. There is a choice of full or weekly boarding for pupils in the Senior School. Day pupils may become boarders temporarily or permanently if the need arises.

All academic subjects have been housed in new or refurbished rooms in the last few years. New facilities for the performing arts were opened by HRH The Princess Royal in 1990. The Grimwade ICT Centre was opened in 1991. The Blatchly Laboratories for Chemistry and Biology were added in 1994 and the Design Technology Centre in 1999.

The Preparatory School is housed in its own buildings on the same campus, while the Nursery and Pre-Preparatory Department enjoys new accommodation adjacent to the main site. The Prep School benefits from all the amenities of the Senior School including the Sports Hall, Swimming Pool, Music School, Performing Arts Centre and Playing Fields.

Admission. Pupils entering the Preparatory School must show language and number skills appropriate to their age. The main entry to the Senior School at 11 is by examination in English, Mathematics and a reasoning test, taken in February. At 13, more pupils enter the Senior School, taking the Common Entrance Examination or the School's own Entrance and Scholarship Examination. Admission to the Sixth Form for girls and boys from other schools is by attainment of the required grades at GCSE, a report from the previous Head and an interview in November. Application forms may be obtained from the Registrar. A registration fee of £40 is payable. (£20 for brothers or sisters.)

Religious Education. There is religious education at all levels in the school and daily chapel services and services on Sundays for different sections of the school; pupils normally attend one Sunday service a term at which their parents are also most welcome.

Careers. There is a well-stocked Careers Room and the school is visited weekly by a professional careers adviser. Computer analyses of interests and aptitudes complement carefully planned advice about GCSE and A Level choices, higher education and professional training.

Curriculum. In the Preparatory School pupils study English, Mathematics (SMP), French, ICT, History, Geography, RE, Science, Music, PE, Art and Design Technology.

Senior School pupils follow a common curriculum in the first two years and an option including Latin, Classical Civilisation, German and Russian is introduced in the third year. Mathematics, English, French, and either separate or coordinated Sciences are taken by all pupils to GCSE level. Apart from these compulsory subjects, pupils are examined in 3 or 4 other subjects chosen from Latin, History, Geography, German, Russian, Design and Technology, Classical Civilisation, Art and Design, Religious Studies and Music.

In the Sixth Form AS and A Level subjects are chosen from the following:

Mathematics, Further Mathematics, Physics, Chemistry, Biology, Latin, Classical Civilisation, Economics, Business Studies, Art, Design Technology, Music, History, Geography, English, French, German, Russian.

In addition to their A Level studies, all Sixth Formers participate in a General Studies course composed of group work, conferences and films designed to complement and broaden the conventional curriculum. This also leads to an AS qualification. A course in ICT is offered in the Sixth Form, as are beginners' courses in Italian and Spanish.

Societies and Activities. All are encouraged to participate in a variety of extra-curricular activities which take place in lunchtimes, after school, at weekends and during the holidays. One afternoon a week is devoted to community service, conservation work, CCF (Army and RAF contingents) and a variety of sports and indoor pursuits.

Drama in the school is particularly strong; continuous activity in this sphere maintains a succession of productions throughout the year, in all age groups. Productions in 2000–2001 included: The Accidental Death of an Anarchist, The Crucible, Guys & Dolls, The Cherry Orchard, Blackadder, Wind in the Willows, A Midsummer Night's Dream and The Night of the Iguana.

Individual lessons are given in all branches of Music, and there are good opportunities for music-making, including Choral Society, Chapel Choir, Chamber Orchestra, Orchestra, Second Orchestra, Concert Bands, Jazz Bands and Rock Groups. In addition there are lunchtime recitals, formal and informal concerts, instrumental competitions, choir tours, and concert visits which pupils are encouraged to attend. Outside the school, concerts are given at Snape Maltings and at parish churches in Suffolk.

The Duke of Edinburgh's Award Scheme, Young Enterprise and the Community Sports Leader Award Scheme are run within the School.

Games. The main team games for boys are Rugby Football, Hockey and Cricket and for girls, Hockey, Netball and Rounders. Alternatives for many in the Senior School include Athletics, Cross-country, Golf, Tennis, Eton Fives,

Soccer, Squash, Polygym, Badminton, Swimming and Riding, also Sailing and Windsurfing which are carried out on nearby Alton Water. Skiing parties travel to America and Europe each year.

The Mermagen Sports Hall, opened in 1993, provides facilities for a wide range of indoor sports and is part of a complex which includes a Polygym and a Cricket Gallery, whose indoor nets function as a centre of excellence for the County as well as the School. There is a heated indoor Swimming Pool, three covered Eton Fives Courts and two Squash Courts.

Fees. Tuition fees. £6,930 pa in the Senior School; £6,231 pa for pupils in the Lower School; £4,809–£4,908 pa for pupils in the Preparatory School; £4,251 pa in the Pre-Preparatory Department

Boarding Fees only. Senior School, full boarding £5,100 pa; weekly boarding £4,404 pa. Lower School, full boarding £4,110 pa; weekly boarding £3,636 pa.

Scholarships (*see* Entrance Scholarship section) **tenable at the School.** Queen's and Foundation Scholarships are available at 11 and 13, carrying up to half remission of tuition fees. Scholarships and Exhibitions may be awarded for music or art as well as for academic excellence. Academic, Music and all-rounder Scholarships are available for external entrants to the Sixth Form. All awards may be held by day-pupils or boarders and may be supplemented by bursaries in case of need.

School Assisted Places (bursaries). These are available on a means-tested basis for entry at 11, 13 and 16.

Leaving Exhibitions. Six endowed Exhibitions of £100 each, Rigaud Prizes of £50 and a Birketts Law Scholarship.

The Old Ipswichian Club celebrated its centenary in 1989. Annual dinners are held in London in April and Ipswich in December. There are clubs for Cricket, Fives and Golf. Teams are fielded against the School in several sports.

Charitable status. Ipswich School is a Registered Charity, number 310493. It exists for the purpose of educating children.

The John Lyon School

Middle Road Harrow Middlesex HA2 0HN.
Tel: 020 8872 8400
Fax: 020 8872 8018

The John Lyon School was established as a Day School in 1876 under the Statutes made by the Governors of Harrow School, in pursuance of the Public Schools Act, 1868.

Motto: *Stet Fortuna Domus.*

Governors: The Governors of Harrow School

Committee of Management:
Professor M M Edwards, JP (*Chairman*)
W D Ashcroft
Dr R J A I Catto
Owain Arwel Hughes
M J Ames
M D Payne
J S Kettle
N W Stuart, CB
The Revd T J Gosden
Dr A B Cooke
Mrs B W Connolly
Mrs S C Hargreaves
C M Nunn

Clerk to the Governors: A J F Stebbings, 45 Pont Street, London SW1X 0BX

Headmaster: **Dr C Ray**, PhD, CPhys

Bursar: The Bursar of Harrow School

Assistant Bursar: C M Eastland

Assistant Staff:
J Barnard, MA, FRCO (*Second Master*)
R I McNae, BSc, CPhys, MInstP (*Director of Studies*)
M J Sadler, BA (*Classics*) (*Registrar*)
P Sanders, BSc (*Head of Science*)
B K Simmons, BSc (*Maths*)
†B Holgate, BSc, CPhys, MInstP (*Physics*)
R V French, BSc, CBiol, MIBiol (*Head of Sixth Form*)
P N B Perdue, CertEd (*CDT*)
J L Irvine, MA (*Modern Languages*)
†R A Shaw, BSc, MA (*Geography*)
D A Rimmer, BSc, MSc (*Head of Middle School*)
Mrs J L Perdue, CertEd
R L Cobb, BEd, BA (*Economics*)
D F Weedon, MA (*Careers*)
C J Jones, CertEd (*Physical Education*)
I R Read, DipAD, ATC (*Art*)
Miss P Waldron, BA (*Head of Junior School*)
N H Parsons, BA (*English*)
†I R Parker, BSc
L D Budd, BA, MA
P M Clarke, BA, MSc (*Learning Strategies*)
G J Ryder, BSc, MA (*Biology*)
S N Hillier, BA
V A Wheaton, BSc, MSc, AKC
N M Pankhurst, BA (*Drama*)
T Mahon, BSc, MA
P Le Berre, MA
S Miles, BMus, ARCO, ARCM, AMusLCM (*Music*)
Mrs I Sassaroli, BA
C H Savill, BA (*History*)
A S Westlake, BA, BA (*Religious Studies*)
D P Bullock, BA
P A Flanagan, BA
R A Freeborn, BSc, MSc (*Information, Communication Technology*)
J R Preston, BSc
Miss E K Sigston, BA (*Head of Outdoor Pursuits*)
C L M Tucker, MA
Mrs E E O'Brien, BA
O S Druker, BMus
Miss E J Bray, BSc, MSc
C D Gladwell, BA
T Pender, BA
A P Wright, BA

Part Time:
Mrs C Smith, BA
Mrs L S Plummer, BA
S T O'Brien, BA

Visiting Music Staff:
V E Davies, BMus (*horn*)
P D Judge, LTCL (*trombone*)
Miss B Copas, LRAM, LGSM (*pianoforte*)
R Boyle, AGSM (*guitar*)
G Mitchell, BMus, DipNCOS (*flute*)
Mrs L Pearce, BA (*violin*)
K Bache, ARCM, LGSM (*trumpet*)
C Grey, BMus, LRAM (*jazz band*)
H Clement-Evans, GRNCM, PPRNCM (*oboe*)
J Nolan, BMus, ARCM (*organ*)
J Holling, DipTCL (*drums*)
Miss S Markham, MMus (*clarinet/saxophone*)
H Clement-Evans, GRNCM, PPRNCM (*oboe*)
A Potts, BSc (*saxophone*)
M Kambo (*Indian music*)

Headmaster's Secretary: Mrs J Horn

There are 525 boys in the School, all day boys.

Admission. The School is open to boys residing within reasonable travelling distance.

There are 72 places each September for boys who will be over 11 and under 12 on their entry into the school. An entrance examination is set in January.

In addition, up to 22 places are available each September for boys to enter the third form. They must be over 13 and under 14. An entrance examination is set in February. There are also places available in the Sixth Form for boys who have five B grades at GCSE.

Fees. The School Fee is £7,335 a year payable in advance in 3 equal payments. It covers the cost of all text books and stationery. Registration Fee £40.

Curriculum. The School Curriculum at present includes Religious Studies, English, History, Geography, Economics, French, German, Latin, Mathematics, Chemistry, Physics, Biology, Art, Music, Design & Technology, Drama, Computer Studies and PE. Religious teaching is undenominational.

Examinations. Boys are prepared for GCSE and able boys take Mathematics a year early. In the Sixth Form four subjects are normally chosen to be studied for AS level in the first year leading to three (or four) A2 levels in the second.

Bursaries. (*see* Entrance Scholarship section) Two bursaries up to 100% of the fees (Beckwith Scholarships) and other smaller bursaries are available - all subject to financial assessment.

Music Scholarships. Scholarships are available at 11+ or 13+.

Governors' Scholarships. Up to ten Academic Scholarships, up to the value of 50% of the annual fees will be awarded to boys entering between 11 and 12 years through the School Entrance Examination and in addition two scholarships of similar value to boys between 13 and 14.

Term of Entry. Normal entry date is in the September term.

School Buildings. The School Buildings are on the West side of Harrow Hill and include usual facilities. Regular additions have been made. In 1973 a wing was built as part of a Development Plan, allowing for the reorganisation and modernisation of existing buildings, which was completed in 1974. In 1981 Oldfield House was built to accommodate the first two years and in 1989 a new assembly hall/theatre/classroom complex called the Lyon Building came into use. A new Sports Pavilion was completed in 1994 and new Science laboratories in 1995. A Sports Complex comprising an indoor swimming pool and sports hall was opened by HRH The Duke of Edinburgh in February 1997. A new computerised Library and a Drama Studio have recently been finished.

Games. The School playing fields are within 10 minutes' walk on the south side of the Hill. In addition, the School is able to use the Harrow School Athletic Track, Golf Course and Tennis Courts.

The main games are Association Football and Cross-country in the Winter Terms, Cricket and Athletics in the Summer Term, supported by Badminton, Tennis, Basketball, Archery, Shotokan-Karate and other games. PE and Swimming are in the curriculum.

Out of School Activities. Boys are strongly encouraged to play an active part in a wide range of activities. There is a School Orchestra, a Junior Orchestra, a Wind Band, a Jazz Band, large and small choirs. Drama, as well as being taught in the curriculum, is developed through House and School Plays. There is the normal range of School Clubs and Societies.

The School takes an active part in the Duke of Edinburgh's Award Scheme. It also uses the Young Enterprise Scheme so that boys can gain early experience of running a small company. Most Lower Sixth Formers take part in a week's residential leadership course in Scotland.

Community Service has been developed through various projects which are undertaken to help the old and the handicapped in the Harrow Area. Each year the school devotes considerable time to fund-raising for a Charity chosen by the boys.

Careers. Advice on Careers is given by the Careers Staff. The School is a member of the Independent Schools Careers Organisation. Specialist advice concerning entrance to Higher Education is given.

The Old Lyonian Association. The Old Lyonians' Association, which was founded in 1902, has always been a strong support to the School. All boys on leaving the school from the Sixth Form become life members of the Association. The Association has its own ground and pavilion at 74 Pinner View, Harrow, and its President is Mr C Nunn.

Entries to Universities. The second year VIth Form on average consists of 70 boys who will usually apply for Degree courses at Universities and of these the great majority are successful. A steady stream of boys is sent to Oxford and Cambridge.

Charitable status. The Keepers and Governors of the free Grammar School of John Lyon is a Registered Charity, number 310033. The purpose of the charity is the education of boys living within reach of Harrow between the ages of 11–18.

Kelly College

Tavistock Devon PL19 0HZ.
Tel: (01822) 813100
Fax: (01822) 612050

Kelly College was founded in 1877 by Admiral Benedictus Marwood Kelly.

Motto: *Fortiter occupa portum.*

Governors:

Chairman: J Q Wright

Vice-Chairman: P Adler

The Rt Revd The Lord Bishop of Exeter
The Revd Preb J E F Rawlings
T L G Landon
Capt M C Clapp, CB, RN
C R Morley
Mrs M Abel
Prof P F W Preece
Mrs J Leverton
Mrs E Loosmore
D W Ball, MBE
Dr H J Ball
Lady Kitson
Mrs A C Mathews
D R Milford (*Chairman, Finance Committee*)
M W Kelham
N R Bomford

Headmaster: **M Steed**, MA, Fitzwilliam College, Cambridge

Second Master: D J Wilson, MA (*English*)

Deputy Head (*Pastoral*): Mrs E A Rowley, BA (*English*)

Deputy Head (*Academic*): T C Jones, BA, BEd (*Mathematics*)

Housemaster, School House: A P Smerdon, BSc (*Geography*)

Housemaster, Courtenay House: C W J Wells, BEd (*Modern Languages*)

Housemaster, Newton House: R B J Huish, BEd (*Biology*) (*Senior Housemaster*)

Housemistress, Newton House: Mrs L B Huish, BEd (*History and Dance*)

Housemaster, Conway House: R J Skillington, BA (*Physics*)

Housemaster, Marwood House: D R Bott, BA (*History*)

Housemistress, Marwood House: Mrs L C Bott, BA (*German*)

Assistant Staff:
S Martin, MA, BSc (*Geography, Master-in-charge of Careers*)
T Ryder, BA (*Director of Studies; Geography and Geology*)
M J Carter, BEd, DipPE (*Physical Education and Biology*)
M R Kent, MSc, KLC, FCollP (*Physics*)
N M Collier, BA (*Art and Design*)
I J A Hardy, BSc (*Maths*)
R G McDermott, MEd (*Design and Technology*)
Mrs G Moore, BEd (*Physical Education and Games Co-ordinator*)
C J Limb, BA (*English*)
N Dunn, BSc (*Chemistry*)
Miss E Rankin, BSc (*Biology*)
Miss J Hasson, BA (*French*)
Mrs A G Shepherd, BA (*Economics and Business*)
Mrs V J Lanyon Jones, CertEd (*SENCO*)
P F Williams, MA (*English*)
Mrs R A Gibbs, BA (*English*)
Mrs S M de Glanville, CertEd (*Mathematics*)
Mrs L E Carter (*Art*)
Mrs J Tosdevin, BA (*Religious Studies*)
Mrs J R Foster, BA (*Spanish*)
Mrs S Collar, DipEd (*English*)
R A Brew (*Director of Swimming*)
Mrs S Bury, BA (*English Support*)
Mrs D Sherrell, BEd (*English Support*)
Miss A Hamilton, BA (*English Support*)
Mrs S Speakman (*Girls Sport*)
Mrs W Langton, MEd (*Girls Sport*)

Music Department:
A M Wilson, BMus (*Director of Music*)
J S Boorer, FTCL (*Clarinet, Flute and Saxophone*)
Mrs S Houghton, ARCM (*Flute*)
D Clayson (*Trumpet and Trombone*)
Mrs O Loewendahl, BMus (*'Cello*)
Roger King (*Guitar*)
Mrs M Mazur-Park (*Piano*)
R Davies, AGSM (*Percussion*)
J Lewington, LTCL, ARCM (*Singing*)
K Garner (*Violin*)
S Williams, FTCL (*Trumpet*)

Registrar and Director of Development: C J Kirwin, MA (*Tel:* 01822 813153/Fax: 01822 612050)

Bursar and Clerk to the Governors: J M Larby

Finance Bursar: Mrs J Padmore

Medical Officer: B G Steggles, FRCS, MBBS, MRCS, LRCP, BDS, LDS, RCS, AKC

Headmaster's Secretary: Mrs S C Harding

There are 360 pupils in the School of whom 160 are girls. There are 185 boarders and 175 day pupils.

Kelly College offers an up-to-date Independent School education in an exciting part of the country. It lies just above the River Tavy on the edge of one of the most beautiful parts of Dartmoor. The M4 and M5 and excellent rail connections make it easily accessible.

A happy atmosphere within a disciplined framework is aimed at, so that caring for others, good manners and a self-respecting appearance, and the habit and enjoyment of sound academic work, develop naturally. Forms are small and much more individual attention is possible than in a larger school, and there is no danger of a boy or girl feeling 'lost'. A highly qualified staff of University graduates prepare boys and girls for the Universities, the professions and industry. All pupils follow a general course, which includes single Sciences to GCSE level, after which there is a wide choice of subjects at 'A' level. Kelly College has a fine games tradition, Academic results have been consistently excellent over recent years. The vast majority of pupils go on to prestigious universities.

Site and Buildings. Kelly College is ideally situated on high and open ground in glorious Devon countryside, a short distance from the attractive market town of Tavistock. The buildings include the School Chapel, Assembly Hall, Library, Reading Room, well-equipped Science Laboratories, the Art and Music School, a new Language Centre, Design Centre and Information and Communication Technology unit, a heated Swimming Pool fitted out for international training, covered Fives and Squash Courts, Gymnasium, Armoury, Miniature Rifle Range, and a newly equipped Adventure Training Centre and Briefing Room. There is a fine School Hall and Central Dining Hall and there are plans for further expansion and development. The School has its own Trout and Salmon Fishing. There are two Senior Boys' Boarding Houses, two Senior Houses for girls and in addition there is a recently opened (1996) Lower School House, Conway, for all Junior Pupils (11-13).

There are 140 boys and girls between the ages of 2½ and 11 at The Junior School, situated half a mile away; boarders are accepted from 9. Kelly and its Junior School are fully integrated and share facilities.

Admission of boys and girls is by the Common Entrance Examination to Senior Schools at the age of 13–14, by School Examination at 11 or 12, or, into the Sixth Form, by interview and a report, including a forecast of good GCSE results from the candidate's present school.

Girls. There are at present 160 girls in the School and special facilities exist for them. We have found that the academic competition stimulates both girls and boys, while the girls have a special part to play in Drama, Music and many outside activities such as Sailing, Riding, Hockey, Tennis, Swimming and Squash.

Term of Entry. Pupils are accepted in all three terms.

Entrance Scholarships. (*see* Entrance Scholarship section) Ten Entrance Scholarships and 4 Music Scholarships of up to half fees are offered for competition each May, an allowance is made for age. Up to four Scholarships of £1,500 pa are for pupils interested in joining the Navy, and these may be awarded on Common Entrance. Foundationerships are available for Founder's kin and for children of deceased Naval Officers. There is a War Memorial Fund from which Bursaries can be awarded to children of Old Kelleians. Further details of help available, particularly for children of Naval Officers or those considering a career in the Royal Navy, may be obtained from the Registrar.

There are Scholarships of up to half fees for boys and girls entering at Sixth Form level. 'All-Rounder', Drama, Art and Science Scholarships are also available throughout the School.

Careers. There is a Careers Department, and practical help is available in the form of personal interviews, a Careers Room containing a wide range of information, and a series of careers courses and work experience ventures. The School is closely in touch with the Independent Schools Careers Organisation and full use is made of aptitude tests and interviews. Information and Communication Technology is fully harnessed in the process of helping boys and girls find careers and university courses.

Combined Cadet Force. There are strong Royal Naval, Army and Royal Marines sections which pupils are encouraged to join. There are miniature and small bore ranges available. The opportunities for sailing, canoeing, subaqua, orienteering, abseiling and other adventure activities, together with strong links with the Royal Navy at Dartmouth, form a particular feature of the School.

Games. Rugby football, cricket, hockey, netball, soccer, athletics, sailing, cross country running, tennis, rugby fives, squash, golf, swimming, judo, badminton, basket-ball and fencing. All junior forms have at least one period of PE every week.

Societies, Clubs and activities. All boys and girls are encouraged to explore new interests and to make the utmost use of their spare time. Societies and Clubs include Literary and Debating, Current Affairs, Drama, Choral and Music, Meteorological, Archaeological, Science, Computer, Astronomical, Survey, Natural History, Rifle, Photographic, Surfing, Fine Arts, Electronics, Amateur Radio and Chess. The school hall is fully equipped for theatrical productions, and the school and houses produce several plays in the course of the year. Musical appreciation is taught and there is a Celebrity Concert Society which parents are also invited to join. There is a joint Town and Gown Kelly Orchestra and Choral Society which gives regular public performances of a high standard. There are ample opportunities for excellent fishing and riding.

Holiday activities. In addition to careers short work courses, there is a wide variety of Royal Navy, Army and Adventure courses taking place in the holidays. Exchange visits to France and Germany are arranged, and there are regular Field Courses in Geography and Biology. Skiing parties go to France every winter.

Dress. The school dress for boys is a blue shirt, grey flannel trousers, pullover and school blazer. The uniform for girls consists of school kilt, white blouse and school blazer.

Fees. The inclusive fees are £14,580 pa for boarders and start at £6,150 pa for day pupils. Music lessons are among the voluntary extras, which are kept to a minimum.

Application. A prospectus and further details may be obtained from the Registrar, who will be pleased to arrange visits for parents by appointment.

Old Kelleian Club: *Gen Sec,* G C L Cooper, Esq, Kelly College, Tavistock, Devon PL19 0HZ.

Charitable status. Kelly College is a Registered Charity, number 306/716. It is a day and boarding school for boys and girls, which also grants maintenance allowances and the provision of assistance for higher education by means of Scholarships, Exhibitions and Means Tested Bursaries.

Kelvinside Academy

33 Kirklee Road,Glasgow G12 0SW.
Tel: 0141-357 3376
Fax: 0141 357 5401

The Academy was founded in 1878. Since May, 1921, it has been controlled by the Kelvinside Academy War Memorial Trust, which was formed in memory of the Academicals who gave their lives in the War of 1914–1918. The affairs of the Trust are managed by a Board of Governors, mainly composed of Academicals and parents.

Motto: AIEN APIðTEYEIN

The Academy is an independent School.

The Governing Body:
Chairman: W Frame, LLB, FRICS, FCIArb

J G Breckenridge
Mrs G Buchanan
T L Craig, MBIM
I C Douglas, BArch, RIBA, FRIAS, MaPS
Mrs M Eadie
Mrs M Falconer, LLB, MA, TQPS
Ms L Hayward
J G Martin
N J McNeill, CA
J S Sinclair
V Skelton, BA (Hons)
J R S Tolmie, LLB
J Turnbull, BSc (Hons)

Secretary to the Governors: Col R C V Hunt

Staff:
Rector: **John L Broadfoot**, BA, MEd

Upper School Staff:
¶I D Lindsay, BSc, BA, DipEd (*Deputy Rector*)
*C Dallas, BSc
*A J Gilliland (*Director of Studies*)
*I Colquhoun, MA
*W Lees, DA
¶G Geddes, MA
*P R Billinghurst, BSc, PhD
*Mrs J Cunningham, BMus (Hons)
B Kelman, BSc
*†R W J Moir, BEd
A G Mulholland, BSc
Mrs P K Williams, BA
†Mrs E Mackie, DA
†D J Wilson, BEd
R D Smith, BA (*OC, CCF*)
†Miss S Crichton, BMus
J Gilius, MA
G Taylor, MA
Mrs G T Ali, MA
J I O Cuthbertson, BSc
A McCann, BSc
Miss A M Dal'Santo, BA
Miss C Massicks, MA
Mrs A Schneeberger, MA
B Farrelly, MA
N Fischbacher, BEng
Mrs H Jephson
S McCallum, BEd
I Nicholson, BSc
S Connor, BEng
Mrs Y Harper, BA
Mrs A Boyle, MA, DipLib
Dr M Given, PhD, BSc
Mrs C Billinghurst, MA
C Lawson, BEd

Chaplain: *Rev D A Keddie, MA, BD (*Careers*)

Bursar: Col R C V Hunt

Assistant Bursar: Mrs M Bennett, MA

Lower School Staff:
Head of Lower School: Mrs T Littlefield, MSc

R A Smith, DPE
Mrs M Jeffrey, DPE
Miss G Cook, CertEd
Mrs L Woore, DPE
Mrs P Campbell, BEd
Mrs K M Fyfe, BEd
Mrs C D Kennedy, MA
Miss R E Patrick, BEd
Miss L Bissett, BEd
Mrs L L McColl, BEd
Miss E Samson, BEd
Mrs S Niewczas, GMus, MMus, QTS
Miss J Salmond, BEd
Mrs B Deutsch, MA

Nursery School Staff:

Miss J E Martin, BEd (*Head of Nursery*)
Mrs J Mann (*Nursery Teacher*)
Mrs J McCreadie (*Senior Nursery Nurse*)
Mrs S Garner (*Nursery Nurse*)

Instrumental Music:
M Ferguson
E Bossley
Mrs J Boddice
A Digger
Mrs S Perricone

Registrar: Mrs L Andonovic, MA

SSI: Capt D Simpson

Kelvinside Academy is a day school for boys and girls (aged 3 to 18) of around 570 pupils.

Girls have been admitted from August 1998, throughout the school.

The main school building is in neo-classical style and Grade A listed but has been extensively modernised within. Further buildings and extensions provide excellent facilities for all subjects and interests, and are symptomatic of the school's progressive approach. The most recent major development has involved a construction of new ICT laboratories and improvements to the Music and Art Departments. The playing fields at Balgray are about half a mile from the school.

Curriculum. Elementary science, technology and computer awareness are taught throughout the Lower School, with French being introduced at the Primary 1 stage. Formal science is started in the Remove (P7) class, together with German and Drama. Latin is offered from the Upper I year. The Course at this point also includes English, History, Geography, Mathematics, Religious Education, Computer Studies, Personal, Social & Health Education (PSHE), Music and Art. Economics is offered as an examination subject from the Upper 3 year and Standard Grade Computing is now a compulsory core subject. The Course leads up to the Standard and Higher Grades of the Scottish Qualifications Authority. In the VIth Form specialised work is undertaken in preparation for the pupil's future career or further study. Pupils are prepared for GCE 'A'level, Certificate of Sixth Year Studies and University Entrance Examinations. Small classes and attention to the individual needs of each child have helped the school to maintain an outstanding record for university entrance.

Combined Cadet Force. All pupils in Upper 3 must join the CCF unless medically exempt. There are RN, Army and RAF sections, and cadets may also join the Duke of Edinburgh's Award Scheme. Membership is voluntary after Upper 3, with those who opt out joining a Liberal Studies programme instead.

Games. All pupils must take School Games unless medically exempt. Rugby and Hockey are played in the winter with Cross-Country running, curling and squash as subsidiary options. Cricket, Tennis and Athletics are the principal summer games with Sailing, Hockey, or Golf as alternatives. The Shooting Team operates throughout the year. In addition to school matches, inter-House competitions are organised in most activities.

Societies. These include Badminton, Drama, Debating, Scientific, Geographic, Mathematics, Computing, Film, Hill-Walking, Art, Scripture Union, Chess, History, Scrabble and Photographic Societies. Ski parties are organised in the holidays.

Music.

In addition to class singing and instrumental tuition, private lessons can be arranged for most instruments. There are Orchestras and Choirs.

Fees (as at March 2000). range from £645 termly in the lowest class to £1,925 termly in the top class.

Admission. Pupils are required to pass an entrance examination before admission.

Scholarships. Scholarships are offered annually to those about to enter the Upper I year. Pupils already at the school are eligible to compete. Further Scholarships are offered to external candidates for entry to the Upper 5 year. Bursaries are also available.

Charitable status. The Kelvinside Academy War Memorial Trust is a Registered Charity, number 11734 (Scotland). The purpose of the Trust is to run a combined primary and secondary day school in memory of those former pupils of the school who gave their lives in the war of 1914–18.

Kent College

Canterbury Kent CT2 9DT.
Tel: 01227 763231
e-mail: registrar@kentcollege.co.uk
website: www.kentcollege.co.uk

The School was founded in 1885, and stands on St Thomas' Hill over-looking the city of Canterbury. In 1920 it was acquired by the Board of Management for Methodist Residential Schools. The Junior School, Vernon Holme, is a mile away.

Kent College was founded for boys only, but has been fully co-educational since 1970. There are 150 boarders and 330 day pupils in the Senior School and 130 pupils in the Junior School, 78 in the Infant Department, together with 27 in the Nursery. There are 150 students in the sixth form.

Although a Methodist foundation, a large proportion of the boys and girls come from non-Methodist homes, and it has always been the policy of the school to welcome boys and girls from overseas as boarders.

Motto: *Lux tua via mea*

Visitor: The President of the Methodist Conference

Administrative Governors:
Dr D McGibney, BSc, MRCP, FFPM (*Chairman*)
H M S Barrett, BA
Mrs H J Brian
Miss J Charlesworth, MA
G A W Connolly, LLB
J Earl, ACIB
K E Elgar, BA, BSc, CChem, FRSC
D J Endersby
C R Evans, MA
Revd D Deeks
B J Haynes, MA, LLB (*OC*)
D F Lander, MRTPI (*OC*)
M G Lang, CQSW
M G Macdonald, MA, LLM
Mrs J McLean
Revd J A Makey
Revd D Marshall
Miss J E Neville
Dr C M Pilkington, BA, PhD
B C Regan, BA, MA
H S Richardson
G Russell, MA
N W Thorne, BEd, FCollP, MSc, FRGS
Miss K J Webster
H F B Weeks (*OC*)
Revd T M Willshaw, MA, BD, PhD
Dr G Young

***Head Master:* E B Halse**, BSc

Deputy Head Master: J W Robson, MA

Second Deputy Head: J Belbin, BA

Senior Teacher: Mrs J Gray, BA

Director of Studies: J Belbin, BA

Marketing Manager: S Kerly, MBE

Chaplain: The Revd E Fletcher, MA (Bristol), BA (Bristol)

Teaching Staff:
G D Colson, BA, MSc, PhD
*D J Perkins, MA
C A Everhart, MusB
D L Allworthy, BSc
*A J Frost, MA
*Mrs C A Baker, CertEd
*J M Coles, BA, MA
R B Grayson, BSc
*Mrs J M Roberts, BSc
A R Corbishley, BA, MA
J Jones, BA, MA
J S Williams, MA
Mrs J M W Haynes, BA, BDA(Di)Dip
*P R Wales, MA, MEd
Mrs F C Hart, BA, MA
*S Worth, MA
*M J Northey, MA
J S J Nickson, BD
Mrs A Tingey, BEd
*T J Williams, BEd
Mrs J L Benge, BA
E D V Young, BSc
R E J Van Hinsbergh, BA
A P Spight, BSc
Mrs B Alonso-Harris, LDA
*M F J R C Sochacki, MA
*Miss I Hemphill, BA
J Burnage, BSc
†S M Howard, BEd
†D J Bunyan, CertEd
D R Montague, BSc, MA
Mrs H A Goddard, BA
S A Fell, BA
Miss R Chohan, BSc
C D T McGarrity, BSc, BA, PhD
Mrs C Rotheram, BA
Mrs R Pollott, BA
Mrs J McRae, BDA
H S A Fido, MA
Mrs C Balsdon, BA
Mrs G Bunyan, BEd
†K R Dorion, BA, MA
Mrs C Maclaren, LADipEurHum

Mrs K L McGibney, BA
Miss H Butcher, BA
G West, MA, LRAM, LTCL
†A Connah, BA, GradDipEd, CertTeach
Mrs J Connah, BSc, GradDipEd
Ms K Karas-Referendian
M Rouse, BSc
Miss S Timmerman
†Ms J Van Deelen, MA
K Wallis, BA
Miss B Whitley, BA

Junior School:
Head Master: A J Carter, BEd

A J J Spence, CertEd (*Deputy Head Master*)
T M Baldwin, BEd
Miss S Colebrook, BEd
Mrs D Everhart, BMus, LRAM
H Ritchie, BSc, CertEd
Mrs A Tingey, BEd
Mrs K Griffiths, DipAD
Mrs J McRae, CertEd, BDA Dip
Mrs E Young, DipEd
Mrs C R Ritchie, CertEd (*Head of Infant Dept*)
Mrs S Henderson, DipEd
Mrs J Gracey, BA
Mrs M Laslett, CertEd
C P Sweet, BA
Mrs R L Fitzgerald, BEd
Mrs B Jones, BA
Mrs J Halse, BSc
Mrs R Pryce, BEd
Mrs C Balsdon, BA
Mrs A Howard, BEd
Mrs H Fairhurst, CertEd
Miss Alexander, BEd
Mrs M S Cettrino, CertEd, BA
Miss G Beare, BA
Mrs K Carter, BEd

Medical Officer: P Livesey, MD, MB, ChB, DObstRCOG

Secretary to the Governors and Bursar: Captain T A Wyndham Lewis, RN

Headmaster's Secretary:
Mrs S Kilbee (*Senior School*)
Mrs G Barry (*Junior School*)

Registrar: Mrs J Simpson

Buildings. Recent additions include two girls' Boarding Houses, a Music Centre with seven Practice Rooms, an Art Centre, Dyslexia Unit, EFL Centre, Drama Studio, Sixth Form Centre, Floodlit Synthetic playing surface for hockey and twelve tennis courts, extra classrooms, laboratories, common rooms and the skilful alteration of the Chapel into a much bigger building to serve as Chapel, Assembly Hall and Theatre. To mark the Centenary, a major development programme was inaugurated which includes an excellent new Library and Reading Room, Careers rooms, a Sports Hall with Squash Courts and a Technology Centre.

Close to the main buildings is the 70-acre Moat Farm purchased in 1952. The farm is managed by a member of the staff. The remainder of the land is used for playing fields and recreational purposes.

The estate at the Junior School is unusually beautiful. The house was originally owned by Sidney Cooper RA and many of the trees and shrubs he planted, some of them rare, survive to make an ideal environment for young children. (See entry under Vernon Holme, Part V).

Curriculum. The curriculum is closely aligned to the National Curriculum but we seek to offer more flexibility and the possibility of a greater range of subjects. All pupils are normally expected to take at least one European language at GCSE. Besides the normal range of basic subjects, the School offers optional courses at examination level in Latin and Greek, Information Technology, Geology, Economics, Politics, Business Studies, Rural Science, Electronics and Psychology.

Pupils are prepared for the GCSE, AS and A2 levels.

It is not the aim to specialise in any one group of subjects, but to provide a balanced curriculum which will give full opportunity for every boy and girl to get a good groundwork of general knowledge and later to develop particular gifts to a high standard.

Most pupils enter the Sixth Form to follow a course of advanced studies, and the majority of these go on to university.

Dyslexia Unit. The school makes provision for a number of dyslexic children of appropriate ability. There is a special unit with qualified staff and in addition the school aims to offer an understanding approach to children with this problem. Our objective is to integrate pupils into the normal curriculum and activity of the school whilst giving them appropriate support within the dyslexia unit.

Pastoral Care. All pupils are placed in the care of a tutor who works closely with the Housemaster and Year Head, liaising with the Head Master on the one hand and parents on the other. The Head Master sees all pupils regularly to discuss their progress. Opportunities are arranged each year to enable parents to meet staff and in addition the Head Master and all Staff are willing to meet parents by arrangement.

Religion. Although the School is controlled by the Board of Management for Methodist Residential Schools, boys and girls of all denominations are accepted. During the week all pupils attend Morning Prayers, and on Sundays there is a service for all boarders either in the morning or the evening. Parents are very welcome at these services. Confirmation classes are arranged in the Spring Term, and a joint Confirmation Service for Methodists and Anglicans is held in the School Chapel early in the Summer Term.

Games and Activities. The school possesses 28 acres of playing fields, 1 floodlit astroturf hockey pitch and 2 Open-air Swimming Pools. The major games for boys are Rugby, Football, Hockey, Tennis and Cricket and for girls Netball, Hockey, Tennis and Rounders. There are also school fixtures in Athletics, Cross-Country, Fencing, Sailing, Swimming, Wind-surfing and Orienteering.

Senior pupils take part in various forms of social service in the city and the School also has its own Duke of Edinburgh Award Group. There is a full range of optional school activities, including Art, Printing, Pottery, CDT, Photography, Riding and Farming. The School has its own farm with plenty of livestock to provide all-year-round interest.

Music and Drama play an important part in school life. Boys and girls work together in school and house plays which are performed each year, and they are encouraged to join the Choral Society, Madrigal Group and Orchestra. Many concerts are given each year, including an annual choral concert in the Cathedral. In addition to class music teaching, individual tuition can be arranged in Piano and Organ and all orchestral instruments.

Admission. Boys and girls are admitted to the Infant Department at age 4 and to the Junior Department at the age of 7. There is also a nursery department which takes boys and girls from 3. The normal age of admission to the Senior School is 11 years. The Entrance Examination takes place in January each year for admission the following September. There is another entry at age 13 and also places are available in the Sixth Form for those wishing to follow 'A' level courses in Arts or Sciences. There are occasional vacancies at other levels.

Fees. Day pupils £8,100 pa. Boarders £14,400 pa. Junior School Boarders £11,076 pa. (These figures are correct from September 2000).

HM Forces: Personnel eligible for the Boarding School Allowance only pay 10% of the total school fee.

Entrance Scholarships (*see* Entrance Scholarship section). Scholarships and Bursaries range in value from one-third to half tuition fee and are awarded each year to 11 and 13-year-old candidates for admission. Sixth Form Scholarships are also offered, and Music, Art and Sporting Scholarships at ages 11–16. The School has its own Assisted Places Scheme and offers such places for children of all ages. Additional bursaries are offered to children who need to board. Selection is made on the results of the Entrance Examination. Full particulars may be obtained from the Headmaster.

Honours. Most school leavers go on to university and up to ten students have secured places at Oxford and Cambridge colleges each year.

Charitable status. The Methodist Secondary Education Trust is a Registered Charity, number 307844. The School was founded to provide education within a supportive Christian environment.

Kimbolton School

Kimbolton Huntingdon Cambs. PE18 0EA.
Tel: (01480) 860505
Fax: (01480) 860386
website: www.kimbolton.cambs.sch.uk

The School was founded in 1600 and was awarded Direct Grant status as a boys' day and boarding school in 1945. Day Girls were first admitted in 1976 and the Pre-preparatory Department (ages 4–7), the Preparatory Department (ages 7–11) and the Senior School are fully coeducational with day boys and girls (4–18) and boarding boys and girls (11–18). As a result of the withdrawal of the Direct Grant the School assumed fully independent status in 1978. There are 96 pupils in the Pre-preparatory Department (48 Day Girls and 48 Day Boys), 172 pupils in the Preparatory Department (78 Day Girls and 94 Day Boys) and 576 pupils in the Senior School (60 Boarders, 238 Day Girls, 279 Day Boys).

Motto: *Spes Durat Avorum.*

Governing Body:

T R Brown (*Chairman*)
J Bates
J B Bourke, MA, MB, BChir, FRCS
C R Boyes
M G Capps
Mrs J Croft
A H Duberly
P S Hamblin
Dr T P Hynes
D N Ireland, MA
J C Mugglestone
S J F Page
Dr A Schofield
P Seabrook
Mrs P W Silby
I Twigden
Dr P Wix

***Headmaster:* R V Peel**, BSc, FRSA

Deputy Headmaster: P J Simpson, MA

Senior Mistress: Miss M Pepper, BA

†A J Bamford, MA
Dr H Barjesteh, BSc, PhD
Miss A V Barnett, BA
Mrs A J Bates, BA
†C J Bates, MA
A J A Beal, BSc, MSc
†Mrs C E Bennett, BSc
†M Bennett, BA, RAS, PDip
Mrs R M Bentham, BA
K D Buckland, BSc
†F G Burns, MA, BEd
Mrs N C Butler, BA
G A Cappi, MA
M Cook, MA
K J Curtis, BSc, CPhys, MInstP
R Davies, BA
Mrs W A Davies, BSc
Mrs C C Elliott, BA
Miss A J Engelhart, BSc
Miss L A Furnival, BA
Revd A P Goodchild, BA
A Gray, BSc
J D Greening, MA
A R J Gunning, MA
M D Hakes, BEd
D Harris, BSc, ARCS
Mrs J Hart, CertEd
S E C Henson, BEd
C J W Horricks, BA
Miss N Hughes, BA
R E Knell, BA
A J M Lawrence, BA
J R Lee, BA
S J Marsh, BSc
Miss C Matthews, BEd
J Norton, BSc
M C Pashley, BMus
Mrs S C Peel, BA
S K Pollard, MA
F Priest, ATD, DipAD
J R Saunders, BA
W J Skinner, MA
Miss K-J Snelson, BA
I W Stokes, BA
J C Stotesbury, BSc
A G Tapp, BEd
C Webb, BSc
R J Wilson, BMetall
S Wilson, BA
Mrs C H Wrench, BA

Preparatory Department:
Head: S E Reeves, DipEd
Deputy: P W Cook, BEd

Miss C Bills, BA
D Buckley, BSc
Mrs J Cole, BA
Mrs J Cook, CertEd
Miss K Forde, BEd, MPhil
Miss D T Lawson, BEd
Mrs L E Reeves, DipEd
M Stott, BEd
Mrs C Wood, BA

Pre-preparatory Department:
Teacher in charge: Mrs E King, BSc

Mrs P Binham, BSc
Mrs E Bradley, BEd
Mrs E J Hartwell, BA
Miss S J Morrell, BA
Mrs F Y Williams, BA
Mrs S Cropper, NNEB
Miss E Rowney, NNEB
Mrs J Laizo, NNEB

Bursar: E F P Valletta, MBIFM

Aims. The School aims to provide a balanced education within a disciplined framework and to encourage students to develop their personalities and potential to the full.

Buildings. The main school building is Kimbolton Castle, once the home of Queen Catharine of Aragon and for 3 centuries the home of the Dukes of Manchester, and now with its Vanbrugh front and Pellegrini murals a building of considerable beauty and architectural importance. There is also on permanent display in the Castle, a fine collection of portraits including some by Lely, Pellegrini, Zoffany and Mengs, and the former Staterooms are study areas for Senior pupils. The Chapel, located in the Castle, is used each day for prayers. In the grounds, the Mews and the Robert Adam Gatehouse have been adapted for school use. There are two large classroom blocks, one of which houses the Mathematics, Geography, Biology and Food Technology Departments. The Donaldson Laboratories for Physics and Chemistry were opened in September 1988, and contain 8 laboratories. The Design Technology Centre has been modernised and extended. The Computer Centre has been built alongside. The School has a fine synthetic-turf hockey pitch. The Lewis hall caters for the performing arts and daily assemblies, and has been completely restructured to provide modern theatre and concert facilities.

A large sports complex, incorporating squash courts, gymnasium, sports hall, multi gym and changing rooms opened in September 1992. A new Art Centre opened in January 1995. A new Library opened in April 1999 and an indoor swimming pool was opened by the Duke of Gloucester in June 2000, as part of the School's quatercentenary celebration.

The Preparatory Department has been recently refurbished and is provided with new classrooms, changing rooms and a hall for music and drama. There is also a gymnasium and specialist science and information technology rooms. The dining facilities and kitchens were upgraded in 1997. A new Pre-Preparatory Department opened in September 1999.

The School Sanatorium is centrally situated.

One boarding house for junior boys and girls across the senior age range, and one senior boys boarding house stand outside the grounds in the beautiful High Street of Kimbolton.

Organisation. The Preparatory Department admits children at the age of 7, 8 or 9 (day pupils only) who are expected to complete their education in the Senior School, whilst the Pre-Preparatory Department caters for children at age 4, 5 and 6. Entry into the Senior School at the age of 11 is open to boarders and day pupils. Suitably qualified post GCSE students are also admitted to the VIth Form.

In the Senior School places are automatically reserved for children from the Preparatory Department whose work reaches a satisfactory standard. There is also a large entry of pupils of 13 from Preparatory Schools. The total number of pupils at present in the Senior School is 576 (60 boarders), with 150 in the VIth Form. In the Preparatory Department there are at present 94 day boys and 78 day girls. There are 48 boys and 48 girls in the Pre-Preparatory Department.

In addition to the boarding houses, there are four Senior houses and one Junior house. Housemasters, assisted by tutors, look after the general well-being and progress of their charges. In the interests of economy and efficiency there is a central Dining Hall.

Work. For the first 2 years in the Senior School there are 3 parallel forms; in the third, fourth and fifth years there are 5 smaller forms and sets for different subjects. Boys and girls entering at 13 from Preparatory Schools join one of the five IIIrd Forms. Until they have taken GCSE all pupils follow a course of general education, and an option scheme is introduced in the IVth Form. In the VIth Forms specialisation occurs, and pupils will usually study four AS subjects from the following list: English, History, Geography, French, Spanish, Maths. (Pure with Mechanics or Statistics), Physics, Chemistry, Biology, Music, Art, History of Art, Food Technology, Design Technology, Economics, Business and Politics. In the Upper Sixth pupils will usually continue with three subjects to A2 level. All sixth formers follow a course in General Studies leading to A2 level.

Most leavers go on to University or to Further Education.

Religious Teaching. Morning prayers are held every morning in the School Chapel, and every pupil in the first three years has one period of Divinity teaching each week. Sunday Services are held in the Chapel for boarders, and occasionally the School worships in the Parish Church.

Games and other activities. The School owns over 160 acres of land, more than 20 of which are laid out as playing fields. The major sports for boys are Association Football, Hockey and Cricket. For girls the main sports are Hockey, Netball and Tennis. Minor sports include Athletics, Lawn Tennis, Swimming, Rifle Shooting, Clay Pigeon Shooting, Squash, Badminton, Basketball and Rounders. Extensive use is also made by the Sailing Club of nearby Grafham Water, both for recreational sailing and inter-school matches. Canoeing is popular in the winter months.

The School contingent of the CCF is a voluntary, keen and efficient body, divided into Navy, Army and RAF Sections, and there is a successful and growing number of participants involved in the Duke of Edinburgh Award scheme. Community Service is an alternative option for senior pupils.

Music and Drama play an important part in the life of the School. There is a Choral Society, two orchestras, several Bands, and ensemble groups. The School Dramatic Society stages plays or musicals each term, with a Shakespearean production in the Courtyard every 3 or 4 years.

There are many other activities and many societies, such as debating, public speaking, Young Enterprise, photography, chess, pottery, family history and philosophy.

Careers. Advice can be sought at any time by pupils or their parents from the Careers Staff, three of whom specialise in university entrance. There is a well-stocked Careers Room, and the School is a member of the Independent Schools Careers Organisation. Fifth formers take the Morrisby careers tests administered by ISCO.

Dress. Boys wear plain grey suits, or blazers and grey flannels. The girls' uniform includes a standard skirt, blouse and blazer.

Admission. (*see* Entrance Scholarship section) Correspondence about entry, whether to the Pre-Preparatory Department, the Preparatory Department or to the Senior School, should be addressed to the Headmaster. The School Entrance examinations at 11+ are held in February when up to five Entrance Scholarships may be awarded. Tests for entry into the Preparatory Department are held in February. Entry at 13+ is usually by the Common Entrance Examination in June, when a number of scholarships are awarded. Candidates also sit the Common Academic Scholarship Examination held in March. The William Ingram Awards are for those at 13+ with strengths in music, art or games. Entry into the Sixth Form is based on interview and GCSE results. There are a number of Sixth Form Scholarships. Arrangements can be made for candidates who are with their parents overseas to take the entrance examination at their own schools.

Fees. The fees are inclusive, and there is no charge for laundry, books, stationery or examination entries.

Pre-Preparatory Department: £1,090, £1,350, and £1,600 per term.

Preparatory Department: tuition £1,960 per term.

Senior School: tuition £2,370 per term; boarding £3,990 per term.

There is a reduction of 2½% when brothers or sisters attend at the same time.

Music Tuition Fee. For individual lessons £140 per term. (A term's notice must be given in writing before a pupil discontinues music lessons.)

Registration Fee. A fee of £40 should be sent when the registration form is completed. This is not returnable.

There is a bursary scheme by means of which up to 30% of tuition fees can be remitted for deserving candidates.

Term of Entry. Most pupils enter at the start of the School year in September, but entry in other terms is also possible.

Old Kimboltonians Association. All correspondence to: The Secretary, OKA, Kimbolton School, Kimbolton, Huntingdon, Cambs PE18 0EA.

Charitable status. Kimbolton School Foundation is a Registered Charity, number 311849. It exists to provide and conduct a school in the Parish of Kimbolton, which shall be a day school or a boarding school for boys and girls.

King Edward's School Bath

North Road Bath BA2 6HU.

Tel: Senior School (01225) 464313; Junior School (01225) 463218; Pre-Prep School (01225) 421681
Fax: Senior School (01225) 481363; Junior School (01225) 442178; Pre-Prep School (01225) 428006
e-mail: headmaster@kesbath.biblio.net
website: www.kes.bath.sch.uk

King Edward's School, Bath, was founded by Edward VI in 1552. Originally a Grammar School, the School was fully independent until 1920, when it accepted Direct Grant status, reverting to full independence in 1976. Originally a boys' school, King Edward's School admitted girls to the Sixth Form in 1986, and then moved towards full co-education in 1997, admitting girls at ages 7 and 11. This process will be complete in 2001.

King Edward's School is a busy day school, with a proud record, steadily enhanced over the past 15 years, of sustained academic achievement (98% of its pupils regularly proceed to universities and institutions of higher education). It is also committed to providing the broadest possible range of opportunities for all its pupils, and a multiplicity of extracurricular activities, trips and expeditions are on offer. The School has a strong commitment to sport, both recreational and competitive, and the arts flourish, with the Annual Arts Festival providing a showcase for talented pupils in art, music and drama.

There are currently 710 pupils in the Senior School (including a Sixth form of 225) and some 186 pupils in the Junior School.

For over 400 years, the School occupied various premises in the city centre, but in 1961 the Senior School moved to a fine fourteen-acre site on North Road, on the south-eastern slopes of the city. This site has been extensively developed in recent years and now boasts superb facilities. The Junior School moved into outstanding new premises here in 1990.

The Pre-Prep School, which caters for children from 3 to 7 years of age, is situated in an elegant Victorian house on the western side of the city.

Chairman of Governors: Prof I D Ford, BSc, MSc, PhD

***Headmaster:* P J Winter**, MA (Wadham College, Oxford)

Second Master: C Rowe, BA

Senior Master: L D L Jones, DLC

Head of Lower School: D J Chapman, BA

Head of Middle School: T P C Snowdon, BSc

Head of Sixth Form: J Turner, BA

Director of Studies: R J Rowe, BA

§Mrs E Azis, BA
Mrs S Bailey, BA
N P C Barnes, MA
§D Bevan, BA
A M Bougeard, BSc
*Mrs P M Bougeard, MA
D L Briggs, BA
*P A Brownrigg, CertEd
*T D Burroughs, BA
T P J Caston, BA
§Mrs J Chapman, BA
§Mrs G Choulerton, CertEd
N M Cox, BSc
M A Cunliffe, MA
*Mrs S M Curtis, BA, MPhil
§Mrs M N Davis, MA
Mrs P A Dennis-Jones, BA
Mrs L Doliczny, BSc
Mrs J Farrant, MA
*Mrs C M Finch, BA
Mrs W J Fletcher, BA
Mrs L Formela-Osborne, BEd
*R Haynes, MA
*B Heywood, BSc
N Hunt, BA
*Ms L Joslin, BEd
*D J Kemp, BEd
*G J F Kilroy, MA
*T W L Laney, BSc
Mrs P Lunter, BSc
A C F Mason, BA
T G Medhurst, BEd
*D Middlebrough, BA
A R Monks, MSc
*L H Newman, MSc, PhD
*M R Pell, BA
Ms T Plews, BSc
Mrs G A Reeves, BA
A D Rice, BA
§Ms J Riches, BA
§Mrs F Rothwell, CertEd
Mrs C A Rowe, BA
J Rutter, BA, BSc
*W R Satterthwaite, MA
Ms L J Saunders, BSc
§Mrs A Sellick, BSc
*P H Simonds, BSc
Ms R L Sonley, BSc
Ms H Stewart-Jones, BA
F R Thorn, BA, PhD
J E G Tidball, BSc
*A W Trim, BA
*A I M Vass, MA
N A Vile, BSc
§Mrs A White
§Mrs J Wilcox, BSc

Director of Music: I D C Phipps, LRAM, LTCL, ARCM

Deputy Director of Music: P C Weaver, BA, FRCO

Head of Careers Education and Guidance: J D Fletcher, MA

Head of Operations & Finance: Ms J I Rowell, MBA, BSc

Registrar and Personal Assistant to the Headmaster: Mrs S E Bury, BSc

Headmaster's Secretary: Mrs A L Plumbridge

Librarian: Mrs J A Ross, BA

Medical Officer: Dr T J Harris, BM, BCh (Oxon), MRCGP

Senior School Chaplain: The Revd S Airey

Junior School:

Head of Junior School: J W Croker, BA

Deputy Head: R D Coleman, BA

Ms J Harrison, DipEd
§M Howcroft, BEd
Mrs C Lewis, CertEd
A J MacFarlan, BA
Mrs E MacFarlan, BEd
Mrs J Munn, MA
D J Orchard, BSc
A Parnell, BSc
Mrs B Poulsom, BA
J Roberts-Wray, BA
Mrs A Sellick, BSc
G Taylor, BA
P Weaver, BA, FRCO
Miss R Whittle, BEd

Junior School Administrator: Mrs V Cross

Junior School Chaplain: The Revd Martin Lloyd-Williams

Pre-Prep School:

Head: Mrs J Siderfin, BA

Miss C Alexander, CertEd, CTh
Miss S Brassington, BA
Mrs S Davies, MA
Mrs K Hale, BEd
Mrs J Jones, CertEd
Mrs J Lewis, BEd
Mrs A Overeynder, BSc

Pre-Prep Administrator: Mrs T Claridge

Buildings. The Senior School is housed in a complex of buildings arranged in three adjoining groups. The Old Building, dating from 1830, provides tutorial accommodation for Sixth Form pupils, the Staff Common Room and completely refurbished Information Technology Centre and Language Laboratory. The Main Building was fully refurbished during the summer 1996, allowing the suiting of the major academic departments. It comprises a Music block, the Wroughton Theatre, Physics and Chemistry laboratories and classrooms, a Biology laboratory, a Geography block, and a Mathematics block. The third group consists of an Art, Craft and Technology Centre and the Willett Hall with adjoining kitchens and servery, which functions as a dining hall, audio-visual centre and lecture hall. The Holbeche Centre houses a Sixth Form Common Room with adjoining kitchen, an extended and modernised Careers and Higher Education Centre, a Drama Workshop, purpose-built Library and various tutorial rooms. There is also a magnificent Sports Hall, together with an artificial playing surface for hockey and tennis.

The pavilion at Bathampton was completed in March 1998.

Admission. While half the pupils come from the City of Bath or its immediate environs, nearly half are resident in the counties of Gloucestershire, Somerset and Wiltshire – a wide catchment area made possible by excellent public transport services and coaches organised by the parents.

Methods of entry.

To the Junior School. From the age of 7 by assessment and interview. The main entry is at the age of 7 or 8 but other vacancies may occur at 9 or 10. Details may be obtained from the Junior School Administrator, North Road, Bath, BA2 6JA. Telephone 01225 463218.

To the Senior School

(1) From our own Junior School, by passing the Senior School Entrance Examination for 11 year-olds.

(2) Pupils from other Primary and Preparatory Schools in the 10–11 age group may be offered fee-paying places on the results of the same examination, held in January of each year.

(3) Older pupils may enter the Senior School, if and where places are available, by sitting an Entrance Examination appropriate to their age.

(4) Students may also seek direct entry into the Sixth Form. Such students are expected to acquire a sound set of GCSE passes before transfer for advanced study. Applicants are interviewed and a reference is sought from their present school.

Application forms and further information concerning entry are obtainable from the Registrar, who will arrange prior visits to see the School. Open Days are held in October and November.

Fees. Senior School: £1,999 per term. Junior School: £1,539 per term. Pre-Prep School (full-time) £1,288-£1,462.

Scholarships. Scholarships and Exhibitions each worth up to £500 per annum are awarded at 11+ level, either for academic excellence or for outstanding talent in another field. Entrance Bursaries may be awarded to children entering Year 7, whose parents are unable to pay the full fee.

Students who perform outstandingly at GCSE may be awarded an Old Edwardians' Scholarship towards the provision of books for A-Level studies.

The Governing Body, to the extent that funds permit, assists parents if they run into financial difficulties during a pupil's schooling. Further details are obtainable from the Registrar.

Curriculum. The School is committed to breadth in education. Seventeen subjects are taught up to GCSE level. A very flexible choice system is introduced in Year 10 so that no doors need be closed before entry into the Sixth Form. All students study all three sciences to GCSE at the Single, Double or Triple Award.

The A-level subjects on offer are English, French, German, Spanish, Latin, History, Economics, Business Studies, Geography, Mathematics, Further Mathematics, Physics, Chemistry, Biology, Technology, Religious Studies, Theatre Studies, Sports Studies, Art and Music; and they may be combined in a variety of ways. In addition, Classical Civilisation, ICT, Philosophy, and Electronics are offered at AS level. In addition, about a quarter of the Lower Sixth Form curriculum is devoted to complementary and general courses. Pupils are encouraged also to enter for A-level General Studies. The Sixth Form Society, comprising all Upper Sixth students, meets each week to listen to a range of eminent speakers or to participate in debate.

Boys and girls are prepared for all forms of Higher Education, especially for Universities and for entry into the Services. The School has a proud tradition of sending a significant proportion of its students to the best universities in the land.

Music, Art and Craft. There is a strong musical tradition in the School. Many instrumental and choral groups afford opportunities to explore differing musical styles. There are Senior, Intermediate and Junior orchestras, Early Music Groups, a Brass Group, a Swing Band, a Chamber Choir and an A Capella Choir. The School is a centre for the examinations of the Associated Board of the Royal Schools of Music and these are held termly. The Chamber Choir undertakes a concert tour in Europe every two years. Music is an enjoyable and highly participative activity.

Every Spring Term over a period of two weeks the annual **Arts Festival** is held. Concerts, recitals, lectures, visits and dramatic productions are held in School and at selected venues in Bath. One highlight is the Chamber Concert held in the elegant surroundings of the neighbouring Holburne Museum. The Festival concludes with an Invitation Concert which seeks to bring together parents, pupils and friends to form a large choir and orchestra for the performance of suitable major works.

Drama. The School has an oustanding dramatic tradition, with two major productions a year. Senior students run a Lower School Drama Club to encourage young talent. The splendid Wroughton Theatre, supported by a full-time technical manager, provides an outstanding facility for productions and concerts of every kind.

Housed in a custom-built suite of studios, the **Art Department** is a centre of excellence, with a fine tradition within the School and the Bath area. Teaching covers fine art, drawing and painting, ceramics and three-dimensional work, printmaking and photography. Art History and critical studies are taught as an integral part of the course and field trips and visits to galleries along with links to practising artists, are encouraged. Sixth Form Art Tours are planned annually. Every year students are prepared for interview at Art School and related courses.

Games. The main playing fields at Bathampton, comprising 17 acres, are attractively situated at one end of the Limpley Stoke valley, about a mile from the School. An All Weather Synthetic Pitch on the main School site has proved to be invaluable for hockey and tennis, and as an intensively used practice area for all games.

The major games are Rugby Football, Hockey, Cricket, Netball and Athletics. Minor sports include Aerobics, Cross-Country, Tennis, Swimming, Soccer, Shooting, Rounders, Fencing, Judo, Badminton, Squash, Golf, Basketball, Dance, Gymnastics, Table-Tennis and Rock-climbing. Each boy or girl has a full games session per week and has ample opportunities to represent the School or to participate in a wide range of inter-Form activities.

Activities. In Year 9, pupils may opt to join the School CCF, founded in 1896 and the oldest in the West Country. The contingent has a fine record of success in regional and national competitions. The CCF provides many opportunities for adventure training and there is an Annual Summer Camp. Each year a number of students win scholarships or cadetships in different branches of the armed services.

There is also a strong tradition of mountain walking and adventure training for pupils who choose not to join the CCF, and trips go to Dartmoor, the Welsh mountains and the Cevennes each year. The School enters two teams into the Ten Tors Competition each year.

School Societies and Clubs. Pupils are actively encouraged to engage in the many out-of-school activities which supplement their more formal education. A wealth of Societies and Clubs caters for every interest and for every age group. An organised programme of Outdoor Pursuits functions throughout the year. Frequent opportunities for travel abroad, especially during the Easter vacation, are provided by School tours or exchanges conducted by members of Staff. The Ski Club visits the Alps or the USA annually.

Pastoral Care is exercised by Form Teachers and Prefects up to Year 11, by Tutors in the Sixth Form, and is coordinated by the Heads of Lower School, Middle School and Sixth Form. The School prides itself on its family atmosphere and the excellent relationships between pupils of all ages and staff. Advice on Careers and entry to Higher Education is readily available. Parents meet Staff at regular intervals to discuss academic progress, or at social functions. Many of the latter are organised by very active parents' committees, and the School, possibly uniquely, boasts a Former Parents' Association which has enjoyed an Annual Dinner for over 20 years.

Dress. Boys in the Main School wear a dark blue blazer and flannels. Younger girls wear a Lindsay tartan kilt, a white open-neck blouse and the school blazer, whilst

Middle School girls wear a grey skirt or grey trousers. In the Sixth Form, boys and girls wear suits of their own choosing, appropriate for formal work. Girls may wear trouser suits.

Junior School. The Junior School is an integral part of the foundation and is governed by the same Board. It joins with the Senior School in major events, such as the Founder's Day Service in Bath Abbey, and shares various games facilities. The work is organised in close consultation with the Senior School and the Pre-Prep to ensure that education provided is continuous and progressive from the age of 3 to 18.

Its curriculum comprises English, Mathematics, Science, CDT, History, Geography, Art, Music, Religious Education, Physical Education, French, Study Skills and Information Technology, and Latin at Year 6.

Music is a strength in the School with all children learning the recorder in Year 3 and violin in Year 4. More than a third of the children learn additional instruments under the tutelage of a strong peripatetic music staff and a majority of children sing in the choir. French is taught throughout the School while purpose-built facilities in Art, Science, Technology and IT, coupled with specialist teaching, ensure high standards of achievement in those areas. The Junior School has developed a reputation in the past few years for dramatic productions of the highest quality and a drama club, which runs throughout the year, is always a popular choice. This School is a very busy one renowned for its extra curricular activities programme. The wide variety of activities on offer include table tennis, gymnastics, fencing, judo, street dance, country dancing, challenge club, environmental club, computer, chess, art and stitchcraft. This is not to mention the various musical and instrumental groups and the many opportunities to play rugby, football, hockey, netball, cricket, basketball, tennis and rounders. All children throughout the School also go swimming at the pool at Bath University. A large number of competitive fixtures are played against other schools in a wide variety of sports and activities and each year group has their own programme of fixtures. Frequent educational trips are arranged in and around the local area and during the summer activities week; residential trips include destinations such as France and Devon. Sporting tours also take place; in the last two years there have been rugby tours to Ireland and Cornwall, and a netball tour this year to the north of England.

The House system plays a strong role in the life of the School. All children belong to one of four Houses and take part in many House events and competitions during the year. These include football, rugby, golf, general knowledge, hockey, unihoc, netball, swimming, tennis, cricket, drama, tabletennis, music and a festival of public speaking.

The main entry is at the age of 7 or 8 but other vacancies may occur at 9 or 10. Applications should be made direct to the Junior School Administrator, North Road, Bath, BA2 6JA

Pre-Prep School. As with the Junior School, the Pre-Prep is governed by the same Board. The former Park School became King Edward's Pre-Prep in July 1999. The aim is to provide access to a balanced and planned programme of learning for all children, which takes into account their individual developmental stage, enables their potential and intellectual growth, and develops each child's potential to the full.

The Nursery class, which takes boys and girls from 3, has its own self-contained unit and playground to cater specifically for the needs of the very young child. Structured play offers children rich opportunities for controlling and shaping what they do. Children may stay all day or attend separate morning or afternoon sessions.

The Pre-Prep caters for children from 4+ to 7+. Children in Reception work on both the Under 5's curriculum and towards Level 1 of the National Curriculum. The aim is that, by the age of 7, children in Year 2 will be achieving at least Level 3 in English, Mathematics and Science.

Applications should be made direct to the Head, Mrs J Siderfin, King Edward's Pre-Prep School, Weston Lane, Bath BA1 4AQ.

Honours. In 2000, there was a pass rate at A-Level of 98% with 65% of grades at A and B. Ninety-eight per cent of all Upper Sixth leavers proceed to Universities or institutions of Higher Education. Twelve students have received offers or conditional offers from Oxford and Cambridge for October 2001.

The Association of Old Edwardians of Bath: *Hon Secretary, L D L Jones, King Edward's School, North Road, Bath BA2 6HU.*

Charitable status. King Edward's School at Bath is a Registered Charity, number 310227. It is a charitable trust for the purpose of educating children.

King Edward's School
Birmingham

Edgbaston Park Road Birmingham B15 2UA.
Tel: 0121-472-1672
Fax: 0121-415-4327
e-mail: office@kes.bham.sch.uk

King Edward's School, Birmingham, was founded in 1552 and occupied a position in the centre of the city until 1936 when it moved to its present 45 acre site in Edgbaston, surrounded by a golf course, lake and nature reserve and adjacent to the University. It is an independent day school with about 890 boys aged 11 to 18. Approximately 20 boys each year receive financial assistance with fees from the Governors' Assisted Places Scheme and the Ogden Trust. The school belongs to the Foundation of the Schools of King Edward VI in Birmingham (two independent and five grammar schools), and its sister-school, King Edward VI High School for Girls, is on the same campus. Academically one of the leading schools in the country, King Edward's is also renowned for its prowess in sport, music and drama.

Motto: *'Domine, Salvum fac Regem'*.

Governing Body:

Professor P A Garrett, BSc, FGS (*Chairman*)
Professor J T Boulton, PhD, HonDLitt, FBA (*Vice-Chairman*)

D Allen, BA, MEd, FRSA
S G Campbell, LLB
Professor E D Ellis, MA, LLM, PhD, Barrister at Law
Mrs M M England, BSc
R J Evans
Councillor L Lawrence, BA(Hons)
Professor T Norris, MA, ScD
G Sanders, MBE, BA
M B Squires, FCA, FCCA, FTII, ACC
M D Stirling, FCA

Secretary to the Foundation: Dr S Grainger

***Chief Master:* R M Dancey,** MA

Deputy Chief Master: G Andronov, BSc

Second Master: D C Everest, DPE

Third Master: K D Phillips, BA

Assistant Teachers:
P H S Lambie, MA
G A Worthington, MA
D C Rigby, MSc
A P Russell, BSc

M L Workman, BA
M D Stead, BA
R W Symonds, BSc
S Birch, BEd
D C Dewar, BSc
P E Bridle, GRSM, LRAM
S E Lampard, BSc
R T Bridges, MA, PhD
D J Hancock, MA, BSc
J R R Emery, MA
S F Owen, MA
T F P Hosty, BA, PhD
J A Cumberland, MA
R N Lye, BA
L W Evans, BA
J P Davies, MA
Mrs T B Hodgin, MIL
I D Loram, BA
J C S Burns, MA
D N D Chamberlain, BSc
Mrs J E Durman, BEd
Mrs C M Southworth, BA
L M Roll, BA
T Mason, BSc
E J Milton, BA
M N A Ostrowicz, BSc
J S Lloyd, CertEd
B M Spencer, BA
J C Hatton, BA

C D Boardman, BSc
S J Tinley, BSc
Miss C M L Tudor, BA
J C Howard, BEd
J Porter, BSc
T A McMullan, BSc
The Revd D H Raynor, MA, MLitt
J G Evans, MSc, PhD
M J Monks, GRSM
R W James, BA
S L Stacey, MA
T F Cross, BSc
R J Deeley, MA
R H C Simpson, BA, MSc
P A Rees, BA
D J Ash, MA
A E D Duncombe, BA
M Daniel, BSc, DPhil
Miss C R Bubb, BA
W-S Lau, MChem
C W Walker, CertEd
H S Smith, BA, PhD
Mrs G D Walster, BA
R J Aydon, BA
Miss L E F Allhusen, BSc
J P Smith, BA
P B Evans, BMus
R J L Lonsdale, BA

Part-time Teachers:

Mrs R A Temperley, BSc
Mrs J R E Herbert, LLAM, ALAM
Miss P Asher, BA
Mrs A Ostrowicz, BA
Mrs J A Matthews, BSc
G Galloway, PhD, MPhilEd
Mrs G Cook, BA

Mrs G Gardiner, BSc, MSc
Mrs G Hudson, BEd
T P Jayne, BA
J R J Herbert, BA
M R Adams, BSc
Mrs G E Savage, BA
Mrs E J Dancey, BPhilEd

Registrar: D H Benson, MA

Careers Adviser: Mrs S Billingham, BA

Librarian: Miss S J Warren, BSc

School Medical Officer: Dr M Forrest, MB, ChB, DRCOG, MRCGP

Visiting Music Teachers:

Piano and Organ:
D Sadler, BMus
S Sadler, LTCL, ATCL
N Argust, FRCO, ARCO, BMus
M Huxley, FRCO, ARCO
Mrs R Storey

Strings:
D Avery, ARCM
Miss J Gubbins, LRAM, ARCM
C Wall
D Carroll

Percussion:
Miss A Oakley, GRSM, ARCM
Miss L Pearcey
C Pick

Woodwind:
J Chater, GBSM, ABSM
E Watson
Miss S Wyatt
C Thompson
Miss A Brooks
Mrs J Schroder
Miss N Waite
Miss A Chadwick
Mrs K Stocks

Brass:
S Dyson
B Hurdley, GBSM
D McNaughton, BA
S Lenton
R Sandland
Mrs M A Brooks

Admission. Candidates for admission must be of good character and sufficient health, and after admission must reside with their parents or guardians, except in cases where special arrangements are approved by the Governors. The names of candidates must be registered at the School before the closing date as stated in the prospectus. Evidence of date of birth and a recent photograph must be produced when the name of a candidate is registered for the examination.

Term of Entry. Autumn term only.

Admission Examination. This examination is held annually for two age groups, one at 11+ for boys who will be 11 but not 12 on 1 September following the examination, the other at 13+ for boys who will be 13 but not 14 on 1 September following the examination. At both 11+ and 13+ candidates take one hour long papers in Mathematics, English and Verbal Reasoning at a level appropriate to the National Curriculum.

A boy who is unsuccessful in the examination at 11+ is not thereby debarred from taking the examination at 13+. 16+ applications are also welcomed.

Fees. £2,072 per term.

With the phasing out of the Government Assisted Places Scheme the Governors have set up their own Assistance Scheme which runs on broadly similar lines to the Government Scheme, offering means tested support to up to 20 boys a year. The scheme targets primarily 11+ entrants but 16+ entrants will also be eligible to apply. In addition, four Ogden Bursaries are available at 11+ for children from families of limited means and who attend a state school.

Curriculum *Lower School* The following subjects are studied by all boys to the end of the third year: English, Mathematics, French, Geography, History, Physics, Chemistry, Biology, (General Science in first year), Latin, Art, Design, Drama, PE and Religious Studies. Music is an obligatory subject to the end of the second year. In addition, boys are required to undertake familiarisation courses in Information Technology. In the Fourth and Fifth year all boys study Mathematics, English, French, Physics, Chemistry and Biology and must choose three other subjects which are taken to GCSE. All boys study German, Spanish or Classical Greek in the third year and may take their choice to GCSE and beyond.

Sixth Form In the Divisions (First Year Sixth) boys choose four from the following subjects for study to A/S level of which three (sometimes four) are carried through to A level.

Ancient History, Art and Design, Biology, Chemistry, Design & Technology, Economics or Business Studies, English Literature, French, Further Mathematics, Geography, German, Greek, History, Latin, Mathematics(M), Mathematics(S), Music, Physics, Spanish, Religious Studies.

In addition, all boys take an A-level in General Studies.

The aim is to produce a broad and well-balanced education consistent with the proposals for a national curriculum.

Scholarships at 11+ and 13+. (*see* Entrance Scholarship section) Up to ten academic scholarships and exhibitions of between one-half and one-eighth fees per annum are offered.

Music Scholarships are also available.

All scholarships are 'indexed' to increase with increases in fees.

Scholarships at 16+. 'Betts Scholarships' of value up to half fees for boys studying Science and Mathematics subjects at A-level, one Finnemore Scholarship for boys studying Arts subjects at A-level of up to half fees.

Games. Rugby Football, Cricket, Hockey, Squash, Basketball, Fives and Lawn Tennis are played. The School has its own swimming pool, all-weather athletics track, games hall and squash courts.

School Club. The School Club is a voluntary organisation covering the following activities: Rugby Football, Cricket, Swimming, Athletics, Basketball, Golf, Hockey, Fives, Tennis, Squash, Badminton, Fencing and Judo, Table Tennis, Bridge, Literary Society, Classical and Junior

Classical Societies, Archaeological Society, Historical and Junior Historical Societies, Parliamentary Society, Economics Society, Musical Society, Dramatic Society, Shakespeare Society, Art Society, Geographical Society, Debating and Junior Debating Societies, Discussion Groups, Christian Union, Scientific Society, Biological Society, Fellwalking Society, Mathematical Society, Meteorological Society, Modern Language Society, Transport Society, Civic Society, Chess Club, Philatelic Section, Photographic Section, School Chronicle, School Newspaper, Anagnostics and Film Society.

CCF. The School maintains Royal Naval, RAF and Army Sections of the Combined Cadet Force.

There is also a Social Service organisation.

Honours. 1991–2000. 25% places at Oxford and Cambridge. 99% of all leavers go on to University, some after a 'year out'.

Forms.

Sixths: Art, English, Classics, Maths, Sci., Mod. Lang., Hist., Geog., Econ. Divisions: Classics, Maths, Sci., Mod. Lang., Hist. Econ. Fifths: 5 forms. Fourths: 5 forms. Upper Middles: 5 forms. Removes: 5 forms. Shells: 5 forms.

Charitable status. Schools of King Edward the Sixth in Birmingham is a Registered Charity, number 529051. The purpose of the Foundation is to educate children and young persons living in or around the City of Birmingham by provision of or assistance to schools, or otherwise.

King Edward's School, Witley

Wormley Nr. Godalming Surrey GU8 5SG.
Tel: (01428) 682572 (Headmaster), 686700 (Bursar), 686794 (Registrar)

The School was founded in 1553 by King Edward VI with the title of Bridewell Royal Hospital. Originally housed at the Bridewell Palace, which was given under Royal Charter to the City of London, the School moved to Witley in 1867, simultaneously changing its name. It became coeducational again in 1952 and will accommodate approximately 500 pupils, equally divided between boys and girls. The School provides both boarding and day education for children between the ages of 11 and 19 years. There are a substantial number of bursaries available to help boys and girls whose home circumstances make boarding a particular need.

President: Her Majesty Queen Elizabeth the Queen Mother

Vice-President: Sir Christopher Walford, MA, DCL

Treasurer and Chairman of Governors: G R A Abbott, MA

***Headmaster:* P Kerr Fulton-Peebles**, MA

Deputy Head: P Tinson, MA

Senior Mistress: Miss M A Fitchett, BSc

Under Master: R Uffold, BEd

Director of Studies: S J Pugh, MA

L G Goodman, BSc
N I Secker, BA
S L Todd, BSc
Mrs F A Reynolds, BSc, DipHE
G M Phillips, BA
R J Bird, BSc
Rev R W E Millington, BA (*Chaplain*)
W Moffat, MA, MSc
B J Turner, MA
N R Fellows, MA
S J Le Butt, BSc
D K Poulter, BSc
Mrs P J Rowell, BA
Mrs M E Wilkes, BEd
Mrs C Waterhouse, BA, NDD
Mrs H A White, BSc
Mrs J Millington, BA
S P Rigney, BA
Mrs L J Parker, BA
S C Pedlar, GRNCM
Mrs G A Pedlar, BA
J G Culbert, BSc
P J Towler, BA
Mrs T A Chapman, MA
K B Forster, BA
P F Innes-Hill, BA
Mrs C J Meharg, BA
Mrs C E Green, BA
D H Messenger, BA
N H Mott, BA
D G Galbraith, BSc
T D Woodhead, BA, LTCL, ARCO, ALCM
P X Pillet, BA, MA
D P Mackey, BSc
Miss J A Thomson, BSc
Miss J A Patton, BSc
Mrs S L Gardiner, BA
Mrs S C Bird, BSc
I E Sharpe, BSc
Mrs K M Goundry, BA
B Doherty, BA
J Warner, BSc
Miss G W Barrow, BSc
Miss A Lyaschenko

Houses and Housemasters/Housemistresses:

Queen Mary House (*Junior Boys*): Mr P Innes-Hill
Copeland House (*Junior Girls*): Mrs S C Bird

Senior Paired Houses:

Ridley (*Boys*): Mr S Todd and St Bridget's (*Girls*): Mrs P Rowell
Wakefield (*Boys*): Mr S Rigney and Elizabeth (*Girls*): Mr & Mrs D P Mackey
Edward (*Boys*): Mr D K Poulter and Tudor (*Girls*): Mrs L J Parker
Grafton (*Boys*): Mr K B Forster and Queen's (*Girls*): Mrs K M Goundry

Medical Officer: P R Wilks, MA, MB, BChir

Bursar: A D Gallie

Headmaster's Secretary: Mrs J Butler

King Edward's School is situated in a well-wooded site of over 100 acres near the Surrey-Sussex-Hampshire border, and is easily accessible by both road and rail. The buildings include the School Chapel, Charter Hall (a modern assembly hall with stage and concert platforms), the Warburg Science School (opened in 1965 and completely refurbished, in 1991 with 9 full-sized laboratories, and well-equipped ancillary rooms), a Mathematics and Computing block built in 1992, both technology and home technology centres, an Art Centre (equipped for Photography, Pottery and Sculpture), an Exhibition Hall, the Countess of Munster Music School (opened in 1963 and including a Concert Hall and Music Library), the Gerald Coke Library, a Sports Centre (opened in 1994) and two other Gymnasia, a dance and drama studio (opened in 1999), an Indoor Swimming Pool, hardplaying and playing fields provision for Cricket, Football, Hockey (boys and girls) and Athletics, and Courts for Tennis, Squash and Netball. From the third form upwards boys and girls live in eight modern, purpose-built paired houses where the accommodation and study areas are completely separate but everyone can come together in the shared communal facilities on the ground floor. The unique paired houses allow boys and girls to mix naturally, and are particularly valued by parents whose sons and daughters attend the school and can be placed in adjacent accommodation. The houses are being continually upgraded and there are new washroom and shower facilities throughout. The refurbishment of the paired house dormitories will commence this year and is part of a rolling programme of improvements. Pupils in the Vth and VIth forms are housed in single or double study bedrooms.

There are 480 pupils in the school, approximately a quarter of whom are day pupils.

The generous staffing ratio and the rather exceptional provision in the School make possible a wide-ranging curriculum, and a real opportunity to live a full life. More than 25 subjects are available at AS and A2 Level. Both the pupils whose interests are academic and those whose bent is less academic find a wide choice of subjects open to them. The great majority of our pupils proceed to the VIth Form and subsequently to higher education.

Places in the School are open to everyone, but it is always kept in mind that the School is a charity whose first purpose is to meet the needs of children who have a particular need for boarding education. Such children are of both sexes, of differing abilities and from every walk of life, and the School seeks to draw as widely as it can to make up its community. It is thus coeducational by conviction, believing that the richer potential of a coeducational environment is desirable for most pupils, and significantly so for the children with whom it is especially concerned.

The School was founded as a result of Christian concern, and it still aims to provide a full education that has a Christian setting, within a caring community. The centre of its spiritual life is the Chapel, where the services are under the direction of the Chaplains, who in turn call on the help of many staff and pupils. Services vary in character although they are based upon the worship of the Church of England. There are both Senior and Junior Christian Unions which meet regularly. Children who wish to do so can join church membership classes which culminate in a Confirmation Service for those wishing to become members of the Church of England.

Children are normally admitted either at 11+ (following an entrance examination) or at 13+ (usually following the Common Entrance Examination) but if there is room they may be admitted at other times, and occasionally a child who should clearly be working alongside older children is admitted at 10+.

The termly fee for boarders in September 2000 is £4,055. This figure includes all boarding and tuition fees, books and games equipment, and the provision of school uniform and games clothing. The day pupil fee is £2,775 including meals and uniform. Individual music tuition in piano, organ, singing and all orchestral instruments is provided at less than cost to all who are prepared to take the trouble to profit from skilled teaching. Over 200 such lessons are given weekly, and the musical side of the School flourishes accordingly.

Some of the pupils may be given bursaries by the Governors. The number and size of the bursaries will depend upon the endowment income available, and they are given at the Governors' absolute discretion. Awards are reviewed annually with regard to parental circumstances and to school fees. They may be given in conjunction with Local Education Authority grants or help from a charitable trust. It is hoped that there will always be as many pupils in the School whose parents are unable to contribute substantially towards the education provided as there are those whose parents are paying full fees from their own resources. The basis on which bursaries are awarded is a combination of the need of the pupil for boarding education, the means of the parent, the support available from other sources, and the contribution that the pupil can make to the school community. It is emphasized that these are not scholarships which a pupil wins by his or her own merits, but a distribution of endowment income to those who need it most. Academic, art and music scholarships, supplementable according to boarding and financial need as described above for bursaries, are offered at 13+ or on entry to the Sixth Form. A limited number of bursaries for the children of Forces personnel are also available.

Charitable status. King Edward's School, Witley is a Registered Charity, number 311997. The foundation exists to provide boarding education for families whose circumstances make boarding a particular need, though the excellent facilities and the high standards of academic achievement and pastoral care make it attractive also to any family looking for boarding education.

King Edward VII and Queen Mary School, Lytham

Lytham Lancs FY8 1DT.
Tel: King Edward site: (01253) 736459
Queen Mary site: (01253) 723246
Fax: King Edward site: (01253) 731623; Queen Mary site: (01253) 781766

The Lytham Schools Foundation was established after a great flood in 1719. King Edward VII School (for boys) was opened in 1908 and Queen Mary School (for girls) in 1930; both were Direct Grant Grammar Schools and with the withdrawal of the Grant became independent. The two schools merged to form a new school with a co-educational intake in September 1999 and will be fully co-educational in September 2002.

The Governing Body includes representatives of the Trust Managers of the Foundation and of the Universities of Lancashire, Liverpool and Manchester, together with co-optative members.

Motto: *Sublimis ab unda.*

Governing Body:

Chairman: Mr W J Bennett, CEng, FICE, FIHT
Vice-Chairman: Mrs M Towers, LLB

Mr B W Bradbury
The Revd C J Carlisle, BEng
Mr W G Cowburn, DipArch, FRIBA, FFB
Mr R N Hardy, LLB
Dr S D A Hayes, MB, ChB
The Revd Canon G I Hirst, BA
Professor J H Johnson, MA, PhD
Mr S Howison, CEng, FRAeS, FIEE, BSc
The Revd C M Porter
Mrs M A L Race, BSc
Dr W J Richards, PhD
Mrs E J Sutton
The Revd D Welch, MA (Oxon)
Mr T Westall, BSc, MICE
Mr E T Woodfine, RD, BA

Clerk to the Governors and Bursar: H E Bracegirdle, FCIS

Staff:

Principal: **Mr P J Wilde**, MA, The Queen's College, Oxford

Head of Senior School (11-16): Mrs S Piggott, BSc Liverpool

Head of Sixth Form: Mr M G Stephenson, BA, St Peter's College, Oxford

Director of Studies: Mr G A Little, BSc Leeds

Art:
*Mr C Wildon, DipAd Wolverhampton College of Art, ATD Birmingham
Miss S Lukasiewiecz, DipAdATC Sheffield College

Business Studies/Economics:
*Mr J A Liggett, BSc Cardiff
Mrs N L Black, BA University Central Lancashire, PGCE Business & Economic Education Lancaster University

Design and Technology:
*Mr P F Klenk, BA Loughborough
Mr T J Green, BEd Manchester Metropolitan
Mr C K Hill, CertEd Birmingham, BA Loughborough

English:
*Mrs E M Antcliffe, BA Liverpool
Mrs K E Busby, BA Liverpool

Mr I R Clarke, BEd Newcastle, MA Lancaster
Mr D G Higgins, BA Strathclyde
Mrs D C Prutton, MA Oxford
Mrs F M Withers, BA Hull

Food Technology: Mrs A M Hoyle, CertEd Elizabeth Gaskell College

Geography:
*Mrs J I K Rimmer, BA London, FRGS
Mrs J A Cooper, BSc Salford

History:
*Mr I D Cowlishaw, BA London
Mrs L Blackshaw, BA Leeds
Mr P Hamer, BA Swansea

Information Technology:
*Mr D G J Culpan, BEng UMIST
Mrs B Duckett, BSc Manchester

Mathematics:
*Mr P J Brotherton, BSc Manchester
Mr W J Birtwistle, BSc, MSc Liverpool
Mr K C Dawson, BSc Manchester Polytechnic
Mr J E D Latham, BSc Bradford
Mrs A Mayes, BSc Newcastle

Modern Languages:
*Mr J G Finney, BA Nottingham
*Mr C W Pickup, BA Liverpool
Mr R P Chester, BA Leeds
Miss E S A Hall, MA Oxford
Miss A C Johnson, BA Durham
Mrs L M Warwick, MA St Andrews
Mrs F M Winterflood, BA Reading
Mrs A Boyes, BA University of Central Lancs (*French conversation*)
Mrs D M Clayton (*French conversation*)
Mrs M Jones (*German conversation*)

Music:
*Mr A C Barratt, BA Open University, GRSM, LRAM, MTC London
Mrs C E Hanlon, BMus Sheffield

Physical Education:
*Mrs K Hanham, BEd University of Sussex
*Mr A M Weston, BEd Chester College
Mr P M Rudd, BSc University of North Wales Bangor
Mrs B Storey, CertEdPE Bishop Lonsdale College Derby
Mr S J Williams, BEd Brighton

Psychology/Sociology:
*Mrs P A Gray, BA Strathclyde
Mrs D Ward, BA University of North Wales, Bangor, MA Lancaster

Religious Studies:
*Mrs J I Pybon, BA Newcastle
Miss J Cooper, BA London

Science:
*Mr A Marikar, BSc London, CBiol, MBiol
Mrs H M Barnsley, BSc University of North Wales, Bangor, BSc Open University
Mrs J M Denver, BEd Nottingham College of Education
Mrs P M Lenning, BSc Leeds
Mrs C Rainforth, BA Open, PGCE (*Secondary Science*)
Mr S N J Smith, BEng Bristol
Mr P Sullivan, BSc Manchester
Mr J M Turner, BSc Sheffield, MSc Salford, CPhys, MInstP

Careers: Mrs S M Hampson, BA Leeds, DCG

Learning Support Co-ordinator: Mrs S Parker, CertEd Newcastle, PGCE Specific Learning Difficulty Edinburgh, AMBDA

Librarians:
Mrs A M Chisholm, ALA College of Librarianship, Wales
Miss J M Clarke, BA Lancaster, ALA College of Librarianship

Situation. The School stands on an impressive 39 acre site overlooking the Irish Sea. The buildings include both main school and specialist libraries; sixteen well-equipped science laboratories; specialist rooms for art, drama and music, design and food technology; resources rooms for English, mathematics and modern languages; a language laboratory; two newly equipped information and communication technology suites; a fitness suite, gymnasium and two sports halls complement the facilities provided by the extensive playing fields. The School owns an outdoor pursuits and residential education centre at Ribblehead in the Yorkshire Dales.

Organisation. There are 700 day boys and girls in the Senior School. On site, there are also a Nursery/Infant School and a Junior School, both co-educational.

The broadly based curriculum, leading to GCSE after five years, comprises the following subjects: art, design and technology, English language and literature, food technology, French, German, geography, mathematics, music, physical education, religious education and the music, physical education, religious education and the sciences (biology, chemistry and physics, which at GCSE include both 'Dual' and 'Triple' options). All pupils take part in games. Most pupils enter the Sixth Form: a full range of AS and A2 subjects, including general studies, is available in very varied combinations. There is a choice of 24 AS/A2 subjects, including the further options beyond GCSE, of business studies, economics, further mathematics, government and politics, psychology, sociology, sport studies and theatre studies. Students are prepared for university, entry to the professions and responsible positions in industrial and commercial life. The School offers comprehensive careers and degree course choice programmes, together with separate weeks of work experience.

Games and Activities. Cricket, hockey, netball and rugby are the main sports, but considerable choice is available including athletics, badminton, basketball, cross-country, golf, tennis, swimming and sailing on Fairhaven Lake nearby. Extra-curricular activities include Duke of Edinburgh Award, mountain biking, canoeing, fell-walking and ski-ing, aerobics, aviation, choir, gymnastics, orchestra and swing band, public speaking and table tennis. Recent productions have included Antigone, Oliver, Bugsy Malone, Our Country's Good and West Side Story.

In addition to outdoor education at the Pursuits Centre, there have been in recent years regular sports tours in the UK and abroad to Ireland, Barbados, Sri Lanka and New Zealand; mountain biking expeditions to Norway, skiing in the Alps and Vermont and scuba diving in the Red Sea and the Mediterranean, cultural trips to Paris and the World War battlefields; student exchanges with France, Germany and with the Czech Republic, art and music tours and a trilingual science symposium.

Admission. Admission to the Senior School is by examination for all pupils, aged 11, held each year in January. Pupils may also be admitted at other ages. Application Forms for admission and further details will be sent on request.

Fees. Senior School: £5,040 pa. Nursery/Infant & Junior Schools £3,470 pa.

Scholarships. A number of Scholarships and Bursaries are offered on the results of the Senior Entrance Examination and include an audition for Music Scholarships. Awards are also available at Sixth Form level.

Charitable status. The Lytham Schools Foundation is a Registered Charity, number 526315. Its aim is to provide a well-balanced academic education catering for the talents, needs and interests of each individual pupil.

King Edward VI School Southampton

Kellett Road Southampton SO15 7UQ
Tel: 023 8070 4561.
Fax: 023 8070 5937
e-mail: registrar@kes.hants.sch.uk.

King Edward VI School was founded in 1553, under Letters Patent of King Edward VI, by the will of the Rev. William Capon, Master of Jesus College, Cambridge, and Rector of St. Mary's, Southampton. The original Royal Charter, bearing the date 4th June 1553, is preserved in the School. The first Head Master was appointed in 1554.

Governors:
W M Cox (*Chairman*)
K St J Wiseman, MA (*Vice Chairman*)
The Lord Lieutenant for the County of Hampshire
Rector of the Parish of Southampton (*City Centre*)
P W Brazier, BSC, FCIOB
D Brown, BSc
R A G Brown, FCA
Dr R B Buchanan, MBBS, FRCP, FRCR
Dr L M Eccles, MBBS, MRCS, LRCP
D English, AIHM
B Gay, BA
I M Hobbins, FIPD
Ms S Jones, BA, MBE
J R-H Martin
Prof B McCormick, BA, MA, PhD
R C Niddrie, FCA
J P Sabben-Clare, MA
A Samuels, LLB
Dr A L Thomas, MA, PhD

Bursar and Clerk to the Governors: Wing Commander V Gage, ACIS, MIMgt, RAF

***Head Master:* P B Hamilton**, MA

Deputy Head Masters:
P A Hartley, BSc
R T Courtney, MA

Registrar: J Gordon, CertEd

Assistant Staff:
R W Allen, BSc
Mrs S L Allen, MA
Sra I S Ariznabarreta
S H Barker, MA
Miss J M Barron, BA
Mlle M Boittin, BA
P A V Braga, MA
Mrs J A Burden
Mrs P E Burrows, MSc
Mrs J M Cole, BA
K P Coundley, MA
Miss S L Crane, BSc, MA
R J Cross, BSc
G T Darby, BA
Mrs C A Davidson, BA
A J Davies, BSc, PhD
P J Day, BSc
Dr H Dean, BSc, PhD
Miss C N du Bosky, BFA
D M Dykes
Dr M E England, BSc, PhD
K N A Esmail, MPhil, PhD
Mrs L J Farnhill, BA
Miss N Fayaud, MA
P H G Ferris, MA
Mrs V L Ferris, BA
J A Fisher, BSc
K A Fitzpatrick
J M Foyle, BSc
J D Gerrish, BSc
A W Gilbert, BA
C E Giles, BA
Miss M F Gouldstone, BA
Miss R M Greenwood, MA
J Hall, MA
M C Hall, BA, ARCO, ATCL
R P Hall, BSc, DipTheol
S G Hall, BSc
P P Harris, MA, MPhil, ARCO
Miss M J Harrison, BSc
G P Havers, BSc
Mrs L C Henderson, BEd
L J Herklots, BSc
Mrs A Hipwell, BA
S R Hoskins, BSc, PhD
G S Hunt, BSc
Mrs J M Hutton, BA
Mrs E B Ingram, MIL, MA
N J James, BA, PhD
P D Jones, BA
D G Kelly, BA
C J Kettle, BA
D Lepping
M W Long, DipAD
Mrs N Lovegrove, BSc
Mrs V C Manson, MCHEM
C B Martin, MA
T Mauger, BA
Mrs C I Mawson, BA
Mrs E Mayes, MA
Miss S S McCarry, MA
S B Morgan, LRAM, LTCL
D Morland, BSc, ARCS
Miss S Noble, BA
M C Orman, CertEd
P S Osman, BA
Miss E L Parker, BSc
R G Patten, BA
Miss C A Peachment, BSc
Mrs E J Poppleton, BA
J G Poppleton, BA, DipRS
D A Price, BA, MIBiol
Mrs J Price, BA
R J Putt, BSc
J A Sampson, BA
Mrs C J Sargeant, L-ès-L, Maitrise
Miss J K Shaw, BA
P Sheppard, BSc
J H H Singleton, BSc
Miss F S Smail, MA
S J Smart, BA
M J Spillett, BSc, PhD
Mrs C L Talks, BA
P B Tasker, BSc
Mrs E J Thomas, BSc
Mrs S C Thompson, BEd
T H Tofts, MA, DipPhil
M A Walter, BSc, MPhil
R J Wilkinson, BSc, PhD
F Winter, BSc
R J L Wood, BEd
G H Wotton, BSc
Mrs G M Wright, BA

There are about 950 pupils in the School, of whom over 260 are in the Sixth Form.

Admission. An entrance examination is held in the Spring Term for boys and girls seeking to enter the First Form at age 11 in the following September. Applications from able under-age candidates will also be considered. In addition, admission into the Third Form takes place at age 13. Smaller numbers of entrants are accepted into the other school years, provided the applicants are of suitable academic ability. Boys and girls also are admitted to the Sixth Form.

Registration for entry may be made at any time on a form obtainable from the Registrar, who can supply current information about fees, bursaries and scholarships.

In order to qualify for entrance to the Sixth Form a boy or girl will normally be required to have grade 'B' or above in six subjects at GCSE, including English Language and Mathematics, and the subjects to be studied at 'A' level, but 'A' grades in French, German and Spanish.

Class sizes average 22; the average size of Sixth Form sets is 12.

Curriculum. All pupils follow a common course in the first two years: this includes French or German or Spanish and Latin, Mathematics and General Science. In years 3, 4 and 5 all pupils study eight 'core' subjects to GCSE: Biology, Chemistry, English Language, English Literature, French, Mathematics, Religious Studies and Physics. In addition there is a range of 'option' subjects: Art, Design and Technology, Economics, Geography, German, Greek, History, Music, Theatre Studies and Spanish. The syllabus leading to the GCSE Examinations, in which most pupils take eleven subjects, is designed to avoid any premature specialisation. Furthermore, there is a wide choice of Advanced Level subject combinations in the Sixth Form and an ambitious programme of General Studies.

On entering the First Year pupils join a form of about 22, with a Form Tutor responsible for their general welfare and progress. The other years are organised on a system of pastoral groups of about 18. Each group has its own Year Head. In addition there is a Head of Lower School who has general responsibility for the first three years; a Head of Upper School and a Director of the Sixth Form, each of whom has similar responsibilities in their respective areas.

Our aim is to provide a congenial atmosphere and a disciplined environment in which able pupils can develop as individuals.

School Activities. Three or four periods a week are devoted in every student's timetable to physical education. Games are regarded as forming an integral part of life at King Edward's, and none is excused from taking part except on medical grounds. The games played in the three terms are rugby football, hockey, cricket and tennis for boys; and netball, hockey, tennis and rounders for girls; other sporting activities include athletics, basketball, badminton, squash, swimming and a number of other games. The School has a large sports hall and a fully equipped fitness studio and an all-weather pitch for Hockey and similar games which provides twelve Tennis Courts in Summer.

A considerable range of societies meets during lunchtime, after school, at weekends and in school holidays, catering for pupils of all ages and many differing tastes. All are encouraged to join some of these societies, in order to gain the greatest advantage from their time at the School. Each pupil receives a term calendar and a copy of 'Sotoniensis', the School magazine, which give details of most society activities.

In addition to a large number of sporting teams representing the School, there are such activities as drama, debating, chess, sailing, collectors' clubs and music. The School has a flourishing choir, as well as two orchestras and a number of smaller instrumental groups. Art and Design and Technology occupy up-to-date premises. The studios and workshops are usually open during lunchtimes and after school. The School has a 250 seat Theatre-in-the-Round.

Fees. The full fee of £2,133 per term can be reduced in appropriate cases by the award of Bursaries and Scholarships. Scholarships are available on entry at age 11 and age 13 and further Scholarships may be awarded during a pupil's career in the School. Some Scholarships are awarded for proficiency in Music.

Charitable status. King Edward VI School Southampton is a Registered Charity, number 306297. The object of the Charity is the provision and conduct in or near the City of Southampton of a school for boys and girls.

King Henry VIII School
(Part of the Coventry School Foundation)

Warwick Road Coventry CV3 6AQ.
Tel: (024) 76673442.
Fax: (024) 76677102

There are 403 day boys and 403 day girls in the Senior School, and 116 boys and 120 girls in the Junior School.

King Henry VIII School was founded under Letters Patent of King Henry VIII, dated 23 July 1545 by John Hales, Clerk of the Hanaper to the King. Today it is an independent, co-educational day school of the highest academic standing. The school is represented on the Headmasters' Conference and on the Governing Bodies Association. The governing body is the Coventry School Foundation, on which are represented Sir Thomas White's Charity, the Coventry Church Charities, Coventry General Charities and Birmingham, Coventry, Oxford and Warwick Universities. There are also several co-opted Governors.

The school moved to its present extensive site in a pleasant part of Coventry in 1885, and the Governors have continually improved, extended and restored the buildings which are well-equipped to cope with the demands imposed by an up-to-date, relevant and challenging curriculum. The science block can have few equals anywhere in the country. The curriculum is broad and balanced, integrating National Curriculum principles and practices where appropriate. The school has extensive playing fields, some of which are located on the main site. Other playing fields are five minutes away by mini-bus.

The Governors have committed themselves to a major building programme at the school. A new Junior School, Dining Room and modern Sixth Form Centre have recently been completed. The English and Modern Languages Departments have been refurbished. Both Senior and Junior Schools have a first rate computer network which is accessible to all pupils. A Sports Hall and new art facility are planned for completion by September 2002.

Examination results at all levels are outstanding, and the School is noted for the excellence of its sport, music and drama. All pupils are encouraged to make a contribution to the extra-curricular life of the school. The school has close connections with many universities including Oxford and Cambridge. The Coventry School Foundation owns an extensive property near Fougères in the Normandy region of France, and all pupils will spend at least one week there during their first two years in the school.

It has also developed a growing reputation for achievement in outdoor education through, for example, the Duke of Edinburgh Award Scheme.

Chairman of Governors: Charles Leonard, Esq

Headmaster: **George Fisher**, MA

Deputy Heads:
Cas Britton, BA
Gethin Lewis, BA

Teaching Staff:
Dr Simon Ainge, BSc *Chemistry*
Mr William Arden, BA *Modern Languages*
Mrs Joanna Batten *School Nurse & PSHE Co-ordinator*
Miss Nicola Baulch, BSc *Mathematics*
Mrs Jan Butler, BA *Music*
Mr Andrew Carman, BA(Econ) *Economics & Business Studies/Events Co-ordinator*
Mr Ray Carnell, BPhil, ALSM *CDT*
Mrs Dympna Cassidy, BA *Classics*
Mr David Charman, BSc *Head of ICT/Timetable*
Mrs Mary Charman, BA *ICT/Law*
Mr David Clarke, CertEd, DipSE *Head of Art*
Miss Cindy Colwell BA *Modern Languages*
Mr Melvin Cooley, BA *Classics; Head of Sherwyn's House*
Mr John Cooper, MA *Head of Mathematics*
Miss Lizzie Coulter, BA, MA, ATD *Art*
Mrs Viv Duckers, MA *English, Press Officer*
Dr Lesley Dunham, BSc, MSc, PhD *Biology/Head of Year 9*
Mr Peter Forse, BA *Head of Sixth Form/History*
Dr Larry Green, BA, MA *English*
Mr John Grundy, BEd *Head of CDT*
Miss Sophie Hall, BSc *Physics*
Mrs Christine Ham, BEd *Physics/Careers/Sixth Form Co-ordinator*
Mr Robert Harwood, LLB *Law*
Mrs Pat Head, CertEd *Physical Education/Deputy House Head*
Mr Andrew Holland, BA *Head of Modern Languages*
Mrs Julie Holland, BA *History*
Miss Lisa Holland *Dance*
Mr Richard Hollingdale, MA, MMus, FRCO, ARCM, LRAM *Director of Music*
Mrs Dorinda Holt, MA *French*
Mr Warren Honey, BSc *Head of Biology*
Mr Robert Howard, BA *Head of Geography/Deputy House Head*
Mrs Barbara Howes, MA *Modern Languages/Head of Year 7*
Mrs Brenda Humphrey, BA *Modern Languages*
Mr John Humphrey, MSc *Head of Chemistry*
Mr Peter Huxford, MA *Head of History/Head of Hales' House*
Mr Peter Jones, BSc (*Econ*) *Head of Economics and Business Studies*
Mrs Hermia Lambie, MA *Classics*
Mr Bernard Lewis, BSc *ICT/Web Site; Examination & Invigilation Scheduler*
Dr Peter Lockyer, BSc, PhD *Mathematics/Librarian*
Mr Peter Manning, BA *Head of Religious Studies*

Mr Ben Masters, MA *English*
Mr Rob McDermott, BEng *Physics/Deputy House Head*
Mrs Pip Milton, BSc *Biology*
Mr Peter Milton, BA *Geography/Head of White's House*
Ms Tracy Moffat, BSc *ICT*
Mr Gary Morgan, BSc *Mathematics*
Mrs Pam Nicholls, BSc *Mathematics*
Mrs Gill Othen, BA *English/Head of Drama*
Mr Andrew Parker, BEd *Head of Boys' PE/Geography*
Mrs Anne Parsons, BA *Head of Home Economics*
Dr Louise Penney, BSc, PhD *Biology and Chemistry/Learning Support Co-ordinator*
Dr Noel Phillips, PhD *Chemistry*
Mrs Amanda Pontin, CertEd *Physical Education*
Mr Ben Poore, BA *English*
Dr Michael Purslove, BSc, PhD *Head of Physics/Health & Safety Officer*
Mr Michael Rees, BSc *Mathematics*
Mrs Lynne Roote, BSc *Mathematics*
Mrs Barbara Seagrave, BA *Girls' PE and Games*
Miss Shelley Simpson, BA *Head of Girls' PE and Games/Geography*
Mrs Chris Spriggs, BSc *Head of Years 10 and 11/Geography*
Mrs Pam Startin *Librarian*
Dr Denise Street, MA, PhD *Chemistry/Head of Year 8*
Mr Terry Street, MA, MInstP *External Examinations Secretary/Physics*
Mrs Susan Swales, BA *Mathematics*
Mr Jeremy Thomas, BA *Head of Classics*
Mr Matthew van Alderwegen, MA *History*
Mrs Laura Vaughan, BA *Modern Languages/Deputy House Head*
Mrs Anne Wade, BSc *Biology/Duke of Edinburgh*
Mrs Jane Whittell, MA *Religious Studies*
Mrs Sue Wilkes *After School Care Supervisor*
Mr Steve Wilkes, BEd *Head of Holland's House/Physical Education/English*
Mrs Helen Wilson *Careers Adviser*
Mrs Mary Woodhouse, BEd *Religious Studies*
Ms Sheila Woolf, BA, MA(*Ed*) *Head of English*

M François Daury *French Assistant*
Fr Kerstin Friedrich *German Assistant*

Junior School:
Headmaster: Mr R Waddington, BA
Deputy Headmaster: Mr V P Broadfield, CertEd
Director of Studies: Mr G Brown, BEd, CertPDE

Staff:
Mrs C Anderson, LRAM, ARCM
Mrs C N Bradley, BA
Mrs J E Coles, CertEd, BPhil, MSc
Mrs V Cooper, BEd
Mr D A Flynn, LLB
Mr R P Fulton, BA
Mrs J Garland, CertEd
Mr B F Hewetson, BA
Mr K Pearson, BEd
Mrs R Poulson, BPhil(Ed)
Mrs J Waddington, BA
Mr A Whittell, MA

Visiting Staff:
Mrs J Halliday, BA
Mrs P J Head, CertEd
Mrs B Seagrave
Mrs J Sewell, BA, ISTC

School Nurse: Mrs J Batten, SRN, DipN

Administration:

Junior School Secretary: Mrs M Sanders

School Treasurer: Mrs C Allen

Curriculum. The Junior School enjoys excellent facilities adjoining the main site which include a Library, an ICT Room with 24 networked PCs, an Art and Design room and a Science and Music Room. Children are accepted by competitive examination from 7+ to 11+. The emphasis is on a broad education based upon the National Curriculum and children are prepared for the Governors' examination for entry to the Senior School.

The Senior School curriculum provides courses leading to the GCSE examinations and GCE AS and A levels. Subjects available currently are Art, Biology, Business Studies, Chemistry, Classical Civilisation, Computing, Technology, Drama, Economics, English, French, Geography, German, Greek, History, Information and Communication Technology, Latin, Law, Mathematics, Music, Religious Studies, Physics and Spanish. Physical Education and Sport are also considered to be a vital part of the curriculum and are available as an AS level option. All students follow a carefully structured PSHE course.

Sciences are taught by subject specialists. New courses in Key Skills/General Studies are being developed.

Games. Rugby Football, Hockey, Netball, Basketball, Cross-Country Running, Athletics, Rounders, Tennis, Cricket, Swimming, Golf, Orienteering and Fencing. Junior School games include Soccer, Rounders, Athletics and Cross-Country Running. In 1986 the Governors took into use the largest artificial turf games area in the country, used mainly for hockey, but providing an additional 24 tennis courts in the summer. This facility is shared with Bablake School.

Scholarships. The Governors award annually a number (not fixed) of entrance bursaries and full scholarships. Full details regarding financial assistance are available from the Headmaster at the school.

School Roll. 806 pupils in the Senior School, equally split between boys and girls, and 247 in the Junior School.

Fees. (September 2001): Junior School £4,140 p.a.; Senior School £5,496 p.a.

Admission. Admission is via the School's own Entrance Examination, held annually in January for entrance the following September. The normal age of entry is 11, but there are smaller additional intakes at other ages, (10, 12 and 13) and also at Sixth Form level. All enquiries about admission to the school should be addressed to the Headmaster. The school is entirely a day school.

Charitable status. Coventry School Foundation is a Registered Charity, number 528961. Its aim is to promote the education, academic, social, physical and moral, of boys and girls and in particular to provide in or near the City of Coventry day schools for boys and girls.

King's College School

Wimbledon Common London SW19 4TT.
Tel: 020 8255 5300
Fax: 020 8255 5309 (Porters' Lodge); 020 8255 5379 (Senior Common Room); 020 8255 5359 (Head Master's Study)
e-mail: admissions@kcs.org.uk; or head.master@kcs.org.uk
website: www.kcs.org.uk

King's College School was founded as the junior department of King's College in 1829. According to the resolutions adopted at the preliminary meeting of founders in 1828, "the system is to comprise religious and moral instruction, classical learning, history, modern languages, mathematics, natural philosophy, etc., and to be so conducted as to provide in the most effectual manner for the two great objects of education – the communication of general knowledge, and specific preparation for particular professions". In 1897 it was removed from the Strand to its present site on Wimbledon Common.

Motto: *Sancte et Sapienter.*

Governing Body:
Visitor: The Archbishop of Canterbury
Chairman of the Governing Body:
C Taylor, MA, LLM

R Ayling
Prof M L Brown, MA, PhD
The Rt Revd Thomas Butler, Bishop of Southwark
A J M Chamberlain, MA, FIA
T A I Fitzpatrick,
P M D Gibbs, MA, FCA
R Gidoomal, CBE, BSc, ARCS, FRSA
J D E Hamilton, FCA
Prof S R Hirsch, MPhil, MD, MRCP, FRCPsych
J M Jarvis, QC, MA
J Keeling, FRICS
H M G King
P Levelle
R S Luddington, MA, MPhil
R G Mathews, FCA
Mrs P Reed-Boswell
The Hon Sir Stephen Richards, QC, BA, MA
G D Slaughter, JP, MA, FRSA
Prof N D J Smith, BDS, MSc, MPhil, FRCR
Prof N H Stern, FBA, MA, DPhil
D G Tilles, BSc, FCMA, AIIMR
Mrs C van Tulleken
Sir Nigel Wicks, GCB, KCB, CVO, CBE

***Head Master:* A C V Evans**, MA, MPhil, FIL

Second Master: D J Grossel, MA

Third Master: K N Hawney, BSc

Senior Masters:
R Cake, BA
B J Driver, BA

Senior Mistress: Miss H L McKissack, MA

Undermasters: to be appointed

Curriculum Director: A R Tilling, BSc

Chaplains:
The Revd S J Robbins-Cole, BA
The Revd R G Stevens, BA

Senior School:

J R Basden, BSc (*Head of Biology*)
N E Edwards, BSc (*Head of Examinations*)
P M Lavender, BSc (*Head of Careers*)
G R Salt, BA
N T Shawcross, MSc

S Foot, BSc (*Head of Chemistry*)
I M Davies, MA
Miss H L McKissack, MA
R J Mitchell, MA (*Housemaster, Maclear*)
A D Nolan, BSc

C M Jackson, MA (*Head of Classics*)
G E Bennett, BA
J R Carroll, MA
M R C Shoults, BA

P R C Powell, MA, MSc (*Head of Economics*)
Dr G M Bamford, BSc, PhD
Mrs C J Shandro, BA
R C Swain, BA

S R J Marshall, MA (*Head of English*)
M D Allen, MA (*Director of College Court*)
R Cake, BA (*Housemaster, Alverstone*)
Ms A C R Edwards, MA
P J Macdonald, MA
F S McKeown, PhD

P S Swan, BA (*Artistic Director in charge of Collyer Hall Theatre*)
Mrs J J Whitaker, BA

P C Guinness, MSc (*Head of Geography*)
M J Chambers, BSc (*Housemaster, Major*)
J A Galloway, BA (*Housemaster, Alverstone*)

A W Thomas, MA (*Head of History*)
Miss R M Davis, BA (*Housemistress, Layton*)
J G Lawrence, BA, MLitt (*Director of Activities*)
Miss M-H Quaradeghini, BA
J G Ryan, BA
N P Tetley, BA

D R Kiddle, BSc (*Head of Mathematics*)
J Aspinall, MA
B J Driver, BA
K N Hawney, BSc
R Hiller, BSc
P J Kite, MA (*Head of Computer Services*)
G C McGinn, CertEd (*Housemaster, Glenesk*)
M P Stables, BA
C J Thomas, BEng
Miss S Walker (*Mistress i/c Rowing*)

S Tint, MA, MIL (*Head of Modern Languages*)
Mrs C R Butler, BA
H Chapman, MA
D A Cooke, BA
Miss F L Cramoisan, MA
S N Hollands, MA
S Marshall-Taylor, BA
Miss R C Peel, BA
Mrs J E Purslow, MA
A R J Swigg, BA
M J Windsor, MA (*Director of IB*)

R W M Hughes, BSc (*Head of Physics*)
G E D Bennett, MA
B C T Goad, BSc
D J Lavender, BA
A R Tilling, BSc

M J Storey, BA, PhD (*Head of Religious Studies*)
S G Else, BA, DPhil
Revd S J Robbins-Cole, BA
Revd R G Stevens, BA

Junior School Tel: 020 8255 5335; Fax: 020 8255 5339; e-mail: jsadmissions@kcs.org.uk

Headmaster: J A Evans, BA

Deputy Headmaster: S M James, BA (*Head of Religious Studies*)

Assistant Headmaster: A D Hein

Senior Subject Master: R K B Halsey, MA, ARCO(CHM) (*Head of Classics*)

C R M Andrews, BSc
Mrs M A Barlow, BEd
Miss C M M Bitaud, BA
Miss J C Brewer, BA
D H Edwards, MA (*Housemaster, Windsor*)
R L Freeman, BA
R Hammond, CertEd (*Housemaster, Tudor*)
J M Harvey, CertEd (*Master in Rushmere*)
S Hassan, MA, MEd (*Housemaster, Norman*)
Miss F C Hutchison, BA
D Jones, BA (*Head of Modern Languages*)
D B Land, BA (*Head of English*)
Mrs G McGee, CTC (*IT Co-ordinator*)
Miss V C Macintyre, BA
Mrs C J Mady, BSc (*Head of Science*)
I D Morris, BA (*Housemaster, Stuart*)
R G Peskett, BScEng

J Poulsom, BA (*Head of Geography*)
M W G Robinson, BA
M W E Snell, BA (*Head of Mathematics*)
E T Watkins, BA (*Head of History*)
Miss S J Woods, BEd

Senior and Junior Schools:

J E Millard, BA (*Director of Music*)
S Porter, BA (*Assistant Director of Music*)
M D Jenkins, ARCM
A E Mason, BA, FRCO
Miss N R Phipps, GMus

Miss D Langenberg, BA (*Head of Faculty of ADT*)
V G Barnes, MA, HDFA, ATD (*Director of Art*)
Miss L S Gillard, MA, ATC (*Head of Junior School ADT*)
J D Broderick, BA
R A Carswell, MA
Miss S Dore, BA
M Fidler, HDFA, ATC
A R Pleace, BSc

J M Atkin, CertEd (*Head of Physical Education*)
C M J Lehane, BA (*Head of Junior School PE*)
J A Galloway, BA (*Master i/c Rugby*)
A D Patterson, BA
W P Waugh, BA
T S Young, BA

CCF Instructor: to be appointed

Administrative Staff:

Bursar: J C S Priston, MA
Head Master's Secretary: Mrs J Fendley, AffIQPS
Junior School Secretary: Mrs J McTavish
Librarian: Miss H J Pugh, BA, ALA

Organisation. KCS is a day school for boys who live at home with their parents. The School consists of a Senior School, which boys enter at 13, and a Junior School, which educates boys aged 7 to 13 in preparation for entry to the Senior School. On entry to the Senior School boys are placed in one of the six Houses. Every boy has a Tutor who is responsible for his progress and welfare throughout his school career.

Admission. Entrance to the Senior School is through the Common Entrance Examination or the KCS Scholarship Examination. Candidates should normally be registered by their tenth birthday, and will be assessed at 11+ with a view to advising parents on their suitability as candidates for KCS at 13+. A number of places are available each year for entry to the Sixth Form. Preliminary enquiries about entry should be made to the Registration Secretary.

Junior School. Entrance examinations, graded according to the ages of the boys, are held in the January and February of the year of entry. Enquiries should be made to the Junior School Secretary. For further details of the Junior School refer to Part V of this book.

Scholarships. 12 Scholarships, with varying values up to 50% of the full tuition fee, may be awarded. One of the scholarships may be awarded to a boy offering Greek who shows particular promise as a classical linguist; two others may be awarded to boys who show particular promise in modern languages or science. The number of Scholarships awarded in any year will vary according to the quality of the candidates. Up to 6 Music Scholarships, with varying values up to 50% of the full tuition fee, may be awarded to boys of high musical ability. Two Art & Design Scholarships may be awarded, with a value up to 50% of the full tuition fee. Candidates for all these awards must be under 14 years of age on 1 September of the year in which they sit the examination. One Organ Scholarship is available in the Sixth Form. Further information on all scholarships is available from the Registration Secretary.

Bursaries. The School has its own bursary fund through which it can offer assistance with fees in case of established need. Boys already in the School take preference in the award of bursaries but some awards may be made to boys entering either the Junior School at 11+ or the Senior School at 13+ or 16+.

Registration. A non-refundable fee of £75 is charged.

Tuition. 2001-2002 fees: £3,310 per term (Senior School). £2,990 (10+, 11+ and 12+ forms in Junior School). £2,650 (7+, 8+ and 9+ forms in Junior School). Individual music tuition is charged separately.

Curriculum. The Middle School provides a 3-year course to the GCSE. In the first year (Fourth Form) boys follow a common curriculum. In the Lower and Upper Fifths the core subjects are English, French, Mathematics, Biology, Physics, Chemistry, Information Technology, PSHE and PE, with options from Art, Classical Civilisation, Design & Technology, Greek, German, Geography, History, Italian, Latin, Music, Religious Studies, Spanish and Russian.

The Sixth Form. The Sixth Form is housed in College Court, a sixth form centre with teaching and seminar rooms, recreation and study areas. College Court also houses the Careers Department as well as the Economics and Information Technology departments. College Court links with Collyer Hall (the theatre/concert/assembly hall) and the Cotman Art Gallery.

Sixth Form Curriculum. Boys can choose to study either the International Baccalaureate or the GCE AS/A2 examinations. Whether they opt for the IB or the AS/A2 programme, they share common ground. This will generally be through a general education programme and extra-curricular activities, including sport, music and drama. College Court, the sixth-form centre, also provides a common base where boys pursuing different courses may meet and forge relationships.

Boys opting for the IB must take 6 subjects: literature; a modern language; a science; mathematics; a humanity (eg History, Geography or Economics); and either a creative subject, a classical language or another of the first 5 categories. 3 or 4 of these subjects are taken at Higher Level, the rest at Standard Level. In addition they must take a course in the Theory of Knowledge and their contribution to extra-curricular activities through Creativity, Action & Service is assessed.

Boys opting for AS/A2 will, in the Lower Sixth, take 4 courses which are examined at AS level at the end of that year; in the Upper Sixth they continue with 3 or possibly all 4 of those subjects, which are examined at A2 level at the end of the year and which will then constitute the full Advanced Level.

The following subjects can usually be taken in appropriate combinations: Art, Biology, Business Studies, Chemistry, Classical Civilisation, Critical Thinking, Design & Technology, Economics, Electronics, English, French, Geography, German, Greek, History, Information Technology, Italian, Latin, Mathematics, Further Mathematics, Music, Philosophy, Physics, Politics, Psychology, Religious Studies, Russian, Spanish, Theatre Studies.

Every sixth-former also participates in a wider educational progboys take Religious Studies and General Studies, which ramme of classes, lectures and activities, which include spiritual and moral issues, a full programme of games and an afternoon devoted to extra-curricular activities.

Religious Education. KCS is an Anglican foundation but welcomes boys from all churches and faiths. The School has two Chaplains. Boys are prepared for confirmation and there is a Chapel for voluntary worship.

Music. There is a purpose-built Music School. Four orchestras, three choirs and two wind bands, as well as various smaller groups and jazz groups, perform a number of major choral and orchestral works each year. Some 40% of the boys have individual music lessons at the School.

Games. After an introduction to a range of games, boys have a free choice of termly game to practise. The games programme includes athletics, badminton, cricket, cross-country running, fencing, hockey, rowing, rugby, sailing, shooting, soccer, squash, swimming and tennis. The School has its own indoor heated swimming pool. The sports hall has a floor area providing 4 badminton courts, as well as volley and basketball, indoor tennis and cricket nets, together with a fitness training room and four squash courts. A new all-weather surface for hockey and tennis was installed at the West Barnes Lane ground in 1998. The School's boathouse is on the Tideway at Putney.

School societies and activities. Every boy is encouraged to take part in extra-curricular activities. Societies meet in the two extended lunch breaks and after school. Friday school finishes early to allow boys to participate in a range of activities like the CCF and voluntary service. There are active drama and debating societies, together with a wide range of other societies.

Numbers. In the Senior School 710: in the Junior School 460.

Honours. Places at Oxford and Cambridge in 2001: 41.

Charitable status. King's College School is a Registered Charity, number 310024. It exists to provide education for children.

King's College, Taunton

Taunton Somerset TA1 3DX.
Tel: Headmaster: (01823) 328210
Bursar: (01823) 328100
Fax: 01823 328202
website: www.kings-taunton.co.uk
Station: Taunton, 1 mile

The School is the oldest school in the Western Division of the Woodard Corporation. Canon Nathaniel Woodard renamed the School King's College in memory of King Alfred, when he bought it in 1879, but its historical links go back to the medieval grammar school which was refounded by Bishop Fox of Winchester in 1522 (he also founded Corpus Christi College, Oxford). In 1869 Lord Taunton moved it from what are now the Municipal Buildings to its present site half a mile south of Taunton.

Motto: *Fortis et Fidelis.*

There are 430 boys and girls in the School, of which 125 are day pupils, and the Sixth Form is 200.

Governing Body: The Provost and Fellows of the Society of SS Mary and Andrew of Taunton

Provost: The Rt Revd The Bishop of Crediton

School Council:
Rear Admiral Sir Robert Woodard, KCVO (*Chairman and Custos*)
T H R Poole, TD, DL
A J Greswell, Esq, DL
Lady Acland, JP
Brigadier A I H Fyfe, DL
Mrs M Bate, JP
The Revd J M Henton, AKC
J L Stace, Esq
C J Parker, FRCS (Urol)
The Revd C H Jobson, MA
Admiral Sir Michael Layard, KCB, CBE
R D V Knight, Esq, MA
C S Martin, Esq, MA
R M Excell, Esq
Canon J Simpson, MA
M C Mowat, Esq, FCA
Sir Gordon Shattock, Kt (*Divisional Bursar*)

Headmaster: **R S Funnell**, MA, Trinity College, Cambridge

Chaplain: The Revd A C Smith

Deputy Headmaster: R A K Mott, BA, PhD

Assistant Masters:
J D Snowden, MA (*Senior Master*)
M T Rogers, MA
J M Crabtree, MA
J W Hudson, BSc
J A Lee, BA
A P McKegney, BA
R J Pocock, BA
B Lewis, BSc, PhD (*Second Master*)
†R H C Poland, BSc
R R Currie, BA
S B Gray, MA (*Director of Studies*)
P A Dossett, BSc
J C Spalding, MA, MLitt
R A Codd, DipPE, BEd
R E F Fitzpatrick, BA
R Llewellyn-Eaton, MA
†D J Cole, BSc
A R Hopwood, BSc
†M A Polley, MA
†Mrs D Polley
†P J Scanlan, MA
†Mrs M J Scanlan, RGN
J A Scott, BSc
J K Round, MA
D R Holmes, BSc, ARCS
†P A Westgate, BA
†J H Griffiths, BTech
C J Albery, BMus
Miss G Fagan, MA
†Mrs K L McSwiggan, BA (*Second Mistress*)
A R Francis Jones, BSc
C G Burton, BSc
Miss R C Davies, CertEd
Miss C G Fisher, BFA
Mrs K E Cole, BA
†H R J Trump, BA
M J Bakewell, BA
J W Grindle, BSc
M M Lang, BSc, MPhil
S A S Worrall, BSc
Miss L E Ellis, BSc
Miss L D Hindley, BA
Mrs J M Chadwick, BA
T K W Hart, BA
Miss C N Mackenzie, BA, DipAD
Mrs M Dominy, BA
S Haste, MSTA, AISC, FIST(*LS*)
P R Pearce, BA
Mrs J M Currie, LLB, CertTEFL
Miss R L Nutt, BA

Director of Music: C K Holmes, BA

Miss D Rees, LRAM, ARCM (*Singing*)
Mrs L Byrt, ARCM (*Oboe*)
M Langdon-Davies, AGSM (*Clarinet*)
Miss S Dawton, BMus, LTCL (*Flute*)
S Anstice-Brown, BMus (*Percussion*)
D Goodier, BEd (*Bass Guitar*)
Mrs L A Langdon-Davies (*Piano*)
T G Bowen, MusB (*Brass*)
C Hearnshaw (*Clarinet and Saxophone*)
P Scott-Wigfield, ARCM, LTCL (*Brass*)
J Crozier-Cole, BA (*Guitar*)
R Cox, ARCM (*'Cello*)
N White, MA (*Saxophone*)
Miss I Fernando (*Double Bass*)
Mrs R Maddock, AGSM (*Violin*)
A Cheshire (*Horn*)

Medical Officers:
Dr P L Squire, MB, BS, MRCGP
Dr Y L Duthie, MB, BS, DCH, MRCGP

Bursar: R J Lee, PhD, CEng, FCIS
Admissions Registrar: Mrs D K Polley
Events Manager: Mrs J M Hake

King's, a community of 430 boys and girls, ensures that each pupil feels at home, gains the self-confidence necessary for success, and learns qualities of independence, leadership and a concern for others. King's provides the highest standards of academic teaching, personal tutoring and careers guidance. Many pupils gain places at Oxford, Cambridge and other leading universities. King's pupils enjoy a superb and exciting range of sporting and leisure activities with many gaining representative honours. King's is renowned for its outstanding performing and creative arts. Full details are to be found in the Prospectus, which may be obtained from the Headmaster.

Admission. All entries are made through the Headmaster. Pupils normally enter between the ages of 13–14 and are admitted via Common Entrance or the Scholarship Examination.

Term of Entry. Pupils are normally accepted only in the Michaelmas and Lent terms.

Fees. The fees are inclusive of all extra charges of general application: Boarders, £4,650 a term; Day Boys, £3,060. The registration fee is £50.

Scholarships (*see* Entrance Scholarship section). For information about Scholarships, please refer to that section.

Old Boys Association. Mr B Sykes, Secretary, The Old Aluredian Club, 1 Church Street, Creech St Michael, Taunton TA3 5PW.

Charitable status. Woodard Schools (Western Division) Corporation is a Registered Charity, number 269669. King's College exists to provide high quality education for boys and girls aged 13–18.

King's School, Bruton

Bruton Somerset BA10 0ED.
Tel: 01749 814200
Fax: 01749 813426

The School was founded in 1519 by Richard Fitzjames, Bishop of London, John Fitzjames, his nephew, Attorney-General, afterwards Chief Justice of the King's Bench, and John Edmonds, DD, Chancellor of St Paul's. It was closed in 1538 on the suppression of the Monasteries, and re-founded by Edward VI in 1550.

Motto: *Deo Juvante.*

Governors:

S J Davie, Esq
N P Evelyn, Esq (*Junior Warden*)
General Sir Alex Harley, KBE, CB
K L Lawes, Esq, FCA
Martin Marriott, Esq, MA (*Senior Warden*)
C S Martin, Esq, MA
Mrs S McKenzie
S R Oxenbridge, Esq
T J Palmer, Esq, CBE (*Chairman of Finance*)
Revd Prebendary J H Parfitt, BPhil, MA
Mrs B Roberts
Air Vice Marshal M M J Robinson, CB, MA
N W Robson, Esq, FCIB
R J Sampson, Esq, FRICS, ACIArb
Air Chief Marshal Sir Peter Squire, GCB, DFC, AFC, ADC, FRAeS, RAF
Mrs M Willson, CertEd

***Headmaster:* R I Smyth,** MA, Emmanuel College, Cambridge

Deputy Headmaster: G J Evans, BSc(Econ)

Registrar: A B Leach, MA

Assistant Staff:

R S Lowe, BSc
R C F Hastings, BSc
C J Jones, BA
P L Davies, BSc
J N P Bennett, BA
M F Parr, MA
N G Watts, MA
S J F Atkinson, BSc
E J Tickner, BA
T V Johnson, CertEd
C S Juneman, MA
P Barnes, BEd
R J P Lowry, BA
J D Roebuck, BA
Mrs M Ashton, CertEd
S W Spilsbury, BEd Tech
D J Friend, BSc
Mrs V G Trenchard, MA
A Atkinson. BSc, PhD
Mrs S M Ryan, BA, MA
Mrs A Crowcombe, CertEd
M J Middlehurst, BA
Mrs G Pryor, BSc
D R Barns-Graham, MA
Miss J R Hodgetts, BA, MA
E A Flitters, BA
Mrs G de Mora, BSc
C H M Oulton, MA
Mrs K Patterson, BA, MA
Miss K A Wood, BA
T Fletcher, BA
P Oldfield, BA
Revd N H Wilson-Brown, BSc (*Chaplain*)
G E Jenkins, BA, PhD
D Warren, BA
F J Llewellyn, BA
Miss E McKnight, BMus
Miss E Stead, BEd
C A Barrow, BA
J P Visentin, BEd
K Pragnell, BA
Mrs D T Paulley
Mrs A Allen, SpLDDip
Mrs C Tickner, BA
Miss A Wickham, BEd
Mrs P M Johnson, BEd
W Hodgson, BA

Houses and Housemasters:
Blackford: J N P Bennett
New: J D Roebuck
Old: M F Parr
Lyon: T V Johnson
Wellesley: Mrs V G Trenchard, MA
Priory: R J P Lowry
Arion: Mrs A Crowcombe

Headmaster's Secretary: Mrs C Ratcliffe
School Secretary: Mrs M Edwards

Medical Officers:
Dr M H Player, BSc, MB, BS, DRCOG, MRCGP
Dr L H Chambers, MB, BS, MDRCOG
Dr U Naumann, FRG, DRCOG, MRCGP
Dr N Gompertz, BSc, MB, ChB, MRCP

Physical Education: C A Barrow, BA

Music:
G E Jenkins, BA, PhD
Miss E Knight, BMus
Mrs S Whitfield, ARCM (*Piano and Theory*)
Mrs F Zagni, MA, BA, LTCL (*Cello and Double Bass*)
J M Padley, BMus, LTCL
Mrs J Beck, BA (*Flute*)
P Caunce (*Violin/viola*)
K R Schooley, MISM (*Percussion and Drumkit*)
P Kelly (*Guitar*)
D Shead (*Trumpet*)
Mrs J Whitteridge, ARCM, CertEd (*Bassoon*)
P Lange, LRAM, ARCM
N Stebbing-Allen (*Singing*)
Mrs A McBride (*Oboe*)
M Walker (*Piano*)

Hazlegrove (*King's Bruton Preparatory School*)
Telephone: 01963 440314 (*Headmaster and Secretary*)
Fax: 01963 440569

Headmaster: The Revd Bramwell A Bearcroft, BEd, Homerton College, Cambridge

Deputy Head: Miss D Lambert, BEd (Hons)

Senior Tutor/Co-ordinator: C J Smith, CertEd

Director of Studies: H D Moore, BSc

Head of Pre-Prep Department: Mrs L Statham, CertEd

Senior Master: A D Telfer, CertEd

Assistant Staff
Mrs S Barns-Graham, BA
Miss K Bartlett, NNEB
Mrs A M Bawtree, CertEd (*Remedial Maths*)
Mrs J A Bearcroft, BEd
Miss S L Benson, MSc
S Bryan, BSc
J P Carnegie, CertEd
Mrs K Cobb, BEd
P Cobb, BA
Mrs A Coyle, BA
Mrs S Cranfield, BEd (*Remedial*)
Mrs T C E Crisell, BA
Mrs A Crowcombe, CertEd
Mme L Edgcumbe
D Ellery, BA
Mrs D Farwell, NNEB
Mrs J Gajraj
Mrs S Gray, BEd
Mrs Gripper
B C Hignell, BA, PGCE
M P Illingworth, MA
Mrs S M Illingworth
J Lambert, BA
Mrs K Lambert, BA
Mrs S J Laver, CertEd
Miss H Lintern
Miss L Messer, BEd
C K Moore, DipEd
Miss E Nash

K Newbitt, BEd
Mrs J K Nutt
Miss M Patel
Miss S Philips
M Psarros, BA, MA
Miss C Seager, BEd
Mrs R Smith, CertEd
Mrs N Smyth
Mrs C Todd, BEd
Mrs S J Threlfall-Eyres, BEd

Assistant Music Staff:
Mrs C Caswell (*flute*)
Mrs D Hann, ARCM (*singing*)
D Kelleher (*guitar and drums*)
P Lange (*piano*)
Mrs S Matthews, ARCM (*piano*)
Mrs B Palmer (*cello*)
B Shanahan (*bagpipes*)
Mrs S Whitfield, BA, ARCM (*piano*)
G Wilkinson, BA, LTCL (*brass*)

School Doctor: J F Hart, MB, BS

School Nurses: Mrs P Dickens, Mrs C Marr

Headmaster's Secretary: Mrs J Cook

School Secretary: Mrs E Viner

Bursar: Capt D Shorland Ball

The number of pupils in the School is 724 (Pre Prep 70 full time and 27 part-time, Junior School 262, Senior School 365.

Buildings. The oldest portion of the Buildings dates from the early part of the 16th century. This, with numerous additions and alterations, forms Old House. New House was begun in 1872, and has been considerably extended since. Priory House is situated in adjacent property acquired in 1942. Lyon House was opened in September, 1954, and extended in 1976 and 1986, and Blackford House in September 1960. Wellesly was opened in 1984 and Arion in 1997. There is a Sanatorium, staffed by a Sister-in-Charge. The Memorial Hall, built by Old Brutonians after the First World War, incorporates a classroom wing, a recital and meeting room and the refurbished and extended Music School. A development programme, completed in 1979, included the extension of the Music School, a large Sports Hall with a theatre-cum-cinema in the same building, and the self-service Dining Hall, built in 1974, which has classrooms and the Norton Library on the first floor. A classroom block, which also includes a centrally located Tuck Shop, leads to the splendid Design Centre opened in 1989 and incorporating all facilities for Design, Technology, Art and Information Technology. An extension to the Design Centre housing a Physics Department and extended Computive facilities was opened in September 1994. A synthetic playing surface for hockey and tennis was opened in September 1995. A new Science Centre for Biology, Chemistry and Home Economics was opened in September 1999. All the boarding houses have been fully refurbished in the last seven years.

Boarding Houses. Old House (M F Parr); New House (J D Roebuck); Priory House (R J D Lowry); Lyon House (T V Johnson); Blackford House (J N P Bennett). Each house has a matron to look after boys' health and clothes. Wellesley House: 13-18 Girls' (Mrs V G Trenchard). Arion Girls, 13-18: (Mrs A Crowcombe).

Co-education. Since September 1969, girls have been admitted to VIth Form courses at the Senior School subject to GCSE level success, either as boarders or day girls. Junior girls from 13 were welcome in September 1997 when Arion House was opened.

The Preparatory School is at Hazlegrove House, Sparkford, 9 miles from Bruton. The fullest cooperation and continuity are ensured between the Preparatory and Senior Schools, boys and girls passing from one to the other having obtained a pass in Common Entrance. As from January 1996 the School has welcomed girl boarders. Hazlegrove House stands in its own large grounds and is splendidly equipped. Recent additions include a Sports Hall, new Science laboratories, a Theatre-cum-Chapel-cum-Assembly Hall, a new Music School, two Squash Courts, a 25 metre indoor swimming pool and an Art and Craft department.

Curriculum. In the Preparatory School the work consists of English Subjects, Latin, French, Mathematics, Science, History, Geography, Scripture, Music, Art, Handicrafts and Computer Studies.

The Senior School is divided into Upper and Lower VIth, four Vth, four IVth and four IIIrd Forms. The subjects taught include RS, English, History, Geography, Politics, Economics, Business Studies, Mathematics, Physics, Chemistry, Biology, Latin, Classical Civilisation, French, German, Spanish, Italian, Music, Art, Technology, PE and Information Technology. National Curriculum GCSE courses are followed up to the Vth Form, after which, in the VI, pupils are able to specialise for subjects at A level, for entry to Universities, the Services and other Careers.

Games. The School games are Cricket, Rugby Football, Hockey and Netball. There is a wide variety of other sports available as options. Rugby is played in the Christmas Term, Hockey in the Easter Term; Cross-Country Running takes place in both. Athletics and Tennis are encouraged in the Summer Term. Girls play hockey in the Christmas term and Netball in the Easter term. There are 2 main playing fields, 17 Tennis Courts, 2 Squash Courts, 2 Fives Courts, a heated open-air Swimming Bath and a Sports Hall. A Hard-Play area with 2 All Weather Hockey Pitches is well-used. A new synthetic playing surface for hockey and tennis was completed in September 1995. A Physical Education course is provided for all pupils. Judo, Basketball, Badminton, Fencing and Golf are actively encouraged.

There is a Combined Cadet Force which all boys and girls are expected to join for a definite period, after which they can undertake other forms of Service in the community. An RAF Section and a RN Section also flourish. There is an excellent Rifle Range, and Army ranges are nearby. A Leadership Training Area was opened in 1984.

Music. Vocal and Instrumental Music has for many years been one of the strong features in education at the School, and pupils are strongly encouraged to learn and appreciate music. Frequent concerts are given by Choir, Orchestra, Dance and Military bands. The Music School, built in 1979, was refurbished during 1992.

Societies and other activities. One afternoon a week and time on 2 other days is devoted to a wide range of activities, including Acting, Archaeology, Archery, Art, Bee-Keeping, Chess, Debating, Electronics, Modelling, Music, Printing, Photography. Design, Technology, Art and Computing are all provided in the Design Centre. The Societies make external visits; exchanges and School journeys abroad are arranged and Lecturers on a wide range of subjects are invited to the School. A Community Service activity provides help in the town and the neighbourhood. Pupils are encouraged to bicycle or walk in the surrounding countryside in their spare time. The Friends' Association provides Travel Scholarships as well as various extra amenities. There are regular School Films.

Worship. Assembly takes place in the Memorial Hall. On Sundays and Thursday mornings the School worships in the large parish church of St Mary, Bruton. Pupils are prepared by the Chaplain for Confirmation in the Autumn Term. There is a flourishing Christian fellowship group.

Scholarships. (*see* Entrance Scholarship section) Scholarships are awarded annually for competition. **For precise details, please refer to the Scholarship section.**

Careers. There is a full Careers Structure with the Head of Careers supported by other masters with specialist knowledge of Industry, University Entrance, GAP year, interview technique and work experience. Pupils have full access to a well equipped Careers Library. The Independent Schools Careers Organisation is fully used and the School enjoys the support of the local Careers Service.

Admission and Fees. No child is admitted to the Junior School before the age of 7½ years, nor to the Senior School before 13. The fees (including necessary Extras, eg Medical Attendance, Sanatorium, Games) for September 2000 are: Boarders – Junior School, from £9,660 pa; Senior School, £13,860 pa. Day Pupils – Junior School, from £6,540 pa; Senior School, £9,750 pa.

Pre-Prep and Nursery. Hazlegrove House, Sparkford, Nr Yeovil. Tel: 01963 440822. Head of Dept: Mrs L Statham, CertEd. The Co-educational Pre-Preparatory School is purpose-built and has specialist staff for each age group. It is situated within the spacious grounds of the Preparatory School with access to its excellent facilities. Ages 3 to 8.

Old Brutonian Association. An edition of the Old Brutonians Register 1911–1979 was printed in 1980. Contact about the Old Brutonian Association can be made to D J C Hindley, JP, MA, at the school.

Charitable status. King's, Bruton is a Registered Charity, number 1071997. It exists to provide education for boys and girls from 3–18.

The King's School
Canterbury

Canterbury Kent CT1 2ES.
Tel: (01227) 595501. Bursar (01227) 595500
Fax: (01227) 595595
e-mail: headmaster@kings-school.co.uk
website: www.kings-school.co.uk

The School is as old as English Christianity. The educational institutions associated from the earliest times with the see and city of Canterbury were gathered by King Henry VIII into an establishment of Headmaster, Lower Master, and 50 King's Scholars, and made part of his reformed Foundation at Canterbury in 1541. King George VI incorporated 'The King's School of the Cathedral Church of Canterbury' by Royal Charter in 1946. A Supplementary Charter of 1992 enabled the School to become fully co-educational.

Visitor: The Lord Archbishop of Canterbury

Governors:

Chairman: The Dean of Canterbury

¶M Herbert, Esq, CBE, MA, FCA
The Revd Canon P G C Brett, MA
¶Sir Robert Horton, LLD, BSc, SM, DCL, FIChemE, CMgt
The Lady Kingsdown, OBE
The Lady Lloyd, MA
C R Prior, Esq, DPhil, PhD
R H B Sturt, Esq, MA
C H Brown, Esq, FRICS
¶The Revd Canon R H C Symon, MA
The Revd Canon M J Chandler, PhD, DipTh, STh
Sir Christopher Chataway, BSc, MA, DLitt
The Ven J L Pritchard, MLitt, DipTh, MA
Mrs M Berg, MSc(Econ)
¶P J Stone, Esq, MA
The Revd R Marsh, BD, MA, AKC, CertEd
¶Mrs S J Gurr, BSc, ARCS, DIC, PhD, MA
O Rackham, Esq, OBE, MA, PhD

Clerk to the Governors: R C A Bagley, Esq, LLB

Governors Emeriti:
¶The Revd Canon D Ingram-Hill, MA, DD
The Rt Hon Lord FitzWalter, JP
¶The Very Revd D L Edwards, DD
Sir Peter Ramsbotham, GCMG, GCVO

***Headmaster:* The Revd Canon K H Wilkinson**, BA, MA, FRSA

Lower Master: B Turner, MA

Senior Mistress: Mrs A L George, BA

Director of Studies: G R Cocksworth, MA

Assistant Director of Studies: A R A Rooke, BSc

Senior Housemaster: S J Graham, MA

Registrar: H E J Aldridge, MA

Head of Sixth Form: C J R Jackson, MSc

Director of Music: S W S Anderson, MA, BMus, ARCM

Head of Orchestral Studies: C Metters, ARCM, HonARCM, HonRAM

Assistant Chaplain: The Revd Dr Iain Bentley, BTech, MSc, PhD

Librarian: Mrs K Hoar, ALA

Bursar: N C Lewis, FCA, ACIB

Medical Officers:
Dr W Lloyd Hughes, MB, BS
Dr J Fegent, MB, BS

Headmaster's Secretary: Mrs L Breaden

M Afzal, BSc, PhD
H E J Aldridge, MA
*J Allday, MA, PhD, ALCM
*S E Anderson, BA
*S W S Anderson, MA, BMus, ARCM
*T J Armstrong, MA
*D M Arnott, BSc, PhD
*Ms C M Astin, MA, LTCL
*C J Banfield, BA, BSc, MA
N J Bell, BSc
J I Bentley, BTech, MSc, PhD
Mrs M-D Bradburn, BA
†P J Brodie, MA, MA(Ed)
Mrs C V Browning, BA
†*H W Browning, MA
*M Bruna, Ldo
*D Cameron, BA
*R Churcher, BSc
G R Cocksworth, MA
Mrs C P Coleman, BA
Mrs J M Cook, BA
R P Cook, BSc
P K Cordeaux, BA
†M P H Dath, L-ès-ScM, M-ès-ScM
Mrs D Davis, MA
A W Dyer, BA
Ms M Edwards, BA
J Evans, BSc, MSc
D J Felton, MA
†P W Fox, MSc
Miss D M Francis, BA
M J Franks, BEd
Mrs A L George, BA
†S J Graham, MA
S A Heath, BA

P G Henderson, BA
C T Holland, MA
*R M Hooper, MA
†Mrs L A Horn, BSc
J M Hutchings, BA
C J R Jackson, MA
T I Jennings, MA
Mrs E S Ladd, BEng
Miss A G Little, MA
M Liviero, DottLing, PhD
A McFall, BSc
Mrs S E Mackenzie, BA
R B Mallion, BSc, PhD, DPhil
H R O Maltby, MA, DPhil
*K E J Martin, BA
S J R Matthews, MA
M J Miles, MA
R B Milford, BA
O G Moore, BSc
†C P Newbury, BA
T Noon, BA, FRCO (ChM)
J W Outram, BA
J R Parker, BSc
T J Parker, MA
N L Phillis, MA
Dr C E Pidoux, MA
A Pollock, MA
*H J Pragnell, MA, ATD
*D J Reid, MA
*Mrs J M Reid, BEd, MPhil
Miss K M Reidy, BA
*R I Reilly, MA, MSc
S J Ripley, BSc, PhD
Miss M Rodes, L-ès-L
A R A Rooke, BSc
G V Solomon, BSc
*Miss J Taylor, BA
*†P Teeton, BA
†Mrs F E Tennick, BA

M J Tennick, BA
T Thomson, MA, DPhil
M Thornby, BSc
B Turner, BA
†Mrs P Wakeham, BA
*R N Warnick, MA
A R Watson, BEd
†Mrs J A Watson, MSc
†Mrs J H Wharfe, BSc
†R C White, BA
*S J Winrow-Campbell, BSc
G D Wood, MA

Music Staff:
*Stefan Anderson, MA, BMus, ARCM (*Director of Music*)
Stephen Matthews, MA (*Academic, Piano*)
Colin Metters, ARCM, Hon ARAM, Hon RAM (*Head of Orchestral Studies*)
Timothy Noon, BA, FRCO (ChM) (*Organist, Academic*)
Andrew Pollock, MA (*Head of Strings*)
Kevin Abbott, DipRCM (*French Horn*)
Rebecca Austen-Brown, BMus (*Recorder*)
Alison Beatty, GRSM, LRAM (*Violin*)
Chris Blundell, GMus, DipMCOS (*Percussion*)
Matthew Booth, MMus, BA, ABSM (*Trumpet*)
Simon Chiswell, GRSM, LRAM (*Bassoon*)
Heather Cleobury, LRAM (*Singing*)
Julia Cleobury, ARCM (*Piano*)
Stephen Cottrell, BA, MMus (*Saxophone*)
Margaret Cowling, GRSM, LRAM, ARCM, FRSA (*Piano*)
Andrew Cunningham (*Saxophone*)
Julie Evans, MA (*Violin*)
Derek Faux-Bowyer, LRAM (*Guitar*)
Felicity Goodsir, GRSM, ARCM (*Flute*)
David Hitchen, GRSM, ARMCM (*Singing*)
Philip Hughes, LRAM (*Piano, Electronic Keyboard*)
Jane Hyland, ARCM (*Cello*)
Roy Jowitt, ARAM LRAM (*Clarinet*)
Katharine Lewis, BA, ARCM (*Singing*)
Roderick Livingstone (*Bagpipes*)
Robin McLeish, BA, BMus (*Piano*)
Mary Morley, BA, DipGSMD (*Harp*)
Henry Myerscough, ARAM, LRAM (*Viola*)
Carol Raby, GRSM, DipRCM (*Clarinet*)
Rosemary Rathbone, LRAM (*Flute*)
David Rees-Williams, BMus (*Piano & Jazz Piano*)
Malcolm Rogers, LRAM (*Guitar*)
Julia Vohralik, MA, ARCM (*Cello*)
David White (*Drum Kit*)
Cliff Willard, LTCL (*Trombone, Tuba*)
John Williams (*Oboe*)
Kenneth Woollam, Hon RCM (*Singing*)

Careers:
J R Parker, BSc
R B Milford, BA
A S Mackintosh, MA (Law)
Mrs D Davies, MA
Mrs L A Horn, BSc

The Junior King's School, Milner Court, Sturry, Nr. Canterbury, CT2 0AY. Canterbury (*01227*) 710245

Headmaster: P M Wells, BEd (Hons) (Exeter)

For details of the Junior King's School See Part V.

Religion. The School has very close links with the Cathedral but there is no denominational requirement for entry.

Numbers and Organisation. The school became fully co-educational in 1990. There are some 754 pupils at King's (606 boarders and 148 day pupils), and some 222 at Milner Court (56 boarders and 166 day pupils), plus 91 in the Pre-Prep.

A pupil's welfare is primarily the responsibility of his/her Housemaster or Housemistress. For individual academic guidance each pupil is further assigned into the care of one of the Tutors in their House. Domestic matters are the concern of the Matron resident in each boarding House. Feeding and medical care are organised centrally.

The School buildings are for the most part within the beautiful and historic Precincts of Canterbury Cathedral and St Augustine's Abbey.

The Houses and Housemasters/Housemistresses are:

School House, Mr H W Browning; The Grange, Mr M P H Dath; Walpole, Mrs J A Watson. Meister Omers, Mr C P Newbury; Marlowe (day), Mr R C White; Luxmoore, Mrs F E Tennick; Galpin's, Mr P J Brodie; Linacre, Mr P Teeton; Tradescant, Mr S J Graham; Broughton, Mrs P A Wakeham Mitchinson's (day), Mr P W Fox; Jervis House, Mrs L A Horn; Harvey House, Mrs J H Wharfe.

Work. All pupils follow a broadly based curriculum for 3 years, at the end of which they sit the GCSE in 9-11 subjects. Pupils take 4 AS levels at the end of Year 12 and 3 A2s at the end of Year 13. Virtually all pupils leave King's for the Universities. The advice of the Careers Department is available at all relevant stages.

Games and Recreation. The major games are Rugby Football, Football, Netball, Tennis, Hockey, Athletics, Cricket and Rowing. Good facilities exist for all the usual sports. A new Recreational Centre including Swimming Pool, Squash Courts and Large Hall opened in 1990. The Milner Hall, opened in 1998, is specifically equipped for Fencing.

Cultural recreations and hobbies are encouraged through some 25 societies managed (with advice) by the boys and girls themselves, and through a programme of "Activities" which occupies one afternoon each week. Lectures and recitals by distinguished visitors take place each term.

King's Week, the School's own festival of Music and Drama, attracts thousands of visitors each summer.

CCF and Social Service. Membership of the Combined Cadet Force is voluntary. The Social Service unit cooperates with kindred bodies in Canterbury.

Music. The strongest encouragement is given to Music, and many entrance awards are available. Details are given in the Music Scholarship section.

Admission. Application should be made to the Admissions Secretary. It is advisable to register pupils at an early age. Admission is normally through the Common Entrance Examination or, if academically able, through the School's own Scholarship Examination. The age of entry is about 13.

Fees. Fees at the Senior School for the September Term 2000 are £5,600 for boarders and £3,910 for day pupils. At the Junior School boarders pay £3,700 and day pupils £2,610.

Entrance Scholarships and other awards. (*see* Entrance Scholarship section) Up to 20 King's Scholarships can be awarded if candidates of sufficient merit present themselves. The examination is held annually in March and is open to boys and girls under the age of 14 on 1st September. The awards are normally up to 50% of the annual fee in every year (more in the case of need). Up to 12 Music Scholarships, up to half fees, are offered each year in February, and Art Scholarships are offered in March. Pupils entering the sixth form may compete for academic scholarships which will be offered as a result of the entrance examination in November. Music and Art scholarships will also be offered for competition in November.

Leaving Gifts and Closed Awards. The School has a number of these.

About 30 offers of admission to Oxford and Cambridge are received each year.

OKS (Old King's Scholars). *Secretary:* M J Hodgson, BA, St Martin's School, Northwood HA6 2DJ.

Charitable status. The Governors, The Headmaster and The Lower Master of The King's School of the Cathedral Church of Canterbury in the City of Canterbury is a Registered Charity, number 307942. It exists to provide education for boys and girls aged 5 to 18 inclusive.

The King's School
Chester

Chester CH4 7QL.
Tel: (01244) 689500
Fax: (01244) 689501

The School was founded AD 1541 by King Henry VIII, in conjunction with the Cathedral Church of Chester. It was reorganised under the Endowed Schools Act in 1873, and by subsequent schemes of the Ministry of Education. The School is now Independent.

Motto: *"Rex Dedit, Benedicat Deus."*

Chairman of the Governing Body: Canon C W J Samuels, AKC

Clerk: R R Williams, FCA

***Headmaster:* T J Turvey**, BSc, DipEd, CBiol, FIBiol, FLS

Assistant Masters:
G J Hutton, BA (*Head of VIth Form; Geography & Economics*)
J E Higgins, BSc, ALCM (*Mathematics*)
K H Mellor, BSc (*Chemistry*)
P A Bradley, BSc, PhD (*Director of Studies, Physics*)
Mrs J M Davies, BEd (*Junior School*)
M V Baker (*Craft, Design, Technology*)
B J W Ball, FTCL, GTCL, LicMusEd (*Director of Music*)
A R Neeves, BA (*Physical Education*)
S Downey, BA (*Art*)
T Keeley, BSc, MIBiol, CBiol (*Biology*)
Mme F Vergnaud, MA (*Modern Languages*)
P S Fentem, BA, (*Classics*)
Mrs C A Hill, MA, MSc (*Mathematics*)
M J Harle, BSc (*Chemistry*)
R G Wheeler, BA (*English*)
Mrs B Roberts, GRNCM, ARNCM (*Junior School*)
A R Price, BA (*Physical Education*)
S Neal, BA (*History*)
M J P Punnett, BA (*Classics*)
Mrs J L Brannan, BSc (*Geography*)
Miss K L Hindley, BA (*Modern Languages*)
C J White, BA (*Religious Studies*)
S A Malone, BEd (*Head of Junior School*)
Mrs A Taylor (*Junior School*)
J H King, MA, MSc (*Geography*)
P D Shannon, MA (*Modern Languages*)
Mrs K J Thurlow-Wood, BA (*Modern Languages*)
H J Duncalf, BEd (*Junior School*)
Miss H D Sayers, BEd (*Junior School*)
Mrs M D O'Leary, BA (*Junior School*)
Mrs J E Meredith, BSc (*Biology*)
Mrs C E Ruston, BA (*English*)
K A Hollingworth, BEd (*Junior School*)
Mrs H M Francis, CertEd (*Junior School*)
B R Lewis, BEng (*Mathematics*)
R D J Elmore, BSc, MIBiol, CBiol (*Biology*)
D Yalland, BSc (*Physics*)
S D Walton, BA, MSc (*Economics*)
N Heritage, BSc, MSc, PhD (*Physics*)
Miss K Z Andrews, BMus (*Music*)
D Murphy, MA, DPhil (*Chemistry*)
Miss D L England, BA (*Junior School*)
J A Hargreaves, MA (*Second Master, English*)
M F Latimer, MA (*Modern Languages*)
D G Lavender, BSc (*Information Technology*)
S J Parry, BA (*Mathematics*)
Miss J M Ledsham, BA (*Modern Languages*)
A H Northcott, BA (*Religious Studies*)
R J P Trevett, MA (*History*)
R D Shaw, BA (*Mathematics*)
S Bosworth, MA, DPhil (*Physics*)
R Parker, BA (*Economics*)
Mrs M Higgins, BEd (*PE*)
Mrs A Hollingworth, BA (*Art*)
M J Hackett, BSc (*Director of Rowing*)
B R F Routledge, MA (*English*)
K J Whiskerd, BA (*Junior School*)

Administration:
Headmaster's Secretary: Mrs H M Hooley, BA
Assistant Secretary: Mrs W Roberts
Junior School Secretary: Mrs S Evans
Bursar: G E Baskerville, FCA
Assistant: Mrs W I Plews
Accountant: Mrs P Hopkinson, ACA
Librarian: Mrs H Holyoak, BSc, ALA
Assistant Librarians:
Mrs M E Hutchings, MA
Mrs C A H Roberts, BSc, ALA

The School, which at present numbers 715, consists of (i) a Junior Department, a School of 8 forms of boys aged 7 to 11 years, which is housed in a separate building, but is run in collaboration with (ii) the Upper School. Boys are admitted to the Upper School aged between 11 and 12, and may remain till the end of the year in which they become 18. Boys in the Junior Department normally move into the Upper School at the age of 11 but must pass the Upper School entrance examination before doing so. Boys and girls are admitted to the Sixth Form on the basis of GCSE results.

The Entrance Examinations for the Junior and Upper Schools are held in the Lent Term. Applications to sit must be made on a form obtainable from the School. The School's own Bursary Trust Fund offers assistance for families in financial need.

The aim of the School is to prepare pupils for admission to the Universities, the professions, commerce and industry, and at the same time provide a liberal education.

School Examinations. The VIth and Vth Forms are examined annually at the end of the Summer Term by the NEAB at 'A' level and the appropriate Examining Boards for GCSE. The subjects of study in the VIth Form are – on the Arts Side: English, French, German, Spanish Latin, History, Geography, Economics, Art, Music, Religious Studies, Politics, Sports Science, Classical Studies; and on the Science Side: Mathematics, Further Mathematics, Physics, Chemistry, Biology. Many combinations of subjects from either Art or Science are possible.

Religious Instruction. All pupils follow a course of Religious Instruction and the subject may be taken at 'GCSE' and 'A' level.

The School is part of the Cathedral Foundation and regularly holds its own services in the Cathedral.

Music. Music is part of the general curriculum for all boys up to the age of 14. After this music may be taken at GCSE and A level. Private tuition in orchestral instruments, piano and organ is available. There is a School choir, Operatic Society, and an Orchestra. There are also Brass, Wind and String ensembles and Swing Band.

Cadet Corps. There is a School detachment of the CCF in charge of a master at the School. Its Headquarters is on the School site.

Fees 2000/2001. For tuition. Upper School £5,751 pa. Junior School £4,401 pa. The School offers a number of its own Assisted places annually.

Scholarships tenable at Universities. – (1) Three Old King's Scholars Exhibitions, of value of £100 pa, for 3 years; (2) Five Robert Platt Exhibitions of £100 pa, tenable for 3 years; (3) Six John Churton Exhibitions of £100 pa, tenable for 3 years; (4) One William Denson Haswell Exhibition of value £40 pa for 3 years; (5) Three

Exhibitions of £100 pa for 3 years awarded by the King's School Mothers' Guild and three exhibitions of £100 pa for 3 years awarded by the King's School Fathers' Association.

Games. Association Football, Rugby, Hockey, Cricket, Rowing, Swimming, Badminton, Basketball, Athletics, Netball, Tennis, Squash, Golf and Volley Ball.

Buildings. At Easter 1960 the school moved into new buildings situated in rural surroundings nearly 2 miles from the centre of Chester. Though the Junior and Upper Schools are on the same site of 32 acres, they are housed in 2 separate buildings each having its own playing fields. On 22 June 1960 the new school was formally declared open by Her Majesty Queen Elizabeth the Queen Mother. In 1964 a new indoor Swimming Bath and Pavilion were opened. All boys are given regular swimming tuition.

More new buildings were added in the 1980's starting with a workshop opened in 1984. On 17 May 1989 Her Royal Highness the Princess Margaret formally opened a development consisting of ten new classrooms, four new laboratories, a music school, an art room, a Sixth Form centre, sports hall, general purposes room for the Junior School, new kitchen, tutorial rooms and offices. In September 1989 the School went from two to three form entry.

In 1994 an extension to the Junior School buildings was completed and from September 1994 boys were admitted at 7.

In 1998 girls were admitted to the Sixth Form.

In January 2000 a new Library/IT Centre was opened.

Old Boys' Association: The School has what is believed to be the country's oldest Old Boys' Association (1866) and the CAOKS is a very flourishing and active body. The present Hon Secretary is Adrian Ackroyd, 2 Heath Road, Upton, Chester CH2 1HU (Tel: 01244 382323; e-mail: aaa@norrad.co.uk).

Charitable status. The King's School, Chester is a Registered Charity, number 525934. The aim of the charity is to provide first class education to all who can benefit from it regardless of their economic and social background.

The King's School
Ely

Ely Cambs CB7 4DB
Tel: Headmaster: (01353) 660701.
Bursar: (01353) 660700
Fax: Headmaster: (01353) 667485; Bursar: (01353) 662187

The school traces its origins back to the 7th century AD and the foundation of the abbey church at Ely, where education was said to have been provided for children. The most famous former pupil is perhaps Edward the Confessor. In 1541 Henry VIII reconstituted the school by royal charter; hence its name. Its statutes were confirmed by Elizabeth I and Charles II. Since 1879 the school has been a registered charity.

Henry VIII stipulated that up to twelve senior boys should be King's Scholars, and in 1973 they were joined by twelve girls, at the request of HM Queen Elizabeth II. The King's and Queen's Scholars, together with the Headmaster, are members of the Foundation of Ely Cathedral - an indication of the continuing strong links between school and Cathedral. The magnificent Cathedral is used, in effect, as the school chapel for regular worship, and the school educates the Cathedral choristers.

The school still uses many of Ely's medieval monastic buildings - as boarding houses, as classrooms and as the dining hall. The 14th century Porta, the great gateway to the monastery, has been converted into a magnificent new Senior School library, fully equipped to give access to electronic information via CD and the Internet. Other new buildings show the continuing and substantial investment in modern facilities: the renovated Georgian villa that now houses the Pre-Prep section of Acremont House; new music rooms and classrooms in the Junior School; a splendidly refurbished senior Art Department; a new Technology Centre and a new senior Music School and Recital Hall which opened in Spring 2001.

The school was one of the first traditional boys' schools to admit girls, in 1970, and is now co-educational from the ages of 2½ to 18. The total roll is about 890, with slightly more boys than girls, and every fourth pupil over the age of eight is a weekly or full boarder. The King's School Ely has a reputation as an exceptionally friendly and welcoming school. Its pupils represent a wide range of ability and interests, from the highly academic to those with predominantly practical or creative talents. The school turns out young people who are considerate, adaptable and self-confident but free of arrogance - and who are often delighted to acknowledge that they have exceeded their own and their parents' expectations.

Visitor: The Rt Revd The Bishop of Ely

Governors:
Chairman: Dr M T Nickson
Vice-Chairman: M V Bright

D A Adams
Sir John Browne
The Very Revd The Dean of Ely
Sir J B Fairbairn, Bt
M H Gruselle
Canon F J Kilner
C R I Matheson
C B Morris
Miss S Rawlings
Canon J Rone
J B Shropshire
Dr K J Skoyles
R P Slogrove
R B Thain

***Headmaster:* R H Youdale**, MA (Emmanuel College, Cambridge)

Deputy Headmaster of Senior School: G Parry, BSc, PhD, PGCE

Director of Studies and Second Deputy Head: G R Hutt, BSc, PhD, AMRAeS

Head of Junior School: A G Duncan, BA, BEd, CertEd

Head of Acremont House: Mrs F A Blake, BA, PGCE

Acting Bursar: R I Morris

Chaplain: The Revd A T D Richards, BA, CTPS, PGCE, FRSA

Marketing and Media Relations Officer: Mrs E M Sayers

Medical Officer: A S Douglas, BMedSci, BM, BS, DRCOG, SPCert

Headmaster's Secretary: Mrs M Fryer

Admissions Secretary: Mrs J Nancollis

Assistant Staff: Senior School:

J R Atkinson, MA
J P A Ball, MA, PGCE
C G Bell, LRAM
Mrs M Blackmore, MA
Miss H Bome, GRSM, LRAM, DipRAM, PGCE
P J Brooke, BA, PGCE
Miss A C Charlton, BEd
P A H Coutts, MA, PGCE
F J L Dale, CertEd, MA, DipTEFL
E J Davis, BA, BA, PGCE
Miss M P Day, BA, LRAM, MTC

Mrs C A Dean, MA, PGCE, CertEd
Mlle N Dignat, UER Let
R P Emms, BA, PGCE
A R Gamble, BA, PGCE
S A Green, DipAD, ATD
G P L Griggs, MusB, GRNCM, FRCO, PGCE
N J G Hammond, BA, PGCE
M G Hawes, BA, PGCE
D J Hodgson, BSc, PGCE
J R E Hooper, BA
Miss J R Howell, BA, PGCE
J Hughes, BSc, PGCE
Mrs E M Hunter, CertEd, BA
H G Ingham, BA
B S Jackson, BEng, PGCE
D Kittson, HND, CertEd, FETC
Miss S E Knibb, BA, PGCE
P A Lott, BSc, PGCE
Mrs J P Mackay, BSc
W J Marshall, BA, MA(*Ed*), PGCE
J A Mascall, BSc, MSc, PGCE, CPhys, MInstP
I A McWhinney, BSc
Miss N C Morrow, MA, PGCE
S L Murfitt, BA, PGATC
Mrs C A Palmer, BSc, AIBMS, CertTEFL, DipSpN
Ms W K Pitt, BEd, PhD
N J Reckless, MA, PGCE
J W Riley, CertEd, MA
G Robertson, BA, AdvDip Speech & Drama, LAMDA
Mrs K M Slater, BA, MA(*Ed*), CertEd
Ms G Smith, MA, MTh, PGCE
A J Thomas, BA, PGCE
N A Tooth, BSc, PGCE
G Wesson, BSc, PhD, DPSE(*Tech*), PGCE
Mrs L A Williams, MA
Mrs L F Wilson
P N Wilson, CertEd, BA
Miss H A Wright, BEd, CertEd

Assistant Staff: Junior School:

D A Boothroyd, BEd
A J Breese, BA, PGCE
S J Buck, BSc, PGCE
Mrs P A Clark, BA, MEd, AdvDip
W S Clement, CertEd
Mrs J K Erskine, BEd, CertEd, RSA, DipTEFL
Mrs P Foulds, BEd
T J O Glenn, BA, PGCE
Mrs M E Gordon Jones, L-ès-L
Miss M R Haigh, CertEd
Mrs J J Hoare, BEd
Mrs A M Humphries, CertEd
Mrs D E Jones, BA, PGCE
Mrs M U Lachlan, LRAM
J A Lowery, BA, PGCE
Mrs A E Maton, HND, SpLDDip
N M Ovens, BA, CertEd
Mrs B A Pope, CertEd
N Porter-Thaw, LTCL, DipTCL
R F Powell, BA, CertEd
Mrs K Prior, SpLDDip
Mrs J C Schaniel, BA, MSc
Mrs A Sutherland, CertEd
N Tetley, BA, PhD, PGCE
J H C Tilly, BA, DipEd
M A Wilkinson, BA, PGCE

Assistant Staff: Acremont House:

Mrs J E Bamforth, CertEd
Mrs C Bloodworth, BTec, Cert in Caring Services
Mrs M Brogan, CertEd (*Head of Nursery*)
Mrs C M Burgess, BA, PGCE
Ms A Byner, BA, PGCE
Mrs C M Cooper, CertEd
Miss J Firstbrook, BA
Miss P Glassbrook, BEd
Miss G Heard, BSc, PGCE
Mrs R J Marshall, CertEd
Mrs H Menarry, BTec, Cert in Caring Services
Miss M Negus, BEd
A G Roberts, BSc, PGCE
Mrs K Wylie, BTec National Diploma
Miss L Foreman, NNEB

In addition 22 visiting music teachers

Organisation and Curriculum. For academic and pastoral purposes the school is divided into three parts. **The Nursery and Pre-Prep** which has its own buildings and grounds at Acremont House in Ely, takes children from age 2½ in its nursery and from Years R to 3 in the Pre-Prep School. The Junior School (Years 4–8) and Senior School (Years 9–13) share a site near the Cathedral.

The curriculum at **The Nursery and Pre-Prep** at Acremont House introduces children to systematic planned learning. Teaching starts from where each child is, in terms of experience and development, not from a pre-determined idea of where they should be. Children are encouraged to express what they have experienced in their growth and learning - in their own way and at an appropriate pace - to help them absorb and consolidate their experience. Teaching is mainly on a class-teacher basis.

The curriculum in the Nursery and Reception classes is geared towards the Foundation Stage laid down by the Government through the Qualifications & Curriculum Authority. Children in Years 1, 2 and 3 follow - and indeed go beyond - the National Curriculum. The areas of learning covered in the Pre-Prep are: Linguistic and literacy, Mathematical, Scientific, Technological, Aesthetic and creative, Physical, Social.

During Year 3 there is constant liaison with Year 4 staff in the Junior School to ensure that children are fully prepared for the next stage of their education.

The Junior School curriculum is planned to give pupils both breadth and depth in their total learning experience. Subject specialists coordinate the work of each department and ensure progression from year to year, though for the youngest pupils teaching is still mainly on a class-teacher basis. From Year 7 all teaching is by subject teachers. Year groups are usually taught in classes based on general ability. Pupils' progress is monitored week by week and reported regularly to parents.

All the foundation subjects are covered in every year, and the whole curriculum is compulsory. French begins in Year 4, as do Information Technology and Technology. The most able pupils study Latin from Year 6. There are specialist teaching rooms to meet the needs of Science, Art, Design & Technology, Information Technology, Drama and Music.

During the school day all children are divided among four co-educational houses for pastoral and competitive purposes; each of these houses is staffed by men and women. The Junior School has three boarding houses: one for girls, one for boys and one for the Cathedral choristers.

The amount of academic choice that pupils can exercise grows as they move through the **Senior School**: options in the Sixth Form are very flexible, and the sets are often small. Up to GCSE (Year 11) there is a compulsory core of English, Mathematics, a course in Religion and Philosophy and Coordinated Science (which is taught as three separate subjects - Biology, Chemistry and Physics - leading to a dual award certificate; triple award sciences are available as an option). For many pupils English is a double subject, as English Literature is taken as a separate examination. Information Technology is delivered through the core subjects. In addition every pupil chooses up to four option subjects from a list of 14 which includes: Art, Business Studies, Drama, English as a Foreign Language, French, Géographie *(Geography taught in the French Language, leading to two GCSEs)*, History, Latin, Music, Spanish, Triple Award Sciences, Design & Technology (Resistant Materials, Food Technology).

The entry qualification for the Sixth Form is five GCSE passes at grade C or above. Twenty-two AS/A2 level subjects are offered in Years 12 and 13.

All Senior School pupils belong to one of seven single-sex houses; three of these (two for boys and one for girls) are for boarders, although day pupils may be attached to them. All day pupils have study space in the school.

Extra-Curricular Activities. Music, art, drama, outdoor pursuits, sports, practical hobbies and interests - all are catered for in a large range of lunchtime and after-hours activities.

The Ely Scheme. All pupils in Year 9 are introduced to the school's distinctive outdoor pursuits programme, the Ely Scheme, which provides a training in practical and personal skills and in teamwork, initiative and leadership. For some pupils it leads on to the Duke of Edinburgh Award Scheme or to specialised activities such as climbing.

Art, Drama and Music. Music is strong, as one would expect in a school that is so closely linked to the Cathedral.

There is a full programme of performances for school and public audiences, and regular tours overseas. Nearly half of all pupils have personal tuition in a musical instrument; many learn two or even three. Well-equipped art rooms and an artist-in-residence inspire painting, sculpture, ceramics and textiles. All parts of the school present plays every year in addition to productions by year or ad-hoc groups.

Games. The main sports are hockey, rugby, netball, cricket, soccer, rounders and rowing - but the emphasis is on choice, and athletics, badminton, tennis, sailing and swimming, among others, are also available. Younger pupils are encouraged to take part in team games, and there is a full programme of fixtures against other schools.

Religious Worship. The Junior and Senior Schools worship regularly in Ely Cathedral. Other services every week are also in accordance with the principles of the Church of England. The Bishop conducts a confirmation service for pupils in the Lent term. There is, however, no religious test of admission to the school: all denominations (or none) are made welcome.

Exeats. Boarders are granted week-end exeats on the written request of a parent or guardian. Weekly boarding is increasingly popular.

Admission. Application forms can be obtained from the Admissions Secretary. Admission to Acremont House is by interview; to Junior School by interview and qualifying examination; and to Senior School at 13+ by the school's entrance examination or an equivalent. There is a registration fee of £25 for each part of the school. Pupils may enter the school at any time, although a September start is recommended; and they may stay at the school until the year in which they become 19.

Scholarships. (*see* Entrance Scholarship section) Scholarships up to a cumulative total of 50% of fees are awarded for achievement and potential in academic work, music, art, design & technology, drama and sports; and for all-round contributions to the life of the boarding community. Choristerships carry a generous remission of fees for as long as the boy remains in the school. Most scholarships are awarded on the basis of examinations held in January or February; Sixth Form scholarships are awarded on GCSE results; choristerships are normally awarded after a voice trial in February.

Fees per term (2000-2001). *Nursery and Pre-Prep:* Nursery places are booked by the session (morning or afternoon) and the day of the week; full care for five days a week would be £1,423 a term. The fee for Years R-3 is £1,535 a term (no boarding). After-school care is available at extra charge.

Junior School: Year 4 £2,236 (day), £3,600 (boarders); there is no Saturday school for Year 4. Years 5 to 8 £2,488 (day), £3,852 (boarders).

Senior School: Years 9 to 13 £3,435 (day), £5,002 (boarders).

Weekly boarding: deduct £85 (Junior School) or £105 (Senior School) from the full boarding rates. Fees for flexible boarding are available on request.

Concessions: for children of the clergy or of members of the armed services, and for third and subsequent siblings of pupils who are already in the school.

Old Eleans. Former pupils receive news of the school and of their contemporaries and are invited annually to events.

Charitable status. The King's School, Ely is a Registered Charity, number 311440. Its aims and objectives are to offer excellence in education to day and boarding pupils.

* Head of Department	§ Part Time or Visiting
† Housemaster/Housemistress	¶ Old Pupil
‡ See below list of staff for meaning	

The King's School
Gloucester (Co-educational)

Gloucester GL1 2BG.
Tel: (01452) 337337
Fax: (01452) 337314

The school was re-founded by Henry VIIIth between the years 1541 and 1547 after the dissolution of the Monasteries, and its life is centred upon the Cathedral, whose Dean and Chapter are the Foundation Governors, and whose Choristers are educated in the School. The historic buildings cluster in a secluded part of the city round the Cathedral and range in date from the 13th century. Within the last few years new science laboratories, a Business Studies centre, indoor sports facilities and a Performing Arts centre have been developed.

The school has been fully co-educational since 1985.

Motto: *Via Crucis via Lucis.*

Governing Body:

Chairman: The Very Revd N Bury, MA, Dean of Gloucester

Canon N Heavisides, MA
Canon R D M Grey, AKC
Canon N Chatfield, MA
Canon C Morgan, MA, MTh
Canon M Irving, BEd
Mrs A Cadbury, OBE, JP, DL
Miss C Holme, JP, LLB
Mr P J M Whiteman, TD, MA
Mr J H Smith, BSc, DipEd
Miss A E Miles, BA
Mr H Chamberlayne, BSc
Mr T Heal, FRICS
Mr A J Siddall, FCCA
Mr N Halls, FCA
Mr P Lacheki, BSc
Mr M Westbury, FCIDB

***Headmaster:* Mr P R Lacey**, MA, FRSA

Deputy Head: Mr D J Evans, MA
Senior Teacher: Mrs J C Gazard, MA

English & Drama:
Miss J Chidzoy, MBBO, MAAD
*Dr M C Craddock, BA, PhD
Mrs L Harrison, BA
Ms C Haines, BA
Mrs K O'Keefe, BA

Mathematics:
Mr P R Lacey, MA, FRSA
*Mr R A Barlow, BSc
Mr A C Sandell, BA, BEd
Mrs N R Lacey, MA

Modern Languages:
*Mr P Arnison, BA
Mr P Irving, BA
Miss A F Williams, BA

Geography:
Mr A Spencer, BSc, PGCE
*Miss C J Barber, BA

History:
*Miss S J Davies, MA
Mr D J Evans, MA
Mrs J M Major, MA

Classics:
*Revd J B P J Hadfield, MA (*Chaplain*)
Mr P J McDonald, BA

Religious Studies:
Mrs J C Gazard, MA
*Mr J M Webster, MA, BD

Economics & Business Studies:
*Mr D A Lloyd, BSc(Econ)
Mr D Burrows, BSc

Art, Design & Technology:
Miss C Billingsley, BA
Mr R J Mansell, BEd
*Mr M Hall, BA

Science:
Mrs D E Field, MSc
*Mr J P Greenfield, MSc, CBiol, MIBiol
Mr S Harrison, MA
Miss G A Loftus, BSc
Mrs B J Rouan-North, BSc
Mr A R Butcher, MSc, CChem, MRSC

Music:
*Mr I R Fox, MA, FRCO, DipEd
Miss S A N Miller, BA, PGCE

Physical Education:
Miss A Williams, BA
*Mr A J Phillips, BSc
Miss J D Fenn, BEd
Mr L E Robson, BEd
Mr C B Stuart-Smith, BEd

Junior School:
Head of Junior School: Mr C Dickie, BEd
Mrs C Bennett, CertEd
Miss J Davies, BA, PGCE
Mrs C J Hadfield, BEd
Mr W R Van der Hart, BEd
Mrs S E Jelf, NNEB
Mrs G M Leigh, CertEd
Miss N Moodie, BEd
Mrs C A Power, CertEd
Mrs G M Rawlinson, CertEd
Miss A F Roberts, BA
Mrs E I Tuffill, BA
Mrs P Williams, NNEB
Mrs A M Wyman, BEd

Special Needs:
Mrs G Bolton, MEd
*Mrs A J Stafford, BEd, BEd(SEN)
Mrs R Stickland, CertEd, TEFL

Personal & Social Education:
*Mrs J C Gazard, MA

Careers:
Mrs D E Field, MSc

Music Department (*Instrumental and Singing Teachers*):
Miss Jill Beddoe, LTCL, ATCL (*Clarinet and Saxophone*)
Mr David Briggs, MA, FRCO, ARCM, FRSA (*Organ*)
Mrs Alice Caterer, BMus, LRAM, ARCM, GRSM (*Piano and Theory*)
Mr Philip Colls, MA, BMus, ARCM, LTCL, CertEd (*Singing and Close Harmony*)
Miss Fay Fisher, LRAM, ARCM (*Oboe*)
Mr Ian Fox, MA, FRCO, DipEd (*Organ, Electronic and Computer Music*)
Mrs Julie Gibbons, BMus, LTCL, CertEd (*Flute*)
Mr Richard Goode, ALCM (*Classical and Rock Guitar*)
Miss J M Greaves, BMus, LTCL, DipASMD (*Voice/Piano*)
Mrs Sally Griffiths, ALCM (*Piano*)
Mr Robert Jones, BMus (*Violin*)
Mrs Juliet Tomlinson, LRAM, RAMProfCert (*Cello*)
Mr Jonathan Trim, BMus, MMus, LRAM (*Violin and String Groups*)
Mr Greg Watson (*Drum Kit*)
Mr Gavin Wells, LRAM (*Brass*)
Mrs Denise Wilman, BMus (*Piano & Keyboard*), LRSM, UTLM, RULM (*Piano & Teaching*), RULM (*Choir-masters*)

Financial Manager: Mr J E Tovey, FFA
Estates Manager: Mr M G Carter, BSc
Registrar: Mrs K O'Keefe, BA

Medical Centre Staff:
Dr I Jarvis, MB, BCh
Sister S Burton, BSc, RGN

Structure of the School. The school provides weekly boarding and day education for boys and girls aged 3–18 years, with boarders usually being admitted in the Sixth Form. The most common ages for entry are at 4, 11, 13 and 16 years. There are 500 pupils in total, including a thriving sixth form of about 100 pupils.

For administrative purposes, the school is divided into the following sections:

Junior School: aged 3–11 (incorporating the Nursery, Wardle House, ages 3–4).

Senior School: aged 11–18.

Junior School (including the Nursery). The Junior School is housed within the main school campus and is staffed by class teachers chosen for their expertise in working with young children. There is a close liaison with the specialist teachers in the senior school to ensure continuity in teaching and the curriculum. The Head of the Junior School is responsible to the Headmaster of King's School for the day to day running of the Junior School. The Junior School shares a common site with the Senior School and benefits from use of the Technology Centre, Gymnasium and Dining Hall, as well as taking part in full school assemblies in the Cathedral. After school care is available.

Senior School. The transition from class teaching to subject based set teaching is carried out gradually to enable the children to feel secure in their educational environment. Pastoral care is form-based with Tutors and Year Heads monitoring the progress of each pupil and liaising closely with parents.

The Senior School is based round the Cathedral buildings with their attractive gardens. Whilst the classrooms afford a sense of history and good learning, as well as having outlooks over the Cathedral Close, the laboratories and Technology suite are housed in modern buildings and are equipped to cope with current curriculum demands. The accommodation is near to playing fields, indoor swimming pool, science laboratories, the Technology Centre and Music School.

The school is proud of its tradition of personal discipline which is based on mutual respect and self esteem. The relationship between pupils and staff is at the same time friendly and well defined. A full time co-ordinator of Personal and Social Education oversees the cross curricular themes essential to the development of the whole person in this challenging world.

The Sixth Form Centre in Dulverton House provides an academic and social focus for senior students.

The Curriculum. Heads of Department are responsible for the teaching of their subjects from the earliest years, in itself an unusual opportunity for establishing continuity of purpose and content.

Formal teaching of modern foreign languages begins at the age of 7 in the Junior School.

A full range of choices at GCSE is available and whilst the National Curriculum is offered, it is by no means compulsory. Every attempt is made to encourage the individual interests and enthusiasms of pupils through a flexible curriculum. Pupils may still opt for Classics as well as Technology. Information Technology is taught at all levels and to all children as an essential cross curricular skill. Physical Education and Business Studies are also offered at GCSE level as well as at A level. Many children take GCSE Music at an early stage of their time in the school, and all take Religious Studies at GCSE. Support is offered to pupils with Learning difficulties through a fully staffed Learning Support Department.

In the Sixth Form there is a very wide range of academic subjects, twenty in all, as well as innovative courses which work towards GNVQ in Business and in Art/Design. All members of the Sixth Form follow a course in General Studies which includes courses in Law, Psychology, Sports Science, Moral Philosophy and IT. All members of the Sixth Form aspire to university courses. The new post-16 curriculum is now in operation.

There is a strong Careers Department which deals with university entrance as well as work experience, careers experience and Service scholarships and cadetships. The school is a member school of the Independent Schools Careers Organisation.

Games and Activities. A full range of games is available with the main games being Rugby, Hockey and Cricket for boys and Hockey, Netball and Tennis for girls. Senior pupils are able to participate in a whole range of minor games including Squash and Badminton, and Athletics is also available. A well equipped Gymnasium and The Riverside Centre provide the focus for Physical Education; Dance is a recent addition to the curriculum.

The school's main playing field, Archdeacon Meadow, hosts the County Cricket Festival each year.

Its proximity to Kingsholm and its special relationship with Gloucester Rugby Football Club has enabled the school to become a centre of excellence in the sport.

The school offers the Duke of Edinburgh Award, a comprehensive outdoor pursuits programme and a wide range of clubs and societies. Annual overseas expeditions go as far afield as The Himalayas and Ecuador.

Music and the Performing Arts. There is a strong tradition of musical excellence as befits a Cathedral Choir School, where all pupils are encouraged to learn and appreciate music. A good proportion of the school receives instrumental tuition and the various choirs, orchestras and ensembles play regularly in the Cathedral, and in the local region. Music Technology includes DAT, MIDI, multi-track, synthesis, sequencing and music publishing. The school is a Choir School and as such provides the trebles for the Cathedral choir, and has a number of music scholarships and bursaries endowed for that purpose. As well as providing a succession of Oxbridge organ scholars, the school provides a full range of musical activities. Tours abroad are also a regular feature.

Dance and Drama are increasing in popularity at the school and productions are arranged in the school hall and Chapter House, as well as in the Cathedral. Both are features of the curriculum throughout the school. The summer Performing Arts Festival has recently become a featured climax to the school year.

Boarding Houses. There are boarding houses for boys and girls situated in the calm of the Cathedral precincts and run very much on family lines with a strong emphasis on pastoral care. Weekly boarding is now offered.

Religious Worship. Whilst pupils from all denominations are welcome, the religious services are in accordance with the principles of the Church of England. Most days start with an Assembly, usually in the Cathedral and of a nature to suit each age group. The boarders have their own services in the Lady Chapel on Sundays.

Admission. Junior School: interview and/or examination. Senior School: CEE or other test appropriate to a child's previous education.

Termly Fees. These are staged according to age: Junior School (day): £1,225–£2,395; Senior School (day): £2,535–£2,925. Weekly Boarders: £4,525.

Scholarships. (*see* Entrance Scholarship section) - Cathedral Choristerships receive a Scholarship worth 85% of tuition fees. Academic scholarships and exhibitions may be awarded at ages 11+, 13+ and for the Sixth Form. Music awards are available to instrumental players of ability and potential. Sports Awards and Governors' Bursaries are also available, as are Special overseas bursaries for Service children.

King's School Society. *Hon Sec:* c/o King's School, Gloucester GL1 2BG.

Charitable status. The King's School of the Cathedral Church of Gloucester is a Registered Charity, number 311745. It exists to provide for the education of Cathedral Choristers and others, within a co-educational environment.

The King's School,
Macclesfield

Macclesfield Cheshire SK10 1DA
Tel: (01625) 260000
Fax: (01625) 260009

Situated in rolling Cheshire countryside on the edge of the Peak District, the School was founded by the Will of Sir John Percyvale in 1502. He founded it as a 'Free Grammar School of the town and country thereabouts, teaching gentlemen's children and other good men's children'.

The Foundation was re-established by the Charter of Edward VI in 1552, giving the school a 'License by Letters Patent for education in grammatical learning and good manners'.

Patron: The Rt Hon The Earl of Derby, MC

Chairman of the Governors: W A Bromley Davenport

***Head of Foundation:* S Coyne**, BSc, PhD, MEd

Senior Staff:

Deputy Headmaster: Dr A Brown, BSc, MSc, PhD

Principal of Boys: W D Beatson, BSc
Principal of Girls: Mrs C M Buckley, BA
Principal of Juniors: G J Shaw, BA
Principal of Sixth Form: I A Wilson, BA

Vice-Principal of Boys: Revd R J Craig, BA, BD
Vice-Principal of Girls: Mrs V B White, BEd, MA
Vice-Principal of Juniors: Mrs P J Aspinwall, BEd
Senior Master: K L Perriss, BEd

Bursar: D O Smith, MInstAM, MIMgt

Mrs L F Adams, BA
T J Adams, BA
M Aiers, BSc, CPhys, MInstP
T H Andrews, MA
C Anson-O'Connell, BA
P J Atkinson, DipTeaching
M Badger, BA
Mrs D C Baker, BA
Dr G N Banner, BA, MA, PhD
Mrs D M Barker, BEd
Mrs J T Barratt, GTCL Hons, LTCL
L A Batchelor, BA
Mrs J Beesley, BA
Mrs C H Bingham, BSc
Mrs L Booker, MMedSci, BA
P P Bradley, BSc, MSc, BA
Mrs H L Broadley, BSc
Mrs J E Brown, BSc
M J Brown, MSc, BSc
D T Browne, BA
C J Buckland, BSc, MSc
Dr B G Caswell, PhD, BSc, CEng, CPhys, MBCS, MInstP
Ms N J Chadwick, BA
Dr A Cohen, PhD, BSc, FRAS
Mrs J Cole, BA
P J Colville, BSc, MSc
Mrs R H Cookson, BA
Mrs A M Cooper, BSc
Mrs V Costello, BA
R G Davenport, BA, MA
P N Davies, BSc
Mrs M A Denovan, PrimTCert
J A Dodd, BSc
J R Doughty, MEd

Miss C E Duff, BEd
Mrs A Eardley, BA
P M Edgerton, MA
B Edwards, BA
B J Ellis, BA
Ms L Farrow, MA
Dr J A Fitzgerald, BSc, MSc, PhD
Mrs M A F Garside, BSc
D Gee, CertEd
A K Green, BA
Mrs G Green, BA
Mrs K Griffin, MA
Dr R Grime, PhD, BSc
P F Halewood, CertEd
A Hallatt, BA
Mrs J Hankinson, TCert
D M Harbord, CertEd, BA
R S Hardman, CertEd
C A Harrison, BSc
M G Hart, MA
J R Hidden, BA
D C Hill, BA, MPhil
Dr C P Hollis, PhD, BSc Hons, CPhys, MInstP
M T Houghton, BA
Mrs C J Hulme-McKibbin, BEd
P Illingworth, BSc, CPhys, MInstP
Miss D Inman, BA
Mrs A M Johnson, BA
G D Jones, BA
Mrs R Jones
A J Jordan, BA
D J Kearney, BA
C E Kingshott, BEd
R J Kitzinger, BA
Mrs A Kuster, BA
G Laurence, MA
Mrs A Lawson, BA
Mrs A Lea, BMus
A Levin, BA

Mrs R Marcall, BA
D R Marshall, BSc
P R M Mathews, DipPE, DipEd
C J Maudsley, BSc
A McInnes, DipPE
J Mellor, Diploma
Mrs A E Mitchell, BSc
Mrs A J Murphy, BA, MA
P Murray, BA
T G North, BSc
J D Nuttall, BA
C O'Donnell, BSc
Mrs E P Olsen, BA
Mrs S E Ord, BA
Dr L C Palazzo, BA, MA, PhD
M Patey-Ford, BA
Dr J R Pattison, PhD, BSc
Mrs E Pentreath, MA
P J Percival, BSc
K L Perriss, BEd
Mrs J E Pullen, BA
Mrs C L Pyatt, GRSM, LRAM
N C J Riley, BSc
Miss A E Rivers, BSc
R D Schofield, BA
P Seddon, NDD, DA, ATDDist
Mrs J E Smith, TDip
Mrs K Stutchbury, MA
Mrs J T Sykes, CertEd
Ms G Taylor, BA
Miss H C Taylor, BA
Mrs C P Thompson, BA
Mrs G D Turner, BA
Mrs L Turner, BEd
F Walker, Licentiate, CertEd
Mrs K Wells, BA
Mrs V B White, BEd, MA
P Williams, BA

Bursar: D O Smith, MInstAM, MBIM

Number in School. Infants 3–7: 46 boys, 30 girls; Juniors 7–11:117 boys, 80 girls; boys 11–16 474; girls 11–16 356; Sixth Form: 178 boys, 119 girls. Total: 1,400.

Organisation. The Foundation is organised in four Divisions: on one site, a Junior Division (co-educational 3–11) and a Girls' Division (11–16); on the other, a Boys' Division (11–16) and a Sixth Form (co-educational 16–18). Each Division is run by a Principal, who is responsible for day-to-day organisation, and the pupils in the 11–16 divisions of the school are taught separately but undertake a number of joint extra-curricular activities (eg music, drama, trips abroad etc.)

The Foundation has one Board of Governors, one Head and one Deputy Head who manage the school and plan regularly with the Division Principals to carry out the aims and objectives of the school. Girls and boys from 3–18 enjoy exactly the same opportunities.

The curriculum for the first three years is broad and common to all, with a second modern language added in the second year.

In Years 10 and 11 pupils choose their own courses within a balanced framework, leading to GCSEs.

Pastoral care is exercised throughout these years by form tutors, year heads and the Principals.

Students are assigned to a personal tutor responsible for a group of 10 or so pupils throughout their VI Form course. Any justifiable combination of available A and AS Level subjects may be pursued, complemented by General Studies and Recreational Activity. In addition to compulsory core units in General Studies, students choose from a wide range of options designed to extend their breadth of cultural interest and intellectual inquiry, whilst Recreational Activities are designed to encourage the positive use of leisure time and offers initial experience in sports and activities new to the individual. Pupils are also prepared for University Entrance Examinations where appropriate.

Arts and Craft. Well equipped art rooms and workshops are also available for use by the members of the Art Club and Craft Societies outside the timetable.

Music. Over 400 pupils receive tuition in the full range of orchestral instruments, the Piano, Organ, Classical Guitar and Singing. An introductory tuition scheme enables all new entrants to assess their talent. There are three orchestras, a Concert-band, a Jazz band and three Choirs, which provide regular performing experience. Pupils regularly enter music profession in addition to those pursuing academic training.

Drama. Theatre Studies is an important creative option at GCSE and A level and covers all aspects of the theatre. Great importance is attached to the regular school plays and musicals, which involve large numbers of pupils and enjoy a distinguished reputation. Pupils regularly take examinations in performance and public speaking.

Games. All pupils take part in games and athletic activity appropriate to the season. Junior School sports include Soccer, Cricket, Netball, Hockey, Tennis, Athletics and a wide range of individual games. In the Senior School, boys' sports include Rugby, Hockey, Cross-Country, Squash, Badminton, Cricket, Tennis, Athletics, Swimming and Basketball; the girls' sports include Hockey, Netball, Tennis, Football and Athletics. In addition there is a varied programme of sports in the Sixth Form, including soccer and such activities as Hill Walking, Caving and Rock Climbing which are actively pursued by boys and girls.

Outdoor Pursuits. There is a regular programme of training in the skills of hill walking and camping for all pupils. In addition, numerous expeditions are arranged in the many favourable areas near the school and also abroad. Sailing and orienteering are popular and the Duke of Edinburgh Award scheme attracts 60 pupils each year.

Clubs and Societies. There is a wide range of other clubs catering for most interests and hobbies.

Religious Instruction in accordance with the principles of the Church of England is given to pupils whose parents or guardians have requested the Governors to provide such instruction for them.

Fees. The tuition fees are £5,340 pa Senior School, £4,215 pa Junior School, £3,555 pa Infants Department. All fees are payable in advance on or before the first day of term.

Financial Support. Bursaries are available for entry at 11 and 13. In addition seven Scholarships are given on performance in the Entrance Examination. Academic, music and organ scholarships are available in the Sixth Form. Funds are available to assist pupils attending courses and field trips and to help in cases of urgent need. Leaving Awards are granted from funds held in trust by the Governors.

Admissions. Admission is normally in September each year through competitive examination for boys and girls aged 7, 8 9, 10, 11 and 13 years, held during the previous February or through the February 13+ Common Entrance Examination for boys and girls at preparatory schools. Girls and boys are admitted to the Sixth Form subject to academic attainment, interview and course requirement. Admission arrangements are advertised and also available on request.

Intermediate admission of new arrivals in the area is possible.

Old Boys' Association: *Hon Secretary,* c/o The

King's School, Macclesfield, SK10 1DA. A gazette and register of names is published regularly.

Charitable status. The King's School, Macclesfield is a Registered Charity, number 525921. It exists for the education of boys and girls between the ages of 7 and 18.

Visit the Website. The award-winning website is found at:
http://www.kingsmac.cheshire.sch.uk

King's School, Rochester
(Co-educational)

Rochester Kent ME1 1TE.
Tel: Medway (01634) 843913
Fax: Medway (01634) 832493
e-mail: walker@kings-school-rochester.co.uk
website: www.kings-school-rochester.co.uk

The School traces its history to 604 AD, when Justus, the first Bishop of Rochester formed a school in connection with his Cathedral. It was reconstituted and endowed by Henry VIII as the King's School in 1542. Fully co-educational since 1993.

Patron: The Lord Bishop of Rochester

Chairman of the Governors: The Dean of Rochester (The Very Rev E F Shotter, BA)

Governors:
The Revd Canon E R Turner, MA
The Revd Canon J M Armson, PhD, MA
The Revd Canon C J Meyrick, MA
E L Darwin, MA, CEng, FICE
The Revd D Crabtree, BSc Econ
Judge L M Grosse, LLB
J W Lord, FCA, ATII
Professor J C Cook, BSc, BS, MD, MRCPsych
The Revd S M Ramsaram, MA, PhD
M J Chesterfield
Ms A J Beazer, CertEd

***Headmaster:* Dr I R Walker**, BA, PhD, LTh, ABIA, FCollP, FRSA

Second Master: Dr R A Suthers, BSc, PhD

Director of Studies: J C Richley, BSc, MA, DMS(Ed), ACP, MCollP

Chaplain and Fourth Master: The Rev P L F Allsop, MA

Senior Teacher: Mrs S E Clements, BSc

Assistant Staff:
Dr C M Woodard MSc, PhD, MRSC
R G Jelfs, BEd
C J L Davies, BSc(Econ)
B W Richter, BA
R J Gosden, BA
Ms R Campbell-Grey, DipAD, SIAD
Miss J Pollard, DipCeramics
B A Roberts, BSc
M E Drury, BSc
The Revd Dr S R Allsopp, MSc, PhD
P W Wallace, BA
C J Halsall, MA, MLitt, DipRSA, DipSocAnth, DMS(Ed)
Mrs C Laws, BA
N J McMillan, BSc
S B Gates, BA
Miss S C K Otaki, MA
A J Robson, BA
W E Smith, BA
Mrs J Fenner, BA
S R Dearnaley, BA
K T Latham, BSc
F G Barr, BSc
I M Parkinson, MA
Mrs C H Lawson, BA
Ms E A Poole, BA, MA
Mrs H M Paulett, BA
C H Page, BA
Mrs L A Kenway, BSc
Mrs T E S Page, BSc
Mrs M Thandi, BA
M Watson, BA
Miss E J Aitken, BEd
G R Brooks, BA
Miss K E Salles, BA
Mrs E A Winstanley, BSc
M Schofield, BA
Mrs J D F Maddocks, BA
Mrs E Gabbitas, BA, ALA (*Librarian*)

Headmaster of the Preparatory School: C J Nickless, BA

Deputy Headmaster: I Rouse, CertEd

Director of Studies: P N Medhurst, BA

Assistant Staff:
D J Oldbury, MA
M R Moss, BEd
Mrs J A Beaney, BEd
Mrs M I Davies, BA
Mrs S Sunderland, BEd
A B Knight, BSc
A K Rumley, BSc, BA
G N Moore, BA
G J Mitchell, BA
P Bellingham, BA
Miss B Cloarec, BA
Miss N J Rigby, BEd
Mrs M M Lapthorn (*Librarian*)

Educational Support Team:

Co-ordinator: C J Steward, BA, RSA, DipSpLD, CertTESOL

Visiting Educational Support Staff:
Mrs J Tooby, BA, RSA, DipSpLD
Mrs M Nickless, CertEd
Mrs A Hodges, BSc, CertSpLD
Mrs R Moss, BA, CertSpLD

Visiting TEFL Staff:
Mrs C Halsall, BA, RSA, DipTEFL
Mrs T Jelfs, BEd
Mrs J Squires, CertTESOL, RSA, CertSpLD
Mrs M McKay, BA, CertTESOL

Headmistress of the Pre-Preparatory School: Mrs A M Parkins, CertEd

Deputy Headmistress: Mrs J Sparkes, CertEd

Assistant Staff:
The Revd C M Haydon, CertEd (*Chaplain*)
Mrs G J Singfield, CertEd
M Malsher, BEd
Mrs A Fisher, DipEd, RSA, DipSpLD
Mrs R Phillips, CertEd
Mrs V A Dunmore, BEd
Mrs H J Pemberton, BA, CertEd
Mrs J Tyson, CertEd

Classroom Assistants:
Miss A Neate, NAMCW, CLANSA
Mrs B Carter
Mrs C Simpson, SRN
Mrs M Harris, SRN
Mr H Carter
Mrs E Franquiera
Mrs T Gilbert, DipCST
Mrs J Hughes
Mrs K New

Educational Support Co-ordinator:
Mrs A Fisher, DipEd, RSA, DipSpLD

Visiting Educational Support Staff:
Mrs S Millward, CertEd, RSA, DipSpLD
Mrs B Lloyd, CertEd, SRN, RSA, DipSpLD
Mrs P Weston, CertEd

Director of the European Initiative:
C J Halsall, MA, MLitt, DipRSA, DipSocAnth, DMS(Ed)

Assistant Staff:
F Wiesner (Pedagogical University, Zwickau)
B Wagner (Leipzig University)
K Neubauer, Lehramt an Grundschulen, Erziehungswissenschaftliche (Fäkultält der Friedrich-Alexander-Universität Erlangen-Nürnberg)

Music Department:

Director of Music:
G R Williams, GRSM, FRCO, LRAM, ARCM

Preparatory School Director of Music:
D J Oldbury, MA

Head of Strings: J M Hines, BA
Head of Woodwind: G R Vinall, BA, LRAM (*Clarinet*)

Visiting Music Staff:
B Hanson, LTCL (*Oboe*)
J M Williams, LTCL (*Bass/Piano*)
C S Banks (*'Cello*)
B Odom, BA (*Voice Training*)
M Hines, AGSM (*Bassoon*)
J Harrison (*Flute*)
S Thorpe, ARCM (*Violin/Viola*)
R Scarff, GTCL (*Percussion*)
C A Hewitt, LTCL (*Keyboards*)
J A Smith, LRAM, LTCL, LMusA (*Piano*)
I S Williams (*Brass*)
B J Kitchin (*Guitar*)

Cathedral Organist and Master of the Choristers: R M Sayer, ARCM, LRAM, FTCL, DipRCM

Bursar and Clerk to the Governors: R Nelson-Gracie, FCA, FIM

Estates Bursar: Lt Col(Retd) R L D Robinson, MIEng, AMICE, MIM

Assistant Bursar: R V Hubbard

Registrar: K J Shave, BSc(Eng), CEng, MICE, MIWEM

Medical Officer: Dr F A Yeates, MB, BS, DRCOG

Nursing Sister: Mrs F M McMillan, AAMS, RGN, RM

The School is situated close to the Cathedral and Castle in the centre of the city and in a secluded conservation area. It enjoys the open spaces of the Precincts and the Paddock, which is one of the school's playing fields. The other playing fields, the Alps, are 5 minutes from the School.

The Main School dates from the mid-nineteenth century but the School also has a number of fine listed buildings from the eighteenth century, and considerable extensions of more recent date. Recent additions include a new £2 million Pre-Prep building and Sports Hall, Prep School Science Block and extension, an additional Biology Wing, new Art Centre and Language Centre, a new Craft, Design and Technology Centre. An indoor swimming pool and a leading edge language laboratory were opened in 1997. New computer laboratories in 1999/2000.

The School numbers almost 700 pupils, of whom nearly 60 are boarders. The school is fully co-educational and divided into a Pre-Preparatory School of 128 pupils (4-8 years), a Preparatory School of 246 (8-13 years) and a Senior School of 308 pupils (13-18 years). This provides 3 units of an intimate size, but which are regarded as a single community working closely together and sharing some activities and staff – for example in music. While catering for the whole of a pupil's career from 4 to 18, there is a large entry of pupils at 11 and 13 who bring experience from other backgrounds, and enjoy the advantages of coming into a stable community with a strong family atmosphere.

The boarders, some of whom are weekly, play an important part in the life of the School. Although a minority, they are a large enough part of the School to make a very significant contribution of their own, and enjoy a more intimate atmosphere than is possible in a larger boarding community.

The ancient connection with the Cathedral, which goes back to the Middle Ages, is still closely maintained. The Dean and Chapter are ex-officio Governors, the Headmaster and King's Scholars are members of the Cathedral Foundation, and the Cathedral Choristers are members of the Preparatory School. The School uses the Cathedral for worship.

Work. In the Pre-Preparatory School, the pupils follow a four year curriculum of Maths, Science, English, Divinity, Geography, History, Information Technology, Science Art and Craft, Design & Technology, Music, Drama and Physical Education. Spoken German lessons taught by native German teachers remain part of the curriculum.

In the Preparatory School the syllabus covers Divinity, English, History, Geography, Mathematics, Information Technology, Science (Physics, Chemistry and Biology), Latin, French, Art and Crafts, Music and Physical Education, spoken German lessons remain part of the curriculum.

In the Senior School, all pupils continue with the same range for the first year, and Computing, DT (Design and Technology) and Drama are introduced as options. In the Fifth forms, where GCSEs are studied, a core of subjects is continued and pupils add a balanced choice of options in preparation for GCSE levels.

In the VIth Form a wide range of AS and A level subjects are available; normally a pupil studies for 4 AS and then 3 A level subjects, and in addition undertakes a programme of General Studies.

All VI formers, who wish to, go on to university or other further education, and are encouraged to think carefully about their ultimate careers. Talks about different types of careers are given by outside speakers, and the advice of specialist careers advisers and the careers masters is available at all stages.

Activities. The School aims to develop pupils through a wide range of activities, both within the School programme and outside it.

There is a large CCF contingent, with Army, Navy and Air Force sections. Strong Service connections locally give particularly wide scope for CCF activities.

Pupils also undertake a variety of activities in Community Service, and participate in the Duke of Edinburgh's Award Scheme.

Out of School there is a range of over 20 school societies, and in the holidays there is a strong tradition of annual cultural and outdoor expeditions in this country and abroad.

Art, Drama and Music. The School sets strong store by the Arts, and uses the comparative proximity to London taking pupils to art exhibitions, concerts and the theatre. The School stages major drama productions each year, recently Iolanthe, Oh What a Lovely War and Macbeth have been the main presentations. There is a strong musical tradition with a wide range of visiting music staff, and pupils are encouraged to learn instruments. In addition to concerts in the School and the Cathedral, the Choral Society and Orchestra give a number of outside performances each year, some by invitation, the choral tradition being strengthened by the presence of the Cathedral choristers in the School.

Games. The main boys' games are Rugby, Hockey and Cricket and for girls' Hockey, Netball and Tennis. Other sports options are Rowing, Athletics, Cross Country, Fencing, Tennis and Swimming, and there are opportunities in addition for Squash, Badminton and Sailing. Physical

Education is a regular part of the School curriculum and all pupils are required to take part in games. 80% represent the school competitively.

Religious Education and Worship. Although there is no denominational requirement for entry to the School, religious instruction is in accordance with the principles of the Church of England. The daily assembly or chapel and the weekly School service on Monday are held in the Cathedral, with the King's Scholars and boarders attending the Cathedral on certain Sundays. The Bishop conducts a confirmation service for school candidates each Lent Term.

Admission. Pupils normally enter the Preparatory School at 8 or 9 after taking the Preparatory School Entrance Examination, but some places are offered at 10, 11 and 12. Entrance to the Senior School is either by Promotion Examination from the Preparatory School, by Common Entrance at 13, or by the school's own examination for pupils who have not been prepared for Common Entrance.

VIth Form entry is on the basis of interview and School report, together with satisfactory GCSE results (a minimum of 5 A-C passes, and grade requirements for some A' level courses).

Term of Entry. Admission is normally in September, but in special circumstances may take place at other points in the school year.

Choristers. Choristers are usually day boys and 40% tuition fee Scholarships are awarded following voice trials held in November and February, together with a satisfactory performance in the Preparatory School Entrance Examination. Under normal circumstances a scholarship will continue until a boy transfers to the Senior School or until he leaves the choir.

Scholarships. (*see* Entrance Scholarship section) *Senior School:* Up to five Major King's Scholarships and five Minor King's Scholarships may be awarded annually. Major Scholarships have a value of 50% and may be up to 100% of tuition fees (means tested above 50%).

Up to five Music Scholarships may be awarded annually on the basis of interview and practical test. One Music Scholarship a year may have the value of a King's Scholarship and others the value of a Minor King's Scholarship. An Organ Scholarship, usually with the status of a King's Scholarship, may be awarded when a vacancy occurs.

One Art Scholarship may be awarded annually with the value of a Major King's Scholarship.

One Sports Scholarship may be awarded annually with a value of 50% of tuition fees.

Governors Exhibitions: These recently added academic awards are available to pupils for the 2000/2001 academic year. A number of Exhibitions are available up to 100% of fees. All are means tested using the same assessment as originally applied to the Government Assisted Places Scheme which they replace.

Preparatory School: Five King's Exhibitions of 50% of tuition fees are available: two for pupils who will be 8 years old by 1 September, and a further three for 10 year olds.

Details of all awards may be obtained from the Headmaster. Additional means tested bursaries may be available.

Remissions. Children of Church of England ministers are given a third reduction in tuition fees.

Children of Service Personnel are given a 20% reduction in tuition fees for the first two years and a 10% reduction in years 3 and 4.

Where parents have three or more children at the school a reduction after the second child of 10% of the youngest child's fees.

Fees (2000/2001). Senior School: Boarders: £15,765 pa. Day Pupils: £9,165 pa. Preparatory School: Boarders: £10,740 to £11,640 pa. Day Pupils: £6,345 to £7,245 pa. Pre-Prep Fees £4,710 to £5,070 pa (Day only).

Charitable status. Rochester Cathedral (King's) School is a Registered Charity, number 307922. It is a charitable trust for the purpose of educating children.

The King's School
Tynemouth

Huntington Place Tynemouth Tyne and Wear NE30 4RF

Tel: (0191) 258 5995

Motto: *Moribus Civilis*

Governing Body: The Provost and Fellows of the Society of S S Mary and Aidan of York

Visitor: The Rt Revd The Bishop of Newcastle
Provost: The Rt Revd Frank V Weston, MA, Bishop of Knaresborough

School Council:
D Bilton, BSc, CEng, MIEE, AMI, MechE (*Chairman*)
D E T Nicholson, MA (*Registrar, The University of Newcastle upon Tyne*)
A M Conn, MA, ACA
S Johnson, CChem, MRSC
The Revd Canon Nigel Stock, BA, DipTheol
F S McNamara, BA
M J Evans, BA
I A Angus, BSc, ARICS
Dr A E Colver, BSc, MRCGP
Ms A Fleming

***Headmaster:* D Younger**, MSc, PhD, DipEd

First Deputy Head: J M Taylor, BSc, BA
Second Deputy Head: Mrs J E Carrotte, BSc, MEd
Head of Sixth Form: J W Forster, BA

Assistant Masters and Mistresses:

B R Cockburn, BA, CertEd
B M Green, BA, MA, CertEd
A Todd, BA, CertEd
D Wager, BSc, DipEd
T S May, BA, MPhil, MBiol, CertEd
S J Pettitt, BEd, MLitt
C Davy, BEd, MEd
W Ryan, CertEd
B J Wood, BSc, CertEd
C Moore, BA, PGCE
Mrs K Davy, MA, PGCE
V Gordon, BSc, PGCE
B J Gibson, CertEd
J Limer, CertEd
Mrs R Dunlop, MA, CertTESOL, CertEd
J H Taylor, MA, DipTh, PGCE
C Johnston, BEd
D H Waters, MA, PGCE
P McCall, BA, PGCE
Mrs C A Rix, BSc, PGCE
K Rix, BA, PGCE
A C Fowler, BEd
P C Hadwin, BSc, PGCE
A E Gerrard, BEd, BA, MA
G R Dickson, BA, MA, PGCE
Revd W D Miller, BA (*Chaplain*)
D Harrison, BA, PGCE
Mrs J H Marsh, DipEd
A Cutting, BA
Mrs K E Rowntree, BSc, PGCE
P A Baxter, BA
Mrs I M Nicholson, BEd, MA
P Angel, MA, BSc, PGCE
Mrs S Perry, BSc, PGCE
Miss V Hansen, BEd
Miss E A Woodhouse, BA, PGCE
Dr A J Cornish, DPhil, BSc
C G Mason, BSc, CertEd
Miss C E Taylor, BA, PGCE
J E Rigg, MA
Miss V Salin, MA, DEA, PGCE
Mrs A Casson, MA, PGCE
P J Nicholson, BA, PGCE
C Brotherton, BA, PGCE, MA
R A Marriott, BA, PGCE
Mrs C Bennett, BA, PGCE
Miss S Murray, BA, PGCE
Dr N J Barker, MMus, PhD
Mrs J Mason, BA (*Librarian*)

Mrs J Mitcheson, BSc, PGCE
A ul-Haq, BSc, PGCE
Mrs J N Liddie, BA, PGCE
G R Daniel, BSc
D P Fitzgerald, BEd

Junior School including Kindergarten:
D J Littlefield, MA, BEd (*Head of Junior School*)
D W Lilly, BEd
Mrs S Ogden, CertEd
Mrs M Varley, CertEd
R Kermode, CertEd
A J Russell, BEd
Mrs H C Baines, BSc, PGCE
Mrs J M Large, BSc, PGCE
Mrs C A McCormick, BEd
Mrs S A Porteous, BA, PGCE
Mrs M Went, CertEd
Mrs C G Stock, BA, PGCE
Mrs V M Boyle, BEd
Miss H Boyle, BTec (*Nursery Nurse*)

Headmaster's Secretary: Mrs S Bethell

Bursar: J Scott-Batey, BEd, FCA

The King's School Former Pupils' Association: M Dyer

Alumni Development Officer: Mrs K E Bilton

General. The King's School, founded in 1860, is the largest member of the Woodard Corporation. It is an Independent Day School for boys and girls aged 4-18. There are approximately 824 pupils in the School: 70 pupils in the Kindergarten (4+ to 7); 140 pupils in the Junior School (7 to 10+); and 612 pupils in the Senior School (11+ to 18) with a Sixth Form of 170. All three sections of The King's School work closely together and enjoy many of the same facilities.

King's endeavours to educate 'the whole person' and so the excellence of our classroom teaching and GCSE and 'A' level results is complemented by a wide range of extra-curricular activities both sporting and cultural.

Teaching is in small groups and all pupils are known individually. As a day school King's aims for a close partnership with parents.

King's is a Christian school and the School Chapel is at its centre, providing a powerful symbol of the School's values and aims.

The School enjoys a remarkably fortunate location: it is situated on the North East coast in the beautiful village of Tynemouth, on direct bus and metro routes from Newcastle and the surrounding areas. There are also private coaches.

Senior School Curriculum. The School aims to give pupils a broad education in general, and in particular to prepare them for public examinations and for entry into Universities (including Oxbridge) and other places of Further Education.

In the first three years all pupils follow a common curriculum consisting of: English, Mathematics, History, Geography, French, Science, Art, Music, Drama, Religious Education, Design/Technology, Computing and Physical Education. Spanish and German are introduced in the Second Year.

In the Fourth and Fifth Years pupils are prepared for a wide range of GCSE options. All pupils in the Fifth Year have a period of work experience immediately after the GCSE examinations.

In the Sixth Form most pupils take four AS level subjects, followed by three or four A2 level subjects in the second year. Practically any combination of subjects is possible and there is no arts-science barrier.

King's maintains excellent links with Industry and is greatly indebted to Parents and the thriving Former Pupils' Association for their assistance in this field.

Careers and University Application. Careers education is provided from the Third Year onwards.

The vast majority of Sixth-formers proceed to degree courses and expert advice is given on University (including Oxbridge) applications.

Games and Physical Education. The programme of games and physical education is designed to provide every pupil with an opportunity to gain satisfaction from participation in sport. King's has busy fixture lists and maintains a high standard at Rugby, Cricket, Netball, Tennis and Hockey (the major team games) as well as at Athletics, Gymnastics, Cross-Country Running, Squash, Soccer, Basketball and Badminton. Facilities are also provided for Golf, Sailing, Canoeing, Swimming, Fencing, Archery and Trampolining.

The School has a magnificent gymnasium and also its own playing fields at Priors Park, virtually adjacent to the main campus. King's fosters close links with local Rugby, Cricket and Tennis Clubs.

Many pupils win selection at county and national level.

Activities. Music and Drama are exceptionally strong at King's as are the numerous other clubs and societies which include: Art; Bridge; Christian Fellowship; Computers; Chess; Dance; Debating; Mineralogy; Orienteering; Ornithology; Photography; Table-tennis; Science; Stained Glass and Board Games.

Many pupils are involved in the Duke of Edinburgh's Award Scheme and in Community Service.

The School organizes annual ski-ing, mountaineering, climbing, and youth-hostelling trips; visits to the Inverclyde National Sports Centre and the Outward Bound Mountain Centre at Ullswater; and a Summer Camp at Portinscale in the Lake District.

The King's School has a field centre, at Alnham in Northumberland, which is used as a base for field study work and for Duke of Edinburgh's Award Scheme activities.

Junior School (including Kindergarten). The Junior School (4+ to 10+ years) is staffed by class teachers specially qualified for work with younger children, though there is close liaison with the specialist teachers in the Senior School to ensure continuity in teaching and the curriculum. The Head of the Junior School is responsible to the Headmaster of The King's School for the day to day running of the Junior School.

The Junior School shares a common site with the Senior School and although housed in separate accommodation with its own classrooms, Library and Design & Technology room, it makes full use of the School chapel, cafeteria, gymnasium, bookshop, laboratories, workshops, playing fields and field centres.

Admissions. Prospectus and Admissions forms can be obtained from the Headmaster's Secretary.

All entries are made through the Headmaster. Pupils are admitted to the Kindergarten on the basis of an interview; and to the Junior and Senior Schools on the basis of performance in the School's examinations in English and Mathematics and an interview with the Headmaster. The main intakes to the Senior School are at 11+ and 13+. For entry at Sixth Form level a minimum of 14 points at GCSE is normally expected in addition to a satisfactory report from a pupil's current Head.

Fees, Scholarships and Bursaries. The full basic fee for a term is currently: Senior School £1,714; Junior School £1,302. Scholarships (including those for Art and Music) are offered for entry to the Senior School at 11+, 13+ and Sixth Form level. Bursaries are available by application to the Headmaster.

Charitable status. The Woodard Schools Northern Division Limited is a Registered Charity, number 269665. It exists to promote education.

King's School, Worcester

Worcester WR1 2LH.
Tel: School Office (01905) 721700
Bursar (01905) 721721
Fax: (01905) 721710

A Cathedral School appears to have existed at Worcester virtually continuously since the 7th century. In its present form, however, The King's School dates from its refoundation by King Henry VIII in 1541, after the suppression of the Cathedral Priory and its school. In 1884 the School was reorganised as an Independent School and in 1944 the Cathedral Choir School was amalgamated with The King's School.

Visitor: The Lord Bishop of Worcester

The Governing Body:
D T Howell, BSc(*Eng*), FCA (*Chairman*)
Miss J R Allen, BA
D Barlow, BA
S J Doughty
Dr B Frellesvig
G A Harris, MA, MBA
Dr J A Harvey, GNSM, LRAM
The Very Revd P J Marshall, BSc
D Mills
The Hon Lady Morrison
The Revd Canon B Ruddock
Mrs S J M Shaw, MSI
R J Slawson
B A Tait, NDD, ATD
D G Wright

Clerk to the Governors and Bursar: J G Bartholomew, MBA, AIMBM, PIIA

***Headmaster:* T H Keyes**, MA

Second Master: T D R Hickson, BA, CPhys, FInstP

Senior Mistress: Mrs P A Stevens, BA, MA

Director of Studies: A J Thould, MA

Assistant Masters:
J L K Bridges, BSc
M W Bentley, CertEd
S R Davies, CertEd
P C Thompson, MA
P J Baseley, DipH/craft
M J Roberts, BSc
J M Roslington, BSc, CPhys, MInstP
Mrs M A Nott, BSc, CBiol, MIBiol
B Griffiths, BTech (*Careers*)
E Reeves, MA
D T Naish, BEd
Mrs C F Roslington, BA
M A Stevens, MA
R A Fleming, BA
D P Iddon, BA
Mrs R C J Diamond, BA
S Le Marchand, BA
R N G Stone, MA
R P Mason, BA
M R Gill, BSc, MA, MSc
Mrs S P Griffiths, BA
Mrs N R Anstey, CertEd
S M Bain, BSc, MSc
M D Rudge, BA
J T Wheeler, BSc, CChem, MRSC
D G Willmer, MSc, PhD
P T Gwilliam, BA, MPhil
Mrs K Appleby, BA
Mrs C M Cox, MA, MSc
R J Davis, BA
Mrs L M Ghaye, BEd, MA
A I Guest, BEd
Mrs S C Allum, BSc
J L Owen, BA
C A Gallantree-Smith, BA
Mrs E R Hand, BA
T R Sharp, MA
Mrs C Painter, BA
Mrs S H Le Marchand, BA
Mrs F L Short, BA
M C Poole, BSc, PhD
Ms C R Harrison-Horácek, MA
*P M Hibbert, BSc
*Mrs T D Marskell, CertEd
Mrs H M Arthur, BSc, CPhys, MInstP
*Mrs P A Edwards, BA, MSc
Mrs J P Maxwell-Stewart, BA
Revd M R Dorsett, BA, MTh, PhD, CertTheol (*Chaplain*)
Miss N Featherstone, BSc
J P Whitehouse, BEd
R P Geary, BSc, CChem, MRSC
A A D Gillgrass, BA
S C Cuthbertson, BA
*C Haywood, BA
A W Longley, BA, MA
S M Atkins, BA
R Jones, BA
*Mrs G Kendrick, BEd
*Mrs M M Longley, BEd
Mrs J Vivian, CertEd
Mrs R J Terry, BA, MA
P S Baldwin, BA
I C Robinson, BSc
M Schramm, BSc
*Mrs S M Beesley, BA
*Mrs J L Guest, BEd
Mrs S Simojoki, BA
O Sucksmith, BA
Mrs J T Golightly, BA
Dr D J Haddock, MA, DPhil (Oxon)
*Mrs C Battrum, BA
Miss J Cooke, BA

Music:
D E Brookshaw, BMus, FRCO
H R Thurlby, LRAM
*D G Phillips, MA, FRCO, CHM, LGSM, ARCM
Mrs V J Gunter, GTCL, LTCL

and 28 Visiting Teachers

The King's Junior Schools

King's St Albans:
Head: R Bellfield, BEd

Deputy: J T Walton, CertEd, FRGS

Mrs A D Walton, CertEd
§Mrs L Jackson, MA
Mrs R Reeves, MEd
D Mews, BA, BSc, CertEd
Mrs C Woodcock, BA, CertEd
Mrs B I Wilson, BA, CertEd
*Mrs N Cain, BA, PGCE
*Mrs P Griffin, BA, BEd
F C McGonigal, BEd
Miss K J Kear-Wood, BSc, PGCE
Mrs J Pitts, BEd
W Toleman, BA
*Mrs M A Keyes, MA

King's Hawford:
Head: R W Middleton, MSc

M I Billen, CertEd
Mrs A Douglas, AMusLCM, CertEd
Mrs J M Tune, BSc
Miss D Churchward, CertEd, DipEd(SEN), MEd, SpLD (RSA)
Mrs S Roscoe, CertEd
R W Figgitt, BA(Ed) (Hons)
§Mrs L Jackson, BA
§Mrs C Heath, BEd

Pre-Prep:
Mrs P M Bradley, BEd
Mrs J N Willis, CertEd
Mrs C A Griffin, BA, PGCE
Mrs H Rankin, BA, PGCE
Mrs G E Riley, BSc, PGCE
Mrs L Baxter, BSc, PGCE

Medical Officers:
Dr M Smith, MB, ChB
Dr A Georgiou, MB, ChB

Sister: Mrs C F Furber, RGN, DipN

Headmaster's Secretary: Mrs C Swainston

The School still occupies its original site south of the Cathedral. The buildings are grouped around College Green and the School Gardens and quadrangles. They range in date from the 14th-century College Hall and Edgar Tower (which contains the school library) through the 17th and 18th century buildings surrounding College Green, to a range of modern, purpose-built accommodation, much of which has been constructed in the last twenty years. Recent additions in a continuing development programme include

Computer facilities, the School Theatre, new teaching and science provision for the Junior School on site, the refurbishment of the Sports Hall, a new covered Swimming Pool, new, upgraded Houses, and extended playing fields and changing rooms.

There are two Junior Schools. King's St Alban's is a large building which stands in its own grounds on the edge of the main school site. King's Hawford is in a spacious rural setting just to the north of the city.

Numbers and Admission. The School has had a mixed Sixth Form for 25 years, and is now mixed throughout. The first girls joined the Junior School at 7+ and 8+ and the Senior School at 11+ in September 1991, and the first 13+ girls entered in 1993. The Junior School has been fully co-educational since September 1993, and the Senior School since September 1995.

King's St Albans has about 180 pupils aged 7–11. King's Hawford has about 200 pupils aged 2–11. The Senior School has about 800 pupils, including 250 in the Sixth Form.

Entrance to the school is by the Junior Entrance Examination at 7, 8, 9 or 11, or by Common Entrance or Scholarship Examination and the School's test at 13. Girls and boys also join the School at VIth Form level; this entry is by test and GCSE results.

Term of Entry. Pupils are normally admitted annually in September.

Religion. The School has a historic connection with the Cathedral. Religious education, given in accordance with the Christian faith, is non-denominational.

Pupils of all denominations and faiths are welcomed.

Curriculum. Pupils are prepared for the GCSE, and A, A/S and S level, or STEP papers, and for entry to Higher Education, the Services, the professions, industry and commerce. The curriculum is designed to give all pupils a general education and to postpone specialisation for as long as possible. Further details will be found in the Prospectus.

Games. The major sports are Rugby, Netball, Hockey, Association Football, Rowing and Cricket: other sports include Tennis, Athletics, Cross Country, Badminton, Rounders, Fencing, Squash, Golf, Swimming, Sailing and Canoeing. PE and games are compulsory for all; a wide choice is offered to VIth Formers.

Other Activities. The School has a Choral Society and two other Choirs, 3 Orchestras and a Wind Band; there are at least nine concerts each year. There are more than a dozen dramatic productions each year, including two or three School plays, of which one is usually a Musical. The School takes part in the Duke of Edinburgh's Award Scheme, there is a CCF and a Welfare and Community Service group. Young Enterprise companies in the Sixth Form are well subscribed and highly successful. A large number of societies and groups cater for a wide variety of other out-of-school activities and interests. The School has an Outdoor Activities Centre in the Black Mountains which is much used both during the term and in the holidays.

Scholarships. (*see* Entrance Scholarship section) Up to 10 Scholarships are awarded at 11+ each year. There are 20 King's Scholarships and two Queen's Scholarships on the Foundation. The Queen's Scholarships are awarded to girls already in the VI Form. Of the King's Scholarships, 3–5 fall vacant each year, and one is reserved in the first instance for Music. Other Scholarships are offered each year at 13+; they may be academic or music awards. Up to four Scholarships cover half tuition fees, and the remainder up to one-third tuition fees. The actual value of awards may be varied in the light of parental means. Scholarships at 11+ are awarded on the basis of the entrance examination and an interview. The 13+ Scholarship Examination is held in February/March and candidates must be under 14 on 1 September following the examination. Entrance Scholarships are also offered at 7+/8+ and at VI Form level.

Fees. *Senior School:* Day pupils, £6,681 pa. *Junior School:* Day pupils, £4,305–£5,811 pa.

Choristers' Scholarships. Entry to the Choir is by means of Voice and Academic Tests which are held annually in December. A high vocal and musical standard is naturally required, and boys must also be of sufficient intellectual ability to hold their own in the Choir and the School. Boys should be 7–9 years old at the time of entry.

The Prospectus and information about Entrance Tests, Awards and Chorister Scholarships can be obtained from the Headmaster's Secretary.

Charitable status. The King's School Charitable Trust is a Registered Charity, number L4/527536/1. It exists to provide high quality education for boys and girls.

Kingston Grammar School

70 London Road Kingston upon Thames Surrey KT2 6PY.

Tel: 020 8546 5875
Fax: 020 8547 1499
e-mail: head@kingston-grammar.surrey.sch.uk

A school is believed to have existed in the Lovekyn Chantry Chapel since the fourteenth century. However in 1561, Queen Elizabeth I, in response to a humble petition from the Burghers of Kingston, signed Letters Patent establishing the "Free Grammar School of Queen Elizabeth to endure for ever". In 1944 the School accepted Direct Grant Status and became fully Independent in 1976. Two years later the School went Co-educational, initially with girls in the Sixth Form, but in the following year joining in the Preparatory and First Forms, to progress through the School. There are still close links with the Royal Borough of Kingston upon Thames, but no residential qualification for entry to the School, which now numbers 392 boys and 214 girls.

Motto: *Bene agere ac laetari.*

Chairman of the Governors: A J H Mercer, BSc, MA, DPhil, CChem, FRSC

Governors:
J A Elvidge, MA, LLB (*Vice-Chairman*)
D Baker, ARICS
L E Bentall
A Clinch, FCIMA, FACA
S B Craig, LLB, FCA
R D Finlay, MA
M Green, MA
D R Hattersley, BSc, ACGI, MICE, FBIM
Mrs J King, LLB
Mrs R E Lipscomb, JP
J Snelling, MCIOB
Rev D C Ward, MA

***Headmaster:* C D Baxter**, MA (Oxon), FRSA

Deputy Head: J R Hind, MA, MEd, PhD *History*
Director of Studies: M Jones, BA, MEd *French*
Director of External Relations: J D Cook, BA, CChem, MRSC *Chemistry*
Head of Sixth Form: Miss D M Williams, BSc *Geography*
Head of Middle School: *R L Barker, BA *English, Careers*
Head of Lower School: Miss P V Crothers, BA *French, German*
Head of Junior School: A M Stribley, BD, AKC *Religious and Personal Education*

Staff:
*Miss R Barnes, BA *English and Drama*
D N Blatchford, BSc *Mathematics*

*N Bond, BA *English and Drama*
Miss S Brosseau, MLEA *French, German*
*D G Buttanshaw, BEd *PE and Mathematics*
*Miss K Challen, BEd *Sports Studies*
M A Chaudhry, BSc, PhD *Mathematics*
Miss L Collison, BSc *Mathematics*
*P J Cooper, MSc *Mathematics*
*Mrs R J Crimes, BA, ATD *Art*
*J M Davies, MA *History*
I Deepchand, BSc *Physics*
J A Dyson, BA *Art*
*Mrs C A Evans, BA, AdvDipEd, MA(Ed) *Geography*
D Farr, BA *Design Technology*
Miss V C Filsell, BSc *Chemistry*
*M Gluning, BSc *Chemistry, Head of Science*
S Hanna, BSc, MSc *Mathematics*
G R J Hemmings, MA *Assistant Director of Music*
*K J Hillary, BA *German*
*Mrs M J Horrocks, BA *French, Spanish*
*C A Jackson, MA, FRCO, ARAM *Director of Music*
*Miss L E M Jowitt, BA, MSc *History, Politics*
A M Langdon, BA, PhD *Mathematics*
*J W M Large, BA *Religious & Personal Education*
Miss R P McCauley, BA *French and Spanish*
D C A Morton, BA *Geography*
*C C Muller, BA *Classics*
*R S Parfitt, BSc, MInstBiol, FLS *Biology*
Miss E Parry, BA *Preparatory Form*
Mrs J V Pearce, BSc *Biology*
Miss V E Penglase, BA *English and Theatre Studies*
Miss C M Rice, BA *French, Spanish*
*P J Ricketts, MA *Economics and Politics*
Mrs A Royce, BEd *Girls' Games*
B J Russell, BEng *Physics*
Mrs M Serjeant, BA, DipLib *Librarian*
*Miss M C Smith, BA *Physics*
J S Smith, BA, MPhil *English*
D A R Sorley, BA *History*
*S R Steele, BEd *Technology*
C D Taylor, MA, MIBiol *Biology*
Mrs C Tullett, DipPE *Physical Education*
D C Wethey, BA *Classics*
T E J White, BSc *Chemistry*
M P Williamson, BEd *Physical Education*
*Mrs J E Wright, BSc *Director of Information Technology*

Bursar and Clerk to the Governors: A G Howard-Harwood, MIMgt, MInstAM

Property Manager: Mr S Braid

Development Director: Mrs J Skeen

Headmaster's Secretary: Mrs A U Stockbridge

Admissions Secretary: Miss J Patterson

Buildings. Starting with the medieval Lovekyn Chapel, the site of Kingston Grammar School has been developed over 400 years to include modern classroom and laboratory facilities. Major recent developments have seen the building of a Library, Studio and Seminar Room, an Art/Technology Centre with an art gallery. Kitchen and dining facilities have recently been upgraded, and all three Science departments have been extended/refurbished. The Chapel has recently been restored as a recital/lecture room, a new History Department building was opened in 1997 and an Information and Communication Technology Centre with a school wide network was installed in 1998. A multi media Modern Languages Centre opened in 1999. The school is easily accessible by road and rail links to Kingston. The 22 acre sports ground includes squash courts, pavilions, cricket nets, an all-weather pitch plus practice area and boat house.

Entry to the School. Admission to the School is by examination: at 10+ and 11+ candidates sit the School's own examination in January for entry the following September; at 13+ candidates sit the Independent Schools Common Entrance Examination in June for entry the following September or the School's own Examination for non-Common Entrance candidates. A large number of girls and boys are also admitted to the VIth Form.

Term of Entry. Apart from occasional vacancies pupils enter in September.

Fees. The basic fee per term is £2,601 for pupils in the Preparatory Year (entry at 10+), and £2,681 for pupils in the Main School (11+ and above); this covers all charges except examination fees and lunch.

Scholarships and Bursaries. (*see* Entrance Scholarship section) The Governors award Scholarships (on academic merit) at 11+, 13+ and 16+, and a number of Bursaries (according to parental means) to pupils entering the School at 11+, 13+ and 16+. Music, Art and Sports awards are also available.

Curriculum. The academic curriculum through to GCSE emphasises a proper balance between varied disciplines and range of intellectual experience, with all taking Maths, English, the three sciences and at least one modern language as part of 10 GCSE subjects. Maths GCSE may be taken early by able candidates. Full careers information and counselling are given, though pupils are encouraged to view academic pursuit as a desirable end in itself, using a profiling process to develop their commitment to study. In the Sixth Form, students choose 4 AS level subjects in the First Year Sixth and 3or 4 subjects for A level. Over 90% of the entire Sixth elect to proceed to higher education, including Oxford and Cambridge Universities.

Care. A pupil's form tutor is responsible for welfare and progress. Heads of Sections coordinate the work of form tutors; the Tutor for Girls has special oversight of the girls and there is a qualified nurse. A School Counsellor visits one day a week to support any pupils who do not feel they are fulfilling themselves in school. Parents' meetings are held annually and pupils receive two written reports per year, in addition to twice termly grade cards. Pastoral evenings are also held, where parents can discuss with each other and staff the difficulties and anxieties faced by young adults.

Games. The school Sports Ground is beautifully situated at Thames Ditton, by the River Thames opposite Hampton Court Palace. Kingston Grammar School prides itself on the large number of pupils who represent Great Britain in Hockey and Rowing.

Hockey (in both winter terms) and Rowing (all the year round) are 'main games'. Cricket (boys) and Tennis (girls) are the 'main games' in the summer. The School also has representative sides in Athletics, Cross-Country, Squash, Shooting, Table Tennis, Tennis and Netball.

Societies. A large number of School Societies provides for the interests of pupils of all ages. They range from Chess and Debating, to Natural History, Shooting and Young Enterprise. The Duke of Edinburgh Award Scheme is popular and overseas travel is a regular feature of many activities. The Music Department has a vigorous programme of concerts and tours to such places as France, Germany, Canada and America.

Combined Cadet Force. The CCF is divided into Army and RAF Sections. A variety of activities ranging from shooting and flying to Outward Bound and Adventurous Training take place. Camps are held in school holidays and pupils attend courses in a variety of subjects. This is an entirely voluntary activity which pupils may take up in the 3rd Form.

Careers. The Careers Staff assist pupils in their choice of options at all levels, and give advice on possible future careers. They are in close touch with employers in professions, commerce and industry, and all fifth formers undertake a period of work experience after their GCSE examinations. An annual Careers Convention is held at the school. Particular attention is given to advice on entry to the Universities to which the majority of VIth Form students go. The School is in membership of the Independent School Careers Organisation and pupils are able to take advantage of several computer assessment programs.

Parents' and Staff Association. The Association exists to further the interests of the School in the broadest possible way and does much to strengthen the links between staff, parents and students. The Sherriff Club and Music Society support the rowing and music of the school respectively.

The Old Kingstonian Association likewise does much to foster a spirit of unity and cooperation. All students are eligible to join on leaving the School. The Hon Secretary is Mr Roger McDaniel, Highlands, The Downs, Givons Grove, Leatherhead, Surrey KT22 8LF.

Honours. An average of 8 or 9 places are gained each year at Oxbridge.

Charitable status. Kingston Grammar School is a company limited by guarantee, Registered in England number 3883748, and a Registered Charity, number 1078461. It exists to enable children to adapt their talents to meet the needs of an ever changing world, whilst holding fast to the principles of self reliance, a sense of responsibility and a determination to seize opportunity.

Kingswood School

Lansdown Bath Somerset BA1 5RG.
Tel: 01225 734200
Fax: 01225 734205

Kingswood is an independent, co-educational and Christian-based school represented on HMC. It was founded by John Wesley in 1748 and moved to its present 218-acre site overlooking Bath in 1851. Kingswood combines academic excellence with a concern for the development of each individual's talents. Boarders and day pupils are fully integrated with the pastoral system centred on seven houses. There are 520 pupils (313 boys and 207 girls) at the Senior School. Kingswood has a boarding and day Preparatory School at Summerhill on the Kingswood Estate with 270 pupils.

Motto: *In via Recta Celeriter*

Chairman of the Governing Body: Mr H R Wright, MA

Hon Secretary to the Governors: Mr J R Monahan, MA, FRICS

***Headmaster:* G M Best**, MA

Senior Deputy Head: The Revd S C Harvey, MA

Deputy Head (Curriculum): Dr Edwina Calvert, MA, BD, DPhil

Headmistress of Kingswood Prep School, Bath: Miss A Gleave, MEd

Chaplain: The Revd M L Wilkinson, MA

Director of Finance: Mr R G Reeson, FCMA

Registrar: Ms A Carlton-Porter

Full-time Teaching Staff:

J C Allison, BEd
Mrs J G Ball, BSc
Miss N J Beale, MA
U K Bergmann, BA
Mrs L N Bland, BEd
Miss R J Bleathman, BA
S J Burgon, BEd, LTCL
R E Burton, BSc
Mrs L J Court, BA
Miss M D Cross, MA
J W Davies, BA
P J Dossor, BSc, DPhil
R Dunster-Sigtermans, MA, FRCO, ARCM
P J Essam, BA, MSc
J R Garforth, MA, BSc
A E Haines, BA
P J Hollywell, BA
G C Hubbuck, BA
Mrs D J Jenner, BA
Miss A A Keam, BA
J R Key-Pugh, MA
J C Kingsnorth, CertEd
R H M Lewis, MSc, BEd
Mrs S J Lockhart, BA, BPhil
R Mainwaring, BA, ALCM
D F Marsham, BSc, PhD
D J Meads, BA
Mrs S J Monks, BEd
G J Musto, BSc
G D Opie, BEd
Mrs J R Opie, BA
Mrs P W Packer, BA
Mrs M K Patterson, MSc
Miss U J Paver, BA
T P R Reeman, BA
M Sealy, GRSM, FRCO(*CHM*), ARCM
N M H Sheffrin, BSc, PhD
D O Sims, BA, BEd
A J P Smith, BA
S R Snowdon, BA
M J Westcott, BEd
Miss A T Wright, BEd

Part-time Teaching Staff:

Mrs F E Best, MA, CChem, MRSC
Mrs N C Duncan, BA
Mrs K Hemmet, BA
Mrs J M Houghton, LLB, MBA
Mrs A G F Lehan, CertEd
Mrs L Prior, CertEd, AMBDA
Mrs J Reeman, BEd
Mrs H Ross-White, BA, ATC

Visiting Music Staff:

D Bevan, MA, BMus *Academic Music*
J V Burchell *Piano*
Mrs G Davies, LTCL, LWCMD *Voice*
R Dorrell, BMus *Brass*
G Harrup, BA, LGSM *Electric Guitar*
M Harvey *Percussion*
A Jenner, ALCM *Guitar*
D Kniveton, BA, LTCL *Flute*
S MacAllister, BSc *French Horn*
Mrs M Montagu, ARCM *Oboe/Bassoon*
Ms S Power, BEd *Cello*
Mrs A Salamonsen, MMus *Violin*
D Seymour, ARCM *Piano*
Dr D V Shepard, BSc, PhD, PGDip, Mtpp *Clarinet/Saxophone*
Mrs P J Wendzina, CertEd *Piano*

Medical Officer: Dr T J Harris, MD, MCh, MRCOG

Site and Buildings. Kingswood occupies 218 acres of superb parkland overlooking the world heritage City of Bath and within easy reach of the M4 and M5 motorways, as well as rail and air links. In addition to the beautiful main Victorian buildings, there is a state of the art Theatre (opened 1995), a a spacious multi-roomed sixth-form centre, a series of specialist buildings for ICT, DT, Art and opened in May 2000, a Music School with its own recording studios, a main teaching complex (which includes eleven science laboratories and recently developed areas for History, Geography, Mathematics, Sports Science and Modern Languages), and a Chapel. There are seven houses and excellent sporting facilities, including a Sports Hall, indoor swimming pool, astro turf, and extensive playing fields. The school also has its own Prep School in a Georgian mansion and award-winning modern buildings in a separate section of the parkland.

Curriculum. Kingswood wants its students to develop lively, enquiring and well-informed minds and the high standard of attainment reached by its pupils has been highly praised. From 11 to 13 pupils follow a broad and balanced curriculum. Each pupil has a tutor to supervise progress and to offer advice and encouragement. At 14 the pupils choose at least eight and up to twelve GCSE subjects to develop their particular talents whilst maintaining a broad range of skills. Most sixth formers specialise in at least three or four subjects and all participate in a General Studies programme. Sixteen subjects are offered at GCSE level as well as over twenty at AS/A2 level, including Politics, Business Studies, Sports Studies and Theatre Studies.

Organisation. *Preparatory:* Kingswood draws its pupils from a wide variety of schools but it also has its own prep school for boarders and day pupils. Kingswood Prep School caters for around 270 boys and girls between the ages of 3 and 11, and offers a variety of activities alongside the academic curriculum. A new boarding house for boys and girls aged 7–11 opened in September 1998. This "family-based" unit of around 20 boarders is cared for by houseparents who also teach at the school. Children from the prep school are expected to move on to Kingswood but parents are advised if children are felt to be academically unsuitable for the senior school.

Westwood: Kingswood operates a junior house for boys and girls aged 11 to 13. This is designed to settle new pupils into the school at 11+ or 12+ and provide the special environment that the younger pupils require before going into senior houses. In effect, it means the pupils enjoy the atmosphere associated with a prep school whilst also enjoying all the facilities of a senior school. Sixth-formers are specially selected to act as elder "brothers/sisters" and prefects to your younger pupils.

Senior Houses: From the age of 13+ pupils are assigned to one of six houses, three for boys and three for girls. The small units of around 50 pupils in each house ensure a good and friendly enviroment. There are also shared social areas in the centre of school as well as the social areas within the houses. It would be normal to have around 160 in the sixth-form, which has its own special building.

Houses. The seven houses are all very distinctive and five are set within their own grounds. One junior house provides sleeping accommodation and recreational facilities for boys and girls under 13. It is run by four resident housestaff, together with assistant housestaff. There are three senior boys' houses and three senior girls' houses, each under a resident Housemaster or mistress and assisted by other teaching staff. Day pupils are attached to a boarding house and share the common room facilities with the boarders. Emphasis is placed on creating a family atmosphere in each house. The school has a number of houses and flats for single and married staff so two-thirds of the staff live on the campus. Relations between teachers and students are exceptionally good.

Sports and Games. The sporting and leisure activities programmes have around 70 activities with particular emphasis on sport, drama, music, art and outdoor pursuits. Sporting activities include athletics, badminton, basketball, cricket, cross-country, fencing, golf, hockey, netball, rugby, swimming and tennis. Other activities range from the Duke of Edinburgh Award Scheme to Computing, from Orienteering to Photography, and Bird Watching to Young Enterprise Companies. Regular group activities in the instrumental field include orchestra, jazz group, string group and wind group. There are also junior and senior choirs and a large-scale choral society. Four dramatic productions take place each year.

Religious Activities. Kingswood welcomes pupils from all denominations. In addition to regular morning worship, there is a wide variety of guest speakers and the Christian Fellowship organises its own events. There are regular fund-raising activities for charities and a Community Service programme. Every year a joint Methodist-Anglican confirmation service is held.

Careers. From the earliest possible age we encourage students to participate in all decisions affecting their future. Our Careers and Higher Education Centre is run by two staff and stocked with a wide variety of information. Kingswood subscribes to the Independent Schools Careers Organisation and has links with local career guidance organisations. Our programme of work experience, followed by all members of Lower Sixth, is aimed at providing experience of the entire process of job application, interview and work itself, and we have established close links with local employers to make all this possible. For the ages 16 to 18 a programme of discussions with visiting employers is reinforced by personal guidance from the Sixth Form Tutor and the Head of Careers.

Leavers. It is normal for all of our sixth-form pupils to go on to university courses.

Fees. The fees for the autumn term 2000 are: Boarding: Prep £3,499; junior £3,999; senior and sixth form £4,999. Day: Prep £1,478; junior and senior (Yrs 7-11) £1,997; sixth form £2,666. TEFL teaching is provided for students who do not speak English as their first language - this is invoiced separately as required.

Entry Requirements. Entry is based on Kingswood's entrance examination, the report of the previous school and a personal interview. Candidates at 13+ may also enter by Common Entrance papers. Entry to the Sixth Form is by a minimum of six or more GCSE passes at grade C or above, plus school report and interview.

Scholarships. (*see* Entrance Scholarship section) Academic scholarships of value up to a maximum of 50% of the full fees are available annually to pupils entering Years 7, 9 and Lower Sixth. "Special Talent" scholarships of a maximum up to 50% of the full fees are also available for pupils entering Years 7, 9 and the Lower Sixth, and are awarded for excellence in a particular field, such as Music, Art and Design or Sport. A number of bursaries are also awarded annually at the discretion of the Headmaster and the Governors. Further details of Scholarships can be obtained from the Registrar.

Charitable status. Kingswood School is a Registered Charity, number 309148. Founded by John Wesley, it maintains its Methodist tradition in providing preparatory and secondary education.

King William's College

Castletown Isle of Man IM9 1TP
Tel: (01624) 822551
Fax: (01624) 824287
e-mail: Principal@kwc.sch.im

King William's College owes its foundation to Dr Isaac Barrow, Bishop of Sodor and Man from 1663 to 1671, who established an educational Trust in 1668. The funds of the Trust were augmented by public subscription and the College was opened in 1833 and named after King William IV, "The Sailor King".

In 1991 the College merged with the Isle of Man's other Independent School, The Buchan School, Castletown which had been founded by Lady Laura Buchan in 1875 to provide education for young ladies. The Buchan School has been reformed as a Preparatory School for boys and girls, boarding and day pupils up to age 11. For further details of The Buchan School, see Part V which relates to Preparatory Schools. The Isle of Man being internally self-governing has a very favourable tax structure and the independence of College would not be affected by changes in UK legislation.

Motto: 'Assiduitate, non desidia'.

Governors:

The Rt Revd The Lord Bishop
The Venerable The Archdeacon
The Director of Education for the Isle of Man
S G Alder, BA, FCA
Mrs J D A Bates, LLB
Prof R J Berry, RD, DPhil, MD, FRCP, FRCR, FFOM
A C Collister
Mrs E J Higgins, BSc, ACA
R P Holland
Mrs J A Holt, MA
Mrs M C James
P P Purcell
C P A Vanderpump, BSc, ACA
Sir David Wilson, DLitt, FBA
N H Wood, ACA

***Principal:* P D John**, BSc

Teaching Staff:

A W Beadle, BEd (*Head of Design & Technology*)
Mrs D M Beckerson, BA (*Head of Art*)
J H Buchanan, BA (*Head of History & Politics*)
S N Cope, BA (*Housemaster, Raglan House*)
Miss R J Corlett, BA (*Head of Senior School*)
Miss A L Crellin, BSc, BEd
Mrs R K Drown, BEd, MSc
Miss D Dubis, BA, MA
G M Garrett, BEd, BA, CMath, MIMA (*Assistant Head Academic Administration, Head of Mathematics*)
P Garrett, BSc, MSc
Rev J R Gulland, MA (*Chaplain*)
J Hazlewood, MA, BSc (*Head of Biology*)
K Holder, BA
M J Hoy, MA (*Head of English*)
Dr C E Humphreys-Jones, BA, PhD (*Housemistress, Barrow*)
R D Humphreys-Jones, BSc (*Assistant Head Director of Studies/Head of Physics*)
M A Jackson, BA (*Head of Modern Languages*)
R J King, BSc (*Examinations Officer*)
Miss B Lace, BSc (*Director of Sport*)
M Leaver, CertEd
A A Maree, BA (*Housemaster, Colbourne*)
Mrs Z McAndry, CertVerse (*Housemistress, School House*)
Dr P H Morgans, BSc, PhD (*Head of Chemistry*)
Miss H E Morton (*Housemistress, Stenning School*)
W D Morton, BSc (*Head of Geography*)
A T Roberts, BA, ARCO (*Director of Music*)
Miss D C Thomas, BSc
M W Turner, BA (*Housemaster, Hunt House/Head of Business Studies*)
Mrs B Van Rhyn, BA, HDE
P Weatherall, BSc (*Information Systems Manager*)
Dr P J Winnett, BA, PhD

Part-time staff:

Mrs B L Bassett, CertEd (*Learning Support*)
Mrs M Gulland, BA
Mrs N A Litton, CertEd
Mrs S A Ross, BEd

School Medical Officer: J E Brewis, MB, ChB

Matron: Sister E Clark, RGN

Bursar and Secretary to the Governors: Captain R James, CBE, RN (Retd)

Assistant to the Principal: Mrs S J Craine

College is set in superb countryside on the edge of Castletown Bay and adjacent to Ronaldsway Airport. The Isle of Man is approximately 33 miles long and 10 miles wide and is an area of diverse and beautiful scenery. The scope for exploration, adventure training and natural history is enormous. The Isle of Man is an unusually safe environment with a very low crime rate.

There are approximately 270 pupils at College and a further 200 pupils at the Preparatory School. Both King William's College and The Buchan School are fully co-educational, girls having been accepted throughout the secondary age range since September 1987.

Entry. New pupils are accepted at any time, but most begin at the start of the September Term. Boys and girls are admitted to the Preparatory School up to the age of 11 at which point transfer to King William's College is automatic. Pupils at both Schools follow the National Curriculum in slightly augmented form. The entry to College including Sixth Form level is by Head's report and, where possible, by interview.

Boarders. There is one Senior House for boys and one Senior House for girls. The living and sleeping accommodation is arranged very largely in study-bedrooms. In 1981 a fine, purpose-built boys' boarding House was opened and modernisation of the remaining accommodation has continued since then.

Each house has its own housemaster or housemistress who is responsible for the well-being, academic and pastoral, of the pupils. He or she is assisted by two or three tutors, of whom at least two are resident. Parents deal with their child's Housemaster or Housemistress on matters of day-to-day routine. Provision is made for boarders from overseas to remain at College during half-term breaks.

Day Pupils. There are two Senior houses for boys, and two Senior houses for girls', each under a Housemaster or Housemistress assisted by a group of Tutors. Day pupils are integrated into the life of the College and play a full part in all activities. They have their own study accommodation in the main school building. Transfer between day and boarding Houses is straightforward and occurs regularly.

Chapel. The College is a Church of England foundation but pupils of all denominations attend Chapel; the spirit of the services is distinctly ecumenical. There is a short daily service for all pupils, and a main service for all pupils on Saturdays. Pupils of non-Christian faith are made welcome and are encouraged to share their beliefs. Pupils are prepared annually for confirmation by the Lord Bishop.

The Curriculum. The Curriculum is designed to provide a broad balanced and challenging form of study for all pupils. At 11 and 12 pupils take English, mathematics, French, science, history, geography, design and technology, ICT, art, music, drama, religious studies and physical education. At 13 there is the opportunity to study from a choice of Creative Subjects, PE, German, Spanish or Latin. A year later a selection of up to ten subjects is made for GCSE.

In the Sixth Form, normal A2 level courses extend for two years and pupils choose three or exceptionally four subjects from a total of eighteen subjects. There is a system of options outside the A2 level courses which allows the breadth of education to be maintained. The College has an excellent record for entry to University. Academic standards are high with over 47% of A level examinations being passed at A or B grade in 2000 and over 80% of pupils gaining 5 or more GCSEs, grades A* to C. Over 90% of our leavers proceed to the university of their choice, before going on to a wide range of professions.

Careers. The College is a member of the Independent Schools Careers Organisation and visits are made three times a year by the Regional Director who conducts interviews and aptitude tests. There is a Careers teacher who also co-ordinates UCAS entries, and a well-equipped Careers Library. There are regular Careers presentations and an established work experience provision.

Music and Drama. There are excellent facilities for drama with House plays and at least one major school production each year, together with regular coaching in Speech and Drama. There are Junior and Senior Bands and Choirs, and a very flourishing Chapel Choir. The House Music competition is one of the many focal points of House activity. There are Senior and Junior School concerts and a Serenade Concert in the Summer.

Games. The College has a strong tradition and a fine

reputation in the major games of rugby, hockey and cricket. There are regular fixtures at all levels for both boys and girls with Isle of Man schools and schools in other parts of the British Isles. Netball, athletics, soccer, cross-country and swimming all flourish and there are both House and College competitions. Senior pupils may opt to play golf on the magnificent adjoining Castletown Golf Links or to sail as their major summer sport. There are approximately thirty acres of first class playing fields, an indoor heated swimming pool which is in use throughout the year, a miniature rifle range, a gymnasium for basketball and badminton with an indoor cricket net, hard and grass tennis courts and two squash courts. Professional cricket coaching continues throughout the year. Girls have the opportunity to play every game and also play rounders and netball.

Other Activities. Every opportunity and encouragement is given to pupils to enable them to develop worthwhile interests and good personal qualities; full advantage is taken of the outstanding natural environment of the Island. There is a wide range of societies and activities to complement academic life. The Art room and Design and Technology workshop and Computer Centre are open at regular times each week and the weekends. Cookery classes are available as an activity and pupils are able to explore the coast and countryside safely by cycle and on foot. The Duke of Edinburgh's Award Scheme flourishes and expeditions are undertaken regularly both on the Island and further afield. One afternoon each week is devoted to Service training through the Combined Cadet Force and the Social Services group. There are strong links with the Armed Services who help regularly with Cadet training. There are regular skiing trips, choir tours and educational trips to the UK and abroad.

Travel. Some boarders come by sea from Heysham or Liverpool using the daily service to Douglas but the majority of boarding pupils and parents come quickly and easily by air from the British Isles and much further afield. They arrive within two kilometres of the College having completed a journey from perhaps the other side of the world without needing to leave an airport building. There are three daily direct flights to and from London (Heathrow), flights from other UK cities, and direct flights to and from Belfast and Dublin. House staff are fully experienced in arranging international flights, visas, etc and younger pupils are met at the airport.

Health. The health of all pupils is in the care of the School Doctor. There is a sanatorium supervised by a qualified nursing sister and high standards of medical care are available at Noble's Hospital in Douglas.

Fees (September 2000). Senior boarders £4,725 per term, Junior boarders £3,935 per term. Senior day £3,360 per term, Junior day £2,570 per term.

A reduction of one third of the fees for boarders and one half for day pupils is allowed for clergy with livings in the Isle of Man. A reduction of 15% is allowed for serving members of HM Forces.

A reduction of 10% is made for the second child, 30% for the third and 50% for the fourth.

Scholarships. (*see* Entrance Scholarship section) There are a variety of Scholarships for pupils entering Years 7 and 9 and Scholarships for Sixth Form entry.

Music Scholarships are available for pupils over 11 on 1st September.

A bursary fund is available to assist with school fees in cases of need.

Further details of the school and a prospectus may be obtained from the Principal to whom applications for entry should also be made.

Charitable status. King William's College is a Manx Registered Charity, number 615 and is operated as a Company limited by guarantee. The College's endowments are administered by Bishop Barrow's Charity.

Kirkham Grammar School

Ribby Road Kirkham Preston PR4 2BH
Tel: (01772) 671079
Fax: (01772) 672747

Kirkham Grammar School, founded in 1549, is an expanding co-educational independent School of 930 pupils aged between 4 and 18. The Senior School of 650 pupils, 75 of whom are boarders, incorporates a Sixth Form of 150, and the Junior School for day pupils, with 280 on roll, housed in splendid purpose-built accommodation. The Headmaster is a member of HMC and a member of the Boarding Schools Association. The school fees are competitive; forces personnel are offered a reduction in the boarding element of the fees; scholarships, exhibitions and bursaries are available at 11+ and 16+. The Boarding House is pleasant and comfortable and is run under the personal supervision of the Boarding Housemaster and his wife, whose residence is attached to the boarding wing of the School.

As well as excellent academic results and a good Oxbridge entry record, Kirkham Grammar School prides itself on turning out rounded, well-balanced and confident young people, the vast majority of whom continue their education at University. The School has a strong Christian ethos, with an emphasis on care for the individual, traditional family values, good manners and sound discipline. It is a friendly close-knit community where staff and pupils work particularly closely together.

Sited amid 30 acres of its own grounds, Kirkham Grammar School boasts some excellent facilities, which include the recent additions of a large multi-purpose hall, a superb floodlit all-weather pitch, a science suite, a Sixth Form Centre and an outstanding new Technology Centre and Languages Centre built in partnership with BAE Systems. An impressive range of extra curricular activities is offered by a School renowned for its sporting prowess, but with strength across the board in music, art, drama, a strong and popular Combined Cadet Force Unit and a flourishing House System.

Chairman of Governors: Mr A B Blackburn

***Headmaster:* B Stacey**, MA (Edin), DipEd (Oxon), FRSA (*History*)

Deputy Headmaster: J R Wood, MA (Cantab), PGCE (*Mathematics*)

Senior Mistress: Mrs J E Taylor, BA, CertEd, AdvDip (*English, PE, PSHE*)

Senior Master: F W Sayer, ACP, LIBiol, CertEd (*Biology, o/c Combined Cadet Force*)

Academic Staff:
Mrs L M Ainsworth, BA (Hons), PGCE (*French*)
Mrs D Airey, BEd (Hons), BDA, TEFL (*Biology, Learning Support*)
J Baron, BSc (Hons), PGCE (*Chemistry*)
Miss L Baxter, BEd (Hons) (*Physical Education, Biology*) (*part time*)
A F Bostock, BA, CertEd (*Design and Technology*)
R J Browning, BSc (Hons), ACCE, PGCE (*Maths, Information Technology*)
J W Callister, BSc (Hons), PGCE (*Physics, Technology*)
Mrs B A Cassidy, BMus (Hons), MEd, PGCE (*Music, Religious Studies*)
J Catterall, LRAM (*Music*)
Mrs P J Cooper, BSc (Hons), PGCE (*Maths*)
Mrs C Copland, ALA (*Librarian*)
S Crowther, BSc (Hons), IEng, MIMechIE (*Design and Technology*)

Mrs A Devine, BA (Hons), PGCE (*French, German and Head of Lower School*)
S F Duncan, BA (Hons) (*History, English, Geography*)
Mrs S K Fletcher, BA (Hons) (*Maths*)
Miss A S Fryer, BSc (Hons), PGCE (*Biology*)
M Gaddes, MA, PGCE (*Physics and Assistant Head of Sixth Form*)
S P Gardiner, BA (Hons) (*Art*)
Mrs I C Gault, CertEd (*Maths*)
Ms K C Gibson, BA (Hons), PGCE, SCITT (*English*)
Mrs J M Glover, BEd (Hons) (*Physical Education, Religious Studies, Geography*)
Dr A C Hall, PhD, Grad RIC (*Chemistry*)
R W Harrison, BA (Hons), BSc (Hons), PGCE (*Geography, Assistant Boarding Housemaster*)
C J Hawkes, BA (Hons), PGCE (*English*)
A M Hill, CertEd LCP (*Design and Technology, Graphical Communication*)
Miss S R Howe, BSc (Hons), PGCE (*Mathematics*)
Mrs Y E Jones, BA (Hons), CertEd (*English*)
Mrs F Lang (*Business Studies*)
A R Long, MA, PGCE (*French, German and Head of Sixth Form, Careers*)
Mrs S P Long, BA (Hons), PGCE (*French*) (*part time*)
M P Melling, BA (Hons), PGCE (*History, Politics and Middle School Careers*)
T P Miller, BA (Hons) (*History*)
R F Noble, MSc, BSc (Hons), PGCE (*Physics*)
S R Painter, BA (Hons), MA (*Art*)
Mrs L Poole, BA (Hons), PGCE (*Drama*)
A T Reid, MA, PGCE (*Maths*)
Mrs D J Rogerson, BA (Hons), PGCE
Dr A B Rollins, PhD, BSc (Hons), PGCE (*Science, Biology, Chemistry, Physics*)
I Rushton, MA, PGCE (*French/German*)
S Sampey, BEd (*English, Games*)
I M Scott, BA (Hons), PGCE (*Geography*)
Mrs M E Scott, BA (Hons), PGCE (*Biology*)
P B Smith, CertEd (*Boarding Housemaster, Chemistry, Physics*)
Mrs J Stanbury, PhD, BA (Hons), PGCE (*Psychology*)
Mrs J K Tabb, BA (Hons) (*Physical Education and Geography*)
B F Taylor, BA (Hons), PGCE (*German/French*)
R D Taylor, DipPhysEd (*PE, Mathematics*)
A E Trenhaile, BA (Hons), MEd, PGCE (*Religious Studies*)
R J Watson, BA (Hons), PGCE (*English, Librarian, Head of Middle School*)
M A Whalley, BEd (Hons) (*Director of PE and Games*)
Mrs B Williams, CertEd, MA (*Religious Studies and PHSE*) (*part-time*)

Housemasters:
Kirkham House: Mr S F Duncan
Fylde House: Mr I M Scott
School House: Mr P B Smith
Preston House: Dr A B Rollins

Junior School:
Head of Junior School: Mrs L A Taylor, BEd, LTCL
Deputy Headmaster: Mr B Edgar, BEd

Staff:
Miss A L Ashton, BEd (Hons)
Mrs A M Atkinson, BEd (Hons)
Mrs W Barton (*Classroom Assistant*)
Mrs C Brindle, CertEd
C Butterworth, BA (Hons), PGCE
Miss E Carr, BEd (Hons)
Miss D Cooper, BEd (Hons)
Mrs H Green, AdvDipEd Primary Education
D Healy, BEd (Hons)
Mrs S Kenmare, BEd (Hons) (*Head of Infant Department*)
Mrs J E Knowles, BEd (Hons)
P Lockett, GRNCM, PGCE (*Head of Music*)
Miss R McKay, BA
Mrs G Morgan, TCert
S J Milner, BEd
Miss R Nixon (*Classroom Assistant*)
Miss F Robles (*French Assistant*)

Musical Instruments Teaching:
Miss J Brierley (*Keyboard*)
W Dowding (*Piano*)
R Evans (*Brass*)
Miss J Jackson (*Violin*)
A G Keeling (*Flute, Guitar*)
Mrs P K Kirk (*Clarinet*)
Miss J Jackson (*Violin*)
Mrs H Shuttleworth (*Singing*)
G Smith (*Brass*)
Miss S Wood (*Percussion*)

LAMDA Teaching: Mrs C Johnson, LLAM (*Speech Training and Drama*)

Bursar: Mrs C E Brown

Headmaster's Secretary/Registrar: Mrs C M Seed
Matron/House Mistress: Miss E McCade
Assistant Matron: Miss M Kennedy

Aims. The School's academic aim is to encourage pupils to extend themselves to achieve the best results of which they are capable in order to acquire the necessary qualifications for entry to higher education or the career they wish to follow. Outside the academic sphere, our objective is to introduce pupils to as wide a range as possible of cultural, sporting and creative activities and to encourage them to participate in those which appeal to them. The School aims to foster an ethos which encourages leadership, self discipline, good manners, cheerful, friendly and supportive relationships and to promote Christian teaching and values within the framework of 'one family'.

Academic Programme. The courses lead to GCSE, A-Level and AS-Level. In the first three years, the basic subjects studied are English, French, Mathematics, German, Geography, History, Physics, Chemistry, Biology, Music, Art, Drama, Information Technology, Design and Technology, and Religious Studies. The first stage of specialisation takes place on entering the fourth form where the core subjects of English, Mathematics and French/German are taught in sets, and there is a further choice of subjects from five option blocks, which include: Art, Design and Technology (Resistant Materials; Graphic Products; Systems), Music, Business Studies, Drama, Geography, History, Information Technology, Religious Studies, German, Biology, Chemistry, Physics and Science.

In the Sixth Form, A and A/S Level subjects are chosen from the following: English, Maths, Further Maths, Biology, Chemistry, Physics, French, German, Art, Music, Design Technology, Geography, History, Psychology, Information Technology, Politics, Theatre Studies, Religious Studies, Business Studies, Physical Education, Electronics (AS only).

In addition all Sixth Formers follow a programme of General Studies and many voluntarily continue in the CCF and/or take up Duke of Edinburgh Award, Young Enterprise or Community Service. Extra tuition is provided for Oxbridge candidates.

Sport. The School has a long and strong sporting tradition and offers the following sports: Rugby, hockey, cricket, athletics, tennis, netball, badminton, squash, swimming and rounders.

Music. There is a very active musical life at the School, with regular Concerts both at lunchtime and in the evening, providing a platform for the Orchestra, Ensembles and Soloists. The School is noted for its fine Choral traditions.

Other Activities. There is a strong Combined Cadet Force contingent, with Army and RAF sections. A large number of societies cater for a wide range of interests including drama, debating, Duke of Edinburgh Award, chess, animal ark, public speaking, German, Italian, philately, climbing, French, Internet and music. A comprehensive careers service is available through the Careers Teachers. The School is an active member of ISCO and is also served by Careerlink.

Admission. Senior School. Four form entry. Pupils are usually admitted at 11 years after passing the entrance examination held in January each year. Some pupils are admitted at 13 via the School's own entrance examination. Admissions to the School in other year groups, especially the Sixth Form are possible. Day/Boarding applications should be made to the Headmaster who will be glad to provide further details.

Scholarships. The School offers an impressive number of Scholarships, Exhibitions and Bursaries which are detailed in a Scholarship Booklet available from the Registrar.

Junior School (4–11 years). The Junior School is an integral part of the School, under the overall control of the Headmaster and the same Board of Governors. The work is organised in close consultation with the Senior School to ensure that education in its broadest sense is continuous and progressive from the age of 4 to 18.

The curriculum is broadly based and balanced. The core subjects: English, Maths and Science will be given priority as set in the National Curriculum. History, Geography, RE, Music, PE and Games will be studied as pure subjects and also as they relate to one another in a cross-curricular manner.

Entry is mainly at age 4 and 9. Application should be made direct to the Registrar, from whom a separate prospectus may be obtained.

Old Kirkhamians Association. For further details contact the Headmaster's Secretary at the School.

Charitable status. The Kirkham Educational Foundation is a Registered Charity, number 526721. The object of the Charity shall be the provision in or near Kirkham of a day and boarding school for boys and girls.

Lancing College

Lancing Sussex BN15 0RW.
Tel: (01273) 452213
Fax: (01273) 464720
e-mail: admissions@lancing.dialnet.com

Founded in 1848 by the Rev Nathaniel Woodard.
Motto: *Beati mundo corde.*

Governing Body: The Provost and Fellows of the Society of SS Mary and Nicolas, Lancing

Visitor: The Rt Revd The Lord Bishop of Chichester

Provost: The Revd Canon John Ratings, MA

School Council:
Chairman: R M Reeve, MA

The Revd Canon John Ratings, MA (*Provost*)
R J C Privett, BA
C E M Snell, IAPS Dip
S J O Gurney, FCA
N A O Bennett, MA
W E Lawes, CA
Mrs C Godman-Law
Dr S Conway, BA, GDAD
D L Godfray, FCII
G Wedlake, Esq
A A Holmes, FCA (*Divisional Bursar*)

Bursar and Secretary to the Council: Mrs P Bulman, FCA

Head Master: **P M Tinniswood**, MA, MBA

Head Master's Deputies:

Second Master: R R Biggs, BSc, MA

Senior Master: C J Doidge, MA

Senior Mistress: Mrs H R Dugdale, MA

President of the Common Room: J L Sherrell, MA

Director of Studies: M C Buck, MA, PhD, FRCO

Director of Extra Curricular Activities: C P Foster, MA

Director of Marketing: R G F Miles, BA

Chaplain: The Revd Roger Marsh, BD, MA, AKC, CertEd

Assistant Staff:
R J Tomlinson, MA
A K Black, MA
D E Austin, BSc, PGCE
C Metcalf, DLC, Loughborough College of Education
D N Cox, MA, FRCO, FTCL, LRAM, ARCM (*Director of Music – College Chapel*)
M F Day, BSc, PhD, MIBiol
P E Lewis, Royal Manchester College of Music, ARMCM, LRAM, FTCL (*Director of Music – Music School*)
R A Wheeler, BSc, PhD, ARCS, DIC
E Fitzgerald, BSc, MPhil
Mrs M A Martindale, MA, MLitt
†D J Wilks, MA
R Bailey, Shoreditch College of Education
†A D B Arnold, MA
J L Sherrell, MA
N A Brookes, MSc
R S Tanner, MA
A P Williamson, MA
M B W Mitchell, MA, DPhil
T H Toon, BA, MBCS
M S W Palmer, BA, PhD
P Dale, BSc, MSc, MIBiol
Mrs A Stone, Dartford College of Physical Education
S W Cornford, MA, PhD
†M J H Smith, BA
†A J Betts, BA, PhD
N P Gwilliam, BEd
†M P Bentley, BEd
Mrs P McLachlan, MA
Mrs A E Tanner, BA
†S R Norris, BSc, PhD
D G Davies, BA
†Mrs C E Palmer, MA
†Mrs C E Meierdirk, BA
Mrs A W Tritton, BSc, MA
Ms J E King, BA, PhD
†Mrs H R Dugdale, MA
Miss K E Vaughan, BA
R G F Miles, BA
T D Watson, MA
Mrs E Furlong, BSc, DPhil
P C Richardson, BA, MA
Miss C M Van der Poll, BA, MPhil

Librarian: Mrs S M Gwilliam, BLS (Loughborough), ALA

Registrar: R J Tomlinson, MA

Head Master's Secretary: Mrs L M B Frean

Medical Officers:
Dr N S Lyons, MB, BS
Dr R M MacLintock, MB, BS, MRCGP, DRCOG
Dr H Bentley, MB, BS, MRCGP, DA, DRCOG

Lancing College is the first of the Schools of the Woodard Foundation.

The School stands on a spur of the Downs, overlooking the sea to the South and the Weald to the North, in grounds of some 550 acres, which include the College Farm.

The main school buildings, faced with Sussex flint, are grouped around two quadrangles on the lines of an Oxford or Cambridge College.

The great Chapel, open to visitors every day, has the largest rose window in the country.

By train, Lancing is 10 minutes from Brighton, 30 minutes from Gatwick Airport and 75 minutes from central London.

The College has extensive laboratories, a purpose-built Music School and two theatres. There are over 330 private studies for boys and girls, many of which are study bedrooms. There is a sports hall, indoor swimming pool and a miniature range. Sporting facilities also include Squash and Fives courts, climbing wall and an All-Weather surface. There is a recently-built Design and Technology Centre with computerised design and engineering facilities. A new library and information centre was opened in March 2000.

Admission. Boys and girls are normally admitted at the beginning of any term between their thirteenth and fourteenth birthdays. Admission is made on the result of either the Entrance Scholarship, the Common Entrance Examination or by private testing. A registration fee of £50 is paid when a child's name is entered in the admission register. Entries should be made with the Head Master, who will assign a House, following as far as possible the wishes of the parents. After a pupil has joined the School, parents usually correspond with the Housemaster or Housemistress directly.

Sixth Form Entry. Applications for entry should be made to the Head Master. Testing takes place in November or by private arrangement.

Houses. There are 400 pupils in the school, accommodated in eight houses: Head's (Mr A D B Arnold); Second's (Mr M P Bentley); School (Dr A J Betts); Field's (Dr S R Norris); Gibbs' (Mr M J H Smith); Teme (Mr D J Wilks), Manor (Mrs H R Dugdale); Handford (Mrs C E Palmer).

Work. The curriculum is designed as far as possible to suit every pupil's potential, and to provide the training required for entry to the Universities, and to a wide range of professions.

In a pupil's first three years the curriculum provides a broad, balanced education without premature specialisation. The total of subjects taken at GCSE is limited to about nine or ten, the object being to promote excellence in whatever is studied and to lay firm foundations for the Sixth Form years.

The following subjects are studied in the Lower School: English Language and Literature, Religious Knowledge, Mathematics, Physics, Chemistry, Biology, French, Spanish, Geography, History, Physical Education, Music, Art, Design and Technology, Latin or Classical Studies, Greek or German. Drama may be taken up in the second year

In the Sixth From there is a choice of 24 subjects which can be studied to A or AS level, together with a wide range of non-specialist courses.

A close connection has been established with schools in Germany and Spain, with which individual and group exchanges are arranged.

Tutorial System. In addition to their Housemaster or Housemistress there are a number of pastoral Tutors attached to each House, and each pupil chooses another member of staff as an academic Tutor at the end of the first year at the College. The academic Tutors main functions are to supervise academic progress and to encourage general reading and worthwhile spare time activities. A pupil keeps the same Tutor until he or she moves into the Sixth Form, where this function is taken over by an Academic Tutor chosen from one of the specialist teachers.

Music and Art form an important part of the education of all pupils. There is a School Orchestra, Chamber Orchestra, Concert Bands and a Choral Society. Organ and Choral awards to Oxford and Cambridge and Colleges of Music are frequently won.

The Art Department has two large teaching studios and a well equipped pottery. The Design and Technology Centre, adjacent to the Science School, provides for a wide range of technical and creative work. Links have been established with local industries, and pupils are involved in business experience through the 'Young Enterprise' scheme.

Other Activities. Boys and girls in their first year are given the opportunity to sample the many activities on offer at the College. A well-organised extra-curricular programme is in place, supervised by the Director of Extra-curricular Activities.

Participation in out-of-school activities is strongly encouraged. Among the School societies and institutions are Debating, Literary, Archaeological, Scientific, Dramatic, and Photographic societies. Up to twelve plays are produced each year and pupils are encouraged to write their own plays and to learn stagecraft.

In the Advent Term the main sports are Association Football for boys and Hockey for girls; in the Lent Term Football and Hockey for boys and Netball for girls. Squash, Fives, Badminton, Basketball, Cross Country and Shooting (indoor and open ranges at the College) take place during both terms for boys and girls, as does Lacrosse for senior girls. Cricket, Tennis, Sailing, Athletics, Rounders and Swimming (indoor heated pool) are played in the Summer term. There is a CCF contingent (with Army, Naval and RAF sections), and a Farming group; and the School takes part in the Duke of Edinburgh's Award Scheme. There is a flourishing Social Service group, which works in the local community and a Social Studies Course, linked with Archbishop Michael Ramsey School in Camberwell.

Careers and Higher Education. There are four careers teachers and a well equipped Careers Library. Over 90% of pupils go on to Universities, and about 15% to Oxford and Cambridge. Careers lectures and visits are arranged throughout the year, and pupils also attend work experience courses arranged by the Independent Schools Careers Organisation.

The **School Fees** which cover all obligatory extras, including medical attention, are termly payable in advance. The only other items of expense are purely optional extras, books, and charges of a strictly personal character.

Apart from the competitive awards listed below, a number of other awards are made to pupils of all round ability who have made outstanding contributions to their present school.

A scheme exists for the payment in advance of a single composition fee to cover a pupil's education during his/her time in the School. Particulars may be obtained from the Bursar.

Entrance Scholarships and Exhibitions (*see* Entrance Scholarship section)

Candidates for the following awards must be under 14 years of age on 1st September in the year of the examination. The age of the candidate is taken into account in making awards. A candidate may enter for more than one type of award, and account may be taken of musical or artistic proficiency in a candidate for a non-musical award; but no one may hold more than one type of award, except in an honorary capacity.

1. About fifteen Open Scholarships and Exhibitions ranging in value from half of the annual boarding fee to £1,000 per year. One of these Exhibitions may be awarded solely on promise in Art.

2. Three or four Music Scholarships ranging in value up to half the annual boarding fee. A number of Exhibitions are also offered to pupils in schools where the time for Music is less than in some others, and where a candidate may have less musical experience but greater potential.

One Professor W K Stanton Music Scholarship of half the boarding fee for a Chorister from Salisbury Cathedral School, or failing that any Cathedral School. A Stanton Exhibition may also be awarded.

3. Two Clergy Exhibitions of the value of £4,000 per year for children of Clergymen of the Church of England.

4. One Naval Exhibition of the value of £2,000 per year for the children of officers or ex-officers of the Royal Navy, Royal Marines, Royal Naval Reserve or Royal Naval Volunteer Reserve.

Entry Forms. For Academic and Music awards: Entry forms are obtainable from the Head Master's Secretary,

Lancing College, West Sussex, BN15 0RW. These forms must be returned to her, with a photocopy of the candidate's birth certificate.

Sixth Form Awards (Boys and Girls). Two Scholarships of the value of £2,200 per year and two Exhibitions of the value of £1,010 per year are available for new entrants to the Sixth Form with special proficiency in Academic Subjects or Music. The candidate's general ability to contribute to the life of a boarding school community will also be taken into account. A small number of Scholarships and/or Exhibitions are also available internally on the strength of GCSE results.

The value of all Entrance Scholarships and Exhibitions may be augmented up to a maximum of two-thirds of the annual fee, according to parental circumstances.

Current Fees, 2000/2001. Boarding £5,250 per term (£15,750 per annum). Day £3,925 per term (£11,775 per annum).

The Lancing Club. *Secretary:* N W R Parker, Esq., 1 New Cottages, Upper Harbledown, Canterbury, Kent CT2 9AT.

Charitable status. Lancing College is a Registered Charity, number 1076483. It exists to provide education for boys and girls.

Latymer Upper School

King Street Hammersmith London W6 9LR.
Tel: 020 8741 1851
Fax: 020 8748 5212

The Latymer Foundation owes its origin to the will of Edward Latymer, dated 1624. It is a boys' Day School of 980 pupils, of whom 360 are in the co-educational Sixth Form. There are also 140 boys in The Latymer Preparatory School which shares the same grounds. (Please see entry in Section V of this Book).

Motto: *Paulatim Ergo Certe*

Chairman of Governors: J Bullock, Esq, FCA, FCMA, FIMC

Co-opted Governors:
Mrs R Caleb-Landy
District Judge S A F Davies, LLM
I S Elliott, Esq, BA
Dr W A D Griffiths, MA, MD, MB, BChir, FRCS, MRCP
Professor A M Lucas, BSc, BEd, PhD, FIBiol, FACE
Professor R N Perham, MA, PhD, ScD, FRS
Wm C Smith, Esq, OBE, JP
B J Southcott, Esq, BSc, AIIMR, ASI
P Taylor, Esq, BSc
T A Woolley, Esq, MA
N L Woolner, Esq, DipArch, RIBA, ARAIA, FRSA
J Wotton, Esq, MA

Clerk to the Governors: S Porter, Esq

***Headmaster:* C Diggory**, BSc, MA, CMath, FIMA, FRSA (Grey College, Durham)

Deputy Headmaster: A L Hirst, MA (Fitzwilliam College, Cambridge)

Assistant Heads:
J G Jeanes, MA, DPhil, FRSA (New College, Oxford)
C I Hammond, BSc, MSc, DipSoc (Grey College, Durham)

Director of Studies: A M Leake, MA (St John's College, Cambridge)

Head of Sixth: C D Chivers, MA (King's College, Cambridge)

Head of Lower School: S P Dorrian, BA (Stirling) (Grey College, Durham; London)

Head of Upper Fifth: S D Weale, MA (Keble College, Oxford)

Head of Lower Fifth: M J Oehler, BSc (Swansea)

Head of Fourth: M B Cliff-Hodges, BA (Cardiff)

Assistant Staff:

Art & Design:
D Mumby, BA (Wolverhampton) *Head of Art & Design*
J Farrar, BA (Camberwell)
Miss P E Hart, BA (Chelsea)
M J Kerrison, BA (Northumbria)

Biology:
R Macklin, BA, MSc (Trinity College, Cambridge) *Head of Biology*
M D Barnett, MA (Trinity College, Cambridge)
G M Hardy, BSc, PhD (Cardiff; Emmanuel College, Cambridge)
N R Orton, JP, BSc, CBiol, FLS, MIBiol (London)
N T Shawcross, BSc (Bristol)
J M Shipway, BSc, CBiol, MIBiol (York)

Chemistry:
B Chaplin, BSc, PhD (Portsmouth; Reading) *Head of Chemistry*
J N Barnett, BSc, ARCS, MSc, DipEng (University College, London)
C I Hammond, BSc, MSc, DipSoc (Grey College, Durham; London) *Assistant Head*
M J Oehler, BSc (Swansea)
P S Sheldon, BSc, PhD (University College, London; Birmingham)
M J Teskey, BSc (Birmingham)

Classics:
M Lewis, BA (Durham) *Head of Classics*
M J Smith, MA (Sidney Sussex College, Cambridge)
Mrs B M Dutrieu, BA (Cardiff)
M G Holmes, BA (Bristol)

Design & Technology:
J Clark, DipTech, MA (Brunel) *Head of Design & Technology*
M P Bennett, BA (Loughborough)
E P Gratwick, BEd (Leeds)

Economics & Business Studies:
M Wallace, BSc (Birmingham) *Head of Economics & Business Studies*
C Ben Nathan, BA, MBA (Exeter; Middlesex)
A M Leake, MA (St John's College, Cambridge) *Director of Studies*
Revd P Simpson, BSc(Econ), MSc, FSS (University College & Queen Mary College, London) *Chaplain*

Computing/IT:
R A Fysh, BSc, MEd (Goldsmiths' & King's College, London) *Head of Computing & IT*
A Gabriel, BA (Kingston)

English:
Mrs P A Fryer, BA (Cardiff) *Head of English*
Mrs S M T Adams, BA, MA (Birmingham; Surrey) *Director of the Arts Centre*
C D Chivers, MA (King's College, Cambridge) *Head of Sixth*
M B Cliff-Hodges, BA (Cardiff) *Head of Fourth*
S P Dorrian, BA (Stirling) *Head of Lower School*
J Green, BA (East Anglia) *Head of Theatre Studies & Drama*
Mrs S J Markowska, BA (Westfield College, London)
B Raudnitz, BA (Bristol)

Miss S Sheringham, BA (King's College, Cambridge)
D Sweetman, BA (Birmingham)

Geography:
D M Williamson, BA, MA, FRGS (Hatfield College, Durham; York) *Head of Geography*
M Cox, BA, MA, FRGS (Plymouth; Institute of Education, London)
M V Green, BSc (London School of Economics)
A L Hirst, MA (Fitzwilliam College, Cambridge) *Deputy Head*
M D Pickering, BA, MSc, FRMetS (Manchester; Kingston) *Head of General Studies*
G J G Willis, BA (Manchester) *Head of Outdoor Education*
J A Wilson, BA (Open University; London) *Examinations Officer*

History & Political Studies:
G W L Bearman, BA (Hertford College, Oxford) *Head of History & Political Studies)*
B J Bladon, BA (King's College, London) *Head of Drama*
J P Foynes, BA, MA (King's College, London)
J S Gilbert, MA (Wadham College, Oxford)
R N Orme, MA (Gonville & Caius College, Cambridge) *Head of History of Art*
Miss M-H Quaradeghini, BA (St Hugh's College, Oxford)
S D Weale, MA (Keble College, Oxford) *Head of Upper Fifth*

Mathematics:
S Wilson, BSc (Royal Holloway College) *Head of Mathematics*
Mrs N Alishaw, BSc, MSc (Kent; Imperial College, London)
M Finnemore, BSc (Imperial College, London)
R K Harris, BSc (Sydney)
W S Macro, BSc, MSc, CMath, MIMA (Nottingham; Open)
S J Nye, BSc (Bristol)
J Payne, BSc (Auckland)
O J Rose, BSc (Queen Mary College, London)
G Sarwar, BSc (Birmingham)
Mrs A B Williams-Walker, BSc, CMath, MIMA (Exeter) *Deputy Head of Sixth*

Modern Languages:
A J Rees, BA (Swansea) *Head of Modern Languages*
Mrs S Andreyeva, BA (Leningrad)
Mrs C Amodio-Johnson (Lecce)
J Gibbons, BA, MPhil, DPhil (Exeter; Hughes Hall, Cambridge; Worcester College, Oxford)
D Gysin, BA (King's College, London)
J G Jeanes, MA, DPhil, FRSA (New College, Oxford) *Assistant Head*
Miss C A Losse, BA, MA (Edinburgh) *Head of German*
M Noble, BA (Southampton) *Head of Spanish*
Miss S Prior, BA (Newcastle)
J Russ, BA (Trevelyan College, Durham)
J Stait, BA (Reading)
S N Ware, MA, MBA (Brasenose College, Oxford; South Bank) *Head of Careers*

Music:
T Henwood, MA, ARCO (Exeter College, Oxford) *Director of Music*
P M Culling, BA (Jesus College, Cambridge)
A Goetzee, MSc, GRSM, ARCM (London)

Physical Education & Games:
A C Simmons, BA, AdDipPastC, DipPE (Open; Exeter) *Head of PE & Games*
J Coulson, BA (Chichester)
M Culverhouse, BA (Kingston)
D McLlachlan, BEd (Auckland)
F C P McMorrow, BEd (Twickenham)

Physics:
M Stenhoff, BSc, MPhil, CPhys, MInstP, FRAS, FRMetS (Royal Holloway & Bedford New College, London) *Head of Physics*
R Clark, HDEd (Durham)
M Morris, MA, MSc (Selwyn College, Cambridge; Jerusalem)
M Pearce, BSc (Brunel)
A Perry, MA, CPhys, MInstP (Fitzwilliam College, Cambridge)
J Ryan, BSc, MSc (Queen Mary College, London)
P P Thomas, BSc (Hull)

Religious Studies & Philosophy:
K Noakes, MA(Theol), MA (Corpus Christi College, Cambridge; Manchester) *Head of Religious Studies & Philosophy*
W Cooper, BA, MPhil (Pembroke College, Oxford)
Mrs C A Macro, BA (Exeter College, Oxford)
A McConville, BA (Fitzwilliam College, Cambridge)

Language Assistants:
Mlle C Horgues (Université de Pau)
Mlle M Robert (Université de Pau)
Srta M Díaz-Parra (Universidad de Sevilla)
Herr R Diesel (Technische Universität Berlin)

Visiting Music Staff:
D J Bourne, GRSM, ARCM (*Trumpet and Tuba*)
G Caldecott, GRNCM (*Piano*)
Miss C Constable, MMus, ABSM (*Cello*)
M Dickinson, BA (*Percussion*)
Mrs L Grattan, BA, ARCM (*Violin and Viola*)
Mrs P Ismay, ARCM (*Clarinet*)
P Jacobs, ARCM (*Piano*)
Miss F Jellard, BA, BMus (*Singing*)
J Lewis, AMusA, BMus (*Saxophone*)
Miss J Lively, AGSM (*Oboe*)
M Kenworthy, BA, ARCO, ALCM (*Piano and Organ*)
Miss J Martin, BMus, FLCM (*Saxophone*)
P McGowan (*Violin and Viola*)
J Martin, BMus, FLCM (*Saxophone*)
G Nash, ARCM (*Trombone*)
B O'Doherty (*Electric and Bass Guitar*)
Miss H Palmer, FTCL (*Oboe*)
C Ramirez, ARCM (*Guitar*)
Miss S Rose, GRSM, ARCM (*Piano*)
Miss J Staniforth, ALCM, LRAM (*Bassoon*)
Miss M Sugars, ABSM (*Horn*)
R Thompson-Clarke (*Cello*)
Miss A Whittlesea, LRAM (*Recorder*)

Administrative Staff:

Executive Director: Mrs S E Smith, MBE, MBA, BEd, MIPD, MIMgt, MIPR
Bursar: P C Cochlin, BA
Registrar: Mrs A Phillips
Librarian: C E Appleton, ALA
School Doctor: M Kaplan, MBBS, MRCGP, DPD, DFFP (*LRCP, MRCS*)
School Nurse: Miss C Farndell, RGN
Head Groundsman: A Beatty

Admission. This is by competitive examination and interview at 11 and 13. Past papers are published and sent to those who register. Details of Open Days and Entry are obtainable from the Registrar. Entry to the Sixth Form is based on interview and conditional offers at GCSE.

Preparatory School. Pupils move to the Upper School from The Latymer Preparatory School as a matter of course. For further details please refer to Section V of this Book.

Scholarships. A substantial number of Scholarships and Awards (Academic as well as for Music, Drama, Art and Sport) are available in addition to Bursaries. Further details are given in the Scholarships section of this Book.

Curriculum. A full range of academic subjects is offered at GCSE and AS and A2 Level. Languages include French, German, Spanish and Italian (European Work Experience and exchanges are run every year), Latin and Greek. Science is taught as separate subjects by subject specialists. Form sizes in the Lower School of around 20 and smaller teaching group sizes ensure the personal attention of staff.

Pastoral Care. The School has a strong tradition of excellent pastoral care. There are three Divisions (Lower School, Middle School, Sixth Form), each led by a Head of Division who is responsible for the pupils in that Division. Teams of Form Tutors deliver a coherent programme which promotes involvement in the community, charity work, and the personal, social and academic development of the Form.

Sixth Form. The large co-educational Sixth Form offers around thirty A Level choices; students opt to take four or five subjects at AS and three or four at A2 Level. Students have the opportunity to undertake work experience in Paris, Berlin, Madrid or New York and receive extensive Careers and Higher Education guidance. All students expect to go on to University or Art College; at least 1 in 10 go to Oxbridge each year. The Sixth Form has use of new Common Room facilities as well as a University and Careers Centre.

Music and Drama. These activities play a large part in the life of the School. There are several orchestras and bands and two major concerts each term. There are five major drama productions each year, and opportunities for all pupils to perform in Gild events. Some orchestral and drama productions are run jointly with The Godolphin and Latymer School. The recently opened Arts Centre houses a new Music School and a 300 seat Theatre in addition to increased facilities for Art.

Sport. There are excellent facilities for Sport. The School has a Boat House on site with direct river access, as well as a large sports hall, squash court and an indoor swimming pool in the grounds. There are playing fields at Wood Lane, near the BBC, and at Whitton. The emphasis is on involvement, participation and choice. School teams enjoy great success in the major sports of rugby, soccer, rowing, cricket and athletics. Other sports such as fencing, swimming and golf cater for individual interests. The School maintains excellent fixture lists for all major sports.

Extra Curricular Activities. There is a wide range of clubs and societies at lunch time and after school. In addition every pupil has the opportunity to have residential experience and to take part in outdoor pursuits as part of the annual School Activities Week. A very active Parents' Gild ensures that nobody is excluded from an activity for financial reasons. The Duke of Edinburgh Award Scheme flourishes in the School with pupils achieving the Gold Award each year.

Charitable status. The Latymer Foundation is a Registered Charity, number 312714. It exists to provide education for children.

* Head of Department	§ Part Time or Visiting
† Housemaster/Housemistress	¶ Old Pupil
‡ See below list of staff for meaning	

Leeds Grammar School

Alwoodley Gates Harrogate Road Leeds LS17 8GS
Tel: (0113) 229 1552
Fax: (0113) 228 5111
e-mail: info@lgs.leeds.co.uk
internet: http://lgs.leeds.sch.uk

Leeds Grammar School continues a 450 year tradition of helping boys achieve their potential from its modern, specially designed site in north Leeds. Consistently ranked as one of the independent boys' schools, it aims to develop boys' confidence, life skills and academic ability.

The School is an independent day school, represented on the Headmasters' Conference and on the Governing Bodies Association. There are approximately 1,000 in the Senior School and 320 in the Junior School.

Motto: *Nullius non mater disciplinae.*

Governors:
Chairman: P N Sparling, LLB
Vice-Chairman: D P A Gravells, JP, MBA, BA

A Barker, OBE, FCA	J Parkinson, BA
Lord Bellwin, LLB, JP	Prof M Losowsky, MD, FRCP
P Chadwick	Prof P A Dowd, BSc, MSc, PhD, CEng
E E Bailey, BChD, LDS, RCS, DOrthRCS	Prof D A Sugden, BSc, MSc, PhD
P Chadwick	E Ziff
A Duckworth	
P Hartridge, FRICS	

Clerk to the Foundation: W M Wrigley, MA

Teaching Staff:

***Headmaster:* Mark Bailey**, BA (Dunelm), PhD (Cantab), FRHistS

Deputy Headmaster: Peter Jolly, BSc

Director of Studies: Eric R Medway, BSc

Director of Operations: Steve Field, BA, CertPE

Head of Sixth Form: Terry J Elsworth, BA
Head of Upper School: Paul R Lunn, BSc
Head of Middle School: Christopher Freeman, MA
Head of Lower School: Geoffrey Thompson, BA
Head of Junior School: John G Davies, BA, DipRE

Heads of Department:

Art, Design and Technology: Ian Setterington, BEd
Biology: Mark Smith, BSc
Careers: David C Bartlett, BSc, PhD, DMS
Science and Chemistry: Ian J Hotchkiss, BSc, PhD, CChem, MRSC
Classics: David Pritchard, BA
Computer Studies: Clive S Fraser, MA
Economic Studies: Christopher J Law, BA
English: Steven W Alderson, BA
French: Deborah England, BA
Geography: Anthony C Wightman, BSc
German: Duncan Moynihan, MA
Historical Studies: Michael J Dickenson, BA, PhD
Mathematics: R Jeffrey Jones, MA, PhD
Music: Andrew Wheeler, GRSM, LRAM, MTC
Physics: Philip J Britton, BA
Physical Education: P Morris, BEd
Religious Studies: Helen Stiles, BA

Senior Housemaster: John Barclay, BA

Housemasters:

Nigel P Day, MA
Kenneth W Depledge, BSc, DipManSt

Martin Knowles, BA
Richard Jackson, MA
Laura Gray, BA
Geraldine Newlyn, BSc
Peter M Spivey, BA
Jonathan D Taylor, BSc

Junior School Housemasters:

Michael Melia, BEd
Mark Heil, BEd
Judy Moynihan, BA

Status. The School reverted to its original Independent status in 1976.

Fees. The present fees are £6,204 a year for the Senior School and £5,214 a year for the Junior School from 5+, and £3,498 a year for Reception (4+).

Facilities. Leeds Grammar School occupies a modern, purpose-built site whose facilities are unrivalled anywhere in the country. The include:

- Specialist suites of teaching rooms for all subjects with the necessary support systems for each faculty.
- Centres for each section of the School, with generous common rooms, locker and cloakroom areas.
- A large assembly hall, capable of accommodating the whole school to reinforce the sense of community.
- A Junior School, having its own identity, its own specialist resources and operating an independent time-table.
- A versatile chaplaincy centre.
- A library incorporating multi-media facilities.
- A dedicated art, design and technology unit.
- A fully resourced music school.
- Extensive playing fields with changing facilities and hospitality areas.
- A large multi-purpose sports complex, including a swimming pool of competition standard.
- Large play and recreation areas for each section of the School.
- Provision for a wide variety of indoor and outdoor extra-curricular pursuits.
- Conservation areas.

Religion. The School has a Chaplain and its own Chaplaincy centre which serves as a focus for worship and pastoral care. Although an Anglican foundation, the School welcomes boys of all faiths and separate meetings are held for Jewish boys, Muslim boys, Hindu boys and Sikh boys.

Entrance Procedure. The entrance procedure takes place in the Lent term for entry the following September and is based upon an examination, an interview and school report. Very young boys are assessed through a series of observed activities. The usual points of entry are 4+ for Reception, 7+ and 8+ for Junior School, 10+, 11+ and 13+ for Senior School. Entry to the sixth form is based upon the attainment of good GCSE grades. New applications are accepted at any time for any age. Details of the entrance procedure together with copies of past papers are available from the Headmaster's secretary.

Awards. Foundation Scholarships are awarded at the 11+ entry and the school is one of a selected number participating in the Ogden Trust Bursary Scheme through which four full fee places are available each year.

Pastoral Care. Junior school boys progress to Senior School, in most cases automatically. Boys entering at 10 or 11 join the Foundation Year or first form which comprises the Lower School section. The Second and Third Forms create the Middle School, and the Fourths and Fifths the Upper School. Heads of Section are responsible for the progress of the boys in their part of the school, and give guidance and advice where necessary. The Form Tutor is directly responsible for the progress of every boy in his or her care.

The School is divided into Houses, three in the Junior School and eight in the Senior School. Each house is under the charge of a Housemaster, assisted by House Tutors. Form Tutors, Housemasters and Heads of Section work closely with the Headmaster and Parents to ensure the well-being of every boy.

Curriculum. In the Junior School boys concentrate upon the core subjects of English, Mathematics and Science. History, Geography, French, Religious Studies, Music, Art and Technology are also taught.

The Foundation Year (Year 6) acts as a transition year preparatory to a five year course beginning in the First Form (Year 7) and leading to the GCSE. Boys follow a broad curriculum, including two foreign languages in Years 7–9.

At the end of the Fifth Form year boys are presented for the GCSE examination.

There are approximately 250 boys in the Sixth Form, where all students study 5 AS levels and 3 A2 levels. It is possible to combine Arts and Science subjects. A General Studies course is offered to all students and most then choose to sit for A Level General Studies. All students also carry out a Community Service assignment.

Games. Rugby Football, Cricket, Athletics, Swimming, Tennis, Basketball, Badminton, Cross-Country, Volleyball, Squash, and Soccer. There is a running track, a swimming pool and a sports centre, including squash courts.

Other Activities. The School's many clubs and societies give boys opportunities for a wide range of out-of-school activities from Mountaineering and Skiing to Choral Singing and Drama. There are regular tours and visits abroad and there are long-established exchanges with French and German schools.

The School has an extensive Arts Programme which covers music, drama, debating and creative art and includes visiting groups with National reputation as well as the students' own contributions.

The School provides a contingent of the CCF (Army & RAF sections), and has a Scout Troop, with Cub Pack and Venture Scout Unit. The School participates in the Duke of Edinburgh Award Scheme.

Scholarships from the School. There are Bursaries available to help boys in the school to undertake projects at home and abroad of a broadly educational nature. Music Bursaries are also awarded.

Old Leodiensian Association. *Hon Secretary:* R S J Tovey, 29 Fastville Terrace, Harrogate, North Yorkshire HG1 3HJ. (Tel: 01423 528300).

Charitable status. Leeds Grammar School is a Registered Charity, number 1048304. It aims to provide the highest quality of education for boys in the Leeds area.

Leicester Grammar School

8 Peacock Lane Leicester LE1 5PX
Tel: (0116) 222 0400
Fax: (0116) 222 0510

Leicester Grammar School was founded in 1981 as an independent, selective, co-educational day school to offer able children in the city and county a first-class academic education. Its founders sought to create a school which would maintain the standards and traditions of the city's former grammar schools lost through reorganisation and develop them to meet the demands of a rapidly changing environment.

Governors:

I D Patterson, LLB (*Chairman*)

C J Castleman (*Vice-Chairman*)
G G Bodiwala, MBBS, MS, FICS, FICA
The Hon Mrs A Brooks
Mrs C Caswell
The Very Revd V F Faull, BA
B Groves
K Julian, MA
Dr D Khoosal, MB, BCh, LLM(RCS), LLM(RCP), FRCPsych
Mrs J Middleton
D V M Mitchell
P L Rose, BA, FCA
Prof J Saker, BSc, MSc
Ms S Shaen-Carter
H C T Staunton
The Rt Revd T Stevens, MA
Prof B H Swanick, BEng, PhD, CEng, FIEE
Prof H Thomason, MSc, PhD, DLC

Bursar and Clerk to the Governors: J R Cox, BSc(Econ)

***Head Master:* J B Sugden**, MA (St Catharine's College, Cambridge), MPhil, FRSA

Deputy Heads:
T R Cawston, BSc
Mrs M Maunder, BA

Head Master, Junior School: H H McFaul, BA, MA

Assistant staff:

T P Allen, BA (*Head of Sixth Form*)
A Baker-Munton, MA, MIL
A R Baxter, MA
R Berry, MA
*J C Christie, BSc
F W Clayton, BA
*Mrs C Crammond, BA
*Dr D M Crawford, BA, DPhil
Mrs A J Davies, BA
†P De May, BA
Mrs S Downs, BEd, CNAA
*A N Duffield, BSc
P Fairclough, BA
Mrs K Farquhar, BA
Dr C W Fearon, BSc, PhD
*D W Gee, City & Guilds Teach Cert, CertEd
R J L Geldard, BA, MA
Mrs B Gott
*M J Gower, BA
M J Gray, BA
*Mrs A L Griffin, BA
†J M Griffin, BA
Mrs H A Griffiths, GNSM
P M Handford, MA
*Mrs B A Harper, BA
*A H J Harrop, MA
Mrs W E Harvey, BA
Dr A Higginson
*C W Howe, BEd, CNAA
Mrs J A Hughes, BA
*P A Kaye, BEng
*R W S Kidd, BA, MA
J Liley
*R I Longson, BA
D M Lupton, BA
*D W Maddock, BA, MA
Miss J Mould, BEd
Mrs E C Nisbet, BEd
Mrs M P Northcott, BA
N Murray, BSc, MA, MSc
C D Paterson, MA
†Miss A M Patterson, BSc
L Potter (*Head of Lower School*)
Mrs A Price, BSc (*Staff Development Co-ordinator*)
Miss K Rayers
*J G Robinson, BA
*D E A Roebuck, BSc, FRSA, CChem, MRSC
Mrs S J Sains, MA
Mrs S L Shales, BSc
B H Shaw, GRSM, ARCM, LRAM (*Head of Instrumental Studies, External Relations Co-ordinator*)
Mrs M Sian, BA
T A Thacker, BEd, CNAA
J S Thomason, BSc (*Assessment Co-ordinator*)
Ms R Thompson, MA (*Head of Middle School*)
Mrs B Wallwork
*Dr D M T Whittle, BMus, PhD (*Director of Music*)
Miss A L Williamson
†D R Willis, BSc
*Mrs C M Young, BA

Visiting music staff:
Miss I Adams
P Adams
N Bullock
J Cherry, DRSAMD, DipRAM, LRAM
N Davis
A de Graeve, BA
K L Hall, GRSM, LRAM, LTCL
Mrs G P Hawkes, BA, LTCL
C Jeans, LRAM
Mrs J Lord, LRAM
Miss S Norris, BA
P J Nuttall, BA
Miss G E Print, BA
K Rubach, ARCM

There are 696 day pupils in the School (296 girls, 400 boys), of whom 162 are in the Sixth Form. A further 250 pupils, aged 3–11, attend the Leicester Grammar Junior School at Evington Hall.

Admission. An entrance examination is held in the Lent Term for boys and girls seeking to enter the Preparatory (10+) and First (11+) forms in the following September. Papers are taken in verbal reasoning, English and Mathematics. Applications from able under-age candidates are also considered. In addition admission into the Third and Fourth Forms takes place at ages 13 and 14 and there is provision for direct entry into the Sixth Form, offers of a place being conditional upon the GCSE grades gained.

Scholarships. (*see* Entrance Scholarship section) Academic, music, art and sports scholarships are offered to the outstanding candidates on examination and the School has some funds available for bursaries. It has always been the policy of governors to try to ensure that children capable of benefiting from education at the School should not be prevented by financial considerations from entry. Registration forms are obtainable from the School Secretary.

Class sizes are about 22 to 24 in the first three years; the average size of a GCSE group is 19, of a Sixth Form group 10.

Curriculum. All pupils in the first three years (and those entering the preparatory form) follow a balanced curriculum covering the National Curriculum core and foundation subjects, religious studies and Latin (Classical Studies in the preparatory form). Classes are split into smaller groups for the creative and technological subjects, so that all pupils can gain practical experience, whether on the School's microprocessors or on its extensive range of musical instruments. From the second year the three science subjects, biology, chemistry and physics, are taught separately. There is no streaming and setting occurs only for mathematics and French. In the Third Year an element of choice is introduced and pupils must opt from a choice of third languages and from a list of five creative subjects.

In years 4 and 5 pupils prepare for GCSE examinations

in ten subjects, as well as doing PE/games. All study a 'core' of seven subjects, English Language and Literature, Mathematics, RE, a modern foreign language and at least two sciences. The range of 'options' includes Art, Biology, Chemistry, Classical Civilisation, Design and Technology, Drama, French, Geography, German, Greek, History, Latin, Music, Physics, Spanish and PE.

Students in the Sixth Form study 4 A/S levels leading to 3 or more A levels from a choice of 19 subjects, including further mathematics, economics, physical education and theatre studies. There is no rigid division between arts and science sides. To ensure that breadth of education does not suffer, a broadly based cultural general studies course leads on to A level General Studies. The school has an excellent record of success at public examinations and university admissions. The Careers Department is very active in giving help and advice to students.

School activities. A broad range and variety of activities complements the academic curriculum. Participation rates are high.

Music, drama and sport form an integral part of life at LGS. Every pupil in the First Year learns a musical instrument and a high proportion continue afterwards with private weekly lessons. The School Orchestra gives two major concerts a year, whilst a training orchestra, a jazz band, a dance band, recorder groups and various chamber ensembles explore other avenues. The School Choir is the resident choir for the Crown Court Services and tours regularly. Links are strong with the Leicestershire School of Music orchestras and several pupils play in national orchestras. Senior and junior drama clubs function throughout the year, a major play or musical and a junior play are staged regularly and house drama extends the opportunity to act to most pupils.

Games are seen as an important means not only of promoting health and fitness but also of inspiring self-confidence. Major games are in Winter hockey, netball and rugby and in Summer athletics, cricket and tennis. Opportunities occur for individuals to follow their interest in badminton, basketball, squash, golf, table tennis, gymnastics, dance, sailing and cross-country running whilst swimming is an integral part of the PE programme. The School's own facilities being limited, it is fortunate in being able to use first-rate local and university facilities; teams represent the School in the main games at all age groups and several students achieve recognition at county or even national level.

Societies and clubs complement these activities, ranging from chess to the Duke of Edinburgh award scheme, history and Lit Soc to model aeroplanes, debating to art, design and technology, for which the workshop and art rooms are usually open during lunchtimes and after school.

The school espouses the principles of the Church of England, teaching the Christian faith, its values and standards of personal conduct, but also prides itself on welcoming children of all faiths, who play a full part in the life of the community. Very strong links exist with Leicester Cathedral, where major services and daily assembly are held. There is a flourishing Guild of Servers and cathedral clergy participate in school life and prepare confirmation candidates.

Responsibility for a wide-ranging system of pastoral care and for the creation of the caring, friendly and disciplined environment, resides in three Heads of School, assisted by form teachers, personal tutors and a very active house system.

Junior School. Entry to the Junior School is by interview and, where appropriate, examination, at 3+, 4+, 7+ and into other school years, when places are available. Pupils are prepared for entry to the Senior School. A balanced curriculum is followed covering National Curriculum Key Stages 1 and 2 and beyond; French (from 5 years), classical studies and ICT are also taught. A wide range of activities complements the academic curriculum, with a strong stress on music and a rapidly growing games programme. The School is a Christian foundation and lays great emphasis upon the pastoral care of young children.

School fees. The fees for 2001/2002 are £1,995 per term for the main school and £1,440 for the Junior School.

Old Leicestrians Association. All correspondence to the Secretary, Richard Longson, at the School.

Charitable status. Leicester Grammar School Trust is a Registered Charity, number 510809. Its aims and objectives are to promote and provide for the advancement of education and in connection therewith to conduct, carry on, acquire and develop in the United Kingdom or elsewhere a School or Schools to be run according to the principles of the Church of England for the education of students and children of either sex or both sexes.

Leighton Park School

Reading Berkshire RG2 7ED.
Tel: 0118-987 9600
Fax: 0118-987 9625

Leighton Park was founded in 1890 with the values of the Religious Society of Friends (Quakers), which appoints 12 of the Governors. The School estate of 60 acres lies on the southern edge of Reading. Reading University is adjacent in Whiteknights Park.

Governors:
Robert J Maxwell (*Chairman*)
Philip M Adler
K Mary Armstrong
Michael D Biddiss
Nigel K Chambers
John E Crosfield
Desmond Harris
Julian P H Harrison
Michael J Hatch
Annette Haworth
John P Hayes
Gillian E Hopkins
Elizabeth F C Whitehouse

Head: **John H Dunston**, MA (Cantab), AIL, FRSA

Deputy Head: Linda Macfarlane, BA (Hons) (East Anglia), MA (King's College, London)

Senior Master: John N Allinson, BA (Liverpool)

Director of Studies: Richard Coupe, MA (University of Wales)

Bursar: Paul Motte, FInstAM, MIMgt

†Roger Aylward, BSc (*Fryer House*)
Nicholas W Bayley, MA (Cantab), DipCouns
Irene Bell, MA (Cantab)
Tony Biggin, BMus, PhD
Zenon Bowrey, BA
Ruth Carter, BSc, MA
Catherine Cremieu-Alcan
Steven Dawson, BA
Baljit Dhadda, BA, MA
Paul Dowdell, BEd, MA
Ann Farmer
†Stephen Field, BA (*Grove House*)
Ulrike Field
†Tim Fulford, MA, BTech (HonsEd), AdDipTech (*School House*)
Sharon George, MSc, PhD
Karen Gracie-Langrick, MA

Richard Griffiths, BSc
Ruth Hamborg, BSc
Geoffrey D Harnett, MA (Cantab)
Thomas D Harrison, BSc
E Brian Hoskins, BSc
Keiko Ikeshiro, BA, MA
Isabelle Impéras-Berrow, BA
Jane Ireland, BA
Bruce Kirk, BA
Richard Lade, BSc
Ann Line, BA
Ray Lovegrove, BA
Ken Lovesy, MA
Jakki Marr, BEd
Ann Munday, BSc
Isabelle Munro
Susan Peel, BSc
Peter A Rado, MA (Cantab)
Claire Reeves, BSc
Alison Reynolds, BA
†Elaine Rimmer, BA, ATC (*Reckitt House*)
Karin Silver, BSc, TEFL
Winsome Simmonds, BA, DipSpecEd
Mark L Simmons, BEd, CertEd
Graham Smith, BA
Christine Smyth, BSc, MSc
Juliet L Straw, BA
Robert Tomlinson, BEd
Nikki Walia, BTech
Nicola Williams, BEd
†Nigel Williams, BA, MA (*Field House*)
Françoise Wilson, BA
Sue Wright, BA
Uta Yardley, BA

Medical Officers:
Dr David Clayton
Dr Deborah Milligan

Librarian: Margaret Coleman, BA, CertEd, CSLS

The School is fully co-educational. Of the 370 pupils, 120 are in the Sixth Form, all of them on 3 or 4 A-level courses. 300 are boys and girls aged 13–18. There are 115 full boarders, 65 weekly boarders, and 190 day-boarders.

Fryer Junior House receives boys and girls aged 11-13, both boarding and day. Fryer numbers are about 70.

Facilities. The School is well laid out, with a large number of separate buildings within the very fine Park. The main classrooms, including the ICT Centre in Old School, are complemented by a Science and Technology Centre, Humanities Centre, Language Block, a Fine Arts Centre, Swimming Pool, Gymnasium and Multi-Gym, Library and Study Centre, and by the distinctive Hall and Music School, which forms the heart of the School's religious and cultural life. A new Drama Studio opened in September 1999.

The Houses are separate buildings. All Sixth formers have studies or study-bedrooms, and all meals are taken in Houses. Housemasters/Housemistresses and their families live in, as well as the House Tutors. The School has a high standard of modern boarding accommodation.

Educational Approach. Leighton Park's religious, social and educational principles reflect a Quaker perception of the best traditions of English education. Through experience of many kinds of excellence, individuals are helped both to discover their own talents and to delight in those of their peers. Within a community free of undue pressures they can become at ease with themselves and others.

The School's framework of good order and responsible behaviour allows the development of that self-discipline which is sensitive to other people's interests. About 10% of the pupils come from Quaker homes. Most denominations are represented among the others. Practical service to the surrounding community is looked on as an important side of education, though it is always voluntary.

All pupils study French and/or German, and have the opportunity to study Latin. Pupils study for nine or ten GCSE subjects. English, Mathematics, a modern foreign language and a Science are core subjects and at least four more optional subjects are selected. All Sixth Form students now study 4 AS levels and then 3 A2 levels in many combinations. About 40% choose a mixture of Arts and Sciences, and over 50% choose Mathematics. The broad General Studies programme complements the Key Skills courses.

Virtually all Sixth Form leavers go on to degree courses, including Oxford and Cambridge. Academic results are excellent.

Academic Structure. Two form entry to Year 7, with at least one additional form joining in Year 9. There is no general streaming in the School, though pupils are setted for mathematics and languages. The VIth Forms are divided into small tutorial groups for specialist subjects, and re-divided into mixed groups for non-specialist subjects.

Leisure Time Occupations. Great stress is laid on education for the right use of leisure time. Hobbies available might include Art, Technology, Painting and other Arts, Pottery, Printing, Canoe-building, etc. Private tuition is available in Singing, Piano and most Orchestral Instruments and most pupils learn at least one instrument. Choral and Orchestral performances are frequent. Drama too is an important activity. Recent productions have included "The Threepenny Opera", "The Duchess of Malfi", "Oliver", "Cabaret", "The Turn of the Screw" and "Bugsy Malone". The School Societies and Clubs reflect other interests such as Chess, Computing, Debating, Electronics, Film, Literary, Natural History, Wildlife and Photography.

Games and Outdoor Pursuits. Games has a balanced place in the overall curriculum. Physical education based on the Gymnasium and Multi-Gym is taught throughout the school. Since almost everyone develops confidence through discovering some physical activity in which to do well, variety is encouraged.

In their first 2 years boys and girls are given training in a wide range of skills. Each learns Swimming and Life-Saving, gains some experience of Canoeing and Sailing, and has a weekend camping and walking. Coaching and practice are given in most games during the course of a year.

Thereafter a pupil may, according to season and availability, choose between Athletics, Basketball, Badminton, Canoeing, Cricket, Cross-Country, Football, Hockey, Rugby Football, Sailing, Squash, Swimming and Tennis, with other possibilities always considered. Girls play Hockey, Netball, Rounders, Tennis and Swimming. Canoeing is a sport in which the School has won considerable distinction including many major trophies. Recent tours have taken hockey, rugby and cricket teams to Hong Kong and Ireland, and, most recently, South Africa. The addition of floodlighting to the astroturf pitch is a recent development. The pitch itself offers full and half size hockey pitches and several tennis courts.

Careers. Advice on careers is available to everyone. A specially furnished Careers Room provides up-to-date information. The Careers staff have extensive knowledge of commerce and industry as well as of the professions. Full use is made of the local Advisory Service and the School is a member of the Independent Schools Careers Organisation and of the Careers Research and Advisory Centre.

Admission. Open mornings for prospective parents and pupils are held almost every week during term time. Visitors always have the opportunity for personal conversation with the Head or Deputy and take a full tour of the school with a present pupil.

Registration may be made at any time. All those who have been registered come to the Park for their interview and entrance test. At the same time their headteachers report on their school work and progress to date. A firm offer of a place may then be made, subject to normal school progress. Other candidates may be transferred to the waiting list for consideration at a later date if a place becomes available. Admission is possible at the age of eleven plus or thirteen plus, or after, if need arises.

Prospective Sixth-formers visit at any time during GCSE courses, and if registered are interviewed and tested. Reference is also made to the head of the student's present school. Those offered Sixth Form places will be confidently expected to achieve at least five GCSE passes at Grade B or above.

Terms of Entry. Pupils are expected to begin their course in the September term. It is only possible to admit pupils at other times in the school year when a particular vacancy arises.

Fees. From September 2001 the following fees will apply: £4,485 (full boarders); £4,035 (weekly boarders); £3,138 (day). Fryer: (age 11–13) £3,813 per term (full boarders), £3,432 per term (weekly boarders), £2,670 per term (day).

Scholarships. (*see* Entrance Scholarship section) Major Awards have a value of 25% of day fees and may be increased to 75% according to family circumstances. They may be awarded for academic achievement or for special talent in Art or Music. There are also minor awards of 15% with additions dependent on family circumstances. Sixth Form Scholarships are available. Exhibitions are also available. Many other pupils also benefit from some form of bursary assistance.

Generous Travel Scholarships are awarded annually to leavers (and exceptionally to others) for adventurous foreign travel.

Old Leightonians. *Secretary:* Philip Gillmor

The Leighton Park Society. *Secretary:* Annabel Leventon.

Parents' Committee. Secretary: Pauline Snyder.

Charitable status. The Leighton Park Trust is a Registered Charity, number 309144. It exists to provide education for young people.

The Leys School

Cambridge CB2 2AD.
Tel: 01223 508900

The Leys is situated less than half a mile from the centre of the university city of Cambridge, close to the River Cam and Grantchester Meadows. The School was founded in 1875 on the initiative of a group of leading Methodists to provide a liberal Christian education, establishing a tradition which has continued unbroken to this day. The School was incorporated as a Charitable Trust in 1878. All the buildings are grouped around the playing field and lie within the estate originally acquired for the purpose; there is a second extensive playing field nearby.

The Leys is a friendly, caring and happy community, large enough to offer many opportunities, but not so large as to lose sight of the individual. The School is fully co-educational; of a total of over 500 pupils, nearly 200 are in the Sixth Form. Girls and boys are accommodated in separate houses. 60% of the pupils are boarders; the remainder, whether home boarders or day pupils, sleep at home but otherwise are able to enjoy all the opportunities of boarding school life.

Motto: *In Fide Fiducia.*

Governors:

Chairman: Lord Lewis, FRS, FRSC

N J M Abbott, MA
¶M A Bishop, MA
J R G Bradfield, CBE, MA, PhD
J Bruce-Ball
J D Callin, FRICS, FRVA
Mrs C Crawford, BA
The Revd R Crewes, MA, BD
Sir Terence English, KBE, BSc, MB, BS, FRCS, MRCP
¶C R Fairey
¶J Hardy, MA, FRICS
¶R B Haryott, BSc, CEng, FICE
G C Houghton, MA
Mrs J Hoy
C M P Johnson, MA, PhD
Rev Ivor H Jones, MA, MLitt, PhD, FRCO
M R Leigh, BA, DipEd
E G Moelwyn-Hughes, MA
¶T N Page, FCA
D Robson, MA
G Smallbone, MA
R D H Walker, PhD
¶P G Watson, MA, MB, BChir, FRCS, DO
Rev K B Wilson, MA, MLitt, PhD
Mrs M Wiseman, BA
The President and Ex-President of the Old Leysian Union.

***Headmaster:* Rev Dr J C A Barrett**, MA

Deputy Headmaster: A W Jessop, MA, PhD

Assistant Teachers:
S H Siddall, MA
J C Harding, MA
J H Aylmer, MA
A S MacGregor, BSc
H A Slatter, MA
A S Erby, BSc
Mrs J W Harding, BA
M A Brown, BSc
P White, BEd
¶E M W George, BEd
Mrs D Morris, MA, MSc, PhD, CMath, FIMA
R Adamson, BSc, PhD
J C Supper, BA
Mrs C M Jackson, BSc, PhD
R A D Hill, BA
D J Nye, BSc
P A Mathieu, BA
Mrs M H O'Keeffe, LLB, ALA
Mrs P B Davis, BA
Mrs S Schilperoort, BSc, MA
M A Waldron, MA
Mrs C E Wiedermann, MA
Mrs P J Jessop, BEd
C I A Fraser, MA
Mrs A P Muston, BEd
Miss C Perri, BA, MA
Mrs E C Butt, BA
W J Earl, BSc
Mrs R E Hill, BA
R H G Jackson, BA
S C Mower, BA
A H Ronn, MA
J M J Deveson, BMus, MMus
G K Howe, BSc, MSc
N M Kelly, BA
L J D Kennedy, BA, PhD
R Silk, BA
Mrs C M Mower, LCE
Revd C J Meharry, BEd
D K Fernandes, BSc
A P Harmsworth, MA
A López, MA
A J Leang, MA, ARCO
Miss C L Sugden, BA, PhD
Miss J Upton, BSc
N G Hawkins, MA
D Bell, MA
S H Dorman, BA, MPhil
A Z Lonnen, BSc
G J Deudney
J M Gibbon
Miss L J McCreath
A L Mutch
Miss A Stern
Miss J Dwyer, BA
Miss K J Rutledge, BSc
I Silk, BA
Miss K Webster, BA
§Mrs J S Fairey, MA
§Mrs C J Illman
§Mrs P C A Taylor, BA
§Mrs S Lambton, BSc
Mrs L H Bernal
Mrs S E Bichener
Miss A Freisenbruch
Miss R L Harvey
Mrs J McPherson
R van de Weyer

Housemasters:
School House: M A Waldron
West House: P A Mathieu

North A House: C I A Fraser
North B House: M A Brown
East House: R A Adamson

Housemistresses:
Granta House: Mrs M H O'Keeffe
Dale House: Mrs D Morris
Fen House: Mrs S Schilperoort

Director of Studies: N G Hawkins

Careers Adviser: Mrs P B Davis

Bursar: E P Magill, CEng, MIMechE

Director of Marketing: J C Supper

Registrar: A S MacGregor

Higher Education Co-ordinator: J C Harding

Chaplain: Revd C J Meharry

Medical Officer: A J Stewart, MB, BCh

Nursing Staff: Sister G Woolley, RN; Sister M A Williams, SRN, SCM; Sister S Smith, RN

Sports Hall Supervisor: C Sneddon

Headmaster's Secretary: Mrs S M Inskipp

Admissions Secretary: Mrs I G S Fenwick, BA

Academic Secretary: Mrs A Page

Administrative Secretary: Mrs K E Potter

Bursar's Secretary: Miss M Buck

There is a continuing development programme involving all areas of the School. Pride of place among the buildings must go to the award winning Design Centre, which contains workshops (metal, plastic and wood), Art School, Ceramics Studio, Electronics Workshop, Computer Centre, School Press, together with facilities for Design, Photography, Cookery and an Exhibition Centre. A Sports Hall and all-weather pitch were completed in 1995 and there are new library facilities.

Other major buildings include the Theatre and Music School, the Science Building and the Queen's Building, comprising classrooms and a drama studio used for both teaching and performances. There are 40 acres of playing fields, an indoor heated swimming pool open all the year, a boat house on the Cam, and synthetic grass tennis courts. The boarding houses have recently been extensively refurbished, and a new wing added to one of the girls' houses.

Admission. Admission for girls and boys is at 11, 12, 13 (main admission), 14 and 16. Registration may be made at any time beforehand. Entrance tests and Scholarship Examinations for 11+ and 13+ entry are held in the February prior to entry. Places in the Sixth Form are available for both girls and boys who have successfully completed their GCSE or equivalent courses elsewhere. Application for admission should be made to the Registrar in the first instance.

Scholarships. (*see* Entrance Scholarship section) Academic Scholarships are available for entry at 11, 13 and for entry to the Sixth Form at 16. Scholarships are also available for entry at 13 in Music, Art, Design Technology, Sport, Drama and All Rounder, and for entry to the Sixth Form at 16 in Music, Art, Sport and Drama. The Scholarship Examinations at 11 and 13 take place in the Spring Term and the Sixth Form Scholarship takes place in the November of the year prior to entry. All Awards range in value up to 50% of the fees payable. The School also participates in the Arkwright Scholarship Scheme, which is an external examination offering Scholarships for those wishing to take Design and Technology in the Sixth Form and who are aiming to read Engineering, Technology or other Design-related subjects in Higher Education. Further particulars may be obtained from the Registrar.

Curriculum. The academic curriculum broadly conforms to the National Curriculum but is not restricted by it. Each pupil has an Academic tutor who, in conjunction with the Director of Studies and the pupil's Housemaster or Housemistress, works to tailor the pupil's programme to suit the needs of the individual wherever possible. Pupils follow a broad programme in the first three years (years 7, 8 nd 9). At the end of Year 9 they choose three from a wide range of GCSE options to add to the basic core of English, Mathematics, Science and a Modern Foreign Language. The GCSE examinations are normally taken at the end of Year 11. Throughout the first five years (to GCSE) pupils are setted by ability for the core subjects. Religious Education and Physical Education are taught throughout the School.

In the Sixth Form, a similar option scheme operates. Pupils choosing from a total of 21 subjects to take normally 4 AS levels in the LVI and 3 at A2 in the following year.

There is a considerable flexibility of combination possible at both levels, and choices are made after consultation between parents, tutors, careers staff and subject teachers.

About 95% of the "A" level candidates proceed to degree courses. A Reading Party for potential Oxford and Cambridge candidates is held during the summer half-term, with distinguished university lecturers, academic tuition and evening concerts or discussions.

Personal and Social Education forms an integral part of the curriculum at all levels. In the Sixth Form a General Studies programme includes a wide variety of courses covering music, drama, architecture, philosophy and communication skills, supplemented by a three day media festival.

The Chapel. The School Chapel is at the heart of the community in every sense. From the time of its Methodist foundation The Leys has been firmly based on non-sectarian Christian principles. It welcomes boys and girls of all denominations and religions, encouraging them to see the relevance of a personal faith of their own. Religious Education forms part of the curriculum. Preparation is also given for Church membership, and a combined confirmation service is held.

Physical Education. The physical education/games programme aims at introducing a wide variety of physical activities. Sports available are Rugby, Hockey, Cricket, Dance, Tennis, Athletics, Netball, Badminton, Basketball, Fives, Gymnastics, Golf, Rowing, Sailing, Karate, Shooting, Clay-pigeon Shooting, Squash, Swimming, Volleyball, Water Polo. Outdoor activities such as Camping, Orienteering, Canoeing, and Climbing are also encouraged through CCF and the Duke of Edinburgh's Award. PE is offered at GCSE and A level. The School has close links with many Cambridge University Sports Clubs, with the Sixth Form competing in University Leagues.

Careers. In the Lower School, careers guidance is provided by Housemasters/mistresses and Academic Tutors, with the support of the members of the Careers Department. Information is easily accessible from the Careers library. In the Lower Sixth, the Careers Department interviews each pupil individually, and encourages them to take advantage of work shadowing and careers courses. Work experience may also be arranged on an individual basis. An annual Careers Forum is organised in the Lent Term of the Lower Sixth. Advice on applications for Higher Education is provided by the Higher Education Co-ordinator with support from academic tutors.

Societies. All are encouraged to participate in out-of-school activities of their choice. These range from Literary, Philosophical, Scientific, Mathematical, Languages, Debating, Music and Drama societies to any of the activities available in the Design Centre, which are available after

School and at weekends. The life of the School is enriched by its proximity to Cambridge; distinguished visiting speakers are available, and pupils are encouraged to go to plays, concerts and lectures in the town.

Combined Cadet Force. There is a contingent of the CCF (Army section), of which membership is voluntary. Camps take place annually, and an Adventure Training week is also undertaken at Easter. There is a miniature range, and a Rifle Club exists for small-bore shooting.

Duke of Edinburgh's Award Scheme. The School is an authorised centre for the organisation of activities within the Award Scheme. Those who choose to may work towards qualifying for the Bronze, Silver or Gold awards in the four sections; service, expeditions, physical recreation and skills or hobbies.

Community Service. The Community Service Group aims to introduce pupils to a range of possibilities for service within the community. They choose from a range of activities including working with the old, young and infirm in cooperation with local groups such as Schools, Hospitals, Rotary and Youth Action.

Fees. Board and Tuition, £14,505 pa (from September 2000). Home Boarding (Day) £6,495–£10,740 pa.

St Faith's Preparatory School is part of the same Foundation. It was founded in 1884 and acquired by the Governors of The Leys in 1938. There are 500 boys and girls, aged 4–13 years. The buildings, which include the Ashburton Hall, opened in 1998, stand in 10 acres of grounds. Full particulars may be obtained from the Headmaster of St Faith's, Mr R A Dyson, BA.

The Old Leysian Union: *Secretary, J C Harding, MA, The Leys School, Cambridge CB2 2AD.*

Handbook and Directory, twentieth edition, 1991.

Charitable status. The Leys School (Cambridge) is a Registered Charity, number 311436. It aims to enable boys and girls to develop fully their individual potential within a School community firmly based on Christian principles.

Liverpool College

Mossley Hill Liverpool L18 8BG.

Tel: 0151-724 4000; 0151 724 1611 (Admissions)
Fax: 0151-729 0105
e-mail: admin@liverpoolcollege.lpool.sch.uk
website: www:liverpoolcollege.org.uk

Motto: *Non solum ingenii, verum etiam virtutis.*

Visitor: The Bishop of Liverpool

President: The Rt Hon The Earl of Derby

Vice-Presidents:

J K Jones, Esq
The Rt Hon The Baroness Young, PC, DL
The Revd Canon Dr D C Gray, TD, PhD, MPhil, AKC, FRHistS
The Rt Hon Lord Hunt of Wirral, MBE
The Rt Revd Nigel McCulloch, MA
District Judge M A W Grundy
District Judge R A McCullagh, MA
H M Alty, Esq, MB, ChB, BDS, FDS, RCS

College Council:

Mrs B M Greenberg (*Chairman*)
D M A Chestnutt, FCA (*Deputy Chairman*)
B S Clarke
Dr E Ward (*Chairman of Academic Committee*)
Dr S Evans, MD (*Chairman of Staff Liaison Committee*)
Mrs S Cunniffe, BDS
I D Hamilton-Burke, FCA
Mrs F S Henderson
J D A Leith
J W Lowe, FCA (*Honorary Treasurer*)
J D Robertson (*Chairman, Preparatory School Committee*)
G N Wood

***Principal:* to be appointed**

Head of Upper School: Mrs C Bradley, BSc (Liverpool)

Mrs K Bamber, BA, BPhil (Liverpool) (*Pastoral Care*)
S P Downes, BSc (Birmingham), PhD (Cambridge) (*Director of Studies*)
Dr B G Hildick, BSc, PhD (Bradford) (*Assessment & Monitoring*)
M K Welland, BSc (Salford) (*Information Services*)
J F Williams, CertEd (Chester College) (*Registrar*)

Chaplain: The Revd E Storey, DRS (Cambridge, BA (Manchester), MEd (Liverpool)

College Counsellor: E B Harvey, MA (London)

Bursar and Clerk to Governors: I N Lightbody

Staff:

M Alexander, BA
T J Belfield, MA
M E Broughton, BA
E Cain, CertEd
R M Carey, MA
D Crassweller, BA, DipLing
A Davies, BSc, MSc
B C Donnelly, BEd
S Doran, BA
S P Downes, BSc, PhD, MBA
C Y Farrell, BSc
L J Flockhart, BEd
J Foster, BA
A Fox, BSc
M R Francies, DASE
R Francis, BSc
R G Freebairn, MA
A Gammon, BEd
J Gardner, MA
S Gifford, BD, MA
L A Goudie, CertEd, JP
P D Greer, BSc
N W Griffith, BA
L A Hamilton, BSc
D Hearne, BA
A Howard, MA
D Jewell, MA
G B Kitching, BA
J Lamb, BSc
E R M Lavin, BA
J L Lishman, BSc
A Markland, MA
R McAlea, MA
I McCormick, BA, MA
C J I McNally, BBS
L M Miller, BSc
R G Moor, BSc
A Mullin, BA
E Othen, MA, MPhil
S Pearson, BA
S Platt, BSc
I G Poole, BA, PhD
I Preston NatDipDesign
P W Purland, BA
T Rooney, BA
B Routledge, MA
J Runacres, MA
P A Ryan, GRSM, ARMCM
C R Seeley, BA, MPhil
S A Simpson
J M E Stephenson, BSc
J M Strauss, BA
J Tegg, BSc
G J Tickner, BEd
A Walker, MA
C Walker, MA
G Walsh, BEd
D Welch, MA
M K Welland, BSc, MSc
J R Wood, MA, ARCM
J Wright, BSc

Prep and Pre-Prep Staff:

Head: S Buglass, MEd
Head of Pre-Prep: Mrs A Parkes, CertEd
Head of Nursery: Mrs B Sproat, CertEd

J Anderson, BSc
D A Buglass, CertEd
B Chew, BA Hons
P A Davey, CertEd
M M Evans, CertEd
M P Fursse, BEd
S E Glaze, BEd
S Gray, BA Hons
N A Hayes, CertEd
B Jones, CertEd
W G Kendall, CertEd
E L Lewis, NNEB
S J Lucas, BA
C Marlow, BA

D McClements, BEd
P McGrath, BEd
G M McGuinness, NNEB
E McLennon, BA
S J Nelson, BEd
M H Oakes, BEd
J Poole, NNEB
A F Russell-Moore, BSc
J Saunders, BSc
J Sayce, BEd
L Strong, BEd
K J Taylor, BEd
M Thomas, BA, MA
E Warbrick, NVQ
A C Wells, BA
A White, BSc
A Whitehead, BEd
M Williams, CertEd
F Wright, BA
M Young, BSc, MA

Music Department:
Director of Music: R M Carey, MA
Assistant Director of Music: J R Wood, MA, ARMCM
Head of Music Technology: P A Ryan, GRSM, ARMCM
Music Coordinator: F A E Wright, BA

Campus and Buildings. The College is situated 4 miles south of the city centre, in 26 acres of wooded grounds and playing fields, adjacent to extensive parkland, and situated in the South Liverpool conservation area. It is easily accessible by public transport or by one of the College buses.

Founded in 1840 with the aim of providing a sound academic and cultural education based on Christian principles, the College has expanded and upgraded the buildings and facilities as a continuous process to keep abreast of curricular developments and to create the optimum environment for a modern multi-faith and multi-cultural educational community. The elegance of the original Victorian buildings has been maintained alongside modern purpose-built facilities, including Science Laboratories for both Junior and Senior pupils, a large, award-winning Design and Technology Centre, a Music Technology Centre and an Information Technology Suite. There is a fine Library with a full-time Librarian; it is open from 8 am to 6 pm every day during term time and for 7 weeks in school holidays. The College also has a Sixth Form Centre. The Junior School has been completely refurbished and the Nursery and Infant School recently extended.

An astro-turf pitch has been added to the extensive playing fields and a Sports Centre was opened in October 1999. There are also plans for a new indoor swimming pool.

Organisation. There are at present approximately 500 day girls and 600 day boys in the school. The College provides a complete and continuous course of education for boys and girls from 3 to 18 years of age in the Preparatory School (3-11) and in Upper School (11–18). Each of the schools has its own Head and staff, but additional specialist teaching is provided in the Prep school in Music, Sport and Modern Languages.

Admission. The main points of entry are at ages 3, 5, 11 and 16 by assessment and/or examination, although pupils are admitted at other ages. Tours of the College may be booked through the Registrar. Male and female students are also accepted into the Sixth Form. Most pupils enter in September although entry at other times is possible, depending on the circumstances.

Scholarships (*see* Entrance Scholarship section). Academic Scholarships, Music, Art and Design Technology Scholarships and College Assisted Places are offered, as are Bursaries for children of Clergy of any religion and of members of the Armed Forces.

The Curriculum. The curriculum retains an emphasis on a rigorous training in academic subjects while allowing scope for individual preferences and vocational and practical subjects. The curriculum to GCSE includes English Language and Literature, Latin, French, German, Spanish, Mathematics, Physics, Chemistry, Biology, Economics, Religious Studies, Information Systems, CDT, Classical Studies, Drama, Art, Music and Physical Education. Information Technology is also taught on a cross-curricular basis.

Advanced Levels and Sixth Form. The majority of pupils proceed into the Sixth Form and nearly all (99%) go on to Universities or pursue other specialist areas, eg Arts, Drama. There is a regular entry to Oxford and Cambridge. While retaining their role as an integral senior part of the community and being required to take some responsibility for the running of the school in a prefectorial capacity, the Sixth Formers enjoy greater freedom and independence. They have separate study rooms, common rooms and a café. All Sixth Form students study four subjects to AS level and then select three to study to A Level. Some will study five and four respectively. All will follow an extension programme. In addition to the subjects offered at GCSE, Greek, Theatre Studies, Business Studies, Music Technology, Geology and Further Mathematics are available at Advanced Level.

Careers. Careers advice and guidance is provided throughout the school by a team of staff with particular experience and expertise in this field. There is a full and active Careers programme of both general instruction and individual, specialist counselling, and a well-stocked Careers room. The College is a member of ISCO. The Head of Careers arranges work experience and work shadowing for Year 11 and Year 12 students within their potential career fields. Particular attention is paid to preparation for University entrance.

Religious Education. All faiths are respected and, although the Chapel remains a focus for Christian worship, assemblies are provided for those of other faiths.

Pastoral Care and House System. The College is divided into four Houses, each with its own Housemaster or Housemistress and Tutors. Pupils join one of the school Houses on entry and continue in it throughout their school career. Close contact is established and maintained between staff and pupils within the Houses. House activities include music, sport and drama. Alongside the Houses and providing a firm infrastructure for academic and pastoral support and guidance is a Tutorial system by year group. Form Tutors and Year Tutors monitor each pupil's progress and give regular advice on a personal and individual basis.

Medical Care. First aid is provided by a team of fully-qualified first aiders.

Reporting. Regular consultations are held with parents to review each pupil's progress and achievement in terms of both ability and effort and in relation to his or her potential: appointments may be made with the Form Tutor or Year Tutor if parents have cause for concern about any aspect of their child's progress.

Sport. For boys the main sports are Rugby, Hockey and Cricket. The main sports for girls are Lacrosse, Hockey, Netball, Tennis and Rounders. For both boys and girls, cross-country races are held in the Lent term and Athletics and Swimming in the Summer. There are many other sports and options.

Music. The College has a strong tradition of excellence in Music. All pupils receive tuition in Music as part of the normal curriculum and many learn at least one musical instrument, including the organ. There are orchestras, bands and other instrumental groups for all ages within the school. Concerts are given regularly on both competitive and informal bases.

Drama. Drama is taught to all pupils up to Year 9. They may then wish to choose a course in Drama for GCSE or Theatre Studies for Advanced Level. School plays and other dramatic productions are staged regularly and as many pupils as possible are encouraged to participate. There is also a House Drama Competition, for which responsibility rests entirely with the members of each House. Staff and pupils in the Art, Music and Drama departments combine to produce a Performing Arts' Evening for parents, guests and students at the end of each school year. The Myriad Theatre Company, based at the College, provides a premier theatrical experience for actors, technicians and musicians.

Activities and Societies. There are more than thirty Societies currently operating: these cover many aspects of pupils' interests from Computing to Classics, from Chess to Debating. Teams from the College regularly participate in Debating competitions, among them the Observer Mace and Cambridge Union. There are flourishing and well-established mixed Cub and Scout troops. Pupils participate in a Community Service Project from Year 9. Over 120 pupils take part in the Duke of Edinburgh Award Scheme.

Activity holidays, Adventure Training and trips abroad which combine recreation and education are organised regularly.

After School Clubs. After School Clubs are provided for children aged 3–11, enabling them to remain on the school premises under qualified supervision until 6.00pm each day.

Combined Cadet Force. The voluntary Combined Cadet Force is one of the largest in the UK and has RN, Army and RAF sections: pupils spend 2 years in one of these sections after a year of pre-CCF training. About 70% volunteer for a further two years.

Tuition Fees per term. Pre-Prep and Nursery £1,295; Preparatory School £1,658, Upper School £2,027. Reductions for brothers and sisters also apply.

Old Lerpoolians. The school fosters and maintains connections with former pupils through the Old Lerpoolian Society and holds regular functions and reunions. Information may be obtained from Mr I N Lightbody, Tel: 0151 724 4000, Ext 225.

Charitable status. Liverpool College is a Registered Charity, number 526682.

Llandovery College
(Coleg Llanymddyfri)

Llandovery Carmarthenshire SA20 0EE.
Tel: Warden (01550) 723000
Bursar (01550) 723044
Fax: (01550) 723049

Llandovery College was formally opened on St David's Day 1848. Founded and endowed by Dr Thomas Phillips, sometime doyen of the Royal College of Surgeons and a distinguished bibliophile, it occupies a fine site amidst magnificent countryside in the small market town of Llandovery. The extensive grounds and playing fields run alongside two miles of the river Towy.

Motto: *Gwell Dysg na Golud. (Better Learning than Riches).*

Visitor: The Rt Revd D Huw Jones, MA, Lord Bishop of St David's

Trustees:
Sir David Mansel Lewis, KCVO, BA, JP, KStJ (*Chairman*)

¶O M R Howell, MA, FCA
¶Major General P R Davies, CB, CIMgt, FIPD, FZS
¶S A Simon
Dr L E Gee, BA, MPhil
¶D E Gravell, MIME
¶D Rhys Jones
Dr T G R Davies, MA, DL
¶P H Jones, FCA
¶Professor R E Mansel, MB, BS, MS, FRCS
A M James, FBIM
H H Thomas, MA
D Phillips
The Revd Janet C Robbins, MA

Hon Solicitor and Clerk to the Trustees: W J Morris, BA

***Warden and Headmaster:* P A Hogan**, MA

Deputy Warden: D S Beck, MA

Senior Mistress: Mrs J D Kendrick, JP

Director of Studies: M H Edwards, MA

Assistant Staff:
C Andras, BA
*G W J Brand, BEd, MA
*T J Cannock, MA
R L Edwards, BA
*G R Evans, BA, MEd
†J D Evans, BA
*C E Griffiths, LWCMD
*Mrs C Hopkins, MA, AMBDA
C N H Jennings, BSc
Mrs S Jones, CertEd
Fr S Leyshon, BA, BTh (*Chaplain*)
†T G Marks, BA
*D G Morgan, BSc
*V A Price, BSc
†A T Rees, BSc
*Mrs D A Rockey, BSc
C J Samuel, BA
Mrs R E Saunders, BSc
¶J C O Thomas, BA
W T Vaughan, BEng
†*N A Watts, AdDip, CertEd
A Wielochowski, MSc
*A G Wood, BA (*Careers*)
*Mrs B Wood, BA, ATC

School Medical Officers:
Dr J Richards, MB, BCh
Dr R W Salt, MB, BCh
Dr J Rees, MB, BCh
Dr M J M Boulter, MA, MB, BS
Dr C R Briscoe, BA, MB, BChir

Bursar: Major W J Evans, MBIM

Director of External Affairs: Mrs C Lamyman Jones

SSI: Capt G C Williams, MBE, BA

College Organisation. Pupils are accepted from the age of 8 into the Junior School. Boys from 11 to 13 are housed in Llandingat and boarders move to Ty Teilo for Forms 4 and 5 (Years 10 and 11). Sixth Form boys are accommodated in single study-bedrooms in Ty Ddewi. Girl boarders occupy Llanover - a purpose built girls' boarding house opened in 1988, while day girls are accommodated in Ty Catrin. Day boys after 13 are accommodated in Ty Cadog.

Currently there are 125 boys and 65 girls divided almost equally between full boarders, weekly boarders and day pupils.

The College employs a catering company and high quality food is served from a modern kitchen.

Curriculum. The following subjects are taught through to GCSE and A-level: Art, Biology, Business Studies, Chemistry, Classical Civilization, Design and Technology, Drama, English, French, Geography, Greek, History, Information Technology and Computer Science, Latin, Mathematics, Music, Photography, Physical Education, Physics, Religious Studies and Welsh.

English as a Foreign Language is available as an optional extra.

The College also welcomes pupils of high intelligence but with moderate dyslexia. Special classes are taught by experienced dyslexia teachers who are always available to offer advice to both pupils and parents.

Entrance Examinations and Scholarships. Examinations for places and awards are set at the ages of 11, 13 and 16 although entrance can be gained at other ages by special arrangement. Pupils from Preparatory Schools would normally be expected to sit the Common Entrance Examination. Dates of the examinations are available from the Warden.

Scholarships. (*see* Entrance Scholarship section) Scholarships up to the value of half-fees are offered as well as bursaries for the sons and daughters of members of the Clergy and Officers serving in the Armed Forces. Carwyn James and Ian Gollop Sports Scholarships are available in the Sixth Form for pupils showing superior sporting skills particularly in Rugby Football and Cricket.

Buildings. The original buildings now contain the Dining Hall (which houses a remarkable collection of paintings) the Library and resource centre, the Warden's Study and administration offices, the Masters' Common Room and dining room, and two of the boys houses.

Around the campus are the new girls house, the senior boys' house, the teaching, science and music blocks, the Health Centre (staffed by fully-qualified nurses), a multi-purpose hall, the CCF headquarters the Design and Technology Centre and the Warden's residence. The new Sports Hall completed in 1991 also houses the Sixth Form Club.

Fees. Current fees are: Boarders £12,468; Day £8,280. Consolidated charge for extras £163 per term.

Chapel. The Chapel which was built in 1934 was the gift of Dr D L Prosser, formerly Bishop of St David's and Archbishop of Wales. In 1990 it was completely refurbished and dedicated to the memory of the donor. The pipe organ, now a fine instrument was completely rebuilt and a specially commissioned stained-glass East window installed. All pupils attend a short act of worship four mornings a week. There is a weekly celebration of the Eucharist. The Chaplain prepares pupils for Confirmation which is administered annually in the College Chapel by the Visitor. Pupils of other denominations are free to attend Sunday Services in Chapels and Churches in the town. The Michaelmas Term ends with a Carol Service.

Drama and Music. As well as being subjects in the school curriculum, Drama and Music feature prominently in the life of the college. Most instruments can be taught privately either by members of the Music Department or by visiting peripatetic teachers. There is a termly concert as well as a series of recitals throughout the year. Pupils are also encouraged to join the Chapel choir. Dramatic productions performed by both pupils and visiting companies are staged regularly.

Career Service. There is a comprehensive Careers Service supported with regular visits by the Regional Director of the Independent Schools Careers Organisation, the Forces Liaison Officers and the Dyfed Careers Service. The department is well equipped to give advice on higher education.

Games. All pupils are required to participate in games unless medically unfit. The College has a long and distinguished reputation in sport particularly in the field of Rugby Football. For boys there is a comprehensive programme of Rugby matches against other schools in the two winter terms and the College also participates successfully in national Seven-a-side tournaments. In recent years boys have regularly won Welsh Schoolboy International Caps. Girls play competitive hockey at school and county level. In the summer term, cricket, tennis and athletics feature as the main sports.

With the advent of the new Sports Hall a whole range of sporting activities are made available including squash, badminton, netball, volleyball, bowling and table tennis.

The College has its own golf course and riding, swimming and clay pigeon shooting are offered at nearby locations.

Archaeology, bridge, chess, photography, model-making and fishing are available for those who wish to participate. Plays performed by pupils and by visiting companies are staged in the College Theatre. A school journal produced regularly since 1886 perpetuates a continuous record of College events.

Outdoor Activities. There is a College contingent of the Combined Cadet Force to which pupils in Years 9 and 10 belong and which is also open to senior pupils. Field days are held throughout the year and annual camps take place in the Easter and Summer holidays. The superb countryside within striking distance of the College lends itself magnificently to outward bound activities such as canoeing, rock-climbing and general expedition work.

The College's indoor shooting range is extensively used. Pupils are coached by the College's SSI and regularly represent Wales in international competitions.

The College participates extensively in the Duke of Edinburgh's Award Scheme. 25 pupils have secured the Gold Award in the last two years.

Regular visits to the theatre are offered throughout the winter season and both skiing and foreign tour holidays are also available. The French department arranges an annual Form 2 holiday and extensive use is made of the twinning arrangement between Llandovery Town and Pluguffan in Brittany.

Parents' Association. An active Parents' Association assists the College by providing such items as minibuses, video cameras and resources for the Library.

Old Llandoverian Society. There is a parent body with branches centred in Cardiff and London.

Charitable status. Llandovery College is a Registered Charity, number 525394. It exists for the purpose of educating children from the ages of 8 to 18.

Lord Wandsworth College

Long Sutton Hook Hampshire RG29 1TB.
Tel: 01256 862201
Fax: 01256 862563
e-mail: admissions@lord-wandsworth.hants.sch.uk
website: lord-wandsworth.hants.sch.uk

Lord Wandsworth College is a co-educational secondary school for 485 pupils between the ages of 11 and 18. There are 215 weekly boarders, 55 full boarders and 215 day pupils.

Motto: *Vincit Perseverantia.*

President: Sir Humphrey Prideaux, OBE, DL, MA

Chairman of Governors: M B Bunting

The Governing Body consists of 8 governors

***Headmaster:* I G Power**, MA

Senior Deputy Head & Foundation Registrar: A J Woolstone, LLB

Deputy Head: A Dyson, CertEd

Bursar: C F Warren

Assistant Staff:
S L Badger, MA
J D Baker, BSc
P Y Booth, BA
J Boyd, CertEd
J P Costain, BA
Miss S Coughlan, BA
Mrs S Dee, BSc
Dr M R Eldridge, BSc, PhD
M J D Featherstone, CertEd
P Finan, BSc
R J Fitzgerald, MA
P M Gilliam, BSc
D F Goldsmith, MA
Miss S Hale, BA
A O F Hamilton, MA
S D Harvey, BSc
R W T Haynes, MA
C C Hicks, MA
D P Ibbotson, BSc
Revd R B Jackson, MA
I S Kerr, MA
R J Kimber, BSc
Mrs D J Last, BA
P A Last, MA

D O C Machin, BA
Mrs J M McKinnon, BA
G J Mobbs, BA
Mrs G R Neighbour
D L Owen, CertEd
D C Pering, MA
Mrs S J Perrett, BA
Mrs L D Power, BA
C H Radmann, BA
T R Richardson, BA Hons(Ed)
M C Russell, BSc
Mrs P Sandham, BSc
G A Silverlock, BEd, MLitt, PhD
G R Smith, BA
P R Waghorn, BEng
E Walker, BSc
R G Walters, BSc
P J Watson, BSc
Miss J M Watt, BA
Mrs S R Weston, BSc
G S Winter, BSc
Mrs C J Wisdom, CertEd, RSA, DipSpLD
C Wiskin

Librarian: Mrs B Males

Medical Officers:
Dr I J Goold, MB, BS, DCH, DObst, RCOG
Dr R Assadourian, MBBS, BSc Hons, MRCGP, DRCOG, DFEP

Location and accessibility. The school is fortunate in that, although it occupies a magnificent rural setting on the edge of the rolling North Downs, it has excellent communications, being five miles from the M3 and under an hour from London, Oxford and the south coast. Access to main line trains and all major airports is quick and easy.

Many pupils come from the surrounding towns and villages around Farnham, Alton, Fleet, Basingstoke, Guildford and Reading, and there is a well-established tradition of such children weekly boarding although living relatively close-by.

History. Lord Wandsworth died in 1912 and left a large sum of money for the foundation of a school. The College that bears his name now occupies a 1,200 acre site in the midst of beautiful Hampshire countryside. The Lord Wandsworth Foundation awards a number of places annually to children who have lost one or both parents.

Mission statement. Lord Wandsworth College is a non-denominational foundation which fosters the intellectual, moral and spiritual development of all the young people in its care. It strives to ensure that each pupil realises his or her full potential within a stimulating environment which emphasises concern for others.

The outstanding features of the school are.

- That almost all academic staff live on campus allowing them to provide both a high level of pastoral care, but also the opportunity for pupils to be able to take advantage of the very wide range of activities on offer.
- That all pupils, whether day, weekly or full boarding, belong to one of the eight boarding houses and are fully integrated into the social life of the school.
- That the school is purpose-built with an outstanding range of facilities for both academic and extra-curricular activities. Recent projects have included the building of a new senior girls' house, refurbishment of boys' accommodation, a new ICT suite and a new music school and performance hall.
- That the school is an unusually unpretentious, caring community. It is a happy and relaxed community; pupils are courteous and loyal.

Curriculum. The aim of the curriculum is to provide a full and flexible range of subjects to fit the needs of each individual. The school's policy is to follow closely the National Curriculum.

Subjects taught to GCSE are: English (Language and Literature), French, Geography, Maths, History, Latin, Classical Civilisation, Drama, Physics, Chemistry, Biology, Spanish, German, Art, Music, Design & Technology and Religious Studies.

Most pupils continue into the Sixth Form where the subjects taught to AS and A2 level are: English, History, Geography, Economics, Business Studies, Classical Civilisation, Music, Latin, French, Spanish, German, Physics, Chemistry, Biology, Maths, Further Maths, Art, Design, Theatre Studies and PE.

All Sixth Formers take a key skills course.

ICT. There is a large networked system across two IT rooms and the Library comprising IBM compatible PCs and various peripherals. All pupils are assigned their own e-mail address and there is daily free access to the Internet. All academic departments and boarding houses own stand alone computers that are used as research resources as well as providing business-standard software applications.

Games. The school lays great store by its games involvement and has a local and national reputation for many of its pursuits. The main boys' games are rugby, hockey and cricket and for girls hockey, netball and tennis are the principal sports. In addition swimming, athletics, squash, badminton, shooting, fencing, golf, cross country running, basketball, canoeing and trampolining all take place and provide teams which represent the school.

Drama. Drama has a high profile within the school and several shows are staged each year. There is a musical production every other year as well as showcases, reviews and workshops. Pupils are encouraged to participate in all fields of drama either acting, writing, set design, lighting, stage management, prop-making or sound.

Music. There is a large variety of instrumental ensembles, including an orchestra, swing band and many chamber groups. Pupils sing in two choirs. Tuition is available in singing, all orchestral instruments, piano, organ, percussion and guitar. Musicians regularly perform formally and informally both within school and at local venues.

Other activities. These include Forestry, Soccer, Bridge, Chess, Pottery, Meteorology, Car Maintenance, Mountain Biking, Karate, Horticulture, Archery, Dance, Electronics, Cookery and Gymnastics.

Pupils in the fourth form are involved for a minimum of one year in the CCF programme which has an Army and Air Force Section. Fifth form pupils and above take part in the very active Community Service programme. All pupils have the opportunity to enter the Duke of Edinburgh Award Scheme.

Organisation. There is a two or three form entry at age 11. For the first two years all pupils are in the co-educational Junior House which has its own buildings and sports fields. At 13 there is another entry, mainly from children who have taken Common Entrance. All houses are in the charge of Houseparents or Housemasters who have five or six additional academic staff to help them as well as two matrons.

Fees. (*see* Entrance Scholarship section) Senior Boarders £4,550 per term. Senior Day Pupils £3,420 per term. Junior Boarders £4,315 per term. Junior Day Pupils £3,250 per term.

Charitable status. Lord Wandsworth College Trust is a Registered Charity, number 272050. It exists to provide education for boys and girls.

Loretto School

Musselburgh Midlothian EH21 7RE.
Tel: School: 0131-653 4444; Headmaster: 0131-653 4441; Admissions: 0131-653 4455
Fax: School: 0131-653 4445; Admissions: 0131 653 4456
e-mail: admissions@loretto.lothian.sch.uk
website: www.loretto.com

Loretto, founded in 1827, is Scotland's oldest Independent Boarding School. The school's early formative influence,

Dr Hely Hutchinson Almond (the Headmaster from 1862-1903), scorned Victorian educational orthodoxies. Dr Almond's strong conviction and belief – in fresh air, exercise, communal singing and the need for the Headmaster to take a central role in the school's pastoral life – can still be seen today. His dislike of constrictive dress and enjoyment of the red jacket are seen and enjoyed by Lorettonians – in today's uniform.

Loretto seeks to foster the partnership between pupil, school and family. Families are welcomed to matches, concerts, plays and to Sunday Chapel. Parents feel very much part of the wider Loretto family.

Motto: *Spartam nactus es: hanc exorna*

Governors:

The Hon Lord Johnston (*Chairman*)
G R G Graham, CBE (*Vice-Chairman*)
W F Bergius
D M Briggs
A J R Brown
R J M Gordon
J F S Gourlay
Sir Angus Grossart, CBE, LLD, FRSE, DL
Mrs G Hinton
J H Hume
Professor J A A Hunter, OBE, FRCP, MD
Mrs S C D Low
Revd A McGregor, QC, BD
Mrs S McLaren
P L Macneal, FRIAS
Mrs P J Saunter, CA
R T M Scott, DL
A R Watt
W Waterhouse
J L E Wotherspoon, WS

Clerk and Secretary: R M Urquhart WS, c/o A & W M Urquhart, Solicitors, 16 Heriot Row, Edinburgh EH3 6HR

Headmaster: **M B Mavor**, CVO (St John's College, Cambridge)

Vicegerent: R G Selley, BEd (*Business Studies*)

Assistant Staff:

G Addison, MA (*English*)
P Angel, BA (*Art*)
P R Aston, BEd (*Head of Technology*)
M J Baker, MA (*Physics; Communication & Resource Centre Co-ordinator*)
Mrs D M Barbour, MA (*Head of English*)
A J R Brown, BA, MA (*English*) (*Director of Activities*)
Dr R H A Brown, BSc, PhD (*Chemistry*)
J D Burnet, MA (*Head of Modern Languages*)
J P Chandler, MA (*History*)
A R Chapman, IEng, MBA (*Technology*)
W E Coleman, MMus (*Director of Music*)
Mrs A Cruickshank, BA (*Geography*)
Mrs C A Cursiter, MA (*Modern Languages*)
D Dugast (*Modern Languages*)
P S Dunn, BSc (*Mathematics*) (*Head of Information Technology*)
I Ebbage, MA (*Head of Classics*) (*Examinations Officer*)
J M Elder, BA, MLitt (*Head of History*) (*Government and Politics*) (*Higher Education Adviser*)
Mrs G Heavyside, BEd (*PE*)
C Hoffland, BSc (*Mathematics and Design*)
M S Jack, BEd (*Science*) (*Head of PE, Director of Sport*)
S J M Lowe, MA (*Modern Languages*)
S Lucas, MLitt (*Special Needs*)
Miss K McGibbons, BA (*Modern Languages*)
H M MacLean, BSc (*Geography*)
D M McLean-Steel, BA (*English and Drama*)
D McPherson, BA (*Classics*)
Miss A Morris, BSc (*Head of Physics*)
Mrs C J Murphy, BSc (*Biology*)
P Murphy, BSc (*Head of Chemistry*)
W J Parkhouse, MA (*Biology*) (*Head of Science*)
D Rossouw (*Sport*)
Revd A J Roundhill, BA (*Chaplain*)
M Seifert, BA, DipPhysEd (*Media Studies, Sport*)
Dr A A Shepherd, BSc, PhD (*Head of Mathematics*)
P A Shepherd, BSc, MSc (*Director of Studies*)
C F Spall, BSc (*Technology*)
M Topping, BSc Hons, PhD (*Science*)
A M Watson, MA (*Head of Art*)
R P Whait, BSc (*Mathematics and Business Studies*)
D R Wylie, BSc (*Head of Geography*) (*Child Protection Co-ordinator*)

Houses and Housemasters/Housemistresses:

Boys:
Hope House: S J M Lowe
Pinkie House: M Topping
Seton House: M Seifert

Girls:
Balcarres House: Mrs D M Barbour
Holm House: Mrs E Middlemass

Bursar: Col W R Hughes, MA

Director of Admissions: Ms H Walker, MA, MSc

Junior School: Vicegerent: R G Selley, BEd

Assistant Teachers:

W D Dickinson, BEd (*Senior Master*)
Miss N Forbes, BEd
K Hutchinson, DipTMus
C R Jones, BSc
Miss S A Kettlewell, BA
M O'Gorman
D H Pearce, BSc
Mrs M Reeves, BSc
J Robertson (*Early Years*)
M J R Rulliere, DUEL
S C Smerdon, BEd
L M Watson, MEd (*Head of Early Years*)
Mrs M Gillies (*Administration*)

Loretto, a non-denominational co-educational boarding school, is 6 miles from Edinburgh. The School makes the fullest use of its proximity to Edinburgh, enabling pupils to take advantage of the music, drama, museums and art galleries of this capital city. The main buildings adjoin the Old Musselburgh Links and face the Firth of Forth, while two of the main boarding houses are in the spacious grounds of the historic mansion of Pinkie House, which is itself a boarding house.

The Senior School consists of approximately 200 boys and 100 girls divided into 6 modern boarding houses fully equipped with dayrooms, common rooms and with individual bedsitting rooms for most VIth Formers.

Academic. GCSE and AS/A levels. Below the VIth Forms the work is arranged to give a sound general education. The subjects taken by all 3rd form pupils are English, History, Latin or Classical Studies, Geography, French, Spanish, Mathematics, ICT, Physics, Chemistry, Biology, Technology, Drama, Art and Religious Knowledge. In the VIth Forms the following subjects are available: Latin, Modern Languages, English, History, Mathematics, Technology, the Sciences, Government & Politics, Business Studies, Geography, Art, Music and Media Studies (AS only). All members of the Lower Sixth Form spend a week attached to an industrial firm as a work experience project.

The School's academic work is inspected by the Scottish Education Department, and courses in all subjects lead towards the GCSE and AS/A levels. The classes are small, so that every boy or girl gets a great deal of individual attention. Work is mainly done in periods of 40 minutes and boys and girls are prepared to qualify for University courses throughout the UK in all the usual subjects.

Recent Developments. In recent years many new developments have taken place. A new Communication and Resource Centre opened in 1999, which combines an extensive reading Library with computer based learning and access to educational websites. The Loretto Music School was opened in June 1990; in addition the new Kenneth Jones 3 manual pipe organ was installed in Loretto Chapel and dedicated in April 1989. The well-equipped Design and Technology Centre was expanded in 1994 to provide more project space for this important subject area. In 1994 a new Sixth Form Social Centre was created in Linkfield, and in June 1995 an all-weather outdoor playing surface, suitable for Hockey and Tennis, was opened.

Religion. Services are held in the School Chapel every Sunday. There are prayers every morning at the Headmaster's 'Double' and there is a midweek service on Wednesday. The services are non-denominational and boys and girls are prepared for confirmation in both the Church of England and the Church of Scotland. They are confirmed at a combined service held in the Chapel. All members of the school are expected to sing in the choir so that the Chapel Services are genuinely congregational.

Music and Drama. In addition to the full school choral singing in Chapel, there are specialist choral and chamber groups which give a number of recitals, formal and informal, both within the School and outside. Many pupils take instrumental music lessons which are taught both by the full-time staff and by twelve visiting teachers. There is a sizeable School orchestra.

The Theatre has also encouraged further development in drama: there is a School play or musical, a Third Form play, a Junior Musical and a pupil-led Lower Sixth play each year offering opportunities both for acting and for stage management in an outstandingly well equipped auditorium.

Games and Exercise. It is a tradition in School that every boy and girl should take regular exercise. These activities at present include: Rugby Football, Cricket, Hockey, Lacrosse, Athletics, Swimming, Fives, Tennis, Squash, Badminton, Sailing, Cross-country and Golf. Good golf courses are easily accessible and the School has a fine tradition in the game. Skiing at the local artificial slope (Hillend) is available. There are also occasional expeditions for Fishing, Climbing, Field Studies, Museum visits, etc. The School encourages overseas tours on a regular basis and teams from Loretto have visited Canada, South Africa, Hong Kong and Barbados in recent years.

The Cadet Force. The School contingent consists of army and naval sections. Training can include Miniature Range Shooting, Orienteering, Expedition Work, Royal Artillery, Signals, Rock Climbing, First Aid, and the Pipes and Drums.

The Pipes and Drums play an important public part within the life of the School and have toured the United States, Belgium, Germany and France. They will play at Lord's Cricket Ground for the South African Test Match in 2001 and played during the Nat-West Final in September 1997 and 1998. They were the only School band to play at Ypres during the special commemoration service on the 80th anniversary of the end of World War I. They regularly Beat the Retreat at Edinburgh Castle and Holyrood Palace and are one of the top School bands in Scotland.

Exchanges have been arranged with pupils in France, Germany, Canada, New Zealand, Australia, and the United States of America.

Health. The School Doctor attends daily, there are full-time Matrons in each of the Houses, and there is a newly refurbished Sanatorium with a fully qualified nurse on duty twenty-four hours a day.

Clothing. The kilt is worn on Sundays by all; the ordinary School dress consists of a white shirt or blouse, open at the neck, dark grey long trousers or a navy blue skirt, and a tweed jacket or distinctive red School blazer.

Leadership and Responsibility. The discipline of the School is firm and in routine matters is maintained by Prefects, Heads of Rooms, and Heads of Tables, who under the Headmaster, Housemasters and Housemistresses have considerable authority. All Sixth Form pupils go on an Outward Bound Teamwork and Leadership Course in the Summer term.

Entrance Examination. Boys and girls are required to pass either the Common Entrance Examination or the Open Assessment Examination in English, Mathematics and Verbal Reasoning before being admitted. Entrance for the Lower Sixth is based on interview and assessment in English, Mathematics and Verbal Reasoning at the School; places are then offered subject to a satisfactory performance at GCSE/Standard Grade.

Day Pupils. The school has provision for day pupils who may wish to board occasionally, and for boarders who may wish a 'flexible' arrangement.

The Junior School is administered as a separate unit enjoys many of the facilities of the Senior School, such as the playing fields, Theatre, Sports Hall, Swimming Pool, Music School and Chapel. The boys and girls are under closer adult supervision than the Senior School but in other respects the system is similar. There are 120 boys and girls aged between 5 and 13. Full boarding, weekly boarding, occasional-boarding and attendance as day pupils are all encouraged.

Fees, etc. Boarding Fees (2000/2001): Senior School, £5,107 per term, Junior School, £3,850 per term. These fees include all the expenses of board, lodging, laundry, most text books, stationery, games material, medical attendance and medicine, CCF, transport to matches and internal school entertainments.

Optional Expenses. These will be kept to a minimum but include: Private Tuition when specially desired; individual voice and instrumental music lessons; extra-curricular visits and expeditions.

Scholarships. (*see* Entrance Scholarship section) The Open Scholarships for Prep School entrants are held in March and are taken at Loretto. Scholarships for other entrants are held during the same week at Loretto. There are also All Rounder, Music and Art Scholarships in recognition of outstanding general, musical, sporting or artistic promise. There are Scholarships for Sixth Form entrants.

Leaving Scholarships. A number of awards are given to assist with university education to those who have 'deserved well of Loretto' in recognition of their loyalty and service to the School.

Old Lorettonian Society: *Secretary, N G C McDowall, Esq, Loretto School, Musselburgh.*

Charitable status. Loretto School is a Registered Charity, number 32383. It exists in order to educate young people in mind, body and spirit.

Loughborough Grammar School

Loughborough Leics. LE11 2DU.
Tel: (01509) 233233/233258
Fax: (01509) 218436

The School was founded in 1495 by Thomas Burton, Merchant of the Staple of Calais, though it is probable that the Trustees of the Town Charity were managing a free school well before that date. The School was moved out to the present site in 1852. It is governed under a Scheme of the Department of Education and Science whereby there are three ex officio governors, five University representatives, one from the Borough of Charnwood, and 16 cooptative governors.

Motto: *Vires acquirit eundo.*

President: Professor D G Crighton

Governors:
P J Tomlinson, Esq, LLB, MA (*Chairman*)
Mrs M J Hanford (*Vice-Chairman*)

Dr A de Bono, MA, MB, BChir, MRCGP
A J Bowen, MA
T G M Brooks, Esq, JP, Lord Lieutenant
Professor S F Brown, BSc, PhD, DSc, FEng, FICE, FIHT
The Rt Hon Stephen Dorrell, MP, BA
A D Emson, Esq, BPharm(Hons), MRPharmS, MCPP
Professor J Feather
G P Fothergill, Esq, BA, FCIM
D Godfrey, BSc, CEng, FIEE
Professor A W F Halligan, MA, MD, BAO, MRCOE, MRCPI
Dr J E Hammond, BDS
P J B Hubner, Esq, MB, FRCP, DCH, FACC, FESC
P E Jordan, Esq, BSc, CEng, FIMechE, FIEE
Councillor A M Kershaw
Mrs G J W Maltby, MA
W M Moss, Esq
Mrs J G E Page, JP
Prof G C K Peach
H M Pearson, Esq, BA, LLB, ACIS
The Rt Revd Tomothy Stevens, Bishop of Leicester
Mrs J M Wales
Professor D J Wallace, CBE, FRS

***Headmaster:* P B Fisher**, MA (Christ Church, Oxford)

Deputy Head (*Administration*): J P Salter, BSc
Deputy Head (*Pastoral*): N Rowbotham, BSc, CChem, FRSC
Head of Main School: J S Weitzel, BSc
Head of Sixth Form: S Leese, BEd, MSc, CPhys, MInstP, FCollP
Director of Marketing: D L Evans, BSc
Chaplain: Revd Canon A J S Cox, MA
Senior Master: D R Horwood, BA, BEd, MSc
Headmaster's PA and Registrar: Mrs D P Briers

Assistant Masters:
D Arkell, BA, LGSM, LTCL
N Bahl, BSc
A W G Ballentyne, MA, MLitt, AssocRHS
G Beazley, BA
D R Bishop, BSc, MSc, CPhys, MInstP
N R Born, MA
M S E Broadley, BA
P D Bunting, MA
A P C Burns, GRNCM
P Calland, BSc
G D Campbell, BA
Miss S Cleveley, BSc
Mrs H J Coles, BA
C V Collington, BA
M J Colliver, BSc
Miss A M Conway, MA
J P Crookes, BSc
Miss P Cumine, BA, MA
Mrs J M Dalton-Pawle, ALCM ARCM, LGSM
P A Davey, MA
C L Davies, CEd, BA
R E Davies, BSc, MSc
A J Dossett, BSc
W Dyson, BA, MA
C B Faust, BSc, MEd, CChem, FRSC
J M Fernandez, BSc
Mrs B Finlan, BA
Mrs H Fisher, BA, MA
Mrs N Gallop, BA
N D Gallop, BA, MA
R T Griffiths, BA
C Groom, PSM
A J Haigh, MA
N Hampton, PhD, MA
R C Healey, PhD, BEng
M R Jennings, BA
M D Johnson, CertEd, LTCL
Dr C E Kelly, BSc
R F Kerr, MA
N Khan, BSc, MSc
P S Lane, BSc, CPhys, MInstP
Mrs E Lax, BA, LTCL
T Lax, LRAM, CertEd, DipMusic
N J Leiper, BSc(Econ), MSc(Econ) (*Head of Careers*)
Miss H Mapplebeck, BA
P Marlow, BSc
B K McCabe, MA
M I McMorran, BSc
J Mellors, BA
D J Miles, BSc
T D Morse, BSc, MSc
D Mouncer, BSc
P O'Connor, CEd
J S Parton, MA
Mrs S Parton, MA
A C Payne, MA, ARCM
M Peake, BA
W M Phillips, BSc, PhD, MIBiol
C A Quarmby, MA
Mrs A Quigley, BA
J M Rees, MA, PhD
N C Roberts, BA, AKC
D Rose, MA
M J Rundle, BEd
C Salt, BA, ARCM, DipRCM
P S Sergeant, BEd, MPhil
P Smith, BEd, MA
D M Starkings, BSc, BA
D W Steele, BSc
B N Symes, BA
D Taylor, BA
Mrs E Thomas, GRSM, ARCM
G P Thomas, MA, MSc, CPhys, MInstP
Mrs V Thompson, BA
H T Tunnicliffe, BEd
P J Underwood, MA, MMus, PhD, FRCO(CHM), FTCL, LRAM, ARCM, ADCM (*Organ & Piano*)
S Vincent, BA
Dr C Walker, MA
A F Walsh, BA, MA
Miss H Walters, MA
R J Willson, MA
G Witts, BSc

Head of Careers: C A Quarmby, MA

Librarian: Mrs V Bunn, ALA

Commanding Officer, CCF: Lt Col G Beazley

Staff Sergeant Instructor (*CCF*): SSI WO1 I G Fraser

Bursar and Clerk to the Governors: K D Shaw, MBE, MSc, FCIS

Medical Officer: Dr A Taylor, MB, ChB, MRCGP, DSSP

School Nurses: Mrs J Bryan, Mrs N Krarup

There are 970 boys in the School, including 50 boarders. There is a Junior School, run co-educationally with The Girls' High School, and this has 264 boys, aged 4 to 11.

Buildings. The School is situated away from the centre of the town in attractive grounds of about 27 acres which contain the beautiful avenues of trees known as the Burton Walks.

The main buildings were erected in 1852 when the School moved from within the town, and these with additions, form three sides of a quadrangle.

There has been much recent building: a Sports Hall and Squash Courts, an Art and Design Centre and Refectory, an English School and Theatre and a Modern Languages building opened in September 2000.

The School has a delightful First Eleven field and a Junior Field of over 13 acres within the precincts. Within 2 miles are well-equipped playing fields extending to nearly 70 acres.

Admission. The School became independent on the withdrawal of the Direct Grant. Entry to the Lower School is from the age of 4. Sixth Form entry dependent on interview and GCSE results.

Boarding Arrangements. Boys are admitted at the age of 10 or over to Denton House (Mr J S Parton), and at 14 they move to School House (Mr M S E Broadley). (Full and weekly).

Fees. In the Upper School, the tuition fee, which includes tuition, books, stationery and examination fees is £5,859 pa. In the Junior School the fee is £4,293 pa. The boarding fee for boys of all ages, which includes laundry, board, medical attendance, totals in the Upper School £10,350 pa. for Full Boarding and £9,144 for Weekly Boarding.

Scholarships. There are a number of Scholarships and Exhibitions at 10+, 11+ and 13+. Dyson Music Scholarships are also awarded at 10+, 11+, and 13+. Some of these will be to a maximum value of one-third fees. There are also a number of bursaries, dependent on parental means.

School Assisted Places. The Governors have introduced a replacement to the Government Assisted Places.

Religious Teaching. The School is undenominational, though there is a strong Christian tradition. The Chaplain is available for boys at any convenient time. On Sundays, Boarders attend the School Chapel, and on request are prepared for Confirmation by the Chaplain.

Curriculum. The aim of the School is to give a good general education to the age of 16, with greater specialisation afterward for those suited to it. From the age of 11 for the first 3 years the course includes French, Latin and the 3 separate Sciences. In Year 8 German and Greek are introduced into the curriculum as choices. In Year 9 there is an option choice of 2 from Latin, Greek, CDT, Art, German. In Year 10 options are chosen for GCSE, the combination may, but need not necessarily, satisfy the National Curriculum. Specialist subjects like Art, Music and CDT may be included in a boy's GCSE choice. The Sixth Form contains 270 boys all progressing to GCE Advanced. In Year 12 four-fifths of a boy's time will be occupied with his 4 subjects being taken for Advanced Subsidiary and in Year 13 he will usually take 3 of them to full GCE Advanced. A wide range of subjects and combinations is available. His remaining time is spent in General Studies and Educational Enrichment.

Games. The major games are Rugby Football, Cricket, Athletics, Hockey and Tennis. There is also a Fencing Club, a Sailing Club,a Swimming Club and a Canoe Club. Many indoor games, including Squash and Badminton are played in the Sports Hall. There are 4 qualified PE instructors on the Staff, and instruction is given in Swimming and Life Saving in the School pool. All boys take part in the major organised games, but seniors with little skill or ability have the choice of changing to other more individual outdoor pursuits when in the VIth Form.

Combined Cadet Force. There is an efficient and keen CCF of about 280 senior boys, run on a voluntary basis, with 14 officers, and the RSM. Boys have the choice of joining the RAF or Army or Naval Sections, and there is a highly proficient Signals Section with a transmitting room. Many varied and adventurous courses are available to members.

Scouts. There is a flourishing Scout Troop with 3 Scouters and 36 boys.

Duke of Edinburgh Award Scheme. Each year a large number of boys earn gold, silver and bronze awards.

Music. There is a Concert Band, a Big Band, Swing Band, two Orchestras and Choir. Visiting instrumental teachers come weekly. Much of this is organised with the Girls' High School.

Drama. A new studio theatre has allowed productions to increase in number and there is a remarkable level of interest from the boys in all aspects of the productions. Again there is collaboration with the High School.

Cultural Activities of all kinds are encouraged. There are numerous School Societies and Clubs, many of which also meet in conjunction with the Girls' High School. Boarders are encouraged to pursue their own hobbies, and no attempt is made to organise every moment of a boy's time.

Careers. Careers Masters are available to advise boys on their futures, with special regard to University or Professional careers. The School is a member of the Independent Schools Careers Organisation.

Academic Successes. Over the last seven years, 1992/2000, an average of 20 boys per year have gained admission to Oxford and Cambridge, and over 98% each year began degree courses at Universities.

Charitable status. Loughborough Endowed Schools is a Registered Charity, number 1081765. It exists to educate children.

* Head of Department	§ Part Time or Visiting
† Housemaster/Housemistress	¶ Old Pupil
‡ See below list of staff for meaning	

Magdalen College School, Oxford

Oxford OX4 1DZ.
Tel: (01865) 242191
Fax: (01865) 240379

Founded in 1480 by William of Waynflete as part of Magdalen College, the school's early Masters, Ushers and pupils include some of the most famous Grammarians of the 15th and 16th centuries such as John Anwykyll and Thomas Stanbridge. Cardinal Wolsey was an early Master, and Sam Mendes a more recent Old Boy. The College choristers have been full members of the School since at least the early 19th century.

In 1987 the School was given separate legal existence by the College as a Company limited by guarantee with charitable status wholly owned by the College.

Motto: *Sicut Lilium.*

Visitor: The Rt Revd The Lord Bishop of Winchester

Governors:
J P Leighfield, CBE, MA (*Chairman*)
G G Audley-Miller, MA
B J Bellhouse, MA, DPhil
L W B Brockliss, MA, PhD
R G Denning, MA, DPhil
D J Eeley, MA
C Y Ferdinand, MA, DPhil
Mrs W E Hart
C J G Ives, MA
G W Neilson, PhD
M J Peagram, MA, DPhil, MBA
B Sutton
Mrs J Townsend, MA, MSc
A W Wyatt

Master: **A D Halls**, MA

Usher: R J Cairns, MA (*History*)

Assistant Staff:
Ms S Allen, BA (*Junior School*)
P Askew, BEd (*Head of Physical Education*)
J R Baker, BSc, MA (*Director of Studies, Mathematics and Physics*)
J N Bates, BA (*Senior Tutor, Geography*)
J Birkin, BA (*Head of Classics*)
C S Bridge, BA (*Head of Business Studies*)
J A Brown, MA (*Physics*)
S J Brown, BSc (*PE and Games*)
D A Brunton, MA, DPhil (*English*)
A C Buckoke, BSc (*Head of Technology*)
Miss J Budd, BA (*Modern Languages*)
C J A Byrne, BSc, PhD (*Head of Chemistry*)
M J Collins, MA (*History*)
A C Cooper, MSc, BA (*Mathematics*)
S J Curwood, BPE (*PE and Games*)
L R Denny, MA (*English*)
A C W Dixon, BA (*Head of Geography*)
T B Earnshaw, MA, MPhil (*Classics*)
Miss J A Ellis (*Junior School*)
P J Emms, BA (*Modern Languages*)
Mrs A L Fairhurst, BA (*Junior School*)
Miss C Gillam, MA, PhD (*Head of English*)
Miss S J Goodgame, BEng, CEng (*Chemistry*)
J H Grundy, BA, PhD (*Head of Sixth Form, Philosophy and Religious Studies*)
R P Harskin, MA, PhD (*Head of French*)
Miss M H Hunter, BSc (*Junior School*)
P A James, MA (*Head of Biology*)
J N Laird, BA (*Head of German*)

C Lowndes (*Head of Computing*)
B Macdonald (*Head of ICT*)
Rev R C Martin, MA (*Chaplain and Head of Religious Studies*)
M T H McNeile, BA (*Junior School*)
A N Middleton, BA (*Head of Mathematics*)
P M Noll, MA (*Head of History*)
M N Pearce, BMus, FRCO (*Director of Music*)
D E Pearson, DipAD, ATD (*Head of Art*)
J F Place, BA (*Head of Junior School and Latin*)
Mrs J R Rowsell, BA (*English*)
Mrs E Rudgard, BA (*English*)
P A Shrimpton, MA, MEd (*Mathematics*)
T Skipwith, BSc (*Biology*)
D L Smith, MBE, TD, MA (*Chemistry*)
P D Smith, MA, LTCL (*Music*)
S A Spowart, BA (*Classics*)
T R Squires, BA (*Mathematics*)
Mrs E Stapleton (*Deputy Head of Junior School*)
Mrs M-R Staton, L-ès-L (*French*)
Mrs T Sulston, BA, ATC (*Art*)
R Teague, BSc (*Mathematics*)
E J White, BSc (*Geography*)
M J Wilkinson, BSc (*Head of Physics and Science*)
R A Winstone, DipPE (*PE and Games*)

Assistant Music Staff:
Dr E M Baird
Ms A Bendy
C Britton
S Cutting
T Dawes
R Dutton
Miss J A Ellis
J Hill
Mrs J Ives
M R Jones
Mrs M A Malpas
Miss A Martin-Davies
R K Stevens
Dr J P Whitworth
S J Wilson
G Williams
Mrs L E Woods

Clerk to the Governors and Bursar: M H Kefford, OBE

Assistant Bursar: Miss S Haynes

Matron: Mrs W M Collier-Parker

Numbers. There are 575 day boys in the School. The Sixth Form numbers 145. The main entry points are at 7, 9, 11 and 13. 16 boys are taken at 7, a further 16 or so at 9, and up to 60 at the age of 11. Up to 25 boys are taken at 13. A limited number of pupils joins the School directly into the Sixth Form. Almost all pupils go on to higher education when they leave.

Pastoral. From 7-10, boys are in form groups of approximately 16. Their form teacher is responsible for day-to-day care, pastoral welfare and academic progress. Boys from age 11 are allocated to one of the six Houses on entry. Houses are divided into four Houserooms. A Housemaster or Tutor in charge of each section is responsible for the pastoral and academic welfare of pupils in his Houseroom. The Senior Tutor, Chaplain and Matron also play their part in the pastoral organisation of the school.

Buildings. The school buildings include a Chapel and Theatre, Library, Classrooms, Science Laboratories, Music School and Art Department. New Science Laboratories were opened in 1991. There are two computer laboratories with a network of RM PCs. A Technology Department opened in 1992. The expanded Junior School was opened in 1993, and new changing rooms and English Department in 1996. New classrooms, Lecture Theatre, Careers Centre and a Sixth Form Centre were opened in September 1998. In June 2001 a £2m Sports Complex will be opened.

Organisation and Curriculum. The curriculum is designed to ensure that all boys study a core of subjects to GCSE level. This core consists of English, French, Maths and Science. In addition, there is a wide variety of options taken by pupils in their GCSE years including Latin and Greek, Geography, German, History, Computing and Art. Most GCSEs are taken in the Fifth year although a few may be taken earlier. There is no streaming and very little setting until the third year.

Mixed Arts and Science subject combinations are common and a boy's A levels are complemented by a wide range of 'minor' (general studies) courses.

Under the new Sixth Form curriculum, many boys take 4 AS and 3 A2s, but a significant proportion take 4 or even 5 AS and A2 subjects.

Careers. There is a well-equipped Careers Room, and there is a team of Careers Staff. Careers Aptitude Tests are offered to all boys in the Fifth Form, and there is a weekly lecture in the Sixth Form.

Games and Societies. In addition to Physical Education which is taught in the curriculum, games play a major part in the School. Major sports are Rugby in the Michaelmas Term, Hockey and Rowing in the Hilary and Cricket, Rowing and Tennis in the Trinity Term. Other sports include Basketball, Fencing, Cross-Country, Sailing and Athletics. There are Army, Navy and Air Force sections of the CCF and a Community Service Organisation. Many boys participate inthe Duke of Edinburgh Award Scheme. Girls from Oxford High School participate in the CCF.

The main playing field, surrounded by the River Cherwell, adjoins the grounds of School House and covers 11 acres. An additional playing field of 13 acres with its own pavilion and changing rooms has been developed at Sandford-on-Thames, three miles from the school.

Music is extremely important in the School and there is a large Choral Society, a Madrigal Group, Senior and Junior Orchestras, a Jazz Band and other ensembles. Many pupils are involved in Drama and there are several productions in the year. There are many other societies and clubs covering cultural and recreational activities.

Fees. The fees for dayboys are £6,525 pa; 7 year olds £4,950. They are payable termly in advance and are inclusive of text-books and stationery. The Registration Fee (non-returnable) is £30.

Admission and Scholarships. (*see* Entrance Scholarship section) Admission at ages 7, 9 and 11 is by a School Entrance Examination held in February each year.

Admission at age 13 is by the Common Entrance Examination for candidates at Preparatory Schools and by a School Entrance Examination held in May each year for candidates at maintained schools. Up to nine scholarships (typically) of £1,000 pa are awarded each year at age 13, and Music Scholarships up to £3,000 pa in total value. A Games Scholarship worth £1,000 pa is awarded to candidates under 14 on 1 September of the year of entry.

In special circumstances awards of bursaries may also be made.

A limited number of boys is admitted each year direct into the Sixth Form after interview and school report. Offers are conditional on good GCSE grades.

Candidates can be registered at any age.

Full particulars can be obtained from the Admissions Secretary.

Term of Entry. Boys enter the School in September. Exceptionally, for example if parents move into the Oxford area, other arrangements can be made.

Choristerships and Exhibitions. There are 16 Choristerships. Entry is by Voice Trial and candidates should normally be between the ages of 7 and 9. For a Chorister half the tuition fee is remitted. All enquiries about Choristerships should be addressed to the Dean of Divinity, Magdalen College, Oxford. Choristers normally continue at the School after their voices have broken. In deserving cases further financial help may be available.

Honours. In the six years 1995–2000 inclusive 76 places have been gained at Oxford and Cambridge universities, and 320 places at other universities, from an average Sixth Form year-group of 70.

Old Waynfletes. *Secretary:* W J Prickett, 2 Southmere, Brize Norton, Oxon.

Charitable status. Magdalen College School Oxford Limited is a Registered Charity, number 295785. Its aims and objectives are to promote and provide for the education of children.

Malvern College

Malvern Worcestershire WR14 3DF
Tel: (01684) 581500
Fax: (01684) 581616
e-mail: inquiry@malcol.worcs.sch.uk

Malvern College was founded in 1862, opened in 1865 and was incorporated by Royal Charter in 1929. Malvern College is co-educational and takes pupils from the age of 3 through to 18.

Motto: *Sapiens qui prospicit.*

Ten members of the Council may be nominated, one each by the Lords-Lieutenant of the Counties of Gloucestershire, Herefordshire and Worcestershire, by the Vice-Chancellors of the Universities of Oxford, Cambridge and Birmingham, by the Service Boards of the Navy, Army and Air Force Departments of the Ministry of Defence, and by the Headmaster and Teaching Staff. Ten members are elected by the Governors, and between six and ten are appointed by the Council.

President and Visitor: The Lord Bishop of Worcester

Council:
N G U Morris (*Chairman*)
Professor K J Davey, OBE (*Vice Chairman*)
L E Linaker (*Treasurer*)
I D S Beer, CBE
R K Black
J B Blackshaw
N R Bomford
P G Brough
Mrs R Dawes, JP
Miss A M Edwards
P H F Edwards
Captain R H Farnfield, RN
The Rt Revd P Hullah
Mrs G J Hylson-Smith
J C Lees
Mrs D Russell
P Temple-Morris, MP
Air Vice Marshal J F H Tetley, CB, CVO
Dr M J Tilby
R T H Wilson

Bursar and Secretary: M Eglington, MA

***Headmaster:* H C K Carson**, BA

Deputy Heads:
W J Denny, NDD, ATC
Mrs M L Kontarines, BSc

Teaching Staff:
R E Allen, BSc(*Econ*), MPhil
Mrs S K Angling, BA
Miss A S L Appleby, BA
Mrs J Bennett, BA
Miss A Bourgouin, DEA
R H Brierly, BEd
P J Chappell, BA
Mrs S E Close, TCertPE
Mrs J Cockbill, MA
G M Cramp, BSc
S Doidge, BSc
M C Frayn, BA(*Econ*)
Mrs R A Gallagher, BEng
J A Gauci, BA
R W German, BSc
Mrs H C Goddard, DipEd, CertTEFL
P Godsland, MA
P J Gray, MA
C Hall, BSc, CBiol, MIBiol (*Careers Master*)
Mrs L M Hallett, BA
M A T Harris, MA
F O Harriss, MA (*Director of Studies*)
M A Hayes
Mrs P G R Heptenstall, License, BTS
Mrs A M Higgins, BA
S C Holroyd, BA
R A Hookham, BA
P Jackson, BSc, PhD
Miss C M Jones, MA
S N Kinge, BSc, PhD
J P Knee, MA
R G Lacey, BSc
Mrs A L Lafferty, BA
M Lakin, BEd
Mrs J S Lamberton, BSc
R A Lister, BA, MTS, PhD
A A G Logan, BA
D G Matthews, MA
D L Mensforth, MA
A J Murtagh, BA
T M Newsholme, BA
D M Penter, BSc, PhD, AKC, FLS
M A L Phillips, BA, FRCO, ARCM
Mrs M T Plant, BS
P I Quickfall, BA (*Senior Tutor*)
Mrs P D Richardson, BA
Mrs H M Robinson, BEd
J A O Russell, BSc, BA
Miss D J Sheppard, BSc
J P Siviter, MA
I D Sloan, ARCM, BMus, CertEd
A Smith, MA
Mrs J J Smith, BSc
R J Smith, BEd
R S D Smith, BSc, MIBiol
S R Spanyol, FTCL, ARCM, LTCL
R P Stafford, BSc, PhD
Mrs S M Sykes, BA
R G Thurlow, MA
R A J Tims, MA
N W L Turner, MA
Miss K Tutcher
Mrs R A Urbainczyk, MEd
T J Urbainczyk, BA
A R Walwyn, BA
M J Weaver, BA
B B White, BEd
R B Winwood, MSc, PhD
R G Witcomb, MA, DPhil, CEng, MIEE

Chaplain: The Revd B E Close, MA
Assistant Chaplain: N A T Menon, MA

Registrar: Mrs S R Jackson, BSc

Medical Officers:
Sarah D Roberts, MB, ChB, MRCGP
D K Payler, MB, BS, LRCP, MRCS, DObstRCOG

Boarding Houses:
Mr J A O Russell (*School House*)
Mr M J Weaver (*Number 1*)
Mr B B White (*Number 2*)
Mrs A L Lafferty (*Number 3*)
Mrs H M Robinson (*Number 4*)
Mrs J S Lamberton (*Number 6*)
Mr R H Brierly (*Number 7*)
Mr R A J Tims (*Number 8*)
Dr R A Lister (*Number 9*)

Day Houses:
Boys: Mr A J Murtagh (*Number 5*)
Girls: Mrs H M Robinson, Mrs P Stagg (*Numbers 3/4 The Lees*)

Malvern College is particularly fortunate in its location. Situated on the lower slopes of the Malvern Hills and close to the centre of Great Malvern, the main College campus commands striking views across the Severn Plain towards the Cotswolds.

Founded in 1865, the College offers coeducation from the age of 3 to 18. There are currently some 773 pupils in the school, 228 of whom are in Hillstone, the Prep School with its Pre-Prep Department, Hampton. At age 13+ pupils join the senior part of the school where there are three girls' boarding houses, one girls' day house and seven boys' houses, one of which is for day boys. The school is justly proud of its high academic standards and of its pastoral care.

Further details of the School are available in the Prospectus which may be obtained by contacting the Registrar.

Curriculum. In the Foundation Year (Year 9), pupils study a wide variety of subjects. Many are introduced to a second modern foreign language. The object of this year (as in extra-curricular activities) is to show pupils as much as possible of what the College has to offer. In the Remove (Year 10) there is a narrowing of choices, though slightly more subjects are maintained here than will finally be taken at GCSE. All pupils take one subject from Art and Design, Drama, Music and Technology. Pupils are carefully advised on choice of subject by their Housemasters/Housemistresses and Tutors in consultation with their parents. At GCSE the following subjects are offered: Mathematics, English (usually plus English Literature), French, Religious Studies (short course, taken in the Remove by many pupils) and Double Award combined Science. There is a choice from: Latin, Greek, German, Spanish, Geography, History. Pupils must also choose at least one subject from: Art and Design, Drama, Music, Technology and GCSE PE to keep their portfolio broad. Most pupils take nine GCSEs in the Hundred (Year 11). It is possible for pupils to take three separate Science GCSEs instead of the Double Award, though for some this means dropping another optional subject.

In the Sixth Form, pupils can choose to study either A-levels or the International Baccalaureate. In the IB, combinations of Art & Design, Biology, Business Studies, Chemistry, Economics, English, French, German, Geography, History, Latin, Mathematics, Music, Physics, Spanish, Technology and Theatre Arts are offered. All pupils take the valuable Theory of Knowledge Course. A-levels are available in the IB subjects (except Business Studies and Theatre Arts) and also Classical Civilisation, Greek, Further Mathematics, Physical Education, Politics and Religious Studies. Pupils take four AS subjects in the Lower Sixth and most drop to three subjects at A level. The timetable allows many different combinations, although a pupil's choice is carefully monitored.

Those taking A-levels take in addition the Sixth Form Skills Course leading to qualifications in the Key Skills of Communication, Numeracy and Information Technology. The course also covers Health Education and university entry and a variety of options including Law, Fitness for Life, Philosophy and Healthy Eating.

Pastoral Care. In addition to their Housemaster/Housemistress and House Tutor, all pupils have a Form Tutor who shares the responsibility for their overall personal development and well-being. Members of the Sixth Form choose their own Tutor.

Health Care. There is a modern and well-equipped Medical Centre staffed 24 hours a day by SRNs.

Coaches. During the school year there are three half-term holidays and about five leave-out weekends. On these occasions, school coaches are run to Cardiff, Exeter, Guildford, London Paddington, Knutsford and Derby, according to demand. Coaches to Heathrow and Birmingham airports run at the start of half term and the end of term.

New Facility. The school has recently opened St Edmund's Hall for Chamber Music and Lectures, while underneath the Cork Centre provides an excellent venue for VIth Form activities.

Activities. The School has a strong tradition of expedition training and outdoor pursuits, including Rock-climbing, Kayaking, Sailing, Mountaineering (Summer and Winter, UK and Abroad). Opportunities exist for the use of the College's cottage in the Brecon Beacons and participation in expeditions in holiday time which take place annually in Scotland in February, and have also gone to Iceland, the Alps, Kashmir, Scandinavia and Ecuador in the Summer. Many of these activities, are integral within the voluntary CCF (which has RM, Army and RAF sections) and Duke of Edinburgh Award Scheme. There is also a flourishing Community Service Organisation.

Art. The Arts Centre has excellent facilities for Painting, Drawing, Printmaking (including etching), Ceramics, Photography and 3-Dimensional Design.

Careers. In the GCSE year pupils sit the ISCO/Morrisby careers guidance tests which assess ability, personality, aptitude and interests. An in depth interview with a tutor helps pupils to make sensible and informed choices about their future. All pupils in the Lower Sixth spend one week away from school on work experience. Pupils may also sit the Centigrade Higher Education questionnaire to support the advice offered by the Head of Careers, Sixth Form Tutor and Housemaster/Housemistress on choice of course at University. Malvern College is a member of the Independent Schools Careers Organisation (ISCO).

Design and Technology. The new Centre ensures that pupils have the opportunity to develop the knowledge and skills offered by this exciting area alongside those of other curriculum subjects. Within Technology there is the opportunity to integrate Design, Business and Industry links, CDT, Food Technology, Information Technology and Textiles. The Centre offers the latest facilities to promote project work in all these areas.

Drama. There is a School Theatre which seats 350 and is in regular use throughout the year. The town Festival Theatre is used for special productions.

Games. Boys play Association Football in the Autumn Term, Rugby Football and Hockey in the Lent and Cricket, Athletics, Tennis and Swimming in the Summer. Girls play Lacrosse, Netball and Hockey in the Autumn and Lent Terms; Athletics, Cricket, Swimming, Rounders and Tennis are their main sports in the Summer. There is a large Sports Hall, Squash and Racket Courts, indoor shooting range, weight-training room and an indoor swimming pool. Boys and girls are also offered Aerobics, Athletics, Badminton, Basketball, Cross-Country Running, Dance, Fencing, Fly-Fishing, Golf, Gymnastics, Hockey, Judo, Kayaking, Polo, Rackets, Sailing, Shooting, Squash, Swimming, Tennis, Volleyball and Winchester Fives. An all-weather sports pitch is due for completion in September 2001.

Music. Malvern has a strong musical tradition. The well-equipped Music School (24 practice rooms, 3 large rehearsal rooms) includes a recording studio and a music technology laboratory. Pupils of all standards are encouraged both instrumentally and vocally, and regular performances (internal and at local venues) are given by orchestras, bands, chamber groups and choirs. The Music Department works closely with the Drama Department and musicals are produced regularly.

Admission. Most pupils are admitted between their thirteenth and fourteenth birthdays and may qualify for admission to the school by a satisfactory performance in either the Common Entrance Examination or the annual Scholarship Examination. Special arrangements are made for pupils who wish to enter from maintained schools.

Pupils are also admitted to the Sixth Form at 16 on the basis of GCSEs, interviews and tests.

Application for admission should be made to the Registrar. A request may be made for a pupil to go to a particular House, and a pupil should be placed on a House list as soon as possible.

Scholarships. (*see* Entrance Scholarship section) The school offers a generous number of Scholarships and Exhibitions at 13+ each year, varying in value according to merit up to 50% of the current fees. Scholarships, but not Exhibitions, are index-linked to fee increases. These awards are given for pupils with academic ability or special talent in Art, Drama, Music, Sport or Technology.

Candidates for 13+ Scholarships must be under 14 years of age on 1 September in the year of the examination but there is no age limit for Exhibitions.

Malvern has a strong Sixth Form entry and a number of separate Scholarships, Exhibitions and Sports awards are available to candidates for Sixth Form places.

Further remission of fees may be possible where financial need can be established.

Fees 2000/2001. The fee deposit payable before entry is £360 and is refunded as a deduction from the final account. The composite fee, inclusive of all obligatory extras, is £5,310 per term. Day fees are £3,860 per term.

Day Pupils and Day Boarders. Day pupils have a shorter day and their fees are £3,365 per term. Day boarders are accommodated in the boarding houses.

The Malvernian Society. On leaving, Malvernians retain contact with the College by joining the Malvernian Society. They also become members of the OM Club which organises various teams and a number of social functions. Secretary of the Malvernian Society: J B Blackshaw (Tel: (01684) 581500). The *Register* (Third Supplement, 1977) and *List of Members* (1996) are available from the Secretary.

Hillstone (Malvern College Junior School) is situated on an adjoining campus and prepares boys and girls primarily for entry to the Senior part of Malvern College. Entries are welcomed at all ages and those who qualify to join the school from age 11 are guaranteed entry to the Senior part of Malvern College at 13. For further details, please see the Preparatory School section, Part V.

Charitable status. Malvern College Incorporated is a Registered Charity, number 527578. It is a charity established for the purpose of educating children.

The Manchester Grammar School

Manchester M13 0XT.
Tel: 0161-224 7201
Fax: 0161-257 2446

The Manchester Grammar School was founded in 1515 to promote 'godliness and good learning' and it has endeavoured throughout its history to remain true to these principles, while adapting to changing times. It is now an independent boys' day school with 1,400+ pupils. Almost all leavers go on to university, about a quarter of them going to Oxford or Cambridge. A well qualified teaching staff of more than 120 men and women provides all pupils with a broad curriculum and rich extra-curricular opportunities.

The tradition of offering places to clever pupils regardless of their background is maintained by MGS bursaries. About a third of the pupils in the school are fee-assisted. They come both from primary and preparatory schools and represent a wide variety of cultural, ethnic and religious backgrounds. Many undertake a long daily journey.

Motto: Sapere Aude (Dare to be wise)

Co-optative Governors:

M I Davis
A M Dean (*Treasurer*)
J B Diggines
W T Hall
Professor T A Hinchliffe
Miss M Hulme
C G Kenyon (*Chairman*)
Joy Kingsley
Mrs F M S Marsh
Sir David Trippier, RD, JP, DL
J P Wainwright
E M Watkins

Ex-Officio Governors: The Dean of Manchester, The President of Corpus Christi College, Oxford, The Lord Mayor of Manchester

Representative Governors of:
Manchester University: Dr R Quayle
Oxford University: Professor A Jones
Bursar and Clerk to the Governors: Mrs G M Batchelor

***High Master:* G M Stephen**, BA, PhD, FRSA

Second Master: P A Laycock, JP, MA

Surmasters:
I Thorpe, MA
N A Sheldon, MA, BSc, MPhil, CStat, MBCS, CEng
Head of Arts Side: N J Munday, BA
Head of Science Side: J S Willson, BSc, DPhil
Head of Middle School: S V Leeming, BSc, CChem, MRSC
Head of Lower School: J W Mangnall, MA

Assistant Academic Staff:

T Ahmed, BSc
R Alderson, MA
Miss R E Aldred, BMus, GRNCM
Miss R E Anderson, BSc
M E Appleson, BA
Miss V E Askew, BSc
G I S Bailey, MA
P N A Baylis, BA
M Bennett, BA
L T Bohl, BA, MA, MEd
R C Bradford, BSc, PhD, MInstP, CPhys
D J Bristow, MA, MA, MIL
D Brown, BD, STM, MLitt
C Buckley, BSc
S J Burch, BSc, PhD, MIBiol
N T Burin, BSc, AFIMA
Mrs H Butchart, BA, LTCL
J A Cantrell, MA, PhD
G E Chandler, MA
E C F Cittanova, L-ès-L, L-ès-L, M-ès-L, DEA
M P A Coffey, MA
J T Coller, BA
Miss A F Crofts, BA
P Crofts, BFA
H S Crowther, BSc, CMath, FIMA
G G Curtis, MA
Mrs E R Dalton, L-ès-L
A J Dean, MMus, ARCM, FRCO
R A H Dean, BA
Mrs L M Dennis, BA
Mrs J Dobbs, BA
A P Dobson, BA, MA
S J Duffy, BSc, MIBiol
P J Dunbar, BA
D Dyson, BA
B S Edwards, MA
M Ellis, BSc, DPhil
R J R Foot
Miss F A Forsyth, MA
S Foster, BA, MA
R J Frost, MA
J C Gibb, MA
R L Hand, BSc, MSc
D F Hares, BSc
W J Hardiman, BA
F Hayes
D G Herne, MA
M S R Hesketh, BSc, MSc
K A Hicks, BSc
A Hodskinson, BSc, PhD
J E M Horth, BA
Mrs H M Hughes, BSc
D G Hutton, BA
G Jackson, BSc
D Jeys, BSc, MA
G R Johnson, BSc
D C K Jones, MA, PhD
D W Jones, BSc
R N Kelly, BA, MA, MPhil
C J E Laithwaite, BA
I Leverton, MA
R Lunn, BEd
M W S MacGillivray, BA
A E McDonald, BSc, PhD
Miss J L McMurray-Taylor, BA
R I A Martin, BA, PhD
N J Matthews, BSc
A A Mayne, BA, MA
Miss A E Mills, BA
Miss R J Minto, BA
D Moss, MA
Miss L J Murphy, BA
G Myers, BA
Mrs J Neilson, BA
Mrs J H Nickson, BA
I W Orrell, BTech
C J Owen, BA
B L Packham, MA, LLB, MIL
T J Pattison, BSc, AFIMA
Mrs E de R Pentreath, MA
A C Pickwick, BSc, MSc, FRAS, AMBCS
P R Ponder, BA
J Potts, BSc
E R Prestwich, BA, BPhil
M R Price, BA
R Price, BA, PhD
G A Read, BSc, PhD
P C Rees, BA
N A Reynolds, BA
L B Rix, BA, MA
Miss H E Sargeant, BA, MA
G E Seel, MA
L J Shaw, JP, BA
J H Shoard, MA
Mrs C Short, BSc
P Shufflebottom, BA
R W Simpson, BA
A M Smith, BA
A N Smith, BA
Mrs L Speed
Mrs P Squires, BSc, PhD
C P Thom, MA
P A M Thompson, BA, DPhil, MA(Ed)
R J Travers, BA
S H Uren, BSc, PhD
N Warrack, BA, MA
J M Webb, MA
P J Wheeler, BSc
D P Whiteley, MA
Miss R G Williams, BA, DPhil
N G Williams, BA
L A Witton, BSc
J N Wood, BSc

Medical Officer: Dr J L Burn, FRCP, FRCPCH

High Master's Secretary: Mrs C Irish

Registrar: Mrs P Hesketh

Registration and Entry. Boys may be registered at any time prior to the Entrance Examination in their year of proposed entry, which is normally at age 11. Some places are available at 13 via the Common Entrance Examination. Entry to the Sixth Form follows interview and appropriate qualifications. Current details are available from the Registrar.

Tuition Fees. From September 2000, £5,400 per annum.

Bursaries. The Governing Body awards means-tested bursaries.

Organisation and Curriculum. The eight unstreamed forms in each of the first two years follow the same broad curriculum, comprising English, Mathematics, Latin, French, History, Geography, General Science, Religious Studies, CDT, Music, Art, Drama, PE, Swimming and Games. From Year 3 there are nine forms in each year and opportunities exist to take up a third language and spend more time on creative subjects and Religious Studies. Significant choices in the curriculum are delayed until the end of Year 4. GCSE in French is taken at the end of Year 4, with other GCSE subjects being examined at the end of Year 5.

In the Sixth Form boys take three A level subjects and, in minority time, study Philosophy, English and a choice of General Studies options.

Pastoral Care. Each form in the school is looked after by a Form Tutor, who is one of the form's subject teachers. The Form Tutor is responsible, with the appropriate senior members of staff, for the academic and general progress of each pupil. Regular written reports are supplemented by Parents' Evenings. The School Medical Room is staffed by a part-time doctor and one full-time and one part-time Nursing Sister. The older pupils selected as prefects are encouraged to help younger pupils in running societies and other extra-curricular activities.

Creative Arts. All pupils experience Music, Art, CDT and Drama within the curriculum, but each of these areas offers large numbers of pupils activities during the lunch-hour and after school. There are choirs, orchestras and instrumental tuition; plays, drama workshops and musicals; clubs for art, pottery, engineering and computer design. There are regular exhibitions and public performances both in school and in public venues.

Sport. All boys take part in timetabled games and the school produces successful teams in most sports. There is a gymnasium and a heated indoor swimming pool. A new sports hall was opened in March 1997 by Michael Atherton, Captain of Cricket at the School, Cambridge University and England. Older boys have a wide choice of sporting activity within the timetable, with some groups travelling to use facilities outside the school.

Outdoor Pursuits. The school has a long tradition of camping and trekking and there are numerous weekend and holiday excursions. Four annual camps cater for the full age range and offer a wide choice of activities. In recent years expeditions have visited the Alps, the Pyrenees, Morocco and Scandinavia.

Foreign Visits. Many trips abroad are organised each year, providing enjoyable holidays of broad educational value. Destinations include France, Germany, Spain, Russia, Italy, Greece, Tunisia, India and China.

Societies and Activities. There are over 50 societies catering for most interests, Chess and Bridge Clubs, and a school newspaper produced by boys.

Prizes and Scholarships. In addition to bursaries, funds are provided for prizes to help deserving pupils with the expense of a range of extra-curricular activities.

Old Mancunians' Association and MGS Parents' Society. The Old Boys' Association has many regional sections. There is an annual Old Boys' Dinner in Manchester. The Honorary Secretary is Mr W T Hall, 38 Broad Walk, Wilmslow, Cheshire SK9 5PL.

The MGS Parents' Society has a membership of pupils, parents and friends and exists to support school activities and promote a programme of social events.

Charitable status. The Manchester Grammar School is a Registered Charity, number 529909. The aim of the School is to prepare able boys from the Manchester area, regardless of their financial background, to proceed to university and make a positive contribution to society in their adult life.

Marlborough College

Wiltshire SN8 1PA
Tel: Main Switchboard: (01672) 892200
The Master: (01672) 892400
The Bursar: (01672) 892390
Admissions (01672) 892300
Fax: Main No: (01672) 892207; The Master: (01672) 892407

Founded 1843. Incorporated by Royal Charter

Visitor: The Archbishop of Canterbury

Council:
President: The Rt Revd The Lord Bishop of Salisbury

P D Orchard-Lisle, CBE, TD, DL, MA, FRICS (*Chairman*)
J D F Dickson, MA (*Chairman of Finance Committee*)
The Very Revd A F Knight, MA
Sir Anthony Greener
The Lady Wakeham, MBE
Lady Appleyard
Field Marshal Lord Inge, GCB, DL
R J H Fleck, LLB
Sir Hayden Phillips, KCB
Mrs J J d'A Campbell, CMG
The Rt Revd Peter Hullah
The Baroness Noakes, DBE
Dr C P M Heath
S R Roger Hurn

Clerk to the Council: R J C Ford

***Master:* E J H Gould**, MA

Deputy Heads:
Mrs R S Groves, BA, PhD
R B Pick, BSc

Director of Studies: A Gist, BA, MA

Senior Master: J P Rothwell, MA

Assistant Staff:
J E Osborne, MA
*D Whiting, MA (*Modern Languages*)
A Clark, BSc, PhD
R T Sanderson, BSc
C T Graham, MA
H O de Saram, MA
†R Jones-Parry, BSc, PhD, CChem, MRSC (*Summerfield*)
*J E Patching, BEd (*Physical Education*)
Ms C C Russell, BA
*J B Selwyn, BSc, MA (*Careers*)
†A J Brown, MA (*Littlefield*)
A S Eales, BMus
†A D McKnight, BSc (*Turner House*)
*R W Nelson, MA (*Director of Music*)

A D Foley, MA
*Rev D J Dales, MA, BD (*Religious Education*)
†C A Fraser, MA (*Preshute*)
†N G Hamilton, BA, PhD (*B House*)
Ms J J McFarlane, BA DPhil
†A W Richards, MA (*C3*)
†N M Allott BSc (*Cotton House*)
*J A Genton, MA (*Science*)
†M J Ponsford, BA, PhD (*Barton Hill*)
†Mrs S M Clark, BA (*Mill Mead*)
P G M Ford, MA
Miss J E Gall, BEd
*J D C Hicks, BA (*Design and Technology*)
†Lady Cayley, MA (*Morris House*)
*D R Smith, MA (*English*)
A K J Yearsley, BA PhD
D Allen, BA, MA
N R Cleminson, MA
*A B D Harrison, BSc (*Mathematics*)
Mrs P J Harrison, BSc
*K J D Richards, MA (*Geography*)
†Ms A D Sharp, BSc, PhD (*New Court*)
P R Adams, BEd
I G Crabbe, MA, FRCO, ARCM
†Mrs G A Patching, BEd (*Elmhurst*)
R Jowett, BSc
Mrs A Korba Jowett, BMet, MMet
*J F Lloyd, BA, MPhil (*Classics*)
†M W McVeigh, BSc (*C2*)
C S Smith, BEng, MSc
Ms L J Playfair, BA
*V J Stokes, BA (*Art*)
S J Ellis, BA
S C Clayton, BA
*S M D Dempster, BA (*Biology*)
R T Markham, BA
*N J Bryant, BA (*Drama*)
M Conlen, BSc
A J Arkwright, BA
Mrs S A Bryant, BA
Mrs W G de Saram, BA, MA, MSc
J P W Dixon, MA
Mrs L F W Ford, MA
*P N Keighley, BEng (*Business Studies*)
E G Nobes, MA
Miss R L Tolputt, BA
N E Briers, BEd
*Miss C A Coates, BSc (*Chemistry*)
*D R Du Croz, MA (*History*)
T J Gibbon, BA
Mrs S L J Greenwood, BSc
†N J L Moore, BSc, MA (*C1*)
T J W Ridley, GRSM
*C E Barclay, BSc (*Physics*)
M A Gow, BA
T E Hare, MA
R D A Lamont, BA
N Nelson-Piercy, BA
W D L Nicholas, BEng
Mrs L J Richards, BSc, PhD
G B Shearn, BSc
R A Cockett, MA
G A Doyle, BSc, MSc, PhD, MRSC, CChem
T G R Marvin, MA
J H Parnham, BA, MA
Miss E Piqué, BA, MA
G R Playfair, BA
*N O R Rosedale, BSc (*Outdoor Activities*)
Miss R Shorrock, BA, MA
Miss C Toomer, GGSM
I R Clarkson, BSc, MPhil
Miss E M Dickson, BA
Miss J A Harrison, BA
A S Jennings, BA
J Cload, ACHE
J A Sheppe, AB, MPhil
M B Blossom, BA
Miss E M Ellwood, BA
J A Hodgson, BSc
Miss R Kettle, BSc
C M McCay, MA, LIB, MLitt
O T Moelwyn-Hughes, BA, LLB, Mst
P J O'Sullivan, BA
R Tong

Bursar: D S Williamson, BA
Chaplain: Rev J G W Dickie, MA, BLitt
Medical Officers:
Dr R Rosalie, MB, ChB, MRCGP, DRCOG
Dr S Hanson, MBBS, MRCGP, DCH
Senior Admissions Tutor: Mrs R S Groves, BA, PhD
Librarian: Mrs P M Lacey, MA
Archivist: T E Rogers, BSc, PhD
Master's Secretary: Miss E H McKerrow, MA

There are approximately 800 boys and girls in the 14 houses in the College. The College is fully co-educational, 13 being the normal age of entry for both girls and boys. A limited number of boys and girls are admitted to the Sixth Form.

Registration. Boys and girls are admitted in the Michaelmas Term on the basis of the Common Entrance examination and Sixth Form examinations. The 13+ Scholarship examination is in February/March and the Sixth Form Scholarship examination is in November.

Scholarships. (*see* Entrance Scholarship section) Scholarships range in value up to 50% of full fees. Augmentation above 50% is available on the basis of need. At least twenty awards are available at 13+,including Music, Art and Sport, and at least six for Sixth Form entry. From time to time there are a number of other special categories of scholarship based upon parental occupation and particular abilities. Anniversary Bursaries, subject to a means test, based on strengths of one or more of academic work, sport, art and music are also available. A number of Children of Clergy Bursaries are awarded on interview and consultation, in addition to the automatic 15% reduction for all Children of Clergy.

Applications and enquiries about entries and scholarships should be addressed to **The Senior Admissions Tutor.**

Universities & Careers. Nearly all pupils who come to Marlborough go on into the VIth Form and virtually all proceed to degree courses. Twenty-seven A and AS level subjects are available in almost any combination in the large Sixth Form, plus additional courses. The Careers Department is modern and well-equipped, and assists Housemasters and Housemistresses in advising boys and girls and their parents as to careers and university choices, in addition to gap year projects.

Extra Curricular. Good games facilities are available with a modern Sports Hall, spacious playing fields, two all-weather pitches, an athletics track and numerous tennis courts. The main games are athletics, hockey, rugby, tennis, cricket and netball; alternative games include lacrosse, soccer, rackets, fives, shooting, swimming and squash. There is a strong Outdoor Activities Department, which offers the Duke of Edinburgh Award as well as climbing, canoeing, sub-aqua and orienteering; the CCF covers adventure training as part of its basic course, with specialist leadership training to a high standard. School Societies offering activities at different levels enable interests to be nurtured and, for those who enjoy country pursuits, the River Kennet and two trout lakes provide fishing and the College has its own beagle pack.

Music. Nearly half the boys and girls play a musical

instrument. There are three school orchestras, a wind band, a chamber orchestra, a brass band, Chapel Choir and a choral society; also numerous small instrumental and choral groups.

Drama. There are over fifteen productions each year, including two school plays, Junior productions and a house drama festival. Many are produced and directed by pupils. The Sixth Form curriculum includes Theatre Studies and Drama is an option at GCSE.

Art and Design. All pupils study Art in their first year and many go on to take the subject at GCSE and A level. The Art School is at the centre of the school and believes that all pupils can acquire a good standard of visual literacy across a variety of artistic disciplines. A new purpose-built centre houses Design, which is taught throughout the school.

Fees. The basic termly fee is £5,470 for boarding and £4,100 for day pupils (in January 2001).

The Marlburian Club, Marlborough College. *Hon Secretary, W J Uzielli, Esq. (From March 2002 M C W Evans, Esq).*

Charitable status. Marlborough College is a Registered Charity, number 309486 incorporated by Royal Charter to provide education.

Merchant Taylors' School

Sandy Lodge Northwood Middlesex HA6 2HT.
Tel: Head Master's Secretary: (01923) 821850
Main switchboard: (01923) 820644
Admissions Secretary: (01923) 845514
Bursar: (01923) 825669
Fax: (01923) 835110

Motto: *Homo plantat, homo irrigat, sed Deus dat incrementum.*

The Governors of the School:
Dr C H Nourse, MA, MB, BChir (Cambridge), FRCP (*Chairman*)
G F Brown
R W E Charlton
M C Clarke, MA (Cambridge), FCA
C P Hare
J R Owens, MA (Oxford), FRSA
Miss M Rudland, BSc
Dr J H S Sichel, MB, BS (London)
M W G Skinner

***Head Master:* J R Gabitass**, MA, St John's College, Oxford

Second Master and Director of Studies: C J J Collier, MA, St Catharine's College, Cambridge

Senior Master: Dr T R Stubbs, BSc, PhD, CBiol, MIBiol

Chief Classics Master: A Woolley, BA

Chief Modern Studies Master: R P S Le Rougetel, MA

Head of Upper School: R L Wilson, MA

Chief Mathematics Master: O L C Toller, MA

Chief Science Master: K G Bridgeman, MA

Head of Middle School: A J Booth, MA

Chief Languages Master: *W R Bingham, BA, PhD

Chief English Master: D G Andrews, BA, MA

Head of Lower School: D Green, MA

Chaplain: The Revd R D E Bolton, MA

Assistant Staff:
Art & Design:
J E Ombler, NDD, ATD (*Head of Art and Design*)
Ms A D Badar, BA
A J D Gerrard, ABIPP

Classics:
A Woolley, BA (*Head of Classics*)
D J Critchley, MA (*Assistant Director of Studies*)
M F Drury, MA (*Head of White House*)
M C Husbands, MA

Economics & Politics:
R P S Le Rougetel, MA (*Head of Economics & Politics*)
J H S Carr-Hill, BSc, MSc
L J Powell, MA, MPhil
C P Sowden, BA, MSc

English:
D G Andrews, BA (*Head of English*)
D C B Brown, BA (*Director of Drama*)
P M Capel, BA
D Green, BA (*Head of Lower School*)
D A Lawrence, MA
C E Roseblade, BA (*Head of General Studies*)
R L Wilson, MA (*Head of Upper School*)

Geography:
D W Trebble, BA (*Head of Geography*)
G P Colley, CertEd (*Head of Manor of the Rose*)
J J B Lawford, BA (*Head of D of E Scheme*)
R D W Laithwaite, BA (*Head of Clive House*)
Mrs S A Scammell, BA

History:
J G Taylor (*Head of History*)
A J Booth, MA (*Head of Middle School*)
J G Brown, MA (*School Archivist*)
J O Morris, BA
S W Stott, BA

Information Technology:
C P Hirst, BA
Dr F R Eade, PhD
S Croxford, LLB

Library:
D M Cook, BA (*Senior Librarian*)
Ms J M Soor, BA (*Second Librarian*)
Mrs P Jones, BA (*Library Assistant*)

Mathematics:
O L C Toller, MA (*Head of Mathematics*)
Miss H L Blatch, BA
D C Bowman, BA, BSc
J A Clifford, BSc
C J J Collier, MA (*Second Master*)
M F Illing, MA (*Head of Andrewes House*)
W S Macro, BSc
J D G Slator, MA (*Head of Mulcaster House*)
P D Wild, BSc, MSc

Modern Languages:
Dr W R Bingham, BA, PhD (*Head of Modern Languages, Head of German*)
R Coode, BA (*Russian*)
Miss V Klein, L-ès-L
Miss H E McCullough, BA
R M McGinlay, MA (*Head of French*)
L Moon, BA (*Spanish*)
T P Rocher, L-ès-L
W G B Stansbury, BA (*Head of Hilles House*)
Mrs H H Tilley, BA
Miss K Trenchard-Morgan, MA
M Turner, BA (*Head of Spencer House*)

Music:
R N Hobson, MA, ARCO (*Director of Music*)
S Groves, BA, ARCO
Mrs J H Stubbs, BMus, ARCO, ALCM (*Assistant to Head of Middle School*)

Physical Education:
C R Evans-Evans, BA (*Director of Physical Education*)
G P Colley, CertEd (*Head of Manor of the Rose*)

Religious Studies:
The Rev R D E Bolton, MA (*School Chaplain*)
S W Stott, BA

Science:
K G Bridgeman, MA (*Head of Science and Commanding Officer, CCF*)
K S Bains, BSc (*Head of Careers*)
T C H Greenaway, BSc

Physics:
N G Blight, MA (*Head of Physics*)
Dr A R H Clarke, MA, DPhil
Ms L A Slator, BSc (*Examinations Officer*)

Chemistry:
A J W Horrox, MA (*Head of Chemistry*)
I Middleton, BA
C P Overton, MSc, MA
M J Reynish, BSc (*Head of Walter House*)

Biology:
N T Richards, BTech, MSc, CBiol, MIBiol (*Head of Biology*)
Dr T R Stubbs, BSc, PhD, CBiol, MIBiol (*Senior Master*)
T G Briggs, BA
T J Smith, BA

Design & Technology:
J B Coleman, MA (*Head of Design & Technology*)
C Forbes, BSc
A S Bannister, BSc

School Counsellor: A J C Dickinson, BA, MEd, ALCP

Visiting Teachers:
R Alston, ARCM (*Piano*)
J Atkins (*Trumpet*)
G Boyd, DipMus (*Double Bass*)
Mrs N S Coleman, CertEd (*Flute*)
A Francis (*Clarinet*)
J Francis (*Saxophone*)
Miss E Frith (*Viola & Violin*)
R Hand, DipRAM, ARAM, ALAM (*Guitar*)
Mrs F Jones, LRAM (*Violin*)
A Keeping, LRAM (*Guitar*)
Mrs R Lambert, ARAM, ARCM (*Piano*)
D Lewis, LRAM (*Brass*)
T Mallett, DipRAM, LRAM (*Bassoon*)
Mrs C Moore (*'Cello*)
Ms PO'Sullivan (*Recorder*)
D Saunderson, GGSM (*Singing*)
N Thompson (*Trombone*)
J West (*Oboe*)
S Yalden (*Percussion*)

Sports:
H C Latchman (*Cricket*)
J Rayden (*Fencing*)
J Shaw (*Hockey & Tennis*)
K Remfry (*Judo*)
L Cole (*Rugby, Hockey, Cricket*)
G Davies (*Rugby*)
K Mardling (*Basketball*)
N Hawgood (*Hockey*)

Bursar: G R H Ralphs

School Medical Officer: Dr W H Bulman, MB, BS

Head Master's Secretary: Mrs S E Hampel

Admissions Secretary: Mrs R Nathwani

Bursar's Secretary: Mrs S Enright

The School was founded in 1561 by the Merchant Taylors' Company, who are still its Governing Body, and strong historical links here have been maintained. In 1933 the School moved from central London to its present attractive, rural setting of 250 acres at Sandy Lodge, Northwood. It is within easy reach of parents in North-West London by car, train or school coach service, as well as a mere half hour from Baker Street and twenty minutes from Heathrow.

There are 770 boys in the School.

Pupils are encouraged strongly, within a supportive system of tutor-groups, to find activities at which they can excel, and to develop confidence in their abilities. The academic achievements of the School are first-rate, and are achieved in a humane, civilised and relatively unpressured atmosphere. There is a clear emphasis to encourage boys to organise much themselves, and to take responsibility for others.

Admission. (*see* Entrance Scholarship section) 11+ Entrance Examination: Four Scholarships, the largest up to the value of one half of the School fee, will be available, together with bursaries depending upon proven financial need which can also be used to increase the value of the Scholarships.

13+ Scholarship Examination: Eleven Scholarships, the largest up to the value of one third of the School fee, will be available together with bursaries depending upon proven financial need which can also be used to increase the value of the Scholarships.

16+ Entrance Examination: One Scholarship up to the value of 15% of the School fee, and one Exhibition will be available.

Lower 6th Internal Exhibition: Four Exhibitions may be awarded at the end of the Lower Sixth year, up to the value of 5% of the School fee.

Music Scholarship Examination: Two Scholarships up to the value of one quarter and 15% of the School fee, will be available, together with two Exhibitions up to the value of one tenth of the School fee. In addition, Music Bursaries are awarded covering the costs of tuition of up to two instruments per individual. These awards are available to candidates at all the usual ages of entry.

Bursaries: Other bursaries are available to assist in cases of special hardship or desert.

Other Awards: There is a generous variety of awards open to Sixth Formers for travel, Outward Bound and Sail Training, as well as Leaving Scholarships to assist at University.

Scholarships at Oxford and Cambridge Universities. At the end of their first undergraduate year, old boys of Merchant Taylors' School are eligible for election to a maximum of three Sir Thomas White Scholarships at St John's College, Oxford, a Matthew Hale at Queen's College, Oxford and a Parkin and Stuart Scholarship for Science or Mathematics at Pembroke College, Cambridge.

Curriculum and Organisation. The course in the lower forms of the School is general, consisting of Divinity, History, English, Music, French, Mathematics, Physics, Chemistry, Biology, Computer Studies, Geography, Art and Design, Design and Technology and Physical Education, with most boys also taking Latin. Greek or German or Spanish is started when 13+ boys enter the school. A boy entering the Lower Sixth embarks upon a two year course in which all boys study four subjects to 'AS' level, followed by three subjects at A2 for most (some continuing with four). In addition, all boys do AS General Studies. A broad system of options is available to him and there is a comprehensive General Studies programme, including Japanese and Mandarin.

Music. Music lessons are arranged for boys who wish for them. The School Choir, the Small Choir, the Orchestra, Wind Band and the Chamber Orchestra give frequent concerts both within and outside the School during the year, and there is a new purpose-built Music School.

Free tuition for one year is available for certain selected boys who wish to start learning an orchestral instrument.

Games and Physical Education. There is ample space at Sandy Lodge for the playing of Rugby Football, Cricket, Hockey, Cross Country and Golf; Fives, Squash and Tennis Courts have been provided and also a running track and new all-weather pitch. The Sports Hall includes an indoor hockey pitch which also accommodates four badminton courts, a multi-gym, a climbing wall and indoor cricket nets. A lake within the School grounds gives facilities for a Sailing Club, canoeing and wind-surfing. Physical Education forms part of the regular work of the School and is included in the curriculum of each Form. There is an indoor Swimming Pool and instruction in swimming is regarded as a necessary part of Physical Education. Instruction in Fencing and in Judo is available.

Service Sections. The School has a Contingent of the **Combined Cadet Force** with RN, Army, and RAF Sections, which includes girls from St Helen's School. There is a miniature Rifle Range for the use of the Contingent, a Duke of Edinburgh Award Group which trains boys for Bronze, Silver and Gold Awards, and the Community Service Group which provides an opportunity for a wide range of activities in the local area. Boys are expected to be members of the CCF, Duke of Edinburgh or Community Service Group for at least two years.

A special feature is a week-long residential holiday for handicapped children every Easter, organised by boys and the girls of St Helen's.

School Societies. There is a large number of School Societies covering a wide field of interests and activities.

Careers. There is a strong Careers Advisory Service, which organizes an annual Careers Convention at the School and a wide range of work experiences.

House and Tutorial Systems. The School is divided into eight Houses. Each House is under the care of a Head of House and a team of pastoral care Tutors, who are responsible for the boys in that House.

Fees. The School Fees for day-boys are £2,840 a term. These cover tuition, lunch and games. There is a registration fee of £50, and an admission fee and deposit of £250, followed by a further deposit of £700, the latter to be set against the first term's fees.

Term of entry. September only unless in very special circumstances.

Charitable status. Merchant Taylors' School Charitable Trust is a Registered Charity, number 1063740. It exists to provide a first-class all-round education for boys, irrespective of their background.

Merchant Taylors' School, Crosby

Great Crosby Liverpool L23 0QP
Tel: 0151-928 3308 (Headmaster); 0151-928 5770 (Bursar); 0151-928 5759 (Registrar)
Fax: 0151-928 0434

The School was founded in AD 1620 by John Harrison, Citizen and Merchant Taylor of London, who bequeathed funds in trust to the Merchant Taylors' Company for the establishment of a School to be called 'The Merchant Taylors' School, founded at the charge of John Harrison', at Great Crosby, where, as his will records, 'my father was born'. In 1878 the School was transferred to its present site. From the time of its foundation until 1910, the School was under the government of the Merchant Taylors' Company, London. The present governing body constituted under the Scheme of 1910 includes representatives of local government, Merchant Taylors' Company, the Universities and the Old Crosbeians' Association and the Old Girls' Association.

Motto: *Concordia parvae res crescunt*

Governors:
S G Povall, Esq, FRICS, FCIArb (*Chairman*)
Prof P Batey
L Colligan, BA
Mrs E M Davies
Councillor T R Glover
R W Harrington, Esq, JP, FCA
Mrs S M I Hetherington, JP
Dr M I Hughes, MB, ChB
F C Mercer, Esq, JP, FCA
Mrs A D Pratt, JP, FCA
A M N Scorah, Esq, MA
Mrs D F Shackleton, MA, MCIH, MAPM
Dr R Thind, MBBS, DMRD, FRCR
Mrs J A Turner
R J Walker, Esq
Capt D A Wallis, RN
K N Wardle, Esq, FCIS, FCCS, FICM, MInstM

***Headmaster:* S J R Dawkins**, MA

Bursar and Clerk to the Governors: P S Gaunt, MA, FCA

Deputy Headmasters:
R J Pickup, BA
A J Whittaker, MA

Assistant Teachers:
J C Ashcroft, BA, MA
D A C Blower, MA (*Head of Sixth Form*)
A P Boardman, BA
J Blundell, BSc
§Mrs I L Callow, Grad. Univ. Heidelberg
Mrs M Casaus, MA
D E Cowling, BSc, PhD
J Coyne, BSc
J Dore, BSc
§Mrs S A Dunning, BA
J P Farrell, BSc, MA
S J Freedman, BSc, CBiol, MIBiol
Miss S M Gibson, BA
Dr J S Gill, BA, MPhil, PhD
Miss T Gonzalez, BA
C A Hall, BA, MSc
A G Heap, BSc, MSc
T W Hildrey, BSc
§H Hollinghurst, MA
D Holroyd, GMus, RNCM, PPRNCM, ARCO (*Director of Public Relations*)
J C Irlam, BSc
P A Irvine, BEd
P Jewell, BSc, MSc, PGCE
S J Kay, MA
Mrs D Knaggs, BSc
P A Lally, BA
P E Leonard, AdvDipMus, FTCL
P Little (*Rowing Coach*)
I W McIntosh, MA
I D McKie, CertEd
Dr N Myers, BA, PhD
J R Park, BSc (*Head of Middle School and Director of Studies*)
Mrs K E Plummer, BA
C D Price, MA
J D Pugh, BA, MA, MEd, MPhil
M Purnell
Mrs E Rea, BA, ALA
D Roberts, BSc
I Robinson, BEd
§F J Rubia Castro
Mrs A C Seddon, BA, MEd
M A C Slemen, BEd, DipPE
Rev D A Smith, BA (*Chaplain*)
Mrs J Smith, BA
P R Spears, BA
Mrs K M Stanley, BSc, MSc
S P Sutcliffe, BA, MA
J E Turner, BA, MA (*Head of Lower School*)
I Wallace, MA
J C Whitehead, BA, DipLI
J D Wild, BA, MEd
Miss T Wilkinson, BA
J H Williams, BA
M I Williams, BSc
S J Williams, BSc

Junior School:
§B P J Ashcroft
B J Bennett, CertEd (*Head*)
Miss L Birch, BEd
Mrs V C Broom, BA, DASE

Mrs A Davies, CertEd
§Mrs D Canter, BA
Miss B Jones, BSc
D I Lyon, BA
Mrs C Martin
A Owens, BEd
M Whalley (*Swimming coach*)
Mrs H White, BA
D K J Youngson, BA

The Upper School consists of about 730 boys, 180 of whom are in the Sixth Form. In addition there is a Junior School with about 170 boys between the ages of seven and eleven.

Since its foundation Merchant Taylors' has sought to provide a Christian, academic, disciplined education for local boys from a wide range of backgrounds. The School has a strong tradition in sport, music, drama, CCF and Scouts and there is a large number of societies which give boys further opportunities to develop their interests. The School has a reputation for academic excellence and the majority of our leavers proceed to degree courses. In the first three years at the Main School boys follow a broad general course of education which includes all National Curriculum subjects and, in addition, a second or third Modern Language and Classics. All boys take nine subjects at GCSE. In addition to the National Curriculum subjects they may choose German or Spanish (French is studied by all boys), Latin and/or Greek. Around 70% take three separate sciences.

In the Sixth Form the following subjects are available at 'A' Level: Mathematics, Further Mathematics, Physics, Chemistry, Biology, Latin, Greek, Ancient History, Classical Civilisation, English, History, Geography, Economics, French, German, Spanish, Design and Technology, Theology, Philosophy, Art, Music, Theatre Studies and Physical Education. In addition, all boys in the Sixth Form follow a course in General Studies which includes Information Technology.

Boys are admitted to the Junior School in their seventh year, and to the Main School at 11, 13 or after GCSE.

Term of Entry. Pupils are accepted each September.

Tuition Fees. Upper School, £4,968 pa; Junior School, £3,564 pa.

Scholarships and Bursaries tenable at the School. - Places are available at 11, 13 and 16 with some School Assisted Places at 11, and Governors' Bursaries based on parental income are also available at 11 and 16.

In addition a number of Merit Scholarships are awarded, based on performance in the Entrance Examination, at a level of one eighth, one quarter or one half fees.

Leaving Scholarships.

A number of awards are available each year to boys proceeding to universities.

Games. Games played are Rugby Football, Cricket, Tennis, Hockey, Athletics, Cross Country and Rowing. There are Wind Surfing and Sailing Clubs, a gymnasium and indoor swimming pool, an Astroturf all-weather surface and six tennis courts. All boys are expected to participate in one of the many games options available throughout their time at the School.

School Societies. A wide range of activities and interests is covered by School Societies.

Music and Drama. About 200 boys receive weekly instrumental tuition and there is a subsidised scheme for beginners on orchestral instruments. There is a School Choral Society, Junior School Choir, Junior and Senior Concert Bands and Jazz Band, all of which perform frequently inside and outside the School, in addition to a number of smaller ensembles.

There are 11 visiting specialist music teachers and close links in Music with our sister school, Merchant Taylors' Girls School. There are also close links with the Girls' School in Drama, which now forms an integral part of the Upper School curriculum as well as being a major extra-curricular activity.

Combined Cadet Force. The School has a voluntary contingent of the Combined Cadet Force with Army, Navy and RAF Sections. There are around 220 members of the CCF, 60 of whom are girls from our sister school.

Old Boys. There is an active Old Boys' Association (The Old Crosbeians) whose Secretary may be contacted via the School and from whom a handbook/register, may be obtained.

Charitable status. Merchant Taylors' School is a Registered Charity, number, 526681. It exists to provide education for local boys.

Merchiston Castle School

Colinton Edinburgh EH13 0PU.
Tel: 0131-312 2200
Headmaster: 0131-312 2202/3
Admissions Co-ordinator: 0131-312 2201
Fax: 0131-441 6060
e-mail: headmaster@merchiston.co.uk
website: www.merchiston.co.uk

The school was established in 1833 and moved in 1930 from the centre of the city out to its present spacious and attractive site, bordered by the Water of Leith and close to the Pentland Hills.

Motto: *Ready Ay Ready.*

Governors:

Honorary President: The Hon Lord Robertson, TD, QC, BA, LLB

Chairman: H C Abram, WS, LLB
Deputy Chairman: P C M Roger, CA

A C W Boyle, MA
J A Aitchison, NDA
I M Riddell, BA, LLB
A E Corstorphine
W M Wilson, CA
A G Mickel
R P Lawson, BA
M N Donaldson, MSc
C M A Lugton, MA
Dr J McClure, MA, DPhil, FRSA, FSAScot
R E M Irving, MA, DPhil
P S Hodge, QC
G Heron, BA, DipPM, FIPD
W M Biggart, BA

Secretary to the Governors and Bursar: D G Smith, BCom, CA

President of the Merchistonian Club: A C W Boyle, MA

***Headmaster:* A R Hunter**, BA Manchester

Deputy Head: K J Houston, BSc Belfast

Housemasters:
Evans: K J A Anderson, MTh St Andrews
Rogerson West: J O'Neil, MA Glasgow
Rogerson East: A W Johnstone, MA Edinburgh
Chalmers East: I S Wilmshurst, MA Cambridge
Chalmers West: G M Lane, BSc Leeds
Pringle Form III: P K Rossiter, MA Oxford
Pringle Forms II + I: P K Hall, MA Oxford

Headmaster's Forum:
Director of Studies: Mrs M Muetzelfeldt, BSc London

Assistant Head, Academic: I G Craig, BSc, MSc Belfast
Assistant Head, Academic: N J Mortimer, MA, DPhil Oxford
Head of Junior School: P K Hall, MA Oxford
Head of Pastoral Care: F N Rickard, BA Hull, ACCEG
Assistant Head, Marketing: T F West, MA Edinburgh

Chaplain: The Revd A S Macpherson, MA Glasgow

Assistant Staff:
J Rainy Brown, BSc Edinburgh *Chemistry Mathematics*
K J Houston, BSc Belfast *Physics*
R J Russel, BSc, PhD Glasgow *Biology, Head of Outdoor Pursuits*
T F West, MA Edinburgh *English*
M C L Gill, BSc, PhD Edinburgh *Head of Chemistry*
J R Hart, BSc Aberdeen *Head of Biology*
J C O Vaughan, BSc Edinburgh *Mathematics*
Mrs M Muetzelfeldt, BSc London *Head of Mathematics*
S D Stranock, BSc, PhD Belfast *Biology*
J K Selby, BA Durham *Modern Studies, Head of History*
P S Williams, BA Leicester *English*
P K Hall, MA Oxford *English*
F N Rickard, BA Hull, ACCEG *English, Head of Guidance*
I G Craig, BSc, MSc Belfast *Head of Science/Technology, Physics*
P K Rossiter, MA Oxford *Head of Music*
Mrs C A Watson, BA Manchester *English, Head of Learning Support*
Mrs M V Prini-Garcia, L-e-L Madrid *Classical Languages, Spanish*
T J Lawson, BA Sheffield, PhD Edinburgh, FSA Scot *Head of Geography*
C W Swan, CertEd Loughborough *Head of Physical Education*
D M Turner, MA Oxford, ARCO *Music, German*
A C N Millard, MA Aberdeen *Geography*
A Watt, BSc Belfast *Head of Electronics; Physics*
S J Horrocks, MA Cambridge *French, Spanish*
P Corbett, MA St Andrews *Head of Languages and French; Latin*
Miss F M Blakeman, DipDes Napier *Art*
I S Wilmshurst, MA Cambridge *Geography*
A W Johnston, MA Edinburgh, MIL *French, Spanish*
A S Macpherson, MA Glasgow *Head of Religious Studies*
K J A Anderson, MTh St Andrews *Religious Studies*
S Campbell, BSc Glasgow *Mathematics*
C L Dinwoodie, MA Oxford *Mathematics*
G M Lane, BSc Leeds *Chemistry*
J R Matthews, TD, BEd Leeds, MCSE, MITT *Head of Computing*
A D Meadows, BSc Manchester *Head of Physics*
C R M Caves, MA Edinburgh *History, Geography*
J A Clifford, BSc Bristol *Mathematics*
C S McIvor, MA Glasgow *History, Politics*
C Smith, BSc Edinburgh *Chemistry*
N J Mortimer, MA, DPhil Oxford *Head of English*
J M V Cordingley, MA London *Art*
J R Károlyi, BA Oxford, PhD St Andrews *French, Spanish*
F Geisler, LA SII/I Bochum *German, EFL*
Mrs F Horrocks, BA South Africa *French*
Mrs M B Watson, BSc Glasgow *Mathematics, Computing*
Miss C A Walker, HNC Napier *EFL*
Miss G A Cordiner, BSc Heriot-Watt *Computing*
D C Rhodes, MA Oxford *Physics*
S M Brown, BSc Edinburgh *Physics*
R A Charman, BA Canterbury *Mathematics, Physical Education*
Miss L A Jordan, BSc Napier *Head of Design Technology*
Mrs A A Niven, BSc Strathclyde, MSc Dundee, PhD Glasgow *Chemistry, Biology*
J O'Neill, MA Glasgow *History, Politics, Modern Studies*
Miss E R Phillips, MA Oxford *English*

Exchange Teachers:
Mr Shengchan Fei, Peoples' Republic of China
Mrs Xiaonan Zhao, Peoples' Republic of China

Student Helpers:
James Webb, Lindisfarne College, New Zealand
Anthony Russell, Sydney Grammar School, Australia

Medical Officers:
Dr H A Chalmers, MB, ChB, DRCOG
Dr T McMillan, MB, ChB, MRCGP, DRCOG

Matrons:
Mrs G A MacKinlay, RGM, RM
Mrs H M Dinnis, RGN

CCF: SSI WOl A Hambling

Administration:
Headmaster's Secretary: Mrs L Blake
Admissions Co-ordinator: Mrs A Richard
Master of Works: D M Stenhouse
Chief Laboratory Technician: Mrs L Scott
Marketing Co-ordinator: Mrs B Lamotte

There are 380 boys in the School, of whom 265 are boarders.

Admission. The normal ages of entry are 8-10, 11 or 12, 13 and 16, though from time to time there are chance vacancies at other ages. Entry at 8-10 is by assessment and interview; at 11 or 12 by means of the Merchiston entrance examination; entry at 13 on the Common Entrance or Merchiston entrance examination. Entry to the sixth form at 16 depends on a successful showing in the GCSE or Standard Grade as well as on interview and a report from the previous school. There are approximately 130 in the sixth form. There are a number of valuable open entrance scholarships (see Scholarship section in this book).

Courses of study. In the lower school the curriculum comprises English, Mathematics, Biology, Chemistry, Physics, History, French, Latin, German, Spanish, Geography, Religious Studies, Art, Music, PE, Electronics, Design and Information Technology. In the middle school a two year course leading to the GCSE is followed, consisting of a core curriculum: English, English Literature, Mathematics, a foreign language (French, German, Spanish), Chemistry, and a wide range of option subjects, including History, a second foreign language, Electronics, Physics, Biology, Computer Studies, Geography, Chinese, Latin, Religious Studies, Art, Design and Music. Most boys take nine subjects. In the two years in the sixth form a boy studies either three subjects to GCE A level or five subjects to SEB Highers. The choice at both levels includes English, Mathematics, Biology, Chemistry, Physics, French, German, Spanish, History, Politics (A level only), Geography, Computer Studies, Latin, Modern Studies (Higher only), Music, plus Design and Art at A Level only. In addition to his main subjects each boy follows a course of complementary studies giving him the opportunity to develop an ancillary skill or interest. These include French for Business Studies, Computer Studies, Music, Design, Art, Presentation and Communication Skills. In the first year of the sixth form all boys undertake a week's career course, a week's leadership course, and those with linguistic skills who are studying Science subjects have additional Science lessons in French and attend a course at the Cité des Sciences et Technologie near Paris. Classes are small throughout the school and all subjects are setted by ability. The school prepares boys for entry to Oxford and Cambridge.

The school makes provision for specialist EFL teaching for foreign students.

Learning Support Provision. Boys with learning difficulties, including dyslexia, enjoy successful careers at Merchiston. Our aim is to enhance self-esteem through genuine praise. We encourage each pupil to find success in his area of strength, whether inside or outside the classroom. The objective is that all pupils have access to a wide and varied curriculum, and that as a result, each discovers his own personal strengths and talents and enjoys the resulting success. The school holds a CReSTeD Category B rating.

Houses. Each of the six boarding houses caters for a particular age group and the atmosphere and activities are tailored accordingly. Special attention is paid by the housemaster and his house tutors to the care of the individual and to the development of both his studies and interests.

Day boys. The life of day boys is fully integrated with that of the boarders; they attend Morning Assembly, use all the house and school facilities, have lunch and tea at school and go home after evening preparation.

Games. The principal games are rugby, played in the Autumn and Spring terms, and in the Summer cricket and athletics. There is a large indoor heated swimming pool and a sports hall, and there are good facilities for tennis, squash, fives, shooting, sailing, ski-ing, badminton and golf.

Music. Music plays an important part in the life of the school. Tuition is available in all keyboard and orchestral instruments and currently about one quarter of the school is learning a musical instrument, and two choirs flourish. There is also a school orchestra, jazz band and pipe band. The choir and instrumentalists frequently go on tour, eg USA, Far East.

Drama. There is at least one major play production a term, with frequent House plays or drama workshop productions in a well-equipped purpose-built theatre.

Art, Craft, Design and Technology, and Ceramics. The art and craft centre offers both within the curriculum and in the pupil's free time scope for painting, pottery, metalwork, woodwork and design work. In addition a new Centre provides courses within the curriculum or in free time in computing and electronics.

Societies. There is a wide variety of clubs: bridge, chess, debating, electronics, film, natural history, philately, photography. Visits to theatres, concerts and exhibitions are a frequent part of a boy's life at Merchiston.

CCF. All boys join the CCF for a period of two years, which includes outward bound activities such as climbing, hillwalking, canoeing, camping. The school is also very active in community service work.

Girls. The school does not take girls but has a special relationship as brother/sister school with St George's School for Girls, Edinburgh and Kilgraston School in Perthshire. This includes alignment of term dates, as well as joint expeditions, concerts, tours, seminars, debating, social events, study courses. Merchiston operates a joint fees scheme with Kilgraston by which there is a reduction of 5% for the second child and 20% for the third when in school at the same time.

Careers advice. A qualified careers adviser leads a team of trained staff to supplement the advice of the Academic Management Team and the Housemasters and House Tutors. Pupils attend lessons in careers as part of their Personal and Social Education Programme in the Middle School and all 5th Form pupils take the Morrisby Careers Aptitude test. The school is a member of the ISCO and all Lower 6th undertake a period of work experience as part of their programme. A designated careers research centre is located in the library complex.

Links with parents. There are regular parent/staff meetings and on all academic and career decisions parents are fully briefed and consulted.

Links with industry. The school runs an imaginative links with industry scheme involving both small and multinational companies as well as professions. The scheme gives the sixth former an opportunity to meet and talk with teams from firms who visit the school.

Health. There is a medical centre in the charge of the school matron and the school doctor visits regularly.

Fees per term from September, 2000. Junior School: Form 1 Boarders £3,500, Day boys £2,300; Forms 2 and 3 Boarders £3,900, Day boys £2,825. Senior School: Forms 4 and above Boarders £5,100, Day boys £3,450.

Reduction of 5% of the fees for the second son and 20% for the third son when in the school at the same time.

There is a reduction of 10% of the fees for sons of serving members of HM Forces, and there are reductions for the sons of clergy and members of the teaching profession.

Entrance Scholarships. (*see* Entrance Scholarship section) Merchiston offers boys a wide range of scholarships and bursaries for entry to the Junior School, Pringle (8-12 years), the Senior School and the Sixth Form. The main categories are academic, all-rounder and music. There are also Prep School Awards for boys entering from prep schools, a Technology Award and a new Community Scholarship for boys living in Edinburgh postcodes. Additional Awards for overseas students include European, Kenyan and Hong Kong.

Scholarships provide discounts of up to 50% off boarding or day fees. Some means-tested bursaries of up to £1,000 per term are also available. Further details can be obtained from the Admissions Co-ordinator.

Entry terms. Autumn, Spring and Summer, where vacancies permit.

Applications. A prospectus and further details may be obtained from the Admissions Co-ordinator. Prospective parents are encouraged to visit the school. Information is also found on our website: www.merchiston.co.uk.

Old boys. The Secretary of The Merchistonian Club, c/o the School. Former pupils include: The Rt Hon John MacGregor, MP; Peter Burt, Chief Executive, Bank of Scotland; John Jeffrey, OBE (ex Scotland XV).

Charitable status. Merchiston Castle School is a Registered Charity, number SCO16580. It aims to give each boy in his way the capacity and confidence to live in an uncertain world and to make that life as rich as possible; more specifically to encourage him to work hard and to take pride in achievement, to think independently, to face up to challenges, to accept responsibility, to show concern for others and to develop wider skills and interests.

Methodist College

Belfast BT9 6BY.
Tel: 01232-205205

Methodist College was founded in 1865 to provide a public school for pupils of all denominations. It was opened in 1868 and has grown to be a very large grammar school with relatively small boarding departments for both boys and girls and with 2 preparatory schools. The Board of Governors consists of 15 members elected by the Conference of the Methodist Church in Ireland (including *ex officio* the President and Secretary of the Church) 6 members appointed by the Department of Education, Northern Ireland, 3 elected parent representatives and 3 elected teacher representatives.

Motto: *Deus Nobiscum.*

Chairman: Professor D Rea, OBE, MSc, MBA, PhD

Honorary Treasurer: J McGarry, ACII, CDipAF, FBIBA

Honorary Secretaries:
The Rev D P Ker, BA, BD
T D Sloan, BSc, CEng, MICE

Principal: **T W Mulryne**, MA, EdD

Senior Vice-Principal: M C Harrison, BA

Vice-Principals:
Mrs M P White, BA
G G Monaghan, BSc
D R S Gallagher, BSc, PhD

Head of Senior School: W J Slater, BEng
Head of Middle School: M A Cinnamond, BA
Head of Junior School: S E Roulston, MA, MEd
Head of Pastoral Care: Mrs F Monaghan, BA
Director of Studies: M A McCullough, BA

Heads of Faculty:

Creative & Performing Arts: J McKee, BEd, MA, PhD
English: Mrs H D Collier, BA, PhD
Environment & Society: Mrs N F M Gallagher, BEd, MA
Languages: to be appointed
Mathematics: A Craig, BSc
Physical Education, Games & Recreational Activities: T D Creighton, BEd
Science & Technology: B R Wheeler, BSc, PhD

Head of Preparatory Department: I R Johnston, BA
Director of Resources: D Wells, DipPE

Registrar: to be appointed

Headmaster's Secretary: Mrs R Wheeler

The School is situated in 14 acres of grounds immediately adjacent to the Queen's University of Belfast. There are 40 acres of playing fields at Pirrie Park, just over a mile away, and a further 12 acres at Deramore Park, at about the same distance, and a Boat House for the Rowing Club on the river Lagan within half-a-mile of the School.

The premises comprise the original College Building, opened in 1868, part of which is used for the accommodation of boy boarders; McArthur Hall, opened in 1891 as a hall of residence for girl boarders; the Whitla Hall, opened in 1935 and capable of seating 800; the Chapel of Unity, built to celebrate the Centenary in 1968; and a fine range of buildings for day school purposes of which three quarters have been built since the Second World War. There are new computer, technology and Science suites; a music department with rooms for individual practice and a range of instruments that includes 2 pipe organs; a fine library; a new Sports Hall; a new Art Department; 2 gymnasia and an indoor swimming pool; and a large number of teaching rooms most of which are adapted for specialist teaching of particular subjects. A VIth Form Centre, with provision for recreational activities, private study and tutorial teaching, was opened in 1972.

Curriculum. With its staff of about 140 full-time teachers the College provides education from the age of 5 to the age of 19 for both boys and girls. In the grammar school, courses lead to the GCSE and 'A' level examinations. English and English Literature, Latin, Classical Civilization, Greek, French, German, Spanish, Russian, Religious Studies, History, Geography, Economics, Political Studies, Mathematics, Physics, Chemistry, Biology, Home Economics, Computer Studies, Technology, Geology, Music, Art, History of Art, Psychology, Drama, ICT are offered in the examinations, and it is possible to arrange for pupils from overseas to be examined in their local languages. A wide-ranging selection of 'general studies' is available to VIth Form pupils alongside their specialist examination work. Religious and Physical Education, Games, Drama, Music and a wide variety of activities ensure that the education given is not limited to intellectual matters and that every kind of talent has an opportunity for development. Boys and girls are prepared for universities in Ireland and Great Britain, for colleges of education and for other forms of professional and vocational training for which a high level of general education is a prerequisite. In recent years about 90% of all leavers have proceeded to degree courses in universities. Each year there is a high success rate of entry to Oxbridge Colleges.

Forms. By reason of its size the School is in a position to offer a wide choice of courses in the senior forms. Advice about these choices in relation to possible careers is given to all pupils by specially trained teachers. Each pupil's progress is kept under review, not only by his or her Tutor, but also by the Head of Form, an experienced teacher in charge of the year group. Senior Tutors are also attached to each year group to ensure that each pupil derives full benefit from the activities the College offers. Careful consideration is given each year to the precise placing of pupils in the next form and parents are consulted where options are to be exercised. Full reports are furnished twice per year and an internal reporting system ensures regular contact with parents throughout the year. The Heads of Form and Heads of Department deal with disciplinary problems, and problems arising from failure on the part of the pupils to work as they should.

Games. Rugby Football, Cricket, Rowing, Hockey, Tennis, Netball, Athletics are among the outdoor activities available. The College has an outstanding record in competitive sport and its former pupils include many notable international players. A heated indoor pool is in daily use at the main School.

Activities. Music and drama are particularly strong. Each year there are 5 or 6 dramatic productions, ranging from large-scale to small and experimental, and involving pupils of all ages. There are 5 choirs, 2 orchestras, a band with some 100 players, and a large number of smaller instrumental groups. In addition to regular recitals in the College, there are major public performances throughout the year, culminating in the Easter Concert which is held on two evenings in the Waterfront Concert Hall in Belfast. Since 1993, the Senior Girls' Choir has been twice Northern Ireland 'Choir of the Year', has been runner-up in the Sainsbury's UK Choir of the Year competition and in 1998 was the overall winner of the Sainsbury's Choir of the Year title, the first school choir to do so. There are some 35 clubs and societies which meet regularly: from Chess, in which the College has an outstanding record to Community Service, Conservation, Electronics, Angling and Debating.

Calendar. The School session opens at the beginning of September, and ends in the last week of June. Holidays totalling about 4 weeks are divided between Christmas and Easter in the way that best suits each year's calendar. Long week-ends are granted at Hallowe'en and at mid-term.

School House. Boys are accommodated to a maximum number of 90 as boarders in the charge of the Senior Resident Master, who is assisted by his deputy, several resident masters, 2 matrons, a nurse, and domestic staff.

McArthur Hall. Girls are accommodated to a maximum number of 70 as boarders in the charge of the Lady Warden, who is assisted by her deputy, several resident mistresses, a matron, a nurse and domestic staff. The very handsome building provides a gracious environment.

Senior boys and girls have individual cubicles and private study places. All boarders are the particular concern of the School Doctor, the Chaplain and his lady assistant. The recreational facilities of a large school are available when day pupils are not present.

Downey House Preparatory School was founded in 1933. There are some 300 pupils and a staff of 16 teachers. The School is in the grounds of the main playing fields at Pirrie Park and the pupils have the full use of these facilities.

Fullerton House Preparatory School received its name in 1950 when the preparatory department of the Grammar School was moved to separate premises in the campus. There are some 300 pupils and a staff of 16 teachers.

Facilities for physical education, swimming and dining are provided in the main College.

The 2 preparatory schools have been allowed to build up their own individual traditions. Under the general supervision of the Headmaster and Governors, the Head of the Preparatory Department has been given as large a measure of autonomy as possible.

Boarders under 11 years of age attend one or other of the preparatory schools.

Fees. The inclusive fees for boarders are: Preparatory £6,125 pa; main school £4,627, or £7,930 for non EU citizens. Membership of the boarding departments is accepted as residence in Northern Ireland.

Fees for individual tuition in music vary according to the instrument studied.

Scholarships. Entrance scholarships of £400 pa are available for first year boarders, and details of these and other awards are available from the Headmaster's Secretary. There is provision on the Foundation for the children of Ministers of the Methodist Church in Ireland.

Admissions. Local pupils are admitted to the Preparatory Schools from the age of 5. Children whose parents are working overseas are admitted as boarders from the age of 8; otherwise it is preferred that boarders enter at 11. The main entry to the grammar school is at 11, for most pupils, on the basis of the Northern Ireland transfer procedure. Application must, however, always be made direct to the College and the choice of pupils admitted rests with the College and not with the local authorities. It is the College's policy to do its utmost to accommodate at later stages the children of parents moving to Northern Ireland, and senior boys and girls who have outstripped the resources of their present schools. Except in such cases, application for the admission of day pupils should be made not less than 6 months before the prospective entry, and for boarders, as early as possible.

Term of Entry. All three, after an interview with the Headmaster.

Charitable status. Methodist College Belfast is a Registered Charity, number X 45039 A. Its aims are to provide education for boarders and day pupils irrespective of their denomination.

Millfield

Street Somerset BA16 0YD
Tel: (01458) 442291
Fax: (01458) 447276
e-mail: admissions@millfield.somerset.sch.uk.
website: www.millfield.somerset.sch.uk

The School was founded in 1935 by R J O Meyer with the philanthropic aim of using its resources to generate places for boys who were gifted but not wealthy. A substantial expansion took place in the 1960's when the School became co-educational. C R M Atkinson became Headmaster in 1971, and carried out a major building programme that established modern purpose-built facilities throughout the academic and recreational areas of the School, including a prize-winning Library and Resources Centre and a large Fine Arts Centre, completed in 1992, a year after his death. Improvements to the campus include a purpose built Mathematics Centre, 550 seater Theatre and new Dining Hall which was opened in May 2001. 8 new boarding houses are currently under construction. The main part of the School is surrounded by over 100 acres of parkland and playing fields, which includes a cross country riding course, stabling for 50 horses, 50m Olympic swimming pool and an indoor tennis centre.

Governors:

Chairman: A E White, CBE

Mrs S Atkinson, JP
Dr M Bailey
Mrs J E Derbyshire
C J Driver
G O Edwards, MBE
The Rt Revd Peter Firth
Sir Peter Kemp
R M Mawditt, OBE
A Patel
D W A Rosser
Mrs R J Saul
D R W Silk, JP, CBE
N Vince

Clerk to the Governors: C R Humphrey

***Headmaster:* P M Johnson**, MA

Bursar: D A P Oddie, MBE, FCMA

Deputy Headmaster: R Decamp, MA

Second Deputy: Mrs S E Langham, BA, JP

Tutor for Admissions: C G Coates, BA, DMS

Teachers:

D J Agutter, BA
T P Akhurst, BEd
Mrs H A Allen, BA
G J Baily, BSc
Mrs S H Banyard, BEd
A R Barker, MA, ARCM
Miss L Berisford, BA
Mrs H J Bevan, CertEd
J A Bishop, BA
Miss A Bland, BA
Revd Canon S F Bloxam-Rose, MA, BTh, PhD
Miss E J Bond, BA
Miss C Bowring, BA
Mrs J Brimacombe, BSc
†¶J A Brimacombe, BSc
¶Mrs K A Buckley, BA
*†R H I Bullock, BEd
D W Burton, MA, DPhil
Mrs C Byrne, BA, MEd
R Cameron, BA
D W Carr, BA
C P Chakabua, DipEd
N A Chamberlain, BSc
I R Chick, BA
S M Coase, MA
†S B Cole, BA
P Cooke, BSc
†P R Cookson, MEd
G Corris, BSc, MSc
G R Cottell, BSc
†A D Curtis, BA
M Day, BA
A H Dearden, LTCL, GTCL
M J Dimery, BEd
P Doran, BSc, ARES
*N R Driver, BSc
S J Dye, BA
†Mrs S M Dye, BA
Mrs J Eagle, BSc
†R A Eagle, BSc, PhD
R M Ellison, BEd
R J Essam, MA
Mrs J M Farthing, BA, LRAM
A T Ford, BA, MEd
*Mrs J A Frampton, BSc
R J Furlong, BSc
†N J Gabb, BEd
*D R Gajadharsingh, BSc
†Mrs L M Gall, BEd
L C Glaser, BSc
M G Godfrey, MA
*L A Green, MA
†T J Greenhill, BSc
D C Griffiths, BA
D J Hacker, HND
J M P Hallows, BSc
Miss V J Harkness, BEd
D Harper, DipAd
W R Harper-Holdcroft, MA
N W Harris, BSc, PhD
Mrs H Heriz-Smith, BA
J M Hill, MTheol, BA
J N Hill, BSc, PhD
Miss R Holland, BA
S Houghton, BA
C J Hughes, AGSM
*M J Hughes, BA
†I M Hunt, BA
*¶Miss L F Jackson, BA
†D G Jarratt, CertEd
†Mrs A K Jeffrey, BA, MEd
T G Johnston, BA
E T Jones, BSc
Mrs P H Jones, BA
Miss V J Kellow, BSc
Mrs L A Kelly, MA
P A Kelly, BA
Miss N Kightley, MSc
†I Kindon, BA
Mrs A M Klemz, L-ès-L
J Knight, BA
*R O Knight, MA
D H Landrock, BEd
*C Lane, MA
Miss N J Lees, BA
A L Lerwill, BEd
M A Lewis, BSc
†Mrs N S Lewis-Williams, BA
S A M Lewis-Williams, BA
†Miss A J Loten, MA
†H R MacNeary, MA
G McBride, BA
*A W McConnaughie, BA, PhD
Mrs M McGlone, MA, DipEd(SpecEd)
Mrs A B Mantell, CertEd

†C A Mantell, BA
P D R Marshall, BSc, DPhil
Miss C E Martin, BA
A P Miller, TCert
M M Milton, BA
A K Mnatzaganian, BA
S K Mottershead, TCert
Miss D L Mugridge, BA
R J Mylne, BEd
P G Neeve, BA(Ed)
*T R Nightingale, MA, DipRADA
Mrs G S Orton, BA, MSc
R Orton, MA
Miss M Osborne, BA
†C I Page, BSc
M A Perry, BSc, PhD
Mrs A V J Phillips, BA
J J Pickles, BSc, GradIMA
J Preston, BEng
†J M Price, BSc, PhD
*R N Ransley, BA
M A Rhind-Tutt, GRSM, ARCM
B G Richardson, MA, MEd
†K Ridgeon, BA
J R Rix, MA
P S Rolf, BA
Mlle P Rouprich, L-es-L
D T Rymer, MA
E J Sanchez, BSc
Mrs A M Scott, BA
A Shaw, BA
†Mrs S I Shayler, BSc, MEd
G T Shayler, BEng
L G Sheills, ARCM
†R W Shilton, MA, PhD
†*S M Shortland, BEd, MSc
C J Skinner, BA, PhD
Mrs S A Skinner, MEd
†M A Smith, BSc
*K G Spears, BSc, MBA, OBE
Mrs M P Speed, BSc
¶R R Speed, MA
E Spring, BA
Mrs L M A Staniforth, MA
†Miss V J Steer, BA, MEd
J R Taylor, BA
A C C Thomas, BEd
*Mrs A Thomas, BA
†D J Trevis, BA, MEd
C Tyler, MSc(Econ)
M T Wadley, TCert
Miss J S Wallace-Mason, BA
R Warman, BSc
Z R Watkins, BSc, PhD
Miss A J Wellman, BSc
*J N Whiskerd, BA
*N E Williams, BA, MPhil
Mrs S H Wilson, BSc
Mrs B E Wood, BA
Mrs H B Wood, CertEd
A R Woods, BA
Mrs S M Woods, BSc
P M Wootton, BA

Houses and Housemasters/mistresses:

Boarding Houses:
Abbey House: Mr and Mrs G T Shayler
Acacia House: Mr and Mrs C A Mantell
Butleigh: Mr and Mrs S B Cole
Chindit: Mr and Mrs H R MacNeary
Etonhurst: Mr I M Hunt
Georgian Cottage: Mr A R Barker
Grange: Mr and Mrs M Day
Holmcroft: Mr and Mrs S M Shortland
Joan's Kitchen: Dr and Mrs R W Shilton
Keen's Elm: Mr and Mrs C I Page
Kingweston: Mr and Mrs T J Greenhill
Martins: Mr and Mrs N J Gabb
Millfield: Mr and Mrs A D Curtis
Orchards: Mr M A Smith
Overleigh: Mr and Mrs S A M Lewis-Williams
Portway: Mr and Mrs A J Gall
St Anne's: Mr and Mrs D J Trevis
Shapwick: Dr and Mrs J M Price
Southfield: Mr and Mrs K Ridgeon
Tor: Miss V J Steer
Walton: Mr and Mrs J A Brimacombe
Warner: Mr and Mrs J M P Hallows

Day Houses (Boys):
Cookson: Mr P R Cookson
Jarratt: Mr D G Jarratt
Bullock: Mr R H I Bullock
Dimery: Mr M J D Dimery

Day Houses (Girls):
Loten: Miss A J Loten
Dye: Mrs S M Dye
Jeffrey: Mrs A K Jeffrey

Coaches:

Cricket: M R Davis, NCA Advanced Coach

Fencing:
Prof N Golding, BAF Diploma, South West Coach
Mrs S Benney, BAF and County Advanced Coach
G Golding, Advanced National Coach

Golf:
D Halford, PGA Coach
Miss K Nicholls, PGA Coach

Hockey:
A Reid, Level 2 Coach
D Wright, Assistant Coach

Judo & Self Defence:
J Robinson, Black Belt
E Poeti, Black Belt (*Karate*)

Netball:
C Morey, Assistant Coach
J Duckett, Assistant Coach
Y Jacobs, Level 2 Coach

Riding:
Director: D O Anholt, BHSI
Assistant Director: Miss P Cruttwell, BHSI, HND Horse Studies
Polo: J Barber

Squash:
J Barrington, SRA National Coach, Former Men's Professional Champion
I Thomas, Intermediate Level III SRA Coach

Swimming:
D F Campbell, ASA Coach
R Thorp, ASA Coach

Tennis:
Director: A A Simcox, Member of Professional Tennis Coaches' Association
Miss I R Wyatt, Coach
Miss J Sinkins, Coach

Trampolining:
R A Dutton, British Trampoline Federation Coach
C Morey, Assistant Coach

The School is fully co-educational with 750 boys and 447 girls; there are 876 boarders.

Housing. The majority of the 22 single-sex boarding houses are situated in or near the School; a small number lie in surrounding villages. They vary in size with the average number being about 45 in boys' houses, 35 in girls'. Houseparents are generally members of the teaching staff and most houses have resident assistant staff. Dormitories for younger pupils are generally smaller than those for older pupils. Sixth formers generally share double study bedrooms. Day pupils are organised into 7 houses, attached to boarding houses for games and activities; they are fully assimilated into all aspects of school life.

The Curriculum. The academic programme is consistent with the broad principles laid down in the National Curriculum pre-16. Thus those moving to Millfield from a wide range of independent preparatory and maintained secondary schools should find both common academic ground and unrivalled choice for GCSE and AS/A2 Level.

All pupils entering the Third Year (at age 13), regardless of ability, study English, Mathematics, three Sciences, at least one language, Technology, Information Technology, Geography, History, Religious Studies, Physical Education, Art and Music. Class sizes average 12 in all subjects. A five-year course in Personal and Social Education (known as 'Choices') is also followed. Each pupil is involved in conservation at the School's 40 acre conservation centre at Worley Hill.

In the Fourth and Fifth Years, all pupils follow courses leading to GCSEs. There is also a wide choice of other subjects available (Art, Business Studies, Economics, Design & Technology, French, Geography, German, Graphic Products, History, Information Technology, Italian, Latin, Music, Physical Education, Religious Studies and Spanish). Pupils take an average of ten GCSEs.

The Language Development Unit provides individual support for all pupils in need of this.

At Sixth Form level, over 40 subjects are on offer leading to AS and A2 qualifications. These include Accounting, Art, Biology, Business Studies, Chemistry, Classical Greek, Communication Studies, Computing, Economics, English Language, English Literature, Food Technology, French, Further Mathematics, Geography, German, Government & Politics, History, Information & Communication Technology, Italian, Latin, Law, Mathematics, Media Studies, Music, Music Technology, Philosophy, Physical Education, Photography, Physics, Product Design, Psychology, Religious Studies, Systems & Control, Spanish and Theatre Studies. Also on offer are the Advanced Vocational Certificate in Education (formerly GNVQ) in Business, Leisure & Recreation and Art & Design. Most students are asked to choose four subjects in the Lower Sixth to AS level, which can lead on to A2 level in the Upper Sixth. In addition all take General Studies to AS level with an option to take this through to A2.

The curriculum offers breadth, depth and flexibility in course choice. Pupils are also prepared for the new World Class Tests and Oxbridge entrance. Arabic and Japanese Certificates, Scholastic Aptitude tests for American Universities, EFL and Language Development Study Support is also available at all levels.

Every pupil is guided through his or her school career by a Group Tutor. Each Tutor cares for between 10 and 14 pupils, taking a close personal interest in each and maintaining regular contact with parents on academic matters.

Games and Activities. Junior pupils are generally required to play the team game of the term; senior boys and girls choose from the following games: Archery, Athletics, Badminton, Basketball, Canoeing, Chess, Climbing, Caving, Cricket, Croquet, Cross Country, Fencing, Fitness Training, Flying, Golf, Gun Club, Hockey, Judo, Karate, Modern Pentathlon, Polo, Riding, Sailing, Shooting, Skiing, Squash, Swimming, Table Tennis, Tennis, Ten Tors Training, Trampolining, Volleyball.

In addition to the above options, boys may choose Rugby or Soccer, and girls may opt for Aerobics, Ballet, Dance, Netball, Rounders or Yoga.

In addition to games all pupils take part in the School's Activities Programme; they choose from a very wide range of 70 activities, including Ballroom Dancing, Climbing, Computer Club, Duke of Edinburgh's Award Scheme, Electric Guitar Making, Horse Riding, Life Saving, Photography, Scenic Design, Social Service, Television Production, Ten Tors Expedition, Water-colour Painting, Young Enterprise Scheme, Zulu Beadwork.

Scholarships and Bursaries. (*see* Entrance Scholarship section) A number of scholarships are available each year for excellence in academic studies, music, art and sport. All-rounder awards are also available for multi-talented individuals. Bursaries are available as an additional support for families in financial need and for the sons and daughters of Service personnel. Further details of all these awards may be obtained from the Tutor for Admissions.

Charitable status. Millfield is a Registered Charity, number 310283. Its aim is to provide independent boarding and day education for boys and girls, and to maintain an extensive system of bursary aid to gifted pupils or those in financial need.

Mill Hill School

The Ridgeway Mill Hill London NW7 1QS.
Tel: 020 8959 1176
Fax: 020 8201 0663
e-mail: registrations@millhill.org
website: www.millhill.org.uk

Motto: *Et virtutem et musas.*

Court of Governors:

Chairman: The Rt Hon Dame Angela Rumbold, DBE, PC

Dr R G Chapman, BSc, MB, BS, FRCGP
Sir Sydney Chapman, RIBA, FRTPI, FRSA, MP
G F Chase, DipEstMan, FRICS, FCIArb
G M R Graham, OBE, BA
E S Harvey, FRICS
H M James, CBE
Mrs A M Morley, LLB
Prof M R E Proctor, ScD
Mrs V Simmons
W Skinner, MA
R L Stewart, MA
Miss J M Taylor, BSc, DipEd
G O Vero, FCA

Company Secretary: Lt Col B Morgan, MSc, BA, FCMA, FCCA

***Headmaster:* W R Winfield**, MA

Deputy Heads:
J F Johnson-Munday, MA (*English*)
Miss J S Herbertson, MA (*French*)

Deputy Head (*External Relations*): P J P McDonough, MA (*History*)

Director of Studies: A C Gaylor, BA (*Mathematics*)

Chaplain: The Revd J T Fields, MA, BD, STM, DipCouns

Assistant Teachers:

Art & Design:
*A D Ross, MA
Miss V C Dempster, BEd

Business Education:
*Miss L H Sharples, BA
P H Edwards, BA
†Mrs V G Miner, MSc
R C Arch, MSc

Classics:
*S T Plummer, BA
Dr C Hobey, BA, PhD

Design Technology:
*†H Barnes, BA *Senior Housemaster*
†Ms B D Banks, BEd

English & Drama:
*T W Corbett, BA *English*
†Miss L J Farrant, BA
J M Lewis, MA *Assistant Director of Studies*
Ms S J Owen, BA
D T Bingham, BA *also Head of Careers*
J R L Orchard, BA
*D S Proudlock, BA *Drama*

Geography:
*N R Hodgson, MA
†D R Woodrow, BA
J R Monaghan, BSc

History & Politics:
*M Dickinson, MA
J D Rees, BA, AKC
A J V McBroom, BA *also Deputy Registrar*

Information Technology:
*M J Northen, BA

Mathematics:
*G Docherty, BSc
P S Bickerdike, BSc
Mrs E A Speed, BSc
D A Robb, BSc, PhD
R P Cross, BSc, CMath, MIMA
S A O'Reilly, MSc, MEd

Modern Languages:
*P R Lawson, MA
†A H Armstrong, BA, PhD
Mrs U Pulham, BA *EFL & SEN*
Miss K Bonnal, Maîtrise-ès-Lettres
Mrs S Stagg, LLB
Miss H D Barnes, MA *Spanish*
Miss C J Lewis, BA *German*
†A R B Phillips, BA

Music: (*with additional visiting teachers*)
R P Allain, BMus, LTCL *Director of Music*
A D Chaplin, BA, ARCM

Physical Education:
†A H Slade, BA *also Maths*
Miss K B Carroll, BA *also Physics*

Sciences:
*D S Hughes, BSc *Science & Biology*
*J G W Watson, BSc *Chemistry*
*P H Thonemann, MA, MPhil *Physics*
T J Chilton, BSc, MA
B J Dickson, BSc
†A Luke, MA
Dr E J M Evesham, BSc, PhD, CBiol, FIBiol
R N R Wallace, BSc
D O Omitowuju, BSc
M C Newman, BSc
G N Saint, BSc
G M Turner, BSc
J H M Widdershoven, MEd

Manager, MHS Enterprises: Miss J Brown

Visiting Music Teachers:
P Butterworth (*Electric Guitar/Bass*)
Mrs V Campbell, LTCL (*Bassoon*)
A Chaplin, BA (*Organ*)
J B Clark, BA (*Guitar*)
Miss M Cotterill (*Voice*)
I E Dalgleish (*Piano/Organ*)
I Fasham, ARCM (*Brass*)
G Holdsworth, BSc (*Clarinet and Saxophone*)
Mrs H Kearns, BA (*Piano*)
Mrs E Partridge (*Violin*)
Miss J E Reed, ARCM (*Cello/Bass*)
M H Robinson (*Trumpet*)
Miss J Shepherd (*Oboe*)
Mrs C Smith (*Flute*)

Officer Commanding CCF: Major H Barnes, BA

Medical Officer: Dr S V Thwaites, MB, BS, MRCG, DO, RCOG

Matron of Sanatorium: Mrs M Moore, SRN, RGN

JUNIOR SCHOOL, BELMONT
The Ridgeway, Mill Hill, London NW7 4ED
Tel: 020 8959 1431; Fax: 020 8906 3519

Master: J R Hawkins, BA

Deputy Master: K J Douglas, BA

Head of Upper School: Mrs L C Duncan, BSc

Head of Lower School: Mrs C A Adler, BA, DipDysInst

Assistant Staff:

Mrs B Ahmed, BA, PGCE (*French*)
C C M Arnold, MA (*Head of Classics*)
Mrs L Bird, BA, PGCE (*Lower School*)
P A Bird, BEd (*Y8 Coordinator*)
Miss L Bomford, BA(Ed) (*Girls Games, Head of Activities*)
Mrs M I Bunce, L-ès-L (*French*)
J Buoy, BEd (*Head of Maths*)
Miss G Carpenter, BA (Hons), PGCE (*Music & Games*)
F I Carr, DipAD (*Head of Art*)
Mrs E Y Carr, BEd (Hons) (*Lower School*)
Miss N Childs, BSc (Hons) (*Lower School*)
Mrs M Clarke, BA, PGCE (*French*)
C Cole, BA (*Head of English*)
Miss E J Culley, BA (*Lower School*)
D W Elder (*Head of PE*)
Miss E Ellis, BA (Hons), PGCE (*Lower School*)
Mrs J Fisher, BEd (Hons), PGCE (*Head of Science*)
Mrs A Gritz, BSc (*Head of ICT*)
A W T Haigh, BSc (*Science, ICT*)
Mrs D Harrison (*Head of Music*)
Mrs M J Hawkins (*Head of PSRE*)
A Hayward, BSc (Hons), PGCE (*Head of Geography*)
D M Hyland, BA (*Head of Design and Technology*)
Mrs C McRill, BA (Joint Hons) (*Head of French*)
Mrs L Mason, ALA (*School Librarian*)
Miss H Miller, BA, PGCE (*Lower School*)
R S Pace, MA (*Head of History*)
Miss K Robinson, BA (Hons) (*Lower School*)
T M Selwood, CertEd (*Physical Education*)
Mrs M L Slade, BEd (*Lower School*)

PRE-PREPARATORY SCHOOL, GRIMSDELL
Winterstoke House, Wills Grove, Mill Hill, London NW7 1QR
Tel: 020 8959 6884; Fax: 020 8959 4626

Head: Mrs P E R Bennett-Mills, CertEd

Deputy Head: Mrs A Attree, CertEd

Assistant Staff:
Mrs L Badger, MontDip
Mrs N Brown, BEd (Hons)
Miss C Clayton, BA (Hons)
Miss G Coleby, BEd
S Kent, GGSM, MA
Mrs S Kirk, BEd (Hons), PGCE
Miss R Mortimer, BEd (Hons)
Miss R Perkins, BEd (Hons)
Miss A Sicka, BA, PGCE
Mrs J Sutcliffe, MontDip
Mrs T Weeks, BA (Hons)

Mill Hill was founded by Samuel Favell (1760-1830) and Revd John Pye Smith (1774-1851) as a grammar school for the sons of Protestant dissenters and opened in 1807. Freedom of conscience, as well as sound learning, has been Mill Hill's "charter" and the policy of the School from its foundation has been one of wide tolerance. In September 1997 the School became fully co-educational.

Location. The School is part of Mill Hill village and is situated in a conservation area, on the borders of Hertfordshire and Middlesex, approximately 12 miles from the centre of London. Set in 120 acres of parkland originally formed by the famous botanist Peter Collinson, the grounds provide a spacious setting for the academic buildings, boarding and day houses and offer extensive facilities for sports and activities.

Buildings. Mill Hill combines a rich traditional heritage with modern educational facilities. The present School House was designed by Sir William Tite, architect of the Royal Exchange, and opened in 1826. Since the late 19th century numerous buildings have been added, including the Chapel, Library, Assembly Hall, Music School and Science Block, with 14 lecture rooms and newly refurbished laboratories. Other additions include the Art and Design Technology Centre, a modern Sports Hall, a Sixth Form Centre a multi-media language centre, two networked IT suites, a music technology centre and a studio theatre.

Houses. There are 600 pupils in the School (460 boys, 140 girls in 2001) of whom around 180 are boarders. There are 4 boarding Houses and 5 day Houses. Day pupils take a full part in the activities of the School.

Admission. Application may be made as early as parents wish. The majority of boys and girls enter at the age of 13. Candidates are selected on the basis of interviews, examination and Heads' confidential reference; successful candidates are given unconditional offers in February for entry in September while others qualify by taking the Scholarship Examination, held annually in January. Pupils not sitting the Scholarship Examination are required to sit the School's own Entrance Examinations which are held in January.

There are two other methods of entry:

(a) A limited number of places are available at 14+. Candidates are selected on the basis of interview, performance in the 14+ Entrance Examination (which is held in January) and a Head's confidential reference.

(b) Sixth Form Entry. Admission to the Sixth Form is open to both boys and girls, from the UK and abroad. Entry requirements are 4 GCSE passes at minimum Grade C plus

3 at Grade B or above, or equivalent qualifications for overseas pupils. More detailed entry requirements for specific A level courses are given in the School's Sixth Form Curriculum Guide. Candidates unable to offer the number of subjects required (eg some overseas candidates) will be considered on their individual academic merit.

Selection is by interview at the School (there are no examinations) and by reference from the candidate's present school. Offers made are conditional on meeting the entry requirements detailed above. Scholarships are awarded on the basis of examinations and interviews in December.

Curriculum. Every effort is made to avoid premature specialisation and in the Lower School all pupils follow a broad curriculum. Pupils are setted separately for core subjects, so that they are able to move at a speed best suited to their ability in different subjects. GCSE French may be taken in the second year, but all other subjects are taken in the third year, in the Fifth Form. Entry to the Sixth Form, from Fifth Form pupils already in the School, is conditional upon a minimum of 3 B Grade and 3 C Grade passes at GCSE.

In the Lower Sixth pupils take a one-year course to AS level in four subjects. In the Upper Sixth they continue with three of these to A level. There is a wide range of subject combinations and pupils are specially prepared in all subjects for Oxford and Cambridge entrance.

A level studies take up approximately 75% of the timetable. In addition Sixth Formers take courses in PSRE, and choose from a wide range of subsidiary subjects, which offer a choice of examinable and non-examined courses including Modern Languages, Art, Music, Cookery, Drama and Computer Studies.

Modern Languages. Mill Hill places emphasis on proficiency in the use of Modern Languages in a vocational context. Full use is made of satellite television and other audio-visual methods. About 20% of the second year take GCSE French one year early and continue in the Fifth Form with AS level. Irrespective of Sixth Form specialisation many choose to take AS levels in French, German and Spanish. Thus a good number of pupils, including Mathematicians and Scientists are competent in their use of a foreign language by the time they leave school. All pupils studying French, German or Spanish are encouraged and helped to spend extended study time abroad under the *European Initiative.*

The European Initiative. One of the distinctive features of the Mill Hill School Foundation is that it provides pupils with an education that is firmly set within a contemporary European context. Over the last 30 years the School has pioneered a number of initiatives, such as seminars, exchange visits, work and GAP year placement in Europe. The range of exchange visits is well established: all first year pupils visit France, Germany or Spain for a three-day stay; there are also term-time exchanges at different ages with schools in Rouen, Nantes, Agen, Almeria and Goslar. In 1997 the European Initiative was recognised by the Central Bureau and Council of Europe by the granting of the European Curriculum Award.

Up to 25 students from the European Continent spend one or two years at Mill Hill. The School also participates in an annual residential seminar week, where pupils and staff from European schools live and learn with Millhillians. Pupils can expect therefore to have first-hand experience of living and working with Europeans together with opportunities to gain qualifications which will enhance a European-based career.

Tutors. Each pupil has a tutor who is responsible for his/her academic progress and pastoral care, and who writes an end-of-term report. Parents are also invited to parents' meetings which are held at least once a year for each year group.

Careers. Mill Hill is a member of the Independent Schools' Careers Organisation (ISCO) and the Careers Department has up-to-date information on entry to and training in most careers. A Careers Room is provided with all the relevant literature, and work experience is arranged during the holidays for individual pupils with firms of their choice. All Fifth Form pupils are interviewed individually to ensure that they choose A level subjects relevant to possible future careers; these interviews are arranged in addition to those requested with Careers Advisers from the ISCO and from the Youth Employment Service. Fifth Form pupils also take an objective personal, academic and vocational test.

Music. The School offers a wide range of curricular and extra-curricular musical activities, including choirs, chamber and full orchestras, wind band and other ensembles. Concerts are given regularly by pupils and visiting professional performers. Pupils are encouraged to perform their own work in regular informal concerts. Individual tuition in most instruments, including voice, is available and instruments may be hired through the School. Free instrumental tuition is available at the discretion of the Headmaster, on the recommendation of the Director of Music. The Music School was recently extended and includes a hard disk recording studio. The Choir recently toured New York.

Art and DT. Pupils in the Lower School study Art and Design Technology and are also encouraged to study Art out of School hours when in addition to normal practical work there are facilities for Oil Painting, Pottery, Modelling, Casting, Printing and Wood Engraving. The Art and Technology Block (fully modernised in 1999) provides facilities for these activities, and for Wood and Metal Work and Design Realisation.

Drama. There is a strong tradition of drama at Mill Hill and in addition to regular School and House plays an annual House Drama Competition is held. Theatre Studies is an option at both GCSE and A level. The Studio Theatre is superbly equipped and offers at least 3 productions each term.

Sport. Every pupil, regardless of physical ability, is encouraged to participate in both individual sports and team games. The major sports for boys are Rugby, Hockey and Cricket and for girls are Hockey, Netball and Tennis. Other opportunities include Aerobics, Athletics, Badminton, Basketball, Cross-country, Eton Fives, Golf, Karate, Sailing, Soccer, Squash and Volleyball. Competition and excellence are valued and the level of professional coaching skills is exceptional. The school has both indoor and outdoor swimming pools, shooting range, all-weather pitch and Sports Hall, with multi-gym and a range of indoor sports facilities. There are strong links with Saracens RFC and special bursaries are available in the Sixth Form for gifted rugby players.

Extra-Curricular Activities. First year pupils are introduced to the range of minor sports (as above) and aspects of adventure training. All pupils are also offered a range of other activities such as debating, drama, modelling, pottery, photography, chess and computing. On Friday afternoons pupils have a choice between CCF (Army, Navy), Community Service, the Orchestra and the Duke of Edinburgh Award Scheme. In addition, many Societies exist to cater for a variety of out-of-school interests and, in particular, the Fifth Form undertake a week's "Challenge of Leadership" course in the summer after GCSE examinations.

Field Studies. Mill Hill owns a property in the village of Dent in the Yorkshire Dales National Park which is visited by the majority of pupils in their first year and used as a centre for geological and botanical field studies for GCSE and A level.

Fees. (2000/2001). £4,980 per term for boarders and £3,260 per term for day pupils which includes the games fee and the cost of most text books and stationery.

Scholarships. (*see* Entrance Scholarship section) The School offers a range of Scholarships and Exhibitions (including Music and Art Scholarships) at 13+ each year, varying in value according to merit up to half the current fees. A number of separate Scholarships and Exhibitions are awarded to candidates for Sixth Form places. There are also a number of special scholarships, bursaries for the children of Old Millhillians, Christian Ministers, members of the Armed Forces and the Diplomatic Services. Details can be obtained from the Admissions Office.

Charitable status. Mill Hill School is a Registered Charity, number 3404450 It exists for the education of boys and girls.

Monkton Combe School

near Bath Avon BA2 7HG.
Tel: Head Master: 01225 721102. Bursar: 01225 721141.
Fax: 01225 721181
e-mail: admissions@monkton.org.uk
website: http://www.monktoncombeschool.com

Monkton Combe School was founded in 1868, and today is one of the best known smaller Independent Schools in the country. The School's aim has always been to provide a broad education designed to enable boys and girls to develop all their potential to the full, with an emphasis on high academic standards. The School's tradition is unashamedly Christian, and every effort is made to relate Christian belief and worship to the needs of daily life.

Patrons:
Admiral Sir Horace Law, GCB, OBE, DSC
The Rt Revd M A P Wood, DSC, MA, RNR
Prof R J Berry, MA, DSc, FIBiol, FRSE
Martin Marriott, Esq, MA
The Baroness Cox of Queensbury, SRN, BSc(Soc), BSc(Econ), FRCN, PhD(Hon)
Lady Stanley, BSc, MSW
The Rt Revd T Dudley-Smith, MA, MLitt
Major-General Sir Philip Ward, KCVO, CBE
The Rt Revd I P M Cundy, MA

Chairman of Governors: P W Lee, Esq, CBE, MA, DL
Vice-Chairman: The Revd J H Simmons, FCCA

Life Governors:
Rear Admiral W J McClune, CB, MSc, MIEE
R D Spear, Esq, JP, MA

Governors:
Major-General (Retd) A N Carlier, CB, OBE, BSc
L E Ellis, Esq, MA, AFIMA, FRSA
Mrs L Gough, JP, RGN, DN, HV
A R Halden, Esq
Mrs J Hepworth, BA
Mrs K A Holt, BA
P R V Houston, Esq, MSc, FCA
Miss J Howell, BSc, AKC
Dr A Kidd, MA, PhD
C P Kimber, Esq, MA, MEd, DipEd
Mrs D Lucas, CertEd
A D Owen, Esq, OBE, MA, HonDSc
P C Poulsom, Esq
R B M Quayle, Esq, MA
The Revd M P Wynter

***Head Master:* M J Cuthbertson**, MA

Deputy Heads:
A D Gorrie, DA, FRSA
T J Dewes, MA, BA

Director of Academic Planning: J P Jenkins, BA, MA

SMT Houseparent: Mrs A Jameson, BA (*Houseparent, Nutfield*)

Senior Academic Tutor: J B Morley, BA (*Houseparent, Clarendon*)

Assistant Staff:
C J H Rogers, BSc (*Assistant Chaplain*)
L J Alvis, BSc
D J Vickery, MA, MEd
M C Garrod, BSc (*Houseparent, School*)
N D Botton, MA
J C Bradby, MA
T W G Baddeley, MA
I D Bygraves, BSc
W O Hanna, MA
D R Jameson, BEd, MA, AIST (*Houseparent, Nutfield*)
P G Bossom, MA
D M Merricks, BEd, MA (*Houseparent, Farm*)
Mrs J R T Gabe, DipRCM, ARCM (Performer's)
J P Jenkins, BA, MA
Mrs A Mills, BEd
I Findlay-Palmer, BSc
Mrs R H Garrod, BEd (*Houseparent, School*)
B J Newman, BMus, FRCO, LRAM
Mrs C M Merricks (*Houseparent, Farm*)
P R Clark
A K Barker, BSc
C M B Newton, BTech
T F Hardisty, BA
D M Conington, BSc
A D McPhee, BA, DipTEFL
R J W Hodge, BSc
J F Perry, BA (*Houseparent, Grove*)
Mrs J J Perry, BAPharm, MRPharmS, DipClinPharm (*Houseparent, Grove*)
S D Solomon, BA, MEd (*Houseparent, Hill*)
P J Woodward, BSc
R K Jeffreys, BSc
Miss A Willis, BSc
S K Skews, LTCL
Mrs L M Vaughan, BA
Mrs A J Weller, BSc
J J Smith, BA
Mrs C S Morley, BEd (*Houseparent, Clarendon*)
P R Harris, CertEd, MA (*Houseparent, Eddystone*)
Mrs P H Harris, BSc (*Houseparent, Eddystone*)
The Revd P Stephens, AGSM, DipTheol (*Chaplain*)
Mrs A J Waddington, BSc
Miss A Willis, BSc
Mrs S A Laing, BEd
Mrs S Cunliffe, CertEd

Visiting Music Staff:
Mrs S M Hollest, GGSM
D C Date, Hon FLCM, GGSM, ARCM, ARCO
P Skelton, BA, LRAM
P Rayner, LTCL, ALCM
Miss S Power, BEd
D Pagett, GRNCM, PGdipRNCM
J Scott
D Kelleher
Mrs G M Davies, LWCMD, LTCL
Mrs J Bateman
Miss A Higgs
Mrs J F Finch, ALCM, LTCL

Headmaster of Junior School: C J Stafford, BA

Head of Pre-Preparatory: Mrs A Russell, CertEd

Medical Officer: Dr N A Gough, MBBS, MRCP, MRCGP, DRCOG, MRCS

Company Secretary and Bursar: T D Sargison, LLB, FCA

Development Director: S J Hausey, BA

Situation. The geographical situation is delightful; the Senior School faces south across the Valley, or Combe, from which the place takes its name, about 200 feet above sea level, while the Junior School is at the top of the hill above, some 400 feet higher, with magnificent views over Avon and Wiltshire.

Organisation. The Junior and Senior Schools each have their own Head Master, staff and full range of facilities. However, they share the same Board of Governors and there are close links between them. About one quarter of the Senior School pupils come from the Junior School; the rest from Preparatory Schools all over the country, State Maintained Schools or from abroad. The Senior School went fully co-educational and merged with Clarendon School, Bedford, in September 1992. The Junior School went co-educational in September 1993.

Numbers. *Junior School:* There are 340 pupils of whom 30 board and 100 are in the Pre-Prep *Senior School:* There are 321 pupils (205 boys, 116 girls), of whom all but 98 are boarders. The Sixth Form numbers 135.

Admission. *Junior School.* The main entry is at age 7, 8 or 9 but every effort is made to accept boys and girls who wish to join at age 10 or 11. Some scholarships are offered. There is also a Pre-Preparatory School organised by the Junior School for boys and girls from 3½ to 7 years old.

Senior School. There is a one-form entry at 11 by means of report and interview and papers in English, Mathematics and a Reasoning Test. The main entry is at age 13 by means of the Common Entrance or Scholarship Examinations. Candidates from State Schools and schools abroad are admitted on the basis of report and interview and papers in English, Mathematics and a Reasoning Test. Entry direct into the Sixth Form is encouraged. Admission is on the basis of report, interviews and a Reasoning Test, and is conditional on not fewer than 5 subjects at grade C or better in GCSE.

Buildings. The Senior School's buildings are of Bath or Cotswold Dale stone. They have been steadily extended and modernised to meet the changing needs of the School. In recent years two new girls' Houses have been built and the boys' Houses have undergone major upgrading and refurbishing.

A new Information Technology Centre, a new Sixth Form Centre, a new Sports Centre a new Drama Studio and a new Shop have recently been opened.

The School has extensive playing fields, an Astroturf all-weather playing area for Hockey and Tennis, Boathouses on the River Avon, 14 Tennis Courts, a covered Rifle Range, a Rowing Tank, a heated outdoor Swimming Pool and 2 Squash Courts.

The Monkton Campaign was launched during 1995 and is designed to assist in the further development of the School over the next few years.

Chapel. There is a full-time resident Anglican Chaplain. The Chapel itself stands in the centre of the School. A short service is held every morning and a School Service, at which parents are welcome, each Sunday. There is a Confirmation Service each year. Pupils of other than Anglican tradition are welcomed to Communion Services.

Houses. The four boys' Houses, the two girls' Houses and the Junior House for 11 and 12 year olds are all under the care of Houseparents, who together with their tutorial teams of colleagues are responsible for the boys' and girls' general welfare.

Day Pupils are fully integrated into the boarding houses and the total life of the School and are encouraged but not obliged to stay until the end of evening prep. Senior pupils are given opportunities for responsibility as School or House Prefects during their sixth-form careers.

Tutor system. Each pupil has a Tutor, normally a member of staff of his or her own choice, who keeps in touch with parents and provides guidance and advice over every aspect of School life and over making choices for the future.

Curriculum. Our aim is to provide a broadly based curriculum in the years leading to GCSE. The curriculum reflects the spirit and fundamental goals of the National Curriculum. Those who show particular ability in French or Mathematics may proceed to work more advanced than GCSE before the end of the Fifth Form year. Personal and Social Education and Physical Education are included.

In the First, Second and Third Forms, all pupils study English, Mathematics and the Sciences with a foundation course comprising at least one Foreign Language, Art, the Classics, Design Technology, Food Studies, Geography, History, Information Technology, Music, PE and Religious Studies. In the Fourth and Fifth Forms, all pupils take GCSE English, Mathematics, and Co-ordinated or Separate Subject Science (Biology, Chemistry and Physics). They choose four other subjects from Art, Business Studies with IT, Classical Civilisation, Design Technology, Drama, English Literature, Food Studies, French, Geography, German, History, Latin, Music, Religious Studies and Sports Studies. In addition, Extra English is available as an option for those with particular needs in this subject.

Most pupils stay on for two years in the Sixth Form. The subjects at present offered at A Level are: Art, Biology, Business Studies, Chemistry, English, French, Further Mathematics, Geography, German, Greek, History, Latin, Mathematics, Music, Photography, Physics, Religious Studies, Sports Studies, Theatre Studies and Technology. As from September 2000, most pupils entering the Lower Sixth will study 4 subjects for one year to AS and continue with three to full A Level. In addition to their A Level subjects, all sixth-formers follow a scheme of General Studies in which they make a choice from a wide range of courses. Pupils also attend courses on world religions, the family, personal finance, self-presentation and interview technique, and a day conference on the "Challenge of Industry". A notable feature of the General Studies programme is the wide variety of lectures and presentations delivered by visiting speakers prominent in their field.

Careers Advice and Staff/Parent meetings. An experienced Careers Teacher works closely with Tutors in advising pupils. There is also a member of staff responsible for advice on higher education and another for links with industry. Parents, Old Monktonians and local people are invited to help pupils in their thinking about careers. The School belongs to the Independent Schools Careers Organisation which arranges Aptitude and Interest tests and whose secretary pays regular visits for interviews. Annual staff/parent meetings are held at the School to discuss pupils' progress. Parents are of course always welcome at other times.

University Entrance. The great majority of leavers go on to degree courses at Universities and Colleges of Higher Education.

Games. Those with particular abilities are encouraged to aim for excellence, but we also believe that regular games and exercise are important for all, helping to build a healthy lifestyle for the future and fostering leadership, teamwork and co-operation. The major sports for boys are: in the Michaelmas Term, Rugby Football; in the Lent Term, Hockey or Rowing; in the Summer Term, Cricket or Rowing. Boys choose either to row or to play Hockey and Cricket, but are allowed to alter their choice during their time at the School. Younger boys are normally required to play the major game of each term but as they become more senior they are allowed a greater degree of choice. During the Michaelmas Term, representative girls' teams are fielded in Hockey. In the Lent and Summer Terms, girls can choose between Netball, Rounders, Rowing, Swimming and Tennis. Representative teams are fielded in all these sports. There are also School teams in Athletics, Basketball, Cross-Country, Fencing, Football, Judo, Squash, Shooting and Swimming.

CCF and Community Service. There are sections for all three Services, besides various specialist activities such as canoeing, climbing and car maintenance. There is also an active Community Service group.

Leisure Activities. Monkton encourages as many worthwhile leisure pursuits as possible. Between 35 and 40 different Activities are offered; up to the age of 15 pupils are expected to be involved in at least one. All pupils keep a

Record of Achievement and discuss it with their Tutors during the term. All the facilities of the School, including the Art and DT Departments, Music Rooms and ICT Centre are available to pupils during their free time. The Choir, Orchestra, Big Band and other less formal music groups play an important part in the School's life and tuition is available in all orchestral instruments. About one-third of the members of the School take music lessons. There is a major School dramatic production in both Lent and Summer Terms. The School is conveniently close to Bath and Bristol for taking parties to concerts and theatres. Some 30 clubs and societies figure on the School List, ranging from the Climbing and Chess Clubs to the Literary Society and the Christian Union. Bible Study groups meet weekly.

Health. The School Medical Officer visits regularly and all boarders are required to register with him. The Medical Centre is under the care of a fully qualified Sister and Assistant who provide a 24-hour service.

Catering. All pupils take their meals in the Dining Hall, with cafeteria service.

Dress. The Clothes List is kept as simple as possible. All required items can be purchased in the School Shop.

Scholarships. (*see* Entrance Scholarship section) Four Anniversary Awards are offered at the age of 11 for open competition each year. They range in value from 50% to 10% of the appropriate fee.

At least ten Scholarships or Exhibitions, including at least two for Music, at least two for Art and at least two for all-round contribution to the life of the School, are offered at the age of 13 for open competition each year. These range in value from 50% to 10% of the appropriate fee.

At least two Scholarships are offered at age 16 for open competition to candidates from other schools for entry into the Lower Sixth each year. Academic, musical or artistic merit and financial need will be taken into account in making such awards. They range in value from 25% to 10% of the appropriate fee.

There is a limited number of endowment funds which provide a few Bursaries to enable pupils to come to Monkton Combe who would otherwise be unable to do so on financial grounds.

Fees. At present (September 2000) up to £5,135 per term for Boarders and £3,504 for Day Pupils at the Senior School (£3,775 and £2,630 respectively for pupils aged 7-13). The Governors are prepared to make a remission of up to one-third of the fee to a limited number of Clergy and Missionaries, on proof of need.

Old Monktonian Club. The Monkton Combe School Register has been fully revised and updated. Details from the Development Office at the School.

Charitable status. Monkton Combe School, a Company registered in England and limited by guarantee (Company Number 3228456), is a Registered Charity, number 1057185. Its aims and objectives are to provide education for girls and boys combined with sound religious training on Protestant and Evangelical principles in accordance with the doctrines of The Church of England.

Monmouth School

Monmouth Monmouthshire NP25 3XP
Tel: (01600) 713143
Fax: (01600) 772701
e-mail: admissions@monmouth.monm.sch.uk
website: www.habs.monmouth-org

The School was founded in 1614, by William Jones, a merchant of the City of London and a Liveryman of the Worshipful Company of Haberdashers, who was born near Monmouth and bequeathed a large sum of money to found a school and almshouses in the town. The School has derived immense advantage from this unusual association with the City of London.

The School is controlled by a Board of Governors appointed variously by the Haberdashers' Company, the Universities of Oxford, Cambridge and Wales, and local representative bodies.

Motto: Serve and Obey.

Chairman of the Governors: Dr C J T Bateman

Ex-Officio: The Master of the Worshipful Company of Haberdashers

[1]J A Ackroyd
P J Attenborough, MA
[1]J E N Bates
[1]Professor P J Bayley
Mrs H M Bosanquet, BA
[1]Dr J M Cook
[1]Councillor W A L Crump
[1]J H W Hamilton
D A Hey
Mrs M Molyneux
[1]Mrs E Murray
P M Oppenheimer
G F Pulman, MA, QC
Professor M W Roberts
[1]Mrs K Spencer
[1]A W Twiston Davies (*Chairman of the School Board*)
Mrs M Wetherell

[1] denotes member of the School Board

***Headmaster:* T H P Haynes**, BA

Second Master: M J Orton, BSc

Director of Studies: S N C Durrant, BA, MA

Head of Sixth Form: M R Christmas, MA

Assistant Staff:
J A T McEwan, BA
D C Adams, MA
†A J Dawson, BSc, MSc
P Dennis-Jones, MA (*Head of Classics*)
Mrs F P Sanders, CertEd
S J Edwards, BA (*Head of Modern Languages*)
G F Edmunds, BSc
J J Hartley, MA (*Head of Geography*)
K A Moseley, BSc, PhD, FRES (*Head of Physics*)
A V Francis, BSc, PhD (*Head of Biology*)
D Owens, CertEd (*Head of Design Technology*)
P C Hunt, GRNCM, LLCM
P Sanders, MA, MSc (*Head of Maths*)
†P Parmenter, CertEd
Miss S J Denner Brown, BA
Mrs M G K Jones, MA
†A N Cochran, BSc, MSc, CEng, MIEE
†J Aguilar, BA (*Senior Boarding Housemaster*)
D J McGladdery, BEd, MA
Mrs J Walker, BEd
†Mrs C J Hartley, BSc
†P D Jefferies, BSc
K J Madsen, BA (*Head of Economics*)
A J Tribe, BA
Mrs P Dollins, BMus
†M H G Hayter, MA
†G D Spawforth, MA
J M Gray, MA, ARCO (*Director of Music*)
J N Exton, DipAD, ACT (*Head of Art*)
D M Vickers, BEd (*Director of Physical Education*)
A J Jones, BA
D Williams, BSc
M D Clarke, BSc, PhD (*Head of Chemistry*)
Ms R M Jennings, BA, MA, PhD
M Metcalfe, BSc
R Howe, BA
†D K Jones, BSc
S Dowling, BA (*Head of English*)
J M Harrison, BA, PhD (*Head of History*)
Mrs A R Callicott, CertEd
M J Tamplin, BSc

L F Taylor, BSc, MSc (*Head of ICT*)
H F Tatham, BA (*Head of Religious Education*)
†J Boiling, BA
†J C Bevan, CertEd
Mrs S G Atherton, BA
N J R Goodson, BSc, CertEd
Miss R A Blacklaws, MA
J M Hart, BSc, MSc
Miss C Lewis, BEd
Miss E K Barson, BSc, MSc
B W Giles, BA
D G Hope, BA
Miss G E Jones, BA
Miss C L O'Brien, BSc
K-A Tiebosch, BA
R Wallis, BA, MSc

THE GRANGE (*Preparatory Department*):
Head: Mrs E G Thomas, BA

D Webb, BEd
P N Morris, BEd
Mrs J A Osborne, BEd
A J Francis, BSc, MSc

Bursar: Mr N G R James, BA, MIPD

Medical Officer: S H D Shaw, BA, BM

There are approximately 585 boys in the School, of whom 145 are boarders. **THE GRANGE,** the School's Preparatory Department, caters for about 88 dayboys aged 7 to 11.

Situation and Buildings. The School was founded in 1614 by William Jones and is one of the schools of the Worshipful Company of Haberdashers. A generous endowment enables the School to provide superb facilities and an excellent academic education whilst keeping fees reasonable. There are many scholarships and bursaries and the Haberdashers' Assisted Places Scheme, which replaced the Government scheme in 1998, ensures that an education at Monmouth School can be available to boys who will benefit from it, irrespective of their parents' income.

The School is enriched by close co-operation with Haberdashers' Monmouth School for Girls in many areas of school life, especially at Sixth Form level.

The School is set in the delightful landscape of the Wye Valley and much use is made of the surrounding countryside for expeditions and other outward-bound activities. There is a strong tradition of music and drama as well as of excellence in sport; a new sports complex was opened in Autumn 1999, a studio theatre in January 2001 and further improvements in the provision for the performing arts and sport are planned for the near future. Other recent developments have included greatly expanded Technology facilities, refurbished classroom blocks and a re-ordered Chapel. The Sixth Form has a dedicated Sixth Form Centre, inaugurated in 1999.

Boarding. The boarding community forms the core of the School. Junior boarders (11 and 12 year olds) are accommodated in St James' House for their first two years and benefit from the care of a dedicated house team who also provide an ambitious and popular programme of extra-curricular activities, tailored to the interests of the age group.

There are four senior boarding houses for boys between 13 and 18. The School has a flexible boarding policy which provides a considerable degree of freedom for families to make boarding arrangements which fit in with their lives, but which encourages boys to take full advantage of the many sporting, cultural and extra-curricular activities for which the School is renowned.

Admission. The main admission points are 7, 11, 13 and 16, but other stages will be considered if places are available. Candidates at 7+ and 11+ sit the School's own entrance tests. At 13+, candidates take either the Common Entrance Examination, the School's own Foundation Scholar ship Examination or its 13+ examination. Entrants to the Sixth Form are accepted either after sitting the Sixth Form Scholarship Examination or on the basis of GCSE results (or equivalent).

Candidates from overseas are welcome. Those whose first language is not English take a preliminary test of proficiency in English before proceeding to the appropriate entrance test.

The School accepts pupils with Dyslexia or similar specific learning difficulties and additional study support is available.

Curriculum. The curriculum is designed to provide both flexibility and breadth and to be in step with the National Curriculum without being constrained by it. Those in Forms 1 and 2 (Years 7 and 8) study a wide range of subjects including Latin, French and combined Science. In Form 3 (Year 9) the three Sciences are taught separately and pupils have the option of starting Greek.

Pupils normally take ten GCSE subjects, four or five of which are of their own choosing. There is a cross-curricular ICT scheme to enable pupils to make full use of the School's extensive facilities.

In the Sixth Form a range of approximately 32 AS subjects is offered along with a Life skills/Key skills programme. This programme and many of the AS subjects are offered in co-operation with Haberdashers' Monmouth School for Girls.

A particular feature of the curriculum is the extensive range of Modern Languages. French is taught at all levels, Spanish is available from Form 2, these along with German and Welsh can be taken at GCSE, and Russian and Italian are also available at AS/A level.

The Chapel. The School is an Anglican foundation and the Chapel plays an important part in its life. All pupils attend Chapel at least once each week and there is a service for boarders on Sundays.

A varied programme of preachers is organised, including clergy and lay people of many denominations. The Archbishop of Wales officiates at the annual Confirmation Service.

Games. The main sports are rugby, rowing, cricket and soccer. Many other sports are also available at a highly competitive level including athletics, cross country running, golf, sailing, squash and swimming. Deveral members of staff have international sporting honours and pupils regularly gain places to represent Wales in a variety of sports.

Activities. There is an extensive programme of activities throughout the School. Pupils in Form 4 and above may join the CCF (Army and RAF sections) which enjoy excellent links with locally based regular and territorial forces. Community Service is a popular option and many boys participate in the Duke of Edinburgh's Award Scheme. There is a very strong musical tradition with many pupils taking part in choirs, orchestras and bands which achieve high levels of success in competitions, and play to appreciative audiences locally and on the regular overseas tours which take place. School musicians have performed alongside professional musicians at such venues as St David's Hall, Cardiff and on national television. Drama is also strong and good opportunities are provided for participation at all levels. A wide range of School clubs and Societies further enriches the life of the School.

Fees. From September 2001: Boarding fee £12,096 pa (including tuition); Day tuition fee £7,257 pa. The Grange fee is £4,977 pa.

Entrance Scholarships. (*see* Entrance Scholarship section) Scholarships are available up to 50% of fees on the basis of performance in the General Entry Test (11+), Foundation Scholarship Examination (13+) and Sixth Form Examination (16+). Bursaries and the Haberdashers' Assisted Places Scheme can also provide up to 100% remission of fees, in certain circumstances.

Old Monmothians. Past members of the School are eligible to join the Old Monmothian Club, which enjoys a close relationship with the School. The Membership Secretary is Henry Toulouse, 3 Monkswell Close, Monmouth NP25 3PH.

Charitable status. William Jones Monmouth Schools is a Registered Charity, number 525616. Its aims and objectives are to provide an all-round education for boys and girls at reasonable fees; also to carry out the Founder's intention that local boys qualifying for entry should not be prevented from attending the School by lack of funds.

Morrison's Academy

Crieff Perthshire PH7 3AN.
Tel: (01764) 653885

Morrison's Academy Boys' School was opened in 1860 with a Girls' Department in 1861, an arrangement which continued until 1889 when a separate school for Girls was opened within the ten acres of the original site. In 1979 these two schools were brought together to become the one Morrison's Academy. The original foundation was possible through the generosity of Thomas Morrison, a native of Muthill who became a builder in Edinburgh and who in 1813 executed a Trust Deed directing that the fee of the reversion of his estate should be used to found and erect 'an institution calculated to promote the interests of mankind, having particular regard to the Education of Youth and the diffusion of useful knowledge . . . a new Institution which may bear my name and preserve the remembrance of my good intentions for the welfare and happiness of my fellow men'. The Academy is an independent school and serves the educational needs of 492 children from 5 years to 18 years, 12% of whom are boarders (8 years to 18 years).

The 332 secondary pupils prepare for Scottish Certification and the usual pattern is for five Higher grades to be attempted. Advanced Higher is offered as post-higher work. Excellent library and study facilities are available.

All children are encouraged to participate in at least some of the co-curricular activities made possible in the extensive playing fields, games complex (including swimming pool), music centre, art studios and laboratories. (*see* Entrance Scholarship section).

Board of Governors:
Chairman: A S F Mair, MBE, DL, BSc, FIMgt

Vice Chairman:
Members:

R B A Bolton, LLB, WS
C P Crabbie
J B Dakers, BSc
N Drysdale, LLB, WS
Professor D R Fearn, BSc, PhD, FRSE
Dr M A Fluendy, MA, DPhil, DSc, CPhys, CClass, FInstP, PRSC, FRSE
J Haggart, BSc
D S McLaren
I Miller
Professor E F Robertson
Mrs A Ross
I Roy, BA, CA
Mrs C M A Simpson, JP, MA

Clerk to Governors: R Mickel, LLB, WS

***Rector:* J B Bendall**, MA, BA
Depute Rector: R J Karling, MA

Head of Primary: Miss M L McCallum, DipCE, NFC

Senior Principal Teachers:
A J Law, MA
J A Harley, MA

Senior Head of Year: Mrs S M O'Grady, BA, MEd

Head of Information & Communications Technology: D Hamilton, MSc, BSc

Heads of Departments:

Art: Miss J Harper, BA
Biology: J B Beedie, BSc
Business Studies: H McMillan, DipCom
Chemistry: M D Hicks, CChem, MRSC
Computer Studies: D Hamilton, MSc, BSc
English: A S Andrews, MA
Geography: D L Allan, MA
History: J A Harley, MA
Mathematics: A E Wrench, MA, BSc
Modern Languages: A J Law, MA
Music: D Laidlaw, DipTMus
Physical Education: D N F Pennie, MA
Physics: P Dyer, BSc

Heads of Year:

Mrs A F Allan, BA
W A Clark, BSc
Mrs E M Fraser, DipCom
Mrs S O'Grady, BA, MEd
G W Young, BSc

Senior Primary Teacher: Mrs L S Anderson, BEd

Housemasters/Mistresses:

Academy House: Mr and Mrs G Wilson
Dalmhor House: Mrs A McIntyre

Charitable status. Morrison's Academy is a Registered Charity, number SC000458. The school is a recognised charity providing education.

Mount St Mary's College

Spinkhill Derbyshire S21 3YL.
Tel: (01246) 433388.
Fax: (01246) 435511

Mount St Mary's College was founded in 1842 by the Society of Jesus in order to provide educational facilities for the growing Catholic population of the country. The manor of Spinkhill in N.E. Derbyshire was the first home of the college and round this nucleus the present school has been built. The Elizabethan manor of Barlborough Hall, some 1¼ miles distant, is the home of the Junior Department of the college.

Motto: *Sine Macula.*

Numbers: College 260. Junior Department 3–11 years: 180. Boarders, Weekly Boarders and Day Pupils (girls and boys) are accepted at the College.

Governing Body:
President: The Very Revd D Smolira, SJ

Chairman: Sir N Adsetts, OBE

Clerk to the Governors: R J Groarke

Rev M Beattie, SJ
Mr J Bergin
Mr A Cooper
Mrs B Hahnel
Bro A Harrison
Mr G W Hodkinson
Mr M McCreton
Mrs E Roch
Mrs J Sanders
The Very Revd D Smolira, SJ (*Provincial*)
Fr P Willcocks, SJ

Superior: The Revd P Willcocks, SJ
***Headmaster:* Mr P MacDonald**, MA (Oxon)

Deputy Head: Mr C Lumb, BSc, MEd (Manchester)

Bursar: Mr C Bogie

Chaplain: The Revd P Willcocks, SJ

Assistant Staff:
S Adams, BEd Hons (Exeter) *Head of PE, Housemaster, Arrowsmith*
Mrs V E Argent, BEd, BA, MA, DipSpNeeds, TEFL, DipSpLD *Head of Learning Support*
Mrs E Bower, BA Hons (Swansea) *TEFL*
G G Brammer, BEd Hons (Sheffield) *Head of Lower School, Geography, Games*
H Cartwright, BA, CertEd (OU) *Head of Careers, Mathematics*
Miss J Corner, MALit, BA Hons (OU) *English*
Miss R Craven, BEd Hons (DeMontfort) *Girls' Games*
Miss N Evans, BA Hons (Reading) *Modern Languages*
J M Fry, BSc, ARSM (London) *Physics*
S Haslehurst, MA (Oxon) *Head of VIth Form, Head of History*
Mrs G Hazlehurst, BSc (Loughborough) *Head of Middle School, PE, PSE Co-ordinator*
Ms L Hobill, BMus, MA (Sheffield) *Director of Music*
P Hulse, MA Dist, BA Hons (Sheffield) *ICT Co-ordinator, Classics*
S M R Jenkins, BEd (Nottingham), MEd, MA, FRSA *Head of English and Drama*
G F Kirrane, BA (Liverpool) *History, English*
M Krlic, BSc (Bath) *Head of Economics*
M Long, BSc (Durham) *Head of Science, Housemaster, Pole*
A P Mulkerrins, BSc Hons (Hatfield Poly) *Head of Biology, Deputy Head of VIth Form, Examinations Officer*
Dr M B Murray, PhD (UMIST), ARIC *Head of Chemistry*)
Mrs A E Nichols, BA Hons (Sheffield), CertTESOL *Head of Modern Languages, Housemistress, Hopkins*
Miss D L Rowe, BSc (Newcastle-upon-Tyne) *Head of Mathematics*
P Scott, BEd (St Paul's), MEd (Sheffield) *Games, PE*
J Stephenson, BTheol Hons (Southampton) *Head of Religious Studies*
T Vickers, BA (Maryvale Institute) *Religious Studies*
Ms D Whetnall *Learning Support, Games*
I M Wilson, BEd (Hallam) *ICT Network Manager*

Headmaster's Secretary: Mrs G Wright

Medical Officer: Dr Palmer

Matron: Miss V Richardson, SRN

CCF: Sq Ldr J M Fry, WO1 G Powell, MISM

Barlborough Hall School:
Headteacher: Mrs W Parkinson, BEd

Category. Co-educational Independent School represented on the Headmasters' and Headmistresses' Conference. Entry to the College from 11+ (Year 7) and to the Junior Department at Barlborough Hall from 3+. Pupils are prepared for GCSE, A Levels and Oxford and Cambridge entry. Entry to the sixth form is accepted on GCSE results.

Aims. Mount St Mary's is a Jesuit school founded upon a philosophy of education inspired by the ideals and thoughts of St Ignatius of Loyola. Care and concern for the individual lie at the very heart of these ideals. We seek to develop the whole person, with Christ as the model for human life. We encourage an appreciation of the needs of others not just in our own community but in the world at large, preparing our pupils for an active life commitment through the development of *'a faith that promotes justice'*. Though essentially a Catholic college, pupils of other religious denominations are welcomed.

Situation. In its own extensive estate of playing fields and farmlands, the College is easily reached from the M1 motorway, Exit 30, and from Chesterfield or Sheffield both some 8 miles away. School minibuses run from Sheffield and other local towns.

Scholarships. Academic Scholarships are awarded at 11+ and 13+ on the basis of performance in the scholarship examinations. Music and Art and Sports scholarships are also available.

Bursaries. In keeping with the school's ethos, bursaries are awarded in cases of proven need.

Organisation. The school is organised into Lower, Middle and Upper Schools, each under its own Head of School who is responsible for overseeing academic progress, pastoral care, recreation and discipline. Heads of School work closely with the Deputy Head.

Boarders are located in one of the boarding areas under the care of a resident boarding housemaster/housemistress, assisted by resident assistant boarding staff. Each boarding area caters for pupils of approximately the same age, but girl boarders have separate boarding accommodation.

Curriculum. The curriculum for the first three years (11-13) broadly follows the National Curriculum at KS3 with the opportunity to pursue a second foreign language and Latin. The KS3 tests in Mathematics, Science and English are taken at the end of the third year (Year 9). Pupils are encouraged to take ten subjects to GCSE which include a core of English, Mathematics, a foreign language and Science. Other subjects are chosen from a range of options. In the 6th form pupils follow AS levels in the L6th (usually four) leading to three A levels at the end of the U6th year. In keeping with the school's Ignatian ethos, all pupils follow a Religious Studies course at every stage. Various special interest subjects are offered in the 6th form such as Astronomy and Amateur Radio. Specialist tuition is available in a variety of musical instruments. Assessment and monitoring of work is built into the tutorial system and reports are sent to parents each half term. Academic excellence and breadth of knowledge are characteristics of Jesuit education and the curriculum is constantly reviewed to ensure that the widest opportunities are available to each pupil.

Religion. Mount St Mary's is a Catholic school and, more distinctively, a Jesuit school. However, pupils of other than Catholic denominations are welcomed. Ignatian principles inform our work in fostering a realistic knowledge, love and acceptance of self and of the world in which we live, and underpin our prime objective: the formation of *'men and women for others'*. Voluntary Masses are available together with other devotional practices. Religious instruction is given throughout the school up to GCSE and at AS and A level. Voluntary Service is undertaken by the 6th form, and the school maintains a strong link with the Jesuit missions in different parts of the world, finding ways and means to further the work of the Society in this field. Many pupils are involved in a GAP year project supported by the Jesuits. Pupils and their parents are expected to recognise and endorse the religious commitment of the college.

Games. The school has extensive playing fields for Rugby, Hockey, Cricket and Football. Rugby is the major sport and the school has a strong regional reputation for the quality of this sport. Cricket facilities are excellent and include Astroturf all-weather practice wickets and indoor practice nets. An all-weather hockey pitch was opened in September 1997. Other sports include Athletics, Swimming (the school has its own indoor pool), Tennis, Basketball, Volleyball, Badminton, Shooting, Netball, Trampolining and Football. The nearby Rother Valley Country Park is used for Sailing, Canoeing and Windsurfing. There is also a Scuba Diving Club. The school has its own well equipped Sports Hall.

Facilities. Amongst the facilities offered are a Television Studio, Observatory, Radio Station, ICT Centre, Music School with 6 practice rooms and Recital Hall, Language

Laboratory with remote Satellite System, Library, Fitness Centre, Heated Indoor Swimming Pool, Sports Hall, Rifle Range, Clay Pigeon Shoot, outdoor Pursuits Centre, excellent all-weather Tennis Courts and 30 acres of games fields. A new Science block opened in September 1994, the all-weather hockey pitch and leisure/sports centre in 1997, and the newly refurbished School Theatre in 1999.

The majority of pupils are housed in en-suite rooms.

Drama. There is an Upper and a Lower School Drama Society which provides major productions in the Autumn and Spring Terms. The new theatre is equipped with computer controlled lighting. There are three plays each year, the major one being in the Spring term. Dramatic productions are of a very high standard.

Combined Cadet Force. Thursday afternoons are devoted to Army and RAF sections of the CCF, compulsory only in Year 10. In addition to Basic Training pupils have the opportunity to take part in Adventure Training, Air Experience Flights and Sailing and Gliding courses.

Special Features. Mount St Mary's has always been known for its homely, family atmosphere. The level of active participation of Old Mountaineers in the life of the school affirms this. Relationships between pupils and teachers are friendly and there are few disciplinary problems. Each pupil benefits from close interest and encouragement throughout the school, and parental involvement is encouraged.

Admissions. Pupils are admitted:

at 11+ via the Entrance and Scholarship Examination taken early in the Spring Term at the College.

at 13+ via the Common Academic Scholarship taken early in the Spring Term at the College or the Common Entrance Examinations taken in the Summer term. 13+ applicants from maintained sector schools are assessed separately on an individual basis.

Into the 6th form on the basis of GCSE results.

Pupils are admitted into other years on the basis of individual assessment and reports from the previous school.

Prospectus. This may be obtained by writing to the Headmaster's Secretary at the College. Parents are welcome to visit either the College or Barlborough Hall.

Leaving Scholarship. The Old Mountaineers Centenary Post Graduate Scholarships are available to those who attend university, and application for these is considered each year.

Charitable status. Trustees for RC Purposes is a Registered Charity, number 230165. Mount St Mary's was founded in 1842 to provide an education for children.

Newcastle-under-Lyme School
(Newcastle-under-Lyme Endowed Schools Charity)

Mount Pleasant Newcastle Staffordshire ST5 1DB
Tel: (01782) 631197

Newcastle-under-Lyme School, which attracts pupils from a large area of North Staffordshire, South Cheshire and North Shropshire, is a co-educational day school for 1,150 pupils aged 7–18. The present School was formed in 1981 through the amalgamation of Newcastle High School and the Orme Girls' School, two schools which were endowed as a single foundation in 1872 under an educational charity scheme for children in Newcastle which has its roots in the 1600s. The two schools enjoyed a reputation for scholarship and for service to the community throughout North Staffordshire, a reputation which has continued with the formation of Newcastle-under-Lyme School. The School is also well known for its high standards in sport, music and drama, which play a major part in the extra-curricular life of the School. The School's structure combines in one school predominantly single-sex teaching between the ages of 11 and 16, within a co-educational environment, with co-education in the Sixth Form. The co-educational preparatory department, Orme House, is adjacent to the Senior School and has some 170 pupils aged 7–11.

***Principal:* R M Reynolds**, BSc, PhD

Vice-Principals:
Miss B M Royle, BSc, MA
J N Tribbick, BA, PhD, LLB

Director of Studies: E M George, BA, MBA

English:
*P A Cash, BA, MPhil
Mrs J K Bell, BA
S Earwicker, BA, MPhil
Mrs B A Godridge, BA
Miss Z R Knowles, BA
O J A Leech, BA
Miss A A Potts, BA
Mrs E Swigg, BA
W D Weigall, BA

History:
*D Dunlop, BA, PhD
D A Cawdron, BA
Mrs J Dawson, BA
Mrs J Steed, BA

Mathematics:
*M Hancock-Child, BA, MA
Ms P Bailey, BA, PhD, AFIMA
Mrs C M Barber, BSc
Mrs J C Cliff, BSc
Mrs J A Cryer, BSc
Miss J M Griffiths, BSc
M J Harris, BSc
Mrs K Ludlow, BSc
C L Swire, CertEd

Computer Studies:
*G W Hall, MA
Mrs J Singleton, BSc

Chemistry:
*M S Snell, BSc
Mrs M M Atkins, BScTech (*Head of Sixth Form*)
J B Ewbank, BSc
Miss J Galvin, BSc
K Healey, BSc

Mrs J M Pinkham, BSc, PhD

Physics:
*Mrs S Bremner, BSc, PhD
A E Baggaley, BSc
T Brazier, BSc
A McDonald, BEng
D A Preston, BSc, PhD

Biology:
*N J Simms, BSc
N C Carter, BSc
D R Pepper, BSc, PhD
Mrs A L Varney, BSc

Geography:
*T P Jowitt, BSc
I J Cartwright, BEd, MA
R G Jones, BA
Mrs F P E Williams, BA
Mrs R Williams, BA

Modern Languages:
*D Brayford, MA, MEd
Mrs H Bayley, BA
R J Hawkins, BA
Mrs C Jones, BA
Mrs V Karpova-Barber, BA
D G Murtagh, BA
I Thompson, BA
Mrs S E Whitehouse, BA
Mrs D A Woodcock, BA

Classical and Theological Studies:
*W J Huntington, MA
J A Pedder, CertEd
Mrs J R Richardson, BA

Economics:
*D N Hartshorne, BSc(*Econ*)
Mrs J A Kelt, BSc(*Econ*)

Art:
*P Dare, BA
Miss S Fiasche, BA

Design and Technology:
*M J Hancock, BEd, MA
Miss S Swan, BEng

Home Economics (Food and Textiles):
*Mrs J A Hopkins, TCert
Mrs J Cox, TCert
Mrs B Jones, TCert

Physical Education (*Girls*):
*Miss E A Webb, BEd, MEd
Mrs J James, TCert
Miss N L Reynolds, BA

Physical Education (*Boys*):
*G M Chesterman, BSocSc
P Goodwin, BA
S A Robson, BEd

Music:
*Mrs S B Helleur, BA, LRAM, LTCL, CertEd
Mrs M L Tebby, BEd, ATCL, LRAM
D G McGarry, DLM
Mrs M Potter, GGSM, ARCM, PGCE

Swimming: P J Butler, FISTC, AIST(LS)

Orme House Preparatory Department:
P C Jerrum, BEd (*Head of Department*)
Mrs E J Bagguley, CertEd, BA
C J Broome, BA
P C Cooper, BEd
Mrs M Daker, CertEd
Mrs H Dickson, CertEd
Mrs J M Parker, BA
Mrs J S Roberts, BEd
Miss K Shipton, BA

Librarian: Miss W F Butler, BA, MA, DipLib, ALA

Buildings and Grounds. Set in 30 acres of grounds, the School is pleasantly situated on high ground in a quiet conservation area close to the centre of Newcastle-under-Lyme. The original buildings still form part of the School and extensions have been added from time to time. A fine new dining hall was opened in one of the wings of the original building, part of the continuing programme of development and refurbishment which was begun when the School reverted to full independence in 1981. The Millennium Sixth Form Centre opened in March 2000 affording spacious new accommodation for senior students. In addition to the well equipped classrooms and Science laboratories, the School has Language laboratories, workshops, a Music School, an Art and Design Centre, two libraries, a gymnasium, and a Sports Centre which includes a sports hall, a weights room and an indoor swimming pool. Computers are accessible in subject areas and in three modern laboratories, where there are 90 machines linked on a network basis. There are also tennis and netball courts and extensive playing fields, providing pitches for cricket, rugby and hockey, adjacent to the School.

Organisation. The School is organised in two sections: a preparatory department, Orme House, which was opened in 1982 and which has 170 pupils in the age range 7 to 11 and the Senior School, with approximately 450 boys and 450 girls. The Sixth Form numbers more than 250 pupils.

Since the amalgamation of the two schools, single sex teaching has been retained in most classes in the first five years of the Senior School. Classes in both the preparatory department and the Sixth Form are fully mixed.

Form Tutors and Year Tutors have particular responsibility for the pastoral welfare of the pupils in their charge.

In the First and Second Forms boys and girls have their own inter-form and inter-house competitions, with separate Junior assemblies. This structure gives to the junior forms a separate identity within the Senior School. The Senior House structure, which extends from Form 3 upwards, consists of four co-educational houses.

Curriculum. A broad curriculum in the first five years has English (Language and Literature), Mathematics, Biology, Chemistry, Physics, and French as core subjects. All pupils also take Latin, German, History, Geography, Religious Education, Music, Art, Home Economics, Design and Technology, ICT, PE, Swimming and Games; Russian and Spanish are introduced as option subjects in the Third Form. All pupils take German, in addition to French, in the Second Form and pupils have the option of taking Biology, Chemistry and Physics as a double award GCSE or as three separate GCSEs in the Fourth and Fifth Forms.

Pupils take nine or ten GCSEs and the great majority will, from September 2000, go on to take four AS Levels, in addition to General Studies in the Lower Sixth Form. Three or four of these subjects will be continued in the Upper Sixth as A2 qualifications.

Optional choices in the Sixth Form include A Level Business Studies, Economics, British Government and Politics, Classical Civilisation, and Philosophy, in addition to AS Levels in the subjects available at GCSE. All pupils follow a course in General Studies and take the NEAB examination at A Level. Pupils are also prepared for Oxford and Cambridge Entrance.

Extra Curricular Activities. The main school games are Rugby, Cricket, Hockey, Athletics, Tennis and Cross-Country for the boys and Hockey, Athletics, Netball, Tennis and Rounders for the girls. Swimming, Waterpolo, Life Saving and Synchronised Swimming also feature strongly and there are usually opportunities for Shooting, Squash, Aerobics, Basketball, Badminton, Golf and other physical activities in the Sixth Form.

There are also strong traditions in both Music and Drama and standards are very high. More than 300 pupils receive instrumental tuition and there are a number of concerts in each year with major performances being given in local churches and in the Victoria Concert Hall in Hanley. There are several major drama productions each year including one each at Senior, Middle and Junior School levels.

The flourishing Combined Cadet Force has naval, army and airforce sections and there is also a large Scout troop, which enrols both boys and girls. Pupils also participate in the Duke of Edinburgh Award Scheme.

Clubs and Societies meet during the lunch hour and after school.

Careers. The School places much emphasis on the importance of careers guidance, both in the GCSE years and in the preparation for tertiary education. The School is an all-in member of the ISCO Careers Guidance Scheme, through which all pupils in the Fifth Form receive a careers report based on tests of ability, personality and aptitude. Pupils receive full advice on applications to Universities and other Institutes of Higher Education.

Honours. Between 1987 and 2000 200 of our students gained places at Oxford and Cambridge, while in 2000, some 95% of all Upper Sixth leavers gained entry to degree courses in Higher Education.

Admissions. Entry to the Prep Department and to the first three forms of the Senior School is by examination only, normally at the ages of 7, 11 and 13. A few candidates are also admitted at 8, 9, 10, 12 and 14. The entrance examinations for these age groups are usually held in January and February for entry in the following September but pupils moving into the area may be considered at other times.

Entry at Sixth Form level is by interview and GCSE qualifications.

Registration forms, and copies of the Prospectus, are available on request.

Scholarships and Bursaries. (*see* Entrance Scholarship section) Six Governors' scholarships are awarded annually on the results of the entrance examination at 11+. Academic and Sports Scholarships are also available for entry at 13+. In addition, a scholarship is awarded at entry at 11, 12 or 13 for Mathematics.

Scholarships are also awarded in Mathematical Sciences and in Physics for the Sixth Form, on the results of Scholarship Examinations.

The Governors have established a Bursary Scheme to assist parents with school fees.

Further details may be obtained from the Principal.

Fees. Senior School £1,594 per term. Preparatory Department £1,410 per term.

Charitable status. Newcastle-under-Lyme Endowed Schools Charity is a Registered Charity, number 5285919. The object of the Schools Charity shall be the provision and conduct in or near Newcastle-under-Lyme of a day or a day and boarding school or schools for boys and girls.

Norwich School

70 The Close Norwich NR1 4DQ.
Tel: (01603) 623194
Fax: (01603) 627036

The School is an ancient foundation. The exact date at which it came into being is unknown, but it is first mentioned in an episcopal charter of 1156. In 1547 it was re-founded and granted a charter by Edward VI. About 4 years later it moved to its present site in the Cathedral Close.

Since 1949, the Worshipful Company of Dyers has taken great interest in the School and given generous building grants. It has 3 representatives on the Board of Governors.

Cathedral Choristers are members of the school. There are approximately 600 boys in the Main School and 150 in the Lower. Girls are admitted to the Sixth Form.

Motto: *Praemia virtutis honores.*

Governing Body:
The Governing Body consists of 22 governors, of whom 8 are representatives and 14 are co-optative.

Chairman: J S Peel, CBE, MC, MA, DL

***Head Master:* C D Brown**, MA (Cantab)

Bursar: N P Cooper, FCA

Second Master: A S Pettitt, MA (Oxon)

Teaching Staff:
*D C Knott, BSc (*Director of Sixth Form*)
¶P D T Cattermole, BSc, PhD
P J Evans, BA
*P F Moore CertEd
*J W Walker, BEd
J E R Waite, CertEd
†R H Bedford-Payne, BA
*E C Dowdeswell, ARCM, GRSM (*Director of Music*)
*P D Goddard, BEd
D R Sturdee, BA
M G Thompson, BSc
M Bhaduri, MSc, PhD
*T J Hill, BSc
†J S Fisher, BSc
†F J McIvor, MA
P J Skinner, BEd
*R C Gardiner, BSc
M James, MA
*N M Plater, MA (*Director of Studies*)
G D Sumner, BEd (*Senior Master*)
A C Yarham, BA
*J F Cullen, BSc
†C Hooper, BA
Mrs A K Coats, BA
†G S P Cardew, BSc
P J Carpmael, MA
*Mrs M C G Phillips, BA
*P E R Badger, BSc
M D Quick, BA, ARCO
†*D P Bateman, BSc
*A Fullwood, MA
†T J W Day, BA
W H J Croston, BA
R M Hudson, BSc
G A Hanlon, BSc
*M D Barber, BA
*S A Kettley, BA
*D N Farr, BA
A L Fisher, BA
J S Stearns, BSc
A J Coull, BA
Mrs A Vincent, MA
*J C Körösi, MBBS, BSc
M Mulligan, BA, MPhil
J Snelling, BSc
Mrs G M Evans, BA
Revd A M R Housman, MA
M A Harley, BSc
Miss A R Whitehead, BSc
*I M Grisewood, BA
*Mrs D Saywack, BA, MA
G M Downes, BA

Lower School:
P M Greenfield, BEd (*Master*)
I K Blaxall, BEd
P R Embling, CertEd
R E Hambleton, BSc, MA
J S G Worton, BSc
Mrs J H Greenfield, CertEd, BA
M Pickering, BSc
C S Cox, BSc
Mrs N B Dunnett, BA
Mrs M J Berry, BA

Medical Officer: Dr J C Bennett, MB, BS

Buildings. The buildings consist of the Chapel, which was built in 1316; the Reynolds Library (1969); 3 blocks of classrooms (the New Buildings 1907, the Dyers Lodge 1953 and 68 The Close); the Fleming science laboratories (1957); the Ethelbert Gateway, which is used as a music room; and School End House, the common room. A large Centre for Advanced Practical Studies was completed in 1976. A new classroom block, three additional laboratories and a new pavilion have been added. In January 1990 the former Bishop's Palace was refurbished to create a lecture theatre, eight classrooms and new VIth Form facilities. 71 The Close has subsequently become the Music School. A new Sports Centre was opened in 1999; in 2000, two further laboratories and a drama studio.

Houses. Boys in the Main School are divided into 7 houses: Brooke House (Mr T J W Day), Coke House (Mr G S P Cardew), Nelson House (Mr R H Bedford-Payne), Parker House (Mr C Hooper), Repton House (Mr J C Fisher), School House (Mr F J McIvor) and Valpy House (Mr D P Bateman). Each house is divided into groups of about 15 boys under a House Tutor. Sixth Form girls are also allocated to Houses.

Midday luncheon, served under the supervision of the staff, is available, as is breakfast.

Admission. Boys are accepted into the School at the beginning of the School year in September on the result of an entrance examination held in the previous spring. Candidates for the Lower School should be between 7 and 10 and for the Senior School between 11 and 13, *at the time of admission*. There are also places for boys under 14 who have reached a good Common Entrance Examination level and for boys and girls who wish to join the 6th Form.

Application for admission should be made to the Head Master on the form obtainable from the School.

Terms and Holidays. The School year begins in September and is divided into 3 terms – Autumn, Spring and Summer. There are approximately 3 weeks holiday at Christmas, 3 at Easter and 8 in the summer.

Religion. The School is non-denominational but has a Church of England Chaplain and daily assemblies in the Cathedral.

Curriculum. The curriculum is planned on the assumption that boys will normally stay at School until they have taken GCE examinations at 'A' level; but all boys take a broad range of subjects at the GCSE level, and may combine 2 Languages with 3 Science subjects and Mathematics. Thus the choice between Arts and Sciences in the 6th Form is deferred until the end of their GCSE year. In the 6th Form a wide selection of A/S and A2 level subjects is offered, and Sciences may be combined with Arts subjects; all 6th Form students are also required to follow a course of general studies.

Computers. The school's Information Technology policy emphasises that computers are useful tools to assist study. Computers are thus widely available throughout the school for classroom use, as a general resource for pupils' research and for administration. There are currently three networks, comprising IBM-compatible personal computers and various peripherals, including laser printers, scanners, a multiple CD-ROM server and fax modems. In addition to the networked resources, every department owns stand-alone computers, with numerous multimedia machines, MIDI hardware and colour printing facilities. There are access points offering fax, e-mail and Internet connections. One network is based around the refurbished IT room, and is used primarily for IT tuition; another network is generally available as a research resource, housed in the School Library; a third network is located in the Lower School. All networks offer business-standard software applications in word-processing, databases and spreadsheets. There is also a selection of graphics, Desk Top Publishing and Computer-Aided Design and Computer-Numerically-Controlled applications which are used extensively in Design and Technology.

Pupils are trained in keyboard skills, the major software applications and various specialised packages. Sixth Form students can work towards qualification in the Certificate of Key Skills for IT.

Career Advice and Selection. As the majority of boys stay into the 6th Form, and well over 90% go on to degree courses, the School provides a Careers advice service of specialised and detailed information. This begins in the Middle 5th and continues through the GCSE level year with interviews and guidance for both those leaving and intending 6th formers. The process is intensified through the 6th to ensure that the scope of varied opportunity is fully considered.

A well-equipped Careers Room is central to this system, operated by the Careers Master. He is assisted by the tutors, who are readily available at the frequent Parents' evenings, and other times by arrangement. Throughout each year, full use is made of the advice and assistance made available by parents, former pupils and local industry, as well as Higher Education and the Armed Services, with many speakers coming to the School. A part of this is the link with Industry and Commerce through the Young Enterprise scheme.

Games and Athletics. The principal games are Rugby Football, Hockey and Cricket. The Athletic sports are held yearly in the Summer term. Athletics, Sailing and Tennis are encouraged during the Summer term and Swimming instruction for the Lower School is arranged during School hours. The range of games activities continues to widen and includes Cross-Country, Fencing, Shooting, Squash, Soccer and Rowing. The School has an astro-turf hockey pitch.

All pupils are expected to take part in the Games and Athletics of the School unless exempted by the Head Master; normally, exemption is given only on medical grounds.

Physical Education. Physical education forms a regular part of the School programme, and is given by fully-qualified members of the staff.

Scouts. The School has its own Sea Scout Group – the 8th Norwich – consisting of a Venture Scout Unit, Scout Troop and Cub Scout Pack. For many years the group has received Admiralty recognition.

Duke of Edinburgh's Award Scheme. Pupils may take part in the Scheme at the bronze, silver or gold level.

School Societies. Pupils are encouraged to take their share in the activities of the various School societies, including the Amnesty Group, Debating, Geographical, History, Photographic, Natural History and the Chess, Computer and Electronics Clubs. Expeditions and trips are a regular feature; there are regular exchanges with two German Schools and with two French Schools.

Drama and Music. The School produces a play each year which, since 1921, has been given, with the co-operation of the Director of the Norwich Players, in the Maddermarket Theatre. Other dramatic activity includes a Junior play and the Lower School performs plays and musicals. The Drama Studio offers further opportunities.

Music forms an important part of the Curriculum; individual instrumental tuition is also arranged. There are orchestras, bands, choirs, jazz bands and a wide variety of music making, both within the School and in the community.

Cathedral and Chapel Choirs. Cathedral Choristers are members of the School. Copies of the regulations concerning their conditions of entry may be obtained on application to the Head Master's Secretary.

There is also a School Chapel Choir, which sings at Sunday services and on special occasions.

Lower School. There is a Lower School for boys between the ages of 7 and 12, under the supervision of Mr P M Greenfield. Promotion to the Senior School is based on each boy's general progress. The School occupies a new purpose-designed building, opened in 1972 and extended in 1991.

Fees. Senior School £5,919; Lower School £5,691.

Entrance Scholarships. (*see* Entrance Scholarship section) The following Entrance Scholarships are available annually if candidates of sufficient ability present themselves for the entrance examinations.

In the Senior School:

(a) *Governors' Scholarships.* At least 3 Scholarships of varying values according to parental means. (These Scholarships are open to boys already in the Lower School.) The maximum value of these awards will be the full tuition fees with a minimum value of £300.

(b) *The Edward Field Memorial Scholarship.* One Scholarship, value according to parental means, available to a boy of 13 already in the School.

(c) *Two Music Scholarships.* Value according to parental means. The maximum value of these awards will be full tuition fees with a minimum of £300.

In addition *King Edward VI Awards* are offered at 11+, 12+ and 16+. These scholarships will vary in value according to parental means.

In Form One of the Lower School:

Governors' Scholarships. 2 Scholarships of varying values according to parental means. The maximum value of these awards will be the full tuition fees with a minimum value of £300.

Also available periodically are (a) *The Morris Armes Scholarship.* Value according to parental means (maximum full tuition fees).

(b) *The Peddie Memorial Scholarship.* Value according to parental means (maximum full tuition fees).

Dyers' Company's Assistance. At the Headmaster's discretion, assistance can be made available to needy pupils.

The Former Pupils' Society is called the Old

Norvicensian Club. *Secretary:* Miss T Wright, c/o Norwich School, The Close, Norwich NR1 4DQ.

Charitable status. Norwich School is a Registered Charity, number 311280. It exists solely to provide education.

Nottingham High School

Waverley Mount Nottingham NG7 4ED.
Tel: 0115-978 6056
Fax: 0115 979 2202

Motto: *Lauda Finem.*

This School was founded in 1513 by Agnes Mellers, widow of Richard Mellers, sometime Mayor of Nottingham. The first Charter was given by Henry VIII, and supplementary Charters were given by Philip and Mary, and by Queen Elizabeth. The School, which remains independent, is now administered under the terms of a scheme issued by the Charity Commissioners.

Governing Body:

The Lord Lieutenant of Nottinghamshire
The Lord Mayor of Nottingham
Three Representatives of the City Council
Two Representatives of the Nottinghamshire County Council
Three Representatives of the City Justices
Four Representatives of the Universities
Eight Co-optative Members
Three members of Parliament for the City

Chairman of the Governors: M H Kidd, FCA

Clerk to the Governors: A B Palfreman, MA, 84 Friar Lane, Nottingham

***Head Master:* Christopher S Parker**, CBE, BA (Bristol), FRSA

Deputy Head Master: P G Sibly, BSc, PhD, ARCM (University College, London)

Senior Master: D I Driver, BSc (Nottingham)

Senior Teacher: K D Fear, BA (Southampton)

Director of Finance and Estates: R G Burdell, ACMA

Head of Sixth Form: J L Wilkinson, MA (St Andrews)

Academic Staff:
F M P Jones, BSc (*Mathematics*)
D Phillips, CertEd (*Mathematics*)
M G Coulam, BSc (*Economics*)
C P Dawson, BSc (*Biology*)
*G J Lewin, MSc, ARCS, DIC (*Physics*)
*R L Nicolle, BSc (*Careers*)
J F W Knifton, MA, (*French*)
*D A Slack, BSc, PhD (*Information and Communication Technology*)
*R G Willan, BA (*Geography*)
*C Lee, DipEd (*Games*)
*R Kilby, BSc (*Mathematics*)
*J A Cook, BSc (*Biology*)
G Douglas, LTCL (*Music*)
P G Morris, BSc (*Physics*)
*A D Holding, BA (*General Studies*)
W P J Ruff, BA (*English*)
A F Wood, BSc, PhD (*Chemistry*)
*R J W Gardiner, BA, CIE (*Art*)
K P Brierley, BSc (*Chemistry*)
M T Cleverley, BSc (*Chemistry*)
A S Winter, BA (*French*)
R J Clarke, BSc (*Mathematics*)
Mrs W M Nicolle, BSc (*Physics*)
R Benson, BSc (*Physics*)
C P Sedgewick, MA (*Geography*)
J T Swain, MA, PhD (*History*)
*Rev S Krzeminski, MTh (*RE*)
S L Williams, MA (*History*)
D J F Woodhouse, BA, ARCM (*Music*)
K C Clayton, BSc (*Biology*)
*G W Woolley, BA (*Design Technology*)
*S Barber, BA (*French*)
P F Carthew, BA, MEd (*History*)
Miss S Willan, BA (*RE*)
*B J Duesbury, BA (*English*)
Mrs C Y Fletcher, BSc, PhD (*Biology*)
Mrs P F Rayner, BA (*Special Learning Support*)
M D Smith, BEd (*PE*)
Mrs P J Gostelow, BSc (*Geography*)
J Lamb, BSc (*Mathematics*)
A V Martin, BA (*Mathematics*)
Mrs M O Mills, BSc (*Mathematics*)
M I Saperia, BSc (*Biology*)
D B Thomas, BEd (*Design Technology*)
R A Gilbert, BA (*Chemistry*)
*D Hecht (Studienassessor) (*German*)
G J Martin, MA (*English*)
G Whitehead, MA (*German*)
*J E Rayfield, BA (*Music*)
*R S Coldicott, BSc, PhD (*Chemistry*)
P J Cramp, BA (*Economics*)
K Weaver, BA (*Mathematics*)
Mrs A Griffin, BA (*German*)
T M Quinlan, BSc (*Biology*)
*M D Bartlett, MA (*History*)
R J Carpenter, BSc (*Physics*)
I F Thorpe, BEd (*Design Technology*)
I P Spedding, BSc (*Mathematics*)
J G Allen, BA (*Mathematics*)
T S Heath, MA (*Geography*)
A N Holman, BA (*Mathematics*)
Ms K Stewart, BA (*English*)
D S Gill, BSc, PhD (*Physics*)
J R Bleakley, BA (*English*)
Mrs K M Costante, MA (*Chemistry*)
Miss E E Hill, BA (*Art*)
*J P Stanley, BA (*Classics*)
S W Schumann (*German Assistant*)
Mrs V J Winter (*French Assistant*)
P D Daley, BA (*Classics*)
D J Poole, MA (*Economics*)
J M Rinder, BA (*Modern Languages*)
Mrs V H Sherwood, MA (*Classics*)

School Nurse: Mrs P H Morris, RGN, FPN

Headmaster's PA/Secretary: Mrs K Holdsworth

Librarian: Mrs M Clark, ALA

Preparatory School:
P M Pallant, CertEd (*Headmaster*)
P Ganley, BEd (*Deputy Head*)
E Jones, BA
Mrs A P Eastwood, CertEd
Mrs L Y Harrison, BA
Mrs H C Davies, BEd
Mrs M Sweeney, BA
P G Martin, BEd
S Doo, BA
R W Fox, BSc
Mrs M Scott-Brown, LTCL

The School was transferred to its present site in 1868 and the premises have been continually improved and extended. The most recent major improvements have been a

Preparatory School; Science Building; Sports Hall; Design and Technology Centre and a Music School. There have also been major developments in the fields of Information and Communications Technology and Language teaching.

Tuition Fees are £1,998 a term Main School. £1,669 a term Preparatory.

Admission. Entrance Examinations are held in January or February each year. Applicants for the Preparatory School should be between the ages of 7 and 11 years, and for the Main School between 11 and 12 years on 1 September of the year of entry.

Organisation and Curriculum. There are 974 day boys, of whom 168 are in the Preparatory School and 232 in the Sixth Form. The Preparatory School (see Part IV) caters for boys who intend to complete their education in the Main School.

The Main School course leads to examinations at GCSE in the normal range of subjects. Boys in the Sixth Form are prepared for the AS and A2 Papers of the GCE, and for 'STEP'. The range of subjects is wide – Latin; Classical Studies; Modern Languages; English; History; Economics; Politics; Design Technology, Geography; Mathematics; Physics; Chemistry; Biology; Music; Art; Philosophy; Religious Studies.

Entrance Scholarships (*see* Entrance Scholarship section). An Entrance Examination is held in January each year for the award of Entrance Scholarships on the Foundation of the School. An additional school fund provides entrance bursaries for boys who receive grants according to their parents' means. Two bursaries are also available each year from the Ogden Trust.

Games. The Playing Fields, covering 20 acres, are situated about a mile and a half from the School with excellent pavilion facilities. There are also indoor cricket nets at the school. The School games, in which all boys are expected to take part unless medically exempted, are Rugby Football (Association Football in the Preparatory School) and Athletics in the winter, and Cricket or Tennis in the summer. Other alternatives provided for senior boys include Cross Country, Squash, Hockey, Association Football, Badminton, Golf, Shooting and Basketball. Swimming forms part of the Physical Education programme.

Combined Cadet Force. The School maintains a contingent of the CCF based on voluntary recruitment and consisting of Navy, Army and Air Force sections. There is a small bore range, and the School enters teams for various national competitions, including Bisley.

Societies. Individual interests and hobbies are catered for by a wide range of Societies which meet in the lunch break or at the end of afternoon school. These include Drama, Modern Languages, Mathematics, Chemistry, Biology, English, Politics, Music and Debating Societies, the Chess Club, the Bridge Club, Christian Union, and the Scout Troop. Over 120 boys a year participate in the Duke of Edinburgh's award scheme. The Community Action Group, the Venture Scouts and other Societies meet jointly with the neighbouring Nottingham Girls' High School.

Music. Apart from elementary instruction in Music in the lower forms, and more advanced studies for GCSE and 'A' level, tuition is offered by 3 full-time and 14 part-time teachers in the full range of orchestral instruments. There are 2 School orchestras of 50 and 30 players, 2 Choirs, a concert band (wind) of 50, a Training Band and Big Band and choral and orchestral concerts are given each year. Four instrumental bursaries, covering fee tuition on one instrument, are available to boys entering Year 7.

Honours. 20 Places at Oxford and Cambridge.

The Old Nottinghamians Society owns a substantial Social Centre at its sports ground. The Hon. Secretary is S Jackson, Lenton House, Cropwell Bishop, Nottingham NG12 3BQ. (Tel: 0115 989 2288).

Charitable status. The Foundation of the Nottingham High School is a Registered Charity, number 528236. It exists to provide education for boys between the ages of 7 and 18 years.

Oakham School

Oakham Rutland LE15 6DT.
Tel: (01572) 758500
Fax: (01572) 755786

Motto: *Quasi Cursores Vitai Lampada Tradunt*

Trustees:
Visitor: Col T C S Haywood, OBE

Chairman: T H White, MA, FRICS

Hereditary Trustee: W F B Johnson

Ex-Officio:
The Rt Revd The Lord Bishop of Peterborough
Air Chief Marshal Sir Jock Kennedy, GCB, AFC, DL
The Very Revd The Dean of Peterborough

Representatives of the Governors of the Foundation:
Sir Clifford Boulton, GCB, DL, MA
Mrs P A G Corah
T F Hart, Esq, MA
Sir Michael Latham, MA, DipEd, DL
Col J M K Weir, OBE, TD, FRICS, DL

Co-optative:
Prof K Baynes
Mrs S K Bickley, BA, CertEd
Dr J M Blatchly, MA, DLitt, FSA
Dr S E Blaza
Mrs G M Harris, MHCIMA
A L Leighton, Esq
Dr D L Smith
M J Swallow, Esq
D W Wilson, Esq

Bursar and Clerk to the Trustees: J R Tomlinson, MA, FCA

***Headmaster:* A R M Little**, MA

Deputy Headmaster: T Manly, BA, MSc

Second Deputy: Mrs J M D West, BSc, DipRSA

Master of Jerwoods: N Davenport, MA

Senior Members of Staff:
Director of Studies: I Robson, MA
Director of Admissions: V J Harvey, BSc
Foundation Director: M V Minshall, BA
Head of Information & Communication Technology: Miss E R Ovenden, BA
Careers: Mrs K A Williamson, BA
Director of Activities: D N Gilvary, MA

Heads of Department:
Economics & Business Studies: R S Williams, BSc, MBA
Science: Dr J K Cheverton, MA, DPhil
Mathematics: Dr G N Thwaites, MA
Geography: A Williams, BSc
Languages: S T Glynn, MA
English: D Jackson, BA
History: Dr S Hyde, MA, DPhil
Facilities Manager: N C Mullinger, BEd
Director of Sports: A C Welch, BEd
Chaplain: The Revd G B McAvoy, MBE, MA

Housemasters/Housemistresses:

Junior School:
Ancaster: Mrs J L Carnell, BA
Lincoln: Mrs A Rawlings, BEd
Peterborough: N Davenport, MA
Sargants: M Durose, BSc

Middle School:
Barrow: Dr S J Miller, BSc, PhD
Buchanans: Mrs P A Craig, BSc
Chapmans: S D Barefoot, MA
Clipsham: M B Rochester, CertEd
Gunthorpe: Miss M E Grimley, BEd
Hambleton: Mrs M Nicholls, BA
Haywoods: S C Northcott, MA
Rushebrookes: D Smith, BA, MPhil
Stevens: S J Burrows, BA/Mrs J Burrows, BA
Wharflands: N S Paddock, BSocSci

Upper School:
Round House: Mrs G Dixon, BSc
School House: J Wills, CertEd

The overall staff pupil ratio is 1:9

Music:
Director of Music: D N Woodcock, MA, FRCO(DipCHM), FRSA
Head of Academic Music: P J Witchell, MA, GRSM, LRAM

Medical Officer: Dr G E McCormack, MB, BS
Personal Assistant to the Headmaster: Mrs J Wood

History. In 1584 Archdeacon Robert Johnson of Leicester, founded "as many free schools in Rutland as there were market towns therein; one at Oakham, another at Uppingham". For 300 years both schools served as humble grammar schools for their respective areas. Oakham remained in essence a small and comparatively local boys' school until 1960 when, first, over a decade the number of boys was almost doubled, and then, following the reversion to full independence in 1970, co-education was introduced throughout the age range (10–19) of the school. Present numbers in the school are over 1,000; boys 500, girls 500; (330 in the Sixth Form). Oakham now combines most successfully its traditional values with an innovative approach.

Buildings and General. In order to meet this rapid expansion the amenities of the school have been transformed and over £25 million has been spent on capital additions and improvements since 1960. Several new boarding houses have been built, others enlarged, and new day houses created. During this period the school has built, in addition, two theatres, a library, science laboratories, a classroom block, an art and design centre, a central dining hall, a music school, and a sports hall with squash courts and indoor swimming pool. The re-designed 'Queen Elizabeth Theatre' was opened by Her Majesty The Queen in November 1984 and has recently been refurbished. Major recent developments include The Merton Building with 24 classrooms for Mathematics, English and History (1991), The Smallbone Library (1994), the Information Communication and Technology Centre (1998) and the Fitness Centre (September 2000). Plans are in place to build an Innovation Centre.

Organisation and Curriculum. There are four Junior School Houses (10–13), ten Middle/Upper School (13–17), and separate Houses for second year VIth Formers, who are thus enabled to lead a less restrictive life and to organise their own commitments to a greater degree. All pupils have a Tutor, who is responsible for generally supervising their work, as well as a Housemaster. The Junior School has a four form entry, and all pupils start French at 11; they have the opportunity of starting a second language (German, Spanish or Latin) at 13 (year 9). When the Preparatory School entry joins the Middle School at 13 there are 6 or 7 forms, some subjects are streamed; in the Fourth and Fifth Forms (years 10 and 11) most subjects are setted up to GCSE. In the Upper School after GCSE the pupil will normally take four AS Level subjects to be followed through to at least three A2 levels. Subjects available are: English, History, Geography, Economics, Business Studies, Computer Studies, Further Maths, Politics, Greek, Latin, French, German, Spanish, Russian, Music, Art and Design, Art History, Theatre Studies, PE and Sports Studies, Design and Technology, Mathematics, Physics, Chemistry and Biology and Ethics and Philosophy of Religion. Pupils are also prepared for Oxford and Cambridge entry, and recent years have brought a steady flow of entries.

Music is an important part of School life, both inside and outside the curriculum. Free tuition on up to two instruments is given to Music Scholars and all other pupils who reach Grade 6 with Merit level of the Associated Board. Chapel Choir, Choral Society, three Orchestras, Concert Band, and various smaller ensembles all flourish vigorously and provide many opportunities for instrumentalists and singers. Choral boarding places to the value of 15% of the full fee are offered to Cathedral and Choir School choristers.

Drama plays an important part in the life of the School with several productions each year. A majority of pupils at all levels takes part in at least one dramatic production a year.

The Richard Bull Centre (Art, Design & Technology), open every day of the week, and at the weekend, offers a wide range of creative activities, including painting, pottery, sculpture, textiles, work in wood, metal and plastics, jewellery making, print-making, computer aided design, electronics, home economics and photography.

Leisure Activities. Different sports vigorously pursued include rugby, soccer, hockey, cricket, athletics, swimming, shooting, tennis, squash, fives, badminton, basketball, netball, fencing, lacrosse, golf and sailing. Many clubs and societies flourish. Various arduous Training Activities are undertaken through the CCF; in particular, the Duke of Edinburgh Award scheme has produced 1000 gold medallists.

Terms of Entry. Pupils are accepted mainly in September for the Winter Term, but a few places may be available for the Spring Term in January.

Fees per term. (*see* Entrance Scholarship section) At September 2000 (£4,970 boarding, £2,970 day).

Honours 1999: 20 places at Oxford or Cambridge, including Organ Scholar at King's College, Cambridge. 95% (62% A & B grade) pass rate at 'A' level. 95%+ of leavers go to University or College. 70 Distinctions and Merits, Royal Schools of Music, Associated Board. 70 Gold Awards of Duke of Edinburgh award scheme.

Charitable status. Oakham School is a Registered Charity, number 527825. It exists for the purpose of education.

The Oratory School

Woodcote Reading RG8 0PJ.
Tel: 01491 680207
Fax: 01491 680020

The Oratory School was founded in 1859, by the Venerable John Henry, Cardinal Newman, at the request of a group of eminent Catholic laymen. The Chaplain apart, the School is administered and staffed entirely by laymen.

Motto: *Cor ad cor loquitur.*

President:
The Duke of Norfolk, KG, GCVO, CB, CBE, MC, DL

Vice-Presidents:
His Eminence Cardinal William W Baum
The Most Rev Maurice Couve de Murville, MA, MPhil, STL
M F S Chapman, TD, MA

Chairman:
J J Eyston, MA, FRICS, KSG

The Governors:

The Rt Revd Mgr R Brown, VG, JCD, KCHS
The Very Revd R Byrne, BD, AKC, Cong Orat
Mrs E M Drew, CertEd, NFF
F J Fitzherbert-Brockholes, MA
C J French
P C H Hasslacher
N R Purnell, MA, QC
C J Sehmer, FCA
Dr R I Simpson, MB, BS
M W Stilwell
Major T E Thorneycroft
T A H Tyler, OBE, BA
D E Wilson, OBE

Clerk to the Governors: A V Phillips

***Headmaster:* C I Dytor**, MC, MA

Assistant Headmaster: J C Harris, BSc, MPhil

Senior Master: P L Tomlinson, MFA

Chaplain: The Revd N C Griffin, BSc, FRSA

Assistant staff:
S A A Bennie, BA
J J Berrow, BA
B W Browne, BSc
P P deW Burr, MA
A N Callan, BSc
M J Crump, BMus
R J Cullen, BSc
Mrs E M Dangerfield, BA
M A Dhillon, BSc
†M J Eastham, BA (*Housemaster, Norris*)
C W Fothergill, BA, MA(Ed)
M H Green, MEd
K Gregory, BSc, MTech
Mrs A E Harris, BA
†T J Hennessy, BA (*Housemaster, St John*)
Mrs P M Hennessy, BA
R L Hey, BSc
A A Hill, MA, AIL
J A Hodgson, BSc
R T H Hood, BSc
N J C Jones, BA, ARCO
I P Jordan, BEd
K Laughton, BA, AIL
A R McBirnie, BA, MMus, PhD, LTCL (*Director of Music*)
E McCarthy, BSc, ACIS
I C McLean, MA, MSc
†A J Nash, MA (*Housemaster, FitzAlan*)
Mrs D A Nash, MA
†M H Povey, BSc (*Housemaster, Faber*)
Mrs R M Povey
D E Riddle, MA
S H Roberts, BA, AIL
R W Sanders, BA, AKC
M A Smith, MA
†P A Thomas, BA, MA(Ed) (*Housemaster, Junior House*)
Mrs E S Thomas, BA, MA
A J Tinkel, MA
N E Topham
H Upton, MA
P R Williams, BA
A J Wilson, BSc
R B Womersley, BEd

Visiting Music Staff:

D Bache, ALCM (*Guitar*)
Miss H Clissold, BMus (*Violin*)
A Handy, ARCM (*Brass*)
R H Herford, MA, GRNCM (*Singing*)
G F Holdsworth, BSc (*Clarinet and Saxophone*)
C C King (*Drums and Percussion*)
Miss E V Krivenko, MMus (*Piano*)
Mrs H Pugh, BA, ARCM (*Oboe*)
S W Rudall, LRAM (*Cello*)
U Underwood (*Guitar*)

Medical Staff:

Dr S A Richards, MA, MB, BChir, DCH (*Medical Officer*)
Mrs P Codner, SRN, SCM (*Sanatorium Sister*)
Mrs J E Tomlinson, SEN (*Staff Nurse*)
Mrs R Hilton (*Assistant Nurse*)

Administrative Staff:

Bursar: to be appointed
Personal Assistant to the Headmaster: Mrs S E Pudney, AIL
School Secretary: Mrs S A Waghorn
PR and Marketing: Mrs J A Dooley

Number in School. There are 400 boys, incorporating a proportion of day boys.

The School is situated in an area of outstanding natural beauty in South Oxfordshire, in grounds of 400 acres. An extensive building programme, which is continuing, has provided modern science laboratories, a new classroom and study wing, a new domestic wing, a theatre, an Art & Design Centre, a Junior Department, 2 new boarding houses, a Music School, a new dining hall, a new Chapel, a Computer Wing and an indoor sports hall incorporating a Real Tennis court. There is also a nine hole golf course. The school also owns a property in Normandy for curricular and extra-curricular study and activities.

Organisation. Four Senior Houses and the Junior House offer boarding facilities for 400 boys. Particular care is taken to provide an environment which facilitates the assimilation of new boys.

Health. The School Medical Centre is under the supervision of a fully qualified resident Sister and the School Medical Officer.

Admission. Boys enter either at age 13 through the Scholarship or Common Entrance Examination, or at 11 by informal interview and exam. A small number of boys are received directly into the VIth Form.

Religious Education is given by the Resident Chaplain with the assistance of members of the lay staff.

Studies. Boys are prepared for A levels on the Oxford and Cambridge Board and GCSE on the Midland Examining Group. A wide range of subjects is offered in the VIth Form. There is no rigid division into Arts and Science subjects; almost any combination of subjects can be taken.

Games. In addition to the main games, Rugby Football, Soccer and Cricket, boys take part in Athletics, Cross-Country Running, Swimming, Tennis, Badminton, Basketball, Squash, Rowing, Golf, Canoeing, Sailing and Real Tennis.

CCF. There is a flourishing contingent of the CCF which, in addition to the basic Army section, includes the following sub-sections: RN, RAF, REME, Signals, Adventurous Training. The Duke of Edinburgh Award Scheme is operated.

Extra-curricular activities. There are frequent theatre outings, visits to museums and art galleries, careers visits, etc., as well as talks and lectures given in the School by visiting speakers. There is a wide range of clubs and societies, and a Young Enterprise Scheme.

Optional Extras. Instrumental Music, coaching in Real Tennis, Lawn Tennis, Squash, Golf, Fencing, Drama and Karate.

Careers Guidance. The Careers Master, together with the Housemasters, provides guidance for boys in their choice of future occupation.

The School is a member of ISCO.

Fees. (*see* Entrance Scholarship section) £5,170 a term for boarders (Junior House, £4,070), £3,625 a term for day boys (Junior House, £2,940). A number of Scholarships and Exhibitions, and Awards in Music, Art and Sport are offered for competition in May. The fees include board, tuition, consolidated extras, and games. An optional insurance scheme is in operation which covers remission of fees in the event of a boy's absence through illness. A full term's notice of withdrawal is required; failing such notice a term's fees are payable. There is a reduction for younger brothers.

The Preparatory School is at 'Great Oaks', a property situated in grounds of 45 acres on the same ridge of the Chilterns, about 2 miles from the Main School, between Cray's Pond and Pangbourne.

The Oratory School Society. *Chairman and Correspondent:* Mr R A Cox, 38 Home Park Road, Wimbledon Park, London SW19 7HN.

Charitable status. The Oratory School Association is a Registered Charity, number 309112. It is a charitable trust dedicated to continuing the aims of its Founder, The Venerable John Henry, Cardinal Newman.

Oundle School

Oundle Peterborough PE8 4EN.
Tel: (01832) 277120 (Headmaster)
(01832) 274536 (Admissions)
(01832) 274014 (School Office)
(01832) 273434 (Bursar)
Fax: (01832) 277128
e-mail: registrar@oundle.co.uk
website: www.oundleschool.org.uk

Oundle School was established by the Grocers' Company with the object of providing a liberal education in accordance with the principles of the Church of England.

Motto: *God Grant Grace.*

The Governing Body of Oundle School

[1]Mr H Whitmore (*Chairman*)
[1]Mr W P Martineau
¶Mr M J W Rogers (*Chairman, Planning Sub-Committee*)
[1]Mr A P Sparks (*2001*)
[1]Mr C D Stewart-Smith (*Chairman, Finance Sub-Committee*)
[1]Mr C Holdsworth Hunt
[1]The Hon Seymour Fortescue
Mrs M E Raker
Mrs G Monk
Mrs A Ponsonby
[1]Mr J Trotter
The Lady Adrian
Mr S F Pott (*Chairman, Estates Sub-Committee*)
Mr N Cheatle

[1]Mr T W N Guinness (*Master of the Grocers' Company*)
[1]Mr J G Tregoning (*Second Warden*)
[1]Mr N J A V Taylor (*Third Warden*)

[1] denotes Member of the Court of The Grocers' Company

Secretary to the Governing Body and Bursar: D H Harris, BSc, FCA

***Headmaster:* R D Townsend**, MA, DPhil (Oxon)

Second Master: R I Briggs, MA (Cantab)

Under Master: N A Brittain, BA (Cantab)

Director of Studies: P P Couzens, BSc (London), ARCS, AFIMA

Senior Chaplain: The Revd I C Browne, MA (Cantab), MA (Oxon)

Head of Laxton: P S C King, BSc (Liverpool), MSc (London)

Medical Officer: Dr D Clayton, MBChB, DRCOG, DCH

Art:
*R J Page, BEd
Mrs S J Hipple, BA, BEd
J D Oddie, BA
J McGowan, BEd
J V Northwood, BA, ALCM
Mrs M P R James, MA
K R Hannis, MA
Mrs D L Watt, MA
J R B Scragg, BA

Classics:
R M Andrews, MA
*P H Barker, MA
Mrs C N Crowe, ALAM
A Martens, BA
A Duncan, DipAct

Drama:
*R M Lowe, BA, DipAct
Mrs J Wright, BA

Economics:
*S D Guise, BA
J D C Gillings, BA
J R O Massey, BSc
D R K Robb, MA

English:
N A Brittain, BA
D W Dew, MA, MPhil
P Roberts, MA (*Publisher*)
Mrs M K Smedley, BA
N J T Wood, BA
*Miss J T Bond, BA
M S Reader, MA (*Deputy Head, Laxton*)
R S Milne, BA
J D J Williams, BA

Geography:
J R Wake, CertEd
J M Taylor, MA
Mrs M S Turner, BA
G Phillips, BA (*Registrar*)
Mrs J H Briggs, BSc
C J Olver, WLIHE
*C W Symes, BSc

History:
D Sharp, BA
C R Pendrill, MA
P J Pedley, BA
R N Mather, MA
I D Clark, BA (*Head of Activities*)
*M A R Collier, MA
A J Armstrong, MA
M P H von Habsburg-Lothringen, MLitt
D Connolly, BA
T S Purser, BA

Mathematics:
R I Briggs, MA
J MacDonald, BA
P P Couzens, BSc, ARCS, AFIMA
D E Butler, MA, MBIM
I A Potts, BSc, BA
A Butterworth, BSc
D A Turner, BSc
*R M Atkins, BSc
N D Turnbull, BA
D B Meisner, MSc, PhD (*Assistant Director of Studies*)
A P Ireson, MA (*Head of Sport*)
Mrs N S Guise, BSc
D P Raftery, BSc
R D J Beever, BSc

Modern Languages:
M N Downes, BA
S T Forge, MA
M B E Maconochie, BA
*S D Johnston, BA (*Head of German*)
*Mrs S R Worthington, BA (*Head of French*)
*P J Lewins, MA (*Head of Modern Languages*)
Mrs N M Mola, BA (*Head of Spanish*)
M P Bolger, BA
Mrs A M Page, MA
C A Baxter, BA
Mrs C R Gent, MA
B Béjoint, L-és-L
Miss E Rochefort, BA, MA
J Röhrborn, MA
Miss E G Fitton, BA
Mrs M McKim, MA

Religious Studies:
M S Steed, MA
Mrs V Nunn, BEd
The Revd I C Browne, MA
Mrs A E Meisner, BA
*The Revd D R H Edwardson, BSc, BA

Biology:
N W Owens, PhD
J F Hewitson, PhD, FIBiol
W F Holmström, PhD
J Hunt, PhD
P S C King, MSc
B McDowell, PhD (*Head of Psychology*)
Mrs M Holmström, MSc
Mrs M G Boyd, PhD
*A E Langsdale, MSc
Miss M C Sylvester-Bradley, BA
P Sanderson, BSc

Chemistry:
G Keeling, PhD (*Proctor*)
*K H Cobb, BSc
R J McKim, PhD, CChem, MRCS, FRAS
R F Hammond, BSc
M A Stephen, PhD
The Hon W Buckley, BSc
B J Evans, BSc

Physics:
P L Hanley, MSc, BEd (*Examinations Officer*)
H N Wells, MA
A B Burrows, BSc
Miss S Overton, BSc
*P C Clark, BSc, ARCS (*Head of Science and Technology*)
Mrs L E Kirk, BSc
J D A Willington, BSc
Miss T I Jenkins, BSc
R Hickox, BSc

Design and Technology:
*A C Gibbings, BEng
C D Humphreys, BA (*Freeman of City of London*)
D A Vincent, CAP, BTS, CAPET
R Johnson, C & G

Information Technology:
*R B Newman, BSc
L P Rooms, CertEd
D F C Fuller, BSc
C Lyon, BA
R J Newman, MSc (*Network Manager*)

Mandarin Chinese:
Lin Da Jiang
Zheng Liang Guo

Learning Support:
*Mrs E H Rayden, BA, DipEdTESI, AMBDA
Mrs A Downes, BA
Mrs J Clay, BA

Library:
*Mrs E P Rooms, ALA

Physical Education and Games:
*C J Olver (WLIHE)
J R Wake, CertEd
Mrs M Layden, CertEd (*Head of Girls' Games*)
Miss R Goatly, BA
J Hyatt, BA
D Nicholson, BSc

The Music School:

Director of Music: G Sutton, MMus
Choirmaster: A M Cleary, BA, ARCO, ARCM
Organist: J C Arkell, BA, FRCO, FTCL, FLCM, FRSA
Assistant Director of Music: Miss S L Johnson, BA (*School Administrator*)
Head of Woodwind: D Milsted, BA, LTCL
Head of Brass: R Kauffman, ARCM
Head of Piano Studies: Mrs N Jones, LTCL, DipRCM, GRSM
Head of Strings: T English, AGSM
And 38 peripatetic teachers

Houses and Housemasters/Housemistresses:
Bramston House: Mr J R O Massey
Crosby House: Mr R M Andrews
Dryden House: Mrs V Nunn
Grafton House: Mr A B Burrows
Kirkeby House: Mrs D L Watt
Laundimer House: Dr B McDowell
Laxton House: Mr A P Ireson
New House: Mrs N S Guise
Sanderson House: Mr D A Turner
School House: Dr J Hunt
Sidney House: Mr R J Page
St Anthony House: Mr M S Steed
Wyatt House: Mrs S J Hipple
The Berrystead: Dr W F Holmströem

Bursar: D H Harris, BSc, FCA
Financial Bursar: Miss L Simpson, FCCA
Assistant Bursar: P Tyldesley, BA, ARICS
Registrar: G Phillips, BA
Communications Officer: Mrs M Smedley, BA
Headmaster's Secretary: Mrs P Barr
Academic Secretary: Mrs A Guy
Administrative Secretary: Mrs M Howe
Bursar's Secretary: Mrs C Webb

Number of pupils (2000–2001): Boarders: 534 boys and 277 girls. Day Pupils: 121 boys and 96 girls

Oundle School originated from the bequest of Sir William Laxton, a native of Oundle, to the Grocers' Company in 1556. In 1876 a decision was made by the Grocers' Company to divide the school into two parts, the original foundation becoming Laxton School and the new boarding school taking over the name of Oundle School. In the 1990s Laxton and Oundle became increasingly integrated, and in 2000 the Governors took the decision to unite the foundations into one School. Its buildings are grouped in various parts of the small market town, and the pupils pass continually through the streets as they go from the boarding houses to their work and games.

The school became fully co-educational in September 1990.

Most day pupils, together with candidates for the junior boarding house, The Berrystead, join the School at eleven having taken English, mathematics and verbal-reasoning tests. Most boarding pupils take the June Common Entrance Examination at thirteen at their preparatory schools before joining in September. A small number of places are available for entry and at other stages, including the sixth form.

The Cloisters houses a number of the main teaching rooms, the Art Studios and the Careers Department. Other teaching rooms are situated in the Needham Building (Physics), opened in 1988, the Sir Peter Scott Building (Biology and Mathematics), opened in 1990, the Gascoigne Building (Modern Languages, Music and Information Technology), refurbished and opened in 1995 and the Palmer Block (Chemistry). The Modern Languages Department is equipped with two language laboratories. The long tradition of Oundle Workshops continues, incorporating courses and projects in Engineering and Industrial Technology and pupils are designing and constructing sports cars and an aeroplane in the Patrick Centre (opened 1998). Facilities in Music include the Frobenius Organ and an electronic Music Studio. The Information Technology Centre includes three fully equipped computer rooms and there are cluster networks around the school. A full school computer network, connecting all school sites, was installed in 1999. A university style lecture theatre is planned for opening in 2002.

An Appeal in 1986 provided a two-roomed Sports Hall built alongside the existing fifty yard Swimming Pool, a new Library, as well as the Needham Building. The School has its own 300 seat theatre, the Stahl Theatre, in which productions of both the School and visiting companies take place. The Chapel was built as a memorial shortly after the Great War and its East windows, designed by John Piper, date from the School's fourth centenary in 1956. Religious instructions accords with the Church of England.

In 1989 the renovation of Fisher and Crosby Houses was completed. The building of the two new girls' houses, Kirkeby and Wyatt, was completed in September 1990. Dryden House was renovated and has taken girls since 1993; similarly New House from 1997 and Sanderson will take girls from 2001. An extension to Laundimer House was added in 2000. The fifteen houses are all independent units, pupils taking their meals in separate house dining rooms.

Laxton Junior (IAPS), caters for 4 to 11 year old boys and girls. Transfer to the senior school is by the normal entrance examination route.

Entrance Scholarships. (*see* Entrance Scholarship section) An extensive series of entrance Scholarships is offered each year to thirteen year olds, including Art, Drama, Technology, General Scholarships (Stainforth and Conradi) and Music awards. In addition, a small number of scholarships are available to eleven year-old boys and girls, and at sixteen to new lower sixth entrants. Full details are available from the School.

Fees. The Oundle School senior boarding fee for 2000–2001 is £16,206; Berrystead 1st Form: £12,378; Berrystead 2nd Form: £14,367; Laxton Day Fee: £8,040; Laxton Junior: £4,845. Details of extras are given in the School prospectus. The registration fee is £75.

Activities. A full range of activities take place and these are intended to be an integral part of the boarding school curriculum. Events in Drama and Music feature prominently in the School calendar, and Art Exhibitions are held in the Yarrow Gallery. A large number of Societies meet on a regular basis. Links have been established with schools in France, Germany, Spain Hungary, the Czech Republic, Russia and China, with annual Exchanges taking place. Pupils are able to participate in the very large number of expeditions and trips in the UK and abroad. There is a flourishing CCF comprising Army, Navy, RAF, Fire and Adventure Training sections and a thriving Duke of Edinburgh scheme is in operation. Community Service plays an important part in school life and much time and energy is devoted to fund-raising activities in order to support national charities as well as holidays run at Oundle for MENCAP and inner-city children.

The main school sports are Rugby, Hockey, Cricket, Rowing, Netball and Tennis, but others available include Aerobics, Athletics, Badminton, Clay Shooting, Cross-Country, Cycling, Fencing, Fives, Golf, Horse-riding, Sailing, Shooting, Soccer, Squash, Swimming and Volleyball. An Astroturf hockey pitch was added to the school's extensive sporting facilities in the autumn of 1995, and a well equipped fitness suite in 1999.

Honours. In the last six years the number of places obtained at Oxford and Cambridge has averaged 24.

Academic Curriculum Third formers (Year 9) take a general course consisting of English, Mathematics, French, Latin, Science (Physics, Chemistry, Biology), History, Geography, Religious Studies, Art, Design and Technology, PE, Music, Drama, Computer Studies and German or Spanish or Greek. The First and Second form curriculum is similar.

The traditional importance of Science and Technology in the Oundle Education is still maintained with all pupils being taught the three sciences to GCSE (Dual Award) and all Third formers spending time in the Workshops gaining a substantial grounding not only in design but also in manufacturing techniques, applied science and craft skills. Courses in Computing and Microelectronics are available at all levels.

Pupils take English, Mathematics, Physics, Chemistry and Biology as the core of their GCSE curriculum and choose a further five subjects from Art, Computing, Design and Technology, Drama, Electronics, French, Geography, German, Greek, History, Latin, Music, Religious Studies and Spanish. Mandarin Chinese and Russian are available as additional subjects.

In the sixth form AS and A levels are offered in Art, Biology, Chemistry, Classical Civilisation, Design Technology, Economics, Electronics, English Literature, French, Geography, German, Greek, Government and Politics, History, Information Technology, Latin, Mathematics, Further Mathematics, Music, Physics, Psychology, Religious Studies, Russian, Spanish and Theatre Studies. Sixth Form pupils take five AS levels in the lower sixth and specialise in three or four subjects in the upper sixth together with a General Studies course.

Charitable status. Oundle School is a Registered Charity, number 309921. The aims of the School are to give its pupils a sense of belonging, expecting them to contribute to the community, to enable its pupils to reach their full academic and intellectual potential, to ensure that they have a sense of accomplishment, and above all to provide them with an overall view of life and sense of values.

Pangbourne College

Pangbourne Reading RG8 8LA.
Tel: (0118) 9842101
Fax: (0118) 9841239

After 75 years as a single-sex boys' school, the College began admitting girls to its Sixth Form seven years ago and has now extended its provision for girls throughout the 11–18 age range. The College was originally founded in 1917 to train boys for a career at sea and the qualities associated with those days are still much valued (involvement, teamwork, leadership, outdoor activities etc). All pupils are prepared for university entrance leading to a wide range of careers.

Motto: *Fortiter ac Fideliter.* (Resolute Through Belief).

Governing Body:
Chairman: ¶M V F Allsop
Vice-Chairman: ¶N J Hollebone
Chairman Finance Committee: D Griffiths

D N Batts, FHCIMA
W P Cooke, CBE, MA
Sir James Devitt, Bt, MA, ARICS
C J T Gould, MA
¶Rear Admiral M G T Harris
¶R I E Knight, MA
¶Admiral Sir Michael Layard, KCB, CBE
Mrs J Marriott
J W Tapner
J C G Trower
Mrs A G Verey
¶R P Wright, Dip Inst du Pantheon, Paris

***Headmaster:* Dr K Greig**, MA (Oxon), PhD (Edinburgh)

Second Master: G Pike, MA (Corpus Christi College, Oxford), PGCE

Assistant Masters:

S M Ball, BSc Hons (Brunel)
Mrs C Bamforth, BA (Cambridge)
R N A Bancroft, BSc (Surrey), PGCE *Housemaster, Port Jackson)*
Mrs S Barton, RSA, DELTA
Mrs C S Bond, BA (London), PGCE
R H A Brodhurst, BA (London), PGCE *Head of History Department*
R Brown, BA (Oxford Brookes), PGCE
Mrs B Callender, BEd (Bulmershe College of Higher Education)
R G C Cheeseman, BEd, CertEd (London), DASE (Bristol) *Special Education Needs Co-ordinator*
P Clark, BA (Nottingham), PGCE, MSc (Manchester) *Head of Business Studies*
Mrs K Clifford, BA (Reading) *Head of Creative Arts faculty*
C J Dossett, MSc (Loughborough) (*Head of PE*)
B Dyer, BEd (Central School of Speech & Drama) *Head of Drama*
Miss C L Dyson, BA (Brunel)
R Everatt, BSc (York), PGCE
D Everhart, MA (Cambridge), PGCE (*Director of Music*)
Ms C M Fletcher, BSc (De Montfort), PGCE (Sheffield)
Dr J H Flint, MA, PhD, PGCE (Oxford) *Director of Curriculum*
R Frowde, BA (Oxford), Associate Royal College of Organists
C Grimble, BA (Manchester), PGCE
Mlle G Guibert
E de la Harpe, MSc(Eng) (Natal)
A Henshilwood, BA (Oxford Brookes), MA (Nottingham)
P Hills *Head of Adventure and Leadership Training, Contingent Commander Combined Cadet Force*
Miss M Hopwood, BA (Staffordshire)
T Lauze, BA (Bordeaux) *Head of French*
M Mackworth-Praed, BSc (Durham), PGCE
C T Martin, BSc (Liverpool), PGCE *Head of Chemistry Department, Head of Science Faculty*
J V Martin, MSc (Liverpool), BEng, PGCE
S N Peberdy, BSc (Keele), PGCE, ALCM *Head of Modern Languages Faculty*
R J H Pickett, BA (Oxon) (*Head of Chemistry*)
R J Pike, BA (Exeter)
J R Powell, GRSM, LRAM, ARCM (*Housemaster of Junior School*)
C Read Wilson, MA (Cambridge), PGCE *Head of Senior School; Head of English/Drama*
D P Rendle, BSc (Durham), PGCE *Head of Geography Department*
P G Savage, BA (Birmingham) (*Housemaster, Macquarie*)
S G Simons, MA, CBiol, MIBiol (Cambridge), PGCE (*Head of Lower School, Housemaster, Parramatta, Senior Housemaster*
Miss S Sinclair *Librarian*
N A Soar, BA (Keele) *Head of English and Drama Faculty*

D W A Somner, BSc *Head of Technology Department*
Mrs R Thake, BA (Durham), PGCE
Ms G Towe, BA (Durham), PGCE
Miss K S Thomas, BSc (Durham) *Head of Mathematics Department*
D J Tooze, CertEd (Borough Road College) (*Housemaster, Hesperus*)
A Vasa, TD, MA (Oxford), DipEd *Head of Physics Department*
M P Walker, BA, PGCE (Wales) *Master i/c Rowing*
P Walker, BEng (Loughborough), MICS, CEng
A C Whale, BSc (Manchester) *Head of Mathology Faculty*
Miss B Wipper, BA (Tuebingen, Germany) *Housemistress, St George*
A Yorath, BSc (Bristol), PGCE

EFL Department:
Mrs M Kudlac, Doctoraal Degree (Utrecht) *Co-ordinator of Overseas Pupils*
Ms V A Clark, BSc (Aston), PGCE

Learning Support Department:
Mrs G M Bovan, BA (Birmingham), PGCE, RSACert
Mrs M Church, BSc (Reading), RSADip
Mrs M F Shave, BEd, RSADip

Chaplain: The Revd B J Cunningham, MA (Oxford)

Bursar: J E Clark

Registrar: Mrs M F Smith

Headmaster's Secretary: Mrs S Belcher, Member, Institute of Linguists

Sister-in-Charge of Sick Bay: Miss A Jiggens, SRN

Number in School. 225 Boarders; 165 Day Pupils

Set in fine grounds of 230 acres, 400 feet above sea level and a mile from Pangbourne village, the College combines a country environment with easy access to London and Heathrow. The extensive school facilities include exciting new Chapel opened March 2000, new IT block, electronics and science laboratories, a new library, art and music schools and new design and technology centre. The performing arts centre contains a school hall/theatre with fly tower. The fully equipped sports hall, all-weather hockey pitch, spacious playing fields, and boathouses on the Thames provide excellent sporting facilities. Pupils are accommodated in five houses (four for boys and one for girls): after the first year they share study bedrooms; single rooms in the Sixth Form. Meals are taken in a central dining hall.

Admission. Senior School entry for boys and girls is at 13 through the Common Entrance or Scholarship Examinations. Sixth Form entry is based on interview, a satisfactory report from the previous school and good examination results. Children normally enter the Junior School at 11+ through an interview and a Cognitive Ability Test (CAT). Prospectus and Registration Form may be obtained from the Registrar who is always pleased to arrange visits to the College.

Scholarships. (*see* Entrance Scholarship section). - Three Academic Scholarships are awarded up to 50% of the fees and four Exhibitions between 10% and 30%. Other awards in Music, Art, Drama, Sport and Technology are available, as are the All-Rounders' Scholarships and Awards which are given to children of outstanding talent, both inside and outside the classroom. The College is a designated Centre of Excellence for the Arkwright Scholarship Trust.

Junior School. Some 60 children, day and boarding, aged 11–13 are looked after in their own delightful country house set in gardens within the main College campus. Fully integrated into the academic, cultural and social life, they have full use of all the Senior School's facilities and its specialist teaching. Awards similar to those mentioned above are also available for Junior School entrants. Pupils transfer automatically to the Senior School without further examination.

Academic Study. The curriculum of the Lower School (11 to 16) is based on the National Curriculum ideal of a 'broad and balanced, education, with an emphasis on diversity of choice for the Sixth Form. There are three basic approaches available when a pupil joins the school. The majority follow a mainstream curriculum covering all the core and foundation subjects of the National Curriculum: English, Mathematics, the Sciences, Technology, French, History, Geography and one 'Arts option' subject chosen from Art, Drama, Music, Religious Studies, German and Latin. A Learning Support Unit, staffed by specialist teachers, is available to help Dyslexics and EFL pupils.

At Sixth Form level there is a choice of 18 'A' levels. To complement these specialised 'A' level courses, all follow a stimulating General Studies course, which includes a Study Skills component.

The College is proud of the quality of its academic and pastoral support system, and each child is guided by a Tutor, a Housemaster/Housemistress and the Director of Studies.

Careers. While the College pursues a deliberate policy of recruiting a broad spectrum of academic ability, it looks for talent of various kinds, believing that its task is to enable each individual to make the very best of his or her potential, no matter where strengths lie.

The Director of Sixth Form Studies and the Careers Adviser work closely with the individual's Tutor to ensure that wise, informed choices are made in the well-equipped Careers Room. The result is that, while the best students will go on to Oxford or Cambridge, the majority will proceed to degree courses at other universities prior to a wide variety of exciting careers.

Games. For a small school Pangbourne has an outstanding reputation for sport, particularly at National levels in several games. A policy of recruiting high-quality, specialist coaches, has led to considerable success in competitive sports in recent seasons. Sports offered include athletics, cricket, cross-country, golf, hockey, judo, lacrosse, netball, rowing, rugby, sailing, shooting, soccer, squash, swimming, tennis.

Adventure Training. The College has always placed great emphasis on teamwork and leadership. There is a full programme of adventure training built into the curriculum from the third form, with week-end and holiday expeditions. Boys and girls can join the CCF which has Army, Royal Navy and Royal Marine Sections. Snowdonia in April and a sea-voyage in the summer holidays are regular features. The school has been chosen by HMS Ocean (Navy's latest helicopter carrier) to be their affiliated school.

Music and Drama. Pangbourne has a long tradition of excellence in Music and Drama. The Music School has its own Recital Room, ideal for internal concerts, and also a newly appointed Recording Studio. The College Choir, Choral Society, Orchestra and Military Band perform regularly within and outside the College. The Choir undertakes a biennial continental tour and more than a third of the school have individual instrument tuition. Drama has an exciting and flourishing tradition and we have a fine theatre fully equipped with computerised lighting and sound systems. School productions run throughout the year at every level.

Clubs and Societies. There is a quiet hour after lunch when societies flourish. There are 30 of them and they vary from Archery to wine, from Architecture to Wargaming.

Fees. At age 11 and 12: Boarders £3,445 per term, Day Pupils £2,500 per term. At 13 and above: Boarders £4,915 per term, Part Boarders £4,290, Day Pupils £3,445 per term. These fees are inclusive of medical attendance, games and most textbooks, and there are no obligatory extras.

Charitable status. Pangbourne College Limited is a Registered Charity, number 309096. The objective is to provide an excellent all-round education for boys and girls between the ages of 11 to 18.

The Perse School

Hills Road Cambridge CB2 2QF.
Tel: (01223) 568300
Fax: (01223) 568293
e-mail: office@perse.co.uk
website: www.perse.co.uk

The Perse School was founded in 1615 under the provisions of the will of Stephen Perse, MD, Fellow of Gonville and Caius College. It is now governed under a Scheme framed by the Board of Education, dated 1910, amended 1918 and 1921.

Motto: *Qui facit per alium facit per se.*

Governing Body:

Representing the University of Cambridge:
Mrs P A Lyon, MA, PhD, Fellow of St Catherine's College

Representing Gonville and Caius College:
R H S Carpenter, MA, ScD, Fellow of the College
D K Summers, MA, PhD, Fellow of the College

Representing Trinity College:
A G Weeds, MA, ScD, Fellow of the College

Co-opted:
A R Cook, JP, FRICS (*OP*) (*Chairman*)
K Barry, MA
A M Booth, MIEE
Mrs J M Brookes
J T Green, MA, PhD
J R Haylock, BSc (*OP*)
The Revd Canon A R Heawood, BA, BD
Mrs M J Macfarlane, MA
H A L H Mumford, MA
G A Pearson, MA (*OP*)
Councillor J E Reynolds
Mrs N M Silverleaf, ACA
Mrs L Swarbrick, MA
D T Ward, FRICS (*OP*)

Clerk to the Governors: G A Ellison, MA

***Head Master:* N P V Richardson**, MA

Deputy Heads:
I Carter, BSc
C P Jeffery, BA

Director of Studies: E C Elliott, MA

Admissions Tutor: R D Crabtree, MA, FRGS

Senior Tutor: M P Nierinck, BA

Registrar: J N Green, MA

Bursar: G A Ellison, MA

Assistant Masters/Mistresses:
Miss G Allnutt, BA (*Biology*)
Mrs C V Auton, DUEL (*Bordeaux*) (*Mod Lang*)
D H J Baker, Diploma, Chester Training College (*Head of Physical Education, Geography*)
P D Baker, BSc (*Mathematics*)
M H Barber, BA (*Geography*)
Mrs C E Bigg, MA (*Mathematics*)
Mrs L J Blaxill, BSc, PhD (*Mathematics*)
P L Bowen-Walker, BSc, PhD (*Biology*)
E K D Bush, MA (*Classics*)
P A Collins, BA (*Head of Modern Languages*)
I R Cooper, BA, MLitt, LRAM (*Director of Music*)
D R Cross, BA (*Head of Geography*)
D F Daniels, BSc (*Head of Maths*)
M R T Donnelly, MA (*Head of Classics*)
Mrs U R Dunn, BSc (*German*)
D McK Gant, MA (*Head of Technology, Physics*)
Mrs J Grant, NDD (*Photography*)
C E J Green, MA (*Head of English*)
Mrs G F Hague, BSc (*Chemistry, Careers*)
Mrs J Harris, MA (*Biology*)
C W Jackson, BA (*Modern Languages*)
D J Jones, BA (*History*)
M Judson, BA (*Head of Art and Design*)
S J Kern, MA (*Classics, UCAS Director*)
Revd B R L Kinsey, MA, BD, MTh, AKC (*Head of Religious Studies, Chaplain*)
W E Kirby, BSc (*Head of Science, Head of Physics*)
Mrs E J Lloyd, BSc, PhD (*Chemistry*)
G L Machin, BSc (*Mathematics*)
M Pitman, MA (*Religious Education*)
C A Proud, BA (*Head of Economics & Politics*)
Mrs J B Pullen, BA (*Modern Languages*)
M Punt, MA, MSc (*Physics, Head of Sixth Form*)
G A Richards, BA (*Music*)
A J Roberts, MA (*Head of History*)
I F S Rossotti, BA (*English, Head of Lower School*)
Mrs A J Rowan, MA (*Physics*)
P J Rowan, BSc (*Head of Biology*)
Mrs J H Smith, BA (*Modern Languages*)
R E Smith, BSc (*Maths, Head of Careers*)
J Southworth, MSc (*Technology*)
P G Spiers, BSc (*Chemistry*)
Miss K E Stamper, BA (*Art & Design*)
W Stevenson, BA, PhD (*History*)
M C Thurston, BEd, MIITTed (*IT and Mathematics*)
Mrs C Tickner, BSc (*Mathematics*)
D Tickner, BA (*English, Head of Middle School*)
D M Tricker, MA, PhD (*Physics*)
H B G Vodden, BA (*Modern Languages*)
M Walker, BA (*Modern Languages*)
R Wareing, BEcon (*Business Studies*)
Mrs E L Welland, MSc, PhD (*Physics*)
S P Wood, BA (*English*)

The main school buildings date from 1960, but these have been considerably enlarged and refurbished in recent years and include a fine multi-purpose hall, a Science Block and IT facility (1996-8), and a Theatre, Art and Design and Modern Languages block (1991). A new Astroturf pitch was laid in 1995, and a Sports Hall and new Sixth Form Centre opened in September 2000, along with the first phase of a new library complex.

The number of pupils in the school is currently about 600, including 25 girls in the Sixth Form.

Education. In the Lower and Middle School a broad curriculum is followed, including PSE at all levels, with choices of options being made at the end of the Second Form (Year 8) and the Third Form (Year 9). All science is taught as single subjects by specialists. In the First and Second Form (Years 7 and 8), pupils study English, French, Latin, History, Geography, Religious Studies, Mathematics, Physics, Chemistry, Biology, Technology, Art and Design, and Music, as well as PE and Games. Options are introduced in the Third Form (Year 9) with the opportunity of taking up Greek, German, Spanish and Classical Civilisation, as well as continuing with Latin, Art and Music. At the end of the Third Form pupils make choices for GCSE. English, English Literature, Mathematics, French, Physics, Chemistry and Biology are compulsory subjects for GCSE, and in addition pupils take three further subjects from Greek, Latin, German, Spanish, History, Geography, Classical Civilisation, Art, Music and Religious Studies. The most able Mathematicians take GCSE Mathematics at the end of the Fourth Form (Year 10), and then take Additional Mathematics at the end of Year 11. In the Lower Sixth Form, students choose four or five AS levels from a wide range, and in addition take part in a Key Skills programme. All Upper Sixth students complete 3 or 4 A2 levels.

The major sports are Cricket, Hockey and Rugby Football; games are played on site on 28 acres of fields. In addition to the major games, there is a wide variety of minor sports catering for all interests. School fixtures and some rehearsals take place on Saturdays, but all timetabled teaching takes place on weekdays only. There is an optional Combined Cadet Force with Royal Navy, Army and Royal Air Force Sections, a Community Service Scheme, and School Scout and Venture Scout Troops. Music, Drama and Art flourish alongside a wide range of school societies, extra curricular activities, holiday trips and exchange visits to France and Germany.

The School has a Preparatory School on a separate site for 170 boys between 7 and 11 (Tel: 01223 568270; Fax: 01223 568273; e-mail: perseprep@aol.com). Headmaster: P C S Izzett, JP, BA, ACP, CertEd. Details are shown in the IAPS section, Part V of this publication.

There is also a co-educational Pre-Preparatory School for ages 3 to 7 (Tel: 01223 568315; Fax: 01223 568316; e-mail: pelicanpp@aol.com). Headmistress: Mrs P M Oates, BEd

Fees (from September 2000). Upper School: £2,229 per term; Preparatory School: £1,998 per term. Pre-Prep: £1,715 per term.

Entrance. The school welcomes applications at 11+, 13+ (boys) and 16+ (boys and girls). At 11+ and 13+ candidates are examined in Mathematics, English and Verbal/non-verbal Reasoning, and given an interview, 16+ candidates are interviewed and given offers based on their GCSE results.

Scholarships. The school awards a number of scholarships and bursaries each year. For details please contact the Headmaster's PA.

Old Persean Society. *Secretary:* J N Green, The Perse School, Hills Road, Cambridge CB2 2QF.

Charitable status. The Perse School is a Registered Charity, number 311434. The School specialises in preparing pupils for University entrance; almost all leavers proceed to degree courses, up to a quarter to Oxford and Cambridge. 81% of all A level entries were awarded grades A or B in 2000.

Plymouth College

Ford Park Plymouth Devon PL4 6RN.
Tel: (01752) 203245 (Headmaster and Admissions); (01752) 203300 (School Office); (01752) 203242 (Bursar)
Fax: (01752) 203246; (01752) 205920 (Headmaster)

The School was formed by the amalgamation in 1896 of Mannamead School, Plymouth, founded in 1854, and Plymouth College, founded in 1877. It is now a co-educational school.

Governing Body:

T E J Savery, MA, LLB (*Chairman*)

D W Luke (*Vice-Chairman*)

The Rt Rev J Garton, The Lord Bishop of Plymouth
Rear Admiral A K Backus, OBE, Flag Officer Sea Training
Professor R J Bull, BSc, FCCA
Captain C M Crawford, MA
R G H Creber, FRICS, FAVLP
M Downward, MA
Mrs N Duncan, LLB
Sir Robert Hicks
K Kite, FRSC, PhD
P H Lowson, FCA
Mrs J McKinnel
R H Midgley, MA
Mrs C Pascoe
Mrs J Paull
C J Robinson, MA
Major General C T Shortis, CB, CBE
Mrs A J Sloggett
B L Spear, ARICS
D J Stark, FCA

Headmaster: **A J Morsley**, BSc, ARCS, CMathFMA, FRSA

Deputy Head:
Miss S J Dunn, BSc

Director of Studies: C R Compton, BA

Assistant Teachers:
J L Arthur, BSc (*Head of Physics*)
R W Fisher, BA (*Master of Lower School*)
M J Allen, BA, TC, St Luke's College, Exeter
D R Nelson, BSc
R A White, BA (*Head of Modern Languages*)
P Dobbs, MA (*Head of Chemistry*)
R Benton, NDD, ATD, Leeds (*Head of Arts and Design*)
M A Probert, BSc (*Head of Information Technology*)
D R Compton, BEd (*CNAA*), FRGS
A J Lewis, BA (*Director of Physical Education*)
C G Shorter, MA (*Head of History*)
J B Phillips, BSc
H R M Clifton, MA (*Master of Middle School*)
M P R Rose, MA
P Davies, MSc, BSc
M A H Bradfield, BA
G K Lang, BA
K C Boots, BA
M R Davies, BTech
J P Gregory, BA (*Head of Economics*)
M E Hodges, BA (*Head of Geography*)
C J Sillitoe, MPhil, MRSC, CChem
G C Strickland, MA (*Head of Mathematics*)
J M Chapman, PhD, ARCS, CBiol, FIBiol (*Examinations Officer & Publicity Secretary*)
Mrs J M White, BA
J W Hocking, BEd (*Head of Design & Technology*)
R Chapman, BEd
S Jordan, PhD (*Head of Biology*)
Mrs B Davies, BA
D J Scoins, MA
J B Jackson, MA (*Head of German*)
C J Hambly, BSc
Miss P J Anderson, MA
Mrs Z P Thurston, BSc
S J Oxley, BA (*Director of Music*)
Miss A C Blunden, BA
M W Baker, BA
G A Ashfield, BA
M Tippetts, BA
G C Roderick, BEd (*Head of Religious Education*)
J Shields, BSc
Miss M D'Souza, MA
R J Prichard, MA (*Head of English*)
R P Robinson, MA (*Head of Careers*)

Part-Time Staff:
Mrs J Pope, MA
Miss N W Davies, MSc, BSc
S J A Terry, MA (*Head of Classics*)
Mrs J E Hansford, BEd
Mrs B C Robinson, BA, CNNA

Headmaster's Secretary: Mrs T Powlesland

Preparatory School:
Headteacher: Mrs P J Roberts, BEd

Deputy Headteacher: C D M Gatherer, BA
Director of Studies: A J S Wayne, BEd

Assistant Staff:
J Perchais, Licencié Lettres, University of Tours, France
P Stephenson, CertEd
Miss L M Cook, CertEd
R D Crawford-Jones, BA
C L R Cottrell, CertEd
P D Raymond-Jones, BEd
H D Law, AMIMechGE, CertEd
Mrs H M Burke, CertEd
Mrs N Aston, CertEd
Mrs S Butcher, BEd
Mrs L H Clifton, CertEd
Mrs P J Avery, BEd
J Ware, OBE, BA, ARAM
Miss J Newnham, BEd
Mrs J Petch, CertEd

Infant Department:

Teacher in Charge: Mrs M C Barker, BA

Assistant Staff:
Mrs J Mills, CertEd
Mrs J Youngs, BA, PGCE
Mrs B Ford, CertEd
Mrs M Mawby, CertEd
Mrs J Wilson, BEd, CertEd
Mrs M Thorpe, CertEd
Mrs C Brooks, ARCM
Mrs R Tall, BA

Bursar and Clerk to the Governors: Colonel (Retd) G H Mills (*Main & Preparatory School*)

Buildings. The Main School stands on high ground in Plymouth. The buildings include Science Laboratories (extended in 1957 and 1984), Art and Craft rooms including extensive facilities for pottery, photography and print-making, the Dining Hall (part of a new block opened in 1961), a new Assembly Hall in which concerts and plays are performed (1974). A well equipped Design and Technology Block was opened in 1979. The grounds in Ford Park include an open-air Swimming Pool, a Small-bore Rifle Range, and Squash Court. Games are also played on 2 other fields to which the boys are transported by coach. The new Sports Hall was opened in 1986. A new library was opened in 1996. An astro-surface was opened in 1989 and currently a new fully equipped swimming pool is under construction.

The Preparatory School is half a mile from the Main School and has its own playing field and swimming pool.

Organisation. Below the VIth Form there is some setting so that pupils may proceed at a pace best suited to their abilities.

Pupils are organised in 6 Houses, and each pupil is under the supervision of a Form Tutor. There is a Chaplaincy team which also has a pastoral responsibility for all pupils. Every pupil is expected to play a full part in games and other school activities outside the classroom.

English (Language and Literature), French, Mathematics, Physics, Chemistry and Biology are taken by all to GCSE. Normally three more are chosen by the pupils.

Sixth Form. The Sixth Form is based on tutor groups with about twelve in each group. Pupils study for four AS levels leading to 3 or 4 A levels and most prepare for General Studies as well. The tutor keeps a pastoral and academic watch on the pupils' performance. Most standard A levels are available.

Sixth Formers are prepared for the Universities, the Services and the Professions; help is given by the Careers Teacher for almost any career, often with the assistance of the Independent Schools' Careers Organisation.

Games. Rugby Football, Cricket, Hockey and Netball are the major sports. There is also Athletics, Badminton, Basketball, Cross-country Running, Sailing, Shooting, Squash, Swimming and Tennis. Games are compulsory but more senior pupils have a wide range of options available to them.

School Activities. There is a contingent of the CCF with Navy, Army and Air Force Sections. There is also a Duke of Edinburgh's Award Scheme. School Societies cover a wide range of activities. A School Yearbook is published annually.

Music. There is an excellent Schola Cantorum which performs in cathedrals. The orchestra plays both light and serious music. These are fed from a junior wind band and string group. Various chamber ensembles are formed ad hoc. There is a choir and a madrigal group performing a variety of music from church to popular as occasion demands. The School provides tuition on all orchestral instruments, including percussion. Guitar and piano lessons are also offered. There are annual music scholarships.

Boarders. In the Main School there are 2 Boarding Houses, Colson House and Mannamead House, each accommodating 40 boys and girls. They are situated close to the school field and are equipped with small dormitories, sickroom, common rooms and games rooms. Feeding is central in the Dining Hall, supplied by a modern, well-equipped kitchen.

Admission. Admission to the Main School is normally based on the College Entrance Examination for boys and girls over 10½ and under 12 on 31 August of the year of entry, but it is also possible to enter at 13 via the Common Entrance Examination. Occasional vacancies are available at other ages. Application forms may be obtained from the Headmaster.

Admission to the Preparatory School is from the age of 3+. Application should be made direct to the Secretary of the Headteacher of the Preparatory School.

Fees per annum. (*see* Entrance Scholarship section) The fees for September 2000 are as follows:

Infant Department: Kindergarten £2,970; Pre-Prep £4,041; Years 1 & 2 £4,245.

Junior Department: Years 3-6 £4,548.

Main School: Years 7-8 £6,147; Years 9-U6 £6,486.

Weekly Boarding: £5,868; Full Boarding: £5,934.

These fees include books, stationery and games. Music lessons are an extra.

Numbers. The School is co-educational - currently there are 570 pupils in the school (176 in the Sixth Form) and of these 157 are girls.

Charitable status. Plymouth College and Mannamead School is a Registered Charity, number 306949. Its aim is to provide private education for boys and girls.

Pocklington School

Pocklington York YO42 2NJ.
Tel: (01759) 303125
Fax: (01759) 306366
e-mail: mainoffice@pocklington.e-yorks.sch.uk
website: www.pocklington.e-yorks.sch.uk

Motto: *Virtute et Veritate.*

Governors:
R E Haynes (*Chairman*)
J L Mackinlay, FCA, FCMA (*Vice-Chairman*)
K Appelbee, OBE, MA
H R L Beadle, MA, DPhil
Mrs J F Bladon
Sir Paul Bryan, DSO, MC
Mrs P Carver
A J C Cochrane, MBE, MA
J E Cox
D M Davis, MP
J A R Dempster
R L Fenton, OBE
Mrs R Hainsworth
The Earl of Halifax, JP, DL
Mrs G Harley, ACA
Revd J Harrison, MA
J P Hewitt

Mrs D Jennings
S P Kamstra, LLB
Prof J A McDermid, MA, PhD, CEng, FBCS, FIEE, FRAeS
Col A C Roberts, MBE, TD, JP, DL, MPhil, PhD, FLS, FIBiol, FCGI, CIMechE
D V Southwell
A R Strugnell, BA, PhD
J E Townend, FCA, MP
Major General H G Woods, CB, MBE, MC, DL, MA, FRSA, FBIM

Clerk to the Governors and Bursar: S N L Fogden, BA, BSc

***Headmaster:* N Clements**, MA, BSc

Assistant Masters:
A M Dawes, BSc (*Deputy Headmaster*)
C J Solomon, MA
D V Rumbelow, MA (*Head of Sixth Form*)
M G Milne, CertEd
G A Sutton, MA, (*Careers*)
R J Peel, BA
D J Parsons, CertEd
S J Bosworth, MA, LTCL
A W Ramsden, BSc
R Smith, BSc (*Director of Studies*)
M J Butcher, BSc
J L Peel, BA, MA
P Edwards, MA
S C Nesom, BA
The Rev M A Smith, MA (*Chaplain*)
P R Horne, BEd
M P Newhouse, CertEd
D Wagstaff, MA
M W Rowe, MA, DPhil
M R Evans, BSc
G Binks, BSc
A W J Heaven, BHum, MA, MCollP
T M Loten, BA
I McDougall, MA
D Watton, BA
I C Sheppard, BSc, ADME (*Head of Fifth Year*)
D B Dyson, BSc, PhD, GRSC
T E W Taylor, MA
Mrs M-H Knights, MA
Mrs P M Baillie, MA (*Director of Pastoral Care*)
N A J Tomaszewski, BA
Mrs M R Peel, BA
Mrs M Newhouse, CertEd
S D Ellis, BA
Mrs C M W Swann, BA (*Head of Fourth Year*)
P J Donaldson, BA
A E Towner, BA
R P Bond, BEd
Mrs S C Beaumont, BSc
Miss A L G Raley, BSc
I J Andrews, BA
M P Aherne, MA, BEd
Miss H V Brown, BSc
M J Davies, BA
D A Galloway, MA
M A Kettlewell, BA (*Director of Music*)
Mrs F B de L Marshall, BA
Miss E J Peden, BA
S D Ward, BSc
P M H L Dare, BA

Part-time staff:
K Robinson, BSc
Mrs P A Boden, BA
Mrs S E Bosworth, BA
Mrs J A McHenry, CertEd
Mrs P J Lochman, BEd
Mrs J E Danby, CertEd
Mrs P M F Bosworth, BA
Mrs S E Elford, BEd, DipRSA, SpLD
Mrs J Kilsby
Mrs S M Green
Mrs A Bond, BEd
Mrs A Greenbank, BA

Junior School:
A R Dennis, BA (*Head of Lyndhurst Junior School*)
G W Stephenson, BSc (*Deputy Head*)
Mrs S E Sumner, CertEd (*Director of Studies*)
B L W Gunter, BEd
Mrs A P Hirst, DipEd
T J Cordery, MA
J R Parker, BA
Miss D H Buckley, BA
Miss A Wilson, BA
Mrs A B Saunders, CertEd
Mrs J A McHenry, CertEd

Boarding Houses:
School: Mr T M Loten
Dolman: Mr R P Bond
Faircote: Mrs S C Beaumont
Lyndhurst: Mr G Binks
Orchard: Mrs M-H Knights

Day Houses:
Dolman Juniors: Miss H V Brown
Gruggen Juniors: I J Andrews
Hutton Juniors: Mrs M R Peel
Wilberforce Juniors: M G Milne

Pocklington School was founded by John Dolman in 1514 as part of a guild whose aims encompassed support for the poor and sick of the parish as well as the foundation of a grammar school "for the bringing up of youth in virtue and learning". The school was thus founded on the basis of a commitment to create opportunity for those who would benefit from the education it provided and who would take their place in a society which was finding itself increasingly in need of an expansion of education. The school values its Christian foundation: pupils and staff of course comprise individuals of different faiths and beliefs but there is a desire to aspire to Christian values. Pupils attend the parish church on a regular basis.

There are currently 733 pupils in the school of whom 154 are at Lyndhurst, the junior school of Pocklington. There is a total of 150 boarders, in 3 senior houses (13-18 years) and 2 junior houses (9-12 years).

The school is set in spacious grounds on the edge of Pocklington, a market town 12 miles east of York. Communications are good, with effective bus service coverage for day pupils and a fast road link to York and the motorway network.

Academic life is at the core of any school and Pocklington's curriculum has been developed to stretch and motivate pupils. Music, drama and art thrive, as do sport, outdoor education, community service, the CCF and an impressive range of other extra-curricular activities. The Tom Stoppard Centre for performing arts was opened in May 2001.

The school recognises the changing nature of modern university courses and career patterns. Sixth Form AS and A2 options are diverse and flexible. There is high quality careers advice. The intention is that Pocklington's education as a whole will provide a sound basis for pupils' lives and careers, in terms not only of qualifications but also of character and experience.

Lyndhurst School. The Junior School, Lyndhurst is situated on the main campus in its own buildings. It has its own identity and specialist resources. A new library and further teaching accommodation was added in 1998 and a new computer suite, music rooms and extended art/design area will be opened in September 2001. The Junior School is two form entry at age 7 and 8 and becomes three forms in years 5 and 6. It is responsible for up to 160 pupils, girls and boys, between the ages of 7 and 11.

Curriculum. Senior School pupils take a full range of subjects in the first 2 years including Sciences, Languages (Latin and French), Humanities and creative subjects (Art, Design and Music). In Year 9 a second modern language (German or Spanish) is also introduced. In Years 10 and 11 pupils take a core of Mathematics, English (Language and Literature), French and Science (80% do separate sciences). In addition they take three options from a wide range of subjects including art, design, drama, geography, German, history, Latin, music, PE, religious studies and Spanish.

In the Sixth Form courses are offered at AS and A2 level in art, biology, business studies, chemistry, design, economics, English, French, mathematics and further mathematics, geography, German, history, Latin, music, physics, politics, religious studies, Spanish and theatre studies. In addition, electronics, environmental science, general studies, IT, PE and video photography are studied at AS level. In the first year of the Sixth Form, pupils are involved in an extensive Community Services programme.

Admission. For entry to the Senior School, boys or girls between the ages of 11+ and 12 take an entrance examination in January; boys or girls between 13 and 14 either Common Entrance or 13+/14+ school entrance examination. Arrangements can be made to admit pupils at other ages. Entry at Sixth Form is subject to GCSE grades.

Admission to the Junior School is by assessment tests in January. The main age of entry is at 7, although children of 8, 9 or 10 may also sit tests for entry.

Fees. Day, £2,252. Boarding, £3,671 per term. These fees include all necessary expenses. Boarders receive free laundry and ordinary medical attention, and there are few extras. Music and singing lessons, £99 per term.

Sports and Societies. Rugby football, cricket, tennis, hockey, athletics, cross country, swimming, squash, badminton, netball, rounders, basketball, gliding, kayaking, trampolining, golf and orienteering. The School has its own mapped orienteering course. Athletic sports are held in June. There are 15 grass and 12 hard tennis courts, 2 squash courts, an indoor heated swimming pool, a gymnasium and a large Sports Hall. Games are played compulsorily on 2 days a week, and there is an afternoon for activities, CCF and Community Service Unit.

School societies include Literary, Debating, Historical, Scientific, Dramatic, Photographic, Chess and Film Societies for Senior School pupils. The school possesses its own cinema projector and a full programme of films, lectures, recitals and concerts is given during the winter terms. Lyndhurst has its own full programme of activities.

Music. There are very wide musical opportunities both for individuals and for ensembles. Over half the pupils learn an instrument or sing. There are ensembles to cover all tastes and styles: orchestral, early music, swing, brass, recorder, rock. Most exist at junior and senior levels.

Religious Life. School services are held in the Parish Church on Fridays and Sundays and there are also voluntary services in the School Chapel. All of these services are conducted by the Chaplain, who is also responsible for preparing boys and girls for Confirmation, and for the organisation of religious education.

Dyslexia Support. Special provision is made for children who are dyslexic. The school has 2 specialist dyslexia teachers who work closely with the teaching staff.

Scholarships and Exhibitions. *Academic.* Scholarships and Exhibitions at 11+, 13+ and 16+ are awarded on the basis either of the school's own scholarship papers (11+, 13+) or of GCSE results (16+). Awards are open to internal as well as external candidates.

Music. Music scholarships and exhibitions are available at all ages, to internal and external candidates. An organ scholarship is also offered.

Charitable status. Pocklington School is a Registered Charity, number 529834. It exists to promote a high quality education for young people.

Portora Royal School

Enniskillen Northern Ireland BT74 7HA.
Tel: (028) 66 322658
Fax: (028) 66 328668
e-mail: mailbox@portora.enniskillen.ni.sch.uk

Founded 1608.

The School buildings were first at the village of Ballybalfour, not far from Enniskillen. In the year 1641 they were removed to Enniskillen itself. The School was removed to new buildings on Portora Hill in 1777, these buildings forming the central block of the old school buildings. Since 1990 all teaching and sporting facilities have been either renovated or rebuilt, and extended. This includes four new Science Laboratories, new Technology and Information Technology suites, an Art & Design Centre, and a Sixth Form Centre. In its earlier days the government of the School was in the hands of the King and the Viceroy, but since the year 1890, the School has been governed and managed under Scheme No. 34 framed under the Irish Educational Endowments Act (1885) and subsequent amending schemes framed under the Act.

Governing Body:

The Rt Revd B D A Hannon, MA, Bishop of Clogher (*Chairman*)
P M C Little, BSc (*Vice Chairman*)
S B Morrow, OBE, BAgr (*Hon Sec*)
T J N Hilliard, JP
J Kerr, CertEd
Revd B A Hunt, BA MTh
Revd Chancellor V E S McKeon, FCA, BD
R L Bennett, MA, DipEd (*Headmaster*) (*ex-officio*)
J C Brady, LLB
Mrs M Cooper, LLB
B Graham, BSc
C R E Parke
E K Rogers, BAgr
R F Toner, BA, FCA
Mrs R Wilkinson, BEd
Revd Precentor B Courtney, MA, BD
H Hamilton, MBE (*Parent Governor*)
Mrs R Armstrong, BSc(Econ) (*Parent Governor*)
W I L Kennedy, BSc(Econ) (*Parent Governor*)
A J Beattie, BSc, DipEd (*Teacher Governor*)
M A Todd, BSc, CertEd, PGCE, CBiol, MIBiol (*Teacher Governor*)
Mrs E B McNeill, MA, DipEd (*Teacher Governor*)
J F Mullan, MPSNI, MRPharmS
Mrs D Frazer, MEd, DipDomSc
R R A Eadie, DL, FRICS
A I A Crawford
J A Collinson, FCA

***Headmaster:* R L Bennett**, MA, DipEd

R H Northridge, BA (*Vice Principal*)

Estates Manager: M R H Scott, MBE, ACIS

Accountant: Mrs A Stronge, ACA, MIATI

Assistant Masters:

T A Elliott, BSc
Revd Canon J D G Kingston, MA (*Chaplain and Second Master*)
W J McBride, BA, LTCL, AMusTCL, LRAM, ARCO
†T R Smith, BEd, DipEd, GradIED, FTC, Prod Eng
†A J Beattie, BSc, DipEd
Mrs M O McCready, BA, DipEd
†J Caswell, BA, CertEd
†R G McNeill, BSc, DipEd
W M Gilfillan, PhD, BSc, CChem, MRSC
R J D Neill, BA, DipEd
Mrs E B McNeill, MA, DipEd
M T Hulme, MA, CertEd, CertCompEd
†M A Todd, BSc, CertEd, CBiol, MIBiol
P S H Johnston, BSc, CertEd
D H Hutton, DA, MAAT, Cert Ed
Miss G A Herdman-Grant, BA, CertEd
Mrs E K Hulme, MA, DipEd, CertCompEd
D K Dempster, MSc, BA, PGCE, MILAM
R J Stewart, MSc, PGCE
J J R Clarke, BEd
S J Gaston, BA, PGCE
J D C Patton, MSc, BA, CertEd
Miss N M Heap, BA, PGCE
D J McLaughlin-Borlace, BA, MSc, PGCE
K A Moore, MA, PGCE
Mrs S McCaul, BA, PGCE
W J Sloane, BSc, PGCE

Numbers. 460 boys.

Situation. The School is situated on an elevated site of 70 acres, on the shores of Lough Erne. Pupils are encouraged to take full advantage of this superb site and the wide area of unspoilt countryside.

The School Buildings. Tuition: a large classroom block, 5 Science Laboratories, Library, Music Centre, Art & Design Centre, Gymnasium, Engineering Laboratory, Technology and Computer Laboratories, and Sixth Form Centre.

Religious Teaching and Practice. This is the responsibility of the School Chaplain. All pupils have at least 2 periods of Divinity a week.

Curriculum and Examinations. Forms 1–3 follow a broad course of general education in the National Curriculum. They choose up to 9 or 10 subjects for study to GCSE level. The range to 'A' level is comprehensive, from the academic to the artistic and technical. University Scholarship work is also undertaken.

Games and activities. A very wide range of outdoor pursuits is followed which take advantage of the School's superb natural environment of rivers, lakes, mountains and forests. Rugby, rowing and cricket are the main team sports. The school has a Gymnasium and heated Swimming Pool, and an all-weather running track. Music and Drama flourish with public performances at least twice each in the year. Amongst the other clubs and societies are the Electronic Society, Debating Society, Chess Club and Squash Club.

Fees. Tuition fee £2,200 per annum. Capital Fee: £45 per annum. Pupils whose parents are EC Nationals do not pay tuition fees.

The Portsmouth Grammar School

High Street Portsmouth Hants PO1 2LN.
Tel: 023 9236 0036
Fax: 023 9236 4256

The School was founded in 1732 by Dr William Smith, Mayor of Portsmouth and Physician to its Garrison, MD of Leyden, and a member of Christ Church, Oxford, to which he left land in trust for the foundation of Portsmouth's first established school.

Motto: *Praemia Virtutis Honores.*

Governing Body:

Chairman: D K Bawtree, CB, BSc(Eng), CEng, FIEE, FIMechE, DL

C C L Andreyev, MA, DPhil
I A Carruthers
Rear Admiral J Chadwick, CEng, FIEE
Mrs J Cockcroft, RGN, FPC, CertEd
C J L Evans, FCA
B N Gauntlett, DipSurv, FRICS
The Right Worshipful The Lord Mayor of Portsmouth, Councillor Barry Maine
Air Chief Marshal Sir Richard Johns, GCB, CBE, LVO, FRAeS, RAF
C H R Niven, MA, DipEd, L-ès-L, D-de-l'U
Sir Leonard Peach, MA, CIPD, CIMgt
M J Pipes, MA, MBA, MInstP
F S K Privett, LLB
Mrs S Quail, BA
Mrs S Resouly, BSc, MRPharmS
Mrs M Scott, BSc
The Provost of Portsmouth, The Very Revd Dr William H Taylor

Clerk to the Governors and Bursar: A P Sullivan

***Headmaster:* T R Hands**, BA, AKC, DPhil

Second Master: P A Smith, BSc

Senior Teachers:
Miss V L Barrett, BA
*Mrs C Giles, BSc
*W M Taylor, BSc, CPhys, MInstP
J P Thomas, BSc

Upper School Staff:

Art & Design:
*P J Tonkyn, MEd, MCSD
Mrs C Derry, BEd, MA
S P H Willcocks, BA

Careers:
A P Savage, BEd

Classics:
*A P Clifford, BA
J E Law, MA, FRSA
Mrs B Richards, BA

Design and Technology:
*C A Dean, BSc
C C Flowers, BEd
A P Savage, BEd

Economics and Business Studies:
*C A Ford, MA
G I Butterworth, BA
Miss D A S Tabtab, MSc

English:
*J E Priory, MA
Miss V L Barrett, BA
Mrs J V Cresswell-Hogg, BA
M D Cawte, MA
†J J Elphick-Smith, MA
A N G Faludy, JP, BA
T McCarthy, BA
Mrs E C Page, PhD, MA

Drama and Theatre Studies:
*D R Hampshire, BSc, BA, ARCS, CBiol, MIBiol
Mrs S M Hague, LLAM
Mrs R Harland
Mrs G Hawkswell, BEd

Food Technology:
Mrs W Whitaker, CertEd

Geography:
*Mrs C Giles, BSc
J P Baker, BSc, MA(Ed), FRGS, FGS
Mrs J K Edwards, BSc
S Horsman, BA
Mrs A D Pollicot, CertEd
†P J B Wright, MA, PhD, FRGS

Government & Politics:
*A J Kittermaster, MA, PhD

History:
*S Lemieux, MA
Miss F E A Bush, BA
T W Butterworth, BA
Mrs S E Palmer, BA
Miss L Pechard, MA

Information Technology:
*A H Harrison, BSc

Mathematics:
*M H McCall, MA, PhD
W J W Arnold, BSc, AFIMA
M J F Core, BSc
D Mountford, BA, MSc, PhD
S L Rowlands, BSc
Mrs D L Spofforth, BSc
J P Thomas
R Thornton, BSc
R H G Wilkins, BSc

Modern Languages:
*N G Waters, BA
R W Bratt, MA (*Assistant Chaplain*)
*Miss C L Coward, BA (*Head of German*)

Mrs L M Gosden, BA
*Mrs C A Gozalbez-Guerola, BA (*Head of French*)
†A R Hogg, BA (*Senior Housemaster*)
Mrs G J Moran
Mrs L Nogueira-Paché, LicSc, MA
*S Page, BA (*Head of Spanish*)
G A Perry, BA
Miss A Qureshi, BA
Mrs M A Stubbs

Music:
*D J Swinson, MA, FRCO, ARCM, LRAM
Miss A D Blackwell, BA, MA, LTCL
Miss J Ingamells, ARCM
D J M Thorne, BA, FRCO, LRAM

Physical Education
*N F C Blewett, BEd, MPEA, DipSP (*Surmaster*)
Mrs D J Blackwell, BEd
Mrs G E Cheesebrough, BEd
M W Earley (*Games Assistant*)
S D Hawkswell, BA
J E Law, MA, FRSA (*Hockey Coach*)
R J Parks (*Cricket Coach*)
Mrs H E Prentice
*Mrs D F Spencer (*Head of Girls' Games*)

Philosophy and Religious Studies:
*The Revd J M Grindell, MA, CertCouns (*Chaplain*)
Mrs S Cussens, BA
Mrs E L Flowers, BEd, CertCouns
G M E Neanon, BA, CPsychol, AFBPS
Miss R J I Richmond, PhD, MA
A R West, MA
Ms G Wilson

Science:
*W M Taylor, BSc, CPhys, MInstP (*Chairman of Science Depts*)
†Miss E J Cox, MSc, CPhys, MInstP
Miss K E Barsby
Mrs M G Bates, BSc
S G Disley, BSc
Miss R M M Duthie, BSc
Mrs M R Habens, BSc, MSc
J K Herbert, BSc
M R Howson, BSc, PhD, CChem, MRSC
J C A Hunt, BSc (*Head of Middle School*)
*N Knight, MA, CBiol, MIBiol (*Head of Biology*)
N O Minns, MSc, CChem, MRSC
*P E Nials, BSc, MA(Ed), CBiol, MIBiol, CertCouns (*Head of Health Education*)
R V Puchades, BSc
O B Robinson, PhD, BA
J P Shepherd, BSc
Mrs K L Sparkes, BSc
*M R Taylor, BSc (*Head of Chemistry*)
Mrs J E Thompson, BSc

Librarian: Mrs M J D Pugsley
Archivist: Mrs C R I Smith
School Medical Officers:
Dr C A Olford
Dr C Foley
Personal Assistant to Headmaster: Miss J E Moody
Admissions Secretary: Mrs G M Williams

Junior School Staff:

Head of Junior School: Mrs P S Foster, CertEd
Deputy Head: A P Laurent, BEd

Mrs D J Blackwell, BEd	Mrs E R Day, BA, CertEd
Mrs S M Capel, MA(Ed)	Mrs S Dipple, BSc, PGCE
Miss C S Chambers, BEd	R A J Evans, CertEd
Mrs J Compton, CertEd	Miss C J Hebdige, BEd
Mrs J Crossley, CertEd	Mrs C Houselander, CertEd
Mrs J E Ingamells, ARCM	Mrs S J Sheldrick, BEd
Mrs D M Lockyer, CertEd	Mrs R Stares, CertEd
A W Marshall, BA	Mrs B E Tilling, BSc
Mrs F Nash, BEd	Mrs S P Tyacke, BEd
Mrs F G Ormrod, BA	J Wadge, BA
G D Payne, BEd	M F Warin, BA
Mrs S Payne, CertEd	Mrs D Willcocks
Mrs K Pratt, CertEd	Miss L Y Wood, BSc
E J P Sharkey, BA	Mrs L Younger
B W Sheldrick, BA	

The School, formerly on the Direct Grant List, assumed full independent status in 1976. It is co-educational throughout. There are 865 pupils in the Upper School and 450 pupils in the Junior School. There are no boarders.

The Nursery School opens in April 2001 and will cater for boys and girls from 2½ years old.

The Junior School numbers 450 boys and girls aged 4-11. It is a thriving, dynamic and popular institution, committed to giving Portsmouth pupils the best possible start to their educational lives. The main ages of entry are 4, 7 and 8, by assessment tests held in January. Occasionally there are places available for intermediate entry. Although promotion to the Upper School is not automatic, it is normal for pupils to move there when they are 11.

Upper School. Admission is by the School's Entrance Assessment at 11, or Common Entrance at 13. Pupils are admitted at other ages, should vacancies occur, subject to assessments and satisfactory reports from previous schools. Admission to the Sixth Form, which numbers 260, is subject to satisfactory standard at GCSE and interview.

Curriculum. Pupils are educated for life as well as public examinations, through initiatives such as The Portsmouth Curriculum in Year 7 and the wide-ranging General Studies Programme in the Sixth Form. The curriculum aims to give a general education and to defer specialisation. After GCSE, pupils enter the Sixth Form, which seeks to prepare pupils for the challenges of a rigorous university education and subsequent competitive employment. Pupils generally select 3 A2 levels and two AS levels from: Art, Biology, Business Studies, Chemistry, Classical Civilisation, Critical Thinking, Design and Technology, Drama, Economics, Electronics, English Literature, French, Geography, Geology, German, Government and Politics, Greek, History of Art, History, Information and Communications Technology, Latin, Mathematics, Further Mathematics, Music, Physical Education, Psychology, Religious Studies and Spanish. The General Studies Programme is mainly taught by outside professionals and is aimed at widening personal and academic horizons. The Sixth Form prepares candidates for entry to Higher Education, and the Careers Department provides close relations with various forms of employment.

Religion. The School has always been closely connected with Portsmouth Cathedral. However, Religious Instruction, given in accordance with the principles of the Christian faith, remains, in accordance with a long tradition of latitudinarianism, non-denominational. The School has a Chaplain and an Assistant Chaplain.

Pastoral Care. Pastoral Care is of paramount importance. Pupils are allocated to one of four Houses on entry. Heads of House and their House Tutors are responsible for the pastoral and academic welfare of all pupils and provide a focal point for communication between teaching staff and parents. Particular emphasis is placed on the triangular relationship between pupil, parents and teaching staff, including a programme of telephone calls from tutors to new parents in which all senior staff and the Headmaster have a monitoring role.

Games. Rugby football, rugby sevens, netball, hockey and cross-country are the main games in Winter and Spring, cricket, tennis, athletics and rounders in the Summer Term. Cross-country running, squash, judo, badminton, basketball, aerobics, swimming, sailing and sea-rowing are also available.

Other Activities. The Combined Cadet Force (which has Army, Navy and RAF Sections) is of particular significance, having produced 3 VCs *inter alia*; liaison with the School's link ship, HMS Invincible, is particularly developed and has been the subject of national press attention. There are opportunities for Adventurous Training, Ten Tors and participation in the Duke of Edinburgh Award Scheme as well as for service to the local community and charity work. Drama flourishes at all levels and Portsmouth's New Theatre Royal provides young performers and technicians with a professional venue for major school productions. Many societies cater for a considerable range of extra-curricular interests. Various holiday activities and visits are encouraged and include many foreign tours for bands, orchestras, choirs and ensembles. The School has a flourishing exchange scheme with French, German, Spanish and American schools. Sports teams have recently gone on tour to South Africa and Barbados.

Fees. (2000/2001). Upper School: £6,000 pa. Junior School: £3,847-£4,266 pa.

Scholarships and Bursaries are available in the Upper and Junior Schools. In the Sixth Form there are awards for academic achievement, academic promise, art, drama, music, sport and all-round ability.

Buildings. Nothing remains of the former Schoolroom, destroyed when the present Junior School, now Grade II listed, was erected on the site of the town fortifications. The Lower Junior School and Senior Schools occupy a unique range of former Barrack buildings in an historic location in the High Street: these are now also listed throughout. In the last decade of the twentieth century there was an emphasis on new buildings: a Music School and Sports Hall (1989), a modern theatre (1990), a sports pavilion (1992) and a Sixth Form Centre (1995). A comprehensive refurbishment of the older buildings was also undertaken including science laboratories (1996 and 1997) and an IT Suite generously equipped by IBM (1998). The most recent acquisition has been the fine Cambridge House Barracks, which not only doubles the space available for teaching and pastoral care, but also gives the School ownership of a harmonious group of historic buildings.

Leaving Scholarships. Occasional awards may be made, at the Governors' discretion, to pupils proceeding to University. The foundation links with Christ Church, Oxford, are maintained by the Allen Exhibition.

Honours. Over 99% of Sixth Formers transfer to University each year, the very large majority to their first-choice university. 14 pupils took up places at Oxford and Cambridge in 2000. Sportsmen include England Cricket Captain Wally Hammond and Athletics International Roger Black. Military distinction in abundance, including 3 VCs (one the first VC submariner), several Admirals, Generals and Air Marshals (including the present Chief of the Air Staff). Medicine is also a continuing theme - from pioneer opthalmologist James Ware to Viagra researcher Ian Osterloh. Arts are well and diversely represented: dramatist Simon Gray, poet Christopher Logue, novelist James Clavell, cathedral organist Christopher Walsh and pop singer, Paul Jones. Civil Servants and Judges and barristers galore, plus entrepreneur industrialist Alan Bristow.

Old Portmuthian Club. This maintains links with former pupils not least by holding reunions in Portsmouth, London and Oxford.

Charitable status. The Portsmouth Grammar School is a Registered Charity, number 1063732. It exists to provide education for boys and girls.

Prior Park College

Bath Somerset BA2 5AH.
Tel: (01225) 835353
e-mail: info@priorpark.co.uk
website: www.priorpark.co.uk

Prior Park College is a fully co-educational Catholic Boarding-and-Day School, which warmly welcomes Christians of other denominations. Founded in 1830 by Bishop Baines, its management, during most of the 19th century, belonged to the Bishops of Clifton. In 1924, ownership and direction of the School passed to the Congregation of Christian Brothers. Since 1981, Prior Park, while cherishing its Catholic character, has been run by the laity, has more than doubled in size and has brought about complete and thorough co-education.

Motto: *Deo Duce, Deo Luce.*

Patrons:
Major General, His Grace The Duke of Norfolk, KG, GCVO, CBE, MC
Rt Hon The Lord St John of Fawsley, PC

Trustees:
His Eminence Cardinal Cormac Murphy-O'Connor, STL, PhL, Archbishop of Westminster
Rt Revd Mervyn Alexander, DD
Most Revd J A Ward, OFM, Cap, Archbishop of Cardiff
The Rt Hon C F Patten, PC, CH
Col R S C Dowden, JP, DL, KCSG
D A Gilmer
F J F Lyons, KSG
M A Sutton, MC, MA, KCSG
C J B Davy, CB
Rear Admiral M A Vallis, CB, FEng

Governors:

C J B Davy, CB (*Chairman*)
Sister Jane Livesey, IBVM, MA (Cantab)
E W Cussen, BSc, FRICS
J A E Evans, MA, FRSA
B A Kelly, QC, MA
Sister Andrea Le Guével, FCJ, MA, MPhil
C W Long, MA, CMG
Fr W M McLoughlin, PhL, BD, MTh, OSM
A J Owen, LLB, FCA
A M Pitt, MA, FCA
M E Thesiger, FCA

Clerk to the Governors: Captain Charles Freeman, FIMgt, Royal Navy

Headmaster: **R G G Mercer**, MA, DPhil

Deputy Headmaster: D G Clarke, BSc (Bradford)

Senior Teacher: Mrs S Ashby, BSc, AdvDipEd (*Housemistress, Fielding*)

Director of Studies: T J Simons, BSc

Chaplain: The Revd J T Shannon, BEd, MPhil

Registrar: Dr Margaret Ruxton, BSc, PhD

Assistant Staff:

Mrs E S Barber, BA
Miss D Barrett, BA (*Housemistress, English*)
D Bevan, MA
T Brierley (*Head of Mathematics*)
S Burt, BSc (*Head of Geography*)
Miss S Button, MA
Mrs J Cocks-Pursall, BEd (*ESL*)
Miss C Cummins, BA
T B Constable Maxwell (*Head of Theology*)
G Davies, BSc, MEd (*Housemaster, Roche*)

Mrs J C Eatwell, BSc (*Head of Economics & Business Studies, Head of Careers*)
Mrs E Farrar, BA (*Head of Language Development Programme*)
Miss R Fox, MA (*Head of History*)
J Fry (*Housemaster, Clifford*)
Miss M Green, BA (*Head of Classics*)
A R J Haines, BA (*ICT Manager*)
A S Hall, BEd (*Housemaster, Baines, Head of Boys' PE & Games*)
T J Hardcastle, BSc (*Head of Chemistry*)
Mrs P M Harper, CertEd
Mrs A Holbrook, ALA (*Librarian*)
D Holland, MA (*Housemaster, Allen*)
Mrs E Jewett, DipEd
Mrs R Kimball, Dip Fine Art
D G Langley, BA (*Head of Drama*)
Mrs S E Lear, BA
Mrs A J Lynch, BA
Mrs K E McCarey, BA (*Housemistress, St Mary's*)
Mrs L Mercer, BA (*Examinations Officer*)
J Moran, BSc
Mrs M E Mudie, BSc
Miss C L O'Brien, BSc
Mrs C Pepler, BA (*Head of Sixth Form Higher Education*)
Miss A Pitt, BA (*Head of Girls' PE & Games*)
G Pruett, BEd (*Housemaster, Burton, Head of Rugby*)
R Robertson, MA, ARCO (*Director of Music*)
Mrs M Robinson, MEd
M Roques, BA, MPhil
Mrs P Rose, BA (*Head of Modern Languages*)
D M Sackett, BA (*Head of Year 7*)
A M Smith, MEd (*Head of Design & Technology; Head of ICT; Key Skills; Head of Sixth Form*
G Smith, BSc, PhD (*Assistant Director of Studies*)
C Spencer, BSc
N J Tattersfield, MA (*Head of English*)
R Trott, BSc, PhD (*Housemaster, Roche*)
Mrs A C Vaught, BA
Mrs A Vick, BA
R L Wells, BSc, PhD (*Head of Science, Head of Biology*)
S A Wilcock, BSc, PhD (*Head of Physics*)
D F Wood, BA (*Head of Art*)
Miss L Young, BSc

Music Staff:
G Austin, ARCM (*Brass*)
P Bradley (*Voice*)
D Bevan, MA (*Academic/Schols*)
Ms R Bevan (*Voice*
Mrs M Buckley, LTCL (*Recorder*)
Mrs A Caunce, GRSM, LTCL, ARCM (*Piano*)
Miss A Grayburn, BA, PGCE, ARCM (*Piano*)
A Haines (*Bass Guitar*)
G Harrup, LGSM (*Accoustic Guitar*)
M Harvey (*Percussion*)
Mrs M Konigsfeldt, GRSM, ARCM (*Piano*)
J Lambert, MA, BMus (*Piano*)
Ms J Mason-Smith, LTCL (*Flute*)
Mrs M Montagu, ARCM, BMus (*Oboe*)
D Pagett, GRNCM, PGDip RNCM (*Clarinet, Saxophone*)
Ms S Power, BEd (*'Cello*)
R White, LTCL (*Violin/Viola*)

Houses and Housemasters/mistresses:

Baines (*Junior House*): Alan Hall
Burton (*Senior day boys*): Giles Pruett
Clifford (*Senior day boys*): Jonathan Fry
English (*Senior day girls*): Angela Vick
Fielding (*Senior day girls*): Susan Ashby
St Mary's (*Senior boarding girls*): Kate McCarey
Allen: (*Senior boarding boys*): David Holland
Roche (*Senior boarding boys*): Robert Trott

Bursar and Clerk to the Governors: Captain Charles Freeman, FIMgt, MInstD

Medical Officer: Dr N Snowise, MA, BM, BCH, MRCGP, DA, DRCOG

Infirmary Sister: Mrs E T McPeake, SRN

Headmaster's Secretary: Mrs L Richards

School Staff Instructor: K Pearn

Number in School. There are 511 pupils in the School, 292 boys and 219 girls. Boarders 13–18: 123; Day 11–18: 388.

Structure of the School. The School provides boarding and day education for boys and girls aged 11–18. The usual ages of entry are 11 and 13, but 6th form boarders and day pupils are also welcome. Boarders are normally not admitted before the age of 13. Each boy and girl between 13 and 18 is a member of a boarding or day House, while younger pupils belong to a co-educational Junior House.

Situation and Buildings. The College is situated on the southern hills of Bath and enjoys a commanding view over the City. Standing in 57 acres of grounds, Prior Park combines a magnificent setting for boarding education with access to Bath and its numerous cultural attractions. Proximity to the M4 and M5 motorways places the College within easy reach of London, the Midlands, the South-West and Wales, while the rail service from London takes approximately 1¼ hours.

The Houses, Administration and College Chapel are to be found in the elegant range of buildings grouped round Ralph Allen's celebrated Palladian Mansion. A major programme of modernisation has provided purpose-built accommodation for residential staff and their families along with comfortable study bedrooms, quiet areas and recreational rooms for the boarders and day pupils alike. Boarding and day accommodation of the highest quality is provided for all girls in The Priory and All Saints at the eastern end of the estate overlooking the valley and the City of Bath. Boys' boarding accommodation is undergoing major refurbishment.

Academic teaching is provided in modern classrooms. These include a Science Block containing seven renovated laboratories. In 1987 a new Art Centre was opened. A Design/Technology Centre was opened in September 1991. New classrooms, a Sixth Form Studies Centre and an outstanding new Theatre were completed in September 1992. A new Music School, including rehearsal rooms and recording studio, was opened in December 1993. The new College library was opened in 1995.

ICT provision includes a suite of computers in the library and ICT room, with permanent links to the internet. Computer access is also available in boarding houses.

The John Wood Chapel and the College Chapel provide magnificant settings for major performances of orchestral and choral music, for which the College has a deservedly high reputation. A magnificent pipe organ was acquired for the Chapel in 1996 after an appeal. Indeed, the College prides itself on its special focus upon the performing and creative Arts.

There are spacious playing fields, including an astro-turf. A heated Swimming Pool is open throughout the year.

Courses of Study. Below the 6th Form the syllabus is broad and specialisation is kept to a minimum. All students study English, Mathematics, the Sciences, a Modern Language and Religious Studies to GCSE. The main 6th form subjects may be selected from: Mathematics, Further Mathematics, Chemistry, Design and Technology, Physics, Biology, English, French, Theatre Studies, Spanish, German, Latin, Greek, Music, Music Technology, Classical Civilisation, History, Geography, Business Studies, Economics, Politics, Theatre Studies, Philosophy, Physical Education, History of Art and Art. Virtually all 6th Form students proceed to courses at Universities, Medical Schools, or other Institutions of Higher Education.

Objects of the College. The College provides a Catholic and Christian education. While the Chaplain serves in a special way the spiritual needs of the boys and girls, great importance is attached to the commitment of all staff to the ethos of the School and, in particular, to the family atmosphere engendered by a resident Headmaster/Housemistress and resident House staff. The School tries to develop to the full the potential of all its pupils, according to their individual abilities, with emphasis being placed on each pupil's academic progress. At a deeper level, we seek to foster the whole person, through the religious life of the School, through Community Service, through shared experiences in sport, music and drama and through a watchful care of each individual's welfare. A Personal Development Programme attempts to equip all boys and girls with information and guidance specifically addressed to contemporary issues and problems.

Admission. (*see* Entrance Scholarship section) The normal method of entry for pupils of 11+ is through the College examination held in January. Most pupils of 13+ enter through the Common Entrance examination. Scholarships are available at 11+, 13+ and 6th form. 6th formers are admitted on the basis of School reports and of attainment at GCSE Level. Scholarships are available to external candidates who have performed well in our 6th Form Scholarship examination. At all ages of entry scholarships in music and art are also available.

Fees (September 2000). Boarding £4,495 per term, Day pupils 13+ £2,495, 11+ £2,395.

Physical Education and Games. Physical Education is included in the curriculum. Games are an important part of the School life. The Main School games are Rugby, Hockey, Cricket, Tennis and Athletics for boys; Hockey, Netball, Tennis and Athletics for girls. There is also provision for Swimming, Badminton, Volleyball, Basketball and Table Tennis, Gymnasium and fitness centre. The school also uses the superb facilities of Bath University nearby.

Wednesday Activities Programme. The voluntary Combined Cadet Force includes all 3 services plus a Signals Platoon and a REME Platoon. Membership is confined to pupils of 15 and upwards. Cadets are encouraged to participate in the Service and Contingent Camps and Courses.

The Duke of Edinburgh's Award scheme operates at all levels up to Gold Award and is an alternative to the CCF. The School has an extensive Community Service programme and it operates its own 'Young Enterprise' scheme.

Activities. Boarders and Day pupils alike partake in a wide range of Activities. Approximately half the boys and girls in the School receive individual tuition in at least one Musical instrument. A lively Music Department promotes further involvement of pupils in a range of Choirs, Orchestra, Junior Orchestra and Band. Drama and Debating feature prominently in the life of the School. There are many practical activities including Pottery, Electronics, Natural History, Technology, Scuba Diving, and the Radio Club. Leisure pursuits include Aerobics, Archery, Chess, Computing, Cross Country and Model Engineering.

Careers. The Headmaster and Careers Staff attach great importance to choices of academic subjects both for GCSE and for Advanced level. Careful guidance is provided on tertiary education and on its relevance to career opportunities and aspirations. ISCO programmes are available to students and there is a well-stocked Careers Library. The development of interview techniques, industrial liaison and work experience are all areas of special focus in our careers programme. The use of computers in careers advice is a major feature at Prior Park. A range of careers software ECCTIST, Which University?, Microdoors and Kudos is used.

PRIOR PARK PREPARATORY SCHOOL. The School is situated at Cricklade, Wiltshire, 35 miles from Prior Park and within easy reach of Swindon BR and the M4. It has ample boarding and recreational facilities for 180 boys and girls aged 7–13+. In addition, a new, purpose-built nursery and preparatory school, "Meadow Park", has been built within the grounds of Prior Park Preparatory School and offers a wonderful educational environment for day children up to the age of six. Extra-curricular activity is an important element and the School has excellent standards in Music, Drama and Sport.

Headmaster: G B Hobern, BA (Hons)

Charitable status. Prior Park College Trustees Limited is a Registered Charity, number 281242. Its aim is to provide independent preparatory and secondary education within the pastoral environment of a Roman Catholic, co-educational school.

Queen Elizabeth Grammar School, Wakefield

Wakefield West Yorkshire WF1 3QX.
Tel: (01924) 373943/369010
Fax: (01924) 378871

The 'Free Grammar School of Queen Elizabeth at Wakefield' is supposed to be the descendant of a School existing in Wakefield in the 13th century, and was founded by Royal Charter in 1591, at the 'humble suit made unto us by the inhabitants of the Town and Parish of Wakefield'. The endowment is largely due to the munificence of George Savile, Esquire, of Haselden Hall, and his sons George Savile and Thomas Savile, whose names may still be read on the exterior of the old School.

Motto: *Turpe nescire.*

Governing Body: The Governing Body, consisting of 15 co-opted Governors and 5 representative Governors, (*including representatives of the Universities of Leeds, Sheffield, Huddersfield and York*), is the Wakefield Grammar School Foundation.

Spokesman: Mrs E G Settle

Clerk to the Governors: R C Hemsley, MA, FCA

***Headmaster:* M R Gibbons**, BA, AKC

Deputy Headmaster: A F Derbyshire, MA, AKC

Director of Studies: L A Hallwood, BSc

Senior Master: M C Winrow, BA, MA, FRGS

G C Anderson, BSc, ARCS
T Barker BSc
Miss A Barnes, BA
A J Barraclough, BSc
D T Benn, BTech
D A Binney, BA
J R Birkinshaw, BTech
D Bunnell, BSc
J P Cholewa, BEd, MA
R D Cowan, MA, MIL
S L Dowson, BEd
P L Dryland BA, ATC
Mrs L J Firth, BA
M Fitzsimons, BA
D R Ford, BA
T H Gibb, BA
A M Goodall, MA, PhD
W W Gough, BSc
D N Gratrick, BSc
J Greenwood, BSc
D H Haigh, BA, ALCM
Mrs V F Halstead, MIL
B P Hamill, BA
J Holt, BSc
G D Howe, BA
R A Hudson, MA
L A Kent, BSc
N A Lambert, BSc
P D Lancaster, BA
W Lobl, BSc
I J Loudon, MA
Mrs V Macklam, BSc
P Mason, BSc
D M Matthews, BSc
M C Parsons, BEd
K J Payne, MA
G Pickersgill, BSc
Mrs J Plaut, BA

J P Preston, BEd
A M Rees, BA
N Rigby, MA
R M Rylance, BA
D B Seal, BA
Mrs H M Sheard, BSc
P Smith, BA
T Spencer, BA, MSc
P W Sutcliffe, BA
G D Tingle, BA
D J Turmeau, BEd, MA, LRAM
Miss C J Walker, MA
D Waters, BA
G W Watts, MA
K S Weston, BSc
Mrs C E Woodside, BEd
R D Woodside, BSc

Headmaster's Secretary: Mrs H C Smith

Junior School:
Headmaster: M M Bisset, BA, MA
Deputy Headmaster: M J Halls, BSc

Mrs C A Blacker, BEd
C Cheffins, BEd, MEd
D G L Collins, BA
J R Coughlan, BEd
Mrs K E Cousins, BEd, LTCL
G N Crowther, CertEd
Mrs C M Downs, BA
P T Ganley, BEd
L W Hanson, BEd
Mrs J A Hill, BA
Miss A Johnson, BEd
Mrs J K Padgett, BA
Mrs P R Perkin, CertEd
Mrs H J Whittamore, BA
D R Wright, BSc, MEd

Headmaster's Secretary: Mrs L H Bisset

Visiting Music Staff:
C J Bacon, GMus
Mrs S T Bacon, GMus
D Beckley, LTCL, FTCL, ARCM
K R Chambers, BA, LGSM
Mrs E Davies, BMus, LTCL, RCST, ITEC
Mrs A Elcock, BSc
G B S Hirst, LRAM, ARCM, LTCL
B Ibbetson, BMus, LRAM
G Lewis
Miss L R Marsh, BA (Oxon), FRCO, ALCM, DipAdvSt(RA)
Mrs J D Maunsell, GBSM, ABSM, LTCL
Ms K Napier, LRAM, DPLM
L Palumbo, GRNCM
M J Roberts, LGSM, DPLM
Mrs S Turmeau, BEd

There are approximately 930 boys in the School (Junior 260 and Senior 670).

The Headmaster is responsible to the Governors for both the Senior and the Junior Schools. Under his general supervision the Junior School (for boys of 7–11 years of age) is separately housed and administered by its own Headmaster. There is a 5 form entry annually into the Senior School.

The Junior School Headmaster is a member of IAPS and full details may be found under the Preparatory Schools section.

Curriculum. In Year 7 of the Senior School all boys follow the same wide ranging common curriculum. In the following year they add German and Latin to the French they are already studying. Boys take GCSE examinations at the end of Year 11. In the Sixth Form boys study subjects in a wide variety of combinations, generally following 4 subjects to AS and continuing 3 to A2 level. All those in the Sixth Form also follow a General Studies course as an additional subject.

An increasing number of subjects in the Sixth Form can be studied with pupils of the sister school, the Wakefield Girls' High School.

Religion. The School is a Christian Foundation and maintains close links with Wakefield Cathedral but there is no denominational bias in either teaching or Morning Assemblies, and those who practise religions other than Christianity are welcomed into the School.

Physical Education and Games. Physical education, under the supervision of the Director and his three full-time assistants, is an integral part of the school curriculum throughout the School. The School has some 37 acres of playing fields, with excellent rugby and hockey pitches in the winter, with four cricket squares, an all-weather athletics track and access to 16 tennis courts in the summer. The school has a six-badminton-court-size sports hall and fully equipped fitness room.

The major games for winter are rugby, hockey and cross country. In the Summer Term cricket, athletics and tennis predominate. All major sports are played to a high level, with boys regularly reaching county and, sometimes, international level.

Table-tennis, basketball, golf, swimming, weight-training, squash and badminton exist at club level, either at lunchtime or after school. Regular competitions take place with other schools.

There is an annual ski trip and the school has a flourishing outdoor pursuits club, where activities are organised weekly during term time and as expeditions during vacations.

Music and Drama. The School has a full programme of musical and dramatic activities, many operating in conjunction with Wakefield Girls' High School. There is a major production each autumn and spring. There are in addition other productions, sometimes Junior or experimental in form.

There is at least one concert each term, designed to reflect the range of musical activity, which is wide and varied, ranging from madrigals through orchestral music to jazz and rock. Activities taking place throughout the year include two orchestras, two concert bands, two swing bands, junior and chamber choirs, together with many smaller groups and chamber ensembles. There is a large team of visiting instrumental staff, and close links with Wakefield Cathedral, where some events take place. The School educates most of the Cathedral choral scholars. A music scholarship is available each year on entry to the Sixth Form.

Societies. These include Art, Chess, Christian Union, Classics, Debating, Drama, Geography, History, Literature, Photography, Angling, Bridge, Fell Walking, Film, Modelling, Table-Tennis, Science, Transport. The '34' Club for senior boys has a number of visiting speakers. The various music groups include Brass, Woodwind, String Ensembles and Choirs. The school also participates in the Duke of Edinburgh's Award Scheme.

Buildings. The main building has been used by the School since 1854. Over the years, the School has expanded greatly, but its core remains the distinguished Early Gothic Revival building, whose architectural merits have been accentuated by extensive stone cleaning and renovation. A gradual programme of building has matched the School's expansion with additions and improvements taking place in most areas. A recent major development was the opening of the Queen's Building named in honour of Her Majesty the Queen who visited the School in 1992 to mark the School's Quatercentenary. The academic year 1998/99 saw the completion of a new Language Suite and new Sports Hall.

Junior School. The Junior School is housed in its own building and enjoys its own specialist facilities; Art Room, DT Room, Hall, ICT Room, Library, Music Room and Science Laboratory.

Entrance. Entry into the Junior School is usually at 7 although places are retained for entry at 8, 9 and 10. Places depend on performance in the entrance examinations held in February, and enquiries for entry at this level should be made to the Headmaster of the Junior School (01924 373821).

Entry into the Senior School is possible from any kind of school and is normally:

(a) at 11 from the Junior School subject to a favourable recommendation.

(b) at 11 from Local Authority or Independent Schools after a satisfactory performance in the entrance examinations held early in the Spring Term.

(c) at 13 from Preparatory Schools after a satisfactory performance in the Common Entrance Examination.

(d) at 16 from any school after a satisfactory performance in the GCSE examinations.

Enquiries about entrance to the Senior School at these or at other ages should be made to the Secretary for Admissions.

Scholarships, Bursaries, etc: The Governors award each year a limited number of Scholarships to boys entering the Senior School at 11. Means and asset-tested Awards are also available under the Wakefield Grammar Schools' Foundation Awards Scheme. Enquiries about these Awards should be made for the Junior School to the Headmaster of the Junior School, and for the Senior School to the Secretary for Admissions.

Choral Scholarships are provided for boys in the Wakefield Cathedral Choir, and enquiry about these should be made either to the Precentor of Wakefield Cathedral, or to the Headmaster of the Junior School.

Leavers. Over 95% of leavers go on to a degree course.

Charitable status. Queen Elizabeth Grammar School is a Registered Charity, number 529908. The School exists to provide an excellent education for your son.

Queen Elizabeth's Grammar School,
Blackburn

Blackburn Lancs BB2 6DF.
Tel: 01254 686300 (Headmaster); 01254 686303 (Bursar)
Fax: 01254 692314
e-mail: headmaster@qegs.blackburn.sch.uk

Blackburn Grammar School was originally a Chantry School founded in 1509 by Thomas, the Second Earl of Derby, and associated with the Parish Church of Blackburn; it was disendowed in the reign of Edward VI, and re-established and constituted a Corporation by Royal Charter in 1567 by Queen Elizabeth. It is now administered by a scheme under the Charitable Trusts Acts dated 1910.

Motto: *Disce Prodesse.*

Chairman of Governors: C T Haworth, LLB

***Headmaster:* D S Hempsall**, MA, PhD, FRSA

Deputy Headmasters:
J Cave, MA
S E Turner, BA

Assistant Staff:
J S Anslow, BSc, MEd
Mrs R Arkwright, DipAD, ATC
Mrs P Brees, BSc
P K Broadhurst, BSc, DMS, TEFL
Dr A M Brown, MA, PhD
M Brown, BEd
A Buckingham, BEd
M E Butler, BA, PhD (*Physical Education*)
P N Carmont, BA
Mrs A M Cherry, BSc
P A Cooper, BSc
Mrs L M Crabtree, MA
R Davies, BSc
Mrs Y A Dickinson, BA
Miss P Disley, BSc
C P J Evans, MA
Mrs E A Evans, CertEd
Mrs M Foxley, CertEd, PGDip (*Complementary Studies*)
L R Fradkin, BEd
Ms J C Frankland, BA
C P Gill, BMus
T R Glover, MA (*Economics*)
I H Gordon, MA (*Head of Junior School*)
J F Grogan, BA
M A Hargreaves, BSc
B G Healey, BA, DipID
P S J Hedworth, BEd, BA (*Chaplain*)
G R Hill, BA, MLitt (*Music*)
M Holden, BSc, FRICS, FSVA
M C Holgate, BA
D Hopkinson, BSc (*Politics*) (*Head of Sixth Form*)
S F Ingham, BSc
P J Johnston, CertEd
Mrs E Kay, BEd
Mrs A Kidd, BA
Miss P A Longworth, BSc
P J Lowe, BSc (*General Studies*)
R Marshall, BSc, MSc, DIC
Mrs P A Maxwell, DipPE
M J McCann, BA, DipPSE (*ICT*)
I Miller, BA
S P Milnes, BA
S J Monk, BA
Miss S E Moynihan, BA
Miss J Nash, BA
S R Northin, BEd (*Careers*)
D N Palmer, BSc (*Mathematics*)
D Parsons, BA (*CDT*)
G G Pearson, MA, PhD (*Biology*)
A F Priory, BA, MA (*Religious Studies*)
A M Rose, BA (*Modern Languages*)
M W Russell, BSc, MA
A Sagar, BSc (*Chemistry*)
S A Smith, BSc
P W Sproston, MA, DipAD (*Art*)
P J Stott, BA
R Stowell, MA, MLitt
Mrs K Taylor, BEd
R M Taylor, MA (*English*)
A M Thirkell, BA, MA
A L Thorpe, MA (*History*)
C J Walsh, BSc
D Westworth, MA
Mrs F Whitham, BSc, MSc
C A Wilson, BA (*Classics*)
N H Wilson, CFA, MCollP
B Woodhead
Mrs C M Woods, CertEd
P H Wooldridge, BSc
A E Young, MA (*Geography*)
Mrs C Young, BEd

Bursar: J Ranford, ACMA

School Secretaries: Mrs D M Tate, Mrs E A Mashiter

Librarian: Mrs C E Baldwin, ALA

School Nurse: Miss C Hargreaves

There are 800 pupils, of whom 140 are in the Junior Department, aged 7–11, and the Sixth Form numbers about 200. Many pupils are bussed-in from a large catchment area.

The Junior School course includes English, Mathematics, Scripture, Geography, History, Elementary Science, Art & Craft, Physical Education, and Music with optional tuition in most instruments.

Boys and girls join the Main School at the age of 11 with a few places at 13+ CE stage and follow a full range of academic and practical subjects up to GCSE.

Boys and girls who enter the VIth Form have a wide choice of Advanced courses, including Classics, Modern Languages, English, History, Geography, Economics, Government, Music, Art, Mathematics, and the Sciences, by means of which pupils are prepared for the universities, the professions and industry.

The School is a non-denominational, Christian school. There is daily worship. Religious instruction forms part of the ordinary teaching of all pupils, except those whose parents express a wish in writing to the contrary.

The School was rebuilt on a new site, facing the attractive grounds of the Corporation Park, in 1883. In 1987 Her Majesty The Queen opened the £3.4M Queen's Wing, which besides providing classrooms also incorporates a library and a language laboratory. In 1989 a new sports hall was built on the sports fields at Lammack. In October 1990, on the school site, a new 25m swimming pool with sophisticated timing facilities was opened. In 1995 a £1.5

million purpose-built Centre, Singleton House, was completed for the Sixth Form.

The main School games are Association Football and Cricket, though Tennis, Rugby and Basketball are among the many other physical activities provided. The 13 acres of playing fields are situated at Lammack, a short distance from the School. They have been extensively developed and improved.

Out-of-school activities are provided for by various societies – Debating, Dramatic, Chess, Geographical, Scientific, Mountaineering and Sailing. A School play and a musical are produced publicly each year while the Choral Society and School Orchestra present one or more concerts. Instruction in the playing of orchestral instruments is provided.

There are educational visits abroad and frequent exchanges with schools in France and Germany.

Fees. Main School £1,818 per term, Junior School £1,430 per term. The School offers Bursaries.

Charitable status. Queen Elizabeth's Grammar School is a Registered Charity, number 1041220. It exists to provide quality education for boys and girls.

Queen Elizabeth's Hospital

Berkeley Place Clifton Bristol BS8 1JX.
Tel: (0117) 929 1856
Fax: (0117) 9293106

Patron: Her Majesty The Queen

By his will dated 10 April 1586, John Carr, a Bristol merchant, made provision for the establishment in the City of Bristol of a bluecoat school on the lines of Christ's Hospital, which was already flourishing in London. The Charter was granted to the School by Queen Elizabeth I on 21 March 1590. Originally composed entirely of boarders, the School continued so until 1920 when foundation day boys were admitted. Direct Grant status was accorded in 1945. The School is now independent.

Motto: *Dum tempus habemus operemur bonum.*

Governing Body:
C E Sweet, MA (*Chairman*)

J G Mason (*Vice-Chairman*)

S M Andrews, MA
Mrs D Bernard, JP
A J Brackin, BA, FCA
J Bretten, MA
Prof J R Farndon, MD, FRCS
R Hamilton-James
Col N King, OBE, MA
Mrs S Lloyd-Smith, PhD
Miss S C Mercer, BA
J G Pickard, BSc
H Roberts
Mrs M Shutt, JP
S C J Williams
R C Zair, BA, FCA

Clerk to the Governors: D W Jones, LLB

Bursar and Assistant Clerk to the Governors:
J W Parker, MIMgt

Office of the Governors, Orchard Street, College Green, Bristol BS1 5EQ (*Tel:* 9290084)

Staff:
***Headmaster:* S W Holliday**, MA

Deputy Headmaster: D H I Cook, MA

Director of Studies: J G Sykes, BSc

Miss J L Aaron, BEng
R Armstrong, BEng
R M A Batchelor, BSc
D M Bateson, BA
Miss N L Baulch, BSc
Mrs F Bean, BEd
M Beet, MA
Mrs L Benson, BEd
J F Brown, BSc
S Bryant, BMus, ARCO
A C M Clements, BSc
T Clements, BA, MA
Mrs S Cosgrove, BSc
R Dixon, BSc
W J Earp, MA
W R Ellis, BSc
Mrs A G Gardner, BEd
J Harford, BSc
Mrs D M Holladay, BA, BPhil
R Houchin, BA
A Hughes, BSc
W C R Husband, MA
D D Jenkins, BSc, PhD
P M Jones, BA
P W Jones, BEd, BPhil
R J Jones, BMus, FRCO, LRAM
P E Joslin, BEd
P J Kirby, BA
C Knight, BEd
Mrs J M Lawrence, BSc
A G Lewis-Barned, BEd
Mrs K Lewis-Barned, BEd, MEd
N Loudon, BA
Mrs S Maltin, BA
J F Mason, BA
P S Mayfield, BA
H Payne, BSc
A Pearson, MA
J D Perkins, MA
Mrs S Pole, BA
D Richards, BSc
P Robson, BA
S P Ryan, BSocSc (*Boarding Housemaster*)
D E Stainer, BA
D A Straun, BA
J N Webster, BSc
Mrs S A Winterson, BA, MA

Visiting Teachers:
Mrs J Browne, LRAM
D Bryant
Mrs C Garland, ATCL, LAMDA
Mrs J George, BA
P Gittings, BSc
S Gore
Miss K Hardman, GRSM
Mrs D Lee, BA
Miss R Phipps, BA
Miss R Stephen
Miss M Thomas, FLCM, ARCM
Mrs M Walker, BA, LTCL
Mrs M Wills, GRSM

Chaplain: The Revd S B Taylor, BA

Headmaster's Secretary: Mrs E Davies

Librarian: P W Jones, BEd, BPhil

Matron: Mrs B A Barlow, BA, SRN, ONC

Medical Officer: Dr B Dunning, MB, ChB, DRCOG

School Marshal: C Wain, BEM

Admission. There are 540 boys in the School, ranging in age from 11 to 18. 60 are boarders and 480 are day boys. Entrance examinations for both 11-plus and 13-plus applicants are held early each year.

Term of Entry. Usually September.

Entrance Scholarships. (*see* Entrance Scholarship section) There are six scholarships to the value of half the tuition fee, four at 11+ and 2 at 13+. These are awarded purely on academic merit for outstanding achievement in the entrance procedures and may carry with them generous assistance for applicants whose parents' means are limited.

Assisted Places. There are many School assisted places for day and boarding applicants. The School has a substantial foundation income and is able to give generous support both to day boys and boarders whose parents' means are limited.

Music Scholarships. Two music scholarships to the value of half the full tuition fee and also free tuition in two instruments are available, one at 11-plus and one at 13-plus. In addition, there is one music scholarship at 11-plus carrying free tuition in two instruments.

Buildings. The School was originally close by the City Centre, but was moved to new premises on Brandon Hill in 1847. A major building and improvement programme, started in 1975 and included new Science laboratories and a new classroom block, a gymnasium with two squash courts, new art and music centres, the acquisition of new playing fields of 18 acres at Failand and the building there of a large pavilion. A new sixth form study and recreation centre was built during 1986 and further staff accommodation was provided. In 1988 the senior boarding accommodation was entirely rebuilt to provide study bedrooms for boys from Year 7 upwards. In 1990 the School completed the building of a theatre and the Technology Department opened in 1992. New Mathematics rooms and further boarding facilities were provided in 1994. Information Technology moved to a new suite in 1997 and the Art School was refurbished in 2000.

Curriculum. Boys are prepared for the GCSE and GCE 'A' level, and for university entrance. The usual school subjects are offered at GCSE level, and the AS/A2 level subjects are: English, Theatre Studies, Economics, Latin, Classical Civilisation, History, Geography, French, German, Art, Music, Mathematics, Further Mathematics, Physics, Chemistry, Biology and Sports Studies. Advanced subsidiary subjects include Drama, Spanish, IT, Electronics and Politics.

Music. There is a School Orchestra, Choir, Brass Group and Wind Band. Music is included in the timetable for all the junior forms. GCSE and 'A' level music is part of the School curriculum, and tuition is arranged for a wide range of instruments. The Choir and Instrumentalists perform regularly and also undertake joint ventures with the independent girls' schools in Bristol.

Art. The Department is well equipped and includes a ceramics section.

Religious Studies. This forms part of the school curriculum. On Sundays the boarders attend a short service at the Lord Mayor's Chapel, and the School Chaplain prepares candidates for confirmation. The School has, however, no official religious affiliation and receives boys of all faiths.

Games. Rugby Football, Soccer, Athletics, Cricket, Hockey, Swimming, Tennis, Badminton, Sailing, Squash, Archery and Fencing.

Dress. Boarders wear the traditional bluecoat uniform on special occasions. Day boys wear either grey flannel trousers and a blazer or a plain grey suit.

General. All parents are encouraged to join the Friends of Queen Elizabeth's Hospital, a society whose aim is to promote a close relationship between parents and staff and to further the welfare of the School. There is a flourishing Old Boy's Society (Secretary: Mr J Moody), which holds regular meetings and circulates a news letter. A panel of Old Boys, formed from all professions, and working with the Careers Master, is available to give advice on careers to boys.

The School has long been known in Bristol as The City School and its links with the Lord Mayor and Corporation are strong. The boarders read the lessons and sing in the Lord Mayor's Chapel, and groups are in attendance for such occasions as Mayor-making and Council Prayers.

The central position of the School, close to the University, the Art Gallery and Museum, the Central Library, the Bristol Old Vic and the Colston Hall, affords ready access to a wide range of cultural facilities which boys are encouraged to use.

Fees. Boarders £3,433 a term, Weekly Boarding £3,123, Day £1,863 a term. Fees include text-books and stationery.

Charitable status. Queen Elizabeth's Hospital is a Registered Charity, number 311732. Queen Elizabeth's Hospital has existed since 1590 to provide an education for boys.

Queen's College, Taunton

Trull Road Taunton Somerset TA1 4QS
Tel: (01823) 272559
Fax: (01823) 338430
e-mail: admissions@queenscollege.org.uk
website: http://www.queenscollege.org.uk

Queen's College is one of the South West's leading independent day and boarding co-educational schools. There is a consistent record of high achievement with the 2000 'A' level results showing an average pass rate of 96% - 100% in 15 subjects. In the same year, an average GCSE pass rate of over 93% was achieved. 45.8% of all papers taken were graded A*/A and 67 of the 91 candidates each gained 9 or 10 A, B, C grade passes.

Although strong in all academic subjects, Queen's expertise also shows in music, drama and the arts. It is not uncommon to see pupils selected for the National Youth Theatre and the National Youth Orchestra.

Queen's College has a well-deserved reputation for the quality of its teaching and all pupils are cared for in small tutor groups. The staff work untiringly to encourage students to develop their personal skills and abilities. The class sizes are well below the national average thus helping develop a friendly, supportive environment. Emphasis is also placed on participation in the Duke of Edinburgh's Award Scheme. All students do Bronze, many do Silver, 90 are currently doing Gold.

The school is controlled by the Board of Management for Methodist Residential Schools and receives pupils of all denominations.

Motto: *Non scholae sed vitae discimus. (We learn not for school but for life).*

Visitor: The President of the Methodist Conference.

Governors:
Chairman: R E Lintott, MA

Rev N J Baker
C J Cutting, FRCS
Revd D G Deeks, MA
J Downton, MA
A Dyke, BA, BArch, RIBA
D R Evans, MA
Mrs H Foster, JP
Dr J M Gibbs, MA, MLitt
Capt P M Gowen, RN
Mrs M Hannam
N Harvey, MP
Rev K S J Hext, MA
T H Lang, FRICS
S A Lawson
L Oldham, FDS, RCS(Eng)
M F Powell, FRICS, FAAW
G Russell, MA
Maj Gen M F L Shellard, CBE
J C G Stocks
P F Watkinson, MA

Honorary Governor: The President of the Old Queenians' Association

***Headmaster:* Christopher J Alcock**, BSc (Hatfield College, Durham)

Chaplain: Revd Robert J Blackhall, BSc, BA (Exeter & Bristol)

Bursar & Clerk to Governors: Andrew S Murray, BSc, CGIA

Domestic Bursar: Ian G Dyer

Admissions: Anne Slocum

Secretary to Headmaster: Wendy Harding

Medical Officers:
Dr David Downs
Dr Gabrielle de Cothi

Sister: Susan Littlejohns, RGN, DNCert

SENIOR SCHOOL:

Deputy Headmaster: Marcus K Paul, BA, MA (Durham & Newcastle)

Deputy Headmistress: Gillian S Paltridge, BEd (Bristol)

Director of Studies: Graham Warner, BSc (Durham)

Staff:
Mandy Adams, BA
Donna Ashman, BA
D Ralph Bates, BEd
Anthony F Bell, BSc
Peter J Bell, BA
Stephen C Bell, MA, FRCO(CHM)
Geoffrey Bisson, BA
Martin G Bream, BA, MIBiol
Vivien Bream, BA, MEd (Psych)
Patricia Burton, BA
John C Chidgey, BA
Carol A Cole, BA
Peter D Cole, DipAD
David J Cooke, BSc
Paul G J M De Jaegar, BSc
Anthony Darby, BSc
Michael Fletcher, BSc
Andrew S Free, BA
Andrew Garton, BA
Keith A Gibbs, BSc
Cherry Grant, CertEd
Sarah J Green
Lindsay Hall, BA
Angus Hamilton, BA
Julie Harrison, BEd
David S Hedges, BA
Lisa Henden, BSc
Timothy P Jolliff, MA
Rhian Jones, BSc
Susan A Lee-Smith, BA
Byron Lewis, MSc
Nigel P Lincoln, BA, MA
Hugh Livesey, BSc
Jennie Lloyd, BEd
Grace Mainstone, BA, LRSM, LTCL
Philip Mann, MNASC
John H Marshall, MA
John J E Marston, BA
Carole Mason, BEd
Christopher Monks, BSc
Ian E Morrell, BEd
Mark Neenan, BEd
Sheila Platt, CertEd
Rachel Poole, BEng
Roger Priest, BA
Jennifer M Robinson, BA
Simon R J Ross, BA
Alan F Sawyer, BA
Angela Snow, DipDolm
Leslie R Stevens, BSc
Michael J Turner, BSc, PhD, CChem, FRSC
Peter J Vicary, BSc
Graham H Warner, BSc
Gillian Watson, BEd
Keith Wheatley, BA
Richard B Wilde, BEd
Michael A Williams, BA, MA
Emily Wiser, BSc

There are 18 visiting music staff.

JUNIOR SCHOOL:

Headmaster: Peter N Lee-Smith, BA

Amanda Adams, BA
Patricia Camera, CertEd
Susan Howard, CertEd
Barbara Johnson, CertEd
Avril Lowes, BEd
Julia Luard, MBDA
Vicky Miller, DipEd
Marion Parr, BSc, MSc
Mervyn K Roberts, CertEd, BEd
Sarah Scutt, BA, MA
David W Sharpe, MA
Michael Stanion, BA
Terence M Stirzaker, CertEd
Margaret Way, LRAM, LGSM, ALAM, AM
Richard B Wilde, BEd

PRE-PREPARATORY SCHOOL:

Headmistress: Elizabeth A Gibbs, CertEd

Diana Henry, CertEd
Sarah Warner, BEd

NURSERY SCHOOL:
Elizabeth Hayes, NNEB, DPQS
Rosemary Wilson, BA

Secretary: Julie Cameron

Number of Pupils. The Queen's College Pre-Preparatory, Junior and Senior co-educational schools are based on the same site with some facilities shared: continuity of education is assured.

The Senior school (11 to 18 years) has 490 pupils of whom 170 are boarders. The Junior school (7 to 11 years) has 135 pupils, of whom 18 board and the Pre-Prep school has a total of 47 pupils (none of whom are boarders). The full College complement of pupils for 2000/2001 is therefore 672. Nursery pupils are additional, attendance being a mix of full and part time.

Situation and Buildings. Queen's College was founded in 1843 within Taunton's Castle walls but was relocated to the south western outskirts of Taunton three years later when the present main school buildings were constructed. It is in a good situation with fine views of the Quantock and Blackdown Hills, within easy reach of Exmoor and Dartmoor, just a mile and a half from Taunton town centre and easily accessible by road or rail, junction 25 of M5 is 2 miles away.

The 1846 original Grade II* listed building contained a School House, the School Hall and a Dining Room. Later a Junior School was added, an indoor heated Swimming Pool and a Music Department.

Over the last twenty years there has been an extensive building programme which has included: nine classrooms for the Junior school, applied science, computer and electronics centre, design area, new changing rooms, day girl and day boy accommodation, enlargement and modernisation of girl and boy boarding houses, school hall for the Junior school, new music school, concert/assembly hall for the Senior school and CDT block. Latest additions are new Sixth Form Centre and, this year, a new Science Block. is about to commence.

Organisation. At Queen's College continuity of education is assured from the Nursery, to Pre-Preparatory and Junior schools and then into the Senior school. As from September 1999 the move from Junior to Senior changed from 12 to 11 years of age.

There are two day boy houses and two day girl houses and each has a House Master/Mistress and assistants. There are two boys' boarding houses and two girls' boarding houses and each is in the care of a House Master and wife together with a resident assistant House Master/Mistress. Tutors are attached to each house and are responsible for academic work. They guide each student through GCSE and 'A' Level choices and in conjunction with one of the Careers Masters and the Director of Studies, the tutor advises them on university selection and choice of career.

Curriculum. To avoid premature specialisation all pupils in the first two years follow a general course of education. In the years preceding GCSE a choice of subjects or 'options' can be made according to interest and level of ability. All take a common core of which religious studies, an art/craft based subject and computer work form a part. Pupils are in sets for mathematics and languages and other subjects are taken in forms which are kept low in number. In the Sixth Form three subjects are studied for 'A' and 'AS' Level from four groups of subjects. The fourth group is devoted to subjects outside a pupil's main field of study.

Out of School Activities. As part of the school routine all members of the lower and middle schools are required to take three occupations per week and time is set aside for clubs such as debating, bridge, computer, chess, photography, radio, or societies such as history, geography or scientific. There is always a large group taking Duke of Edinburgh Awards and over 260 Queen's pupils have now achieved their Gold Award.

The Art and Design Centre provides for art, woodwork, pottery, screen printing, fabric work, dressmaking, plastics and metalwork.

Music and Drama. There is an orchestra of over sixty, a large choir, madrigal group and band. The Music school has excellent facilities and is very well situated. There is a strong tradition of drama and the club offers two major productions a year as well as entering local festivals in drama and dance.

PE/Games. The playing fields of Queen's are both extensive and adaptable: we have 30 acres to use. In the Autumn term the grass area forms 5 rugby pitches and a small hockey pitch. The Spring term sees most of these being converted to hockey pitches; however, 2 rugby pitches remain for Rugby Sevens.

The Summer term makes maximum use of the grass

area: 2 grass volleyball courts, a 400m athletics track and numerous rounders and cricket pitches.

The two artificial playing areas are very frequently used. Both the Astroturf and the red gravel pitch are used for hockey daily in the Autumn and Spring terms and are of such quality that Queen's has often been called upon to host County hockey tournaments. Both pitches are converted to tennis courts in the Summer, the Astroturf containing 12 courts. In the Summer this gives us a total of 24 tennis courts.

The hard court surface in the middle of the field is used for netball in the Spring term and for tennis in the Autumn and Summer terms. Alongside this area are cricket nets for use in the Summer term.

The Sports Hall is used for the following activities: gymnastics, trampolining, basketball, badminton, volleyball, indoor hockey and indoor tennis. There are 2 squash courts adjoining the Sports Hall, a multigym and table tennis tables on the balcony overlooking it. Within the complex is an indoor heated pool that is used at various times for swimming from Pre-Prep through to Sixth Form lessons. Team swimming, canoeing and sub aqua are regular activities throughout the year.

Admission. Education at Queen's can start at 2½ years on entry to the Nursery. The majority of pupils join the Pre-Preparatory school from the age of 4 years. Junior school pupils start at age 7. Entrance is by examination and those who are successful in gaining places to the Junior school transfer without further test to the Senior school. There are places for boys and girls at the age of 13 from Preparatory schools who take the Common Entrance examination. A limited number enter the Sixth Form direct on GCSE Level results.

Scholarships. (*see* Entrance Scholarship section) 11+ and 10+ (Music only) scholarships are awarded in January, 13+ in February/March and Sixth Form in November. Academic Scholarships by examination – half, third or quarter fees for students of proven academic ability in one or more subjects. Up to 8 day and 5 boarding academic scholarships for students aged 8+, 11+ and 13+ on 1 September in year of entry. Eight Sixth Form scholarships are also on offer.

Music Scholarships – half, third or quarter fees for the most gifted scholars including free tuition in one or two instruments. Up to 8 scholarships for talented musicians aged 10+, 11+, 12+ and 13+ at the projected time of entry to the college. Three Sixth Form entry scholarships are also available plus an Organ award.

Sports Scholarships – half, third or quarter fees for students of best ability. Up to 6 scholarships for talented students with proven sports ability aged 11+ and 13+ at the projected time of entry to the college. Sixth form scholarships included.

Fees per term 2000/2001. Pre-Preparatory school £852 to £885 (day pupils only); Day Pupils Junior from £963 to £1,821; Boarders Junior from £1,968 to £2,845. Day Pupils Senior £2,280-£2,652; Boarders Senior £3,459-£4,047. These fees include all necessary expenses: books, stationery etc.

Charitable status. Queen's College, Taunton is a Registered Charity, number 310208. The College is a leading Charitable Trust in the field of Junior and Secondary education.

* Head of Department § Part Time or Visiting
† Housemaster/Housemistress ¶ Old Pupil
‡ See below list of staff for meaning

Radley College

Abingdon Oxon. OX14 2HR
Tel: (01235) 543127 (Warden); 543122 (Bursar); 543000 (General Enquiries)
Fax: (01235) 543106
website: www.radley.org.uk

St Peter's College, Radley, was founded by the Rev William Sewell, Fellow of Exeter College, Oxford, to provide an independent school education on the principles of the Church of England. It was opened on 9 June 1847, and incorporated by Royal Charter in 1890. It stands in a park of some 700 acres.

Motto: *Sicut Serpentes, sicut Columbae.*

Visitor: The Rt Revd The Lord Bishop of Oxford

Chairman: M E L Melluish, OBE, MA

Council:
J H Pattisson, MA (*Vice-Chairman*)
J W Tapner, LLB
W A B Smellie, BA, FRCS
I A Balding, LVO
C G Clarke, FCA
M E Hodgson, MA, ARICS
R E Morris Adams
D A Peck, MA
The Rt Revd D H Bartleet, MA
Sir Richard Wilson, GCB, LLB, MA
T O Seymour, MA
J P Barron, MA, DPhil, FSA
M J W Rushton, BA
R C B Henson, BA
A L Robinson
J C Hedger, CB, MA
Sir Tim Rice

***Warden:* A W McPhail**, MA

Sub-Warden: H H Aird, MA

Director of Studies: A E Reekes, MA

Second Master: C J Butterworth, MA

Assistant Masters:
J K Mullard, BA
R Pollard, MA
J P Wylie, BA
M J Harris, MA
C W Hastings, MA
M F Dean, BA
†M J S Hopkins, BA (*E Social*)
A C Wallis, BSc, PhD
G Wiseman, BA
J C Nye, MA
C R Barker, BA
P Russell, MA, DPhil
J F le Manac'h, BA
V S Clements, BSc
C A Milward, MA
†B J Holden, BTech (*D Social*)
M R Wright, BSc
J R Summerly, BA, PhD
R J Freeman, BA
Mrs J A Wright, BA
W J Bamforth, BA
†R A Holroyd, MA (*B Social*)
M P Horsey, CertEd
J F C Nash, MA
S Rathbone, BA
P W Gamble, MA
I P Ellis, BA, DipRASchls
R E Schofield, MA
†W J Wesson, BA (*A Social*)
S Barlass, BA
†I R Davenport, BA (*F Social*)
A J McChesney, BSc
Mrs A C Steer, MA
C M Bedford, BA, PhD
Mrs M E H Craig, BA
N Murphy, BA
I S Yorston, MA
D P Corran, BA
R M C Greed, BSc
†H D Hammond, BSc (*G Social*)
M J Moore, MA
N W K Morgan, MA
†S C I Jones, BA, MSc (*C Social*)
Mrs C D Sargent, MA, ALA (*Librarian*)
W O C Matthews, BA
T R G Ryder, BA, MFA
†D C K Edwards, MA (*H Social*)
R A King, BSc, MRSC, CChem
S A Thorn, BSc, PhD
R A Ball, MA
J M Sparks, BSc
Miss J A Lueck, BA
S A Hall, BA, MPhil, PhD
S E Hearsey, BSc
N J Weaver, BA
M K T Hindley, MA

M V Hubbard
Miss R A Pickup, BA
Miss F M C Church, BA, MPhil
M R Jewell, BA
Mrs J A L Longworth, BA (*Foundation Director*)
E J Wolstenholme, BSc, PhD
L G Bartlett, BA
M G Bemand, MMath
F E J Wawn, MA
R Johnson, BSc
J R W Beasley, MA
J S Whitehead, MA, MPhil, PhD
C R Martin, BA
J G Power, BA
Mrs E C Williams, BA
I K Campbell, BA
Mrs S Pullen, BA
E B S Bowles, MEng

Chaplain: The Revd Canon R A Stidolph, GBSM, ARCM, ABSM

Assistant Chaplain: The Revd P F Boyden, BSc, AKC, MA, MLitt

Music:
Precentor: J Madden, MA, LRAM, LMusTCL
A J A Williams, MMus, DipRAM, GRSM, LRAM
Miss S-L Naylor, MA

There are 26 peripatetic music staff.

Bursar and Secretary: R P L Beauchamp, BA, MICE

Medical Officer: Dr D M Otterburn, MB, BS, MRCP

General Arrangements. There are 620 boys in the School. On admission, boys enter one of the 8 houses known as Socials. Two of the Socials are 'in-College'; the other 6 are close together within the grounds. All meals are served in Hall on a cafeteria system.

Admission to the School. Boys are admitted between the ages of 13 and 14 in the Michaelmas Term, and qualify by taking either the Common Entrance Examination or the Entrance Scholarship Examination. Entrance forms can be obtained from the Warden's Secretary. All entries are made through the Warden. A registration fee of £50 is payable when a boy's name is entered. This fee is not returnable. Registration does not guarantee a place in the School. Three years before a boy is due to come, a Final Acceptance Form will be sent to parents for whose sons a place can be guaranteed. An Entrance Fee of £300 is payable on acceptance.

Entrance Awards. (*see* Entrance Scholarship section) Up to fifteen Entrance Scholarships and Exhibitions, varying in value from half fees to £1,000 a year are offered for competition in February or March. Scholarships for instrumental playing, one of half fees, one of up to half fees, two of one-third fees and one of one-quarter fees, and several Exhibitions are offered annually. Two Art Scholarships, of half fees and £500 pa, are also offered, as are two Sports Awards, each of quarter fees. Candidates must be under 14 on 31st August in the calendar year in which they sit the examination. All awards may be supplemented by a bursary in case of financial need.

'Latymer' Bursaries for sons of country clergymen in the Diocese of Oxford are available from time to time. Particulars are available from the Warden.

In addition to the above, a number of Bursaries have been endowed by the War Memorial Fund. Preference is given to the sons of Old Radleians. Application should be made to the Hon Secretary of the Fund: A E Money, Radley College.

Work. In the Shells, Removes and Vth Forms the usual general subjects are taught.

In the VIth Form a boy can specialise in a combination of Classics, Modern Languages, English, History, Geography, Geology, Science subjects, Mathematics, Economics, Music, Art or Design, leading to AS/A2 examinations.

Careers. Advice and assistance is available to all boys on a wide range of career possibilities through the Careers Master. The School is a member of ISCO (The Independent Schools Careers Organisation) and close connections are maintained with the professions, with firms and with the Services. Visits and talks by experts in these fields are a special feature.

Games. In the Michaelmas term Rugby Football is the School game. In the other 2 terms the 'wet-bobs' row; the 'dry-bobs' play Hockey and Soccer in the Lent term, Cricket, Athletics and Tennis in the Summer.

The playing fields are close to the main buildings.

The College has its own boathouse, and the use of a stretch of the river Thames below Nuneham Courtenay. The VIII's compete in the appropriate regattas.

There are two all-weather Hockey Pitches, 3 soccer pitches, an Athletics Track, 5 Squash Courts, a Rackets Court, 2 covered Fives Courts, 20 Hard Tennis Courts and a 9-hole golf course. There is a large, well-equipped Gymnasium and an indoor, heated Swimming Pool attached to a multi-purpose Sports Hall. All these sports are represented by School teams and there is also a Sailing team. Swimming and Judo are taught by fully qualified instructors. Boys may play Real Tennis in the court in Oxford.

The College has a pack of beagles which hunts twice a week during the winter months.

CCF. All boys, in their third or fourth term, join the Radley College Contingent, Combined Cadet Force (Army, Navy and Air Sections). They work for the Proficiency examination, which can take up to 4 terms. When they have passed Proficiency and done a week's Corps Camp in the holidays they may opt out of the Corps or stay on in a special section for further training. Over 20 options are open to those who opt out of the Corps. These include such activities as Social Services, Computing, Electronics, Photography and Printing.

School Charges. The fees are £16,410 pa (inclusive of Medical Attendance). Lessons in Pianoforte, and other musical instruments are given at a charge of £17.20 a lesson. There is available a system of insurance against loss of fees caused by illness, accident, or infection. Particulars can be obtained from the Bursar.

Charitable status. St Peter's College, Radley is a Registered Charity, number 309243. It exists for the purpose of the education of youth in general knowledge and literature and particularly and especially in the doctrines and principles of the Church of England.

Ratcliffe College

Fosse Way Ratcliffe on the Wreake Leicester Leicestershire LE7 4SG.
Tel. School Office: (01509) 817000;
Headmaster: (01509) 817006
Fax: (01509) 817004
e-mail: registrar@ratcliffe.leics.sch.uk
website: ratcliffecollege.com

The School was founded in 1844 and opened in 1847; the original buildings by A W Pugin were erected with funds provided by Lady Mary Arundel of Wardour, who also bequeathed money for subsequent extensions.

Motto: *Legis plenitudo charitas.*

Governing Body:
The Provincial and Consultors of the Rosminian Order, who act as permanent governors together with additional governors who hold office for a period; the present additional governors are:

R Brucciani, OBE, DL
R W Gamble
Dr R Graham-Brown

B N Kennedy
M Linnett
Mrs A Niland
Lady A-M Ralph Kerr
Professor M Scott (*Chairman*)
A R Weston

***Headmaster:* ¶Mr P Farrar**, MA

Deputy Head: Mrs J P Clayfield, BSc Hons

Senior Teachers:
Mrs T Gamble, BEd
G J Sharpe, BA, MBA
Dr P Tickle, BTech, MEd, PhD, MRSC, CChem

Rector: Fr P Sainter, BSc, BPhil, MA, STL

Chaplain: Sister A P Pereira, CTC

Bursar: A Nutter, BSc, ARICS

Teaching Staff:
Mrs J Ackerley, BA
Miss K Alexander, BSc
Mrs L D Arnold, BSc, MPhil
R Ayton, BA
M Balmbra, BSc (*o/c Army Section*)
*P Banks, BA (*Media Studies, English*)
Mrs P Bentley, BA
Mrs E A Boldrin, BA
Miss L Brown, BA
*Dr M Burns, BSc, MSc, PhD (*Biology*)
Miss J A Callaghan, BA
Mrs C Caven-Henry, AISTD
*Mrs S Clay, BA (*Special Needs Co-ordinator*)
*Mrs S Cushing, BA (*Languages*)
T B Davis, DipArch, RIBA (*Head of Year 9*)
Mrs C L Dwyer, BA
A K Dziemianko, BSc
Mrs L Eccles, BA
*J Echevarría, BA, MA (*Religious Studies*)
Mrs C Freeman, CertEd
J A Green, BEd, MEd
Mrs M Hanks, BSc (*Head of Year 10*)
*G Higham, BSc (*Mathematics*)
R M Hughes, BA, QTS
*M P Jones, BA (*Director of Music*)
*O P Jones, BA (*Physical Education*)
J C Lillywhite, BA, MA, DPhil
*S M Lomax, MA, BSc (*Physics*)
P McCrindell, BA (*Head of Year 11*)
*H C Midgley, BA, MEd, JP (*Information Technology/ Assistant Director of Studies*)
C S Millar, BSc
Miss K A Newton, BMus
Mme A Oliviero
Mrs C M J Peel, BEd
Mrs S Rankine, BEd (*Head of Nursery & Reception*)
*S Richardson, BA (*Art and Design*)
Mrs S M Roberts, BA
Mrs L Robinson, BA
Mrs V Robinson, BA
J Satterthwaite, NDD, ATD
M Sleath, BSc (*Head of Year 12*)
Mrs H Smith, BSc
*T Stanford, BA, BEd, MA, MEd (*English*)
Mrs C Stocks
Mrs S Strutt, BSc
*Mrs A Taylor, BEd (*Director of Sport & Activities*)
N Taylor, BEd (*Boys Boarding Master*)
*R W Thomas, BSc (*Economics/Careers*)
*Mrs K Tomlinson, BA Hons (*History*)
N J Walsh, LLB
Miss R Warner, BSc
*P R Watson, BSc (*Geography*)
Mrs E White, BSc
I White, BEng
Mrs S A Worsnop, BSc
Miss A Wright, BA

Medical Officer: Dr T Jennings

Senior Nursing Sisters:
Mrs V Bowman, RGN
Mrs J Galbraith-Marten, RGN
Mrs G Myring, RGN

Librarian: Mrs G C Burton, BLibStud

Laboratory Technicians:
Mrs A Heywood, MISCT
Mrs S Widger

The Preparatory School: Grace Dieu Manor, is a separate establishment near Whitwick. It houses some 345 boys and girls. (Headmaster: Mr D Hare, BA).

Aims and Organisation. The first aim of Ratcliffe College is to provide a deeply Christian environment in which each pupil may develop his or her talents generously for the glory of God and in the service of the Community and in so doing achieve happiness.

The School is fairly small so that the religious community, the lay staff, and the boys and girls form a close-knit family. Interest in each individual is furthered by arranging the School into year groups each under the care of a Master and his assistant for the boys, and House Mistresses for day and boarding girls, helped, in the Main School, by prefects and monitors. Priests from the Community act as chaplains to each of the year groups.

The discipline of the School is under the general supervision of the Deputy Head: the main end to which discipline is directed is the right use of liberty and the development of character and personality.

The pupils are also organised into Houses, but these function chiefly in the field of games.

Admission. There are currently 572 pupils in the School, of whom one-third are girls and over 100 are boarders. The age of entrants (boys and girls) is currently 3-18. Boarding girls and boys are accommodated in separate wings and are under the supervision of a resident House-mistress/Housemaster. The 13-year-olds coming from Preparatory Schools are required to pass the Common Entrance Examination. Other entrants are required to sit an appropriate entrance examination for their age group set by the school. Applicants to enter the Sixth Form must have satisfactory GCSEs.

Term of Entry. Pupils are admitted in all terms.

Fees. The fully inclusive boarding fee for the Summer Term 2001 is £3,838. This fee is subject to such termly increase as may prove necessary. There is a registration fee of £50. Additional charges are made for private music lessons and for Home Economics provisions.

Entrance Scholarships. (*see* Entrance Scholarship section) Academic awards are offered annually at 11, which are held for two years, reviewed at the age of 13. The papers are aimed to assess basic literacy, numeracy and intelligence, and can be tackled by any pupil who has followed a normal junior school curriculum.

The basic subjects of the 13+ Scholarship examination are English, History, French, Mathematics, Science and a general paper.

Candidates are encouraged to attempt the Scholarship papers at about 13 and allowance is made for boys and girls who are on the young side.

Candidates must be over 12½ and under 14 years of age on 1st May. Entries must be in by 31 January. Additional scholarships are offered for Sport, Music and Art at the discretion of the Headmaster. Forces and sibling discounts are also available.

In the Sixth Form, Scholarships are awarded to pupils who show outstanding results at GCSE.

Further particulars can be obtained from The Registrar, Ratcliffe College, Fosse Way, Ratcliffe on the Wreake Leicester LE7 4SG.

Site and Buildings. The College is situated on the A46 7 miles north of Leicester. The main buildings surround a quadrangle and contain the School Chapel, dormitories, Art Department, Library, dining hall and recreation rooms. The Computer Centre is also housed in the main buildings together with a media and editing suite. A complex of buildings nearby houses the majority of the classrooms arranged in sets of 3 or 4 to accommodate the boys and girls in each of the pre-GCSE years. There is also a centre containing further classrooms, five Science Laboratories, Home Economics, Language Centre and History specialist rooms. Close to these are an extensive Music department with its own Concert Hall, and a Sports complex comprising of a multi-purpose Hall, Gymnasium, covered heated Swimming pool and Baspograss all-weather pitch. There is a Design Technology Centre where pupils can study all aspects of art and design, including computer aided design, ceramics, art and the history of art. The Theatre is reserved for lectures and dramatic productions. Each year group in the Main School has the use of three recreation rooms: the Sixth Form has its own recreation centre. There are study bedrooms for Fourth, Fifth and Sixth Form pupils. 'The Newman', a purpose-built Junior block provides younger day pupils up to Year 7 with the extra care and attention they require. The Junior Department while having its own separate area, uses all the facilities of the Main School. As part of the Governors' development plan, a Year 5 class for 9-year-olds and a Nursery School for children aged 3–5 opened in September 1998, and was followed by Year 1 and Year 4 classes in 1999. Classes for children in Years 2 and 3 now complete the provision for children aged 5-11 in the Junior department.

Studies. The School prepares boys and girls for universities and colleges of higher education, and provides a sound training for any business career. Up to GCSE there are three or four sets in each core subject, the aim being to cater as far as possible for the individual requirements and capabilities of boys and girls at every stage within a flexible system, but without specialisation below the Sixth Form. A wide range of option subjects is available. In the Sixth Form it is possible to study a wide variety of combinations of subjects. In 1999, GNVQs in Computing and Business Studies were introduced. The majority of Sixth Form boys and girls proceed each year to various universities.

Careers. There is a fully equipped Careers Room and five members of staff have special responsibility for careers advice. The School is a member of the Independent Schools Careers Organisation.

Games and other activities. The playing fields cover about 100 acres which surround the School buildings. The major School games include Rugby Football, Hockey, Netball, Cricket, Tennis, Swimming and Athletics. The School has a 'Baspograss' all weather hockey pitch, covered heated swimming pool and offers a wide range of evening, Saturday morning and weekend activities.

The School has a School Choir and two Bands. Crafts and Hobbies are encouraged and there are various clubs and societies. Dramatic productions take place regularly. The School runs a CCF contingent, offering both Army and RAF contingents, a Scout Group, and a Voluntary Service Unit. Students also participate in the Duke of Edinburgh Award Scheme.

Charitable status. Ratcliffe College is a Registered Charity, number 527850, founded for the education of children.

Reading Blue Coat School

Holme Park Sonning Berks, RG4 6SU
Tel: 0118 944 1005
Fax: 0118 944 2690
e-mail: headsec@blue-coat.reading.sch.uk

The School was founded in 1646 by Richard Aldworth, a merchant of London and Reading, and a Governor of Christ's Hospital. It is governed by the Trustees of Reading Municipal Church Charities. There are 600 pupils (aged 11–18) including a co-educational Sixth Form. The School is situated in 46 acres of grounds and riverside woods near the village of Sonning, four miles east of Reading and within easy access to Heathrow and the M4, M3 and M40.

Visitors to Trustees:

Vice-Chancellor of Oxford University
President of St John's College
Warden of All Souls' College

Chairman of Governors: B S Walsh

***Headmaster:* S James W McArthur**, BSc, MA, CertEd, FCollP

Deputy Headmaster: G J Best, BA, PGCE
Second Deputy: P E Firebrace, CertEd, BA
Senior Tutor: J M Storey, CertEd, BEd (*CNAA*)
Academic Director: A R W Taylor, BSc, MSc, PGCE, MIBiol
Staff Tutor: Mrs C Sams, CertEd

Staff:

Mrs S M Adams, BA, PGCE
M J Baker, BA, PGCE
Mrs A Bawden, BA, PGCE
A I Beddoe, CertEd
Mrs L J Bennett, BEd
Revd N J Bennett, DipTheol, CertPastCoun, BA (*Chaplain*)
Mrs C L Black, BA, PGCE
P S Bodinetz, BA, PGCE (*Registrar*)
J Bowler, BA, PGCE, LTCL, ARCM (*Director of Music*)
A T Brown, BSc, CertEd
J P Brown, BSc, PGCE
D Brunt, BSc, PGCE, MSc
J D Bruce, BSc, DipEIA, PGCE
S D Burke, LaCompl, PGCE
S J Cook, BA, CertEd
D N Cottrell, CertEd
Dr S Crook, BSc, PhD, PGCE
Dr S M Dimmick, BSc, MSc, DipEd, PhD
R N Ennis, BA, PGCE
W M L Evans, BA, PGCE
A T Fowler, BA, MA, PGCE
J F M Gooddy, MA, PGCE
Mrs S A Head, MA
J S Holdaway, BEng (Hons), PGCE
Mrs M J Holden, BEd, MIITT
I P Holleley, BA (*Director of Arts and Culture*)
E R Hooper, BA, MA, DipEd, GDIESE
J S Imeson, CertEd
Mrs K S Lambert, BA, PGCE
R W A Line, MA, FRCO, PGCE
A J Maddocks, BA
G H Martin, BSc, PGCE
Miss I Matteudi, L et Maît d'Anglais, PGCE
T B Nutt, BSc, PGCE, MIBiol
T R O'Brien, BSc, PGCE, ARCS
A M Pett, BSc, PGCE
Mrs S A Price, MA
P A Reedman, BLib, PGCE
Mrs L J Richardson, BA
S S Roberts, BSc, PGCE
Mrs C Ross, BA, PGCE
S W Sadler, BA
D L Salmon, MA, ComputingDip, PGCE
Dr F Santos, BSc, MSc, PhD
D H R Selvester, BA, PGCE
Mrs L R I Smart, BA, PGCE
Mrs J P Smith, BSc, PGCE
Mrs H Taylor, BSc (Hons), PGCE
Mrs J Turton, BSc, PGCE
T C Walford, BSc, PGCE
R J Wallis, BA
P J van Went, MA, CertEd

Miss T van der Werff, MA, PGCE
M D Wadsworth, BSc (Hons), PGCE
D C Williams, BA, PGCE
Mrs J Warwick, BA, ALA (*Librarian*)

Bursar: J G E Jacob, BSc (Hons), MIMgt
Headmaster's Secretary: Mrs R H Grimmett
Admissions Secretary: Mrs V M Frost
School Nurses:
Mrs L Chandler, BSc (Hons), RGN, RSCN
Mrs G F Montgomery, RGN

Aims. The School aims to provide a stimulating and friendly atmosphere in which each pupil can realise his or her full intellectual, physical and creative potential. Pupils are encouraged to be self-reliant and adaptable, but we hope that they will learn the basis of good citizenship founded on honesty, fairness and understanding of the needs of others.

Our School is a Church of England Foundation, and emphasis is placed on Christian values and standards. Confirmation classes are taken by the Chaplain.

Buildings. As the first phase of an ambitious development programme a new 12 laboratory Science Centre has been built (2001). This accommodates all teaching of Science, including Geology. Provision for the teaching of all other subjects is of a high standard. Well-equipped Computer Rooms, Music School, Art and Drama Studios and DT Workshops are available to all pupils.

Curriculum. The first and second years provide a broad foundation, with a wide variety of subjects, including two foreign languages, Music, Art, Information Technology, Craft, Design and Technology. In the Third Year there is some provision for choice, and in the Fourth Year subjects are chosen for GCSE courses with English, Mathematics, Science and a language being compulsory. A wide range of subjects is offered to 'A' level, with most pupils going on to University courses, and several go on to Oxford and Cambridge.

Sixth Form. The co-educational sixth form centre accommodates 200 students. Day girls are fully integrated into all activities. In addition to the examination courses, all sixth formers follow the General Studies AS level course and Key Skills.

Games and Activities. A wide range of sports and activities is offered within the curriculum. From the Fourth Year, pupils may choose their sport and regular school fixtures are arranged. Full advantage is taken of the River Thames and rowing is a popular sport for both boys and girls. The main boys' games are Rugby and Hockey in the Christmas Term, Soccer and Hockey in the Easter Term, and Cricket and Athletics in the Summer Term. Girls play Netball and Hockey. Other sports on offer include Fencing, Squash, Basketball, Tennis and Swimming.

The Cadet Force is voluntary with Army, RAF and RN Sections. Camping and adventure training activities take place during holidays and at week-ends. Non-CCF pupils have a wide range of other activities, including the Duke of Edinburgh Award.

Music and Drama enjoy a high profile in the life of the School. Well over a third receive individual instrumental lessons and pupils are encouraged to join in activities such as the Choir, Orchestra, Wind Band, Brass Group, Jazz and Swing Bands. Concerts and plays are presented regularly.

Admissions. The main entry is in September between ages of 10 and 12 by entrance examination taken the previous January. Entry at other levels will be considered, including at 13+ for Preparatory School boys who are required to sit the Common Entrance Examination. Entry to the Sixth Form for girls and boys is by GCSE results and interview. The Foundation makes provision for awards of scholarships and bursaries including Music Awards, based on merit and need.

Fees. From September 2001: £2,510 per term.

Charitable status. The Reading Municipal Church Charities is a Registered Charity, number 309023. Its aim is the provision of secondary education for pupils aged 11 to 18.

Reed's School

Cobham Surrey KT11 2ES.
Tel: (01932) 869044

Reed's is a boarding and day school for boys with girls in the VIth form, founded by Andrew Reed in 1813 and incorporated by Act of Parliament in 1845 under the presidency of the Archbishop of Canterbury, the Duke of Wellington and the Marquis of Salisbury. When the School was founded, its facilities were reserved for boys and girls whose fathers had died. In 1958 the School expanded and all boys, and 6th Form girls became eligible for entrance in the 1990s. Foundation awards are still granted each year to boys and 6th Form girls who have lost the support of one or both of their parents.

Patron: Her Majesty The Queen

Presidents:
G M Nissen, CBE
Mrs S I Barnett, OBE

Governors:
Viscount Bridgeman (*Chairman*)
J D Andrewes, MA, FCA
U D Barnett
T S B Card, BA
Mrs C E Cator
I P Evans, OBE, MA, PhD, CChem, FRSC, DIC
R S Fidgen, FRICS
J W Flecker, MA
D V Harvey, JP
J R McMillan, MA
M W P Noakes
Mrs A F Noakes
The Revd T D Page, MA
The Revd Dr J E Platt, MA, MTh, DPhil
L A Ponsonby
P D Reed
Miss K Richardson, MA
J B Rogers

***Headmaster:* D W Jarrett**, MA

Second Master: G R Martin, BA

Senior Master: R M Garrett, BA

Chaplain: The Revd A J Clarke, MA

Assistants:
R A H Warnock, BA
E M Hearle, BEd
N I Heather, MSc
M D Hewett, BA
R Coulson, FRCO, GRSM, ARCM, LRAM
R E Nicholson, BA
T R Newton, BSc
D H Hamilton, BA
†I A Clapp, BEd
†M C Vernon, BSc
†C Sandison-Smith, MA
Mrs M Francis, BA
Mrs A Springett, BA
†P P Davies, MA
†P R Kemp, BEd
Miss A N Johnson, MA, FRSA
R I Blewitt, BA
†G P Daniel, MA
†P M Laycock, BSc, BA
Mrs J S Motson, BSc
M J Macdonald, BEd
†M A Pitts, BEng
K S Motson, BMus
M V Holdsworth, BEng
Mrs R Mills, BA
Mrs C Kemp, BA
A R W Balls, BEd
D J Crowther, BSc
G I McCutcheon, BSc
D H Phillips, PhD
Mrs J Shelton, BA
Mrs E Gahan, BA
P-J Coehlo, BSc
B J Edwards, BA
Mrs J A Lawrence, BA
A J Perry-Adlam, BA
J A Rollinson, BSc
L Michael, BA
C S Thomson, BA

Visiting Music Teachers:
W McAlpine, FGSM
A Watkiss
P Stevens, BA, ARCM
W Chew, ARCM

Ms L MacAulay, ARCM
P Newton, BMus
Ms S Malcolm, BMus
J Dunning
M Coudon

Bursar & Secretary to the Governors: A D Bott, FCCA

Medical Officer: R Draper, MB, ChB, DCH, DRCOG, DA, MRCGP

The School is situated near Esher in 40 acres of heath and woodland. It can be reached in 30 minutes by train from Waterloo and is within half an hour's drive of both London Airports.

To the original buildings have been added in the last 15 years a Sixth Form House, Chemistry laboratories and Computer Centre, two Artificial Turf Hockey Pitches, an Assembly Hall, a swimming pool and sports complex, a new library and a new teaching block for the Physics, Mathematics and History departments, and new Music School. There are 440 pupils, just under a third of whom are boarders, divided among 5 senior houses, Blathwayt, Bristowe, Capel, Mullens and School House, and one junior house, The Close, for those under 13. There is also a separate Sixth Form House. Admission at the age of 13 is normally by the Common Entrance examination; admission at the age of 11 or 12 is by means of the School's own examination, normally taken at the School. There is admission into the VI Form for boys and girls.

Pupils can be accepted into Reed's School at the beginning of all three terms, although the January intake is small and the April intake minimal. The School has 30 Dutch day pupils, boys and girls, who are partly integrated into the School's academic, games and activities programmes. They follow a Dutch curriculum in French, German, Dutch and Mathematics.

Pupils are prepared for GCSE and GCE, A/S and A levels for University Entrance, and for entry to the Services, professions and industry. The games are Rugby Football, Cricket, Hockey, Athletics, Tennis, Swimming, Squash and Sailing. The School has its own Combined Cadet Force with RAF and Army sections. Duke of Edinburgh Awards can also be taken at Bronze, Silver and Gold levels. The Governors offer grants to enable pupils to attend language courses abroad and outdoor training courses during the holidays.

Pupils are all involved in a wide-ranging Activities Curriculum. There is also a wide range of Inter-House competitions. There is a School Choral Society and Orchestra, and a Chapel Choir which is regularly invited to sing locally.

Religious instruction is in accordance with the principles of the Church of England, and an annual Confirmation Service is held in the School Chapel for which pupils are prepared by the Chaplain. Pupils may not be withdrawn from religious instruction or from normal services in the Chapel.

The fees are £13,578 pa for boarders over 13, and £11,253 for boarders in the junior house. There are no compulsory extras. The fees for day boys are £10,263 for boys over 13 and £8,439 for boys under 13, both inclusive of meals. All boarders may exercise a weekly boarding option.

The National Curriculum is broadly followed in Years 7 to 9 and early specialisation is avoided. There is a Careers Master who advises pupils and arranges suitable visits and interviews and a master who specialises in advice on University degree courses. The School is a member of the Independent Schools Careers Organisation.

The main responsibility for each pupil is undertaken by his Housemaster, supported by a Tutor. The health of the pupils is in the care of the School Doctor, and a State Registered Nurse is in charge of the Medical Centre.

Scholarships. (*see* Entrance Scholarship section)

All applications should be made to the Admissions Secretary, Reed's School. All other enquiries should be addressed to the Headmaster's Secretary.

Charitable status. The London Orphan Asylum (Reed's School) is a Registered Charity, number 312008. Its aims and objectives are to provide boarding education for pupils who have lost the support of one or both parents.

Reigate Grammar School

Reigate Road Reigate Surrey RH2 0QS
Tel: (01737) 222231
Fax: (01737) 224201

The School was originally endowed through a bequest in 1675 by Henry Smith, Alderman of the City of London.

Chairman of Governors: Dr Alan Whitworth

***Headmaster:* D S Thomas**, MA, ARCO

Deputy Heads:
K A Knapp, BSc, PhD (University College, London)
L N Emerson, MA (Fitzwilliam College, Cambridge)

Assistant staff:
R A Rooth, DipEd
A K Reid, BEd
D N Watkins, BSc
P J R Chesterton, BA
D C R Jones, MA
M S Russell, BEd
J A Harwood, BSc
†A J Whiteley, BEd
A J Manfield, BSc
†C S Nicholson, BSc
†D G Bader, BSc
M D Hallpike, CertEd
†M G Cline, BA
Mrs L J Stephens, BEd
P G Stephens, BSc
Mrs J R Manfield, BA
J H Worthen, MA
J W Grant, BA
†V J Robinson, BA
A M Proudfoot, BSc, PhD
P M Wilson, BEd
A A Powell, BD, AKC
Miss S J T Freeman, ATC
J O'Hara, BSc
Mrs F A Gunning, MA
†W H Edwards, BA
P F Tinney, BA
J M Sergeant, BSc
D J Bishop, BEd, MEd
A R Matthews, MA
A B Richards, BA, MSc
Mrs E J Mitchell, BEd
Mrs E L Bader, BEd
S A Kerr, BA
T R Fearn, BSc
Miss V Goldbold, BA
Mrs B M Goode, BSc
C G Coughlan, BEd
Miss J Willis-Bund, BA
C Daws, BA
Mrs P A Tucker, BA
Mrs N M-J McVitty, Licence d'Anglais
N M Lee, BA, BD
S J M Wakefield, BA, PhD
P J O'Brien, BA
Mrs G C Dexter, BA
Mrs K Ellis, BA
Miss C J Allen, BA
J P Bird, BA, ARCM
Miss F G Carn, BSc
Miss S L Kumpel, BA
Miss R E Thomas, BSc
Mrs J Gonsalves, GRSM, ARCM
Mrs S M Cantor, RSA TCert
M J Ellis, ADCM, FRCO, CHM, GRSM, ARCM
Mrs J S Hails, BSc
Mrs A J Davies, BEd
Mrs J M O'Dwyer, BSc
R D Appleton, BA
Miss S Branston, BA
M J Buzzacott, BA
Mrs S Cowell, BSc
Miss A K Furley, BA
P G Goldbrum, BSc, MSc
Miss E C Holland, BA
Miss K M Modha, BA
Miss H Poullain, BA, MA
Miss L A Yeomans, BA, MA
Dr S Lawson, BSc, PhD
M Wood, BA, ATCL
T Wright, BA, MA
N C Roberts, BA

Visiting Music Staff:
Mrs S N Beddy, GRSM, LRAM, ARCM
G Bolton, ARCM
Mrs J Healey, BSc
Mrs N Whitson, GRSM
G Williams, GRSM
D Humphries, AGSM
P Kaye
P A Legg, ALCM
Ms M McGuire, BA
Mrs L J Myall, GLCM
Ms C Stapel
Mrs J Fitzgerald
W Goddard
Ms S Kirkup
Ms S Russell

Bursar and Clerk to the Governors: D J Imrie, MA

Medical Adviser: Dr P Lambourne, MB, BS(*Lond*), DRCOG

Headmaster's Secretary: Mrs C A Harrison

Reigate Grammar School is an independent co-educational day school of 800 pupils with 230 in the sixth form. Boys and girls enter the School by competitive examination at the age of 10 or 11, and at 13 through the Reigate Grammar School Scholarship Examination, Common Entrance or School 13+ Examination. A number of boys and girls also join the sixth form at the age of 16.

Aims. To continue the traditions of the Grammar School in providing an excellent all-round education to talented pupils from a wide range of social backgrounds. To stimulate intellectual curiosity, enabling pupils to achieve their academic potential. To provide a disciplined and caring environment that will encourage boys and girls to develop into morally and socially responsible young people. To provide all pupils with the essential skills and experiences that will equip them for the world outside school.

Religious Education. The School values its historic links with St Mary's Parish Church and provides an education based on sound Christian principles. The School meets in three sections for Morning Assembly which is usually held in the Parish Church or the School Concert Hall. All boys and girls are expected to attend daily Assembly and Religious Education lessons unless specifically exempted by the Headmaster at the request of their parents.

Organisation and Curriculum. In the First and Second Forms all pupils follow a common curriculum. Towards the end of the third form year, following consultation between staff and parents, pupils choose the subjects which they wish to take for the GCSE examination. The sixth form timetable is designed to allow a wide range of possible combinations of subjects and also includes a comprehensive programme of General Studies.

Physical Education. A variety of team and individual games and sports is offered, including athletics, badminton, basketball, cricket, cross-country running, gymnastics, hockey, netball, rugby, soccer, squash, swimming and tennis. There is a heated open-air swimming pool attractively situated in the grounds and a large sports hall. The Hartswood Sports Ground, with 33 acres of playing fields, pavilion and all-weather pitch, is situated about 2 miles south of the main school site.

Music. There is a Director of Music who is in charge of two choirs, a swing band, and two orchestras. Arrangements can be made for individual instrumental tuition. Concerts and musical productions are held regularly in the school concert hall and local churches. The subject is taught at GCSE and 'A' level.

Careers. There is a Careers Centre and members of the Careers Department provide information and advice about all aspects of careers and courses in higher education. They also offer guidance to students about their choice of sixth form courses. The vast majority go on to university degree courses.

Other activities. The CCF is open to pupils in the fourth, fifth and sixth forms. There are Royal Navy, Army and RAF sections. The Duke of Edinburgh Award Scheme is also a very popular activity with a wide range of choice. Community Service activities are being developed within the school, to involve all pupils. The Drama Department presents a series of major productions throughout the year. There are numerous school societies and boys and girls are encouraged to take part in their activities.

Fees per annum. There is a registration fee of £25. The tuition fees (from September 2001) are £7,278 per annum. A number of entrance scholarships are awarded each year and a limited number of bursaries will be available to assist parents who suffer financial hardship during their son's or daughter's school career. The School offers a number of 'School assisted places' and other scholarships for talented pupils. These are means-tested and aimed at those candidates who could not otherwise attend the School. Information about scholarships and School assisted places is available from the Headmaster to whom all enquiries concerning admission should be made. The entrance examination for pupils aged 10 and 11 is held early in January each year.

Charitable status. Reigate Grammar School is a Registered Charity, number L5.312030 A/1. Its aim is to provide high-quality education for boys and girls.

Rendcomb College

Cirencester Gloucestershire GL7 7HA.
Tel: (01285) 831213
Fax: (01285) 831331
e-mail: info@rendcomb.gloucs.sch.uk
website: www.rendcomb.dircon.co.uk

Rendcomb College was founded in 1920 by Noel Wills. It is a member of the Governing Bodies Association and the Headmaster is a member of The Headmasters' Conference. A new Junior School opened in September 2000. (Further details at the end of the entry).

The Governors:

Dr H T H M Phelps, DCL, BA, FCIT, FRAeS (*Chairman*)
Sir Michael Angus
M D Birchall
W E Brown
D P J Cairns, FRICS
Miss E Castle, BA, JP, OBE
Mrs A Copley, MA
P N H Gibbs, MA
Mrs P Hornby
T J Page, BSc, FIPD
S D E Parsons
A O H Quick, MA
The Ven H S Ringrose
H C W Robinson, BA, DipFM
A T K Smail, SCA
St J S L Thomson, BA, ARICS
Major M T N H Wills, DL
The Hon R I H Wills, BA
R H Wills

Headmaster: **G Holden,** MA, FRSA St Andrews University

Deputy Headmaster: H Morgan, BA Bristol University (*History*)

Senior Master: C J Wood, MA, CChem, MRSC Exeter College, Oxford (*Head of Science/Chemistry*)

Director of Studies: P Sykes, MSc Loughborough University (*Mathematics*)

Senior Academic Tutor: Mrs D Dodd, BA Victoria University, New Zealand (*English, Theatre Studies, Housemistress Godman House*)

M H Graham, MA Gonville and Caius College, Cambridge (*History and Library*)
M S Griffiths, BA Wolverhampton Polytechnic (*Art*)
J G Williams, BSc Manchester University (*Housemaster, Stable House/Mathematics*)
D B White, BA, LRAM Durham University (*Housemaster, Old Rectory/Director of Music*)
J H Stutchbury, BSc York University (*Biology*)
Mrs J D Stutchbury, BA Leeds University (*Head of English as a Foreign Language*)
Mrs E Young, BA, RSADipTEFL
I G Patterson, BSc Lancaster Polytechnic, MIITTed (*Head of Information Technology*)
A St J Brealy, BA St Andrews University (*Geography and Mathematics/Assistant Housemaster Old Rectory*)

Mrs N A Gill, BA Manchester University (*Head of Geography/Housemistress, Park House*)
Miss R E Houghton, BA Exeter University (*Head of German/Assistant Housemistress, Godman House*)
Mrs D Botham, MA St Catherine's College, Cambridge (*Physics/Assistant Housemistress, School House*)
Mrs S R Blackwell, DipAD (Fashion & Textiles) St Martin's School of Art, London (*Art, Design and Textiles*)
D Whitehead, GRSM (Hons), ARCM Royal College of Music, Manchester (*Assistant Director of Music/Assistant Housemaster School House*)
M Slark, BA, University of Hull (*Business Studies/Housemaster, Lawn House*)
Mrs S M Westhead, CertEd Sussex University (*Physical Education*)
B L North, BA, BPhil University of Liverpool (*Head of French/Housemaster, School House*)
C Vuolo, BSc University of London (*Biology and Head of PE/Assistant Housemaster Stable House*)
Mrs K Ewing, BA Warwick University, MA Oxford Brookes (*Head of English and Drama*)
Mrs J Gibson, BSc, CChem, MRSC Edinburgh University (*Chemistry and Physics*)
M Debenham, MSc Liverpool University (*Physics and ICT*)
Mrs K-L Bates, CertEd, FAETC, MWATD, ISTD (*Dance*)
Miss V A Hatton, BA Birmingham (*French/Assistant Hoiusemistress Park House*)
P Dodd, MA Selwyn College, Cambridge (*English/ Assistant Housemaster Lawn House*)
Mrs E M Ramsay, BA Liverpool (*Food and Nutrition*)
K Taplin, BA London Bible College (*Chaplain/RE and PSE*)
Mrs S Cuthbert (*Learning Support*)

Head of Junior School: A Palmer, BEd St Paul's College, Cheltenham, MA Open University

Mrs B Mayoh, BSc, PGCE
Mrs K Carden, BEd Hons
Mrs C Audritt, BA, PGCE
Mrs K Hume, BSc, PGCE
Mrs J Palmer, CertEd

Bursar: Lt Col The Hon J F A Grey, MIMgt
Marketing Director: Dr P Shackel, BSc, PhD Aston University
Headmaster's PA: Mrs S Downie
Admissions Registrar: Miss J L Pratt
Bursar's Secretary: Mrs K Lawson
Accountant: Mrs K M Collins
Medical Officer: Dr S W Drysdale, MB, ChB, MRCP
Sister: Mrs J Pritchard, GRN
Assistant Sister: Mrs J Hunt, GRN

Visiting Music Staff:
Mrs J Baldwin (*Oboe and Bassoon*)
P Cordell (*Electric Guitar*)
M Rogers (*Violin and Viola*)
P Dunn (*Guitar*)
Mrs G Day (*Piano and Clarinet*)
Mrs S Day (*Piano, popular styles*)
C Green (*Saxophone and Brass*)
Mrs J Morris (*'Cello and Singing*)
C Shiner (*Brass*)
Mrs S Day (*Jazz Piano*)
G Watson (*Drums*)
Mrs T McIver (*Flute*)

Situation and Buildings. Rendcomb overlooks the River Churn in the heart of the Cotswolds, five miles from Cirencester and ten miles from Cheltenham on the A435. It is easily accessible from the M4, A40 and M5. The College is set in 200 acres of parkland rich in wildlife.

Numbers. There are 130 boys and 110 girls, who either fully board, weekly board or are day pupils. Flexible boarding is available.

Admission. Pupils normally join at 11, 13 or 16 to enter the Sixth Form. The entrance examination for entry at 11 is taken at Rendcomb and comprises three papers: English, Mathematics and Verbal Reasoning. At 13 pupils are admitted by Common Entrance or Rendcomb Examination, and at 16 by interview, school reports and GCSE results.

Character. Rendcomb is the right size for everyone to grow in confidence and ability. The College week is designed to combine academic studies with a wide variety of activities and sports.

We encourage pupils to achieve the best possible academic results and to find out what they are good at. We want them to care for other people and their surroundings, and to enter the world of work, of marriage and of family life, with confidence and sensitivity.

Rendcomb provides a stable, disciplined and structured way of life to sustain hard work, with fine opportunities for developing talent outside the classroom. Facilities for study and leisure are superb, helping prepare students for University and independent living.

Curriculum. Pupils are prepared for GCSE and 'A' level examinations and for university entrance. They go on to a wide range of careers in the professions and services, commerce and industry, and in agriculture.

In the first two years there is a broad course of studies including Religious Studies, English, French, History, Mathematics, German, Geography. Music, Art, Craft, Design & Technology, General Science, Drama, Games, PE, ICT and PSME.

In the third year, Science is studied as separate subjects and all pupils study a short course GCSE in ICT.

In the fourth and fifth years pupils are offered a range of options and most take ten subjects at GCSE.

'AS' Level courses are provided in English, History, French, German, Geography, Business Studies, Mathematics, Physics, Chemistry, Biology, Art, Music, Theatre Studies, PE and Music Technology. Most pupils take four AS levels. Three of these are continued in the second year of the Sixth Form to A2 level.

University Entrance. A high level of academic achievement is maintained, and in recent years over 95% of leavers have gone on to a Higher Education.

Careers. There is a Careers Room which offers comprehensive current information on both careers and higher education and experienced staff are available for further information, consultation and advice.

Careers advice is available for all pupils throughout their stay at Rendcomb. It is particularly important when selecting subjects for GCSE and A level. Rendcomb uses the Centigrade System as part of the Higher Education Applications Procedure to assist Lower 6th Form pupils in selecting universities and degree courses. Work experience takes place during the Lower 6th Year and all pupils will take part in an 'Understanding Industry' conference during their time in the 6th Form.

Religious Education Church Services take place on Sundays and during the week in the fine 16th Century Parish Church, which also serves as the church for the small village of Rendcomb. Pupils are required to attend a short service on two days in the week and boarders attend a Morning Service on Sunday. There is an annual Confirmation and the Chaplain also runs Rendcomb's Personal and Social Education Programme. He is available as a listening ear to all members of the school.

Music, Art and Drama. The Arts Centre stands at the centre of the school site. It is equipped for Art, Music, Design, Pottery and Textiles.

Art is taught to all pupils for at least three of their years at Rendcomb and they may use the facilities at other times as an activity or for recreation. A special studio is dedicated to pupils studying 'A' level Art and professional artists teach alongside the Director of Art to provide balanced, relevant and up to date teaching. Visits are undertaken to a wide range of art galleries.

There is a high standard of instrumental and choral performance. Individual tuition is available in all instruments and voice. There are many opportunities to play and sing throughout the year at Rendcomb and at other venues.

Plays are staged in the well-equipped fine Victorian Orangery. The Rendcomb site also lends itself to producing open air plays during the summer term. All kinds of productions are staged at Rendcomb from full scale performances involving large numbers of pupils and staff to the regular junior play and small plays and reviews produced by pupils. Recent productions include Plunder and Annie. There are also performances by visiting companies and frequent trips to theatres in London, Stratford, Bristol, Oxford and Cheltenham.

Drama is offered at GCSE and Theatre Studies may be studied at A and AS level.

Sport. The games fields are excellent and a large majority of members of the school represent Rendcomb at one or more sports in their age group. There are cricket, hockey, netball and rugby tours.

An all-weather playing surface represents an important training advantage in hockey and tennis at Rendcomb; it complements the seven hard and one grass tennis courts already in use. There are two squash courts, four badminton courts in the sports hall, an open-air swimming pool and climbing wall. Football, archery, clay pigeon shooting and horse riding are also popular.

Living Accommodation. Rendcomb has excellent accommodation for both boarders and day pupils. Each pupil in the Fourth Form and above has a comfortable single study bedroom and there are spacious Common Rooms and excellent social facilities. Sixth formers enjoy their own centre, with TV, Satellite TV, video, games room, dance area and bar.

Scholarships. (*see* Entrance Scholarship section) There are a number of valuable scholarships available at all ages of entry for pupils with special academic, artistic, dramatic, musical or sporting abilities.

For further details and information about Scholarships apply to the Admissions Registrar, Rendcomb College, Cirencester, Glos GL7 7HA. Tel: (01285) 831213.

Fees.

Years 1 and 2 £3,420 per term (Boarding); £2,600 (Day)

Years 3–6A £4,900 per term (Boarding); £3,480 (Day).

Fees are payable termly in advance, by the first day of term. The Governors reserve the right to charge interest at up to 2% per month on fees not paid by this date. For information on monthly and other payment schemes please contact the Bursar.

The premium for a pupil's personal accident insurance scheme is included.

The registration fee is £35.

The Junior School. The Junior School opened in September 2000 and now has classes for four to eleven year olds. The main entry points are at four years by interview with the Headmaster and at seven years by examination, interview and school report.

For pupils in Reception, the Curriculum is based on an extension of the Government's learning goals including social, emotional and physical development. Junior 1 and 2 are largely class teacher taught with Junior 3 to 6 operating a degree of subject specialism. A wide range of subjects are taught including ICT, Drama, French and Latin.

The pupils have an opportunity to perform in a music concert and an annual play. There are annual soccer and cricket tours.

Each pupil has an Education Profile with targets and there are regular Grade cards and parent/teacher meetings.

After-school clubs run Monday to Thursday, from Top of the Pops Dancing to Chess, Fencing to Clay Shooting. The use of College facilities by the Junior School, from the Astro-turf to the Multi-media Suite, raises the standard of activities. The Junior School also has its own facilities including an adventure playground.

Enquiries should be directed to the Admissions Registrar on 01285 831213.

Charitable status. The Trustees of Rendcomb College is a Registered Charity, number 311713. The aims and objectives of the Charity are the provision of boarding and day independent education.

Repton School

Repton Derby DE65 6FH

Tel: Headmaster: (01283) 559220

Bursar: (01283) 559200

Fax: (01283) 559210 (School); (01283) 559223 (Headmaster)

website: www.repton.org.uk

Motto: *Porta vacat culpa.*

Repton School was founded in 1557 under the Will of Sir John Port, of Etwall, Derbyshire. His executors purchased the remains of Augustinian Repton Priory which had been established in the 12th century and therein the School was started.

The central features of its buildings are still the Priory and Cloister Garth.

The School is now governed by a scheme drawn up under the Endowed Schools' Act in 1874 and subsequently amended.

Repton is 8 miles from Derby and 4 from Burton-on-Trent.

There are at present 363 boarders and 166 day pupils in the School.

Governors:

[1]The Countess of Loudoun
[1]The Earl of Carnarvon
[1]Lord Gerard
Sir Richard Morris, CBE, FEng (*Chairman*)
J M Fry
W A W Bemrose
J K Bather
Mrs G M Hutchinson
Dr K J Dell
Prof J H D Eland
Professor Dr Dr G Pulverer, FRC, FRSM
Brigadier C E Wilkinson, CBE, TD, DL
R A Litchfield
Lt Col J D Hetherington
D B Wilkinson, MA
Miss S R Cameron, BA
R J R Owen
A Lee, MA
B A Gray
P McLoughlin, MP
Prof D Wallace, CBE
P M Village, LLB
Mrs A E Hill, JP

[1] denotes Hereditary Governors

***Headmaster:* G E Jones**, MA

Second Master: P D Silvey, BA

Senior Mistress: Mrs R E Harris, BA

Director of Studies: J C Driver, BSc

Director of Admissions: J McLaren, MA

Assistant Masters:

J McLaren, MA (*Careers Master*)
C R Carrington, BSc, ARCS
T D H Scott, MA
R S Thompson, BA
A A Cox, MA, FRGS (*Careers Master*)
P N Bradburn, BSc
M R H Wimbush, BSc
G B Attwood, BA, MSc, CMath
C M Keep, MA
M Stones, BA
C J Price, BSc
A F Mylward, MA

N G Bennett, CertEd, RSADipSpLD
J H Bournon, BA (*Director of Art and Design*)
N J Kew, BA
J Plowright, MA
D Morris, BSc
S J Clague, BSc
T P Cosford, BA
R J Hillier, MA, PhD
J G Golding, BA
P V Goodhead, MA
Mrs S M Q Nield, BA
F J Rule, BSc
Mrs G E Snelson, CertEd
Mrs S A B Tennant, BA
Mrs C E Goodhead, BSc
H G Gould, PhD, MSc, CPhys, MInstP
The Revd R L Short, MA (*Chaplain*)
A J Smith, BSc
R H Dacey, GRSM, FRCO, LRAM, ARCM (*Director of Music*)
G Lawrence, MA
E J Wheeldon, BA
T J Collins, BA
M M Carrington, BSc
R G Embery, BA
T B Blain, MA
Mrs M J Blain
D S Newman, BA
J C Sentance, MA
K J R McCallum, BA
F P Watson, BA
Miss A E Carter, BSc
P J Griffiths, MSc
M A Sanderson, BSc, LRSM
Miss K E Dalton, BA
Miss M K Emuss, BA
B J Fogarty, MA
S Earwicker, MPhil
T Bayley, BSc

Assistant Music Masters:
D C Hadwen, ARMCM
N J Firth, GBSM
N C Millensted, FTCL, LRAM, ARCM, LTCL
P J Williams, MA, GRSM, FRCO, LRAM

Bursar: R G Silk

Medical Officer: Dr L M O'Hara, MB, ChB

Boarding Houses:
School House (*A F Mylward*)
The Priory (*J G Golding*)
The Orchard (*T P Cosford*)
Latham House (*Dr R J Hillier*)
The Mitre (*T J Collins*)
New House (*N J Kew*)
The Abbey (*Mrs C E Goodhead*)
The Garden (*Mrs S M Q Nield*)
Field House (*Mrs S A B Tennant*)

Admission. The usual age for entrance is about 13½ years. Application for admission should be made to the Headmaster. There is a registration fee of £30. Candidates must normally have passed the Common Entrance Examination at their preparatory schools, but there is also an entrance examination for candidates not being prepared for the CEE.

Fees. Boarders – £5,025 per term; day pupils £3,725 per term. Additional expenses (for books, stationery, pocket money, etc.) need not, after the first term, exceed £100 per term.

There is a Bursary Fund from which grants in the form of remissions from full fees may in certain circumstances be made. No remission of fees can be made on account of absence.

Scholarships. (*see* Entrance Scholarship section) Academic scholarships and exhibitions are awarded annually after a competitive examination, senior in November, junior in February. Their value varies between 50% and 10% of the fees, but the value of an award may be increased where need is shown. *C B Fry Awards:* Up to 5 Awards are made annually (worth 20% of the Repton boarding fee) to candidates exhibiting outstanding all-round potential. Music, Art, Information and Design Technology scholarships are also offered, awards being made if work of sufficient merit is offered.

In addition, there are nominated foundation scholarships, endowment fund bursaries and Old Reptonian Society exhibitions, which can be awarded without examination. Allowances may also be made for the sons and daughters of members of the Armed Forces.

Entry forms and further particulars relating to all the above awards may be obtained from the Headmaster.

Organisation and curricula. Normal point of entry to Repton is September of Year 9, but an increasing number of pupils join for the Sixth Form.

The curriculum in Year 9 is very broad so that pupils are able to make an informed choice of GCSE subjects at the beginning of Year 10.

All pupils study Mathematics, English, French and Science to GCSE. Science is offered as a dual award GCSE; the more able pupils are entered for examination in the three separate sciences. Pupils also take GCSE's in three or four optional subjects; these are chosen from Art, Design Technology, Business Studies, Information Technology, Drama, German, Spanish, Greek, Latin, Classical Civilisation, Geography, History, Music, Religious Studies and PE.

In the Lower Sixth form, pupils have the opportunity to study up to five AS level courses, although the norm is four. In the Upper Sixth the majority of pupils will choose to continue with three of these through to A level, although some will choose to offer four or five.

AS level courses are offered in all subjects available to GCSE, plus Economics and General Studies. Most of these courses can be continued to A level, although Drama and Religious Studies are not taught beyond AS level.

Teaching in the Key Skills is an integral part of all courses, and some pupils are prepared for assessment in Communication and Information Technology.

All pupils follow a Study Skills course at the beginning of their Lower Sixth year. Potential Oxbridge candidates are identified by the end of their first terms in the Sixth Form, and are prepared for interview.

Chapel services are those of the Church of England, and boarders are expected to attend a service every Sunday unless specially excused. A Confirmation is held each year.

Other activities. Every opportunity and encouragement are given to pupils to develop their creative faculties in art, music, drama and design and technology. There are numerous School societies, covering a wide variety of interests.

Games and sports. Cricket, association football, hockey (three all-weather pitches), netball, rugby, fives, squash rackets, tennis (2 indoor courts and 14 hard courts), cross country running, athletics, sailing, climbing, canoeing and swimming. Ample facilities are provided for physical education including a Sports Hall, a Gymnasium and an Indoor Swimming Pool.

Combined Cadet Force. The School maintains a contingent of the Combined Cadet Force and every pupil is a member for two years. Older pupils may leave the CCF and undertake Community Service or remain in the CCF to take part in Duke of Edinburgh, or specialise as instructors as an alternative.

Organisation and Curriculum. Repton is co-educational and all pupils belong to a house, which is regarded as their home in their time at school. The housemaster or housemistress, who has overall responsibility for a pupil's work and development, lives in the house and all meals are taken within the houses. The three girls' houses, The Abbey, The Garden and The Field, have been purpose-built and offer a high standard of accommodation.

Old Reptonian Society. All boys and girls who leave Repton become members of the Old Reptonian Society which has branches all over the country. Annual dinners and other regional social functions provide an opportunity for them to maintain and renew old friendships. Old Reptonian football, cricket and other sporting clubs are also keenly supported, and provide opportunities for young players to enjoy amateur sport at its best. Repton has been a frequent winner of the Arthur Dunn Cup, and also won the Cricketer Cup in the year of its inauguration. The Secretary of the Old Reptonian Society is J R Muir, 6 Chestnut Way, Repton, Derby.

Repton Preparatory School and Pre-Preparatory School are situated at Foremarke Hall, about three miles from the main school. There are at present 86 boarders and 200 day boys and girls, plus 87 pre-prep day boys and girls. Pupils are currently taken from the age of 3 and prepared for entrance to Repton and other schools. Academic Scholarships are offered and the examination is in February.

Further particulars may be obtained from The Headmaster, Paul Brewster, Foremarke Hall, Milton, Derbyshire DE65 6EJ.

Charitable status. Repton School – Sir John Port's Charity is a Registered Charity, number 527177. It exists to provide high quality education for boys and girls.

Robert Gordon's College

Schoolhill Aberdeen AB10 1FE.
Tel: (01224) 646346
Fax: (01224) 630301

Motto: *Omni nunc arte magistra.*

The College was founded as a residential establishment in 1729 by Robert Gordon, a member of a well-known Aberdeenshire family, who made his fortune as a merchant in the Baltic ports. In 1881 it was converted into a Day School, but a boarding facility was re-established for a very small number of pupils from 1937 to 1995. Formerly a grant-aided school in receipt of a Direct Grant from the Scottish Education Department, the College became a fully independent school on 1st August, 1985, though retaining its statutory link with The Aberdeen Educational Endowments Scheme 1958 (amended 1985). It has been fully co-educational since 1992.

Governors:
Convener of Grampian Regional Council (*ex officio*) and representative of the following bodies: Grampian Regional Council (*3*), University of Aberdeen (*2*), Aberdeen Presbytery of the Church of Scotland (*2*), Aberdeen Endowments Trust (*2*), Gordonian Association (*2*), Seven Incorporated Trades of Aberdeen (*1*), Trades Unions (*1*), Chamber of Commerce (*1*), and not less than 4 nor more than 6 co-opted members.

Chairman of Governors: Professor Graeme R D Catto, MD, DSc, FRSE, FRCP, FRCPE, FRCPG

***Headmaster:* Brian R W Lockhart**, MA, DipEd

Deputy Head: Jennifer M S Montgomery, MA, DipEd

College Secretary: Robert M Leggate, MA, CA

Assistant Heads:
G J Urwin Woodman, MA, MEd
Rona B Livingstone, BSc, FSA(*Scot*)
Michael S Elder, MA

Head of Junior School: Ian M Black, MA

English:
Ian Gotts, MA, MLitt, PhD (*Head of Department*)
Diana C Gotts, MA, DipEd
Roderick W Richmond, MA, DipEd
Michael S Elder, MA
Lynda Turbet, BA, MA
Louise M R Webster, MA
Shona M Bruce, MA, MEd
Iain Major, MA
Fiona Wilson, MA
Patricia Horne, MA

Geography:
Howard O Smith, BSc (*Head of Department*)
Stuart W Robertson, MA
Kerry Scott, MA

History:
Philip J Skingley, BA, MEd (*Head of Department*)
Sally Watson, BA
Kenneth J Wright, MA
Alison Raby, MA
Kathleen Hudd, BA

Mathematics:
Valerie M Thomson, BEd (*Head of Department*)
Elizabeth M Riddell, BSc
Arthur Jamieson, BSc
Fiona M Robertson, MA
Walter S Craig, MA, DipEd
Deidre L Latimer, BSc
Elaine Pascoe, BEd
Lorna Taylor, MA
Eileen Smith, MA

Physics:
Stuart Farmer, BSc (*Head of Department*)
Graham P Sangster, BSc
Sheila B Sanderson, BA
Chandralekha Khaund, BSc, MSc
John Thomson, BSc
Sandra Lonie, BSc, MSc
Jane Kennedy, PhD, MA
Christopher Spracklin, BSc, PhD

Chemistry:
Robert Graham, BSc, PhD (*Head of Department*)
Gordon B Aitken, BSc, PhD
John Duncan, BSc
Kevin S Cowie, BSc
Christopher Spracklin, BSc, PhD
Jane Kennedy, PhD, MA

Biology:
Bruce B Simms, BSc, PhD, DipEd (*Head of Department*)
David A Horne, BSc
Margaret Houlihan, BSc
Rona B Livingstone, BSc, FSA(*Scot*)
Wendy MacGregor, BSc
Gail Kemp, BSc

Classics:
Allan M Bicket MA, MLitt (*Head of Department*)
G J Urwin Woodman, MA, MEd
Anne C Everest, MA
Allan B Girdwood, MA, PhD

Modern Languages:
Thomas C Cumming, MA, DipEd (*Head of Department*)
Marilyn Lowdon, MA
Daniel Montgomery, MA, DipEd
Alice Huddart, MA, DipEd
Derek A Harley, MA, DipEd
Phyllis Johnstone, MA
Catherine Richmond, MA, DipEd

Art:
Andrew L Hopps, BA (*Head of Department*)
Fraser Beaton, DA
Caroline Chinn, DA
Sally Somers, DA
Fiona Michie, DA

Technical Subjects:
David McLaren, DipTechEd (*Head of Department*)
Colin J Lavery, BSc, DipTechEd
Ross Murdoch, BEd

Economics and Business Studies:
Andrew Slater, DipComm, DipM, ASCA, BA (*Head of Department*)

Michele Ramsay, BA
Scott McKenzie, BA

Computing Studies:
James Bisset, MA, MSc (*Head of Department*)
Fiona M Currie, BSc
Caireen McDonald, BA

Music:
Leslie M Inness, BMus (*Head of Department*)
Rhonda E McColgan, LTCL
Kevin Haggart, BMus, MM
Kevin Cormack
P Louise A Counsell, AGSM
Rachel Mackison, GRSM

Physical Education:
Andrew Dougall, DPE (*Head of Department*)
Sheila McNaught, BEd
Colin B Filer, BEd
Evelyn J S Scotland, DPE, DCE
Emma Eddie, BEd
Stephen Newton, BSc

Religious Education:
Anthony Luby, BEd, MPhil, DipEd (*Head of Department*)
Joyce Wintour, MA
David Starbuck, MA

Careers/Guidance:
Anne Everest, MA (*Principal Teacher, Careers*)
John Thomson, BSc (*Principal Teacher*)
Sheila Sanderson, BA (*Principal Teacher*)
Daniel Montgomery, MA, DipEd (*Principal Teacher*)
Kevin Cowie, BSc (*Principal Teacher*)
Shona Bruce, MA, MEd
Fraser Beaton, DA
Colin Filer, BEd
Phyllis Johnstone, MA

Network Manager: Gordon Crosher
Network Manager's Assistant: James Florence
Admin Systems Supervisor: Kelly Paterson
Administration/Exams: Roderick Richmond, MA, DipEd (*Principal Teacher*)
Outdoor Education: Stuart U Robertson, MA (*Principal Teacher*)
Learning Support: Aileen Howie, MA

Junior School:
Gavin Calder, MA (*Deputy Head*)
Peter D C Wilkinson, DCE, BA
Graham Bowman, MA, MEd
Alexander Robb, BA
Julie Mitchell, BEd
Maureen R Glegg, DPE (*Swimming/Games*)
Anne McDonald, DipEd
Veronica S McGillivray, DPE (*Science*)
Karen B Thomson, DipEd
Ailsa Reid, BEd
Helen Stuart, BEd
Tracey J Geddes, MA
Matthew Northcroft, BEd
Lorraine Wright, MA
Vivien Scott, BEd
Sheila Leheny, MA (*Learning Support*)
Rosemary Elliott-Jones, LTCL (*Music*)
Carole Nicoll, MA (*French*)
Jane Livingstone, BA, DPE (*Swimming/Games*)
Daphne Mallia (*ICT Co-ordinator*)
Sophie Malins, BEd
Geetha Clark, BA

Infant Department:
Head of Department: Varie Macleod, BEd
Carol Ferries, MA
Maureen Drummond, DipEd
Susan Rust, MA

Nursery: Ann Gauld, DipEd, AssEdEE

Nursery Nurse: Anne Marie Gove, NNEB

School Nurse: Shan Elliot, RGN

School Librarian: Elaine Brazendale, MA, ALA

Assistant Librarian: Penny Hartley, BA

Headmaster's Secretary: Ann Gannon

Admission. The College is divided into two sections – the Junior School – 440 pupils (Primary – Classes 1–7) and the Senior School – 950 pupils (Secondary – Forms I–VI). The normal stages of entry are to Primary 1, Primary 6 and Secondary I.

Entry to Primary 1 (age 4½–5½ years) is by interview held in February, and to Primary 6 (age 9½–10½ years) by Entrance Test held in February.

Entry to Secondary I is by an Entrance & Scholarship Examination held in January.

Entry at other stages depends upon vacancies arising, and the offer of a place is subject to satisfactory performance in an Entrance Test and interview.

Nursery. There is also a Nursery Unit (age 3–5) for some 40 children.

Fees. Junior School – P1 + 2 £3,320 pa P3–7 – £4,610 pa. Senior School – £5,330 pa. These fees are inclusive and cover Games. Pupils provide their own books.

Scholarships. A significant number of scholarships are awarded to pupils entering SI on the basis of performance in the Entrance & Scholarship Examination and of financial need. Two major scholarships are awarded to pupils entering S5 tenable for 2 years, and twenty major scholarships are awarded to pupils entering the Sixth Year. In total some 25% of pupils in the secondary department receive financial help.

Buildings. The centre block was erected in 1732, but there have been many modern additions. The College is fully equipped with Assembly Hall, Library, Laboratories, Art Rooms, Computing areas and Workshops. There are 2 Gymnasia and a Swimming Pool at the School. A new playingfield was opened in 1992 on a 40 acre site 3m from the school incorporating first-class accommodation and facilities, including an astroturf all-weather sports surface. A new five-storey teaching block incorporating a Dining Hall, seating 300, was opened in 1993, and a new Library and Information Centre in 2000.

Curriculum. In the Junior School the usual subjects of the primary curriculum are covered with specialist teachers in Art, French, Computing, Music and Physical Education in Primary 6 and 7. The first 2 years of the Senior School have a general curriculum; after that some specialisation is permitted, and courses are provided in Classics, English, Mathematics, Physics, Chemistry, Biology, Human Biology, Modern Languages (French, German, Italian), History, Geography, Modern Studies, Music, Art, Drama, Religious Studies, Computer Studies, Information Systems, Technical Subjects, (Technological Studies, Graphic Communication), Economics, Accounting and Finance and Business Management. Pupils are prepared for the Scottish Qualifications Authority examinations which lead directly to university entrance. All pupils have classes in Religious Education and Physical Education. Special courses are run for 6th Year on entrepreneurship, philosophy, leadership, psychology, sociology, ceramics, photography, electronics, word processing, survival cooking and European Computer Driving Licence (ECDL).

Examination results are among the best in Scotland, with 96% annually going on to University, some 20% of these beyond Scotland.

Games. Rugby, Hockey, Cricket, Netball, Tennis, Athletics, Cross-Country Running. A wide range of other sports is offered – Badminton, Basketball, Volleyball, Golf, Squash, Skiing, Swimming, Orienteering, Hill-Walking.

Extra-Curricular Activities: There is a Contingent of the Combined Cadet Force (Army and RAF sections) and a Pipe Band. Participation in the Duke of Edinburgh Award Scheme is consistently strong. The Choir, Concert Band and Orchestra play a prominent part in the life of the School, as do a Literary and Debating Society, which meets weekly, and a Dramatic Society, which presents at least one play or operetta each year. Many other clubs and societies flourish, making over 50 in all.

Charitable status. Robert Gordon's College is a Registered Charity, number SC000123. It exists to provide education for boys and girls.

Rossall School

Fleetwood Lancs FY7 8JW.
Tel: (01253) 774201
Fax: (01253) 772052

Motto: *Mens agitat molem.*

Rossall School was founded in 1844 on the coast of Lancashire. It is incorporated by Royal Charter, granted in 1890, and is under the management of a Council.

Governors:
The Earl of Derby, President of Corporation
¶R P Shepherd, Esq, DL

Council (*ex-officio Governors*)

T R A Groves, Esq (*Chairman*)
Mrs H Woods, BA (*Vice-Chairman*)

¶S G Lee, Esq	¶J M Pickering, Esq
¶R C Rawcliffe, Esq, MA, FCA	¶J W Cowpe, Esq, BA
	¶M J Reece, Esq, MA
D R W Silk, CBE, JP, MA	A S Airey, Esq, BA
The Hon Mrs Justice Steel, DBE	Mrs J A Bruck, JP, BSc
	D J Craven, Esq, BCom
¶P J C Bagot, Esq, FCA	Mrs J A Eaves, BSc, CQSW
¶A N Stephenson, Esq, MA	The Rt Revd R Ladds, SSC, BEd, LRCS, FCS
Mrs A E Bott, JP	
Mrs H N Trapnell	¶J Parr, Esq
¶J Coulson, Esq, LLB	Mrs C Preston, BSc, ARICS
¶C C Fayle, Esq, BSc, CEng, MIMechE	

Secretary to the Corporation and Council: B E Clark, Esq, MBE

Principal: R D W Rhodes, JP, BA

***Headmaster:* G S H Pengelley**, BA, PGCE

Deputy Heads:
Pastoral: *†M Holder-Williams, BA, MA, PGCE *History*
Staff Development: *Mrs J C Briggs, BA *English*
Curriculum: *D J Fowkes, BSc, PGCE *Science*

Assistant Masters and Mistresses:
†J C Roberts, BA, FRGS, CertTEFL *Geography*
A D Todd, CertEd *PE*
†R N S Leake, BSc, PGCE, MIBiol, CBiol *Biology*
*R V W Murphy, MA, DPhil, DipEd *Mathematics*
†*Miss K M Plant, MA, CertEd *PE*
*P T J King, BEd *Technology*
†*J A Ralph, BA, PGCE *English/General Studies*
J M Foster, LTCL *Instrumental Music*
†*Mrs A Jurczak, CertEd, DipRE *Language Development*
†M G Roberts, BSc, PGCE *Science*
*M B Searle, BA, PGCE *Modern Languages*
Mrs T Marsh, BEng, PGCE *Mathematics*
*Miss J P Kent, BEd, BA, MA, IntroCertTEFL
†*C P Drew, BA, PGCE *Geography*
*C Egdell, BSc, PGCE *IT, Physics, KS3 Science Co-ordinator*
Mrs J Evans, BEd, RSADipTEFL *EFL*
Z Siddique, BEng, PDipPGCE *Mathematics*
Mrs C S Wolstencroft, BA, RSACertTEFL, MEdTESOL *EFL*
†M J Eddon, BSc, PGCE *Mathematics*
†Mrs R Fowkes, BA, PGCE *Geography*
*Mrs S E Roberts, MEdESL, CertEd *ESL*
Miss J Mercer, BSc, PGCE *Science*
I Moore, BA, PGCE, TESOL *English & IT*
P D Benson, MSc, BSc *Mathematics*
D G Boothroyd, MA, BA, BEd *English*
Miss E Bukovinszki, BSc *Student Teacher*
L Condon, BA, PGCE *English*
Miss P M Fitzgerald, BSc *Chemistry*
Miss H M Gibson, MA, PGCE *Modern Languages*
A M Jackson, BA *Modern Languages*
N A Lister, FRAS *Researcher in Residence*
*T J Strain, BEd, HND *Economics/Business Studies*
*Revd R Taylor, BA, BD, PGCE *Chaplain*
Miss A M Woods, BA, PGCE *English*
Mrs R Barker, BA, CertTEFL *English*
Miss S Bathe *FLA*
*G W Cassidy, BA, FRCO(CHM), PGCE *Music*
S L Corrie, BMus *Music*
P E Crawford, BDS, PGCE *Biology*
Mrs S J Cross, BA, PGCE *English*
Dr D Dohmen, PhD, PGCE *Modern Languages*
A Fairhurst, BA, PGCE *Geography*
S P Hoffman, BA *Economics/BS*
*Miss E L Jones, CertEd *Girls' Games*
Miss M Magneron *FLA*
Mrs J Mickiewicz, BSc, PGCE *HE/BS*
*Miss H J Mountstephen, MA, BA *Art*
A Norton *History*
J L Riding, BEng, PGCE *Science*
Miss I H Riley, BA, CertTEFL *English*
D Rose, BA, CertTEFL *History*
Miss A M Strachan, BSc *Mathematics*

*Mrs B A King, BEd *Home Economics*
T L Briggs, FFB, MSA, DipID *Art*
Mrs J Searle, BA, PGCE *Modern Languages*
L M K Brown, BA, MA, DipWSET *Physics*
R W F Oakley, PhD, BSc *Physics*
†Mrs S Holder-Williams, BA, RSADipPA *Art*
Miss J M Rowe *Independent Listener*
Mrs S Shepherd *Dance*
Mrs N Sinclair *Mathematics*
M Nelson *Rugby/Sports*
Mrs S Alonso, UGDFL, AIOL, CertEd *Spanish*
Mrs L Jeffery *Mathematics*

Instrumental Music:
§A G Keeling, BMus, MMus, FTCL, FLCM *Flute, Composition*
§I Forgrieve, GMus (RNCM), PPRNCM *Percussion*
§C Masters *Guitar*
§Mrs H Clarke, CertEd *Piano*
§A H Lingings, ARCM *Piano*
§Miss P Holt, BA *Cello*
§Mrs S Gent, GTCL *Clarinet*
§B Harrison *Woodwind*
§Miss J Wunderley *Voice*
§P Lyon, GRSM, FRCO, ARMCM, LTCL *Piano*
†Mrs S Ralph *Bassoon*
§C J Andrews, BA, LTCL *Brass*
†Mrs S L Eddon, GRSM, LRAM, PGCE *Music, Piano*
§Mrs R E Bridge *Piano*
Miss E Keaton *Voice*

UK Marketing Manager: D Gore

Librarian: Mrs A Norton

Commercial Director: P Wright

Director, International Study Centre: M Hamlett, MEd

Medical Officer: Dr P G Carpenter, MB, ChB, MRCGP, DRCOG, FPA

Consultant Dental Surgeon: Dr Robert I Bland & Associates

Term of Entry. Any term in the year for boys and girls aged 11+ and 13+; September only for those aged 16+.

Academic Curriculum. All entrants are expected to take a broad based curriculum prior to the selection of a nine subject two year course leading to GCSE. Options include English, Mathematics, French, History, German, Geography, Physics, Chemistry, Biology, Domestic Science, Craft and Design, Art, Religious Studies, Information Technology, Economics, Business Studies and Music.

In the Sixth Form, after GCSE a two-year course leads to GCE 'A' Level. All entrants to the Sixth Form are expected to offer three subjects from the wide choice available: Arts and Science subjects can be combined in certain cases. These main subjects are supplemented by courses in 'minority subjects'. Rossall also offers the **International Baccalaureate,** a two year course of study that meets the needs of well motivated students, offering academic rigor, breadth and coherence. It is a highly effective and very successful preparation for university and the world of employment. It is recognised by prestigious universities world-wide such as Oxford and Cambridge, The Sorbonne, Heidelberg and Yale. The majority of the Sixth Form go on to degree courses at a University or to other courses of Higher Education; but the education given is broad enough to offer a good start to those seeking direct entry to careers in the fields of Commerce, Business, the Armed Services, and the Police, etc.

Special arrangements are made for those who seek entrance to Oxford and Cambridge by any of the various routes.

Scholarships and Bursaries. (*see* Entrance Scholarship section) Up to three Trapnell Scholarships (value full fee) for a candidate aged 11 or 13 who shows high academic ability in any subject though preference will be given for promise in Mathematics and/or Science. Ten valuable Open Scholarships (up to 75% of the Basic Fee) are offered by special examination each February/March for those still under 14.0 on 1st September. Junior Scholarships are also awarded to those performing well in the 11+ Entrance Examination.

Four Music Scholarships (up to 75% of the Basic Fee) are offered for instrumentalists who enter at the age of 11, 13 or 16; these awards also include free tuition in two instruments.

One Art and Design Scholarship of value up to 50% fees.

Substantial Bursaries, limited in number, are available for children of the Clergy and of parents serving in the Armed Services.

Ten Governors Academic Awards for direct entry to Sixth Form (up to 50% of fee with additional Bursary in cases of particular need).

The following special awards are for competition by examination and interview: For children aged 11+ or 13+ who can show boarding need the Jackson Scholarship (up to full fee dependent on parental income).

For children of good character and wide-ranging interests educated in the UK or Kenya the Newell Scholarship (£1,740 pa).

For children 'worthy of encouragement' the Watson-Smith Scholarship (£750 pa).

The Arts, Science and Technology. Facilities are available for use both inside and outside the normal school time-table.

A flourishing Music Department, housed in the Thomas Beecham Music School, provides individual tuition to approximately one-third of the school. The Chapel Choir sings weekly choral services of a high order in the magnificent Chapel of St John Baptist, and are engaged in a busy performing schedule, which includes an overseas tour. The Orchestra, Jazz Club, Concert Choir, Chamber Choir, Middle School Choir and numerous ensembles have many and varied performing opportunities throughout the year. A large scale choral work is performed each year with professional orchestra and there is a series of professional concerts promoted each year. Stage musicals are also a regular feature.

The Science Schools have nine laboratories for the three sciences as well as a full complement of lecture/demonstration rooms. Each year a large number of students move on to continue their training in Engineering, Medicine, Agriculture and other branches of Applied Science, as well as the Pure Sciences. The School also has its own field study centre, and Astronomy Club.

IT Suite. Rossall commissioned its new Department of Information Technology and Computing. The new area creates a bespoke learning environment in the north end of the Science and IT Block. The "Genesis Cluster" comprises 27 state of the art Pentium III computers, each with its own scanner, fingerprint recognition security login and installed with latest software (including Microsoft Office 2000), running in a secure Windows NT network environment. The facility includes fast colour laser printing, daily back-ups, automatic virus interceptors, daily updated internet filters (to restrict pupils from accidentally wandering into inappropriate areas of the internet) with automatic internet activity logging and a host of security measures including 24 hour CCTV and alarm links direct to the local Police Force. New schemes of work throughout the age ranges have been created and a new A Level course in IT has now begun. IT is now an integral component in many academic disciplines.

The Design & Technology Centre, together with the adjoining Derby Arts Schools, offers pupils an opportunity to undertake a wide range of creative projects utilising traditional and modern techniques. Links to the Computer Suite enable pupils to access CAD and Graphic Design packages.

The Home Economics Department offers excellent facilities for both boys and girls to undertake courses in cookery and for girls to acquire skills in dressmaking.

The Modern Language Laboratory allows pupils of all ages to practise their conversation and pronunciation in French and German.

All Departments have ready access to teaching aids, such as video-recorders and the various types of projection equipment.

The House System. All children are members of a House which affords a recognisable social unit when they are not in the classrooms. There are 2 boys' boarding houses, and 1 boarding house for girls; also 2 for day-boys and 1 for day-girls. Boys and girls entering at the age of 11 spend two years in either James House or Osborne House. With the exception of Osborne and James Houses all boys and girls are accommodated in studies shared with others of the same age. Boarders sleep in small dormitories until they reach the Sixth Form, when study bedrooms are available for their last one or two years.

Housemasters, Housemistresses or Houseparents have overall responsibility for each boy's or girl's welfare and general progress; they or their Deputies are available at all times for consultation and advice. Full use is made of the School's careers advisers and of the Masters in charge of University and Polytechnic Admissions.

Maltese Cross House: Mr & Mrs M Holder-Williams

Mitre and Fleur-de-Lys House: Mr and Mrs J Ralph
Pelican House: C P Drew
Rose House (girl boarders): Miss K M Plant
Spread Eagle House: Mr and Mrs M G Roberts
James House: M Eddon
Dolphin House (day girls): to be appointed
Osborne House: Mr and Mrs R N Leake
Dragon Crescent House: Mrs R Fowkes

Religious Instruction. Rossall was founded as "The Northern Church of England School" and Chapel services remain an important part of every student's life. The Chaplain (assisted in his ministry by a former chaplain) exercises a pastoral role throughout the School. Each February a service of Confirmation is held in the Chapel. Pupils of other denominations are made warmly welcome.

Games. The 45 acres of playing fields allow all boys to play cricket, rugby, association hockey and lawn tennis; girls to play association hockey, netball and tennis. The sea-shore at low-tide offers a mile of sand which is used for the unique game of Rossall Hockey as well as other forms of exercise and relaxation. The 25-metre heated indoor pool is used for informal and competitive swimming throughout the year. Squash courts, Fives courts and Gymnasium are used throughout the day. Tennis is also played on hard courts during the summer. An all weather playing surface provides an international size Hockey pitch in winter and twelve Tennis courts in summer. An indoor climbing wall has recently been completed.

The CCF, Rossall Award and related activities. - During Year Nine boys and girls take part in the Service and Community Programme which introduces them to a variety of outdoor activities which include Orienteering, Canoeing, Camping, Windsurfing and Sub-Aqua.

In Years 10 and 11 pupils may join the CCF or continue on the Service and Community Programme. Rossall was the first School to form its own Corps (in 1860). A first-class miniature range is also in the grounds. A number of School and private boats sail regularly on the protected waters of the Wyre Estuary. There are regular opportunities for flying at RAF Wood Vale, near Southport.

In the Sixth Form, the emphasis on activities available to boys and girls is on service and leadership. Many do social service among the elderly and disabled in the neighbourhood. Some serve as NCO's in the CCF and as leaders in the Service and Community Programme. Others perform various duties to maintain different School organisations. Many boys and girls take part in the Duke of Edinburgh's Award Scheme.

Choice activities and Clubs. At various times throughout each week there are opportunities to opt for one of the following activities: drama in one of the productions regularly produced on the two stages; golf on one of the excellent local courses; astronomy in the School's Observatory with a fine 6 inch telescope; electronics in a laboratory set aside for this purpose; computer printing; debating; photography; chess; driving lessons.

Fees (at September 2000). Boarders: £4,725 per term. Day Pupils: £1,725 per term. For 11+ entrants to Osborne and James Houses, Boarders: £3,250 per term, day pupils: £1,625 per term.

Admission. All applications for entrance should be made to the Headmaster. On registration a fee of £30 will be charged. Applicants will be put in touch with a Housemaster or Housemistress as soon as appropriate. All enquiries about Scholarships and Bursaries and other awards should be addressed to the Headmaster.

Access. Motorway: 15 minutes from the M55 (spur off M6). Railway: Blackpool North (6 miles). Air: Manchester International Airport 55 minutes by road.

Rossall Preparatory School. Rossall has its own Preparatory School situated within the same grounds. (Full details will be found under the Preparatory School Section). There is also a Pre-Preparatory Department for day-boys and day-girls aged 2–7.

The Rossallian Club. (General Secretary: John Dewhurst, Rossall School, Fleetwood, Lancs FY7 8JW.) This Old Boys' Club keeps a record of more than 5,000 members and co-ordinates the activities of eight Branches. A Newsletter is published twice each year.

Charitable status. The Corporation of Rossall School is a Registered Charity, number 526685. It aims to provide a sound Christian education for boys and girls.

Rougemont School

Llantarnam Hall Malpas Road Newport S Wales NP20 6QB

Tel: (01633) 820800
Fax: (01633) 855598
e-mail: Thehead@rsch.co.uk

Governors:

Chairman of Governors: Mr I S Burge, Solicitor, former parent

Mr D Blayney, Solicitor
Mr C Bridgeman, Civil Engineer
The Revd Canon A Charters, MA, former Headmaster, King's School, Gloucester
Mrs S Evans, Teacher, Parent
Mr A W Graham, JP, FRICS, Chartered Surveyor, Parent
Mr T R Harker, Dental Surgeon, Parent
Mr P Lambert, Company Director
Mrs E Mais, Former Lower School Teacher
Archdeacon R H Roberts, CB, MA, Chairman of OFWAT
Mr I G Short, Company Director, Parent
Miss J Sollis, Careers Advisor/Educationalist
Mr M Tebbutt, Company Director
Mrs A C Thomas, JP, Former Parent

***Headmaster:* Mr Ian Brown,** DipPE

Assistant Headteacher: Dr D Wade, MA, BEd, CertEd, CertMaths *Mathematics*
Curriculum Co-ordinator: Mr M James, BEd, BA, BSc, CBiol, MBiol *Head of Biology*
Pastoral Co-ordinator: Mr J E G Worth, BA, PGCE *Head of Geography*

Senior Tutor (Years 3-6): Mrs L C Turner, BEd *English*
Senior Tutor (Years 7-9): Mr R M Wilkinson, MA, PGCE *Head of English*
Senior Tutor (Years 10-11): Mr G E Prothero, BA, CertPE *French, German, PE*
Senior Tutors (Sixth Form):
Mr R Carnevale, BSc, PGCE *Head of Physics*
Mrs E Ferrand, BEd (Hons) *Head of Mathematics*
Senior Mentor: Mr I R Kelly, BA, PGCE *Head of German*

Mrs S Ashton, BSc, PGCE *Mathematics*
Mr B Avis, MSc, InstP, PGCE *Physics and IT*
Miss E A Barnes, BEd *Girls Physical Education*
Mr K Bell, BA, PGCE *Physical Education*
Mrs K Benson-Dugdale, BMus, MA, PGEM *Head of Music*
Mr A L Bitvus, BSc, PGCE *Mathematics*
Mrs J Bolwell, CertEd *Junior School Class Teacher*
Mrs N Busschaert *French Assistant*
Mr J Clarke *English, Duke of Edinburgh Award Coordinator*
Mrs M Dimmock, CertEd *Part Time EFL Teacher*
Mr N George, CertEd *Junior English, History, Physical Education*
Mr R Georgious, BSc, PGCE *Economics and Business Studies*

Miss V Gibson, BA, ACT *Art (part-time)*
Mrs J Greenaway, CertEd *Junior School Class teacher*
Mr J Hardwick, BSc, PGCE *Biology, Chemistry*
Mrs J E Harris, CertEd, DipTheol *Head of Religious Studies, PSE Co-ordinator*
Mrs H Hoffmann, MA, BA, PGCE *English (part-time)*
Mr A H Marsden, BA, PGCE *Head of Physical Education*
Mrs M Martin, BMus (Hons), LTCL(TD) *Music*
Mr J McLoughlin, BSc *Head of Science and Chemistry*
Mr B W Minshall, BA, PGCE *Junior School Class Teacher*
Mrs E Mintowt-Czyz, ALA *Librarian*
Mr L Mintowt-Czyz, BA, BTec, PGCE *Head of Art*
Mrs D Morgan, BA, PGCE *Head of French*
Miss S Northam, BSc, PGCE *Mathematics*
Mr F C Pearce, BSc, PGCE *Head of Information Technology*
Mrs M Pettit, BSc, PGCE *Physical Education*
Mrs C E Poore, BEd *Physical Education, Science, Mathematics, KS2 Co-ordinator*
Mrs K Pugsley, BEd *Junior School Class Teacher*
Mrs J L T Rimell, BA, PGCE *English, Drama (part-time)*
Miss H Roberts, BA, QTS *Junior School Class teacher*
Mrs P Rogers, BSc, PGCE *Head of Geography*
Mr S Rowlands, BA *Teaching Assistant*
Miss A Rust, BA *Physical Education, History*
Mrs C Sims, BA, PGCE, AMBDA *Dyslexia Unit*
Mr H Singer, BA, PGCE *Head of Design & Technology*
Mrs R M Taylor, BA, PGCE *English, Dyslexia Unit*
Mr A J Twelftree, BA, PGCE *Head of Humanities, History*

Lower School:

Mistress in charge: Mrs N Rice, BA, PGCE

Kindergarten Supervisor: Mrs C Townsend

Miss A Ali, NNEB *Nursery Assistant*
Mrs A Barry, ACP *Year 1 Class Teacher*
Miss S Brean, ACP *Year 1 Class Teacher*
Mrs N Bunn *Class Helper*
Mrs S Burgess, NNEB *Nursery Assistant*
Mrs A Burridge *Class Helper*
Mrs J Farouzan, NNEB *Nursery Assistant*
Mrs S Hotchkiss, BA, QTS *Year 2 Class Teacher*
Mrs L Miah, BA, QTS *Year 1 Class Teacher*
Mrs C Monk *Reception Class Teacher*
Mrs S Morgan *Class Helper*
Mrs T Mountford *Year 2 Class Teacher*
Mrs S Neale, NNEB *Nursery Assistant*
Miss H Netherway, NNEB *Nursery Assistant*
Mrs N Noor, BA, PGCE *Reception Class Teacher*
Mrs J Smith, TTC *Year 1 Class Teacher*
Miss M Verrier, BA *Reception Teacher*
Mrs G Walshaw, SRN *Class Helper*

Rougemont was founded in a house of that name immediately after the First World War as a co-educational day school taking children through to grammar school entrance at 11. It moved to Nant Coch House (the present Lower School) just after the Second World War and grew to about 200 pupils.

In 1974 the school was re-founded as a Charitable Trust. Since then it has bought extensive new buildings and has over 680 pupils on role in Lower School (Nursery to Year 2), Middle School (Years 3–8) and Senior School (Years 9–13).

The Middle and Senior School moved to a new site at Llantarnam Hall, a large Victorian mansion set in 50 acres of grounds between 1992 and 1995. The grounds have been landscaped to provide playing fields and a building programme begun that will provide permanent facilities on the site. During 1998 a Liberal Arts area including Sports Hall, Music suite and Drama Studio was completed. In 1999 a new classroom block and library was completed and in 2000 additional classrooms together with Art studio were built.

Admission to the Lower, Middle and Senior Schools is by interview and subject to vacancy. Entry to the Sixth Form is dependent on GCSE results.

The following paragraphs refer to the Senior School although peripatetic specialists work in both and there is some inter-change of teachers.

Curriculum. Pupils follow a wide syllabus to 14. For the two years to GCSE pupils study nine subjects of which English Language and Literature, Mathematics, a language, science and a humanities subject are compulsory. 16 subjects are available.

Sixth Form. 14 AS/A2 levels are available. Sixth form pupils have their own common room and study area. All Sixth Form pupils also follow a General Course and take part in a range of extra-curricular activities and games.

Religion. Rougemont School has no direct affiliation to a Christian Church or denomination. However, the religious instruction, corporate worship and moral value system of the School is based on that of the broad tradition of the mainstream Christian Churches. All pupils are expected to take part in school assemblies and acts of corporate worship which have their roots in the Christian tradition.

Careers. The School belongs to the Independent Schools Careers Organisation. The Senior teachers advise on all aspects of further education and careers.

Music. These are specialist teachers of music and a number of peripatetic teachers covering the range of orchestral instruments. There are choirs and instrumental ensembles for all ages.

Drama. In addition to the Lower School's Spring Festival and the Senior School Eisteddfod, one major play and one musical are performed each year.

Elocution and Dance. Visiting staff hold weekly classes for LADA courses, ballet and modern dance.

Sport. The School is developing its own facilities at Llantarnam Hall but also uses facilities at nearby sports clubs which offer a full range of activities for all major sports.

Clubs. A wide variety of extra-curricular activities and clubs are available at lunch time and after school, as is supervised prep.

Duke of Edinburgh Award Scheme. This is a very successful activity within the school and over 52 pupils have gained the Gold Award.

Entrance. By interview and assessment.

Scholarships. An annual scholarship examination is held. Awards are available at 11, 13 and for the Sixth Form.

Former Pupils. The Former Pupils' Society hold annual reunions and matches between FP's and pupils.

Further information. A prospectus and other details are available from the Admissions Secretary (Tel: 01633 820800). E-mail: rougemont@rsch.co.uk.

Charitable status. Rougemont School is a Registered Charity, number 532341. It exists to provide education for boys and girls.

* Head of Department	§ Part Time or Visiting
† Housemaster/Housemistress	¶ Old Pupil
‡ See below list of staff for meaning	

The Royal Belfast Academical Institution

College Square East Belfast BT1 6DL.
Tel: (02890) 240461.

The School is under the management of a Board of Governors constituted under a scheme authorised by the Privy Council in Ireland. Twenty-four Governors are elected by members of the Institution, 3 are co-opted, and there are 2 parent and 2 teacher Governors.

Founded in 1810, the Institution was until 1849 a College as well as a School and had Faculties of Arts and Medicine; on the foundation of the Queen's College, now The Queen's University of Belfast, it became a School offering grammar school courses.

Motto: *Quaerere Verum.*

Board of Governors:
Chairman: Dr R J Rodgers, MA, FRSA

Vice/Chairman: A W Kinnaird, OBE, BAgr, BSc, FRICS

Secretary to the Governors and Registrar: J D Marshall, ACIS

***Principal:* R M Ridley**, MA

Vice-Principals:
M Gillan, BSc, MSc
C A McKinstry, BEd, PGDipGC

Dean: B J Todd, BA, MEd, PGCE

Head Masters of Departments:
F A Ormsby, MA (*English*)
A D Smyth, BSc (*Science*)
R J Maxwell, BA (*Languages*)
T S Bowles, BA (*Geography and Economics*)
D R J Carruthers, BSc, PhD (*Mathematics*)

Assistants:
J E McCullough, BA
I J Laverty, BSc, MRCS, DipEd
D A Haslett, BA, DipEd
W R Bennett, BA
D I Ritchie, BSc
J D Collins, BA, DipEd
C E Maitland, BA, DipEd
R J McGrath, BSc
R W S McMurray, MSc, DipEd
C M Macauley, MA
D G Reilly, BSc, PGCE, PGDipGC
R McB Davren, BSc
W J Collins, BSc, MSc, DipEd
C A Gault, BSc, PGCE
P Cupples, BA, PGCE
E T Foster, BA, MLitt, PGCE
R T Meek, BSc, PGCE
D J Madill, BA, PGCE
D Weir, BSc, DBA
J N O'Reilly, DipAd, ATD
B S Connell, BA
R G Pattinson, BA, PGCE
W O'D Jacques, BA
Mrs O M Campbell, BA, DipEd
Miss E R Mahoney, MSc, PGCE
N Ternahan, BA, PGCE
I W Condron, BSc, PGCE
P M Bolton, MA, BMus, PGCE
G I V Hamilton, BSc, PGCE
Mrs M A O'Fril, MBA, BSc(Econ), PGCE
Mrs C A B Wright, BA
Mrs J A Muise, BSc, PGCE
R E Cotter, BA, MIL, DPhil
Mrs C Kennedy, BEd, PGDipGC
B McD McLaughlin, BEd
R J Wilson, BEd, PGDSc
N McClements, BSc, PGCE
Mrs F C Eakin, BSc, MSc, PGCE
I R H Gray, BSc, PGCE
J B Peak, BA, PGCE
Miss S M Taggart, BA, CISM, PGCE
A R Monteith, BEng, PGCE
D J S Wilson, BA, PGCE
S S Reid, BA, PGCE
D S Scott, BSc, DIS, PGCE
R K Hedley, BSc, MSc, PGCE
N D Carson, BEng, MSc, PGCE
Miss W E Graham, BA, MA, PGCE
Miss V H Lyttle, BA, PGCE
A R Douglas, BSc, DIS, PGCE
G T Monteith, BEd
Miss K Andrews, BSc, PGCE
T A Hamilton, BA, PGCE
B P Waring, BA, PGCE
C J Greer, BSc, PhD, PGCE
Miss K R Coles, MA, PGCE
J H Seath, BD, PGCE
T H Lynn, BSc (Hons), MSc, PGCE

Preparatory School:

Head Master: W A O Armstrong, BA

Senior Assistant: R M Guy, BEd

Miss J Miskelly, TCert
S A Allen, BEd
S Markwell, BEd
Mrs R Watson, BEd
G W Francey, BA
V Sinclair, BA
Mrs D Wallace, BEd
Mrs A S H Morwood, BEd
Miss H E Wedlock, BEd, MEd
Miss D Robinson, BEd

The School occupies an 8-acre site in the centre of the City on which its first buildings were erected; major additions in 1983 and 1991 provide modern and specialised facilities. In addition to 40 Classrooms, there are seventeen specialist laboratories, Art suite, Technology and Design Centre, Music suite, a Careers room, a Computer department, a new Sports Hall, fitness suite, gymnasium, indoor heated swimming pool, fifty classrooms, a Common Hall with extensive stage facilities, a Dining Hall, an excellent library. There is also a very well-equipped Sixth Form Centre with study and social accommodation. There is a Boat House on the River Lagan.

For the first 3 years boys normally follow a common curriculum: in the fourth year the curriculum is still general but certain options are introduced, and at the end of the fifth, boys sit the examination for the Northern Ireland GCSE. Subjects studied at 'A' level in the Sixth Form include English, Modern History, Geography, Economics, French, German, Spanish, Greek, Latin, Technology, Mathematics, Physics, Government and Politics, Chemistry, Biology, Music and Art.

Rugby Football and Hockey are played in the winter; Athletics, Cricket and Tennis occupy the summer months; Badminton, Fencing, Shooting, Rowing, Squash and Swimming (including Water-polo and Life-saving) take place throughout the year. Teams representing the School take part not only in matches and activities within the Province, but also in events open to all Schools in the United Kingdom. There are numerous Clubs and Societies, a School Orchestra, Choir and Band, a contingent of the Combined Cadet Force, Scout and Venture Scout units and a Community Service Group.

Over 95% of each year's leavers go on to universities or to full-time courses in other institutions of higher or further education. In addition to a large number of prizes throughout the School, endowed Scholarships are offered in the Sixth Form which are tenable for travel or at University.

Candidates for admission to the Main School should be under 12 on 1 July of the year of admission and applications must be received by mid-February. Boys who are regarded by the Department of Education for Northern Ireland as qualified for grammar school education have their Tuition Fee paid by their local Education and Library Board. There is an annual capital fee of £570. Scholarships are awarded by the School to boys whose work shows outstanding progress during their School career.

Leaving Scholarships. There are offered each year up to 8 Sir Joseph Larmor Exhibitions, 2 Porter Exhibitions, 4 Hyndman Scholarships, 1 Trevor Nicholl Scholarship, 1 C L Handforth Prize and a James Moore Exhibition.

Preparatory School. This is set in 6 acres of ground in South Belfast. Admission is mainly at 5, but can be at any age depending on availability of places. The Annual Fee is £1,700.

Old Instonians' Association. *Hon Sec:* D Jardin, 5 Elmwood Pk, Lisburn, Co Antrim BT27 4AX.

The Royal Grammar School
Guildford

High Street Guildford Surrey GU1 3BB.
Tel: Headmaster: (01483) 880608.
School Office: (01483) 880600
Fax: (01483) 306127
e-mail: tmsyoung@mail.rgs-guildford.co.uk
website: www.rgs-guildford.co.uk

Governing Body:

Chairman: ¶K G Stephens, PhD, CEng, CPhys, FIEE, FInstP

Vice Chairman: D A R May, ACII

¶K T Ash, MBE
M Blocksidge, MA
Mrs J E Bratley
Mrs C Cobley, MIPM
The Reverend R L Cotton, MA, DipTh
Professor W Gelletly, OBE, PhD, CPhys, FInstP
B Hartop, BSc
A D Jenkins, MA
¶J N Martin, FICE, FIStructE, FEng
The Mayor of Guildford
The Earl of Onslow, High Steward of Guildford
J McCann
H J Pearson, MA, PhD, CMath, FIMA
¶J E Rule, FCA
Mrs C Stevens, CC
¶R C G Strick, MA, DLitt(Hon)
A J P Vineall, MA
Ms R J Walker, PhD, MA (Oxon), ACIS
N A White, PhD, MSc, CEng, FIMechE

Governor Emeritus: ¶J F Brown

Bursar and Deputy Clerk to the Governors: I C A Watson

***Headmaster:* T M S Young**, MA

Second Master: R Griffin, MA

Director of Studies: J A Simpson, BEd, MIBiol, AdDipEd, MSc, MPhil, CBiol

Third Master: A R Rattue, MA

Assistant Staff:
D H B Jones, BSc
A J W Thorn, MA
A T J Evans, ARCS, BSc
C J Pafford, BA
R E J Seymour, BEd, FRGS
P R Clark, MA
A G Kittow, BSc, MSc
S B R Shore, BEd
R D E Mant, BA, AMITD
E J Badham, ARCS, BSc, CBiol, MIBiol
Mrs M C Booth, BEd
C J Grace, BA, LTCL, AMusLCM
P J Hosier, BA, MEd
O C Lawson, BSc
G E Schofield, BEd, MA
Mrs E L Sharp, BA
Mrs E D McIntyre, MA
P H White, MA
W D Cowx, BSc, MSc
D J Woolcott, BA
Mrs J R Beattie, BA
G M Knight, BA
A Attenborough, MA
Mrs P C E Hemment, BSc
M R Jenkins, BSc
L M Holland, BSc
A C Evans, BEd
J R Saxton, MA
A N Rozier, BA
M P Richardson, MA
Mrs E Fischbach, BSc
M J Jennings, BA
J A Ross, MA
Lt Col G T Ardrey, MA, CEng
S G Thornhill, MA, DPhil
A Wain, LLB, MA
Mrs S J Lingard, BSc
T D Milton, BEd
Mrs R Downey, BA
A M J Curtis, MA
Mrs M R Goodman, BA
Mrs A Hurst, BA, ALA
Rev J Whitaker, MA
Mrs S A Ford, BEd
R A Nicholson, BEd
A H Dubois, BSc
M G Paterson, BA, MPhil
Mrs S Shattock (*Industrial Fellow*)
R B Meadowcroft, BA, MA
E Kinsella, BSc, PhD
Mrs K Handley, BSc
P A Le Bas, MA, DPhil, STL
Mrs S Rowlatt, BA, MA
G O Jones, BEd
J A Casale, BSc, MBA
D Rowlands, MA
M A Burbidge, BSc
D H Chambers, BMus, PCASS
Mrs J C Crouch, BSc
R Corthine, MA
P G Nathan, BA
Mrs D Whitehead, BTech
I Wilkes
Miss J E Nash, BSc, PhD
J P Danks, BSc, DPhil
J B Kelly, BA, MA
Mrs B J Norton, BMus, ARCM
H J P Ionascu, BMus, ARCM
A Marshall-Taylor, MA
T Arrand, BA
N E Wild, BA
A Facchinello, BA
J W Pressley, MA
Mrs J Bodmer, BSc, PhD
G J Kerr, BSc
S J H Yetman, BSc
S M Adams, BA
Miss A M Conway, MA
Mrs M Ford, BA

The Royal Grammar School has occupied its fine Tudor buildings in Guildford's High Street for nearly five centuries.

It was founded by Robert Beckingham in 1509 and established by King Edward VI's Charter of 1552, which decreed that there should be '. . . one Grammar School in Guildford . . . for the Education, Institution and Instruction of Boys and Youths in Grammar at all future times for ever to endure'. Among the first in the country to be purpose-built, the original buildings contain a remarkable Chained Library, which is now the Headmaster's Study.

The Royal Grammar School of the late 20th century is a day school for about 840 boys, some 250 of whom are in the Sixth Form. The age range is 11 to 18. It occupies a large site in the centre of Guildford. As well as the Chained Library, the Old Buildings contain the Careers Centre, the Sixth Form Common Room and the Music and Art departments. The New Building, opened in 1965, contains Great Hall, the Library, the Dining Hall and kitchens, the Gymnasium, the Language Laboratory and a large number of classrooms and laboratories. A continuous programme of building development has recently provided a Drama Studio, excellent facilities for Science and Technology, a Sculpture Studio and a large Resources Centre and Study Area. There are on-site facilities for training and coaching in various sports; most games teaching is at the splendid RGS sports ground at Bradstone Brook near Shalford. Transport to the games afternoons is provided.

The Royal Grammar School has a well-deserved reputation for academic excellence. Virtually all its sixth-formers comfortably pass at least three A levels and gain entry to higher education. About a quarter of them go on to Oxford and Cambridge.

In the first three years (Years 7, 8 and 9 nationally), all boys follow a common curriculum embodying the programmes of study for Key Stage 3 of the National Curriculum. The subjects studied are English, French, Geography, History, Latin, Maths, Information Technology, RE, PE, Art, Music and Science with Technology, which includes aspects of Astronomy, Earth Science, and Biotechnology. In the third Year (Year 9) all boys choose between German and Greek and study the separate sciences and Technology.

In the fourth and fifth Years (Years 10 and 11) all boys follow a broad and balanced curriculum and take at least nine GCSEs which include English, Maths, French and Science. In addition, all boys take RE, PE and Games. A course in Study Skills, Problem Solving and Personal, Social and Health Education is taught through a timetabled tutorial programme. After the GCSE examinations, all boys participate in the work experience programme.

In the Sixth Form, in addition to the subjects already mentioned, boys may take Classical Civilisation, Electronic Systems and Economics through to A level and Drama, Geology, Politics, ICT, PE and Spanish to AS level. Although many boys prefer a predominantly Maths/Science or Arts choice of subjects, there is no Arts/Science barrier, and more or less any combination is possible. There is an enterprising programme of Sixth Form General Studies organised in conjunction with Tormead School for girls.

The Royal Grammar School is not a specifically religious foundation, but Religious Education (non-denominational) is naturally an integral part of the School's curriculum. RE periods are compulsory at all levels in the School, although parents with conscientious objections may ask the Headmaster for alternative arrangements to be made. The school day normally begins with Assembly at which every boy is required to be present. The short Act of Worship which usually comprises Assembly is a Christian one. The School also holds annually its own Carol Service, Commemoration Service and Remembrance Service. The School is closely linked with Holy Trinity Church, a few yards down the High Street.

Each boy's progress through the School is monitored with care, and there is a system of regular checks involving the Careers Department in conjunction with a boy's parents. Below the Sixth Form a boy is looked after mainly by his Form Tutor; in the Sixth there is a system of tutor groups. All boys belong to one of the six Houses, which exist mainly to provide a framework for competitive sport, but which also give further pastoral care opportunities.

The School's day is from 8.45 am to 4.00 pm. There are no lessons on Saturdays.

Clubs and Societies flourish. Activities include Bridge, Chess, Computing, Debating, Electronics, Model Railway, History, Geography and Philosophy. There is a Scout Group, a Combined Cadet Force contingent, and participation in the Duke of Edinburgh's Award Scheme. Many boys play musical instruments and there is a School Orchestra, a variety of instrumental groups and a strong Choral Society. There are frequent opportunities for boys throughout the school to participate in dramatic productions. The Christian Union is extremely active.

The School's principal games are rugby, hockey and cricket, although as boys move up the School their sporting options widen considerably. Sports available include tennis, swimming, cross-country running, shooting, sailing, athletics, golf, squash, basketball, football and badminton. The School has recently produced sportsmen of international status in rugby, cricket, shooting, athletics and weight-lifting.

Boys may be considered for entry to the Royal Grammar School at any age between 11 and 18. The usual ages of entry, however, are at 11 from the maintained primary schools, 13 from the Preparatory Schools and 16 into the Sixth Form. Applicants aged 11 take the School's entrance examination early in the year of entry: Preparatory School boys take the Common Entrance examination after 11 or 12+ assessment.

The Headmaster is pleased to meet parents, arrange for them to see the School, and discuss the possibility of their son's entry to the School. Appointments may be made through the Headmaster's Secretary, who will supply the School's prospectus on request.

Scholarships. (*see* Entrance Scholarship section) Details of Scholarships and Bursaries are also available from the Headmaster's Secretary.

The termly fee, inclusive of all tuition, stationery and loan of necessary books, is £2,623.

Term of Entry. New boys are admitted in September of each year.

Preparatory Department. Lanesborough (see Part V of this Book) is the preparatory department of the RGS.

Old Boys. The Membership Secretary of the Old Guildfordians' Association is D H B Jones, BSc at the School.

Charitable status. The King Edward VI Royal Grammar School, Guildford is a Registered Charity, number 312028. It exists to provide education for boys from 11 to 18.

Royal Grammar School
Newcastle upon Tyne

Newcastle upon Tyne NE2 4DX.
Tel: 0191-281 5711
Fax: 0191-212 0392

The Royal Grammar School was founded and endowed in the early 16th century by Thomas Horsley, and by virtue of a Charter granted in 1600 by Queen Elizabeth it became 'the Free Grammar School of Queen Elizabeth in Newcastle upon Tyne'. It has for centuries valued its close links with the city and region, and its Governing Body consists largely of representatives of Local Authorities and Universities.

The School benefits from its central position, being within easy walking distance of the Civic and City Centres and of Newcastle's two Universities, and linked with the whole region by easily accessible rail, bus and metro services.

The School is a Day School for boys, with girls in the Sixth Form; there are about 1,050 pupils (including 145 in the Junior School). Some bursaries are available.

Governors:

N Sherlock, DL, BA (*Chairman*)

D L Taylor, MA (*Vice-Chairman*)

Dr M J Atkins, MA, DPhil
Councillor G W Douglas, BA, DipEd
B D Ebbatson, BA, MIL, DAES
Professor R G Egdell, MA, DPhil, CPhys, MInstP
J J Fenwick, DL, MA
P C Moth, MA
Dr K J Neill, MBBS, FRCA
Dr J R Patterson, MA, DPhil
Councillor N Povey
Councillor A W Purdue, BA, MLitt, FRHist
Professor C B Riordan, BA, PhD
L P Shurman, MA
Professor W J Stirling, MA, PhD, CPhys, FInstP
P A Walker, BA
S E Wood, BA, LLB

Clerk to the Governors and Bursar: R J Metcalfe, MA, FBIFM

***Headmaster:* J F X Miller**, MA

Second Master: J R Armstrong, MA

Assistant Staff:

Art:
*K Egan-Fowler, BA
S J Crow, BA
Mrs M Elliott, DipEd
§Mrs J R Sheppard, BA

Biology:
*T J Bolton-Maggs, MA
M H Bell, BSc, PhD
Miss S L Deliss, BSc
P M Fernandez, BA
Mrs J A Malpas, BSc

Chemistry:
*N R Goldie, BSc (*Head of Science*)
*Mrs J W Collins, BSc, MSc
Mrs C H Goodman, BSc
A D Law, BA
A J Pulham, BA, DPhil
Mrs S J Syers, BSc
§Mrs J M MacGregor, BSc

Classics:
*Mrs C N Astington, BA
T C Clark, BA (*Head of Lower School*)
E H T Noy Scott, BA
S J W Squires, MA
§M A Griffiths, MA

Computing:
*D J Lawson, BSc

Economics/Politics:
*R C M Loxley, BSc
G F Keating, MA
J D Neil, MPhil
P Shelley, BA, MSc

English:
*S J Barker, BA, PhD
Mrs H Jones-Lee, BA, DPhil (*Head of General Studies*)
Mrs J Ross, BA
D A Rothwell, BA
Miss C Shephard, BA, MA
J S G Thomas, MA (*Head of Drama*)
Mrs C Thomson, BA

Geography:
*D A Wilson, BSc
M G Downie, BA
Mrs R J L Laws, MA
A O Newman, BA

History:
*B Mains, BA, DPhil
M Bond, BA
O L Edwards, BA
J Ferstenberg, BA
P J Saint, BA
S E Tilbrook, BA

Mathematics:
*P J Mitchell, MA, MSc, DPhil
A Delvin, BSc, MSc
W Gibson, BA
T E Keenan, BSc
Mrs P E Perella, BA, MSc
E D Renshaw, BSc
D J Ridley, BA
Mrs E Temple, BSc
S D Watkins, BSc (*Head of Middle School*)

Modern Languages:
*Mrs P A Sainsbury, BA
Mrs L M Boucaud, BA
Miss C L Crossley, BA
Miss S Demoulin, DEUG
Mrs H A Murphy, MA (*Head of French*)
M C Oswald, MA (*Professional Development Co-ordinator*)
D M Walton, BA
§M Metcalf, MPhil

Music:
*N T Parker, BA
A A Bird, BMus, LRAM (*Director of Studies*)
Miss A P Graham, BMus

Physical Education:
*P J Ponton, BA, DLC
G Bradley, BSc
F Dickinson, BEd
D W Smith, BEd (*Senior Master*)
P D Taylor, CertEd, DipPE
§R V MacKay, ILAM Leisure, CC Leisure

Physics:
*E T Rispin, BSc
A N Baker, BSc
J L Camm, BSc
G D Williams, BSc
P Wilson, MSc

Religious Studies:
*H H H Baker, MA (*also Third Master and Head of Upper School*)
D J Merritt, MA (*Counsellor*)

Technology:
*I Goldsborough, BEd, MSc
S Gooch, HND, BEd
Mrs C A Pipes, BA

Junior School:
R J Craig, BEd (*Headmaster*)
J K Wilkinson, BEd (*Deputy Head*)
Mrs C S Daly, BSc
Miss R Irving, BA
Mrs V James, BA
Mrs B Joy
A J Spencer, BSc, PhD
J S Wood, BA

School Medical Officer: Dr M A Borthwick, MB, BS, MRCGP

The accepted date for the foundation of Newcastle RGS is 1545 and so for 450 years and on six different sites the school has been of major educational importance in Newcastle and in the North East as a whole. It currently has 915 pupils in the Senior School (11–18) and 140 in the Junior School (8–11).

Work. The aim of the curriculum up to Year 11 is to offer a general education, culminating in GCSE in a wide range of subjects. All boys study English, French, Mathematics, Biology, Physics and Chemistry to this level and three further examination subjects are taken at GCSE level from Art, Classical Studies, Economics, Geography, German, Greek, History, Latin, Music and Technology. Additionally there is a programme of Art, Music, IT and Technology for all in Years 7 to 9.

Sixth Formers will normally choose 4 subjects for study to AS level in the Lower Sixth, and in the Upper Sixth 3 subjects to A level, most combinations from the following list being possible: Art, Biology, Chemistry, Classical Civilisation, Economics, English, French, Geography, German, Greek, History, Latin, Mathematics, Further Mathematics, Music, Physics, Politics, Psychology, Religious Studies, Technology. Philosophy is one of several subjects available as an AS in the Lower Sixth. There is a substantial course of General Studies available including such options as Arabic, GCSE Physical Education, and Spanish or Italian.

Almost all sixth-formers go on to University, and success in gaining entry at Oxford and Cambridge has been an outstanding feature of the school's record.

Physical Education. All pupils are required to take part in a Physical Education programme which, up Year 10, includes Rugby Football, Cricket, Athletics, Gymnastics, Swimming. At the upper end of the School a wider range of activities is offered: in addition to the above pupils may opt for Badminton, Basketball, Climbing, Cross-country Running, Fencing, Fitness training, Hockey, Karate, Orienteering, Squash, Tennis, Volleyball. A wide range of activities is available to all through voluntary membership of various Sports Clubs.

Activities. Art, Drama and Music are strong features in the life of the School, all of them over-flowing from scheduled lessons into spare-time activity. There are two school orchestras, 2 wind bands, a jazz band and various other instrumental ensembles. There are two productions in the theatre in most terms. Numerous societies meet in the lunch-break or after school, some linked with school work but many developing from private enthusiasms. There is a Duke of Edinburgh Award programme. There is an entirely voluntary Combined Cadet Force Contingent. Annual overseas visits include ski-parties and exchange arrangements with schools in France and Germany.

Supervision and Pastoral Care. Each pupil is within the care of (a) Form Supervisor and (b) Tutor. The latter will normally be associated with the pupil throughout their school career, and the aim is to forge a personal link with pupils and their families.

The Careers programme begins in Year 9; in Year 11 and the 6th Form every possible care is taken to advise each pupil individually about Careers and Higher Education.

The School's Medical Officer is available regularly for consultation, and organises conferences and lectures on subjects within his sphere; there is also a School Counsellor.

Buildings. Most of the School's buildings date from 1907 and are described by Pevsner as "friendly neo-Early-Georgian". Recent years have seen many developments and improvements, including the rebuilding of the indoor swimming pool in 1990, the opening in February 1996 of a new Sports Centre, a new Science and Technology Centre which opened in 1997, and new Maths and ICT departments in 1998.

Junior School. The Junior School is separately housed in Lambton Road opposite the Senior School playing fields. Junior School boys use the Senior School laboratories, Sports Centre, Swimming Pool, games fields and dining hall. The basic subjects of English and Mathematics are taught by Form Teachers, while Environmental Studies, French, Science, Religious Education, Music, Art and Physical Activities are taken by specialists. Modern methods are blended with a sound and tried traditional approach.

Entrance. Entry is by examination. No waiting list is kept. Application forms available from the Admissions Secretary.

Junior School (a) At 8+. The Junior School examination is held each January for boys who will be 8 on 1 September of the year in which entry is desired. Applications by 13 January. There is a small entry at 9+ also by examination in January.

Senior School (b) At 11+. The Senior School examination is held each January for boys who will be 11 on 1 September of the year in which entry is desired. Applications by 15 December (later application at School's discretion).

(c) At 13+. An entrance examination is held each February, or entry at this age may be through the Common Entrance Examination (usually in February). Applications by 15 December (later application at School's discretion).

(d) At 16+. Applicants are considered for direct entry to the 6th Form if their GCSE results are likely to form an adequate basis.

The examinations for entry at 8+, 9+ and 11+ include a paper in arithmetic and an English comprehension and composition paper. Sample questions will be sent on receipt of the completed application form. Further details of the examination at 13+ are available on request.

Term of Entry. Autumn only.

Fees (2000-2001). Full fees are £5,139 pa (Senior School), £4,284 pa (Junior School).

Some bursaries, awarded on the basis of parental income, are offered; bursaries include some awarded by the Ogden Trust, which may cover all fees and expenses depending on parental income. Details are available from the Bursar.

Charitable status. Royal Grammar School, Newcastle upon Tyne is a Registered Charity, number 528148. It is a Charitable Trust for the purpose of educating children.

Royal Grammar School
Worcester

Upper Tything Worcester WR1 1HP
Tel: (01905) 613391
Fax: (01905) 726892
e-mail: office@rgsw.org.uk
website: www.rgsw.org.uk

The School was founded ante 1291, received its Elizabethan Charter in 1561 and was granted its 'Royal' title by Queen Victoria in 1869.

Motto: *Respice et Prospice.*

Governing Body:
The Six Masters of Worcester
N L Collis (*Chairman*)
I L Carmichael, BSc, AIMechE
P T Sawyer, FRICS
W B Stallard, MA, LLB
M B Tetley, FCA
P C Underwood, JP, MInstBm

Nominative:
R I Ingles, MA (*Old Elizabethans*)
N W Tanner, PhD (*Oxford University*)
R H Rowden (*City of Worcester*)

Co-opted:
Mrs J Douglas-Pennant
R G Fry, OBE
A Lee
C W Parr
T G Walker, FCA, FBIM

***Headmaster:* W A Jones**, MA

Second Master: P J Lee, BA

Senior Master: N W Lowson, BA

Section Heads:
S C Woolcott, BA (*Sixth Form*)
R J Michael, MA (*Middle School*)
R H Savage, BSc (*Year Nine*)
R L Blackbourn, BSc (*Lower School*)

Assistant Masters:
B M Rees, BA
A R Millington, BSc, MIBiol
M J Ridout, BA, MSc
D J Cotterill, BEd
B J Hughes, BSc, PhD
C D A Carter, BSc
J G Wilderspin, BSc, ARCO
M D Wilkinson, BSc
J M Shorrocks, BSc, BA
J H Croasdell, BEd
H Groves, MA
M J Sledge, MA
J N Waller, MA
R Cartwright, DipTEd, AMIBF
T S Curtis, BA
M D Ralfe, MA
S D Howells, BA
C S Kelly, BEd
I Venables, BA
M H Vetch, MA
P J O'Sullivan, BSc
P Roberts, BA, ALA
R C Tarry, BSc
C N Wright, BA
R D Burt, MA
J P R Newton-Lewis, BA
S C Brough, BEd
P Dent, BSc
S N Alexander, BA
D J Ward, MA
J D Moffatt, BA
S R Ravenhall, BA
C M Hamilton, BA
R T Gibson, MA
P H Mullins, BSc, PhD
Mrs D A Dawson, BEd
G Emerson, BA
G W Hughes, BEd
R N Berry, BSc
I J Connor, BSc
M M Fairweather, MA
S J Osmond, MA
R J Stanyer, BSc
J S Wilson, BA
R Turner
D Ayling, MA
J E Collings, BA
Miss E Lindgren, BA
Miss A J Bollons, BA
P J Day, MA
J C Friend, BSc
P Newport, BA
T A Smith, BEng
J Stow, BSc
R J Wiebkin, BA
A P Wilson, MA
G M Cramp, BSc
T J B Hallett, BA
M G Skinner, BA

Preparatory School:
R E Hunt, BA (*Head*)
J L Wickson, BA
P R Hitchcock, BEd
A M Sinton, BEd
Mrs M Yarnold, BEd
T C Barnes, MSc
A C Hymer, BA
Miss C H Darge, BA
Mrs H L Baverstock, BA
J Holtby, BA

Pre-Preparatory School:
Miss A D Gleave, BEd
Mrs A Fincher, NNEB
Miss J Houlton, NNEB
Miss J Allen-Griffiths, BA

Mrs V Bradley, BA
Mrs M-C Egginton, BSc
Mrs M E Windsor, CertEd
Mrs D Bennett
Miss N Evans, BA
D Coggins, BA
Mrs A E Parish, BEd
Mrs L Gundersen, BSc
Mrs S Coleman, BA
Dr R Scase, PhD
Miss E M Bussey, BEd
Miss P Davies, BEd

Bursar: Cdr M J Sime, CDipAF, FIMge, RN

Situation and Buildings: The School is situated a few minutes' walk from the centre of the City and convenient for rail and bus stations. The older buildings date from 1868. Substantial benefactions by the late C W Dyson Perrins provided a fine Assembly Hall and Science Laboratories and, more recently, a Sixth Form Centre, Dining Hall, Design Centre, Lecture Theatre and Sports Hall have been constructed. The playing fields are close by and the School has good use of the local swimming pool.

Organisation: The School is divided into an 11–18 senior school (718 boys), an 8–11 prep school (121 boys) and a new 3–8 pre-prep (165 boys and girls). The senior school, including 202 sixth-formers, is divided into four sections, Lower (Years 7 and 8), Year 9, Middle (Years 10 and 11) and Sixth Form, with a senior member of staff responsible for each. The basic unit is the form, and the form tutor, under the Head of Section, is responsible for all day-to-day matters relating to the pupils in his charge. In addition, all pupils are placed in one of eight Houses which exist mainly for internal competitive purposes, but which do provide an important element of continuity throughout a pupil's career at the School.

Aims: A high level of academic achievement is sought within a caring and civilised society. By placing emphasis on a wide range of sporting and other activities, we aim to extend our pupils in as many ways as possible. Overall, we offer a balanced and challenging education which will stand our pupils in good stead in their future careers and within the community at large.

Curriculum: Pupils follow a common curriculum for the first three years which includes the usual academic subjects, plus IT, Design Technology, Music and PE. The GCSE option arrangements (Years 10 and 11) allow a wide choice, subject to final selection giving a balanced curriculum which does not prejudice subsequent career decisions. Normally 9–10 subjects are studied: English, Mathematics, French and Science being setted and compulsory, plus three from German, Latin, Spanish, Geography, History, RE, Music and Design Technology. Most members of the Sixth Form study four subjects to 'AS' level and three to A2 level. In addition to those subjects studied at GCSE level, Economics and Business Studies, PE, ICT, Ancient History and Politics can be taken up.

Careers: The School is a member of ISCO; the well-equipped Careers Rooms are readily available and the Careers Master is responsible for ensuring that all pupils receive basic careers education, and, subsequently, access to all the necessary information and experience on which a sound decision may be made regarding future career and Further or Higher Education.

Physical Activities: The School aims to satisfy a wide range of sporting interests and abilities. Rugby Football is the main Winter Term activity; Association Football and Cross-Country Running are the main outdoor Spring Term sports and Cricket, Athletics, Swimming and Rowing have a full programme of fixtures in the Summer Term. Basketball and Badminton share priority in the Sports Hall throughout the year, though serious cricket coaching is given throughout the winter months. Tennis, Golf, Hockey, Fencing and Squash are also offered.

Outdoor Pursuits. Combined Cadet Force and Duke of Edinburgh's Award Scheme: all pupils may choose to join one or the other at the beginning of Year 10. The strong CCF comprises Royal Navy, Army and Air Force Sections and all cadets receive instruction in shooting. Good opportunities exist for attachments to regular units in UK and abroad, for flying training, for leadership training and for Adventure Training. Those who choose the Duke of Edinburgh Scheme can work for the bronze, silver and gold awards, and undertake Adventure Training, and Community Service.

Other Activities: There is a wide range of Clubs and Societies. All lower school pupils receive drama lessons as part of the curriculum and school productions take place each term. School music is also strong: in particular, there is a fine organ, a wind band, brass ensemble, madrigal group and an Early Music Consort. The School fosters a range of international links including regular exchanges with schools in France, Germany and Spain.

September Admission is by our own examination held in February, mainly at 11+. However, we also examine at 12+ and 13+. Pupils are also admitted into the Sixth Form on the basis of GCSE results, an interview and a test. Exceptionally, pupils can also be examined and admitted at any time of the year. Admission to the Preparatory School is at age 8, 9 or 10 after examination.

Fees: September 2000 £1,612–£1,932 per term (no extras).

Scholarships, Bursaries. Scholarships are available at age 11 and 13, irrespective of parental means. Major Scholarships give one-half and one-third remission of fees. There are also a number of minor scholarships worth one-sixth remission. Bursaries are also available according to parental means. Similar facilities are available for entry into Sixth Form. When making awards, note is taken not only of academic ability but also of potential in one or more of the School's main activities. Further particulars can be obtained from the Registrar, Mrs L Horne.

Charitable status: Royal Grammar School, Worcester is a Registered Charity, number 527527. The aim of the charity is the education of boys, and of girls up to the age of 8.

The Royal Hospital School

Holbrook Ipswich Suffolk IP9 2RX
Tel: 01473 326200

The Royal Hospital School is a co-educational boarding school with 680 pupils aged 11 to 18. Founded at Greenwich in 1712 by the Crown Charity, Greenwich Hospital, it moved to its present 200 acre purpose-built site on the banks of the Suffolk Stour in 1933.

The School is magnificently situated and well equipped. All boarding accommodation and teaching areas have been refurbished during the last decade and recent additions include a purpose-built Technology Centre, Computing and Food Technology areas and an all-weather sports surface. A Sixth Form Centre will open in September 2001.

The facilities for sport and leisure are of the highest order. There is a nine hole golf course, ninety acres of playing fields, a sports hall, heated indoor swimming pool and squash courts. The School has a strong sailing tradition with a fleet of dinghies on the adjacent reservoir as well as yachts and dinghies in our own creek giving access to the River Stour and the North Sea at nearby Harwich.

The School has a particular musical tradition with a fine choir, an orchestra and band. Almost half the pupils are involved in music on a regular basis. The Chapel is of cathedral proportions and has one of the finest organs in England.

Whilst the School is open to children from all backgrounds the parent charity, Greenwich Hospital, awards bursaries to the children and grandchildren of seafarers. Half fee scholarships are awarded for academic excellence, music, art, sport and an interest in things maritime, as well as into the Sixth Form for candidates gaining 6 or more 'A*, A' grades at GCSE and following interview. Day places are also available for Sixth Form entry.

Visitor: HRH The Duke of York

Director of Greenwich Hospital: D C R Heyhoe, Esq

Chairman of Governors: T Fellowes

***Headmaster:* N K D Ward**, BSc

Deputy Headmaster: J M Gladwin, BSc

Chaplain: The Reverend Dr C E Stewart

Senior Master and Registrar: M L March, JP, BEd

Senior Mistress: Mrs H Anthony, BA

Director of Studies: S R Letman, BA, MA

Head of Sixth Form Studies: Dr P M Chapman, BA, MA, PhD

Teaching Staff:
*C F Morgan, BA
*C J Chick, BSc
*P H Crompton, GRNCM
S P Durrant, BA
L Thompson, BEd
*P Hall, MA
A G Tottle, BSc
*D W Hawkley, BA
*¶M A Callow, BSc, MA
*¶R Trowern, BSc
P A Surzyn, BSc
*S R Warr, MA, ACP
†A J Loveland, BSc, MA (*Collingwood*)
*H Yates, BSc
*L Dryden
A J Wilding, BEd
S J Barley, BSc
L R Menday, AIST
†J R Dugdale, BEd (*Anson*)
*D D Harrison, BA MA
S F Walker, BA
*J C Herbert, BSc, MA
*Mrs C Herbert, BSc
P E Creasey, CEng, MIEE, AIST
Mrs R Gladwell, BSc, MA
*P G A Mussett, BSc
Dr D S Stratford, DSc, BSc
Mrs K V Wilkinson, BEd, GIBio
*I V Simmons, BA
R Jones, ARCM
†Mrs J Hillard, DipEd (*Howe*)
P McCaffery, BMus, LRAM, ARCM
*L G Frost, BEd, BSc, MA
†C A Rennison, BSc (*Hawke*)
P Madge, BA
*G D Ravenhall, BA, ATD
C Boughton
†Mrs D M Clayton, DipEd (*Blake*)
*Dr F M Kirk, BA, MA, PhD
S M Lovell, BSc
*P Hardman, BSc
†M H Godfrey, BSc (*Nelson*)
†Mrs S Godfrey, BA (*Nelson*)
Miss C Hinchliffe, BSc
Mrs S Bruce, DipEd
Mrs J Wilby, BA
Miss L Castaldo, BA(Ed)
Mrs D Dean, BA
†Mrs J Fuschillo, CertEd (*Hood*)
*M Hart, DipM
Mrs N Mann, MA
Mrs A Pearson, BEd
†B Hocking, BEd, MEd (*St Vincent*)
*A Gloag, BA
Mrs D Hitchin, BA
D Simmons, BEd
P P Malone, BSc
†Miss S J Bourhill, CertEd (*Cornwallis*)
Miss L M Porter, BA
Miss A Lynn, MA
D Cousins, BA
Miss N A Belle-Isle
Mrs G Miller, MA
R J Mann, BA
†S Matthews, BA (*Drake*)
†A Evans, BA, BSc (*Raleigh*)
D Miles, MA
S Fairclough, BA

Bursar: R J Crick
Librarian: Miss R Gitsham, BA
Roman Catholic Chaplain: Fr Michael Ryan

Boarding Houses. There are eleven boarding houses, all modernised to a similar high standard to allow younger pupils to live in clusters of four and with double or single rooms for older pupils. In the Upper Sixth boys and girls join 'Nelson' where the regime aims to prepare them for life after school. Pupils at this stage have single rooms.

The Curriculum. The School follows the main elements of the National Curriculum. At eleven there are usually four forms, rising to five or six by Year Nine. The School aims class size not to exceed 24 and in most cases forms of 20 to 22 are the norm. Pupils are streamed and in many cases setted for subjects from the outset. All pupils are expected to follow GCSE in a minimum of 8 subjects with most taking 9 or 10.

Entry into the Sixth Form is as a result of gaining a minimum of 8 points at GCSE (where Grade C equates to 1 point). For students who do not feel suited to conventional Advanced Level courses the School offers Advanced VCE Business. All other students will follow AS and A2 courses from a wide range of options. In addition it is also possible to follow an Advanced Level General Studies course.

Careers guidance. From Year 9 onwards there is a continuous service both inside and outside the curriculum. All pupils take part in a Personal and Social Education course and are offered expert careers help by the Careers Master and by outside specialists. Much information on careers and higher education is available via the computer network.

Religion. There is a Chapel which holds well over a thousand. Inter-denominational services are held and Roman Catholic pupils are able to regularly attend Mass. The Chaplain prepares candidates for Confirmation annually and every School day begins with an act of worship.

Facilities. The School is situated on a magnificent 200 acre purpose-built campus overlooking the River Stour. There are 90 acres of playing fields and the main sports coached are rugby, soccer, hockey, netball, cricket, athletics, cross country, rounders, tennis and swimming. A newly opened all-weather surface is much used. The swimming pool offers opportunities for canoeing and sub-aqua as well as the more usual pursuits. There is a nine hole golf course and the School has extensive sailing facilities on the River Stour and on the nearby Alton Water Reservoir where every pupil has the opportunity to learn to sail. A new Library, a Technology Centre and three Computing Centres have been added to the School's facilities in the recent past.

CCF and Community Service. All pupils join the Combined Cadet Force in Year 9 and are able to choose between Army, Naval, RAF and Royal Marine Sections. The emphasis is on adventurous training at all levels and The Duke of Edinburgh Award Scheme thrives within the School. Staff and pupils operate the Holbrook Auxiliary Coastguard Station and there is a thriving St John Ambulance Brigade unit. The Community Action Team is actively involved in a wide range of activities.

Music and Drama. As well as the choir and chamber choir which perform both nationally and internationally there is a fine marching and concert band as well as an orchestra. Peripatetic teachers offer tuition in a wide range of instruments and the School organ is one of the finest in Europe, much used by pupils as well as professional performers. Talented performers are offered free instrumental tuition. There is a popular annual house singing competition and choir and band concerts attract large audiences.

A wide range of drama is on offer; as well as drama within the curriculum there is at least one school play and a major musical each year. There are also junior plays and an annual inter-house Drama Festival.

Further Education. The majority of pupils move onto University upon completion of Advanced Levels. Annual awards are made to assist successful students at University.

The School is particularly proud of its links with HM Forces, and particularly the Royal Navy. A number of students progress to Dartmouth and elsewhere after University.

Travel. Coaches are organised by parents to the South and South West of England. The School provides the services of an International Co-ordinator to oversee the travel arrangements of all pupils living overseas and they are collected from Heathrow at the beginning of every term. Tickets for national and international travel can be booked through the School.

Admission. Entry to the School is at 11, 13 and 16 with small numbers joining at 12 and 14. The entrance examination takes place at the end of January and may be taken in conjunction with Common Entrance. Entry into the Sixth Form is by way of GCSE results following an interview with the Headmaster and senior staff.

Fees. (*see* Entrance Scholarship section) At the Royal Hospital School the fee includes all school uniform, sports clothing, accommodation, food and tuition. The current maximum fee for UK residents (1999-2000) is £3,693 per term. The day fee is £2,394 per term. For non UK residents the fee includes ESL tuition and travel to and from Heathrow and is £4,027 termly. Fees are generally set a little above forces BSA and for the children and grand-children of seafarers not in receipt of this allowance the fees are assessed by Greenwich Hospital on the basis of family income up to a maximum of £3,134 per term. Subsequent eligible children will usually pay a fee of £330 pa.

Scholarships. Up to 10 half fee scholarships are awarded annually into Years 7 and 9 for academic excellence, musical, artistic talent, for sport and for an interest in things nautical. Minor (25%) Scholarships are also available. Additionally, free musical tuition is offered to pupils of high ability. Candidates entering the Sixth Form with 6 or more A grades (minimum of 1 A*) may be offered half fee academic scholarships.

Charitable status. The Royal Hospital School is owned by Greenwich Hospital which is a Crown Charity. The School exists to provide education for boys and girls aged from 11 to 18.

Rugby School

Rugby Warwickshire CV22 5EH.

Head Master: Tel: (01788) 556216; Fax: (01788) 556219

e-mail: head@rugby-school.warwks.sch.uk

Bursar: Tel: (01788) 556261; Fax: (01788) 556267

e-mail: bursar@rugby-school.warwks.sch.uk

Registrar: Tel: (01788) 556274; Fax: (01788) 556277

e-mail: registry@rugby-school.warwks.sch.uk

Website: www.rugby-school.warwks.sch.uk

Motto: *Orando Laborando*

Rugby School was founded in the year 1567 by Lawrence Sheriff, native of Rugby, one of the Gentlemen of the Princess Elizabeth, a Grocer and Second Warden of the Grocers' Company. The School was endowed with estates in the neighbourhood of Rugby and in London. In 1750 the School moved to its present site on the edge of Rugby town. Between 1809 and 1814 the Head Master's House, School House and the Old Quad were built. Under Dr Arnold and subsequent Head Masters, including two later Archbishops of Canterbury, Rugby was influential in establishing the pattern of independent education throughout the country.

There are currently 770 pupils, including 275 girls and 175 day pupils. The proportion of girls in the School will rise in September 2002, when an existing boys' House becomes a new girls' House.

Rugby values scholarship, team work in games, music and drama, and qualities of leadership and self-reliance in the pupils. Rugby prides itself on a sharp edge of academic excellence but its aim, as a fully coeducational school, is to encourage cooperation, seeing a wide range of enterprises through to their conclusion, an awareness of the wider world and a lively approach to a very broad range of opportunity. The boys and girls who come to Rugby are expected to have a go at a variety of things. As they leave they should feel ready for (almost) anything; that they have stretched themselves and have been asked to do a great deal; and finally that along the way life at Rugby has been fun.

Governing Body:

Sir Ewen Fergusson, GCMG, GCVO (*Chairman*)
W M T Fowle, Esq (*Deputy Chairman*)
Professor H F A Strachan
M J Aldridge, Esq, FRSM
Mrs J Leslie, JP
Miss E Llewellyn-Smith, CB
A P Shearer, Esq, FCA
Mrs E A Malden, MA
Dr P J Cheshire
Professor N W Gowar, FRSA, FIMA
R S Broadhurst, Esq, FRICS
The Lord Lieutenant of the County of Warwick, M Dunne, Esq, JP
The Rt Hon Lord Lang of Monkton
Mrs P Williams
The Rt Revd D A Urquhart
Mrs J Bailey

Bursar and Clerk to the Governing Body: G M Randall, MA, FCA

Estates Bursar: C P Daw, BA, DipArch, RIBA

Medical Officers:
Dr P J Kilvert, BSc, MB, BS, DRCOG, DCH
Dr R M Bryant, MB, ChB, DRCOG, DA, FFARCSI

***Head Master:* P S J Derham**, MA

Deputy Heads:
J P Allen, MA, CChem, FRSC
D Livingstone, BSc, PhD

Director of Studies: Mrs S K Fletcher, BA

Registrar: Mrs H A Morrish, MA, ACIB

Assistant Teaching Staff:

Chaplaincy:
The Revd R M Horner, BSc (*Chaplain*)
Miss K Bohan, MA, MAT, BD (*Assistant Chaplain*)

Classics:
M J Taylor, BA, ALCM (*Head of Department*)
Miss E Mills, BA
A P Walker, MA
H Price, MA

Design:
C P John, BA, FRSA (*Director of the Design Centre*)
P A Byrne, BA (*Head of D & T*)
R B Drennan, DSD, CDS (*Director of Drama and Media*)
Miss K M Atkin, BA
M Howard, DipAD
P D Richard, BSc
Miss S J Sharrard, MA
M R Williams, BA
B E Gurah, BA (*Jewellery*)
Mrs S E Phillips, BA (*Ceramics*)
Miss L J Pilcher, BDes (*Photographer in Residence*)
P Deller, BA (*Head of Art*)

Economics and Business Studies:
M E Ronan, MA (*Head of Department*)
J A H Lewis, BA
P J Rosser, BA
H G Steele-Bodger, MA
B Walton, BSc

English:
J B Cunningham-Batt, BA (*Head of Department*)
Miss H E Alexander, MA
Mrs E M Barlow, BA
A Fletcher, MA
A Golding, BA
Ms J James, BA
A J Naylor, BA

Geography:
J C Evans, BA (*Head of Department*)
D Livingstone, BSc, PhD
Miss A J V Moreland, BEd
Mrs S A Rosser, BEd
A E Smith, BSc, MPhil, PhD, FRMetS, FRGS

History:
E A V Beesley, BA (*Head of Department*)
P W Dewey, BA
Mrs S K Fletcher, BA
J R Moreland, MA
J D Muston, MA, MPhil, DPhil

Information Technology:
S D Carter, BSc (*Head of Department*)
C A Burton, BSc, PhD, MIITT
J S Heir, BSc

Mathematics:
G A M Newth, MA
D G Dachtler, BSc
C J Edwards, MA
Mrs J Fielden, MA
G J Hedges, MA
E D Hester, BA (*Head of Department*)
R G Murray, BSc
D A Shinkfield, BSc
R W B Williams, MA
S Hill, BSc

Modern Languages:
S Sommer, MSc (*Head of Department*)
J M Burns, MA
Mrs W J Corvi, BEd
N D Jarvis, BA, MA
J P King, MA
Mrs A C Leamon, BA, MA, PhD
M G P T Leverage, MA
Mrs C A M O'Mahoney, BA
J C Smith, MA, DPhil
Mrs S Sommer, MA
Mrs C Williams, L-ès-L, M-ès-L
G J Winter, MA

Music:
A P Crook, MA, BMus, ARCO, LRAM (*Director of Music*)
G D Bevan, MMus, BMus, ARCO(CHM), ARCM (*Assistant Director of Music*)
T W Bentham, BA (*Head of Brass*)
A C Broadbent, LRAM (*Head of Strings*)
R F Colley, MA, DipRAM, LRAM, ARCM (*Pianist and Composer in Residence*)
M C Martin, BMus, LTCL (*Music Studio & Cello*)

Physical Education:
F J Hemming-Allen, BEd, MEd (*Director of Physical Education and Sport*)
M K Coley, BSc (*Director of Boys' Games*)
Ms L J Yates, BEd (*Director of Girls' Games*)
Miss A J V Moreland, BEd

Politics:
R D R Ray, BSc(Econ), FRGS (*Head of Department*)
P W Dewey, BA
M G Taylor, MA

Science:
N A Fisher, BSc, MSc, CPhys, MInstP (*Head of Science and Physics*)
N J Morse, BSc, PhD, CChem, MRSC (*Head of Chemistry*)
J Winchester, BSc
J P Allen, MA, CChem, FRSC
B R Allen, BA
J P Bartle, BSc
Miss P C Chubb, BSc
J H G Jarvis, BSc, MSc
Mrs F M Myers, BSc
M R Pattinson, MA, CBiol, MIBiol
P D Richard BSc
P J Robinson, BSc, PhD, CPhys, MInstP
J L Taylor, BA, BPhil, DPhil
M Walsh, BSc, DPhil
T M White, BSc
J D Wright, BSc
N Hampton, MA, PhD (*Head of Biology*)

Development Office: G M Helliwell, MA (*Appeal Director*)

Careers and Higher Education: Mrs J C Phelps
Rackets Professional: P J Rosser, BA
Sports Centre : H D P Bennett (*Manager*)

Situation. Rugby is situated near the junction of the M1 and M6 motorways and is not far from the M40. It is just one hour by hourly rail service from London (Euston) and is close to Birmingham International Airport as well as being within easy reach of Heathrow. Though the School is close to the countryside and has a 150-acre campus with a full range of facilities and games fields, it is essentially a town school and has the practical advantages of links with industry and opportunities for experience and service in a very real world.

Facilities. The main classroom block, the Macready Theatre, the Chapel, the Temple Reading Room and Gymnasium were designed by William Butterfield and to these have been added further buildings of architectural distinction, among them the Temple Speech Room and the Science Schools.

Since then there have followed new Science Laboratories, the Careers Centre, Drama Studio, Multi-media Language Laboratory, IT Centre, Geography Schools, micro-electronics centre and floodlit astroturf pitches for hockey, tennis and netball.

Other developments include a Sports Centre, opened by HRH The Duchess of Kent in 1990, and a cross-curricular Design Centre (this includes a television studio), in which all boys and girls take courses. Some 18 different activities, including Art, silver-smithing, computer-aided Design, Science and Information Technology, Business Studies, television production, ceramics, wood and metal work and Domestic Science are on offer, both within the curriculum and in free time.

The School is fully networked and a phased programme of introducing laptop computers throughout the school is in progress. A phased programme for the redevelopment of the Science Schools is also underway.

Boarding Houses. All boarding houses undergo a continuous programme of improvement. The aim, already achieved in most Houses, is to provide small dormitories of 4 to 6 in the first two years and study-bedrooms thereafter. Meals are eaten in House Dining Halls.

Boarding Houses (boys)	Tel: Rugby (01788)
Cotton: Mr Christopher John	556110
Kilbracken: Mr Neil Jarvis	556130
Michell: Mr Colin Edwards	556140

School Field: Mr Guy Steele-Bodger 556160
School House: Mr Bob Williams 556170
Sheriff: Mr David Shinkfield 556180
Tudor: Dr Andrew Smith 556220
Whitelaw: Mr Malcolm Burns 556230
Day Boy House
Town: Mr John Moreland 556210
Boarding Houses (girls)
Bradley: Mrs Monica Barlow 556100
Dean: Mrs Chantal Williams 556120
Rupert Brooke: Mrs Sally Rosser 556150
Stanley (Sixth Form only): Mrs Jane Phelps 556200
Day Girl House
Southfield: Mrs Frances Myers 556190
Junior Day House (boys and girls)
Marshall: Miss Alison Moreland 556240

A few boys and girls are day pupils in Boarding Houses. Tudor House becomes a girls' House in September 2002.

GCSE. All the usual subjects are offered as well as German, Russian, Spanish, Latin, Greek, CDT, Art and Music.

AS/A2. AS/A2 level is offered in all the GCSE subjects as well as in Design, Economics, Business Studies, Ancient History, English Language, Theology, Media Studies, Theatre Studies, History of Art and Politics. Nearly all boys and girls go on to Higher Education and about 22 to 24 go on to Oxford or Cambridge each year.

There are several learned societies and each subject invites distinguished speakers to the School. Rugby has mounted two international colloquia recently and has put on major exhibitions in the Science Schools, the latest of which has been 'Design at Work'.

Religion. Divinity is taught in the curriculum for the first three years. There is a theological society and careful preparation for confirmation as well as a regard for quite a wide variety of faiths and backgrounds. There are three short services during the week and, in a typical half-term, compulsory School Matins on two Sundays, a choice of Eucharist or Forum (a talk) on two Sundays and a voluntary Eucharist on one Sunday.

Sport. Sports include Athletics, Badminton, Basketball, Cricket, Cross-country, Fencing, Football, Golf, Gymnastics, Hockey, Judo, Lacrosse, Netball, Rackets, Riding, Rugby, Sailing, Squash, Swimming and Tennis.

Activities. There is a Director of Activities and all boys and girls are encouraged to undertake a full programme of extra-curricular activities. The School aims to ensure that music touches the lives of all pupils as well as catering for outstanding musicians. With School, House and visiting productions and a very well-equipped theatre, drama is already well to the fore. Other activities include Ballet, Canoeing, Camping, CCF, Choirs, Climbing, Duke of Edinburgh's Award, First Aid, Orienteering, Pottery, Sculpture, Target and Clay-pigeon shooting, Silver-smithing, Social Service and Television Production. The aim is to give all boys and girls a wide variety of experience so that they can excel in a few things but understand and develop some appreciation of most areas.

Entry. Entry for boys and girls is ultimately at 13 by Common Entrance or by Scholarship or – for those living abroad or attending international schools – by interview, report and specially designed tests. All 13+ boarding applicants take a pre-assessment test five terms before they join the School, following which firm places are offered subject to passing Common Entrance. A similar test will be available to latecomers. Day pupil places are offered two years before entry, following a similar pre-assessment test, and are also subject to success at Common Entrance.

Boys and girls also enter the VIth form on the basis of interviews and a report from the current school, or by scholarship.

The Junior Department. At age 11 boys and girls enter Marshall House as day pupils by taking an examination. Bursaries are available at this level. There is one class of 11-year-olds and one of 12-year-olds. Classes run from 8.45 am to 3.30 pm. A full programme of extra-curricular activities is offered, most of it based on the Senior School's extensive facilities. Much of the teaching is done by staff from the Senior School but Marshall House has its own Head.

Foundation. Up to 14 Major Foundationerships (giving free tuition) and 28 Minor Foundationerships (giving tuition at half-fees) are offered under the School's Foundation to day boys and girls entering Town House and Southfield at 13.

Further details of the Scheme of Foundationerships may be obtained from the Registrar.

Scholarships (*see* Entrance Scholarship section). At least twelve academic Scholarships are offered annually to boys and girls entering at 13. The examination takes place at Rugby in May.

Sixth Form academic Scholarships are also offered to boys and girls to enter the Upper School. The examination takes place at Rugby in November for entry the following September.

Music Scholarships, Jeremy Smith String awards, Art Scholarships, Design Scholarships and Sports Scholarships are also offered annually.

A Leigh Thomas Bursary is offered to assist boys or girls born and living in Wales to enter Rugby.

Augmentation of Scholarships. Any Scholarship can be augmented if the financial circumstances of the parents make this necessary. Notice of intention to apply for such augmentation must be given at the same time as application for the Scholarship.

Fees. The consolidated 2001 fee for boys and girls (boarding and tuition) is £5,460 per term. (Optional charge for Instrumental or Singing Tuition: £155 per term). The basic 2001 fee for Town House and Southfield is £3,280 per term.

Further Information. Full information about the School's aims, its academic curriculum, facilities and activities will be found in the School's prospectus. Inquiries and applications should be made in the first instance to the Registrar who will be pleased to arrange for parents to see the School and to meet members of the staff and the Head Master.

'I learned at Rugby what I do not think I could have learned as well anywhere else – how to learn anything I wanted'. (A Major Foundationer).

Charitable status. The Governing Body of Rugby School is a Registered Charity, number 528752. It exists to provide education for young people.

Rydal Penrhos School

Pwllycrochan Avenue Colwyn Bay LL29 7BT.
Tel: (01492) 530155
Fax: (01492) 531872
e-mail: info@rydal-penrhos.com

In 1995, two historic schools, Rydal founded in 1885 and Penrhos College founded in 1880 joined together to become one of the leading Boarding and Day schools in the North West. Rydal Penrhos is essentially coeducational although pupils aged 11-16 years are taught in single sex classes. The Sixth Form is fully coeducational and so too is the Preparatory School. A £3 million capital investment programme was initiated by the school in 1998 adding extensive new facilities to the already splendid campus.

Motto: *Veritas Scientia Fides (Truth Knowledge Faith)*

The Governors:
Chairman: D L Wigley, MA, MSc
Vice-Chairman: Mrs M E Davies, BA, JP

Principal: **M S James**, MA (Oxon), MSc, MPhil, FIMgt

Vice Principal: P J Bendall, BSc

Chaplain: The Revd K Tewkesbury, MTh (Oxon)

Bursar: J N Barry, BA

Situation and Buildings. The School is built on rising ground within the conservation area of Colwyn Bay, a small rural town overlooking the Irish Sea. The Snowdonia National Park with the many opportunities it affords for extensive and exciting extra-curricular activities is within easy reach. The School is easily accessed via excellent transport provision including the A55 Express Way, regular rail services and Manchester International Airport (1 hour's drive).

The excellent teaching accommodation includes 9 laboratories, dedicated study areas for senior pupils, specialist Art, Music and Design Technology centres, and a Lecture Theatre. There is a new state of the art Library and Resources centre, and a new Information Technology suite. The new Sports Hall and Astroturf pitches enhance the already extensive sporting facilities. Phase 2 of the Millennium Development Plan includes a new dining hall and additional facilities for music and drama.

Boarders are accommodated in fine houses which are separate from the main buildings. The residential facilities (recently refurbished) are of a superior quality and comprise in the main single, double and triple bedrooms. The Preparatory School which takes boarders from 7 years (day pupils from 2½ years) is on an adjacent site.

Numbers and Organisations. There are 455 pupils in the Senior School, 225 boys (74 boarders) and 229 girls (92 boarders). This includes 148 in the Sixth Form. There are 3 boarding houses for boys and 3 boarding houses for girls. Each house is supervised by resident houseparents with the assistance of a team of tutors and matrons. The houses are fully self-contained although pupils use a central dining hall. There are two dedicated Upper Sixth houses, one for boys and one for girls.

Religious Aims. Rydal Penrhos is a Methodist foundation although pupils are interdenominational. Prayers are held daily with boarders attending a Sunday service. There are wide ranging styles of worship and once a month pupils are encouraged to attend a local church of their own faith.

Curriculum. Boys and girls are taught in single sex classes between the ages of 11-16. It is fundamental to school policy that whilst the National Curriculum is shadowed, it is also supplemented to afford extra opportunities and choices to the pupils. The extended day and boarding tradition allows pupils more breadth and depth to their study.

On entry at Year 7, pupils study Art, Biology, Chemistry, Physics, English, French, Geography, History, Latin, Mathematics, Religious Studies, Information Technology, Music, Physical Education, Design Technology and Personal and Social Education.

Years 10 and 11 constitute Key Stage 4 (KS4) of the National Curriculum and in Year 10 the core subjects are English, Mathematics, Biology, Chemistry, Physics, ICT, a modern foreign language and Religious Studies. In addition, the majority of pupils will choose two further subjects from the following: Art and Design, Business Studies, Design Technology, Drama, a second foreign language, Home Economics, Geography, History, Latin and Music to complete their GCSE options. During KS4, all pupils participate fully in both Physical Education and a Personal and Social Education programme.

The Sixth Form. The Sixth Form at Rydal Penrhos is particularly strong. Pupils are expected to have Grade C or above in at least 5 subjects at GCSE before embarking on the two-year A level course. With a wide range of A level options available, pupils have the advantage of choosing courses which reflect their own particular strengths and interests. Options include Art and Design, Biology, Business Studies, Chemistry, Design Technology, Economics, English Literature, French, Geography, German, History, Home Economics, Information Technology, Latin, Mathematics, Music, Physical Education and Sports Studies, Physics, Psychology, Religious Studies and Sociology.

Additionally, all Sixth Formers follow a skills-based course leading to the Diploma of Achievement. The wide range of study includes practical skills (car maintenance and cooking), Communication Skills (effective discussion and note taking skills, public presentation skills), Numeracy (handling statistics, analysing data, budgeting and finance), Information Technology (word processing and graphics, databases and spreadsheets) and PSE/RE (Philosophy of Religion, relationships and sexuality and health issues).

Sports and Activities. All pupils undertake a balanced programme of both sporting and non-sporting extra-curricular activity. The aim is to provide a wide variety of opportunities to learn various skills and to suit different aptitudes. The importance of competitive sport is recognised. Principal games include Rugby, Cricket, Netball, Hockey, Athletics and Tennis. In addition there are ample facilities for Swimming, Squash, Volleyball and Gymnastics. Pupils compete with success at both national and international level.

The School's coastal location within a few miles of Snowdonia National Park allows for a full programme of adventurous activities, including mountaineering, climbing and canoeing. The Duke of Edinburgh's Award is very well supported by pupils. The School has a strong reputation for sailing, and is recognised by the RYA (Royal Yachting Association) as a training centre. The School hosts and organises national sailing events.

The Arts. The School has a fine tradition in both Music and Drama and pupils are actively encouraged to develop an enthusiasm for the performing arts. Tuition across the widest possible range of musical instruments is available and there is a particularly active choir. Regular concerts are given by the orchestras and the swing band. Music scholarships are available.

The Senior and Junior Dramatic Societies give regular performances throughout the year. A particular feature is the annual House Drama Competition which involves many members of the School. Stagecraft is a popular extra-curricular activity. Sets are always ambitious and pupils have access to sophisticated lighting systems.

The Arts Centre (Art, Pottery, Photography, Fashion Design) and the Design-Technology Centre (Woodwork, Metalwork, Design) all add to the school's wide ranging facilities.

Careers. Professional staff are responsible for advising on Careers and Higher Education, and the school has a well-equipped Careers Centre to support this function. Each year pupils taking GCSE levels undergo the Morrisby tests in order to help them make the right A level subject choices. All pupils in Year 11 have access to work experience and the School holds a regular Careers Convention and Industrial Conference. Mock Interviews are arranged with local businesses and the professional community and pupils have regular personal tutorials.

Admission. Pupils can be admitted at the beginning of any term after their 11th birthday although by far the largest entry is in September. Entry is normally via the School's Entrance Examinations or the Common Entrance Examination.

Scholarships. (*see* Entrance Scholarship section) A number of valuable entrance scholarships, exhibitions and bursaries are awarded annually by examination for excellence in academic studies, music, art and sport. These are available for entry between the ages of 11 and 16. Sons and daughters of Methodist and Anglican Ministers are admitted at substantially reduced fees and a number of Services Bursaries are available. A limited number of means tested Bursary Awards are available for able students.

Fees per annum. Boarding: Years 7 and 8 £11,733; Years 9-13 £13,260. Day pupils: Years 7 and 8 £7,695; Years 9-13 £8,232.

Rydal Penrhos Preparatory School. This is situated close to the Senior School and is therefore able to share its facilities. Teaching between the two parts of the school is also closely co-ordinated.

Charitable status. Rydal Penrhos School is a Registered Charity, number 525752. The aim of the charity is the education of young people.

Ryde School with Upper Chine

Queen's Road Ryde Isle of Wight PO33 3BE.
Tel: (01983) 562229
Fax: (01983) 564714
e-mail: school.office@rydeschool.org.uk
website: www.rydeschool.org.uk

Ryde School was founded in 1921 by William Laxon McIsaac and moved to its present site in 1928. In 1994, it was joined by Upper Chine School.

The School is fully co-educational at all levels. There are some 420 pupils between the ages of 11 and 18 in the Senior School, and some 250 aged 3 to 11 in the Junior School which shares part of the same site. There are full and weekly boarders who board on the Bembridge site (see below). The remainder are day pupils from the Island, with a small handful commuting on a daily basis from the Portsmouth area.

Motto: *Ut Prosim.*

Visitor: The Bishop of Portsmouth

Governors:

Chairman: D J Longford, BSc

Vice-Chairman: M J Flux

Hereditary Governor: R McIsaac, MA

Honorary Governors:
Mrs J G McCue, BSc
G W Searle, MA

The Venerable K M L H Banting
I J Clarke, LLB
P J Donaldson, FRCS
R J Fox, MA, CMath, FIMA
Mrs S Glasgow
Ms D Patterson, MA, FRSA
A N Porteous, FCA
Major General M S White, CBE, CB
S Willy, ACIB

Clerk to the Governors: P C Taylor, FCA, JP

***Headmaster:* Dr N J England**, MA, DPhil, St Catherine's College, Oxford

Deputy Heads:
G J Price, MA, PGCE, St Edmund Hall, Oxford
Mrs J Till-Dowling, BA, MA, PGCE, Pembroke College, Cambridge

Senior School:
M Bannister, BA, MIEE, CertEd
N Brady, BA, PGCE (*Head of Economics and Business Studies*)
Miss C Burroughs, MA
A R Cantwell, MA, PGCE (*Head of Sixth Form and Head of History and Politics*)
Miss M E Daniel, BSc, PGCE (*Head of Geography*)
Mrs S Davis, MA, FSBT (*Head of Sixth Form*)
Dr J A Deeny, BSc, DPhil, PGCE
Mrs C Doe, BSc
K J Dubbins, BEd
Mrs S E Evans, BA (*Director of Drama*)
Mrs B Field, CertEd, AdvDipSN
M J Glasbey, BSc, PGCE (*Head of Year 9 and Head of CDT*)
P K Griffiths, BA, MA, PGCE
A Grubb, BMus, PGCE (*Director of Music*)
Miss P J Harrison, BA, PGCE
A G Higgens, BSc, QTS
R Hoare, BA
Mrs H Laurie, CertEd, BDADip
Revd J Leggett
M E Mairis, BA, PGCE
S J McCabe, BA, PGCE (*Head of Mathematics*)
S M Mead, BEd (*Head of Year 11 and Head of Chemistry*)
Mrs A M Mellor, CertEd
J H Mitchell, BHum, PGCE (*Head of Boys' Games and PE*)
Mrs M E Moorman, BEd (*Head of IT*)
Mrs S M Mundy, DipEd
L O'Brien, BA, MA, PGCE
C M Ody, BA, PGCE (*Head of Year 7 and Head of Modern Languages*)
Mrs P A Parry, BA, MA, CertEd (*Head of Year 10 and Head of English*)
Mrs S Patel, BSc, MSc, HNC, FIMLS, PGCE
A Penalva
B W Penn, BSc, CBiol, PGCE (*Head of Science, Biology and Psychology*)
S M J Peskett, MA, PGCE
Mrs T M Phipps, BA, PGCE
Mrs B Preston, CertEd (*Head of Girls' Games and PE*)
Mrs S Prewer, BEd
B V Price, CertEd (*Contingent Commander CCF*)
Mrs R Runnette, BEd, CertEd
Mrs D M Shepherd, CertEd
Mrs J Sheridan, BA, CertEd
I Stewart, MEd, LLB, PGCE, CertTEFL
Mrs B Sutton, CertEd
C G S Trevallion, BSc, PGCE
Mrs R Tweddle, GTCL, LTCL (*Choral Director*)
Mrs K Vowell, BSc, PGCE
Mrs J A Wadsworth, BA, PGCE
M D Wallace, BA
D J A Weatherston, CertEd (*Head of Year 8*)
M C Williams, BSc, PGCE (*Head of Physics*)
Miss G M Wright, MA, CertEd (*Head of Art*)

Junior School:

Head: H Edwards, BSc, PGCE

Deputy Head: D B Napper, BA, DLC, Loughborough College

A Bentley, BSc, PGCE
P Craig, BSc, PGCE
Mrs A Lascelles, BA, Cert Ed
Ms J McKay, BEd
Miss D J Meadows, BEd, FLS, MIMgt
M Miller, BA, PGCE
Mrs I Oakley, CertEd
Miss W Owen, BA, PGCE
K Smith, CertEd, AMusLCM
Miss A Sparrow, BA, PGCE
Mrs A van der Merwe, BA, PGCE

'FIVEWAYS' Nursery and Pre-Prep:

Head of Fiveways: Mrs S A Davies, BEd

Mrs L Ball, BEd
Miss K Clarke, NNEB
Miss S Crocker, BTec, NatDip Nursery Nursing

Mrs J Edwards, BSc, PGCE
Mrs S Ellis, NNEB
Mrs B Eustace, NNEB
Miss D Gillam, BEd
Miss S Glover, NNEB
Mrs S Hawker, BA, CertEd
Miss V Lovell, BEd
Mrs S Luke, BMus, PGCE
Mrs P Ong, Dip in Pre-school Practice

Situation and Buildings. The School stands in its own grounds of 17 acres in Ryde overlooking the Solent, and is easily accessible from all parts of the Island and the near mainland. It is within walking distance of the terminals which link Ryde to Portsmouth by hovercraft (10 minutes) or catamaran (15 minutes). In recent years there have been many additions to the School buildings. Since 1989, a programme of new building and conversion has provided an Art and Design Centre, a Sports Hall, a Music School, a new classroom block for languages, a new Science Block and a Sixth Form Centre. A new teaching block of eight Senior School classrooms and a library has recently been opened.

Organisation and Curriculum. The School aims to provide a good all-round education based upon Christian principles, and enjoys an enviable reputation on the Island for high standards both inside and outside the classroom.

In the Junior School strong emphasis is laid on basic skills and on proficiency in reading, writing and number work. Pupils are prepared in this way for entry into the Senior School, and, following a recommendation from the Head of the Junior School, they are offered places in the Senior School at the age of 11.

The programme of work in the Senior School is designed to provide as broad an education as possible up to the end of the Fifth year. The subjects taught to GCSE level are English, Mathematics, Physics, Chemistry, Biology, French, German, Spanish, Latin, Geography, History, Business Studies, Art, Music, Physical Education, Religious Education, Drama and Craft, Design and Technology. All pupils also follow a programme of Religious Education, Health Education and Games.

In the Sixth Form pupils are normally required to select three or four subjects at A or A/S level from a wide choice. In addition, pupils may follow a General Studies course, designed to add breadth to their academic studies. Courses lead to entrance to universities, the Services, industry and the professions. The Careers Department provides advice and guidance to all pupils.

Tutorial System. Each pupil has a tutor who is responsible for his or her academic and personal progress and general pastoral welfare. The tutorial system encourages close contact with parents, which is further reinforced by parents' meetings which are held at regular intervals. The School aims to maintain sound discipline and good manners within a traditionally friendly atmosphere.

Games. The main games in the Senior School are rugby football, hockey, cricket and athletics for the boys, and netball, hockey and athletics for the girls. In the Junior School, Association football is also played. Other games include basketball, fencing, golf, swimming and tennis. Regular matches are arranged at all levels against teams both on the Island and the mainland.

Music and Drama. The Music School incorporates practice and teaching facilities and a well-equipped recording studio. The School has a flourishing choral tradition, with opportunities for participation in a variety of choirs and instrumental groups. Concerts and musical plays are performed in both Senior and Junior Schools, and concert tours abroad have taken place in recent years. Full-length plays are produced each year by both Senior and Junior Schools, and special attention is given in the English lessons of the younger forms to speaking, lecturing and acting. Public speaking is a particular strength. In addition to a newly refurbished theatre and a smaller studio theatre on the Ryde site, the School now enjoys the use of the Ryde Town Theatre.

Activities. There are many societies which cater for a wide range of individual interests. The School has a contingent of the Combined Cadet Force with Royal Navy and Royal Air Force sections. Sailing, canoeing, gliding, and other forms of venture training are strongly encouraged. The School runs a Community Service Scheme which operates with local charitable organisations. Holiday visits and expeditions are regularly arranged, and there are opportunities for exchange visits with schools on the continent.

Boarding. Boarding for both boys and girls is available for pupils on the Bembridge campus which offers approximately one hundred acres of playing fields and woodland overlooking Whitecliff Bay and Culver Cliff, some six miles from Ryde. Transport is provided to and from Ryde for the school day.

Fees. Tuition: Nursery (full day) £795, (half day) £480 Form 1 and Reception £950 per term, Junior School, £1,670–£1,720 per term; Senior School, £1,900 per term. Boarding (excluding tuition fee) Senior School (full) £1,980, (weekly) £1,740 per term. Boarding Junior School (full) £1,715, (weekly) £1,510. A reduction in Tuition Fees is made for brothers or sisters (10% for a second child, 20% for third or fourth children) who are in attendance at the School at the same time.

Scholarships and Bursaries. (*see* Entrance Scholarship section) The School offers a number of Ryde Assisted Places. These are awarded to suitable candidates either internally or from outside the school. These places are means tested. Some scholarships are also awarded on merit.

Charitable status. Ryde School is a Registered Charity, number 307409. The aims and objectives of the Charity are the education of boys and girls.

St Albans School

Abbey Gateway St Albans Herts AL3 4HB.
Tel: (01727) 855521
Fax: (01727) 843447
e-mail: hm@st-albans-school.org.uk
website: www.st-albans.herts.sch.uk

The origins of the School date back, according to tradition, to the monastic foundation of 948, and there is firm evidence of an established and flourishing school soon after the Conquest. Following the Dissolution, the last abbot, Richard Boreman, sought a private Act of Parliament to establish a Free School. Charters, granted to the Town Corporation by Edward VI and Elizabeth I, together with endowments by Sir Nicholas Bacon from the sale of wine licences, secured the School's continuance.

Visitor: The Rt Rev The Lord Bishop of St Albans

Governors:
Chairman: R B Sharpe, FCA

The Mayor of St Albans	A K Gray
The Dean of St Albans	I F Jennings
The President of the Old Albanian Club	B S Kent, BA
	D C Lindsell, FCA
J Barber, PhD	A R M Little, MA
Mrs V Y Barr	Mrs J Mark, MA
Cllr R Blossom	Prof R C Munton
Dr M J Collins	P Parry
Ms S Connor	D Pepper, FRICS, FSVA
G R Dale, MA, MIPM	Prof H Thimbleby
P J Dredge	

Bursar and Clerk to the Governors: Lt Col R M G Brooks, BSc(*Eng*)

***Headmaster:* A R Grant**, MA, FRSA

Second Master: S A Corns, MA

Senior Master: D R Ireson, ARCM, CertEd

Director of Studies: S W Dolan, MA, DPhil

Senior Tutor: A P S Talbot, BA

Head of Middle School: P R Byrom, MSc

Head of Lower School: R Scase, DipPE, BEd

Assistant staff:

Mrs K M Bailey, BSc, PhD	P McGrath, BA
E J Beavington, BSc	C M Mannall, BSc
R T Bendon, BA, ADipEd	T J Martin, BA
Mrs V A Bird, BA	A C R Mason, BA
I J Black, MA	H Modak, BA
Miss L J Bloomer, BA	I Murray, BA
Mrs C C Bolton, BA	M A Pedroz, MA
J S Burrowes, BEd	Mrs D S Percival, MA, MIL
N J Cassidy, BA	Mrs E O Perrottet, AGSM
I Charlesworth, MA	A S Postill, MSc
Mrs H E Conway, MA	A J Rees, BSc
Mrs E W Davies, BA	Mrs L R Reid, BSc
M E Davies, MA	A J Rylatt, BEng
R Dear, MA	Mrs S G F Scase, BA
J E Duffield, BA	A J Smith, BEd
Mrs S D Frearson, BSc	G L Smithson, BSc
S R Gell, BA	Mrs L L Stanbury, BSc
C P A Gould, BSc	Mrs M O Stratton, MSc
R C S Grant, BA	P N Stubbs, MA
Mrs V H Graveson, BA	Mrs J H Swain, MA
Miss J M Grieveson, BA	D Swanson, RADA
G C Higby, MA, PhD	P W Taylor, BEd
C C Hudson, BSc	S J Terrell, BA, MPhil
Mrs L V James, AIL	C S Tolman, BA
T N Jenkins, BA, MFA	P P Wade-Wright, BSc
A K Jolly, BA	G J Walker, BA
Miss D Lawlor, MSc	D A Webster, BEng
P A Legouix, MSc	N A Wood-Smith, BSc, FSS
E J Logan, BA	R C Wright, BA
D K McCord, BMus, ARCM	P G Yates, A CertEd

Chaplain: The Revd Dr C D Pines, BA, MB, BS

Medical Officer: Dr P E Skelton, MB, BS

RSM: Capt K J Everitt

Visiting Staff:

Poet-in-Residence: J D Mole, MA

Music:

J Acton
N Buick, DipMus, RSAM
P Cox, BA, PGrad, DipABSM, LTCL
C Forshaw
M Foster, GGSM
S Laffy
Mrs P Manning, GRSM, ARCM
Mrs K Parker, GRSM, ARCM
Mrs E O Perrottet, AGSM
Mrs R Runcie, LRAM, ARCM
Miss J Spotswood, GTCL
M Vishnick, LLCM, ALCM
Mrs M Winfield, MA, LRAM

St Albans is a day school of about 700 pupils which, after being for many years part of the Direct Grant System, reverted to full independence. Girls were admitted into the Sixth Form in September 1991. Its atmosphere and ethos derive from its long tradition and its geographical position near the city centre of St Albans in close proximity to the Abbey and overlooking the site of the Roman City of Verulamium. Whilst maintaining a high standard of academic achievement, it offers wide opportunities for development in other fields, and a strong emphasis is laid upon the responsible use of individual talents in the service of the community.

Buildings. For more than 3 centuries the School was in the Lady Chapel of the Abbey. It moved in 1871 into the Monastery Gatehouse, a building of considerable historic and architectural interest where teaching still continues. Since 1900 extensive additions have been made, including, most recently, the award-winning Hall, the Language Laboratory, Library, Art School and IT, Design and Technology Centre and new Science laboratories.

The School has close historical ties with the Abbey, and by permission of the Dean the nave of the Abbey is used regularly for morning prayers.

Admission and Fees. The majority of boys enter at the age of 11 or 13 but there are also entries at 16, when girls are also admitted; candidates are accepted occasionally at other ages. For the main entry at 11 an examination in basic subjects is held at the School each year, normally in January, and parents of interested candidates should write to the School for a prospectus and application form. Candidates at 13 enter through the Common Entrance examination, and conditional offers of places are normally made about one year before entry, following a preliminary assessment. Ideally parents should apply to the School at least 2 years in advance for entry at 13.

The fees for the year up to April 2001 are £7,305 pa.

Pupils are admitted only at the start of the Autumn Term unless there are exceptional circumstances.

Bursaries and Scholarships. (*see* Entrance Scholarship section) Some assistance with tuition fees may be available in cases of proven need from the School's own endowments. Such Bursaries are conditional upon an annual means test and will be awarded according to a balance of merit and need. Numerous scholarships, worth up to 50% of fees, are awarded on academic merit at each age of entry, and Scholarships in Art and Music are offered to entrants at 13+ who show exceptional talent. Internal Bursaries from a fund established to the memory of John Clough, a former Director of Music, are awarded annually to pupils who show musical talent.

Curriculum. The curriculum for the first three years is largely a common one, and covers a wide range. All boys study two languages and three sciences, and devote some part of their timetable to Art, Drama, Music, ICT and CDT. Mathematics GCSE is taken at the end of the fourth year, and in the fourth and fifth years a system of compulsory subjects and options leads in most cases to the taking of at least a further eight GCSEs. In the Sixth Form most pupils study four subjects at AS level in the Lower Sixth Form and three or four A2s in the Upper Sixth. In addition, all pupils take General Studies either as an AS or a full A level and are prepared for Key Skills qualifications. The choice is wide, and the flexibility of the timetable makes it possible for almost any combination of available subjects to be offered.

Virtually all Sixth Form leavers go on to universities or other forms of higher education, a good proportion to Oxford or Cambridge.

Out-of-school activities cover a wide range, and there are clubs and societies to cater for most interests. Several of these are run in conjunction with other schools. Musical activities are many and varied and include regular concerts and recitals by the School Choir, Choral Society and ensembles and by professional artists. Plays are produced 3 or 4 times a year either in the New Hall, the English Centre Studio Theatre or in the Open-air Theatre, and there is ample opportunity for creative work in the Art school, the

Workshops or the Printing Press. There is a strong contingent of the CCF with sections representing the Army and RAF. Other groups train under the Duke of Edinburgh's Award Scheme and do various forms of social service and conservation work in and around the city of St Albans. The School owns a Field Centre in Wales which is used for research and recreation in holidays, as part of the Lower School curriculum and as a base for field studies and reading parties. The School also owns a working 400 acre farm within 3 miles of the school where new playing fields, extending to 45 acres, are due to open in 2002. The new grounds include an Astroturf all-weather pitch.

Games. The main games are Rugby Football, Hockey, Cross-country, Cricket, Tennis and Athletics, with a range of other sports, which includes Association Football, Squash, Shooting, Sailing, Swimming, Orienteering, Basketball, Golf and Table Tennis. The playing fields are within easy reach of the School, and the spacious and pleasant lawns on the School site, stretching down to the River Ver, provide room for Tennis Courts, Cricket Nets and a Shooting Range.

Enquiries about entry should be addressed to the Headmaster's Personal Assistant.

Information about the Old Albanian Club may be obtained from its secretary, R L Cook, 1 Pondswick Close, St Albans (Tel: 836877).

Charitable status. St Albans Grammar School is a Registered Charity, number 310005. The aims and objectives of the charity are to provide an excellent education whereby pupils can achieve the highest standard of academic success, according to ability, and develop their character and personality so as to become caring and self-disciplined adults.

St Bede's College

Alexandra Park Manchester M16 8HX.
Tel: 0161 226 3323
Fax: 0161 226 3813

Motto: *Nunquam otio torpebat*

Foundation: St Bede's was founded in 1876 by Bishop Herbert Vaughan, who later, as Cardinal Archbishop of Westminster, went on to found Westminster Cathedral. From small beginnings the College has grown and changed whilst remaining faithful to Bishop Vaughan's ideals. Over 500 priests have received their early training at the College; although the number of priests on the staff has been reduced in recent years our religious faith remains central to the life of the College.

Throughout the many changes that have taken place since its formation the College has remained true to its founder's intention: to provide a thorough academic education for Catholic children, in an atmosphere of stability, care and concern.

We therefore seek the highest standards of performance so that pupils are stretched to, but never beyond, their personal limit. The provision of this education within a Catholic environment remains one of the chief characteristics of the College. High expectations of personal behaviour and discipline are rooted in our faith.

The College was one of the first Catholic schools in the country to enter the Direct Grant system. St Bede's was the only school which opted to retain that independence when the Catholic secondary schools in Manchester were reorganised in 1976.

The Governors introduced co-education in 1984, so that they could offer girls from Greater Manchester and beyond the benefits of a Catholic Grammar School education. The curriculum has been widened considerably and a major building programme undertaken, including a new Technology Suite, a new Library and a major extension to the Prep School and a new IT Suite opened in January 1996.

Size: The rapid growth of recent years enables us to offer 975 senior school places (300 of them in the Sixth Form).

Most pupils enter St Bede's at 11+ by taking the College Entrance Examination. Of those who apply, approximately one quarter are admitted. There are occasional vacancies in other age groups, and there is an additional intake of students from outside the College into the Sixth Form each year.

Governors:
Chairman: Rev J Austin, MA,
Vice-Chairman: H B Ellwood, PhL, BA, RIBA

Rt Rev Mgr J Allen, STL, PhL
Rt Rev T J Brain, Bishop of Salford
A Carr, LLB
Rt Rev Mgr T Dodgeon, MA
Mrs L Edwards
Mrs C Finnigan, LLB
S Harrold, BSc, PhD
M G Hartley, MScTech, PhD, DSc, FIEE, CEng
His Honour Judge G W Humphries
G. Lanigan, FCA
A J Keegan, BA
R Machell, MA, LLB, QC
Dr Susan O'Driscoll, BSc, MBBS
K O'Flynn, MB, BCh, BAO, FRCS, FRCS(Urol)
Rt Rev Mgr M Quinlan, VG, DCL, RD
Very Rev J C Rigby, RD

***Headmaster:* J Byrne**, BA, MEd

Deputy Headmaster: T G Barnes, MA

Deputy Head: Mrs R Meehan, GRSM

Director of Studies: S Duggan, MA

Assistant Staff:
Mrs N Alderson, BA
Mrs S Alexopoulos
Mrs M Andrews, CertEd
Mrs C Aspinall, BSc
S Bargery, BSc
Mrs P Beattie, BA
J M Berry BA
J J Bowden, BA
Miss P Brammer, BSc
M Cahill, MSc
Mrs M Cobbold, MA
Mrs M Collins, BEd
Mrs M Conway, BA
A Dando, BSc, PhD
Miss R Darby, BMus
Mrs E Denby, BA
Mrs M Di Mauro, MSc, PhD
Miss J Doroszkiewicz, BA
Mrs E Duffy, MA
M J Duffy, BSc, PhD
Mrs M Duffy, BA
S Duggan, MA
J Dumbill, BA
S Fallon, BEd
T Fisher, CertEd
Mrs J Flood, BA
J Gibson, MA
D Grierson, MA
J Harrison, APS
Mrs M Harter, BA
Mrs M Hazell, MA
A Hennigan, BEd
Miss C Hennity, BSc
Mrs P Jackson, BA
L Jones, BA
Miss A Jordan, BA
D Kearney, BA
Mrs H Knight, MA
J Lalley, BSc
Mrs N Lavorini, BEd
P Lee, MA
P J C Loader, BSc
Mrs R Lockett, BA
D McCotter, BSc
P McDaid, BSc
S McGleenan, BSc
K McKeogh, MA, MBA
Miss S Mansfield, BA
P B Maree, BA
J Martin, BSc
B Mistry, BSc
T Moore, BA, BSc
Mrs G Morris, BEd
J Moynihan, BA
J Murphy, BA
M Nally, BSc
Mrs E O'Neal
B Peden, MA
H Peers, BA
Mrs S Pike, BSc
Mrs S Quirk, BSc
K Rafferty, BEd
Miss H Roberts, BA
I Service, MA

J F Stienne Lic d'Anglais, Maitrise d'Anglais
M Taylor, BA
C Toner, MA
Mrs M Vidouris, BA
G Walker, MA
Mrs J Wallwork, BA
H Weiss, BEd
Mrs A Wood, BA

Clerk to Governors: Rev B N Jackson

Bursar: J L Fletcher, FCA

Medical Officer: Dr Po Chan

Organisation. There is a common curriculum in the Lower School and a wide choice of optional subjects in the Middle School. Students must normally possess seven GCSE passes (grades A*–C) before they are admitted to the Sixth Form where they usually take four subjects at AS level in L6 plus 3A2 subjects in U6. The subjects available are: Classics, Modern Languages (French, German, Spanish), English, History, Business Studies, Economics, Politics, Theatre Studies, English Language, Religion, Geography, Mathematics, Further Mathematics, Physics, Chemistry, Biology, Geology, Art, Music and Sports Science.

Entrance. The College Entrance Examination normally takes place on the last Saturday in January and is open to Catholic boys and girls who will not have reached the age of 12 by 31st August in the year of the examination. Christians of other denominations are also welcomed. Details of the examination and copies of past papers may be obtained from the Headmaster's Secretary. Occasional vacancies occur in other years. There is also direct entry to the Sixth Form for boys and girls who expect to obtain good GCSE results. Interviews are held from the beginning of the Easter Term.

Awards

Sixth Form Scholarships. Each year the Governors provide a number of scholarships and bursaries for Catholic boys or girls from other schools, who would like to enter the Sixth Form at St Bede's. The scholarships are awarded both on the basis of interview and performance in an examination which is held in January and according to financial need. Further details may be obtained from the Headmaster's Secretary.

Music Scholarship. The Governors award at least one half fee Music Scholarship to a pupil entering the Upper Third. Details of the award may be obtained from the Headmaster's Secretary.

St Bede's Educational Trust. St Bede's College Educational Trust awards a large number of bursaries to Catholic pupils of good academic ability who can demonstrate financial need. At present one third of pupils are in receipt of means-tested bursaries.

Music. In the first three years, pupils have two periods of music per week, thus obtaining a thorough theoretical introduction to the subject as well as ample opportunity for practical experience. They learn to read music fluently by playing the recorder, and study the lives and music of the major composers. From the fourth year, it becomes an optional subject for those taking it to GCSE and A level.

Instrumental tuition is available in string, woodwind and brass instruments. The College Orchestra meets once a week and there is a keen Early Music ensemble. Each year there is a full programme of evening concerts, as well as a popular series of lunchtime recitals given by staff and pupils.

Art. The Art and Craft Department has mirrored the growth of the College as a whole, with increased facilities and a widening curriculum, which now includes pottery, textiles and photography, with the specialist facilities to support the many enthusiastic pupils who follow these courses. In addition to our pottery, dark room and general art rooms for the main school, there are three rooms reserved exclusively for Sixth Form use. Independent of the main Art rooms, these give Sixth Formers a better opportunity to study the subject at a more mature level. All pupils take Art in the first three years, with GCSE and A level courses as options thereafter. The Department includes design as an important subject, and offers courses in the History of Design and (to A level) in the History of Art and Architecture and in Embroidery.

Drama. We stage two productions each year in late November and March. There are also one act plays for younger pupils and occasionally some open-air productions. Every two years we stage a drama festival, which is particularly successful in encouraging participants from all levels at the College.

Games. The Physical Education curriculum includes Badminton, Basketball, Netball, Volleyball, Cross Country, Gymnastics, Swimming, Rounders, Cricket, Tennis, Athletics, Rugby, Soccer and Orienteering. We have extensive facilities which include a modern Sports Hall, a weight training room and a new multigym, 13 acres of playing fields and tennis and netball courts. On any Saturday there may be over three hundred pupils representing the College and 20 members of staff on duty, supported by large numbers of parents.

Other Activities. A wide range of expeditions and excursions are organised each year as part of our programme of activities. Every summer there is an activities holiday in the Lake District for First Year boys and girls, giving them a chance to live for a week under canvas and enjoy activities like canoeing, orienteering, fell-walking, rock-climbing and pony-trekking. Over twenty staff and a number of Sixth Form volunteers supervise the holiday.

There are regular trips to the Continent. Other extra-curricular activities include: Debating and Public Speaking, Drama, Theatre Visits, Orchestra and Choir, Chess, Photography, Community Service, Geological Society, Computing Group, Scientific Societies, Orienteering, United Nations Group, Politics Group, St John's Ambulance, Pottery Groups, Quizzes, Art Club.

Fees. The tuition fees in the academic year 2001–2002 will be £5,232 per annum.

Careers Education. The Careers Room with its library contains an extensive range of literature on Careers and higher education opportunities and is open every day and manned by two members of staff with responsibility for careers guidance. We make extensive use of computer based information sources and in particular of the Prestel Database, in addition to the many printed guides, brochures and prospectuses.

Every two years a Careers Convention is organised for pupils from Upper Fourth to Sixth Form and for senior pupils a three day higher education conference is organised every February.

Honours. 12 Oxford and Cambridge offers for 2001.

Charitable status. St Bede's College Limited is a Registered Charity, number 700808. Its aims and objectives are the advancement and provision of education on behalf of St Bede's College.

* Head of Department § Part Time or Visiting
† Housemaster/Housemistress ¶ Old Pupil
‡ See below list of staff for meaning

St Bees School

St Bees Cumbria CA27 0DS.
Tel: (01946) 822263
Fax: (01946) 823657
e-mail: mailbox@st-bees-school.co.uk
Website: www.st-bees-school.co.uk

Motto: *Expecta Dominum.*

Founded by Edmund Grindal, Archbishop of Canterbury, in 1583. Now conducted as a co-educational independent school under a scheme approved by The Charity Commission.

Governors:

Chairman: W Lowther, Esq, OBE, JP
Deputy Chairman: D G Beeby, Esq, FCA

The Rt Revd The Lord Bishop of Carlisle
J A Cropper, Esq, BA, FCA, The Lord Lieutenant of Cumbria
D T Johnston, Esq, OBE, AADipl, FRIBA
Professor H F Woods, BSc, BM, BCh, DPhil, FRCP
Mrs A Metcalfe-Gibson
N A Halfpenny, Esq, BSc, MSc, MBIM
M P T Hart, Esq, FRICS, DipQS
G R Smith, Esq, BSc
Mrs C T McKay
G W Lamont, Esq, FCA, FCCA, ACIS, MIMgt
C R C Tetley, Esq, BA
Mrs M A I Creed
J Bryson, Esq
J H Hunter, Esq
A P Fox, Esq

***Head:* Mr P J Capes**, BSc

Deputy Head (*Marketing & Development*): *P J Etchells, BSc, PhD

Deputy Head (*Academic*): F A Winzor, BMet, PhD

Deputy Head (*Administration*): J W Rowlands, MA

Assistant Masters/Mistresses:

*A C Payne, BA
¶†D W Davies, BSc (*Housemaster of Abbots Court*)
*H M Turpin, GNSM
*T M Elvin, BSc
*A J Parker, MA, MSc
J E Knewstubb, BA, AIL
†*H L Lewis, Cert Ed (*Housemaster of School House*)
Mrs T Messenger, BA
*M R Davey, Cert Ed
*A J H Reeve, BA, PhD
Mrs G F Hudson, MA
Miss J L Dyer, BSc
*Mrs B E Stephenson, BA
*Mrs J Wharrier, CertEd, DipSpLD
Mrs V Carter, BA, MSc, ARCM
†*A J Hannah, BA (*Housemaster of Grindal House*)
Mrs P M Davies (*Housemistress of Abbots Court*)
†*J M Mellor, BA (*Housemaster of Bega House*)
*J D Evans, MA
E J Berwick, BSc
Mrs J A Hendry, LLCM
†¶Mrs S K Hannah, BA (*Housemistress of Grindal House*)
Mrs A J Denyer, BA
Miss S L Deakin, BA
*Mrs J A Carnegie, BA
†Mrs W Mellor (*Housemistress of Bega House*)
†Mrs C S Lewis (*Housemistress of School House*)
M R Lewis, MSc
M A Williams, BA
*M K Midwood, BA
S McNee, BA
Miss S M Telford, BA
G R Ayers, BSc, MSc, PhD
†Mrs C M Dearden, CNAA (*Housemistress of Lonsdale House*)
M Ollis, BA
R W D Notman, BCom
Mrs S J Evans, BEd
Mrs C O Reed, BSc
T H Bell, BSc
Miss P A Close, MA, MPhil

Chaplain: *Canon P R Bryan, BA

Medical Officers:
G J Ironside, MB, ChB, MRCGP, DRCOG
F C Ironside, MB, ChB, MRCOG, MRCGP

Bursar: ¶D F Lord

Registrar: Mrs H C Miller

Head's Secretary: Mrs E M Smith

Situation and Buildings. The School stands in 150 acres of the attractive Valley of St. Bees, half a mile from a fine sandy beach and on the western edge of the Lake District National Park.

The principal older buildings, including the Chapel, Library, Art & Design Department, Gymnasium and Swimming Pool are of St. Bees sandstone and are situated on a raised terrace overlooking the main playing fields. The original school-room, which dates from 1587, now forms one side of a quadrangle and is used as the dining hall. A recent programme of expansion and modernisation has transformed the domestic and teaching accommodation and enhanced the cultural and sporting amenities.

Recent developments include a Business Management Centre which is used jointly by the school and industry. In September 1997, an International Centre opened providing specialist education in English for overseas students. A fully refurbished Music School opened in Summer 2000.

Organisation. There are 300 pupils aged 11–18, and each member of the School is the responsibility of a Housemaster or Housemistress and a personal tutor. There are three Houses for boys and two for girls. All senior boarders have study bedrooms while junior boarders have small dormitories. Boys and girls who live close to the School are accepted as day pupils and the school also admits weekly boarders. The school operates an extensive bus service.

Religion. The Chapel stands at the centre of the School buildings and there are short services on week-days before morning school. The Vicar of the Parish is the Chaplain and on certain Sundays the School attends Morning Service in the Parish Church, The Priory.

Aims. The purpose of the School is to provide an education based on Christian principles, which will enable each pupil to develop his or her individual talents to the full. Particular emphasis is placed on academic excellence, good personal relationships and strong pastoral care. Thriving artistic, dramatic and musical traditions coupled with a wide range of sporting facilities help to avoid any narrow specialisation.

Curriculum. The curriculum provides GCSE courses in English, Latin, French, Spanish, History, Geography, Mathematics, Physics, Chemistry, Biology, Information Technology, Home Economics, Art, Physical Education and Music; option systems permit pupils to select the combination of subjects best suited to their abilities. Most members of the Sixth Form will study four subjects at AS level and three at A2 level together with Key Skills to level 3 and virtually all proceed to higher education. There is a highly successful Dyslexia and Learning Support Unit and Specialist EFL tuition is also provided.

Careers. The School is a member of the Independent Schools Careers Organisation and members of the Staff are responsible for providing specialist advice on careers and higher education and for developing links with industry and commerce. The Head, Housemasters and Housemistresses are also involved in this work and there is regular contact between parents and staff so that progress, future options and career plans can be discussed.

Games. The major sports for boys are Rugby Football, Cricket and Athletics. The girls play Hockey, Netball and Rugby 7's, and are given a wide choice of games during the Summer Term, including Cricket. Many senior girls gain coaching and umpiring qualifications. Many County and Regional Representatives in all major sports and several National athletes. A large number of other sports flourish; the School has its own Golf Course, indoor heated Swimming Pool, large multi-purpose Sports Hall, and courts for Eton Fives, Squash Rackets, Tennis and Badminton.

Other activities. There is a wide variety of societies and clubs and each pupil is encouraged to develop cultural interests. The school offers an extensive and varied weekend programme for boarders.

Music. The School possesses a strong musical tradition and a large proportion of the pupils receive tuition in an instrument. In addition to the orchestra and choir there are strings, brass and woodwind ensembles. Keyboard players have access to a Willis organ. The Choir and instrumentalists perform regularly at the school and in the locality and there are frequent concert tours of West Germany. There are close links with drama.

Drama. Drama is part of the junior curriculum and each year there are several productions involving all age groups.

Combined Cadet Force and St Bees Challenge Award. Pupils are members of the CCF for three years and may choose to extend their service while they are in the Sixth Form. There are Army and RAF Sections and all cadets receive instruction in Shooting. Advanced courses are available in Leadership Training. Courses in flying and pilot training are also arranged. The St Bees Challenge Award is a tailor-made Duke of Edinburgh equivalent.

Outdoor Activities. The School makes full use of its unique location between the Lakeland Fells and the sea and outdoor activities are encouraged for the enjoyment that they give and the valuable personal qualities which they help to develop. Adventure Training is part of the curriculum for junior pupils. A number of members of Staff are experts in mountaineering and water sports and all pupils have opportunities for receiving instruction in camping, canoeing, hill walking, orienteering and snow and rock climbing. There are annual ski-ing parties to Europe.

Admission. Candidates for entry at age 11 or 13 sit the Scholarship and Entrance Examination in February. Boys and girls from Preparatory Schools take the Common Entrance Examination for entry to the School at age 11 or 13. Entry to the VIth Form is dependent on interview, school report and the gaining of a minimum of five GCSE passes. The Head is prepared to give individual consideration to candidates entering at other ages.

Scholarships and Bursaries (*see* Entrance Scholarship section). Junior Scholarships to the maximum value of half fees are available to pupils who are entering the first year and are under the age of 12 on 1st September and to pupils entering the third form who are under the age of 14 on 1st September. Music Scholarships up to half the value of the fees are available at the ages of 11, 13 and 16. Academic and Art Scholarships and Sports Bursaries are available to pupils entering the Sixth Form.

The School also offers a limited number of means-tested Bursaries.

Fees. Senior Full Boarders £4,833 per term; Weekly Boarders £4,436 per term; Junior Boarders £3,537 per term, Junior Weekly Boarders £3,124 per term; Senior Day Pupils £3,176 per term; Junior Day Pupils £2,573 per term.

Registration. A fee of £30 is payable at the time of registration.

Former Pupils. The St Beghian Society. *Secretary:* J E Bell, Esq, St Bees School, St Bees, Cumbria. Tel: (01946) 822254. Handbook and Register of Members. Latest Edition 2000.

Further Particulars from The Registrar, St Bees School, St Bees, Cumbria, CA27 0DS. Tel: (01946) 822263. Fax (01946) 823657. E-mail: helen.miller@st-bees-school.co.uk

Charitable status. St Bees School is a Registered Charity, number 526858. It exists to provide high quality education for boys and girls.

St Benedict's School

54 Eaton Rise Ealing London W5 2ES.
Tel: Headmaster's Office: 020 8862 2010
School Office: 020 8862 2000
Fax: 020 8862 2199
e-mail: headmaster@stbenedicts.org.uk

Motto: *A minimis incipe.*

The School traces its history back to the foundation of the English Benedictine Community of St Gregory at Douai in 1606. St Benedict's was founded in 1902 by Abbot Hugh Edmund Ford to provide in London a Catholic education on Benedictine lines. The School occupies an attractive site in West London. The number of pupils is 560, including 42 girls in the Sixth Form. Boarders are not accepted. There is also a Junior School of some 220 boys between the ages of 4 and 11.

Governing Body: The Abbot & Community of Ealing Abbey, assisted by a lay Advisory Body.

***Headmaster:* Dr A J Dachs**, MA, PhD (Cantab), FRSA

Deputy Headmasters:
M L Barber, MA, MSc
Dom Andrew Hughes

Director of Studies: C Windmill, BSc, ARCS

Procurator: Dom Philip Austen, BA

Assistant Masters:

Dom Thomas Stapleford, BA
Dom Alban Nunn, MMus
W J Twist, MA
I D Stephen, BSc(Econ) (*Careers Master*)
R J Nonhebel, BA
R A Hardman, BA
P Koenig, ATD
R V Irons, MA
P J Halsall, BA
P A Dixon, ISM
M Nalewajko, MA, MEd
P A F Thomas, BA
A J Murphy, BA, BD, MA
J P McCumisky, BA, MA
C S Gasiorek, BEd, MSc
B A Bennett, BSc, MSc
T J Ennis, BA, MA
F Grogan, BA
N H Hull, BSc, MSc, MA
Ms K M Ravenscroft, BEd
W Voice, BA (*Games Master*)
T J Summerfield, BA
S Scicinski, BSc, MSc
P J C Davies, BA, BA
R G Simmons, BA
I S Maines, BSc, MSc, PhD, CChem, MRSC
J P Foley, BA
Mrs R M Babuta, BA, MLitt
Mrs A Baxter, BA
P Daly, BA, MA
J W Singer, BSc (Econ), MSc
Miss S K Cook, BA

R J J Nicholson, BA, ARCO (*Director of Music*)
H M Gunasekara, BSc
P D McCabe, MA
Miss J McKenzie, BA
A J Rees, BSc
D P Seed, BEng
G R Harwood, BSc, MSc
E O Brooks, BA
Miss L McGill, BA
M Watts, MA
Miss R Anderson, BSc
J Bonfiglio, BA
Miss H Devine, BSc
M E Knights
M McEnery, BA, MBA
Miss E Fordyce, BMus
R Grennan, BA
D Little, BA
D C C Mochan, BA
E Pauletto, BSc
Miss E M A Stewart, BA
Mrs O Kirtchuk, BA

Assistant Music Staff:
R Childs, LRAM
Miss E Jackson, GMus, ARCM
A Pledge, FRCO, LRAM, ARCM
L Sollory, ALCM
Miss R Gibson, BMus
L Taliotis, BA, DipRAM
Miss H Rhodes, BA, PPRNCM
I Marcus
P Jaekel, GRSM, LRAM, ARCO
D Field, GLCM, LLCM, MMus

Accountant: Mrs C de Cintra, BA, ACA (*Tel:* 020 8862 2190)

Accounts Assistants: Mrs H Mortemore, Mrs H Shah, Mrs M Moore

Properties Manager: R Ferrett, MASI, ACIOB

Headmaster's Secretary: Ms P Kalli (*020 8862 2010*)

School Secretaries:
Mrs C Irwin-Childs (*020 8862 2000*)
Mrs D Blondiau

Librarian: Mrs S Mortimer

Technicians:
Mrs M Teegan
H Patel, BSc
Miss D Martin
J Hatch

Combined Cadet Force: Major T Summerfield

Old Priorian Association: Dr J L Kearns (*Hon Secretary*), c/o The School

Admission to the School is in September at the age of 11, by interview and special examination. There is a further entry at 13 by the Common Entrance Examination or the School's own examination. Both girls and boys are admitted to the Sixth Form, subject to good GCSE results. Application for admission should be made to the Headmaster.

Religion. A specifically Christian and Catholic atmosphere is fostered through contact with the monastery. There are regular periods for liturgy, both formal in the Abbey Church and informal in small groups.

Curriculum. For the first years all boys study a common curriculum including Latin, French, Art, Music and Technology. In the third year additional languages are offered, Greek, German and Spanish. All proceed to GCSE in nine or ten subjects. A wide choice is available at A Level and AS level. Pupils are also prepared for Oxford & Cambridge entrance, where there is an impressive record.

Religious Studies are undertaken by all in every year. The Sixth Form is large, about 180, and almost all proceed to University or further education.

Physical education and Games are part of the curriculum throughout the School. Rugby and cricket are the two principal games but other sports are also fostered, particularly tennis, swimming, athletics, karate, volleyball and table-tennis. The School has 15 acres of playing fields nearby at Perivale. An indoor Sports Centre and Art and Design rooms were completed in 1991.

School activities include Combined Cadet Force, Duke of Edinburgh Award Scheme, and opportunities for social work with the elderly and disadvantaged. Drama is strong with annual major productions. The Musical tradition is firm; almost any instrument can be learnt and activities include choirs and two orchestras. Public concerts are held several times each term. Art is outstanding, with several pupils passing from the Sixth Form to Art Colleges each year. All the usual societies are encouraged Debating, Literary, Scientific, Computing. Considerable use is made of opportunities available in London for visits to concerts, theatres, museums and art galleries. In the nature of a wholly day school, contact with parents is frequent and regular.

Careers. There is a Careers Centre with experienced Careers staff and work experience in appropriate fields is organised. Close contact is enjoyed with the Services.

Honours. We continue to have a strong Oxbridge entry each year.

Fees. Registration and Entrance Fee: £20. Tuition fees are £2,400 per term.

Charitable status. St Benedict's is a Registered Charity, number 242715. Its aim is to promote the Christian and Catholic education of young people.

St Columba's College

King Harry Lane St Albans Hertfordshire AL3 4AW
Tel: 01727 855185
Fax: 01727 863997
e-mail: domstephen@sccoffice.prestel.co.uk

St Columba's College has been under the care of the Brothers of the Sacred Heart (New England Province) since 1955 and is a Roman Catholic, selective boys school, but with about one third of its pupils coming from other denominations and faiths. Brothers and lay teachers (now in the majority) work together with pupils and parents to provide a Christian education based on traditional values, balancing a friendly community with sound discipline and academic rigour.

The College and its Preparatory School stand in their own grounds overlooking the picturesque vale of St Albans and the Roman settlement of Verulamium. A purpose-built Science and Technology Centre was built in the 1980s and work has recently been completed to provide a new Sixth Form Centre, extended facilities for the Preparatory School, a new Dining Hall and improved facilities for Music. The next major element in the development plan involves extension of the ICT facilities and this will begin in July 2001.

Motto: *Cor ad cor loquitur*

Governors:

J Magee, ACIL, FCILA (*Chairman*)
A Fay, BComm, FCA, MBIM (*Vice-Chairman*)
P Cahill, BL, Barrister at Law
Mrs G Cummings, JP
Dom Stephen Darlington, OSB, BA
Br R Breault, SC, MA
P B Fisher, MA
M Freeley, Esq
C Hancock, Esq
Br Louis Laperle, SC, MA, MBA
P J McKay, BSc, ACA
Br R Reinsant, SC, BA, MA, CAGS
K Rudd, Esq

Dean, Trustee: Br R Reinsant, SC, BA, MA, CAGS

***Head Master:* Dom Stephen Darlington,** OSB, BA

Second Master: D Shannon-Little, CertEd, BA

Director of Studies: S D M Danes, MA
Head of Sixth Form: I T Nash, BSc
Senior Master (Admissions): A K Smith, DLC, CertEd

Housemasters:
P J Baker, BSc (*More House*)
R J Byrne, BSc (*Alban House*)
S J D'Souza, BSc (*Fisher House*)
D Gaze, MA (*Becket House*)

Teaching Staff:
P R Allington, BA, LRAM (*Head Master's assistant for Academic Development*)
J Ashmore, BEd, MA
P J Baker, BSc
P Beaton, BA (*Head of Careers*)
Mrs L Bills, BA, LGSM
Miss J Bonsey, BA
M Burke, BA
R J Byrne, BSc
Miss M Casson, BA
Mrs P Cockman, BSc
Miss A Cowdery, MA
S D M Danes, MA
T P Dennehy, CertEd, BA (*Head of Physics*)
I Devereux, BEd (*Head of Mathematics*)
J D Dolman, BSc (*Head of Geography*)
M Drugan, BEd (*Head of Design Technology*)
S J D'Souza, BSc
Mrs B Elliott, MA (*Head of Spanish*)
Ms G Garrier, L-es-L
D Gaze, MA (*Head of German*)
Mrs J Greaves, BSc
Mrs L Groom, BA, ALCM
Miss S Jasieczek, BA (*Head of French & Modern Languages*)
P M Jones, BA, MA (*Head of History*)
M H Kempson, MA
Mrs A Kipling, BA (*Head of Art*)
Br I Lane, SC, BA
G E Lawson, BSc
Mrs M Lawson, BEd (*Head of English*)
S M Leadbetter, BA, MA (*Director of Curriculum Information Technology*)
Mrs C Lee, BA
A Lowles, BEd
Mrs P MacKenzie, MA (*Director of Music*)
Miss S M McGleave, BA, MA, CertRE (*Head of Religious Studies*)
I T Nash, BSc
A L G Nevard, BSc, PGTC, SpLDCert (*Head of Learning Support*)
Mrs K Panayides, CertEd, BA
Mrs G Pilditch, BA
Br R Pinette, SC, BA, MA, MEd
Br R Reinsant, SC, BA, MA, CAGS
M Robins, BEd, MEd (*Head of Sociology*)
Mrs J Sage, MA, DipLib (*Head of Library*)
J G Sapsford, BSc (*Head of Chemistry*)
D Shannon-Little, CertEd, BA
Br D St Jacques, SC, BA, MA
M Swales, BSc
P Toney, BEd (*Director of Sport*)
T J Turner, BA (*Head of Economics*)
Br P Vaillancourt, SC, BA, MA
Mrs M Walker, BSc (*Head of Science*)
E Waters, BA
R C Whiteman, BA (*Head of Classics/Latin*)

Examinations Officer: M D Lyons, BSc

Accounts Manager: Mrs G Consterdine, BA, ACA

Head Master's PA: Mrs R Crowley

Registrar: Br D Bessette, SC, BA

School Nurse: Mrs C Newton, SRN

Business Manager: Br R Champagne, SC

Estate Manager: M Owen

Head of Prep School: E F Brown, BEd, MA

Senior Master: J L Lewis, BEd
Director of Studies: Mrs M Shannon-Little, BEd
Head of Pre-Prep: Mrs S Edmonds, MA

Teaching Staff:
B Alexander, HDipEd
Mrs P Almond, BA
Mrs L Bills, BA, LGSM
Mrs L Brown, BEd
Mrs S Burgon, BA
Br I Chabot, SC, MA
D Edwards, BEd (*Head of PE and Games*)
Mrs K Fahy, BSc(Ed), MEd
Mrs B Fullard, CertEd
M Gale, HDipEd
Br T Greer, SC, MART, MAChSP, PastMin (*Head of RE*)
Mrs U Kelly, BSc
Mrs L Latham, BA, PGCE
Mrs P MacKenzie, MA (*Director of Music*)
Mrs H McLeod, MA, ALA
Miss E Paradine, BEd
Mrs J Perkins, NNEB
Mrs J Pumo, BA, NDD
S Riddett, BHMS
Mrs N Sells, BA
Mrs D Sumpter, BA
A Tucker, CertEd, DipEd
Mrs L Turley, BEd
Mrs E Williams, CertEd
Mrs A Wynn-Owen

The Music Department is assisted by visiting instrumental teachers.

Entry. The school admits boys from 4-18. Currently there are 240 boys in the Preparatory School (including the Pre-Prep Department), aged 4-11, and 550 boys in the College, aged 11-18. Pupils are accepted in September. The main entry for the Senior School is at 11, by Entrance Test and interview, with a significantly smaller group entering at 13+ (CEE). Occasional entry, during an academic year, is possible only in exceptional circumstances if a place becomes available.

Scholarships. Academic Scholarships are awarded at 11, 13 and for the Sixth Form. Additionally, the College offers two Music Scholarships per year.

The Curriculum. This is kept as broad as possible up to GCSE, pupils usually taking 9 subjects from the traditional range of Arts and Science options. There are 20 A Level (A2) subjects for pupils to choose from, many of them also available as a fourth option up to AS. Sixth Form education is complemented by a Key Skills course which aims to develop further the pupils' abilities in the fields of ICT, communication and numeracy. The vast majority of the Sixth Form go on to University, including Oxford and Cambridge.

Careers. The school is a member of ISCO; the well equipped Careers Room is readily available and the Careers Master is responsible for ensuring that all boys receive all the necessary advice to make informed decisions on subject selection, university entry and subsequent careers.

Pastoral Care. St Columba's is a Roman Catholic school and, though it admits some boys who are not

Catholic, its ethos is rooted in the Catholic tradition. The spiritual and moral well-being of our pupils is a matter of primary importance for all of our staff, the majority being tutors. The four Housemasters and their teams are supported by a Chaplain and a full-time Counsellor. Their work is co-ordinated by the Second Master. Relations between the school and parents are very open - a strength of the College - and they are in regular contact with each other in monitoring the progress of the boys. The school seeks to nurture the academic and personal talents of each individual.

Sport. All boys participate, and the school has a strong sporting reputation. A rich variety of sports is available, including Rugby, Basketball, Soccer, Tennis, Cricket, Athletics, Swimming and Cross Country. For Sixth Form boys, not selected for the major sports, an even wider range of activities is available. Facilities include a large gymnasium and sports field on site. We also make extensive use of pitches, athletics track, swimming pool and a golf course which are all immediately adjacent to the College site.

Clubs and Activities. The school offers a mix of activities both at lunch-time and after school. These include sports clubs, drama, art, chess, computing, Young Enterprise and many others, as well as a variety of academic and social clubs. There are a number of music ensembles, including a choir, orchestra and jazz band. There are currently three choirs of hand-bell ringers.

CCF. In 2000, the College launched a Combined Cadet Force which includes an Army and an RAF section. We employ an SSI (a School Staff Instructor). The Duke of Edinburgh Award Scheme now comes under the same management.

Preparatory School. St Columba's College Preparatory School is on the same site as the College and shares many of its facilities. The school has a strong family atmosphere, providing a secure and purposeful environment in which expectations are high. It admits boys only, by examination and interview. Admission to the Preparatory School does not guarantee admission to the College; this may be obtained only by passing the Entrance Examination.

Fees per annum. £5,610

Charitable status. St Columba's is a Registered Charity (Brothers of the Sacred Heart Foundation for Education), number 231733.

St Columba's College

Whitechurch Dublin 16.
Tel: Dublin 353-1-4906791 (Warden)
353-1-4931551 (Staff)
Fax: Dublin 353-1-4936655

Motto: *Sicut Columbae.*

St Columba's College was founded in 1843 by the Rev William Sewell, the Lord Primate, the Earl of Dunraven and others. The College was incorporated by Royal Charter in 1913.

Visitor: The Most Rev Dr R H A Eames, Archbishop of Armagh and Primate of All Ireland

Fellows:

R G H Roper
The Most Revd D A Caird, DD
H D Thompson, MA, BAgricSc
The O'Morchoe
Dr Brian L Bond, BA, BAI, PhD, CEng, FIEI, MICE, ACIArb
Mrs Ann Budd, MA, HDipEd
J N White
Mrs A C Kennedy
J R E Bewley (*Chairman*)
Professor M G T Webb, MB, MPhil, FRCPI, FRCPsych, FTCD
Mrs J M C Pettigrew
W R Ellis
C D S Shiell
Mrs P MacCarthy-Morrogh
R H Simpson, BBS, FCA
Mrs K M Erwin, MA

***Warden:* T E Macey**, MA, CertEd

Sub-Warden: R M McMullen, BA, AgrB, HDipEd

Bursar: J K Bailey

Accountant:

Assistant: Mrs M Heffernan-Kelly

Assistant Staff:

The Rev M R Heaney, MA, HDipEd (*Chaplain and Careers*)
P J L Gray, BA, HDipEd (*Registrar*)
†N F D Falkiner, BA, HDipEd, LLB (*Archivist*)
J M Fanagan, MA, HDipEd
†P J Jackson, BSc, HDipEd,
H M Dockrell, BA, HDipEd
†F H Morris, BA, HDipEd
J R Brett, MA, HDipEd
P R Watts, DipArt (*Pottery*)
J M Girdham, BA, HDipEd (*Librarian*)
†Mrs F H Morris, BA, HDipEd
†D C Sherwood, BA, HDipEd
B A Redmond, BTech (*Woodwork & Design*)
G R Bannister, MA, PhD, HDipEd
C F T Jenkins, ARCM, ARCO, LTCL, ALCM, ARIAM (*Precentor*)
A F F Cox, BA, HDipEd
†L Canning, BA, HDipEd
Miss A Maybury, BA, HDipEd
Miss A Kilfeather, BA, HDipEd
J J Stone, BSc, PhD, HDipEd
Dr M Singleton, BSc, MSc, PhD
P G McCarthy, BA, HDipEd
Mrs M O'Connor, BA, HDipEd
†Mrs D Sherwood
†Ms S McEneaney, BA, PGCE
Mrs F G Heffernan, CertEd, ACLD, ARTI
Mrs T Cahill, Dip Sports Science
J G Farrelly, BA, DSS, HDipEd
F X Nathan, BA, HDipEd
Mlle A Courtay, BA, HDipEd
N D R Atkinson, BA, HDipEd
Miss B M Buckley, BA, HDipEd
Miss D Cullen, BEd (*Art & Design*)
D Higgins, MA, HDipEd
Mrs P Macey, Dip Fine Art, DipADT
Ms N Forrest, BA, HDipEd
J Zlnay, BSc(Ed)
Mrs S Hutchinson-Edgar, BA, HDipEd
P Cron, MA, NDip
H de Jong (*Hockey*)
S McArdle, NCEHS
Mrs K Lovatt, NCEHS, ITEL
J May, NCEF
J Morrissey, NCEF
A Grundy, HonVCM, FTCL, LRSM, ALCM (*Guitar*)
A P McKeever, BA, DipCounsPsych, LGSM, FTCL, LRSM (*Piano and Organ*) (*Assistant Organist*)
Ms M Barnecutt (*Flute*)
Miss G Malone Brady, LRAM, ARCM (*Piano*)
R Boyle, ALCM (*Brass*)
M Carey, BA, LGSM (*Violin & Piano*)
Miss M Brown, BA, ARIAM (*Violin*)
Ms S McManus (*Singing*)

Medical Officer: Dr D Taylor, MB, MICGP
Warden's Secretary: Ms I Hasslacher, BA, HDipEd
Infirmary Sister: Mrs Catherine Donnelly, SRN, RGN
Assistant: Mrs A Hackett, RGN

The College is a co-educational boarding school, with a number of day boarders, for about 300 pupils. It is situated on the slopes of the Dublin Mountains about 7 miles south of the city overlooking Dublin Bay in an estate of 138 acres.

Having occupied its present site for 146 years, the College combines the best of architecture old and new.

Recent additions include a new Library and Reading Room, a sports hall, a computer centre, a Careers Library and a new Arts Centre.

Admission. Application for admission should be made to the Warden. There is a registration fee of £25. Entrants from Preparatory Schools take the Common Entrance Examination. There is a junior House for entrants between the ages of 11 and 13 years.

Curriculum. In the Upper School, a wide choice of subjects and a large number of courses are available for the Irish Leaving Certificate. This examination keeps many options open for third-level colleges. It is the qualifying examination for entry to Irish universities and is acceptable (with requisite grades) to the faculties of almost all British universities. The Irish Junior Certificate is taken in the third form.

Religious Teaching. Chapel services and religious instruction are based broadly upon the liturgy and doctrine of the Church of Ireland. Boys and girls of other denominations and faiths are included.

Other Activities. Music, Art, Pottery and Woodwork (which are part of the curriculum in the Lower School) and Drama, Debating, Photography, Computers and various other clubs and societies function at all levels.

Games and Pursuits. Rugby Football, Hockey, Cricket, Athletics, Cross-country Running, Farming, Tennis, Squash, Badminton, Basketball, Golf, Swimming, Canoeing, Hill-walking and Orienteering.

Fees. Senior House: IR£7,590 pa. Junior House IR£5,298 pa. Day Boarders IR£4,665 pa. Day Pupils IR£3,465 pa.

The above fees are expressed in Irish £s. Fees may be paid in the sterling equivalent.

Entrance Scholarships. (*see* Entrance Scholarship section) Pennefather and Bowles Scholarships. Three or more awards from a Major Scholarship, Minor Scholarships and Exhibitions, each tenable for four years, will be offered after an examination held in May. The examination papers may be taken at Preparatory Schools. One Old Columban Scholarship is offered. Senior School Scholarships and Junior School Exhibitions are also offered. Special fees are available for the sons of Clergy of the Church of Ireland and other Bursaries are granted by the Fellows (details from the Warden).

Leaving Scholarship. Norman Scholarships, for two years or more at all university colleges in Britain and Ireland, are open to the sons and daughters of Clergy of the Church of Ireland.

St Columba's Old Pupils' Society. Old Columban Society. *Hon Secretary:* J M Girdham, St Columba's College.

Charitable status. College of St Columba is a Registered Charity, number 4024. Its aims and objectives are the provision of Secondary Education facilities.

St Columba's School

Duchal Road Kilmacolm Renfrewshire PA13 4AU
Tel: 01505 872238
Fax: 01505 873995
Junior School Castlehill Road Kilmacolm Renfrewshire PA13 4EQ
Tel: 01505 872768
e-mail: stcolumba@rmplc.co.uk
website: www.stcolumbas.renfrew.sch.uk

St Columba's School is a non-denominational co-educational school, founded in 1897, with a roll of 670 of which 370 are in the Senior Department. It has an excellent academic reputation but additionally encourages the development of the individual through participation in sport, music and drama. The school is also extremely strong in the Duke of Edinburgh Award Scheme.

Over the past few years much investment in capital projects from a Games Hall to Science Laboratories has greatly enhanced the school and its facilities in a wide range of curricular subjects. A new Music, Art and Technology Block opened in January 1999, followed by a new Library in the Autumn of the same year. 2001 saw the opening of the new Primary School costing £1 million, and an Astroturf Hockey/Tennis area.

Rector: **Mr A H Livingstone,** BSc (Hons Mathematics), DipEd

Depute Rector: Mrs J Wallace, DipPE (Dunfermline), DipSpecNeeds

Head of Primary School: Mrs D Grant, DipPrimEd, DipAdvProfStudies, Dip Management in Education

Deputy Head of Primary School: Miss E Paton, DCE Infant Mist Endorsement, AssocBDA

Chairman of the Board of Governors: Mr R M Kennedy, TD, FCCII, FLIA

Business Manager/Bursar: Mr A Gallacher, CA

Secretary to the Rector: Mrs D Motherwell

Entry. This is by formal entrance test and interview with the Rector or Head of Primary School.

Curriculum. St Columba's follows a Scottish curriculum presenting pupils for S-Grade, H-Grade and CSYS examinations. Over 90% of leavers move on to university including Oxford and Cambridge.

Fees. For the academic year 2000/2001 the termly fees for Prep are £575, Primary 1 £1,117, Primary 2 £1,215, Primary 3 £1,337, Primary 4 £1,417, Primary 5/6 £1,493, Transitus to Senior VI £1,667. No major scholarships are available.

Organisations. The school is broken up into four Houses for both pastoral and competitive purposes. Each house has a Housemaster or Mistress as well as pupil Captain and Vice Captain. Career guidance is done through the House System or via ISCO.

Charitable status. St Columba's School is a Registered Charity, number Ed Cr 35129/SCO 12598. It exists to provide education for pupils.

St Dunstan's College

Stanstead Road London SE6 4TY.
Tel: 020 8516 7200
Fax: 020 8516 7300
website: www.stdunstans.org.uk

Motto: *Albam Exorna.*

The College originated in the Parish of St Dunstan-in-the-East, part of the Tower Ward of the City of London; and as early as 1446, Henry VI declared the parish school to be one of the efficient grammar schools of the City.

St Dunstan's College was refounded in Catford in 1888.

Chairman of the Governors: Professor A J Bellingham, CBE, FRCP, FRCPath

Deputy Chairman: ¶Sir Paul Judge, FRSA

List of Governors:
Professor Harry Allred
¶The Revd J Andrews, MA, FRSA

Eddie Bell
Lady Florette Boyson
P L Coling, FRICS, ACIArb
Alderman Sir Roger Cork
Mrs Judy Davies
The Revd Canon Peter A Delaney, FSC, AKC
The Rt Hon The Lord Ellenborough
¶Philip France
Alan Gordon
Peter Lincoln
Mrs Kate Price
¶Colin Watts

Clerk to the Governors and Bursar: Colonel N Wallace

***Headmaster:* D I Davies**, MA, FRSA

Deputy Head: Mrs J D Davies, BSc

Head of Junior School: J D Gaskell, CertEd

Director of Studies: M Blocksidge, MA
Head of Sixth Form: Mrs M A Lipton, BSc
Head of Middle School: ¶B Harrild, BA
Head of Lower School: ¶S D Thorogood, BA

Assistant Masters and Mistresses:

M J Adams, BA
*¶G N Alderman, BEd
*Mrs R D Allen, BA
R J Alton, BA, MSc
N Amy, MA
R Austin, BSc
A M Banks, BSc
*Mrs H S Baptiste, BSc
Miss S Bennell, BEd
*R R D Bodenham, BSc
*I P Burgess, BSc
Ms M Callaghan, BA
Mrs M Cole, CertEdQualSpLD
*P F Davis, MA
A Dickson, BEd
R A Duckworth, CertEd
Mrs E G Emes, BSc, MSc
*J D Foster, BA
P A Glavin, BA
P Glyne-Thomas, BA
P M Gobey, GRSM, ARCO, ARCM
*D C Gordon, MA
Mrs E P Gray, BSc
Mrs A Hallett, BEd
*N A J Harper, MA, FRCO
*Mrs G L Holmes, DPSE, CertEd
*W J Holroyd, BA, AKC
S G J Huet, BEd
Mrs A G Hughes, BEd
Miss E Hulls, BA
Mrs P Hunt, CertEd
*G Hunter, BA
Miss A C Iglesias, BA
A H Isaachsen, BEd
Miss L M Jackson, DipEd
Mrs J P Kerr, MA, ARCM, AGSM
*J P Kitchingman, BSc
Mrs I Lambert, Leipzig University
R W Lea, BA, BEd
M J Leang, BSc, MA, AKC
Mrs A M Lewis, BEd
C E W Lowe, BA
A J Miller, BSc, PhD
M Moffet, BSc
Mrs F Montaigu, DipAD
Ms H Morris
M J Muchall, BA, MA
Miss M V Neal, BSc
*¶J M Newman, BA
Ms J Oliver, BA
*C J Osborne, BEd
Mrs S J Parratt, BEd
M Patel, BSc, PhD
Ms J Pavell
A J Pearson, BSc
G A Pickett, BSc
*Mrs K A Plummer, BA
Mrs S P Poole, CertEd
*P D Powell, MA
T G Pratt, MA
Miss H J Priestley, BEd
*M E Punt, BA, MSc
Ms J Reeves, BA
Miss D Reid, BEd
C M Rimmer, BEd
Mrs S Sanbrook-Davies, LRAM
A Schofield, MA, FRSA
*A D Sharp, MA
M E O'Shaughnessy, BA
Mrs H A M Smith, BA
Miss S L Stapleton, BA
*R E Stevens, BSocSc
Mrs K L Stevenson, ALA (*Librarian*)
N R Taylor
Mrs K E Vinson, BA, HDFA
A M Wilkins, BA
G C Willatt, BEd
Mrs D H Wood, CertEd
Miss L J Woodburn, BSc
Mrs L P Woodhams, BA
M Workman, BA
Ms E Yemenakis, BA

Headmaster's Personal Assistant: Mrs Penny Phillips

College Registrar: Mrs Maura Bacca

Junior School Secretary/Registrar: Mrs Rosemary Scard

College Secretary: Mrs Lorraine Currie

College Doctor: ¶Dr D G Thompson

Buildings. The College is a large group of mainly Victorian buildings, about 3 minutes' walk from Catford and Catford Bridge railway stations.

In addition to classrooms the buildings include the Great Hall, Refectory, Sixth Form Common Room, Libraries, Theatre, Art School, DT Centre, Projection Room, Physics, Chemistry and Biology Laboratories, Swimming Pool and Rugby Fives Courts. An additional building for the Preparatory Department was provided in 1968 and further extensions comprising laboratories and a music centre were brought into use in 1972. Further classrooms were added in 1997. New Changing Rooms, incorporating a specially designed climbing wall, were built in 1989. A new suite of three Biology Laboratories above renovated cloakrooms and toilet facilities was brought into use in 1992 and substantial developments for specialist Technology accommodation have recently been completed.

A Pre-Prep was opened in 1994 and a new Sports Hall in 1996.

Organisation and Curriculum. The College is divided into a Junior School of some 320 pupils from 4–11 which includes a Pre-Prep of 111 pupils from 4–7 and a Preparatory Department of 210 pupils aged 7–11. The Junior School is a member of IAPS. The Senior School consists of a Lower School, Middle School and Sixth Form of together approximately 660 pupils aged 11–18.

The academic life of the Junior School includes the best of the National Curriculum with great attention given to the fundamentals of English, Mathematics and Science. French is taught throughout the Junior School. A friendly, caring and stimulating environment is encouraged with home and school working in close partnership. In the Senior School account is taken of a pupil's individual tastes and aptitudes and a considerable choice of studies is permitted. The curriculum includes RS, English, Drama, History, Economics, Political Studies, Business Studies, Geography, Latin, French, German, Spanish, Mathematics, Physics, Information Technology, Chemistry, Biology, Art, Music, Design Technology, Physical Education and Personal and Social Education.

In the Sixth Form a wide variety of A levels is offered and every pupil proceeds to University.

Other Activities. The more formal work of the classroom is supplemented by other activities which aim at the widening our pupils' outlook and developing their special interests.

Pupils are encouraged to participate in regular community service, often through locally based organisations. Every year the College supports specific fund-raising activities for the benefit of charities.

The chief games are cricket, rugby and association football for boys and hockey, swimming and netball for girls. In the Lent Term there is cross-country running and fives. There are also facilities for tennis, swimming, water-polo, basket-ball, chess, squash racquets, judo, badminton, golf, sailing, shooting and a wide variety of other sports for boys and girls in the Sports Hall.

The College supports a strong contingent of the Combined Cadet Force (Army and Navy sections) which is open to pupils in the Upper School; motor maintenance, rock climbing, work with wireless and other signallers' equipment, sailing and preparation for the Duke of Edinburgh's Award, are among the various activities provided by the CCF. Parents are strongly advised to allow their children to make use of the opportunities which the Corps offers for the development of initiative, leadership and a sense of responsibility. Attendance at the School's Annual CCF Camp is regarded as an essential part of training.

Numerous other activities include the Armstrong (Science) Society, Bridge Club, Chess Club, Christian Union, Classics Society, Computer Club, Craft Club, Debating Society, Dramatic Society, English Society, Electronic Workshop, Geographical Society, Mathematical Society, Modern Languages Society, Musical Society and Natural History Society.

There is a College Choir which is open to pupils from all parts of the school. In addition there is a Prep Choir and a Chamber Choir. There are three orchestras, a string orchestra, two wind bands and a jazz group. Individual tuition in a musical instrument is available.

Entrance. Pupils are generally admitted in September at the age of 4, 7, 11, 13 or 16. The younger and older pupils are assessed in individual interviews but at 11+ there is an Entrance Examination, held annually in January, consisting of papers in English and Arithmetic and Verbal and Abstract Reasoning tests.

Entrance Scholarships (*see* Entrance Scholarship section). There are various Foundation Scholarships and Bursaries awarded on academic merit.

Fees. The consolidated fees (including lunch) are from £1,631 to £2,311 per term.

Old Dunstonian Association. There is a thriving Old Dunstonians Association to which parents are strongly encouraged to subscribe on behalf of their sons and daughters so that they may leave the College as life members.

St Dunstan's College Family Society. The Society is open to all parents, Old Dunstonians and other friends of the College; it supports College activities and affords opportunities for social gatherings.

Charitable status. St Dunstan's College is a Registered Charity, number 312747. It exists to provide education for boys and girls.

St Edmund's College

Old Hall Green Ware Herts SG11 1DS.
Tel: (01920) 821504
Fax: (01920) 823011
e-mail: registrar@secware.demon.co.uk
website: www.stedmundcollege.org

Motto: *Avita pro Fide.*

Saint Edmund's College has two roots. The first is the English College at Douai, founded by Cardinal Allen in 1568. This College was peopled by fellows, tutors and students exiled from Oxford University, and was established to educate Catholic priests and laymen. The College was forcibly closed during the French Revolution and the staff and students returned to England. The second root is Silkstead School founded during the 1640s; this School had moved to Old Hall Green by 1769. The students evicted from Douai joined the boys of the Old Hall Green Academy in 1793 and the combined establishment was put under the patronage of the Saint on whose feast day the union took place – Saint Edmund of Canterbury.

Patron and President: Cardinal Cormac Murphy O'Connor

Governors:
J I O'Mahony, BSc(Econ), FCA (*Chairman*)
H M Burgess, BSc (*Deputy Chairman*)
J Gillham, MA, LLB
The Revd D Sheehan
Dr John Tudor, MB, MA, MRCS, LRCP, DRCOG, FFR
Dr T H McLaughlin, PhD, MA
Ms P Bessey, BSc, FFB, RIBA, MRAE
Mrs M Edmondson, BA, DipEd, DipCG
J L Lipscomb, MA, MSc
The Revd Canon M Brockie, JCL
S Szemerenyi, MA
D B A Hirst, FCA

Clerk to the Governors and Bursar: G T Black, ACIS, ACIB

***Headmaster:* D J J McEwen**, MA (Oxon), FRSA

Deputy Heads:
Mrs J Neal, BA
D R Black, BSc, MPhil, PhD, LTCL

Priest in Residence: Revd M Pinot de Moira

Head of Centre for Advanced Studies: J Sheridan, BSc, MA

Assistant Staff:
†Mrs P H Pond, BSc
†D A Gallie, KM, BEd
†C M Jenkinson, BEd
†Mrs M C Lewis, MSc, FZS
†Mrs J A Ball, CertEd
J Vaughan-Shaw, BA
K M Hall, MA
J A Hayes, MA
A A Drew, BSc
A L Moss, BEd
Mrs T King, BEd
Mrs P T Parker, BA
A J Sleight, BEd
G Lewis, BA
R T Armour, BA
Mrs C M Hugo, CertEd, DipRSA
Mrs L Blackburn, BA, DipRSA
J J Kinoulty, BSc
J Fogarty, FCH, FRSA
Mrs J Morley, BA, HND
The Revd M Pinot de Moira (*Priest in Residence*)
J W Morley, BA
R M Lewis, BEd
N Cattermole, BEd
Mrs E Sheridan, BSc
Miss A Bell, BA, MA
Mrs B Howitt, BA (*Matron*)
Mrs C MacDonald, BA
J Stypinski, BA
P Bates, BA
Mrs H Clark, BSc
P Davies, MA
Mrs C DeVito, BA
Miss K Grice, BA
E Higgins, BSc
Miss E King, BSc
Miss P Moakler, BA
Miss R Osborough, MA

St Hugh's:
†Mrs D M Elliott, BSc
A J Robinson, BEd
S A Gibbons, BA
Mrs P M Davies, CertEd
Mrs A Parsons, CertEd
Mrs E Brooks, DipEC
Mrs B McDonald, CertEd
Mrs P Wheldal, CertEd
Miss N Rogers, NNEB
Mrs H McCallion (*Assistant*)
D J Brinsdon, RCM, ARCM
Mrs Y Elliott, BA
N Martin, MA
Mrs S Mills, BEd
Mrs C Wadsworth, BA

Music Staff:
D Wadsworth, BEd
N D Howard, BA, LTCL, FRCO

Library: Mrs S Gribben, BA

Information Technology Manager: S Winfield

Careers Staff: Mrs M P O'Shea, BA

Medical Officers:
Dr T Reynolds, MB, ChB
Dr P Lancaster, MBBS, DRCOG, FPCert
Dr M Partington, MB, ChB

Infirmary:
Mrs A Hartfield, RGN
Mrs J Izzard, RGN
Mrs P Jenkins, RGN

Archivist: D A Gallie, KM, BEd

Registrar: R Parsons, BA, MA

CCF: Squadron Leader A A Drew

St Edmund's and St Hugh's (prep school) are situated in over 400 acres of parkland on the A10 London-Cambridge road, approximately 25 miles north of the capital. At present there are 300 boys and 240 girls aged between 3 and 18 day, 7 and 18 boarding.

Admission. (*see* Entrance Scholarship section) Pupils are admitted at the ages of 3, 5, 7, 11, 13 and 16, although entry is always considered at other ages. The College offers some Music and Academic Scholarships, and Bursaries to the value of a maximum of 50% of the fees. Applications should be made to the Registrar.

Fees. Day Pupils: £2,440–£2,675; Weekly Boarders: £3,510–£3,985; Full Boarders: £3,780–£4,275; all depending on age of the pupil. There are reductions for families of HM Forces and for younger brothers and sisters.

Organisation. All pupils follow the National Curriculum. At the end of NC Year 11, pupils take GCSE examinations in all courses that they have followed, usually more than is required by the National Curriculum.

In Rhetoric (Sixth Form) students will study four AS Levels in the Lower Sixth and 3 A2's in the Upper Sixth. A GNVQ's are offered in Business and Art and Design.

Courses are also available in Law and Theology. Tuition is provided for entry to Oxford, Cambridge and other Universities.

Religious Instruction. St Edmund's is a College for those of the Christian faith who would appreciate the values of Catholic education. All pupils receive instruction in Christian doctrine and practice from lay teachers. GCSE Religious Studies, AS Theology and Maryvale Certificate Course in Christian Faith are entered. Importance is attached to the liturgical life of the College and the practical expression of faith.

Games and Activities. Great importance is attached to games and physical education throughout the College. All pupils are required to participate in a variety of sports on two afternoons a week. The major sports for boys are soccer, rugby, cricket and athletics, while for girls they are hockey, netball, rounders and athletics. The other sports available are cross-country, tennis, swimming, basketball, badminton, volleyball, squash and croquet. A large sports hall, swimming pool, tennis and squash courts, weights room, together with 400 acres of grounds provide ample facilities. Some fixtures take place at the weekends.

There are many extra-curricular activities including regular concerts and dramatic productions. The CCF - RAF and Army sections -, Community Service and Duke of Edinburgh's Award Scheme play a prominent part in developing a self-reliant and confident individual. Time is also set apart for the many clubs and social activities that take place.

Careers. There is a fulltime Careers teacher and Careers Library. The College is in membership with the Independent Schools Careers Organisation. Careers advice is available to pupils from the age of 13. There are regular careers lectures and visits to industry and Universities. Work experience is organised for Lower Sixth. There is a Neighbourhood Engineering Scheme and CREST. Centigrade and Oasis testing is also available.

St Hugh's School exists on the same estate. It consists of a Nursery, Infants and Junior School for pupils from 3 to 11, which feeds into the Senior School at 11. The pupils are able to make use of many of the amenities of the Senior School such as Science Laboratories, Swimming Pool and Sports Hall. There is no boarding at St Hugh's.

Charitable status. St Edmund's College, Ware is a Registered Charity, number 311073. It aims to provide an education for Catholics and other Christians between the ages of 3 and 18.

St Edmund's School
Canterbury

Canterbury Kent CT2 8HU
Tel: (01227) 475600
Fax: (01227) 471083

Motto: *Fungar Vice Cotis*

The School, which is named after the great scholar-saint, St Edmund, Archbishop of Canterbury 1234–1240, was founded in 1749 and was transferred from London in 1855, mainly through the munificence of the Rev Dr Samuel Warneford, to its present 60 acre site on an out-lying spur of the Downs, a mile from Canterbury. It commands a marvellous view of the Cathedral and the city of Canterbury, and is only 5 miles distant from the sea. The 1855 main building, constructed of Kentish ragstone, is praised in Pevsner's *Building of England.* Many other buildings have been added and there has been considerable development in recent years, including a new Junior School wing in 1998.

The school is owned by St Edmund's School Canterbury, a charitable company limited by guarantee registered in England and Wales.

Patron: The Lord Archbishop of Canterbury

Governors and Directors:

Chairman: Professor J F J Todd, BSc, PhD, CChem, CEng
Vice-Chairman: Mr P R J Holland, MA

Mr R Bristow, BA, MSc, DipFE, Dip Counselling
Mr M J Bukht, OBE, BA, FRSA
The Revd Canon M J Chandler, PhD, STh, DipTh
Ms E M Kerr, BA (Hons)
Mrs M L Lacamp, CertEd (London), DipRSA
Brother Christian Pearson, SSF, MA
Mr M C W Terry, FCA
Mr R N L Tyndale-Biscoe, BSc, CEng, MICE
Mrs E K Wicks, SRN
Mrs A A Williamson, JP, BSc, FRSA

***Headmaster:* Mr A N Ridley**, MA (Oxon)

Master of the Junior School: Mr R G Bacon, BA (Dunelm), PGCE

Chaplain: The Revd R L Hawkes, CertEd, BEd Hons (Leeds)

Head of Finance and Estates: Mrs M Stannard, FCA

Deputy Head: Mr D E Knight, BA Hons (Leeds)

Senior Mistress: Mrs J E Mander, BSc Hons (Nottingham), FEDA

Director of Studies: Mr H W Scott, BSc (Surrey)

Assistant Staff:

[1]*Art:*
*Mr D Griffiths, BA Hons (Brighton)
Miss Z J Fountain, BA Hons (Staffs)
Miss S C Passmore, MA (Birmingham)

Business Studies:
*Mr G A Wallace, BEd, DipA (Sunderland)

Classics:
*Mr I F Thompson, MA (Cantab), LRAM

Curriculum Support:
Mrs S Williams, BA Hons (Nottingham), DipSpLD(RSA), DipTEFL

[1]*English:*
*Mr J P Dagley, MA (Oxon), MA (Kent)

Miss C M Ballantyne, MA (Oxon)
Mr R H Brookeman, DipEd (Loughborough)
Mr I F Narburgh, MA (Edinburgh)
Mr R M Parsons, BEd (Winchester)
Mrs J C Wilkinson, MEd (Bristol)

EFL:
Mrs W Scott, MA (Kent)

Geography:
*Mr S H A Hollingshead, BA Hons (Nottingham), FRGS
Mr P J L Mighell, MA (Oxon), ARSGS

History, Government and Political Studies:
*Mr D E Knight, BA Hons (Leeds)
Mr L G Foody, BSc (London)
Mr R A Robinson, BA Hons

[1]*Information Systems:*
*Mr E J Gaskell, BA Hons (Leeds)
Mr S H A Hollingshead, BA Hons (Nottingham), FRGS

[1]*Mathematics:*
*Mrs J E Mander, BSc Hons (Nottingham), FEDA
Mr C D Barnard, BEd (London)
Mr A W J Middleton, BA Hons (Kent)
Mrs C O Periton, MA (Christ Church), BA (OU), BEd (Leeds)

Modern Languages and European Studies:
*Mr T J Barnett, BA Hons (Southampton)
Mr M B H Jeffrey, BA Hons (Kent), AIL
Mr I F Thompson, MA (Cantab), LRAM
Mrs I G Wallace, BA Hons (Anglia)

[1]*Music:*
*Mr I P Sutcliffe, BA Hons (Huddersfield), PGCE (Lancaster)
Dr A R Braddy, PhD (Goldsmiths), MA (City), BA Hons, ABSM (*Head of Strings*)
Mr S J Payne, BA Hons, MA, LTCL, ARCM, PGCE (*Head of Academic Music*)
Mr S J Wassell, ARCM, LTCL, CertEd (*Head of Brass, Wind, Percussion*)

Visiting Music Staff:
Mr K Abbott, ARCM *French Horn*
Ms M Bartlette, ALCM, LLCM(TD) *Violin*
Mrs R Cane, BA Hons *Piano*
Mr J E Colbourne *Percussion*
Miss E de la Porte, ARCM, LRSM *Piano*
Mrs J D Evans, MA, BSc Hons *Violin*
Mr D E Fauxbowyer, LRAM *Guitar*
Mrs A Fidler, LRAM (*Bassoon*)
Mr D A Flood, MA, FRCO(ChM) *Piano*
Mr P Freeman, GLCM, LLCM(TD), AdvCertPerf *Clarinet, Saxophone*
Mrs V Jones, LRAM *Piano*
Mrs K Le Page, MMus, FTCL, DipTCL, LTCL (*Oboe*)
Mrs K Lewis, BA, ARCM *Voice*
Mr C J D Lister, LRAM *Voice*
Mr R McLeish, MA, BMus *Piano*
Miss M Morley, BA Hons, DipOrchStudies *Harp*
Miss R A Rathbone, BA Hons, LRAM *Flute*
Mr D Rees-Williams, BMus, GRSM, ARCM *Piano*
Mr I Swatman, BA Hons, DipNCOS *Clarinet/Saxophone*
Mr R Turner, ARCM *Trombone*
Mrs K Upton, LRAM, ARCM *Trumpet*
Mrs R Waltham, DRSAM *Cello*
Ms F Whiteley, LRAM *Violin*
Mrs S Willmoth, BA Hons (*Flute*)

[1]*Physical Education:*
*Mrs J C Wilkinson, MEd (Bristol)
Mr R H Brookeman, DipEdPE (Loughborough)
Mr J J Cattell, BA (Leeds)
Miss T M Cliff, CertEd (Sussex)
Mr M C Dobson, BA Hons (Christ Church)
Mr A W J Middleton, BA Hons (Kent)

[1]*Religious Studies:*
*The Revd R L Hawkes, CertEd, BEd Hons (Leeds), MA (Kent)
Mr S H A Hollingshead, BA Hons (Nottingham), FRGS

[1]*Science:*
*Dr R Barnes, BSc, PhD (Bristol)

Biology:
*Mrs K M E Barnard, BEd (London), MISTC
Miss H E Faulkner, BSc (St Andrews), MSc (London)
Mr H W Scott, BSc (Surrey)

Chemistry:
*Dr R Barnes, BSc, PhD (Bristol)
Mr R E Barham, BA Hons (Dublin)
Mrs K M E Barnard, BEd (London), MISTC
Miss J Morley, MChem (Manchester)
Mr D G Whitehouse, BSc (Nottingham)

Physics:
*Dr J C Horn, BSc, PhD (Leeds)
Mr M G S Hawkins, MA (Cantab), MSc (Kent)
Mr G Monk, BSc (Kent)
Mr D G Whitehouse, BSc (Nottingham)

[1]*Technology:*
*Mrs K L Thrush, MSc (Christ Church)

Design & Graphics:
*Mr S R Lund, CertEd (Loughborough)
Mr P Gadenne, MCSD

Food:
*Mrs K L Thrush, MSc (Christ Church)

Theatre Studies:
*Mr R M Parsons, BEd (Winchester)
Miss C M Ballantyne, MA (Oxon), CertTEFL
Mr I F Narburgh, MA (Edinburgh)

[1]denotes Department serving both Senior & Junior Schools.

Additional Responsibilities:
Careers Adviser: Mr P J L Mighell, MA (Oxon), ARSGS
Director of Marketing: Mr M B H Jeffrey, BA Hons (Kent), AIL
Director of Music: Mr I P Sutcliffe, BA Hons (Huddersfield), CertEd
Director of Sport: Mrs J C Wilkinson, MEd (Bristol)
Public Examinations Officer: Mr D G Whitehouse, BSc (Nottingham)
Hall Manager: Mr M G S Hawkins, MA (Cantab), MSc (Kent)
Hall Technical Director: Mr G N Hawkins, BSc (London), ARCS
Higher Education Adviser: Mr J P Dagley, MA (Oxon)
Officer Commanding CCF: Lt Col C D Barnard, BEd (London)
President of Common Room: Mr D Kefford, DipPE, CertEd (Exeter)
President of Games: Mr D E Knight, BA Hons (Leeds)

Junior School:

Director of Studies: Mr M G B Walters, BA Hons (London)
Senior Master: Mr T Hooley, MA (Cantab) (*Latin, General Subjects*)
Head of Lower School: Mrs J A Radford, CertEd (London) (*Form 1*)
Head of Pre-Prep Department: Mrs J M Frampton-Fell, CertEd

Preparatory:
Mrs A S Atkins, BEd Hons (Christ Church)
Mr R Austen, BEd Hons (Bulmershe) (*Mathematics*)
Miss H A Dixon, BA Hons (Kent), PGCE (*Form 2*)

Mrs M Duke, MEd (Exeter) (*Curriculum Support*)
Mr M G S Hawkins, MA (Cantab), MSc (Kent) (*IS, Physics*)
Mr T Hooley, MA (Cantab) (*Latin, General Subjects*)
Mrs C A Hutchinson, CertEd (London) (*Form 3*)
Mr D Kefford, DipPE, CertEd (Exeter) (*Mathematics, Games*)
Mrs W L Kefford, MIBSC (*PE, Games*)
Mrs R H Kroiter, BA Hons (Liverpool) (*EFL*)
Mrs C M Lawrence, BA (Christ Church) (*English*)
Mr J Newton (Collegiate School, Wanganui, New Zealand)
Mr D G C Parry, BA Hons (London), PGCE (*French, Latin*)
Mrs A Pearce, CertEd (*Form 3*)
Mr T J Pearce, ACertCM (Christ Church) (*Religious Studies, General Subjects*)
Mr C Penn (*Games, PE*)
Mrs M P Scott, BA Hons (East Anglia), PGCE (*Form 3, Science*)
Mr E J Southey, CertEd (Dartford) (*History, PE, Games*)
Mrs E A Swallow, MA, BEd (Durham) (*Form 2*)

Abingdon House (*Pre-Prep*):
*Mrs J M Frampton-Fell, CertEd (*Owls*)
Miss R-M Bradley (Montessori, Black Rock) (*Wrens*)
Mrs L C Deed (Montessori, London) (*Nursery*)
Mrs H M Thompson, BEd (Birmingham) (*Robins*)

Choristers:
*Mr D A Flood, MA (Oxon), FRCO(ChM) (*Cathedral Organist and Master of Choristers*)
Mr T Noon, BA (Oxon), FRCO(ChM), ARCM (*Assistant Cathedral Organist*)

Headmaster's Secretary: Mrs E M Narburgh

Junior School Master's Secretary: Mrs Y King

School Secretary: Mrs W J Fitzpatrick

RSM: WO2 J O'Sullivan

From its inception St Edmund's has maintained the highest in educational standards for all its pupils and, to this day, it retains its rooted traditions of purposeful endeavour and a high quality of caring.

It has been able to build continuously on its Christian foundation whilst developing into an exciting but well-ordered school of some 530 boys and girls.

The school enjoys a commanding site at the top of St Thomas' Hill overlooking the city and cathedral of Canterbury and adjoining the University of Kent. Behind its magnificent facade there lies a happy and busy boarding and day community which is committed to excellence in all that it undertakes, and which is large enough to provide a rich variety of opportunities, yet small enough to maintain the strong family ethos for which it has become renowned. The gifted academic, the talented artist, the promising musician, the devotee of sport, as well as those who are still identifying their talents, all find support and skilled teaching to cultivate their aptitudes to the fullest extent. Pupils are very much encouraged to develop their individuality and to do so in an atmosphere of civilised tolerance towards others.

Whilst the school is modern in facilities and forward looking in its curriculum, great stress is laid on such traditional virtues as courtesy, honesty, self-discipline and smartness of dress.

Organisation. The junior and senior schools are very closely integrated, sharing many of the same facilities, and affording continuity of education throughout the age range of 3 to 18. The Junior School, which educates the choristers of Canterbury Cathedral, has about 50 boarding boys and girls, 130 day boys and 95 day girls. The Senior School (13 years and upwards) contains about 50 boarding boys, 100 day boys, 90 day girls and 40 boarding girls.

The Senior School is divided into four Houses: Baker, Wagner, Warneford and Watson, the respective House-masters each being assisted by a team of Deputies and Tutors.

The Chapel. All pupils attend at least two of the morning services a week. There is a variety of Sunday services, attendance at most of which is voluntary. Parents are always welcome, especially to the regular family communions. Confirmation is conducted annually by the Archbishop of Canterbury (as Patron of the School) or by the Bishop of Dover acting on his behalf; the candidates are prepared by the School Chaplain. The school carol service is held in Canterbury Cathedral, by kind permission of the Dean and Chapter.

Academic Organisation. In the Pre-preparatory and Junior Schools the curriculum provides a firm foundation in all academic subjects in line with the National Curriculum requirements. French and Latin are also taught in the Junior School. All pupils are prepared for the Common Entrance Examination with the most able given the opportunity for Senior School Scholarships.

In the first year of the Senior School (Year 9) pupils follow a core curriculum in English, Mathematics, French, Physics, Chemistry, Biology, History, Geography, Art, Music, Information Technology, Religious Education, PSE and Physical Education, Drama, Technology (Resistant Materials), Food Technology, Graphics, German and Latin are options.

GCSE core subjects are: English, English Literature, French, Mathematics and dual award Sciences. Options include Latin, German, History, Geography, Art (Ceramics), Art (Drawing and Painting), Technology (Resistant Materials), Food Technology, Graphic Products, Music, Drama and Religious Studies.

The following subjects are offered for AS/A2 Level examinations: Art and Design, Biology, Business Studies, Ceramics, Chemistry, Design and Technology, English Literature, French, German, Geography, Government and Political Studies, History, Mathematics and Further Mathematics, Music, Music Technology, PE, Physics and Theatre Studies.

Pupils in the Lower Sixth are expected to study four AS Levels, most then proceeding to three A2 subjects in the Upper Sixth. A General Studies programme and a Key Skills programme are also integral parts of the Sixth Form curriculum.

Comprehensive reports are sent at the end of each term. A system of interim reports, as well as regular parents' meetings, ensures close communication with parents.

Buildings and facilities. Over the past twenty years there have been extensive additions to the school's buildings and facilities: a new Junior School building, a new Sixth Form Centre, the main hall with tiered auditorium and exhibition area, the splendid sports hall, the technology department, additional classrooms and major extensions to the science, art, information technology, music, girls' boarding and pre-prep departments are in addition to the refurbishment of older buildings to suit the modern world, whilst retaining the secure atmosphere of tradition and stability.

Careers and Higher Education. The school is affiliated to the Independent Schools Careers Organisation and the Careers Research and Advisory Centre. Pupils have the opportunity to undergo careers aptitude testing in the GCSE year, and all pupils are assisted in finding a placement for a week's work experience in the GCSE year. The careers and higher education staff give all possible help in the finding of suitable careers and in selecting appropriate universities and colleges of further education. Most 'A' Level candidates go on to degree courses after leaving school; others join Art or Music colleges.

Music. There is a continuous programme of music

tuition from the age of 6. A very high standard of music is maintained and there are numerous ensembles, both large and small. 60% of pupils learn at least one instrument. Tuition is given in piano, organ and all orchestral instruments. Parents are invited to join the flourishing choral society. Music scholars benefit from an exciting programme of seminars and London concerts (of which full details may be obtained from the Director of Music).

Sport. Association football, hockey, cricket, athletics, tennis, squash and (for girls) netball and rounders are the principal sports but there are opportunities for many other forms of exercise, including cross-country running, golf, badminton, basketball, volley ball, swimming, fencing, weight training and sailing. The large playing fields adjoin the school buildings. There is an open air heated swimming pool. The sports hall is well-equipped and includes a multi-gym room. There are eight tennis courts (both hard and grass), a golf course and a rifle range. The school has access to the climbing wall, the gym and the astroturf pitch at the University of Kent.

Activities. For those in the first four years one afternoon a week is given over specifically to a broad range of activities. A number involve helping the local community, while other pupils learn new skills, eg bridge, golf, fencing, electronics, desk top publishing or photography. Over 80 different activities have been offered during the last four years.

In the second year all pupils join the Combined Cadet Force, a highly successful unit commanded by one of the masters and administered by an ex-regular army sergeant major. The CCF is renowned for its shooting. There is an annual camp in the summer and an adventurous training camp at Easter, attendance at which is voluntary. Cadets may remain in the CCF for the duration of their school career if they wish, and are encouraged to do so if contemplating a career in the armed forces.

Pupils may also participate in The Duke of Edinburgh Award Scheme, Young Enterprise and the British Association of Young Scientists. There are regular ski and field trips, choir and music tours, and sports tours.

Health. The school sanatorium is modern, and staffed by state registered nurses at all times. The health of the boys and girls of both Junior and Senior Schools is supervised by one of the leading local practitioners under the NHS.

Junior School. The Junior School is in membership of the IAPS and prepares boys and girls for the Senior School. It is self-contained and has its own classrooms, dormitories, playing fields, etc. Applications for admission should be addressed to the Master of the Junior School. See Part IV.

Choristers. The thirty choristers of Canterbury Cathedral are all members of the Junior School. They board in the Choir House (in the Cathedral Precincts) in the care of Houseparents appointed by the school. All their choral training is undertaken in the Cathedral by the Organist; the remainder of their education takes place at St Edmund's. Admission is by voice trial and academic test. Enquiries should be addressed to the Master of the Junior School or to the Cathedral Organist.

Admission to Senior School. Entry at 13 from preparatory schools is through the Common Entrance Examination. Candidates from other schools will be tested appropriately or may be accepted on the basis of school reports. There is also a large entry of pupils into the Sixth Form, usually on the basis of GCSE grade estimates from their present school.

Admission to Junior School. Entry at any age from 3-12. Candidates will sit entrance tests and all prospective pupils will be interviewed.

Chorister admission. St Edmund's is the school of the Canterbury Cathedral choristers. For details of the voice trials please contact the Master's Secretary.

Time of admission. September entry is preferred and encouraged, though pupils will be admitted at other times as appropriate.

Fees (2000/2001). Senior School: boarders, £5,214 per term; day pupils, £3,365 per term. Junior School: boarders, £3,645 per term; day pupils, £2,565 per term. Pre-preparatory £1,817; Reception £1,338; Nursery £1,033 (mornings only £555). Music fees: £134 per term. Extras have been kept to the minimum.

Entrance scholarships (*see* Entrance Scholarship section). The school offers various awards at 11+, 13+ and 16+ each year. Academic, Music, Art, Drama, Sports and All-Rounder scholarships of up to half fees are offered. Full details are available from the School Secretary.

Bursaries and Fee Concessions. Bursaries and fee concessions are available to the sons and daughters of clergymen serving the Anglican Communion, former pupils, members of the armed forces and diplomatic personnel. The School was originally founded to provide a free education for the fatherless sons of the clergy of the Church of England and the Church in Wales and still accepts applications from boys and girls for Foundationer status. Applications should be made to the Headmaster.

The St Edmund's Society (for former pupils). *Secretary:* F Dowling, 42 St Johns Road, Swalecliffe, Whitstable, Kent CT5 2RH.

Charitable status. St Edmund's School Canterbury is a Registered Charity, number 1056382. It exists to educate the children in its care.

St Edward's School

Oxford OX2 7NN.
Tel: Warden (01865) 319323; Bursar (01865) 319321
Registrar (01865) 319200
Fax: (01865) 319202

St Edward's School was founded in 1863 by the Rev. Thomas Chamberlain. Originally the School buildings were in New Inn Hall Street, Oxford. In 1873 it was removed to Summertown, and the present School was built by the Rev A B Simeon.

Motto: *Pietas Parentum.*

Visitor:
The Rt Rev The Lord Bishop of Oxford

Governing Body:
Sir Bob Reid (*Chairman*)
H W Bolland, Esq, BA
H L J Brunner, Esq, MA, DL
M Daymond, Esq
R W Ellis, Esq, CBE, MA
G Fenton, Esq
M P Gretton, Esq, MA, FNI
The Revd R G Griffith-Jones, MA
M G Hay, Esq, BA, PhD, MBA
Mrs A Holloway, BM, MRCGP
C I M Jones, Esq, MA, FRSA
I M Judge, Esq, MA
P M Oppenheimer, Esq, MA
G B Palau, Esq
Mrs J M Peach, MA, DPhil
R G P Pillai, MB, BS, FRCS
Mrs C R Repp, MA, DPhil
D A Roe, Esq, DLitt, MA, PhD
M P Stanfield, Esq
H E P Woodcock, Esq, MA

***Warden:* D Christie**, BA, BSc(Econ)

Sub-Warden: T A James, BSc, MSc

Director of Studies: D M Cundy, MA, CMath, FIMA

Assistant Masters:

R D Aldred, BA
R A L Anderson, MA
S R Arnold, BA
J V Baker, BSc, MIITT
O S Bartholomew, MA
B S Bramley, BSc
Miss J W Casely, MA
J Cope, BA, MA
N H Coram-Wright, MA
E C Danziger, MA, BA, MEd
R Dodds, BSc
Miss J Dowman, BSc, MSc
Miss E M Dowse, BA
D Drake-Brockman, BA
R E Fletcher, BA, MA, MLitt
D R Gibbon, BSc
J W Gidney, MA, Lic Phil
Miss S F Gill, MA, BSc
Mrs S D Greaves, DMS, DipSpLD
N E Grimshaw, MA, DA, ATD, FRSA
P Harper, BA
I Hart, BSc, PhD
P M Herring, MA
M J Hiner, MA
G J Hoskins, BA
R McA Hughes, BMus, LTCL
E T Hunt, BA, MA
Mrs N F Hunter, BA
Ms S J Hutchinson, BA
K N Jones, MA, DPhil
A J Kerr-Dineen, MA
P A Kitovitz, BA, MSc
D M Lauder, MA
P Lloyd-Jones, DipFA
Mrs L A Lyne, MA
Ms L Maycock, BA, DipRADA
J P B McNamara, MA, FRCO
D S Moore, BSc, PhD, AKC, CChem, MRSC
A Murray, BSc, PhD
J R Murray, BA, MA
G E Nagle, MA, DPhil
R T F Pleming, MA
B J Pyper, DipArt & Design
N R Quartley, BA
G R Rigault, L-ès-L
I R M Rowley, MA, ALCM
B C I Ryan, BSc
Miss T J Ryan, BA
Miss C S Schofield, MA
M I Sellen, BA, MMus, ARCM
K J Shindler, BA
Miss J M Smart, BA
Miss D J Smith, BA
J N Tucker, MA, PhD
Miss L F S Warren, BSc
A J Wiggins, MA
D P G Wiggins, BSc
K A Williams, BSc, PhD
Rev D S Wippell, BSc, MA

Houses and Housemasters/Housemistresses:

Cowell's: C J Lush, MA
Sing's: V Abigail, BA
Field: J H W Quick, BA
Macnamara's: Mrs A Wilkinson, BSc, MEd
Apsley: J P Middleton, BA
Tilly's: P A Jolley, BA, BEd
Segar's: Revd A D G Wright, MTheol
Kendall: C F Baggs, BSc
Oakthorpe: Mrs J Young
Corfe: Mrs S J Kerr-Dineen, MA

Administrative Officers:
Bursar: S Withers Green, MA, ACA

Registrar: Mrs E A Brooks

OSE Secretary: The Revd D S Wippell

Examinations Officer: W M Boswell, MA

Librarian: Mrs P J James

Medical Officers:
Dr P H Roblin, MA, MB, BCh, MRCP, DCH, MRCGP
Dr S Perryer, MB, BS, MRCP

CCF, SSI: Major C J J Johnston

The School stands in its own grounds of over 100 acres, 2 miles north of the centre of Oxford. There are about 600 pupils, of whom about 180 are day pupils. The proportion of girls to boys in each year group is about 3:7.

The school's academic buildings, Chapel, Hall, Library, Dining-Hall and six boarding houses are on the east side of the Woodstock Road. On the west side are the playing fields, the sports complex and four boarding houses. A subway connects the two parts of the campus.

There is a continuing programme of renovation and development of all facilities. In the academic year 1999-2000 the school has opened a new boarding house and a new sports complex, developed in conjunction with Esporta plc. This includes a Sports Hall, indoor swimming pool, multi-gym, 3 squash courts and 4 indoor tennis courts. The extensive playing fields include 12 tennis courts, a new Golf course and an Astroturf hockey pitch. Rowing takes place on the Thames at Godstow, and sailing on Farmoor Reservoir.

Pastoral Care. All pupils are members of one of the 10 Houses (3 for girls and 7 for boys) and are under the pastoral care of a Housemaster or Housemistress and their tutors (at least one for each year group within the house).

Academic Work. Boys and girls entering the Shells (Year 9) follow a wide common course of study. The only choice to be made at this stage is between studying German, Spanish, or Ancient Greek. In the following two years (Fourth and Fifth forms) pupils follow courses leading to 9 subjects at GCSE. In the Sixth Form pupils are expected to study 4 or 5 subjects in the first year, and proceed to at least 3 A Level subjects. A wide range of courses is available, including A Level courses in Design and Politics and AS courses in Archaeology and Philosophy. Progress at all stages is monitored by a comprehensive reporting and tutorial system, with important elements of pupil self-assessment.

Careers and Higher Education. The Careers Department is staffed by two teachers, and draws on the expertise of ISCO for Careers advice and psychometric testing. It runs sessions on the University application procedure and interviews, as well as a highly participative 'Challenge of Management' conference. There is a programme of work experience for Fifth form pupils, and Lower Sixth pupils take part in the Young Enterprise Scheme.

Music. Pupils may learn vocal and instrumental music – piano, organ, strings, woodwind and brass instruments. There is a school orchestra and a chamber orchestra, a Concert Band, Jazz Band and Chamber groups, a Chapel Choir and a Chamber Choir. There can be about 50 concerts of varying scales given by pupils during a year.

Games and Activities. The School offers a wide variety of sports and extra curricular activities, including Rugby Football, Hockey, Cricket, Rowing, Athletics, Netball, Squash, Swimming, Tennis, Cross-country running, Sailing, Fencing, Clay Pigeon Shooting, Golf, Soccer, Judo, Basketball, Canoeing, Rock-climbing, Chess, Bridge and Community Service. There is a Combined Cadet Force; its Air Force section offers opportunities for pupils to fly.

Admission to the School. Registration forms can be obtained from the Registrar. There is a registration fee of £50. Boys and girls are expected to take the Common Entrance Examination or Scholarship in their last Summer term at their Preparatory School. Separate assessment arrangements can be made for applicants from schools not preparing candidates for the Common Entrance Examination. Lower Sixth scholarship and entrance examinations are held in November prior to entry; offers of places in the sixth form are subject to good performance in GCSE.

Entrance Scholarships. (*see* Entrance Scholarship section) Open Scholarships and Exhibitions varying from 10% to 50% on merit plus the possibility of up to an additional 50% dependent on need, assessed by means test. Awards are available for those offering an all round contribution to the school. There are two HM Forces exhibitions. A number of music scholarships are available each year, as are art awards.

Bursaries of up to 30% of current boarding fees are available for children of clergy.

Continuation scholarships may be awarded for the last two years at Preparatory School. These may be worth up to 60% fees at the Prep School and 20% fees at St Edward's.

Scholarships for entry to the Lower Sixth are also available.

School Fees. Boarding, Tuition and Maintenance £5,410 per term; Day Pupils (including subscriptions and meals) £3,995 per term.

Charitable status. St Edward's School is a Registered Charity, number 309681. The aims and objectives of the School are to provide education for pupils between the ages of 13 and 18.

St George's College

Weybridge Surrey KT15 2QS.
Tel: (01932) 839300
Fax: (01932) 839301

Founded by the Josephite Community in 1869 in Croydon, the College moved in 1884 to its present attractive grounds of 100 acres on Woburn Hill, Weybridge. Within its particular family orientated ethos, the College seeks to encourage a wide, balanced Christian education in the Catholic tradition encouraging excellence and achievement across a broad spectrum of academic, sporting and extra-curricular activities. Almost all pupils move on to higher education, gaining places at a wide range of institutions including Oxford and Cambridge. The College is co-educational throughout the school.

Motto: *Amore et Labore.*

Governing Body:
Chairman: N N Twist

Governors:

Rev M R Connor, CJ
Rev R D Hamilton, CJ
M J G Henderson
Rev J R Lear, CJ
Rev W M Muir, CJ
Mr O'Sullivan
Mrs D S Phillips
Mrs K Quint
J F Rourke

Clerk to the Governors and Bursar: P J Fletcher, ACIS

***Headmaster:* J A Peake**, MA (Oxon), PGCE

Staff:
R Ambrose, BA(Ed)
Mrs J A Andrew, BSc
Mrs A L Barnett, BSc
R Bawtree, BSc, ALSPT
Mrs M Bigwood, BSc
Mrs J M Bourne
D J Bradford, BH, PGCE
Ms S E Bray, BA, PGCE
G J Bunting, MA
Mrs P Chambers, BA
Miss T A Cooke, BSc, MS, PGCE
Miss O H Cooper, BSc, PGCE
Mrs L Courtney
J M Cunningham, BA, PGCE
J E H Davies, BA, PGCE
Dr J Drayton
C Dunning
Sr Kitty Ellard, SIJ (*Chaplain*)
A Fairhurst, BA
Miss S Frawley, MA, MPhil
E Fry (*Registered Tennis Professional*)
Mrs F L Gabriel, BA
Ms P George, BA, MA, BEd
R M Godsmark, BSc
Miss A H Gooda, BA
P J Graves, BA
R P Grimmer, BSc, PGCE
C G Gunn, BSc
A M Gunning, BA, PGCE
Mrs G Hale, BA
Miss S Hall, BSc
B Hanson, BSc
S M Hardy, BA, PGCE
Mrs C E Hughes, BA
Fr P C Hunting, CJ, MA
J Hyzler, BA
Mrs S M Knights, BSc, PGCE
P C Lamb, BA, MA, PGCE
Mrs M Lamey, BSc, MInstP
Mrs H J Lane, BA
Mrs L G Lane, BA
A J Leadbetter, BSc, PGCE
R E Lee, BSc, PGCE
Ms L Lever, BA, PGCE
Mrs P A Lightfoot, BA
Miss F E MacAlpine, BA
Miss S J Marlow, BA
P R Marshall, BA, ACertM
H P McHugh, MA
Miss J F May, BA, PGCE
Mrs J M Maynard, BA
Ms E O'Brien, BA
J A P O'Brien, BEd
D G P Ottley, CertEdPE
Mrs C M Parnham, BEd, CertEd
M Parnham, BSc, BA, PGCE
Mrs W A Pereira, CertEd, AMBDA
Miss E L Procter, BSc, PGCE
A J Reynolds, BA, PGCE
Mrs B A Sanders
M A Saxon, BA, MA (*Deputy Head*)
M A Schofield, BA
D G Skeat, BSc
Mrs H A Smith, BEd, MA
Mrs M Simons, BA, ALA (*Librarian*)
Mrs J A Spenceley, BSc
Mrs I E Stait, BA, PGCE
T Sweeney, BA, MA
K Taggart, BEng, PGCE
F J Tavares, BA
Mrs C S Thorne, BSc
M P Tiley, MA
A Topliss, BA, PGCE
Mrs S Turner, BA
R von Reibnitz, BA
S C Walford, BA, PGCE
G P Walters, BSc
A Watters, BA, DBA, PGCE
Mrs M Weaver, BSc
Mrs H West, BA
A Witter, MA, MPhil
Mrs A V Wood, BSc, MA, PGCE (*Director of Studies*)
Ms S Wood, BA, HDE
S J Woolnough, BA, PGCE
M P Work, BA
Mrs K York, BSc

Marketing and Development Manager: Miss C A Murgatroyd, BA

Headmaster's Secretary: Mrs C A Greenwood

Matron: Mrs A Sweeney, BSc (School Nursing), RGN

Director of Music: C D Knights, ARCM
Assistant Director of Music: P M Aspden, BMus, FRCO

Naomi Arundel *Piano/Accompanying*
Charlotte Aspden *Piano*
Geoffrey Boyd *Double Bass/Piano*
Chris Clarke *Classical Guitar*
Jo Colledge *Voice*
Jenny Gibbs *Violin/Viola*
Peter Greenhalgh *Piano*
Valerie Gregory *Piano/Violin*
Lee Halestrap *Electric Guitar*
Richard Halliday *Trombone/Tuba*
Martyn Hayward *Clarinet/Saxophone*
Stephen Hiscock *Percussion*
Julie Holland *Clarinet/Saxophone*
Martin Hooley *Violin/Viola*
Louise Howden *Bassoon*
Chris Hurn *Cello/Piano*
Anthony Lee *Piano*
Flario Matani *Classical Spanish Guitar*
Craig Rickards *Saxophone/Clarinet*
David Rix *Clarinet/Saxophone*
David Smith *Flute*
Grierson Smith *Bagpipes*
Robin Smith *Trumpet*
Erik Stams *Percussion*
Luke Stevens *Flute*
Phillida Thompson *Recorder/Flute*
Pam Wedgwood *French Horn/Piano*
Julian West *Oboe/Piano*

There are approximately 900 boys and girls in the school. Entry is normally at age 11 (First Year), 13 (Third Year) or 16 (Sixth Form).

Term of Entry. Students are accepted in September each year. Entry is also possible during an academic year if a place is available.

Entrance Scholarships (*see* Entrance Scholarship section). Academic Scholarships are awarded at 11, 13 and for the Sixth Form. Additionally, the College offers Music, All Rounders and Art Scholarships.

Bursaries. Bursaries are allocated in the case of

proven financial need. The College has its own in-house Assisted Places Scheme. Further information is available from the Bursar.

Facilities. A process of redevelopment has resulted in state-of-the-art provision for Technology and Theatre Studies. Recent refurbishment has also provided modern facilities for Music, Languages, English, Mathematics, Biology and Geography. There is an extensive Arts Centre, an impressive library with Internet access and CD-Rom, a Sixth Form Study Centre and a large indoor Sports Hall with an adjacent fitness training room. The College has 19 tennis courts, including three international standard grass courts and an impressive four-court Indoor Tennis Centre. In addition there are three new Resource rooms, networked computers – e-mail for all students, and new floodlit netball courts. The College Boat Club is situated nearby on the Thames.

The Curriculum. This is kept as broad as possible up to GCSE, with a balance between Arts and Science subjects. Students usually take a maximum of 10 GCSEs, A level candidates may choose from over 20 subjects. The vast majority of the Sixth Form goes on to university including Oxford and Cambridge.

Careers. Guidance is given throughout a student's career but particularly in making GCSE, A level and university choices. The Careers Co-ordinator has a modern well stocked Careers Room and makes effective use of COA testing, portfolios, work experience, trial interviews, Challenge of Industry days and computer software.

Art. The Art Department attracts large numbers of students at GCSE and A level who achieve consistently high results in public examinations. A large proportion of A level candidates successfully apply to Art Colleges, often each receiving several offers in this highly competitive field.

Music. Music plays a vital part in school life. There is a wide range of music-making encompassing early music, madrigal groups, jazz, rock, African Drumming as well as more traditional ensembles, orchestras and wind bands. The choir and orchestra give regular performances (including radio broadcasts), and tour Europe annually. Tuition is available on all orchestral instruments from a team of 36 visiting specialists who teach over 400 students each week. Students play in youth orchestras including the NYO and have gained scholarships to the major conservatoires.

Responsibility and Service. Many boys and girls belong to the St Vincent de Paul Society, a Catholic organisation involved in social work, engaged in care for the elderly at home or in old people's homes, as well as the mentally and physically handicapped. Each Easter and Summer groups of Sixth Formers accompany handicapped people on visits to Lourdes. Pupils find these activities a rewarding exercise in Christian service. The Prefect system and the mentor system offer positions of responsibility to the oldest pupils. The Duke of Edinburgh's Award Scheme is encouraged and there is a flourishing College Council.

Pastoral Care. The spiritual, moral and academic well-being of the students is the concern of every member of staff at the College. Nearly all staff act as Group Tutors with particular responsibility for the daily care of their students and for forging links with parents. Each Year Group is led by a Head of Year, and the Chaplain has a general pastoral role. All groups have a day of retreat away each year. The College also has four Houses to which the students are affiliated and all students have one period per week as part of their PSE programme.

Extra Curricular Activities. There is a wide and growing range of clubs and societies taking place both at lunchtime and after school. In addition to music and sport, a broad range of interests is catered for such as the Science Club, Cookery, Young Enterprise, Philosophy and Model Clubs. Amnesty International is represented and cultural trips for the Sixth Form are arranged through the Byzantian Society.

Sport. All students participate and there is a variety of sports: rugby, hockey, netball, cricket, tennis, rowing, and rounders, plus a wide range of other activities such as golf, athletics, badminton, horse riding, basketball and cross-country. Each student has the opportunity to develop his or her own talents in small coaching groups. The College has its own boat house on the Thames, nineteen tennis courts (including four indoor), a flood-lit artificial pitch with viewing stand, floodlit netball courts, six artificial cricket nets, one main pavilion and two smaller cricket pavilions, eight rugby pitches. The College has access to the Junior School heated swimming pool. All facilities are of a very high standard in an attractive setting. Overseas tours to South Africa, Australia, Portugal and Ireland have been completed recently by hockey, tennis and rugby teams. Attendance at national hockey finals is an annual event and the College hosts a very popular U18 Hockey sixes every year. International honours have recently been gained in hockey, cricket, rowing and tennis.

Preparatory School. St George's College Junior School is located nearby in Thames Street, Weybridge, formerly the site of St Maur's School, and is co-educational, catering for boys and girls from 3 to 11.

Fees per term. £1,300 to £2,650

Charitable status. St George's College Weybridge is a Registered Charity, number 1017853 and a company limited by guarantee. The aims and objectives of the Charity are the Christian education of young people.

St John's School

Leatherhead Surrey KT22 8SP

Tel: 01372 373000 Switchboard; 01372 372021 Headmaster; 01372 372016 Bursar

Fax: 01372 386606

e-mail: secretary@stjohns.surrey.sch.uk

website: www.stjohns.surrey.sch.uk

Founded 1851. Royal Charter, 1922.

St John's School was founded in North London in 1851 for the education of the sons of Anglican clergy. The move to Leatherhead was made in 1872 and a Royal Charter was granted in 1922. The School has grown to 440 pupils, including about 20 Foundationers, sons and daughters of clergy, and is coeducational in the Sixth Form.

Motto: *Quae sursum sunt quaerite.*

Patron: HRH The Duchess of Gloucester

Visitor: The Lord Archbishop of Canterbury, DD

The Council:

Chairman: M E Doherty, FCA

Vice-Chairman: Major General M J P Hunt, OBE, FRSA (*OJ*)

A M Airey, LLB (OJ)
R H Alcock
S G G Benson, MA
E H Cruickshank, BSc, PhD
The Rt Rev The Bishop of Dorking
R G Fentiman, BA, BCL (OJ)
P G Gardner, FRICS (OJ)
R M Gordon Clark, LLB (OJ)
Mrs J Grant Peterkin, BA
The Rt Rev The Bishop of Guildford
The Rt Hon The Earl of Kinnoull
R G Notley, MS, FRCS, (OJ)
A J Peake, FCA (OJ)
Mrs P L Privett, JP
Mrs G Rivers
P H Thorne, BA (OJ)
D J Woodhead, BA, FRSA

Bursar and Secretary to the Council: Miss J Robertson, BA, DMS

***Headmaster:* C H Tongue**, MA, Jesus College, Cambridge

Deputy Headmaster: S Morris, MA, St John's College, Cambridge

Assistant Staff:

*R B Hughes, BA, MA
†P C Noble, BSc
B W Stevens, BEd
P F Lutton, MA, ARCO, ARCM
*P D Wells-Cole, BA, MA
J Nuttall, BSc, MSc, PhD, BPhil (*Director of Studies*)
I Ruddlesdin, BSc
†A B Gale, BSc, CPhys, MInstP
*A J Phillips, BA
†A P King, BA, FSA
C G Boden, BSc
*Mrs J E Phillpotts, MA
*B M Joplin, MA
*M W Clarke, BSc
Mrs D J Burgess, BSc
*Mrs V A Shore, MA
Miss J A Belfrage, BA
*Mrs L S Culm, BEd, DipRSA (SLD), AMBDA
†*R C B Clark, BA, MBA
*M T Dawson, BEd
†Miss R Sullivan, BSc
*Miss S Hunter, BA, MA
*The Revd M J Lawson, MTh (*Chaplain*)
J A McKellar, BEng
†*S M Antwis, BSc
*P M Goodyer, BA
*B Noithip, BA, BMus
*D F Parker, BSc
M Rogers, BSc
*Mrs A V Davie, BA
*R W L Allen, BA
P L Eversfield, BA
Miss M M E Kidwell, MA
*J A Lockwood, BEd
*J M Thorne, BA
P J Toal, MA
*A Bass, BEd
*J Burrell, BA
Miss R Crabtree, MA
D J Hepworth, BA
Miss N S K Hague, BA, MSc
*A L Morgan, BA
P Reilly, BSc, MA, PhD

Administrator: S Mayes
Librarian: Mrs S Todd, BA, ALA
Archivist: J C Stuttard, MA, MSc
Medical Officer: F G C Meynen, MB, BS, DRCOG, FRCGP
Sanatorium Sister: Miss J Peace, RGN, NDN
CCF Contingent Commander: Major R E Jones, WG

Boarding. Full and weekly boarding places are available.

Houses. There are three boarding houses for boys: West (R C B Clark), East (S M Antwis) and Churchill (A P King). There are three day houses for boys: North (P C Noble), Surrey (to be appointed) and Montgomery (A B Gale). There is one day and boarding house for girls: Hallaton (Miss R Sullivan).

Buildings. The School occupies a 50 acre site in Leatherhead within easy reach of the M25. The original 19th century buildings form an open cloistered quadrangle, comprising the boarding and day houses, the oak-panelled dining hall, the assembly hall, and the original chapel (now the library). Extensive development of the site has included a heated indoor Swimming Pool, an Art Centre and Music School, superbly equipped DT workshops, science laboratories, a Sports Hall and a Communications Centre, including an extensive ICT suite, English department classrooms, a multi-media studio and Sixth Form Study Centre. Current developments include a new Theatre, Sixth Form Social Centre and all-weather pitch.

Religion. As a Church of England Foundation, St John's has always had a special place for worship in the life of the School, and is particularly fortunate in its fine modern Chapel.

Curriculum. On entry into the Fourth Form, all boys follow a general course of English, Mathematics, Religious Education, French, German or Spanish, Physics, Chemistry, Biology, Geography, History, ICT, PE, Music, Art and Design Technology, with Latin as an option.

In the second year, boys begin their GCSE courses. Every boy studies English, Mathematics, Science and a modern language. Other GCSE subjects are grouped into option blocks and include Religious Studies, French, German, Spanish, History, Geography, Latin, Art, Design Technology and Music. Religious Studies ICT and PE are continued as non-examined subjects.

In the Sixth Form, boys and girls begin their Advanced Subsidiary and Advanced Level courses, choosing four subjects in the first year. Subjects are grouped into option blocks and include: English, Mathematics, Religious Studies, French, German, Spanish, History, Geography, Geology, Latin, Biology, Chemistry, Physics, ICT, Business Studies, Economics, Psychology, Physical Education, Art and Design, Design Technology, Drama, Film Studies and Music.

In addition, each student in the Sixth Form follows a General Studies programme, with the twin aims of encouraging an interest in different aspects of culture and society and developing communication and other key skills, alongside a course on entry to Higher Education.

Music. There is a strong musical tradition. The Chapel Choir, 60 in number, contributes effectively to the worship in Chapel and travels widely at home and abroad. Many boys and girls study musical instruments and are encouraged to participate in the school orchestra, wind band, string quartets, choral society, madrigal society, jazz band and rock groups. There are regular informal concerts to encourage informal performance.

Art and Design Technology. The Art and Design facilities and the Technology workshops are used extensively in class and in extra-curricular activities. Standards are high; students contribute to exhibitions and a few artists progress to Art College.

Drama. Drama plays an important part in the life of the School, with most boys and girls taking to the stage at some point during the year. At least nine productions, including School and House plays, are staged each year.

Information and Communication Technology. The School continually upgrades the hardware and software connected to the extensive network system. There are four dedicated ICT classrooms and every other classroom is connected to the network. All boys and girls have access to the facilities in class, in extra-curricular activities and in their own time for research and preparation.

Debating. The School competes in national and regional competitions and other inter-school events. There are inter-House competitions at junior and senior level each year.

Careers. All boys and girls are advised on their Advanced Level and Higher Education courses. ISCO careers aptitude tests are offered, as are regular careers evenings and visits. There is a work experience programme and an annual 'Challenge of Business Management' conference.

Sport. Cricket, Rugby Football and Soccer are the major sports for boys, with Hockey and Netball for girls. Many other sports flourish, including Hockey, Tennis, Fives, Squash, Fencing, Judo, Swimming, Sailing, Badminton, Table tennis, Athletics, Volleyball, Basketball, Cross Country Running and Shooting.

Combined Cadet Force. The contingent comprises RN, Army and RAF sections. All boys join the CCF in their second year and are required to serve for 4 terms. During this time, cadets train for the Services Proficiency Certificates and may prepare for the various stages of the Duke of Edinburgh Award Scheme. Termly Field Days, annual camps and courses are an integral feature of CCF training. Adventure Training expeditions take place each year in more remote areas of the country. After the period of compulsory service, boys elect to continue in the CCF or move to the Community Service Unit. Girls may opt to join the CCF in the Sixth Form.

Admission: Boys are required to take the Common

Entrance Examination, unless they have previously satisfied the Examiners in the Scholarship Examination. No boy is admitted under the age of 13 or over 14 years except in special circumstances. The Prospectus and Application Forms may be obtained from the Headmaster's Secretary. Academic, Music, Art and All Rounder Scholarships are available.

For Sixth Form admission, boys and girls take tests and have interviews in the November before their entry into the Sixth Form. There are Academic, Music, Art and All Rounder Scholarships available at this stage. Day and Boarding places are available. Details of Open Days and admission may be obtained from the Headmaster's Secretary.

Foundationerships. In accordance with the Foundation of St John's, places are available for sons and daughters of Anglican clergy who are resident in any Diocese of the Church of England or the Church in Wales and who are engaged in the Ministry of the Church. These Foundationerships are awarded on the result of the Common Entrance or Scholarship Examination, or Sixth Form entry tests. Remission of fees may be up to 90%. Grants from other sources may also reduce the outlay on fees.

Term of Entry. The only term for entry, except in special circumstances, is the Autumn term.

Scholarships. (*see* Entrance Scholarship section) The following awards are offered to those entering the School:

Under 14:

1. Academic: Three Scholarships of 50%; three Exhibitions of 25%; one Science Exhibition of 25%; one Arts Exhibition of 25%.
2. Music: One Scholarship of 50%; two Exhibitions of 25%.
3. Art: Three Exhibitions of 25%.
4. All-Rounder/Sports: Eight Exhibitions of 25%.
5. Common Entrance: Two Exhibitions are offered to candidates performing exceptionally well in the Common Entrance Examination.

Sixth Form.

1. Academic: 2 Scholarships of 50%; 2 Exhibitions of 25%.
2. Music: 1 Scholarship of 50%; 1 Exhibition of 25%.
3. Art: 2 Exhibitions of 25%.
4. All Rounder/Sports: 4 Exhibitions of 25%.

For boarders the award will be a percentage of the total boarding fee, whereas for day pupils it is a percentage of the day fee. The percentage stated represents the maximum value of each Award.

The Entrance Scholarship Examination is held at St John's in February/March. Candidates must be under 14 on 1 September in the year of entry, unless special permission is obtained from the Headmaster.

All-Rounder Awards take into consideration a boy or girl's personality and leadership potential, together with a combination of their sporting, musical, artistic, dramatic and other relevant achievements. Testing for Under 14 awards take place in March and for the Sixth Form awards in November.

Fees. Boarders £4,400 per term, Day Boys £3,100 per term.

Old Johnian Society. Contact the Secretary, Philip Morgan, at the school.

Charitable status. St John's School is a Registered Charity, number 312064. It exists to provide a first class education for children.

* Head of Department	§ Part Time or Visiting
† Housemaster/Housemistress	¶ Old Pupil
‡ See below list of staff for meaning	

St Lawrence College

in Thanet Ramsgate Kent CT11 7AE.
Tel: (01843) 592680 (Headmaster)
(01843) 587666 (Bursar's Office)
Fax: (01843) 851123

Motto: *In bono vince.*

St Lawrence was founded in 1879 and incorporated in 1892.

It aims to

(i) provide an academic, orderly, active, caring and Christianly–conscious community; small enough to establish 'family' ties and large enough to stimulate high achievement —

(ii) develop a balanced sense of confidence, a spirit of service, a healthy curiosity for the contemporary world and a sensitivity for the best in our heritage —

(iii) give opportunities to appreciate excellence and sound judgement, initiative and integrity, tolerance and courtesy —

(iv) permit a continuity of education from 3 to 18 years for boys and girls, day and boarding.

The Senior, Middle and Junior Schools stand on the same estate. Full particulars from the Headmaster's Secretary. There are 300 pupils in the Senior School (13-18) (with 120 in the VIth Form), 90 in the Middle School (11-13) and 100 in the Junior School (3-11).

The Council:
President: Sir Kirby Laing, JP, MA, FEng, DL

Vice-Presidents:
The Rt Hon The Baroness Cox, BSc, MSc, FRCN
D I A Hamblen, CB, OBE, MA
R Q Drayson, DSC, MA, FRSA
Sir Martin Laing, CBE, MA, LLM, FRICS
C A H Lanzer, MA
B G Smallman, CMG, CVO, MA

Members:
D M F Scott, MA
S Webley, MA (*Chairman*)
M G Macdonald, MA, LLM
M Iliff, MSc, ACA
Mrs I B Neden
A T Emby, FCA
Dr R L Cornwell, DVSc, PhD, FRCVS
The Rev D C L Prior, MA
Dr G H Mungeam, MA, DPhil
Mrs G E Page,
Mrs A E Driver, BA
Miss S A Ross, BSc, FRSA

***Headmaster:* M Slater**, MA (St Edmund Hall, Oxford)

Master of the Middle and Junior Schools: R Tunnicliffe, BEd, MA(Ed)

Deputy Head: R F Crittenden, MA (*Physics*)

Chaplain: The Revd D J Peat, BA, MA

Housemasters (*Senior and Middle Schools*):
J M Harper, GRSM, LRAM, ARCM, LGSM (*Bellerby; Music*)
Miss P Savill, BA (*Laing; Mathematics*)
N O S Jones, BA (*Newlands-Deacon; Head of Games*)
T A Clarke, BSc, MSc, PhD (*Lodge; Head of Biology*)
E B Gill, BSc, PhD, CChem, MRSC (*Manor-Grange; Head of Chemistry*)
R A Bendall, BA (*Tower; German, French*)
T Moulton, BA (*Middle School; History, English*)

Assistant Staff:
D A Scales, BA, PhD (*Director of Studies; Head of Classics*)
Mrs B N Birchley, BSc (*Senior Mistress*)
S A Clarkson, BMus, FRCO, ARCM (*Director of Music*)
C A Baker, BA, PhD, AKC (*Head of Geography*)
J M Lewis, BA (*Head of Maths*)
D E Fletcher, BA (*Classics; CCF*)
M P M Watson, MA (*Head of English*)
A P Brown, BA (*Head of History*)
E B Gill, BSc, PhD, CChem, MRIC (*Head of Chemistry*)
P N W Birchley, BSc, MSc, PhD (*Head of Science/ Curriculum Development*)
J C Evans, BEd (*Design Technology*)
Mrs J A Green (*Home Economics*)
G P Simmons, MA (*Geography*)
Miss N Christie, BSc (*Science*)
A G Rudall, BSc (*Chemistry*)
Mrs J Vint, BSc (*Spanish, French*)
W G Higgins, BA, PGCE (*Modern Languages*)
P W Graham, BA (*Spanish, French, Head of Modern Languages*)
Mrs S A Barnsley, BSc (*Business Studies/Mathematics*)
I D Dawbarn, BA, MSc (*Mathematics*)
M J Grace, BSc (*Head of Information Technology, Mathematics*)
Mrs G C Harris, BSc (*Chemistry, Mathematics*)
S M McDonald, MA (*Latin, Greek*)
Mrs A Bickle (*Pottery, Dyslexia*)
Mrs H L Belasyse-Smith (*Speech and Drama, EFL*)
S Smith, BA (*English*)
Miss S Cutler, BA (*English*)
I M Anderson, MA (*Economics*)
P A Geall, BA (*Modern Languages*)
Mrs D B Paynter, BA (*Library*)
Mrs P A McKenna, CertEd (*EFL*)
N Cavaglieri (*SSI*)
Mrs A J Fletcher, BEd (*Marketing*)
R P Dubieniec, BA (*Head of Design Technology*)

Visiting Staff:
S G Urwin, ARCM, AGSM (*Guitar*)
D W White (*Percussion*)
Mrs J Cullis, ARCM (*Violin, Viola*)
A L Upton (*Violin, Brass*)
J M Gallagher (*'Cello*)
E Retallick (*Piano*)

Master of Middle and Junior Schools: Mr R Tunnicliffe, BEd, MA(Ed)

Deputy Master: Mr R E Muncey, BEd

Assistant Staff (Junior School):

Mrs A G Burgess, TCNFF, ACP	J M Gallagher, LTCL, LGSM (*Cello*)
Mrs S C Gayton, BEd, DipPE	G Urwin, ARCM, AGSM (*Guitar*)
Mrs R J Guest, CertEd	Mrs K Upton, LRAM, ARCM (*Piano*)
Mrs S Lawrie, CertEd	R Jones, GGSM (*Piano*)
Miss T Limbrick, MA, BA, PGCE	Mrs J Evans, LRAM, GRSM (*Piano, Violin*)
Mrs V S Marks, CertEd	D W White (*Percussion*)
Mrs J A Rampall, CertEd	A L Upton (*Brass*)
M R E Watling, BMus, PGCE	

Matron: Mrs D Aldred

Secretary to the Council and Bursar: J P Marshall

Medical Officers:
Dr Susan Goldberg, BSc, MB, BS, MRCGP
Dr Alan Cunard, BSc, MB, ChB

Location. The College stands on an estate of 150 acres in Thanet, on the coast between Ramsgate and Broadstairs, facing South towards the English Channel, about 120 feet above sea level. The area is one of the driest and sunniest parts of the UK, with 15 miles of impressive chalk cliffs, sandy beaches, sites of geological significance, an estuary, nature reserves and a busy yachting marina. Ramsgate, as a limb of Sandwich, a town that preserves its medieval and Elizabethan buildings, was one of the original Cinque Ports. The College is 100 minutes from London, 30 minutes from Canterbury and 30 minutes from the Channel Tunnel.

The Chapel stands at the centre of College life. The College is a Church of England School with an Evangelical commitment. A brief service is held on weekday mornings before lessons. There is a communion service followed by a compulsory main service on Sundays. Many Lawrentians have entered the Ministry and there has always been a strong bond with Missionary Societies. Services take a variety of forms with frequent pupil participation. The Chaplain prepares pupils for confirmation each year. There is a flourishing Christian Union. The Community Service Scheme gains much of its impetus through the Chapel. Pupils of other denominations and faiths are accepted at the College.

The Senior School Curriculum. There are 25 Subject Rooms; a language laboratory, suites for Computer Studies and Home Economics, a Music School, an Art, Pottery and Photographic Centre, 10 Science Laboratories and Lecture Rooms, Workshops, 2 main Libraries, a large theatre hall and a new Technology Centre.

The maximum class size is about 20, with much smaller sets in the VIth Form. There are 3 streams in each year with considerable mobility and setting. The following subjects are available to GCSE.

English Language, English Literature, History, Spanish, Geography, German, French, Latin, Classical Civilization, Greek, CDT, Home Economics, Art/Pottery, Mathematics, Physics, Chemistry, Music, Biology, Information Technology, *Religious Studies.

(*Usually taken a year early)

Information Technology and CDT are now core elements in the curriculum for Forms I to III.

Pupils are normally expected to take 4 subjects in the Lower VI (AS Level) and continue with 3 of these in the Upper VI (A2). The subjects from which a choice may be made are as follows: English Literature, French, German, Spanish, Latin, PE, History, Classical Civilisation, Religious Studies, Geography, Economics, Information Technology, Art, Business Studies, Mathematics, Pure Mathematics, Music, Statistics, Chemistry, Physics, Biology, Mechanics, Theatre Studies.

Most combinations of these subjects are available, though there will be some restriction on the fourth choice in the Lower VI.

Occasionally a pupil may take more or fewer subjects; we carefully advise pupils who are considering this possibility.

Two periods of General Studies and, in the Lower VI, two further periods (IT/CDT or Home Economics or Art/ Pottery) are attended in addition to A Level work. These periods are usually drawn from the following subjects: Careers, Drama, Economics, English GCSE, Health Education, Mathematics GCSE, Music, Psychology, Relationships, Religious Studies, Science in Society, 20th Century History.

Houses. There are 2 Boarding Houses for boys, 2 for Boarding and Day girls, 2 for Day Boys and a Middle School for the 11-13 age group. Here the process of development is strongly marked as individuals learn to adapt to the needs of others, progress towards self-discipline and relate their physical being to the whole personality. From Junior Common Room and Dormitory to individual Study Bedroom, pupils gradually gain more responsibilities, privileges and independence.

Tutoring System. Each pupil is assigned to a member of staff by his or her Housemaster for the initial stages of academic and pastoral supervision. Pupils meet their Tutors at least once a week. Three times a term marks and effort are recorded in each subject on Tutor Sheets which are sent home to parents. The sheets are scrutinised by Housemaster and Headmaster. Various follow-up procedures are adopted to encourage pupils to maintain their best efforts.

Health. If a pupil is ill, immediate attention is available: there is a secluded Sick Bay under the care of qualified nurses. The School Doctor calls daily and is available for any emergency.

Meals. There is a modern Self-Service system, organised by experienced caterers. A wide choice of meals is available. Each House is given a specific arrival time so that meals are civilised and leisurely.

Games. There are 35 acres of playing fields, a large gymnasium, a multigym, 2 squash courts, 11 hard tennis courts, badminton, basketball and netball courts, an all-weather surface for hockey, netball and tennis, hard surface cricket nets, a miniature shooting range and an indoor heated swimming pool, as well as an Astroturf hockey pitch with floodlights.

The major games are: Rugby, Netball, Hockey, Cricket, Tennis and Athletics. Other games include: Cross-Country, Cycling, Badminton, Basketball, Swimming, Squash, Sailing, Shooting, Golf, Riding.

The College is a well-known Hockey School. The annual Public Schools Oxford Hockey Festival was created and administered by the College in post-war years. There is an annual Preparatory Schools Hockey Festival at the College in the Easter holidays. Games remain an exciting and essential part of College life. Many are highly competitive and produce high standards. They do not however displace academic or cultural interests. The academic high-flyer, the musician, carpenter or regular supporter of the Social Service Scheme, is as much respected for his talents as the games player.

Activities provide vital areas where diverse talents can be realised. There is a strong Music and Drama tradition. Three major concerts, Choral and Orchestral, as well as a number of invitation Concerts, are held each year. In the Combined Cadet Force the emphasis is on Camps, Adventure Training, First Aid, Life-Saving, Map Reading and opportunities for leadership. Other activities include; Chess, Bridge, Science Society, Computing, Electronics, the Duke of Edinburgh Award Scheme, Natural History Society and the Social Service Scheme.

Careers. The College maintains a well-stocked Careers Centre which is always open. Vth Formers are encouraged to take Intelligence Tests and Aptitude assessments, to supplement career courses at school and advice from Careers' Master, Housemaster and Heads of Departments. Most pupils leave to take up degree courses at Universities or to join the Services, business and industry. A number go to Oxford and Cambridge each year.

Admissions. Boys and girls are accepted at the following ages; at 11–13 into the Middle School (mainly from Maintained Primary Schools after internal assessments, reasoning tests and interview) at 13 into the Senior School, at 14 (to begin a 2 year course to GCSE after internal assessments and school reports) and at 16 (for direct entry to Sixth Form 'A' Level courses after reports on projected GCSE Level results and interview).

Term of Entry. Pupils of suitable ability admitted in any term if space is available.

Scholarships. (*see* Entrance Scholarship section) A limited number of Scholarships are awarded for outstanding merit to boys and girls on entry to the Senior School at 11, 13 and 16. Awards at other points of entry may be considered. Scholarships are awarded at 8 in the Lower School.

The value may range from 10% to 50%, depending on ability and performance.

Some Music Scholarships are also available at similar points of entry and of similar value. Music scholars should be at a minimum Grade 5 in performance. They receive instrumental tuition fee and have obligation to orchestra and choir.

Bursaries. In accordance with tradition children of Clergy and Missionaries and of serving members of HM Forces will be considered for bursaries. Bursaries for the former can be up to 50%. Parents in HM Forces pay the Services Boarding School Allowance plus 10% of our main boarding and tuition fees. Parents with more than one child in the school pay 75% fees for the second child, and 50% for the third and subsequent children.

Fee. A Registration Fee of £50 is payable with the form of application for admission. Fees are payable in advance each term. The Fees per term are: 11–13 years in the Middle School: Boarders £3,905, Day £2,425. Senior School: Boarders £5,180, Day £3,325.

Individual Private Tuition £27.70 per hour. Individual Instrumental Music £26.70 per hour (10 half-hour sessions per term).

Old Lawrentian Society. *Hon Sec:* Christopher Dell, 122 Botany, Kingsgate, Kent CT10 3SE.

The Junior School. The Junior School is co-educational with 16 boarders and 89 day pupils, with an additional 28 children attending the Nursery. It is on the same campus as the Senior School but has an independence with its own Master and staff. Some of the Senior School facilities are shared – for example, CDT, Science Department in Years 7 and 8, Home Economics, Astroturf, heated swimming pool, dining hall – giving the prep school many advantages.

Children can enter from age 3 in the Nursery School. Boarders are taken from 7.

Pupils are prepared for KS1 and KS2, PESE, and Common Entrance, if required.

Up to two major scholarships are awarded at 7+, tenable while in the Junior School, and at 13+ up to two major scholarships are awarded for entry into the Senior School – thus providing a continuous education through to 18.

There is a strong pastoral concern which follows the welfare of each pupil. The Headmaster, together with the Boarding, Parents and other residential staff and matrons provide a caring environment for the boarders.

A wide selection of extra-curricular activities are on offer to develop an interest in hobbies and other skills. The school also encourages pupils to explore their faith and relationship with God.

Charitable status. St Lawrence College in Thanet is a Registered Charity, number A307921. It exists to provide education for children.

St Mary's College

Crosby Merseyside L23 3AB
Tel: 0151-924 3926.

St Mary's College was opened by the Christian Brothers in 1919 at the invitation of Archbishop Whiteside of Liverpool, who felt it was of paramount importance that the Catholic boys of this locality should have the benefits of Grammar School education. The school has been fully co-educational since September 1989.

Motto: *Fidem Vita Fateri.*

Governors:

Chairman: Prof T Bell, FEng, PhD, CEng, FIM

Mrs M Flanagan, LLB
Fr P Harnett, SCJ
H Hitchen, FCA
F Hughes, MA
Professor A H Hudson, MA, LLB, PhD
P Keith
The Revd T Kelly
The Revd N Livingstone, BA
Councillor P McVey
The Revd J O'Sullivan, BA
Councillor Mrs P M Parry
E P J Murgatroyd, BSc

***Headmaster:* W Hammond**, MA (Scholar of Jesus College, Cambridge)

Deputy Heads:
Mrs J Marsh, BA, MSc
G Prendergast, BSc

Bursar: S B Brady, FCA

Senior Teacher: S White, BSc (*Head of Middle School*)

Head of Lower School: Mrs M M O'Neill, BA

Assistant Teachers:
Mrs B Baden, BA
Miss C Ball, BA
Mrs S Bartolo, BEd
Mrs L Bennett, BEd
Mrs J Bibby, BEng
A Byers, BA
Mrs H Carey, BA
S Christopherson, BSc, PGCE (*Head of Boys' PE and Games*)
J P Clucas, BA, MEd (*Head of English Department*)
D Colford, BSc
Mrs J Davies, BA
J Devitt, MPhys
L Doherty, BEd (*Head of Third Year*)
M Duffy, BSc (*Head of Biology Department*)
P Duffy, MPhil (*Head of Religious Studies Department*)
R W Duxfield, BSc (*Head of Physics*)
S C Emery, BA (*Head of Music*)
Mrs B Fletcher, BA
Mrs E Ford, BA
Mrs C Gibbon, BEd
Mrs K Gilbert, BEd
P Hale, BSc
Mrs A Hayes, BSc
J J Hayes, BA
A R Hyland, BA, MPhil (*Head of German Department*)
M Ireland, BEng, MSc
R S Johnston, BSc
Mrs M C Jones, BA
Mrs C Killen, BEd
J G King, BEd, MDes (*Head of Design and Technology Department*)
Mrs K Lane, BEd (*Head of Girls' PE and Games*)
T G Lane, BSc, PhD
P Lyons, BA
N A McCallen, MSc (*Head of Comp Studies*)
P E McColgan, MA
Miss A McDonald, CertEd
Mrs M McKean, BA (*Head of German*)
Mrs F McMillan, DipPhysEd
D Magill, BA (*Head of French Department*)
Miss J Mueller, MEd
E P J Murgatroyd, BSc (*Head of Chemistry Department*)
A J Murphy, MA, PhB, DipRelSt
P Nagington, BEd, MDes (*Head of Second Year*)
E O'Neil, BSc
J F O'Neill, BA (*Head of Spanish Department*)
R I Parr, BA
S Picewicz, CertEd
H Piotr, BSc (*Head of Geography Department*)
P N Richardson, BA
N C Rothie, BA (*Head of History Department*)
H Sage, BSc (*Assistant Head of 4th/5th Year*)
Miss J Simpson, BA (*Head of Business Studies*)
G Smoult, BA
K A Sprakes, BSc, PhD (*Head of Mathematics Department*)
Mrs R Steele, BA
Mrs J Thomas, BSc
Mrs A Whelan, MA (*Head of Art Department*)
C D Wilkinson, BA
S Wilson, BEng

Preparatory Department:

Head of Preparatory Department: Miss B May, BEd, CertEd, DipManagement

Assistant Teachers:
Mrs A Abbott, CertEd
G Bates, BA, PGCE
Miss C A Boggiano, BA
Mrs C Carter, LLB, PGCE
A M Chambers, CertEd (*Head of Infant Department*)
Mrs M P Dixon, CertEd
Mrs L Gallagher, CertEd
M Hewlett, CertEd
Miss D J Marrs, BEd
Mrs A M Melia, BEd
J B Mitchell, BEd
J Moran, BEd
Mrs C Murphy, CertEd (*Deputy Head*)
N J Webster, CertEd

Claremont House:
Miss A Sankey, BEd
Mrs S Seiffert, NNEB (*Head of Nursery*)
Miss M Bell, NNEB
Mrs A Fielding, NNEB

Preparatory Department. Open to boys and girls up to the age of 11. There is an Early Years Unit comprising baby unit and kindergarten. Pupils are admitted to the Preparatory Department after an interview at 4, 5 and 6 years of age and by examination in the other year groups. An agreement must be signed by the parent or guardian undertaking that the pupil shall attend until the end of the School year in which he or she attains the age of 11. Admission to the Preparatory Department does not guarantee admission to the Senior School; this may be obtained only by passing the Entrance Examination.

Curriculum. The Mount has a strong family atmosphere, providing a secure and lively environment in which expectations are high. The school takes what is best from the National Curriculum and follows an enhanced programme with greater emphasis on the 3 Rs and fostering self-discipline.

Sciences play an important part in the curriculum. Sport and Music are particularly strong. Tutoring in a wide range of musical instruments is provided. French and Spanish are taught in small groups from Year 1.

The Headmistress of the Preparatory School, Miss B May will be pleased to meet you and show you round.

The Senior School admits pupils at 11 both from The Mount and from Primary Schools over a wide area.

Senior School. Fully coeducational since September 1989. An Entrance Examination is held in January each year for pupils wishing to enter the Senior School. Generally speaking pupils must be between the ages of 10½ and 12 on 1 September of the year in which they wish to enter the School. There is also a 13+ entry.

There are no boarders.

Curriculum. The course includes English Language and Literature, French, German, Spanish, History, Geography, Classical Studies, Latin, Physics, Chemistry, Biology, Mathematics, Information Technology, Art, Music, Design and Technology and Physical Education. A broad curriculum of 14 subjects is followed for the first 3 years. In the 4th and 5th years, pupils normally take 10 subjects at GCSE including either single Sciences or Dual Award. All pupils in the 4th and 5th year study for GCSE Religious Studies and a Euro-qualification in Information Technology. In the VIth Form there are Advanced courses in all the subjects mentioned above. Economics and Business Studies, and Drama may also be taken to 'A' level and all VIth Formers take A level General Studies. The Sixth Form options system is flexible allowing combinations of 3, 4 or 5 A levels.

St Mary's is a pioneer school on Merseyside in the inclusion of orchestral music as a normal feature of the School curriculum. All pupils are given the opportunity to play a musical instrument. The School Band and Orchestra give an annual Concert in the Liverpool Philharmonic Hall and win regional contests and undertake tours abroad.

Religious Education. The course followed is that devised by the Archdiocese of Liverpool. In the VIth Form, Religious Education is continued to a more advanced level and integrated with social work for the handicapped and deprived.

Careers. The College works in full partnership with the Independent Schools Careers Organisation. Arrangements are made each year for interviews for Vth Formers to which parents are invited. VIth Formers are interviewed several times to help them choose appropriate courses at University or in Higher Education. Advice is given to 3rd year pupils in choosing options. There is a Lower Sixth Work Experience Scheme.

Games. Games periods provide opportunities for Rugby, Cricket, Hockey, Netball, Squash, Golf, Cross-Country, Tennis and Basketball. Girls main games are Netball and Hockey. There is an adjacent modern Sports Centre.

Activities. Some 40 extra-curricular activities and societies are available, including the Duke of Edinburgh's Award Scheme.

Combined Cadet Force. There is a very active Combined Cadet Force which contains Army and Air Force sections. Membership of the Combined Cadet Force is voluntary.

Numbers. There are 643 pupils in the Senior School and 302 in the Preparatory Department.

Fees. A Registration Fee of £40 is payable with the form of application for admission.

The fees are currently about £4,770 in the Senior School and £3,153 in the Preparatory Department and £3,093 and £2,826 in Reception and Kindergarten respectively.

Open Academic Scholarships. There are up to six Open Scholarships based on performance in the College Entrance Examination, wotth up to half fees. The awards are based on academic merit alone and are irrespective of income.

Sixth Form Scholarships. Edmund Rice Scholarships (up to half fees) are available on merit, and are awarded on the basis of a Scholarship Examination in January.

School Assisted Places - Edmund Rice Junior Scholarships at 11+. These are income-related and are open to pupils whose parents' joint income would have brought them within the Government scheme.

St Mary's College Association. St Mary's College Association, 17 Moor Lane, Crosby, Merseyside L23. Tel: 0151-924 1774.

Charitable status. The Congregation of Christian Brothers Trustees is a Registered Charity, number 254312. The aims and objectives of the Charity are to advance religious and other charitable works.

* Head of Department § Part Time or Visiting
† Housemaster/Housemistress ¶ Old Pupil
‡ See below list of staff for meaning

St Paul's School

Lonsdale Road Barnes London SW13 9JT.
Tel: 020 8748 9162
Fax: 020 8748 9557
e-mail: hmsec@stpaulsschool.org.uk
website: www.stpaulsschool.org.uk

St Paul's School was founded in AD 1509, by John Colet, DD, Dean of St Paul's. An ancient Grammar School had previously existed for many centuries in connection with St Paul's Cathedral, and was probably absorbed by Colet into his new foundation. Colet laid down in the original statutes, still preserved at Mercers' Hall, that there should be 'taught in the scole children of all Nacions and Countres indifferently to the Noumber of a CLIII', the number of the Miraculous Draught of Fishes. There are still 153 Foundation Scholars, in a school of 800 pupils, in addition to about 440 pupils in the Preparatory School. Colet appointed 'the most honest and faithfull fellowshipp of the Mercers of London' as Governors of his School. The Governing Body has been extended to include 6 University Governors and other nominees. The School was moved from its original site adjoining the Cathedral to West Kensington in 1884 and to its present position on the River Thames at Barnes in 1968. A history of the school entitled 'A miraculous draught of fishes' by A H Mead was published in 1990.

Motto: *Fide et literis.*

Governors:

Chairman: D A Tate, Esq, OBE
Deputy Chairman: ¶Sir David Rowland, Kt

Master and Wardens of the Mercers' Company:
¶R C Cunis, Esq
A E Hodson, Esq
Wing Commander M G Dudgeon, OBE

Appointed by the Mercers' Company:

J J Fenwick, Esq, DL
The Hon H W Palmer
Mrs Coral Samuel, CBE
D N Vermont, Esq
D C Watney, Esq
J A Watney, Esq

Appointed by the Mercers' Company in consultation with the University of Oxford:

Dr J P Barron, MA, DPhil, FSA
Professor I Grant, DPhil, FRS

Appointed by the Mercers' Company in consultation with the University of Cambridge:

¶Professor P A Cartledge, PhD, FSA
Professor P E Easterling, MA

Appointed by the Mercers' Company in consultation with the University of London:

Professor C S Peckham, CBE

Clerk to the Governors: C H Parker, MA

***High Master:* ¶R S Baldock**, MA

Surmaster: B Taylor, MA

Director of Studies: P Woodruff, MA, MSc

Undermasters:
R G Jaine, BA, FRGS
B J O'Keeffe, MA
P J King, MA
T L Peters, BSc
A G Wilson, BA

Housemasters:
G S Miller, BSc, MA, MInstP, CPhys (*School House*)
P A Collinson, MA (*Colet House*)

Art:
§J R Crocker, BA
§Mrs P C Holmes, BA, UED
*N W Hunter, BA (Hons), MEd
§Miss E A Mackinlay, BA
I J Tiley, MA, ATC

Classics:
¶R S Baldock, MA
D J Cairns, MA
J N Davie, MA, BLitt
*Ms C J I Butler, MA
¶P J King, MA
S A May, MA
A G Wilson, BA

Economics:
A H Ellams, MA
*R D Jones, MA
M R Mikdadi, BSc, MSc, MBA
E A du Toit, BPE

English:
D G R Bussey, MA (*University Entrance*)
P R J Hudson, MA
J S Lowden, MA
G May, BA
Miss J McLaren, MA
B J O'Keeffe, MA
J A Sutcliffe, BA
*J C Venning, MA

Geography:
*Rev N K Hinton, BSc, MA (*Assistant Chaplain*)
D H Howell, BA, FRGS
P S Littlewood, BSc, MSc (*General Studies*)
Mrs S M Nichol, BA, MSc

History:
C Dean, MA
*M G Howat, BA
M K Lawson, BA, DPhil
Mrs S Mackenzie, MA
K R Perry, BA
N J Sanderson, BA

Mathematics:
*M V Bradley, MA
R J Gazet, MA
M L Harvey, BSc
G Leversha, MA, PhD
A J Mayfield, BSc, MSc, DPhil
T C I Morland, MA
P W Motion, BSc
T L Peters, BSc
D M Rollitt, BSc
M J R Slay, BA, MSc
P Woodruff, MA, MSc

Modern Languages:
R P Bailey, BA
Miss J M Ball, MA
Mrs M-J Gransard, L-ès-L
†P A Collinson, MA
*J-L González-Medina, BA, MA, DPhil
D J M Hempstead, BA, MPhil (*French*)
Mrs E D J Hess, MA, MLitt
*P E Maudsley, BA (*German*)
B Taylor, MA
R J Thompson, BA (*Italian*)
P S Vanni, MA
E J T Williams, MA (*Drama*)

Sciences:
*M J Beard, BA (*Chemistry*)
*P J C Boddington, BSc (*Biology*)
B Brook, BSc, PhD
C G Henderson, BSc, PhD
Mrs A Jeffery, BSc
M Kondrollochis, BSc, PhD
N A Lamb, BSc, PhD
C R Lawrence, MA, PhD
Mrs R S M Peach, MA
†G S Miller, BSc, MA, MInstP, CPhys
*I Poots, BSc, PhD, CChem, MRSC (*Science*)
§P S Rodgers, BSc, PhD, CChem, MRSC
C A P Sammut, BSc, MSc
I C Vinall, MA, PhD (*University Entrance*)
A P Weeks, MA, PhD
*K P Zetie, BA, MA, DPhil (*Physics*)

Physical Education:
R G Harrison, BSc
*R G Jaine, BA, FRGS

Technology:
*P F Bullett, MA, MEd, PhD (*Director, Technological Studies*)
*K M Campbell, BEd (*Design Technology*)
*O V Avni, BSc, ARCS (*Electronics*)
*R A Barker, MA (*Computing*)
*C J Fry, MA (*Control Technology*)
*D J May, BA (*Director of ICT*)
*A E Goodridge, BA

Music:
*P M Tatlow, MA, MMus, ARAM, FTCL, ARCM, LGSM
P W Gritton, BA, LRAM
R D A Wedderburn, MA, GRSM

Chaplain: *Revd S E Young, BD, AKC, BPhil

Pastoral Chaplain: Revd J F Ganga, BA, MA, BSS

Bursar: Air Commodore D J Loveridge, OBE, FRAeS, FBIM, MCIPD

Medical Officer: Dr O G Evans, BSc, MBBS, MRCP

Counsellor: Prof R Bor, CPsychol, AFBPsS, UKCP

Librarian: Mrs A Aslett, BA, ALA

Colet Court *St Paul's Preparatory School*
Tel: 020 8748 3461
Fax: 020 8563 7361
e-mail: HMsecCC@stpaulsschool.org.uk

Headmaster: G J Thompson, BA, MEd, CBiol, MIBiol, FLS, FCP, FRSA

Deputy Headmaster: P A David, BEd

Director of Studies: K F Sharpe, BA

Director of Administration: A P C Fuggle, MA

Head of Juniors: G E Nava, BSc

P J Berg, ARCM, FRCO
K M Campbell, BEd
D Carroll, BA
Miss S E B Clarke, NDD
P S Evans, BA
A E Goodridge, BA
Mrs A J Gordon, BA
Mrs B A Gordon, BA, DipEd
Mrs R A Gutch, BA
T J Harbord, CertEd
The Revd G Holdstock, MA
N E L Howe, BEd
Mrs S M Humphrays, CertEd
I T Hunter, GTCL, ARCO
Miss S Judson, CertEd
Mrs K A Kent, CertEd
Miss S E J Lohn, BSc
I StJ Maynard, BEd
Mme V C M Nolk, L-ès-L
Mrs J S Olney, BEd
Mrs R Perry, BEd
J A J Renshaw, BA
P H Reutenauer, L-ès-L
Mrs W K Seigel, CertEd
R Stanton, BSc
Mrs A Thompson, CertEd
G Tsaknakis, BSc
Miss S Wilson, BEd

Application for Admission to St Paul's is to be made on a form to be obtained from the Admissions Office. Candidates at 13+ take the Common Entrance Examination in June prior to entry in September. A few Sixth Form places are also available.

Fees. There is a registration fee of £100.

A Deposit of one third of the termly day fee is required when a parent accepts the offer of a place for his son after interview. The Deposit will be returnable if the boy fails to reach the necessary standard in the entrance examination or when the final account has been cleared after the boy leaves St Paul's.

The Basic Fee from September 2000 is £10,365 a year for St Paul's. This covers Tuition, Games, Loan Books, Stationery, Libraries, Medical Inspection, a careers aptitude test in the GCSE year, certain School publications and Lunch, which all boys are required to attend. Charges are made for the purchase of some books (which become the personal property of boys) and Public Examination Fees.

There are facilities for up to 60 boarders (ages 11 to 18) and boarding is flexible allowing boys to go home at weekends as they wish. The Boarding Fee is £5,280 a year from September 2000 in addition to the Basic Fee.

Foundation Scholarships. (*see* Entrance Scholarship section) For details see relevant section in this Book.

Other Scholarships. Music: A number of Foundation Music Scholarships are available at St Paul's each year. Candidates are expected to have attained at least grade VI on their principal instrument. A Dennis Brain Memorial Scholarship is available from time to time and a Sharp scholarship for entry to St Paul's at 16+. South Square Choral Awards are offered each year in conjunction with Colet Court for treble voices of age 8, 9 or 10.

Bursaries: A small number of bursaries is available whereby the school maintains the spirit of the former Government Assisted Places scheme. The bursaries are means-tested and boys joining Colet Court at 10+ or 11+, or St Paul's at 13+ or 16+ are eligible.

South Square Art Scholarships. One or more scholarships are available each year to boys who have taken GCSE to assist them in following a career in practical art. These scholarships can be awarded either during the candidate's A Level course at St Paul's, or later at a recognised Art College, or at both.

Arkwright Scholarships. The School is a member of the Arkwright Scholarship Scheme which offers financial assistance to sixth-formers who intend to pursue a career in Engineering, Technology, or other Design-related subjects.

Leaving Scholarships or Awards. A number of Prize Grants and Exhibitions (including the Lord Campden's exhibitions, founded in 1625 by Baptist Hicks, Viscount Campden) are given by the Governors every year to boys proceeding to Oxford or Cambridge or to any other place of further education.

Curriculum. All boys follow a broadly based course up to GCSE. Thereafter in the Eighth Form, AS and A level subjects are so arranged that boys can combine a wide range of Art and Science subjects if they so wish, eg History can be studied with Physics and Mathematics or Classics with Mathematics, or Chemistry and Physics with French. AS and A level Art and Music can be fitted in with most other subjects.

Games. In addition to Rugby Football, Cricket and Rowing, Fencing, Swimming, Fives, Athletics, Golf, Tennis, hard and grass, Sailing, Judo and Squash are offered. The School has its own Swimming Pool, Fencing Salle, Tennis, Squash, Fives and Rackets Courts (new December 2000), and its own Boat House. The Games Centre also comprises a Sports Hall and Gymnasium. The Sports Hall is equipped for Tennis, Badminton, Basketball and indoor Cricket nets. There are Cricket and Rackets Professionals.

Music. Tuition is available in piano, organ, harpsichord, all the standard orchestral instruments, jazz, bagpipes and the Alexander Technique. There are three choirs, two orchestras, several jazz bands and a wealth of small ensembles. New purpose built Music School and Recital Hall opened in Autumn 1999.

School Societies. There is a wide choice of more than 30 Societies, including Musical, Artistic and Dramatic activities, Debating, Historical and Scientific Societies, Politics and Economics, Bridge, Chess, Natural History, Photography, European Society, a Christian Union and Social Service.

The Preparatory School (Colet Court) adjoins St Paul's School. For details see part V.

Charitable status. St Paul's School is a Registered Charity, number 312749. The object of the charity is to promote the education of boys in Greater London.

St Peter's School

York YO3 6AB.
Tel: 01904-623213
Fax: 01904-640973
e-mail: enquiries@saintpeters.york.sch.uk

Founded in 627 by Paulinus, first bishop of York, St. Peter's is one of Europe's oldest schools. It provides both boarding and day education for boys and girls from 13 to 18. St Peter's School has an excellent record of accademic achievement. Its adjacent junior school, St. Olave's, admits boarding and day boys and girls from 8 to 13.

Motto: *Ingredere ut proficias super antiquas vias.*

Governors:

Major General D M Naylor, CB, MBE, DL (*Chairman*)
M W Bainbridge, Esq
Mrs C Blenkin, BSc
S M Burn, Esq, LLB, TEP, ACIArb
R A Elliott, Esq, FCA, MLIA
Canon P J Ferguson, MA, FRCO(CHM)
Mrs P Hewish
Lady Ingilby
Brigadier P Lyddon, MBE
N A McMahon Turner, Esq
Prof N J Maitland, BSc, PhD
J Pike, Esq
Mrs E M Reid
Mrs C Rymer, JP, MBE
P N Shepherd, Esq, HND, DipPM
G B Smalley, Esq, OBE, TD, ACID
R J Wilson, Esq, MA
R Wood, Esq

Clerk to the Governors: R C Dixon, BA

***Head Master:* A F Trotman**, JP, MA

Deputy Headmaster: R C Perry, MEd

Director of Studies: D J Watkinson, BSc

Senior Chaplain: The Revd J Daly, MA

Assistant Staff:

Mrs J Bainbridge, BA
L Bass, MA
C Blood, ARCM
Miss J Cawsey, MA
*M Dawson, CertEd
R W Doyle, BSc
*R C G Drysdale, MA
M J Duffy, BA
M A Edwards, BSc
Miss E Ellis, BA
A W Ellis-Davies, BSc
Mrs P A Fletcher, CertEd
S M Gair, MA
M J Grant, BA
C W Hall, MA
M Hall, BSc
Miss S J Hall, MSc
Dr R Hockenhull, PhD, PGCE
*C A Hodsdon, BA
Mrs M Hopkinson, MA
Mrs J Houghton, BA
Mrs J M Houghton, BA
*R H Hubbard, BSc (*Head of Careers*)
D J Hughes, BA
*M W Johnston, BA
*M R T Jones, CertEd
I H Lancaster, BSc
*M C Lawrence, MA
Miss A Lewis, BA
M A Lodge, BA
*I M K Lowe, BA
N A Matkin, BSc
M A Monteith, BSc
Miss A F Moore, BA
*D K Morris, BSc
A Murray, MA
*P D Northfield, BSc
J A Owen-Barnett, BA
M Painter, BA
*D M Paterson, BA
J Pennington, BMus
A W Rogerson, MA
*A Severn, BA
Mrs W M Shepherd, CertEd
R G Shread, BTech, MSc
*D J Spencer, BSc
Mrs L Stark, BSc
P J Stephen, BEd
*P Taylor, MA
P C Taylor, BA
*Miss G Terry, MA
R Tildesley, BSc
Mrs A Tooby-Smith, BA
R Wallace, BSc
Mrs S M Watkinson, BA
Mrs M C Wike, BSc
*A P Wright, BMus, LRAM (*Director of Music*)

Houses and Housemasters/mistresses:

Girls' Boarding Houses:
Dronfield: Mr and Mrs M J Grant
The Rise: Mr and Mrs C Hall

Boys' Boarding Houses:
Linton: Mr and Mrs R Doyle
The Manor: Mr P J Stephen

Day Houses:
Clifton: Mrs M C Wike
Grove: Mr M A Monteith
Queen's: Mrs J Bainbridge
School House: Mr N A Matkin

Temple: Mr M A Edwards

The Junior School (St. Olave's):
Master: T Mulryne, MA, BEd, DipPE

Deputy Head: Mrs S Jackson, BA

Director of Studies: Mrs L Garner, MA

Lay Chaplain: A P Hughes, BA

Assistant Staff:
C E Benson, BA
P C Brooks, BEd
A Cannons, BEd
Mrs A L Daish, BA
*Mrs Y E Dyson, BEd
*Miss S-J Fell, BEd
*Ms S E Gilford, MA
C Hald, BSc
Mrs S E Horton, CertEd
S G Humphries, BA
*Mrs D J Jones, BEd
Ms M K Lamb, LRAM
*C W R Lawrence, BSc, MIBiol
Mrs E K Monteith, BEd
J Moors, BA
P D Oldham, BEd
B A Owen, BSc
Miss J Pickles, BEd
Mrs S E Rose, BA
Mrs C F J Round, BA
¶K J Sargeant, CertEd
N B Savage, BEd
*J W Slingsby, BEd
*Mrs F J Stasiak, BA
*Mrs H E H Whiteley, BA

St Olave's Houses and Housemasters/mistresses:

Junior Boarding: Mr and Mrs J W Slingsby
Day Houses:
Ainsty: Mrs S E Horton
Elmet: Miss S-J Fell
Fairfax: Mr C W R Lawrence
York: Mr P C Brooks
Boarding: Mr J W Singsby

Clifton Preparatory School:
Headteacher: Mrs P M Arkley, MA, BSc, CertEd

Mrs F Bonas, NNEB
Mrs E J Harrison, BEd
Mrs V Knighton, MA, PGCE
Mrs A R Oldham, BA, PGCE
Mrs M H McCulloch, MA, BEd
Mrs M E Rees, CertEd
Mrs G D Spaven, CertEd
Mrs S Taylor, CertEd
Mr C Tidswell, BEd
Mrs M Trotman, MA, PGCE
Miss T E J Ward, BA, PGCE
Mrs L Wilson, ARCM, CertEd

Bursar: Major P B Jelbert, FCMA, MIMgt

Medical Officer: Dr D S Kemp, MBBS, MRCGP, DRCOG

Assistant: Dr S Fathea Zam, MA, MB, BChir, MRCGP, DRCOG

Archivist: J V Mitchell, CertEd

Librarian: Mrs A J M Pedley, MA, ALA

St Peter's is fully co-educational with 486 boys and girls. In addition, there are 328 girls and boys in the Junior School. There are 121 boy boarders, 60 girl boarders and 299 day boys and 224 day girls. There are four boarding and five day houses for St Peter's pupils and 2 boarding and 4 day houses for St Olave's pupils.

Buildings and facilities. The School occupies an impressive site with a large complex of buildings and playing fields stretching down to the River Ouse.

A large sports centre was opened in 1974, and another development in 1984 provides for the teaching of science, electronics, computing, design and technology in the most up-to-date conditions. There is also a fine drama centre, music school, well-equipped art and pottery department and a superb new library.

Entrance. Pupils are admitted through the School's entrance examinations held in January (13+) and February (16+). Entry to other years is also possible when vacancies occur. St Olave's entrance examinations are held in January (8+) and February (10+ and 11+).

Scholarships (*see* Entrance Scholarship section). Various academic and music scholarships (and awards for instrumental tuition) are available.

Bursaries may be given to supplement scholarships and other awards in cases of need.

Curriculum. A very broad middle school curriculum includes information technology, music, physical education, craft, design and technology, and courses in personal and social education.

Nearly all pupils proceed into the sixth form, and 'A' level courses in all subjects studied for GCSE and in economics, politics, business studies and further mathematics are available. 'A' level general studies courses are followed by all.

Academic and pastoral care. A comprehensive house and tutorial system throughout the School and interim assessments and reports during the term ensure the closest interest of all the teaching staff in pupils' academic and general development.

Religious education and worship. Religious studies are a part of the curriculum, and Chapel is seen as an opportunity for pupils to be made aware of the School's Christian heritage and helped to grow in that faith.

Careers and university entrance. The School is an 'all-in' member of the Independent Schools Careers Organisation, and the careers staff are always available for consultation, maintaining an extensive library relating to careers and higher education.

Games and Physical Education. Physical education is part of the curriclum. There is an extensive games programme and excellent sports facilities. Rugby football, netball, hockey, cricket and rowing are major sports, and many other options including swimming (in a heated indoor pool), athletics, cross-country, shooting, basketball, climbing, squash, badminton, tennis, association football, trampolining and weight-training.

Combined Cadet Force. A flourishing and voluntary CCF contingent, with army and air sections, allows the pursuit of many activities including a full programme of holiday camps and courses.

Music. Musical ability is encouraged throughout the School. There is an orchestra, band, choir, choral society and various smaller groups, with concerts as a regular feature of the school year.

Tuition in all instruments is available, and GCSE and 'A' level music courses may be studied.

Art. Drawing, painting, print-making, pottery and sculpture may all be taken up both in and out of school hours in a well-equipped department. In 1996, 1997 and 1998 all GCSE entrants received A* grades.

Drama. The School has two theatres: the Memorial Hall and the smaller, more flexible Drama Centre. There are various productions through the year giving opportunities both for acting and back-stage skills.

Clubs and societies. Many societies flourish including chess, debating, discussion groups, bridge, etc. Also, use outside school hours of such facilities as workshop, electronics laboratory, computer department and art studio is encouraged.

Travel and expeditions. Recent holiday opportunities, which are frequently available, have included skiing trips, hill-walking and climbing in Snowdonia and the Scottish Highlands and expeditions to the Sahara, Iceland, Greece, Norway, France and the USSR.

The Friends of St Peter's. Parents are encouraged to join the Friends, a society whose aim is to promote a close relationship between parents and staff and to further the welfare of the School.

The Old Peterites. The honorary secretary of the Old Peterites' Club is: P J Netherwood, Esq., 4 Moor Lane, Haxby, York YO3 8PH (Tel. 01904 783550).

Fees. From September, 2000, inclusive fees per year are as follows:

III–V forms: boarding £12,228, day £7,119
VI form: boarding £12,555, day £7,476

These fees cover all costs (including books and stationery) except individual music lessons, external examination fees and day pupils' lunch charge.

Prospectuses of St. Olave's (see also Part V) and St. Peter's, containing full details of the two schools, scholarships, entry requirements, etc., are available on request, or visit our website at: www.saintpeters.york.sch.uk.

Charitable status. St Peter's School is a Registered Charity, number 529740. Its aims are to promote education.

Sedbergh School

Sedbergh Cumbria LA10 5HG.
Tel: 015396 20535 (Headmaster).
Tel: 015396 20303 (Bursar).
Fax: 015396 21301
e-mail: HMsedbergh@aol.com
website: www.sedbergh.sch.uk

Sedbergh School was founded in 1525 by Dr Roger Lupton, Provost of Eton, and endowed by him with lands connected with a chantry, probably for the souls of his kinsmen. Today, Sedbergh School aims to offer a blend of academic learning and all-round development of the individual through a strong and caring House system and a wide range of exciting and challenging extra-curricular activities. It is known for its excellence in sport, art and music, magnificent location and happy atmosphere.

Motto: *Dura Virum Nutrix*

The Governing Body:
R S Napier, MA (*Chairman*)
The Most Revd and Rt Hon The Lord Archbishop of York, represented by The Lord Bishop of Bradford
Her Majesty's Lieutenant of Cumbria, J A Cropper, BA, FCA
M P Adams
Mrs S E Bagot
R W Brock, MA, DPhil
Mrs S K Buckley, BDS, LDS, DOrth, RCS(Eng)
R deC Chapman, MA
J Guthrie, MA, FRICS
P T Johnstone, ScD
S A M Rayner
A O Robertson, OBE, LLB
N P G Ross, MA
Mrs P V Smith, CBE, JP
Admiral Sir Jock Slater, GCB, LVO, ADC

Clerk to the Governors and Bursar: N A H McKerrow, MA (Cantab), FRSA

Assistant Bursar: P W Whittaker

***Headmaster:* C H Hirst**, MA

Second Master: J O Morris, BSc

Senior Housemaster: †E A D Campbell, BA
Senior Mistress: Mrs S L Hirst, BEd
Director of Studies: J M Sykes, BSc, MSc
Senior Tutor: *S M Manger, BA
School Chaplain: †*The Revd C D Griffin, BA
Director of Marketing: P M Wallace-Woodroffe, BA

Assistant Staff:
*D M Andrew, MA (*Director of Music*)
*G Aveyard, DipAD, HDipDes
†G T Ayling, MA
*M R Baggley, BSc
Miss D Benson, BSc
*J C Bobby, BA (*Director of Sport*)
D C Bowker, MA
N H Brown, BSc
Mrs L le M Campbell, BA, MA
*L W Catlow, BA, PhD
G A Clarke, BA
Miss H J Crawshaw, BEd
H R Davies, BSc
Mrs S J Davies, BSc
Mrs S A Doherty, GRNCM
J E Fisher, BSc
Mrs S A Griffin, BA
Mrs M E Griffiths, BA, DAA (*Archivist & Librarian*)
*D J Harrison, BA
R C J Hartley
*T Jeffries, BSc
P J N Knowles, BA, DPE
R Kooper, MA
A R Lewis, BPhil
†P Meadows, MA
Mrs C M Morgan, BSc
*C R I Morgan, MA
†J R D Morgan, BA
I J Platt, BA
*M M Priestley, BA, MA
*M A F Raw, MA
†P H Reynolds, BA, MEd
†M P Ripley, MA, DPhil
Mrs J V Rowbotham, BEd
*S M Smith, MA
H M Symonds, BA (*Careers Master*)
Mrs D K Thomas, MA
R H Thomas, BSc
*M J O Valentine, BA
D T Vigar, BA (*Admissions Tutor*)
†Mrs S J Wallace-Woodroffe, BSc
C P Webster, BSc

Medical Officer: Dr P R C Dowse, MB, BAO, BCh, MA

Headmaster's Secretary: Miss A J Bird, BA

There are 370 pupils in the School, of whom 360 are boarders distributed among 7 boarding houses and 2 junior houses (8 to 12 year olds), where the pupils live, eat all their meals and have their studies/bed sitting rooms.

The School is fully co-educational, 8 to 18.

Pupils are looked after in their Houses by a Housemaster or Housemistress, the House Matron and a House Tutor, who keep in close touch with pupils' parents. If the pupils are ill, they are treated in the School Sanatorium, which is managed by fully qualified staff. The present House staff are:

Senior:
Evans E A D Campbell
Hart The Revd C D Griffin
Lupton Mrs S J Wallace-Woodroffe
Powell M P Ripley
School P Meadows
Sedgwick G T Ayling
Winder J R D Morgan
Junior:
Cressbrook P H Reynolds

The academic curriculum is designed to give pupils a thorough grounding in essential subjects and to delay as long as possible the need to specialise. In the VIth Form, a flexible system makes possible a large number of combinations of A and AS level subjects, while in addition all pupils study English, Divinity, Current Affairs and a number of options, ranging from Russian to Computing, Electronics to Music. There are also various academic societies (eg Art, History, Music and Science), and a programme of Civics Lectures throughout the year. The

School has excellent computing facilities and a Modern Language Laboratory.

The School lays emphasis on introducing pupils to the Christian faith. Confirmation services for both the Church of England and the Church of Scotland are held each year. Howeve r, the School welcomes pupils of all denominations. It is usual for pupils to attend a service in Chapel on Sundays; each day begins with an assembly in Powell Hall and ends with prayers in the Boarding Houses.

Sedbergh tries to develop as many as possible of the pupils' individual skills and talents and to introduce them to a wide range of hobbies and activities.

Art and Design Centre. The Art School includes Studios for Painting, Pottery and Sculpture, Photographic Darkrooms and an Exhibition Gallery. The Design Centre provides multi-media workshops and Design Studios with CAD/CAM, and digital editing facilities. All pupils work in the studios and workshops as part of the curriculum, and have opportunities to do so in their spare time. Also in the Centre is a Lecture Theatre with facilities for video, films and drama.

Music. Musical activity is encouraged at all levels. There is a Chapel Choir and a Choral Society which performs 2 major works each year. An Opera is produced in alternate years. Instrumentalists may join the Orchestra, String Orchestra Junior or Senior Bands and Jazz Orchestra, and there is a considerable amount of music making in small ensembles. Music lessons, given by full-time music staff and visiting teachers, are offered for the usual orchestral and keyboard instruments. Many pupils study Music at GCSE, AS and A level. A series of Subscription Concerts brings distinguished artists to the School and there are regular School concerts throughout the year. Music Scholarships are available.

Drama. As well as visits to theatres there are usually two School plays a year and one Junior production; there are also House plays and year-group productions. Houses also organise entertainment for their own parents and pupils, usually plays, songs and revue sketches.

The Setting. The School capitalises on its beautiful situation in the Yorkshire Dales National Park and has a very active Natural History Society, which manages three conservation sites in the area; it also runs numerous expeditions on the fells and in the Lake District. The programme includes Geography and Biology Field Courses, Adventure Training and CCF camps, Climbing, Potholing, Canoeing and Sailing trips. It also includes major expeditions abroad; musical, geographical, historical, sporting and pure adventure. Pupils may enter for the Duke of Edinburgh's Award Scheme. The School has an Adventure Training Centre in the Highlands of Scotland.

CCF. The School CCF has Army, Navy and Air Force Sections, and as well as undertaking Basic Training it gives boys and girls an experience of camping and preliminary instruction in Shooting in its miniature range. Rifle Shooting is encouraged and a high standard is achieved both on the miniature and open ranges. The School is a regular winner of major trophies at Bisley. There is a flourishing CCF Marching Band and Corps of Drums which regularly tours the country and overseas.

Games. There is an extensive programme of games, almost all of which are open for boys and girls. The main games are Rugby Football (played in both Winter terms), Hockey, Cricket, Netball, Fives, Cross-country Running, Athletics, Tennis, Swimming (the indoor 25 metre heated pool is open all the year round), Squash and Soccer. There is a Gymnasium, modern Sports Hall and all-weather surface..

There are opportunities for Sailing and Fishing, and School societies make provision for many other activities including Debating, Natural History, Archaeology, Geology, Photography and Art.

Fees. The Registration Fee is £50 which is paid at the time of Registration. The senior tuition and boarding fee is £15,495 pa (for Day Boys the fee is £11,460 pa) In addition there are voluntary fees (£146 per term for Instrumental Music and £28 per term for CCF). Tuition and boarding fees for boys in Cressbrook House £11,175 per annum (for day boys in Cressbrook House £8,385 per annum). For Danson House £9,690 for boarders and £6,600 for day boys.

Bursaries and Scholarships. Numerous Scholarships and Exhibitions are awarded annually to those revealing academic excellence or talent in Music, Art and Sport, as well as all-round ability. All such awards can be supplemented up to the value of the full fee by a further Bursary award, which will be based upon the financial circumstances of the candidate's parents. All Scholarship examinations are held at the school in the Lent Term annually. Full details available from The Headmaster's Secretary.

Application for admission. *Senior School:* Application for admission at any age should be made to the Headmaster. At the age of 13 it is usual that a pupil would sit Common Entrance or Scholarship. Pupils are also accepted into the Sixth Form on the basis of GCSE level results.

Cressbrook House. A separate boarding and day house for 50 pupils aged 11-12. To be admitted a pupil must sit the Entrance Examination held at the School in February. Junior Bursaries are available to those whose parents would encounter considerable hardship in the payment of school fees.

Danson House.

A boarding and day house for pupils aged 8-10. Admission is by interview and assessment.

The Old Sedberghian Club (c/o Malim Lodge, Sedbergh School, Sedbergh) flourishes and has branches all over the world.

Charitable status. Sedbergh School is a Registered Charity, number 1080672. It exists to provide boarding education and pastoral welfare to pupils from the ages of 8 to 18.

Sevenoaks School

Sevenoaks Kent TN13 1HU
Tel: (01732) 455133
Fax: (01732) 456143
e-mail: enq@admin.soaks.kent.sch.uk

Sevenoaks School is an independent co-educational School. Founded in 1432.

Motto: *Servire Deo Regnari Est.*

Governing Body:

Hereditary Governor and President: Rt Hon Lord Sackville, Lord of the Manor of Knole

Chairman: R P Wilkinson, OBE, BA

Governors:

J J Adler, JP
C J Bailey, MSc, AMIEE
Dr K C Draper, MB, BChir
A C V Evans, MA, MPhil, FIL
Professor G Fleet, MA, PhD, DPhil
Lady Harrison
Mrs E Hoodless, CBE, BA, DipAppSocStud, JP
Capt J D W Husband, OBE, RN
Sir Michael Jenkins, OBE, MA
Mrs D McEuen
R S Norman, BA, FCA
R Sackville-West, MA, MSc
The Rt Revd B A Smith
¶L C Taylor, MA
Mrs P C Walshe
Mrs F Weston, BA
J C Wilson, MA, PhD

Clerk to the Governors and Bursar: J P Patrick

Academic Staff:

***Headmaster:* T R Cookson**, MA

Undermaster: ¶J B Guyatt, MA

Registrar and Deputy Headmaster: M J Bolton, BA

Deputy Headmistress: Miss T M Homewood, MA, BSc

Senior Master: A P F Theaker, MA, FRGS

Senior Mistress: Mrs J C Hackett, BA

Chaplain: The Revd N N Henshaw, BA

Assistant Teachers:
R H Atherton, MPhil (*Mathematics*)
Mrs S Austin, BA (*French*)
P R Bassett, MA (*Mathematics*)
*R C Bourlet, BA (*French, German, Spanish*)
Miss M T Boyd, BSc (*Mathematics*)
Ms A J Brookfield, MA (*English*)
Miss H E Brown, BA (*Chemistry*)
*M J F Brown, BSc, PhD (*Geography*)
J N Burger, BA (*Mathematics*)
*Miss A Buxade Del Tronco (*Spanish*)
I C Campbell, BSc (*Biology*)
E C Coles, MEng (*Electronics & Design Technology*)
N K Connell, BEd (*French*)
Miss M T Connolly, BSc (*Physics*)
G Coupe, MA (*Art*)
Miss F J Dodsworth, BA (*French/Spanish*)
Miss A Downton, BA (*French & Spanish*)
*Miss J E Fenn, MA (*History*)
*D Fenwick, BSc (*Electronics and CDT*)
*A P Forbes, BA, LRAM (*Music*)
Mrs C E Forbes, BEd, AIST (*Physical Education*)
*P Ford, BSc (*Computing*)
*Miss K Fox, Staatsexamen (*German*)
Miss A A Franks, MA (*Mathematics*) (*Director of Administration*)
T B Fugard, PhD (*Mathematics*)
S A Gent, MA (*History*)
*J W Grant, BA (*Drama*)
*C D Greenhalgh, BA, PhD (*English*)
R Hackett, BSc, PhD, CEng (*Mathematics and Chemistry*)
P Harrison, MA (*English*)
N T Haworth, BA (*History/ Geography*)
Mrs C J Henshaw, BA (*English*)
*Revd N N Henshaw, BA (*Chaplain, Religious Studies, Humanities*)
J A Hewitt, BA (*Economics & Business Studies*)
D I Hewson, BA (*Economics & Business Studies*)
P T Hill, BEd (*Physical Education and Geography*)
¶J F Hills, BA (*French*)
Mrs B Hobbs, BA (*Art*)
*D A Holland, MSc (*Mathematics*)
P M Hornsby, MSc (*Computing & IT*)
Miss N J Horsley, MA (*Physics*)
Miss E S Kemp, BSc (*Mathematics*)
A J Kennedy, MA (*Physics*)
Mrs J L Kiggell, BA, ARCM, AMus, TCL (*Music*)
T A Kiggell, MA (*French & German*)
Miss E J King, BA (*Classics*)
P I Kino, BA (*German*)
*G E Klyve, DPhil (*Classics*)
T G Lacey, MA (*History*)
Miss J Y Lee, BA (*Classics*)
P G Leese, MSc (*Mathematics*)
*Mrs J A Lenferna de la Motte, BLibSc (*Librarian*)
Miss E J Lewis, MA (*English*)
†Mrs K Lewis, BSc
*T C Lewis, BSc (*Physical Education*)
*P J Lloyd, BSc (*Biology*)
Mrs A C McEwen, BA (*French*)
Mrs S E Mann, BA (*French and Spanish*)
Mrs A J Maynard, BA (*French*)
A Merson-Davies, BSc (*Biology*)
L N Morgan, BSc, PhD (*Chemistry*)
Mrs E J Mount, BEd (*Physical Education*)
Miss K-M Newton, BA (*Drama*)
Miss J R Nowicki, BA (*English*)
N J O'Donnell, BEng (*Physics*)
R Otley, BA (*Economics & Business Studies*)
*S M Owen, PhD (*Chemistry*)
Mrs J A Penney, BSc(Ed) (*Chemistry*)
Mrs K L Pitcher, BSc (*Biology*)
A J Presland, BSc (*Mathematics/ Computing*)
*B Richards, BSc, PhD (*Physics*)
R M Ruge, MA (*French and German*)
*P M Shakespeare, MA (*CDT*)
S J Sharp, MA, PhD (*Physics*)
A W Skinnard, MA (*RS/ Philosophy*)
†A C Smith, BComm (*Economics and Business Studies*)
D M Smith, BA, MPhil, PhD (*History*)
†Mrs A M Stuart, BSc (*Biology*)
T Stuart, BA (*Biology*)
Mrs P Styles, BA (*Dorton House Tutor*)
C J Tavaré, MA (*Biology*)
S C Taylor, BA (*Classics & Philosophy*)
Miss H P Tebay, MA (*Mathematics*)
*C M Thomas, BA (*Art*)
Miss J E Thomas, MA (*History and Careers*)
*Mrs S E Tierney, BA (*French and Russian*)
*J P S Toy, MA (*Economics & Business Studies*)
†M M Turnbull, BA (*Geography*)
Mrs B Walpole, BSc, MPhil, MIBiol (*Biology*)
Miss E M Weaver, BA (*Chemistry*)
Miss C F Williams, BA (*English*)
G P Williams, BSc, PhD (*Maths*)
A G L Wilson, BA (*English*)
R C Woodward, BSc, MA, ARCS (*Chemistry*)
Miss W J Worham, BA (*Religious Studies*)
P F Young, BMus, ARCO (*Music*)

Part-time Staff:
Mrs K Agarwal (*Hindi*)
O Barratt, BA (*Art*)
J D Britten, MA (*English & French*)
Mrs R Campbell, BA (*English*)
Mrs R Chard, BA (*Classics*)
Mrs E Connell, BSc (*Mathematics*)
B T Corbishley, BEd, CertEd (*Design*)
Mrs L A Fisher, BA (*Mathematics*)
Mrs J Fitzsimmons, CertEd (*Mathematics*)
§Mrs M Gower (*Japanese*)
†Mrs R A Greenhalgh, BA (*Spanish*)
R B Hebbert, BA (*Sailing*)
A R Hopf, MA (*EFL & Dyslexia*)
Mrs W Huang (*Mandarin*)
Mrs E Kelly (*Russian*)
C Kent (*Modern Greek*)
§Mrs Y Knott (*Japanese*)
§D Merewether (*Photography*)
§Miss L Millar (*Weaving*)
§A C Mitchell, BA (*Film/ Video*)
§S Okkenhaug (*Norwegian*)
§A Penfold, MNASC (*Shooting*)
Mrs E Salomaa-Jago (*Finnish*)
§Mrs M Schofield, CertEd (*Italian*)
Mrs E E Taylor (*Swedish*)
Mrs J Tucker-Hargreaves (*Dutch*)

Library Staff:
Head of Library: Mrs J A Lenferna de la Motte, BLibSc

Library Assistants:
Mrs P Kino, BA
Ms C Woodhouse, BA
Mrs S Birch, BA
Mrs S Heath, ALA
Mrs B Nash, BSc(Econ)

Bursar: J P Patrick
Administration Bursar: P Vaughan
Finance Bursar: Mrs J M Wilson
Headmaster's Secretary: Mrs H F McMillan

History, Site and Buildings. Founded in 1432, the School is one of the three oldest lay foundations in England. A variety of endowments and benefactions strengthened the School over the next few hundred years, but the first building of note was that designed by the Earl of Burlington in 1718. The 20th century has brought rapid expansion. Recent developments include a new Sixth Form Centre, International Centre, Dining Hall, Centres for Mathematics and Modern Languages and all weather running track. The School today occupies 95 wooded acres, alongside the 1,000 acres of Knole Park that look south over the Weald of Kent. The School's easy access to London (half-an-hour by train), Gatwick Airport (half-an-hour by car) and Heathrow Airport (one hour), and to the M20 and the Channel Tunnel and ports, has encouraged the development of the boarding element and of the School's valued international outlook.

General Ethos. Sevenoaks offers a uniquely balanced community providing an environment which will help boys and girls to be fully prepared for the needs of young adults in modern society. It is genuinely co-educational. We believe this is in the best interest of both boys and girls academically and socially. We are a large, mixed boarding and day school and welcome the advantages that this presents to both. Set in a beautiful campus-like environment at the top of the town and on the edge of Knole Park, we are continually searching for new ways of helping the young, both within the curriculum and in out-of-school activities. At the same time we run a rigorous games programme, competing with the top HMC schools in the south-east of England. Entry for day or boarding children is at 11+, 13+ or in the Sixth Form.

Structure of the School. The most important element in our day pupil system of pastoral care is the House Tutor Group. Tutors meet their charges every morning, watch over their academic and general well-being and are the School's main channel of communication with parents. There are seven boarding houses which cater for boys and girls at different points of entry. To ensure that every pupil receives the maximum possible help, direction and encouragement, there are also six Divisional Headmasters/Headmistresses (one in the Junior School, three in the Middle School and two in the Sixth Form) who keep in close touch with their boarding house staff and day house tutors and confer weekly with the Headmaster. Pastoral groups are single-sex in the Junior and Middle School, but the Sixth Form Day Houses are mixed, as are all teaching groups.

The School has its own Chaplain and Religious Studies Centre. Religious Studies is taught throughout the School and the "Church in the School" holds services in St. Nicholas' Church or Knole Chapel which are both close by.

The Junior School (11–13) has a wide range of amenities and activities designed to meet its special needs, but it is an integral, much valued part of the main school. To enrich the education given at this stage several non-academic subjects are studied to help develop interests, skills and talents which can then be further extended in subsequent years. Pupils have ready access to all the academic, sporting and creative facilities of the School.

Particular care is taken to foster good work habits in preparation for the Middle School, yet these two crucial years are passed in a friendly environment where pastoral care is highly developed and the opportunities for enjoying academic studies abound.

The separate Junior Boarding House, Lambardes, caters for some twenty eleven and twelve year old boys and girls.

The Junior School Society, known as the Young Sox, is enormously active, organising frequent trips to destinations at home and abroad, visits to London theatres, museums and so on, and a host of other activities. The recreation room, with its many absorbing games, acts as the social centre. The whole Junior School comes together twice a week for formal assemblies.

The Curriculum.

Junior School. At 11, about half the entry of 60 is male and half, female. Pupils take one of French, German or Spanish together with English, Maths, Latin, History/Geography, RS, Science, PSD, Music, Drama, Art, Pottery, Design Technology, Electronics, Computing and Physical Education.

Middle School. About 75 new pupils enter the school at 13, via Common Entrance, Scholarship or by transfer. There are seven Third Forms this year. All pupils take English, Maths, a modern language and all three sciences, plus various combinations chosen from History / Geography / Classical Civilisation / Latin / Greek / French / German / Spanish / Music / Art / Design / Drama / Computing / Electronics, to GCSE. Work in Mathematics, Sciences and most languages is in sets according to ability. Through the last two years the brighter students are challenged by wide programmes, while there is provision for the more average to be supported by a narrower range of key subjects up to GCSE.

Upper School. Nearly all pupils go into the Upper School. About 85 boys and girls join each year just for the Sixth Form to follow the broad programme of the International Baccalaureate. The Diploma programme requires pupils to study six subjects, three at Higher level with three at Standard level. The six subjects should include English, a modern language, a humanity, a science and Maths. The following courses are currently offered: English, French, Spanish, German, Russian, Mandarin, Japanese, Italian, History, Geography, Economics, Business and Organisation, Philosophy, Psychology, Information Technology in a Global Society, Classical Civilisation, Physics, Chemistry, Biology, Design, Electronics, Maths, Maths Studies, Maths Methods, Theatre Arts, Art, Latin and Greek. It may be possible for other subjects, particularly modern languages, to be taken by special arrangement. Students will also follow a course in Theory of Knowledge, participate in CAS (Creativity, Action and Service) and complete a 4,000-word Extended Essay in order to qualify for the International Baccalaureate Diploma.

Physical Education. For boys and girls, sport figures prominently in the life of the School. The PE department organises a varied programme and the school has a fixture list in the following games: Rugby, Cross Country, Association Football, Badminton, Cricket, Athletics, Squash, Tennis, Netball, Sailing, Hockey, Basketball, Shooting and Table Tennis. There are many other games and activities including: Swimming, Volleyball, Golf, Aerobics, Weight-training, Canoeing, Cycling, Gymnastics and Riding. The Marley Sports Centre provides excellent facilities indoors, whilst there are three covered tennis courts (in addition to nine outdoor courts) for coaching and playing all the year round. There is a 6-lane athletics track, an all-weather pitch and some sixteen pitches outdoors. There are five members of the PE Department who, together with many academic staff, are responsible for games. Both boys' and girls' teams have an unusually high number of competitive external fixtures.

The Johnson Library. Centrally located on the campus is the Johnson Hall housing the School Library. It is fully computerised with 18 networked computers offering CDs, a wide range of computer applications, E-mail, Internet and a catalogue of 32,000 books and other media. The library is open 12 hours a day Monday to Friday, and Saturday to 1600hrs. A mezzanine floor with 80 places offers pupils a quiet, supervised area in which to study. Author visits, book fairs and festivals are arranged throughout the year. A collection of antiquarian books in the Sennockian Library is available for research.

Music, Art, Workshop, TV, Drama. Provision is made for tuition in individual instruments. The Music School, the Art Rooms, and the Workshops are open out of school hours and many pupils regularly use them. The School has a television studio with CCTV and videotape recording facilities, which is used both for creative and for teaching purposes, and a Design Centre. The Sackville Theatre flourishes both as the Drama teaching centre and as a venue for school and professional productions.

The School runs a ten-day Summer Arts Festival at the end of the Summer Term. This has become an important cultural festival in the local community as well as being a stimulating experience for the pupils, whether as organisers, performers or audience members.

Information Technology. 250 PCs are on a Local Area Network spanning the School campus, allowing access to any of a number of fibre-optically linked Servers. WWW Internet, centralised CD-Rom interrogation, library information, World Wide E-mailing are available to all. Students have access to information systems which form an integral part of everyday use of IT across all areas of the curriculum.

Medical Arrangements. The School Medical Officer cares for boarders and they must be registered with him under the National Health Service. Each boarding house has a sick room and a House matron. The School Matrons are State Registered Nurses and, under the guidance of the School Medical Officer, are available for first aid and general advice for all pupils, day and boarding, in the Medical Centre.

Clubs and Societies. There are currently over 50 clubs and societies. Among these are: Aerobics, Amnesty International, Astronomy, Art, Badminton, Barber-shop, Basketball, Blues Band, Canoe, Chemistry, Chess, Choir, Christian Fellowship, Computer, Cross Country, Cultural Awareness, Dance, Debating, Films, Fives, Guitar, International Club, Maths Club, Model United Nations, Modern Languages, Orchestra, Photography, Poetry, Rock-climbing, Shooting, Sixth Form Film Society, Spanish, Swimming, Sub-Aqua Diving, Tennis, Theatre Technicians, Volleyball, Workshops, Young Sennockians.

Responsibility and Service. All pupils from the 4th year join either the Voluntary Service Unit or the Combined Cadet Force (Army, Navy, RAF sections). The Voluntary Service Unit was established in 1960 and now incorporates all the town's schools. The Unit hopes to give pupils an understanding of society by directly involving them – through practical service – with the elderly, physically and mentally handicapped and young people in care. The CCF places considerable emphasis on leadership training and expeditions.

The School was one of the original participants in the Duke of Edinburgh Award Scheme. It has a licence to operate the Scheme. Some 120 pupils are enrolled in the award.

International Outlook In 1962 Sevenoaks School pioneered an International Sixth Form House for Boys and in 1977 opened a sister Girls' International House. Fully integrated into the School, these Sixth Form houses offer the opportunity for our own pupils to mix with bright young people from different cultural backgrounds, to live and learn and grow up with them, and also for a controlled experiment in responsible self-government less easy to attempt in 'traditional' boarding houses.

The School gives great emphasis to exchanges, believing they are the key to successful language learning. There are long-established links with several European schools. After a short taster exchange in the Second Year with Ecole Saint Martin de France in Pontoise, the Third Year exchange is an integral part of the School's curriculum. Pupils who are in one of the two link classes take part in a three-week term-time exchange with either the Ecole Saint Martin or the Institut des Chartreux in Lyon. All other pupils either participate in a shorter term-time exchange or have a two-week holiday exchange with the Institut des Chartreux. The Fourth Year is reserved for German and Spanish exchanges with the Goethe Gymnasium in Ibbenbüren and Cerrado De Calderon in Malaga. There is also a Russian exchange with a school in Perm. Pupils who continue to study one or more languages in the Sixth Form are offered exchanges with our other partner schools in Hamburg, Lyon, Brussels and Zaragoza.

Careers. The School prides itself on the advice and guidance it offers to pupils about higher education and careers, not only when they are at the School, but after they leave, too. Each pupil has individual interviews, aptitude tests and group advice from the Fourth Year upwards. A work experience week is organised for Fifth Formers, along with a Careers Evening at which many careers are represented. In the Sixth Form each pupil has two individual interviews with the Careers Staff and there are several talks by the Careers Department to each year group on applying to higher education. Each Wednesday, speakers from a career area of a university visit the School to talk and advise. There is also extensive preparation for Oxbridge applications, and interview training for all Second Year Sixth is available.

Post Sevenoaks. In a year group of 210 pupils, 98% go on to a degree course, either immediately or, for a minority of 30%, after a 'gap' year. Over 40 pupils gain Oxbridge places each year. About 24% go on to university to read Science, Engineering or Medicine, 39% Social Science subjects, 5% languages, 20% humanities. The rest are admitted to a wide variety of other degree courses, some in the United States and other countries.

ADMISSIONS/ENTRY/FEES.

Entry. Normal entry ages are 11+, 13+ and 16+, into the First, Third and Sixth Forms, and a small number are admitted at the other levels. At 11, pupils are admitted on the basis of a competitive examination held in January, together with an interview and Headmaster's report. At 13, those in prep schools take the Independent Schools' Common Entrance Examination in June or, for others, our own Senior Entrance Examination. At 16, pupils are admitted into the Sixth Form on the strength of their GCSE results or equivalent overseas qualifications (a minimum of seven passes is required, of which at least three must be grade A), interview and Headteacher's report, or through the Scholarship examination. There are boarding and day places for boys and girls at all ages. All applications for entry should be addressed to the Registrar.

Fees. Boarders £15,219. Day Pupils £9,270 (including lunch). Fees for pupils entering directly into the Sixth Form are £16,482 and £10,533 respectively.

Scholarships (*see* Entrance Scholarship section) 2000: Up to FIFTY Awards available at 11+, 13+, Sixth Form. For:

1. Outstanding academic ability or promise either generally or in one subject:
2. Outstanding ability in Music (separate Awards available).
3. Outstanding ability in Art (separate Awards available at 13+ and Sixth Form only).
4. All round qualities of character. The Pipemakers' Scholarships, including a number at Sixth Form level, are awarded specifically for this.

Major Scholarships are normally to the value of one-half of the day fee, but may be augmented in case of need. Minor Scholarships are normally to the value of one-third of the day fee, but may be augmented in case of need.

Foundation Scholarships are normally to the value of 15% of day fees.

The Sixth Form Scholarship examinations are held in November each year, all others during the Lent Term.

Charitable status. Sevenoaks School is a Registered Charity, number 307923. Its aims and objectives are the education of school children.

Sherborne School

Sherborne Dorset DT9 3AP
Tel: (01935) 812249
Fax: (01935) 810422
e-mail: registrar@sherborne.org
website: http://www.sherborne.org

The origins of Sherborne School date back to the eighth century, when a tradition of education at Sherborne was begun by St Aldhelm. The School was linked with the Benedictine Abbey, the earliest known Master was Thomas Copeland in 1437. Edward VI refounded the School in 1550. The present School stands on land which once belonged to the Monastery. The Library, Chapel, and Headmaster's offices which adjoin the Abbey Church, are modifications of the original buildings of the Abbey.

Royal Arms of Edward VI: *Dieu et mon droit.*

Governors of the School:

Chairman: Sir John Weston, KCMG
Vice-Chairman: Professor R Hodder-Williams, MA, PhD

Ex-officio:
The Representative of Her Majesty's Lord Lieutenant for the County of Dorset, Captain Michael Fulford-Dobson, CVO, JP, RN
The Representative of The Bishop of Salisbury, The Rt Revd John Kirkham, MA, Bishop of Sherborne
The Vicar of Sherborne, The Revd Canon E J Woods, MA, FRSA

Co-optative:
C R J Eglington, Esq
H P Stewart, Esq, LLB, FCA
J A Watney, Esq
G E Gilchrist, Esq, MA, TD, FCIB
Sir John James, KCVO, CBE, FRICS
C C W Taylor, Esq, BPhil, MA
Mrs Dora Morton, BA
Lady Williams, MBBS, MRCP, DObst, RCOG, DCH
M Beaumont, Esq
J Vintcent, Esq
D Burgess, Esq

Bursar and Clerk to the Governors: Air Commodore J B Thorne, OBE

***Headmaster:* S F Eliot**, MA

Second Master: W A M Burn, MA

Senior Master: I R Elliott, MA

Director of Studies: D S Smart, MA, CMath, FIMA

Housemasters:
Abbey House: W J Murphy-O'Connor, MA (01935 812087)
Abbeylands: M A Weston, MA (01935 812082)
The Digby: A C Morgan, BSc, MSc (01935 812687)
The Green: G D Reynolds, MA (01935 810440)
Harper House: S Tremewan, BA, PhD (01935 812128)
Lyon House: P S Francis, MA (01935 812079)
School House: P J Watts, BSc (01935 813248)
Wallace House: S P H Haigh, MA (01935 813334)

Staff:

Revd C W M Aitken, BA (*Chaplain*)
R D Ambrose, MA, AFIMA (*Head of Mathematics*)
Mrs A J Barker, BA (*English as a Second Language*)
D G N Barker, MA, PhD (*Classics*)
R W Bool, BA (*Geography*)
G Brière-Edney, BSc (*Geography*
M J Brooke, MA (*Head of Classics*)
D C Bryson, BA (*Modern Languages*)
W A M Burn, MA (*Modern Languages*)
D B Cameron, MA (*Modern Languages*)
D P K Carling, MA (*English and Theology*)
P R Chillingworth, BA (*Head of Design Technology*)
S J Clayton, CertEd (*Physical Education*)
M J Cleaver, BA (*Classics*)
J I W Davies, ARCM (*Music*)
A M Davis, DipEd (*Mathematics*)
Fräulein U E Dedek (*Modern Languages*)
D J Dunning, BA (*Head of Theology*)
D S Edwards, BA (*Economics & Business Studies*)
I R Elliott, MA (*Chemistry*)
P C Ellis, BMus, GRNCM, ARCO (*Head of Music*)
P S Francis, MA (*History*)
R C F Gardner, BSc, PhD (*Head of Chemistry*)
R Gibson, MA (*Biology*)
M J Goold, MA (*Art*)
S P H Haigh, MA (*English*)
C G B Hamon, PhD, CChem, MRSC (*Chemistry*)
A M Hatch, BA (*Geography*)
D Hedison, BSc (*Head of Economics & Business Studies*)
B A M Henry, BSc, MSc, PhD (*Biology*)
B J Holiday, MA (*Head of English*)
Ms S Melvin, MA (*Economics & Business Studies*)
Miss K L Millar, BA (*Head of Geography*)
A D Millington, BSc (*Physics*)
J S Mitchell, BSc (*Physics*)
A C Morgan, BSc, MSc, FRSA (*Mathematics*)
W J Murphy-O'Connor, MA (*History*)
Miss E M A Newton, BA (*Theology*)
M D Nurton, DipEd (*Theology*)
A R Oates, BA, MLitt (*Modern Languages*)
M P O'Connor, BA (*English*)
J-M Pascal, DEA, PhD (*Modern Languages*)
R G Patterson, BLitt, BA (*English*)
M A Pryor, BSc (*Mathematics*)
G D Reynolds, MA (*History*)
Mrs K L Reynolds, LLB (*English*)
H W Ridgeway, MA, DPhil (*Head of History*)
D J Ridgway, BSc (*Head of Biology*)
P Riley, BSc (*Head of Physics*)
G T W Robinson, BA (*English, Head of Drama*)
P Rogerson, MA (*Classics, Head of Careers*)
J Salisbury, BEd (*Technology*)
D A Scott, BEd (*Head of Physical Education*)
S M Skinner, ARCM (*Music*)
D S Smart, MA, CMath, FIMA (*Mathematics*)
A J Stooke, BA (*Head of Art*)
J R Storey, BA (*Classics*)
P T Such, MA, PhD (*Head of Modern Languages*)
J A Thompson, BA (*Mathematics*)
S Tremewan, BA, PhD (*Classics*)
M F Wade, MA, PhD (*Mathematics*)
J J B Wadham, BSc, PhD (*Biology*)
R M Warren, BA (*History*)
D A Watson, BSc (*Chemistry*)
P J Watts, BSc (*Physics*)
M A Weston, MA (*Modern Languages*)
G A F Wilkinson, BA, BSc, FBIS, LTCL (*Music*)
J G Willetts, BA, CPhys, MInstP (*Physics*)

Director of ICT: A M S Masterson, CCNA, MCSE, BTec, MISM

Medical Officers:
S G F Cave, BSc, MB, ChB
G Miles, MA, MB (Cantab), BChir, DA, DRCOG

Sister: Mrs S E Hancock, RSCN

Headmaster's Secretary: Mrs F Mill-Irving (01935 812249)

Sports Centre Manager: M D Nurton, DipEd(PE) (01935 810459)

Sports and Uniform Shop: A Willows (01935 810506)

Registrar: M J Cleaver, BA (01935 810402). Fax: (01935 810422). E-mail: registrar@sherborne.org

Situation. The School lies in the attractive Abbey town of Sherborne. By train, Salisbury is forty minutes away, London and Heathrow two hours.

Organisation. There are about 490 boarders and 30 day boys accommodated in eight houses, all of which are within easy walking distance of the main school.

Admission. Entry is either at 13+ through the Common Entrance and Scholarship examinations or at 16+ after GCSE.

Parents, who would like to enter their sons for the School, or have any queries, should contact the Registrar.

Boys can be entered either for a particular House or placed on the general list.

Visits. Visits can be arranged at any time of the year by ringing the Headmaster's Secretary on (01935 812249).

Scholarships/Exhibitions. (*see* Entrance Scholarship section) Sherborne offers a wide range of scholarships and exhibitions, Academic (May), Music (February), Art and All-Rounder (March), and Early Promise (October). Candidates should be under 14 on 1 September in the year of entry. Further details of all these awards are available from the Registrar.

Sixth Form Entry. Places are available for boys who wish to join the Sixth Form for two years. Both the entrance and scholarship examinations take place in January. There are up to two full fees worth of scholarships offered annually. Also available, for good A level candidates, are the Arkwright Scholarship for Technology and the Walford Award for those who excel at rugby or cricket.

Curriculum. All pupils follow a broadly based curriculum for their first three years to GCSE. In the Sixth Form boys study at least three A levels and one AS level drawn from 27 A level and 30 AS courses, as well as some non-specialist courses designed to broaden the scope of their studies. Some of these courses are run jointly with Sherborne School for Girls.

Careers and Universities. The Careers Department has an enviable reputation. Boys experience work shadowing programmes in the fifth and lower sixth forms – these are followed by careers conventions, university visits, parents' forums and lessons in interview techniques. There is an encyclopaedic, fully computerised Careers' Room with regularly updated contacts with those at university and at work. The department has visited all universities and places of higher education. Virtually all leavers go on to university.

Pastoral Care. The boys in each house are in the care of a Housemaster and his wife, and a resident matron. The School Chaplain also plays a major role and will talk with a boy whenever required.

Tutor. Each boy has a personal Tutor who not only monitors his academic progress but provides a useful contact point.

Religion. Theology courses are designed for each academic year. There is a wide variety of weekday and weekend services, which are held in the School Chapel or in Sherborne Abbey. Holy Communion is celebrated every Sunday and on some weekdays, including a Friday night candlelit Eucharist service. Boys are prepared for confirmation by the School Chaplain.

Community Service. Boys take part in a busy programme aimed at encouraging a sense of responsibility towards the local community. Entertainment, fund-raising and assistance are organised for the elderly and handicapped in and around Sherborne.

Art. The Art School is well-known and highly regarded. The core disciplines are based around the study of fine art and architecture. Alongside these, there are extensive print-making facilities, photographic dark rooms and the opportunity for boys to work in computer-aided design, film and media studies, history of design and museum and heritage studies. The annual study tour to Europe or last year to New York allows all boys to appreciate culture in an international context. The Art School moves to a new site in September 2001 allowing it to expand further.

Music. There is a strong music tradition in the School – over 400 music lessons take place every week. There are two full orchestras, various chamber music groups, many different types of Jazz band, a brass group, a swing band, Chapel choir and a choral society. Many of these groups tour both home and abroad. Numerous concerts, recitals and musical productions are held throughout the year. Lunch time concerts take place every Friday. Regular subscription concerts are given by visiting professional musicians.

Drama. Drama productions of all kinds are a major feature of school life, from large scale musicals to classical drama, substantial modern works and fringe performances. The sophisticated technical resources of the Powell Theatre attract adventurous programmes from professional touring companies.

Information Technology. The main network links all academic departments, boarding houses, Library and the Careers room.

Sports. There are over fifty acres of sports fields, where, at any one time, seventeen various games or matches can take place. Other facilities include an astroturf pitch, twenty tennis courts, rugby fives courts and a shooting gallery. Within the School's sports centre there is a sports hall, a twenty-five metre swimming pool, a multigym and squash courts. A wide variety of sports and activities are offered including athletics, badminton, basketball, canoeing, cricket, cross-country, fencing, rugby fives, golf, hockey, riding, rugby, sailing, shooting, soccer, sub-aqua, swimming and tennis.

Societies and Activities. Numerous academic societies meet regularly throughout the term. Other activities and clubs take place on Wednesday afternoons and whenever time allows. They include: angling, astronomy, bridge, chess, computing, debating, fishing, instrument making, modelling, model railways, photography, typing, woodland management and a Young Enterprise company.

The Duke of Edinburgh's Award Scheme is well supported. Expeditions are organised to Scotland, the Lake District, Wales, Exmoor and Dartmoor. Boys also take part in the annual 'Ten Tors Challenge'.

Membership of the Combined Cadet Force is voluntary – however the Army, Navy and Royal Marine sections usually attract about 150 boys each year. A large number of trips and camps are arranged during the term time and the holidays.

Development Programme. The new Chemistry and Physics Centre was opened in Summer 2000. The Art and Technology departments are being extended and refurbished, and the present Chemistry and Physics laboratories converted into classrooms for other departments. A long-term permanent fundraising programme is in place.

Old Shirburnian Society. Secretary: Cdr R L Warren, Old Shirburnian Office, Sherborne School, Dorset DT9 3AP. Tel/Fax: 01935 810557. e-mail: OSS@sherborne.org

Girls' Schools. There is close liaison with the neighbouring girls' schools, which allows us to offer many of the real benefits of co-education with all the advantages of a single-sex secondary education. As well as the Joint Sixth Form academic courses with Sherborne School for Girls, drama, music and social activities are arranged throughout the year.

Fees. For the academic year 2000/2001, the termly fee is £5,450 for a boarder (£4,085 for a day boy).

Charitable status. Sherborne School is a Registered Charity, number 1081228 and Company Limited by Guarantee, Registered in England and Wales, number

4002575. Its aim and objectives are to supply a liberal education in accordance with the principles of the Church of England.

Shiplake College

Henley-on-Thames Oxon RG9 4BW.
Tel: 0118 940 2455
Fax: 0118 940 5204
website: shiplake.org.uk

The College was founded in 1959 and occupies the buildings and grounds of the historic Shiplake Court. The policy has always been to have small classes and to achieve the maximum results with a minimum of fuss.

Motto: *Exemplum docet.*

Governing Body:

Chairman: B N Gilson, CA(SA)

A J Adams
J B Bowcock, MA, FICE, FIMechE
N K Cook, BSc
J W R Goulding, MA
R C Lester
The Hon Sir William McAlpine, Bart
Lady Phillimore
R W Phillis, BA, FRSA, FRTS
T N Rosser, OBE, DFC
D Tanner
J P Turner, BSc, FCA
D S Williamson, BA

Bursar and Clerk to the Governors: T J Mansergh, MA (Cantab), FICE

***Headmaster:* N V Bevan**, MA (Balliol College, Oxford), CertEd (Cambridge)

Deputy Head: B P Edwards, MA, PGCE (Cambridge)

Director of Studies: R T Mannix, BSc (London), PGCE (Bath)

Senior Master/Director of Music: M L Woodcock, CertEd (Oxford)

Chaplain: The Revd R P Prance, BTh (Salisbury Wells)

Teaching Staff:
†C E Alcock, BA, PGCE (Reading)
J Blunsdon, BSc (Reading), PGCE (Cambridge)
†N J Brown, BA, PGCE (East Anglia)
G Cassells, BEng (Bradford)
†A R Cheadle, MA (Reading), BComm (Rand)
Mrs L G Cook, BA (OU), CertEd
P M Davey, BEd (London)
D G Dovaston, BSc, PGCE (Aston)
Miss L E Eccleston, MA, PGCE (Edinburgh)
M Edwards, BA (Southampton), PGCE (East Anglia), MBA (Reading)
Miss S K Ellis, BA (Durham), PGCE (Cambridge)
†P C J Gould, BEd (*Reading*)
Mrs C M Gray, BA (WSCAD), PGCE (Reading)
Mrs C M Healy, BA (Durham), PGCE (Cambridge)
P G Hose, BA Exeter)
A F J Hunt, BEd (S Australia)
D I S Jacklin, BSc, PGCE (Rand)
G S Lawson, BSc (Swansea), MSc, MPhil (Southampton), PGCE (OU)
A K Lewis, BHum (St Mary's), PGCE (West London)
L S McDonald, BA, PGCE (Oxford)
Miss S J McKenna, BEng (Bradford), PGCE (Worcester)
S J O'Brien, DipTchg, TTC (Auckland, NZ)
J R Seaton, CertEd (Bristol)
Mrs V J Smallman, BEd, CertEd (Nottingham), DIPSE, SEN LD, TCWWLLD (Reading)
R C Snellgrove, BSc, PhD (CNAA)
D C Stoker, BA (Coventry), ATD, PGDip (Birmingham)
P J F Webb, BA (OU), CertEd (Borough Road)
†G P Wells, BHum (London), PGCE (Loughborough)
D Wilson, MA, PGCE (Oxford)

Part-time Staff:
Mrs A M Sadler, PGCE (OU)
Mrs J A Smail, BA (London), PGCE (Oxford)
Mrs M P White, BA (Reading)

OVS Secretary: M L Woodcock, CertEd

Registrar: Mrs A M Lazur
School Medical Officer: Dr A J M Terris, MB, BS, MRCP
Sister: Miss W J Robinson, RGN, NDN
School Secretary: Mrs R S Jones
Music Secretary: Mrs C Jacklin
Careers Secretary: Mrs J K McCoy
Shop Manager: P Emerson

The College was founded in 1959 on the banks of the River Thames, 2½ miles upstream from Henley. The policy has always been to have small classes and to achieve the maximum results with a minimum of fuss.

Academic. In Year 9 a broad curriculum ensures that pupils lay strong foundations in a wide range of subjects and that they are able to make an informed selection of subjects for GCSE. Pupils normally sit a minimum of 8 GCSEs in Year 11.

In the Sixth Form pupils select up to four subjects, from a choice of fifteen, at AS Level. They may then continue with all four subjects. For a small group of pupils, not qualifying for AS courses, the College provides a programme of retake GCSEs and new GCSEs such as Business, Media and Sports Studies.

Games. All boys play Rugby football in the autumn term. In the spring term boys play Hockey or row, and in the summer term there is the choice of Cricket, Tennis, Rowing or Sailing. The school has 3 Boat Houses, 2 Squash Courts, a Swimming Pool, a Fitness Room, a Sports Studio, a .22 Shooting Range and regular access to Hockey Astroturfs. There are also some Soccer fixtures. There is a large Sports Hall. The girls enjoy a mixed programme of activities using nearly all of the sporting facilities available.

CCF. Most boys join the CCF for a minimum of 2 years. There are Navy, RAF and Army sections. The School was one of the first to join the Duke of Edinburgh's award scheme and about a third of the pupils take part on a voluntary basis.

Other activities. There are numerous activities in which pupils are expected to join. These include Music, Art and Pottery, Literature, Photography, Public Speaking, Young Enterprise, Computers, Sailing, Canoeing, Climbing and the School Newspaper. There are School Plays, Interhouse Debates, Concerts and a programme of cultural events in the Tithe Barn Theatre.

Religion. The School is Church of England. Pupils attend services in the Parish Church. The School Chaplain also co-ordinates the School's Personal and Social Education Programme.

Careers. There is an experienced Careers Adviser and particular attention is paid to the choice of University and career from Year 11 onwards. The School is a member of ISCO.

Developments. Over the past nine years the College has spent over five million pounds on building developments. Recently new accommodation has been provided for Business Studies, English, Geography, History, Learning Support, Media Studies and Modern Languages with additional provision of Information Technology. Boarding accommodation is also subject to a regular programme of refurbishment.

Houses. In a small school of just 280 boys and 6 girls there is strong house spirit with competitions organised for arts and games. On admission a pupil enters one of five houses. One is reserved for day boys, another is for weekly boarders, one for full boarders and two which offer a more flexible arrangement based on remaining at school for at least four weekends each term.

The girls have separate study facilities in a house which has weekly boarders. Each House is in a separate building with its own Housemaster and resident staff. The typical house will have 5 year groups of 12 pupils in each year (9-13). All meals are served in the Great Hall on a cafeteria system.

Admission. A prospectus and admission forms can be obtained from the Registrar. All entries are made through the Headmaster. Boys admitted between the ages of 13 and 14 normally qualify by taking the Common Entrance Examination. Pupils entering from the maintained sector sit Mathematics and English only. A small number of places are available for boys and girls to enter the Sixth Form.

All prospective entrants to Shiplake College are interviewed and full consideration is always given to those with learning difficulties but who have other talents which they can develop at school.

Scholarships are offered to outstanding sportsmen, artists or musicians at Year 9 level and in the Sixth Form for all academic subjects.

Fees. There is an inclusive fee of £4,800 per term for boarders and £3,238 for day-pupils. This covers all compulsory extras, such as laundry, books, visits, subscriptions to Boat Club, and most of the learning support provision.

Charitable status. Shiplake College is a Registered Charity, number 309651. It exists to provide education for children.

Shrewsbury School

Shrewsbury Shropshire SY3 7BA.
Tel: (01743) 280500 (Switchboard); 280525 (Headmaster); 280820 (Bursar); 280550 (Registrar)
Fax: (01743) 340048 (Headmaster); 243107 (Bursar); 351009 (Registrar)
e-mail: headmaster@shrewsbury.org.uk
website: www.shrewsbury.org.uk

Shrewsbury School was founded by King Edward VI in 1552 and augmented by Queen Elizabeth in 1571. In 1882 it moved from the centre of the town to its present site overlooking the town and the River Severn.

Motto: *Intus si recte, ne labora.*

Governing Body:

Chairman: Sir David Harrison, CBE, FEng

Professor P Goddard, FRS
His Honour Judge A S Booth, QC
R H M Tildesley
Cllr K Brennand
Cllr Mrs A M Woolland
M N Mitchell, MA, ACIS
N C F Barber, MA
Sir David Lees, FCA
J R G Wright, MA, DL
The Revd H St J S Corbett, MA
The Lady Davies
Sir David Barnes, CBE
W A J Pollock, FCA
A G A Hillman, ACA
A Haining
Mrs V Tuck, BA, MA, MIL

Headmaster: **J W R Goulding**, MA

Bursar and Clerk to the Governors: I P Somervaille, CBE

Assistant Masters:
[2]S F Adams, MA, MSc
A J Allott, MA
J C Armstrong, BA
R Auger, MA (*Director of Studies*)
J Balcombe, BSc
G M Barnes, BSc
[2]†M J Barratt, BA
S D Baxter, MA
†G St J F Bell, BA
A D Briggs, BSc, PhD
J R Burke, BSc
[2]P F Cann, MA, PhD
R E D Case, BA
M D H Clark, BA
M R Clarkson, BA
C W Conway, MA (*Senior Tutor & Head of Careers*)
[2]S H Cowper, MA
[2]P T C Cox, MA
[2]M J Cropper, MA
N P David, BSc
Miss L R Davies, BA
M D Dickson, BEd
A L M Dunn, MA
C J Etherington, BA
†P A Fanning, MA
†D R Field, MA
R E W B Field, MA (*Registrar*)
Miss E M A Finch, BSc
[2]T R Foulger, BSc, PhD
S A A Fox, BA
[2]J Godwin, MA, PhD
Mrs S L Hankin, BA
M H Hansen, BSc
A W Hayes, BSc
[2]S Hellier, BA
†S M Holroyd, BA
†M A C Humphreys, MA
†R N R Jenkins, OBE, MA
R J Kendall, BSc
†D Kirkby, BSc
M W Knox, BA
[2]I H W Lacey, MA
†P H Lapage, BA
M J Lascelles, BA
M E Ling, MA
A C Machacek, MPhys, DPhil
[2]C J Minns, MA, PhD
Mrs J E Morgan, BA
T S Morgan, BSc, PhD
[2]M M Morrogh, BA, PhD
†M A J Mostyn, BA, MA(Ed)
M A Orviss, MA
R Pagnamenta, BA, MEng
H R W Peach, BA
J C Peat, BA
R G Roscoe, MA
C M Samworth, BSc, PhD
W J D Sayer, MSc
[2]M Schutzer-Weissmann, MA
†M J Tonks, BA
[2]M Twells, MA
P R Vicars, MA
I J Walton, BSc
T D J Warburg, MA
A S M Went, BA
[2]T C Whitehead, BA
Rev G J Williams, MA (*Chaplain*)
J M Williams, BSc
G C Woods, MA (*Second Master*)

Houses and Housemasters:

School House: G StJ F Bell/S A A Fox
Rigg's Hall: M A J Mostyn
Ingram's Hall: M J Tonks
Moser's Hall: D R Field
Severn Hill: S M Holroyd
Churchill's Hall: P H Lapage
Oldham's Hall: R N R Jenkins
Ridgemount: M A C Humphreys
The Grove: P A Fanning
Porthill (*Day Boys*): M J Barratt
Radbrook (*Day Boys*): D Kirkby

Music:
[2]J F Moore, BA, LRAM (*Director*)
C Q Argent, MA, ARCO
D M Joyce, DipRCM, ARCM
Mrs D B Nightingale, MTD, LTCL

Art:
[2]P N Woolley, BA, MFA
Miss C M Pringle, BA

Craft and Design:
T Kidson, BEd;
[2]D Nickolaus, CertEd

Physical Education:
[2]P R Scales
A P Pridgeon

[2] denotes Head of Faculty

Visiting American Master: J C Dewis, AB (Harvard)

School Doctor: Dr P S Bennett, MA, MB, BCh (Cantab), MRCGP

Dental Adviser: R J Gatenby, BDS, DGDP, RCS

Number in School. There are 700 boys in the School (556 boarders and 144 day boys).

Admission to the School. Boys are admitted at 13, or (direct to the VIth Form) at 16. Most boys start in September. There are also a few admissions in January. Entrance Forms and other information can be obtained from the Headmaster or from the Registrar.

Entry at 13. Boys usually take the Common Entrance Examination in the term preceding that in which they wish to come, or the Scholarship Examination in May. The School has its own entrance test for boys who have not followed the Common Entrance syllabus.

Scholarships. (*see* Entrance Scholarship section) The Scholarships are inflation-linked. In 2001 the Governors expect to offer 4 Scholarships to the value of Half Fees, and the same number to the value of One-Third Fees.

In addition, they offer 2 Scholarships of Quarter Fees, 7 Exhibitions of at least £1,000, 4 Music Scholarships up to the value of half fees, and one Art Scholarship up to the value of one-quarter fees.

VIth Form Entry. Direct entry to the VIth Form depends on an interview and examination at Shrewsbury and a favourable report from a boy's present school. Entry at this age is intended principally for boys who have been educated at day schools and want 2 years' experience of boarding away from home before going on to a university. Scholarships worth half fees are available for outstanding candidates. There are also two Sixth Form Music Scholarships up to the value of half fees.

Buildings. Over the last few years a thorough refurbishment programme for all Houses has been carried out. A new building for Science and Information Technology opened at the end of May 1996. The School has a continuous programme of refurbishing academic facilities. A new Music School, including an auditorium and a large ensemble room, was opened in February 2001.

The Moser Library houses The School Library, the Moser collection of water-colours, and the Ancient Library. Its medieval manuscripts and early printed books make it one of the 3 or 4 really important scholarly libraries in the possession of a school: it is unique in possessing entire and exactly as it was, the original collection of books owned by the School in Stuart times.

Courses of Study. To avoid unduly early specialisation, all boys follow a general course as far as the GCSE level Examinations. In the VIth Form it is usual to study 3 subjects to 'A' level and one to AS level. The number of combinations of subjects for which it is possible to opt is very large. Key Skills and General Studies are included in the new curriculum from September 2000.

On the whole the School acts on the assumption that well-tried traditional methods of teaching work best. A full-time European Liaison Officer has been appointed to heighten awareness of Europe. There continues to be an increasing emphasis on Information Technology.

Games. Rowing, Cricket, Association Football, Swimming, Cross-country, Rugby and Eton Fives. The School has its own indoor Swimming Pool, Gymnasium, Multi-gym, Miniature Rifle Range, all-weather playing surface, Tennis Courts, Squash Courts and Fives Courts. The River Severn flows just below the Main Building and the Boat House is within the School grounds.

Activities. New boys are introduced to the history and surroundings of the School and are also offered the chance to try out a considerable range of new activities. They are provided with a variety of outdoor activities via either the Combined Cadet Force or a non-uniformed outdoor pursuits section. The programme of activities and opportunities continues to broaden as a boy moves up the School and includes The Duke of Edinburgh Award Scheme.

Art and Design. Art and Design are taught to all boys in their first year. For those not doing GCSE or A level courses they subsequently become activities followed mainly, but not exclusively, out of school hours. The Art and CDT centres are available 7 days a week. The CDT department offers the chance of advanced design work and of creative work in materials as diverse as silver and glass-fibre. 'A' and GCSE level design are also offered.

Societies. These range from Literary, Political, Debating, Drama and Language societies to those catering for practical skills like Printing, Electronics or Canoe-building. Hill-walkers and Mountaineers make use of the unspoilt country on the doorstep and of the Welsh hills. In addition to two major School productions, most Houses produce a play each year.

Music. Teaching is available in any orchestral instrument, as well as the Piano and Organ. The charge for this is £13.20 per lesson, £12.15 per lesson for second and subsequent instruments. Regular Choral, Orchestral and Chamber Concerts are given by the boys. In addition concerts are given during the winter months by distinguished visiting artists.

Field Study Centre. Shrewsbury owns a farmhouse in Snowdonia used at weekends throughout the year as a base for expeditions.

Careers. There is a full time Careers Master. All boys are offered the Morrisby Aptitude Tests and the services of the Independent Schools Careers Organization.

Social Service. In association with other schools in the town, boys play an active part in caring for the old and needy in the Shrewsbury area.

Shrewsbury House. Founded in Liverpool as a Club for boys in 1903, it was re-built as a Community Centre in association with the Local Authority and the Diocese in 1974. There is residential accommodation in the Centre and groups of boys from the School have the opportunity to go there on study courses.

School Charges. Fees are £5,325 per term. The fees include tuition, board and ordinary School expenses and there are no other obligatory extras, apart from stationery. The registration fee, which is non-returnable, is £20. Day Boy fees are £3,750 per term. Application for reduced fees may be made to the Governors through the Headmaster.

Old Boys' Society. Most boys leaving the school join the Old Salopian Club. Secretary: J P Lazarus, c/o The Cottage, 17 Ashton Road, Shrewsbury SY3 7AP.

Charitable status. Shrewsbury School is a Registered Charity, number 528413. It exists to provide secondary education.

Silcoates School

Wrenthorpe Wakefield WF2 0PD.
Tel: (01924) 291614
Fax: (01924) 368690/368693

Silcoates was founded in 1820 on its present site, 2 miles north-west of Wakefield. While retaining its links with the Church through the Governing Body and the provision of bursaries for children of ministers, the object of the school is to provide a broad education for boys and girls of all denominations and faiths.

Motto: *Clarior ex ignibus.*

Board of Governors:

Chairman: P B H Johnson, MA

Vice-Chairman: Dr M Beddow, MA, PhD

The Revd G M Adams, BA, MBA, CertEd
Professor J C G Binfield, OBE, MA
W J Bramley
J H Bryan, LLB
The Revd A G Burnham, BA
Dr P H Clarke
D J Figures, MA
The Revd T D Fletcher, JP, BA
R S Hanson
The Revd A Harrison, BA
B T Herbert, MA, LLB
The Revd Brenda L Hill, JP
Mrs A M Johnson, MA, ALA
J R Lane, LLB, AKC, TEP
P Lenton, JP
Dr J D Nelson
J E Payling, MA, FCA
P A Shipley
E V Willings, BChD
The Revd Mrs B Willis, MA, BEd

Staff:

***Headmaster:* A P Spillane**, BA (*English and Latin*)

Deputy Headmasters:
D A Curran, BSc (*Geography*)
S Fox, MA (*French, German and Latin*)

Head of Junior School: R H Wood, BEd, MA

Professional Development Co-ordinator: Miss H M Wren, BA, MA (*Religious Studies*)

Chaplain: *The Revd A J L Jones, MA, LTh, MRInstPhil (*Religious Studies*)

Assistant Staff:
*L B Brown, BTech (*ICT*)
Mrs L Burdekin, CertEd (*Junior Subjects*)
*R M Carey, BA (*English*)
Mrs K Clark, BSc (*Biology*)
J C Clewarth, BEd, MEd (*Deputy Head of Junior School*)
*D Coll, BEd (*Physical Education and Games*)
Mrs S Coll, BA (*Modern Languages and Latin*)
D B Coulson, BSc (*Biology*)
G L Cox, GTCL, LTCL (*Admin Co-ordinator, Housemaster of Spencer's House*)
Mrs R L Dews, BEng (*Mathematics, Examinations*)
Mrs L C Dinmore, ARCM, CertEd (*Music*)
R Elliston, BA (*English*)
R J Fenn, BEd (*Geography and English, Head of Third Form, Housemaster of Evans'*)
*R Greenwood, BEd (*Art*)
*R J Greenwood, BA, MA (*Economics*)
Mrs J Hall, BA (*Spanish and French*)
*N M Halsey, BA (*Design & Technology, Housemaster of Moore's*)
*A M Hammond, BA (*French and German*)
D O Hardy, LGSM (*Music*)
P L Harrison, BEd (*Design & Technology, Careers*)
Mrs M Hayes, DipAD, SIAD (*Art*)
T W Hilling-Smith, BA, MA (*Mathematics*)
M D Jeanes, BSc (*Mathematics*)
S J Knowles, BSc (*IT Co-ordinator*)
Mrs J M Le Grâs, CertEd, BEd, MA (*Junior Subjects*)
*D G Mann, BA (*Director of Music*)
Mrs K March, BEd (*Science & Physical Education*)
Ms C A Marsh, BEd (*Religious Studies, History & Geography*)
*T J Mills, BEd (*Head of First Form*)
*J M Newell, BSc, CPhys, MInstP (*Physics, Head of Science, Housemaster of Yonge's*)
Mrs J M Newell, BA (*English, History and Geography*)
Miss E L Nuttall, BA (*Physical Education & Games*)
S Ogden, BSc (*Physical Science*)
G E M Openshaw, BA (*English*)
*N Owen, BA (*Geography*)
Mrs S Parkin, BA (*Spanish & French*)
*Miss H M Peach, BA (*Physical Education and Games*)
R C Peacock, BSc (*Chemistry*)
J R L Piggott, BSc (*Junior Subjects*)
B G Pye, BEd (*Design & Technology, Head of Fourth & Fifth Forms*)
*D J Raggett, BSc (*Mathematics*)
*P A Richards, BSc (*Chemistry, Head of Sixth Form*)
Miss L C Roberts, BA (*Junior Subjects*)
T J Roberts, BA (*Drama and English*)
*Mrs B W Shaw, BA (*French and German*)
*L J Shears, MA (*History, Head of Second Form*)
Miss C Smith, BEd (*Junior Subjects and English*)
M N Surr, BA (*Economics & Business Studies*)
Mrs D J Townsend, BSc (*Mathematics, Senior Girls' Mistress*)
T Verinder, BA (*History*)
Miss G Walker, BSc (*Junior Subjects*)
N P Ward, BEng (*Physics*)
*P V Watkin, BSc (*Science*)
G Wetherop, BA (*Junior Subjects, Junior School Curriculum Co-ordinator*)

Bursar & Clerk to the Governors: D Dinmore, MBE, MCIPD, MIMgt
Outdoor Pursuits: J C France, PhD, BSc
Librarian: Mrs J D Spillane
Estates Manager: F Bradshaw
Finance Manager: A Gracie
Headmaster's Secretary: Mrs M I Butterfield, CertEd
Registrar: Mrs C Wade
School Secretary: Mrs L M Nutbrown
Bursar's Secretary: Mrs S E Beverley
Accounts Assistant: Mrs K B Cade
Accounts Secretary: Mrs J Raywood
Matron: Mrs L Cotterill, RGN
Computer Officer: J Wilson, BSc
Biology Technician: J C Nelmes
Chemistry Technician: Mrs L Denton
Physics Technician: N Cooke
Design Technician: D C Carr

Admission. There are 670 pupils in the school. Boys and girls are admitted to the Junior School at the age of 7, and further entries take place between 7 and 14. Places are available for girls and boys wishing to study for an 'A' level course in the Sixth Form. The School also provides a pre-preparatory education for boys and girls from 2 to 7 years, at Sunny Hill House School and St Hilda's School, Horbury, which also offers education for girls from 7 to 11.

Entry. Entrance Examinations take place in January for admission the following September.

Fees. Fees for 7 and 8 year old pupils £4,026 per year; 9-10 year old pupils £5,376 per year; 11-18 year old pupils £6,798 per year. These are inclusive and there are no extra payments except for private music lessons or personal expenses.

Curriculum. All pupils sit a minimum of 9 GCSEs and 4 A levels, and the vast majority go on to degree courses. A level subjects are Mathematics, Physics, Chemistry, Biology, History, Geography, Economics, Religious Studies, Spanish, PE, Business Studies, English Language, English Literature, French, German, Music, Art, Design and General Studies. The summer of 1991 saw the completion of a magnificent new building which houses Science, Design Technology, Information Technology, Mathematics, Careers Department, a Study Centre and the Library. All other academic departments have been relocated and improved.

Religion. Pupils are prepared by the School Chaplain for confirmation into all branches of the Christian Church.

Games and Activities. School games are Rugby Football, Hockey, Cross Country, Squash, Athletics, Cricket, Tennis, Netball, Badminton, Golf and Swimming. There are over 30 acres of playing fields. The School has a squash court, and an indoor swimming pool, and a nine-hole golf course. The Sports Hall is large enough for four badminton courts or indoor cricket and tennis practice. Every boy and girl is encouraged to learn to swim and to enter for the Amateur Swimming Association's Proficiency Examinations. The School Camp at Lake Windermere is used for outdoor activities and a full programme of training leading to the Duke of Edinburgh Awards is available.

The School possesses Junior and Senior Libraries. The Sixth Form Society offers cultural and social studies talks by visiting speakers. Parties of pupils regularly visit repertory theatres and art galleries throughout the north of England. Drama flourishes, with a variety of large-scale and small-scale productions each year.

Tuition in a wide variety of musical instruments is available in the Music School. Pupils are encouraged to perform in concerts, in choirs, instrumental groups, and in the School Wind Band. Over two hundred instrument lessons are taught each week.

Pastoral Care. Girls and boys between ages of 7 and 11 are under the supervision of the Head of the Junior School and his assistants. From the age of 11 pupils are allocated to one of the Senior Houses and each member of the academic staff is assigned a position of responsibility in one of these Houses. In addition, pupils between 11 and 16 are assigned to a Tutor, who supervises their academic progress and general welfare. Sixth Formers choose a member of staff to act as their Tutor who gives advice on choice of university courses or professional careers. Careers guidance is provided by the Careers staff and a well equipped Careers Room is available for reference. All pupils are offered the services of the Independent Schools' Careers Organisation; an extensive programme of work experience is organised for Lower Sixth Formers. Community Service is encouraged in the Sixth Form.

Entrance Scholarships. (*see* Entrance Scholarship section) Substantial bursaries are available for the sons and daughters of Ministers and Missionaries of the United Reformed Church or of the Congregational Church, and of other recognised Christian denominations. Academic and Music Scholarships are offered at 11+ and above; Sixth Form entrants are eligible for these awards.

Charitable status. Silcoates School is a Registered Charity, number 529281. It aims to provide a first class education for boys and girls.

Solihull School

Solihull West Midlands B91 3DJ
Tel: 0121-705 0958 (Headmaster); 0121-705 4273 (Admissions); 0121-705 0883 (Bursar)

The School was founded in 1560, with income from the Chantry Chapels of Solihull Parish Church.

Motto: *Perseverantia.*

Chairman of the Governors: Air Vice-Marshal J W Price, CBE, DL

Bursar and Clerk to the Governors: B H Bartlett

***Headmaster:* J A Claughton**, MA, Merton College Oxford

Second Master: P J Griffiths, MA

Senior Master: R J Melling, BSc

Master of the Middle School: M Goatham, BA

Master of the Lower School: R J Willshire, MA

Master of the Junior School: A Brindley, BSc, MA

Director of Studies: B D W Chacksfield, MA

Assistant Masters:

M K Ayers, MA
D M Harding, BSc, BA
B L Thomas, BA, MEd
Revd N A Cluley, BA (*Careers Master*)
P T Holt, MA
D R Miller
M H Dodgeon, MLitt, BA
J Lloyd, BSc
B Wormald, BSc
B Blessed, BSc
L C Garrett, BSc
M K Swain, BA
R M Melhuish, LLB
M R Brough, BA, MPhil
Mrs M A Barrett, BA, MEd
A Dunn, MA
B J Keylock, BA
J J Nickson, MA
H J Thomas
J C Loynton, BEd, MA
P D Brattle, BSc
P J Irving, BA, ARCM, FRCO
D R Aldis, MA
J Troth, PhD, BSc
Mrs C D L Davies
G A Ginns, BEd
J H Belcher
L A Benge, BA, BEd
C H Jones, BEd
Mrs L M Fair, BA
R V Smith, BSc
Mrs S Wolffe, CAP, BA, MIL, MSc
M J Covill, BSc
D M Rowson, PhD
Mrs R A Barralet, BA
S A Morgan, BA
D M Phillips, BA
J McGowan, MA
Mrs A C Roll, BA
Mrs H Sinclair, AGSM, ATC
G P Reddington, BA
M J Garner, BSc
N W S Leonard, BEd
D Reardon, BSc
H Moore, MA
Revd A C Hutchinson, BA, MEd
Mrs L J Brough, BA
Miss D H Weston, BSc
Miss P J Davies, GBSM
P Jackson, BSc
S A Hart, BA
S D E Bromley, BA
Mrs U Mynette
Miss S Heyes, BA
Mrs B Belcher
J N J Roberts, BA
Mrs C Steele, BEd
Miss L J Standley, BA
M P Babb, BSc
A Byrom, BEng
Miss L M Carter, BSc
Miss J C Frampton, BA
Miss L M Moore, BMus
N A Weedon, BEd
S J Perrins, MA
L Bradley, DipAD
M Allen, BEd
D A O'Neil, BA
T P Edge, BA
Mrs J Warlsnck, BA
P D Hall-Paliner, BA
Mrs C Topping, MSc
A Wild, BSc
Mrs G Byrom, BSc
P Delaney, BA
P Gunning, BA
Mrs R Hadley, BEd
M Worrall, BA

Director of Music: S J Perrins, MA, FRCO

Director of Art: L Bradley, DipAD

Director of Physical Education: S A Morgan, BA (Loughborough)

CCF: Lieut Colonel D R Miller

SSI & RQMS: I N Swift

Medical Officer: Dr P J Travis, MB, ChB, DRCOG, MRCGP

School Matron: Mrs E Haynes, RGN

Headmaster's Secretary: Mrs K Roberts, BA

Admissions Secretary: Miss B H Burton

Bursar's Secretary: Mrs S Pheasey, MA

Librarian: Miss A M Vaughan, BA

General. Solihull is an Independent Day School, represented on the Headmasters' Conference and the Governing Bodies' Association. The School is of Church of England foundation, but there is no religious bar to admission. Chapel services are held each day and, for pupils, their families and friends, on Sundays during term. There is a strong choral tradition.

Situation. The School stands in 50 acres of grounds in the centre of Solihull. It fronts the Warwick Road and is within a mile of the M42 (Junction 5). There is easy access by road and rail. The School has a further 12 acres of playing fields one and a half miles away.

Buildings. School House is the original victorian building erected when the school moved to its present site in 1882. Since then the centre of the school has moved to the buildings around the quadrangle and this will be greatly enhanced in 2001 by the conversion of the present Big School into a modern high tech library with large computer rooms attached. This is made possible by the building of a new Big School which will also provide modern facilities for drama and school concerts as well as accommodate the whole school for assemblies. This multi-million pound development continues the tradition of the last decade which has seen the modernisation of the Science block and School House, the building of extra laboratories, a modern languages wing, an astroturf and three squash courts and the extension and refurbishment of the Design and Technology Centre. Art has moved to new accommodation and the Junior School has new buildings.

General Organisation. The number of boys in the School is roughly 870, and there are 70 girls in the VIth Form. The School is divided into the Junior School (for boys under 11), the Lower School (for boys aged 12 and 13), the Middle School (for boys of 14 and 15) and the Upper School (for boys over 15 and VIth Form girls). Each division is to an extent self-contained within the general body of the School. There are Houses (with Upper, Middle, Lower and Junior divisions) for games and other corporate activities.

Admissions. The limits of school age are normally 7 and 19 years. School Entrance Examinations are held for boys aged 11 and 13 in January, and for those aged 7, 8, 9 and 10 in March, for entry in the following September, which is the ruling date for the above ages. English and Arithmetic are the only compulsory subjects up to age 11. Boys over 13 are also admitted on the results of the Common Entrance Examination. Latin is not compulsory at this age. Further details are available from the Admissions Secretary.

Fees. Tuition: £1,845 per term (£1,430 per term for boys aged 7-10). Lunch charges: £1.60 per day Junior and Lower Schools, £1.90 per day Middle and Upper Schools. There are few obligatory extras.

Curriculum. Our aim is to provide a broadly based programme, following the main aspects of the national curriculum; and to offer a suitable range of public examinations, which will lay firm foundations for the degree courses to which nearly all leavers proceed.

In the Junior School particular emphasis is placed on establishing good standards in the core subjects – and there are specialist areas for Art, Design and Technology and Music. In the Lower School, all pupils have at least one year of Latin. German and Spanish are option subjects. French, Maths, English, Physics, Biology and Chemistry remain compulsory to GCSE – and three other subjects are chosen, from a good range of options, to supplement these. A minimum of six passes at GCSE is required for entry to Sixth Form courses, which consist of four subjects at AS level and an enrichment programme. We attempt to cater for all combinations of A levels, which include Art, Biology, Business Studies, Chemistry, Classical Civilisation, Design, English, Economics, French, Geography, German, History, Latin, Mathematics (and Further Mathematics), Music, Psychology, Physics, Religious Studies and Spanish. All these subjects can be taken to A level, plus Sports Science, Theatre Studies, Information Technology, Photography at AS level.

Religious Studies, Education for Citizenship and Information Technology are also important aspects of the programme.

Games are considered an integral part of the School curriculum, and all pupils up to and including the Upper VIth are required to take part unless debarred on medical grounds. The principal games, which are organised on the House and Set system, are Cricket, Rugby Football and Hockey. Subsidiary sports are Basket-ball, Squash, Swimming, Athletics, Shooting, Tennis, Badminton and Sailing. All boys in the Middle, Lower and Junior Schools have Physical Education as part of their normal school routine. Four of the Masters are trained PE Instructors. Sixth Form girls have their own games arrangements with a full programme of fixtures against local schools.

CCF. Boys of 14 and over are eligible. Membership is not compulsory and no boy need serve for more than 9 terms. Girls may also join the unit. The contingent includes Army and Air Force Sections. Shooting is organised by the CCF and there is an indoor Rifle Range on the premises.

An adventure organisation, known as Terriers, exists for younger boys.

Out-of-School Activities. These include Choral, Orchestral, Debating, Dramatic, Literary, Geographic, Photographic and Scientific Societies, a Chess club, etc. These are open to pupils of all ages. The School has its own fully equipped Mountain Centre in Snowdonia and Sailing facilities in Solihull itself. The School also participates in the Duke of Edinburgh Award Scheme.

Scholarships. (*see* Entrance Scholarship section) A number of Free Places covering full Tuition Fees, and other Scholarships, are available each year. Most of these awards will be to boys between the ages of 11 and 12 and will be available equally to outside candidates and to boys already in the School. A small number will be awarded to boys taking the entrance examinations at 13. Two of the awards available for boys between 11 and 13 will be reserved for those who show special promise in Music. Up to date details are available in the year of admission.

The P R Ansell Mathematics and Science Scholarship, covering the full cost of tuition, and the Old Silhillians' Bushell Scholarship, are competed for annually for entry to the VIth Form. Sixth Form Scholarships are also available for Music, Art and Design.

Assisted Places. The School has its own Assisted Places Scheme. 14 places are available at 11+ and 2 at 13+.

Admission to the Sixth Form. Girls and boys are admitted to the VIth Form at the age of 16 for the 2-year course leading to GCE at 'A' level. Selection is by interview and Head's report and is conditional on GCSE results gained before admission.

Careers Advice. The School is a member of the Independent Schools Careers Organisation, through which each boy in his GCSE year takes a series of career aptitude tests. In addition, computer software may be used by any pupil seeking advice. Other facilities available include work experience courses, careers talks and a careers evening.

Honours. An average of thirteen places at Oxford and Cambridge and over 100 places at other universities per year, including Academic, Choral and Instrumental awards.

Old Silhillians Association. *Secretary:* A J Richardson, Memorial Clubhouse, Warwick Road, Knowle, Solihull. The aim of the Old Silhillians is to support and maintain links with the School. They also have their own clubhouse and extensive sports facilities.

Charitable status. Solihull School is a Registered Charity, number 529056. It exists to provide high-quality education for pupils between 7 and 18 years old.

* Head of Department	§ Part Time or Visiting
† Housemaster/Housemistress	¶ Old Pupil
‡ See below list of staff for meaning	

Stamford School

Stamford Lincolnshire PE9 2BS.
Tel: (01780) 750300
Fax: (01780) 750336
e-mail: headss@stamfordschool.lincs.sch.uk

Founded by William Radcliffe, of Stamford, 1532.
Motto: *Christe me spede*

Chairman of the Governing Body: M E Llowarch, Esq, FCA

Vice-Chairman: Air Vice Marshal P Dodworth, CB, OBE, AFC, BSc

***Principal of the Stamford Endowed Schools:* Dr P R Mason,** BSc, PhD, FRSA

***Vice-Principal and Head:* P T Fraser,** MA

Director of Studies: J Crampin, MA, MBA

Senior Teacher: W C Chadwick, MA
Head of Sixth Form: R D A Haynes, BEd
Head of Middle School: J W Dawson, MA
Head of Lower School: M R Barton, DLC
Head of Preps: P P Wiggin, BSc, MSc
Marketing Co-ordinator: A Gombault, MA
Chaplain: The Revd M R Ruff, BD, AKC
Director of ICT: N A Faux, MA

Assistant Staff:
G Woolf, BA
G T Earl, BSc
A G Summers, MA
S Walker, DLC, MDAS, CGLI
J R Speak, MA, MSc
B J Mailley, BA
G E Morgan, BA
K J Chapman, BEd
E J Holt, BSc
G Froggett, BA
M G Sawyer, BSc, CBiol, MIBiol
C V Killgren, BA
D Lennie, BA
D F Williams, CertEd
R J B Henry, BEd
L H Phillips, BEd
N S Taylor, BA
J P Hodgson, BSc (*Boarding Housemaster, Byard House*)
J M Livingstone, BA
P G Raymond, BA
M J Blissett, BA
M C Caseley, MA
A J McGarry, BA, MA
G P Brown, MA
J M Backhouse, BEd
Mrs V C Lacey, BA
J E Culley, BA
G Mitchell, BSc
S O'Grady, MA, BSc
J A Lyons, BEd
Miss V A M Rainforth, BSc
A R Wilkes, MA, BD
S J Mills, MA (*Boarding Housemaster, Brown House*)
G A Bucknell, BSc
K J Mills, BA
R A Brewster, BSc
Miss C A Legard, BA
D Johnston, BA
A N Pike, BA
N J Porteus, BSc, MIBiol, CBiol
Mrs J E Lloyd, BA
N C Crawley, CertEd
Dr R G Gosling, BSc, PhD
Miss L Tankaria-Clifford, BA
Mrs A J M Holland, BA
Dr I G Young, BSc, PhD
D J Laventure, BA
Mrs H L Nutting, CertEd
Mrs C Walklin, DipEd
Miss C Witham
A Satherley

Part-time teaching staff:
Dr J C Dodd, BA, PhD
Mrs H M Chew, BA
Mrs N A Cliffe, BSc
Mrs S M Fisher, CertEd
Mrs J C Fox, BA
Mrs C A Robertson, MA
Mrs M Rigg, BSc
Mrs I Roberts, MASc
Mrs D E Watson, BA
Mrs C Nolan, BA
P J Stevens, BSc

Director of Music for the Stamford Endowed School: P J White, MA, MEd, LMusTCL
Band Master for the Stamford Endowed Schools: D J Walker, RMSM
Head of Strings: D Leetch, GRSM, LRAM
Director of Chapel Music: D L Brown, BMus, ARCO, LRAM

Visiting Music Staff:

Violin:
Mrs S Thomas, GTCL, LTCL
Mrs E Anderton-Taylor, BA
Cello:
Mrs R Hardy, GRSM, ARMCM
Mrs K Bentley, GTCL, LTCL
Guitar: C Bell, LRAM, ARCM
Electric Guitar: N Gray
Clarinet: Mrs H J Brown, BA
Saxophone: P Casson
Flute: Mrs L Price
Oboe: G Brown, BMus
Bassoon: Mrs A McCrae
Piano:
J W Dobson, ARCM
Mrs L Williamson
Mrs M Maclennan, LRAM, ARCM
A Hone, BMus, ARCM, ARCO
P D Burnham
Organ: M Duthie, BSc, ARCO
Percussion: A Burgoyne
Trombone: S Tate-Lovery, BA
Singing: Mrs M Bennett, LRAM, LTCL
Kit Drum: S Andrew
Double Bass: Mrs K Bentley, GTCL, LTCL

Medical Officer: C S Mann, MB, ChB, BSc

Introduction. Stamford School is one of three schools within the overall Stamford Endowed Schools Educational Charity, along with Stamford High School (girls) and Stamford Junior School, the co-educational Junior School.

Buildings and Grounds. Stamford School dates its foundation to 1532. The grounds include the site of the Hall occupied by secessionists from Brasenose Hall, Oxford, in the early 14th century. The oldest surviving building is the School Chapel, which was formerly part of St Paul's Church, but which from 1532 until restoration in 1929 was used as a schoolroom. Extensive additions to the School continued to be made throughout the nineteenth and twentieth centuries. In 1956 the Old Stamfordians gave the School a swimming pool as a war memorial. The science school was built in 1957 and extended in 1973 when a new dining hall and kitchens came into use. A music school was built in 1977 and extended in 1984. A further extensive development programme was begun in 1980 and included the building of one new senior boarding house (Browne), opened in 1981, and extensive and comparable provision in the other (Byard). School House was converted principally into a sixth form teaching centre. In the autumn of 1983 a mathematics and computer centre was completed, as were additional project rooms and laboratories in the science school. The new art and design centre came into use in 1987 and the library was refurbished in 1998. Reorganisation in 2000 resulted in new classrooms and the development of an administration centre.

School Structure, Admissions and Curriculum. The school consists of around 700 boys divided into Lower School (11–14), Middle School (14-16) and Sixth Form. The Heads of each section, with their assistants and Form Tutors monitor the academic progress of each boy and manage the pastoral arrangements. Entry to the school is at 11 but boys are considered at any age. A number join at age 13 or directly into the sixth form.

The National Curriculum is broadly followed but much more is added to the curriculum to make it stimulating and rewarding. Information Technology, Art & Design and

Design Technology form an integral part of the curriculum and from Year 8 boys may begin German or Russian. All boys are prepared for a complete range of GCSE examination; the great majority of them continue into the sixth form and then onto higher education.

In the sixth form of about 200 students the time-table is so arranged that a wide range of combinations of subjects is possible. In partnership with Stamford High School all sixth form students can choose from the full range of subjects available across the two schools, which allows a total of 28 subjects to be offered.

Activities. Art, Music, Drama, Games and Physical Education form part of the normal curriculum. There is a choral society, an orchestra, a band and a jazz band, and a robed chapel choir. The musical activities of the school are combined with those of its sister school, the Stamford High School for Girls under the overall responsibility of the Director of Music for the Endowed Schools. The school maintains RN, Army and RAF sections of the CCF and there is a rifle club. A large number of boys are engaged at all levels of the Duke of Edinburgh's Award Scheme.

The school plays rugby football, hockey, cricket, tennis, golf. The athletics and swimming sports and matches are held in the summer term. In winter there is also badminton, cross-country running and basketball. Four squash courts were built in 1973. A full-sized astroturf hockey pitch suitable for most sports was opened in 1983 and a new sports hall in 1985. There are many school clubs and societies.

Close links are maintained with the local community. The school welcomes performances in the hall by the music societies of the town and uses the excellent local theatre in Stamford Arts Centre for some of its plays.

Careers. The school is a member of ISCO and has a team of careers staff headed by Mr A Gombault. There is an extensive new careers library, computer room and interview rooms.

House Structure and Activities. Boarding:
Byard House (11-14) Mr J P Hodgson
Browne House (15-18) Mr S J Mills

Competition in games, music and other activities are organised within a day house system. Day housemasters with their assistants monitor boys' commitments to the wider curriculum and act as counsellors when boys need to turn to someone outside the formal pastoral and disciplinary system.

Admission. The main point of entry is at age 11. Application forms for admission may be obtained from the school office. The school's entrance examinations take place late January, but arrangements may be made to test applicants at other times. Entry into the sixth form is considered at any time. Boys who are making good progress in the Junior School move on to Stamford School at age 11 without having to take further entrance tests.

Fees (September 2000). Registration Fee £50. Acceptance Fee £250.

Tuition Fee: £1,944 per term. Boarding Fee: (including tuition) £3,768 per term.

These fees include stationery, text books and games. School lunches for day boys are at additional charge.

Scholarships. (*see* Entrance Scholarship section) There are foundation awards on entry at age 11 and up to four awards into the sixth form. These can be for art or music as well as for academic work.

Charitable status. As part of the Stamford Endowed Schools, Stamford School is a Registered Charity, number 527618. It exists to provide education for boys.

Stockport Grammar School

Buxton Road Stockport Cheshire SK2 7AF.
Tel: 0161-456 9000 Senior School
0161-419 2404 Headmaster's Secretary
0161-419 2401 Bursar
0161-419 2405 Junior School
Fax: 0161-419 2407
e-mail: sgs@stockportgrammar.co.uk

Stockport Grammar School, founded in 1487 by Sir Edmond Shaa, has been in continuous existence since then under the patronage of the Worshipful Company of Goldsmiths. The school has been co-educational since 1980.

Stockport Grammar School's examination results are consistently among the best in the country.

The present buildings reflect the Governors' primary concern to provide the best modern facilities required for a large day coeducational community. The school's long term plan ensures that these facilities are continually improved and extended.

Motto: *Vincit qui patitur.*

Patron: The Prime Warden of the Worshipful Company of Goldsmiths

Governing Body:
C E Speight, FCA, ATII (*Chairman*)
M J Garner, BSc, FRICS, ACIArb (*Vice-Chairman*)

R H Astles
Mrs C H Beatson, MA
J C P Blunden-Ellis, BSc, MSc (*The Alan Sykes Trust*)
P A Cuddy, BA, FIMgt, FIPD
E D Foulkes, LLB
N G Henshall, MA (*Teaching Staff*)
P M Kershaw, ASLTC, JP
R J Griffiths, BA, JP (*Old Stopfordians' Association*)
Dr N L Reeve, BSc, MB, ChB (*University of Manchester*)
R L E Rimmington, BA, FCA
Mrs A Mack (*Ephraim Hallam Educational Foundation*)
B Tomlinson, FCA
R P Yates
The Worshipful The Mayor of Stockport
Dr E M Morris

Clerk to the Governors and Bursar: J H Leay, BA

***Headmaster:* I Mellor**, MA (Sidney Sussex College, Cambridge)

Deputy Headteacher and Proctor: J P Ashcroft, BSc, MA

Deputy Headteacher and Director of Studies: Mrs M Harris, MA

School Chaplain: Revd E Leaver, MA

Assistant Masters and Mistresses:

G J Affleck, BA
*Mrs A H Armitage, BA
Mrs C A Beckett, DipAD
Mrs S L Belshaw, BA
*J P Bird, BA
Mrs M A Blackburn, BSc, FRGS (*Head of Upper School*)
*J Boulding, BSc
Mrs S J Braude, BA
A Brett, BA
Mrs H K Bridges, BSc, MIBiol
I H Bruce, BSc
A B Cheslett, BSc, MSc
Mrs C E Condliffe, GRSM, ARMCM
Miss G A Cope, BA
M J Cowling, BSc, PhD
S R Cross, BA
Mrs S Farrar, BA
Mrs A M Fitton, BSc
Mrs F S Forbes, BA
Miss B Garnier, MSc, BSc
Mrs K L Garrett, BSc
Mrs V E Garrett, BA
*P L Giblin, MA, MEd
P J Grant, BSc
A T Gregg, BSc (*Head of Middle School*)
A S Hanson, BEd

Mrs D L Harris, BSc
Miss R E Haskins, BA
*A C Heath, BSc
*S E Helm, DipAD
Miss K Hickey, BA
Mrs A C Hicks, BA, FRGS
Miss M E Higgins, BSc
Mrs D Hill, BA
Mrs M S Hirst, MA
K A Hollin, BSc, MSc, PhD (*Careers*)
*R Howarth, BA
*D W Howson, MA
Miss C R Hughes, BSc
Miss H M Johnson, BSc
Mrs R G Johnson, BA, MA (*Careers*)
Mrs H Jones, BA
Mrs G J Kelly, BA
Mrs H F Kennedy, GNSM, ARCM, LRAM
W Krywonos, MSc, PhD
Mrs L Lammas, BA
Ms H R Lawson, MA
Mrs G M Lockwood, MA
Mrs C L Marshall, BSc
D S Martin, MA, FRGS
*S M Massey, BEd
Miss E A Mellor, MA
N P Mellor, BA, MA
J R Metivier, BSc, PhD
*D M Mort, MA
P T Moylan, BA
*Mrs C S Muscutt, BA
Miss N Otte, BA
Miss K Owen, BA
T E Palfreyman, BA, MA
Mrs L S Pearson, BA
S E Pettigrew, BSc
Miss C E Pye, BSc
Miss F Rankin, BSc
Miss G I A Shaw, BA
*D Short, BSc, MEd
*S J D Smith, BA, PhD
Mrs M Swift, BSc
A C Thorley, BA
Miss J Thornton, BA
P A Urwin, BA
P Walker
R W Wallington, BSc (*Head of Lower School*)
Mrs J White, BA
Mrs K Wilkinson, BA
Miss L Williams, BA
Miss S Withington, BEd
*C J Wright, BA
R Young, BEd

Director of Music and Organist: *J J Towers, BA

Development Director: Mrs C Henstock

Systems Manager: P Roebuck, BSc

Librarian: Mr R Turner, BA, DipLib, ALA

Headmaster's Secretary: Mrs J E Baker

Junior School Staff:
Headmaster: L Fairclough, BA
Deputy Head: Mrs G Taylor, BEd

Assistant Masters and Mistresses:
Miss L Booth, BA
Mrs H C Carroll, BEd
G Clayton, BSc
Mrs R J Cole, BA
Ms M T Fagan, BEd
Mrs C A Hampson, BA
Mrs A L Hardy, BEd
Mrs C M Haworth, CertEd
D E Jones, BEd
Mrs J L Lowe, CertEd
D J Makinson
Mrs P Martin, BEd
Miss J K Meek
Mrs J Mercer, BA
S Meredith, BA
Mrs K V Roberts, BEd
Mrs R P S Scott, BA
Mrs H Shanks, CertEd
Mrs A Smith, BEd
Mrs J M Swales, BA
Mrs V L Thomas, BSc
Mrs L J Turner, BEd

Stockport Grammar School aims to provide the best all-round education to enable boys and girls to fulfil their potential in a friendly and supportive atmosphere. The backbone of the school is academic excellence, with a clear framework of discipline within which every activity is pursued to the highest levels. With over 1,450 pupils between 4 and 18 years, including over 400 in the Junior School and 280 in the Sixth Form, entry is at 4, 7, 11 and 16. At age 11, there are six classes of 25 divided evenly between boys and girls.

THE SENIOR SCHOOL. Boys and girls are admitted at the age of eleven by competitive Entrance Examination. This is held in late January or early February, for admission in the following September. Open mornings are held on Saturdays in November and January. Occasional vacancies are considered on an individual basis and a few places are available in the Sixth Form each year. Visitors are always welcome to make an appointment to see the school.

Curriculum. The emphasis is on how to learn. The GCSE philosophies are introduced in the first three years as part of a broad general education. The sciences are taught as separate subjects and all pupils study Latin, French and German. Extensive use of visual aids and modern techniques has not altered the emphasis on secure and sound academic rigour which is at the heart of the academic tradition. Much importance is placed on homework. On entering the fourth year, at the age of 14, pupils retain a core of subjects but also make choices, so that the particular aptitude of each can be developed to the full. GCSE examinations are taken in the fifth year; the percentage pass rate has not been less than 97%. In 2000 it was over 98% with 65% of entries gaining an A* or A grade. On entering the Sixth Form, at the age of 16, pupils take four AS Advanced Level courses. The pass rate at Advanced Level was 97% in 2000, with 67% of all entries gaining the top two grades, with an average of over 23 UCAS points per candidate. The School has a good record of success in the entrance examinations and all Sixth Form pupils proceed to Honours degree courses.

Art. A high standard is set and achieved. There are facilities for all aspects of two-dimensional work and textiles, plus a fully equipped ceramics area and a sculpture court. There are regular exhibitions in the School's Brooke Gallery.

Music. The curriculum provides a well-structured musical education for the first three years. GCSE and Advanced Level are offered for those who aspire to a musical career as well as for proficient amateurs. Three main areas of musical ensemble - choirs, orchestras and wind bands - are at the centre of activities with opportunities open from the First Year to Sixth Form. Emphasis is on determination, commitment and a sense of team work. All ensembles are encouraged to reach the highest standards.

Drama. A particularly strong tradition has been fostered over many years and regular productions involve all year groups. Drama is part of the English curriculum in the first three years and there are drama clubs, trips to local theatre groups and workshops in school.

Physical Education. The Physical Education curriculum is diverse, with activities including aerobics, ball skills, badminton, basketball, dance, gymnastics, health-related fitness, squash, swimming and volleyball. The main winter games for boys are lacrosse and rugby, and for the girls are hockey and netball. In the summer, boys concentrate on cricket and athletics, whilst the girls focus their attention on tennis, athletics and rounders. Up to 350 pupils represent the school at Saturday fixtures and the teams have an excellent reputation, gaining success in regional and national competitions.

Information Technology. Two dedicated Computer Suites accommodate full classes, each pupil having access to a Pentium PC on the school's site-wide network. All pupils have their own password and email address, and are able to use the Internet for research. The rooms are available to everyone as a computer resource at lunch-times and after school. Information Technology skills are taught as part of the curriculum, and academic departments incorporate the use of computers into their everyday lessons, although the subject is not studied for public examination. By the time they leave the school all pupils should be computer-literate.

Houses. Every pupil is a member of one of the four Houses which each have eight House staff. The Houses organise and compete in a wide range of sporting and non-sporting activities.

Clubs and Societies. The School has many active clubs and societies covering a wide variety of extra-curricular interests, for example, debating, where Fifth and Sixth Formers have the opportunity to participate in up to four Model United Nations Assemblies each year.

Visits. Well established language exchange visits are made every year to France and Germany, in addition to hill walking, camping, mountaineering, skiing, sailing and cultural trips. The school also has a centre at Wasdale in the Lake District.

Assembly. Formal morning assemblies are held daily for all pupils; there are separate Jewish and Muslim assemblies. House assemblies which include Junior school pupils are on Wednesdays: the Sixth Form have a fortnightly assembly.

Pastoral Care. Form Teachers get to know each pupil in the form individually, and are supported by Year Heads and by the Head of Lower School (years 1 to 3), the Head of Middle School (years 4 and 5) and the Head of Upper School (the Sixth Form).

Discipline. This is positive and enabling. Much importance is attached to appearance and to uniform, which is worn throughout the school.

Fees. For 2000–2001, the Senior School fees are £1,725 per term.

Bursary Scheme. The school's own Bursary Scheme aims to provide financial assistance on a means-tested basis to families who have chosen a Stockport Grammar School education for their children. Details available from the Bursar.

STOCKPORT GRAMMAR JUNIOR SCHOOL. - With its own Headmaster and Staff it has separate buildings and a playing field on the same site. The Junior School has boys and girls between the ages of 4 and 11 years. Entrance is by observed play at the age of 4 years into two Reception forms, and by examination in February for an additional form at the age of 7. All pupils are prepared for the Entrance Examination to the Senior School at the age of 11. See also Part VI.

The Junior School buildings provide special facilities for Art, Technology, Music and computing. In 1993 a new reception classroom and infant craft and library areas were opened. A major extension opened in September 1997 adding more classrooms, a new front entrance, a central paved courtyard, and a secure parking area near the Senior School buildings. The winter games are soccer, hockey and netball, with cricket and rounders being played in the summer. There are swimming lessons every week; other activities include the gym club, life saving, athletics and chess. There are clubs running each lunchtime and after school for both infants and juniors. Matches are played every Saturday against other schools in the major sports. Many pupils have instrumental music lessons and there is an orchestra, band, recorder group and a choir. The musical, held in May each year, is a very popular event in which all pupils participate. Visits are made annually to Paris at Easter and to the Lake District in May. Short annual residential visits are introduced from age 7. For 2000–2001, the Junior School fees are £1,329 per term.

Charitable status. The Stockport Grammar School is a Registered Charity, number 525936. The objectives of the Charity are the maintaining of a public secondary school for boys and girls as day scholars.

Stonyhurst College

Stonyhurst Lancashire BB7 9PZ.
Tel: (01254) 826345. Admissions: (01254) 827093
Fax: (01254) 826732/826370 (Admissions)
Rail Station: Preston 12 miles

Stonyhurst College is staffed by lay men and women and Jesuits and is the property of the Society of Jesus. It stands in its own estate in the beautiful Ribble Valley on the slope of the Longridge Fells, ten miles from the M6 motorway, and just over 1 hour by car from Manchester International Airport.

In 1993 the College celebrated the four hundredth anniversary of its foundation at St Omers in France. In 1994 it celebrated the two hundredth anniversary of its move from the Continent to its present site.

Motto: *Quant je puis.*

Governors:
President: Very Rev D Smolira SJ

Chairman: Rev Fr K Fox, SJ
Deputy Chairman: M J Prior

Miss B M Banks
W P Boylan
Revd M B Flannery, SJ (*Superior*)
R Eastwood
Revd P Hamill, SJ
Sister F Orchard, IBVM
T O Mayhew

***Headmaster:* A J F Aylward**, MA (Oxon)

Deputy Head: L E McKell, MA

Assistant Headmaster: J D Hopkins, BA

Director of Studies: S P H Andrews, BSc, MA

Assistant Staff:
P R Ansell, BA (*Head of Modern Languages*)
Major A Barber (*Cadet Corps*)
T J Bayley, BSc
T A Bell, MA, DPhil (*Poetry Playroom Master*)
Mrs A Bidwell
J D Blore, BSc
D B Channing, BSc
S J Charles, MSc, BA (*Rhetoric Playroom Master and Head of PE and Games*)
J Cook, BA
L Crabtree
Mrs R Crossley, BA (*Head of Careers*)
L A Crouch, BA (*Head of English*)
I Cunliffe, BSc, MBA
Mrs H C Davies (*Head of Special Educational Needs*)
D A Eachus, BTech (*Head of Design & Technology, Grammar Playroom Master*)
Mrs H L Flatley, BSc, MSc
P J Gavin, BSc, PhD (*Head of Physics*)
M Gibson (*Head of Information Technology*)
Miss E L Gierat, BA
B C Glover, BA
Mrs C Hartley, BA
N Henshaw, BA
R A Highcock, BMus (*Director of Music*)
P E Hodkinson, BSc, MSc
R J Holland, BA
Mrs A Jackson, BA
A Jackson, BA
H Kaaber, BSc
D N Knight, BA (*Librarian*)
T P Layzell, ALCM, BSc, PhD (*Head of Chemistry*) (*Syntax Playroom Master*)
J H Lennox, BEd
S Lewis, BA
Mrs C M Markarian, BSc, MSc
K Morgan, BA, FRCO, LRAM, LTCL
S J Oliver, BA
F J O'Reilly, MA, CertObsAst (*Head of Classics*)
Miss C E S Oxley, BA, MSE (*Lower Line Girls' Deputy Housemistress*)
Miss A Padilla
Mrs G P Parkinson, BA
Miss J M Parkinson, MPhil, MA, BA
R A Pearce, MA, BLitt
Mrs J E Pierce, BA, BSc(Econ) (*Head of Economics & Business Studies*)

Revd M Power, SJ
D N Rawkins, BSc (*Head of Mathematics*)
D C Ridout, BA (*Head of Politics and General Studies*)
A Roberts, BA
D G Roberts, PhD, MSc, BSc
Mrs J Robinson, BEd
S D J Roche, BSc
J M B Sharples, BA
Mrs R Shipley (*Higher Line Girls' Deputy Housemistress, Games*)
M A Thompson, BSc, PhD, GRSC
Mrs L W Timmins, BA
M J Turner, MA (*Head of History*)
Mrs F Verner
Mrs M Wainwright, BMus (*Senior Girls' House Mistress*)
T J Warner, BSc, PhD (*Head of Biology*)
P A Warrilow, BD (*Head of Religious Doctrine/Day Pupil Master*)
N C Willetts (*Syntax Playroom Master*)
Mrs I M Williams, BEd
Mrs K Wright, BA
A Young, BA (*Head of Art, Lower Grammar Playroom Master*)

Visiting Music Staff:
W Ashton, BMus, LRAM (*Piano*)
I Barker, ALCM, LTCL, LLCM (*Guitar*)
D Barron (*Flute/Saxophone*)
J T Boden, AMusLCM (*Brass*)
I Coburn (*Double Bass*)
Mrs A Coburn, ARMCM (*Head of Strings*)
I Forgrieve, GMus, RNCM, PPRNCM (*Head of Percussion*)
P Green halgh, BMus, ARCM, ALCM (*Piano*)
Miss P Hyde, LRAM, DipRAM (*Singing*)
Mrs B Ingleby, LRAM (*Oboe*)
Mrs J Moon, BA, ALCM (*Singing*)
Mrs M Rigby, GRSM, ARMCM (*Violin*)
Ms L Shaw, BEd (*Violin/Viola*)
P Stacey, PPRAM (*Violin*)
L Wood, GNSM (*Cello*)
Mrs P J Wood, GMus, LTCL (*Head of Woodwind*)

Bursar: J Ridley, BA, MBA, FCMA

Director of Admissions and Development: P A Anwyl, MA

Registrar: Mrs G Bentley

Domestic Bursar: Miss F V Ahearne

Headmaster's Secretary: Mrs E Blackall

College Doctors:
J Saunders, MB, ChB, MRCGP, DRCOG, CertFPA
R Higson, MB, ChB, MRCGB

Senior Nursing Officer: B M Capps, BGA, DOHN

Assistant Matrons:
Mrs A Pearce, RGN
Mrs D Robinson, RGN

ST MARY'S HALL, Stonyhurst Preparatory School (*Boys and girls 6-13*)
Headmaster: M E Higgins, MA, BEd
Chaplain: Rev Fr A Howell, SJ

Aims. The School curriculum is intended to reflect the ideals of the founder of the Jesuits, St Ignatius Loyola: the importance of trying to find God in all things; the development to the full of each individual's talents whatever his or her gifts; the need for thoroughness and breadth in learning, helping pupils to think for themselves and to communicate well; above all an awareness of the needs of others. We aspire for our pupils to be men and women of competence, conscience and compassion.

Religion. The College is Roman Catholic and strives to educate its pupils in the principles and practice of their Faith. Christians of other denominations are welcomed and encouraged to be active in the school's worship and spiritual life.

Organisation. There are 385 pupils in the College, with 220 in the adjacent preparatory school, St Mary's Hall, which admits boys and girls from 5 to 13. A significant proportion of the boys joining the College from the South of England come from the Jesuit Preparatory School, St John's Beaumont in Old Windsor which is part of the Stonyhurst Foundation. There are 95 day pupils. The school is now fully co-educational from 13 to 18. The pastoral care is based on 5 year groups called 'Playrooms' each of which is in the care of married Playroom staff assisted by others including a Jesuit priest acting as Chaplain to the year. The younger girls are in the care of resident married House-parents and occupy their own designated area of the College. A resident Housemistress takes particular responsibility for the boarding and day girls in the Sixth Form. The Health Centre is self contained but within the main building; medical care is available on a 24 hour basis.

Academic organisation. A broad curriculum is offered up to GCSE in an attempt to avoid undue specialisation at an early age. There are 24 A Level subjects available and all Sixth Formers must follow a course in Morals and Ethics. Academic progress at all ages is monitored on a regular basis by tutors, and progress reports are sent to parents throughout the term. There are two central IT resource centres with Video Conferencing facilities. Sixth Formers have their own IT resource centre and networked computers in their rooms with e-mail and controlled internet facilities. Recent developments have created the highest quality teaching areas across the whole curriculum, with a particularly impressive Science Department and provision for the Performing Arts. Staff from the Special Needs Department are available to give help and support where required and TEFL classes are held on either an individual or group basis without extra charge.

Music, Art, Design and Technology. These subjects form an integral part of the curriculum. All pupils entering the School must learn an orchestral instrument at the College's expense in their first year and the opportunities for both formal and informal music are extensive: there are several orchestras, a Concert Band, small string ensembles, a Choir and other groups. Design and Technology is taught to all first year pupils along with Art, prior to the choice of GCSE subjects; the facilities for both these subjects are outstanding thanks to recent developments. Drama is strong and there are opportunities for taking part in a wide range of dramatic productions throughout the year either in our own Theatre or in the nearby Centenaries Theatre at St Mary's Hall.

Games. The main games are Rugby Football, Cricket, Hockey, Netball and Athletics, but it is our aim to offer the widest possible range of sporting and recreational opportunity to all pupils. In addition to playing on our own golf course, pupils can take part in Soccer, Tennis, Badminton, Squash, Fencing, Basketball, Netball, Clay Pigeon Shooting, Sub Aqua and Cross Country. Our indoor six lane swimming pool offers first class opportunities for both competitive and recreational swimming, and the Sports Hall provides the usual range of indoor activities. An aqueous-based all weather pitch has just been opened.

Cadet Corps and Other Extra Curricular Activities. In their second year all pupils are members of the Cadet Corps, which introduces pupils to a number of activities such as canoeing, orienteering, climbing, trekking and shooting, in addition to an extensive programme of Army-based training. After the second year, membership of the Cadet Corps is by selection; it is invariably over-subscribed. An active Outdoor Pursuits Department offers opportunities for climbing, sailing, fell-walking and caving; the Duke of Edinburgh Award Scheme is very popular with boys and girls at all ages.

Voluntary Service. Active work in the Community is a hallmark of Stonyhurst's commitment to others. Weekly programmes of community work are arranged and thousands of pounds a year are raised for charitable causes, in particular the College's own annual holiday for children with disabilities.

Higher Education and Careers. On average over 95% of our leavers go on to higher education either in the UK or abroad with an average of 10% to Oxbridge. Our Careers department, based on a well-stocked Careers library with both video and computer facilities, enables pupils to be fully informed about university choices and tutors are actively involved at all stages in the decision making. Careers conferences are regularly organised.

Fees. The termly boarding fee for 2000/2001 is £4,980; weekly boarding £4,487; the day fee is £3,006.

Bursaries and Scholarships. (*see* Entrance Scholarship section) A large number of bursaries and scholarships are awarded each year at all age levels including the Sixth Form. Bursaries are intended for pupils likely to benefit from a Stonyhurst education and to contribute to it, and whose parents are unable to pay the full fees. Scholarships are awarded on the basis of academic achievement or potential after competitive examinations in May. Scholarships are also available in Music, Art, and Art and Design. Some All-Rounder awards are also made each year. Details of all these awards can be gained by application to the Headmaster.

Admission. Enquiries about admission should be addressed to the Director of Admissions. Candidates entering at 13+ are normally required to pass the Common Entrance Examination, but alternative Tests are available for candidates from maintained schools or from abroad. Applications for Sixth Form boarding and day places for girls and boys are particularly encouraged.

Charitable status. Stonyhurst College is a Registered Charity, number 230165. The Charity for RC Purposes exists to provide a quality boarding and day education for boys and girls.

Stowe School

Stowe Buckingham Bucks MK18 5EH
Tel: (01280) 818000
Fax: (01280) 818181
e-mail: enquiries@stowe.co.uk

The School is adamant that very bright children should receive a highly academic education without losing touch with their less formally intelligent peers or losing out on the full breadth of a boarding curriculum. Its aim is to do the best by every child, and to do so by mixing very different children together and ensuring that all discover and win recognition for at least one special talent, so that all gain confidence in their own various abilities and respect for those of others.

The School was founded in 1923. The main mansion, originally Stowe House, the seat of the Dukes of Buckingham and Chandos, was finished about 1770 from designs by Robert Adam and other distinguished 18th century architects. The landscaped grounds of 750 acres around the House are now in the care of the National Trust.

Motto: *Persto et Praesto.*

Visitor: The Rt Revd The Lord Bishop of Oxford

Governing Body:
The Rt Hon Sir Nicholas Lyell, MA, QC, MP (*Chairman*)
N W Berry
M Bewes, MA
J G Cluff
The Revd J J M Fletcher, MA
C Honeyman Brown
Mrs G Hylson-Smith, BA
Sir Richard Kleinwort, BA
R D Lord, MA
A J Macintosh, MA
P L Morris, MA
Professor H F A Strachan, PhD
C J Tate, BA, MIMC
P J Thorogood
E R Verney, BA, FRICS
C H Walton, MA
Mrs H E W Williams, MA
A J Wing, MA, DM, FRCP

Secretary to the Governors: N Coulson

***Headmaster:* J G L Nichols**, MA

Deputy Headmaster and Admissions Tutor: C J Edwards, MA

Senior Master: Mrs R E Masters, BA, PhD

Director of Studies: S G A Hirst, BA, MA

Assistant Staff:
R R Akam, BSc
Mrs S L Akam, BA
P C Armstrong, BA
The Revd S N Austen, BSc, BA (*Chaplain*)
S J B Ayers, BA
D S Barr, BA, MA
Miss F A Baddeley, BA, MA
M J Bevington, MA
Mrs D C Bisp, DipPE
P M Board, BA
M A Carpenter, BA
Miss L M Carter, BSc
S O Collins, MA, CPhys, MInstP
P V Cottam, MA
G A Cottrell, MA
A Dalton, BA
B J Davey, GRSM, LRAM
P StJ Davies, BSc
B G Durrant, BA
M Edwards, BSc, BA
A G Eve, BA, DipCDTE
Miss Z J Fairbairn, MMus(RCM), BA, ARCM(PG), LGSM
P A S Farquhar, MA
D Fletcher, BEd
Mrs B Fox, CertEd
C G Gleeson, BA
Mrs F M Green, BA
J C Green, MA, GRSM, FTCL, LRAM, ARCM (*Director of Music*)
Miss L J Greatwood, BSc
S Grimble
Mrs J L Hamblett-Jahn, LLB
J E C Henderson, MA
B Hogan, BSc
Miss T L Hooker, BA
G M Hornby, MA, DPhil (*Senior Tutor*)
A Hughes
D W James, BSc, PhD
B L Johnson
C H Johnson, MA
A McDaid, BEd
I J McKillop, BA, Dip Art & Design
S H Malling, BEd, MSc, CPhys, MInstP
A G Meredith, BA
I Michael, BEd
J S Moule, BA
A K Murray, BSc
Mrs K M Noble, BSc
B H Orger, BSc, PhD
M Pitteway, BCom
S J Plummer, BEd
C C Robinson, MA, MPhil
P S Ruben, BSc, MPhil, MBA
B Sandow, BSc
R J S Secret, ARAM
D A Stephenson, MA
Miss K J Sumner, BSc
R C Sutton, BEd
J M Tearle, BA
C J A Terry, BSc
Miss A J Thistlewood, BSc
E S Thompson, BA, MPhil
W E H Vernon, BSc
M Waldman, MSc, PhD
M D G Wellington, BSc
L E Weston, DipPE, CertEd
A J Wharton, BTh
D J Woods, BA
I O Young, MA

Medical Officer: R W E Harrington, MB, BSc, MRCGP, DObst, RCOG, DFFP

Bursar: R Litherland, MA

Assistant Bursar: M V Cardy

Stowe is a country boarding school with boys from 13 to 18 and girls from 16 to 18. The number of pupils in the School is 580, comprising 518 boarders and 62 day pupils. About 50 new girls and 20 boys (boarding and day) are accepted each year for 2 year A level courses.

Houses. There are 8 Boys' and 2 Girls' Houses, 6 of which are within the main building or attached to it and 4 at a short distance from it.

Boys' Houses
Bruce House Mr I Michael
Temple House Mr J E C Henderson

Grenville House Mr D Fletcher
Chandos House Mr A Dalton
Cobham House Dr D W James
Chatham House Mr W E H Vernon
Grafton House Mr C H Johnson
Walpole House Mr J S Moule
Girls' Houses
Nugent House Mrs B T Fox
Lyttelton House Mrs J L Hamblett-Jahn

The Curriculum allows boys to enjoy a wide variety of subjects before they settle down to work for their GCSEs (nine) taken in the Fifth Form. A flexible Options system operates at this stage. Most boys and girls will go on to take 4 AS and 3 A levels. Throughout the School, boys and girls have a Tutor to look after their academic welfare and advise them on further education. A course in Visual Education was introduced in 1996 for boys and girls in their first years at Stowe. It promotes an understanding of Stowe's architecture and landscape gardens in particular and the built environment in general.

The School has an International Awareness Programme which aims to encourage pupils to improve their knowledge, understanding and experience of life within an international context.

Art, Design and Information Technology. All boys are introduced to these in their first year at Stowe. IT is delivered across the curriculum, not as a separate subject. The Art School and Design Workshops are popular both for those pursuing hobbies and for those studying for formal examinations. Traditional skills are covered alongside more modern techniques such as computer aided design and desk top publishing.

Music and Drama. Music and Drama both flourish as important and integral parts of the School's activities both within and outside the formal curriculum. There is plenty of scope in the School Orchestras, Jazz Band, Clarinet Quartet, Choirs, School plays, House plays and House entertainments. The timetable is sufficiently flexible to allow special arrangements to be made for outstanding musicians. Drama Clubs and Theatre Studies groups have two fully-equipped theatres at their disposal.

Careers Guidance. Pupils are provided with a variety of opportunities which allow them to make sound career decisions. Seminars, Gap advice and an interview training programme are all offered, and in addition all Stoics are registered with the Independent Schools Careers Organisation (ISCO), entitling them to a wide range of services, including the Morrisby aptitude assessment, careers experience courses and specialist advice. The Careers Centre is extremely well resourced, with a suite of computers and appropriate software, video facilities and a wealth of literature. Every encouragement is given to regular visits to the Centre during a pupil's time at Stowe and parents are always welcome to attend Careers events and to spend time using the available resources.

Religion. The School's foundation is Anglican and this is reflected in its chapel services on Sundays. Pupils of other faiths and other Christian Churches are welcomed and in some cases separate arrangements are made for them on Sundays. Every pupil attends the chapel services on weekdays.

Games. The major sports for boys are rugby, hockey and cricket, and the other sports range from badminton, basketball, cross country, football, Eton fives and fencing in the winter to athletics, swimming, tennis, sculling, sailing and golf in the summer; there are inter-school fixtures in all these sports.

The major sports for girls are hockey, lacrosse, netball and tennis, and the other sports are similar to the boys.

The School enters national competitions in many sports and encourages pupils to challenge for representative honours. The School has a heated 6-lane 25m indoor swimming pool, a sports hall, squash courts, Eton Fives courts, a weight training/fitness room and a flood-lit Astroturf pitch which provides 12 tennis courts in the summer. There are also 11 hard tennis courts available all the year round, plus netball courts, 4 outdoor basketball courts, an athletics track, an indoor shooting range, a clay-pigeon shooting tower, a nine-hole golf course, where the National Prep Schools (IAPS) annual tournament is played, and extensive playing fields for rugby, hockey, football, cricket and lacrosse. Sculling, canoeing, sailing and fishing take place on a lake within the Landscape Gardens.

Other Activities. Pupils complement their games programme with a large variety of extra-curricular activities, including clubs and societies. Stowe's grounds lend themselves to outdoor pursuits such as fishing and clay pigeon shooting, and horse-riding takes place at Stowe Ridings a short distance away. The School has its own pack of Beagles. On Mondays a special activities programme is based on Outdoor Pursuits (Combined Cadet Force with all three service arms and the Duke of Edinburgh Award Scheme), Community Service (in the neighbourhood) and Leadership skills.

Fees. The School Fees for tuition, board and lodging for the academic year 2000/2001 are £16,545 pa, and £12,405 pa for day pupils payable termly in advance. Nine months before the term of entry parents are asked to pay an advance deposit; this deposit is credited to the final term's fees. A full term's notice is required before the removal of a pupil.

Scholarships and Allowances. (*see* Entrance Scholarship section) Scholarships and Exhibitions are available for award on the results of competitive examinations held in the Spring term prior to entry. These can be as much as one half of the boarding fee. Stowe, together with almost all HMC Schools, is a signatory to the ACES agreement which restricts awards to that maximum level in order to release funds for assistance in cases of need. Subject to means testing, fee support for scholars can be augmented in this way. In addition, Music and Art Scholarships and Exhibitions are available. Roxburgh Awards are open to boys and girls who gain entry to Stowe via a good all-round performance on an Entrance Examination, and who also show particularly striking qualities such as leadership, commitment or a flair for communication.

A few Bursaries are available each year to pupils who could not remain at Stowe without financial assistance and who have proved themselves to be of outstanding character. Certain Memorial Bursaries are also available.

Admission. Boys and girls can be registered at any age. Full details can be obtained from the Registrar, who will supply entry forms. The School is always prepared to consider applications from boys to enter the School at 14 if they have been educated overseas or in the maintained sector. The date of birth should be stated and it should be noted that boys are normally admitted between their 13th and 14th birthdays.

The Old Stoic Society. *The OS Registrar* is John Bridgwood, The Old Stoic Society, Stowe, Buckingham MK18 5EH

Charitable status. Stowe School Limited is a Registered Charity, number 310639. Its aims and objectives are the education of children at an independent boarding school.

* Head of Department	§ Part Time or Visiting
† Housemaster/Housemistress	¶ Old Pupil
‡ See below list of staff for meaning	

Strathallan School

Forgandenny Perth PH2 9EG.
Tel: 01738-812546
Fax: 01738 812549
e-mail: secretary@strathallan.pkc.sch.uk

Strathallan School was founded by Harry Riley in 1912 and moved to its present site in Forgandenny, Perthshire in 1920. The School is fully co-educational and numbers 437 pupils, of whom 92 are day pupils and 345 are boarders.

Motto: *Labor Omnia Vincit.*

Governors:

Chairman: C D Pighills, MA

A A Arneil, FRICS
G I Bennet, MA, FCA, MSPI
J A R Coleman, ARICS
J W Dinsmore, FRICS
P J M Fairlie
Professor P Gifford, MA
J B Gray, CA
J S Hunter, BCom, CA
I Q Jones, MA, LLB, WS
Mrs C C Laing
Lady Lane, BSc, DLD, FRSE
Professor R Leake, MA, DPhil
A Logan
Judge J McKee, QC, RD
W A McMillan, BL
Professor H G Miller, OBE, BSc, DSc, FIBiol, FIC
M I Patterson, BA, CA
R S Peters, MA
D O Sutherland, MA, LLB, NP, MSI
E G M Targowski, QC, LLB Hons
Dr A P D Wilkinson, BSc, MB, ChB
D L Young, BArch (Hons), DipArch, RIAS, RIBA

***Head Master:* B K Thompson**, MA (Oxon)

Assistant Staff:

Mrs E M Adam, MA
Mrs D J Balnaves, MA
D J Barnes, BSc, PGCE (*Second Master*)
G A Bolton, BA, MSc
J S Burgess, BSc
Dr D J Carr, BSc, PhD, PGCE
R C Caves, BEd
W A Colley, BA (*Riley House*)
C N Court, BEd, MPhil (*Freeland House*)
Mrs M-L Crane, BA, PGCE
Miss S Dewar, BA, DipEd
Mrs A Dorward, DipPhysEd
N T H Du Boulay, BA
Mrs C A C Duncan, MA
A L K Dutton, CertEd
Miss E A England, MA, PGCE
P M Evans, BA (*Woodlands House*)
R H Fitzsimmons, MA
J R Fleming, BEd
Mrs S E Fleming, BEd
D R Giles, BA (*Nicol House*)
J Goddard, BSc, PGCE
Mrs E W Hamilton, MA
D M Higginbottom, MA
Mrs J Higginbottom, MA
Mrs D S Hunter, DA
Miss J S R Hutcheon, DipPhysEd
Mrs A Ingram Forde, BA
P J S Keir, BEd
E G Kennedy, BA, PGCE
I W Kilpatrick, BA, PGCE, MEd (*Simpson*)
G Kitson, BSc
A J M Lunan, BEng
Mrs J L Martin, BSc, DipEd
Miss A J Mason, MA, PGCE
J McCann, BEng
Dr D McDougall, BSc, PhD, PGCE
Mrs I I M McFarlane, MA, CertSpLD
Miss V S M McKay, BEd, DipLib/Inf
A E C McMorrine, DA
Miss J L Morrison, BEd
Miss S U NiRiain, BSc
Mrs F M Ninham, MA
Revd R G Pickles, BD, MPhil (*Chaplain*)
Mrs C Pillar, MA
R J W Proctor, MA
Mrs D L Raeside, BSc, HDE(PG)
C A C Raitt, BSc, PGCE
D G Read, MMus, FRCO (*Director of Music*)
G R M Ross, BSc, MSc
J D Salisbury, MA, PGCE
P Shields, MA, PGCE
Miss L J Smith, BA, BEd (*Senior Mistress/ Registrar*)
N Smith, BSc, BA
D R Sneddon, BSc, DipEd, BA
A C W Streatfeild-James, MA, PGCE
Mrs K Streatfield-James, BA, PGCE
Mrs J A Summersgill, BSc
P R Summersgill, MA, PGCE (*Director of Studies*)
A Thomson, BA
Dr A M Tod, BA, PhD
M R Tod, BSc
P M Vallot, BSc
C N Walker, BSc (*Director of Studies*)
R C A Walmsley, BA
Mrs J A Watson, BA
A Watt, BComm, HDE (*Ruthven House*)
M Wilson, RN

Chaplain: Revd R G Pickles, BD, MPhil

Director of Music: D G Read, MMus, FRCO

Art: A E C McMorrine, DA

Bursar: K G Legge, MIPD

Medical Officers:
J Sinclair, MB, ChB, DCH, DRCOG, FPCert
A Falconer, MB, ChB, MRCGP, DRCOG, FPCert

Situation. Strathallan is located a few miles south of Perth in the village of Forgandenny. It occupies a glorious rural location, situated in 150 acres of richly wooded estate on the northern slopes of the Ochils and overlooks the Earn valley. At the same time, Strathallan is within easy reach of the international airports – Edinburgh (45 minutes) and Glasgow (1 hour) – and Perth (10 minutes) with its mainline railway station and shopping facilities.

At the centre of the School is the main building which dates from the 18th century and was formerly a country house and home of the Ruthven family. The School continues to invest in its outstanding facilities. Recent additions include modern laboratories, a Theatre, Computer Centre, Library, Design and Technology Centre, Sports Hall, Astroturf pitch, Medical Centre and Art School. All boarding houses provide modern accommodation, with a single study bedroom for every pupil after their first senior year.

Aims. At the heart of the School's philosophy is the commitment to provide opportunities for every boy and girl to excel; to help them make the most of their abilities within the framework of a caring environment.

Organisation. The School is primarily a boarding school yet also takes day pupils who are integrated into the boarding houses. There are four Senior Boys' houses (Ruthven, Nicol, Freeland and Simpson) with approximately 60 in each. There are two Girls' houses (Woodlands and Thornbank) accommodating 70 in each. All boarding houses have their own resident Housemaster or Housemistress, assisted by House Tutors and a Matron.

The Junior House, Riley, is designed to cater for boys and girls wishing to enter the School from Primary Schools at 10+. Riley is run by a resident Housemaster and his wife, assisted by tutors, two of whom are resident, and a resident Matron. After Riley, pupils move directly to one of the Senior houses.

Riley is situated within its own campus, yet also enjoys the facilities of the main School. It has its own Common Room, Library, dormitories and music practice rooms.

The whole School dines centrally and there is a choice of hot and cold meals as well as vegetarian options. All boarding houses have their own tuck shop and "brew rooms" for the preparation of light snacks.

Religion. Strathallan has a resident Chaplain who is responsible for religion throughout the School. Services take place during the week and on Sundays.

Curriculum. Pupils entering the School at 11 are placed in Form I, whilst those who join at 13 are placed in the IIIrd Form where they will be setted by ability for their core subjects. Up until the IVth form, all will follow the same broad curriculum which comprises English, Mathematics, French, German/Spanish, Latin, Physics, Chemistry and Biology, History, Geography, Computing, Design Technology, together with Divinity, Personal and Social

Education, Art, Drama, Music and Physical Education. Instruction in French and Latin begins in Form I.

In the IVth and Vth forms, pupils select nine subjects for GCSE. All the above subjects (plus Business Studies and Greek) are available at this level.

A satisfactory performance at GCSE (a minimum of five passes or equivalent) qualifies a boy or girl for entry to the VIth form where he or she prepares for AS and A2 examinations in three or four subjects, or five subjects at Scottish Higher. Scottish Higher examinations are generally taken at the end of the Upper Sixth year. AS and A2 examinations are taken in the Lower and Upper Sixth.

In the VIth form, there is greater flexibility in the range of courses available and full details of these are issued to parents in advance. Potential Oxbridge candidates are identified in the Lower VIth form and additional tuition is provided. On average, more than 95% of senior pupils go on to University.

Each pupil is allocated a tutor who is a member of the academic staff and one of the duty staff of the boarding house. The tutor monitors the academic progress of the boy or girl and is responsible for discussing their three-weekly reports with them. Teacher:Pupil ratio: 1:7.

Games. The main School games are rugby, cricket, hockey, netball, athletics and tennis, and standards are high. Other sports include skiing, squash, football, fencing, judo, swimming, golf and cross-country running.

Strathallan has two squash courts, 18 hard tennis courts, an astroturf, a heated indoor swimming pool, sports hall, gymnasium and a fitness and weight training room. The sports hall comprises a basketball court, three badminton courts, a rock climbing wall as well as facilities for six-a-side hockey and indoor cricket coaching. Sailing, canoeing and skiing are recognised pastimes, and a large number of pupils participate in School ski days in the Spring term. Strathallan also has its own six-hole golf course and trout fishing is available in the grounds.

Activities. All pupils are encouraged to take part in a range of activities for which time is set aside each day. Among the activities available are dance, drama, pottery, chess, photography, shooting (both clay pigeon and small bore) and fishing. There are also several societies and a full programme of external speakers who visit the School. Boys and girls keen to do so, work towards awards under the Duke of Edinburgh Scheme. They are also encouraged to take part in Community Service.

Music. The vibrant Music department has its own concert room, keyboard room and classrooms, together with a number of individual practice rooms. Music appreciation and singing are included in the timetable, and music may be taken at GCSE, Higher and AS/A2 Level. There is a choir, choral society, traditional music groups, a jazz band, wind band and two orchestras. A house music competition takes place annually and there are regular concerts throughout the term. Individual tuition is available for virtually all instruments. Recitals and visits to concerts in Edinburgh, Perth and the environs are arranged. The School has an outstanding Pipe Band and a resident full time Pipe Major.

Art. Art is recognised as an important part of the School's activities and there are opportunities to study the subject at GCSE and AS/A2 Level. Pupils benefit from regular art trips abroad and have the opportunity to exhibit their work both locally and further afield. A new purpose-built Art School opened in 1999, featuring facilities for ceramics, sculpture and print-making.

Drama. Drama thrives throughout the School and the department makes full use of the new theatre. There are senior and junior performances each year as well as inter-House drama competitions. Pupils are encouraged to take responsibility for all aspects of production and there have been workshops from visiting groups. The School also provides tuition in public and verse speaking and pupils regularly win trophies at the local festivals.

Combined Cadet Force. There is a large voluntary, contingent, of the Combined Cadet Force with Naval, Army and Marines Sections. The School has a motor launch on the Forth and there is also a covered miniature shooting range and an assault course.

Careers. Careers guidance begins in the Vth Form. The Careers Adviser maintains close links with universities and colleges and regularly visits industrial firms. There is a dedicated Careers Library, well-stocked with prospectuses, reference books and in-house magazines. Strathallan is a member of the Independent Schools Careers Organisation, a representative of which visits regularly.

All pupils have the opportunities to gain work experience in the Vth form, after their GCSEs. There is also a GAP year programme which provides placements for pupils to work overseas prior to going to university, either with other schools with whom Strathallan has links, or with organisations such as Operation Raleigh or Project Trust.

Pastoral Care. There is a strong emphasis on pastoral care. The School has drawn up its own welfare guidelines in consultation with parents, governors and Tayside social services. It has also appointed a trained child protection co-ordinator and counselling is available through various channels.

Medical Centre. Strathallan has its own purpose-built Medical Centre with dedicated male and female wards, plus consulting and treatment rooms. There is 24-hour care available for all pupils with a nursing sister living on-site. The School's Medical Officers visit four times a week, and physiotherapy and chiropody also take place in the Centre during term time.

Entrance. Junior Entrance Examination – Boys and girls are admitted to the Junior School (Riley House) at either age 10, 11 or 12. An Entrance Examination common to all ages is held in early Spring each year. It is based on the Primary School Curriculum and no knowledge of foreign languages is required.

Entry to the Senior School – Candidates for entry into the Senior School at 13 may enter via either the Open Scholarship examination (February), Common Entrance (June) or specially prepared papers (arranged with parents and present School).

VIth Form – Boys and girls may also enter at VIth form level, either via the VIth Form scholarship examination (which takes place in November) or on the basis of a satisfactory School report and GCSE/Standard Grade results.

In all cases, pupils are accepted in September, January and occasionally April of the academic year.

Scholarships. (*see* Entrance Scholarship section) The number and value of the scholarships available for entry to Riley, the IIIrd Form or Lower VIth Forms depend upon the abilities of the candidates. Awards of up to 50% of the full fee are available and can be supplemented by bursaries if genuine need can be shown. Candidates must be under 14 years of age on 1 September for the Open Scholarship examination and under 12 on 1 September for the Junior entrance examination.

Each year a number of Music and Art scholarships are offered which can be up to 50% of the fees and 'All rounder' awards are also available. Bursaries, under the School's Ochil Trust scheme may be available to those who have gained places in the normal way. Eligibility is determined by a means test.

Fees per year (1999/2000). Junior School (Riley House): fees are £10,485 boarding and £7,146 day. Senior School: fees are £14,040 boarding and £9,672 day.

Prospectus. Up to date information is included in the prospectus which can be obtained by contacting the Registrar. The school has a website: www.strathallan.co.uk.

Charitable status. Strathallan is a Scottish Charity dedicated to Education.

Sutton Valence School

Sutton Valence Maidstone Kent ME17 3HL.
Tel: (01622) 842281

Sutton Valence has over 400 years of proud history behind it. Founded as a small grammar school in 1576 by William Lambe under Charter of Queen Elizabeth I, the last hundred years have seen constant growth and innovation. After the First World War there were 160 boys on the school roll: today there are 407 boys and girls. The school occupies an area of about 100 acres on the slopes of a high ridge, with unequalled views over the Weald of Kent, and in the historic, beautiful and safe village of Sutton Valence: an environment in which it is easy to learn and to grow as a human being. Recent additions to the facilities include an IT Suite and Sixth Form Common Room. A large sports hall and fitness complex is due for completion in January 2001. Various clusters of IT facilities support an innovative approach to this key discipline.

In September 1995, Underhill, a thriving Preparatory School of 300 pupils, became the Junior School to Sutton Valence. Underhill occupies its own secure and attractive site one mile from the neighbouring village of Chart Sutton and provides a strong, caring education for children between the ages of 3 and 11.

Motto: *My Trust is in God alone.*

Visitor: The Lord Archbishop of Canterbury

Foundation: United Westminster Schools

Governing Body:
B F W Baughan (*Chairman*)
E R P Boorman, MA
Mrs S B Bracher, MA, MBE
P Cockburn, FCIB
Ven Patrick Evans, Archdeacon of Maidstone
T F Godfrey-Faussett, MA, FIPM
J J Knott, BA
M A Maberly
F V Morgan, BSc, MEd
C J Saunders, MA
E Watts, OBE, BA, FRSA
Mrs V Wilson, BA

***Headmaster:* J Davies**, MA

Deputy Headmaster: T Wilbur, BA (*History*)

Director of Studies: D E Clarke, BSc, CBiol, MIBiol (*Head of Biology*)

Assistant Staff:
W K Piper, BA, BEd, AMBDA (*Head of Learning Support*)
P J Harcourt, MA, MIL (*Modern Languages*)
C F G Parkinson, TD, BA (*Senior Master; Economics/Mathematics*)
C W W Wilson, BA (*Head of History, Head of 2nd Year*)
G R Piper, BSc, MInstP, CPhys (*Head of Science; Head of Physics*)
E L Stanley, BA (*Head of Economics; Careers/Universities Master; Head of Year 5*)
I S Hendry, MA (*Head of Modern Languages*)
M D Willdridge, BA (*Head of Art*)
†Mrs S C Rawlings, BA (*Modern Languages*)
P J Horley, BA, ARCO, ALCM (*Deputy Director of Music*)
D A Cooper, BEd (*Head of Chemistry, Assistant Head of 6th Form*)
Mrs K L Jackson (*Head of Home Economics, Head of 4th Year*)
Miss S A Boddy, BA (*Director of Development; History; Games*)
Mrs A Jefferson, BSc, BA (*Head of Mathematics/PSHE, Head of 6th Form*)
S P Hiscocks, BSc, PhD (*Chemistry, Webmaster*)
†R H Carr, BA (*Religious Studies/Humanities and Games*)
Miss F Clayton, BA (*Head of English*)
W D Buck, CertEd (*Head of Sport; English, Religious Studies*)
Mrs J P A Fletcher, BSc (*Chemistry, Head of 1st Year*)
A S Hall, BA (*Head of PE and Sports Studies*)
Miss E J J Mitchell, MA (*English, Media Studies*)
J R Walsh, MSc (*Biology*)
D J J Keep, BEd (*Head of Design Technology*)
Miss P C Tragett, BSc (*Mathematics*)
Mrs S Anstey (*EFL*)
Miss A J Brown, MA (*Modern Languages*)
J C Harding, MA (*English and Theatre Studies, Head of Drama*)
D Holmes, LRAM (*Head of Strings*)
†S J Marriott, GTCL, LTCL (*Director of Music*)
Mrs A Brenchley (*Head of Girls' Games*)
J McCormick, MA (*Classics*)
†Mrs M T Hall, BEd (*Geography, Head of 3rd Year*)
Miss B Adzic (*Chemistry and Biology*)
B R Calderwood, BEd (*Head of IT*)
A P Hammersley, BSc (*Biology*)
Mrs R Hine, BSc (*Head of Geography*)
C R Jenkins, BA (*English and Media Studies*)
R Lindley, BEng, PhD (*Physics*)
J D Peverley, BSc (*Sports Studies*)
Miss S K Roberts, BSc (*Mathematics*)
J F Stephens, BSc (*Mathematics*)
Mrs A F F Wilkinson (*Girls' games/extra-curricular activities*)
Mrs B J Piper, BA (*Art*)
Mrs C J Kitchen (*Mathematics; Examinations Officer*)
F B Oliver, BA (*Design Technology/Work Experience*)
Mrs A M Buck (*Home Economics*)
Mrs A Brenchley, CertEd (*Head of Girls Games and PE*)
Mrs S Anstey (*EFL/Community Service*)
†Mrs F Wilbur

Visiting Staff:
M Eden, LRAM (*Guitar*)
M Hunt, GGSM (*Clarinet/Saxophone*)
Mrs E Field, ARAM, GRSM, LRAM, ARCM (*Singing/Piano*)
Mrs P Fisher, GRSM, ARCM (*Brass*)
Mrs A Hutchinson, MA, MSc, CertEd (*Flute*)
Mrs S Marshall, LRAM (*Oboe*)
Mrs C Saunby, GRSM, LRAM, DipRAM (*Piano*)
R Scarff, GTCL (Hons), LTCL (*Percussion/Piano*)

Mrs L Rylands (*Typing*)
Mrs R Faulkner, BA, CertEd (Cambs), BDA(DI) (*Learning Support*)
Mrs P Stileman, MAFCollP (*Learning Support*)

Administrative Staff:
Bursar: A J Hutchinson, MA, FCA
Estates Bursar: Mrs R Harrison
Headmaster's Secretary: Mrs M Noar
Admissions Secretary: Mrs K Taylor
PA to Bursar: Mrs A Smith
Book-keeper: Mrs C Box
School Medical Adviser: Dr I Roberts, MB, BS, DRCOG, MRCP(UK)
School Fees Administrator: Mrs J Holderness
CCF Adjutant: Capt B W Miller
Clerk of Works: M J Shewbridge
Caterer: J R Devine

Curriculum Organisation. The academic curriculum is under constant review, with the object of achieving a balance between the needs of the individual and the demands of society, industry, the universities and professions. Classes are small and the ratio of graduate teaching staff to pupils is approximately 1:10.

In forms 1 and 2 (years 7 and 8: age 11 and 12) the National Curriculum is broadly followed, covering English, Mathematics, Sciences (Chemistry, Physics, Biology), Modern Languages (French is compulsory, and a second language chosen from German, Spanish and Latin), Humanities (History, Geography, Religious Studies), Design Technology, Food Technology, ICT, Creative and Expressive Arts (Art, Music, Drama), Physical Education.

The National Curriculum is broadly followed in form 3 (year 9: age 13+) where subjects offered are the same as forms 1 and 2. However, the syllabi are designed to cater for not only those who enter form 3 via forms 1 and 2 but also the large number of pupils who join the school at 13+.

In forms 4 and 5 (years 10 and 11) pupils usually study eight or nine subjects to GCSE level. These are divided between the core – English and English Literature, Mathematics, a Modern Language (French, German or Spanish), Science (Chemistry, Physics, Biology are all studied and taken either separately or as a Dual Science award), Religious Studies, PSHE and ICT - and option groups. Each option group contains a number of subjects, offering a choice which allows every pupil to achieve a balanced education whilst, at the same time, providing the opportunity to concentrate on his or her strengths. Subjects on offer are History, Geography, Economics, Business Studies, a second Language, Latin, DT, Home Economics, Art, Music. In addition, all pupils follow a cross-curricular ICT course which results in a short course GCSE qualification.

In the two years covered by the lower and upper sixth (years 12 and 13) pupils study four, or occasionally five, subjects at AS level. AS level subjects are arranged in five option groups. Pupils continue with three or occasionally four subjects in their final year, and are well positioned to meet the entrance requirements of the universities and professions.

All those who have no computing qualification take an appropriate course.

Potential Oxbridge candidates are identified in the lower sixth year and appropriate tuition is arranged.

European Dimension. Recent years have seen a considerable expansion in the provision for foreign exchange with schools in France and Germany. Regular cultural and sporting exchanges, particularly to Holland, Germany and Italy, are also very much part of the School's policy.

Choice of Subjects. Decisions regarding option choice for GCSE and "A" level are taken only after extensive consultation with both pupils and parents. Separate booklets on GCSE and "A" level options are available.

Setting, Promotion, Reporting. In forms 1–5 Mathematics is setted; in forms 4 and 5 English and Science are also setted. Otherwise subjects are not setted. In forms 1–3 a top group is selected.

The minimum qualification for entry into the Sixth Form is normally considered to be five B/C grade passes at GCSE level. Academic progress is monitored by Housemasters/mistresses, and at regular intervals throughout the term every pupil is graded for achievement and effort in every subject. Every term full subject reports are written on all pupils, except at the end of the Lent term when pupils in years 1-4 receive a short report.

Computing and Information Technology. In addition to an excellently equipped Computer Room, the School has developed a campus-wide network in recognition of the fact that the computer/word processor is one of key cross-curricular tools in all pupils' education.

The school network serves twelve academic departments, the library, the staff common room and Heads of Department. It provides open access for pupils in the Computer Room and various 'clusters' around the school via IBM-PC compatibles working on industry-standard software. Pupils are encouraged to use recommended palm-top machines in conjunction with the school network

Other computers provide for specialist tasks; these include a fully networked suite in the library with full CD-ROM, sound-card and interactive learning facilities, a CAD system, a meteorological monitoring system and video captive facilities.

Higher Education and Careers. Sutton Valence has a fine modern and well-equipped Careers Room in the new Sixth Form Centre which incorporates a Careers Library and computerised systems to help in degree and career selection.

Every pupil sits a series of aptitude and ability tests during the two years prior to GCSE. This is followed by a thorough interview with specially trained members of staff in conjunction with the Kent Careers Service, when suggestions are made for Sixth Form academic courses and possible degrees/careers to be explored.

In the Sixth Form further interviews are conducted, advice is given on university and college applications and a range of Careers Lectures and visits are laid on. At the end of the lower Sixth year a whole week is devoted to the choosing of degree courses or careers.

The Careers Master is assisted by at least four other members of staff with expert knowledge across the careers board.

Music. Music plays a very important part in the life of the school, and we have a deservedly fine reputation for the quality and range of our music-making. There is a fine modern Music School which contains a Concert Hall, five teaching rooms, ten practice rooms and an ensemble room.

About half the pupils learn a musical instrument; there are three choirs, an orchestra, wind band, jazz band, assorted pop groups and a very full termly programme of concerts. Music tours to Europe have been arranged, and the Music Society organises a programme of distinguished visiting performers every year.

Drama. As with Music, Drama is extremely active in the school. Each year, at least a third of the school will be involved in up to seven productions. Every year there will be a Junior, Middle School and Senior production. In addition, there are many smaller scale productions, theatre workshops run by professional producers, Reviews and Cabarets. The school also enters productions for national competitions.

Sport and Physical Education. Despite our comparatively modest size Sutton Valence has a deserved reputation as a strong sporting school, competing most successfully with others and in open Championships in seventeen sports. 30 pupils currently have representative honours at County, Regional and National levels.

With 40 acres of playing fields, one of the best cricket squares in Kent, a floodlit Astroturf pitch for hockey, heated swimming pool, fives, tennis, netball and squash courts, a six-hole golf course and gymnasium, there is a tremendous range of choice for both boys and girls, all of whom will be involved in sport on at least two afternoons of every week. Our facilities will be greatly enhanced early in January 2001 with the opening of a large modern sports hall and fitness complex.

Additional sports, such as fencing, football, judo, horse riding and volleyball are offered through our activities programme and in afternoon/evening sessions with professional coaches.

Pastoral System. The School is split into Year Groups - from 1st to Upper 6th. Each year group has a Head of Year and within each year group, pupils are split into Tutor Groups. Pupils meet with their Tutor (a member of the teaching staff) twice a day and this allows their progress to be regularly monitored as well as giving pupils an opportunity to seek guidance. The continuity of meeting tutors twice a day gives Tutors an indepth knowledge of the strengths and weaknesses of each pupil. In addition to monitoring academic progress, Tutors can help pupils develop their potential through the Personal, Social and Health Education (PSHE) programme.

The Chapel of St Peter. The Christian faith has been the foundation of the School for many centuries. This is expressed today by the prominence given to daily worship in the chapel and by the presence of a resident chaplain who is a priest in the Anglican Communion.

The spiritual growth of pupils is believed to be as important as their academic, social or physical development, and all pupils, whether day or boarding, are encouraged to participate actively in Chapel life and are exposed to visiting preachers from a wide range of religious backgrounds. The boarders have regular Sunday evening sung Eucharists to which parents are most welcome.

Community Service, CCF and Duke of Edinburgh's Award Scheme.

All pupils are expected to join one or more of the service schemes offered by the School. The CCF, with Army, RAF and Royal Navy sections, are popular and successful and offers a wide variety of activities through regular camps, adventure training, field weekends and range days. The Duke of Edinburgh's Award Scheme is, similarly, well supported. Others participate in community service activities whereby pupils visit local primary schools, undertake charity work and help out with local conservation projects.

Clubs and Activities. Time is specifically set aside each week for clubs and activities. Every pupil spends time pursuing his or her own special interests, and with up to forty clubs or activities from which to choose, the range and scope is obviously very wide. In addition, various school societies and some other activities take place out of school hours.

Entrance Scholarships. (*see* Entrance Scholarship section) Scholarships and Exhibitions (up to a maximum of 50% of the day or boarding fees) are available in Drama, Music, Art and Sports. "All-Rounder" Awards were introduced in 1998. Junior and Senior Academic Scholarships are also available. All Awards are now index-linked to fee increases.

Fees. (*see* Entrance Scholarship section) Boarders £3,710–£4,940 per term. Day pupils £2,330–£3,160 per term plus £127.50 per term for lunches.

Instrumental Music. £120 per term.

Extras. Music Lessons, Judo, Fencing, etc. Books, stationery and clothing are charged for as supplied. A small charge is also made for entry at each stage to the Duke of Edinburgh's Award Scheme. Any other extras are those expenses personal to the individual. School transport is available from areas across Kent costing up to £200 per term.

Charitable status. United Westminster Schools is a Registered Charity, number 309267. Its aims are to promote education.

Taunton School

Taunton Somerset TA2 6AD.

Tel: (01823) 349200; Headmaster (01823) 349224; Admissions (01823) 349223

e-mail: enquiries@tauntonschool.co.uk

Motto: *Ora et Labora.*

Taunton School is a friendly, purposeful co-educational boarding and day community with high academic standards and a full extra-curricular programme. We enable our pupils to develop their talents to the full, and to learn habits of self-discipline that will stand them in good stead in Higher Education and professional training. The School is exceptionally well-equipped and attractively situated with extensive grounds. It has three parts: the Senior School (13–18) of about 470 pupils (with a Sixth Form of 200 plus), the Preparatory School (7–13) of about 330, and the Pre-Preparatory and Nursery (3–7) of about 140. Each section has a distinct persona within the whole family, but the School has the advantage of offering a co-ordinated curriculum and identical terms and holidays.

Governors:

President & Chairman: Major General Barry M Lane, CB, OBE

Deputy Chairman: Mrs Jane E Barrie, BSc, ARCS, FSI

Honorary Life Vice Presidents:
Dr John M Roberts, CBE, MA, DPhil
William R G Pearse, Esq, FCA

Treasurer: David T Watson, Esq, MA, FCA

The Revd W Ray P Adams, BA
Brian P Bissell, Esq, MBE, MA, BD
Michael H N Button, Esq, FCA
John D T Cooper, Esq
Mrs Christine Glover, MA (Oxon), ACA
Dr Anne C Grocock, MA, DPhil
Air Vice Marshal Peter Harding, CB, CVO, CBE, AFC, FRAeS
Dr Christine Z Pfeifer Harrison, MB, BS, MRCGP
Mrs Gillian Hylson-Smith, BA Hons
Alan M Large, Esq, LLB
Maj Gen Antony Makepeace-Warne, CB, MBE, BA
Geoffrey A Matthews, Esq, BA
Dr Stuart R Milligan, MA, DPhil
David A Sizer, Esq, FRICS
Michael J O Willacy, Esq, CBE, FCIPS
Mrs Joan M R Williams, LLB, AKC

Clerk to the School Governors: David J A Taylor, Esq, GradICSA

***Headmaster:* Julian P Whiteley**, BSc, MBA

Deputy Headmaster: John A Carrington, MA

Second Deputy: Miss Bridget M Goldsmith, BSc

Director of Studies: Neil Mason, BSc

Director of Recreation: Richard B Jowett, BSc

Chaplain: The Revd David R Owen, BA

Assistant Staff:
†Rob E Abell, BSc
Mrs Christabel Ager, BA, ALA (*Librarian*)
Mrs Sophie Anderson, BA
†Derek Baty, Cert Ed
†Jimmy M H Beale, BSc (*Careers Adviser*)
David J Bearman, BSc
*Mrs Joan Bird, CertEd (*Head of Home Economics*)
*Martin A Bluemel, MA, CChem, MRSC
Mrs Louise Bolland, BA
Mrs Elaine Bowyer, BSc, MSc
A John M Brown, MA
*T Mark Chatterton, BA (*Head of History*)
Mike J Cook, BSc
Mike D Copleston, BA
Philip Cutts, MA
Gareth E Doodes, MA
Dr Maureen E Ervine, MA
Mrs Sue Falkingham, BEd (*Head of Spanish*)
*John H Fisher, MA (*Head of ICT*)
*Mrs Gill Foster, BA (*Head of English*)
*Jeremy D Foster, BSc (*Head of Technology*)
Antonio Garcia, CertEd
Paul Gibson, BSc
*John G Gillard, MA, MSc (*Head of Mathematics*)
Simon J D Gulliver, BSc
*Dr John Guntrip, BSc, CBiol, MIBiol (*Head of Biology*)
*Alistair J Hallows, BSc (*Head of Sixth Form*)
*Trevor J Hill, BSc (*Head of Physics and Science*)

Simon T Hogg
Mrs Fiona S Holford, BA (*EFL*)
Ron J Hornsby, BMus
†Miss Judy F Iredale, BA (*Head of German*)
Clive Large, BA, MA, MBA
Mrs Jeanne Leader, BSc
†Mrs Carol A Manley
Mrs Mary P Mason, GRSC
†Keith Moore, MA
†Mrs Lynne Moore, BEd, DipEd
Mrs Rosemary M Nash, BA
Ian D Piper, BSc
*Roger Priest, BA (*Head of Classics*)
†Stephen E Pugh, BSc
†Dr Jane Roberts, BSc (*Head of Geography*)
†Declan C Rogers, MA
Miss E Mags Rowles, BA
*Miss Meryl Z Smart, BEd (*Head of Theatre Studies*)
Dr Mark P Tanner, MA, FTCL
†Hugh K C Todd, CertEd (*Head of Physical Education*)
Mrs Susan Treseder, MEd
Mrs Lucy Turner, BA
*C Philip Tyack, MA, BMus (*Director of Music*)
†Mrs Marie-Christine Tyack, Licence et Matrice (*Head of French*)
Mrs Sandra E G Wickham, DipPE
*D Ian Wilton, DipAD, ATD (*Head of Art*)
David J Yates, BPhil (*Learning Support*)

Headmaster's Secretary: Mrs Carol Cotton
Admissions Secretary: Mrs Chris Skinner
Bursar's Secretary: Mrs E Ann Spurway
School Secretary: Mrs Sue Goodall
Medical Officer: Dr James E Davidson, MB, ChB, DObst, RCOG

Situation. The School stands in its own grounds of over 50 acres on the northern outskirts of Taunton, within easy reach of some of the most attractive countryside in England. Taunton is exceptionally well placed on the M5 and the Paddington to Penzance main line with easy access to all parts of the British Isles and Heathrow.

Facilities. The School moved to its present site, the Fairwater estate, in 1870 to a fine range of buildings purpose built in the Gothic style. The original house, Fairwater, dating from 18th century is a boys' boarding house. The Wills family, notably Lord Winterstoke, made a series of munificent gifts including the Chapel (completed in 1907), a Library, and two boys' boarding houses, Wills East and Wills West.

A separate Science Building was added as a War Memorial after the Great War, and subsequently extended. Building has proceeded continually as a result of good housekeeping and appeals, adding specialist teaching facilities, including a Technical Activities Centre, and two purpose-built girls' boarding Houses. A policy of continuous modernisation has seen additions to the Houses, and in 1998 further accommodation for boarding girls. There have also been improvements to the Science laboratories and other teaching facilities. The Preparatory School was rebuilt in 1994/95 (see separate entry under IAPS section, Part V). A new Arts Centre was built in 1995.

Worship. The Chapel plays a central role in the life of the community. The School is no longer denominational and welcomes members of all Christian beliefs, or other faiths. There is a daily service, and a service on Sundays for all boarders in residence. The Chapel Choir plays a major role in the enhancement of worship. The present Chaplain prepares candidates for confirmation and celebrates Holy Communion for all who are in good standing with their denomination, and preparation for Free Church membership is also arranged.

Curriculum. In the first year of the Senior School the timetable sets out to give a wide experience of subjects, including the separate sciences.

Nine GCSE subjects are offered with English (Language and Literature), Mathematics, French and Science (Biology, Chemistry and/or Physics) as a core, and a choice from Art, Business Studies, Design & Technology, Drama, Geography, German, History, Latin, Music, PE, Religious Studies and Spanish.

Twenty-three subjects are offered at AS & A2 level, the latest additions being Theatre Studies, Physical Education and Psychology, with the majority of Sixth Formers aiming at university or college entry. GNVQ ICT is also offered.

Careers. Careers advice is an important part of school life with work experience for all in the Lower Sixth. The Head of Careers and Director of Studies advise on applications for Higher Education.

Music. Music plays a vital part in the life of the School: about one third of the pupils take lessons in a great variety of instruments, and there are choral groups, orchestra, windband, ensembles, and a jazz band.

School Societies. Everyone is encouraged to participate in extra-curricular activities and a wide range is offered including debating, drama, the Duke of Edinburgh's Award Scheme, Combined Cadet Forces, public service and astronomy. The School has a distinguished international debating record and is well known for its initiatives and original work in Radio-Astronomy.

Games. The School has a distinguished record in games and has strong fixture lists. The principal games are rugby, hockey, netball, cricket and tennis, with excellent facilities also for squash, badminton and basketball. The School has a shale and an artificial turf hockey pitch. The latter provides twelve tennis courts in the Summer. There are outdoor and indoor heated swimming pools. The Sports Hall is equipped with an up-to-date Fitness Suite, climbing wall and a wide range of indoor games. Pupils also take part in athletics, cross-country, canoeing, sailing, riding and golf. There is also a miniature rifle range. The School's philosophy is to encourage athletic excellence whilst remembering that these activities are essentially for recreation.

Medical. The School Medical Centre provides the medical service for the whole School community, and is staffed by qualified nurses under the supervision of the School Medical Officer who visits daily.

Admission. The main ages of admission are 3, 7, 9, 11, 13 and 16, but entry at intermediate ages is also possible. Prospectuses and registration forms are available from the Admissions Secretary, who will also be pleased to arrange visits (01823-349223).

The Admissions Secretary at the Preparatory School will be pleased to assist with enquiries for children up to the age of 13 (01823) 349209.

Entry at 13. The Taunton School Scholarship Examination is held annually in February or March, and is open to all candidates under the age of 14 in the following September.

Other candidates attending Preparatory Schools would be expected to take the Common Entrance Examination in June. Candidates who have not been prepared for Common Entrance would be required to attend for interview, and may be asked to sit an assessment.

Members of Taunton Preparatory School proceed to the Senior School on the basis of a Record of Progress.

Entry to the Sixth Form. Entry to the Advanced Level course will normally be conditional on a minimum of 5 GCSE passes at grade A to C, but again, interview and report play an important part in determining the offer of places.

Scholarships and Exhibitions. (*see* Entrance Scholarship section) *13+ Open Scholarship.* A number of Scholarships of up to half fees and Exhibitions are awarded at the age of 13.

The examination is held at Taunton School in the Spring, as announced in the Independent Schools Year Book for Examination Group B. Papers may be sent to candidates' Preparatory Schools if it is wished to sit the examinations there. The compulsory subjects are English, Mathematics,

French, Science, History, Geography, Religious Studies and a General Paper, with optional papers in Latin, Greek, Spanish, German and Design & Technology.

Sixth Form Scholarships. These are awarded annually to outstanding boys or girls who will be taking GCSE examinations in the current year, and who are regarded by his or her Headmaster or Headmistress as strong University candidates. Candidates are required to attend for interview in November.

11+ Scholarships and Exhibitions. A number of Scholarships and Exhibitions are awarded to boys and girls under the age of 12 on 1st September of the year of entry. The examinations are held at Taunton School in January.

Music and Art at 13+ and Sixth Form level. A number of Scholarships and Exhibitions are offered in both Music and Art each year. These do not form part of the Open Scholarship Examination. Details may be obtained from the Admissions Secretary (01823) 349223.

Sport. Up to 2 Scholarships are offered at 13, and 2 Scholarships to candidates for the Sixth Form. Details from the Admissions Secretary (01823) 349223.

Bursaries. Ministerial Bursaries may be offered to the sons and daughters of Ministers of all recognised denominations, from the age of 11, on condition that the candidates satisfy the academic requirements of the School.

Service Bursaries are available for the children of Service families.

Fees per term. As at September 2000 (inclusive). Senior School Boarders, £4,695, Day, £2,995.

Taunton Preparatory School Boarders: £2,010 to £3,655; Day: £1,195 to £2,415; Pre-Preparatory and Nursery: £780. There are generous rebates for families with more than one child in the school.

Charitable status. Taunton School is a Registered Charity, number 1081420. It exists to provide education for boys and girls.

Tettenhall College

Wolverhampton West Midlands WV6 8QX.
Tel: (01902) 751119
Fax: (01902) 741940

Tettenhall College was founded in 1863 by a group of Wolverhampton businessmen to provide a school for sons of nonconformists. Tettenhall is now co-educational and an interdenominational school, providing a quality education from nursery to university entrance.

There are about 460 pupils, of whom 90 are Boarders.

Motto: *Timor Domini Initium Sapientiae.*

Governors:

Chairman: P Brown, OBE, MA

Vice-Chairman: Revd Prebendary G Wynne, MTh, BSc(Soc), BD, AKC

P H Creed
K S Geekie
Mrs C Hammond, BA
M Kersen
R McKenzie, BSc, CEng, FICE
Mrs D Margetts
Mrs J Parker, SRP, MCSP
G B Price
Professor R E Smallman, CBE, BSc, PhD, DSc, FEng, FRS
J A Sower, FCCA
Mrs G M Sower, BA
R A Street, ACIB
Mrs V Vaughan-Hughes
R J Whild, ARIBA
Miss M Whild, BA, DipArch, RIBA
J F Woolridge, CBE, BSc

***Headmaster:* P C Bodkin**, BSc, PhD

Second Master: R A Roberts, MA, LLM, PhD, JP

Teaching Staff:

G L Andrews, BA
M J Barraclough, BA
Mrs S Blake, BA, MA
Miss J Bohr, MA
D J Butler, BA
P I Cochrane, C in E
Mrs H Compain-Holt, MA
W G Cullis, BA, CBiol, MIBiol
M Davis, BSc
C J Evans, BSc, MIBiol, MCollP
G P Evans, BSc
Mrs P A Evans, BA
Mrs E J Gwilt, BSc
P J Higgins, BA
Mrs M E Johnson, C in E
P J Kay, BA
R M Leighton, BA
C D McCrea, BEd, MEd
A R Mottershead, BEd, PhD
The Revd N Murphy
Mrs V J Prentice, BSc
G J Raine, BA
Mrs A A Ridyard, BA
Mrs E Seed, CinE, DipSpNeeds, CertSPLD
Mrs D E Spencer, BEd
Mrs C A Squire, BA
Mrs J L Taylor, C in E
Miss M D Uttley, BA
I F Wass, BEd
Mrs C E Whiting, BSc, BEd
Mrs G O Whitmore, BSc
Y Zhang, BEng, MEng, PhD

Head of Lower School: P I Cochrane, C in E

Visiting Teachers: 12 staff provide Music tuition and 1 takes pupils for Speech training

Clerk to the Governors: M J Kilvert

Bursar: Mrs C E Jones, FMAAT

Medical Officers:
Dr J J Bright
Dr A Williams

School Nurses:
Mrs C Wagstaff
Mrs L Hazeldine

Situation and Buildings. Three miles west of the centre of Wolverhampton in the old village of Tettenhall, the school stands in 33 acres of extensive gardens, woods and playing fields.

The original building contains the Boys' Boarding House, the Dining Hall, the Chapel and also Big School which is now the School Library.

A new Girls' Boarding House was built in 1989 and another one was purchased in 1990.

The Towers, acquired from the Thorneycroft Estate in 1942, houses the Lower School form rooms, the Music Department and a fine theatre built in the nineteenth century. A new Lower School building is to be opened in September 2002.

The Maurice Jacks Building incorporates five excellent Science laboratories, administrative offices, a staff common room and form rooms.

Other amenities include a Sixth Form Centre, an Information Technology Network, a Home Economics Centre, a separate Art Department, a Resources Room, a covered, heated Swimming Pool, a Sports Hall and courts for Netball, Tennis and Squash. There are two Cricket squares and playing fields for Rugby, Soccer, Hockey and Athletics.

Religion. Services in the College Chapel are interdenominational.

Entry. The school accepts girls and boys. Entrance to the Upper School (age 11–18) is normally by way of assessment in Mathematics, English and Verbal Reasoning. Pupils at independent preparatory schools take the Common Entrance Examination. By arrangement with the Headmaster, pupils may be interviewed and tested according to their individual needs. Assessments are set by the Head of Lower School for pupils between the ages of 7 and 11. These can be taken in any term by appointment.

Organisation. Upper School (Years 7 to 11 and the Sixth Form) and Lower School (Years 3 to 6) are each divided into 4 Houses which compete in activities, work and games. The Drive School comprises a Nursery, Kindergarten, Reception and Years 1 and 2.

Upper School Curriculum. GCSE may be taken in the following subjects: Art, Biology, Business Studies, Chemistry, Economics, English, French, Geography, German, History, Information Studies, Mathematics, Music, Physics, Physical Education and Religious Studies.

In the Sixth Form various combinations of subjects are possible, and AS and A level courses offered include Art, Biology, Business Studies, Chemistry, Economics, Electronics, English, French, Geography, German, History, Law, Mathematics, Music, Physics, Performing Arts and Sports Science.

Careers. Extensive advice is given by the Careers Teachers and the local Careers Service.

Societies and Activities. All pupils are encouraged to become fully involved in the life of the community and to play a part in the social and cultural organisations.

Pupils take part in the Duke of Edinburgh Award Scheme, working for Bronze, Silver and Gold Awards, and members of the Social Service Group help those in need in the neighbourhood.

Full facilities are provided for Badminton, Basketball, Canoeing, Chess, Computer Studies, Drama, Karate, Dance, Pottery, Snooker and Table Tennis. There are numerous clubs and societies that meet regularly. Speech Training is also available for those who want it. Excursions are frequently arranged to places of special interest for those doing Business Studies, Geography, History, Science and Technology, and foreign journeys have, in recent years, regularly included visits abroad and exchanges with schools in Bensheim and Bremen. School plays are produced each year; there is a house festival of Performing Arts and the Music Department is strong.

Lower School. Lower School is housed separately in The Towers but enjoys the facilities of Upper School for Art, Music and Science. Upper School Staff help with games and specialist teaching.

Years 3 to 5 are taught mainly by their Form Teachers. Particular attention is paid to standards in English and Mathematics. French is taught from the age of seven and German from Year 6.

Athletics, Cricket, Netball, Hockey, Rounders, Rugby, Soccer, Swimming and Tennis are the main sports and all pupils have PE and two afternoons of games each week. Extra-curricular activities include Badminton, Bridge, Chess, Computing, Dance, Drama, Squash and Table Tennis. Music and the playing of musical instruments is strongly encouraged.

The Drive School. The Drive, the pre-preparatory department for pupils aged 2 to 7 years is accommodated within a new purposely designed building adjacent to The Towers. The emphasis is on the three Rs. The Humanities are approached through topic work; Science and Technology is experienced "hands on". Activities include Art and Craft, Music, PE, Dance and Swimming.

Fees (*see* Entrance Scholarship section) (per term): Year 7 and above Boarders £3,834, Weekly Boarders £3,190, Day Pupils £2,319. Below Year 7 Boarders £3,148, Weekly Boarders £2,554, Day Pupils £1,856. The Drive School £1,102-£1,466.

The Old Tettenhallians' Club. Correspondence should be addressed to Mr L N Chown at the College.

Charitable status. Tettenhall College Incorporated is a Registered Charity, number 528617. It exists to provide a quality education for boys and girls.

* Head of Department § Part Time or Visiting
† Housemaster/Housemistress ¶ Old Pupil
‡ See below list of staff for meaning

Tonbridge School

Tonbridge Kent TN9 1JP.
Tel: (01732) 365555

Founded by Sir Andrew Judde. Chartered by King Edward VI, AD 1553.

Motto: *Deus dat incrementum.*

Governors: The Master, Wardens, and Court of Assistants of the Worshipful Company of Skinners.

***Headmaster:* J M Hammond**, MA

Second Master: N M Lashbrook, BA

Assistant Staff:

A L Austin, BA
M S V Bardou, BA
C M Battarbee, BA
The Revd S M Beaumont, BD
P J Belbin, BSc, MEd (*Careers*)
Miss L D Benson, MA
M H Bishop, BSc
J Blake, BA, MSc
R J Bradley, BSc (*Computing and IT*)
Mrs P Brandling-Harris, BA, DipSpLD
D R Braybrook, MA, DPhil
M S Bull, DipPE
C J Burnand, BA, MSt
P S D Carpenter, MA (*English*)
Mrs C H Chisholm, BA
D J Clack, ARCM
M J Clugston, MA, DPhil
J C Cockburn, BA (*Art*)
Mrs T E M Coomber, L-ès-L
D Cooper, BA (*History*)
H Davan Wetton, HonDMus, MA, ARCM, ARCO(ChM) (*Music*)
K J Davis, BSc (*Art and Technology*)
D Dixon, BA (*Design Technology*)
R J Dunn, MA
A J Edwards, MA
C J Ellott, LLB
H B Evans, MSc, PhD
R H Evans, MA
D L Faithfull, BTech, MSc, MIEE (*Electronics*)
R L Fleming, MA
G P Gales, BEd (*Physical Education*)
J D Gibbs, MA, LLB
C M Henshall, BA (*Geography*)
R D Hoare, MA (*Modern Languages*)
J S Hodgson, BA
J N Holmes, MA, LRAM
Mrs D M Hulse, MA
I R H Jackson, MA, PhD
T C R Jones, MA
J D King, MA, PhD
Miss M S Laing, GGSM, ARCM, LRAM
Miss E Lambert, BSc, PhD
A J Leale, BA
N Leamon, MA
R I Longley, MA
N J Lord, MA (*Mathematics*)
I N Lucas, BSc
I S MacEwen, MA
J H Maynard, BA
P McManus, BSc (*Director of Studies*)
M I Morrison, BA (*Drama*)
W E Moss, BA
Miss K E Moxon, MA
R W G Oliver, MA
The Revd T D Page, MA (*Chaplain*)
P W G Parker, MA
P Pattenden, MA, DPhil
A E L Pearson, BMus, LRAM, ARCM
J E Perriss, BA
I R Pinkstone, BSc
K P Rea, MA
T W Richards, BA
P M Ridd, MA (*Science and Biology*)
D M Robins, MA
Miss M Robinson, MA
M G Rowan, MA, FRGS
A P Schweitzer, MA
J B Smith, MA
L S Steuart Fothringham, MA, FRCO
R J Stevens, DipPE, BEd
J S Taylor, MA, DPhil (*Classics*)
P B Taylor, BA
D H Tennant, BSc
Miss E J V Thomas, BA
L Thornbury, DipDrama
R D Tillson, MA (*Economics*)
P A Todd, BA
S M Wainde, MA (*Spanish*)
N C Waite, BSc (*Physics*)
A K Wallersteiner, MA
D R Walsh, MA
D L Williams, GRSM, ARCM, LRAM
A F Worrall, BA, PhD (*Chemistry*)
C E Wright, BA (*German*)

Administration:

Bursar: R E E Hart, OBE, JP
Assistant Bursar: D J C Dickins, MBE
Librarian: Mrs B Matthews, ALA
Headmaster's Secretary: Mrs J Marchant
Admissions Registrar: D M Robins, MA
Admissions Secretary: Miss R Hearnden
Clerk to the School: E J Smalman-Smith, MA

Tonbridge School was founded in 1553 by Sir Andrew Judde, under Letters Patent of King Edward VI. The Charter ordained that the Governors of the School after the death of the Founder were to be the Worshipful Company of Skinners, one of the oldest City Livery Companies. Sir Andrew, himself a distinguished member of this Company, left property in the City of London and in the Parish of St Pancras as an endowment for the school.

The School occupies an extensive site of about 150 acres on the northern edge of the town of Tonbridge, and is largely self-contained within that site. The central buildings of the present school date from the second half of the nineteenth century, a time in which the school grew considerably in size and importance.

There has been much further building in the twentieth century, including a new boarding House in 1990. A £20m development programme, which involves both new building and the creation of additional or improved facilities within the existing buildings, was initiated in 1991. The first phase of this programme, resulting in new and enlarged accommodation for three academic departments, was completed in 1992, and a new Biology Department was built in 1993. The second phase included a new Social Centre, and a Lecture Theatre (both completed in 1994). In the third phase, a major new Arts and Technology Centre, providing new accommodation for Art, Technology, Electronics and Computing, as well as a substantial extension of the Music facilities, was opened in the summer of 1996. The final phase includes a 400-seat Theatre, opened in 2000, and a Sports Hall (2003).

Tonbridge is a Christian foundation, and the services in the splendidly restored Chapel (1995) are an important and regular part of school life. The whole school gathers for a short service or assembly on most weekday mornings. Boarders attend a full choral service each Sunday.

There are 720 boys in the School, aged between 13 and 18, of whom 420 are boarders and 300 are day boys. There are seven boarding Houses, each with a complement of about sixty boys, and five day boy Houses. Each boarding House has its own dining room, kitchen and domestic staff, and boys take their meals in their own Houses.

Boarding Houses. School House (Mr A J Edwards); Judde House (Mr M S Bull); Park House (Mr P B Taylor); Hill Side (Mr P W G Parker); Parkside (Mr A P Schweitzer); Ferox Hall (Dr I R H Jackson); Manor House (Mr M G Rowan).

Day Boy Houses. Welldon House (Mr A K Wallersteiner); Smythe House (Mr D L Williams); Whitworth House (Mr I S MacEwen); Cowdrey House (Mr J H Maynard); Oakeshott House (Mr P A Todd).

Admissions and Scholarships (*see* Entrance Scholarship section) The great majority of boys join the school at the age of 13, having gained admission through the Common Entrance Examination or the school's own Scholarship Examination (held in early May). About 140 boys are admitted at the age of 13 each year. A few places are available for entry to the Sixth Form at the age of 16. Except in special cases, entry is in September only.

Up to 36 scholarships are offered for award each year. In a typical year there are awarded some 21 academic scholarships, 9 or 10 Music scholarships, and 4 or 5 Art or Technology scholarships. A number of Choral Boarding places, with a value of one sixth of the fees, are also offered each year for award to Choristers of Cathedral or other Choir Schools. The value of any scholarship awarded may be increased, by any amount up to the full school fee, if assessment of the parents' means indicates a need.

Registration of a boy as a potential candidate for admission to the school at the age of 13 should be made as early as possible, and preferably not later than three years before the date of intended entry. Applications for Sixth Form entry may be made at any time up to the end of April in the year in which entry is desired in September.

Each year all candidates for 13-year old entry in September are invited to spend two days at the school in March, just after the end of the Tonbridge Lent Term, and those who will be boarders spend the night in the boarding House they intend to join. The boys greatly enjoy this visit, and it contributes to the ease with which they settle in September.

Academic Life. All boys entering the school at the age of 13 join one of the six Third Form sets of about 23 boys each. They are taught most subjects in these groups which are broadly streamed, but they are separately setted for mathematics and for foreign languages. In the Fourth Form and above, all subjects are taught in subject-specific sets: the average set size in the Fourth and Fifth Forms is 17, and in the Sixth Form 9.

In the **Third Form,** in addition to the usual range of academic subjects, all boys take courses in Art, Music, Drama and Technology (including Design & Technology and Electronics).

The curriculum in the **Fourth and Fifth Forms** is designed to offer flexibility both of choice and pace, so that boys can choose a programme which suits their own inclinations and needs. Many boys take some GCSE examinations at the end of the Fourth Form year, and the remainder of their examinations in the Fifth Form: others take the majority of their GCSEs at the end of the Fifth Form year. For most boys, then, the Fifth Form is a mixed economy – in some subjects continued work towards GCSE, in others more advanced work as a preparation for Sixth Form study.

A course in Information Systems is followed by all boys in the Third, Fourth and Fifth Forms.

In the **Sixth Form** all boys study four subjects to AS level in the Lower Sixth, and then either three or four subjects to A level in the Upper Sixth. The choice of subjects is wide, and the timetabling allows virtually any combination to be taken.

The school believes strongly in the importance of general education; throughout the Fifth Form year, all boys attend a Seminar programme to extend their intellectual horizons and attitudes in preparation for the Sixth Form. This programme develops in the Lower Sixth where, in small groups each led by a member of staff, boys experience group exercises, lectures and discussions whose object is the enlargement of their ethical, cultural, scientific and political awareness. In the Upper Sixth the Seminar programme consists of a series of talks by distinguished visiting speakers drawn from the worlds of politics, economics, academia, the arts and the media. Special arrangements are made for the preparation of candidates for admission to Oxford or Cambridge.

All boys in the Lower Sixth Form spend a week of work experience during the holidays. There is a Careers Adviser on the school staff.

Sport. The school's facilities include about 100 acres of playing fields, a heated indoor swimming pool, an all-weather athletics track of county standard, three hard playing areas for hockey and tennis (two of them Astroturf), squash courts, fives courts and a rackets court. Sailing takes place at Bough Beech reservoir. The school offers expert coaching in some 20 sports.

A distinctive feature of Tonbridge sport is that a very large number of boys have the opportunity to represent the school – not only the top sportsmen but also the average players. It is not uncommon for nearly half the school to be involved in representative matches on one afternoon: in the Michaelmas Term, for example, the school fields up to 23 XVs. There are also House Leagues in the main sports, which offer a particular opportunity to those who do not play in the major school teams.

Activities and Trips. Both Music and Drama play a major part in the life of the school. There is a strong tradition of musical excellence, and over half of the boys in the school learn a musical instrument: there are three orchestras, several bands, and many smaller ensembles. The Chapel's four-manual Marcussen organ is internationally famous and the Chapel Choir is much in demand to sing services outside the school. There are weekly performance opportunities for boys (the School has three fine Bosendorfer grand pianos) and a large-scale choral/orchestral concert every term. Composition flourishes; the Sibelius 7 program has made this activity accessible to a large number of boys. A fully equipped recording studio is much used by Jazz and Rock groups. Two or three plays are produced each term, and a year's programme includes senior and junior school plays, several House plays, smaller-scale productions by particular groups of boys, and usually a play in French or German. There are strong links with local Girls' Schools, and the new Theatre provides excellent opportunities for pupils to work with a range of visiting companies. Boys may gain experience not only as actors, but also as directors or as members of the technical teams. There is an annual Arts Festival - a week of events including Drama, Music, Art and Literature.

One afternoon each week is devoted by all boys to activities wholly separate from their academic and sporting programmes. The choice of activities is wide, and includes participation in the Community Service Group, the Duke of Edinburgh's Award Scheme, and the three sections of the CCF.

There are about 35 school societies and clubs which hold regular meetings. A Societies Fair is held at the beginning of each school year.

A large number of expeditions, trips and exchanges is organised each year, with full staff supervision. There are annual exchanges with schools in Paris and Hamburg; study trips to France, to Greece or Italy, and to America; Sixth Form reading parties; and a wide range of other academic, cultural, musical, and sporting tours. In the Easter holidays between 15 and 20 such trips are regularly organised by the school in this country and abroad.

Each year Easter and Summer holiday courses for children and adults are offered at the school in some 40 sports, crafts, and educational activities.

Annual School Fees. Boarders, £16,767; Day Boys, £11,847.

Charitable status. Tonbridge School is a Registered Charity, number 307099. It exists solely to provide education for boys.

Trent College

Long Eaton Nottingham NG10 4AD.
Tel: Headmaster: (0115) 8494949
General enquiries: (0115) 8494949
Bursar: (0115) 8494920
Registrations' Secretary: (0115) 8494950
Fax: (0115) 8494997
e-mail: enquiries@trentcollege.nott.sch.uk
website: www:trentcollege.nott.sch.uk

The Foundation Stone of Trent College was laid by the Duke of Devonshire in 1866 and the School opened two years later. The School was founded by Cecil Wright.

Motto: *Fons vitae sapientia.*

Governing Body:

President: His Grace The Duke of Devonshire, PC, MC

Chairman: Mrs S Rose, LLB

Dr B R Allen, MB, ChB, FRCP
G D Bates
Mrs W E Cooke, BSc
Professor C Day, CertEd, LRAM, MA, DPhil, PhD, FRSA
Mrs A Ferdinand, BSc
Prof M W Fowler, BSc, PhD, CIBiol, MIBiol, FIBiol, FRSA
Mrs E A Gregory, BSc, ACIS
B L Harris, BA, MBA
The Revd Dr J Kelly, PhD, BTh, LLB
M C McDowell, ACC
R W Nelson, LLB
Mrs P Spaven, BSc, PGCE
A D Swallow (*Chairman, Finance Committee*)
Mrs M J Thornhill, MA
The Revd A F Walters, ACP, CertEd

Senior School Staff:

***Headmaster:* J S Lee**, MA, St Edmund Hall, Oxford (*Physics*)

Director of Human Resources: Mrs W M Robinson, MA (*Business Education*)
Director of Marketing: P D McKeown, BA (*Business Education*)
Director of Studies: M C B McFarland, BA (*History*)
Deputy Head/Head of Sixth Form: G C Sharpe, BSc, MSc, MRSC, CChem (*Chemistry*)
Head of Main School: D Collingwood, BA, BEd, CBiol, MIBiol (*Biology*)
Head of Lower School: K G Edgar, BSc (*Geography*)
Director of Information Systems: M A Cowie, BSc, MEd (*Information Technology*)
Senior Boarding Housemaster: S Ryder, BA (*English*)

Assistant Housemistress of Bates House: Miss E A McKenzie, BA (*History and English*)
Housemaster of Blake House: M C Phillips, BA (*Geography*)
Housemistress of Cavendish House: Mrs H E Pickup, BA (*French and Spanish*)
Housemaster of Hanbury House: A S Jones, BSc (*Mathematics*)
Housemistress of Martin House: Mrs L E Wilbraham, BA (*Geography*)
Assistant Housemaster of Shuker House: A R Bradshaw, BA (*Head of Spanish*)
Housemaster of Wright House: G W Thompson, BSc (*Design*)
Houseparent of Catterns: Mrs J Rimington

Assistant Teachers:
S D M Barnett, BSc (*Head of Mathematics*)
A M Benstead, BA, MA (*Head of PE*)
Ms A C Berry, BSc (*Mathematics*)
Mrs F A Brimblecombe, BSc (*Mathematics*)
Mrs L S Cassidy, BSc (*Chemistry*)
D A Curtiss (*Head of Brass*)
R L Dolby, MA (*German and French; Higher Education*)
Mrs G M P Drummond, MA, BMus, DPhil (*Music*)
Ms N J Duguay, BA (*Head of Theatre Studies*)
D A Dunford, MA (*English*)
Mrs E D Dunford, BA (*English*)
M R Field, BA (*History*)
Mrs E D Fisher (*Theatre Studies*)
Mrs J A Gale, BEng (*Mathematics*)
S C Gorman, BA (*Design and ICT; Co-ordinator of Expeditions*)
M D Grindle, BSc (*Physics*) (*Director of the Wortley Sixth Form Centre*)

The Revd T R Haggis, MA (*Chaplain*)
J T Jordison, BA (*Geography*)
P D Kelly, BSc, PhD (*Head of Chemistry; Head of Academic Administration*)
Mrs L M L Leadbetter, BA (*Modern Languages*)
F W B Leadbetter, MA (*Head of Classical Civilisation*)
Ms E L Matthews, BSc (*Biology*)
Mrs J McFarland, BSc (*Biology*)
Ms C Mackay, BSc (*Mathematics*)
P J Millward, BA, FRCO (*Choirmaster*)
D W Mitchell, MA
J E Morley, BSc, PhD (*Physics*)
W G Pedley, BA, PhD (*Head of Modern Languages*)
D W Pinney, BSc, CBiol, MIBiol, DipEd (*Head of Biology*)
J Prince, BSc (*Head of Technology*)
P D Redfearn, BA, ARCM (*Director of Music*)
K Rimington, BA (*Head of English*)
A F Rolt, CertEd, MA (*Director of Sport*)
Ms J Rutter, BSc (*Head of Girls' Games*)
Mrs L A Ryder, GRNCM (*Music*)
I R Sanderson, MA (*French and ICT; Director of Resources*)
P Saville, BA (*Head of Design*)
P A Shuttleworth, BSc (*Head of Geography*)
Miss M L Smith, BA (*PE*)
D Sprakes, DipAd, ATD (*Head of Art*)
D J Tidy, BEd (*Head of Business Education & Careers*)
Ms S Turner, BSc (*Chemistry*)
P L Wearn, BSc (*Head of Physics*)
M H Westhead, MSc (*Information Technology*)
Mrs E Woods, BSc (*Mathematics*)
T P Woods, MA, DPhil (*Head of History*)
Miss A G Wright, BA (*Head of German*)

Part-time Teachers:
Mrs G Everrett, BEd (*Learning Support*)
Mrs C S Grindle, BSc (*PE*)
Miss V M Lee, BA (*Art*)
A S Northeast, MA (*Art*)

Foreign Language Assistants:
Senorita E A Vicente (*Spanish*)
Mrs U Hobday (*German*)
Mrs G Mesbah (*French*)

Instrumental Teaching Staff:
Miss M H Coupe, GRSM, ARMCM, DipPerf Berlin (*Piano*)
E Dring (*Brass*)
D E Gore (*Guitar*)
Mrs S J Grange, BA, LRAM (*Piano and Strings*)
S G Hicking, LRAM (*Flute*)
Mrs E Keeley, BA (*Flute*)
D J Kennard, BEd, LRAM (*Woodwind*)
P Lacey, GBSM, ABSM, LTCL (*Brass*)
Mrs A R Lewin, LWCMD (*Violin, Viola*)
I A Otley, DipEd (*Clarinet, Saxophone*)
D Pikett (*Double Bass*)
Mrs U E Redfearn, Grad Hanover (*Violin*)
P M Scott, GRSM, ARMCM (*Oboe, Recorder*)
Mrs M G Sharpe, BA (*Piano*)
M Sillitoe (*Percussion*)
Mrs A M Stephen, BA, LRAM (*Piano, Voice*)
Mrs T Teasdale-Firth, GBSM, ABSM (*Violoncello*)
Mrs B Walker, LCCM (*Piano*)

Bursar: W Mulvenney, BA
Finance Bursar: D R Spicer

School Doctor: Dr J G Crompton, MB, BS

School Sister: J van Craeyenest, SRN, Mssch, MBchA

School Staff Instructor, CCF, and Health & Safety Officer: A J McIntyre, WO2
Cricket Coach: J A Afford (*ex Nottinghamshire and England*)

Junior School Staff:

Headteacher: Mrs A Beardsley, BEd

Assistant Teachers:
R Davies, BA (*Year 3*)
Miss L Draper, BA (*Year 1*)
Mrs J Hancock, BEd (*Year 2*)
Miss P Marlow, BSc (*Reception*)
Miss L Pattison, GRSM (*Music Co-ordinator, Year 4*)
Miss L Rigley, BA (*Year 5*)
Dr S Turner, BSc, PhD (*Year 6*)
Mrs G Veasey, CertEd (*Head of Nursery*)

Part-time teachers:
Mrs C Chivers, BEd (*Dance*)
Mrs B Nielsen, BSc (*French*)

Situation. Trent College is situated in 45 acres of attractive grounds, approximately midway between Nottingham and Derby, on the edge of the town of Long Eaton which has a population of approximately 35,000.

Pupils. In September 1999 the School opened its own Junior School, The Elms, which caters for 170 children from the age of 3 to 11. From September 2001 The Elms begins a phased increase to two-form entry. The Senior School is divided into three key parts. Firstly the Lower School (11-13) with around 150 pupils, including some boarders. Pupils then move on to the Main School (13-16) with about 270 pupils. There are 5 Houses, 3 co-educational Day Houses and a Boys' Boarding House and a Girls' Boarding House. Finally the pupils move up to the Sixth Form of around 200 pupils where there is no house system. There are two Boarding Houses, one for boys and one for girls.

Ethos. Trent is a selective and academic school, with considerable competition for places. Traditional standards of morality, considerate behaviour and compassion for others less fortunate are emphasised within a Christian framework. Trent has a boarding school ethos, which means that the day pupils may stay in school until 6.00 pm on each weekday, five lessons are taught on Saturday mornings (except for those in the Lower School) and there are games for the vast majority on Saturday afternoon. With a well-coordinated and imaginative programme of week-end activities, involving trips away and the use of the school's own facilities, Trent is committed to 'full boarding'. However, we appreciate the changing needs of parents and therefore we also offer flexible boarding, where pupils can go home after their commitment on Saturday or stay and join in the weekend activities.

Buildings. Trent makes very good use of the original School building which contains the 5 main School Houses, the Chapel, the Dining Hall, the Teachers' Common Room, the Sixth Form Club and the School Administration. There has been an impressive development programme over the 15 years with the addition of an Art, Design & Technology Centre, a new Sixth Form Boarding House, a new Biology Centre, a new Pavilion, new teaching facilities for Modern Languages and History, a new Business Centre and most recently a new Sixth Form Centre which was completed in October 1999.

Academic. Whilst taking full note of the implications of the National Curriculum, Trent has its own curriculum to GCSE. All pupils will take Maths, English (Language) and English Literature at GCSE. On top of this, six additional GCSEs will be taken from a wide range of options. In the Sixth Form every pupil will take four Advanced GCE AS subjects; the more able may take further courses selecting from a wide range of options. In the Sixth Form great emphasis is placed on the Sixth Form Skills Programme. The vast majority of the pupils leaving the school proceed to degree courses at university, several each year gaining places at Oxford or Cambridge.

Games. The major sports, played on three afternoons a week, are rugby football, hockey and cricket (for boys); hockey, netball and tennis (for girls). There are facilities for swimming, athletics, squash, fencing, tennis, badminton, basketball, cross-country, soccer and shooting. There is great emphasis on all pupils being given the chance to develop their sporting talent, whatever their level, and the School, with its large number of teams, tries to provide as many as possible with the opportunity of representing the School. A second astroturf and a second hard play surface were opened in January 1995.

Music and Drama. Many pupils learn musical instruments and a large number play to a very high standard. With a First, an Intermediate and a Junior Orchestra, together with several other bands and ensembles, all musicians, no matter what their standard or age, are given every opportunity to perform with others in a group. An early experience of public performance helps maintain the overall high standard of musicianship.

There is a whole range of dramatic productions each year, either using the May Hall Stage or Understage or the Melton Studio Theatre, so that as many as possible are given the chance of developing any dramatic talent.

Societies. Tutors encourage their tutees to make good use of the many and varied societies and activities which are on offer either at lunchtime, late afternoon or early evening. This area of the school is flourishing and helps pupils develop broad interests.

Service Activities. On one afternoon each week, every pupil in Year 10 and above must opt for one 'Service' activity. These choices include: CCF (Army or RAF section), Community Service, Duke of Edinburgh Award, Adventure Training, Life Saving and Scouts. All members of Year 9 follow the Trent Award (an activity which develops their self-reliance and enterprise). Many of the Service Activities, particularly CCF, Duke of Edinburgh Award and Scouts, organise exciting holiday activities.

Expeditions. Trent over the last few years has established an impressive record of organising overseas mountaineering/trekking expeditions: Iceland (1988); Siberia (1990); Pyrenees (1991); Iceland (1991); Belize (1992); Canadian Rockies (1992 and 1995); Iceland (1994), Greenland (1999); Iceland (2001); Canoeing in Canada (1994) and Greenland (1997), Norway (1998).

Art, Design, Technology and Computing. Art, Design, Technology and Computing flourish at Trent, both as academic subjects and interests. Out-of-class involvement is strongly encouraged and, in recent years, Trent has established a most successful record in regional, national and international competitions with a number of impressive successes including: Top Prize in the European Design Competition in Brussels (1989); Top Prize in the national Young Engineer of Great Britain (1990) and the Young Electronic Designer (1999); Top Prize in the European Science & Technology Exhibition in Zurich (1991); a winner at the 43rd International Science & Engineering Fair in Nashville (1992); Top Prize and runner-up in the national U16 Section of the Young Engineer Competition (1992 and 2000), prizes in both the U16 and the Senior Young Engineer Competition every year from 1992.

Fees (2000). Junior School: £3,780. Lower School Day: £6,732. Lower School Boarding: £8,942, Main School Day: £7,473. Main School Boarding: £11,608 (flexible) or £12,567 (full). All prices are per year.

As far as possible we aim to make fees all-inclusive and only charge for genuine extras.

Admission. Entry to the Junior School is either at Nursery, Reception or Year 3. All pupils are assessed, and entry can be assured at any time during the year. Most pupils enter the Senior School in September, although it is possible for entry to take place at other times in the year.

Lower School (11+ entry): c 80 places, boarding and day, are available each year. Entry is decided as a result of a competitive examination held in late January or early February.

Main School (13+ entry): 30 places, predominantly boarding entry. Usually these places are awarded as a result of an applicant's performance in the Common Entrance or Scholarship Examination.

Sixth Form Entry (16+): there are approximately 35 places (split equally between boarding and day) available each year for girls. There are approximately 15 places (split equally between boarding and day) available each year for boys. Places are awarded following an interview and the receipt of a confidential report from the applicant's present school, but are ultimately conditional on a satisfactory performance at GCSE.

Scholarships. (*see* Entrance Scholarship section) A large range of Scholarships is available.

Awards are made for excellence in Music, Drama, Art, Sport and Academic ability at 11+, 13+ and 16+.

At 13+ further awards are made in Design and Technology, and Information Technology. There are also boarding awards for those who could make an all-round contribution, and special consideration is given to those with a parent in the Services.

At 16+ additional awards are available in Business Education.

Bursaries are also available to those in need of extra financial support.

The value of an Award depends on the age of the child, their ability and whether they are a day pupil or a boarder.

Full details on all scholarships, examinations and entrance procedures are available from the Registrations Secretary: Tel 0115 849 4950.

School Prospectus. A prospectus and registration details may be obtained from the Registrations Secretary, Mrs Phillips (Tel: 0115 849 4950). Parents are encouraged to visit the School and appointments may be made by contacting Mrs Phillips.

Old Tridents' Society. Most pupils who leave the School join this active Society. The Society's Administrator, Alan Seldon, may be contacted at the School's address.

Charitable status. Trent College Limited is a Registered Charity, number 527180. Its aims are to provide education for boys and girls between the ages of 3 and 18.

Trinity School
Croydon

Shirley Park Croydon CR9 7AT.
Tel: 020 8656 9541
Fax: 020 8655 0522

The School was founded by Archbishop John Whitgift in 1596. Its name was Whitgift Middle School from 1857 until 1954. The full title of the school is Trinity School of John Whitgift

Motto: *Vincit qui Patitur.*

Visitor: His Grace The Archbishop of Canterbury

Governing Body:

Chairman: Sir Douglas Lovelock, KCB

The Bishop of Croydon (*The Rt Revd Dr W Wood*)	Clr R W Coatman, MBE, JP, FRICS, FIArb, MRSH
The Vicar of Croydon (*The Revd Canon C J L Boswell*)	Prof J W Dougill, PhD, FEng
	Clr M A Fowler, FCA, FCIArb

V F Long, FCIB
A D Sexton, BA
D W North, BSc(Eng), ACGI, MICE
Mrs J Manklow
Clr T Letts
Dr A Orchard, MBBS, DObst, RCOG
Prof A H Windle, PhD, FIM, FRS
P Squire, MA
Clr H Malyan

Clerk to the Governors: R J Smith

***Headmaster:* C J Tarrant**, MA, BD

Deputy Headmaster: J W Watson, MA

Second Deputy: M J Horrocks-Taylor, BSc, MEd

Senior Master: T A W Cattell, MA

Director of Studies: G P South, MA, PhD

Head of Sixth Form: N H Denman, MA

Head of Middle School: I A Jardine, BA

Head of Junior School: R Brookman, BSc

Senior Mistress: Mrs K A Goldsmith, BEd

Tutor for Admissions: B Widger, DLC

Assistant Staff:
M I Aldridge, BEd
*E M Alexander, BEd
M Asbury, BSc
M S Asquith, BA, MA, PhD
D Bell, BA, ATC
J Bird, BSc
D S Brand, BEd
R Brookman, BSc
C R Burke
J-L Cantor, L-ès-L, MA
M J Case, BA
T W Chesters, BSc
I W Cheyne, DipPE
S W Christian, BA
*A P Colpus, BSc
Miss D M Contreiras, BA
K A Cooper, CertEd
G A Crouch, CertEd
A F Davey, BSc
D J de Warrenne, ARCM, LGSM
M J Dodd, BSc, PhD
*A B Doyle, MA, MA
D O Dyer, BSc
R H Ellson, BA
R G Evans, BSc
Mrs S L Flynn, BSc
*M P Geoghegan, CertEd
*T M Glynn, BA
D Harley, BSc
Ms M K Harrop-Allin, BSc, MSc, PhD
*J Janda, BA, ATC
I Jeeves, PhD, DIC, CChem, MRSC
Mrs C S Jennings, BSc
M V Johnson, BSc
*E Jones, BEd
M J Judge, BEd
Mrs B C Langford, MEng, MICS
D A Lawson, BEd
*R E Lee, MA
Miss G MacArthur, BA
O McDevitt, BA
*F S Macdonald, BA, MA
P March, BA
Mrs D R M March, L-ès-L
S R Margetts, BA
*I G Marsh, BEd, DipPE
*C Marvin, BSc
*P Mazur, BA, MA
Mrs C Morgan, BA
N E Oldham, BA
Miss H T Painter, BA
J M Peake, BA
N Peters, BA, MA
*G J Powell, MA
P J Radford, BSc
Miss J A Rand, BA
*N W Rivers, BSc
S Robertson, DRSAM, DipMIT
Miss A A Rogers, BA
Ms K A Rossé, BA
Miss J M Rowley-Jones, BMus
*P H Rule, BSc
*C T Shanks, BSc, PhD
*J Stone, MA
*R M Sutton, BSc, MA
*D J Swinson, MA, FRCO, ARCM, LRAM
Miss E Teale, BSc
*J G Timm, BA
W S Tucker, BSc
*D G Urmston, BA, MSc
J K Waller, BA, BA, MSc
J P Whyatt, BA
R J Wickes, BSc
S H Wilberforce, MA
Mrs L Wilson, BEd

Librarian: Mrs M Fletcher-Hale, BA, DipLib, ALA

The School, one of the three governed by the Whitgift Foundation, is an Independent day school with 870 boys, of whom 250 are in the VIth Forms. The School aims to give a wide education to boys of academic promise, irrespective of their parents' income.

Buildings and Grounds. Trinity School has been in its present position since 1965, when it moved out from the middle of Croydon (its old site is now the Whitgift Centre) to a completely new complex of buildings and playing fields on the site of the Shirley Park Hotel. The grounds are some 27 acres in extent, and a feeling of openness is increased by the surrounding Shirley Park Golf Club and the extensive views to the south up to the Addington Hills. There are additional playing fields in Sandilands, ten minutes' walk from the school.

The resources of the Whitgift Foundation enable the school to provide outstanding facilities. All departments have excellent and fully equipped teaching areas.

Admission. The main ages of admission are at 10, 11 and 13. Entry is by competitive examination, for which applications are accepted until shortly before the examinations, which are held during the Spring Term. Entries into the Sixth Form are welcomed. The school attracts applications from over 150 primary and preparatory schools.

Fees. The fees are £7,305 for the academic year 2000–2001, and cover tuition, books, stationery and games.

Fee Remission. *Bursaries:* Around a third of parents receive a bursary for their sons. These are awarded when a boy joins the school. A proportion of pupils have a free place.

Entrance Scholarships: Academic, music (instrumental), sports, art and technology scholarships are awarded to boys who show outstanding promise. They are awarded without regard to parental income, and are worth a percentage (maximum one-half) of the school fee throughout a boy's career.

Organisation and Counselling. The school is divided into the Junior School (National Curriculum years 6 to 9), the Middle School (10 to 11), and the Sixth Form. The teacher in charge of each section works with the team of Form Tutors to encourage the academic and personal development of each boy. There is frequent formal and informal contact with parents.

There is a structured and thorough Careers service, which advises boys at all levels of the school and arranges work experience and work shadowing.

While the academic curriculum is taught from Monday to Friday, there is a very active programme of sports fixtures and other activities at the weekend and all boys are expected to put their commitment to the school before other activities.

Curriculum and Staffing. The school is generously staffed with well qualified specialists. The organisation of the teaching programme is traditionally departmental based. The syllabus is designed to reflect the general spirit of the National Curriculum while allowing a suitable degree of specialisation in the Middle School.

The normal pattern is for boys to take 9 or 10 GCSE subjects, and to proceed to the Sixth Form to study an appropriate mixture of A and AS level– subjects, complemented by a wide-ranging General Studies programme, before proceeding to university.

Games and Activities. Rugby Football, Hockey, Cricket and Athletics are the main school games. Many other sports become options as a boy progresses up the school. Games are timetabled, each boy having one games afternoon a week.

At the appropriate stage, most boys take part in one or more of the following activities: Community Service, CCF, Duke of Edinburgh Award Scheme, Outdoor Activities. There are many organised expeditions during the holidays.

Music. Music at Trinity has a national reputation, and every year Trinity Boys' Choir is involved in a varied programme of demanding professional work, for example, at Henry Wood Promenade Concerts, the Royal Festival Hall, the Coliseum, Fairfield Hall and on radio and television. Trinity Choristers, who specialise in religious music, hold an annual residential Easter Course at a British cathedral. Choral Scholarships are awarded annually and enable boys to receive additional professional voice training without charge. Many boys learn at least one musical instrument, and a large visiting music staff teach all orchestral instruments, piano, organ and classical guitar. There are several orchestras, bands and other instrumental groups for which boys are selected according to their ability.

Drama. There are two excellently equipped stages in the school and a lively and developing programme of formal and informal productions directed by boys and staff. Drama forms part of the formal curriculum in years 6 to 9.

Art and Design Technology. As well as the formal curriculum, which has led to 70% of the school taking a GCSE in art or design technology, boys are encouraged to make use of the excellent facilities to develop their own interests.

Charitable status. The Whitgift Foundation is a Registered Charity, number 312612. The Foundation now comprises the Whitgift Almshouse Charity for the care of the elderly and the Education Charity which administers three schools.

Truro School

Truro Cornwall TR1 1TH
Tel: (01872) 272763
Fax: (01872) 223431

Truro School was founded in 1880 by Cornish Methodists. In 1904 it came under the control of the Board of Management for Methodist Residential Schools and is now administered by a Board of Governors appointed by the Methodist Conference. Although pupils come from all parts of the country and abroad, the roots of the school are firmly in Cornwall and it is the only HMC school in the county.

The religious instruction and worship are undenominational though the school is conscious of its Methodist origins.

There are about 760 pupils in the senior school (11+ and above), of whom about 120 are boarders. There are another 200 pupils at Treliske, the Preparatory department, where boys and girls may start in the pre-prep section at the age of 3.

The school is fully co-educational throughout and there is a strong VIth form of some 240 pupils.

Motto: *Esse quam videri.*

Visitor: The President of the Methodist Conference

Administrative Governors:
Chairman: J R Heath, BA
Vice-Chairman: D J Jewell, MA, MSc, FRSA
Deputy Chairman: B M Grime, MSc(Eng), FEng, MIMechE, MIEE

Lady Banham, JP
J S Baxter, BA, DipEd, MBIM, FRSA
R R Cowie, FCA
Rev S B Dawes, MA
Rev D Deeks
C N Harding, BSc
Mrs E A Malden, MA
Mrs C R Roberts, BEd
G Rumbles
G Russell, MA
C S F Smith, DipArch, RIBA, FFB
Mrs J Toms
District Judge C J Tromans, MA, FRSA
Rev D W Watson

***Headmaster:* P K Smith**, MA, MEd

Deputy Heads:
S Price, MA
Mrs P A Harris, BA

Director of Studies: N J Baker, BSc (Econ)

Chaplain: R J Buley, MA

Head of Science: Dr P D Allen, BSc, MSc, PhD

Boarding House Staff:

G J Neill, MA (*Poltisco*)
Mrs M A Gould, CChem, MRSC (*Pentreve/Malvern*)
J Triggs, MA (*Trennick*)

Heads of Year:

Dr C J Blake, BSc, PhD (*6th Form*)
J L Worthington, BA (*Assistant, 6th Form*)
P H J Collenette, MSc (*5th Form*)
Mrs U A Hold (*4th Form*)
J R A Golds, MA (*3rd Form*)
Mrs C Thompson, BSc (*1st and 2nd Forms*)
S A Collinge, BSc (*Assistant, 1st and 2nd Forms*)

Heads of Department:

D R Heseltine, CertEd (*Art*)
G Baines, BA (*Biology*)
M W D Thompson, BA (*Chemistry*)
R A Dunbar, MA (*Classics*)
A Mulligan, BA (*Drama*)
T R Tall, BEd (*Design and Technology*)
J C Cornish, BA (*Economics, Business Studies and Politics*)
Mrs S Spence, MA (*English*)
P H J Collenette, MSc (*Geography and Geology*)
Dr P J Flood, BA, PhD (*History*)
I K Hardwick, MA (*Mathematics*)
M Homer, BA (*Modern Languages*)
D J Spedding, MusB, GRSM, ARMCM (*Music*)
G C Whitmore, BEd (*PE and Games*)
Dr P D Allen, BSc, MSc, PhD (*Physics*)
C Case, MTheol (*Religious Education*)

Treliske:

Headmaster: R L Hollins, BA, BEd, CertEd
Deputy Headmistress: Mrs J P Grassby, MEd, CertEd, CAP
Senior Master: R Lear, BPhil(Ed), CertEd, DipMathsEd
Head of Pre-Prep Unit: Mrs A Allen, CertEd

Bursar and Clerk to the Governors: A M Jones

Doctor to the Boarding Pupils: Dr P Short

Number in School. Senior School: 775 pupils, 487 boys, 288 girls; 664 day, 111 boarders. Junior School (Treliske): 144 pupils, 89 boys, 55 girls; 138 day, 6 boarders. Pre-prep: 59 pupils, 34 boys, 25 girls.

Boarding. The boarders at Treliske live in a family atmosphere and the domestic routine is supervised by the Headmaster and his wife.

At Main School girl boarders live in Pentreve/Malvern, a newly refurbished house supervised by married couples. Junior Boy boarders are accommodated in a separate modernised house, Poltisco, on the main school site. Boys in forms 4, 5 and 6 live in the Main School (Trennick House), again supervised by residential married couples. Pupils eat in the central dining room with a cafeteria system. There is a School Medical Centre on site.

Campus and Buildings. Treliske's campus is built around a country house acquired by the school in the 30s. It has an indoor heated swimming pool, a large assembly hall and extensive areas for science, computing, art and crafts, as well as two modern Sports Halls. The purpose-built Pre-prep unit opened in September 1991.

The Main School occupies an outstanding site overlooking the Cathedral city and the Fal Estuary; it is only five minutes from the centre of the city but the playing fields reach into the open countryside. The school is excellently equipped. There is a first class Library, extensive science laboratories, excellent Technology and Art facilities, a Computer centre, two language laboratories, music school, upper and lower sixth form centres and a range of classroom blocks. Sports are well served by a covered swimming pool, two large sports halls, squash and tennis courts and 30 acres of playing fields. September 2001 saw the opening of a fine new block containing six classrooms, a drama centre and the Burrell theatre. An attractive chapel provides a focus for the life of the school.

Organisation and Curriculum. Pupils are unstreamed in the first three years except for French, German and Maths from Form 2. The academic programme is conventional and the school follows the National Curriculum. All pupils take the basic subjects including the three sciences, design and technology and two foreign languages until the end of the third year when the students adopt their own balanced GCSE programme. GCSE subjects taken include English Language, English Literature, French, German, Latin, Geography, History, Religious Education, Music, Art, Design and Technology, PE, Physics, Chemistry, Biology, Mathematics. All pupils take Music, Religious Education and Physical Education at most stages and games appear in the timetable for the first five years. 6th formers are encouraged to use their free periods to participate in Physical Recreation. They are usually studying for four AS levels in the Lower 6th and these include English, History, Geography, Geology, Mathematics, Further Mathematics, Design and Technology, Art, Music, Religious Education, Physics, Chemistry, Biology, Economics, French, German, Spanish, Business Studies and Politics. General Studies include modules on Careers, Religious Education and Creative Studies. It is likely three subjects will be most commonly continued into the Upper 6th at A2 level. The vast majority of sixth formers go on to further education when they leave.

Out-of-School Activities. Extra-curricular life is rich and varied. There is a choir, school orchestra, a jazz group and a brass band. Facilities such as the ceramics room, the art room and the technical block are available to pupils in their spare time. A huge variety of activities includes fencing, archery, climbing (2 indoor walls), squash, sailing, golf, basketball, clay-pigeon shooting, surfing, spinning, photography and many others. Many boys and girls take part in the Ten Tors Expedition, an exceptional number are engaged in the Duke of Edinburgh Award Scheme, as well as local Community Service, and the Young Enterprise Scheme. Computing and electronics are very well catered for. Chess has traditionally been strong and the School has recently been very successful in national competitions. The School's model engineering group have had considerable national success. The School has an outdoor activities centre on Bodmin Moor and pupils have a chance to spend time there during the course of their education at the school.

Games. All the major team games are played. Badminton, cross-country, hockey, netball, squash and tennis are available throughout most of the year. Rugby and Girls Hockey are played in the Michaelmas Term and Soccer and Netball in the Lent Term. In the summer, cricket, athletics and swimming are the major sports. The covered pool is heated.

Scholarships. Truro School was once a Direct Grant Grammar School and most pupils join at the age of 11. There are vacancies for entry at other ages, particularly at 13 and 16. Scholarships are available and also a limited number of places under the School's own successor scheme to Government Assisted Places.

Fees. Main School Boarders £3,840 per term, Day Pupils £1,987 per term. Treliske Boarders £3,332 per term, Day Pupils £1,817 per term. Pre-prep pupils £1,209 per term.

Academic results. A number of pupils proceed to Oxbridge every year and well over 100 to other degree courses. The 2000 A level pass rate was 98.2%, with 69.5% at A and B grades. At GCSE the 2000 "pass" rate was 96.2% with over 50% at grades A* and A.

There is a strong Old Pupils' Association with centres locally, in London and in the Midlands. The Truro School Society associates parents, staff, old pupils and friends of the school.

Charitable status. Truro School is a Registered Charity, number 306576. It is a charitable foundation established for the purpose of education.

University College School

Frognal Hampstead London NW3 6XH.
Tel: 020 7435 2215
Fax: 020 7431 4385

University College School is a day school providing places for 700 boys in the Senior School and 220 boys in the Junior Branch.

Established in 1830 as part of University College, London, the School moved to its present site in Hampstead in 1907. Though now independently governed, UCS has sustained by continuous reinterpretation many of the ideals of its founders. Its basis remains the provision of the widest opportunities for learning and development without the imposition of tests of doctrinal conformity but within a balanced and coherent view of educational needs and obligations. This in turn rests on the recognition that care for a boy's social, moral and spiritual upbringing is a shared responsibility between home and school, an understanding fostered by mutual trust and regular communication. Thirdly, the distinctive ethos of the School stems from the conviction that a positive, lively and humane community, both within and beyond the School, can only be created by the liberal encouragement and disciplined fulfilment of the diversity of gifts among its individual members.

It is in this spirit that the School day begins with a short Assembly.

Council:

Chairman: Sir Victor Blank, MA

Honorary Treasurer: J Waddington Esq, MA, FCA

Professor I M Barron, Esq, MA
P Bayvel, PhD, BSc(Eng)
Professor P B Boulos, MS, FRCS, FRCS(Ed)
Mrs R Deech, MA
W H Frankel, Esq, OBE, BA
Sir Alan Greengross, MA
A G Hillier, Esq, BA, MBA
C Holdsworth Hunt, Esq
C Holloway, Esq, MA
Dame Tamsyn Imison, BSc
Sir Brian Leveson, QC
D J N Nabarro, Esq, MA, MBA
A P M Orchard, PhD, MA
Lady Winston, MA

***Headmaster:* K J Durham**, MA, Brasenose College, Oxford

Vice-Master: J L Older, BSc

Director of Studies: T A Morris, BA

Senior Master: D J Colwell, BA, PhD

M Alsford, BSc
Mrs K J Anthony, BA
E A Barnish, BA
I A Barr, MA
B J Bateman, BEd
S M Bloomfield, BA
C Bowes-Jones, BEd

J M Bradbury, MA, GBSM, ABSM
P Briercliffe, BA
S J Button, BA
R H Chapman, BSc
M P Collins, BA
Mrs G M Cooper, BEd
I A Cornish, CertEd
A Davis, BSc
R A Digby, BA (Hons)
Miss L A Dolata, BSc, MSc
D W J Edwards, BA
Mrs H Eggleton, BA, MIL
P R Eggleton, BEd
P Ellis, MA
G C Fisher, BSc
S A P Fitzgerald, BA
I C Gibson, MA
A J Gowlett, BSc
[2]G J Greenhough, BA, MA, MLitt
A P Haggar, BEng
D Hall, BA
S J Hann, HND
R A K Hawkins, BTech
S Hawley, BSc
Miss R Hemming, BA, BMus, MSc
M J Hitchcock, BA
C Hoile, BA
G Hudson, BSc
J M L Hudson, BA, MSc
Mrs K Hudson, BA
R Hyde, MA, MA
Mrs S Ingram, BSc
Mrs A H Isaac, BA, MA
S M Jacobi, MA, PhD
C A Letchford, MA
G W Lewis, MA, PhD
M B Lewis, BA
Mrs E B Lusty, MA
C P Mahon, BSc
M J Matuszak, BSc
Mrs R McCann, BA
M A McElroy, BSc, MA, ARCS
K McLaughlin, MA
N W McNaughton, BA(Econ), MSc
Mrs G Mori, L-ès-L
C M Myles, BA
N R Peace, BSc, MA
[2]G A Plow, MA, MA
D P Rance, CertEd
C M Reynolds, BSc, MSc
P Richards, BA, MA
D A Robb, PhD, BSc (Hons)
[2]T Roberts, BA, DPE
S Rynkowski, CertEd
M V Smith, DipAD, ATC
Mrs P R Spencer, BA
A J Steven, BA
I A Stroud, BA
Miss E M Thompson, MA
A G Vaughan, BA
M J Walsh, BEd
A R Welch, BEd, MSc, CBiol
S T Wells, BSc, ARCS
[2]A Wilkes, BA
D J Woodhead, BA
[2]A Woolley, BA, DPhil
T F Youlden, BA, MSc

[2] denotes Deme Warden

Bursar: C M Clark, BSc, FCA

Headmaster's Secretary: Mrs S E Lobatto

Consulting Physicians:
Dr E Laleye
Dr J Sheldon

Junior Branch
11 Holly Hill, NW3 6QN. Tel: 020 7435 3068

Head Master: K J Douglas, BA, CertEd

Deputy Headmaster: B Duggan, CertEd

Deputy Head (*Curriculum*): Mrs S E Martin, BSc

M A Albini, MA, BSc
Mrs R Beedle, BSc, MSc
Mrs L Biriotti, DipArch
M Cassell, BSc
Mrs J M Eggleton, BEd
Mrs H L Gregory-Judd, BA
Mrs Y P Gregory, BEd
A P Haggar, BEng
Mrs C Hopkins, GGSM
W G Jones
M Lall-Chopra, BA
Miss L Lipman, BA (Hons)
P Messingham, BSc
D C Quy, BA
Miss K Thomas, BA
Mrs T C Thomas, BA
A G Walliker, BHum, BA

Headmaster's Secretary: Miss J C Wormald
Consulting Physician: Dr M McCollum

Entry. Entry is in September only.

Admission. Boys are normally admitted to the Senior School at either 11+ or 13+. Admission at 11+ is either by promotion from the Junior Branch or by examination held in January of the year of entry. Admission at 13+ is by the Common Entrance following the UCS Preliminary Assessment, and interviews. These are held two years prior to entry. A substantial deposit is required when a place is accepted which will be credited against the first term's account. Bursaries and Grants are available where financial need can be shown.

Applications for entry should be made to the School Secretary at any time up to mid-September two years prior to admission (13+), or the beginning of December preceding the proposed year of entry (11+). There is a registration fee of £50.

The Lower and Middle Schools. The Curriculum is designed to provide a broad range of knowledge and experience for all boys over the 5 years from 11 to 16. In the first 2 years boys take English, French, Geography, History, Mathematics, Biology, Physics, Chemistry, Latin, Art, Design Technology, Drama, Music, Information Technology and Personal and Social Education. At 13+ they add a further subject choosing two from Latin, Greek, German, Spanish and Civics. Some modifications are made one year later according to aptitude and ability but most boys offer 9 subjects at GCSE.

The VIth Form. All boys take 4 subjects to AS Level in the Lower Sixth, with the option of narrowing to 3 in the following year.

AS level subjects may be chosen from: Art, Biology, Chemistry, Design & Technology, Economics, English, French, Further Mathematics, Geography, Geology, German, Greek History (Early Modern or Late Modern), Information Technology, Latin, Mathematics, Music, Philosophy, Physics, Politics, Spanish, Theatre Arts.

Boys in the VIth Form have their own spacious study and social areas in the VIth Form Centre, opened in 1974, and have the major responsibility for its use and upkeep. Senior Tutors, in collaboration with the Careers Master, provide detailed advice for each boy about the selection of courses at Universities and other further education opportunities as well as ensuring that a boy's course in the VIth Form meets the entrance requirements of his intended future course and professional career. The enormous majority of leavers go on to degree courses.

Boys are prepared for entrance to Oxford and Cambridge. Tuition is on a seminar basis.

Pastoral Care. In the Lower School (11+–12) boys are cared for by form teachers, Heads of Year and the Warden of the Lower School. The Middle and Senior Schools are divided into 5 Demes, each under the supervision of a Deme Warden. Many activities outside the classroom are organised by Demes, but the primary responsibility of the Deme Warden is to maintain a personal relationship with each member of his Deme, constant throughout a boy's school career. Consequently, in all important pastoral and disciplinary matters he deals directly with the boy in consultation with parents and other teachers and is answerable to the Headmaster for the general welfare of his Deme.

In addition to parents' evenings, parents are encouraged to consult informally with teachers about any issues that arise with their sons. A Parents' Guild exists to promote the general welfare of the School.

Careers. Boys are guided by means of interviews and tests towards careers appropriate to their gifts and personalities. Boys are given opportunities to attend holiday courses directed towards specific careers. To this end also, visiting speakers are invited to the School and there are frequent Careers Conventions. There is a full Careers Library and a comprehensive programme of Work Experience. The Parents' Guild and Old Boys also provide advice and support.

Physical Education and Games. There is a new Sports Hall and boys have periods of Physical Education within their normal timetable.

The School playing fields cover 27 acres and are situated a mile away in West Hampstead. In addition to grass surfaces, there is a large all-weather pitch and two fully refurbished pavilions. The major sports are Rugby Football in the Autumn Term and Cricket and Tennis in the Summer. In the Spring there is an open choice between Soccer, Hockey and Cross Country Running. The School has its own Tennis and Fives courts at Frognal, together with an indoor heated Swimming Pool. Other sports include Fencing, Athletics, Squash, Badminton, Basketball, Fives and outdoor pursuits.

Music and Drama. There is a strong musical tradition at UCS and many boys play in the Orchestras, Wind Band and a great variety of groups and ensembles. Choral music is equally strong and Jazz is a particular feature. Instrumental tuition is given in the Music School, opened in 1995, and this and Ensemble Groups are arranged by the Director of Music.

The School Theatre, opened in 1974, is the venue for a range of Drama from major productions to experimental plays, mime and revue. An open-air theatre was completed in 1994. A regular programme of evening events is arranged for the Autumn and Spring terms.

In both Music and Drama, there are many opportunities for collaboration with South Hampstead High School.

Other School Societies. These cover a wide range of academic interests and leisure pursuits, including the Duke of Edinburgh Award Scheme. There is a very active Community Action Unit, which works locally in Camden and regular fund-raising Schemes for both local and national charities are launched at the School.

Development Programme. The School has recently completed a major upgrading and building programme. This programme included the provision of 13 new classrooms, a lecture theatre, computer laboratory, two further science laboratories, new central library and music school and a lecture theatre. The Technology Block and School Theatre were also extended and upgraded. A range of important refurbishments are now underway before we embark upon another major building programme in 2001/2002.

Fees. The charge of £3,050 (Junior Branch £2,850) per term includes all fees save those payable in respect of music and other private lessons, and books.

Entrance Scholarships. (*see* Entrance Scholarship section) A number of Scholarships may be awarded at 11+ to boys whose performance in the UCS Entrance Examination is outstanding. Scholarships and Exhibitions are also awarded for Music.

The Junior Branch (See part V). The Junior Branch is housed in separate buildings at Holly Hill, a few minutes' walk from Frognal. Like the Senior School, its main purpose is to provide full scope for the steady maturing of a boy's personality and capacity and for the preparation of boys for the Senior School in order to ensure a continuity of care, stimulation and reasoned discipline. It has its own Library, Computer Room and Laboratory and shares with the main School the playing fields and Sports Hall. A specialist building accommodates Art, Craft and Technology.

Boys are admitted at the ages of 7+ and 8+. Admission is by preliminary examination and interview. Applications should be made to the Headmaster's Secretary, The Junior Branch, 11 Holly Hill, Hampstead, at least a year in advance. There is a registration fee of £50.

History. An illustrated History of the School from 1830 to 1980 was published in 1981 and is available on request from the School Office, price £5.00 including postage.

Old Pupils' Society (Old Gowers). A copy of the UCS Register 1925-1988 is obtainable from the School Office, price £5.00 including postage.

Charitable status. University College School (Hampstead) is a Registered Charity, number 312748. Its aims and objectives are the provision of the widest opportunities for learning and development of boys without the imposition of tests and doctrinal conformity but within a balanced and coherent view of educational needs and obligations.

Uppingham School

Uppingham Rutland LE15 9QE.
Tel: (01572) 822216
Fax: (01572) 822332 (Headmaster). 821872 (Bursar)
e-mail: admissions@uppingham.co.uk
website: www.uppingham.co.uk

Uppingham School was founded in 1584 by Robert Johnson who obtained a grant by Letters Patent from Queen Elizabeth I. For 300 years Uppingham remained an unremarkable local Grammar School until the arrival of Edward Thring in 1853, during whose Headmastership it was transformed into one of the foremost public schools of the time. His pioneering beliefs in the values of an all-round education still mark the school strongly today.

The Governing Body:

Chairman: ¶C C Williams
Vice-Chairmen:
¶W D Fulton, JP, DL, FCA
¶The Rt Hon Stephen Dorrell, MP

The Rt Revd The Lord Bishop of Peterborough
The Very Revd the Dean of Peterborough
W F B Johnson
¶T D Melville-Ross
Mrs P T Helps
Dr Muriel Walker
¶C L McRitchie Pratt, MA, ACIS
P J Attenborough, MA
C L Mitchell
V S Anthony, BSc(Econ), Hon FCP, HonDocEd, FRSA
W J A Timpson
¶R J S Tice, BSc
Mrs C Shadla-Hall
Sir Thomas Kennedy, GCB, AFC
Prof E C Cocking, FRS
¶L J Wigglesworth
Lady Goldring, JP
¶A J Trace, QC
Mrs J Richardson, MA
S Darlington

Bursar/Finance Director, Clerk to the Trustees: Ms S A Buxton, MA, ACA

***Headmaster:* Dr Stephen C Winkley**, MA, DPhil

Deputy Head: Ms S J Thomas, BA

Director of Studies: M R J Burton, MA

Senior Mistress: Mrs W F McLachlan, BSc, CBiol

Registrar: J P Rudman, MA, BEd

Chaplain: The Revd B E Close, MA

Assistant Staff:

Art, Design & Technology:
*S Sharp, BA
*A Wilson, BA, FRPS
J A Davison, BA
S T Hudson, BA
Mrs J D Miller, BA
C Simmons, BSc

Biology:
*N K de Wet, BSc
†P L Bodily, BSc, MEd, CBiol, MIBiol, AIB
Mrs W F McLachlan, BSc, CBiol, MIBiol
V R Muir, BA
Miss A S Roebuck, BSc

Chemistry:
*Dr M A Thompson, BSc, PhD
Dr S A Cotton, BSc, ARCS, PhD, DIC, CChem, FRSC
C J Middleton, BSc
Miss A Williams, BSc

Classics:
*G S Tetlow, MA
S Bolderow, BA, MStud
J Dowman, MA
†Mrs K J Gaine, MA
Miss C A Horrex, BEd
T J Montagnon, BA
Ms S J Thomas, BA

Economics & Business Studies:
*A C Hunting, DMS
C W Kealy, BComm
T J Montagnon, BA
†M J Priestley, BA
E J Young, BA

English:
*Dr J N Waddell, BA, PhD
D A McLachlan, MA
C R O'Hanrahan, BA
Mrs N L Reihill, MA
I M Rolison, BA
Mrs P J Stocker, BA
Dr G A Tresidder, MA, PhD

Geography:
*Mrs N L Hunter, BA
Miss C J H Barker, BA
†P R Green, MA
A G Hancock, MA
†N S Merrett, BEd

History:
*T P Prior, MA
N A Browne, BA
M R J Burton, MA
T Makhzangi, BA
J D Shipton, BA
J S Wilson, BA
†Mrs E A Worthington, BA

History of Art:
†*D S R Kirk, BA
J D Shipton, BA

Information Technology:
*C J Ramsdale, DLC
A P Skailes, BSc
Miss S Webster, BSc

Learning Support:
*Mrs N Hulbert, MA
Mrs J L Pigott, CertEd
§†Mrs J S Broughton, MA, DipRS
§Mrs M P Cuccio
§Mrs P J Land, BA, DipRSA

Library:
H H S Spry-Leverton, BLib

Life Skills:
¶R A S Boston, BSc, DICTA
Mrs W F McLachlan, BSc, CBiol, MIBiol

Mathematics:
*J Lickess, BTech
T P J Clarke, BSc
A R W Dawe, BSc
Mrs M A Eales, BSc
†P Gomm, BSc
Miss O Langton, MEng
A P Skailes, BSc

Modern Languages:
*P Stocker, BEd, FIL
*Mrs H M Draper, BA
*I R Worthington, MA, Lic-ès-L
†M R Broughton, MA
M R Fries, MA
D J Jackson, BA
Mrs E M A Nicholls, BA
D S Northwood, MA
Mme N C Poole, MA
C C Stevens, MA
†R M B Wilkinson, MA

Music:
*D R Evans, MA, GBSM
P M Clements, BA, ARCO, FRCO
†S K Drummond, DRSAM, ARCM
A Ffrench, PGDip, GSMD, AGSM
†Mrs A W Priestley, LTCL
S A Smith, BA, CNAA
A Tester, BA

Physical Education:
†*K G Johnstone, BEd
†N A Gutteridge, BEd
B T P Donelan, HND
Miss C A Horrex, BEd
Mrs S M Singlehurst, BEd, MSc

Physics:
*Dr F J Clough, BSc, PhD
*J E T Sidders, BA
†W S Allen, BEd
B J Fell, BA
M J Lang, BEng
§Dr M E Sewter, BSc, PhD

Political Studies:
*T P Prior, MA
†M J Priestley, BA

Religious Studies:
*B Cooper, BA

Theatre Studies:
*J D Freeman, BA
Mrs H Freeman, Dip Drama
N M D Parkin, BA
A J Swift, BA

Visiting Music Staff:
Mrs E Atkins
Mrs M Bennett, LRAM, LTCL
Miss L Coffin, FTCL, AGSM
†Mrs T M Drummond, GRSM, LRAM
N France
Mrs L H Ffrench, GRSM, LRAM
J Goldmark
Mrs A J Green, GGSM
Mrs J T Holmes, LRAM
K Learmouth, ALCM
P R Merry, MMus, LRAM
S Morris, BMus
T O'Rourke
D N Price, LRAM
K E Rubach, ARCM
Miss K F Stretton, BA, MA
Miss J Thoday, ARAM
T G Waddington
Miss S E Wain, BMus
Miss S J Waters, GRSM, LRAM, ARCM, MTC
M Westlake, AGSM
J A Whitworth, MA, ARCM

General Information. Uppingham School is a full boarding school for boys and girls aged 13–18.

Many of the distinguishing characteristics of Uppingham School today were determined under the Headmastership of the great educationalist Edward Thring: that Houses should be small and family-like; that boys (and now girls) should have privacy; that an all-round education should be offered to a broad range of pupils and that children are happier and learn better in inspiring surroundings.

The School's buildings are concentrated in two central groups. One contains the Chapel, Memorial Hall, Old Schoolroom, the Library, Music School and classrooms, the other comprises the indoor swimming pools, gymnasium, Sports Hall, the Armoury and Shooting Range, Leonardo Centre, Woodfield, the Maths, Economics and Computer Centre and Theatre. Ranged around these, like a university campus, are the thirteen boarding houses, each with its own garden, recreational facilities and dining room.

Particular features of the School are its strong commitment to music, drama, art, design and technology and sports. Uppingham is a Church of England foundation and the whole school meets in the school's Chapel four or five times a week. Numerous clubs and societies flourish at the School including several debating forums. Girls and boys may choose between CCF and Community Service, and The Duke of Edinburgh Award Scheme is very popular. There is also a large Sixth Form Centre open four evenings a week for social occasions and which also contains reading and computer rooms.

There are around 660 pupils in the School, of which some 330 are in the Sixth Form. Over 90% of the School's pupils are full boarders. Girls have been accepted into the Sixth Form since 1975 and make up around 40% of the Sixth Form numbers. About 6% of the School's pupils are foreign nationals, mainly from the European Union, Eastern Europe and South East Asia.

Uppingham is a small market town set in beautiful countryside in Rutland. It is about 90 miles north of London and midway between Leicester and Peterborough on the A47 road. It is roughly equidistant from the M1 and A1/M11, and the new A14 link road has made connections with the Midlands and East Anglia easier and faster. It is served by Kettering, Oakham and Peterborough train stations.

Academic Matters. In 2000, the A-level pass rate was 97.7% with 65% of subjects being graded A or B and an average UCAS score per student of 23.4 (23.1 in 1998). With a staff:pupil ratio of almost 1:8 all subjects enjoy the benefits of small class sizes and a wide range may be taught. 28 different A-level subjects and 20 GCSE subjects are offered.

Until GCSE, specialisation is minimal and pupils normally take a minimum of 9 subjects. Most subjects are setted individually. All members of the Sixth Form study four AS levels in the Lower Sixth and three or four A levels in the Upper Sixth which are complemented by an extensive General Studies programme and a wide variety of extra-curricular activities.

The progress of all pupils is monitored by an assigned Tutor and their Housemaster or Housemistress, as well as by a system of regular reviews and reports from subject teachers. Parents and pupils may also call on the School's Higher Education and Careers advisers. At all stages of a pupil's career, the Housemaster keeps in touch with parents regularly.

Nearly all students go on to further education although some choose to go directly into careers. The School offers advice on planning GAP years to many leavers each year. A sizeable number of students are prepared for and accepted at Oxbridge.

Pupils have access to a beautiful central Library, as well as extensive, more specialist libraries for most subject departments.

For those with learning difficulties the School has trained staff to help with special education needs and any pupil may use the services of a professional psychologist or the School's trained counsellor.

Boarding. There are 14 boarding houses, which are dotted around the town and school estate: 10 for boys, 3 for sixth form girls, and one house, Samworths', for 13-18 year old girls. Samworths' admits its first girls in September 2001. Houses are kept small and are usually home to no more than 50 children, 45 in the case of 6th Form girls' houses. All students eat their meals in their own house dining room and are joined at lunch by teaching and non-teaching staff.

Almost all boys have their own private study upon arrival and by the time they reach the Sixth Form, they can choose to share or have their own study bedroom. Almost every girl entering the 6th Form has a study bedroom to herself if she wishes.

Much of the non-teaching life of the School is organised around the houses and they engender strong loyalties. In addition to excursions and social events, there exists a long-standing tradition of house drama productions, music concerts, artistic displays, as well as inter-house debating and sports competitions.

The resident Housemasters and Housemistresses are helped by a team of four tutors who are signed to particular pupils. They assist with monitoring academic progress and social development.

The Houses and Housemasters are:
Brooklands Peter Green
Constables Nic Merrett
Fairfield (Girls) Stewart and Tessa Drummond
Farleigh Neil Gutteridge
Fircroft David Kirk
Highfield Richard Wilkinson
Johnson's (Girls) Mark and Julia Broughton
The Lodge (Girls) Katharine Gaine
Lorne House Keven Johnstone
Meadhurst Martin and Alison Priestley
Samworths' Elizabeth Worthington
School House Phillip Gomm
West Bank Steve Allen
West Deyne Peter Bodily

Music. Uppingham has always had a very distinguished reputation for music since being the first school to put music on its curriculum for all pupils. The School has an outstanding Chapel Choir, numerous orchestras and chamber groups, four bands, a concert club and many thriving musical societies and rock groups. A busy programme of weekly recitals, house and year-group concerts and larger public performances in the UK and abroad offer pupils of all abilities regular chances to perform and nearly two thirds of pupils learn an instrument. A large number of visiting music staff enables pupils to receive conservatoire-style tuition at the school.

Among recent achievements are a record-breaking number of Oxbridge Choral awards in the 1990s, a best-selling CD in 1997 and 1998 and winning the Schools Chamber Music Competition three years in succession.

Further enquiries may be made directly to the Director of Music (extension 4028).

Sports and Games. All students participate in sports or games three time a week. Approximately thirty sports are offered, ranging from Aerobics to Scuba diving. The major sports are Rugby, Hockey, Cross-Country, Cricket, Tennis and Athletics for boys and Lacrosse, Hockey, Cross-Country, Netball and Tennis for girls. Shooting, Climbing, Fencing, Sailing and Golf are further sports which have a strong tradition.

There are over 60 acres of playing fields including the Upper, dedicated to First XI Cricket. There are also 2 Astroturf surfaces, a hard-play area for Hockey and some 26 Tennis courts as well as courts for Squash. In addition to the sportshall and gymnasium, the Sports Centre also houses swimming and diving pools and a well-equipped fitness room.

All these facilities are open 7 days a week under the guidance of the Sports Centre manager and his appointed staff. The School usually has a number of pupils representing the regional or national teams in a variety of different sports. In 1999 the Captain of the England U18 rugby team was at Uppingham School.

Further enquiries may be made directly to the Director of Sport on 01572 823977.

The Leonardo Centre. This award-winning Art, Design and Technology Centre was opened in 1995 at a cost of over £1.6 million and was designed by Old Uppinghamian, Piers Gough, CBE. The glass-fronted structure allows a broad range of creative activities to take place in a single uncompartmentalised space and thereby stimulate each other. The Leonardo Centre houses a Fine Art and Printing space, studios for Design, Electronics, Ceramics, Sculpture, Photography, Television studio and Sound engineering, workshops primarily for wood, metal and plastic, and teaching rooms dedicated to History of Art. The Sunley Gallery is used to display the work of pupils, staff and other artists. The Centre is manned and open seven days a week and is open to all pupils, whatever their public examination options.

Admission. Boys and girls may be registered for admission at any time after birth. A formal letter of a place is conditional on the pupil achieving our academic requirements for entry and to our receiving a satisfactory report from the present school.

Admission to the Senior School is at 13 (the 4th Form), and 16 (Sixth Form). Most boys and girls at 13 will take the Common Entrance Examination. If candidates are at a school which does not prepare for Common Entrance, they would be required to sit our own entry tests. Places for girls, and a limited number of places for boys are available at sixth form. Admission at this level is dependent on tests and interviews at Uppingham, and a satisfactory performance in GCSE.

Parents may ask for a boy or girl to be registered for a specific boarding house, or parents may ask for guidance from the Headmaster or Registrar.

From 2001, Uppingham is taking girls, from the age of 13, into Samworths'.

It is occasionally possible for boys and girls to enter the school other than in September at the age of 13 and 16. Inquiries and requests for information about admissions should be addressed to The Registrar (extension 4019).

Scholarships (*see* Entrance Scholarship section). A large number of scholarships are awarded annually. At 13, boys and girls may apply for Academic (ISEB Common Scholarship), All-Rounder, Art/Design and Music Scholarships. At 16 Art/Design and Music Scholarships are awarded. All scholarships are worth from 10% to 50% of the fees.

For details of scholarships please contact the Admissions Secretary (extension 4039).

Fees. For the academic year, 2000/2001 the boarding fee is £5,425 per term. The day fee is £3,800 per term. There is a scheme for paying fees in advance; further details may be obtained from the Finance Manager (extension 4007).

Former Pupils. All pupils may become life members of The Uppingham Association on leaving the School. 6,700 Old Uppinghamians are currently registered and enjoy regular gatherings at social, sporting and other occasions at the School, in the provinces and abroad. Enquiries may be made directly to the Secretary to the Uppingham Association (extension 4014).

Charitable status. The Trustees of Uppingham School is a Registered Charity, number 527951. It exists to provide education for boys and girls.

Victoria College
Jersey

Jersey Channel Islands
Tel: (01534) 638200
Fax: (01534) 727448

The College was founded in commemoration of a visit of Queen Victoria to the Island and opened in 1852. It bears the Arms of Jersey.

Motto: *Amat Victoria Curam*

Visitor: Her Majesty The Queen

Governing Body:

Chairman: R Pirouet
Air Chief Marshal Sir Michael Alcock
Senator L Norman
P Le Brocq
S Austin-Vautier
Dr J Platt
Mrs J Gindill
R Pittman

Headmaster: **Robert Cook,** BEd (Hons), FRSA

Vice Principal: T A Packer, BSc, MSc, CPhys

Assistant Staff:

G D Adeney, MA
Mrs J E Averty, CertEd
M J Bithell, CertEd
Ms H Blake, BSc
G Bloor, BD, AKC
A Blythin, BSc
B F Carolan, BA
J P Clark, MSc
Mrs J E Crosby, BA
Mrs L Curgenven, BSc
Ms M A Morrison, BA
D A R Ferguson, DPE (*Sports Manager*)
P T Germain, CertEd
Miss N Good, BA
P J Gray, BSc
A R Hamel, MA
I A Hickling, BSc, MSc
R A Hopkin, BSc, CertEd
S Jones, BA
L Keenan, BSc, MA
Mrs P Le Feuvre, BA
E G Le Quesne, MA, DipEd
J F Le Quesne, CertEd
L Manning, BA
P Marshallsay, BA
Mrs D B Montgomery, BA
Ms J Mulliner, BA
Miss S Newall, BA
G O'Hagan, MA
Miss A Perestrelo, BA
A G Pickup, BSc, MIBiol
Mrs P Ramsden
J Randles, BA
G D Reakes, BA, DipEd
D J Rotherham, BEd, FRGS
P J Shaw, BEd
I Simpson, BSc
S Stevenson, BA
R L Stockton, BA
Mrs A C C Swindell, BA
M Talibard, MA
Mrs M Taylor, BSc
E M Tully, MA, MSt

Preparatory School:

P Stevenson, BSc, CertEd (*Headmaster*)
B J Arnold
J R Collinson, BEd
Miss D Creigh, BEd (Hons)
Mrs V Crowe
J Curtis
S Dewhurst, BA (*Deputy Headmaster*)
Mrs H Gunton, BA (Hons)
Mrs K Hay, BSc, MPharms
Mrs A Hossard, BSc (Hons)
Mrs R Hayhurst
D J Le Boutillier, CertEd
Miss A S Martin, CertEd
D Pateman, BA (Hons)
W Waymouth, BEd

Medical Officer: Dr C R Grainger, Medical Officer of Health and Principal School Medical Officer

There are at present 620 boys in College and 276 in the Preparatory School and 90 in the Pre-Prep. Boys in their first two years at College constitute the Junior School.

The fine original building of 1852 with its Great Hall, libraries and classrooms is now the centre of new teaching accommodation including classrooms, a Drama Workshop, an Art School and a superb Science Block that was opened by Her Royal Highness The Princess Anne. A VIth Form Library and new Music and Drama Centre were opened in Summer 1977. A new Computer Suite was opened in 1992. A refurbished theatre was re-opened in 1996. The College is built in pleasant grounds above the town of St Helier and looks south over the sea.

There are playing fields adjacent to the School including a new astro-turf hockey pitch and in the grounds the Worrall Memorial Swimming Pool, the Miniature Range, Squash Courts and the Scout Hut. A new Art Suite and Design Technology Centre opened in 2000. A Sports complex and swimming pool is currently under construction.

Education. There is an emphasis on academic success, nearly all boys go on to Universities in the UK. The curriculum conforms to the requirements of the National Curriculum. In the Junior School all boys follow the same timetable which includes Religious Education, English, Mathematics, French, a second Modern Language, History, Drama, Geography, Science, Music, Art and ICT. In the Lower School, the aims of the curriculum are to stimulate enthusiasm and develop an all-round competence.

Thereafter the basic curriculum includes Religious Education, English, Mathematics, French, Sciences and ICT. In addition, a boy selects from optional subjects those which best suit his natural talents, the choice being guided by teaching staff in consultation with parents. The options are so arranged that a boy is not faced with an irreversible choice below the VIth Form.

There is no division into Arts and Sciences VIths and boys may take any selection of A level subjects suited to their objectives and abilities. All take a course of General Studies and Key Skills.

At all ages there is opportunity for voluntary work, Music and the Arts, and these, with other subjects, are also encouraged by numerous School Societies.

Prizes. The Queen gives three Gold Medals annually for Science, Modern Languages and Mathematics as well as two Prizes for English History. The States of Jersey offers a Gold Medal and a Silver Medal annually for French. There is an award given to the boy achieving the top score in Year 7 Entrance Examination called the St Mannelier et St Anastase Gold Medal.

Preparatory School. The College has its own Preparatory School which stands in the College grounds. Boys, on passing the Entrance procedure, progress to the College at the age of 11.

Admission. The age of admission is 11 years though boys are accepted at all ages. Entrants must pass the College Entrance Examination but boys entering at age 13 take Common Entrance.

Annual Fees. The annual tuition fees are £2,665 for College, and £2,400 for the Preparatory School.

Physical Education and Games. Physical Education is included in the timetable of all boys. The College places some emphasis on sport and each year it has sports tours to different European countries, and to the United Kingdom.

The principal games in the winter are Association Football, Rugby, Hockey, Squash; and in the summer Cricket, Swimming, Shooting, Tennis and Athletics.

Matches at all games are played with Elizabeth College, Guernsey and College sides visit the mainland for matches against English Independent Senior Schools.

The College has a CCF Contingent with an authorised establishment of 50 in the Army Section, 80 in the RAF Section and 60 in the RN Section. It is commanded by Lieutenant Colonel R L Stockton.

There is a large and flourishing Scout Troop which continued active throughout the war and has been in existence for over 70 years.

Leaving Scholarships. There are a number of Scholarships (of varying amount). The Queen's Exhibition is tenable for three years at a University. The Wimble Scholarship, the Sayers Scholarships and the Baron Dr Ver Heyden de Lancey Scholarship each of up to £750 a year, tenable at British Universities, and the Rayner Exhibitions are recent additions to the rich endowment of Scholarships enjoyed by the College, for Jersey-born boys.

Warwick School

Warwick CV34 6PP.
Tel: (01926) 776400
Fax: (01926) 401259
e-mail: enquiries@warwick.warwks.sch.uk

Warwick School can produce documentary evidence that suggests its existence in the days of King Edward the Confessor, and it probably dates from 914. In 1123 the School was granted to the Church of St Mary of Warwick. In 1545 King Henry VIII increased and re-organised the endowments. The School subsequently moved to the Lord Leycester Hospital. In 1571 it moved to another site within the boundaries of Warwick, and in 1879 to its present site south of the town on the banks of the Avon.

Motto: *Altiora Peto.*

Governing Body and Staff:

Chairman of the Warwick School Committee: Professor E W Ives, BA, PhD

The Right Honourable the Earl of Warwick

The Lord Lieutenant of the County of Warwick

The Worshipful the Mayor of Warwick

Dr A J Barker
The Revd Canon D Brindley
P G Butler, Esq
Dr H Butters
R V Cadbury, Esq
F R Chandley, Esq
Mrs J A Edwards
J E Francis, Esq, FCA
Mrs P Goddard
R J Grant, Esq
G B Guest, Esq
D Hanson, Esq
Mrs M B Haywood
Dr J M Henderson
Mrs C Jennings
C R Mason, Esq, CBE, FCIPS
Mrs V Phillips
K Rawnsley, Esq, JP
K C K Scott, Esq
M L Shattock, Esq, OBE, MA
R A Stevens, Esq
N F J Thurley, FRICS
M O Travis, Esq, FCCA
Professor R H Trigg, MA, DPhil

Foundation Secretary: A Bligh, Esq, BSc, FCA

***Headmaster:* P J Cheshire**, BSc, PhD

Deputy Headmaster: S H L Williams, BSc, MA

Senior Masters:
M J Green, MA
P J O'Grady, MA

Art:
*R Flintoff, BA
Mrs J R McBrien, BA
D J Snatt, BA
G Ward, MA (*Housemaster, School House*)

Classics:
Mrs C A Ellison, BA
R Hudson, MA
*J E P Morris, MA
D C Menashe, BA

Information Technology:
*D Seal, BSc
P Nield, MBA, BSc

Design and Technology:
*R A Bradley, BEd
I B Armstrong, BSc
A Hartley
J D Stone, BSc

Drama:
*J R Daws, BA
Mrs P Orme, MA

Economics:
M J Green, MA (*Senior Master–Personnel, Head of Sixth Form*)

*D E J J Lloyd, BSc
D J Barr, BA

English:
C E Thomas, BA
Mrs L M Haines, BA
G I R Ogdon, MA
Miss L Pearson, BA
*G S Wilson, MA, PhD

Geography:
*S R Chapman, BA
T J Jefferis, BSc
I B Moffatt, ACP (*Master in charge of Games*)

History:
*J N Jefferies, MA
C G J Gibbs, BA
T A C Butcher, BA
D A Pyrah, MA
S Wheeler, MA (*Master of the Scholars*)
P E Wheaton, BA

Mathematics:
J A Hanson, MMath
R A Chapman, BSc
J W Clift, MA, MPhil
*R R Cousins, MA, PhD
C G Daniel, MSc
A Debney, BSc
G Guidici, BA (*Careers*)
P J O'Grady, MA (*Senior Master–Academic Administration*)
D J Shield
M W Shield, BA

Modern Languages:
*E J Hadley, MA (*Modern Languages*)
*Mrs E M Halborg, MA (*German*)
M M Jackson, BA
C G McNee, BA (*Head of Upper School*)
Miss C C Morel, Lic
*Mrs B Rossay-Gilson, BA (*French*)
R J Thirwell, BA (*Head of General Studies*)
Miss A Williams
*Miss J A Wiltsher, BA (*Spanish*)

Music:
*T G Barr, BA
C P Russell (*Master i/c Brass*)
R G Appleyard, GBSM
Mrs R Jefferies, MMus
C H Watmough, BA, FRSA

Physical Education:
T Hoyle, BA (*Head of Lower School*)
B Emmerson
*G A Tedstone, BEd
M T Byrne, BSc

Religious Education:
*The Revd A W Gough, BA
Mrs Z Russell-Wilks, BA

Science
W G Adams, MA
J A Cooper, MA
*I S Dee, BA (*Biology*)
*P J Duckworth, MA (*Physics*)
*R W Fair, BA, PhD (*Chemistry*)
G N Frykman, MA
P A Johnson, BSc, AMITD
W M Newton, BSc, PhD
*A J Reilly, BA (*Science*)
Mrs S L Sephton, BEng
P A Snell, BSc
Mrs M Yates, BSc (*Head of Middle School*)

Curriculum Support:
Mrs L A Bain, BSc, TEFL
Miss R Baseley

Junior School:
D J Rogers, BA (*Headmaster*)
J L Elston, BEd (*Deputy Head*)
Miss G E Beck
Miss A J Bond, MA
Mrs A Bungard
Mrs D Caswell, BEd
Miss R Deer, BA
S Gray, CertEd, DTM, MITD
T C Lewis, CertEd
K Marshall, BEd
N J Oakden, BA
Mrs C O'Grady, BEd
Miss J L Ward, BA
Mrs A C A Williams, BMus
Mrs A E Wilson, BEd

Commanding Officer, CCF: Major P A Johnson

R.S.M.: J Pipitone

Bursar: N G R Stock, BSc, ARICS

Librarian: Mrs L Lucas, ALA

Assistant Librarian: Mrs H Laws

Medical Officer: Dr A Parsons

Headmaster's PA: Mrs C Dixon

Headmaster's Secretary: Mrs D Jones

Warwick School is an Independent day and boarding school for boys. There is a Senior School of about 800 boys, age range 11 to 18 years, and in the Junior School, age range 7 to 11 years, there are about 200 boys. There is boarding accommodation for about 60 boys (Junior and Senior).

The School Buildings and Grounds. The school is situated on the outskirts of Warwick town with fine views over the River Avon and Warwick Castle. In 1879 the school moved into its present buildings designed in a rococo Tudor style with 50 acres of playing fields attached to the school. Many buildings have been put up over the years. There is a programme of continuous development. In the last few years this has improved and extended the boarding, indoor sports facilities, music, drama and teaching facilities; most recently a new Sixth Form Centre, an ICT and Library Building, a Performing Arts Centre, Music Department and Arts Building for History and Geography.

Admission is by entrance examination set by the School. Entry to the Junior School is at the ages of 7 (about 40 boys) and 8 (about 10 boys) with only a few places available at 9 and 10. Entry to the Senior School is at 11 (about 100 boys), 12 (about 5 boys) and 13 (about 30 boys). The examinations at 11 and 12 include a Verbal Reasoning Test and tests in English and Mathematics. The examination at 13+ is based on the syllabus for the Public Schools Common Entrance examination.

Curriculum. The aim of the school is to provide a broadly based education which allows pupils to achieve academic excellence. All pupils are encouraged to develop their individual talents to the full and to accept responsibility for themselves and others.

In the Junior School the curriculum aims to give a firm grounding in the National Curriculum foundation subjects English, Mathematics and Science. A range of other subjects including History, Geography, Technology, French, IT and Religious Education are taught throughout the school with some degree of specialisation in the last two years. French is taught throughout as is Art, Music and Physical Education. In the Senior School the curriculum offers a range of options but there is a core curriculum of English, Mathematics, French and Science (including Physics, Chemistry and Biology as separate subjects) up to GCSE which all boys take in their fifth year. Boys continue into the sixth form where A levels or AS levels are taken after a two year course. There is a wide range and programme of General Studies. The curriculum is designed to give all boys a broad general education and to postpone any specialisation for as long as possible.

Games and other activities. Active interest in out of school activities is much encouraged. Winter games are Rugby football, hockey and cross country running. These are played in the Michaelmas and Lent Terms. Summer games are cricket, tennis, athletics and swimming. Archery, badminton, basketball, clay pigeon shooting, golf, rifle shooting, squash and volleyball are played throughout the year. There are fine sporting facilities in the new indoor Sports Complex, including a new 25m 6-lane Pool and Sports Hall.

There are usually some 30 different clubs and societies active in school life. There is a CCF contingent (with army and RAF sections) an outdoor activities group and a Voluntary Service Group linked with the local community. Other activities include drama, music, amateur radio, poetry and sailing.

Religious teaching. The Chapel Services and teaching are according to the Church of England, but there are always pupils of other denominations and race and for these other arrangements may be made. Pupils attend services on two mornings a week and boarders the service on Sunday. The Chaplain prepares members of the school for Confirmation each year, the Confirmation Service taking place in the Lent Term.

Boarding. There is boarding for both Junior and Senior School boys. Boys may be weekly or full boarders. Boarding can sometimes be arranged for day boys to accommodate short term parental requirements. There is also an opportunity for an extended day facility.

Fees. Tuition: £4,911–£6,315 pa. Boarding: £6,165 (weekly) – £7,092 (full). Optional: private tuition in piano, violin, cello, woodwind, brass, guitar, organ and percussion

Scholarships: Up to ten Scholarships giving up to half fee remission are available for award on the results of the entrance exam at 11+. In addition at 11+ there are two music Scholarships to 50% of the fee. At least four Scholarships including Scholarships for music up to half fees remission are available to be awarded on the examination at 13+. At least two Scholarships giving up to 2/5 fee remission are awarded on examination on entry into the Sixth Form. A bursary may be awarded to increase the value of any award where need is shown.

Warwick Foundation Places. The School benefits from a scheme offering the possibility of free places depending on level of parental income.

Warwick Foundation Places (unrestricted) are offered each year at the following ages: 10 places at 11+; 2 places at 12+; 2 places at 13+; 2 places at 16+.

Warwick Foundation Town Places (restricted to those living within the town of Warwick, an area embracing the old Borough of Warwick (predominantly CV34)) are offered each year at the following age: 3 places at 11+.

Remission of fees will be according to an agreed scale depending upon gross parental income. Warwick Foundation Places are awarded on the results of entrance examination and interview at 11+, 12+ and 13+. The qualifications to be eligible for an award at 16+ are at least 5 GCSE grade B's with grade A/B in those subjects or allied subjects which are to be studied in the sixth form.

Boys already in the School can be recommended for Warwick Foundation Places at 12+, 13+ and 16+ without being examined.

Warwick Town Foundation Scholarship at 11+. One full fees Scholarship may be awarded on the results of the entrance examination held in January. The Scholarship may only be awarded to a boy from a maintained school living within the town of Warwick representing the area embracing the old Borough of Warwick (predominantly the postal code CV34). The Scholarship is not means tested and is awarded for merit in the examination, on school report and on the interview.

Old Warwickian Association. There is a flourishing Old Warwickian Association with a club, The Portcullis Club, in the centre of Warwick and a thriving Rugby Club with its own ground. There are regular OW events at the school. Secretary: D M Phillips, 13 Oakdene Close, Claverdon, CV35 8PL.

Charitable status. Warwick Schools is a Registered Charity, number 538775. It exists to provide high quality education.

Wellingborough School

Wellingborough Northamptonshire NN8 2BX.
Tel: 01933 222427
Fax: 01933 271986
e-mail: headmaster@wellingboro.fsnet.co.uk
website: www.wellingboroughschool.org

The endowment of this School was first set aside for charitable purposes in the year 1478. Further land, purchased from the Crown, was granted by Letters Patent in the reigns of Edward VI and Elizabeth I. The endowment was confirmed as being for educational purposes by an Order of the Lord Keeper of the Great Seal in 1595. The School moved to its present site in 1881 upon which new and improved buildings have from time to time been added.

The School offers day co-education for boys and girls from the age of 3 to 18. The School is firmly wedded to Christian principles, to equality of opportunity and the enrichment of individuals in the community. The School is divided into a Pre-Preparatory School (3–8: 160 pupils), the Junior School (8–13: 250 pupils) and the Senior School (13–18: 340 pupils).

Motto: *Salus in Arduis.*

Chairman of the Governors: R A Swindall, FRICS

A W Bailey
J W Brant
W T G Clifton
L E Eadon
R G Foulkes, MA, PhD
Mrs E Higgins
J J H Higgins
Major D F Hooton, OBE, TD, DL, JP
B Huckle
K C Lowe, PhD
C A Odell
Mrs P A Perkins, OBE
P S Phillips, MA, FCA
Mrs P E Ritchie
J E Saxby
M E Sneath
A Warwick, JP
C A Westley

***Headmaster:* F R Ullmann**, MA, late Scholar of Trinity College, Cambridge

Deputy Headmaster: G R Bowe, BA, University of Kent

Deputy Headmistress: Mrs N Webb, MA, St Hilda's College, Oxford

Assistant Staff:
†*M H Askham, BEd
Mrs S M Barnhurst, BSc
†R C Batley, CertEd
Mrs F J Burgess, BEd
S M Cook, BSc
†J A Dutfield, CertEd, DAD
†N J Elbourne, BA (*Director of Activities*)
*D Ellison, ATC (*Head of Art*)
*R A Farey, BSc (*Head of Science/Physics*)
Mrs J A Gormley, BA (*Head of English*)
J Gray, BSc
Mrs C R M Grove, BA
*J R Haste, CertEd (*Head of Design Technology*)
*J H Hughes, BA (*Head of Geography*)
Mrs P Imms
Miss C S Irvin, BSc
D Jameson, MA, GTCL
A Jones, BSc
P A Knox, BEd
R C Lithgow, MSc
*J P Maddox, MA (*Head of Mathematics*)
P R Marshall, BA (*Director of Music*)
*C Martin-Sims, BSc, MSc, BA (*Head of Drama*)
Mrs R E Maynard, MA
Miss K L Mills, BA
G B Moss, BA (*Director of Sport*)
*M A Nugent, BA (*Head of Modern Languages*)
D A Ramsden, BA (*Head of History and Politics*)
Mrs C H Richbell, BA
K M Seecharan, BSc
Mrs K A Shutt, BSc
Mrs R A Shuttlewood, BSc, MSc
Mrs B Strange, MA (*Dyslexia*)
Miss A C Sweby, BA
M E Thompson, MA (*Librarian*)
Revd M J Walker, MA
*J R Ward, BSc, PhD, MA (*Head of Chemistry*)
Miss K E Wilson, BSc
Mrs J Wood, BA

Housemasters/Housemistresses:

Cripps' House: N J Elbourne
Fryer's House: K M Seecharan
Garne's House: M H Askham

Marsh House: Mrs R E Maynard
Parker-Steynes: J H Hughes
Platt's House: J A Dutfield
Nevill House: Miss K E Wilson
Weymouth House: Miss K L Mills

Manager of Information Systems: P B Waugh, BEd

Head of Careers: Mrs E P Farey, CertCG, MICG, MIMgt

Instrumental Music Teachers:
Keyboard:
Mrs S M Astbury, LRAM, DipEd
Mrs M Boniface, ARMCM
S Garfirth, DipRCM, ALCM
Mrs M E Vinton, BA (Mus)

Strings:
S Garfirth, DipRCM, ALCM
Mrs C A Malitskie, BA, DipRAM, LRAM
Mrs C Nash

Woodwind:
Mrs H C Barlow, BSc
P F Baxter
Mrs S Healey, MA, GRSM, ATCL, ARCM
Miss K Keeble, ProfCertRAM, LRAM, DipNCOS
B G Riches
Mrs M E Vinton, BA(Mus), CertEd
E Williams, HonFTCL, FRSAMD

Brass:
S Turnbull, CertEd

Guitar:
K Learmouth, ALCM, CertEd

Organ:
D Jameson, MA, GTCL
S T Johnson, BA, ARCO

Percussion:
J E Wears, LTCL

Singing:
Mrs M Boniface, ARMCM
D Jameson, MA, GTCL
Miss A Pyke, BA, LTCL
Miss F Y Whelan

Junior School:
Headmaster: G R Lowe, BEd

Deputy Headmistress: Mrs J M Wratten, CertEd

Director of Studies: N R Grove, MA, BA, Dip Art & Design, CertEd

K M Campbell, MA, CertEd
Mrs S Campbell, BSc, CertEd
Mrs D Claber, CertEd
Miss C J Dodsworth, BA
Mrs C Handford, CertEd
M R Lower, BA
C J Owen, BA
Mrs K A Owen, BSc
S A Prall, DipEd(IAPS)
Miss R J Sanders, MA
P A Shouksmith, BSc

Pre-Preparatory School:
Headmistress: Mrs J D Jones, CertPDE
Deputy Headmistress: Mrs J A Askham, BEd
Mrs J E Bennett, NNEB, CertEd
Mrs M E Campbell, BTec
Mrs B E Forrest, CertEd
S Garfirth, DipRCM, ALCM
Mrs S E Lowe, CertEd
Mrs J A Panter, BA
D C Popplewell, BA
Mrs S M C Sandall, NNEB
Miss V J Scouse, BEd
Mrs C H Waite, BEd
Mrs A E Wood, CertEd
Miss L A Woolhead, NNEB
Miss A-M Ystenes, NNEB

Bursar and Clerk to the Governors: M J Skidmore, ACIB
Headmaster's Secretary/PA: Mrs A Whittington

Sanatorium Sister: Mrs S Lock, RGN, OND

Officer Commanding CCF: Commander N J Elbourne

Wellingborough is situated 63 miles from London, 10 miles east of Northampton. Close to the main railway line from St Pancras to Leicester and Sheffield, it is served by an excellent network of motorways and dual carriageways connecting the A1, A14 and the M1.

Buildings and Organisation. The School occupies a fine site on the south of the town, and stands in its own grounds of 45 acres. In the Senior School there are five boys' houses and three girls' houses, organised on boarding house lines. Each house has about 45 pupils. The Sixth Form numbers around 130 pupils, 90% of whom go directly to higher education.

Admission at 13+ for boys and girls is by means of entry tests and interview or the Common Entrance Examination from preparatory schools. Direct entry into the Sixth Form is on the basis of an interview, school report and likely GCSE results confirmed before entry. Please note that A level courses begin in June after GCSE examinations.

The Junior School, while sharing some of the facilities of the Senior School, has its own buildings and classrooms on the east side of the campus. The Pre-Preparatory School occupies its own modern purpose-built buildings.

The main school buildings include an ICT study centre, a library, assembly hall, careers room, chapel, and three classroom blocks including seven science laboratories and the information technology department. There is a design technology centre, music school, modern languages centre, sports hall and central dining hall.

Religion. Religious teaching is according to the Church of England. Pupils attend a mixture of morning prayers and longer services on weekdays, and a morning service on some Sundays during term. The Chaplain prepares members of the School for confirmation each year, the confirmation service taking place in the Lent Term.

Curriculum. In the Pre-Preparatory School and the Junior School the curriculum is an enriched version of the National Curriculum. French and Latin are also taught in the Junior School.

In the first year of the Senior School (Shell form) pupils follow a core curriculum in English, Mathematics, French, Physics, Chemistry, Biology, History, Geography, Design Technology, Art, Music, RE, Information Technology and PE. German and Latin are both options in this year. GCSE courses are offered in English, English Literature, French, Mathematics and dual award sciences. Options include separate Sciences, Latin, German, History, Geography, Art, Design Technology, Music, Drama, PE and Religious Studies.

The following subjects are offered for A level examination: Art and Design, Biology, Business Studies, Chemistry, Design Technology, English Literature, French, German, Geography, History, Mathematics and Further Mathematics, Music, PE, Physics, Politics and Psychology. Information Technology, Drama, Economics, English Language and Religious Studies are offered as freestanding AS levels.

Music, Drama, Art, Design. The Music School contains a central teaching room and several practice rooms. Professional tuition is given on all instruments and there are chapel and concert choirs, junior and senior bands and a school orchestra.

Concerts, school and house drama productions and lectures are held in the School Hall, which has well-equipped stage facilities. The Richard Gent Design Centre offers workshops and studies for design technology and ceramics. Two-dimensional art has recently been given its own building. Pupils are encouraged to make full use of these facilities in their spare time.

Sport. The playing fields, over 40 acres in extent, are used for association football, cross country, rugby, athletics, cricket and tennis, and include a nine hole golf course. Girls' games in the winter are hockey and netball. On the school site are also astroturf pitches, five all-weather tennis courts, two squash courts, shooting range, gymnasium and sports hall. The latter has four badminton courts, indoor cricket nets and facilities for fencing, table tennis, basketball, weight training etc.

Other Activities. After two terms in the Senior School pupils join the Combined Cadet Force (RN, Army, Commando or RAF Section) or concentrate on the Duke of Edinburgh's Award Scheme. Training is given in first aid, map reading and orienteering, and camping expeditions take place at weekends. There is an annual CCF camp and there are opportunities for band training, open range shooting, REME work, canoeing and sailing.

Pupils may take part in community service work in the town and various societies and clubs cater for a wide range of extracurricular interests.

Careers. Guidance is available to all pupils on further education and careers prospects through the Head of Careers and other members of staff. The School is a member of the Independent Schools Careers Organisation.

Scholarships. (*see* Entrance Scholarship section) - Foundation Scholarships are offered to external candidates for entry to the Junior School at 11+. At 13+ entrance scholarships are offered to pupils entering the Senior School. At 16+ two Hawkes Scholarships are offered. Music scholarships are available at 13+ and 16+ for candidates of outstanding ability and musical potential. Art scholarships are awarded sometimes at 13+ and at 16+. Sports awards are awarded at 13+ and at 16+.

Bursaries. Some bursaries are available for candidates who can make an outstanding/special contribution to the School where there is a proven case of financial need. All awards are subject to satisfactory performance both academically and in other respects.

Further details and application forms for all the above awards may be obtained from the Headmaster.

Fees per term. Senior School: Day £2,290. Junior School: £2,140. Pre-Preparatory School: £1,270. Fees include most extras apart from instrumental lessons (£120 per term), public examination fees and books.

Admission. Applications should be made to the Headmaster for entry of boys and girls at 13+ and for direct entry into the Sixth Form. Enquiries concerning entries between the ages of 3 and 7 should be addressed to the Headmistress of the Pre-Preparatory School and entries between the ages of 8 and 12 to the Headmaster of the Junior School.

Term of Entry. New pupils are accepted at the beginning of any term. The largest entry is in September each year.

Old Wellingburian Club. All former pupils who have spent at least one year in the School are eligible for membership. Correspondence should be addressed to the OW Club Secretary at the School.

Charitable status. Wellingborough School is a Registered Charity, number LA/309923A/2. It exists to provide education for boys and girls from the age of 3 to 18.

* Head of Department	§ Part Time or Visiting
† Housemaster/Housemistress	¶ Old Pupil
‡ See below list of staff for meaning	

Wellington College

Crowthorne Berkshire RG45 7PU.
Tel: The Master (01344) 444010, Registrar (01344) 444012,
Bursar (01344) 444020, Reception (01344) 444000

Incorporated by Royal Charter, dated 13 December 1853.

Visitor: Her Majesty The Queen

President: HRH The Duke of Kent, KG, GCMG, GCVO, ADC, DL

Vice President: Sir David Scholey, CBE

Ex-Officio Governors:
The Archbishop of Canterbury, PC, PhD
The Duke of Wellington, KG, LVO, OBE, MC

Governors:
H J H C Hildreth, MA
H M P Miles, OBE
J A Hopkins, MA, LLB
Lady Renton of Mount Harry
D R W Silk, CBE, JP, MA
R J B Yeldham
Admiral Sir Jeremy Black, GBE, KCB, DSO
Professor Sir Gareth Roberts, FRS
Sir Michael Spicer, MP
Mrs G duCharme, MA
General Sir Edward Jones, KCB, CBE
D J Cowley
The Rt Revd D J Conner, MA
A G Bruce
Dr A Borges
Mrs V Mitchell

Clerk to the Governors: M C Gowar, MA, FTII

***Master:* A H Monro**, MA (Pembroke College, Cambridge)

Second Master: J D Martin, BA

Administrative Assistant to the Master: R E Coleman, MA

Director of Studies: P Hucklesby, MA

Assistant Staff:
R M S Fox, BA, MPhil
*J R P MacArthur, BA
¶C M St G Potter, BSc
R J W Walker, MA
†R C Auger, MA
*M B Lovett, BA, MA
J N Jones, BSc
*A Carter, BSc, MSc
†K M Hopkins, BSc
A C Taylor, BSc, MPhil
†D A Burns, BSc, MSc
†Rev D M Outram, BA, BD
J J Breen, MA, BA
*I C E Mitchell, BSc
†T J Head, BA
†¶R I H B Dyer, BA
†A R Dewes, MA
M Farrington, BSc, MSc, PhD
*M N Halpin, MSc
D G Grainge, BSc
J A Groves, BSc
*J L Price, BA
Mrs L P Walker, MA
R J Williams, BSc
P G Shilston, MA
R R Foskett, MA
*N B Ritchie, MA
Mrs E M Hood, BSc, PhD
Mrs A M Francis, BA
A J Welby, BA
*M G Fowler, BA
†J C Rawlinson, BSc
†A R Taylor, BA
G C Nurser, BEd, MA
C M Oliphant-Callum, MA
*Mrs J T Lunnon, BA
†I M Henderson, BA
Ms C J Evans, BA
B N Roth, BSc, BA, AFIMA
†N C Lunnon, BSc
†M T Boobbyer, BA
E J Heddon, FIEIE, MIPD
†P G S Boscher, BA, PhD
†¶P T Galley, BSc, DIC, PhD, ARCS
M J Sayer, MA
*J A F Jeffrey, BA
C J Hooper, BA
S D Laverack, BSc, PhD
M C F Fielder, MA
Mrs C J Blunden-Lee, BA (Open), CertEd, DipRSA, SpLD, CertTEFL

*D H Lang, BSc
M J Oakman, BA
J R Williams, MA
S W Lockyer, BSc
¶S S-M Cheung, BSc
R L Humphrey, BA
C J Hutchinson, BSc
R F J Tear, BSc
S H Dean, BSc
E D Fountain, BEcon, LLB, MPhil
A Edgar, BEng
M Hynd, MA
M J D Ellwood, BEd
Mrs B F Boscher, BA
N J Diver, BA
Mrs E A Stevens, BSc
Miss M Jones, BSc
M D Chesterman, BA, DipEd
Miss F E Sutherland, BA, MA
J White, BA

Chaplain: *The Revd R J Warden, BA, MA

Music:
J D Holloway, MA, ARCO (*Director*)
H J Adcroft
J D Oakes, ARCM
M J Kelly, ARCM, DipRCM
S R J Williamson, MA, FRCO
Plus 25 visiting instrumental teachers

Art:
C K P Thomas, MA, MFA (*Director*)
Miss C Harrison, BA
Ms S A Lang, BA
Ms A Hall, BA, MLitt
J Grater, BA, MA

Drama:

PE:
†G Waugh, BEd

Commanding Officer CCF: Major E J Heddon, MBA, MIPD

Librarian: Ms J L Shepherd, BA, ALA

Bursar: M P Sherwin, BSc

Accountant: J A L Ferns

Works Bursar: G Burbidge, MCIOB

Facilities Bursar: Mrs T A Evans

Estate Manager: M F Brandom, BA, BSc

Medical Officer: A P McG Greig, MB, BS, DCh, DRCGP

Sanatorium Sister: Mrs J L Whalley

Registrar: Mrs S F Sparks

Assistant to the Registrar: Mrs P Gatland

Master's Secretary: Mrs J M Radford

College Secretary: Mrs T A Kennedy

Wellington College was founded by public subscription as a memorial to the Great Duke. It was granted a Charter in 1853 and took its first pupils in 1859. In the early days of the school there were strong connections with the Army. Today, the school's connection with the Army is much less strong although places continue to be reserved for the children of deceased officers (Army, Navy or Royal Air Force) who apply to be Foundationers.

The school is set in a woodland estate of 400 acres and has 800 pupils of whom 50–55 are girls on a two year A level course. The great majority of pupils board but there are about 150 day pupils, approximately half of whom become boarders in the Upper School. About 400 boys are boarded in eight houses in the main College buildings. The remainder are in six separate houses in the grounds of the College. The girls have their own separate boarding house, Apsley.

On entry to the school, a new pupil will go straight into his House. In most Houses, he may well be in shared accommodation in his first year and will then move to his own room. Day pupils are spread among the boarding Houses and thus play a full part in the life of the school.

Houses and Housemasters are: Benson, R I H B Dyer; Stanley, R C Auger; Talbot, Dr P G S Boscher; Anglesey, A R Taylor; Beresford, T J Head; Blücher, M T Boobbyer; Combermere, N C Lunnon; Hardinge, I M Henderson; Hill, P T Galley; Hopetoun, G Waugh; Lynedoch, Rev D M Outram; Murray, J C Rawlinson; Orange, K M Hopkins; Picton, A R Dewes; Apsley (girls), D A Burns.

There is a central dining hall with modern kitchens and serveries. Meals are taken here on a cafeteria basis by most of the pupils although three Houses outside the main buildings have their own dining facilities. The school has its own Medical Officer and a 22 bed Sanatorium constantly staffed by fully qualified nursing staff. The Houses in and out of College have their own Housekeepers and domestic staff.

Academic Work. Academic standards are high: GCSE & A Level pass rates are in the 94–99% range, and nearly all boys and girls go on to university. There is a good rate of entry to Oxford, Cambridge, Durham, Edinburgh and many other good universities. Most work takes place in modern specialist blocks near to the main buildings. The principal one, Queen's Court, also contains a theatre. The Science laboratories have all been recently refurbished and a modern building, the Kent Building, houses a well equipped Design and Technology Centre and a Micro-technology Centre encompassing computing and electronics. A new Art School and Physics Laboratories have been built on sites near to the Kent Building. The old Art School in the main buildings has been converted into a new lecture room and conference room.

The school is divided for teaching purposes into the Lower School (Blocks II & III), the Middle School (Block I) and the Upper School (Lower Sixth and Sixth). The GCSE is taken in the Middle School. All the usual subjects are taught in the Middle and Lower Schools, including three separate sciences. In Block III the following subjects are taught: Divinity, English, History, Geography, French, Mathematics, Physics, Chemistry, Biology, Art, Music, IT, Electronics, Design and Technology. Not all boys are required to study Latin, but most do. Greek, German and Spanish are taught, too. In Block II there are six "columns" of options which allow boys some choice outside the four main subjects.

In the Upper School, a wide range of AS and A level choices is available. These include all the usual combinations but at least one-third of our boys and girls do a combined Arts/Science grouping.

Extra Curricular Activities. All boys on arrival join the Junior Society which introduces them to a wide variety of activities. Art, Music and Drama are outstanding. A Creative Writing Group meets regularly, and a literary magazine, the Wellingtonian, is edited by pupils.

Other Societies include: Art, Astronomy, Chess, Bridge, Classics, Debating, Film, Golf, Mathematics, Music, Natural History, Opera, Photography, Pottery, Sailing and Science. There is a scholarly society called the Phoenix (membership by invitation only) and a wine-tasting society called the Noble Rot. There are regular visiting lecturers on a variety of topics, an Artist in Residence, and master-classes in Art, Music/Drama and Literature.

Throughout the College, a conscious effort is made to provide all boys and girls with a programme of personal development which includes experience of management and team-building and leadership training.

Wellington has been a Round Square school since 1995; the Round Square is made up of schools from around the world which are all pledged to foster international standing and to educate through service at home and overseas.

Games. The school has a national reputation for prowess in games, at the moment particularly in Rugby, Hockey, Cricket, Shooting, Swimming and Athletics.

There are great opportunities for boys to represent the school in teams; for instance we regularly field up to 24 XVs in Rugby. Other games flourish too, offering a wide chance of active involvement. Girls too have a wide range of opportunity. The school has excellent sporting facilities with over 80 acres of playing fields, an 'all weather' pitch for hockey and all-weather tennis courts. There is a Sports complex which incorporates a rackets court, three fives courts, five squash courts, an indoor pool and a large Sports Hall. This has a main hall 37m × 32m in size in which a wide variety of indoor games may be played as well as specialist weight training and rock climbing areas. A nine-hole golf course is under construction; it will open in 2001. The normal pattern of boys' games is rugby in the Michaelmas Term, hockey, football and cross country in the Lent Term and cricket, athletics and swimming in the Summer. Other games include rackets, squash, basketball, tennis, sailing, football, shooting, fencing, karate, golf, badminton, canoeing, fives, sub-aqua and volleyball.

Admission to the School. Most boys enter the school in September when they are between 13 and 14 years of age. There are a few places available for boys for entry to the Sixth Form at 16+. Girls enter at 16+ to the Sixth Form. Applications for registration should be addressed to the Registrar, or in the case of Foundationers, to the Bursar. On registration, a small fee is charged which entitles a child's name to remain on the register until two years or so before entry is due. At this point, we ask for a confirmation of entry. The school keeps in touch with parents of children registered through a regular newsletter. After registration, and if entry has been confirmed, a place is guaranteed, subject to satisfactory results in the Scholarship, Common Entrance or other entry exams. Upon confirmation of entry, an entrance fee of £300 is charged of which £225 is returned on the pupil's final fee account. Girls' entry is by competitive exam in the November before admission, supplemented by individual interviews. Boys applying for entry to the Sixth Form are interviewed in the spring of the year of entry.

Scholarships. (*see* Entrance Scholarship section) There are nineteen Scholarships and Exhibitions offered. In the academic field, the top four Scholarships are for 50% of the fees; there are up to seven of 30% of the fees, and eight Exhibitions of 15% of the fees. Two Major Music Scholarships of 50% of the fees and a number of minor awards will be awarded if boys of sufficient ability present themselves. There will be Art and Design and Technology awards of 15% of the fees if there are candidates of sufficient merit. Art, Design and Technology and Music candidates must satisfy our general entry requirements. Scholarships of all values may be augmented where the financial situation of the parents makes this necessary. Candidates must be under 14 on 1st September in the calendar year in which they sit the examination. For girls entering at 16+ there are three academic awards (one of 50% and two of 30% fees) and one music award of 50% fees.

Fees. In 2000/2001 the termly fees for boarders are £5,460 and £4,095 for day pupils. For pupils in the Lower Sixth and Sixth Forms, there is an additional charge of £74 per term. Separate charges totalling £155 per instrument are made for musical tuition. The school runs an attractive fees in advance scheme for parents with capital sums available.

Old Wellingtonian Society. The OW Society has branches in ten countries, clubs representing ten different sports, around 7,000 members (including 500 girls) and a Secretary based at College (Tel: 01344 444069; Fax: 01344 444007.

Charitable status. Wellington College is a Registered Charity, number 309093. It exists to provide education for boys, with girls in the Sixth Form.

Wellington School

Wellington Somerset TA21 8NT
Tel: (01823) 668800
Fax: (01823) 668844
e-mail: admin@wellington-school.org.uk
website: http://www.wellington-school.org.uk

The School first opened in 1837 as a private school, and was refounded in 1879. In 1908 it was reorganised under the Charitable Acts with an Independent Governing Body, holding Direct Grant status from 1945 until 1978. Subsequently the School has expanded and has been fully coeducational for twenty years.

Motto: *Nisi dominus frustra.*

Governing Body:

Chairman: P H Lee, CB, MBE
Vice-Chairman: Mrs S E Watts
Vice-Admiral Sir Edward Anson, KCB
J H Butler
D J Fasey, ACIB
Prof M P Furmston, TD, MA, BCL, LLM
Col R A Hooper, RM, MA, FRSA
D O Joseph, MA, BA
Mrs R Lawrence Mills, BSc
Revd Preb C J B Marshall
J A G Moore, OBE
G N R Morgan, TD, FRICS
G Ridler, BSc
Mrs C Seymour
Mrs A M Smith, BA
D T Trist, MRPharms
E J Warren
D Wheeler

Clerk to the Governors: G E Moody, MA

***Headmaster:* A J Rogers**, MA, FRSA

Deputy Head: R S Page, MA
Assistant Deputy Head: Mrs L A Jones, BA
Head of Lower School: T J G Scott, BA, MA
Director of Studies: I F Loudon, MA

Assistant Academic Staff:

A Anderson, BA
D R Armitage, BSc
C F Barratt, BSc
*Mrs A E Bazley, BEd (*Girls' PE and Games*)
†T M Bazley, BA (*Richards*)
*Mrs J C Bernard, BA (*Home Economics*)
*J F Bird, BA (*Classical Studies*)
M J Blackmore, BA
M Bradbury, BA
J H Bradnock, MA, BA
Mrs L Burton, BA
Miss K A Butt, MA, BA
†A R Carson, BSc (*Darks*)
Dr S Chalk, BSc
Miss M Collins, BA
A R Crozier, BSc
†Mrs L Davey, BSc (*Rowan*)
†A N Denham, BA (*Lights*)
C R J Dew, BSc
*R Dixon, BSc, MSc, MIBiol (*Biology and Co-ordinator of Sciences*)
†R M Eastmond, DipPE (*Oak*)
I J Everton, MA, PhD (*i/c Activities*)
Mrs J H Gane, BA
Mrs B Hall-Palmer, CertEd, MIL, DipTrans
*The Rev J P Hellier, BD, AKC, CF (*Chaplain and RE*)

Miss F E Hobday, MA
Mrs J Hogg, BA
Mrs M E Kerslake, MA
†Mrs J F Kingston, BSc (*Gillards*)
Miss V Knowles, BSc
†*M A Leins, BSc(Econ), LTCL (*Economics, Careers*) (*Beech*)
†J Leonard, BA (*Howard*)
†Mrs L E Leonard, BA (*Linden*)
D R Lungley, BSc, PhD (*OC CCF*)
Miss R L Marsden, BA
N McGuff, BSc(Ed)
D Millington, BA, MSc (*Information Technology*)
†*L C Neville, BEd (*Maths*) (*Willows*)
P F Norman, BA
†*P M Owen, MA, PhD (*Physics*) (*Hardwick*)
Mrs S Page, MA
*J A Paltridge, MA, MSc, MEd (*Modern Languages*
†P M Pearce, BA (*Talbot*)
C J Petley, BSc, MSc
S C Phippen, BA
A J Pizii, BEd
M H Richards, BEd (*Boys' PE and Games*)
Mrs L K Richold, CertEd, DipTEFL
Mrs S Rogers, BA
B A Ryder, BEng
Miss C L Ryder, MA
*Mrs H M Sail, MA (*Geography*)
A Salt, BA
†Mrs H Salter, BA (*Price's*)
I A Sarginson, BSc
*J P W Shepherd, MA (*English*)
Miss K N Simpson, BA
*K Smith, BA (*Director of Art*)
A W Stevenson, MA (*Director of Drama*)
T P Sutton-Day, BPhil(Ed)
P J Swan, MSc
Mrs A H Thorne, BSc
†Miss S F L Toase, BSc, GIBiol (*Avenue*)
*A J Trewhella, BA, ARCO (*Director of Music*)
†Mrs R Turner, BA (*Fox's*)
*E G Whall, BSc
Mrs S E White, ARCM
*G H Woodward, BA, MLitt (*History*)
Mrs J A Woodward, BSc

Assistant Music Staff:

Mrs P Adie, MBE, LRAM (*Voice*)
Mrs A Caunce, GRSM, ARCSM, LTCL, ARCM (*Piano*)
Mrs R Cox, ARCM, DipPRCM (*Cello*)
Mrs A Ennis, DipTCL, PGCE (*Violin, Viola*)
Miss I Fernando, LRAM (*Double Bass*)
H D H Elkington, MA (*Flute*)
Mrs K Jasper, ARCM (*Piano*)
Mrs D Jerrold, ARCM (*Oboe, Bassoon*)
Miss A Kimber, BA, FTCL, ARCM, CertEd (*Flute*)
M A Leins, BSc, LTCL (*Classical Guitar*)
S Phippen, BA, LTCL, PGCE (*Piano*)
Miss C D Rose, BA, PGCE (*Clarinet*)
K Schooley (*Percussion*)
J Small (*Guitar*)
C Taylor (*Brass*)
T Waller, MA, BMus (*Piano*)
N White, BA, PPGSM (*Saxophone*)
Mrs S E White, ARCM, DipRCM (*Saxophone, Clarinet*)
Mrs H Wickham, DRSAM, LRAM (*Flute*)
Mrs V Williams, ARCM (*Brass*)

Bursar: Cdr R D Coupe, OBE, RN
School Administrator: P J Swan, MSc, FIMA, CMath
Registrar and Headmaster's PA: Mrs C Jones, BA
Medical Officer: Dr J G Scott, MBBS, DRCOG
OC CCF: Lt Col D R Lungley, BSc, PhD
CCF SSI: RSM G T Farrar

Situation. Located on the southern edge of Wellington, at the foot of the Blackdown Hills with their familiar Monument to the Great Duke, this fully coeducational School is equidistant from Tiverton Parkway and Taunton Railway Stations. The M5 approach road (Junction 26) is within a mile. Currently there are 850 pupils, of whom 20% board.

Buildings. The School has witnessed an extensive building programme over the last twelve years, the new buildings having been carefully and tastefully blended in with existing architecture. The Great Hall, built in 1925, also houses the Gymnasium, and the Chapel, completed in 1931, is centred in the heart of the School as a memorial to those former members of the School who fell in the Great War. In 1964 an addition was made to the Corner Block, with further classrooms for Geography, Classical Studies and Economics.

1984 saw the creation of the Duke's Building, housing a new, enlarged Library, a Resources Centre, a Sixth Form Centre and Staff Common Room. This was followed 2 years later by a spacious, well-equipped Design and Technology Centre, containing workshops, computer facilities and Home Economics laboratories. Shortly afterwards old buildings were imaginatively converted to extend the Music School and provide an Art Centre. In January 1990 the John Kendall-Carpenter Science Centre was opened, with state-of-the-art laboratories and a Lecture Theatre, while in 1992, Maths and Modern Languages were brought to the door of the 21st century with the total modernisation and refurbishment of the New Northside Building, including European satellite television down-links. The last three years have seen the development of 2 new IT suites to be used for teaching and private study. In addition, provision for changing and leisure facilities for day pupils, as well as boarding facilities, are undergoing a rolling programme of expansion and modernisation. A new sports complex is scheduled for the Millennium and a Junior School opened in September 1999, taking children from the age of 3 years.

Grounds. There are 12 hectares of playing fields including 'play deck' tennis courts, an all-weather hockey pitch and six further new tennis courts/four netball courts. Squash courts, changing rooms and a climbing wall were added recently to the outdoor swimming pool.

Houses. There are separate Houses for boys and girls, and for Seniors and Juniors. All Houses have their own changing, work and recreational facilities.

There is a central Dining Hall and all meals are served on a cafeteria basis. The School also has its own well equipped laundry.

All pupils are full members of the School; the day pupils being regarded as boarders who sleep at home. There is a fully equipped Sanatorium, with a trained staff under the direction of the School Medical Officer.

Academic Organisation. The School is divided into Upper, Middle and Lower strata.

The Upper School consists of the U6th and L6th which are divided into Tutor Groups to monitor academic progress. All the standard subjects are available to A level, and although it is normal for a group of related subjects to be chosen, it is possible for students to select unusual combinations. It is expected that all will start on 4 A Levels, with most reducing to 3 subjects for the U6 year. Subsidiary general subjects are also studied in the L6 year, including Key Skills Level Three in IT. Almost all then enter universities.

In the Middle School pupils spend three years preparing for GCSE. The Third Form year is a preparatory year for the two year GCSE course during which all subjects on offer are taught to all pupils. In the Fourth and Fifth Forms all pupils study English Language and Literature and Mathematics, with at least one foreign Language, and 6 options from separate sciences, Physics, Chemistry, Biology or Balanced Science, French, German, Spanish,

Latin, Classical Studies, Geography, History, Art & Design, Music and Design & Technology. The top set Mathematicians take GCSE a year early in the Fourth Form and study Additional Mathematics during the Fifth Year.

In the Lower School boys and girls spend 2 or 3 years, entering at 10+ into the Preparatory Form or 11+ into the First Form. The emphasis in the Prep Form is upon the basic subjects of English and Mathematics, although a very wide range of subjects is offered.

Religious Education is part of the curriculum in the Lower and Middle Schools. The School is Christian in tradition and there is a short Act of Worship in the School Chapel on each weekday with a longer Sunday service. The content and form of these services are based on contemporary Anglican procedures. Attendance is expected although sensitivity is shown towards pupils of other faiths, who may be exempted.

Music. Private Tuition is offered in piano, organ and all string and wind instruments. A modern three-manual organ is available for organ pupils. Practice rooms are available and group or individual tuition may be arranged. Instruments may be borrowed from the School. There are several activities in which pupils are encouraged to take part: Choral Society; Chapel Choir; School Choir; Full Orchestra and Junior Orchestra; Brass Ensemble and Recorder/Woodwind groups. A fine Steinway piano is available for the most able pianists and regular termly concerts are held in the Great Hall, Small Hall or in the Chapel. Once a term a visiting professional musician is invited to perform in concert. A large number of pupils are entered each term for the Associated Board Examinations.

Physical Education and Games. Besides its own playing fields, swimming pool, squash courts and fitness room, the School uses the facilities of the Wellington Sports Centre each week. All pupils play games regularly, unless exempted for medical reasons, and Physical Education takes place in the Gymnasium and as part of the normal timetable for Prep to Fifth Forms. All pupils learn to swim and are granted the opportunity to take part in as many sports as possible. In the winter term, rugby, hockey and squash are the main sports; in the spring term hockey, netball, cross-country running and squash; in the summer term athletics, cricket, tennis, swimming and rounders. Team practices/matches mainly take place on Wednesday and Saturday afternoons.

Out of School and CCF Activities. All pupils from the Fourth Form upwards either join the large CCF contingent, with both army and naval sections, or are engaged in other activities on a weekly basis, ranging from community services and conservation, to gardening and stage crew. Outward Bound Activities, both within the CCF and as part of the flourishing Duke of Edinburgh Award Scheme, are very popular, with many trips organised. The CCF also has a highly respected Corps of Drums, which frequently features in local ceremonial events. Societies, in addition to the above, include Art, Bridge, Chess and Drama at various levels, Cookery, Computing and others.

Admission. (a) **Lower School Entrance.** The age range for the examination for boarders and day pupils is over 10 and under 12 by 1 September of the year of entry. If pupils are under 11 they will normally spend a year in the Preparatory Form.

(b) **Common Entrance.** This examination takes place at the pupil's Preparatory School during the term before registration for entry, and arrangements are made by the Preparatory School. Other entrants at this age are by interview.

Academic Grants. As well as a number of Scholarships, up to 20 reduced fee places are given annually to those academically able pupils whose parents would not otherwise be able to meet the fees.

Careers. A complete careers guidance service is offered in a well equipped suite of Careers Rooms. Mr M A Leins, in charge of Careers, is in close contact with the Independent Schools Careers Organisation.

Fees. From September 2000 the fee for boarders is £3,505 per term, which includes tuition, board, laundry, mending, medical attention and Sanatorium, stationery and games. The termly fee for day pupils is £1,921. For all pupils there is a registration fee of £20.

Extras. Apart from purely personal expenses, the termly extras are private music lessons from £98 to £130; Activities and CCF £4 and £8 respectively. Boarding House subscription £7. EFL lessons are charged a small amount.

Scholarships. The equivalent of seven Tuition Scholarships are available at Lower School Entrance level, and a number of bursaries are available in the Sixth Form. All Service children receive a bursary. Music Exhibitions are available for outstanding musicians from the age of 10.

Charitable status. Wellington School is a Registered Charity, number 310268. It aims to provide a happy, caring coeducational day and boarding community, where pupils are provided with the opportunity of making best use of their academic experience and indeed the School enrichment activities, in order to enhance their overall preparation for life after the age of eighteen.

Wells Cathedral School

Wells Somerset BA5 2ST
Tel: (01749) 672117 (Head Master)
Tel: (01749) 672263 (Bursar)
Fax: (01749) 670724

In the 12th Century there was a Cathedral School in Wells providing education for choir boys. Today, Wells Cathedral School is fully coeducational with nearly 800 pupils, day and boarding, from the age of 3 to 18.

Governors:
The Dean and Chapter of Wells, The Very Revd R Lewis (*Chairman*)
The Revd Canon M Matthews
The Revd Canon P Woodhouse
The Venerable R Ackworth
Mr D C Tudway Quilter
Dr David Atterton, CBE
Mrs Rosie Inge
Mrs Stella Clarke, JP
Mr M Willey
Mr P McIlwraith
Mr T Peryer

Development Trustees and Consultants:
Lord Rees-Mogg
Lord Marmaduke Hussey
Sir Roger Young
Mr Brian Beazer
Professor Yfrah Neaman, OBE
Mr John Vallins, OBE
Dr Janet Ritterman
Lord Armstrong of Ilminster

Head: **Mrs Elizabeth Cairncross**, BA (University College, London), PGCE

Deputy Headmaster: C Cain, BA
Second Deputy: Mrs D Davies, BA (York), MEd (Warwick)
Director of Music: Mrs Dorothy Nancekievill, BA, BMus

Senior School:
Mrs A M Armstrong, BMus, LRAM, PGCE
Dr P J Arnold, MA, DPhil
M J Ashton, BA
J Attwater, BA (Oxon)
J R Barnard, BSc
Mrs H Bennett, BA

Miss J Blythe, BSc(Ed)
D Byrne, Dip (Moscow Cons), ARCM, ARAM, DipRAM
Mrs N A M Connock, BSc
Dr I Davies, DMus, MA (Cantab)
Mrs S C Dawson, BEd
C S Day, BA
P Denegri, FTCL, LTCL
Miss S G I T Domalski-Hall, BA
Mrs M Edwards, HECert
Mrs S Evans, ALA (*Librarian*)
Mrs M C Fielding, BSc
Mrs P J Garty, BSc
D Gowen, BA
Dr R Henson, GRLC, PhD
Dr A K Hignell, PhD
K H Humphreys, BSc
Miss S Jameson, BSc
A G Jones, BA
Miss C L Jones, BA(Ed)
D Jones, BSc
A J Keep, BA, MA
A M Laing, MA (Cantab)
Miss C Lord, ARCM, Juillard Diploma
J C C Machling, BMus
B Marsden, BA (Hons)
C Masters
Dr H Murphy, PhD, MA, BMus, LRAM
Dr K Murphy, PhD, MMus, BA
Mrs D Nankerbille, MA, BMus
D O'Hara, CertEd, DipEd
K Padgett, BSc
Mrs G A Pearson, BEd
W C R Robbetts, BA, MEd, MIBiol
D Rowley, BSc
Mrs S G Rowley, BA
Miss A Smith, BA (Hons)
Mrs S E Smith
K D Sowden, BEd
M C H Stringer, DipEd
S Tapner, BSc
M Theodorou, BA
Mrs D Tinker, BSc
Miss K Trego, BA
Mrs A-L Tyler, BA (Hons)
J D Walkey, MSc, FSS
D Williams, BA (Hons)
Mrs J S Wyatt, BA, PGCE, ADT

Part-time Staff:
R J Baker, MA (Oxon)
R A Barnes, LLB, BEd
P L Bishop, BA (*Registrar*)
Mrs J M Bocquet, BSc
Mrs L J Bridson, BA, PGCE
Mrs D Bucknall, BSc
M Cornelius
Dr N H Day, PhD, MMus, BMus, APRS
Mrs S Day, BSc
Mrs D L Fried-Booth, BA
D C Hansom
J M Hard, MSc, CBiol, MIBiol (*Careers Consultant*)
Mrs F L Meare, MIL
C Mitchell, BA
Miss B Murray, GRSM, ARCM
Mrs J Obradovic, LTCL
P Silverwood, ICA
Miss A J Simper, BSc
Mrs L E Walkey, CertEd
A N Walsh, BA
P Yates

Junior School:
The Head of Junior School: N M Wilson, BA, PGCE

Deputy Head: Mrs J Barrow, BEd

Mrs J Burns, Central School of Speech and Drama
Miss A Clark, BEd
Miss V Clarke, BEd
J Davis, BEd
Mrs E Drabble, CertEd
Mrs J Edmonds, BSc, ALCM
Mrs P Evans, BEd
Mrs J Ford, BA
Mrs D King-Holford (*House Parent of Polydor House*)
Mrs E Lord, BEd
Miss A Maidment, BEd
D Pittard, BA Hons, PGCE
Miss K Summers, BEd
Mrs K M Thomas, CertEd
Mrs J Tucker, DipEd
J Wells, BEd (*House Master of Polydor House*)

Bursar and Clerk to the Governors: Mr S J Drabble, BSc
Financial Controller: Mrs P J Smart
Headmaster's Secretary: Mrs Barbara Smith
Publicity Officer: Tony Bolton
Development Director: Mrs S O'Sullivan, MICFM
Sister i/c Sick Bay: Mrs R G Bevan, SRN, FAETC

General. There is a Senior and Junior School with a total of 751 boys and girls aged from 3 to 18. Boarders number 244, whilst the remainder are day pupils. Once accepted, a child normally remains in the School without further Entrance Examination until the age of 18+. There are 359 girls of whom 137 are boarders. They join in all activities but there are also opportunities for separate interests.

Fees. (From September 2001) Nursery (3-4): £655 termly charge for 5 sessions per week excluding lunches. Pre-Prep (4–7): £1,300 per term; Boarders (7–11): £4,095 per term; Day: £2,455 per term. Boarders (11–14): £4,728 per term; Day: £2,775 per term. Boarders (15–18): £4,850 per term; Day: £2,880.

Scholarships (*see* Entrance Scholarship section) **and Entrance.** Scholarships are awarded as a result of Entrance and Scholarship Tests taken in January at the School. These consist of tests and interviews, whilst also considering any specialist gifts or aptitudes.

Sixth Form Scholarships are awarded on the basis of rigorous interview and a confidential reference from the applicant's current school.

Cathedral Choristerships are awarded as the result of a Choral Trial. Applicants should be between 8½ and 10½ at the time of the Trial. Entrance Tests can be arranged in any term and special arrangements can be made for children overseas.

Situations and Buildings. The mediaeval city of Wells, with its famous Cathedral and a population of only 10,500, is the smallest city in England. It is just over 20 miles from Bath and Bristol where there is a good rail service, and easily accessed from the M4 and M5 motorways. The School occupies all but one of the canonical houses in The Liberty. This fine group is planned to keep its mediaeval and 18th Century atmosphere while providing for the needs of modern boarding education. There are modern classrooms and science laboratories built amongst walled gardens. A Sports Hall provides indoor facilities for Tennis, Badminton, Cricket, Basketball, Volley Ball, Hockey, Five-a-Side Football, Climbing and Multi-gym. There are Theatrical and Concert facilities, a new Music Technology Centre, a Computer Studies Centre, Home Economics Centre, Art, Design and Technology Department, Drama Studio, Library, Sixth Form Centre, 25 metre Swimming Bath, Tennis and Netball courts, three sports fields and an all-weather hard play area.

There is one Boarding House in the Junior School and a further eight in the Senior School, four for boys and four for girls, the most senior pupils having study-bedrooms. The aim is to give security to the younger and to develop a sense of responsibility in the older.

Organisation and Curriculum. Despite its national and international reputation, the School has retained close links with the local community, and its fundamental aim is to provide all its pupils with an education consistent with the broad principles of Christianity. More specifically, the School aims to be a well-regulated community in which pupils may learn to live in harmony and mutual respect with each other and with the adults who care for them. The curriculum has been designed to enable all children who gain entry to the School to develop fully all their abilities, and to take their place in due course in tertiary education and the adult community of work and leisure. There are three Forms at 11, and four at 12, 13, 14 and 15 before the Sixth Form. Forms are limited to a maximum of 25. Two years before GCSE a tutorial system is introduced whereby some ten boys and girls are the responsibility of one member of Staff for academic progress to GCSE. Pupils then choose a subject faculty for sixth form tutoring in similar groups.

The emphasis is on setting by ability in particular subjects rather than streaming. There is every attempt to avoid early specialisation. All take Mathematics, English, double Science, and a foreign language to GCSE. There is a Sixth Form of some 170 taking 'A' Level courses in all major academic subjects.

Many places have been gained at Oxford and Cambridge in recent years and most Sixth Formers leave for some form of higher education (98% in 1998).

Societies. There is a wide range of indoor and outdoor activities in which pupils must participate, although the choice is theirs. Outdoor education is an important part of the curriculum. Besides a Combined Cadet Force with Army and RAF sections and a Duke of Edinburgh Award scheme, activities as diverse as chess and kite making, photography, sailing and golf are also on offer. Ballet and riding lessons are also arranged.

Music. The School is one of four in England designated and grant-aided by the Department for Education to provide special education for gifted young musicians, who are given substantial financial assistance. Wells is unique in that both specialist and non-specialist musicians are able to develop their aptitudes within a normal school environment. These talents are widely acknowledged by audiences at concerts given by pupils from Wells throughout the world.

There are over 160 talented pupils following specially devised timetables which combine advanced instrumental tuition and ensemble work with academic opportunity. More than half of the School learns at least one musical instrument. Violin is taught to all children in the Pre-Prep as part of the curriculum. Pupils receive the highest quality teaching, often leading to music conservatoires and a career in Music. Central to specialist music training are the opportunities to perform in public and there is a full concert diary. There are also regular concerts by the many ensembles in the School.

For further details write to: The Registrar, Wells Cathedral School, Wells, Somerset BA5 2ST.

The Wellensian Association. Chris Neave, Chairman, Old Wellensians, Wells Cathedral School, Wells, Somerset BA5, 2ST.

Charitable status. Wells Cathedral School Limited is a Registered Charity, number 310212. It is a charitable trust for the purpose of promoting the cause of education in accordance with the doctrine of the Church of England.

West Buckland School

Barnstaple Devon EX32 0SX.
Tel: (01598) 760281
Fax: (01598) 760546
e-mail: johnvick@westbuckland.devon.sch.uk

West Buckland School was founded in 1858 "to provide a first class education at reasonable cost". It has always stressed the importance of all-round character development alongside good academic achievement, with the size remaining small enough to allow plenty of attention to individual needs and talents.

West Buckland Preparatory School educates children between the ages of three and eleven. There is strong co-operation and support between the schools, which share the same grounds, so making the transition as easy as possible.

West Buckland is fully co-educational.

Motto: Read and Reap.

President: Vice Admiral Sir Anthony Tippet, KCB, CIMgt

The Governing Body:

Chairman: P D Orchard-Lisle, CBE, TD, DL, MA, FRICS

Vice-Chairmen:
The Countess of Arran
W H G Geen

Governors:
D G Avery
Dr L M Baggott, MSc, PhD
R F Banbury
D L Cummins
C R Evans, MA
Lady Gass, JP, MA
G G Harrison, BSc, FRICS
J W J Milton
Mrs R Morgan
H J Pedder
The Revd R D Simpson, MA, MLitt
Dr R Thomas, CBE, BA

***Headmaster:* J F Vick**, MA, St John's College, Cambridge

Deputy Head: D A Clark, BSc, Sheffield

Director of Studies: C J Burrows, MA, Exeter College, Oxford

Second Deputy Head: Mrs C Tibble, BA, Open University

Headmaster, Preparatory School: A D Moore, BEd

Chaplain: The Revd A M Kettle, MA

Housemaster/Housemistress:

Mrs R H Berry, MA Bristol (*Brereton House*)
J Whitfield, BSc Lanchester Polytechnic (*Courtenay House*)
Mrs S G Fowles, BSc Exeter (*Fortescue House*)
J T B Clark, BEd Reading (*Grenville House*)

Assistant Staff:
Miss E K Barson, MSc
Mme M LeBarth, L-ès-L
V P Berry, MA
M T Brimson, BA
Mrs J E Brock, MA
Mrs P A Brown, BSc
Mrs P M Bryars
Mrs J F Bunclark, MA
Dr C R Byfleet, MA, PhD
A J Calder, BSc
Miss A L Callow, BSc
A J E Cameron, MA
R W L Carter, BA
R D Clarke, BA, BEd
B M Coates, MA
R N T Cook, BA
P H Davies, BSc
C H Dawson, BSc
R A Durrant, BSc
A D Evans, BEd
C Gambles, BSc
M J Greer, BA
Mrs S P Hartnoll, BEd
Mrs Y Helicon, BA
A P Hooper, BSc
Mrs J M Hopkins, BA
D M Hymer, BSc
The Revd A M Kettle, MA
R D Mace, BA
Miss E Mackay, CertEd
Miss K P A MacBride, BA
N Minard, BA
D W Minns, BEng
J R Moor, MA
Dr A K Percival, BTec, PhD
P J C Ponder, BEd
S J Prior, BSc
Mrs A L Pugsley, BA
M Richards, BMus, MMus
M A Ryan, BA
I S Seager, GradDipArch, CertEd
Miss D J Sharman, BSc
M G Stuart, BA
M J Tucker, CertEd
Mrs J Whittal-Williams
L Whittal-Williams
D A Wilson, MA
Mrs V Wilson, BEd
Mrs A V Wyatt, BEd

Visiting Music Staff:
Mrs P Adie, MBE, LRAM (*Singing*)
Mrs B Bradley-Bailey, BMus (*Choir*)
K Chetwin (*Guitar*)
Mrs S Cole (*Piano*)
Mrs J Crew, LTCL (*Viola/Cello*)
I H Goodliffe, DipEd (*Clarinet/Saxophone*)
Mrs S Cole (*Piano*)
Mrs V Hind, BA, LTCL (*Oboe/Viola da Gamba*)
Mrs A Hughes, LTCL (*Piano*)
D Moreton (*Double Bass*)
Mrs C Nicholls, BA (*Flute*)
Mrs A Olver, LRAM, ARCM, GRSM, ABRSM (*Piano*)
Mrs S Robinson, BMus (*Violin*)
C Taylor (*Brass*)
B Waring (*Percussion*)

Bursar: Cdr A R Jackson, MILT, MInstAM
Assistant Bursar (*Finance*): Mrs R A Priscott, CT, ABRSM
Domestic Bursar: Miss M Y Duke, MHCIMA
Bursar's Secretary: Mrs P Alldis
Fees Secretary: D Foster
Headmaster's Secretary: Mrs H M Clark
Assistant Secretaries:
Mrs Y Reed
Mrs J L Schumacher

Medical Officer: Dr C A Gibb, BMed, BM, DA, MRCGP, DRCOG, DPD

School Sisters:
Mrs C E Pouncey, RGN
Mrs G M Rowland, RGN
Mrs R L Withecombe, RGN

Houseparents:
Mrs L A Brimson, BA
Mrs S Marston
Mrs J E Moor
Mrs A Seager

Librarian: Mrs J A Thayre, ALA

Situation. The School stands in its own grounds of 100 acres on the southern edge of Exmoor. Barnstaple is 10 miles away and the M5 motorway can be reached in 40 minutes. Boarders arriving by train at Exeter station are met by coaches.

Buildings and Grounds. The central range of buildings, dating from 1860, still forms the focus of the school. A major reconstruction has created a performing arts centre. Other major developments and improvements include a sixth form centre, mathematics and physics centre and new boarding houses for boys and girls. A new Preparatory School classroom block and IT Centre opened in September 1999. The grounds offer many sports facilities, including a 9 hole golf course and an indoor heated 25 metre swimming pool.

Admission. Boys and girls are admitted as boarders or day pupils. The present number of pupils is:
115 boarding
562 day

Entrance to the Preparatory School is by interview and assessment. Entry to the Senior School is by examination at 11 and 13, or to the Sixth Form upon interview and school report. Entry at other ages is usually possible, and arrangements are made to suit individual circumstances.

Fees per term. Senior: Boarding £3,400 to £3,915; Day £2,210; Preparatory: Boarding £2,515 to £2,940; Day £960 to £1,750. Nursery £2.55 per hour (including lunch).

Bursaries and Scholarships (*see* Entrance Scholarship section). Several scholarships are offered at 7, 11 and 13, ranging in value from 20% to 50% of fees. Candidates must be under 8, under 12 or under 14 years of age on 1st September.

Bursaries are available to pupils of all ages in urgent financial need, dependent upon achievement and parental income.

A Trust Fund provides special bursaries for Sixth Form boarders and day students.

Curriculum. In the Preparatory School the main emphasis is upon well-founded confidence in English and Mathematics, within a broad balance of subjects that adds modern languages to the national curriculum. Careful attention is given to the development of sporting, artistic and musical talents.

In the Senior School breadth is complemented by specialisation. The national curriculum is expanded by extra attention to the three separate sciences from year 7 upwards and to languages, French, German and Spanish, while there is flexibility within the choice of GCSE subjects to allow for individual strengths and preferences. A wide range of A level subjects is offered to sixth formers, whose results uphold the high academic standards of the School.

Careers. The Careers Staff advise all pupils upon the openings and requirements for different careers. They make full use of the facilities offered by the Cornwall and Devon Careers Ltd.

Games and Leisure Activities. The School has a strong sporting tradition. Rugby football, cricket, netball, hockey, tennis, squash, swimming, cross-country, golf, athletics, shooting and many other sports offer opportunities for inter-school and inter-house competition and for recreation. All members of the school are encouraged to develop interests in such pursuits as art, chess, debating, drama and many others.

Music. Over 120 members of the school receive instrumental tuition on all instruments. They are encouraged to perform in concerts, in choirs and instrumental groups. Music Technology is a strong feature of the department's work.

Adventurous Pursuits. Much use is made of the proximity of Exmoor. All boys and girls receive instruction in camp craft, first aid, and map reading. The Combined Cadet Force has Army and Royal Air Force sections, and offers a range of adventurous and challenging pursuits. Many boys and girls succeed at all levels in the Duke of Edinburgh Award Scheme each year.

Religion. The tradition is Anglican but other denominations and religions are welcome. Services of worship are held throughout the week including Sundays. Many services are held at East Buckland Church. The Chaplain prepares boys and girls for confirmation every year and can be found in his room by anyone who needs personal help or advice.

Attitudes and values. The School sets out to be a friendly and purposeful community in which happiness and a sense of security are the foundation on which young lives are built. At all levels members of the school are asked to lead a disciplined way of life, to show consideration for others, to be willing to be challenged and to recognise that the success of the individual and the success of the group are inextricably linked.

Charitable status. West Buckland School is a Registered Charity, number 306710. Its purpose is the education of boys and girls from 3 to 18.

Westminster School

17 Dean's Yard Westminster London SW1P 3PB
Tel: 020 7963 1042 (Head Master)
020 7963 1003 (Registrar)
020 7963 1028 (Bursar)
020 7963 1050 (Common Room)
020 7821 5788 (Westminster Under School)

Westminster School, which was attached to the Benedictine Abbey of Westminster, was re-founded by Queen Elizabeth I in 1560, and soon afterwards the original 40 Queen's Scholars began to be outnumbered by boys not on the Foundation. The present number of boys and girls is about 670.

Motto: *Dat Deus Incrementum.*

Visitor: Her Majesty The Queen

Governing Body:
The Dean of Westminster (The Very Revd A W Carr, MA, PhD)
The Dean of Christ Church (The Very Revd J H Drury, MA)
The Master of Trinity (Professor A K Sen, FBA)
The Revd Canon N T Wright, MA, DPhil
The Revd Canon M J Middleton, BSc, MA
D H Rice, MA, BPhil
Professor Sir Elihu Lauterpacht, CBE, QC
M C Baughan
T M Robinson, MA
S J B Langdale, MA
C N Foster, FCA
Mrs W E K Anderson, MA
Professor L N Johnson, FRS

Dr P Chadwick, MA, PhD
Professor C R W Edwards, MA, FRCP
The Lord Lester of Herne Hill, QC
Dr A Borg, CBE, PhD, FSA
The Lord Lawson of Blaby, MA, PC
I W Harrison

Secretary to the Governing Body and Bursar: D R Chaundler, OBE

Head Master: **T Jones-Parry**, MA

Under Master: E A Smith, MSc

Master of The Queen's Scholars: J B Katz, MA, DPhil

Director of Studies: Mrs F M R Ramsey, MA, DPhil

Registrar: J M Curtis, MA

Assistant Staff:
C Clarke, FRSA (*Senior Tutor*)
D L Edwards, MA
R R Stokes, MA
G Griffiths, BA
P J Needham, BSc, PhD
R M Tocknell, MA
J E C Arthur, MA
C R L Low, MA
Mrs J L Cockburn, MA
G J Bartlett, MA
M C Davies, MA
P D Hargreaves, MA
A E A Mylne, BA
R J Pyatt, MA
C D Riches, BEd
S C Savaskan, BA, MMus, PhD
W D Phillips, MSc, PhD
M N Robinson, BA
R Dudley-Smith, BSc
H A Aplin, BA, PhD
Miss G M French, MSc, GRSC, FRSA
A L Bateman, DipAD, ATD
R R Harris, MA
G P A Brown, BA, DPhil
G K Jones, MA
N A Stevenson, BSc
Mrs D J Harris, MA
J J Kemball, BSc
S Craft, BA
J R G Beavon, BA, PhD, CChem, MRIC
M K Lynn, MA
Miss C Harrison, BA
J C Troy, BSc(Econ)
D J Vincent, BEd, IEng, MIET
S N Curran, BA
R J Hindley, BA
Mrs A Jørgensen, BTec, MA
A R Morris, BA, MSc, PhD
K D Tompkins, BA
G StJ Hopkins, BA
Mrs J A Lambert, BSc, MSc
D R Hemsley-Brown, BSc, AMIE
J N Hooper, BA
J Kershen, MA
Miss L D Choulerton, BA
N J Hinze, BA
Miss G E Hodges, BA
Mrs S M Jackman, ARCM, LRAM
N G Kalivas, BSc, DPhil
K D McAllister, LRAM, DRSAM
Miss T E L Morris, BA
R P Rees, BA
M Feltham, BA
J M Barot, BA, MSc
T H Mordecai, MA
A H N Reid, BSc, PhD
Mrs F G Smart, BA
Miss G D Ward-Smith, MA, PhD
J C Witney, MA
Mrs J I Cogan, BA
F H Eveleigh, BA
K A P Walsh, BSc
T A Kennedy, BA
Mrs L J Newton, BSc
Miss J E Richardson, BA
Mrs E Brown, BA
P D MacMahon, BA
Miss L Turner, BA
R Huscroft, BA, MA
A Johnson, BA
M J Milner, MA
M Boulton, PhD
J T Harvison, MA
P Hartley, PhD
J A Ireland, MA
J Moston, MA
S Warr, BA

Chaplain: The Revd T H Mordecai, BA, MA

Director of Music: G StJ Hopkins, BA

Librarian: F H Eveleigh, BA

Archivist: E A Smith, MSc

Mistress in charge of girls: Mrs D J Harris, MA

Westminster Under School

Master: J P Edwards, BA, MA

Deputy Head:

Assistant Staff:
Mrs G Howarth, MA
Miss S E K Corps, BSc
Ms Y Colebatch, BA
A J Downey, BA
R C Bennett, MSc, BEd
B E M Evans, CertEd
S R H James, BA
J S Walker, BEd, LRAM (*Director of Music*)
D G Kay, MA, L ès L
P Russell, BA
K G Bamford, MA, MLitt
P Rupar, MA
Miss C Léonidas, L ès L
Miss M J Walker, BSc
B H Evans, BEd
Mrs H M Arthur, CertEd
Mrs C Dunning, BEd
A Paterson, BFA (Aut)
M Snell, BA
Mrs P McLean, BEd, MA
Ms F Illingworth, BA
N Tumber, MA
E Jolliffe, BA, MMus
Mrs C Stevens, BSc

The Foundation of Queen Elizabeth I consists of 40 Queen's Scholars who board in College. The admission to vacancies (averaging 8 yearly) is by open competition in an examination named The Challenge held in May each year. The value of The Queen's Scholarship is half the current boarding fee, but this may be supplemented up to the value of the full boarding fee if there is financial need.

There are also some additional means-tested bursaries awarded to boys who come high on the list.

Candidates sit The Challenge Examination in May for admission in late August of the same year. They must be under 14 years of age on 1 September in the year of entry.

Bursaries are offered to Sixth Form entrants. Music Scholarships and bursaries are also offered to 13+ entrants. Information about all scholarships and bursaries from the Registrar.

Applications for Admission should be made to the Registrar, Westminster School, Little Dean's Yard SW1P 3PF (020 7963 1003). The age of admission for boys is normally from 13–14 years. Entrance is obtained through The Challenge or the Common Entrance Examination. A number of boys and girls (boarding and day) are admitted in the VIth Form in the Autumn term; details are available from the Registrar in the summer of the year preceding entry. Some bursaries are available for this entry.

The Boarding Houses (apart from College, which is confined to The Queen's Scholars) are as follows: Grant's (Boys) – Mr G Griffiths, 2 Little Dean's Yard; Rigaud's (Boys) – Mr J E C Arthur, 1 Little Dean's Yard; Busby's (Mixed) – Mr A E A Mylne, 26 Great College Street; Liddell's (Boys) – Dr A R Morris, 19 Dean's Yard; Purcell's (Girls) – Mr R R Harris, 5 Barton Street.

The Day Houses are as follows (although some Day Boys and Girls are also attached to Boarding Houses): Ashburnham – Mr G K Jones, 6 Dean's Yard; Wren's – Mr K D Tompkins, 4 Little Dean's Yard; Dryden's – Mr R M Tocknell, 4 Little Dean's Yard; Hakluyt's – Mr J J Kemball, 19 Dean's Yard; Milne's – Mr J C Troy, 5A Dean's Yard.

Fees. (*see* Entrance Scholarship section) Boarders: £5,570 per term. Day pupils: £3,858 (inclusive of lunch). VI Form Entry (Day) £4,184. VI Form Entry (Boarders) £5,570.

A Preparatory Department, (Day Boys only). In September 1981, the Under School moved into larger premises in Vincent Square, Westminster, overlooking Westminster School's playing fields. In the new building the Under School has 260 pupils; entry at 7, 8 and 11. Some full Bursaries are available at 11+. The latter is mainly for boys from primary schools. All enquiries should be addressed to the Master (Mr J P Edwards), Westminster Under School, Adrian House, 27 Vincent Square, SW1P 2NN. (Tel: 020 7821 5788). Fees £2,668 per term.

Charitable status. St Peter's College Westminster is a Registered Charity, number 312728. The school was established under Royal Charter for the provision of education.

Whitgift School

Haling Park South Croydon CR2 6YT.
Tel: 020 8688 9222
Fax: School Office 020 8760 0682; Headmaster: 020 8649 7594

Foundation. The Whitgift Foundation originated in 1596 and the School was opened by Archbishop Whitgift in 1600. It is an Independent Day School.
Motto: *Vincit qui patitur.*

Visitor: His Grace The Lord Archbishop of Canterbury

Governing Body:
Five Governors are appointed by the Archbishop of Canterbury, 2 by the London Borough of Croydon and 4 by co-optation. The Bishop of Croydon and the Vicar of Croydon are Governors ex officio.

Chairman of the Court of Governors: Sir Douglas Lovelock, KCB

Deputy Chairman: Cllr R W Coatman, MBE, JP, FRICS, FIArb

Chairman of Estates and Finance Committee: V F Long, FIB

V F Long, FCIB
Prof J W Dougill, MSc, PhD, FEng, FCGI
A D Sexton, BA
M A Fowler, FCA, FCIArb
The Rt Revd Dr W D Wood, Bishop of Croydon
D W North, BSc(Eng), ACGI, MICE
The Revd Canon C J Luke Boswell, Vicar of Croydon
Cllr T Letts
Dr A S Orchard, MBBS, DObst, RCOG
Prof A H Windle, PhD, FRS, FIM
P J Squire, MA
Cllr H Malyan

Clerk to the Governors: R J Smith

***Headmaster:* C A Barnett**, MA, DPhil, Oriel College, Oxford

Second Master: J M Cox, BSc, PhD

Deputy Headmaster: P J Yeo, BA

Senior Master & Head of Upper School: G P Lloyd, BA, MSc

Senior Master: P B Sutherland, MA

Proctor: D E C Elvin, BSc, MSc

Head of Lower School: Miss M L Guest, BD

Management Co-ordinator and Head of Activities: P J Dunscombe, BSc

Assistant Teaching Staff:

D A Aldridge, BA
D J Arnall, BEd
D W Attfield, BSc
J Backhouse, MA
S A Beck, BEd (*Deputy Head of Lower School, Head of First Form & Registrar)*)
D Bowers
W P Brierly, BSc
M Brown, BA (*Head of History*)
R V Brown, IFSTA
D J Byrne, MA
M J Callow, MA
J P D Cannon, BA, PhD, MPhil
I B Carnegie, MA, LRAM (*Head of Performing Arts*)
J Cathcart, BA
Miss A Chaudhry, BSc
S A Collins, BA (*Head of Geography*)
S D Cook, BA (*Head of English*)
P J Dibsdall, BSc
R J Dinnage, BA
Mrs G L Edens, BA
D J Edwards, BA
L Faux-Newman, BSc, PhD
P C Fladgate, BEd (*Senior Housemaster*)
Miss A M V Froehlich, BSc
P L Gibson, BA
B Graoui, BSc
B G Griffiths, MA (*Co-ordinator of Human Resources & Learning Development*)
Miss F M Harrison, BA
C J Harwood, BSc (*Head of Computing*)
Mrs A V Hemsworth, BA (*Head of Italian*)
Mrs S M Hooker, MA (*Head of Careers*)
M W Hoskins, BA (*Head of Economics & Business Studies*)
J Humphrey
Mrs D Jenner, MA
R B Johnstone, BEd (*Head of Design Faculty*)
Mrs J Jordan, BEd
Mrs B A Keating, BA
L D Kelly, BSc
S P Kelly, BA
Miss C M Kennedy, BSc
C J Kibble, BEd (*Director of Sport*)
I H Latif, BSc
Miss C J Leman, BA (*Head of PSHE*)
Miss C Léonard, L-ès-L, M-ès-L
B Lewis, BA (*Head of Art and Design*)
Dott P Liberti, U de Studidi Udiree
T J Lindsay, MA (*Head of Fifth Form*)
S W Litchfield, BEd
P M Lloyd, BSc, PhD (*Head of Chemistry*)
R W Macklin, MA
R F Martin, MA
Miss B A McDonald, MA
R L C McDonald, BA
R M C McGrath, BA (*Head of Classics*)
D F Melotte, NDD
A Moncrieff, BSc
M J Mooney
N P Morgan, BA (*Housemaster, Mason's*)
Miss C Morley, BA
Mrs C A Mulley, BSc
D M Munks, MA, MSc, LRAM, ARCO (*Head of Mathematics*)
Mrs K Nash, BA (*Head of German*)
P J Nicholls, BSc
A Norris, BA (*Head of Games*)
M Ofner, PhD, MAG, TEFLDip (*Head of Bilingual Studies*)
A G Osborne, BA (*Head of Physical Education*)
J Owen, BSc, PhD
C Pates
A J Pearson, BSc
D A Penman, BSc, PhD
W J Penty, BA (*Head of Modern Languages & Head of French*)
J D C Pitt, BA (*Head of Sixth Form*)
Mrs E P Polovinkina, MSc
Miss E Poole, MA
Miss V S Pownall, BA
Mrs F Pritchard, BA
Miss V Ramsden, BSc, MSc
Miss C Range, Diploma, Speech & Drama
Mrs A-M C Rigard-Asquith, L-ès-L, M-ès-L
J H L Roberts, CertEd
Mrs J Rubin, CertEd

D T Schaefer, BA
D J Selby, BA
C D Shaw, BA
T C W Shaw, MA (*Head of Religious Studies*)
K A Smith, BA
Mrs A Starmer, BSc (*Head of Biology*)
Mrs L E Strevens, MA
C G Tinker, PhD, GRSM, ARCM (*Director of Music*)
Miss S Tucker, BA
Miss S Wall, BSc
H L Wallis, MA, PhD
D Ward
Mrs D Watts, BA (*Head of Third Year*)
D M White, MA
Mrs R Whitfield, DipRCM
D R Williams, BTech
P S Wilson, MA (*Head of Drama*)
P Winter, GBSM, DipNCOS (*Head of Strings*)
A Wood, BSc, AKC (*Head of Science & Head of Physics*)
M G Yates, BSc

Bursar: R S Hills, MInstAM, MIMgt
School Medical Officer: Dr C J Wilcock, MBBS
Headmaster's PA & Marketing Manager: Mrs C McCormack, DipM, ACIM

Numbers. There are 1,100 boys on roll, 740 in the Senior School and 360 in the Junior School.

Buildings and Grounds. The School has buildings of great character, opened in 1931 and situated in some 45 acres of attractive parkland with extensive playing fields. The original park, sited around a fine quadrangle, includes Big School, classrooms for most Arts subjects and Mathematics. 1990 saw the completion of a very substantial and superbly equipped extension which links Science, Computing, Design Technology and Art and also incorporates a large new Library.

Other separate buildings include the Junior School, the Sports Hall, a Drama Studio and the Music School. Sports facilities include a heated Swimming Pool, courts for Fives, Squash and Tennis and an all-weather Hockey pitch.

Aims. The School offers a challenging and balanced education which will prepare its pupils for adult responsibility in the modern world. It aims to combine high academic achievement with the all-round development of the individual through games and co-curricular activities, and a strong encouragement of the pursuit of excellence.

Admission. Entry for boys aged 10, 11, 12 or 13 is by competitive examination and interview. Admission is on the basis of performance in the School's entrance tests and on an assessment of a boy's potential to contribute to, and benefit from, the extra-curricular programme and the wider life of the School. The majority of boys enter at 10 or 11. Application forms may be obtained from the School Office.

Fees. The fees for the academic year 2001–2002 are £6,699 and cover tuition, books, stationery, and games. A substantial number of Bursaries is awarded each year according to need.

Scholarships. For entry at the age of 10 or 11, approximately 40 awards carrying partial remission of fees are offered to candidates of outstanding merit in the Selection Tests. For boys entering at the age of 13, awards may be offered to candidates who do outstandingly well in a special Scholarship Examination. Entrance to this examination is limited to boys who have previously been firmly registered to come to Whitgift as the parents' first choice of school. At all ages, boys may be considered for all-rounder awards or for scholarships in particular subject areas as well as for academic scholarships. For music awards and Scholarships, see "Music" below.

Curriculum. In the first three year groups a general preparation is given. With a few exceptions, boys take all of their GCSE examinations in the Upper Vth Form. There is no early specialisation but various options are available, with a particularly wide range of languages, including Japanese, available. There are bilingual sections in French and German.

In the VIth Form, 'A' and 'AS' level subjects can be taken in a wide range of combinations. Pupils are also prepared for the Oxford and Cambridge entrance procedures.

Organisation. The academic progress of boys in the First and Third forms is under the supervision of the Head of the Lower School and that of the Fifth and Sixth Forms under the supervision of the Head of the Upper School. Pastoral matters are dealt with by the respective Heads of Year and their assistants. Boys are allocated to eight Houses, which have Upper and Lower School sections, and Housemasters have general responsibility for supervising pupils' development in co-curricular activities. Boys in the Upper Fifth and Sixth forms have a personal tutor to whom they can turn for help and advice if required.

Religious Education. Every attempt is made to stress the relevance of religious thought to modern living. Although the School has a close link with the Anglican Church, teaching is given in an ecumenical spirit.

Physical Education. All boys, unless excused on medical grounds, take Physical Education, Swimming and organised games, ie Rugby, Hockey, Cricket and Athletics, and many options are available. Facilities are provided for Badminton, Basketball, Fencing, Fives, Soccer, Squash, Tennis and Shooting and a range of other sports.

Music. All 10 and 11 year old entrants learn a musical instrument for the first term free of charge and, thereafter, private tuition is available in school time. Boys perform in various choral and instrumental ensembles. Concerts are regularly held and opera and musicals are performed each year. Awards carrying free instrumental tuition are available to musically talented pupils, either on admission or subsequently. Music scholarships are also awarded.

Other activities. There are a Combined Cadet Force, with specialist Royal Navy, Army and RAF sections and a Duke of Edinburgh's Award group. There are a large number of play productions (more than ten a year) and boys are encouraged to join some of the many School societies. Field courses and foreign exchange visits are regularly arranged in the holidays, and there is a very large number of link schools in many parts of the world.

Careers Advice. There is a well-equipped Careers Room and a very full service of guidance is offered over choice of career and courses in higher education. The vast majority of pupils go on to universities and colleges after leaving school.

Charitable status. The Whitgift Foundation is a Registered Charity, number 312612. It exists to provide education for boys.

William Hulme's Grammar School

Spring Bridge Road Manchester M16 8PR.
Tel: 0161-226 2054 2058 2087
Fax: 0161-226 8922
e-mail: enquiries@whgs.co.uk
website: www.whgs.co.uk

The School was founded by the Hulme Trust and opened in January, 1887.

Motto: *Fide sed cui vide.*

Governing Body:
Chairman: J D Marsden

Vice-Chairman: Canon M Arundel, MA

Dr M N Bhattacharyya, FRCOG
D D Boddington, BSc, ARICS
D A Boothman, FCA
D W Homer, JP
C F Jeanes, OBE, MA
J M Shorrock, QC
A D Sturrock, LLB
Mrs M J Taylor, OBE, BA, DipEd
E Thorp
P F Veitch, FCA
Professor T W Warnes, MD, FRCP

Governors Emeriti:
E B Jackson, FCA
C B Muir, OBE

Clerk to the Governors: J M Shelmerdine

***Headmaster:* S R Patriarca,** BA

Deputy Headmistress: Mrs G M Brown, BSc (*Mathematics*)

Deputy Headmaster: M P Jones, BA (*Politics & History*)

Senior Master: A Simkin, MA (*Director of Studies, Chemistry*)

Senior Tutor: Mrs T Pollard, BEd (*Physical Education*)

Assistant Staff:

Mathematics:
*M R Booker, BSc, AFIMA
†M D Wood, BSc (*House Master, Dalton*)
†L Sharp, BSc (*House Master, Heywood*)
Miss J F Smith, BSc (*House Mistress, Gaskell, Deputy Head of Sixth Form*)
G Addison, BSc
Miss H P Kelly, BSc
Mrs B M Beardwood, BSc

English:
*T P Heavisides, BA, MA
A E Watson, BA, MA (*i/c General Studies*)
Mrs J F Swindlehurst, BA
M C Gorman, BA
J R Wise, BA (*Drama*)
Miss J A Milligan, BA (*Junior Drama*)

History:
*P J Callaghan, MA
Miss S R Tandon, BA (*i/c PSHE*)
Miss C A Volante, BA

Geography:
*J H Hardy, BSc (*Warden, Outdoor Pursuits Centre*)
H N Veevers, BSc (*Head of Sixth Form, Head of Geology*)
G H Jones, BA (*Head of Middle School*)
Miss A J Raw, BSc (*Careers Adviser*)
Miss H Edwards, BA

Economics:
P R Hewston, BA (*i/c Economics*)
P R Amuzu, BA

Classics:
*M H Gracey, MA, MLitt
C MacLachlan, MA, BLitt (*Co-ordinator of IT and Examinations Officer*)
Mrs J A Worthington, BA (*i/c Oxford & Cambridge Applications*)

Physical Education:
*C H Seddon, BEd
Miss J Barlow, BEd
G J Muckalt, BA

Modern Languages:
*J G Hofton, BA
†D M Fisher, BA, OC, CCF (*House Master, Fraser*)
P M Bull, BA (*Head of Spanish*)
A C Crane, BA (*Deputy Head of Lower School*)
Miss C S Lambert, BA, MPhil, PhD (*i/c German*)
Srta S Reyero-Cascallana, BA
Ms K J Marsh, BA

Religious Education:
B S Swales, BA
Miss F T Doyle, BA

Music:
*P W Goodwin, ARMCM, ARNCM
Miss E N Nuttall, BA

Art and Design:
*N P Dunn, BEd (*House Master, Byrom*)
G L Bennett, BA
D M Cailey, BA
G N Grant, DLC

Physics:
*M I Barker, BSc, PhD
J H Thomson, BSc
D M Martin, MA, DPhil, PhD
Mrs J E Picken, BA, MA

Chemistry:
*A Greenall, GRIC, FCS
Mrs S M Watson, BSc

Biology:
*R S Moore, BSc
†D A Myers, BSc, MSc, MIBiol (*House Master, Whitworth*)
Miss E L Matthews, BSc (*Assistant Warden of Outdoor Pursuits Centre*)

Preparatory Department:

Mrs C G Wilson, BA (*Head of Department*)
Miss E P Cole, BSc (*Deputy Head of Department*)
Mrs A McKay, BEd
Mrs P Ferguson, CertEd
Miss T Alexander, BA
Mrs M P Cross, BA
Mrs J Howles, NNEB, ADCE
M T R Jones, BSc
Mrs M Lomas, CertEd
Mrs L McConnell, DOSEd, CertEd
Mrs J Robertson, BA
Mrs C Iddin, MIDTA, ISTD, RAD
Mrs T Chidley, CertEd

Librarian: Mrs M Evans, BA, ALA

Bursar: Wing Commander P D G Milloy, MEng, BSc

Medical Officer: A Wilson, MB, ChB

Organisation. In the Main School there are 577 pupils of which 411 are boys and 166 are girls. There are no boarders. The Preparatory Department caters for pupils from 3 to 11 years of age and boasts excellent purpose-built facilities in the Main School building. A Nursery Department, which caters for children aged 6 months to 3 years, opened in April 2000. There is a broad curriculum for all pupils on entry in Year 7, with an increasing number of options available leading to 9 GCSEs being taken at the end of Year 11. In the Sixth Form the opportunity is given for specialisation in Art, Biology, Government and Politics, Chemistry, Classics, Combined English Literature and Language, Design Technology, Economics and Business Studies, English Literature, French, Further Mathematics, Geography, Geology, German, History, ICT, Mathematics, Music, Physics, Religious Studies, Spanish and Theatre Studies.

The school occupies a spacious campus in South Manchester with good sports fields, a swimming pool and sports hall. A modern languages centre was opened by HRH The Princess Royal in June 1993 and there are also modern ICT facilities. The sixth form have a purpose-built centre and there is a large school library.

Entrance. Entry to the Preparatory Department is dependent upon satisfactory performance in Entrance Tests and an interview with the Head of the Preparatory Department. Boys and girls are admitted to the Main School between the ages of 10 and 12 on the results of an examination held at the School in January. At 11+ there is a Governors' Bursary Scheme depending on income, and at 16+ the Governors award a limited number of Sixth Form Scholarships. All pupils must be of an acceptable academic standard.

Independent Status. The School resumed its former Independent Status in 1976 when the Direct Grant was withdrawn.

Out-of-School Activities. The main School games, Cricket, Rugby Union, Football, Hockey and Netball, are played, unless pupils are medically exempt. Tennis, Athletics, Swimming, Badminton and Squash are additional activities. There is a Combined Cadet Force, membership of which is voluntary. Music, both Orchestral and Choral, and Drama have a firm and traditional place in the School. There are also a number of other societies for varied interests.

Music Scholarships. Several Music Scholarships are awarded annually.

Field Study Centre. The School owns a property in Wensleydale which is used at week-ends throughout most of the School Year as a base for Expeditions, Academic and Cultural Studies and Field Courses.

Fees per annum. From September 2001 fees range from £3,156 (Reception class) to £5,475 (Grammar School), exclusive of lunches. No extras are charged.

Old Hulmeians' Association. *Secretary:* Mr A P Marsden, 93 Hulme Hall Road, Cheadle Hulme, Cheshire SK8 6LF.

Charitable status. William Hulme's Grammar School Foundation is a Registered Charity, number 510668. The object of the charity is the provision and conduct in or near Manchester of a day school for boys and girls.

Winchester College

College Street Winchester Hampshire SO23 9NA.
Tel: 01962 621100 (Headmaster and Admissions)
01962 621200 (Bursar)
Fax: 01962 621106

Winchester College – 'the College of the Blessed Virgin Mary of Winchester near Winchester' – was founded in 1382 by William of Wykeham, Bishop of Winchester. Wykeham planned and created a double foundation consisting of 2 Colleges, 1 at Winchester and the other (New College) at Oxford. The 2 Colleges are still closely associated.

Motto: Manners Makyth Man.

Visitor: The Lord Bishop of Winchester

Warden: The Rt Hon Viscount Younger of Leckie, KT, KCVO, TD, DL

Sub-Warden: The Rt Hon The Earl Ferrers, MA, DL

Fellows:
M H Keen, MA, DPhil, FRHistS, FSA
Sir David Calcutt, QC, MA, LLD, MusB, FRCM
Miss C M Kay, MA
The Rt Hon Sir Martin Nourse, MA
R T Fox, CBE, MA, FCIB
A J Ryan, MA, DLitt, FBA
A C V Evans, MA, MPhil, FIL
D A Quayle
Sir Andrew Large
D R Helm, DPhil
Professor D C Hanna, PhD, FRS

Secretary and Bursar: W G F Organ, OBE, CDipAF, FIMgt

***Headmaster:* E N Tate**, CBE, MA, PhD

Second Master: R J Wyke, MA

Senior Master: P M Keyte, MA

Registrar: D J Baldwin, BA

Assistant Masters:
M D Fontes, BA
R D H Custance, MA, DPhil
A J P Ayres, MA
R A Conn, BA
R F Bottone, MA, BMus, FRCO
P J Krakenberger, MA
M R S Nevin, BA
J R Havil, BSc, MSc, PhD
Rev J D Smith, MA, DPhil
G Robinson, BSc
N Fennell, MA
P V A Williams, MA, PhD
G Eyre, MA
J D Falconer, MA, ARCM
T P J Cawse, BSc
C J Tolley, MA, DPhil, FRCO
S P Anderson, MA
S J Bailey, BEd, PhD
A Morgan, DipAD
R S Shorter, ARCS, PhD, MInstP, CPhys
A C Sinclair, BA
L Mackinnon, MA, MLitt
B J A Tanter, MA
A P Wolters, BSc, PhD, MRSC, CChem
Rev J M Kerr, MSc
L C Wolff, MA, FRSA
T R V David, MA, MSc
C H J Hill, MA
G J Penney, BSc
K M Pusey, MusB, GRSM, ARMCM
G A Brook, BSc, MEd
P A Nash, BA, ARCM
M D Wallis, MA
P J Metcalfe, MSc (*Econ*)
A S Leigh, MA
Mrs B L H MacKinnon, BA, PhD
N I P MacKinnon, BA
Mrs C A Cooper, BA
P J M Roberts, MA
C F Upton, BSc
W E Billington, MA MICE
P G Cornish, BA, MMus, FTCL, ARCM
Rev R G A Ferguson, LLB
J M Cooper, BSc, PhD
D J Ceiriog-Hughes, MA, PhD
W G Day, MA, PhD
Miss C J Ovenden, MA
A P McMaster, BSc
T J Parkinson, BA
P S A Taylor, BA
I E Fraser, BSc
L N Taylor, BA
Rev N C A von Malaisé, MA
S K Woolley, BA
N R Chippington, BA
M D Hebron, BA, DPhil
J G Webster, BA, DPhil
P H Williams, BA
A R Johnson, BA
P J M Cramer, MA, PhD
C Cai, BA, MA, PhD
R J Clarkson, BSc, PhD
C J Good, BEd
J E Hodgins, BSc, PhD
G J Watson, BA
M G Armstrong, MA
Miss N C Christian, BA, PhD
J P Cullerne, BSc, DPhil
Miss P S Hill, BA, MFLE
C S McCaw, BSc, DPhil
T N M Lawson, BA
A D Adlam, BMus (Han)
Miss J F Avery, MSc
D A Smith, BA, PhD
J S Price, BA
A P Dakin, BA
Miss H R Fox, MA
M Romans, BA
Y W Ooi, BA, MB.BS
J McManus, MSc
Miss A L Keep, BA, MSc

Headmaster's Secretary: Mrs S E Rae

The School is divided into 3 blocks: IVth Book (Junior, Middle, and Senior Part) where a general curriculum including a full range of academic subjects as well as certain arts, crafts and skills is followed to GCSE; Vth Book, which is a transitional stage; and VIth Book where full A Level courses are done. The higher forms are arranged in 3 groups: Classical (A ladder), Modern (B ladder), and Science (C ladder). On all ladders it is possible to study a variety of combinations of subjects, including some combinations of arts and science subjects.

Physical Education, Art, Technology and Music are

additionally taught on an extra-curricular basis, as well as in the timetable, and there are opportunities to pursue them all throughout a boy's school life.

Scholarships, (*see* Entrance Scholarship section) **etc.** The election of scholars and exhibitioners takes place in May each year. Full particulars of the examination are obtainable from the Headmaster.

About 14 scholarships and 6 exhibitions are awarded each year. There are 70 scholars, who live together in College; the annual fee payable for a scholar is half the full boarding fee, but this may be wholly or partly remitted on grounds of need. Exhibitions are tenable in Houses; the maximum value of an exhibition is one third of the full fee, either boarding or day. Two Malory Exhibitions are offered each year to 13 year olds from State schools. Details from the Headmaster.

Music Awards. Information about Music Awards will be found in the appropriate section of this book.

Sixth Form entry. Up to four awards are offered each year to boys joining the Sixth Form from other schools. Examinations and interviews for both awards and places take place in Winchester in late January each year. Enquiries should be sent to the Registrar.

Commoners. The 2000/2001 fee for boarding Commoners is £17,319 pa, £16,455 for day boys, and there is an entrance fee of £300. There are about 60 Commoners in each House, and the present Housemasters are:

Chernocke House (A):	R S Shorter
Moberly's (B):	P J M Cramer
Du Boulay's (C):	P J Metcalfe
Fearon's (D):	D J Ceiriog-Hughes
Morshead's (E):	S J Bailey
Hawkins' (F):	N I P MacKinnon
Sergeant's (G):	J M Cooper
Bramston's (H):	P A Nash
Turner's (I):	N R Chippington
Kingsgate House (K):	W E Billington

A boy's name cannot be entered before he reaches the age of 8; application should be made direct to a Housemaster or to the Registrar as soon as conveniently possible after the boy's eighth birthday. Housemasters do not normally allot firm vacancies until boys are 10½/11 and it is wise to make alternative arrangements until a promise of a vacancy has been given. The Headmaster has from time to time a Nomination for a House at his disposal, and the Registrar keeps a Reserve List; parents wishing to enter the name of a boy aged 10½ or more should write to him. Candidates for Nomination are usually expected to take the scholarship examination in the summer term.

A few day boy Commoners are also admitted; details can be obtained from the Headmaster.

The usual age of entry to the school is between 13 and 14, but exceptions may be considered in special circumstances.

The entrance examination covers the normal subjects; particulars and copies of recent papers may be obtained from the Headmaster.

Term of entry. Normally September.

Old Boys' Society, Wykehamist Society. *Secretary:* P S W K Maclure, 17 College Street, Winchester SO23 9LX.

Charitable status. The Warden and Scholars of Winchester College is a Charity. It is exempt from registration, being named as an exempt charity in Schedule 2 of the Charities Act 1960, and therefore has no registration number. The objects of the charity are the advancement of education and activities connected therewith.

* Head of Department § Part Time or Visiting
† Housemaster/Housemistress ¶ Old Pupil
‡ See below list of staff for meaning

Wisbech Grammar School
(Co-educational Day School)

North Brink Wisbech PE13 1JX
Tel: Senior Dept: (01945) 583631.
Junior/Infant Dept: (01945) 475101
Fax: Senior Dept: (01945) 476746
Junior/Infant Dept: (01945) 475101
website: www.wgs.cambs.sch.uk

Senior Department (Years 7 to 13).

The School was founded in 1379 above the South Porch of the Church of St Peter and St Paul, Wisbech. Co-education is well established and this is reflected in the equal numbers of boys and girls who make up the School population. There are now 600 boys and girls in the Senior School, aged from 11 to 18, including more than 160 in VI Form. The Junior & Infant Department has 160+ boys and girls aged from Reception to age 11.

The School was substantially rebuilt in 1991 when 19 new classrooms wereadded, together with specialist rooms for computers and electronics, an assembly hall and a sports hall. More recently the design technology facilities have been extended and upgraded, a sports pavilion added and a business centre completed (September 2000). The ongoing development programme will see rebuilding of the old pavilion and a performing arts centre (including a music school) should be completed for September 2003. Substantial investment has been made in the latest network computers and a recent major award from the Wolfson Foundation has added further to the School's resources in this area.

Governing Body:

Chairman: J A Hazel, FRICS, FNAEA
Vice-Chairman: A D Salmon, FCA

Dr D Barter, MB, BS, FRCP, DCh
P Dennis, AMICE
Mrs J Easter, FCCA
H A Godfrey
F A N Grounds, MA (Cantab), ARICS, MRAC
C H Hutchinson, BSc
Dr C F Kolbert, MA, PhD (Cantab), DPhil (Oxon), FCIArb
Mrs M Sackrée, BA
Dr F Sconce, MB, ChB
J E Warren

Nominated by the Master of Magdalene College, Cambridge:
R L Skelton, MA, CEng, FIChemE, MIMechE, FINucE

Bursar and Clerk to the Governors: Miss E P Thuburn

Teaching Staff:
***Headmaster:* R S Repper**, MA (Oxon), FIMgt

Deputy Headmaster: L J Haslett, BA (Hons), DPhil

Deputy Headmistress: Miss C M Noxon, BA

Senior Master: *D G Bradley, BA

Head of Sixth Form: *A W Ayres, BA (Oxon)

Director of Studies: *R C Baum, MA (Cantab), MInstP, CPhy

Assistant Staff:
*P B Bannister, ACP, CertEd
Miss M P Barrington, CertEd
*R J Baty, BA
§Mrs R Baum, MA (Cantab)
Mrs F Bliss, BTec
Mrs Z R Booth, BSc
§J E Breeze
†M C Burns, BSc, MPhil

§Mrs M Calton, BSc
T D Chapman, MA (Cantab)
A P Clarke, MA, MEd
T W Claydon, BSc
Miss A M Clayton, BA
*A E Clemit, MA
Mrs C R D Clemit, MA
*Mrs S D Cooper, BA
*K S Doman, MA (Cantab)
M L Forrest, MA (Cantab)
Mrs S L Freakley, BA
D S Garfoot, BA
†S J Gough, BA
R W Greenwood, BA (Oxon)
Mrs D A Gridley, BSc
*Miss S E Harris, BEd
*¶Mrs M Hartigan, MIHEc
*G E Howes, BSc
¶§Mrs J Jarvis
N Kay, BA
*Miss R Keep, BA
P J King, MA (Oxon)
§Mrs J E Littlechild, BEd
*K J Mann, BA, PhD
R W Morgan, BSc
*A D Norburn, BMus, LTCL, ALCM
*Mrs S O'Brien, DipEd
D L Penny, BSc
Mrs J Perkins, BSc
R K Powis, BSc
Mrs S A Ramsay, MA
Mrs J T Reavell, BA
†Mrs E R Snow, MIL
*M P Stump, BA
*M J Wager, BA
Mrs B A Waling, GTCL, LTCL, ATCL
*P J A Webb, BA
B P Wiles, BSc
K L Wood-Smith, BSc

Headmaster's Secretary: Mrs J R Calton

Admissions Secretary: Mrs J Handley

Junior & Infant Department (*Reception to Year 6*)

Head: Mrs C Cranwell, CertEd

§Mrs S Borrmann, BEd
Mrs R Brown, CertEd
G Chilton, BA
Mrs A Dennis, CertEd
Mrs A Fuller, CertEd, NFFTC
Mrs T R Linford, BEd
Mrs C C R Mayer, MA
Mrs J McAdam, BA
Mrs G D Reinbold, MA (Cantab)
Mrs G Stapleton
Mrs J Stonham, CertEd

Learning Support assistants:
Mrs R Bingham
Miss S Croot
Miss L A Daw
Miss J Gibbs
Mrs L Gray
Miss A Poll
Miss S M Whitwell

Secretary: Mrs J Stiles

SENIOR SCHOOL.

Situation. The School occupies a position in the centre of Wisbech on a 26 acre site which therefore provides generous playing field accommodation.

Whilst strong links have been maintained with Wisbech and District other boys and girls travel from as far away as Hunstanton, King's Lynn, Whittlesey, Ely, Long Sutton and Peterborough. There are school buses from a number of these destinations and villages en route. For the large number of pupils who continue with activities after school there are late buses to most destinations.

Entry. The main intake is at 11+ by competitive examination. Places can also become available at other stages. Sixth Form entry is on the basis of GCSE results and interview.

There are a number of Governors' Assisted Places and School Bursaries at 11+, 12+, 13+ and for entry into the Sixth Form. Boys and girls are prepared for the GCSE, A-level and entry to Universities.

Academic Organisation. There is a sound academic curriculum. All pupils receive a thorough grounding in mathematics, English, French, German, science, information technology, history, geography, music, technology (resistant materials, computer aided design, textiles and home economics), art and religious studies. For GCSE boys and girls study English, mathematics, and then choose six more subjects from a list of fifteen. This selection must include at least one science, although many take the three separate sciences, one language and one humanities subject. There are 21 different subjects available at A-level.

Physical Education and Games. The main games for boys are rugby and hockey in the Christmas and Easter terms respectively, together with cricket and athletics in the Summer. Girls play hockey and some netball in the first two terms, tennis and athletics in the Summer. For boys and girls above Year 9, who are not involved in a major team game, there is a large range of options including basketball, volleyball, squash, multigym, swimming and badminton. The School enjoys regular use of a covered swimming pool and an Astroturf pitch, both of which are adjacent to its own facilities.

There are many opportunities for pupils to represent the School at sport via the extensive fixture programme with other schools in Cambridgeshire, Norfolk and Lincolnshire.

Activities. All pupils are encouraged to take part in one, or more, of the many activities, clubs or societies which form an essential part of the School's programme. As well as the usual games practices and music and drama rehearsals there are information technology, electronics, photography, Christian Union, public speaking, Duke of Edinburgh Award, Young Enterprise, debating, skiing (dry slope), chess, scrabble and the School Magazines. The art and the technology facilities and maths help club are also available throughout the lunchtimes.

Information Technology. The School has three dedicated computer rooms with network computers running industry standard products such as *Microsoft Office* and *Adobe Photoshop.* In addition there is a suite of personal computers connected to the same network, for careers and sixth form use, and a number of other computers around the school which connect virtually every academic department to the network. Staff and pupils are therefore able to use a vast range of programs and information from almost any point in the school. There are 80 computers for use by pupils and these facilities are available during the whole of each day until 5.30 pm.

The introductory programme, which all pupils follow in their first three years at the school, enables them to experience some typical commercial applications such as mail merge, stock control and invoicing. Students may choose information technology at GCSE or A level. Alternatively sixth formers may usefully follow the RSA Integrated Business Technology course to levels two and three, a much sought after qualification in the commercial world, together with their A level subjects.

Technology. All pupils receive a broad introduction in their first year. A whole afternoon (2 hours) per week is set aside and the year is divided into four 8 week blocks of work in resistant materials, computer aided design ,home economics and textiles. These courses continue throughout the School and each subject is available at GCSE and A Level. There has been considerable investment in equipment in the recently extended technology block. This has allowed further development of the work in electronics. Due to a generous donation from the Stationers' Company, the School is also able to offer further advanced work in textiles using the newly installed automatic photo-silkscreen printing equipment.

Music and Drama. Lessons on a wide range of instruments are available to all boys and girls. There are various group musical activities including a school orchestra, woodwind ensembles, chamber choir, and junior and senior choruses. Each year two major stage performances are given, one of which is a musical. Recent productions include The Sound of Music, Antigone, Oh

What a Lovely War, The Boyfriend, Grease and Fame.

Trips Abroad. These are popular; in recent years parties of pupils and staff have visited Austria (skiing), USA, the Black Forest, Sweden, Denmark, the USSR, China and Iceland. There are strong exchange links with Willibrord Gymnasium, Emmerich in Northern Germany and Institution Ste Ursule in France, with many pupils participating each year. Year 8 boys and girls visit a chateau in Normandy each year and lower sixth students studying French may undertake work experience placements, during their Easter break, in Brittany.

Old Wisbechians Society. This is a thriving organisation which has several hundred members. Further information about the Society can be obtained from the Admissions' Secretary at the School, to whom requests for the School magazine, Riverline, should be sent. The interests of the Society are furthered by The Old Wisbechians Cricket Club.

Honours. 12 students obtained places at Oxford and Cambridge in the last three years.

JUNIOR & INFANT DEPARTMENT (Reception to Year 6). The refounding of this section of the School, after a break of more than 50 years, took place on 3 September 1997, and has grown from 83 to 160+ pupils with boys and girls from Reception to Year 6.

Great emphasis is placed on the acquisition of the basic skills in reading, writing and number. A high standard of work is expected from the children in all areas of the curriculum which includes Mathematics, English, Science, RE, Art, Music, Drama, Geography, History, IT, French, PE, Swimming and Games.

The Junior School pupils benefit from being part of an established senior school and so have access to many of the excellent facilities that already exist there. The computer suite, a science laboratory, sports hall and theatre are availabe to the Junior Department. Specialist teaching is offered in Music, Design Technology, PE and Games, Information Technology and Drama. Many girls and boys are involved in peripatetic music lessons. Opportunities for performance in Drama and Music are regular features of the school year.

There are many sporting opportunities with a full timetable of fixtures each term, when pupils are involved in games against other schools. The main sports played are netball, hockey, rugby, tennis and athletics.

There is a very varied after school programme giving children the opportunity to develop sports and leisure skills, artistic and musical talents. A supervised homework club is also available each day.

School field trips, activity days at the local museum and visits by theatre groups and speakers from outside all form an important part of the curriculum.

Entry. Generally children can be admitted to the Reception class in September, at the beginning of the school year in which they reach the age of five. All children registering are invited to spend part of a day with the School during which time they are assessed in a manner appropriate to their age.

All enquiries for the Junior & Infant Department should be addressed to the Secretary, Wisbech Grammar School Junior & Infant Department, North Brink, Wisbech, Cambs PE13 1JX. Tel/Fax: 01945 475101.

Charitable status. The Wisbech Grammar School Foundation is a Registered Charity, number 311433. It exists to promote the education of boys and girls.

Wolverhampton Grammar School

Compton Road Wolverhampton WV3 9RB.
Tel: 01902 421326
Fax: 01902 421819
e-mail: wgs@wgs.org.uk
website: www.wgs.org.uk

Wolverhampton Grammar School was founded in 1512 by Sir Stephen Jenyns - a Wolverhampton man who achieved success as a wool merchant, became a member of The Merchant Taylors' Company then Lord Mayor of London. He decided to benefit his home town by founding a school "for the instruction of youth in good manners and learning". The school retains close links with the Company.

Wolverhampton Grammar School is now an independent, selective day school for girls and boys aged 11-18 which places scholarship at the heart of a challenging all-round education. Students come from a wide catchment area throughout the West Midlands, Staffordshire and Shropshire.

Governing Body:

Chairman: His Honour Malcolm Ward, MA, LLM (OW)

Vice-Chairman: Mrs P Earle, OBE, JP

The Mayor of Wolverhampton (*ex officio*)
D Berriman, FSVA (OW)
Professor J S Brooks, BSc, PhD, DSc, CEng, CPhys, FInstP
Professor L N Brown, OBE, MA, LLM, Dr en Dr (OW)
A C Flockhart, BSc, CA
Professor W R Garside, BA, PhD
B Gilmore, CB, MA (OW)
Mrs D M Griffiths, JP
D J Hughes, MA
Miss J Iles, BA (OW)
Dr C H Nourse, MA, FRCP
Dr J Orledge, MBBS
E A Sergeant, BSc, CEng, MIMechE (OW)
Dr S Walford, MA, MD, FRCP
P E J White, FInstMgt (OW)
T J G Whitmarsh, PhD
Mrs C Wood, JP
Mrs J C Wrigley, JP

***Head:* B St J Trafford**, MA, MEd, PhD, FRSA

Deputy Head: A J Pattison, MA, PhD, FRSA

Assistant Staff:

Mrs C A Ambrose, BSc
N J C Anderson, BSc
D R Barlow, BA, STB, MDiv
B M Benfield, BA
A J Bennett, BSc
N J Bradley, BSc, PhD
R J Brandon, MA
Mrs S F Brentnall, BA
Mrs E P Brown, BA
T J Browning, BSc
J-P Camm, BSc, PhD
A P Carey, BSc
R B Charlesworth, BA
Mrs V E Chilvers, BSc
D N Craig, MA
Ms M B Craig, BA
N H Crust, BA
J D Edlin, BSc, PhD
F A Foreman, BSc, CChem, MRSC
Miss C E Gooch, BMus
Mrs P D Grigat, Erstes und Zweites Staatsexamen
Mrs H Hills, BSc
P A Hills, BA
S Hinchcliffe, BA, PhD
B C Hoffmann, BA
J Holroyd, MA, MLitt
S Hope
Mrs C A Howlett, BSc, MEd
J M Johnson, BSc
Miss R E Johnson, BA
P Johnstone, BA
D Jones, MA, DMS
L J Judson, BSc
Miss H Kostyrka, BA
J O Linton, MA
Mrs F L Lister, BSc, MSc
Ms S P B MacDowall, MA, DMS
C D McKie, MA
Miss R Maisey, BA

C W Martin, MA, PhD
P A Merricks-Murgatroyd, BA
Mrs R F Millard, BSocSci
Mrs K Muir, BA
N P Munson, BSc
C O'Brien, BSc, PhD
T D Page, BA
R A Pawluk, GRAM, LRAM, LTCL, ALCM
Miss L C Pearson, BA
J W Perkins, BA
J G Phillips, BSc
Mrs C A Preston, BSc
A A Proverbs, BA
V P Raymond-Barker, BA
S Roberts, MA, PhD
A N Smith, BSc
Mrs P Stokes-Smith, BEd
K Stott, BSc
Ms R E Sutcliffe, BA
Mrs A-M Tarr, Mâtrise
R J Tarr, BA
I Tennant, MA
Mrs O Trafford, ATD
I H M Tyler, BA
K Uppal, BA
Mrs D M Ward, MA
The Revd P R Whale, MA, BSc, BD, PhD

Bursar: Mrs M Wilmot

Headmaster's Secretary: Mrs J E Boss

Buildings. The school's original impressive Victorian buildings have been improved and augmented over the years in an on-going programme to provide up-to-the minute facilities for students. The school has a purpose-built music suite; a magnificent Sixth Form Centre was completed in 1995; a Sports Centre and flood-lit astroturf pitch provide some of the best facilities in the area while the early 20th century Merridale and Caldicott Buildings house laboratories that have been refurbished to the highest modern standards. The ICT suite was updated in Summer 2000. Language laboratories have video facilities, satellite TV, and PCs. The recently renovated Jenyns Library for First to Fifth Formers - with multi-media room, networked computers with internet access and CD-ROMS, videos and magazines - is adjacent to the new Sixth Form centre and library. Total book stock is 25,000 volumes.

Admission. Boys and girls usually enter the school in September. The school's own entrance tests are held in the preceding January following registration at the end of December. The principal age of entry is at 11 with small entries at 12 and 13. A significant number of boys and girls join the school in the Sixth Form: offers of places are made subject to GCSE results and interview. Transfers at other ages can be made by arrangement, subject to availability of places.

Fees. In 2000/01, £2,140 per term.

Entrance Scholarships. (*see* Entrance Scholarship section) Following the January entrance tests, up to six Governors' Academic Scholarships (two half-fees, four quarter-fees) are awarded to the highest-placed candidates at 11+ and one Scholarship (one-third fees) is offered at 13+. Two Scholarships are available to students wishing to enter the Sixth Form by transfer (one-quarter fees plus further means-tested assistance) based on interviews and a reference from the applicant's existing school. There are two music scholarships of ¼ remission of fees at 11 and 16 plus free music tuition within the school on the instrument of the student's choice.

Assistance with Fees. As the Government Assisted Places Scheme, in which Wolverhampton Grammar School was heavily involved, is phased out, the Governors now offer means-tested Aided Places to children who can demonstrate academically and personally that they will benefit from the opportunity of a WGS education. The school is also pleased to offer two Ogden Trust Bursaries for State School applicants, giving up to 100% of fees, travel, uniform and extra-curricular activity allowances. References are also sought from the child's current school and teachers/coaches where relevant.

Curriculum. In the first three years students study a broad curriculum of English, Maths, three Sciences, History, Geography, Art, Information Communication Technology, Design Technology, Theology & Philosophy, PE & Games and Music, in addition to French, German and Latin. In the fourth form students pursue a core of English Language and Literature, three separate Sciences, Mathematics and at least one Modern Language. There is a wide range of additional optional subjects, and most students take ten GCSEs. 90% of students proceed to the Sixth Form to take three or four subjects at AS/A2 and some 98% continue in Higher Education, including a number of students who go to Oxford or Cambridge.

Games and Outdoor Activities. A 'sport for all' attitude exists in games and PE, where the staff endeavour to match the student to a sport or activity in which they can succeed. There is a commitment to the highest standards of skill and sportsmanship but the emphasis is also placed on enjoyment. The 4th Wolverhampton (Grammar School) Scout Troop is open to all students and celebrated its 70th birthday in 2000 and the school participates in the Duke of Edinburgh's Award Scheme at Bronze Level. Students find that there are opportunities to undertake field trips, foreign exchanges and expeditions throughout their schooldays.

Special Needs (Dyslexia). THE WGS OPAL (OPportunities through Assisted Learning) PROGRAMME which started in September 1998 is designed to allow bright children with Specific Learning Difficulties (Dyslexia) to enjoy the challenge of a first-rate academic education. Thanks to the generosity of Mr and Mrs Guy Hands, an OPAL Scholarship will be offered to a 2001 entrant to the programme.

Arts and Other Activities. The Music Department runs several choirs, bands and orchestras which practise and perform regularly to popular acclaim. Theatre is an integral part of the vibrant arts policy at the school which mounts three full-scale drama productions yearly involving students of all ages as actors, technicians, stage managers, set and costume makers and directors. The Art Department exhibits regularly and currently has an artist-in-residence. There is a wide variety of extra-curricular clubs and activities giving students the opportunity to discover and cultivate new interests, both inside and outside the classroom. A Community Service programme and an active student Charity Fund-raising Committee ensure that all students are involved in working for the good of others.

Pastoral Care. The school is proud of the pastoral care and support it offers to its students. In the Lower and Middle Schools care is provided by a form tutor under the overall responsibility of the appropriate Heads of Schools. Regular consultations are held with parents supported by full and frequent reports. An important forum is the Student Council which consists of elected representatives from all year groups who are encouraged to voice concerns and suggest improvements to the running and organisation of the school. The weekly meetings, with the Head plus one other member of staff in attendance, are run by an elected Chair and Secretary.

Charitable status. Wolverhampton Grammar School is a Registered Charity, number 529006. It is an independent selective co-educational secondary day school. Its philosophy places scholarship at the heart of a challenging education which promotes achievement through active involvement. It seeks to develop self-awareness and a sense of responsibility, values both individuality and altruism, and fosters the spirit of community traditional to the school.

* Head of Department	§ Part Time or Visiting
† Housemaster/Housemistress	¶ Old Pupil
‡ See below list of staff for meaning	

Woodbridge School

Woodbridge Suffolk IP12 4JH.
Tel: (01394) 385547
Fax: (01394) 380944
e-mail: @woodbridge.suffolk.sch.uk
Motto: *Pro Deo Rege Patria.*

Governing Body: The Trustees of The Seckford Foundation

Chairman: Air Vice-Marshal P J Goddard, CB, AFC, FRAeS, RAF (Retd)

***Headmaster:* S H Cole**, MA, CPhys, MInstP, PGCE

Deputy Head: M R Streat, MA, PGCE

Director of Studies: J R Mileham, BSc, CertEd

Senior Mistress: Mrs D E Piper, BA

Senior Master: C H Pluke, BSc, UED

Chaplain: The Revd M E Percival, BSc, MA

Assistant Staff:
M A Weaver, BA, DipEd
M A Mitchels, MA, CertEd
A D Maude, BSc, DipEd
J R Penny, MA, CertEd
Miss C A Pendal, BA, CertEd
I T Saunders, BTech
S J Ashworth, BSc, PGCE
A H Garfath-Cox, BA, MEd, MIITT, CertEd
G B Bruce, MA, CertEd
Mrs K Pluke, BA, CertEd
R F Broaderwick, MA, PhD
Mrs K M Shelley, CertEd
Miss S Theasby, BA, PGCE
C N Warden, BA, PGCE
M R Ringer, BEd, CertEd
S E Cottrell, BEd, CPhys, MInstP
R E Fernley, BA, PGCE
Mrs V Jones, BA, ATD
Mrs P Morgan, BA, PGCE
R A Rabjohn, BSc
A P Jackson, BSc, PGCE
Miss J A Gill, MA(Ed), BEd
Mrs E A M Davidson, DipMusEd, RSAMD
G P Sagar, MCCEd, CertEd
Miss S A Chuter, CertEd, BEd
Mrs J M Hudson, BA, ALA
Mrs C R Marlowe, MA
J A Hillman, BSc, PGCE
Miss H V Richardson, BA, PGCE
J H Stafford, ARCM
Mrs V R Porter, BEd
Mrs S Morbey, GLCM, ARCM
Mrs A P Willett, CertEd, AdDipEd(SEN)
R A Carr, BA, ATC
B T Edwards, BA
Miss S K Lee, BSc, PGCE
C P Seal, BA, PGCE
P A Trett, BSc, PGCE
Miss C V E Shepherd, BA, PGCE
N E Smith, BA, PGCE
Mrs C A Weaver, BA, CertEd
Mrs S Cartwright, BA
Miss A H Berry, BA
Mrs S J Booth, ARCM, ATCL
Miss L R King, BA, PGCE
Dr L V Rickard, BSc, PhD, PGCE
M Bosworth, BA, PGCE
J Dickin, BA
Miss M Dunn, BA, PGCE
Mrs W McNally, BSc, PGCE
Mrs E Mitchells, BA, PGCE
Dr J Wharam, BSc, PhD, PGCE
Mrs C Odedra
Mrs N Ingold, CertEd
Mrs M Wellings, BA, PGCE
J Percival, BA
Mrs E K Bambridge, BSc, PGCE
Mrs D Marshall, BA, PGCE
D Cook, BSc, PGCE
Mrs L A Bloxham, CertEd

THE ABBEY (*Woodbridge Junior School*)
Tel: (01394) 382673

Master: N J Garrett, BA, PGCE
Second Master: Mrs C M T Clubb, BEd
Director of Studies: Miss J A Golding, BEd

Assistant Staff:
A H A Clarke, ARCM, GRSM, PGCE
C J French, BA, PGCE
Mrs J King, BEd (*Head of Pre-Prep*)
Mrs A Mason, CertEd
M D Staziker, BEd
Mrs S M Whymark, CertEd
Mrs P Salmond, CertEd
Mrs A M McGlennon, BA
Mrs L Graham, BSc, PGCE
Mrs C A Youngs, CertEd
R D O Earl, BA, PGCE
Mrs L Routledge, DipEd
Mrs E Brooking, CertEd
D A Graham, BEd
Mrs S J E Woolstencroft, BA, PGCE
Mrs P Ibison, CertEd
Miss S K Olliff, BA
Mrs R Walker, BEd
R M Heazlewood, BEd
Miss F S K Pinching, MA
Mrs C R Hayhow, MSc, CBiol, MIBiol
Mrs M Burgess-Simpson, CertEd, DipSEN

Bursar: D S Haynes, MA, MSc
School Medical Officer: R P Verrill, MBBS, MRCEP, DRCOG, FPCert
Registrar: Mrs J Rodgers

Number in School. In the age range 11–18 there are 299 boys (of whom 22 are boarders) and 286 girls (of whom 16 are boarders). At 4–11 there are 157 boys and 125 girls.

History and Buildings. Woodbridge School was founded in 1662. The scholars were to be taught, "both Latin and Greek until that thereby they be made fit for the University (if it be desired), but in case of any of them be unapt to learn those languages . . . they should be taught only Arithmetic, and to Write, to be fitted for Trades or to go to Sea". They were also to be "instructed in the principles of the Christian Religion according to the Doctrine of the Church of England".

For 200 years the School existed in cramped quarters in the town until its incorporation with the Seckford Trust. Endowment income then enabled it to move to its present undulating site overlooking the town and the River Deben, and to begin the steady expansion and development which have accelerated over the last 25 years. A full modernisation programme has been carried out and new buildings include an Art and Technology Centre, a Sixth Form Centre, a large Sports Hall, Sailing Centre, a fine Music School and a Science Block. A new Library, Information Technology, Modern Languages, English and Mathematics building was completed in September 1994, and an All-Weather hockey pitch in September 1995. The Day House Rooms were redeveloped and refurbished in 1999; Queen's House officially opened its new 150 seater hall in January 2000; a new changing room complex, opened in 2001, preludes the next stage of development.

Woodbridge has had close links with the local community and through its outstanding Music and Science with Finland, France, Spain and The Netherlands. Since 1974 girls have been admitted throughout the School which is now fully co-educational, with equal numbers of boys and girls.

Organisation. The Senior School numbers 299 boys and 286 girls with 38 boarders and a Sixth Form of 170. *Boarders.* There is a coeducational Sixth Form Hall of Residence. *Day pupils.* A House system exists with a Junior House for 11 year old entrants and 4 other Houses for those from 12–16. All Sixth Form day pupils are based in the Sixth Form Centre.

Careers. The school is a member of the Independent Schools Careers Organisation, whose regional secretary visits regularly. Parents are encouraged to enter their children for the ISCO Aptitude tests in Year 11.

Games and Activities. Sailing, shooting and hockey are real strengths. In addition the main games are rugby and netball in the winter; cricket, tennis, athletics, swimming and rounders in the summer. The Sports Hall has facilities for badminton, basketball, volley ball, table tennis, trampoline, gymnastics, cricket, hockey and other indoor sports. There is a first class Combined Cadet Force with Army, RAF and Royal Navy Sections. There is a large variety of clubs and societies including the Duke of Edinburgh's

Award Scheme. All 11 and 12 year olds follow the Seckford Scheme.

Chapel and Religious Education. A section of the School attends Chapel most days and the Chaplain is responsible for RE throughout the School. On some weekday evenings and Sunday mornings every term a service is held, and a Confirmation Service is held annually.

Admission. The majority enter the Senior School at 11 through the School's own examination, interview and report. At age 13 entry is through the School's own or the Common Entrance examination. Entry to the Sixth Form is based on interview and GCSE results. Admission to The Abbey is at any stage from the age of four.

Scholarships. (*see* Entrance Scholarship section) These are awarded on the results of the annual entrance examinations at 11+ and 13+. At 16+ Scholarships are awarded on the basis of interview. There are several Music and one Art Scholarship each year.

The Abbey Prep School is centred in a beautiful house dating from the 16th century in the town, adjacent to which two large new buildings have been added. Taking pupils from 7–11, it has full use of the Senior School swimming pool, sports hall, tennis courts, etc.

Queen's House, the Pre-Prep Department for pupils aged 4–6, opened in 1993 in its own building on the Woodbridge School site.

Fees and Remission of Fees. Due to its generous endowment, the School is able to offer remission of part of the fees to pupils whose parents have incomes in the lower and middle ranges. These awards are termed "Marryott Bursaries".

Situation. Woodbridge is an attractive country town on the River Deben, opposite the site of the famous royal Saxon ship burial at Sutton Hoo. Timber-framed buildings dating from the Middle Ages and Georgian facades draw many visitors to the town throughout the year. Excellent sailing facilities are available on the River Deben. Woodbridge is seven miles from the Suffolk coast and close to the continental ports of Felixstowe and Harwich. The rail journey to London is less than an hour.

Charitable status. The Seckford Foundation is a Registered Charity, number 214209. Its aims are to give education for "poor children" by the provision of scholarships and fee remissions out of charity funds, and to maintain "the elderly poor" by providing a subsidy out of the charity for the Almshouses and Jubilee House.

Woodhouse Grove School

Apperley Bridge West Yorkshire BD10 0NR.
Tel: (0113) 250 2477
Fax: (0113) 250 5290

Woodhouse Grove is situated in spacious, well-kept grounds on the slopes of the Aire Valley and within easy reach of Bradford and Leeds. The moors are within view and the Dales National Park is not far away.

The School was founded in 1812 for the education of the sons of Wesleyan ministers but now welcomes members of all denominations, both as pupils and as staff. It is fully co-educational, taking pupils from the age of 3–18.

Motto: *Bone et fidelis.*

Visitor: The President of the Methodist Conference

Administrative Governors of the School:

G B Greenwood, JP (*Chairman*)

J S Brodwell, LLB
Mrs E E Cleland
K Davy, OBE, JP
R Davy, JP
Revd D Deeks, MA
Miss E Evans, BSc, FRSA
Mrs M A M Greaves, MA, JP
Dr G H Haslam
A S P Kassapian
Revd A G Loosemore, MA, BD
Mrs E A McCarthy
Dr J M Moore
W A Nunn
S C Rawson, FCA
P Robertshaw
Q L A Robinson, MB, ChB, FRCAnaes
G Russell, BA
Brigadier D W Shuttleworth, OBE
Revd P Whittaker, BA

Secretary, Methodist Residential Schools: G Russell, BA

Staff:

***Headmaster:* D C Humphreys**, BA

Deputy Headmaster: M L Pearman, MA

Second Master: J K Jones, CertEd

Director of Studies: Dr J A Wilson, BSc, PhD

Head of Lower School: J C Cockshott, CertEd

Head of Upper School: D N Wood, BA

Head of Sixth Form: Mrs E Enthoven, BSc

Chaplain: Revd R G Morton, BA

Bursar and Clerk to the Governors: Lt Col P D T Irvine, OBE

House Heads:

P Maud, BA (*Stephenson*) *Learning Support*
A Jarvis, BA (*Findlay*) *German, French*
D C Hole, BSc (*Towlson*) *Chemistry*
R I Frost, BEd (*Vinter*) *PE and Geography*
Mrs G Wilkinson, MEd (*Atkinson*) *Physics*
*A S Zammit, BSc (*Southerns*) *Physics*

*Mrs E Ainscoe, MA *Biology*
Miss K Austin, BEd *PE and English*
*J A Baker, CertEd *Design Technology*
*J C L Bolt, BA *Art*
Dr S Boyes, BSc, PhD *Chemistry*
Mrs G Bruce, BA *Spanish*
Mrs F J Callan, BA *French & German*
*P C Clare, DMS *Business Studies*
*J F Clay, BA *History & Politics*
*A J Copping, MA *English & Theatre Studies*
A N Crawford, BA, ARCO *Music*
Mrs C Currier, BSc *Physics*
Mrs M Foody *Dyslexia Unit*
*G D Garner, CertEd *English and RS*
Mrs A Gingell, BSc *Biology & ESL*
R M Golen, BA, LLB *English*
*J P Heyes, MA, MSc *Mathematics*
*E R Howard, BA, BEd *PE & History*
Mrs F L Hughes, BEd *French*
*A Jennings, BA *Religious Studies*
*Mrs J Johnston, MA *Music*
Mrs J Knowles, CertEd *Girls' PE*
Miss S McBrinn, BA *Geography*
Mrs S McCallion, MA *Art*
G Mitchell, BA *English & Games*
Miss A Middleton, MA *Business Studies*
P J Moffatt, BA *Geography and History*
*Mrs E M Mollard *PE, Mathematics, PSE*
*M F Munday, BA *Geography*
Miss L Oakley, BA *English*

*Mrs V Othick, BA *ICT*
Miss K Page, BA *Business Studies and IT*
*A C Peel, BA *German*
Mrs S Richardson, BEd *Learning Support*
R Rich, BA *Art*
J Robb, BA *Religious Studies*
Miss E Rowley, BA *Drama, English*
Mrs A Sellars, BSc *Mathematics*
Miss H Senior, BA *PE & Biology*
Mrs D L Shoesmith-Evans, BA *History*
W T Shorey, BTech *Chemistry*
*B D C Stone, BA *French*
P M Wightman, BSc *Mathematics*

Headmaster's Secretary & Registrar: Miss A Peebles

Brontë House:

Headmaster: C B F Hall, LLB, PGCE

Ashdown Lodge:

Headteacher: Mrs C Robinson, CertEd

Numbers. There are 615 pupils in the Senior School including 100 boarders and 150 students in the VIth Form. Brontë House (7–11) has 160 pupils including 8 boarders. Ashdown Lodge (3–7) has 140 day pupils.

Buildings. The buildings are spacious and well-equipped. A large Business Management Centre was opened in September 1989 for the teaching of Business Studies, Information Technology and Modern Languages. This is equipped with a Language Laboratory, satellite dishes, computer rooms and a Midbank. Though the School is divided, for the sake of convenience and competition, into Houses, there is central administration under the general control of the Headmaster, Deputy Headmaster, Bursar and Heads of Schools. There are good Science laboratories, well-equipped DT and Art Centres and a spacious Music Block. There is also a large heated indoor Swimming Pool and three squash courts.

Sport and Music. Playing fields adjoining the School cover about 40 acres. Cricket, Hockey, Netball, Rugby, Squash, Basketball, Athletics, Swimming, Tennis and Rounders are the main games, and there are eight all-weather Tennis Courts. There is also a large gymnasium and an indoor Cricket School.

There are 3 Orchestras, many ensembles, several Choirs and a Concert Band. Many pupils take extra instrumental lessons.

A new sports centre and centre for the performing arts is planned for completion within three years.

Curriculum. Boys and girls enter the Senior School at the age of 11, 13 or 16 and the curriculum is arranged to provide a continuous course from Ashdown Lodge, through Brontë House and upwards through the Sixth Form to University entrance. Special support is available for dyslexic pupils. For GCSE, all pupils take the following core subjects, (English, French, Maths, Science - Dual Award, IT), together with three others chosen from German, Geography, History, Art, CDT, PE, Spanish, Drama, Music. In the Sixth Form each pupil selects 4 subjects from 22 possible options for study at AS and A2 level. In addition, all Sixth formers take a two-year course in General Studies (Key Skills). The Vocational A Level is available in Business.

A school-wide IT network, full-time IT Director and IT Technician, state of the art PCs ensure that all pupils enjoy access to excellent IT facilities.

Sixth Form Entry. Places are available for students who want to come into the School at the Sixth Form stage to take A levels or the Vocational A Level in Business.

Entrance Awards (*see* Entrance Scholarship section) are available at 11, 13 and 16. Several Music and Art Awards are made each year at all ages. Means-tested bursaries are available and special allowances for children of Methodist Ministers and Service Personnel.

Term of Entry. Pupils are normally accepted in September, though special arrangements may be made for entry in other terms. This applies to Woodhouse Grove, Brontë House and Ashdown Lodge.

Brontë House (named after Charlotte Brontë who was a governess at a house on the same site, and after her parents who were married from the Main School) is a Preparatory School and takes boys and girls, both boarding and day, from the age of 7.

Ashdown Lodge opened in September 1993 to extend the family of Woodhouse Grove to the pre-preparatory age range of 3 to 7, takes boys and girls on a day basis only.

Fees per term. Boarders: £3,870-£3,900 (Main School), Day pupils: £2,230-£2265 (Main School); Boarders: £3,460-£3,525 (Brontë House), Day pupils: £1,800-£1,950 (Brontë House); Day pupils: £1,330-£1,550 (Ashdown Lodge). Fees include meals, books, stationery, examination fees and careers tests.

Extra Subjects – Piano, Violin, Viola, Violoncello, Organ, Flute, Clarinet, Oboe, Trumpet, Trombone, Horn, Saxophone, Bassoon, Guitar, Percussion, Singing, Speech and Drama Training, Dancing, Judo, extra sports coaching.

Old Grovians Association. *Secretary:* D I Littlefair

Charitable status. Woodhouse Grove School is a Registered Charity, number 529205. It exists to provide education for children.

Worksop College

Worksop Nottinghamshire S8O 3AP.
Tel: (01909) 537100
Headmaster: 537127
Fax: (01909) 537102

Foundation. Worksop College is the last of the Woodard (Church of England) Schools to be founded personally by the 19th Century educationist Canon Nathaniel Woodard, who died between the School's foundation in 1890 and its opening in 1895.

Motto: *Semper ad Coelestia.*

Governing Body:
The Provost and Fellows of the Midland Division of the Woodard Schools.

Visitor: The Rt Revd The Lord Bishop of Lichfield

Schools Council:
The Revd Canon W Weaver, BA, DB (*Provost*)
D B Moody, MA (*Custos*)
R P H McFerran, BA (*Vice-Custos*)
Mrs A F Broughton
His Honour Judge J V Machin, LLB
T D Fremantle, MA
C H D Everett, CBE, MA
P Roberts, FCA
Dr J H Anderson, MB, CHB, MRCPsych
Prof D E Luscombe, DLitt, FBA
Mrs J C Richardson, JP, BA
M A Chapman, MLIA
Sir David Naish, DL
C W Reynard, BA
Mrs I M Brown, JP
R C Theobald, BA
The Ven R F Blackburn, MA

***Headmaster:* R A Collard**, MA, Sidney Sussex College, Cambridge

Deputy Head: C T Callaghan, MA, BA (*Modern Languages*)

Director of Studies: P Seery, MEd, BSc (*Chemistry*)

Senior Mistress: Mrs E A Warner, CertEd (*Physical Education*)

Chaplain: Revd P Finlinson, MA

Assistant Staff:
A Angelosanto, BSc (*Head of Chemistry*)
Mrs W H Bain, BA (*English*)
Mrs C A Barnacott, BA (*French, Latin*)
R K Bateman, BA (*Head of Economics, Head of Careers*)
P Batterbury, BSc, MEd (*Biology/Chemistry*)
Mrs C M Beckett, BA (*English*)
P J Beckett, BSc (*Mathematics*)
Mrs A Beeson, CertEd (*Business Studies & Economics*)
Miss R Bellamy, BA (*English and Girls' Physical Education*)
P Boxall, BA (*Director of Music*)
Mrs S Brock, BA (*Physical Education, Geography*)
Mrs J Collard, BA (*History*)
R C J Costin, MA, FRCO (*Music*)
Ms M Daniell, TESOL (*English*)
Mrs H S Dodd, BEd (*English*)
J A S Driver, BSc (*Biology*)
G R Duckering, BEd (*Head of Technology*)
Miss S E A Edwards, BA (*History*)
M Fagan, BEd (*Mathematics*)
N R Gaywood, BSc (*Director of Physical Education*)
M K Gillard, BSc (*Chemistry, Physics*)
Mrs A A Gray, BEd (*English*)
A C Hall, BSc (*Head of Mathematics*)
C J Hamlet, BSc (*Physical Education and Mathematics*)
M A Holterman, BA (*Design Technology*)
H G Jackson, BSc (*Head of Physics*)
A James, MA, BA (*English*)
Dr S E James, PhD, MA, MSc (*Mathematics and Head of General Studies*)
S Jordan, BSc (*Head of Geography*)
A B B Kenrick, BA, ATD (*Head of Art and Design*)
N A K Kitchen, MA (*Head of History*)
T P Larkman, BSc (*Geography*)
Mrs K J Lindsay, BEd (*English*)
Mrs P Parkinson, BA (*Head of Modern Languages*)
C G Paton, BA (*Modern Languages*)
Ms S J Price, BA (*Head of English*)
M C Richardson, BA (*Business Studies/Economics*)
W G Robinson, BSc (*Mathematics*)
Miss D L Sawoscianik-Murray, BA (*Art & Design*)
R B Skinner, BSc (*Head of Science and Biology*)
Mrs E Sutton, L-ès-L (*Modern Languages*)
B A van den Berg, BA (*History*)
L Waller, BSc (*Physics*)
Dr S Woodward, PhD, BA (*Latin*)

School Doctors:
Dr L J Millar
Dr J Edbrooke
Dr J Fulton

Old Worksopian Society Secretaries: C H Murphy and M Fagan

Ranby House Preparatory School:

Headmaster: A C Morris, BEd

Deputy Head: D W T Sibson, BA

Chaplain: The Rev R A Whittaker, MA

There are 370 pupils in the College of whom about one third are girls.

Situation. The College is situated in its own estate of 300 acres with extensive playing fields and an 18-hole golf course. It is on the edge of Sherwood Forest, a mile or so south of Worksop in North Nottinghamshire, overlooking the Clumber and Welbeck Estates, to both of which the pupils have free access. Lying close to the M1 and A1 and only 7 miles from Retford on the main East Coast Inter-City route from London to the North, the College is easily accessible by road and rail from most parts of the country. It is also well placed for contact with the universities, museums, theatres and cultural life of Nottingham, Sheffield, Leeds, York and other cities in the region.

Buildings. Earlier buildings include the Chapel, the Great Hall, the Main Quadrangle of classrooms and boarding Houses, a well-equipped Theatre, an Art School, including excellent Textiles and sculpture areas. In recent years modernisation and refurbishing of the earlier buildings has been accompanied by considerable further building. The indoor heated Swimming Pool, Science Laboratories, a Gymnasium, an additional Boarding House, new Kitchens, Music School, Drama Studio, Special Needs, Computer rooms, an Assembly Hall and a new Design Centre.

Houses. There are 7 Houses:
Mason – Mr W G Robinson
Pelham – Mr P Batterbury
Talbot – Mr C G Paton
Shirley – Mr A James/Dr S E James
Portland – Mr N A K Kitchen
Derry – Mr P J Beckett
Gibbs – Mrs W H Bain

The 4 boys' Boarding Houses, a girls' House and a co-educational Day House are all in the main College. The girls' Boarding House is in a separate building. The housemaster or housemistress, assisted by the house tutors, associate tutors and academic tutors, has the principal responsibility for the individual welfare and programme of the boys or girls in the house, with whom they are in constant contact. At the same time the compactness of the buildings makes it easy for boys or girls to seek advice from other members of staff, in particular the Chaplain, and to make friendships with boys or girls in other houses as well as their own.

Religion. The Anglican religion is at the centre of the School's life, in Chapel services and throughout the school routine. A genuine effort is made to show that Christianity remains a vital response to the challenges of the 21st Century. While the great majority of pupils are Anglican, pupils of other creeds and faiths are also welcome, not least for the distinctive vision of God which they contribute to the School's experience.

Curriculum. Because the College enjoys the ratio of 1 teacher to fewer than 10 pupils, close attention can be given to individual needs at every level. The Curriculum is designed to give pupils as wide an education as possible in the first three years, leading to the GCSE examinations in the VIth form, a broad range of A and AS level examinations is available including English, History, Geography, French, Spanish, Latin, Mathematics, Physics, Chemistry, Biology, Further Mathematics, Business Studies, Economics, Divinity, Music, Art, Design, Theatre Studies, ICT, Physical Education and General Studies, as well as Advanced GNVQ Business.

About 97% of VIth form leavers go on to Higher Education.

Music. A large Music School containing a recital and rehearsal room with a capacity of 150, 10 teaching and practice rooms with pianos and a Music Library is the focal point for the Director of Music and a large visiting staff.

Art. The Director of Art has at his disposal 2 large studios for painting and drawing, a room for graphics, textiles and sculpture areas and a library and teaching room.

Design and Technology. A purpose-built Technology

Centre has facilities for design, the use of computers and areas for work in metal, wood and plastic.

Drama. There are 2 fully-equipped theatres and plays involving boys and girls are put on 3 or 4 times a year.

Physical Education and Games. Physical Education, under the supervision of the Director is an integral part of the curriculum for a pupil's 5 years. The major games for boys are Rugby (Michaelmas Term), Hockey and Cross-Country (Lent Term), and Cricket, Athletics, and Swimming (Summer Term). For girls, they are Hockey (Michaelmas Term), Netball (Lent Term) and Tennis, Athletics and Swimming (Summer Term). Pupils are also encouraged to play other sports (Badminton, Basketball, Golf, Sailing, Soccer, Squash, Sub-Aqua, Tennis, Volley Ball, Water Polo, Weight Lifting) and, as they become more senior, are permitted to specialise in them rather than in the main games if they choose.

Activities. In their first year all pupils are taught life-saving, first-aid and other basic skills. There is then the choice of joining the CCF or voluntary community service. There is training in camping, orienteering, climbing, canoeing, motor engineering, shooting (the school has its own 25-yard range), signalling, and survival swimming. Boys and girls have all these options as well as the chance to take part in the Duke of Edinburgh's Award Scheme.

One afternoon a week is also set apart for Societies and Hobbies. These include Archery, Art, Board Games, Bridge, Boat Maintenance, Bookshop, Chess, CDT, Computers, Creative Fabrics/Dressmaking, Dance, Drama, Duke of Edinburgh, Conservation Work, Radio Control Cars, Golf Coaching, Mountain Bikes, Model-kit Making, Photography, Theatre Technical Staff, Wildfowlers, Horse Riding, Fishing, Karate, Shooting, Music Group.

Ranby House. Rather under a third of the boys and girls in the School come from Ranby House, the preparatory school for Worksop, which is about 4 miles from the College and offers boarding and day education to boys and girls from 7–13. It also has a Pre-prep Department.

Fees. Autumn Term 2000: £4,525 (Boarders). £3,100 (Day Pupils).

Scholarships. (*see* Entrance Scholarship section) Scholarships and Exhibitions may be awarded annually, examination in February. (Candidates must be over 12 and under 14 on 1 May in the year of entry.) Sixth Form Scholarships are held in February each year.

Music Scholarships, Art Scholarships, Sports Awards and Golf Awards are also available.

The value of an award may, in special cases, be increased if the financial circumstances of the parents make this necessary.

A number of Bursaries are awarded to the children of Clergy and to children of members of Her Majesty's Armed Services on the basis of financial need.

Term of Entry. The main intake is in September each year, but pupils do join at other times. Pupils for September from preparatory schools will join through either the Entrance Scholarship or the Common Entrance Examination. Other Entry Tests are held at the College in February and April for 13+ applicants from the maintained sector. Increasingly boys and girls are joining the College after GCSE to study in the VIth form.

Charitable status. Worksop College is a Registered Charity, number 269671. It exists for the purpose of educating children.

Worth School

Turners Hill West Sussex RH10 4SD.
Tel: (01342) 710200
Fax: (01342) 710201
e-mail: office@worth.org.uk
Internet: www.Worth.org.uk

Worth is one of the youngest schools whose Head is a member of HMC. A Catholic boys' boarding and day school welcoming all Christians, Worth is a learning community in which it is easy to know and be known, offering each pupil a high level of pastoral care, the best of modern education and the spiritual depth of a Benedictine monastic order. The monastery was founded in 1933, using a country house and 500 acres of Sussex parkland. In 1957, the monastery became independent and Worth admitted the first boys to its own Senior School in 1959.

Continuous investment: More recent developments include the opening in September 1996 of Austin House (a building designed to provide a comfortable home for younger boys aged 11–12), new squash courts and a refurbished Study block and Science laboratories. St Bede's, one of the boarding houses, has now moved into new, brightly furnished accommodation. Following a successful appeal, a new Performing Arts Centre and Music School and a new Day House were opened in 1999. Existing facilities include a Technology centre, 2 IT Network rooms with numerous IT clusters in classrooms around the school, a sports hall, learning resources centre and private study bedrooms for Sixth Formers. Perhaps the most striking and important 'new' building in size and significance since 1933 is the modern Abbey Church.

One school: The opening of Austin House is evidence of Worth's commitment to a 'one school' approach with the Junior and Senior schools combining to form an 11–18 year school in which all pupils have the same teachers, share facilities and equipment, resulting in closer integration.

Welcoming all Christians: The great majority of boys at Worth are from Roman Catholic families but there are a number of Christians from other denominations. Equal members of the community in every way, non-Catholic boys have no difficulty integrating in the school and bring a different perspective which is most welcome. The School Chaplaincy team includes an Anglican Chaplain, as well as Catholic Chaplains and lay members.

Committed to Boarding: Although a new Day House has been opened to better meet the specific needs of the day boys (13-18) in the school, the ratio of boarding to day remains at 4:1.

The Abbot's Board of Governors, comprising both monks and laity.

President: Rt Rev Dom Stephen Ortiger, MA, STB, OSB

Chairman: R Barker, MA

A Boys
Dom James Cutts, CertEd, OSB
M Gairdner, BA, FCA
M Haan, FCA
Sister Margaret Mary Horton, CRSS
Dom Luke Jolly, BA, OSB
Sister Frances Orchard, IBVM
A Randag, MA
Mr K Smyth
Dom Kevin Taggart, MA, OSB

Clerk to the Board: Colonel C Champion

***Headmaster:* Dom Christopher Jamison**, MA (Oxon), BA (London)

School Bursar: Mrs A Higgs, BSc, ACA

Headmaster's Secretary: Mrs P B Lownsborough

Deputy Headmaster (*Development*): P J Armstrong, MA
Deputy Headmaster (*Curriculum*): F W Belcher, BSc, DipEd

Members of Staff:
R J Acworth, BEd
Mrs A J Adams, BA, PGCE
A Ali, BSc, PGCE
P R Ambridge, BA
A J Arratoon, DipAD, ATC
A J Baars, BMus, ARC, PGCE
Dom Mark Barrett, MA
D R Beale, BSc, MSc, PGCE
Mrs V M M Bird, MA, PGCE
Mrs M S Burridge, BA
Miss H-C Burt, BATheol, PGCE, MTh
C D Chalcraft, BA, PGCE
Mrs A L R Childs, Lic-es-Lettres Eng
N W D Connolly, BA
Mrs J Cook, BEd, OCR, DipSpLD
J Denman, BSc
S P Doerr, BA, CertEd
B Doggett, BSc, PhD
J L Dowling, BEd
B Dunhill, BA
Mrs A Fagan, NDD, ATC
M T Fagan
A J K Farquhar, MA
Mrs M I Fieldhouse, BSc, DipEd
P R Green, DipEE, PGCE
Dom Charles Hallinan, MA
P M Hearn, CertEd
Dom Bede Hill, MA (*Chaplain*)
Mrs P Kelley, CertEd, DiDip
B Klopper, BA, BA (Hons), BEd, HDE
R Knowles, BA
H J Loubser, HED
P P Macklin, BA, PGCE
M D Margrett, MA
Dom Martin McGee, MA
N McLaughlan, BA, PGCE
Mrs C Miller, BA, (*Librarian*)
P S Miller, MA, PhD
A J Mitchell, BSc, PGCE, (*Head of Games*)
M W F Oakley, BA, MMus, PGCE (*Director of Music*)
C Parsons, BSc, PGCE
Dr D Pring, MA, PhD, PGCE
G T Robertson, CertEd
P I Robinson, MA, CertEd
D W Smith, MSc
S R Smith, BA, PGCE
A G Taylor, BA, PGCE
Mrs P Taylor, BA
G Teasdale, BEd
Mrs J Ward, BEd, MA
P J Williams, BSc, PGCE

Medical Officer: Dr W C Smith, MB, BS, D(*Obst*)RCOG
Mrs J Cowan, SRN, HV
Mrs E Gubbin, SRN

ADMISSION POLICY.

Entry to Austin House. Boys are admitted at 11 years and 12 years. There is an entrance examination in February in the year of entry. Remedial assistance is available for those with specific learning difficulties and a good IQ.

Entry at 13+. Boys take the School's own entry tests in February, or the Scholarship Examination.

Scholarships (*see* Entrance Scholarship section). Scholarships are awarded annually, varying in value from 15% to 50% of the annual fees. The examination for Year 9 entrants is held each spring term and candidates must be under 14 years of age on 1 September of the year in which they take the examination. Scholarships are also available for boys entering Austin House at 11+ through the entrance examination in February. Sixth Form Scholarships are awarded to boys aged 16, based on good GCSEs and an interview. Music Scholarships are available on entry at all levels.

Fees per term. Senior Boarding £4,936; Junior Boarding £4,442. Senior Day £3,589; Junior Day £3,230.

For further information on Admissions please contact Mrs N Robinson on 01342 710231.

EDUCATION. Worth offers students an education based on five key features:

Work. In the Senior School, students take up to nine subjects at GCSE. The compulsory core is: English, French or Spanish, Mathematics, Religious Studies, Science. The options include: Art, Business Studies, Drama, Geography, History, Latin, Music, Spanish and Technology. Tuition is available (for an additional fee) in German, Greek, Italian and Chinese to GCSE and A level. There is a choice of 20 subjects at A level, including relatively new courses in Media Studies, Physical Education, Theatre Studies, Electronics, Philosophy, Psychology. Virtually all students go on to university. Sixth Form students may also choose to study for Oxbridge entrance and about 10% are successful.

The Worth Information Technology Project has made the computer an integral part of the study of every subject at every level, not by building a computer centre but by building computers into every aspect of learning. There are over 120 'curriculum' computers in the school with a ratio of nearly 1 computer to every 4 boys. Internet access and e-mail is available to all pupils. The Worth web site may be found at www.Worth.org.uk.

Careers education is an integral part of Fifth and Sixth Form life. Worth has a fully resourced Careers Room with weekly Careers sessions for members of the Lower Sixth. ECCTIS+ and other software are available on the IT Network and the school is a member of the Independent Schools Careers Organisation.

Play. Sport is an important part of Worth life, with opportunities to pursue all major team sports, in some cases to county and national levels. Each year, over 20 boys represent Sussex in their chosen sport. Rugby and soccer are the main winter games and cricket, athletics and tennis the main summer games. Other sports played at competitive level include fencing, squash, basketball and roller hockey. Minor sports are also available through school clubs. There is a seven hole golf course and a small indoor heated swimming pool. In their free time boys can take advantage of the hard play area and the sports hall for rollerblading, five-a-side football, basketball and other games.

Music is a popular activity. There is a flourishing choir that is involved in tours and recordings as well as regular appearances in the Abbey Church. The Choir sings in various Cathedrals each year and undertook a tour to Japan in 2001. Parents and local friends as well as students join the Choral Society for at least two concerts each year (performing such works as Requiems by Faure and Gounod, and the St Cecelia's Mass). The School orchestra performs regularly during the year within the school and beyond. The annual House Music competition provides all pupils with an opportunity to perform competitively, celebrating the abilities of others. The Worth Abbey Community Orchestra gives two concerts a year.

Drama also flourishes with regular productions at all levels, from two man plays to 'whole school' productions. In the summer of 2000, a party of over 70 students from Worth and Burgess Hill School took a combined drama and rugby touring party to Australia and Hong Kong. During the three week tour, the party staged three separate theatre productions, in three different venues and played seven rugby matches. Many of the boys who went on the tour were involved in both the rugby and theatre productions. The new Performing Arts Centre was opened in September 1999 comprising a Theatre studio, Drama office and Workshop, Recording Control room, rehearsal rooms, an Ensemble room and Music classrooms.

One afternoon a week every boy participates in an activity, ranging from silversmithing to Indian cookery and clay pigeon shooting. Worth is a centre for The Duke of Edinburgh Award Scheme; the Bronze Award is achieved by most boys and over 200 boys have achieved the Gold Award.

Love. Care of the boys is a central concern throughout the School. Each boy is a member of a House and has a personal tutor who monitors work progress and assists the Housemaster and his team with overall care. The Benedictine tradition of community life underpins all this. Many staff families live on-site and parents are welcomed as integral to the school. There are regular points of contact, with parents' conferences, meetings, social events and active support from the Friends of Worth (a parents' association).

The school has a long tradition of community involvement, reaching out to others through an extensive voluntary service programme taking place on a weekly basis, involving a large number of students.

Morality. The monastic community at Worth is committed to the Rule of St Benedict and it is this moral and spiritual ethos on which the school community was founded, providing stability in the moral confusion of our rapidly changing world. This sense of stability and a high level of pastoral care provides an enriching and secure environment in which boys can live, as boarders and day pupils. The curriculum also provides opportunities for open discussion of moral issues, following a personal and social education syllabus.

Religion. We believe that each person is on a spiritual journey through life and that the school should support them wherever they are on that journey. There are prayers each day in Houses and Mass every Sunday for those boarding over the weekend and for local families. Religious Studies is a core GCSE but is also a popular option at A level. Beyond this simple framework, the Chaplaincy Team of monks, a Church of England Chaplain and lay people provide a variety of opportunities for students, staff and parents to meditate and to worship, to retreat and to travel. There are annual pilgrimages to Lourdes and the Holy Land.

Worth's special quality is that all five of the above features are first equal in importance. Some people are better at one feature than another but, as a community, we promote each feature equally, identifying and developing each boy's potential. If Worth had a motto it would be: "The glory of God is a person fully alive".

Charitable status. Worth Abbey is a Registered Charity, number 233572. Its aims and objectives are to promote religion and education.

Wrekin College

Wellington Telford Shropshire TF1 3BG.
Tel: (01952) 240131
Fax: (01952) 240338. Headmaster: 415068

Wrekin College was founded in 1880 by Sir John Bayley and in 1923 became one of the Allied Schools, a group of six independent schools including Canford, Harrogate, Riddlesworth Hall, Stowe and Westonbirt.

Motto: *Aut vincere aut mori.*

Visitor: The Rt Revd The Lord Bishop of Lichfield

Governors:
C Rogers-Coltman, MA (*Chairman*)
The Viscount Boyne
J Ellison, FCA
¶P R Dutton
A C U Evans
¶D S Hewitt, FCA
Mrs P Holt
Mrs M T Gwynne, BVSc, MRCVS
Mrs E Moore, LLB
C Reynolds-Jones, TD
A Stilton, MA
M P Willcock
N Coulson, MA, MBA (*Secretary*)

Headmaster: **Stephen Drew**, MA, MEd St Catherine's College, Oxford

Deputy Heads:
H P Griffiths, BSc, PhD
A J H Fisher, BA

Senior Mistress: Mrs S E Clarke, BA

Bursar: C McCulloch

Deputy Bursar and Enterprise Manager: B Crone

Marketing Manager: Mrs S Benwell

Assistant Staff:
J Ballard, BSc
†P J Berry, BA
J L Bridges, BA
Miss R Callard, BSc
G E Cowley, BSc
Mrs L J Drew, BA
†R G Edrich, JP, BA, PhD, FRSA, FRGS
†R C Graham, BSc
†H R Gray, BSc
J Hill, BA
†A R Hurd, BSc
D A Johnson, BA, FRGS
Mrs K M Johnson, BA, MPhil
Mrs H King, BSc
E S Lee, MA
M B Marshall, BA, ARCO, DipMus
D McLagan, BA
R D Morris, BA
F Murton, BMus, LRAM, LTCL, ARCO
A Palmer, CertEd
Mrs M Pattinson, MA
J Pitts, BSc
E Roberts, BA
†A Savage, BSc, DLC
D R Styles, BSc, MA, CPhys, MInstP
Miss C Thompson, BA
C J Tolley, BSc
Miss F L Toomey, BSc
M R Watson, BA
M de Weymarn, BA
D J Winterton, BA
Miss A M Wooller, MA

Learning Support:
Mrs C A Graham, BSc
Mrs B Harbron, BA, CFPS
Mrs F L Lovatt, CertEd

Secretary OWA: M Joyner, BSc

Visiting Music Staff:
Mrs C Benson, AGSM (*Singing*)
D F Bill (*Clarinet & Saxophone*)
A L Hughes, BEd, LRAM (*Guitar*)
Miss H Ing, GBSM, ABSM (*Oboe*)
A Inglis, BMus (*Brass*)
C J Jones, BMus (*Piano*)

T L D Jones, CertRMSM (*Clarinet*)
A Kennedy, BA, BMus (*Violin*)
Miss S A Lane, ARCM (*Flute*)
Mrs C Oldham, GBSM (*'Cello*)
P Parker (*Guitar*)
G Santry (*Drums*)
R Smythe, LRAM (*Piano*)
Mrs G L Styles, BMus, ALCM (*Piano*)

Visiting PE Staff:
Mrs C A Ritchie-Morgan
Mrs C Cartwright (*Netball*)
J Field (*Basketball, Cricket & Squash*)
B Foulkes (*Cricket*)
K Holding (*Fencing*)
Mrs C Still (*Gymnastics*)
P C Tudor (*Cricket*)

Medical Officers:
Dr S Mohammad, BSc, MBBS

CCF: SSI & Outward Bound Instructor:
RQMS, E J Fanneran, late RA

Headmaster's Personal Assistant: Mrs J M Leeke
Headmaster's Secretary: Mrs K Cooke

The College, known locally as 'the School in the Garden', is situated in an estate of 100 acres on the outskirts of the market town of Wellington. We pride ourselves on the excellent quality of our people, as well as the excellent quality of our facilities, and we measure our achievements not only by our outstanding examination results, but also by the whole development of individuals within the school. Being a relatively small school, about 350 pupils, the quality of relationships is good and enables a purposeful atmosphere to prevail in which students can achieve their potential, both in academic and extra-curricular activities. We are splendidly equipped with many modern facilities including a new purpose built Theatre and a double Sports Hall, together with all the expected classrooms and ICT facilities. Teaching is expert and disciplined. Co-educational for a generation, there are 6 Houses which cater for both Day and Boarding pupils and this includes a specially dedicated Junior House for the 11 to 13 intake. Everyone eats together in a central Dining Room and there is a Medical Centre available to all pupils. The Chapel is central to the school both geographically and in the impact it makes on the ethos of the College.

Admission. Boarders and day pupils are admitted at 11+ or 13+ after passing the Common Entrance Examination or an alternative entry test in the case of pupils not at Preparatory Schools. There is also a VIth Form entry. The school has been co-educational since 1975.

Term of entry. The normal term of entry is the Autumn Term but pupils may be accepted at other times of the academic year in special circumstances.

Fees. Registration Fee, £40; Boarding Fee, £4,360 per term (13–18); £3,960 per term (11–13); Day Fee, £2,280 per term (11–13); £2,640 per term (13–18). Private tuition may be arranged at an extra charge. Music Fees are £115 per term.

The School Curriculum is framed to meet the needs of the GCSE Examination, AS and 'A' levels. In the Upper School boys and girls are prepared for entrance to Oxbridge and other Universities. Every pupil has an academic tutor. Expert careers advice is given and all members of the Fifth Form take an aptitude and assessment test before selecting their 'A' levels. The school's careers staff organise work experience for Sixth Form pupils. Regular careers lectures take place in the two winter terms and there is an annual Careers Fair in the Summer Term. Links with businesses in the Telford Enterprise Zone are strong. Special courses in study skills and interview techniques are conducted in the Sixth Form. All pupils undergo a counselling course on important moral and social issues and Sixth Form pupils take part in a Leadership Course.

Games and Activities. We are particularly strong in Netball and Cricket, and the main games for girls are hockey, netball, tennis, athletics and rounders; for boys, rugby, soccer, hockey, cricket, tennis and athletics. Many other sports are available, including squash, basket-ball, volley-ball, cross country, fencing, shooting, climbing, badminton, sailing, canoeing and swimming for both boys and girls. On Tuesdays or Fridays, pupils select from a large range of other activities. Over one hundred pupils are involved with the Duke of Edinburgh Award Scheme and there is a growing tradition of Community Service. There is also a Combined Cadet Force.

Art, Crafts, Music and Drama. There is a flourishing tradition of all these at Wrekin. Art, Pottery, Multi-media Design-Technology and Music are all taught in the junior forms and it is hoped that everyone will continue with one of these creative activities throughout his or her time at the school. All can be taken at GCSE and 'A' level. There is a large Choir and Orchestra and other instrumental and Jazz Bands. Many plays are performed by Houses, year groups and at school level.

Scholarships, (*see* Entrance Scholarship section) **Exhibitions and Prizes.** Academic Scholarships and Exhibitions, open to boys and girls under 12 or under 14 on 1 September in the year in which the examinations are held, are offered annually. Sixth Form scholarships are awarded to candidates entering Wrekin after GCSE. These are awarded in advance, based on GCSE predictions of at least six A grades and following an interview at the school. Valuable Music Scholarships, and Exhibitions are awarded annually. Bursaries are awarded to candidates who offer outstanding ability in games. Music and Art examinations and assessments take place in the Lent Term and are open to pupils for entry at all levels of the school. There is an important link with the Services and bursaries are available to support the sons and daughters of service personnel. Particulars of all scholarships and awards may be obtained from the Headmaster.

Old Wrekinian Association. A flourishing Wrekinian Association of over 3,500 members exists to make possible continuous contact between the School and its Old Pupils, for the benefit of both and to support the ideals and aims of the school. It is expected that boys and girls will become members of the Old Wrekinian Association when they leave Wrekin.

Charitable status. Wrekin College, Wellington, Co Ltd is a Registered Charity, number 528417. It exists to provide independent boarding and day coeducation in accordance with the Articles of Association of Wrekin College.

Wycliffe College

Stonehouse Gloucestershire GL10 2JQ.
Tel: (01453) 822432
Fax: (01453) 827634
Tel/Fax: Common Room (01453) 822793
e-mail: senior@wycliffe.co.uk
internet: http://www.wycliffe.co.uk

Founded in 1882 by Mr G W Sibly, Wycliffe was placed on a permanent foundation under a Council of Governors in 1931.

President: Dr J G Collingwood, BSc, DSc(Hons), FEng, FIChemE

Chairman of Governors: S P Etheridge, MBE, TD, JP, MBA, FIFP, CFP, FCII, FLIA, ALIA(Dip), ACIArb

Vice-Presidents:
Dr H G Mather, MA, MD, FRCP
K H Plested, JP, FRICS

Vice-Chairman: Air Chief Marshal Sir Michael Graydon, GCB, CBE, FRAeS

M L Blinkhorn, FRICS
Capt N B M Clack, MA, MSc, CEng, MIEE, FBIM RN(*Retd*)
Lt Col D A R Clark
S C Coombs, BA, MPhil
Major General G B Fawcus, CB MA
Mrs K R Fife, BSc, MRPharms
S J Fisher, LLB
Mrs S V Fisher, JP
A R Kirby, LLB
Mrs S J Pontifex, BSc, ARICS
W M J Pope, FCA
J H Powell-Tuck, FRICS
J C H Pritchard, DipM, MIMC, MCIM, MIMgt
M M Rushbrooke, MA
Mrs M H Sutton, MA
J R E Williams, FCA

Secretary to the Council: Lt Col S J A Flanagan, MC

***Headmaster:* Dr R A Collins**, MA (Cambridge), DPhil (Oxford)

Second Master: C R C Tetley, BA (Durham)

Senior Mistress: Mrs M J Hardwick, MA (Glasgow)

Senior Master: K Melber, BA (London), DASS

Head of Sixth Form/Head of Higher Education and Careers: J M Hardwick, BA (York)

Director of Teaching: M Scott-Baumann, MA (Cambridge), MA (London)

Director of Learning and Research: Mrs K Davies, MA (Oxford)

Director of Studies: P Woolley, BA (Kent)

Senior Tutor: D A Pemberton, MA (Shakespeare Institute, Birmingham)

Director of Foundation Years: M G Clarke, RSA, CertTEFLA

Associate Chaplain and Head of RE: D J Elliott, BA, MSt (Oxford), DipJewSt (Oxford Centre for Hebrew & Jewish Studies)

Senior Housemaster: G P Buckley, BA (OU), MinstSRMDip, MILAM

House Staff:

Mrs L M Atkins, BA (University of Wales, Aberystwyth)
Mrs E A Buckley, BSc (University of Wales, Aberystwyth)
P Hale, BSc (Warwick)
J Hardaker, BA (Manchester Metropolitan)
Mrs S R Jeffreys, BSc (Leicester)
Mrs J A Krolikowski, BSc (Surrey)
R J Pavis, BA (Durham)
P Woolley, BA (Kent)

Support Staff:

Mrs J M Frith, BEd (Southampton)
Dr J Hudson, MA (Oxon), PhD
S Davies, BSc (Bristol)
Miss A J Bamford, HNC
C Dainton, BA (OU), CertEd
T Dyer, BSc(Eng) (Bath)
S Garley, BAF
Mrs H M Hackett, BA, MSc (London)
J Herniman, BSAC
Dr D Farmer, BSc (Sheffield), PhD
Mrs A C Banyard, HNC
D A Clark, BSc, MNASC, DipSportPsych

Teaching Staff:
B E Shakeshaft, BSc (Sussex)
K W Long, BSc (Birmingham), MIBiol, CIBiol
A Mason, DLC, CertEd (Loughborough College)
I T Dunbar, BA (Oxford)
P J Spicer, JP, BSc (London)
T H Jones, BA (Keele)
Dr A D Gazard, BSc, PhD (Leeds)
W E Henley, BA (OU), MSc (York), MIITT, LRPS
C G Swain, MA (Oxford), FRCO
D J Frith, MA (Oxford)
G J Wheeler, BEd (London)
S N Bird, BA (Portsmouth)
A M Golightly, BA (Drama Centre, London)
M A Floyer, MA (Oxford), MPhil
M J S Hackett, BSc (London)
Mrs J M Macgregor, BSc (Bath)
Major P N Rothwell (*OC CCF*)
Mrs C V Collins, MA (Oxon), DIDipSpLD
D S Jeffreys, BSc (Leicester), PGCE
Miss C E Wellington, BA (Brunel)
Mrs K L Page, BA (Salford), RSA, CTEFLA
Miss A E Beech, BSc (Natal)
R L Hudd, BSc (Cheltenham & Glouchester CHE)
Mrs S E Kessler, BA (Leeds)
N P Migallo, BSc (London), ARCS (Keele)
P Nutter, BA (Lancaster)
D Morrish, SRA Level III Advanced
Mrs A M Lauppe, BA (UWE, Bristol)
S Hill, BA (Wolverhampton), RSADipTEFL
R C Pearse, BEd (Wolverhampton)
Mrs A M Creed, BSc (Sheffield), CertEd
Mrs E A Dancer, BSc (London), DASS
Mrs R M Guest, BEd (De Montfort)
W H Helsby, BA (Newcastle), RSADipTEFL
M J Kimber, New Zealand Coaching Cert, ECB Level 1, RFU Levels I & II
S Taranczuk, BMus (Hull), MMus, ARCO

Part Time Teaching Staff:

G J H Roberts, MA (Oxford), MSc, CMath, MIMA
S J Hubbard, BA (Gloucester College of Art)
Mrs S I Goodwin, CertEd (Lady Mabel College of PE)
Miss J Broadbank, BEd (Westminster College, Oxford)
Miss A M Fowler, MIL, RSACertTEFLA
Mrs S E Harrison, MA (London), DipTEFL
B Norbury, BSc, BEd, TTHD, MEd
Mrs L A Wong (Warwick)
Mrs H P Williams, BA (Leicester)

Librarian: Mrs J M Frith, BEd (Southampton)

Director of Marketing, Admissions & Development: Ms M L Z Bailey

Registrar: Mrs L d'Abo

Headmaster's PA: Mrs R Whitworth

Staff Common Room Secretary: Mrs P Hanson

Visiting Staff:

Music:

P Bassett, ARCM, DipEd (*Oboe*)
Mrs H Barry (*Bassoon*)
J Carter, DipRAM (*Piano*)
I Dollins, BMus, ARCM (*Piano and Voice*)
W Duggan (*Clarinet*)
S Ellsmore, ARCM (*Voice, Organ & Piano*)
Mrs V Green, GRSM, ARCM, LRAM (*Piano/Double Bass*)
Mrs N Higginson, GRNCM, FLCM (*Flute*)
J Lambert, MA, BMus (*Piano*)

N Nash (*Saxophone*)
Miss J Orsman, GBSM (*Violin*)
P Reynolds (*Guitar*)
Mrs P Smith (*Percussion*)
Col W P Thomas, MIM (*Brass*)
Miss J Tomlinson, GRSM, LRAM (*Violoncello*)

Engineering Projects:
T Dyer, BSc(Eng)
C Dainton, BA (OU)

Medical Officers and Staff:
Dr S Anslow, MB, ChB, MCCGP, DRCOG
Dr J Sivler, MB, ChB, DRCOG
Dr I D Lake, MB, MRCGP, FPCert
Dr L A Lake, MB, FPCert, DRCOG, DPD
Mrs M E J Cocks, RGN, SCM

Administration:

Bursar: Lt Col S J A Flanagan, MC

Assistant Bursar (*Financial Accountant*): A C Golding, FCA

Domestic Bursar: Mrs D Tetley

Bursar's Secretaries:
Mrs A Edwards
Mrs C Coleman

Caterer: Mrs M R Adams, LHCIMA, MICA

Junior School: (*see also Part V*)

Headmaster: R Outwin-Flinders, BEd (Hons)

Deputy Head and Director of Studies: P Arnold, BA (London), PGCE (Leeds)

House Staff:
Mrs U Milner
Mrs A Johnson
J F Coombs, BEd
M F Davies, CertEd
D K Fisher, CertEd
Mrs K Coram, BA

Head of Pre-Prep: Mrs D E Tucker, CertEd

Nursery: Miss A King (*Montessori*)

Assistant Staff:
S J Arman, BEd Hons
Mrs L Askew, LLAMDA
Mrs A Bevan, CertEd
P Duffy, BMus, GBSM, ABSM, PGCE
R Gaunt, BA (*QTS*)
Mrs S I Goodwin, CertEd
Mrs C Graham, BSc, PGCE, CertSpLD
Miss N Harrison, BA
Mrs P Latham, BEd, CertEd, CertSpLD
Miss S Merrett, BEd
J D Newns, CertEd
R E Rennicks, CertEd, BA
R Stevenson, CertEd, DipMathsEd
Mrs L Swift, CertEdSpLD
Mrs L Virgoe, DipRBS, AISTD
Mrs N C Warden, BEd
Mrs S Warren
Mrs J Wood, CertEd
Mrs C Woodhouse, BEd (Hons)

Registrar: Mrs D Outwin-Flinders, BEd

Headmaster's Secretary: Ms M A G Thorn

Catering Manager: Mrs S Robertson

Senior Matron: Mrs W Jestice

Location. 2 miles from M5 (J.13): Stonehouse Railway Station 200 metres; London Paddington under 2 hours; London Heathrow 90 minutes; Bristol Airport 50 minutes; Birmingham International 60 minutes. The Junior School (under its own Headmaster) is on a separate adjacent campus with its own extensive facilities, including a recently opened Performing Arts Centre and new Dining Hall.

Organisation. Senior School 13–18. 269 Boys, 137 Girls, two-thirds Boarding. Sixth Form number some 210: Class sizes vary from 3–17 pupils. Junior School 3–13. 220 Boys, 160 Girls.

Admission. At any age following interview and assessment, via numerous Scholarships and Awards; via Common Entrance or Scholarship examinations at 13/14; via GCSE or Scholarship examinations into the Sixth Form. Application to the Headmaster who is personally concerned about each student and available to meet any parent.

Religion. Interdenominational, all faiths welcome. Confirmation classes; Christian Fellowship group and daily worship in keeping with this generation are an integral part of College life.

Houses. Boarders reside in seven Houses. There are three new Sixth Form Halls of Residence each with Study Bedroom with en suite facilities. New Boarding House for 46 boys sharing twin en suite study bedrooms opened Spring 1998.

Tutors. Each student has a House based tutor in the Lower School and a subject based tutor in the Sixth Form. Thus supported by Housemaster/Housemistress Tutor, Chaplain and Head of Year each student may gain maximum advantage towards personal fulfilment in a community noted for its friendly and caring support.

Medical Centre. 24 hour attendance by qualified staff in a well equipped separate Sanatorium. The Health Centre is in the same street. Healthy food is prime consideration. Special dietary requirements for health or faith satisfied through a new £1m 21st Century Kitchen and Dining Hall.

GCSEs are usually taken three years after 13+ entry. Traditional subjects, including five Modern Languages - French, German, Spanish, Italian and Russian, may be studied. Design and Technology, Computing, Physical Education and Drama are also available as GCSE options. Textiles, Astronomy and Psychology will also be available at GCSE to members of the Lower Sixth.

Development Sixth. A unique Course is provided for those in need of an additional year post GCSE but prior to the full two-year A-Level course. It may also be used as an alternative to the A-level course leading directly to qualifications accepted by industry, commerce and most institutions of Higher/Further Education. Parts of the course may also be continued with A-levels. Options include English for Business; Mathematical Problem-solving; Business Studies; Media Studies; Science, Health and Safety.

A-Levels. As from September 2000 the new Advanced Supplementary and A2 Level specifications are in operation. As a general rule students will choose four, or occasionally five, AS subjects to study in the Lower Sixth. Most students will then continue to study the second year in three subjects to A2 Level. Apart from the traditional subjects, the following will also be on offer to A2 Level from September 2000: Art and Design, Design and Technology, Psychology, Business Studies, Media Studies, Political Studies, Theatre Studies and Physical Education. Additional subjects to AS Level will be Classical Civilisation, Computing, Critical Thinking and Philosophy.

Scholarships and Awards. (*see* Entrance Scholarship section) Thanks to the generosity of Governors and Old Wycliffians, a large number are available offering up to 50% of the fees. These may be supplemented in cases of financial need.

For 13+ entry a candidate must be under 14 on 1st September of year of entry and sit the examination in early summer.

For 16+ entry, examinations are held in the Autumn prior to arrival or by arrangement.

At other ages, applications to be made to the Headmaster

Awards are made to candidates with academic talent or potential and also specifically in Music; Art; Design Technology; Drama; Sport; Squash, Rowing, Fencing.

Special awards are also available to (a) students with a good reform background, (b) those with all round merit, (c) children of retired or serving members of the Services, (d) good Common Entrance candidates highly recommended, (e) children of teachers/clergy, (f) vegetarians.

Physical Education. Classes are part of the curriculum. Facilities are available for Rowing, Rugby, Hockey, Fencing, Soccer, Netball, Squash, Badminton, Basketball, Swimming, Scuba Diving, Cricket, Tennis, Athletics, Health and Fitness, Shooting, Adventure Training, Cross Country.

Training for Service is available via the Combined Cadet Force, Scout Troop, Venture Scouts, Duke of Edinburgh Award Scheme, Leadership Courses.

International Travel is regularly organised for varied groups whether musicians, scouts or cadets and arduous training is available in the UK. Pupil exchanges are arranged for those studying foreign languages.

School Societies. Among 90 available are Drama Workshops; Stage Management; Philosophy; Language; Debating; Archaeology; Pottery; Craft; Computing; Electronics; Shooting; Choral, Instrumental Music; First Aid; Cookery; Dance and a Sixth Form Club.

Sunday Specials are organised for Boarders.

Music. A purpose-built music school with enthusiastic staff enables high standards to be achieved. Music is taken at GCSE and A-Level and several pupils each year continue their music studies at the Conservatoires and Universities. There are several choirs, orchestras and three Bands, and Associated Board Examinations are taken every term. The College hosts professional concerts and dramatic productions annually.

Careers Guidance. A vital department which is recognised as a centre of excellence. The College is a member of the Independent Schools' Careers Organisation and the Careers Library is well-equipped with information on careers and entrance to Higher Education.

British College Holidays. Wycliffe offers some of the most exciting vacation courses available in England for foreign students between the ages of 7 and 18. We also offer a comprehensive **EFL** programme all year-round.

Teacher Training. Wycliffe has been selected as a training centre for teachers, reflecting the high esteem in which the College is held.

Fees from September 2000. Boarders £4,815–£5,750 per term. Day pupils £3,385–£3,510 per term. Junior School: Boarders £2,665–£3,445 per term. Day pupils £1,495–£2,375.

Extras are kept to a minimum but may include sanatorium charges, expeditions, certain Society subscriptions, Games Fund and EFL.

Old Wycliffians Association, "OW Society", *Hon Secretary:* F M L Smith, Wycliffe College.

Charitable status. Wycliffe College Incorporated is a Registered Charity, number 311714. It exists to provide education for boys and girls.

Yarm School

The Friarage Yarm Stockton-on-Tees TS15 9EJ
Tel: (01642) 786023
Fax: (01642) 789216

Yarm School, a co-educational day school, was established in its present form in 1978. It has its own co-educational Preparatory School for pupils from 4 to 11 years of age.

Governing Body:
Chairman: D G Blakeley, JP, MA

Mrs H R Andrews
J C Baggaley, MA
M M Bisset, BA
His Honour Judge J de Guise Walford
C F Owen, FCA
W R Pickersgill, MCIBS
Dr E Pugh, MB, ChB
J R H Sale, BA
Mrs M F Veitch, MB, BCh

***Headmaster:* D M Dunn**, BA

Deputy Headmaster: D G Woodward, BSc

Director of Studies: M Wilson, BSc

Head of Sixth Form: M Ford, BSc

Senior Masters:
†R A Brown, BSc *Head of Fourth Year*
J J Logan, JP, MA

Headmaster's Secretary: Mrs J Hill

§Mrs B Abbott, BA
P R Bailey, BA
Miss K von der Becke, MA
†*G C Booth, MA (*Head of Fifth Year*)
P J Connery, MA
*G B Cooper, BSc
§Mrs K Crabtree, BA
*S H A Crabtree, BSc (*Head of Careers*)
*E M Craig, BA
Mrs K Crewe-Read, BA
Mrs H A Crick, BSc
*P E Crookes, MA
§Mrs R M Crookes, BA
T J Day, CertEd
*J R C Doherty, BSc
*†D V G Dunn, MA (*Head of Second Year*)
†S Edwards, BA, MPhil (*Oswald Housemaster*)
V J Feeney, BSc
*Mrs L Findlay, CertEd
T L Foggett, BA, BSc
Miss J A Fraser, BSc (*Head of First Year*)
*S C Gibson, BEd
P V Hampson, BSc
*R J L Harandon, MA, MPhil
Mrs S J Hardy, BA (*Deputy Head of Sixth Form*)
S P Hardy, BEd
C H Hart, BSc
Frau J Heinen, Studienassessorin
†M H Hilton, BA (*Bede Housemaster*)
*H A Killick, BA, MPhil
Dr M Kirk, BSc
†Mrs L Kneale, BA (*Head of Third Year*)
†Miss G Lumley, CertEd (*Aidan Housemistress*)
Miss S J Marshall, BSc
*M J McNulty, BSc
*Mrs J Nixon, BA
Mrs S Rea, BA
*C Read, MSc
Miss N E Redhead, BEd
Miss C E Rhodes, BSc
I Stewart, BSc
P Telfer, BA
*C Thomas, BEd
S Thompson, BSc
§Mrs C Trinder, BA
*R G N Webb, BA
†S Whitehead, BEd (*Cuthbert Housemaster*)
*B D R Wilson, BA
Miss J Woinson, BA

Bursar: Dr S C Palmer, MA, CEng, FIMechE

Preparatory School:

Headmaster: P M Garner, MEd

Deputy: Mrs L Jessup, CertEd
Head of Studies: S G Pearce, BA, BEd
Head of Early School: Mrs W Young, MA(Ed)

Mrs B Abbott, BA
M R Beecroft, BEd
Mrs H Brooks (*Teaching Aide*)
§Mrs J J Catterall, CertEd
Mrs R Cooper (*Teaching Aide*)
M Crewe-Read, BSc
C R Davis, BEd
Mrs G Denney, Dip Teaching
Mrs P De Martino, CertEd
Miss K J Dickenson, BA
Mrs R M Greenwood, BA
J Grundmann, BSc(Econ)
§Mrs C M Gledhill, BEd
Mrs A J Gray, BEd
P Hardy, BA
Mrs M E Hodgson, CertEd
Mrs E Lickess, BA
S Mudd, CertEd
A M North, BA, MSc
§Mrs C A Pearce, BA
Miss J V Renwick, BEd
Mrs J Richardson, BEd
W Richardson, BEd
Miss A Russian, MA
Mrs G Selby (*Teaching Aide*)
§Mrs S Snape, BA, PGDSpLD
Miss H E Utridge, BA
Mrs A White, BEd

There are about 840 pupils in the School including 310 4 to 10 year olds who are in a separate Preparatory School. There are about 170 in the Sixth Form. The school is fully co-educational.

Situations and Buildings. Yarm is an attractive market town on the edge of the Cleveland/Teesside conurbation giving easy access to both town and countryside. The North York Moors National Park is only 15 minutes away.

The School occupies two adjacent sites on the outskirts of Yarm: the buildings of the original Yarm Grammar School (founded 1590, oldest building dated 1884) and The Friarage, comprising an eighteenth century mansion and several other buildings, set in attractive grounds bordering the River Tees. A classroom block to house the English, History and Geography departments was completed in 1988 and September 1992 saw the completion of a sports hall and squash court, a 600-seat theatre with adjacent music facilities and purpose built accommodation for modern languages. A new science block containing facilities for computing and geology in addition to the normal provision for physics, chemistry and biology was completed in May 1996. An exciting new electronics and technology centre opened in April 1997. There is a self-contained sixth-form centre and a new sixth form library was opened in 2000. The School possesses about 26 acres of playing fields, several tennis courts and a multi-gym. The Preparatory School has its own accommodation which includes a gym, a school hall and specialist facilities for art, technology and computing. A new dining hall and kitchens were added for the start of the 1996/97 school year.

Admission. Pupils are admitted at 11 by means of the School's own Entrance Examination, or at 13 through Common Entrance. Direct Sixth Form Entry is dependent upon GCSE results and interview. The Preparatory School has its own entrance procedures. Academic scholarships are offered at 11-plus, 13-plus and for sixth-form entry. Music Scholarships can be won at any age. There are also a number of bursaries.

Curriculum. The School's academic reputation in the Cleveland area is high and virtually all leavers go on to take university degrees. In the Preparatory School the curriculum is both wide ranging and demanding. Whilst the basics in English and Maths are given great emphasis, the Sciences, Technology and Modern Languages also form an important part of the time-table. In the First Year all pupils study the following subjects: English, Maths, Physics, Chemistry, Biology, Technology, German or French, Latin, History, Geography, Information Technology, Art, RE and Music. Setting by ability takes place in Mathematics, English and in Modern Languages. In the Second Year many pupils begin a second Modern Language and setting in the Sciences is also arranged. GCSE is taken as a two year course comprising seven compulsory 'core' subjects (English, English Literature, Maths, German or French, Physics, Chemistry and Biology) and 3 or more 'options'. Options can usually be selected from French, German, Latin, Classical Studies, Greek, History, Geography, Information Technology, Technology, Design and Realisation, Art, Music and Religious Studies. The more able pupils (perhaps a third or more of a 'year group') will take Maths and a foreign language a year or more early enabling them to take these subjects to levels beyond GCSE whilst still in the Fifth form.

In the Sixth Form A-levels are selected from about twenty options. All Lower Sixth students take 4 AS levels and 3 or 4 A2's in the Upper Sixth. General Studies is also taught in the Upper Sixth.

Modern languages are enhanced by means of regular exchanges with 'twin' schools in France and Germany. Teams entered for nationwide Mathematics and Science/Technology competitions have won several awards in the last three or four years.

Organisation. Pastoral care is based on both a year group and a House system. Every pupil belongs to one of four Houses for his/her whole school career. Houses exist to promote competitions, sports events, charity fund-raising etc. Each pupil also has a personal Tutor and Head of Year whose task it is to look after all the pupils within a given year group. Sixth-formers have the opportunity to serve as House Monitors and School Prefects.

Games and Activities. Rugby, hockey, rowing and netball are the School's main winter games and there are representative teams in these sports for all age levels. In the summer cricket, tennis and athletics become the major sports. In addition canoeing, squash and cross-country are also pursued at inter-school level throughout the year. Several other games are available as options.

There are many School societies. A great deal of extra-curricular activity is centred on the Duke of Edinburgh Award Scheme. Rock climbing, canoeing and other aspects of outdoor education are given some prominence and residential weekends at an outdoor pursuits centre are a fixed part of the curriculum. There is a flourishing CCF contingent (membership, though popular, is entirely voluntary). School excursions are frequent and very varied. Expeditions in recent years have travelled as far as India, America and Guyana. Drama (at least three major productions a year) and Music (several choir and orchestral concerts are given each year) are given every encouragement and have a strong following. Activities which are an extension of Art or Technology or Biology also flourish particularly well.

Religion. The regular services in the Parish Church are a feature of the School's corporate life and though the services are Anglican in style, the School is an inter-denominational community comprising pupils of both Christian and non-Christian backgrounds.

Fees. (*see* Entrance Scholarship section). Senior School fees vary according to the year of study and are £2,160 per term. Preparatory School fees start at £1,490 per term (7+) and Pre-Prep (Early School) at £1,270. Lunches are extra at about £1.80 per day.

Academic Scholarships are offered at 11+ and for sixth-form entry (a major award could amount to a one-third reduction in fees). The School makes available a small number of bursaries to cover special circumstances.

Former Pupils. Past members of the School are eligible to join the Former Pupils' Society whose Hon Secretary may be contacted via the School Office.

Charitable status. Yarm School is a Registered Charity, number 507290. It exists to provide quality education for boys and girls.

Headmasters' Conference: Schools in Europe

Aiglon College

1885 Chesières-Villars Switzerland
Tel: 41 24 496 6161
Fax: 41 24 496 6162
e-mail: info@aiglon.ch
internet: www.aiglon.ch

Aiglon College is a British (HMC, ECIS accredited) co-educational boarding school founded in 1949 by John Corlette.

The School is governed by the Board of Governors of the Aiglon College Association, which is registered as a charitable trust in Switzerland, the United Kingdom, the United States, Canada and Holland.

Chairman of the Governors: The Revd Norman Drummond

***Headmaster:* The Revd Dr J Long**

Deputy Headmaster (Curriculum): P Crute
Deputy Headmaster (Pastoral): D Rhodes
Headmaster of the Junior School: D Boutroux
Director of Admissions: Mary Sidebottom
Director of Finance & Administration: R Huxford
Director of Information Systems: J Hibbins

Houses and Houseparents:

Senior School:
Alpina: Mr and Mrs Teal
Atitlan: Mr and Mrs Beata
Belvedere: Mr and Mrs Gillmore
Clairmont: Mr and Mrs Hall
Delaware: Mr and Mrs Tysoe
Exeter: Mr and Mrs Thomson
Chantecler: Mr and Mrs Stevenson

Junior School:
La Baita: Mr and Mrs Boutroux
La Dacha: Miss Kellett-Smith

There are approximately 62 full-time qualified Assistant Staff, and 14 part-time and visiting staff. Pupil enrolment is 335 from approximately 58 nations.

Aiglon's aim is to provide, within a safe, caring and supportive framework, a challenging and rigorous education in intellectual, physical, moral, emotional and spiritual self-discipline and self-discovery. Students should be equipped individually and collectively with the initiative, integrity and perspective to become positively motivated contributors to the world community.

Aiglon has a Christian tradition and pupils attend regular services conducted by the School Chaplain; however children of all faiths are welcomed.

Situation. The School stands in the village of Chesières on a sheltered south-facing slope in the Swiss Alps, at a height of 4,000 feet (1,200 m) overlooking the Rhône Valley to the Dents du Midi and the Massif du Mont Blanc, and is 80 minutes by road or rail from Geneva airport. There are 7 senior boarding houses and a separate Junior School. Facilities include an outstanding new teaching building, opened in 1996, housing science laboratories, a computer centre, a music department with recording studio and mathematics classrooms. In addition there are language laboratories, a newly extended art school, three libraries and a variety of sporting surfaces. The school also has access to swimming pools, a skating rink, sports centre with indoor tennis and squash courts, and extensive ski slopes.

Curriculum. The school is divided into Junior (approx ages 9 to 13), Middle (13 to 15) and Upper (15 to 18) schools. The reception class (9–11) is a bilingual (French/English) section. In the rest of the school all courses except foreign languages are taught in English. There is a Special English Section for overseas students whose English needs improvement. All students are advised on and prepared for GCSE and A level examinations and all but a few go on to university in Britain, the United States or elsewhere in the world.

Activities. All students are required to participate in outdoor activities, organised by fully-qualified sports and expeditions staff. The main sports are basketball, soccer, tennis, volleyball, squash, swimming, athletics and skiing in the winter months.

Character training through adventure is a special feature of life at Aiglon, and weekend expeditions in the mountains, on skis, on foot and on bicycles take place throughout the year. Once a term there is a Long Expedition, lasting three days. In the Winter Term this is on skis, usually with a mountain hut or hostel as a base. The school is also a centre for the Duke of Edinburgh Award Scheme. In the Autumn Term, the school is divided into groups for cultural expeditions to European cities of note such as Basel, Lucerne, Strasbourg, Venice, Florence, Rome and Stratford.

The pupils are encouraged to employ their leisure time creatively. Crafts and hobbies are pursued through a system of 'Options'. These include Astronomy, Ceramics, Art, Canoeing, Drama, Music, Cookery, Philosophy, Ecology, Photography, Silk Painting, the Yearbook and Choir. Aiglon is a committed and active member of the Round Square: an international group of schools committed to the educational principles of Kurt Hahn and to an active programme of international community service and educational exchange.

Admission is through the school's entrance tests or the Common Entrance Examinations and a small number of places is also available in the Lower VIth for candidates with good GCSE qualifications.

Fees and Fixed Charge (to cover extras):

SFrs 39,000 per annum for boarding preparatory form to SFrs 60,000 per annum for pupils over 13 years of age.

(Fees are subject to change).

Scholarships. (*see* Entrance Scholarship section) Scholarships equivalent to approximately 50% remission of fees are offered annually. Bursaries are also available for deserving candidates who do not qualify for a scholarship. Awards are made on the results of Common Entrance and/or the Aiglon entrance exam, school recommendation and interview.

Further information may be obtained from The Headmaster, Aiglon College, 1885 Chesières-Villars, Switzerland. Telephone: 41 24 496 6161. Fax: 41 24 496 6162.

"The Aiglon College Alumni Eagle Association" consists of former pupils and friends. Contact Jaime Tackett of the External Relations Office for information on Alumni Affairs.

The British School of Brussels

Leuvensesteenweg 19 3080 Tervuren Belgium.
Tel: (02) 766 04 30
Fax. (02) 767 80 70
e-mail: principal@britishschool.be
website: www.britishschool.be

Patrons:
His Excellency the British Ambassador to the King of the Belgians
His Excellency the Belgian Ambassador to the Court of St James

Chairman of the Board of Trustees: Tony Beck

Chairman of the Board of Management: Peter Akers

***Principal:* Jennifer Bray**

Creation. The British School of Brussels (BSB) was founded in 1969 as a non-profit making organisation in Belgium and was opened in 1970 by HRH The Duke of Edinburgh. It is run by a Board of Trustees and a Board of Management, comprising distinguished British and Belgian citizens from both the professions and the world of business, together with parent and staff representatives.

Site. The School occupies a beautiful site of 120 hectares, surrounded by woodlands and lakes near the Royal Museum of Central Africa at Tervuren, which is 30 minutes by car from the centre of Brussels. The site belongs to the Donation Royale, the foundation which manages the estates left to the Belgian people at the beginning of the century by King Leopold II.

Buildings. The school has excellent facilities and almost all buildings have been fully refurbished within the past ten years. In the secondary section these include a prestigious science and maths centre with eight laboratories, a new wing with four art studios and three technology workshops, comprehensive languages and humanities suites, two dance and drama studios, and four networked ICT rooms. In addition, there is a large and popular self-service Cafeteria for the whole School. Use of the extensive sports facilities (gymnasium, grass pitches, all weather floodlit training area, tennis and squash courts, indoor sports hall) the Auditorium and Arts Centre, together with the programme of Adult Studies courses, make the School a focal point for the local and international community.

Organisation. BSB is a coeducational day school for students from 3 years to 18 years with 1,100 currently on roll: there are 160 students in the Sixth Form. Its own creche - the Kinder Crib - was opened in 1999 for 40 children under the age of three. Entry throughout is non-selective and students are accepted regardless of race, colour or creed. 60% of the students are British and over 65 other nationalities are represented. The UK National Curriculum and Curriculum 2000 are followed as a minimum entitlement and courses lead to GCSE and GCE A and AS Level public examinations, as well as to Vocational A levels. Provision is also made for Oxbridge tuition. There is a Learning Support Department, headed by an Educational Psychologist, and also a school Counsellor.

Sports and Extra Curricular Activities. A wide range of competitive sports is offered: athletics, cricket, cross-country, gymnastics, hockey, rugby, soccer, swimming and tennis - as well as recreational activities such as basketball and golf. The School participates successfully in the International Schools Sports Tournaments. There are very many opportunities for involvement in music groups - in orchestras, concert bands and instrumental ensembles - as well as in dramatic performances including student-directed productions. There are also numerous opportunities for overseas travel and school journeys.

Careers. Advice on careers, as well as on higher and further education opportunities, is of vital importance to expatriate students. The School takes part in many careers conventions, as well as hosting its own annual Careers Week and welcoming numerous university tours.

Past Students' Association. The "15 Club" c/o The British School of Brussels.

The British School in The Netherlands

Senior School (11-18 years) Jan v Hooflaan 3 2252 BG Voorschoten THE NETHERLANDS
Tel: 31 (0)71-5602222
Fax: 31 (0)71-5602200
Junior School (3-11 years) Vlaskamp 19 2592 AA Den Haag
e-mail: Info@britishschool.nl
website: www.britishschool.nl

The British School in The Netherlands (BSN) was founded in 1935 since when it has grown into a school of over 1450 pupils from nursery (age 3) to Sixth Form (age 18). Although the majority of pupils are of British origin, the School truly serves the international community, with children from over 50 other nations. The School is established under Dutch law as a non-profit making Association administered by a Board of Governors. It is independent and non-denominational, though close ties are retained with the UK and with other overseas British and international schools and it is inspected by UK education officials.

The School aims to develop the potential of its pupils by providing a caring environment, in which they are offered the widest possible educational opportunities. Pupils are helped to develop their powers of reasoning, increase their knowledge and become aware of the importance of their individual contribution and responsibility to society. All are encouraged to aim for excellence and to respect one another. These aims will be achieved only in a happy school whose pupils join with high expectations and where they are encouraged in the belief of their fulfilment.

A new Junior school building was opened in September 1997, purpose built for children aged 3 to 11 years on a green field site close to the centre of The Hague. In 1998 it won an Award from the Dutch Government for the best school building in The Netherlands. The new school is built in a crescent shape so that all the light and airy classrooms face on to the extensive grounds. A Foundation School was opened in The Hague in 2000 which caters for nursery and reception classes (ages 3 to 5). This newly refurbished building is situated in the city and has excellent space for the children to develop in early education skills. The Senior School already occupies a large green field site in Voorschoten (a small town just north of The Hague) and enjoys excellent facilities which support the comprehensive educational and recreational programmes. Each School has a Headteacher, and a Principal has overall responsibility for both these schools as well as a small school in Assen in the north of the Netherlands. All of the 180 teachers are fully qualified and are mostly recruited from the United Kingdom.

An independent School bus service links the schools and covers most of The Hague, Voorburg, Leidschendam, Wassenaar, Voorschoten as well as parts of Rotterdam, Rijswijk, Leiden, Amsterdam and Zoetermeer.

The School was inspected by HMI in November 1996 using the inspection criteria for Independent Schools. The report stated that the School "exceeded national expectations in all core subjects" and "results at GCSE and A level are high, well above the national average".

Pupils follow challenging programmes of study based on the National Curriculum but with an added international dimension. All pupils study English, mathematics, science, technology, history, geography, music, art and physical education from the age of five years. Dutch is taught from the age of five and French from ten years, then, at 12 years in the Senior School, Spanish and German are added. Pupils prepare for the GCSE (at 16+) and A and A/S Level examinations at 18 years, chosen from a wide variety of subjects including theatre studies and psychology. The School has a long and proud record of success in these public examinations with the majority of pupils entering universities and other higher education establishments all over the world.

Excellent facilities are available at the School for indoor and outdoor games, including rugby, hockey, aerobics, tennis, athletics, judo, football, basketball, volleyball and gymnastics. Fixtures are arranged with local clubs and other schools, including annual tours and tournaments in the United Kingdom and elsewhere in Europe.

The School takes pride in its regular participation in the annual Model United Nations Conference in The Hague and mounts a full programme of field and activity trips in The Netherlands, the United Kingdom, France, Switzerland, Spain and Germany, capitalising on its central location in Europe.

To ensure that each pupil is known individually, and cared for, there is a pastoral system which begins with the form teacher, who is responsible to a year group leader. Together they work to care, support and guide the individual in all aspects of school life. Success is achieved only through close cooperation between home and school, a positive learning environment and high standards of discipline.

Admission is granted at any time in the school year following an interview with the parents and applicant. Great care is taken to ensure the academic and social integration of the child. Special provision is made for pupils with learning difficulties. Any child with Special Needs will be considered according to the School's policy on Special Needs Provision, which is available on request. Specialist help is provided throughout the School for pupils requiring individual tuition in English as an Additional Language.

PRINCIPAL: MR TREVOR ROWELL, BOERDERIJ ROSENBURGH, ROSENBURGHERLAAN 2, 2252 BA VOORSCHOTEN. TEL: 071-5602251 AND FAX: 071 5602290.

The Foundation School (age 3–5 years), Tarwekamp 3, 2592 Den Haag. Tel: 070 315 4040. Fax: 070 315 4054.

Junior School (age 5–11 years), Vlaskamp 19, 2592 AA Den Haag, The Netherlands. Tel: 31 (0)70-3338111 and Fax: 31 (0)70- 3338100.

Senior School (age 11–18 years), Jan van Hooflaan 3, 2252 BG Voorschoten. Tel: 31 (0)71-5602222 and Fax: 31 (0)71- 5602200.

Charitable status. Vereniging The British School in The Netherlands is a Registered Charity, number V409055. It aims to offer a British education to international children living temporarily or permanently in The Netherlands.

The British School of Paris

38 Quai de l'Ecluse 78290 Croissy sur Seine FRANCE
Tel: 01 34 80 45 90
Fax: 01 39 76 12 69
e-mail: bsp@fr.inter.net
website: www.eccis.org/bsp

Chairman of Governors: J R Bouscarle, CBE

Principal: **M W Honour**, BA (Hons), MSc

Number of Pupils. 700 (Boys and Girls)
Fees. From FF70,000 per year.

The British School of Paris caters for English-speaking children of over 30 nationalities (about 65% are British) from ages 4 to 18. It is a non-profit association in France and is managed by a Board of Governors under the patronage of His Excellency the British Ambassador.

The school is on two campuses in the western suburbs of Paris. The Junior School occupies a beautiful wooded site overlooking the Seine valley and has many modern facilities including an indoor swimming pool and a play area with synthetic turf. Studies are based on the British National Curriculum with emphasis on English, Maths and Science, and of course, the French language. Various sports, music and drama and many extra curricular activities are also provided.

At the Senior School modern facilities include four spacious laboratories, a refectory and a sports hall. Students enter at the age of 11 and for the first three years, a broad general education is maintained in line with the National Curriculum. Pupils are prepared for the GCSE and A Level examinations in a comprehensive range of subjects.

Music and drama are encouraged; the music centre has teaching and practice facilities and a well-equipped electronic studio. Specialist teachers visit the school to provide individual lessons in a wide range of instruments. Highly professional drama productions, ranging from Shakespeare to musicals such as "My Fair Lady" take place in a local theatre. The school's membership of the International Schools Theatre Association enables pupils to take part in drama workshops in a variety of countries.

The school has had considerable sporting success over the years, winning the International Schools' Sports Tournament competition in girls' field hockey, and boys' rugby. Our international fixture lists provide an incentive to gain a place in school teams. As well as local matches our teams travel regularly to Belgium, Holland, Germany, Britain and Austria and, on occasions have been as far afield as the Czech Republic and Canada.

The British School is co-educational throughout with almost equal numbers of boys and girls. Each section has about 350 pupils, with a two form entry into the senior school. Most are day pupils, although a number of senior school pupils live, under school supervision, with carefully chosen French and occasionally English, "host families". This is of particular interest to pupils who come to Paris to do their A Levels and especially if they are studying French.

Small overall numbers, modest class sizes and a supportive pastoral system, mean that new pupils integrate quickly and find themselves well motivated in their work. Academic standards have improved steadily in recent years and compare favourably with good academic schools in England. Ninety percent of sixth formers go on to higher education in Britain and elsewhere, with a regular intake to Oxford and Cambridge.

International School of Geneva

62 route de Chêne CH-1208 Genève Switzerland
Tel: (022) 787 2400
Fax: (022) 787 2410

The Foundation of The International School of Geneva.

Director General: **Donald Billingsley**

The Foundation serves the international community of Geneva by providing education on three campuses accommodating 3,400 students aged 3-19.

The school was founded in 1924 to create the world's first international school, committed to promoting international understanding and values now incorporated in the ideals of the United Nations organization. This philosophy guides the daily life of the school community.

Today the school serves about 120 nationalities in a multi-lingual, pluralistic community. Its educational programmes, based on a multi-cultural view of the world, promote the development of the whole child with an emphasis on learning to learn. The curriculum has been designed to provide breadth and balance within a commitment to the achievement of excellence. Its internationally recognised standards allow children to transfer easily between school systems. Tuition is offered in English and French and students are encouraged to maintain contact with their mother languages.

The school has a major campus in Geneva, another in Founex in the Canton of Vaud and a third, smaller primary campus next to the United Nations. It is housed in accommodation that ranges from listed historic buildings to modern purpose-built accommodation that attracts international interest.

The school pioneered the development of the International Baccalaureate which now forms the basis of its university preparatory programme in the senior secondary school in a complete range of subjects. The school also prepares students for the International GCSE, the Swiss federal Maturité and the French Baccalauréat. Its graduates have entered leading universities in most countries of the world, many reaching positions of great distinction. This academically-oriented programme is supplemented by extra-curricular activities in which the arts, music, theatre and a variety of sports are prominent.

Serving an internationally mobile community, the school is prepared to accept students throughout the year based on previous academic records and recommendations.

Chartered and supervised by the Swiss Federal authorities, it has not-for-profit status and is governed by a Board of elected parent members and representatives of local authorities. The school is accredited by ECIS and MSA.

The International School of Paris

6 Rue Beethoven Paris 75016 FRANCE
Tel: 1.42 24 09 54; Primary School: 1.42 24 43 40
Fax: 1.45 27 15 93
Primary School: 96 Bis Rue du Ranelagh 75016 Paris

President of the Board of Directors: Mr R Gren

Headmaster: **G F Jones**, MSc

Principal of Lower School: Mrs Elizabeth Hickling

Enrolment: 415 day pupils, boys and girls.

The School was founded in 1964 as a non-profit-making school to cater for the various educational needs of the international diplomatic and business communities in Paris, within an international framework. It has expanded steadily since then and now contains 415 pupils, all day, in a co-educational environment, between the ages of 3 and 18. It is administered by a Board of Trustees, made up of leading figures in diplomatic and banking circles, and parents, and is accredited by the French law of 1901, by the New England Association of Schools and Colleges and the European Council of International Schools. The Headmaster is also an Overseas Member of HMC.

The schools are centrally situated about 15 minutes' walk apart in the much sought-after residential environment of the 16th "arrondissement" of Paris, close to the Trocadéro. This enables the pupils to make the best use of the marvellous cultural setting in which they are placed.

The educational policy of the school is to prepare pupils in the best possible way for their future studies and careers, in whatever country they may be (and there are 47 nationalities represented), while at the same time providing a firm and supportive community as an attachment when they may have led a less stable life before.

The teaching medium is English, but all pupils have an hour of French every day. Special care is taken with those from non-English speaking backgrounds. After a broad general education in the Primary and the Middle Schools, the majority of pupils then sit the International GCSE examinations, followed by the International Baccalaureate, as we believe that these examinations give the broadest possible base and equip the pupils best for their University studies. Fourteen subjects are currently on offer for the International Baccalaureate exam and all pupils in their last two years take a wide-ranging course on the Theory of Knowledge and prepare an extended essay on a subject that interests them. The aim is to make use of the best aspects of the British, American and French systems, as well as the unique features of the Paris environment. Academic standards are high, with an 86% success rate in last year's International Baccalaureate Diploma examinations.

The school possesses a small gymnasium of its own, but also has the use of other sporting facilities and there are active basketball, soccer and athletic clubs, both during and after school hours. Pupils are encouraged to participate in a wide range of extra-curricular activities, sporting, dramatic, musical and cultural.

Because of the need to serve the mobile International Community, admission is permitted at any time during the school year, provided that places are available and the Director of Admissions is satisfied with the results of an entrance test and interview, as well as the receipt of a satisfactory report from the previous school. Where English is not the pupil's mother tongue, the school must be sure that the pupil will benefit from an English language education, if necessary with the help of expert EFL Staff.

King's College

Paseo de los Andes 35 Soto de Viñuelas 28761 Madrid Spain
Tel: (34) 918-034 800
Fax: (34) 918-036 557
e-mail: soto@kingsgroup.com
website: http://www.kingscollege.es

King's College is a British co-educational day and boarding school founded in 1969. The Headmaster is an overseas member of HMC, while the school is a member of COBISEC, ECIS and NABSS.

The school is governed by the School Council composed

of distinguished members from the business and academic communities.

Chairman of the School Council: Sir Mervyn Brown, KCMG, OBE

Headmaster: **C T Gill Leech,** MA (Cantab)

Deputy Headmaster: P R Cook, BEd Hons (Nottingham)
Head of Primary: Ms A Gasca, CertEd (London)
Head of Spanish Studies: A Ortega, Lic Ciencias (Madrid)

There are 85 fully qualified staff, 55 women and 30 men, of whom a total of 69 are British. Pupil enrolment is 1,300 (665 boys and 635 girls), including 30 boarders.

The aim of King's College under the key phrase of its Charter "A British Education in Spain for Europe and the World", is to provide students with a fine all-round education while fostering tolerance and understanding between young people of different nationalities and backgrounds.

The school caters for children of about 30 nationalities between the ages of 18 months and 18 years.

Situation. The school is situated in a residential area about 25km to the north of Madrid near the Guadarrama mountains, but well connected to the city centre by motorway. It stands on a 12 acre site and there is an optional comprehensive bus service connecting the school to the city of Madrid and its outlying residential areas.

The Boarding House is located on two floors of the school's west wing and has a capacity for approximately 50 pupils.

The school has extensive, purpose-built facilities which include 7 science laboratories, 2 libraries, art studio and 2 computer centres with multimedia stations. The sports facilities include a 25 metre indoor heated swimming pool, a floodlit multi-purpose sports area, football pitches, basketball and tennis courts, a gymnasium with fitness centre and a horse riding school.

Curriculum. King's College follows the English National Curriculum leading to (1)GCSE, AS Level and GCE "A" Level examinations. There are Induction English Classes for children over the age of 7 who need to improve their English while gradually integrating into the mainstream of the school. There is also a Spanish section for pupils wishing to follow the Spanish Baccalaureate from the age of 16 (Y12). All pupils learn Spanish. Pupils are well advised on Higher Education, and the majority go on to university in Britain, the United States and Spain, amongst other countries.

Activities. King's College has choirs, musical ensembles and Drama Groups, which participate in numerous events throughout the year. Pupils are encouraged to explore their capabilities in the areas of music and the arts from a very early age.

Sports play an important role at the school and pupils, who are required to attend physical education classes at all stages of their studies, are encouraged to take part in the inter-house tournament and local competitive events. King's College currently has football and volleyball teams participating in local leagues at Provincial level, and also takes part in inter-school championships in swimming, athletics and cross-country.

There are a series of optional classes which include horse riding, ballet, judo, Spanish dancing, swimming, tennis, piano, violin (Suzuki method), musical initiation, and creativity workshops.

Admission. Pupils entering the school at the age of 7 or above are required to sit entrance tests in English and Mathematics and possibly other subjects, while younger candidates are screened by an Educational Psychologist. For those applying to the Sixth Form, admission depends on the results of the (I)GCSE examinations, or equivalent.

Fees. School fees range from Ptas 196.500 to Ptas 421.750 per term, excluding lunch and transport. Boarding fees are 311.000 Ptas additional per term.

Scholarships. The school offers scholarships to Sixth Formers selected on academic merit.

Further information may be obtained from The Admissions Officer at the School.

St George's British International School

Via Cassia La Storta 00123 Rome Italy
Tel: (0039) 063086001
Fax: (0039) 0630892490
e-mail: secretary@stgeorge.school.it
website: www.stgeorge.school.it

Visitor: HBM Ambassador to Italy.

Principal: **Brigid Gardner, MA**

Assistant Staff: 55 full-time and 4 part-time teachers, all fully qualified (95% British and high percentage from Oxford or Cambridge).

Enrolment: 580 pupils, ages 3 to 18; approximately 35 in each Primary and 45 in each Secondary year-group, evenly balanced boys and girls; 80 in the Sixth Form.

Founded in 1958, St. George's is a fully independent school owned by a non-profit-making Association and run as a limited company. Its purpose is to provide for the international community of Rome a British-system education, with a full academic programme, enriched by extra-curricular activities, good pastoral care and encouragement of self-discipline and independence. Children come from over 60 nationalities, the majority having had all their education in English, and a large number would expect to stay at St George's until completion of their school years.

The 15 years of schooling incorporate the work of British primary and secondary schools, leading to GCSE and International Baccalaureate in all standard subjects. Maximum class size is 25, with key subjects divided into smaller 'sets' in the secondary age-group, according to ability. Special care is taken over the teaching of English, whether mother-tongue or English-as-an-Additional-Language. The School organises many educational trips, to take advantage of its splendid location. Most children go on to university or other further education, the majority to the UK with an average of 8% to Oxbridge.

The school owns its 14-acre site on the north-west side of Rome, with 19 school buses serving all principal residential areas of the city. Facilities include a full range of standard and specialised classrooms, gymnasium, a library with first class internet facilities, 5 science laboratories, 4 ICT/technology rooms and 3 art/design studios. The music and drama departments are very active and sports facilities are considerable, with an athletics track, rugby, cricket and football fields and all-weather courts for tennis, volleyball and basketball.

The school year runs from early September to late June, Mondays to Fridays, with many activities in breaks and after school. Admission is dependent on interview, reports from previous school and a screening test. Entrance is possible at any time of the year. Fees are set in Euros and adjusted each year in the light of inflation.

2000 GCSE results. 94% pass rate grades A, B or C with 50% grade A.

2000 International Baccalaureate. 86% awarded diploma. 25% gained 36 points or more (pass 24 points). Average diploma score: 33 points. Average UCAS points per candidate: 23.4.

Headmasters' and Headmistresses' Conference

Additional Membership

The Constitution of the Headmasters' and Headmistresses' Conference provides that the membership shall consist mainly of Headmasters and Headmistresses of Independent and Assisted Places Schools. At the same time, it is held to be a strength of the Conference that its membership should include also a limited number of Headmasters of schools of Voluntary or Maintained status. There is therefore provision for the election of Headmasters of schools other than Independent or Assisted Places when it is felt that their contribution to education makes their membership appropriate.

Headmasters elected in this category are in every way full and equal members of the Headmasters' and Headmistresses' Conference; but their schools are not included in the section of the Independent Schools Year Book which gives detailed particulars of the Independent and Assisted Places Schools.

The following is a list of Headmasters in this special category of the membership:

J C McIntosh, obe The London Oratory School, Seagrave Rd, London SW6 1RX, 020 7385 0102.

P J Mawby, The Royal Grammar School, East Road, Lancaster, LA1 3EF, 01524 32109.

K Starling, The Judd School, Brook Street, Tonbridge, Kent TN9 2PN, 01732 770880.

C D Barnett, Bishop Wordsworth's School, The Close, Salisbury, Wilts SP1 2EB, 01722 333851

R Sommers, Gordano School, St. Mary's Road, Portishead, Bristol BS20 9QR, 01275 842606.

Dr E M Sidwell, Haberdashers' Aske's Hatcham College, Pepys Road, New Cross, London SE14 5SF, 020 7652 9500.

M Thompson, St. Ambrose College, Hale Barns, Altrincham, Cheshire WA15 0HE, 0161 980 2711.

C J Cleugh, St. Anselm's College, Manor Hill, Birkenhead, Wirral CH43 1UQ, 0151 652 1408.

J Waszek, St. Edward's College, North Drive, Sandfield Park, West Derby, Liverpool L12 1LF, 0151 281 1999.

A Jarvis, St. Olave's GS, Goddington Lane, Orpington, Kent BR6 9SH, 01689 820101.

M Brooker, King Edward VI Camp Hill School, Vicarage Road, King's Heath, Birmingham B14 7QJ, 0121 444 3188.

J Hughes, The English Martyrs School and Sixth Form College, Catcote Road, Hartlepool TS25 0AA, 01429 273790.

M Cooper, Latymer School, Haselbury Road, Edmonton, London N9 9TN, 020 8807 4037.

D Mulkerrin, Gordon's School, West End, Woking, Surrey GU24 9PT, 01276 858084.

Overseas Schools in Europe

The Headmasters of the following Schools are overseas members of the Headmasters' and Headmistresses' Conference.

Europe

Aiglon College, 1885 Chèsieres-Villars, Switzerland
R McDonald

British School of Brussels
Ms J Bray

British School in The Netherlands, The Hague
R T Rowell

British School of Paris
M Honour

Kings College, Madrid
C T Gill Leech

St Julian's School, Portugal
Acting Head

St George's English School, Rome
Mrs B Gardner

St Edward's College, Malta
W Dimech

The International School of Geneva
G R Walker

Headmasters' and Headmistresses' Conference: Overseas Schools other than in Europe

Africa
Falcon College, P. O. Esigodini, Zimbabwe
P N Todd
Diocesan College, Rondebosch, SA
Acting Head
Peterhouse, Marondera, Zimbabwe
M W Bawden
St Alban's College, Pretoria, 0040
G R R Nupen
St Andrew' College, Grahamstown, SA
Anthony R Clark
St George's College, Harare, Zimbabwe
B Tiernan
St Stithian's College, Randburg, SA
D B Wylde
Hilton College, Natal 3245, SA
M J Nicholson
Michaelhouse, Balgowan, Natal
R D Forde

Australia
Ballarat & Clarendon College, Victoria
D S Shepherd
Brighton Grammar School, Victoria
M S Irwin
Brisbane Boys' College, Brisbane
M Norris
Camberwell Grammar School, Canterbury, Victoria
C F Black
Canberra Grammar School, Redhill, ACT
A S Murray
Caulfield Grammar School, East St. Kilda, Victoria
S H Newton
Church of England Grammar School, Sydney, NSW
R A I Grant
Christ Church Grammar School, Claremont, W. Australia
Acting Head
Cranbrook School, Sydney, NSW
J Madin
The Geelong College, Geelong, Victoria
Dr P Turner
Geelong Grammar School, Corio, Victoria
N Sampson
Guildford Grammar School, Western Australia
K Walton
Haileybury College, Keysborough, Victoria
Dr R J Pargetter
Hale School, Wembley Downs, West Australia
R J Inverarity
Ivanhoe Grammar School, Victoria
R D Fraser
Kinross Wolaroi School, NSW
A E S Anderson
Knox Grammar School, Wahroonga, NSW
P J Crawley
Melbourne Grammar School
A P Sheahan
Mentone Grammar School, Mentone, Victoria
N Clark
Newington College, NSW
M H Smee
Pembrooke School, South Australia
M Lamb
St Peter's College, St. Peter's, S Australia
R L Burchnall
Scotch College, Adelaide, S Australia
K Webb
Scotch College, Hawthorn, Melbourne, Victoria
Dr F G Donaldson
Scotch College, Torrens Pk, S Australia
A G F Fisher
Scotch College, W Australia
Revd A P Syme
Scots College, Sydney NSW
Dr R L Iles
The Southport School, Southport, Queensland
B A Cook
Sydney Grammar School, NSW
Dr J T Vallance
Trinity Grammar School, Summer Hill, NSW
G M Cujes
Wesley College, Melbourne
D Loader
Westbourne Williamstown Grammar Schools
G G Ryan

Bermuda
Saltus Grammar School
N Kermode

Brunei
Jerudong International School, Bandar Seri Begawan
D Wilkinson

Canada
Brentwood College School, Vancouver Island
W T Ross
Hillfield Strathallan College, Hamilton, Ontario
W S Boyer
Ridley College, Ontario
R P Lane
St Andrew's College, Aurora, Ontario
E Staunton
Upper Canada College, Toronto
J D Blakey

Hong Kong
Island School
D J James
King George V School
D S Cocks

India
Assam Valley School, 784101 Assam
L Fox
Bishop Cotton School
K Mustafi
Lawrence School, Sanawar
Acting Head
The Scindia School, Gwalior
A N Dar
The Cathedral and John Connon School, Bombay
Mrs M Isaacs

Indonesia
The British International School, Jakarta
Principal

New Zealand
Christ's College, Christchurch, Canterbury
R A Zordan

King's College, Auckland
J Taylor
The Collegiate School, Wanganui
J R Hensman
Scots College, Wellington
I McKinnon

Malaysia
Kolej Tuanku Ja'afar
P D Briggs

Pakistan
Aitchison College, Lahore
Shamim Khan

Portugal
St Julian's School (See Europe)
F D Styan, O.B.E.

South America
Academia Britanica Cuscatleca, El Salvador
G Hobson
Markham College, Lima, Peru
W J Baker
St Andrew's Scots School, Buenos Aires, Argentina
Acting Head
St George's College, Quilmes, Argentina
N P O Green
St Paul's School, Sao Paulo, Brazil
R Benammar
The British Schools, Montevideo, Uruguay
C D T Smith

USA
St. Mark's, Massachusetts
A J de V Hill

ALPHABETICAL LIST OF SCHOOLS

HEADMASTERS' CONFERENCE (PART 1)

* denotes HMC schools reckoned to be co-educational

GEOGRAPHICAL LIST OF HMC SCHOOLS

Avon
Schools formerly listed under Avon will be found under Somerset

Bedfordshire
Bedford School
Bedford Modern School

Berkshire (see also Oxfordshire)
Bradfield College
Douai School
Eton College
Leighton Park School
Oratory School
Pangbourne College
Reading Blue Coat School
Wellington College

Buckinghamshire
Stowe School

Cambridgeshire
Kimbolton School
King's School, Ely
Leys School
Perse School
Wisbech Grammar School

Channel Islands
Elizabeth College, Guernsey
Victoria College, Jersey

Cheshire (see also Merseyside)
Cheadle Hume School
Grange School, Hartford
King's School, Chester
King's School, Macclesfield
Stockport Grammar School

Cleveland
Yarm School

Cornwall
Truro School

Cumbria
St Bees School
Sedbergh School

Derbyshire
Abbotsholme School
Mount St Mary's College
Repton School
Trent College

Devon
Blundell's School
Exeter School
Kelly College
Plymouth College
West Buckland School

Dorset
Bryanston School
Canford School
Sherborne School

Durham
Barnard Castle School
Durham School

Essex
Bancroft's School
Brentwood School
Chigwell School
Felsted School

* denotes Greater Manchester

Gloucestershire
Cheltenham College
Dean Close School
King's School, Gloucester
Rendcomb College
Wycliffe College

Hampshire
Bedales School
Churcher's College
King Edward VI School, Southampton
Lord Wandsworth College
Portsmouth Grammar School
Winchester College

Greater Manchester (see Lancashire)

Herefordshire and Worcestershire
Bromsgrove School
Hereford Cathedral School
King's School, Worcester
Malvern College
Royal Grammar School, Worcester

Hertfordshire
Aldenham School
Berkhamsted Collegiate School
Bishop's Stortford College
Haberdashers' Aske's School
Haileybury
St Albans School
St Columba's College, St Albans
St Edmund's College, Ware

Humberside (North)
Hymers College, Hull

Isle of Man
King William's College

Isle of Wight
Ryde School with Upper Chine

Kent
Kent College, Canterbury
King's School, Canterbury
King's School, Rochester
St Edmund's School, Canterbury
St Lawrence College, Ramsgate
Sevenoaks School
Sutton Valence School
Tonbridge School

Lancashire (see also Merseyside)
Arnold School, Blackpool
* Bolton School
* Bury Grammar School
* Chetham's School of Music
* Hulme Grammar School, Oldham
King Edward VII and Queen Mary School, Lytham St Annes
* Manchester Grammar School
Queen Elizabeth Grammar School, Blackburn
Rossall School
* St Bede's College
Stonyhurst College
* William Hulme's Grammar School, Manchester

***Greater Manchester (see Lancashire)**

Leicestershire
Leicester Grammar School
Loughborough Grammar School
Oakham School
Ratcliffe College
Uppingham School

Lincolnshire
Stamford School

London (see also Essex, Middlesex, Surrey)
Alleyn's School
Bancroft's School
City of London School
Colfe's School
Dulwich College
Eltham College
Emanuel School
Forest School
Harrow School
Highgate School
The John Lyon School
King's College School, Wimbledon
Kingston Grammar School
Latymer Upper School
Merchant Taylors' School
Mill Hill School
St Benedict's School, Ealing
St Dunstan's College
St Paul's School
University College School
Westminster School

Merseyside
Birkenhead School
Liverpool College
Merchant Taylors' School, Crosby
St Anselm's College
St Mary's College, Crosby

Middlesex
Hampton School
Harrow School
John Lyon School
Merchant Taylors' School

Norfolk
Gresham's School, Holt
Norwich School

Northamptonshire
Oundle School
Wellingborough School

Northumberland see Tyne and Wear

Nottinghamshire
Nottingham High School
Trent College
Worksop College

Oxfordshire
Abingdon School
Bloxham School
Magdalen College School
Radley College
St Edward's School
Shiplake College

Rutland see Leicestershire

Shropshire
Ellesmere College
Shrewsbury School
Wrekin College

Somerset
Bristol Grammar School
Clifton College
Colston's Collegiate School
Downside School
King's College, Taunton
King Edward's School, Bath
King's School, Bruton
Millfield
Kingswood School
Monkton Combe School
Prior Park College
Queen's College, Taunton
Queen Elizabeth's Hospital
Taunton School
Wellington School
Wells Cathedral School

Staffordshire (see also West Midlands)
Denstone College
Newcastle-under-Lyme School

Suffolk
Culford School
Framlingham College
Ipswich School
Royal Hospital School
Woodbridge School

Surrey
Caterham School
Charterhouse
City of London Freemen's School
Cranleigh School
Epsom College
Frensham Heights
King Edward's School, Witley
Kingston Grammar School
Reed's School, Cobham
Reigate Grammar School
Royal Grammar School, Guildford
St George's College, Weybridge
St John's School, Leatherhead
Trinity School, Croydon
Whitgift School

Sussex (East)
Brighton College
Eastbourne College

Sussex (West)
Ardingly College
Christ's Hospital
Hurstpierpoint College
Lancing College
Worth School

Tyne and Wear
Dame Allan's School
King's School, Tynemouth
Royal Grammar School, Newcastle-upon-Tyne

Warwickshire
Rugby School
Warwick School

West Midlands
Bablake School
King Edward's School, Birmingham
King Henry VIII School
Solihull School
Tettenhall College
Wolverhampton Grammar School

Wiltshire
Dauntsey's School
Marlborough College

Worcestershire (see *Hereford and Worcester*)

Yorkshire (North)
Ampleforth College
Ashville College
Bootham School
Giggleswick School
Pocklington School
St Peter's School, York

Yorkshire (South) (see also Derbyshire)
Birkdale School, Sheffield
Mount St Mary's College

Yorkshire (West)
Ackworth School
Batley Grammar School
Bradford Grammar School
Leeds Grammar School
Queen Elizabeth Grammar School, Wakefield
Silcoates School
Woodhouse Grove School

Ireland

Bangor Grammar Scthool
Belfast Royal Academy
Campbell College, Belfast
Clongowes Wood College, Co. Kildare
Coleraine Academical Institute
Methodist College, Belfast
Portora Royal School
Royal Belfast Academical Institution
St Columba's College, Dublin

Scotland

Daniel Stewart's and Melville College, Edinburgh
Dollar Academy
Dundee High School
Edinburgh Academy
Fettes College
George Heriot's School, Edinburgh
George Watson's College, Edinburgh
Glasgow Academy
Glasgow High School
Glenalmond College
Gordonstoun School
Hutchesons' Grammar School, Glasgow
Kelvinside Academy
Loretto School
Merchiston Castle School
Morrison's Academy, Crieff
Robert Gordon's College, Aberdeen
Strathallan School

Wales

Christ College, Brecon
Llandovery College
Monmouth School
Rougemont School
Rydal Penrhos School

Entrance Scholarship Announcements for 2001/2002

Abbotsholme School (see p 1). Scholarships of up to half fees are awarded annually to candidates aged between 10 and 13 intending to enter Forms One, Two or Three. Awards at each level are reserved for those showing outstanding ability in Art and Music. VI Form Scholarships are also available on the basis of GCSE Level results, school reports and interview. Bursaries may also be granted to members of the clergy or the teaching profession, or in cases of financial hardships.

All applications should be made to the *Headmaster*.

Abingdon School (see p 3). The following awards (all of which are means-tested) are available to candidates aged between 12 and 14 (except music and Sixth Form awards):

Foundation Awards: One Mercers' Company Scholarship: up to an entire tuition fee. One Duxbury Scholarship, reserved for boarding candidates, (may be awarded for music): up to half of the total tuition and boarding fee. A number of other awards and one Sixth Form Scholarship: up to half the tuition fee.

One Art & Design and up to three Music Scholarships: up to half the tuition fee. A number of Music Exhibitions.

All awards entitle the holder to a nominal fee remission of £200 per annum plus fee remission dependent on financial need. Tenure of awards is conditional upon continued good work and behaviour, and holders of music and design scholarships, in particular, are expected to play prominent parts in their respective specialities.

Arkwright Scholarship: The school subscribes to the scheme run by the Combined Trusts Scholarship Trust, under which one Design and Technology scholarship, up to the entire tuition fee subject to parental need, can be available for an entrant to the Sixth Form.

Further details from the Headmaster.

Ackworth School (see p 5). Academic Scholarships worth up to 50% of the boarding or day fee are awarded annually. At ages 11+, 12+ and 13+ the awards are made on the basis of performance at the Entrance Tests and a subsequent interview.

At Sixth Form level an offer of a Scholarship is made to applicants with outstanding prospects at GCSE. This offer is confirmed once the results are published and subsequent to an interview with the *Headmaster*.

Bursaries are also available for Members or Attenders of the Society of Friends and in other cases where need can be shown.

Aldenham School, Elstree, Herts (see p 6). Scholarships and Exhibitions are awarded to boys and girls who have demonstrated outstanding achievement and who have the potential to make a special contribution to the School. There are also opportunities for Music, Art, Sport and Design Technology. This will usually be in the academic field. Bursaries are available to help boys and girls who will benefit from education at Aldenham but whose parents would not otherwise be able to afford the full fees. A Scholarship automatically carries a 15% discount of fees and an Exhibition a discount of 7½%. The parents of Scholars and Exhibitioners may be eligible for a Bursary which is subject to a simple means test and to the availability of funds. They will normally have first call on Bursary funds. Bursaries vary from 1/6 to 2/3 of fees. At 11, Academic Scholarships are awarded by means of testing and interview; at 13 by competitive examination taken as an alternative to Common Entrance; at 16 by GCSE results and interview.

Alleyn's School (see p 7). The following scholarships are offered annually for open competition in the entrance examination for fee payers held each year in February, simultaneously for entrance at 11 and 13.

(1) At least 12 Major scholarships of half the full fee, the majority awarded at age 11, but one at least awarded at 13. A Music Scholarship will also be awarded and a number of Bursaries are available.

Candidates should be under the ages of 12 and 14 respectively on 1 September.

(2) Sixth Form Scholarships and Bursaries are available for suitable applicants.

Further particulars from the Headmaster, to whom application forms should be sent by 1 January.

Ampleforth College (see p 10). Scholarships are awarded annually on the result of examinations and interviews held at Ampleforth.

First Year entry: up to six Major Academic Scholarships from a maximum of half fees, and up to eight Minor Scholarships are offered. Two Major Music Scholarships are also offered. All candidates should have reached their 12th birthday and must not have passed their 14th birthday on 1st September following the Scholarship examination. In assessing the candidates account is taken of their age. The examination is normally held in the second week of May.

VIth Form entry: Scholarships are awarded to boys of outstanding academic ability. The examination and interviews are normally held in January.

All Scholarships are awarded on the basis of academic excellence. Award winners who need further help are invited to apply for bursaries.

For further details apply to the *Admissions Office*.

Ardingly College (see p 11). A number of Scholarships and Exhibitions are offered for annual competition. They include Academic, Art, CDT, Drama, Music and Sports Awards and Ashdown Awards for all-rounders for those entering at both 13+ and 16+. The Junior School offers Academic, Art, Music and Sports Awards at 11+ with Academic and Music Awards for the under-11s. Some Junior School awards are tenable in the Senior School and others are for the Junior School years only. Along with other HMC schools, the maximum value of a scholarship is 50% of the basic fees p.a. but all may be supplemented by a means-tested bursary if need can be shown.

Ardingly is one of the selected schools for Barclays Bank Educational Awards.

A limited number of bursaries (value up to 50% of basic fees p.a.) are available for the Children of the Clergy.

Please address all enquiries about admissions, scholarships and bursaries to either Junior or Senior Schools to the Registrar (tel. 01444 892577/fax 01444 892266/e-mail registrar@ardingly.com)

Arnold School (see p 13). Several Scholarships (including those for Music) for entry at 11 and in the Sixth Form. Further particulars from the *Headmaster*. (01253 346391)

Ashville College (see p 15). Eight Scholarships worth up to half the tuition fee are awarded annually on the results of the Entrance Examination. Candidates must be under the age of 12 on 31st August of that year.

Candidates who do particularly well in the Common Entrance examination at 13 years can also be considered for the award of a Scholarship.

Apply to the *Headmaster, Ashville College, Harrogate, N. Yorkshire*.

Bancroft's School (see p 18). The School awards up to twelve Scholarships worth 50% of the fees, and up to six Bancroft's Assisted Places, which are means tested, at age 11 as a result of its Entrance Examination in January. Two of the Scholarships may be Music Scholarships. There are five Scholarships worth 50% of the fees for Sixth Form entrants.

Barnard Castle School (see p 21). Scholarships are awarded on the results of the Entrance Examinations held in March, giving partial exemptions from the payment of school fees. The Governors may provide maintenance allowances for boys who need financial assistance.

Particulars from the *School Secretary.*

Bedales School (see p 24). Separate from the Music Scholarships, are general Academic Scholarships at 13+ and 16+, Drama, Art and Design Scholarships at 16+ (up to half the value of fees). For full details of the Scholarships and timing of assessment, please apply to the Registrar.

Bedford Modern School (see p 25). Harpur Scholarships are offered at age 11 and 13, giving assistance on an income basis, and are open to Day Boys.

Bedford School (see p 26).

(1) Up to nine scholarships at 13+ offering remission of tuition and boarding fees ranging from 50% to one quarter. All except one of these awards are offered annually and one is awarded on the basis of all-round qualities rather than purely academic performance.

(2) Up to six minor awards and a number of Common Entrance exhibitions ranging in value from £900 p.a. to £500 p.a. awarded annually at 13+.

(3) One scholarship for a new entrant to the Sixth Form of up to one-third of tuition and boarding fees, awarded in alternate years. Certain of the awards available at 13+ are also available to new entrants to the Sixth Form.

(4) An Organ Scholarship for a boy entering the School at 16+ who has passed the Associated Board Grade 8 Organ Examination, and/or has reached diploma standard. This award offers remission of up to half tuition and boarding fees.

(5) A number of major and minor Music scholarships, with remission of up to one half tuition and boarding fees, plus free musical tuition. In addition, up to three Music exhibitions offering free musical tuition.

(6) One Major scholarship for Art, Drama or Technology of up to one third of tuition and boarding fees, and two exhibitions of £500 p.a.

(7) All-round awards offering remission of up to 25% of tuition and boarding fees for boys who expect to achieve at least 60% in CE and who are notably talented at sport, music or drama.

(8) Two major scholarships are available for candidates entering the Preparatory School at age 11, with fee-remissions of up to one half of tuition and boarding fees. Two minor scholarships are available with fee-remission of up to 25% of tuition and boarding fees. Exhibitions of £500 p.a. are also available. These are tenable in the Preparatory School only.

For full particulars, apply to *the Registrar, Tel. Bedford (01234) 362200.*

Leaving awards may be made from the Elger Bequest to assist boys to go to Cambridge and from other benefactions to go to Oxford and other universities.

Berkhamsted Collegiate School (see p 30). Entrance scholarships are awarded thus:

The Marshall Scholarship at 11+ for £1,000 p.a. for boys on entry to Y7.

The Major School Scholarship at 13+ for up to half tuition fees for boys on entry to Y9.

The Edward Penny Scholarships at 13+ for £1,000 p.a. each, on entry to Y9 from a maintained school, with preference given to a candidate from Berkhamsted.

The Methuen Scholarship at 13+ for £1,000 p.a. on entry to Y9 (with preference given to an intending boarder).

The Benson-Cooke Scholarship at 13+ for £500 p.a. for boys on entry to Y9 (with preference given to sons of medical doctors and army officers).

The Figg Sixth Form Scholarship at 16+ for £750 p.a. on entry to the Sixth Form (with preference given to boys joining the Sixth Form from another school). The Award will be determined by achievement at GCSE.

More information about Scholarships and Bursaries may be obtained on application to: *The Deputy Principal's Secretary, Berkhamsted Collegiate School, Castle Street, Berkhamsted, Herts HP4 2BB.*

Bishop's Stortford College (see p 35). Scholarships and Examinations are awarded at three levels VIth Form and under 14 in the Senior School, under 12 in the Junior School. The main awards are (1) Scholarships up to a maximum of full fees, (2) other Scholarships and Exhibitions, maximum value £1,000 (3) Music Awards of similar values. There are special Awards for pupils of Free Church Ministers and a Lloyd's Cuthbert Heath Centenary Bursary for candidates needing financial asssistance.

Bloxham School (see p 38). Scholarships and exhibitions are awarded on the basis of a competitive examination. The value of these awards is up to 50% of fees according to academic merit, but they may be augmented up to 100% of fees, either boarding or day, according to the financial needs of parents.

Among the awards offered are Roger Raymond Scholarships and John Schuster Scholarships (reserved in the first instance for Sons of Clergy or of members of the teaching profession). Boarding exhibitions may be awarded to sons of members of the HM Forces on the grounds of academic and/or all-round merit and promise.

Awards are made for all-round academic performance but subject Scholarships may be awarded for promising performances in a particular subject area. There are Art and Design Awards and Music Awards with free instrumental tuition. The auditions for the latter will be held in February/ March 1999.

Chapel Centenary Awards of up to £3000 per year may be awarded to good candidates of less than Exhibition standard on the basis of academic, musical or artistic performance or all-round merit and promise.

Day-boarders are eligible for all awards at equivalent value related to day-boarder fees. Candidates should preferably be under 14 of September 1st. An age allowance is made to young candidates.

Sir Lawrence Robson Scholarships or Exhibitions are awarded each year to Sixth Form entrants. The value of these will be up to 50% of fees (up to 100% in cases of financial need). Candidates must be under 17 on September 1st. The examination will be held at the beginning of February.

Further details may be obtained from the *Headmaster.*

Full details may be obtained from the Bursar, *Bloxham School, Banbury, Oxon OX15 4PE*

Blundell's School, Tiverton (see p 39).

(1) Open awards. About ten awards of up to 100% of tuition fees.

(2) Foundation awards. Up to four awards covering tuition fees. Preference given to day boys resident in the Ancient Borough of Tiverton for at least three years.

(3) Music and Art awards. Several awards of up to 100% of tuition fees, based on Common Entrance or Scholarship examinations and practical demonstrations of ability.

Open, Music and Art awards may be supplemented by the Head Master from funds at his disposal.

Two military bursaries of 25% of tuition fees, are awarded each year. Blundell's participates in the IAPS and Sons of School Master's schemes; and may be able to offer bursaries to sons and daughters of clergy.

Full details may be obtained from the *Head Master, Blundell's School, Tiverton, Devon EX16 4DN.* Tel: 01884-252543.

Bootham School, York (see p 42). John Bright Boarding Scholarships: up to four awards can be made of value up to 50% of full fees. (A Bursary supplement can be made and is means-tested). Two scholarships are available at 11+, two at 13+ for boys and girls.

Major and Minor Scholarships of up to half fees are available at 11, 13 and for Sixth Form entry.

Music and Art Scholarships of up to 50% fees are awarded at 11+, 13+, 16+.

Other awards can be made for entrance candidates at the Headmaster's discretion.

All awards are based on an evaluation of achievement and potential in candidates and are open equally to boys and girls.

Scholarship examinations and interviews are held in February (11+), March (16+) and May (13+).

A number of bursary awards is also made annually. Full details of all the above from the *Headmaster*.

Bradfield College, Berks (see p 44). Awards will be made annually on the results of a competitive examination held at Bradfield each year in the Lent Term on the following basis: Up to 15 Scholarships of between 10% and 50% of full fees.

Further Honorary Awards conferring the status and privileges of a scholar.

The value of an award may be increased where need is shown. Candidates must be under the age of 14 on 1 September. Further information and entrance forms can be obtained on application to the *Head Master, Bradfield College, Reading, Berkshire RG7 6AR*.

Brentwood School (see p 47). On the Entrance Examination at 11: 6 Foundation Scholarships are awarded: 2 Full; 1 of £3,489 p.a; 3 of £1,983 p.a. 3 Boarding Scholarships of £1,512 p.a. at 11 or 13 on the Common Entrance Examination; 3 Music Scholarships at £1,446 p.a. 1 Art Scholarship of £1,140 p.a. at 16 and 1 Toleman Scholarship at 16. 2 Music Scholarships at £1,140 and 2 Foundation Scholarships of £1,889 for girls at 11. Further Details from the *Headmaster*.

Brighton College (see p 48). The following awards are offered annually:

TWELVE academic scholarships to pupils entering the College at age 13 (Candidates should be under 14 on June 1st of the year of entry). Entries must be in by May 1st.

Continuation Scholarships: Up to four Continuation Scholarships are offered each year to pupils aged 11+ at certain Preparatory Schools. These are worth 20% of fees for two years at the Prep. School and guarantee an award of 20% of fees at Brighton College. They *may* be matched by an award of a similar amount from the Prep. School.

One or two *Gill Memorial Scholarships* for the sons of Regular Army Officers (serving or retired) up to a maximum of £1,000 p.a.

A number of *Art and Music Scholarships* are available. These can also be awarded to pupils entering the Sixth Form.

Lloyd's Cuthbert Heath Memorial Bursary worth up to £1,000 p.a. awarded to a pupil wishing to enter the College at 13 who has a positive contribution to make to the life of the College, and whose parents would otherwise be unable to afford the fees.

A *Cooper Rawson Bursary* for sons of Clergy. An award of up to £1000 p.a. can be considered by the Committee which meets in June each year.

Up to four *Sixth Form entry Scholarships*. Candidates to take papers in two A-level subjects plus general paper. Entries by November 1st.

Further particulars can be obtained from *The Headmaster, Brighton College, Eastern Road, Brighton BN2 2AL*.

Latest School fees: Full boarders £11,385 p.a. Weekly boarders £10,185 p.a. Day pupils £7,485 p.a.

Bristol Grammar School (see p 51). The Upper School offers eight academic scholarships to entrants at 11+. These scholarships are quite separate from the Schools assisted places. The scholarships are currently valued at £100 per term, subject to regular review. They are awarded on academic merit and are irrespective of parental means.

Bromsgrove School, Worcestershire (see p 53). The following awards are made on the results of open examinations held at the School in January. Major Scholarships (full tuition fees) which will be awarded at 13+; a number of Scholarships and Exhibitions to the value of half the tuition and boarding fees awarded at 11+ and 13+; a significant number of bursaries for pupils of academic, athletic, musical or all-round ability awarded at 11+ and 13+; a Music Scholarships (half tuition fees and free tuition in two musical instruments) and a number of Music Exhibitions up to the value of half tuition fees awarded at 13+. Sixth Form Scholarships, Bursaries and Exhibitions are also available up to the value of sixty percent of the tuition and boarding fees. Full particulars from the Headmaster, Bromsgrove School, Worcestershire.

Bryanston School, Blandford (see p 55).

(a) Eight Academic, one Art, one Technology, four Music and up to four Sport Scholarships are available annually for entry at 13+. In addition, there are *Richard Hunter All-rounder* awards open to competition for the same range of pupils.

(b) Two Academic and two Music Scholarships, as well as (usually) two Udall Awards for Sport, are awarded for entry to the Sixth Form.

Academic, Music and Sport Scholarships are worth up to 50% of boarding fees. Art and Technology Scholarships and *Richard Hunter* Awards are worth up to 33% of boarding fees. All scholarships may be supplemented by means-tested bursaries.

Campbell College, Belfast (see p 58). The following open scholarships are offered for competition in May or June each year to boys under 14 years of age on the 1st June: *Boarders:* 1 open scholarship of up to 50% boarding fees and 1 of up to 25% boarding fees. *Dayboys:* 2 open scholarships of up to 100% tuition fees (if receiving the L.E.A. grant of £1,550). *Music:* 1 scholarship of up to £200 pa (or *pro rata* in the case of a day boy) with free tuition in Music and 2 Exhibitions of £50 with free tuition in Music. Apply to the *Headmaster, Campbell College, Belfast.*

Canford School, Wimborne (see p 60). *Scholarships.* It is Canford's policy to encourage excellence and to enable pupils to come to the school who, without the assistance of a scholarship, would not be able to do so. In accordance with the agreement of the majority of HMC schools, Canford limits the value of any one scholarship to 50% of the fees. All Canford's scholarships are indexed as a percentage of the fees so that their relative value remains constant throughout the scholar's school career.

Open Scholarships: 13+: Scholarship examinations are held in February/March and awards are made as follows: a number of academic scholarships ranging from 50% to 10% of the fees; a number of music scholarships ranging from 50% to 10% of the fees; one Royal Naval scholarship of 20% to the son/daughter of a serving Naval Officer; one or two art scholarships worth in total 20%; a number of Assyrian scholarships, for a broad contribution of high quality to school life and a sound academic standard, ranging from 40% to 10%; one Canning Memorial Bursary of £100 p.a. for sons/daughters of Old Canfordians. Candidates must be under 14 on 1st September in the year of their examination. All 13+ scholarships are tenable with effect from the September of the year in which they are awarded.

Open Scholarships: 16+: The School offers a number of academic and music scholarships each year to entrants at sixth form level. Each scholarship may be worth up to 50% of the fees. The examination is held in the November prior to entry.

Bursaries: Bursaries for the sons/daughters of clergymen of the Church of England are available; these are awarded on interview and record, and candidates must pass the June Common Entrance Examination. Bursaries are also sometimes available from the School where the financial need of the parents has been established.

Further details about any awards can be obtained from *The Registrar*.

Caterham School (see p 62). Fifteen *Academic Scholarships* of up to half the tuition fee are available for boys and girls joining the Preparatory School at 10 and the Senior School at 11, 13 and 16. Internal candidates may apply for scholarships at 10 and 16. At 10 and 11 the award is based on the School's own entrance examination and at 13 on the Common Entrance Examination.

Governors Boarding Scholarships of up to 75% of the boarding fee are available. Assisted Places Scheme boarding candidates may also apply for this award.

Eynon Scholarships are reserved for the sons and daughters of Old Caterhamians from 11+. The value of these scholarships are up to half the tuition fee and not less than £300.

Foundation Bursaries are available to the sons and daughters of Ministers of the United Reformed and Congregational Churches. Bursary awards are also available for Ministers of some other denominations.

For further particulars apply to *The Headmaster, Caterham School, Caterham, CR3 6YA.*

Charterhouse (see p 64).

For entry at 13+

At least 12 Foundation Scholarships and 5 Exhibitions are offered annually. Of the Scholarships 6 are major Foundation Scholarships of value HALF FEES. The examination is held in May.

In addition a Benn Scholarship is offered for proficiency in Classics.

A Peter Attenborough Scholarship is awarded annually to a candidate who demonstrates all-round general competence and distinction.

The Sir William Blackstone Award is offered to sons of lawyers – for details see Educational Awards section.

For entry into the Sixth Form

The following awards are offered annually:

Academic Four Peter Newton Scholarships for those who are financially unable to come to the school without a scholarship.

Three Sir Robert Birley Scholarships – up to one-third of the fees.

A number of Exhibitions.

In addition Music and Art Scholarships are offered (see relevant sections).

All Scholarships may be increased to the value of the FULL SCHOOL FEE in cases of proven financial need.

For full details apply to the *Admissions Secretary, Charterhouse, Godalming GU7 2DX.*

Cheadle Hulme School (see p 66). (Day and Boarding Co-Ed).

One or more Niel Pearson or School Scholarships or either 50% or 25% of tuition fees offered to candidates for entry into the VI Form who show outstanding promise in Music, Drama or the Arts.

Particulars may be obtained from *the Registrar.*

Cheltenham College (see p 67). The College offers academic awards to boys and girls entering at 13+ and into the Sixth Form: awards may reach 50% of the current fees. Awards are similarly offered to boys and girls demonstrating excellence in Sport, in Leadership and in All-round Potential. Awards are also made for Art, Design Technology and Electronics.

Chigwell School (see p 70). Sixth Form entrance interviews are held throughout the year, principally in November and January and there are generous Academic, Art and Music Scholarships available. Music Scholarships are also offered from 11 years of age. A competitive examination for Academic Scholarships is held each year during the Lent term for pupils of 7, 11 and 13. Up to three Scholarships are offered at 7 years of age, up to twelve Scholarships are offered at 11 years of age and two Scholarships at 13 years of age.

Further details from the Headmaster, Chigwell School, High Road, Chigwell, Essex IG7 6QF.

Christ College, Brecon (see p 72). Up to ten academic scholarships and exhibitions, tenable at 11+, 13+ or 16+, and ranging in value from 10 to 50% of the fees, are offered annually. In addition, three scholarships are awarded each year to those entering the Sixth Form, each worth £1500 a year: A *Lord Brecon*, a *Roydon Griffiths* and a *G John Herdman* Scholarship. There is also one Frederick A Pike Scholarship for entry to the Sixth Form, preference being given to a candidate born or living in Cardiganshire. Two Sixth Form sports awards and one or more *WAG Fryer* all-rounder (13+) awards are offered each year. 10% bursaries are available for sons and daughters of personnel serving in the Armed Forces. There is a remission of 25% of the fees for the sons and daughters of Clergy. Music Scholarships are also available. The value of any award may be augmented in case of need. Scholarship examinations are held at Christ College in early February (11+) and late February/early March (13+). Age limits: seniors under 14 and juniors under 12 on 1st September in the year of examination. Further details from *The Headmaster, Christ College, Brecon LD3 8AG.*

City of London Freemen's School, Ashtead (see p 76). Corporation Entrance Scholarships are offered as follows:

At 8+: four awards annually to the value of one third tuition fees on the basis of 8+ Entrance examinations.

At 13+: two awards at one third tuition fees annually on the basis of 13+ Scholarship examinations.

For Sixth Form entry: at least ten awards annually to the value of two thirds tuition fees or more awards of lesser value pro rata on the basis of Sixth Form Entrance Scholarship papers.

City of London School (see p 77). Six Corporation Scholarships, to the value of up to half the cost of school fees at any time, are awarded annually at the 11+ stage either from primary or preparatory schools. Four Corporation Scholarships, of the same value, are awarded annually to boys under 14 on 1 September. The scholarship examinations are held in early February. At least 1 scholarship a year is a Music Scholarship. Two Exhibitions, to the value of one third the cost of school fees at any time may be awarded in place of any one Scholarship.

Clifton College (see p 78). Entrance Scholarships. Candidates must be under 14 on 1 September. Boys and girls who are already in the School may compete. At least ten awards may be made. In accordance with guidelines laid down by the Headmaster's Conference, the maximum scholarship will not exceed 50% of the fees, though awards will be augmented by a Bursary if need is shown.

There are special awards available for the sons and daughters of Old Cliftonians for boys and girls who are resident in or at school in Scotland, Ireland, Wales, Lancashire and Cheshire (Wall-Marston) and for the son or daughter of a journalist or other person engaged in the newspaper industry in the counties of Avon, Gloucestershire, Somerset, Wiltshire or Dorset (Bristol Evening Post).

Particulars of the conditions of examination from *The Headmaster, Clifton College, Bristol BS8 3JH*

Scholarships are also awarded to boys and girls to enter the VIth Form.

Cranleigh School (see p 85). Cranleigh offers the following Awards annually for entrance at age 13; candidates must be over 12 and under 14 on 1 September. *Academic and Art Awards* (examination in February): four Scholarships of half fees and eight other Scholarships of up to one-quarter fees which may include one for special ability in Mathematics, and Closed Awards for the sons of Regular Commissioned Officers on the active list of the Royal Navy, Army or Royal Air Force, sons of Clergy of the Church of England and sons of members of the public services. One of the one-quarter fee Scholarships may be reserved as an Art Scholarship if a suitable candidate comes forward. Closed Awards are termed Exhibitions. *Music Awards* (examination in February): one or two Scholarships of half fees and two Scholarships of up to one-quarter fees depending on the merit of candidates. Music Scholarships include free musical tuition. Cranleigh also offers up to six *Academic* and two *Music* Scholarships of one-quarter fees to boys and girls entering at *Sixth Form* level (examination in November).

Further details and closing dates may be obtained from the *Admissions Secretary, Cranleigh School, Cranleigh, Surrey GU6 8QQ, telephone (01483) 273997.*

Culford School (see p 88). Culford School has its own Assisted Places Scheme (CAPS) with means tested scholarships at 8+, 13+ and Sixth Form.

Scholarships valued at up to 50% of the tuition fees are awarded according to merit, following examinations for 8+ and 13+ held in March and for 16+ held in December. Jubilee Scholarships at 11+ and 13+ are offered as closed awards to schools participating in the Jubilee Scholarship scheme.

For further details apply to *The Registrar, Culford School, Bury St. Edmunds, Suffolk IP28 6TX.* Tel: 01284 729308. Fax: 01284 728631.

Dauntsey's School (see p 92). Scholarships and Exhibitions are awarded on examinations held in November (Year 12), January (Year 7) and February (Year 9) for the following September.

Full particulars are available from the *Academic Registrar* at the School.

Dean Close School, Cheltenham (see p 94). A competitive examination is held annually at the school in February/March. All awards are open to both boys and girls. Candidates must be under 14 on 1 September in the year of the examination. The following Scholarships are on offer:

Governors' Open Scholarships.

Fergus McNeile Scholarships for children of Clergy and Missionaries.

W A M Edwards Science Scholarships for VIth Formers to read Science.

Daisy Cross Arts Scholarships for VIth Formers to read Arts subjects.

Scholarships and Bursaries for the children of Schoolmasters and those serving in H.M. Forces.

Awards are also offered at 11 to children entering from the maintained sector by way of the Junior School.

Denstone College (see p 96). A generous range of Academic, Music, Art and CDT Scholarships are available. Clerical Bursaries are available for the sons and daughters of Clergy. Further particulars about these Awards may be obtained from *The Headmaster, Denstone College, Denstone, Staffordshire, ST14 5HN.*

Downside School (see p 99). Downside makes the following awards at 13+:

One Major Scholarship of half fees
Two Minor Scholarships worth one-third fees
Several Exhibitions
One Mathematics Scholarship
One Classics Scholarship
One Art Scholarship
One or more Music Scholarships or Exhibitions
Several Choral Exhibitions.

In addition to the above-mentioned scholarships, an award, known as the Denis Agius Award, may be made to a candidate who, though not quite strong enough to win an academic award outright, shows outstanding all-round ability.

Academic awards are available for entry into St Oliver's on the basis of examinations held in late February/early March.

6th Form Scholarships up to half fees are awarded on the basis of examinations in late January.

The number and size of awards in any particular year is at the discretion of the Head Master. In addition, the Trustees reserve the right to increase, reduce, combine or divide any award(s) at their absolute discretion. The tenure of Scholarships awarded on entry to St Oliver's is usually for the last two years in St Oliver's; awards at 13+, or into the Sixth Form, are intended to be for the duration of a holder's education at Downside.

Dulwich College (see p 100). A number of Scholarships will be awarded on the results of the combined Entrance and Scholarship Examination to be held in the Lent Term. These Scholarships are available for competition for all new boys entering the College between the ages of 10 and 14 years on 1 September. Two Scholarships will be instrumental music scholarships and one for excellence in art. One boarding bursary of half the boarding fee (at present £6,318 pa) will be offered to a successful Scholarship candidate.

These scholarships will be for either half or one third the tuition fee, which is currently £6,318 pa. In cases of special need, the value of the Scholarship can be increased.

In addition one or two C D Broad Scholarships of £600 pa, the Dr H M Fisher Scholarship of £600 pa, the Alleyn Club Scholarship of £450 pa and a number of Bursaries can be awarded.

Each year the Governors also award some Scholarships to boys already in the School entering the First Form, at the age of eleven.

For post-GCSE entrants a number of Bursaries are available including the Colonel W E Grey Bursary, the Stephen Howard Bursary, The Peter B Mudge and Margaret E Mudge Bursary and the Roger Looker Bursary. Assessment for these Bursaries and for the Harry Carr Gibbs and Pewterers' Scholarship will be on the basis of academic potential and of financial need.

All Scholarships are available for day boys, boarders and weekly boarders and will be continued until the boy leaves the College, subject to satisfactory progress and conduct. Candidates should be registered for the Entrance and Scholarship Examination by 31 December.

Further particulars from *The Master, Dulwich College, London SE21 7LD.*

Durham School (see p 104). A generous range of Academic, Music, Design & Technology and Art Scholarships are available. Up to six King's Scholarships are awarded to pupils aged 13 to a possible maximum value of 50% fees for a boarder or a day pupil, which can be increased in case of need, while the Burkitt Scholarships are availabe for those seeking entry to the Sixth Form. Small Exhibitions are available to pupils aged 11. Clerical Bursaries are available for the sons of Clergy.

Further particulars about these Awards may be obtained from the Headmaster, Durham School, Durham DH1 4SZ.

Eastbourne College (see p 105). Entrance Scholarships and Exhibitions are offered up to 50% of the fees if candidates of sufficient merit present themselves.

Candidates must be under 14 on 1st September.

Entry forms for scholarships and exhibitions can be obtained from: The *Headmaster, The College, Eastbourne, E Sussex BN21 4JX.*

The Edinburgh Academy (see p 107). A number of Scholarships are offered for award to candidates of very high ability. These will include four A L F Smith Scholarships, of half the Tuition Fees (plus a quarter of the Boarding Fee where relevant), offered for academic merit, or for music or art, to boys not already attending the Academy. They can be increased to three-quarter fees at need. One is reserved for candidates from State Schools (Scottish Primary 7 or equivalent). The Examination is held about the end of February and candidates must be under 14, and should normally be over 11½, on 1 March. Further details from *The Registrar, The Edinburgh Academy, Edinburgh, EH3 5BL.*

Elizabeth College, Guernsey, CI (see p 109). One or more Boarding Scholarships may be awarded annually by the Gibson Fleming Scholarship Trust. There is no upper limit to the value of these Scholarships which will be adjusted to the need of the parent. The trustees take the general personal qualities of candidates into account as well as their academic performance. The full details may be obtained from the *Principal*.

Ellesmere College, Shropshire (see p 111. Five Scholarships (2 of not more than 50% fees pa, and 3 of not more than 25% of fees, 2 Musical Scholarships of not more than 50% fees, several choral exhibitions of value up to 25% of fees, and one art exhibition of up to 25% of fees pa). In cases of need, all these awards may be supplemented further. Regional and Foundation Awards are also available.

Application forms are obtainable from the *Head Master*.

Eltham College (see p 112). Up to ten entrance scholarships awarded on the entrance examination for boys of 11: annual value not less than one third of tuition fee and augmented according to income: tenable for 7 years.

A number of Sixth Form scholarships, usually 10, tenable for 2 years to value of half tuition fees.

Further details from the *Headmaster*.

Epsom College (see p 115). Candidates may compete for one or more of the following types of Award: Academic Scholarships, Music Scholarships, Art Scholarships, All-Rounder Scholarships, and Sports Scholarships. There are generally about 30 Awards. The value of a Scholarship may be up to 50% of the initial fees. Some Awards are open only to the sons and daughters of Doctors. Candidates must be under 14 on 1st September or entering the Sixth Form.

Eton College (see p 117). The examination for King's Scholarships is held at Eton in May. Candidates need to be registered only a few weeks before. Candidates must be under 14 (and over 12) on 1 September.

Subjects of Examination: All candidates take the following four papers: English, Mathematics A, General I (general questions requiring thought rather than knowledge) and Science. Each must also offer *THREE or more* of the following, their choice to include at least *one language* – French (written, aural, oral), Latin, Greek, Mathematics B, History and Geography, General II (Literature, the Arts, moral and religious issues, etc.)

In assessing the candidates the examiners may take age into account.

A King's Scholarship is normally tenable for five years.

The value of the Scholarship varies according to the Scholar's financial need, but is never less than half the full fee. Full particulars and Entry forms may be obtained from *The Registrar, Eton College, Windsor, Berkshire, SL4 6DB.*

Exeter School (see p 119). Academic Scholarships are offered annually to pupils who excel in the School's entrance tests and/or scholarship examination. Music and Art Scholarships are awarded annually following audition/assessment and are conditional on applicants achieving the School's academic requirements for entry. A number of Governor's Awards may be offered to pupils whose parents are unable to afford the full School fees and who show academic potential and a talent perceived to be of benefit to the School.

At age 7 – one Academic Scholarship offering a discount of up to 15% off tuition fees throughout the Preparatory School.

At age 11 – up to two Academic Scholarships offering a discount of 10-50% off tuition fees. Up to three Academic Exhibitions offering up to 10% off tuition fees.

At age 12 – up to two Academic Scholarships offering a discount of 10-50% off tuition fees. Up to two Academic Exhibitions offering up to 10% off tuition fees.

At age 13 – one Academic Scholarship offering a discount of 10-50% off tuition fees. Up to three Academic Exhibitions offering up to 10% off tuition fees.

Felsted School (see p 121). Academic Entrance Scholarships are awarded annually varying in fixed value up to 50% of the fees. Music, Art and CDT Scholarships are awarded up to the value of 50% of the fees. Bursaries are available to increase the awards in case of need up to 100% of the fees in certain cases. Entrance Scholarship candidates must be under 14 on 1st September following the examination which is held in May. Scholarships are also awarded at 11+ at Felsted Preparatory School and these may be carried through to the Senior School. Academic Sixth Form Entrance Scholarships are available (one at 50% and two 25%) as well as Art, Music and CDT Scholarships up to the value of 50%. The examinations for the Sixth Form Scholarships take place each November and February. Arkwright Foundation Scholarships are also available to talented students in Design at 16+. Foundation awards which recognise all round ability or specific ability in one area are available on entry at 11, 13 and 16 years old. Full particulars from the *Headmaster, Felsted School, Dunmow, Essex.*

Fettes College (see p 123). Scholarships up to the value of 50% of the fees are available for candidates age 10–13 and also for entry to the Sixth Form. The Examinations for candidates aged 10–13 is held in February/March and those for Sixth Form entrants in November.

Foundations Awards and Bursaries are available to those candidates whose parents cannot meet the full value of the fees. The value of these awards depends upon parents' financial means and they can cover the entire boarding fees. These awards are made not only on the basis of academic standard but also on the ability and enthusiasm of the candidates to contribute strongly to the sporting and cultural activities of the School.

Music Scholarships of up to the value of 50% of the fees are available.

Bursaries provide 12.5% reduction in fees for children of members of H M Forces.

Preparatory School Continuation Scholarships are available to boys and girls at Preparatory Schools aged under 12 on 1st September.

One scholarship is available annually for sons or daughters of regular officers in H M Forces.

Bursaries are available which automatically provide a 12.5% reduction in the fees for children of members of H M Forces.

Special consideration is given to children of Clergy.

Full details of all awards are available from *The Headmaster, Fettes College, Edinburgh EH4 1QX.*

Forest School (see p 125). A Scholarship examination is held at the School in January for the awarding of up to 12 Scholarships or Bursaries to cover full fees. Candidates must be under 12 on 1st September each year. There is further provision for Sixth Form, Music, Art, Boarding and Old Forester Scholarships. Full details are available from the *Warden*.

Framlingham College (see p 126). Many Scholarships are available up to 50% of the fees. a) For 13+ entrants, scholarships are awarded on the basis of an examination held at the College in May. Papers are set in English, Maths, French, Science, History and Geography. Latin, Greek, German and Spanish are options. Some awards may also be made on an outstanding performance in Common Entrance and the Albert Memorial Scholarships exists to recognise an all-rounder who is likely to do well academically but contribute outstandingly in other areas, too. The Porter Science Scholarship is examined separately in March and seeks a 13+ student with particular flair. Assisted Places are available for qualifying applicants. b) Some Sixth Form Scholarships are available for 16+ entrants of high academic promise and are awarded on the basis of GCSE results and interviews. c) Scholarship auditions for Music and Drama are held in March; Art Scholarships are awarded by portfolio and interview. d) Pembroke Scholarships, constituting 100% of the tuition fees and which are intended for students who live in designated areas of Suffolk, are advertised as and when they become available and are awarded to pupils at 13+ or 16+.

Frensham Heights (see p 128). A limited number of scholarships may be awarded each year for academic distinction or exceptional promise in music and art at 11+, 13+ and for Sixth Form entry. Some bursaries are available in cases of financial need.

Giggleswick School (see p 133). Generous academic scholarships and exhibitions are offered for boys and girls as boarding or day pupils. The examinations are held in February and may be taken at age 8 and 10/11 for Catteral Hall, and at age 13 and for 6th Form entry to Senior School. Scholarships and exhibitions are also available for Music, Art, Sports and General Distinction, and for Drama and Design and Technology (these last two for 6th Form entrants only). A number of Continuation Scholarships are also available. A leaflet containing full details of the awards and examinations can be obtained from the *Director of Studies*.

Glenalmond College (see p 136). The Entrance Scholarship Examination is held each year in February/March. Up to 10 Open Scholarships and Exhibitions ranging in value from 10% to 50% of the fees are offered for competition each year. Also available annually are about 5 Music Scholarships worth up to 50% of the fees. Awards are also made for Art. Clergy Bursaries for the sons and daughters of Clergy are also available, as are Bursaries for the children of serving Armed forces families.

Junior Scholarship candidates must be under 14 on 31 May of the year of entry. A short statement showing the scope of the examination will be forwarded on application, and copies of last year's papers may be obtained. Open Scholarship candidates will be examined at their Preparatory Schools, but may be required to come to Glenalmond after this examination for interview and further examination. For further particulars application should be made to *the Warden, Glenalmond College, Perthshire.*

Gordonstoun School (see p 138). *Junior Scholarship Competition* for boys and girls under the age of 14.3 on September 1st in the year of entry.

The competition is designed for the selection of boys and girls either who are outstanding in one or two areas or with all-round gifts. Evidence of high academic promise will be required. Candidates are required to take the following papers: English Language, French, Mathematics, General Paper, General Science, Latin (optional).

Junior All-Round Scholarships. In addition to academic awards, the School offers All-Round Scholarships each year. Candidates for these are expected to take the academic scholarship papers and make a respectable showing in them although not necessarily of scholarship standard. In addition, they should have clear strengths and considerable potential in areas beyond the classroom, particularly those of a sporting or creative nature.

Sets of the last two years' papers are available on request. Several Scholarships are available; their value is up to half fees but these can be augmented in cases of need. They are for the duration of the pupils' time at Gordonstoun but subject to periodic review.

The Scholarship takes place during the Spring Term. Papers are taken at the candidates' schools, either at the end of February or for the first week in March and short-listed candidates are invited to come for interviews in mid-March.

Sixth Form Scholarship Competition. Several scholarships, tenable for two years, are awarded annually. These are for pupils of real academic ability who will also make a contribution to the wider aspects of Gordonstoun life. The normal maximum of any award is 50% of the School fees although this may be augmented in cases of need.

Certain specifically endowed awards are available from time to time and the School, through the generosity of an Education Trust, awards scholarships for those who show particular qualities of Leadership.

Further information and entry forms are available from the *Headmaster*.

Gresham's School, Holt (see p 142). An Open Scholarship examination is held each year at Gresham's in late February or early March. Candidates must be under 14 on 1st September in the year of entry. Scholarships available are:

The Edinburgh Scholarship (Fishmongers' Company) of 50% of fees.

The Fishmongers' Scholarship of 50% of fees.

In case of financial need and subject to a means test, the value of the above two Scholarships can be increased to 100%. This is in accordance with an agreement between all HMC schools.

One Open Fishmongers' Scholarship of one third of annual fees.

One Open Fishmongers' Scholarship on one quarter of annual fees.

Either One County Scholarship of 20% or current annual senior day pupil fees. OR Two County Scholarships of 10% of current annual senior day pupil fees.

Those applying must have been resident in Norfolk for the previous five years.

There are 3 Continuation Scholarships for pupils with 2 years remaining at their Prep Schools to the value of one quarter of the Gresham's Senior day pupils' fees. Continuation scholars may sit for an open award at 13. If successful the higher award will stand.

Two Academic Scholarships of one quarter of annual fees. One Drama Scholarship is available of one quarter of the fees at 13+ and Sixth Form level, and 3 scholarships for both Art and Music of one-quarter of annual fees. There is also available a Sixth Form Sports Scholarship of £500 per annum funded by The Inchcape Trust and one Swatland/Uccelli Science Scholarship of ¼ fees.

Particulars from the *Headmaster, Gresham's School, Holt, Norfolk.*

Haileybury (see p 146). Numbers of generous Academic Scholarships are available to boys and girls each year at Haileybury for those entering the school at the following levels: into the Russell Dore Lower School at 11+, into the Main School at 13+ and into the Sixth Form at 16+.

Scholarships may be awarded for outstanding work in any one subject or for a high general standard. They are tenable for the whole of a pupil's career, subject to a level of progress and application befitting a scholar.

There are also numbers of Music and Art Scholarships available annually, as well as All Rounder Awards. The latter are available either to those who are considered a 'near miss' for academic scholarships and music or art awards, or else to those who can show, in addition to academic strength, outstanding 'all-round' potential as might be demonstrated in music, games, drama or art.

The maximum value of any award is 50% of the fees. All awards are measured as percentages of the fees and are effectively index-linked. Awards can be further supplemented by bursaries in cases of demonstrable financial need.

A scholarship brochure is issued annually in the Autumn and this provides all appropriate information regarding dates and application procedure. This can be obtained from Nick Gandon, The Registrar, Haileybury, Hertford SG13 7NU. He will be pleased to discuss with parents any aspects of the scholarship procedure.

Hampton School (see p 148). At least three Scholarships remitting ⅓ of school tuition fees and at least two Exhibitions remitting ⅙ of fees are awarded annually for entry at age 13. Five Scholarships remitting ⅓ of fees and two Hammond Scholarships (Geographically restricted) remitting ½ of fees are awarded for entry at age 11. The value of all awards may be increased in cases of need. Further details from the *Headmaster.*

Harrow School (see p 150). The examination takes place annually in March at Harrow. About 12 Scholarships and Exhibitions are open for competition to boys who will be under 14 on 1st July in the year of the examination. The Awards range in value from half fees to £100 pa. Up to 8 Scholarships each year can be supplemented to the full amount of the school fees in cases of proved financial need. These supplementable Scholarships are awarded only to boys of high academic ability. In addition for Music there is one Head Master's Scholarship of half fees per annum, one Basil Umney Scholarship of half fees, and one Domus Exhibition of £600 pa. Full particulars and forms of application can be obtained from *The Headmasters' Secretary of Harrow School, 1 High Street, Harrow-on-the-Hill.*

Hereford Cathedral School (see p 151). A number of Scholarships and Exhibitions of a value of up to one third of the tuition fees, are available for meritorious performance in the Common Entrance Examination for 13-year-old entrants and in the Spring Junior Entrance Examination for 11-year-old entrants. Candidates for Cathedral Choristerships may be given similar awards for musical ability and promise. Full details from the *Headmaster.*

Highgate School (see p 153). Up to eight Foundation Scholarships are offered annually to external candidates; the maximum award is half-fees, but any scholarship may be increased in case of need. For those joining the School at age 13+ the examination is part of the entry procedure in January/February. Boys transferring from Highgate Junior School are also eligible for scholarships and are considered separately.

At least two Music Scholarships are offered each year, and the holders also receive free tuition in one instrument in school.

Full details of Scholarships and Bursaries may be obtained from the *Headmaster's Secretary.*

Hurstpierpoint College (see p 159). Scholarship examinations are held annually in May, and Scholarships and Exhibitions ranging from one-half to one-fifth of the fees are offered. Candidates must be under 14 on 1 June of the year of entry. Music Scholarships ranging from one-half to one-fifth of the fees are offered in February/March for entrance into the Junior and Senior Schools the following September. Full details may be obtained from the *Headmaster.*

Ipswich School (see p 164). Queen's and Foundation Scholarships are awarded at 11 and 13, carrying up to half remission of tuition fees, and there are smaller Exhibitions. Scholarships and Exhibitions may be awarded for Music or Art as well as for academic excellence. Academic, Music and All-rounder Scholarships are available for external entrants to the Sixth Form. For further particulars apply to *The Headmaster, Ipswich School, Suffolk, IP1 3SG.*

The John Lyon School (see p 166). Up to 12 academic scholarships are awarded at 11+ and up to two at 13+ on the strength of a boy's performance in the entrance examinations. The value of these awards ranges from 25% to 50% of the school fees.

In addition, two Beckwith Scholarships worth up to 100% of the fees are offered each year and these are subject to financial assessment.

Kelly College (see p 167). Examinations will be held in May. 15 Scholarships of up to half fees may be awarded, including 4 for Music and 4 for pupils interested in joining the Royal or Merchant Navies. The latter may also be awarded on Common Entrance.

All-Rounder Scholarships are awarded in which all-round ability, including leadership and games is taken into full account.

Sons of Naval Officers and sons of Old Kelleians are eligible for certain reductions in fees.

Candidates must be over 12 and under 14 years of age on 1 June. Entries must be in by 24 April.

Further particulars can be obtained from *The Headmaster, Kelly College, Tavistock, Devon.*

Kent College, Canterbury (see p 170). The Entrance Examination is held in February. A number of scholarships at 11+ and 13+ are offered each year, ranging in value from full tuition fee to one-third tuition fee. A Sixth Form Scholarship is also offered on the results of the GCSE exams. Music Scholarships are offered on the basis of an audition taken later in February; candidates for these must take the normal examinations.

Full particulars may be obtained from the *Headmaster.*

Kimbolton School (see p 172). Up to five Scholarships are awarded at 11+ to those candidates who perform with distinction in the Entrance Examination.

Further Scholarships, known as William Ingram Awards, may be awarded at 13+ to those who perform well in the Common Scholarship Examination or in Common Entrance. A number of awards at 13+ are reserved for candidates with strengths in music, art and games.

Sixth Form Scholarships and Exhibitions are awarded to those who achieve outstanding results in GCSE.

King Edward's School, Birmingham (see p 176). *Scholarships at 11+ and 13+* Up to three open full fee scholarships are offered annually. Up to ten major scholarships and exhibitions of between half fees and £300 pa are also offered. These scholarships may be increased to full fees in cases of financial need.

Music and Art Scholarships and exhibitions are also available.

All scholarships are indexed to increase with increases in fees.

At 16+ 'Betts Scholarships' of value up to full fees for boys studying the Sciences at 'A' level and one Finnemore Scholarship for boys studying Arts subjects at 'A' level of up to half fees.

King William's College, Isle of Man (see p 206). Scholarship Examinations in late February or early March. Academic, Open (boys under 12 on September 1st): one free place, two half-fees, a number at 10% reduction augmentable up to full fees in case of need. Academic, non-Manx (boys under 12 on September 1st): a number at 10% reduction, augmentable. Two Sixth Form Boarding Scholarships (half-fees). Music Scholarships: 10% reduction, augmentable. Notice of intention of applying for augmentation must be given at the time of application but, if financial need occurs later, the Trustees will always consider augmentation of any award holder's scholarship.

There is a separate boarding scholarship scheme for boys in their last year in Manx Primary Schools run in conjunction with the Isle of Man Board of Education.

Further particulars may be obtained from the *Principal.*

King's College, Taunton (see p 186). Scholarships up to the value of a half-fee place are available to boys and girls who are under 14 on 1st May. Major academic awards, a major Science Scholarship and Classics Exhibition are awarded to candidates of sufficient merit, as well as all-rounder awards (Haywood and Barrow), CDT exhibitions and Art exhibitions. Music Scholarships up to half-fees are held in February, and at Sixth Form level Academic, Music and Sporting Scholarships are available. A limited number of half-fee places are awarded to sons of clergy. Full details of awards are available from the *Headmaster.*

King's School, Bruton, Somerset (see p 187). Examinations will be held annually at King's School during May to decide the following awards:

Up to seven Open Scholarships or Exhibitions worth up to 50% of current fees. Major Scholarships are worth 50%, Minor Scholarships 25%, and Exhibitions 12.5% of fees. These may be increased in value as a bursary.

Candidates must be under 14 on September 1st of the year in which they sit the examination. Compulsory papers will be set in English, Mathematics, French (including an oral examination), Science (which will include questions on Physics, Chemistry and Biology), History, Geography, Religious Studies and a General Paper. Candidates may also offer optional papers out of Greek, German and Latin. A cognitive ability test will be set. All candidates will also be interviewed by the Headmaster and allowance will be made for age.

Two Nangle Scholarships, each worth £200 per annum, for mathematical and geographical ability. These may be awarded on the basis of performance in the Open Scholarship.

and during February/March to decide the following awards:

Up to four King's Music Scholarships, worth from 10% to a possible 50% of current fees.

One Blackford Scholarship for a pupil from the Junior School of £150 per annum.

At least two Scholarships of 25% of fees each will be offered annually, to be awarded for *All-round Ability* for pupils sitting the Scholarship Examinations or for good Common Entrance candidates.

Two Art/Technology Scholarships worth 12.5% of current fees.

Sixth Form Scholarships: Academic Scholarships, worth up to 50% of current fees, are awarded following an annual examination held during the month of November. *One Art Scholarship*, worth up to 33% of fees and *Music Scholarships*, also worth up to 33% of fees, may be awarded to pupils entering the Sixth Form.

Further information, application forms and copies of past papers may be obtained from the *Registrar*.

The King's School, Canterbury (see p 189). Up to 20 King's Scholarships are offered annually for competition in March to pupils under 14 on 1 September in year of entry. The awards will be between 30 and 50% of the annual fee in every year and will be 'inflation proof'. Further assistance above 50% is available but would depend on parental income. A good many other scholarships and exhibitions are awarded on the results of the examination for King's Scholarships.

For details of Music Scholarships see that section.

A scholarship leaflet is issued annually in the Autumn, and may be obtained from the *Admissions Secretary*.

King's School, Ely (see p 192). Entrance Scholarships and Exhibitions (ie scholarships of lesser value) recognise exceptional promise in academic work, Art, Design & Technology, Drama, Music or Sports.

Boarding awards may be offered from Year 4 upwards to pupils who will contribute strongly to the overall life of the boarding community. The total value of scholarships will not normally exceed 50% of fees.

Junior School Academic Awards are for the two final years of the Common Entrance course. A competitive examination is held in January each year and successful candidates will enter Year 7 the following September.

Middle School Awards are for the three years leading to the GCSE examinations and are made on the basis of a competitive examination in February. Successful candidates will enter Year 9 the following September.

Sixth Form Awards are for the two years of the AS/A2 course and are made on the basis of GCSE results. Provisional awards are made before Easter and confirmed when the results are published.

Art and Design & Technology Awards are made for Year 7, Year 9 and Year 12 entry and candidates are invited to the School in February for interview.

Music Awards are available for choral and/or instrumental excellence, including organ-playing and normally include free weekly tuition on two musical instruments. Candidates for entry into Year 7 and Year 9 are invited to the School for auditions in February and in November for entry into Year 12 the following September.

All Choristers of Ely Cathedral are full boarders of the Junior School and receive a scholarship of two-thirds of the fees while they remain in the choir. Bursaries worth one-third of the appropriate fees are available if a boy continues into the Senior School.

Sports Awards are open to boys and girls with potential for major county, regional or national representation or with all-round sporting excellence. Reports will be sought from the candidates' coach(es) and practical tests, if required, will be held at the school in February.

Full particulars of all awards are available from: *The Admissions Secretary, The King's School, Ely, Cambridgeshire CB7 4DB. Tel: 01353 660702.*

King's School, Gloucester (see p 194). Open Scholarships providing free tuition at this Cathredral School may be awarded to outstanding boys and girls at age 11 and 13. A number of lesser Exhibitions are also available at this age. Scholarship examinations are held annually in March. One or two awards may be made to candidates on the results of the Common Entrance Examination at age 13. Music Exhibitions are available at age 11, 13 and in the Sixth Form.

Choral Scholarships for Cathedral Choristers are available for boys between 7 and 9½.

Full particulars from the *Headmaster*.

King's School, Rochester (see p 198). Five King's Scholarships of 50% of tuition fees and five Minor King's Scholarships of 25% of tuition (and boarding) fees may be awarded annually. King's Scholars become members of the Cathedral Foundation.

Candidates are normally expected to be under 14 years old on the 1st September of the year in which they sit the examination. Allowance is made for age.

Candidates will be expected to sit the Common Entrance Examination in June or, if not prepared for this, may take the King's Senior School entrance Examination in May.

Five Governors' Exhibitions, all means tested, are available up to 100% of tuition fees. Five King's Exhibitions of 50% tuition fees are available, two at 8+ and three at 10+.

Details of Music and Art Scholarships are given elsewhere. A scholarship brochure, and further information, may be obtained from *The Headmaster, King's School, Satis House, Boley Hill, Rochester, Kent, ME1 1TE. Tel: 01634 843913. Fax: 01634 832493.*

King's School, Worcester (see p 202). There are 20 King's Scholarships on the Foundation, of which 3–5 fall vacant each year, one being offered in the first instance for Music. They are of a minimum value of half fees, the actual value will depend on the financial means of the parent. One full fees and two half fees Scholarships are offered. A few Exhibitions of a minimum value of £905 are also available, for which preference is given to the children of clergy. The Scholarship Examination is held in February/March, and external candidates must be under 14 on 1 September. Full particulars may be obtained from the *Headmaster*.

(For particulars of Choristers' Scholarships (age 8–9½), apply to the *Precentor, 2 College Green, Worcester*).

Kingston Grammar School (see p 203). At age 11 there are up to 10 half fee Academic Scholarships, including a Hans Woyda Memorial Mathematics Scholarship, awarded on the results of the Entrance Examination in mid January.

Two half fee scholarships are available for entry at age 13+. Scholarships are also awarded to entrants to the sixth form, following a written examination, interview and successful GCSE results.

Two half fee music scholarships, including free tuition in one instrument, may be awarded at 11+ or 13+. Similarly two Art scholarships may be awarded at 11+ or 13+ following interview and submission of a portfolio.

Further particulars may be obtained from the *Registrar*.

Lancing College (see p 210). Candidates for the following awards must be under 14 years of age on 1st June in the year of examination. The age of the candidate is taken into account in making awards. A boy may enter for more than one type of award, and account may be taken of musical or artistic proficiency in a candidate for a non-musical award; but no boy may hold more than one type of award except in an honorary capacity.

(1) About fifteen Open Scholarships and Exhibitions ranging in value from half of the annual boarding fee to £950 per year. One of these Exhibitions may be awarded solely on promise in Art.

(2) Three or four Music Scholarships ranging in value from half the annual boarding fee. A number of Exhibitions are also offered to boys in schools where the time for Music is less than in some others, and where a boy may have less musical experience but greater potential.

One Professor W. K. Stanton Music Scholarship of half the boarding fee for a Chorister from Salisbury Cathedral School, or failing that any Cathedral School. A Stanton Exhibition may also be awarded.

(3) Two Clergy Exhibitions of the value of £3,900 per year for sons of Clergymen of the Church of England.

(4) One Naval Exhibition of the value of £1,700 per year for the sons of officers or ex-officers of the Royal Navy, Royal Marines, Royal Naval Reserve or Royal Naval Volunteer Reserve.

Entry Forms

For Music awards: Entry forms are obtainable from *The Head Master's Secretary, Lancing College, West Sussex, BN15 0RW.*

For Academic awards: These may be obtained from *The Head Master's Secretary, Lancing College, West Sussex, BN15 0RW.*

Sixth Form Awards (boys and girls)

Two Scholarships of the value of £2,000 per year and two Exhibitions of the value of £1,000 per year are available for new entrants to the Sixth Form with special proficiency in Academic Subjects or Music. The candidate's general ability to contribute to the life of a boarding school community will also be taken into account. A small number of Scholarships and/or Exhibitions are also available internally on the strength of GCSE results.

Latymer Upper School (see p 212). The Latymer Foundation funds scholarships for up to half fee remission, at the three levels of entry to the School (11+, 13+ and co-educational Sixth Form). Scholarships are awarded on academic merit, and some are reserved for Music, Drama, Art and Sport.

The Edward Latymer Bursary Fund exists to provide financial support both to the parents of those applying for entry to the School and for parents who find themselves in financial difficulties whilst their sons or daughters are at the School.

Further details are available from *The Registrar (020 8563 7707; registrar@latymer-upper.org).*

Leicester Grammar School (see p 215). Academic scholarships (12½%, 25% and exceptionally 50%) are available at all ages from 11+ upwards and are given on the results of the Entrance Examination (or, at VI Form entrance, GCSE results). Music scholarships are also available, awarded following audition, as are a small number of art scholarships, awarded on examination and portfolio.

Leighton Park School (see p 217). Several Major Awards each year, minimum value 25% fees, increasing to 75% fees according to family circumstances. Also Minor Awards of 15% fees and Exhibitions of 10%. All these Awards may be given for special talent in Art or Music as well as in academic work. Candidates, who must be under 14 on the following 1 September, are invited to the school for testing in English, Mathematics, French, Science, General Paper and a further subject of the pupil's own choice. Full particulars should be obtained from the *Headmaster, Leighton Park School, Reading,* before 31 December.

The Leys School (see p 219). *Entrance Scholarships* The Examination for Scholarships and Exhibitions will be held in the Spring term. Candidates must be under 14 on 1 August: allowance is made for age. Up to 14 awards are offered each year, the value being expressed as a percentage of the fees: Scholarships up to 50% and Exhibitions. There are Music Scholarships, also, up to half-fees (plus free tuition on two instruments). The examination will be held in February. Awards are also offered for Art. Scholarships of up to 50% of fees are available in the Sixth Form. The School also participates in the Arkwright Award Scheme for Technology. Full particulars may be obtained from the *Headmaster.*

Llandovery College (see p 223). *Thomas Phillips Scholarships* (of value up to half fees) are awarded as a result of the entrance examinations held in late January for entry at 11+ and 13+. Candidates from Preparatory Schools may alternatively sit the Common Entrance Examination in June.

Sixth Form Scholarships are held in late January.

Carwyn James and Ian Gollop Scholarships are offered for pupils having superior sporting skills, particularly in Rugby Football and Cricket. Aptitude tests are normally held each February. Candidates are also encouraged to sit the academic scholarship examinations.

Full particulars from *The Warden.*

Lord Wandsworth College (see p 224). Scholarships of between 10% and 50% of the consolidated fees are awarded annually. These consist of: First Form – Academic, Drama and Music; Third Form – Academic, Drama, Music, Art, CDT and All-Round Awards; Sixth Form – Academic, Drama, Music, Art, CDT and All-Round Awards.

Further details may be obtained from the *Headmaster.*

Loretto School, Musselburgh, Midlothian (see p 225). Loretto is pleased to announce a number of major Scholarships, Exhibitions and Bursaries.

Open Scholarships: *Forbes Mackintosh* Memorial Awards of up to 50% fees, Open Exhibitions of up to 33% fees and Open Bursaries of up to 10% fees.

Closed Scholarships: available to those not currently attending a Prep School.

Services Scholarships and Bursaries: Scholarships are available to Services children of sufficiently high academic standard.

Bursaries: In the event of financial difficulty, a number of Loretto Bursaries may be available either to stand on their own or to supplement Scholarships and Exhibitions.

Music Scholarships: to be awarded if the standard of performance is sufficiently high.

Piping Bursaries: to be awarded after competitive trials on the Highland Bagpipe at Loretto.

Art Bursaries: to be awarded in recognition of outstanding artistic promise.

Candidates must be over 12.10 and under 14 years of age on 1 September. Entries must be in by 6 February.

Further particulars can be obtained from the *Headmaster.*

Magdalen College School, Oxford (see p 229). At age eleven 17 Assisted Places are offered under the Government's Scheme, awarded on a combination of academic merit and financial need. Candidates should take the School Entrance Examination in February, consisting of papers in English, Mathematics and Verbal Reasoning, and be under 12 on the subsequent 1 September.

At age 13, 5 Scholarships of up to £1,000, but capable of increase up to half fees in case of need, are awarded each year on the results of a two day scholarship examination in March. Candidates should be under 14 on the subsequent 1 September. Closing date for entries 1 February. At age 13 4 Assisted Places are available on the results of the School Entrance Examination in English, Maths, Verbal Reasoning and a foreign language for candidates from state schools. The 13+ Examination is held in May.

Further information can be obtained from the *Master's Secretary, Magdalen College School, Oxford OX4 1DZ.*

For details of Choristerships (for boys aged 8 to 10) application should be made to the *Dean of Divinity, Magdalen College, Oxford OX1 4AU.*

Malvern College (see p 231). The Porch Memorial Award, which consists of a scholarship of 50% of the fees, which may be increased by a means-tested bursary of up to 25% of the fees, is offered for a candidate of outstanding ability. Up to 20 other academic awards are offered. They range from Scholarships of up to 50% of the fees to Exhibitions of a lesser value. Music Awards of up to 50% of the fees and one Art Scholarship of up to 30% of the fees are also offered. There are also two Art Exhibitions of lesser value. Scholarships, but not Exhibitions, are linked to the fees and are increased automatically each time the fees are increased.

Candidates must be under 14 years of age on 1 September in the year of the examination. Entries must be in three weeks before the examination.

Sixth-Form Scholarships are available. Please consult the Registrar for details.

Further particulars may be obtained from the *Headmaster, Malvern College, Malvern, Worcestershire WR14 3DF.*

Marlborough College (see p 234). The College offers Open, Foundation (Clergy) and Armed Services closed scholarships. All are index-linked to the fees. Candidates must be under 14 on 1st September.

At least 12 academic scholarships and exhibitions altogether will be available, the value of any award depending on merit and need. The merit component will range up to 50% of the fees. Awards will be eligible for augmentation above 50%, dependent on family financial circumstances, by means of bursaries.

Sports awards are also available.

In addition to Open Scholarships there are Foundation Scholarships for children of Clergy, and these may be supplemented by grants from the College's Children of Clergy Fund. (The minimum grant from this fund is 15% of the fee.)

There are also closed awards for children of Officers in HM Forces. Details of those available each year are available from the Senior Admissions Tutor.

The closing date for entries is February.

For Art and Music Scholarships, see separate lists.

There are also scholarships available for Sixth Form Entry.

A Scholarship Prospectus and copies of past papers may be obtained from *The Senior Admissions Tutor, Marlborough College, Wiltshire, SN8 1PA.*

Merchant Taylors' School (see p 236). Entrance scholarships are awarded at 11, 13 and 16 on the results of examinations held in January and March. Their maximum value is one half of the day-boy fee, but if there is financial need this can be increased, even up to full fees. For Music Scholarships, see separate list. Details from the *Admissions Secretary, Merchant Taylors' School, Sandy Lodge, Northwood, Middlesex HA6 2HT. Tel. 01923 845514.*

Merchiston Castle School (see p 239). Scholarships are offered for competition at 11+, 12+, 13+ and Sixth Form level. Junior examinations (Academic and All-rounder) for boys aged between 10½ and 12 are held in February, when Scholarships up to a maximum of 50% may be awarded. Main School Examinations (Academic and All-rounder) are held in February/March when Scholarships up to a maximum of 50% may be awarded. NB for Main School Awards, candidates must be under 14 on 1st February. All-rounder scholarships assess academic ability and two specialisms eg Music, Sport, Drama etc. One Sixth-Form scholarship up to a maximum of 50% of fees may be awarded to a boy not already at Merchiston who wishes to follow a 2-year programme leading to A level. Major Scholarships may be increased up to 75%, subject to means testing. Further particulars may be obtained from the *Admissions Co-Ordinator.*

Millfield (see page p 243). Scholarships. The Governors offer the following awards each year:

Academic: up to 30 scholarships for entry into the third form, and a further 25 for entry into the Lower Sixth form.

Music: 15 Scholarships for entry into either the third or Lower Sixth form.

Art: 3 Scholarships for entry into either the third or Lower Sixth form.

All awards are in the form of a percentage of current boarder or day fees to a maximum of 50%. Further remission of fees is possible where financial need can be established.

Mill Hill School (see p 245). Ten academic awards up to 50% of fees and a number of Music Scholarships and Exhibitions are awarded annually. Candidates must be over 12 and under 14 on 1st June, with examinations and auditions taking place in January. Bursaries are also awarded to sons and relatives of Old Millhillians; sons of Christian Ministers and to candidates with outstanding qualities of character and general ability, even though they may not be of Scholarship standard. There are also two major Sixth Form Scholarships awarded annually and a number of Bursaries awarded according to parental circumstances and financial need.

Monkton Combe School (see p 248). Four Anniversary Awards are offered at the age of 11 for open competition each year. They range in value from 50% to 10% of the appropriate fee. At least ten Open Scholarships are offered at age 13 (including at least two for Music, at least two for Art and at least two for All-round contribution to the life of the School) of value ranging from 50% to 10% of the appropriate fee. Additional bursaries are available to supplement Scholarships in case of need. Candidates must be under 14 years of age on 1st September. Further particulars and copies of specimen papers can be obtained from the *Head Master's Secretary.* At least two Sixth Form Scholarships are also offered each year, ranging in value from 25% to 10% of the appropriate fee; details can be obtained from the *Head Master's Secretary.*

Monmouth School (see p 250). A generous number of Entrance Scholarships are awarded on the School's General Entry Examination (held in February) for boys entering at the age of eleven, on the Foundation Scholarship Examination (held in February/March) for boys entering at the age of thirteen, and the Sixth Form Scholarship Examination (in March). In cases of need, Scholarships may be augmented by a Bursary.

At eleven: 1. Open Scholarships to the value of ½ fees, whether for dayboys or boarders.

2. Further Scholarships and Bursaries, including those from the Old Monmothian Scholarship Fund, will be awarded, their value being determined and annually adjusted according to parental need. If candidates of sufficient merit present themselves, two bursaries will be reserved for sons of serving members of HM Armed Forces.

At thirteen: Foundation Scholarships up to the value of ½ total fees are normally reserved for intending boarders not at the time pupils of Monmouth School. Candidates must be between the ages of 12 and 14 on the first day of September following the examination.

Sixth Form Scholarship awards of up to ½ fees for day boys or boarders. Candidates to be under the age of 17 on the first day of September following the Scholarship Examinations.

Morrison's Academy (see p 252). *Sixth Form Scholarships.* Two Scholarships are awarded after examination and interview in June. Not less than 50% of tuition fees will be paid while consideration will be given to other course-related expenses (visits, field work, etc.). Full details from *The Rector, Morrison's Academy, Crieff PH7 3AN.*

Mount St Mary's College (see p 252). Three Entrance

Scholarships are offered annually, awarded by examination in the Spring Term before entry. Nominal value of Scholarships may be supplemented by bursary up to full fees according to need. Other bursaries occasionally available. Full details can be obtained from the *Headmaster, Mount St Mary's College, Spinkhill, Via Sheffield S31 9YL.*

Newcastle-under-Lyme School (see p 254). The following Scholarships and Bursaries are available.

Governors' Scholarships: One Scholarship of value £1,200 per annum for up to 7 years and 5 Scholarships of value £800 per annum for up to 7 years to be awarded on the results of the 11+ Entrance Examination.

The J. C. Bamford Scholarship: Value £100 per annum for up to 3 years, to be awarded to a candidate on entry at 11, 12 or 13 for Mathematics.

The Robert S. Woodward Scholarships: 1, or 2 Scholarships, value of £1,000 per annum, to be awarded annually to pupils entering, or in the Sixth Form for outstanding performance in the field of Mathematical Sciences.

The J.C.B. Sixth Form Scholarship: 1 Scholarship, value of £250 per annum, to be awarded annually to pupils entering, or in the Sixth Form, for outstanding performance in Physics and Applied Mathematics.

Bursaries: The Governors have established a Bursary Scheme to assist parents with school fee.

Further details may be obtained from *the Principal, Newcastle-under-Lyme School, Mount Pleasant, Newcastle, Staffordshire, ST5 1DB.*

Norwich School (see p 256). Entrance Scholarships are awarded annually on performance in the entrance examination to the Senior School in the Spring Term. There are 3 Governors' Scholarships. The maximum value of all these awards is the full tuition fee. The Edward Field Memorial Scholarship (value according to parental means) is awarded annually to a boy of 13 already in the School. There is a special examination. Apply to the *Head Master.*

Nottingham High School (see p 258). Part-Scholarships of a fixed sum may be awarded. They are not linked to parental finances and will normally continue throughout a boy's school career. Application does not have to be made for part-scholarships as these are awarded at the discretion of the Headmaster, subject to entrance examination performance and interview. Following the ending of the Government Assisted Places Scheme, Nottingham High School has introduced its own Bursaries to be awarded to boys entering the Senior School at either age eleven or sixteen. In addition, two Ogden Trust Bursaries are now to be awarded each year. All Bursaries will be awarded at the Headmaster's discretion and will normally continue until a pupil leaves the School.

Oakham School (see p 259). Over £350,000 per year is currently devoted to academic, music, art, drama, chess and organ scholarships and exhibitions. An extensive range of awards is offered annually for competition by boys and girls entering aged 11 and 13 and into the Sixth Form. Further particulars about age limits and examination dates may be obtained from the *Registrar, Chapel Close, Oakham, Rutland LE15 6DT.*

Oratory School, Woodcote (see p 260). A number of Scholarships and Exhibitions of varying values, not exceeding half fees. Awards in Mathematics, Music, Art and Sports. Particulars from the *Headmaster.*

Oundle School (see p 262). An Open Scholarship Examination is held at Oundle for boys and girls under fourteen on the 1st September. Allowance will be made for age. (The Preliminary takes place in February each year). These Scholarships are tenable during the whole of the pupil's time at the School, provided progress is satisfactory. Successful candidates are assured of a place in the School regardless of whether their names are previously registered for a vacancy or not.

Fifteen Scholarships, ranging in value from 50% to 25% of the fees. *The Grocers' Scholarship* is elected annually after completion of one year in the School.

Two General Scholarships (Conradi and Stainforth) of value up to 25% of the fees awarded to candidates with high academic ability who will also contribute significantly to school life.

Two Junior Scholarships for eleven year old boys and girls of value up to 50% of the fees.

Two Sixth Form Scholarships of up to 50% of the fees for boys and girls. The examination is taken in November prior to entry the following September.

Further particulars can be obtained from *The Academic Secretary, The School, Oundle, Peterborough PE8 4EN.*

Pangbourne College (see p 264). Six Scholarships: one of two-thirds and two of half the value of current fees, the rest up to the value of £900 a year each. Papers are written in candidates' own schools but all candidates are interviewed at Pangbourne College, usually in the year before they sit the examination. Additional awards are reserved for candidates of exceptional musical or artistic ability. Music or Art Scholarship candidates are required to visit the College by arrangement with the Headmaster. They may either take the scholarship papers or be elected to awards on a combination of proven musical or artistic ability and promise and a commendable performance in the appropriate Common Entrance Examination.

Plymouth College (see p 267). For boys and girls entering at 11 there are 3 Major Scholarships (£1,200 pa) and 3 Ordinary Scholarships (£900 pa). Two of these six awards are restricted to pupils coming from Plymouth College Preparatory School. Awards are made on the basis of the Entrance Examination.

At 13+ there is one more Major and one more Ordinary Scholarship and these are awarded on a Scholarship Examination.

For those entering the Sixth Form two further awards are made based on GCSE results.

There are 6 Scholarships and Awards for Art, Music and Sport 3 of these are awarded at 13 and three to Sixth Form entrants. The value of these are up to £1,200 pa.

Further information from the *Headmaster.*

Pocklington School (see p 268). Scholarships and Exhibitions are awarded annually to boys from Preparatory Schools of value ranging from Full Tuition Fees, including one for Music of up to £500 pa. Applicants for these awards will be required to come to Pocklington School in February/March to take the Scholarship examinations. They must be under 14 on 1st September following. The School Entrance Examination (for the 11+ age group) will be held in February and up to 6 Scholarships and Exhibitions are awarded annually, from Full Tuition Fees. In all cases application should be made to the Headmaster before 1st February. Sixth Form Scholarships available to boys and girls joining the school for their 'A' Level course.

Portsmouth Grammar School (see p 271). *Scholarships and Bursaries*: The School offers scholarships at 7+ and 8+ on the basis of the Junior School Entrance Assessments. In addition, a small number of Scholarships, each amounting to no more than 10% of full fees, are awarded to outstanding candidates in the 11+ Entrance Assessments. All candidates are automatically considered for Scholarships, which are awarded entirely on academic merit; no application is required.

Ogden Trust Educational Bursaries, worth up to full fees, are offered at 11+ to outstanding candidates with parents of limited income from state primary schools. Limited additional assistance through the award of Foundation Bursaries is also available.

Scholarships from the A D Nock Trust are offered at 13+ to both Common Entrance candidates and existing pupils.

Academic Scholarships and Bursaries are awarded for entry to the Sixth Form to candidates with outstanding results at GCSE.

Prior Park College (see p 273). An entrance examination is held in January each year and is linked to Scholarships at 11+. Scholarships are awarded annually to external candidates for 13+ entry and the examination is held during May. Sixth Form Scholarships are held in February.

The following awards will be offered annually:

Scholarships up to a maximum of 50% of day fees.

Candidates must be under 14 years of age on September 1st following for the May Scholarship and under 12 years of age on September 1st following for the January Scholarship.

Further details obtainable from the *Headmaster.*

Queen Elizabeth's Hospital, Bristol (see p 278). *Entrance Scholarships.* There are six scholarships to the value of half the tuition fee, four at 11-plus and two at 13-plus. These are awarded purely on academic merit for outstanding achievement in the entrance procedures and may carry with them generous boarding assistance for boarding applicants whose parents' means are limited.

Queen's College, Taunton (see p 279). Queen's College Scholarships – 10+, 11+ and 12+ scholarships are awarded in January, 13+ in February/March and Sixth form in November.

Academic Scholarships by examination – half, third or quarter fees for students of proven academic ability in one or more subjects. Up to 8 day and 5 boarding academic scholarships for students aged 8+, 11+ and 13+ on 1 September in year of entry. Eight Sixth form scholarships are also on offer.

Music Scholarships – half, third or quarter fees for the most gifted scholars including free tuition in one or two instruments. Up to 8 scholarships for talented musicians aged 10+, 11+, 12+ and 13+ at the projected time of entry to the college. Three Sixth form entry scholarships are also available plus an Organ award.

Sports Scholarships – half, third or quarter fees for the students of best ability. Up to 6 scholarships for talented students with proven sports ability aged 11+, 12+ or 13+ at the projected time of entry to the college. Sixth form scholarships included.

For further information apply to the *Headmaster.*

Radley College (see p 281). Scholarships and Exhibitions are awarded annually in February or March. Awards range from half fees to £1,000 pa. They may be supplemented by a bursary where necessary. Candidates must be under 14 on 31st August. Part I of the examination will be sat at preparatory schools; selected candidates will be called to Radley for Part II. Further details from *The Warden's Secretary.*

Ratcliffe College (see p 282). Scholarships are offered at 11 and 13.

The basic subjects of the examination are English, History, French, Mathematics, Science and a General Paper. Candidates are encouraged to attempt the Scholarship papers at about 13 and allowance is made for boys and girls who are on the young side. Candidates must be over 12½ and under 14 years of age on 1st May.

In the Sixth Form scholarships are awarded to pupils who show outstanding results at GCSE.

Further particulars can be obtained from *The President, Ratcliffe College, Fosse Way, Ratcliffe-on-the-Wreake, Leicester LE7 4SG.*

Reed's School, Cobham (see p 285). Open Scholarships and Exhibitions are offered each year, the maximum value of any award being half fees per annum. There is also a VI Form Scholarship available to boys and girls up to half fees in value. The examination takes place in February. All enquiries should be addressed to the *Headmaster.*

Substantial Foundation Awards are offered to boys who have lost one or both their parents, the value of these awards varying in relation to the circumstances. Applications for entrance as foundationers should be sent in the first instance to the *Secretary to the Governors, Reed's School.*

Rendcomb College (see p 287). There are 13 major academic scholarships including one free place (Noel Wills Scholarship). There are also major scholarships in Music, Art and Sport and a number of minor scholarships in Music (including choral), Art, Sport and Performing Art. Bursaries are available for children of members of HM Forces.

Further details may be obtained from the Headmaster's Secretary.

Repton School (see p 289). Up to 14 academical Scholarships and Exhibitions are awarded annually in May. Their value varies between 50% and 10% of the fees. Music Scholarships (in February) and Art Scholarships (in May) are also offered. The value of any award may be increased where need is shown. Apply the *Headmaster, Repton School, Derby DE6 6FH.*

Rossall School (see p 293). The following are offered for competition every year in February/March: 1 Trapnell Scholarship (value full boarding fee plus certain extras including school uniform clothing and replacement) intended principally for promise and ability in Mathematics or Science; 1 Jackson Scholarship (value full boarding fee plus allowance for extras, clothing and travel), based on character, personality and range of interests as much as on academic ability; 10 Open Scholarships; 1 Art and Design Scholarship and up to 4 Music Scholarships of value up to 75% basic fee according to ability of those selected. Music Scholars also receive free tuition in 2 instruments. Candidates must be over 12.9 and under 14 at 1st September. Allowance is made for age. Scholarships may be awarded on the results of the 11 year-old Entrance Examination. Bursaries are awarded each year either on the Scholarship or on the Common Entrance Examination to children of Clergy, where need is shown. Service Bursaries are awarded for the children of members of H M Armed Forces and may be up to 30% of the basic fee. One Newell Scholarship of £1,740 pa is awarded on record and interview to a boy or girl of good character and wide ranging interests educated in UK or Kenya; 2 Watson-Smith Scholarships of £750 pa for pupils who are worthy of encouragement. Apply to the *Headmaster, Rossall School, Fleetwood.*

Royal Grammar School, Guildford (see p 298). King's Scholarships and Scholarships are awarded in recognition of outstanding academic merit, and vary in value from 50% to 10% fee remission. For boys entering the First Form at 11 there is a competitive examination in English and Mathematics, held in mid-February. For boys entering the Third Form at 13 there is a two-day examination covering all Common Entrance subjects, held in February or March.

For full details of these and of arrangements for boys entering the School at 11 and 16, write to the *Headmaster.*

The Royal Hospital School, Ipswich (see p 302). Up to 10 50% Scholarships awarded annually at 11/12/13+. 7 for Academic Excellence; 2 Musical Scholarships; 1 Art Scholarship.

Additionally 2 at 16+, one for outstanding GCSE results and one Eastern Electricity Scholarship for a girl entering sixth form and likely to study Engineering at University.

Full details may be obtained from the *Headmaster's Secretary:* Telephone 01473 328342.

Rugby School (see p 304). Up to thirty Scholarships are offered annually at 13+ and 16+. These include Music, Design and Art Scholarships.

Entrance Scholarships at 13. The examination is held at Rugby in May for entry in September.

Up to fifteen scholarships are offered ranging from 50% to 15% of the fees.

Candidates must be under 14 on September 1st in the year of the examination.

16+ Scholarships are offered for both boarding and day places. The examination takes place in November for entry the following September.

Music Scholarships. A number of awards up to 50% of

the fee are made. The examination at 16+ takes place in November and at 13+ in February, both for entry in September, in conjunction with the appropriate Academic Scholarships.

Design Scholarships & Talbot Kelly Art Scholarships of 10% are offered with the examinations again taking place in conjunction with the appropriate Academic Scholarships.

Augmentation of Scholarships. All Scholarships, except the Talbot Kelly Art Scholarship, can be augmented if the parental circumstances made this necessary. Notice of intention to apply for such augmentation must be given at the same time as application for the Scholarship.

Further information, including the closing date for entries, can be obtained from the *Registrar, School House, Rugby School, Rugby CV22 5EH.*

Rydal Penrhos (see p 306). Up to 10 open scholarships and exhibitions ranging up to half-fees are offered by examination in February each year. At least two of them are reserved for music and art & design. Candidates must be over 12 years 6 months and under 14 years of age on 1st September. Additionally, there are three Sixth Form Scholarships for girls and boys seeking entry at this point.

For full details of all these awards, please apply to the *Headmaster's Secretary, Rydal School, Colwyn Bay, Clwyd, LL29 7BT.*

Ryde School with Upper Chine (see p 308). Bursaries are awarded to suitably qualified candidates who are already attending the school or pupils who apply from outside. Bursaries are means tested. Further details from the *Headmaster*.

St Albans School (see p 309). There are numerous scholarships worth up to 50% of fees awarded on merit at each age of entry.

St Bees School (see p 313). Scholarships and Exhibitions to a maximum of half fees are awarded to candidates under the age of 12 on 1 September. All candidates must take the papers in English, Mathematics, Science and French, together with the combined paper in History and Geography. An optional paper is set in Latin.

Substantial bursaries are available.

St Columba's College (see p 317). Pennefather and Bowles Scholarships. Three or more awards from a Major Scholarship, Minor Scholarship and Exhibitions, each tenable for four years, will be offered after an examination in May which may be sat at preparatory schools. The values of the awards are one-third, one-quarter and one-sixth of the annual fee respectively. One Old Columban Scholarship is also offered. Candidates must be under 14 years of age on 1 June. The closing date for entries is 1 May.

Junior School Exhibitions may be awarded on the result of the Junior School Entrance Examination held at the College in April for those entering at 11 or 12 years of age.

A Senior School Scholarship Examination is held in January for those entering the College after 'O'-level.

Further particulars and copies of specimen papers at £2 per set can be obtained from the *Warden, St Columba's College, Rathfarnham, Dublin 14.*

St. Dunstan's College (see p 318). Up to 8 Foundation Scholarships awarded on the entrance examination results for boys of 11; 2 may be for full remission of fees, the remainder for half fee remission. There are a number of Bursaries which may be awarded in cases of financial need, or to augment the Foundation Scholarship.

A number of Sixth Form Scholarships and Bursaries may also be awarded. Further details from the *Headmaster.*

St Edmund's College, Ware (see p 320). Scholarships which vary between one-third and one-half of the basic College fee for boarders or day pupils, fall into 4 classes: (1) for pupils entering the College from St Hugh's, (2) for pupils entering the College from other schools at the age of 13, (3) for pupils entering the College at 11+, (4) 6th Form Scholarships. Further details may be obtained from the *Headmaster*.

St Edmund's School, Canterbury (see p 321). Various scholarships and exhibitions of up to one half of the fees (which may be supplemented by bursaries at the Headmaster's discretion) are awarded on entry at the following ages:-

Academic: 11 (Junior School), 12/13 (Senior School), 16 (Sixth Form).

Music: 11 (Junior School), 12/13 (Senior School), 16 (Sixth Form).

Art and Design: 12/13 (Senior School), 16 (Sixth Form). Also at 11 (Junior School) to candidates who show exceptional talent.

Sport: 12/13 (Senior School), 16 (Sixth Form). Also at 11 (Junior School) to candidates who show exceptional talent and achievement.

All-Rounder: Awards are available at 11, 13 and 16 to candidates whose combination of talents marks them out as gifted all-rounders. They must be established academics and in addition show particular talent in music, drama, art or sport.

Details are available on request of scholarships, bursaries and fee concessions available to sons and daughters of the clergy, former pupils, diplomatic personnel and armed forces personnel. Concessions are also offered to third and subsequent children from the same family.

St Edward's School, Oxford (See p 324). Up to fifteen scholarships and exhibitions, with a maximum value of 50% of fees; Service Exhibitions of at least 10%; examination in mid-May. Music scholarships (up to 50% of the fees) awarded annually on examination in February. Clergy Bursaries of 30% of full fees may be awarded at the Warden's discretion. Means-tested supplements may be available. Art awards are considered in May at the same time as academic scholarships.

For full particulars apply to the *Registrar*.

St George's College, Weybridge (see p 326). Up to fifteen scholarships may be awarded annually.

Three *Major Scholarships* of 50% of tuition fees will be awarded at 11+, one of which must be awarded to a boy at Woburn Hill School.

Two *Leavers' Scholarships* of 25% will be awarded at 11+ to boys entering St George's College from Woburn Hill School.

Two *Minor Scholarships* of 25% will be awarded at 11+ to boys entering St George's College from Woburn Hill School.

Two *Minor Scholarships* of 25% will be awarded at 11+ to boys entering St. George's College from other schools.

Five *Major Scholarships* of 50% will be awarded at 13+ for entry to the Third Form of St George's College.

Three *Scholarships* of 50% may be awarded to boys entering the Sixth Form.

Details may be obtained from the *Headmaster.*

St John's School, Leatherhead (see p 327). The Governing Council of St. John's School, Leatherhead is pleased to announce the following awards which will be on offer to external candidates from 1993.

Academic (Under 14) 3 Scholarships 50%; 3 Exhibitions 25%; 1 Science based Exhibition 25%; 1 Arts based Exhibition 25%.

Academic (Lower VI) 2 Scholarships 50%; 2 Exhibitions 25%.

Music (Under 14) 1 Scholarship 50%; 2 Exhibitions 25%.

Music (Lower VI) 1 Scholarship 50%; 1 Exhibition 25%.

Art (Under 14) 1 Scholarship 50%; 1 Exhibition 25%.

Art (Lower VI) 2 Exhibitions 25%.

All-Rounder Awards (Under 14) 2 Exhibitions 25%.

For boarders the percentage award will be a percentage of the total boarding fee whereas for day pupils it is, of course, only the percentage of the day fee. The percentage stated represents the maximum value of each Award.

Candidates for the Under 14 Awards must be under 14 on 1 September 1993, unless special permission is obtained from the *Headmaster.*

All-Rounder Awards will take into consideration a boy's academic performance and personality together with a combination of his sporting, musical, artistic, dramatic, and other relevant achievements. Candidates should sit special examinations in Mathematics, English (similar to Common Entrance) together with a Verbal Reasoning Test on Monday 10 May, but may also sit the main Scholarship examination from 11–13 May if they wish to be considered for an academic Award.

Forms of entry containing further details may be obtained from: The *Headmaster, St. John's School, Leatherhead.*

St Lawrence College, Ramsgate (see p 329). A limited number of Scholarships are awarded for outstanding merit to boys and girls on entry to the Senior School at 11, 13 and 16. Awards at other points of entry may be considered. Scholarships are awarded at 8 in the Junior School.

The value may range from 10% to 50%, depending on ability and performance.

Some Music Scholarships are also available at similar points of entry and of similar value. Music scholars should be at a minimum Grade 5 in performance. They receive instrumental tuition fee and have obligations to orchestra and choir.

In accordance with tradition children of Clergy and Missionaries and of serving members of HM Forces will be considered for bursaries. Bursaries for the former can be up to 50%. Parents in HM Forces pay the Services Boarding School Allowance plus 10% of our main boarding and tuition fees.

St Paul's School, Barnes, SW13 9JT (see p 333). A few Foundation Scholarships may be awarded to boys aged 11 on the basis of internal examinations. Examinations for the Senior School are held in May. Candidates must be under 14 on 1 September. One or two Senior Scholarships may be awarded to external candidates for the A-level course. There are 153 Scholars at any given time and about 30 vacancies arise each year. Subject to merit up to 6 of the Junior Scholarships at the Senior School may be awarded with a minimum of 50% remission, irrespective of the parental means. The value of the other Foundation Scholarships depends upon parental circumstances and ranges from a minimum of fifteen per cent to the full Tuition Fee and 50% of the boarding fee. Further particulars from the *Bursar*.

St Peter's School, York (see p 335).

Scholarships at 13: those doing very well in the third form entrance tests are invited to compete for scholarships. Various scholarships up to half tuition fees are awarded annually by examination in March. To qualify for an award a candidate must be under 14 on 1st September in the year of the examination. Minor scholarships may also be available for former pupils of York Minster School and the children of clergy.

Scholarships for the sixth form: scholarships of up to half tuition fees are awarded annually and are tenable for the two sixth form years. An examination and interviews are held in March.

Full particulars from the *Head Master's Secretary*.

Sedbergh School (see p 337). Major and Minor Scholarships and Exhibitions may be awarded annually as a result of examinations held in February.

Scholarships are available at three points of entry to the school:

Scholarships at 11 for entry into Cressbrook House.

Scholarships at 13 for entry into the senior school.

Scholarships at 16 for entry into the Sixth Form.

In addition to scholarships available for academic excellence awards are also available for achievement and all round potential in Music, Art and Sport.

All awards may be supplemented by means of a bursary according to parental need.

Further particulars and specimen papers are available from: *The Headmaster, Sedbergh School, Sedbergh, Cumbria, LA10 5HG.*

Sevenoaks School (see p 338). Over fifty Awards available at: 11+ (Junior School), 13+ (Middle School), Sixth Form.

For;

Outstanding academic ability or promise either generally or in one subject;

Outstanding ability in Music (separate Awards available);

Outstanding ability in Sport (separate Awards available);

Outstanding ability in Tennis (separate Awards available).

All round qualities of character. The Pipemakers' Scholarships, including one girl and one boy at Sixth Form level, are awarded specifically for this;

Candidates proposing to study for the International Baccalaureate in the Sixth Form;

Major Scholarships are normally to the value of one half of the day fee, but may be augmented in case of need.

Minor Scholarships are normally to the value of one-third of the day fee, but may be augmented in case of need.

Foundation Scholarships are normally to the value of £1,400 per annum.

Applications should be made to the *Registrar, Sevenoaks School, Sevenoaks, Kent* by 31st December for all Junior Awards; 31st January for 13+. Applications for 6th Form awards should be made to the 6th Form Registrar by 30th September.

Sherborne School (see p 342). The following awards are offered. Open Scholarships: four at half fees (including the Alexander Ross Wallace Scholarship): two at quarter fees and eight Exhibitions at one-fifth fees and a further two major Scholarships (Bow) for boys living within 20 miles of Sherborne. In awarding one of these Exhibitions regard will be paid to special proficiency in Science. (In addition all rounder (Jeremy Irons) Exhibitions are available to good Common Entrance candidates who show ability in disciplines that are not necessarily found in the classrooms.) Closed Awards: Raban Exhibition of 10% of fees for the sons of serving or ex-service officers, a Nutting Exhibition of 10% of fees for sons of RN Officers. All candidates must be under 14 on 1st September. Music Scholarships: up to three full fees worth of Scholarships may be awarded each year. (In addition one Marion Packer Scholarship of £600 p.a. for an outstanding performance on the piano may be offered.) Those awarded Scholarships receive free instrumental tuition.

Art Scholarships and Exhibitions of half to one-eighth fees are offered.

Sixth Form Scholarships: up to two full fees scholarships are offered annually.

The following awards are also available for good A-level candidates: The Arkwright Scholarship for Technology and the Walford Award for candidates who excel at rugby or cricket.

In common with most other HMC Schools the maximum value of any award is 50% of the fees but this may be supplemented in cases of financial need.

Further particulars and copies of specimen papers can be obtained from the *Headmaster's Secretary, Sherborne School, Dorset DT9 3AP. Tel: (01935) 812249. Fax: (01935) 810422.*

Shrewsbury School (see p 345). The Examination is held during the Summer Term. Seventeen Scholarships are open to competition. Four are to the value of half fees, and the same number to the value of One-Third Fees. Two are to the value of One-Quarter Fees. These Scholarships guarantee the same proportion of a boy's fees throughout his time at Shrewsbury.

There are also up to seven Exhibitions of at least £1,000 pa, four Music Scholarships up to the value of Half Fees and one Art Scholarship up to the value of one-quarter fees.

Candidates must be under 14 on 1 September, following the examination.

Four Sixth Form Scholarships and two Sixth Form Music

Scholarships are offered to boys entering the School after GCSE.

Full particulars from the *Registrar, The Schools, Shrewsbury* (Tel: (01743) 280550).

Silcoates School (see p 346). Substantial bursaries are available for the sons of Ministers and Missionaries of the United Reformed Church or of the Congregational Church. Scholarships are available for open competition by examination each year for candidates aged 11 and for external candidates only at the age of 13, the rate of which is a maximum half fee. Candidates from outside the school who do not win a scholarship may be granted entrance on their performance in these examinations. Bursaries for boys and girls who obtain high grades at GCSE level and wish to undertake an 'A' level course, are available to pupils within and outside the School; the bursaries will amount to a minimum of half the tuition fee.

Music Scholarships (index-linked) are offered at 11+ and above. Award holders enjoy free music tuition.

Solihull School (see p 348). Twelve Scholarships, including four covering the full cost of tuition, may be awarded to boys between the ages of 11 and 12. Two awards are available to candidates taking the 13+ examination. Three awards will be reserved for boys showing special promise in music. Up to date details are available in the year of admission from the *Admissions Secretary, Solihull School, Solihull, West Midlands B91 3DJ.*

Stamford School (see p 350). There is at least one Foundation Award into the Senior School, which can be for full fees and up to four Awards into the Sixth Form. These can be for Art or Music or for exceptional ability in Sport as well as for academic work. Additionally one scholarship of £500 and exhibitions of £250 are offered each year to boys under 14 on 1 September. For further particulars apply to the *Headmaster, Stamford School, Lincolnshire.*

Stonyhurst College (see p 353). Open Major and Minor Scholarships are awarded annually at 13+ on the result of an examination held at Stonyhurst in May. These vary in value up to a maximum of half fees. Open Major and Minor Music scholarships are also awarded in February. Sixth-form academic scholarships, scholarships for Art and Design and Technology and All-rounder awards are also made.

For further details please apply to the *Headmaster.*

Stowe School (see p 355). At least 15 Academic Scholarships and Exhibitions to a maximum of half fees; several Music Awards to a maximum award of one half of the fees, and several Art Scholarships to a maximum value of one quarter of the fees are available annually. There are a number of Memorial Scholarships and Bursaries available from time to time. Awards may be supplemented by means of a bursary according to parental need.

Entry forms may be obtained from the *Registrar.*

Strathallan School, Forgandenny, Perthshire (see p 357). The number and value of the Scholarships depend upon the standard shown by the candidates; the awards are given as a percentage of the fee and can range from 8% to 50% or more for outstanding candidates if genuine need can be shown. Awards are also made to Junior Entrance candidates. The examination for this is specifically designed for candidates from Primary Schools. In addition to the above, the Strathallan War Memorial Scholarship, minimum value £350 pa, is offered every 5 years. There is also an annual Music Scholarship which can be up to 50% of the fees for a suitable candidate. Special consideration will be given to violinists.

Candidates must be over 12 and under 14 years of age on 1 September for the Senior examination and over 10 and under 12 on 1 September for the Junior examination.

Up to four 6th Form Scholarships are offered each year of value at least half the current fee.

Further particulars and copies of specimen papers can be obtained from the *Headmaster's Secretary, Strathallan School, Forgandenny, Perth, PH2 9EG.*

Sutton Valence School, Kent (see p 359). Scholarships (up to a maximum of two-thirds of the boarding fees), Exhibitions, Music and Art Scholarships, may be awarded annually for candidates who are under 14 on the following 1st September.

Junior Scholarships (for candidates who will be aged between 11 and 12 on 1 September) are competed for annually in February, shortly after sitting the Junior Entrance Examination.

All awards are now linked to fee increases.

Further details may be obtained from the *Headmaster.*

Taunton School (see p 361). VIth Form Scholarship of full or part remission of tuition fees are awarded each year to an outstanding boy or girl entering the VIth Form from another school.

Up to five Open Scholarships giving full or partial remission of tuition fees offered annually.

Awards may also be given for Music and Art.

Limited number of Bursaries available to sons and daughters of Ministers.

Further details from *the Headmaster.*

Tettenhall College (see p 363). Lower School Awards (value up to two-thirds fees) and Upper School Scholarship (value to the two-thirds fees) may be offered to outstanding boys and girls from either state or independent schools. Sixth Form Scholarships (value up to two-thirds fees) are available for boys and girls joining the VIth form after taking GCSE elsewhere.

Tonbridge School (see p 364). Up to twenty one academic Scholarships (awarded by examination in May); up to nine Music Scholarships (examination in early February); up to five Art or Technology Scholarships (examination in early February).

The value of any Scholarship awarded may be increased, by any amount up to the full school fee, if assessment of the parents' means indicates a need.

Choral Boarding Exhibitions, with a value of one sixth of the school fee, are offered each year for award to Choristers of Cathedral or other Choir Schools.

Candidates for all awards must be under 14 on 1st June of the year in which they sit the examination. Entries for awards may be made at any time until three weeks before the examinations.

For boys over 10 and under 11 on 1st September, two Junior Judd Scholarships are awarded, tenable at a local preparatory school. Candidates must be attending a County or Voluntary Primary School and normally resident within ten miles of Tonbridge Parish Church. Junior academic and music awards may be made to 10 or 11 year old sons of needy parents in fee-paying Prep Schools. They are awarded as either 'Continuation' or 'Advance' Scholarships by competitive examination in February two years before entry to Tonbridge.

Entry forms and full particulars of all Scholarships may be obtained from the *Admissions Secretary, Tonbridge School, Tonbridge, Kent TN9 1JP. Tel: 01732 304297; email: admissions@tonbridge-school.org*

Trent College, Long Eaton, Nottingham (see p 366). Awards are made for excellence in Music, Art, Sport, Drama and Academic ability at 11+, 13+ and 16+.

At 13+ further awards are made in Design and Technology, and Information Technology. There are also boarding awards for those who could make an all-round contribution, and special consideration is given to those with a parent in the Services.

At 16+ additional awards are available in Business Education.

Bursaries are also available to those in need of extra financial support.

The value of an Award depends on the age of the child, their ability and whether they are a day pupil or a boarder.

Full details on all scholarships, examinations and entrance procedures are available from the *Registrations Secretary:* Tel: 0115 849 4950.

Trinity School (see p 368). Up to thirty Entrance Scholarships are awarded annually to boys applying at 10+, 11+ or 13+. Boys must be of the relevant age on 1 September of year of entry. Awards are based on the results of an entrance examination and interview. Scholarships are also available for entry to the Sixth Form, based on GCSE results. The value of the Scholarship is up to half of the school fee and this may be supplemented up to the value of the full fee if there is financial need.

University College School (see p 371). A number of Scholarships will be awarded to boys whose performance in the UCS Senior School Entrance Examination is outstanding. These awards are largely Honorary though they will cover all textbook charges incurred by Scholars throughout their careers at the School. Similar awards will be made to boys in the Sixth Form at the Junior Branch on the basis of their performance in the special end of year examinations. Scholarships are held subject to a boy's satisfactory progress and behaviour.

Uppingham School (see p 373). At least twelve academic scholarships and exhibitions worth between one-half and one-tenth of the fees will be awarded annually, if suitable candidates present themselves. Up to ten music scholarships may also be awarded. Academic and music scholarships for Sixth Form entry are also awarded in November. All academic awards and music scholarships may be supplemented at the School's discretion in cases of need. Scholarships for art and design/technology are also available.

Davies Exhibitions are available to the sons of clergymen and other bursary assistance is occassionally available.

Full details of all scholarships, examinations and procedure may be obtained from the *Headmaster's Secretary.*

Warwick School (see p 377). At least 18 Scholarships are available to be awarded each year with values ranging up to 50%. In addition, a number of Assisted Places and Bursary Awards are also available.

(*a*) 11+ & 12+ – At least 10 Scholarships giving up to 50% fee remission are available for the award on the results of the Entrance Exams at 11+ and 12+.

(*b*) 13+ – There are at least 4 Scholarships up to half fees remission which are available to be awarded on the Examination at 13+. This examination is based on the Common Entrance syllabus. The range of options in the Schools Scholarship examinations ensures that candidates can show particular skills in Music and Art. A scholarship may thus be awarded on the basis of either of these two subjects.

(*c*) 16+ – At least 4 Scholarships are available giving up to 40% fee remission. These are awarded based on the Sixth Form Scholarship Exmination.

Scholarships are not means tested, but a Bursary may be awarded to increase the value of an award where need is shown.

Bursaries may be awarded in instances where need is shown and the Governors operate a generous Bursary scheme for Boarders where need is shown.

Further details about these awards may be obtained from the *Headmaster, Warwick School, Warwick CV34 6PP (Tel: 01926 492484).*

Wellingborough School (see p 379). Scholarships and Exhibitions are offered annually. Awards are based on the Common Entrance Examination held in June for candidates under 14 on 1 September following. Candidates who have not been prepared for the Common Entrance examination may be allowed to sit a restricted range of papers. Entries are required by the end of April.

Three Foundation Scholarships are offered annually. The examination is held in January for candidates over 10 on 1 March. Entries are required by the end of December.

Information relating to Music Scholarships is given in that section.

Further details and application forms may be obtained from the *Headmaster, The School, Wellingborough, Northants.*

Wellington College, Berks (see p 381). A total of nineteen entrance scholarships or exhibitions may be awarded. Of these, fifteen are academic awards for boys entering at aged 13 and consist of four scholarships of 50% of fees, three of 30% and eight of 15%. One of these minor exhibitions may be awarded for Art. Two academic awards are reserved for boys entering Eagle House Preparatory School from the maintained sector and remain tenable at Wellington. Three academic awards are available for girls entering at aged 16. The remaining awards are for Music. One 50% fee scholarship may be awarded to a girl entering at 16 and two are available for boys entering at 13. The remaining exhibitions are also for boys at 13. Candidates for all awards at 13 must be under the age of 14 on 1st September. For further information apply to *The Registrar, Wellington College, Crowthorne, Berkshire RG45 7PU.*

Wells Cathedral School (see p 385). Scholarships and Exhibitions are offered to those who show outstanding ability on the Entrance Scholarship Tests held in February at the School. At least three full Scholarships and two Exhibitions are offered annually between the ages of 11 and 13. Auditions are held over the same weekend for those seeking places as specialist musicians.

There are 70 Department of Education and Science (DES) places available at the School which are normally awarded, for which children become eligible at the age of 11. A further eight places are awarded to the Sixth Form each year at the time of entering the Lower Sixth. DES awards are dependent on parental income for help with tuition fees.

Assistance is also available from the Department of Education and Science (DES) for specialist musicians entering each year.

Ex Choristers also qualify for bursaries to help with tuition or boarding fees for the remainder of his time at the School.

Further details may be obtained from *The Headmaster, Wells Cathedral School, Wells, Somerset BA5 2ST. Tel: (01749) 672117 or Fax: (01749) 670724.*

West Buckland School (see p 387). Up to six scholarships are awarded for entry at 7, 11 or 13, ranging in value from 20% to 50% of the day or boarding fee. The maximum may be increased in case of financial hardship. Candidates must be under 8, under 12 or under 14 years of age on 1st September following the examination, which will take place in March.

Sixth form scholarships of similar value are also offered.

Westminster School (see p 388). An Examination (The Challenge) will be held in May to elect The Queen's Scholars. There are 40 Queen's Scholars in College and the average number of Scholarships awarded annually is 8. The value of a Scholarship is half the current boarding fee, but this may be supplemented up to the value of the full boarding fee if there is proven financial need. All Queen's Scholars board in the College. **Boys who do not wish to board may be candidates for an Honorary Scholarship which carries a small award (worth £1050 for 1999).**

There is also a number of means-tested bursaries for boarding or day places awarded on the basis of ability and need. **Parents wishing to apply for financial assistance must complete an assessment form which is available from the Registrar and should be returned to the Head Master by the 31st March preceding the examination.**

For further information write to the Registrar, Westminster School, Little Dean's Yard, London SW1 3PF (Tel: 0171-963-1003).

Whitgift School (see p 390). Up to 5 Whitgift Foundation scholarships are awarded at age 10 with up to seven being available at age 11. Further scholarships are also available at age 13 and at Lower Sixth level. Awards for music, art and design, design technology and all-round ability are also available.

Winchester College (see p 393). The Scholarship examination (Election) is held in May each year, and an average of 14 scholarships are awarded. The Scholarships have a value of half the full fee, but this may be supplemented, in cases of financial need, up to the amount of the total school fee. Scholars live together in College and must board.

On the same examination there will be awarded about six Exhibitions of a maximum value of one third of the full boarding or day fee. Exhibitioners live with Commoners in boarding houses. There are also Music Exhibitions about which enquiry should be made to the Master of Music. Candidates for these who are not taking the Scholarship Examination will be required to take the entrance examination.

Candidates must be over 12 and under 14 on 1st September.

Further particulars and copies of specimen papers can be obtained from *Mr Peter Roberts, Master in College, Winchester College, College Street, Winchester, Hampshire SO23 9NA.*

Up to four *Sixth Form Scholarships* may be awarded each year to external candidates. Further particulars from the *Registrar* (address as above).

Wolverhampton Grammar School (see p 396). Up to six Governors' Scholarships (two half-fees, four quarter-fees) will be awarded to the highest placed candidates in the January 11+ entrance examination and subsequent interview. One scholarship will be offered at 13+ (one-third fees), also awarded on the basis of the January examination and interview. A Music Exhibition (quarter-fees) will be offered to an outstanding performer at 11+ or 13+. For further particulars apply to the *Headmaster.*

Woodbridge School (see p 398). Academic Scholarships are available for entry at 11, 13 and 16. Art and Music awards are also available.

Woodhouse Grove School, Apperley Bridge, Bradford, Yorkshire (see p 399). Entrance Scholarships are available at 11 and 13. A Music Scholarship and Exhibition may be awarded each year. Further details can be obtained from the *Headmaster.*

Worksop College (see p 400). Scholarships (up to half fees pa), and Exhibitions (up to half fees pa) may be awarded annually by Examination in May. All particulars from the *Headmaster.*

Bursaries may be given in addition to Awards if the financial circumstances of the parents make this necessary. Application for such an increase in the event of an award being made should be sent to the Headmaster at the time of entry.

Sixth Form Scholarships. Several VI Form Scholarships are available each year, for which there is an examination for external candidates in February. For further information, please contact the *Headmaster's Secretary.*

Sports Awards, to the value of up to 25% fees pa, available for entrants at 13+ and at Sixth Form Examinations in March and May. For further details contact the *Headmaster.*

Worth School (see p 402). At 11+: Awards of up to 50% of annual fees, based on tests in English, Maths and Verbal Reasoning, held at Worth in February.

At 13+: Seven or eight awards, varying in value from 15% to 50% of annual fees. A special award of 25% of annual fees may be awarded to any candidate who does well in Science and Mathematics. Worth is part of the Common Scholarship Scheme and exams take place at Worth in February.

At 16+: Sixth Form scholarships of a value up to 50% of annual fees. These awards are based on a good school report, good GCSE grades and interview.

Wrekin College, Wellington, Shropshire (see p 404). Examinations for Entrance Scholarships are held annually in March. All candidates must be under 12 or under 14 on 1st September in the year in which the examinations are held. There are a minimum of two Music Scholarships a year worth a maximum of half of the school fees. Music scholars and exhibitioners receive free tuition in music.

Art Scholarships worth a maximum of half fees are available, as are bursaries for sons and daughters of serving members of the armed forces. Wrekin Scholarships of up to three quarter fees for children from maintained schools are awarded annually. Bursaries may be given for outstanding ability in games.

Full particulars may be obtained from the *Headmaster.*

Wycliffe College (see p 405). At least five Scholarships and Exhibitions being up to 50% of school fees. These include a WA Sibly Scholarship (for vegetarians), and an F A Wilson Scholarship for Art or Music (preference being given to vegetarians or boys with a food reform background). Additionally, a number of Exhibitions are offered for Music. Candidates must be under 14 years of age on 1 September in the year in which they sit the Examination. Pearson Bursaries may be awarded to boys of all round merit whose parents cannot afford full fees, and all Scholarships and Exhibitions will be expressed as a percentage of school fees and will now be increased proportionately when fees rise. They may also be *supplemented* where there is a clear case of *financial need.*

A 'Ward' Leaving Scholarship to St John's College, Cambridge, may be awarded twice in every 3 years.

The income from the Edwards Bequest provides Scholarships for boys, who would not otherwise be able to do so, to extend their VIth Form courses.

For particulars apply to the *Headmaster, Wycliffe College, Stonehouse, Glos.*

Yarm School (see p 408). Several (usually six each year) Academic Scholarships, up to the value of one-third of the full fee, are awarded to boys as a result of their performances in the 11+ Entrance Examination (held late January) or in the 13+ Common Entrance. Academic Scholarships for sixth-form entrants (boys and girls) are available, performance in GCSE being the yardstick. Competition is strong and a major award generally calls for 10 GCSEs at A grade. Additionally there is a generous Exhibition for a pupil showing exceptional promise in mathematics.

The school also offers Music Scholarships which provide for a reduction up to half fees although most major awards are at the level of one third of fees plus free instrumental tuition. Candidates for a major awards are normally expected to offer a minimum of two instruments or one instrument plus voice. Music Scholarships can be awarded at any stage in the pupil's school career and modest awards can be upgraded in the light of further outstanding progress.

A limited number of Bursaries are available to assist in cases where family resources do not allow full fees to be paid. Such awards are not dependent on academic ability beyond the requirements to pass the standard entrance examination. Bursaries can be combined with scholarships.

Aiglon College, Switzerland (see p 410). Scholarships equivalent to approximately 50% remission of fees are offered annually. Bursaries are also available for deserving candidates who do not qualify for a scholarship. Awards are made on the results of Common Entrance and/or the Aiglon entrance exam, school recommendation and interview.

The British School in The Netherlands (see p 411). Two Tercentenary academic scholarships to the value of the full school fees may be awarded annually to suitable sixth form candidates.

ACADEMIC SCHOLARSHIP GROUPS 2002

Heads of both preparatory and senior schools should do their best to ensure that parents observe the convention that a scholarship offered in the first group must be accepted or refused before the examinations for the second group begin.

Group A. Week beginning 25 February. Closing date for entries 4 February. Aldenham; Ampleforth; Bedales; Bradfield; Bromsgrove; Caterham; Christ College, Brecon; Chigwell; Clayesmore; Cranleigh; Dauntsey's; Dean Close; Denstone; Eastbourne; Epsom; Giggleswick; Glenalmond; Gordonstoun; Haileybury; Hereford Cathedral School; Hurstpierpoint; Kimbolton; King's School, Rochester; King's College, Taunton; Kingston Grammar School; Lancing; Lomond School; Lord Wandsworth; Loughborough Grammar School; Oratory; Oswestry; Ratcliffe; Reed's School; Rendcomb; Repton; Rossall; Rydal Penrhos; St David's; St Edmund's, Canterbury; St George's, Weybridge; St John's; St Lawrence College, Ramsgate; St Peter's, York; Sedbergh; Stowe; Sutton Valence; Trent: Uppingham; Worksop; Worth.

Group B. Week beginning 4 March. Closing date for entries 11 February. Berkhamsted; Bishop's Stortford; Bloxham; Blundell's; Bootham; Cheltenham; Canford; Clifton; Exeter; Fettes; Framlingham; Gresham's; Harrow; Ipswich; King's School, Canterbury; King's School, Ely; King's School, Tynemouth; King's School, Worcester; Kingswood; Leighton Park; Loretto; Magdalen College School; Marlborough; Merchiston; Monmouth; Plymouth; Pocklington; Prior Park; Queen's, Taunton; Radley; Rannoch; R.G.S. Guildford; Sevenoaks; Strathallan; Taunton; Trinity School; Wellington College.

Group C. Week beginning 6 May. Closing date for entries 15 April. Abingdon; Ardingly; Bedford; Bryanston; Charterhouse; Downside; Ellesmere; Eton; Felsted; Hampton; Kelly College; King's College School; King's School, Bruton; Malvern; Milton Abbey; Monkton Combe; Mount St Mary; Oundle; Pangbourne; Rugby; St Edward's, Oxford; St Paul's; Sherborne; Shrewsbury; Stonyhurst; Tonbridge; Westminster; Winchester.

Group D. Week beginning 13 May. Closing date for entries 22 April. Brighton; Millfield.

Schools that advertise scholarship dates outside the group system: Abbotsholme; Ackworth; Alleyn's; Ashville; Austin Friars; Barnard Castle; Bancroft's; Birkdale; Brentwood; Bristol Grammar School; Churcher's College; City of London; Claremont Fan School; Culford; Dollar Academy; Dulwich; Durham; Elizabeth College; Eltham; Emanuel; Frensham Heights; Friend's School, Saffron Walden; Highgate; John Lyon; Kent College; K.E.S. Birmingham; K.E.S. Witley; King's School, Gloucester; Kirkham Grammar, Preston; Latymer Upper School; The Leys; Merchant Taylors'; Mill Hill; Oakham; Perse School; Portsmouth G.S.; Ratcliffe College; Rishworth School; Royal Hospital School; Royal Wolverhampton; St Albans; St Bede's; St Bees; St Dunstan's; St Edmund's College, Ware; Sidcot School; Solihull; Stamford; Stewart's Melville College; University College School; Warwick; Wells Cathedral School; West Buckland; Woodbridge; Woodhouse Grove; Wrekin; Wycliffe.

COMMON ENTRANCE EXAMINATION DATES 2002

11+ 28-29 January 2002 | 12+/13+ 25–28 February 2002 | 12+/13+ 27–30 May 2002

NOTE: 1. Fees quoted by Schools may be for the year 2000/2001 or for the year 2001/2002, unless stated. Readers should check with individual Schools, if uncertain.

2. Schools are reminded of the policy of the Headmasters' and Headmistresses' Conference that "All Schools should operate a common date for eligibility for Scholarships i.e., under the age of 14 on 1 September in the year of the examination". HMC Manual of Guidance, page 40. "6.2.1. Academic Awards".

Musical Scholarships

For fuller information and dates of vacancies, application should be made to the School concerned.

Abbotsholme School
At least one Music Scholarship for up to half fees — with free tuition in two instruments. Candidates must be under 14 on the date of the examination. Further details from the Headmaster.

Abingdon School
Two Music Scholarships entitling the holder to a nominal fee remission of £200 per annum plus fee remission up to the value of one-half of the tuition fee, on a means-tested basis, plus free tuition on up to three instruments, and, when appropriate, one Duxbury Scholarship.

Music Exhibitions giving free tuition on one or two instruments may also be offered.

The above awards are normally made to 13 year old candidates, but can, exceptionally, be made at an earlier or later age.

Further details from the *Headmaster*.

Ackworth School
Up to four Musical Scholarships worth up to 50% of fees are usually awarded at 11, 13 or 16+. The awards are made on the strength of a ½ hour audition and recognise achievement and potential preferably in two instruments. Free tuition in one or two instruments is also offered to promising musicians who do not gain an award.

Aldenham School
Scholarships and Exhibitions are available at 11+, 13+ and 16+ for Music under the same terms as for academic awards. Free Tuition is given to Music Scholars. The Forsyth Grant Organ Scholarship is associated with the fine organ in the School Chapel and is designed to encourage young organists. Any combination of choral and instrumental ability may be offered for the audition.

Alleyn's School
At least one Scholarship value half of the current fee per annum. One W J Smith Memorial Bursary will be awarded to a promising sixth form musician in need of financial aid.

Ampleforth College
Major Awards are offered to a maximum of half fees; some Minor awards are also available. All scholarships carry free music tuition. 13+ candidates should normally have reached their twelfth birthday and not have passed their fourteenth birthday on 1st September following the examination. For 16+ candidates the respective limits are normally their fifteenth and their seventeenth birthdays. Entry forms may be obtained from the Admissions Office.

Ardingly College
Up to ten Music awards may be made each year to those who show that they will have an active contribution to make to the musical life of the School, not only as soloists on their own particular instruments, but in ensemble work, orchestras, choirs and productions, etc. Six of these awards may be to the value of 50% of fees p.a., two being reserved for orchestral string players and two for choristers in attendance at schools which are in membership of the Choir Schools Association. All awards include free music tuition. Any combination of instrument(s) and/or voice may be offered and, although it is hoped that candidates will offer a good standard of playing/singing, beginners who show really good potential and enthusiasm may be considered.

Two Choral Scholarships may be offered for boys entering the Sixth Form. These may be worth 33% of fees and carry free singing/instrumental tuition for two instruments.

Ashville College
One Music Scholarship is available each year, and general scholarships are open for Music also.

Bancrofts School
Two Music Scholarships which cover half fees and extra music tuition.

Bedales School
Scholarships (up to the value of half fees) are awarded each year to outstanding musicians for entry at 8–12, 13+ and 16+. Means tested bursaries are also available to those of proven need.

Bedford Modern School
A music scholarship up to a maximum of £1,000 together with free tuition on one musical instrument or free vocal tuition.

Bedford School
A number of major and minor Musical Scholarships with fee remissions of up to one half, plus free musical tuition. In addition, up to three Music exhibitions offering free musical tuition.

Berkhamsted Collegiate School
The Music Scholarship at 13+, up to £1,500 pa plus free instrumental tuition. For boys on entry to Y9 (Instruments at Grade 5+).
The Webb Sixth Form Music Scholarship at 16+ for a £700 contribution towards music tuition. The award will be determined by audition on two instruments and held through Y12 and Y13.

More information about Scholarships and Bursaries may be obtained on application to: *The Deputy Principal's Secretary, Berkhamsted Collegiate School, Castle Street, Berkhamsted, Herts HP4 2BB.*

Bishop's Stortford College
Music candidates, instrumental and choral, can compete for all major awards at VIth Form level, under 14 and under 12.

***Bloxham School**
Up to 50% of fees with free tuition and music (up to 100% dependent on financial need). Scholarships, Exhibitions and Chapel Centenary Awards. Musical ability taken into account in Open Scholarship and Common Entrance Examinations.

***Blundell's School**
At least two awards generally made, worth from 25% to 100% of tuition fees. Interested parties should contact *the Director of Music.*

Bootham School
Up to four Music Scholarships of up to half fees are awarded at 11 and 13. The scholarships are given in recognition of achievement and potential in musical ability, and are then confirmed by a competent result in Common Entrance or the Bootham Entrance Exam.
Musical ability is also noted in connection with other Entrance Scholarships.
Muscial awards of other value can be made. All awards can be supplemented by bursaries when appropriate.

***Bradfield College**
Up to 4 Music Scholarships of between 20% and 50% of full fees plus free tuition on up to three instruments.

Brentwood School
Three Music Scholarships of £1,446 pa and free music tuition on up to two instruments may be offered on examination at the School before February Common Entrance Examination. Candidates must be over 11 and under 14 years of age on or before 1st September. One

* Music is taken into account in ordinary Scholarship Examinations.

Music Scholarship for Girls of 11 (£1,446 pa). Entries must be in by January 1st. Further details from the Headmaster.

Brighton College
A number of scholarships and exhibitions will be offered each year to candidates showing outstanding ability in Music. Examinations and interviews will be held at the College in January or February for candidates intending to enter at 13+ in the following September. The value and number of the awards will depend on the calibre of the candidates. These awards are available also to pupils entering the College in the Sixth Form.

Bristol Grammar School
Two Music Scholarships are awarded at 11+ with free tuition in instrument of choice (or voice) throughout school career. In addition, one music scholarship on similar terms is awarded at 13+ and at 16+.

Bromsgrove School
Two Music Scholarships of one-third of tuition fees, one at Sixth Form level and one for any age; two Exhibitions of one-tenth of tuition fees, for candidates under 14. The award also include free tuition on two instruments.

***Bryanston School**
Four Junior and two Sixth Form Music Scholarships, worth up to 50% of boarding fees, plus free music tuition. All scholarships may be supplemented by means-tested bursaries.

Canford School
A number of Music Scholarships ranging from 50% to 10% of the fees, with free tuition on two instruments, are awarded at 13+. VIth Form Entry: A number of Scholarships are available worth up to 50% of the fees.

Caterham School
Music Scholarships are awarded at 11, 12 and 13. They are currently worth up to £500 per annum plus free tuition on up to two instruments.

Sixth Form Music Bursaries are worth up to 25% of the tuition fee plus free tuition on up to two instruments.

***Charterhouse**
At 13+ *entry*. A number of Major Music Scholarships are offered worth up to HALF FEES. The examinations are held at the school in February.
Sixth Form entry. Three Music Scholarships are offered annually. These are normally awarded in Autumn. In addition, there is the John Pilling Organ Scholarship, worth HALF FEES, and the Peter Oundjian Strings Scholarship which is offered in alternate years.
Music tuition is free for Music Scholars.

All Scholarships can be increased to the value of the FULL SCHOOL FEE in cases of proven financial need.

For details write to the *Admissions Secretary, Charterhouse, Godalming, Surrey GU7 2DX.*

Cheltenham College
Music Scholarships and Exhibitions up to a maximum individual value of 50% of the fees may be awarded annually at 13+ and for entry into the Sixth Form.

Chetham's School of Music
Entry is by audition only; all who are selected (at any age between 8 and 16) qualify for grants from the DFE under the "Aided Pupil (Music and Ballet) Scheme". Parental contributions are calculated according to means, and parents on low incomes qualify automatically for full fee-remission. The Bursar will be glad to advise about the scales.

Chigwell School
Generous Music Scholarships are available at all ages.

Christ College, Brecon
Up to 8 Scholarships in total are available each year, for award at 11+, 13+ or 16+ ranging in value from 10 to 50% of the fees, together with free tuition on one instrument. The value of any award may be augmented in case of need.

City of London Freemen's School
The following music awards are made for pupils of up to 13+ — either from outside — or within the existing pupil body:
— one Music Scholarship to the value of half tuition fees with free instrumental tuition.
— one Music Exhibition to the value of one-third fees with free instrumental tuition.
Details may be obtained from the Director of Music, and applications should be in to the School by 1st February.

City of London School
One Instrumental scholarship, to the value of two-thirds the cost of school fees or 2 exhibitions to the value of one-third the cost of school fees each are awarded annually. Choristers of the Temple Church and of the Chapel Royal, who must also satisfy the School's entrance requirements receive bursaries from the respective choirs while they remain chorists.

Clifton College
Awards for Music of up to half fees, with free tuition in two instruments. Music awards are also available for entry to the Sixth Form.

Cranleigh School
Cranleigh offers Music Awards annually for entrance at age 13: one or two Scholarships of half fees and two of up to one-quarter fees depending on the merit of candidates; Scholarships include free musical tuition. Examination in February; candidates should be over 12 and under 14 on 1 September and should have passed Grade IV–VIII or be at that standard. Instrumentalists present two contrasted pieces, SR and ET; singers, one prepared song and SR; all take written paper on general musical knowledge. Potential musicianship is considered an important factor. In addition, candidates sit either the Academic Scholarship or the CEE. Choristerships (free tuition in singing and one instrument) are offered to local boys aged 7–13 to sing treble with the Chapel Choir. Further details and closing dates may be obtained from the Admissions Secretary, Cranleigh School, Cranleigh, Surrey GU6 8QQ, telephone (01483) 273997.

Culford School
Two awards are made up to the value of 50% of the tuition fee for a Musical Scholarship to a pupil entering at 13+ and one award is made at 11+.

Dauntsey's School
Musical ability or potential is considered for any Awards, at all ages. The Benson Music Scholarship is awarded at 13+, and the Logsdon Exhibition may also be awarded. Details from the Academic Registrar.

Dean Close School, Cheltenham
Major Scholarships in Music (including Organ). Tenable for whole school career. All music tuition is free to all Music Scholars and Exhibitioners.

Denstone College
Instrumental and Choral Scholarships of up to not more than 50% of the fees are available. In cases of need these Awards may be supplemented with Bursaries.

Douai School
One or two music scholarships are offered each year to pupils entering the school at third form level from preparatory schools. An outstanding candidate may be awarded the total value of the scholarship which is equal annually to one term's fees in the September term of the year of the award, but this amount may be divided between two good applicants. Candidates must be over 12 and under

* Music is taken into account in ordinary Scholarship Examinations.

14 on the date of the examination. Further particulars may be obtained from the Headmaster.

Downside School
Music Scholarships worth up to half fees, and Choral Exhibitions (for boys who will sing at Mass with the Schola Cantorum in the Abbey Church on Sundays and Feast Days) worth up to 10% of fees, are awarded annually after competitive auditions which take place in February.

Dulwich College
Two Instrumental Scholarships of one half of the tuition fee plus free music tuition. The award may be increased in case of need. Age limit under 14 on 1 September. Examinations in the Lent Term. Two contrasted pieces required. SR ET Short viva voce. Second instrument welcome. The College offers outstanding facilities and opportunities for musical performance. Candidates must take the Dulwich Entrance and Scholarship Examination.

Durham School
Various Music Scholarships and Exhibitions are available at 11, 13 and 16 to a maximum value of half fees. The voice may be offered as an instrument. All holders of Music Awards receive free instrumental tuition.

Eastbourne College
Instrumental or Choral Scholarships up to the value of 50% of fees are also offered.

The Edinburgh Academy
One Music Scholarship annually to the value of half fees (boarding or day). Free tuition in two instruments.

Ellesmere College
Music Scholarships of not more than 50% fees, several choral Exhibitions of up to 25% of fees. In cases of need, all these awards may be supplemented further. Tenable while candidate remains at school, subject to progress.

Eltham College
Four Music Scholarships of not more than 50% of fees usually at ages 11 and 16. Candidates are auditioned and also need to sit the entrance papers.

Emanuel School
Up to 2 scholarships at each age group of 10/11, 13+ and 16+. Their value is up to 50% of fees and free music tuition on one instrument.

Epsom College
Music candidates compete for all Open Scholarships. Music can be offered at a lower level as part of a candidature for an All-Rounder Award. Candidates must be under 14 on 1st September or entering the Sixth Form.

Eton College
Up to 8 Music Scholarships are awarded annually: four of half fees and four of one-sixth fees. All awards carry remission of instrumental lesson fees up to two hours tuition per week. All these awards may be supplemented up to the value of the full fee in cases of need.
In addition there are several Music Exhibitions carrying remission of the fees for instrumental lessons. Last year 14 awards in all were made.
Special consideration will be given to cathedral choristers who would still be able to sing treble in the College Chapel choir.
Further particulars and entry forms from *The Registrar, Eton College, Windsor, Berkshire, SL4 6DB.*

Exeter School
Music Scholarships are offered annually following auditions in February and are conditional on applicants achieving the School's academic requirements for entry.
The *Sammy Sargent Music Scholarship,* the top scholarship award made to an outstanding Music scholar, may be awarded at age 11, 12, 13 or 16 and has a value from 25-50% off tuition fees.
At ages 11, 12, 13 and 16 – One Music Scholarship offering a discount of 10-50% off tuition fees. Music Exhibitions offering smaller discounts and/or free music lessons may also be awarded. Free music lessons may be offered in addition to a Music Scholarship, Music Exhibition or other award.

***Felsted School**
Music Entrance Scholarships of up to 50% of fees are available at 13+ and for entry into the Sixth Form.

***Fettes College**
Music Scholarships of up to the value of 50% of the fees are available to instrumentalists at any age between 10 and 16; high musical potential is sought. The standard required at age 13 is normally at least Grade 5 in the main instrument. Promising string players, however, of a more modest standard at present and ex-cathedral choristers will be considered with interest.

Forest School
Up to the equivalent of 4 Music Scholarships to cover half tuition fees may be offered annually to candidates aged 11, 12, 13 or 16 on 1st September of the year concerned.

***Framlingham College**
Music Scholarships are available with a normal maximum of 50% of the tuition fee coupled with free music tuition.

Frensham Heights
One or more Music Scholarships, may be awarded annually.

Giggleswick School
A number of Music awards are available from age 10 for Catteral Hall, and at 13+ and Sixth Form for the Senior School. Award holders receive free musical tuition.

Glenalmond College
About five scholarships worth up to half fees per annum (which may be increased in the case of need).
Awards may be available to boys or girls at 12+, 13+ or Sixth Form. Candidates will usually offer two instruments at least to Grade V. Promising string players and singers will be considered with great interest. Award holders receive free musical tuition.

Gordonstoun School
Junior Music Scholarships. Candidates for Music Scholarships at this level should be of Grade 6 standard or above on any musical instrument or Grade 5 standard in two instruments and to qualify for admission to the School. The maximum value of Music Scholarships is half fees but this can be augmented in cases of need.
Senior Music Scholarships. Music Scholarships are offered to boys and girls entering the School at Sixth Form level. Candidates should be at least approaching grade 8 standard on one instrument. The normal maximum of a music scholarship is 50% of the fees but his may be augmented in cases of need. Intending applicants or their parents are advised to contact the School's Director of Music before submitting an entry form.

Gresham's School
For 13+ entry three music Scholarships of either one half or one quarter of annual fees. For one of these preferences will be given to a good organist, who would be encouraged to assist local churches.
For Sixth Form entry up to three Scholarships of one quarter of the annual fees.

Haberdashers' Aske's School, Elstree
One Bursary available at age 11+, up to £900 p.a. Free tuition in one instrument.

Haileybury
Up to five awards worth up to half fees per annum (which

* Music is taken into account in ordinary Scholarship Examinations.

may be increased in case of need). Proficiency in one or two instruments is expected. Choral ability is an advantage. Free tuition in two instruments. Instrumental Awards are also available, worth free tuition in 2 instruments.

Hampton School
Two instrumental Scholarships of ⅓ fees pa, plus free instrumental tuition. Also one Choral Scholarship of ⅓ fees in conjunction with the Chapel Royal.

***Harrow School**
For Music there is one Head Master's Scholarship of half fees, one Basil Umney Scholarship of half fees and one Domus Exhibition of £600 pa.

Hereford Cathedral School
Substantial reduction of tuition fee available for Cathedral Choristers. See main School announcement. Up to four Music Exhibitions are awarded each year as a result of auditions held in the first half of the Spring Term. Details are available from the Director of Music. Two Sixth Form Music Scholarships are also available.

Highgate School
Two Scholarships. Free tuition in one instrument.

At least two scholarships ranging in value from 25% to 50% of fees with free tuition in school on one instrument. Awards are made to candidates of outstanding ability or potential

Hurstpierpoint College.
Four or more music awards ranging in value from one half to one-fifth of the fees, and two choral awards in Junior School. Free tuition in two instruments.

Ipswich School
Music auditions for promising instrumentalists are held in February. For 11+ entrants these are held at the same time as the February entrance examination. Music awards to those under 14 on the 1st September wishing to enter the Third Form are made conditional on a satisfactory showing in either Common Entrance or the school's entrance and scholarship examination. The highest awards carry one-half tuition fees but may be supplemented by bursaries in cases of proven need. Sixth Form Music Scholarships are also available.

The John Lyon School
Music Scholarships up to 50% of the school fees plus free tuition on two instruments are offered at 11+ and 13+.

***Kelly College**
Several up to half fees. Instrumental and Choral. Free tuition in 2 instruments.

Kent College, Canterbury
Music Scholarships of one-third and two-thirds tuition fee are offered in conjunction with the February Entrance Examination for candidates aged 11–13. Free tuition on two instruments is offered to Music Scholars. Full particulars may be obtained from the Headmaster.

King William's College
Several of nominal value 10% of the fees, but augmentable. Free music tuition. Instrumental with Choral. Whole school career. Reasonable educational standard required.

King's College Taunton
Instrumental Scholarships and Exhibitions are held in February. Awards to the maximum value of half-fees and include free instrumental tuition in up to two instruments.

King's College School, London
Up to 6 Music Scholarships, of varying values up to 50% of the full tuition fee, may be awarded to boys of high musical ability. Candidates must be under 14 years of age on 1 September of the year in which they sit the examination. One Organ Scholarship is available in the Sixth Form. Further information is available from the Music Secretary or the Registration Secretary.

King's School, Bruton
Music Scholarships varying from 50% to 10% of the fees.

King's School, Canterbury
Up to 12 Music Scholarships are offered annually for competition in January or February to pupils under 14 on 1 September in year of entry. They range in value up to half fee and carry free tuition in 2 instruments. A good many further awards are available, sometimes tenable in conjunction with the Regular Music Scholarships: the system is flexible, and enquiries should be addressed to the Director of Music. There are special Bursaries for members of Canterbury Cathedral Choir, each of total value £100 pa, granted by the School and the Dean and Chapter conjointly. Free tuition in 2 instruments.

A Scholarship leaflet is issued annually in the Autumn, and may be obtained from the Admissions Secretary.

King's School, Ely
The boy choristers of Ely Cathedral are all full boarders in the Junior School. Choristers receive a scholarship of two-thirds of their fees while they remain in the choir. Bursaries worth one-third of the appropriate fees are available if a boy continues into the Senior School. A voice trial for selection of choristers is held at the end of the Michaelmas term or the beginning of the Lent term for boys who will be aged eight the following September.

Entrance Scholarships and Exhibitions (i.e. scholarships of lesser value) are awarded during the Lent Term to candidates showing exceptional promise in music. Awards are available for choral and/or instrumental excellence, including organ-playing and may represent up to 50% of fees and normally include free weekly tuition on two musical insturments. Candidates for entry into Year 7 and Year 9 are invited to the School for auditions in February and in November for entry the following September into Year 12. A brochure giving full details is available from: *The Admissions Secretary, The King's School, Ely, Cambridgeshire CB7 4DB. Tel: 01353 660702.*

King's School, Macclesfield
Three Music Scholarships are available in the Sixth Form for instrument or singing.

King's School, Rochester
Up to five Music Scholarships and an Organ Scholarship may be awarded annually.

One Music Scholarship may have the value of a King's Scholarship of 50% of tuition fees. The Organ Scholarship will have the value of King's Scholarship. Free tuition on all instruments studied is given to holders of major and minor awards.

The Scholarships, available from 11+, will be awarded after an examination, usually in February, consisting of aural, sight reading and practical tests, and a viva voce. In addition, candidates will be expected to be of Grade 5–6 standard and capable of passing Common Entrance if 13+ or a genuine 'A' Level candidate if 15+

The *Peter Rogers* Scholarship of £3,500 per annum is awarded from time to time to assist an exceptionally talented musician.

Choral Scholarships of 40% of tuition fees for Cathedral Choristers aged 8–10 are awarded for the Preparatory School. The Scholarships may continue into the Senior School.

Details of Academic and Art Scholarships are given elsewhere. A scholarship brochure, and further information, may be obtained from *The Headmaster, King's School, Satis House, Boley Hill, Rochester, Kent, ME1 1TE. Tel: 01634 843913. Fax: 01634 832493.*

* Music is taken into account in ordinary Scholarship Examinations.

***King's School Worcester**
Scholarships of half the full fees for Cathedral Choristers (age 8/9½). One King's Scholarship and other awards each year for music (age 13+), also possibly at 8+/9+/11+. Bursaries for ex-choristers.

Kingston Grammar School
Two half fee instrumental Scholarships plus free tuition on one instrument. Auditions are in early February for candidates who are applying for entry at either 11+ or 13+.

***Lancing College**
Three or four Music Scholarships or Exhibitions ranging in value from half the annual boarding fee. A number of Exhibitions are also offered to boys in schools where the time for music is less than in some others, and where a boy may have less musical experience but greater potential.

One Professor W K Stanton Music Scholarship of half the boarding fee for a Chorister from Salisbury Cathedral School, or failing that any Cathedral School. A Stanton Exhibition may also be awarded.

Latymer Upper School
Music Scholarships are available at the three levels of entry to the Upper School (11+, 13+ and Sixth Form). These are worth between one quarter and one half of fee remission. Music Scholars are expected to take a leading part in the musical activities of the School. A Music Scholarship also covers the cost of tuition on either one or two instruments. Music Awards are available for gifted musicians who just fail to qualify for a Scholarship and cover the cost of the tuition on either one or two instruments.

***Leighton Park School**
Major awards of 25%–75% fees, and minor awards of 15% fees, are available for Music and for other subjects.

Leicester Grammar School
Up to four scholarships are offered at any age. The scholarships are given on audition in recognition of achievement and potential in musical ability and are confirmed by a pass in the Entrance Examination.
All awards can be supplemented by bursaries when appropriate.

***The Leys School**
Awards of up to half-fees, index-linked. A reasonable academic standard required either in CEE or Scholarship Exam. Free tuition in up to 2 instruments. Music Scholarships are also available to Sixth Form Entrants.

Llandovery College
Candidates for Music Scholarships, which may be awarded at any age, must achieve satisfactory academic results, will be interviewed by the Director of Music and be called upon to demonstrate their choral and/or instrumental abilities. Free tuition is offered on one instrument.

Lord Wandsworth College
Music Awards are made annually at all stages of entry to the College. Further details may be obtained from the Headmaster.

Loretto School
Scholarships of up to one half of the annual fee and Exhibitons of up to one third fees are offered and free tuition on up to three instruments. A major Organ Scholarship is also available. Full particulars are available from the Admissions Tutor.

Magdalen College School, Oxford
Music Scholarships up to £2,500 pa in total value are offered each year at age 13 on an examination held at the School in March. Award holders also receive free tuition in one instrument.

Malvern College
Music Awards of up to 50% of the fees are offered. Free tuition. Scholarships, but not Exhibitions, are fee-linked.

Marlborough College
Up to six instrumental/choral scholarships/exhibitions are offered for competition each year in February to boys and girls at 13+. Up to four instrumental/choral equivalent awards are available for pupils entering the Sixth Form each September. The awards will be worth up to 50% of full fees depending on merit, augmented by bursarial assistance in cases of need. Scholars will receive free tuition on up to three instruments. At least grade 5 Merit or Distinction will be expected on the principal instrument of 13+ candidates: grade 7 to 8 Merit or Distinction for Sixth Form candidates; ability on a second instrument will be helpful but not essential. The examination will include two contrasting pieces on the main instrument and supporting skills will be tested. There will be a viva voce but no written test. Special consideration is always given to cathedral choristers and their potential for the Chapel Choir, even if their instrumental attainment has not reached the appropriate grade level.

Award winners must pass Common Entrance in June, unless they qualify for entry in the academic scholarship examination. They must be under 14 on 1st September.

Boys and girls should apply direct to the Director of Music for a preliminary audition (01672 892481). General information and registration forms are obtainable from the Senior Admissions Tutor, Marlborough College, Wiltshire SN8 1PA (01672 892300).

Merchant Taylors' School
The awards in music offered annually to boys at 11, 13 and 16 include two Scholarships up to the value of one quarter of the School fee, together with two Exhibitions up to the value of one tenth of the School fee. In addition, all award-holders receive free instrumental and/or singing tuition for up to two instruments per individual. Details from the Admissions Secretary, Merchant Taylors' School, Sandy Lodge, Northwood, Middlesex HA6 2HT. Tel 01923 845514.

Merchiston Castle School
Music Scholarships up to a maximum of 50% of full fees, plus free tuition on up to two instruments, may be awarded to suitably qualified candidates. Music Bursaries are available covering free tuition on up to two instruments. A Piping Bursary, covering tuition fees on the Bagpipes only, is also available to a suitably qualified candidate. (Applications by mid January).

Millfield
15 awards for entry into either the third or Lower Sixth Form.

Mill Hill School
One to four Music Scholarships or Exhibitions up to the value of 1/3 of the fees may be awarded to instrumentalists of outstanding potential. Auditions at the School are normally held during the Academic Entrance Scholarship Examinations (see p 419). Free instrumental tuition may be offered in addition to or in place of Awards.

***Monkton Combe School**
At least two instrumental Scholarships (see details under Entrance Scholarships). Free tuition in two instruments. Examination in February.

Monmouth School
Music Scholarships and Bursaries may be awarded at 11 and 13 up to the value of one-half fees and carrying free instrumental tuition. Sixth form organ or instrumental scholarships also available.

Norwich
Two Music Scholarships: value according to parental means. The maximum value is full fees, the minimum £300 p.a. Assistance is also given for instrumental tuition.

Cathedral Choristers hold Chorister Bursaries to the

* Music is taken into account in ordinary Scholarship Examinations.

value of 50% of fees. Further assistance in cases of need is possible.

Oakham School
A significant proportion of the Scholarship fund is devoted to Music Scholarships for candidates entering the school at 11, 13 or into the Sixth Form. The value and number of awards are determined by the standard of entries. Free instrumental tuition is given to award-holders and to pupils who have passed Grade 6 merit or above. 5% remission of full fee is offered to Cathedral and Choir School choristers.

Oratory School, Woodcote
All annual scholarships are open to music candidates. Awards include free music tuition.

Oundle School
Six Music Scholarships of half the school fees or a greater number of Minor Scholarships and Exhibitions, including the Manners Wood Scholarship for a string player. Bursaries available in certain cases.

Pangbourne College
Several Music Scholarships of up to the value of 50% of College fees are offered annually. All awards carry free tuition on two instruments.
Candidates should be approximately Grade V standard or above on their main instrument. A second instrument, or experience as a chorister is an advantage. String players will be given special consideration for an award even if the standard is below Grade V provided that sufficient potential is shown.

Candidates should be under fourteen on September 1 in the year of entry. The exact date of the Scholarship Examination, which is in early March, may be obtained on application. Music Scholarships are also available for entrance to the Junior School at the age of eleven.

Plymouth College
One internal Scholarship of £240 pa awarded at the end of the First Form Year.

One internal Scholarship of £480 pa awarded at the end of the Second Form Year.

One Open Music Scholarship (age 13+) of up to £750 pa.

Pocklington School
One Scholarship/Exhibition of up to £500 pa and/or Free tuition in one instument. Candidates must take February CEE.

Portsmouth Grammar School
A variable number of Scholarships is available at 13+, depending upon the quality of applicants. A major Scholarship of 50% of full fees may be awarded to an outstanding young musician. There are up to two Scholarships at Sixth Form level. Candidates are obliged to attend for tests, interview and audition on two musical instruments.

Prior Park College
Awards are available at three levels of entry: a Junior Scholarship (for entry at age 11) worth up to 50% of day fees, a Major Scholarship (for entry at age of 13) worth up to 50% of day fees, and a 6th Form Scholarship worth up to 50% of day fees.

Queen Elizabeth's Hospital, Bristol
Two music scholarships to the value of half the full tuition fee and also free tuition in two instruments are available, one at 11-plus and one at 13-plus. In addition, there is one music scholarship at 11-plus carrying free tuition in two instruments.

Queen's College, Taunton
Music Scholarships – half, third or quarter fees for the most gifted scholars including free tuition in one or two instruments. Up to 8 scholarships for talented musicians aged 10+, 11+, 12+ and 13+ at the projected time of entry to the college. Three Sixth form entry scholarships are also available plus an Organ award.

***Radley College**
Instrumental Scholarships, one of half fees, one of up to ½ fees, two of ⅓ fees, one of ¼ fees, and several Exhibitions are offered annually and further awards may be made if there are enough candidates of sufficient merit. Free tuition. Further details from the *Warden's Secretary*.

Reed's School
Any of the existing Scholarships and Exhibitions may be awarded for music.

Rendcomb College
Available at 11, 13 and 16. At least three major open scholarships. Several minor scholarships, valued at £900 per annum, including choral scholarships for gifted singers. Audition and interview take place at Rendcomb, and further details can be obtained from the Headmaster, Rendcomb College, Cirencester, Glos GL7 7HA. Tel Cirencester (01285) 831213.

***Repton School**
Up to 5 awards, one for string players; maximum value half fees. Free tuition in Music.

***Rossall School**
Up to 4 Instrumental Music Scholarships value of which varies from 50% to 15% of the Basic Fee according to the merits of the candidate. Awards include free tuition in two instruments.

***Royal Grammar School, Guildford**
Available at 11 and 13. One King's Scholarship for music, and a number of music Scholarships. Values vary from 50% to 10% fee remission. It is hoped that at least one major award can be made each year to a boy of outstanding musical potential entering the First Form at 11.

Rugby School
A number of Music Scholarships up to 50% of the fees plus free Music tuition are offered both at 13+ and 16+. The examinations are held at Rugby in February for the 13+ and November for the 16+. These awards may be augmented in cases of need. Details from the Registrar, School House, Rugby School, Rugby, CV22 5EH.

***Rydal Penrhos**
One or more Music scholarships may be awarded each year. These carry up to one-third remission of school fees plus free tuition on one instrument.

St Albans School
A variable number of awards of not less than 12½% of fees is offered for internal candidates or for pupils entering at 13+.
Internally awarded bursaries of up to a value equivalent to free musical tuition are offered to pupils from each year in the school. These awards are re-assessed at 13+ and 16+.

***St Bees School**
Music Scholarships up to half the value of the fees are awarded to candidates under 12 or under 14 on 1st September or to candidates for entry into the Sixth Form.

***St Columba's College**
Exhibitions, number not limited, £100 pa tenable for 4 years. Free tuition in one instrument.

St Edmund's College
Several scholarships of ½ and ⅓ fees are offered, all with free instrumental tuition. Music scholarships may be held with academic scholarships also up to ½ fees. Awards are made after examination in January at age 11–13 (Grade 5 is the minimum standard) and for entry into the sixth form

* Music is taken into account in ordinary Scholarship Examinations.

(Grade 8 standard required). Scholarships may exceptionally be awarded below the age of 11 to suitable candidates. A second instrument/singing is useful and special consideration may be given to orchestral instrumentalists and organists.

St Edmund's School, Canterbury
Scholarships and exhibitions of up to one half of the boarding or day fees (which may be supplemented by bursaries at the Headmaster's discretion) are available for applicants aged 11–16. The Scholarship also covers the cost of occasional lessons with London teachers for pupils reaching a sufficiently high standard. Music Scholars are expected to take a full part in the School's instrumental and choral ensembles, and attend concerts specified by the Director of Music, either locally or in London (the cost being covered by the Scholarship).

Examination requirements: Candidates should be at least Grade 5 standard at age 13. Two contrasting pieces on 1st instrument, 1 on 2nd. Scales, sight-reading, aural tests. Melody repetition, clapping rhythms, viva voce and musical tests covering basic rudiments and their application.

St Edward's School, Oxford
Music scholarships of up to 50% of full fees will be awarded each year to candidates of sufficient merit.

St John's School, Leatherhead
One Music Scholarship of value 50% of the tuition fee. Two Music Exhibitions of value 25% of the tuition fee. Free tuition in music.

***St Lawrence College, Ramsgate**
Music Scholarships are available at 11, 13 and 16. Awards at other points of entry may be considered.

The value may range from 10% to 50%, depending on ability and performance.

Music scholars should be at a minimum Grade 5 in performance. They receive instrumental tuition fee and have obligations to orchestra and choir. Preference is given to vocalists and string players.

St Paul's School
Several Foundation Scholarships and other scholarships and exhibitions are offered. The value depends on parental circumstances and may, in the case of Foundation awards, amount to full fee remission. One Sharp Scholarship is awarded at 16+. One Dennis Brain Scholarship is available on an irregular basis. Up to three South Square Scholarships may be awarded annually, in conjunction with Colet Court, for boys aged 8, 9 or 10 to sing in the Chapel and elsewhere with St. Paul's Chamber Choir. Instrumental awards at Colet Court for boys aged 10 or 11 may be converted to Foundation awards at St Paul's after a further audition. Free tuition for Foundation Scholars in two instruments.

Candidates for Scholarship entry at age 13+ must be aged under 14 on 1st September 2001.

Full particulars available from the Director of Music, St Paul's School, Barnes, London SW13 9JT.

St Peter's School, York
Various music awards up to half tuition fees are available for entrants to the third or sixth forms each year. Additionally, up to five pupils in each Senior School year may hold an award which carries with it free tuition in a musical instrument. Interviews and auditions for these awards are held in February or early March.

Full particulars from the Head Master's Secretary.

Sedbergh School
Musical Scholarships up to the value of half fee are offered for competition. Music scholars are usually offered free tuition in two instruments.

The Director of Music will be happy to meet prospective candidates at any time.

Further details may be obtained from the Headmaster.

Sevenoaks School
Several music awards are available each year, the number depending on the quality of the applicants. Usually about a dozen awards are made. The awards range in value up to one half of the day fee plus free music tuition in two instruments and are available to pupils entering at 11+, 13+ or 16+. Interviews and auditions are held in the Lent term. Full details from The Registrar.

Sherborne School
Up to three full fees worth of Scholarships may be awarded each year. In addition one Marion Packer Scholarship of £600 p.a. for an outstanding performance on the piano may be offered. Those awarded Scholarships receive free instrumental and tuition. The examination takes place in February.

Shrewsbury School
Four Scholarships up to the value of half fees. Music scholars are entitled to free tuition on two instruments.

Two Sixth Form Music Scholarships up to the value of half fees.

Silcoates School
Music Scholarships (index linked) are offered at 11+ and above. Award holders enjoy free music tuition.

Solihull School
One Full and two 50% Music Scholarships awarded annually. Age 11-13. Free tuition in one instrument.

Stonyhurst College
One or more music Scholarships offered annually on a generous scale related to parents' income and boy's talent.

***Stowe School**
Several Scholarships and Exhibitions are available to the maximum value of one half of the fees. Boys should be under 14 on 1st September. Those hoping to receive a major award should be at least Grade V standard on an orchestral instrument. There is no written examination but candidates should be prepared to sight-read and do ear-tests to the required standard as well as perform prepared pieces. There will also be an extensive interview with appropriate members of the music department. The Director of Music will be pleased to meet prospective candidates at any time. Full details may be obtained from: The Registrar, Stowe School, Buckingham MK18 5EH.

Strathallan School
Music Scholarship up to the value of 50% of the full boarding fee with free music tuition, are offered annually to candidates of suitable ability who should normally be under 14 on 1 September.

Sutton Valence School
Awards up to the value of 75% of the day or boarding fee are available at 11+, 13+ and into the Sixth Form. Free tuition in two instruments given.

Taunton School
Any of the existing Scholarships and exhibitions may be awarded for Music. Free tuition in orchestral instruments.

Tettenhall College
Two music scholarships (up to the value of two-thirds fees) may be awarded with free tuition.

Tonbridge School
Up to nine Music Scholarships (which include free instrumental tuition) are awarded each year. The value of any Scholarship awarded may be increased, by any amount up to the full school fee, if assessment of the parents' means indicates a need.

In addition, a number of Music Bursaries, giving free instrumental tuition, can be awarded each year.

* Music is taken into account in ordinary Scholarship Examinations.

Choral Boarding Exhibitions, with a value of one sixth of the school fee, are offered each year for award to Choristers of Cathedral or other Choir Schools. Candidates for music awards must also satisfy the academic entrance requirements of the School through the Common Entrance Examination or Scholarship Examination.

Full particulars of all Scholarships may be obtained from the Admissions Secretary, Tonbridge School, Tonbridge, Kent TN9 1JP. Tel. 01732 304297;
email: admissions@tonbridge-school.org

Trent College
There are several awards for Music available at 11+, 13+ and 16+.
The value of an Award depends on the age of the child, their ability and whether they are a day pupil or boarder.
We also offer free tuition to a number of deserving musicians each year.
Full details on all scholarships, examinations and entrance procedures are available from the Registrations Secretary, Tel: 0115 849 4950.

Trinity School, Croydon
Music Scholarships are available of up to 50% of full fee, supplemented up to the value of full fee in cases of financial need, with free tuition in one or two instruments. Boys are required to play two pieces on principal instrument and show academic potential in the Entrance Examination. Awards are available for all instruments and singing ability can be taken into consideration. Further details from the *Director of Music.*

University College School
One Scholarship or a number of Exhibitions will be awarded for Music after auditions in the Spring Term. Details of these special awards and their values are available from the Director of Music. In cases of need, Music Scholarships may be supplemented from the Bursary Fund.

Requirements: Two contrasting pieces on main instrument and, if possible, a demonstration of some ability on a second. Ear tests, sight-reading and viva. Singing is welcome as an additional accomplishment. Successful candidates will be required to play full part in the musical life of the school. The Director of Music is pleased to answer queries at any time. Candidates must not be over 14 or under 12 on 1st September of the year in which they take the examination. All Music Scholars/Exhibiters will be required to qualify academically for the Senior School.

Uppingham School
Up to twelve Scholarships of up to one half of the fees. Music Scholarships (for entry into the Sixth Form) are also awarded in November.

An indefinite number of Music Exhibitions may be awarded, granting free tuition on all instruments.

All Music Scholarships may be supplemented at the Schools' discretion in cases of need.

Warwick School
Music Scholarships are available to candidates entering the School at 13+. The awards are up to a value of 50% of the tuition fees and are based on the overall performance in the School Scholarship exam together with evidence of Scholarship ability in the Music option section of the Scholarship Exam. All Scholarships awarded on the basis of Music ability may be supplemented by Bursaries in cases of need. Further details available from the *Headmaster, Warwick School, Warwick, CV34 6PP (Tel: 01926 492484).*

***Wellingborough School**
One or more Scholarships at each level of entry, 13+, 14+ and Sixth Form.

***Wellington College**
A total of six Music awards is available, one of 50% fees for a girl entering at aged 16 and two of a similar value for boys at aged 13. There are three lesser awards, one of them tenable through Eagle House Preparatory School. Successful candidates are given free music tuition on up to two instruments; in certain cases this concession may be extended to deserving cases who fail to win an award.

Wells Cathedral School
A number of Music Scholarships and Exhibitions are available depending upon the standard and quality of applicants. Musical Scholarships can be up to 60% of specialist music fees.

In addition, the School is one of only four in England designated by the DES providing specialist musical education. The DES therefore provides generous assistance with tuition, boarding and music fees for up to 50 gifted musicians; grants being linked to parental income.

Cathedral Choristerships are awarded annually between the ages of 8½ and 10½, which normally provide 40% of boarding and tuition fees.

Ex Chorister Bursaries. On ceasing to be a Chorister, boys are eligible for an ex Chorister Bursary giving 8% of tuition or boarding fees.

Further details may be obtained from The Headmaster, Wells Cathedral School, Wells, Somerset BA5 2ST. Tel: (01749) 672117 or Fax (01749) 670724.

***West Buckland School**
One scholarship, value 20% to 50% of fees, for entry at the age of thirteen.

Westminster School
Several awards up to the value of half the current boarding or day fee, including free music tuition, are offered annually **with the possibility of additional means-tested bursaries up to a maximum of full fees**. The closing date for entries is early in January. Candidates, who must be under 14 years of age on the following 1st September, must subsequently take either the Common Entrance or gain admission through the Scholarship Examination, The Challenge. The Director of Music, Guy Hopkins is happy to give informal advice to possible applicants. For further information write to the Registrar, Westminster School, Little Dean's Yard, London SW1P 3PF (Tel: 0171-963-1003).

Whitgift School
A number of music scholarships and awards (for free instrumental tuition) are available up to the value of half the school fees to young musicians with outstanding potential. The closing date is mid January with auditions shortly after that date. Further details available from the Music Administrator.

***Winchester College**
At least six instrumental Exhibitions are available annually, normally worth up to half the boarding or day fee, with free instrumental tuition on two instruments. In cases of financial need additional bursary grants can be considered. One award may be reserved for Winchester College Quirister. In addition, one award may be available for entry at Sixth Form level. Successful candidates are generally at the level of Grade VI–VIII distinction. Music award tests take place in early February (each year). Music can also be offered as an option in the academic scholarship examinations in May.

The award of all music exhibitions is conditional upon candidates satisfying the academic requirements for entry into the school. For 13+ entry, candidates must be under 14 on 1st September of the year they come into the school.

The Master of Music – Mr K M Pusey – is pleased to answer queries and to see prospective candidates at any time. Full details available from the Secretary, Winchester College Music School, Culver Road, Winchester, Hampshire SO23 9JF.

Wolverhampton Grammar School
Musical Scholarships. A Music Exhibition (quarter-fees)

* Music is taken into account in ordinary Scholarship Examinations.

will be offered to an outstanding performer at 11+ or 13+. For further particulars apply to the Headmaster.

Woodbridge School
Music Scholarships and Bursaries are available, ranging from 25% of fees plus free music tuition to free music tuition.

Woodhouse Grove School
Instrumental scholarships and exhibitions given to promising musicians. The range of awards is from exhibitions for free music tuition to scholarships of up to half fees.

Worksop College
Instrumental Scholarships and Exhibitions up to 50% fees. Entry forms and further details about the Scholarships are available from the Headmaster's Secretary (01909 537127).

Worth School
At 11+, 13+ and 16+: Awards of up to 50% of annual fees. Exhibitions are also offered giving free instrumental/vocal tuition.

Wrekin College
At least two Instrumental or Choral Scholarships worth a half and a third of the school fees. Free tuition in music.

Wycliffe College
Instrumental – Scholarships and Exhibitions with a total value of £1,000. Free tuition in music.

Yarm School
Several music scholarships are awarded each year up to a maximum value of a one third fee reduction. Free instrumental tuition is usually included. Music scholarships can be applied for at any age.

SCHOOLS IN EUROPE

The British School of Brussels One Scholarship awarded annually value £3,000 per annum.

Art and Design & Technology Scholarships

For fuller information and dates of vacancies, application should be made to the School concerned.

Abbotsholme School
At least one Art Scholarship or Bursary is available per year for up to half fees. Candidates must be under 14 on the date of the examination. Further details from the *Headmaster.*

Abingdon School
One Art and Design Scholarship, entitling the holder to a nominal fee remission of £200 per annum plus fee remission up to the value of up to one half of the tuition fee, on means-tested basis, is offered annually to 13 year old candidates. Further details from *the Headmaster.*

Ackworth School
Up to two Art Scholarships of up to 25% of fees are awarded at 11 or 12. The awards are made on the strength of a 3 hour Art Scholarship examination and the submission and discussion of a portfolio of work, all of which must be supported by competent performance in the Entrance Tests.

Aldenham School
A small number of awards at 11+, 13+ and 16+ are available each year. These are based on the candidates portfolio and a short exercise at the school on a mutually convenient date.

Ardingly College
Two entrance scholarships in Art may be awarded annually. Both awards may be worth up to 50% of fees per annum. Both 13+ and sixth form entrants are eligible. Candidates will be interviewed by the Director of Art and will be expected to bring a portfolio of their work with them. They will also be expected to do a practical test. Art may be taken in its widest sense and any form of two or three-dimensional work which shows candidates' interests and ability is acceptable.

Bedales School
Art, Design and Drama Scholarships are awarded at 16+. Full details from the Registrar.

Bedford School
One minor scholarship for Art, Drama, Design Technology or Information Technology, value up to one third of tuition and boarding fees, and two exhibitions of £500.

Berkhamsted Collegiate School
The Art Scholarship at 13+ for min. £500 pa but variable according to merit, for boys on entry to Y9.

More information about Scholarships and Bursaries may be obtained on application to: *The Deputy Principal's Secretary, Berkhamsted Collegiate School, Castle Street, Berkhamsted, Herts HP4 2BB.*

Bishop's Stortford College
Art candidates can compete for all major awards at VIth Form level, under 14 and under 12.

Bloxham School
Art and Design Scholarships up to 50% of fees (up to 100% dependent on financial need). Scholarships, Exhibitions, Chapel Centenary Awards. Artistic ability taken into account in Open Scholarship and Common Entrance Examinations. Further details from the *Headmaster, Bloxham School, Banbury, Oxon, OX15 4PE.*

Blundells School
At least one award, sometimes more, of at least 25% of tuition fees. Details from *the Head Master.*

Bootham School
Up to two Art Scholarships of up to half fees are awarded at 11 or 13. The scholarships are given in recognition of artistic ability and potential but must be supported by a competent performance in Common Entrance or the Bootham Entrance Exam.

Awards can be supplemented by bursaries when appropriate.

Bradfield College
Up to 5 Art/Design and Technology Scholarships of between 10% and 50% of full fees.

Brentwood School
One Art Scholarship of £1,446 pa offered at 16. Further details from *the Headmaster.*

Brighton College
A number of scholarships and exhibitions will be offered each year to candidates showing outstanding ability in either Art or Design & Technology. Examinations and interviews will be held at the College in January (Art), May (CDT) for candidates intending to enter at 13+ in the following September. The value and number of the awards will depend on the calibre of the candidates. These awards are available also to pupils entering the College in the Sixth Form.

Bryanston School
One Art and one Technology award, value up to one-third current fees awarded on practical tests during examination.

Canford School
One Art Scholarship worth 20%, or two of 10% of the fees, is offered annually.

Charterhouse
Two Art Scholarships are offered for entry at 13+ as a result of an examination held at the school in February. In addition two Art Scholarships are offered for Sixth Form entry; the examinations for these awards will normally be held in the Autumn. All Scholarships can be increased to the value of the FULL SCHOOL FEE in cases of financial need. For details write to the *Admissions Secretary, Charterhouse, Godalming GU7 2DX.*

Cheltenham College
Art Scholarships may be awarded annually. Candidates should demonstrate ability in as many fields as possible, but particularly in drawing. Scholarships are also available in Design Technology and Electronics. Awards may reach 50% of the current fees and are available at 13+ and for entry to the Sixth Form.

Christ College, Brecon
One Art Scholarship may be awarded each year at 13+, up to the value of 50% of the fees.

Clifton College
A number of Art awards are made annually, including the Roger Fry Scholarship which is worth 50% of fees. Candidates must by under 14 on 1st September.

Cranleigh School
Each year, one one-quarter fee Scholarship may be reserved as an Art Scholarship if a suitable candidate comes forward. Examination in February; candidates sit either the Academic Scholarship or the CEE and must be over 12 and under 14 on 1st September. Further details and closing dates may be obtained from the Admissions Secretary, Cranleigh School, Cranleigh, Surrey GU6 8QQ, telephone (01483) 273997.

Culford School
One award is made up to the value of 50% of the tuition fee for an Art and Design & Technology Scholarship to a pupil entering at 13+.

Dauntsey's School
Any of the Awards, at 11+, 13+ and 16+, may be gained by a

candidate offering Art/Design. The Logsdon Exhibition may also be awarded. Details from the Head Master.

Dean Close School
An Art Exhibition or Bursary may be awarded. This is based on the candidate's portfolio, an interview with the Director of Art and a drawing test at the School.

Douai School
One or two art scholarships are offered each year to pupils entering the school at third form level from preparatory schools. An outstanding candidate may be awarded the total value of the scholarship which is equal annually to one term's fees in the September term of the year of the award, but this amount may be divided between two good applicants. Candidates must be over 12 and under 14 on the date of the examination. Further particulars may be obtained from *the Headmaster.*

Downside School
At least one Art Scholarship or Exhibition is awarded annually following the submission of a portfolio and an interview/assessment in May.

Dulwich College
At least one Art Scholarship annually to the value of one half of the tuition fee. The award may be increased in case of need. Age limit under 14 on 1 September. Examination in Lent Term. The successful candidate is likely to be one who, besides showing promise, is able to demonstrate that art is a predominant interest in his leisure time. A portfolio must be submitted and those called for interview will be expected to undergo a practical test. Candidates must take the Dulwich College Entrance and Scholarship Examination.

Durham School
Art and Design & Technology Scholarships and Exhibitions are available at 11, 13 and 16 to a maximum of half fees.

Eastbourne College
Up to 50% of the fees may be awarded per annum, in the form of Art Scholarships.

Ellesmere College
One or two Art Exhibitions awarded each year in May on the basis of an exam and a portfolio of pupil's work.

Emanuel School
At least one Art Scholarship is available at each age group of 10/11, 13+ and 16+. The value is up to 50% of fees.

Epsom College
Art candidates compete for all Open Scholarships. They should submit a varied portfolio of about 15 pieces of work and they will then be invited to Epsom to discuss their work at interview and to do an object drawing. Candidates must be entering the Sixth Form or under 14 on 1st September.

Exeter School
One Art Scholarship is offered annually following an assessment and is conditional on applicants achieving the School's academic requirements for entry. This scholarship offers a discount of 25-50% off tuition fees. Art Exhibitions offering smaller discounts may also be awarded.

Felsted School
Art and CDT Entrance Scholarships of up to 50% of the fees are available at 13+ and for entry into the Sixth Form. The School is a participant in the Arkwright Foundation Scholarship Scheme for Talented Students in Design at 16+.

Forest School
One Art Award to cover up to 50% of the fees is offered annually.

Framlingham College
Art and Design Scholarships of up to 50% of tuition fees are offered at 13+ and 16+. Applicants are invited to visit the school during the Lent term and will be expected to present a portfolio of work.

Frensham Heights
One or two Scholarships may be awarded annually for outstanding ability or potential in the creative or performing arts.

Giggleswick School
Art Scholarships and Exhibitions are available at either 13+ or Sixth Form level.

Glenalmond College
Boys and girls are invited to apply at 12+, 13+ or Sixth form. Awards may be up to 50% of fees.

Gordonstown School
One Art bursury (tenable for one or two years only) of up to £1,000 per annum is on offer each year.

Gresham's School
For 13+ entry one Open Scholarship of one half annual fees or two Open scholarships of one quarter annual fees.

One open Fishmongers' Scholarship of one third annual fees to a pupil of artistic and musical promise but with priority in Art.
For Sixth Form entry up to 3 Scholarships or one quarter of the annual fees.

Haileybury
Art Scholarships of up to half fees are available.

Hurstpierpoint College
One Art Scholarship awarded on the basis of a reasonable Common Entrance result and presentation of a folio of drawing and/or paintings.

Ipswich School
Pupils submit a portfolio of their work at the time of their entrance examination. The highest awards carry one-half tuition fees but may be supplemented by bursaries in case of proven need.

Kelly College
One Scholarship is offered annually of up to 50% of fees to boys and girls under 14 on 1st June. Candidates must either sit the Academic Scholarship Examination or reach the qualifying standard in the Common Entrance Examination. Candidates are invited to bring a portfolio or other examples of their work, and will take a practical test on the day to show their ability in drawing and painting. In addition they will be expected to submit a drawing assignment on a specified subject, details of which will be sent to candidates three weeks before the examination.

Exhibitions and Sixth Form Awards may also be available on the same basis.

Entry forms and further particulars can be obtained from: The Headmaster, Kelly College, Tavistock, Devon PL19 0HZ.

King's College, Taunton
Art & Design and Technology Scholarships. Applicants are invited to visit the school during the Lent term with a portfolio of work. Appointments may be made with the Headmaster's Secretary.

King's School, Canterbury
Art Scholarships are available to candidates of outstanding ability. Candidates must be under 14 on 1 September in year of entry. Further details from the Admissions Secretary.

King's School, Ely
Entrance Scholarships and Exhibitions (ie scholarships of lesser value) are awarded during the Lent term to candidates showing exceptional promise. Awards, which may represent up to 50% of fees, are made for Year 7, Year 9 and Year 12 entry and candidates will be invited to the School in February for interview with relevant Head of Department. A

brochure giving full details is available from: *The Admissions Secretary, The King's School, Ely, Cambridgeshire CB7 4DB. Tel: 01353 660702.*

King's School, Rochester
One Art Scholarship may be awarded annually and may have the value of a King's Scholarship of 50% of tuition fees.

The Scholarship will be awarded on the basis of an examination, usually in February, and a portfolio of the candidate's work.

Candidates will be expected to be capable of passing the Common Entrance Examination if 13+ or give evidence of being a genuine 'A' Level candidate if 15+.

Details of Academic and Music Scholarships are given elsewhere. A scholarship brochure, and further information, may be obtained from *The Headmaster, King's School, Satis House, Boley Hill, Rochester, Kent, ME1 1TE. Tel: 01634 843913. Fax: 01634 832493.*

Kingston Grammar School
Two Scholarships of half fees may be awarded at 11+ or 13+ following interview and submission of portfolio.

Latymer Upper School
Of the scholarships (up to half fee remission) funded by The Latymer Foundation a number are reserved for Art. Applicants will be expected to show at interview a full portfolio, including examination work and showing the breadth and depth of their artistic achievement. They should aim to demonstrate experience, qualifications and activity in recent years in and out of School, as appropriate, as well as their specific interests. Details are available from the Registrar 020 8563 7707.
e-mail: registrar@latymer-upper.org

Leighton Park School
Major awards of 25%–75% of fees, and minor awards of 15% are available for Art and for other subjects.

The Leys School
Art Scholarships are available at 13+ and 16+ to suitable candidates.

Llandovery College
Arkwright Technology Scholarships are awarded by special examination. Candidates should have a strong all-round science background.

Lord Wandsworth College
Art and Design & Technology Scholarships are offered to entrants to the Third Form and Sixth Form. Further details may be obtained from the Headmaster.

Loretto School
Art Scholarships are available at 13+ to suitable candidates. Portfolio and interview. Full particulars are available from the Admissions Tutor.

Malvern College
One Art Scholarship of up to 30% of the fees and two Art Exhibitions of lesser value. Scholarship, but not Exhibitions, is fee linked.

Marlborough College
One scholarship is offered annually at 13+. The merit component will range up to 25% of the fees. An Award will be eligible for augmentation above 25%, dependent on family financial circumstances, by means of bursaries.

Candidates will be required to bring their portfolio for discussion. It should contain a range of studies, colour work, objective drawing, imaginative work and indeed anything found to be visually interesting. Promise as well as achievement will be taken into account.

Award winners must pass Common Entrance in June, unless they qualify for entry in the Academic Scholarship Examination. However, they will be judged for the art scholarship entirely on the strength of their promise as artists. They must by under 14 on 1st September.

One Sixth Form Scholarship is offered annually and is worth 25% fees. This award may be augmented above 25% dependent on family financial circumstances, by means of bursaries.

Details of the Art Scholarships can be obtained from The Senior Admissions Tutor, Marlborough College, Marlborough, Wiltshire SN8 1PA.

Merchant Taylors' School
A scholarship may be awarded for Art on entry into the Lower Sixth. Both internal and external candidates are eligible. The maximum value is one half of the day-boy fee, but if there is financial need this can be increased, even up to full fees. Details from the Registrations Secretary, Merchant Taylors' School, Sandy Lodge, Northwood, Middlesex HA6 2HT. Tel: 01923 820644.

Merchiston Castle School
One Art and Design Scholarship up to 50% of full fees may be awarded (Applications by mid January). Candidates are required to submit a portfolio of work though promise, as well as achievement, is taken into account. Candidates will also be expected to achieve a sound academic standard. The Colin Paton Technology Award up to 50% of full fees is open to boys aged 13+, 14+, and 16+ who can demonstrate a technological aptitude, particularly in Electronics. (Interview flexible). The Arkwright Scholarship for Sixth Formers is awarded for Engineering, Design, Technology.

Millfield
3 awards for entry into either the Third or Lower Sixth Form.

Monkton Combe School
Of the ten Open Scholarships offered at least two may be offered for Art.

Oakham School
Art and Design, and Design and Technology Scholarships and Exhibitions may be awarded to candidates entering Oakham at 13 years of age. The normal academic entry requirements must be satisfied. Candidates will be required to submit a representative folder of their work together with a completed set project and come to Oakham for interview in February.

Art and Design and Design & Technology Scholarships to the total value of one third tuition fee are offered to candidates entering the Sixth Form. They are intended for those who wish to follow an A Level course in Art or Design and Technology, with the aim of taking up a career in these fields. Candidates will be required to submit a representative folder of their work, together with a completed set project, and come to Oakham for interview in November, and to qualify academically.

The Oratory School
Any of the existing Scholarships and Exhibitions may be awarded for Art.

Oundle School
Two Art Scholarships to the value of one third of the fees. Two Technology Scholarships to the value of one third of the fees.

Plymouth College
One Open Art Scholarship (age 13+) of up to £750 pa.

Portsmouth Grammar School
Art Scholarships are available at Sixth Form level.

Prior Park College
An Art Scholarship is available to exceptionally able applicants at ages 13+ and 16+. An Art Exhibition (minor Scholarship) is available to exceptionally able applicants at age 11+, who may then become eligible for the 13+ Scholarship when they reach the appropriate age.

Radley College
One Major Scholarship of half fees and the Bain Clarkson Scholarship of £500 pa will be offered annually. Candidates must be under 14 on 1 September. Further details from the Warden's Secretary.

Reed's School
Any of the existing Scholarships and Exhibitions may be awarded for Art and Design Technology.

Rendcomb College
Available for entry at 11, 13 and 16. At least two major open scholarships. Several minor scholarships at £900 per annum. The examination takes place at Rendcomb, and further details can be obtained from the Headmaster, Rendcomb College, Cirencester Glos GL7 7HA. Tel.: Cirencester (01285) 831213.

Royal Grammar School, Guildford
One Art Scholarship is available annually.

Rugby School
Design Scholarships & Talbot Kelly Art Scholarships (10% of the fees) are available for entry at 13+ and 16+. Details from the *Registrar, School House, Rugby School, Rugby, CV22 5EH.*

Rydal Penrhos
One or more art and design scholarships may be awarded each year. These carry a remission of up to one-quarter of the school fees.

St Albans School
At least one Scholarship worth not less than 12½% of fees is offered for internal candidates or for pupils entering at 13+.

St Edmund's School, Canterbury
Awards of up to one half of the boarding or day fees (which may be supplemented by bursaries at the Headmaster's discretion) are available for pupils entering at 13 or into the Sixth Form. The departments cover drawing, painting, sculpture, ceramics, photography, printmaking, textiles, and design and technology. Art may also be taken as part of the academic scholarship examination. A candidate offering art will be expected to produce a folio of recent work.

St John's School, Leatherhead
One Art Scholarship to value 50% of the tuition fee. One Exhibition at 25%.

Sedbergh School
Art Scholarships to the value of £3,000 are offered for competition.

Sherborne School
Art Scholarships and Exhibitions from half to one-eighth fees are offered. The examination takes place in March.

Arkwright Design and Technology Awards are also available.

Shrewsbury School
One Scholarship up to the value of one-quarter fees.

Stonyhurst College
Stonyhurst offers Scholarships in Art & Design and/or Design & Technology. Applicants are invited to submit portfolios of their work, personal as well as set pieces, which demonstrate a lively interest in and enthusiasm for the subject(s). There should also be evidence of proven ability through a variety of media and approaches. Portfolios should be sent or brought by the applicant early in May.

Stowe School
Art Scholarships to a maximum value of one quarter of the fees are offered in March. Candidates should normally be under 14 years of age on the 1st June. Candidates will be assessed on the quality of a portfolio of work and on performance in a day's practical test at Stowe. Painting, graphics and printmaking are the main courses offered but candidates are free to submit work in any areas of Art and Design though evidence of sound objective drawing must be shown. Full details may be obtained from: The Registrar, Stowe School, Buckingham MK18 5EH.

Sutton Valence School
Any of the existing Scholarships and Exhibitions may be awarded for Art.

Tonbridge School
Up to five Art or Technology Scholarships are awarded annually. The value of any award may be increased by any amount up to the full school fee if assessment of the parents' means indicates a need.

Candidates for Art Scholarships will be assessed by interview and practical assessment in early February. A representative portfolio of previous work will be requested together with two pieces of work done in advance of the examination.

Candidates for Technology Scholarships will be assessed by interview and written examination in early February. A portfolio will be requested as evidence of design and/or manufacturing skills.

Candidates for these awards must also satisfy the academic entrance requirements of the school through Common Entrance or the academic Scholarship examinations.

Full particulars of all Scholarships may be obtained from the *Admissions Secretary, Tonbridge School, Tonbridge, Kent TN9 1JP. Tel: 01732 304297;*
email: admissions@tonbridge-school.org

Trent College
Awards are available in Art at 11+, 13+ and 16+ and at 13+ and 16+ awards are available in Design and Technology.
The value of an Award depends on the age of the child, their ability and whether they are a day pupil or a boarder.
The school is also a member of the National Arkwright Scholarship Scheme.
Full details on all scholarships, examinations and entrance procedures are available from the Registrations Secretary: Tel. 0115 849 4950.

Uppingham School
Scholarships of up to half of the fees may be awarded for Art, Design and Technology. Full details may be obtained from the Headmaster's Secretary.

Warwick School
Art Scholarships are available to candidates entering the School at 13+. The awards are up to a value of 50% of the tuition fees and are based on the overall performance in the School Scholarship Exam together with evidence of Scholarship ability in the Art option selection of the Scholarship Exam. All Scholarships awarded on the basis of Art ability may be supplemented by Bursaries in cases of need. Further details available from the *Headmaster, Warwick School, Warwick CV34 6PP. (Tel: 01926 492484).*

Wellingborough School
One Art Scholarship is available annually.

Wellington College, Berks
Of the entrance scholarships one exhibition may be awarded for Art. Art is also taken into account for the aged 16 girl entry.

Wells Cathedral School
Discretionary Art Scholarships may be awarded. Art candidates compete for all open awards.

Further details may be obtained from The Headmaster, Wells Cathedral School, Wells, Somerset BA5 2ST. Tel: (01749) 672117 or Fax (01749) 670724.

Whitgift School
A small number of Art and Design Technology awards are

available to promising pupils. Please apply to the Registrar for further information.

Woodbridge School
An Art Scholarship to the value of 25% fees is available annually.

Worksop College
Awards will be announced at the same time as the academic scholarships. They will, however, be subject to an acceptable Common Entrance standard.
Folios should be sent to the Director of Art *by 7 May.* Candidates will be called to the school in *May.* They will be required to take a practical examination and, in some cases, a written examination in English comprehension and composition.
Entry forms, available from the *Headmaster's Secretary,* should reach the school *by 15 April.*

Wrekin College
Wrekin College Scholarships of a maximum of half of the fees may be awarded annually to pupils entering at any level in the school.

Yarm School
One art and one technology scholarship are available each year for sixth form entrants. Maximum value is a one third fee reduction.

Educational Awards

Enquiries are often made whether any schools either offer awards solely or primarily for the children of members or former members of the Services, Clergy, etc, or give special consideration to such children in the matter of reduction fees. This list does not claim to be a complete list of schools which offer such awards; up-to-date information may be obtained from the School concerned.

BEDFORDSHIRE

Bedford School

(1) One Fitzpatrick Scholarship for which preference is given to the sons of clergy.
(2) One Philip Blackwell Scholarship for the sons of Old Bedfordians.
(3) A number of Services Bursaries are available for the sons of serving members of the armed services. These offer 10% remission of tuition fees and 20% remission of boarding fees.
(4) Bursaries are also available for the sons of teachers in IAPS and HMC schools.
(5) Harpur Bursaries (Assisted Places) are available for Bedfordshire day-boys at 11+, 13+ and 16+, and Bedford School Bursaries for boys of the same age living outside the county.

BERKS

Eton College

Apart from the King's Scholarships, Music Scholarships, Sixth Form and Junior Scholarships described in the main entry, Eton offers the following Bursaries:

(1) A small number of Camrose and certain other Bursaries are available to any boy who would be unable, without financial assistance from the School, to receive education at Eton. The sons of clergymen, of university or school teachers and of other professional parents are particularly sympathetically considered. Bursaries are awarded according to need and may be worth up to one half of the School fee.
(2) War Memorial Bursaries, of similar value to Camrose Bursaries, are available on the same terms to sons and grandsons of Old Etonians.

Wellington College

Foundation Scholarships for sons of deceased Army Officers, also open and closed Scholarships.

BUCKS

Stowe School

At least 15 Entrance Scholarships and Exhibitions are offered annually to a maximum value of half fees. In conjunction with the majority of HMC schools Stowe is a signatory to the ACES agreement which limits awards to this level thus releasing money for additional exhibitions and bursaries according to parental need. Awards are also available in Art and Music. Roxburgh Scholarships are available for boys who gain entry at near scholarship standard. Candidates should be under 14 years of age on 1st September. Full details may be obtained from: The Registrar, Stowe School, Buckingham MK18 5EH.

CAMBRIDGESHIRE

King's School, Ely

A 10% discount in fees is available from age 4 upwards for childen of clergy serving the Christian faith, brothers and sisters of a child already in the school and boarders who are children of service personnel in receipt of BSA.

The Leys School

Certain awards for sons of Methodist Ministers and of Methodist families are available. The Bisseker Memorial Bursary is also available from time to time, for sons of Old Leysians. Special consideration is given to the sons and daughters of members of HM Forces.

CLEVELAND

Yarm School

Ethel Walton Bursaries are available to assist parents in difficult circumstances educate boys at Yarm School. Competitive Academic Scholarships offering up to a one third reduction in fees are available at 11+, 13+, 16+ and in the Preparatory School.

CUMBRIA

St Bees School

Substantial Bursaries are available.

Sedbergh School

Grants are made from the Sedbergh School Education Fund to sons of Old Sedberghians. The Headmaster has at his disposal other funds to help with the expenses of educating boys at Sedbergh.

DERBYSHIRE

Abbotsholme School

Concessions are available to children of members of the Clergy and the teaching profession.

Trent College

Two Albert Ball Scholarships for sons of RAF officers of £250 pa: 2 scholarships reserved for the sons of clergy, or half fees. The Kenneth May Award (value £250) is awarded on evidence of qualities of leadership together with games ability.

DEVON

Kelly College

Reduction of fees are made to sons/daughters of naval officers, schoolmasters and clergy according to need. Sons/daughters of naval officers killed on active service may be offered Foundationerships.

Plymouth College

Bursaries of up to two-third fees, together with various similar Scholarships, including one of £300 for the son of an OPM (Old Boy).

West Buckland School

Concessions are made to the children of clergy and of members of HM Forces.

DORSET

Canford School

One Royal Naval Scholarship worth 20% of fees pa for the son/daughter of a serving Naval Officer.

Bursaries for the sons of clergymen of the Church of England will be offered; these are awarded on interview and record, and candidates must pass the June Common Entrance Examination.

Sherborne School

Exhibitions are available for the sons of serving or ex-service officers, for the sons of R.N. officers and bursaries for the sons of Church of England clergy.

DURHAM

Durham School

Bursaries are available for the sons of Church of England clergy. Further particulars from the Headmaster.

ESSEX

Felsted School

Special Bursaries for sons of Clergy in the County of Essex and Diocese of Chelmsford.

GLOUCESTERSHIRE

Cheltenham College
Dill Memorial Scholarship awarded every 3 years – open in the first instance to descendants of the Prince of Wales Leinster Regt (Royal Canadian) and the E. Lancs. Regt. and to pupils from N. Ireland.

The Boyes' Scholarhip is awarded in the first instance to sons and daughters of serving members of Her Majesty's Forces.

Dean Close School
One Scholarship of 50% for sons and daughters of Clergy. Children of Schoolmasters, if awarded one of the 3 Open Scholarships (each worth 50% of the current fees), are awarded an extra 15%. Two Service Scholarships each at 18% of the current fees. Details of the allowances available to children of Clergy and for a third child will be made available on application to the School.

HAMPSHIRE

Lord Wandsworth College
Foundation places are available to pupils who have lost one or both parents through death, divorce or separation. Apply to the Foundation Registrar for full details.

Winchester College
Grants are made from the War Memorial Education Fund, primarily to the sons of Old Wykehamists. Particulars may be obtained from the Headmaster.

HEREFORD-WORCESTER

Hereford Cathedral School
Reduction of fees is made to the children of stipendiary clergy within the Diocese according to need.

King's School, Worcester
Several Exhibitions are available, for which preference is given to sons of clergy.

HERTS

Aldenham School
Special Bursaries of up to two-thirds of fees are available each year. These are for boys and 6th Form Girls who can show financial need and who are likely to make notable contributions to the life of the school.

Bishop's Stortford College
Richard Morley Scholarship available to sons of Free Church Ministers. A Lloyd's Cuthbert Heath Bursary is awarded annually to a boy in need of financial assistance who is likely to make an outstanding contribution to school life.

Haberdashers' Aske's School, Elstree
A number of Governors' Bursaries are awarded at age 11+, value £900 pa (occasionally more), to boys who score well in the School Entrance Examination and prove financial need. Open equally to boys already in the School and to those applying from other Schools. One Bursary is reserved for Music.

Haileybury
Scholarships, Exhibitions, All Rounder awards and Bursaries. Some Bursaries give preference to sons of serving and deceased officers. Reductions for sons of Clergy are considered.

St Edmund's College
Reductions are offered for sons and daughters of serving members of the armed forces and also for sons and daughters of school teachers.

ISLE OF MAN

King William's College
Three Hughes-Games Bursaries of £225 a year for sons of Naval Officers. Reduction of one half of the day-boy fee, one-third of the boarding fee for sons of Clergy resident in Isle of Man.

KENT

Kent College, Canterbury
A number of scholarships at 11+ and 13+ are offered each year, ranging in value from one-third to full tuition fee; a Sixth Form Scholarship is also offered on the results of the GCSE exams. Some Bursaries are available to assist with boarding fees for Assisted Place holders. Bursaries are also available for the children of Methodist Ministers.

King's School, Rochester
Reductions for sons of clergy (C of E) of $33\frac{1}{3}$% of tuition fees.

Service Personnel are allowed a 20% reduction in tuition fees for the first 2 years and 10% for the next 2 years.

Parents with three or more children at the School are allowed a reduction after the second child of 10% of the third child's fees, 20% for the fourth child and 40% for the fifth child.

St Edmund's School, Canterbury
Academic, Music, Art, Sport and All-Rounder scholarships are available at ages 11, 13 and 16. Bursaries and fee concessions are also granted to the children of former pupils, clergy, members of the armed forces, diplomatic personnel and to the third and subsequent children of the same family in the school at the same time. The School was originally founded to provide a free education for the fatherless sons of the clergy of the Church of England and the Church in Wales and still accepts applications from boys and girls for Foundationer status.

Applications should be made to the Headmaster.

St Lawrence College, Ramsgate
Scholarships and Bursaries. In the Senior and Junior Schools, on evidence of need, Bursaries of up to $^1/_3$ of the fees for children of clergy and missionaries, and of 10% for children of serving members of HM Forces.

Sevenoaks School
Five Assisted Places and a limited number of Bursaries are available each year in addition to the scholarship seperately announced.

Sutton Valence
One or two Clothworkers' Bursaries to the value of £500 per annum are available to boys entering the Sixth Form.

LANCASHIRE

Rossall School
A number of clerical bursaries, awarded on a means test to sons of Clergy who can sustain a proportion of the Fees themselves but who need extra help.

The bursaries rise to meet increases in the Fees.

Stonyhurst College
A large number of Bursaries up to half fees are awarded annually to boys in need of financial assistance and who are likely to make a good contribution to the life of the school.

LEICESTERSHIRE

Loughborough Grammar School
Not less than 2 scholarships for VIth Form Boarder entrants for sons of regular service personnel.

LONDON

City of London Freemen's School
A large number of Bursaries from Livery Companies are also available, mainly to sons and daughters of Freemen of the City.

Eltham College
Funds can be made available for sons of Missionaries and for sons of Ministers of other denominations. Please contact school for further details.

Forest School
Reductions for children of the Clergy.

Highgate School
A limited number of sons of Anglican clergy are admitted at half the Tuition Fee.

King's College School, Wimbledon
Bursaries and special grants for the sons of clergy of the Church of England.

Latymer Upper School
The School has its own bursary fund through which it can offer assistance with fees. The Parents' Guild and the Old Latymerian Association also provide bursaries to assist with school trips, tours and exchanges.

Mill Hill School
Exhibitions for sons of Christian Ministers. Scholarships and Bursaries for sons and relatives of Old Millhillians.

NORTHANTS

Oundle School
One Scholarship of £600 pa for the son of an Officer in the Royal Navy or Marines; when vacant (about every 5 years). Bursaries of varying value are available each year to assist the parents of boys and girls who would not otherwise be able to send their sons/daughters to Oundle.

NOTTS

Trent College
Boarding Awards for children of clergy and children of retired, deceased or active members of the armed services. On evidence of need Bursaries might be available to increase the grant.

Worksop College
Sons of clergymen may be taken at reduced fees.

OXFORDSHIRE

Bloxham School
Preference for some awards is given to the children of Clergy and members of the teaching profession. Preference for Raymond Scholarships is sometimes given to residents of North Oxfordshire. Boarding exhibitions can be awarded to the children of members of HM forces on the grounds of merit or promise.

St Edward's School
Clergy Bursaries of up to 30% of full fees may be awarded at the Warden's discretion.

SHROPSHIRE

Ellesmere College
Reduction in fees for sons of the clergy. Foundation and Regional awards for sons of parents of limited means.

Wrekin College
Special bursaries are available for sons and daughters of serving members of the armed forces.

SOMERSET

Clifton College
Special awards are available for the sons and daughters of old Cliftonians.

The Birdwood Award, for sons and daughters of serving members of HM Forces, is awarded on the result of the Entrance Scholarship exam.

King's College, Taunton
Academic, Music and Haywood and Barrow (all-rounder) Scholarships are available with awards of up to half-fees. A limited number of bursaries up to the value of half-fees are awarded to sons of the clergy. The Old Aluredian club awards bursaries of £750 per annum from time to time from its Benefit Fund.

Kingswood School, Bath
Special provisions are made for the children of Methodist Ministers and consideration may also be given to the sons and daughters of clergymen of other denominations, with a reduction in fees according to circumstances.

Two or three Scholarships covering full fees may be awarded each year to children of Methodist Ministers.

Monkton Combe School, Bath
In the Senior and Junior Schools remission of up to 1/3 of the fees is made to children of clergy and missionaries on proof of need.

Monkton Combe
Remission of up to one-third of the composite fee to a limited number of sons of Clergy and Missionaries on proof of need and this may be increased for Scholarship winners.

Taunton School
A limited number of bursaries for sons of clergy carrying a remission of up to half fees. One award given annually to the son of a member of the banking profession if there is a candidate of sufficient merit. In certain cases, assistance with education of sons of Old Boys.

STAFFORDSHIRE

Denstone College
Bursaries are available for the sons and daughters of the Armed Forces and Clergy.

SUFFOLK

Culford School
Generous Bursaries are available to members of the Armed Forces.

Framlingham College
Special bursaries available for the sons and daughters of serving members of HM Forces.

SURREY

Caterham School
Foundation bursaries are available for the sons of Ministers of the United Reformed and Congregational Churches. With the help of the Milton Mount Foundation, the value is up to 80% of the Boarding Fee.

Charterhouse
For sons of lawyers a Sir William Blackstone Award is offered annually to boys when aged 11 for entry to Charterhouse at the age of 13.

For details write to the *Admissions Secretary, Charterhouse, Godalming, Surrey GU7 2DX.*

Cranleigh School
Annual Closed Awards for sons of Regular Commissioned Officers on the active list of the Royal Navy, Army or Royal Air Force and sons of Clergy of the Church of England and sons of members of the public services. Further details may be obtained from the Admissions Secretary, Cranleigh School, Cranleigh, Surrey GU6 8QQ, telephone (01483) 273997.

Epsom College
Scholarships and bursaries for children of the medical profession and sometimes for children of solicitors.

Reed's School
A large number of Foundation awards are made each year to boys who have lost one or both parents, or whose parents are divorced or separated or whose home life is for some special reason, either unhappy or unsatisfactory. The values of the awards vary according to the circumstances. Enquiries should be addressed to the Secretary to the Governor's, Reed's School.

St John's School, Leatherhead
Special Scholarships and Foundationships for the sons and daughters of the Clergy.

Whitgift School
A large number of scholarships and bursaries are available each year courtesy of the Whitgift Foundation.

SUSSEX (EAST and WEST)

Ardingly College
One Scholarship to the value of 15% of fees pa for the Children of Clergy. This Scholarship carries the automatic award of a Clergy Bursary (up to 50% of fees pa). Two other Clergy Bursaries are available each year.

One Scholarship to the value of 15% of fees pa for the Children of Serving Members of HM Armed Forces.

One Scholarship to the value of 15% of fees for the child of an Old Ardinian.

Brighton College
Three or 4 Gill Memorial Scholarships offered in the Senior School and one in the Junior School for sons of regular Army officers (serving or retired). Fee concessions may also be made to sons of clergy of the Church of England where there is financial hardship. Cuthbert Heath Memorial Bursary available 3 years out of 5 for pupils who have a positive contribution to make to the life of the College.

Eastbourne College
Remission of fees is available for a limited number of sons of Clergy and Old Boys. Bursaries may also be awarded if a clear need for boarding education can be shown.

Hurstpierpoint College
There are Bursaries based on Common Entrance results and a means test for the sons of serving and retired Servicemen, and there are 3 Bursaries a year for award to the sons of Clergy.

Lancing College
Exhibitions annually for sons of Clergy, value up to £3,900 pa each. One Exhibition annually for sons of Navy or R Marine officers, value £1,700 pa.

WARWICKSHIRE

Rugby School
Awards, subject to availability of funds, are made to parents whose circumstances change whilst their children are being educated at the School. Certain of the funds devoted for this purpose give preference to the sons and daughters of former pupils. There is also some association with the Services. All such awards are subject to a means test.

WEST MIDLANDS

Solihull School
Reduction of 50% for sons of the clergy.

Tettenhall College
Reduction in fees for the children of clergymen and members of HM Forces.

WILTSHIRE

Dauntsey's School
Scholarships and Exhibitions are awarded on examinations held in November (Year 12), in January (Year 7) and February (Year 9) for the following September.

Full particulars are available from the Academic Registrar.

Marlborough College
The College offers a range of academic, music and art Scholarships at both 13+ and 16+, and sports awards at 13+, all of which are awarded as a result of competitive assessment. In addition, scholarships are available each year for children of Clergy, for whom there is an automatic remission of 15% of fees, with additional assistance as necessary. Other endowed scholarships and bursaries, and closed awards for children of Armed Forces personnel, are available from time to time when vacant.

YORKSHIRE (NORTH, SOUTH and WEST)

Ashville College
Special bursaries are available for the sons and daughters of Methodist ministers, and reduced boarding fees for the sons of serving members of HM Forces.

Bootham School
Bursary help may be available to sons and daughters of Quakers, or those in social or educational service. Further details from the Headmaster.

Giggleswick School
Discount available for children of HM Forces entering the Third or Sixth Forms.

Woodhouse Grove School
Special assistance is given to the children of Methodist ministers (to boarders and day pupils) and to boarders who are sons and daughters of serving members of HM Forces.

IRELAND

The Royal Belfast Academical Institution
One Scholarship normally of £27.50 pa for sons of clergymen, awarded on academic performance at the end of the first year.

SCOTLAND

Fettes College
Scholarships are available annually for sons or daughters of regular officers in HM Forces. Bursaries are available which automatically provide a 12.5% reduction in the fees for children of members of HM Forces. Special consideration is given to children of Clergy.

Glenalmond College
Scholarships are available for open competition, but in the award of one preference is given to sons or daughters of Service personnel. Special bursaries available for sons and daughters of clergy.

Gordonstoun School
Bursaries are available through the Heath Jary Sheridan-Patterson Trust up to one third of the fees for the sons or daughters of Royal Navy or Merchant Navy personnel.

Other bursaries are available to children of Service personnel.

Other specific awards are made from time to time and details of these are available from the Headmaster.

Loretto School
A number of Bursaries are available to sons and daughters of the Clergy. A limited number of Services Bursaries is available from time to time. In circumstances of special need, contact the Headmaster.

Merchiston Castle School
Community Award: One Scholarship up to 50% of full fees (up to 75% means tested), providing financial support to boys who would otherwise not be able to attend Merchiston, is available to candidates aged 8–18 years living in Edinburgh and surrounding area (EH postcode). Assessed by interview in conjunction with Entrance or Scholarship examination. (Application by mid January).

Trust Applications: The School can apply to charities on behalf of prospective pupils.

Forces: 10% fees remission is given to sons of members of HM Forces.

Hong Kong/Europe/Kenya/India: One All-Rounder Scholarship award for each country given either to a scholar or a boy who would otherwise not be able to attend Merchiston.

A number of other bursaries are available on application in cases of special need.

Morrison's Academy
A number of bursaries are available after examination each year. These will be awarded to pupils about to embark on the 'O' grade course (Secondary Form 3). The bursaries are income related and are restricted to pupils who are within daily travelling distance of the School. Further details from The Rector, Morrison's Academy, Crieff PH7 3AN.

In special circumstances consideration will be given to pupils at other stages.

WALES

Christ College, Brecon
There is a 25% fee remission for sons and daughters of the clergy, and 10% bursaries are available each year for the children of serving members of the armed forces.

Llandovery College
Forces bursaries are available for the children of serving members of the armed forces.
Sons or Daughters of the Clergy from the Province of Wales are eligible for a reduction of one third of the fee. A special Bishop Prosser Scholarship title is available for candidates from the Diocese of St. David's.

Monmouth School
Two bursaries are reserved for sons of serving members of HM Armed Forces on the 11-year-old General Entry Examination.

Rydal Penrhos
Reductions for sons and daughters of Ministers of the Methodist and Anglican Churches. Bursaries for sons and daughters of serving members of the armed forces.

BELGIUM

The British School of Brussels
Assisted places are awarded in accordance with need.

PART II

Schools appearing in Part II are those whose Heads are members of the Girls' School Association

The Abbey School

Kendrick Road Reading RG1 5DZ
Tel: 0118 987 2256

Founded 1887. Incorporated 1914

Council:
President: C F Taylor, Esq, OBE, DL
Chairman: Mrs F M Rutland, MA
Vice-Chairman: A J Kerevan, Esq, FCA

Professor R W Ainsworth, BA, DPhil
W Barclay, Esq, MA
Mrs J D Belcher, JP, MA, FRSA
Mrs C S Bevan, BSc, ACA, ATII
Mrs E H W Curran, BA
R G Griffiths, Esq
I C Kemp, Esq, MB, MRCP, MRCGP, DCH, DOBST, RCOG
Dr C F Print, DBA, ACMA, ADipC
The Revd Canon B Shenton
Mrs H M Smith
Dr B J Snell, BSc, MB, BS, MCopth, DO
Mrs A Stephens
P D Thomson, Esq, BSc, MIPM
Mrs S S van den Bos, MA, BSc
N Vaughan, Esq, MNASC
Mrs S Whitfield, MA (Cantab)

Staff:
***Headmistress:* Miss B C L Sheldon**, BA, ACE (Birmingham), CertEd (Hughes Hall, Cambridge)

Deputy Headmistress: Ms J E Harris, BA, MEd (Birmingham)

Mrs J K Arnold, BSc (Reading)
Miss K F Arnold, BEd (College of St Mark & St John, Plymouth)
Miss R J Arnold, BEd (Oxford)
Mrs C T Ayles, BSc (Leicester)
Mr N J Balchin, BSc (Bristol), BA (Open University)
Mrs H S Ball, BEd (King Alfred's College, Winchester)
Mrs J L Barton, MA (Oxford)
Miss J R Beer, BA (Leeds)
Mrs A Blaseby, BA (Reading)
Mrs W Bond, BA (University College, Cardiff)
Mrs J M Boot, BA (London)
Miss E R Boswell, BA (Worcester College, Oxford)
Mrs E A Boyle, BSc (North Staffordshire Polytechnic)
Miss A Bright, BA (York)
Mrs K E Bull, BSc (Birmingham)
Mrs C A Burn, BEd (Bedford College of Higher Education)
Mrs C I Butler, BEd (Reading)
Miss M L Caley, BA (Portsmouth Polytechnic)
Mrs Y J Charlesworth, BSc (Reading)
Mrs P Cody-Singer, BA (Loughborough)
Mrs S L Colebrook, BSc (Sheffield)
Miss A Davies, BA (Sussex)
Mrs M M Delaney, BSc (London)
Mrs B Downes, BA (Durham)
Mrs S M Elder, DipEd (Dunfermline College of Physical Education)
Mrs M Farsch, MA (Reading)
Mrs K E I Florey, BA (University College, Cardiff)
Miss R H L Floyd, BEd (Bedford College of Physical Education)
Mrs S H Flynn, BA (Roehampton Institute)
Mrs M B Giblin, Lda en Filosofia y Letras (Salamanca)
Mr M Giles, BA (Wales)
Mrs L H Glithro, BSc (St Andrews)
Mrs S M Goodenough, BSc (London)
Mrs J L Gray, BSc (Reading)
Miss E L Hadfield, BSc (University College, Chester)
Mr C A Hammond, BA (Reading)
Mrs J A H Harrison, BSc (Warwick)
Mrs K Haywood, MA (Paris), Licence d'Anglais (Paris)
Mrs S L Heard, BA (Huddersfield)
Mrs J H Hill, BA (London)
Mr E J Hills, BSc (Dundee)
Dr A E Holland, BA (Manchester), PhD (Reading)
Mrs C E Hudson, BA (Birmingham)
Mrs V A Hughes, BSc (Lancaster)
Mr W Hunter, BA (York)
Mrs R Jennings, BA (Birmingham)
Mrs L A M Johnson, L-ès-L (Rennes), MA (Manchester)
Mrs R M Johnson, BSc, ARCS (London)
Mrs P J Kemp, BA (London), MA (Reading)
Mrs V Lakin, BEd (Reading)
Miss B M Laverack, BSc (London)
Mrs J Lesbirel, BEd (University College, Cardiff)
Mrs M A Lovett, JP, BA (Durham)
Mrs E Lowth, BA (St Hugh's College, Oxford)
Mrs L A Lyle, BA (Belfast) MLitt (Newcastle)
Mrs S A McCaig, BSc (Hull)
Mrs M McCallum, Lda en Filosofia y Letras (Barcelona)
Mrs D M McDougall, BA (Bristol)
Mr J L Maingot, BA (London)
Mrs J A Marks, BA (University College of Wales, Aberystwyth)
Mrs W I Mitchell, CertEd (Notre Dame College, Liverpool)
Mrs C A Nelms, BSc (Southampton)
Mrs J Page, BSc (London)
Mrs J C O Palfrey, Teacher's Certificate, Diploma in Theology (London)
Mrs S M Parsons, CertEd (Bath College of Education)
Mrs F M Pateman, BEd (Sheffield)
Mrs K Pinto, BSc (Sussex)
Miss A Quinn, BEd (Bedford College of PE)
Ms G M Reilly, BSc (Dublin)
Miss P S Roberts, BSc (London)
Mrs B A Salisbury, ARCM, LRAM
Mrs H S Scourse, BSc (Belfast)
Mrs M R Shepherd, BA (Southampton)
Mr J M Singer, BA (Nottingham)
Mrs D Smailes, CertEd (St Hild's College, Durham)
Miss J A Snaith, BEd (Bedford College of Higher Education)
Mrs P M Solomons, BSc (Bristol)
Mrs J M Stanbrook, CertEd (Reading)
Mrs K Staub-Leigh, BA (Reading)
Mrs R Steele, BA (Reading)
Mrs S A Stone, BSc (London)
Mrs A-M Sturrock, BEd (College of St Mark & St John, Plymouth)
Mrs T Sweby, BSc (Reading)
Miss S E Talbot, BA (London)

Mrs K Thomas, BSc (Robert Gordon's Institute of Technology)
Mrs J F Thomson
Mrs J A Trott, BSc (London), MPhil (Newnham College, Cambridge)
Mrs J C Tuckett, MA (Cambridge)
Mrs J E Turkington, MA (Lancaster)
Dr L Walker, BSc (Glasgow), PhD (London)
Mrs S Watt, FCA
Mrs V F Whistance, BSc(Econ) (University College of Wales, Aberystwyth)
Mr S D Willis, BA (St John's College, Cambridge)
Miss V J Woodley, BA (Hull)
Ms S J Young, BA (Durham), LTCL

Visiting:
There are 19 Visiting Music Staff and a Teacher of Speech & Drama

Bursar: Mrs V M Haywood, MA, MIPD, MBIFM

Number of girls. 990.
Church of England Foundation.

The School is situated in 6 acres of grounds. Many improvements and extensions to the buildings have been added: an extensive science block, a separate VI form suite, six computer rooms, two school libraries, a music centre with rooms for class teaching and individual instrumental teaching, and two large assembly halls. There is a Modern Language Centre with language laboratories. The school has an indoor heated swimming pool. The Junior Department has its own buildings, including science laboratories, music facilities, computer room and fine assembly hall.

Education. The course provides for a balanced academic education up to University and Oxbridge entrance. Subjects taught include: Religious Studies, English, History, Geography, Sociology, Economics, Business Studies, French, German, Spanish, Latin, Greek, Mathematics, Physics, Chemistry, Biology, Computing, Psychology, Drama, Art and Design, Food Technology, Textiles, Music, Physical Education including swimming, dance, gymnastics, hockey, netball, rounders, athletics, tennis and rowing.

Extra Subjects. Pianoforte, Violin, Violoncello, Double Bass, Flute, Clarinet, Oboe, Cornet, Trumpet, Horn, Trombone, Euphonium, Tuba, Saxophone, Percussion, Speech and Drama.

Academic scholarships (*see* Entrance Scholarship section). Scholarships are available at ages 11 and 16, including a Wolfson Bursary offering an award of one third fees. Music Awards are also offered at ages 11 and 16. The School has its own Assisted Places Scheme.

Postal Address: The Abbey School, Kendrick Road, Reading RG1 5DZ.

Telephone: 0118 987 2256

Charitable status. The Abbey School is a Registered Charity, number 309115. The School exists to educate academically able girls.

Abbots Bromley
(School of St Mary and St Anne)

See under School of St Mary & St Anne, page **701**.

* Head of Department	§ Part Time or Visiting
† Housemaster/Housemistress	¶ Old Pupil
‡ See below list of staff for meaning	

Abbot's Hill

Bunkers Lane Hemel Hempstead Herts HP3 8RP
Tel: (01442) 839107 (both Junior & Senior Schools)
Fax: (01442) 269981
e-mail: registrar@abbotshill.herts.sch.uk
website: www.abbotshill.co.uk

Founded 1912
Motto: *Vi et Virtute*

Chairman of the Governing Body: G Corbett, MA (Cantab), MSc

***Headmistress:* Mrs K Lewis**, MA (Cantab), BSc (Open), PGCE

Deputy Headmistress: Mrs S Robinson, BA (Hons) (Herts), CertEd

Headmistress of Junior School, St Nicholas House: Mrs B Vaughan, CertEd

School Chaplain: The Vicar of St Mary's Church, Apsley

Bursar: Mr Charles King, FCMA

Abbot's Hill School day, weekly, and flexible boarding for girls aged 11–16. The school is noted for its family atmosphere, small class sizes, and the individual attention afforded to each pupil. The school offers a broadly based education, which enables girls to achieve their maximum academic potential. It has a strong tradition of developing all round skills and confidence in each pupil.

Premises. The school is set in a Victorian country house within 70 acres of parkland near Hemel Hempstead. The grounds have impressive facilities for Science, Art and Craft, Information, Communication Technology, Music and Sport.

Location. Excellent road and rail networks link the school with major motorways (M1/M25), 35 minutes by train to Central London. Heathrow and Luton Airports are 35 minutes by car.

Philosophy. Each girl is recognised as an individual and they are encouraged to expand their knowledge and capabilities to the maximum of their potential. With small classes and a high teacher-pupil ratio, the school aims to develop the academic and creative talents, social skills and confidence of each pupil. Every girl benefits from being known personally by the Headmistress and teaching staff who seek to create a happy and caring environment.

Curriculum. During the first three years, a broad programme based on the National Curriculum is followed, encompassing both academic and creative subjects. Each girl's potential and progress is carefully monitored by both teaching staff and a personal tutor. Subjects studied include English, Maths, Science, French, Spanish, Geography, History, Information and Communication Technology, Religious Studies, Music, Personal, Social and Health Education, Art and Design, Cookery and Home Economics, Physical Education and Child Development.

In Years 10 and 11 a core GCSE curriculum of 6 subjects is followed with girls choosing up to three further subjects. English as a Foreign Language and Extra English are also available.

Religion. Abbot's Hill is a Christian foundation. Children of all faiths are welcome at the school and all religious observations are respected.

Boarding and Day Options. Boarding at Abbot's Hill has evolved over the years to offer the maximum flexibility to parents. The school offers Weekly, Flexible and Daily boarding as well as Day pupils. The school day accommodates the needs of all pupils. Whichever option is chosen every girl benefits from being part of a small close knit community.

Music. The school has a very strong Music Department, with the School Choirs and Orchestra performing regularly in concerts, recitals, plays, musicals and various functions throughout the year. During the Year 2000 pupils from Abbot's Hill took part in Millennium celebrations at the Royal Albert Hall, St Paul's Cathedral and St Albans Cathedral. The Senior Choir also embarked on a singing tour of Canada during the summer of 2000.

Sports. The school has a strong sporting tradition. There is a well equipped gymnasium, lacrosse pitches, grass and hard tennis courts (indoor and outdoor), and a heated swimming pool. The main sports played are Lacrosse, Netball, Athletics, Tennis, Rounders and Swimming. Tennis coaching is available throughout the year on the indoor courts. All girls are encouraged to participate in the sporting opportunities at Abbot's Hill and currently there are a number of girls who have reached County and National standard in selected sports.

Extra-Curricular Activities. Many activities and clubs are held outside of school and these vary in range from Dance, Art, Photography, Duke of Edinburgh Award Scheme, Music, Speech and Drama and all sports.

Sixth Form and Beyond. In Years 10 and 11 girls are prepared to make decisions regarding their future academic career. They are encouraged to think beyond their GCSE results and to decide whether they would like to study for A level courses. A Sixth Form Forum is held every year and many schools are invited to Abbot's Hill to exhibit their Sixth Form Courses.

Admission. Admission to Abbot's Hill is by Entrance Examination, a report from the Junior school and Interview. Girls are admitted to the school at ages 11, 12 and 13. Bursaries and scholarships are available.

Fees. (*see* Entrance Scholarship section) Weekly boarders £4,500. Flexible boarding fees depend on the number of nights boarded. Day Pupils £2,720 per term.

Junior School. The Junior School of Abbot's Hill is St Nicholas House. Situated in the grounds of the Senior School, St Nicholas House provides nursery, pre-prep and preparatory education for girls aged 3–11 and boys aged 3–7. Please see separate entry under the IAPS section, Part V of this Book.

Further information. Abbot's Hill welcomes visits from prospective parents and pupils. If you would like to visit the school, please telephone the Registrar for an appointment on 01442 839107.

Charitable status. Abbot's Hill Charitable Trust is a Registered Charity, number 3110533. It exists to provide high quality education for children.

Adcote School for Girls

Little Ness Near Shrewsbury SY4 2JY
Tel: (01939) 260202
Fax: (01939) 261300
website: www.adcoteschool.co.uk

Motto: *Nisi Dominus Frustra.*

Visitor: The Bishop of Lichfield

Board of Governors:
President: Mr D H Peters, OBE
Chairman: Mr L R Jebb, MA
Vice-Chairman: Mrs S Draper, BEd

***Headmistress:* Mrs A E Read**, MA (Open), BSc (Birmingham), PGCE (Cambridge)

Director of Studies: Miss L Hudson, BEd (Bedford)
Senior Teacher: Miss E Stephenson, BSc (City), PGCE (London)
Housemistress: Mrs S Smithyman, BEd (CNAA)
Head of Junior Department: Mrs A Ravenscroft-Jones, BEd (Birmingham)
School Chaplain: The Revd L Foster

Staff:
Mr D Austin, MSc (Portsmouth), BSc (Lancaster), BA (Open), PGCE (Reading)
Mr A Batchelor, BSc (Wales), PGCE (Bath)
Dr D Bonella, PhD (London), BSc (Southampton), PGCE (Middlesex)
Mr R Bonella, MA (London), MSc (Loughborough), BSc (Southampton), PGCE (Wolverhampton)
Mr P Bullough, BA (Sheffield), PGCE (Bristol)
Mrs S L Dever, BA (Reading), PGCE (Leeds)
Mrs R Dyas, BSc (Liverpool), PGCE (Wolverhampton)
Mr R Gwillim, BA (Greenwich), PGCE (Aberystwyth)
Miss N Halford, BA (Exeter), PGCE (UEA)
Mrs A Knox, BEd (Bath)
Mrs C Lapage, MA (Wales), BMus, PGCE, ARCO
Mrs F Nicholson, BEd Hons (Liverpool)
Mrs H Reidy, BA (Sheffield), PGCE (London), RSA Diploma Specific Learning Difficulties
Mrs J P Sambrook, University of Liverpool Teacher's Certificate
Mrs M Wilford, University of Munster Teacher's Certificate
Miss L Wilson, BSc (Bangor), PGCE (Bangor)
Mrs G C Wragg, DipAD (Exeter) ATC (Hornsey)

Adcote is a Boarding and Day School for girls aged 4–18 (weekly boarders welcome). It was founded in 1907 and became an Educational Trust in 1964. The main house, a Grade I listed building acknowledged to be one of the finest works of Norman Shaw, RA, stands in 27 acres of landscaped parkland with extensive views to the Welsh Hills.

Recent developments include a third specialist Science Laboratory; Sixth Form Centre; Re-designed and refurnished Junior Department; Art/Craft Department, in the latter multi media work in ceramics, print making, graphics, photography and fine art are offered; and an expansion in the Technology Department which includes a new Food Technology Room. There is a well equipped Gymnasium, Lacrosse and Athletic Fields and three hard Tennis Courts.

Great importance is attached to developing the talents and character of each girl. There are a wide range of extra curricular activities available including Sporting Clubs; Instrumental Music; School Choir; Duke of Edinburgh Award Scheme; Motor Vehicle Studies; Riding; Speech and Drama; Dance; Archery; Clay Pigeon Shooting.

A wide range of subjects are offered to both GCSE and A level and small classes and high teacher pupil ratio of 1:9 ensure good academic results.

Termly Fees: (for 2001/2002). Day Girls from £1,355 to £2,510; Weekly Boarders £3,280 to £4,065; Full Boarders £3,610 to £4,455. Reductions are made in fees of second and subsequent sisters. Bursaries are available for children from Service families.

Scholarships for academic excellence.

Prospectus and further details may be obtained from the Headmistress.

Charitable status. Adcote School Educational Trust Limited is a Registered Charity, number 528407. It was founded to provide boarding and day education for children.

The Alice Ottley School

Worcester WR1 1HW
Tel: (01905) 27061; Bursar (01905) 21394

Badge: *Lilium Candidum*
Motto: *Candida Rectaque*

Visitor: The Right Revd The Lord Bishop of Worcester

Governing Body:
Chairman: The Rt Hon The Lord Sandys, DL

Mrs C F G Anton, MA (Cantab)
Miss S M Chapman, BA
Mr F H Briggs, BA, FCA
Sir Geoffrey Dear, QPM, DL, LLB
Mr J Del Mar, BSc
Mrs M Goodrich, MA (Cantab)
Mr K D Harmer
Mr D R Harrison, LLB
Mr A C S Hordern, FCA
Sir Anthony Hughes
Lady Mynors
Mr T J Patrickson
Sir Michael Perry, CBE
The Ven Dr J Tetley

Secretary to the Council and Bursar: Mr S B Cusack

***Headmistress:* Mrs M Chapman,** MA (Aberdeen), DipEd, NPQH

Deputy Heads:
Mr Q N Brewer, BEd (Birmingham), MA (Open)
Miss M Morrow, BEd (Leeds), MEd (Belfast)

Head of Junior School: Miss J A Layfield, BEd (CNAA)

Hon Chaplain: The Reverend S Currie, MA (Oxon), MA (Cantab)

Staff:
Mrs J Allison, BSc (Birmingham) *Biology*
Miss R I Atkinson, BEd (CNAA) *Home Economics, Careers*
Mrs C R Bayliss, MA (Aberdeen), LLCM *Music*
Mrs A M Barrett, BA (Birmingham) *Religious Education, Careers*
Miss R S Briggs, BSc (Bath) *Natural Sciences*
Mrs L J Cameron, BSc (St Andrews) *Botany*
Mrs G Cartwright, BSc (Aston) *Chemistry*
Mrs V D Chatwin, BA (Oxon) *Classics*
Mrs J Cormack, MA (Aberdeen) *Geography/History*
Mrs J L Cowton, BA (Birmingham) *French, Head of Year*
Miss K M Dale, BEd (Bath) *Textiles*
Mrs D J Davies, BSc (London), ARCS *Physics*
Mrs M Deighan, BA (Manchester) *English*
Miss E A Dovey, MA (Oxon) *History*
Miss N Estaun (University of Valladolid) *Spanish*
Mrs J M Evans, BA (Open), ABSM *Music*
‡Mrs S J Farr, CPE (Chelsea) *Physical Education*
‡Mrs A Fitch *Physical Education*
‡Mrs M R Fox *Textiles*
Mrs J S Garratt, BSc (Bristol) *Geography, ICT*
Mrs J F Glover, BSc (London) *Mathematics, Head of Year*
Mrs H Green, MA (Heidelberg) *German*
Mrs M R Hatch, BSc (Aston) *Mathematics, Head of Year*
Mrs S C Hobby, BA (Leicester) *English*
Miss E J W Holwill, BSc (London) *Geography*
Mr A J Horton, BA (Bristol Polytechnic) *French*
Mr M A Howard, BTech (Brunel) *Design Technology*
Mrs C A Hunter, BA (Leeds) *Art*
Miss M E John, BSc (Wales) *Mathematics*
Mrs L Kettle, BEd (Madrid), MA (Murcia), MSocSci (Birmingham) *Spanish*
Miss S J Lambert, BA (Oxon) *Mathematics*
Mrs J Marks, BEd (Sussex) *Physical Education*
Miss J E Marsh, BA (Wales) *Religious Education*
Mrs J F McCreath, BA (Exeter) *French*
Miss J R Pearson, BA (London) *History*
Mr M L Pegg, BA (Birmingham), MA (Reading), ARCO, ARCM, ABSM *Music*
‡Mrs S E Perks *Art, Head of Year*
Mrs J M Peters, BA (Open) *Economics, Business Studies*
Mrs S J Price, BA (Liverpool) *French and Russian*
Miss S J Richards, BSc (Durham) *Mathematics*
Mrs S D K Ridgway, BA (Keele) *Classics*
Miss S Roberts, BSc (South Bank, London) *Physical Education*
Mrs A C Taylor, BSc (Leeds), PhD (London) *Science*
Mrs L F Taylor, BSc (London) *Chemistry*
Mrs M Thompson, BA (Open), CPE (Dartford) *Mathematics*
Mrs A R Threadgold, BA, MA (Birmingham), BEd (CNAA) *English*
Miss E H Tyler, BA (Kent), MA (Warwick) *German*
Mr M P Williams, BEd (Birmingham), CPhys, MInstP *Physics*
Miss A Wilson, CPE (Dartford) *Physical Education*

Visiting Staff: Music
Mrs M Bridger, GRSM, LRAM, ARCM
Mrs A Grew, GMus
Mrs D Gwilt, LTCL
Mr M Harrison
Mrs P Harrison, GTCL, LTCL
Mr T Hunt, GRSM
Mrs J C Jones, BA (Birmingham), ARCM, ABSM
Mrs J Jones, BA
Mrs C Kennedy, BMus (London)
Mrs P Moore, MA (Edinburgh)
Mr M Schellhorn, BA, BMus (Cantab), ARCM
Mrs M Thompson, BMus (Sheffield)
Mrs M Willmot, LRAM
Miss E Winscom, BA (Bristol)

Junior School Staff:
‡Mrs P M Arr
Mrs L Bayly, BEd (Worcester)
‡Miss C Burbidge
Mrs S Graty, BA(Ed) (Worcester)
‡Mrs A M Hale
‡Mrs J M Jarvis
Mrs A M Jennings, BEd (CNAA)
Mrs A Webster, BEd (Exeter)
Mrs G Williams, BEd (Birmingham)

‡ denotes Dept of Education Certificate

The Alice Ottley School is an independent day school for girls from age 3-18. We aim to provide the best possible education for all our girls in a community based on trust and mutual respect. By combining excellent academic standards with a varied programme of activities, pupils may enjoy a rewarding and challenging school environment. We value all types of contribution and achievement within a single sex environment, where girls are free to develop self-confidence and self-awareness in readiness to face the demands of the modern world.

Admission. The School has its own Entrance Examination from 6+. Sixth Form entry is by examination and interview, conditional on five GCSE passes at A*-C.

Excellent Facilities. The School occupies spacious Georgian buildings close to the city centre, with easy access to the railway station. These have been extensively modernised to include a newly furbished Modern Languages suite of rooms and first class accommodation for

Home Economics and Textiles. There is a separate Science block, a Design and Technology wing, a Lecture Theatre, an indoor Sports Hall and a Performing Arts Studio. The Junior School, Springfield, is located nearby in its own grounds. There are 650 girls in the School, with 122 in the Sixth Form and 150 in Springfield.

Sixth Form Centre. The Sixth Form students have their own separate accommodation in St Oswald's, a house close to the main school buildings. This consists of two common rooms, a study area, seminar teaching rooms and a kitchen.

Curriculum. The School aims to provide an all-round education, enabling each girl to reach her full potential. A broad and balanced programme is followed to the age of fourteen and the Option scheme for GCSE in Year 10 is arranged to ensure that each girl has a balanced programme without premature specialisation.

At A Level a wide range of subjects is offered, including a comprehensive General Studies programme. The School has an excellent record of entries to Oxford and Cambridge and to other universities and colleges of education.

Activities. Music plays an important part in the life of the School and tuition is given in most instruments. There are two orchestras and a strong choral tradition. Lacrosse, Hockey, Netball, Tennis, Rounders, Athletics and Badminton are all played, with the school teams achieving excellent results in local and national competitions. There are frequent Drama productions, usually in co-operation with the neighbouring boys Grammar School. Girls are also encouraged to be aware of the needs of others, and every year thousands of pounds are raised for charities, local, national and international. A wide range of activities is on offer at lunchtimes and after school, from Archery to Art Club and from Technology to Trampolining. Many of the older students participate in the Duke of Edinburgh's Award Scheme and the Young Enterprise Business Scheme.

Staff organise many overseas trips for pupils and recent visits have included the study of Art and Architecture in Florence, a Business Studies and Economics trip to New York and skiing trips to America and Austria.

There are annual language exchanges with schools in France and Spain.

A supervised Homework Club is run in the main Library every day from 4.00 to 5.30 pm.

School Fees. Tuition fees £1,059 to £2,276 per term, inclusive of lunch, books and personal accident insurance. There is a special rate for the daughters of stipendiary Clergy, and a reduction for sisters.

Scholarships. The School awards a number of scholarships to the value of one-third fees at 11+ in academic subjects and in Art, Music and Sport. Academic and practical scholarships are also awarded for entry into the Sixth Form.

Charitable status. The Alice Ottley School is a Registered Charity, number 527532. It exists as a day school for girls.

Amberfield School
Ipswich

Ipswich Suffolk IP10 0HL
Tel: (01473) 659265
Fax: (01473) 659843
e-mail: registrar@amberfield.suffolk.sch.uk
website: http://www.amberfield.suffolk.sch.uk

Chairman: R D Thomas, Esq

Governors:
J Chalmers, Esq
A Lang, Esq, MA, MBA, MCIBS
M P Gotelee, Esq
Rev Canon G L Grant, MA
Mrs R Brooke
F Madden, Esq, TD, LLB
Mrs J Mills, DipAD
G Hall, Esq,
Mrs A Healey
J S Richardson, MA
Mrs J M Van Den Bergh, LLM

***Head Mistress:* Mrs M L Amphlett Lewis**, BA

Head of Junior School: Mrs G Hadwen, CertEd

Management Team:
Mrs K Waring, BSc (Hons)
Mrs M Winders, CertEd
Mrs L Woodhouse, CertEd

AMBERFIELD SCHOOL. Amberfield is an independent day school for girls aged 3–16 years and boys aged 3–7 years.

It is a small school of approximately 300 pupils. Its size is one of its great strengths: we can build a close-knit community based on Christian precepts; have an effective pastoral care system and enable pupils to participate fully in a wide range of sporting and cultural activities.

Education is a partnership with parents. We create an environment that is safe and happy, in which academic and social skills, individual talents and consideration and sensitivity to the needs of others are developed.

We are justly proud of the achievements of our pupils, whether those achievements come in the form of a full set of GCSE A* grades, or in seeing a pupil grow in confidence and ability through help from the school's Special Needs Department.

SCHOOL LIFE. Amberfield School nestles in pleasant woodland on the edge of Nacton village, near Ipswich. Benefiting from its peaceful, out-of-town location it is nonetheless well placed for major routes including the A12 and A14. The school also provides bus services from Long Melford, Woodbridge, Felixstowe, Stowmarket and Ipswich.

There are modern, purpose-built classrooms and laboratories in addition to the original buildings and all rooms are light, airy and well equipped. Within the grounds there is a full range of outdoor sports facilities including tennis courts and recently-constructed, high quality hockey pitches and athletics facilities.

THE SCHOOL DAY. For all children the school day begins at 8.50 am and ends at 3.45 pm.

Supervised team activities and clubs take place at lunch times and after school. Homework supervision is provided up to 5.30 pm for a small daily charge.

The School is made up of three parts – Senior School, Junior School and Nursery School. Entry for Seniors is by interview and test, normally held at the beginning of the Spring Term. New Junior pupils spend a day with us before joining. In the Nursery School girls and boys attend on a full time basis or by sessions in new purpose-built accommodation.

CURRICULUM. Amberfield's academic life is not confined to the National Curriculum but this forms the basis of the school's teaching.

Junior School pupils undertake Key Stage 1 testing in addition to regular monitoring. In the Senior School the rigours of GCSE requirements keep us close to the National Curriculum.

For each year group there is regular testing, two full reports and a parents' evening.

A broad range of subjects is offered at GCSE.

Amberfield has an enviable track record in all subjects including Physics, Chemistry, Biology and Astronomy, which are taught as separate sciences. Computers are used throughout the curriculum from age 3 and in a structured Information Communication Technology course for all pupils, leading to GCSE for those who wish to pursue it.

Careers advice is provided to help girls select the most appropriate subjects for their planned career path. The Careers Room contains a well stocked library of information including videos and a computer database. It is available to senior girls at all times.

PASTORAL CARE. Maintaining the highest standards of pastoral care is at the heart of Amberfield's philosophy. This is crucial to each pupil's self-confidence and hence to their success. Every effort is made to ensure pupils are happy and at ease with school life.

Form teachers are the backbone of the pastoral care system. By developing an open and trusting relationship with their pupils, form teachers can provide a receptive ear and the essential support and help that may be required. Parents are kept informed so that the school and family can work in partnership.

CREATIVE LIFE. Artistic talent and practical skills are encouraged at all ages. Original and exciting work is produced in our Art, Textiles and Home Economics Departments; there is a large choir and orchestra, plus opportunities to dazzle in Drama or Debating. A variety of activities including Drama, Country Dancing and Ballet are offered in the Junior School.

SPORT. Sport is an important part of life at Amberfield. Physical fitness is essential to our well-being and pupils benefit greatly from the experience of working as a team.

With dedicated sports teaching, pupils from age 9 participate in strong Hockey and Netball teams. There is Tennis coaching for all pupils, yielding excellent results. A full range of sporting activities, from Athletics to team games, enables all pupils to find their forte.

Many of our girls have been chosen to represent the county in Tennis, Hockey, Netball and other sports, including Golf and Squash.

SCHOLARSHIPS. Academic, Art and Music Scholarships are awarded annually at 11+ and 13+.

BURSARIES. Five Junior School Bursaries are available annually.

Charitable status. Amberfield School is a Registered Charity, number 731980. It exists to provide education for girls from 3 to 16 and boys from 3 to 7.

Ashford School
Kent

East Hill Ashford TN24 8PB
Tel: (01233) 625171
Fax: (01233) 647185
e-mail: registrar@ashfordschool.co.uk
website: www.ashfordschool.co.uk

Ashford School is part of the Church Schools Company.

Chairman of School Council: Mr J E Hosking, BSc, CBE, JP, DL
Vice-Chairman: Mrs A A C Cottrell, JP

Council Members:
Mr H N L Blenkin, QPM
Mrs Sarah Cavell
Mrs M F de Courcy, BSc
Mr J Elias, BA
Mr R I Henderson
Mr C M Jackson, MA, HonMEP
Mrs J G Loudon
Mr P Massey
Mrs E Rose
Professor J H Strange, BSc, PhD, CPhys, FInstP

***Headmistress:* Mrs P M Holloway**, MSc (Oxon) (*Geography*)

Deputy Heads:
Mr R Yeates, BA Hons (*Music*)
Mrs M Williams, BSc Hons (Liverpool) (*Chemistry*)
Mrs J Crouch, BA Hons, PGCE (Keele)

Assistant Staff:
Miss L Allen, BA Hons (London), PGCE (*Modern Languages*)
Mrs M Bee, BA Hons (East Anglia), CertEd (*History*)
Mrs E D Breen, BA Hons (Leeds), PGCE (*English & Drama*)
Mrs J Brentnall, BA Hons (East Anglia) (*German & EFL*)
Mrs S Brown, BA, TCert (Durham) (*Mathematics*)
Mrs A Burrill, BA Hons (Wales), PGCE, MA (Kent) (*English*)
Mrs B J Davies, BA Hons, MA, CertEd (Cambridge) (*English and Careers*)
Mr B J Fehr, BMus (London), ARCM (*Music*)
Mr P Ford, BA (Newcastle) (*IT*)
Dr S Goldwin, PhD (London) (*Biology*)
Mrs J Gore, BSc (London) (*Physics*)
Mr G S Gould, BEd Hons (Liverpool) (*Mathematics*)
Mr C R Hartley, CertEd (*Technology*)
Mr D Hill, ABSM, GRSM (*Music*)
Mrs M C Hill, L-ès-L (*Modern Languages*)
Mr C Howard, BSc Hons (Salford), CertEd, MIBiol, CBiol (*Biology*)
Mrs J James, Teachers Cert (*PE*)
Mrs M Jarrett, BSc Hons (London) (*Mathematics*)
Mr J Jones, BA Hons (Open University) (*Chemistry*)
Mrs G P Kemp, BA Hons (London), PGCE (*Modern Languages*)
Mr J Knight, City & Guilds TC Nat Dip Design
Mrs F Lees, BA Hons, PGCE (*Technology*)
Mr P Limmer, MA Hons (Oxon) (*Geography*)
Mrs H Lazenby, BArch (Lima) (*Modern Languages*)
Mrs V Lingwood, IMA, Teachers Cert (*Food & Nutrition*)
Mrs C Ludlow, BSc Hons (London) (*Chemistry*)
Mrs A Le Rossignol, PGCE, BA Hons, PGCADE (*Art*)
Mrs P Mantell, BSc Hons (Bristol) (*Physics*)
Dr J Marks, PhD (London), BSc (*Biology*)
Mr G Marsh, BA (Portsmouth) (*Economics & Business Studies*)
Mr B J Mead, BSc (London), PGCE (*Geography*)
Mrs Metherell, BA Hons (Wales), PGCE (*Classics*)
Mrs G Miles, BSc Hons (Notts) (*Mathematics*)
Mrs R Moorat, BEd (*Modern Languages*)
Mrs A Oliver, WADA, DipLLCM
Mrs S Overy, BSc Hons (Oxon), PGCE (Cambridge)
Mr A F Palmer, AKC, CertEd (Christchurch) (*Religious Education*)
Miss S Rea, BEd Hons (*PE*)
Mr G Reynolds, CertEd (*Art*)
Mrs P Simmonds, BA Hons (Leeds), PGCE
Miss E Spittal, MLitt (Oxon), MA Hons (St Andrews) (*English*)
Miss L Stanley, MA Hons (Oxford), PGCE
Mr F B Stockwell, MSc (Kent), BSc (London), PGCE (*Physics*)
Mrs J Watson-Bore, BA Hons (Newcastle-Upon-Tyne,) MA (London) (*English*)
Mrs J M Wilkes, BA Hons (Reading), PGCE (*Classics*)
Mr R Wordsworth, BSc Hons (Kent) (*Mathematics*)

Visiting Music Staff:
Mr S Dandridge

Mr J Dawson
Mrs R Dolby, BA
Lady Nicollette Douglas
Mr M Estes
Mrs J Gow, GRSM, LRAM
Mr D Green
Mrs F Hardy, LRAM, ARCM
Miss J Hollis, BMus, GTCL, LTCL
Mr M Kime
Mr C Reid
Mr J Tagford
Mrs F Thornby
Mrs C Thorneloe, ARCM
Mrs R Waltham

Nightingale House (*for Years 1–6*):
Mrs C Collins, DipEd (Sheffield)
Mrs D Emery, TCert (Stockwell Coll, Bromley)
Mrs J Gardiner, BA Hons, PGCE
Mrs A H Gould, BEd Hons (London)
Miss P M J Hoad, TCert (Froebel Inst, London)
Miss S Munro, BEd Hons (London)
Mrs P O'Hara, BEdDip Music (West Sussex Inst of HE)
Mrs L Playford, CertEd (Bedford College of PE)
Mrs M Radcliffe, BA Hons (London)
Mrs M Roylance, CertEd (Bristol)

Bridge House (*Nursery and Reception*):
Miss G Andrews
Miss K Athow, NVQ11
Mrs R Beard, NNEB
Miss C Blundell, BTech
Miss Z Gibbons, BTech
Miss J Lovell, NAMCW
Mrs J Keech
Miss D Pool
Mrs S Pratt, NAMCW
Mrs A Pritchard, NAMCW
Mrs F Russell, NNEB
Miss A Shires, NVQ11
Miss C Sutton, BTech
Miss M Titchmarsh, BTech
Miss N Wade-Cache, NNEB
Mrs M Willetts, BTech

Secretary to the Headmistress: Mrs S Mason
Marketing & Public Relations: Mrs S Boyce

Ever since 1898 Ashford School has been offering a broad yet academically demanding curriculum to girls, designed to foster a spirit of enquiry, active concern for others and thoughtful self-confidence. There are 380 girls in the Senior School of whom 120 are in the VI Form and about 90 are boarders. Nightingale House (for Years 1–6) and Bridge House (Nursery and Reception classes) have 170 pupils with boarders amongst the 9 and 10 year-olds. The School's ethos is founded upon traditional Christian values but welcomes girls of many faiths, whose culture and practices are respected and supported.

The Senior School curriculum constantly evolves to keep abreast of good modern practice and new technology, while maintaining a firm base in the more traditional disciplines, such as Latin. Up until the end of the V Form (Year 11), girls follow a broad curriculum, to keep their options open. In addition to the core subjects – English, Mathematics, at least one Modern Foreign Language and all three Sciences – girls study additional languages, History, Geography, Classical Civilisation, Religious Studies, Information Technology, Food Studies, Art and Textiles, Music, Drama and Physical Education. Throughout the Senior School, subjects are set by ability – not streamed – and there is a strongly pastoral tutorial system. Whenever possible, ways are found to link the School's curriculum to local businesses and to the needs of the community. VIth Form linguists, for example, provide translations for the Red Cross. There are three Artists in Residence – a sculptor, a print-maker and a stained-glass artist – who run workshops for the girls as well as placing the School's Art studies into a 'real world' context.

External Examinations. At Key Stage 4 there is a full choice from all subjects for GCSE; most girls take between 8 and 10 subjects in the V Form, perhaps adding to these in VI Form. Many A Level combinations are available to the VI Form, of whom over 95% go on to Higher Education before entering a varied range of vareers including advertising, banking, engineering, journalism, law, management, the media, medicine, veterinary science. There is a consistently high external examination success rate and girls are prepared for Oxbridge in all subjects.

Facilities include 9 laboratories, a music wing, gym and sports hall, heated indoor swimming pool, purpose-built refectory, large library, computer centre, language laboratory, technology centre and Sixth Form Centre. There are Senior and Junior choirs and orchestras.

Boarders. Our boarding houses offer a friendly and supportive environment. Clubs and activities include jazz, swimming, video-making, art, cookery, drama, and a range of sports.

Entry requirements: school report, tests and interview for the Sixth Form, supporting six or more A-C grades at GCSE. Written tests at 11 and 13. Test and interview for Junior Department at 7, informal interview at 3 and 5. Academic and Musical scholarships.

Location and Travel. The School is set in 23 acres of grounds, in the town of Ashford, which is an hour's train journey from London, and 20 minutes from Canterbury and Folkestone. Many of the boarders have parents working abroad, and comprehensive travel and escort arrangements are made for those using the main airports and channel ports. Day girls come from a large surrounding area making use of the local bus and train network. Ashford's International Passenger Station makes travel to the Continent uncomplicated and speedy for flexi-boarders from Lille, Bruxelles and Paris.

Fees. (*see* Entrance Scholarship section)
Senior Boarder: £4,830 per term
Senior Day: £2,780 per term
Junior Boarder: £4,161 per term
Junior Day: £2,110 per term
Pre-Prep: £1,333 per term
Nursery: from £412 per term
Prospectus available from the Registrar, Stephanie Boyce.

Charitable status. Ashford School Kent is a Registered Charity, number 1016538. It exists to provide education for girls only, aged between 3 and 18 years and to assist the local community where possible with the hire of school facilities and participation in local activities.

The Atherley School (CSC)

Grove Place Upton Lane Nursling Southampton SO16 0AB
Tel: 023 8074 1629
Fax: 023 8074 1631

Motto: *Abeunt Studia in Mores*

Governing Body: The Council of the Church Schools Company

Patron: The Rt Revd The Lord Bishop of Winchester

Chairman of the Local Council: Professor M J Clark

Head: **Mrs Maureen Bradley**, BEd, MEd

Head of Junior School: Mr Andrew Moy (Froebel Institute)

The Atherley Senior School is Southampton's only independent senior school for girls from 11–18 years. It aims to educate girls within a Christian framework. Academic standards are high, maintaining the school at the forefront of the Government league tables for Hampshire. The school links pupils, parents and staff into a team encouraging individual talent, responsibility and self-esteem.

The Atherley Junior School is co-educational from 3–11 years with special emphasis being placed on modern languages from the age of 5 and the provision of facilities for an extended day to 5.30 pm.

The School is sited in 30 acres of parkland on the outskirts of Southampton; it is conveniently located on the road to Romsey close, to the M27/M271 junction. The Junior School is housed in modern, single-storey classroom blocks. The Senior School is housed in new purpose-built accommodation. The adjacent Elizabethan manor house, a Grade I listed building, has been refurbished to provide a centre for the Sixth Form, music and drama. The school's catchment covers a wide area and is served by a popular school bus service extending to Lymington, Salisbury, Winchester and Fareham. More than three-quarters of the senior girls use this service.

Fees. (*see* Entrance Scholarship section) A registration fee of £25 is payable on application. Tuition fees per term: Mornings only for children under 5 years £589, Reception, Years 1 & 2 £1,345, Year 3 to 6 £1,665, Senior School £1,885. There are Church Schools Foundation Assisted Places available at ages 11 and 16. Where there are two or more members of one family attending the School at the same time, the following reduction in fees will be given: for the second child 5% per term; for the third and any subsequent child 10% per term. These fees include text-books and school stationery. Scholarships are available at 11+ and 16+, and the school operates an Assisted Places scheme. Extra subjects include Instrumental lessons, for which the termly fee is £100; Speech and Drama lessons, for which the termly fee varies depending on group size, and Tennis Coaching during the Summer term. Public Examination fees are paid separately.

School Lunch is compulsory.

School Hours. Senior School 8.40 am to 3.45 pm; Junior School and Preparatory Department 8.30 am to 3.30 pm (to 5.30 pm by arrangement).

Terms. There are 3 terms, with a half-term holiday each term.

Scholarships. Entry into Year 7 and Year 12: academic, music, art, drama and sport.

The Old Atherleian Association: Enquiries c/o the school.

Charitable status. The Church Schools Company is a Registered Charity, number 1016538. The school aims to educate girls within a Christian framework.

Badminton School

Westbury-on-Trym Bristol BS9 3BA.
Tel: (0117) 905 5200
Fax: (0117) 962 8963
e-mail: registrar@badminton.bristol.sch.uk
website: www.badminton.bristol.sch.uk

Motto: *Pro Omnibus Quisque: Pro Deo Omnes*
Founded 1858, Non denominational.

Board of Governors:

Vice Presidents:
Professor Sir Mark Richmond, BA, PhD, ScD, MRCPath, FRS
Mrs P Stone, MA
A M Urquhart, Esq, OBE, BA

Chairman: Professor R Hodder-Williams, MA (Oxon), FRSA

Vice-Chairman: Mrs A Bernays

The Hon Mrs N Appleby
P Ashmead, Esq
Mrs A Bernays
J G Brown, Esq, FCA, ATII
P Forrest, Esq, FRSM
Mrs S Laing, MA, PGCE, RSA, DipTEFLA
I J Leslie Esq, MChOrth, FRCS
Mrs V Murrell-Abery, MA, AcDipEd, DipCG, MICG
P O'Connor, Esq, BSc, FCA
The Hon Mrs V Pelham, SRN
Prof C A Seymour-Richards, MA, MSc, PhD, DM, FRCP
Miss M A Winfield, BA, PGCE

Clerk to the Governors, Secretary and Bursar: Mr R N Cook, FCA

Headmistress: **Mrs J A Scarrow,** BA (Manchester)

Deputy Head: Mrs C Bateson, BA (London)

Head of Sixth Form: Miss J Wakeham, BA (Lancaster)

Head of Boarding: Mrs C Thornberry-Stoker, BA

English:
Miss L Taylor, BA (Oxon) *English*
Miss J Wakeham, BA (Lancaster)
Mrs R Robertson, MA (Newcastle)
Mrs A Mackay, BA (Queensland)
Miss C Sammons, BEd (Wales) *Drama*

Mathematics:
Mrs A E Cobby, BSc (Exeter) *Mathematics*
Mrs P Eveleigh, BSc (Exeter)
Mrs J Mackay, BA (Open)
Miss N Bass, BSc (Bristol)

Science:
Mr D Amies, BSc (Nottingham), MSc (E Anglia) *Head of Science*
Dr C Enos, BSc, PhD (Swansea) *Chemistry*
Mr P Foster, BSc (London) *Physics*
Mr D Williams, MSc (Warwick)
Mrs A Thomason, BSc (Bristol) *Biology*
Mr G Stinchcombe, MSc (Bristol)
Mrs J E Jones, DipHEc, (Cardiff) *Home Economics*
Mrs G M Dunphy, MA (Dublin) *Computing*
Miss A Black, BA, MSc (Oxford)

Modern Languages:
Mrs J Wake, BA (Nottingham), MA (Bristol) *Head of Modern Languages*
Mrs C Turner, L ès L (Metz)
Mrs A Pattison, Licence d'Anglais (Reims)
Mrs A Webb, DEUG, MA (La Sorbonne), PGCE (UWE)
Miss S J Whyatt, BA (London) *German*

Classics:
Mr M Belfield, BA, MLitt (Bristol)
Mrs R Summers, MA (St Andrews)

Humanities:
Mrs V Drew, BA (Wales) *History and Careers*
Mrs C Bateson, BA (London)
Mrs J C Ellis, BA (Bristol) *Geography*
Mrs F Annear, BA (Durham)
Mrs D Betterton, BA (Exeter) *Economics*
Mrs M Evans, MA (Oxon) *Religious Education*

Music:
Mr C M Francis, BA (Bristol)
Mr W Goodchild, BA, LCSM (East Anglia) (*Piano*)
Mrs H P Potter, BA (Bristol), ALCM, ARCM

Creative Arts:
Mr P Rock, BA (Newcastle) *Art*
Miss C Chapman, BA (West of England)
Miss A J Cozens, BA (Bristol)
Ms S Clothier, BA (Brighton)

Physical Education:
Mrs S A Myers, CertEd (Bedford) *Games*
Miss R Lee, BA (Cardiff)
Miss J Nicholas, BEd (Plymouth)
Mrs J I Winn, CertEd (Bedford)
Miss T Trevaskis, BA(Ed) (Exeter)

Staff of the Junior School:
Mrs A Lloyd, CertEd (Oxon), LGSM *Head*
Miss E K Thomson, CertEd (Bristol)
Mrs M Holdsworth, MA (Angers)
Mrs V Swerdlow, BSc (Bristol)
Miss H Spratt, BA (West of England)
Mrs M Turner, BSc (Leicester)
Mrs S Lyons, BEd (Chester)
Miss R Webb, BEd (Plymouth)
Mrs A Cannon, BA (Oxon)
Miss E Feakin, BA (Durham)

Extra Curricular Staff:
Mrs C Barratt, BMus (London), ARCM
Miss C Black, BA (Reading), ALCM *Violin*
Mr D Brown, BA (Leeds CM) *Jazz Guitar*
Miss L Clarke, MSTAT *Alexander Technique*
Mrs K D Dyer, BSc (Liverpool), LTCL *Piano*
Mr K Figes, LGSM *Saxophone*
Mrs J Francis, GRSM, ARCM *'Cello*
Mr S Gore *Drum Kit*
Mrs N Higginson, GRNCM, ABSM, FLCM *Flute*
Mr M J Kearley, LRAM, ARCM, LLCM *Piano*
Miss R Kerry, BA (Bath), CTABRSM
Mr A King, GBSM, LTCL *Oboe*
Mrs D Lee, BA (Cantab) *Bassoon*
Miss J Levine, BA (Bath)
Mrs A Little, BMus (London)
Mr J Little *Orchestral Percussion*
Mrs D McAdam, BMus (Sheffield) *Singing*
Mrs E Melville, ALCM, LLCM *Violin, Viola*
Mr D Pagett, GRNCM, PGDip *Clarinet*
Ms A M Parker, ALCM *Clarinet*
Mrs J Phillips, BA (Reading) *Singing*
Miss C Reynolds, BMus, ALCM
Miss R Skinner, BA (Bristol) *Singing*
Mr J Taylor, BA (Exeter) *Jazz Piano*
Mr J Thomas, BEd *Harp*
Mrs T White, ARCM *Horn*
Mrs M F Wills, GRSM, ARMCM *Double Bass*
Miss A Wiseman, BMrs (Birmingham Conservatoire) *Brass*
Miss J Yard, BA (Bath), LLCM *Guitar*

Mrs S M Fallon, BA, DipEd, LGSM *Speech and Drama*
Mrs J Tuckett, LLAM *Speech and Drama*
Mrs E Lloyd, LLAM, LGSM
Mrs P Jenkins *Self Defence and Judo*
Mr D Hunt *Fencing*
Mr S Veira *Kick Boxing*
Mr G Laird *Golf*
Miss K Clark *Tennis*
Mr V Reed *Tennis*
Mr R Conway *Tennis*

Resident Housestaff:
Mrs S Callister, DipDomSc, PGCE
Ms R Boyd, BEd (Durham), MA (York)
Miss E Austin, BA (York)
Miss E Thomson, CertEd
Miss T Trevaskis, BA(Ed) (Exeter)
Miss D Moriarty, BA (Leeds)
Mrs S Holdaway, BSc (Open)
Mrs A Pascual, BA (London)
Miss J Hart, BA (Nottingham)

School Doctor: Dr D Kershaw, MB, ChB, MRCGP

School Sisters:
Mrs S Sabido, SRN, SCM
Mrs E Ritchie, RGN, SCM

Registrar: Mrs F A Hazell

Domestic Bursar: Mr C Atkinson

Pupils: Boarding, Senior 160, Junior 10. Day, Senior 130, Junior 90. Total 390

Staff: Full-time teaching 45, Part-time teaching 12. Teacher Pupil ratio is currently 1:7

Age range of pupils: 4 to 18

Entry requirements: Common Entrance or Badminton Entrance Examination. Sixth Form entry requires 6 GCSEs at Grade B or above.

Fees per term (September 2001): *Day* Senior £2,900, Junior £1,600–£1,975, *Boarding* Senior £5,150, Junior £3,500.

Educational Philosophy of Badminton School. The style of Badminton is a combination of discipline and warmth, where the parameters are firm and there is a welcome absence of pettiness. Staff/pupil relations are mature and friendly, based on the principle of courtesy and mutual respect. High standards are expected for both work and behaviour: the pursuit of excellence and all round ability are equally valued. Pupils work hard, play hard and lead busy and active lives, which aims to keep them happy and fulfilled. Constant encouragement is the key to their success in a good learning climate which helps to develop their self-confidence and their self-discipline. A girl's academic progress is carefully monitored by a regular grading system for achievement (A–E) and effort (1–5). Head Girls and House Captains take responsibility for a number of duties such as supervising prep, but enjoy little real power. The school encourages regular contact with and support from parents, and there is a flourishing PTA. Girls wear school uniform except in the Sixth Form.

Academic. Badminton has a fine academic record at GCSE and A and levels and believes in the pursuit of academic excellence without cramming. Girls are expected to produce results according to their ability and to develop their individual talents. The GCSE and A Level pass rate exceeds 97%, and all of the Sixth Form go on to degree courses, including Oxford and Cambridge. The school currently offers 18 subjects at GCSE and A Level: most of the girls take 9 GCSE Levels and go on to take 4 AS and 3 A Levels in the Sixth Form. Mathematics and Science are particularly strong. Class size is 18 in the main school, and about 12 in the Sixth Form.

There is a full general studies course in the Sixth Form which includes Health Education, Politics, Model United Nations, European Youth Parliament, First Aid, Computing, Information Technology and additional languages. The Careers section is particularly strong.

Educational Facilities. The School is well equipped with classrooms, including a large modern block containing 8 science laboratories and domestic science facilities: a Creative Arts Centre, several computer rooms, a languages' listening room, theatre, gymnasium, 7 tennis courts, playing fields, heated indoor swimming pool, Casson Library, fiction library, numerous satellite libraries, eight common rooms, an extended and refurbished Sixth Form Centre opened in 1999 and 2 Music Schools.

Music and Creative Arts. It is the policy that all girls are involved in the creative arts, both within the curriculum and as extracurricular activities, and the School attaches great importance to the development of musical and artistic talent. Badminton has an excellent tradition in Music having three Orchestras, numerous ensembles and four choirs. There is a wide choice of Creative Arts – Art, Drama, Pottery, Light Crafts, Textiles, Printmaking, Design, Jewellery-making, Photography, Speech and Drama. It is policy that all girls are involved in the creative arts, both within the curriculum and as extracurricular activities, and the School attaches great importance to the development of musical and artistic talent. There are several dramatic productions every year and girls have the chance to produce, direct and stage-manage house plays: there are also joint music and drama productions with boys' schools.

Clubs and Societies. Science, Politics, Young Enterprise, Langages Vivantes, Geographical, Mathematical, Debating, Public Speaking, Social Service, Drama, Art, Librarians, Historical, Young Engineers, Model United Nations, European Youth Parliament, Christian Union.

Games and Activities. The School offers hockey, tennis, netball, swimming, athletics, rounders, squash, gymnastics, badminton, volley ball, trampolining and enters for county trials where appropriate. Optional extras include self-defence, fencing, riding, driving, golf, judo and skating. All girls participate in activities which include the full choice of games and creative arts as above and boarders have the opportunity of additional activities at the weekend. The Duke of Edinburgh's Award is taken by over half the pupils. There are regular trips abroad to European countries, especially for art, history, music, geography, skiing, and exchanges with trusted schools in France, Germany and Spain.

Badminton is fortunate in being in a university city; regular visits are arranged to concerts, lectures and theatres, including municipal and civic activities, and there is considerable contact with the University and outside visits to industry and universities; girls attend short courses on Industry. There is a flourishing Social Services Group, where girls help in primary schools, day nurseries, and with elderly people, gardening and cooking.

Entry. (*see* Entrance Scholarship section) Entry to the Junior School is by personal interview, English, Mathematics and reasoning tests; to the Senior School it is by Common Entrance or Badminton entrance examination for girls aged 11–13. The Headmistress likes to see all girls and their parents before entry where possible. Entry to the Sixth Form requires a minimum of six passes at GCSE, Grade B or above. Scholarships of up to half fees are offered both for entrance to the Senior School and the Sixth Form for academic excellence, music, art and all-round ability. Bursaries are usually reserved for girls already in the School.

Charitable status. Badminton School Limited is a Registered Charity, number 311738. It exists for the purpose of educating children.

* Head of Department	§ Part Time or Visiting
† Housemaster/Housemistress	¶ Old Pupil
‡ See below list of staff for meaning	

Bedford High School

The High School Bedford MK4O 2BS
Tel: (01234) 360221
Fax: (01234) 353552
e-mail: head@bedfordhigh.co.uk
website: bedfordhigh.co.uk

This School is part of the same foundation as Bedford School for Boys endowed by Sir William Harpur in 1566.

***Headmistress:* Mrs G Piotrowska**, MA Cambridge

Deputy Headmistress: Mrs J Carwithen, BSc London

Head of Junior School: Mrs J Boulting, NFF

Head of Sixth Form: Mrs V Stewart, BSc Leicester

Staff:

Religious Education:
*Mr P Fricker, BA Dunelm
Mr N Sydenham, BA Sheffield, MA King's College, London

English:
*Mrs S Mason-Patel, BA Dunelm
Mrs J Harper, BA Birmingham
Mrs C Oldfield, BA Manchester
Mrs A Hepworth, BA Liverpool
Mrs J Marriott, BA Manchester
Mrs D Clifton, BA Bristol

ESOL:
*Mrs C Wrangham-Briggs, BSc(Econ), RSADipTEFL, MA
Mrs J Greening, BA, BPhil, DipTEFL
Mrs N Harbour, CertEd, BPhil, TEFL/TESL
Mrs H Wright, BA, RSA, DipTEFL

Drama and Dance:
*Mrs D Morgan, BEd Exeter, MA Open, CertEd
Mrs L Atkinson, DipEd Nottingham, Dip LCDD, AISTD, Reg Teacher RAD
Mrs F Kemp, MA Leeds
Miss L Bream, DipLCD, AISTD
Mrs H Cameron-Kettle, BEd
Miss H Dennis, LRAD
Mrs C Riddington-Smith, Acting Diploma, Bristol Old Vic
Miss P Hardy, BA London

History:
*Mrs K Fricker, MA, BLitt Oxon
Mrs E Godbolt, BA London
Mrs E Hall, BA Bristol

Geography and Geology:
*Mrs D Whiteley, BSc London
Mr B Purser, BSc Sheffield
Ms H Rose, MA London, FRGS, BA London
Mrs J Pendry, BSc Bristol

The Business, Economic & Political Studies Department:
*Mr J Lawrence, BA Leicester, MA London
Mrs L Proud, BA Newcastle, MSc London
Mrs A J Pollard, BA Portsmouth Polytechnic, MA De Montfort

Careers:
*Mrs A Samuel, BA Leeds, PGCE Exeter, ACCG
Mrs L M Davies, BSc Wales

Classics:
*Mrs J Morris, MA Cantab

Modern Languages:
*Mrs L M Barnes, BA London
Mrs G Davis, BA Cantab (New Hall), MA
Mrs J Chadwick, BA Oxon (St Hugh's)
Miss M Gómez-Alonso, Licenciatura en Filologia Inglesa, Madrid
Mrs L Cebula, BA Reading
Mrs D M Arrowsmith, MA Nottingham
Miss V Videt, Maitrise es Lettres Université d'Orleans
Mrs L A Chalmers, BA Bangor
Mrs J E Scopes, BA Nottingham
Mrs A Humphrey, Licence es Lettres, Sorbonne, Paris

Mathematics:
*Mr I C H Pullen, Msc, BA Open, BEd Cantab, CertEd
Mrs J McKinney, BSc Queens Belfast
Mrs S J Lockwood, BSc Nottingham
Mrs K Nicholls, BSc UCW Aberystwyth
Mrs J Carwithen, BSc London
Mrs H Pennington, MEng Durham
Mrs M Hardman, BSc Salford, PGCE
Mrs C Bawden, BSc Loughborough, CertEd

Science:
*Dr W Smith, BSc London, PhD London, CPhys, MInstP (*Head of Science and Physics*)
*Mrs A Jackson, BSc Sussex (*Head of Chemistry*)
*Mrs S Wiggins, BSc Newcastle (*Head of Biology*)
Mrs J Uden, BSc Southampton
Mrs L Davies, BSc Wales
Mrs M Samuels, BEd Cantab
Dr A J Gedge, BSc, PhD Nottingham
Mr G Burden, BSc London
Mrs V J Stewart, BSc Leicester
Mrs J Lowrie, BSc Aberdeen, MSc London
Mr I Gordon, BSc, AdvDip
Mrs C Powis, BSc, DipEd
Mrs S Sellars, BSc Nottingham
Dr V Kambhampati, BSc UCL, MSc Birkbeck College, London, PhD Southampton

Technology:
*Mrs K Macaulay, BEd, Northumbria
Mrs C Anthony, CertEd London
Mrs M Appleby, BEd Leeds
Mrs G Appleby, BA University of Massachusetts
Mrs D Buthee, BA Birmingham Polytechnic
Mrs A Goodman, BEd Thames Polytechnic
Mr D Leitner, MSc Herts, ProfCert RAM Music Technology
Mrs G Surtees, BA Manchester, CertEd

Art:
*Mrs S Jones, National Diploma in Design, Art Teacher's Diploma, Art Teacher's Certificate (Manchester)
Mrs P M Ville, Art Teacher's Cert Durham
Mrs A Larter, BA Manchester

Junior School:
Head: Mrs J Boulting, National Froebel Foundation

Staff:
Mrs C Royden, BEd De Montford (*Deputy Head of Department*)
Mrs C G Bridgeman, BSc Leeds
Mrs L Parker, BMus Manchester, GRNCM, ARNCM
Mrs M Butt, BA London
Mrs P Burgess, CertEd London
Mrs K Nicholls, BSc UCW, Aberystwyth
Mrs J Saghri, BEd Bedford
Mrs C Anthony, CertEd London
Mrs D Parkman, BSc Loughborough
Mrs B Weltz, BA University Hall, Oxon

Music:
*Mr P J Bond, GRSM, Manchester, ARMCM (*Director of Music*)
*Mr D P Williams, BA Southampton, LRAM, ARCO (*Assistant Director of Music*)
Dr S J Weston, MPhil, PhD Leicester, GRSM London LTCL, Professional Certificate, RAM (*Head of Instrumental Teaching*)
*Mrs L Parker, BMus Manchester, GRNCM, ARNCM *Class teaching, piano*
Miss D Anderson, BMus London, LRAM *Double Bass*
Miss E Attwood, LRAM, ARCM, FTCL, FLCM *'Cello, Piano*
Miss P Baldwin, ARCM, CertEd Nottingham *Flute and Recorder*
Miss J Benham, BMus London, LRAM (*Teacher's and Performer's Dip*) *Piano*
*Mrs P Bennett, GGSM *Flute*
Mr R Childs, LRAM *Percussion*
Miss E Foggin, GMus, RNCM, DipAdvStudies Manchester *Brass*
Mrs L Forbes, MA Oxon, Dip RAM *Oboe*
*Mrs H Goldsmith, BMus London, LGSM *Flute*
Mr P Gyles, GTCL, LTCL *Violin, Viola*
Mrs C Harrison, LRAM, LCST *Piano*
Miss K Hills, GRSM London *Bassoon and Flute*
Miss R Hoskins, BA Newcastle, ARCM, MSTAT *Piano*
Mr F Jenkins *Saxophone, Clarinet*
Mrs C John, GRSM London, LRAM, ARCM, MTC *Clarinet and Piano*
Mr D Leitner, MSc, ProfCertRam *Guitar, Electronic Music*
Mr P Mourant, BMus Cardiff, LTCL, ACWCMD *Brass*
Mrs S A Odom, GRSM London, LRAM, Professional Certificate RAM *Piano, Theory*
Mr M Phillips, BMus RCM, ARCM *Trumpet*
Miss A Trentham, MMus Eastman School NY, GLCM *Harp*
Mrs A Warburton, GRSM Manchester, ARMCM *Piano, recorder*
Mrs J Welsh, LRAM, LTCL, ATCL, ALCM *Recorder, Singing*
Mrs D Williams, BA Southampton, ATCL *Violin, viola*
Mrs T Wood, BA London, LRAM *Piano*
Miss C L Woodhouse, BMus Manchester, Orchestral DipGSMD *Piano*

Modern Language Assistants:
Mrs S Locke *German*
Mrs M Johnson *French*
Miss G Fernandez Sanz *Spanish*

Physical Education:
*Mrs J Axford, BA Exeter

Mrs L Darbon, CertEd Chelsea College of PE
Mrs I Whale, Chelsea Coll of PE
Mrs C Whitaker, BA, QTS Brighton
Miss D Harris, BEd De Montford
Miss S Godson, BA Newcastle
Mrs E Singfield *Rowing Coach*
Mrs S Bullerwell, CertEd Liverpool

Administrative staff:

Bursar: R E V Clark, MSc, BA, BSc
Assistant Bursar: Mrs C P Galley
Bursar's Financial Assistant: Mrs M Gardiner
Headmistress's Personal Assistant: Mrs D Malone
Registrar: Mrs H Tench
Librarian: Mrs S E Coleman, BA (Hons) Manchester, ALA
School Nurse: Mrs R Neal, SRN
School Doctor: Dr J Butlin, MBchB, MRCGD, DRCOG

Housemistresses:
The Quantocks: Mrs A Laing, BA Newcastle
Wimborne Grange: Mrs L Darbon, CertEd Chelsea College of PE
The Chilterns: Miss P Jackson, NNEB *Housemother*

Average number 880.

Introduction. Bedford High School was founded in 1882 as part of the Harpur Endowment. The school has a long tradition of academic excellence, diversity of opportunity and the highest standards in pastoral care.

Following a broad, general education a choice may be made from 15 GCSE subjects, 30 A Levels and an Information Technology Course. Academic results are consistently high. Recent refurbishment has resulted in a total of 11 laboratories to accommodate the large numbers taking Sciences for A Level. Modern Foreign languages enjoy excellent results. The Creative Arts and ICT are particular strengths. The recent installation of superb ICT facilities, fully networked enabling fast access to the Internet, illustrates a commitment to the future. With 23 acres of playing fields, 11 grass and two hard tennis courts, an indoor swimming pool and the river nearby, the provision in sports is outstanding. Teams excel in lacrosse, hockey, tennis and netball and the school has an enviable reputation for swimming and rowing.

There is an emphasis on the importance of realising individual potential. Careers guidance and preparation for Higher Education begin at the age of 13 years. A programme of personal development and health awareness is conducted by form tutors. Almost all in the Sixth Form continue their education at university with a number of Oxbridge entrants each year.

The on-site Junior School provides an ideal foundation, fostering an enquiring mind and establishing good study skills, within a caring atmosphere. Juniors have the benefit of specialist teachers and use main school facilities whilst enjoying their own purpose built accommodation.

Extra-curricular activities (43), are diverse: examples include chess, cricket, dance, fencing, harp, internet club, rock band, madrigal group, youth action, Duke of Edinburgh, Combined Cadet Force and Young Enterprise.

Boarding. Weekly, full and flexible boarding are offered. The boarding houses have recently been refurbished and extended to the highest standards. A full range of weekend activities is provided and included within the fees, with transport supplied at the beginning and end of terms. Centrally sited in Bedford, the school is convenient for all London airports.

Entrance Examination. Entrance Examinations are held in January for entry the following September. Entrance to the Sixth Form is by GCSE results, report and interview.

Scholarships and Bursaries. Scholarships are awarded for academic excellence at 11+, 12+ and 13+ and also on entry to the Sixth Form.

Harpur Bursaries are available from 11+ onwards for those residing in Bedfordshire.

Bedford High School Bursaries are awarded on the same basis to girls living outside the area covered by Harpur Bursaries.

Fees. Annual Tuition Fees: Junior School £4,749; Upper School £6,699.

Annual Boarding Fees: £5,655; Weekly Boarding £5,523.

Charitable status. The Bedford Charity (The Harpur Trust) is a Registered Charity, number 204817. It exists to provide a high quality education for girls.

Bedgebury School

Bedgebury Park Goudhurst Kent TN17 2SH
Tel: (01580) 211221
Registrar: (01580) 211954
Fax: (01580) 212252
e-mail: info@bedgeburyschool.co.uk
website: www.bedgeburyschool.co.uk

A full and weekly boarding and day school for girls aged 2½–18 and boys aged 2½–7½

Motto: *Service not Self*

Bedgebury concentrates on developing the full potential of each girl in its care, through inspiring enthusiasm and motivation, building confidence and emphasising achievement. The curriculum offers a wide range of GCSE and A Level subjects, together with a good range of vocational courses for Sixth Formers and unparalleled extra-curricular activities. At heart a boarding school, Bedgebury offers the flexibility of full or weekly boarding as well as offering day girls a way of life, not just an academic programme. Academic progress is monitored closely by Year Heads supported by form tutors. Boarders are looked after by a team of experienced house staff including two qualified nurses.

Governing Body: Church Education Corporation Ltd (*founded 1900*)

Head Office: Bedgebury School, Goudhurst, Kent

Governing Council:
President: Mr B W Guest
Vice-President: Air Vice Marshal J M Stacey, CBE, DSO, DFC
Chairman: Mr J Marsh

Mr J M Midgley
Mrs R McMurray
Lady Warren
Mrs F Nowne
Mr A Fellows
Mrs R M Baker
Mr R G Sinclair-Smith
Mrs P Hardingham
Canon P T Mackenzie
Miss J R Binstead
Mr M K G Scott
Mrs J E M Webb

***Headmistress:* Mrs H Moriarty**, BA Hons (Trinity College, Dublin), MA

Deputy Head: Mr A Simmons, MA

Head of Junior School: Mrs B Canham, JP, BA Hons, PGCE (Froebel)

Head of Administration & Clerk to the Governors: Mr J N Willoughby, FCIS

Chaplain: The Revd N Gallagher, BD Hons (London), BA Hons (Open), CertEd (Birmingham), AKC

Head of Sixth Form: Miss Z Axton, BSc (Liverpool), PGCE

Head of Sixth Form Boarding: Mrs E Lewis, MA (Reading), TCert

Senior Housemistress: Miss R Bradley, BA Hons (London), PGCE

Senior School Staff:

Mrs J Alder, CertEd (Birmingham), TEFL (RSA) *EFL Co-ordinator*
Miss Z Axton, BSc (Liverpool), PGCE *Head of Sixth Form and Careers*
Mrs M Beckett, BA Hons (Sussex), MA (Simon Fraser), PGCE (London), CertModDrama (Sussex)
Miss R Bradley, BA Hons (London), PGCE *Senior Housemistress; Head of Classics*
Mrs C Budd, BEd (Homerton) *Head of Key Stage 3; Latin and History*
Mrs D V Coley, BA Hons (Nottingham), MA (London), DipRE, Dip Media Studies *Head of Year 9, Head of Communication Studies*
Mr D Colpus, BSc Hons, PGCE (Soton) *Head of Information & Communication Technology*
Miss V Cox, BEd Hons (Bedford) *Head of Physical Education*
Mrs S Cross, BEd Hons (Sussex), DipRSA *Head of Business Studies*
Mrs C Davidson, BA Hons (Brighton), MLC, DipCounselling *Head of Outdoor Pursuits*
Mrs S Evans, BA Hons (Oxford), PGCE *Head of English*
The Revd N Gallagher, BD Hons (London), BA Hons (Open), CertEd, AKC *Chaplain and Head of History*
Mr B Gipps, FTCL, ARCO(CHM), ARCM, LRAM *Director of Music*
Mrs J Haworth, BA (Open), CertEd (Southampton) *Head of Geography*
Mr B Hodgson, BA Hons (Maidstone), TCert *Head of Art*
Mrs L A Hodgson, TCert, AMBDA *Head of Learning Support*
Mrs C Houchin, Licence ès Lettres (Bordeaux) *Head of Modern Languages*
Mr J Kirsopp, TCert (London) *Head of Technology*
Mrs E Lewis, MA (Reading), TCert *Head of Sixth Form Boarding; Home Economics*
Mrs C Pollington, LCGL, Dip Fashion (C & G) FE, CertEd *Head of Key Stage 4; Head of Fashion*
Mr J Stacey, BSc, MSc (London), FLS, CBiol, MIBiol, PGCE (Soton) *Director of Studies and Head of Science*
Miss D Williams, BSc Hons (Exeter), PGCE (Wales) *Head of Mathematics*

Assistant Teachers:

Miss K Avery *Ceramics*
Mrs M Beckett, BA Hons (Sussex), MA (Simon Fraser), PGCE (London), CertModDrama (Sussex) *English and Theatre Studies*
Miss J Blair, BSc Hons (Ulster), PGCE (Leeds) *Chemistry*
Miss A Bowen, BA Hons (Liverpool), PGCE *English*
Mrs S Brown, BA Hons (Wales), Inst of Ling F Dip in German *Head of Religious Education and Key Skills Co-ordinator; Business Studies*
Mrs W Dersley, BSc (Open), PGCE *Mathematics*
Miss J Gorrie, CertEd (Cambridge) *Lacrosse*
Mrs S Griffith, BA (Madrid), CertEd (Thames) *Spanish*
Mrs E Hutchins, BSc Hons (Surrey), PGCE (Brunel) *Physics*
Ms H J Manfield, BSc, DipEd (Wales), DipEcol (Kent) *Biology*
Mrs M Mitchell, CertEd (London), AMBDA *Learning Support*
Mrs R Mitchell, BSc Hons (Keele), PGCE (Manchester) *Science and Mathematics*
Miss S Reeves, BA Hons, PGCE *Modern Languages*
Mrs S Roddie, BA Hons (Camberwell) *Art and Ceramics*
Miss K Stone, BSc Hons (Bedford) *Physical Education*
Mrs S Thorpe, BA Hons (Oxford), PGCE (Leeds) *Mathematics*
Mrs E Tamburrini, BSc Hons (London) *Business Studies and Secretarial*
Miss J Tucker-Williams, BA Hons (Herts) *Jewellery)*
Mr M Williams, BMus Hons (Durham), FRCO, MTC, FLCM, GRSM, ARCM *Music*

Junior School Staff:

Mrs Z Armitage, CertCambInstitPE *Kindergarten Class Teacher*
Mrs M Bell, MA (Oxford) *General Subjects*
Mrs J Betteridge, CertEd (Avery Hill) *Year 3 Class Teacher; Library*
Mrs B Canham, JP, BA Hons, PGCE (Froebel) *Head of Junior School; English*
Mrs P Collins, CertEd (London) *Physical Education*
Mrs E Deacon, Montessori Diploma *Kindergarten Class Teacher*
Mrs C Gray, LRAM, GRSM, ARCM *Music*
Mrs C Hurst, CertEd *General Subjects*
Mrs J Kitchin *Classroom Assistant - Reception*
Mrs C Houchin, Licence ès Lettres (Bordeaux) *French*
Mrs B Marsh, CertEd (Sussex) *Year 1 Class Teacher*
Mrs J Moody, BEd Hons (Brighton) *General Subjects*
Mrs K Paton *Classroom Assistant - Kindergarten*
Mrs S Roddie, BA Hons (Camberwell) *Art and Technology*
Mrs J Rummery, CertEd (London) *Year 2 Class Teacher; Curriculum Co-ordinator for Pre-Prep*
Mrs L Shaikh, BA Hons (Brighton), PGCE *Year 3 Class/ English Teacher*
Mrs C Spink *Classroom Assistant - Reception*
Mrs S Stevens *Classroom Assistant - Kindergarten*
Mrs P Thomas, BA Hons (London), PGCE *Reception Class Teacher*
Mrs J Usherwood, CertEd (Portsmouth) *Curriculum Co-ordinator; Science and Mathematics*

Boarding Staff:

Miss R Bradley, BA Hons (London), PGCE *Head of Main School Boarding*
Mrs E Lewis, MA (Reading), TCert *Head of Sixth Form Boarding*
Miss S Broomfield *Assistant Housemistress*
Miss L Farley, BA Hons (Wales) *Assistant Housemistress, Sixth Form*
Miss E Grayson, BA (Queensland) *Assistant Housemistress*
Mrs L Hodgson, TCert, AMBDA *Assistant Housemistress*
Miss S Lloyd, NNEB Dip *Assistant Housemistress*
Mrs M Martin *Sixth Form Housemistress*
Miss S Morshead *Student Housemistress*
Miss S Pugh *Assistant Housemistress*

Riding Centre:
Mr S Gregory, BHSAI (IT) *Director*
Miss C Booth Jones *Secretary*
Miss H Fawcett, BHSAI *Instructor*
Mrs M-A Horn, BHSII, BHSI (SM & T) *Senior Instructor*
Mr L Townsend, BHSAI (IT) *Instructor*

Visiting Staff:
Miss K Bennetts, BA Hons, LTCL *Recorder & Guitar*
Mr N Boyd-Cox, *Oboe and Flute*
Miss J Coleman, AISTD *Ballet*
Mrs J Dammers, LRAM *Cello*
Miss S Downey *Gym Club*

Mr D Ecott, LGSM *Brass*
Mr P Fields, ARCM *Violin*
Mrs V Haynes, ARCM *Cello*
Mrs H Kershaw, BEd Hons *Piano*
Miss H Parsons, BMus Hons, LRAM *Saxophone and Clarinet*
Mrs K Pusey, GGSM, PGCE *Singing*
Miss A Pyne, ProfCert Hons, LRAM *Flute*
Mrs S Reeve, ALCM, LLCM(TD), LGSM, LLAM *Speech & Drama*
Mrs M Riley, BA Hons, PGCE, LTCL *Piano*
Mrs L Robinson, BA Hons, RSADip *Learning Support*
Mr R T Scarff, GTCL Hons, LTCL *Percussion*
Mr J Walker, MA, DipEd, CertEd *Learning Support*
Miss A Watson, DipPhysEd, DyslexiaDip *Learning Support*

Sanatorium:
Senior Sanatorium Sister: Mrs C Slade, RGN, RMDipM
Relief Sanatorium Sister: Mrs C Wilson, SRN

Location and Travel. Bedgebury is situated in the heart of the Weald of Kent one hour's journey from London by rail, ninety minutes from Gatwick airport and two hours from Heathrow (an escort service is arranged to and from the airports). Six return daily minibuses, run by the school, service the Weald of Kent and East Sussex.

The Senior School, for children 11 to 18 years is centred around a magnificent country house which was the former home of Viscount Marshal Beresford, one of Wellington's distinguished Generals during the Peninsular Wars. The School is set in spectacular grounds of 200 acres together with a 22 acre lake.

The Junior School for children aged 2½ to 11, is set in the grounds a quarter of a mile from the Senior School. It is purpose built and was opened in September 1998. The light, airy classrooms provide specialist facilities in Science, Music, Art and Information Technology together with two halls for physical activities, drama and dance.

Entrance and Fees. There are 394 girls in the school 38% Boarding, 62% Day). Girls sit written papers for entry to the School from age 9 onwards and are interviewed by the Headmistress. A Scholarship Entrance Examination is taken and awards of up to one-third day fees are available. The De Noailles Trust funds bursarial assistance for the daughters of Church of England Clergy. Details of scholarships (including Sixth Form Awards, and Academic, Music, Drama, Art, Riding and PE Scholarships) may be obtained from the Headmistress. There are fee reductions for daughters of service personnel, and some Music and Art bursaries are available in addition to Scholarships.

Fees 2000/2001. Boarders: £3,320–£5,040 per term (age 8–18). Includes all boarding and tuition fees, books, laundry, incidental meals.

Day Girls: £760–£3,130 per term (age 2½–18). Day Boys: £760–£2,660 per term (age 2½–7½). Includes tuition fees, books and incidental meals.

Facilities and Activities. Bedgebury's specialist facilities include a purpose built Arts Centre; a networked Information Technology facility, Physics Laboratory; a Grade 5 Approved British Horse Society Equestrian Centre with two indoor schools and stabling for 60 horses together with a full cross country course; a 22 acre lake for sailing, windsurfing and canoeing; a 15 stage assault course, climbing wall and abseil tower; open-air heated swimming pool; extensive sports fields for lacrosse, hockey, tennis and cross country running. The Sixth Form boarding house has 60 university style single study bedrooms.

Curriculum. In the Junior School the children are encouraged to develop a love of learning through a broad curriculum with the emphasis on literacy and numeracy. We seek to provide the best educational experience for the children within a friendly family atmosphere. In the Senior School girls are prepared for the GCSE examination. A core curriculum of English Language and Literature, Mathematics, a Language, the pure Sciences (Chemistry, Biology, Physics), and a Humanity plus PE and PSE is maintained up to and including Year 11. Careers guidance is given to help with GCSE option choices, and again before entering the Sixth Form. Specialist Learning Support is available. The wide range of A Levels (21 subjects) is complemented by a choice of vocational courses including BTEC National Diploma in Business & Finance (Equestrian), BHSAI, RSA Secretarial and City & Guilds Fashion Diploma. Careers guidance throughout the Sixth Form prepares girls for choices about university entrance and careers.

All girls in Year 9 and again in the Lower Sixth follow weekend personal development and leadership training courses designed to encourage the girls to work together as a team; to bring out leadership qualities and decision making abilities; to increase self confidence for the individual and encourage communication and empathy amongst the group.

Ethos. Building Confidence, Inspiring Enthusiasm, Emphasising Achievement.

Bedgebury aims to provide an excellent and challenging education in accordance with the principles of the Church of England, although girls of all denominations and faiths are welcome.

For further information telephone Mrs Alison Donelan, The Registrar on 01580 211954 for a prospectus and an appointment to visit.

The School is a member of the Girls' Schools Association, the Boarding Schools' Association and the Governing Bodies of Girls' Schools Association (GBGSA).

Bedgebury School Old Girls' Association: *President:* Mrs H Moriarty (Headmistress).

Charitable status. Bedgebury School (Church Education Corporation) is a Registered Charity, number 306308A/1-CD(LON). It exists to provide a widely based Christian education.

Beechwood Sacred Heart

Pembury Road Tunbridge Wells Kent TN2 3QD
Tel: (01892) 532747
Fax: (01892) 536164

Beechwood is an independent day and boarding school for girls 11-18, with an integrated Preparatory School for girls and boys aged 3-11. Of the 300 pupils, approximately 60 are boarders. Founded in 1915 by the Society of the Sacred Heart, it has been a lay school since 1973, retaining a sound Catholic tradition while welcoming pupils from all nations and creeds.

Governors:
Father J K Taggart, OSB (*Chairman*)
Mr D Abrams
Mr B Ansell
Mrs S Chapman-Hatchett
Mr D W Chard
Mrs S Clark
Dr D Findley
Mr P Holland
Mrs M F Mason
Mr B Melbourne-Webb
Mr G A Rodmell

Company Secretary and Clerk to the Governors: Mr A J G Harvey

***Head:* Mr Nicholas Beesley,** MA (Oxon)

Deputy Head: Miss Madeleine Moore, BA (Hons), PGCE *English, Drama*

Staff:

Mr Michael Awdry, BA (Hons), PGCE *Art & Design*
*Mrs Maria Bird, CertEd, BA, BEd (Hons) *Art & Design; Careers*
Mr John Buckle, MSc, PGCE *Physics*
Mrs Valerie Byrne, BSc (Hons), MIPD *Business Studies*
Mrs L Clack, BA (Hons), PGCE *History*
Mrs Imelda Connell, BA (Hons) *EFL; Spanish*
*Mr Paul Cotton, BA (Hons), PGCE *Geography; DoA*
*Mrs Lucia Crewdson, BSc (Hons) *Mathematics; SVP*
Mrs Philippa Drury, CertEd *Science; Biology; PSHE*
*Mrs Patricia Findley, BSc, PGCE *Science; Chemistry*
*Mrs Diane Fowling, BA (Hons) *Modern Languages*
Miss Mary Fox, BA (Hons) *Law*
Mrs Imogen Janke, Staats Examen *German; Spanish; Latin*
Mrs Brigitte Jenner, Lic d'Ang *Modern Languages*
Mrs Virginia Letchworth, PGCE, PGDipSLD (Dyslexia) *Learning Support Co-ordinator*
*Mrs Carol Mitchell, BA, PGCE *Physical Education*
Mr David Molloy, DMS, ACCA *Accountancy*
Mr R Ormrod, BA (Hons), CertEd *English*
*Mrs Candida Prodrick, BD, PGCE *Religious Education; Charities; Old Girls Assoc*
Mrs Diana Ringer, BSc (Hons), PGCE, MSc *Mathematics*
Miss Celia Roe, BSc (Hons), PGCE, TEFL(Dip) *EFL*
*Mrs Sandra Truman, MA *English; Drama*
*Miss Lynda Wallens, BEd (Hons) *Information Technology; Curriculum Co-ordinator*
Mrs Heather Warburton, BSc, PGCE *Biology*
Mrs Rosemary Snook *Tennis Coach*
Mrs Molly Wood *Laboratory Technician*

Preparatory School:

Head: Mrs Susan Deeks, BEd (Hons), CertEd

Mrs Sandra Blacker, MA, BSc, PGCE
Mrs Rosemary Cazalet, CertEd *Food Technology*
Mrs Lucinda Coombes, BEd
Mrs Madeline Gammie, BA (Hons), PGCE
Mrs Helen Hunter, CertEd
Mrs Cheryl Jude, Montessori DipEd
Mrs Hilary Richardson, CertEd *PE*
Mrs Meryl Scott, CertEd
Mrs Susan Shepherd, SocSc (Hons), PGCE
Mrs Susan Skomorowski, BA (Hons), CertEd, DipEd
Mrs Karen Atkinson (*Classroom Assistant*)
Miss Tracy Bartlett (*Classroom Assistant*)
Mrs Lorna Reed (*Classroom Assistant*)
Mrs Karen Gillett, BA (*Nursery*)
Miss Jayne Richards (*Nursery*)

Boarding and Pastoral Staff:

Head of Boarding: Miss Madeleine Moore, BA (Hons), PGCE
House Mistress (Seniors): Mrs Sue Dyke
House Mistress (Middles): Miss Mary O'Brien
House Mistress (Juniors): Mrs Sandra Newman
School Nurses: Mrs Anne Bishop, SRN; Mrs Elizabeth Hassan, SRN
Assistant House Mistresses:
Mrs Catherine Hamilton
Mrs Ros Love
Miss Rachelle Maillard

Administration:

Director of Finance: Mr Andrew Harvey
Accounts Manager: Mrs Ruth Fowler
Registrar: Mrs Sue Dyke
Head's Secretary: Miss Liz Milner
School Secretary: Mrs Ros Couldwell
Facilities Manager: Mrs Deirdre Peachey
School Housekeeper: Mrs Sandra Newman
Chef: Mr Brian McLellan-Dunn
Maintenance:
Mr Trevor Foster
Mr Michael Grote

Pastoral care. At Beechwood we educate in a happy relaxed atmosphere, with values based on traditional Christian principles. A strong partnership between family, staff and pupils encourages every child to develop and to excel at their individual talents. Small numbers allow for individual pastoral care with effective, careful monitoring of academic and social progress.

Curriculum. A broad curriculum is followed throughout Key Stage 3 with a wide range of choice of subjects at GCSE and A level.

The Performing Arts of Music, Drama, Modern Dance and Ballet are an important part of life at Beechwood. More than half the pupils have extra lessons in instrumental music and opportunities to perform are wide and varied. Pupils of all ages and abilities are encouraged to take part in a wide variety of dramatic activities, often presented as full-scale productions. Emphasis is always on full participation and confidence building.

Modern Languages have a dominant place in the curriculum. There is a foundation Latin course in Year 7, with French, Spanish and German available to GCSE, AS and A level.

Information Technology is provided as a cross-curricular discipline throughout the school. ICT skills are taught as part of the curriculum from an early age and techniques acquired in lessons are quickly used as tools for projects and coursework in all areas of the school programme.

Our own integrated Learning Support Unit caters for pupils with dyslexia and other mild specific learning difficulties, and offers a comprehensive Study Skills Course at all levels.

School facilities. Academic facilities include: library, up-to-date computer room, modern well-equipped science building, language and business centre, art and pottery studio, food technology room, music auditorium, drama and dance hall. Sports facilities include: hockey and football pitches, netball, basketball and tennis courts, heated outdoor swimming pool, gymnasium, playing fields. We encourage our pupils to participate in a wide variety of sporting experiences, the emphasis always being on fun and participation. Recent sporting successes include being Kent county champions in basketball at four different age levels.

Scholarships. Academic, Art, Drama, Music and Sports Scholarships are available at 11+ (Year 7), 13+ (Year 9) and 16+ (Sixth Form). Sixth Form scholarship day is in November, 11+ and 13+ scholarship day is in January each year.

Entry requirements. The school is non-selective academically, selection for entry being based on interview with the Headmaster (where possible), previous school report and a confidential reference. All enquiries and applications should be addressed in the first instance to the Registrar.

Fees per term. Full boarders £3,605-£4,650; Weekly boarders £3,090-£4,135; Day pupils £1,480-£2,850.

Charitable status. The Sacred Heart School Beechwood Trust Limited is a Registered Charity, number 325104. It exists principally as a private girls day and boarding school, both for primary and secondary education.

* Head of Department	§ Part Time or Visiting
† Housemaster/Housemistress	¶ Old Pupil
‡ See below list of staff for meaning	

The Belvedere School (G.D.S.T)

17 Belvidere Road Princes Park Liverpool L8 3TF
Tel: 0151-727 1284
Fax: 0151-727 0602
e-mail: enquiries@belvedere.gdst.net
website: gdst.net/belvedere

Founded 1880

This is one of the 25 schools of The Girls' Day School Trust. For general information about the Trust and the composition of its Council, see p 532. A more detailed prospectus may be obtained from the school.

Local Governors:
Chairman: Miss J Robson, FRCS
Professor L Archibald, BA, PhD
Ms A C Brook, BA, MIMgt, FRSA
Mrs K Butcher, BA, MSc
Professor C Gaskell
Mrs R Hawley, BA
Mrs S Malthouse, BA
Mr R Miller, BSc
Mrs G M Perrin, MA, BLitt

Headmistress: **Mrs G Richards**, BA, MEd (Wales) *History*

Senior Department:
Deputy Head Mistress: Miss E M H Owen, BSc (Nottingham) *Geography*

Senior Mistress: Miss A J Povall, BSc (Liverpool) *Geography*

Head of Sixth Form: Miss J D Tyndall, BD (London), AKC *Theology*

Teaching Staff:
Mrs M W Anderson, BSc (Liverpool) *Physics*
Mrs C L Beard, BA (Birmingham) *German, Spanish*
Mrs A Beddard, BEd (Liverpool) *Physical Education*
Miss C M Bolton, BA (Birmingham) *Latin and Russian,* MA (Liverpool) *Classics*
Mr G Bonfante, BSc (Southampton) *Biology*
Miss J Brown, BSc (Warwick) *Mathematics*
Miss N Buckland, BA (Liverpool) *Business Studies*
Mrs C Clapham, DipAD, Fine Art, (Newcastle) *Art and Design*
Mrs M M Close, BA (Manchester) *History*
Mrs M Cowan, BSc (Leeds) *Chemistry*
Mrs J Davies, CertEd (Durham) *Physical Education*
Mrs L Davies, CertEd (Sussex) *Physical Education*
Mr P Elliott, BA (Sheffield) *Philosophy*
Mrs K Foley, BA (Nottingham) *Sociology/History*
Mrs S Freeman, BSc (Manchester) *Art and Textile Design*
Miss J K Gordon-Brown, BMus (Edinburgh) *Music*
Mrs B Green, MA (Glasgow) *English and History*
Mrs J Hargreaves, BSc (Huddersfield) *Geography*
Mrs L Higgins, BA (Open University) *Mathematics*
Mrs A M E Hogan, BA (Newcastle) *English*
Mrs P Howell, BSc (London) *Mathematics*
Mrs H M Hunter, BSc (Sheffield) *Biochemistry*
Mrs J Ireland, BA (Liverpool) *English and German*
Mr S King, MA (Aberdeen) *History*
Mrs R Matthews, BA (Manchester) *French*
Miss A V McCombe, CertEd (Edinburgh College of Domestic Science), BSc (Open) *Home Economics*
Mrs A McGregor, MA (Liverpool) *English Renaissance Literature;* BA (Open University) *Literature*
Miss K M Nolan, BSc (Manchester)
Miss H Paterson, BSc (London) *Geography, MSc* (Liverpool) *Environmental Assessment, Oxbridge Co-ordinator*
Mrs B Pollard, BA (London) *English*
Mr R D Pritchard *Mathematics*
Mrs A E Ramkaran, BSc, (London), PhD (Liverpool) *Biology*
Mrs B Rigby, BSc (Manchester) *Chemistry*
Mr C J Ritchie, MA (Leeds) *Spanish and French*
Mrs H Roberts, BMus (Dublin), LRAM, ARCM *Music*
Miss B A M Rouse, BSc (Liverpool) *Biochemistry*
Mrs M Smith, BSc (Newcastle-upon-Tyne) *Mathematics, MSc* (Liverpool, Hope) *IT*
Mrs J Taylor, BA (Reading) *English; MA* (Lancaster) *Theatre Practice*
Ms H Ward, BA (Liverpool) *Art*
Mrs J L Williams, BA (Liverpool) *French*

Junior Department:
Head of Junior Department: Mrs C Hazlehurst, CertEd (Liverpool)

Deputy Head of Junior Department: Mrs K Smith, BEd (Liverpool) *Environmental Science*

Miss R Brittain, BA Hons, PGCE (Sheffield Hallam)
Mrs W Hill, BEd (Liverpool)
Mrs R McConomy, BEd (Sheffield)
Mrs A Moffitt, BA Hons (Roehampton Institute)
Miss M Nugent, BEd (Liverpool) *Primary Education*
Miss C J Thompson, BA (Northumbria) *History of Modern Art, Design and Film*
Mrs M Williams, BA (Bath) *European Studies (French)*

Nursery:
Head of Nursery Unit: Mrs G Breen, CertEd (Normal College, Bangor)
Mrs D Roberts, NNEB
Miss J Ellis, NNEB

Visiting Staff:

Pianoforte: Miss C Chong, GMus, GBSM, LTCL

Strings: Miss G Burgess; Mrs F Vella Johnson

Singing: Miss J K Gordon-Brown, BMus, ARCM

Brass: Mr I Anstee, GRNCM

Woodwind:
Mrs S Francis, BA *Music*
Miss K Slack, BMus, GRNCM

Guitar: Mr R Smith

Oboe: Miss C Walker, BA

Percussion: Miss R Wright, GRNCM

Speech and Drama: Mrs C Parsons

Dance: Miss C Duffy

French Conversation: Miss A Saulnier

German Conversation: Mrs I Callow

Spanish Conversation: Mr C Alvarez

Headmistress's Secretary: Mrs P A Capper

Admissions Secretary: Miss H Starmer

Administrative Officer: Mrs K Crewdson

Teaching Resources: Mrs M Traynor

School Administrator: Mrs K Cull

Recruitment Officer: Mrs C Adnett

School Doctor: Dr G Inatimi

School Nurse: Ms D Divito

Librarian: Mrs L Redfern

Computer Technicians: Ms J Backstrom; Mr M Draycott

Science Technicians: Mrs J Huyton, Mr M Evans, Mr K Hornby

Junior School Assistants: Mrs V Giddings, Mrs E Roberts, Mrs D Roberts, Miss J Ellis

The school was opened in 1880 and the original buildings are still in daily use. Facilities have expanded considerably since then, including new Kitchen and dining facilities, a Technology House, a Music House, Computer Suite and Sixth Form Centre. The building programme includes a Sports Hall, new nursery and a Performing Arts Centre. The Junior Department is housed in a separate house a few minutes walk from the main school. There are 600 pupils in the school, including a Sixth Form of 100 and a Junior and Nursery Department of 150 (age range 3–11).

Physical activities include lacrosse, netball, tennis, rounders, gymnastics and many others. There are facilities on site for netball, tennis and lacrosse; facilities for athletics and swimming are a short distance away. The catchment area includes Liverpool and surrounding areas: Widnes, Runcorn and Warrington. The school is well served by public transport in addition to school coaches.

Curriculum. The school provides an environment in which girls of all ages work hard to develop their abilities. The curriculum provides a wide general education and specialisation is deferred as long as possible. Emphasis is placed on all-round personal development within this framework. Girls are prepared for GCSE and AS and Advanced Level examinations in a wide choice of subjects. In addition to Advanced Level courses the Sixth Form girls study a variety of general subjects and they have the opportunity to do voluntary service and to organise clubs, plays and societies with younger girls.

Fees. From September 2000: Senior School £1,680 per term; Junior Department £1,220 per term; Nursery £980 per term.

The fees cover the regular curriculum, school books, stationery and other materials, choral music, games and swimming, but not optional extra subjects or school meals except for Nursery.

The fees for extra subjects, including instrumental music, speech and drama, are shown in the prospectus.

Thanks to a partnership between the Girls' Day School Trust and the Sutton Trust, an educational charity founded in 1997 by the philanthropist Peter Lampl, the Belvedere School at Senior level (11-18 years) is an open access independent school.

An open access school accepts pupils on academic merit. Pupils are offered places on the basis of their performance in the entrance procedure and no account is taken at this stage of their parents' finances. The Trust will then look at whether the parents can afford the fees and if families cannot they will be given financial help as necessary, up to a free place.

Scholarships. There are at present a number of Scholarships for entry to the Sixth Form and at 11+.

Meetings of Old Girls are held annually.

The Parents' and Friends' Association enables parents to meet informally and several social events are organised each year.

Charitable status. The Belvedere School is one of the 25 schools of the Girls' Day School Trust which is a Registered Charity, number 1026057. The aim of the Trust is to provide a fine academic education at a comparatively modest cost.

Benenden School

Cranbrook Kent TN17 4AA
Tel: (01580) 240592

Council:
Mrs C E A Nunneley, MA (*Chairman*)
M O Coates, Esq, FRICS (*Vice-Chairman*)
J G Sanger, Esq, MA, MBA, FCA (*Finance Director*)
D C Bonsall, Esq, MA, LLM
H R Collum, Esq, FCA
Mrs S H Doyle
C J Driver, Esq, MPhil, BA, BEd, STD
Mrs R J Johnston
Miss D M Lavin, MA, DipEd
M K H Leung, Esq, BA, DipSoc
C H Moore, Esq, BA
H Salmon, Esq, BA
M C Sargent, Esq
Mrs I R Shackleton, LLB
J V Strong, Esq, ARICS
B V R Thomas, Esq, MA
Mrs T R Winser, MA
The Chairman of the Benenden School Trust: A V Georgiadis, Esq, MA, MBA
The Chairman of the Benenden School Parents' Association: Mrs S H S Simpson
The Chairman of the Benenden School Seniors' Association: Countess C Grocholska

Secretary to the Council and School Bursar: R Dalton Holmes, Esq, TD

***Headmistress:* Mrs C M Oulton**, MA (Oxon), PGCE

Deputy Head (*Director of Studies*): D A Harmsworth Esq, MA (Oxon)

Deputy Head (*Administration*): The Revd Dr H M D Petzsch, MA (Edinburgh), BD, PhD

Housemistresses/masters:
Guldeford: T A J Dawson, Esq, BSc (London), MA (Open), DipAdvStats (Oxon) (*Mathematics*)
Hemsted: Mrs M Cass, CertEd (*Information Technology*)
Norris: Miss E D McMeechan, MA (Aberdeen) (*French*)
Echyngham: Mrs R van der Vliet, BA (UCW Aberstwyth) (*Modern Languages*)
Medway: Miss A Steven, BA (Bristol) (*English/Physical Education*)
Marshall: J Watts, Esq, MA (Oxon) (*History*)
Founders':
Beeches: Mrs F Breeze, BA (Oxon) (*Classics*)
Elms: Miss S J Hatt, MA (Kent), BA (*English*)
Limes: Mrs S J Perry, BSc (Liverpool) (*Science*)
Oaks: Mrs E M Sanders, MA(TCD), MA, MPhil (Nottingham), DipEd (Belfast), AFBPsS, CPsychol (*English*)

School Chaplain: Revd A C V Aldous, BA (Southampton)

Administrative Staff:
Bursar: R Dalton Holmes, Esq, TD
Deputy Bursar: A G Parsons, Esq
Facilities Manager: C K Hayman, Esq
Domestic Bursar: J L Peters, Esq

Registry:
Mrs D Price (*Development Director*)
Mrs E A Ward (*Admissions Secretary*)
Mrs J Hayter Johnson (*Seniors' Officer*)
Dr A W Bailey, BA (Penn), PhD (*Fundraising Officer*)
S Thorneycroft (*Marketing Assistant*)

Secretariat:
Mrs J A Sullivan (*Headmistress's Personal Assistant*)
Mrs G D B Trott (*Bursar's Secretary*)

§Mrs A G Pissarro (*School Secretary - termtime*)
§Mrs C A Cooper (*School Secretary - holidays*)
Mrs T Johnson (*Development Director's Secretary*)
Mrs D M Benson, LTCL, FTCL (*Music Administrator*)
§Mrs M E Murphy (*Careers Administrator*)
§Mrs S Roberts (*Common Room*)
§Mrs N K Wood, BA (Cornell) (*Deputy Heads' Secretary*)

Accounts:
A G Wilton, Esq (*Accountant*)
Mrs S E Lock (*Deputy Accountant*)
Mrs B Tanner-Tremaine, BSc(Econ) (London) (*Assistant Accountant*)

Medical:
Dr A M Wood, MB, ChB, MRC Psych (*Medical Officer*)
Sister J L Mallion, RGN
Mrs A Blythe, RGN
Mrs K Brown, SEN
§Mrs J M McDonnell, SRN

Academic Staff:
English:
N van der Vliet, Esq, BA (UCW, Aberystwyth)
Mrs M M M du Plooy, BSc (Stirling), BEd (Sussex), CertEd, MA (London)
Miss S J Hatt, MA (Kent), BA
Mrs E M Sanders, MA(TCD), MA, MPhil (Nottingham), DipEd (Belfast), AFBPsS, CPsychol
Mrs R Smith, BA, MPhil (Oxon)
Miss A Steven, BA (Bristol)
A R Stiller, Esq, MA (Oxon)
§Mrs S Elkin, BA, MA (Open)

Mathematics:
Mrs D G Swaine, BSc (Wales)
Mrs V A Burgess, BSc (Dunelm)
Mrs E Thomson, BA (Cape Town Technical)
§B A Clough, Esq, BSc (London)
§Mrs M A Pook, BSc (Sheffield)

Science:
Dr P F Lewis, BSc, PhD (London), ARCS, DIC, CBiol, MIBiol
Dr N J Dowrick, BA (Oxon), DPhil (Oxon)
Mrs J Hall, BSc (London)
S C Heron, Esq, BSc (London)
Dr R J Hill, BSc, PhD (Warwick), CChem, MRIC
Mrs S J Perry, BSc (Liverpool)
§Dr F Westcott, BSc (Liverpool), PhD
§Mrs A Linney, BSc (Birmingham)

Modern Languages:
Mrs E F Shellard, L-ès-L (Sorbonne)
Mrs J Beloso-Forbes, BA (London)
J D Crouzet, Esq, M-des-L, L'èsh (St Etienne)
Mrs M S Curran, BA (Oxon)
Mrs A Jarman, BA (Oxon)
Miss E D McMeechan, MA (Aberdeen)
Mrs R van der Vliet, BA (UCW Aberystwyth)
P Walls, Esq, BA (Wales), MPhil (Leeds)
Mrs I Willison, BA (Leicester)
§Mrs M Best, MPhil (Innsbruck)
§Miss R Domingo Chaves, Lic-ès-Lettres (Madrid)
Mrs L Pagotto, Lic-ès-Lettres (Metz)
§Mrs F Powell, Lic de Geog (Sorbonne)
§Mrs S Li, BA (Quinghai)

Classics:
Dr D R Marsh, BA (Nottingham), PhD (London)
Miss L Boyce, MA (Oxon)
Mrs F Breeze, BA (Oxon)
D A Harmsworth, Esq, MA (Oxon)
Mrs P Wileman, BA (Nottingham)

Economics:
Mrs B Cocksworth, BSc (London)
C E Williams, Esq, BSc (Southampton)

Geography:
C E Williams, Esq, BSc (Southampton)
Miss C M Moat, BA (Nottingham)

History and Politics:
J Watts, Esq, MA (Oxon), BPhil (York)
Miss K M Dobson, BA (Newcastle)
Mrs C M Oulton, MA (Oxon), PGCE
The Revd Dr H M D Petzsch, MA (Edinburgh), BD, PhD
Mrs B Scopes, BA (Kent)
Mrs I Denny, BA (Bristol), MA (Kent)

Religious Studies:
Mrs J F Duncan, MA (St Andrews)
Revd A C V Aldous, BA (Southampton)

Art & Design:
R S Leighton, Esq, BA (Stourbridge)
Mrs P J Futrell, BA (Middlesex Polytechnic)
Mrs J L King, BA (Nottingham Trent) (*Textiles*)
§S H Mansfield, Esq, BA (Staffs) (*History of Art*)

Design and Technology:
A Vincent, Esq, BA (Manchester Poly)
Mrs L F Palmer, BA (Camberwell)

Information Technology:
A D Sanderson, Esq, BSc (Warwick), MSc (Bath)
Mrs M E Cass, CertEd (*Information Technology*)

Speech & Drama:
Mrs V Whitelaw, MA(Ed) (Open), DipCS, DipDa (London)
Mrs D Caron, BA (Loughborough), LGSM
G R Lee, Esq, CertEd (Roehampton)
§Mrs R J Clements, BA (Open), BEd
§Miss A L Wickens, LLAM, LAMDA

Music:
E S Beer, Esq, MA (Oxon), LRAM
Mrs C Harmsworth, ARCM (*Violin*)
Mrs V Lewis, ARCM, DipRCM (*Piano/Cello*)
S J Wallace, Esq, BMus (London), BSc (City)
§Mrs C Alexander, LRAM, ARCM (*Cello/Bass*)
§Ms P Calnan, ARAM (*Violin*)
§Miss E Clarke, LTCL (*Singing*)
§Mrs N M Davis, LRAM (*Piano*)
§P Dhasmana, Esq, BMus (Sydney), MMus (RCM) (*Flute*)
§A Geary, Esq, GLCM (*Percussion*)
§A W Haigh, Esq, ARCM, LRAM (*Piano*)
§M D Hines, Esq, AGSM (*Bassoon*)
§Miss D M Maxwell, GGSM, AGSM (*Piano*)
§Mrs G A Mendes, GHSM, LTCL (*Recorder*)
§Miss J M Miller, AGSM (*Singing*)
§D Murphy, Esq, AGSM, MMus (*Violin & Conducting*)
§Mrs S Purton, LRAM (*Oboe/Piano*)
§Miss E J Roberts, GRNCM, PDOT, GSMD (*Horn*)
§Miss L F Temple, LRAM, ARCM (*Brass*)
§Mrs J Tilt, GGSM, LRAM (*Singing*)
§Mrs C Wheadon, BA (Colchester) (*Flute*)
§P Williams, Esq, CertEd (*Saxophone*)
§Miss A Wynne, BA (Birmingham) (*Harp*)

Physical Education:
Miss V A Sawyer, MBA (Keele), BEd (Reading)
Miss E M Brown, BA (Brighton)
Miss W K Reynolds, BEd (Liverpool Moores)
Mrs Y Reynolds, CertEd (Dartford College of PE)
J Mitchell, Esq, BA (Bedford) (*Squash, Tennis*)
Miss J E Chapman (*Sports Centre Supervisor*)
§D Weighton, Esq, DipPhysEd (Strathclyde) (*Tennis*)
§M D Geer, Esq (*Swimming Coach*)
§J Chorley, Esq (*Fencing*)
§R F Armstrong, BJA Coach BASI (*Judo, Self Defence*)
§Mrs K A Atterton (*Keep Fit Association Teaching Cert*)
§Miss J Wilson, ISTD, LCDD (*Ballet*)
§Mrs R M Elliott, RAD, ISTD (*Tap*)

Careers & College Guidance:
§Mrs I Denny, BA (Bristol), MA (Kent)

Special Needs:
§Mrs J H Edwards, BEd (London), MEd (UCNW), TCert, DipPsych

Librarian: Miss A Morley, BA (Brighton), ALibA, MA (Sussex), DipTEFL, DipPub

Our aims. Benenden School aims to give each pupil the chance to develop her potential to the full within a happy and caring environment. We want her to feel ready to take on whatever challenges lie ahead and able to make a positive difference to the world, whether that is at work or at home or both. Whilst we aim to help each girl to achieve her best possible results in public examinations, we also emphasise the importance of spiritual growth and of developing as a person, in confidence, culture, compassion and social skills. We want to encourage each pupil to develop as an individual as well as a responsible and caring member of a community.

We aim to do this by providing:

- a full and balanced curriculum and a very wide range of extra-curricular activities, designed to promote academic, creative, physical, spiritual and social development;
- well-taught, well-differentiated lessons in good, up-to-date facilities;
- individual academic and pastoral care;
- appropriate university and careers guidance;
- opportunities for leadership within the school;
- a culture of praise, encouragement and support within a framework designed to develop self-discipline;
- the experience of learning to live with other people which a full boarding school can provide.

General Information. The School is an independent girls' boarding school standing in its own parkland of 240 acres. In the heart of the Kentish Weald, it is easily reached by road, or by rail to the neighbouring main line station at Staplehurst, and is well placed for the air terminals of Gatwick and Heathrow, the continental ferry ports of the South East coast and the Channel Tunnel (Ashford International).

The School provides education for girls between the ages of 11 and 18 years. There are 450 students at Benenden; all are boarders and they come from a wide range of backgrounds.

Girls are taught by highly qualified full-time staff of over 50 men and women, together with some 40 part-time specialists, many of whom are leaders in their particular fields.

Each student belongs to a House in which she sleeps and spends much of her private study and leisure time: it is, in effect, her home from home. There are six Houses for 11 to 16 year olds, while Sixth Form students live in the Founders Sixth Form Centre in one of four Sixth Form houses.

Each House has a resident Housemistress or Housemaster, who is also a member of the teaching staff and responsible for the academic and pastoral well-being of each student in the House. Much of the day-to-day work is shared with Assistants and Day Matrons, while other non-resident members of the teaching staff are Personal Academic Tutors.

The School's facilities have been greatly improved in recent years with the construction of a new science and medical centre in 1988, an indoor swimming pool and sports hall opened in 1990 and a technology centre completed in 1991. A Sixth Form Centre opened in September 1993 and was extended in 1997. A new Study Centre is presently being built to provide state-of-the-art classrooms equipped with the latest computer technology, library and IT Centre. Phase One of the Study Centre opens in autumn 2001.

For physical recreation there are nine lacrosse pitches, 13 all-weather tennis courts, sports hall containing a further full sized tennis court, an indoor heated swimming pool, a gymnasium (also used for badminton, volley ball, netball and fencing), two squash courts and a grass running track.

The School is a Christian community, based on Anglican practice, and the ethos of the School reflects Christian principles. Members of other communions and beliefs are welcomed to the School and every effort is made to help them in the practice of their own faith, in an atmosphere of respect and toleration for the views of others.

Entrance to the School is after internal assessment at Preview Weekend, but dependent upon candidates meeting the School's standard at 11+, 12+ and 13+ Common Entrance or in entrance papers. There is also a small intake at Sixth Form level, with competitive entry by the School's own examination. All of the School's students are expected to qualify for degree courses, leaving School with at least three A levels and at least eight subjects at GCSE. A full careers programme is a key component of the Personal Development Programme, aimed to foster the widest range of skills.

The core subjects up to GCSE are English, mathematics, science and modern languages. The compulsory balanced science course ensures that all three sciences are studied (either for single sciences at GCSE or for Dual Award), and every student studies in Key Stage 3 at least two of the three modern languages offered in addition to Latin. Cross-curricular skills and the balancing of theoretical concepts with practical applications are actively encouraged. The ability to work independently is critical to enjoyment and success, and students are given every opportunity to acquire appropriate study habits. The curriculum is under constant review and development, reflecting national initiatives and the aspirations of staff and students.

Benenden believes in close cooperation between School and parents and there is regular contact with them. Formal reports are sent at the end of every term. Parents are encouraged to visit the School for concerts, plays and other events, as well as to take their daughters out for meals or weekend exeats.

The Benenden School curriculum is as follows: LOWER SCHOOL: English, mathematics, biology, chemistry, physics, French, German or Spanish or Classical Greek, Latin, geography, history, religious studies, art & design including textiles, design technology, information technology, drama, music, physical education.

GCSE CORE: English, mathematics, biology, chemistry, physics, French.

GCSE OPTIONS: German, Spanish, Classical Greek, Latin, geography, history, religious studies, art, textiles, design & technology, music, drama & theatre arts.

A LEVEL OPTIONS: English language and literature, English literature, mathematics, further mathematics, biology, chemistry, physics, French, German, Spanish, Greek, Latin, classical civilisation, economics, geography, history, politics, religious studies, art & design, history of art, music, theatre studies, design and technology.

(All students' programmes also include careers education, information technology, physical education, religious education, personal, social and health education).

Sport. Lacrosse, tennis, swimming, netball, rounders, badminton, athletics, volleyball, squash, basketball, gym, dance, fencing, trampolining, aerobics.

Opportunities in music. Tuition is available in all orchestral and keyboard instruments as well as singing. Numerous opportunities exist for instrumental and choral performance. The School is home to a full youth symphony orchestra, and in which students from other schools also play. Benenden also enjoys a strong choral tradition and hosts recitals by musicians of international calibre.

Opportunities in speech and drama. Students are able to pursue drama as an extra-curricular activity throughout their School career by participating in drama workshops, House and School plays. Speech and drama lessons are available and students are prepared for both English Speaking Board and LAMDA examinations. There are two debating societies and students compete at the Oxford and Cambridge Union debating competitions. Sixth Formers are encouraged to run drama and debating clubs.

Optional Extras. Speech and drama, ballet, tap, modern dance, brass, guitar, percussion, piano, string, voice, woodwind, squash, tennis, fencing, judo, self-defence, yoga, riding, clay pigeon shooting, Duke of Edinburgh Award Scheme, foreign languages.

Fees. £5,650 per term (September 2000) payable before the start of term, or by the School's Advance Payment of Fees Scheme.

Scholarships. (*see* Entrance Scholarship section) The School offers annually the following entrance scholarships.

Academic & Music Scholarships to girls under the age of 14 on 1 September following the examination. Sports, Art & Design and Technology scholarships are also offered to girls entering LVth (13+) year group. Academic, music and art scholarships are also offered to those entering the Sixth Form. Upper School Academic, Art & Music internal awards are offered annually.

Prospective parents are encouraged to visit the School, either individually or with others at a prospective parents morning. Prospectuses and full details of entry and scholarship requirements may be obtained from the Admissions Secretary.

Charitable status. Benenden School (Kent) Limited is a Registered Charity, number 307854. It is a charitable foundation for the education of girls.

Berkhamsted Collegiate School

Kings Road Berkhamsted Hertfordshire HP4 3BG.
Tel: (01442) 358166/7
Fax: (01442) 358168

Motto: *'Festina lente'*

Patron: Her Majesty The Queen

The Governors:

¶Mr P J Williamson (*Chairman*)
¶Mrs A F Moore-Gwyn (*Vice-Chairman*)
¶Mrs F M Altman
Dr V J L Best
Mr C J Butcher, Fellow of All Souls, Oxford
Mr R de C Chapman
Mrs J Dunbavand
¶Mr D G Flatt
Mr C N Garrett
Mr R G Groom
Mr J N P B Horden, Fellow of All Souls, Oxford
Mr M P Horton
Mr J D Lythgoe
Mr K J Merrifield
Mr A H Noel
Mrs R Randle
Mrs H Rost
Mrs J Sewell
Miss S E Wolstenholme

Clerk to the Governors & Business Director: Mr P Maynard, RD, FCIS

***Principal:* Dr P Chadwick, MA, PhD, FRSA**

Deputy Principals:
Dr H Brooke, BSc, PhD
Dr P G Neeson, BSc, PhD

Head of Sixth Form: Dr J S Hughes, BSc, MSc, PhD

Senior Master: †Mr C Nicholls, CertEd

Director of Studies: Mr W R C Gunary, BSc

Teaching Staff:
Mrs L J Allen, MA, DipEd
Mrs H R Andrews, BA
Dr J W R Baird, BA, PhD
Mrs E A Baker, BA
†Mr M E Batchelder, CertEd, DipEd, MA
Mr R Batstone, MA
*Mr T H Bendall, MEd
Mrs K Bly, BA
Mrs J A Brannock Jones, BA
Mrs L C Briand, BA, DipTESOL
*Mr J R Browne, BA, FRCO, FRSA
†Mr G R Burchnall, BEd
*Mr F Charnock, CertEd
*Dr E J Chevill, BA, BPhil, PhD, AKC, MMus
Mrs S A E Clay, Dip Central School of Speech & Drama, CertEd
Miss F Colyer, Teacher's Diploma, LGSM
†Mr D J Coulson, BEng, MEng, CEngIChemE
Mr P C Cowie, MA
†Mrs M A Crichton, MA
†Mr S J Dight, BA, DipEd
Mr P E Dobson, BSc, LChem, MRSC
Mrs A M Doggett, BSc
*†Mr C H Eaton, BSc
Mr A J R Esland, MA, MMus, PGCE
*Mrs B Evans, MA
Mr B P Evers, BA
Miss J F Freeman, BA, MA
Mrs D Galloway, MA
Ms F M Garratt, BSc
Miss L Gent, BA, MA
Miss A Gold, BA
Revd S Golding, BA, CertEd, DipPastStuds
Mr T A Grant, MA
Mr M J Green, BSc, HDE
*†Mrs J A Hallett, MA
Mr M I Hamilton, BSc, DipEd
Mr J C Harber, BA (Hons), PGCE
*Miss J Hart, BA
Miss M Hatley, BSc (Hons)
Mrs A Hatton, BA
Mr C J Hayward, BA
†Mrs E M Hines, BA
†Mrs S L Horsnell, BSc
Mrs H I S Howgate, BEd
Mrs J I Jenkins, BA
†Mr P C Jennings, BA
Mrs T K Kelly, BEd
Miss E Kennedy, BSc
Mrs P Kent, CertEd
*Mrs W L Keppel, BSc
*Miss S B Kirton, BA, MA
Miss L Lewin, BEd
Mr J A Leyland, BA
Mrs E M Lindop, BA
*Mr T D Lines, BA, MA, MEd
Mr P R Luckraft, BA
Mrs B S Macgregor, CertEd
Mr A Mackay, BSc, MA
Mr R J McIlwaine, CertEd
†Mr T J McTernan, BA, MA
Mr R H Mardo, BSc
Mr M S Metcalfe, BSc, MInstP, CPhys
Mrs R E Miles, BSc
†Mr R K Mowbray, MA
Mrs A Mulcahy, DipEd, MIL
†Mr R F Newport, BA
Mrs B J Newton, MA
Mrs S Nicholls
Mrs V A Ostle, CertEd
Mr M A Pearce, BA
Mr M S Pett, BA
*Mrs A M Pike, CertEd, RSADipSLD
Mr A P Powles, BSc
Mr S J E Rees, BA
*Mr D G Richardson, BSc
Mrs E A Richardson, BSc
*Mr P T Riddick, MA, MSc
Miss C L Ringrose, MChem
*Mrs A R Roberts, BA
*Mr D K Roberts, BSc
†Mrs E A Roberts, BA
Miss P J Rowan, BA
†Mrs C G Ryder, BSc
Mrs S C Sansome, BSc
†Mr D H Simpson, CertEd, AdvDipDesTec
*Miss A E Smith, BEd
Mrs S Sneddon, BEd
Miss D H Spain, BA
Mr M Sparrow, BA
†Mr N Stevens, BA
*†Mr I R Stewart, BA, MA
Mr R Thompson, BA
Mr M J Thum, MA
†Mr W A Webb, BA, BEd, MEd
†Mrs L Wheater, BSc
Mrs J M Wild, GLCM, ALCM, LLCM(TD)
Mr D J Wiles, BSc
Mrs P Williams, CertEd
Miss T J Woolley, BA, GradIPD

Visiting Staff:

There are 30 visiting music staff and the following instruments are offered in the school: acoustic guitar, bagpipes, bassoon, cello, clarinet, double bass, electric guitar, euphonium, flute, French horn, harpsichord, jazz piano, oboe, organ, percussion (*including kit drumming*), piano, recorder, saxophone, trombone, trumpet, tuba, viola and violin.

Librarian: Mrs S Bartlett, BA, ALA

Chaplain: The Revd S Golding, BA

Medical Officer: Dr N Ormiston, MBBS, MRCP, DRCOG

Principal's Secretary: Mrs N M Golder (*Tel:* 01442 358002; Fax: 01442 358003)

Deputy Principal's Secretary: Mrs S Ruggles (*Tel:* 01442 358161; Fax: 01442 358162)

History. In 1541 John Incent, Dean of St Paul's, was granted a Licence by Henry VIII to found a school in Berkhamsted, Incent's home town. Until the end of the 19th Century Berkhamsted School served as a grammar school for a small number of boys from the town, but over the last century it has developed into a school of significance. In 1888 the foundation was extended by the establishment of Berkhamsted School for Girls. In 1996, these two schools formalised their partnership to become Berkhamsted Collegiate School, offering the highest quality education to pupils from ages 3 to 19.

There are 300 pupils in the flourishing co-educational Sixth Form; between the ages of eleven and sixteen 350 boys on Castle Campus and 250 girls on Kings Campus are taught in single-sex groups; and 400 pupils from ages three to eleven attend the Preparatory School. The Principal is a member of both HMC and GSA.

Aims. The School seeks to enable pupils to achieve their full potential. In addition to the development of the intellect, social, sporting and cultural activities have an important part to play within the framework of a disciplined and creative community based on humane Christian values. It is important that pupils come to value both the individual and the Community through School life. The School seeks to encourage spiritual and moral values and a sense of responsibility as an essential part of the pursuit of excellence.

Organisation. The School stands in the heart of Berkhamsted, an historic and thriving town only thirty miles from London. It enjoys excellent communications to London, the airports, to the Midlands and the communities of south Buckinghamshire, Bedfordshire and Hertfordshire.

The original site has at its heart a magnificent Tudor Hall used as a Schoolroom for over 300 years, which is still in use. The complex of other buildings are from late Victorian to modern periods and of architectural interest (especially the Chapel which is modelled on the Church of St Maria dei Miracoli in Venice). There are new Science laboratories, Library and Learning Resources Centres, Information Technology suites, Sixth Form centres, Careers library, Dining hall, Medical centre, House rooms, Deans' Hall (an Assembly/Concert Hall and Theatre) and Centenary Hall (a very modern 500 seat Lecture Hall also used for concerts and theatre productions). Recreational and sports facilities include extensive playing fields, a listed indoor swimming pool, an open-air heated swimming pool, Fives courts, Squash courts, Tennis courts, two Gymnasia, Drama studio, Music school and Art studios.

The Berkhamsted Collegiate Preparatory School is housed in separate buildings nearby, including a nursery. The school is fully co-educational from Y1 to Y6.

For further information see under IAPS section, Part V of this Book.

At age 11, boys and girls transfer into **single-sex senior schools** on adjacent sites, where they are taught separately up to GCSE. Pupils are supported by a coordinated pastoral system and extra-curricular activities take place across the campuses.

At age 16, pupils join the **fully co-educational Sixth Form,** which offers an extensive ranage of 'A' level subject choices with highly experienced staff and impressive teaching facilities. Clubs, societies, sports, work experience and community service all complement a stimulating programme of activities, which provide students with valuable opportunities for responsibility and enhance their university applications. Careers guidance and personal tutoring are offered throughout the Sixth Form.

Day and Boarding. Pupils may be full boarders, weekly/flexible boarders or day pupils. The two Boarding houses, accommodating boys and girls separately, are well equipped and within a few minutes walk of the main campus. There are 100 boarding places. Day pupils come from both Berkhamsted and the surrounding area of Hertfordshire, Buckinghamshire and Bedfordshire.

Pastoral Care and Discipline. The main social and pastoral unit is the House; the Head of House and House Tutors provide continuity of support and advice and monitor each individual pupil's progress.

The aim is to encourage self-discipline so that pupils may work with a sense of responsibility and trust. Those rules which are laid down cannot cover every contingency but, generally, pupils are expected to be considerate, courteous, honest and industrious. Any breach of good manners or of common sense is a breach of the School Rules, as is any action which may lower the School's good name. Bullying is regarded as a most serious offence. Alcohol, proscribed drugs and smoking are banned. Every member of the School is expected to take a pride in his or her appearance and to wear smart school uniform.

There is a Medical Centre with qualified staff. The School Medical Officer has special responsibility for boarders. A qualified Counsellor is available to all pupils for confidential counselling. The school also has a full-time Chaplain.

Curriculum. The curriculum includes: English, English Literature, Mathematics, Physics, Biology, Chemistry, History, Geography, Religious Studies, French, Latin/ Classics, German/Spanish, Music, Art, Design and Technology. Up to eleven subjects may be taken for GCSE. In the Sixth Form 'A' levels are offered in around 27 subjects, complemented by AS General Studies. Pupils are prepared for university entrance, including Oxbridge. All pupils are taught computer skills and have access to Information Technology centres.

Sport and Leisure Activities. A number of different sports are pursued including Athletics, Badminton, Cricket, Cross Country, Eton Fives, Fencing, Golf, Hockey, Judo, Lacrosse, Netball, Rowing, Rugby, Shooting, Soccer, Squash, Swimming and Tennis. The School also has use of the local Sports Centre. Team games are encouraged and pupils selected for regional and national squads.

There is a flourishing Duke of Edinburgh Award Scheme at all levels. The CCF, community service, work experience and 'Young Enterprise' are offered, along with clubs for gymnastics, drama, computing and technology. Regular school theatre productions, orchestral and choral concerts achieve high standards of performance.

Careers. A team of advisors, internal and external, is directed by the Head of Careers. Heads of House supervise applications for higher education. Parents and pupils are encouraged to consult them and the Careers advisors. The great majority of leavers proceeds to university and higher education.

Entry. Entry to the Preparatory School is from the age of 3 onwards and pupils transfer to the Senior School at age 11. Entry to the Senior School is from 11. The School's Entrance Assessments and an interview are required. Those working towards the Common Entrance Examination can sit this examination in addition to the School's Assessment. Sixth Form entry normally requires at least 3B and 2C grades at GCSE. Entry is normally in September but a few places may be available for the Spring or Summer Terms.

Scholarships and Bursaries. Details of the range of awards (eg music, art, academic) can be obtained from the School.

Fees. Day Pupils: Nursery £1,381, Preparatory £1,662–£2,219 per term; Senior: £2,655–£3,122 per term. Boarding Pupils: £4,499–£4,966 per term.

Old Berkhamstedians. Hon Secretary: Mr J Bale, The Spinney, 128 Horsham Road, Cranleigh, Surrey GU6 8DY. Tel: 01483 274439.

Charitable status. Berkhamsted Collegiate School is a Registered Charity, number 311056. It is a leading Charitable School in the field of Junior and Secondary Education.

Birkenhead High School (G.D.S.T.)

86 Devonshire Place Prenton CH43 1TY
Tel: 0151-652 5777.

Founded 1901

This is one of the 25 Schools of The Girls' Day School Trust. For general information about the Trust and the composition of its Council, see p 532. A more detailed prospectus may be obtained from the school.

Local Governors:
Chairman: Miss B Lloyd, BArch, JP

Mr B J Cummings
Mrs J Greensmith, DL, BCom
Prof R S Jones, MVSc, DrMedVet, JP, FRCVS, DVA, MIBiol
Mrs I Love, MA, JP
Mr G Nissen, CBE, MA
Mrs C Owen
Mrs J Timms, MA, DASS
Mr B Trepess

***Headmistress:* Mrs C H Evans**, BA (Wales) *Economics*

Deputy Head: Miss G A Shannon-Little, BA (Manchester) *English Language and Literature*

Senior Mistress: Mrs N I Matthews, BSc (Sheffield) *Mathematics*

Senior School Staff:
Miss P Bromwell, BSc (Newcastle-upon-Tyne) *Psychology*
Mrs L P M Butler, BA (Swansea) *Latin/Greek*
Mrs B A Carrington, BA (Reading) *History*
Mrs N Clarke, BA (Sunderland Polytechnic) *Fine Art*
Mrs M A Concannon, Certificate in Physical Education (Liverpool)
Mr C B Cooke, BA (Bradford) *Russian/French*
Mrs E Davey, MA (Oxford) *Geography, Dip History* (Liverpool), Dip Soc Admin (LSE)
Miss J Devlin, BSc (Belfast) *Geography*
Dr G Ffrench, BA (Open University) *Combined Studies, MEd* (Manchester) *Aesthetic Education, PhD* (Manchester) *Philosophical Aesthetics*
Mrs L C Fraser, BSc (Leicester) *Mathematics*
Mrs C Frowe, Licence (Metz) *English*
Mrs C M Greenwood, BA (Open University) *Humanities*
Mrs S J Guest, Certificate in Physical Education (Liverpool)
Mr J Halsall, MA (Cambridge) *Social & Political Science*
Dr G R G Hayhurst, BSc, PhD (Liverpool) *Zoology*
Miss G L Humphreys, BSc (Dundee) *Physics*
Mrs M Huntriss, BSc (Durham) *Mathematics*
Mrs O Kahn, BA (Witwatersrand, S Africa) *English*
Mrs K J Kelly, BA (Swansea) *English Literature*
Mr A J Leeder, BSc (Birmingham) *Biological Sciences,* MSc (Durham) *Ecology*
Mrs S E Lindsay, BSc (Reading) *Microbiology*
Mrs A C Lock, BA (Liverpool) *English Language and Literature*
Mrs C Lowry, BSc (Liverpool) *Physics*
Mrs S Mathieson, BA (London) *History, MA* (Open University) *Education*
Mrs J E Milligan, BSc (Manchester)*Geography*
Miss P Mooney, BA (Liverpool) *Fine Art, Sculpture*
Mr C Nolan, MA (Cambridge) *Modern and Medieval Languages*
Mrs I M Nolan, BA (Exeter) *Music,* LGSM
Mrs L Owen, BSc (Liverpool) *Chemistry*
Mrs B Parry-Jones, BSc (Aberystwyth) *Zoology*
Mrs C P Richards, BEd (Didsbury) *Physical Education*
Mrs J Richards, BA (Liverpool) *Medieval and Modern History*
Mrs C Richardson, BA (Oxford) *Chemistry*
Mrs A Rigby, BA (Manchester) *French and German*
Miss E Roberts, BEng (Leeds)
Miss S Robinson, BA (Northumbria) *French/Spanish*
Mrs J V Rogers, BA (Liverpool) *French*
Mr T Sanderson, BSc (Liverpool) *Chemistry/Physics*
Mr B J Wilson, BA (Lampeter) *Theology*

Junior Department:

Head of Junior Department: Mrs M Watson, BA (Open University) *English*

Deputy Head of Junior Department: Mrs J Palmer, CertEd (Bristol)

Miss M Aitken, BA (Liverpool) *English Language & Literature*
Mrs B M Coyne, BA (London), PGCE (Durham), MA (Liverpool) *English Literature, History and Local History*
Mrs A E Derbyshire, BA (Open University), TCert (Chester)
Mrs J Hillock, Teaching Cert (Lancaster)
Mrs P Hodgson, BEd (Liverpool)
Mrs P Moss, BSc (Birmingham) *Psychology*
Mrs E Murphy, BEd (Liverpool) *English and Education*
Mrs S Nance, CertEd (London)
Mrs R O'Connell, BEd (Matlock)
Miss J M M Parry, NFF Certificate, CertEd (London)
Mrs S Shute, MEd (Liverpool)
Mrs S Williams, BEd (Crewe & Alsager) *PE/Geography*
Miss J Yardley, BA (Liverpool) *Music*

Part-time Staff:
Mrs A Clements, BA (Leicester) *Latin*
Dr H W Davies, BSc, PhD (University of Wales) *Physics*
Miss L Dawes, BA (Manchester) *Three Dimensional Design*
Mrs A G Hogg, MA (St Andrews) *English Language and Literature*
Mrs C Holloway, BEd (Leeds) *Music*
Mrs A J Johnson, Certificate in Physical Education (Liverpool)
Mr O A Jones, BA (Cardiff College of Art) *Fine Art*
Mrs M J Jones, BSc (Birmingham) *Biology*
Mrs C A Kingsland, BSc (Liverpool)
Mrs J Lappin, BSc (Liverpool) *Mathematics*
Mrs J Lloyd, BA (Open University) *English Literature*
Mrs H McCarthy, BEd (Huddersfield) *Business Studies and Technology*
Mrs P Meredith-Davies, BEd (St Katharines) *Theology*
Mrs J Martindale, BA (Sheffield) *Music/Russian*
Mrs B Murthwaite, Baccalaureat Philosophie (France)
Mrs A Nathan, BA (York) *English/Music,* MA (Open) *English*
Mrs K Ollerhead, BA (Hull) *History*
Mrs E A Soane, MA (Edinburgh) *Medieval Studies*
Mrs J Taylor, DipPE (Liverpool)
Mrs J Thompson, BA (Leeds) *French*

Visiting Staff:

Piano:
Miss J Faulkner, ARMCM, ARMCMM

Mrs S Howard, BA, ARCM
Mrs J M Lampard, ARCM, LRAM, LTCL, CertEd
Mrs V Maclean, ARMCM, ARCO

'Cello:
Mrs C Jones

Violin:
Mr R Hebbron

Violin/Viola:
Mrs C Hebbron, ARCM

Clarinet/Saxophone/Guitar:
Mr E Walpole

Flute:
Mrs J Oade
Mrs E D Thompson

Brass:
Miss J Baker

Percussion:
Miss R Wright

Singing:
Mrs J Rotheram

Speech and Drama:
Mrs V Sanders, TCert
Mrs S Beer, MA (Cantab) *Modern and Medieval*

Ballet:
Miss G Morgan-Hayes

School Doctor: Dr P Nuttall, MBchB, DRCOG, FPCert

Headmistress's Secretary: Mrs M Wainwright

Admissions Secretary: Mrs V Emmitt

Assistant Secretaries:
Miss R Lang
Mrs C Pickles

School Administator: Mrs M Greenhalgh

Administrative Assistant: Mrs E Pettigrew

School Nurse: Mrs C I E Johnston, RSCN

Chartered Librarian: Mrs M Hogan, BA, ALA

The School was opened in September 1901. It is situated at 86 Devonshire Place, Birkenhead in a residential area. The catchment area includes Birkenhead, Wallasey and Wirral and the school is easily accessible from all districts. The Junior Department and Nursery have separate buildings in the School grounds.

Number of pupils: Senior School: 611, age range 11–18 years, including 162 Sixth Form. Junior Department 289, age range 3+–11 years. The normal ages of entry are at 3+, 4+, 7+, 11+ and Sixth Form. Admission is by the school's own entrance examination.

The school is well equipped with a hall, library, computer suite, design and technology workshops, drama studio, art facilities, 8 science laboratories, specialist music facilities and Sixth Form Centre. The Sports Building has a large Sports Hall and a 25m swimming pool.

There are 9 tennis courts, some are floodlit and an all-weather pitch.

Physical activities include lacrosse, hockey, netball, tennis, rounders, gymnastics, dance, volleyball and many others.

A large number of girls participate in the Duke of Edinburgh's Award Scheme at Bronze, Silver and Gold levels.

Curriculum. The curriculum is planned to provide a wide general education which includes Music, Drama, Art and Physical Education and defers specialisation as long as possible. All academic subjects are included. Girls are prepared for the GCSE and AS/A2 level examinations and for university entrance. A wide choice of course is offered in the Sixth Form and all girls are expected to proceed to university, college or some other form of higher education.

Visits to theatres, concerts, art galleries, museums, lectures and conferences are arranged frequently for a wide age range.

School uniform, black and white, is worn up to the end of Year 11.

The School Captain is elected to office. Each girl is encouraged to exercise responsibility for herself, and for others if she so wishes.

The Sixth Form girls have their own accommodation and are not required to wear uniform. It is hoped that the Sixth Form will be a bridge between school and the next stage of education or training and that it will foster independence and self-reliance. Sixth Form girls have many opportunities to run clubs and societies, organise concerts and produce plays.

A flourishing Parents' Association provides opportunities for parents to meet informally, and many social and cultural activities take place each year.

Meetings of Old Girls are held annually in Birkenhead and London.

Fees. From September 2000: Senior School £1,680 per term; Junior Department £1,220 per term; Nursery £908.

The fees cover the regular curriculum, school books, stationery and other materials, choral music, games and swimming, but not optional extra subjects or school meals.

Fees for extra subjects, piano, strings and woodwind instruments, speech and drama, are shown in the prospectus.

Following the ending of the Government Assisted Places Scheme, The Girls' Day School Trust has made available to the school a substantial number of scholarships and busaries. The bursaries are means tested and are intended to ensure that the school remains accessible to bright girls who would profit from our education but who would be unable to enter the school without financial assistance.

Bursaries. Bursaries post-entry are available in cases of financial need. Application should be made to the Headmistress.

Scholarships. These are at present available to internal or external candidates scholarships for entry at 11+ or to the Sixth Form.

Charitable status. Birkenhead High School is one of the 25 schools of the Girls' Day School Trust, which is a Registered Charity, number 1026057. The aim of the Trust is to provide a fine academic education at a comparatively modest cost.

Blackheath High School (G.D.S.T.)

Vanbrugh Park London SE3 7AG
Tel: 020 8853 2929
Fax: 020 8853 3663

Founded 1880

This is one of the 25 schools of The Girls' Day School Trust. For general information about the Trust and the composition of its Council, see p 532. A more detailed prospectus may be obtained from the school.

Local Governors:
Revd H Burgin, FISW (*Chairman*)
Mrs P M Clarke, LLB (Leeds)
Dr P Faid, PhD (Newcastle)
Mrs R Smith, BA
Dr P Broadhead
Mr G Davis
Mrs B Huish

Headmistress: **Mrs E A Owen**, BA (Liverpool), PGCE

Deputy Head: Miss M Judge, BA (Newcastle), Licence-ès-Lettres, Maîtrise (Sorbonne), PGCE

Senior Teacher: Mrs S Clements, BSc (Southampton), PGCE

Head of Junior Department: Mrs N Gan, CertEd (Exeter)

Assistant Staff:

English:
Miss L Martin, BA (London), MA (London), PGCE
Mrs D Jurksaitis, BA (Manchester), MA (Sussex), PGCE

History:
Mrs C Maddison, BA (Staffs), PGCE
Mrs R A Hibberd, BA (York), PGCE

Geography:
Mrs R Ware, BA (London), PGCE

Economics & Business Studies:
Dr H Allen, BSc (London), PhD (Oxon) (*Head of Middle School*)

Modern Languages:
Mrs C Lamb, Doctorat ès Lettres (Sorbonne)
Mrs S Bond, BA (Sheffield), PGCE
Mrs P Perry, MA (Oxon)

Classics:
Miss S Williams, BA (Cantab), PGCE (*Head of Upper School*)

Mathematics:
Mr M Thunder, BSc (Manchester), PGCE
Mr P Garner, MA (Cantab), BA (Cantab), PGCE

Science:
Mr C Rostagni, BSc (London), CertEd
Mrs S Clements, BSc (Southampton), PGCE
Mrs C Dons, BSc (Otago), DipEd
Dr M Harman, BSc, PhD (Glasgow), PGCE
Miss L Chu, BSc (Kent), PGCE

Information Technology:
Dr H Allen, BSc (London), PhD (Oxon)

Music:
Mr Y S Yeo, BA, MMus (London), CertGSM, PGCE
Mr E Bennett, BA (Bristol), LGSM

Design Department:
Mr P De'Athe, CertEd, BEd (London)
Mrs M Aspden, BA (London), PGCE
Miss A London, BA (Leeds), PGCE

Physical Education:
Miss L Jones, BEd (London)
Miss D Gill, CertEd (London)
Mrs J Hrebien, BSc (Loughborough), PGCE

Junior Department:
Mrs J Collinson, BEd (Dartford), NNEB
Miss A Drummond, BA (Newcastle), PGCE
Mrs J Evans, BEd (London)
Miss E Groves, CertEd (Dartford)
Mrs M Hazell, BEd (London)
Mrs J Lines, BEd (London)
Mrs P Lobb, CertEd (London), BA (Open)
Mrs F Lynn, GRSM (London)
Miss L Mitcham, BEd (London)
Miss R Monkman, BEd (London)
Miss C Murphy, BEd (London)
Mrs W Neill, BA (Liverpool), PGCE
Miss R Nichols, BA (Ontario), PGCE
Mrs K Phillips, BA (Tasmania), DipEd
Mrs V Rickus, CertEd, BEd (Oxon), MA (London)
Mrs C Soan, DipMus (Huddersfield), PGCE
Ms M Sochocka, CertEd (London)

Visiting Staff:
Piano:
Mr B Dix
Miss P Fry, LRAM
Miss C Venton

Oboe: Ms L Foster

Bassoon/Recorder: Ms J Rowan

Brass: Mr W Spencer

Trombone: Mr W Spencer

Clarinet: Mr M Foster

Violin: Miss A Morrison, DipMusEd

Cello: Mrs Bowler

Flute:
Mrs S Searchfield, BSc
Miss P Fry, LRAM

Saxophone: Mr E Bennett, BA (Bristol), LGSM

Singing: Miss A Gilchrist

Percussion: Mr A Jackson

Double Bass: Mr C Yule

Guitar: Miss A Dixon, BHum, LTCL

Information Systems Manager: Mr D Nott, BSc (Reading)
School Administrator: Mr A W L Sutherland, MBE
School Doctor: Dr J Parker, MB, BS
School Nurse: Mrs A Tormey, SRN

Blackheath High School, founded in 1880, is a successful academic school which offers a broad and stimulating curriculum in a warm and friendly environment. Admission, which is by examination and interview, is competitive and bursaries and scholarships are available. The school is a member of the GDST and GSA.

Middle School girls (11–14) enjoy a strong cross-curricular element in their studies and at GCSE level a wide variety of subjects is offered, including the separate sciences and Latin. After A-level, almost all pupils proceed to higher education; many achieve success in joining highly competitive professions. Pastoral and careers education is strong and full use is made of the many facilities which London affords. The sense of community is striking.

The school moved in 1994, after 100 years on its original site, to a spacious and elegant new home comprising both purpose-built and historic buildings just off the A2 near Docklands, Greenwich and the Blackwall Tunnel. Pupils do, in fact, come from a wide area stretching from Kent to north of the River Thames. The expanding Junior Department moved into the refurbished Wemyss Road site at Christmas 1994. Public transport is excellent and the school is easily accessible by train, bus or private car. These moves reflect a major investment and will enable pupils to be offered really excellent facilities in convenient and attractive buildings.

Visitors are always welcome and the Headmistress likes to discuss each girl's particular needs individually with pupils and parents. Please telephone the Admissions Secretary who will be delighted to offer further information.

Curriculum. In both Senior School and Junior Department the programme of study follows the normal pattern of subjects; specialisation is deferred as long as possible and emphasis is placed on all-round personal development within a framework of disciplined learning. Games are taken seriously and played both on site and at our nearby playing fields which boasts a recently purpose-built sports pavilion. Girls are prepared for the GCSE and Advanced Level examinations in a wide range of academic subjects. Systematic careers advice is available and the curriculum enables pupils to prepare for many forms of higher or further education and so for a wide range of careers.

Fees. From September 2000: Senior School £2,044 per term; Junior Department £1,588 per term. Nursery £1,200 per term.

The fees cover the regular curriculum, school books, stationery and other materials, choral music, games and swimming, but not optional extra subjects or school meals.

The fees for extra subjects, including piano, strings, wind instruments and speech training, are shown in the prospectus.

Bursaries. Following the ending of the Government Assisted Places Scheme, the GDST has made available to the school a substantial number of scholarships and bursaries. The bursaries are means tested and are intended to ensure that the school remains accessible to bright girls who would profit from our education but who would be unable to enter the school without financial assistance.

Scholarships. (*see* Entrance Scholarship section) There are at present available to internal or external candidates a number of Scholarships for entry at 11+ or to the Sixth Form.

Charitable status. Blackheath High School is one of the 25 schools of the Girls' Day School Trust, which is a Registered Charity, number 1026057. The aim of the Trust is to provide a fine academic education at a comparatively modest cost.

Bolton School (Girls' Division) (Independent, formerly Direct Grant)

Bolton Lancs BL1 4PB
Tel: (01204) 840201

Trustees:
The Lord Haslam of Bolton
Sir A Cockshaw, BSc, HonDEng, FEng, FICE, FIHT
B H Leigh-Bramwell, Esq, MA
His Hon Judge J M Lever, QC
M E Tillotson, Esq, TD, JP, MA

Emeritus Governors:
The Lord Haslam of Bolton
T S Glaister, Esq
Cllr J C Hanscomb, CBE, MA (Cantab)
Alderman Mrs B A Hurst, MBE
M E Tillotson, Esq, TD, JP, MA

Governors:
Sir A Cockshaw, BSc, HonDEng, FEng, FICE, FIHT *Chairman*
G Banister, Esq, MSc, LDS, VU (Manc)
Mrs C Boscoe (*Parent Governor*)
R J Byrom, Esq, JP, BA(Arch), MPhil, RIBA, FSVA, FCIArb
R J Duggan, Esq, BSc
Mrs S E Fisher, MSc, MBChb, BDS, PDSRCS, FRCS
M T Griffiths, Esq, BA, FCA
The Hon Mrs M J Heber-Percy
Ms S K Hodgkiss, DL
Mrs L A Hopkinson, BEd (*Parent Governor*)
P Jarvis, Esq, CBE, BA
B H Leigh-Bramwell, Esq, MA
His Hon Judge J M Lever, QC
Mrs W P Morris, OBE
Mrs G E Sidebottom
Mrs S R Tonge, JP, DipHorb

Clerk and Treasurer: R T Senior, BA

Headmistress: **Miss E J Panton**, MA (Oxon)

Deputy Headmistress: Miss J M Dickinson, BSc (London)

Director of Studies: Mrs P M Fairweather, BA (Oxon)

Senior Mistress: Mrs C A Brown, BA, PhD (Manchester)

Head of Sixth Form: Mrs V Hanrahan, BSc (London)

Head of Fifth Form: Mrs P Keenan, BA (Leeds)

Head of Middle School: Mrs R J Garthwaite, BA (Hull)

Upper School:
English:
Mrs G Wallwork, BA (Manchester), *Head of Department*
Mrs H M Bardsley, BA (Sheffield)
Mr M G Eccles, MA (York)
Mrs R E Hadjigeorgiou, BA (Manchester)
Mrs J M Hancock, BA (Manchester)
Mrs J Kingsford, BA (London)
Mrs E A Lowe, BA (Manchester)
Mrs V Millington, BA (Manchester)
Mrs J T M Sowerby, BA (Oxon)

Mathematics:
Mrs V Hanrahan, BSc (London), *Head of Department*
Mr E T R Aldred, BEd (Manchester), MSc (UMIST)
Mrs K A Baldwin, BSc (Sheffield)
Miss J M Dickinson, BSc (London)
Mr K M Graham, BEd (Manchester Metropolitan)
Mrs E M Hayes, BSc (Salford)
Mrs L D Kyle, BSc (St Andrews) *Second Mistress*
Mrs C Y Ward, BSc (Nottingham)

Science:

Biology:
Miss M Corkill, BSc (Birmingham), MSc (Dunelm) *Head of Department*
Miss H J Beresford, BSc (Aberystwyth)
Mrs S A Berne, BSc (Leeds)
Miss A R Forsyth, BSc (Manchester)

Chemistry:
Mrs J M Appleyard, BA (Cantab) *Head of Department*
Mrs K B Blagden, BSc (Sheffield)
Mrs P M Fairweather, BA (Oxon)
Mrs S O'Kelly, BSc (Manchester) *Head of Key Stages 3 & 4, Science*

Physics:
Mrs P A Oldershaw, BSc (Nottingham), MSc (Salford) *Head of Department*
Mrs C E McCann, BSc (Dunelm)
Dr J S Morris, BSc, PhD (Cardiff)

Psychology:
Mrs C Bell, BA (Bolton)

Technology:
Mr P J Linfitt, BSc, MEng (Manchester) *Technology Co-ordinator*

Design Technology:
Mr P J Linfitt, BSc, MEng (Manchester) *Head of Department*
Mrs R E Langley-West, BA (Sheffield City Polytechnic)

Food Technology:
Mrs I M H Smalley, BSc (Manchester) *Head of Department*
Mrs C S Haslam, BEd (Newcastle)

Information Technology:
Mrs P M Fairweather, BA (Oxon) *Director of IT Development*
Mrs L Hayes, BA (Bolton) *Head of Department*
Mrs M E Brown, BSc (Hull)
Mrs J C Cunningham, BSc (Leeds)
Mrs L J Whitehead, BA (Nottingham)

Textile Technology:
Mrs A Tankard, AdvDip (Open) Technology, CertEd (Manchester)

Art:
Mrs J Cole, BA (Manchester) *Head of Department*
Mrs T J Fisher, BA (Wolverhampton)
Miss T N McKay, BA (Leeds Metropolitan), MA (Chelsea College of Art)

Modern Languages:
Mrs A M Hutchings, MA (Manchester), L-ès-L, M-ès-L (Dijon), *Head of Modern Languages*

French:
Mrs A M Hutchings, MA (Manchester), L-ès-L, M-ès-L (Dijon) *Head of Department*
Mrs R J Garthwaite, BA (Hull)
Mrs A J Kolot, MA (Glasgow)
Mrs B A Lowe, BA (Nottingham)
Mrs J Patterson, BA (Nottingham)
Mrs A Shafiq, BA (Leeds)
Mrs P Sheaff, BA (Oxon), MA (*Manchester*)
Mrs P A Taylor, BA (London)

German:
Mrs R O Artley, BA (Birmingham) *Head of Department*
Mrs A J Kolot, MA (Glasgow)
Mrs B A Lowe, BA (Nottingham)
Mrs P Sheaff, BA (Oxon), MA (Manchester)

Spanish:
Mrs A Shafiq, BA (Leeds) *Head of Department*
Mrs J Patterson, BA (Nottingham)

Classics:
Mrs R Wainwright, MA (Edinburgh) *Head of Department*
Mrs J D Partington, BA (Birmingham), *Classics and Examinations Officer*

General Studies:
Mr A B Davies, BA (Wales) *Acting Head of Department*

Physical Education:
Mrs K A Heatherington, BA (Manchester) *Head of Department*
Miss A Donaghy, BEd (Liverpool John Moores)
Mrs P M Hall, CertEd (Nonington College of PE)
Mrs M McCulloch (IM Marsh College of PE)
Miss K J Watson, BEd (Liverpool John Moores)

Careers and Higher Education:
Miss J M Dickinson, BSc (London), *Head of Department*
Mrs K Bell, Careers Assistant
Mrs C Sutcliffe, Careers Assistant

Business Studies:
Mrs L C Rixon, BSc (Cardiff)

History:
Mrs S A Heap, BA (Liverpool) *Head of Department*
Miss S L Cottam, MA (St Andrews)
Mrs D C Curtis, BA (Nottingham)
Mr A B Davies, BA (Wales)
Mrs J Head, BA (Bristol)

Geography:
Mrs P Keenan, BA (Leeds) *Head of Department*
Mrs C E McLellan, BA (Birmingham) *Sixth Form Curriculum Enrichment Co-ordinator*
Mrs K J Shaw, BSc (Sheffield)
Miss S E Wells, BA (Lampeter)

Religion and Philosophy:
Mrs C A Brown, BA, PhD (Manchester), *Head of Department*
Miss S H Clarke, BA (Southampton)
Mrs L Foster, BA (Manchester)
Mrs C Greenhalgh, BEd (Manchester)

Music:
Mr J A Davenport, MA (Cantab), FRCO, ARAM, LRAM *Head of Department*
Miss C Tope, BA Music (Manchester)
Mrs C J Whitmore, BA (Oxon)
Mr J Bernardin, BA *Percussion*
Mr J Bleasdale, BA (Salford), LLCM *Guitar*
Miss E Caton, GRNCM, PPRNCM *Clarinet, Saxophone*
Mr S Death, BSc Music, PPRNCM *Pianoforte*
Mrs K P Dewhurst, BMus (Manchester), PGCE *Pianoforte*
Mr P Fowles, BA (Bolton), ALCM, LLCM, ATCL *Guitar*
Miss H Francis, LRAM, ARCM, ABSM *Singing*
Miss J Gleeson, GRNCM *Violin*
Mr P Morrison, MA, GRNCM, FRCO *Piano, Organ*
Mr R W Proudman, GMus, PGDip, RNCM *Clarinet*
Miss E Ringrose, GRNCM, PPRNCM *Oboe, Bassoon*
Mrs A C Swinford, GRSM *Piano*
Ms R M Thompson, GRNCM *Violin*
Mrs E C Tristram, GRNCM *Flute*
Mrs S L Walker, GRNCM, PPRNCM *Flute*
Mr M Wildgust, GMus, PGCE, ARCM, LTCL *Brass*

Lower Schools:
Junior Department (*Age 8–11*)
Acting Head of Junior Department: Mrs K M Critchley, BEd (Liverpool)

Mrs A J Forshaw, BA (Dunelm)
Miss G Harrison, BA (Liverpool)
Mrs C Haynes, CertEd (Edge Hill College)
Miss B A Howard, BEd (Exeter)
Mrs B J Tatlock, TCert (Sydney, Australia)
Mrs M Worsley, MA (Ulster)
Classroom Assistant: Mrs M S Drinkwater, BA (Ulster)

Beech House (*Age 4–8*)
Head of Beech House: Mrs H Crawforth, BEd (Cantab)

Mrs K L Aldred, BEd (Nottingham)
Mrs C Brown, MEd (Manchester Metropolitan)
Mrs D Ganley, DEUG (Dijon) *French*
Mrs C J Glaister, CertEd (Chester College)
Mrs S Gliddon, BEd (Lancaster)
Mrs H Holt, BEd (Cantab)
Miss L C Rotheray, BEd (Liverpool)
Mrs A V Ryder, BEd (Cantab)
Mrs M Turner, BSc (Open), Cert Ed (Christ Church College)

Nursery Nurses:
Mrs C Naughton, NNEB
Mrs L Prasad, BTecDip
Miss L Williams, NNEB
Classroom Assistant: Mrs L Oldham

Librarian: Mrs L M Frew, BA, ALA (Newcastle Polytechnic)
Assistant Librarian: Mrs J Groves

Secretarial Staff:
Headmistress's Secretary: Mrs S Bourne

School Secretary and Secretary for Admissions: Mrs L Graham

Secretaries for Lower Schools:
Mrs A Bradbury
Mrs A Devine

Curriculum Support Staff:
Mrs J Stone, BSc (Hull), *Curriculum Support Manager, Senior Science Technician*
Mr I M Austen *Network Manager/ICT Technician*
Mrs V Birkenhead *Senior Staff Assistant/ICT Assistant*
Mrs A Carroll *Chemistry Technician*
Miss P Cook *Textile Technology Assistant & Staff Technician*
Mr R Hesketh *Performing Arts/AV Technician*
Mrs C Kelly *Food Technology Assistant*
Mr V Marsden *IT Technician*

Mr L Marsh *Design Technology Assistant and Staff Technician*
Mrs P Rushton *Art Assistant*
Mr P Stulock *Science and Audio-Visual Technician*
Mr K West *Physics Technician/Demonstrator*
Mrs J Whitehead *Assistant to Examinations Officer & Staff Technician*

Medical Staff:
Mrs G Grundy, SEN
Mrs C A Taylor, SRN, NNEB
Mrs J Grice, *School Counsellor*

Bolton School Girls' Division was founded in 1877 as the High School for Girls and quickly gained a reputation for excellence. In 1913 the first Viscount Leverhulme gave a generous endowment to the High School for Girls and the Bolton Grammar School for Boys on condition that the two schools should be equal partners known as Bolton School (Girls' and Boys' Divisions). It is within this spirit that the school now has a significant number of joint activities and benefits from shared facilities with the Boys' Division while offering its pupils all the advantages of single sex education.

Facilities. The two Divisions with their Lower Schools (separate Junior Department and a mixed Preparatory Department), occupy a superb 32 acre site. The Girls' Division has a Great Hall to seat 900 people, two fully computerised libraries, with a full time and a part time librarian, a newly refurbished theatre, eight laboratories, three Information Technology rooms, a Design Technology Suite and many well-appointed specialist teaching rooms. Our computer network extends across more than 160 PCs. These allow pupils access to basic software, CD-ROMS and the Internet in the Libraries, Careers Room, the Computer Suite and several departmental areas. The Sixth Form Suite includes a kitchen and a study area with seven computer work stations all linked to the school network. The Language Bureau with its impressive range of audio, video and interactive computerised materials in 13 languages provides pupils with further opportunities for speaking and listening practice. The Careers' Department has a resource centre giving access to all the latest information. This, too, is fully staffed by two experienced assistants. Besides having its own gym, the Girls' Division shares the modern sports hall, swimming pool and Sports Pavilion with the Boys' Division. In addition to these excellent facilities for Physical Education, the school has an outdoor pursuits centre at Patterdale in the Lake District which is used regularly by girls from the Junior and Senior schools for a wide range of activities.

Beech House (Preparatory Department) has 200 children aged between 4 and 8. It offers a rich combination of new approaches and traditional methods. Specialist teaching is provided for older pupils in Physical Education and Music and all children are taught French. There is a PC in every classroom and, in addition to its own resources, Beech House benefits from use of Senior School facilities such as the swimming pool, computer rooms, theatre and Arts Centre.

The Girls' Junior School, of 150 pupils, has its own suite of rooms (including a computer room with 16 networked PCs), within the main building. There are two classes in each of years 4, 5 and 6 (8–11 years). Besides following the National Curriculum, pupils have additional opportunities. The many clubs and wide range of extra curricular sport ensure a full and well balanced programme.

The curriculum in the Senior School encompasses all the National Curriculum but also offers the study of two modern languages, the classics and a wide range of modules in Technology. At age 11 all girls follow a similar weekly timetable. The twelve subjects offered are: Art, English, French, Geography, History, Classical Studies, Mathematics, Music, PE, RE, Science and Technology. The list, however, does not fully show the great variety of opportunities available which also include: Athletics, Biology, Business Studies, Chemistry, Dance, Drama, Earth Science, Electronics, Food Technology, Gymnastics, Information Technology, Lacrosse, Netball, Physics, Resistant Materials Technology, Rounders, Swimming, Tennis and Textiles Technology. This breadth is maintained to GCSE with a second language, German, Latin or Spanish, being offered in Year 8.

There is extensive choice at GCSE. All follow a common core of English, English Literature, Mathematics, Information Technology and, either Dual Award or separate Sciences together with non examined courses in PE and Religion and Philosophy. Students take 10 subjects at GCSE: the core subjects plus options chosen from Art and Design, Biology, Business and Communication Systems, Chemistry, Food Technology, French, Geography, German, Greek, History, Latin, Music, Physics, Religious Studies, Resistant Materials Technology, Spanish and Textile Technology. Essential balance is maintained by requiring all to include one Humanity and one Modern Language but the choice is otherwise entirely free.

In the Sixth Form flexibility has always been a key feature. This is even more true for the new AS/A2 courses which started in September 2000. Students choose from a list of 30 different Advanced Subsidiary courses. Breadth is promoted further by our complementary Enrichment Programme. All students have the opportunity to follow a range of non-examined courses as well as Physical Education (sports include golf, climbing, aerobics and self-defence). Links beyond school include Community Service schemes, Young Enterprise groups as well as opportunities with Understanding Industry and Work Experience.

Teaching in the Sixth Form is in small groups. Students have greater freedom which includes wearing their own clothes, exeat periods and having a common room and private study facilities. There are opportunities for students to assume a variety of responsibilities both within the school and in the wider community. Increasing personal freedom within a highly supportive environment helps students to make the transition to the independence of the adult world.

Music and Drama are popular and students achieve the highest standards in informal and public performances. The wide variety of concerts and productions may take place in the Arts Centre, which was opened in 1993, the Great Hall or the fully-equipped Theatre all of which make excellent venues for joint and Girls' Division performances.

Personal and Social Education, PSE is targeted in a variety of ways and co-ordinated centrally. Some issues may be covered within schemes of work while others will be discussed in the informal atmosphere of form groups led by the form tutor. Those areas which require specialist input are fitted into longer sessions run by experts from outside school.

The Careers Department helps prepare students for adult life. The extensive programme starts at 11 and includes communication skills, work sampling, and support in making choices at all stages of schooling. In addition girls prepare their curriculum vitae and applications to Higher Education with the individual help of a trained tutor.

Extra-curricular activities. The acquisition of the lease on Patterdale Hall in the Lake District has led to an expansion of the school's outdoor pursuits programme. Activities include sailing, orienteering, abseiling and gorge walking. Awards are regularly made to enable individuals to undertake a variety of challenging activities both at home and abroad while every year over 40 pupils embark on the Duke of Edinburgh Award Scheme. In addition to the annual exchanges for Modern Languages students we also offer a wide range of educational and recreational trips both at home and abroad. All have the opportunity to follow a wide range of non-examined courses of their choice plus Physical Education.

Entrance to the school is by Headteacher's report, written examination and interview in the Spring term for girls aged 8 and 11. New girls are also welcomed into the Sixth Form. Total numbers in the Senior School are 800 of whom 211 are in the Sixth Form. Almost all students (95%) go on to Higher Education (15% to Oxford and Cambridge).

A significant number of Governors' Foundation Grants have been created in response to the loss of the Assisted Places Scheme. As one of the first schools to benefit from The Ogden Trust, we are now able to offer a further six bursaries.

Fees (September 2000): £5,664 per annum in Senior School; The Junior and Preparatory Schools £4,188 per annum. (Fees include lunches).

Charitable status. The Bolton School is a Registered Charity, number 526618. Bolton School leads the way in the provision of an excellent education for pupils aged between 4 and 18 years.

Bradford Girls' Grammar School

The Grammar School for Girls Bradford Yorkshire BD9 6RB

Tel: (01274) 545395

Established under a Scheme of the Endowed Schools' Commissioners on 5 August 1875, now administered under a Scheme of the Charity Commission of 13 April 1983. Incorporated 4 November 1879, under the Charitable Trusts Act, 1872. The Charter of Incorporation was granted by Charles II to the Bradford Grammar School in 1662.

Governors:

P Clough, Esq, JP, FCIS, (*Chairman*)
J K Clayton, Esq, FRCOG
Mrs B M Curtis
Mrs P Gadsby-Peet
J M Holmes, Esq (*Vice Chairman*)
Dr R Killick, BA, PhD
D Trevor Lewis, Esq, LLB
E Marshall, Esq, MInstM
Miss S Pattison
S Pearson, Esq, FCA, FCCA
Mrs S A Weatherall
Mrs J L Whitehead, JP, ATD

***Headmistress:* Mrs L J Warrington**, MEd

Assistant Staff:

Senior School Heads of Department:

Mrs A Ashton, BSc (UMIST) *Chemistry*
Mrs B Beverley, BSc (Bradford) *Psychology*
Mrs E Brooke, BSc (Bristol) *Chemistry*
Miss J Edwards, BA (Warwick), MA (Leeds) *French/Spanish*
Mrs S M Empson, BSc (Liverpool) *Physics*
Miss J Everington, BEd (Nottingham) *Human Movement and Geography*
Mr P Groves, BA (Newcastle upon Tyne), LTCL *Music*
Mr C Hannam, BSc(Tech) (Sheffield) *Material Science*
Mrs J M Harland, Certificate in Teaching (Ilkley College of Education) *Food Technology*
Mrs J Hemsley, BA (Liverpool) *Economics*
Mrs C M Hinkles (Dartford College of PE) (University of London CertEd)
Mrs R Macdonald, BAS (University of Queensland) *Japanese*
Miss R Meadows, BA (East Anglia) *Economics/English*
Mrs C A Morley, BSc (Bradford) *Mathematics*
Mrs C Morrel, BA (Leeds) *Fine Art*
Mrs M Muirhead, BA (Hull) *Russian*
Mr G M Nicholas, BA (London) *Classics*
Miss J H Robson, BA (London), MA (Leeds)
Mrs C Rowe, BSc (Bradford) *Business Studies*
Mr J Ryan, BSc (Leeds), MEd (Leeds) *Ecology*
Mrs J R Smethurst, BA (Nottingham) *History*
Mrs L Stead, BSc (Manchester) *Geography*
Mrs J C Warham, BA (Reading), MA (Leeds) *English Language and Literature*
Mr D J Webster, MSc (Bradford) *CDT*
Mrs S Whitfield, MSc (London) *Mathematics*
Mrs A Wicks, BA (Bristol) *French*
Mrs C A Willey, BA (London) *German/English*

Preparatory School:
Mrs C Hardaker, CertEd (Leeds)

The School, founded in 1875, stands in an estate of 17 acres on the outskirts of the City. There is a programme of constant renewal and extension of buildings and facilities. In recent years a Sixth Form College was opened in a new building adjacent to the main school, and a Sports Centre with Hall and 2 Squash Courts was completed. A building housing eight additional teaching spaces and a glass covered atrium was completed during 1996.

The facilities in the school include 11 Science Laboratories, Language Laboratories, Craft, Design and Technology Centre, Information Technology Centre, libraries and heated swimming pool.

The Junior School is housed in a separate building and has been further developed in 1999. In 1983 remodelled attics were made into a library, laboratory and music rooms, and in 1992 extensive refurbishment created additional space for art, science, technology and information technology.

Physical Education is well established and facilities include gymnasium, nine tennis/netball courts, two hockey pitches and athletics areas. The Junior School has its own tennis/netball court and a gym for the very young.

Music and Drama are well established and there is a Senior Dramatic Society and two Orchestras, together with instrumental groups and choirs.

In 1999 a new kitchen and dining room was built between Lady Royd and the main school building.

The number of pupils in the School is approximately 884 with over 250 in the Junior School.

Tuition Fees. The fees include all subjects of tuition and stationery. The fee in the Senior School is £1,995 per term. Bursaries have been given by the Governors in the Senior School each year beginning September 1976. These are of varying amounts and may include 1 entirely free place. Junior School for girls from 3–11 years of age £1,443 per term. Kindergarten for girls aged 3 £1,218 per term. Music fees, according to instruments.

The hours of attendance: Monday to Thursday (inclusive) 8.35 am–12.30 pm, and 1.45 pm to 3.50 pm. Friday 8.35 am to 12.30 pm, and 1.20 pm to 3.30 pm. The School is open on Friday afternoon for preparation and games.

Examinations. Public examinations are taken in the Upper Fifth and Sixth Forms at GCSE, Advanced, and Scholarship standards, according to the requirements of individual pupils.

Charitable status. Bradford Girls' Grammar School is a Registered Charity, number 528674. It exists to provide high quality education for girls.

Brighton and Hove High School (G.D.S.T.)

The Temple Montpelier Road Brighton East Sussex BN1 3AT
Tel: (01273) 734112
Junior Department: Radinden Manor Road Hove E Sussex BN3 6NH
Tel: (01273) 505004

Founded 1876
This is one of the 25 schools of The Girls' Day School Trust. For general information about the Trust and the composition of its Council, see p 532. A more detailed prospectus may be obtained from the school.

Local Governors:
Chairman: Mrs S Cordingly
Mr D Angel, CBE, BSc(Econ)
Lady Bryson
Councillor Mrs P A Drake
Dr D Funnell
Mrs M Greig
Mr S Neiman
Mr D Pierce
Mr D E Stevens
Councillor Mrs P Stiles

***Headmistress:* Miss R A Woodbridge**, BA (York), MA (London) *History*

Senior School:
Deputy Headmistress: Mrs C Coleman, MA (Oxford) *French & German*
Senior Mistress: Miss S Olejnik, BEd (Sussex) *Physical Education*

Teaching Staff:
Mrs K Ashdown, BA (Bristol) *English*
Mrs J B Baker, BSc (Sussex) *Physics*
Mrs J Berry, BSc (Nottingham) *Maths*
Mrs G Burnet-Smith, Licence (Bordeaux) *French*
Mrs M A Burton, MSc (Birmingham) *Chemistry/Mathematics*
Mr S Cannon, BA (Cambridge) *Natural Sciences*
Ms M Casey, BA (Sussex) *French European Studies*
Miss B Castaing, MA (Université de Pan et de l'Adour) *English*
Mr C Condon, BA (Exeter) *German*
Mrs J Conway, BSc (Bristol) *Biology*
Mrs G Cook, BA (Durham) *French and Spanish*
Ms J Croydon, BA (London) *Fine Art*
Mr K Crump, BEd (Nottingham Trent), MEd (London), Dip in Computing
Miss M Davies, BEd (Cardiff) *Religious Studies*
Mrs J Doughty, BA (Reading) *History*
Mr D Eastwood, BSc (Sussex) *Mathematics & Physics*
Mrs S Fairhurst, BMus (Birmingham) *Music*
Mrs A Foss, MA (Sussex) *Language/Art*
Miss W Fox, BA (Durham) *Latin with Greek*
Mrs K Fumagalli, BSc (Exeter) *Chemistry*
Miss S Garlick, BA (Oxford) *History*
Ms L Guthrie, BA (Newcastle) *3-D Design*
Mrs C Guy, BEd (Oxford) *Technology*
Mrs E Harrison, BSc (Edinburgh) *Chemical Physics*
Mrs M Horrocks, BA (London) *Latin*
Mrs K Howell, BSc (London) *Geography*
Mrs A Kilding, BA (N Stafford) *Geography*
Mrs M A Lorimer, IECert (Liverpool) *HE*
Mr P Marsh, BSc (Sussex) *Biochemistry*
Mrs S Mashford, BSc (Manchester) *Biochemistry*
Dr M Mason, BA (Dublin), BPhil (Liverpool), PhD (London) *Geography*
Mr R McGrath, BSc (Swansea) *Economics*
Mrs S Meeks, BA (Reading) *Mathematics*
Mrs A O'Callaghan, BSc (Loughborough) *Mathematics*
Mrs E Osborne, BEd (Sussex) *Physical Education*
Mrs C M Rotondo, BA (Cardiff) *French, Italian*
Mrs C Schilt, BA (London) *English & Drama*
Mrs M Schofield, BA (Bangor) *English*
Mr G Sherwood, BA (York) *History/English*
Ms E Stannard, BA (Southampton) *Drama, Theatre & TV*
Dh Suddhacitta, BSc (London) *Chemistry*
Mrs S Thomas, BEd (Sussex) *Physical Education*
Ms D Wallace, BEd (Brighton) *Religious Studies*
Mrs A Wetson, BSc (Birmingham) *Biology*
Mrs M Wogan, BA (Open University) *Mathematics*
Mrs S Wood, BA 3-D Design (Camberwell School of Art & Crafts) *Ceramics*

Junior Department:
Head of Junior Department: Miss C Vickers, BEd (Bristol)
Mrs K Al-Najjar, GRSM, ARMCM, ATCL
Miss N Alty, BA (Kingston)
Ms L Amos, BA (Durham)
Mrs D Booth, IECert (IM Marsh)
Miss G Bradnam, BEd (West Sussex IHE)
Mrs H Freedman, MA (Glasgow)
Mrs S Hindell, IECert
Miss A Kilpatrick, BEd (Brighton)
Mrs S Lacey, IECert (Brighton)
Mr N Ludlam, BEd (Newland Park College)
Miss A Perryman, BEd (Portsmouth)
Miss L Petrie, BSc (Cheltenham & Gloucester IHE)
Mrs A Sams, IECert (Gloucester)
Mrs J Stephenson, BEd (Exeter)
Mrs J Taylor, BA (Sussex)
Mrs M Woodward, IECert (Portsmouth)
Mrs P Wright, BSc (Ulster)

Visiting Music Staff:
Piano:
Mrs A Wicks, BA (Durham), LTCL
Mr A LeClercq
Ms J Duncan, LRSM

Violin and Viola:
Miss S Voigt, DipRCM
Ms H Browne, ARCM

'Cello: Mrs A Copley, MA (Krakow)

Flute/Recorder: Miss C Munro, BA (Birmingham), ABSM, ARCM, GBSM

Oboe: Mrs J Caws, ARCM

Clarinet: Mrs L Morsi, BA, MA(Ed)

Bassoon: Ms S Martin, BA (UCW), LTCL

Brass: Mr E Maxwell, BA (Sussex), DipRCM

Guitar: Mr B Ashworth, LLCM(TD)

Recorder:
Mr A Roach, BMus (Guildhall), LGSM
Mrs M Sanger, BA

Singing:
Miss S Mileham, BA (Sussex)
Ms J Money, BMus (London)

Saxophone/Keyboard/Music Technology:
Mr J Slade, DipMus (Brighton)

Drums: Mr P Solomon

School Administrator: Mr K Revell

Secretary of Old Girls' Association: Mrs J Moss

School Medical Officer: Dr M Karnicki, MB, BS, DRCOG

The school, which opened in 1876, stands in its own grounds in the centre of the new city of Brighton and Hove. It is about half-a-mile from Brighton Railway Station and pupils come in from Lewes, Haywards Heath and Lancing by train. It is easily reached by bus from all parts of Brighton and Hove.

There are about 475 girls in the Senior School, including 90 in the Sixth Form, and 300 in the Junior Department (ages 3–11) which moved to newly furbished premises in Radinden Manor Road in 1997. The Senior School is in the Temple, a gentleman's residence built by Thomas Kemp in 1819. It has been considerably altered and enlarged by a science wing in 1961, a new gymnasium/hall, a canteen and a converted art, technology, mathematics and computing centre. A Sports Hall will be added shortly. There is a self contained, newly converted Sixth Form House and the school owns a Field Centre on the River Wye in mid-Wales.

Curriculum. The school course is planned to provide a wide general education which includes Music, Art, Drama, Computing, DT, Home Economics and Physical Education. Girls are prepared for the General Certificate of Secondary Education and in the Sixth Form a wide choice of subjects is offered in preparation for universities, schools of medicine, colleges and other forms of professional training. In addition to their Advanced Level subjects girls take Key Skills courses and can choose work experience as an option.

Gardens with hard netball and tennis courts adjoin the Temple and the school also has an all-weather hockey pitch at the Junior Department site with further facilities for hockey, rounders and tennis. Gymnastics and dance are also taught with swimming for junior forms, and senior forms choose from activities including badminton, squash, swimming, aerobics and self-defence.

Fees. From September 2000: Senior School £1,680 per term; Junior Department £1,220 per term. Nursery £980 per term.

The tuition fees cover the regular curriculum, school books, stationery and other materials, choral music, games and swimming but not optional subjects or school meals.

The fees for extra subjects (instrumental music and speech and drama) are shown in the prospectus.

Scholarships and Bursaries. Following the ending of the Government Assisted Places Scheme, the GDST has made available to the school a substantial number of scholarships and bursaries. The bursaries are means tested and are intended to ensure that the school remains accessible to bright girls who would profit from our education but who would be unable to enter the school without financial assistance.

A few Trust Scholarships are available on merit, irrespective of income, to internal or external candidates for entry at 11+ or to the Sixth Form.

Charitable status. Brighton and Hove High School is one of the 25 schools of the Girls' Day School Trust, which is a Registered Charity, number 1026057. The aim of the Trust is to provide a fine academic education at a comparatively modest cost.

The Brigidine School

Queensmead King's Road Windsor Berkshire SL4 2AX
Tel: 01753 863779
e-mail: mbcairns@brigidine.windsor-maidenhead.sch.uk

An Independent Day School administered by a Local Governing Body under the Trusteeship of the Sisters of St Brigid.

Governors:
Chairman: P Blake, Esq
Sister Theresa Kilmurray (*Provincial*)
Dr W J Baker
Mrs S Burns
Sister Margaret Creagh
G Franklin, Esq
Mrs M G Hindmarsh
Mrs R Dwane (*Clerk*)

***Headmistress:* Mrs M B Cairns**, BSc, TCert, FRSA

Deputy Headmistress, Senior School:

Senior Department Staff:
Mrs J Aellen, BSc, PGCE
Mrs M Bacon, BA, CertEd
Mr B A Cannon, BA, DipEd
Mrs J Cooper, CertEd, BEd
Mrs C Cottingham, BEd
Mrs S Davies, TCert
Miss M Diver, BA, CertEd
Mr P Fletcher, BA, MA
Mrs K A Forshaw, BSc, CertEd
Mrs M Goldspink, BA, PGCE
Mme F Gordon-Smith, Cert d'ET, L-ès-L
Ms W Grantham, BA, PGCE
Mrs M Hargreaves, BA, PGCE
Ms E Hart, BEd
Mrs E Hawkes, CertEd, AdvDipEd, GradDipEd
Mrs K Holloway, BSc
Mrs G Lilley, BSc, PGCE
Mrs M Llewellyn, MEd, CertEd, AMBDA(Teaching)
Mrs C Mackenzie, BA, CertEd
Mrs D Mallinson, MA, TCert, BEd
Mrs M Morris, BA
Mrs M Penrose, BA, CertEd
Mrs J Peppiatt, CertEd
Mrs S Perrett, BSc, TCert
Mrs T Pinsent, BA
Mrs P Plant, BPharm, PGCE
Mrs E Quick, CertEd
Mrs D W Reay, TCert
Mrs H Rees-Williams, BA, PGCE
Miss B Roberts, MA Hons, PGCE
Dr M Sachania, BA, MA, PGCE
Miss S Stephenson, CertEd
Mrs J Symon, TCert, SpLD
Mrs G Ward, NDD, ATD
Mrs A White, TCert
Mrs J Willcocks, BSc, PGCE

Junior Department:
Head of Department: Mrs A Bradberry, TCert

Mrs S Bond, BSc, PGCE
Mrs M Edge, CertEd
Sister Margaret Fingleton, CertEd
Mrs S Goddard, HND Community Artist
Miss J Hughes, BA, QTS
Mrs P Kilkenny, BEd, CertEd
Mrs T Lega, CertEd
Mrs M Lindsay, BEd, CertEd
Mrs S March, BEd
Mrs T Milton, CertEd
Mrs R O'Hara, BSc, PGCE
Miss J Perrett, BA

Nursery Assistant: Mrs M Jernigan

After School Assistants:
Mrs J Moore
Miss N Nyiri

Administration Staff:

Bursar: Mrs R Dwane
Accountant: Mr M Studd, FCA

Secretary to the Headmistress: Mrs N Walsh
School Secretary: Mrs A Coward
Librarian: Mrs H Houliston
Lab Technicians: Mrs P Ives; Mr D Jordan

Age Range: Girls, Nursery and Junior: Rising 3 years to 11 years. Boys: Rising 3 years to 7 years. Girls, Senior 11+–18 years

School Hours: 3–11 years 8.45 am–3.30 pm. 11+–18 years 8.45 am–3.55 pm.

The Brigidine School was established in Windsor in 1948 by the Congregation of the Sisters of St Brigid. Today, under lay headship and trusteeship of the Order, it continues its Roman Catholic foundation whilst welcoming children of all other denominations and faiths.

It offers a broad education in a friendly, caring atmosphere and caters for children with a wide range of abilities and talents. It provides support and opportunities for each girl to develop her full potential as a unique individual so enabling her to become a confident, compassionate and accomplished young adult.

The full curriculum is available to all pupils with girls studying, on average, nine GCSE subjects in Years 10 and 11. The very able girls may take 10 or 11 subjects at the end of their course. Our Sixth Form offers a very good range of subjects at Advanced level.

There is a wide range of extra-curricular activities with tuition in ballet, modern dance, speech and drama and musical instruments being available. Sporting extras on offer include tennis coaching, trampolining, short tennis, rowing, yoga, self defence, aerobics and fitness training. All pupils are encouraged to participate.

Admission. The usual ages for entry are rising 3, 8, 11 and 16, but entry can be at any stage. From 8 years old, the pupils are interviewed and assessed prior to entry.

Fees. (September 2000). Registration (non-returnable) £40. Senior Department including Sixth Form £2,135 per term. Junior Department, Years 4, 5 & 6 £1,740; Years 2 & 3 £1,590; Year 1 £1,490; Reception & Nursery £1,475. Nursery, Part-time £810 per term.

Charitable status. The Brigidine School is a Registered Charity, number 232463. It exists to provide quality education for girls.

Bromley High School (G.D.S.T.)

Blackbrook Lane Bickley Bromley Kent BR1 2TW
Tel: 020 8468 7981
Fax: 020 8295 1062
e-mail: bhs@bro.gdst.net

Founded 1883

This is one of the 25 schools of The Girls' Day School Trust. For general information about the Trust and the composition of its Council, see p 532. A more detailed prospectus may be obtained from the School.

Local Governors:
Chairman: Mr A J Gore, BA
Mr B D Dance, MA
Mrs M L Elkington, BA
Mrs P Miles, GGSM, FRSA
Mr P Ralph, BA, FCA
Mrs G F Roberts, BA

Headmistress: **Mrs L Duggleby, BA** (York), DipSSG, DipEdLead

Deputy Head: Mrs S Mitchell, MA (Oxon) *English*

Senior Teacher: Miss J A Butler, BEd (Sussex) *Pastoral Head of Middle School*

Teaching Staff:
Ms L Ashley, MA (Oxon) *History*
Ms K Bennett, BEd (Greenwich) *Technology*
Mr T J E Brasier, BA (Hull), MA (CNAA) *Head of History/Government and Politics/Business Studies*
Mr G Buckley, BSc (Salford) *French and Spanish*
Mr D P Burt, MA (Royal College of Art) *Photography*
Mrs S Churchill, CertEd (Dartford) *Physical Education*
Mrs F J Clark, BD, MA (London) *Religious Studies*
Mrs S E Clarke, BSc (York) *Mathematics*
Mrs J M Cumming, CertEd (Liverpool) *Head of Physical Education, Pastoral Head of Upper School*
Mrs J Dick, BSc (London) *Biology, Head of Sixth Form*
Mrs A M Dolan, BSc (Nottingham) *Head of Science and Biology*
Mrs J Edwards, MA (Oxon) *English*
Mrs N Gilbert, BSc (London) *Mathematics*
Mrs P J Grier, MA (Edinburgh) *Geography, Head of Careers*
Mrs M A Hart, BA (Sheffield)
Mrs D Harvey, BA (Austria) *German*
Mrs S Harwood, BA (Essex)
Mrs P T Haslam, BA (Warwick) *Mathematics, Examinations Officer*
Miss D Hewitt, MA (Edinburgh) *French and German*
Mrs G Hilder, BSc (London) *Economics/Business Studies*
Mrs R A Hinton, BA (London) *Head of Geography*
Miss G Hoar, BA *PE, History, Head of Physical Education*
Mrs M Hood, BA (Hull) *French*
Mrs H Hopper, CertEd (Leicester) *Art and Ceramics*
Mrs C D Horseman, GGSM *Music*
Mrs B J Howarth, Teaching Certificate (Manchester) *Food Studies*
Miss C Hurst, BA (Brighton)
Mrs C A Jenner, BA (Warwick) *English*
Mrs C A Kempton, BSc (London) *Head of Chemistry*
Mrs A Lessiter, BEd (London) *Mathematics*
Mrs J Littlewood, MSc (London) *Mathematics*
Mrs E Lucking, GRSM, LRAM *Music*
Mrs G Marshall, MSc (London) *Chemistry, Key Skills Co-ordinator*
Mr P Marshall, MA (LSE), MA (London) *History*
Mr T Masters, BA (Greenwich) *Head of Design Technology*
Mrs E P Moore, BA (Wales) *English*
Mr G G Morgan, BA (Sheffield Hallam)
Mrs E B Muchajer, BA (London) *Head of French*
Mrs J W Murphy, BA (Open) *Politics/Business Studies*
Mrs A Parrington, BA (Reading)
Mr G E Phillips, BSc (LSE)
Mrs L Platt, CertEd (Garnett College) *ICT Co-ordinator*
Mrs K Ridgeway, BMus (Sheffield) *Director of Music*
Mrs E Russell-Mitra, BA (London) *English*
Mr A Sheppard, GRSM, LRAM *Music*
Miss C Smith, BSc (Warwick) *Mathematics*
Mrs J M Smith, BSc (Bristol) *Head of Mathematics*
Mrs P L Taylor, BA (Kent) *Head of English*
Mrs C Thomson, BSc (London) *Head of Physics*
Mrs E Thornburrow, BSc (York) *Physics*
Dr E R Trotter, BSc (Aston), PhD (*Liverpool*) *Biology*
Mr W Walker, BA (Open) *Physics, Information Systems Manager*
Mrs I Weston, BA (Reading) *Head of Modern Languages, Deputy Head of Sixth Form*
Mrs N Wolf, M-ès-L (Tunis and La Sorbonne) *French*
Mr G Wright, BSc (Loughborough)

Modern Languages Assistants: Conversation
Mrs D Halls *German*
Mrs D Harvey, BA, DipEd (Austria) *German*
Mrs D Smith *French*
Mrs M Kidner *Spanish*

Junior Department:
Head of Junior Department: Mrs D Pratt, CertEd (Sheffield)
Deputy: Mrs D F Brown, BEd (London)
Head of Prep Dept: Mrs J A Evans, BSc (Bristol)

Assistant Staff:
Mrs D L Batten, BEd (South Bank)
Mrs A C Botham, BSc (Loughborough) *Physical Education*
Mrs L Clare, GTCL, LTCL (*Music*)
Mrs E Durrant, BEd (Sussex), DipEd (London)
Mrs A Fagan, Teacher's Certificate (Leeds)
Mrs C Goodson, BEd (Surrey)
Miss A Greenway, BSc (UCL)
Mrs M Higham, BEd (Avery Hill)
Mrs A Lawrance, Teaching Certificate (Eastbourne)
Mrs A Lee, CertEd (London) *ICT*
Mrs J Newman, BEd (Middlesex)
Miss H Porteous, BA (East Anglia)
Miss A Pugh, BA (Leicester), PGCE
Mrs P A Rowe, MA (Glasgow) *French*
Mrs S Sommers, BEd (South Bank)
Mrs C M Thomas, BA (Greenwich)
Mrs J Timberlake, BEd (Thames)
Mrs E Verlander, Teacher's Certificate (London)

Classroom Assistants:
Mrs M M Beveridge, PPA
Mrs A Bush, DPP
Mrs C England (*City & Guilds Learning Support*)
Miss M J Harper, NNEB
Miss M Hollman, NDCS

Visiting Staff:
Brass:
Mr J Warburton, ARAM

Cello:
Ms A Lines, AGSM

Clarinet:
Miss J Hyland, GLCM, ALCM
Mr T Hyland, AGSM
Miss D Lesley, BMus, CertEd
Mr A Sheppard, GRSM, LRAM

Double Bass:
Mr R Chilton, GRNCM

Flute:
Mr T Hyland, AGSM, Teaching Certificate
Miss L Pocknell, FTCL, LTCL
Mr A Sheppard, GRSM, LRAM
Mrs J Allan, GRSM, LRAM, LTCL

Guitar:
Mr R Chilton, GRNCM

Harp:
Miss N Jenkins, BSc, LTCL, LGSM

Keyboard:
Miss D Lesley, BMus, CertEd

Oboe:
Mrs S Grint, GRSM, LRAM, ARCM

Percussion:
Ms J Dyer, GRSM, LRAM

Piano:
Mrs E B Lucking, GRSM, LRAM
Mrs M Woodall, BMus
Miss Y Harris, GGSM, ATCL
Mrs J Allan, GRSM, LRAM, LTCL
Mrs C Horseman, GGSM

Recorder:
Mrs J Allen, GRSM, LRAM, LTCL

Saxophone:
Mr A Sheppard, GRSM, LRAM
Miss D Lesley, BMus

Theory:
Miss J Hobbs, GGSM
Mrs M Woodall, BMus

Violin and Viola:
Miss J Hobbs, GGSM
Mr N Woodall, BMus, ARCM
Miss A Sharova, HonARAM, Dip (St Petersburg)
Mr D Blew, GTRCL, LTCL, ARCM

Voice:
Mrs B Howard, BMus
Mrs S Harpham, ARCM
Miss T Penwarden, DipTCL

Speech and Drama:
Mrs M Ball, BA (Trinity Dublin), LGCM, PQVS *English*
Miss S Hart, BA (Goldsmiths) *Performing Arts*
Ms L Wakeling, BA (Kent) *Performing Arts*

Administration:

School Administrator: Miss M Phelan

Librarian: Mrs S Goulding

Bursary:
Mrs J Dabrowska
Mrs S Driscoll

Secretariat:
Mrs C Collier
Mrs K Davies
Mrs S Davison (*Junior School*)
Miss P Henley
Mrs J Mitchell
Mrs M Stagg (*Head's Secretary/Office Manager*)

School Doctor: Dr B Choong, MBBS, BSc, DRCOG, DCH

School Nurse: Mrs C Cattigan, RGN, SCM

Technical Staff:
Mr P Coates (*DT Technician*)
Miss E Costa, BSc (London) (*Biology*)
Mrs J Lyons, HNC (*Chemistry*) (*Senior Technician*)
Mr F Taylor (*Physics*)

Resources Officers:
Mrs J Lett
Mr S Loxley

ICT Technicians:
Mr J Riddle, BA (Greenwich)
Miss M Patel

Senior Caretaker: Mr J George
Assistant Caretaker: Mr K Lake
Head Groundsman: Mr V Bartley
Catering Manager: Mr B Bishop

Founded in 1883 by the Girls' Day School Trust, Bromley High School was originally situated in the centre of Bromley. In 1981 it moved to Bickley to occupy new buildings set in 24 acres of beautiful grounds.

There are 576 girls in the Senior School, including 103 in the Sixth Form. The Junior Department numbers 314 pupils aged between 4 and 11.

Sharing the same site, the buildings of both departments provide excellent facilities, the Junior School having been substantially extended in September 1993 to provide an ICT centre, library and large assembly hall in addition to specialist rooms for Technology and Art and several well equipped form rooms. A music wing with recital room and practice rooms was opened in Autumn 1998.

The Junior School curriculum includes English, French -

taught from the first year in school by a specialist member of staff - Mathematics, History, Geography, Religious Education, Drama and Music, taught in the newly opened Music wing, and German in Year 6. Science, ICT, Technology, Art and Physical Education are taught in specialist rooms. Extra curricular activities are very important: sport thrives, with girls gaining success at local, county and national level; there are regular musical and dramatic performances, in French as well as English and many visits, field trips and holiday activities are organised.

The Senior School houses seven laboratories, some refurbished in August 1997, a large, well-stocked library/ resource centre, a careers room and specialist library as well as specialist teaching rooms for Art, Technology and Ceramics, (all built and equipped Spring 1996), Geography and Food Studies. Full use is made of audio-visual equipment for the teaching of Modern Languages, including satellite. The Music School includes an octagonal recital room and small practice rooms; Music Techno logy is available as a GCSE and A or A/S Level option. The main ICT suite consists of two teaching rooms fully equipped with networked PCs. Other networked machines are distributed throughout the school and clusters can be found in the Art/Design Technology wing, Modern Languages and the recently upgraded Library, as well as some non-specialist teaching rooms. All PCs have permanent access to the Internet through a high speed leased line. The school can be found on the World Wide Web at: http:// schoolsite.edex.net.uk/77/.

Sports facilities include a large, well-equipped gymnasium, an athletics track, three hockey pitches (one of which is all-weather), netball and tennis courts and a fine indoor heated swimming pool, and a newly laid Astroturf pitch. The school enjoys a first-class record of sporting success and the Sports Hall was opened in 1997. New Dining Room facilities were completed in 1996.

The school provides an environment in which girls of all ages work hard to develop their abilities. Academic studies are of paramount importance and standards are high with a curriculum making equal provision for arts, sciences, practical and creative subjects. Careers education has a high profile and the school is a member of ISCO.

The large Sixth Form enjoys a wide GCE Advanced Level and AS Level curriculum, a broad provision for minority studies, opportunities for taking responsibility and for travel to Europe and beyond; video-conferencing facilities are available to support distance learning. In addition to the many sports available in the senior school, including archery and fencing, sixth-formers are able to play golf and squash and to row with the school Rowing Club. Almost all the Upper Sixth go on to higher education and each year girls maintain our established "Oxbridge" tradition. Applications for Sixth Form entry are welcome.

A great emphasis is put on an enthusiastic involvement in music, art, sport, drama and community activities. The school has a high local reputation for its annual dance production and holds several sports championships. Major school concerts are organised at venues such as the Royal Albert Hall, St Martin-in-the-Fields and Southwark Cathedral.

All extra-curricular activities flourish in this lively community where Young Enterprise, work experience, work shadowing, Neighbourhood Engineer and teacher placement schemes have considerable support. Both the Bromley High School Association and the Old Girls' Association support the school most generously. Girls enjoy contributing to local, national and international charities and to community service. They are prepared for all standards of the Duke of Edinburgh Award Scheme and there is a keen interest in environmental issues. There are many clubs in which girls of all ages take a share of responsibility. There are regular exchanges to France, Germany and Spain as well as annual Geography and Biology field trips and annual ski-trips to popular European resorts. World Challenge expeditions have visited Uganda, Malaysia and Ecuador and will visit Thailand in the Summer of 2001. Annual Music Tours have travelled to Australia, Venice, Malta and South Africa, with the 2001 Tour planned to the United States. The Year 6 and 7 Music Tours have visited Paris and Brussels, with the 2000 Tour planned for Normandy.

The school is well served by public transport and the Bromley High School Association arranges a private coach service over an extensive area.

Fees and Financial Assistance. From September 2000: Senior School £2,044 per term; Junior Department £1,588 per term.

Fees cover tuition, stationery, textbooks and scientific and games materials as well as entry fees for GCSE and GCE Advanced Level examinations. Extra tuition in music and speech and drama is available at recognised rates.

Bursaries. Following the ending of the Government Assisted Places Scheme, the GDST has made available to the school a substantial number of scholarships and bursaries. The bursaries are means tested and are intended to ensure that the school remains accessible to bright girls who would profit from our education but who would be unable to enter the school without financial assistance.

Scholarships. There are scholarships for the most successful candidates in the 11+ examination, and for entry into the Sixth Form. There is also a music scholarship at 11+ and in the Sixth Form, and Sport and Art Scholarships in the Sixth Form.

Charitable status. Bromley High School is one of the 25 schools of the Girls' Day School Trust, which is a Registered Charity, number 1026057. The aim of the Trust is to provide a fine academic education at a comparatively modest cost.

Bruton School for Girls

Sunny Hill Bruton Somerset BA10 0NT
Tel: (01749) 812277
Fax: (01749) 812537
e-mail: Brutonschoolforgirls@btinternet.com
website: www.brutonschool.co.uk

Boarding, weekly boarding and day.
Founded in 1900.

Chairman of Governors: Mr M S Persson
Vice-Chairman of Governors: Mrs J Montgomery

***Principal:* Mrs Barbara Bates,** BA, MA, MIMgt, FRSA

Senior Staff:

Vice-Principal: Mrs Daphne Maclay, MA
Head of Preparatory School: Mr David Marsden, JP, BSc, CertEd, DipIT
Bursar: Mr J R M Hill, OBE

A preparatory, senior school and sixth form college of over 500 pupils, of whom almost 150 board, with recent significant developments to buildings, facilities and curriculum. An outstanding location in beautiful countryside, yet accessible by nearby road and rail links to London, Bristol, Bath, Salisbury. The School is set on a 40 acre campus.

Structure. There are 3 elements of the School.

Sunny Hill Preparatory School has its own specialist accommodation with over 120 pupils from 3 to 11 years. There is a nursery and pre-prep department. Small orderly classes develop strong learning habits and make the most of these inquisitive childhood years. Girls explore the exciting world of science, information technology, French, music and creative arts. Mathematics and English programmes build firm foundations for purposeful learning.

Bruton Senior School is a very successful 11 to 16 school of 320 pupils with a 97% A to C pass rate in up to 10 GCSE subjects. 21 GCSE subjects are offered and Information Technology is seen as an important 'transferable skill' developed across the curriculum. Mathematics, modern languages and sciences are 'set' individually to maximise pupil potential. About 8% of girls are from overseas and have specialist EFL tuition, and pupils with academic potential but specific learning difficulties benefit from support specialists.

Bruton College for Sixth Form Girls, with 115 students, is an innovative approach to pre-university study, with tutorial support and individual study programmes. The College has a considerable reputation for academic achievement, "oxbridge", and university entrance. Cultural and social skills are developed to enhance independence and career ambitions. An ethos of unobtrusive supervision encourages students to take responsibility for their own study programmes within an agreed framework. An extensive range of 'A' levels is enhanced by cultural activities, extension studies, and extra curricular programmes which include driving tuition. Career and Higher Education advice feature prominently at this stage and are reinforced by our association with various professional bodies, and a well-equipped careers resource centre.

Residential accommodation is available from 7 to 18 years and reflects changing expectations of girls according to age, and a flexibility to reflect the needs of busy families. There are three boarding houses. A close family atmosphere of warmth and security is offered by the Preparatory School. Senior girls gradually move from small dormitories to individual cubicles in Year 11 and are cared for by Housemistresses and assistant house staff. Sixth formers occupy a separate hall of individual rooms with washbasin, telephone and computer terminal, and enjoy a degree of freedom that reflects our aim to bridge between 'school' and 'university'. Full, weekly and occasional boarding is available, and with no compulsory Saturday schooling, parents can choose the frequency of visits and exeats. A varied and stimulating programme of activities is offered each weekend.

The Medical Centre is staffed by well-qualified Sisters who provide 24 hour care and are supported by Bruton Surgery.

A high standard of catering is available and specific dietary needs are provided for.

Extra-curricular Activities. Art, drama, music and sport feature strongly. There are opportunities for choral and instrumental performances at all levels. The success of the Art department is reflected by additional activities which have drawn boys from other schools and adults from within the community to participate in photography, painting, sculpture etc. Drama, public speaking and theatre studies are offered to all girls from the age of 11, and the school has several productions each year. Sports-women frequently represent the county and attend national competitions; tennis coaching and horseriding are offered year-round, in addition to a full fixture list of competitive matches. However an important philosophy of the school is respect for sport as healthy recreation, therefore a choice of non-competitive activities including modern and classical dance, fencing, martial arts and yoga etc, and individual exercise regimes are available in the Fitness Suite and Dance Studio. There is a popular Duke of Edinburgh's Award programme and students can also attend training as Army Cadets.

Pastoral Care. In the Preparatory School small form groups under the guidance of class teachers promote self-esteem and motivation of individual girls where positive achievement, in all aspects, is rewarded. Senior girls are vertically grouped into four Halls with a system of tutors who closely monitor each girl's progress and pastoral needs. Sixth formers are guided by their own tutors who monitor academic progress, assist with university applications and support the students' welfare. A lively and social ethos exists which encourages the development of independent, confident and purposeful young women.

Fees per term. Senior School: £2,250 (day); £3,870 (boarding). Prep School: £1,700 (day); £3,320 (boarding). Pre-Prep: £1,450.

Scholarships and Entry. Bruton School for Girls has a range of generous scholarships and awards at all entry levels. The criterion for scholarship awards to a maximum of 50% fees is based on academic excellence. In addition exhibitions and awards are offered on the basis of aptitude in particular areas, eg music, art, drama etc. Further details are available from the Registrar.

There is open entry into the pre-prep and preparatory schools. Girls are assessed for entry into the Senior School by our own examinations and interviews. Entry into the Sixth Form College is by interview and subject-specific-testing.

Location. The school is 4 miles from Wincanton and the M3/A303 corridor between London and the South West. It lies 25 miles south of Bristol and Bath and within 40 miles of Salisbury and the south coast. The Paddington London railway to Exeter and Plymouth is 1 mile away and the line to Waterloo is 12 miles - the school offers minibus connections. Students can also be collected from Heathrow Airport (2 hours). A network of daily buses also serves the school.

Charitable status. A Company Limited by Guarantee, number 4094352. UK Registered Charity, number 1085577.

Bury Grammar School (Girls)

Bridge Road Bury Lancs BL9 0HH
Tel: 0161 797 2808
Fax: 0161 763 4658
e-mail: info@bgsg.bury.sch.uk
website: http://www.bgsg.bury.sch.uk

Motto: *Sanctas Clavis Fores Aperit*

Chairman of Governors: Mr J A Rigby

Bursar and Clerk to the Governors: Mr D A Harrison, BSc(Econ), FCA

Headmistress: **Miss C H Thompson**, BA

Deputy Headmistresses:
Mrs G G Burton, BSc (London)
Mrs L D Billinge, BSc (Leicester)

Senior Teachers:
Mrs E J Schofield, MA (Manchester)
Mrs P Wells, BSc (Liverpool), MSc (MMU)
Mrs J S Skinner, BA (London)

Heads of Departments:
Mr L R Bergin, BA (Hull) *Economics and Business Studies*
Mrs D Brooks, CertEd (Northern Counties College) *Technology, Food & Textiles*
Mrs C Buckley, BSc (Hull) *Physics*
Miss J E Cardno, BSc (London) *Biology*
Miss J D Cebertowicz, BA (Bath) *Art and Design*
Miss S Davenport, BA (London) *English*
Mrs A E Grant, BA (Southampton) *Geography*
Mrs Y G Hanham, BSc (Salford) *Mathematics*

Miss B G Hill, CertEd (Bedford College) *PE*
Mr D Jones, LCG (Leeds) *D and T*
Mr M Joyce, MA (Oxon) *Modern Languages*
Mr S Keene, BSc (London), BA (Open) *IT*
Mrs L C A Kerr, BA (Manchester) *RS*
Mrs V Livsey, BA (Liverpool) *German*
Miss H C Lunt, BA (Manchester) *Classics*
Mrs J I M Stafford, MSc (Newcastle) *Chemistry*
Mrs D Stoddard, GNSM, LRAM, ARCM *Music*
Mrs S Thorpe, BA (Salford) *Politics*
Mrs H Ward, BA (Leicester) *History*

Head of Sixth Form: Mrs J S Skinner, BA (London)
Head of Upper School: Mrs R Rosenthal, BSc (Manchester)
Head of Middle School: Mrs J Larby, BA (London)
Head of Year 7: Mrs S C Trethewey, BA (Bangor)

Kindergarten and Junior School:
Mrs D E Robinson, CertEd (Didsbury) *Kindergarten*
Miss V Woodward, CertEd (Edge Hill College) *Junior School*

The Girls' School was founded in 1884 as the Bury High School for Girls and became, a few years later, the Bury Grammar School. The school maintains high academic standards and traditional grammar school values – sound learning, sensible discipline and good manners – whilst encouraging each girl to develop her individual talents and abilities as far as she can in a lively environment which strives to respond to the challenge of change.

In September 1997 the Junior School moved into new, purpose built premises adjacent to the distinctive Edwardian building which dates from 1906. The school is conveniently situated near the centre of the town and the bus-rail interchange. Facilities are regularly improved and updated; significant additions and modifications to our buildings have been made in recent years including the Dorothy Lester Library with an attached Resource Centre, new Sports Hall, new Humanities block, computer rooms and additional specialist teaching rooms for Science, Design and Technology, Textiles, Home Economics, English and Music. The Swimming Pool has been completely refurbished.

The new Junior School houses eight classes of girls aged seven to eleven. The School is purpose built and self-contained on the Senior School site, and has shared use of the Roger Kay Hall, Gymnasium, Sports Hall, computer rooms and swimming pool. The large and attractive classrooms, Music Room and large Library/Computer suite provide a comfortable and pleasant environment in which to learn and work.

The curriculum is broad and balanced in the first five years of the Senior School. All girls follow courses in ICT, Design Technology, Latin and a second Modern Language in addition to the traditional curriculum. Traditional teaching methods are combined with pupil-centred learning work, group work, investigative work and a problem solving approach.

The Key Skills are developed; pupils are encouraged, through a variety of cross curricular projects, to seek solutions to problems which are real to them and to take an ever increasing responsibility for their own learning.

Physical Education and Music are well established; in recent years the School has been represented in National Netball and Swimming Championships and on County Netball, Swimming, Tennis and Badminton teams. Each year the Festival Choir competes internationally and in the UK. There are two orchestras and a chamber group. The Chamber Choir regularly sing BBC Radio 4 Morning Service.

The School co-operates with Bury Grammar School (Boys) for dramatic and musical productions, and other extra-curricular activities. The Sixth Form common rooms are open to both boys and girls.

Public examinations are taken in Years 11, 12 and 13, according to the requirements of individual pupils. There is a wide choice of subjects in the Sixth Form and each year all or virtually all students proceed to degree courses at prestigious universities, including Oxford and Cambridge. The School achieves high pass rates in public examinations.

These successes and initiatives, along with PSE, careers advice and extra curricular activities–clubs, visits, holidays in England and abroad, charity work and school productions, offer wide educational opportunities and encourage links to be forged with industry and commerce and with the community in Bury and beyond.

The Junior School is following the recommendations and programmes of study of the National Curriculum orders. Recording and assessment procedures are also being followed. The curriculum includes the three core subjects and Design/Technology, ICT, History, Geography, Religious Education, Art and Craft, Music and Physical Education. Particular emphasis is placed on the teaching of basic skills in reading, writing and mathematics. The aim is to provide a broad and balanced education and to give each girl the opportunity to develop her full potential. The combination of a dedicated staff and good facilities has allowed girls to maintain the high academic standard expected of them and to respond well to a variety of challenges.

The School has a Kindergarten for boys and girls from the age of 4–7 which offers spacious accommodation within the main building. Both Kindergarten and Junior School departments share the excellent sports facilities, the Computer rooms and Assembly Hall whilst maintaining the atmosphere of a primary school in the self contained units. The numbers at present are 175 in the Kindergarten Department, 176 in the Junior School and 730 in the Senior School.

Scholarships. At 11+ the Governors offer one Kay Scholarship, an Ogden Trust Bursary and a number of means-tested bursaries.

Fees. Kindergarten £3,189 per annum. Junior School £3,402 per annum. Senior School £4,770 per annum.

Charitable status. The Governors of Bury Grammar Schools is a Registered Charity, number 526622. Its aims and objectives are to maintain high academic standards and traditional grammar school virtues – sound learning, sensible discipline and good manners – whilst encouraging each girl to develop her individual talents and abilities as far as she can in a lively environment which strives to respond to the challenge of change.

Casterton School

Kirkby Lonsdale Carnforth Cumbria LA6 2SG
Tel: (015242) 79200
Fax: (015242) 79208

The School was founded at Cowan Bridge in 1823 by the Reverend W Carus Wilson for the education of daughters of the clergy and was moved to Casterton in 1833. In 1921 daughters of the laity were first admitted and the school is now an Independent Senior School for approximately 340 girls. There is a Preparatory Department which also admits day boys up to the age of 11.

Governing Body:
Chairman: J D Clark, Esq, CertEd with Dist, FRSA
Vice-Chairman: Mrs G M Hunter, JP

District Judge G R Ashton, LLB
J K Chew, Esq
Mrs J Cawley

Mrs M Crisp, BSc, PGCE, DGCE
Dr P A L Faux, MB, ChB, DMRD
P V Hoyle, Esq, FCIS, ATII
Miss J Laycock
His Honour Judge A J Proctor, MA, LLM (Cantab)
Mrs E Raitt, BA Hons, PGCE, AdvDip in Educational Management
P Thurnham, Esq, MA, FInstMechEng
C J Weir, Esq, MA (Oxon)

Visitor: The Right Rev The Lord Bishop of Carlisle

Staff:
***Headmaster:* A F Thomas**, MA (Cantab)

1st Deputy Head: Miss C L Summerhayes, BEd Hons (Leeds) *Religious Studies*

2nd Deputy Head: Mrs P A Gee, MA (Oxon), BA (Open), PGCE (Cheltenham) *History*

Assistant Deputy Heads:
Mrs D Lomax, BSc Hons (Durham), PGCE (Cambridge) *Geography*
Mrs G A Sykes, BSc Hons (Exeter), PGCE (Sheffield) *Mathematics*

Miss G Aldcroft, BA Hons (Liverpool) *Lacrosse*
Mrs J Aveyard, BA Hons (Wimbledon), PGCE (Leeds) *Art*
Miss J Barmstone, BEd Hons (St Paul & St Mary, Cheltenham), BTec *Physical Education*
Mrs J Barmstone, CertEd *Business Studies*
A Bell, BSc Hons (St Andrews) *Science*
Mrs C E Birtwistle, BA (Open), BSc (Edinburgh), PSC, RMCS *Typewriting & Word Processing*
Mrs J A Blackmore, MA (Central England), BA Hons (Leeds), PGCE (Liverpool) *Art*
Miss C E Bloomfield, BA Hons (Lincolnshire & Humberside), PGCE (Leeds) *Junior subjects*
Mrs J Bowden, BSocSci (Birmingham), PGCE (Avery Hill) *History and Sociology, Keyskills Co-ordinator*
Mrs V Bray, CertEd (Matlock) *English*
D C Chapman, MA (Oxon), LRAM Teaching Dip *Music*
R Christie, BSc Hons, PhysEd (Loughborough) *Prep School*
I L Cochrane, BSc Hons (St Andrews) *Mathematics*
Mrs C A Cochrane, MA Hons (St Andrews), AIL German
Mrs C Y Cookson, CertEd (Lancaster) *Junior Subjects*
Mrs A Cox, BEd (Liverpool), CertEd (Chester) *Mathematics and Outdoor Pursuits*
Mrs S Cox, CertEd (I M Marsh) *Physical Education*
Mrs K J Culshaw, BEd Hons (I M Marsh) *Physical Education*
Mrs V Eden, CertEd, Dip in Ceramics *Ceramics*
Mrs E Edmonds, BA (Keele) *English*
Dr P Ellis, PhD (Reading), BA (Manchester), MA (Univ of Manitoba), Cert Ed (Dundee) *English*
Miss K Fisher, LTAReg *Tennis*
Mrs G A Green, BA (Bristol), CertEd (Birmingham) *Economics, Business Studies*
Miss S L Haddrill, BA (Open), CertEd (Durham) FIST *Biology*
Mrs M Hamilton, DipMusEd (RSAM) *Music*
Miss P A Hayward, BA Hons (Durham) *Latin and EFL*
Mrs H Hill, CertPhysEd (Anstey College) *Physical Education*
Dr J L Howard, C.Chem MRIC, PhD (Salford), CertEd (Lancaster)*Chemistry*
Mrs G M Hoyle, BEd Hons (Southampton), CertEd (King Alfred's College) *Head of Preparatory School*
Mrs H M Hughes, CertEd (Darlington) *Prep School*
D Kay, MSc (Bradford) *Mathematics*
P Keay, PGCE (St Martins), MA Textile & Design (London) *Textiles*
J W P Leahy, BA Hons, PGCE (Bangor), Dip Hum (Aberystwyth), MPhil (San Diego) *History, Careers*
Mrs N Marriott, BA Hons (Birmingham), PGCE (Leeds) *Drama*
Dr M Martin, MSc (UMIST), PhD, CertEd (Manchester) *Physics*
Ms V May, CertEd (Madeley College of Education) *Prep School*
Miss S B Nelson, BHSII *Riding*
Mrs J F L Nott, L-ès-L (Anglais) *French*
Mrs V A Parkinson, BEd (Manchester) *Home Economics*
Mrs C Peek, BA Hons (Bangor), CertEd (Liverpool) *French*
Miss C Pelufo, BA Hons (Valencia) *Spanish*
Mrs G M Pinkerton, MA (Lancaster), BA Hons (Wales), CertEd (Reading) *English*
Mrs A Pioch, CertEd (Leeds) *Prep School*
Miss A C Rigby, CertEd (Gloucester College) *Home Economics*
Miss S Robinson, BHSPI *Riding*
Mrs J D Rollings, BEd (Bedford) *Physical Education*
Miss H L Rowland, BA Hons (Nottingham), PGCE (Nottingham) *Geography*
R J Sanders, BSc (Liverpool), PGCE (Chester) *Biology*
Mrs S Scott, BTech (Lancaster) *Nursery*
Mrs J M Slater, BA Hons (St Martin's, Lancaster) *Prep School*
Mrs P Sneddon, BEd (Nevilles Cross), RYASI, PE *Sailing*
Mrs P J Symonds, BSc Hons (Durham), PGCE (Oxford) *Information Technology*
Miss D Vernon, MA(Ed) (Open), BA Hons (Open) *Learning Support*
Mrs A M Weir, LGSM Hons *Drama*
J Westall, ALCM, GLCM *Music*
Mrs J Wheeler, MA (Aberdeen) *French*

Headmaster's Secretary: Mrs M Holden

Chaplain: The Revd P S Atkinson, BD, AKC (London), MA (Durham) *Religious Studies, Dip RE* (London)

Medical Officer: Dr P J I Hall, MB, ChB, MRCGP

Senior House Mistress: Miss H Whitfield, CertPhysEd (Anstey College)

Head of Junior House: Mrs C Y Cookson, CertEd (C Mason)

Sanatorium: Sister M King, RGN

Number of girls. There are 333 girls in the School, of whom 215 are Boarders, 5 Weekly Boarders and 113 are Day Girls.

Situation. The School is situated in South Cumbria in the vale of the River Lune, 1½ miles from Kirkby Lonsdale, on the edge of the Lake District but only 7 miles from the M6.

School Buildings etc. The Junior House stands in its own grounds a few minutes walk from the main buildings and has accommodation for 60 boarders, weekly boarders and day girls. Girls under 12 years live here in the charge of a Housemistress and Housematrons. All lessons are in the main school building but the Juniors spend their leisure hours in their own House.

The main school buildings have accommodation for 260 boarders and day girls with an age range of 12 to 18+. Girls over the age of 12 years enter one of the 5 School houses. Each House has its own dormitories and sitting room and the girls are in the charge of a Housemistress. The Senior girls have separate VIth Form Houses.

Apart from boarding accommodation, the main buildings include Gymnasium Hall, Libraries, Classrooms, Home Economics Centre, a Commerce Room and Music Wing. A purpose-built Science and Mathematics block opened in 1995. There are Pottery and Sculpture Rooms, two Computer rooms, Language Laboratory, Theatre, New Creative Arts Centre and Sixth Form study area.

A separate Preparatory Department caters for day boys and girls up to the age of 11 and for boarders (girls only) between the ages of 8 and 11.

Education. The education includes; RE, English, History, French, Geography, Economics, German, Spanish, Latin, Mathematics, Physics, Chemistry, Biology, Computer studies, Business Studies, Music, Art, Physical Education, Home Economics and Drama.

Examinations. Pupils are prepared for GCSE and 'A' level examinations, the Universities (Entrance and Scholarships) and the examinations of the Associated Board of the Royal Schools of Music.

Age of Admission. Entrance can be considered at any age - there is an Entrance Examination for applicants from the age of 8 upwards.

Extras, which are optional include instruction in a wide range of musical instruments, singing, speech and drama, riding, tennis coaching, ballet

Termly rates for these, and tuition and boarding fees, are available from The Headmaster on request. Details of scholarships are also available on request.

Clergy Daughters. There are Bursaries available for the daughters of clergy. The number is now limited and grants can be offered only as vacancies occur.

Gymnastics and Games. These form part of the normal curriculum and include Hockey, Netball, Lacrosse, Tennis, Rounders, Athletics and Swimming. There are hard tennis courts in the grounds of the main building and a covered heated swimming pool.

Fees per term: Senior Boarding, £4,290; Senior Day £2,640. Junior Boarding: £3,675; Junior Day: £2,292; Junior Weekly Boarding £3,582; Pre-Prep £1,218-£1,365.

Casterton School Old Girls Association: *Secretary:* Miss J Laycock, Hillcrest Cottage, Cherry Clough, Denshaw, Saddlesworth, OL3 5UE.

Charitable status. The Governors of Casterton School is a Registered Charity, number 1076380. The school was originally founded for the education of Clergy daughters, but is now open to pupils of all creeds.

Central Newcastle High School (G.D.S.T.)

Eskdale Terrace Newcastle-upon-Tyne NE2 4DS
Tel: (0191) 2811768/2813811
Junior Department West Avenue Gosforth, Newcastle-upon-Tyne NE3 4ES Tel: (0191) 2851956
Junior Department
Chapman House
Sandyford
Newcastle-upon-Tyne NE2 1NN
Tel: (0191) 2126910

Founded 1895

This is one of the 25 schools of The Girls' Day School Trust. For general information about the Trust and the composition of its Council, see p 532. A more detailed prospectus may be obtained from the school.

Local Governors:
Chairman: Mr J Cawood
Mrs P Denham, BSc, PhD
Mr M F Downing, MSc, FLI, FRSA
Mrs J MacGregor, JP
Mr D Fleming
Dr J Buchanan
Mrs A Darling, JP
Dr R H F Carver
Cllr K Taylor
Mrs M Martin

***Headmistress:* Mrs L J Griffin**, BA Hons (Wales) *English, BPhil* (York) *Medieval Studies*

Deputy Headmistress: Miss J M Rycroft, BA Hons, PGCE (Lancaster) *Chemistry*

Second Master: Mr M Tippett, MA Hons (Oxford), PGCE (Cambridge) *Classics*

Head of Sixth Form: Mrs L J McKay, BA Hons (Oxford), DipEd (Birmingham)

Mr M R Allender, MA (Cambridge), PGCE (Oxford) *History*
Miss H E Andrews, BA Hons, PGCE (Durham), PGDip (Northumbria) *French*
Mr J Armstrong, MSc (Newcastle-upon-Tyne) *Psychology*
Mrs J Atkinson, BA Hons Sport & Recreation (Madeley College), PGCE (Carnegie School of Human Movement) *Physical Education*
Mrs J M Ayton, BA Hons, CertAdEd (Newcastle-upon-Tyne) *Geography*
Mrs B Bailey, BSc Hons (Newcastle-upon-Tyne), PGCE (Bristol) *Mathematics*
Mrs C M Ballantyne, GRSM, ARMCM (Manchester), IECert (Leeds) *Music*
Mr A J Beale, BA Hons (Newcastle-upon-Tyne) *Classics*
Mrs M Brock, DipAD (Sunderland College of Art) *Art/Design*
Ms J Clare, BA Hons, PGCE (Warwick) *English*
Dr H E Coapes, BSc Hons, MSc, PhD (Newcastle-upon-Tyne) *Chemistry*
Mrs N Cording, BSc Hons (York), PGCE (Newcastle-upon-Tyne) *Mathematics*
Mrs E Coulton, MA, PGCE (Oxford) *Physics*
Mrs N Crotty, BA Hons (Oxford), PGCE (Nottingham) *Classics*
Mrs G Denmark, BEd Hons (Cambridge), CertEd (Bedford) *PE*
Mr J Donneky, BSc Hons (Durham), MSc (Newcastle Polytechnic), MA (Durham) *Science*
Mrs D L Edmonds, BA Hons (Newcastle-upon-Tyne), PGCE (Cambridge) *Geography*
Miss A Featonby, BSc Hons (Liverpool), PGCE (Lancaster) *Sports Science*
Mrs J Fitzpatrick, BSc Hons, DipEd (Newcastle-upon-Tyne) *Biology*
Mr L Fox, MA Hons, PGCE (Lancaster) *German*
Mrs L Gardham, BA Hons (Leeds), PGCE (Warwick) *History*
Dr J M Germain, BSc Hons, PhD (Newcastle-upon-Tyne) *Chemistry*
Mrs D Goddard, SRN, CertEd, HECert *Biology*
Miss A Goldie, BA Hons (Dundee) *Art/Design*
Mr R Gooding, BA Hons Music (Keble College, Oxford), PGCE (Durham) *Music*
Mr A Gouge, BA Hons (Newcastle-upon-Tyne), PGCE (Sunderland) *Economics*
Ms J Greenwood, BA Hons ADB (Brentwood), PGCE, MEd (Newcastle), MA (Nottingham) *English*
Mrs C Hayward, Teacher's Certificate (Bedford College) *Physical Education*
Mrs A M Holloway, BA Hons, PGCE, LGSM (Leicester) *English*
Mrs J M Hoodless, BA Hons, PGCE (Newcastle-upon-Tyne) *French/German*
Mrs K A Howard, BSc (Bradford), PGCE (Leeds) *Mathematics*
Mrs S Hurst, BA Hons, PGCE (Newcastle-upon-Tyne) *English*
Mrs R Jameson, CertPE (IM Marsh College) *Careers*
Mrs S Lishman, MA Joint Hons (St Andrews), CertEd (Newcastle-upon-Tyne) *French/German*
Mr J McKay, BA Hons (Oxford) *Classics*

Mrs A Mateos, BA Hons (Leon, Spain), MA (Durham) *Spanish*
Mrs S May, BSc Hons (Aberystwyth), DipEd (Newcastle-upon-Tyne) *Mathematics*
Miss D J Moorhouse, BSc Hons, PGCE (London) *Physics*
Mrs M M Ollerenshaw, Dip (Monte Carlo) *French Conversation*
Mrs B Prince, BEd (Newcastle-upon-Tyne) *Mathematics*
Mrs H Ranson, BSc Hons (Bristol) *Biology/Physics*
Mrs B Rankin, BA Hons, DipEd (Newcastle-upon-Tyne) *Art/Design*
Mr J Rankin, BA Design Hons (Dundee), MA *Art & Design*
Mrs M Robinson, BA Hons, DipEd (Newcastle-upon-Tyne) *Geography*
Mrs J M Robson, BA, PGCE (Newcastle-upon-Tyne) *English/Religious Studies*
Ms A Schulte *French/German*
Mrs M H Shrubsall, BSc Hons (Sussex), PGCE (Newcastle-upon-Tyne) *Information Technology*
Mrs E Silipo, BSc Hons (London) *Physics*
Mrs C M Southward, BSc Hons (Newcastle-upon-Tyne), Teaching Certificate (Dortmund) *Mathematics*
Dr A Spector, BA Hons, PhD (Leeds) *Philosophy*
Mrs P Stanwick, BA Hons (Birmingham) *Information Technology*
Ms M Wilde, Dip (Argentina), EFL (Newcastle-upon-Tyne) *Spanish*
Mrs E M Wilkins, BSc Hons, PGCE (Bristol), MEd (Newcastle-upon-Tyne) *Geography*
Mr D J Wilson, BA Hons (Wales), PGCE (Lancaster) *RS and Philosophy*
Mrs L Wilson, BA Hons (Cambridge), PGCE (Oxford) *Biology*
Mrs D Wright, BA Joint Hons (*Newcastle-upon-Tyne*), PGCE (Durham) *English*

Junior Department:
Head of Junior Department: Mrs A Lomas, BA, PGCE (Manchester)
Mrs J Anderson, CertEd (Ripon)
Mrs S Ashmore, CertEd (Birmingham), BA (OU)
Mrs H Barnes, CertEd (Durham)
Mrs R Booth, BMus (Manchester), PGCE (Cambridge)
Mrs H N Burchall, CertEd (Sheffield)
Miss L E Hunter, BPhil (Newcastle-upon-Tyne), CertEd (Hull)
Mrs S Jones, BSc Hons, PGCE (Durham)
Mrs M McGrady, BEd Hons (Northumbria)
Mrs H Pearson, BEd (Newcastle-upon-Tyne)
Mrs N Peruzzo, BA Hons (Durham), PGCE (Newcastle-upon-Tyne)
Mrs L Rae, DipPrimEd (Hamilton)
Mrs P Roberts, BA(Ed) Hons
Mrs J Robson, CertEd (Northumberland)
Miss L Taylor, BA Hons (London), PGCE (Leeds)
Mrs S Thomas, BEd Hons (Leeds)
Mrs C E Wilkie, CertEd (London)
Miss C Williams, BSc Hons (York), PGCE (Plymouth)
Miss C Wilson, BSc Hons (Durham), PGCE (Newcastle-upon-Tyne)
Miss S Hadden, BTec
Mrs K Kendra, BTec
Miss M Murray, GNVQ Level 3
Miss F Toothill, NNEB, BTec

Visiting Staff:
Mr B Alimohamadi, LGSM, BA, CertEd *Flute*
Mrs S Bladon, BA Hons, DipILM, LRAM, ALCM *Singing*
Mrs J Craig, BA, LTCL *Cello/Double Bass*
Ms J D'Ambrosie, DipMus *Violin/Viola*
Mrs A Doig, BMus Hons *Piano*
Mr J Ferguson, LTCL *Guitar*
Mrs H Gilfillan, BMus, PGCE *Oboe/Bassoon*
Mrs L Northey, LTCL, LGSM, ALCM *Piano/Clarinet*
Mr R Northey, LTCL, LGSM, LLCM *Piano/Brass*
Mrs J R O'Connell, BA, ARCM, LRAM *Piano*
Miss S Parker-Forster, BA *Violin/Viola*
Mr M Shillito, LRAM *Flute/Horn*
Miss C Dalby, LGSM *Speech and Drama*
Mrs T Hagger, LTCL, LGSM, ALCM *Speech & Drama*
Mrs S Fear, BA Hons, CertEd, LGSM, VSP *Speech & Drama*

Administration Department:
School Administrator: Mrs C Gaughan
School Doctor: Dr G P Rye, MB, BS
School Nurse: Mrs G Gordon, SRN, SCN
Headmistress's Personal Assistant: Mrs G Lord
Admissions Secretary: Miss J Howe
School Secretary: Mrs B Office
P/T Admin Assistants: Mrs J Toman, Mrs A Shields, Mrs V Bowman
F/T Admin Assistant: Mrs D Bates
Domestic Bursar: Mrs A M H Perry, MHAIMA
Information Systems Manager: Mr C Cording
Computer Technician: Mr A Basak
Resources Officer: Mr J Hawdon, CGLI 726 & 736 TechCert
Resources Assistant: Mrs N Davison
Laboratory Technicians:
Mrs C Mudd, ONC, HNC Chemistry
Mrs I Sproat, CGLI, 755 TechCert
Mrs J Slater
Librarian: Mrs C Elliott, BA, ALA

Number of pupils approximately 983.

Senior School 648 (aged 11–18 years of whom 159 are in the Sixth Form).

Junior Department 335 (aged 3–10 years).

The Central Newcastle High School is one of the 25 schools of the Girls' Day School Trust, an organisation which for well over a century has promoted the education of girls.

Early pupils were among the first women to gain university degrees and enter the professions. The school maintains these high academic standards and almost all leavers go on to degree courses. The school aims at a wide social blend of pupils and various forms of assistance with fees are available.

Girls are encouraged to develop many talents: music is strongly encouraged. The standard of sport is extremely high with a great measure of success in local and national competitions. National level has been reached at tennis (LTA School of the Year 1997-8), netball, cross country and squash; coaching and extra clubs are available and girls are selected for county squads in a variety of sports. The school was awarded the Sportsmark Award in 1999. There have been many recent additions and improvements, including a Music School and Sports Hall which were completed in July 1994. A new Sixth Form Wing was opened in September 1998 and additional Junior School premises for the 8-11 year olds opened in September 1999 in Sandyford. A nursery was added to the Infants section which will continue to occupy the former Junior Department building in Gosforth.

Curriculum. The regular school curriculum covers a wide range of academic subjects, including a variety of languages. Art and Music are encouraged and there has been considerable investment in computer technology. Philosophy is taught at Year 7 as well as in the Sixth Form. Girls are prepared for GCSE and all gain certificates of competence in computing. In the Sixth Form 26 subjects are offered at AS and most can be continued to A level. Virtually all girls proceed to degree courses: medicine and law are popular choices. The girls are involved in a wide variety of activities beyond their academic studies, ranging from Duke of Edinburgh Award to Poetry Society, Greek Drama to Community Service.

Fees. From September 2000/2001: Senior School £1,680 per term; Junior Department £980-£1,120 per term.

The fees cover the regular curriculum, school books, stationery and other materials, choral music, games and swimming, but not optional extra subjects or school meals. The fees for extra subjects, including instrumental music, speech and drama and, in the Junior Department, dancing, are shown in the prospectus.

Following the end of the Government Assisted Places Scheme, the GDST has made available to the school a substantial number of scholarships and bursaries. The bursaries are means tested and are intended to ensure that the school remains accessible to bright girls who would profit from our education but who would be unable to enter the school without financial assistance.

Bursaries. These are available before or after entry throughout the Senior School and application should be made to the Headmistress in cases of financial need. All requests will be considered in confidence.

Scholarships. These are at present available to internal or external candidates and are for entry at 11+ or to the Sixth Form.

Charitable status. Central Newcastle High School is one of the 25 schools of the Girls' Day School Trust, which is a Registered Charity, number 1026057. The aim of the Trust is to provide a fine academic education at a comparatively modest cost.

Channing School

Highgate London N6 5HF
Tel: 020 8340 2328 (School Office); 020 8340 2719 (Bursar)
Fax: 020 8341 5698
e-mail: admin@channing.co.uk
website: www.channing.co.uk

Governors:
Mr G A Auger, FCCA (*Chairman*)
Mr S Barber, BSc(Econ), FCA
Mr S M D Brown, JP, BA (Durham)
¶Miss C E A Budgett-Meakin, BA (Kent)
Mr J M Burns, MA (Oxon)
¶Miss J A M Davidson, BSc (London)
¶Dr A P Hogg, MA (Oxon), PhD (Lond)
Mrs J A G Kennedy, OBE, MA (Oxon), CEng, MICE, ACIArb
Mrs V A Schilling, MCSP
Mr L P Shurman, MA (Oxon) (*Vice-Chairman*)
Mr M Steiner, MA (Oxon)
¶Dr K J I Thorne, MA, PhD
Dr A G White, MB, ChB, FRCP, DPhysMed
Dr D J Williams, MB, BCh

Bursar/Clerk to the Governors: Lt Col G H Miller

Bursar's Secretary: Mrs L Davies

Headmistress' Secretary: Mrs S Kelliher

School Secretary (*Senior School*): Mrs A Sherriff

School Secretary (*Junior School*): Mrs C Gibbons

Nurse: Mrs S Golding

Academic Staff:

***Headmistress:* Mrs E Radice**, MA (Oxon) *English*

Deputy Head: Mrs G Long, MA (London) *Classics*

Assistants (*Senior School*):
Mr J Andrews, BSc (Sheffield) *Economics and Mathematics*
Miss T Bailey, BA (Melbourne, Australia) *PE*
Miss A Bally, BA (Bath Academy of Art) *Pottery*
§Mrs J Benson, BA (Sussex) *English*
*Mrs D Bicknell, BSc (Durham), MEd *Head of Science, Biology*
Mrs D Bond, BA (Cantab) *French and Head of Sixth Form*
Mrs H Brazier, BA (London), MA (Open) *English Literature*
Mr D Coram, BA (Durham), MA (London) *Classics*
*Mr R Crawford, MA (London) *Head of Art*
§Ms A Derbyshire, BA (Central School of Art & Design) *Art*
Ms C Derckel, MA *French*
*Dr M H Ferguson, MA (Oxon), PhD (Reading) *Geography*
*Miss J Fox, BEd (London) *History and Political Studies, Head of Upper School*
Mr M Fouilleul, BA (Manchester) *French and Spanish*
Miss S-L Fung, BSc (Coventry) *Physics*
§Mrs N Giles, BSc (Bristol) *Mathematics*
§Mr K Gilley, BA (Oxon) *RE*
*Miss J Greedy, BA (Reading) *History and Head of Political Studies*
Mrs R J Harper, BA (Kent), ALAM *English*
Mr M Holmes, BSc (City of London Polytechnic) *Information Technology*
*Mr R Jacobs, BA (Oxon) *Physics*
Mrs G Johnson, MPhil, BSc (London) *Biology*
*Mr R Jones, MMus, BMus (London) *Director of Music*
*Mrs M Karatas, BSc (Otago, NZ) *Head of Chemistry*
Mrs R Laurie, BA (Reading) *English*
*Miss T Lederer, BEd (CNAA) *PE*
*Miss V Marsden, MA (Cantab) *Classics*
Mrs C Older, BA (Sussex) *Mathematics and Head of Middle School*
Miss C Packer, BSc (UCL) *Chemistry/Key Skills Coordinator*
Miss E Paske, BA (Liverpool) *Pure Mathematics*
§Mrs E Pencharz, BDSC (St Andrews) *Mathematics*
Miss H Peters, MA (Cantab) *English and Theatre Studies*
Miss J Pinney, BA (Cantab) *Biology*
*Mrs V Renaudon-Smith, BA (Keele) *French/English, Head of Modern Foreign Languages*
*Mrs R J Roots, MA (Sussex) *English*
Mrs S Scamell, BA (Birmingham) *Geography*
Mr N Shah, BSc (Bristol) *Mathematics*
*Mrs C Soto, BA (London) *Spanish*
§Ms H Speight, MA (Sussex) *History, Head of PHSE*
*Ms A Stoeckmann, MA (Westfaelische Wilhelms) *German*
Miss T Sutton, BMus (London) *Music*
*Mrs K Thonemann, BA (Oxon) *Mathematics*
Miss S Watchorn, BA (York) *PE*
Miss M Wharmby, BA (Loughborough), ALA *Librarian*
Miss R Wood, MA (Edinburgh), MSt (*Oxon*) *French*

Junior School:

Head Teacher: Mrs J Newman, BEd (Cantab) *Geography*
Deputy Head: Mrs J Todd, BA(Ed) (Herts)

Miss J Evans, BEd (Dundee College) *Form Teacher, Year 3*
Miss K Hilton, BSc (Birmingham) *Form Teacher, Year 5*
Miss A Phipps, BEd (Middx Polytechnic) *Form Teacher, Reception*
Mrs H Reznek, BEd (Hertfordshire) *Form Teacher, Year 2*
Miss R Sutherns, BA(Ed) & Welsh (Wales) *Form Teacher, Year 1*
Mrs J Todd, BA(Ed) (Hertfordshire) *Form Teacher, Year 6*
Miss R Johnson, MA (City University) *Head of Music*
Miss S Watchorn, BA (York) *PE*

Mrs C Brierley *Classroom Assistant*
Mrs D Orrell *Classroom Assistant*
Mrs J Ridett *Classroom Assistant*

Visiting Staff:

Mr S Allen, ARCM *Clarinet*
Mrs K Brown, GMus, RNCM, PPRNCM *Saxophone*
Mrs P Capone, AGSM *Piano*
Mr J Dobson, ProfCert (RAM), LRAM *Piano*
Mrs E Dobson, GBSM, ABSM, DipNCOS *Cello*
Miss R Edmunds, DipRCM *Bassoon*
Miss S Egan, BA (Cantab) *Voice*
Mr N Foster, BA, RSAMD *Percussion*
Mr A Khan, LTCL *Guitar*
Mr R Martyn, AGSM, LRAM *Brass*
Mrs C H Mendelssohn, LRAM *Violin*
Miss M Pepper, LTCL *Cello*
Miss C Philpot, ARCM *Oboe*
Miss H Rochelle, GTCL *Flute*
Mr J Sampson, BMus, ARCM *Violin and Viola*
Miss L Skriniar, DipTCL *Voice*
Miss J Stein, LTCL, GTCL, FTCL *Flute*
Miss S Thurdow, MMus, BMus *Clarinet*
Miss J Watts, FRCO, GRSM, LRAM *Piano*

Founded in 1885, Channing is a day school for girls aged 4 to 18, approximately 350 in the Senior School (Sixth Form 81 girls) and 160 in Fairseat, the Junior School. It is situated in Highgate Village, in extensive and attractive grounds, and offers a balanced education combining a traditional academic curriculum with modern educational developments. The complex of old and new buildings has been constantly adapted to provide up-to-date facilities, and there are strong links with the local community and with Highgate School.

Entry is by test and interview at 4, 11 and 16, and there are occasional casual vacancies. Fairseat girls sit the entrance examination to the Senior School to qualify for a place, and usually transfer there. Forms and teaching groups are limited in size to allow for close working relationships between girls and senior staff; the Head teaches all pupils in their first year and in the Sixth Form. Every girl follows a core curriculum in line with the National Curriculum, with plenty of opportunities to develop strengths in Classics, Modern Languages, Music and Art/Design and Drama. Option blocks in the Sixth Form and for GCSE are designed according to the current needs of each year group.

In accordance with Channing's Unitarian foundation, the religious teaching is of a liberal Christian character. All girls attend Religious Education lessons and morning assembly.

The Physical Education curriculum covers a wide variety of sports, and girls take part in the Duke of Edinburgh Award Scheme. Young Enterprise flourishes in the Sixth Form, and there are joint orchestral concerts with Highgate School, as well as a joint choral concert and joint dramatic productions.

Further information can be obtained from the school prospectus and the Sixth Form Handbook, available from the School Office.

Particulars of scholarships and bursaries. (*see* Entrance Scholarship section)

Fees as at January 2001. Junior School. Reception Class to Year 6: £2,210 per term. Senior School. Years 7 to 13: £2,400 per term.

Charitable status. Channing House Incorporated is a Registered Charity, number 312766. It aims to provide full-time education for girls aged between 4 and 18 years.

The Cheltenham Ladies' College

Bayshill Road Cheltenham Glos. GL50 3EP
Tel: (01242) 520691. Bursary (01242) 253233
Fax: (01242) 227882

Since 1853 the College has been one of the world's leading girls' schools. Today it has a reputation for academic excellence and provides an education within the traditions of the Church of England. It is our aim that all students leave College with the qualifications and the depth of knowledge, the range of skills and the personal qualities needed for modern life. Moreover, that they take with them warm friendships and cherished memories that will last a lifetime.

The Council:
Chairman: R Bernays, Esq

Representative Members:
Dr J B Morrison
Dr D Sutton

Elected Members:
The Hon M Beloff, QC
Mrs B M V Blackburn, MBE
Mrs S J Briscoe
Lord Peter Chadlington
Dr M Corley
C D Croker, Esq
Mrs J De Swiet
Mrs J A Eldridge, JP
D A E Finch, OBE, MA
Lady Gass, OBE, MA
J Hall, Esq
Canon Heavisides, MA
Admiral Sir Peter Herbert, KCB, OBE, CBIM, MINucE
Mrs J Hillman
Mrs J Kingsley
F E Maidment, Esq
Mrs H Maunsell, OBE
Mrs K Philp
P Randall, Esq
Mrs J M Richardson, FCA, JP
Ms H E Stone, BSc, CEng, FICE
Mrs J M Whiteman, RIBA, AADipl
R N A Wood, Esq

Bursar and Secretary to the Council: A J Siddall, Esq, FCCA

Deputy Bursar and Deputy Secretary to the Council: C C Shergold, Esq

Principal: **Mrs Vicky Tuck**, BA, MA, MIL

Vice-Principal: Mrs M Pimenoff, MA

Deputy Principal (*Pastoral*): Mrs S Roberts, MA

Director of Studies: Mrs J Abbotts, MEd

College Chaplain: The Revd A David Barlow, MA

Admissions Tutor: Mr J R Carpenter, BA

Heads of Divisions:

Sixth Form College: Miss C J Kirk, BA

Upper College: Mrs D J Vass, BA

Lower College: Mrs R J Hope, MA

Teaching Staff:

Art:
*Mr G Shaw-Rutter, BEd
Miss F James, BA, MA

Mrs F Richardson, BA
Mr A Richardson, BA
Mrs D Rowell, BA
Mr A D Watt, BA
Mr M Wilde, BA

Classics:
*Mr J R Holland, BA, MA, MSc
Miss S Buttery, BA, MLitt
Miss L Eveille, BA, ABSA, Companion of the Guild of St George
Mr F C Hepburn, MA, MLitt, FRSA
Mrs C Weston, MA

Drama:
*Miss J Bond, NCSD, LUDDA, IPA
Mr C H R Moss-Blundell, RBTC Dip
§Miss T M L Black, CertEd, AGSM
§Mr R Hugenin, BA
§Mr A Richards, MLitt, CertEd, LGSM
Mrs A Wilson, NCSD, LUDDA
§Ms A McKie, LUDDA
§Mrs P Deacon-Jones, LRAM, NCSD, LUDDA, IPA
Mrs E Sharples, DipRADA
Miss J C Garratt, BA (*Director in Residence*)
Miss G Greeph, LUDDA

Economics:
*Mr A R Hodge, BSc, MA, MPhil
Mr M H Barker, MA
Mrs R Cole, BA

English:
*The Revd H R Wood, BA
Mrs L M Armitage, BA
Ms K Bourne, BA
Mr J R Carpenter, BA
Mrs A G Roberts, MA
§Mrs C S de Piro, MPhil, BLitt
Mrs S Roberts, MA, DipRSA
Mrs S W Rudge, BA
Mrs E Sanderson, BA
§Miss A Silk, BA
§Mr R H Stuart, MA, BLitt
§Mrs T Wood, BA, CTEFLA
§Mrs K Bywater, MA
Mrs K Adam, BA
Miss R Livingston, MA

Geography:
*Mrs L M King, BA
Mr R Homan, BA
§Mrs E M S Bailey, BSc
Miss J S Tudge, BA
Mrs D J Vass, BA
Miss R M Smith, BA

History:
*Mrs S Lancashire, BA
Mr M R Bower, BA, MPhil
Mr G Bott, BA, MSocSc (*Head of Careers*)
Mrs H G Bradley, BA
Mrs J Derbyshire, BA
§Mrs H J A More, BA (*Government & Political Studies*)
Mrs J N Wright, MA
§Mrs E Smith, BA

Technology:
§Mrs S Bocchi
Mrs I Mitchell, DSc, CertEd
§Mrs V S Ripley, BEd
Mrs A E Jackson, BSc
Mr V Stannard, BA, PGDip

ITIS:
*Dr R I Reeves, BA
Mr A J Fayter, BA, MSc

Mr N G Watson, BEd
Mrs T Shaw, BA

Mathematics:
*Mrs B M Winn, BSc
Mrs J A Dorling, BSc
Mrs A Churchill, MA
Mrs D J Clarke, BSc
Mr I Clarke, BSc
§Mrs L Fletcher, BEd
Miss S M Jones, BSc
Mrs M E Millward, LCI
Mrs C M Pellereau, BSc
Mrs S E Silcock, BSc
Miss M Thomas, BSc
§Mrs A Abrams, MA
§Dr B Ralph, PhD

Modern Languages:
*Mrs J S Bott, BA
§Mrs E Brooke, BA
§Mrs Y Burch, BLi
§Mrs M Cole, MA, MPhil
§Mrs G Crofton, BA
Miss E Díaz, LFI, LFH
Dr P F N di Robilant, BA, MA, MPhil
§Mrs V M Kean, BA
§Mrs S A Lesniowski, BA
Mrs A Lillis, BA
Mrs J Palmer, BA
§Mrs U Proctor
Mrs J Snell, L-ès-L
Mrs J Abbotts, BA, MEd (*Director of Studies*)
Miss S Irmscher
Dr C Quirighetti, BA, PhD

Music:
*Mr D Hawley, BMus (*Director of Music*)
Miss J M Upton, GRSM, LRAM (*Flute, Piano, Head of Wind*)
Mrs N C Alsop, BA, ARCO, LTCL (*Organ*)
Miss V C Butler, MMus, GRSM, DipRCM (*Clarinet*)
Miss S L Harper, GRSM, ARCM, DipRCM (*Violoncello, Head of Strings*)
Mr A A MacLean, DipMusicEdRSAMD, LTCL, FTCL (*Piano, Head of Keyboard*)
Miss C J E Piper, BMus, LRAM, ARCM (*Violin & Viola*)
Mr R S Raby, GMus (*Piano & Harpsichord*)

Visiting Music Staff:
Mrs L H Adams, BA, LTCL (*Flute*)
Miss I Bailey, LCCMD, LTCL, LRAM, LGSM (*Piano*)
Mrs J Baldwin, ALCM, LLCM (*Oboe*)
Mr J Baldwin (*Clarinet & Saxophone*)
Mrs S Blewett, FTCL, LTCL, LWCMD (*Flute*)
Miss J Boardman (*Bassoon*)
Mr G Bowles (*Saxophone & Clarinet*)
Mrs P Bowyer, LTCL, GTCL (*Flute*)
Mrs F M Brown, MA, FRCO, LRAM (*Piano*)
Mr J Carter, DipRAM (*Piano*)
Mrs G Day, GRSM, LRAM, ARCM (*Clarinet, Piano & Recorder*)
Mrs C E Gibbons, CertEd (*Clarinet*)
Mr R Goode, ALCM (*Guitar*)
Ms J Greaves (*Singing*)
Mrs C J Hepburn, MA, FRCO, LRAM, LGSM (*Piano & Flute*)
Mrs A Howarth, BA (*Piano*)
Mrs L Jennings, BMus, ARCM (*Piano*)
Miss C Johnstone, BA, DipNCOS (*Violoncello*)
Mrs A A MacLean, DRSAMD (*Violin*)
Mrs Y Mathers, BMus, LGSM (*Piano*)
Miss B Mills (*Solo Singing*)
Mrs C Neale-Brown, MSTAT, GRSM, LRAM (*Alexander Technique*)

Mr R O'Connor, BA, LTCL (*Piano*)
Miss C M Paterson, MA, FLCM, ARMCM, LTCL, AMusTCL, ALCM (*Solo singing & Piano*)
Mrs J Reynard, GRSM, LRAM (*Piano*)
Miss P Rowley, LRAM, ARCM (*Piano*)
Mr A W Schaaf, BA, BEd, LRAM, ARCM (*Saxophone*)
Mr D Seacome, CertEd (*Percussion*)
Mrs P Smith (*Drum Kit*)
Mrs J M Statham, ARCM (*Violin*)
Mrs A Thistlethwaite (*Singing*)
Miss A Trentham, MMESM, GLCM (*Harp*)
Mrs J Tribe, LTCL, CertEd (*Flute, Recorder & Viol*)
Mrs T White, ARCM (*French Horn*)
Mrs F Wild, LRAM (*Piano*)
Mr M Willett, BA (*Double Bass*)
Mr I A Willox, BA (*Bagpipes*)

Physical Education:
*Mrs S J Matthews, BEd
Miss V J Freeman, BSc
§Mrs J Land, CertEd
Miss E M Morris, BA(Ed)
Mrs P Penhale, CertEd
Mrs J Roberts, CertEd
§Mrs C J Whiting, BEd
Miss C Brotherhood, BA
Miss P Thomas, BSc

Outdoor Education Co-ordinator: Mrs S T Vincent, BEd

CLC Sports Centre
Manager: Mr P Turnbull, ILAM, RLSS

Religious Studies:
*Mr L Winkley, MA
§Mrs M Turner, BA
The Revd A D Barlow, MA
§Mrs V Gregory, BA
§Mrs G Grove, MA
Mrs M Pimenoff, MA

Science:
*Miss J R Adams, BSc

Biology:
*Mr R A C Turner, MA
Mrs A West, BSc
Mr J C Davies, BSc
Mrs F Dooley, BSc, MSc
Mrs R J Hope, MA
Mrs J A Martin, BSc, MA, CBiol, MIBiol
Miss C Poole, MA(Ed), BSc, CBiol, MIBiol
§Mrs A Thiselton, MA
Dr H K Laver, BSc, PhD

Chemistry:
*Dr Joan Flower, BSc
Mrs C W Bate, BSc
Miss J E Davies, BSc
Miss C J Kirk, BA
§Mrs J McAllister, BSc
Mrs A Millington, BSc

Physics:
*Miss J R Adams, BSc
Mrs V A Baxter, BSc
Mrs R Kaye, BSc
§Mrs J Knott, MSc, BSc
§Mrs J F Neale, MA, BSc
Mr W H Potts, MSc, BSc
Miss N Rouse, BEng

Higher Education Adviser: Mrs D Rowell, BA
Assistants: Mrs A West, BSc, Miss J S Tudge, BA, Mrs V A Baxter, BSc, Miss S M Jones, BSc, Mrs H Bradley, BA

Careers:
*Mr G Bott, BA, MSocSc
Mr R Raby, GMus
Mrs J Snell, L-ès-L

Counselling:
§Mrs M Westbrook
Mrs J Roberts

PSE & Combined Studies:
Miss T M L Black, CertEd, AGSM

Administrative Staff:
Administration Services Manager: Mrs J E Jones, CertEd
Principal's EA: Mrs S Turner, BA
Registrar: Mrs P Cochrane
Administrative Officer: Miss J E Craig, BSc, PGDip

Library: Mrs J M Johnstone (*Librarian/Archivist*)

Chairman of the Medical Committee & Consulting Physician: Dr P Roscoe, BSc (*Hons*), MB, ChB, FRCC (Edin)

House Doctors and Medical Inspection:
Dr D G Price, BSc, MB, BS, DCH
Dr Susan Court, BSc, MB, BS
Dr R Hyatt-Williams, MRCS, LRCP, LMCC, CSPQ
Dr Jean Thompson, MB, BS
Dr Sarah Youngs, MBCH, DROG, DFFP

The pattern of day-to-day life revolves around two centres which complement each other – the College teaching buildings and the Boarding and Day Girl Houses. College is divided into three divisions – Lower College for girls in years 7–9, Upper College for girls in years 10 and 11, and Sixth Form College. The latter normally contains about 300 girls and nearly all proceed to degree courses.

Admission. Girls normally enter the College between the ages of 11 and 13+, although older girls are accepted into the Sixth Form for Advanced Level studies.

Numbers. Day 220, Boarding 630.

Terms. The College year of 36 weeks is divided into three terms, beginning in September, January and April.

Fees. Day £3,525, Boarding £5,445 per term. Sixth Form Day £3,525; Boarding £5,445. Some extras, eg music, riding are charged.

Ethos. We seek to develop the talents of each girl and provide an environment in which girls can achieve the very highest standards in what they choose to do. Although a large school the units within it are small: there is a friendly, openness about College which makes it a very happy place to live and learn.

Pastoral Care. The systems of pastoral care are exceptionally good. Each girl is looked after by her Housemistress and a Tutor. All Tutors are full time members of the academic staff and will advise girls on matters relating to their academic work and progress, including university advice and applications. Sixth Form Housemistresses teach an academic subject. As well as members of staff each house employs 4 other adults to help look after the girls. The level of pastoral care is very high indeed.

Buildings. The main building is built in a Gothic revival style, and its interior decorations owe a great deal to the Arts and Crafts Movement. With three Libraries, 17 laboratories, 5 networked computer rooms, an Electronics workshop, Language laboratory, a new £4m Art Wing, and fully equipped careers and university advice library, the resources available to pupils are constantly kept up to date.

Houses. Farnley Lodge, Glenlee, St Austin's, St Helen's, St Margaret's, Sidney Lodge are junior boarding houses. Beale, Cambray, Elizabeth and St Hilda's are Sixth Form houses. Bayshill, Bellairs, Glengar and St Clare are Day Girl houses.

Music, Drama and Dance. 800 individual music

lessons take place each week, and there are generally five choirs and five orchestras running at any time. 450 girls have individual drama lessons in addition to the large number of productions put on each year. Dance and gymnastics are also available.

Sport. The main sports are hockey, lacrosse, netball, swimming, athletics but the College provides what girls enjoy and about 40 sports are offered, including rowing, cricket, soccer, squash, tennis and golf. The aim is to encourage girls to enjoy physical exercise and take up an interest which will last throughout their life. There is a large and superbly equipped sports centre and fitness suite. The College owns its own Riding Centre set in 1500 acres of beautiful countryside.

Health. Each house has its own doctor, and College has its own Medical Centre staffed 24 hours a day by fully qualified nurses. Full medical records are kept by the College and medical attention is always available in the Boarding Houses and in the College Medical Centre.

Scholarships and Bursaries. (*see* Entrance Scholarship section) A centenary scholarship of half the annual fees and up to 20 other scholarships, including Music and Art, are offered annually. There are leaving Scholarships for girls entering Universities.

Former Pupils, known as The Guild. There are 9,000 former pupils throughout the world, and they are a valued source of help to present girls, particularly in providing work-shadowing and careers advice.

Charitable status. The Cheltenham Ladies' College is a Registered Charity, number 311722. It exists to provide a high standard of education for girls.

City of London School for Girls

St Giles' Terrace Barbican London EC2Y 8BB
Tel: 020 7628 0841
Fax: 020 7638 3212
e-mail: info@clsg.org.uk
website: www.clsg.org.uk

Motto: *Domine Dirige Nos*

Staff:
***Headmistress:* Dr Y A Burne**, BA, PhD (London), FRSA

Deputy Headteachers:
Mr W A Douglas, BA Hons (Oxon)
Mrs H Kay, BSc Hons (Sheffield)

Head of Sixth Form (*Years 12 & 13*): Miss M J Gelling, BA Hons (Hull), FRGS
Head of Senior School (*Years 9, 10, 11*):Mrs P R Restan, BA Hons (Nottingham)
Head of Lower School (*Years 7 & 8*): Mrs F M Angel, BA Hons (Bournemouth)

Heads of Department:

English:
Mrs G Guest, BA (Otago, New Zealand), BA Hons (London)

Drama:
Mr S Morley, DipCCSD (Acting) Full Equity Member

Classical Languages:
Miss P Perkins, BA Hons (Durham) DipEd

Modern Languages:
Mrs S Chatterton, BA Hons (Bristol)

French:
Mr G Tyrrell, MA (Oxford Brookes)

German:
Mrs M Baack, BA Hons (Bristol)

Russian:
Mrs N Foreman, Moscow Pedagogical Institute

Spanish:
Mrs Y Jenner, BA Hons (London)

Geography:
Mrs E A Wren, BA Hons (Liverpool), FRGS

History:
Mr B Burnham, MA Hons (Aberdeen), MLitt (Oxon)

Religious Education:
Miss B K Kelly, BA Hons (Durham) (*and Head of PHSE*)

History of Art:
Mrs D M B B Southern, MA (Edinburgh)

Economics/Politics:
Mr A C Genillard, BSc Hons (Brighton)

Mathematics:
Mr R Hale, BSc (Liverpool), MA (London)

Science:
Mrs D Barry, BSc Hons (London), MA (Institute of Education, London)

Chemistry:
Mr M J Tyler, CChem, MRCS (*Chemistry*)

Physics:
Ms E Starck, BEng Hons (Sussex)

Biology:
Dr S J Goddard, BSc Hons (Leeds), PhD (Leicester), FLS, FLZ

Art:
Miss J Curtis, BA Hons (London, St Martin's School of Art), ATC (London)

Technology:
Mr T J Collins, BSc Hons (Loughborough)

Music:
Mrs M Donnelly, BEd Hons (London) (*Director of Music*)

Physical Education:
Mrs A MacLean, CertEd (Dartford)

Careers:
Mrs C E Lipman, BA Hons (Manchester)

Preparatory Department:
Mrs C Thomas, BA (Open University), CertEd

Bursar: Colonel E L Yorke

Headmistress's Secretary: Miss L Clarke

Admissions Secretary: Mrs V S Sampson

School Doctor: Dr D Soldi, MB, ChB, DCH

School Sister: Mrs S J O'Hea, SRN

This School was established by the Corporation of London, in conformity with the wishes of the late William Ward, as expressed in his Will, dated 3 June 1881, namely: 'That the School shall correspond, as near as may be, to "The City of London School", now belonging to and managed by the Mayor and Commonalty and Citizens as a place of education of boys and making all proper allowances for the difference of the sexes' shall provide for 'the religious and virtuous education of girls, and for instructing them in the higher branches of literature and all other useful learning'.

The School Course includes English Language and Literature, History, Geography, Religious Studies, Latin, Greek, French, German, Spanish, Russian, Italian, Mathematics, Biology, Chemistry, Physics, Economics and Politics, Art, Music, Singing, Technology, Physical Education, Classical Civilisation, Design Technology, History of Art and Theatre Studies.

Pupils are prepared for the General Certificate of Secondary Education and for Advanced Supplementary and A2 Level Examinations offered by EDEXCEL, OCR and AQA. They are also prepared for Entrance to Oxford, Cambridge and other Universities. The VIth Form courses are designed to meet the needs of girls wishing to proceed to other forms of specialised training.

Girls are admitted at 7 and 11 years of age, and to the VIth Form: for girls over 11 years old, vacancies are only occasional. The entrance examination for 7 and 11 for admission in September, will usually be held in the Spring Term. Admission to the Sixth Form is also by written examination and interview.

Applications for 11+ should reach the Admissions Secretary by the previous 1st December and for 16+ by the end of October.

The School Tuition Fees, are: (1) Preparatory Department, £2,592 per term including lunch; (2) Main School, £2,592 per term excluding lunch.

The Extra Subjects include Pianoforte, Violin, Cello, Flute, Clarinet, Organ, Guitar, £141 each a term; and group instruction in Guitar, £72 a term (fees all payable in advance). Special arrangements are made on request for tuition in other instruments.

Cafeteria lunches at £141 per term are available to the Main School. Pupils in the Preparatory Department are expected to take school lunch for which there is no extra charge. After school supervision is also available at £100 per term until 6 pm.

Facilities are provided for outdoor and indoor games and the School has its own indoor Swimming Pool. Extra curricular activities in the lunch hour or at the end of afternoon school include Debating, Football, Drama, European Society, Technology, Fencing, Netball, Gymnastics, Swimming and Tennis. Guest speakers are frequently invited to meetings of Societies. There are also Junior and Senior Choirs, a Madrigal group, First and Second Orchestras, a Wind Ensemble, a Chamber Orchestra and a Swing Band. Lunch hour music recitals, with visiting professional players, are encouraged. Many girls take the Duke of Edinburgh Award Scheme at bronze, silver and gold.

Scholarships tenable at the School. The School has a variety of generous academic, art and music scholarships for entry at both 7+ and 11+ and is fortunate in receiving generous support from many Livery Companies and the Corporation of The City of London in this regard. Scholarships are also awarded at 16+ for entry to the Sixth Form.

Further details of the awards available may be obtained from the Admissions Secretary at the school. Bursaries are awarded on entry at 11 and 16 to those in financial need. As part of the Ogden Trust the school will offer two girls, in 2002, full bursaries. A Centenary Scholarship is also available offering up to full fees for an outstanding candidate needing financial support.

* Head of Department	§ Part Time or Visiting
† Housemaster/Housemistress	¶ Old Pupil
‡ See below list of staff for meaning	

Clifton High School

College Road Clifton Bristol BS8 3JD
Tel: (0117) 973 0201 (Upper School); (0117) 973 8096 (Lower School); (0117) 973 3853 (Bursar)
Fax: (0117) 923 8962
e-mail: admissions@chs.bristol.sch.uk
website: www.chs.bristol.sch.uk

Clifton High School, founded in 1877, is an independent school offering a first-class education to girls and boys in the Lower School (3-11) and girls only in the Upper School (11-18). Family boarders are accepted in the Sixth Form from the age of 16 years.

Governing Body (*School Council*):

President: Dr R Gliddon, BSc, PhD
Vice-President: Mrs V H W Stevenson

Mr D A G Bayliss
Mr G K Cairns, FCA
Mr J Curran, OBE, FCA
Ms K Das, LLB
Mr F W Greenacre, BA, FMA
Mr S C Hegarty, LLB
Mrs J M Huckman, MCSP, SRP
The Revd Canon P F J Johnson
Dr S E Lloyd, BEd, PhD
Mr W G Mather, MA, FIA
Mr A C Morris, MA, FCA, FSS, FRSA
Prof B Sandhu, MBBS, MRCP, MD
Miss L A Seager, MBA, BA
Mr H Stebbing, BSc, FRICS, FBIFM, FRSA, FICPD
Mr A L Stevenson, FCA
Mrs G L Wynick, RGN, DipN

Headmistress: **Mrs Colette Culligan**, MEd (Bristol), PGCE

Head of Upper School and Sixth Form: Dr A M Neill, PhD (UCW Aberystwyth), PGCE

Head of Lower School: Mr A J Richards, MBE, BSocSc Hons (Birmingham), PGCE

Upper School Staff:

Deputy Head: Mrs E A Anderson, BSc Hons (Nottingham), PGCE

Senior Teachers:
Mrs C Campion-Smith, MA (Cantab), PGCE
Dr G Hallett, PhD (Durham), MRSC, CChem

Art & Design:
*Mrs J Wolf, BA (OU), CertEd (Homerton College, Cambridge)
Miss S Duncan, BA Hons (Bristol), PGCE, DipExtStudies *also Key Skills Coordinator*

Business Studies:
Mr P G Jackson, BA (University of Westminster), PGCE *also Information Technology*

Careers:
*Mrs L M Broomsgrove, BSc (Exeter) *also Science & Mathematics*

Classics:
*Mrs B Bell, BA Hons (London), PGCE
Mrs A Foakes, BA Hons (Leicester), PGCE
Mrs A Tyler, BA Hons (Cardiff), PGCE

Design & Technology:
Mrs H D Brain, CertEd (Elizabeth Gaskell College, Manchester)
Mrs L Short, BA (University of West of England)

Drama:
*Mrs G Malpass, BA Hons (London), PGCE *also Theatre Studies*
Mrs S Swallow, MA Hons (Edinburgh), PGCE *also Theatre Studies and English*

English:
*Mr T C Beddow, MA (London), PGCE
Mrs M C Culligan, MEd, PGCE
Mrs S P Hosty, MA (Kingston), DipTEFL *also SENCO*
Mrs J P Pritchard, BA Hons (Exeter), PGCE *also Drama*

Geography:
*Mrs S Leafe, BSc Hons (Bristol), PGCE
Mr R Heath, BSc (UCL), PGCE *also Diploma of Achievement*

Government & Politics:
*Mrs K Barker, MSc (Bristol), BA Hons (Bristol), PGCE, DipInfTech, DipSocAdmin *also History and Head of Library*

History:
*Mrs V Edwards, BA Hons (East Anglia), PGCE *also PSE*

Home Economics:
*Mrs H M Davies, CertEd (Ilkley College of Education)

Information Technology:
*Mr G A A Taylor, BA Hons (York), PGCE
Mr R Hardie, BA Hons, QTS (University of West of England)

Mathematics:
*Miss B Norman, BSc Hons
Mrs C Campion-Smith, MA (Cantab), PGCE
Mrs E A Anderson, BSc Hons (Nottingham), PGCE
Mrs M Higgins, MA (Oxon) *also PSE*
Mrs K Packer, BSc Joint Hons (Newcastle), PGCE

Modern Languages:
*Dr E M Dand, PhD(Bristol), PGCE *Head of Modern Languages/French*
Mrs B Charlton, Licenciatura Filologia (Barcelona) *Spanish*
Mrs J Evans, BA Hons (Lancaster), PGCE *French*
Mrs A Ferragut, BA (Kingston on Thames College of Technology), PGCE *French and Spanish*
Mrs A Holloway, BA (Oxon), PGCE *German*
Mrs P M Winter, BA (Durham), PGCE *French*

Assistants:
Mme C Bouyer Chapman *French*
Miss B Iglesias *Spanish*
Miss C Stoecker *German*

Music:
*Mr J F Palmer, BA Hons (Reading), ARCM, PGCE *Director of Music*
Mrs D A Shippobotham, DipEd, DipMus (Wales) *also PSE*

Physical Education:
*Miss K Price, BEd Hons (Sussex Chelsea College of PE)
Mrs D J Kingston, BEd Hons (Cambridge Bedford College of PE)
Mrs V Williams, CertEd, DipPE (Bristol)
Mrs J Winn, CertEd (Cambridge Bedford College of PE)
Miss E Young, BEd Hons (Greenwich)

Personal & Social Education:
*Mrs A Crossley, BEd Hons, MA (London) *also Government & Politics, Classical Civilisation and French*

Religious Studies:
*Revd Z M Helliwell, BD (London), ALBC, ALCM, PGCE
Mrs J Awolola-Hill, BEd, CertEd (Birmingham)

Science:
*Mrs H M Webster, BSc Hons (Bristol), DipEdBiol *Head of Science, Biology*
*Dr G Hallett, PhD (Durham), MRSC, CChem *Chemistry*
*Mr Z Dif, BSc, PGCE *Physics*
Mrs J Heckford, BSc Hons (Bristol), PGCE *Biology*
Mr T Hilton, BSc (Loughborough), DipIS *Chemistry*
Dr A M Neill, PhD (UCW Aberystwyth), PGCE *Biology*)
Mr M Welton, MSc (Exeter), PGCE *Physics*

Lower School Staff:

Deputy Head of Lower School: Mrs J Denham, BEd Hons (South Glamorgan Inst of Higher Education)
Head of Preparatory Department: Mrs M A Valitis, CertEd (St Mary's Training College, Newcastle)
Head of Nursery Department: Mrs F J Mather, CertEd (Homerton College, Cambridge), CertAPS

Junior Department:

Miss E Beveridge, BA Hons (Leicester), PGCE
Mrs A Dobson, BA, ALA *Librarian*
Mrs A Fowler, MSc (Aston), BSc Hons (Bristol), PGCE, ALCM
Mr T George, BSc Hons (University of West of England)
Miss J M Hayton, BEd (Nottingham), CertEd (Bishop Grosseteste, Lincoln)
Miss S Hill, BEd Hons (University of West of England)
Mrs A M Holland, BEd Hons (Homerton College Cambridge)
Mrs J Knott, BEd (Bristol)
Mrs S Lloyd, BEd (UWE), CertCouns (*Learning Support*)
Mr A Lucas, BA Hons (University of West of England), PGCE
Mrs S Murphy, BA Hons (Bristol), PGCE
Mr D J E Pye, BA Hons (West London Inst of Higher Education), PGCE
Mrs J J Williams, CertEd (Sheffield College of Education)
Miss S Williams, BSc Hons (Bristol), PGCE (Queen's, Belfast)

Preparatory Department:
Miss R S Clay, CertEd (Crewe & Alsager College)
Mrs E Hales, BSc Hons (Reading), PGCE
Mrs K G M Harrold, BA Hons (Southampton), PGCE
Mrs S J Jones, BA (Bristol), PGCE
Mrs M Moggridge, CertEd (Redland College, Bristol)
Mrs J Nangia, CertEd (Northumberland College of Education)
Miss H Phillips, BEd Hons (Winchester)
Mrs A K Roberts, BSc Hons (Southampton), PGCE
Miss J Sayers, CertEd (Homerton College, Cambridge)

Nursery Department:
Mrs T Arthurs, CertEd (Lady Spencer Churchill College, Oxford)
Mrs E A Osborne, BEd (Bath College of Higher Education)

Classroom Assistants:

Junior Department: Mrs S Furneaux

Preparatory Department:
Mrs L Banfield, NNEB
Mrs G Lambert
Mrs F Perkins
Mrs V Stanley, CertEd
Mrs B Williams, NNEB

Nursery Department:
Mrs G Brown
Mrs A Godshaw, NNEB
Mrs E Park, PPA
Mrs A Trembath, NNEB

Visiting Staff:

Mr D Ashby, ARCM, FLCM, LRAM *Flute*

Miss M Baker, GTCL, LRAM, ALCM *Clarinet*
Miss C Black, BA, ALCM *Violin*
Mrs R Carpenter, BMus *Piano*
Mrs M Chave, LTCL *Piano*
Ms D Dixon, LRSM *Violin*
Mrs N Gittings, ARCM, DipRCM *Violin, Junior Orchestra*
Mr P Gittings, ARM, DipRCM *Oboe*
Miss C Glover *Singing*
Mr S Gore *Drums*
Miss S Grundy, BA, LRSM *Flute*
Mr D Hobourn, GTCL, FTCL, ARCO *Piano*
Miss C Johnstone, BA, DipNCOS *Cello*
Mrs D Lee *Bassoon*
Mr G Lewis, LTCL *Brass*
Mrs C M Moule, CertPerfTCL *Clarinet/Saxophone/Keyboard*
Miss J Norman *Singing*
Mr S Robshaw *Contemporary Guitar*
Mrs V Shelton, LRAM, LTCL, ATCL *Piano*
Mrs J Sidgreaves, GRSM, ARCM *Violin and Viola*
Mrs H Vale, LRAM, ARCM *Piano*
Mrs L Worley, LRSM *Singing*

Speech & Drama: Mrs L Barnes, ALAM

Tennis: Mr V Reed

Bursarial Office:
Bursar: Mr R Smith
Domestic Bursar: Mr E Gardener
Fee Administrator: Mrs T Gajewski, BA Hons (OU)
Payroll Administrator: Miss M Burton
Bought Ledger Administrator: Mr A Wilford

Headmistress' Office:
PA to Headmistress: Mrs J Howard-Brown
Admissions Secretary: Mrs H Thomas
Assistant to Headmistress' PA: Mrs V Houlford

Upper School:
Secretary to the Head of Upper School & Sixth Form: Mrs T J Scales

School Office:
Receptionist: Mrs N L Cross
Database Administrator: Mrs C Smith

Lower School Office:
Secretary to Head of Lower School: Mrs E J Hill
Secretarial Assistant: Mrs M Coles

Matrons:
Mrs A Skeen, RGN
Mrs S Clifton, RGN

Technicians:
Mrs G Brewer, FIMLS *Science*
Mr A Wilkes *Science*
Mr G Litjens, BA Hons (OU), PGCE *Information Technology*

Catering Manager: Mr R Kellaway

Maintenance Staff:
Mr P Holmes (*Head Caterer*)
Mr G Hooper
Mr M Hewitt

Aims. The school aims to provide each pupil with an excellent education in a wide range of subjects in a happy, secure and stimulating environment. Individual talents and interests are fostered and a broad spectrum of extra-curricular pursuits offered, with particular emphasis on sporting and practical activities. Emphasis is placed on self-discipline, courtesy and consideration for others, good moral values and attitudes and the development of self-confidence, self-reliance and initiative.

Organisation and facilities. The school occupies a splendid site in Clifton, near the Downs and Suspension Bridge. It is organised in two sections: The Upper School for girls from 11 to 18 (340 pupils) and the Lower School for girls and boys from 3 to 11 incorporating Nursery (40 pupils), Preparatory (120 pupils) and Junior (220 pupils)

Departments.

The Lower School shares many Upper School facilities but maintains its own identity, with each of the three individual departments housed in its own spacious Regency building. The facilities and accommodation are first class including recently refurbished Science Centre with 7 laboratories, well stocked libraries and ICT resources rooms, Sixth Form Centre and a complex for the creative arts. Sports facilities include a heated 25m indoor swimming pool, gymnasium and floodlit netball courts on site, together with a new partnership with Bristol University including an indoor tennis centre (4 courts) and 2 artificial turf hockey pitches.

Curriculum. The Lower School offers an excellent academic, social and moral foundation.

The Nursery, in its secure atmosphere, encourages learning through imaginative play, art and craft, cookery, percussion, singing, woodwork and gym, leading to pre-reading and early writing skills.

The Preparatory Department, working in an informal atmosphere within a structured framework, focuses on high standards of literacy and numeracy, stimulating the children's minds through creative work and challenging projects. The curriculum includes ICT, Science, History, Geography, Drama, Art, Music, PE, Swimming and Games.

The Junior Department. Children are given a strong grounding in English, Mathematics, Science, ICT, History, Geography, Music, Art, Drama, Design Technology, Religious Studies, Gymnastics and Games (Netball, Hockey, Rugby, Football, Tennis, Cricket and Athletics).

French, Latin and Swimming are taught throughout the Junior Department by specialist teachers from the Upper School. A wide range of extra-curricular activities are on offer including Chamber Choir and Orchestra, ICT, Speech and Drama, fencing, craft and an array of sports clubs.

Outdoor pursuits take place at weekends and include canoeing, abseiling, caving, archery and orienteering. Regular visits to the local area and overnight stays take place throughout the year. Children in the Junior School also have the opportunity to go on an annual ski trip.

Upper School. Throughout the Upper School, girls have a personal tutor who monitors their academic and social welfare. In Years 7 to 9 all girls study a broad and balanced curriculum, subjects include English, Mathematics, Physics, Chemistry, Biology, ICT, History, Geography, Religious Studies, one or two modern languages (French, German, Spanish), Latin/Classical Studies (with opportunity to study Greek from Year 9), Drama, Music, Art & Design, Technology (Textiles, Resistant Materials and Food), Physical Education and Personal and Social Education (PSE). In Years 10 and 11, Physical Education and PSE form part of the general programme. For study at GCSE there is a common and balanced core of English, Mathematics, Science (Double Award or three separate sciences), a modern foreign language and ICT (Short Course), in addition to which girls may select subjects based on their interests and career plans.

Sixth Form. The Sixth Form is a thriving centre of excellence within the school, the students playing an important part in the whole school community, developing their leadership skills with the younger pupils. Students have a free choice from 25 Advanced Level subjects including all those offered at GCSE level as well as Government & Politics, Theatre Studies, Business Studies, Economics, Sport Studies and Further Mathematics. Almost all go on to university, the most able being encouraged to apply for Oxbridge entrance. All Sixth Form students take part in an Enrichment Programme designed to offer breadth and a range of experiences. Key Skills evidence can be accessed through this programme in addition to Advanced level studies.

Family boarding. Clifton High School offers a unique opportunity for Sixth Form students (especially those from overseas) to board, full-time or weekly, with families known to the school. The school Matron acts as liaison officer and oversees the welfare of both the students and the host family.

Physical Education. Pupils are encouraged to challenge themselves physically. In addition, to the school's traditional activities of hockey, netball, swimming, athletics, rounders, tennis and gymnastics (BAGA), specialist staff teach a wide variety of other activities including volleyball, basketball, soccer, cricket, aerobics and trampolining. Fencing and self-defence are optional. Pupils regularly gain county and national honours.

Music and Drama. Virtually any instrument, including voice, may be studied, with over 50% of pupils having individual lessons. Associated Board examinations are taken. There are opportunities to belong to orchestras, wind bands and choirs, performing in a variety of concerts and choir tours. In Speech and Drama, a large number of pupils enter LAMDA examinations. Each year there is both a Lower and Upper School major production, as well as numerous smaller ventures such as a House Drama Competition.

Social services and extra-curricular activities. Pupils have a strong sense of social responsibility and are actively involved, often in their House groups, in various local and national charity fundraising events, annual collection amount to several thousand pounds (£6,000 last year). There is a lively extra-curricular activities programme both in the Lower and Upper sections of the school, responding to pupils' interests. There are over 20 clubs currently running including Scottish Dancing, Pottery, Science, Debating and Public Speaking, Christian Union, and Mathematics. Girls regularly take part in the Duke of Edinburgh Award and Young Enterprise Schemes.

Admission and scholarships. Registration forms and further details are available from the Admissions Secretary. Entry to the Lower School is by informal assessment. Entry to the Upper School is dependent on the results of an entrance examination. Academic Scholarships are awarded each year at Year 7, Year 9 and at Sixth Form level, some school assisted places and John James scholarships (means tested) are available for girls entering at Year 7. Music scholarships are also available.

Fees. Full details are available from the school. Tuition fees per term range from £780 in the Nursery to £1,930 in the Upper School. In addition, family boarding fees per term are £1,405 (full boarding) and £970 (weekly boarding). Discounts are given for siblings currently in the school.

Charitable status. Clifton High School is a Registered Charity, number 311736. It exists to provide first-class education for pupils aged 3 to 18 years.

Cobham Hall

Cobham Nr Gravesend Kent DA12 3BL
Tel: (01474) 823371 (School)
Fax: (01474) 825902/825904/825906
e-mail: cobhamhall@aol.com
website: www.cobhamhall.com

Founded 1962.

Governing Body:
Miss C Cawston (*Chairman*)
The Earl of Darnley
Col P Davies, MBE, BA, FIMgt, DipEd
R P Mountford, Esq
C Sykes, Esq
Mrs A Travis
Mrs N Phillips
Mrs A T T Rottenburg
Mrs L Ellis
S Mole, OBE
Mrs C Balch
Ms P Bristow, BSc
Mrs M Griffin

Staff:
***Headmistress:* Mrs R J McCarthy**, BA (Leeds)

Deputy Headmistress: Dr S Coates-Smith, PhD (London), PGCE (Kent)

Senior Mistress: Mrs N D Laughland, BSc (Sheffield), PGCE (London)

English:
Dr J Payne, PhD (USA)
Mr A Pinchin, MA (Cantab)
Mrs C Tribe, BA, PGCE (Loughborough)

EFL:
Mrs C Kemsley, BA, HDip/DipTOEFL (Dublin)
Mrs Z Child, BA (Brno)

Susan Hampshire Dyslexia Centre:
Mrs C Ostler, CertEd (Bishop Otter), ATSBDA
Mrs H Long, BSc (Surrey), PGCE (Reading), CertSpLD

Mathematics:
Mrs S Vale, BSc, PGCE (Manchester)
Mrs M Martin, BSc (Loughborough)
Mrs W Barrett, BSc (London)

Chemistry:
Mrs N Laughland, BSc (Sheffield), PGCE (London)
Mr R Calladine, BSc (Bath), PGCE (London)

Physics:
Dr S Coates-Smith, PhD (London), PGCE (Kent)
Mrs W Barrett, BSc (London)
Mr R Calladine, BSc (Bath), PGCE (London)

Biology:
Dr P Smith, PhD (London)
Mrs S Miles, BSc (London)

Information and Communications Technology:
Mr J Hillman, BA, CertEd

Computer Technician:
Miss K Waller, MA (Canterbury)

History:
Miss M Parsons, BA (East Anglia)

Geography:
Mr J Long, BA (Natal)

French:
Miss E Negus, BA (Bristol)
Mrs A Smart, BA (Belfast)

Spanish:
Mr C Thorne, BA (Bristol)
Mrs A Smart, BA (Belfast)

German:
Mrs M Bromham, CertEd, TEFL (London)

Russian:
Mrs Z Child, BA (Brno)

Classics:
Mrs I Giles, MA (London)

Business Studies:
Mrs L Levett, MA (London)

Economics:
Mr A Pinchin, MA (Cantab)

Art and Design:
Mrs J Mason, MA, RCA, BA (London)
Mr B Blunden, NDD, DipEdCeramics (London)
Mrs K Walsh, BA (Hons), CertEd

Physical Education:
Miss C Hough, BEd (London), CertEd
Mrs M Martin, BSc (Loughborough)
Mr S Kitcher

Music:
Mrs D Wallace, BMus (London), LRAM, LTCL(Perf), LTCL(MusEd)
Mrs G Coppack, ALCM

Theatre & Drama Arts:
Mrs C Tenison-Smith, NCSD, DipEd, LUD (London)

PSRE Coordinator:
Mr A Pinchin, MA (Cantab)

Careers and Higher Education Adviser: Mrs L Levett, MA (London)

Librarian: Mrs M Digby

Housemistresses:
Mrs M Ackers, DipPE (Chelsea)
Miss D Pretty
Mrs L Levett, MA (London)
Mrs C Ostler, CertEd (Bishop Otter), ATSBDA

Sanatorium:
Nurse V Dyke, SEN
Nurse J Kember, SEN
Nurse G Powell, SEN

School Doctors: Meopham Surgery

Visiting Staff: There are visiting staff for Piano, Oboe, Violin, Viola, 'Cello, Double Bass, Flute, Guitar, Saxophone, Ballet, Tennis, Aerobics and Karate.

Administration:

Bursar: Mr N Powell, MIMgt, DipEng

Registrar: Mrs S Ferrers

Headmistress' PA: Mrs D Usher

Headmistress' Secretary: Mrs S Gilroy

Accounts Clerk: Mrs I Burton

Bursar's Secretary: Mrs B Taylor

Cobham Hall is an international boarding and day school for 200 girls aged between 11 and 18.

Situation. The School is set in 150 acres of parkland. Situated in North Kent close to the M25, adjacent to the M2/A2. Forty minutes from London, 55 minutes Heathrow, 40 minutes Gatwick, 60 minutes Dover. Escorted travel to and from airports can be arranged.

School Buildings. This beautiful 16th century historic house was the former home of the Earls of Darnley. There are many modern buildings providing comfortable accommodation for study and relaxation. Brooke and Bligh Houses are separate buildings, within the school's grounds, for the upper and lower Sixth forms. In Brooke House each girl has her own study bedroom, some with shower rooms en suite and in Bligh House the girls are accommodated in study bedrooms of up to three. Both Houses have a large common room with TV and video, a kitchen, payphones and computer room.

Admission. Admission is by the School's own entrance examination which can be taken at the annual Newcomers' Weekend in January or at a girl's own school. Girls normally enter the School between the ages of 11+ and 13+ and follow a course leading to GCSE level at the end of the fifth year and A Levels at the end of the seventh. Girls wishing to enter the Sixth Form should achieve at least five GCSE or equivalent examination passes at Grade C or above.

Scholarships. (*see* Entrance Scholarship section) Scholarships are available for 11+, 12+, 13+ and 16+ entry.

Curriculum. The School is a centre for the GCSE and A level examinations. It has well equipped science laboratories; Physics, Chemistry and Biology can be studied to university entrance besides Languages, Mathematics, and a wide range of Arts subjects. The average number of GCSE passes is 9. There is a course of General Studies for all girls in the Sixth Form, in addition to their A level studies. The range of subjects and specialist teaching is exceptional for a small school.

Reports are issued three times a year and parents are always welcome to come and discuss their daughter's progress.

Sporting and other activities. The School's main sports are Tennis, Swimming, Athletics and Netball. There are 7 hard tennis-courts, 6 netball courts, a large, indoor multi-sports complex, including dance studio and a heated indoor swimming pool, which is in use throughout the year. Horse riding may be taken as an 'extra', and a wide variety of extra-curricular activities is available.

Careers. A full-time Careers' Adviser provides Careers and Higher Education guidance within a comprehensive careers' programme. On average, 95% of the Sixth Form go on to university.

Round Square. The School is a member of this international group of schools, which acknowledge and practise the style of education developed by Kurt Hahn. Annual conferences are attended by a school delegation including sixth formers; in recent years these have been in Australia, America and Germany. Students have the opportunity to visit other member schools on an exchange programme as well as visit other countries by taking part in project and relief work organised by the Round Square International Service.

Health. There are resident trained nurses giving 24 hour medical care. The Sanatorium is regularly attended by the School Doctor.

All Terms. Girls have two Exeat Weekends and a Half Term holiday. There is escorted travel to and from London Victoria and the airports for younger girls.

Fees per term. Day girls: £2,950-£3,650. Boarders: £4,700-£5,400.

Old Girls' Association. Known as Elders, this is a flourishing organisation with a representative committee which meets regularly in London. Annual events include social gatherings in London and at the School. The Chairman is Sheila Buchanan.

Charitable status. Cobham Hall is a Registered Charity, number 313650. It exists to provide high quality education for girls aged 11–18 years at Cobham Hall.

Colston's Girls' School

Cheltenham Road Bristol BS6 5RD
Tel: (0117) 9424328
Fax: (0117) 9426933
e-mail: cgs.admin@btconnect.com

Motto: *Go and do thou likewise*

Colston's Girls' School was founded in 1891, through the generosity of the Society of Merchant Venturers. For over 100 years, generations of girls have received a broad, academic education which has enabled them to take their place in a modern and changing world.

The School occupies its original building in Cheltenham Road and its many modern additions include a Modern Languages and Music Centre, a well-equipped Sports Hall, newly refurbished libraries, Wolfson laboratory and Geography rooms. There are also specialist rooms for teaching information technology and design/technology and an Apple Macintosh and PC networks.

Governing Body:

Chairman: Mr R M McKinlay, CBE, FEng, HonDTec, BSc, ARTC, FRAes

Vice-Chairman: Mrs G E Woolley, BSc, DipEd

Professor R Bailey-Harris
Mr A R E Brown, MA
Miss A Dixon, BSc, MEd, FIBiol
Mrs C B Evans, BSc
Mrs G Hebblethwaite, MBE
Mr C R T Laws
Mrs S Lucas
Mr G A Matthews, BA Hons
Mr J J D McArthur, BA Hons
Mr D M Parkes
Brigadier H W K Pye
Mr T Smallwood
Mrs J Wade, MSc, FIMgt
Mrs C Webb, MSc

Clerk to the Governors: Mrs W Wetton, BA Hons (Open University)

***Head Mistress:* Mrs Judith Franklin**, BA Hons (Wales)

Deputy Head Mistress: Miss Anne Hughes, BA Hons (Dunelm)

Chaplain: The Rev Ray Brazier

Faculty of Creative and Aesthetic subjects:

Miss M Viney, BA Hons (Wales) (*Head of Faculty*)
Mrs V Ford, CertPE (Bedford)
Miss D Fretten, BA Hons (University of The West of England)
Miss A Hughes, BA Hons (Dunelm)
Mrs S Johnson, DipPE (Dublin College of PE)
Mrs K Kigwana, DipAD (Bath Academy of Art)
Mrs D Lee, MA (Cantab)
Mr A Mackenzie, GRNCM
Mrs L M A Nunn, Dip Art & Science of Movement (Nonnington College)
Mrs J E Rossiter, BSc Hons (Surrey)
Miss J Simmons, BA Hons (Exeter)

Faculty of English:

Mrs A J Boyce, BA Hons (Wales) (*Head of Faculty*)
Mr A Coveney, MA (Cantab)
Mrs J P Franklin, BA Hons (Wales)
Mrs J J Geyl, BA (University of New South Wales) (*Director of Studies*)
Mrs J Hook, BA Hons (Bristol)
Mrs J Steer, BA Hons (Toronto)

Faculty of Humanities:

Mr R J Wilkinson, MA (Cantab) (*Head of Faculty*)
Miss D M Ace, BA Hons (Wales)
Mr P G Barker, BSc Hons (Bristol)
Mr G B Butcher, MA (Oxon)
Mrs A Greenslade, BSc Econ Hons (London) (*Examinations Secretary*)
Mrs G Halliday, MA (Cantab), MA (Oxon)
Mr A Perry, BA Hons (London)
Mrs R A Robinson, BEd Hons (Bristol)
Mrs R J Routledge, BSc Hons (Sheffield)

Faculty of Mathematics:

Miss A Taylor, BSc Hons (Reading) (*Head of Faculty; Head of Upper School*)
Mr P Cooksey, BA Hons (Exeter)
Mrs J J Duncan, BA (Open University) (*Head of Lower School*)
Mrs C Jones, BEd Hons (St Paul's & St Mary's, Cheltenham)
Mrs M Parsons, BSc Hons (Bristol)

Faculty of Modern Languages:

Miss V M Kies, BA Hons (Warwick), L-ès-L, M-ès-L, DEA (France) (*Head of Faculty*
Mrs A Chapman, BA Hons (Birmingham)
Mrs C Davenport, BA Hons (Bristol)
Miss H Hinksman, BA Hons (Birmingham) (*Head of Careers*)
Mrs G Opstad, MA (Oxon)
Mrs M Smith, BA Hons (Bristol) (*Head of Sixth Form*)
Miss R Smith, BA Hons (Dunelm)

Faculty of Science:

Dr M W Tideswell, PhD (London) (*Head of Faculty*)
Mrs P Colman, BSc Hons (Wales)
Mrs P Lenney, BSc Hons (Leeds)
Mr W P B Moggridge, BSc Hons (Hull)
Mrs E P Perry, BSc (London)
Mrs L Webber, MA (Cantab)

Visiting Music Staff:

Mr P Anstey (*Double Bass*)
Mr T Clarke, MA (*Guitar*)
Mrs D Cresswell, BA, PPRNCM (*Voice*)
Dr K Cullen (*Recorder*)
Mrs J Francis, GRSM, ARCM (*Cello*)
Mr B Hewlett (*Harmonica*)
Mrs A Howell, BMus, FRCO, LGSM (*Piano*)
Mr D Kenna, ALCM, ABRSM (*Piano, Jazz Piano*)
Miss K Latham, ARCM, LRAM (*Violin*)
Mr D Lawrence (*Brass*)
Mrs D Lee, MA (Cantab) (*Bassoon*)
Miss E Palmer, ARCM (*Woodwind*)
Miss R Skinner (*Voice*)
Mr M Thomas, LGSM, LLCM (*Flute*)
Mr B Waghorn (*Clarinet, Saxophone*)
Miss A White, BMus Hons (*Viola*)
Miss C White (*Percussion*)

Technical Support Staff:

Mr P Britten, BA Hons (Open University)
Mrs G Miller, BSc Hons (Open University)
Mrs P Prewett
Mrs C Saunderson, BA Hons (Open University)

Librarian: Mrs A Richardson, BA Hons (Open University)

Administrative Staff:

Head Mistress' Secretary: Mrs W Wetton, BA Hons (Open University)
School Secretary: Mrs B Allen
Accounts Office: Mrs B Singleton, Mrs A Cottrell, Miss J Parry
Receptionist: Mrs S Andrews

Admission. There are about 460 girls in the School, aged from 10 to 18 years including a sixth form of 100. Admission at the age of 10 or 11 depends on the result of an entrance examination and interview held each spring for the following September, although girls may be admitted further up the School subject to test, interview and satisfactory school reports.

The School has participated in the Government Assisted Place Scheme but now may award some School Assisted

Places. A few bursaries are also available for girls in senior forms who find themselves in need of financial assistance to continue with the school course. These bursaries have been made possible through the generosity of benefactors, past pupils, staff and parents, and their value depends on parental income.

Sixth Form. The sixth form plays a vitally important role in life of the school. The girls are treated as young adults, have their own Common Room and other privileges. Pupils are prepared for university, colleges of higher education and for entry into the professions. Girls in the Sixth Form compete very succesfully in the Young Enterprise Scheme. The school is now a Young Enterprise Registered Centre.

Curriculum. We aim to provide stimulating and exciting learning environments to encourage all pupils to progress, providing a balance between encouraging the individual talents of girls and enabling them to work in harmony with one another. We aim to help each girl to lead as full and as satisfying an adult life as possible and this necessarily includes preparation for a career. The school offers all subjects in the National Curriculum and in addition subjects which enrich and extend the girls' academic experience, such as Latin and a second Modern Language. In being given specialist teaching from the first year girls can benefit from the enthusiasm of their teachers for their subjects

Teachers of the first year cooperate in many ways, building links between subjects, with the aim of integrating girls into an environment which seems to them very different from their junior school. Individual disciplines, however, remain paramount. Later, the disciplines are strongly specialist, and the school has many teachers who are active in their own subject outside school.

All girls take nine or ten GCSE courses chosen to maximise sixth form, and hence options career choice. The School's Head of Careers is always available for advice and discussion.

GCSE subjects include: English Language, English Literature, History, Geography, Religious Studies, French, German, Spanish, Russian, Latin, Mathematics, Double Science, Art, Music, Food, Technology and Physical Education.

Advanced level subjects in the sixth form include: English, History, Geography, Business Studies, Religious Studies, French, German, Spanish, Russian, Latin, Classical Civilisation, Chemistry, Biology, Physics, Art, ICT, Geology, Music, Food and Nutrition, Design Technology, Theatre Studies, Sports Studies, Psychology.

All girls take an additional RSA qualifications in Information Technology. Some additional GCSE courses are available. A certificated course in Japanese is also offered. Gymnastics, Dance, Swimming, Hockey, Netball, Tennis, and Athletics are included in the curriculum for all girls, with clubs or teams in all these activities. After the first four years, girls have a wider choice of physical recreation which includes Badminton, Squash, Aerobics and Tone-Zone.

The tradition of music is very strong with over fifteen performing groups, and drama productions are a regular feature of school life.

Scholarships and Assisted Places. (*see* Entrance Scholarship section) At 11+ Assisted Places are available and academic scholarships, endowed by the Society of Merchant Venturers and The John James Educational Trust. Music Exhibitions are also available.

Scholarships are available for sixth form study which may amount to £1,500 for the two year Advanced level course. The competition for these is held in the Spring term and is open to girls already in the school and to those intending to enter in the following September. Details of the Wolfson, Jenner and Bathurst Scholarships, and other information on sixth form studies, is contained in a separate booklet, available from the school.

Fees. The fees are £1,610 per term and for the 10+ preparatory form £1,085 per term and are payable termly and in advance. They cover the regular curriculum including associated school visits, school books, stationery, medical inspections and fees for such public examinations as are taken on the advice of the Head Mistress.

The Colston's Girls' School Old Girls' Society. Mrs R Trowbridge, c/o Colston's Girls' School.

Charitable status. Colston's Girls' School is a Registered Charity, number 1079551. It has existed since 1891 to provide an education for girls.

Combe Bank School

Sundridge Sevenoaks Kent TN14 6AE
Tel: (01959) 563720/564320/562918
Fax: (01959) 561997

Council of Management:
Chairman: J B Sullivan, Esq

Mrs E Allibone
Mrs S Arnott
Mrs D Basden-Smith
Mrs J Branson
K T Coles, Esq
C G Court, Esq
P Evans, Esq
Father R Harvey
R I Lynam, Esq
R McVean, Esq
Mrs D Mills
D Nichols, Esq
R Partridge, Esq
S Prebble, Esq

Bursar: Hugh V C Phillips, MIPD, MIMgt

Senior School Staff:

***Headmistress:* Mrs R Martin**, MEd, NPQH

Deputy Head: Mrs J Bateman, TCert

Senior Mistress: Mrs E Bird, BSc, CertEd *Head of Geography*

Heads of Departments:
Mrs L N Ah-Sun, L ès L CAP *Languages*
Miss P J Anderson, BSc *Biology*
Mrs J Bateman, TCert *Head of Mathematics*
Mr M Broderick, BSc Hons, MSc, PGCE *Science*
Miss M Carter, CertEd *History*
Miss J Davis, BEd *PE*
Mrs J Dixon, BEd, MA *Business Studies*
Mrs K Harris, BA, PGCE, CTC(Merit) *English*
Mrs B Hooper, DipEd
Mrs M Howard, BA, TCert *Chemistry*
Mrs A Jagelman, CertEd *Home Economics, Textiles & Biology*
Mrs M Martin, LGSM, NEA *Drama and Theatre Studies*
Mrs J Redpath-Johns, BA, PGCE *Joint Head of Art*
Miss G Roberts, GRSM Hons (London) *Music*
Mrs M Southgate, BA Hons, PGCE *Religious Studies*
Mrs L Tunstall *Joint Head of Art*
Mrs E B Wynes, CertEd *Office Management*

Headmistress of the Preparatory School: Mrs R Cranfield, TCert, Froebel

Deputy Head: Mrs E Dale, CertEd (Homerton College, Cambridge)

School Chaplain: Father Duncan Lourenz

Combe Bank is an independent day school for girls. Founded in 1868 by the Society of the Holy Child Jesus, in 1972 the Combe Bank Educational Trust was established to administer the schools. As a Roman Catholic Foundation the School aims to provide a Christian education for girls of all denominations and to encourage each girl to develop her individual talents to the full.

The School occupies beautiful buildings including some designed by Roger Morris in 1720 and a Library decorated by Walter Crane. It is set in 27 acres of parkland. There is a school chapel in which voluntary Mass and Holy Communion are celebrated. There are 400 girls, equally divided between the schools.

Entrance is by interview and assessment to Preparatory School from 3–11, to Senior School at 11+ by School's examination, at 13+ by CE, School's examination or assessment, and 16+ by interview and 6 GCSE grades A–C for 3 A Levels.

Entrance Scholarships. (*see* Entrance Scholarship section) Up to seven scholarships are awarded worth up to 50% of tuition fees at 11+.

Sixth Form Scholarships. Up to two scholarships worth half day fees.

Fees (2001/2002). Senior School £2,460 day, Prep School from £1,100–£2,775 per term.

Curriculum. Girls are prepared for GCSE Examination Groups and A Levels and GNVQs, and in the Sixth Form for University Entrance, also for qualifications of the Royal Society of Arts. The Examinations of the Associated Board are taken in Music and of the Guildhall in Speech and Drama. As well as the usual subjects girls study Home Economics, Information Systems, Business Studies, Music, Drama, German and Spanish. In the Sixth Form they may study Sociology and Business Studies as well as the usual A Levels, some AS Levels, GNVQ level 2 and 3 in Health and Social Care, Leisure and Tourism, typing, office practice, shorthand, word processing. Dyslexic girls are accepted subject to receiving special help provided in school by qualified teachers.

Games. Winter games are hockey, netball, cross country running and uni-hoc, and summer games are tennis, rounders and athletics. Swimming all year round (indoor pool). Girls also take part in gymnastics, badminton, volleyball, table tennis, trampolining, judo and dancing.

Pastoral Care is mainly in the hands of Form Tutors. They are assisted by the Careers Mistress, Religious Studies Department and School Chaplain.

Charitable status. Combe Bank School Educational Trust Limited is a Registered Charity, number 1007871. The aim of the School is to provide a sound education for girls aged 3 to 18.

Cranford House School

Moulsford Wallingford Oxfordshire OX10 9HT
Tel: (01491) 651218

Members of the Board of Governors:
H M Thomas, Esq, MA (*Chairman*)
Mrs C G Bomford
Mrs P M Copestake
I Mavroleon, Esq
J B McBroom, Esq, BSc
Mrs S C Salvidant, BEd Hons
Mrs P Thomson

***Headmistress:* Mrs Alison B Gray**, BSc (St Andrews), PGCE (Edinburgh)

Deputy Head and Head of Junior School: Miss M Johnstone, CertEd (London)

Head of Senior School: Miss R Williams, BA Hons (Cardiff), PGCE (Institute of Education, London)

Head of Kindergarten: Mrs J Simmons, NNEB (Clifton)

Senior Teacher: Miss E Scoates, BSc Hons, MPhil (Reading), PGCE (Oxon)

Bursar and Clerk to the Governors: Mrs R J Huntington

Senior School Teaching Staff:
Mrs S Armitage, CertEd (London)
The Revd L Cook, MA Hons (Oxford)
Mr P Futcher, BMus, PGDip (Surrey), PGCE (Kent)
Mrs E H Goodall, BA Hons (Reading), DipEd (Oxford)
Mrs A B Gray, BSc (St Andrews), PGCE (Edinburgh
Mrs M Hancock, BSc Hons Physics (London), PGCE (Reading)
Mrs E Hoyle, BSc Hons (Bristol), MSc (Imperial), PGCE (Reading)
Mrs J P Jennings, BA Hons Modern Languages (Oxford), PGCE (Reading)
Mrs H Russell, BA Humanities (Open), CertEd Home Economics (Bristol)
Miss E A Scoates, BSc Geography, MPhil (Reading), PGCE (Oxford)
Mrs C Shaikh, CertEd (Oxford)
Mrs L Shepherd, CertEd (Cambridge)
Mme C Robichez, BA French and English (Sorborne)
Miss R Williams, BA Hons History (Cardiff), PGCE (Institute of Education, London)

Junior School Teaching Staff:
Mrs R Bickham, BA Hons (Oxon), PGCE (Oxford)
Mrs A J Cheeseman, BEd (London)
Mrs P A Conie, CertEd (Bristol)
Mrs E Gardner, BSc (Manchester), PGCE (Southampton)
Mrs R Gregory, CertEd (London)
Mrs L Hatch, CertEd (West Midlands)
Miss M Johnstone, CertEd (London)
Mrs J Lake, BA Hons (London), PGCE (Westminster College, Oxford)
Mrs S Maw, BEd Hons (Wales)
Mrs S McNaught, BEd Hons (Southampton)
Mrs H Osborn, CertEd (Hull)
Mrs F Weikert, CertEd (London)

Kindergarten Teaching Staff:
Mrs A Bateman, NVQ Level III in Child Care and Education
Mrs J Simmons, NNEB (Clifton)
Mrs N J Pearce, NNEB (North Tyneside)

Learning Support:
Mrs R Hall, CertEd (London), RSADip for Teachers of pupils with Specific Learning Difficulties
Mrs P Jackson, CertEd (Leeds)

Visiting Staff:
Mr C Bache *Saxophone and Clarinet*
Mr D Bache, AICM *Guitar*
Mr J Boughton, BA Hons, ALCM *Piano & Recorder*
Miss E Carter, ARCM *Singing*
Mrs E Holman, GRSM, LRAM, DipNCOS *Cello & Piano*
Miss A Pickering, LLCM(TD), ALCM *Flute*
Mrs M Thorns, BMus, CertEd, LRAM *'Cello and Piano*
Mr N Somerville, BA *Brass*
Miss S Warnes, GRSM, LRAM *Violin*
Mr W R Burnside, Int Judo CertEd, British Judo Blackbelt 5th Dan
Mr T Murrell, Part II LTA Coach (*Specialist Tennis Coaching*)

Administrative Staff:
Bursar: Mrs R J Huntington

Bursar's Assistant: Mrs E Hayward
School Secretary: Mrs A J Howell-Pryce
Headmistress's Secretary: Mrs S Colton
Admissions Secretary: Mrs C Isherwood

Ancillary Staff:
Kindergarten Assistant: Mrs P-A Mills
Classroom Assistants:
Mrs W Rant; Miss N Brown; Mrs E Sherston
Laboratory Technician: Mrs C Boucher

Cranford House is an independent day school for 265 pupils, girls aged 3–16 and boys 3–8.

Fees. £447–£2,050 per term.

In the Lower Junior School the emphasis is on the basic 3 R work with a gradual widening of horizons through the full range of of National Curriculum subjects. In the Senior School, every girl follows a course leading to GCSE, choosing ten out of sixteen subjects. Class music, speech and drama, art and technology lessons are included in the curriculum, while instrumental music, judo and riding are available as extras. There are both Junior and Senior Orchestras and Choirs and the Senior Choir tours abroad on a regular basis.

The school has extensive recreational and games fields. In winter, hockey and netball are played, the summmer sports are tennis, athletics and swimming in the school's heated outdoor swimming pool. Classes also have a weekly lesson of gymnastics and modern educational dance. Dramatic, musical and dance productions are an important aspect of school life.

School transport runs from Caversham and Henley and public service vehicles operate between Didcot and Moulsford via Wallingford and Reading and Moulsford via Pangbourne.

Our aim is to encourage pupils not only to achieve the best possible academic results but to become responsible and useful citizens, happy, and with a high degree of self esteem – adaptable and equipped for life in the new millennium.

Charitable status. Cranford House School Trust Limited is a Registered Charity, number 280883. It exists to provide a caring community which aims to strike a balance between traditional approach and the wider ranging demands of the National Curriculum.

Croham Hurst School

79 Croham Road South Croydon CR2 7YN
Tel: 020 8686 7347 (School); 020 8680 3064 (Head)
Fax: 020 8688 1142
e-mail: CrohamH@.aol.com

Independent Day School for Girls
Motto: *Finis Coronat Opus*

Members of the Council:

Chairman: Mr P Longfield, FCIB

Vice-Chairman: Mrs M E Carter-Pegg, NFF

Governors:
Mr J D Adams
Dr S Ali, MBBS, MRCP(UK)
Mrs F Bayliss, NFF
Mrs D Brent, BSc, FCA
Mr D A de Moraes
Mr H Duncan, BSc, MCIOB
Mr J Kidd, ACIB
Councillor M Mead
Mr M D Plater, FRICS, IRRV, MCIArb
Miss D C Raine, BSc, PGCE
Mr D F Simmonds, BA, ACMA
Mr M T W Turner

Staff:
***Head:* Miss S C Budgen**, BA (Exeter)

Deputy Head: Mrs S J Riley, BSc (Reading)

Senior School Staff:

Mr S Addis, BA (Bristol)
Mrs A Allan, MA (Edinburgh)
Mrs M Allan, MA (St Andrews)
Mrs A Barwell, BA (London)
Mrs S Blake, BA (Central St Martin's College, London)
Mrs M Bourne, CertEd (Avery Hill College of Education)
Mrs B Bradley, BEd (Avery Hill College of Education)
Mrs J Cadman, BA (OU)
Mrs S Cowley, BA (London)
Mrs L Farley, BA (Reading)
Mrs S Garcia, BEd (Ontario)
Mrs M Glass, L ès L (Nantes)
Mrs P Goodwin, CertEd (Dartford College of Ed)
Miss J Hammett, BSc, MSc (Imperial)
Mr I Harding, BA, MA (York)
Dr D Hardy, BSc (Newcastle), PhD (London)
Miss A Higeuras, BA (Jaen University, Spain)
Mr M Jenkins, BSc (Hull)
Mrs P Jenkinson, BEd (London)
Mr C Jones, BSc, FCollP (Leicester)
Mrs C King, BSc (Bristol)
Mrs A Lauer, CertEd (Seaford College of Education)
Mrs C Leak, CertEd (Cheshire County Training College)
Miss T Logan, BEd (Bedford College)
Mr R McCann, AdvDip (South Bank Polytechnic), TCert (De La Salle College, Manchester)
Mrs A McKinlay, BHum (London)
Mrs L Miller, BEd (Thames Polytechnic)
Mrs A O'Regan, Licence de Langues Modernes (Algiers)
Mrs S Paterson, MA (Edinburgh)
Mrs D Payne, BA (OU)
Mrs L Pearson, BA (OU)
Mrs S Peate, BA (Bristol)
Mrs E Poore, GRSM, MEd, LRAM
Miss J Redfern, BEd (Gloucester College of Education)
Mrs B Scott, MA (Glasgow)
Miss G Smith, BSc (London)
Mrs J Smith, BA (London)
Miss P Stone, GRCM, ARCM
Mrs A Trouncer, BA, MA (Oxford)
Mrs C Vigurs, BA (London)
Mr N Walker, BSc (St Andrews), MA (Manchester)
Mrs J Wright, BSc (Sussex)

The Junior Department "The Limes":
Head: Mrs L J Stringer, CertEd

Mrs J Atkinson, CertEd (Maria Grey College of Education), DipSpLD
Mrs W Bevan, BA (Portsmouth Polytechnic), PGCE (Roehampton)
Mrs E Bird, CertEd
Mrs I Cheshire, DPP
Mrs G Foster, CertEd (Froebel Institute)
Mrs M Irvine, BEd (Bristol)
Mrs B Lee, NNEB, Cert in Child Care & Education (Croydon College)
Miss P Lowe, BEd (Oxford Polytechnic)
Mrs S Mackenzie-Carmichael, CertEd (Bognor Regis College of Education)
Mrs S Macklin, BSc (Skidmore College, New York)
Mrs E Massey, BA (Edinburgh)
Mrs C Milburn, CertEd (Brighton College of Education)
Mrs C Nolan, BA (Southampton)
Miss H North, NNEB (Croydon College)

Miss J Pegler, DipRBS (TTC), (Royal Ballet School), PGCE (Brunel University)
Mrs C Petrie, BEd (Southbank Polytechnic)
Miss M Prescott, BEd (Southbank Polytechnic)

Visiting Staff:
Mrs H Butterworth, GRSM, ARCM
Mrs M Carter-Pegg, NFF
Mrs J Cox, LRAM, LTCL
Mr D Cox, FTCL, LTCL
Miss N Hawkins, GLCM, FLCM
Mrs S Koeze, NFF
Mrs C McNaughton, BA, ARMCM
Mrs G Nunn, ARCM
Mrs S Pearn, ARCM
Mr R Randall, BMus, ABSM
Miss C Schroder, ALAM
Mrs J Sutherland, GRSM, ARCM
Miss C Thompson, BMus (Hons)
Mrs L Wilde, ARCM
Mrs A Winter, GRSM
Mr R Willey, ARCM

Administrative Staff:

Bursar and Clerk to the Council: Mr G M Flook, BA

Secretaries: Mrs S A Jones, Mrs L Kellaway, Mrs L Patacchiola, Mrs C Perrott, Miss P Rowland

School Librarian: Mrs L Brettle

Technicians: Mrs J Harvey, Mrs P Keating, Mrs B Wheeler, Mrs K Damerell, Mrs M Collins, Mrs J Beaven, Mr G Bottle

School Nurse: Mrs E Brown, SRN

School Medical Officer: Dr M A Whitehead, MB, BS, DRCGO, MRCGP

Founded in 1899, Croham Hurst School occupies an attractive open site and is easily accessible by public transport. The 550 girls come from all districts of Croydon, from Streatham and North East Surrey, North West Kent and the Sutton/Wallington area.

The school has a Christian ethos but welcomes girls from all faiths.

Aim. By placing the individual at the heart of the curriculum, Croham Hurst aims to develop the full potential of each girl.

Facilities. The Senior School and the Junior School, known as "The Limes", are housed on the same site and amenities include the heated swimming pool, gymnasia, hard courts and playing fields. Croham Hurst's extensive facilities also include libraries, a science block, art and drama studios, information communication technology and technology rooms and a fine music suite. A new Design and Technology block opened in Autumn 2000. The Junior School has a nursery unit, library, IT room with Internet access and Design Technology room.

Curriculum. From the age of 3+, girls at Croham Hurst are educated in a lively, stimulating environment, where the emphasis is on promoting enthusiastic and active learning. This is sustained in the Senior School by a broad curriculum in the first 3 years where National Curriculum subjects are supplemented by Classical Civilisation, German, Latin, Spanish and Textiles. An extensive range of option courses is offered, leading to examinations at GCSE and A Level in 23 subjects including Psychology, Economics, Theatre Studies and Business Studies. Learning is supported by small teaching groups and the flexibility to provide 'tailor made' timetables to accommodate the needs of the individual.

Croham Hurst has a proven record of excellent public examination results and an established tradition of university entrance, including Oxbridge.

Activities. Girls' personal talents and interests can be extended through an exciting programme of extra-curricular activities. Clubs include Aerobics, Algebra, Debating, Drama, Information Technology, Public Speaking, Scrabble and Trampolining.

Music and Drama productions are important fixtures in the school calendar and the girls are involved in the varied cultural and sporting House activities. Pupils can be prepared for LAMDA and instrumental examinations. In addition, a large number of school visits are organised which take advantage of the exhibitions, lectures, concerts and theatre offered by London and local venues. School journeys and foreign exchanges planned for 2001-2002 include those to France, Belgium, the USA and Peru.

Scholarships. (*see* Entrance Scholarship section) Academic scholarships at 11+ and 16+.

Entrance. Entrance is by interview and testing relevant to age. The main entrance times are at 3+, 4+, 7 and 11 years of age and also into the Sixth Form.

Bursaries. Some bursaries are available at 11+ and 16+ and at other ages at the Governors' discretion.

Fees. Ranging from £1,245–£2,080 per term.

Associations. There is a flourishing Old Crohamians' Association which organises regular functions and an active and supportive Parents' Guild.

Charitable status. Croham Hurst School is a Registered Charity, number 312609. It exists solely to provide an excellent education for girls.

Croydon High School (G.D.S.T.)

Old Farleigh Road Selsdon South Croydon CR2 8YB.
Tel: 020 8651 5020
Fax: 020 8657 5413
e-mail: info2@cry.gdst.net

Founded 1874

This is one of the 25 schools of The Girls' Day School Trust. For general information about the Trust and the composition of its Council, see p 532. A more detailed prospectus may be obtained from the school.

Local Governors:
Chairman: Mrs L J Barnett

Mr G Black
Mr A K Carey
Mrs A Cooper, MBE
Councillor Mrs A Fraser
Dr S Lowe
Mrs V Maltby
Mr G McConnell
Miss J M North, OBE
Mrs C Walker

***Headmistress:* Miss L M Ogilvie**, BSc (Edinburgh), MSc (Calgary), FRMetS *Geography*

Senior School:
Deputy Headmistress: Mrs D Stainbank, BSc (Sheffield), MA, FRSC *Chemistry*
Senior Mistresses:
Mrs M Casebourne, BSc (Durham) *Biology and Human Biology*
Mrs J E Evans, BSc (Nottingham) *Mathematics*

Teaching Staff:
Mr J L Baker, BA (London) *French and German*
Mrs S Beck, BEd (West London) *Physical Education*
Mrs E Berner, BA (Oxford), MA (Oxford) *History*
Mrs R E Bingham, BSc (Loughborough) *Physical Education*

Mrs S A Bowes, BA (Cambridge) *Economics and Careers*
Mrs A M Butler, NDD, ATC (Portsmouth College of Art) *Art*
Mrs E J Coleman, BEd (Brighton) *Physical Education and Information Technology*
Mrs S F Collins, BSc (Liverpool), MA (Open) *Mathematics*
Mrs S Dassie, CertEd *Physical Education*
Mrs J E Davies, MA (Oxford), ARCM *Music*
Mr M P Dodsworth, BA (University of Wales) *History*
Dr L E Dorgan, BTech (Brunel) *Chemistry*
Miss A L du Plessis, BA (Leeds) *History*
Miss M Emberson, BSc (Kings), MSc (South Bank) *Mathematics*
Mrs L K Eynon, CertEd (Thomas Polytechnic) *Information Technology*
Mr G Farrelly, BSc (Birmingham), MTh (London) *Mathematics*
Ms J Forshaw, BA (Oxford), MA (Bristol) *English*
Miss J Guppy, MA (Sussex) *Mathematics*
Mrs L Hale, BA (St David's) *English*
Mrs C A Heath, BSc (London), PhD *Physics*
Mrs P A Hinton, LRAM, ARCM, GRSM *Music*
Dr G Hülsmann-Diamond, DPhil (Westfälische) *German*
Miss H M Lambert, BA (London) *Latin*
Mrs V M Leang, Licence-ès-Lettres (Lille) *French*
Mrs A B Lee, MSc (London) *Geography*
Miss H M Leeming, MEng (Birmingham) *Information Technology*
Mrs A Leonard, MA (St Andrews) *Geography*
Mr D P Lock, BA (London) *Geography*
Mr B McVicar, MSc (Surrey) *Chemistry*
Mrs P J Massey, BSc (Reading) *Biology*
Miss T J Miller, BEd (de Montfort) *Physical Education*
Miss C J Muller, BSc (London) *Biology*
Mrs T Munro, BEd (Leeds) *Drama*
Mrs E L M Orange, M-ès-L (Sorbonne, Paris) *French and German*
Mr R Paler, BA (Kent), MA (London) *History, Government & Politics*
Mrs J E Pascoe, BA (East Anglia) *English*
Miss M Peacey, BA (Lancaster) *Religious Studies*
Mr I Porter, BA (London) *Information Technology*
Miss S Richardson, BA (Manchester) *Art*
Mrs S A Roberson, BSc (Nottingham) *Biology*
Mrs C S Runalls, BSc (Portsmouth) *Physics*
Miss G Saudek, BA (Cambridge) *English*
Miss A E Seaborn, BA Textile Design (Winchester College of Art) *Art*
Mrs M R Semos, BSc (Bristol) *Biology*
Miss J Silcox, BSc (London) *Biology*
Mrs L Simpson, BA (Bombay), MPhil (Sussex) *English*
Mrs L C Sinclair, BA (Birmingham) *German*
Mrs P Smee, BEd (Cheltenham) *Religious Studies*
Mrs M Thomas, BSc (London) *Chemistry*
Mr J P Vickery, BA (Oxford) *Government & Politics, English*
Mrs S E Wilkinson, BA (London) *French*
Mrs E Williamson, MA (University of Western Ontario), LLB (London) *Latin*
Mr J F Wilkey, BEd (Avery Hill) *Design Technology*
Mrs A M Wood, BSc (Manchester) *Physics*
Mr S J Woodley, BSc (Kent) *Chemistry*

Junior Department:
Head of Junior Department: Mrs S A Grunberg, BSc (London)
Deputy: Mrs A E Lawson, BEd (Exeter)

Mrs M Bamfield, MPhil (London), TDip
Miss S Brock, NNEB
Mrs J Bunner, CertEd
Mrs M B Cooper, CertEd
Mrs A J Garrard, CertEd
Mrs J Harris, TCert
Mrs H C Holland, TCert
Miss A-M Malloy, DipEd (Natal)
Mrs J Masson, BA (Open), BEd (South Bank)
Mrs M E Mooney, BA (Open), DipEd
Mrs C J Moulder, TCert
Mrs M Y Oatway, CertEd
Mrs P J Putman, TCert
Mrs R Troop, CertEd
Mrs A E Tugwell, TCert (Dartford College of PE)

Visiting Staff:
Flute:
Mrs J Cox, LTCL, ARCM
Miss H Foster, GRSM, ARCM

Oboe:
Mrs H Butterworth, GRSM, ARCM

Piano:
Mr B Ellsbury, ARCM, LTCL
Mrs L Strange, LRAM, LRSM
Mrs J Sutherland, ARCM, GRSM

Clarinet and Saxophone:
Mr D A Cox, LTCL, FTCL

Clarinet & Saxophone:
Mr D Harrison, LGSM

Violin and Viola:
Mrs C Dillon, LRAMAM
Mrs S Hackett, LRAM
Mrs P Wyatt, ARCM

'Cello:
Miss R Ford, BMus, LRAM
Miss L Nagioff, DipASOP

Double Bass and Piano:
Mrs C Hibberd, GRSM, LRAM, ARCM

Trumpet and Cornet:
Mr M Hinton, ARCM

Bassoon:
Mrs A Lakin, GRSM, LRAM

Horn:
Mr K Abbott, DipRCM (*Performers*)

Trombone and Tuba:
Mr D Scott, DipRCM (*Performers*)

Guitar:
Miss G Brown, LRAM

Percussion:
Mr M Kruk

Singing:
Miss C Daniels
Mrs T Glynne-Jones

Speech and Drama:
Mrs A Crichton, LGSM
Mrs O Murphy, BA (Oxford)
Mrs R Rokison, Rose Bruford Diploma, LCST

German Conversation:
Mrs R M Horner

French Conversation:
Mrs B Simms
Miss E McVicar (Maine, France)

Spanish Conversation:
Miss M-C Santos, BA (Open)

Librarian: Mrs W J Roberts, ALA, MSc(Econ)

School Administrator: Mrs M Lynn

Administrative Staff:
Mrs J Bewhay

Mrs B Congram
Mrs K Cownie
Mrs A Harris
Mrs S Hart, BA
Mrs K Hill
Mrs J Slaughter
Mrs S Davenport, CertEd (Portsmouth) (*Headmistress's Secretary*)

ISM: Mr O Asenguah, BSc

Laboratory Technicians:
Miss P Salmon, BTec HNC
Mr M Chambers
Mrs S Hayes
Mrs A Highfield
Mrs S Rose
Mrs J Thacker

Teaching Resources Officer:
Mrs E Woodward
Mrs E Szilagyi

Junior Department Ancillaries:
Mrs C Botterill
Mrs B Davies
Mrs C Drew
Mrs C Durling
Mrs B Rowe, NNEB

School Nurse: Mrs T Edwards

Medical Officer: Dr Valerie Gallagher

The school opened in 1874 and moved in 1966 to its present site of over 20 acres at Selsdon on the edge of the Green Belt, two miles south of Croydon. Pupils travel from a wide area, many using the excellent public transport network. There are around 600 pupils (aged 11–18) in the Senior School, including around 180 in the Sixth Form and 300 (aged 3–11) in the Junior Department which has its own nursery and is in an adjacent building on the same site. Main points of entry are at age of 3, 4, 5, 7, 11 and 16 but girls are accepted at any stage subject to availability of space. The school has its own entrance tests.

The Senior School buildings, which were purpose built, have been expanded over the years and include specialist music rooms, a drama room, language laboratory, 4 computer rooms (1 in Junior Department) 10 science laboratories, design technology room and a recently refurbished sports block incorporating sports hall, gym, indoor swimming pool, fitness room and dance studio. The school is surrounded by spacious playing fields including netball/tennis courts, athletics track and hockey pitches. An all weather pitch is planned for autumn 2001. The Sixth Form have their own suite of rooms, including a common room and quiet study area, adjacent to the school library. Students in the Sixth Form are not required to wear uniform.

Curriculum. Girls choose 9 GCSE subjects and all take a a ½ GCSE in IT with the aim of providing a broad and balanced core curriculum at this stage to keep career choices open. At AS and A level there is a wide range of subjects including Government and Politics, Economics, Latin and Physical Education. Almost all girls proceed to University, including Oxbridge.

The emphasis is on a high level of academic achievement, through the development of independent learning, whilst encouraging all girls to participate in the wide ranging extra-curricular life of the school, and to have fun. The many activities include choirs, orchestras, Duke of Edinburgh's Award, debating, drama and a wide range of sports where girls are regularly successful at County and National level. There are opportunities for study, music and recreational trips abroad.

Fees. From September 2000: Senior School £2,044 per term; Junior Department £1,588 per term.

The fees cover the regular curriculum, school books, stationery and other materials, choral music, games and swimming, but not optional extra subjects or school meals.

Optional extra subjects include instrumental music and speech and drama.

Following the ending of the Government Assisted Places Scheme, the GDST has made available to the school a substantial number of scholarships and bursaries.

Bursaries. The bursaries are means tested and are intended to ensure that the school remains accessible to bright girls who would profit from our education but who would be unable to enter the school without financial assistance. These are available before or after entry throughout the senior school and application should be made to the Headmistress in cases of financial need. All requests will be considered in confidence.

Scholarships. There are at present available to internal or external candidates a number of scholarships for entry at 11+ or to the sixth form.

Charitable status. Croydon High School is one of the 25 schools of the Girls' Day School Trust, which is a Registered Charity, number 1026057. The aim of the Trust is to provide a fine academic education at a comparatively modest cost.

Dame Alice Harpur School

Cardington Road Bedford MK42 0BX
Tel: (01234) 340871
Fax: (01234) 344125
e-mail: admissions@dahs.co.uk

Dame Alice Harpur School. Foundation – The Harpur Trust

School Committee of Governors:

Chairman: Mr A P Hendry, CBE
Vice-Chairman: to be announced

Mr P Buckley, FRICS
Mr F D G Cattley, FCA
Mrs H A Didier, SRN, RSCN, SCM, MTD, Dip Nursing
Miss J Lawley, BA
Dr D W Monk
Mrs C Polhill
Mrs A M Roberts, JP
Mr C G Rose
Mrs A R Watson, JP

Clerk to the Governors and School Bursar: Mr S Frater, JP, MIPD, MIMgt

Staff:

***Headmistress:* Mrs J Berry,** BA, MEd

Headmistress of the Junior School: Mrs S Braud, BA, NPQH

Deputy Headmistresses:
Mrs C Catlow, CertEd, ACP
Mrs F McGill, BEd

Assistant staff:

Mrs B Ansell, CertEd
Mrs J Armitage, BSc
Mrs E Baker, DipEd, LUDDA
Mrs G Barrell, BSc
Mrs J Beale, BSc
Miss C Benfield, BA
Mrs G M Berkley, BA
Mrs V Bryant, BA, MA
Mrs L Burton, BEd
Miss E Calvert, BA
Mrs C Chapman, BEd, DipSpLD

Mrs J Chubb, BSc, MEd, CChem, MRSC
Mrs L Clarke, BSc
Mrs F Clements, BSc
Miss I Crocker, BSc
Mrs J Davies, BA
Mrs D Day, BA
Mrs G Deverson, BA
Mr M Faulkner, BA, MA(Ed)
Mrs C Fourey-Jones, Lic-ès-Let
Ms S Gibson, BA
Mr G Goodwin, BSc
Miss C Gough, BA
Mrs A Grafton, CertEd
Dr A Grant
Mr J F Handscombe, BSc
Mrs S Hardy, BA
Mrs E Harling, BSc
Mrs J L Holmes, CertEd
Dr R Hopkin
Mrs R E Houghton, BA, MA
Mrs G Hubbard, BSc
Mr D Jackson, CertEd
Miss L Jameson, BA
Ms J Kilcoyne, BA
Mrs A B Lambert, BSc
Mrs D Langford, BA
Mrs T Lennie, BA, MPhil
Mrs E Lewis, CertEd
Mr K Leyland, BA
Mrs A Lippett, Lic-ès-Let
Mrs E Mapes, BEd
Mrs F Marquand, BA
Mrs J McCardle, BEd
Mrs S McPhail, BA
Mr L Miller, MA (Hons Fine Art)
Mrs P Milton, BEd
Mrs J Moore, BA
Mrs A Myers, CertEd
Mrs P Mylott, CertEd
Mrs E Need, BA
Miss T Newman, BA
Miss E North, BSc
Mrs E Pagliaro, BEd
Mrs J Paradiso, BSc
Dr L Penney
Mrs S Perren, CertEd
Mrs C Randall, BEd
Mrs V Redford, LLAM
Mrs R Reed, BA
Mr G S Roberts, BSc, MInstP, CPhys
Mrs G Rowland, BSc
Mrs C Salusbury, CertEd
Ms V Sanders, MA
Mrs K Scorer, BEd
Miss P Seath, BA
Miss G Stuart, BA
Dr S Sullivan
Mrs N Summers, BA
Mrs C Taylor, BA
Miss N Tekell, BSc
Mr G Thompson, BA
Miss E Turner, BA
Mrs D West, BA
Mrs L Whapples, BSc
Mrs E Williams, CertEd
Mrs S Willis, BLib
Mrs J Wootton, BSc
Mrs S Wright, BEd
Mrs D York, BA

Full Time Music Staff:
Mrs S Aylen, BMus, MA, ALCM, ARCM
Mr L Howard, BMus

Visiting Music Staff:

Flute:
Mrs A Davies, GLCM, LLCM(TD) (*also Piano, Clarinet and Theory*)
Mrs E J Howard, ARCM, DipRCM

Oboe: Mrs J Payne, ARCM, LTCL, MInstAM (*also Recorder*)

Clarinet: Mr F A Jenkins (*also Saxophone*)

Percussion: Mr R Childs, LRAM, GRAM

Brass: Mr P Rudeforth, BMus, LRAM

Guitar: Mr P Davies, ALCM, ONC, HNC

Violin and Viola:
Miss J Board, LRAM
Mrs K Collison, BMus, DipRAM
Mr P Thompson, ATCL
Mrs J Yeung, BA, CTABRSM

'Cello:
Mr L Howard, BMus (*also Piano*)
Mr J Metzger, BMus

Double Bass: Miss D Anderson, BMus, LRAM

Piano:
Mrs S Aylen, BMus, MA, ALCM, ARCM
Mrs I Evans, ARCM, GRSM (*also Theory*)
Mrs C Harrison, LCST, LRAM
Mr L Howard, BMus
Mrs J Howson, GRSM, ARCM, LRAM (*also Clarinet*)
Mrs C Macdonald, BA (*also Clarinet*)
Mrs J Payne, ARCM, LTCL, MInstAM (*also Oboe and Recorder*)
Ms G Ram, BMus
Mrs J Sparrow, LRAM

Bassoon: Mrs P Babbington

Voice: Mrs C Radok, CertEd

Visiting Drama Staff:
Mr R Anderson, BA
Miss D Burns, LLAM, AISTD
Miss A Lewis, BA

PE Coaches:
Mrs S Bullerwell, CertEd, LTA, ACA
Ms A Calder, FIST, AISC
Mr A Hassan
Mrs J Larman, CertEd
Mr S McMenamie
Ms S Noble

Language Assistants:
French: Mlle L Mulat
German: Mrs H Harris
Spanish: Mrs A Kitson

Number of girls 953.

The School is attractively situated on the South Bank of the River Ouse. The Senior School offers excellent facilities for all curriculum areas, together with a spacious and well-stocked library, Sixth Form Centre, Sports Hall, indoor swimming pool, and floodlit all-weather sports pitch. The Junior School occupies Howard House, which is set in attractive gardens opposite the Senior School campus, and offers its own wide range of accommodation including a magnificent newly-built Hall, Library, Science Laboratory, Computer Room, tennis/netball courts and Coach House suite which serves as a Year 3 base.

The School provides a broad education for able girls aged 7-18. Subjects offered at the different stages include English, French, German, Spanish, Latin, Greek, Economics, Business Studies, History, Politics, Geography, Religious Studies, Mathematics, Physics, Chemistry, Biology, Art, Information Technology, Creative Textiles, Food Technology, Design Technology, Music, Drama, Theatre Studies and Physical Education. Every pupil follows a programme of Personal and Social Education appropriate to her age. An extensive range of extra-curricular activities is available. Senior pupils have the opportunity to participate with the boys of Bedford School in the joint Combined Cadet Force, French Society, Science Forum and in the popular Harpur Trust Debating Society.

Bursaries. A candidate for entry to the Senior School may apply for a Bursary Award, which takes into account not only her academic ability but also her family's financial circumstances.

Holidays. About 3 weeks at Christmas, 3 weeks at Easter, and 7/8 weeks in the summer.

Fees. Tuition Fee: Junior School (7–10 years) £4,503 pa; Senior School (11–18 years) £6,216 pa. Registration and Entrance Examination Fee: £25.

The Dame Alice Harpur School Association. Hon Assistant Secretary, c/o the School.

Charitable status. The Bedford Charity (The Harpur Trust) is a Registered Charity, number 204817. It exists to promote the highest standards in education.

* Head of Department
§ Part Time or Visiting
† Housemaster/Housemistress
¶ Old Pupil
‡ See below list of staff for meaning

Dame Allan's Girls' School

Fenham Newcastle upon Tyne NE4 9YJ
Tel: (0191) 2750708; Bursar (0191) 2745910
Fax: School: (0191) 2751502
website: www.dameallans.newcastle.sch.uk

The School was founded in 1705 by Dame Eleanor Allan and in 1935 was moved to Fenham on a site of 13 acres.

Governors:
Chairman: Mrs D J Salmon
Vice-Chairman: Mr G S Brown

Ex-officio:
The Lord Mayor of Newcastle upon Tyne
The Provost of Newcastle
The Vicar of the Parish of St John

Mrs M E Slater
Miss M Foster, BA, FRGS
Mr C J Hilton, MA
Dr J A Hellen, MA, DPhil
Mrs M Kindred
Prof P D Manning
Mr W Miles, MA, LLM
Mr L Cassie, MA, MEng
Mr G Smith
Mr T St A Warde-Aldam
Mr E Ward
Mr M Bird

Clerk to the Governors and Bursar: J Fleck, ACMA

Staff:

***Principal:* Mr D W Welsh**, MA

Vice-Principal: Mrs E D Wheeler, BA, MSc(Econ)
Director of Studies: Mrs J Middlebrook, BA
Head of Sixth Form: Mrs E J Hilton, BSc, AHA, MEd
Assistant Head of Sixth Form: Mr D C Henry, BSc

In addition there are 33 full-time members of staff and 4 part-time.

There are approximately 440 girls in the School which has a three form entry of some 60 girls at 11+. With the Boys' School, which is in the same building, it shares a mixed Sixth Form and a mixed Junior Department (8+–10+).

The Main School follows the normal range of subjects, leading to examination at GCSE. Distinctive features are a Language Awareness course in Year 7 and a thriving Dance Department (leading to GCSE and A Level Dance qualifications).

Most girls stay on into the Sixth Form and from there normally go on to Higher Education.

Buildings. In the last 6 years, developments have included a Sports Hall, new Science Laboratories, additional classrooms, Computer Resource Centre and Sixth Form Centre.

School Societies. The current list includes: Outdoor Pursuits (including Duke of Edinburgh Scheme), Choirs, Orchestra, Drama, Computing, Art, Christian Fellowship, Amnesty International, History, Science, Mathematics, Dance, Public Speaking, Debating, Desktop Publishing.

Pastoral. Each girl is placed in the care of a Form teacher who oversees her progress and development. In the Sixth Form she has a Tutor who is responsible for both academic and pastoral care.

Careers. There is a structured programme, beginning in Year 9 and with a significant contribution from Tyneside Careers.

Sixth Form. In 1989 the Sixth Form was merged with that of our brother School, giving both Schools the rare constitution of single-sex education (11 to 16) with a coeducational Sixth Form. The Head of Sixth Form is Mrs E J Hilton who will welcome inquiries concerning admission.

Physical Education. Hockey, Netball, Tennis, Gymnastics, Athletics, Fencing, Badminton, Squash, Swimming. The playing fields adjoin the school. Instruction in swimming is given at the Fenham Hall Baths. Dance is particularly popular.

Admission. Governors' Entrance Scholarships and Bursaries are awarded on the results of the Entrance Examination held annually in the Spring Term at all ages from 8+ to 13+. Bursaries are available to pupils aged 11+ and over on entry.

Fees. Full fee £5,022 per annum; Junior Department £3,954 per annum.

Dame Allan's Old Girls' Association: *President,* Julia Weatherall, 11 Princess Mary Court, Jesmond, Newcastle upon Tyne NE2 3BG.

Charitable status. Dame Allan's Schools is a Registered Charity, number 1084965. It exists to provide education for children.

Derby High School

Hillsway Littleover Derby DE3 7DT
Tel: (01332) 514267

Founded in January 1892; taken over from the Church Schools Company in 1910 by a local Governing Body. In 1959 the school became associated with the Woodard Corporation

Foundation Governors:
B A Ashby, FRICS
The Revd E Palmer
J G R Rudd, FCA
Mrs E Wassall, JP, MA

Governors
Chairman: Mr G Rudd

Mrs J A Thompson
S A Irish, LLB
H M L Jenkins, DM, FRCOG
R M Faithorn, MPhil, BA, PGCE
Mrs M Moore
Miss E Evans, DSc, BSc
Revd W Weaver, BA, BD
A Blackwood, MSc
Dr J Moore, MB, ChB
Dr R Verma, MB, ChB, FRCA
Mrs S Cornish

Treasurer: M R Hall, FCA, FCMA, FCT

***Headmaster:* Dr G H Goddard**, DL, FRCS, CChem, FRSA

Deputy Head: Mrs M Viles, BA, MEd (Nottingham), PGCE (Cambridge) *History*

Mrs J Allcorn, BEd Hons (Nottingham) *RE, PSE*
*Mrs A Arthey, BA (Birmingham), PGCE (Nottingham) *French and German*
Mrs J M Bingham, BSc Hons (Leicester) PGCE (Nottingham) *Chemistry and Careers*
*P R Birchall, PhD (Bristol), PGCE (Nottingham) *Geography*
Mrs L M Boreham, BA Hons (Sheffield), PGCE (Nottingham) *French and German*
Mrs T Bullas, CertEd, BEd Hons (Nonington College) *PE*

Miss V Burford, BA Hons (Cambridge), PGCE (York)
Mrs C Cleave, BSc Hons (Exeter), PGCE (Cambridge)
*Mr B Cleary, BEd (Durham) *English and Drama*
*Mrs S Collingwood, BA Hons (York) *Biology*
Mrs N Driver, BEd Hons (Lancaster) *RE, PSE*
Mrs J E Else, DipPE (Sheffield) *Physical Education*
Mrs G Follows, BEd Hons (Warwick), CertEd *Biology*
Mrs D C Folwell, BSc (Special) London CertEd (Leicester) *Information Technology, Computing and Mathematics*
Mr P Gould, GRSM, FRCO, ARAM, LRAM, ARCM, DipEd
Mrs I Hall, GRSM, ARMCM
Mrs L Hamblett, BSc (London), PGCE (Derby) *Mathematics*
Mrs J Hancock, BEd Hons (Crewe & Alsager College) *PE*
*Mrs S K A Harding, Pre Dip, Dip AD (Fine Art) (Sunderland School of Art), CertEd (Trent Polytechnic) *Art*
*Mrs L Hough, BSc Hons (Brunel) *Design Technology*
Mrs M Jack, BA Hons (Southampton), CertEd (Manchester) *Music*
Mrs V Lucas, BA Hons (OU), TCert *Mathematics*
Mrs J E Nelmes, BSc Hons (London) PGCE (Nottingham) *Chemistry and Physics*
*Mrs M O'Neill, BA Hons (Leeds), PGCE (Leeds) *Economics, Geography and Careers*
*Mrs A Penny, BA Combined Hons (Birmingham), PGCE (Loughborough), MEd (Nottingham) *Director of Studies*
Mrs C E Read, BA Hons (Reading), PGCE (London) *English*
*Miss C Riley, BSc Hons, PGCE (Leeds)
*Miss J Robertson, BSc Hons (Hull), PGCE (Birmingham) *Mathematics*
Mrs J Robson, CertEd (Durham), DipPDE, MEd (Derby) *History, Geography*
Mrs J Sample, BSc Hons (Durham), PGCE (Cambridge) *Mathematics*
Mrs M Seaby, BA Hons (Lancaster), MA (Nottingham), PGCE (Sheffield) *English*
*Miss F Sharrock, BA Hons (Hull), PGCE (Keele) *History*
*Mrs D G Stringer, BEd Hons (Cardiff) *Food Technology*
Mrs P Sutton, BA (OU), TCert (Brighton) *Biology*
Mr M Thomas-Goddard, BSc Hons, SRD *Food Technology*

Visiting Staff

Music:
Mrs G A Barker, TCert (Manchester)
Ms Cunningham
Mrs D Gould, CertEd
Miss E Gould, GMus, RNCM, PPRNC
Mrs D Hinds, BEd
Mrs M Marubbi
Mr J Mewitt
Mrs Prockter, BA Hons (Dunelm)
Mrs J Rawson, CertEd, DIDip *Special Needs Education*
Mrs Solomon, MA, BA, LTCL
Mr Susans, TCert
M G Smith, GRSM, DipEd (London)

Junior School:
Mr A Boyer, BEd Hons (Derby)
Mr J Dabell
*Mrs K M E Carey, BEd (Liverpool) Chester College
Mrs C A Alvis, BEd (Nottingham)
Mrs K Hughes, BEd Hons (Worcester College of Higher Education)
Mrs M Joyner, ALCM, LRAM, Teaching Cert Music (Nottingham)
Mrs A Payne, BSc Hons
Mrs J Swainston, BEd Hons (Sheffield)
Miss G Temple-Smith, HND, FBS, HNC, PGCE (Loughborough)
Mrs M Thomas-Goddard, BSc (London), SRD
Mrs A Whirledge, BEd Hons (Derby)

Kindergarten:
*Mrs C J Barton, CertEd (Coventry)
Mrs P R Charge, CertEd (Poulton-le-Fylde)
Mrs M Dickinson, CertEd (Derby)
Mrs L Brebner, DipEd (Jordan Hill College, Glasgow), ITC (Notre Dame College, Glasgow)
Mrs M Hannaford, BEd Hons (Derby)
Miss M Buckley, BEd Hons (Derby)
Miss A Jeffs, BSc(QTS(*Hons* (Newman College of Higher Education)

Chaplain: The Revd A Matthews

Bursar: Mrs S Marson

Headmaster's Secretary: Mrs M Bennett

Number of pupils 600.

The School gives Church of England teaching, but children may be withdrawn from Religious Education on the written request of parent or guardian.

The Senior School Course includes Religious Education, English subjects, Mathematics, German, French, Economics, Biology, Physics, Chemistry, Domestic Science, Art, Music, Drama, Information Technology, and Physical Education.

There is also a Kindergarten and Junior School to which boys are admitted.

Examinations. The School prepares girls for GCSE and Advanced level examinations, the Associated Board of the RCM and RAM examinations and RSA qualifications in IT.

Games. Hockey, Netball, Tennis, Swimming, Athletics and Short Tennis.

Charitable status. Derby High School Trust Limited is a Registered Charity, number 527185. It exists to provide education for children.

Downe House

Cold Ash Thatcham Berks RG18 9JJ
Tel. (01635) 200286
Fax: (01635) 202026
e-mail: correspondence@downehouse.berks.sch.uk
website: www.downehouse.net

Founded 1907

Visitor: The Right Reverend Richard Harries, The Lord Bishop of Oxford

Governors:
Chairman: G Inge, Esq, FRICS

L E Ellis, MA
Mrs C Hughes, BA
Mrs P Hunt, BA
Mrs R J Louth
J R C Lupton, Esq, LLB
D Male, Esq, CBE
R D Marsh, Esq, LLB
Dr D E Miller, LLB, MBBS, FRCA
R Parry, Esq, LLB
Mrs P Penney, BA
E Pfaff, ESQ, BA, LLB, JD
N M S Rich, Esq, CBE, MA, FCA
The Revd Canon Scott-Dempster, MA

***Headmistress:* Mrs E McKendrick,** BA (Liverpool)

Deputy Head: Mrs A Gwatkin, MA (London)

Senior Mistress: Mrs J Wood, BSc (Leicester)

Assistant Head: Mrs M Moore, CertEd (Gypsy Hill Training College)

Director of Studies: Mr J Bayliss, MA (Cantab)

Director of Public Relations: Mrs A Gwatkin, MA (London)

Housemistresses:

Aisholt: Mrs P Kelly, BA (Worcester)
Ancren Gate North: Mrs P J Plass, BSc (Leeds)
Ancren Gate South: Mrs J A Shone, BA (King Alfred's, Winchester)
Holcombe: Miss V Barnes, BEd (Dunelm)
Tedworth: Mrs W D Nurser, BA (Birmingham)
Darwin: Mrs R A Burns, BA (St David's College, Wales)
Hill House: Mrs F V Capps, CertEd (Bedford College)
Hermitage House: Mrs M Moore, CertEd (Gypsy Hill Training College)
Willis West House: Mrs B Wells-West, BA (Rhodes)
Willis East House: Miss A Proctor, BA (Oxon), MSc (Dunelm)
York House North: Mrs L Whalley, BA (Open), MA (Salford)
York House South: Dr F Parsons, BA (Birmingham), PhD
French House: Mrs J C Howard, BA (Manchester)

Heads of Department:

English: Mrs C A Miller, BA (London)
History: Mr A J Hobbs, MA (Cantab)
Classics: Mrs J Twaits, MA (Cantab)
Religious Studies: Dr F Parsons, BA (Birmingham), PhD
Modern Languages: Mr G D Salter, MA (Oxon)
Geography: Mr C J Rogers, MA (Oxon)
Social Sciences: Mr M D Turner, MA (Oxon)
Science: Mrs J D Kingland, BSc (London)
Biology: Miss D Hicks, BSc (London)
Chemistry: Mr I R Watson, BA (Cantab)
Physics: Mrs J D Kingsland, BSc (London)
Mathematics: Mrs K A Henson, BA (Oxon)
IT Co-ordinator: Mrs M J Lawler, BSc (Liverpool)
Technology: Mrs A K Dibble, BSc (Birmingham), AdvDipEd
Food: Mrs C D Petter, CertEd (Liverpool)
Textiles: Mrs B M Jones, Dip in Theatre Design (The Welsh College of Music & Drama)
Music: Mr A B Cain, ARAM, FTCL, FLCM, LRAM, ARCM
Art: Mrs S J Scott, BA Textiles (Birmingham Polytechnic)
History of Art: Mr P S Risoe, DipAD Painting (Chelsea School of Art)
Drama & Theatre Studies: Mrs M Scott, BEd Drama & English (Brisbane)
Physical Education: Mrs L J M Rayne, BEd (Brighton)

Photography: Mr G Roberts, LMPA, MFEP
Personal & Social Education: Mrs P Kelly, BA (Worcester)
Learning Support:
Mrs P Commins-Gregg, BA (Wales), DipSpLD
Mrs S Harniman, BSc (Wales), RSA DipSpLD
Careers: Mrs R Oldham, BSc (Bristol)
The Medical Department: Mrs C Clouting, RGN

Bursar: Mr A J Pitchers

Registrar: Mrs C Cook

Numbers on role. 516 Boarding girls; 14 Day girls.

Age Range. 11–18.

Downe House is situated in 100 acres of wooded grounds, five miles from Newbury and within easy reach of Heathrow Airport. The school's proximity to the Universities of Oxford and Reading allows the girls to take part in a rich variety of activities outside the school.

Buildings. There are Junior Houses for girls aged 11+ and 12+, and five mixed-age Houses for those between 12 and 16. Two of the mixed age houses have been rebuilt in the last two years and the remaining houses have been refurbished. When girls enter the Sixth Form they move into Sixth Form Houses where they have study bedrooms and facilities appropriate to their needs. All the Housemistresses are members of the teaching staff and are responsible for the co-ordination of the academic, pastoral, social and moral development of the girls in their care.

The school buildings include Science Laboratories built in 1990, Art School, Music School, indoor Swimming Pool and Squash Courts and Library. The games facilities are excellent and a new Sports Hall is currently under construction opening in September 2001. The school has two Concert Halls which are used for lectures, concerts and plays.

Religion. Downe House is a Church of England school having its own chapel, which girls attend for daily prayers and for a service of either Mattins or Evensong on Sunday. Holy Communion is celebrated once a week and girls are prepared for confirmation if they wish. Other denominations are welcome. Arrangements are made for Roman Catholics to attend Mass.

Curriculum and Activities. The curriculum includes the study of English, History, Geography, Religious Studies, French, German, Spanish, Italian, Latin, Greek, Mathematics, Physics, Chemistry, Biology, Computer Studies, Technology, Music, Art, Theatre Studies, Food and Nutrition and Textiles. In addition, Classical Civilisation, Business Studies, Politics, Economics and History of Art are offered at 'A' Level as well as General Studies, which is taken by all Sixth Formers. Leiths "Food & Wine" Certificate is also offered to girls in the Sixth Form. Girls are prepared for GCSE and 'A' Level examinations, with all girls going on to University or some other form of Higher Education.

ITC skills are being developed across the years and all girls have an e-mail address which is popular.

All girls in the Lower Fourth, aged 12, spend a term at the School's House in France in the Dordogne, to study French and increase European awareness.

A Careers Specialist gives help to the girls in selecting their careers and a Careers Room is available to all ages.

There are many extra curricular activities, including a variety of musical instruments, Fencing, Drama, Sub Aqua, Pottery, Woodwork, Photography, Art, Craft, Singing, Speech & Drama Training, Cookery, Clay Pigeon Shooting, Rowing, Model Making and Self-defence. There is a regular programme of varied Weekend Activities, including the Duke of Edinburgh Award Scheme. Expeditions abroad such as World Challenge which develops leadership qualities are offered alongside Young Enterprise which offers an insight into Business Practice at home.

Fees. The fees currently stand at £5,300 per term for Boarders and £3,842 for Day Girls.

Admissions. Girls may enter the school at 11+, 12+ or 13+ after assessment, interview and Common Entrance. A few girls annually are given places, on interview and entrance test, to follow the 'A' Level Course in the Sixth Form.

Application for entry should be made well in advance. Prospective parents are asked to make an appointment to see the Headmistress, at which time they are offered a comprehensive tour of the school.

Scholarships. (*see* Entrance Scholarship section) The Governors offer a limited number of Open Scholarships at 11+, 12+, 13+ and for entry to the Sixth Form. Two Music Scholarships and two Art Scholarships are generally awarded as well as minor scholarships and exhibitions in each age group.

Seniors' Bursaries are available for the daughters of 'Old Seniors' if their parents are in need of financial assistance.

Charitable status. Downe House School is a Registered Charity, number 1015059. Its aim is the provision of a sound and broadly based education for girls, which will fit them for University Entrance and subsequently for a successful career in whatever field they choose.

Dunottar School

High Trees Road Reigate Surrey RH2 7EL
Tel: (01737) 761945
Fax: (01737) 779450
e-mail: info@dunottar.surrey.sch.uk
website: www.dunottar.surrey.sch.uk

Independent School for Girls (Day)

Governors:
Chairman: Miss J Buchan
Mr T Benton
Mr C Dixie
Mrs C Kewell
Mrs N Kohn
Mr N Pinks
Mr G Richardson, FRICS
Dr M Sage
Mr T Seckel
Sister Jean Sinclair, BSc
Mr P White
Mr R Wilman

Clerk to the Board: Mrs J M Kefford

***Head:* Mrs J Hobson**, MA (Cantab), PGCE

Senior Management:

Deputy Head: Mrs T McKee, BSc Hons (London), ARCS
Head of Junior Department: Mrs M Hammond, MA (Surrey), BEd (Surrey), CertEd
Head of Sixth Form: Mrs A Smith, MEd, BSc Hons (Dundee), DPSE, MIBiol, CBiol

English Department:
Mrs S E Das Gupta, BA Hons (London), PGCE *Head of Department*
Miss T Katesmark, BA Hons (Surrey), PGCE
Mrs A Mundy, BA Hons (Manchester), PGCE
Mrs C Turner, BA Hons (London), PGCE
Mrs S Watkins, LGSM DipActing (Webber-Douglas Academy)

Mathematics Department:
Mr M Elliott, MA (Cantab), PGCE *Head of Department*
Mrs M Gannon, BEd Hons (London), CertEd
Mrs J Hobson, MA (Cantab), PGCE
Miss C Massey, BS (University of Massachusetts) Mathematics & Earth Science

Science Department:
Mr H Loughlin, BSc Hons (Durham), PGCE, CChem, MRSC, MCoT *Head of Department and Senior Chemist*
Mrs A Smith, MEd, BSc Hons (Dundee), DPSE, MIBiol, CBiol *Senior Biologist*
Mrs A Hanzal, BSc Hons (London), PGCE *Physics*
Dr L Peat, PhD (Manchester), MSc (British Columbia), BSc Hons (Leeds) *Biology*
Miss C Venton, BSc Hons (Southampton), PGCE *Physics*

Modern Languages Department:
Mrs K Fekete, BA Hons (Sussex), AIL, *German, Russian Studies, French, Head of Department*
Mrs W Leighton-Porter, BA Hons (Exeter), PGCE *Latin*
Miss C Venton, BSc Hons (Southampton), PGCE *Spanish*
Mrs C Welch, L-ès-L, CAPES (Sorbonne, Paris) *French*
Mrs M Wilson, MA (Liverpool), BEd Hons (Leeds), CertEd *Spanish, French*

Information Technology Department:
Mr M Woodward, BEd Hons (Surrey), MIITT, FIST, MSTA *Head of Department*
Mrs M Gannon, BEd Hons (London)

Design Technology Department:
Mr P Anspach, MCSD, CertEd *Head of Department*

Geography Department:
Mr S Hirst, MA (Syracuse), BA Hons (Witwatersrand) *Head of Department*
Mrs E Rudolf, MA, BSc Hons (London), PGCE (Exeter)

Economics and Business Studies Department:
Mr M Goss, MA (Surrey), BA Hons (Warwick), PGCE

History Department:
Mrs M Kennedy, BA Hons (Newcastle), PGCE, CFPS (Bristol), ACCEG (Kent) *Head of Department*
Mrs J Boden, MA (St Andrews), PGCE
Miss C James, MA (Lancaster), BA Hons (Exeter), PGCE

Sociology Department:
Mrs M Kennedy, BA Hons (Newcastle), PGCE, CFPS (Bristol), ACCEG (Kent) *Head of Department*
Mrs J Boden, MA (St Andrews), PGCE

Art Department:
Mrs A Sillifant, CertEd *Head of Department*
Mrs M Baker, BA Hons (Bath Academy), PGCE

Music Department:
Mr W T Lamont, BMus (London), PGCE *Director of Music*
Mr C Thompson, BA Hons (East Anglia), MTC *Singing*

Peripatetic Staff:
Mrs J Benson, LRAM *Violin/Viola*
Mr J Brown, RAM, GRSM, LRAM *Piano*
Mr D Duffel *Guitar*
Miss E Laurens, DipRCM *Performance and Brass*
Mr R LeServe, ALCM, LLCM *Clarinet/Saxophone*
Mr G Morrison, GGSM, DipAdvanced Studies Performance *Flute*
Miss L Nagioff, DipNCOS *'Cello*
Miss S Nolan, GRSM, LRAM, PGCE *Percussion*
Mrs C Walford, AISTD *Dance*
Mrs S Watkins, LGSM, DipActing (Webber-Douglas Academy) *Speech and Drama*

Physical Education Department:
Mrs L Baxter, BEd Hons (Exeter) *Head of Department*
Miss K Hoskins, BA Hons, QTS (Brighton)
Mrs E Pieters, BA Hons, QTS (Brighton)

Religious Studies Department:
Miss C James, BA Hons (Exeter), MA (Lancaster), PGCE

Home Economics Department:
Mrs G Faulkner, CertEd *PSE Co-ordinator*

Careers:
Mrs M Gannon, BEd Hons (London), CertEd

Work Experience Co-ordinator:
Dr L Sundström, PhD (Helsinki), MSc (Cantab), BSc Hons (St Andrews)

Junior Department:

Mrs M Hammond, MA (Surrey), BEd Hons, CertEd *Head of Department*
Mrs J Beach, DipEd, CertEd
Mrs H Butt, BEd Hons (Sussex), CertEd
Mrs R Chapman, BTec, Cert in Childcare
Mrs E Denny, BA Hons (Leicester)
Mrs J Emburey, BEd Hons (W Sussex Inst of Education), CNAA
Mrs J Lynch, BSc Hons (Hull), PGCE

Mrs M McIntyre, BEd Hons (Cheltenham), CNAA
Mrs S Robinson, CertEd
Mrs D Hack *Nursery Assistant*

Administrative Staff:

Bursar: Mrs J M Kefford
Premises and Resources Manager: Mr M Carey
Headmistress's Secretary, Admissions: Mrs S Horsman
School Secretary: Mrs J Jones
Bursar's Secretary: Mrs C Aris
Laboratory Technicians: Mrs J Brown, Mrs S Evans
School Nurse: Mrs L Kelly
Computer Technician: Mrs S Ameen, BSc (Basrah), MIEE

Dunottar is a day school for some 410 girls, between the ages of 3 and 18. The School was founded in 1926 and became an Educational Trust in 1961. It is situated in 15 acres of gardens and playing fields on the outskirts of Reigate, convenient to mainline stations and bus routes. Development over the years has provided additional classrooms, art and craft studio, audio visual rooms, careers room, Assembly hall, music rooms, Sixth Form common room and 25 metre heated indoor swimming pool. The school is fully networked and has excellent IT facilities including a dedicated computer suite. A new Science Block opened in the early 1990's, and a new block of eight classrooms opened in 1997. Dunottar commences a major development programme in Summer 2001 that will provide pupils with a new auditorium, a state-of-the-art Sports Centre, new Sixth Form facilities and ultimately a purpose-built Arts and Sixth Form Centre.

Aim. The School's aim is to enable each girl, in a happy and controlled environment, to achieve her full potential academically and personally. She will be taught and encouraged to work hard, to discipline herself, to make the most of her opportunities, while recognising and responding to the needs of others. High standards of behaviour are maintained. Parents receive detailed reports twice yearly, and a number of brief Intermediate Reports. They have regular opportunities to discuss progress with teachers, and appointments can be made at any time to see the Head. There is a flourishing Friends' organisation.

Religion. The School holds the Christian ethos paramount and welcomes children from any denomination or none.

Curriculum. Seventeen GCSE, and twenty A Level subjects are on the curriculum, which is planned to provide a broad education and to preserve a balance between arts and science subjects. Early specialisation is avoided, though some subject options become necessary from the beginning of the GCSE year. Subjects include Religious Studies, English Language and Literature, French, German, Spanish, History, Geography, Latin, Mathematics, Biology, Physics and Chemistry taught for the Dual Award examination, Business and Economics, Design Technology, Information Technology, Theatre Studies and Sociology. There are regular exchanges with France, Germany and Spain. The School has very strong sporting and music traditions. Teaching is given in a wide range of musical instruments and girls are encouraged to join the School orchestras and music groups. There are a number of School choirs. Instruction is available in Drama and Dance, and in a wide variety of musical instruments. Drama and music performances are given frequently. There are excellent on-site games facilities including a large indoor heated swimming pool and playing fields. The school holds the prestigious Sportsmark Award for its commitment to sport. A great number of extra-curricular activities are provided and the School participates most successfully in The Duke of Edinburgh Award Scheme at Bronze, Silver and Gold levels.

Careers. Advice is provided at each key stage of education. Girls are encouraged to research and discuss career plans and opportunities with staff and work experience is offered in a variety of careers.

Physical Education. Sports and games are an important part of School life, and there are excellent facilities for tennis, badminton, rounders, lacrosse, netball, volleyball, hockey, fencing, croquet, gymnastics, athletics and swimming. Year 11 and Sixth Formers take part in activities at the local leisure centre.

Examinations taken. GCSE and 'A' Levels, Associated Board of the Royal School of Music, London Academy of Music and Dramatic Art, Imperial School of Dancing, Royal Society of Arts.

Admissions. Entrance examinations are held in January prior to entry the following September. Early application is advised. Girls are accepted directly into the Sixth Form.

Scholarships. The following Scholarships are awarded annually: eight scholarships at 11+ up to the end of year 11, open to both new and present pupils, are awarded as a result of competitive examination. Two Music Scholarships, usually one at 11+ and one at 14+, are awarded running for seven and four years respectively. These are open to new and current pupils. The prestigious John Zinn Scholarship is awarded annually to the prospective Sixth Form student who submits an entry for best original piece of work during her GCSE year. Other awards are in the form of a reduction in fees for the Sixth Form course.

Further particulars may be obtained from the Headmistress's Secretary who will also arrange an appointment to visit the School and meet the Head.

Charitable status. Dunottar School Foundation Limited is a Registered Charity, number 312068. It exists to provide high quality education for girls.

Durham High School for Girls

Farewell Hall Durham DH1 3TB
Tel: (0191) 384 3226
Fax: (0191) 386 7381
website: www.dhsfg.org.uk

Governing Body:

Chairman: Mr W Hurworth

Mrs A M Chapman, BA
Dr W D Corner, FInstP
Dr R Etchells, MA, BD, DD
Mrs V Hamilton, MA, MEd
Mr G Johnson, BA
Mr P A Lucas, AIB
Canon A J Meakin, TD, MA
The Rt Revd Alan Smithson, MA, Bishop of Jarrow
Mrs G Walker
Canon D Whittington, MA
Mr P Wills, ELS Membership

***Headmistress:* Mrs A J Templeman, MA, DipTh** (Oxon) *Classics*

Deputy Headmistresses:
Miss C P Chapman, MA (London) *History*
Mrs V A Dunsford, BA (Manchester) *French*

Head of Junior House: Mrs M Stone, BEd (Oxon)

Bursar: Mrs S Ruskin, FCA

Senior House:
Dr J M Andrews, BA (York), MSc (Bristol), DPhil (York) *Physics*
Miss J A Barrow, BA (Leeds) *French, Italian, German*
Mrs J Bell, CertEd (Manchester) *Art & Textiles*

Mrs E A Bennett, BA (London) *English*
Mrs T S Bickerdike, BSc (Dunelm) *Mathematics*
Mrs M I Brown, BA (Hull), MSc (LSE) *History*
Mrs P M Burton, BA (Dunelm) *French*
Mrs S M Butler, BA (Dunelm) *Religious Education*
Mrs P G Clarke, BSc (Cork) *Physics*
Mrs D L Close, BSc (Dunelm) *Biology*
Mrs B J Cook, BEd (Dunelm) *Mathematics*
Mrs C I Creasey, BA (Dunelm) *Geography*
Mrs J E Drew, BA (Dunelm) *English*
Mrs V M Dyson, BA (Dunelm), LTCL *Music*
Mrs S A Egglestone, BEd (Dunelm) *ICT*
Mr M Getty, BA (Northumbria) *Business Studies & Economics*
Mrs S Griffiths, BA (York) *Music*
Mrs J M Hush, BSc (Open) *Mathematics*
Mrs M P Jakeway, BSc (Hull) *ICT*
Mrs S E Jones, BA (Sussex), MA (CNAA) *History*
Mrs E R Morgan, BA (Keele) *French*
Mrs P Neary, BA (Open) *Physical Education*
Mr J Neeson, MA (Manchester) *Art*
Mrs A P Parks, BA (Open) *Careers, Religious Education*
Mr N Raine, BSc (Newcastle), BEd (Sunderland) *Design & Technology*
Mrs K M Roberts, BA (Newcastle) *English*
Mrs C Smale, BSc (Dunelm) *Chemistry*
Mrs M M Thomas, MA (St Andrews) *French*
Mrs M M Tomlinson, BSc (Newcastle-upon-Tyne) *Biology*
Mrs J S A Topping, BEd (Liverpool) *Physical Education*
Miss Z I V Tucker, BA (Dunelm) *Physical Education*
Mrs I Woodland, MA (Cantab) *Geography*
Mrs D J Woodman, BA (Newcastle) *Classics*
Mrs C W Wright, MA (Oxon) *Mathematics*

Junior House:
Mrs G Settle, BEd (Leeds) *Deputy Head*
Mrs K A Anderson, BEd (Durham)
Mrs E K Darnton, BSc (Huddersfield)
Mr R Dellar, MSc (Birmingham)
Mrs J Dilley, CertEd (Sussex)
Mrs C J Harding, CertEd (Durham)
Mrs G H Hudson, BEd (Bristol)
Mrs K M Jackson, CertEd (Durham)
Miss H Johnston, BA (Humberside)
Miss K A Longstaff, BA (Central Lancashire)
Mrs P M Matthews, CertEd (Leeds)
Mrs L Mock, BA (Dunelm)
Miss R A Owen-Barnett, BA (Loughborough)

Junior House Support Staff:
Miss V Bennett, NNEB, ADCE (Darlington)
Mrs S J Elphick, SRN
Miss A Gowland, NNEB (Durham)
Miss A Pinnington, NNEB (Durham)

Visiting Staff:
Miss C Ashley, BA *Brass*
Miss V Bojkova, Dip In Conducting & Piano *Singing*
Mr M Dick *Percussion*
Miss S Innes, BMus, LRAM *Violin & Viola*
Mrs D Neat, ARCM *Flute*
Mrs J Provine, MMus *Violin & Viola*
Mrs J H Reid, LRAM, ARCM *Piano*
Mr P Richardson, DRSAMD *Cello*
Mr G Ritson, GRNCM, PPRNCM *Brass*
Miss R Shuttler, BM, MMus, LTCL *Piano*
Mrs M Taylor, LTCL, ARCM *Oboe and Piano*
Miss R Thodey, BD, LGSM *Classical Guitar and Lute*
Mrs J D Wakefield, Gold Medal LAM *Speech & Drama*

Administrative Staff:

Headmistress's Secretary: Miss J Robson
Deputy Bursar: Mrs A Williams
Database Mgr/JH Secretary: Mrs M Collinson
Librarian: Mrs J Durcan, ALA
Financial Assistant: Mrs K A Halliday
Catering Manager: Mrs M Lupson
Senior Technician: Mrs M A Bartley
ITC Systems Manager: Mrs J Boam
Laboratory/JH Assistant: Mrs W Crabtree
Technician: Mrs E Bates
Receptionists: Mrs W Hedley, Mrs K M Wesson
Head Caretaker: Mr K Riding
Assistant Caretaker: Mr D Wilson

Number on roll. 520 day pupils.

Age range. Seniors: 11–18. Juniors: 4–10. Nursery: from age 3.

Normal ages of entry. 3, 4, 10, 11 and 16.

Entry requirements. Assessment, formal testing and interview. Sixth form entry is dependent on the level of achievement at GCSE.

Extra subjects. Elocution and Music (piano, strings, brass, woodwind), Singing.

Fees as at 1 February 2001. Seniors: £1,930 per term. Juniors: £1,260–£1,695 per term.

Durham High School for Girls aims to create, within the context of a Christian ethos, a secure, happy and friendly environment within which pupils can develop personal and social skills, strive for excellence in academic work and achieve their full potential in all aspects of school life.

- Small classes and individual attention.
- Highly qualified, specialist staff.
- Excellent examination results.
- Continuity of Education 3 to 18 years.
- Entry at 3, 4, 7, 9, 10, 11 and 16.
- Purpose built accommodation including Sports Hall and Sixth Form Suite.

Junior House (age range 3-11 years). A new purpose-built Nursery opened in September 1997, providing a stimulating environment for children aged 3-4 years.

Junior House follows a broadly based curriculum to enable children to enjoy every aspect of learning and discovery. Form teachers encourage a high standard of achievement and promote a feeling of warmth and security.

Extra-curricular activities include: Choirs, Instrumental Tuition, Young Textiles Group, Drama, Gymnastics, Netball, Tennis, Karate and Dance.

Regular visits are made to the Theatre, Museums and places of educational interest.

Senior House Curriculum. The *curriculum* is designed to be enjoyable, stimulating and exciting, providing breadth and depth in learning.

- Wide choice of options at GCSE and Advanced Levels.
- Languages: French, German, Italian, Latin and Classical Greek.
- Separate Sciences.
- Personal and Social Awareness programme.
- Careers Education and Guidance.

Extra-curricular activities include regular visits abroad, foreign exchanges, visits to the theatre, art galleries, museums and concerts. There is also a thriving programme of Music, Drama and Sport, as well as flourishing Duke of Edinburgh Award and World Challenge Schemes.

The Sixth Form. The Sixth Form of 80 girls takes a full and responsible part in the life and organisation of the school. A wide range of A and AS level subjects is available. Girls take 4 or 5 subjects in L6, 3 or 4 in U6.

Scholarships and Bursaries. At 11+ a number of academic Open scholarships are offered and bursaries are available in cases of financial need. There is also the Barbara Priestman award of £600 per annum for daughters of practising Christians. Scholarships (academic and music) are awarded at 11+ and financial help is available at all stages from age 11.

At 16 there are a number of academic scholarships

available to external and internal candidates. Music scholarships are also available at 16+, as well as a Sports Scholarship and an Art Scholarship.

Transport. Transport is available from all local areas and the school is also accessible by public transport.

The Headmistress is always pleased to welcome parents who wish to visit the school. For further information and a full prospectus please contact the School Secretary: tel: 0191 384 3226; fax: 0191 386 7381; website: www.dhsfg.org.uk; e-mail: headmistress@dhsfg.org.uk.

Charitable status. Durham High School for Girls is a Registered Charity, number L3/527374 A/1. Its aim is to provide a high standard of education.

Edgbaston High School

Westbourne Road Birmingham B15 3TS
Tel: 0121 454 5831
website: www.edgbastonhigh.bham.sch.uk

President: The Rt Hon Sir Stephen Brown, PC, Hon LLD

Vice Presidents:
Sir Dominic Cadbury, BA, MBA
Mrs S M McIlveen, MB, ChB, DRCOG
Mrs E M Davies, MA (Cantab)

Council:
Chairman: Mr I Marshall, BA
Deputy Chairman: Mrs J L Rothwell, BSc(Econ)

Mr D J Cadbury, MSc, DSW, CQSW
Mrs V J Fuller
Mr P B Hodson, MA (Cantab)
Mr A L Jones, BA, FCA
Dr J F C Olliff, FRCR
Mr A D Owen, OBE, MA (Cantab), HonDSc
Mr P C Stone
Miss S Thomas, LLB
Mr G H Tonks, BSc, FCA

Representing the Old Girls' Association: Mrs E J Taylor

Representing the Friends of Edgbaston High School: Mrs J Littlejohns

Secretary to the Council and Bursar:
Lt Col C Warren

Auditors: Messrs Baker Tilley & Co, Chartered Accountants

Registered Office: Westbourne Road, Edgbaston, Birmingham

School Staff:

***Headmistress:* Miss E M Mullenger**, BA English, Wales, FRSA

Deputy Headmistress: Ms K Barnett, BA, MA English, Birmingham

Pastoral Deputy: Mrs C L Jones, BSocSc, Sociology, Birmingham

Miss W Austen, GBSM, ABSM
Mrs A C Ballinger, BEd, Mathematics, Birmingham
Ms N L Barnard, BA, French, Birmingham (*part-time*)
Mrs S A Barnes, BEd, Dress and Textiles, Bath College of Higher Education
Mr M G Birks, BA, English, Birmingham
Mrs J D Blake, BSc, Earth Sciences, Open University
Miss A G Bosc, BSc, Biological Sciences, Birmingham (*part-time*)
Mrs E A Boyce, BA Mathematics, Open University, DipEd, Dunfermline College, Edinburgh (*part-time*)
Mrs M C Bustillo Sanchez, BA, English, University of Salamanca (*part-time*)
Mrs J Coley, BA, History, Reading (*part-time*)
Dr D M Comis, PhD, BSc, Zoology and Comparative Physiology, Birmingham
Dr F Cook, PhD, Solid State Physics, Warwick, MA, Natural Sciences, Cambridge (*part-time*)
Mrs J Cox, BSc, Physics, Birmingham
Mr M L Dukes, BA, Graphic Design, Wolverhampton Polytechnic
Mrs C A Evans, CertEd, Birmingham Polytechnic (*part-time*)
Mrs I S Field, BA Classics, Birmingham (*part-time*)
Dr H Gay, PhD, BSc, Zoology, London
Miss Z L Graham, BSc Design Technology, Sheffield Hallam University
Mrs A E Gunning, BA, Spanish, Birmingham
Mrs C Handley, BA, German, Leicester
Miss M Harper, GRNCM, ARMCM
Miss J P Harrison, BA, English and Music, Southampton, MA, Shakespeare Studies, Birmingham (*part-time*)
Miss K E Haynes, MEd, Birmingham, BA Mathematics, Warwick
Mrs H Howell, GBSM, ABSM
Miss A L Joyce, Teacher's Certificate in Home Economics, Sheffield Polytechnic
Mrs M Kent, BSc, Mathematical Statistics, Birmingham (*part-time*)
Mrs A Lacey, BSc, Biological Sciences, University of East Anglia
Mrs M Lea, BSc, Chemistry, Sheffield
Mrs C Lund, MA, Cheltenham & Gloucester College of Higher Education, BA, Divinity, Wales
Mrs L Maile, BA, History and English, Cambridge College of Arts & Technology (*part-time*)
Miss K E Mayer, BSc Mathematics, Birmingham
Miss C Mellor, BA, French/Home Economics, Surrey
Mrs S Mobley, BSc, Geography Aberystwyth (*part-time*)
Mrs S L Palfrey, BSc Mathematics, Nottingham
Mrs M S Petchey, MEd, Birmingham, BEd French Leeds (*part-time*)
Mr C J Proctor, BA, English Literature, Swansea
Miss F Richards, BSc, Zoology, Bristol, BA, 3D (*Interior*) Design, Birmingham Polytechnic (*part-time*)
Miss R Richardson, BA, History, Reading
Mrs J Ruisi, BEd, Social Psychology and Sport, Sussex (*part-time*)
Miss C Simpson, BA, Art History, Leicester, Diplomas in Graphic Design & Illustration, St Martin's School of Art
Mrs D Snabel, BA, English, Leicester
Mrs P J Speer, BA, Education, Open University, Teacher's Certificate, Birmingham Polytechnic
Mrs K J Stocks, BMus, Birmingham, ARCM (*part-time*)
Mr M Tomaszewicz, BSc, Biochemistry, Birmingham
Mrs W V Trotman, BA, French, Manchester
Mrs H Watts, BA, Geography, London
Miss C E Woods, BA, Physical Education, Warwick

Librarian: Mrs S E Sansom, BA, Music, Bangor, ALA
Library Assistant: Mrs J Hall, BSc, Mathematics, University of Surrey

Language Assistants:
French: Mrs J Wilkinson
German: Mrs C Kuhn

Laboratory Technicians:
Mrs L Moon, BA, Open University, MISct, RegScTech
Miss S M Pinkess

Technical Assistants:
Mrs A Dolby
Mrs C Smith

Preparatory Department:

Head of Department: Mrs L Bartlett, MA Education, BPhilEd, Warwick

Deputy Head of Department: Mrs T Norris, BA Open University, TCert Bordesley College of Education, ACP

Mrs V Alderson, CertEd, City of Birmingham College of Education
Mrs S Amann, BA, English, Birmingham, PGCE, Birmingham
Mrs A Barker, BA, History, Nottingham, PGCE, Manchester
Mrs A R Bradford, BSc, Chemistry and Zoology, Bristol; Dip Soc Studies, Southampton, PGCE, Birmingham Polytechnic
Mrs A M Collins, BEd, Birmingham, Teachers' Cert, Dudley College of Education
Mrs S Draper, BSc, Geography, PGCE, Swansea
Mrs S Dudley, CertEd, French, Northumberland College of Education (*part-time*)
Mrs A L Gelderd, BSc Zoology and Psychology, Leeds
Mrs E E Halling, BA, QTS, Warwick
Mrs C M Hamilton, BSc, Geography and Geology, Manchester, PGCE, Southampton
Miss S Hazlehurst, BA, QTS, Warwick
Mrs V M Heaselgrave, CertEd, Bishop Grosseteste Lincoln, DipSLD (*part-time*)
Miss A Hornsby, CertEd, West London Institute
Mrs J Knott, BA, History and French, PGCE, Birmingham
Mrs R Murray, BA Ancient History/Archaeology, PGCE, Birmingham
Miss S Neale, BEd Biological Science, Worcester College of Higher Education
Miss V Orchard, BEd Environmental Studies, Birmingham Polytechnic
Mrs P H Ritchie, BSc, Micro Biology, Glasgow, Primary Teaching Diploma, Dundee College of Education
Mrs S Robinson, Teacher's Certificate, Westhill College
Mrs S Wight, BEd, Birmingham, BTh, Southampton

Classroom Assistants:
Mrs I Goulding, BTEC National Diploma
Mrs C Mills, NNEB
Mrs J Russon

Technician: Mrs S Lees
Secretary: Mrs L Barton
After-School Supervisors:
Ms D Hill
Mrs C A Francis
Miss K Wagstaff

Pre-Preparatory Department:

Head of Department: Mrs L Bartlett, MA, Warwick

Teacher-in-charge: Miss K Baulke, BEd, Queen's University, Ontario, Canada

Mrs A Hartland, BEd, Theology, Education, Birmingham
Mrs D A Kennedy, BEd, West Midland College of Higher Education
Mrs K Paine, BSc, Chemistry, Birmingham, PGCE, York
Mrs M Smith, CertEd, St Paul's College, Rugby
Mrs J Troughton, TCert, Wall Hall College

Nursery Nurses:
Mrs E Barnsley, DPQS
Mrs H Coulson
Mrs A de Salis, NNEB

Nursery Assistants:
Mrs J Collenette
Mrs J Corbett
Miss T Hale

Visiting Staff:
Ballet: Miss D Todd

Classroom Assistant:

After School Supervisors:
Mrs D Cox
Mrs E Ashford Cottrill
Miss L Morris

Special Subjects:

Head of the Music Department: Miss M Harper, GRNCM, ARNCM

Assistant:
Miss W Austen, GBSM, ABSM

Pianoforte:
Mrs H Howell, GBSM, ABSM
Mrs L Kitto, GBSM, ABSM, LTCL
Mrs J Gopsill, LRAM
Mrs C J Purkis, GBSM, ABSM, LRAM
Mrs S Reid, LRAM, ARCM

Flute:
Mrs A Humphreys, ARCM
Miss S Johnson, ARCM
Miss H Jones, BA

Oboe/Recorder: Mrs K J Stocks, BMus, ARCM

Clarinet/Saxophone: Miss C Pountney, LTCL

Bassoon: Mr P Brookes, GBSM, ARCM, DipOrchStudies

Violin: Mrs S Gough, BA, ARCM

'Cello: Mrs R Storey, BA, ARCM

Guitar: Mrs N Dinnigan, BA, ABSM

Singing: Mrs M Truelove, GBSM, ABSM

Brass: Mrs S Dyson, AGSM

Recorder: Miss W Austen, GBSM, ABSM

Percussion: Mr S Street

Swimming: Mrs B Parton, ASA Teacher's Certificate

Fencing: Professor P Northern, BAF

Catering Officer: Mr S Watson, MHCIMA

Matron: Mrs G L Taylor, RGN, SCM

Headmistress's Secretary: Mrs J A Harley

Registrar: Mrs S E Mason

This independent day school, founded in 1876, attracts girls both from the immediate neighbourhood and all over the West Midlands. They come for the academic curriculum, the lively programme of sporting, creative and cultural activities, and for the individual attention and flexibility of approach. There are some 940 day girls, aged two and a half to eighteen years.

Personal relationships at EHS are of paramount importance. Parents, both individually and through their association, give generously of their time to support our activities; while staff, through their hard work and good relationship with the girls, create an atmosphere at once orderly and friendly.

Organisation and Curriculum. There are three departments working together on one site which caters for over 900 girls aged two and a half to eighteen. One of the features of EHS is the continuity of education it offers. However girls can be admitted at most stages. Staff take special care to help girls settle quickly and easily. Pupils enjoy a broadly based programme which substantially fulfils the requirements of the National Curriculum and much more.

The Pre-Preparatory Department, known as Westbourne, offers facilities for about 100 girls aged two and a half to five in a spacious, purpose-built, detached house.

The staff aim to create an environment in which they can promote every aspect of a girl's development.

The Preparatory Department accommodates over 350 girls from 5+ to 11 in up-to-date facilities, among them a new IT suite, Science Laboratory, Library and Design Technology Centre. A full curriculum, including English, Mathematics, Science and Technology, is taught throughout the department.

The Senior School caters for about 500 girls aged 11+ to 18. Girls follow a well-balanced curriculum which prepares them for a wide range of subjects at GCSE, Advanced and Scholarship Level.

Examination results are very good with high grades distributed across both Arts and Science subjects. Almost all the girls in the Sixth Form of over 100 proceed to Higher Education. Every year girls obtain places at Oxford and Cambridge.

Extra Curricular Activities. Girls can take part in a broad range of activities including art, ceramics, dance, drama, Duke of Edinburgh Award, music, sport and Young Enterprise. There are clubs during the lunch hour and after school. Instrumental music lessons are available. There is a strong music tradition in the school. Girls go on visits, foreign exchanges and work experience in this country and abroad. We encourage girls to think of the needs of others.

Accommodation. There is a regular programme of improvements to the buildings. The Pre-Preparatory and Preparatory Departments have recently been refurbished and the Music Department doubled in size. In September 1993, new Science Laboratories and classrooms, as well as a new teaching area for Information Technology, were opened in the Senior School. In 1996 the Sixth Form Centre was completely refurbished. The school has its own indoor swimming pool, 12 tennis courts and 8 acres of playing fields.

Location. The school is pleasantly situated next to the Botanical Gardens in a residential area, 1½ miles south-west of the city centre. It is easily accessible by public transport and also has its own privately run coaches.

Fees. Pre-Prep mornings only £720; 5 days £1,130; Prep £1,180–£1,655; Seniors £1,795.

Scholarships and Bursaries. (*see* Entrance Scholarship section) Scholarships are available at 11+ and 16+, including two for Music (see relevant section). Sports Scholarships are also offered in the Sixth Form. A bursary fund exists to help girls enter the Sixth Form and to assist those whose financial circumstances have changed since they entered the Senior School.

Further information. Full details may be obtained from the school. Parents and girls are welcome to visit the school by appointment.

Charitable status. Edgbaston High School for Girls is a Registered Charity, number 504011. Founded in 1876, it exists to provide an education for girls.

Farlington School

Strood Park Broadbridge Heath Horsham West Sussex RH12 3PN.

Tel: (01403) 254967
Fax: (01403) 272258
e-mail: TheOffice@Farlington.W-Sussex.sch.uk
website: farlington.w-sussex.sch.uk

Founded 1896

Motto: *Vive ut Vivas*

Governing Body:
Council of twelve Members
Chairman: K J Johnson, OBE

***Headmistress:* Mrs P M Mawer,** BA, PGCE

Deputy Heads:
Mrs A J Darnton, BA, CertEd
Mrs C Stanton, CertEd

Director of Studies: Mrs V A Scott, BA, MA(Ed)

Senior School Teaching Staff:
Mrs G Aguilar, MIL, FETC, DipTran
Mr T Allen, BSc
Mrs A J Binns, BA
Mrs J Bray, BA
Mrs S E Brinsley, BA, TEFL
Mrs J M Browne, CertEd
Mrs J Byford, BA
Mrs L Carvell, BA
Mrs O Clifford, BA
Mrs J Cronin, RSA Teacher's Cert
Mrs E A Dale, L-ès-L
Mrs J M Dilliway, M-ès-L
Mrs P Elborn, LRAM
Mrs S T Farman, BA, MA
Mrs E A S Garrett, BSc, MA
Mr R S Gibbs, BEd
Mr A Guyton, BSc
Mrs J Hansell, BMus, LTCL
Mrs L Hawkins, BEd
Mrs J A Hewitt, BA, MA(Ed), ACCEG
Mrs S J Humphries, BA
Mrs V A Kelly, BA
Mrs V M Kidd, BA
Miss J M Lewis, BA
Mrs M A Lloyd, BEd
Mrs S Lympany, MSc
Mrs A Malleson, CertEd
Mrs E McLeish, BSc
Mrs C M Moult, NFU Teacher's Cert, ALCM
Mrs C Nasskau, BA
Mr A Parkin, BSc
Mrs S M Pearson, BSc
Mrs M Potter, BA, TEFL
Miss S J Saward, BA, LTCL
Mrs J A Smith, BEd
Mrs R Sprey, BA
Mrs C Tagg, BA
Mr D H Thomas, BA
Mrs M Wallace, BA, MA
Mrs R G Woodhatch, BSc
Mrs J Yazicilar, GTCL, LTCL
Mrs S Zanger, BEd

Preparatory School Staff:

Head of Prep School: Mrs J Baggs, BA, CertEd

Mrs E Booth, LGSM
Mrs R H Branton, BA, PGCE
Mrs E M Burke, DRSAMD, PGCE
Mrs P A Cochrane, BA, PGCE
Mrs L Cooper, ALAM
Mrs B Dodd, CertEd
Mrs M Hobbs, BA, DipEd
Miss J Houzego, BEd
Mrs J Marten, CertEd
Mrs C A Osborne, BA
Miss N J Patching, ANEA
Mrs L J Strivens, BEd
Miss G S Welsh, BA

Bursar: Mr H Kersey, ACIS
Registrar: Mrs C George

Boarding Staff:
Mrs J Yazicilar *Housemistress*
Mrs J Cronin *Assistant Housemistress*

Nursing Staff:
Mrs C A Clifton, SEN
Mrs J A Wood, SRN

Doctor: Dr J M Mulvey, MA, MBChB, DRCOG, DCH, MRCGP

The School. The official foundation of Farlington School (then Farlington House) was in 1896 at Haywards Heath. The school moved to its present site in 1955. It is situated in 33 acres of beautiful parkland on the Sussex-Surrey border. It has a small farm run by the girls, two lakes, sports and recreational facilities.

We have approximately 410 girls aged from 4 to 18. Girls can board from the age of 9, on a full or weekly basis, or attend as day girls. All are equally important members of the school community. We have a new building to accommodate the increase in our Preparatory School, a purpose-built Science Building, new IT facilities, making the pupil to computer ratio 6:1 and a new Sports Hall with facilities for badminton, volleyball, netball and basketball. A Sixth Form Centre is being built in 2001.

Curriculum. We aim to provide a broad and balanced curriculum for all age groups. Our academic standards are high, and we encourage girls to raise their own expectations of achievement. Our approach involves good teaching practice coupled with clearly set targets and positive encouragement throughout every girl's school life. The rewards are good examination results: a 99% pass rate at 'A' Levels, with 66% at A & B grades, and 96.6% A* to C grades for GCSE in 2000. Over 95% of our sixth formers go on to university or other degree courses.

Important though academic standards are, education is more than examination results: we aim to educate the whole child. We are concerned to encourage spiritual, physical and personal development, as well as academic achievement.

Spiritual awareness, care for others, tolerance and compassion are the basis of our religious education. We are a Church of England foundation, but we welcome all faiths. There is an assembly each weekday morning, and boarders are given the opportunity to attend a service at a church of their choice on Sundays. Work for charity and service to the community are part of the ethos at Farlington.

Farlington's emphasis on care and guidance in personal development is underlined in our tutorial system. Each girl is placed in a tutor group where she is given individual attention. Tutors liaise with other members of the teaching staff, boarding staff (where appropriate) and parents. They monitor academic progress and extra-curricular activities. Each week a tutor period is devoted to the discussion of a wide range of topics within our personal and social education programme (PSE), including moral issues, personal relationships, health education and study skills.

Extra Curricular Activities. Opportunities for pursuing activities of all sorts exist after school and during lunch hours. Every member of staff runs an activity, which involves her (or him) in a different kind of contact with the girls. Some are physical activities, such as the Duke of Edinburgh Award Scheme, step classes, orienteering; others are more creative like Art or Drama club. Musical activities are popular, or then again, girls can become debators or join the Chess Club.

A wide range of sporting activities is available and the school enjoys considerable success at county and national level in many sports. We have been the National Schools' Riding Association Champions for six consecutive years. There is a strong drama and music tradition within the school. All girls are encouraged to take at least one activity, and there is also supervised prep until 5.45 pm.

Admission (*see* Entrance Scholarship section). Admission is by the school's own entrance examination and interview. Academic and Music Scholarships are available at 11+ and Sixth Form entry.

Fees per term. Prep School from £1,220–£2,110; Senior School (day girls) £2,545; (weekly boarding) £3,255–£4,020; (full boarding) £3,340–£4,105.

Charitable status. Farlington School is a Registered Charity, number 307048. It exists to provide education for girls.

Farnborough Hill

Farnborough Hampshire GU14 8AT
Tel: (01252) 545197/529811

Motto: *In Domino Labor Vester Non Est Inanis*

Board of Governors:

P M Wilson, Esq (*Chairman*)
Mrs E M Halford (*Deputy Chairman*)
Sister R E Alexander, RCE
Sister Anne-Marie, CRSS
Ms P A Cole
Dr R A Hancock
Mrs E Lockett
Ms J Mackett
M A Murphy, Esq
Sister J Shannon, RCE
Mrs C Siebert
Ms J Sloane

Headmistress: **Miss J Thomas**, BA (Kent), MA, PGCE (London)

Deputy Head: Mrs A Griffiths, BEd (Roehampton Institute), MA (Surrey)

Senior Teacher: Mrs H Kippin, BSc (Southampton), PGCE (Bristol)

Assistant Staff:

Mrs V Alexander, BSc (Aberystwyth), BSc (Surrey), PGCE (Nottingham) *Psychology and Mathematics*
Mrs J Anthony, BSc (Nottingham), PGCE (Sheffield) *Physics*
Mrs A Barr, BSc (Leeds), DPSE (Preston Polytechnic) *Mathematics*
Dr J Beaver, BSc, PhD (Reading) *Chemistry*
Miss J Beill, CertEd (Bedford), *Physical Education*
Mrs A Berry, CertEd (Sussex) *Physical Education*
Mrs S Bond, CertEd (Sheffield College) *Art*
Mrs S Burtsell, CertEd (Battersea) *Design & Technology*
Mr P Butler, BA (Leeds), PGCE (Reading) *French and Classics*
Mrs R Byrne, BA (South Glamorgan Institute), Art Teacher's Cert (Goldsmith's College) *Art*
Mrs L Cadby, BA, MEd (City University, New York) *Information Technology*
Miss E Casey, BA (Exeter), PGCE (Roehampton) *French*
Mrs N Cooke, L-ès-L (Bordeaux), TCert *French*
Mrs L Craven, BA (Berkeley), MA (Kent), PGCE (Oxford) *English*
Miss K Davis, BSc (London), PGCE (Surrey) *Mathematics*
Mrs A de Winter, BA, PGCE (Liverpool) *Careers*
Miss R England, BA (Roehampton), PGCE (Brighton Polytechnic) *Physical Education*
Mr D Fanshawe, BA (Hull), MSc (Portsmouth Polytechnic), PGCE (Trinity and All Saints) *Spanish and French*
Mrs A Fawkner-Corbett, L-ès-L (Sorbonne) *French*
Miss D Franzoni, BEd (Central School of Speech & Drama) *Drama*
Mrs L Glover, BEd, CertEd (Sedgley Park) *Religious Education*
Mrs S Gregory, MA (Cambridge), PGCE (Moray House) *French and Italian*

Mrs E Hales, BEd (Southampton), CertEd (London) *Geography*
Mrs C Hall, BA (London), PGCE (Southampton) *Classics*
Mrs D Harding, BSc, CertEd (Loughborough) *Mathematics*
Mrs F Hatton, BEd (London) *Biology and Chemistry*
Mrs S Hayes, BSc (Leicester), PGCE (Ripon and York St John) *Biology*
Mr J Hewitt, BA, PGCE (Leeds) *History*
Mrs M Holliss, BSc (Swansea), PGCE (West London Institute) *Mathematics*
Mr K Johnson, MA (Cambridge), DipEd (Oxon) *Classics*
Miss S Lane, BA (Newcastle), MA (Surrey), PGCE (Hull) *German*
Miss D Lewis, BA (Exeter), BPhilEd (Warwick), PGCE (Chichester) *Religious Education*
Mrs S Macey, BSc (UMIST), PGCE (Cambridge) *Chemistry*
Mrs S McIntyre, BA (Southampton), DipEd (London) *Geography*
Mr K McSteen, BEd, MA (Southampton) *Design & Technology*
Mrs E Nelson, BSc (St Andrews), CertEd (Dundee) *Mathematics*
Mrs L Newman, GTCL, LTCL, LRAM, CertEd (Leeds) *Music*
Mrs S Park, BA, MPhil (Cardiff), PGCE (Swansea) *English*
Mrs V Peters, BA, PGCE (Leicester) *Economics and Geography*
Mrs R Robbins, BA, PGCE (Bristol) *English*
Mrs J Russell, BA, MA (London), TCert *English*
Mrs A Smith, MA, PGCE (Cantab) *Mathematics*
Mrs F Soakell, BSc (Manchester), PGCE (Manchester Polytechnic) *Physics*
Mrs L Storrie, BSc (Salford), PGCE (Manchester) *Biology*
Mrs R-M Thomson, CertEd (Chelsea) *Physical Education*
Mr J Venables, BMus (Huddersfield), PGCE (Roehampton) *Music*
Mrs L Walker, BA, ArtTCert (Goldsmith's College), CertHistArt (Southampton) *Art and Design*
Mr R Wellington, BA (Exeter), PGCE (Birmingham) *Theology*
Mrs D Woodham, BA, PGCE (Nottingham) *History*

Librarian: Mrs E McElwee

Matron: Miss V Cunningham, RN

Bursar: Cmdr A Woolston, CDipAF

Development Director: Mrs J Evans, MInstSMM

Counsellor: Miss A Downes, BATheol, HDipEd (Maynooth), DipPsychotherapy and Counselling (London)

School Secretary: Mrs L Parsons, PESD

Farnborough Hill is an independent day school for 500 girls aged 11 to 18. It is housed in the former home of the late Empress Eugenie of France to which a purpose built school has been added. Facilities include science laboratories, technology workshops, chapel, refectory, indoor heated swimming pool, gymnasium, art rooms, information technology facilities and extensive playing fields.

Although within a few minutes walk of both Farnborough Main and Farnborough North railway stations, the school is situated in 63 acres of parkland and woodland with magnificent views over the Hampshire countryside. Pupils come from Hampshire, Surrey and Berkshire with many travelling by train or by school coach.

The school was established in Farnborough in 1889 by The Religious of Christian Education and is now an educational trust. Although a Roman Catholic foundation, the school welcomes girls of other Christian denominations and religious faiths provided that they participate in the religious activities of the school and respect its Christian ideals.

Farnborough Hill is committed to the education of the whole person in an environment based upon Christian values. Each pupil is valued for herself and helped to develop all her talents, grow in confidence and learn leadership skills.

Academic standards are high with pupils usually taking ten GCSE subjects. In the Sixth Form the majority of students take three A Levels and then go on to Higher Education. The school is a member of ISCO and there is a well equipped Careers Department and a specialist Careers teacher.

The school offers a wide range of extra-curricular activities and is especially renowned for its reputation in sport and in the creative arts. Many girls take individual tuition for speech and drama or a musical instrument and perform in choirs, orchestras and drama productions.

Entry is by examination taken in January for the following September. The school offers academic, music and sports scholarships and also bursaries for parents who are in need of financial assistance.

Tuition fees: 2001/2002, £2,175 per term.

Further information. The prospectus is available from the Development Director. The Headmistress is pleased to meet prospective parents by appointment.

Charitable status. The Farnborough Hill Trust is a Registered Charity, number 1039443. Its aim is to educate the whole person through academic achievement, personal development and values based in Catholic Christian tradition.

Farringtons and Stratford House

Chislehurst Kent BR7 6LR
Tel: 020 8467 0256

Board of Management for Methodist Schools

Governing Body:
Chairman: Mr B C Drury, JP, MA, MEd
Vice Chairman: Mrs D Forsyth, BA

Members:
W Allen, Esq
E D Barkway, Esq, CBE
D G Cracknell, Esq, LLB
Revd David G Deeks, MA
Mrs G W A Dempster
Miss M Faulkner, BSc
Mrs E Giles, MA
A Glover, Esq, BSc, FIMgt
Mrs R Howard
Revd H S Richardson, MA
Mrs H S Richardson, BA
G Russell, Esq, MA
J M Sennett, Esq, MA
Mrs M Setchell, BA
P M Walker, Esq

Bursar and Clerk to the Governors: Mrs J Niggemann

***Headmistress:* Mrs C James**, MA (Liverpool and London)

Deputy: Mrs S Worth, BA Hons, PGCE

Chaplain: Revd Dr M Eggleton, BA Hons, DMin

Head of Junior Department: Mrs R E Stokes, CertEd

Director of Admissions: Mrs F Horton

Department of English:
*Mrs J A Bennett-Hunter, BA (Dublin), MA (Leicester) *Librarian*
Mrs J Ward, BA (Wales), PGCE

Department of Mathematics:
*Mrs P MacKillican, BSc Hons, PGCE (Reading)
Mrs N Groocock, BEd (Keele)
Mrs J W S Baillie, BEd Hons (London)
Miss A C Smith, BSc Hons, PGCE

Department of Science:
*Mr D Ellerington, BSc (Cardiff), BA, MA, PGCE
Mr R H A Flack, BSc (Reading)
Mrs B I Holland, BSc (Cardiff), DipEd
Mrs W K Stanford, BSc (London), MSc (Birmingham), PGCE

Department of Modern Languages:
*Mrs E J Y Bromfield, BA (Kent)
Mlle F Bondonneau, L-ès-L
Mrs C Higgins, BA (London), PGCE
Mrs M Haynes *French Conversation*
Mrs S Wolage *German Conservation*
Mrs J E Cliff, MA, PGCE

Department of Humanities:
Revd Dr M Eggleton, BA Hons, DMin
Mrs J A Barter, BA Hons (Bristol), PGCE
*Mrs A R T Springer, BA (Dunelm), PGCE
Mrs J W S Baillie, BEd (London)
Mrs D Fraser *Typing*
Miss Sovismova

Department of Technology:
Mr T Hadwin, BA (Leeds)
Mrs R Lewis, MA (London)
Mrs L D Matthews, CertEd (Newcastle)
Miss S Thorne, BEd (London)
Mrs J Fairley, DipEd

Department of Performing Arts:
*Mr I Reed, BA (Open), ARCM, LTCL, CertEd
Mr G J Davy, MA
Mrs J Lee, GTCL, LTCL *Organ*
Miss E Banks, BEd Hons

Department of Sport:
Mrs L Long, BEd (Bedford)
Mrs G Ody (*Acting Head of Sport - Maternity cover*)

Junior School:
*Mrs R E Stokes, CertEd (London)
Miss J Cox, BEd Hons
Mrs H M Wood, BA Hons (Loughborough), PGCE
Mrs P F Garrett, BA (Sheffield)
Miss M R Horner, CertEd
Mrs E M Osborn, BA (Durham), PGCE
Mrs M H Thompson, BA Hons, PGCE
Mrs W Reed, LTCL, CertEd
Mrs J Rotter, LTCL, PGCE
Mrs J Goatcher, BEd Hons (Sussex)
Mrs A J Jones, BEd Hons (Cambridge)
Miss E Nichols, BEd Hons (Durham)
Miss V Bloomfield, CertEd
Mrs Burns, DipEd
Miss Buckley, DipEd
Mrs Champness, BA Hons, PGCE
Mrs J M Hook, BEd Hons
Miss J Richards, BA Hons, PGCE
Mrs N J Tetley, BA Hons

Housemistresses:
Mrs D Fraser *Senior Resident Mistress*
Miss C Davis, BA Hons
Mrs S Firth, BA Hons, PGCE
Mrs A Yule

Nursery:
Mrs S M Bainbridge, BA Hons, PGCE (*Teacher in charge*)
Mrs L McEntee
Mrs K Band

Farringtons and Stratford House is situated in 26 acres of green belt land in Chislehurst, which provide attractive surroundings while still being within easy reach of London (20 minutes to Charing Cross), the South Coast and Gatwick (45 minutes) and Heathrow airport via the M25 (1 hour).

The School is committed to providing a first-class education for girls of all ages in a caring community which supports all its members and helps each pupil to achieve her full potential both academically and personally. There is a healthy balance between Day Girls and Boarders (who are accepted from the age of 7), and there are opportunities for Day Girls to be flexible Boarders when required. For Junior day girls after school care is available until 6 pm.

The curriculum offered is that of the National Curriculum, with a wide range of GCSE and Advanced level subjects available. More than 90% of Sixth Form leavers customarily go on to degree courses at Universities or Higher Education Colleges. Academic standards are high from a comprehensive intake of girls and in 2000 ran at 84% of all Year 11 girls securing 5 or more A*-C grades and an 82% pass rate at A level.

The excellent facilities include a new Technology building, a large recently built Sports Hall with Dance Studio and Weights Room, splendidly-equipped Science and Modern Language departments, well-stocked libraries, CD-ROM computers, Careers Room, heated swimming pool and extensive playing fields, as well as our own School Chapel, where the School comes together for a few minutes each morning.

The main sports are lacrosse, netball, tennis, swimming and athletics, but badminton, volleyball and table-tennis are also undertaken and other extra-curricular activities available include the Duke of Edinburgh Award Scheme, Young Enterprise, various choirs and instrumental ensembles, gymnastics, jazz-dance, ballet, drama club, fencing, etc.

To obtain a prospectus and further information or to arrange a visit, contact the Registrar.

Charitable status. Farringtons and Stratford House is a Registered Charity, number 307916. It exists solely to provide a high quality, caring education for girls.

Francis Holland (Church of England) School
Regent's Park

Clarence Gate Ivor Place London NW1 6XR
Tel: 020 7723 0176
Fax: 020 7706 1522

Founded 1878

Patron: The Right Revd and Right Hon the Lord Bishop of London

Council:
Chairman: Lady V France, OBE, MA
Vice Chairman: Mr H M Neal, CBE
Prof J Caldwell, BPharm, PhD, DSc, HonMRCP, CBiol, FIBiol, MInstD
Dr C Carpenter, BA, MA, PhD
Mr M Clarfelt, MA
Prof J C Foreman, DSc, PhD, MBBS, FIBiol
Mr R E Gourgey
Mrs A Grainger, LLB
Mrs V V R Harris, MA, PhD, FCCA
Mr C J P Iliff, MA
Mrs CLongworth, BA Hons
Miss S Mahaffy, BA Hons

Mr I A N McIntosh, MA, FCA
Mrs B Mathews, BA, FCA
Ms A Millett
The Hon Mrs F F B Morgan, MA
Mr A C E Sandberg, BSc
Lady Staughton, BA, JP
Dr S Watkinson, MA, PhD
Dr G Young, MB, BS, DCH

Bursar and Secretary to the Council: Mr C Martinson
The Bursary, Francis Holland Schools, 35 Bourne Street, London SW1W 8JA
Tel. 020 7730 8359

***Headmistress:* Mrs G Low**, MA (Oxon)

Deputy Headmistress: Miss J B Addinall, MA (Cantab), PGCE

Senior Mistress: Mrs F J Forde, CertEd (Dartford College)

Teaching Staff:
Art:
Miss B Conway, BA (Edinburgh), PGCE (Moray House College of Education)
Miss H Gardner, BA Hons (Nottingham), PGCE
Miss J Orr, BA (NkU), MA (Sussex)
Dr R Chaplin, BA, MA, DPhil
Miss V Taylor

Careers/Librarian:
Mrs E L S Kelly, BA (Leics), DipLib, ALA

Classics:
Mr D Piper, BA (London), PGCE
Miss J B Addinall, MA (Cantab)
Mrs M Alderson, BA (Bristol)
Mrs C Griffiths, MA (London)

Economics:
Miss J Green, MA (Cantab), MSc (London)

English:
Miss M Williamson, BA (London)
Mr N E Marsh, BA (Sussex), MPhil (London)
Mrs K F Oakley, BA (London)
Mrs N Foy, MA (London), PGCE

Geography:
Miss S Harrison, BSc
Miss J Green, MA (Cantab), MSc (London)
Mrs F Forde, CertEd (Dartford College)

History:
Mrs P C Edgar, BA (London)
Mr H Clayton, BA (Liverpool)
Mr J Skidmore, BA (Oxon), PGCE
Mrs J Piercy, BA (London)

History of Art:
Dr R Chaplin, BA, MA, DPhil

Information Technology:
Mr N Evans, BA DipRSA, CertEd
Mr P Phillips, BSc, CertEd

Mathematics:
Mrs B Dilan, BSc (Queensland, Australia)
Mr R Jacks, BSc (London), MSc (Bristol)
Mrs T Jensen, BSc, BEd (Newfoundland), PGCE
Mrs R Salter, MA (Cantab)
Mrs A Stiff, BA (Liverpool), PGCE
Miss A C Williams, BSc (Durham)

Modern Languages:
Mrs B Edwards, BA (Hull)
Miss J A Birkett, BA (London) *French*
Mrs F Bryant, Lehrerin für Grund-und Hauptschulen (Bonn) *German*
Dott M Cicora, (Milan), Instituto Universitario Lingue Moderne *Italian*
Miss M Gustave, BA (Montpelier), MA (Montpelier) *French*
Mrs D Safarian, BA (Reading) *Italian/French*
Mrs N Bullock, Titulo de Licendiada en Filosofia y Letras (Salamanca), MA (Madrid) *Spanish*
Miss C Mendiaux, BA (Université Libre de Bruxelles)

Music:
Mrs E Rolfe Johnson, BMus (London)
Mr P Thorne, BA (Oxon), MMus (UEA), PGCE (Keswick Hall)

Visiting:
Mr K Abbs *Clarinet/Saxophone*
Ms J Birtchnell *Cello*
Miss R East *Violin*
Miss F Firth *Voice*
Ms L Friend *Flute*
Mr C Glynn *Pianoforte*
Mrs C Hall *Voice*
Miss N Kennedy *Voice*
Mr M Lloyd *Trombone*
Ms J McLeod, ARCM *Music Theory*
Ms T Mukai *Flute*
Mr C Noulis *Pianoforte*
Mr D Parsons, ARCM *Guitar*
Mr P Robinson *Voice*
Miss C Summerhayes, AGSM *Piano*
Also visiting teachers for: Recorder, Other instruments, Aerobics and Alexander Technique, according to demand.

Physical Education:
Mrs E Searle, BEd
Miss J Murphy, BA Hons (Swansea), PGCE (UCL)
Mrs S Drummond, CertEd (Neville's Cross)
Mr M Stepinac, AFA, BAF

Psychology:
Mr P Sandison, MSocSci, MCertEd

Religious Education:
Miss H M Last, BA (Hull)
Mrs J James, BD, MA, PGCE

Speech and Drama:
Mr A Allkins

Science:
Mrs A Berberian, BSc (London) *Chemistry*
Mr M G Taylor, BSc (Exeter) *Physics*
Mr A E Lowe, BSc (London) *Physics*
Mrs J Pan, BSc *Biology*
Miss D Andrews, BSc (Cardiff), PGCE (Cambridge)
Miss H Stossel, BSc Hons (Durham), PGCE (Cambridge)
Mrs S Drummond, CertEd (Neville's Cross)

Laboratory Technicians:
Ms C Sule
Mrs G Unwin

School Counsellor: Mrs D Robotham

Registrar: Mrs S Bailey

School Secretary: Mrs R Kernot

School Keeper: Mr V Sheriffs

Catering Manager: Mr S King

Resources Support: Mrs E Sheriffs

There are about 380 day girls and entry by examination and interview is normally at 11+, with a small number joining at 16+ for the Sixth Form. The school was founded in 1878 and is affiliated to the Church of England, but girls of all Christian denominations and other faiths are accepted.

Curriculum. Girls are prepared for GCSE, A and AS

Levels, and for admission to Universities, and Colleges of Art, Education and Music. Games are played in Regent's Park and full use is made of the museums, theatres and galleries in central London. Extra lessons are available in Fencing, Music, Pottery, Speech and Drama, Alexander Technique. For the first five years, to GCSE, girls follow a broad curriculum and normally take 9 or 10 GCSE subjects. Careers advice is given from the third year, and all pupils receive individual guidance through to the Sixth Form. In the Sixth Form a wide choice of Advanced Level subjects is combined with a general course of study. All girls are expected to stay until the end of the Advanced Level course.

Scholarships and Bursaries. (*see* Entrance Scholarship section) One Music Scholarship of value up to one-quarter of the current school fees for seven years at 11+.

Two Sixth Form Scholarships of value one half of the current school fees for two years.

Bursaries are available to girls in the school according to need, and there is a remission of one third of the school fees for the daughters of clergy.

The current fees are £2,440 per term.

Situation. The school is situated just outside Regent's Park and is three minutes from Baker Street and Marylebone stations. Victoria and Hampstead buses pass the school. 00MC

Charitable status. The Francis Holland (Church of England) Schools Trust Limited is a Registered Charity, number 312745. It exists to provide high quality education for girls and religious instruction in accordance with the principles of the Church of England.

Francis Holland (Church of England) School
Sloane Square

39 Graham Terrace London SW1W 8JF
Tel: 020 7730 2971
Fax: 020 7823 4066

Founded 1881

Patron: The Right Reverend and Right Honourable The Lord Bishop of London
Council:
Chairman: Lady France, MA (Oxon), OBE
Vice Chairman: Mr H Neal, CBE, BSc(Eng)

Lady Appleyard, MA (Oxon)
Prof J Caldwell, BPharm, PhD, DSc, HonMRCP, CBiol, FIBiol, MInstD
Dr C Carpenter, BA, MA, PhD
Mr M Clarfelt, MA
Mr R Gourgey
Mrs A Grainger, LLB
Mrs V Harris, BA, MA, PhD, FCCA
Mr C Iliff, MA
Mrs C Longworth, BA
Miss S Mahaffy, BA (Oxon)
Mrs B Mathews, BA, FCA
Mr I McIntosh, MA, FCA
Ms A C Millett, BA
The Hon Mrs F Morgan, MA
Mr A C E Sandberg, BSc, FEng, OBE
Mr C Sheridan
Lady Staughton, BA, JP
Dr S C Watkinson, MA, PhD
Dr G Young, MB, BS, DCH, MRCPCH

Bursar and Secretary to the Council: Mr C Martinson, BSc, The Bursary, Francis Holland Schools, 35 Bourne Street, London SW1W 8JA. Tel: 0171-730 8359

***Headmistress:* Miss S J Pattenden**, BSc (Durham)

Deputy Headmistress: Mrs S Pepper, MA (Oxon)

Second Mistress: Miss S Majury, BSc (London)

SENIOR SCHOOL
Full Time:
Mr P Bartolomei, BEd (Perth) *Physics/Science*
Mrs S Boase, MA (Oxon) *Mathematics*
Mrs D Burnham, BA (Leeds) *Classics*
Mr C Chisnall, BSc (UC Wales, Aberystwyth) *Computer Science*
Miss Z Connolly, BA (Cantab) *Classics*
Miss J Ellinsworth, BA (Liverpool) *English*
Mrs M Gepfert, BA Maths (Essex), MSc (*Computing*) *Mathematics*
Miss W Grimshaw, BA (Manchester) *History*
Mrs R Hardy, MA (Oxon) *History*
Mr M Hill, BA (Durham), MSc (London) *Geography*
Mrs R Keown, BSc (Durham) *Physics/Science*
Miss M McLaren, BSc (Glasgow) *Chemistry/Science*
Miss A McLean, BSppSc (Melbourne) *Physical Education*
Mrs A Margetson, PECert, Australian CPE *Physical Education*
Mrs L Pollock, BA (Durham) *English*
Miss D Powell, BA (York) *Biology*
Miss A Stevenson, BA (London) *French and Spanish*
Miss E Tobin, BA (Oxon) *French*
Miss H Vickery, BA (Cantab) *Music*

Staff (*Part-Time*):
Dr G Allen, BA, DPhil (Oxon) *Chemistry/Science*
Mr C Bartram, BSc (Portsmouth) *Biology/Science*
Miss S Bryant, BA, ATC *Art*
Miss S Carr-Gomm, BA (UEA), MA (London) *History of Art*
Miss A Diaz, BA (London) *Spanish*
Mrs R de Pelet, MA (Edinburgh) *English*
Ms J de Rome, BEd (London), CertEd (Homerton) *Art*
Miss K Ferguson, DipMusEd, LRAM, PGCE (Glasgow) *Junior Music*
Mrs C Grant, BA (London), PGCE (London) *Geography*
Mrs P Hartwig, NDD, ATD (Bristol) *Art*
Mr E Henderson, MA (Dundee) *Economics*
Mrs P Homer-Norman, BA (Exeter), MA *English*
Miss D Kaleja, I and II Staatsexamen *German*
Mme A Lenec'h, Licence (Rouen), MA (Connecticut), USA) *French*
Mrs S Lucas, BA (London), MPhil (London) *Religious Studies*
Mrs O Madden, BSc (Edinburgh) *Mathematics*
Mrs V Mrowiec, BEd (Liverpool) *Physical Education*
Mrs S Pepper, MA (Oxon) *History*
Mrs C Remy-Miller, BSc, MSc (France) *French*
Mrs B Ross, ARCM, LRAM, GNSM *Music*

JUNIOR SCHOOL
Head of Junior School: Mrs M Bown, DipEd (Bishop Otter), CertEd, SRN

Full time:
Mrs V Adamson, BA (OU), CertEd
Miss K Brown, BA (Nottingham)
Mrs J Collett-White, CertEd (Canada)
Mrs K Collins, BA (Bloemfontein)
Mrs G Fall, CertEd (Liverpool)
Miss E Gallagher, BEd, CertEd (London)
Miss M Gallagher, CertEd (London), DipMathEd
Miss E Horn, NNEB, DBH
Mrs E Morgan, CertEd, Junior/Secondary Maths (Trent Park), FLCM, LTCL

Miss C Rolls, BA (London)
Mrs H Russell, Montessori Primary Teaching Cert

Staff (visiting):
Miss R Acworth, BA, MA (London), MMus (Glasgow) (*Singing*)
Ms M Beattie, GGSM *Harp*
Mr Y Bouvy, CertAdvStudies, RAM, Diplôme d'État de Professeur de Musique (*Flute & Piano*)
Miss C Constable, MMus (London), BMus, ABSM (*Cello/ Piano*)
Miss B Corsi, FTCL (*Clarinet*)
Mr R Hammond, BSc, DipRCM (*Trumpet*)
Mrs V Hitchen, RBS, TTCDip, Children's Examiner, RAD (*Ballet*)
Miss S Jamieson, GGSM (*Piano*)
Miss M Leaf, BA (London) (*Speech & Drama*)
Miss E Littlewood, GGSMD (*Singing*)
Mr R Mann *Karate*
Mr S Mantas (*Chess*)
Mrs C Norman (*Scottish Dancing*)
Mr A Sadiq (*Fencing*)
Ms A Sharova (*Violin*)
Mrs S Shaub, LRFM, GRFM (*Piano*)
Miss J Smith, GGSM, LGSM (*Violin*)
Mr J Sparks, BA, MA, FCCM (*Guitar*)
Miss J Stoneham, BA (*Percussion*)
Miss V Taylor (*Pottery*)

Librarian: Miss S Bassington, BA (London), DipLib, MLS, ALA

Lab Technicians: Mr M Holden; Miss P Taplin

Computer Technician: Mr P da Costa, BSc

Registrar: Mrs P Woollard, BA, MA (London)

School Secretary: Mrs E Atkinson

Numbers and age of entry. There are 415 Day Girls in the School and entry by the School's own examination is at 4+ for the Junior School (ages 4–11), 11+ for the Senior School (ages 11–18) (member of London Schools consortium) and 16+ for Sixth Form.

Curriculum and Aims. The school aims to provide a broad general education and girls are prepared for GCSE, AS and A level and admission to Universities and Colleges of Art & Music. Full advantage is taken of the school's proximity to museums and art galleries.

Junior School. There is a Junior Department attached to the school.

Religious Education. The school's foundation is Anglican but girls of other faiths are welcomed.

Physical Education. Hockey, Netball, Volleyball, Gymnastics, Athletics, Tennis and Swimming are taken. Senior girls have a choice of other activities as well including Squash, Step Aerobics, Jazz and Rowing. Optional activities open to girls are Karate, Fencing, Rowing and Jazz.

Fees 2001-2002. £2,305–£2,710 per term.

Scholarships and Exhibitions. (*see* Entrance Scholarship section) There are the following competitive awards each year: One Scholarship at 11+ of value one-quarter fees. Two Sixth Form Scholarships of value half of the current School Fee for two years.

Remission. For daughters of Clergy there is a remission of one-third of the School Fee.

Charitable status. The Francis Holland (Church of England) Schools Trust Limited is a Registered Charity, number 312745. It exists to provide high quality education for girls.

Gateways School

Harewood Leeds LS17 9LE
Tel: (0113) 288 6345
Fax: (0113) 2886148

Governing Body:
Chairman: M Shaw, Esq, LLB Leeds

The Hon Justice J Black, BA York
Miss E M Diggory, BA, FRSA London
J D Halliday, Esq, ACA Bishop Thornton
Dr Shirley Lee, BSc, Northumberland
R Marsh, Esq, BSc, FCA Leeds
K G Nussey, Esq, Bramham
G Phillips, Esq, BSc Leathley
Col A Roberts, MBE, TD Leeds, ADC, DL, PhD, FCGI
Professor D Shorrocks-Taylor, Leeds
Mrs F T Thomason, MA Harrogate
J D Turner, Esq, FCA, Scarcroft
Victor H Watson, Esq, CBE, DL, MA, LLD East Keswick

Staff:
***Headmistress:* Mrs D Davidson**, BA Hons, MEd

Deputy Headmistress – High School: Mrs K T M Matthews, BSc Hons, PGCE *Mathematics*

Head of Preparatory School: Mrs J Pardon, BSc, PGCE, MA

Deputy Head of Preparatory School: Mrs S Bassitt, BEd Hons *Form Lower II*

Miss N Adams, BA Hons, PGCE *Form Lower III*
Mrs J Adamson, CertEd *PE*
Mr S Archer, MA, PGCE *Classics and French*
Mrs E A Bottomley, BEd *Physical Education*
Mrs G A Brennan, BA Hons, PGCE *French and Spanish*
Mrs F S Broers, BA Hons, PGCE *History*
Mrs R Burton, BSc Hons, PGCE *Chemistry*
Mrs L Casper, CertEd, AdvDipSecEd *Business Studies, GNVQ, Careers*
Mrs A Davies, MA, FTCL *Music*
Mrs G Dowlman, BA Hons, PGCE SecEd, Cert PrimEd *English and Drama*
Mrs G Dunlop, NVQ 111 *Nursery*
Mr P Dutton *Director of Music*
Miss T A Elliott, BA Hons *Lower III*
Mrs V A Evans, BA, CertEd *Biology*
Mrs D L Fellerman, BA Hons, PGCE *Art and Design*
Mrs S M Finan, BEd Hons *Physical Education, History*
Mr K Fineran, BSc, PGCE *Physics*
Miss E M Green, CertEd, DPSE *Learning Support Co-ordinator*
Mrs B Harrad, BA Hons, PGCE *Classics*
Miss A Hebden, BA Hons *Lower II*
Mrs G M Holloway, CertEd *Reception*
Mrs S Hopkins, CertEd *Lower I*
Mrs J Johnson, MBA, BSBA, PGCE *Mathematics*
Miss A Khan, MA, BA, PGCE *English*
Mrs P Macklin, BSc *Mathematics*
Mrs B J Massey, BA Hons, PGCE *Geography*
Miss S Maynard, BA Hons *Technology*
Mrs J Ralph, BA, MA, PGCE *German and French*
Mrs L Sagar, BA, CertEd *Lower I*
Miss S Scaife, BA, PGCE *Transition Class*
Mrs A Starkey-Smith, BEd *Upper II*
Miss J Suggitt, BEd *Upper I*
Miss J Thomas, BSc, PGCE *Science*
Mrs L Thompson, BA, MA, PGCE *Art*
Mrs K Titman, BEng, PGCE *Technology, Information Technology*
Mrs A Tunley, BA Hons, CertEd *Religious Studies*

Mrs J Unwin, DipEd *Music*
Mrs L Williams, BA Hons, PGCE *English & Theatre Studies*

Visiting Teachers:
Mrs W Crawford, LTCL *Classical Guitar*
Mrs P Dunford *Singing*
Mrs J A Emerick, BA Hons *Drama*
Mrs E Green, ARMCM(T), ARNCM(P) *Violin*
Mr D Highley, GCLCM *Guitar*
Ms S Ladds, ATCL, DRSAMD *Cello*
Mrs D Lee, Teaching Diploma *Clarinet*
Mr D Longden, GCLCM *Jazz and Contemporary Piano*
Miss J Maxwell, CertEd *Dance*
Mrs J Miller, CertEd *Flute and Oboe*
Mrs L Sturge, CT ABRSM *Recorder*
Mr R Winckless, GCLCM *Brass*

Business Manager: Mrs A J Cooper

Registrar and Headmistress's Secretary: Mrs N D Harris

Gateways was founded in 1941. It is an independent day school for 450 girls aged 3 to 18. There is a Preparatory Department for girls aged 3–11 and boys 3–7, housed in a purpose built building.

The school, which has been much extended, is based in the dower house of the Harewood estate, and is situated in its own grounds in a country area half way between Leeds and Harrogate on the A61.

It is a Christian foundation but welcomes girls of all faiths and denominations. Girls are encouraged to develop their talents and to feel that they are valued for their contribution to the life of the school community.

The Curriculum. The curriculum, which is kept under review, includes all the subjects of the National Curriculum, and also Latin, a second modern language, music, drama and sports. There is a wide choice of subjects to study to Advanced level and pupils are prepared for University entrance. Advanced level courses are enriched with a programme of general studies and the opportunity to follow additional courses which lead to GCSE or GNVQ qualifications. There are opportunities for girls throughout the school to experience the Arts, Music, Drama and a range of physical education and sports in addition to their core and foundation subjects.

Buildings. There are well equipped modern science laboratories, a Design and Technology Building and a Performing Arts Centre. All subjects have specialist rooms which include a newly updated information technology centre. The school has lacrosse/hockey pitches, an athletics track, netball and tennis courts and a gymnasium on site. A purpose-built Sports Hall opened in the Spring Term 2000. The Library and some classrooms are situated in the original building.

Extra-Curricular Activities. There are a large number of clubs and societies which meet in the lunch hour or after school. In addition to the school games teams, there are choirs, an orchestral group and instrumental lessons. Girls work for the Duke of Edinburgh Awards Scheme and there are regular outdoor pursuits and expeditions culminating in a World Challenge expedition to Honduras. Overseas stays include skiing, language and cultural experiences. Young Enterprise, work experience and community service are available for more senior girls.

Scholarships (*see* Entrance Scholarship section) For details see the relevant section.

Fees. High School £1,850; LIII, UII, LII, UI £1,515; Transition/LI, Reception £1,195; Gatehouse £1,026 full day or £717 mornings.

Charitable status. Gateways Educational Trust Limited is a Registered Charity, number 529206. It exists to offer a broad education to girls, where they are encouraged to strive for excellence to the best of their ability.

The Girls' Day School Trust

100 Rochester Row London SW1P 1JP
Tel: 020 7393 6666
Fax: 020 7393 6789

Secretary: J C Boal, BA, BPhil

Schools. Royal High School, Bath, Birkenhead High School, Blackheath High School, Brighton and Hove High School, Bromley High School, Croydon High School, Heathfield School (Pinner), Howell's School, Cardiff, Ipswich High School, Kensington Preparatory School, The Belvedere School (Liverpool), Central Newcastle High School, Norwich High School, Nottingham High School for Girls, Notting Hill and Ealing High School, Oxford High School, Portsmouth High School, Putney High School, Sheffield High School, Shrewsbury High School, South Hampstead High School, Streatham Hill and Clapham High School, Sutton High School, Sydenham High School, Wimbledon High School.

For full particulars of these schools, see separate entries.

Each school has an individual prospectus which may be obtained from the Headmistress.

The following are some particulars of the Trust and of its schools as a whole:

Patron: HRH Princess Alice, Duchess of Gloucester, CI, GCB, GCVO, GBE

President: Dr Marilyn Butler, MA, DPhil

Vice-Presidents:
Lady Alethea Eliot
Mrs C G Hardie, MA, PhD
Sir Douglas Henley, KCB, BSc(Econ), HonLLD
Dr A P Hogg, MA, PhD
Dame Rosemary Murray, DBE, DL, BSc, MA, DPhil, HonLLD, HonDSc, JP

Council:
Chairman: Mrs E Elias, MA

Mr D Angel, CBE, BSc (Econ)
Mrs A Beleschenko, BSc, MPhil
Ms A Biss, BSc(Econ)
Mrs J Bridgeman, CB, BA, FRSA
Mr S W Dance, BSc, ARICS
Mr D C Fildes, OBE, MA, HonLiHD
Mrs J H Galbraith, MA
Sir Douglas Henley, KCB, BSc (Econ), Hon LLD
Mrs J R R MacGregor, JP
Mrs V A V Maltby, MA
Mr G M Nissen, CBE, MA, HonFRAM
Mr J R Peers, MA
Mrs G M Perrin, MA, BLitt
Mr P P Ralph, BA, FCA
Mrs R Smith, BA
Dr J H Sondheimer, MA, PhD
Baroness Warnock, DBE, MA, BPhil
Dr P T Warren, CBE, MA, PhD
Mr R J Wilson, MA, FRSA

The Trust was founded in 1872 and was a pioneer of education for girls. Today there are nearly 18,500 pupils in its 25 schools.

The schools are divided into Senior and Junior departments except in the case of Kensington, which prepares girls for entry to other senior schools. The age of entry to the **Senior School** is normally 11 but the schools admit also direct into the **Sixth Forms** and there may be occasional vacancies at other stages. Admission to the **Junior**

Departments occurs at various ages between 4 and 9. Details of requirements for entry at all stages may be obtained from the individual schools.

The schools of the Trust have always stood for both high academic standards and for a broad general education. Girls achieve outstanding results in both GCSE and GCE 'A' level examinations and most continue to higher education. The courses are kept under constant review and all the schools are benefiting in stages from an extensive building programme.

Tuition Fees. The Trust endeavours to keep its fees down to the minimum in order to make a Trust education practicable for as many families as possible. The fees are as follows from September 2001:

Senior Departments. In the London area, £2,208 per term; outside the London area, £1,814 per term.

Junior Departments. In the London area, £1,715 per term; outside the London area, £1,317 per term. Boarding £3,564 (Royal High School, Bath).

The fees cover the regular curriculum, public exam fees, Personal Accident Insurance, books, stationery and other materials, class music, games and swimming but not lunch. (There are separate scales of fees for the Junior school at Kensington).

Tuition, for which extra fees are charged, is given in a number of optional extra subjects, e.g. instrumental music, and at some of the schools in such activities as judo, fencing and golf.

Scholarships and Bursaries. Following the ending of the Government Assisted Places Scheme, the GDST has made available to the schools a substantial number of scholarships and bursaries. The bursaries are means tested and are intended to ensure that the schools remain accessible to bright girls who would profit from our education but who would be unable to enter the schools without financial assistance.

The Godolphin and Latymer School

Iffley Road Hammersmith London W6 0PG
Tel: 020 8741 1936. Bursar: 020 8563 7649
Fax: 020 8746 3352

Motto: *Francha Leale Toge*

Foundation: Godolphin and Latymer, originally a boys' school, became a girls' day school in 1905. It was aided by the London County Council from 1920 onwards and by the Inner London Education Authority when it received Voluntary Aided status after the 1944 Education Act. Rather than become part of a split-site Comprehensive school it reverted to Independent status in 1977.

Governors:
Chairman: Mrs L Patten, BA

Mrs E Attenborough
Dr J S Axford, BSc, MD, FRCP
Lady Butler, BA
Mrs C H Collins, BA
Mr T R Cookson, MA
Mrs C Davies, BA, ATD
Professor Susan Greenfield, CBE, MA, DPhil
Mr C S H Hampton, BA, FCA
Mr G M Nissen, CBE, MA
Her Hon Judge V Pearlman
Mr R D Sidery, BSc(Econ), FCA, FCMA, MIMC
Mrs B Stout-Hammar, BA
Miss J M Taylor, BSc

Clerk to the Governors: Mr M Gairdner, BA (Cantab), FCA

Staff:
***Head Mistress:* Miss Margaret Rudland**, BSc (London)

Deputy Head Mistress: Miss C R Mercer, BA (London)

Senior Mistresses:
Mrs C Parker, MA (Oxon)
Miss J A Hodgkins, BEd (CNAA)

Teaching Staff:
Miss S Adey, BEd (Brighton)
Mrs S Andreyeva, BA (Leningrad)
Mrs C J Armstrong, DipAd, ATD (London)
Miss A J Arthurton, BSc (Bristol)
Mrs S Banks, Licence d'ensignement-Es-Lettres (Paris)
Mr P Barnes, BSc (London)
Mr A Belfrage, CertEd (Leeds), Dip Computer Ed (WLIHE)
Mr J F Bell, BA (Cantab), MA (Sussex)
Mrs M A Beresford, BA (Lancaster)
Dr P Bickley, BA (London), PhD (London)
Miss M J Biggs, BA (Camberwell)
Miss C S P Bircher, BEd (De Montfort)
Mrs J Bostock, Teacher's Cert (Worcester), BEd (Surrey)
Mrs C Brady, BA (London)
Mrs J Capper, BA (London)
Miss A M Clark, BA (Oxon)
Mrs M Cockbain, MA (Oxon)
Miss S K Cox, BA (Edinburgh)
Miss K Cripps, MA (Cantab)
Mrs G Cuming, MA (Sorbonne)
Mr A Davies, BA (Cardiff Institute)
Mr Q J Davies, MA (Keele)
Mrs D Dawe, BA (Oxon)
Mrs K Dawrant, BSc (Dundee)
Mrs A Devadoss, BSc (London)
Miss C Drennan, BA (Oxon)
Mrs A M Duffy, BA (Oxon)
Mr J Escott, MA (Cantab)
Mrs U D Fenton, Diploma (PH Freiburg)
Miss J M Field, BSc (Leicester)
Mr M Fitzmaurice, MA (Cantab)
Mr B Fleming, DipAD (Exeter College of Art and Design)
Mrs C Franklin, BA (Reading)
Miss N Freshney, BSc (Leicester)
Miss S V R Fryer, BA (Bristol)
Mrs C E C Gatward, BA (Oxon)
Miss J Gibbon, BPhil (Oxon), BA (Oxon)
Miss E M Gil Rivas, BA (Southampton)
Mrs S E Guy, BA (Camberwell)
Mrs E C Hahn, BA (York)
Miss C M Hall, BSc (Sussex)
Miss T Hanley, BA (Cardiff)
Miss K Healy, BA (Leicester)
Mrs B M Henry, BSc (London)
Mrs R J Hollis, BSc (Portsmouth Polytechnic), PhD (Birmingham)
Miss G Hulme, BSc (London)
Miss J Ingham, BSc (London)
Miss A H Jacobs, BA (Cantab)
Dr I W Jones, BSc (Liverpool), MSc (Cardiff), PhD (CNAA)
Mrs S Kinross, BA (Exeter)
Mr E W M Kittoe, BSc (London)
Mrs C Lee, MA (Institute of Education), BEd (Exeter)
Mrs C Lewis, BA (Coleraine)
Miss S C Lowden, BA (Durham)
Miss J P Lowndes, BA (Reading)
Mrs J M Mackenzie, BA (Southampton)
Mr P McGuigan, CertEd (St Mary's, Twickenham), BA (OU)
Mrs H Mason, BA (Durham)
Mrs R O S Michael, BSc (Liverpool, John Moores), MSc (Brunel), PGCE (Rochdale)

Mr J R Mills, MPhil (Cantab), BA (Oxon)
Mr J T Morris, BSc (Sussex), MSc (Imperial College)
Mrs M Nott, BSc (Sussex)
Mrs D O'Connor, BSc (Galway), MSc (Birkbeck)
Mrs V A Owen, BSc (York)
Mrs F Payne, MA (Oxon)
Mr S Raleigh, BA (Cantab)
Mrs P Ranaraja, CAPES d'Anglais
Miss J Reid, BA (Liverpool)
Mrs S H Rendall, BA (Manchester)
Mrs E A Rooke, BSc (London)
Miss A M Salmon, BA (London)
Miss P M Shadlock, MA (Sheffield), BA (London)
Mrs E A Shaw, BA (Cantab)
Miss J M Stevens, BA (London)
Mrs J A Stobbart, BA (Norwich School of Art), PGCE (Birmingham Polytechnic)
Miss S von Haniel, MA (Edinburgh)
Ms J A Waltham, BSc (Manchester)
Mr D White, BSc (Leeds), MEd (Warwick)
Mr N S White, BSc (London)
Dr K M Wolfe, BD (London), Dip Theology (Geneva), DipEd (London), PhD (*London*)
Mrs J Wright, BEd (Bath College)

Visiting teachers in Music and Speech Training:
Mrs P Belcher, BA (Exeter)
Miss E Bell, LTCL, LLMC(TD), ALCM
Miss L Bradbury, BMus (London)
Mrs J Clark-Maxwell, BMus (London), LTCL
Miss V L Galer, BA (York)
Miss S C Graham, LRAM, GRSM
Miss P Hodgson, GMus, RNCM
Miss F A Harrison, GRSM, DipRCM
Miss R A Latham, BMus, ARCM
Miss B McGregor, ARCM
Mrs E Mantle, MA (Sussex), BA (Middlesex Polytechnic)
Miss C Morphett, BMus (Sydney)
Miss V L Munday, BMus (Sydney), MMus (Australian National University)
Mr J M O'Donnell, BSc (York)
Mr D Neville, BA (Royal College of Music)
Miss B O'Neill, FTCL
Miss H Palmer, FTCL, GTCL, LTCL
Miss H Pegler, BA (Trinity College of Music)
Mrs S Plumley, GTCL
Miss A M Pope, MA (Oxon), ARCM
Mrs C M Raeburn, BA (Oxon), ARCM
Miss J Ryan, DipRCM
Miss J A Staniforth, GRSM
Miss E A Stanley, ARCM
Miss J Underhill, BMus (Surrey)
Mrs P Whinnett, GMus, RNCM
Miss S K Willis, BMus, DipRCM
Mrs E Wu, ARCM

Finance Bursar: Mrs D Hrynkiewicz, BSc (Kingston), FCCA

Estates Bursar: Mr C Holton, JP, BA (Lancaster)

Registrar: Mrs F R Beckwith

Head Mistress's Secretary: Mrs V S Cox, BA

School Doctor: Dr L B Miller, MA (Cantab), MB, BChir, DRCOG, MRCGP

School Nurses:
Mrs C A Owen, SRN
Mrs S Stannard, RGN

Godolphin and Latymer is an independent day school for 700 girls, aged 11 to 18. The school stands in a four acre site in Hammersmith, near Hammersmith Broadway and excellent public transport. The original Victorian building has been extended to include a gymnasium, pottery room, computer studies room and language laboratory. Buildings opened in 1991 offer science and technology laboratories, art studios, a dark room and an ecology garden. This redevelopment enabled a refurbishment of the Library and Music and Drama facilities. In 1993 a grass playing field was converted to an all-weather surface for hockey and tennis. In Autumn 2000 we opened a new building to provide a Sixth Form Centre, specialist room for Technology and Pottery, four classrooms and a servery.

The Godolphin and Latymer School aims to provide a stimulating, enjoyable environment and to foster intellectual curiosity and independence. We strive for academic excellence, emphasising the development of the individual, within a happy, supportive community.

Girls are expected to show a strong commitment to study and are encouraged to participate in a range of extra-curricular activities. We aim to develop the girls' self-respect and self-confidence, together with consideration and care for others so that they feel a sense of responsibility within the school and the wider community.

Pastoral Care. The school has a close relationship with parents, and every member of the staff takes an interest in the girls' academic and social welfare. Each girl has a form teacher and there is a Head of Lower School, Head of Middle School and a Head of Sixth Form.

Curriculum. We offer a broad, balanced curriculum including appropriate education concerning personal, health, ethical and social issues. During the first three years Religious Studies, English, French, Classical Studies, History, Geography, Mathematics, Physics, Chemistry, Biology, Information Technology, Food and Nutrition, Art, Music, Technology, Drama and Physical Education are studied. In Year 8 there is a choice between Latin and German and in Year 10, for GCSE, German is available again, together with Russian, Spanish and Classical Civilisation. Most girls take nine subjects to GCSE.

All subjects offered at GCSE level are available at AS and Advanced Level, with the addition of Ancient History, History of Art, Drama, Italian, Philosophy and Politics. Sixth Formers also follow a General Studies programme, including a weekly lecture given by outside speakers.

The Sixth Form. The new Sixth Form facilities include a Common Room, Work Room and Terrace. The 200 girls in the Sixth Form play an important role in the school, taking responsibility for many extra-curricular activities, producing form plays and organising clubs. They undertake voluntary work and lead our social service programme. Most proceed to Higher Education degree courses (including an average of 15 a year to Oxford and Cambridge).

Careers Advice. A strong careers team offers advice to girls and parents. Our specialist room is well stocked with up-to-date literature and course information, and lectures and work shadowing are arranged.

The Creative Arts. Music and Drama flourish throughout the school. We have two large music studios and 16 smaller soundproofed rooms for group and individual work. There are three choirs, an orchestra and several small ensembles, and a joint orchestra and choral society with Latymer Upper School. Individual music lessons are offered in many different instruments. Each year there is a pantomime, form play competition, and Lower Fifth and Sixth Form plays as well as the school production. Venues out of school have included the Cochrane, Lyric and Westminster Theatres, and the Edinburgh Festival.

Physical Education. Physical Education is a vital part of a girl's development as an individual and as a team member. Younger girls play hockey, tennis, rounders and basketball, but in the senior years a wider range of activities is offered. There is a fitness room and gymnasium.

Swimming and rowing are also popular sports and we use the Latymer Upper School pool and boathouse.

Extra-Curricular Activities. The many opportunities for extra-curricular activities include the British Association of Young Scientists, Public Speaking, Computing, Chess, the Young Enterprise Scheme, Debating, Classics Club and the Duke of Edinburgh Award Scheme.

Activities outside the School. We organise language exchanges to Hamburg, Paris, Nantes and Moscow, a musical exchange to Hamburg and work experience in Germany, France and Spain. There is also an exchange with a school in New York. Each year, Year 9, girls ski in the USA and there are study visits to Spain and History of Art visits to Paris, Bruges, Venice, Florence and the Sinai Desert.

We take advantage of our London location by arranging visits to conferences, theatres, exhibitions and galleries. Field courses are an integral part of study in Biology and Geography.

Admission. Girls are normally admitted at age 11 (First Year Entrance) or into our Sixth Form. Examinations for First Year entrance are held in January and for the Sixth Form in November. There are occasional vacancies in other years. Entry is on a competitive basis.

Fees. (*see* Entrance Scholarship section) Fees are at present £7,935 p.a., but may be raised after a term's notice. Private tuition in music and speech training are extra. Lunches are available as an option.

Uniform. Uniform is worn by girls up to and including Year 11.

Bursaries. School bursaries towards the cost of fees are available.

Charitable status. The Godolphin and Latymer School is a Registered Charity, number 312699. It exists to provide education to girls aged 11 to 18.

The Godolphin School

Milford Hill Salisbury SP1 2RA
Tel: (01722) 430500. Preparatory School (01722) 430652
Fax: (01722) 430501
e-mail: admissions@godolphin.wilts.sch.uk
website: www.godolphin.org

Motto: *Franc Ha Leal Eto Ge* (Frankness and Loyalty be Yours)

Founded by Elizabeth Godolphin in 1707; date of the will of the Foundress, 24 June 1726; a new scheme made by the Charity Commissioners and approved by HM, 1886, and re-issued by the Charity Commissioners in February 1986. The Godolphin School is an independent boarding and day school for girls aged 11–18, and has its own purpose-built preparatory day school for girls from the age of 3½. Of the 413 girls in the senior school, over 100 are in the Sixth Form.

Governing Body:

G Fletcher, Esq (*Chairman*)

P N Aitken-Quack, Esq
R C R Blackledge, Esq, MA, FSA
M R T Bryer Ash, Esq
Mrs S Herd
Mrs Susan Key, BSc
J S Lipa, Esq, LLB, MJur, FINZ, ICFM
The Revd Mary Macvicar, MA
Rear Admiral S L McArdle, CB, LVO, GM, JP
Miss J M McCallum, BA
S G Metcalf, Esq, MA
M J Nicholson, Esq
The Revd Canon J Osborne, BA, MPhil
Mrs Sarah Streatfeild
Mrs Susan Thomson
Mrs T Watkins, BA

Bursar and Clerk to the Governors: T R Cottis, Esq, MBE

Assistant Bursar: J Walsh

***Headmistress:* Miss M J Horsburgh**, MA (Oxon)

Deputy Heads:
Mrs J Escott, BA (Warwick) *Senior Mistress*
S D Loxton, Esq, BEd (Sussex), MPhil (Hull) *Director of Studies*

Admissions Secretary: Mrs D Baker

Staff:

Religious Studies:
*F R Spencer, Esq, BA (Essex), BTh (Southampton)
S D Loxton, Esq, BEd (Sussex), MPhil (Hull)
Mrs C Shereston, BA (New Mexico, USA)

Philosophy:
S D Loxton, Esq, BEd (Sussex), MPhil (Hull)

Psychology:
Miss A Bowler, BA (Manchester), BA (Wimbledon)

English:
*S Lycett, Esq, BA (Sheffield), BPhil (York)
Mrs J Carlisle, BA (London)
Mrs S Jeffries, MA (Oxon)
Mrs M Johns, BA (Wales)

History:
*Miss J Miller, BA (Belfast)
Mrs T Cotton, BA (London), MA (York)
Mrs S Eggleton, MA (Aberdeen)
Miss M J Horsburgh, MA (Oxon)

Business Studies and Economics:
*D J Miller, Esq, BA (Nottingham)
D Overall, Esq, BSc (Leeds), BSc(Econ) (London)
Miss N Reilly, BEd (Huddersfield)

Geography:
*Mrs A Powis, CertEd (Durham)
Mrs D Osborne, BEd (Southampton)
Miss S Stone, BSc (Wales)

Classics:
*Miss A Codd, MA (Oxon)
Mr P Farrier, BA (Durham)

Modern Languages:
*Mrs S Smith, MA (Cantab) *Head of German/Spanish*
*Mrs P A Wain, BA (Manchester) *Head of French*
Mrs L J Cherry, CertEd (London)
Mrs C Dunning, Licence-ès-Lettres (Bordeaux)
M Dunning, Esq, MSc (Southampton)
Mrs J Escott, BA (Warwick)
Ms M A Cibis, BA, MA (Sheffield)

Mathematics:
*J I Wain, Esq, BSc (Exeter)
Mrs L Conrad, BSc (Liverpool)
Mrs K Healey, BSc (Bristol)
Miss R C Nicholls, BSc (Exeter)
Miss N Reilly, BEd (Huddersfield)
Mrs J L Robson, BSc (Bristol)

Science:
*A J Brown, Esq, BSc (Dunelm) *Head of Chemistry & Science*
C M Burrows, Esq, BSc (Birmingham)
R J W Hodge, Esq, BSc (Dunelm) *Head of Physics*
*Miss J Hopper, PhD (London) *Head of Biology*
M E Adams, Esq, BSc (Newcastle)

Miss S Flower, BSc (London)
Mrs E Newman, BSc (East Anglia)
Mrs C Walsh, CertEd (York)

Technology:
*M Berry, Esq, BEd (Leeds), MA (Open)
Mrs A Schwarz, BEd (Nottingham)

Information and Communication Technology:
*D Overall, Esq, BSc (Leeds), BSc(Econ) (London)
Mrs S Eggleton, MA (Aberdeen)
Mrs W Laptain, BEd (Manchester)
D J Miller, Esq, BA (Nottingham)
Miss J A Thomas, BEd (Worcester)
Miss N Reilly, BEd (Huddersfield)

Art and Design:
*W Cherry, Esq, BA, ATD (Liverpool)
Miss A Bowler, BA (Manchester), BA (Wimbledon)
N Eggleton, Esq, BA (London), ATC
Miss P Fletcher, BA (Liverpool)
Mrs J G Whiteley
Miss E Findley, BA (Leeds Metropolitan)

Music:
*Mrs E Sharp, Diploma in Music Education (Dartington), CertEd (Exeter)
Miss O Walsby, BA (Dunelm)
Mrs M Brookes, CertEd

Instrumental Staff and Ensemble Coaches:
Mrs M Brookes, CertEd
Miss S Cox, BA
Mrs A Felton
C Hobkirk, Esq, BA(MusEd), ARCO
D Kennell, Esq
Mrs J Littlemore, BMus, LRAM
Mrs C Long, GTCL, LTCL
Mrs L Margetts, GRNSM
M Marshall, Esq, MMus, BA (Oxon), LGSM
P Moore, Esq, BMus, LRAM, LGSMD
R Preston, Esq, RMBS (Retd), MISM
P Price, Esq, LRAM, LTCL, ALCM
J Sharp, Esq, RMBS (Retd), MISM
Miss C Stevens
Miss S Stocks, LRAM, LGSM
Miss V Walton, ALCM, LLCM, GLCM
C Watts, Esq, MA, CertEd, LGSM
M Wilkinson, Esq, CertEd
Miss R Wright, BA (Cantab), PGDip, RNCM

Physical Education:
*Mrs S Everatt, BEd (Bedford College)
Miss H Carruthers, BEd (De Montfort, Bedford)
Miss S Rook-Blackstone, BA (Brighton)
Miss J A Thomas, BEd (Worcester)
Miss A J Wells, BA (Manchester), PGSC Physical Education

Drama:
*R J Luetchford, Esq, BEd, MA, CertEd (Southampton)
Miss N Strode, BA (Cardiff)

EFL Coach: Mrs M Dance

Speech and Drama Coach: Mrs M Ferris, LGSM, LTCL

Chaplain: The Revd Canon D Slater, DipECPE, KC

Librarian: Mrs H Clarkson, BSc (Bristol), ALA

Senior Tutor and Higher Education Adviser: C M Burrows, Esq, BSc (Birmingham)

Careers Adviser: Ms V Griffith, BA

Middle School Tutor: Mrs L Conrad, BSc (Liverpool)

Junior School Tutor: Miss J Miller, BA (Belfast)

Further Learning: Mrs D Bentley

Housemistresses and Deputy Housemistresses:
School House: Mrs L Cherry, CertEd (London) Mrs C Shereston, BA (New Mexico)
Douglas: Mrs P Loxton, CertEd (Sussex) Miss E Findley, BA (Leeds Metropolitan)
Hamilton: Mrs W Laptain, BEd (Manchester) Mrs G Wasley
Methuen: Mrs S Moore, BEd (Liverpool) Miss J Tatem, BEd (Southampton)

Development Director: Miss M Driver, BA (Leeds)

Sanatorium:
Mrs A M Oldbury, RGN
Mrs M Thompson, RGN
Mrs S Lewis

The School stands in 16 acres of landscaped grounds on the edge of the historic cathedral city of Salisbury, overlooking open countryside.

A strong academic life combines with thriving art, music, drama and sport. A five studio art centre provides superb art and design facilities. Sixth formers regularly undertake external art commissions (eg for Salisbury District Hospital). 85% play musical instruments with numerous public performances including regular European music tours. A superb 300-seat Performing Arts Centre complements the Science and Technology Centre, Information Technology Suite and Language Laboratories to offer comprehensive state of the art facilities.

A dedicated Sixth Form Centre provides a focus for careers and higher education advice, as well as specialist study areas and well equipped recreational areas.

Four family-run boarding houses (including Sixth Form House) are comfortable, friendly and have a genuinely homely atmosphere. Fifth year upwards can choose between single and double study bedrooms.

Religious Instruction is that of the Church of England.

Curriculum. High academic standards (36.2% A level passes at A grade and 63.3% A-A* grades at GCSE in 2000) are combined with a wide range of additional subjects which include computer literacy, non-examination languages, Duke of Edinburgh awards, etc. 24 subjects are available at A Level; virtually all students continue to higher education including Oxbridge, art colleges and music conservatoires. Numerous links with industry include a well established work shadowing scheme and Young Enterprise. Exceptional range of clubs, societies and weekend activities, open to both day girls and boarders. CCF introduced in September 2000.

Physical Education. Good sporting record with pupils regularly selected for county and national teams. 22 sporting options include lacrosse, hockey, netball, tennis, athletics, swimming, gymnastics, dance, rounders and cross-country. Each girl is encouraged to find at least one sport she really enjoys during her time at the school.

Entrance Examination. Generally through Common Entrance Examination for Girls' Schools Ltd at 11+, 12+ and 13+. Godolphin's own examination and interview for Sixth Form candidates.

Scholarships. (*see* Entrance Scholarship section) (*a*) 11+, 12+ and 13+ Academic, Art (13+ only), Music and Sports Scholarships are awarded for outstanding merit and promise. It is likely that a music award would only be made to a candidate who has attained at least Grade 4 standard on one instrument.

(*b*) Sixth Form Academic, Art, Music and Sports scholarships are also available.

(*c*) Six Foundation Scholarships, each worth 70% of the fees, are available from time to time to able candidates from single parent, divorced or separated families who have been brought up as members of the Church of England.

(*d*) Old Godolphin Association Scholarship, available from time to time to the daughter of an Old Godolphin.

Fees per term. Boarders £5,080, Day Girls £3,070, Prep School £1,255-£2,458. Fees include tuition, textbooks, stationery, sanatorium, laundry, and most weekday and weekend clubs and activities.

Extra Subjects. Individual tuition in music, speech and drama, Japanese, Mandarin, Russian, Italian, tennis, fencing, judo, EFL and learning support.

Old Godolphin Association: *Secretary*, Miss H Duder, Keith Cottage, Cold Ash, Thatcham, Berkshire RG18 9PT, or via Development Office, Tel: 01722 430570.

Charitable status. The Godolphin School is a Registered Charity, number CR 309488. Its object is to provide and conduct in or near Salisbury a boarding and day school for girls.

Greenacre School for Girls

Banstead Surrey SM7 3RA
Tel: (01737) 352114
Fax: (01737) 373485
e-mail: Headmistress@greenacre.surrey.sch.uk

Motto: *Fides et opera*

Council:
Chairman: H A J Watson, Esq, BSc, CPhys, FInstP

Mrs E Booker
Mrs F Brookwell, IPD
Mrs M Cairns, BSc, FRSA
E Engel, Esq, ARICS
Dr S Macrae, BEd, MSc, PhD
Mrs A Marshall
A Oakley, Esq
Dr R Prentis, BSc, PhD
Miss C Ryland
D Smith, Esq
R Steward, Esq, FCIS

Bursar and Clerk to the Council: Miss K A Scott, AInstAM(Dip)

***Headmistress:* Mrs P M Wood**, BA Hons Hull

Deputy Headmistress: Mrs E M Jones, BA Hons Bristol (*English*)

Teaching Staff:
Mrs F Alford, BSc Hons Birmingham, PGCE (*Geography*)
Miss C Axcell, BA Hons New College, Oxford, PGCE (*Mathematics*)
Mrs G Brinded, BEd Manchester, CertEd (*English*)
Mrs K Brooks, BSc Hons Salford, PGCE (*French and German*)
Mrs Y Burnett, BA Hons London, CertEd (*English*)
Mrs E E Bye, BSc Wales, DipEd (*Biology*)
Mrs L Chessell, BSc Hons Durham, PGCE (*Mathematics*)
Mrs M Y Emery, BA Hons London (*Spanish*)
Miss A English, BA Hons Cambridge, PGCE (*Music*)
Mrs D R Fewtrell, BA Hons Swansea (*French*)
F K Gillespie, Esq, BA Hons, PGCE (*Business Studies*)
Mrs E Hannah, AGSM, CertEd (*Speech & Drama*)
Mrs J Hirst, BA, CertEd (*Junior Form Mistress*)
Ms S Howes, BSc Hons Greenwich, PGCE (*Biology*)
Mrs D Jenner, MA Hons St Andrews, PGCE (*History*)
Miss M C Kirk, BA Hons Liverpool, PGCE Oxford (*English*)
Mrs F Lewis, BA Hons Loughborough, PGCE (*Art*)
Mrs H J Mann, BEd Hons Furz (*Religious Studies*)
Mrs C A Matthews, BEd (*PE*)
Mrs S Parker, BEd Roehampton (*Junior Form Mistress*)
Mrs R M Pedrick, BA Hons Durham (*French*)
Mrs E N Redshaw, BA Hons Cambridge (*Geography*)
Mrs E Samuels, CertEd Sussex, Chelsea College of Physical Education (*PE and Junior Form Mistress*)
Mrs L Shakeri, IIP (*Photography*)
Mrs G Skidmore, BSc Hons Edinburgh, CertEd (*Mathematics*)
Mrs A Smith, BEd Hons Chelsea College (*Physical Education*)
Mrs G Strange, BSc Hons, PGCE Sussex (*Physics*)
Mrs R Tisdall, BEd Hons, National Froebel Foundation CertEd (*Head of Junior Department*)
Mrs C A Vaughan, BA Hons, Bristol, CertEd (*French*)
Mrs E Vicars, BSc Hons London (*Chemistry*)
Mrs M Walsh, BA Hons, MSc, PGCE (*ICT*)
Mrs J Windett, BEd Hons Crewe and Alsager (*Junior Form Mistress*)
Miss H Wood, GRSM, ARCM (*Music*)
Mrs M Wraith, HND, CertEd (*Art & Textiles*)

Nursery:
Mrs K F Sutton-Smith
Miss E Makins
Mrs F Saunders
Mrs L M Tyer, SRN

Assistants:
Mrs A Bentley
Mrs J Melville
Mrs V Tann

Laboratory Assistant: R Hindley, Esq

Visiting Teachers:
P Aslangol (*Cello*)
Mrs B Bates (*Guitar*)
Mrs J Jones (*Singing*)
Miss C Lyon (*Clarinet*)
Mrs H McMeechan (*TEFL*)
Mrs A O'Gorman (*Flute/Singing*)
Mrs J M Treagus, GTCL, ALCM (*Piano*)
Mrs H Weller (*Piano*)
Miss M Wildbur (*Violin*)

Secretary to the Headmistress: Miss E A Inman, BSc Hons

Assistant to the Bursar: Mrs A Wills

Welfare to pupils & Office Assistant: Mrs J Rawlins

Greenacre School welcomes girls from three years of age through to A level education. From the nursery class to the Sixth form the girls are encouraged to develop their own talents, and believe that success is achievable. The examination results for 2000 were excellent - 100% pass rate at A level and 96% A-C grades at GCSE. These results show the hard work and dedication of both pupils and staff.

Over recent years we have built a Sports Hall with four classrooms, a Science Building, which consists of four laboratories, prep rooms and a lecture theatre and a two classroom extension to the Junior Department. Alongside this we have created a lovely playground for the children. There is a covered swimming pool and sports field. Plans are always being formed to provide the best resources we can for the pupils at Greenacre.

The school has a relaxed atmosphere in a friendly and pleasant environment, where the girls are happy to work hard and join in with the many activities the school has to offer. The dedicated staff encourage the girls to participate in a variety of clubs as well as end of term plays, Business Incentive schemes and Duke of Edinburgh awards.

We believe that at Greenacre we are ready to take on the challenges of the 21st century.

Fees. Day Girls £1,250–£2,150 a term, including lunches, except Sixth Form.

Scholarships. (*see* Entrance Scholarship section) For details, see relevant section of the book.

Charitable status. Greenacre School for Girls Ltd is a Registered Charity, number 312034. It exists to provide education for girls.

Guernsey—The Ladies' College

Les Gravées St Peter Port Guernsey Channel Islands GY1 1RW
Tel: (01481) 721602
Fax: (01481) 724209
e-mail: Ladycoll@btconnect.com

Motto: *Fais ce que dois, advienne que pourra*

Chairman of the Board of Governors: Deputy W M Bell

Senior School:
Principal: **Miss M E Macdonald**, MA (Hons) (St Andrews), DipEd (Oxon)

Deputy Principal: Mrs R Cook, BSc (Hons) (Swansea), PGCE, MEd (Exeter)

Art and Design:
Miss B Chmiel, BA Hons (Exeter), PGCE
Mrs M A Bairds, NDD (Bournemouth Municipal College of Art and Technology)
Miss L Tillotson, BA Hons (Preston), PGCE

Classics:
Miss J E M Geach, MA, (Oxon), PGCE
Miss H Weston, BA Hons (Lancaster), PGCE

Drama:
Mr B Cornelius, BA TDipA (London), DipEd, LSDA (Tasmania)
Mrs K Tucker, BA(Ed) (Edith Cowan University, Perth, Australia)

Economics and Business Studies:
Mrs A Niven, MA(Econ) (Edinburgh), ACIB
Mr E Adams, BA(Econ) (Kingston), PGCE (London)

English:
Mrs C Hargreaves, BA Hons (Manchester), MA (*Hull*), MEd (Leeds)
Mr J M Henderson, BA Hons (Leeds), PGCE
Mrs J Massey, BA Hons (OU), CertEd (Oxford)
Miss S Robertshaw, BA Hons (London), PGCE
Miss H Weston, BA Hons (Lancaster), PGCE
Mrs K Tucker, BA(Ed) (Edith Cowan University, Perth, Australia)

Geography:
Mrs M Brogan, BSc Hons (Exeter), PGCE
Mrs E S Webster, BEd Hons, (Reading), Teacher's Certificate
Mrs J Le Poidevin, CertEd (Portsmouth College of Education)

History and Government & Political Studies:
Mrs S E Mathieson, BA Hons (Leicester), PGCE
Miss H Weston, BA Hons (Lancaster), PGCE

Mathematics:
Mr R S Harbour, BSc Hons (Dunelm), FRAS
Mrs M Brogan, BSc Hons (Exeter), PGCE
Mrs J Haskins, BSc Hons, (Cardiff)
Mrs M A Ozanne, CertEd (King Alfred's College, Winchester)
Mrs C Rabey, MA (Cambridge), BA, PGCE
Mrs Walton

Modern Languages (*French, German, Italian*):
Mrs J Sproule, MA (Edinburgh), PGCE
Mrs S Devine, BA Hons (Manchester), PGCE
Mrs V Hanna, BA Hons (Bedford College, London)
Mr Y Thoz, L-ès-L (Rennes), CAPES

Music:
Director of Music: Mrs H M Grand, BMus Hons (London), PGCE, MBA (Leicester)
Mr J M Henderson, BA Hons (Leeds), PGCE

Physical Education:
Mrs R F Dovey, BEd (West Sussex Inst of Higher Education)
Mrs J Le Poidevin, CertEd (Portsmouth College of Education)
Mrs S M Wheeler, CertEd (Chelsea College, Sussex)

Religious Studies:
Mr J M Henderson, BA Hons (Leeds), PGCE
Mrs J Le Poidevin, CertEd (Portsmouth College of Education)

Sciences:
Miss S A Robilliard, BSc Hons (Southampton), PGCE, ChMRSC
Mrs R Cook, BSc Hons, (Swansea), PGCE, MEd (Exeter)
Mr P Davis, BSc Hons (Birmingham)
Mr C Grant, BSc Hons (Liverpool), PGCE
Miss S Khan, BSc Hons (Liverpool), PGCE
Mrs P Knight, BSc (Portsmouth Polytechnic), PGCE
Mr P Rigby, BSc Hons (St Andrews), PGCE
Mr A M Wade, BSc Hons (Cardiff), PGCE

Information Technology:
Mr A Wade, BSc Hons (Cardiff), PGCE

Design and Technology:
Miss L Tillotson, BA Hons (University of Central Lancashire), PGCE

Careers Guidance:
Mrs E S Webster, BEd Hons (Reading), TCert

Librarian:
Miss C Le Ray, BA Librarianship, Associate Library Association ASL

Laboratory Assistants:
Mr S Hodgson
Mrs R Wolfe

Administrative Staff:
Bursar and Clerk to the Governors: Mrs J Allett
Secretary to the Principal and Registrar: Mrs C Wood
College Secretary: Miss R McClean
Receptionist: Mrs S de Carteret

Junior School:
Mistress in Charge: Mrs P A Cann, BA Hons (King's College, London), BEd, MEd

Mrs S Anthony, Teacher's Certificate (Charlotte Mason College)
Mrs R E Bishop-White, CertEd (Jordanhill College, Glasgow)
Mrs C Guibert, BEd (St Mary's, Twickenham)
Miss R Le Lievre, BA Hons (Christ Church College, Canterbury)
Mrs V K Joyce, BEd Hons (De Montfort University, Bedford)
Mrs S Spurrier, BEd Hons (Westminster College, Oxford), SRN (King's College, London)
Miss C Beaton, BA Hons (Roehampton, University of Surrey)
Miss E Wilkins, BA Hons, PGCE (University of Wales)
Mrs M D Blin-Bolt, BA, PGCE

Part-Time Staff: Mrs J McCord, CertEd (Redland College, Bristol)

Administrative Staff:

Secretary to Mistress in Charge: Mrs V Lawton

The College was founded in 1872 as an independent school with a non-denominational Christian ethos. It is now Direct Grant with approximately one third of the pupils in the Senior School holding State Scholarship places. The College aims to achieve high academic standards and at the same time maintain the traditional values of courtesy and consideration for others.

Number of girls. Senior School: approximately 350, with 80 in Sixth Form. Junior School: approximately 150.

Curriculum. The Junior School(Melrose) offers a caring environment in which pupils from 4+ to 11 years are given a sound foundation in the traditional skills of reading, writing and number work. In addition they study Science, History, Geography, Music, IT and Art. French, Religious Knowledge, PE and Drama form part of the general curriculum.

The Senior School has a selective entry and places are only given to those applicants who have achieved a satisfactory result in the College entrance tests. In the first three years, all girls follow a broad general curriculum, including Latin, and start German as a second modern language in addition to French. Seventeen subjects are offered at GCSE.

The Sixth Form curriculum is essentially an academic one. Twenty-two subjects are offered at A Level and it is expected that the majority of Sixth Formers will proceed to Higher Education.

The College operates a Sixth Form Partnership with the local HMC School, Elizabeth College. Students can choose their A Level subjects from the combined provision of both schools and may opt, if they wish, to study one or more subjects at Elizabeth College. Boys from Elizabeth College may likewise opt to study a subject offered at the Ladies' College. The Ladies' College provides tutorial guidance and pastoral care for all the girls regardless of where they are taught for A Level.

Music. There is a high standard of music at the College, which has an orchestra, choir, madrigal group, wind-band and recorder group. Instrumental lessons are available from the College staff and from peripatetic teachers.

Sport. The College has an unusually large gymnasium and has its own outdoor heated swimming pool. In addition to the usual sports of hockey, netball, rounders, tennis, swimming and athletics, the school offers badminton, fencing, dance and trampolining.

Drama. The College offers Drama at GCSE and Theatre Studies at A Level in the Sixth Form. Extra-curricular Drama flourishes with school productions taking place two or three times a year.

Extra-curricular activities. The Duke of Edinburgh's Award Scheme is well supported as is the Young Enterprise Scheme. Pupils are also involved in work in the community and in fund-raising for charity.

Entry procedure. All applicants must initially contact the College Registrar (Registration Fee £75).

Tuition Fees. Senior School, £960 per term; Junior School, £1,070 per term.

Scholarships. (*see* Entrance Scholarship section) For details of Scholarships see relevant section.

* Head of Department	§ Part Time or Visiting
† Housemaster/Housemistress	¶ Old Pupil
‡ See below list of staff for meaning	

Guildford High School (CSC)

London Road Guildford Surrey GU1 1SJ
Tel: (01483) 561440
Fax: (01483) 306516
e-mail: registrar@ghs.surrey.sch.uk

Motto: *As one that serveth*

Established in January, 1888

Governing Body: The Council of the Church Schools Company.

Patron: The Rt Rev The Lord Bishop of Guildford

Local Council:
Chairman: Mr D P G Cade

Mrs M E Bland
Miss A Bowey
Mrs C Cobley
Revd R Cotton
Professor M Cox
Dr D Faux
Mrs J Ferretter
Mrs L M Keat
Mr D J A Morgan
Mrs R Scott
Baroness Sharp of Guildford
Mr B Yendole

Staff
***Headmistress:* Mrs S H Singer**, BA (Open University) *Mathematics*

Deputy Heads:
Mrs F J Boulton, BSc (Cardiff), MA (London) *Science*
Mr S J Callaghan, BA (Durham) *Modern Languages*

Head of Junior School: Mrs M I Shepard, BA (OU), CertEd (Bishop Grosseteste College)

Art & Design:
Mr I A Charnock, BA (University of Wales, Bangor), MA (London)
*Mrs E M Henley, BA (Leeds), MPhil (Leeds)
Miss M Sikkel, BA (Chelsea School of Art)

Classics:
Mrs R Arnold, MA (Oxon)
*Miss C J Currie, MA (St Andrews)
Mrs M J Wernham, BA (Reading)

Design & Technology:
Mrs J M Bancroft, BA (OU), CertEd (Madeley), Dip D & T (Roehampton) *Head of Years 10 & 11, Head of Food & Textiles*
Mrs W A Bengoechea, BEd (Bath)
*Miss S M Earley, BSc (Dundee)

Economics:
*Mrs C J Richards, BA (Dublin)

English & Theatre Studies:
*Mrs S A Stewart, BA (London), MA (London)
Mr J C Baddock, BA (UCL)
Ms A L Fenton, BA (University of Wales, Aberystwyth)
Miss A Gordon, MA (Aberdeen)
Mrs K Hack, BA (University of Wales, Swansea)
Miss V J Hallam, BA (Leeds)
Mrs N J Lewis, BA (York)

Geography:
Mrs R V Carr, BEd (Cambridge)
*Miss C F Grindrod, BSc (London, Wye College)
Mrs S E Jacot, BA (Durham)

Mrs P A Thomas, BSc (London, Guildhall), MSc (University of East London)

History & Politics:
*Mrs J E Hellier, BA (Durham), MA (London)
Mrs S Meakins, MA (Cambridge)
Mrs A Minear, BA (Exeter)
Mr R J K Sheard, BA (York)

Information Technology:
*Dr S J Bancroft, BSc, PhD (Birmingham), MIMechE, CEng
Mrs E A Cross, BSc (Surrey)

Mathematics:
*Mrs J A Aughwane, BSc (Loughborough University of Technology)
Mrs E Bearpark, LLB (Hull)
Mrs K M Denny, BSc (London)
Mrs S M Norris, BSc (Warwick)
Mrs D Patteson, BSc (London)
Mrs G T Rackham, BSc (Sheffield)
Dr F Turner, BSc, PhD (UMIST)

Modern Languages:
Mrs M Arnold, BA (London)
Dr D J Beer, BA (Oxon), MA (London), PhD (London)
*Mrs M J Bell, MA (London), BA (Southampton)
Miss K A Buckley, BA (Exeter) *Head of Sixth Form*
Mr R Mantle, MA (Oxon), MLitt (Glasgow)
Miss C M Motte, Maîtrise (Strasbourg)
Mrs C A Salisbury, BA (Hull)
Mrs A B Taylor, BA (Rome)
Mrs L M Taylor, BA (Exeter)

Music:
Mrs L Cawley, BA (OU)
Mr M F Suranyi, BA (Durham)
*Mr G A Thorp, MA (Cantab), FRCO
Mrs P L Wood, GRSM, LRAM, MTC

Physical Education:
Mrs M Clifford, CertEd (Neville's Cross College, Durham)
Ms S M Cornwall, BA (University of Wales)
*Mrs L Fitzroy-Stone, BEd (Bedford College)
Mrs J Kemp, BEd (Brighton Polytechnic)
Mrs K L Nanson, BEd (Bedford College)
Miss M Young, BEd (University of Wales, Bangor)

Psychology:
*Dr J E Boyd, BSc (Newcast;e), PhD (London, King's College)

Religious Studies:
Mrs M J Barnes, BA (Bristol)
Mrs A E Gillingham, BA (Westminster)
*Mrs J A Wagstaff, BA (University of Wales, Lampeter)

Science:
Mrs E Carter, BSc (Sheffield)
Mrs W Cocks, BSc (Leeds), MSc (Oxon), ACE (Oxon) *Head of Year 7*
Mrs B I A Davies, BSc (London, King's College)
*Mrs C A Fuller, BSc (Newcastle)
Dr K D Fuller, MSc (Reading), PhD (Reading) *Head of Physics*
Miss C J Guthrie, MA (Cambridge)
Mrs C R Kittow, CertEd (Homerton College, Cambridge) *Head of Years 8 & 9*
Mrs P McCormack, BSc (University of Wales, Cardiff)
Miss S H Onslow, BSc (Surrey)
Dr H Prideaux, BSc (Durham), PhD (Southampton)
Mrs G A Scott, BSc (Surrey)
Dr F M N Zumpe, BSc (Witwatersrand), PhD (London) *Head of Biology*

Junior School:
Miss S J Bauchop, BEd (Leicester)
Mrs J A Bottomley, BA (Birmingham)
Mrs S E Chapman, BEd (DeMontfort)e)
Mrs M B Crowley, BSc (London)
Mrs J Dobell, CertEd (Bradford)
Mrs J M Dubery, CertEd (Bristol)
Miss B E Ellis, BEd (Surrey)
Miss M Erdmann, CertEd (Germany)
Mrs J E Flood, BA (Reading)
Mrs D C Hall, BA(Ed) (Exeter)
Miss R K Hinkley, BEd (De Montfort)
Mrs D M Jones, CertEd (St Mary's, Bangor)
Mrs E A Lloyd, BA (Reading)
Mrs R Melville, CertEd (Philippa Fawcett College, London)
Miss C E Pow, BA (University College, Chichester)
Ms N-A Sloane, BEd (Kingston)
Mrs H M Stamp, BEd (East Anglia)
Mrs A Stewart, MA (Glasgow)
Mrs A Taylor, BSc (Manchester Polytechnic)
Mrs Y M Warren, BSc (University of Wales, Cardiff)

Careers: Mrs S M Goodsir, BA (Leicester)

Librarian: Mrs Y A Skene
Assistant Librarian: Mrs M D B Olive

Visiting Staff:

Speech and Drama:
Mrs Y Craven, LLAM, LAMDA
Miss T Quinn, FVCM (Hons), LVCM (Hons), LGSM, LLAM

Music:

Piano:
Mrs M I Baxter, BSc, ARCM
Mrs D Dawkins, LRSM, LTCL
Mrs P M Morley, ATCL, ARCM, GRSM
Mrs M Roberts, BA, ARCM, LRAM
Miss V C Rowe, GRSM

Singing:
Ms N Long, MM, BA
Mrs S M Hellec-Butcher

Head of Strings & Cello:
Mrs A Scott, LRAM, DipRAM

Violin and Viola:
Mrs S B Dewey, LRAM
Mr B Lloyd Wilson, MA, AGSM, ARCM
Mrs S Thomas, ARCM, LRAM
Miss C A Wioehrel, Grad (Lucerne)

'Cello:
Ms C Alexander, ARCM, LRAM
Miss E Whipple, AGSM

Double Bass:
Miss N Bailey, ARCM, LRAM

Guitar:
Mr P L Howe, ARCM

Harp:
Mrs J Carr, BMus

Flute:
Mrs D Ball, LTCL
Miss R E Chappell, AGSM
Mrs F J Howe, ARCM

Oboe:
Miss J Lees, ARCM

Clarinet and Piano:
Mrs J Dodd, LRAM, ARCM

Clarinet:
Miss C Henry

Bassoon:
Miss A Meadows, GRSM, ARCM, LRAM

Brass:
Mr B J Ray, ARCM

Saxophone:
Mr S D West, GTCL, LTCL

Recorder and Harpsichord:
Miss P Cave, LRAM, GRSM

Percussion:
Mr N Marshall

Guildford High School is a day school for academically able girls. Enthusiasm and love of learning are encouraged through a broadly-based curriculum which goes well beyond examination requirements. Extra-curricular activities are seen as an essential element in a well-balanced education. The school is a Church of England foundation and has a deep concern for each girl's personal development.

The curriculum is designed to provide a broad academic education without early specialisation. It includes English, History, Geography, Economics, French, German, Italian, Spanish, Russian, Latin, Greek, Mathematics, Information Technology, Physics, Chemistry, Biology, Music, Art and Design, Design Technology, Food Technology and Physical Education. All girls attend Religious Studies lessons. Pupils are prepared for the General Certificate of Secondary Education, for General Certificate of Education Advanced Level and for Oxbridge entrance.

Sixth Form. There is a strong Sixth Form and most girls take four AS Level subjects from the wide range offered and continue with 3 of these subjects to A Level. They also follow a General Studies course and a continuation course in a modern language if they are not involved in A level or GCSE language. Virtually all girls proceed to University or to other areas of Higher Education. The Sixth Form have their own accommodation, which has been extended and refurbished as part of a major development plan.

Music. There is a lively musical tradition and girls are encouraged to play musical instruments and to join one of the orchestras or the wind bands. They are prepared for the Associated Board Music and Speech and Drama examinations.

The Duke of Edinburgh Award Scheme, run jointly by parents and teachers, offers opportunities for developing character through service, skills and expeditions.

Physical Education. Lacrosse, netball, tennis, rounders, athletics, gymnastics, swimming, badminton and basketball. Sixth Formers have a wider choice and may use facilities at the University and Sports Centre.

Situation and Facilities. The school is pleasantly situated near the centre of Guildford on a bus route and close to London Road Station; frequent trains to the main station provide links over a wide area. Facilities include libraries, eleven well-equipped laboratories, an Information Technology Centre, a Design Technology Centre, Art and Design Studios, a Food Technology Room, Music Rooms, Music Technology Studio, a Careers Room and Dining Hall. There is a new Gymnasium, indoor Swimming Pool and four-acre playing field.

The Junior Department, which combines a warm, caring atmosphere with a stimulating environment, offers careful preparation for entry to the Senior School. A new Junior School building was opened in September 1993, as part of a major development plan.

Number on roll. 900 day girls.

Age range. 4 to 18 years.

Normal ages of entry. 4, 7 and 11 years and Sixth Form level.

Admissions. The school sets its own entrance examination. Academic standards are high.

Fees. Termly fees (September 2000): Lower Junior £1,358, Upper Junior £1,847, Senior £2,288. Text books and stationery are provided.

Extra Subjects. Instruments (orchestral) £104, Speech & Drama £52.

Bursaries. (*see* Entrance Scholarship section) Available at Sixth Form level.

Charitable status. The Church Schools Company (to which Guildford High School belongs) is a Registered Charity, number 1016538. Its aims and objectives are to provide pupils with a sound education based on and inspired by Christian principles.

The Haberdashers' Aske's School for Girls

Aldenham Road Elstree Herts WD6 3BT
Tel: 020 8266 2300
Fax: 020 8266 2303

Motto: *Serve and Obey*

This School forms part of the ancient foundation of Robert Aske and is governed by members of the Worshipful Company of Haberdashers, together with certain representatives of other bodies.

Clerk to the School Governors: Mr J P R Mitchell

***Headmistress:* Mrs P A Penney**, BA (Bristol), FRSA, FIMgt, MInstD

Deputy Headmistress: Miss B O'Connor, BA (Oxon)

Deputy Headmistress: Mrs A Hale, BA (Dunelm)

Bursar: Mr P B C Collins, MA (Oxon)

ICT Manager: Mr K O Lewis, BSc (Aston), MEd

Teaching Staff:

Art:
*Miss S Monelle, BA (Reading)
Miss L A Powell, Dip (Swansea Coll of Art), Teaching Cert of University of Wales
Mrs P White, BA (Sheffield School of Art & Design)

Careers:
*Mrs R A Balfour, BA (Bristol)

Classics:
*Mrs R Battersby, MA (Cantab)
Mrs R A Balfour, BA (Bristol)
Miss B O'Connor, BA (Oxon)
Miss S M Williams, MA (Cantab)

Computer Studies:
*Mr A R Thacker, BSc (Manchester)

Craft Design and Technology:
*Miss S McCarthy, BSc Hons (Brunel)
Miss L Grover, BA, QTS (Middlesex)
Mr R W Thacker, AdvDip (Brunel)

Economics:
*Mr M Catley, BSc (LSE)
Mrs S Cowley, MA (Cantab)

English:
*Miss A M Harvey, MA (Oxon)
Mr T W Blaikie, BA (Lond)
Mrs S Collins, MA (Edinburgh)
Dr C Harraway, BA (Exeter)

Micc C MacDonald, BA (Kingston, Ontario)
Miss F Miles, BA (Cantab)
Mrs A Yates, BA (London), MA (London)

Geography:
*Mrs S M Wood, BA (Hull), FRGS
Mrs S Murphy, BSc (Notts)
Mrs V J Robinson, BA(Econ) (Sheffield)
Mrs A Wooding, BSc (Manchester), MSc (London)

History:
*Mrs A Pearson, BA (Dunelm)
Mr P Harper, BA (Oxon)
Miss C Thompson, BA (Exeter)

Library:
Mrs A Fynes-Clinton, BA (Canterbury, New Zealand), DipLib
Mrs R Gosden, BA (Kent)

Mathematics:
*Mrs V P Mayer, BSc (*London*)
Mr T Bowley, BA (*Oxon*)
Mrs C Godfrey, BSc (Leicester)
Mrs M Hodgskin, BA (Open University)
Mrs A Kingsley-Smith, BSc (Lond)
Miss E Paske, BA (Liverpool)
Mrs K Roantree, BA (York)
Mrs M Smith, BSc (London)
Mr A Thacker, BSc (Manchester)

Modern Languages:
*Mr L J Bardou, L ès L, Dip et Sup, CAPES (Sorbonne), MPhil (Sussex)
Mrs A M Dennis, BA (Notts)
Mrs S Dexter, BA (University of Milan)
Mrs I Fanning, Lic Artes (University of Buenos Aires)
Miss J Gershon, MA (Bristol)
Mrs M Gradon, L-ès-L (Lille)
Mrs L Grieder, BA, MLitt (Bristol)
Mrs A Hale, BA (Dunelm)
Miss G Mellor, BA (Exeter)
Mrs K Nabarro, BA (British Columbia)
Mrs F Ray, L-ès-L Matrise, CAPES
Mrs E Saint-Dizier, L-ès-L (Toulouse)
Mrs M I Walmsley, BA (Birmingham)

Music:
*Mr A Mitchell, BA, LLCM
Mrs L Bernays, BA (Oxon)
Miss A Turnbull, LRAM

and 21 Visiting teachers

Physical Education:
*Miss A M Saunders, IM Marsh Coll of PE, BEd (Liverpool)
Mrs H Birkett, BEd (Bedford PE College)
Miss R Edbrooke, BEd (Bedford PE College)
Miss L Priest, BA(Ed) (Exeter)
Mrs K P Miller, BA (Warwick)
Mrs P A Newton (Cert of Cambridge Institute of Education)
Miss L Youds, BEd (Brighton)

Religious Studies:
*Mr P Moriarty, MA (Oxon)
Miss C Hughes, BA (Oxon)
Miss V Thompson, BA (Oxon)

Science:
*Mrs M R Brown, BSc (Aberdeen)
Mrs J Dabby-Joory, BSc (Southampton)
Mrs R J Goodby, BSc (London)
Mrs B Grey, BA (Keele)
Mrs J E Jones, BSc (Lond), CBiol, MIBiol
Mrs V Leigh, BSc (London)
Miss Z Makepeace, MChem (Oxon)
Mrs J McNally, BSc (Hatfield), CChem, MRSC
Mrs S C Mitchell, BSc (Manchester)
Miss K Phillips, BSc (Bristol)
Mrs C Redding, BA (Cantab)
Dr M Venables, BA (Oxon), PhD (Birmingham)
Mrs M Weaver, BA (Open Univ)

Lower School:
*Mrs D Targett, Teacher's Cert (Oxon)
Mrs R Blum, CertEd (Trent Park College of Education)
Miss E Burman (Surrey)
Mrs P A Dear, BSc (Univ College of Wales)
Mrs M Galvin, BEd (London)
Mrs S Hart, BEd
Mrs K Herridge, CertEd (Whitelands College)
Mr N Hobley, BSc (Oxford Brookes)
Mrs J Kirk, ARCM
Miss K McNerney, BSc (Newcastle)
Mrs E Murdoch, CertEd, DipEd
Mrs I Neve, BA (University College of North Wales)
Mrs C W Pepper, CertEd (Lond)
Mrs S Rose, BEd (Cantab)
Miss S Skidmore, BA (Exeter)
Mrs S Swain, BA (London)
Miss C Yates, BEd (Surrey)

Personal Assistant to the Head Mistress: Mrs B Cohen

The School moved in September 1974 to the Aldenham Estate, and stands in 56 acres of park and woodland adjacent to Haberdashers' Aske's School for Boys. It is served by an extensive school coach service throughout Hertfordshire, parts of Middlesex and North London.

The School is open to girls between the ages of 4 and 18. There are 1,140 day girls. There are excellent sports facilities including a Sports Hall, a double gymnasia and a heated indoor swimming pool. There is a large well-equipped library, a new Technology building, extensive science laboratories, an IT suite, two modern languages laboratories, and a new Art/Music school was opened in 1995. The curriculum comprises all the usual school subjects with provision for separate Sciences throughout the School. At Advanced Level the curriculum covers Classics, Economics, Humanities, Mathematics, Modern Languages and Science. Pupils are prepared for GCSE and for University entry. Sixth Form students are not required to wear uniform and have their own common room complex.

Fees. Upper School £2,175. Lower School £1,840. A number of Scholarships and Bursaries are given annually.

Charitable status. The Haberdashers' Aske's Charity is a Registered Charity, number 313996. It exists to support schools at Elstree and Hatcham.

Haberdashers' Monmouth School for Girls

Hereford Road Monmouth NP25 5XT
Tel: (01600) 711100
Fax: (01600) 711233
e-mail: admissions@hmsg.gwent.sch.uk
website: www.habs-monmouth.org

Motto: *Serve and Obey*

Trustees: The Worshipful Company of Haberdashers

Governing Body:
Chairman: Dr C J T Bateman
The Master of the Worshipful Company of Haberdashers, ex officio

J A Ackroyd, Esq
P J Attenborough, Esq, MA
J E N Bates, Esq
Professor P J Bayley
Mrs H M Bosanquet, BA
Dr J M Cook
Cllr W A L Crump
J W W Hamilton, Esq
D A Hey, Esq
Mrs M Molyneux
Mrs E Murray
P M Oppenheimer, Esq, MA
G F Pulman, Esq, MA, QC
Professor M W Roberts
Mrs K Spencer
A W Twiston Davies, Esq
Mrs M Wetherell

Clerk to the Governors: P J C Metcalfe, Esq, FCA

Bursar: Wing Commander David Charlton

***Headmistress:* Dr Brenda Despontin**, BA Hons, MA, PhD (Wales) Psychology, PGCE (Bath), MInstMgt

Deputy Headmistress (*Curriculum*): Mrs S M Green, BA Hons Geography, PGCE (Wales)

Deputy Headmistress (*Pastoral*) with responsibility for the Sixth Form: Dr R A Weeks, BSc Hons, PhD (Birmingham) *Chemistry*

Head of Upper School: Mrs C D Trayler-Smith, BA Hons, ATD (Wales)

Head of Middle School: Mrs O E Davis, BSc Joint Hons (Salford)

Head of Year 7: Mrs J A Ward, MA (Oxon) *German*

Heads of Department:

Art:
Mr A E Bethell, ATD, NDD (Manchester)

Careers:
Mrs D E Hudson, BSc Hons (Exeter)

Classics:
Mrs P A Biddle, BA Hons (Bristol), Dip of Institute of Linguists, PGCE (*London*)

Computer Studies:
Mrs D Walmsley, BSc, MPhil, MBCS, CEng

Design Technology:
Mr P Williams, BA Hons, ATD (Birmingham)

Drama & Theatre Arts:
Miss S Slingo, BEd Hons (Wales), LRAM, CertEd

Economics and Business Studies:
Mrs L M Read, BA Hons (Wales)

English:
Mrs L C Ramsden, CertEd (London)

Geography:
Mr J Terry, BSc Hons (London)

History:
Mrs K MacDonald, BA (Manchester), PGCE (Wales), MSc(Econ) (Wales

Home Economics:
Mrs M Cornelissen, BEd Hons (Plymouth)

Mathematics:
Mrs A Evans, BSc Hons (London)

Modern Languages:
Mrs S L Coutts, MA (St Andrews)

Director of Music:
Miss A Randles, BMus (London), LRAM, LTCL

PSE:
Mrs M E Allen, BSc Hons (Birmingham), PGCE (London)

Physical Education:
Miss R V Parry, BA Hons (Bedford), PGCE (Bedford)

Psychology:
Mrs D M Moore, BA (Open University), CertEd (Birmingham)

Religious Studies:
Mr J M Lewis, BDiv MTh, PGCE (Wales)

Science:
Dr P M Davies, BSc Hons, PhD (Wales) *Physics*

Special Needs & TEFL: Mrs D Mori, DipSEN (Wales), DipTEFL, PGCE

Preparatory Department – (*Gilbert Inglefield House*)
Mrs R Vigrass, BA Hons, PGCE (London) *Head of Preparatory Department*

Head of Boarding:
Mrs J James, BA Hons (Edinburgh) *Geography*

Librarian:
Mrs F Green, ALA

Haberdashers' Monmouth School for Girls is one of the two schools of the Jones's Monmouth Foundation, arising from a bequest of William Jones, Merchant, in 1615, and administered by the Worshipful Company of Haberdashers. The School stands high on the outskirts of the town of Monmouth, in the beautiful countryside of the Wye Valley.

There are about 575 girls in the Main School with a Sixth Form of 158. Pupils from 7–11 have their own modern Preparatory Department of 107 girls on site. Thriving Boarding Community with accommodation on the school site, includes a Junior House and modern Senior House with study bedrooms.

A £2 million Science Building opened September 1994, updated Sixth Form block in 1998 and new Music rehearsal rooms in May 1999. Classrooms and laboratories are extensive, with special Sixth Form provision. Specialist workshops are provided for DT and Drama. Full use is made of the ample sports facilities; spacious playing fields, tennis courts, sports hall, indoor swimming pool and gymnasium are all adjacent to the School.

The School has a Christian foundation and girls are encouraged to attend the places of worship of their own denomination; the majority attend the parish church.

A large and fully qualified staff of graduates teaches a modern curriculum, which aims to achieve high academic results within a broader education, acknowledging our cultural inheritance and technological and social needs.

Classics is taught throughout the School. At examination level, are offered Latin GCSE, Latin AS/A level, Classical Civilisation AS/A level. Ancient Greek is offered at Sixth Form level only.

Almost all pupils progress to Higher Education. With ample careers advice, girls are aware of the scope of degree subjects; several annually enter Oxford and Cambridge.

Every encouragement is given to creative and practical work, especially Music and Drama. Girls frequently attend concerts, plays and exhibitions, and an active interest is taken in industry and management. Local businesses lend support to the School's Young Enterprise schemes.

Girls participate in the Duke of Edinburgh Award scheme, help in the community and many also belong to local voluntary organisations.

Main sporting activities include lacrosse, netball, tennis, rowing, fencing and dance; many played at County and National level.

Fees. (*see* Entrance Scholarship section) (As from September, 2001). Tuition £1,869–£2,366 per term. Boarding £1,885 per term.

Entry is usually at 7, 11, 13 or post GCSE, although occasionally other vacancies occur. Entrance to the first class of the Main School is by examination in January; scholarships and bursaries are awarded at this age, 13+ and for the Sixth Form.

Tests for entry to the Preparatory Department for girls of 7 years are held in the Spring Term.

Prospectus, etc. on application to the Admissions Secretary.

Haberdashers' Monmouth School for Girls Old Girls' Association.

Secretary, Mrs J Mace, c/o Haberdashers' Monmouth School for Girls, Monmouth. The OGA Annual General Meeting is held at the school on second Saturday in November.

Charitable status. Jones's Grammar School Foundation is a Registered Charity, number 525616. The object of the Foundation shall be the provision and conduct in or near Monmouth of a day and boarding school for boys and a day and boarding school for girls which schools (hereinafter referred to as "the schools") shall respectively be called The Haberdashers' Monmouth School and The Haberdashers' Monmouth School for Girls.

Harrogate Ladies' College

Clarence Drive Harrogate North Yorkshire HG1 2QG
Tel: (01423) 504543
Fax: (01423) 568893
e-mail: enquire@hlc.org.uk
website: www.hlc.org.uk

Board of Governors:
P Taylor, Esq, JP, FCA, ATII (*Chairman*)
A J Armitage, Esq, FCCA, FIPA, FICM
Mrs S Baron, DipCOT
Mrs M Dance, MA (Oxon), JP
Mrs J Hepworth, BA
E Robinson, Esq, MA (Oxon)
D Simpson, Esq
J P Spens, Esq
Mrs C Tennant, MA, PGCE
R Tennant, Esq

Secretary to the Governors and General Manager of Allied Schools: N Coulson, Esq, MA, MBA

***Headmistress:* Dr M J Hustler**, BSc, PhD

Deputy Head: Mr D C Andrews, BA(Mus)

Head of Boarding: Miss P J Shield, BEd (Lancaster), TCert

Head of Sixth Form: Mrs P D Jervis, BA (Sheffield), PGCE (*Head of English*)

Full-time staff:
Mrs C S Alp, GRSM, LRAM, LGSM
Mrs K E Baskerville, BA (Leeds), PGCE
Mrs M Bond, BA (Notts)
Miss N J Butters, BA (Leeds), PGCE, MMedSci (Sheffield)
Mrs J D Chapman, BSc (Birmingham), CertEd (Leeds), PGCE
Mr D Chubb, BSc (Leeds), PGCE
Miss H Clothier, BA (Salford), PGCE
Miss V C Cooper, BSc, PGCE (Manchester), MEd (*Leeds*)
Miss H Eastwood, BEd (Bedford)
Mr D Gilbert, Dip Dramatic Art (RADA), LADA Gold Medal (Hons)
Mr J Gillespie, BSc (Durham), PGCE
Mrs G F Heyes, BA (London), BA (Open University), GIMA
Mrs A Hickling, BEd (Worcester)
Mr R Horton, BSc (Dunelm), PGCE
Mrs F Irvine, BEd *PE with Science*
Mrs J List, BA (York), PGCE
Miss T-S Mutchell, BSc (York), PGCE
Mr P Pritchard, BSc (Exeter), PGCE
Miss J Roberts, BA (Nottingham), PGCE
Mrs A J Saunders, BSc (York), PGCE
Mrs A Simmonds, MA (Cantab), PGCE
Mr T Skelling, BEd (Crewe & Alsager)
Mr K Slingsby, MA (Cantab), PGCE
Mr A C Staniland, BA (Leeds), PGCE
Mr A J Stretton, FTCL, GTCL, LTCL, PGCE
Mrs K E Sutton, BA (Newcastle), PGCE
Mrs C Upton, MA (Cantab), CertEd
Mrs C Viner, BA (London), PGCE
Miss A White, BSc (Bristol), PGCE
Miss K Williams, BEd Art (Leeds), CertEd

Part-time Staff:
Mrs G A Andrews, BA(Mus) (Reading)
Miss M Bovino, BA(Mus)
Mr R Britton, BA(Mus)
Mrs M A Bushby, BA (Leeds), LTCL
Mr D Chappel, BSc (Hull)
Mr D Clarke, BSc (Leeds), MSc
Mrs P Coghlan, ALCM, LAM, LAMDA
Mrs S C Coulbeck, BA (Belfast), DipEd
Mrs K L Dammone, BA (Hull), MA (Leeds), PGCE
Mrs W Dishman, BA (Manchester), MA (Lancaster), PGCE
Mrs C K E Faber, BA (Cantab)
Mrs D Griffin, BA (W Surrey)
Miss S E Harbisher, BEd (Liverpool)
Mrs S Hey, CertEd
Lady S E Hill, BA (Leeds), AYAS, LAM, Gold Medal (Hons)
Mrs J Jackson, BA (Open University), LRAM
Mr J Johnson, BA (Ripon & York), PGCE
Mrs B Jones, BSc (Leics), PGCE
Mrs E Livesey, BA (Preston), PGCE
Miss E Lloyd, BA(Mus)
Mrs C Martin, BA (Leeds Poly), PGCE
Mrs J M Middleton, AIDTA (Hons), RSA, YMCA, MIPR
Mrs D Murray, BA (Cardiff), MA (Bretton Hall), PGCE
Mrs B A Pankhurst, GRSM, ARMCM
Mrs M Parker, BA Fine Art (Newcastle), ATD, PGCE (Bristol)
Mrs L C Parsons, MA(Ed), CertEd
Mr I Peak, BEd, LGSM
Mrs J E Power, City & Guilds Teaching Certificate
Mrs F C Pygott, GRSM, ARMCM
Mr A P Selway, FRCO, GRSM, ARMCM, LRAM
Mrs M C Smith, GRSM, LRAM
Mrs L A Taylor-Parker, LRAM
Miss N Woods, BA(Mus)

Medical Officer: Dr S O'Neill, MB, BChir, MA, DRCOG

Health Centre Sister: Mrs B B Dean, SRN

Chaplain:

Bursar: Mr J D Hart, FIMgt, MInstAM, MBA

Assistant Bursar: Mrs A Adams

Pupils' Accounts: Mrs J Hatcher

Bursar's Secretary: Mrs P Tucker

Headmistress's PA: Miss C J Walshaw, BA (Leicester)

Receptionist: Mrs M Thewsey, BEd (Reading)

Assistant Secretary: Mrs R Coughlan

Librarian: Mrs F Brady, BSc (LeedsPoly)

Housemistresses:
Miss D Easterbrook (*Oakdale*)
Mrs L C Parsons (*Lancaster/York/Clarence*)
Miss P J Shield (*Lincoln East/Lincoln West*)
Mrs J Bailey (*Tower*)
Miss V Cooper (*Lancaster*)

Highfield Preparatory School:

Head: Mrs P Fenwick, CertEd
Deputy Head: Mrs P Grimsditch, CertEd

Full-time staff:
Mrs S Gladstone, BA (Newcastle)
Miss J Walton, BA(Ed) (Durham)
Miss S Howarth, BSc (Worcester College), PGCE
Mr T Marshall, BEd (Cambridge)
Mrs K Reeves, CertEd
Mrs J Rennison, NNEB

Part-time staff:
Mrs V Pickard
Mrs A Cook, BSc (York), PGCE
Miss V Robinson, RAD Teacher Training
Miss A Kennedy, TCert
Mrs M Scrimger, BEd
Mr N Dunne

Numbers and Location. Harrogate Ladies' College is a Boarding and Day school for 365 girls aged 10–18. Situated within the College campus, Highfield Prep School, which opened in 1999, is a Day prep school for nearly 100 boys and girls between the ages of 4-11. The College is situated in a quiet residential area on the Duchy Estate about 10 minutes walk from the town centre and is easily accessible by road and rail networks. Leeds/Bradford airport is 20 minutes' drive away. Harrogate itself is surrounded by areas of natural interest and beauty.

Accommodation. Approximately two thirds of the pupils are full or weekly boarders. Pupils enter 'Oakdale', the boarding house for 8–13 year olds and then progress to one of the five main houses on site. Upper Sixth Formers enjoy a greater sense of freedom in their own accommodation called 'Tower House'. This contains a large, modern kitchen, comfortable lounges and relaxation areas and all girls have individual study bedrooms. Each house has a Housemistress and Assistant Housemistress who are responsible for the well-being of the girls.

Curriculum and examinations. The College aims to provide a broad-based curriculum for the first three years in line with National Curriculum requirements. This leads to a choice of over 20 subjects at GCSE and A Level mainly using syllabuses of the Northern Examination and Assessment Board (AQA). Each girl has a form tutor who continuously monitors and assesses her development.

Facilities. The central building contains the principal classrooms, hall, library, and dining rooms, and a VI Form Centre with studies, seminar rooms, kitchens and leisure facilities. The College Chapel is nearby. An extension provides 8 laboratories for Physics, Chemistry, Biology and Computer Studies. There is a computer network of 90 plus Pentium PCs throughout the school. Additional facilities for specialised teaching include a language laboratory, studies for Art, Pottery, Design and Technology, Drama and also for Home Economics and Textiles. The College has its own amateur radio station. There is a well-equipped Health Centre with qualified nurses.

Sport. The College has its own sports hall, a full size indoor swimming pool, gymnasium, fitness centre, playing field, 9 tennis courts and 2 squash courts. Girls are taught a wide range of sports and may participate in sporting activities outside the school day. Lacrosse and netball are played in winter, and tennis, swimming and athletics are the main summer physical activities. Extra-curricular sports include horse riding, golf, badminton, sub-aqua, windsurfing, skiing, self-defence, judo, sailing and canoeing.

Sixth Form. The College has a thriving Sixth Form Community of 120 pupils. Girls may follow their chosen courses of AS/A Levels or follow the Advanced VCE Business qualification for 2 years. They also follow a General Studies course covering a wide variety of subjects, and there is a broad range of general cultural study. In preparation for adult life, Sixth Formers are expected to make a mature contribution to the running of the school and many hold formal positions of responsibility. Personal guidance is given to each girl with regard to her future plans and most pupils choose to continue their education at University.

Religious Affiliation. The College has a Church of England foundation although pupils of other religious denominations are welcomed. Religious teaching is in accordance with the principles of the Church of England and all girls attend Chapel services. A school confirmation is held each year in the chapel and girls may be prepared for acceptance into membership of churches of other denominations.

Music. A special feature is the interest given to music and choral work both in concerts and in the College Chapel, and the girls attend frequent concerts and dramatic performances in Harrogate. There are Junior and Senior choirs, orchestra, string, wind and brass groups.

Scholarships. Open scholarships including music scholarships and exhibitions are awarded annually on the results of an examination held each Spring term and there are also several awards to girls already in the School.

Fees as at September 2000. Boarding £4,155 per term; Weekly Boarding £4,155 per term; Day £2,545 per term. There is a reduction for a girl joining her sister in the School. The fees cover most normal school charges. Individual tuition in a musical instrument, Dance (Ballet/Tap/Modern), Riding or Diction is an extra charge.

Entry. Entry is usually at age 11, 13 or at Sixth Form level. Entry is based on the College's own entrance examination and a school report. Sixth Form entry is conditional upon GCSE achievement and an interview with the Headmistress.

Charitable status. Registered Charity, number 529579. Harrogate Ladies' College exists to provide high quality education for girls.

Headington School
Oxford

Oxford OX3 7TD
Tel: (01865) 759100
Admissions: (01865) 759113
Fax: (01865) 760268
e-mail: admissions@headington.org
website: www.headington.org

Patrons:
Sir Michael Atiyah, OM, PRS, MA
Sir Roger Bannister, CBE, DM, FRCP
The Rt Hon Lord Robert Blake of Braydestron, MA, BLitt, FBA
The Rev Canon N Macdonald Ramm, MA

Council:
Chairman: Mrs C Wood, MA, VetMB, MRCPath, MRCVS
Vice-Chairman: Mr S P B Capel, LLB

Mr W G Alden, MA, MBA
Mr R G Barnes, BSc, MBA
Mrs T Boswood, BA
Miss E Castle, BA, JP

Dr R P R Dawber, MA, MB, ChB, FRCP
Mr R C H Genochio, MA
Mrs J H Hearnden, NFF
Mrs R C Miles, MA, ACA
Mr G A Paine, JP, FCA
Dr J M Peach, BSc, MA, DPhil
Mrs E M Rawling, MA, MBE
Mr D S Ridout, MSI
Mr P G Saugman, MA, OBE
Dr R Stewart, BA, MSc, PhD
Mrs R J S Talbot Rice
Prof G Upton, MA, MEd, PhD, CPsychol, FBPSS

Secretary to the Council: Mr John Clark, MA

Staff:

Head Mistress: **Mrs H A Fender**, BA Hons (Exeter) *History*

Deputy Headmistress: Mrs J Bulkeley, BA Hons (Oxon) *Economics*

Assistant Head and Director of Studies: Dr J Jefferies, BSc Hons, PhD (Exeter)

Assistant Head and Head of 6th Form: Mr M Farmer, BA Hons (Portsmouth) *Economics*

Head of Boarding: Mrs A Tear, Diploma (Textiles) (Leicester)

Junior School Tutor: Mrs E Gittins, BD Hons (London), PGCE (Cambridge

Senior School Tutor: Dr P Smaldon, BSc (Swansea)

Bursar: Colonel A Brett, BSc

English:
Mrs J A Whitehead, BA Hons (Exeter), PGCE (London) *Head of Department*
Mrs N Archer, BA Hons, PGCE (London) *Head of Drama*
Miss S R Duff, CertTEFL (*part-time*)
Mrs K Hegarty, BA Hons, DipEd (Queens Belfast)
Mr P Waddleton, BA Hons, MA (Oxford Brookes), PGCE (Westminster College) *CTEFL*
Miss L R Wilkinson, BA Hons, PGCE (Reading)
Mrs J French, BSc Hons (Nottingham), DipEd (Birmingham) (*part time*)
Mrs K Pigott, BA (Cape Town)
Mrs C Dawson, BSc (London), RSADipSpLD, Cert in Counselling, SEN

Mathematics:
Mrs C Knight, BSc (Strathclyde), PGCE (Westminster College) *Head of Department*
Mrs R Bowen, MA (Oxon), PGCE (Oxon)
Mrs C Tilley, BSc Hons (Aberystwyth)
Mrs J Fouweather, BSc Hons, PGCE (Hull) (*part-time*)
Mrs A Hutchison, MA Hons (Glasgow), PGCE (Jordanhill) *part-time*
Mrs J Bulkeley, BA Hons (Oxon) *Economics*
Mrs S Long, BSc Hons (Birmingham)

Information Technology and Business Studies:
Mr M Howe, BA Hons, PGCE (East Anglia) *Head of Department*
Miss S R Duff, BTec, HND, CertTEFL, FAETC (Oxford College of FE) (*part-time*)
Mrs R Kitto, BA Hons (Open University), TEFL (*part-time*)
Mr M Farmer, BA Hons (Portsmouth), PGCE
Mr M Chandler *Systems Manager*

Economics:
Mrs J Bulkeley, BA Hons (Oxon)
Mr M Farmer, BA Hons (Portsmouth), PGCE

Modern Languages:
Dr G Delaney, BA Hons (Manchester), PhD (Warwick), PGCE (Bristol) *French & German, Head of Department*
Mrs C D Cruz, MIL, PGCE (London) *French and Spanish*
Mrs G H Earle, MA (Oxon), DipEd (Oxford) *French and Spanish, Head of Spanish*
Mrs S Hallas, BA Hons, PGCE (Leicester) *French*
Frau C Kirchlechner, DiplPsych (Munich) (*Assistant*)
Mme C Mazou, Licence (Orleans), PGCE (Westminster College) *French* (*part-time*)
Mrs J Longley, MA (Oxon, RSACert, TEFLA (London)
Mrs E Whiteley, BA Hons, PGCE (London) *French and German* (*part-time*)

Science:
Mrs M L Goodhead, BSc Hons (Leicester), MSc (London) *Head of Physics, Head of Department*
Mrs C Al-Sabouni, BA Hons (Open University), PGCE (Oxford)
Mr A Ashley, BSc Hons (Newcastle), MA (Keele), PGCE (Leeds)
Dr H Brooks, BSc Hons, PhD, PGCE (London)
Mrs C Canlan-Shaw, BSc Hons (Loughborough), PGCE (Roehampton)
Miss L I Davis, BSc Hons (Open University), CertEd (Durham) (*part-time*)
Mrs S Eden, MA (Cantab), CertEd (Cambridge)
Mrs S Helby, BSc, CertEd (Birmingham) *Head of Chemistry*
Dr K Krebs, MA, DPhil (Oxon), CertEd (Bangor) *Head of Biology*
Dr P Smaldon, BSc (University College of Swansea, South Wales) (*part time*)

Classics:
Mrs C A E Hamand, BA Hons (Dunelm & London), PGCE (Birmingham) *Head of Department* (*part-time*)
Miss G Hutchinson, BA Hons (Keele), PGCE (Nottingham)

History, Politics and Law:
Mrs J Ormston, BA Hons, PGCE (London) *Joint Head of Dept*
Mrs S Wilkinson, BA Hons (Newcastle), PGCE (Oxford) *Joint Head of Dept*
Mrs H Fender, BA Hons (Exeter), PGCE (London)
Mrs E Parkes, BA Hons (Hull), PGCE (Leicester) (*part-time*)
Miss M Macaskill, BA (Honshaw, Exeter), PGCE in Legal Practice (*part time*)
Mr A Ashley, BSc Hons (Newcastle), MA (Keele), PGCE (Leeds) *Psychology*

Geography:
Mrs L Newman, BA Hons, PGCE (Exeter) *Head of Department*
Dr J Jefferies, BSc Hons, PhD (Exeter)
Mrs H Brewin, BSc Hons (Nottingham), PGCE (Durham) (*part-time*)
Mrs M A James, BA Hons, PGCE (London) (*part-time*)
Mrs C E Moffat, BA Hons (Leicester), MA (Northumbria), PGCE (Liverpool) (*part-time*)

Religious Studies:
Mrs E Gittins, BD Hons (London), PGCE (Cambridge) *Head of Department*
Mr I Price, BA Hons (Wales), MA (London), PGCE (Greenwich)

Home Economics:
Mrs J M Taylor, DipEd (Bath) *Textiles, Head of Department*
Mrs J Amos, BEd (Newcastle) *Food and Nutrition*
Mrs C Stevenson, CertEd
Mrs A Tear

Art and Design and Art History:
Mr M Taylor, BA Hons (Coventry) *Head of Department*
Mr N James, BA Hons (Cheltenham & Gloucester College), PGCE (Surrey)
Miss M A MacDonald, DipArt (Edinburgh) PGCE (Birmingham)

Dr D B Morrish, BA Hons (York), MA (Kent), DPhil (York) (*part-time*)
Mrs A Turner, BA Hons, PGCE (Reading) (*part-time*)

Physical Education:
Mrs J Wareham, BEd Hons (Bulmershe College, Reading) *Head of Department*
Mrs M Buswell, CertEd (Bedford) (*part-time*)
Mrs J Collinson, BA (Open University), CertEd (Dartford)
Mrs S Israel, CertEd (Bedford) (*part-time*)
Mrs J Roche, CertEd (Bedford) (*part-time*)
Miss S Mitchell, BEd Hons (Durham) *Director of Rowing*

Music:
Mr M Paine, BA Hons, ARCM, PGCE (Reading) *Director of Music*
Mr J Penman, BMus, MMus, PGCE
Mrs S Chappell, BA (Colchester) *Head of Music, Junior School*
Miss C Goble, BMus Hons (Southampton)

Theatre Studies:
Mrs S Pelling, LGSM, FRSA *Head of Department*
Miss B Hines, BA (*part time*)
Mrs S Lowe, AGSM (*part time*)

Housemistresses (*Boarding*):
Senior Housemistress: Mrs M Rodgers, CertEd (Liverpool), BSc (Open University)

Celia Marsh Housemistress: Mrs S Long, BSc Hons (Birmingham)

Junior Housemistress: Mrs S Hawkins

Visiting instrumental music teachers:

Piano:
Mr R Leigh Harris, MMus, GRSM, PGCE
Mrs S Chappell, MA (Reading), BA Hons (Colchester)
Mrs K Suter, GRSM, LRAM, ALCM
Mrs M Cooper
Miss F Hedges, MA (Oxon), PGCE
Ms S Stowe, ARCM

Strings:
Miss I Knowland, LRAM
Mrs G Warson
Mr O Bonnici
Mrs V Kay
Mrs P Chilcott

Woodwind:
Mrs J Cairns, GLCM, ALCM
Miss C Goble, BMus Hons
Mrs S Nichols, GRSM, LRAM (*piano*), ARCM (*oboe*)

Brass:
Mr D McNaughton, BA Hons

Guitar:
Mr M Ridout, GRSM

Percussion:
Mr I Dawes

Singing: Mrs A Rogers, GRSM, LRAM

Visiting Coaches:
Fencing: Mr A H Jones, AFA
Rowing:
Miss S Mitchell, BEd Hons (Durham) (*Director of Rowing*); Mrs C Partridge
Dr A Green
Mr B Gibson
Mr J Broadhurst
Miss T Crosland
Tennis: Mrs J Hobbs; Mr R Watkins
Trampolining: Miss S Costigan, BTA; Miss J Spurling, BTA
Judo: Mrs L Scarlett, BJA
Badminton: Mr I Grierson, BA
Volleyball: Mr G Slater, BVA
Basketball: Mr S Cruz, BBA
Swimming: Mrs T Bremble; Mrs J Smith; Miss L Smith, BEd Hons (Cheltenham)
Aerobics and Gymnastics: Miss L Smith

Administrative Staff:
Catering Manager: Mr P Rowcliffe, AHCIMA, MISM
Housekeeper: Miss S Brown
PA to the Headmistress: Mrs C Colley
Assistant Secretary: Mrs E Reed
Admissions Registrar: Mrs J E Pennington
Assistant Registrar: Mrs A Baxter
Assistant Bursar: Mrs K Hoy, BSc, ACA
Bursar's Secretary: Mrs L Painter
Bursar's Assistants:
Mrs A Mercier
Mrs J Miller
Swimming Pool and Sports Hall Manager: Mr G R Arman

Medical Staff:
School Doctors:
Dr G E Sacks, MB
Dr H M Merriman, MB, BS, FFARCS, MRCGP, DRCOG
Sanatorium Nurses: Mrs C Martin, SEN, Mrs C Allen, RN, RM, DipHE

Junior School

Head: Mrs R Faulkner, CertEd (Lancaster)

LIII (*10+*):
Miss E Gibbs, MA (York), PGCE (Reading)
Mrs K Smith, BEd Hons (Westminster College, Oxford) (*Deputy Head*)

UII (*9+*): Mrs E Newton, CertEd (Culham College of Education)

UII (*9+*): Miss C Davies, BEd Hons (Westminster College, Oxford)

LII (*8+*): Miss S Cousins, BA Hons (Hull), PGCE (Leicester)

LII (*8+*): Mrs R Morton-Jack, Montessori Dip, CertEd (Froebel)

Form I (*7+*): Mrs S Lifely, BEd Hons (Oxford Brookes)

Form I (*7+*): Mrs C Marshall, BEd Hons (Oxford Brookes)

Transition (*6+*): Dr L E Hughes, BSc Hons, PhD (Aberystwyth), PGCE (Westminster College)

Kindergarten (*5+*): Mrs S C Slater, MA, DipEd, PGCE (Aberdeen)

Pre-Kindergarten (*4+*): Mrs R Griffiths, CertEd (Cambridge)

Nursery (*3+*):
Mrs M Kempton, BA Hons (Nottingham), PGCE (Bristol)
Miss C Tebbitt, NNEB

Physical Education: Mrs L Smith, BEd Hons (Cheltenham)

Class Music: Mrs Chappell, BA (Colchester)
French: Mrs M Blanc, Licence et CAPES d'Anglais

Other teaching staff:
Mrs C Delderfield, BEd (Cambridge)
Mrs Paplomatas, CertEd (Westminster College)
Mrs R M E Ford *Ballet*
Mrs D Goddard

Administrative Staff:
PA to the Head: Mrs J E Kitching
School Secretary: Mrs A Blanchard

Headington School Oxford is a boarding and day school for 600 girls from 11 to 18, with a separate Junior School of a further 230 pupils with girls from 3 and boys from 3 until the age of seven. Girls may board from the age of nine. Weekly boarding is a popular option throughout the school.

History. The school was founded in 1915 and moved to its current buildings in 1930. It is one of the UK's top 100 academic schools, and yet is dedicated to providing a broad education, in which other attributes such as music, art, sport and drama play an important role. The school is situated in 26 acres of grounds, one mile from the centre of Oxford and just under 60 miles from London. It is a Church of England Foundation but girls of all denominations are actively welcomed.

A steady programme of building and upgrading has ensured excellent facilities for both living and working. A major three year £2.3 million development programme is currently underway, with a major new teaching block for Mathematics and Humanities opening in 2001, a Performing Arts Centre in 2002 and an extension to the Music Department in 2003. Over the past decade, other building works have included a new Sixth Form Centre, a sports hall (including a 25m indoor swimming pool) and fitness centre and, in 1998, a large art and design centre with studios, gallery areas, CAD and dark room.

All girls continue to higher education, with most studying for degrees in subjects as diverse as civil engineering, medicine, architecture and textiles. Detailed assistance on choice of universities is given in the Sixth Form through specialist computer programmes and careers tutors. The careers programme is in place throughout the school, with plenty of individual help as the girl reaches her GCSE years. Much use is made of Headington's proximity to London, Stratford and particularly Oxford. There are regular trips for all age groups to theatres, concerts, lectures, museums and galleries, while Oxford acts as a magnet for many visiting speakers, who can often be persuaded to include Headington in their itinerary.

Curriculum. In the **Senior School,** the National Curriculum is broadly followed up to GCSE level. In addition all girls take a three year course in Latin, from 12–14, and take either German or Spanish for one year before they all choose their GCSE subjects. All girls take GCSE in English, French, Mathematics and Science (Single or Dual Award) and half or full GCSEs in Information Technology. Up to four other subjects are chosen from Geography, History, Spanish, German, Greek, Latin, Classical Studies, Religious Studies, Music, Drama, Art and Design, Food, Textiles. As non examination subjects girls also take Religious Studies, Personal and Social Education and Physical Education. Most pupils stay to take A Levels at Headington and are usually joined by another 20 or so new pupils, some of whom will come from overseas. With the changes to the A Level curriculum in September 2000, girls now study four or sometimes five subjects during the first year of Sixth Form, reducing these to three for the second year. 30 subjects are currently available.

Parents are kept closely informed of their daughter's progress. Regular parent meetings are held.

There is a very high standard of Physical Education. The school "match" sports are hockey, netball, tennis, athletics, basketball, volleyball and swimming with teams regularly becoming County champions, and with girls playing in County and regional teams. The Headington School Boat Club, founded in 1992, now ranks near the top of the national schools' rowing league, with pupils representing Great Britain and rowing at international events.

A purpose built music school ensures a high standard of music within the school, with a large number of girls playing a wide variety of instruments to an advanced level. There are a number of orchestras, choirs and ensembles and joint musical events with other local schools often take place. The Chamber Choir regularly goes on foreign tours (in 2000 to Prague) and full operatic productions take place regularly. The Chamber Choir's most recent CD achieved considerable critical acclaim.

Dramatic productions range from Shakespeare to Ibsen, with girls involved in all aspects of stage management from lighting to box office. Numerous smaller productions take place throughout the year and at all ages, and Drama may be taken as a GCSE option, with Theatre Studies popular at A level. The Debating Society is also popular.

Extra-curricular activities and clubs are vital to school life and all day girls are welcome to stay on into the evening to participate. A wide range are on offer, including Young Enterprise, a thriving Duke of Edinburgh Award Scheme, the British Association for Young Scientists and the Council for Education for World Citizenship. Girls also take part in Model European Parliaments, which attract delegates from throughout Europe. There is also a strong tradition of community service, with numerous charity events as well as the opportunity, in the Sixth Form, to help in local hospitals, schools for the handicapped and charity shops. Sixth Formers also organise a Christmas charity fair each year, which raises several thousand pounds.

Boarding Houses. Boarding houses recently underwent a major re-organisation, in order to create greater opportunities for each age group as they move up the school. The youngest pupils (from 9 to 13) are housed in a comfortable Edwardian family home, with small dormitories and plenty of emphasis on helping each child to enjoy life at school at her own pace. Pupils from 13 to 16 move into a more modern boarding house, taking gradually more responsibility for their leisure time and increasing work load. The Sixth Form Centre is the final element of the reorganisation, offering a secure link between school and university. Many pupils are weekly boarders but a substantial number remain in school for weekends, when a full programme of activities, both in and out of the school, are arranged. Day girls may board for the occasional night.

Uniform. A new uniform was introduced in September 1998 and has been well received. Girls may choose from a number of options, with two styles of blue checked skirt, navy trousers, a jumper or sweatshirt and an enormously popular "fleece", as well as a blazer for formal occasions. Girls in the Sixth Form wear their own clothes.

Entrance. Application forms for places may be obtained, together with the prospectus, from the Admissions Registrar. Entrance to the Junior School is taken in order of application and is subject to an interview and, for pupils aged 7+ upwards, a short test. Entrance to the Senior School is by examination: Common Entrance Examination for 11+, 12+ and 13+, and school's examination for 14+ and 16+ ages. Early application is advised and applications should be made at least a year before the proposed date of entry. There is no entry at 15+ or 17+ (GCSE and A Level Years).

Fees per term for September 2000. Senior School: Boarders Upper III Form – VI Form £4,235; Day Girls, UIII Form – VI Form £2,320.

Junior School: Lower III £1,915; Boarders Lower III £3,980; Upper II £1,670; Boarders Upper II £3,710; Transition, I and Lower II Forms £1,490; Pre-Kindergarten and Kindergarten £1,260; Nursery £1,070.

Registration Fee. £40 (UK) and £60 (Overseas)

Overseas Examination Fee. £50

Deposit. £250 (UK) and £500 (Overseas).

Charges for optional extra subjects. Piano, String, Woodwind and Brass instruments £155 per term; Extra Art £60 per term plus materials; Fencing, £82 per term; Group Tennis £11 per hour and individual Tennis £21 per hour; Rowing £133 per term. Junior School After Care Scheme £4.50 per session or £6 on an occasional basis.

Scholarships. (*see* Entrance Scholarship section) As a result of a £1.2 million bequest to the school in 1998, a number of means tested scholarships are offered at 11+ and into the Sixth Form, each worth a minimum of 20% and a maximum of 50% of day or boarding fees. In addition a number of open scholarships are offered at either 11+, 12+, 13+ and the Sixth Form.

Charitable status. Headington School, Oxford Limited is a Registered Charity, number 309678. It exists to provide quality education for girls.

Heathfield School
Ascot

London Road Ascot Berkshire SL5 8BQ
Tel: (01344) 898343
Fax: (01344) 890689
e-mail: admin@heathfield.ascot.sch.uk
website: www.heathfield.ascot.sch.uk

Chairman of Council: Mrs J Tulk-Hart

Council:
Mr A B V Hughes
Mrs D G Dollar
Mrs J Deedes, BA
Mr I A D Pilkington
Mr J F Meighan
Professor S J Eykyn, FRCP, FRCPath, FRCS (*The Viscountess Dilhorne*)
Dr A E C Letley, PhD, MA, MPhil
Nina Campbell
Mr R Wreford
Mr C Kindersley
Mr H Munro
Mr T Cross Brown, MA
Mr A Deal

***Headmistress:* Mrs H Wright**, MA (Oxon)

Director of Studies: Miss L Morrison, BA (Strathclyde), MA (London)

Senior Mistress: Mrs J Dickens, BA (London)

Chaplain: The Revd F Otto, MA (Oxford), Cert Theol (Oxford)

Bursar: Mr R Tierney, BSc (Durham)

Science:
*Mrs A Palles, MSc (London) *Biology*
Mrs S E Rossell, BSc (London) *Biology*
Mrs J Kemp, BSc (London) *Biology*
Mrs H Hesp, BSc (Manchester) *Physics*
Mrs J A Smith, BEd (Reading) *Chemistry*
Mrs J Stephen, BEd (Bristol) *Chemistry*
*Mrs J Knight, BSc (London) *Mathematics*
Mrs S Brain, BSc (London) *Mathematics/Physics*
Mrs M A Samuel, BEd (Wales) *Mathematics*
Miss C Edwards, BA (Liverpool) *Mathematics*
Dr J D Godolphin, BSc, PhD (London) *Mathematics*
Mrs M Nicholls, BSc (London) *Mathematics*
Mrs J Skinner, CertEd (Worcester) *Business Studies/Computers*
Mrs L Wilson, BSc (Paisley) *Senior Laboratory Technician*
Mrs M Girdler *Laboratory Technician*
Mr R Hesp, BSc (Manchester) *Physics Technician*

Humanities:
*Mrs L Ranscombe, BA (London) *English*
Mrs J Dickens, BA (London) *English*
Mrs J Banks, BA (Durham), MA (London) *English*
Miss J Major, BA (Southampton) *English*
Mrs J Phillips, BA (London) *English*
Mrs J Morgan, RSA Diploma *Curriculum Support*
*Mrs M Brown, BA (University of Wales) *History*
Miss L Morrison, BA (Strathclyde), MA (London) *History*
Mrs G Moore, BA (London), MA (Open) *History/Classical Civilisation*
Mrs C Green, BA (Bristol) *History/Classical Civilisation*
*Mrs H Edge, BA (Liverpool) *Geography*
Mrs S E Ingram, BEd (London) *Geography*
Miss K Slocock, BA (Durham) *Religious Studies*
Mr T Murden, BA (Lancaster) *Economics*
Dr R Priest, MA (Leeds), PhD (Open University) *History of Art*
Mr P S Veal, LLM (Reading) *Law*

Languages:
*Mrs C Strudwick, L-ès-L (Sorbonne) *French*
Mrs R Lankshear, M-ès-L (Pau) *French/Spanish*
Mrs M C Davies, L-ès-L (Besançon) *French*
Mrs H Wright, MA (Oxon) *French/German*
Mrs M Curtis-Weight, MA (St Andrews) *Spanish*
Mrs R E Edwards, BA (Trieste) *Italian*
Mrs J M Rogers, MA (Kiel) *German*
Mrs J Moss, BA (London) *Latin*
Mrs E Viegas-Whitaker, BA (Lisbon) *Portuguese*
Mrs K Forrester, BA (Tokyo) *Japanese*
Miss M Ortega *Spanish Assistant*
Mlle S Ducla *French Assistant*

Arts:
*Mrs S Richardson, BA (Newcastle), MA (Reading) *Art*
Mrs K Curwin, BA (Glasgow School of Art) *Art and Photography*
Mrs W L Butler, CertEd (Newland Park) *Ceramics*
Miss C Davison, BA (Liverpool) *Art*
Mrs J Stephens, BA (London) *Drama*
Miss L Porter, BA (York) *Drama*
Miss N Vinson, BA (West Sussex Institute) *Dance and Drama*
Mrs C Smith, TCert HE & Ed (London) *Cookery*

Music:
*Mr E F Patterson, MA (Oxon), MMus (London), AKC, LRAM, ARCM *Director of Music*
Miss P S Gee, BMus (London), DipRCM, ARCM *Assistant to Director*
Part-time teachers for instruments

Sport:
*Miss E Cooney, BA (Brighton) *Physical Education*
Mrs S Bettison, DipEd (London) *Physical Education*
Miss L Jordan, BEd (de Montfort) *Physical Education*
Professor J Parkins, Maitre d'Armes de L'Acad d'Armes de France *Fencing*
Miss S Marsh, BA, WLA, LTA *Tennis*
Mr P Downs, PTCA, LTA *Tennis*
Mr D Gill, BTCA, LTA *Tennis Coach*

Administration:
PA to Headmistress: Mrs J Westwood
Registrar: Mrs A Norris
School Secretary: Mrs L Barber
Administrative Secretary: Mrs A Di Simone
Bursar's Assistant: Mrs L Farrin
Bursar's Secretary: Mrs W Reeves
Librarian: Mrs K Bramley, MA (Univ of Wales)
Housekeeper: Mrs D S Fossey
Caterer: Mrs J Scriven

Pastoral:
Mrs E Hill, SRN, DNCert *Head of Pastoral Care/Health Education*
Mrs V Viljoen, RGN *Deputy Nursing Sister*
and a team of year housemothers
Miss E Pointon *Head of Boarding*

Number of Pupils. 230

Heathfield School, founded in 1899, is one of the few remaining girls' schools where every pupil is a full boarder. Set in 35 acres, the school is 40 minutes from London and within easy reach of airports. The original Georgian house has been extended over the years and facilities now include a new science block, art studios, a recently extended upper-sixth house, a superb sports hall and a new indoor swimming pool. The school has a beautiful late Victorian chapel, the foundress's first addition.

Heathfield is unashamedly comfortable but competitive and academically rigorous too. Emphasis is always on individual achievement and depth, an ethos underlined by excellent, highly-qualified teachers. The staff:pupil ratio is 1:7. While the more traditional subject combinations remain most popular, there is also excellence in art, drama and music. Twenty-four subjects are offered at A level including Law, Economics, Business Studies, Media Studies, Theology and Japanese. Academic results are consistently impressive and all girls go on to higher education, including Oxbridge.

Boarding accommodation is excellent, more than two thirds of the pupils having single bedrooms. The Upper Sixth live in a separate, self-contained house which encourages them to prepare for the relative independence of university. Pastoral care throughout the school is recognised as outstanding, with year heads and form staff, tutors, two resident SRNs and eleven resident house mothers all playing their part.

Computers, CD-ROMS and the Internet are used in a wide variety of academic areas as well as outside lessons. The sports hall is always a hive of activity and there are many other extra-curricular activities, also frequent museum and theatre trips to London and elsewhere, workshops, field trips and work experience abroad for linguists. At Heathfield the day does not finish at 4pm, nor the week on Friday.

Entry for the majority of pupils is at 11, a few girls join at 12 or 13 or come into the Lower Sixth for A level studies. Junior entrants take assessment papers set by the school and also the appropriate Common Entrance examination. Entry into the Lower Sixth is via predicted GCSE grades and tests in intended A level subjects. A number of academic, music, art, drama and sports scholarships for entry to the Junior School and the Sixth Form are awarded each year.

School fees per term. £5,425

Charitable status. Heathfield School Limited is a Registered Charity, number 309086. It exists to provide boarding education leading to tertiary education for girls aged between 11 and 18.

Heathfield School Pinner (G.D.S.T)

Beaulieu Drive Pinner Middlesex HA5 1NB
Tel: 020 8868 2346

Governing Body:

Mr T R Angear, BA, MBA, FRSA (*Chairman*)
Mrs H C Tucker, BA (*Vice-Chairman*)
Dr D Amin, MB, BS, DCH, DRCOG, DCH, DGM, MRCGP
Ms A Biss, BSc
Mrs S Clark, BA
Mrs F Davies, BSc(Econ)
Mr A S Lee, MA
Miss A Norris, BSc
Mr J Orchard, BA, DipArch, RIBA

Headmistress: **Miss C M Juett**, BSc (London) *Geography*

Deputy Headmistress: Ms K Hollingdale, BA (East Anglia) *Literature and French*

Senior Staff:
Mrs F Bard, BA (Southampton) *Spanish with French*
Mrs J Bénard, BA (Warwick) *French*
Miss J Borg, BA (Reading) *Classics*
Mrs V Burden, BA (Open University) *Science*
Mr M Chanter, BSc (Brunel) *Politics & Modern History*
Mrs A Corcut, BA (London) *English*
Mrs C A Daniels, BA (Open University) *Mathematics*
Mrs L Estruch, BSc (Manchester) *Chemistry*
Mr I Fielder, BSc (Bristol) *Physics*
Mrs J Fish, BEd (Cambridge) *Geography*
Mrs J Gillard, ATD (London) *Art*
Mrs M E Goodhew, BA (London) *English*
Miss C Goring, BA (Cardiff) *History*
Mrs V E Holmes-Neeld, BA (Birmingham), MA (London) *Religious Studies*
Miss H Hopkins, BA (Surrey) *PE and History*
Mrs E Humble, BSc (Cardiff) *Mathematics*
Dr M Izen, BSc (Glasgow), PhD (Nottingham) *Molecur Biology*
Mr M Jimson, TCert (Nottingham), DipCDT (Brunel) *PE & Science*
Miss S Johnson, BEd (De Montfort) *Physical Education & Mathematics*
Ms A Jones, BA (Chelsea School of Art) *Graphic Design*
Dr A Khan, BSc (London), PhD (London) *Chemistry*
Mrs M Lalor, BSc (University of West Indies) *Mathematics*
Miss L Lambie, BA (Leicester) *French and Italian*
Mrs M Leach, MA (Bucharest) *English and German*
Mrs N Lister, BA (Kent) *English & American Literature*
Mrs M Lorente-Moltó, TCert (Valencia, Spain), Cert of Proficiency in English (Cambridge)
Mrs S J Millar, BEd (London) *English*
Mrs L M Mitchell, BA (Middlesex) *Economics*
Mr R J Pimlott, BA (Middlesex) *Geography*
Mrs C J H Rankine, BEd (Wales) *Geography and Careers Adviser*
Mr D Rogers, BA (Cambridge) *Classics*
Mr D Rubin, MA (Glasgow) *French and Russian*
Mrs R Safarfashandi, BSc (Essex), MSc (Loughborough) *Chemistry*
Mrs F J Sinclair, BEd (Worcester) *Fashion and Fabrics*
Miss J Smallwood, BEd (Liverpool John Moores) *Physical Education and Science*
Ms L Smith, BSc (Open University) *Psychology, MA* (Open University) *Education*
Mrs P Smith, CertEd (Brighton) *Mathematics*
Mrs S B Thomson, BEd (London) Natural Science, MEd (London) *Computer Education*
Mrs J Uhart, BA (Open University) *Humanities*
Mrs J Viney, L-ès-L (Sorbonne) *English*
Mrs K Walley, BA (Oxon) *Physics*
Mr S Werner, BMus, BA (Cardiff) *Secondary Music Education*

Junior Department:

Head of Junior Department: Mrs C McCulloch, BA (Leeds)

Mrs D C Bell, CertEd (Essex)
Mrs J Brown, CertEd (Camb Inst)
Mrs P Daniells, CertEd (London)
Miss K L Higginson, BEd (University of Hertfordshire)
Mrs E Ibie, BEd (North London)
Mrs V G Marsh, BEd (London)
Mrs L Palmer, BSc (Westminster) *Natural Science & Computing*
Miss J Parker, GTCL, LTCL, DipRCM (Royal College of Music)

Mrs J West, BSc (Liverpool John Moores)
Mrs V M Woods, BA (Nottingham)

Number of Pupils: 558

Heathfield School was founded in Harrow in 1900; it moved to its present location in September 1982, and became a member of the Girls' Day School Trust in September 1987. The School is situated on a nine-acre site, including 6 tennis courts and playing fields, and is well served by trains and buses, the nearest stations being Eastcote and Rayners Lane.

The accommodation includes six Science Laboratories, a separate Music School, Technology Workshop, four Computer Rooms, Art Rooms, Textiles Room, Geography Room, Careers Centre and a large Learning Resources Centre. The Junior Department is housed in new purpose-built separate accommodation where there are 11 classrooms, a Hall, Library and specialist rooms for Music, Science and Techology. A new indoor Swimming Pool, Sports Hall and Senior Library were opened in January 2000. They are to be followed by a Centre for the Performing Arts, Dining Room, suites for Art, DT, Textiles, Mathematics and Careers plus 3 new laboratories.

Girls enter the School in the Junior Department at 3+, 4+ and 7+, or the Senior School at 11+ and 16+. The School provides a general education up to GCSE and GCE AS/A2 Level and also offers a wide range of trips, visits and extra-curricular activities. All Sixth Form leavers continue to Universities, including Oxford and Cambridge.

A special feature of the school is its happy, caring and friendly ethos and its family atmosphere.

Admission. An Entrance Examination is held each January for girls wishing to enter the School in the following September. Sixth Form places are available for girls who have reached a certain standard at GCSE.

Following the end of the Government Assisted Places Scheme, the GDST has made available to the school a substantial number of scholarships and bursaries. The bursaries are means tested and are intended to ensure that the school remains accessible to bright girls who would profit from our education but who would be unable to enter the school without financial assistance.

Vacancies for pupils other than at 3+, 4+, 7+, 11+ or 16+ are occasionally available.

Fees. (as from September 2000) Senior School £2,044 per term; Junior Department: £1,588 per term for 4+–10+, and £1,200 for 3+, including lunches.

Prospectus and registration forms may be obtained by writing to the Secretary for Admissions at the school.

Charitable status. Heathfield School, Pinner is one of the 25 schools of the Girls' Day School Trust, which is a Registered Charity, number 1026057. The aim of the Trust is to provide a fine academic education at a comparatively modest cost.

Hethersett Old Hall School

Hethersett Norwich NR9 3DW
Tel: (01603) 810390
Fax: (01603) 812094
e-mail: prospectus@hohs.co.uk
website: www.hohs.co.uk

Chairman of Governors: H M G Speer, Esq

Headmistress: **Mrs J M Mark**, BA (London)

Deputy Headmistress: Mrs N Kay, MA, PGCE (Leeds)

Head of House Staff: Mrs S Adams

Bursar: Mrs D Kay

Headmistress's Secretary: Mrs S Mander

Registrar: Mrs J Smith

HETHERSETT OLD HALL SCHOOL, founded in 1928, lies between Norwich and Wymondham, off the A11, in 14 acres of attractive grounds.

The school is an educational trust administered by a Board of Governors in membership of the GBGSA. The Headmistress is a member of the GSA, SHA and ISIS.

The school provides flexi-boarding and day education for 250 pupils aged between 4 and 18 years old.

Boys are accepted in the new Pre-Prep Department at the age of 4, but proceed to either Preparatory schools or the maintained sector at the age of 7.

Boarders live in the main house and in the new Sixth Form house, in the care of resident house staff who organise varied and interesting evening and weekend activities. Nearly half the boarders have single or double study bedrooms.

AIMS. Each girl is encouraged to develop her academic, creative and practical skills and to become self-reliant, adaptable, tolerant and concerned for others.

CURRICULUM. Girls from the Pre-Prep Department will be expected to sit and pass the Entrance Examination for the Junior Department alongside external candidates for entry at 7+. The Junior Department provides direct entry to the main school, emphasising a thorough grounding with many opportunities for creative work and music. Girls have access to the main school's specialist facilities.

The senior school teaching is by graduate and trained specialist staff. For the first three years, an unusually wide range of academic, technological and creative subjects is taught in small teaching groups. In the third year girls are guided in their choice of GCSE subjects. Careers advice is given at each stage.

SIXTH FORM. A wide range of A and A/S level subjects is offered. Most Sixth Formers go on to university. Some choose vocationally-orientated careers in business or community care as an optional career path. Examination results at GCSE and A level have been consistently good.

BUILDINGS AND FACILITIES. Excellent teaching facilities have been added to by an on-going building programme. In recent years, the Wolfson science laboratories, the sports hall and indoor swimming pool have been completed. Also a new art and technology building with photography dark room, and humanities classrooms.

RECREATIONAL ACTIVITIES. The school offers a wide range of recreational activities and optional extras which include music, sport, community service and The Duke of Edinburgh Award Scheme.

ENTRANCE. Entry is by the school's own examination or the Common Entrance and interview. Entry to the Sixth Form is by interview, school record and assessment. Particulars of the school are available from the Registrar.

SCHOLARSHIPS. (*see* Entrance Scholarship section) Academic: two at 11+; one boarding scholarship from 11+ to 13+, up to 3 at Sixth Form. Two Jubilee Bursaries also available at 11+ (means tested).

CHARITABLE STATUS. Hethersett Old Hall School is a Registered Charity, number 311273. It exists to provide a high quality education.

* Head of Department	§ Part Time or Visiting
† Housemaster/Housemistress	¶ Old Pupil
‡ See below list of staff for meaning	

Highclare School

10 Sutton Road Erdington Birmingham B23 6QL
Tel: (0121) 373 7400
Fax: (0121) 373 7445
e-mail: abbey@highclareschool.co.uk
website: highclareschool.co.uk

Founded 1932

Highclare School is an independent day school for girls from 18 months–18 years and for boys aged 18 months–11 years and a co-educational Sixth Form.

Governors:
Mr J A Barrett (*Chairman*)
Mr J T Duff
Mr I Hazel
Mrs P Mayall
Mr B Pattni
Dr N Speak
Mrs L Flowith
Mr R O Dauncey
Dr A P Parnell
Mrs S Watson
Mr K Brown

***Headmistress:* Mrs C A Hanson**, BSc Hons (Nottingham)

Deputy Headmistress: Mrs L Edwards, BA Hons (Swansea), PGCE

Head of Senior School: Mrs P Petersen, BA Hons (Hull), PGCE

Head of Junior and Preparatory School: Mrs B Twivey, CertEd (Birmingham)

Head of Highclare Woodfield: Mrs L Jude, CertEd (Chester)

Head of Highclare St Paul's: Mrs J Anderson, DipEd (Moray House)

Head of Sixth Form: Mrs G Gately, BA Hons (Leicester)

Head of Nursery: Mrs J Laker, NVQ3

Examinations Secretary: Mrs L Clifford, CertEd (Birmingham)

Careers Department:
Mrs K Rivett, BEd (Birmingham), CertEd

Art:
*Mrs H Suter, BA Hons (Birmingham), PGCE
Mrs H Good, BEd Hons (Worcester)

Biology:
Mrs M Bellshaw, BSc Hons (London), PGCE
Mrs K J Flavell, BSc Hons (Wolverhampton), PGCE

Business Studies and Law:
Mrs L J Embury, LLB Hons (Wolverhampton)

Chemistry:
Mrs B J Brown, BSc Hons (Nottingham) PGCE

Computer Studies:
Mrs M Morris, ANCM
Mrs H Geddes

English:
*Mrs S Riley, BA Hons (Leicester), PGCE
Mrs S Gregory, BA Hons (Durham), PGCE
Mrs K M Quirke, BEd Hons (Leeds)
Mr R Seal, BA Hons (Birmingham), PGCE
Miss L Weston, BA Hons (Leicester), PGCE

French:
Mrs P K Litting, BA Hons (London Ext), PGCE
Mrs A Owen, BA Hons (Leicester)

Geography:
*Mrs P Petersen, BA Hons (Hull), PGCE
Mrs M White, BA Hons (Manchester)
Mrs K Rivett, BEd (Birmingham), CertEd

German:
Mrs M Ford, BA Hons (Liverpool), PGCE
Mrs J Unsworth, BA (Bristol), PGCE

Health and Social Care:
Mrs A Sargent, SEN

History:
Mrs L Edwards, BA Hons (Swansea), PGCE
Mrs K Thomas, BA Hons (Reading), PGCE

Home Economics:
Mrs N Watts, CertEd (Liverpool)

Mathematics:
Mrs S Cook, BSc Hons (Nottingham), PGCE
Mrs A Toley, BSc Hons (London), PGCE
Mrs T Lennox, BSc (Sheffield), PGCE

Music:
Mrs R Salt, BMus Hons, GRSM, ARMCM
Mrs A Bownass, BSc (Econ) (Swansea), PGCE

Physical Education:
Mrs L Benson, BPhil Hons (Warwick), CertEd (London)
Mrs L Clifford, CertEd (Birmingham)
Mrs E Cunningham, BA (Leeds), PGCE
Miss Y Lloyd, BEd Hons (London)

Physics:
Mrs J Baker, Goldsmiths (London), CertEd
Mrs P Cheney, GradInstP

Religious Education:
Mrs J Bazen, BA Hons (Durham), DipEd

Sociology:
Mrs G Gately, BA Hons (Leicester)

Speech Training and Drama:
Mrs J Agnew, BA (Open), LLAM
Mrs P Nixon, LLAM

Junior School Staff:
*Mrs B E Twivey, CertEd (Birmingham)
Mrs J Anderson, DipEd (Edinburgh)
Miss J Arnold, BEd Hons (Newman College)
Mrs A J Bownass, BSc(Econ) (Swansea), PGCE
Mrs H Hew, BEd, CNNA (Birmingham)
Mrs E Higginbotham, CertEd
Mrs H Jones, BEd, Distinction in Practice of Education
Mrs C Mackay, BEd Hons (Wales), CertEd (Cardiff)
Mrs J Medina, CertEd (Avery Hill)
Mrs S Nash, CertEd (Durham), DipPrimScience (UCE)
Mrs J O'Connor, CertEd (Bordesley College)
Mrs L Parkes, BA Hons (UCE)
Mrs S C J Pears, BSc Hons (Leeds), PGCE (Open)
Mrs W Pestridge, BA Hons (Wolverhampton), PGCE
Mrs M Pollard, TCert (Nottingham College)
Mrs E Riley, MEd (Birmingham), CertEd (W Midlands)
Mrs J Robinson, BA (Open), PGCE
Mr M Robinson, BEd Hons, CertEd (ONC)
Mrs V Shields, CertEd (Northumberland)
Mrs S Zoulias, BEd Hons (Wolverhampton)

Preparatory Department Staff:
*Mrs L Jude, CertEd (Chester)
Mrs A Clark, BEd Hons (Leeds), CertEd (Bingley)
Mrs J Colman, BA (Open), CertEd (Oxford)
Mrs V Commander, BSocSci (Birmingham), PGCE (Leicester)
Mrs M Craddock, BEd
Mrs D Dyal, BA Hons (Open), CNNA, NNEB
Mrs S H Gething, CertEd

Mrs H Goldsworthy, CertEd
Mrs J Harris, NNEB
Mrs S Hayward, BSc Hons (UMIST), PGCE (Manchester)
Mrs B Mandley, CertEd (Keele)
Mrs M Moore, Catholic TCert in RE (Birmingham)
Mrs J Spargo, BEd Hons (Wolverhampton)
Miss K S Stamps, BA Hons (UCE), PGCE
Mrs L Stewart, BEd Hons (Westhill)
Mrs C Weston, BEd Hons (Oxford)
Mrs J Wilson, CertEd (Birmingham)
Mrs D N Williams, CertEd (Oxford Polytechnic)
Mrs S White, NVQ3, CCEBirmingham)

Nursery and Care Scheme:
Mrs J Laker, NVQ3 (*Manager*)
Miss R Dodd, NNEB (*Deputy Manager*)
Miss N Christie, BTech (*Deputy Manager*)

Location. The School is situated on three sites on the main road (A5127) between Four Oaks, Sutton Coldfield and Birmingham. The girls' Junior and Senior Department and co-educational Sixth Form, occupying a former Benedictine Abbey, is on direct train and bus routes from Birmingham City Centre, Tamworth, Lichfield and Walsall. There are school buses from Coleshill, Four Oaks, Aldridge, Streetly, Tamworth and Lichfield to all three sites. We operate an extended day from 8.00 am until 6.00 pm for the parents who require it and holiday cover.

Number of pupils: Approximately 800 day pupils.

The school is divided into four departments:

Nursery and Preparatory Department (Age 18 months to 7 years, girls and boys).

The Nursery caters for children from 18 months to 3 years and although an independent unit it has the support of the facilities and resources of the Preparatory Department. The staged development programme stimulates and encourages children providing a natural progression of continuous educational care.

The Preparatory Department staffed by qualified teachers and NNEB nursery nurses caters for children from 3 to 7+ years. Because of small classes staff are able to devote a great deal of attention to each child thus encouraging both confidence and independence. A wide variety of well balanced activities ensures that each child is given every opportunity to develop his/her physical, social and academic potential to the full. The Department is able to provide a secure and stimulating introduction to school life with much emphasis being placed on Maths, English and Science at Key Stage 1.

Junior Departments (7+ to 11 years). Girls and Boys on separate sites. (Entry by School's own assessment procedure).

The Junior Departments with classes of 20 pupils follow National Curriculum guidelines. Pupils are taught as a whole class or within ability groups using a combination of traditional and modern methods. Much emphasis is placed on the teaching of English and Mathematics where work takes account of the National Numeracy and Literacy Strategies, Science and ICT. (Pupils have the benefit of specialist tuition in Science, French (from age 7), PE and Music and ICT in Year 6. Thus a solid foundation is established for an easy, natural transition to Senior School.

Other foundation subjects are taught by subject.

Many extra curricular activities are open to pupils in the Junior School. These include choirs, orchestra, windband, recorder club, speech and drama, dance, chess and scrabble clubs. In addition a wide range of sporting activities are pursued, led by the school's PE staff, with the assistance of tennis, football and cricket coaches.

Senior Department. (Age 11 to 16, Girls). (Entry by School's own examination).

Highclare provides all the benefits of a small school with only 40 pupils in each year group. This enables us to focus on the individual within a caring environment, stretching the very able and encouraging those less gifted.

The full curriculum is covered in KS3 and GCSE subjects are chosen from Geography, History, Religious Education, Art, Music, Home Economics and a second modern language, which are studied with the core subjects English, English Literature, Mathematics, Dual Certificate Science, a modern language and Information Technology.

In addition to their examination studies, girls also study PSE which includes careers guidance, industrial awareness, health education and citizenship. Physical Education is also an important part of the curriculum.

Pastoral care has a high priority within the school as do extra-curricular activities. Through these we aim to ensure that all students reach their full potential and gain confidence as everyone meets success in at least one area of school life.

Co-educational Sixth Form. Age 16+

The Sixth Form timetable is structured to meet the individual requirements of each student. The school has a strong academic tradition and students may select from a wide range of 'A' and 'AS' level subjects. Those students seeking a vocational course may choose to combine an 'A' level with an Advanced VCE in Business or Health and Social Care. Opportunities for leadership and community service are an integral part of the Sixth Form life and enable the students to develop into mature and responsible citizens.

Examinations. *GCSE:* OCR including CLAIT I & II, EDEXCEL, AQA (NEAB/SEG).

GCE: EDEXCEL, AQA (NEAB/AEB), OCR, GNVQ Business, Health & Social Care.

Music examinations: Associate Board of Royal School of Music.

Elocution and Drama: LAMDA.

Sport. The flourishing Sports Department has a gymnasium and sports fields. Activities include hockey, netball, swimming, rounders, tennis, athletics, football, cricket, cross-country, trampolining, badminton, dance and gymnastics.

Extra-curricular activities include orchestra, windband, choirs, debating society and tuition is available in a variety of musical instruments and singing. Speech and drama are also available and community service is encouraged. Holiday activity courses are also arranged.

Entrance Scholarships. Entrance scholarships are available each year for the 11+ age group. These will be awarded to the best all-round candidates, consideration being given to girls exhibiting special academic qualities and having artistic or sporting talents. There are also scholarships for the Sixth Form.

Fees range from, £1,100 per term to £1,960 per term.

School Aims.

- To provide high quality teaching and to encourage independent learning within a secure and happy environment.
- To motivate each individual pupil to achieve her (his) full all round potential.
- To develop the values of self-respect and self-discipline, alongside tolerance and respect for others.

Charitable status. Highclare School is a Registered Charity, number 528940. It exists to provide education for children.

* Head of Department	§ Part Time or Visiting
† Housemaster/Housemistress	¶ Old Pupil
‡ See below list of staff for meaning	

Hollygirt School

Elm Avenue Nottingham NG3 4GF
Tel: 0115 958 0596

***Headmistress:* Mrs M I Connolly**, BA, MPhil, MIMgt, DipAGMS

Deputy Headmistress: Mrs M P Worth, BSc (Hons) (London) *Chemistry*

Senior School:

Director of Pastoral Care and Careers: to be appointed

Heads of Faculty:

Languages/Humanities: Mrs C E L Williams, MA (Oxon), DipEd (Oxford), Cert Local History (Nottingham) *Head of History*
Mathematics/Sciences: Mrs C E Barker, BSc (Hons), PGCE (Bristol) *Head of Geography*
Design and Technology: Mrs C L Ellis, CertEd (Leeds) *Head of Design & Technology*

Assistant Staff:
Mrs S W Atherton, MA (Oxon), PGCE (Oxford) *Head of Science Department, Biology*
Mr R A C Bill, BEng (Liverpool) *Head of IT/IT Co-ordinator/Network Manager/Physics*
Mrs E Freemantle, CertEd (Lady Mabel, Sheffield) *Physical Education*
Mrs S M Freeston, CertEd (York) *English*
Miss J A Holmes, BA (Hons) (Newcastle), PGCE *French and German*
Mrs A E Hughes, MA (Cantab), ARCM
Miss M Ifould, BEd (Ilkley), Diploma in Careers Education *Head of Physical Education & Outdoor Pursuits*
Mrs A Justice, BEd (Hons) (Warwick) *Religious Studies*
Mrs S Kelham, CertEd (Exeter) *Mathematics, Religious Studies*
Mrs B McEwen, BA (CNAA, Cheltenham), PGCE (Leeds) *Art and Design, Design and Technology, Textiles*
Miss J C Melia, BEd (Hons) (Warwick) *Head of English*
Mrs J E M Parry, BSc (Hons) (London) *Mathematics, General Studies*
Mrs S C Price, BSc (Hons) (York) *Chemistry*
Mrs E F Smith, BSc Hons (Loughborough), PGCE *Head of Mathematics*
Mrs A R Standing, BA (Hons) (Newcastle), PGCE (Leeds) *Head of Art and Design, Design and Technology*
Mrs E A Thomas, BSc, CPhys, MInstP, CertEd (Edinburgh) *Physics, Design Technology*
Mrs M A Turner, BSc (Hons) (Durham), PGCE (Oxford)
Mrs A M Whitaker, BA (Hons) (Coventry), PGCE (Huddersfield) *Head of Foreign Languages, French, German*

Science and Technology Technician: Mr R Arnold, BA (Hons), BTECNat (Science)

Network Manager: Mr P Fisher

Junior School:
Head of Junior Department: Mrs J Holberton, BSc (Hons) (London), MSc (Hull), PGCE (Hull)

Curriculum Co-ordinator: Mrs F Young, BSc (Edinburgh), PGCE (London)

Assistant Staff:
Mrs E K A Baker, BEd (Hons) (Oxford)
Mrs J Beardsley, BEd (Middlesex)
Mrs P Carter, BEd (Hons) (Reading)pen), CertEd, Montessori Dip, CertTEFL
Mrs E J Redburn, CertEd (London)
Mrs D Sowerby, BA (Hons), DipEd (Keele)
Mrs J Tilley, MEd (Minnesota), CertEd (London)
Mrs H Nicholson, NNEB (Nottingham)

Mrs S Griffiths, BA (Hons) (Plymouth) *Swimming*
Mrs C Gibson, CertEd (Coventry) *325 Club*
Mrs S Walker *325 Club Assistant*
Mrs C Twite *325 Club Assistant*

Visiting Staff:
Mrs M A Land, Gold Medal LAM, Member of Society of Teachers of Speech and Drama *Speech and Drama*
Miss H Davies, BMus, LRAM, PGCE *Piano*
Miss J Horrocks, GRSM, ARCM *Clarinet*
Miss J Parsons, BA (Hons) (CNAA), PGCE (Manchester) *Flute*
Mrs L C Roe, GRNCM *Singing*
Mrs C A Seedhouse, BMus (Sheffield), CertEd (Nottingham) *Violin*
Mr G Truman, LRAM *Trumpet*

Bursar: Mrs D M Zinsaz, BA (London)

Registrar & Headmistress' Secretary: Mrs J M Swain

Receptionist: Mrs P Bonner

Marketing and PR: Mrs A Mullins, BEd (Hons) (Nottingham)

Hollygirt School is a day school, founded in 1877 occupying buildings which were originally large private houses, now suitably adapted, together with large purpose built accommodation, close to the City centre. The playing fields are at Lady Bay some three miles from the School: in addition the school has the use of Nottingham University's Sports Hall, swimming pool and athletics track. There are 340 girls in the School between the ages of 3 and 16 of whom 110 are in the Junior Department.

The School is administered as a charitable trust and it aims to provide an education with emphasis on the needs and abilities of individual girls. In addition to academic success, the School is concerned with the spiritual, moral, cultural and physical development of each girl as she is prepared for the opportunities, responsibilities and experience of adult life. All girls are encouraged to take a positive and enthusiastic approach to whatever they undertake, whether in form, games or leisure activities. Extra help in Mathematics and English is given on an individual or small group basis.

After leaving Hollygirt the majority of girls proceed to A-Level courses or Intermediate/Advanced GNVQ courses in the sixth forms of other independent day and boarding schools. Others go to the local sixth form colleges.

Curriculum. The curriculum includes English, Double Award Science, Mathematics, French, German, Design Technology, Art, History, Geography, Religious Studies, Information Technology, Music and Physical Education.

Games. Hockey, netball, athletics, cross country running, tennis, basket and volleyball, unihoc, rounders, football, softball, badminton and swimming.

Careers. A programme of careers advice begins in Year 9. The School is a member of the Independent Schools

Careers Organisation which offers careers guidance to parents, staff and girls in member schools.

Extra Curricular Activities. These include Orchestra, Choir, Duke of Edinburgh Awards, Basketball Club, Dance and Drama Workshops, a programme of sports matches, an annual production, and lunchtime clubs that have included Local History, Latin, French, Computing, Art, Cookery and Table Tennis. School travel opportunities have included Ski-ing in France, and Canada, Music in Canada, and visits to France, Germany, India, Nepal and China

Admission. Entry to the Preparatory Form (4 years), is dependent on readiness for school and availability of places, for Years 1 and 2 on availability of places. Girls entering Years 3, 4, 5, 6 spend a day in School during which informal testing takes place. Entry to the Senior School is at 11+ (Year 7) although places occasionally become available in other years. Early in the Spring Term preceding entry, applicants are required to sit the School's entrance examination.

Fees. Junior Department: £1,277 per term; Senior Department: £1,689 per term. Speech and Music tuition are extra at £98 per 10 lesson term.

Hollygirt Old Girls Association (HOGA). The Secretary, Mrs S Williams, can be contacted via the school.

Charitable status. The Rhoda Jessop Educational Charity is a Registered Charity, number 508617. The aim is to provide an all round education which will prepare a girl for today's competitive, uncertain and rapidly changing world.

Holy Child School

Sir Harry's Road Edgbaston Birmingham B15 2UR.
Tel: 0121-440 4103/0256
Fax: 0121-440 3639

Roman Catholic School for Girls aged 2–18 and Boys aged 2–11.

Trustees of Holy Child School:

Chairman: Mr C P King, FCA
Vice Chairman: Mr H J Harper, DipArch
Sister M Dinnendahl, SHCJ
Mrs A O'Meara, LLB
Mr M J Sheehan, CEng, MIMechE
Mr N R Thompson, FRICS

Governors of Holy Child School:
Chairman: Miss V J Evans, CBE
Vice Chairman: Mr H J Harper, DipArch

Mrs J Bryer, MA
Mrs M Davison, BA
Mrs F J Evans
Mr P Fuller
Mr S Gilmore, LLB (London)
Fr Michael Miners
Mr T J P Ryan

Clerk to the Governors: Mrs M Davison, BA Hons (Trinity College, Dublin) *Modern Languages*

Bursar: Mrs M Graham, MIPM

Representing the Old Girls' Association: Mrs A Sheehan, c/o Holy Child School

Representing the Friends of Holy Child School: Mrs N Broadbridge

Staff:
***Headmistress:* Mrs E Brook**, MA, BEd Hons

Deputy Head: Mr J Fagan-King, MA (Lancaster), BEd (Liverpool) *Divinity, English*

Senior School:

Mrs S Bassett, BSc Hons (Wales), PGCE, DipP&P
Mr P Byrne, BSc Hons (Cardiff) *Economics*
Miss J Dale, CertEd (Exeter)
Mrs M E Davis, BEd, CertEd, DipProfStudEd, UCE (*Senior Teacher*)
Mrs M Douglas, BEd Theology (Newman College, Birmingham)
Mr A Flood *ICT Manager*
Mr A Harding, BSc, MInstP, CPhys (Chelsea College of Science & Technology, London) *Physics*
Mrs C Jones *Laboratory Technician*
Mrs L Kennedy, BSc Hons (Exeter), CertEd (Leicester)
Miss A Lendinez-Pacheco, MA (Barcelona) *English Philogy*
Mrs J Littlewood, GNSM, CertEd (Didsbury College, Manchester)
Dr V Long, BSc Hons, PhD, PGCE (Birmingham)
Mr C F Lucas, BSc Hons (Birmingham) *Biochemistry*
Mr P Mannion, DipPE (Twickenham)
Mr R Mayer, BA (Leeds), MA (Birmingham)
Mrs L O'Day, CertEd (Northern Counties College)
Mrs K Parish, CertEd (Chelsea College, Sussex)
Mrs S Sandys, Diploma in Language Studies (Oxford Poly)
Mrs M E Stubbs, BA Hons (Birmingham) *Modern Languages*
Mr J Thomas, BSc Hons, DipEd (Wales)
Miss S Vann, BEd Hons (De Montfort, Bedford)

Preparatory School:
Deputy Headmistress: Mrs A E Cleary, CertEd (Newman College, Birmingham)
Mrs M Brett, CertEd (Crewe and Alsager College)
Mrs J Pearson, CertEd (North London Polytechnic)
Miss M Sutton, CertEd, BEd Hons (University of Central England)
Mrs G Hogan, BEd Hons (Liverpool), CertEd (Digby Stuart, London)
Miss D Kelly, CertEd (Bordesley College of Education)
Mrs P Skrybant, BEd Hons (Newman College, Birmingham)
Miss A Stewart, DipEd (Aberdeen College of Education)
Mrs J Yewdall, CertEd (Newman College, Birmingham)
Mrs R Bird, NNEB *Kindergarten Manager*
Miss S Joyce, NNEB
Miss E Conway, NVQ3
Miss K Hill, NVQ2
Miss E Jackson, NVQ3
Miss L Brotherhood *Trainee*
Miss H Bush *Trainee*
Miss I Hughes *Trainee*
Miss C Malley *Trainee*
Miss J Mooney *Trainee*
Mrs S Lakin *Classroom Assistant*
Mrs R Lenihan, NNEB *Nursery Assistant*
Miss J Williams *NVQ3 Classroom Assistant*
Mrs S Wilson *Classroom Assistant/After Care Assistant*
Mrs S Williams *Classroom Assistant*

School Chaplain: Fr Richard Dinnis

Visiting Tutors:
Mrs D Wills, ALAM, LLAM (*Speech & Drama*)

Tutors also visit the school to teach dance, singing and the following instruments:
Violin, Flute, Guitar, Piano, Clarinet, Saxophone, Oboe

Administration Staff:

Assistant Bursar: Mrs S Thompson
Secretary: Mrs C Wright
Preparatory School Secretary: Mrs J Jeffries

Location. The school, founded on its present site in 1936 by the Sisters of the Society of the Holy Child Jesus, stands in 14 acres of parkland in the pleasant suburb of Edgbaston, only 2 miles from the centre of Birmingham. As well as beautiful formal gardens there are extensive playing fields and excellent astro-turf tennis courts. There are frequent bus services into the centre of Birmingham with good connections to other parts of the West Midlands.

Organisation and Curriculum. There are approximately 102 girls in the Senior School (age range 11–18) and 140 in the the Preparatory School which also accepts boys (age 18 months - 11). The School also has a purpose built nursery for children of 3 and 4 and a Kindergarten aged 18 months and 3 which is open for 48 weeks of the year from 8am to 6pm. After school care facilities are available up to 6.00 pm if required.

The School offers Christian education with a European dimension. Languages are part of the core curriculum from age 8 to 18 and the school has strong links with Europe. Worship is based on the Roman Catholic tradition but applications from members of other Churches and Faiths are welcomed.

The school has a strong academic tradition and records of success at all levels are consistently high. There is an extensive programme of careers education and advice, and most Sixth Formers who leave the school go on to University or other higher education. Girls frequently obtain places at Oxford and Cambridge. A wide range of subjects is available for GCSE and A-level with good facilities, including well equipped Science Laboratories, Language Resource Room, Information Technology facilities, gymnasium and library.

Extra-curricular activities. These include a wide range of clubs. Individual tuition is offered in Speech, Ballet, Singing and Instrumental music.

Entry. Entry to the Preparatory Department and Nursery is by interview and day visit and to the Senior School by school report and examination at 11+. Scholarships are awarded at 7+, 11+ and 13+, and Sixth Form Scholarships are available for 16+ entrance.

Scholarships (*see* Entrance Scholarship section) For details, see the appropriate section.

Bursaries may be awarded in cases of special need.

Fees. Day pupils range from £1,140 to £1,878 per term.

Further Information. Full details may be obtained from the school. Parents and girls are welcome to visit the school by appointment in addition to general open day visits.

Charitable status. Holy Child School is a Registered Charity, number 518009. It exists to provide education for children.

Holy Trinity College
Bromley

81 Plaistow Lane Bromley Kent BR1 3LL
Tel: 020 8313 0399
Fax: 020 8466 0151
e-mail: info@htc-bromley.co.uk
website: www.holytrinitycollegebromley.co.uk

Roman Catholic School for 560 Girls

Governors:
Mrs S Clarke, BA Hons, PGCE (*Chairman*)
Dr E T MacCann, MB, BCh, BAO, DRCOG (*Deputy Chairman*
Mr A J Baulf, FCA, FCCA
Mr R D Collins, FRICS, FCIArb, MBAE, FBEng, FInstD
Miss M Connell, MA (Oxon)
Mr J Dunne, FICA
Mr D Maguire
Mr D Mahony
Mr T May
Canon P Pearson (*Parish Priest*)
Sr Jeanne Madeleine Timmins, BA Hons, PGCE

***Headmistress:* Mrs Janet Dunn**, BDiv Hons, PGCE

Deputy Head: Mrs S M Aldhouse, BSc Hons, CertEd

College Chaplain: Mr M J Côté, MA, BA

Senior School Teaching Staff:

Miss N Billington, BA Hons, MA, ARCM, PGCE *Head of Music*
Mr M Biltcliffe, BA Hons, PGCE *Head of Drama*
Mrs C Bowden, CertEd *Food Technology/Textiles*
Mrs M Briggs, BSc Hons, MSc *Mathematics*
Mrs E Bromfield, BA Hons, PGCE *Head of Languages*
Mrs C Fallows, BA Hons, PGCE *French*
Miss M Fowler, BA Hons, PGCE *Head of English*
Mrs P Garton, BSc Hons, PGCE *Physics, Chemistry, General Science*
Mrs S Hearn, BSc Hons *Biology, Science, Geography*
Mr A Kemp, BA Hons, MA, PGCE *Head of History*
Mrs H Knowd, BEd Hons *English, Head of Sixth Form, i/c Key Skills*
Miss S Lilley, BEd Hons *Head of Physical Education*
Mrs J Long, BA Hons, PGCE *German*
Mrs A Lowles, BA Hons, ATC *Art*
Dr C Lyons, BSc Hons, PhD *Chemistry, Head of Science*
Mrs G Malcolm, BA Hons, MSc *Head of Mathematics, Head of Upper School*
Mrs L Moule, BA Hons, PGCE *Head of Religious Education/Senior Pastoral Head*
Mrs E North, CertEd *Mathematics, Examinations Officer*
Mrs J Norton, BA Hons *Religious Studies/History*
Mrs P Payne, BA Hons, CertEd *English*
Mrs M Plummer, BA, LCCI *Business Studies/i/cCareers*
Mrs R Ssemuyaba, BA Hons, PGCE *Information Technology*
Mrs J Tilley, BA Hons, PGCE *Physics/Technology*
Miss D Tonkins, BA Hons, PGCE *Psychology, i/c Special Needs support*
Mrs A Valentine, BSc Hons, PGCE *Physics/General Science*
Mr J Wanstall, BSc Hons, PGCE *Head of Information Technology*
Mrs R Warwick, BSc Hons, MSc, PGCE *Head of Geography*
Mrs M Williams, BSc Hons *Head of Lower School/Science/Biology*
Mr M Wilson, BA Hons, PGCE *Head of Art*

Preparatory School (*including pre-school Nursery*):

Teaching Staff:

Head: Mrs M E Titterington, BA(Econ) Hons, PGCE

Mrs S Bishop, CertEd *Year 1 Teacher*
Miss M E Bruton, NNEB *Nursery Nurse in Reception*
Mrs D M Clark, CertEd *Year 2 Teacher, KS1 Co-ordinator*
Miss C Clarke, BA Hons, HDipEd *Year 4 Teacher, Language Co-ordinator*
Mrs G Dalziel-Jones, BEd Hons *Reception Teacher*
Mrs C E Goodridge, CertEd *Year 3 Teacher*
Miss K Kilgallon, CertEd *Year 5 Teacher*
Mrs L Knight, CertEd, BEd Hons *Mathematics*
Mrs R McKay, BSc Hons *Year 6 Teacher/KS2/Maths Co-ordinator*
Mrs J M McMillan, BEd Hons *Year 6 Teacher*
Mrs P G Moore, CertEd *Year 1 Teacher*

Mrs S Norbury, CertEd, BEd *Year 4 Teacher*
Mrs V G O'Keeffe, CertEd *Year 2 Teacher*
Mrs M A Partridge, GRSM, ARCM *Music*
Mrs D Perry, CertEd *Teacher/Reading & Nursery Music*
Miss B A Rickwood, CertEd *Year 3 Teacher*
Mrs R H Thomas, BA Hons *French*
Mrs E M Twohig, BEd Hons, CertEd *Year 5 Teacher/IT Co-ordinator*
Mrs A Vinales *Classroom Assistant in Reception*
Mrs T A Wells, CertEd *Reception Teacher*
Mrs C Williams, CertEd *Year 6 Teacher*
Mrs Z R Williams, BSc Hons, PGCE *Science*

Nursery:
Mrs E Barker *Nursery Assistant*
Mrs R Barker *Nursery Assistant*
Mrs K Coley *Nursery Assistant*
Mrs J Grainge, DNN (NNEB) *Nursery Teacher*
Mrs E M High, DPP *Nursery Teacher*
Mrs A F Roberts, ALA, NVQIII *Nursery Teacher*

Administration/Support Staff:

Prep & Senior School:
Bursar/Clerk to the Governors: Mr C Allies
Finance Officer: Mrs P Goode
Admissions Secretary: Mrs S Tomlinson
Premises Manager: Mr B North

Senior School:
Headmistress' Secretary/Admin Officer: Mrs A Crosbie
Librarian: Mrs A High, ALA, BA
Laboratory Technician: Mrs F Durand, IUT (France)
IT Assistant: Mrs J Douse, BSc Hons, CertEd, DipIT
Secretary/Reception: Mrs P Girling
Welfare Supervisor/Reprographics: Mrs D Sloane
Welfare Assistant: Mrs M Corrie-Walker
Welfare/Support Assistant: Mrs D Cormack

Prep School:
Welfare/Reading: Mrs A Burfield
Reception/Welfare: Mrs J Crisp
Admin Assistant/Reprographics/Welfare: Mrs P Jefferies
School Secretary: Mrs A Sneary
Welfare Assistant: Mrs M Corrie-Walker
Welfare Assistant: Mrs J Whinder, BEd

Caretakers/Groundsmen:
Mr R Colyer
Mr E Thorpe

Holy Trinity College is a Catholic day school founded in 1886 by members of the congregation of French Trinitarian Sisters whose aim was to offer an excellent education for young girls and to develop and deepen in their pupils the awareness of God's love. Today, under lay headship and trusteeship of the Order, it continues its Roman Catholic foundation whilst welcoming pupils of other denominations and faiths sympathetic to our Christian ethos. As a member of the worldwide Trinitarian Community our school is marked by love, respect for each other and an understanding of essential human dignity. All pupils, from preschool to the Sixth Form, are valued as individuals and motivated to achieve their very best across a rich and wide-ranging curriculum experience. The school provides a stimulating and caring environment in which our pupils succeed and where they regularly receive recognition for personal achievement whatever their individual talents and skills. Small teaching groups enable girls to achieve excellent academic results which take them into higher education and the professions. The College has a well-defined and strong pastoral system.

Buildings and facilities. Situated on a fifteen acre site within easy walking distance of central Bromley, the College's original eighteenth century mansion now forms part of a large modern complex. There is a music block, heated open-air swimming pool, hockey pitches, tennis and netball courts and an extensive track and field area. Recent improvements include a newly refurbished Year 11 Common Room, new shower and changing rooms, Upper Prep unit, Sixth Form Suite, Prep Library, Music and Science laboratory and the introduction of stricter security measures.

Curriculum. Full details may be found in the College prospectus. Art, Drama, Music and Sport are important subjects. The Preparatory Department numbers 270 girls and there are between 40-70 girls and boys in the Nursery during an academic year. French is taught throughout the College from Nursery upwards. Ballet is taught as part of the PE curriculum from Nursery to Year 3 inclusive. Girls in Years 5 and 6 benefit from the use of Senior School specialist facilities including Food Technology, Science, IT and Design Technology. Many subjects in the Prep School are taught by specialist teaching staff. The Senior School with 270 pupils has two-form entry. Girls are grouped by ability and interest into smaller sets in most subjects. In KS3 a broad and challenging curriculum which includes and extends the National Curriculum is offered to all pupils. All girls sit the Religious Studies GCSE in Year 10. In KS4, a common core plus three further option-choice subjects leads to GCSE covering a range of sixteen subjects. The average number of GCSE subjects studied is 10. At AS and A2 level candidates choose from a wide range of subjects including Art, Biology, Business Studies, Chemistry, Computer Studies, English, French, Geography, German, History, Mathematics, Music, Physics, PE, Psychology, Theology and Theatre Studies. Students are prepared for University entrance including Oxbridge. Information Technology courses leading to Key Skills examinations are offered. There is a structured programme of careers education and advice from Year 9 to Year 13. The College has a consistently excellent record of academic success and all-round achievement.

Extra curricular activities. Girls are encouraged to make full use of the College recreational facilities and there are a number of clubs and sports which are a regular feature of lunchtime and after-school activity including music, art, language, debating, dance, gym, computer, trampolining, swimming, tennis, netball and hockey. Drama and Music have a high profile and singers and instrumentalists are invited to join the various choirs, ensembles and orchestra. Advantage is taken of the College's proximity to London to visit theatres, museums and art galleries and to attend conferences. Regular field courses are arranged for the geographers and biologists and staff accompany pupils abroad during the school holidays for a range of vocational and academic pursuits. The College is well-supported by the Parent Teachers Association. The College operates an associated after-school club, Après HTC, which offers a range of after school facilities for pupils of the school and affords working parents an extended school day.

Admission. (*see* Entrance Scholarship section) Every girl seeking admission into Years 7-11 is required to sit an entrance examination and attend an interview. An entrance examination is held each January for girls seeking entry into Year 7 the following September. The Sixth Form Scholarship examination is held each January for students seeking entry into Year 12 the following September. Year 12 students are admitted on the basis of their public examination results and an interview. Music and academic scholarships are available at Years 7 and 12 entry. Following the demise of the Assisted Places Scheme the College established a Bursary Scheme to enable talented girls from families with modest income to take advantage of the education offered at HTC. A limited number of bursaries are available to girls entering Year 7 and Year 12. For further information and a prospectus, which includes admission details for HTC's Prep and pre-school (to which boys as well as girls are admitted until the age of 5 years); please contact the Admissions Secretary.

Fees per term. Nursery £130-£145 per session per term; Preparatory School £1,517-£1,559; Senior School £2,020-£2,054.

Charitable status. Holy Trinity College Bromley Trust Limited is a Registered Charity, number 1015230. Its aim is to provide an excellent broad-based education for girls aged 2½ to 18 years and pre-school education for boys aged 2½ to 5 years within a caring Christian environment.

Holy Trinity School
Kidderminster

Birmingham Road Kidderminster Worcs DY10 2BY
Tel: (01562) 822929
Fax: (01562) 865137

***Headmistress:* Mrs E Thomas**, CertEd, CTC

Deputy Headmistress: Mrs G Coen, BA

School Chaplain: The Revd D Lamb, BA

Senior School Staff:
Mrs M Bishop, BA (Hons)
Mrs E Booton, BA (Hons)
Mrs C Cooper, Licence de Lettres (*French*)
Mrs M Crowther, BEd
Mr M Dunnington, CertEd
Mrs C Foord, BA (Hons), PGCE
Mrs P Foulds, MPhil, CertEd
Mrs C Glover, BA
Mrs S Harris, DipEd
Mr P Jackson, CertEd, BPhil
Mrs J Mackie-Smith, BA (Hons)
Mr P Mackie-Smith, FRICS, PGCE
Mrs P Meredith, BSc
Mrs J Morris, CertEd
Mrs H Perks, GRSM, LRAM, DipEd
Mrs V Preston, BSc
Mme A M Robinson, BA
Mrs M Skinner, CertEd, CTC
Mrs G Smith, BSc Hons)
Mrs M Spears, BSc (Hons)
Mrs J Thomas, BEd
Mrs S Webb, BSc, PGCE

Lower School Staff:
Mrs E Bemand, BEd (Hons)
Mrs J Brotherton, CertEd
Mrs H M Fathers, BEd
Mrs J Ferris, BA (Hons), PGCE
Mrs E Morgan, CertEd
Mrs M Phillips, BA (Hons)
Mrs M Robinson, BA (Hons), PGCE
Miss L Ridley, BEd (Hons)
Mrs S M Smith, CertEd
Mrs K Wilkin, BA (Hons), PGCE

Nursery School Staff:
Mrs S Dipaola, PPADip
Miss L Gismondi, BTec
Miss E Mansell, BTec
Mrs M Polito, PPADip
Mrs L Young, BSc, PGCE, Montessori Diploma

Baby & Toddler Unit Staff:
Miss G Carter, BTEC
Mrs G Edgar, BTEC
Miss J Gallagher, NNEB
Miss D Hart, BTec
Miss L Prescott, BTEC
Mrs C Simpson

Elocution/Ballet/Music:
Miss M Brockway, ARAD
Miss A Brown, LLAM, ABBO
Mrs J Fisher, CertEd
Mrs A Lipman, LRAM
Mr D Payne, BA
Mrs C Quekett, CertEd
Ms C Stober, LTCL
Mrs C Vetch, GTCL, LTCL
Mr D Whitehouse, ABSM
Mrs M Willmott, LTCL

Administrative Staff:
Bursar: Mr I Crowe, ACIB
Bursar's Assistant: Mrs T Irving
Headmistress'/Admissions Secretary: Mrs G Harrison
School Secretary: Mrs J Dixon
Business Development Manager: Mrs K Watts
Receptionist: Miss C Curtis
Lab Technician: Mrs P Plant

Auxillaries:
Miss H Drew, Montessori
Mrs H Taylor

Introduction. Holy Trinity School is a multi-denominational day school, administered by a board of trustees. The school believes strongly in the continuity of education. Girls are welcomed into the school from three months to eighteen years and boys from three months to eleven years. High educational standards are set and a happy environment provided for students to fulfil their potential. The school's broad education is based on high academic principles with strong pastoral care, preparing every student for university and adult life.

Location and transport. The school is within easy access of Kidderminster town centre and there are frequent train and bus services. A school coach collects children from Lye, Stourbridge and surrounding villages.

Organisation and curriculum. The school is divided into five main sections:

Baby and Toddler Unit - boys and girls
Nursery - boys and girls
Lower School - boys and girls
Senior School - girls only
Sixth Form - girls only

The school welcomes visitors. Parents are encouraged to talk with staff and to allow their children to spend time in an appropriate class to judge for themselves the exceptional opportunities on offer. With the emphasis on a broad, balanced education, there is a wide range of subjects available at GCSE. Most children sit eleven GCSE subjects.

Eighteen subjects are offered at A level with all national curriculum Key Stages followed in the lower and senior schools. Throughout the senior school, girls are set for core subjects and on entry they are assigned to one of the four houses. Reports are sent to parents on a half termly basis to help monitor progress, with two full reports annually. The school holds two official parents' evenings a year to allow direct discussion with all subject staff, but parents are always welcome to discuss their child's progress.

Admissions. Formal entrance/scholarship examinations are held in January for entry to the Senior School and the Sixth Form in September. Transfers can be made from other schools throughout the year. Prospective pupils spend two days in school prior to the offer of a place.

Scholarships. Academic, music and sporting scholarships are available at 11+ and 6th form. A limited number of Holy Trinity Assisted Places (based on the Government Assisted Places Scheme) are also available.

Buildings. The school is housed on one campus with connecting buildings. Recent improvements include a newly re-furbished dining room, senior school library and computer suite. The indoor swimming pool, classrooms and science laboratories provide excellent accommodation, which are conducive for learning.

Extra Curricular Activities. Students' talents and interests are extended through an exciting programme of activities. Extra curricular activities include fencing, self defence, science drama, public speaking, choirs, orchestra, Duke of Edinburgh Award Scheme, ballet, art, chess, cookery, dance, fitness, Latin, netball, gymnastics, speech and drama, ornithology and many more. The Lower Sixth participates in the Young Enterprise Business Scheme. For all students, pre-school and after-school care and homework clubs are available on a daily basis.

Charitable status. Holy Trinity School is a Registered Charity, number 517893. It exists to provide quality education for girls and boys.

Howell's School Llandaff (G.D.S.T.)

Llandaff Cardiff CF5 2YD
Tel: (029) 2056 2019
Fax: (029) 2057 8879
e-mail: headsec@how.gdst.net

Founded 1860. **Day School for Girls**

The Governing Body.

The school, together with the other schools of The Girls' Day School Trust, is administered by the Trust, the Trust being Trustee.

Howell's School, Llandaff was opened in 1860 as a school for girls. It was built by the Drapers' Company from the endowment left by Thomas Howell, son of a Welshman, merchant of London, Bristol and Seville and a Draper, in 1537. In 1980 the Council of the Girls' Public Day School Trust became the Trustee. The aim of the Trust is to provide a fine academic education at a comparatively modest cost. The school's own Governing Body includes nominees of the Drapers' Company and the University of Wales, Cardiff, all appointed by the Council of the GDST.

Governors:
Chairman: Mr N W Sims, MBE, FCA

Mr J Cory, DL, JP
The Very Reverend A R Davies
Mr J A N Devereux
Miss E Edwards, BSc
Mr D C Fildes, OBE, MA, HonDLitt
Professor I Finlay, FRCGP, MRCP, FRCP
Mrs V Harpwood, MA, LLM
Mrs L James, BSc(Econ), JP
Mrs J Jenkins, RGN, RM
Mrs M E Jones, JP
Mr D W C Morgan, OBE, DL
Ms L Quinn, MSc
Lady S W Reardon Smith
Sir Donald Walters, LLB

***Headmistress:* Mrs C J Fitz**, BSc (Tasmania), BSc (London) *Biology, Chemistry*

Deputy Head: Mrs S Davis, BSc (London) *Geology*

Full-time Teaching Staff:
Mrs E Barton, BA (Reading) *French*
Mrs E A Bevan, BA (Wales) *Physical Education*
Miss M Brewer, BA (Oxon, MA (Oxon) *French*
Miss D S Cook, BSc (Wales), CMath, MIMA *Mathematics*
Mr S G Crump, BA (University of CE, Birmingham), MA (Birmingham) *English*
Mrs S W Dafydd, BA (Wales) *Welsh*
Mrs C Darnton, BEd (Wales) *ICT*
Mrs H Davies, BA (Wales) *History*
Miss A E L Eddy, BA (Adelaide) *German*
Mrs S A Eddy, BA (Cardiff Institute), PATC *Art*
Mrs S M Evans BA (Southampton) *Religious Studies*
Dr J G Everett, BSc (Bristol), PhD (Wales) *Physics*
Mrs L S Finch, BSc (Wales) *ICT and Science*
Mrs M Gent, MSc (Swansea), MEd (Cardiff) *Chemistry*
Mrs C Gorno, BA (Wales) *French*
Mrs J C Guy, BA (Leicester) *English*
Mrs C Hamlett, BA (Bristol) *Classics*
Mrs S J Jenkins, BA (Wales) *Classics*
Mrs C W Jones, BEd (Barry) *Physical Education*
Mrs J King, BA (Exeter), MSc (Southampton) *Mathematics*
Dr R D Knowles, BA (Wales), MA (London), PhD (London) *English*
Mr R McPartland, BA, ATC (London) *Art*
Mrs S E Marusza, BSc (Wales) *Biology*
Mrs J S Maurice, MA(Ed) (OU), BSc (Keele), MSc (OU) *Biology*
Mrs W J Moyle, BSc (Swansea) *Mathematics*
Mrs E A Phillips, BA (Wales) *Music*
Mrs J A Poyner, BSc (Exeter) *Mathematics*
Mrs G L Prys-Davies, BA (Wales) *Welsh*
Mrs A Rees, BA (Wales) *English and Drama*
Dr S Southern, PhD (Durham), BSc (Stirling) *Chemistry*
Mrs J G Sully, MA (Wales) *History*
Mr J A Summers, MSc, BSc (Wales) *Physics*
Mr D G Thomas, MA, BMus (Wales), ARCO, ARCM *Music*

Part-time Teachers:
Mrs Y J Baker, BEd (Sussex) *Physical Education*
Mrs A Brown, BA (Aberystwyth), MEd (Cardiff) *Geography*
Mrs P M Churchman, MSc (London), MA(Ed) (OU) *Physics*
Mrs R Davies-Schöneck, Staatsexamen (Freiburg) *German*
Mrs C A Elmes, BSc (Swansea) *Mathematics*
Mr D T Evans, BSc Econ (Wales) *Business Studies*
Mrs R Gaskell, BA (Reading) *French and German*
Mrs C George, BA (Exeter) *History*
Mrs J House, BA (Wales) *Geography*
Mrs E L Jenkins, BSc (Cardiff) *Science and Biology*
Mrs K T Jones, MA (Glasgow) *English and Drama*
Mrs A Madeley, BA (Combined Hons), (Birmingham) *Physical Education*
Mrs E R H Pexton, CertEd (Wales), ACCEG *Home Economics and Careers*
Mrs S E Richards, BA (Wales) *English*
Mrs A Russell-Jones, BA (London Bible College), ThM (Atlanta) *Religious Studies*
Mrs A M Tudor, BSc(Econ) (Wales) *Geography*
Mrs E J Walters, BA(Econ) (Sheffield), MSc (Wales) *Geography*
Mrs J A Walters, BSc (London) *Biology*
Mrs M Williams, BA (Cambridge) *Classics*

Junior Department:
Mrs M S Davis, BEd (Kingston), MA(Ed) (OU) (*Head of Junior School*)
Mr I Beckett, BLib (Wales)
Mrs J Davies-Edwards, TTC (Wellington)
Mrs T Davies, BEd (Wales)
Mrs M Dunstan, CertEd (London), BA (Wales)

Mrs J Eager, BEd (Roehampton)
Mrs S M Jones, BEd Hons (Wales)
Mrs J A Lund, BEd (Rolle College)
Mrs B Ludlam, CertEd (Wales)

Visiting Music Teachers:
Piano:
Mr S Shewring, BMus, LRAM, ARCM, FTCL, LGSM
Mrs C Oakes, LRAM, ARCM
Mrs J M Phipps, BMus, LRAM, ATCL, DipMus

Violin/Viola:
Mrs G Williams, AGSM
Miss M Mattison, LRAM

Cello:
Mr A Davies

Double Bass/Bass Guitar:
Mr W Graham-White, GWCMD, DipEd

Flute:
Ms J Groves, LWCMD
Mrs S Buckland, BMus, LTCL

Oboe:
Mrs B James, BPharm, MEd, PHC, PGCE

Clarinet:
Mrs L Dunstan, BMus, LRAM, ARCM Examiner, Ass Board, RSM
Miss R Bradshaw, BA

Bassoon:
Mr M Bowen, LRAM

Saxophone:
Mr M Ronchetti, FRAM

Trumpet:
Mr D Wright, GMusRNCM, PPRNCM

French Horn:
Mr S Morgan

Trombone:
Mr D Smith

Timpani/Percussion:
Mr P Girling, BA

Tuba:
Mr M Thistlewood, BMus, ACP

Voice:
Miss P A O'Neill, DipMus
Mrs J K Woolveridge, BMus, LRAM

Guitar:
Mr C Ackland, GRSM, LRAM, LTCL

Visiting Drama Teacher:
Mrs S Cooksey, CertEd, LWCMD, LGSM

Teaching Support Staff:
Mrs A Ballantine
Mrs M Crowe
Miss A Gallon
Mr G Jones
Mr J Leat
Mrs C Maidment
Mr P Maurice
Mrs G Stevens
Mr R Thomas

Head of Learning Resources: Mrs P Williams

Marketing Officer: Ms J Sanders, MA

Information Systems Manager: Mr C Hardisty

Nurse: Mrs B Budd

School Medical Officers:
Dr F J F Matthews
Dr L M Tapper-Jones
Dr J D Westlake

School Administration:

School Administrator: Mr J S Williams, BSc (Wales)
Deputy School Administrator: Miss J M Ballinger
Clerk to the Governors and Head's Secretary: Mrs C Castle
Junior School Secretary: Mrs C A England
Administrative Assistants: Mrs E Fitzgibbon, Mrs J Walters, Ms S Powell
Administrative Officers: Mrs D Scourfield, Mrs P Chamberlain
Catering Supervisor: Mrs E Newton
Caretaker: Mr M J Caswell
Assistant Caretakers: Mr A Harrison, Mr D Morris
Groundsman: Mr C Walden

Howell's School, Llandaff is an academically selective independent school for 740 girls aged from 3–18. The Nursery Unit for girls of 3+ was opened in September 1997. The school is situated within easy reach of the Cardiff city centre and set in 18 acres of grounds. The splendid grey stone building, designed by Decimus Burton which has been expanded and modernised is still the focal point of the school. In addition there are four large Victorian houses which provide excellent accommodation for the Junior School, the Sixth Form and the Music School. There are extensive facilities in all subjects. The new Sports Complex was opened in May 1997 and the school now has the best sporting facilities in the area.

Curriculum. All National Curriculum subjects including Welsh are taught at Key Stages 1, 2 and 3. In addition girls in the Junior School study French and in the Senior School two European languages and Latin. Girls are encouraged to see learning as an exciting process and to have an inquisitive and creative attitude. Active learning styles are seen as an essential part of classroom experience. A broad list of AS and A2 subjects is available in the Sixth Form. All girls take the Key Skills Course. Examinations in all AS subjects are taken at the end of Year 12. The majority go on to Higher Education. There is a comprehensive careers programme for everyone from age 3 to 18.

Extra-curricular activities. There are a number of opportunities to develop musical, dramatic and sporting talents from an early age. Girls take part in the Duke of Edinburgh Award Scheme from Year 10, in debating and public speaking competitions, in community service and in the Young Enterprise Scheme in Year 12. Eisteddfodau are held in both the Junior and Senior Schools annually.

A substantial number of bursaries are available. These are means tested and are intended to ensure that the school remains accessible to bright girls who would profit from our education but who would be unable to enter the school without financial assistance.

Details of scholarships, bursaries and music exhibitions are available, on request, from the school.

Fees. From September 2000. Senior School Day, £1,680 per term. Junior Department £1,220 per term. Nursery £980 per term. The school's own examination for entry at 11+ is held in early February. A number of suitably qualified pupils are admitted each year to the large Sixth Form.

Charitable status. Howell's School Llandaff is a Registered Charity, number 525757. Its Trustee is the Girls' Day School Trust (1872), a Limited Company registered in England No 6400C. A Registered Charity number 306983. The aim of the Trust is to provide a fine academic education at a comparatively modest cost.

Hull High School
(CSC)

Tranby Croft Anlaby East Yorkshire HU10 7EH
Tel: 01482 657016

Under the Management of the Church Schools Co Ltd.
Motto: *The fear of the Lord is the beginning of wisdom*

Governing Body: The Council of the Church Schools Company

***Headmistress:* Mrs M A Benson**, BA (Hull)

Deputy Headmistress: Mrs I E Nixon, BA, MA (York)

Secretary: Miss J E Phillips

The School was opened in 1890 and currently numbers about 420 pupils. It is in membership of the Girls Schools Association.

Kindergarten. Boys and Girls are accepted into the Kindergarten from the age of three and remain there until an appropriate point, following their fourth birthday. A wide range of learning activities is offered and individual attention is paid to each child. All the basic pre-school skills are covered in preparation for entry to the Reception Class of the Junior Department.

Junior School. This is also for boys and girls from the ages of four to eleven. **Lower Juniors** covers the Reception and DES Years 1 and 2, leading up to Key Stage 1 Level.

Upper Juniors take children from the age of 7+ to the age of 11. The education is essentially class teacher based but gradually the children are prepared for the Secondary Stage by using specialist rooms for some subjects and the staff have the support of Senior specialist teachers in some areas. The children become the youngest members of the four School Houses.

The Kindergarten, Lower and Upper Juniors are housed in a purpose built block which was added to the School in 1982. Light and airy rooms are well equipped and give a very happy environment in which to learn.

The Senior School. 11+ to 18+ covers the main curriculum for everybody in the first three years, including Art, Biology, Chemistry, English, French, Geography, German, History, Home Economics (Food & Textiles), Information Technology, Latin, Mathematics, Music, Physics, Physical Education and Religious Studies.

For DES Years 10 and 11 two year courses leading to GCSE examinations are offered with full guidance provided for the selection of subjects to form each girl's programme of studies.

Sixth Form. Applications are welcome from both internal and external candidates to join the Sixth Form where the teaching groups are usually small enough to provide individual attention but large enough to provide inter-action of discussion and ideas. There are separate facilities in a Sixth Form Centre.

Admission. To the lower part of the School by assessment and testing (up to Year 2) and by more formal tests and examinations from the age of eight onwards.

Sporting Activities. Appropriate games and sporting activities are offered for each age range. The main Senior sports are Hockey, Netball, Cross Country in the winter months, Tennis, Rounders and Volleyball in the summer. The School also has facilities for Athletics, Badminton, Table Tennis and Trampolining. Swimming lessons are available at the nearby Haltemprice Sports Centre for all children aged 7+ to 12+ and as part of the Physical Recreation periods for the more senior members of the school.

Extra subjects. The following subjects are available: Pianoforte, Violin, 'Cello, Double bass, Flute, Clarinet, Trumpet, Trombone, Percussion, Speech and Drama. (Fees on application).

Registration Fee. A non-returnable fee is required when an application is submitted.

Fees. Fees range from £3,273 to £5,112 per annum, and are subject to annual review. There is a fee reduction for additional children in the same family.

Scholarships. A small number of Scholarships is awarded annually on the basis of entrance examinations and also for girls entering the Sixth Form. Children of Clergy are offered a fees remission up to a third of fees.

Charitable status. Hull High School (as a member of The Church Schools Company) is a Registered Charity, number 1016538. It was founded to further education based on Christian principles.

The Hulme Grammar School for Girls
Oldham

Chamber Road Oldham Lancs OL8 4BX
Tel: 0161-624 2523
Bursar: 0161-624 8442
Fax: 0161-620 0234
e-mail: Enquiries-Girls@hulmegrammarschools.org.uk

Motto: *Fide sed cui vide*
Founded under the Endowed Schools Act 1887, opened in 1895.

Governing Body: As from 29 March 1977 there are 15 Governors, 10 appointed by the previous Governing Body, 5 representative Governors appointed by local authorities

Chairman: Mrs Rosemary Brierley, JP, BA

Vice Chairman: Barrie Williams, LLB

Honorary Treasurer: Andrew Scholes, AMCST

John Ainley
Mrs Elizabeth M M Boon, MBE
Stuart Brook, ACIB
G Malcolm George
David J Illingworth
Mrs Barbara Jackson
Mrs Sylvia Jackson
Graham F Partington
Kenneth Stocks
Raymond J Whitehead, OBE
Graham Winterbottom

Clerk to the Governors: H David Moore

***Headmistress:* Miss M S Smolenski**, BSc (Manchester)

Deputy Headmistress: Mrs R M Mannell, BA (London)

Senior Mistresses:
Miss S E Shepherd, BA (Royal Holloway College, London) *French*
Mrs C A Wilkinson, BSc (Liverpool) *Mathematics*

Assistant Staff:
Mrs B J Allwood, MA (Oxford) *German*
Miss E S Anderson, BEd (Sheffield Hallam) *Physical Education*
Dr P Beagon, MA, DPhil (Oxford) *Classics*
Mr J M Bibby, BSc (Aberystwyth) *Chemistry*
Mrs M Birch, BA (Manchester) *History*
Mrs F M Bradbury, TCert (Liverpool) *Physical Education*

Mrs R J Broadbent, MA (Oxford), ARCO, ARCM *Music*
Mrs R Chester, BSc (Hull) *Biology*
Miss T Chung-Li, BEd (Chester) *Preparatory School*
Mr J A Condliffe, BSc (Manchester) *Mathematics*
Mr C Z Cook, BA (Liverpool) *English*
Mrs M Crossman, BSc (Manchester), MEd (Manchester) *Physics*
Mrs C Davies, BA (Kent) *English*
Mrs T Dent, BA (Open University) *Mathematics*
Mrs R M Dixon, BA (Liverpool) LRAM *Music*
Miss C W Duffy, BA, MPhil (Aberystwyth) *History*
Mrs Z Fleming, Teacher's Certificate (Edge Hill College) *Preparatory School*
Mrs E E Greer, DipPE (Dublin) *Physical Education*
Mrs K Gregson, BSc (Lancaster) *Biology*
Mrs R Hall, BA (Birmingham), MTh (Nottingham) *Religious Studies*
Mrs J Harrison, BSc (Durham) *Mathematics*
Miss J Hathaway, BA (Swansea), MEd (Durham) *English*
Mrs C Headdock, BA (London) *Modern Languages*
Mrs D Howarth, BSc (Manchester Metropolitan) *Home Economics*
Mrs C Jones, BA (Open University) *Home Economics*
Mrs T Kershaw, BA (Salford) *Modern Languages*
Mrs J King, BA (Reading) *English*
Mrs A J Kremnitzer, BSc (Aberdeen) *Chemistry*
Mr P Langdon, BEd (Manchester Metropolitan) *Information Technology*
Mrs D Maders, BSc (Leeds) *Chemistry*
Mrs C W Maitland, BSc (Sheffield) *Preparatory School*
Mrs E H Marsland, BSc (Hull) *Mathematics*
Mrs C E Morrison, BA (Nottingham) *Classical Studies*
Mrs H J Murray, BA (Durham) *Modern Languages*
Mrs A M Newby, BSc (Brunel University) *Design and Technology*
Mrs B A Parkinson, BSc (Liverpool) *Geography*
Mr R Parr, BA (Leeds) *English*
Mrs A D Pearson, Teacher's Certificate (Chester College) *Preparatory School*
Mrs S M Poyser, Teacher's Certificate (Yorkshire College of Education and Home Economics) *Home Economics*
Mrs P T Ramotowski, BSc (London), BA (Open University) *Biology*
Mrs A G Robinson, MSc (Manchester), BSc (Babes-Bolyai) *Physics*
Mrs E M T Schofield, BEd, CNAA (Westminster College, Oxford) *Preparatory School*
Mrs C Shuttleworth, BA (Leicester) *English*
Mrs S M Stafford, BSc (Hull) *Physics*
Miss M Stevenson, NDD, ATD (Sheffield) *Art and Design*
Mrs J Sullivan, BSc (Salford) *Chemistry*
Mrs D Thurrell, NDD, ATD, (Manchester) *Art and Design*
Mrs S Titmuss, BA (Manchester) *History*
Mrs S Toole, BSc (London) *Biology*
Mr G I Wailes, BA (Sheffield Hallam) *Business Studies and Economics*
Mrs S Watt, BA (Manchester), MEd (Leeds) *Geography*
Mrs D V Wheldrick, BA (Preston Polytechnic) *Information Technology*
Mrs J Wood, BA (Leeds) *Religious Studies*

Medical Officer: Dr D Bayman, MB, ChB, DRCOG

Nurse: Mrs A Baulk, RN, School Nurse Certificate

School Secretaries:
Mrs P M Mullin
Mrs J Tattersall

Receptionist: Mrs P Haigh

Housekeeper: Mrs A Gorton

The Hulme Grammar Schools were opened in 1895, one for girls and the other for boys. The Girls' School moved to new buildings adjoining the Boys' School in 1925. There has been a steady development of the School's facilities since the 1970's and these now include a refurbished indoor heated swimming pool and a sports hall, improved Sixth Form facilities as well as additional laboratories, two computer rooms and new dining facilities. A new wing, containing a specially designed music room and other classrooms opened in 1988 allowing the school to expand from two to three form entry. Other sports' facilities include grass and all-weather hockey pitches and 5 hard tennis/netball courts. A joint Library shared with the Boys' school opened in September 1997.

The school is situated within easy reach of the town centre. It is well served by public transport and special buses to the surrounding areas and is within easy reach of the M60.

The Preparatory School (Estcourt) for 100 girls was extended in 1984 by the building of two new classrooms. Entry is by examination at the age of 7 years. There are approximately 500 girls in the Senior School, entry for which at 11 years old is by examination and interview. In 1999 Werneth Preparatory School joined the Hulme Grammar Schools and takes girls and boys from Nursery to Year 2.

In the first five years of the Senior School the curriculum is a broadly based one avoiding too much specialisation and preserving a balance between Arts and Science subjects. 19 subjects are offered at GCSE level and 22 subjects at AS and A level. All girls in Years 12 and 13 take General Studies and Key Skills as examination subjects. Annually, over 95% of A level leavers go on to Higher Education. Each year a number of girls gain places at Oxford and Cambridge Universities.

A wide range of extra curricular activities, including BAYS, Duke of Edinburgh Award Scheme, Young Enterprise and Community Action are offered. Instrumental lessons (string, woodwind and brass) are taken as extras.

Fees. Senior School £4,743 pa; Preparatory School £3,393 pa (2000–2001).

Bursaries are awarded in the Senior School from the Governors' Bursary Fund on the basis of merit and need. Other financial assistance may be available, including assistance to girls entering the Sixth Form. Leaving Exhibitions are awarded by the Governors, to girls going on to Higher Education.

Charitable status. The Hulme Grammar School for Girls is a Registered Charity, number 526636. It exists to provide a balanced academic education for pupils between the ages of 7 and 18 years. The present schools opened in 1895, though there was an earlier foundation in 1611.

Ipswich High School (G.D.S.T.)

Woolverstone Ipswich 1P9 1AZ
Tel: (01473) 780201
Fax: (01473) 780985

Founded 1878

This is one of the 25 schools of The Girls' Day School Trust. For general information about the Trust and the composition of its Council, see p 532. A more detailed prospectus may be obtained from the school.

Local Governors:

Chairman: The Hon M J Ganzoni

Mrs N R Alcock
D Brown, BA, DMS
S Clark, BSc, FRICS, ACIarb
Mrs J H Galbraith, MA

Mrs M E Hallett, MCSP, SRP
Miss C L Marx, FRCS
E J Smitheram, BSc
Mrs S Vermont, MA
P V Weir, LLB
R Williams, MA, MSc
H T Wykes-Sneyd, FRICS, NDA, FAAV

Headmistress: **Miss V C MacCuish**, BA (London) *Modern Languages*

Deputy Head: Miss V A Davis, BSc (London), ARCS *Chemistry*

Senior School:
Teaching Staff:
Mrs J Andrews, BSc (Exeter) *Mathematics*
Mrs M E Bailey, BA (London) *English*
Mrs H J Beales, BA (Oxon) *Mathematics*)
Mrs S N Blaxill, BSc, MPhil (Leeds) *Chemistry*
Mrs E M Brooking, TCert (Bristol) *Home Economics*
Mr P Butlin, BSc (Durham), MA (OU) *Chemistry*
Mr P W Clayton, BA, LRAM, MPhil (Sheffield) *Music*
Mr P Constantine, TCert (Loughborough) *Design Technology*
Mr R G Crosby, BSc (London) *Economics*
Mrs B M Curran, MA (St Andrews) *French*
Mrs A M Dane, BEd (London) *Art*
Mrs C F Davis, BA (Middlesex) *Art*
Mrs E Dew, BSc (Reading) *Mathematics*
Mrs D Double, MA (Stuttgart) *German*
Mrs L Eastwood, BSc (Leeds) *Biology*
Mrs B J Emmott, BSc (Bradford) *Mathematics*
Miss H M Farrell, BMus (Edinburgh) *Music*
Mrs A M Forrest, MSc (Kent) *Physics*
Mrs F Garnham, BSc (Leeds) *Physics*
Mrs C E Gay, BSc (London) *Physiology*
Mrs P Grimwade, BA (London) *English*
Mr J C G Groslin, BA (Hull) *French*
Mrs G Hannemann, BA (Leeds) *French*
Mr K Hannemann, MA (Georgia, Augusta) *German Conservation*
Miss V L Hughes, BA (Liverpool) *Physical Education*
Mrs R C Kemsley, BA (Durham) *History*
Mrs J R J Kermath (Baccalauréat) *French Conversation*
Mrs S A Laws, BA (Hull) *Theology/English*
Mrs S J Letman, BA (Wales) *English*
Miss J C MacKenzie, BSc (Western Australia) *Geography*
Miss L Meek, BA (London) *Drama*
Mrs J S Noble, BSc (Reading) *Geography*
Mrs M Pineo, TCert (Bedford) *PE*
Mrs C A Poppy, MA (London) *Art*
Mrs A Pratt, BSc (Brunel) *Biology*
Dr S J Ridd, MA (Oxford), PhD (Cambridge), *Classics*
Mrs S L Sharpe, BSc (London) *Biology and Chemistry*
Mrs C Sim, BSc (Durham) *Physics*
Mrs S Steer, BA (London) *English*
Mrs B F Sturgeon, BA (Exeter) *French*
Mrs C Taylor, BSc (East Anglia) *Chemistry*
Mrs J Thomson, MA (St Andrews) *German*
Miss L Waghorn, BEd (Bedford) *Physical Education*
Mrs M Warner, BEd (Bristol) *Home Economics*
Mrs J F Westlake, BA (Southampton) *History*
Mrs K Yates, BSc (London) *Mathematics*

Junior Department:
Head of Junior Department: Mrs C I Stephenson, TCert (London)

Mrs S E Aldred, TCert (Cambridge)
Mrs R T Baldwin, BEd (Liverpool)
Miss S J Clarke, BEd (Exeter)
Mrs J E Cook, TCert (Surrey)
Mrs N J Greenwood, BEd (Cambridge)
Mrs S Lazar, TCert (London) *Physical Education*
Mrs D M Lewis, TCert (London)
Mrs P Milner-Smith, TCert (London)
Mrs C Morton, TCert (Dundee)
Mrs S Rea, BMus (Sheffield)
Mrs K Rose, TCert (Edinburgh)
Miss V J Swales, BEd (Derby)
Mrs S H Thompson, BA (Open University)
Mrs L S Thomson, BEd (Coventry, University of Warwick)

Visiting Staff:
Prof R J Bales *Fencing*
Mrs M Catchpole, GNSM *Violin*
Miss E A Chappell, LRAM, GRSM *Piano*
Mrs J Derrick, BA *Piano*
Mr G P Gillings *Percussion*
Mrs D Hemmings, LRAM *Clarinet*
Mr J W Hemmings *Brass*
Mr J Hughes *Cello*
Mr C H Irwin, BA (Cantab), ARCM, ARCO *Bass, Cello, Organ*
Miss J Parrott, PPRNCM *Singing and Piano*
Mrs M P Pells, LRAM *Cello*
Mrs J Ridley, LRAM, ARCM *Violin*
Mr A D Smith, LRAM, ARCM *Flute*
Miss M Tricker, BMus (London), DipRCM *Oboe*
Mr C Wybrow, BMus (Wits) *Clarinet and Saxophone*

School Doctor: Dr P Exley, MB, ChB

School Administrator: Mrs S E Leask, BA

Secretary: Mrs R Rooke

Ipswich High School was founded in 1878 and from 1907 to 1992 occupied a site in a residential area of north Ipswich. Planning restrictions prevented further expansion on the site and in September 1992 the school moved to Woolverstone Hall, some four miles south-east of Ipswich, where there are greatly improved facilities. The eighteenth-century Hall, a grade I listed mansion, provides the Sixth Form Centre, library, some teaching rooms, offices, kitchen and dining room, while other, later buildings house spacious accommodation for other departments and activities. The Junior Department enjoys its own modern building. A splendid new sports hall and theatre have been built and a covered heated swimming pool is planned for the millennium. All rooms have wide views over the Orwell estuary or the surrounding parkland, covering more than eighty acres.

There are currently approximately 700 girls in the school, including a Junior Department of 220 girls aged 3½ to 11 and 100 in the Sixth Form.

Curriculum. The curriculum is broad and challenging and the girls take nine subjects at GCSE. A wide variety of Advanced Level courses is offered and almost every girl goes on to higher education as a preparation for careers in, for example, medicine, engineering, veterinary science, languages, law, media, business and design.

The girls are offered an extensive programme of extra-curricular activities and the school has strong traditions in Art, Drama and Music and a commitment to the Duke of Edinburgh Award Scheme. The grounds allow ample space for hockey, netball, tennis, rounders, cross country and athletics and there is a very full fixtures list for school teams. Instrumental lessons, singing, drama, sailing and fencing are offered as extra subjects.

Fees. From September 2000: Senior School £1,680 per term; Junior Department £1,220 per term.

The fees cover the regular curriculum, school books, stationery and other materials, examination fees, careers guidance, choral music, games, but not optional extra subjects or school meals.

Bursaries. Following the ending of the Government Assisted Places Scheme, the GDST has made available to the school a number of scholarships and bursaries. The bursaries are means tested and are intended to ensure that the school remains accessible to bright girls who would profit from our education but who would be unable to enter the senior school without financial assistance.

Scholarships. Academic Scholarships are offered at 11+ and for the Sixth Form, and Music Scholarships are available at 11+.

Charitable status. Ipswich High School is one of the 25 schools of the Girls' Day School Trust, which is a Registered Charity, number 1026057. The aim of the Trust is to provide a fine academic education at a comparatively modest cost.

James Allen's Girls' School (JAGS)

East Dulwich Grove London SE22 8TE
Tel: 020 8693 1181
Fax: 020 8693 7842
website: www.jags.org.co.uk

Governing Body:
Miss Joanna Dodson, MA, QC
Mrs Mary Francis, MA
Mr Ram Gidoomal, BSc, ARCS, FRSA, CBE
Mr Peter Hogarth, FCA
Lord McColl of Dulwich, MS, FRCS, FACS, FRCSE (*Chairman*)
Dr Gordana Milavic, FRCPsych
Mrs Alison Miles, BA
Mr Nigel Pantling, BA
Mrs Heather Rankine, BDS
Professor Colin Roberts, PhD, FIEE, FInstP
Mr Christopher Smith, BA, FCA, AIPM
Ms Katharine St John Brooks, BA
Dame Valerie Strachan, BA, DCB

Clerk to the Governors and Bursar: Mr John Reid, ACIB, MIMgt

Deputy Bursar: Mr Kevin Barry, ACA

Development Director: Miss Alison Graham, BA Hons, MA, FRSA

Headmistress: **Mrs Marion Gibbs**, BA Hons, MLitt (Bristol), FRSA

Teaching Staff:

Deputy Head: Mrs Vikki Askew, MA Hons (Edinburgh) *History*

Mrs Jill Adepegba-Ogidan, BSc Hons (Liverpool) *Biology, Careers Adviser*
Miss Helen Adie, BA Hons (London) *Drama and English*
Mr Timothy Askew, BA Hons (Oxford) *History*
Mrs Hélène Bardell, Licence-Maitrîse (Poitiers) *French*
Mrs Wendy Barratt, BSc Hons (Kent) *Biology*
Mrs Corrine Barton, BA Hons (Sheffield) *Head of History and Politics*
Miss Sarah Bedford, MA Hons (Cambridge) *English*
Mrs Joanna Billington, BA Hons (Middlesex) *Drama*
Mr Timothy Billington, BA Hons (London) *German, French, ICT*
Mrs Beatrice Blake, Dotoressa (Bocconi-Milan) *Italian*
Mr Rupert Bond, BMus Hons (London), LRAM, DipNCOs *Director of Music*
Miss Antonia Buccheri, BSc Hons (Manchester) *Mathematics*
Mrs Anita Carpenter, BEd (Liverpool John Moores) *Head of Physical Education*
Mr Andrew Carter, BA Hons (Central St Martin's) *Art*
Miss Rebecca Cartwright, BA Hons (Oxford) *History and Politics*
Mrs Isabelle Clapon, Licence (Nancy) *French*
Miss Louise Cook, BA Hons (Wolverhampton) *Technology*
Miss Elinor Corp, BA Hons (Bristol) *Music*
Mrs Helen Cousins, BEd (London) *Physical Education*
Mrs Elena Crompton, Staatsexamen (Bonn) *Head of German*
Mrs Mehri Davarian, BSc Hons (Greenwich) *Physics*
Mrs Margaret Davis, BA Hons (Newcastle) *Geography*
Mrs Helen Dixon, MA (St Andrews) *French*
Miss Melanie Duignan, BA Hons (Newcastle), MA (Manchester Metropolitan) *English*
Mr Mark Dunford, BA Hons (London Slade School) *Head of Art*
Mrs Frances Eastwood, BA Hons (Oxford) *English*
Mrs Rachel Edwards, BA Hons (Cambridge) *English*
Miss Sarah Ellard, BA(QTS) (St Mary's) *Physical Education*
Mrs Katharine Firth, BA Hons (CNAA) *Art*
Ms Sara Glover, BSc (London) *Head of Mathematics*
Mrs Clare Grant, BSc Hons (Sussex) *Chemistry*
Mrs Charlotte Griffiths, BEd (Lancaster) *German*
Mr Thomas Hamilton-Jones, BA Hons (Oxford) *Head of Economics*
Mrs Jennifer Hanner, BSc Hons (London), DPSE *Head of Biology, Head of Sixth Form*
Mrs Marilyn Harper, MA (Cambridge), FRCO, GRSM, ARMCM *Music*
Mrs Joyce Hawting, BA Hons (London) *History*
Mrs Catharine Henley, MA (Canada) *Mathematics, Classics*
Miss Maria Hernandez, BA Hons (Pais Vasco), MA (London) *Spanish*
Mrs Victoria Hibdige, BA Hons (Central England) *Art*
Mr Andrew Hicklenton, BSc Hons (Southampton) *Physics*
Dr Meridel Holland, MA (Cambridge), PhD (Harvard) *English*
Mrs Jennifer Holman, BA Hons (London) *Head of History of Art, Senior Teacher*
Mrs Alison Hooper, BEd Hons (Cambridge) *Head of Drama*
Mr Robert James, BA Hons (London) *English, Senior Teacher*
Mrs Pauline Jeljeli, MA Hons (Oxford) *Mathematics*
Miss Wendy Johnson, BEd Hons (London) *Physical Education*
Mrs Ruth Jones, BA Hons (Durham), MA (Southampton) *Classics*
Mrs Christine Kent, BSc (London) *Chemistry*
Dr Sarah Knight, BSc Hons, PhD (London) *Chemistry*
Mrs Jean Larkman, BA Hons (Open), MCSP *Mathematics, Head of Years 10-11*
Mrs Ellie Latham, BSc Hons (London) *Physics*
Dr David Lazar, BSc Hons (London) *Economics*
Miss Catherine Ledsham, BA Hons (Cambridge) *English*
Miss Georgina Legg, BA Hons (Sussex) *French*
Mrs Nobuko Leslie, LLB Hons (Tokyo) *Japanese*
Mrs Deborah Lewis, BA Hons (Sheffield) *Head of Religious Studies*
Miss Paula Limbert, BA Hons (Bradford) *French and Russian*
Mr John McClafferty, MA (Cambridge) *English*
Ms Paula McCormick, BA Hons (London) *Design Technology*
Mrs Rosemary McCormick, BMus (London) *Music*
Mrs Ann Massey, BA Hons (Oxford) *History*
Mrs Cherie Millsom, BA Hons (Sheffield) *Classics, Religious Studies*
Mrs Jennifer Milner, MA, BLitt (Oxford) *French, Head of Modern Languages*
Mrs Greta Mountain, BSc (Nottingham) *Chemistry, Head of Science*

Miss Fiona Murray, BEd Hons (London) *Physical Education*
Mrs Kathryn Norton-Smith, BA Hons (Birmingham) *Drama*
Mrs Gillian Oxbrow, BSc Hons (Exeter) *Mathematics, Head of Years 7-9*
Mrs Janet Parkinson, BA Hons (Belfast) *Head of English*
Mr John Pattison, BSc Hons (Newcastle), MA (Lancaster) *Mathematics*
Mr John Putley, BSc Hons (Nottingham) *Head of Physics*
Mrs Roberta Rosen, BSc(Spec) (London), AKC *Head of Geography*
Mrs Josephine Ruscoe, BA Hons (London) *Classics*
Mr Peter Sanders, BSc, MSc (London) *Computer Studies, Information Systems Co-ordinator*
Mrs Frances Shaw, MA (Oxford) *Head of Classics, Philosophy*
Miss Helen Side, MA (Cambridge) *Spanish*
Miss Pauline Simpson, MA (Cambridge) *Mathematics*
Mrs Pamela Swindell, BA Hons (Sheffield) *Religious Studies*
Miss Alexandra Tann, BA Hons (London) *Religious Studies*
Mrs Olivia Thompson, MA Hons (Edinburgh) *Italian*
Miss Natalie Tozer, BSc Hons (Bristol) *Mathematics*
Ms Karen Trinder, BSc Hons (York) *Biology*
Mr Robert Wallace, MA (Birmingham), MBA (Nottingham) *Head of Technology*
Miss Heather Webb, MA (Oxford) *Head of Chemistry*
Mr Laurence Wesson, BSc Hons (London) *Head of Biology*
Dr Julian Willard, MA (Oxford), MTh, PhD (London) *Religious Studies, Philosophy*

Librarians:
Mrs Cynthia Pullin, BA Hons (York), DipLib
Mrs Jean Hedden, BA (OU)
Mrs Stephanie Grant, BA Hons (Anglia)

School Secretary: Mrs Yvonne Tilt

Registrar: Mrs Julie Ellis

School Nurses:
Mrs Judith Sherlock, RGN
Mrs Karen Cattenach (*part-time*)

The school was founded in 1741 as part of the Foundation of Alleyn's College of God's Gift and is the oldest independent girls' school in London.

JAGS is set in 22 acres of grounds in the heart of Dulwich, with extensive playing fields and long-established Botany gardens. The school buildings include well-equipped modern library, 13 laboratories, a recent purpose-built suite of language laboratories, 6 art rooms, 4 computer rooms, Design & Technology workshops, indoor swimming pool (to be replaced in 2001), Sports Hall with squash courts and fitness room, a professionally-managed theatre and a Music School. The Sixth Form Centre has its own tutorial rooms, common rooms and Lecture Theatre.

There is a four-form entry at 11 and JAGS has about 750 pupils with 200 in the Sixth Form. About two thirds of girls come up from our junior department, James Allen's Preparatory School (qv) with about a third entering from other preparatory and primary schools.

Girls follow a broad curriculum with a wide choice of GCSE options, structured to ensure a balanced programme. Advanced Level courses are available in all the usual subjects as well as Classical Civilisation, Greek, Latin, Russian, Spanish, Italian, Economics, Philosophy, Music and Theatre Studies. All Sixth Form girls take a General Studies course which includes Ethics, Politics, and Public Speaking. A modern foreign language is studied by all in the Lower Sixth year and full use is made of satellite TV and audio aids. Special provision is made for pupils preparing for Oxford and Cambridge entry.

The extra-curricular programme is a key part of the JAGS education. The excellent Prissian Theatre enables first class, full scale drama productions, while the active music department plays a central role, offering 3 choir schools, 4 orchestras, 2 brass ensembles, 4 wind ensembles plus jazz and big bands. A great variety of other interests is encouraged, from Duke of Edinburgh's Award, debating, photography, and the Literary Society, to politics, the Polyglots Society and Amnesty International. Exchange visits to Russia, France, Germany, Italy, Spain and the USA are regularly organised. The choirs, orchestras and sports teams also visit overseas. Community Service plays an important part in school life, and there are partnership activities with other local schools and organisations.

Sports are well catered for. Hockey, netball, gymnastics, dance, tennis, rounders, swimming, athletics and self defence are curriculum subjects, with opportunities for fencing, football, badminton, sailing, ice-skating and riding.

Individual lessons in Instrumental Music and Speech and Drama are available (fees on application).

Fees. (a) Registration fee, £30; (b) £2,568–£2,664 per term.

Admission. Girls are admitted at 11+ and 13+ and also into the Sixth Form.

Entrance Examination. Every candidate for admission will be required to pass an examination, graduated according to age. For details and method of admission apply to The Registrar, Mrs J Ellis.

Scholarships (*see* Entrance Scholarship section) Up to twenty Foundation Scholarships are awarded every year to girls of 11 years of age on entry to the School. Sixth Form scholarships are also available. Scholarships are awarded for academic ability and for Music and Art.

All Scholarships are augmented by a means-tested element in cases of need.

Following the demise of the Government Assisted Places Scheme, the School has introduced James Allen's Scholarships to continue to enable talented girls from families of limited means to enter JAGS.

Charitable status. James Allen's Girls' School is a Registered Charity, number 312750 and exists for the purpose of educating girls.

Kent College Pembury

Old Church Road Pembury Tunbridge Wells Kent TN2 4AX

Tel: (01892) 822006
Bursar: (01892) 820220
Fax: (01892) 820221
e-mail: admissions@kentcollege.kent.sch.uk
website: www.kent-college.co.uk

Kent College Pembury is a day and boarding school, offering continuous education from ages 3 to 18. A happy school with high academic standards, the school provides for the educational and cultural needs of day students and boarders from all over the world. Set in beautiful countryside, just 35 miles from London, students benefit from high teaching standards in a superbly equipped environment, within a caring Christian community. All girls participate in the imaginative programme of music, drama, sports, clubs, societies and other activities.

Board of Governors:

Chairman: Mrs P J Darbyshire

Vice-Chairman: Mrs M Richards

Mrs A Bolton, MA, MBA, PGCE
Mrs J Bridgeman, CB
The Revd D Deeks
The Revd H D Gardner, BAF rtd, ALCM
P T Hardiman, Esq
Mrs A P Harvey, SRN, RSCN, SMB
Mrs K High, MA (Oxon), ACA
Mrs V Knight, BA (Oxon)
C Lendrum, Esq
P McManus, Esq, BSc (Hons), PGCE
J Morgan, Esq
D P Rendell, Esq, MA (Oxon), PGCE
Dr J Ronder, BSc, MBBS, MRCPsych
G Russell, Esq
H Shaw, Esq
T Sturgess, Esq, ALA

***Headmistress:* Miss Barbara J Crompton**, BSc, DipEd, CPhys, MInstP, FRSA

Chaplain: The Revd Dr J Quarmby, BSc (Hons) Bath, MTh Cardiff, PhD Bath

Business Director and Clerk to the Governors: Mr C Hinks, MA Oxon, DipM, MCIM

Director of Studies: Mrs D Hatcher, BEd (Hons) Chester College of Education

Senior School Staff:
Mrs J L Ash, BA (Hons), PGCE Leeds (*History*)
Mr N Ashton, BA (Hons) Worcester College of Higher Education, PGCE London (*Head of Drama*)
Mr R Bayliss, BSc (*Hons*) Southampton, PGCE Exeter (*Head of Mathematics*)
Ms E A Benfield, BA Birmingham, MA London (*English as a Foreign Language*)
Miss K Bond, BA (Hons), PGCE Exeter (*Head of Religious Education and PSE*)
Mrs K Bradley (*Aerobics Tuition*)
Mr A P Brook, BA (Hons) London, MA University of North London, PGCE Greenwich (*Drama*)
Mr G G Bullough, BSc (Hons), PGCE University College, Swansea (*Head of Science*)
Miss A M C Church, BA Oxford, PGCE Birmingham (*Head of English*)
Mrs V Fitzpatrick, BA (Hons) Liverpool, PGCE, MA King's College, London (*French*)
Mme M-T Ford, MA (Hons), Paris-Sorbonne (*Head of Modern Languages*)
Dr J E Goddard, MSc, PhD London (*Mathematics*)
Miss P Greenwood, CertEd London (*Drama*)
Mrs A Hall, TCert Digby Stuart, BA, MA London (*English Support*)
Mrs L Hallam, BA (Hons) Southampton (*Spanish and French*)
Mrs M Hambleton, BA (Hons) Reading, PGCE London (*Head of Geography*)
Mrs K E Harman, BEd (Hons), CertEd Sussex (*Physical Education, Activities Co-ordinator*)
Mr P A Hatch, BMus (Hons) Manchester (*Music*)
Mrs F Hedgeland, BA, MA (Cambridge), PGCE (Cambridge), DipM (Chartered Institute of Marketing) *English*
Mrs M Heslop, BA (Hons) York, PGCE Cambridge (*Head of History, Head of Sixth Form*)
Mrs M Hoiles (*Drama*)
Mrs J Horbury, BA (Hons), Newcastle, DipEd, Durham (*Director of Music*)
Mrs N Ingham (*Trampoline Tutor*)
Mrs J Kashima, Dip in Teaching Japanese as a Foreign Language (Inst of Int Education) *Japanese*
Mrs P R Kemp, BA (Hons), PGCE Hull, CertEd (*German and French*)
Mrs T Kitteridge, BA (Hons) Brighton (*Physical Education and Mathematics; Head of Lower School*)
Mr J S N Lang (*Life Saving*)
Mrs J Lashbrook, BA (Hons) Portsmouth, PGCE Sheffield (*Humanities*)
Miss R E Lawrence, BA (Hons) Oxford (*Head of Physics*)
Miss J Linden, TCert (*Drama*)
Mrs M McCall, Dip Home Economics Bath College of Education (*Technology, Textiles, Careers; Head of Upper School*)
Mrs C Metcalf, BSc (Hons, MEd, PGCE London and Reading (*Head of Economics and Business Studies*)
Mrs C M Moreton Jackson, MA, DipEd London (*Head of Classics*)
Mr R F G Nash, MA (*Cantab*), DipEd University of East Africa (*Head of Chemistry*)
Miss A Neve *Housemistress*
Dr O O'Connor, PhD, BA (Hons) Dublin, PGCE Greenwich (*Science*)
Mrs B Packman, BSc Thames Polytechnic (*Head of IT*)
Mrs I Payne, BA, DipSocSci, DipEd Belfast (*Mathematics*)
Mr A Pitman, MA (Sunderland), CertEd (Keele) *English*
Miss E Powell, BSc (Hons) Reading, PGCE London, DipBusAd (*Geography, Housemistress*)
Mrs J Robinson, CertEd East Sussex College of Education (*Head of Technology*)
Miss J Ross, BEd (Hons), Belfast (*Head of Physical Education*)
Mr M J Sainsbury, BA (Hons) London (*Head of Art*)
Miss M D Saville, BA (Hons) College of Ripon & York St John (*Art, Housemistress*)
Mrs G E Shukla, BEd Bradford College, PGCE Reading (*Careers Coordinator*)
Mrs A Stone, BEd I M Marsh College of Physical Education (*PE*)
Mrs S Waller, ALA (*Librarian*)
Miss R A Young, BSc (Hons) Roehampton (*Additional Support Tutor*)

Visiting Instrumental Staff:
There are 12 visiting Instrumental staff

Medical Officer: Dr N M Welch, MB, BS
Nursing Sister: Mrs J M Devine, RGN

Housemistresses:
Mrs V Cowan
Miss A Neve
Miss E Powell
Miss M Saville

Administrative Staff:
Marketing Manager: Mrs S Rowse
Registrar: Mrs D Sainsbury
Headmistress's Secretary: Mrs A Winchester
School Secretary: Mrs J Hazell
Receptionist: Mrs A Linford
Accounts Secretary: Mrs P Payne
Business Director's Secretary: Mrs J Miles
Staff Secretary: Mrs V England
Laboratory Technician: Mr M Dolan
General Manager: Mrs S Gadd
Catering Manager: Miss J Veitch
Site Manager: Mr M Cooper
Duke of Edinburgh Award Scheme: The Revd S Morrell
Accounts Assistant: Mrs G Revell

Ethos and Aims. A happy school with high academic standards, we welcome girls from a range of abilities and backgrounds. Kent College Pembury provides an environment in which individual achievement is nurtured. While working towards academic qualifications, students can discover their strengths through an extensive programme of extra-curricular activities. All girls are taught to contribute to the community. We aim to empower students to be adventurous and positive, to develop self-reliance and the confidence to take risks. They can look forward to the future with optimism, find fulfilment in their lives and develop rewarding careers.

Location and Facilities. The Junior School (ages 3-11) and the Senior School (ages 11-18) share the site which is set in 75 acres of beautiful green countryside in Pembury, three miles from Royal Tunbridge Wells. It is just forty minutes to London by train and within easy reach of Gatwick, Heathrow and Luton airports, channel ports and the Channel Tunnel. An escort service to London and the airports operates at the beginning and end of terms. The school campus comprises an elegant Victorian manor house and purpose-built modern facilities, including boarding houses, a music school, science block, Sixth Form Centre, and an indoor heated swimming pool and new sports hall. A new theatre will be completed in January 2002. A campus-wide network of computers provides the latest software with e-mail for all students, Internet access and CD-ROM databases. Boarders enjoy modern, comfortable accommodation and all benefit from healthy, award-winning cuisine. The Junior School is a striking purpose-built building, offering a family boarding unit with after school care.

Curriculum. In the first years of the Senior School all girls follow a wide curriculum which includes academic as well as creative and practical subjects. They learn keyboard skills and are encouraged to develop confidence in the use of computers and technology. At GCSE level, all girls take English language, English literature, mathematics, science, and select up to four other GCSE option subjects. At 16+, the majority of girls take the two-year Advanced Level course in three or four subjects. Approximately half the girls take at least one science subject and all follow a structured Curriculum Enrichment programme. In addition to A Levels, students can take the prestigious Leith School's Basic Certificate in Food and Wine. All students are given extensive careers and higher education advice and academically able students are prepared for admission to Oxford and Cambridge. The majority of students proceed directly to universities and colleges of higher education.

Sport. Sporting activities include hockey, netball, rounders, basketball, football, athletics, cross-country, water sports, horse riding, swimming, tennis, trampolining, dance and self-defence. The school has a reputation for achievement in inter-school matches and talented athletes can enter county competitions. The superb facilities include an indoor heated swimming pool, sports hall and spacious grounds with a variety of courts and pitches.

Extra-Curricular Activities, Music and Drama. The school prides itself on offering an extensive programme of extra-curricular activities at lunchtimes, after school and at weekends which are open to day girls and boarders. All pupils are expected to take part in at least two after school activities from a list which includes sports, water sports, jazz dance, pottery, horse riding, choirs, orchestra, first aid, Duke of Edinburgh Award, photography and glass painting. There are frequent visits to London theatres and overseas trips in the holidays. The school has a record of success in public speaking and a reputation for high standards in music and drama. There are opportunities for girls of all ages to take part in drama productions. A new theatre will be completed in January 2002.

Christian Community. Kent College was founded by the Wesleyan Methodist Schools' Association in 1886 and is now an interdenominational Christian school, welcoming girls of all faiths and backgrounds. The school continues to benefit from having its own resident Chaplain. There are Christian assemblies on weekdays and a school service each Sunday.

Entrance. (*see* Entrance Scholarship section) The main entries to the Senior School are at 11+, 13+ and 16+. Entrance is by the school's own Entrance Examination or Common Entrance, interview and a report from the previous school. Academic scholarships are awarded to outstanding entrants at 11+, 13+ and 16+. Music and drama awards are also available. Girls wishing to study A Levels are required to gain at least five GCSE passes at grade C or above. Boarders are welcomed from age 8.

Fees per term. Senior Full Boarders £5,025; Weekly Boarders £4,900;, Day £3,110. Junior Full Boarders £3,860, Weekly Boarders £3,560, Day from £1,420. There is a 25% discount for Forces' personnel. Discounts also available for daughters of clergymen and sisters.

Charitable status. Kent College Pembury is a Registered Charity, number 307920. It exists for the education of children.

Kilgraston School
Society of the Sacred Heart Foundation

Bridge of Earn Perthshire PH2 9BQ
Tel: (01738) 812257
Fax: (01738) 813410
e-mail: mkeay@kilgraston.pkc.sch.uk (Headmistress' Office)
bursar@kilgraston.pkc.sch.uk (Finance Office)
ahughes@kilgraston.pkc.sch.uk (Registrar)
mling@kilgraston.pkc.sch.uk (Senior Resident Mistress)
mfgibbons@kilgraston.pkc.sch.uk (Deputy Head)
akellaway@kilgraston.pkc.sch.uk (Head of Grange)
bursar@kilgraston.pkc.sch.uk (Estate Manager)
athomson@kilgraston.pkc.sch.uk (Domestic Manager)
website: www.kilgraston.pkc.sch.uk

Girls Independent Boarding/Day School

Chairman of Board of Governors: Mr Michael Munro

***Headmistress:* Mrs J L Austin**, BA (Hons)

Deputy Head: Miss M F Gibbons, MA (Hons), MEd, PGCE

Senior Resident Mistress: Miss M Ling, BSc (Hons)

Bursar and Secretary to the Board: Mr B Farrell, BComm

Director of Studies: Mrs C A Lund, BA (Hons), MA, MEd, PGCE

Teaching Staff:

Mrs A Bluett, BA (Hons) *French, Housemistress*
Miss S Bone, BEd (Hons) *PE*
Mrs J Carmichel, LLB, PGCE *Junior School*
Mr A Dempster, BSc (Hons) *Mathematics*
Mrs H A Dempster, BA (Hons), DivAdvEdSt *Computing*
Mrs P Ferguson, MA (Hons), CertPriEd *Junior School*
Mrs S Gruson-Stokes, BA *French*
Mrs K Guthrie, MA (Hons), PGCE *English as a Foreign Language*
Mrs M Halmarack, BA (Hons), MSc *Biology/Junior School Residential Mistress*
Miss J Harrod *Speech & Drama*
Mrs M Hulme-Jones, MA (Hons) *German/French*
Mrs A Kellaway, BEd *History, Modern Studies, Junior School*
Mrs H Lawrenson, BA *English/Classics*
Mrs J Lee, BEd (Hons) *Physical Education*
Mrs T M Little, MA *English/Religious Education*
Miss A M Losty, BSc *Chemistry, Housemistress*
Mrs C A Lund, BA (Hons) *History/Careers*
Mrs M McCabe, MA *Spanish/French/Religious Education*
Mrs F McCarthy, BEd (Hons), DipDyslTher *Learning Support*
Mrs C McIntyre, BSc (Hons) *Physics*
Mrs A Mailer, DipArt *Art & Design*

Mrs L Marshall, BMus (Hons) *Music*
Dr J Moiser, DD *Religious Education*
Dr H Moseley, PhD, BSc (Hons), PGCE *Biology*
Ms A R Neilson, DipArt *Art & Design*
Mrs S Nicol, DipDomesticSc *Home Economics*
Mrs C O'Hare, BA (Hons) *Geography*
Mrs S Osborne, CertPriEd *Junior School*
Mrs L Oswald, BEd (Hons) *Mathematics*
Mrs J Reilly, LTCL *Music*
Mrs S E Rhodes, DipPhysEd *Physical Education*
Mrs M Rose, DipComm, PGCE *Business Studies*
Mrs S Rossi, MA, PGCE *Junior School/RE*
Mrs M Saunders, BA (Hons) *English*
Mrs V Sherwood, BEd, Nat Dip Rec & Leisure *Geography/ Outdoor Education*
Mrs V E Whiteside, BSc *Mathematics*

Also visiting staff for counselling and for ballet, highland dancing, percussion, clarsach, guitar, strings, piano, woodwind, etc.

Religious Affiliation: Roman Catholic (Other denominations welcomed).

Age range of pupils: 5 to 18 (Boarding 8–18).

Number of pupils enrolled as at 1.1.2001. 245. Sixth Form 53; Lower School 112; Junior School 80

Average size of class. 15

Teacher/Pupil ratio: 1/8

FOUNDATION. Founded in 1920 by the Society of the Sacred Heart the school moved from the original site at Edinburgh to Kilgraston in 1930. Today, under lay management, Kilgraston is part of the international network of Sacred Heart schools in the trusteeship of the Society of the Sacred Heart and run according to its educational aims and philosophy. It welcomes girls of all denominations.

CURRICULUM. Educational excellence is the school's first priority and students are presented for the Scottish Examination Board examinations at Standard and Higher Grade, in which good grades ensure university entrance. In Sixth Year there is an option to upgrade results or to add to these with Advanced levels. Results are impressive with around 90% of our leavers having university places.

Entry requirements and procedures. To Junior School – Interview and Assessment. To Senior School – Interview, School Report, Common Entrance or own Entrance Examination.

Range of Fees as at 1.1.2001. Boarding £3,770–£4,520 per term, Day (inc lunch) £1,535–£2,665 per term.

Scholarships. (*see* Entrance Scholarship section) Scholarship and entrance examinations are held in February each year. As well as for academic achievement, Scholarships are offered in Art and Music. There are also awards for Riding and Tennis.

Examinations and Boards offered. Scottish Qualifications Authority Standard and Higher Grades and GCE Advanced level (UCLAS/Oxf/NEAB(JMB) Boards), LAMDA, Associated Board, ISTD, RSA, SCOTVEC.

FACILITIES. Kilgraston's aim is to encourage a LOVE OF LEARNING, a SPIRIT OF ADVENTURE and OPENNESS OF HEART. With about 240 pupils, one of the great advantages is its size and the school has the atmosphere of an extended and happy family. Assembly is held on four mornings each week and House Meetings once weekly. Small classes and a favourable staff/pupil ratio mean that pupils receive plenty of individual attention and care both in their lessons and in their personal lives. With a Georgian mansion as its main building, the school's excellent facilities encourage sports enthusiasts, with all weather floodlit courts, playing fields and a superb sports hall in its 72 acre grounds. All pupils from the age of 12 have single bedrooms, while younger pupils are in small dormitories. Pastoral care is excellent, with residential staff caring for boarders outside of school hours, and Housemistresses and House Tutors liaising with Form Teachers. A qualified nurse and assistant are resident in the school infirmary, and the doctor makes a weekly visit. Kilgraston's Art Department is widely recognised and many pupils have followed very successful careers in this field after Art College. The well equipped Music Department encourages group and individual talent and Speech and Drama is popular with much success in the LAMDA (London Academy of Music and Dramatic Art) Examinations. A modern extension houses superb science laboratories, computing (all pupils on 'E Mail' with new systems installed in 1999), mathematics, needlework, cookery and common rooms, as well as sixth form study bedrooms. Activities available include tennis, hockey, netball, volleyball, badminton, gymnastics, athletics, modern dance and ballet, Scottish country and Highland dancing, karate, riding, swimming, golf, windsurfing, squash, archery and skiing. The Duke of Edinburgh's Award Scheme promotes a variety of pursuits and hill-walking, rock-climbing expeditions and skiing in the Southern Grampians and the Cairngorms are popular at weekends. In 2000 the School Ski team came 4th in the British Championships. The Grange, our Junior School, imaginatively converted from the former stables and opened in 1993, is a vital part of Kilgraston. Members of the Upper 3rd (Primary 7) automatically take the Entrance Examination for entry to the Senior School. Each year a small number of overseas students come to Kilgraston and take, very successfully, the Cambridge preliminary test, Cambridge 1st Cert, Cambridge Advanced cert, and London Chamber of Commerce Test in Spoken English : IELTS; examinations in English as a Foreign Language. They enjoy experiencing another culture whilst making lasting friendships. The school's location just south of Perth, and close to the M90, makes it easily accessible by rail, road and air –Edinburgh Airport is less than an hour's drive.

Charitable status. The Society of the Sacred Heart is a Registered Charity, number SCO 03316. Its aim is to develop a LOVE OF LEARNING, a SPIRIT OF ADVENTURE and OPENNESS OF HEART.

King Edward VI High School for Girls

Birmingham

Edgbaston Park Road Birmingham B15 2UB
Tel: 0121 472 1834
Fax: 0121 471 3808

(Independent, formerly Direct Grant)

Governing Body: The Governors of the Schools of King Edward VI in Birmingham

Headmistress: **Miss S H Evans**, BA (Sussex), MA (Leicester), PGCE

Assistant Staff:
Mrs K F Aldridge, BEd (Birmingham)
Mr N J Argust, BMus (Birmingham), FRCO, PGCE
Mrs R M Arnold, BA (Oxon), PGCE
Miss B Ashfield, BA (Oxon), PGCE
Mrs J L Bagnall, BSc (Sheffield), PGCE
Mrs I Bannister, Teacher's Certificate (Philippa Fawcett College)
Mr R P Barrett, BA (Leeds), PGCE
Mrs S J Burns, BSc (Oxford Brookes), PGCE
Mr T O Cooper, BA (Bristol), PGCE

Mrs M V C Crossley, L-ès-L, PGCE
Mrs J M Darby, MA (Oxon), PGCE
Miss L M Dovey, MA (Oxon), PGCE
Mrs P M Eames, BA (Birmingham), PGCE
Miss E M Edwards, BEd (Bristol)
Mrs C D Flint, BA (Manchester), PGCE
Mr N Freeman-Powell, MA (Oxon), PGCE
Miss S M Gray, MA (Cantab), PGCE
Dr C E Gruzelier, MA, PhD (Oxon)
Mrs F Hall, BA (Oxon), PGCE
Mrs J Herbert, ALAM, LLAM
Mrs S J Holland, BA (Birmingham), PGCE
Mr R M Hopkinson, BSc (Hull), MSc (London), PGCE
Mrs C M Hosty, BA (York), PGCE
Mrs L H Hutton, MSc (Durham), PGCE
Miss D H Jackson, BA (Lancaster), PGCE
Mr H J Kavanagh, BA (Cantab), PGCE
Mrs J J Kerridge, Teacher's Certificate (Elizabeth Gaskell College)
Miss V Krutin, BA (Bath), PGCE
Miss R Laurent, DEUG (Mulhouse), PGCE
Mrs D A Leonard, BEd (Leeds)
Mrs J K Lessar, BA (Leeds), PGCE
Mr F Mackinnon, BA (Strathclyde), PGCE
Mrs J E Moule, BA (Durham), PGCE
Miss A J Norris, BSc (Birmingham), PGCE
Miss J Oldfield, BSc (Durham), PGCE
Miss R L Reeve, BSc (Birmingham), PGCE
Mrs P J Rutter, BSc (Birmingham)
Mrs K Sangha, BA (Warwick), PGCE
Mrs B E Sheldon, BSc (Nottingham), PGCE
Mrs S K E Shore-Nye, BA (Swansea), PGCE
Mrs J C Smith, CertEd (Bedford College of PE)
Dr B L Tedd, BSc (London), PhD (Leicester), PGCE
Miss O N Terry, BA (Cardiff), PGCE
Mrs M Vickery, BSc (Hull)
Miss A C Warne, BA (Birmingham), PGCE
Mrs J Whitehead, BSc (Birmingham), PGCE
Mrs Z K Williams, BA (Brighton), PGCE
Mrs L Workman, BA (Durham), PGCE
Mrs S M Wright, BA (London)
Mrs A Young, BA (Birmingham), PGCE

Librarian: Mrs A Z Moloney, BA, MA, PGCE

Secretaries: Mrs C L Tovey, Mrs S J M Jones

Matron: Mrs M Knight

Founded in 1883, the School moved in 1940 to its present buildings and extensive grounds adjacent to King Edward's School for Boys. There are 540 girls from 11 to 18 years of age, all day pupils.

Curriculum. The curriculum is distinctive in its strong academic emphasis and aims to inspire a love of learning. The purpose of the curriculum is to help girls realise their full potential. Excellence is sought in aesthetic, practical and physical activities as well as in academic study. Our aim is to achieve a balance of breadth and depth, with dropping of subjects postponed as long as possible so that girls may make informed choices and have access to a wide range of possible careers.

In **Year One** all girls take English, Mathematics, separate Sciences, Religious Studies, French, History, Geography, Music, Art and Design, Information Technology, Games, Swimming, Dance and Creative Skills.

In **Years Two and Three** all girls take English, Mathematics, Separate Sciences, Religious Studies, French, Latin, History, Geography, Music, Art and Design, Information Technology, Physical Education, Creative Skills.

Core subjects in **Years Four and Five** are English Language, English Literature, Mathematics, Biology, Chemistry, Physics, Latin, French. Girls then choose from 3 option blocks their other GCSE subjects. Greek or German can be taken as a two year GCSE course.

In the **sixth form** girls choose for AS and A2 from a wide range of subjects, all Arts, or all Sciences or a mixture of the two. Some subjects are taken jointly with King Edward's School. Stress is placed on breadth at this level. All girls take General Studies at A-level (normally as their fifth subject) with courses for all in English, Mathematics and Languages (Spanish, Russian and Italian can be begun). Various philosophical, scientific and practical topics are explored by all in short courses.

All girls follow a course in personal decision-making in which they explore and discuss a wide range of issues which call for personal choice and which helps develop life skills.

Religious and moral education are considered important. Academic study of them is designed to enable girls to be informed and questioning. In the last two years courses (apart from the choice of Religious Studies at GCSE or 'A' Level) are designed as part of the General Studies programme. There is no denominational teaching in the school in lessons or morning assembly. Girls of all faiths or of none are equally welcome.

Girls take part in Physical Education, until the Upper 6th Form where it is voluntary, with increasing choice from gymnastics, hockey, netball, tennis, rounders, dance, fencing, badminton, squash, swimming, athletics, basketball, volley ball, self-defence, aerobics, archery, health related fitness. We have our own swimming pool, sports hall and extensive pitches, including two artificial hockey areas.

In addition to the music in the curriculum, there are choirs and orchestras which reach a high standard. These are mostly joint with King Edward's School. Individual (or shared) instrumental lessons, at an extra fee, are arranged in school in a great variety of instruments. Some instruments can be hired. Individual singing lessons can also be arranged.

A large number of clubs (many joint with King Edward's School) are run by pupils themselves with help and encouragement from staff. Others (eg Drama, Music, Sport) are directed by staff. Help is given with activities relating to the Duke of Edinburgh Award scheme. Some activities take place in lunch hours, others after school and at weekends.

As part of the school's commitment to developing an awareness of the needs of society and a sense of duty towards meeting those needs, girls are encouraged to plan and take part in various community service projects as well as organising activities in school to raise money to support causes of their choice.

A spacious careers room is well-stocked with up to date information. Individual advice and aptitude testing is given at stages where choices have to be made. One member of staff has overall responsibility but many others are involved with various aspects. Girls are encouraged to attend conferences, gain work experience, make personal visits and enquiries. Old Edwardians and others visit school to talk about their careers. There is good liaison with universities and colleges of all kinds. Normally all girls go on to higher or further education, most to universities. An exceptionally wide range of courses is being taken by Old Edwardians.

Admission of Pupils. Entry is normally for girls of 11 into the first year of the school in September. Applications must be made by 17th January 2002 for entry in September 2002. Girls must have reached the age of 11 years by 31st August following the examination. Girls up to 1 year younger than this can be considered in some circumstances; parents of such girls must communicate with the headmistress in the previous autumn term. Girls are examined at the school in English, Mathematics and Reasoning. The syllabus is such as would be normally covered by girls of good ability and no special preparation is advised.

Girls from 12 to 15 are normally considered only if they move from another part of the country, or in some special circumstances. Applications should be made to the headmistress in writing as soon as the move is planned. Such girls can be admitted at any time if there is a vacancy.

There is an entry into the sixth form for girls wishing to study four main 'A' Level subjects and General Studies. Application should be made to the Headmistress as early as possible in the preceding academic year.

Fees, Scholarships and Assisted places. (*see* Entrance Scholarship section) Fees are £1,896 for the summer term 2001.

The equivalent of up to a total of two free place scholarships may be awarded on the results of the Governors' Admission Examination to girls entering the first year. These are independent of parental income and are normally tenable for 7 years.

For girls entering the school at age 16 a one half fee scholarship is available.

Governors' Assisted Places are available for girls entering the first year and additional places are available for girls entering at 16+. These are means tested.

The Headmistress will be pleased to provide further information.

Charitable status. The Foundation of the Schools of King Edward the Sixth in Birmingham is a Registered Charity, number 529051. The purpose of the Foundation is to educate children and young persons living in or around the city of Birmingham mainly by provision of, or assistance to its schools.

The King's High School for Girls

Warwick CV34 4HJ
Tel: (01926) 494485
Fax: (01926) 403089
e-mail: khsw@primex.co.uk

Chairman of Governors: Mr J E Francis

Governors:
The Earl of Warwick
The Lord Lieutenant of Warwickshire
The Mayor of Warwick
Dr A J Barker, BA (Cantab)
Canon D Brindley, BD, MTh, MPhil, AKC
Dr I Butters, MA, DPhil, FRHistS
Mr R V Cadbury, MA (Cantab)
Mr P M Davies, BA
Mrs P Deeley, LLB
Mrs J Edwards, BA, MBA
Mr R J Grant, BEd
Mr D E Hanson
Councillor M B Haywood
Professor E W Ives, BA, PhD, FRHistS
Mrs S James, BSc, ARICS
Mrs J Khan, BA, MA, MEd
Mrs J Marshall, BA
Mr C R Mason, CBE, FCIPS, FRSA
Mrs V Phillips
Mr K Rawnsley, JP
Mr K C K Scott
Mr M L Shattock, OBE, MA (Oxon)
Mr A F Thurley, FRICS
Professor R H Trigg, MA, DPhil (Oxon)

Secretary to the Governors: A Bligh, BA, FCA

Staff:
***Head Mistress:* Mrs E Surber**, BA, MA

Deputy Head Mistress: Mrs C J Russell, MA (Cantab)

Head of Sixth Form: Miss H L Lenygon, BA (London)

Key Stage 4 Co-ordinator: Miss R Court, BSc (London)

Key Stage 3 Co-ordinator: Miss E J Waite (Bedford)

Careers Co-ordinator: Miss J Dormer, BA (Durham)

Head of Science: Mrs R Chapman, BA (Oxon)

Staff Admin Co-ordinator: Mrs C M Horn, BA (Sheffield)

Examinations Secretary: Mrs L Y Sherren, BSc (Sheffield)

Religious Education:
*Miss B Hollingworth, BA (Birmingham)
§Mrs S E Lampitt, BA (Durham)

English:
*Miss M Clark, MA (Oxon)
§Mrs C Andrews, MA (Edinburgh)
§Mrs K Greaves, BA (East Anglia)
Miss A J Smith, MA (Edinburgh)
Miss H A Young, BA (York)

History:
*Miss H L Lenygon, BA (London)
Mrs C Watts, BA (Bristol)

Geography:
*Mrs R Gloster, BSc (Liverpool)
Mrs J Sarson, BA (Durham)
§Mrs E A Thornton, BA (Nottingham)

Business Studies:
Mrs R Gloster, BSc (Liverpool)

Modern Languages:
*Mr E W MacFetridge, BA (Coventry)
*Mrs R King, MA (Cantab)
§Mrs D M Emms (Mainz)
§Mrs J Hardy, BA (Bristol)
Mrs C M Horn, BA (Sheffield)
Miss M E Forde, BA (Oxon), MA (Birmingham)
Mr C Pulford, BA (Leeds)
Miss J Wake, BA (Southampton)
§Mrs G N Parsons French Conversation
§Mrs Williams Spanish Conversation

Classics:
*Mrs J Nicolson, BA (Leeds)
Miss J A Dormer, BA (Durham)

Mathematics:
*Miss R M Court, BSc (London)
Miss U Birbeck, BA (Warwick)
Miss P Edwards, BSc (Warwick)
§Mrs A M Hill, TCert (Goldsmith's, London)
Mrs S Munday, BSc (London)
Mrs L Y Sherren, BSc (Sheffield)

Computer Studies:
*Mrs P Prance, BSc (Warwick)
Mrs A Byrne, BSc (Coventry)
§Mrs A MacDonald, ACII
Mrs C J Russell, MA (Cantab)

Sciences:
*Mrs A M Smith, BSc (Liverpool)
*Mr R A Smith, BA (Oxon)
*Mr R Wythe, BSc (London)
Dr P M Boulton, BSc (London), PhD (Birmingham)
Mrs R Chapman, BA (Oxon)
Mrs K M Evison, BSc (Birmingham)
Mrs J M Grant, BSc (Durham)
Dr E H F McGale, BSc (Liverpool), PhD (Manchester)
Mrs B Stewart, BSc (Manchester)

Home Economics:
*Mrs J Andrews, BSc (Bristol)

Art and Design:
*Miss S J Lewis, BA (Wales) (*also Design Technology Co-ordinator*)
§Mrs J R McBrien, BA (Manchester)
Miss N K Smethurst, BA (Sunderland)
Mr N Walker, BSc (Brunel)

Physical Education:
*Miss E J Waite (Bedford)
Mrs L Aymes (Anstey)
§Mrs C Best
§Mrs S Hoyle, MS, BEd (Anstey)

Music:
*Miss M Crayston, GRSM, ARMCM, BA(Mus) (Manchester)
Mrs G Jones, ARCM, BA (Leeds)

Visiting Music Staff:
Piano: Mr C Druce; Mr A Etherden
Piano/Violin: Mrs R Dawkins
Clarinet: Miss A Hill
Oboe/Flute: Mrs L Bausor
Recorder/Flute: Mrs L Knowles
Violin: Mr R Meteyard
'Cello: Mrs M Todd
Woodwind/Brass: Mrs S Lucas
Bass/Singing: Mrs J Rigby

Head's Secretary: Mrs M Hooper

Staff Secretary: Mrs G Brown

Registrar: Mr A Sherren

Bursar: Mrs D Johnson

Receptionist: Mrs G Timmis

Matron: Mrs S Ward

Librarian: Mrs E Alkhalaf, ALA

Secretary of Old Girls' Association: Mrs J Edwards

The school, which opened in 1879, is of the same Foundation as Warwick School (for Boys) and Warwick Preparatory School. It was formerly a Direct Grant Grammar School. There are 550 girls from 11–18 years of age. Extensive re-development in the last decade has ensured that the school has superb facilities.

Curriculum. The curriculum aims to give students as broad an education as possible and all pupils study two modern languages and Latin. ICT is used across the curriculum. Girls are prepared for GCSE and A Level with all proceeding to university. The majority of girls also participate in musical activities and many take Associated Board examinations. Some sixth form activities, such as Young Enterprise, are done in conjunction with our brother school, Warwick. Many girls belong to the school's unit of the Duke of Edinburgh's Award Scheme.

All girls are encouraged to participate in school affairs from their first year. Senior girls are invaluable in taking responsibility for younger girls and for organising activities with the local community. This is facilitated by the school's location in the town centre. Nearby sporting facilities, including a sports hall, ensure a generous allocation of time for students to pursue gymnastics and dance, netball, hockey, tennis, rounders, athletics, badminton, basketball, volleyball and football with impressive results.

Fees, Scholarships & Bursaries. Tuition £1,928 per term. Music: Brass, Pianoforte, Strings, Woodwind, Guitar, Drums, Singing £130 for 10 lessons. Scholarships are available on entry at age 11. Warwick Foundation Awards are available on entry at 11+ and also in the Sixth Form.

Admission Girls are required to take an entrance examination. Some places are available for Sixth Form entry.

Charitable status. King's High School is a part of the Warwick Schools' Foundation which is a Registered Charity, number 528775. The aim of the charity is "to provide for children (3–18) of parents of all financial means – a high proportion of whom shall come from Warwick and its immediate surroundings, but subject to satisfying academic standards where required – education of academic, cultural and sporting standards which are the highest within their peer groups."

The Kingsley School

Beauchamp Hall Beauchamp Avenue Leamington Spa Warwickshire CV32 5RD
Tel: (01926) 425127
Fax: (01926) 831691

Independent Day School for Girls aged 2½ to 18, and boys up to 7 years, founded in 1884 and ISJC accredited.

Council:
President: Lady Butler

Vice-Presidents:
The Lord Bishop of Coventry
J E C Tainsh, DA (Dundee), FRIBA

Chairman: Mr W Preston

Vice-Chairman: Dr S Hill, MA, MPhil, PhD, FSA, FSA(Scot)

Mrs P Birt
Lady Butterworth, BA
Mrs V C Davis
S G Evans, FRICS
Mrs G Glover
A G S Griffith, FBIM, ACIOB, MA, PM
Mrs M Hicks, CertEd
Dr S J Hill, MA, MPhil, PhD, FSA, FSA (Scot)
Mrs R Lea
A J Lord
P S Sanghera, BA
Mrs R Skilbeck, BDS
The Revd G Warner, MA

***Headmistress:* Mrs C A Mannion Watson**, BA, MSc(Ed)

Deputy Heads:
Mrs A Greensmith, GRSM, LRAM (*Pianoforte*), LRAM (*Vocal Studies*) (Royal Academy)
Mrs J Burn, BA, PGCE

Head of Junior School: Mrs A Clark, BEd, HDipRE
Head of VIth Form: Miss R Dyson, BA (Reading), PGCE (Hull), Dip in Counselling (Warwick)

Staff:
Religious Studies:
§*Mrs E Mackenzie, BPhil, MEd, CertEd

English:
†*Mrs C Robbins, BA (York), MPhil (Oxford), PGCE (Warwick)
Mrs R J Dyer, BA (Reading), PGCE (Nottingham)
Mrs R Dennill, BA, HDE (Natal)
Mrs A Hamilton, BA, PGCE
Mrs K Todman, BA, PGCE

History:
*Mr J Goode, MA (Cantab), PGCE (Cantab)
Miss R Dyson, BA (Reading), PGCE (Hull), Dip in Counselling, Warwick
§Mrs S Waterson, BA (Warwick), PGCE (Warwick)

Geography:
*Mrs J Bailey, BA
Mrs H Lewis, BA, PGCE (Aberystwyth)
Mrs D Frydman, BSc, CertEd

Economics and Business Studies:
*Mrs C Murphy, BA (Ealing)
§Mrs L Fletcher, LLB (Coventry), PGCE (London)

Classics:
*Mr A J Dean, MA (Oxon, Jesus College), DipEd (Edinburgh)
§Mrs A Ingham, BA (Bristol), PGCE (London)

Modern Languages (French, German, Italian, Spanish):
*Mrs F M Harris, MA (Cantab), PGCE (Warwick)
Ms A Fretwell, BA (Oxon)
Mrs S E Jessett, BA, PGCE (Warwick)
Mrs K Baker, BA (Wales), PGCE (London)
Mrs S Robinson, BA Hons (Leeds), PGCE

Mathematics:
*Mrs M Sheldon, BA (Cardiff), DipEd Dunelm (Durham)
Mrs S Morris, BSc (Wales), CertEd (Leicester)
†Mrs J Sanders, BSc (London), CertEd (Sheffield)
†Mrs R M Bott, BSc (London), Cert in Counselling Skills
Mrs C Pearson, BA (Open University), CertEd (Cheltenham)

Science:
*Mrs J Hilton, BSc (Birmingham), PGCE (Birmingham), CPhys, MInstP
*Mrs K Molloy, BSc, PGCE (Warwick), MEd (Open University) (*Chemistry*)
Mrs S Old, BSc (Sheffield), PGCE (Warwick)
Mr R E Eldridge, BSc (Birmingham), CChem, MRSC, CertEd
Mrs S Croft, BSc, PGCE
Mrs C Duke, BSc, PGCE
Mr P Harris, BSc, PGCE
Dr C Robertson, BSc, PhD, PGCE
Mrs K Hall, BSc, PGCE
Mrs L Trow, BSc (Glasgow), CertEd

Information Technology:
*Mrs J Jones, BEd (Birmingham), CertEd, DipRSA
Mrs J M Smart, DipRSA, TDipITS (JEB)

Careers:
Mrs H Lewis, BA, PGCE (Aberystwyth)

Home Economics:
*Mrs S Bresnen, CertEd (Llandaff College of Education)
§Mrs C Davies, BEd (Gloucester)
§Mrs R Williams, BEd, (Sussex), CertEd (London)

Performing Arts:
*Mr A Brade, BEd, FNCM, LLCM, ALCM, CertEd (*Director of Music and the Performing Arts*)
*Mrs J Walton, BEd (London) (*Drama*)
Mrs A Vallance, BA, IDTA (*Dance*)
§Mrs J Parkinson, ALAM (LAMDA)
Mrs A Greensmith, GRSM, LRAM (*Pianoforte/Vocal Studies*)
§Mr C Langdown, MMus, GRSM, DipRCM, ARCM (*Piano & Music Theory*)
§Mr R Meteyard, AGSM (*Violin/Viola*)
§Mrs L Bausor, CertEd (Sheffield), ATCL (*Flute, Oboe*)
§Mrs P McKie, BA, ALCM, PGCE (*Flute/Recorder*)
§Mrs S Russell, GRNCM, LRAM, LGSM (*Percussion*)
Miss C Robinson, BMus
Mr T Meryon, BMus (*Guitar*)
Mrs M Walton, BMus (York) (*Violin*)
Mrs C Wimpenny, GBSM, ABSM (*'Cello/Double Bass*)
Mr P Staite, BMus (Birmingham) (*Piano*)
Miss B Morley, BA (*Head of Vocal Studies*)

Art:
*Mr J Gaskin, Dip AD, Post Diploma Fine Art (Loughborough)
§Mrs P Davies, DA (Glasgow), ATC (London)

Physical Education:
†*Mrs S Bates, BA (Open University), CertEd (I M Marsh, Liverpool)
†Mrs C J Hoare, DipPE (Bedford), APSMT (Wales)
§Mrs P Rogers, BEd (Cambridge), CertEd (Bedford)
Mrs F Fisher, CertEd (London)

Psychology: Mrs S Minton, BA, MEd

Duke of Edinburgh Award Scheme:
Mrs S Palliser, CertEd
Mr T Palliser

Junior School:
Mrs A Clark, BEd, HDipRE
Mrs G Adair, BN, PGCE
Miss A Bond, MA Hons (St Andrews), PGCE
Mrs I Bull, CertEd
Mrs Y M Hargreaves, NNEB (Solihull College)
Mrs J Kay, GNSM, LRAM, CertEd
Mrs F Kishor, BSocSc (Birmingham), PGCE
Mrs K Liverton, BA (Birmingham), PGCE (Warwick)
Mrs P Parton, CertEd (Hull)
Mrs S Jones, BEd, PGCE
§Mrs D Heawood
Mrs L Sims
§Ms J Marsh, BEd (Leeds)
Mr R Band, BEd

Bursar: I D Squire, FCA
Assistant Bursar: Mrs A Reddin
Bursar's Assistants: Mrs J Bostock, Mrs B Davis
Reception/Secretary: Mrs M Wright
Headmistress' Secretary and Registrar: Mrs D A Eady
School Secretary: Mrs C A Watson
School Nurse: Mrs O Hodgson, RSCN

Technical Support:
Mrs J Kelway
Mrs A Platt
Mrs L Litchfield
Mrs J Sanders

Health & Safety Adviser: Ms B Port, BSc, MIOSH

Kingsley is a selective independent ISJC accredited day school for girls between 2½ and 18 and boys from 2½ to 7 years. It has a long history of success in every area of the curriculum and its traditions and ethos combine to make it a happy and secure environment for its 560 pupils. The school is basically a Christian foundation but welcomes pupils of different faiths. Since 1884, Kingsley has upheld traditional values in a happy, purposeful and well-disciplined environment. It enjoys an enviable teacher:pupil ratio of 1:10 and every student is recognised as an individual.

The Junior School provides a secure, well-structured and carefully balanced education for 150 pupils. Emphasis is placed on essential skills but all areas of the National Curriculum are covered in depth and opportunities are provided for foreign visits, field trips and many extra-curricular activities. SAT and Scholarship results are very good.

The Senior School provides a wide range of GCSE subjects including 3 separate sciences, 4 modern languages, Latin, Computer Studies, Physical Education, Drama, Dance and Music. Academic standards are high with the 2000 results showing a 95.10% pass rate at grades A*-C with an average of 8.7 passes per girl at this level. In the Sixth Form of over 100 girls a choice of 22 'A' level subjects is offered including Psychology, Computing,

Music, Theatre Studies and Sports Studies. Latest results show a 98.8% pass rate with an average of 3.3 passes per student. Most girls go on to University including Oxbridge.

Music, Drama and Dance flourish throughout the school and benefit greatly from the new Performance/Sports Hall. Sport is well catered for and pupils regularly represent Warwickshire. Kingsley boasts highly successful competitive riding teams which have won both the National Schools' Cross Country and National Jumping Championships. In 2000, the School organised an Inter Schools' Junior Jumping Competition at Stoneleigh with over 150 entrants. There is a wide variety of clubs and societies including a thriving Duke of Edinburgh's Scheme in which over 100 Gold Awards have been gained. An extensive range of field courses, educational exchanges and expeditions is organised in Britain and overseas (eg in the Summer of 1997, 20 girls took part in a 'World Challenge' expedition to Zimbabwe and 10 students went to the Pindos Mountains in Greece for their Duke of Edinburgh Gold expedition). In 1999 26 girls took part in a World Challenge expedition to Rajasthan. In 2001, 20 will visit Zimbotnam. Every girl can find something in which to participate with enthusiasm and success.

Academic, Art, Music and Drama Scholarships are available at 7+, 11+ and 16+. New Kingsley Awards at 7+, 11+ and 16+ replace Government Assisted Places. Private transport serves a wide area and after school care is available. Please visit and see what Kingsley has to offer.

Charitable status. The Kingsley School is a Registered Charity, number 528774. It exists to provide high quality education for girls aged 2½ to 18 and boys up to 7 years.

The Lady Eleanor Holles School

Hanworth Road Hampton Middlesex TW12 3HF
Tel: 020 8979 1601
Fax: 020 8941 8291

This Independent Girls' School derives its endowment from a Trust established in 1710 under the will of Lady Eleanor Holles. The Cripplegate Schools Foundation has administered the Trust since 1711 when the original school for girls was founded in Cripplegate in the City of London. It is governed under schemes of the Charity Commissioners (1868, 1875), and the Ministry of Education (1905, 1910, 1933). The present school in Hampton accommodates about 900 girls, aged from 7 to 18 years.

The Cripplegate Schools Foundation

Chairman of the Foundation: A Cowen, Esq

Vice-Chairman: Mrs J Ross, BSc, CIPFA

Governors:
Mrs J Birch
J Boodle, Esq
D J Bradshaw, Esq, CC
M Breckon, Esq
Professor J R Cash, BSc, ARCS, PhD (Cantab), FIMA, CMath
Mrs P C G Longmore, MCSP
Mrs M I Nagli
The Revd K Rumens, The Rector of St Giles, Cripplegate
Mrs T Wallendahl

Clerk to the Governors: N B Noble, Esq, OBE, FCIS

***Head Mistress:* Miss E M Candy**, BSc London, (Westfield College), FRSA

Deputy Head Mistress: Mrs L C Hazel, BA (Hull)

Senior Mistress: Miss M E Beardwood (Dartford College of Physical Education), BA (OU), MA (Reading)

Assistant Staff:
Senior School:

Art and Craft:
Miss S Pauffley, BA London (Goldsmiths' College)
Mrs M Barclay, DipAD (Hons), ATC (Hornsey College of Art)
Ms K Jeffery, BA (Leicester) *History of Art*
Miss H Peat, BA (Loughborough College of Art and Design)
Mrs G Taylor, BA London (Birkbeck College), MA (Institute of Education)

Classics:
Mrs R Iredale, BA (Bristol)
Dr A Arrighi, BA, MA (Pisa)
Miss K C Eltis, BA Oxon (Balliol College)
Miss S Ferro, BA Oxon (St Anne's)
Mrs L C Hazel, BA (Hull)
Mrs S Welsh, BA (Leicester)

Design Technology (including Home Economics):
Miss A M Travers, BEd (Surrey)
Mrs A M Angliss, BEd Dublin (Trinity College)
Miss A C Avenido, BA (de Montfort)
Mr A M Kerr, BA (Brunel)

Economics:
Miss A J Matthews, BA (Leicester)
Miss D A Self, BSc (Brunel)

English:
Miss S Gamblin, BEd Cantab (Newnham College), MA (London, Institute of Education)
Mrs M Eskenazi, BA (Wales), MA (Hull)
Mrs M Fare, Dip Central School of Speech & Drama
Mrs C L Gilroy-Scott, BA (Birmingham)
Miss C J Hendry, BA (Bristol)
Mrs J Morris, BA London (King's College)
Mrs A Pearce, BA (Exeter)
Mrs C Richardson, BA (Reading)
Mrs V K Whittingham, BA (Reading)

Geography:
Mrs S E Coggin, BA (Swansea)
Mrs L M McAteer, BA (Leicester)
Mr R Malewicz, BSc London (London School of Economics)
Miss E C Wood, BA (Newcastle)

History:
Miss L Gordon, BA Oxon (St Hilda's College)
Mrs K L Donald, BA (Birmingham)
Mrs E Hossain, BA (York)
Mrs B M E Jones, BA (Reading)
Miss C S T Ryton, MA (Aberdeen)

Information Technology:
Mrs C Norgate, BSc (Manchester)
Mrs M Barclay, DipAD (Hons), ATC (Hornsey College of Art)
Miss M Beardwood, MA (Reading), BA (OU), (Dartford College of Physical Education)
Mrs F M Wimblett, BSc London (Royal Holloway)

Mathematics:
Mrs J B Painton, BSc (Southampton)
Mrs J Fairhurst, BSc London (Imperial College), MA (Lancaster)
Mrs C Gibney, BA (Open)
Mrs M D King, BSc (Swansea)
Mrs S Leigh, BSc (Edinburgh)
Mrs C Norgate, BSc (Manchester)
Mrs A C Patrick, BA (Bristol)
Miss C Swainston, BSc (Surrey)

Mr M J Williams, BA (City of London Polytechnic)
Mrs F M Wimblett, BSc London (Royal Holloway)

Modern Languages:
Mrs E D Hanna, BA (Reading) *French*
Mrs J A Basannavar, BA (Bristol) *German*
Ms S A Buckley, BA (Sheffield)
Mrs E De Lorenzo, BA (Exeter) *Spanish*
Mrs A Dietz, BA (Sussex) *French*
Mrs N L Fahidi, BA (Leeds) *French*
Mrs R A M Johnson (Cologne) *German*
Mrs D Kuehn, BA (Aix-en-Provence) *French*
Mrs K M Munday, BA (Manchester) *German*
Mrs G M Piquet-Gauthier, Maîtrise De Langues Vivantes (Montpelier) *French*
Mrs N Rees, BA Cantab (New Hall) *Spanish*
Miss D L Robbins, MA (St Andrews)
Mrs C Tait (Cologne) *German*
Mrs A M Walter, BA (Liverpool) *Russian and German*
Mrs L Wilson (Minsk) *Russian*

Music:
Director of Music: Mrs P Woollam, MMus (Reading), LRAM, ARCM
Mr B Hughes, BA Oxon (Exeter College), MMus (London)
Miss N C Woodcock, BA (Southampton)
Miss H Attfield, LRAM *Singing*
Mr G Beebee, LTCL *Wind Band, Recorder*
Mrs M Beebee, ALCM *Clarinet*
Miss K Fotherby, BMus *Clarinet*
Mr A J Gee, BMus *Double Bass*
Miss A Harris, AGSM *Violin, Viola*
Miss K Howell, LRAM, GRSM *Pianoforte*
Mrs D L Hume, DSCM *Violin*
Mr R Kennedy, ARCM, DipRCM *Brass*
Miss A Meadows, GRSM, ARCM, LRAM *Bassoon*
Mr R Millett, Dip RCM Perf Percussion
Miss S Morfee, ARCM, LTCL *Flute*
Miss S Morley *Harp*
Mr A Parkinson *Saxophone and Clarinet*
Mrs P A Phillips, GRSM, ARCM Pianoforte
Mr Julian Rolton, AGSM (Teaching) *Pianoforte*
Miss P Scott, BMus, LRAM *Cello*
Miss J Soane, GTCL *Voice*
Mrs A Storer, LRAM *Pianoforte*
Miss H Storer, ARCM *Oboe*
Miss T Williams *Guitar*

Natural Sciences:
Mrs S Stephens, BSc London (Imperial College) *Physics*
Mrs L Baker, BSc (Sussex) *Biochemistry*
Mrs H Beedham, BSc (Hull), MSc (Kingston) *Chemistry*
Mr M J Crewe, BSc (Birmingham) *Physics*
Mrs K M Ellis, BSc (Durham) *Physics*
Mrs B L Flood, BA Oxon (St Hugh's College) *Chemistry*
Miss H C Gibson, BA Oxon (St John's College)
Miss M A James, BSc (Bristol) *Biology*
Mrs J Johnston, BSc (Hull), BA (OU) *Biology*
Mrs J Monteil, BSc (Swansea), MSc (London) *Psychology*
Miss S S Ostrander, BSc (Bristol)
Miss R Parker, BSc (Manchester) *Chemistry*
Mrs J Roberts, BSc London (Westfield College) *Chemistry*
Mrs S Thackray, BSc London (University College) *Chemistry*

Physical Education:
Mrs W V Vye (I M Marsh College of Physical Education)
Miss J Bexon, BEd (Warwick)
Mrs B Crockford, CertEd (Chelsea College of PE) *Rowing*
Miss J Maguire, BA(Ed) (Exeter)
Miss M J Waters, BEd (Bedford College of HE)

Religious Education:
Mrs J Perkins, MPhil, BA (Exeter)
Mrs T Millington, BEd (King Alfred's College, Winchester)

Careers Advice:
Miss A J Matthews, BA (Leicester Polytechnic)

Junior Department:
Head of Department: Mrs J A Cowper, DipEd (Edinburgh), MEd (Nottingham)

Assistant Staff:
Mrs J E Allden, BSc (London), MSc
Mrs J Baker, BA (Hull)
Miss V M Barnes, BA (Kingston)
Mrs M Crowley, BA (Exeter)
Mrs J Fairlamb, MA (Edinburgh)
Mrs J Gazetas, BSc (Newcastle)
Miss J Grant, (*Teachers' Cert*)
Mrs A E Haynes, BA (Southampton)
Mrs C Lyne, (Dartford College of PE), BA (OU)
Mrs J Ormerod, AGSM
Mrs A J Willmott, BEd (Whitelands College)
Miss R K Webster, BA (Exeter)

Administration:
Bursar: N B Noble, Esq, OBE, FCIS

Facilities Manager: D A Curtis-Donnelly, Esq

Head Mistress's Personal Assistant: Mrs A M Stribley

School Secretary: Mrs M Mathews

Registrar: Mrs R D'Albert

Medical Adviser: Dr S J Bowskill, MB, BS (London)

School Nurse: Mrs M J Court, SRN

The school dates from 1711 and is named after its benefactress The Lady Eleanor Holles who directed that the surplus from her Will should be used to establish a school for young girls. Originally in the Cripplegate Ward of the City of London, it moved in the nineteenth century to Hackney and then in 1937 to Hampton. The present, purpose-built, school was opened by Princess Alice, Duchess of Gloucester and accommodated 350 pupils. Numerous additions to the building and the acquisition of more land have enabled the school to increase in size to some 720 girls who enjoy a wealth of specialist facilities and the use of 30 acres of playing fields and gardens. Nine science laboratories, two large libraries, an Art Block, a Design and Technology suite, a Music and Drama wing, extensive IT and multi-media language facilities and a dedicated Careers area are complemented by grass and hard tennis courts, netball courts, 5 lacrosse pitches, track and field areas and a full-sized, indoor heated swimming pool. A Boat House, shared with Hampton School, was opened in October 2000 and the Sports Hall will be ready for use in September 2001.

The School's Statement of Purpose embodies the original aim, rage to encourage every girl to develop her personality to the full so that she may become a woman of integrity and a responsible member of society. It also emphasises the value of a broad, balanced education which gives due importance to sport, music and the creative arts in general whilst providing the opportunities for girls to achieve high academic standards within a framework of disciplined, independent study.

The Curriculum. In DfEE Years 7-9 contains two modern, foreign languages, two years of Latin, experience of the separate sciences, dedicated IT lessons and a PSE programme which continues throughout the school. Selection rather than specialisation for GCSE allows girls to respond to individual abilities and attributes whilst the School's scheme ensures that every girl continues to experience a broad education in which as few doors as possible are closed. A large sixth form of about 190-200 girls enables a wide choice of Advanced and Advanced Subsidiary subjects to be offered by the School. Most girls will study four or five subjects at Advanced Subsidiary level, proceeding to A level with three or four and all are entered for the A level General Studies examination. All sixth form students move on to further training, the majority to universities and there is a sizeable Oxbridge contingent annually. The formal Careers programme which begins in Year 9, before GCSE choices are made, continues throughout the school and uses external specialists, parents and past pupils, ECCTIS and other computer programmes as well as the School's own, trained staff.

Extra-curricular activity includes a wide variety of sport, with many girls representing their county, and some, the country. There are two orchestras, a chamber group, numerous ensembles and choirs including an award-winning Madrigal choir. Young Enterprise companies, The Duke of Edinburgh Award Scheme, Service Volunteers, opportunities for skiing, travel abroad on cultural and linguistic pursuits, leadership and adventure courses and many clubs and societies provide a wealth of opportunity for those who wish to be involved.

The Junior Department (190 pupils aged 7–11) is accommodated in a separate building in the grounds. It is an integral part of the whole school community and uses some specialist facilities.

Entrance. All applicants must sit the School's competitive entrance examinations, which are held in November (Sixth Form) and January (11+) each year for admission in the following year. Pupils may enter the Junior Department from the age of 7, and the Senior School at 11 years. Girls with good academic ability may apply for direct entry to the Sixth Form courses. Some Academic and Music Scholarships are available for both internal and external candidates at 11+ and Sixth Form entry stages and the Governors of the Cripplegate Schools Foundation offer a small number of Foundation Entrance Bursaries which are available to girls of suitable academic standards. The amount of assistance is calculated on a sliding scale which is related to family income.

Fees. (*see* Entrance Scholarship section) Registration and Entrance Examination £50. Termly: £1,855 in the Junior Department; £2,460 in the Senior School, inclusive of Books, Stationery, Games and Public Examination fees. Younger sisters of pupils already in the School are eligible for certain reductions.

Optional Subjects. Individual lessons in instrumental Music – £129 per term. Rowing £129 per term, Speech and Drama from £59 per term and Chess £30.50 per term.

Former Pupils Association: The Holly Club Address for communications, Secretary of The Holly Club, c/o The School.

Charitable status. The Cripplegate Schools' Foundation is a Registered Charity, number 312493. The Foundation is now responsible only for The Lady Eleanor Holles School which exists to provide education of a high standard to girls between the ages of 7 and 18.

La Sagesse Junior and High School

Newcastle upon Tyne

North Jesmond Newcastle upon Tyne NE2 3RJ
Tel: Senior: (0191) 2813474
Junior: (0191) 2815308

Motto: *Deo Soli*

La Sagesse Junior and High School educates girls from the age of 3-18 years. The foundation of the school is Catholic and Christian and the mission statement echoes the key elements of care, respect, truth and justice. The fundamental aim is to educate the whole child in a supportive yet challenging environment. Academic results are excellent. The school retains traditional values whilst also being forward looking. Pastoral and monitoring systems are very thorough and effective. Opportunities abound for sporting and creative activities and personal development is advanced with trips abroad, outdoor activities and involvement in charity work. The Sixth Form is strong and active with excellent all round provision. The grounds, buildings and facilities are extensive and impressive. The catchment area is wide but access is easy by road and rail because of the proximity to Metro, bus and train routes.

President: The Rt Rev Ambrose Griffiths, OSB Lord Bishop of Hexham and Newcastle

Council:
Reverend Sister Sheila Mary (*Chairman*)
Mrs F McGhee (*Vice Chairman*)
J T McLoughlin, Esq, BA
Dr M C Robinson, MBBS, FRCPath
Sister M Seddon (*Mother Provincial*)
J Adams, Esq, LLB
H Menon, Esq, BSc Hons, LLB
Dr A Walsh, MRCD, FRCPsych
Mrs K McCourt, MEd, CertEd, BA Hons, DipN (London), RGN, RM, RCNT, RNT
Mrs J Plasom-Scott, BA, ACA

Secretary to the Council: Mr J Anderson, LLB

Auditor: A A E Glenton, Esq, TD, FCA

***High School Headteacher:* Miss L Clark**, BEd Hons, MA

Deputy Headteacher: Miss H C Thompson, BA Hons, PGCE

Senior Teachers:
Head of Years 7-9: Dr C Whitford, BSc Hons, PhD, PGCE *Science*
Head of Years 10-11: Mrs K Eyre, BA Hons, PGCE *Head of Geography*
Head of Sixth Form: Mrs M McHugh, CertEd, BA *Drama/English*
Head of Marketing and Fundraising: Mrs M Morris, BA Hons, PGCE, MEd

Staff:

Art and Design:
*Mrs H Ketchin, NDD, ATC
Mrs A Pye, DAES

Business Studies:
Mrs K Thomas, CertEd, BA

English:
*Mrs V Boyle, BA Hons, PGCE
Miss T Hutson, BPhil, TCert
Mrs H Pitkethly, TCert

Geography:
Mrs M Gibson, TCert

History:
*Mrs J Pearson, BA Hons, PGCE

Home Economics:
*Mrs C Nevins, TCert

Information Technology:
*Mrs D Rabot, GradDip Music, PGCE, MA(Ed)

Mathematics:
*Mrs J Mee, TCert
Mr M Rye, BA Hons, QTS
Mrs J Moore, BSc Hons, PGCE

Modern Languages:
*Mrs A Potter, BA Hons, PGCE *Head of Modern Languages*
*Mrs M Henderson, BA Hons, DE *Head of French*
Mrs G Montague, BA Hons, PGCE *Spanish*

Music:
*Miss J MacNaughton, BA Hons, PGCE

Physical Education:
*Mrs J Atkinson, BA Hons, PGCE
Mrs B Laidler, Bedford College of PE

Science:
*Mrs J Pritt, BSc Hons, DipEd *Head of Science*
*Dr M Brookes, BSc Hons, PhD, PGCE *Head of Biology*
*Mrs E Lambert, BSc Hons, MSc *Head of Physics*
Miss K Brown, BSc Hons, PGCE *Science*
Dr C Whitford, BSc Hons, PhD, PGCE *Science*

School Chaplain: Sister Ancilla, BEd Hons

Office Staff:
Headteacher's Secretary: Miss K Turner

Secretary/Receptionist: Mrs J Thompson

Business Manager: Mr M Duke

Accounts Assistant: to be appointed

Technicians:
Senior Science Technician: Miss H Coulter
Science Technician/Resources: Mr L Camsell

Junior School Headteacher: Mrs A Ellis, TCert, LRAM

Staff:

Mrs K Craig, ARAD, FIDT *Senior Teacher*
Mrs H Fletcher, BA, MEd, TCert *Senior Teacher*
Mrs L Bartram, TCert
Mrs C Bell, BEd, TCert
Mrs C Edge, BEd Hons, TCert
Ms C Graham, BEd Hons
Mrs J Hunter, TCert
Mrs A Joyce, MA, BA Hons, TCert
Mrs P Kennedy, TCert
Mrs C Wilkinson, TCert

Headteacher's Secretary: Mrs J Polsinelli

Ancillary Staff:

Miss S Brennan
Mrs T McQuade

Visiting Staff:
Mrs N Hodgson, TCert, LGSM
Mrs M Smith, BMus Hons, TCert, LTCL
Mrs E Mellor, CertEd (Bretton Hall)
Ms L Sharman, BA, AGSMD
Mrs M Smith, BMus Hons, TCert, LTCL
Mrs C Summers, BA Hons, PGCE
Ms M Thomas, BA Hons

Numbers. There are 294 in the Senior School and 129 in the Junior School.

La Sagesse is a Christian School with a Catholic foundation which welcomes girls of all faiths. From this foundation emanate its basic values of care, justice, respect and truth. The education provided is in line with the National Curriculum. Teaching and learning is positive and dynamic. Girls progress and achievement are closely monitored in order to foster continuous development. Each girl is valued as an individual and is supported by an extremely well structured pastoral system. Examination results at all levels are excellent and objective tests such as ALIS, Yellis and NFER are evidence of the considerable 'value added' factor produced by the school. The school is situated in magnificent grounds close to Newcastle and has an impressive range of facilities. Opportunities abound for all manner of extra curricular and sporting activities. Classes are small and staff are talented, committed and exceptionally hard working.

La Sagesse is a school where children are happy to learn.

Charitable status. La Sagesse Convent High School (Newcastle upon Tyne) Limited is a Registered Charity, number 503958. It aims to provide girls of 3 to 18 years with a sound academic education in a caring and Christian atmosphere.

Laurel Park School

4 Lilybank Terrace Glasgow G12 8RX

See Hutchesons' Grammar School, HMC section, Part I of this Book.

Lavant House Rosemead

Lavant House Chichester West Sussex PO18 9AB
Tel: (01243) 527211
Fax: (01243) 530490
e-mail: office@lhandr.demon.co.uk
website: http://www.lhr.w-sussex.sch.uk

Governors:

Chairman: Mr R Hoare, OBE, MA (Oxon)

M E Emmerson, Esq
D M Green, Esq, MA (Cantab), FCollP
The Revd Canon J F Hester, MA (Oxon)
C P Horsley
N W Hudders
R H Malcolm-Green, Esq, CEng, BSc (London)
Mrs R M Moriarty, MA (Oxon)
Mrs S Revell
Mrs J Schofield, MA (Cantab)

Associate Member:
C Doman, Esq, MA (Oxon) *Solicitor*

Bursar and Clerk to the Governors: Mrs M Lowe

***Headmistress:* Mrs M Scott,** MA (Cantab)

Director of Studies: Dr N Sturt, BA (London), PhD

Head of Junior School: Mrs M E Gardner

Lavant House Rosemead is an Independent School of 150 pupils, of whom approximately a quarter are boarders. Day girls are accepted from age 5–18 and boarders from the age of 11. The school was founded in 1952 with the aims of combining a high level of academic education with a wide range of general activities in a family environment.

Situation and Buildings. The school stands in its own grounds of 14 acres at the foot of the Downs, 3½ miles from Chichester. The main school is housed in a listed 18th Century building of Sussex flintstone, and all other blocks are set within walled gardens and old yew hedges. The school rents a further 50 acres for grazing horses.

Curriculum. Girls work towards an average of 8-10 GCSE passes in a wide choice of subjects; similarly at A (and AS) Level a wide variety of subject combinations can be offered. The Junior School (Stanier House) has specialist teaching in Mathematics, English, Science, French, Music, Computers and PE.

Careers Guidance. University and Careers guidance is given by VIth form tutors.

Religion. The school has strong affiliations with the Parish and the girls walk to the 16th Century village church for special school services. Girls can be prepared for Confirmation in the parish and all denominations attend the assemblies in the school.

Games. Gymnastics, Swimming, Tennis, Hockey, Netball, Rounders, Badminton, Volleyball and Athletics; own heated outdoor swimming pool, specialist netball courts.

Extra-Curricular Activities. Own stables for livery, riding lessons, hacking, shows; Duke of Edinburgh Award Scheme. Regular chamber concerts, excellent choir; drama is very popular with two full scale productions each year.

The School has four minibuses which are available to transport girls to and from school. If parents wish, day girls can stay on for tea/overnight.

The Boarding Life. Qualified housestaff, nurse, weekend activities/trips include ice-skating, swimming, dance, cinema etc, all available off-site. Flexi-boarding as required. Separate Sixth Form accommodation and facilities.

Termly Fees. From September 2000: Day: £1,180 (infants) to £2,375 (seniors). Boarding - day rate plus £1,760. A 50% returnable deposit is charged for overseas pupils.

Admissions. Entry to the senior school is usually by written tests and activities on an entry assessment day in March, combined with Key Stage 2 SATs results. Requests for full details should be made to the Headmistress's Secretary.

Charitable status. Lavant House School Educational Trust Limited is a Registered Charity, number 307372. It exists to educate girls and foster social and moral growth based on clear Christian principles, in a caring family environment.

Leeds Girls' High School

Headingley Lane Leeds LS6 1BN
Tel: (0113) 2744000
Fax: (0113) 2752217

Motto: *Age quod Agis*

Governing Committee:

Appointed by Leeds Girls' High School:
Mr J M Ainsley
Mrs A F B Portlock, FCA
Mr R I Bairstow
Dr A Cooke, MBChB, MRCGP, DRCOG
Mr P A H Hartley, CBE (*Chairman*)
Mr S Johnson, CBE
Mr P D Lawrence
Mrs S Moore
Mr K Morton, ARICS
Miss B Neale, BSc
Mr D Pickersgill, FCA (*Treasurer*)
The Revd Canon Graham Smith

Appointed by Leeds University:
Professor C Leigh, BA, PhD

Clerk to the Governors and Bursar: Mr R G Hancock, MA, FCIS, MIMgt, MCIPD

Head: **Mrs S Fishburn,** BSc (Birmingham)

Assistant Head: Mrs P M McClive, BA (Leeds)

Senior School:

Senior Teacher: Mr B Brindley, BA (Warwick), MBA (Bradford)
Senior Teacher: Mrs C D Bamforth, BEd, MEd (Leeds)
Head of Sixth Form: Mrs L J Wood, MSc (York)
Head of Middle School: Mrs M Kelbrick, BEd (Manchester)
Head of Lower School: Mrs J C Apps, BSc (Leeds)

Art and Design:
Miss P A Davis, BA (Manchester) *also Design & Technology*
Mrs J Smith, BA (Liverpool)

Classics:
*Mrs A R Bowers, BA (London) *also Careers Team Leader*
§Mrs P Coningham, BA (Cantab)
§Mrs J Halliwell, BA (Leicester)

Design and Technology:
Mrs A M Clements, BSc (LMU) *also Business Studies and IT*

Drama:
*Mrs P S Hutley, BA (Worcester)
Miss A Andrews, BA (Kent) *also English*

Economics and Business Studies:
*Mr B Brindley, BA (Warwick)
§Mrs J A N Street, BA (Manchester)
Mr M K Walczak, BA (Wales)

English:
§Mrs M A Doyle, BA, MA (Essex)
Mrs S Harrison, BA (Lancaster)
Mrs M E Hall, BA (Lancaster)
*Mrs J J Kerr, BA (Hull)
Miss S Longfield, BA (Oxon)

French:
Mrs J Beck, BA, MA (London)
*Mrs B Gilbert, MA (Leeds)
Mrs M Hutson, BA (Newcastle)
§Mrs P A Walker, BA (London)

Geography:
*Mrs M A Carr, BA (Leeds) *also Design and Technology*
Mrs R Rothwell, BSc (Manchester)

German:
§Mrs H Inglis, BA (Durham)
*Mr D Stovell, BA, MEd (Keele), MSc
§Mrs E Whittaker, BA (Birmingham)

History:
*Mrs A J Chadwick, BA (Hull)
§Mrs E Sampson, BA (Sheffield) *also Business Studies*
Miss E M Wall, BA (London)

Home Economics:
Mrs M J Kelbrick, BEd (Manchester)
§Mrs M Senior, BA (OU) *also Design & Technology*
§Mrs H Smith, CertEd (Leeds) *also Design & Technology, Art and Information Technology*

Librarian:
Mr P A Harris, BA (Leeds)

Mathematics:
Mrs C D Cleverley, BSc (London)
§Mrs M Grainger, BSc (London)
Mrs S E Howe, BSc (Bristol)
Mr A M Pollard, BSc (Durham)
*Mr A P Pearson, BSc (Bristol)
§Mrs J Studholme, BSc (CNAA)

Music:
Mrs R Hindmarch, BMus (Manchester)
*Mrs K E L Staggs, BA (Oxon)

Physical Education:
*Mrs K A Nash, BEd (CNAA)
Mrs C D Bamforth, BEd, MEd (Leeds)
Mrs C Johnson, BEd (IM Marsh)
Miss J Lynam, BEd Hons (Cheltenham & Gloucester)

Politics:
Mr P Chappell, BA (Durham), MA (Leeds)

Religious Studies:
Mrs C M Calvert, BA (London)
*Miss S P Matthews, BA (Nottingham)

Science:

Biology:
Mrs G E Hall, BSc (Leeds)
*Mrs C H Jagger, BSc (Hull) *also Head of Science*
§Mrs P Philips, BSc (Manchester)
Mr A Shaw, BSc, MSc (Leeds)
Mrs L J Wood, MSc (York) *also Industry Liaison Officer*

Chemistry:
Mrs J C Apps, BSc (Leeds)
Dr P J Battye, BA (Lancaster), PhD (Exeter)
*Mrs K H McDougall, BSc (Newcastle)
Mr D Swain, BSc (Manchester)

Information Technology:
*Mrs K Davidson, BEd, MSc (Queen's)

Physics:
Mrs S L Andrews,, BSc (Durham) *also Mathematics*
Mrs J R Briant, BA (Keele)
*Mrs H Spencer, BSc (Manchester)

Full time staff 49; Part-time staff 13

Junior School, Ford House:

Head: Mrs P E Addison, BA (OU)

Mrs A Andrews, BEd (Leeds)
Ms P Barnett, CertEd (Bingley)
Mrs J E Briggs, BA, MA (Oxon)
Miss R Dunn, BA (Lancaster)
Miss M B Ellen, BA (Leeds)
§Mrs C Hilditch, MEd (Leeds)
Miss E Jeffries, BEd (Leeds)
Mrs R J Morgan, BEd (CNAA)
Mrs M Dolan, BA (Leeds)
Mrs R H Roberts, MEd (Leeds)
§Miss V M Strachan, BA (York)
Mrs C J Wainwright, BA (Manchester)

Full-time staff 11; Part-time staff 2

Preparatory School, Rose Court:

Head: Miss A L Pickering, BEd (Newcastle)

§Mrs D L Barnes, BA (Nottingham)
Mrs A Campbell, DipEd (Aberdeen)
§Mrs A Furbank-Lee, CertEd (Sheffield)
Mrs V H Lee, CertEd (Leeds)
Mrs D Lipinski, CertEd (Didsbury)
Mrs K Newman, BSc (Manchester)
Mrs G A Ramage, CertEd (Leeds)
Mrs R C Scholey, BEd (Leeds)
Mrs P White, BEd (Leeds)

Full-time staff 7; Part-time staff 3

Visiting Staff:

Bassoon: Ms S Hardwick, BA, LRSM, PGCE
Brass: Mr P Milner, PPRNCM
Cello:
Mrs S Ladds, ALCM, DRSAMD
Mrs J Maslin, LRAM
Clarinet: Mrs C Turner, BA
Flute: Miss H Smith, LTCL
Guitar: Mr R Britton, BA
Harp: Mrs P Radford, MSc
Oboe: Mrs J Stretton, FTCL, GTCL, LTCL
Organ & Piano: Mr M Aston, MA, ARCM
Percussion: Mr D Sales, BMus
Piano:
Mrs M Garbutt, ARMCM
Mrs A Wright, BA
Saxophone & Piano: Mr O Whawell, BA
Theory & Recorder: Mrs H Oliver, GBSM, ABSM
Singing:
Mrs J Edwards, ARCM, LRSM
Ms S Estill, MA, MMus
Violin:
Mrs A J Major, BSc, LGSM
Mrs I Sidebottom, GRSM, ARMCM
Speech & Drama:
Mrs Groves
Mrs Ballantyne

Accommodating 968 pupils (968 girls), the School is an Independent (ex Direct Grant) day school founded in 1876. Key features are high academic standards, care for the individual and a wide range of extra-curricular activities. A happy and stimulating environment encourages pupils to develop to their full potential, able to make a valuable contribution to society. The pass rate in 1999 at GCSE was 99.26% of which 73.23 achieved grade A and starred A grades. At Advanced Level the pass rate was 98.20% of which 71.95% was at A or B grade.

The school accepts girls 3–18. The Preparatory School (Rose Court) is for pupils aged 3–7 and the Junior School (Ford House) for pupils aged 7–11. Entry to the Senior School is usually at age 11 though occassionally vacancies arise in other age groups. Sixth Form applicants are welcome. Scholarships, including Music Scholarships, are available, regardless of parental income.

All sections of the School enjoy excellent provision for sport, music and drama, including a new purpose-built drama studio. In the Senior School other facilities include 10 science laboratories, 2 spacious libraries and 3 well-equipped computer rooms.

The school is situated in its own grounds of about 10 acres, 2 miles from the city centre and close to the University. Pupils travel from a wide catchment area using public transport or private buses organised by the School's Transport Coordinator.

Fees for 2000/2001. Senior School UIII to Upper VI £5,871; Junior School £4,278; Preparatory School £3,927.

Charitable status. Leeds Girls' High School is a Registered Charity, number 1048719. It exists to provide a high-quality education for children from Leeds and surrounding areas.

Leicester High School for Girls

454 London Road Leicester LE2 2PP
Tel: (0116) 270 5338

Board of Governors:
Chairman: M Barton, Esq, FRICS
Acting Clerk to the Governors: Mrs M Law
Mrs M R Banks, MBE, MEd
P S Bonnett, Esq
Mrs D R Davidson, BSc
Mrs H Dunham, BA
The Hon R T Fisher, MA
M Gray, Esq
The Very Revd D N Hole, HonDLitt
G E Jones, MA
D C Macqueen, Esq
T B Nightingale, Esq, MA, FCA
R W Pain, Esq, FCA

P S Parsons, Esq, FRICS
The Rt Revd Tim Stevens, The Bishop of Leicester
H C Stevenson, Esq
Dr N H Walker, BSc, PhD, FLS

Secretary to Leicester High School Charitable Trust Ltd: Mrs J Greasley, FCCA

Headmistress: **Mrs P A Watson**, BSc Hons (Reading)

Deputy Head: Mrs S M Rankin, CertEd (Liverpool), MEd (Sheffield)

Examination Officer: Mr M Joannou, BSc Hons (Salford), MEd (Leicester)

Senior Mistress: Mrs P J Prescott, BSc Hons (Cardiff)

Senior Department:

Assistant Staff:
Miss H W Ball, MSc (Bradford)
Mrs M R Ball, CertEd (Bristol)
§Mrs S Berridge, BA Hons (Kent)
Miss E Brooks, BEd Hons (Bedford)
§Mrs D Brunning, MA Hons (Oxon)
Mr T P Bureau, MA Hons (Edinburgh)
Mr A Chappell, BSc Hons (Leicester)
Mr S Dyer, BA Hons (Lancashire)
Mrs M E Evans, BA Hons, MA (London)
§Mrs J Farrell, BA Hons (Birmingham)
Miss C Fox, BA Hons (Dunelm)
*§Mrs B M Gill, BA Hons (Hull)
§Mrs M Gillam, BSc Hons (Nottingham)
§Miss E Graff-Baker, MA (Oxon), ARCM
§Mrs R Hall, BSc Hons (Aberystwyth)
Mrs R Hall, BSc Hons (London)
Mr B D Holness, BSc Hons (Southampton)
§Mrs M H Hoskins, BEd (Dunelm)
Miss H M Kesterton, BA Hons (Edinburgh)
§Mrs B L Krokosz, BA Hons (Coventry)
*Mrs H Lee, BSc Hons (Sussex)
§Mrs L C Martin, BA Hons (London), DipPsy
Ms J M Moore, BA Hons (Leicester)
§Mrs D A Morgan, BSc Hons (Warwick)
*Mrs C D Morton, MEd (Nottingham), LRAM
§Mrs W E Noble, CertEd (Keele)
Miss N Overall, BA Hons (Luton)
*Mrs C A Page, BA Hons (Liverpool)
Miss S M Pawley, BA Hons (Sheffield), MSc (Loughborough)
Mrs L P Pearson, BA Hons (Leicester)
Mrs H Rees, BA Hons (Birmingham)
*Mrs J M Robbins, Dip in Art (Edinburgh)
Mrs D J Robertson, BEd Hons (Reading)
Mrs A K M Shelton, MA Hons (St Andrews)
§Mrs E A Smith, DipPE (Lady Mabel College)
Mrs K Smith, CertEd (London)
*Mrs I Stanyer, BEd Hons (Warwick)
Mrs G Unsworth, CertEd (Leicester)
*Mr A C Wells, BSc Hons (Loughborough)
Mrs S D Wood, Diplome d'Etudes Francaises, Universite de Poitiers, CertEd (Liverpool)

Bursar: Mrs M Law
Headmistress's PA: Mrs L McMorran
Librarian: Mr M Lilley, BLib Hons (Aberystwyth)
Assistant Librarian: Mrs M Pritchard, BSc Hons (Bristol)
Accountant: Mrs J T Greasley, FCCA
Accounts Assistant: Mrs E J MacKay
Registrar: Mrs L Barnette
School Secretary: Mrs S Parkinson
IT Systems Manager: Mrs J Kirkwood
Laboratory Technician: Mrs A Hulls

Visiting Staff:
Mrs A Baker, LTCM *Clarinet/Flute*
Mrs J Bound, GBSM *Piano*
Mrs S Constantine-Smith, Dip(LSC), Dip(BMN), Member of RAD
Ms J Farrell, BA Hons (Birmingham) *Piano*
Miss S Garratt, BA *Speech & Drama*
Miss E Graff-Baker, MA (Oxon), ARCM *Violin*
Miss R Guillain, GSMD, LAMDA, EMPA, IDTA *Speech and Drama*
Mrs R A Houghton, FISTD, ARAD *Ballet*
Mrs S Jacobs, GRSM, LRAM *Violin*
Mrs W M Philpott, BA Hons, PGCE, LTCL *'Cello*
Mr D B Rowe, ATMInstF *Percussion*
Mr B Starbuck *Speech & Drama*

Junior Department:

Head of Department: Mrs C A Jolley, BEd Hons (Sheffield)
Deputy Head: Mrs E H O'Kane, CertEd (London)
Senior Teacher: Mrs P Wilson-Clark, CertEd (Bingley)

Mrs A C Berry, BA Hons (Leicester)
Mrs S J Davies, BEd Hons (Exeter)
Mrs E J Johnson, NNEB
Mrs W Knight, BA Hons (Stoke on Trent)
Mrs J Rodgers, NNEB
§Mrs E A Smith, DipPE (Lady Mabel College)
Mrs J Vick, BA Hons (Leicester)
Mrs D Wood, NNEB

Ancillary Staff:
Mrs M Bale
Mrs B Edwards
Mrs B K Goodrich, BA Hons (Loughborough), ATD, CLAIT
Mrs E M Hay, DipPrimEd (Scotland)
Mrs D Swepson

Leicester High School is a well established day school for girls situated in pleasant grounds on the south side of the city. Founded in 1906 as Portland House School it now comprises a Junior Department of 130 girls (3–9 years) and a Senior Department of 305 girls (10–18) sited on the same campus.

The school offers an academic education of a high standard, and the Sixth Formers almost invariably go on to Higher Education. It is a friendly community where an emphasis is placed on honesty, integrity and respect for the views of others. Class size is kept small so that there is every opportunity for each girl to achieve her full potential while developing the self confidence and self discipline to help in her future.

The Headmistress is responsible for both junior and senior departments. The staff are well qualified specialists and the school is renowned for both its academic excellence and extra-curricular programme. At the moment 20 subjects are offered at GCSE level and 22 subjects at A level.

The premises are a combination of modern purpose built units and the original gracious Victorian house, skilfully adapted to its present purpose. The facilities of the school have been systematically improved over the past ten years and most recently the school has undergone an exciting building programme. This includes a drama studio, music room, three fully equipped computer rooms, plus extra science laboratories and subject teaching rooms. A purpose-built library and resource centre was opened in the summer of 1999.

The school is a Trust with a Board of Governors. It is in membership of the GBGSA and the Headmistress belongs to the GSA.

Admission. All candidates over the age of 7 are required to pass an entrance examination for admission into the Junior and Senior sections. Entry into the Senior Department would normally be at 10+ or 11+ but entry at other ages is considered. There is also direct entry into the

Sixth Form dependent on GCSE results. Entrance into the Kindergarten Unit is by assessment. A registration fee of £25 is payable for all applicants aged 6 or more.

Religion. Religious instruction is based on that of the Church of England, but members of other denominations and faiths are welcome.

Scholarships. (*see* Entrance Scholarship section) These are awarded annually to girls of 11+ on entry into the Senior School through the Entrance Examination. A Music scholarship, Sixth Form Bursaries and Sixth Form Scholarships are also available.

Extras. Individual Music lessons, Speech and Drama, and Ballet are offered.

The Headmistress is always pleased to meet parents of prospective pupils and to show them the school. All communications should be addressed to the Headmistress from whom prospectuses, application forms and up-to-date details of fees may be obtained.

Charitable status. Leicester High School Charitable Trust Limited is a Registered Charity, number 503982R. The Trust exists to promote and provide for the advancement of education based on Christian principles according to the doctrines of the Church of England.

Lodge School

11 Woodcote Lane Purley Surrey CR8 3HB
Tel: 020 8660 3179
Fax: 020 8660 1385

Lodge School comprises Silverdene Lodge (mixed infants), Downside Lodge (co-educational prep) and Commonweal Lodge (senior girls only). Commonweal and Downside Schools merged in 1997 after 80 years of separate existence as a girls' school with a junior department and a boys' prep school, respectively.

Governors:

Chairman: Ann Stranack, BA (Hons)
Vice-Chairman: Anthony Carter-Clout

Pauline Cardwell
Roger Chapman, MBE, MA, FCA
Martin Harper, MCIOB
Anne Horne, BA
Sheila Lord
Dr Rosemary Northfield, DIH, FFOM
Andrew Pickering

***Principal:* Miss P A Maynard**, BEd (Hons), MA

Commonweal Lodge:
Senior Mistress: Mrs L Bailey, BSc Hons (Sussex)

Mrs G Arnold, BSc Hons (Cardiff)
Mrs L Bailey, BSc Hons (Sussex)
Mrs S Baldwin, BSc Hons (London)
Mrs E Baughan, CertEd (London)
Mrs A Bottiglia, BA Hons (St Martins School of Art & Design)
Mrs E Cheyne, CertEdPE (Camb Inst of Ed)
Mrs D M Duncan, Teachers Cert (Manchester)
Mrs D Edmunds, BA Hons (Exeter)
Ms C Fournès, BA (Toulouse), PGCE (Sussex)
Mrs H Gibson
Mrs D Glover, BEd (London)
Mrs B Hanson, BSc Hons (London)
Mrs D Jones, CertEd (London)
Mrs U Kendall, BSc(Econ) (London)
Mr R Killick, BA Hons (London)
Mrs C Lipscombe, BA (Open University), CertEd (London)
Mrs V Miall, BEd Hons (Nottingham)
Mr E Phillips, MSc (London)
Mrs P Vogel, BEd Hons (London)
Mr J Wilson, RSAMD, RCM

Downside Lodge:
Senior Master: Mr S Speer, BEd Hons (London)

Mrs A Cooper, BEd (Exeter)
Mrs J Edwards, BA, PGCE (Bedford)
Mrs A Harrington, BEd Hons (Canterbury)
Mr P Hider, BEd Hons (Westminster College)
Mrs F Leadbetter, CertEd (Birmingham)
Mrs S Moses, BSc (Open University)

Silverdene Lodge:

Mrs E Bruton, NNEB *Kindergarten*
Miss R Jones, NNEB
Mrs V Leonard, CertEd (London), Froebel Cert
Mrs S Stoby-Cater, BEd Hons (Southampton)
Mrs H Wiggins, CertEd (Bristol)

Special Support Staff:
Miss J Fry, CertEd (London), Froebel Cert

Technical: Mrs J Al Bandar, BSc (Aberdeen)

Secretary: Mrs D A Rawlinson

Finance Manager: Mr A Earl, ACMA

Lodge School is located off Foxley Lane in a private residential road. There are extensive playing fields and attractive garden areas. The grounds are edged by mature trees providing a tranquil, virtually traffic-free setting.

Sport is taught by specialists and all the children have the benefit of the excellent facilities including two gymnasia, two swimming pools and equipment for all major boys' and girls' sports and games.

There are four laboratories, three of them new, and science and IT, with 2 new suites totally refurbished in 1999, are strong at all levels. Music concerts and drama productions are held throughout the year and all children are given the opportunity to perform.

Admission. Pupils are admitted at any time if there are vacant places. An assessment is made during a day visit at most levels, though an examination is set at 7+ and 11+. Silverdene takes boys and girls from the age of 3. An extended day is available from 8.00am to 6.00pm if required.

Curriculum. The National Curriculum Key Stages are incorporated into the teaching and the examinations are sat at the appropriate times. Boys and girls are prepared for entrance examinations, although girls may transfer directly into the senior school. Two modern languages are taught, separate sciences at GCSE and 'A' level, and small group sizes provide stimulation for able pupils and support for those with moderate learning difficulties including dyslexia.

Aims. All pupils are encouraged to use their abilities to the full, mentally, physically and spiritually. The Schools are undenominational but seek to inculcate a sound standard of values based on Christian principles and School Assembly and religious education are a vital integral part of the school life. Pupils are given a knowledge and understanding of other faiths and cultures and are expected to contribute to the life of the school and to succeed in some aspect of it.

Fees. The fees range from £1,130 to £1,950 per term, Nursery class £600/£950 (normal school day).

Scholarships. Scholarship examinations for boys and girls at 7+ and for girls at 11+ are held in January. Music Scholarship at 11+.

Commonweal Lodge Old Girls' Association is called Old Knots. *Secretary,* Julie Paice, e-mail: oldknots@hotmail.com.

Charitable status. Lodge Educational Trust Limited is a Registered Charity, number 312610. It exists to provide independent education for girls and boys to the age of 11 and girls to the age of 18.

Loughborough High School

Burton Walks Loughborough Leicestershire LE11 2DU.
Tel: (01509) 212348
Fax: (01509) 215720

Loughborough High School is part of Loughborough Endowed Schools. The Grammar School is the brother school and the co-educational junior school is known as Fairfield. We enjoy a very old foundation, for in 1850 the upper school for girls came into existence thus making Loughborough High School the first girls' grammar school in England. In 1879 the school moved to its present site in Burton Walks. The High School enjoys excellent facilities, which are being added to and improved continuously.

Loughborough High School is an 11 to 18 school of approximately 560 day girls with a large sixth form numbering some 160. At the High School we aim to provide an excellent academic education in a caring atmosphere. Since we are a comparatively small school, we are able to know our pupils as individuals and this engenders a strong community spirit. In providing a scholarly education in a disciplined atmosphere we hope to enable each girl ultimately to enter the career of her choice. Academic work and the pursuit of the best standards of which a pupil is capable is central to our philosophy but we also believe that the personal and social development of each individual pupil is of great importance. The school offers a wide range of cultural, recreational and sporting activities and there are clubs and societies for virtually all tastes and interests (many in the Senior School are joint with Loughborough Grammar School). We trust that all will discover and develop their individual talents and interests as they progress through school. Further details about the school can be obtained by contacting the school's secretary.

Governors: P J Tomlinson, Esq, LLB (*Chairman*)

A J Bowen, Esq, MA
T G M Brooks, Esq, JP
Prof S F Brown, BSc, PhD, DSc, CEng, FICE, FIHE
Dr A de Bono, MA, BChir, MRCGP
The Rt Hon S Dorrell, MP, BA
A D Emson, Esq, BPharm(Hons), MRPharmS, MCPP
Prof J Feather, BLitt, MA, PhD, FLA
G P Fothergill, Esq, BA, MInstM
D Godfrey, Esq, BSc, CEng, FIEE
Prof A W F Halligan, MA, MD, BAO, MRCOG, MRCPI
Dr J E Hammond, BDS
Mrs M B Hanford
Dr P J B Hubner, MB, FRCP, DCH
P E Jordan, Esq, BSc, CEng, FIMechE, FIProdE
Councillor A M Kershaw
Prof J Laybourn-Parry, BSc, MSc, PhD, DSc
Mrs G J W Maltby, MA
W M Moss, Esq
Mrs J G E Page
Prof G C K Peach, DPhil
H M Pearson, Esq, BA, LLB, ACIS
The Rt Revd T Stevens, Bishop of Leicester
Mrs J M Wales
Prof D J Wallace, FRS

Bursar and Clerk to the Governors: Mr K D Shaw, MBE, MSc (Cranfield), FCIS

Headmistress: **Miss J E L Harvatt**, BA, Hons University of London (*Westfield College*) *German*

Deputy Head: Miss E Steel, BSc Hons (Nottingham) *Geography*

Senior Mistress: Mrs P M Armstrong, BA Hons (Keele) *History*

Assistant Staff:
Mrs J M Atherton, BA Hons (Durham) *French*
Mrs H L Baker, BEd Hons (Bedford College of Education) *Support Co-ordinator*
Dr A P Bean, BMus, LRAM, PGCE, AMusD
Mr J W Bean, LRAM, LGSM(MT), CertEd *'Cello*
Mr P W Blissett, CertEd (Shoreditch College of Education) *Information & Technology*
Mrs K Burns, BA Hons (Birmingham), LLCM *Violin and Viola*
Mrs R M Butterfield, MA Hons (St Andrews), MLitt (Oxon) *History*
Mrs S K Cameron, BSc Hons (Aberystwyth) Geography and Geology
Mr G M H Carter, GLCM, ARCO *Piano and Singing*
Mrs S E Cheeseman, MA Hons (Oxon), ALCM *Music*
Mrs C Craig, BSc Hons (Manchester) *Biochemistry*
Mrs J V Darby, BA (Loughborough), CertEd (Radbrook College) *Domestic Science*
Dr J Downing, BSc Hons (Bristol) *Chemistry*
Dr E C Eadie, BA Hons (Birmingham) *History*
Mrs G P Fernandez, BSc Hons (Liverpool) *Mathematics*
Miss S Finch, BSc Hons (London) *Geography*
Mrs J Firth, Diploma Yorkshire Training College of Housecraft, (Leeds) *Domestic Science*
Mrs M Ghaly, BSc Hons (Teesside) *Chemistry*
Mrs A Gillies-Loach, GMus (Huddersfield), LRSM, LTCL *Flute*
Miss R C A Goodwin, BA Hons (Wales) *English*
Mrs A E Gray, BSc (London) *Economics*
Mrs S Harrison, BA Hons (Sheffield) *Mathematics*
Mrs E Heap, BA Hons (Leicester) *English*
Dr A Henshaw, MA Hons (Oxon), DPhil (Oxon) *Classics*
Mrs S R O Henson, BA Hons (Loughborough) *Fine Art*
Dr S Jackson, BSc Hons, PhD (UMIST) *Chemistry*
Mrs P J Kent, BA Hons (Bristol) *Classics*
Mrs L Lofthouse, BSc Hons (Warwick) *Mathematics*
Mr S G Lofthouse, BSc Hons (Warwick) *Information & Computer Technology & Mathematics*
Mrs B Lott, BA Hons (Sussex) *French*
Mrs C Lundie, BA Hons (Leeds) *French*
Mrs S E Meadows, BA Hons (Durham) *English and Religious Studies*
Mrs K Merritt, BEd Hons (Bedford College, de Montfort) *Physical Education*
Miss N Mitchell, BA Hons (London) *History*
Mrs P V Needham, BTheol (Geneva) *Theology*
Miss C E Nelson, BSc Hons (Manchester) *Chemistry*
Mrs J Piggott, BEd Hons (Sheffield) *Mathematics*
Mrs J M Pirie, BA Hons (Exeter) *English*
Mrs M A Reilly, BSc Hons (Surrey) *Home Economics*
Mrs J Richardson, BA Hons (Loughborough) *Sculpture*
Mrs J Roberts, BA Hons (Newcastle), MA (Loughborough) *German*
Miss J Roper, GRSM, ARMCM, ACertCM *Flute*
Miss P Ross, BA (Open), *Design Technology*
Mrs M Rowley, BA Hons (London) *English*
Mrs C M Simmonds, GRSM, LRAM, ARCM *Piano*
Mrs S M Singlehurst, BEd Hons (Liverpool Polytechnic) *Physical Education,* MSc (Loughborough University) *Physical Education and Sports Science*
Mrs C A Smith, MA Hons (Oxford) *French*
Mrs M Starkings, BSc Hons (Nottingham), BA (Open) *Physics*
Mrs A M Steele, BSc Hons (Leeds) *Agricultural Science*

Mrs M Sterry, MA (Edinburgh) *French/Spanish*
Mr J R Stoeter, BSc Hons (Leicester) *Mathematics*
Mrs M E Thirlwell, BA Hons (Leeds) *English and Theology,* MTh (University of Nottingham) *Theology*
Miss C E Todd, BSc Hons (Manchester) *Biology*
Mr R W Tomblin, MA Hons (Oxford) *French*
Miss Z A Walsh, BEd Hons (Bedford College, De Montfort) *Physical Education*
Miss D E J Wassell, BA Hons (Leeds) *English*
Miss S Weaver, MA (London), GTCL, FLCM *Music and Violin*
Mrs A R Wilkins, BA Hons (London) *German*
Mrs B Woodward, BA Hons (Essex) *Physics*
Mrs N J Young, BA Hons (East Anglia) *English*

Librarian: Mrs P E Hodgson, ALA
Matron: Mrs A Durning, RGN
Secretary: Mrs P M Brown

Assistant Secretaries: Mrs L A Bentley, Mrs S Cassidy

Doctor: Dr A M Bagley, MB, CHB

School Curriculum. Religious Studies, English, History, Geography, Economics, French, German, Spanish, Greek, Latin, Classical Civilisation, Mathematics, Chemistry, Physics, Biology, Music, Technology (Food, Textiles, Design and Information, Computer Technology), Art and Design, Gymnastics, Modern Dance, Games (hockey, netball, tennis, rounders, swimming and athletics). Careful note is taken of the National Curriculum though we deviate from it in some respects in order to give greater flexibility to the students' choice of subjects at GCSE level and to include some subjects not included in the National Curriculum.

Fees. Term Fees £1,779. Additional Fees, Music (individual instrumental lessons), £69–£137.

Entrance Awards and Music Scholarships. (*see* Entrance Scholarship section) School Assisted Places replace the Government Assisted Places.

Charitable status. The Loughborough Endowed Schools' Company, number 4038033, is limited by guarantee and registered in England. It is also a Registered Charity, number 1081765.

Luckley–Oakfield School

Wokingham Berks RG40 3EU.
Tel: (01189) 784175

Governing Body:

Mr D Houghton, MSc, DIC (*Chairman*)
Mr D Cook
Mrs J Farmer
The Revd G Herbert, MA
Dr J Ledger, BSc (Hons), MSc(Eng), PhD, FIMgt
Dr J Orr, MBBS, DRCOG
The Lady Remnant
Mr S Richmond
Mrs R Stevens, FCA
Mr M Walker, MA, BSc, FRES
Mr T Workman

***Headmaster:* Mr R C Blake**, MA Oxford, MPhil Southampton *History*

Deputy Head: Mrs J A Stewart, BSc Birmingham *Physics*

Staff:
Mrs S Allen, City & Guilds *Food Technology*
Mrs J Amos, BA, Charles University, Prague *German*
Dr R Archer, PhD, Warwick *Mathematics*
Mr G Bell, BA (Hons) Lancaster *History/Sixth Form Housemaster*
Miss A E Caldwell, BSc (Hons) Hull *Geography*
Mrs D Chacko, BA (Hons) Nottingham, MA London *German, Housemistress*
Mrs H Chaddock, BA (Hons) Swansea *Physics*
Mrs H Clements, BA (Hons) Swansea *Geography/French*
Mrs P J Creech, CertEd Bristol *IT/Business Studies*
Mrs S Dixon, BA (Hons) Central Lancashire *Art/Senior Housemistress*
Mrs J M Eastaugh, BSc (Hons) Leicester *Mathematics*
Mrs D Etherington, BA (Hons) Exeter *English*
Mrs C Gadsby, BSc (Hons) Nottingham *Chemistry*
Mrs B Gathercole, BA Theology (Nottingham) *Religious Studies*
Mrs S Gibson, BSc Bath College of Higher Education *Food & Textile Technology*
Mrs P A Higginson, BSc (Econ) (Hons) Aberystwyth *Economics/Business Studies*
Mrs S Hills, BEd (Hons) Leeds Polytechnic, MSc City *Physical Education*
Mrs M Kempton, BEd (Hons) London, BA (Hons) Reading, MA, Reading *English*
Mrs D Mason, BEd (Dual Hons) Sheffield *Biology/Chemistry/Head of Lower School*
Mrs K McGonnell, BEd (Hons) Exeter *French*
Dr M B McLeod, BSc (Hons) Southampton, MSc, PhD Birmingham *Biology*
Mr J Moss, MA, BA (Hons) Aberystwyth *Fine Art/Art History*
Mrs Z Percival, BSc Crewe & Alsager College *Science*
Miss E Reeves, BSc Hons (Cheltenham & Gloucester College of HE) *PE*
Mrs V Routledge, BA (Hons) Birmingham *Head of Modern Languages*
Mrs S Sayer, BA (Hons) Durham *French/Spanish*
Mrs M Sherwood, MA Cantab *Mathematics*
Mrs M Smith, BSc (Hons) Bradford *Psychology*
Mr K Stewart, MA Reading, BSc Birmingham, CEng, MBCS *IT*
Mrs F Sutherland, BD (Hons) London, MA *Drama/Theatre Studies*
Mrs E Thomas, BA (Hons) Lancaster *Head of English*
Mrs M Vogel, BEd (Hons) East Anglia, LGSM *Music*
Rev J Wakeling, CertEd Cambridge, DipRS London *Chaplain/RS/PE*
Mrs M Wilson, BA (Hons) York *Mathematics*
Mrs J Wood, BA (Hons) Lancaster, MA (OU) *History/Head of Sixth Form*

Bursar: Mr M Browning, ACIB, MIMgt, MIITT, MRIPHH

Registrar: Mrs B Remmington

School Secretaries: Mrs M Cope, Mrs J Leatherby

Headmaster's Secretary: Mrs N Hall

Matron: Miss P L Stuart, SEN

Resident Sixth Form Housemistress: Mrs J Bell

There are 280 girls (67 boarders) in the school, aged 11–18. The normal age of entry is at 11 by the school's own entrance examination and interview, but older pupils are admitted when there are vacancies. Girls are prepared for GCSE, Advanced Subsidiary and A2 examinations, for University entrance, and entry to other forms of Higher Education. There are excellent facilities for the Sciences, Food & Textiles Technology, Art and Crafts. The lower school curriculum includes French, German and Information Technology. Girls take Double Award Science GCSE incorporating Physics, Chemistry and Biology. The three sciences are popular subjects at 'A' Level.

Sixth-formers have their own purpose-built house, with studies and study bedroom accommodation. The Sixth

Form Housemaster and his wife live in this block and are houseparents to the girls. Senior girls take on various responsibilities and a number become School Prefects.

The school stands in 22 acres of grounds with its own games pitches, tennis courts and heated covered swimming pool. There is a large well-equipped Sports Hall. The main games are hockey, netball, tennis, rounders and athletics.

About half of the girls learn musical instruments and the school has two choirs, an orchestra, a wind band and smaller instrumental groups. Lessons for pianoforte, wind and stringed instruments and singing are available as extras. Other additional subjects include German conversation, Spanish and Speech and Drama.

Boarders and day girls are encouraged to join in the activities period between 4.00–5.30pm on weekdays when a wide range of options is open to them, such as riding, aerobics, badminton, CCF, and the Duke of Edinburgh Award Scheme.

The school is small enough to give individual pastoral care and large enough to offer a full spread of academic and leisure pursuits. There are day, weekly boarding and full boarding places, and this gives a great degree of flexibility to parents, particularly those who have to spend periods abroad.

The school has an evangelical Church of England foundation, but girls of all denominations are welcomed. Christian values shape the ethos of the school. There is a regular Sunday Service for boarders.

Fees. Boarders – £4,377 per term. Weekly Boarders – £4,039 per term. Day Girls – £2,565 per term.

Bursaries. Scholarships are awarded at 11+ on the results of the Entrance Examination, and re-awarded for entry to the Sixth Form. A music scholarship is available at 11+.

Chairman of the Luckley-Oakfield Old Girls' Association (LOOGA).

Mrs S Lunn, 25 Brooklyn Drive, Emmer Green, Reading, Berks.

Charitable status. Luckley-Oakfield is a Registered Charity, number 309099. It offers day and boarding education for girls on the basis of Christian values.

Malvern Girls' College

Malvern Worcestershire WR14 3BA
Tel: (01684) 892288
Fax: (01684) 566204
e-mail: registrar@mgc.worcs.sch.uk
website: www.mgc.worcs.sch.uk

This Independent Boarding School was founded in 1893

Visitor: The Right Reverend The Lord Bishop of Worcester

Council:
Chairman: A G Duncan, Esq

Members:
Mrs A Berington
Mrs P Birchley
Mrs S A E Bradford
P N Guy, Esq, FCA
Lady Harrison, MA, DipEd
Dr J L Jones, BEd, MEd, MBA, PhD
R S Kettel, Esq, FCA
Sir Nigel Nicholls, KCVO, CBE, MA
R N Philipson-Stow, Esq, DL, FCA
Dr T Price, MA, BM, BCh, FRCP
J R D Scriven, Esq, MA
R H Tedd, Esq, QC, BCL, MA
Mrs G Wagstaffe, MA
Prof C Whitehouse, BSc, PhD

Secretary to the Council and Bursar of the College: S W Hesketh, Esq, BSc, CEng, FCIS

***Head:* Mrs Philippa M C Leggate,** BA York, MEd Bath, PGCE Bristol

Deputy Head: The Revd P D Newton, BA, MPhil, PGCE Southampton

Senior Mistress: Miss S M Tudsbery Turner, TD, LRAM, ARCM

Head of Sixth Form: Miss P Drew, BA, York

Head of Middle School: Mrs M Taylor, BSc Nottingham

Head of U3/L4: Mrs L Brighton, BEd Birmingham

Chaplain: Revd F Middlemiss, BA Manchester, PGCE

Curriculum Director: Dr S B Munday, BA Hons, PhD Open

Librarian: Ms R Jones, BSc, PGCE

Careers Adviser: Mrs S Matthews, BA, PGCE Leeds

Computer Administration: Mrs J Palmer

Registrar: Mrs S Chance

Headmistress' Secretary: Mrs L Burman

Medical Officer of Health: Dr G W Williams

Sanatorium: Sister P Tavender

Housemistresses:
Ivydene Hall: Mrs S Pallett
The Mount: Mrs E Prophet
The Benhams: Mrs E Rambridge, MA, PGCE
Hatfield: Mrs I M Lloyd, CertEd

Sixth Form House Tutors:

Poulton:
Revd F Middlemiss, BA Manchester, PGCE

Greenslade:
Miss H Vose, BA Portsmouth

Avenue Annex: Miss N Watson, CertEd

Heads of Department:

English:
Mrs L Melhuish, MA, BA Hons London, PGCE Cambridge

History:
Miss C E Walker, BA, MA, Oxford, Somerville, PGCE

Geography:
Mr A Hutchings, BSc, MEd

Religious Studies:
Mrs H Jeys, BA, PGCE

Classics:
Mrs A C Dicks, BA, Leicester

Modern Languages:
Mrs A E Crowther, BA Southampton, PGCE *French*
Mrs C Flannigan, BA, PGCE *Spanish*
Mrs S M Matthews, BA Leeds, PGCE *German*

Mathematics:
Mrs M Perkins, BSc Reading, PGCE Oxford

Information Technology and Computer Studies:
Mr M A Wilson, MusB, Manchester, PGCE

Economics:
Miss Z Lewis, BSc Wales, PGCE

Natural Sciences:
Dr J A Hutton, BSc, PhD, CChem, MRSC, Reading *Head of Chemistry*

Mrs I J Carmichael, BSc Reading, PGCE *Head of Physics*
Miss C Evans, BSc Hons, PGCE *Head of Biology*

Home Economics:
Mrs L Tonner, BEd Worcester

Art:
Mrs H Vale, Dip Art, BA Cheltenham, PGCE Birmingham

History of Art:
Mr E D E Thomas, MA Edinburgh, MA East Anglia

Music:
Mr D Evans, MA, GBGSM, PGCE

Drama:
Mrs J Fisher, BEd, LRAM Central School of Speech & Drama

Physical Education: Mrs J Smallwood, CertEd Bedford College

Outdoor Pursuits: Miss S Cole, BA Liverpool, PGCE Lancaster

General. Malvern Girls' College is situated in one of the most beautiful areas of Britain, at the foot of the Malvern Hills. Founded in 1893, Malvern Girls' College is an independent girls' boarding school, with a longstanding reputation for academic excellence, and a commitment to providing a well-balanced education in which outstanding opportunities in sport, music, drama and art help to develop the whole person as an individual.

There is no single blueprint for a 'Malvern Girl'. Every girl brings her own special personality and talents to the College, where the individual contribution matters. Visitors comment on the College's welcoming and friendly atmosphere and the tremendous self-esteem each girl seems to enjoy.

Numbers and Accommodation. There are 420 girls aged 11–18, 350 boarders and 70 day girls.

Fees. From September 2000, Boarders £5,300 per term, Day Boarders £3,525 per term. Sixth Form Boarding £5,800 per term and Sixth Day Boarders £3,900 per term.

School Facilities. The College facilities are attractively located in some 30 acres of land. They include extensive classrooms, laboratories and specialist areas for art, drama, music, technology and computing. A new Science Education Centre was opened in October 1998 which provides excellent facilities for the teaching of the sciences and reinforces a long tradition of excellence in science. There is also considerable investment in Information Technology. A strong musical tradition exists in the College with more than three quarters of pupils playing at least one instrument.

The College boasts a large and comprehensive Art department with an extended Sixth Form studio where Sixth Formers enjoy their own working area. There is also a large and light art studio for the Middle School and an Art & Technology Resources Library.

Sport. The College has been awarded the Sports Council's Sportsmark Gold Award for the second time for its physical education provision in teaching more than 21 sports, which include athletics, gymnastics, lacrosse, hockey, squash, badminton, netball, riding, rowing, rounders, swimming and tennis. Facilities include a heated indoor swimming pool, astro-turf games pitch and squash courts.

Pastoral Care. House activities and pastoral care are designed to provide a happy and secure environment. Boarding life revolves around the six Houses, including Ivydene our Junior House for 11-12 year olds, three other Middle School Houses, The Benhams, The Mount and Hatfield, and two Sixth Form Houses Poulton and Greenslade. Day boarders are regarded as full members of the Houses and take part in all House activities.

There is close liaison between home and school, with Housestaff keeping parents informed about their daughter's welfare. Our system of pastoral care provides a number of avenues that girls may follow if they need help or support. No girl is left alone if she is struggling with a personal or academic problem. All members of staff actively support the concept that pastoral care is everyone's responsibility.

Religion. The College has a specifically Christian tradition but girls from all religious communities and from non-religious backgrounds are warmly welcomed and every effort is made to provide a sympathetic environment in which each person may practice her own faith and develop her own beliefs.

Community Service. Girls are encouraged to take part in community service. Every year members of the Sixth Form undertake a week's community service placement around the UK. Many other activities are undertaken throughout the year where girls are able to become involved with and to help those in need.

Extra-curricular Activities. There is a busy and varied weekend programme of activities, including abseiling, canoeing, dry slope skiing, rock climbing, photography, watersports and expeditions leading to the Duke of Edinburgh Award.

Examinations. Girls are prepared for GCSE and Advanced Level examinations, university entrance and scholarship examinations. Girls are also able to take the examinations in Music, Speech and Drama of the Associated Board of the Royal Schools of Music.

Health. There is a dispensary in each House, as well as a Health Centre with qualified medical staff available 24 hours a day.

Scholarships/Bursaries (*see* Entrance Scholarship section). The College offers Academic Entrance Scholarships and Exhibitions up to 50% of fees at 11+, 12+ and 13+, as well as entrance awards for excellence in Art, Music and Physical Education. Scholarships are also awarded to girls entering the Sixth Form.

Admission. Admission is through the College's own examinations, or through Common Entrance examination, together with an interview with the Head. Girls normally enter the College at ages 11, 12, 13 and also at Sixth Form level.

Old Girls' Association. The Old Girls' Association is an association run by Old Girls, based in College. It helps to keep them in touch with each other and what is happening at College. There are over 3,500 members world-wide with a network of overseas and UK area representatives.

The OGA holds two reunions every year, one in May at College and one in November elsewhere in the UK.

Charitable status. Malvern Girls' College (1928) Limited is a Registered Charity, number 527513. It exists for the purpose of educating girls.

Manchester High School for Girls

Grangethorpe Road Manchester M14 6HS.
Tel: 0161 224 0447
e-mail: admin@manchesterhigh.co.uk
website: http://www.manchesterhigh.co.uk

Board of Governors:

Chairman: Miss G Hush, MBE, MA

Dr C Beeson, BA, PhD, FRNCM
Mr V N Bingham, OBE, MA, FIPD
Mr R J Chapman, MA, DipArch, RIBA, FHospE
Mr A Clarke, FCA
Mrs B M Fleming, MMus, LRAM
Mrs B Harris, BA

Her Honour Judge L Kushner, LLB, QC
Mr A B Murray, CA, ACMA, FIMI
Professor A Pearson, BSc, PhD
Mr V Ruia, BA
Mrs C V F Sargent, BSc
Mr F R Shackleton, MA, LLM
Mrs C Walker, BA
Mrs A M Wilkinson, NFF, CertEd

Hon Treasurer: Mr A B Murray, CA, ACMA, FIMI

Clerk to the Governors and Bursar: Mr D A Abbott, BA, DipM

School Medical Officer: Dr J E Miller, MRCGP, DRCOG, DCH, MFFP

***Head Mistress:* Mrs C Lee-Jones**, MA, MIMgt, FRSA

Deputy Head Mistresses:
Mrs S M Smith, BSc (Leeds), MEd (Bristol)
Ms H Huber, BA (Manchester), Dip Management of Education (Manchester Metropolitan)

Senior Teachers:
Miss S E Coulter, BEd (Liverpool) *Head of Preparatory Department*
Mrs A Wells, BA (Essex) *Director of Academic Development*

Staff:
Miss R Aldridge, BA (London)
Mrs R Ashworth, BSc (Newcastle), MSc (City)
Mr M K Barlow, BA (Manchester)
Mrs B Bates, BA (Manchester)
Mrs C Bennett, BSc (Staffordshire)
Mrs J Bold, BA, MA (Huddersfield)
§Mrs F Brown, BA (Nottingham)
Miss P Catlow, BSc (Manchester)
*Mrs A G T Chambers, BA (West Surrey College of Art & Design), ATC
*Mr J Clarke, BA, MPhil (Manchester)
Miss L Cooke, BSc (Wales)
Mrs M Cornell, BA (London) (*Head of Sixth Form*)
§Mrs D Crichton, BA (London)
*Dr S Crook, BSc, PhD (Dundee)
Mrs B E Davies, DipAD (Birmingham)
Miss S A L Davies, BA (Cardiff)
Mrs E T Downie, BSc (Edinburgh)
*Mrs G M Edgar, CertEd (Manchester)
Mrs P Elcombe, BMus (Manchester), ARCM
Mrs P J Flatman, CertEd, PE (Bedford)
§Mr P J Flynn, BSc (London)
Mrs J L Fordham, CertEd (Manchester)
Mrs A Frood, BSc (Liverpool), MA (OU)
Miss C Griffiths, BSc (York)
Mrs J R Heydecker, BA (Leicester)
*Mrs J M Hillier, BSc (London), MSc
Dr R E Hoban, BSc, PhD (Newcastle)
*Mrs M G Hobson, BSc, MA (Salford)
Mrs V Horsfield, BA (Durham)
Miss P M Hunt, MA (Manchester)
Miss A M Jackson, BA (Middlesex)
Mr D L Jones, BSc (Manchester)
Mrs P A Kellett, CertEd PE, (Bristol)
*Miss A M Kilgarriff, CertEd, PE (Hull)
Mrs E Knox, BA (Manchester)
§Mrs C M Lomas, MA (Oxon)
Mrs P Mahey, BA (Central England)
Miss R McGrath, BA (London)
Miss L McNabb, BEd
Mrs A Morris, MA (Oxon), BD (London)
Miss J Parker, BSc (London)
Mrs S C Peake, CertEd, PE (London) (*Head of Upper School*)
§Mrs C J Pollock, MA (Glasgow), MIL
Miss E M Pope, MA (Oxon)
Dr C M Poucher, BSc, PhD (Leeds)
Miss R E Pownall, BSc (Manchester)
Dr E Pratt, MA, PhD (Cantab)
*Mrs H Rix, BSc (London)
*Mrs P L Roberts, BA (Durham)
Miss A F Robertshaw, BA (Hull)
*Mrs K Rundell, BMus (Manchester)
Mrs P Scott, BA (Duncan of Jordanstone College of Art)
*Miss C Stark, BA (Bristol)
Mrs J M Thickbroom, BSc (London)
Mrs C A Thomas, CertEd, BA (OU)
Mrs E Thornber, BA, MPhil (Manchester)
§Mrs D E Troth, BA (Exeter)
§Mrs C M Tynan, BA (York)
Mrs T Wainwright, BA (Liverpool)
§*Mrs E Wallace, BA (London), MEd (Manchester)
*Mr P R Warburton, BA (Portsmouth Poly), MPhil (Leicester)
*Miss J Welsby, BA (Manchester)
*Mrs L A Witton, BA (Leeds)
§Mrs J L Youngjohns, MA (Oxon)

Preparatory Department Staff:
Mrs K Alcock, CertEd (Dudley)
Mrs A Allman, Teacher's Dip (Sedgely Park)
Miss P M Bristow, BEd (Manchester)
Miss S Diamond, BEd (Cantab)
Miss J D'Vigne, BEd (Bangor)
Mrs M Foley, CertEd (Phillipa Fawcett College)
Miss I P Head, CertEd (Caerleon)
Miss C L Payne, BEd (Liverpool John Moore's)
Mrs J C Philip, BA (Manchester)
Mrs A Taylor, CertEd (Didsbury College)
Mrs M A Young, BEd (Cheltenham)

Senior Secretary: Mrs B K Gorvin, BSc (Leeds)

Librarian: Mrs R E Russell, ALA

Manchester High School for Girls is a day school for students aged 4 to 18. The School provides an academic education which is both dynamic and forward-looking, and which produces students who distinguish themselves in many professions. There is a well-structured, supportive guidance system. A broad range of subjects offers challenging learning activities which extend students' knowledge and skills beyond the National Curriculum. An exceptional programme of lively extra-curricular activities and educational visits helps to develop personal strengths and communication skills. Students achieve impressive performances at GCSE and A Level. Almost all leavers go on to university.

The Preparatory Department forms an integral part of the School but has its own purpose-built accommodation comprising eleven classrooms, two assembly halls and resource areas including a computer suite and libraries. Admission is by means of an assessment for Infants and an entrance examination in Mathematics and English for Juniors. Girls may enter at ages 4, 7, 8 or 9. There are occasional vacancies at intermediate ages.

Many pupils join at the age of eleven. The School sets its own entrance examination in January for vacancies the following September. School Bursaries are available for a limited number of pupils annually. Scholarships may be offered to candidates who show exceptional performance in academic work and/or music. The Sixth Form welcomes applicants at age 16. Sixth Form assessment is by interview and GCSE qualifications.

Learning is supported by an exciting learning environment. This includes IT suites, a specialist Music Block, an indoor swimming pool, all-weather sports pitches, refurbished science laboratories, a Sixth Form Centre and a multi-purpose auditorium. The School benefits from proximity to stimulating cultural and intellectual events in Manchester and its universities. Instrumental and Speech & Drama lessons are optional extras.

Further details and a prospectus are available from The Registrar.

Charitable status. Manchester High School for Girls Foundation is a Registered Charity, number 532295. The aim of the charity is the provision and conduct in Manchester of a day school for girls.

Manor House School

Manor House Lane Little Bookham Surrey KT23 4EN
Tel: (01372) 458538

Motto: *To Love is to Live*

Governors:
Chairman: Mr R F C Zamboni, FCA
Vice-Chairman and Treasurer: Mr R L Jennings, BSc, FCA, FTII, ATT

Dr M L Birtwistle, MB, BS, DA
Mr R E Blackmore, FRICS
Mr J Bostock, FCMA
Miss S Bradley, BA (Hons), PGCE
Mr W Broughton, MA
Miss J Brown, BD
Mr M J Easun
Lady Hunt
Mr L Kaczykowski (*Parent Governor*)
Mr I McArdle, MA, RA, RIBA, FRSA
Mrs L A Mendes, BA (Hons)
Mrs J Paterson (*Parent Governor*)
Mrs J Phiri, Froebel CertEd
Mrs P Voy, RGN

***Headmistress:* Mrs L A Mendes**, BA (Hons)

Deputy Headmistress: Mrs A Morris, BSc (Hons), PGCE

Senior Mistress: Mrs P Stribley, BA (Hons)

Senior Department:

Religious Studies:
Mrs M Williams, BA (Hons), PGCE
Miss M Collett, BEd (Hons)

Art:
Mrs T Williams, BA (Hons), PGCE

Biology:
Mrs J Hall, BSc, PGCE

Chemistry:
Mrs G Gibson, BEd (Hons), CertEd

Computers:
Miss T Barton, BA (Hons), PGCE

Drama:
Mrs S Roberts, LAMDA
Mrs J Sinnamon

English:
Mrs W Boulton, BA (Hons), BEd (Hons)
Mrs P Stribley, BA (Hons)

French:
Mrs L Hulme, MA, DipEd, PGCE
Mrs E Landon, MA (Oxon), PGCE
Mrs J Lelong, Dip Bilingual Studies

Geography:
Mrs J Elkes BA (Hons), PGCE

German:
Mrs M Darke, BA (Hons), PGCE

History:
Mrs M Parkhouse, BA (Hons), PGCE

Home Economics:
Mrs K Tercan, BEd (Hons)

Latin:
Mrs E Rogers, BA (Hons), CertEd

Mathematics:
Mrs A Morris, BSc (Hons), PGCE
Mrs J Nelson, BSc (Hons), PGCE

Music:
Miss L Macaulay, ARCM, CertEd
and 9 Peripatetic staff

Physics:
Mrs H Broadhurst, BSc (Hons), PGCE

Physical Education:
Miss S Munro, BA (Hons), PGCE
Miss C Poultney, BEd (Hons)

Junior Department Staff:

Mrs J Cho, BEd (Hons)
Mrs A Coleman, CertEd
Miss E Denby, BEd (Hons)
*Miss J Gay, BA (Hons), PGCE
Mrs P Harryman, CertEd
Mrs V Kyte
Miss C Mayhook, BA (Hons), PGCE
Mrs C Polley, BA (Hons)
Mrs I Rodwell, BEd (Hons)
Mrs A Taylor, BA (Primary Education)
Miss J Thompson, BEd (Hons)
Miss C Voy, BA(Ed) (Hons)

Boarding House Staff:

Mrs A Plugge
Mrs K Wood, SRN
Miss E Denby, BEd (Hons)

Business Manager and Company Secretary: Mr T Wynne

Admissions Secretary: Mrs J Clifford

Manor House is an independent school for girls between the ages of 2 and 16 years. Founded in 1927, the school is a charitable trust situated in a Georgian building and set in seventeen acres of parkland within easy distance of London. Our own minibuses meet the trains at Effingham Junction station and collect pupils from other points before school each day. Manor House is a day school with a day boarding system (8 am to 8 pm).

The School has three new Science Laboratories and a recently completed multi-purpose hall. The School has an open-air heated swimming pool and five tennis courts, two of which are floodlit, with all-weather surfaces. The grounds have hockey and rounders pitches.

The girls follow a wide curriculum throughout their school career and generally take 9 GCSE subjects which must include English, Mathematics, Science and a modern language. Girls are expected to partake fully in the life of the school and develop their individual talents in Drama, Music and Sport. Tuition is available for a wide range of musical instruments including piano, flute, brass, saxophone, violin, cello, guitar and clarinet. The school has a successful choir and instrumental groups.

The aim of the school is to create a secure and firmly disciplined environment where each girl can achieve her individual academic potential. Manor House is a Christian non-denominational school but has close links with the Church of England. A Manor House girl is confident and outgoing with a strong sense of values and the ability to succeed in her chosen career. Girls are encouraged to be independent and to take responsibility for themselves and others.

Admission is by entrance examination at 7+ to the Junior Department and 11+ to the Senior Department. Junior and Senior Department Scholarships may be awarded as a result of these examinations. Entry at other ages is subject to availability of places and is determined by assessment and interview.

Fees. (*see* Entrance Scholarship section) Tuition Fees £500 to £2,180 per term; Day Boarding Fee £290 per term; Weekly Boarding Fee £955 per term.

Charitable status. Manor House School is a Registered Charity, number 312063. It exists for the promotion of children's education according to their academic, social, sporting and musical abilities.

The Mary Erskine School
Edinburgh Merchant Company Schools

Ravelston Edinburgh EH4 3NT
Tel: 0131-337 2391
Fax: 0131-346 1137
e-mail: principal@maryerskine.edin.sch.uk
e-mail: schoolsecretary@maryerskine.edin.sch.uk
website: www.maryerskine.edin.sch.uk

Governing Council:
Chairman: Mr Iain Gotts

Clerk to the Governors: Mr J Kerr

***Principal:* Mr J N D Gray**, BA

Bursar: Mr I McGregor, MA (Hons)

Senior School:

Deputy Head: Mrs N S Rolls, BSc
Assistant Deputy Head: Mrs J E R Barton, MA (Hons)
Assistant Head Teacher: Dr D J Waugh, MA (Hons), PhD, DipEd
Assistant Head Teacher: Mrs M P Bryden, MA, DCE
Assistant Head Teacher: Mrs J Dormand, BSc (Hons), CertEd
Assistant Head Teacher: Dr I R Scott, PhD, FRSA, CertEd

Art:
*Mrs A C Henderson, BA (Hons), PGCE
Mrs J A Read, DA, CertEd
Miss F J Lindsay, BA, PGCE

Biology:
*Miss J M Houston, BSc (Hons), PGCE
Mrs J D Fraser, BSc, CertEd
Mrs A L Macleod, BSc, PGCE
Miss C Oxley, BSc (Hons), PGCE

Business Studies:
*Mrs F Monk, BA (Hons), PGCE
†Miss R A McBeath, DipC, CertEd (*Head of House - Appin*)

Chemistry:
*Mr P Wilson, MA (Hons), PGCE
Dr E Murray, BSc, PhD, PGCE
Mrs C Murdie, BSc (Hons), PGCE
Ms R Blair, BSc, PGCE

Classics:
*Miss A E Cowperthwaite, MA (Hons), CertEd
Mrs C D'Arcy, BA, PGCE

English:
*Mrs A Drew, BA (Hons), PGCE
†Mrs A Holt, BA (Hons), PGCE, ALCM (*Head of House - Lochaber*)
Mrs J E R Barton, MA (Hons), CertEd
Mrs M P Bryden, MA, CertEd
†Miss C S Firth, MA (Hons), PGCE (*Head of House - Torridon*)
Mrs C Gray, MA, CertEd (*Careers*)
Ms L Rickis, MA (Hons), PGCE
Miss L Marshall, BA (Hons), PGCE
Mrs M Richmond, BA, DipEd
Dr D J Waugh, MA (Hons), PhD, DipEd

Geography:
*Mrs J A Wright, MA (Hons), DipEd
Ms K S S Nicholson, MA (Hons), PGCE
Miss J F Pollitt, MA (Hons), PGCE
Mrs J Watson, MA (Hons), PGCE

History:
*Mrs E P Trueland, MA (Hons), DipEd
Miss G Akhtar, BSc (Hons), PGCE
Ms L J Buckle, MA (Hons), PGCE
Dr I R Scott, MA (Hons), PhD, FRSA, CertEd

Home Economics:
*Miss Y McCann, MSc
Mrs N L Murray, BA, PGCE

Mathematics:
Mrs J Dormand, BSc (Hons), CertEd
Mrs J Fritchley-Simpson, BSc, PGCE, PGDip
Mrs K L Munro, MA (Hons), DipEd
Mrs N S Rolls, BSc
Mrs D H Sharp, MA, BSc (Hons), DipEd, LRAM
Ms P Wilson, BSc (Hons), PGCE
Miss J Summers, BSc (Hons), PGCE

Modern Languages:
*Mr M G Chittleburgh, MA (Hons), DipEd
Mrs S Old, MA (Hons), DipEd
Ms J H Bremner, MA (Hons), PGCE
Mrs G H Dixon, MA (Hons), PGCE
Mrs E R Hyslop, MA (Hons), DipEd
†Mrs J Lowe, MA (Hons), CertEd (*Head of House - Kintyre*)
Mrs M L Thornton, MA, DipEd
Mrs A T Mallon, MA (Hons), PGCE
†Mrs P McInally, BA (Hons), PGCE (*Head of House - Ettrick*)
Miss J Scott, MA (Hons), PGCE

Music:
*Mrs M H Mitchell, LRAM, DipEdMus
Mrs S Headden, DRSAM, DipEd

Physical Education:
*Mrs V G Thomson, BEd, BSc
Mrs L C Thomas, DPE
Mrs S Borthwick, BEd
Miss F Gardner, BA, PGCE
Mrs J L Brown, BEd
Mrs K A Mundell, BEd
Miss C Lampard, BEd

Physics:
*Mr J Herbison, BSc (Hons), DipEd
†Mrs M A Fotheringhame, BSc (Hons), PGCE (*Head of House - Galloway*)
Mrs M Marshall, MSc, PGCE

Religious Studies:
Mrs V Walker, BSc, BD, PGCE

Technology:
*Mr D K Bowen, BA (Hons), ATC
Miss C A Boyle, BSc (Hons), PGCE, MSc

Learning Support:
Mrs M Brown, MA (Hons), DipEd, DipEdPsych
Mrs B J Wright, BSc, RSADip

Junior School:

Head Master: Mr B D Lewis, BA
Deputy Head: to be appointed
Deputy Head (Early Education): Mrs M M Rycroft, DipCe

The Mary Erskine School was founded by Mary Erskine and the Company of Merchants of the City of Edinburgh in 1694. It is therefore one of the oldest schools in the UK endowed specifically for girls. Known in its early years as 'The Merchant Maiden Hospital', its aims were to educate and care for the daughters of City Burgesses who found themselves in reduced circumstances. Throughout its history, the school has been administered by the Edinburgh Merchant Company. In November 1989 this authority was devolved to the Erskine Stewart's Melville Governing Council.

The school, named the Mary Erskine School in 1944 to mark the 250th anniversary of its foundation, has been housed on various sites in the city - the Cowgate, Bristo, Lauriston and Queen Street - and the buildings are depicted on the engraved glass panels in the entrance hall and on the far wall of the Assembly Hall.

Since 1978 the school has been twinned with Daniel Stewart's and Melville College, Queensferry Road. Through this arrangement, the Senior Schools are separate and single-sex but are each led by the Principal, while all the girls and boys below the age of 12 are educated together in The Mary Erskine and Stewart's Melville Junior School. Pupils from each school come together in the Combined Cadet Force, in orchestras, choirs, drama and musicals and in numerous outdoor education projects.

The Mary Erskine & Stewart's Melville Junior School. (1,176 pupils). Girls and boys are educated together from 3 to 12. The Preparatory and Nursery Department (up to Primary 3) is situated in the Mary Erskine School grounds at Ravelston, where a new Nursery and Preparatory building was opened in 1991, while boys and girls from Primary 4 to Primary 7 are taught on the Stewart's Melville site at Queensferry Road. Normal entry points are Nursery, Primary 1, Primary 4 and Primary 6. The school is remarkable for the breadth of its educational programme and the quality of its cultural activities.

The Senior School (671 Girls – 646 day, 25 boarders). The school curriculum corresponds predominantly with practice in Scotland. Girls generally sit the public examinations prescribed by the Scottish Qualifications Authority.

Forms I and II follow a broad curriculum, whereby girls are equipped to pursue all routes to Standard Grade. In Form III girls commence eight Standard Grade courses, including English, Mathematics, a modern language, at least one Science, a "humanities" subject. In Form V the majority of girls take 5 subjects at Higher level. Girls are expected to achieve their full potential by the well established Learning Support Department. The majority will continue their studies for a Sixth Year, usually for the Advanced Higher, to provide a firm foundation for degree courses in Scotland and England. Most girls proceed to such courses.

In October 1966 the school moved to purpose-built accommodation on the magnificent 38 acre site adjoining Ravelston House. The playing fields at Ravelston underpin a fine tradition in hockey and tennis. The school buildings command splendid views of the nearby city and castle. Physical Education facilities include two gymnasia, grass hockey pitches and running track, an excellent all-weather hockey pitch, and two groups of hard tennis courts. A state-of-the-art astroturf hockey pitch was constructed in 1998 and a Sports Hall was completed in 2000. In 1991 a well-equipped Technology Centre was opened by HRH Prince Philip, the Duke of Edinburgh. 1996 saw the opening of The Pavilion, a splendid new facility which provides the Sixth Year girls with a Common Room and Study Area during the week and also is available to parents and friends as a coffee area on Saturday mornings and other times when sports events take place.

The Science block was completely refurbished in the 1996/97 session, providing 8 laboratories, 2 preparation rooms, 3 staff bases and a chemical store.

In 1997 the Art Department was completely refurbished. The girls enjoy first class facilities which help them develop diverse artistic talents. There is a specially designated area for Form VI girls, many of whom proceed to Art colleges, as well as dark room facilities for keen photographers.

The Music Department possesses fine facilities in Ravelston House and the school enjoys a notable reputation for the quality and range of its musical activities. The attractive School Hall offers good facilities for drama and there are frequent productions involving girls of all ages.

The Combined Cadet Force comprises an army and an airforce section. Girls are regularly selected for the Shooting VIII which competes annually at Bisley. The combined Pipe Band has an international reputation and girls in the Highland Dancing team also achieve frequent success in competition. Many girls participate in the Duke of Edinburgh Award Scheme, as well as in hillwalking and other forms of outdoor recreation. Each week the school offers to girls a variety of extra-curricular clubs and societies ranging from curling to cross-stitch.

The school has a sophisticated system of Guidance. Form I tutors, led by the Head of Year, help girls to make the transition from Junior School to Senior School a happy experience. During the next four years girls belong to one of six 'vertical' houses. The Head of House liaises closely with colleagues on each girl's academic progress, teaches the personal and social education programme received by girls in the house and encourages each girl to derive a maximum benefit from the school's extra-curricular programme. The sixth year is a genuinely co-educational experience, both academically and pastorally, in partnership with the sixth formers of Stewart's Melville College. Each student belongs to a co-educational tutor group. While girls sustain their loyalty and commitment to The Mary Erskine School, they are equally at home in the Sixth Year Centre of the boys' school. We see Form VI as a preparation for university, when girls and boys assume greater responsibility for their academic programme and their career aspirations. All girls in the school receive guidance and help from the well-established careers department.

A boarding house (Erskine House) was opened in 1981 with accommodation for approximately 30 girls in small, brightly decorated, study/bedroom units. The girls share dining and recreational facilities with the Stewart's Melville boarders in Dean Park House.

Fees. Termly tuition fees range from £1,194 (Nursery) to £1,818 (Senior School). A full school lunch is provided for all girls who opt for it, in which case an adjusted composite fee is charged to parents. The Senior School boarding-and-tuition fee is £3,808 per term.

Awards. Two Dux Prizes and University Bursaries are awarded annually to girls in Form VI for outstanding academic work. The Jubilee Scholarship, endowed by the Former Pupils' Guild, and the 240th Anniversary Prize are awarded annually to girls moving from Form V to Form VI.

There are three Entrance Scholarships, one Mackay Scholarship, one Wolfson Scholarship and one Merchant Company Schools Appeal Scholarship with a value of up to 40% of fees. There are also a number of Mary Erskine

Academic Awards. Application forms and full particulars can be obtained from the Principal. There are also two Travelling Scholarships.

There are a number of means-tested academic bursaries for pupils who apply for entry at any stage.

The Mary Erskine School Former Pupils' Guild. - *Secretary:* Mrs J Ferrington, The Mary Erskine School, Ravelston, Edinburgh EH4 3NT.

Charitable status. The Merchant Company Education Board is a Registered Charity, number Ed CR4551A. It is a leading charitable school in the field of Junior and Secondary education.

Marymount International School

George Road Kingston upon Thames Surrey KT2 7PE
Tel: 020 8949 0571
Fax: 020 8336 2485
e-mail: admissions@marymount.kingston.sch.uk
website: www.marymount.kingston.sch.uk

An Independent boarding and day school for girls aged 11–18. A member of GSA, ECIS and MSA (USA).

Headmistress: **Sister Rosaleen Sheridan,** RSHM, MSc Psychology and Social Sciences (University of Dublin)

Number of Pupils. 210, including 104 boarders.

Established in 1955 by the Sisters of the Sacred Heart of Mary, Marymount International School is an independent day and boarding school for girls, aged 11–18 (grades 6–12), representing approximately forty different nationalities. The school is within a half-hour's drive of Heathrow Airport and conveniently located for M25/A3 road links.

The school aims to provide an intellectually stimulating and emotionally secure environment in which the academic, social and personal needs of each individual student may be met. Education is seen as a continuous process of growth in awareness and development towards maturity in preparation for participation in the world community. Small classes enable students to attain their full personal and academic potential. Each student's schedule is individually tailored to the subjects she wishes to follow. The overall student:teacher ratio is 12:1 and the average class size numbers 14 students.

Entry requirements and procedures. Previous reports, teachers' recommendations and interview.

Facilities in the beautiful seven-acre campus include a £1 million block which comprises Library, Computer Centre and classrooms, as well as a Sports Hall, Auditorium, Art Studio, Language Laboratory, Science Centre, Music Centre, Design Technology Centre and tennis courts. A new boarding wing was completed in 1995 incorporating additional facilities for day and boarding students alike.

An integral part of the school programme each year is the option to visit a variety of foreign locations to learn about the history and culture of the area. For 2001 the choice was Greece and Les Collons (Switzerland).

Examinations. Students are prepared for the International Baccalaureate Diploma (ages 17/18, grades 11–12) by the IB Middle Years Programme (ages 11–16, grades 6–10). Marymount was the first British school to be accepted to teach the MYP, and now offers students an IB curriculum from ages 11–18 (grades 6–12).

The IB diploma syllabus leads to UK university admission and US college credit. On average, ninety-eight percent of graduates go on to third level education in the UK and abroad.

Fees per Term (2001/2002). Day students £3,210 (grades 6–8) – £3,566 (grades 9–12); Five-day boarders £3,546 to £3,665; Seven-day boarders £3,626 to £3,745.

Charitable status. The Institution of the Religious Sisters of the Sacred Heart of Mary Immaculate Virgin is a Registered Charity, number 228365. It exists for the promotion of education.

The Maynard School
(Sir John Maynard's Foundation)

The Maynard School Exeter EX1 1SJ
Tel: (01392) 273417
Fax: (01392) 496199
e-mail: office@maynard.co.uk
website: www.maynard.co.uk

Endowed 1658.

The Governors:

Appointed by the Governing Body of St John's Hospital:
R Dunsford, Esq
Mrs K Gardner
Mrs J P Regan
R D Thomas, Esq, FRICS, FAAV (*Chairman*)

Co-opted by the Governors:
Mrs V M Clarke
Mrs C Harding
Mrs T Murray

Appointed by the Exeter City Council:
P J Brock, Esq
Mrs J Jones
Prof M R Macnair
G A F Owens, Esq
Mrs J M Richardson

Appointed by the Devon County Council:
Mrs D Bess
B C J Hughes, Esq

Parent Governors:
J Hopkins, Esq
Dr C Sheldon

Staff Governors:
Miss L Millar
Mrs P Wilks

The Right Worshipful, The Mayor of Exeter (*ex-officio*)

Clerk to the Governors: T A Hughes-Parry, Esq

Headmistress: **Dr Daphne West**, BA, PhD, LTCL

Deputy Head: Mrs A Boyce, BSc (Exeter) *Biology*

Senior Mistress: Miss M Ellis, MA (Cambridge) *Physics*

Head of Junior Department: Mrs F Goulder, CertEd *Mathematics*

Head of Sixth Form: Mrs P Wilks, MA (Oxford) *History*

Staff:
Dr A A Allen, BSc, PhD (London) *Chemistry*
Miss G Bailey, BSc (Manchester) *Physics*
Mrs G Batting, BEng (Exeter) *Chemistry/Physics*
Dr J Burgess, BA, PhD (Reading) *Classics*
Mrs M H Coaton, MA (Oxford) *French*
Mrs I T Colley, BEd Hons (*Lang & Litt*), MA (*Contemporary Drama*), LRAM (*Speech & Drama*)
Mrs G Dunton, BA (Open) *Junior Department*
Mr C J Earle, BA, (Open), FIMA *Mathematics*
Mrs J Elson, BSc, MPhil (London) *Geography*
Mrs S Fanous, BEd (Keele) *Home Economics*
Mrs C M Gabbitass, BSc (Loughborough) *PE*

Mrs A J Horton, BSc (Exeter) *Mathematics*
Mr N V Horton, BA (Bristol), ARCM *Music*
Mrs S Hurved, BSc (Exeter) *Chemistry*
Mr S Janssens, BA (Birmingham) *Classics/History/English*
Mrs C M Jenking, BSc (London), CBiol, MIBiol *Biology*
Mrs R Z Langley, MA (Wales) *English and Drama*
Dr P Le Gallez, BA (Bristol), MA, PhD (*Exeter*) *English*
Mrs J M MacBryde, BSc (London) *ICT*
Mrs V Martin, BA (Hull) *English*
Mrs L Masson, BSc (Pietermaritzburg), PGCE (Exeter) *Junior Department*
Miss L Millar, BEd (Belfast) *PE*
Miss S Reeder, BSc (Swansea) *Biology*
Mrs C Roche, BSc (Exeter) *Mathematics*
Miss N Rogers, BA (Exeter) *Religious Education*
Mrs C Rowe, DipEd (Edinburgh) *Junior Department*
Dr P Rudling, BA (Cambridge), PhD *Psychology*
Mrs F Smart, BSc (Exeter) *Mathematics*
Mrs M Tudge, BEd (Exeter) *Art*
Mrs W Weir-Jones, BSc (Bath) *Home Economics*
Mrs J West, BA (Wimbledon School of Art) *Art*
Mrs P Wilks, MA (Oxford) *History*
Mrs S Wood, BA (Exeter) *PE*

Part-time Staff:
Mrs C L Austin, GRSM, LRAM *Music*
Mrs M E Cameron, L-ès-L (Paris and Lille) *French*
Mrs J Dawick, BA (London) *History*
Mr C Dunlop, BA (Durham) *German*
Mrs A Govier, BA (Exeter) *Spanish*
Mrs G Hedges, BSc (Exeter) *Design Technology*
Mrs J M MacBryde, BSc (London) *ICT*
Mrs M McKenzie, MA (Munich) *German*
Miss D Middleton, BA (London), ATCL *Music*
Miss J Periss, BSc (University of Wales) *Junior Department*
Mrs O Saunders *French Assistant*
Mrs K Smiley, BA (Oxford) *Classics*
Mrs V Smithers *Speech & Drama*
Mrs J Tew, DipGraph (Hamburg) German Assistant
Mrs G Wade, BA (Open) *History*
Miss S Way, BEd (Goldsmiths) *Performing Arts*
Mrs D Williams, BA (St Paul's & St Mary's, Cheltenham) *Geography*
Mrs M Williams *Spanish Assistant*
Mrs S Woolley, MA (Oxford) *French*
Mrs A Wride, BA (Exeter) *Economics*

In addition there are 13 Visiting Music Staff and 4 Visiting Coaches for extra-curricular activities.

School Secretary: Mrs G West

Assistant Secretaries: Mrs T Taylor, Mrs C Waugh

Domestic Bursar: Miss J Beever

Marketing Officer: Mrs S Bromwich, BA (Exeter)

Medical Officer of Health: Dr C Sheldon

School Counsellor: Mrs P Lawford, Diploma in Counselling

Ethos. A warm-hearted, challenging school for able girls, the Maynard provides a rich breadth of curriculum and encourages individual talent and confidence. It is non-denominational and values the contribution made by pupils of other faiths. A daily Assembly is held, and the spiritual and moral development of each pupil is furthered by a carefully-planned pastoral programme. Extra-curricular activities foster concern for others as well as the development of personal giftedness in Music, Art, Drama, Sport etc.

Numbers. There are approximately 480 day girls in the School – 280 in the Main School and 90 in the Junior School. The Sixth Form numbers 120 girls. Help with fees is available through Governors' Assisted Places – up to 10 each year.

Curriculum. The curriculum is academically strong, maintaining a good balance between Arts and Science subjects. Music, Drama and Sport are particular strengths; full scope is given to creative and practical activities, as well as IT skills. The School prepares all girls for the Universities, especially Oxford and Cambridge. A carefully developed programme of careers advice, begun at 13+ and continuing through to the Sixth Form, ensures that all pupils are individually guided in subject options etc with their long-term career interests at heart.

School Buildings. The School is situated in an attractive conservation area five minutes from the centre of the City. The extensive buildings include a separate Sixth Form Centre; a brand new purpose-built block for Science (9 laboratories), Mathematics, Design and Technology, and Information Technology; well-equipped Food & Nutrition and Textiles Rooms; Music and Art Rooms; two specialist Geography Rooms, a large Gymnasium, and impressive Sports Hall which provides full-scale indoor facilities for sports. The Junior Department is situated in a detached building in the grounds, and is fully equipped for the education of girls aged 7–10 years.

Admission. All admissions are subject to an Entrance Examination graduated according to age and are held in January each year for entry in the following September.

Examinations. Candidates take 9 or 10 subjects at GCSE (Boards: EDEXCEL, MEG, NEA, SEG) and 3 or 4 at Advanced Level (Boards: AEB, EDEXCEL, MEG). Pupils are fully prepared for Oxford and Cambridge University Entrance.

Scholarships. (*see* Entrance Scholarship section) Up to 10 Governors' Assisted Places awarded annually to applicants ranging from 11+ through 12+ and 13+ to Sixth Form. Wolfson Foundation bursaries are awarded at Sixth Form level. Up to four Governors' Leaving Exhibitions (value £90) are awarded in the Upper Sixth year. Music Scholarship and Bursaries are available.

Physical Education. Hockey (outdoor and indoor), Netball, Badminton, Basketball, Volleyball, Fencing, Dance and Gymnastics are offered in the winter terms; Tennis and Rounders are played in the Summer Term. Training is given in Athletics and regular instruction in Swimming as part of the normal timetable for all girls during the Summer Term. Besides its excellent indoor facilities and the three hard courts in its own grounds, the School is close to three heated swimming pools and an Astroturf playing area, within a few minutes' walking distance of the School. The school has an extensive fixture programme in Netball, Hockey, Indoor Hockey, Badminton, Basketball, Tennis, Swimming, Athletics and Rounders. Teams have regularly reached national standard.

Further Information. The Prospectus, Governors' Assisted Places information and details of fees are available from the Marketing Officer, Mrs Susie Bromwich. Visitors are welcome by appointment.

Old Maynardians' Society. *Secretary:* Mrs Jane Jones, 5 Matford Avenue, Exeter, Devon

Charitable status. The Maynard School is a Registered Charity, number 306726. It exists to provide quality education for girls.

* Head of Department § Part Time or Visiting
† Housemaster/Housemistress ¶ Old Pupil
‡ See below list of staff for meaning

Merchant Taylors' School for Girls

Crosby Liverpool L23 5SP
Tel: 0151-924 3140

The Merchant Taylors' School for Girls of the Foundation of John Harrison Crosby, Liverpool.
Motto: *Concordia Parvae Res Crescunt*

Governors:
Chairman: S G Povall, Esq, FRICS, FCIArb
Chairman of Finance: F C Mercer, Esq, JP, FCA
Prof P W J Batey, BSc, MCD
Mrs E Davies
Clr T R Glover
Mrs S Hetherington, JP
Dr M Hughes, MB, ChB
Mrs A D Pratt, JP, FCA
A M N Scorah, MA
Mrs D Shackleton
Dr R Thind, MBBS, DMRD, FRCR
Mrs J Turner
Captain D A Wallis, RN
K N Wardle, Esq, FCIS, FCCS, FICM, MInstM
R J Walker, Esq, CEng, MIMechE

Bursar & Clerk to the Governors: P S Gaunt, Esq, MA, FCA, The Merchant Taylors' School, Crosby, Liverpool, L23 0QP

***Headmistress:* Mrs J I Mills**, BA Hons (York)

Deputy Headmistress: Mrs J C Moon, BSc Hons (Sheffield)

School Staff:
Art & Craft:
Mrs D Rees, BA (Tex) ATD (Nottingham)
Miss L McWatt, BA Hons (Bristol)
Miss D Graham, NatDip in Design (*part-time*)

Biology:
Mrs J O Leeder, BSc Hons (Birmingham)
Mrs R E Fairburn, BSc, MSc (Liverpool)
Mrs S Rice-Oxley, BSc Hons, (UCNW) (*part-time*)
Mrs G Mitchell, BSc Hons (Exeter)(*Part-time*)
Mrs J Johnson, MA (Oxon) (*part-time*)

Chemistry:
Mrs D Galbraith, BSc Hons, PhD (London)
Mrs M J Williams, BSc Hons (Manchester)
Mrs P Colvin, MA (Oxon)
Mrs B Miller, BSc Hons (Bristol) (*part-time*)

Classics:
Mrs F J M Williams, MA (Oxon)
Mrs A Wadsworth, BA Hons (Durham)
Miss F Gow, BA Hons (Oxon)

Drama:
Mrs D A Wigmore, BA (Wales)
Mrs A Dalton, BA Hons (Wales)

Business Studies:
Mrs A H Irwin, BA Hons (Preston)

English:
Mrs A Stubbs, BA Hons (Manchester)
Mr D Donnan, BA Hons (Cantab)
Mrs G Enstone, BA Hons (Sussex), BPhil (Liverpool)
Mrs M Myring, MPhil (Bangor), BA Hons (UCNW), MA, SDYC
Mrs D A Wigmore, BA (Wales)
Miss H Standard, BA Hons (Warwick)
Mrs D V Butler, MA (Liverpool) (*part-time*)

French:
Mrs Y Whalley, BA Hons (Leeds) *French & Spanish*
Mrs S E Clarke, BA Hons (Liverpool)
Mrs M Tweddell, BA Hons (Liverpool)
Mrs F Menzies, CLA
Mrs A-M Davey (*part-time*)
Mrs S M Thompson, BEd Hons (Liverpool) (*part-time*)

Geography:
Mrs M Hart, BA Hons (Liverpool)
Mrs H M Peppin, BSc Hons (Leeds)

German:
Mrs J Garside, BA Hons (Newcastle) (*part-time*)
Mrs I Callow, Staatsexamen, Heidelberg (*part-time*)
Mrs S M Thompson, BEd Hons (Liverpool) (*part-time*)

History:
Mrs J Nicholson, BA Hons (East Anglia)
Mr S Cox, BA Hons (Warwick)
Mrs P Richardson, BA Hons (Liverpool)
Mrs C Grindley, BA Hons (Leeds) (*part-time*)
Mrs F Miller, BA Hons (Leeds) (*part-time*)

Home Economics:
Mrs B Jones, BEd (Liverpool)
Mrs S Phillips, CertEd (Leeds)

Information Technology:
Mr J Hood, BA Hons (Humberside)

Librarian:
Mrs A Barry, BLib (Aberystwyth)

Mathematics:
Mrs V E Jopling, BSc Hons (Sussex)
Mr M Wood, BSc Hons (Aberystwyth)
Mrs H F Hurst, BSc Hons (Keele)
Mrs J C Moon, BSc Hons (Sheffield)
Mrs A Jordan, BSc Hons (Edinburgh) (*part-time*)
Mrs P M Carter, BSc Hons (Liverpool)
Mrs A Stevens, BSc (Nottingham)

Director of Music: Mrs J Thompson, BMus Hons (Wales), MA

Head of Music: Mrs M L Bush, BMus Hons (Wales)

Visiting and Part-time Music Staff:
Mr D Bridge *Guitar*
Mr J Powell *Brass*
Mrs E Halls, ARMCM, CertEd *'Cello*
Mrs D Kirby, ARCM, LTCL, CertEd *Clarinet*
Miss D O'Hara, GRNCM Hons *Piano*
Mrs T Parker, LRAM *Oboe*
Mr W M Turner, LRAM, TchqCert *Voice*
Mrs K L White, ARMCM Dip *Flute, Violin*

Physical Education:
Mrs A P Stenson (IM Marsh College of PE)
Mrs L Dickinson (IM Marsh College of PE)
Miss E Jones, BEd Hons (Liverpool)

Physics:
Mrs F Rossington, BSc Hons (Reading)
Mrs B A Large, BSc (Liverpool)
Mrs J E Custard, BSc Hons (Lancaster)
Mrs A Jordan, BSc Hons (Edinburgh) (*part-time*)

Politics:
Mrs J Nicholson, BA Hons (East Anglia)
Mr S Cox, BA Hons (Warwick)

Religious Studies:
Mrs M Dodds, BA Hons (Newcastle)
Mr E Wilson, MA (Durham)

Spanish:
Mrs C Y Whalley, BA Hons (Leeds)
Mrs J Doyle, BA Hons (*part-time*)

Junior School 'Stanfield':
Head of Junior School: Mrs K Kelly, BA, DipEd, LGSM
Deputy Heads:
Mrs C M Ashworth, CertEd (Leeds)
Mrs E Hooton, BA Hons (London)

Mrs C Copping, BA Hons (Manchester)
Mrs J Harman, CertEd (C F Mott)
Mrs S E Healy, CertEd (Cambridge)
Mrs A Kynaston, CertEd (Sheffield)
Mrs K MacKenzie, CertEd (Bristol)
Mrs A M H Millen, MA (Edinburgh)
Mrs J Roberts, BEd Hons, (Lancaster)
Mrs L Rothwell, CertEd (*part-time*)
Mrs C Seddon, BEd (IM Marsh)
Miss R Walker, BA Hons (Nottingham)
Miss K Wilson, NNEB (*KG Assistant*)
Miss A Williams, NNEB (*KG Assistant*)

Secretary: Mrs M Kennedy

Resident Piano Teacher: Miss D Hill, LRAM, ARCM

Visiting Music Staff:
Mrs E Halls *'Cello*
Mrs K White *Flute*
Mr A Wilson *Clarinet/Flute*

Administration:

Secretary to Headmistress and School Secretary: Mrs N Marshall

School Secretary: Mrs J Murphy

Assistant Secretaries:
Mrs S Nield
Mrs S Cadwallader
Mrs P Scott (*part-time*)

Lab Technicians: Mrs J Walsh, Mrs R Garvey, Mrs J Heckford, Mrs S Childs, Mr S Coughlan, Mr T Browne

The School was opened in 1888 on the site which had been occupied by the Boys' School for over 350 years; the original grey stone building, erected in 1620, is still in daily use. Extensions have been made from time to time including a Fitness Suite, Science Laboratories and Sixth Form Centre. The Centenary Hall provides exciting accommodation for concerts, plays and as a Sports Hall. The School is beautifully situated in its own grounds, about 8 miles from Liverpool and within 10 minutes walk of the sea. There are Netball and Tennis Courts on the premises and a playing field a short distance away.

The Infant and Junior Classes are carried on in a separate self-contained building near to the Main School.

There are at present 920 pupils in the School. Children are received in the Kindergarten from the age of 4½ years.

The girls receive a broad academic education – subjects included in the curriculum are Religious Studies, British Government and Politics, Information Technology, Drama, Theatre Studies, Economics, English Language and Literature, History, Geography, French, Latin, German, Spanish, General Studies, Biology, Physics, Chemistry, Mathematics, Art, Home Economics, Music (Vocal and Instrumental) and Physical Education. Visual aids and sound and television broadcasts are used to full advantage.

School Fees. Junior School – £1,140 per term. Middle and Senior School £1,656 per term. Junior School – Music, £115 per term. Senior School – Music, £115 per term (subject to revision).

Examinations. Pupils are prepared for the General Certificate of Secondary Education and for University entrance examinations.

The Music Examinations taken are those of the Associated Board of the Royal Schools of Music.

Parents' Association. *Hon Sec* Mrs S Lennon, 1 Holborn Drive, Ormskirk, Liverpool L39 3AR.

Old Girls' Association. *Hon Secretary:* Mrs S Duncan, 'Fairhaven', The Serpentine South, Liverpool 23.

Charitable status. Merchant Taylors' Schools is a Registered Charity, number 526681. The object of the Charity is the provision and conduct in or near Crosby of a day school for girls.

Moira House Girls School

Upper Carlisle Road Eastbourne BN20 7TE
Tel: (01323) 644144
Fax: (01323) 649720
e-mail: head@moirahouse.co.uk
website: www.moirahouse.e-sussex.sch.uk/moirahouse

Established 1875
Motto: *Nemo A Me Alienus*

The Council:
Chairman: Miss M G Platt, *Accountant and Former Pupil*
Chairman of the Finance Committee: Ms J A Jackson-Hill, *Company Director and Former Pupil*
Dr J A Clarke, MB, CHB, DObst, RCOG, FPACert, Cert Accr, BSMDH, DPD, *Parent of former Pupil*
Mrs S-A Dennis, MIPA, *Partner, Public Relations company*
Mrs I Glaister, *Lecturer in Physical Education and former Pupil*
Mr K T Macdonald, CA, ATII, *Parent of former Pupils*
Mr R O Plail, *Consultant urologist; parent of pupil*
Mrs C Turner, *Former Pupil*
Miss F Waymer, MA, *Former Pupil*

The Common Room:
***Principal:* Mrs A Harris**, BEd Hons, ARCM *Music*

Deputy Principal: Miss T Why, CertEd, BEd Hons, CAPS *Personal & Social Education, Art*

Bursar and Secretary to the Council: Mr D Ingham, BSc, ACA

Chaplain: The Rev Canon G Rideout, BA, MTh

Senior School:
Senior Mistress: Miss P S Merritt, BA Hons, MA, PGCE *Geography*

Miss G Aitken, MA, PGCE, RSA, DipTEFL, AMBDA *English, Special Needs*
Mr K Ashby, BA *Director of Studies, Mathematics*
Mrs J Bailey, BEd Hons *Physical Education, Business Studies*
Mr H Barlow, BA, CertTEFL *Careers Counsellor*
Mrs J Bastide, BA Hons, PGCE, DipRE *English*
Mrs S M Bourn, DipArt, PGCE *Design Technology, Art*
Miss K Chapman, BA, PGCE *Director of Drama*
Mrs G Clare, BA, CertEd *Mathematics*
Mrs R Curtis *Art*
Mrs C Dunn, CertEd *Science, PSE*
Miss R Harris, BA Hons, PGCE *German*
Mrs H Harrison, ASA *Swimming, PE*
Miss P Hibbs, BEd Hons *History, English, Religious Studies*
Mr A Hodge, BSc Hons, PGCE *Chemistry*
Mr A Horvath, MTh Hons, PGCE *Religious Education, PSE*
Miss S Hurst, BA Hons *Physical Education*
Mrs J Lambert, BA Hons *Mathematics*
Mrs A Lucarotti, BA Hons, PGCE *Head of Modern Languages*

Mrs J Markland, CertEd *French*
Mr C O'Reilly, BA Hons, PGCE, TEFL *Spanish, French*
Mr P Parfitt, BA Hons, MMus *Director of Music*
Mrs B Power, C & G Cert, CertEd *Information Technology*
Mrs L Pyle, BEd *Physical Education*
Mrs G Y Rich, BSc Hons *School Librarian, Mathematics*
Mrs J Ritzema, BA Hons, CertEd *English*
Mrs S Robinson, MIScT *Laboratory Technician*
Mr L V Schulze, BSc, BEd *Physics, Head of Science*
Miss J Scott, MA *Languages*
Mrs J Taylor, BA Hons, PGCE *History, Politics*
Mrs J A Wood, BSc Hons, PGCE *Geography, Science, PSE*
Mr S Wood, MA(Ed), BA Hons, PGCE *Business Studies, Mathematics*
Mrs C Woodward, CBiol, MIBiol, CertEd *Biology*

Junior School:
Head of Junior School: Mrs J Booth-Clibborn, CertEd, CertEng

Assistant Mistresses:
Mrs C Comber, CertEd, DMS *Junior 2*
Miss S Dix *Nursery*
Mrs J Gough, BA(Ed) Hons *Junior 4*
Ms C Gowers, NVQ, City & Guilds *Nursery Manager*
Mrs V Harper, CertEd *Junior 3*
Mrs M Horvath, BEd Hons *Reception, English*
Mrs W Lambert, BA Hons, PGCE *Physical Education*
Mrs J Long, CertEd *Junior 1*
Miss H Rowe, BA Hons Mus, PGCE, MusEd *Music*
Mrs D Shephard, BEd Hons *Mathematics, Science, Junior 6*
Mrs J Soan, BA Hons *Physical Education, English, Junior 5*

Houses:
Deputy Principal: Miss T Why, CertEd, BEd Hons, CAPS

School House:
Miss P Hibbs, BEd Hons *Senior Housemistress*
Mrs M Jervis, CertEd *Housemother*

Boston Sixth Form House:
Mrs J Markland, CertEd *Senior Housemistress*
Miss J Scott, MA *Assistant Housemistress*

Dunn House (*Day Girls*):
Senior Tutor: Mr S Wood
Tutors: Mrs S Bourn, Mrs C Woodward, Mrs J Bailey

Visiting Teachers:
Mrs B Ashby, GGSM *Oboe, Piano*
Miss A Back, GGSM, LGSM, DipPCS *Flute, Piccolo*
Mrs J Bending, BA Hons, CTEFLA *EFL*
Mrs E Buckland, AISTD *Dance*
Mr J Chappell *Percussion*
Mrs M Cooper, DipRCM(Performers), DipRCM(Ten) *Violin*
Mr P Cosford, FISTC, MBTCA, Level 2NCA Coach, RFU Coach *Tennis Coach*
Miss E Godier, GLCM, LLCM(*TD*), ALCM, PGCE *Clarinet, Piano*
Mrs S Huxley, BA Hons, PGCE *Speech & Drama*
Miss HLatimer *Junior Music Group*
Mrs J Lindley *Dance*
Mrs E J Mansergh, FTCL, ARCO *Piano*
Mrs D Maxwell, GGSM, AGSM *Piano*
Miss R Rork, PGCE, CLCM, LGSM *Clarinet, Saxophone*
Mrs C Stuart-Pennink, ARCM *'Cello*
Mrs E Vegh *Piano*
Mrs A Wilks, BA Hons, LTCL, PGCE *Piano*
Miss A Wynne, BA Hons, MMus *Harp*

School Doctor: Dr K Leeson, MBBS, DCH, DRCOG, FPACert

Senior Sister: Mrs S J Day, RGN, CertHEd

Sisters:
Mrs L Lane, SRN
Mrs I Hatton, RN

Assistant Bursar: Mrs S Weldon

Principal's PA: Miss S Busby

School Secretary: Mrs C Smith

Junior School Secretary: Mrs J Hafernik

Development Manager: Mrs J Potts

Secretary, Old Girls' Club: Miss T Why

Accounts: Mrs J Hollister-Sheppard

Foundation. Moira House was founded in 1875 in Croydon. After 7 years the School moved for a brief period to Bournemouth and then came to its present site in 1887. Its founders, Mr and Mrs Charles Ingham were regarded in their time as gifted pioneers in the field of female education. In 1947 the School was converted into an educational trust. It is represented on the Girls' Schools Association, the Boarding Schools Association and SHMIS.

Situation & Facilities. The School is situated on high ground in Eastbourne, near Beachy Head, with views over the sea. The grounds open directly on to the Downs which provide magnificent walking country and offer opportunities for expedition work and field studies. There are extensive playing-fields with facilities for Tennis, Hockey, Netball and Athletics. The school is a founder member of The David Lloyd Club, an Eastbourne centre for squash, tennis and badminton. We have our own 25 metre, indoor heated swimming pool.

Each subject has its own resource base, double subject rooms being allocated to each academic area. There are also 4 laboratories, 3 computer centres, 2 libraries, a Design Technology centre, a well-equipped gymnasium, an art studio, music studio, and a hall, which can be quickly converted into a concert room or dance-drama studio. We are fortunate in that Eastbourne is a thriving cultural centre containing 3 theatres, an art gallery and a concert hall.

Faith. The School is inter-denominational. On Sundays the majority of the School attends Family Service at the Parish Church and the Youth groups. Arrangements are also made for girls of other faiths to attend their own services. The School chapel is always open for private devotion. The Chaplain prepares girls for confirmation.

Organisation.

Junior School: The Junior School has provision for 120 pupils day girls starting at 2 and junior boarders starting from the age of 8.

Senior School: The Senior School has provision for 100 boarders and 150 day girls.

Boarding Houses: There are two boarding houses, including a separate VI Form House. Each house has a Senior Housemistress and Assistant Housemistress most of whom are teachers in the school. In boarding at the school, emphasis is placed upon a full range of organised activities, both in the evenings and at weekends.

*Day Houses:*There are two Day Houses for Day Girls. Dunn House is for those girls in the First to Fifth Forms, and Boston House for the Sixth Form.

Curriculum.

Junior School: We offer a wide curriculum, whilst preparing for transfer to the Senior School.

Senior School: The formal academic course follows the normal curriculum in Arts and Sciences to GCSE, A/S and 'A' level and University Entrance. At GCSE we offer English, English Literature, Mathematics, Biology, Chemistry, Physics, Science, French, German, Spanish, Latin, History, Geography, Religious Studies, Music, Drama, Art and Design, Design/Technology and Information Systems.

VI Form: A levels are offered in English Literature, IT,

History, Geography, French, German, Spanish, Music, Theatre Studies, Art, Mathematics, Further Mathematics, Accounting, Chemistry, Physics, Biology, Business Studies. A/S levels are offered in English Literature, Geography, French, German, Spanish, Music, Mathematics, Chemistry, Physics, Biology, ICT, Business Studies.

Careers' Counselling. We have a strong programme of Careers' Counselling, which starts in our IIIrd Year and concludes as our girls go off to university. This personal programme of Careers' Counselling has been developed by our Careers' Counsellor, Howard Barlow, well known for his lecture work in this vital area and as author of *How to Pass A Levels and GNVQs and University Places 1997 and 1998.*

Drama and Music. Drama and Music have always been strengths of Moira House. We are aware of the part Speech and Drama play in the development of clear communication and creative expression. Girls are encouraged both to appreciate and to perform. There are a number of School productions and concerts each year, and the school choirs take part in performances throughout Sussex. We also enter the local festival of Music and Drama and our proximity to Glyndebourne gives the girls a chance to have their first taste of opera at an early age. As well as regular class music lessons, there is every opportunity to learn a musical instrument, and the exams of the various musical examining bodies are taken. Overseas tours to Europe and Australia have also taken place.

Physical Education and Sport. There is emphasis on sport and Physical Education. The main sports are Swimming, Netball, Tennis, Athletics and Hockey, and teams represent the School in these sports. In addition coaching is given in Sailing, Riding, Squash, Dance, Golf and Badminton. We have a biennial Hockey and Netball Tour to the USA, Barbados, Europe or Australia.

Activities. Activities are considered an essential part of the curriculum. A wide range of activities is offered, including: Drama, Music, Trampolining, Weaving, Needlework, Pottery, Bridge, Chess, Local History, Library, Sailing, Down-walking, Environmental Studies, Poetry/Play Reading, Table-tennis, The Duke of Edinburgh's Award, the Young Enterprise Scheme and Debating. Girls are also encouraged to be aware of the needs of others. Old people and disabled people are visited on a regular basis and senior girls work with local charities. There are annual expeditions both within this country and to Europe and the School has links with French and German schools of a similar nature to ours.

Health. The school doctor holds a weekly surgery at the School and there are Sisters in charge of the sickbay.

Entry. Entry is by Examination and Interview. For the Senior School the Common Entrance Examination is preferred, but the school does also have its own Entrance Examination.

Entrance to Junior School at any age.

Entrance to Senior School usually at 11–13+ and 16+.

Scholarships/Bursaries. (*see* Entrance Scholarship section) Ingham Scholarships are offered each year for entry into the Senior School (25%-50%) and Sixth Form (up to 75%). In addition there are also Swann Exhibitions, for excellence in Music, Art, Drama and Sport (15%-25%), and Junior Scholarships. Daughters of Old Girls of the School, and daughters of members of the Services, are eligible for a 10% Bursary.

Fees per term. From September 2000: Boarding: £3,725–£4,800. Weekly Boarding: £3,400–£4,300. Day: £1,230–£2,900.

Charitable status. Moira House School is a Registered Charity, number 307072. It exists to provide quality education for young women.

More House School

22–24 Pont Street London SW1X 0AA
Tel: 020 7235 2855; Bursar: 020 7235 4162
Fax: 020 7259 6782
e-mail: office@morehouse.org.uk
website: www.morehouse.org.uk

Governing Body:
Chairman: Mr T Read, BA

Canon V Berry
Mrs J Booth, LLB
Mr M Broadbent
Mr J Davidson, BA
Mrs A Fitzwilliam-Lay
Mr M Greville-Hordern
Mrs C King, BA (Cantab)
Countess C Preziosi, PL (Malta)
Mrs S Taylor
Mr J Wilson

***Headmistress:* Mrs L Falconer**, BSc (London)

Deputy Head: Mr S Fletcher, MA (Oxon), MMus (London)

Senior Mistress: Mrs K Howe, MA (Edinburgh)

Bursar: Mr J Temple, FCIB

Chaplain: Canon V Berry

School Secretary/Admissions: Mrs P Usher

Admin Assistant: Mrs S Queen, LLB

Laboratory Technician: Ms J Kakkonen, BSc (Bristol)

Staff:
Mrs E Allen, MA (Courtauld) (*History of Art*)
Ms A Baeza, LLB, MA (London) (*Spanish*)
Mrs A Blenkinsop, BA (Newcastle) (*Mathematics, Latin*)
*Mrs R E Breakwell, BA (Newport) (*Art*)
Miss H Carslake, MA (Cantab) (*Classics*)
*Mrs F Casalaspro, CertEd (London) (*Physical Education*)
Miss J Crowe, BSc (Aberdeen) (*Chemistry*)
*Mrs C Dawson, BA (London) (*English*)
*Mr J E Drew, BSc (London) (*Geography*)
Mr M Ginever, BSc (Exeter) (*Mathematics*)
Mrs M Haig, MA (Glasgow) (*History, Geography*)
*Mr J Hancock, BA (London) (*History*)
Mrs R Hartley, BSc (London) (*Physics*)
*Mr J E Howard, MA (Oxon) (*French, Spanish*)
Mrs K Howe, MA (Edinburgh) (*French*)
*Mr M R Keeley, BMus (London) (*Music*)
*Mr A Lloyd, BSc (Birmingham) (*Physics*)
*Mrs P A Maudsley, BA (London) (*German*)
*Miss S Mold, BEd (Cantab) (*Mathematics*)
Mrs W L Norman, BSc (Newcastle) (*Biology*)
Mrs V Parrott, BA (London) (*French*)
Ms P Revell, BA (Wellington) (*Economics, Politics*)
Mr N Ruscoe, LLAM, CertEd (Birmingham) (*Drama, English*)
Mrs S Skinner, BA (Aberdeen) (*Art*)
*Mr P Thompson, BA (Manchester) (*Religious Studies*)
Ms V Westfold, BA (Manchester) (*English, Careers*)
Miss A Whalley, BSc (Liverpool) (*Biology*)
Mr G Young, BA (York) (*ICT Support*)

Peripatetic staff:
Mrs T Henderson, ISTD (*Dancing*)
Professor J A Parkins, Diplomé de l'Académie (*Fencing*)

More House is an Independent Day School of up to 240 girls between the ages of eleven and eighteen. It occupies two adjoining houses, conveniently situated in Knightsbridge, retaining many of the original architectural features, but modernised to include laboratories, a computer room, common rooms, study room and computer room for the sixth form, a chapel, a library and a newly refurbished gymnasium. More House is a small and happy community in which a generous teacher:pupil ratio allows the talents of each girl to flourish with all the stimulus and encouragement that she needs. The maximum class size is normally twenty, streamed where necessary in mathematics, science and languages. The majority of girls leaving the sixth form proceed to Higher Education, including Oxbridge, and then to careers in every field.

A Catholic Foundation, More House was opened in 1953 by the Canonesses of St Augustine; since 1969 it has been under lay management as a charitable trust and with a Board of Governors which has always included parents of present pupils. The School attracts pupils from the international community in London and girls from many different nationalities are members of More House.

Places at the school are usually awarded on the basis of an interview, a report from the candidate's previous school, and an examination held in January each year. Girls who join us in the sixth form are required to have achieved grades A-C in at least six subjects at GCSE Level.

Instrumental tuition is available in school and in recent years the School Choir has given performances in Rome, Malta, Madrid and the USA. Full advantage is taken of the school's position in Central London and we organise regular visits to lectures, galleries and exhibitions.

Extra-curricular activities include Music, Drama, Sport, Dance and the Duke of Edinburgh Award Scheme.

The Curriculum. The school curriculum offers a wide range of subjects at all levels. In the first two years all girls study Mathematics, Science, English, French, Latin, History, Geography, Religious Studies, Information Technology, Drama, Art, Physical Education and Music. Spanish or German is added in the third year, giving the possibility of taking two modern languages at GCSE, where the core curriculum of Mathematics, Science, English Language and Literature, French and Religious Studies is supplemented by three further options.

The Advanced Level courses offered are structured around each girl's choice of subjects, new options available at this stage being History of Art, Politics and Economics; further breadth of study is achieved through the General Studies programme. Each subject has its own specialist rooms and for Physical Education the sport and leisure facilities available in the neighbourhood are used in addition to the school's gymnasium.

Fees. £2,530 per term including lunch, textbooks, stationery and some educational visits. Academic Scholarships may be awarded on entry at 11+ and in the Sixth Form.

Charitable status. More House Trust is a Registered Charity, number 312737. It exists to provide an academic education for girls aged 11 to 18 within the framework of a Catholic Day School.

Moreton Hall

Weston Rhyn Oswestry Shropshire SY11 3EW
Tel: (01691) 773671
Fax: (01691) 778552
e-mail: forsterj@moretonhall.org

Moreton Hall was founded in 1913 by Ellen Lloyd-Williams (Aunt Lil) in Oswestry and moved to its present location in 1920. In 1964, the school became an educational trust. Although the school is predominantly boarding, a number of day pupils are admitted each year.

Governing Body:

Chairman: M N Mitchell, MA, ACIS

R Auger, MA
G J Beasley
G Bridgeland, MA
M Deere, BSc, MEng
Mrs J France-Hayhurst, LLB Hons
Mr J M Gourlay
Mrs M Job
Dr J M Marchant, MA, FFARCS
Mrs K Neilson
Mrs D Rylands
D Tucker, MA

Principal: **Jonathan Forster**, BA, FRSA

Deputy Head (Academic): Michael Hartley, MA, MEd
Deputy Head (Pastoral): Diane Rogers, BSc

Bursar: P Lamb

Teaching Staff:

†*Pia Abbott, BA Drama, Housemistress:* Gem House
Toby Belfield, BA, MA *Mathematics*
Anne Brown, BA, BEd
Leslie Cadwallader, BA *Head of History*
Jillian Cantrill, BSc *Biology*
Georgina Copestick, CertEd *Assistant Housemistress, Norton-Roberts House, Mathematics*
Jacqueline Devey, BA *French and Spanish*
Carolynne Edwards, BEd *GNVQ Co-ordinator*
Ian Edwards, MA *Head of History of Art*
Lesley Eyre, BA *Head of French*
Jillian Field, BEd *Head of Home Economics*
†*Ian Fitton, BSc Mathematics, Housemaster:* Norton-Roberts House
†Patricia Fitton, RGN *Housemistress, Norton-Roberts House, PSE*
Sylvia Grace, BA *Head of Moreton 1st*
Pamela Hillier, BSc, PhD *Biology, ICT Co-ordinator*
Sarah Hughes *Assistant Housemistress, Pilkington House, RE, English*
Elizabeth Killen, BEd Physical Education, English, Resident House Tutor: Gem House
Deidre Kok, BSc *Physics*
Robert Knill, DLC *Mathematics*
Karen Malin, BA *English*
†*Anne McCall, BSc Science, Housemistress:* Lloyd-Williams House
Rona McKechnie, MA *Careers Advisor, History*
Richard Meyer, GMus *Director of Music*
John Nanson, BA, MA *Head of Geography*
†*Elspeth Nolan, BA Librarian, Housemistress:* Charlesworth House
Timothy Nolan, BEd *ICT*
Hilary Prescott, BA *English*
Anne Rincon *Assistant Housemistress, Charlesworth House*
Anne Simpson, BA, MA *Head of Modern Languages*
Christopher Steare, BA *Head of English*
†*Sally Tester, BEd Head of Physical Education, Housemistress:* Pilkington House
Carla Tonks, BA, MA *Religious Studies, English*
Tracey Virr, GTCL *Assistant Director of Music*
Paul Warren, BA *Head of Classics*
Mark Whitworth, LSIAD, BEd *Head of Art*
Andrew Wilkinson, BSc *Head of Science*
Geoffrey Williams, BA *Head of Mathematics*

Part-time:

Catherine Ashworth, BEd *Business Studies, GNVQ*
Susan Aston, BA *Latin*
Janet Barlow, BA *Special Needs*
Karen Booth, HND *Business Studies*

Anne Brown, BA, BEd *Geography*
Victoria Eastman, BA *German*
Andrea Greaney, BA, MA *French*
Merriel Halsall-Williams, BA, LGSM, ALAM, FESB *Spoken English*
Karen Hatcher, BA *German*
Eva Jordan *Russian*
Vivien Lewis, BA *English*
Stephen Welti, PTCA, LTA *Professional Tennis Coach*

School Doctors:
Dr J Greaves, MA, MBChB, MRCGP, DRCOG
Dr J Roberts, BA, MA, BMBCH, MRCP, DRCOG, MRCGP, DFFP
School Sister: to be appointed

Entry Requirements. From September 2000 girls aged 9 and 10 were admitted to the new junior department (Moreton First). Girls are admitted to the school, normally in September at the age of 11, either by Common Entrance or by the School's entrance examination which is held at the end of January each year. This examination requires no knowledge of foreign languages and is designed to test potential ability rather than factual recall. This examination can be taken by pupils at 10+, and with supplementary papers at 12 and 13. Candidates from preparatory schools may enter through Common Entrance if they so choose at 11, 12 and 13. Sixth Form entrance is by examination and interview, and numbers are limited. All applications should be addressed to the Principal.

Scholarships. A number of scholarships worth between 10% and 50% will be made to pupils at 11+, 12+ and 13+. Sixth Form Scholarships and bursaries, given in memory of Miss Bronwen Lloyd-Williams, are awarded to girls entering Lower VI or to assist a pupil in the school to complete her education. Awards for Music, Drama, Art and for outstanding sporting talent are made at 11+, 12+, 13+ and 16+.

Curriculum. Going well beyond the National Curriculum, some 20 subjects are available at GCSE, varying from traditional academic subjects such as Latin and the Sciences, to practical subjects such as Drama, Dance and Physical Education. Modern Languages available include French, German, Spanish and Russian. 'A' levels in History of Art, Social Biology, Business Studies and Theatre Studies extend the range of the curriculum as does GNVQ Leisure and Tourism (level 3). Information Technology is a compulsory subject up to Sixth Form, optional thereafter.

Examinations offered. GCSE (MEG, SEG, NEAB, London), 'A' level (Oxford, JMB, London). RSA (Computer literacy), ABRSM (English Speaking Board), LAMDA. Over three quarters of second year VIth form go on to University.

Member of GSA, GBGSA, ISCO, ISIS.

Religious activities. Church of England but ecumenical in approach. Weekday service, longer service on Sunday, visiting preacher.

Academic, Sporting and Extra Curricular facilities. Moreton Hall is engaged in an ambitious development programme and has facilities of the highest quality designed to provide the right environment for the education of girls in the twenty-first century.

Younger girls are housed in the Norton and Roberts building under the supervision of two resident housemistresses and matrons. The building is designed to create a family atmosphere with dormitories split into smaller units, close to common rooms, washrooms and staff accommodation.

As pupils progress up the school, the dormitories are gradually replaced by double and finally single study bedrooms, as girls move from middle school houses to the second year sixth house, Lloyd-Williams. Here, within the structure of a boarding school, senior girls are given the necessary freedom to prepare for the next stage in their career: university.

The new laboratories, Information Technology rooms and Art and Design Centre are housed within a short distance of the central classroom, careers and library complex.

In 1999 a new ICT development plan was implemented to network classrooms, libraries and laboratories linked to a new ICT Centre. In 2000 all classrooms, libraries and boarding houses were networked. All Sixth Formers have internet access from their study bedrooms.

An exceptionally well equipped Sports Centre comprising a sports hall and floodlit tennis courts along with a heated swimming pool, tennis courts, nine hole golf course and playing fields are set in one hundred acres of beautiful parkland at the foot of the Berwyn hills. The school offers a wide range of sporting options, including Lacrosse, Netball, Hockey, Cricket, Tennis and Athletics. Sailing and Riding are also popular.

The Musgrave Theatre, Outdoor Theatre and Music School stimulate theatrical and musical activities ranging from house plays, lunchtime shows and jazz evenings through to ambitious school plays and orchestral concerts. A studio theatre was completed in 2001. Great emphasis is placed on girls taking part in as wide a range of extra-curricular interests as possible.

Moreton Enterprises offers the girls real business experience. Supervised by professional advisers, Moreton Enterprises runs the tuckshop, payphones, HSBC Bank recording studio and new radio station.

Boarding houses at Moreton Hall are all linked informally with houses at Shrewsbury School, pupils meeting regularly for social and cultural occasions.

A limited number of day girls are admitted each year.

Old Moretonian Association. Secretary: Miss A Pinder, c/o Moreton Hall.

Charitable status. Moreton Hall Educational Trust Limited is a Registered Charity, number 528409. It exists to provide a high quality education for girls.

The Mount School, York

Dalton Terrace York YO24 4DD
Tel: (01904) 667500
Headmistress's Secretary (01904) 667508
Bursar (01904) 667504
Fax: (01904) 667524
e-mail: Registrar@mount.n-yorks.sch.uk
website: http://www.mount.n-yorks.sch.uk

Motto: *Fidelis in parvo*

The Mount is an Independent Quaker Boarding and Day School, going back to 1785. Girls of all faiths and none are welcomed, although our intake is predominantly British and Christian. Stress is laid on sound academic standards in the context of a broad general education. Most girls proceed to degree courses at University or elsewhere. Our aim is to educate the whole person and to value everyone. The Mount stands in extensive and beautiful grounds close to York's historic centre. It has close links with the other Quaker school in York, Bootham. There are combined activities for all ages and particularly in the Sixth Form.

Committee of Management:

Clerk: Geoffrey Hutchinson
Hon Treasurer: Sheila Grant
Deputy Clerk: Stephen Parry
Secretary: Anne Bolton

Peter Addyman
Simon Crosfield
Leah Dalby
Sheila Fisher (*Old Scholar*)
Jane Holloway (*Friends of The Mount*)
Brian Jardine
Howard Masters (*Co-opted*)
Richard Platt
Joy Saunders (*Old Scholar*)
Elizabeth Schweiger
Stephen Parry
Stephen Nuthall
Raymond Williams

Staff:

Headmistress: **Diana J Gant**, BD (Hons) London, PGCE Canterbury

Senior Director: Sarah E Hebron, BA (Hons) CNAA, PGCE London

Director – Boarding: Iona J McLeod, TLD University of Cape Town

Director – Curriculum: Sarah Sheils, BA (Hons) York, MA York, PGCE Leeds

English:
Lydia Harris, BA (Hons) Wales, PGCE Keele
Jeni Wetton, BA (Hons) Open University, MA Leeds
§John Keely, BA (Hons) York, PGCE College of Ripon & York St John
§Beverley Wilson, BEd (Hons) Leeds

Mathematics:
Michael W Moon, BSc (Sp Hons), PGCE Sheffield
Denise Hall, BSc (Hons) London, PGCE Glasgow
Christine Andrews, BA (Hons) Bristol
§Bridget Bullivant, BSc (Hons), PGCE Sheffield

Modern Languages:
Jean Drysdale, MA (Hons) St Andrews, DipEd Edinburgh
Janine Von Bertele, BA (Hons), PGCE Nottingham
Wendy A Thompson, CertEd Edge Hill College
§A Susan Snell, MA (Hons), TCert, DipEd Aberdeen
§Christine Clayton, Inst Ling Cert

Latin, Greek and Classical Studies:
A Rosemary McEvoy, BA (Hons) Lancaster, PGCE Nottingham
§Jane Fineron, BA (Hons) London

Science:
Rosalind Fitter, BA (Hons) Oxon, MSc Liverpool, MIBiol
Mike Atkinson, BSc (Hons) Birmingham, PGCE College of Ripon & York St John
Valerie J Hood, BSc Leeds, DipEd Oxon
Catherine Morris, BSc (Hons), PhD London, PGCE Newcastle
Anthony Welbrock, BSc (Hons) Edinburgh
§Bridget Bullivant, BSc (Hons), PGCE Sheffield

Religious Education:
Judith Campbell, BEd (Hons) East Anglia
Christine Andrews, BA (Hons) Bristol
Vivien Moon, BA (Hons), PGDipEd Sheffield

History:
Sarah E Hebron, BA (Hons), CNAA, PGCE London
Sarah Sheils, BA (Hons) York, MA York, PGCE Leeds
Gerry Hallom, BA (Hons) York, PGCE Huddersfield

Geography:
Vivien Moon, BA (Hons), PGDipEd Sheffield
Carol Whitfield, BA (Hons) London, PGCE Newcastle upon Tyne

Art & Design:
Sian Gabraitis, BA (Hons) Bristol, PGCE Cardiff
§Joanne Harmon, BA (Hons) Surrey Instit, PGCE Middlesex

Design Technology:
Rachel Martin, BA (Hons), PGCE College of Ripon & York St John, MSc Huddersfield
§Guy Dixon

IT:
Anthony Welbrock, BSc (Hons) Edinburgh

Music:
Derek Chivers, BA (Hons) York, DPhil Keele, PGCE Open
Sandra J Miller, GGSM (Hons), LTCL, MTC London

Economics:
§Sue Barlow, MA St Andrews, PGCE Birmingham

Sociology:
Gerry Hallom, BA (Hons) York, PGCE Huddersfield

Physical Education:
Jennifer Lyall, BSc Chester, PGCE Ripon & York St John
§Fiona Crompton, CertEd IM Marsh College of PE
§Lynne Marsh, CertEd IM Marsh College of PE
§Judith Pearson, CertEd Bedford College of PE

Careers:
Sarah Sheils, BA (Hons) York, MA York, PGCE Leeds

English as a Foreign Language:
§Christine Morris, BA (Hons) Leeds, TEFL

Dyslexia:
§I Lynn Gagg, CertEd Worcester College of Education

Librarian:
§Rowena White, BA (Hons), DipHE Loughborough, ALA

Tregelles (*Junior Department*)

Head of Department: Jan Wilson, BEd Durham, AdvDipEdMan Open University
Mary Anderson, CertEd Hull
Lynne Atkinson, CertEd Didsbury College of Education, Manchester
Marie Durkin, BA (Hons) Leeds, PGCE Lincoln, MA York
Justine Greenhalgh, BEd Chester College
Gillian Scott, BEd Kingston
E Victoria Smart, BA (Hons) College of Ripon & York St John
Jane Thorn, BA (Hons) Lancaster, PGCE Leeds
Jacky Timbrell, BEd Leeds
§Veronique Weller, L-ès-L

Nursery:
Helen Kingsley, BA College of Ripon & York St John, NNEB
Patricia Brook, GNC
Karen Vasey

Learning Support:
§Mary Elliot

Non-Teaching Assistants:
§Valerie Blackburn
§Karen Garrity
§Win Jones

After-School Care Staff:
§Gillian Finney
§Hilary Fryer

Housemistresses:
Senior Resident: Iona McLeod, TLD University of Cape Town
College House: Jennifer White; Elizabeth Barrell, BSc Aberystwyth
School House: Iona McLeod, TLD University of Cape Town; Nicola Upton, BA (Hons) York

Resident Graduates:
Anne-Marie Hannett, BSc (Hons) Bradford
Jean Stokes, BA (Hons) Aberystwyth

Health Centre:
Angela Wardale, SRN, SCM
Valerie O'Brien, RGN, ONC

Medical Officer: Dr Hazel Brown, BM, DRCOG

Visiting Staff:
Aurélie Breton *French Assistante*
Kathrin Stock *German Assistentin*
Malar Ware *Word Processing/Shorthand*
Isobel Dunn, ARAD *Ballet*
Della Horn *Riding*
Gina Huntington *Tennis*
Brian Matless *Fencing*
Elizabeth Matthews *Duke of Edinburgh Award*
Andrea Cundell, BA *Ceramics*
Lesley Mayo, BA *Photography*
Kim Gibson *Textiles*
Karen Thomas *Creative Studies*

Piano:
Christina Blood, DRSAM, ARCM Glasgow
C Jayne Cole, GRSM, LRAM, ARCM
Kathryn Coombes, BMus (Hons) Sheffield, LRAM, LTCL, PGCE London

Strings:
Margaret Bryan, BA (Hons) York, PGCE York
Susan Mills, BA (Hons) Open

Woodwind:
Colin Allison
Angela Anelay, BMus, LTCL, MA, PGCE
Frances Beatty, BA (Hons) Bretton Hall, DipMusTech York, LTCL
Louise Evans, BA (Hons), LTCL
Emma Leaman-Brown
Katharine White, BA (Hons)

Brass:
Derek Chivers, BA (Hons) York, DPhil Keele, PGCE Open University

Percussion:
Michael Stier

Guitar:
Andrew Normandale

Singing:
Sandra J Miller, GGSM (Hons), LTCL, MTC London
C Jayne Cole, GRSM, LRAM, ARCM

Speech & Drama:
Margaret Hillier, BA (Hons) Leicester, BEd Toronto

Administrative Staff:

Bursar: Anne Bolton, MA Cantab, PGCE, MBA London
Finance Officer: David P Leonard, CEng, MICE, MIStructE
Finance Assistant: Lorraine Miller
Administrative Assistant: Julia Hampshire
Bursar's Secretary: Jeanne R Roddam
Headmistress's Secretary: Norma Wright

Assistants:
Michele Drasdo
Andrea Sparks
Jennifer White
Receptionist: Sally Knowles
Admissions: Gillian Porteous
Marketing Officer: Jane Holloway, BA (Hons) Leeds, PGCE Ripon & York St John
Tregelles Secretary: Elizabeth Farrington
Assistant Secretary: Janet Harris

Catering Managers: Emma Skirrow, Mary Woolen
Domestic Services Manager: Christine Myers
Laboratory Technicians:
Mandy Burns
Linda Oldfield
Maintenance Manager: Philip Paxman
Maintenance Staff:
Richard Smith
Malcolm Turpin
Head Gardener: Kevin Upton
Groundsman: Stephen Midgley

Numbers on roll: 75 Boarding, 15 Weekly boarding, 255 Day.

Age range: 11–18.

Normal age of entry: 11, 13 or 16.

Method of Entry: Interview, School's own examination and former Head's report.

Curriculum and Aims: Wide basic curriculum–Arts, Languages, all Sciences, Mathematics. The School aims to provide a friendly ordered community in which girls learn to work hard, to recognise a sound set of values and to make the best use of their individual gifts.

Extra subjects: (in addition to a wide curriculum). *Crafts:* eg ceramics, textiles, photography, Dancing: as required; *Languages:* eg Spanish. *Music:* piano, brass, strings, wind (Associated Board examinations). *Speech and Drama:* (Examinations of Guildhall School of Music and Drama). *Sports:* eg fencing, riding and trampoline.

Special Facilities: Science and Maths Complex. Music School. Excellent Art and Design Centre. Language Laboratory. Large indoor heated Swimming Pool, Grass Tennis Courts and Playing fields adjoining School building and 2 computer suites. New Sports Hall, and newly refurbished English department with Drama Studio opened in September 2000.

School Fees. Senior School: From September 2001 the fees are £4,265 per term for boarders Years 7 and 8 £3,316; Years 9 to 13 £4,560. £2,860 per term for day boarders. Additional charges are made for private lessons, craft materials, external examination fees, outside lectures and concerts. Further details about registration, offers of places and Awards may be obtained from the Registrar.

Tregelles Junior Department: 2001 termly fees for the Junior Department are £1,325 for Infants (4 to 7 years) and £1,740 for Juniors (7 to 11 years) amd £1,130 for the Nursery class. Government Nursery Vouchers are accepted in part payment.

Composition Fees Scheme. Parents are encouraged to consider paying School Fees by lump sum in advance. This can generate considerable reductions in the overall cost. The acceptance of a Composition Fee Payment is not a guarantee that a place can be offered at the appropriate time, but such payments are normally transferable between schools. Composition Fees may be accepted at any time prior to the probable date of entry and may be supplemented by additional payments either prior to or during the child's schooling. Further particulars are available from the Bursar.

Scholarships: (*see* Entrance Scholarship section) Academic Scholarships at 11, 13+ and 16. Awards also for Music and Art. Bursaries are also available; children of members of the Society of Friends are charged according to parental income.

Mount Old Scholars' Association. *Hon Secretary:* Caroline Bayes, 25 Woodfield Park, Ledstone, Amersham, Bucks HP6 5QH.

Tregelles. Tregelles, which is the Co-educational Junior Department for day children aged 3 to 11 years, shares the ethos of the Senior School, to encourage and develop the potential of the individual. There is a creative and stimulating learning environment which promotes the exploration of skills and the development of confidence.

Academic standards are high and progress is carefully observed. Extension to Nursery and two-form entry at Reception from September 2000.

Charitable status. The Mount School, York is a Registered Charity, number 513646. It exists to provide education for girls from 3 to 18 and junior boys.

The Newcastle upon Tyne Church High School

Tankerville Terrace Newcastle upon Tyne NE2 3BA
Tel: (0191) 2814306
Fax: (0191) 2810806

Motto: *Vincit Omnia Veritas*
Founded in 1885.

Governing Body:
President: The Lord Bishop of Newcastle

Governors:
Chairman: Mrs G Gilthorpe, BSc
Mrs B Bryant
Mrs J M Collinson, BL
The Very Reverend N G Coulton
Mr D Cuthbertson, FCA
The Reverend D R J Holloway
Mr J A McIntosh, MA, FCA
The Right Reverend Paul Richardson
Mr A J Serfontein
Mr P H Southern, FRICS

Senior Management:
***Headmistress:* Mrs L G Smith**, BA (London), FRSA, FIMgt, PGCE

Deputy Head Mistress: Mrs Y Fleming, BA (Dunelm), DipEd Management, PGCE

Headmistress of Junior School: Mrs J Gatenby, BA (Dunelm), PGCE

Bursar: Mr P J Keen, FCCA

Head of Infant Department: Miss J A Cunningham, BPhil (Newcastle), TCert

Head of Sixth Form: Mrs J R Smith, BA Hons (Dunelm), PGCE

Teaching Staff:
Mr A Bolton, BSc Hons (Loughborough), PGCE
Mrs P A Breakey, BEd (Roehampton Institute of FE)
Miss S E Carolan, MA (Glasgow), PGCE
Miss C Chapman, MA (Aberdeen), PGCE
Mrs C Charlton, BA (Newcastle), PGCE
Miss E M Cornish, BEd (Hons) (Northumbria)
Miss J Coulson, BA (Oxon), PGCE
Mrs L F Crawford, BSc (Edinburgh), PGCE
Miss L Dalton, BA (Hons) (Birmingham), PGCE
Miss N Eddy, BEd (Hons) (*Primary*) (Edinburgh)
Mrs A J Emmett, BEd (Newcastle)
Mrs F R Evans, BSc (Cardiff), PGCE
Mrs R Fairless, TCert
Mrs P Y Farrin, MSc (Newcastle), PGCE
Mrs A J Farrington, TCert, AMBDA
Mr L J Fleck, BA (Oxon), PGCE
Mrs W Gardiner, BSc (Sheffield), PGCE
Mrs J Gardner, BEd (Hons) (Primary) (Northumbria)
Mrs P M Halliwell, TCert
Mrs A L Hardie, BA (Hons) (Oxford), PGCE
Mrs S M Harris, BSc (Hons) (Newcastle), PGCE
Miss S King, BA (London), PGCE
Mrs B Mayhew, BA (Newcastle), PGCE
Mrs A J Morgan, MA (Newcastle), DipEd
Mrs J M Mumford, BA (Oxon), DipEd
Miss C Oates, BA, QTS (Leeds)
Mrs C Oliver, MA (Hons) (Institute of Linguistics), PGCE
Mrs C Packham, BSc (Birmingham), PGCE
Mrs K Peart, BA (Sunderland)
Mrs M Quince, MA (France)
Dr D P Raymond, BSc, PhD, CChem, PGCE
Mrs A M Roe, BA (Hons) (Newcastle), PGCE
Mrs J Rollings, TCert
Miss J P Ross, BA (Hons) (Newcastle), PGCE
Miss J Scott, BEd (Hons) (Leeds Metropolitan)
Mrs S Scott, BEd (Hons) Primary (Northumbria)
Mrs J A Spencer, BSc (Warwick)
Mrs J K Thew, BA (Hons) (Durham), PGCE
Miss K Thompson, BSc (Hons) (St Andrews), PGCE
Mrs S Timney, BEd (Newcastle)
Mrs D L A Wade, BSc (Nottingham), PGCE, MEd (Newcastle)
Mr J G Wells, BA (Hons) (Trent Poly), PGCE
Mr P G W Wood, MA, DipTh (Oxon), PGCE
Miss D Young, BEd (Sheffield)

Music Department:
Mrs G M Blazey, BMus, CertEd (Cape Town), MA(-MusEd) (Leeds)
Mr M O'Brien, LLB, LSF, LTCL, PGCE

In addition there are 14 peripatetic Teachers

Physical Education:
Mrs D Chipchase, PGD
Mrs M C Johnson
Mrs D Chappell
Mrs J Gordon

Home Economics:
Mrs H McLean

Administrative Staff:

School Secretary: Mrs N Quince
Junior School Secretary: Mrs B Cooper
Secretary: Miss D M May
Secretary: Mrs M Watson
Bursar's Assistant: Mrs B Cavanagh

Ancillary Staff:

School Nurse: Nurse S Foster
Senior Laboratory Technician: Mrs L Lant
Assistant Laboratory Technician: Miss R Lakey
IT Systems Manager: Mr S Farrell
Reprographics Technician: Mrs J Kirkup
Art Technician: Mr S Valentine, BA (Hons) (Wolverhampton)
Nursery Officer: Mrs J Goodwill
Nursery Assistant: Miss K Bendelow
Auxiliary/Teacher's Helpers: Ms S Beach, BA (Hons) (Northumbria);
Mrs S Glover, BA (Hons) (Durham)

The Newcastle upon Tyne Church High School has been part of Newcastle life since 1885, when it was founded by the Church Schools' Company.

The aim of the school is to develop in every pupil a sense of her own self-worth, a respect for others and a desire fully to realise her own individual potential. We aim to provide a secure, happy family atmosphere and believe this is a positive benefit in achieving our excellent academic results. It is the friendliness of the Church High School, together with its insistence upon high standards of work, behaviour and appearance, which most readily characterises it and upon which its reputation is founded. As an Anglican Foundation the school encourages all girls to develop spiritual awareness and moral values, and to understand and to respect Christianity and the faiths of others. Girls of all races and religions are welcome as part of the school community.

The school is situated in a residential suburb of Newcastle upon Tyne, less than a mile from the city centre. The main building was purpose-built in 1889 and three further buildings –Tankerville, Haldane and Westward - complete the school. The Junior School building, recently extended, is in its own grounds next door and includes a new Science Laboratory, Library, Craft, Design and Technology Room and Infant and Junior Halls. Our Nursery is housed at the rear of Westward. In the Senior School, a New Wing housing Art and Food Technology suites and additional classrooms was opened in September 1999 and further refurbishment plans are already under consideration.

The school shares a two-pitch playing field with the Central Newcastle High School and uses the local swimming baths. The school has an extremely impressive record of success in sporting events. We are proud that a large number of our girls represent the City and County teams in netball, hockey, tennis, swimming and athletics, and that some have been National representatives across a variety of sports. The school runs a thriving Duke of Edinburgh Award Scheme programme.

Academic standards are high. The A Level and GCSE pass rates are consistently in the 90%s. As the majority of Senior School pupils have been in our Junior School, these results are testimony to the excellent preparation girls receive there. Excellent careers guidance and university applications advice means that more than 75% of girls gain places at their first choice universities.

Fees. Registration fee, £20.

Nursery £1,220 (full time) per term, Infant Department and Junior School £1,300. Senior School £1,730 per term. Reduced fees for daughters of Clergy.

Scholarships. (*see* Entrance Scholarship section) At least two 11+ Scholarships, worth 50% of the fees, and three Exhibitions, worth 33% of the fees, are available. There is a Music Exhibition at 11+.

New Hall

New Hall School Chelmsford Essex CM3 3HT
Tel: (01245) 467588
Fax: (01245) 464348

ACADEMIC YEAR 2000-2001

***Headmistress:* Sister Anne-Marie**, CRSS, MA (Cantab), PGCE (Newcastle)

Headmaster of Preparatory School: Mr D Silver, BEd

Deputy Head: Mr D Callender, BA

Bursar: Mr A M D McKechnie, DipNEBSM, IM

Other Senior Staff:
Mr S Woodgate, BSc (Aston), PGCE, CBiol, MIBiol

Heads of Academic Departments:
Religious Studies:
Ms K Edwards, BA (UEA), PGCE
English:
Mrs A Harris, BA (Nottingham), MPhil, PGCE
Mathematics:
Mr C R F Tye, BSc (London), Dip Mathematical Management (*MA*)
Information Technology:
Mr W Chaplin, BSc (APU), PGCE
History:
Mrs C Wren, BA (Warwick), PGCE (Cambridge), MHist (Warwick)
Geography:
Mr T Davies, TC (London)
Language and Classical Studies Faculty:
Mrs A Snaith, BA (Bristol), MA (*UEA*), DEA (Sorbonne)
Sciences:
Dr J Williams, BSc (Sussex), MSc (Bristol), PhD (Bristol)
Home Economics:
Miss J Harris, CertEd (Sheffield), BA (OU)
Performing Arts Faculty:
Mr B Harte, Dip Perf Theatre Arts (Guildford)
Art Design and Technology:
Ms D M Colchester, DipAD, ATD
Economics and Business Studies:
Mrs R Sharpe, BEd (Bristol), BA (OU)
Careers:
Mrs K Wintersgill, CertEd, DipPSE
Special Education Needs:
Mrs A Howarth, CertEd, BA (Open), MEd
Physical Education:
Miss Z Cox, BSc (Brighton), PGCE (Christ Church College, Canterbury)

Pastoral Care:

Housemistresses:
More House: Mrs C Webb, BA (Birmingham), PGCE (Newcastle)
Dennett House: Miss M Morrow, BEd (Leeds), DASE, MEd (Queen's, Belfast)
Hawley House: Mrs M Murray, BA (Open), DipEd (Dundee), DipMaths
Campion House: Mrs P Bright, CertEd (Leeds)
Heads of Year:
Sixth Form: Mrs J Hopkinson, BSc (London)
Acting Year 11: Mrs K Wintersgill, CertEd, DipPSE *Head of Careers*
Year 10: Miss M Morrow, BEd (Leeds), DASE, MEd (Queen's, Belfast)
Year 9: Mrs M Murray, BA (Open), DipEd (Dundee), DipMaths
Year 8: Mrs R Chaplin, BA (Warwick), PGCE (Swansea), BDA Dip
Year 7: Mrs S Strudwick, BEd (Cantab)

Chaplaincy Team:
Sister Diana, CRSS
The Revd A Rose
The Revd J Harvey
Medical Department:
Medical Officer: Dr M Edelsten, MB, ChB
School Nurse: Sister Mary Matthew, RGN
New Hall Voluntary Service:
Chairman: Mrs J Jennings (*parent*)

We believe that New Hall, a Catholic boarding and day school, enables pupils to meet confidently the challenges of the wider world. Here pupils from all traditions are educated in an environment where academic excellence is achieved. This is brought about in surroundings where relationships are based on the Gospel values of trust and respect. Our aim at New Hall is to build a community of faith, a community of committed students, and always to be looking outward to the wider world.

A Broad and Balanced Curriculum. We believe that the key values underpinning the curriculum for each pupil are that it should be broad, balanced and appropriate, and it must involve the student actively in her learning.

To prepare them for a fast-changing world, we introduce girls to a wide range of concepts, skills and knowledge. Our aim is to go beyond the requirements of the National Curriculum to provide a wider range of choice and more depth in studies.

New Technology and Traditional Skills. Changes in the world of work mean that it is vital that every pupil be competent in the use of technology. The school has recognised this and invested heavily in the latest equipment. Pupils use computers to research topics, log data and present solutions. We believe that technology is a tool to aid education and to prepare pupils for life in the 21st century. Girls also need to develop competence in more traditional skills. The library is a multimedia resource centre with CD ROM computing facilities. It is open to pupils late into the evening and throughout the weekend. Here students can learn to use periodicals, to skim and scan books and to extract information from a variety of sources.

First-Rate Facilities. The school is determined to provide first-rate facilities. These currently include: 6 full-sized laboratories for Science; 3 large Information Technology suites as well as the provision of computers in many departments; a purpose-built Performing Arts centre including Dance, Music and Drama facilities in addition to a recording studio; various Art and Design studios in an environment which inspires creativity; sports facilities that are constantly being improved. Currently these include an indoor swimming pool, a well-equipped gymnasium, a sports hall, ten hard courts for tennis and netball and three pitches used for hockey and athletics.

A Community of Faith. At the heart of our foundation lies the faith that is essential to the character of the school. While the school is a Roman Catholic community, it embraces pupils of different religious beliefs. The spiritual development of all those at New Hall, including girls from a number of Christian denominations and other faiths, is of the highest importance.

The Performing Arts. Many girls enjoy the creative arts and benefit from the talents they can develop in this area. Our modern purpose-built Performing Arts centre, Walkfares, allows girls to participate in Music, Drama and Dance within the curriculum and also outside the classroom. Many leisure-time activities take place in Walkfares. Choirs, instrumental groups and ensembles meet regularly to perform all kinds of music from the Blues to Mozart. Girls can film and record their performances in the school's own recording studio. New Hall runs drama workshops for all ages and many of these lead to public performances ranging from major productions to small studio plays. In addition to timetabled Dance lessons, girls can enjoy lessons in Ballroom, Contemporary, Tap and Ballet. The Performing Arts faculty works as an integrated unit and many activities will combine elements of all three areas: Dance, Drama and Music.

Clubs and Interest Groups. School societies and clubs abound at New Hall. The school caters for every interest from the historical to the scientific, and from public speaking to computer design. For girls who enjoy Art, there is the opportunity to be creative with pottery, fabric work, sculpture and painting. The school's darkroom allows pupils to pursue an interest in photography. Girls can improve their language skills by watching carefully selected foreign television and videos.

Activities. At weekends both boarders and day girls can enjoy the many activities organised within the houses and use all of the facilities on the campus. They can also take part in visits run by the Entertainment Society. The school's location close to London and the motorway system makes it possible for New Hall to arrange visits to historic, cultural and recreational sites. Many foreign students particularly appreciate the chance to see more of England.

Day Girls. We seek to integrate day girls fully into the life of the school. We encourage them to stay for tea and to join in the wide range of activities on offer after lessons. The school provides a supervised study room where they can complete their homework. Many travel to school on the daily buses. One way in which we integrate pupils is by ensuring that all houses are made up of both day girls and boarders.

Weekly Boarding. Many parents feel that weekly boarding offers their daughters the opportunity to experience the fun of boarding and the full range of New Hall's activities while keeping close links with home. Girls with a long journey daily and those approaching public examinations find the chance to live at New Hall during the week very attractive. They see this as a step to a more independent life as well as a chance to spend more time with their school friends. Their parents often appreciate the change from acting as their daughter's chauffeur and see weekly boarding as the best of both worlds.

Full Boarding. For full boarders, the school becomes their home away from home. We aim to provide an environment where friendships flourish and girls enjoy companionship and security. The house staff recognise their special responsibility for those who do not have daily contact with their parents. They do their utmost to guide and direct those in their care. Full boarding can provide a stable and secure education for children whose schooling would otherwise be interrupted. It is the logical answer for parents living overseas. However, many girls who live locally also opt for full boarding as it can provide a very special experience of living with others. Full boarding is fun! Many activities are arranged at weekends to keep boarders happy and well occupied. At the same time, girls are given a fair degree of privacy and are given the chance just to enjoy one another's company.

An International Community. We welcome a number of girls of other nationalities at New Hall. Pupils enjoy the diversity to be found within the community. Living alongside girls from other countries offers all pupils the chance to learn from the richness of other cultures. The teaching of English as a Foreign Language is available to support and encourage students from overseas. The extra assistance we provide helps these girls to integrate quickly into mainstream classes and to enjoy their stay in Britain.

High standards of care. There are four houses within the school, based on pupil's age groups: the junior house for eleven and twelve year olds; two houses for the thirteen to sixteen age group and, finally, a sixth form house. This arrangement allows staff to focus on the needs of particular age groups. It also helps girls to mix with pupils from other years and gives them a sense of progression. The house system provides every girl, whether she is a boarder or a day girl, with a social base within the school. The houses are smaller groups within the larger community where strong bonds can develop. A team of resident and non-resident staff provides continuous care for the girls in their charge.

Service to others. The New Hall Voluntary Service (NHVS) responds to the needs of the local community. Sixth Form volunteers lead the action groups. Girls come to appreciate the needs of a variety of people – the elderly, the handicapped, the lonely and the terminally ill. They become aware of the importance of commitment, dependability and service.

Visits, Expeditions and Events. Many older students join the Duke of Edinburgh Award Scheme. The award aims to develop young people not only physically and mentally, but socially as well. Service to the local community is therefore a vital component of this scheme. Girls attend courses such as those given by the Fire Service and the Police. They develop initiative and a spirit of adventure on the highly enjoyable expeditions to untamed areas of the country.

We foster many social and educational contacts with other schools. This leads to debates, workshops, competions at regional and national levels and special occasions including the annual Ball. Social opportunities also include mixed choirs, discos, field trips and combined religious events.

Our staff arrange many overseas visits which take place during half-term and the holidays. These reflect the broad range of interests nourished at New Hall. Recent trips have included the study of business in Prague, art in Paris and classical antiquities in Tunisia. There are language exchanges with schools in France and Germany as well as European work experience for older students.

Careers and Higher Education. The school pays great attention to helping pupils prepare for university and the world of work. There is a programme of guidance led by the Head of Careers and the tutors, who have particularly strong links with the wider community. We believe that all pupils are entitled to comprehensive, up-to-date information on education, training and employment opportunities. The school recognises that girls need a variety of knowledge, work experience and specialist support in order to make informed choices.

Fees per term (September 2000). Day £2,900; Weekly Boarding £4,330; Full Boarding £4,470.

Entry requirements. Own entrance papers, plus reports, and if possible interview. Please note that further information on the curriculum and a copy of the prospectus is available from the Registrar.

Scholarships. (*see* Entrance Scholarship section) Details about Scholarships can be obtained from the School and are also contained in the Scholarships section of this Book.

Pupil numbers (senior school – girls 11 to 18). Day 267; Weekly Boarding 35; Full Boarding 74.

Charitable status. Canonesses of the Holy Sepulchre is a Registered Charity, number A229288 A/1. Its aim is the education of children within a Christian environment.

Northampton High School

Newport Pagnell Road Hardingstone Northampton NN4 6UU
Tel: (01604) 765765
Fax: (01604) 709418
e-mail: admin@northamptonhigh.northants.sch.uk

President: The Right Revd The Lord Bishop of Peterborough

Governing Body:
Appointed by the Peterborough Diocesan Board of Education:
Lady Wake (*Chairman*)
R Alcock, Esq
J Barker, Esq
The Bishop of Brixworth
J Bonner, Esq
M Brown, Esq
E Cripps, Esq
R M J Fountain, Esq (*Vice Chairman*)
Mrs S Hunt
Mrs E Kelly
Professor M King
Mrs S Moody
Mrs C Pearce
M J Percival, Esq
Mrs D Runchman
M Stanton, Esq
Mrs M Young

Appointed by the Northamptonshire County Council:
J Davis, Esq
Mrs M Gaskell
S Ohri, Esq

Staff:
Head Mistress: **‡Mrs L A Mayne**, BSc (Bristol) *Mathematics*

Deputy Head Mistress: ‡Ms C Marten, BA (Birmingham) *English*

Senior Teacher: ‡Mrs L Davies, BA (Sheffield) *German/French*

‡Mrs H Anderson, BA (Birmingham) *Art*
‡Dr C Archer, BSc (Royal Holloway), PhD (London) *Biochemistry*
‡Mr W Asbury, BSc (Sheffield) *Physics*
‡Mrs K Attridge, BA (Leicester) *Design Technology*
‡Mrs E Bevan, (Loughborough) *Physical Education*
‡Miss M Binns, BA (Birmingham) *History*
‡Mrs J Birch, BA (Kingston) *Art*
‡Mrs R Boyce, BA (Lancaster) *German/French*
‡Miss G Brindley, BA (Central England) *Music*
Miss A Buxton, BA(Lib) (Wolverhampton/Cumbria) *Librarian*
‡Miss S Casson, BA, MA (Edinburgh) *Latin*
‡Mr G Chamberlain, BSc (Hull) *Geography*
‡Mrs D Claridge, BEd (Manchester) *Physical Education*
‡Mrs K Corbett, MA (Glasgow) *Classics*
‡Mrs J Coupland, BA, MA (Oxford) *French and German*
‡Mrs K Cowell, BEd (Birmingham) *Mathematics*
‡Mr R Cox, BA (Open University) *Biology*
‡Miss L Cramp, BA (Bangor) *English*
‡Mrs J Davis, CertEd (Ilkley College) *Food, Textiles & Design Technology*
‡Mrs J Drew, BA (Cardiff) *Music*
‡Mrs G Drinkwater, BSc, BA, MSc (Leeds) *Mathematics*
‡Mrs J Edge, BA, DipEd (Cardiff) *English*
‡Mrs S Ellam, BSc (London) *Mathematics*
‡Mrs S Emmins, BA (Leeds) *French, German and Russian*
‡Miss C Fletcher, BA (Northampton) *Drama*
‡Mr G French, BA (London) *English*
‡Mr J Glover, BA (London) *Religious Education*
Mrs Guiberteau, *French Assistante*
‡Mrs P Guy, BA (Open University) *Special Needs*
‡Mrs S Hakes, *Physical Education*
‡Mrs A Halstead, BA (London) *English*
‡Mrs M Haycox, BA (Bangor) *Religious Education*
‡Mrs J Hennessy, BA (Leicester) *Art*
‡Mrs D Hill, BA (Leeds) *French*
‡Mrs H Hill, BA (Kent) *History*
‡Mr T Hoddle, BA (London) Computer Education
‡Mr T Holden, BA (Birmingham) *Spanish*
‡Mrs P James, BSc (Aston) *Chemistry*
‡Mrs I Lamas-Fentanes, BA (Warwick) *Spanish and French*
‡Mrs S Lamb, *Religious Education*
‡Mrs M Langhorn, BSc (Coventry) *Geography/Economics*
Ms L Leach, BA, MA (Nene College) *Drama*
Mrs J Leaviss, BSc (London), BA (Open University) *Mathematics and Science*
‡Mrs J Leech, BA, MA (Oxford) *French*
‡Mrs R Littlewood, BEd (Liverpool) *Physical Education*
‡Mrs A Mayhew, BSc (London) *Biology*
‡Miss J Mollard, BA (Cantab), MA (*London*) *English*
Mrs S Moss, BEd (Keele) *Home Economics*
‡Mrs C Petit, BA (Kingston) *Economics*
‡Mrs R Pointer, BSc (York) *Chemistry*
‡Mr G Powell, BSc (Aberystwyth) *Biology*
‡Mrs P Swift, BSc (Leicester) *Geography*
Mrs C Turner, BSc (Nottingham) *Physics*
‡Mr N Versey, BSc (Warwick) *Mathematics*
‡Mr L Walker, BA (London) *Classics*

‡Miss C Ward, BA (Oxford) *History*
‡Mr R Wells, BSc (Nottingham) *Design & Technology*
Mrs C White, BSc (Nottingham) *Mathematics*
‡Mrs C Wilson, BA (Dublin) *English*

Junior School:

Headmistress: ‡Mrs W Nugent, BSc (Leicester)

Deputy Headmistress: ‡Miss E Savage, DipEd (Leicester)

‡Mrs G Allport, BA (Kent)
‡Mrs J Arrowsmith, BEd (Sheffield)
Miss K Borley, NNEB
‡Miss S Bull, BA (Warwick)
‡Mrs J Cooper, BA (Nottingham)
‡Miss E Galvayne, BEd (Sunderland Polytechnic)
‡Mrs L Green, BA (Manchester Polytechnic)
‡Mrs J Hamilton
‡Mrs P H Jolley, BA (Open Univ)
‡Mrs C Miller, GTCL (London)
‡Mrs L Monk
‡Mrs S Norris, BEd (Cambridge)
‡Mrs E Parry, CertEd
Mrs J Petts, NNEB
‡Mrs R Platt
Mrs J Purvey-Tyrer, BEd (Ripon and York St John)
‡Mrs H Russell, MA (Edinburgh)
‡Mrs O Schumskij
‡Mrs E Shaw, (Birmingham)
‡Mrs J Stock, BEd (CNNA)
‡Mrs J Stone, BA (Canterbury)
‡Mrs S Turner, BA (Sussex) *English/History*

‡ denotes holder of Teacher's Certificate or Diploma

Visiting Staff:
Brass: Mr M Howard
Cello: Mrs C Jones
Clarinet and Saxophone: Mr B Gates, LGSM, BA
Drum Kit: Mr A Faulkner
Flute and Clarinet: Mrs S Clarke
Flute, Clarinet and Saxophone: Mr D Garland
Flute, Clarinet and Jazz Saxophone: Mr P Egan
Guitar (*Classical*): Mr B Duncan
Piano:
Mrs P Dibben, LRAM (*and Oboe*)
Mrs J Evans
Mr P Cunningham
Singing: Ms S Jelley
Violin & Viola: Miss S Cameron, BA

The School, opened in 1878, is an Anglican Foundation Independent day school formerly Direct Grant. Scholarships are offered at 11+ and Sixth Form. In addition, we now offer bursaries to supersede the Assisted Places scheme.

It is located on a 27 acre site on the southern edge of the town. Extensive purpose-built accommodation includes 8 well-equipped laboratories, art, home economics, textiles, information technology, music, design technology, modern languages and other specialist rooms for all curriculum areas. A large library with computer facilities for independent study is also provided.

The Junior School adjoins the main buildings and has its own hall, dining facilities, library and practical rooms for Science and Design Technology. There are computers in all the classrooms.

There are splendid sports facilities on the site. These include a 27m swimming pool, badminton, squash, netball and tennis courts and hockey pitches.

Girls are prepared for GCSE and Advanced Level examinations and almost all go on to universities and other institutions of higher education.

The Junior School takes children from the age of four years and there is a nursery class for three year olds.

Fees. At September 2000: Upper School £1,950 per term. Lower School £1,425 per term. Nursery £1,300 per term.

Old Girls and Associates. *Secretary:* Mrs A Rodwell, Northampton High School, Newport Pagnell Road, Hardingstone, Northampton NN4 6UU.

Charitable status. Northampton High School is a Registered Charity, number 309929. It exists to provide education for girls.

North Foreland Lodge

Sherfield-on-Loddon Hook Hampshire RG27 0HT
Tel: (01256) 884800
Fax: (01256) 884803
e-mail: nflodge@rmplc.co.uk

Motto: *Bene Agere Ac Laetari*

Board of Governors:

Chairman: Mrs S Thorne

M R L Astor, Esq
I Curry, Esq
C Donald, Esq
N Fisher, Esq
Mrs E Hughes
Mrs T Jackson, BSc (London)
Brigadier N Prideaux
The Hon F J Pym
Mrs G Stanley
C H Tongue, Esq

Bursar and Secretary to the Governors: Mrs G Iddeson

***Headmistress:* Miss S R Cameron,** BA Hons (London)

Deputy Headmistress: Mrs C Hamilton, MA (Cantab), PGCE

Religious Knowledge:
Miss J Bowden, MA Hons (Oxon), PGCE
Miss J Smart, BA Hons (Stirling), DipEd

English:
Ms H Morland, BA Hons (Hull), MA, PGCE (Nottingham) (*Head of Department*)
Mrs S J Cooper, BA (Swansea), DipEd
Miss F Mackay, BA Hons (Ulster), PGCE
Mrs S Nicholson, BA Hons (Manchester), PGCE

History:
Mr J N Sumner, MA (Reading), PGCE (*Head of Department*)
Mrs S Collins, BA (Open), CertEd

Geography:
Miss J Davies, BSc (University of Wales), PGCE (*Head of Department*)
Mrs H Freitag, BA Hons (Liverpool), PGCE

Politics and Sociology:
Mr J N Sumner, MA (Reading), PGCE

Business Studies:
Mr P Crouch, MA (Cantab)

Modern Languages:
Mrs E A M Redfern (Université d'Aix-en-Provence) *French* (*Head of Department*)
Mrs S Collins, BA (Open), CertEd *German*
Mrs A Foubister (Instituto de Ensenanza Media Jovellanas) *Spanish*
Mrs D Cook (Université du Mirail, Toulouse), PGCE *French*

Mrs C Hamilton, MA (Cantab), PGCE *French/Spanish*
Mrs I Garbett, BA Hons (Ulster), PGCE, CTESOL *Spanish*
Miss J Smart, BA Hons (Aberdeen), DipEd *French*

Latin & Classical Studies:
Mrs E McGibbon, BA Hons (UCL)

Mathematics:
Mr J Rowell, BSc, PGCE (*Acting Head of Department*)
Mrs P Edworthy, BSc (Wales), PGCE, DipSpLD
Ms C Quirk, BEng Hons, PGCE
Miss E Hughes, BSc Hons (Keele), PGCE

Science:
Dr A Shah, BSc (Nairobi), PhD (Belfast)
Mrs J Ross, BSc (Liverpool), CertEd
Mrs J Kirsch, BSc (Birmingham), PGCE
Mrs A Curtis, BA (Open), BSc (Anglia)

Information Technology:
Mrs L C Hunt, MA (Reading), CertEd

Home Economics:
Mrs J Taylor, Teaching Cert (Manchester) (*Head of Department*)

Art and History of Art:
Mrs P Downing, TCert (*Head of Department*)
Mrs E Alsbury, BA (Trent Poly), CertEd, CertSpLD
Mr A Hosking, TCert (CNAA)
Mrs N Levick, BA Hons (London), MA (London)

Performing Arts:
Miss E Barter, MA (Cantab)
Mrs S Cooper, BA Hons (Swansea)
Mr A Fielding, BA (Central)
Mrs S Nicholson, BA Hons (Manchester)
Mrs G C Fulbrook, MMus (Reading), ARCM, LRAM
Mrs M Lucas, DipMus, CertEd (Milton Keynes)
Miss C Smith, DipMus (Univ of Wales), GWCMD
Miss V Pearson, ARCM, PerfCert(RAM), LTCL

Learning Support and EFL:
Mrs F Harte, CertEd, DipSpLD, AMBDA
Mrs J Jones, BSc, DipSpLD
Mrs L de Albuquerque, CertEd, RSA CELTA
Mrs J Kennedy, CertEd, DipSpLD
Mrs P Edworthy, BSc (Wales), PGCE, DipSpLD

Physical Education:
Mrs N Dangerfield, BEd Hons (Sussex) (*Head of Department*)
Mrs K E McNamara, BA (Warwick), QTS
Mrs T Coussins, BEd (Bishop Otter College)
Mrs R Hill, HND (Crewe & Alsager College of HE)
Miss R Smith, BEd Hons (Greenwich)

Laboratory Technicians:
Mrs S Cocks
Mr R Hopgood

Housemistresses:
Mrs S Nicholson *Buckfield*
Mrs I Garbett *Lydney*
Mrs N Dangerfield *Upper Sixth*
Mrs A Curtis *Lower Sixth*
Mrs H Tooze *Set 1*

School Nurse: Mrs T Elphick, RGN

Headmistress' Secretary: Mrs J Watkins

Registrar: Miss F Mackay

Admissions Secretary: Mrs A Ryan

Bursar's Secretary: Mrs E Burt

School Secretary: Mrs G Karmy

North Foreland Lodge was founded in 1909 in Kent by Miss M Wolseley-Lewis. The school moved to Hampshire in 1947 and now occupies a 90 acre site in parkland between Reading and Basingstoke, and close to the M3, M4 and M25.

Numbers in school: 180 girls. 155 boarders, 25 day.

Age range: 11–18

Method of entry: 11+, 12+ and 13+ Common Entrance with interview, and for A-Level courses.

The school aims to provide a balanced education and to encourage each girl to achieve her full potential, not only in the academic field, but also in sport, art and music. The staff pupil ratio is 1:7. All girls follow a common core curriculum for the first three years, consisting of all basic subjects, including English, Mathematics, three Sciences, IT, Latin, Modern Languages, Art and Music. A wide range of options is available at GCSE AS and A level. There are two careers advisers on the staff and most girls proceed to university.

The girls spend part of the year in Switzerland at NFL Chaumont, the school's centre in Europe.

The original manor house provides boarding accommodation for the younger girls. Various new additions have been built over the years to provide modern facilities, including a music wing, chapel/assembly hall, four laboratories, new classrooms and a sports hall.

Fees per term. Boarding: £5,200. Day £3,200.

Scholarships. (*see* Entrance Scholarship section) A variety of entrance Scholarships at 11+, 12+ and 6th Form level.

Charitable status. North Foreland Lodge Limited is a Registered Charity, number 307333. Its aims and objectives are to provide a full education for girls between the ages of 11 and 18.

Northlands School

Roma 1210 1636 Olivos Pcia de Buenos Aires Argentina
Tel: (00 54 11) 4 711 0011
Fax: (00 54 11) 4 711 0022
e-mail: info@northlands.org.ar
website: http://www.northlands.org.ar

Founded in 1920, Northlands School is dedicated to providing students with a fully bilingual education in English and Spanish to the highest international standard.

Situated in Olivos, a picturesque suburb to the north of the city of Buenos Aires, the school buildings surround attractive gardens and they have been continually up-dated. The school grounds enclose an excellent range of purpose built facilities. There are more extensive sporting facilities at a nearby site.

Highly qualified teaching staff from Argentina and overseas create a basis for a rich and stimulating learning environment and ensure that the outstanding record of academic achievement is maintained.

Number of Pupils: 1,100
Motto: *Friendship and Service*

Chairman of the Board of Governors: Jane Turner de Beller
Vice Chairman of the Board of Governors: Patricia Lopez Aufranc

***Principal:* Dr Susana Price-Cabrera,** BSc, PhD, FEdTC, PGDPC
Secondary Head of Section: Prof Melanie Bulgheroni
Director of Studies, Careers and General Studies: Lic Fernanda A de Moreno
Academic Director: Leslie Fearns, BA, PGCE
IB Coordinator: Prof Marcela Scarone
IGCSE Co-ordinator: Lic Patricia Benmergui

Senior School Responsibilities:

English: Alistair Summers, BA, PGCE
Spanish: Prof Norma Bianchi de Vigna
French: Prof Armelle Maudet
Mathematics: Irene Owen
Sciences: Prof Marcela Scarone
Information Technology Co-ordinator: Alejandro Pedrosa
Humanities: Prof Maria del Carmen Risolia de Capurro Robles
Economics and Business Studies: Dr Raymond Day
History: Leslie Fearns, BA, PGCE
Geography: Anne Smith, BSc
Music: Humberto López
Theatre Arts & Public Speaking: Maria Benaglia, BA
Art: Lucila Linik, BA
Graphic Designer: Prof Monica de Gregorio
Physical Education: Lic Vivian Tait and Prof Moira Pearson
International Department: Lic Laura Lanosa
Extra-Mural Studies: Prof Maria Jose Maciel
Extra-Curricular Activities: Lic Maria Andrea Búsico

Primary Head of Section: Barbara Brizuela, MA

Kindergarten Head of Section: Prof Susan Arndt de Lamas

Philosophy and Aims. The aim of the School is to give all pupils the opportunity to realise their full potential. The School constantly investigates new approaches to enrich the students' education, inspire creativity and to foster a genuine enthusiasm for learning. Great importance is attached to the development of personal initiative, sound judgement and leadership skills.

By offering a bilingual curriculum and an ethos which respects cultural diversity, Northlands is able to maximise learning opportunities for every student. The School firmly upholds its traditional motto of "Friendship & Service" and pupils are encouraged to develop social awareness and to live by a clear moral code.

Curriculum. The *Primary Section* offers a fully integrated English and Spanish curriculum which combines the compulsory elements of the Argentine system and the best of the UK National Curriculum with a strong language support unit for new pupils. Through responding to a wide range of mathematical stimuli and children's literature, strong emphasis is placed on numeracy and literacy, developing an awareness of the richness and creative use of Language together with the practical application of numbers. The key components of Biology, Physics and Chemistry are taught using a hands-on approach with specialist resources. Primary students have access to new laboratories. From Year 1 (6 year olds) instrumental lessons (violin) are an intrinsic part of our flourishing and innovative Music Programme.

In the *Secondary Section,* Northlands offers a fully integrated Spanish/English curriculum that exceeds national requirements. The curriculum has been structured to achieve a harmonious relationship between content and skills to promote positive group work, independent learning and the self-confidence to welcome change as a positive challenge. Cross-curricular school-based projects are designed to develop a range of interdisciplinary skills.

Students are prepared for the International General Certificate of Secondary Education (*University of Cambridge Examinations*), followed by the International Baccalaureate Diploma and the Argentine *Bachillerato.* Provision is made in differentiated courses and materials to allow for varying styles and rates of learning, as well as for the needs of children from other countries and educational backgrounds. The programme is tailored to provide a broad and balanced education and to ensure that national and international requirements for Higher Education are met. Recent graduates have gained places at the Universities of Oxford and Cambridge (UK), Princeton and Harvard (USA) and other distinguished seats of further education.

The International Students' Department caters for the special requirements associated with living and studying in a foreign country. The Department aims to help non-Spanish speaking pupils to quickly acquire a working command of the language in order to facilitate their integration into the main student body. Students from overseas and their families are also encouraged to share in social, cultural and sporting activities.

Physical Education. Physical Education is an integral part of the curriculum and the standards attained are excellent. The main sports include hockey, volleyball, rugby, football, athletics, swimming, softball and tennis. Facilities include the School sports ground in the outskirts of town as well as the sports field, swimming pool and multi-purpose courts on the Olivos site. The Senior teams participate in national tournaments and international tours.

The Music Department has a full academic programme and offers instrumental tuition as part of the curriculum in the Primary Section. Various choral concerts and musical dramas are presented each year and the Senior Choir performs in the provinces and internationally.

Drama, Public Speaking and Debating. Recent activities, such as hosting the 1998 World Debating and Public Speaking Championships, have positioned Northlands at the forefront of these disciplines in Argentina. The Senior Debating Team achieves impressive results at international events, as do the younger teams in inter-school competitions. These activities are bilingual (English/Spanish).

Extra Curricular Activities. There are over 40 activities on offer, including instrumental lessons, sport, computing, photography, horseback riding, fencing and Scottish dancing. There are also organised visits to museums, art galleries, exhibitions and plays. Regular field trips are organised to nature reserves and the provinces.

The International Exchange Programme. The Exchange Programme has been established with eminent schools in England, USA and Australia to prepare pupils effectively for life and work in a global society. The short-term exchanges enable students to visit and study at an overseas school and stay with a foreign family for up to 6 weeks, and in return to host their exchange partners during their visit to Northlands. This provides a fascinating and character strengthening experience for the participating students and is a most effective means of improving their language skills. The interaction with visiting exchange students raises cross-cultural awareness in pupils throughout the School and promotes understanding of international issues.

Facilities. The curriculum is dynamic, evolving to cover the needs of tomorrow's student, with up-to-date Information Technology being used in the educational process at all levels. There are three fully equipped computer labs offering high quality workstations, network access at every terminal and in many classrooms, with up-to-date software including the most popular business and educational programmes. Northlands provides full Internet access to students for their personal research, and private e-mail addresses to all staff and students on campus. After learning basic computer skills, pupils are taught how to use hardware and software as tools for other subject areas such as Science, Mathematics and the Humanities. New multi-media centres have been installed in the Primary Section, the Senior Library, and the Kindergarten.

The School has five excellent Science Laboratories, three of which were installed in 1996 and fitted with state-of-the-art equipment from the USA and UK. There are also dark room facilities, audio-visual laboratory, a preparation room and specifically programmed computers available for science work.

The Library is fully modernised and houses an extensive

collection of fiction, non-fiction and reference books in both English and Spanish. In the Library, many computers are networked to the Internet as well as the School's own Intranet. The Primary Section Library is also equipped with computers and an exciting range of reading materials to complement the Home Reading Scheme and the Longman Book Project.

The Art Studios have the capacity to accommodate a range of media including graphic design, jewellery-making and pottery.

The School Year. The academic year runs from March to December and is divided into two terms. The first term begins at the beginning of March and ends in mid July; the second term is from August to mid December. Each term is divided by a half-term break of a week.

Admission. Northlands accepts pupils from the ages of 2 to 5 years in Kindergarten, 6 to 10 years in Primary, 11 to 13 years in the Middle School and 14 to 17+ in the Senior School. The School sets its own entrance examinations.

Scholarships. Scholarships of up to 50% are available for highly gifted students. Awards are based on results of examinations in Oral and Written English, Written Spanish, Mathematics and Perceptual Reasoning. The examinations are held in October, prior to admission for the following academic year.

Fees (2000). Kindergarten: US$240-540 per month (increases by year level); Primary School: US$560-735 per month (increases by year level); Middle School: US$935 per month; Senior School: US$1,045 per month.

North London Collegiate School
(The Frances Mary Buss Foundation)

Canons Edgware Middlesex HA8 7RJ
Tel: Senior School: 020 8952 0912; Junior School: 020 8952 1276
Fax: 020 8951 1391

Established 1850 by Frances Mary Buss. Regulated under a Scheme made by the Board of Education 6 May 1910 and revised 1938 and by The Charity Commission in 1981 and 1993.

North London Collegiate School provides an academic education for girls.

President: HRH Princess Alice, Duchess of Gloucester

Vice President: Mr Brian Moorhouse, Barrister, FCIS

The Governing Body:
Mr I McGregor, MA (*Chairman*))
Mrs D M Phillips, MA (*Vice Chairman*)

Mr D Abbott
Professor R Barnett, BA, MPhil, PhD, DLitt(Ed), FRSA, FSRHE
Mrs M Bunford, JP
Mr J Catty, FCA
Councillor Mrs J Cowan
Mr D S R Finning, MA, FICA
Mrs C Froomberg, MA, FCMA
Mr J L Hammond, MA, MSc
Ms L Hill, BSc, MBA
Ms J Johnson, MPhil
Mr S N Kamath
Dr M Mays, BA, MA, PhD
Mr J Renshaw, FRICS, FCIOB
Judge G Rivlin, QC
Mr M V Sternberg, MA, LLM
Ms H Stone

Bursar and Clerk to the Governors: Miss V Wall, FCCA

***Headmistress:* Mrs Bernice McCabe**, BA, MBA, FRSA

Deputy Headmistress: Mrs B J Pomeroy, BSc (Nottingham)

Deputy Head: Mr O Blond, BA (Essex)

Head of Sixth Form: Mr J Morrow, BA (Oxon), MA (Wake Forest, NC)

Upper School Tutor: Mrs M E King, BA (Exeter)

Middle School Tutor: Mrs P S Tabraham, CertEd (Liverpool)

Head of Junior School: Mrs D Francken, BA (Illinois), MA (Chicago)

Higher Education Advisor: Mrs K M H Merino, BA (Bristol)

Careers Advisor: Mrs E A Yates, BSc (Salford), DipCGG

Heads of Academic Departments:

Religious Studies: Mrs J M Locke, BEd (Edinburgh)

English: Mrs H A Turner, MA (Cantab)

Drama: Mrs J Podd, BA (Lancaster)

History and Government & Politics: Mr C Vernon, BA (Oxon)

General Studies: Mr M Burke, BA (Newcastle), MA (Durham)

Geography: Miss M Wheatley, BSc (London)

Economics: Mrs G Hurl, BSc (Liverpool), MSc (London)

Classics: Mrs M A Fotheringham, MA (Oxon)

Modern Languages and French: Mrs S Nistri, DottLett (Florence)

German: Ms A M Cain, MA (Cantab)

Spanish: Mrs K M H Merino, BA (Bristol)

Russian: Mrs T Kinsey, BA (Tver)

Italian: Mrs S Nistri, DottLett (Florence)

Mathematics: Mrs J F Huntly, BSc (Leicester)

Science: Mrs C A Stegmann, MSc (London)

Biology: Mrs E A M Hanson, BSc (London)

Chemistry: Mrs J P Mason, BSc (Sussex)

Physics: Mr A P Wingfield, MA (Oxon)

Information Technology: Mrs A E Martin, BA (Oxon)

Design Technology: Mr C Greensted, MA(London)

Art: Mr T Hardy, BA (Fine Art) (Middlesex)

Music: Mr D G Podd, MA, BMus (Cardiff)

Physical Education: Mrs G James, CertEd (Liverpool)

PA to the Headmistress: Mrs J C Dudley

*The pupil teacher ratio is 11:*1

North London Collegiate School combines all the beauty of a rural setting with the convenience of being only a short distance from the heart of London. The school provides an ambitious education for girls from a wide range of social backgrounds. The very best of academic teaching is coupled with the widest range of extra-curricular activities to help the pupils achieve the best of themselves.

There are 1,000 girls at NLCS: 60 in the First School, aged from 4+ to 7, 180 juniors, aged from 7–11, and 760 in the Senior School, 11–18, of whom 230 are in the Sixth Form.

NLCS draws on a rich tradition. It was founded by Miss Frances Mary Buss in 1850 to provide an education for girls that would equal that of boys and produced many of the first women graduates.

The school's academic record is outstanding; the Daily Telegraph described it as the most consistently successful academic girls' school in the country, and it achieved the best A level results of any school in 1999. In 2001 the school was especially proud of its success in having a record 36 girls receive conditional or unconditional places at Oxbridge.

The facilities at the school are first class, designed to offer the girls every opportunity to develop themselves both academically and socially. These facilities include lacrosse pitches and tennis courts and a new Sports Centre with indoor swimming pool and fitness centre.

The Performing Arts Wing includes a Drama Studio for both rehearsal and performance: on two recent occasions the plays the girls have produced have moved on to the Edinburgh Fringe. Music is strong, with opportunity for all to take part in choirs and orchestras, and includes challenging music for the most able with such events as the National Chamber Group competition where the school has won the Founder's Trophy as the most successful competing school on several occasions. On the campus are a Music School, Drawing School and Design Technology Block, all situated around the lake, where waterlilies in the summer make it the ideal place to relax during the long lunch interval. Alternatively, girls may visit the recently-opened library, where they can make use of a huge collection of books, videos and CD-ROMs, now housed in a beautifully light and spacious four-floor building.

The school is open to visitors on 6 October and 3 November 2001. Visitors are welcome to see the First & Junior Schools in the morning and the Senior School in the afternoon. Mid-week visits can be arranged by appointment.

Bursaries. A number of bursaries are awarded to girls who do well in the 11+ test whose parents can demonstrate financial need.

Scholarships. (*see* Entrance Scholarship section) Scholarships are awarded on performance on entry to the Senior School; some are specifically for those talented in Music.

Fees. At September 2001. Senior School: £2,536 a term. Junior School: £2,151 per term.

Charitable status. The North London Collegiate School is a Registered Charity, number 1025776. It exists to provide an academic education for girls.

Northwood College

Maxwell Road Northwood Middlesex HA6 2YE
Tel: (01923) 825446
Fax: (01923) 836526

An independent day school for girls
Motto: *Nisi Dominus Frustra*

Council of Governors:
Chairman: Mr D Dixon, MA
Mrs S V Black, JP, LCST
Mrs S Burrell, BA
Lady Dyson, LLB, LLM
The Hon Lady Goodhart, MA (Oxon)
Mr G Hudson
Mr A Mansell
Mrs S Marris, BSc
Mr K Patel, BSc, MBBS, FRCS(orl)
Mr P Phillips, MA (Oxon)
Mr H Shaw
Mr J Soughton, FCA
Mr K Wild
Mr P J Willoughby, FCA, JP

Clerk to the Governors: Mr C Siggs

***Headmistress:* Mrs A Mayou**, MA (Oxon)

Deputy Headmistress: Mrs E Skelton MA (St Andrews), DipEd (Edinburgh)

Director of Studies: Mr S Brant, MA (Oxon), PGCE (London), FCSM, FGMS, FFCM

Bursar: Mr C Siggs

Head of Lower School: Mrs N Asquith, BSc Hons (Birmingham), PGCE (Bristol)

Head of Upper School: Mrs H Shama, BA Hons (Liverpool), PGCE, AdvDipMaths (OU), MA(Ed) (OU)

Head of Sixth Form: Miss J Jackman, BA (Manchester)

Head of Junior School: Mrs J Johnson, CertEd (London)

Assistant Staff:

Art:
Mr D Edes, BA Hons Graphic Design (Exeter)
Miss F Clark, BA Hons (London), PGCE (London)
Mrs S Deamer, BEd Hons (Lancaster), BA Hons (Manchester Polytechnic)

Business Studies & Economics:
Miss J Jackman, BA (Manchester)
Mr H Jones, BSc Hons (University of Wales), PGCE (Manchester)

Careers:
Mrs C Marsh, BA (Birmingham)

Classics:
Miss S Parnaby, BA (Dunelm)
Mr R Morris, BA Hons (London), PGCE (St Mary's)

Design Technology:
Mrs J Onslow, BEd (Bath), Cert in Secondary Maths (Chelmer Institute)

English:
Mrs B Luck, BA (OU), CertEd (Birmingham)
Mrs C Coveney, MA (Warwick)
Mrs C Evans, BA (London)
Ms S Ahmed, BA Hons (Essex), MA (London), PGCE (Cambridge)
Mrs C Spears, BEd (Exeter)
Mrs L Spicer, BEd (Westminster)

Geography:
Miss J Jackman, BA (Manchester)
Mrs A Spicer, BSc (LSE)
Miss C Foster, BSc Hons (Manchester Metropolitan), PGCE (Cambridge)

History:
Mr R Elliott, BA (Southampton)
Mrs E Ryan, BA (London)

Home Economics – Food & Textiles:
Mrs J Ronson, BEd (Liverpool)
Mrs J Onslow, BEd (Bath)

Information Technology:
Miss K Winn, BA (Liverpool)
Miss C Foster, BSc Hons (Manchester Metropolitan), PGCE (Cambridge)

Mathematics:
Mrs F Teskey, BSc (Aston)
Mrs H Shama, BA (Liverpool)
Mrs C Morgan, BA Hons (OU), PGCE (St Mary's Twickenham)

Mrs P Spikings, BSc Hons (Nottingham)
Mrs J Onslow, BEd (Bath)
Mr J McKenna, BS (CNAA) (Hendon Polytechnic), PGCE (Isleworth)

Modern Languages:
Mrs E Greenley, BA (Newcastle)
Miss C Quirk, MA (Liverpool)
Mr D Ezekiel, BA Joint Hons (Manchester), PGCE (Cambridge), MA (London)
Mrs E Skelton, MA (St Andrews)
Mrs D M Smith, BA (Hons) Applied Language Studies (Thames Valley University)
Mrs C Weeks, MA (Oxon), PGCE (Oxon)

Music:
Mr P J Williams, GLCM, LLCM, (TD), ALCM
Mrs S Gouldstone, BEd Hons (Cantab)

Physical Education:
Mrs P Nunn, CertEd (Birmingham)
Ms S Bisset, BEd Hons (Exeter), MEd (Brunel)
Miss L Nash, BEd Hons (Exeter)
Miss K Summerlin, BSc Hons (Teeside), PGCE (Exeter)

Religious Studies:
Miss L McAvoy, BA Hons (Cambridge)
Mrs G Mead, BA Hons (Kent), PGCE (Canterbury)

Science:
Mrs N Asquith, BSc (Birmingham)
Mrs V Brandon, BSc (Liverpool)
Mr S Brant, MA (Oxon)
Mrs A Evans-Evans, BSc Hons (Manchester), PGCE (Manchester)
Mr D Jensen, BSc Hons (Manchester)
Mrs H Levy, BSc (Witwatersrand)
Mrs G Bignell, BSc (London)
Mrs V Rowntree, BSc (Bristol), PhD (Chelsea College)
Mrs F Sykes, BSc Hons (Leicester)

Theatre Studies & Drama:
Miss C McCoy, BA Hons, PGCE, MA (Central School of Speech & Drama)
Ms S Ahmed, BA Hons (Essex), MA (London), PGCE (Cambridge)

Librarian: Miss M Edmonds, BA Hons (London Polytechnic), Library & Information Cert (de Havilland College), PostGradDip (North London), Chartered Librarian

Junior School:
Mrs J Adams, BA (Hull)
Mrs J Barraclough, BEd (College of St Paul & St Mary, Cheltenham)
Mrs E Bradley, CertEd (All Saints College, London)
Mrs P Cooper, BA (Nottingham)
Mrs M Coulson, AGSM Hons (Trent Park College)
Miss E D'Souza, BSc (Birmingham)
Mrs H Frankland, TCert (Cambridge Instit of Ed), BA (OU), LRAM
Mrs C Jones, CertEd (Twickenham)
Mrs J Jones, CertEd (Rolle College)
Miss J Knight, BSc Hons (Southampton)
Mrs P Prime, Teacher's Certificate (Stranmillis College, Belfast)
Mrs C J Simister, MA Hons (Cambridge)
Mrs H Stewart, BA (Bath)
Mrs M Thomas, CertEd (Bristol)
Miss N Wragg, BEd Hons (Brighton)

Nursery Teachers:
Mrs P Cooper, BEd Hons (London)
Mrs J Read, CertEd (Manchester)

Visiting Staff:
French Conversation: Mrs C Anderson
German Conversation: Mrs C Shirmeister
Spanish Conversation: Mrs C Gauci
Ballet: Miss J Mitchell, LRAD, ARAD
Judo: Mr K Remfry, Black Belt, 6th Dan

Music:
Mr J Bridge *Horn, Trumpet, Trombone*
Mr R Childs, LRAM *Percussion*
Mrs R Ferguson, GradCMRE *Violin*
Mrs H Frankland, BA, LRAM *Piano*
Mrs J Gallagher, BA (Reading), LRAM *Violin, Viola*
Mr P Godfrey, MA, ARCO *Piano*
Mr L Hague *Guitar*
Mrs R Hinman, BA, LRAM *Voice/Piano*
Mrs J Maclean, BSc, LTCL *'Cello*
Mr P Noble, BA (Kent) *Flute*
Mrs J Rippon, LRAM, ARCM *Piano*
Miss K Samways, BMus (Hons) *Clarinet/Oboe/Saxophone*
Miss K Turner, GRSM (Hons), ARCM *Violin*

Foundation. The College was founded in 1878 by Miss Catharine Buchan-Smith. There are now 758 girls in the School aged between 4 and 18 years, plus 25 in the Nursery aged 3+.

Location. Northwood is 14 miles from Central London and is served by the Metropolitan Line and several good local bus services. A supervised school bus service brings girls through Edgware, Canons, Stanmore, Hatch End, Queensbury, Kingsbury, Kenton, Harrow, Pinner, Borehamwood, Elstree, Radlett, Bushey, Chorleywood and Rickmansworth (4 routes).

General Information. The College is divided into five sections: the Nursery (Redington), Pre-prep (Vincent), Junior School, Senior School and Sixth Form, all of which are located on the same site. The Nursery, Pre-prep and Junior School occupy their own self-contained buildings.

All parts of the school are equipped with specialist subject facilities. In addition to standard classrooms, the Senior School is equipped with a well-stocked Library, three art rooms, eight laboratories, an assembly hall, drama studio, and specialist centres for Technology, Modern Languages, Music, two newly equipped computer rooms and the Sixth Form Centre. The sporting facilities include a Sports Hall and adjoining indoor 25 metre six-lane swimming pool. This facility is used by girls from all sections of the school.

The attractive grounds include gardens, five hard tennis/netball courts, a hockey/rounders field and a field for junior games. The pre-prep stands in its own grounds.

Aims. The aims of the College are: to foster a love of learning through an excellent academic education, to develop creative and sporting talents, to encourage initiative, independence and self-confidence in a friendly and supportive community and to promote traditional values of social responsibility and concern for others.

We hope each girl will develop her talents to the full within the framework of a disciplined community where courtesy, consideration and sensitivity to the needs of others are highly valued. Above all, it is hoped that a girl leaving Northwood College will have the confidence to succeed at whichever career she realistically chooses, the ability to adapt to an ever-changing world and the strength of character to uphold values and standards.

Examinations. Pupils are prepared for the General Certificate of Secondary Education, for 'A', and A/S levels and for University Entrance.

Curriculum. The College offers all National Curriculum subjects. In addition, French is taught from the age of 7, Latin from 12, Spanish and German from 13. Drama is taught throughout the school. A very wide range of 'A' level subjects is available in the Sixth Form.

Scholarships. Two academic scholarships and a music scholarship are awarded annually to girls entering Senior

School and three academic scholarships are awarded to girls entering the VI Form. Please contact the Head Mistress for details.

Music. There are two school orchestras, a wind band and three school choirs. Concerts are held each term and there is a music competition. Girls may take instrumental lessons with visiting staff and are prepared for the Associated Board's examinations.

Drama. There is one major dramatic production in both Junior and Senior schools each year. Girls may take individual drama lessons with visiting teachers.

Physical Education. Trained Staff teach Gymnastics, Games and Swimming. Hockey and Netball are played during the winter months; tennis and rounders in the summer. Swimming is taken all the year round. Senior girls are able to explore other sports.

Fees (from September 2000). Tuition, £4,338–£6,567 per annum. Nursery £1,220 per term.

Charitable status. Northwood College is a Registered Charity, number 312646. It exists to provide education for girls between the ages of 3 and 18 years.

Norwich High School (G.D.S.T.)

95 Newmarket Road Norwich NR2 2HU
Tel: (01603) 453265
Fax: (01603) 259891

Founded 1875

This is one of the 25 schools of The Girls' Day School Trust. For general information about the Trust and the composition of its Council, see p 532. A more detailed prospectus may be obtained from the school.

Local Governors:

Chairman: Dr A L Bushell, CEng

Mrs D Alston, BSc
Mr I Corsie, BSc, CEng, FICE, MIHT
Mrs A de Las Casas, SRN, SCM
Mrs J H Galbraith, MA
Dr K Harrison, MB, BS, MRCGP
Miss M Jarrold, MA (Cantab)
Mr G Jones, BA, MBA
Mr J Turner, FCA
Mrs S Watkins, DBO

***Headmistress:* Mrs V C Bidwell**, BA (Newcastle-upon-Tyne) *Modern Languages*

Deputy Headmistress: Mr S D Kavanagh, BA (Leicester) *Geography*

Teaching Staff:
Mr R S Allpress, BSc (London), MA (Ed) (Leeds) *Mathematics*
Miss C Avery, BA (Oxford) *English*
Mrs J C Bagshaw, BA (Anglia Cambridge) *Modern Languages*
Mrs J Barham, BA (Manchester) *Geography*
Miss A Bell, BSc (York) *Mathematics*
Mrs H J Bignell, DipAD *Art*
Dr A S Blanchard, BSc (London) Biology, PhD (East Anglia) *Biochemistry*
Mrs L Burnell, BA (Ulster) *History*
Mrs S J Byrne, BA (Leeds) *History*
Mrs L Chapman, BA (Manchester) *English*
Mrs S Cooper, BA (Oxford) *Classics*
Miss K A Crossfield, BSc (East Anglia) *Chemistry*
Mrs B A Crouch, BA (Sheffield) *English Language & Literature*
Mrs S J Day, BA (Kent) *Physical Education*
Mrs E Dromgoole, MA (London) *Art & Design*
Miss C Durrant, MA (Oxford) *English*
Miss K Farrage, BA (Reading) *Geography*
Mrs E M Fisher, BA (London) *Modern Languages*
Mr G W Foulkes, BSc (Bangor) *Electronic Engineering*
Mrs C A Goodby, BA (Leeds) *English*
Mrs E Groves, BSc (Durham) *Psychology*
Mr R C Hart, BA (Nottingham), MA (London) *History*
Mrs T R Hewett, BEd (Ripon & York St John) *Religious Studies*
Mr D Y Hopkins, BSc (London) *Physics*
Mrs O Howe-Browne, BA (London) *Spanish*
Mrs J M Ingham, BA (London) *Classics*
Mr W N Jepson, BA (Aberystwyth) *Visual Art*
Mr J H King, BSc (Hull) *Chemistry/Second Master*
Mrs R E King, BSc (London) *Mathematics*
Mrs J M Lane, BSc (Liverpool), MA (*East Anglia*) *Mathematics*
Mr R K Malton, BA (Ripon & York St John) *Design Technology*
Mr A Martins, MA (Leeds) *History*
Mrs A E McCourt, BA (Keele), MSc (*East Anglia*) *Chemistry*
Mr S Morling, BA (Lancaster) *Economics*
Mr R Murray, BSc (Reading) *Zoology*
Mrs G Muse, BSc (Newcastle-upon-Tyne) *Physics/Director of Studies*
Mrs C H M Norris, BA (London) *Modern Languages*
Mrs S C Nursey, CertEd (Bedford) *Physical Education*
Mr S Orton, MA (Cambridge) *Music*
Mr J W Reed, Teaching Certificate (Shoreditch) *Craft, Design & Technology*
Mrs H Roebuck, BTech (Bradford) *Applied Biology*
Mr P Rothwell, BEd (Manchester) *Craft, Design & Technology*
Miss J Sandford, BSc (Reading) *Geography*
Mrs B Searle, BA (UEA) *History*
Mr C Shannon, BA (Worcester College, Oxford) *Theology*
Mrs G Slater, BA (Oxford) *Physics*
Mrs J Slater, MA (Bath) *English*
Miss D Smith, BEd (De Montford) *Physical Education*
Mrs I M Smith, BA (Bristol) *Modern Languages*
Miss S P Smith, BA (Birmingham) *Modern Languages*
Mrs C Spurr, BA (Durham) *Geography*
Mrs E A Thurlow, BA (Cambridge) *Classics*
Mrs J Todd, BSc (Nottingham) *Mathematics*
Mrs A S Turner, BA (Wales) *Modern Languages*
Mrs J Turner, BA (UEA) *History of Art*
Mrs A E W Vincent, BSc (St Andrews) *Zoology*
Mrs J Walmsley, CertEd (Sheffield) *Physical Education*
Mrs H Weiland, BA (Cambridge), MA (London), LRAM *Music*
Mr R Windle, MSc (Reading) *Chemical Education*

Junior Department:
Head of Junior Department: Mrs J Marchant, BA (London) *English, MPhil* (London) *Cultural History*

Mrs C M Abhay, BA (London) *French*
Mrs C Ackroyd, BSc (Wales)
Miss A L Brand, BA (Anglia Polytechnic University)
Mrs R J Cordiner, BA (Open)
Miss S A Gothard, CertEd (London)
Mrs R A Green, CertEd (Nottingham)
Mrs C Moir, BA (Leeds)
Mrs M Pattinson, CertEd
Mrs G S Pilgrim, CertEd (Cambridge)
Dr J R Taylor, BA, PhD (East Anglia)
Mrs J Whiffen, CertEd (Dartford)

School Librarians:
Mrs J L Adnams, BA (Reading), MA (Sheffield), ALA
Mrs P Bull, CL, ALA

Visiting Staff:
Piano:
Mrs V Denny, LRAM, GRSM, MTC (London)
Mr C Green-Armytage, GRNSM, BMus, MMus
Mrs S Wilson, BA, BMus (Arkansas)
Mrs E R Yelin, ARCM, Teaching Certificate

Violin/Piano/Theory: Mrs E Smith, BA, MA, PGCE

Strings:
Mr C Clouting, LRAM, GRSM
Mr S Gallagher, BA
Mr R Rose, ARCM
Mr D Storer, LTCL, GTCL

Woodwind:
Mrs B L Jennings, ARCM, LGSM, DipEd
Mrs S Knights, GGSM, ARCM, PGCE
Mr C S Knights
Ms A Bryant, GRSM, LRAM

Brass:
Miss L Roberts, AGSM, ARCM, Dip NCOS

Singing:
Miss E A Smith, DipMusEd, RSAM, ALCM

Percussion:
Mr Shaw, NAPT Reg

Fencing:
Mr A Sowerby

Step Aerobics:
Miss J O'Mahony

Speech Therapy:
Mrs C McClennan

School Doctor: Dr K Harrison, MB, BS, MRCGP

Senior School: about 650, aged 11–18 years, of whom about 160 are in the Sixth Form.

Junior Department: about 250, aged 4 to 10 years.

Norwich High School was opened in 1875 and draws its pupils in almost equal numbers from the city of Norwich and the county of Norfolk. It stands in about 12 acres of grounds on the main Newmarket Road, a mile-and-a-half from the city centre.

In addition to the main buildings, which are attached to a very distinguished Regency house – built in 1820 – there is a Junior Department with many specialist rooms, a sixth form centre, a music school, a spacious sports hall, performing arts centre and a covered and heated swimming pool. All the playing fields are around the school, and a wide range of indoor and outdoor physical activities are offered, including tennis, rounders, badminton, gymnastics, dance, netball, lacrosse and athletics.

Admission. All girls are tested prior to entry and the normal ages of admission are 4, 7, 11 and 16. Occasional vacancies may occur at other ages.

Curriculum. The curriculum is planned as a continuum and on the assumption that all girls remain at the school to take A levels. The school has always prided itself on providing a liberal education and preparing girls for admission to the universities, professions, commerce and industry. A wide range of subjects is available including 21 at both A level and GCSE, and in the sixth form all girls are encouraged to study widely in addition to their examination subjects.

Information systems. A new network has recently been installed which means that the whole school is cabled for the computer network, shared by both senior and junior departments. In addition to the two senior and junior IT rooms, there is a room in the sixth form centre to allow students to work independently. The library has access to the network, as do laboratories and all the teaching rooms. In addition the libraries have computerised catalogues and there is a large number of CD Rom multimedia players in the school. Computers are widely used for teaching and teaching administration and girls are taught Desk Top Publishing, Computer-Aided Design and business applications. Satellite Television is used in sixth-form modern language teaching as are the two computerised language laboratories.

Careers Education and advice. A carefully planned Careers Education programme commences in Year 9 encompassing sessions on decision making, information seeking and the development of communication and interview skills. The majority of Sixth Formers enter Higher Education for which they receive comprehensive guidance and preparation from their tutors, the Head of Sixth Form and the Careers Department. The Careers Room is fully stocked with up-to-date information. ECCTIS and other databases are in regular use. Advice is also given by visiting speakers, as well as delegates to the Careers Afternoon and Higher Education Fair. Girls undertake work experience and job shadowing in addition to the Young Enterprise Scheme.

Extra-curricular activities. In keeping with the liberal tradition of the school these are extensive. Music, sport and drama are all strong features of the school and orchestras, musical ensembles, plays and teams are well supported. Many girls participate in the Duke of Edinburgh's Award Scheme, Young Enterprise business scheme, rowing and orienteering clubs, and activities such as debating, chess, photography, Amnesty International, Christian Union and life saving.

Fees. From September 2000: Senior School £1,680 per term; Junior Department £1,220 per term.

The fees cover the regular curriculum, school books, stationery and other materials, choral music, games and swimming, but not optional extra subjects or school meals.

The fees for extra subjects, including piano, string, wind and brass instruments, are shown in the prospectus.

Financial Assistance. The GDST has made available to the school a substantial number of scholarships and bursaries.

Bursaries. These are available on or after entry to the Senior School and applications should be made to the Headmistress in cases of financial need. All requests are considered in confidence. Bursaries are means tested and are intended to ensure the school remains accessible to bright girls who would profit from our education, but who would be unable to enter the school without financial assistance.

Scholarships. Various scholarships are available to internal or external candidates for entry at 11+ or to the Sixth Form.

Charitable status. Norwich High School is one of the 25 schools of the Girls' Day School Trust, which is a Registered Charity, number 1026057. The aim of the Trust is to provide a fine academic education at a comparatively modest cost.

Notre Dame Senior School

Burwood House Cobham Surrey KT11 1HA
Tel: (01932) 869990
Fax: (01932) 860992

Notre Dame is a Catholic Day School for Girls established in Cobham in 1937 by the Sisters of the Company of Mary.

Governors:

Chairman: Mr Glen Travers
Deputy Chairman: Miss Suzanne Ormsby, LLB

Sister Anne Bayley, ODN
Mr Brian Mepham, FCA
Mr Timothy Moles, BA
Sister Frances Orchard, IBVM
Mrs Trudy Wykes, CertEd

Bursar & Clerk to the Governors: Mr Alexander Bradshaw, DMS, MIMgt, FISM

***Headmistress:* Mrs Margaret McSwiggan,** MA

Deputy Headmistress: Mrs L Crighton, BA (Hons), PGCE
Assistant Deputy Head: Mrs V Cochrane, BEd, Cert in Counselling
Head of Sixth Form: Mrs I Oettinger, CertEd
Pastoral Assistant: Sister Catherine McLenaghan, ODN

Staff:

Miss J Banks, BA (Hons), PGCE *Geography*
Mrs S Barney, ASA FIST, TCert *Swimming Coach*
Mrs J Benny, CertEd *Art*
Mr F Budge, BA (Hons), PGCE, DipBusEd *Information Technology*
Mrs A Butcher, BEd *Mathematics*
Mr M Coackley, BA (Hons), PGCE *History*
Mrs A Cox, BA (Hons), PGCE *French, Spanish*
Dr A Cripps, BSc, MSc, PhD *Biology, Psychology, Technology*
Miss C Davis, BA (Hons), PGCE *Art*
Mrs S Duckworth, BA (Hons), TESOL *English as a Foreign Language*
Mr R Fenton, BMus (Hons), PhD *Music*
Miss C Fuller, BA (Hons), PGCE *English*
Dr V Gibb, PhD, BEd, MPhil, PGCE *Business Studies*
Miss C Graham, BA (Hons), PGCE *Drama, English*
Miss M Grzesik, BA (Hons), PGCE *French and Spanish*
Mrs P Hall, CertEd *Design Technology*
Mrs K Hammond, BEd (Hons) *Physical Education*
Mrs C Hearne, BA (Hons), PGCE *French and German*
Mme M-J Herring, BEPC *French*
Miss F Hickey, BA, MA (Hons), DipTeaching *Information Studies*
Mrs B Hilder, BA (Hons), PGCE *Classics*
Mrs E Hope, BSc (Hons), ARCS *Biology*
Mrs C Jackman, BSc (Hons), PGCE *Mathematics*
Mrs Y Jackman, CertEd *Design Technology*
Miss S Kielty, BA (Hons), PGCE
Mrs A Lovett, BSc (Hons), PGCE *Physics, Technology*
Mrs H Marsh, BA (Hons), PGCE *Physical Education*
Mrs C Mosley, BSc, PGCE *Physics*
Mr N Moughtin, BA (Hons), PGCE, MEd *History, Politics*
Mrs I Oettinger, CertEd *German, Head of VIth Form*
Mrs M Rowe, BA, HDipEd, PGCE *Religious Education, English, History*
Miss S Russell, BSc (Hons), PGCE *Geography*
Mrs K Rylance, BSc (Hons), PGCE *Biology & Chemistry*
Mr S Seidler, BD (Hons), PGCE *Religious Studies*
Mrs L Shore, BSc, MSc *Mathematics*
Mr M Smith, MA, PGCE *Mathematics*
Mrs V Szambowski, BSc (Hons), PGCE *Chemistry*
Miss M Taft, BA (Hons) (Oxon), PGCE *English*
Mrs S Treherne, ALAM, LGSM *Drama*
Mrs M Turner, BA (Hons), PGCE *English, French*
Mrs S Whittaker, BEd (Hons), SENCO

Associate Staff:

Secretaries:
Miss B Riddell
Admin Assistant: Mrs A Saunders
Librarian: Mrs P Whitlock
Laboratory Technicians:
Mrs V Catalano
Mrs J Matkin
School Nurse: Mrs J Bonney, SRN, RSCN

Foundation. Notre Dame School was established in 1937 by the Sisters of the Company of Mary, Our Lady who have a four hundred year old tradition of excellence in education worldwide. The Sisters of the Company of Mary continue to play a very important role in the pastoral life of the school ensuring that the ethos is maintained. Through the Company of Mary the school has well-established links with schools in France, Spain and the USA.

Notre Dame is a Catholic school which welcomes families from all religious denominations. Whilst helping our Catholic children to deepen their understanding of our faith we teach universal tolerance and understanding of all religious beliefs. The school provides a friendly and caring environment in which every girl is encouraged to fulfil her potential. There are approximately 340 girls aged from 11 to 18 in the Senior School. Notre Dame Preparatory School occupies the same site and has approximately 360 girls from 2½ to 11.

General information. Located in tranquil rural surroundings, easily accessible by road and served by an extensive network of school coaches, Notre Dame boasts comprehensive facilities for the pursuit of academic work, drama, music, art, sports and other activities. Facilities include a heated indoor swimming pool, sports hall, well-equipped science laboratories and an extensive computer network. A beautiful Chapel is located in the heart of the school.

Curriculum. All pupils follow a broad curriculum leading to the achievement of up to 10 GCSEs. In addition to the core subjects of English (literature and language), Mathematics, Science and Religious Studies, girls may choose to take French, German, Spanish, Latin, History, IT, Geography, Drama, Music, Art, Food and Textiles Technology and Physical Education. In the Sixth Form most girls will take four AS level and three A level subjects chosen from a large range of options. All girls are prepared for university entrance (including Oxbridge).

Extra-curricular activities. Notre Dame excels in swimming and netball and offers a wide range of other sporting activities including tennis, athletics, gymnastics, badminton and rounders. The school boasts thriving Drama and Music Departments with all girls having the opportunity to participate in productions, various choirs and musical ensembles ranging from the chamber orchestra to rock groups. All girls take part in a weekly activities programme. Other ongoing extracurricular activities include Duke of Edinburgh Award Scheme, Young Enterprise and community service within the local parish.

Admission. Admission is normally at 11+, although girls may be admitted at other ages subject to an entrance examination and the availability of places. Two academic scholarships are awarded at 11+ based on the entrance examination. Scholarships are also awarded to girls entering the Sixth Form. Short-term bursaries may be made available to assist parents in times of personal financial hardship. Approximately half our intake at 11+ comes from Notre Dame Preparatory School.

Fees. The fees are £2,375 per term.

Charitable status. Notre Dame Senior School is a Registered Charity, number 238228. It exists to provide education for girls.

* Head of Department	§ Part Time or Visiting
† Housemaster/Housemistress	¶ Old Pupil
‡ See below list of staff for meaning	

Nottingham High School for Girls (G.D.S.T.)

9 Arboretum Street Nottingham NG1 4JB
Tel: (0115) 941 7663
Fax: (0115) 924 0757

Founded 1875

This is one of the 25 schools of The Girls' Day School Trust. For general information about the Trust and the composition of its Council, see p 532. A more detailed prospectus may be obtained from the school.

Local Governors:
Chairman: His Honour Judge John Hopkin, DL
Deputy Chairman: Councillor M W Suthers, OBE, MA (Cantab)
Mrs J Bridgeman, CB, BA
Dr F Coutts, MBChB, DObst, RCOG
Mr R Freeston, FRICS
Professor S J Harris, BA, MA, PhD
Mr J E Madocks, CBE, DL
Mrs J Munro, BSc, FKC
Mr J G Nowell, BSc, FCA
Professor P Rubin, MA, DM, FRCP
Mr R M Stevenson, HonOBE, MA

***Headmistress:* Mrs A C Rees**, MA Hons (Oxford) *Physics*

Deputy Head: Mrs D Sprague, BA (Leeds) *German and Russian*

Senior Mistress: Mrs J E Peters, BA (Leeds) *French*

Assistant Staff:
Miss J Abbott, BEd (Bedford) *Physical Education*
Mrs K M Anderton, BSc (Liverpool) *Mathematics*
Dr I Arthurson, BA (Keele) *History and English,* PhD (Keele) *History*
Mrs C L Asher, FTCL
Mrs F C Austin, BSc (Dunelm) *General*
Mrs C S Beckett, BA (Lancaster) *French,* MA (*Nottingham) Modern German Literature*
Mrs S Bell, BSc (Nottingham) *Physics*
Mrs S E Beynon, BA (London) *French*
Mrs M J Biggs, BSc (Leeds) *Mathematics*
Mrs V M Bird, CertEd (Sussex) *History and Religious Education*
Mrs V E Black, BSc (Nottingham) *Chemistry*
Mrs H Boldt, BA (Fachhochschule Koln Polytechnic) *Translating*
Mrs M Booth, BA Hons (Leeds) *English*
Mr T P Browne, BA (Huddersfield) *Music*
Mr G W Campion, BSc (Nottingham) *Metallurgy, Diploma Religious Education*
Mrs M Cassidy BSc (Manchester) *Geography*
Mrs H M Coombs, MA (Cantab) *English*
Mrs J M Cooper, BA (London), MA (Loughborough) *English and Education*
Mrs J R Couch, BSc (Sheffield) *Geography*
Mrs M Crittenden, BSc (Sheffield) *Zoology,* MSc (Toronto)
Mrs I F E Dance, BA (Aberystwyth) *Geography*
Mrs D I Daw, BA (Leeds), ALCM (London) *Theology, Music*
Mr W A Dyas, BA (Stirling) *Sociology/Psychology,* MEd (Nottingham) *16+/Post Compulsory Education*
Mrs S Erde, BA *Physics/Theoretical Physics*
Dr A N Finnis, MA (Flinders - Australia), *French, Spanish, German,* PhD (*Cantab*) *Linguistics*
Mrs J E Fishel, BSc (Salford) *German/Spanish*
Mrs H M Fisher, BA (Exeter) *French/Spanish*
Mrs G A Flint, BEd (Bristol) *Home Economics, DPSE* (Nottingham Trent) *Design Technology*
Mrs S Folwell, BEd (Cantab) *History*
Mrs E A George, BA (Liverpool) *Geography*
Mrs A Hall, BSc (Hull) *Mathematics*
Mrs J J Harris, BSc (London) *Chemistry*
Mrs P A Higgins, BEd (Bishop Lonsdale) *Physical Education*
Mrs C Hill, BA (Open) *Education and Food Technology*
Mr P Holden, BSc (London) *Chemistry/Physics*
Mrs C Howard, BMedSci (Nottingham) *Biochemistry*
Mrs M-J Hughes, MA (St Andrews) *Economics/Philosophy*
Mrs R N Hulme, BA Hons (Newcastle-upon-Tyne) *Biochemistry*
Mrs W A Hunter, BA (Essex), MA (Nottingham)
Mr S Imms, BA (Wolverhampton) *Fine Art*
Mr M J Jessop, BEd (Sussex) *Physical Science*
Mrs O Jose, BA (Nottingham) *English,* MA (Nottingham) *Linguistics*
Mrs J Kelly BA (Lancaster) *Religious Studies*
Mrs W Kitchen, BA (York) *Economics*
Mrs J E Lowden, BA (Leeds) *English*
Mr D A B Machell, MA (Cantab) *Modern & Medieval Languages,* BMus (Dunelm), FTCL LTCL (*CMT*) LTCL, LMus, TCL *Music*
Miss P A Messenger, BSc (Liverpool) *Mathematics,* MEd (Nottingham)
Mrs J Moore, BA (Bristol) *Classics*
Mrs C Nicklin, BMus (Surrey)
Miss P A Osborn, BA (Loughborough) *Textiles/Fashion,* ATD
Mrs L M Ovadia, BA (Aberystwyth) *French*
Mrs M Owen, MA (Glasgow) *English Literature and Language*
Mrs E J Parkin, BSc (Leicester) *Biological Sciences*
Miss S C Peacock, BSc (Nottingham) *Mathematics*
Miss S D Penfold, Bedford College of Physical Education, Teacher's Cert
Mrs P Porter, BA (Nottingham) *French/Russian*
Mr S W Price, BA (Oxford) *Engineering Science*
Mrs S E Robins, BA (Nottingham) *English/American Studies,* MA (Nottingham), *American Literature*
Mrs J M Rodgers, BA (Oxon) *Zoology*
Miss G Scott, BA (London) *History*
Mrs J Skinner BEd (Exeter) *Physical Education*
Mr J E Smith, BEd (Nottingham Trent) *Technology for Schools,* MEd (Nottingham)
Miss S M J Taylor, BSc (London) *Mathematics*
Mrs J Thieme, BA (London) *Latin*
Miss C D Thomas, BSc Hons (Coventry) *Chemistry and Physics*
Mrs M G Thomas, BA (London) *Latin*
Mrs J Towle, BSc (Leeds) *Zoology*
Mr J A Turner, BEd (Trent Polytechnic) *Technology*
Mrs W Vivian, BSc (N Staffs Polytechnic) *Computing Science*
Miss N A White, BEd (Nottingham Trent) *Design Technology*
Mr G A Whittaker, BA (Hull) *English, French*
Mrs R A Wilson, BSc (Nottingham) *Zoology,* MEd (Nottingham)
Miss L Wooliscroft, BSocSc (Birmingham) *Economics*

Junior Department:
Head: Mrs M J Renshaw, BSc (Bristol) *Biochemistry*
Deputy Head: Miss S Stokes, BA (Open) *Psychology*
Mrs C M Edley, BA (Open) *Ed Studies & Literature,* CertEd, AdvDipEd, CLD
Miss P Edwards, BEd (Canterbury, Christ Church, New Zealand)
Mrs S Everett, CertEd (Bishops Lonsdale)
Mrs E K Fulton, BEd (Cantab) *Drama*
Miss L Gledhill (Manchester Metropolitan) *Primary Education with Physical Education*
Mrs J M Hamilton, BEd (London) *Geography*

Miss C R Hill, BA (Bradford) *Interdisciplinary Human Studies*
Mrs J A Holborow, CertEd (Leicester)
Mrs G M James, BA (Open) *Education Studies*
Miss P J Needham, BSc *Combined Science* (Brighton), MSc *Social Science* (Reading
Mrs J A Price, BSc (Froebel) *Geography and History*
Mrs C Rayfield, BMus (Birmingham)
Miss A Robinson, BSc (London), Teacher's Certificate *Plant Biology,* PGCE
Mrs C A Sheffield, Teacher's Certificate (Leeds)
Mrs A M Suttill, TCert (Ripon)

Visiting Staff:
Piano:
Mrs H Fox, ALCM
Mr K Leese, GRSM
Ms V Locock, LRAM
Mrs G M Roddis, BA (Exeter), LTCL *Music*

Violin, 'Cello and Double Bass:
Mrs S Foxley, BA (Nottingham) *Music*
Mr S A McCoy, MMus, ARCM *Classical Guitar*
Mrs M McGinnes, DipRCM Teach/Perf
Mr E Wileman, LRAM

Brass:
Mr G Truman, LRAM

Woodwind:
Mr T P Browne, BA (Huddersfield) *Music*
Mrs S Cordon, ALCM, LLCM(TD)
Mrs J Nabarro, LTCL
Mrs A J Quine, LRCM

Percussion:
Mr M Sillitoe

Singing:
Ms C L Asher, FTCL

Speech Training:
Mrs R J Valentine-Hagart, Dip in Dramatic Art

Sport:
Mrs H A Hill
Mrs A Malik
Mr R J Mewett

Support Staff:

School Administrator: Miss S P Gamble
Administrative Officer: Miss K M Harris
Secretary to the Headmistress: Mrs N E Hudson, BA
Senior Department Admissions: Mrs M L Shaw, BA
Junior Department Secretary/Admissions: Mrs S Eustace
Librarian: Mrs C Huett, ALA
Assistant Librarian: Mrs V M Jackson
Information Systems Manager: Mr P R Day
ICT Technician: Mr M Rolfe

Language Assistants:
French: Mlle G Martin, Mlle N Fontaine
German: Fraulein A Silbert
Spanish: Senorigna E M Asensio Vincente, Senorigna S Fernandez

Laboratory Technicians:
Mr C C Baldwin, BSc
Mrs R Chapman
Mrs V M P Gudgeon
Mrs J Maltby
Mrs A Wade

Design Technology Technician: Mr J Clarke, BEd Hons (Nottingham Trent) *Design & Technology*

Junior Department Classroom/General Assistants:
Mrs A L Bell
Mrs H M Lawson, BA, PGCE
Mrs P Onions
Mrs P Wood

Administrative Assistants:
Mrs E I K Collingwood
Mrs M T Roebuck
Mrs J A Staniland

Teaching Resources Officer:

Teaching Resources Assistant: Miss S Turton

After-school Supervisor: Mrs V M Jackson

Medical Centre: Doctor: Dr Hobson, MB, BS, DRCOG, FPCert

Nurses:
Mrs L Newton, RGN
Mrs S J Wilding, RGN

The school was opened in 1875. It is situated in Arboretum Street on a site adjoining the Arboretum and conveniently near the city centre, with easy access from all surrounding areas. It is well served both by public transport and by special buses.

In the Senior Department there are about 850 pupils, including well over 260 in the Sixth Form. There is an Infants and Junior Department of about 280, aged 4 to 11. Entry to the school is mostly at 4, 7, 11 and 16 years.

The school buildings are partly former private houses, suitably adapted, and partly modern, purpose-built accommodation. A few years ago a major building programme involved the building of a new Junior Department and improvements to the facilities of the Senior Department. In the Senior Department there are 9 laboratories, a lecture theatre, drama studio and spacious library, as well as Information Technology, Design Technology and Home Economics rooms, a music house and other specialist teaching accommodation. The current building programme includes an atrium entrance for girls and a new dining hall for the 2001 Autumn Term.

Facilities for physical education include all-weather courts, Sports Hall with attached Fitness Suite and gymnasium on site and playing fields which can be reached by bus. Girls have the opportunity to learn swimming, gym, dance, netball, hockey, tennis, rounders, cricket, badminton, volleyball, aerobics and many other activities. A recreational course including ice-skating, bowling, yoga, self-defence and step-aerobics is offered in the 6th form.

The Junior Department has its own science laboratory, music rooms, hall, art room and library and is well-equipped with computers.

Curriculum. The curriculum is designed to give a broad academic education with scope for the development of individual interests. Full note is taken of the National Curriculum throughout the school and in the Senior Department girls are prepared for GCSE, A and AS levels and almost all girls proceed to university. A wide choice of courses is offered and Art, Technology, Music, Drama and Physical Education are an integral part of the school curriculum.

Tuition in most instruments can be arranged. There are two orchestras, a concert band and several groups and choirs in the Senior Department and a choir and orchestra in the Junior Department.

Fees. From September 2000: Senior Department £1,680 per term, excluding lunch. Junior Department: £1,220 per term, including lunch.

The fees cover the regular curriculum, school books, stationery and other materials, class music, games and swimming, but not optional extra subjects.

The fees for extra subjects, including instrumental music and speech training, are shown in the prospectus.

Assisted Places. Following the ending of the Government Assisted Places Scheme, the GDST has made available to the school a substantial number of scholarships and bursaries. The bursaries are means tested and are intended to ensure that the school remains accessible to bright girls who would profit from our education but who would be unable to enter the school without financial assistance.

Bursaries. These are available after entry throughout the Senior Department and application should be made to the Headmistress in cases of financial need. All requests will be considered in confidence.

Scholarships. The Girls' Day School Trust makes available to the school a number of scholarships each year for entry to the Senior Department at both 11+ and direct into the Sixth Form. The maximum value of a Trust Scholarship is normally half the current tuition fee. Scholarships are awarded solely on the basis of academic merit and no financial means test is involved.

Charitable status. Nottingham High School for Girls is one of the 25 schools of the Girls' Day School Trust, which is a Registered Charity, number 1026057. The aim of the Trust is to provide a fine academic education at a comparatively modest cost.

Notting Hill and Ealing High School (G.D.S.T.)

2 Cleveland Road Ealing W13 8AX
Tel: 020 8997 5744

Founded 1873

This is one of the 25 schools of The Girls' Day School Trust. For general information about the Trust and the composition of its Council, see p. 532. The following are additional particulars and a more detailed prospectus may be obtained from the school.

Local Governing Body:
Mrs S Stirling, BA (*Chairman*)
Mrs E Baron, MA
Professor J Bately, CBE, MA, FKC, FBA
Mrs J MacGregor (*Council Representative*)
Professor Susan Malcolm, MA.PhD, FRcPath
Mrs J Moir, BA
Mr J Newbegin
Mrs L O'Sullivan, BA, PGCE
Mrs G Simmonds, BSc
Councillor A C B Young, BVMS, MRCVS

***Headmistress:* Mrs S M Whitfield**, MA (Cambridge) *Natural Sciences and Physical Anthropology*

Senior School:
Deputy Head: Miss L Ashley, BSc (London), PGCE, *Social Sciences and History,* MSc (Econ)
Senior Teacher: Mrs H Strange, BSc Hons (Durham), CBiol, MIBiol *Biology*

Mrs S A M Ashby, MA (Auckland) English, BA (Wellington) *Latin and English*
Miss L Asher, BSc (Loughborough), PGCE *PE and Sports Science*
Miss R Bailey, BA (Oxford) Literae Humaniores, PGCE
Mrs A Bray, MA (St Andrews) *English*
Mrs P Butler, MA (London) *Science Education*
Mrs J Butcher, BA (East Anglia) *Politics and History*
Mrs K Clarke, MA (Oxford), PGCE *French and Spanish*
Miss R Clark, BA (Cambridge), PGCE *Natural Sciences*
Miss S Cohen, BEd Hons (London) *Geography/Geology*
Ms H Critcher, BSc (London) *Mathematics*
Mr S L Dace, MA (Oxford), PGCE *English*
Mrs E Da Costa, BA (London) *English*
Mr I Davidson, BSc (Edinburgh) *Physics/Mathematics*
Miss M Di Paola, BA Hons (East London), PGCE *Fine Art/Art & Design*
Ms C Douglas, Diploma in Specific Learning Difficulties
Mrs D Geary-Jones, BA (Leeds), PGCE *Music/Theology*
Mrs S Gerlis, BA (Manchester), PGCE *Spanish/French*
Mr P Harrison, MSc, BA (Hons) Fine Art, PGCE *Information Technology*
Mrs P Hurd, Chelsea Diploma, ATC
Mrs M-J Jeanes, MA (Oxford), PGCE *Natural Sciences*
Mrs C Johnson (Salzburg), City & Guild Teaching Qualification *English and German*
Mrs S Lawrence, BA (Leeds) *Spanish*
Miss J Lee, BSc (Brunel) *Physical Education & Geography*
Ms J Lucas, BA (Reading) *Art, History and French; BTec NatDipl Art & Design; PGCE Art & Creative Arts*
Mrs C Maynard, BA (Leicester), PGCE *Geography*
Mr W McInally, BEd (Northumbria) *Design and Technology*
Mrs M McKeigue, BSc (London) *Mathematics*
Mr J Moore, BA (Leeds), PGCE *Economic and Social History*
Ms H Niko, BA (Birmingham) American Studies, PGCE *English*
Mrs H Patterson, BA (London), MA(Ed) (London), PGCE *History*
Miss S Plowden, BA (Edinburgh)
Mr A Phillips, BMus, MMus (London) *Music*
Mrs G Phillips, MA (Cambridge), PGCE *Geography*
Mrs J Phillips, BMus (London) *Music*
Miss S Potter, BA (Dartington), PostDip in Theatre Direction *Theatre Studies*
Mr P Quarmby, BSc (Durham) *Mathematics/Psychology*
Mrs L Rhys, MA (Oxford) *History*
Mrs J Scott, BEd (Sussex) *Human Movement*
Mrs M Sergeant, MA (Cambridge), PGCE *Classics*
Mr G Sinclair, AGSM, (Guildhall), CertEd
Mrs J A Sinclair, BSc Hons (Durham) *Physics*
Mrs F Singer, MA (Aberdeen), MEd *German and French*
Mrs S Singer, BA (Durham) *French and German*
Mr D Soares, BA (Cambridge), PGCE *History and Philosophy of Science*
Ms J Uhart, BA (OU) Humanities, Dip in Art & Design (Guildford) *History of Art*
Mr P Warne, BSc (London) *Zoology,* BSc (London), PGCE *Chemistry*
Mrs S Worley, BSc (Sheffield) *Zoology and Botany*
Mrs L Wright, BSc (Durham), Natural Sciences, PGCE *Mathematics*

Junior School:
Head of Junior and Preparatory Departments: Mrs P Lynch, MA Hons Psychology (St Andrews), PGCE (Goldsmith College)

Ms S Beck, BSc, PGCE (Leicester) *Mathematics*
Mrs D Bryant, BA, Teaching Certificate *Psychology*
Mrs S Burke, BA Hons (Leicester), PGCE
Mrs M J Conroy, BA (London), PGCE *Music/teaching in Senior School*
Mrs G M Grabowska, CertEd, DipPriSci, CPDev
Mrs M Halberstadt, CertEd
Mrs K Leafe, CertEd (London)
Miss S Lister, BA Hons, PGCE *English*
Miss C Loftus, BA (Roehampton), PGCE *History and Education*
Miss L Murdoch, BEd (Edinburgh)
Miss C Palmer, BEd (Oxford Brookes)
Ms S Silva, BEd *Education/Drama*
Mrs J Stepan, CertEd
Miss J Taylor, BA (Warwick), PGCE *History*
Mr L Temple, BA (Cambridge) *English Literature, Drama*
Mrs S Vao, TCert (New Zealand), TchrsCdDip (distinction)

Visiting Staff:
Piano:
Mrs E M Curran, MGR
Mr H Aston
Ms B Mikhail
Violin, Viola:
Mr J Humphries, BA, FISTC
Ms H Stanley
Mrs K Schofield
'Cello:
Mr A Manoras, LRAM
Miss A Ashton
Double Bass:
Ms L Heath
Flute:
Ms S Morfee
Mrs N Robertson
Oboe:
Miss R Broadbent
Clarinet:
Miss L Atkinson
Bassoon:
Mrs S Price
Saxophone:
Miss J Ng
Brass:
Miss M Sugars, GBSM
Guitar:
Mr J Clark
Singing:
Miss M Langfield
Miss M Cotterill
Miss E Harries
Speech and Drama:
Ms J Fielding
Mrs C Legge, LGSM

School Administrator: Mrs C Bates, BSc, BA

Admissions Secretary: Mrs A Enright

School Librarian: Ms P Lyon, MA (Cambridge), ALA *English*

Information Services Manager: Mr A Dickson

School Doctor: Dr Margaret Lauder, MB, BCh, DCH, DObst, RCOG

The school was opened at Notting Hill in 1873 and moved to Ealing in 1931. Ealing Broadway station is nearby, and buses pass the door. Although most girls come from Ealing, many come from outside the Borough, where there are good transport links. There are approximately 830 pupils, of whom 560 are in the Senior School (140 in the Sixth Form) and 270 in the Junior department.

The buildings have been added to over the years. There is a large development programme underway which is partially completed, and is being paid for centrally by the GDST under its normal budgeting arrangements. The Junior department now has its own computer suite, as well as the computers which are already in each classroom. The Senior school has three computer rooms, with two computers in each Science laboratory and a number of others in various departments. The entire system is networked, and ICT is used across the curriculum as well as being taught as a distinct subject. There is central CD ROM selection, and the newly refurbished library provides additional computer use. Pupils are taught to use the Internet efficiently and wisely, and its use by individuals is monitored by modern regulatory software. Internet research is widespread.

Sport is taken seriously, but enjoyment at all standards is also encouraged. There is specialist teaching throughout the school, and the Senior school makes use of the facilities at Brentham Club, with whom we have recently gone into a form of partnership. Netball and hockey are the main winter sports, with tennis, athletics and rounders in the summer. Gymnastics are very popular, and there is an excellent gym squad. An indoor swimming pool is planned; at present we use a pool nearby for Juniors and as an option from Year 10 together with other local amenities.

Curriculum. The curriculum includes a wide range of academic and practical subjects, with nineteen offered at A/S and A2 level, including History of Art, Government & Politics and Theatre Studies. It is not compulsory, but students are strongly advised that at least one A/S subject should be in contrast to the others. Girls take nine subjects at GCSE, including a compulsory core of English Language and Literature, Mathematics, Double Award Science and a Modern Language. All girls study Latin and two Modern Languages up to Year 9, and may choose all of these at GCSE. Many girls come from families with a second language at home, and may take that language at GCSE and A level outside school at some point. In the Sixth Form, we also have a General Studies programme and will in future be giving students the opportunity to develop much further the effective key skills for employment.

The school is proud of its standards in Art, Drama and music, as well as in traditional academic fields. Many girls take private tuition leading to examinations at LAMDA and The Royal Academy of Music.

To complement the academic curriculum, all girls throughout the school also follow a programme of personal and social education, which includes health issues, study skills, relationships, careers advice, interview techniques et cetera.

Virtually all girls proceed to higher education. Most girls go straight to university (including Oxbridge and various medical schools); some attend Art College first. Many girls take a year off before going to university.

Fees. From September 2000: Senior School £2,044 per term; Junior School £1,588 per term.

The fees cover the regular curriculum, school books, normal examination fees, stationery and other materials, choral music, but not optional extra subjects or school meals.

The fees for extra subjects including instrumental music, speech and drama, are shown in the prospectus. Certain off-site sports are charged for separately if taken, as are school trips.

Bursaries. Following the ending of the Government Assisted Places Scheme, the GDST has made available to the school a substantial number of scholarships and bursaries. The bursaries are means tested and are intended to ensure that the school remains accessible to bright girls who would profit from our education but who would be unable to enter the school without financial assistance. Application should be made via the school.

Scholarships. These are available to internal or external candidates for entry at 11+ or to the Sixth Form. They include academic scholarships, and for the Sixth Form, awards for Physical Education, Drama, Art, and an All-rounder scholarship. At the age of 11 there is in addition a Music scholarship.

Charitable status. Notting Hill and Ealing High School is one of the 25 schools of the Girls' Public Day School Trust, which is a Registered Charity, number 1026057. The aim of the Trust is to provide a fine academic education at a comparatively modest cost.

Ockbrook School
Derby

The Settlement Ockbrook Derbyshire DE72 3RJ
Tel: (01332) 673532
Fax: (01332) 665184
website: ockbrook.derby.sch.uk

Founded in 1799.

Independent Day and Boarding School for girls aged 3–18. Member of GBA, GBGSA in addition to GSA.

Motto: *In Christo Omnia Possum*

Governing Body:

Chairman of Governors: Mrs O M Dean, BA

Mr R F Acton, BA, FAIA, FInstAM
Mr J A Caborn, LLB, LLM, ACII
Mrs O M Dean, BA
Mrs S Handley
Mrs B Heppell, BSc
Mr G Hinchliffe, BA, MEd
Dr G D Lamming, FRCOG, LRCP, MRCS, MBBS
Mr J Luke
Revd W J H McOwat
Mrs J Morten
Prof J Y Muckle, MA, PhD
Revd D Newman, BA, BSc
Dr W A Rosslyn, BA, MPhil, PhD
Rev H Smith, BA, CertTheol
Mr J Thompson, FCA
Mr D Woods, BA, BSc

Clerk to the Governors: Miss P J Harrold, BA

Staff:

Head Teacher: **Denise P Bolland**, BA, MSc (Brunel), MIMgt *Physics*

Deputy Head: Mrs J Gwatkin, BEd (Birmingham) *Physical Education*

Deputy Curriculum: Mrs A Logie, BA (Hull) *Geography*

Assistant Teachers:
Dr S Allen, PhD, BSc (Salford) *Chemistry*
Mrs C Beckett, BA, MA (Nottingham) *French/German*
Mrs E S Berry, BEd (Derby) *Primary*
Miss J Biss, BA (Warwick) *Mathematics*
Mrs J Brown, BSc (London) *Physics*
Miss M Burton, BA (Exeter)
Mrs D Callaghan, BA, MA (Nottingham) *German/French*
Mrs S Chamberlain, BA (Oxon), MA (Nottingham) *History*
Mrs J Clark, BA (Open) *ICT, Drama, PSE*
Miss S Crompton, BEd (Manchester) *Primary*
Mrs F Faulkner, BSc (Newcastle), MA (Nottingham) *Technology/ICT*
Miss C Griffiths, BEd (Derby) *Primary*
Mrs K Hawkins, CertEd (Sheffield) *Head of Early Years - Year 2*
Ms J Holditch, BA (Liverpool) *History*
Miss A Hoskin, BSc (London) *PE/Games*
Mrs E A Hoyle, BA (London) *French*
Miss S Jones, BA (Scarborough) *Primary*
Mrs G Lloyd, BEd (Nottingham)
Mrs H Marsden, BA (Derby) *Primary*
Mr G Maskalick, MA (Carnegie) *Music*
Miss F McCreddin, BA (Reading) *Art and Design*
Mrs I Mellors *French Conversation*
Mrs S Mitchell, BA (Hull) *English*
Mrs J Mullineux, BEd (Bedford College) *PE*
Mrs A Newton, BSc *Mathematics*
Mrs E S Newton, BEd (Nottingham) *Primary*
Mrs Y Oakes, BA (Derby), ALAM *Theatre Studies*
Mrs P Parker, CertEd (Coventry) *Primary*
Miss C Renow, BA, MEd (Nottingham) *History*
Mr J Robertson, BA (Central England) *Primary*
Mrs L Shaw, DipPE (Dunfermline) *Head of Years 3-6*
Mrs R Shock, MA (London) *French, Italian*
Mrs M Smith, MA (Birmingham) *English*
Mrs S Smith, BSc (Wales) *Geography*
Mrs B Thornton, BEd (Derby) *Primary*
Mrs S Throssell, BSc (Durham) *Science*
Mrs R Turner, BEd (Sheffield) *PE/Games*
Miss A Tooley, BA (Stirling) *Economics & Information Technology*
Mrs P Wakeman, BA (Newcastle) *Business Studies, Economics*
Mrs M Watkins, BA (Leeds) *French/Spanish*
Mrs J Whitaker, MSc (Leicester) *Biology*
Mr D Williams, BEd (Wales) *Primary*
Mrs W Wilton, MEd, BPhil (Nottingham) *Mathematics*

Personal Assistant to The Head & Admissions Secretary: Miss J Dawes, BA

School Administration: Miss D Webster

Financial Manager: Mrs J Harrison, DMS

Boarding House Staff:
Mrs M Griffin *Assistant Housemother*
Mrs M Smith *Housemother*
Miss S Hawkshead *Assistant Housemother*

Medical:
Dr D Disney, MB, ChB, MRCGP, DPCOG, DPD
Dr M Keeling, BSc, BMedSci, BM, BS, DCH, MRCGP, DRCOG
Dr R James, MB, ChB, MRCGP, DPCOG
Dr J Rivers, BPharm, MSc, MB, ChB, MRCGP, DRCOG
Mrs W Holmes, EN

Classroom Assistants:
Miss D Archer, NNEB
Mrs G E Ellis, CertEd (Sheffield)
Mrs J A Hamper, NNEB
Mrs J Harvey
Mrs L Holmes, NNEB
Mrs A Kenyon
Mrs S Smithson
Mrs J Howes, RDSA

Technicians:
Mr A Haw, BSc (Manchester)
Mrs L Kendall, BSc (Manchester)

Visiting Music Teachers:
Mrs M Eades, BA (Durham), DipEd, ARCO *Piano/Violin*
Mrs J Franklin *Cello*
Mrs J Fraser-Burton, GBSM, ABSM *Voice*
Mrs J Geary, GGSM, PGOS *Strings*
Mr M Johnson, HonVCM, AVCM, SVCM, TCert *Guitar*
Mrs J Millensted, GRSM, LRAM *Voice*
Mrs C Morgan, BMus (Manchester), GRSM, ARMCM *Oboe/Piano*
Mrs A Negus (University of Performing Arts, Stuttgart) *Woodwind*
Mr M Thorpe *Woodwind*
Mr G Truman, LRAM *Brass*

Situation. Situated in the heart of the Midlands, Ockbrook School lies between the historic towns of Derby and Nottingham and is easily accessible from motorway networks, rail and air transport. The School is set in a superb rural position overlooking the Trent Valley and it is surrounded by its own estate including landscaped gardens, grounds, playing fields and farmland. This setting and the high standard of facilities within it provides an excellent environment for learning... free from urban noise and distractions.

Pupils. There are approximately 490 pupils, girls aged 3–18 who are divided between the Primary (3–10) and Senior (11–18) Departments. Boarders are accepted from the age of 11 years.

Ethos. The pursuit of excellence is our central ethos. This is realised through a twin track pupil development strategy...educating each pupil to realise their capabilities and achieve their personal best, and providing the motivation to attain the highest grades in GCSE and AS/A2 level examinations.

Ockbrook combines tradition with a clear understanding of the demands of the world in which we live. We aim to engender a strong sense of self-worth, self-assurance and confidence and to guide each pupil towards developing into responsible, socially aware and mature young adults.

We believe that education should be a partnership between School, pupils and parents. To this end we provide comprehensive feedback on progress in the classroom and welcome family and friends at our extra-curricular drama productions, concerts, sports events and acts of worship.

We hope that you will join us and experience our sense of purpose, achievements and commitment to our ethos.

Curriculum. *Primary Department*

Early Years (Ages 3–5). A dynamic programme of language, numeracy and scientific activities provide a secure foundation for later conceptual development.

Key Stage 1 (Years 1 & 2). The core subjects of Mathematics, Science and English are covered in addition to nine other subject areas including French and Information Technology.

Key Stage 2 (Years 3–6). Study for the core of subjects continues with additional experience in nine other subjects including Dance, Drama and Gymnastics.

Teachers' assessments are carried out throughout both Key Stages and form the basis of internal assessment procedures for entrance to the Senior Department at 11+.

Senior Department

Lower School (Years 7–9). Pupils study the core of subjects and a broad range of additional subjects including Information Communications Technology, Drama and PSE (Personal & Social Education). In Year 8 all pupils study German in addition to French.

Upper School (Years 10–11). At GCSE level all pupils study for Mathematics, English Language and English Literature, plus six or more additional subjects chosen from a wide range of options.

Sixth Form. Students usually study for 4 AS Levels in the Lower Sixth and proceed to 3 A2 subjects in the Upper Sixth. A wide range of subjects is available. Great emphasis is placed on the Key Skills Programme which helps to develop the competences so necessary for adult life, whilst adding to the breadth of study. The vast majority of pupils leaving the Sixth Form proceed to higher education, including Oxbridge.

Sport. New Sports Complex opened in March 1998. Netball, hockey, and cross country are the main games of the School. In addition there is also a strong tradition in athletics, swimming and rounders. A rapidly expanding programme of outdoor pursuits is also available for pupils which includes sailing, water-skiing and golf. Teams of various ages, in most sports, have full fixture lists with neighbouring schools and the School is proud of its County and National representatives.

Activities. The Duke of Edinburgh's Award Scheme is available to pupils over the age of 14, together with a wide range of trips and outdoor holidays, walking, canoeing and skiing. Other activities include Young Enterprise, World Challenge Expeditions, Guides, Cycling Proficiency, chess, debating, and 40 other clubs or societies.

Music and Drama. Many pupils learn musical instruments and a large number play to a high standard. Opportunities are provided by the Primary and Senior choirs, orchestras, guitar club, handbells, recorder group, strings group, windband and madrigal group. There is a wide range of dramatic productions each year providing as many pupils as possible with the chance of developing any dramatic talent.

Art & Design & Technology. Great emphasis is given to the development of creative talent both as academic subjects and interests. Out of class involvement is strongly encouraged.

Fees (2001). Senior Day Pupils £5,490 pa. Sixth Form Day Pupils £5,640 pa. Primary Day Pupils £3,960–£4,260 pa. Boarders £4,740 in addition to tuition fees.

Admission. Ockbrook is an academically selective School with considerable competition for places. Most pupils enter in September, although it is possible for entry to take place at other times in the year.

Primary Department. Entry is decided as a result of a combination of interview, assessment day and school report (if applicable).

Senior Department. Entry is decided as a result of a combination of interview, assessment day, school report and entrance examination held in the Spring term.

Sixth Form. Entry is decided as a result of a combination of interview, school report, and ultimately a good performance in the GCSE examinations.

Scholarships. A range of scholarships are available for 11+ entry and Sixth Form entry. Full details are available from the Admissions Secretary.

School Prospectus. A prospectus and registration details may be obtained from the Admissions Secretary, (Tel: 01332 673532; Fax: 01332 665184; Website: ockbrook.derby.sch.uk) Parents are encouraged to visit the School and appointments may be made by contacting the Admissions Secretary.

Charitable status. Ockbrook School is a Registered Charity, number 251211. Its aims are to provide an education for girls between the ages of 3 and 18.

The Old Palace School of John Whitgift

Croydon Surrey CR0 1AX
Tel: 020 8688 2027
Fax: 020 8680 5877

Governing Body:
Chairman: Sir Douglas Lovelock, KCB

Cllr R W Coatman, JP, FRICS, FCIArb, MBE, MRSH
Cllr T Letts
Mr V F Long, FCIB
Prof J W Dougill, PhD, FEng, FCGI
Mr A D Sexton, BA
Mr M A Fowler, FCA, FCIArb
The Rt Rev Dr Wilfred Wood (*The Bishop of Croydon*)
Mr D W North, BSc(Eng), ACGI, MICE
The Revd Canon Colin J Luke Boswell (*The Vicar of Croydon*)
Dr A S Orchard, MBBS, DObst, RCOG
Prof Alan H Windle, PhD, FRS, FIM
Mr P J Squire, MA
Cllr H Malyan

Headmistress: **Mrs E J Hancock**, BA (Nottingham), PGCE

Deputy Heads:
Mrs E J Pearce, MA (Oxford), PGCE
Mrs J Trodden, BSc (London), PGCE

Art:
Mrs G Crozier Meares, BA (Birmingham), MA (Sussex) CertEd
Mrs C Langley, MA (Edinburgh), TCert Art (London)

Business Studies:
Mr N Watson, BA (Hull), PGCE
Mr D Wilkins, BSc (London), PGCE

Classics:
Miss A Bertram, MA Hons (Cambridge), PGCE
Mrs S Crampton, BA Hons (Sydney), MAT (Harvard)
Miss S Funnell, MA (Oxford), PGCE

English:
Mr D Keith, MA (Oxford), PGCE
Miss J French, MA (Oxford), PGCE
Mrs A Jones, BA (Leicester)
Mrs A Lister, BA (London), MA (London)
Miss A Radelat, BA (Bristol), PGCE
Miss K Wall, BA (Oxford), PGCE

Geography:
Miss J Carlsson, BA (London), PGCE
Mrs A Ford, BA (Durham), PGCE
Mrs M Salter, BSc (Salford), PGCE

History and Politics:
Miss E Phillips, BA (Oxford), PGCE
Mrs S Benson, BA (Exeter), PGCE
Mrs L Jeffries, BA (London), PGCE

Home Economics:
Mrs K Williams, TCert (Manchester) *Food & Nutrition*
Mrs S Pressney, BA (Leeds), TCert Art *Textiles*

Information Technology:
Miss H Lewis, BA (Birmingham), RSA Teacher & Trainer Diploma ICT
Mrs K Burdett, BSc (Lancaster), PGCE

Mathematics:
Mrs L Colbeck, BSc (London), PGCE
Mrs C Kneller, BSc (Kent), PGCE
Miss L Moffett, MA (Edinburgh), PGCE
Mrs J Pearce, MA (Oxford), PGCE
Miss K Stewart, BSc (Stirling), PGCE
Miss G Rees, BA (Open University), TCert
Mrs J Greenfield, BSc (Southampton), PGCE

Modern Languages:
Mrs J Simpson, Cert d'Etudes Litteraires Generales Licence ès Lettres (Sorbonne), PGCE (London)
Mrs C Barnard, BA Combined Honours (Dusseldorf), PGCE
Mrs J Hollingum, BA (London), PGCE
Mrs A Liddle, BA (Southampton)
Mrs L Mazzeo, BA (Wales), PGCE
Miss C Pepin, BA (Bristol), PGCE
Mrs C Periton, BA (London)
Mrs C Young, Licence es Lettres (Toulouse), DipPolSci
Miss C Poirier, Diplome de la Licence d'Anglais (Angers), PGCE

Music:
Mrs C Jewell, MA (St Andrews), PGCE
Miss V Lloyd-Richards, BA (Cambridge), PGCE
Mr J Core, GTCL (London), LTCL, PGCE

Physical Education:
Miss S Poole, CertEd (Durham)
Mrs A Eley, BSc (Loughborough), PGCE
Miss J Hall, BEd (Greenwich)
Mrs J Sugarman, CertEd (Brighton)

Religious Studies:
Mrs J Mulrenan, BA (Cardiff), DipEd

Science:

Physics:
Mr C Barwell, BSc (Southampton), PGCE
Miss R Jackson, BSc (Durham), PGCE
Mrs C Sandhu, BSc (Bombay), BEd
Mrs J Trodden, BSc (London), PGCE, CPhys, MInstP

Biology:
Mrs P Shaw, BSc (Leeds), PGCE
Dr J Bannister, BSc (Sheffield), PhD (Leeds), PGCE
Mrs M Mayers, BSc (London), PGCE

Chemistry:
Dr L Nicolas, BSc (Sheffield), PhD (London), PGCE
Mrs J Gradon, BA (Cambridge), PGCE
Mrs C Marren, BSc (Swansea), PGCE
Miss G Storey, BSc (Bristol), PGCE

Technology:
Mr J Plater, MA, BEd (Southampton), MSD-C
Miss A Nariapara, BSc (Loughborough)

Careers: Mrs S O'Hanlon, BSc (London), PGCEon

Preparatory Department Coordinator:
Mrs J Eden, CertEd (Rolle College), RSADip(SpLD)

Pre-Preparatory:
Mrs C Munro, CertEd (Sussex)
Mrs C Blok, BEd (London)
Mrs J Bushin, CertEd (Bristol)
Mrs S Keanie, CertEd (Froebel)
Miss C Rogers, BEd (London), TCert, PGCE
Mrs G Stone, BEd Hons (Cambridge)

Classroom Assistants:
Mrs H Gittings, Pre-School Learning Alliance - Foundation & Curriculum
Mrs E Marshall
Mrs A Grant
Mrs J Russell
Mrs C Schad, BA Hons (London)
Mrs J Tooze
Miss S Brown

Preparatory:
Miss F Clements, MA (Oxon), MMus (Sheffield), PGCE
Mrs A Frost, BSc (Birmingham), PGCE
Mrs J Goatcher, BEd (Sussex)
Miss N James, BSc (Loughborough), PGCE
Mrs M Moore, BA (Reading), PGCE
Mrs A Palmer, CertEd (Roehampton)
Mrs C Pederson, DipEd (Edinburgh)
Mrs M C Sarkis, BA (London), DipMRS, PGCE
Miss R Scott, BEd (London), CNAA
Miss M Simpson, ALCM, BMus (Huddersfield)
Miss S Walker, TCert (Nottingham)
Mrs T Wallis, BEd (Oxford)

Peripatetic Music Staff:

Piano:
Miss J Williams, GRSM, ARCO, ARCM
Miss J Bruce, RCM
Mrs C Tinker, DipArts Music Grad Dip Arts Music, LRAM, ARCH

Violin:
Mrs P Craft, LGSM
Mr D Giles, LTCL

Flute:
Mr S Dean ARCM, LGSM

'Cello:
Mrs D Elliott, BA (London)

Double Bass:
Mr C Canonici

Oboe:
Mrs H Wilson, LRAM, RAM

Clarinet:
Mr L W Jones, DipM&D

Guitar:
Mr W Baulch, LLCM

Brass:
Mrs T Golding, GGSM Hons, DipNCOS

Percussion:
Mr S Pachnine

Bassoon:
Miss J Bruce, RSM

Speech & Drama:
Mrs E Weatherill, BEd, LRAM, LGSM
Mrs H Jerome, LLAM, Teacher's Diploma

Administrative Staff:

Bursar: Mr G C Kellas

Headmistress's Secretary: Mrs F Evison

Secretaries: Mrs D Halsey, Mrs S Stark

Old Palace School of John Whitgift is a girls' independent day school with 850 girls on roll aged 4-18, 550 in the Senior School and 300 in the Preparatory School. It is situated on the site of the Old Palace of the Archbishops of Canterbury in the heart of Croydon. It is well served by public transport being within walking distance of main line stations, bus routes and tram routes.

The School was founded in 1889 by the Community of the Sisters of the Church. It became a member of the Whitgift Foundation in 1993. The School aims to provide education to the highest academic standards and to develop the individual talents of each girl to the full within an environment of mutual respect and support.

Facilities. The original Grade 1 listed - English Heritage - buildings have been enhanced by a science block of seven well-equipped laboratories, an Arts and Technology Annexe comprising very good facilities for art, music, drama and design technology. Four computer rooms are fully networked with internet access. There are sports facilities on site for netball, gymnastics, tennis and a new swimming pool was opened in 1999.

A purpose-built Preparatory Department opens in Summer 2001 giving good sized classrooms, facilities for music and computing and a library to complement the existing science and art rooms.

New sixth form accommodation in the Shah Building is planned for September 2001, including a dining room, PE area and ICT/Resources Room.

Curriculum. *The Preparatory Department* follows a wide curriculum in a friendly and cheerful atmosphere. At four years old the girls are received into Reception classes and are quickly introduced to the skills of reading and number. In the Junior years the girls are progressively introduced to specialised teaching in French, Science, ICT and Music. Girls are carefully prepared for the Senior School entrance examination.

The Senior School curriculum for ages 11-16 is based upon traditional disciplines but keeps abreast of modern developments. All subjects are taught by well qualified specialist staff. Girls study French and Latin together with a third language from Classical Greek, Italian, Russian, German or Spanish. Information Technology is taught as a separate skill and is also integrated within subjects. Design Technology, Textiles and Art are studied by all girls and are available within the GCSE option choices. Extra-curricular activities thrive with three orchestras, four choirs, over 100 girls gaining Duke of Edinburgh awards each year, dramatic performances in each age group, debates, and support for charities through Caritas. Visits enhance the curriculum in many subjects and girls studying languages have the opportunity to stay in the relevant country. There is a wide programme of visits and musicians have recently travelled to Belgium, Venice and Hungary. There is a strong house system.

Sixth Form. Most girls remain at Old Palace for their AS/A2 level studies. New students integrate quickly and become happy and committed members of the School community. A wide range of A and A/S levels are offered with girls studying four subjects in the first year. An enrichment programme provides guidance in study skills, key skills, and careers and opportunities for sport, community service and General Studies. Girls take part in Young Enterprise and World Challenge. Almost all girls proceed to university, including Oxford and Cambridge, to read subjects as diverse as, for example, drama and veterinary science.

Admissions. Girls are normally admitted at 4, 7, 11 and 16 with occasional vacancies at other ages. At 4 years old admission is by interview and assessment, at 7 and 11 by examination and interview and at Sixth Form by interview and GCSE results.

Scholarships and Bursaries. Girls of outstanding merit in the 11+ entrance examination will be offered scholarships of up to 50% fee remission. Bursaries are also awarded on the 11+ entrance for families who need financial assistance. Up to a quarter of girls in the senior school are awarded a bursary place including some who have a free place.

Fees per annum. Senior School £5,748; Preparatory School £4,209.

Fees cover tuition, stationery, text books and examination entries. Extra tuition is available in music and speech and drama.

Charitable status. The Whitgift Foundation is a Registered Charity, number 312612 which administers three schools.

Oxford High School (G.D.S.T.)

Belbroughton Road Oxford OX2 6XA
Tel: (01865) 559888
Fax: (01865) 552343

Founded 1875

This is one of the 25 schools of The Girls' Day School Trust. For general information about the Trust and the composition of its Council, see p 532. A more detailed prospectus may be obtained from the school. The school operates on three separate sites with Pre-Prep at The Squirrel, Junior Department at Greycotes and Seniors at Belbroughton Road.

Local Governors:

Chairman: District Judge A Campbell, DL, MA

Mrs J Bale
Mrs J Flemming
Mrs J H Galbraith, MA
Dr M Griffin, MA, DPhil
Mrs M C Shannon
Mr J Smith, JP, FRICS, FCIArb
Dr G A Stoy
Ms M Talbot, BA, BPhil
Mr A Wain, BSc (Econ), ACMA, MIMC
Mrs P West, MA

Headmistress: **Miss O F S Lusk**, BMus (Victoria, NZ)
Music

Deputy Headmistress: Mrs D Rose, MA (Cantab) *History/ Politics*

Director of Studies: Miss E M Edgar, BSc (London), CBiol, MIBiol *Biology*

Senior Department Staff:
Mrs J Bastow, BA (London) *Geography*
Mrs P Bennett, BSc (London) *Mathematics*
Miss S E Berry, BA (Cantab) *Biology*
Mrs W Burdett, BSc, MSc (London) *Chemistry*
Mrs H M Cave, BA (York) *English and Drama*
Mrs D Clark, NDD (Exeter) *Art*
Mrs J Clewett, TCert
Miss N R Copeman, BSc (Coventry) *Mathematics*
Mrs P J Cullerne-Bown, MA, MPhil (Oxon) *English*
Mrs O Curry, MA, MSc (Oxon) *Biology & Chemistry*
Miss J Davies, GRSM, ARCO, LRAM *Music*
Miss S J Derrick, BEd (Chelsea and Sussex) *Physical Education*
Mr T J Dougall, MA (Oxon) *History*
Mrs S Douglas, MechScience Tripos, MA (Cambridge *Physics*
Miss P Dunn, BA (Oxon), MA (Essex) *Spanish and French*
Mrs S C L Earley, BA (Nottingham) *Russian*
Miss A M Edwards, MA (Cantab), CBiol, MIBiol *Biology*
Dr A Fearnhead, BA (Oxon), DPhil *Mathematics*
Miss R M Fijalkowski, MA (Oxon) *Classics and French*
Mrs A Finch, BSc (London) *Geography*
Miss E E Forbes, MA (Oxon) *Classics*
Mrs F J Foster, MA (Oxon) *French and Italian*
Mr M W Gallacher, MA (Oxon) *Economics*
Ms M Girling, BA (Oxon) *English*
Mrs S Harskin, DEUG (Bordeaux)
Mrs P Hook, CertEd *Physical Education*
Mr A S Lewis, BA (Birmingham) *Mathematics*
Ms S McCabe, BSc (Paisley) *Information Technology*
Mr R McGeorge, BA (East Anglia), MPhil (Cambridge) *Geography*
Miss S McGowan, BA (London) *German and French*
Mrs A J B McNeillie, BSc (Aberdeen) *Mathematics*
Miss R Mallard, BA (Bristol), MA (Oxon) *English*
Mrs C M H Mayr-Harting, BA (Liverpool) *Classics*
Ms E Meloni, MA (London) *Applied Linguistics*
Mrs P L Melville, BSc (Leeds) *Physics*
Miss M R Mills, BA (Leicester), MA (Birmingham) *French*
Miss E M North, BA (London) *History*
Miss C J O'Neill, MA (Oxon), MA (London) *English*
Mr R Packard, BA (Lancaster), MA (Leicester) *Religious Studies*
Mrs C Powell, BEd (Cheltenham & Gloucester) *PE*
Mrs A K Quick, BA (Manchester) *Drama*
Miss A M Raw, BA (Newcastle) *Design Technology*
Miss R Rutty, BA (Kingston Poly) *Art*
Dr S Smith, MA (Oxon), DPhil *History*
Mr R C Spikes, MA (Oxon) *Music*
Miss A Stewart, MA (Manchester) *Textiles*
Mrs J Stone, MA (Oxon) *Biology*
Mrs J M Waller, BSc (London) *Chemistry*

Modern Language Assistants Conversation:
Ms E Meloni *Italian*
Mrs L Checkley *Russian*
Miss A Geremia *French*
Mrs G Thomas *Spanish*
Mr R Koglbauer *German*

Visiting Staff:
Piano:
Mrs H J Donald, GTCL
Mrs M Rosenberg, ARCM, LRAM
Miss M Lake, LRAM
Mrs K Suter, LRAM, GRSM

Viola: Mrs H Haskell, ARCM

Violin:
Mrs S Reynolds, GRSM, LRAM
Mrs H Haskell, ARCM

'Cello:
Mrs J Dallosso
Mrs V Findlay
Mrs K Suter, LRAM, GRSM

Oboe: Mrs C King, BA, PhD

Double Bass: Dr S Kershaw

Harp: Mrs R Bartels

String Coach: Mr P Davies

Flute:
Mr C Britton, BA (Birmingham)
Mr P Foster, LTCL
Mrs C Woodward, ARCM

Saxophone: Mr P Foster, LTCL

Clarinet:
Mrs D Brittain, ARCM
Miss M M Lake, LRAM

Brass: Mr R E Cutting

Harp: Mrs R Bartels

Recorder: Mr C Britton, BA (Birmingham)

Singing:
Mrs P Martin-Smith
Mrs R Landin

Speech and Drama: Mrs J Clewett, TCert

Administrative Staff:
Administrator: Mrs C Parker, CDipAF
Headmistress's PA: Mrs G Whitaker
Senior Admissions Registrar: Mrs S M Maund
Finance Officer: Mrs E Baird
Administration/Teaching Resources Officer: Miss S Warren
Receptionist: Mrs S Perry
School Computer Manager: Mr S Rundle, AIMgt
Librarian: Mrs E Sloan, ALA
School Doctor: Dr C Godlee
School Nurse: Mrs C A Collinge, BSc (Leeds)
Technicians:
Mr C Barlow
Miss K Bell, BA (Open), TEC
Mrs J Brown, CertEd
Mrs C Carder
Ms E Hedges
Mr O Tulloch

Junior Department:

Head of Junior Department: Mrs J Scotcher, BSc (Southampton), CertEd (Brunel)

Deputy: Mrs F S Thomson, BA (Birmingham)

Assistant Staff:
Mrs B Austin, BEd (Chelsea)
Miss K Banwell, BA (Warwick)
Mr T J Cooper, MA (Oxon), MA (Leeds)
Mrs R Davis, BA (Oxon), MA (Oxon)
Mrs S Gibson, CertEd
Mrs E F Gorick, CertEd (Avery Hill College)
Mrs L Lewis, BEd (Bedford)
Mrs K E McMichael, CertEd (Maria Grey College)
Mrs J M Morris, BA (Bristol)
Ms L Mullaney, BEd (Ilkley)
Miss R Nunn, BA (Roehampton)
Mrs C M L Patchett, BSc Hons, PGCE
Mrs C L Pope, BA (London)
Mrs Powlett Smith, CertEd (Homerton)

Miss E Swift, BEd, PE (Chichester)
Miss B Thomas, BA (Bath)
Mrs C Thomas, CertEd (St Luke's College)
Mrs J Waite, BEd (Worcester)
Mrs B Winearls, MSc (Oxon)
Mrs S Young, CertEd

Formroom Auxillaries:
Mrs S Gibson, CertEd
Mrs J Hammond, NNEB
Mrs M J Lewis

Visiting Staff:
Mr R Cutting
Mrs M Ford
Mr P A Foster, LTCL
Mrs C J Goodall, BA (Oxford), MA (London)
Mrs M A Malpas, BLitt, MA (Oxon)
Mrs P A Miller, BA (Exeter), LTCL
Mrs F R Potter, BA (Durham)
Mrs J P Quillen, AB (Harvard-Radcliffe)
Mrs S C Reynolds, GRSM, LRAM
Mrs J Richardson, BMus (Surrey)
Mrs M Rosenberg
Mrs C Sadler, GGSM, CertEd
Mrs K Suter, GRSM, LRAM, ALCM
Mrs R Van Der Werff

Administrative Staff:
Administrator: Mrs S Cox, BA (Reading), PGDE
Administrative Assistant: Mrs C Ogle
Caretaker: Mr D Joyce
After School Care Supervisor: Mrs M J Lewis
After School Assistant: Mrs J Hammond

Pre-Prep Department:

Head: Mrs R Beale, CertEd

Assistant Staff:
Mrs A Beveridge, CertEd, MEd
Mrs R David, TCert (Nursery)
Miss J Day, TCert
Mrs V Ellis, BA
Mrs J Honeyman, Teaching Diploma
Mrs T Poyntz, NNEB
Mrs C Stephenson, BEd
Mrs C Waller, Teaching Diploma

Classroom Assistants:
Miss N Bagshaw
Mrs M Baker, PPA
Mrs S Costar
Miss C Douglas-Jones, NNEB, MontDip
Mrs G Stephens, PPA
Mrs M Wakefield
Mrs G White, NNEB

Visiting Staff:
Mrs R Astley *Special Needs*
Mrs S Coates *Recorder*
Mrs M Colgrove *Ballet*
Miss L Haigh *Singing*
Mrs McMillen *Speech and Drama*
Mrs J Quillen *Violin*
Mrs K Suter *Piano*

Administrative Staff:
Administrative Officer: Mrs S Fitz-Gibbon
After School Care: Mrs P Smith

The school was opened in 1875. It is now situated in Belbroughton Road, off the Banbury Road, about 2 miles from the centre of the city. The school recently merged with two neighbouring preparatory schools to provide education in the Pre-Prep Department at The Squirrel (boys and girls 3–7 years), the Junior Department at Greycotes (girls 7–11 years), with the Senior Department (girls 11–18 years) at Belbroughton Road. Major refurbishment at The Squirrel and Greycotes has now been completed. On the Senior Department site there is a Sports Hall and separate purpose-built centres for Music and Art and Design and Design Technology and a Sixth Form Centre. There is also a well equipped ICT centre, an additional central IT and AV resource centre attached to the Library and a computer centre for Science. The whole school is networked for computers. Over the next year the Senior Department will be provided with a new Music School, indoor Swimming pool and other facilities.

There are about 550 pupils in the Senior Department of whom 150 are in the Sixth Form. There is provision for entry at the Sixth Form stage. The Pre-Prep and Junior Departments number about 340. Admission is at 3+, 4+, 7+, 9+, 11+ and 16+.

Curriculum. The curriculum is broadranging with the full range of subjects on offer including Ancient Greek, Russian and Drama. There is an emphasis on using ICT across the curriculum. Girls are prepared for GCSE, and AS/A Level, and for university entrance and scholarship examinations. Generally nearly 30% proceed to Oxbridge each year. Many girls also take the examinations of the Associated Board in Music, and in Speech and Drama. Many girls belong to the Duke of Edinburgh's Award Scheme, take part in Young Enterprise, and belong to the Combined Cadet Force along with Magdalen College School.

Physical activities include Hockey, Volleyball, Trampolining, Badminton, Gymnastics, Netball, Tennis, Athletics and Swimming. The school has its own outdoor swimming pool, sports hall and hard courts in the school grounds and extensive playing field. Senior girls have the use of a squash court close to the school.

Fees. From September 2000: Senior School £1,680 per term; Junior Department £1,220 per term. Pre-Prep Department: Nursery (mornings only) £490 per term, 4-7 year olds £1,220 per term.

The fees cover the regular curriculum, school books, stationery and other materials, Choral Music, Games and Swimming, but not optional extra subjects or school meals. Lunch (currently £115 per term) is compulsory for girls up until Year 9, and for new entrants to the Junior Department at Greycotes. The fees for extra subjects, including Instrumental Music, Singing, Speech and Drama, are shown in the prospectus.

Bursaries. Following the ending of the Government Assisted Places Scheme, the GDST has made available to the school a substantial number of scholarships and bursaries. The bursaries are means tested and are intended to ensure that the school remains accessible to bright girls who would profit from our education but who would be unable to enter the school without financial assistance. Bursaries are available before or after entry throughout the Senior School and application should be made to the Headmistress in cases of financial need. All requests will be considered in confidence.

Scholarships. There is at present available to internal or external candidates a number of academic and music scholarships for entry at 11+ or to the Sixth Form.

Oxford High School Old Girls' Association. Secretary: Mrs J Birch, 15 Cunliffe Close, Oxford OX2 7BJ.

Charitable status. Oxford High School is one of the 25 schools of the Girls' Day School Trust, which is a Registered Charity, number 1026057. The aim of the Trust is to provide a fine academic education at a comparatively modest cost.

Palmers Green High School

Hoppers Road London N21 3LJ
Tel: 0181-886 1135

Founded 1905
Motto: *By Love Serve One Another*

School Council
Chairman: Mrs B D Smith
Mrs M J Dunn
Mrs J Knuth, NNEB
D Lewis, Esq, ACIB
Mrs M Lucey, MA (Oxon)
Mrs J Mayhew, CertEd
D Orfeur, Esq
D B Smith, Esq, FRIBA
M Richman, Esq
J Zinkin, Esq, FAC

Head Mistress: **Mrs S Grant**, BMus Hons (University College of Wales, Aberystwyth)

Deputy Headmistress: Mrs P Simmonds, MA (Oxon), BSc (London) (*Mathematics*)

Head of Lower School: Mrs J Hart, BEd Hons (Southampton), MSc, DipRE (*Form Teacher, Senior 4*)

Staff:
Mrs A Atkinson, BEd (*Nursery Teacher*)
Mrs S Banks, NNEB (*Nursery Assistant*)
Miss A Barrett, Teacher's Cert (Trent Park College, London) (*Form Teacher for Prep 3 and Head of Prep Department*)
Mrs H Bhundia (*Auxiliary Assistant, Lower School*)
Mrs I Bidewell, BA (University College, Dublin). Higher Diploma in Education (*Geography*) Form Teacher for Senior 1
Miss L Birri, Teacher's Cert (Newman College). Form Teacher for Prep 2
Mrs S Borkowski, Teacher's Cert (Maria Assumpta College) (*Physical Education*)
Miss D Capp, BA Hons (Brighton) (*Physical Education, Form Teacher S3C*)
Mrs A Cook, Teacher's Cert (London) (*Religious Education and Careers*)
Mrs C Doe, BA Hons (East Anglia) (*Head of English*) (*Form Teacher, Senior 5*)
Mrs L Dufton, BA Hons (Middlesex) (*Form Teacher for Junior 2*)
Ms M Dutton, DipAD Fine Art (Chelsea School of Art and Arts Teaching Diploma) (*Art*)
Mrs G Gabzdyl, BA Hons (London) (*Head of History*)
Mrs T Gully, BSc Hons (London) (*Information Technology and Business Studies*)
Mrs S Hagi-Savva (*Nursery Assistant*)
Mrs E Hall, BA Hons (West Surrey) (*Lower School Art*)
Mrs E Hassan, *Lower School Auxiliary Assistant*
Mr D Healey, MA, CertEd, DipAD, DipCDT (London) (*Design and Technology*)
Mrs J Kobylanski, BSc Hons (Chelsea College of Science & Technology) (*Mathematics, Form Teacher for Senior 3K*)
Mrs E Kocen, BA Hons (London) (*German*)
Mrs M Lawrence, BSc Hons (*Sheffield*) (*Science and Personal and Social Education*)
Mrs A Lee, BEd (Birmingham) (*Form Teacher for Junior 3*)
Mr J Matthews, BMus Hons (Cardiff) (*Head of Music*)
Mrs A Mielniczek, BA Hons (London), MA (London) (*English*)
Miss J Newman, BA Hons (London) (*French*)
Miss F Notley, BA Hons (Durham) (*Form Teacher, Senior 1*)
Miss V Penglase, BA Hons (London) (*Performing Arts Coordinator, Form Teacher for Senior 4*)
Ms K Roy, BA Hons (East Anglia) (*Head of Modern Languages, Form Teacher for Senior 2*)
Mrs C Shaw, BSc Hons (Warwick) (*Mathematics*)
Mrs R Smith, BA Hons (Manchester) (*Science Coordinator*)
Mrs M Suleyman (*Auxiliary Assistant Lower School*)
Mr C Vincent, BSc Hons (Swansea), DipCEG (*Head of Careers Education & Guidance, Life Skills, Work Experience and Geography*)
Mrs J Wakeley, BEd Hons (London) (*Head of Physical Education and Outward Bound Education*)
Ms C Walker, BEd Hons (*Form Teacher for Prep 1*)
Mrs S Worringham (*IT Support Assistant*)

Visiting Staff:
Instrumental Tuition:
Clarinet: Miss R Chard, LRAM
Recorder/Flute: Mrs E Marshall, BMus Hons, ARCM
Piano: Mrs S O'Conner, LRAM
Violin/: Mrs S White, GRAM
Ballet and Speech & Drama: under the auspices of the Vallé Academy

Bursar: Mr M Hanks, ACIB
Headmistress' PA/Office Manager: Mrs M Harding
Assistant Secretaries:
Mrs J Brown
Mrs S Davies
Accounts Assistant: Mrs A Monty
Laboratory Technician: Mrs C Stow, BA Hons (Open University)

Palmers Green High School is a girls' independent day school for up to 350 girls aged 3–16 in Winchmore Hill, North London. It is well served by a number of bus routes and close to British Rail Stations in Winchmore Hill and Palmers Green. Southgate, on the Piccadilly Line is the nearest Tube Station.

The School was founded by the late Alice N Hum in buildings in Green Lanes, Palmers Green and transferred to Avondale Hall on its present site in Hoppers Road, Winchmore Hill in 1918.

The School's motto 'By Love Serve One Another' was carefully selected by Miss Hum to reflect her deep Christian convictions derived from her membership of the Society of Friends (Quakers).

The ideals of integrity and care implicit in that philosophy have been maintained by succeeding generations of teachers in the face of changing standards and are still a vital part of the School's ethos.

Palmers Green High School continues to provide the warm and sympathetic environment of a small school in which both sound academic and personal development go hand in hand. The School aims to foster and maximise the individual talents of each girl while encouraging her to think independently, act in a responsible way and acquire self-discipline.

During the past eight years, seven building phases have provided for the re-building and extension of the school's major facilities. These modern facilities include a new Preparatory Department, Computer, Technology and Science Laboratories, Performing Arts Suite, Library, Pottery and Photography areas and a new administrative block. A new sports hall and theatre as well as new catering facilities have also been completed.

The games facilities used are among the best in the area, covering a wide range of sport – from hockey to golf, canoeing to ice-skating. Outward bound courses are organised on a regular basis and this wide range of sporting activities forms the basis for the study of a GCSE in

Physical Education at the age of 14 and the Bronze and Silver Awards of the Duke of Edinburgh Scheme.

The Academic Nursery is situated half a mile from the main school in modern premises. There is a qualified teacher in attendance at all times as well as two assistants. Pupils follow a stimulating but demanding curriculum for preparation for the main school.

The curriculum, embracing the National Curriculum, is designed to give a broad education in which the active acquisition of skills, as well as knowledge is encouraged. Children are familiarised with computers from the Preparatory Department upwards with all pupils taking the RSA Computer Literacy and Information Technology Certificate by the age of 14.

Educational visits to take advantage of the facilities of London in particular are considered important and are often arranged.

The performing arts are encouraged in the school and each term sees a large number of pupils taking part in plays, musicals and concerts, including the House Music Competition and the Dame Flora Robson Drama Competition.

Careers education is an integral part of the timetabled curriculum from 11–16 and all pupils participate in careers lectures, exhibitions and work experience placements.

Pupils are prepared for up to 10 GCSE subjects, with a view to continuing their studies to A level and beyond.

Fees at present £725 per term for the Nursery; £1,235 Prep; £1,570 Junior; £2,100 Senior.

Scholarships. There are Entrance Scholarships and Bursaries to the Senior School as well as Music Awards.

Entrance. Admission to all forms is by test and interview, the main intake being at 3+, 4+ and 11+.

Charitable status. Palmers Green High School Limited is a Registered Charity, number 312629. It exists to provide a high standard of education for girls.

Parsons Mead

Ottways Lane Ashtead Surrey KT21 2PE
Tel: (01372) 276401
Fax: (01372) 278796

Independent Day School for Girls 3–18. Member of GBGSA and GSA.

Governing Body:

Chairman: Miss J Burnell, BSc, MIBiol, FRSA

Mrs S Butcher (*representing the PTA*)
Mrs L Cartwright-Taylor, BSc, MSc, PhD, MBA
A Coles, BA (Hons), MA
Mrs E P Crips Villiers (*representing Old Girls' Association*)
P E Firth, Esq
R Lynch, Esq
D Mitchell-Baker, Esq, CEng, MICE
Mrs E R Oliver, BA
A Smith, Esq, FIIMR, FCIM, FFA, FCEA, MSI, CMC, MIMC, MIRM, MICM, DPhil, MA, MBA, CPhys, FInstP, FIMA, FSS
H Ward, Esq, PhD, BSc(Eng), FInstD, FInstMan, DIC, ACGI, CEng
A S Way, Esq, MSc, CEng, MIEE
Mrs J E Widman

Secretary to the Board of Governors and Bursar: Mrs M Wright

Academic Staff:

Headmistress: **Mrs P Taylor**, BA (Hons) Dunelm

Deputy Head: Mrs R Wilson, BA (Hons)

English:
Mrs R A Driver, BA (Hons) Dunelm
Mrs M G Turner, BA (Hons) Warwick
Mrs E M Jolly, BA (Hons) London (*Drama*)

Mathematics:
Mrs T McKee, BSc (Hons) London
Miss C Workman, BEd (Hons) London
Mrs R Allen, BA (Hons) Oxon
Mrs A Langridge, BSc (Hons) Liverpool
Mrs J Robinson, BSc (Hons) Open University

Languages:
Mrs J Shiret, BA (Hons) Newcastle
Mrs J Watney, BA (Hons) Reading
Mrs B Wheatley, Studienassessorin Berlin
Mrs C Leighton, BA (Hons) Dunelm
Mrs L McKay, BA (Hons) Wales

Humanities:
Mrs J Bennett, BA (Hons) Sheffield
Mr M Ingall, BSc Bristol
Mrs J Morgan, BA (Hons) Wales, MA Kingston
Mr P Chatterton, BA Newcastle
Miss M Collett, BEd London
Miss S Porter, BSc, DipASS, PGCE Open University

Science and Design Technology:
Mr R Kernley, BSc (Hons) London
Mrs L Boardman, BSc (Hons) Exeter
Miss C Workman, BEd (Hons) London
Mrs B Welton, BSc (Hons) York
Mrs R J Coleman, BA (Hons) Open University
Mrs M Dawe, BEd (Hons) Cantab

Music:
Mrs D Stirling, GTCL, LTCL, ATCL (London)

Physical Education:
Miss S M E Dudgeon, BEd (Hons) Exeter

Careers:
Mrs L A McKay, BA (Hons) Wales

Librarian: Miss B A Dawson, MA Lancaster, DipLib Leeds

Head of Junior Department:
Mrs J Ince, CertEd

Junior Department Staff:
Miss J Dibbs, CertEd Nonington
Mrs M Frye, CertEd, PDE
Mrs J Orgill, BEd (Hons) Wales
Miss C Page, BEd (Hons) Cantab
Ms M Reynolds
Mrs V Reynolds, BA (Hons) Brunel
Mrs A Rogalska, BEd London
Miss C L Russell, BSc (Hons) City University
Mrs G A Sims, LTCL
Mrs V Straszewski, CertEd
Miss M Totten, BSc Reading
Miss C Pewtress, NNEB

Boarding House Staff:
Miss B Dawson, MA Lancaster, DipLib Leeds

Nursing Sister: Mrs C Collins, RGN

Domestic Bursar: Mrs J Mountford, MHCIMA

Headmistress's Secretary: Mrs P J Stubbs

Old Girls' Association: Miss Louise Firth, c/o Parsons Mead.

Number of Pupils. 300 (including 2 Boarders), about 125 of whom are in the Junior Department. Entry from 3+ upwards is by School's own assessment.

The Buildings. The original house is now the main building with the School Office and dining room. The teaching facilities, Science Laboratories, Art Room, Food and Textiles Rooms, Library and Information Technology Rooms are all of modern design. A Drama Studio opened in 1993. The Junior Department is separately housed on the same campus in a new building completed in early 1998. A new Sixth Form Centre was opened in September 1998.

The School stands in 12 acres of wooded grounds which incorporate gardens, playing fields, tennis/netball courts, heated swimming pool and a sports hall. The school has easy access to the M25 (exit 9).

The curriculum includes English Language and Literature, History, Geography, French (from 3 years of age), Latin, ICT, German, Mathematics, Biology, Chemistry, Physics, Music, Drama, Art, Textiles, Food Technology, Religious Studies, Gymnastics and Games. Spanish, Business Studies and Psychology are added subjects in the VIth Form. In the VIth Form, girls are prepared for 'A' levels and Key Skills. Instrumental Tuition, Speech & Drama, Tennis coaching and Dancing are extras.

Examinations. Pupils are prepared for Key Stage 1 and 2 Tests, GCSE and 'A' level examinations, and for University entrance, including Oxford and Cambridge.

Educational expeditions to London and other places of interest at home and abroad are arranged. There is a French exchange.

Fees per term. (*see* Entrance Scholarship section) *Senior School:* Day £2,070. *Junior School:* Day £1,190-£1,795. *Under 5 years: on application.*

Charitable status. Parsons Mead Educational Trust Limited is a Registered Charity, number 312062. It exists for the furtherance of education.

The Perse School for Girls

Union Road Cambridge CB2 1HF
Tel: (01223) 454700 (Headmistress's Secretary); (01223) 454701 (Bursar)
Fax: (01223) 467420
e-mail: PerseGirls@aol.com
website: www.perse.cambs.sch.uk

Founded 1881

Governors:
Mr R F Blanchard
Mr S R R Bourne
Mr A K Brett
Dr M C Carpenter, PhD
Mrs P Cleobury
Dr A Crowden
Miss J Gough, MA
Dr D J Howard, PhD
Dr M F Hunt, PhD
Mrs S McMullen
Dr W J Macpherson, MA
Colonel M Payne
Mrs S Stopford
Dr G Sutherland, MA, DPhil (*Chairman*)
Mrs R Thackray
Dr R M Williams

Clerk to the Governors: Mrs D E Cook, ACIB

Headmistress: **Miss P M Kelleher**, MA (Oxon), MA (Sussex)

Deputy Headmistress: Dr C Mullen, BA, PhD (London) *French & Latin*

Senior Staff:
Mrs C M Beadle, BA (York) *Chemistry, Year Head*
Mr R Bett, BA Hons (Loughborough) LTCL *CDT, Technology Co-ordinator*
Mrs J Bragg, BSc Hons (Sussex) *Biology, Year Head*
*Mr J Brown, GradMechEng *DT*
*Miss M Chambers, BEd Hons (Bristol) *Physical Education*
Mrs D Clements, BSc (Stamford), PGCE (Cantab) *Head of Junior School*
*Miss E Cook, MA (Oxon) *Mathematics*
*Mrs G Dambaza, BA (Cantab) *Physics*
Ms V Demidova, BA (Herzen University), PGCE (Nottingham) *Russian*
*¶Mrs M Dicken, MA (Oxon) *History*
*Mr M Everett, MA (Cantab), MMus (Surrey) *Music*
*Mrs L Handcock, BSc Hons (Exeter) *Information Technology*
*Mr B Heyes, BA Hons (Leeds ATC) *Art and Design*
*Mrs B Horley, BA Hons (Birmingham), MA (OU) *Religious Education/PSE Co-ordinator*
*Mrs D Jimenez, BA Hons (Manchester) *Spanish*
*Miss K King, BSc Hons (Sussex) *Chemistry*
Mrs E Langworth, BA Hons (Warwick) *History, Year Head*
*Mrs C Lemons, Agrégée, M-ès-L (Bordeaux), CAPES *French*
Mrs L Lloyd, MA (Oxon) *Biology, Year Head*
*Mrs S Lynn, BSc Hons (Bristol) *Chemistry, Head of Science*
*Miss F Mason, BEd Hons (London) *Drama*
Mrs S Miller, BA Hons (Hull) *Archivist and Librarian*
Miss K Milne, BEd Hons (Cantab) *Deputy Head of Junior School*
Mr V Minei, BSc Hons (OU) *Italian*
Miss B Pankhurst, BA (Cantab), MA (McMaster) *English, Head of Sixth Form*
Mrs A Rushen, BA Hons (Reading) *Geography, Year Head*
Mrs M Thomas, BA (Northwestern Ill) Illinois State Teachers' Cert *German*
*Mrs A Thompson, BA (Liverpool), MPhil (Oxon) *Classics*
*Miss B J Whitehead, MA (Cantab) *Geography*
*Mrs S Williams, BSc Hons (Manchester) *Biology*
Miss E Wood, GRSM, ARMCM *Music, Projects Manager*

Secretary: Mrs L Crilley, BA Hons (OU)

Bursar: Mrs D E Cook, ACIB

The Senior School comprises about 550 girls between the ages of eleven and eighteen. There are 52 full-time and 22 part-time teaching staff and 27 peripatetic music staff. The Junior School has about 160 girls between the ages of seven and ten with 11 full-time staff. Some Senior School staff teach also in the Junior School. The School's own entrance tests are held annually for applicants at 7, 8, 9, 10 and 11. There is also regular entry at the Sixth Form stage, on the results of interviews and GCSE examinations.

Extras. Individual music lessons in most instruments, speech and drama.

Fees. From September 1st 2000: Junior School £1,794 inclusive per term. Senior School £2,124 inclusive per term.

Exhibitions and Bursaries. One Exhibition is offered annually by Trinity College, Cambridge, to a girl going up to Oxford or Cambridge. The Perse School for Girls' Appeal Fund Trust, set up in 1977, with a further Bursary Fund established in 1997, administers bursary funds for pupils in the Senior School. A few Sixth Form Scholarships were introduced in 1993. Bursary information may be obtained from the Headmistress.

School Curriculum. The Senior School prepares girls for the universities and professions and for the GCE and GCSE examinations There is a three-form entry. Forms are unstreamed with setting in some subjects. In the first three years pupils acquire knowledge and basic skills in a wide range of subjects chosen from the finest traditions and promoting newer technologies. A second Modern Language (German, Italian, Russian or Spanish) and Latin are introduced in the second year. At GCSE the compulsory core consists of English, English Literature, Mathematics, French, Second Language, Biology, Chemistry and Physics. The options, of which girls normally choose three, include History, Geography, Religious Studies, Latin, Greek, Design and Technology, Information Technology, Art, Drama, Music and Textiles. Courses in Physical Education and General Religious Education continue throughout the Middle School, together with PSE and Careers Guidance (introduced in the third year). Class excursions, fieldwork, foreign exchanges, clubs, activities, and large scale projects enrich the curriculum. Individual music lessons and speech tuition are also available.

In the Sixth Form AS/A2 courses are offered in the following subjects: English, Emglish Language and Literature, Mathematics, Further Mathematics, Computing (AS only), Biology, Human Biology, Chemistry, Physics, Psychology, Economics, Geography, History, Theology, Classical Civilisation, Latin, Greek, French, German, Italian, Japanese (AS only), Russian, Spanish, Design and Technology, Art, Music, Theatre Studies, Textiles and General Studies. Students have traditionally chosen to broaden their Sixth Form studies and can choose up to five subjects at AS in the first year, reducing to three or four A levels in the second year. In addition, Key Skills will be delivered through a compulsory General Studies programme leading to AS or A level. Students may also choose certificated courses from a Complementary Studies programme: Foreign Languages at Work (FLAW) in French, German, Italian and Spanish, further GCSE subjects in the Creative Arts and Technology, Classical Greek, and Japanese, and Cambridge Information Technology. All students participate in Creative Activities which offers sporting and leisure activities as well as cultural pursuits. European Work Experience is available for linguists.

The School is a member of ISCO and has links with Cambridgeshire Careers Guidance. An extensive careers programme, including individual counselling, enables students to make informed choices about Higher Education and Careers.

The Junior School curriculum includes Religious Education, English, Mathematics, Information Technology, History, Geography, French, Science, Art, Design and Technology, Music, Drama and Physical Education. Recorder, violin, 'cello and speech and drama classes are available in addition to individual music and speech tuition.

It is possible for a few Sixth Form girls to board with families in the town. Boarding arrangements are the responsibility of parents but require the approval of the Governors and Headmistress.

Buildings and facilities. The School's facilities include 8 well-equipped laboratories, 3 language laboratories, 2 computer rooms, a drama studio, a DT workshop, netball and tennis courts and hockey pitches. The Bedson Music Wing provides 18 individual teaching rooms. The Junior School building has been completely re-built and was re-opened in January 2001.

Old Persean Guild. *Secretary:* Miss M Monnier, c/o The Perse School for Girls, Union Road, Cambridge CB2 1HF.

Charitable status. The Perse School for Girls is a Registered Charity, number 52213, established to educate girls.

Peterborough High School

Westwood House Thorpe Road Peterborough PE3 6JF
Tel: 01733 343357. Bursar: 01733 355720
Fax: 01733 355710
e-mail: phs@peterboroughhigh.peterborough.sch.uk
website: www.peterboroughhigh.peterborough.sch.uk

Independent School for Girls, belonging to the Eastern Division of the Woodard Corporation

School Council:
Chairman: R B Yates, Esq, FCA

The Reverend Canon T R Christie, MA (*Provost*)
Miss L Ayres, LLB
Mrs I Coles
Mrs J Cook
Mrs S Farrow
Mrs L Frisby
The Revd Dr E Hebblethwaite
Dr C J Howe, MA, DPhil, FLS
Mr S R Howell
Mr S J Russell (Registrar)
Air Commodore M C G Wilson, RAF (Retd)

***Headmistress:* ‡Mrs Sarah A Dixon**, BA Hons (Warwick)

Deputy Headmistress: Miss P M Facy, BEd Hons (Madeley College) *Home Economics*

Director of Studies: Mrs S M Butter, BA Hons (London), MPhil (Manchester)

Head of the Junior School: Mrs P L Seabrook, BEd Hons (London)

Staff:
Mrs A Z Atreides, Montessori Diploma
Mrs A M Axe, BA Hons (Birmingham) *Physical Education*
Miss G Batey, BA Hons (OU) *Preparatory Department*
Mrs M Beardshaw, BA Hons (London) *Classics*
Mrs L Boyle *Preparatory Department*
Mrs T Brooker, BEd Hons (Northampton) *Preparatory Department*
Mrs R Burrell, BEd Hons (Lancaster) *Preparatory Department*
Miss S M Clarkson, BA Hons (Cantab) *History*
Mr D C Coleman, MA (Oxon), BLitt *English*
Mrs P Cooper, BEd (Cambridge), DipEd (Bedford) *Business Studies*
Mr P Cotton, MA (Cantab) *Religious Studies*
Mrs P Dangerfield, BEd Hons (Manchester) *Business Studies and IT*
Ms T Doyle, MNATD *Speech & Drama*
Mrs J Evans, Licence Limoges *French*
Miss C L Foster, BSc Hons, MSc (Leeds) *Science*
Mrs S J Hall, BSc Hons (UEA) *Chemistry*
Mr A Harwin, BA Hons (Norwich) *Art*
Miss H J Hathaway, BEd Hons (York) *Preparatory Department*
Mr D Hodges, BA Hons (London) *Geography and History*
Mr A Jackson, BA Hons (Warwick) *German*
Mr C King, BSc Hons, CMath, MIMA (Keele) *Mathematics*
Mrs B A Laing, BA, DipRSA Drama (Edinburgh) *Director of Drama*
Miss R Lowman, BA Hons (Roehampton) *Preparatory Department*
Miss R J Mayle, BA Hons (Reading) *Geography*
Miss J McNeal, BA Hons (Dunelm) *English*
Ms L Nicol, BA Hons (Exeter) *French*
Miss C Penfound *Preparatory Department*
Mr M Ratchford, BA Hons (York) *Preparatory Department*

Mr G Reaks, BA Hons (Birmingham) *Music*
Mrs P Samuels, LGSM *Speech and Drama*
Mrs M Sharp, CertEd, NFF Assoc member in Early Years (Glasgow) *Preparatory Department*
Ms E Shaw, BA Hons (Birmingham) *Art*
Miss C Taylor-Ward, BEd (Nottingham Trent) *Preparatory Department*
Miss J L Wildman, BEd Hons (Bedford) *Physical Education*
Mrs S Wilkinson, CertEd *Mathematics*
Mrs L D Willey, CertEd *Biology*

Music Department:
Mr M Vessey, CertEd (London) *Director of Music*
Miss C J Wood, AGSM, DipNCOS *Head of Instrumental Tuition*
Mrs H Bell, DipMus (OU), ATCL, MusEd *Flute*
Mrs K L Norton, GRSM, ARCM *Piano/Singing*
Mr L Dash, BMus Hons, LCM, DipHE *Percussion*
Mrs N Attwell, CertEd (Bristol) *Piano*
Miss B Prettejohn, LRAM *Violin and Viola*
Mr C Radford, LRSM *Woodwind*

Boarding House:
Mr & Mrs J Axe (*House Parents*)
Mrs J Payne (*Matron*)

Administrative Officers:
Bursar: Major T J Batchelder, ACIS
Headmistress's Secretary/Registrar: Mrs A Field
Accounts: Mrs P Chapman
Administration Assistant: Mrs J Percival
Catering Manager: Mrs Z Clark
Medical Officer: Dr A M O'Reilly
Laboratory Technician: Mrs P Reid
ICT Technician: Mr D Still
Reprographics: Mrs V Tobin

Peterborough High School is an Independent School for girls aged 3 to 18 and for boys aged 3 to 11 years. The School was founded in 1895 and admitted to the Eastern Division of the Woodard Corporation in 1968. There are at present 330 pupils, of whom 30 are boarders.

Situation and Buildings. The School is located in beautiful secluded grounds, near the centre of Peterborough, 50 minutes by fast train from King's Cross and easily accessible by road from the A1 and A47. The elegant Victorian house which formed the original School is now the centre of a modern purpose-built complex of classrooms, well-equipped laboratories, Music School, Gymnasium, Art Block, Sixth Form Centre, Library and a new ICT Suite with 'state of the art' facilities.

Boarding. Weekly, termly and flexi-boarding are available to girls, all of whom have study bedrooms. Both boarding houses are adjacent to the main school buildings. Single rooms are available to girls in the Fifth and Sixth Forms, if they so wish.

The Preparatory Department. Boys and girls are admitted into the Reception Class from the age of 3+. Most classes in the Preparatory Department are taught by Form Teachers. Specialist teachers are introduced to add variety and depth to the general, broad-based curriculum. Numerous extra-curricular activities are offered throughout the year. Before and after-school activities and supervisory facilities are available.

The Senior School. The curriculum of the main school is characterised by small classes and an emphasis on individual guidance and target-setting. A balanced programme of forms of knowledge and areas of experience leads to high achievement at GCSE in up to ten subjects. English, Mathematics, Science, Religious Education, Games and PE, remain compulsory throughout; Languages, History and Geography, Art (including Textiles and Pottery), Classical Civilisation, Music, Drama and Physical Education form the matrix of options. Unusually, both German and French are studied from Year 7.

Pupils are selected from the entrance examination and thereafter are in unstreamed tutor groups, although there is setting in Mathematics and Science.

In September 2000, the school opened a large, new ICT suite with state-of-the-art equipment. All classrooms are networked. ICT skills are central to the work of every department, and co-ordinated to allow the girls to build up CLAIT certification in several modules by the end of Year 11. Specialist laboratories for all sciences and for languages are provided.

The Sixth Form offers AS and A2 courses in English Literature, Mathematics, Biology, Chemistry, Physics, Physical Education, Geography, History, French, German, Classical Civilisation, Art, History of Art and Music. In addition, new 6-unit Advanced GNVQs in Performing Arts and Travel and Tourism have been launched. General Studies courses include Philosophy, to which eminent practitioners from the university contribute.

All Sixth Form students follow an intensive tutorial programme in the skills and techniques of study, and build up a portfolio of achievement in the newly defined Key Skills. The destination of most Sixth Formers is university.

As a school with pupils from Reception, older girls have many opportunities to develop a sense of involvement and responsibility, and carry out valuable service in the wider community of the city during the Sixth Form. Business sense is developed through the Young Enterprise scheme, in which the school has reached the national final.

A thoughtful and balanced programme of personal and social education operates throughout the school, and includes careers advice and guidance.

Religion. Weekly Communion Services are held in the School Chapel. Arrangements are also made for termly boarders to attend local churches, including Peterborough Cathedral, or to worship in the School Chapel on Sundays. Special arrangements are made for daily Muslim worship.

Music and Drama. The music of the school, in particular its choral tradition, is renowned, the choir having sung in the cathedral, churches over a wide area, including Paris, London, and Cambridge college chapels. Tuition in piano and all orchestral instruments can be arranged. Major theatrical and musical productions take place several times a year, and the school enjoys its links with amateur theatre in the city. Standards are extremely high.

Games and Physical Education. The pupils play and work hard, achieving outstanding success in team sports and athletics. Many girls have represented the County, the region, and even England. The school estate is spacious, with several pitches, tennis courts and an athletics track. The Olympic standard sporting facilities of the city are within easy reach for swimming and major athletic events.

Extra-curricular activities. Many clubs and societies operate in extra-curricular time, and field visits and excursions illuminate classroom work. Exchange schemes for French and German operate on an annual basis to Lyons and Augsburg. Sixth Form work experience is possible in Augsburg. Many pupils undertake the Duke of Edinburgh Award Scheme at both Bronze and Gold levels, with outstanding success.

Scholarships. Academic and Music scholarships are available. Please apply to the Headmistress for details.

Westwoodians' Association. Hon Chairman: Miss E Combridge, Brownlow Farm, Creeton, Grantham, Lincs NG33 4QB.

Charitable status. Peterborough High School, as part of the Woodard Schools (Eastern Division) Limited is a Registered Charity, number 269667. It is an independent school which exists to promote the education of girls aged 3-18 and boys aged 3-11.

Pipers Corner School
High Wycombe

Great Kingshill High Wycombe Bucks HP15 6LP
Tel: (01494) 718255
Fax: (01494) 719806

Visitor: The Rt Rev The Lord Bishop of Buckingham

Board of Governors:

Chairman of Governors: The Countess of Buckinghamshire

Air Vice-Marshall D G Bailey, CB, CBE, RAF(Retd) (*Vice-Chairman*)
Mrs B Y Boyton, CertEd, DipEd (*Vice-Chairman*)
B Callaghan, Esq, FCA
R Corner, Esq
M F T Harborne, Esq
D B Jones, Esq, MPhil
Professor P B Mogford
J H Phimester, Esq

***Headmistress:* Mrs V M Stattersfield**, MA (Oxon), PGCE

Deputy Head: Mrs H Murphy, MA (Oxon), PGCE

Bursar and Clerk to the Governors: Colonel R Maxwell, MBE

Pipers Corner is a boarding and day school for 400 girls aged 4 to 18 years. Situated in its own 36 acres of Chiltern countryside, the school campus includes a modern Performing Arts Centre and excellent sports facilities.

Pipers is easily reached from London, and from Heathrow, Gatwick and Luton airports. Overseas boarders can be escorted to and from airports. Weekly boarding is a popular option with some girls travelling from our wide catchment area. School coaches are available from the Beaconsfield, Penn, Haddenham, Wendover, Princes Risborough, Marlow, Gerrards Cross, Chesham and Amersham areas.

We warmly welcome visitors to Pipers Corner, which provides a secure and happy environment in which each individual is helped to fulfil her potential and to emerge with maturity, confidence and a sense of independence.

In addition to girls chosen for academic ability, Pipers invites you to apply if you have an interest in the expressive arts and sport. A broad and balanced curriculum is followed, supported by expert careers advice. Every girl is encouraged to achieve her personal and academic potential in an atmosphere which combines good order, friendliness and courtesy.

Our Pre-Prep department for 4-6 year olds is flourishing and pupils progress through the Prep Department to the Senior School. Girls are encouraged to achieve high standards and small classes ensure attention to individual growth.

We have a thriving Sixth Form which provides a wide range of A level courses including Business Studies as a vocational A level. All girls are prepared for Higher Education in the friendly, lively, challenging atmosphere which prevails.

A full programme of extra-curricular activities is offered and experience of the wider community is gained through travel opportunities.

Qualified resident nursing staff ensure high standards of health care. Housemistresses arrange weekend activities and aim to give boarders a warm and secure environment.

We aim to achieve both success and happiness for each girl here in our care.

Termly Fees: (Autumn 2000) (*see* Entrance Scholarship section) Boarders: £3,395–£4,075; Weekly boarders: £3,350–£4,025; Day girls: £1,125–£2,445.

Charitable status. Pipers Corner School is a Registered Charity, number 310635. It exists to provide high quality education for girls.

Polam Hall

Darlington DL1 5PA.
Tel: (01325) 463383

Founded 1848.
A boarding and day school for 500 girls

Governors:
Mr W A Goyder, MA, LLB (Cantab) *Chairman*
Professor G R Batho, MA FRHistS
¶Mrs D M Bateman
Mrs K A Bonas
Dr M M Carr, MD, BSc, FRCP
Mrs E G Crossley, BA
Mrs S Earle
Mr D W France, FCIB
Mrs R H Gray
Mrs J Johnson
Mr R S Long
¶Miss D H Mounsey
Mr C D W Pratt, BSc
¶Mrs M L Pratt
Dr M Richardson
Mr R Tonks
Mr F Turnbull, MBE, FCCA

***Headmistress:* Mrs H C Hamilton**, BSc Hons (London) *Mathematics*

Deputy Headmistress: *Mrs J R Taylor, BEd Hons (London), FRGS *Geography*

Bursar and Clerk to the Governors: Mr M N Carr, ACIB

Polam Hall is an Independent School for Girls founded in 1848. The school has long been interdenominational. There are now 420 day and 40 boarding pupils; 186 of these are juniors.

The school stands in 20 acres of parkland, but is still within 5 minutes walking distance of the town centre. The mainline station, the A1 and Teesside Airport are only minutes away giving excellent access for both overseas and local students.

The main Hall contains administrative offices, Art Centre, Library, Music Department and CDT Centre. There are separate, well-equipped Laboratories, Gymnasium and Domestic Science area as well as a fully equipped computer room. The school has an excellent theatre, seating in excess of 200 people, where drama and musical productions of a very high standard are held.

There is a separate sixth-form centre providing study rooms and common rooms, and the Junior School is in a separate building within the school grounds.

The Junior School (aged 4-11) is closely integrated with the Senior School. All pupils follow a mixture of a formal and informal education. An internal examination is taken at age 11 for entry into the Senior School. There are many extra individual lessons available privately, including speech, piano, cello, violin, flute, clarinet, trumpet and guitar, fencing, ballet, modern and tap dancing.

Entry to the Senior School is through examination. All girls are expected to work towards between 9 and 11 subjects for GCSE. A choice from among 20 subjects is available with individual needs being catered for and extra subjects can be added in the Sixth Form.

The Sixth Form is divided into small tutorial groups with

a large number of subjects available, including Physics, Chemistry and Biology, Mathematics, Statistics, English, German, French, Spanish, History, Economics, Geography, Home Economics, Music, Art, Theatre Studies, History of Art, English Language. Educational visits are regularly arranged to various points of interest around the area. There is a Careers room where personal advice is available together with an Annual Careers Convention. The number of students going on to College and University is high - 100%.

Girls who board are arranged in small groups under the individual care of a housemistress who takes a close personal interest in the girl's welfare.

A wide range of activities is available to the girls with fixtures made for lacrosse, hockey, netball, tennis, rounders and athletics matches. In addition girls do gymnastics and modern dance. There are also opportunities for judo, riding, fencing, basketball, volleyball, trampolining and swimming. There is a Brownie pack for the junior girls and senior girls may enter for the Duke of Edinburgh Award Scheme. A high emphasis is also placed on community service.

Scholarships are awarded at 9+, 11+, and 13+. At 16+ there are a variety of awards available. Music Awards are available at 11+, 13+ and 16+.

Fees. Senior Day £1,905 termly; Senior Boarding £3,890 termly; Junior Day £1,376 termly; Junior Boarding £3,144 termly.

PHOSA Polam Hall Old Scholars' Association. *Secretary:* Mrs C Steele, Glen View, Piercebridge, Darlington, Co Durham.

Charitable status. Polam Hall School Limited is a Registered Charity, number 527369. Its aim is to provide, maintain, and carry on a school for the education of children.

Portsmouth High School (G.D.S.T.)

25 Kent Road Southsea Hampshire PO5 3EG
Tel: 023 9282 6714
Fax: 023 9281 4814

Founded 1882.

This is one of the 25 schools of The Girls' Day School Trust. For general information about the Trust and the composition of its Council, see p 532. A more detailed prospectus may be obtained from the school.

Patron: The Right Revd The Lord Bishop of Portsmouth

Local Governors:
Mr J R Bannell, FRICS
Mrs A Barnes
Miss A E Clarke, BA, JP
Mr M C Craft, MA
Rear Admiral I A Forbes, CBE
Mr N Jonas, OBE, DL, MA
Mrs R B Raper, JP
Mrs J Round, BA, MA(Econ), CDipAF, FIMgt
Dr J Sondheimer, MA, PhD
Mrs A Stoneham, MA, MSc

***Head:* Miss P Hulse**, BA (Open University) *English*

Deputy Head: Mr C J Campbell, BSc (Aston), MSc (Surrey) *Chemistry*

Senior Teacher: Mrs S Lloyd, BA Hons (Open University) *English*

Senior School:
Teaching Staff:
Mrs C Baczynski, BSc (Leeds) *Mathematics*
Mr J R Barrett-Danes, BA (Bristol Polytechnic) *Art*
Mr R Bramall, BA (Oxon), BSc (London) *Politics and Economics*
Mrs A Brooks, BEd (Southampton) *Art*
Mrs K Brown, BSc (London) *Geography*
Mrs P Brown, MA (Oxford) *Mathematics*
Mrs B Cant, MA (Glasgow) *German*
Mrs C Chadwick, BSc (Southampton) *Biology*
Mrs A Clark, CertEd (Cambridge) *PE*
Mr P D Collins, BSc (Southampton) *Mathematics*
Mrs R Comrie, BA Hons (Manchester)
Mrs E P C Coombes, BA (Open) *Chemistry*
Mrs G W Dearsley, LRAM, GRSM (London) *Music*
Mrs D E Dey, BA (Manchester) *French and Spanish*
Mr B D Diffey, BSc (London) *Physics*
Mrs S E Ellam, Diploma in Physical Education (Birmingham) *PE*
Mrs S M Fothergill, BSc (Wales) *Biology*
Mrs C Griffiths, BSc (London) *Mathematics*
Miss M Hainsworth, BA Hons (De Montfort University) *Dance & Drama with Literature*
Mrs S Hayes, ARCM Singing, CertEd *Music*
Mrs A Hooper, BA (Nottingham) *German*
Mrs A K Hoyle, BA (North Staffordshire) *English*
Mrs A M Hunter, BSc (York) *Biology and Careers*
Mrs E Jennings, BA (Oxford) *History*
Mr B C Jones, BA (Liverpool) *Spanish, French*
Miss L Knight, BEd (London) *Design & Technology*
Mrs S B Lovering, BSc (Portsmouth) *Chemistry*
Mrs N C Marriott, BA (Cardiff) *Spanish and French*
Mrs A Mason, BA (South Bank) *French and Spanish*
Mrs S Nelson, BEd (West Sussex/HE) *Physical Education*
Mrs S A Ridley, CertEd (Sarum St Michael) *Religious Knowledge*
Mr J D Smith, BSc (Southampton) *Physics and IT*
Mrs S Spender, CertEd (Bedford) *Physical Education*
Mrs R Thornton, BA (Sheffield) *Classics*
Mrs H J Trim, BSc (Southampton) *Geography*
Mrs E S Turner, BSc (London) *Geography*
Mr M J Vale, BA (Cambridge) *History*
Dr L Watson, BA (Southampton), PhD (London) *Classics*
Mrs Y Williams, BA (York) *English*
Miss H Wolseley, BA
Mrs E A Wood, BSc (St Andrews) *Chemistry and Physics*

Junior Department:
Head of Junior School: Miss P Kirk, BEd (Exeter) *English*
Mrs S Band, CertEd (Bedford) *Physical Education and English*
Mrs G W Byrne, BA (Portsmouth), DipCPC *English and Music*
Mrs C Collins, CertEd (St Osyth's)
Mrs S M Essex, CertEd (Leicester), DipRSA(IT) *Mathematics*
Mrs C Fontana, BA (Durham), DipMaths, DipDrama *English*
Mrs A Good, BA Hons (Nottingham) *History*
Mrs C Hadfield, CertEd (London), ALCM, Dip Management Studies *Mathematics*
Miss A Hills, BEd (London), Cert Music Education(TCM) *Music and Education*
Mrs S M Holding, CertEd, Certificate in Early Education
Mrs S B Jackson, CertEd (Brighton) *Biology*
Miss E Jupp, BA Hons (Southampton) *English & Archaeology*
Mrs M Saulet, CertEd (Maria Assumpta) *Geography and Music*

Visiting Staff:
Pianoforte:
Miss K Kingsley, GRSM, LRAM

Mrs L Beck
Violin and Viola: Miss K Robertson, GRSM, LRAM
'Cello: Mrs S Towner, ARCM
Flute: Mrs C Nicholson, FLCM, LRAM, LTCL, LLCM
Clarinet: Mr R Blanken, GRNCM, ARCM
Singing: Mrs S Hayes, ARCM
Guitar:
Mr J C Albert, TPCB
Mr N Worley, LTCL
Recorder: Mr C Burgess, LTCL
Oboe: Mrs A Clements, BEd Music
French Horn and Trumpet: Mrs B Bartholomew, LRAM, LTCM
Double Bass: Mr A Osman, GRSM, CertEd
Percussion: Mr R Huggett
Harp: Miss J Walters
Speech and Drama:
Mrs C Sinclair, LGSM, AGSM, ALAM, DipEd
Ms M Collinson, BA Hons (Hull)

School Administrator: Mrs G Owen
Head's Secretary: Mrs W Crellin
School Doctor: Dr J Thompson

Portsmouth High School, founded in 1882, draws pupils from a wide area of Hampshire, West Sussex and the Isle of Wight as well as from Portsmouth itself. It stands less than a mile from Portsmouth and Southsea station and is served by frequent town and country buses. Of its 610 pupils, 401 are in the Senior School, including 100 in the Sixth Form. The Senior school is accommodated in the original building which has been considerably extended in recent years to meet the needs of the modern curriculum, while the Juniors (209 girls, aged 4 to 11) are located 5 minutes walk away in a fine period house with extensive gardens and a range of indoor and outdoor facilities to stimulate the pupils' development. The school has 4 hard tennis and 6 netball courts, and additional games facilities are hired nearby for tennis, lacrosse and swimming.

There is an active Guild for former students which holds autumn and summer reunions. Details regarding the Guild are available from the Guild Secretary, c/o Portsmouth High School. Information regarding Old Girls can be found in the supplement to the School Magazine, copies of which can be obtained from the School.

Curriculum. The course is planned to give a well-balanced general education. In addition to academic subjects, a range of Physical Education options is taught and girls take part in choral, orchestral and dramatic activities. Pupils are prepared for GCSE and 'A' levels in a wide range of subjects, and for entrance to universities, schools of medicine and music, and other forms of higher education. Sixth Form students do not wear uniform and have a recently modernised separate Sixth Form Centre with a large common room and kitchen, study rooms and IT room. They are trained to work independently by having free periods in school and a free afternoon for home study.

Fees. From September 2000: Senior School £1,680 per term; Junior School £1,220 per term.

The fees cover the regular curriculum, school books, stationery and other materials, choral music, games and swimming, but not optional extra subjects or school meals.

The fees for extra subjects, including individual lessons in instrumental music and speech training, are shown in the prospectus.

Bursaries. Following the ending of the Government Assisted Places Scheme, the GDST has made available to the school a substantial number of scholarships and bursaries. The bursaries are means tested and are intended to ensure that the school remains accessible to bright girls who would profit from our education but who would be unable to enter the school without financial assistance.

Scholarships. There are at present available to internal or external candidates a number of scholarships for entry at 11+ or to the Sixth Form.

Charitable status. Portsmouth High School is one of the 25 schools of the Girls' Day School Trust, which is a Registered Charity, number 1026057. The aim of the Trust is to provide a fine academic education at a comparatively modest cost.

The Princess Helena College

Preston Hitchin Hertfordshire SG4 7RT
Tel: (01462) 432100
Fax: (01462) 431497
e-mail: head@phc.herts.sch.uk
website: www.phc.herts.sch.uk

Motto: *Fortis qui se vincit*
Founded 1820. Incorporated by Royal Charter 1886.

Patron: Her Majesty the Queen

President: HRH Princess Alice, Duchess of Gloucester

Vice-President: Miss Mary Beattie, MBE, JP, DL

Governing Body:
Chairman: Lady Staughton, JP
Vice Chairman: Rear Admiral N J Wilkinson, CB, FIMgt
Honorary Treasurer: C Beer, Esq, MA (Cantab)

Clerk to the Governors and Bursar: Mr Christopher Marley

***Headmistress:* Mrs Anne-Marie Hodgkiss**, BSc Econ (London), PGCE

Deputy Head: Mrs Françoise Austin, L et Dipl ès Lettres (Sorbonne, Paris)

Director of Studies: Mr Keith Miller, MA (Herts), BEd

Senior Housemistress: Ms Susan Harr, BA (Leics)

School Matron: Mrs Peggy Edwards, SRN, RMN

School Medical Officer: Dr Christine Ryecart, MB

Secretary to the Headmistress: Mrs Elizabeth Madden

Old Girls' Secretary: Mrs C Murray, 29 Binden Road, Shepherd's Bush, London W12 9RJ.

Foundation. The Princess Helena College is a small boarding and day school. It was founded in 1820 to educate as future governesses the daughters of deceased Anglican Clergy and of Naval and Military Officers who had died for their country in the Napoleonic Wars.

In 1879 HRH Princess Helena, third daughter of Queen Victoria, bestowed upon the School its present title. Her association with the College began in 1868 and lasted until her death in 1923.

The College is at Temple Dinsley, an historic and beautiful estate of 183 acres, situated in the village of Preston, near Hitchin, on a northern ridge of the Chiltern Hills.

Facilities. The main building, a Queen Anne mansion of 1712, was enlarged by Lutyens in 1909, when the gardens were designed by Miss Gertrude Jekyll. The Dower House, also a Grade II listed building, opened in January 1992 as a new Sixth Form House, following extensive renovation and the building of a new wing.

The historic houses are complemented by modern classrooms, science laboratories, a superb sports hall and a well equipped Design Technology Centre.

Curriculum. Throughout the school pupils are provided with the skills needed to thrive in the 21st Century. The lower school curriculum consists of English, French,

Latin, German, Mathematics, Information Communication Technology, Biology, Physics, Chemistry, History, Geography, Religious Education, Music, Art and Design and Technology. There are also programmes in Personal and Social Education and General Studies. Most orchestral instruments are taught and girls are entered for the examinations of the Associated Board of the Royal Schools of Music.

Prior to the Sixth Form, girls choose their GCSE subjects, following much consultation with staff and parents. On average, girls study between 8 and 10 GCSE subjects. The pass rate A*-C is 96% with 43% of the GCSEs being passed at A* or A grade. A comprehensive careers programme is undertaken and ICT skills are further developed for all pupils.

In the Sixth Form, A Level courses are available in all the main academic subjects. The success rate A-E is 94% and 90% of pupils go on to university. Comprehensive careers support is provided.

Religion. Girls attend the nearby village church of St Martin's in Preston, which is also used for the school's Confirmation Services. Although the school's affiliation is to the Church of England, girls of other denominations and religions are welcomed.

Games. In addition to timetabled lessons, there are sports activities each weekday after school and on Saturdays. Girls participate in a wide range of sports, but lacrosse and netball are the main competitive games in winter, tennis and athletics in summer. A heated outdoor swimming pool is used from April to October.

Extra-Curricular Activities. There are regular concerts and plays and many girls participate in the Duke of Edinburgh's Award. Other evening and weekend activities include drama, cookery, decorative craft, debating, riding, gardening, aerobics, trampolining and desk-top publishing.

We enjoy the benefits of our proximity to London and Cambridge and frequent visits are made to the theatre, art galleries, museums and other places of interest.

Leave. Boarding arrangements are flexible and weekly boarding is also well established.

Parents' Meetings. Meetings are held with the parents, or guardians, of each year group each year. At other times parents are encouraged to see the Headmistress to discuss their daughter's progress.

Admission. Candidates for entry take either the Common Entrance Examination at 11, 12 or 13 years of age, or The Princess Helena College's own Entrance Examination. Sixth Form places are conditional on GCSE results.

Fees. (*see* Entrance Scholarship section) Boarders: Years 7 and 8 £3,520 per term; Years 9, 10, 11 and Sixth Form £4,420 a term. Day girls: Years 7 and 8 £2,365; Years 9, 10, 11 and Sixth Form £2,985 a term (excluding some books). Some scholarships (worth 50% of annual fees) are available for academically able pupils. Bursaries are available for those with special talents in music, art or individual academic subjects.

Access. Visitors travelling by car from London take the A1 to Stevenage North, Junction 8 (signed to Luton Airport) and follow signs to Hitchin until a large roundabout is reached. They take the second exit to Gosmore and stay on that road for about 3 miles until the village of Preston is reached. The College main gates are on the left, past the village green. The village, Preston, lies 8 miles east of the M1, 2 miles west of the A1 and 3 miles south of Hitchin, which is 32 minutes from London by the faster trains from King's Cross Station and 39 by the faster trains from Cambridge.

Charitable status. The Princess Helena College is a Registered Charity, number 311064. It was founded in 1820 for the purposes of education.

Prior's Field

Godalming Surrey GU7 2RH
Tel: (01483) 810551
Fax: (01483) 810180
e-mail: admin@priorsfield.demon.co.uk

Motto: *We live by admiration, hope and love.*
Founded in 1902.

Board of Governors:
Chairman: Commander R W Kent, MA, RN

Mr M Burton-Brown, TD, MA (*Deputy Chairman*)
Mr A M Christie
Mr M H Cooke, BA
Mrs C W J Formstone, HDCR
Miss J I Hall, MA
Miss E A S Hannay, MA
Mr A L Hodges, BCom
Miss A Huxley
Mrs D H Jerwood, MA
Mr C J D Robinson, TD, BA
Mrs J J Thorpe, MA
Mrs S C Witheridge

***Headmistress:* Mrs Jenny Dwyer**, BEd (Hons) (Cantab)

Deputy Headmaster: Antony Hudson, MA, PGCE

Director of Studies: Mrs Jennifer Carter, BA, CertEd *Head of Geography, Head of Sixth Form*

Bursar and Clerk to the Governors: Col Jack Stenhouse, OBE, MVO, MBA

Chaplain: The Revd John Fellows, MA

Academic Staff:

Mrs Amelia Allen, MA, PGCE *Head of Mathematics*
Stephen Barnett, MSc, LRPS, PGCE *Head of Science, Photography*
Mrs Mary Claire Cook, BEd, CertEd *Geography, Charity Organiser, Head of Upper School*
Mrs June Darling, CertEd *Physical Education*
Mrs Clare Dollard, CertEd *Head of Physical Education*
Mrs Susan Eaton, BA, PGCE *French, Spanish*
Mrs Celia Ellis, BSc, PhD, PGCE *Biology*
Mrs Andrea Fairbairn, BA *Mathematics*
Miss Karina Gabner, MA *Head of Art*
Mrs Nicolette Gunn, CertEd *French, Word Processing, Careers*
Mrs Julia Harrington, BA, PGCE *History, Religious Studies*
Miss Myrna Harris, PhD, BA, PGCE *English*
Mrs Marilyn Hawkswell, CertEd *Business Skills*
Terence Henderson, BA, CertEd *Media Studies*
Mrs Susan Holmes, BA, CertEd *Economics, Business Studies and Politics*
Mrs Catherine Humphreys, BSc, PGCE *Science, ICT*
Mrs Rosemary Ingram, BA, PGCE *Head of History*
Mrs Phyllis Langcake, BSc, DSSPT *Science*
Mrs Emma MacMillan, BMus, LRAM, ARCM *Head of Religious Studies*
Ms Rita McGeoch, MA, MLitt, PGCE *Head of English*
Mrs Valerie Page, BA, PGCE *English*
Ms Melanie Pencycate, BA, PGCE *Psychology*
Mrs Beatrice Rapine-Baldwin, MA *French*
Mrs Joy Rennie, BA *Design Technology, Resistant materials*
Martin Rossetti, MGCP *ICT Systems Manager*
Mrs Anne Sheldrake, CertEd *Mathematics, ICT*
Mrs Janet Smith, MA, CertEd *Head of Modern Languages*
Mr McDonald Smith, PhD, BSc, PGCE *Chemistry*
Mrs Melanie Thorne, MA, LGSM *Head of Music, Flute, Saxophone*

Mrs Susan Townsend, DipFurtherEd, CertEd *Head of Design Technology, PSE, Young Enterprise*
Mrs Linda Valentine, DipAD, LDC, PGCE *Ceramics*
Miss Rosemary West, BSc, PGCE *Mathematics*
Mrs Christine Yates, CertEd *Design Technology, Food & Textiles*

Visiting Staff:

Mrs Hazel Bagley, MA, PGCE, RSA, DipSpLD *Dyslexia Support*
Mrs Deirdre Ball, LTCL *Flute*
Mrs Nicola Castle, LLB, DipEd, AMBDA *Dyslexia Support*
Mrs Nicola Fournel, BAMus *Piano*
Mrs Cherry Gay, DipEFL *EFL*
Miss Celia Harrisson, FLCM, LLCM, ARCM, LGSM, CertEd *Singing*
Miss Lucy Hill, FTCL, LTCL *Violin*
Mrs Helen Hollowood, GRSM, ARCM *Oboe, Music Theory*
Mrs Fiona Howe, ARCM *Flute*
Mrs Sally Lagan *German*
Darren Lucas *Guitar*
Douglas MacMillan, FTCL, FLCM, LLCM(TD), AMusLCM *Recorder*
Mrs Margaret Parke, LGSM, LTCL *Instrumental Accompanist*
Mrs Lynne Sharratt, ARCM, GRSM, PGCE *Clarinet*
Miss Jayne Spencer, AGSM, LGSM, ALCM *'Cello*
Mrs Jean Stevens, BEd *Instrumental Accompanist, Piano*
Paul Wardell *Tennis Coaching*
Ian Young *Percussion*

Administration:

Headmistress' Secretary: Mrs Karen Bryant
Registrar/Marketing Assistant: Mrs Jane Gallie
School Office Manager: Mrs Deborah Speirs
School Secretary: Mrs Margaret Elliott, BA
Assistant Accountant: Mrs Diane Cant
Bursary Assistant: Mrs Carol Harding
Bursar's Secretary: Mrs Dawn Stenhouse
Accountant: Miss Sue Collins
Sanatorium Sister: Mrs Eileen Snow, RGN

Housemistresses:
Head of Boarding: Mrs Myrna Harris, PhD, BA, PGCE
VIth Forms: to be announced
Ist-Vth Forms: Mrs Theresa Vowles

Assistant Housemistresses:
Miss Catherine Spicer

Librarian: Mrs Jill Lewis
Laboratory Technician: Mrs Joanne Slaytor
ICT Technician: Mrs Adele Godden

Numbers: Boarders 36, Weekly Boarders 58, Day Girls 172.

Age range: 11–18

The School was founded by Julia Huxley, mother of Aldous and Julian, to provide a broadly based education of very high standard; this remains our aim today. We work in small groups and strive to develop the full potential of each girl in all areas in a happy, friendly atmosphere.

The original buildings were designed by Charles Voysey and the garden by Gertrude Jekyll. Additions in recent years have been a completely new teaching block, which incorporates a new Art and Craft centre, the VIth Form House, the Music School and new CDT rooms. In addition to classrooms, the main building now includes a newly-designed Drama studio and Technology area.

Weekly boarding is a very popular option for many of our girls and boarders are placed in the care of the Housemistress. Bedrooms are generally of between one and four girls, the younger girls being in the larger rooms with many senior girls having single study bedrooms. Sixth form boarders reside in a separate sixth form house where they lead more independent lives under the supervision of the resident sixth form Housemistress. Throughout the boarding houses the emphasis is on friendliness, helpfulness and the creation of a warm, supportive environment which enables the girls to mature into caring and independent adults.

The juniors follow a general curriculum including Spanish, ICT, Design and Technology, Art and Craft, as well as all the 'core' subjects. The seniors are prepared for GCSE and the new Curriculum 2000 in the sixth form. In the sixth form minority subjects are also available, such as DT or Art for Fun. Girls are prepared for Oxbridge entrance, other universities, Art College, and many other areas of higher or further education. Careers advice is included in the timetable for all girls. In addition, visits are arranged to university open days, and the school also arranges talks by visitors from a wide range of professions, whilst fifth formers are encouraged to join a work experience scheme after GCSE examinations.

Music flourishes throughout the school. A wide range of instruments is taught, and more than half the girls take individual lessons. Girls are prepared for written and practical music examinations of the Associated Board of the Royal Schools of Music. Individual singing lessons are also available and girls have the opportunity to join the junior and chamber choirs. The jazz band has toured Northern Italy and the orchestra gives regular concerts.

Girls may join various clubs ranging from Craft and Drama to Photography and Computing. Older girls can join the Duke of Edinburgh Award Scheme and Young Enterprise. Outings are arranged for boarders at weekends, whilst throughout the year there are numerous educational visits to theatres, local factories, etc.

Lacrosse, hockey, netball, swimming, tennis, athletics and rounders are our main games, but there are many opportunities for other sports as well. The school is situated in 25 acres, and games take place in the grounds. In addition, the sixth form use the nearby Charterhouse Sports Centre. Our new sports hall is now open. Tennis coaching is available throughout the year. Coaching in golf, fencing, self-defence and aerobic training is also available. Ice skating, bowling and swimming take place at the Guildford Spectrum for all pupils who are interested and the equestrian team practises locally and competes in 'eventing'.

Access: The school is situated between Godalming and Guildford and is less than a mile from the A3. Godalming and Guildford are the nearest railway stations, and we are conveniently placed (via the A3 and M25) for both Heathrow and Gatwick Airports. At the start and finish of term, girls may be escorted to, or met from, either airport or railway station.

Admission is by the School entrance examination. Open days are held every term and individual visits are arranged at parents' convenience by the Registrar.

Scholarships/Bursaries. (*see* Entrance Scholarship section) The Governors offer for annual competition at 11+ two academic Scholarships, one of 50% of school fees and the other of 25% of school fees. Art, Music and Drama Scholarships are also available, either one at 25% or two, one at 15% and one at 10% of school fees. There is also a 10% reduction in fees for the daughter of an old girl. Fee reductions are offered to service families and siblings. Scholarships are available for entry to the sixth form.

Fees at 1 January, 2001: Boarders £4,396 per term; Day Girls £2,940 per term.

Charitable status. Prior's Field is a Registered Charity, number 312038. It exists to promote education and to offer and provide Scholarships, Exhibitions, Prizes and Awards at any school carried on by the Trust.

Putney High School (G.D.S.T.)

35 Putney Hill London SW15 6BH
Tel: 020 8788 4886
Fax: 020 8789 8068
e-mail: putneyhigh@put.gdst.net
website: www.gdst.net/putneyhigh

Founded 1893

This is one of the 25 schools of The Girls' Day School Trust. For general information about the Trust and the composition of its Council, see p. 532. A more detailed prospectus may be obtained from the school.

Local Governing Body:
Mr A Chubb
Mr C E Gallop, MA
Mrs J Hargadon
Mrs S Kwok, BSc
Miss J Lee, NFF
Mrs S Michie
Mrs D Mitchell, BE, CEng, MICE, MIEI
Mr P Ralph
Mr C Roshier, MA, FCA, MSI
Mrs G Tyrrell

Headmistress: **Mrs E Merchant**, JP, BSc (Sheffield) *Chemistry*

Senior School:
Deputy Head: Mrs M A Chandler, MA (Glasgow) *French and History*

Miss A Ames, BSc (London) *Molecular Biology*
Mrs P Arthur, MA (Oxford), MSc, PGCE (London) *Mathematics*
Mrs A Balabanovic, BSc (Belgrade) *Chemical Engineering*
Mrs A Barrett, BA (London) *English & Psychology*
Miss N Bassam, BSc (London), MA (London) *Economics, Area Studies*
Mr G Bowen, BSc (Aberdeen) *Biochemistry*
Mrs A P Boyes, BSc (London) *Physics*
Mr J E Bright, MA (Cambridge) *Applied Biology*
Ms N Bright, MA (Middlesex) *Geography*
Ms J Brown, BA (Cambridge) *Modern Languages*
Mr R Carter, MA (Cambridge), FTCL, ARCM, LTCL *Music*
Mr M D Chandler, MA (Brunel) *Technology*
Mrs C Christie, BA (London), PGCE (Cambridge), MPhil *Classics*
Miss P Coate, MA (Oxford) *French & Spanish*
Miss S E Cockburn, BA (Cambridge) *English/History of Art*
Mr I Crane, BSc (Durham *Mathematics & Philosophy*
Miss J A Dampier, BA (Exeter) *English and Philosophy*
Miss M Diaz Parra, Degree (Seville) *Modern Languages*
Miss B Doe, BA (Warwick) *English & European Literature*
Ms P Flannery, MA (London) *Text & Performance Studies*
Miss G Gallego, Psychology Degree (Madrid)
Mr K Halon, BA (Oxford) *English Language & Literature*
Miss J Hardie, BA (Cambridge) *Physics & Chemistry Metallurgy*
Miss D Hawkins, BEd (Bedford) *Human Movement Studies & Science*
Mr A Haworth, BA (Gloucestershire), MA (Royal College of Art) *Fine Art*
Mrs M L Hayes, CertEd (Anstey College) *Physical Education*
Miss J A Heap, BEd (Cambridge) *Religious Studies & Education*
Ms J Holl, BA (Reading) *French*
Miss F H Howard, BA (Newcastle) *Design in Industry*
Mrs G John, BSc (Exeter), MSc, MSc *Mathematics*
Ms M K Johnston, BA (Leicester) *Geography*
Mrs J J A Khan, MA (Oxford) *Modern History*
Mr E Krastev, Diploma (University of Sport, Bulgaria)
Ms J Lawrence, MA (Surrey), CertEd, BEd, BD *Educational Studies*
Mrs A Marr-Johnson, BA (York) *English & Related Literature*
Mrs L M Matley, MA (Oxford) *Modern Languages*
Ms M Mescall, BEd (Surrey) *Home Economics*
Ms C Mouton-Muniz, DEA (Toulouse) *Sciences de la Terre*
Miss C Mulderrig, MA (Oxford) *Modern Languages*
Mr N Murray, BA (Camberwell), PGCE (London) *History of Drawing & Printmaking*
Miss J D Nicholls, BA (Bristol) *Music*
Ms A Noble, MA (Cambridge) *Classics*
Mrs C O'Donoghue, BA (Cheltenham & Gloucester) *Geography & English*
Miss C Osborne, MA (Sussex) *History of Art*
Mlle C Pamart, Maitrise Degree (Orleans)
Mrs J Y Patton, MA (Oxford) *French and German*
Mrs S Rosier, BSc (Durham) *Natural Science*
Mrs V Ross-Russell, BA (Manchester) *Geography*
Miss J S Sharp, BA, MLitt (Newcastle) *English*
Mrs P Sharp, BSc (Sheffield) *Mathematics*
Miss A J Simmons, BA (Bristol) *History*
Mr J Skinner, BSc (London) *Chemistry*
Mrs F Summers, MA (Cambridge) *Economics/Mathematics*
Mrs G Witty, BA (Liverpool) *Latin*
Mr P Wootton, BA (East Anglia) *History*

Junior Department:
Head of Junior Department: Miss C J Attfield, CertEd (London), JP
Deputy Head of Junior Department: Mrs G Al-Samerai, CertEd (Cambridge)

Mrs A F Balcerkiewicz, CertEd (Cambridge)
Mrs A Davies, MA (Oxford) *Modern History*
Miss R Fabian, Teaching Certificate (Brighton)
Miss B Hattaway, BA (Auckland) *English*
Mrs J A Melvin, BEd (Cambridge) *Geography*
Miss F Morrison, BA (Leicester) *Geography*
Mrs E Myers, BA (Reading) *English*
Mrs P Preston, CertEd (Belfast)
Mrs P Proctor, CertEd (London)
Mrs G Sandham, BA (Surrey) *Educational Studies*
Mrs V Styles, BSc (Nottingham) *Zoology*
Mrs A Taylor, BA (Whitelands) *History*
Miss D H Thompson, Teaching Certificate (Cambridge)
Mrs V M Webb, BEd (California) *Psychology and Drama*
Mrs R Wyatt, BSc (London), PGCE (Hull) *Mathematics & Psychology*

Visiting Staff–Instrumental Music:
Ms M Dodge, BEd (Cambridge) *Music, Flute*
Mrs S Duller *Harp*
Miss J Edwards, ARCM, RCM *Violin*
Mrs L Forbes, LRCM *'Cello*
Mr P Gilham, LRAM *Voice*
Ms S Grealy, LRAM, ARCM *Flute*
Ms J Holland, LRAM *Clarinet*
Ms G James, AGSM *Double Bass, Flute*
Mrs M Johnston, ARCM, GRSM, LTCL *Piano*
Miss A Kane, ARCM *Voice*
Mr S Keogh, GGSM, ARCM *Trumpet*
Miss J Larrad, LTCL *Guitar*
Miss J R Lively, AGSM *Oboe*
Mr B Norbury, BA (Oxford) *Music, Recorder*
Mr R Skirrow, ARCM, Diploma RCM *Percussion*
Mr F Watson, RCM *Horn*
Mr G E Williams, RCM *Saxophone*
Mrs J Winchester, LRCM, LTCL, ARCM *Bassoon*

School Administrator: Mrs L Kelleher

Secretary to the Headmistress: Mrs J Sharman
School Doctor: Dr G Provost

The school, which opened in 1893, is situated about half way up Putney Hill, and near bus routes 14, 37, 39, 74, 85, 93 and 337, a short distance from East Putney Station (District Line). There are frequent trains from Waterloo to Putney (Network South East) Station.

There are about 800 pupils, of whom 540, including a Sixth Form of 140, are in the Senior School (ages 11–18) and 260 in the Junior Department (ages 4–11).

Recent extensions include Computer Laboratories, to which all classrooms are being networked, a Design Technology centre and a hall for the Junior Department. There are 7 well-equipped laboratories, a modern three-storey classroom building, a specialist Music Block and new Art Block.

An extension to the Junior Department, consisting of a Science room and three additional classrooms, was added in 1993. A new Sports Hall was built in 1995. The Senior School Hall has been refurbished.

The grounds provide on a single site spacious gardens, netball and tennis courts (2 floodlighted), rounders pitch and Sports Hall. Sports facilities at the local Leisure Centre, Thames Rowing Club and Barn Elms are used for a variety of sports. The school has its own boats and special links with Belgrave Harriers for athletics and Mayfield Gym Club. The Sixth Form have a choice of physical activities including netball, tennis, trampolining, badminton, rowing, multigym and swimming. They can also undertake a course to qualify as Community Sports Leaders. Girls can join a number of sports clubs, including Aerobics, Dance, Gym, Sports Acrobatics, Badminton, Fencing, Netball and Tennis.

Curriculum. The curriculum is planned to provide a wide general education which includes Technology and Information Technology. Girls are prepared for the General Certificate of Secondary Education at 16+. In the Sixth Form they may choose between many combinations from a range of 25 AS/A Level subjects and can be prepared for university entrance and scholarship examinations. They all go on to higher education or training, and guidance on careers is given. There are flourishing extra-curricular activities including Music, Drama, Sport and the Duke of Edinburgh Award Scheme.

Fees. From September 2000: Senior School £2,044 per term; Junior Department £1,588 per term.

The fees cover the regular curriculum, school books, stationery and other materials, Choral Music, Games and Swimming, but not optional extra subjects or special sports. All pupils below the Sixth Form take school meals for which the current charge is £110 per term.

The fees for instrumental tuition are shown in the Prospectus.

Financial Assistance. The GDST has introduced its own Bursary Scheme now that the Government Assisted Places Scheme has been discontinued. The Bursary Scheme is means-tested and enables the school to accept bright girls whose parents would not be able to afford the fees.

Scholarships. There are at present, available to internal or external candidates, a number of scholarships for entry at 11+ or to the Sixth Form.

A Music Scholarship (up to half fees) is also available at 11+.

Charitable status. Putney High School is one of the 25 schools of the Girls' Day School Trust, which is a Registered Charity, number 1026057. The aim of the Trust is to provide a fine academic education at a comparatively modest cost.

Queen Anne's School

Caversham Reading Berkshire RG4 6DX
Tel: 0118 918 7300; 0118 918 7400 (Bursar)
Fax: 0118 918 7310
e-mail: admis@queenannes.reading.sch.uk

Motto: *Quietness and Strength*
Founded in Westminster 1698. Incorporated 1706.

Reconstituted 1873. Established at Caversham 1894.

Governing Body of The Royal Foundation of Grey Coat Hospital:

Chairman of Queen Anne's School Council: Mrs P Morgan, MBE, JP

Governors:
Mr R G Armstrong
Mr D Bruce
Mr J Claughton, MA
Mr R H Clutton, CBE, FRICS
Mrs M Gale, MA
Mr M D Grundy, BA
Mrs C A Hopkins, OBE, MA, LLB
Prof B Kemp, BA, PhD, FSA, FRHistS
Lady Laws, BLitt, MA
Mrs C I Obolensky, BA, MIPM
Mr R Palmer
Mr C J Perrin, MA
Miss A Price, BA, MBA
Mrs J Randle
Professor P T H Unwin, MA, PhD
The Revd Canon R Wright, BA

Clerk: Mr R W Blackwell, MA

***Headmistress:* Mrs D Forbes**, MA

Deputy Headmistresses:
Miss N Coombs, BEd (Bishop Otter College)
Mrs J L Furlonger, BA, PGCE (London)

Head of Sixth Forms: Mr J Owen, BA (Oxon), MA (Reading), PGCE (Reading)
Head of Fifth Forms: Mrs C Haley, BA (Reading), PGCE (Cantab)
Head of Fourth Forms: Mrs I Kenyon, BA (Sheffield)

Housemistresses:
Michell: Miss J Lewis
Holmes: Miss M Stamp
Wisdome: Mrs H Avramakis
Maddock and Ffyler: Mrs C Munro
Webbe: Miss S Wilkinson
Wilkins: Mrs R Hooper

Heads of Department:

The Revd Mrs H Benson, BA (Manchester), PGCE (Cantab), DipHE (Bristol) *Religious Studies*
Mrs L Cook, BA (Open Univ), PGCE (IM Marsh College) *Theatre Studies*
Mrs M Devereux, BSc (London) *Physics*
Mr A D H Garner, MA (Cantab) *Classics*
Mr D J Gathercole, MA (London) *Art*
Mrs E Green, MA, PGCE (Reading) *English*
Mrs C Haley, BA (Reading), PGCE (Cambridge) *Geography*
Mrs B Hough-Robbins, BA (Cardiff), PGCE (Bristol) *Modern Languages*
Mrs H Marvin, BSc, PGCE (Brighton Polytechnic) *PE*
Mrs D C Nightingale, MA (Oxon), PGCE *Mathematics*
Mrs B Orpwood, HNC (LRSC), PGCE (Reading) *Chemistry*
Mrs J Reason, BEd (Reading) *Computer Studies*

Mrs C Sharpe, BA (East Anglia), PGCE (Newcastle) *History*
Mrs S M Twitchett, BSc (Bristol), PGCE *Biology/Careers*

Music:
Miss F Brewitt-Taylor, BA (Liverpool), MA (Nottingham), PGCE (Liverpool), ARCO *Class and Chapel Music*

Chaplain: The Rev Mrs H Benson, BA

Bursar: Lt Col K R Whiteman

PA to Headmistress: Mrs A Witkowski

Registrar: Mrs E Brunwin

Marketing: Miss S Thomas

School Secretary: Mrs S Mansfield

Administrative Secretary: Mrs T Armstrong

School Doctor: Dr F Aitken, MBBS (London), MRCS, LRCP, MRCGP, DCH, DOpst, RCOG

Resident Nurse: Miss S Eatwell, SRN

Queen Anne's is pleasantly situated just north of Reading and within easy reach of London and the airports. A boarding and day school, it provides an all-round education for girls aged 11-18. Founded in 1894 by the Grey Coat Hospital, it was started as "a boarding school in the country" and maintains its links with Grey Coat Hospital School and Westminster. There are 320 pupils, two thirds of them boarders, who enjoy the friendly atmosphere and wide range of opportunities available.

Pastoral organisation. Each girl is housed in a comfortable House on the campus, either boarding or day, in the care of a Housemistress and Assistant Housemistress. The Sixth Form are in two purpose built Houses which aim to provide a bridge between school and university. A full programme of weekend and evening activities is arranged for all boarders and day girls, if they wish. Full and flexible boarding are provided.

Curriculum. All girls follow a broad and varied curriculum up to GCSE. Separate sciences as well as Dual Award are taught; Spanish or German may be taken from Year 8; Latin is also studied from Year 8. Music, art, drama, CDT, cookery and textiles form part of every girl's timetable until the end of Year 9. Information technology is taught throughout the school. A wide range of A Level subjects is offered. A programme of personal and social education is followed by all girls.

Careers. 100% of girls go on to university. Advice for university entrance is thorough and the careers advice begins in Year 9.

Extra-curricular activities. Queen Anne's is well-known for its prowess in lacrosse (National Champions on many occasions) but opportunities for sport are many, including rowing in the nearby Thames. Music and drama are both strong, offering many chances for participation. The Duke of Edinburgh Award, Young Enterprise, dance, riding, social activities and much more enrich the pupils' lives.

Admission. Girls are admitted at any age by our own examination or by Common Entrance at 11, 12 or 13. Sixth Form places are offered on the basis of GCSE results.

Scholarships (*see* Entrance Scholarship section). The top scholarship is worth full tuition fees; other scholarships are awarded for excellence in any field for girls at 11, 12 or 13+. Sixth Form scholarships are also available. All scholarships are open to internal and external candidates.

Fees. Boarding: £14,910 per annum; Day girls £10,080 per annum.

Charitable status. The Royal Foundation of The Grey Coat Hospital is a Registered Charity, number 312700. Its aims and objectives are the provision and conduct of two schools for girls in which religious instruction in accordance with the doctrines of the Church of England shall be given.

Queen Margaret's School

Escrick Park York YO19 6EU
Tel: (01904) 728261

Motto: *Filia Regis*

Board of Governors:

Chairman: Mrs Eleanor King

Mrs A Bates
The Revd Rachel Benson
Brigadier M A Charlton-Weedy
C D Forbes Adam, Esq
W T Hartley, Esq
The Hon Mrs F Horton
D A Kerfoot, Esq
C P Moorhouse, Esq
D T Sheppard, Esq
R J Shephard, Esq
Sir Jack Whitaker, Bt

School Solicitor: M A Chidley, Esq, Messrs Addleshaw, Booth & Co

School Accountant: R L Hudson, Esq, Pricewaterhouse-Coopers

Company Secretary & Clerk to the Governors: M D Oakley, Esq, Crombie, Wilkinson & Oakley

***Headmaster:* G A H Chapman**, MA (Oxon), DLitt et Phil (SA), FRSA

Deputy Head: Mrs J King, BA Hons, PGCE (Liverpool)

Bursar: Miss P J Lacy, ACA

Director of Studies (*Timetable*): C S Nettleship, MMus (University College, Cardiff)
Director of Studies (*Curriculum*): Miss A S Buchan, PhD (Leeds), BSc (Hull), PGCE
Head of Sixth Form: M T Baker, BA (London), CertEd, AdvDipEd

Chaplain: The Revd R L Owen, BD (Wales), PGCE

Doctor: Dr S J Butlin, MBChB, DRCOG, DCH

Art:
*M P Baby, MA (Leeds), DipAD (West Surrey College of Art)
Miss H L Colman, MA (Newcastle), BA Hons (Leeds), PGCE
Mrs L J Heaton, MA (Leeds), BA Hons (Trent Polytechnic)

Careers:
*Ms R S Jones, MA (Leeds), BA Hons, PGDCG (Birmingham), NVQ4 (TDLB)
Ms B O'Donnell, BSc Hons (Manchester), PGCE

Classics:
*Mrs J Muir, BA Hons (Bristol), PGCE
W M Grant, MA Hons (St Andrews), PGCE

Design and Technology:

Drama:
*Mrs V J Chapman, BA Hons (Natal), PGCE
Miss L R Durrani, BA Hons (Middlesex), PGCE

Economics and Business Studies:
*Mrs S M P McDougall, BA (Oxford Polytechnic), PGCE

English:
*Mrs N J L Onyett, BA Hons, DPhil (York, PGCE
I Giles, BA Hons (Sussex)
Miss J V Ball, BA Hons (Polytechnic of Wales), PGCE
Miss M L Burns, BA (Kingston), PGCE

Mrs J M Fairley, MA (Montreal), BA Hons (York), MEd (Sheffield)

Food Technology:
*Miss G M Rickard, BEd (Manchester)
Mrs S A Winrow, CertEd (Manchester)

Geography:
*Mrs E Layfield-Bell, BA Hons (Sheffield), PGCE
Ms L Watkins, BSc Hons (Leicester), PGCE

History and Politics:
*Mrs C E S Batten, MA (Michigan), BA Hons (Queens Belfast), PGCE, DASE
R P Dockerill, MSc (London), BA Hons (Durham), PGCE
Mrs G F Hobson, BA Hons (Nottingham), PGCE
Mrs J Rayner, BA Hons (Hull), PGCE

History of Art:
*Ms H Moore, MA (UCL), BA Hons (Bristol)

ICT:
*Mrs M Anastasi, BSc Hons (Open)
Mrs R E Airey, RSA Teaching Cert

Technicians:
Mr G Mark, BScEE, MCSE
Mr G M Howe

Mathematics:
*Mrs B S Reynolds, BSc (Newcastle), PGCE
Mrs C I Herbert, BSc Hons (Leeds), PGCE
Mrs J A Edwards, BSc Hons (Dunelm), CMathMIMA, PGCE
Mrs B A Shaw, BEd (Leeds)
Mrs K Tse, BSc Hons (Manchester), PGCE

Modern Languages:
*Mrs E A Hughes, BA Hons (Reading), PGCE (*French*)
M T Baker, BA (London), CertEd, AdvDipEd (*French, Spanish*)
Miss A J Evans, BA Hons (Newcastle), PGCE (*French, Spanish*)
*Mrs B Kirkham BA Hons (Halle, Germany) (*German*)
*Mrs V A Knott, BA Hons (London), PGCE (*Spanish*)
Mrs I L Leaf, BA (Lyon, France), PGCE (*French*)

Language Assistants:
Mrs I Gibson (*German*)
Miss C Jannin (*French*)
Miss L López (*Spanish*)
Mrs M Ward (*French*)

Music:
Director of Music: C S Nettleship, MMus (University College, Cardiff)

Miss A V Walker, MA (York), BA Hons (York)
M Ward, BMus Hons (Sheffield), LRAM, PGCE

Part-time staff:
C Allison (*Bassoon, Clarinet*)
Miss A Aslin, BMus Hons (London), ALCM (*Harp, Piano*)
F Ayres (*Percussion*)
N A Bellamy, BA Hons (Dartington, Exeter), RCO (*Piano*)
Mrs C Blood, ARCM, DRSAM (*Oboe, Piano*)
Mrs D Clough, BA (York) (*Flute*)
Miss L Evans, BA Hons (Huddersfield), LTCL (*Flute*)
P Laidlaw, BA Hons (York) (*Piano*)
J Mackenzie, BEng Hons, FTCL, FLCM, LGSM, LRAM, MIFireE (*Guitar*)
Mrs D Pomfret, LGSM, DipEd (*Piano*)
Miss M Roycroft, BMus Hons, RNCM, PPRNCM (*Cello, Bass*)
Mrs J Sturmheit, GGSM, MTC (*Singing*)
P Titcombe, BA Hons (York) (*Piano*)
Miss C Vaughan, BA Hons (Leeds) (*Clarinet, Saxophone*)
S Wade, BA (Leeds) (*Brass*)
Mrs C Ward, BMus Hons, LRAM, LTCL, PGCE (*Piano, Violin*)
Music Assistant: Mrs M Nettleship

Physical Education:
Director of Sport and Games: Miss A Davies, MEd (Wales), CertEd (Wales), PGCE
Miss A K Froggett, BA Hons (Wales), PGCE
Mrs J M Norman, CertPE (Bedford CPE)
Miss J N Pratt, BA Hons (Trinity & All Saints, Leeds), PGCE
Miss J L Whay, BEd Hons (IM Marsh, Liverpool)
Miss F J Whittle, BEd Hons (Bedford CPE)
Dance: Mrs S P Hewgill, ISTD, RAD
Riding: Miss G Sanders, BHSAI, CertEd
Tennis: Mrs C Place, LTA Coach, CertEd (Bedford CPE)

Religious Studies:
*The Revd R L Owen, BD (Wales), PGCE (*Chaplain*)

Science:
*Miss A S Buchan, PhD (Leeds), BSc (Hull), PGCE (*Chemistry*)
*Mrs S H Bullock, BSc Hons (Dunelm), PGCE (*Biology*)
S M Corcoran, BSc Hons (Leeds), PGCE (*Chemistry*)
Ms J L Heyes, BSc Hons (Kent), PGCE (*Physics*)
Miss A Lawrence, BA Hons (York), PGCE (*Biology*)
N J Millward, BSc Hons (Manchester), PGCE (*Physics*)
Mrs E A Morton, BSc Hons (London), PGCE (*Chemistry*)
A Rayner, BSc Hons (Hull), PGCE (*Physics*)
Mrs M Scott, PhD, BSc Hons (Wales) (*Biology*)

Pupil Support:
Mrs B L Gregory, MA (York), CertEd
Mrs S Hubberstey, BEd (Cambridge), CertEd
Ms M Tate, CertEd (Leeds)

Examinations Officer: Mrs M Perry

Librarian: Mrs P J Powell, DipLib (Cape Town), BA (Bulmershe)

Administrative Staff:
Headmaster's Secretary: Miss F C Jones
School Secretary: Mrs P S Cockroft
Admissions Secretary: Miss R Buckley
Administrative Assistant: Mrs M Perry
Receptionist: Mrs K Chambers

Bursar's Assistants: Mrs A E Wharton, Mrs L A Walton
Clerk of Works: Mr W Hulley
Functions Manager: Mr M W Territt

Resident Housemistresses:
UVI Mrs J Rayner/Miss L K Crawford
LVI Mrs J Hildyard/Miss H Ouadi
V Miss J L Whay/Mrs S D Mirza
IV Mrs J M Fairley/Miss L R Durrani
III Mrs J King/Mrs H Tarleton
II Miss C M Goddard/Miss D Moffatt
I Mrs S P Hewgill/Mrs W Lawson

Additional Assistant Housemistresses:
Miss C Jannin
Miss L López
Miss L Ober

Gap Student: Miss C Simoni

Medical Centre:

*Mrs G M Swinglehurst, RGN
Ms P V Gage, RGN

Foundation. Queen Margaret's School was established in Scarborough in 1901 by the Woodard Foundation. Following evacuation to Pitlochry during the First World War and to Castle Howard during the Second, the school came to Escrick Park in 1949.

In 1986, on the initiative of the Parents' and Friends' Association, a new company was established, which is registered with the Charity Commission.

Situation. Surrounded by sixty-five acres of parkland in the Vale of York, Queen Margaret's occupies a gracious country house with an attractive range of buildings linked to the main school. Girls live in year groups with broadening facilities and privileges each year. The first year girls live in Red House and the sixth form girls have study bedrooms in Cloisters, Carr House and adjacent cottages.

Numbers. Boarding: 327, Day: 37

Admission is by Entrance Examination at 11+, and by Common Entrance at 12+ and 13+. There is also entry at 16+.

Fees. Boarding: £4,408, Day: £2,793.

Curriculum. All girls follow a broad curriculum for three years before selecting an average of nine GCSE subjects taken from a wide range of core and optional courses, providing all the strengths of the National Curriculum without its restrictiveness.

The Sixth Form at Queen Margaret's is strong. Most girls stay on from the fifth year and are joined by pupils from other schools, making a total sixth form of over 100 girls. Over 20 subjects are offered for A and AS level in a wide variety of Arts and Science subjects. Candidates are prepared for all University entrance including Oxbridge. At all levels high academic standards are achieved.

Classrooms are modern and well equipped and ICT provision is widespread and up-to-date. There are seven new science laboratories. Art, Design & Technology is located in a new purpose-built centre. Pottery, sculpture, textile and fabric design, printing and photography as well as drawing and painting are on the curriculum. A Home Economics Department gives pupils the opportunity to study for examination or for leisure.

Drama is important in the curriculum and school productions are mounted regularly. In addition girls can take classes in modern, tap and ballet dancing and individual tuition is available. Music plays a major role in school life at Queen Margaret's and there are three full time and twenty specialist music teachers on the staff. There are two orchestras and two bands, smaller ensembles, rock bands, chapel choir, choral society and junior choir. The school's choir provides the music for services in Chapel as well as the Parish Church and local concerts and regularly sings in York Minster and occasionally abroad.

Games. Games and Physical Education are an integral part of the curriculum. The school has first-class facilities for games including astroturf, sports hall and competition swimming pool. All-weather courts ensure year-round tennis of a high standard, and there are two squash courts and a nine-hole golf course. Main activities are lacrosse, hockey, netball, tennis, rounders, swimming and athletics with fixtures at all ages against schools and clubs of all types. Other clubs and societies cater for fencing, badminton, rowing, canoeing, shooting and skiing.

The Riding School is situated within the grounds adjacent to the main school campus and offers riding to girls of all standards from beginners to Pony Club B Test level. In the Sixth Form a Horse Knowledge and Riding course can be run for girls who would like to take the British Horse Society examinations.

The School is divided into six Houses which compete in Games, Music, Drama, and other activities. Girls take part in the Duke of Edinburgh Award Scheme at Bronze and Gold level.

Scholarships. (*see* Entrance Scholarship section) Awards are made at 11+, 12+, 13+ and 16+. Music and Art Scholarships are also available. For further details apply to the Admissions Secretary.

Queen Mary's School

Baldersby Park Topcliffe Thirsk North Yorkshire YO7 3BZ

Tel: 01845 575000
Fax: 01845 575 001
e-mail: admin@queenmarys.org
website: www.queenmarys.org

A School of the Northern Division of the Woodard Corporation.

Provost: The Rt Revd F V Weston, Bishop of Knaresborough

Chairman of Governors: The Hon Mrs Susan Cunliffe-Lister

***Head of Senior School:* Mrs M A Angus**, MSc, CertEd, DipCEG

Head of Preparatory School: Mr I H Angus, MA, HDipEd

Director of Studies: Mrs M Mead, BSc (Hons), PGCE

Miss E Abrahams, Montessori Diploma *KS1 Teacher*
Mrs M A Angus, MSc, CertEd, DipCEG *Careers*
Mr J Arnold, BA (Hons), QTS *Head of ICT*
Miss R Blades, BSc (Hons), PGCE *Year 4 and Design Technology*
Mr N Carter, GRSM, ARCM, LRAM, LGSM, PGCE *Director of Music*
Mrs P Coghlan, ALCM, LAM Gold Medal *Speech & Drama*
Mrs J Coles, BEd (Hons) *Year 5 & Science*
Mrs D Coull, BA (Hons), PGCE *English*
Mr A Cowey, BEd (Hons) *KS1 teacher and KS1 Co-ordinator*
Mrs E Cragg-James, MA *Head of Modern Languages*
Mrs M Creyke, CertEd *Head of Home Economics*
Mrs M-J Foster, BA, PGCE *Head of Early Years*
Mrs S Ford, BA (Hons), PGCE *English*
Mrs V Foulser, BA (Hons), MA, PGCE *Head of Religious Studies*
Mrs D Gormley *Careers/Work Experience Co-ordinator*
Mrs M Grant, MA, PGCE *Special Educational Needs Co-ordinator*
Mr A Grey, MA (Oxon), PGCE *Head of English*
Miss D Hannam, BEd (Hons) *Physical Education*
Mrs J Hartley, Dip Un d'Etudes Literaire L en L *French*
Miss A B Hayes, BA (Hons), ATD *Head of Art & Design*
Miss H Hepworth, CertEd *Head of Physical Education*
Mrs E Hopkins, CertEd *Biology/Modular Science*
Mrs M Jandrell, BA, PGCE *English*
Mrs V Jessop, BA (Hons), PGCE *Geography*
Miss L Leigh, MA (Cantab) *Head of Classics*
Mrs K Manson, BSc (Hons), PGCE *Mathematics*
Mr P Nuttall, BSc (Hons), PGCE *Biology/Head of Science*
Miss A Pearson, BA (Hons), PGCE *Head of History*
Mrs A Petty, CertEd *Special Educational Needs*
Mrs C Phillips, BEd, CertEd *French*
Mrs C Punshon, BA (Hons) *French*
Mrs A Ryan, GNSM, ARCM, MTC *Assistant Director of Music*
Miss V Salmon, BEd *Year 3*
Mr M Walker, BSc (Hons), PGCE *Head of Chemistry and Physics*
Mrs C Wiggins, BSc (Hons), PGCE *Head of Geography*
Mrs S Wilcox, BEd (Hons) *Year 5 and Key Stage 2 Co-ordinator*
Mrs R Wrigley *Learning Support*

School Chaplain: The Revd N Sinclair
School Administrator Mrs M F Atkinson

Financial Secretary: Miss L Davies
School Nurse: Mrs A Price, RGN
Senior Matron: Mrs J Barker
School Outfitters: Mrs E Simpson
Riding Instructress: Mrs P Ashworth

Queen Mary's is an all girls boarding and day school for pupils aged 7 to 16. We have co-educational Early Years and Pre-prep departments for day pupils aged 3 to 6+. Our total school roll is currently 270.

Queen Mary's is situated at Baldersby Park in a beautiful Grade 1 Palladian mansion, with 50 acres of grounds, including formal gardens, playing fields, and a riding menage. Despite its idyllic surroundings, it is only 2 miles from Junction 49 of the A1 and within ten minutes of Thirsk railway station. York and Harrogate are within easy reach and so are Leeds/Bradford and Teesside airports. Six minibuses, each covering a twenty five mile radius, transport girls to and from home on a daily basis.

The Curriculum. The National Curriculum forms the basis of what we teach, and all our pupils sit Key Stage tests at the appropriate age. However, we offer our pupils much more in terms of breadth and depth of learning. We give generous time to core subjects, English, mathematics, science and modern languages, but we place strong emphasis on the supporting subjects - geography, history, religious education, classics, ICT, design technology, music, art and a varied programme of physical education. Classes are kept deliberately small, which means that every girl can receive plenty of support from her teachers. We have an excellent learning support department for those pupils who have specific learning difficulties. Each girl receives weekly tuition in our main computer room which has 18 networked computers and a smart-board. Our software is excellent and our hardware is up to date. Our school-wide network extends to all the laboratories and classrooms and each girl has her own e-mail address and filtered access to the Internet. The two years leading up to GCSE are full and focused, with most girls taking ten subjects at GCSE. Our public examination results are outstandingly good and we are one of the highest achieving non-selective schools in the country.

Pastoral care. We are a school of the Woodard Corporation, an Anglican foundation which promotes Christian education and high academic and pastoral standards within all its schools. All girls in school have personal tutors who oversee the academic, social and emotional development of each of their tutees. Building self-confidence and developing the individual talents of each pupil is seen as a vital aspect of the education we offer. We encourage each girl to be self-reliant from an early age and we foster in our pupils a real concern for the needs of others. Girls in their final year at Queen Mary's undertake a number of important responsibilities to help the school community function smoothly.

Boarding. Queen Mary's offers a number of boarding options to suit the needs of parents and their daughters. Those who choose to board may be weekly or full boarders. We consider the experience of boarding to be valuable for all girls and, when space permits, day girls may board on a nightly basis to fit in with extra-curricular commitments or parental need. The boarding accommodation is all within the main building and the girls find their dormitories cheerful and comfortable. The full boarders, who stay at weekends, enjoy lots of very varied activities and trips, often much to the envy of those who go home. The senior matron, together with her colleagues, looks after the general health of the girls, while the school nurse and the school doctor oversee all medical care.

Extra-Curricular Activities. An impressive range of extra-curricular activities is available to all members of the school community. Choral and orchestral music are both huge strengths of the school but our sport is good too with hockey, lacrosse and netball being played in the winter terms and tennis, rounders and athletics in the summer. Facilities include a modern indoor swimming pool. Drama, debating and Duke of Edinburgh's Award at bronze level are highly popular choices and our new, all weather outdoor riding menage allows more than 70 girls to ride each week.

What happens after GCSE? Queen Mary's has no VIth Form and we see this as a real strength of the school. We offer specialist careers' advice throughout the senior school and well informed support to the girls as they seek to make application to their new schools and colleges. Many will opt for boarding. Each senior girl is able to choose a school or VIth form college which can offer her exactly the courses and educational environment she requires for her VIth form studies. A healthy proportion of the girls join their new schools as scholars. A few girls will embark on GNVQs or vocational training. We currently have Queen Mary's girls in the VIth form of over 30 different schools and colleges.

Entrance. By interview and placement test. Entry can be at most stages, subject to availability. An up to date prospectus will be despatched immediately on request. Our website (www.queenmarys.org) also provides useful information.

Fees. Nursery: £10.50 per half-day session; Reception: £1,250 per term; Pre-Prep: £1,500 per term; Years 3-6: £2,275 Day, £3,550 Boarding per term; Years 7-8: £2,450 Day, £3,750 Boarding; Years 9-11: £2,780 Day, £4,080 Boarding per term.

Extra subjects per term. Music £145, Speech and Drama £40, Riding £12 per lesson.

Scholarships. Scholarships are offered at 11+, 12+ and 13+ to those candidates who show particular academic flair or have special talent in music or art. Examinations are held early in the Spring term.

Queen Mary's Association. Old girls of the school can make contact with the secretary of the Queen Mary's Association via the school office.

Preparatory School. For information about the Preparatory School, please refer to entry in the IAPS section.

Charitable status. Queen Mary's School is a Registered Charity, number 269665. It exists to educate children in a Christian environment.

Queens College, London

43–49 Harley Street London W1G 8BT
Tel: 020 7291 7070
Fax: 020 7291 7099
e-mail: queens@qcl.org.uk
website: www.qcl.org.uk

The College was the first institution to provide higher education and proper qualifications for young women. It was founded in 1848 by F D Maurice, Professor of Modern History at King's College and in 1853 received the first-ever Royal Charter for Women's Education. Today it is a thriving school of 375 girls from 11–18.

Patron: Her Majesty Queen Elizabeth, The Queen Mother

Visitor: The Rt Revd and Rt Hon the Lord Bishop of London

Council:

Chairman: Professor J Somerville, MD, FRCP, FACC

The Revd David Burgess, MA (Oxon), FSA
Mrs J Campbell, CMG, MA (Oxon)
The Lady Chorley

Bernard Clow, FCA
Mrs D Davis, BA (Manchester)
Lady Hopkins, AADip, HonFAIA, HonFRIAS
Mrs J Howarth, MA (Oxon) *Fellow of Girton*
Nicholas Inge, BA (Oxon)
Dr C Kenyon-Jones, MA (Oxon)
Mrs J M Pulay, MA (Oxon)
Mrs C M Rumboll, CertEd (Cambridge), DipSoc (London)
Tom Shebbeare, CVO, BA (Exeter)
Mrs S Stopford, AB (Radcliffe), BA (Cantab) (*Representing the Staff*)
David Summerscale, MA (Cantab)
Mrs T Williams

Secretary to the Council: Mrs E C Chesswas, BA (OU)

Principal: **Miss M M Connell**, MA (Oxon)

Senior Tutor: J S Hutchinson, MA, MSc
Deputy Senior Tutor and Senior Mistress: Mrs L Foord, MA
Curriculum Tutor: Miss A Lang, BA
Director of Studies: Mrs S Harrison, MA
University and Library Tutor: Mrs E Relle, MA, PhD
Examinations Tutor: J P Gray, MA, PhD
Administration Tutor: Miss T Millar, BEd
Bursar & Secretary to the Council: Mrs E C Chesswas, BA (OU)

Lecturers and Teachers in College and School:
E D Bird, BA (Wimbledon) *ICT/Art/Modern Languages*
Mrs C Briscoe, BA (London) *English/Theatre Studies/Drama*
Miss A Carlier, BA (Oxon) *Religious Studies*
S Dawoodbhai, BSc (Plymouth) *Mathematics*
Mrs R de Gomez, BA (Sheffield) *Spanish/French*
Miss C de Sybel, BA (Cantab) *Piano/Theory*
Miss P Dhillon, BSc (Durham) *Physics*
J T Donovan, BSc (London) *Mathematics*
Mrs B Edlin, MA(TCD) *German/French*
Miss F Elderkin, BSc (Exeter) *Biology*
J D Ferrar, BA (Cantab) *English/Drama/Media Resources Officer*
N G Flower, BA, BSc (OU) *ICT*
Mrs L Foord, MA (St Andrews), MA (London) *French/Japanese*
J P Gray, MA (Oxon), PhD (London) *Art/History of Art/Examinations Tutor*
Miss L M Hardwick, BA (Cantab) *Italian/French*
Mrs S Harrison, MA (Oxon) *Classics*
J S Hutchinson, BA (London), MA (London), MSc (Kingston) *Classics/ICT*
Mrs M Jones, MA (Oxon), MSc (UCLA) *Chemistry*
Mrs M Kateck, BA (McGill), MA (London) *History*
Miss A Lang, BA (Oxon) *Classics/Mathematics*
Miss U J M Lynam, BA (Oxon) *Italian/French*
A Marchant, BSc (London) *Biology*
Miss R Martinez, BA (Kent), MA (Birmingham) *Art/History of Art/Junior Mistress*
Miss T Millar, BEd (Durham) *Physical Education*
Mrs E Murray, BSc (Wales) *Biology/Science*
Mrs N Peace, BA (St Petersburg) *Russian/French*
Mrs E Relle, MA, PhD (Cantab) *English/Theatre Studies*
J R Rose, BA (Kingston) *Music*
Mrs P H O Sperling, BA (London), FRGS *Geography/RS*
Miss L M Walker, BA (Oxon) *English/Drama*
Mrs A M Wells, BSc (Canterbury, NZ) *Mathematics/Economics/PE*
P C Wilford, BA (Newport) *Art*
D Willows, BA (York), MA (London) *History*
Miss E D M Woodhouse, MA (Oxon) *English/Drama*
Mrs H Yorston, BSc (Bristol) *Mathematics*

College Librarian: Mrs J Fitz Gerald, MA (Cantab)

College Archivist: Mrs M Poulter, BA (Wales), DAA

Part Time:

Mrs S C Atkins, BA (Oxon) *Classics/Careers*
Miss N Daines *Dance*
Mrs S C Deans, MA (Oxon) *Geography*
Miss A F Goodall, DipBAF, DipAAI, HonRCM *Fencing*
Mrs D F Gumpert, BD (London) *Religious Studies*
Mrs C M Huckin, BEd (Sussex) *Physical Education*
Mrs J Kazai, BA (Kumamoto) *Japanese*
Miss C Lax, LRAM, LTCL *Director of Music (Administration)*
Mrs L Penny, MA (Oxon) *Classics*
P Solomons, BA (Oxon) *French*
C A F Stephens, BA (Oxon) *Government/Politics*

Visiting Music Staff:
Miss S Blair, GRSM, LRAM *Piano*
A Caldon, DipRAM *Brass*
Miss S Hambleton-Smith, LRAM *Guitar*
Miss C Lax, LRAM, LTCL *Principal Accompanist/Piano/Singing*
Miss R Palmer, LRAM *Violinng*
Miss J Phillips, DipRCM *'Cello*
P Robinson, FTCL, LLCM *Woodwind/Theory*
Miss C de Sybel, BA (Cantab) *Piano/Theory*
Miss I Tasic, BMus *Harp*
A Timperley, LTCL *Clarinet/Saxophone*

Administrative Staff:

Bursar: Mrs J Marsden
Admissions Secretary: Mrs S Hoenderkamp
College Nurse: Miss S P Hutchison, BA (Victoria, NZ)
Finance Officer: Mrs L Thompson
General Office Manager: W Leigh Knight
General Office Assistant: Miss A Goodhart, BA

Support Staff:

Laboratory Technician: Mrs L Austin, HNC
Senior Laboratory Technician: K P Anderson, OND
Network Manager: S A Mya, BSc (Mandalay), BSc (QMW)
College Warden/Maintenance: M Kevin

Numbers: There are over 375 girls in the College, aged from 11 to 18, of whom 95 are in the sixth form.

Situation: The College is situated in Harley Street in central London. The 18th century buildings have been well modernised with facilities for Art, Drama, six new Science Laboratories and well equipped laboratories for ICT, Modern Languages and Music.

Admission: This is by the London Consortium entrance examination and interview. Girls are admitted at 11, 12, 13 and 14 to begin to prepare for GCSE courses and at 16 to A Level courses; ie the school grows larger at the older age-range.

Curriculum: The College provides an academic curriculum preparing girls for the General Certificate of Secondary Education and for GCE Advanced Levels, AS Levels and Oxford and Cambridge Entrance. There is a wide range of subjects at A Level including Computing, and most girls go on to further education. Music, Art and Drama are important activities and the College takes full advantage of London's theatres, concerts, lectures, museums and galleries. Physical Education includes netball, hockey, tennis, swimming, dance, gymnastics and fencing. The College is an Anglican foundation but is open to all denominations.

Scholarships. Some Scholarships, up to half fees, are available for girls entering the Sixth Form. Girls can apply for all subjects including Art and Music.

Fees. £2,815 a term.

Charitable status. Queen's College, London is a Registered Charity, number 312726. It exists to provide education for girls.

Queen's Gate School

133 Queen's Gate London SW7 5LE
Tel: 020 7589 3587
Fax: 020 7584 7691

Governors:
Lady Dowson, MBE (*Chairman*)
Mrs James Cran
Mr David Hurst
Miss Jenny Lee
Mrs Elizabeth-Ann Reed
Mrs V Russell, JP
Sir Graham Wilkinson, Bt

Staff:
Principal: **Mrs A Holyoak**, Inst of Educ Cert, London

Head of the Senior School: Miss M Skone-Roberts, BSc, PGCE, LTCL

Senior Mistress: Miss E de Leeuw, BA Hons

Art and Design:
Mrs L Campbell, MFA
Miss S Marinkov, BA (Hons), PGCE

Art, History of, Careers:
Miss E de Leeuw, BA (Hons)

Physics:
Mrs L Kidd, BEd (Hons)

Biology:
Miss K Rees, BSc (Hons), PGCE
Mrs B Rennie, BSc (Hons), PGCE

Chemistry:
Mr A Ellison, BSc (Hons), PGCE, CChem, MRSC

Classics:
Dr T Bell
Mrs N Clear, BA (Hons), PGCE

Computer Studies:
Mrs I Jones, BA (Hons), PGCE
Miss T McGregor, BA

Design and Technology:
Mrs B Polanski, BA, ATC, PGCE

Drama and Speech Training:
Miss S Linstead, MA
Miss R Nelhams, BA (Hons), PGCE

English:
Mrs P Bleazard, BA (Hons), PGCE
Miss S Osbourn, BA (Hons), PGCE
Miss L Huxtep, BA (Hons), PGCE

Special Educational Needs:
Mrs K Kindersley, BA (Hons), PGCE
Mrs T Lynsky

French:
Mrs T Delbarry, L-ès-L Moderne
Mr J Addy, BA (Hons), PGCE

Geography:
Mr M Crundwell BSc, MPhil
Miss S Gamm, BSc (Hons), CertEd, MIEnvsc

German:
Miss B Gusenheimer, MA

History:
Mrs J S Ditchfield, MA
Miss N Don, BA (Hons), PGCE

Italian:
Mrs M G Simkins, Dr Mod Lang Milan

Mathematics:
Miss S Badger, BSc (Hons), PGCE
Mrs B Breedon, MSc, BEd

Music:
Mrs E Burgess, BA, BEd

Physical Education:
Miss G Kenny, BEd
Miss M Bax, BA (Hons)

Religious Studies:
Mrs N Clear, BA (Hons), PGCE

Sociology:
Mrs S Shuckburgh, BA (Hons), PGCE

Spanish:
Miss S Gomez, Licenciada en Filologia

Laboratory Technician: Mr D I Swan, BSc

Librarian: Mrs L Lancashire, BA (Hons)

Fencing: Prof J Parkins, Maitre de l'Academie d'Armes de France

Junior School:
Headmistress: Mrs N Webb, BA (Hons), PGCE

Form Tutors:
Mrs S Neale, BEd, ARCM, LTCL
Miss C Harris, CertEd
Mrs V Feeny, CertEd
Mrs M Wallace, BA
Miss K Greenwood, BEd (Hons)
Mrs E Colquhoun, CertEd
Miss A Dimmer, BEd (Hons)
Mrs G Bilbo, BSc, PGCE
Miss A Gallway, BA (Hons)

Drama & Speech Training:
Miss R Nelhams, BA (Hons), PGCE

French: Miss V Dinga, Licence de Psychologie

Music Staff:

Clarinet & Saxophone: Mr M Ford, FTCL
Flute: Miss S Moore, BMus, DipARCM
Guitar: Mr S Carpenter, BMus, AGSM
Piano: to be appointed
Miss S Birchall, ARCM
Miss M Squires, BMusEd, DScM, Montessori Dip
Recorder: Mr A Robinson, AGSM
Violin: Miss S Coates, BMus, DipARCM
Cello: Miss C Constable, MMus HonsRCM, PGDip
Horn and Piano: Miss H Shillito, BMus RCM (Hons)

Bursar: Miss V Butler
Registrar: Mrs A James
School Secretary: Mrs A Nissen, BSc(Econ), DipEd

Queen's Gate School is an independent school for girls between the ages of 4 and 18 years. Established in 1891, the school is an Educational Trust situated in three large interconnecting Victorian Houses within easy walking distance of Kensington Gardens, Hyde Park, the gardens of the Natural History Museum and many of the main London museums.

The aim of the school is to create a secure and happy environment in which the girls can realise their academic potential and make full use of individual interests and talents. We have few rigid rules, encourage the development of self-discipline and create an atmosphere where freedom of thought and ideas can flourish.

Close co-operation with parents is welcomed at every stage.

Girls follow as wide a curriculum as possible and generally take GCSE in 8 or 9 subjects which must include English, Mathematics, Science and a modern language.

A full range of A level subjects is offered.

Admission is by test and interview in the Junior School, The London Day Schools' Consortium Entrance examination at 11+, The School's own Entrance examinations for second, third or fourth year entry. Applicants for the VIth Form are expected to have passed five GCSEs at A-C Grade with A grades in those subjects they wish to pursue to A level. They study for 4 or 5 A/S levels in the first year and 3 A levels in the second.

There is no school uniform except for games and gymnastics, but the girls are expected to wear clothing and footwear suitable for attending school and taking part in school activities.

Games. Netball, Hockey, Tennis, Swimming, Athletics, Basketball and Volleyball.

Fees. There is no registration fee. Entrance fee: £25 for Junior and Senior School, £25 for VIth Form. Tuition fee: apply to the school.

The Queen's School
Chester

City Walls Road Chester CH1 2NN
Tel: (01244) 312078
Fax: (01244) 321507

Founded 1878

Governing Body:
Chairman: Mr P A W Roberts, MA, FCA

Deputy Chairman: Mrs H McNae, BA, JP

Mr G C Adnitt, FRICS
The Right Reverend The Lord Bishop of Chester
Mrs E M Barnes, BEd, MEd
Mrs E Bolton
Mrs E J Brown, CPFA
Mr D T Doxat-Pratt, ARIBA
Mrs S P Jones, CC
Dr C H Laine, MB, ChB, MSc, FRCR
Mrs S Lloyd, BA
Mrs D McConnell, CBE, DL
Mrs S Seys-Llewellyn, DipEd
The Revd Canon J M Roff, BSc
Mr E B Walton

Clerk to the Governors: B Dutton, FCA, 37–43 White Friars, Chester. Tel: Chester 312351.

***Headmistress:* Miss D M Skilbeck**, BA

Deputy Headmistress: Mrs S Sheedy, BSc

Secretary: Mrs S E Salter

Assistant Secretary: Mrs J Taylor

Bursar: Mrs M Kelly

Bursar's Assistant: Mrs S Hughes

Administrator: Dr L Rees, PhD

Domestic Bursar: Mrs C Reynolds

Assistant Teachers:
English:
Mr R Ainsworth, BA (Durham), BPhil (Newcastle), ACP
Mrs W Beynon, BA (Liverpool), RSA Dip TEFL
Mrs S Chafer, BA (Wales)
Mrs C Holland, BA (Birmingham)
Mrs K Roden, BA Hons (Open)

Religious Education:
Mrs B Lloyd, BD (London)
Mrs H M Morris, CertEd, AdvDip Curriculum Studies

History:
Mrs P Tolley, BA (London)
Mrs J M Roberts, BA (Newcastle-upon-Tyne)
Mrs P M Jones, BA (Liverpool), DipRDov

Geography:
Mrs E D Rowland, BSc (London)
Mrs M O Selby, BA (Liverpool)
Miss R Fox, BA Hons (Exeter), PGCE

Classics:
Mrs E A Jevons, BA (Southampton)
Mrs E M L Griffiths, MA (St Andrews)
Mrs F M Culver, BA (Newcastle)

French:
Mrs M B Chorley, BA (Manchester)
Miss M J Hemming, MA (Birmingham)
Miss P Heaney, BA (Sheffield)
Mr McEwan, MA (St Andrews)

French Conversation: Mrs E Shannon, L-ès-Lettres, Mâitrise, PGCE

German:
Mrs P Maddocks, BA (London)
Mrs W Marshall, BA (Bangor)

German Conversation: Miss S Kuschke

Italian: Mrs S J Bowden, BA (Manchester)

Spanish: Mrs E Shannon, L-ès-L, Mâitrise, PGCE

Mathematics:
Mr I J Armstrong, BSc (Durham)
Mrs S Osborne, BSc (London)
Mrs S Sheedy (*Deputy Headmistress*)
Mrs S Stinson, BSc (London)
Mrs A Carter, BSc (Liverpool)
Mrs J O'Donnell, BSc Hons (Lancaster), PGCE

Physics:
Mr C V Cook, BSc (Wales)
Mrs P Moate, BSc (Nottingham)
Mrs P Steventon, BSc (Exeter)
Dr K Hill, PhD, BSc (London)

Design Technology:
Mrs P Moate, BSc (Nottingham)
Mrs S Bright, BA Hons (Leicester)

Chemistry:
Dr K R Young, PhD, MEd (Liverpool), CChem, MRIC
Dr C P Johnson, PhD (London)
Dr J Martin, PhD, BSc (Salford)
Mrs K Campbell, BSc Hons (Edinburgh), PGCE

Biology:
Miss S Woodland, MSc (York)
Mrs E L Jones, BSc (Bristol)
Mrs S M Swift, BSc (London)
Mrs I J Harrison, BSc (Liverpool)

Information Technology: Miss J L Bartle, BA (Bangor)

Economics:
Mrs J Falcon, BA (Open University)
Mrs L Cracknell, BA (Nottingham)

Current Affairs & Careers: Mrs J Falcon, BA (Open University)

Home Economics:
Mrs G Hoyle, CertEd (Madeley)
Mrs M Leigh, CertEd (F L Calder)

Art:
Mrs F Blything, BA (Manchester)
Mrs A J Latham, BA (Loughborough College)

Music:
Mrs J Bartai, GTCL, LTCL
Mr C Pilsbury, FTCL, ARMCM, LTCL

Pianoforte:
Miss R Jones, GMus, RNCM, LRAM, ARCM, FLCM

Violin & Viola:
Mrs J M Holmes, MusB (Manchester), GRSM, ARMCM

Cello: Mrs C E Jones, BA (Glasgow), LGSM

Woodwind:
Mrs E Dutch, BA (*Bristol*), ARCM
Ms R M Lyons, BAMus (Liverpool)
Mr R Hinde
Miss K Turner

Singing: Mrs F Cooke, BA (Cambridge)

Brass: Mr A M Lewis

Speech and Drama: Mrs A Mistry, LGSM, ALAM

Physical Education:
Mrs C E Moore, CertEd (Coventry College)
Miss J Huck, BA Hons (Nonington College)
Mrs L Waring, BEd (IM Marsh College of Physical Education)

The Junior Department at Nedham House, 57 Liverpool Road, Chester:
Miss J D Dewhurst, BEd (Oxford Polytechnic), MEd (Manchester)
Miss S M Paice, CertEd (Goldsmith's College, London)
Mrs S Lindop, BEd (Cambridge)
Mrs P Williams, BEd (Chester)
Mrs J M Holmes, BMus (Manchester), GRSM, ARMCM
Mrs M D Meredith, CertEd (C F Mott College of Education)
Mrs C Tottey, BEd (IM Marsh College of Physical Education)
Mrs S Shearlock, BA (Manchester)

The Preparatory Department at Sandford House, 55 Liverpool Road, Chester:
Miss R R Morgan, BA (Wales)
Mrs D G Heron, BEd (St Katherine's College, Liverpool)
Mrs B Arkley, CertEd (Durham)
Mrs D Thomas, BEd (Sussex)
Mrs F Carder, BEd (Exeter)

The Buildings. The original school assembly hall, built on land given by the Duke of Westminster in 1882 when Queen Victoria became the first patron, has been enlarged and extensive alterations have been made to improve and modernise the old buildings. There is a well-equipped science block, a Sixth Form Centre and a Learning Resource Centre. The principal playing field adjoins the School, below the City Wall. There is an all-weather practice pitch. The Lower School, divided into 2 departments, is housed in separate buildings. It has a large garden and playing field of its own, where the school swimming pool is situated.

Number of Pupils. 652.

Admission. The school's own entrance examination for the Upper School is held in the Spring Term and candidates should be under the age of 12 on 1 September in the year of admission.

All girls admitted are expected to remain at school until they have completed the 2 years Sixth Form Course.

Nedham House. Girls not already in the School are tested each year for admission to Nedham House. These are occasional vacancies.

Preparatory Department. Girls are admitted from 4–8. Assessments held in Spring Term.

Application forms may be obtained from the Secretary.

The Curriculum includes the usual academic subjects. Languages include French, German, Spanish and Latin. Greek may be started in the fourth year. There is a small Language Laboratory. Full attention is paid to the teaching of both arts and science subjects throughout the School. Music may be studied for the A Level and GCSE examinations and girls learning an instrument may be entered for the examinations of the Associated Board of the Royal Schools of Music. There are Choirs, Orchestras and Instrumental Ensembles.

Games. Hockey, Lacrosse, Netball, Tennis. Private tennis coaching can be arranged. The school has 2 playing fields and an indoor, heated swimming pool.

Religious Teaching is undenominational although the School is associated with Chester Cathedral in which two services are held each year.

Examinations. Pupils are prepared for the General Certificate of Secondary Education and Advanced Level examinations and for entrance to Oxford and Cambridge.

Scholarships. 1. A scholarship instituted in commemoration of Queen Victoria's Jubilee, awarded to the Sixth Form pupil who does best in the yearly examination: the holder to be called the Queen's Scholar. 2. Four Hastings Scholarships giving exemption from tuition fees and 2 for half-fees. 3. One Chester Blue Coat Exhibition awarded annually. Value £200 per year. The holder must have been born in, or currently be resident in the City of Chester, defined by the 1974 boundary. 4. A limited number of bursaries will be awarded each year from The Queen's School Centenary Bursaries Fund. Application forms and further particulars can be obtained from the Secretary. 5. A University Scholarship of £30 a year, founded by Miss Nessie Brown, is tenable at a college of Oxford or Cambridge University.

Present Fees. Upper School: £5,550 per annum. Lower School: £3,360 per annum.

Music Lessons. All instruments £123 per term.

Cost of Lunch. Upper School £1.75 per day, Junior £1.65 and Preparatory Department £1.60.

Payment of Fees. All fees to be paid at the National Westminster Bank, St John Street, Chester, to the account of the Queen's School, Chester. No fees will be received at the School. Accounts (including dinner bill) will be sent to parents and guardians at the opening of each term, and prompt payment is requested.

A term's notice of the intention to remove a pupil must be given in writing to the Head Mistress; otherwise payment for the next term will be required. No one is entitled to claim remission of fees on account of absence from school through illness, but parents may insure themselves against absence with a firm of underwriters; particulars of the scheme can be obtained from the Secretary.

The Governors reserve the right of requiring the withdrawal of a pupil at their discretion without any assignment of cause.

Visiting Hours. The Head Mistress is at home to receive parents who wish to see her during term time between 1.30 and 3.30 on Tuesday afternoons. Annual Open Days held in November for Senior School and Lower School. Evening for prospective Sixth Formers held in March. Taster days arranged to suit pupils of all ages.

The Queen's School Association (Old Girls). *Secretary:* Mrs M Miln, 3 Boughton Hall Drive, Great Boughton, Chester CH3 5QG.

Charitable status. The Queen's School, Chester is a Registered Charity, number 1081/06. It exists to provide education for girls.

* Head of Department	§ Part Time or Visiting
† Housemaster/Housemistress	¶ Old Pupil
‡ See below list of staff for meaning	

Queenswood

Hatfield Hertfordshire AL9 6NS
Tel: (01707) 602500
Fax: (01707) 602597
e-mail: go@queenswood.herts.sch.uk
website: www.queenswood.herts.sch.uk

Founded 1894

Governors:

Chairman: C G Sneath, FCA
Vice-Chairman: Mrs J K King

The Revd Dr J C A Barrett, MA, FRSA
M Beggs (*Chairman of Fellowship*)
Miss C Davies
A K Dawson, MA
Professor R Eatock Taylor, MA, PhD, FEng, FIMechE, FRINA
Mrs M C A King, BA, ACA
Dr A M Lee, PhD, BA, FIPD
G Morton-Smith, BSc, FRICS
Dr A E Ormerod (*Fellowship Representative*)
H T Porritt, BSc(Eng), ARSM, FCA
Sir William Purves, CBE, DSO
Dr J M Riley, MA, BA, PhD (Cambridge)
G Russell, MA
C P Smith, FCA
The Lord Stamp, MD, MSc, FRCP
W J Sykes, Esq
Miss P M Wrinch (*OQA Representative*)

***Principal:* Clarissa M Farr**, BA Hons, MA, PGCE

Clerk to the Governors and School Bursar: Mr A P H Dunlop, MIPD, MIMgt, CDipAF

Deputy Principal (Pastoral): Mrs D M Clinton, BEd, CertEd

Deputy Principal (Academic): Mr R J Morgan, BA Hons, MA, PGCE

Housemistresses:
Upper Sixth: Mrs G M Dawson
Lower Sixth: The Revd Shirley Clayton
Clapham North: Miss P Dixon
Clapham South: Ms J Lodrick
Hartley: Mrs D M McMahon
Waller: Miss S Cannon
Upper Trew: Mrs V Castle

Administrative Staff:
Principal's PA: Miss H Langdon

Registrar: Mrs S K Wood

Marketing Manager: Ms J Rushton, MSc, BEd, DipM, MCIM, AMIPR

Activities Development Manager: Miss E A Needham

Finance Manager: Mrs T Elmer

Accounts Manager: Mrs D Willmott

General Office Secretaries: Mrs M Park, Mrs S Barber

Medical Staff:
Dr R J Elder, MB, ChB, MRCGP, DCH
Mrs R Marlow
Mrs H McMillan

Counsellor: Mrs P Thomas

School Shop Manageress: Mrs V Castle

Maintenance Manager: Mr B Owens, MICW, ACIOB

Estate Manager: Mr P Grigg, NDT

Catering Manager, Scolarest: Mr D Penlington

Teaching Staff:
Religious Studies:
*Miss F J E Gunn, LIB Hons (Exeter), PGCE
The Revd Mrs S Clayton, BA Hons (Westminster College, Oxford), CertEd (*Chaplain*)

English:
Mrs G Bonwick, BA Hons (Bradford), TESOL (*TEFL*)
Ms C M Farr, BA Hons, MA (Exeter), PGCE
Mrs T P Filskow, BA Hons (Manchester)
Mr S D Gifford, BA Hons (N Wales), MA (Massachusetts) (*Librarian*)
Mrs M A Gourd, BA Hons (Nottingham), MA (London), PGCE
Mrs L V Jones, ARCM, CertEd (*Special Needs*)
Mrs D M McMahon, BA Hons (Liverpool)
*Mrs H Ness-Gifford, BA Hons (Exeter), PGCE (*Head of English*)
*Miss A Parker, BA Hons (Wales), PGCE (*Head of Drama*)
Mrs K M Tudor, BA Hons (Leicester), PGCE

History:
*Mrs E M G Roberts, BA Hons (Nottingham), PGCE
Mrs F Williams, BA Hons (Oxford), PGCE

History of Art:
*Mrs E M Butterworth, BA (Open)

Economics:
*Mrs V A Challacombe, MA (Cantab)
Mrs G M Dawson, BSc Hons (Cardiff)

Speech & Drama:
Mrs G Butlin, LLAM, ALAM (*Speech and Drama*)
Mrs N J Dearnley, RegMCSLT, ALAM, LLAM, ATCL (*Speech and Drama*)
Mrs B Thomas (*Speech and Drama*)

Geography:
*Miss H Hoyle, BA Hons (Oxon)
Mrs A M Allsop, MA (Cantab), PGCE
Miss P Sex, BA Hons (Swansea), PGCE

Modern Languages:
*Mr A G M Barthelemy, L ès L, M ès L (Lyons), MIL
Mrs G M Darabi (*Italian*)
Miss P Dixon, BA Hons, PGCE, MIMgt
Miss C Friadeisen (*German Assistant*)
Miss W Gabarre Yáñez (*Spanish*)
*Ms J S Gandee, MA (Cantab), PGCE
Miss L Harvie, MA Hons (Aberdeen), PGCE
Miss T Hinterreicher, MagPhilt (Saltzburg), CertEd
Miss C Marchand, L-ès-L (Savoie) (*French Assistant*
Mr R J Morgan, BA (Wales), MA, PGCE
Miss E T G Silvestri, BA Hons (Kent), PGCE
Miss N Gabarre Yanez (*Spanish Assistant*)

Science:
Mrs M Adcock, BSc Hons (Manchester), MEd (Cantab), PGCE
*Mrs M F T Davidson, BSc Hons (Leicester), PGCE
Mrs H Giachardi, BSc (Leeds), PGCE, CBiol, MIBiol
Miss T Grove, BSc Hons (Reading), PGCE
Mr D A King, MA Hons (Cambridge), PGCE
Mr M A J Lock, BSc (London), MSc (Reading), PGCE
Mrs D M Rowe, BSc Hons (Bristol), PGCE

Science Technicians:
Mrs D Becker
Mrs C Culshaw
Mrs K J Hyat
Mrs M Moolenaar
Mrs M Osborn

Information Technology:
Miss A Evison, CertEd, DipITE, MA (Kings)
*Mr M Henderson, BA, BEd (Queensland, Australia)
Mr A Lim, BSc (Durham), BA (Wolverhampton)
Mr M McDonald, BSc (Open)

Mathematics:
*Mrs P M Clark, BSc Hons (Liverpool), PGCE
Mr P Vincent, BA Hons (East Anglia), PGCE
Mrs G M Wilson, BSc Hons (Leicester), PGCE
Mr M H Worrall, MA (Cantab), BA (Leeds)

Music:
*Mr S D M Potts, BMus Hons (Nottingham) (*Director of Music*)
Head of Academic Music: Mrs P J Woodhouse

Mr J Blaskett, GRSM, FCSM, LRAM, ARCM, PGCE (*Chapel Organist*)
Miss V Ronchetti, BMus (Manchester), GRSM, ARMCM (*Head of Strings*)
Ms J Lodrick, BA Hons (Chichester), PGCE

Instrumental Staff:
Miss D Anderson, BMus Hons, Performance, LRAM (*Double Bass*)
Ms S Burnett (*Bassoon*)
Miss J Clarke, BA Hons, GTCL, FTCL, LTCL (*Piano, Flute*)
Miss H L Cheng, MMus, ARCM, DipRCM (*Piano*)
Miss B Copas, LRAM, LGSM (*Piano*)
Mr R Drew (*Percussion*)
Miss R Fulgoni, BA(Mus), RNCM (*Violin*)
Mr T Gucklhorn, LTCL, FTCL
Ms C Kelbie, GLCM Hons, TCM, FLCM, LLCM, ALCM
Mr J Kirby, LRAM, GRSM Hons (*Piano*)
Ms S Pilgrim, ARCM, DipRAM (*Singing*)
Mr R Ralph, Prof Cert RAM (*Piano*)
Ms J Rees, ARCM, GRSM (*Singing*)
Ms J Spotswood, GTCL Hons, LTCL
Mrs B Stewart, BMus Hons, LRAM
Ms G Thoday, LRAM (*Cello*)
Miss A Turnbull, LRAM (*Oboe*)
Ms R Whiffen, GMusHons, PARNCM, PPRNCM(Chamber), PGRNCM (*Clarinet, Saxophone*)
Miss K Wilkinson, BMus, FLCM, ARSM (*Flute*)

Art and Design:
Miss J Atkinson, BA Hons (Edinburgh), MA (Royal College of Art)
*Mr J Hills, BA Hons (Reading), MA (London), PGCE

Design & Techology:
Miss S Cannon, BSc Hons (Brunel), CertEd

Physical Education:
Mrs D M Clinton, BEd (Leeds)
Miss M Cunningham, BSc Hons (Loughborough), PGCE
Miss M Merrigan, BSc (Loughborough), PGCEe)
Miss F Neil, BEd Hons (Exeter)
Miss S Thorp, BEd (Exeter), MSc (Springfield College, USA) (*Director of Sport*)

Peripatetic Staff:
Miss L Christian, BPhil Hons, FISTD, DipLCD, Enrico Ceccetti Dip (*Dance*)RAD (*Dance*)
Miss A Holmes, BTF Coach (*Trampolining*)

Tennis:
Mrs K Bachelor, LTA ECA Coach
Mr M Dunkley, LTA CCA Coach
Mrs P Hall, LTA CCA Coach
Miss T Lilley, LTA CCA Coach
Mr A Phillips, LTA ECA Coach
Mr A Pinter, LTA CCA Coach, Hungarian Professional
Mr J Trehearn, LTA Performance Coach (*Senior Coach*)
Miss M Wainwright *Visiting Tennis Professional*

Careers: Mrs J Kilsby, BA Hons (UCL), PGCE

Librarians:
Mr D S Gifford, BA Hons (N Wales), MA (Massachusetts)
Mrs J M Roser, BEd (London)

Artists in Residence:
Miss R Adams, BA Hons (Liverpool), PGCE (*Art*)
Mr N Kelley, BA Hons (Oxon) (*Drama*)

Driving Instructors:
Mrs S Fennessy
Mr B Wallis

Queenswood is a modern independent boarding school for senior girls, beautifully sited in 120 acres of green belt, 17 miles north of central London with easy access to motorways, rail services and airports. Queenswood offers full and day boarding with activity weekends, home weekends and flexi weekends. Activity Weekends could include trips or inter-house drama and music festivals. During flexi weekends for those girls who choose to stay in school, there are many activities on offer - clubs, workshops and outings - as well as the chance to relax with friends after a busy week.

As well as a beautiful site, Queenswood has excellent educational facilities: a magnificent library with 20,000 items and a CD-ROM server; a large and well-equipped science block; a fine arts centre containing a concert hall, 36 music teaching and practice rooms and art, design and pottery rooms. A modern teaching block comprises eight departmental suites including a language laboratory fitted with video and satellite access. The school has a high performance computer network using fibre optic links between buildings. CD-ROMs are available across the network from a CD-ROM server as well as several standalone machines. Information Technology is integrated across the curriculum. Girls are taught ICT in timetabled lessons in Years 7, 8, 9, 10 and the Lower Sixth and its use is encouraged, as appropriate, in all subjects. The school has introduced laptop computers into three year groups and is part of the Microsoft AAL initiative. There is Internet access to all our networked computers.

Over one quarter of the 380 pupils are in the Sixth Form following the new Curriculum 2000 programme. All Sixth Formers continue to do languages. 97% of the girls will go on to do degree courses at university. Careers advice begins in Year 8 with work shadowing and continues throughout the school. In Year 11 and the Lower Sixth work experience, a careers convention, Young Enterprise, Young Engineers and leadership training are arranged.

Entrance to Queenswood is by the Independent Schools Examinations Board or Queenswood Entrance Examination and interview at 11+ or 13+ and by examination and interview into the Sixth Form. The curriculum is broad and goes beyond National Curriculum requirements. The graduate staff are highly qualified and girls are prepared up to Oxford and Cambridge entrance standards.

The school is of Christian foundation, interdenominational, with its own Chapel which plays a central part in community life. As a school which welcomes girls of all faiths, spiritual welfare is a priority, as part of the school's emphasis on pastoral care.

The international aspect of the school is a strength. Teacher exchanges with Australia and resident Spanish, French and German assistantes enrich the experience within the school. Pupils can spend a term in schools in Canada, Australia, America, South Africa and New Zealand. Many girls take two modern languages at GCSE: French and either German or Spanish. Regular overseas visits take place – for example, the Queenswood Singers visit to European countries, linguists to Spain, Cuba and France, tennis players to Portugal, hockey players to South Africa and New Zealand, ski trips, the Queenswood Raven

Exploration Society expeditions to Kenya and Nepal, and Art historians visit Florence and Paris.

Physical Education and sport are an important part of the curriculum with the emphasis on health-related fitness and sport for all. The Queenswood/LTA Tennis Centre includes 12 'fast-dry' green clay courts as well as 16 astroturf courts and indoor acrylic courts, providing for the complete development of players for the modern game at this centre of excellence. The astroturf hockey pitch, seven grass pitches, athletics field, palaestra and indoor swimming pool, fitness suites and gymnasium provide opportunities to participate in many sporting activities at all levels or just for fun.

Nearly two-thirds of the girls study a musical instrument. The two orchestras, ensembles, choirs and chamber choir regularly perform at prestigious venues at home and abroad and have performed at the Barbican and Queen Elizabeth Hall. There are annual school drama productions as well as studio presentations throughout the year preparing pupils for GCSE Drama and A level Theatre Studies. Inter-house Music and Drama Festivals are annual events.

Girls may take part in the The Duke of Edinburgh Award Scheme to bronze and silver level. Community Service encourages the girls to consider those less fortunate than themselves.

Generous Scholarships up to 50% of full fees are offered to girls under 14 and to those entering the Sixth Form. Tennis scholarships and bursaries, sports scholarships, music scholarships and creative arts scholarships are also offered; the Winifred Turner Open Music Scholarship has a value of up to two-thirds full fees. The Dame Gillian Wier Organ Scholarship is valued up to 50% of full fees. There is also an Old Queenswoodians' Bursary, for the close relative of old students. Entrants at 11+ and 13+ can also be considered for an All-Rounder Scholarship.

A prospectus with full details is available on request. You are encouraged to visit Queenswood and meet the Principal, staff and pupils.

Fees (September 2001). Full Boarders: Sixth Form £16,680; Years 9–11 £16,680; Years 7–8 £15,330. Day Boarders: Sixth Form £11,295; Years 9–11 £10,815; Years 7–8 £10,350.

Old Queenswoodians' Association (OQA) has over 3,000 members, organised in regional branches throughout the UK and in America, Canada, Australia and South Africa. The OQA can be contacted through the School.

Charitable status. Queenswood School Limited is a Registered Charity, number 311060, which exists to provide high quality education for girls.

Redland High School

Redland Court Bristol BS6 7EF.
Tel: (0117) 9245796
Fax: (0117) 9241127

Motto: *So hateth she derknesse*

The School was founded in the year 1882, and established at Redland Court in 1884. The aim for which the School was instituted was to provide for the girls of Redland and its neighbourhood a non-denominational public school education of the highest class, fitting pupils for home life, for professional life, or for the Universities.

President: Dr Beryl Corner, JP, MD, BS (London), FRCP, MRCP
Vice President: Mr J P Wynne-Willson, MA (Oxon)

Council:
Mr P J F Breach, BA Hons, FCA, ATII, ACT, IIMR (*Chairman*)
Dr M A Hollingsworth, BSc (*Eng*), PhD, MRALS (*Vice-Chairman*)

Mr D Brake
Mrs E Corrigan, MBA, BA Hons, SRN
Mrs A Ebery, BA Hons
Mrs C Fleming
Mr A J Light, JP, BSc
Sir Alexander Macara, FRCP, FRCGP, FFPHM, DSc(Hon)
Mrs C Melvin, BA Hons
Mrs S Perry
Mr J R Pool, MBE, FRICS, MA
Mrs P Pyper, MA
Mr D Tyrrell
Mr M Whife

***Headmistress:* Mrs Carol Lear**, BA Hons (London), PGCE (Bristol)

Deputy Head: Mrs P Davidson, BA Hons (Bristol), PGCE (Bristol)

Full-time Staff:
Mrs S M Argent, BA Hons (Worcester College of HE), PGCE (Exeter) *Geography*
Mrs S E Barnes, BA (Bloemfontein) *Mathematics*
*Mrs S K E Belfield, BA Hons, PGCE (Bristol) *Classics*
Mrs M H Bennett, BEd Hons (Exeter) *French*
*Mrs D Clarke, BSc (Bristol), PGCE (Cambridge) *Biology*
*Mr J N Davies, MA, BMus Hons, FRCO, PGCE (University College, Cardiff) *Music*
Mrs L Davies, BA Hons (Kent), PGCE (Bristol) *English*
*Mrs J R Dixon, MA (Cantab), PGCE (London) *History*
Miss C M Douglas, BA Hons (Keele), PGCE (Cardiff) *French*
*Miss H A Drew, BA Hons (Leeds), PGCE (Cambridge) *Theology and Religious Studies*
Miss A L Earle, BA Hons (Brunel University College) *History*
*Mrs L D Fletcher, BEd Hons (London) *Chemistry*
Mrs P M Hamilton, BA Hons (Belfast), PGCE (Oxford) *Joint German/French*
Miss L A Hipkins, BA(Ed) Hons (Exeter) *PE & Science*
Mrs B J Icke, CertEd (Goldsmith's College London) *Art*
*Mr J E Icke, BEd Hons (Goldsmiths College, London) *Art*
Mrs E A Jones, MSc, BSc (Glasgow), PGCE (Bristol) *Mathematics*
Mrs P F Lambert, CertEd (Southampton) *Physical Education*
Miss E J Lanyon, BA Hons (Cardiff Institute of Higher Education) *Physical Education/Careers*
*Miss P J Lord, CertEd (Bedford College of Physical Education) *Physical Education*
Miss S McCormack, BA Hons (Manchester), PGCE (Cambridge) *English*
Mrs K M McMahon, BA Hons (Birmingham) *German/French*
*Mr N McPherson, BA (Cambridge), PGCE (Cheltenham) *English*
*Mrs D F Myram, BSc Hons (Nottingham) *Physics/Mathematics*
*Mrs J Neil, MSc, BSc Hons (Lancaster), PGCE (Edinburgh) *Geography*
*Mrs S M Owst, BSc Hons, PGCE (London) *Mathematics*
Mr M D Redman, BA Hons (Bristol), BEng Hons (Manchester), FRCO, PGCE (Bath) *Music*
Mr M A K Sloan, BSc Hons (Bristol), PGCE (Edinburgh) *Physics*
Mrs V Walden, BA Hons, PGCE (London), MA *Classics*
Miss A J I Wilson, MA (St Andrews), PGCE (Christchurch) *English*
Mrs H Woods, BSc Hons (Cardiff) *Chemistry*

*Mrs S S Wright, BA Hons (Southampton), MA (Reading), MPhil (Southampton) *French*
*Mrs J E Yarrow, CertEd (Gloucester College of Education) *Technology - Food*

Part-time Staff:
Mrs D L Alderson, BSc Hons (Reading), PGCE (Leicester) *Geography*
Mrs F Bailey, BA Hons, PGCE (York) *Biology*
Mrs K Buff, BA Hons (Bristol), PGCE (Bristol) *Business Studies*
Mrs M J Coutanche, Licence d'Anglais (Nantes) *French Assistante*
Mrs L Gillion, CertEd *Religious Education*
Ms L Harper, BA Hons (Reading) *Psychology*
Mrs D A Horsted, BSc Hons (Nottingham), PGCE (Southampton) *Biology*
Ms M B Isglesias, BA Hons, PGCE (Pontevedra) *Spanish Assistant*
Mrs T L Jones, BEd Hons (Bath College of Higher Education) *Technology - Fashion/Textiles*
Mrs E de la Fuente Lewis-Smith, Licenciada en Filosofia y Letras Valladolid, MIL *Spanish*
Mrs T J Owen, BEd Hons (Bristol Polytechnic) *Design Technology*
Mrs M Pinnock, TCert (London) *Home Economics*
Mrs K Roberts, BA, MA (Bern) *German assistant*
Mrs J E Sheather, MA Hons (Oxon), DipEd (London) *Classics*
Mrs A Stean, BSc Hons (Leicester), PGCE *Combined Sciences*
Mrs K M Wallace, BSc (Leeds), PGCE *Mathematics*
Mrs D J Yamanaka, BSc Hons (London) *Information Technology/Computer Studies*

Junior School:
Head: Mrs M Lane, CertEd

Full-time Staff:
Mrs A Adachi, BA Hons (Bristol), PGCE *Music*
Mrs J Ashill, BEd Hons (Swansea Institute of Higher Education)
Mrs A E Cartwright, BEd (Oxon)
Mrs H Farion, BEd (Plymouth) *Primary Education*
Mrs K E George, BSc Hons (Bristol), PGCE (Southampton)
Mrs R Hayward, CertEd
Mrs J M Hunt, CertEd
Ms K Lashley, BA Hons (Carmarthen), PGCE
Mrs D Murley, BEd Hons (Brighton)
Mr A Sandars
Mrs E Scott, BA (Durham), PGCE *German/Spanish/Latin*
Ms K Siggers, BSc Hons (Portsmouth), PGCE *Geography*
Mrs R L Sutor, BEd Hons (UWE)

Visiting Staff:
Miss M Baker, GTCL, LRAM, LTCL, DipEd *Clarinet*
Mr J Berry, BEd, MEd, ARGM *Brass*
Ms V Bremner, BA Hons, ATCL, ALCM *Singing*
Mrs K Gilbert *Speech & Drama*
Mr A Gleadhill *Percussion*
Ms S Grundy, BA, LRSM *Flute*
Miss V Hodges, BA Hons, ALCM *Clarinet*
Ms C Johnson, BA Hons *Music, Piano*
Mr A King, GBSM, ABSM, LTCL *Oboe*
Mrs I Miller *Bassoon*
Mrs S Phipps, LRAM *Flute, Saxophone*
Mrs A M Rump, GGSM *Cello/Double Bass*
Mr G Smith, LRAM *Violin, Viola*

Librarian: Mrs C J Spalding, BA Hons (Hull)

Tennis Coach: Mrs E Jefferies

Headmistress's Secretary & PA: Mrs A O'Callaghan

School Secretaries:
Mrs K Harvey
Ms C Jenner

Junior School Secretary: Mrs L Stannard/Mrs P McCarter

Bursar and Secretary to the Council: Mr N P Blampied, BA Hons (Kent) Accountancy & Law

Development & Marketing Officer: Mrs J Butterworth, BSc (London)

ICT Systems Manager: Mrs J Duddridge

Redland is an Independent School for girls between the ages of 3 and 18, with approximately 170 Juniors and 500 Seniors. All girls are given a broadly based education aimed at developing the ability and potential of each individual. The school is a friendly, purposeful, disciplined and caring community.

The Junior School is housed in three Victorian houses close to the Senior School. The National Curriculum is followed and there is a carefully maintained balance between the sciences and the creative arts. Music is a particular strength of the school. All pupils have access to Pentium PCs which are based in a purpose-built ICT suite. A wide variety of sport is taught. Junior School pupils are often able to make use of Senior School facilities and all Junior School pupils swim once a week. Older girls have opportunities each year to visit an Outdoor Centre in Devon or to visit a European country.

The Senior School is situated in a beautiful eighteenth-century mansion to which additional classrooms and excellently equipped laboratories have been added. There is a flourishing Art department housed in an Arts Centre, a Music Suite, an ICT Suite, a Technology Workshop, a well-equipped Home Economics unit and a fine gymnasium with a large stage, well designed for dramatic productions. Early 1999 saw the opening of the new ICT block with fully networked Pentium PCs and Microsoft Office software. The school is in the forefront of ICT education. Girls throughout the school can learn a wide variety of musical instruments and there are Junior and Senior choirs and orchestras. Wide reading and individual work is strongly encouraged and there is generous library provision in both schools. At the end of the fifth year the girls take nine or ten subjects in the General Certificate of Education. Girls who enter the Sixth Form have the exclusive use of the Mary Crook Study Centre which provides excellent facilities and spacious accommodation for teaching and study; two common rooms are also available where the girls can relax and enjoy an informal atmosphere. The Sixth Form do not wear uniform and are encouraged to develop their independence by sharing responsibility in the day to day running of the school thus helping in the transition between school and university. The Senior School has a well established link with a school in Marburg, Germany and pupils take part in the annual Bristol/Bordeaux exchange. Other educational trips are organised and girls may take part in the Duke of Edinburgh's Award Scheme, and the Young Enterprise Scheme.

The school curriculum consists of Religious Education, English Language and Literature, Drama, French, German, Spanish, Greek, Latin, History, Geography, Mathematics, Computer Studies, Design Technology, Biology, Chemistry, Physics, Textiles, IT, Art, Home Economics, Craft, Class Singing and Musical Appreciation including aural training, and Physical Education which includes Gymnastics and Dancing, Hockey, Netball, Athletics, Tennis, Badminton, Fencing, Cricket and Swimming. Additional subjects available in the Sixth Form are Business Studies, Government & Politics, Psychology, Theatre Studies, Environmental Biology, Classical Civilisation and History of Art.

Fees per term as at September 2000. Senior School

£1,780 per term which includes stationery, books and examination fees. Junior School graduate from £1,052 to £1,250 per term. Nursery fees will be charged pro rata, dependent on the number of half days attended.

Scholarships. (*see* Entrance Scholarship section) Particulars of Scholarships including School Bursaries and Music Scholarships in the school will be given on application.

Charitable status. Redland High School is a Registered Charity, number 311734. We hope to provide a broad and balanced education which will enable each girl to reach her potential, help her to form secure relationships and provide her with the skills and qualifications for a career and for creative leisure.

The Red Maids' School

Westbury-on-Trym Bristol BS9 3AW
Tel: Headmistress (0117) 962 2641.
Governors' Office: (0117) 929 0084
Fax: (0117) 962 1687

Founded, 1634

The School was founded in accordance with the terms of the Will of John Whitson, an Alderman of the City and County of Bristol, and is the oldest girls' school in the country. It is a Day and Boarding School providing a grammar school education for girls aged 11 to 18 with a separate junior school for day girls aged 7 to 11. It was on the Direct Grant List of the Department of Education and Science before it became fully independent.

Governing Body:
Chairman: A K Bonham, BA, FCA, DL. Nine Governors nominated by the Trustees of the Bristol Municipal Charities. Three Governors may be nominated by the Bristol Education Authority. Four co-opted Governors.

Medical Officer: Dr A Tavare, MB, ChB, MRCGP, DRCOG

***Head Mistress:* Mrs I Tobias**, BA (New Hall, Cambridge)

Deputy Headmistress: Mrs W Griggs, CertEd, BA (Homerton College, Cambridge) *Mathematics*

Assistant Teaching Staff:
Mrs R G Brown, BSc (University of Hull) *Mathematics*
Mr S Browne, GRSM, LRAM, ARCM (Royal Academy of Music) *Music*
Mrs A Costen, MA (Somerville College, Oxford) *English*
Miss L E Crossley, BA (University of Wales, Trinity College) *Drama, Theatre Studies and English*
Mrs V Dixon, BSc (University of Manchester) *Mathematics*
Mrs A Farthing, CertEd, MA (Elizabeth Gaskell College of Education Manchester) *Textiles*
Mrs W B Gillman, BA (University of Bristol) *Economics*
Mrs J Goulden, BA (University of Warwick) *History*
Mrs G Hayward, CertEd (Lady Mabel College of Physical Education) *Physical Education*
Mrs E Hinkins, BEd (Cheltenham & Glos College of Higher Education) *Physical Education & Careers*
Dr E Johnstone, MA, PhD (University of St Andrews) *Mathematics*
Miss A Jones, BSc (University of Salford) *Physics*
Mrs V Macdonald, BSc (University of Liverpool) *Chemistry*
Mrs E A Nair, BA (University of Bristol) *Classics*
Mrs S C North, BA (University of Exeter) *French and Spanish*
Mrs M Palmer, BEd (Bath College of Higher Education) *Music*
Mrs M R Piolle, BA (University of Kent) *French*
Mrs P C Robinson, MA (New Hall, Cambridge) *English*
Mrs G M Ross, BSc (University of London) *Physics*
Mrs J Stokes, BEd, MA (Bristol Polytechnic) *Design Technology*
Mrs S Sutherland, CertEd (Institute of Education, University of Bristol) *Art*
Mrs K A Webster, BSc (University of Manchester) *Biology*
Mrs P West, BSc (University of Bristol) *Geography*
Mr J Williams, BSc (University of Wales, Cardiff) *Mathematics*
Mrs P Willis, CertEd (Northern Counties College) *Home Economics*
Mr R Wood, BA (University of Exeter) *Spanish*
Mrs C Woodman, GBSM (Birmingham School of Music) *Music*
Mrs P Wooff, BSc (University of Sheffield) *Biology*
Mrs A E Wookey, CertEd (Lady Mabel College of Physical Education) *Physical Education*
Mrs V Woolford, CertEd (Redland Training College) *Religious Education*

Housemistresses:
Miss J M Anderson, GRSM, LRAM, LTCL (Royal Academy of Music) *Music*
Miss J K Horwood, BA (University of Plymouth) *Careers*
Mrs Y Penn, BEd (University of Wales) *ICT, Mathematics*

Part-time Staff:
Mrs J Browne, LRAM *Flute*
Mrs T Davies, BA (University College of South Wales & Monmouth) *Religious Education*
Mrs E J Dodds, BA (University of Lancaster) *History*
Mrs J Evans, BMus, ARCM *Flute*
Mrs J Francis, GRSM, ARCM *'Cello*
Mrs M L Gitahi, BA (University of Exeter) *Russian*
Mrs H Goodman, GRSM, ARCM *Violin and Viola*
Mrs J Gupta, BA (University of Manchester) *Italian*
Mr B Hewlett *Harmonica*
Mrs S Higgins, BSc (University of Hull) *Chemistry*
Mrs S Hopkins, BA (University of London) *English*
Mrs G Jones, BSc (University of Wales, Aberystwyth) *Chemistry*
Mr J Little, BSc *Percussion*
Mrs C Loveless, BA (St Hilda's College, Oxford) *German*
Mrs S E Merelie, BA (University of Liverpool) *Geography*
Miss E Palmer, ARCM *Oboe and Bassoon*
Mrs J Parsons, BA (University of Swansea) *French and Latin*
Mrs C Parker, BMus, ALCM *Flute*
Mr T Parker, BMus, MMus *Singing*
Mrs M E Pinnock, CertEd (Seaford College) *Home Economics*
Miss J Ratcliffe, BA (Bristol Polytechnic) *Art and Ceramics*
Miss M Rhind, BSc (University of London) *Biology*
Mr P Riley, BA, ARCM *Piano*
Mrs J M Smith, BA (University of London) *Geography and History*
Mrs A Tyler, BA (University of Wales, Cardiff) *Classical Civilisation*
Mr J Whipps, ALCM, FLCM *Guitar*
Mrs T White, ARCM *Brass*

Head of Junior School:
Mrs G Rowcliffe, BEd (University of Bristol)

Assistant Teachers:
Mrs L Brown, BSc (University of Leicester)
Mrs F Clarke, Li-ès-Lettres (Université de Tours)
Mrs M Edbrooke, BEd (King Alfred's College, Winchester)
Mrs S Hiley, BSc (University of Lancashire)
Mrs J Noad, BA (University of Wales, Swansea)

Numbers. There are 380 day girls and 80 boarders in the Senior School and 80 day girls in the Junior School with ages ranging from 7–11.

Curriculum. Subjects taught include Religious Education, English, History, Geography, French, German, Italian, Latin, Russian, Spanish, Economics, Mathematics, Philosophy & Ethics, Sciences (Physics, Chemistry, Biology), Technology, Home Economics, Textiles, Art, History of Art, Music, Drama, Games, Dance, Business Studies, Information Technology, Classical Civilisation, Theatre Studies, Gymnastics and Swimming. Girls are prepared for the General Certificate of Secondary Education and GCE Advanced level of OCEAC, NEAB and AEB and for entrance to the Universities and other places of further education.

Religious Instruction. The School is undenominational. The Boarders attend a Church of England Service on Sundays, and girls, whose parents so desire, are prepared for Confirmation. Special arrangements are made for Roman Catholics and girls of other faiths.

Fees. Fee-paying Boarders £10,380. Day Girls, £5,190. The only extras are piano lessons, clarinet, flute, viola, french horn, oboe, bassoon, violin, 'cello, saxophone, singing, trumpet, guitar, £127 per term, and for Speech and Drama lessons.

Admission to Junior School. Entrance examinations are held at the end of January for girls aged 7–10 to select day girls for admission the following September.

Admission to Senior School. Entrance examinations are held at the end of January for girls aged 10½–11½ to select girls for admission the following September. There are entries at 11, 12, 13, 14 and to the Sixth Form. For full particulars about fees, Scholarships and admission procedure application should be made to the Headmistress.

Scholarships. (*see* Entrance Scholarship section) - Priority is given to children of one-parent families. Open Scholarships and School Assisted Places will be offered in 2002. Grants are made from the Perry Bequest to enable girls who could not otherwise have done so, to proceed to further training or to complete their VIth form course. There are two Music Scholarships each covering two instruments.

General Information. The School stands in its own grounds of 12 acres in a suburb of Bristol. The playing fields and school gardens are adjacent to the classrooms and boarding houses. Games played are: Netball, Volleyball, Hockey, Squash, Basket Ball and Badminton in the winter. Athletics, Rounders, Tennis and Swimming in the summer. There is a Guide Company, Young Enterprise, Young Engineers, choirs and orchestras, and there are numerous societies. The School year consists of about 36 weeks, with a half-term holiday each term when the girls go home. Lunch is available for day girls at a small charge. The school meals are carefully planned. Red Maids are taken to the theatre, lectures and to concerts in Bristol. The Duke of Edinburgh Award Scheme is encouraged. There is a separate boarding house for VIth form with single cubicles or study/bedrooms, and other houses for the Junior and Middle school boarders. On special occasions the boarders wear the traditional school uniform which consists of straw bonnets with white linen fichus and aprons over red dresses. There has been continued expansion of facilities over the years. A new Technology/Creative Design/Science extension was completed in 1990, the Sixth Form Centre was opened in 1994, a new Sports Hall was opened in 1997 and a Performing Arts Centre was opened in 1999.

Charitable status. The Red Maids' School is a Registered Charity, number 311733. It has existed since 1634 to provide an education for girls.

Roedean School

Brighton BN2 5RQ
Tel: (01273) 603181; Admissions: (01273) 667626
Fax: (01273) 680791
e-mail: admissions@roedean.co.uk
website: www.roedean.co.uk

Founded 1885.
Incorporated by Royal Charter 1938.

President: Lord Renton of Mount Harry, PC

Vice-Presidents:
Mrs S Fowler-Watt (OR)
The Rt Hon Baroness Chalker of Wallasey, PC, FSS (OR)
Dr J M Peacey, MB, BS, MRCGP (OR)

Chairman of Council: B J Hanbury, Esq

Vice-Chairman of Council: Dr J M Peach, BSc, MA, DPhil

Council:
G Able, MA, MA
R J Blackburn, Esq, MA, FCA
Ms J M Briggs, MA, PGCE, AdvDipBFM (CIPFA)
Dr E A Brumfit, MA
Mrs W Challen (OR)
M L Hepher, Esq, FIA, FCIA, ASA, FLIA, CBIM
Mrs M-G Hodgson (OR)
R H A Jenkyns, MA, MLitt
R Jonas, RICS
Mrs A T D Macaire (OR)
T P Pope, FCA
Mrs P Sinclair, JP (OR)
Mrs C C Taylor, BA (*OR*)
Dr J H Thomas, BSc, PhD
Major General E G Willmott, CB, OBE, MA, FICE

Clerk: J D Craig, Esq, 190 Strand, London WC2R 1JN

President of the ORA: Mrs P Wheatley

Staff:
Head Mistress: **‡Mrs P Metham**, BA (Bristol)

Deputy Head and Director of Studies: ‡Mr J M Farmer, BSc (London)

Bursar: Mr J E Hynam, MPhil, BEd, ACP, MIMgt

Heads of Department:

MATHEMATICS:
*Mr P W Tarbet, BSc (Durham), FRAS

ENGLISH:
*‡Mrs S A Packer, BA (Oxon), MA (Carleton)

NATURAL SCIENCES:
Head of Science: *‡Dr P Carpenter, BSc, PhD (Aberystwyth)
Biology: *Miss A C Fraser, BSc (London)
Chemistry: *‡Mr A S England, MA (Cantab)
Physics: *Dr D Fisher, BSc, PhD (London)

MODERN LANGUAGES:
Head of Modern Languages: *‡Mrs M Landivar, BA (London), MA (Sussex)

HUMANITIES:
*‡Mr R Castleden, MA, MSc (Oxon), FGS, FRGS

History:
Mr J M Davis, BA (Lancaster), MA, MSc (London), ARHistS

Geography:
*‡Mr R Castleden, MA, MSc (Oxon), FGS, FRGS

Religious Education:
*‡Mrs M E Sitwell, BEd (Sussex) (*Lay Chaplain*)

Classics:
*Mrs M Davis, BA (London)

ART, DESIGN AND TECHNOLOGY:
*‡Miss C Harfleet, NDD, ATD (London), AdvDipTech

BUSINESS EDUCATION:
Head of Business Studies: Miss J Hayward-Voss, BA (Brighton)
Head of ICT & Computing: Mrs R Saunders, BSC
Economics: Mr P Ellis, BSc

PERFORMING ARTS:

Dance:
Miss S Stidston, LISTD, AISTD, RAD

Music:
*Mr P Brough, MA (Oxon)

Speech & Drama:
*‡Mrs K P Armes, BEd, CSSD, MA(Ed) (Southampton)

PHYSICAL EDUCATION:
*‡Mrs A F Romanov, BA (OU)

Careers Administrator: ‡Miss S Epps, BEd (Sussex), DipPE (Bedford), Dip School Lib

‡ denotes Training Diploma

Introduction Roedean is primarily a boarding school, with 400 boarders aged 11–18. Day places are also offered throughout the school. Founded in 1885, the school moved to its present site on the Sussex Downs, overlooking the sea, in 1898. The school buildings are set on a 40 acre site dedicated to sports and leisure use and surrounded by a further 75 acres of farmland.

Roedean has excellent road and rail links to London and is within easy reach of Gatwick and Heathrow Airports.

Philosophy. Roedean provides a 'whole life' education. The basic philosophy of the school is to offer every girl the opportunity to develop her full potential in a setting that provides for intellectual, physical, social, personal and moral growth. The school is particularly strong academically and has always had a reputation for high standards which is borne out year after year by excellent examination results.

The boarding approach is ideally suited to carry out the school's 'whole life' philosophy by providing a rich and balanced programme of learning and activities in a context which is structured yet informal. Day girls benefit from this ethos and are well integrated into the House system. The single sex environment has particular advantages for girls; it prevents stereotyping, raises expectations and develops self confidence by offering many opportunities for leadership and responsibility.

Curriculum. Girls are given a structured grounding in basic skills and offered a very broad programme of knowledge and experience. Subject specialists work together in a coordinated approach to achieve maximum reinforcement and continuity across 23 subjects. The benefits of traditional subjects, including Latin, are balanced by Computer Studies, Design and Technology and Information Technology.

Each girl's GCSE programme is individually tailored to provide a broad, balanced education and to ensure that requirements for Higher Education are met.

Our strong VIth Form offers an extensive range and combination of A and AS Levels covering 27 subjects.

We have developed a strong link with Sussex University enabling our most able Sixth Formers to study undergraduate modules alongside their AS and A level courses.

Extra Curricular Activities and Physical Education. The range of music, art and design, speech, drama and dance opportunities within the curriculum are further supported by optional private tuition and club activities. The school is particularly strong in music (choirs and orchestras), drama, dance and debating.

The school has an excellent record in the Duke of Edinburgh Award Scheme and Young Enterprise Business Scheme which offer girls opportunities to develop a spirit of discovery and independence and encourage links with the wider community.

Lacrosse, netball, hockey, tennis, swimming, athletics, cricket and rounders are the principal sports with badminton, basketball, volleyball, squash, trampoline, gymnastics, fencing and karate also available. Inter-school fixtures are part of all the major sport programmes and girls are encouraged to enter local, county and national tournaments.

Boarding. The House system is designed to provide the supportive and caring environment necessary for each girl to develop both as an individual and a member of the community.

Our four Main School Houses (for girls 11+ to 16+), our two 6th Houses - Keswick and Lawrence - each have a resident Housemistress through whom there is close liaison between parents and school. Facilities range from bedrooms for 3 or 4 girls to individual study bedrooms for UV and VIth Form girls.

Continuity of individual guidance and care is ensured by the school's tutorial system. Tutors monitor each girl's academic progress and involvement in extra curricular activities and liaise with House Staff on a regular basis to maintain a balanced, realistic timetable which meets the individual's needs and abilities.

Health. The School Health Centre is run by a Registered General Nurse who is assisted by a team of similarly qualified nurses. Two doctors (one male and one female) visit the School and hold clinics regularly each week. They are "on call" in case of an emergency.

Religion. The School welcomes students of all religious denominations. Arrangements are made for Anglicans to be prepared for Confirmation, for Roman Catholics to attend Sunday Mass locally and for Jewish girls to receive instruction. The demands of the School programme do not permit girls below the Sixth Form to fast.

Facilities. Over 140 internet computers offering schoolwide integrated learning, Design and Technology Centre, Humanities Centre for History, Geography and Economics, Performing Arts complex, Main Library and Resources Centre. Multi-purpose Sports Hall, 13 hard tennis courts, heated indoor swimming pool, squash courts, ample playing fields.

New facilities: science block with 6 laboratories for Chemistry and Biology (Physics laboratories in main building); Multimedia Languages Centre; Business Education Suite; indoor cricket facilities in Sports Hall.

School Year and Leave Out. There are three terms, beginning in September, January and April. The summer holidays last eight weeks and the other two up to four weeks each. Girls go home for half term and there are two weekend exeats on specified dates. The school provides a full boarding programme, but there is considerable flexibility to accommodate the individual needs of families and girls may be taken out on most weekends.

Admission. Entry at 11+, 12+ and 13+ is through the Common Entrance Examination or Roedean Entrance Examination. A number of suitably qualified girls are admitted each year to the VIth Form.

Scholarships and Bursaries. (*see* Entrance Scholarship section) Scholarships are awarded each year after a competitive examination held in January for candidates under 14 on 1 September in year of entry and in November for VIth Form entrance.

Entrance Scholarships will normally be worth up to one half of the fees. Music Scholarships and two Major

Exhibitions are also offered. In exceptional circumstances further finance by way of a bursary, may also be available.

A number of special bursaries are available for day pupils.

Fees. Boarders £5,575 per term. Day Girls £3,420 per term. For girls entering the VIth form from other schools, there is an additional charge of £80 a term. Parents who wish to pay a single composition fee should apply to the Bursar.

Extra fees are charged for individual tuition in musical instruments, speech training, ballet and some athletic activities.

For further details please contact the Admissions Officer.

Charitable status. Roedean School is a Registered Charity, number 307063. It exists to provide quality education for girls.

The Royal High School Bath (G.D.S.T.)

Lansdown Road Bath BA1 5SZ
Tel: (01225) 313877
Fax: (01225) 465446
e-mail: royalhigh@bath.gdst.net
website: http://www.gdst.net/royalhighbath

The Royal High School, Bath was created in September 1998 through a carefully planned merger between two long-established and highly successful neighbouring girls' schools on Lansdown Hill – Bath High School and the Royal School. The Junior department, numbering approximately 300 girls from Nursery (3 years) to Year 6 (11 years) is accommodated on the Hope House site, which provides beautiful enclosed gardens, elegant Georgian buildings and outstanding facilities for Science, Information and Design Technology, Art, Music and Physical Education. The Senior department accommodates approximately 600 girls aged from 11 to 18 on an extensive campus, about half a mile further up Lansdown Hill. Its facilities include a new Sports Hall, a new suite of Science Laboratories and newly developed Art, Music, Library and Technology facilities. The School is one of the 25 schools of The Girls' Day School Trust and is unique in offering high quality boarding facilities for about 100 girls. For general information about the Trust and the composition of its Council, see p 532.

Governors:

Chairman: General Sir Robert Pascoe, KCB, MBE

Mrs S Chivers
Dr M Ede, MA, DPhil
Major General G Ewer, CBE
Mr A Giles, DSE, CE
Mr M King
Lt Col J Mills, MBE, MIPR
Professor J P McGeehan, PhD, MIEE, MIERE, CEng, FRSA
District Judge S Raskin
Mrs J Robb
Mrs A Rowley, JP
Miss J Sadler
Brigadier M Strudwick, CBE
Dr D M Sweetenham
Mr J J Thring
Baroness Warnock, DBE, MA, BPhil, DipEd
Councillor Mrs M Wheadon, MA
Captain J Worlidge, LVO, RN

Headmaster: **Mr James Graham-Brown**, BA (Hons), MPhil *English*

Deputy Heads:
Mrs Christine Edmundson, BMus (Hons) (London), LRAM, ARCM *Music*
Mrs Isabel Tobias, BA (Hons) (Cambridge) *English*

Senior School Staff:
Mrs P Anderson, BSc (Hons) (Manchester) *Home Economics*
Mrs A Bernard, LTCL (Trinity College), Cert of Arts (Bristol) *Music*
Ms S Bicheno, MA(Ed) (Open), DipMaths (Sussex), CertEd (Chelsea College of PE)
Mrs C Bown, BA (Hons) (Exeter) *Spanish and French*
Mr C Bray, BA (Hons) (Sheffield), BPhil(Ed) (Warwick) *Religious Studies*
Mrs D Burman, LGSM (London) *Drama and Theatre Studies*
Dr J Chamberlain, BSc (Hons) (Bristol), PhD (Bath) *Microbiology*
Mr M Cockerham, MA (Hons) (Cambridge), ARCO, ARCM, LRAM *Music*
Mrs R Cole, BEd (Hons) (Bedford) *Physical Education and Geography*
Mrs A Corrigan, MA (Hons) (Oxford) *Mathematics, Economics and Politics*
Mrs D Cowell, BSc (Hons) (London) *Animal Science*
Mrs M Davis, MA, Maitrise de Lettres (Universite de Montpelier) *French*
Mrs D Dellar, BEd (Hons) (Exeter) *Mathematics*
Mrs C Doyle, BA (Hons) (Aberystwyth) *English*
Mrs E Ellison, BSc (Hons) (Bristol) *Pharmacology*
Mrs J Everson, BSc (Hons) (Aberystwyth) *Geography*
Miss E Fisher, BA (Hons) (Coventry) *Fine Art*
Mr B Follansbee, BA(Hons) (New Hampshire), MA (London) *History/Archaeology*
Mrs A Ford, BEd (Hons) (Bath) *Textiles*
Mrs S Gilmour, BSc (Natal) *Mathematics and Geography*
Mrs R Glover, BA (Hons) (Oxford) *Geography*
Dr M Golder, BA (Hons), PhD (Manchester) *Biblical Studies*
Mr D Goodman, BA (Hons) (East Anglia) *Economics and Sociology*
Mrs S Gosling, BSc (Hons) (London) *Geography*
Mrs S Grist, CertEd (London) *Home Economics*
Dr S Gurr, BSc (Hons), PhD (Salford) *Chemistry*
Mrs H J Harker, BSc (Hons) *Architecture*
Mr G Harris, BSc (Hons) (Durham) *Physics*
Mrs W Hartley, BA (Hons) (Newcastle) *Classics*
Mrs K Harvie, BSc (Hons) (Glasgow) *Mathematics*
Mrs J Hicks, ATD (Bath Academy) *Art*
Mrs C Hobbs, BSc (Hons) (Exeter), MEd (Bath) *Chemistry and Sociology*
Dr S Howarth, BSc (Hons) (Leeds), PhD, GCScE (London) *Biology*
Mrs C Hynes-Higman, BA (Hons) (London), MEd (Bath) *French and German*
Mrs R Johnson, BA (Hons) (Surrey) *Mathematics*
Miss S Kerr, BEng (Hons) (Brunel) *Manufacturing & Engineering Systems*
Mrs R Key-Pugh, MA (Hons) (Oxford) *Physics*
Miss T Knevett, BA (Hons) (East Anglia) *English and Drama*
Mrs L Lethby, BSc (Hons) (Leeds) *Chemistry*
Mr D Mather, BA (Hons) (Leeds) *Spanish and French*
Mr A Melton, BEd ((Bristol), BTech (Hons) (Brunel) *Design and Technology*
Mrs A Ockwell, BA (Hons) (Belfast), MSc (Oxford) *History*
Mrs J Palmer, BSc (Hons) (Leicester), MEd, AFIMA *Mathematics*
Miss E Pawlowski, MA (Bremen) *English*

Mr G Preedy, DipATD (Kent Instit of Art & Design) *Art*
Miss E Purves, BA (Hons) (Hull) *German*
Mrs S Reeves, BA (Hons) (Durham) *Latin/Greek*
Mrs M Rhys, BSc (Hons) (Exeter) *Biology*
Ms C Rich, BEd (Hons) (Leeds) *Physical Education*
Mrs F Ryan, BA (Cork, Ireland), *Modern Languages*
Mrs A Sammes, BSc (Hons) (London) *Biology*
Mrs G Sansbury, BA (Bristol), LCST *Individual Needs*
Miss R Sara, BSc (London), MSc (Reading), AKC *Chemistry*
Miss S Scriven, BSc (Hons) (York) *Mathematics*
Mrs J Side, BA (Hons) (Manchester) *Spanish and French*
Mrs A Smerdon, BA (Hons) (Oxford) *English*
Mrs S Toogood, CertEd (London) *Physical Education*
Miss S Turner, BA (Hons) (Birmingham) *History and Sport*
Mrs C Venables, BA (Hons) (West London College of Art & Design) *Sculpture and Fine Art*
Mrs J Vickerman, BA (Hons) (Southampton) *Modern European Studies*
Mrs R Wagstaff, BA (Hons), MA (Exeter) *French and Spanish*
Mrs A White, Licenciada-en-Letras (Universidad de Concepcion, Chile) *Spanish*
Mrs J Woodward, BA (Hons) (Oxford) *History*

Senior Librarian: Mrs C Kneebone

Junior School:
Head: Miss L Bevan, BA (Hons) (Aberystwyth) *English*

Staff:
Miss N Ackland, BEd (Hons) (Winchester) *Geography*
Mrs N Bishton, ARMCM (Royal Manchester College of Music), CertEd (Bath)
Mrs S Boyce, BA (Hons) (Aberystwyth) *English and Art*
Mrs M Bright, TCert, BA (Open University) *Educational Studies*
Mrs K Cavill, BA (Hons) (London) *Geography*
Miss E Cooper, CertEd (Bristol) *Geography*
Mrs A Hale, DRSAM, DipMusEd (Royal Scottish Academy of Music and Drama) *Singing and Piano*
Mrs J Hallett, Teaching Cert (Derby) *Physical Education and Geography*
Mrs S Hirst, Teaching Cert (Bangor) *English*
Miss R Howe, BEd (Hons) (Bath) *Science*
Mrs L Hunt, Teaching Cert (Oxford) *Biology*
Miss S Lloyd, BEd (Hons) (Edgehill) *History/Education*
Mrs H Miller, BA Primary Ed (Bristol) *History*
Mrs S Phillips, BEd (Bath) *Humanities*
Mrs T Saunders, CertEd (Newcastle)
Mrs B Sheppard, Teaching Certificate (Bath)
Mrs P Willars, Teaching Certificate (London)

Junior School Classroom Assistants:
Mrs M Crozier
Mrs S Dark
Mrs D Davies
Mrs R Goulding
Mrs M Murray

Junior Department Secretary: Mrs J Virley

Head of Boarding: Ms S Bicheno

Boarding Staff:
Years 5-10
Senior Housemistress: Mrs R Pereira
Resident Housemistress: Miss S Kerr
Assistant Housemistress: Miss J Stephens
Years 11 and Sixth Form
Senior Housemistress: Mrs W Goodman
Resident Housemistress: Mrs S Graham
Resident Housemistress: Mrs R Johnson

Resident Boarding Staff:
Mrs E Joy
Mrs N Stocker

Resident Boarding Assistants:
Miss T Whiteford (*UK*)
Miss E Watts (*NZ*)

Visiting Staff:
Mr B Barnes, BMus (Hons) (Glasgow), LGSM, LTCL (*Recorder*)
Miss H Barnett, GRSM, LRAM (Royal Academy of Music) *Music*
Mr S Buck, LTCL (*Flute, Saxophone, Percussion*)
Mr V Burchell (*Piano*)
Mrs W Carter, LRAM, LGSM (*Speech & Drama*)
Mr P Clare (*Judo*)
Mrs F Clements, LTCL (*Cello*)
Mrs J Crompton, ARCM, GRSM (London) (*Piano, Violin*)
Mrs J Finch, ALCM, LTCL (*Oboe*)
Mr P Gittings (*Piano*)
Mr A Graham, LTA (*Physical Education*)
Mr D Green (*Keyboard*)
Mrs A Hamilton (*Violin*)
Mr M Harvey (*Percussion*)
Mrs M Henneveld (*Guitar*)
Mrs A Higgs (*Brass*)
Mr D Kniveton, BA (Hons) (Bath), LTCL (*Flute*)
Mr W Lynn, BA (Hons) (Bath) (*Brass*)
Mrs P Minns, TCert (Coventry) (*Drama & Dance*)
Miss S Norris (*Gymnastics Coach*)
Mrs M Osborne, BA (Hons) (London) (*Flute, Recorder*)
Mr D Pegler, BA (Hons), MusEd, ALCM (*Saxophone, Clarinet*)
Mrs J Phillips (*Singing*)
Mr G Pike, BA (Hons) (London) Music, LTCL (*Clarinet*)
Mr A Reining, LRAM, CertEd (*Piano*)
Mr P Sweet (*Guitar*)
Mrs G Thursfield, LRAM (*Piano, Clarinet*)
Mrs J Trevithick (*Speech & Drama*)
Mr A Webb, LTCL (*Trumpet, Recorder*)
Mrs D Webb (*Ballet, Modern Dance*)
Mrs P Wendzina, CertEd (Bristol) (*Piano*)
Mrs F Zagni, BA (Southampton), MA, LTCL (*Cello*)

Medical Centre:

Dr C Stagg, MRCGP, DRCOG *Visiting Medical Officer*
Dr L Leach, MBBS, DRCOG, MRCGP *School Doctor*
Sister F Close, SRN (*Relief Sister*)
Sister J Greene, SRN (*Sister*)

Administration:

School Administrator: Mr R Hulley
Headmaster's Secretary: Mrs J Morris
Information Systems Manager: Mr C O'Mahony, BA (Hons) (Australia Catholic University) (*Information Technology*)

Curriculum. Education of a high academic standard is achieved through the constructive partnership between highly qualified staff and a commitment to hard work and sound learning by the girls. A wide choice of subjects is offered at both GCSE and 'A' Level. Creativity, technological skills and independent thought are encouraged. The majority of girls move on to university courses ranging from Medicine to Music and Economics to English, whilst some others choose vocational careers in Physiotherapy, Nursing or Banking. Each year a number of candidates gain entry to Oxford or Cambridge.

Extra-curricular Activities. A wide-ranging programme of extra-curricular activities is a distinctive feature of the school. Lunch-time and after school clubs available to all pupils, include aerobics, pottery, gymnastics, computing and photography. Opportunities exist for participation in a range of choirs, orchestras, music groups, sports teams and the Duke of Edinburgh Award Scheme. There is also an exciting programme of Saturday morning activities, available to all girls, some of which offer additional qualifications and skills in areas such as Information Technology, First Aid, Speech and Drama and Dance. Numerous cultural and historical visits, including exchanges and visits abroad, figure regularly in the school's calendar. Concerts and plays feature frequently in the school's life.

Boarding. All boarders from 8-16 years old are housed within the main school building, sharing comfortable, well equipped rooms with girls of their own age. Sixth Form boarders are accommodated in a modern self-contained centre with single or double bedrooms with their own study facilities. A 10% discount is offered for boarders whose parents are serving members of HM Forces. The school is the only one in the GDST to offer a boarding experience and special transfer arrangements are available for any girls who have a boarding requirement.

Fees. From September 2000: Senior School Day from £1,540 per term; Senior School Boarding £3,300 per term; Junior Department £1,120 per term; Junior School Boarding £3,300 per term. The fees cover the regular curriculum, school books, stationery and other materials, but not optional extra subjects. For boarders, fees are all inclusive except for optional activities and extra subjects.

Bursaries. Following the ending of the Government Assisted Places Scheme, the GDST has made available to the school a substantial number of scholarships and bursaries. The bursaries are means tested and are intended to ensure that the school remains accessible to bright girls who would profit from our education but who would be unable to enter the school without financial assistance.

Charitable status. The Royal High School is one of the 25 schools of the Girls' Day School Trust which is a Registered Charity, number 1026057. The aim of the Trust is to provide a fine academic education at a comparatively modest cost.

The Royal Masonic School for Girls

Rickmansworth Park Rickmansworth Herts WD3 4HF
Tel: (01923) 773168
Fax: (01923) 896729
website: url:www.royalmasonic.herts.sch.uk

Governing Body: Royal Masonic School Co. Ltd

Chairman of Governors: Mr K S Carmichael, CBE, FCA, FTII

Trustees and Governors:
Colonel R K Hind
Dr G J Piller
Sir Gerard Vaughan

Governors:
The Rt Hon The Earl Cadogan
The Countess of Eglinton & Winton
Miss W J Forrester
Rev P Hemingway
Mr M B Jones
Mr R Morrow

***Headmistress:* Mrs I M Andrews**, MA (Oxon), FRSA

Deputy Headmistress: Miss L A H Reading, BSc (London)

Deputy Headmistress: Miss B E Newell, BA (Open), CertEd

Head of Preparatory Dept: Miss L E Beckett, BEd (Bucks)

Head of Sixth Form: Mrs J Stearn, BA Hons (Herts)

Chaplain: The Reverend M Horton, LLB, BTheol (Cuddesdon)

Business Manager: Lt Commander R S Sidebotham, BSc

Bursar: Mr I J Mackenzie, CEng, MIEE, MIMgt

Personal Assistant to the Headmistress: Mrs M Beresford

Admissions Secretary: Mrs G Braiden

Housemistresses:
Atholl/Sussex House: Mrs J Scholes
Connaught House: Miss M Drury
Cumberland: Miss A McDonald
Moira House: Mrs J Faherty
Ruspini House: Miss D Norman
Zetland House: Miss K Lord
Alexandra House: Mrs M Abel
Cadogan House: Miss P J Watson

Teaching Staff:
Mrs L C Adamson, BA (West Sussex Institute) *English*
Mrs A Barnes, MA (Dunelm), BA (Exeter) *History*
Mrs S Barton, BSc (Wales) *Mathematics*
Miss L E Beckett, BEd (Bucks) *Head of Prep Dept*
Mr E Bigden, BA (East Anglia) *Head of English*
Mrs N Bigden, MSc (London) *Mathematics*
Mrs N Bloor, Maîtrise ès Lettres (Bordeaux, France) *French and Spanish*
Mrs S Booth, BA (Bristol) *Politics and History*
Miss K S Brierley, BSc (Durham) *Mathematics, Psychology*
Mrs A Brown, BA (Reading) *Deputy Head of Prep Dept*
Miss A M Bryant, CertEd, DipCGE *Careers*
Mr D Buddie, BSc (Dundee) *IT Coordinator*
Miss J Bush, BEd (Kingston) *Prep Dept*
Miss B A Champion, BA (London), PGCE *History & Economics*
Mr A Colville, BA (Nottingham) *Modern Languages*
Mrs A Considine, BA (London) *Classical Studies*
Mrs E A Couldridge, MA (London) *Geography (Head of Department)*
Miss L P Cowburn, BA (Open) *English, Library*
Miss C E Cranmer, BA (Durham) *English*
Mrs L Daniel, BSc (Bristol) *Biology*
Miss M Dines, BA (Bucks) *Design Technology*
Miss M Drury, Certificate in Art & Science of M'ment PE
Mrs J Duggan, MA (Oxon) *Chemistry*
Mrs J Faherty, CertEd *PE and Geography*
Miss C Frossard, Licence (Strasbourg) *Modern Languages*
Mrs E Fulker, DipTEFL, DipSpLD *Special Needs*
Mrs S J Gandy, Dip Art & Design *Art (Head of Department)*
Mrs E A Griffin, BA (York) *Prep Department Special Needs*
Mr M Handford, CertEd *Design Technology*
Mrs D Headen, BEd (Newcastle) *Home Economics*
Dr B C Hellyer, BA (London), MSc, PhD, FRAS *(Head of Science)* Physics
Mrs A Hitchcock, BA (Wales) *Prep Department*
Revd M J Horton, LLB, BTheol (Cuddesdon) *Religious Studies*
Miss J Hurt, BA (Brunel) *Physical Education*
Mrs N Isherwood, CertEd *Drama*
Mrs N Jones, LIQPS, Further Education Teachers' Cert *Secretarial Studies (Head of Department)*
Mrs M Kenny, CertEd *Prep Dept*
Mrs P Kenyon, BA (Keele) *Biology and Geology*
Ms J Lee, MA (Trinity), LRAM, CertRAM *Music*
Mr A Leech, BA (West of England) *Art*
Miss S M Lloyd, BA (Surrey) *Home Economics*
Miss A McDonald, ARCM, ABSM *Music*
Miss J Matthews, BSc (Kent) *Physics*
Mrs S Mealing, CertEd *Prep Dept*
Mrs V Merrett, JEB Teachers' Diploma *Secretarial Studies*

Mrs J D Newby, CertEd *Physical Education*
Miss B E Newell, BA (Open), CertEd *Psychology*
Miss D Norman, Teaching Diploma (Australia) *Prep Dept*
Miss S Palmer, BA (Somerset) *Textiles*
Mrs K Patel, BSc (London) *Mathematics*
Mrs B M Prescott, CertEd *Head of Physical Education*
Mrs A Ralph, BSc (Lancaster) *ICT*
Mrs J E Raphael, BA (Birmingham) *English*
Mrs A Ratcliffe, BA (Dunelm) *History* (*Head of Department*)
Miss L A H Reading, BSc (London) *Science*
Mrs M A Rogers, CertEd *Prep Dept*
Mrs E J Scholes, CertEd *PSE & PE*
Mrs A Short, BSc (Bristol) *Mathematics* (*Head of Department*)
Mrs C A Simpson, BSc (Reading) *Geography*
Mr P Slade, BA (Oxon) *Chemistry*
Mrs D Smith, BA (Open), BSc (London) *Prep Dept*
Mr L J Smith, MA (Kingston), BA (Open), LTCL, FTCL, CertEd *Director of Music*
Miss R J Smith, BSc (Nottingham) *Biology*
Miss H S Stanley, BEd *PE Department*
Mrs J P Stearn, BA Hons (Herts) *English*
Mr R E Stengel, BA, (Manchester), KDS (Munich), MCollP, PGCE *German*
Miss B A Stevens, BA (Aberystwyth) *Geography*
Mrs M Tamura, Licence ès Lettres (Rennes Univ, France) *Head of French*
Miss P J Watson, BTech (Bradford)
Mrs P Wootton, CertEd *Prep Dept*
Mrs K Young, BSc (Notts) *Mathematics*
Mr N M Young, MA (Oxon) *Classics*
Miss E A Zeronian, BA(Ed) (Durham) *Prep Dept*

Visiting Music Teachers:
Mr D André *Brass*
Mrs J Bush, LRAM *Singing*
Mrs D Cooke, ARCM *Piano*
Mr P Hewitt, GTCL, FTCL *Piano*
Ms H Lang, FTCL, LTCL *Flute*
Mr C Lawrance *Guitar*
Miss R Le Good, LRAM *Violin*
Ms J Paul, GRSM, LRSM, ARCM, ARCO
Mr N Penfold, MA, BMus *Woodwind*
Miss A Tunnicliffe *Drum Kit*
Mr T Turton, LWCMD *'Cello*
Mr E Ware, DipRMA, LRAM *Flute, Piano*
Mr D Wright *Woodwind*

Visiting Drama Teacher:
Mrs M Coulson, AGSM, Teachers' Dip
Mrs Y S Sampson, BA (Middx)

Medical Staff:
Dr A C K Savani, LRCP, MRCS *School Doctor*
Sister S M Mackenzie, RGN *Nursing Sister*
Sister M Burrows, RGN *Nursing Sister*
Sister C Wilcock, RGN *Nursing Sister*
Mrs J Jury *Nursing Assistant*

There are 750 pupils in school, of whom 200 are in the Preparatory Department and 130 in the 6th Form. 250 of the current school population are boarders and integration of day girls and boarders is achieved through the allocation of all girls to one of the main School Houses. The proportion of boarders to day pupils increases as girls come up through the School.

Premises and Facilities. Founded in 1788, the School came to Rickmansworth in 1934. It stands in 300 acres of parkland on an attractive site overlooking the valley of the River Chess. The buildings are spacious and well-appointed. They include an excellent 6th Form Centre, a well-equipped modern Science building, a Chapel and Library of exceptional beauty.

A new Sports Hall is finished and equipped to the highest international standards. There is a heated indoor swimming pool, 12 tennis courts, 4 squash courts and superb playing fields.

Location. Central London is 15 miles to the south and Amersham is just north of the town. The M25 is 1 mile from the school and links it to London (Heathrow) – 30 minutes, London (Gatwick) – 50 minutes and Luton Airport – 30 minutes. London Underground services (Metropolitan Line) and British Rail from Marylebone enable Central London to be reached by train in 30 minutes.

General Curriculum and Aims. The first three years of Senior School provide a broad general education which fulfils the requirements of the National Curriculum and reaches beyond it. As well as the traditional academic subjects of English, Mathematics, Science, History, Geography and Religious Studies, girls learn Design & Technology and Information Technology. Language Studies begin with French and Latin. In Year 9 German and Spanish are available for the more able linguists. Art & Textiles, Home Economics, Keyboarding, Music, Physical Education and Personal and Social Education are included in every girl's timetable.

GCSE options are chosen from among all the subjects taught in Years 7 to 9 and new possibilities, such as Child Care and Drama are introduced at this stage. Most pupils take nine GCSE subjects and girls are guided in their choices by form and subject teachers, in full consultation with parents.

The Sixth Form. The School offers a wide range of A and A/S Level subjects in flexible combinations. Politics, Economics, Geology and Psychology are all new additions to the curriculum at this stage. There are also practical and vocational courses leading to GNVQ qualifications. These enable those girls with less academic interests to enjoy the advantages of a sixth form education. Most sixth formers go on to higher education.

Religion. In the School Chapel services are held according to the rites of the Church of England. Special arrangements are made for girls of other faiths. At Assembly each day a short act of worship is included.

Health. The School Doctor attends the Medical Centre regularly. There are three Nursing Sisters and a Medical Assistant.

Admission. Applications should be made to the Admissions Secretary. The School sets its own entrance examinations at all levels. New boarding and day pupils are accepted into the Sixth Form where there is a wide range of opportunities for girls of all abilities.

Scholarships. (*see* Entrance Scholarship section) A number of scholarships are available at 7+, 11+ and 16+, and some bursaries. The former are for open competition; the latter are restricted to certain categories of pupils in need. There are a number of Foundation Scholarships available at 11+ for the daughters of freemasons. Based on academic ability, they are for boarding places only.

Fees per annum at January 2001. Seniors – Boarders £11,094; Weekly Boarders £11,019; Day Pupils £6,750. Juniors – Boarders (Years 3 and 4) £6,588; (Years 5 and 6) £6,828; Weekly Boarders (Years 3 and 4) £6,513; (Years 5 and 6) £6,753. Day Pupils (Years 3 and 4) £4,134; (Years 5 and 6) £4,254. Pre-Prep (Years Reception to 2) £3,474 (day only). Free places available for daughters of freemasons in need of assistance.

Charitable status. The Royal Masonic School Limited is a Registered Charity, number 276784. Its aims are the advancement of education.

Royal School Haslemere

Farnham Lane Haslemere Surrey GU27 1HQ
Tel: 01428 605805
Fax: 01428 607451
e-mail: admissions@royal.surrey.sch.uk
website: www.royal.surrey.sch.uk

Headmistress: **Mrs Lynne Taylor-Gooby,** BEd, MA

Deputy Head: Mrs Karen Owen, BEd (Hons)
Director of Studies: Mrs Ros Davies, BSc

Admissions Registrar: Mrs Helen Schuyleman (*Tel:* 01428 605805, Ext 252)

Foundation. The Royal School, Haslemere, was formed in 1995 as a result of a merger between The Royal Naval School for Girls, Haslemere and The Grove School, Hindhead. It is an independent school for girls aged between 4–18 who attend as day pupils or as weekly or full boarders. It has its own nursery taking children from age 3.

Situation. The Royal School is situated in an area of outstanding natural beauty on the outskirts of the country town of Haslemere, less than an hour by road and rail from central London, Gatwick and Heathrow. It is set in a 30 acre site and has excellent facilities housed in a blend of Edwardian and modern buildings.

Its Junior School at Hindhead is also situated in a wooded 30 acre site with a brand new teaching block.

Numbers. Total numbers of pupils are 334 of which 36 are in the 6th form.

Admission. Entrance to the Junior School is by day visit and individual assessment. Entrance to the Senior Department of The Royal School is by the School's own entrance examination at 11+ or at 13+. There are a number of academic scholarships at 11+ together with those in Dance, Drama, Sport, etc. There are also a number of major academic scholarships available at 6th form level.

Curriculum. The full range of subjects is studied both at GCSE and A level. The girls are prepared for a maximum of 10 GCSE subjects. 99% of our sixth formers go on to study degree courses at university.

Games. Netball and lacrosse are played in the Autumn and Spring terms. While tennis, athletics and swimming are the activities of the Summer term.

Extra Curricular Activities. The School provides a wide range of extra curricular activities of both sporting and cultural varieties. Girls participate in the Duke of Edinburgh Scheme. A full programme of events is organised for the boarders each weekend.

Transport. The School has a large fleet of minibuses with daily runs that cover the surrounding area fully. Transport for boarders is available to and from central London and its airports.

Fees. Junior School £1,698–£2,121 per term. Senior School £2,736–£2,895 per term. Boarding £1,647 per term.

Charitable status. The Royal School is a Registered Charity, number 312060. It aims to provide an outstanding education for girls.

* Head of Department § Part Time or Visiting
† Housemaster/Housemistress ¶ Old Pupil
‡ See below list of staff for meaning

Rye St Antony School

Pullen's Lane Oxford OX3 0BY
Tel: (01865) 762802
Fax: (01865) 763611
e-mail: ryestantony@btconnect.com
website: www.ryestantony.co.uk

Rye St Antony is an independent Catholic Boarding and Day School, founded in 1930.
Motto: *Vocatus Obedivi*

Governing Body:

Chairman: Mrs J Ward, BEd
Vice-Chairmen:
Mr C G Briscoe, MA, ARIBA
Mr D G Heynes, FCA

Mr S Calnan
Dr T M M Czepiel
Mr S A Fox
Mrs E Kenworthy-Browne, BA
Mr P Mackenzie-Smith
Mr T J Morton
Mrs J Townsend, MA, MSc
Dr M Vohrah, FRCA

Adviser to the Governors: Dom H Wansbrough, OSB, MA, STL, ISS

Clerk to the Governors: Mr A C Sinclair

***Headmistress:* Miss A M Jones**, BA (York), PGCE (Oxon)

Deputy Headmistress: Miss K Roberts, BEd (Liverpool) *Religious Education, Sixth Form General Studies*
Director of Studies: Dr C Rosser, BSc, PhD (Leeds), MSc (Oxon) *Information and Communications Technology*

Senior Department Staff:

Ms A Bell, BA (Cantab), MPhil (Jussieu, Paris and Trinity College, Dublin), PGCE (Cantab) *French*
Mrs M Birtill, MA (Glasgow), DipEd (Edinburgh) *Spanish, Information and Communications Technology*
Mrs S Byrne, BEd (Liverpool), BA (Open) *Drama*
Mrs K Campbell, Staatsexamen (Bonn) *German*
Mrs A Chance *Learning Support*
Mrs P Clark, BSc (Reading) *Mathematics*
Mrs M Conway, MA (Ulster), MEd (Queen's, Belfast), CertEd (London) *History*
Mrs M Evans, BSc, DipEd (Oxon) *Mathematics*
Mrs P Evans, BA, MA (Open), CertEd (Leeds) *Religious Studies*
Mrs M Ewart, BA, DipEd (Queen's, Belfast) *English*
Mrs E Fever, BSc, CertEd (Southampton) *Mathematics*
Miss D Furphy, BA (Manchester), MA (Queen's, Belfast), PGCE (Ulster) *History*
Mrs A Garside, BA (Kent), PGCE (Bath), CETHIC (Oxford Brookes) *Geography*
Mrs J Gooch, BA (Dublin), PGCE (Oxon) *Learning Support*
Mrs H Good (Japan) *Japanese*
Mr N Hamper, BA (Slade), MA (Royal College of Art) *Art and Design*
Mrs K Harman, BSc (Cardiff), RSADipTEFLA (Bournemouth) *English as an Additional Language*
Mrs G Harrison, BA (Manchester) *English*
Dr C Heath, BSc, PhD (Warwick), PGCE (Portsmouth) *Chemistry*
Revd T Herbst, BA (Santa Barbara, California), MA (Berkeley, California), MDiv (Berkeley) *Religious Studies*
Miss B Hines, BA (London), PGCE (Oxon), LGSM *Drama*

Mr R Hypher, BSc (McMaster, Canada), BEd (Queen's, Canada) *Physics*
Mrs C Lau, BA (Hong Kong), MA (Oxford Brookes) *Chinese*
Mrs A Lucas, CertEd *Home Economics*
Mrs P Matfield, BA (Dartington) *Drama*
Mr J Mitchard, MA (Kent), PGCE (Cantab) *Learning Support*
Mrs A Newsome, BSc, MSc (London), PGCE (Reading) *Geography*
Mrs J Owens, BSc (Aberystwyth), CBiol, MIBiol, PGCE (Lancaster) *Biology*
Miss C Peck, BEd (Leeds) *Physical Education*
Miss L Peck, BA, PGCE (Leeds) *Physical Education, Geography*
Mrs S Puri, BEd (Liverpool) *Learning Support*
Miss H Rakowski, MA (Oxon), PGCE *Music*
Mr J Rawlinson, BA (Wolverhampton), PGCE (Liverpool), MEd (Oxon) *Art and Design*
Mrs E Roberts, BA (York), PGCE (Cantab) *English*
Mrs A Robson, BA (Otago, New Zealand), PGCE (Christchurch, New Zealand) *Latin*
Mrs S Savery, BA (Cantab), CertEd (London) *Economics, Business Studies*
Mrs G Sheppard, BA (London), PGCE (Oxon) *French*
Mrs F Stuart, MA, PGCE (Oxon), ARCM *Music*
Mrs J Thompson, BSc (St Andrews), PhD (Oxon) *Learning Support*
Miss H Tomlinson, BEd (Brighton) *Physical Education*
Miss H Turner, BSc (Loughborough), PGCE (Cantab) *Physical Education*
Mr A Vesty, BSc (Manchester) *Chemistry and Physics*
Mrs C Walker, Maitrise (Sorbonne, Paris), PGCE (Southampton) *French, Spanish*

Junior Department Staff:
Miss K Dooley, HND (Liverpool), PGCE (Nottingham)
Mrs A Dyar, MontDip (Dublin)
Mrs A Gillespie, BA (Cardiff), PGCE (Oxon)
Mrs J Haigh, BSc (London)
Mrs H Holland, BA (Oxford Brookes), CertEd (Warwick)
Lady Fiona Kildare, DipRSA, SLD
Mrs J Marecki, BEd (Oxon)
Mrs C Pattinson, DipEd (Bedford)
Mrs M Pettifor, BA (Manchester), PGCE (Oxon)
Mrs J Rawlinson, BA (Open), BEd (Oxon), CertEd (Bath)

Nursery Department Staff:
Mrs I Fenton, MontDip (London)
Mrs H Moorhouse, BA, MSc (Bangor), PGCE (Oxon)
Mrs E Stevens
Miss D Waters, PPA

Visiting Music Staff:
Ms A Bendy, LTCL, DipMusEd *Guitar*
Miss A Brittain, ARCM *Singing*
Mr K Fairbairn, AGSM *Percussion*
Mr P Foster, LTCL *Saxophone*
Miss L Haigh, BA (Durham) *Singing*
Miss E Hodson, MA, DPhil, PGDip *Violin and Viola*
Mr D Horniblow, BSc (Guildhall) *Woodwind*
Mr D McNaughton, BA *Brass*
Mrs P Miller, BA, LTCL *Clarinet*
Mrs C Rees, BMus(Ed), SRAsT *Oboe, Piano*
Miss A Strevens, BSc(Mus), SRAsT(M) *Flute*
Mrs M Woodcock, ARCM *Piano*

Librarian: Mrs E Kirby, BA (Manchester)

Medical Adviser: Dr C Pyper
School Nurse: Mrs S McIlvenna, RGN

Administrative Staff:
Bursar: Mr A C Sinclair
Assistant Bursar: Mrs T Hudson

School Secretaries:
Mrs M Hulme
Mrs G Hughes-Jones
Mrs E Kerry
Mrs S King
Mrs E Taylor

Rye St Antony was founded in 1930 by Elizabeth Rendall and Ivy King, two school teachers who reached the decision to start a school of their own during a visit to Sussex and the Church of St Antony in Rye, in commemoration of which the School was named. In 1939 the School moved to its present site, 12 acres of exceptionally beautiful grounds a mile to the north east of the centre of Oxford on Pullen's Lane, a quiet lane overlooking the city.

A steady programme of building and refurbishment has provided excellent teaching and residential facilities, all the twentieth century buildings being carefully harmonised with the architecture of the original handsome Victorian houses. King House was opened in 1986, the Art, Design and Technology wing in 1989, the Information and Communications Technology unit in 1991, the new wing of the Rendall Building in 1993 and the Sumpter Building with its Science laboratories in 1995. The most recent development has been the extension of the computer network throughout the School into all teaching and boarding areas, and a new Performing Arts building is currently being planned.

The School is highly regarded for its happy and purposeful atmosphere, its strong sense of community and its emphasis on the value of each member of the community as an individual. Pupils are helped to understand their strengths and weaknesses and the reasons for their successes and failures; they are encouraged to accept challenges and learn initiative and independence. They also have many opportunities to contribute to decision-making for the School, thereby learning how to play an active part in the school community and in future communities to which they will belong.

The School offers boarding and day places for girls aged 5-18, some day places for boys aged 5-8, and in Beech Tree Nursery School whole-day and half-day places for boys and girls aged 3-5. Short-stay and occasional boarding arrangements, varying in length from a single night to a whole term or more, can be made according to need.

Religious Life. The School's sacramental life is of fundamental importance, the Eucharist in particular uniting the School with Christ and his Church and giving a focus to prayer, both liturgical and private. Several Oxford priests regularly celebrate Mass for the whole School on special feast days and at the beginning and end of each term; they also celebrate the Sunday Masses, form Masses and weekday Masses. Religious Education is an integral part of the curriculum throughout the School, and all pupils are involved in the Christian life of the school community, not least its liturgical celebrations.

Senior School Curriculum. Academic standards and expectations are high, girls are offered many opportunities in music, art, drama and sport, and there is a busy programme of evening and weekend activities.

In the Senior School all girls follow a broad and balanced common course for the first three years, comprising English, Mathematics, Physics, Chemistry, Biology, Religious Education, French, Latin, History, Geography, Technology, Information and Communications Technology, Art, Music, Drama and Physical Education. Spanish is offered from Year 9, and there is a cross-curricular Health Education programme.

Twenty plus subjects are offered at GCSE level. For the two-year GCSE course girls usually study 10 subjects, a mixture of options and core subjects (including Co-ordinated Science, a double award subject).

In the Sixth Form girls typically study four AS subjects in the first year of Sixth Form and continue with three of these subjects as A2 subjects in the second year, thus completing Sixth Form with certification in 3 A Level subjects and an additional AS subject. Through a popular General Studies programme, each member of Sixth Form works towards her Diploma of Achievement and Key Skills certification.

Careers Guidance. The School's careers advisory service provides help and guidance for all girls, and there is a formal programme of careers advice throughout Years 9, 10 and 11 and Sixth Form. All girls go on to university and are helped to investigate thoroughly the Higher Education and careers options open to them, careful guidance being given concerning their applications and interviews. The support of the Headmistress, the Deputy Headmistress and other senior staff is available at all stages. Work experience placements are organised, and girls are encouraged to make particular use of this option at the end of their GCSE courses. The School belongs to the Independent Schools Careers Organisation and benefits from its many services. Visiting speakers give lectures on various Higher Education and careers topics; visits to appropriate conferences and exhibitions are arranged; and the School organises and hosts a biennial Careers Convention. In the careers library is a wide range of printed, video and computer-based information.

Junior School Curriculum. The Junior School and Senior School are closely linked, and Junior School pupils are steadily introduced to the specialist teaching and facilities of the Senior School. In the early years the teaching of most subjects is undertaken by the class teachers. In Years 5 and 6 girls are taught by subject teachers, some of whom also teach in the Senior School, and this arrangement gives girls the benefit of specialist teaching and encourages them to develop a feeling of confidence and continuity when the time comes for them to move into the Senior School. Use of the Senior School facilities is particularly valuable in Science, Art, Music, Physical Education and Drama. There is a Junior Library in Langley Lodge, and older Juniors may also use the King Library in the Senior School.

Performing Arts. The School has a strong tradition of debating and public speaking, and girls have many successes to their credit in city, county and regional competitions. A major drama production each year, and various smaller presentations give girls the opportunity to develop their skills in performing, directing, lighting, sound, stage design, costume design and make-up. There are frequent visits to Stratford, London and regional theatres including the Oxford Playhouse and some girls perform at the Playhouse in the annual schools' gala. The majority of girls learn one musical instrument and some learn two or more; there are two choirs, one orchestra and several smaller ensembles, and some girls are members of the Oxford Girls' Choir, the Oxford Youth Chamber Choir, the Oxford Schools' Symphony Orchestra, the Oxfordshire Youth Orchestra and the Thames Vale Orchestra. Instruments learnt include piano, violin, viola, 'cello, flute, oboe, clarinet, trumpet, bassoon, saxophone, French horn, guitar and percussion. Through musical productions, concerts and the liturgy there are many opportunities for girls to contribute to the musical life of the School. In both Drama and Music, pupils take the Guildhall School of Music and Drama examinations.

Sport. The School has good playing fields, all-weather hard courts and an outdoor heated swimming pool. The principal winter sports are netball and hockey; the principal summer sports are tennis, swimming, athletics and rounders. Girls compete regularly in local, county and regional tournaments.

Duke of Edinburgh's Award. The School has an outstanding record in the Duke of Edinburgh's Award, each year about 35 girls achieving the Bronze Award, 20 girls or so achieving the Silver Award and 20 or more girls achieving the Gold Award. The purpose of the Award is to give challenge, responsibility and adventure to young people, thus encouraging them to develop initiative and team skills.

Visits. Fieldwork, conferences, lectures, art exhibitions, plays and concerts give girls an interesting programme of visits within the UK. Visits abroad include study courses, exchanges, sports tours and skiing holidays, and the School regularly hosts visiting groups from schools overseas.

Health. The School Nurse works closely with the School Doctor who holds a weekly surgery at the School and who also sees girls at her nearby Health Centre. Dental and orthodontic treatment can be arranged locally, and the John Radcliffe Hospital is five minutes away.

Admissions. Admission to the Junior School is by interview and the School's own entrance tests. Admission to the Senior School is by interview and entrance examination (Common Entrance at 11+). Admission to the Sixth Form is by interview, school report and GCSE results. Scholarships are available at 11+ and 16+.

Fees per term. Full Boarders £3,150-£3,695; Weekly Boarders £2,975-£3,445; Day Pupils £1,265-£2,115.

Charitable status. Rye St Antony School Limited is a Registered Charity, number 309685. Its purpose is the furtherance of Christian education.

Sacred Heart Beechwood

Please see entry for Beechwood Sacred Heart.

St Albans High School

3 Townsend Avenue St Albans AL1 3SJ
Tel: (01727) 853800

Motto: *The fear of the Lord is the beginning of wisdom*

Visitor: The Right Reverend The Lord Bishop of St Albans

Council:
The Very Reverend The Dean of St Albans (*Chairman*)
Mrs J Banful
Dr P Barrison, MBBS
D M W Bolton, Esq, MA, FRSA
Mrs J F Boulton, ARICS
Mrs J Burns
Dr A Denham
S C de Galleani, Esq
T de Pencier, Esq
A Detheridge, Esq, MA, AFIMA
M D Lockhart, Esq, AIM
Miss R Musgrave, MA
Mrs M Ormiston
Mrs M Oxley
Cllr D B Phillips
M Rayner, Esq, MB, FRICS
Mrs S Williams
Mrs J Woolley

R Brooks, Esq, LLB (*Clerk to the Governors*)

‡***Head Mistress:*** **Mrs Carol Y Daly**, BSc Nottingham

Assistants:
‡Mrs A Adlam, BSc Southampton, MSc London

‡Dr G Alderton, BSc, PhD Leeds
Mrs M Allan, DipEd Jordanhill
‡Dr J Armstrong, DPhil Cambridge
Miss M Bacon, BEd Exeter
Mrs L Bamford, BA Humberside
‡Mrs B Batchelor, BA London
§Mrs D Browne, BEd Sussex
§Mrs W Burdett, Teacher's Dip in PE Chelsea College
‡Mrs P Chapman, BSc Nottingham
‡Mrs S Cooper, BA Exeter
‡Miss D Coxon, BSc De Montfort
‡Miss C Cozens, BSc Exeter
Mrs E Davies, BA Warwick
*‡Mrs G Davies, BSc, MSc Wales
‡Mrs J Day, BSc Swansea
Mrs J Dennick, BA Open
‡Mrs S Devlin, BSc Cork
§Mrs H Doherty, Cert Ed London
§‡Mrs S Dover, BSc London
*‡Mrs S Dunkerley, MA London *Head of Junior Department*
‡Mrs S Edwards, GRSM
‡Miss J Fielden, BSc Wales
‡Mrs J Fingland, BA Leicester
*‡Mrs R Frost, MA(Ed) Open, BEd Dundee, BA Open
‡§Mrs P Gibbons, BA London
Mrs S Gilchrist, DipEd Jordanhill
‡§Mrs T Gott, BSc London
‡Mrs B Goulding, MA(Ed), BA Sheffield
Mrs M Harcourt, BEd Cantab
Mrs J Houston, CertEd Brighton College of Education
‡Mrs E Johns, BA Aberystwyth
*‡Miss H Jones, MA London
‡Mrs H D Kain, BSc Sussex
*‡Dr S Legg, BSc Birmingham, DPhil Oxford
‡Mr J Lisher, BA Oxford
§‡Mrs V Loffler, BSc London
*‡Mrs J Longbourne, BA Sussex
Mrs M Longmuir, DipEd Jordanhill, Cert of PE Dunfermline
‡Mrs E Lusty, BA Cambridge
§Mrs J Lyal, BEd Sussex
‡Mr S McGuinness, BA Manchester Polytechnic
Mrs S Mason, BEd Homerton
*‡Mrs C J Mead, MA Cantab
‡§Mrs B Mitchell, BSc Sheffield
§‡Mrs M H Newton, BSc London, DipArch UCL
‡Mrs A Norton, BA Bristol
Mrs C Nudds, BEd London
§‡Mrs S Oldfield, BA Hons London
‡Mr L O'Neill, BA, MA(Ed) *Director of Studies*
Mrs K Osborne, BEd Hons London
*‡Mrs M Patel, BA Wales
‡Mrs E Pyett MA Leeds
‡Mr S Ramsbottom, BSc Reading
Mrs A Reid, BEd Herts College of HE
‡Miss S J Riley, BA London *Deputy Head*
‡Mrs L Robson, MA Cambridge
*§‡Mrs A Sawyer, BSc London
Mrs H Scott, Teacher's Cert, Home Econ St Osyth
Mrs A Shackley, CertEd Herts College of HE, LRAM
‡Mrs K Smith, BSc, UMIST
*‡Dr N Springthorpe, BMus, PhD, FLCM, CertRCM Surrey
*Mrs J Spyropoulos, NDD Art Teacher's Cert London
‡Mrs A Stevens, BA Durham
§M Strange, MSc, BSc London
§‡H Swain, MA, BA Cambridge
Mrs C Sykes, CertEd Homerton College, Cambridge
*‡Mrs G Thompson, BA London
‡Mr I Thomson, BA London
*‡Miss K Tovey, BA Warwick
‡Mrs S Watts, BA Hons London
‡Mr C White, BSc London
‡Mrs T Wood, GNSM, ARCM, LRAM
‡Mrs C A Wright, BA Ulster
‡Miss J Wright, BA Durham
§‡Mrs C Wybraniec, BSc Birmingham

Chaplain: The Revd Diane Fitzgerald Clark

Visiting Staff:
Music:
§Mr B Booth *Percussion*
§Mrs K Bradley, LRAM *Violin*
‡Mrs V Brill, BA, GLCM, LLCM *Recorder and Flute*
‡Mrs C Brittain, ARCM *Flute*
§Miss F Bryan, GGSM, DipRAM *Bassoon and Clarinet*
§Mr J Cherry, DRSAMD, DipRAM, LRAM *Flute*
‡§Miss J Cutler, GTCL, LTCL, PGCE *Violincello and Double Bass*
‡§Mrs E Fagg, LRAM, GRSM, MTC *Piano*
§Miss J Faulkner, LRAM, ARAM *Violin*
§Mr I Gammie, MA, ALCM *Guitar*
§Mr G Hunt, AGSM *Piano*
‡Mrs J Jasinski, LTCL *Violin*
‡Mr S Jones, GTCL, LTCL, MTC *Singing*
§Miss E Lane, GRSM, ARCM *Singing*
§Miss H Leek *Piano*
§Miss J Miller, BMus, LGSM *Oboe*
§Mr I Muncey, AGSM *Trumpet*
§Mr M Onissi, LTCL *Saxophone and Clarinet*
§Mrs E Perrottet, AGSM *Brass Instruments*
§Lady R Runcie, Hon ARAM, LRAM, ARCM *Piano*
§Miss A Tysall, BMus *Piano*
§Mrs B Valdar, AGSM *Clarinet*

Mrs A Tett *Music Administrator*

Physical Education:
§Mrs L Helps, member of British Tennis Umpires Association
§Mr L Larson
§Mr M Johnson, 1st Dan Judo Coach
§Mr J Smith *Badminton Coach*

Speech & Drama:
Mrs I Lake
Mrs L Samson

Librarian: §Mrs E Blower, BA Open ALA

Technicians:
Mrs C Munro *Physics*
Mrs C Chaytow *Biology*
Mrs M Ruebotham *Chemistry*
Mr P Gauntlett *IT Resources Technician*
§Mrs W Hyams *Art*

Administration:
Bursar: Mr D A Matthews, FCA

PA to Bursar: Mrs S Pentecost

Domestic Bursar: Mrs H Ware

Welfare Assistants Junior House:
Mrs D Foddering
Mrs S Holmwood

Headmistress's Secretary: Mrs E Roberts
School Secretary: Mrs J Herbert
Admissions Secretary: Miss S Nicholls

‡ denotes holder of Teacher's Diploma or Certificate

St Albans High School is a day school for 780 girls aged between 4 and 18. Since its foundation in 1889, it has been closely linked with the Cathedral and Abbey Church of St Alban and the Christian ethos is very important in the life of the School. Services are held regularly in School or at the Abbey. The School is only a few minutes' walk from the town centre.

The Junior Department, which is for girls aged 4–11, numbers 216. There are 9 full-time and 4 part-time members of staff. The department has its own buildings and play areas. The curriculum covers all the primary school subjects in the National Curriculum through a modern and lively approach.

The Senior School has facilities for the teaching of a wide range of subjects. There are eight modern science laboratories, a Design and Technology Centre, a Drama Studio, an Assembly Hall with a fully equipped stage, specialist rooms for computers, art, music, textiles, home economics and all the usual academic subjects. The curriculum, which is kept under review, includes all the subjects of the National Curriculum, and also Latin, a second modern language and drama. There is a well stocked library and a Sixth Form Centre to accommodate some 156 girls at the top of the School.

Girls are encouraged to participate in a wide range of extra-curricular activities, among which sport and music feature strongly as well as the Duke of Edinburgh's Award Scheme, Young Enterprise and Community Service, some of which are organised jointly with St Albans School. Pastoral care is important at all levels of the School and girls are encouraged to feel that they are valued for their contributions to the life of the School community.

In the grounds of the Senior School there is a modern Sports Hall and a heated swimming pool. The main games field is ten minutes' walk from the School and there are eight hard tennis courts, two lacrosse pitches and a pavilion.

Pupils are prepared for GCSE examinations at the age of 16, for Advanced Level examinations, for Oxford and Cambridge entrance and for the examinations of the Associated Board of the Royal Schools of Music.

Fees, which are inclusive, are: Reception £1,560 per term, Junior department (7–11) £1,650 per term, Senior School (11–18) £1,980 per term. Private music lessons, special tennis coaching, School meals, daily School coaches are all optional extras.

Scholarships. (*see* Entrance Scholarship section) A Music Scholarship is awarded annually at age 11 and an Academic Scholarship at ages 11+, 13+ and 16+. There are a few bursaries to assist in cases of hardship and special terms are offered for daughters of the clergy.

Admission. Pupils are normally admitted in September at the age of 4 and 7 for entry to the Junior House, 11 for the Senior School and 16 for the Sixth Form. Offers of places in the Sixth Form are provisional until the results of the GCSE examinations are known: girls are required to have a minimum of 6 subjects with A or B grades including A or B grades in the subjects to be taken at Advanced Level. Entrance examinations are held in the Lent Term for admission in the following September.

Charitable status. St Albans High School for Girls is a Registered Charity, number 311065. It exists to provide an education for girls "in accordance with the principles of the Church of England".

St Andrew's School
Bedford

Kimbolton Road Bedford MK40 2PA
Tel: (01234) 267272
Fax: (01234) 355105
e-mail: standrews@standrewsschoolbedford.com

Founded 1897
Motto: *Non Sibi Sed Deo et Alteria*

Governing Body:
Chairman: Dr G M Yerbury, MB, BS, MPhil, FRCPCH

Clerk to the Governors and Company Secretary: Ms J F Lisle, FCA, BSc Econ

Staff:
***Headmistress:* Mrs J E Marsland**, BPhil(Ed)

Mr P Barlow, BSc (*Chemistry/Physics*)
Mrs F Boland, BSc, PGCE (*Mathematics*)
Mrs L Coldwell, BEd (*Physical Education*)
Mrs H Hull, CertEd (*Textiles*)
Mrs V Humphries (Slade School of Art) (*Stage Design*)
Mr C Jones, BEd (*Mathematics/ICT*)
Mrs J Leitner, LRAM, GRSM (*Music*)
Mrs C Long, BA, PGCE (*German/History*)
Mrs J Mould, BSc, PGCE, AdvDipTec, DPSE (*Technology*)
Mrs J Randall, MSc, DipEd (*Geography*)
Mrs H Ryan, BEd, CertEd (*Middle School Science*)
Mrs S Shepherd, BSc (*Mathematics*)
Mrs J Smithson, BA, PGCE (*History, Religious Education*)
Mrs A Sprake, BA, PGCE (*English*)
Mrs C Thomas, BEd (*English, Careers*)
Mrs S Tribe, MA, PGCE (*Modern Languages*)
Mrs F Turner, CertEd (*Physical Education*)
Mrs C Wedge, BSc, PGCE (*Biology/Chemistry*) (*Deputy Head*)
Mrs J Whittaker, BA (*Drama*)
Mrs H Wittering, CertEd (*Food Technology*)

Preparatory Department:
Head of Department: Mrs C Murphy, CertEd

Mrs D Berrington, CertEd
Mrs J Crawford, BEd
Mrs H Darbon, CertEd
Mrs J Ebbs, CertEd
Mrs E Jackson, BA
Mrs H King, BEd

Pre-Preparatory Department:
Head of Department: Mrs C Matthews, BEd

Mrs W Armitage, CertEd
Mrs T O Dell, BA, PGCE (*Psychology/Child Development*)
Mrs J Russell, BSc, PGCE

Nursery Department:
Head of Department: Mrs S Bingham, MA, Montessori International Diploma

Learning Support Department:

Mrs L Ledsom, CertEd, DipSpLD
Mrs J Prentice, CertEd, DipSpLD
Mrs J Wainwright, CertEd, DipSpLD (*Dyslexia*)

Librarian: Mrs Y Owen, CertEd

There are a number of visiting Music staff and Speech and Drama staff, offering a wide range of individual tuition.

Dance: Mrs H Redish, RA Diploma (*Teaching*)

St. Andrew's is a small day school for girls from the ages of three to sixteen and boys from three to eight who are taught in small classes.

A 19th Century house is at the heart of the School, which has expanded to provide modern facilities to meet the demands of the National Curriculum and beyond. The Preparatory Department occupies separate accommodation. The Nursery/Pre-Prep buildings cater for boys as well as girls.

The School prepares girls for the GCSE examinations and further education in the Sixth Form of local Independent Schools, Upper Schools or Colleges. There is an extremely wide range of extra-curricular activities, which includes sport, music, drama and the Duke of Edinburgh Award Scheme.

For further details contact the School Office, Bedford (01234) 267272. Fax: (01234) 355105. E-mail: standrews@standrewsschoolbedford.com.

Charitable status. St Andrew's School (Bedford) Limited is a Registered Charity, number 307531. It offers a broad based education to pupils of all abilities, who are encouraged to strive for excellence in all they do.

St Antony's-Leweston School

Sherborne Dorset DT9 6EN
Tel: (01963) 210691
Fax: (01963) 210786
e-mail: st.antony@virgin.net
website: www.leweston.co.uk

Independent, Boarding, Flexi-Boarding and Day School for Girls aged 11–18 with separate, purpose-built, Co-ed Preparatory School for boys and girls aged 2½–11 on same campus. Roman Catholic foundation but all denominations welcome. Excellent academic reputation and strong Sixth Form.

Governing Body:
Mr Paul Burns *Chairman*
Mr E W Ludlow *Deputy Chairman*
The Revd Father Alexander George, OSB
Sister John Bosco
Mrs R Berry
Mr J S Black
Mr M A Sutton, MA, Notary Public (Oxon)
The Very Reverend Keith Collins
Rear Admiral James Carine
Mr P Austin
The Countess Charles de Salis
Mrs B Wingfield Digby
Mrs J Townsend
Mr C Stunt
Mr D J Bilbé
Mr P C Mott, QC

Head: **Mr H J MacDonald**, MA (Oxon, PGCE *Latin, Greek, Ancient History*

Deputy Head: Mrs P A Hooper, BA Hons (Cardiff), PGCE (Bristol) *Director of Boarding, Classics*

Bursar: Mr J Macfarlane, CDipAF, MIMgt, AHCIMA (*Tel:* (01963) 210765)

Development Director: Mrs S J Eagles, MIPR (*Tel:* (01963) 210783). e-mail: development-director@stantonys-leweston.fsnet.co.uk

Teaching Staff:
Miss R Britton, BMus Hons, PGCE Pianoforte *Director of Music*
Mrs R Peacock *Head of Drama*
Miss R Dodd, BSc (Durham), EFL, RSA Prep, EFL
Mrs S E Keen, BA Hons (Birmingham), PGCE (Bristol) *Head of Department, French*
Miss M Meadows, BA Hons (Manchester), PGCE (London) *French*
Mrs S O'Connor, BEd Hons (London) *German, French*
*Mrs J Hopkin, BA Hons (Exeter), PGCE (Leeds), Head of Sixth Form, Geography
Mr D N Barlow, BSc Hons (Nottingham), MSc (London), PGCE (*Birmingham*) *Head of Department, Geography*
*Mr A Ashwin, BEd Dip in Economics (Goldsmiths, London), GenCert in Horticulture (Royal Horticultural Society) *Director of Studies, Economics, Mathematics and History*
Mr J Cross *Mathematics, Head of Department*
*Miss J Kelly, BEd Hons (Leeds), Catholic Teacher's Cert (Leeds) *Head of Department, Religious Studies*
*Miss P L Haywood, BSc, PGCE *Head of Department, Biology*
Mrs P Walden, BSc Hons (London) *Physics*
Mr J Sherwood-Taylor, BA (Open Univ), MSc (York), Cert Ed *Chemistry, Head of Department*
Dr O Kemal, BSc Hons, PhD (London), PGCE *Chemistry, Physics*
Mrs E C Williams, BA Hons Graphic Information Design, PGCE (Manchester) *Teacher in Charge, Art*
Mr A Barnes, Dip AD Hons (Portsmouth School of Art), MA History of Art (Royal College of Art) *History of Art*
*Miss K N Mullen, BEd Hons (Sussex University), CertEd (Chelsea School of Human Movement/Brighton Polytechnic) *Head of Department of Physical Education*
§Mrs S Gardner, RSA Teacher's Diploma *Typing*
§Mrs E Norman, ARCM (Guildhall School of Music) *Music* (*Viola*)
§Mrs N Price (Royal College of Music), ARCM, LRAM, GRSM Hons *Music* (*Piano, Bassoon*)
§Miss M Nightingale, Dip of Music in Education (Dartington College), LGSM (Guildhall School of Music) *Music* (*Recorder*)
§Miss K E Evans, BMus Hons (University College of North Wales) *Music* (*Flute*)
§Mrs J Dams, ARCM (Royal College of Music) *Music* (*Flute and Piano*)
§Mrs K Sheppard, ARCM (Royal College of Music) *Music* (*Horn, Trumpet, Trombone*)
§Mr C Daly, Cert Ed, LRAM *Music* (*Guitar*)
§Mrs N Leadbetter, AGSM (Guildhall School of Music) *Music* (*Violin*)
Miss A J Kelly, BA Hons (Southampton) *Music* (*Piano, Clarinet, Violin, French*)
§Mr P Shutler *Music* (*Piano, Accordian*)
§Mrs J Fenton, ARCM, (Royal College of Music) *Music* (*Singing*)
§Mr N Boothroyd, ARCM (Royal College of Music) *Music* (*'cello*)
§Mrs W Bednall, BA Hons (Southampton), ALCM *Music* (*Piano*)
§Miss D Laxton, RAD *Ballet*
§Mr J Candor (*Clarinet*)

St Antony's-Leweston School welcomes girls of all abilities as full Boarders, Flexi-boarders or as Day pupils between the ages of 11 and 18 years. Admittance is by means of Common Entrance at eleven but girls are also admitted at twelve or thirteen.

Situated in 40 acres of beautiful Dorset parkland, 3 miles south of Sherborne, the School offers all the advantages of both the traditional and modern in education with excellent facilities, particularly in the Sciences and Design & Technology.

Founded by the Sisters of Christian Instruction in 1891, the School is a Catholic School but has a large percentage of pupils from other denominations. There are 250 girls in the School of whom 120 are boarders. The ethos of the School is based on a wide social mix with a spread of talents, firm but friendly discipline and a keen sense of Christian and moral values. The Head is forward looking with a strong sense of leadership and vision. The School has a resident Chaplain and girls are expected to attend Chapel once a week. Preparation for confirmation is available for both Catholic and Anglican pupils.

The academic standard of the School is high. Top of DfEE league tables for GCSE results in Dorset in 2000. At both GCSE and A Level pass rates are consistently over 95% and the School's reputation for excellence in Music and Drama runs parallel with academic achievement in Sciences and The Arts. The real success of the School, however, is achieved by realising the full potential of each individual girl, whether they are high fliers or not. Very good for academic added-value. Each year girls gain places at Oxbridge and go on to read a wide range of degrees at all the major universities.

Teachers are dedicated and imaginative, including specialist teachers for Dyslexia and EFL. The School's special quality is its ability to encourage in each pupil a sense of her own worth and ability. Girls are outgoing, well-mannered and unstuffy. While Leweston has a high proportion of Day Girls, the School is fully committed to boarding offering a wide programme of activities in the evenings and at the weekends. Riding is especially popular. Annual prestigious Dressage Competition.

The School has close links with Sherborne School and Milton Abbey and there are many combined social, recreational, musical and cultural activities between the Schools. Sherborne is an attractive historic abbey town with few of the distractions of a large city but at the same time is served by regular Network Express trains to and from London and good road links to Salisbury, Exeter and Bath. The School's facilities are among the best in the West Country. There is a fine Astro-turf all weather sports pitch, Design and Technology Centre, modern Senior Science Centre, arts studio, health centre, heated swimming pool, sports hall, multi-gym, squash courts, tennis courts and extensive well-maintained grounds and playing fields.

St Antony's-Leweston Preparatory School (IAPS). St Antony's-Leweston Preparatory School is situated on the same campus offering continuity of education for girls from two and a half to eighteen years, with boarding provision for girls from 7. Boys from three to eight. Excellent early years provision including French from 3 years, beautifully situated Nursery and weekly Parent/Toddlergroup. Headteacher: Mrs Lynn-Marie Walker (Tel: 01963 210790).

Scholarships. (*see* Entrance Scholarship section) - Generous Scholarship provision including Academic, Music, Sport, Art and Drama.

Further particulars may be obtained on application to the Head or Admissions Tutor.

Fees per year. Boarding £13,539; Day £8,919. Flexi Boarding (including supper) £19.50 per night.

Charitable status. St Antony's-Leweston School Trust is a Registered Charity, number 295175. It is a charitable foundation set up for educational purposes.

St Catherine's School

Bramley Guildford GU5 0DF
Tel: (01483) 893363
Fax: (01483) 899608

Founded as a Church of England School for Girls in 1885.

Governing Body of St Catherine's School:

Ex-officio Members:
The Lord Bishop of Guildford
The Archdeacon of Surrey
The Chairman of the Surrey County Council

Governing Body of Bramley:
Chairman: Mr R W Lilley

Vice-Chairman: M A McLeod, FRICS

C M R Campbell, Esq, MA
Mrs K M Clayton
Dr O Darbishire, MA
Mrs E R W Dent
P W G DuBuisson, Esq, FCA
Mrs S M Fowler-Watt
R W Lilley, Esq
M A McLeod, Esq, FRICS
G G Moore, Esq, MA, FCA
Dr J F McGowan, FRCA
Prof G A Parker, PhD, CEng, EurIng, FIMechE, MASME
Mrs E S Reed
S E Sexton, Esq, ARCS, BSc
N E L Thomas Esq, FSVA

***Headmistress:* Mrs Alice Phillips**, MA (Cantab)

Deputy Head & Head of Boarding: Mrs G Bucknall, BSc (Wales), PGCE (London)
Head of Junior School: Mrs K M Jefferies, BSc (Bridgewater, Massachusetts), PGCE (London)
Director of Studies: Miss W Griffiths, BSc (Wales), PGCE
Senior Housemistress: Mrs M J Banks, BA (London), PGCE
Director of Music: R E Gillman, MMus (London), RCM, FRCO, CHM, ARCM, PGCE
Chaplain: The Revd Canon Colin Tickner
Bursar: Mr A Oakley, FCCA, ACIS
Headmistress's Secretary: Mrs W A Waite

Senior School:
Mrs J Allen, BA (London), BA (Courtauld Institute) *History of Art*
Mrs J Arrick, BSc (Liverpool), PGCE *Psychology*
Mrs K J Atkins, BSc, PGCE, ARCS (London) *Physics*
Mrs M J Banks, BA (London), PGCE *French*
Mrs A Baxter, MA (Edinburgh), PGCE *Modern Languages*
Mr A Beety, BSc (Sheffield), PGCE *Mathematics*
Miss N Bennett, BA (Wales), PGCE *Physical Education*
Mrs A Blake, LTA, CCA, SRA Advanced Coach *Tennis/Squash*
Miss F Bolton, MA (Oxon), PGCE *German and French*
Mrs S Brunskill, MA (Oxon) *Business Studies & Economics*
Mrs G Bucknall, BSc (Wales), PGCE *Biology*
Mrs E Campbell, MA, CertEd (Glasgow) *Modern Languages*
Mrs S Cannon, BA (Anglia) *PHSE & General Studies*
Miss R Chaplin, BA (Exeter), PGCE *French/Spanish*
Mrs J Collins, CertEd (Bath College), MIHec *Home Ecomomics & Textiles*
Mrs J Craig, BEd, CertEd (Edinburgh) *English*
Miss V A Cranwell, BEd (Brighton) *PE & Mathematics*
Mrs L Crispin, BA (Manchester) *Textiles*
Mr C Curtis, BSc (UMIST), PGCE *Chemistry*
Mrs G David, BA (Manchester), PGCE *History*
Mrs J Davies, CertEd (St Osyth) *Home Economics*
Mrs A Davis, MA (St Andrews), PGCE *French*
Mrs C L De Vilo, BA (UCL), DipFr *English*
Mrs R Folley, BEd, DipEd (Chelsea) *Physical Education*
Mr P Friend, BSc (Lancaster), PGCE (St Martin's) *Mathematics*
Mrs F Gane, BA (London), CertEd *History*
Miss R Garcia, BA (Oviedo) *Spanish*
Mrs M Gartland, CertEd (Bognor Regis) *Physical Education*
Mr R E Gillman, MMus (RCM), FRCO, (CHM), ARCM, PGCE *Music*
Mrs M Green, LLAM, LALAM *Drama and Theatre Studies*
Miss W Griffiths, BSc (Wales), PGCE *Biology*
Mrs S J Hall, BA (London), PGCE *Modern Languages*
Mrs P Hallam, BA (Birmingham) *Classics*
Mrs P Harris, BSc (Edinburgh), PGCE *Biology*
Mrs A Hawtin, BSc, PGCE (Reading) *Biology*
Dr J Haystead, BA (Reading), PhD (Aberdeen) *Development Secretary*

Miss E Hayward, BEd, CNAA (West Sussex Institute of Higher Education) *Religious Studies*
Miss J Hilvert, BA (London), PGCE, MA (Middlesex) *Director of Drama*
Mrs N E Hompstead, BEd (Wales), CertEd *Chemistry*
Mrs J Keane, MA (Greenwich), TEFL (Trinity), AMBDA *SENCO*
Miss K Keane, BA (Humberside), PGCE *French and Business Studies*
Mrs S Kelsall, MA (Open), BSc (Brighton), PGCE *Mathematics*
Miss C Komor, BEd (Wales) *Home Economics*
Miss T Kuchmy, BMus (Manchester), PGCE, GRNCM, ARNCM, LRAM, ARCM *Music*
Mrs J B R MacIntyre, BSc, DipEd (Edinburgh), BA (Open) *Mathematics*
Mrs R C S Matfield, BSc (Surrey), MSc (London), PGCE *Biology and General Studies*
Mr F R McDonald, BSc (London), MSc (CNAA) *Biology and Chemistry*
Mrs K Meredith, BA (London), AKC, PGCE *Classics and PSHE*
Dr C A Mills, BA (Hull), MA (McMaster University), PhD (London), PGCE *Classics*
Miss R Morgan, BA (London), DCG *Careers*
Mrs S Murray, BSc (London), AKC *Physics*
Mrs A G Palmer, BA (Southampton), ARCM, CertEd *Religious Studies & Music*
Miss R Percy, BA (Oxon), PGCE *Music*
Mrs A M Phillips, MA (Cantab) *English*
Dr K Puech, BSc (Dublin), PGCE (King's, London) *Physics*
Mrs C Rose, BA, PGCE (Nottingham) *History*
Mrs B Rounce, CertEd (Portsmouth College) *Science*
Mrs G Scahill, BSc (North Staffordshire) *Information Technology*
Mrs J Silk, DipAD (Bath Academy of Art) *Art and Ceramics*
Mrs C Silver, BSc, PGCE (Durham) *Mathematics*
Miss S Slater, BA, MA (Durham) *English*
Miss H Smith, BA (Brighton) *Physical Education*
Mrs J Smith, BSc (St Andrews), PGCE *Information Technology*
Mrs A W Stagg, BA (London) *Geography*
Mrs A Stortt, BSc (Exeter), PGCE (London) *Geography*
Miss V Vinen, BA (Plymouth), PGCE (London) *Art and Design*
Mr D Weightman, BA (Surrey Institute) *Photography*
Mr A White, BA (Winchester) *Design & Technology*
Mrs A White, BSc(Econ) (Wales), PGCE *Geography*
Mrs A Williams, BEd (Wales), CertEd *English*
Mrs N Wynne, MA (Cantab), PGCE *Mathematics*
Miss A Youens, BA (Open), CertEd *Mathematics*

Boarding Staff:
Housemistresses:
Symes: Miss K Keane
Bronte: Miss C Komor
Keller: Miss A Youens
Sixth Form: Mrs S Cannon, Mrs A White

Housematron: Mrs G Sanchez

Sanatorium Sisters:
Miss S Barber, RGN
Mrs L Green, RGN
Mrs P Colloby, RGN

School Housemistresses:
Ashcombe: Mrs A Williams
Merriman: Mrs F Gane
Midleton: Mrs N Hompstead
Musgrave: Mrs A Stortt
Russell-Baker: Miss V Vinen
Stoner: Mrs M Banks

Catering Manager: Mr W McGregor

Librarian: Mrs S Lawrence, ALA

Junior School:
Mrs R Brown, CertEd (Portsmouth) *General Subjects*
Mrs J C Hager
Mr M Hardman, BA (York), PGCE
Mrs D Hodgkiss, CertEd (Winchester)
Mrs K M Jefferies, BSc (Bridgewater, Massachusetts), PGCE (London)
Mrs H Johnson, BEd (Lancaster) *PE*
Mrs A MacVean, BEd (King Alfred's College, Winchester) *General Subjects*
Mrs T Marmion, BEd (Exeter) *General Subjects*
Mrs L Marriott, CertEd (Cambridge) *General Subjects*
Mrs E Moore, BEd (Exeter)
Mrs J Parker, BEd (Strathclyde) *General Subjects*
Mrs S Platt, CertEd (Leeds) *General Subjects*
Mrs F Thomas, BA, TTC (New Zealand) *General Subjects*
Mrs P Topham, GMus, RNCM, PGCE *Music*
Mrs F S Wright, CertEd (London) *General Subjects*
Mrs R Young, BEd (Sussex)

Nursery Assistants:
Miss K Brindley, NNEB
Miss J Fuller, BEd (Birmingham)

Visiting staff teach piano, string, wind instruments, brass, percussion, ballet, speech and drama.

Outstanding A Level results in August 2000 have again secured a place for St Catherine's School, Bramley among the very best in the highly competitive league of single sex girls' schools. A long record of success in public examinations has enabled more and more St Catherine's leavers to gain places in top universities, in competitive disciplines like medicine and veterinary science, law and languages. This success comes not only as a result of the fine quality of the teaching, but is also due to the individual attention received by every girl. St Catherine's places great emphasis on creating a happy environment where every girl is encouraged to work hard to maximise her talents. A network of Housemistresses and House Tutors provides pastoral support; the atmosphere is friendly, but high standards of behaviour and good manners are expected. The curriculum is broad and varied, and all pupils participate in many challenging and rewarding extra-curricular activities, at the same time raising impressive sums of money for charity each year.

A major programme of building and refurbishment has seen extensions to both Junior and Senior schools in recent years. The magnificent new Millennium Building opened in September 2000 with new classrooms for classics and languages, two new Chemistry laboratories, a Language Laboratory and a Sixth Form workroom with IT and audio facilities. The Main School boarding houses have also been refurbished, and the days of enormous dormitories for up to ten girls have gone forever. In their place are smart common rooms with kitchen facilities, a games room and study bedrooms for two to four girls.

St Catherine's has an unrivalled reputation in art, music, sport and drama; whatever her level of expertise, every girl is encouraged to take part in sport, and a large number go on to represent the county in netball, lacrosse, swimming, squash and athletics. In recent years, over a dozen St Catherine's girls have played at national level, and last season, Katy Bennett played alongside her PE teacher in the senior England lacrosse team.

Music is an important feature of school life, with several choirs, an orchestra and two concert bands practising each week, and performing regularly. The highlight of last year for many of the senior Chamber Choir was Russell Watson's CD. They accompanied him on two pieces, and were later invited to appear on television with him. Almost half St Catherine's girls learn to play a musical instrument, and there are flute choirs, recorder groups and ensembles to cater for all levels of ability.

The popular House drama competition, held in the Autumn term every year, is seen as a challenge by the Sixth Form, who not only write the plays, but also organise the production from start to finish. The highlight of the drama calendar is the school production, this year *Daisy Pulls it Off.* There are also Sixth Form "Plays in a Day", polished performances by GCSE Drama and A Level Theatre Studies students, and Speech and Drama lessons throughout the school. GCSE Photography is a popular option amongst Sixth form girls, and art, pottery and design flourish, with after-school clubs for the Middle School. The annual Fashion Show gives GCSE pupils the opportunity to present their coursework in an imaginative way to the rest of the school and parents. The Upper Five Art group won a major prize at the Tate Modern last May for their pottery. As a result St Catherine's now has an Anthony Gormly signed print on display, and an Artist in Residence for two terms who has masterminded a huge mural which will be hung in the Dining Hall.

The Junior School offers a full academic and games curriculum. It aims to support families in helping younger pupils develop a strong sense of values, high standards of behaviour and consideration for others, as well as excellent academic success. Girls are accepted from the age of 4, with many more joining the school at 7, to benefit from the specialist teaching, combining the best traditional methods with modern technology to prepare them for the Entrance Examination to the Senior School at 11+.

St Catherine's is fortunately situated in extensive grounds, at the heart of the attractive Surrey village of Bramley. Guildford, with its excellent facilities, and main line station (Waterloo 35 minutes) is close by. Access to Heathrow and Gatwick via the A3 and M25 is good, and travel arrangements are made for overseas boarders.

Fees from January 2001. Day Girls (including lunch): Reception Class £1,340 per term, Kindergarten £1,625; Transition £1,915; Junior School £2,215; Middle and Senior School £2,680.

Boarders: Middle and Senior Boarding and Tuition £4,405 per term; Juniors Boarding and Tuition £3,965.

Entry (*see* Entrance Scholarship section). This is by Entrance Examination held in January. The Junior School also holds its entrance tests in January.

Entrance Scholarships are offered at 11+, together with a number of Sixth Form scholarships of one third fees. A number of music exhibitions, providing music tuition, music and instrument hire are also offered. A Sixth Form Art Scholarship is available.

Prospectus and School Visits. Please apply to the Registrar. The Headmistress will be pleased to see parents by appointment.

Charitable status. The Corporation of St Catherine's, Bramley is a Registered Charity, number 1070858. It exists to provide education for girls in accordance with the principles of the Church of England.

* Head of Department	§ Part Time or Visiting
† Housemaster/Housemistress	¶ Old Pupil
‡ See below list of staff for meaning	

St David's School
Ashford

Church Road Ashford Middlesex TW15 3DZ.
Tel: (01784) 252494; 240434 (Junior School); 240680 (Bursary)
Fax: (01784) 248652

Board of Governors:

Chairman: Dr W A Stevens

Dr C J Barton
Mr S Bhasin
Miss C Cawston
Mrs A Lacey
Mrs E M Masson
Mr P R Withers Green
Mrs P Wood

Adviser to the Governors: Mr N Finlayson

***Head:* Ms P Bristow**, BSc Hons (London), PGCE (London *Chemistry*

Deputy Head: Mrs Janet Mackenzie, MA (Glasgow) *French and German*

Head of Junior School: Mrs Pauline G Green, AdvDip (London), CertEd

Bursar: Mr William Hanlon, BA Hons (Ulster), MBA (Lancaster), PGCE, ADSE

Senior School Teaching Staff:

Miss T Adams, BA Hons (Coventry), PGCE *Technology*
Mrs C S Atkins, BEd Hons (London), CertEd (Cambridge) *Head of Physical Education/Duke of Edinburgh's Award Organiser*
Mrs D E Bishop, BA Hons (Wales), PGCE *Head of History, Day Girl's Coordinator*
Mrs M J Bruce, BSc Hons (Bristol), RSA Cert, TEFL *EFL*
Mrs P Carr, BEd Hons *Head of IT*
Mrs L Clark, BEd (London) *Food Technology*
Mrs C Coldicott, DipAD, PGCE *Head of Art*
Mrs A Davey, BEd (Dunfermline) *Physical Education*
Mrs C Davies, BA *Spanish*
Mrs A Deighton, BA, PGCE, RSA Cert, TEFL *Psychology/EFL*
Mrs M R Dent, BSc (Reading), PGCE (Southampton) *Head of Mathematics and IT*
Ms M Flieger *German/French*
Miss S Funnell, BA, PGCE *English/Drama*
Mrs A Garrett-Cox, BEd Hons *Mathematics*
Mrs A Gittins, BEd *PE (part-time)*
Mr I Goodridge, BSc Hons (Surrey), PGCE (London) *Business Studies*
Mrs J Green *Housemistress/Matron*
Mrs R Hill, BA Hons, PGCE *Music (part-time)*
Mr D Hymers, BA, PGCE Hons (Canterbury), MA *History*
Mrs J Jarrett, CertEd *Learning Support (part-time)*
Mr N G Jones, BSc Hons, MSc (Wales) *Head of Science/Biology*
Mrs C Khoo, BA, PGCE *Geography*
Mrs A Kjoller, BDS (Copenhagen), PGCE *Biology*
Ms V Mercieca, MSc, BSc *Physics*
Ms M A Muir, BA Hons (Open University), CertEd *English*
Dr A Nitkunan, MSc, PhD *Chemistry/Science*
Mrs B Reeves, RSACertTEFL *EFL*
Miss H M Richards, BMus (Cape Town), LTCL *Head of Music*
Miss I Schmidt, BA Hons, MA (London), PGCE *Head of Modern Languages*
Mrs M J Smith, CertEd (London), RSA/CTEFLA *Chemistry (part-time)*

Miss J Stranaghan, BA Hons (Belfast), PGCE *Head of English*
Mrs H Taylor, BA Hons (London), PGCE *French*
Mr P J Taylor, BSc Hons (Sussex), MEd (Brunel) *Physics*
Miss G Tucker *Housemistress*
Ms A Wilson, BA, PGCE *Art (part-time)*
Mr P Wilson, BEng (Nottingham), PGCE *Mathematics*

Visiting Music Staff:
Miss I K Attwater, GGSM, LGSM *Piano*
Mr M Baigent, GMusRNCM *Piano/Recorder*
Ms V Bajic (DipMus, Belgrade) *Piano*
Mr I Brener, BSc Hons *Singing*
Mrs B Cotes, (Trinity College of Music) *Classical Guitar*
Mrs C Forkes, BA Hons (Kingston) *Flute*
Ms B Grant, CertEd, AGSM *Strings (violin)*
Miss Y Gray, Licentiate (Trinity College, London) *Singing*
Mr J Marshall, LLCM(TD) *Piano*
Mrs V Stephen, GRSM, ARCM *Violin/Viola*
Mrs S L Trower, LRAM, ARCM, CertEd *Cello*
Ms N C Warren, DDME, BA, DipEd, MIEx *Clarinet/ Saxophone/Recorder*
Mr J West, BA Hons *Oboe*

Mrs A Blair, BEd Hons (Roehampton), MA, RSA (DSLD), DIT *Learning Support Unit*

Secretaries:
Admissions Registrar: Mrs D Hinton
Personal Assistant to Head: Mrs M Chapman
Senior School Office: Mrs S Ross
Marketing Officer: Mrs P Bradshaw

Bursary:
Accountant: Ms B Allen, DipCom (Open), FCA
Assistant Accountant: Mrs S Lawrence
Personal Assistant to the Bursar: Mrs R V Wallace

Medical Officer: Dr H Surtees, MB, BS (London)

St David's is an Independent School for Girls founded originally in London in 1716 and under the patronage of Her Majesty The Queen. Moving to Ashford in 1857 it now has plenty of room to breathe and play, in an oasis of 30 acres only 35 minutes by direct rail link from the City. Heathrow Airport is 15 minutes' car drive away, as are the main motorway systems linked by the M25. As a modern school in historic surroundings, St David's offers all the benefits of an 'all through' school, catering for girls from age 3 to 18. The Junior School goes up to age 11.

The School maintains a close dialogue with parents about their daughters' successes and problems, believing that praise and positive thinking are possibly the most powerful influences it exerts.

We aim to enable each individual to develop their talents to the full in a happy, caring environment upheld by a strong moral framework.

The General Curriculum includes English, Drama, Theatre Studies, Spanish, French, German, History, Geography, Mathematics, Physics, Chemistry, Biology, Religious Education, Information Technology, Business Studies, Food Technology, Art and Design, Class Singing, Musical Appreciation, Composition and Aural Training, PE, Swimming and Tennis. We have a Learning Support Unit on site. Most girls enter for 9 GCSE subjects. We have a 100% pass rate.

Duke of Edinburgh Award Scheme. There is a long standing commitment to this Scheme, because it promotes initiative, survival techniques, public service and the spirit of adventure.

St David's loves singing and all forms of instrumental music and revels in creative, artistic work.

The girls are also sports-minded. There is particular pride in our sponsored national and international gymnasts.

Hockey and netball are our Winter games: athletics and rounders in the Summer. Our own lake offers the opportunity to canoe. Swimming is available locally.

Sixth Formers have a wide variety of individual, pair and group sports available both on site and locally.

Sixth Form: Years 12 & 13. The one hundred strong Sixth Form runs on co-educational lines through a consortium arrangement with Halliford Boys' School. Mixed classes are conducted in both schools: some social time is also shared. At least 20 subjects are on offer at AS and A level, plus 'minority time' courses.

Most students are aiming for Universities: those who are not are equally welcome. We have a 94% plus pass rate at A level.

Girls of many nationalities are already enjoying their education here and our location, as well as our flexible boarding, encourages a cosmopolitan approach to life.

Parents should satisfy themselves that a guardian is appointed if their daughter joins St David's as a Boarder (ages 10 to 18).

Fees. (*see* Entrance Scholarship section) For September 2001: Boarders £4,190 per term; Weekly Boarders £3,930 per term; Senior Day Girls £2,390 per term; Junior Day Girls £1,790 per term; Reception Classes £1,410 per term; Nursery £18 per session.

Charitable status. The Most Honourable and Loyal Society of Ancient Britons is a Registered Charity, number 312091. It exists to provide high quality education for girls from the United Kingdom and abroad.

St Dunstan's Abbey

The Millfields Plymouth Devon PL1 3JL
Tel: (01752) 201350 (2 lines)
Fax: (01752) 201351

St Dunstan's is a Church of England Day and Boarding School for Girls. Founded in 1850 and then run by Anglican Sisters, the school has been under secular control since 1956. It has a high academic standard but is also proud of its caring atmosphere and its record of helping girls who have not realised their potential in other schools.

Visitor: The Right Reverend The Lord Bishop of Exeter

Governing Body:
Chairman: Mr M J Willacy, CBE
Vice Chairman: Mrs K Bairstow
The Right Reverend The Bishop of Plymouth
The Revd R J Carlton
Mr J A Constable, FRICS, JP
Mrs M Drake
Mr A Gough
Mrs J Haddon
Miss A Holt
Mr C A Howeson
Mr Lucas
Mrs P Phillips
Prebendary S Philpott
Mrs P Porter
Mr R J Rowden
Mr P J Russell
Mrs M Stoyel
Mr M Thompson
Mr B Walton
Miss S Wing
Miss A C C Wright

Staff:
***Headteacher:* Mrs B K Brown,** BA Hons

Deputy Head: Mrs S Knight, BEd Hons

Administrative Staff:
Bursar: Mrs L Killick
Bursar's Assistant: Mrs A Ellis
Headteacher's Secretary: Miss N Abery
Bursar's Secretary: Mrs A Asprey
Admissions Secretary: Mrs J Learmouth
School Secretaries: Mrs A Morris, Mrs S Cooper

Housemistress: Mrs J Penman
Matron: Mrs E Read

The School is situated close to Plymouth City centre in grounds of over 4 acres. It is close to the railway station and within walking distance of the bus station. The school moved to a new site in April 1996. It has a capacity of about 450 students and places for about 60 boarders in newly renovated accommodation. The boarding is flexible, offering accommodation from one night to full boarding in single study bedrooms.

Specialist teaching is available for non-English speakers and those with dyslexia. The sixth form is housed in a purpose-built Sixth Form Centre and is particularly strong for the size of the school.

Entrance to the Universities; GCSE and GCE 'A' level; the Associated Board of Music; The Guildhall School of Music and Drama; The Royal Academy of Dancing. Time Subjects help in the training of girls towards responsible citizenship.

The Flying Start Nursery is a school for boys and girls from 3 months to 4½ years of age. It is run by a well-qualified and experienced staff.

Girls normally enter the pre-Kindergarten class at the age of 4½ and pass into the Senior School at 11, having passed the entrance examination.

The Preparatory Department benefits from large airy classrooms that are pleasant to work in. High standards are expected of the preparatory girls who are taught good study habits and a love of learning.

Senior School new applicants are expected to reach an acceptable standard in the Entrance Examinations. The secret of the school's success lies in the small group sizes and happy atmosphere, this being particularly beneficial to those who are uneasy in large institutions.

Sports Activities include hockey, netball, tennis, rounders, swimming, athletics, sailing, archery, fencing, dry-slope skiing in addition to gymnastics. The school enters teams in Local School Tournaments, and has a gym club.

Musical activities include several school choirs and an orchestra. The School is affiliated to the Royal School of Church Music.

Extras include tuition in piano, guitar, violin, woodwind, diction, dramatic art, ballet, tennis coaching and English as a second language. Also, the famous London Theatre Company, The **Italia Conti** Academy, founded in 1911, has appointed St Dunstan's Abbey as an associated school. We can now offer, at weekends, tuition in all aspects of theatre training, singing, dancing and acting.

Fees per term. (Day) – Pre-Kindergarten, Kindergarten, Transition, L Prep and U Prep £1,166, Preparatory Department, Forms I and II £1,439, Senior School, Form III £1,785; Senior School, Form IV and above £1,953; Full Boarding (excluding tuition) £1,675; Weekly Boarding (excluding tuition) £1,318.

Scholarships. (*see* Entrance Scholarship section) Up to five open academic, music, art, drama and sports scholarships may be awarded annually on the results of an Examination held in February of the year of proposed entry at 11+. Two open Sixth Form scholarships may be awarded on the results of GCSE. Discretionary scholarships awarded for music and physical education. A new scholarship available is a drama scholarship in collaboration with the Italia Conti School.

Applications for admission should be addressed to the Admissions Secretary, and the Registration Form (sent upon request) should be completed and forwarded with the appropriate Registration Fee of £50.00. Early application is advised.

St Elphin's School

Darley Dale Derbyshire DE4 2HA
Tel: Matlock (01629) 733263
Headmistress: 732687
Bursar: 732314
Fax: (01629) 733956

Church of England Independent Boarding/Day School for Girls, in association with the Woodard Corporation.
Motto: *Nisi dominus frustra*

Patrons: The Bishops of Blackburn, Chester, Derby, Liverpool and Manchester

Trustees:
T H B Bowles, Esq, MA
Mrs R Chambers
R N Horne, Esq, JP

Chairman of the Governors: The Revd Canon J C Tomlinson

Governors:
T H B Bowles, Esq, MA (*Vice-Chairman*)
Mrs F Cannon, JP, DL, RGN, OHN
Mrs R Chambers
The Revd A Entwistle, BA, MEd, FRSA
The Rt Revd D C Hawtin, MA
Mrs K Hodkinson
R N Horne, Esq, JP
The Revd G C Matthews
Mrs L Moir
P J Moore, Esq
G L Preston, Esq, BA
The Very Revd Dr S S Smalley
Mrs M Smith, BEd

Co-opterd Governors:
The Revd Canon W Weaver, BA, BEd
Mrs D Ambrose

Parent Governors:
Mrs R Cable
Mrs L Sutton

School Solicitor: J B Naylor, 21 Palmyra Square, Warrington, Cheshire

School Accountants: Voisey & Co, Winmarleigh Street, Warrington

Secretary to the Governors: Mrs M Hunter

***Headmistress:* Mrs E Taylor**, BSc, MA, PGCE

Deputy Head: Dr D J Mouat, PhD, BSc, PGCE
Director of Studies: Dr D J Mouat, PhD, BSc, PGCE
Chaplain: to be appointed
Bursar: Mrs W M Renshaw
Registrar: Dr N Ogden, PhD, MEd, BA

Teaching Staff:

Art & Design:
Mrs E Hughes, BA, PGCE
Miss G Jones, BA, PGCE

Business Studies:
Mrs S J Taylor, BSc (Econ), PGCE
Mrs S Dakin, BA, PGCE

Dr N Ogden, PhD, MEd, BA
Mrs S J Spriggs, BSc, PGCE

Classics: Mrs P A Miles, BA, PGCE

Drama: Mrs D Botham, BA, PGCE

English:
Mrs V A Hodgson, BA, PGCE
Mr P Franks, BA, PGCE
Mrs E Prince, BA, PGCE, BDAD

Geography: Mr A K Coutts, BA, MSc, PGCE

History:
Mr P Franks, BA, PGCE

Information Technology:
Mr A K Coutts, MSc, BA, PGCE
Mrs S Dakin, BA, PGCE
Mrs S J Taylor, BScEcon), PGCE

Mathematics:
Mrs J A Corfield, BSc, PGCE
Mrs S J Spriggs, BSc, PGCE

Modern Languages:
Mrs G Martin, BA, PGCE
Mrs P K Outram, BA, PGCE
Miss R Xianyu (*Chinese*)
Mrs C Bathie, BA, PGCE (*Private German Lessons*)

Music:
Mr A J Teague, MA, FRCO, LRAM, PGCE (*Director of Music*)

Visiting Music Staff:
Miss D Buckley, BMus, ARMCM (*Clarinet, Saxophone, Bassoon*)
Mr N Clarke, BA, ARCM, CertAdvStud (RCM) (*Violin*)
Mrs R Dobbin, ARCM, LTCL (*Violin*)
Mrs S Hardie, LTCL, GGSM, PGCE (*Piano*)
Mrs B M Heap, BA
Mrs H Jenkinson, GRSM, ARMCM, LTCL, DipEd (*Piano & Recorder*)
Mrs F Jones, LTC, LWCMD (*Clarinet & Flute*)
Mr P Mold, TCert (*Piano & Recorder*)
Mrs M Mugnaini
Mr A Noble, DipRCM, ARCM, LWCMD, LTCL (*Piano and Cello*)
Miss D Saville, GRSM, ARCM, PGCE (*Cello & Bass*)
Mr B Towse, CertEd, LGSMDip (*Brass*)
Mrs K Ward, BEd (*Flute*)
Mrs R Wolfe, GRSM, LRAM (*Violin*)

Physical Education:
Miss C Jefferies, BA, PGCE
Mrs C James, TCert
Mrs J Davies, CertEd
Mr D Keal, LTA Coach

Visiting PE Staff: Mr R Lock (*Self Defence*)

Religious Studies:
Mrs W J Kenyon, BEd

Sciences:
Miss C Pilkington, BSc, PGCE (*Biology*)
Dr M Dinsdale, PhD, BSc, PGCE
Mr G T J Mayo, BSc, MIM (*Chemistry*)
Dr D J Mouat, PhD, BSc, PGCE (*Chemistry*)

Speech and Drama:
Mrs D Botham, BA, PGCE

Technology:
Mrs E Hughes, BA, PGCE (*Textiles*)

Infant/Nursery/Junior School Head: Mrs R E Duff, TCert

Junior School Form Teachers:
Miss M A Hall, BEd
Miss R Smith, BA, PGCE
Mrs K Gardiner
Mrs J Henson

Infant & Nursery Department:
Mrs R E Cuff, TCert
Miss E Boyer
Miss R Figg
Mrs S R Gregory
Mrs D Hewitt, TCert
Miss K Martin
Miss A Mellor, NNEB
Miss K McLennan

Careers:
Mrs S Dakin, BA, PGCE

Library: Mrs J Whiteside

Dyslexia/Special Needs: Mrs E Prince, BA, PGCE, BDAD

EFL: Mrs M-C Bogie

Housemistresses:
Mrs A Phillpot
Mrs J Hablehames
Miss G Jones, BA, PGCE
Miss C Jefferies, BA, PGCE
Miss R Xianyu

Sanatorium: Mrs J M Mitra, SRN, TCert

School Doctor: Dr P WS Lingard, MB, ChB, MRCGP, DRCOG

Administration:
School Secretary: Mrs H Fairley
Examination Officers:
Mrs P K Outram, BA, PGCE
Mrs E Wass, BA, DipEd
Laboratory Assistant: Mrs K Barrett
Clerical Assistant: Mrs J Davies, TCert

Visiting Teachers:
Mrs M Abrahams, BA, PGCE
Miss D Aldred (*Dance*)
Mrs E Hooper, BSc, PGCE (*Mathematics*)

St Elphin's is a boarding and day school for girls in the heart of the Peak District. The School is easily accessible from the north or the south of the country and is within easy reach of two airports.

We aim to challenge and stretch every pupil, providing a curriculum which is a mixture of traditional and modern. Latin is available as well as Computing, GNVQ Business Studies and Young Enterprise. During an extended day there is provision for further modern language study, a range of sports and leisure activities, public speaking and debating, Duke of Edinburgh's Award Scheme, Speech and Drama, instrumental music, choirs and orchestras.

The girls play tennis, hockey, netball, badminton and basketball, and take part in athletics. Many compete at county and national level. The swimming and life-saving programme is a speciality of the school and part of the curriculum of every pupil from the age of 5 upwards. Many pupils are interested in equestrian sports and we have a special relationship with the Red House Stables, which runs the country's most prestigious carriage driving centre.

Our Sixth Formers regularly gain places at either Oxford or Cambridge and all go on to higher education, some at places abroad.

The School maintains small classes and through a careful pastoral system attends meticulously to the needs of the individual. Specific learning problems such as dyslexia are quickly diagnosed by our specialists and each child works to an individual programme supervised by experienced staff.

The boarding accommodation, ranging through small

dormitories for the very young pupils, refurbished private cubicles with washbasins, rooms and networked study bedrooms for the Sixth Form, makes our school a beautiful and homely base for pupils who must live far from parents, or who choose to practice their independence. Boarders flourish in the working environment created by a team of experienced House staff.

The Junior School is well-provisioned with computer room, library facilities for each year group, music and CDT rooms. Specialist teachers enrich the Junior School curriculum and the pupils have full access to senior facilities for sports, drama, art and home economics.

Religious Instruction is that of the Church of England and is in the hands of the Chaplain and other qualified members of Staff. Girls are prepared for Confirmation every year.

Fees. Boarders £12,372-£13,572 per annum (Seniors). £10,278 per annum (Juniors). Day Girls £7,206 per annum (Seniors). £4,176–£5,676 per annum (Juniors). There are special bursaries for the daughters of Clergy in the 4 beneficiary dioceses of Manchester, Liverpool, Chester and Blackburn and reductions in fees for Church of England clergy daughters. Fees are inclusive of most extras. There is a 5% reduction for weekly boarders, and service families are offered a discount of at least 10%.

Scholarships. (*see* Entrance Scholarship section) On the results of examinations held annually in January, awards are available to external or internal candidates. These include special awards for daughters of clergymen of the Church of England. The School also offers Sixth Form scholarships and two Performing Arts scholarships of £1,500 per annum, plus free tuition in one or two instruments.

Entry. Infants (Girls and Boys from 3 years) interview only. 7+ – 10+ Junior Entrance Examination. 11+ – 13+ Senior Entrance Examination. All details about entry are available from the Headmistress's Secretary.

Charitable status. St Elphin's Church of England School is a Registered Charity, number 527183. Its aims and objectives are to provide a Christian-based broad education for girls.

Saint Felix School

Southwold Suffolk IP18 6SD
Tel: (01502) 722175
Fax: (01502) 722641

Motto: *Felix Quia Fortis*
Founded 1897

***Head:* Mr R Williams**, BSc

Heads of Department:

Mrs J E Alker, BSc Hons (CNAA) (Liverpool) *Physics (Head; Science)*
Miss M F D'Alcorn, BA Hons (Birmingham), MA (UEA) *Careers and History*
Mrs A Freeth, CertEd (IM Marsh College of PE) *Physical Education*
Mrs L Leicester, Licence Es Lettres (Grenoble) *French, Modern Languages*
Mr I Lomax *Design and Technology*
Mrs L Roberts-Rossi, BA Hons (Leicester) *Art & Design*
Mrs S E Smith, MA (Cantab) *Classics*

Music Department:
Director of Music: Mr V Scott, BA Hons (Liverpool), DipEdMus

Housemistresses:
Bronte: Mrs J Camburn, BSc Hons (Loughborough)
Somerville: Miss K Parkhouse,BA (Bangor)
Fawcett: Mrs W Holland, Headmistress, St George's/Mr P Holland, BSc
Fry (*UVI House*): Mrs A Freeth, CertEd (I M Marsh College of PE)
Gardiner (*LVI House*): Miss K Chapman, BSc (St Andrews)
Clough: Miss S McIntosh, BA Hons (Glamorgan)

Sanatorium Sister: Mrs A Carr, RN

Registrar: Mrs M A Feilden

Saint Felix stands in seventy-five acres of campus a mile and a half from the sea on the road that leads from the A12 to Southwold. Here, a hundred years ago, Margaret Isabella Gardiner founded a school where girls would be treated as reasonable beings; we honour that idealism today as we prepare girls to campaign in a competitive world. Saint Felix has all the facilities that you would expect of a top-flight girls' independent school – laboratories, technology workshops, drama studio, indoor swimming pool, squash courts. But more important, we create an environment where each individual may discover where her natural talents lie and where she can develop them to the full. While we help each girl towards the achievement of the qualities she needs for success in later life (100% A Level, A & B Grades 81% and 93% GCSE pass rates, A* & A 43% in 2000, sixty-five Gold Duke of Edinburgh awards in five years), we encourage her to enjoy learning for its own sake. From the day she joins us we make sure that every girl feels she is a valued and irreplaceable member of the community. Day girls are fully integrated in the life of the boarding houses. Sixth Formers live in separate lower and upper sixth Houses with single study bedrooms. Virtually all our girls go on to degree level courses.

Scholarships. (*see* Entrance Scholarship section) The School offers academic Scholarships of 33% of fees and Exhibitions of 20% on entry at 11+, 12+, 13+ or into the Sixth Form. The Hess Music Scholarship, for outstanding promise in music, is awarded annually. Value 33% of the fees. Drama and PE Scholarships are also available. Services discounts may be available.

Fees. Board and Tuition £3,935-£4,635 (Boarder), £2,430-£3,060 (Day).

Number of girls in School. 160.

Charitable status. Saint Felix School is a Registered Charity, number 310482. It exists to promote excellence in education for girls.

St Francis' College
Letchworth Garden City

The Broadway Letchworth Herts SG6 3PJ
Tel: (01462) 670511
Fax: (01462) 682361

Governors:
C G Nott *Chairman*
G Williams *Deputy Chairman*
Mrs P J Barlow
Mrs S Boardman
Miss J Bond
Miss E Ismay
Dr J Leigh
P McKay
B L Purser
Dr S Richardson

J M Stevens
Sister Joan Yates

Headmistress: **Miss M Hegarty**, BA, HDipEd, DMS

Deputy Headmistress: Dr P Gough, BA, MA, MTh *English*

Headmistress of Preparatory Department: Mrs C Whitty, CertEd

Bursar: Mr A Nutter, BSc, ARICS

Sixth Form Co-ordinator: Mrs A Cotterell, BA, DipEd *Geography*

School Chaplains:
Father Christopher Burgess
The Reverend Nicholas Setterfield

Full-time teaching staff:
Mr H Aitchison, BA, PGCE
Mrs M Campbell, BA, PGCE *Head of English*
Mrs C Clothier, BSc, MEd *Head of Biology/Teacher of Science*
Mrs A Cotterell, BA, DipEd *Head of Geography/6th Form Co-ordinator*
Mr B J Eaton, MA, BEd *Head of Religious Studies*
Mrs S Edgar, BA, PGCE *English/Careers*
Mrs M Fenton, BA, MA, PGCE *Head of History*
Mrs A Gillan, BSc, PGCE *Geography/Humanities*
Miss M Linacre, BSc, CertEd *Head of Mathematics*
Mr A Mallett, NDD, ATD *Director of Art*
Miss F McClymont, LTCL, GTCL, ARCM, PGCE *Director of Music*
Mrs M O'Leary, BSc, PGCE *Head of Chemistry/Teacher of Science*
Mrs S Pope, BEd, AdvDipIT *Head of IT/Technology Co-ordinator*
Miss S Roberts, CertEd *Head of Physical Education*
Miss V Semmens, BBS, DipBusAdmin, TTC *Economic/ Business Studies*
Mr P Taylor, BA, PGCE, DPSE *Head of German; English*
Mrs K Tipping, BSc, PGCE, MBA *Head of Science/Head of Physics*
Mrs J Whyte, BA, PGCE *Head of Foreign Languages*

Part-time teaching staff:
Mrs S Barfoot, BA *Science*
Mrs M Drew, CertEd *Physical Education*
Mrs C Guevel-Badou, BSc, PGCE *Mathematics*
Mrs L Hetherington, BA, PGCE
Mrs B Holland, BSc, DipEd *Science/Biology*
Mrs C Moore, BA, PGCE, TEFL, TESL *Director of International Sixth/English*
Mrs C Scupham, BA (Hons), DipEd *Latin*
Mrs A Taylor, BSc, PGCE *Mathematics*
Mrs R Thompson, BA, PGCE *French*
Mrs C Turner, CertEd *Physical Education*

Preparatory Department Staff:
Mrs C Whitty, CertEd *Headmistress/Teacher Prep 4 & 5*
Mrs S Bromelow, BA, CertEd *Senior Mistress/Year 2*
Mrs R Dowell *Classroom Assistant*
Mrs D Vaughton, CertEd *Reception*
Mrs J White, CertEd *Prep 4*
Mrs M Rayner *Classroom Assistant*
Mrs D Hunt, DipPrimEd *Prep 3*
Mrs H Stone, CertEd, MEd, AdvDipEd *Prep 6*
Mrs W Bailey, CertEd *Prep 5*
Mrs A Glew, BA, PGCE *Prep 6*
Mme A Greenhalgh, BA *French*
Miss S Neave, LAMDA *Speech & Drama*
Miss S Roberts, CertEd *PE/Games*
Mrs M Drew, CertEd *Swimming/PE*
Mrs C Turner, CertEd *Swimming/PE*
Mr P Cousins, FRCO, ARCM *Music*
Mrs A Byatt, CertEd *Kindergarten*
Mrs A Shiel, CertEd *Kindergarten*
Mr H Aitchison, BA, PGCE *Speech & Drama*
Mrs N Parsons *Classroom Assistant*
Mrs E Turner, BA, QTS Hons *Year 1*
Mrs H Wilderspin *Classroom Assistant*
Mrs B Hook *Classroom Assistant*

Residential staff:
Miss L Shields
Miss P Johnson
Mrs S Reed, CertFET, TEFL, BPhil, *Head of Boarding*

Visiting staff:
Mrs R Baldwin, BA, LTCL *Violin/Voice*
Mrs M Callaghan, DipEdPrim *EFL*
Mr C Crosby, BSc, ARCM *Oboe*
Mr H Gurden, ARCM *Brass*
Miss R Holbrow, GLCL, ALCM, LLCM, PGCE *Saxophone/Clarinet*
Miss D Jellis, LISTD, AISTD, SCLDD *Ballet and Tap*
Mr K Keightley, ARMC *Piano*
Mrs A Kelly, ARMC *Violin*
Ms C Lax, LRAM, LTCL *Singing*
Mr P Maundrell, GTCL, FTCL, LTGL, CertEd *Piano*
Mr N Pearce, BSc, PGCE *IT Consultant*
Mr M Stone *Guitar*
Mrs P Trussell, DipRSA, TEFL *EFL*
Mrs S York, LTCL, BSc, MSTAT *Flute/Alexander Technique*

Secretarial/Support Staff:
Mrs S Cain *Headmistress' Secretary/Admissions Secretary*
Mrs W Roskilly, BA *Prep Department Secretary*
Mrs Y Deards *Reprographics*
Mrs D Gilbert, BSc *Laboratory Technician*
Mrs M Valsecchi *Laboratory Technician*
Miss L Holmes *Assistant to Bursar*
Mr V Holder *Payroll Assistant*
Mrs T Dickerson *Bursar's Secretary*
Mrs M Langley *Receptionist*
Mrs E Swain *Receptionist*
Mrs C Clayden *Admin Assistant*
Mr D Daniels *Caretaker*
Mrs K Goude *Reception*
Mr D Swain *Reprographics*

The College was founded on its present site in 1933 by Sister Elizabeth of the Trinity, one of the Sisters of Charity of Jesus and Mary, an order of Roman Catholic Sisters based in Belgium. It grew steadily and flourished for the next fifth years until 1983 when the Belgian Order decided to reduce its educational commitment in the United Kingdom. The College was taken over by a newly formed Educational Charity, The St Francis' College Educational Trust, and is administered by a Board of Governors. St Francis' College is a member of the Governing Board of the Girls' Schools Association and of the Association itself. The College is also ISJC accredited.

Within the ethos of the College the aim is to provide a modern education based on Christian principles. Pupils receive close individual care promoting spiritual, moral, intellectual and physical development. The College recognises the unique qualities of each pupil and encourages social responsibility and respect for others. With its Roman Catholic foundation and heritage, St Francis' is a Christian community, ecumenical in outlook, which has always welcomed pupils from other faiths. Religious Education plays a vital part of life in the College and remains part of the curriculum for all girls in the College. Organised community service is an important feature of the extra-curricular life of the College for pupils from Year 10 and 11 and girls in the Sixth Form.

Education is about encouraging talent and developing new interests. Small classes ensure that each girl is given individual attention and a professional and dedicated staff enable pupils to achieve success in a wide range of areas both academic and extra-curricular. St Francis is committed to the provision of an all-round education where each girl is valued and each can contribute towards enriching the life of the community. There are 325 pupils on roll of whom about 50 are boarders.

Girls are prepared for GCSE and Advanced Level examinations as well as for Oxford and Cambridge entrance. The majority of girls take 10 GCSE subjects and stay on into the Sixth Form from where they proceed to University and Higher Education. The Sixth Form is housed in a newly-created Sixth Form centre, with common rooms, quiet study areas and tutorial offices.

Entrance to the College is by examination but due importance is also attached to school reports and interviews. Scholarships are available for entry at 7, 11, 13 and 16+.

Fees per term from September 2000 (*see* Entrance Scholarship section). Kindergarten from £415 (half-day) to £1,120 (full day including lunch); Reception (including lunch) £1,370; Preparatory Department from £1,650 to £2,050 (day) and £3,020 (weekly boarding) to £4,110 (full boarding). Senior School Day £2,230 to £2,630, and from £3,640 (weekly boarding) to £4,740 (full boarding).

Charitable status. The St Francis' College Trust is a Registered Charity, number 287694. It has charitable status on three counts: it advances education, it provides an education founded on strong Christian ethos and it also helps many of its pupils financially by means of Scholarships and Bursaries.

St Gabriel's School

Sandleford Priory Newbury Berkshire RG20 9BD
Tel: (01635) 40663
Fax: (01635) 37351

Church of England Independent Day School for Girls.
In membership of GSA, GBGSA and IAPS.
Numbers on roll 450

Patron: The Right Reverend Richard Harries, Bishop of Oxford

Chairman of Governors: Mr Paul Goble, FAA

Governing Body:
Mrs S Bowen
Mr N Chapman
Mr A C Cooper, FCA
Mr N Garland, BSc
Mr P Goble, FAA (*Chairman*)
Mr A Hills
Dr L J King, MD
Mrs N Lee, LLB
Revd Mrs J Ramsbottom
Mr M Scholl

Principal: Mr A Jones, LTCL, LWCMD

***Head:* Mrs J A Parsons**, CertEd London

Senior School Teaching Staff:
Mrs M Bayly, BA (Hons), PGCE *Latin*
Mrs R Black, BD (Hons), PGCE *Religious Studies*
Mrs S Cocker, BA (Hons), PGCE *History*
Miss S Davies, BA (Hons), PGCE *English*
Mrs D J Duff, BA (Hons) Liverpool, PGCE *Geography*
Mr I Edwards, BSc (Hons), PGCE *Head of Mathematics*
Mrs H Everett, BSc (Hons), PGCE *Chemistry*
Mr A Gibson, BSc, PGCE *Physics*
Mrs S Gillow, BSc, PGCE *Physics*
Mrs J Gustard, BSc (Hons), PGCE *Head of Sixth Form, Head of Science, Biology*
Miss K Hill, BA (Hons), PGCE *PE*
Miss A Keenleyside, BEd *Art & Design*
Mrs H Kinloch, MA (Hons), DipEd *Head of Middle School & Modern Languages*
Mrs S Kirke, MSc, BSc (Hond) *Psychology*
Mrs G Langley-Smith, Teaching Dip *Home Economics*
Mrs S J Lumley Kreysa, BA, CertEd *PE*
Mrs J Luton, BA (Hons), PGCE *Drama*
Mrs P Lyons, BA, PGCE *Business Studies*
Mr J M Mannion, BA (Hons), PGCE *Information Technology Coordinator*
Mrs B March, BA (Hons), PGCE *English & SEN*
Mrs H E Norris, MA, ALA *Librarian*
Mrs R Owen, BA, DipEd *Religious Studies & SEN*
Mrs P Parrington, CertEdHE *Technology Coordinator*
Mrs J A Parsons, CertEd *Head of Senior School & Mathematics*
Mrs R Payton, BA, PGCE *Classics and History*
Mrs P Peacock, BSc (Hons), CertEd *Mathematics*
Mrs H Porter, BSc (Hons), PGCE *Biology & Chemistry*
Mrs A Raine, BA (Hons), PGCE *French and German*
Mrs C Reseigh, BA (Hons), PGCE *French*
Mrs J Rowntree, GRSM, ARCM, PGCE *Head of Music*
Miss C A Searle, BEd *Head of PE*
Mrs S Sim, BSc (Hons) *Mathematics*
Mrs V Smith, MA, BEd (Hons) *English & Drama*
Mrs V Tierney, BA (Hons) *Art*
Mrs S Vines, BEd *HE Food & Textiles*
Mrs V Weston, BA (Hons), PGCE I>Classics
Mrs P Willetts, BA (Hons), PGCE *Geography*

Junior School Teaching Staff:
Mrs J H Felton, BEd (Hons), MA *Headmistress*
Mrs P A Baker, BEd (Hons), CertEd *Form Tutor Year 6S*
Mrs A A Cope, CertEd *Form Tutor Year 5S*
Miss E Lee, TCert *Form Tutor Year 6G*
Mrs C Moriarty, BEd (Hons), CertEd *Form Tutor Year 3S*
Mrs A Pasternakiewicz, BEd *PE Department & Form Tutor Year 5G*
Mrs R Robinson, BEd *Special Needs Department & Form Tutor Year 5F*
Miss A Smith, MA(Lit), BEd (Hons) *Form Tutor Year 3G*
Mrs M G Smith, CertEd, Dip Teacher of Deaf *Form Tutor Year 4G*
Miss C Townley, BA (Hons), PGCE *Form Tutor Year 4S*

Pre-Prep Department:
Mrs D Atkinson *Classroom Assistant*
Mrs J Bindloss Gibb, CertEd, Special Needs Diploma, Form Tutor Year 1G
Mrs S Bowden *Classroom Assistant*
Mrs C Charlton *Classroom Assistant*
Mrs P Dixon, CertEd *Pre-Prep Coordinator, Form Tutor Year 2G*
Mrs S Gimingham, BSc (Hons), QTS *Form Tutor Year 1S*
Mrs J Greenfield, CertEd *Form Tutor Reception G*
Mrs S Harding, Cert Learning Support *Teaching Assistant*
Mrs C Hedges *Classroom Assistant*
Mrs L Kuehnel, Cert Learning Support *Teaching Assistant*
Mrs K Lock, BA, CertEd *Form Tutor Year 2S*
Miss C Molyneux, Montessori DiptEd, RDSA *Nursery Teacher*
Mrs E J Spragg *Classroom Assistant*
Mrs G Tilley *Classroom Assistant*
Mrs A Toms, Cert Learning Support *Teaching Assistant*
Miss C Wilson, PGCE *Form Tutor Reception S*

Visiting Music Staff:
Mrs H Bartley *Violin*
Mrs Bevan *Harp*
Mr T Bryanton, CertTCM *Guitar*

Mrs J Oppenheimer, MA (Hons), AGSM&D *Singing*
Mr S Parker, ALCM, LLCM *Clarinet & Saxophone*
Mrs M Parkinson, LTCL(T) *Piano*
Mr D Reynolds, ARCM, LTCL *Recorder*
Mr N Streeter, CertEd *Percussion & Orchestra*
Mrs S Stringer, DipMusEd, RSAM *Piano*
Mr P Tarrant, ARCM, CertEd *Brass*
Miss C M Tyler, GRSM, ARCM *Piano*
Mrs A Williams, LRSM, GRSM *Cello*

Technicians:
Mrs P Bird (*Science*)
Mrs K Cook (*Art*)
Mrs K Pusey (*IT*)
Mrs A Warwick (*Science*)
Mrs S Yeoman (*Technology*)

Administrative Staff:

School Secretary: Mrs L Barlow
Bursar's Assistant: Mrs P A Jones
Bursar's Office Assistant: Mrs S Thomas
Registrar: Mrs J M Morris, BA (Hons)
Bursar & Clerk to Governors: Mr P P Sanders-Rose, JP, MA
Junior School Receptionist: Mrs P Williams

Chaplain: The Reverend Mrs Rita Ball

Visitors to St Gabriel's quickly recognise that this is no ordinary school. From Nursery to Sixth Form they are struck by the enthusiasm and sense of purpose of both staff and pupils. Some parents choose us because of our reputation for achieving exceptional academic standards, others welcome the individual attention which is given to all pupils.

The friendly and confident manner of our pupils is a reflection of the secure and caring environment in which they work. All pupils have the opportunity to take part in a wide variety of individual and team sports, music and creative arts. An extensive range of extra curricular activities are offered - well over 50 each week.

Each of our pupils is unique and our primary objective is to develop individual strengths and interests. These culminate in the high quality of our GCSE results, which in 2000 was 93.5% A*-C with an average of 9 passes per girl. Our new Sixth Form is gathering strength, catering for a broad choice of individual subject requirements aimed at university entrance. The year 2000 produced some fine A level results with the pass rate at 96% and 49% of grades at A or B.

Fees: From £1,630–£2,329.

Charitable status. S Gabriel and Falkland S Gabriel Schools is a Registered Charity, number 325060. It exists to provide education.

St George's School
Ascot

Ascot Berks SL5 7DZ
Tel: (01344) 629900
Fax: (01344) 629901
e-mail: office@stgeorges-ascot.org.uk

Member of GSA, GBGSA, BSA

Governors:
Mr J S Calvert *Chairman*
Mr G W P Barber, MA (Oxon), LVO
Mrs C Borwick, MSc, AMBDA, DipCST
Dr S Dalley
Mrs P J Everett, CertEd
Mr B Gallacher, OBE
Mr P Granger, FCA
The Hon R W Jackson, BA, ACA
Mrs A Laurie-Walker, BSc, MSc
Mr J B MacGill, MA (Cantab)
Mr J M G Markham, FCA

***Headmistress:* Mrs J Grant Peterkin,** BA Hons (Dunelm), PGCE

Deputy Head: Mrs J Tucker, MA (Oxon), PGCE *English*

Academic Senior Mistress: Mrs S van der Veen, MA (Oxon), MA (Warwick), DipEd *External Examinations Officer, French, German*

Pastoral Senior Mistress: Mrs F Booth, BA Hons (Southampton), PGCE *Head of Boarding, Film Studies*

Head of Sixth Form: Mrs C N Dyer, BA Hons (OU), MA (Edinburgh), PGCE *History*

Staff:
Mrs B Baker, PGDipSpLD, TDipITS, TDipWP *Office Applications and IT*
Mrs Y S Barratt, BA, PGCE *Geography*
Mrs J Bennett-Rees, BSc Hons, MA, CertEd *Mathematics*
Mrs M-C Bissinger, Licence d'anglais *French, Head of Alexander House*
Mrs E Brown, BEd *English, RS, Librarian, Careers*
Mrs P Came, PGDVS, LRAM, LLAM, GSMD *Speech and Drama*
Ms J M Cauldwell, BSc, MSc, MA TCert *Mathematics and IT*
Mr I Charnock, BA, PGCE *History of Art*
Miss S Cole, BA, MA, PGCE *English, Head of Darwin House*
Mrs J Crossley, BA Hons, PGCE, RSA DipEd in Drama *Drama*
Dr C Cushing, BA, PGCE, PhD *English*
Mrs M L Edwards, BA, CertTEFLA *French and TEFL*
Mrs C Evans, BA, PGCE *German*
Mrs C A Fidler, BA, PGCE *Art*
Mrs J A Fitton, BSc, MPhil, DIC *Biology and Chemistry*
Mrs M Fitzgerald, Dip *Speech and Drama*
Miss L Fontes, BA, PGCE *Classical Civilisation, Latin, French*
Mrs H Forbes, MA, PGCE *History*
Mr C Foreman, MA (Durham), BSc Hons (Edinburgh) *Economics, History*
Mrs S Foster, CertEd *Home Economics, Head of Churchill House*
Mr I Frankland, BEd *Physics*
Miss K Gilbert, BA Hons, PGCE *Textiles*
Mrs V J Green, MA, PGCE *Mathematics*
Ms J Gregory, BA, MA, PGCE *Art*
Ms J Gregson, BMus, CertEd, ARCM *Music*
Mrs J Hadnagy, MA, TCert *Chemistry and Physics*
Mrs J Hayward, DipTh, CertEd *Religious Studies*
Mr I G Hillier, FLCM, GLCM, LLCM, FCSM *Director of Music*
Mrs B Hughes, DipTEFL *TEFL*
Mrs J M Kennedy, BA *Geography, Head of Becket House*
Mrs C Lilley, BSc Hons, PGCE *Mathematics*
Miss K Lofthouse, Army PT1 Cert *Physical Education*
Mrs G Lovell, BA Hons, PGCE *Religious Studies, IT*
Mrs W Moyles, BEd *English, History*
Mr N Mohammad, HDipE, MA, BSc *Mathematics, ICT*
Mrs S Parry, BA, MPS *Spanish and French*
Mrs V Potter, BA, PGCE *French, History*
Mrs D Shaw, DipPE *Physical Education*
Mrs J Spooner, BSc *Science*
Mrs R Tear, BSc, PGCE *Science*
Miss T Whitmore, BEd *Physical Education*

Mrs A Wood, MA, CertEd *Junior Latin/Classics*
Miss H Woodruff, BMed *Music*
Mrs I Wright, BA *Drama*

Visiting Music Staff:
Miss A Barker, LTCL, ALCM *Clarinet and Saxophone*
Miss M M Bishop, ARCM, CertEd *Piano*
Mr J B Clark, BA *Guitar*
Mr D J Daniels *Wind Instruments*
Miss L Deacon, GRSM, LRAM *Cello*
Mr D A Edwards *Trumpet*
Mrs E Lee, MMus *Piano*
Mrs R A Merchant, BA Hons *Piano*
Mr S Perkins, BMus *Violin*
Miss S Salo *Harp*
Mr R S Smith *Percussion*
Mr M Stanley, BMus, ARCM *Piano*
Mrs A P Watson, BMus *Singing*

Pastoral Staff:

Pastoral Senior Mistress: Mrs F Booth, BA, PGCE

Housemistresses and Resident Tutors:
Mrs M Crowcroft, DipPE, TCert *Main School (2nd & 3rd Years)*
Mrs A Farmer *E N Loveday (Sixth Form)*
Miss K Gilman, BSc Hons (Loughborough) *Physical Education and Assistant Housemistress*
Mrs P Harrison-Sims *Main School (1st Years)*
Mrs S Hillier, BA, TCert *(5th Years) (Head of PSE)*
Miss A Morgan, MA Hons (Dundee), PGCE *Art, Assistant Housemistress*
Miss V Shipley *(4th Years)*

Pastoral Assistants:
Miss E Lockett
Miss C Woodhill

Bursar: Mr N C Fleming, CEng, MIMechE, CDipAF
Bursar's Assistant: Mrs A Pearce
Bursar's Secretary: Mrs S Moody

PA to the Headmistress and School Secretary: Mrs S A Burn

Admissions Secretary: Mrs J Gillate

School Doctor: Dr L Gardner, MB, BS

School Nurse: Mrs S Horth

Housekeeper: Mrs S Brownbridge

St George's is a School with approximately 135 boarders and 150 day girls. There are 75 in the sixth form. The UVIth run their own house as an independent unit. The small size enables Mrs Grant Peterkin to take a personal interest in each pupil. The school work is planned to give a sound general education for girls in classes of 15–20, which are 'streamed' or 'set'. A high academic standard is maintained without subjecting the girls to undue pressure and there is a happy and friendly atmosphere.

The School stands on high ground with lovely views in a beautiful estate. There are 8 hard tennis courts, a heated swimming pool, an extensive sports field for lacrosse and athletics and a magnificent Sports Hall opened in May 1992. There are four science laboratories, music school and computer rooms. There is a computer network which provides each girl with her own e-mail address, computer/network access from every classroom, common room and senior bedroom. The girls also have their own voice-mail.

The health of the girls is under the supervision of a registered nurse and the school doctor attends at least twice a week.

Curriculum. The curriculum includes English Language, English Literature, Drama and Theatre Studies, Mathematics, Information Technology, Combined Science, Biology, Chemistry, Physics, Latin/Classics, French, German, Spanish, Geography, History, Economics, Politics, Religious Studies, Art, History of Art, Textiles, Home Economics, Music, PE. Girls are prepared for GCSE, and, in the Sixth Form, for Advanced GCE, AS and A2 examinations, as well as for Oxbridge entrance. Girls throughout the school also work towards the examinations of the Associated Board of the Royal School of Music, LAMDA in Acting and Verse and Prose, and Computer Literacy and Information Technology. Girls are given full advice about careers and Higher Education.

At weekends girls take part in a wide variety of recreational activities including drama, art, music, pony treks, cooking, photography, sport, Duke of Edinburgh Award Scheme, first aid courses, school matches and visits to theatres and concerts, art galleries etc in London. Girls are encouraged to follow some form of social service. Girls may keep pets at school.

Entrance. Applicants take the Common Entrance examination for Girls' Independent Schools. The normal age range is 11+, 12+ and 13+. VI form entry requires at least 6 GCSE grades of C/B or better, with preferably B/A in subjects to be studied at A-level.

Fees. £4,990 per term boarding, £3,195 per term day.

Scholarships. Scholarships are available for outstanding potential as evinced by examination results. Music scholarships and instrumental awards are also available.

Extra Subjects. Other languages, Music (most instruments), Speech and Drama, Ballet, Modern Stage and Tap Dancing, Individual Tennis, Fencing, Archery and Golf, Dry Skiing, Riding, Skating and Yoga.

Charitable status. St George's School Ascot Trust Limited is a Registered Charity, number 309088. It exists to provide Independent Secondary Girls' Education.

St George's School for Girls
Edinburgh

Garscube Terrace Edinburgh EH12 6BG
Tel: 0131-332 4575
Fax: 0131 315 2035

Council:
Chairman: Sir William Reid, KCB, LLD, FRCPE, FRSE
Vice Chairman: Dr P Thomas, BSc, PhD
Mr H F Ballard, LLB, CA
Mrs S Edward, LLB
Mr J S Graham, BA
Mr C D G Guest, FRICS
Mrs W K Henderson, MHCIMA, MREHIS
Dr M M Macartney, MBChB, DPD, FRCGP
Mr A McGlynn, BA, MPhil
Ms E Mendl, BSc Hons, MSCP, SRP
Professor P Peattie, FRSA, MHSM, BSc, RGN, RSCN, RNT
Mrs A Smith, QC
Mr A R Steedman, MCIBS
Mr P L Wilson, BSc, MA, FIMgt, FIPD
Dr P Wyld, MB, ChB, FRCP (Glasgow), FRCP (Edinburgh), FRCPath, FFPM

Secretary and Treasurer to the Council: Mr M F Sinclair, MA, CA

Staff:

***Head Mistress:* Dr Judith McClure,** MA, DPhil (Oxon), FRSA, FSA Scot

Deputy Headmistress: Mrs E M Davis, BA (Hull), PGCE

Director of Studies: Mrs H A Mackie, BA (Birmingham), PGCE

Head of Primary and Early Years: Miss E K Childs, DipPrimEd, CertPrimSc

Head of Guidance: Miss P Lancaster, MA (Aberdeen), CertEd

Facilities Director: Miss M Imlah, MA (Aberdeen), MHCIMA

Academic/Exam Co-ordinator: Mrs A Armstrong, BSc (Hons), PGCE

Deputy Head of Lower School: Mrs M Rushworth, DipEd, DipRSA

Assistant Staff Upper and Lower Schools:
Mrs F Aiken
Dr J M C Alison, BSc, PhD (Edinburgh), BA (OU), PGCE *Physics*
Mr R H Allison, MA (St Andrews), BPhil (Oxon), CertEd *Classics, Co-ordinator of Extra-curricular Activities*
Dr J Arrowsmith, MA, MSc, DLitt, CPsychol, DipRelEd *Psychology*
Miss K Bargeton, BEd (Moray House) *Physical Education*
Miss M Bowman, MA (Hons), PGCE *English*
Mrs J Boyle, BSc (St Andrews), MSc(Ed) (Edinburgh), PGCE (Cambridge)
Miss S Brotchie, DA, PGCE (Edinburgh) *Textiles*
Mrs E J Bryce, MA (St Andrews), PGCE *Mathematics, Assistant Head of Sixth Form*
Mrs R W Carrington, BSc (London), PGCE *Biology, Head of Sixth Form*
Mrs A Comerford, BA, PGCE (London) *French and Italian*
Mrs G Corbett, BSc (Edinburgh), PGCE *Chemistry*
Ms B Doherty, MA, PGCE *French*
Miss K M Doig, BEd (Moray House) *Physical Education*
Dr F R Dorward, MA, PhD (Edinburgh) *Head of Spanish*
Miss N Doubble, BSc (Hons), PGCE *Biology*
Mrs I M Duncan, BA (Open University), Cert Ed *Head of Biology and Duke of Edinburgh's Award Scheme*
Mrs A B Edwards, BA (Dublin), DipEd *German and French, Joint Chairman of the European and Internaional Society*
Miss L C Emslie, DRSAMD (Glasgow), CertEd *Music*
Mrs C Erdal, BA (Bristol), MEd (Edinburgh), PGCE *English, Head of Careers*
Mr J J Fairhurst, BSc (Heriot-Watt), CertEd, CChem, MRSC, FRSA *Head of Chemistry and School Industry links*
Mrs J T Forbes, MA (Aberdeen), DipEd *English and RE, Year Tutor*
Mrs P J Foster, BArch (Edinburgh), PGCE, AdvDip *Head of Design Technology, Young Enterprise Co-ordinator*
Mrs H A Gilchrist, MA (Edinburgh), PGCE *Mathematics, Assistant Director of Studies and Mathematics*
Miss H B Gillard, MA (St Andrews), PGCE *Head of English and Drama*
Mrs L Gilmour, BSc (Hons), PGCE *Mathematics*
Mrs E M Grady, BSc (Hons), PGCE *Chemistry*
Mrs M E B Hall, BSc (St Andrews), PGCE *Biology and Young Enterprise, Head of Lower School*
Mrs J M Houston, DipPE (DCPE) *Physical Education*
Mr J Hughes, BEd *Director of ICT*
Miss H S Keenan, MA (Hons), PGCE *Classics*
Miss N L Kerr, BEd (DCPE) *Head of Physical Education*
Mrs A King, MA (Edinburgh), PGCE *Art*
Mrs K Knowles, BSc (Aberdeen), PGCE *Information Technology*
Mrs S Knox, BA (Exeter), PGCE (London) *Art and English*
Mrs A Lawrence, BA (Hons), DipEd *English*
Miss M E Loughran, MA (Hons), PGCE *Mathematics*
Mrs A Martinez, RSAPrepCertTEFL, RSADipTEFLA, Teacher of English to Students of other Languages
Mrs E McIlmoyle, BA (Belfast), PGCE *Geography*
Mrs C McInally, MA (Hons), PGCE *Mathematics*
Miss C M McNulty, MA (Edinburgh), PGCE *Italian and German*
Miss P M Paterson, BA (Strathclyde), DipLib *Librarian*
Miss E Patrick, MA Hons (St Andrews) *History*
Mrs D H Patterson, BSc (Edinburgh), PGCE *Physics*
Mrs E Peckham, MA, DipEd *Geography*
Mr P K Redfern, BMus, ARCO *Director of Music*
Mr P Ricca, BSc, HND, PGCE *Economics & Politics*
Miss A Rodriguez, BA
Miss C Savage, MA (Edinburgh) *Head of Geography*
Mrs K M Shaw, Diploma in Home Economics, C & G *Embroidery, Home Economics*
Mr N H Shepley, MA (Cantab), MEd (Edinburgh), CertEd *Head of History and Modern Studies*
Mrs P Sinclair, BSc (Edinburgh), PGCE *Chemistry and Lower School Science Co-ordinator, Co-ordinator of Community Links*
Miss N Smith, MA, PGCE *History and Modern Studies*
Mrs P R Spence, BA (Liverpool), PGCE *Head of Art*
Mrs C W Steedman, BEd (MHCE) *Physical Education*
Mrs L Steedman, CertEd (Moray House)
Mrs S Stenhouse, BA Hons (Napier), PGCE (Strathclyde)
Mrs K Y Stirling, BA, PGCE *English*
Ms J Stronach, BSc *Mathematics*
Mrs E Tait, BEd (Dunfermline) *Physical Education*
Mrs C Tate, Licence ès Lettres (Paris, Sorbonne), Agrégation d'Anglais *French*
Mr P Thomson, DipMusEd, PGCE (RSAMD) *Music*
Miss A Tomlinson, MTheol, PGCE *Religion/Philosophy*
Mrs E Traynor, MA (Edinburgh), PGCE *Head of German*
Mrs M E Walker, CertEd (Durham) *French and Learning Support, Joint Chairman of the European and Industrial Society*
Ms S Wall, BA, PGCE *Geography*
Mrs R Wearmouth, BA (Warwick), PGCE (Edinburgh) *English & Drama*
Dr S R Wherrett, BSc, PhD (*Reading*), PGCE *Head of Physics and Educational Administration* (*Internal*)
Mrs A Williams, MA (Oxon), DipEd *Director of Chinese Centre*
Dr B M Winning, BSc, PhD, PGCE *Biology*
Mrs G M Young, MA (Edinburgh), DipEd *Assistant Librarian*

Primary School:

Mrs M A Adams, BAMusEd (Kingston upon Thames), PGCE *Primary*
Miss A Bell, MA (Hons), PGCE *Primary*
Mrs L M S Bird, MA (Hons), PGCE, Montessori International Teaching Diploma
Miss L R Danzig, MA, PGCE *Learning Support*
Mrs H A Finlayson, MA (Edinburgh), PGCE Primary
Miss J M Forbes, Diploma in Primary Education, National Froebel Certificate, Infant Mistress and Nursery School Endorsement
Mrs S E Hay, BEd (Edinburgh) *Primary*
Ms B Hill, BEd *Primary*
Miss A Hippisley, BEd (Cambridge) *Primary*
Miss M Kidd, Diploma in Primary Education, National Froebel Certificate, Infant Mistress and Nursery School Endorsement
Mrs A E Lyburn, Diploma in Primary Education *Head of Lower Primary*
Mrs S Masson, GGSM, PGCE *Music*
Mrs M Munro, DipEd (Edinburgh)
Dr D E Oswald, BSc (Hons), PhD *Primary*
Mrs M J Peden, BA (Edinburgh), PGCE (Primary)
Ms V A Pickup, CertEd, BEd *Primary*
Mr R Porteous, BA, PGCE *Primary*
Mrs K E Rankin, MA (Aberdeen), PGCE (*Primary*)
Miss E S Ray, Diploma in Primary Education

Mrs T Robertson, BEd Primary
Mrs L Roger, MA, PGCE *Primary*
Mrs M Rushworth, Diploma in Primary Education *Deputy Head of Lower School*
Ms L Schwarz, BA, PGCE *Primary*
Miss J Stark, BEd (Edinburgh) (*Primary*)
Miss K Tulloch, LLB Hons (Aberdeen), PGCE
Mrs F C White, BSc (Glasgow), PGCE

Early Years:

Mrs E Stewart, MEd (Edinburgh) *Head of Early Years*
Mrs J Anderson, DipEd
Miss H Hyland, BEd (Hons)
Miss L Jack, HNC (*Childcare/Education*)
Miss M I Robertson, NNEB, ND, RSH
Miss L Service, HNC (*Childcare/Education*)
Mrs S Stewart, NNEB, SEN
Mrs J Watson, NNEB, ND

Visiting Music Teachers:

Piano:
Mrs E A Bannatyne, BA (Moscow), MMus
Miss M Dunbar, DipMusEd (RSAM), ARCM
Mrs A R Hardman, LRAM
Miss A Lewis, AGSM
Mrs S MacLeod, BA
Mrs L Redfern, BMus Hons (Edinburgh), LRPS

Flute:
Ms A Higgins, BMus Hons (Edinburgh)
Miss S Evans, BA, PGPerf

Oboe:
Miss R E Pollard, BA

Clarinet/Saxophone:
Miss R Cohen
Mrs A J Murray, LRAM, ARCM
Ms J Nicholson, GRSM (Hons), DipRCM
Ms S A Smart

Bassoon: Miss V Dyason, BA, MMus, RSAMD, BA (Hons)

Violin/Viola:
Miss J Carpenter, LRAM
Miss A E M MacDonald, ABSM
Mr R W Long, ARCM, DipRCM, ACT *Head of Strings*
Mrs P Murray, DRSAMD, PGCE

Violoncello: Miss P Hair, DRSAMD

Double Bass: Mrs C Melrose, DRSAMD

Trumpet/Trombone: Mr M Bennett, RNCM (Perf), BSc

French Horn: Ms J Johnstone

Guitar: Mr J M Watson, MMus (Perf), BA (MusPerf), LTCL, ALCM

Celtic Harp (*Clarsach*): Miss S Askew, MMus, BA

Percussion:
Mr G Williamson
Mr J Pouter, BA (Hons), CPGS

Recorder:
Mrs S Masson, GGSM, PGCE
Miss S Evans, BA, PG (Perf)

Singing:
Mrs E A Bannatyne, BA (Moscow), MMus
Miss A Lewis, AGSM
Mrs S Macleod, BA (Hons)

Headmistress's Personal Assistant: Ms D Thomas

Leader of After School Care: Mrs S Anderson

After School Care Assistant: Mrs S Mohamed

St George's was founded in 1888 to provide a full education for girls and to take the lead in the advance of the women's educational movement in Scotland.

There are 565 girls in the Secondary Department and 327 in the Primary Department, 68 in the Nursery; 902 Day, 58 Boarding.

The age range covered is from 5–9 in the Primary Department and from 9–18 in the Secondary Department. Entry at 5 (Interview), at 9 (Interview and Test) and at 11 (Interview and Test). The Nursery Department accepts girls and boys between the ages of 2 and 5.

St George's is administered by its own Council and is on the Register of Independent Schools and its Head is a member of the Girls' Schools Association. It stands in its own extensive grounds which include Hockey and Lacrosse pitches, one of which is floodlit and all-weather, and 12 Tennis courts. There is also a purpose-built Centenary Sports Hall, which contains a main sporting area large enough for five Badminton Courts and marked out for indoor Hockey, Lacrosse, Volleyball, Basketball, Netball and Tennis. In addition there are two Squash Courts. A new St George's Centre has recently been completed.

In 1991 the purpose-built Robertson Music Centre provided an auditorium with seating for 200, 12 music cells and two classrooms. The Upper School Science Laboratories have been completely refurbished, and there is an extensive IT network with Internet access.

St George's prepares pupils for Standard Grade, the Scottish Higher examinations and for the GCE 'A' level. Approximately 8 pupils a year enter Colleges in Oxford and Cambridge.

Well over 95% of leavers proceed to degree courses at University.

Fees and Charges (the Session has 3 Terms). Registration Fee: The registration fee of £30 must accompany the Application Form. Tuition and Boarding Fees (per term): Tuition fees, U4–U6 £1,900; Remove-L4 £1,725; Primary, 3, 4, 5 and 6 £1,350; Primary 2 £1,170; Primary 1 £1,025; Nursery £595 morning; £400 afternoon; £995 9am–3pm; £1,540 9am–6pm; Nursery (2-3 years) £310–£460. Boarding fees (in addition to the tuition fee) £1,900. Plus £75 Fabric Fee per term at all stages.

When three or more sisters are pupils at the same time, the third and subsequent sisters will receive a discount of one-third on class fees. A comparable discount is given where families have three children at St George's and the Edinburgh Academy at the same time. A limited number of Scholarships and Means-Tested Bursaries will be available for entry into L4 (S1/Yr8), U4 (S2/Yr9), L6 (S5/Yr12) and U6(S6/Yr13).

Text books are provided by the School without charge for use during the Session. Extra subject fees are paid in full for each pupil.

Extra Subject Fees. Extra subject fees (per term) Pianoforte £148, Recorder charged according to number in group and length of lesson, Solo Singing £148, Riding by arrangement, Speech Training £27.50, Curling by arrangement, Photography £95 (per term), Judo £45 per term.

Charitable status. St George's School for Girls is a Registered Charity, number 8667 Scotland. It exists to promote educational excellence for girls.

* Head of Department	§ Part Time or Visiting
† Housemaster/Housemistress	¶ Old Pupil
‡ See below list of staff for meaning	

St Helen and St Katharine

Abingdon Oxon OX14 1BE.
Tel: (01235) 520173
Fax: (01235) 532934
e-mail: info@sthelens.demon.co.uk
website: www.sthelens.oxon.sch.uk

The School (which was founded by the Community of S. Mary the Virgin, Wantage in 1903) is a Church of England Independent School for day girls. There are 595 girls of whom 154 are in the Sixth Form.

Governors:
Mrs P Cakebread (*Chairman*)

Mrs R Anthony
Prof K M Burk
Miss J E Cranston
Mr H W P Eccles, QC
Dr S V Evans
Lady C Goodhart
Mr D Lea
Mr T A Libby
Mrs D M May
Mrs M A R Varju
The Revd Flora Winfield
Mr J J H Wormell

Bursar and Clerk to the Governors: Lt Col A Douglas, MA (Cantab), FIMgt

***Headmistress:* Mrs C L Hall**, MA (Oxon)

Deputy Headmistress: Mrs R Gunn, MA (Cantab)

Chaplain: The Revd Pauline Seaman, BD, AKC (London)

Head of Upper School: Mrs V Burbank, BA (Bristol), PGCE

Head of Middle School: Mrs C Townsend, BA (London), PGCE

Head of Lower School: Mrs C Shebbeare, BA (Exeter), M-ès-Lettres (Strasbourg), PGCE

Staff:

Religious Studies:
The Revd Pauline Seaman, BD, AKC (London), PGCE
Mrs J White, BA (Southampton), PGCE

English:
Mr K Durham, MPhil (Liverpool), PGCE
Mrs C Nash, MA (Oxon), PGCE
Ms J Atyeo, BA (Leeds), PGCE
Miss S Matthews, MA (Birmingham)
Mrs R Robinson, JP, BA (Hull), PGCE
Mrs J Murphy, BEd (London)
Mrs V Webb, BA (Oxon), PGCE

Business Studies:
Mrs N King, BA (Oxford Brookes)

Classics:
Mrs D Bennett, MA (Oxon), PGCE
Mrs E Poole, MA (Cantab), CertEd
Mr R Batters, MA (Cantab), PGCE
Mrs D Dicks, MA (Natal)

Modern Languages:
Mrs L Astbury, BA (Birmingham), PGCE
Mrs Y Hurrell, MA (London), PGCE
Mrs M Lynes, LAUREA, BA (Milan), PGCE
Mrs C Friend, MA (Oxon), MA (Reading), PGCE
Mrs C Shebbeare, BA (Exeter), M-ès-Lettres (Strasbourg), PGCE
Mrs A Waissebein, LFR (Lisbon)
Dr G Clark, MA (Cantab), DPhil (Oxon), PGCE
Mrs I Foster, BSc (Peru), MA (Reading), CertEd

Geography:
Mrs V Burbank, BA (Bristol), PGCE
Mrs E Gale, BSc (Manchester), PGCE
Mrs J Grey, BSc (Manchester), PGCE
Mrs L McLaughlan, MA (Glasgow), CertEd
Mrs C Townsend, BA (London), PGCE

History:
Mr G Williams, MA (Cantab)
Mrs S Green, BA (Oxon), BA (Open)
Mrs E Poole, MA (Cantab), CertEd
Miss A Murphy, BA (Oxon), PGCE

Mathematics:
Dr P Secker, PhD (Birmingham)
Mrs S Govier, BA (Reading), DipEd
Mr D Ireland, BSc (Leicester), FRAS
Mrs A Jennaway, BSc (Bristol), PGCE
Mrs B Owen, BSc (Southampton), CertEd, LRAM
Mrs H Rich, BSc (Herts), MEd (Kent), PGCE
Mrs C Russell, BSc (London), PGCE

Science:
Mrs K J Edwards, BSc (Nottingham), PGCE
Mrs J Bell, BSc (Bristol), MSc (Oxon), PGCE
Mr M Rich, MA (Oxon), MA (Kent), PGCE
Mrs E Rossington, BA (Oxon), PGCE
Mrs J Armstrong, BSc (Leeds), PGCE
Dr T Bainbridge, BSc (Leeds), PhD (London)
Mrs H Rich, BSc (Herts), MEd (Kent), PGCE
Mrs A Watson, BSc (Bath), PGCE
Dr M Forrest, PhD (Newcastle)
Mrs S Woollacott, BSc (Bristol), PGCE
Mrs R Gunn, MA (Cantab)
Mrs J Peat, BSc (Bristol), PGCE

Art and Design:
Mrs J Jackson, DipArt and Design (Bristol), ATC
Mr K Stiles, BA (Falmouth), PGCE
Miss O Sutherland, BA (Loughborough)
Ms P Ellis, MA (London)
Mrs J McDonald, BA (Exeter), CertEd
Miss A Wardell, BA (Derby)

Technology:
Mrs J Jackson, Dip Art & Design (Bristol), ATC
Mr J Naisby, ONC App Physics, HNC Mech Eng, BTec Electronics
Mrs H Rich, BSc (Herts), MEd (Kent), PGCE
Miss O Sutherland, BA (Loughborough)
Miss A Wardell, BA (Derby)

Food Studies:
Mrs P Adams, CertEd (Gloucester)

Information Technology:
Mrs J Simpson, BSc (Victoria, NZ)
Mrs R Gunn, MA (Cantab)
Mrs J Dunwoody, CertEd (Dartford)

Physical Education:
Mrs J Dunwoody, CertEd (Dartford)
Mrs S Evans, CertEd (IM Marsh), CPE
Mrs I Harrison, CertEd (Kirkbyfields, Liverpool)
Miss J Hunt, BEd (St Mark & St John)

Year 5 Class Teacher: Mrs H Townsend, BEd (Oxon)

Year 6 Class Teacher: Mrs E Gale, BSc (Manchester), PGCE

Library:
Mrs S Harries, BA (Birmingham), MA (London), PGCE, DipLib, ALA
Mrs K Gray, BSc (Manchester)

Music:
Mr A Tillett, BMus (Birmingham), LRAM, ARCM
Mrs E Oxley, MA (Oxon), PGCE
Mr A Bottrill, MA (London), GGSM
Mrs M J Bevan (*Harp*)
Mr R E Cutting (Kneller Hall) (*Brass*)
Ms J Evans (*Double Bass*)
Mrs C Filleul, ARCM (*Violin, Viola and Guitar*)
Mrs V Findlay, MA (Glasgow), LRAM (*Cello*)
Mr P Foster, LTCL (*Flute and Saxophone*)
Mrs H S Haskell, ARCM (*Violin and Viola*)
Mrs E Hutchings, GTCL, LTCL, LRAM (*Piano*)
Mrs Kanerick (*Singing*)
Mrs C King, MA, PhD (*Oboe*)
Mrs C Manship (*Organ*)
Miss R E Martin, AGSM (*Singing*)
Mrs S Mears, MA (Oxon), LRAM, PGCE
Mr T Palmer (*Percussion*)
Miss F Parker (*Horn*)
Mr N Somerville (*Trombone*)
Mrs M R Thorne, BAMusEd, LGSM (*Clarinet*)
Mr R Thorne (*Flute*)
Miss K S Wills, GTCL, LTCL (*Flute and Recorder*)

Modern Dance:
Mrs J Stew, AISTD, RAD Reg teacher
Miss H Reynolds

Careers:
Mrs J Armstrong, BSc (Leeds), PGCE
Mrs L Evans, BA (Swansea), PGCE
Ms A McGrath, BA (Oxon), MA (Open), PGCE

Medical:
Dr H Hodgson, MBBS
Nurse K Ashton
Nurse A Dexter
Mrs F Campbell, BEd (Durham)

The School is located on the outskirts of Abingdon with easy access from Oxford and surrounding villages. It is situated in extensive grounds which include tennis and netball courts, lacrosse pitches, athletics track and a heated open-air swimming pool.

The original building dates from 1906 with extensions being added at various times over the past 40 years. The School has an ongoing building programme which saw the completion of a purpose built concert hall in 1992. Additional science laboratories were completed in September 1997 and a new Sixth Form Centre opened in January 1999. A new building was opened in September 2000 housing the English and Modern Languages Departments. Specialist rooms exist for Art, Food Studies, Geography, Information Technology, Pottery and Technology. These are complemented by a careers room, a library, Science laboratories, theatre and a gymnasium and sports hall for indoor games.

The School encourages girls to maintain a broad and balanced curriculum as long as possible. Subjects included in the curriculum are: Art, Biology, Chemistry, Drama and Theatre Studies, Economics, English Language, English Literature, Food Studies, French, Geography, German, Greek, History, History of Art, Information Technology, Italian, Latin, Mathematics, Music, Physical Education, Physics, Politics, Pottery, Religious Studies, Spanish and Technology.

There is a strong musical tradition in the school with many girls learning at least one instrument. Tuition is provided in all major instruments including the harp and organ. There are three orchestras, five choirs and numerous ensembles.

Mutually beneficial interchanges exist with two local boys' schools giving opportunities for joint activities in music and drama. For selected subjects in the Upper School girls are taught with boys from Abingdon School, extending the choice of courses available.

A programme of personal and social education encourages girls to care for themselves and others. Social service is emphasised and all pupils are encouraged to take part in the wide range of extra-curricular activities available at the School including: The Duke of Edinburgh Award Scheme, Young Enterprise, debating, fencing, modern dance, sailing and rowing.

The School has its own Chapel in which a weekly Eucharist is offered to staff and girls.

Admission is at 9+, 10+, 11+ and 16+. An entrance examination is held in January for 9+, 10+ and 11+ for admission in the following September. Girls are accepted into the 6th Form on the basis of their GCSE results and an interview. There may be occasional vacancies in other years of the school.

Bursaries are awarded at 11+. Governors' Scholarships are awarded at 11+ and 16+; Music Scholarships are available at 11+ and are awarded to girls already in the school from 14+.

Fees. £1,979 per term.

Charitable status. The School of St Helen and St Katharine Trust is a Registered Charity, number 286892. The Trust was established to promote and provide for the advancement of education of children in the United Kingdom and elsewhere. Such education to be designed to give a sound Christian and moral basis to all pupils.

St Helen's School for Girls

Northwood Middlesex HA6 3AS
Tel: (01923) 843210
Fax: (01923) 843211

Founded 1899.
Independent Boarding and Day School for Girls.
Member of GSA and GBGSA.

Council of Governors:

Chairman: Miss R Faunch, BSc (Manchester)
Professor B Aylett, MA, PhD (Cantab), FRSC, CChem (nominated by the University of London)

Mr D Bucks, FCA
Mr M Clark, MSc (London)
Mrs J Davies
Mr H Forsyth
Professor V Isham
Mrs J Kirchheimer
Mrs J Lewis
Mrs A Little
Miss J Priestley, SRN
Mrs A Roberts, MA (Oxon)
Mr T R Roydon, BSc (London), MBA (Pittsburgh)
Dr M Stanley, BSc (London), PhD (Bristol), MB (Adelaide), MA (Cantab) (*Nominated by the University of Cambridge*)
Mrs C Thompson, BA, FCA

Staff:
***Head:* Mrs M Morris**, BA Hons (London)

Deputy Heads:
Mrs P Cullen, MSc (London)
Mrs J Roseblade, MA (London)

Head of Sixth: Mrs J Taylor, BA (Cantab)
Head of Upper School: Mrs E Cadman, BSc (London)
Head of Middle School: Mrs L Landsman, BA (Dublin)
Head of Junior School: Mrs C Thorburn, MA (London)

Head of Little St Helen's: Mrs G Gosling, CertEd

Asst Head of Sixth: Mrs M Bowman, BEd (Leeds)
Asst Head of Upper School: Mrs A Fairweather, MA (Edinburgh)
Asst Head of Middle School: Miss A Pitt, BSc (Leicester)
Asst Head of Junior School: Mrs J Williamson, GTCL
Asst Head of Little St Helens's: Miss A Dhar, BA

Professional Development Manager: Mrs A Weaver, MA (St Andrews)

English & Drama:
Director English and Drama: Dr T Kingston, BA, PhD (London)
*Ms M Flatto, BA (Manchester) (*Head of Drama*)
Mrs V Beckley, BA (Leeds)
Mrs R Hershman, CertEd (Froebel)
Mrs K Martin, BA (Oxon
Mr A Newton, MA (London)
Mrs D Sinclair, MA
Mrs A Thomas, BA (London)
Mrs J Threlfall, BA (Leicester)
Mrs S de Vaux-Balbirnie, BA (Reading)

Mathematics:
*Mr N Tully, BSc (York)
Mrs E Cadman, BSc (London)
Mrs J Creed, BSc (London)
Mrs L Landsman, BA (Dublin)
Mrs J Malcolm, BA (Oxon)
Mrs M Moore, BA (Cantab)
Mrs T Onac, BSc (London)
Mrs A Pateli, CertEd (St Mary's College)
Mrs J Vann, BSc (London)

Science:
Acting Head of Science: Mrs S Williams, BSc (Exeter)

Biology:
*Miss V Marro, BSc (London)
Mrs P Cullen, MSc (London
Miss R Lee, BSc (Liverpool)
Miss M Stretton, BSc (York)
Mrs H Wooldridge, BEd (Dundee)
Dr A Young, BSc (Leeds), PhD (Reading)

Chemistry:
*Mr N Parry, BSc (Bangor)
Mrs J Arthur, BSc (Reading)
Mrs J D Barnatt, BSc (Dunelm)
Mr C Foster, BSc (Brunel)

Physics:
*Mrs S Williams, BSc (Exeter)
Mrs J Barnatt, BSc (Durham)
Mr D Floyd, BEd (Ontario)
Miss K Johnston, MSc (St Andrews)
Mrs S Wardley, BSc (Southampton)

Modern Languages:
Head of Modern Languages: Mrs M Gerry, MA (Oxon)

French:
*Mr E Terris, BA (London)
Mrs D Clayden, BA (Leeds)
Mrs M Gerry, MA (Oxon)
Mrs B Priestman, MA (Edinburgh)
Ms N Stephenson, MA (Cantab)
Mrs A Twining, BA (London)
Mrs J Warton, L-ès-L (Nancy)

German:
*Ms N Stephenson, MA (Cantab)
Mrs A Fairweather, MA (Edinburgh)
Mrs K Forman, BSc (Surrey)

Italian:
Mrs N O'Hagan, CertEd

Japanese:
Mrs M Ishikawa, MA (London)

Spanish:
*Mrs J Orme, BA (Dunelm)
Mrs D Clayden, BA (Leeds)
Mr R Oliver, BA (Manchester)

Art:
*Ms E Senior, DipAd, BA
Mrs F Ames, BA (Open)
Mrs N Beckett, NDD
Miss C Ng, BA (York)

Economics & Business Studies:
*Mrs M Bowman, BEd (Leeds)
Mrs F Britten, BEd (UWE), BSc (OU)
Mrs A Fairweather, MA (Edinburgh)

Careers:
*Miss E McKinley, BA (Heriot-Watt)
Mrs M McIntosh, TCert (London)

Classics:
*Dr G Sharples, BA, PhD (London)
Mr S Jenkin, BA (Oxon)

Design and Technology:
*Mr B Gee, MA (OU)
Mr A Johnson, BSc (Essex), MSc (Aberdeen)
Mr R Shaikh, BA (Brighton)
Miss K Weston, BSc (Nottingham Trent)

Geography:
*Miss E Rynne, MA (London)
Mrs C Beake, BA (London)
Miss A Pitt, BSc (Leicester)

History and Politics:
*Mrs C Hill, BA (Newcastle)
Mrs F Ames, BA (Open)
Mr R Oliver, BA (Manchester)
Miss M Palmer, BSc (Brunel)
Mrs J Taylor, BA (Cantab)
Mrs A Weaver, MA (St Andrews)

Home Economics:
Mrs M McIntosh, TCert (London)

Information Technology:
*Mr N Schofield, BA (OU)
Mr A Johnson, BSc (Essex), MSc (Aberdeen)
Miss C Ng, BA (York)
Mr R Shaikh, BA (Brighton)
Mrs T Dombey *IT/Curriculum Support*

Music:
Director of Music: Mr R Lambert, MA (London)
Mrs R Yates, GRSM, LRAM, ARCM

Visiting Music:
Miss H Astrid, DipRAM *Singing*
Mrs A Brennan, BMus *Violin/Viola*
Miss L da Silva, BMus Hons, LRAM *Recorder and Theory*
Mrs L Fletcher, GRSM, ARCM *Piano*
Mr A Francis, LRAM *Clarinet*
Miss E Frith, BMus Hons, DipGSMD *Viola/Violin*
Mrs S Furzey, ATCL, ALCM *Piano*
Mr A Gathercole, GGSM, ALCM *Brass*
Miss K Grace, GTCL *Flute*
Mrs E Grant, LLCM, A(Mus)LCM *Piano*
Miss R Hilser-Smith, BMus *Flute*
Miss V Kavina, GTCL *Violin*
Mrs S Lawman, ARCM, GRSM *Piano, Singing*
Mr I Marcus *Saxophone*
Mr N Martin *Drums*
Mrs S Martin, BA, PGCE, RSAMD *Oboe*
Mrs J Maclean, LTCL(TD) *Cello*
Mrs S Murdoch, LRAM, ARCM *Piano*

Mr T Parks, BMus, ARCM *Head of Piano*
Miss M Pollock, DipMusEd, RSAMD, CertAdvStudies (GSM) *Bassoon*
Mr E Rance, LGSM *Classical Guitar*
Mr N Thompson, ALCM, LLCM(TD), GLCM, PHTL *Brass*
Miss S Turner, BMus, DipRCM *Flute*
Miss J Wilson, BMus, LGSM *Double Bass*

Physical Education:
*Mrs R Jackman, CertEd (Bedford)
Miss S Heath, MA (London)
Miss V Hill, BSc (Brunel)
Mrs L Liddelow, BA (Exeter)
Mrs E Muddiman, BA (Leeds)
Miss C Ng, BA (York)

Religious Studies:
*Miss V Chamberlain, MA (Cantab), MA (Oxon)
Miss Y Cawdell, BA (Durham)

Library:
*Ms E Howard, BA, ALA Chartered Librarian
Mrs S Gleave
Mrs G Hill, BA, DipLib
Mrs J Turnbull

Junior Department:
*Mrs C Thorburn, MA (London)
Miss F Bristow, BEd (Worcester College)
Mrs K Buchanan
Mrs E Crawford
Mrs K Delaney, BA (Cardiff)
Miss G Furphy, BEd (London)
Mr M Hoffman, BA (S Africa)
Mrs J Huntingdon, BEd (Australia)
Mrs R Jackman, CertEd (Bedford)
Mrs S Kneller, MA (Open)
Mrs N Lawson, BA (Bath)
Miss H Murfet, BMus (Bangor)
Mrs M Pratt, BEd (Australia)
Miss M Schrinner, BEd (Australia)
Miss R Shillinglaw, BEd (Chester College)
Mrs L Wilkinson, BA (Warwick)
Mrs J Williamson, GTCL
Mrs L Wood, BA (Ambassador College)

Little St Helen's (Pre-Preparatory Department):
*Mrs G Gosling, CertEd
Mrs E Crawford
Miss L Crocker, BEd (Cantab)
Miss T Denham, NNEB
Miss A Dhar, BA
Miss D Donaghy, BA (Cantab)
Mrs A Ebbutt, LRAM
Miss V Matthews, BA (Hull)
Miss C Sewell, BEd
Mrs P Spokes

Welfare Officer: Mrs M da Rocha

Boarding:

House Mistresses:
Mrs H Wooldridge, BEd (Dundee)
Mrs B Priestman, MA Hons (Cardiff)

Assistant House Mistress:
Miss M Stretton, BSc (York)

Housekeeper: Mrs I Leach

Independent Listener: Dr C Herbert

Administration:

Bursar and Clerk to the Council: Mrs F Button, BSc (Leeds), MBA
Accountant: Mrs P Durrant
Domestic Bursar: Mrs L Toms
Registrar: Mrs P Witterick
Network Manager (Admin): Mrs P Goodman
PA to the Head: Mr D McLaren
PA to Bursar: Mrs T Bunting
Head's Secretary: Ms J Coleman
Secretary to Head of Junior School: Mrs J Botten
Secretary to Head of Little St Helen's: Mrs L Jones
Administrative Assistant (Marketing): Mrs L Gower
Senior Administrative Assistant: Mrs V London
Administrative Assistants: Mrs R Disney, Mrs C Sampson, Mrs L Quilley
Accounts Office: Mrs C Jay, Mrs J Mahon
Stationery: Mrs E Green

Technicians:
AV Technician: Mrs J Dean
Design Technology: Mr A Nice
Art Technician: Mrs S Page
Junior School: Mrs J Webb
Science: Mrs A Hewlett, Mrs Z Alidina, Mrs E Jacob, Mrs C Nichols, Mrs R Roberts

After School Assistants: Miss J Bressloff, Mrs K Brown

School Doctors:
Dr P R Goodwin, MB, BS
Dr C Etherington

School Nurses: Mrs J Dibbo, RGN, Mrs S Shackman, RGN
School Counsellor: Miss L Mass

St Helen's School has a commitment to academic excellence that has given us an enviable reputation for over 100 years. We provide an excellent academic education for able girls, developing personal integrity alongside intellectual, creative and sporting talents. The staff are highly qualified and enthusiastic, the facilities are excellent, discipline is good and we know and care for every individual pupil.

Above all we encourage all the girls at St Helen's to chase their dreams and achieve a successful and fulfilling life.

The school is divided into three departments; Little St Helen's (4+–7), Junior School (7+–11) and Senior School (11+–18), enabling continuity and progression in the education of every pupil. Main entries are at 4+, 7+, 11+ and 16+.

St Helen's has an excellent academic record and girls achieve outstanding results in public examinations at all levels. In our flourishing Sixth Form there are approximately 170 girls who choose from over twenty Advanced Level courses. 98% of girls proceed to University and we send a significant proportion to Oxford and Cambridge each year.

The curriculum is designed to enable every girl to achieve intellectual and personal fulfilment and to develop her talents to the full. We support the aims of the National Curriculum, but offer a wider range of subjects and teach to greater depth, so enabling the girls to explore their interests and talents. The staff are subject specialists whose aim is to inspire a love of their subjects in the girls. They help the girls to learn how to study independently and develop good study habits, through stimulating and rigorous teaching. All girls study two modern foreign languages together with Latin. Science is taught throughout as three separate subjects. We expect the girls to study with commitment and we attach particular importance to the diligent and prompt completion of homework assignments. Music, Art, Drama and Sport are all an integral part of the life of the school and involve every girl. Many also take extra instrumental Music, Ballet, Speech and Drama lessons and Games coaching.

Girls take a full part in the broader life of the school and, through extra-curricular activities, discover interests to complement their academic achievements. Clubs and societies abound and we have a flourishing programme of optional outdoor and adventurous activities. A vertical House system also thrives which girls help to run, and all participate in inter-house competitions.

St Helen's is easily accessible using the Metropolitan Line. Northwood Station is less than five minutes from the school.

St Helen's runs extensive and flexible coach services from the surrounding districts.

St Helen's is close to Heathrow and also accessible from Gatwick, Luton and Stansted airports.

Our popular day boarding programme allows girls to extend their day in the safety of the school environment until parents can collect them. Our highly qualified staff involve the girls in many activities, such as baking, games and paper craft, and enable them to complete their homework before they go home. Day boarding is housed in the Junior School and the boarding houses, in familiar surroundings and tea and supper are provided.

Fees. Registration Fee UK £50; Overseas £60; Weekly Boarding Fee with tuition (Senior School) £3,997 per term; Full Boarding £4,144 per term; Little St Helen's, including Lunch and Ballet) £1,587 per term; Junior School (Year 3 & 4, including Speech & Drama) £1,754; (Years 5 and 6) £1,708 per term; Senior School £2,200 per term.

Scholarships. Academic Scholarships are awarded for girls entering the Sixth Form and Entrance Scholarships at 11+. Music Exhibition at 11+ and Art Exhibitions at 11+, 16+, Leader-Baker Scholarship awarded every four years at 14+. Bursaries are available.

St Helen's Old Girls' Club. *Secretary:* Mrs Sally Fleming, 2 Moneyhill Road, Rickmansworth, Herts WD3 2EQ.

Charitable status. St Helen's School for Girls is a Registered Charity, number 312762. It exists to provide quality education for girls.

St James's School

West Malvern Worcs WR14 4DF
Tel: (01684) 560851
Fax: (01684) 569252
e-mail: kershawhm@aol.com
website: http://www.st-james-school.co.uk

An Independent Boarding School for up to 150 girls, age range 10–18 years

Visitor: The Lord Bishop of Worcester

Council: Sir John Harvey-Jones, KB, MBE (*President*)

Sir Ralph Anstruther, Bart, KCVO, MC, DL, BA
C R Sandison, Esq, FCA
Mrs E J Anson, JP
S Driver White, Esq
B Woodall, Esq (*Chairman*)
Dr J M Moore, JP, MA, PhD, FRSA
A W Twiston-Davies, Esq

***Headmistress:* Mrs S Kershaw**, BA (Hons), PGCE York, FRSA

Director of Studies: Mrs R Hayes, BA (Hons) Reading, PGCE, MA Open, FRGS

Clerk to the Council and Financial Bursar: Mr D Boorn

Chaplain: Revd C Attwood, BA (Hons) Bristol, MA (Hons) Oxford, Cert Theol

Heads of Department:

English:
Mrs A Fearnside, BA (Hons) London, CertEd

Humanities:
Mrs R Hayes, BA (Hons) Reading, PGCE, MA Open, FRGS

Business Studies:
Mrs M Walker, BA (Hons) Reading, CertEd

Languages:
Mrs B Wadman, Licence d'Anglais Rennes (*French*).

Mathematics:
Miss L Turner, BSc (Bristol), MSc (Loughborough)

Science:
Mrs C M Panter, BSc (Hons) Newcastle, PGCE (*Biology*)

Director of Art:
Mrs K Shindler, BA (Hons) Cheltenham, MA (RCA), CertEd Birmingham

Design & Technology:
Mr M Tebbett, BEd Wales, CertEd

Music:
Mrs L Lindner, TLD (University of Cape Town), Teachers Licentiate Dip

Physical Education:
Mrs K Bevan, BEd(PE) (IM Marsh College)

Senior House Tutor:
Mrs H A Churchill, CertEd (Birmingham)

Sanatorium Sisters:
Sister S Richmond-Allen, SRN
Sister G McLean, SRN

Number in School. There are 100 boarders and 40 day girls.

Ideals. To give to each girl that education which will best prepare her for a full life in the working world which she will enter; to provide the freedom to develop and gain self-confidence within a well-structured, caring community, and to enable her to undertake responsible, self-disciplined study, born of a joy of learning in the widest possible sense.

Site. On the Western slopes of the Malvern Hills, commanding impressive views of the Welsh mountains. The grounds extend to over 45 acres.

Accommodation. Junior and Middle School Houses, and Senior Houses with single study-bedrooms in the Sixth Form.

Special features of the buildings are a new Sixth Form Centre, The Harvey-Jones School for international business (opened September 1998), a fine Science Block, up to date Language Laboratory, Library, purpose-built 250-seat Theatre, The Oakdene Centre for Music & the Performing Arts (opened September 1998), Art and Pottery studios, heated outdoor Swimming Pool and full provision for Tennis, Hockey and Athletics. Other sports are available.

Indoor Recreation Area. This includes well furnished rooms for games, crafts, discussions, television, record playing and a Quiet Room which houses a Junior Library. The aim is to encourage varied use of leisure-time.

Curriculum. A full range of academic subjects is offered in the Humanities, Languages, Science and Technology up to Advanced Level. This includes a Vocational A level in Business. The School also has a rich tradition in Music, Art and Drama.

The Sixth Form. The School has a large Sixth Form proportionate to its size.

Fees (include lunches and most books). Boarding/Weekly Boarding £4,655 per term; Day £2,250 per term for Years 6 to 11 and £3,050 for Sixth Form.

Scholarships and Bursaries. General Scholarships and individual subject scholarships, including VI Form awards, are offered annually. Particulars from the Development Director.

Entry. Common Entrance Examination or the School's own Entrance Papers, with interviews. VI Form entry dependent on interview, report from present school and GCSE results.

St Joseph's Convent School

Upper Redlands Road Reading RG1 5JT
Tel: (0118) 966 1000
Fax: (0118) 926 9932

Motto: *Optima Deo*

Patron: The Bishop of Portsmouth

Board of Governors:
R E Poole (*Chairman*)
Rev Mother Provincial, Sisters of St Marie Madeleine Postel
Sister Magdalena, Sisters of St Marie Madeleine Postel
P Grainger
R C Hadaway
P Parratt
W Walker

Bursar: Mr R Vaux

School Secretary: Mrs J A Paul

Staff:
***Headmistress:* Mrs Veronica Brookes**, BEd Hons

Deputy Headmistress: Mrs H J Trapani, MA, PGCE
Head of VIth Form: Mrs D Mason, BEd Hons
Director of Studies: Mrs C Turner, BSc
Head of Prep Department: Mrs E Burgin, MA
Heads of Faculties:
Science/Maths: Mr I Cooling, BSc Hons
Creative Arts: Mrs J Tinker, BEd
Communications: Mrs M Evans, MA

Nature of tuition. classes/tutorials/small groups.
Average size of class. 20.
Teacher/student ratio. 1:10.
Fees per term. Senior £1,865; Junior £700–£1,110.
Courses offered. GCSE, A/S and A Level courses.
Scholarships. The school awards a number of scholarships each year. These are given on entry to the Senior Department and in recognition of excellence at GCSE. Scholarships are also given to girls in respect of the contribution that they are prepared to make to the school during their Sixth Form life.

St Joseph's is an independent day school for girls aged 3–18 years. The school was founded in 1894 by the Sisters of St Marie Madeleine Postel and welcomes girls of all denominations and faiths. There are some 500 pupils on the school roll, making it large enough to offer a varied curriculum and excellent facilities but small enough to foster a strong sense of community.

St Joseph's is situated in the university area of Reading, convenient to the town centre and the M4. The Preparatory Department is housed in a purpose built complex, designed with the needs of small children in mind, which is adjacent to the Senior Department campus. Its proximity to the Senior Department enables resources to be shared, such as the Information Technology Suite and the indoor swimming pool. Classrooms and laboratories throughout the school are well equipped and within the grounds there is a full range of outdoor sporting facilities.

At St Joseph's we work in partnership with our parents. We create an environment that is safe and happy, in which academic and social skills, individual talent and consideration of the needs of others are developed. We are justly proud of the achievements of our girls, whether in the form of GCSE or A Level results or in seeing them grow in confidence and develop as young adults.

St Joseph's academic life is not confined to the National Curriculum, but this forms the basis of the school's teaching. Preparatory Department pupils undertake Key Stages 1 and 2 testing in addition to regular monitoring. In the Senior Department the rigour of GCSE, A/S and A Level requirements keep us close to the National Curriculum. For each Year Group there is regular testing with a Parents' Information Evening at the beginning of each academic year, plus two Consultative Evenings to discuss performance.

Academic standards are high and nearly all our Sixth Formers go on to university.

Artistic talent and practical skills are encouraged at all ages. Original and exciting work is produced in Art/Textiles, in CDT and Home Economics.

The school has a strong music and drama tradition. There are various orchestras, musical groups and choirs. The girls regularly give concerts and there are many opportunities to take part in Drama, Dance and Debating.

Sport is an important part of life at St Joseph's. A full range of activities, from Athletics and Swimming to team games, is offered. Girls are regularly chosen to represent their county in Athletics, Swimming, Tennis and Hockey.

Form Tutors form the backbone of the pastoral care system at St Joseph's. By developing an open and trusting relationship with their pupils, they can provide a receptive ear and the essential support and help that may be required.

Admission to the Preparatory Department is by interview. Entry to the Senior Department is by examination and a report from the pupil's previous school. Good GCSE grades, plus a report from the previous school, are required for admission to the Sixth Form.

Charitable status. St Joseph's Convent School Reading Trust is a Registered Charity, number 277077. It exists to promote and provide for the advancement of education of children and young persons.

St Leonards–Mayfield School

The Old Palace Mayfield East Sussex TN20 6PH
Tel: (01435) 874623 (Headmistress and Secretary) 874600 *(School)*; 874614 *(School Office)*
Fax: (01435) 872627
e-mail: enquiry@stlm.e-sussex.sch.uk
website: www.stlm.e-sussex.sch.uk

St Leonards–Mayfield School is a Roman Catholic boarding and day school for girls, based on the Old Palace of the pre-Reformation Archbishops of Canterbury. It reflects the independence and breadth of vision of Cornelia Connelly, the foundress of the Society of the Holy Child Jesus, who was invited, in 1846, to come to England to create schools for the education of Catholic girls. Her American background and broad European cultural experience underpinned an amazingly forward looking and challenging concept of education.

The school of today seeks to combine these traditions to prepare girls to 'meet the wants of the age', to bring a thoughtful and Christian perspective to all areas of life, and to develop their own gifts and those of others to the fullest possible extent. It seeks to establish a supportive and compassionate community, in which each girl is encouraged to grow into a true acceptance of herself, with the inner security which comes from a knowledge of the love of God.

Governors:
Sister Anne Murphy, SHCJ (*Chairman*)
Mrs Audrey Butler
Mr Crispian Collins
Mrs Jane Cutler
Sister Mary Hilary Daly, SHCJ
Mr John Dilger
Sister Maria Dinnendahl, SHCJ
Mr Richard Hazle
Professor Christopher Howe
Mr George Hubbard
Mrs Sara Hulbert-Powell
Sister Christina Kenworthy-Browne, IBVM
Sister Judith Lancaster, SHCJ
Mr Julian Lee
Mrs Jane Stockdale

***Headmistress:* Mrs Julia Dalton**, BA (York)

Deputy Heads:
Mrs A Barker, BSc
Mrs M D McGovern, BA

Bursar: Mr Rowland Leigh, FCA

Teaching Staff:

Religious Studies:
*Mr P L Oxborrow, BA, MA
Miss C M Clay, BA
Mrs C Reade, BA
Mrs C M Wethered, MA

English:
*Mrs K M P Cornish, BA, MA
*Mrs M M C Crane, MA, MA
Mrs I J Bradford, BA, MA
Mrs A Brasted, LGSM, BA
Mrs M McCarthy-Marshall, BA, MA

EFL:
*Mrs E R Atherstone, BA, DipTEFLA
Mrs J Carter, BA
Mrs H Frias del Rio, BA

Classics:
*Mrs M C Boothroyd, BA, MA
Mrs J I Morton, MA
Miss G J Reed, BA

Modern Languages:
*Mr J M Plant, MA, MA
Mrs R E Boumediene, BA
Mrs P A M Crook, MA
Mrs F B Haslegrave, BA
Mrs M L Hockton, L-és-L
Miss C Scully, CertEd
Mrs A Stride, BA
Mrs A C von Wulffen, MA

History:
*Dr P S Tosoni, PhD
Miss C M Clay, BA
Mrs E N Davies, BA

Economics:
Mr P Allen, BSc, MA

Geography:
*Mrs A J Rae, MA
Mrs F M Morris, BEd
Mrs C A Turner, BA

Mathematics:
*Mrs H McDougall, BSc
Mrs C A Baker, BEd
Miss J P Eales, BEd
Mrs S Maclean, BSc
Mrs G J Sargent, CertEd

Information Technology:
*Mr M Fradd, BSc
Mr T J Parker, CertEd, BA

Sciences:
*Mrs L A Morcombe, BA
Mrs K E A Blackman, BSc
Mrs G Brennan, DipEd
Mr M Fradd, BSc
Mrs S J Holmes, BSc, MSc
Mrs I M Osprey, BSc, MIBiol, CBiol
Mr T J Parker, CertEd, BA
Miss T A Rakowska, BSc
Mrs S E Tosoni, BSc

Commercial Studies:
Mrs J Uren, RSA TLOS, CommTDip, CertEd

Food & Nutrition:
Mrs S Rothero, BEd
Mrs M A Easteal, DipEd, BSc

Art & History of Art:
*Mr P A Joy, ICAD, NDD, ATD
Mrs F Joy, ATD, MEd, MA
Miss A Coombes, BA

Ceramics:
Mrs C F Allen, NDD
Mrs R Webber, CertEd

Craft, Design & Technology:
Mr C F Harper, CertEd, Dip D & T

Drama & Theatre Studies:
*Mrs G P Moore, TDip Sp & Dr
Miss S B Aldous, BEd

Physical Education:
*Mrs S E Taylor, CertEd
Miss H Calvert, BA
Mrs A J Douch, BEd
Mrs F M Morris, BEd
Mrs J Nevill, BA
Miss B Ward, BEd

Careers:
Mrs E N Davies, BA

Duke of Edinburgh Award Scheme:
Mrs G J Sargent, CertEd

Records of Achievement & Work Experience:
Mrs E J Stewart Malir, DipPE

Music:
Director: Mr J L Thomas, MA, FRCO, FTCL, GTCL, LRAM

Housemistresses and Houses:

Mrs L Fawls *St Dunstan's*
Mrs B J Flanagan *Chapel*
Mrs A Brasted *St Thomas's*
Mrs P Crook *St Edward's*
Miss L Evans *Connelly*
Mrs E J Stewart Malir *Gresham*
Mrs G Brennan *Lower School*

Secretary to the Headmistress: Mrs J P Field-Brodie

Registrar: Miss S G Murphy, BA, MBA

School Doctor: Dr A Coates, BM, DROCG (Dip Therapeutics)

Matron: Mrs G Osborne, RGN

There are 400 girls (about 50% are boarders) in an age range from 11–18, with 140 of these in the VI Form.

Organisation. There are boarding houses for years 7 & 8, for years 9 & 10, for year 11 and for the Sixth Form. There are two day houses for year 9 and above; lower school day girls are integrated with the boarders.

Curriculum. In the first three years the curriculum seeks to establish a good foundation in the different disciplines, to encourage initiative, investigation, and many varieties of creative activity, and the growth of self-discipline, self-motivation. The core for GCSE comprises English Language, English Literature, Mathematics, a modern foreign language, Physics, Chemistry and Biology, either as three separate subjects, or in double-certificated Balanced Science, and Religious Studies. Three further subjects may be chosen freely from fifteen possible options. About twenty five subjects are offered for AS & A2 level. The importance of non-examination subjects is stressed, together with the need to develop inter-personal skills, to take responsibility for younger members of the school and those they help in the neighbourhood, and to achieve a proper balance between work and leisure. Virtually all proceed to higher education, over 90% to university.

The standard of Music is high; there are five choirs and two orchestras, and individual tuition is available in a large number of instruments. Various teams and individuals play different sports at county, regional and national level, to a very high standard. There are many opportunities for drama, with excellent standards attained in productions directed by staff, and by the girls themselves.

The school has a Music school; the Concert Hall is used for both Music and Drama. There is an indoor heated 25 metre swimming pool, in use throughout the year; there are two gymnasia, hard courts and playing fields, and an all weather pitch. Sports include hockey, netball, tennis, rounders, athletics, swimming, gymnastics, volleyball, and many types of dance; at VI form level squash, sailing, golf are the possible options. A riding sand school and cross-country course serve horseriders well.

Admission. At ages 11–13 Common Entrance Examination; at 14 (exceptionally) on school report: at 16 (for VI Form Course) 5 good passes in GCSE, and report from present head.

Fees. (*see* Entrance Scholarship section) Boarders £4,686 per term, Day girls £3,124 per term, Registration fee £50 (£75 overseas). Scholarships are offered for achievement and potential in academic subjects, in music and in art.

Charitable status. St Leonards-Mayfield School is a Registered Charity, number 1047503. It exists to provide education for girls.

St Margaret's School
Bushey

Merry Hill Road Bushey Herts WD23 1DT
Tel: 020 8901 0870
Fax: 020 8950 1677

Founded 1749
Motto: *Sursum corda Habemus ad Dominuum*
The School is constituted as follows:

Patron: Her Majesty The Queen

President: The Rt Revd C Herbert, Bishop of St Albans

Vice-Presidents:
The Lord Archbishop of Wales
The Lord Archbishop of York
The Lord Bishop of London
The Chaplain of the Fleet
The Chaplain-General, Army
The Chaplain-in-Chief Royal Air Force
C A McLintock, CA
M H McQueen, Esq, LVO, MA

Committee:
Treasurer and Chairman: The Rt Revd D J Farmbrough, MA

Vice-Chairmen:
Lt Col D H C Thrush, TD
Mrs G Pazzi-Axworthy, LLB

Members:
Miss J Alderton
Miss E V Andrews
P R Faulkner, FRICS, FAAV
The Rev Canon F Foster
P W Morriss, CA
The Revd O R Osmond
J P Read, FCA
Miss M Rudland, BSc
Mrs A K Stewart

Staff:

***Headmistress:* Miss M de Villiers**, BA (UCT), STD

Deputy Head: Mrs J L Duncan, BSc (St Andrews)

Bursar: Mr N De Lord, BSc (Cardiff), HND
Director of Studies: Mrs E Jarvis, MA (Birmingham), LGSM, PGCE
Pastoral Co-ordinator: Mrs J Sanders, BSc (London), PGCE
Examinations Officer: Mr R Aniolkowski, BSc (Leeds), PGCE, MInstP

English:
Mrs E Jarvis, MA (Birmingham), LGSM
Mrs J Cox, BA (Durham), PGCE
Mrs R M Brennan, BEd (Winchester)
Miss K Day, BA (York), PGCE
Miss A Pateman, BA (Edinburgh)

Mathematics:
Mr M Ferris, BSc (Bristol), PGCE
Mrs G Cook, BEd (London)
Mrs J L Duncan, BSc (St Andrews), DipEd
Miss D Thompson, BA, MSc (London), PGCE

Art & Design:
Mrs L Lusher, NDD, ATD (Leicester)
Mrs R Howard, MA (Edinburgh), PGCE

Biology:
Mrs J Sanders, BSc (London), PGCE
Mrs S Wood, BSc (Salford)

Careers: Mrs B Foster, BA (New York)

Chemistry:
Mr G Hall, BSc (Reading)
Mrs T Feldman, BA (Oxon), MA, MSc (London)
Mr I Gill, BSc (Bristol), PGCE

Classics:
Miss C Hannan, MA (Cantab), TEFL
Mrs S Butcher, BA (Reading), PGCE
Mrs M P Small, BA (Keele), CertEd

Information Systems:
Mrs E Nutt, IPM
Mr D Nelson, CertEd, DipEd

Drama:
Mrs E Janacek, BA (Herts), BEd

Business Studies & Economics:
Mrs C Rees, MA (Leicester)

Geography:
Mr C Knox, BA (Middlesex), PGCE
Mr P Crewe, MA (La Trobe), DipEd

History:
Dr J Wheaton, BA, PhD (Manchester)
Miss J Chatkiewicz, BA (Wales), PGCE

Home Economics:
Mrs C Timms, BEd (Bath), MNATHE

Modern Languages:
Mrs S Hudson, BA (Manchester), PGCE
Mrs E Norman, BA (London)
Mrs P Tyers, BA (York), PGCE
Mrs E Serrano, BA (Madrid)
Miss L M H Shaw, BA (Exeter), PGCE

Music:
Mr I Hope, BMus (Edinburgh), PGCE, LTCL
Mr M A Hammond, BA (Cantab), PGCE, FRCO, LRAM

Physical Education:
Mrs D Pimlott, BEd (Eastbourne)
Miss M Monk, BEd (Bedford)
Mrs S Adams, BEd (Bedford)

Physics:
Mr R Aniolkowski, BSc (Leeds), PGCE, MInstP

Religious Studies:
Mr D Dicks, BA, BTh, HPTC

Merry Hill Teaching Staff:
Mrs A Talbot, BA (Cantab), CertEd
Miss D Harvey, BA (OU), CertEd
Miss S Carr, BA (Southampton), PGCE
Mrs P Edward, CertEd (Middlesex)

Infant Department:
Mrs E Merrin, CertEd (Manchester)

Mrs S Kingsford, MA (Brunel)
Mrs M Leigh, Montessori Teaching Diploma

Senior School Housemistresses:
Gordon: Mrs J Sanders, BSc (London), PGCE
Nicholson: Miss J Chatkiewicz, BA (Wales), PGCE
Raleigh: Mr I Gill, BSc (Reading)
Wesley: Miss A Pateman, BA (Edinburgh)

Assistant Housemistresses: Mrs C Maclean; Mrs V Morley

Lower School and Merry Hill Housemistress: Miss J Chatkiewicz, BA (Wales), PGCE

Matron:
Mrs L Eastland

Housekeeper: Mrs H Green

Bursar's Assistants:
Mrs A L Upton, Mrs J A Felts, Mrs A Smith

Registrar/Head's Secretary: Mrs H Baldry

School Secretary: Mrs A Artime

Assistant Secretary: Mrs J Davies

Sanatorium Sister: Mrs P Beazley, RGN, SCN, ONC

Laboratory Technicians:
Mrs C Day
Mrs H McKenzie

Established in 1749, St Margaret's School is an Independent school for girls aged 4–18 years. Day places with Boarding and Weekly Boarding available to girls in the Senior School. Although an Anglican foundation, pupils of other faiths and customs are welcomed.

The school enjoys a rural aspect, situated in 72 acres of playing fields and woodland, while at the same time within easy access of central London, a 40 minute tube journey from Stanmore. Close to the M1 and M25 junctions it is in an ideal position for travel to Heathrow Airport (35 minutes) and on British Rail (10 minutes to Watford).

The school has a broad, balanced curriculum and a strong academic tradition with a very good GCSE, A level and Oxbridge record. Each year girls proceed to a wide range of courses at Universities and Colleges of Further Education. Education takes place in small classes in a caring and supportive community. Enrolment to St Margaret's is by interview at 4+, 5+ and 6+ and via the school's own Entrance Examination and interview at 7+, 11+ and 13+. Sixth Form places are conditional on GCSE results. Scholarships and Bursaries are available.

Recent new additions to the buildings have included an Art and Design block, an IT centre and newly upgraded library. Boarding accommodation has been upgraded to provide comfortable, modern facilities. There is a fees reduction for siblings, Forces and Anglican clergy children and school coach transport is available.

Pupils take advantage of a full and varied programme of music, dramatic and sporting opportunities. The Duke of Edinburgh Award is popular and enjoys wide participation among the girls. Language Exchange trips abroad are a regular feature of the annual calendar. The presence of a substantial boarding and weekly boarding community means that there is a wide range of extra-mural activities available to all. A strong Old Girls Guild and Parents Association contribute in a positive way to the life of St Margaret's.

Fees. (*see* Entrance Scholarship section) Senior and Lower School: Boarding £4,695 per term; Day £2,755 per term. Preparatory: Day £2,410 per term. Transition: £2,195 per term. Infant: £1,785 per term.

St Margaret's Guild (Old Girls' Association). *Secretary:* Mrs J Wilson, 43 Chase Ridings, Enfield, Middx EN2 7QE. Guild Membership available to any old girl of St Margaret's School.

Charitable status. St Margaret's School Bushey is a Registered Charity, number 1056228. It exists to provide high quality education for girls.

St Margaret's School
Edinburgh

East Suffolk Road Edinburgh EH16 5PJ
Tel: 0131-668 1986
Fax: 0131-662 0957

Honorary President: The Rt Hon The Lord Mackay of Clashfern

Board of Governors:
The Rt Hon Lord Cullen, LLB, FRSE (*Chairman*)
Mr K Aitken
Mrs K Fairweather
Mr R Fife
Mr M Chiappelli, CA
Mr R Nimmo
Mrs Anne Pollock, LLB
Mrs P Walsh
Mr R Watson
Mr D Wilkinson, CA
Mr N Weibye

***Principal:* Miss Anne Mitchell**, MA

Deputy Principal (*Curriculum*): Mr Colin Smith, MA

Deputy Principal (*Guidance*): Mrs Sally Duncanson, MA

Deputy Principal (*Finance and Administration*) and Secretary: Mr S Newton, BA

Heads of Department:

Art:
Mrs F Shaw, BA, PGCE

Business Studies & Computing:
Mrs C A B Young, BA, DipCommerce

Careers:
Mrs A Hood

Classics:
Dr I C Mantle, MA, BA, PhD, PGCE

Drama:
Mrs J Douglas

English:
Mrs L Rodger

Geography/History/Modern Studies:
Mrs M E Muggridge, MA

Learning Support:
Mrs C Brotherston, BA Hons, CertEd
Mrs J Goodall, BA, DipEd, CertTESOL

Mathematics:
Mrs J Gilmour, BSc Hons, DipEd

Modern Languages:
Miss E Duncan, MA Hons

Music:
Mrs D Millar

Physical Education Department:
Miss C Robertson, BA, PGCE

Science Department:
Mr R Dickson, BA, MEd, DipEd, CBiol, MIBiol *Head of Department*

Dr S E Chesher, BSc, PhD, CertEd *Head of Chemistry*
Mr I W Moffat, BSc, CertEd *Head of Physics*

Junior School:
Head of Junior School: Mrs M B Saunders, MA, DipEd

From January 1998 St Margaret's School merged with St Denis & Cranley School.

St Denis & Cranley School was an amalgamation itself of two Edinburgh girls' schools of long-standing traditions, St Denis founded in 1855 and Cranley founded in 1871.

The combined school is called St Margaret's School Edinburgh and has its main base at the existing St Margaret's site. The increased pupil numbers and the greater financial strength have enabled the combined school to develop a richer curriculum, provide better facilities and ensure a strong future.

The merger brings together the shared traditions of schools committed to providing education to girls on the south side of Edinburgh.

St Margaret's was founded in 1890 as an independent school to provide education for girls aged 5 to 18 years. There are now approximately 620 pupils who range in age from 3 to 18 years and include both day girls and boarders. The chief aim of the school is to help girls to develop their own talents and personalities and, by individual assessment, to provide a course for each girl which suits her particular interests and abilities and enables her to achieve her personal best. Girls are encouraged to have high expectations of themselves.

The main complex of School buildings is situated in a quiet road in South Edinburgh, readily accessible by public transport from all parts of the city and surrounding districts. There is a separate Senior College for the education of older pupils (S5 & 6).

Boarders. There is a Boarding House, St Hilary's for girls aged 10 upwards. The girls participate in a variety of local activities and at weekends visits are often arranged to places of interest in and around Edinburgh. It is less than 5 minutes walking distance from the main School buildings and the girls enjoy all the amenities of the capital city and its cultural life.

The Nursery and Preparatory Department. The Nursery accepts girls and boys between the ages of 3 months and 5 years. The Preparatory Department comprises Primary 1 and 2 classes. Boys can continue up to age 8.

The Junior School (Girls only). There is an intimate friendly atmosphere conducive to learning. As with the Preparatory Department regular meetings are held at which parents have the opportunity of meeting members of staff and each other. Reports of progress are issued regularly, and parents may consult the Principal or the Head of the Junior School about their daughters' education and development at any time.

The Senior School (Girls only). In the Senior School classes are unstreamed, but setting in some academic subjects is introduced enabling every girl to progress at the pace most suited to her own ability. As in the Junior School, reports of progress are issued regularly and parents may consult the Principal at any time.

In the First and Second Years most subjects listed can be studied, but some are available to older girls only. At the end of the Second Year girls take eight subjects in which they are prepared over a period of two years for the National Qualifications Examinations at Standard Grade.

Senior College (S5 & S6–Ages 16 to 18). The Senior College was established in 1984. The aim is to provide a more adult atmosphere for pupils during the last two years of their school careers, thereby helping to bridge the gap between a controlled school environment and the independence of student or business life. The emphasis is on preparation for Higher Education. Smaller tutorial groups are arranged and pupils are also encouraged to develop a mature attitude towards the planning of their own studies.

Courses are individually tailored with students taking Intermediate 2, Highers, or a combination of both in S5, and Highers and/or Advanced Highers in S6. Subjects on offer are the same as in S3 and S4 with the addition of Accounting & Economics, as well as a variety of General Interest courses, some of which follow a modular pattern certificated by SQA. Pupils continue to have Social Education, but the scope is widened to include Current Affairs and Political Awareness. Careers advice is given on an individual basis, and students are involved in work experience programmes in S5, and encouraged to go on visits to Unversities, Colleges or businesses to help them decide on the next stage of their careers.

Curriculum. Tuition is available in the following subjects: English, History, Geography, Modern Studies, Latin, Greek, French, German, Spanish, Mathematics, Statistics, Computer Studies, Accounting, Economics, Chemistry, Physics, Biology, Music, Home Economics, Art and Crafts, Religious Education, Physical Education, Business Management, Word Processing, Drama and Social Education.

The School is generously staffed with fully qualified, registered teachers, who prepare the girls for entrance to the Universities, including Oxford and Cambridge, and for other forms of Higher education, and for professional training of all kinds.

Candidates are entered for the following examinations: National Qualifications Standard Grade, Higher and Advanced Higher; the Examinations of the Associated Board of the Royal Schools of Music.

TEFL specialist help is available for pupils whose first language is not English and individual courses can be arranged.

Career Guidance. There is a specialist member of staff with responsibility for careers guidance. Detailed and individual guidance is given on university selection and all forms of higher education. There is also close liaison with the local Careers Office and aptitude tests are available.

Music and the Arts. There are two school orchestras (Junior and Senior), a wind band and recorder groups. Tuition is available in piano and in most string and wind instruments. Girls are prepared for the Examinations of the Associated Board of the Royal Schools of Music and the Choirs, Junior and Senior, have had considerable success in local and national competitions.

There are facilities for Arts and Crafts, including well-equipped studios, a photography dark room and a pottery kiln. An imaginative Art Display can be seen annually.

Physical Education. The gymnasium is well-equipped and use is made of the excellent facilities at the University of Edinburgh. School teams compete in Hockey, Lacrosse, Swimming, Tennis, Rounders, Netball, Athletics, Ski-ing and Riding and facilities are also available for Fencing, Squash, Dancing and Gymnastics. Class swimming instruction is given from Primary 3 to 7 and as an option further up the school.

Riding is a popular activity with many of the boarders and arrangements can be made for them to have instruction. The facilities of the Meadowbank Sports Centre and the nearby Commonwealth Swimming Pool are used by both day girls and boarders, as is the Hillend dry ski slope.

Leisure Activities. Girls are encouraged to use their leisure time wisely and to develop interests and hobbies. They have a wide choice of clubs and societies including the Literary and Debating Society and Clubs for Computing, Electronics, Films, Photography and Gymnastics. The Duke of Edinburgh's Award Scheme is also in operation. Many girls take part in voluntary or community service. The enthusiasm of the Charities Committee gives everyone a sense of social involvement.

Expeditions to places of interest and visits abroad are regular features of each year's programme.

Scholarships. (*see* Entrance Scholarship section) See appropriate section.

Development Trust. A Development Trust was formed in 1967 in order to launch an appeal for funds to carry out a programme of capital development. An annual Continuation Committee ensures that parents of each new intake of pupils, who are benefiting from the generosity of previous donors, may also have the opportunity to contribute.

Former Pupils' Club. The School has a Former Pupils' Club which maintains links between School and its old girls. Social functions are arranged several times a year and news of former pupils is published in the FP section of the School Magazine.

Charitable status. St Margaret's School Edinburgh Limited is a Registered Charity, number CR 38971. St Margaret's exists for the purpose of giving girls a sound preparation for life.

St Margaret's School
Exeter

147 Magdalen Road Exeter EX2 4TS.
Headmistress/Admissions Secretary: Tel: (01392) 491699
School Office: Tel: (01392) 273197
Bursar: Tel: (01392) 277132
Fax: (01392) 251402
e-mail: mail@stmargarets-school.co.uk
website: www.stmargarets-school.co.uk

Woodard Corporation (Western Division)

Headmistress: **Mrs M D'Albertanson**, MA

Deputy Headmistress: Mrs D Williams, BA

Director of Sixth Form Studies: Mrs F E Scott, BSc

Chaplain: The Revd R Barrett

Headmistress's Secretary and Admissions Secretary: Mrs C Clapp

General School Secretary: Mrs D Masters

Foundation. St Margaret's was founded at the turn of the century and has always had a strong Church of England tradition and links with the Cathedral. In 1968 the School was brought into association with the Woodard Corporation, and in 1975 it became incorporated into this large group of independent schools.

Situation. St Margaret's is situated a mile from the City Centre. The School consists of 8 large Georgian Houses in the Magdalen Road area. There is a Gym, Assembly Hall, specialist rooms and hard courts for tennis and netball. Playing fields are available in the locality for games. A new Performing Arts Centre was opened in 1997, and a Learning Resources Centre was opened in September 1998.

Numbers. Total number of pupils 430. There are 85 pupils in the Sixth Form.

Admission. Entrance is by the School's own examinations, held in the Spring Term prior to entry in September. Entrance tests are from the age of 7 to the Junior House, through to the Lower 6, subject to GCSE results and report. Tests can be arranged at other times. Music and clergy bursaries are available, and Academic Scholarships are offered at 6th Form level.

Religious Life of the School. As a Woodard school we follow the principles of the Church of England, and the school has a Chaplain and all other faiths are respected.

Inspection. A team from the Independent Schools Inspectorate visited the school in October 2000. In the summary it was stated that "pupils leave the school as confident, mature, friendly and lively young adults" and that "public examination results are good".

Curriculum. Full ranges of subjects are studied at GCSE, AS and A2 levels. There are fully equipped Science laboratories, Home Economics and Information Technology centres.

All girls take the RSA and IBT courses in computer literacy. French, Spanish and German are available at GCSE and A level. St Margaret's specialises in music, art and drama There are three school orchestras, three choirs, Chamber ensembles and jazz groups. The school enjoys national recognition for music and choral work and have produced their own CD. The Senior Choir has sung in Venice in Saint Mark's Basilica and regularly sing in Exeter Cathedral. Musical tuition can be offered in any instrument. Over 40 peripatetic teachers are available for lessons.

Games. Competitive netball, hockey, tennis, rugby and rounders are played. Gymnastics, dance and swimming are part of the curriculum and there is a range of extra curricular sporting activities.

Extra-Curricular Activities. The school provides a wide range of activities. There are frequent visits to theatres, art galleries and other places of interest. Foreign exchange visits to Germany, Spain and France are organised. Achievement in adventure training is a strength of the school and teams are entered for the Ten Tors expedition on Dartmoor. There have been successful expeditions to Everest Base Camp and, as part of the Duke of Edinburgh Award scheme, girls travelled to Malawi in 2000 and a tour of India is planned in the school's centenary year of 2002. The Duke of Edinburgh scheme offers girls the opportunity to work towards Bronze, Silver and Gold awards. St Margaret's has its own CCF (Combined Cadet Force) contingent.

Careers Advice. A fully stocked careers library with Internet access, and guidance and information is available. There is also a programme of work experience for 5th and 6th year pupils and opportunities for Service to the Community.

Scholarships and Awards. Scholarships are available to girls who demonstrate outstanding academic, music, art or drama ability. There are School Council Awards for parents not able to fund the full school fees. Reductions are available for the daughters of Clergy.

Fees per term. (*see* Entrance Scholarship section) Senior £1,824; Junior £1,500.

Charitable status. Woodard Schools (West Division) St Margaret's Exeter is a Registered Charity, number 269669. St Margaret's offers a stimulating and challenging academic education within a caring Christian environment. The school seeks to develop the potential of each girl giving her the confidence to respond to the responsibilities and opportunities offered by society.

St Margaret's School for Girls
Aberdeen

17 Albyn Place Aberdeen AB10 1RU
Tel: (01224) 584466
Fax: (01224) 585600
e-mail: info@stmargaret.aberdeen.sch.uk

Founded in 1846.

School Council:
J J Carter, OBE, BA, PhD (*Chairman*)
J P Grant, BL, CA

Dr D W G Gray, MBChB
Mrs H A B Harper
B Hay, MA, CA
Mrs J Hessing, MEd
J Johnston, MA, CA
Mrs M Laing, MA
E G Mackenzie, LLB, NP
C Milton, MA, PhD
Mrs A Mulvie, BA, MSc, DMS, FIPD
P Stephen, RIBA, ARIAS
J Stevenson
The Rev A Wilson, MA, BD (*ex officio*)
President of the Former Pupils' Club (*ex officio*)

Auditors: KPMG, Chartered Accountants

***Headmistress:* Mrs Lyn McKay**, BA (Hons), PGCE, ACCEG

Deputy Headmistress: Miss F E G Carey, MA *French*

Senior Staff:
§Mrs A Christiansen, DipPE *Physical Education*
*Miss K Cowie, BA Hons *Art*
Mrs E Crisp, BA *Geography*
Mrs P Davey, BA *Geography, Modern Studies*
*Dr E Dunkley, MA *French, German*
§Mrs L Forman, DipHome Econ *Food Technology*
§Mrs D Fraser, DipPE, BEd (Hons)
Mrs J Garrett, BA (Hons) *Religious Education*
Mrs L Gurney, LTCL *Woodwind*
Mrs S Kennedy, MA (Hons) *English*
Mrs A Leiper, MA, DipEd *English, Library*
Mrs S Lynch, MA *German, French*
*Miss W Main, BA *Latin, Classical Studies*
*Dr R Masson, BSc *Chemistry*
*Mr M McColgan, MA *History*
§Mrs G Millar, BSc *Physics, Careers*
Mr R Minett, MA *German and French*
Mrs S Morrison, DRSAM, ARCM *Music, Piano*
Mr I Murray, BSc *Computing/Information Technology*
*Mrs G Parker, DipPE *Physical Education*
§Mrs E Petrie, DSD, Dip Speech & Drama *Speech and Drama*
§¶Mrs N Pirie, DipPE *Physical Education*
Mrs N Pont, MA *Mathematics*
*Dr S Purves, BSc *Biology*
Miss S Reid, BA, LTCL *Strings*
Mr D Ross, BSc *Physics*
§Mrs J Slater, DipComm *Word Processing/Keyboard Skills/Office and Information Studies,Accounting*
§Mrs D Smith, DA *Art*
§Mrs P Snape, BSc *Biology, Chemistry*
Mrs J Stephen, DipPE *Physical Education*
*Mrs S Stirton, MA *Mathematics*
§Mrs H Thomson, BEng (Hons)
*Mr A Tulloch, LRAM, ARCM, LTCL *Music, Piano*
Mrs C Williamson, DipPE *Physical Education*
*Mr J Witte, MA *English*

Junior Staff:
¶Miss F Black, BEd
Mrs M Black, DPE
§Mrs L Easton, BEd
*Mrs J Fowlie, DipEd *Head of Department*
Mrs M Hendry, MA, Cert in PrimEd

Preparatory Staff:
Miss E Beattie, BEd Hons
Miss A Bibby, DPE
¶Mrs A Brown, MA
*Mrs K Cable, DPE *Head of Department*
§Mrs C Capstick, NNEB
Mrs M Chapman, DipEd
§Mrs E Cordiner, LTCL *Music, Piano*
Mrs E Findlay, DPE
Mrs M Leiper *After School Child Cover*
§Mrs M Massie, Nursery Nurses Cert *Nursery Assistant*
§Mrs K Marino *After School Child Carer*
Mrs L Williamson, MA, DPSE, SEN *Learning Support*

Bursar: Mr G Brown

Administrative Staff:
¶Mrs J Lawrie *Headmistress's Secretary*
Mrs S Mair *Secretary*
Mrs G Smith *Secretary*
Mrs K Torpey *Assistant Bursar*
Mrs S Ingram *Reprographic Assistant/Playground Supervisor*
Mrs M Punton *Laboratory Technician*

There are also visiting instrumental teachers for strings, brass and percussion and two modern language assistants.

Founded in 1846, St Margaret's School is the oldest all-through girls' school in Scotland and a member of the Girls' Schools Association. Education is provided for around 400 girls from 1 Prep to VIth Year. There is a Nursery School within the main building to which boys and girls are admitted from the age of 3 years.

St Margaret's School is conveniently situated in the west end of Aberdeen. The School's excellent facilities include spacious, well-equipped Science laboratories, a congenial library, an attractive Music Suite, an Art studio, a fine gymnasium and extensive playing fields at Summerhill. A new music suite, classroom wing and fifth laboratory were opened in August 1996. The Computer Laboratory was updated in 1998, when the whole school was networked.

Aims. The aims of the School are to provide the sound academic education essential for entry to higher and further education, to industry, commerce, and the professions, to develop an appreciation of the Arts, and to give each girl an education appropriate to her abilities in an atmosphere conducive to the full development of her personality.

Girls are expected to show courtesy and self-discipline at all times and are encouraged to assume responsibility and have fun.

Curriculum. Girls are prepared for Standard grade, Intermediate 2, Higher and Advanced Higher examinations of the Scottish Qualifications Authority. RSA Word Processing is also available. National examinations can be taken for awards in piano, speech and life-saving.

The curriculum includes Art, Biology, Chemistry, Computer Studies, Drama, English (language and literature), French, Geography, German, History, Latin, Mathematics, Modern Studies, Music, Office and Information Studies, Physics, Physical Education, Religious Education, Social and Personal Development and Word-Processing.

Girls are encouraged to take part in extra-curricular activities which include piano, speech, dancing, swimming, drama, debating, computer club, Young Engineers Club, Scripture Union, Junior and Senior Orchestra, woodwind ensemble, Junior and Senior Choir, Duke of Edinburgh's Award Scheme, Young Enterprise and Young Investigators.

Admission. Girls are admitted to the School by test and interview.

Fees. (*see* Entrance Scholarship section) These include tuition fees, SQA examination fees and all books and materials for nursery and preparatory classes and are payable termly with an option to pay monthly. A reduction is made when three or more sisters attend at the same time.

Fees per term. Nursery School (3 year olds) £538; Nursery (4 year olds) £1,044; 1 Prep £1,016; 2 Prep £1,173; 3 and 4 Prep £1,510; Junior £1,611; I to VI Senior £1,772. Music Fees £100.

Charitable status. St Margaret's School for Girls is a Registered Charity, number SCO 16265. It exists to provide a high quality education for girls.

Saint Martin's
Solihull

Solihull West Midlands B91 3EN
Tel: 0121 705 1265
Fax: 0121 711 4529

Motto: *The Grace of God is in Courtesy*

Founded 1941

Chairman of Governors: Mr W I Jollie, LLB

Headmistress: **Mrs J R Taylor**, BEd (London), MA (Dunelm), MIMgt, FRGS

Deputy Headmistress: Dr S Gait, BSc (Leicester), PhD (Liverpool)

Independent Day School for girls 3 to 18.

Staff:
English:
Mrs E Allen-Back, MA (London), PGCE
Mrs P Hill, BA (Wales), PGCE
Mrs V Llewellyn, MA (Edinburgh), PGCE

Modern Languages:
French: Mrs C Gibney, DUT (Nancy), MIL, PGCE
French & Spanish: Mrs E R Allin, MA (Oxon), PGCE
French: Mrs M F Hawkins, BA (Bristol), PGCE
French Conversation: Mme Claude Terrot
German: Mrs R Garrett, BA (Wales), CertEd

Classics:
Mr K Carroll, BA (Nottingham), PGCE
Mrs L Beaumont, BA (Manchester), PGCE

History:
Mrs B A Morris, MA (Swansea), PGCE
Mrs A Hanson, BA (Oxon), CertEd

Geography:
Mrs M Gosling, BSc (Newcastle), MPhil (Nottingham)
Mrs F Fowles, BA (Durham), MSc (Reading), PGCE

Religious Knowledge:
Mrs J Tucker, MA (Oxon), BLitt

Mathematics:
Mrs H Barber, BA (York), PGCE
Dr S Gait, BSc (Leicester), PhD (Liverpool)
Ms S Hussain, BSc (Leicester), PGCE
Mrs R Lawson, BEd (Warwick)
Mrs M Thompson, BA (Open), CertEd

Information Technology:
Mr D Pohl, BEng (Warwick), PGCE
Mrs J Potter, BA (Oxford Brookes), PGCE
Mrs C Warwick, BSc (Coventry), PGCE

Science:

Biology:
Mrs J Morris, BSc (Nottingham), PGCE
Mrs J Parker, BSc (Reading), PGCE

Chemistry:
Mrs B Ridley, BSc (Wales), PGCE

Physics:
Mr B Southgate, BSc (Manchester), PGCE
Mrs C Dodson, BSc (Leeds), PGCE

Business Studies and Economics:
Mrs J Potter, BA (Oxford Brookes), PGCE

Technology:
Mrs E Enderby, CertEd

Art and Design:
Mrs L Dougall, BA (Essex), PGCE
Mrs L Winnett, BEd (Sheffield), CertEd

Speech and Drama:
Mrs C Kimpton, NCSDD, LUD (Dramatic Art), LRAM
Mrs J Plain-Jones, BA (Hertfordshire), CertEd

Music:
Mrs F Mortimer, GBSM, ATCL

Dance:
Miss M Gillott, Dip of London College of Dance and Drama, CertEd, Licentiate ISTD

Physical Education:
Mrs J Elston, CertEd (Bedford College)
Mrs B Waters, CertEd (Bedford College)
Mrs H Burgess, BA (Birmingham), PGCE
Mrs H Levenger, AIST
Mrs S Trenchard, BEd (London)
Mrs H Bradbury, AIST, MSTA

Judo: Mr R Knight, CertEd, BJA Black Belt 4th Dan

Junior School
Head of Junior School: Mrs K Woods, BA (Lancaster), PGCE

Mrs J Docker, CertEd
Mrs D Gregory, BEd (Bristol)
Mrs J Hill, CertEd
Mrs C Johnson, CertEd
Mrs C Metcalfe, BPhil (Warwick), CertEd
Mrs M Schofield, BA (Durham), PGCE

Preparatory Department
Head of Preparatory Department: Mrs L G Whittingham, CertEd

Mrs L Campbell, CertEd
Mrs G Ginns, CertEd
Miss E Lewis, BSc (Portsmouth), PGCE
Mrs W Maggs, CertEd
Mrs E Rowley, CertEd
Mrs R Smith, CertEd
Mrs S Rintoul, CertEd

Librarian: Mrs K Butcher, ALA

Bursar & Clerk to the Governors: Mr M Llewellyn, FCIS

Saint Martin's, which was founded in 1941, is a well established day school for approximately 540 girls situated in a beautiful twenty acre site in the south of Solihull. Solihull is about 8 miles from Birmingham and is on the edge of a rural district within very easy reach of Warwick, Coventry and Leamington Spa.

In addition to the main school buildings which are attached to the very fine Grade II listed Malvern Hall, there are separate, self-contained buildings for the Preparatory and Junior Departments; the Sixth Form is housed in recently renovated and extended listed buildings near to the main school. All playing fields, including tennis and netball courts, are on the premises and an exceptionally wide range of indoor and outdoor activities is offered. In addition, the all-weather facilities at nearby local sports and activities centres are frequently used. A 25 metre indoor swimming pool was opened in November 1999.

The school enjoys well resourced, specialist accommodation for teaching science, music, art, drama and technology and there is a rolling programme of improvements to the buildings. The School has refurbished and much improved the facilities for the teaching of Information Technology: the Preparatory and Junior Departments have networked computer rooms and the Senior School has been re-equipped with a network of industry standard machines. A new Junior Science Laboratory has been built recently and Senior Science laboratories are currently being refurbished. A new Senior Library was provided in 1994.

Girls receive a broad academic education with considerable opportunities for the development of individual interests and good academic standards are maintained. Emphasis is placed on hard work, discipline and independent learning. Courses leading to GCSE examinations are offered in all the usual subjects as well as Information Systems, German, Latin, Classical Civilisation, Art and Music and all girls are required to continue with Mathematics, English Language, English Literature, a modern language and all three sciences. Classes are not streamed, but some subjects are taught in ability sets. In the Sixth Form, the majority of girls will study four Advanced Subsidiary subjects in the first year and complete three Advanced Level courses in the second year chosen from the same range as is offered at GCSE, with the addition of Economics, Business Studies and General Studies. In addition, there is a wide range of extension studies available. The majority of girls go on to higher education and all senior pupils receive extensive careers education and advice and all take part in work experience in the Fifth and Lower Sixth Forms.

Sport, music, drama and public speaking are all strong in school: plays and concerts are held throughout the year at all ages and a very large proportion of girls study at least one instrument. A large selection of other extra-curricular interests is catered for ranging from French and Chess for younger girls to Young Enterprise and the Duke of Edinburgh's Award Scheme for the seniors. Clubs and societies are encouraged. There are opportunities for voluntary service within the local community and regular field trips and school trips abroad are undertaken.

Admission is by assessment for girls aged 5–7 and by interview and examination for older pupils. Girls are admitted to the Sixth Form on the basis of GCSE results and interview. A number of scholarships, including one music scholarship, are awarded annually for admission at 11+ and two scholarships worth up to 50% of fees are awarded to girls entering the Lower Sixth or to enable a girl in the school to complete her education.

Scholarships. (*see* Entrance Scholarship section) See relevant section.

Charitable status. Saint Martin's (Solihull) Limited is a Registered Charity, number 528967. It exists to provide education for girls.

St Mary's Convent School

Mount Battenhall Worcester WR5 2HP
Tel: 01905 357786
Fax: 01905 351718
e-mail: head@stmarys.org.uk
website: stmarys.org.uk

Independent Catholic Day School for girls (aged 2½ to 18) boys (2½ to 8).

Board of Trustees:

***Headmaster:* Mr Christopher Garner, BA Hons**

Deputy Headmistress: Mrs D O'Keeffe, BA Hons

Head of Preparatory School: Mrs S Cookson, BEd Hons

Bursar and Clerk to the Trustees: Mr M D Oakley

Senior School Staff:

Mrs E Amos, BSc Hons
Mrs S Barrie, BA Hons
Mrs M Burnham, MEd
Mrs J Chaundy, MA
Mrs E Cox, BA Hons
Mr S B Gater, BSc
Mrs A Gilks, CertEd
Mrs K Greenfield, BA Hons
Mrs A Hines, BA Hons
Mr A Howe, BSc Hons
Mrs C Howe, BA Hons
Mrs F Hudson, BA
Mrs E Hughes, BEd
Mrs J Hunt, BA
Mrs J Lewis, BSc
Miss L McGeown, BEd Hons
Mrs L Morris, BSc Hons
Mrs C Oliver, BA Hons
Mrs C Rodgman, BEd
Mr G Stokes
Mrs N Thomas, BA Hons
Mr M Wall, GTCL
Mr S Warburton, BA

Preparatory School Staff:

Mrs S Chance, CertEd
Mrs J Clinton, NNEB
Mrs M Hamill, BA Hons
Mrs B Lumb
Mrs E Marshall, BEd
Mrs N Lynas, BA Hons
Mrs M Wall, CertEd
Mrs C Way, BTec
Mrs M Williams, CertEd

Administrative Staff:

School Secretary: Miss C Hitchen
Clerical Assistant: Miss B Prescott
Clerical Assistant: Mrs C Goode
Laboratory Assistant: Mrs L Newell

Foundation. The school was founded by the Sisters of St Mary Madeleine Postel in 1934 to offer a Christian education. It is a Catholic foundation which offers a warm welcome to those of other denominations. There has been a lay Head since 1986 and the school is now controlled by a Trust comprising members of the Order and lay people who delegate the running of the school to the Head.

The school is about one mile from the centre of Worcester and set in extensive grounds. There is a 6.5 acre sportsfield close by as well as a dri-play hockey pitch, netball and tennis courts.

Children may enter the kindergarten from the age of two and a half and boys are accepted up to the age of 8. Children over the age of 7 take an entrance test. At 11 girls transfer to the Senior School if there has been satisfactory progress in the preparatory department. Girls from other schools take an entrance examination at this point. Girls are prepared for GCSE examinations in all the usual subjects. A levels are offered to those whose performance at GCSE indicates the potential for success in subjects already studied plus Political Studies, Economics and Further Maths. There is also a comprehensive programme of General Studies at this level.

The National Curriculum with tests at the various key stages is being observed. St Mary's exists to offer the best in Christian pastoral care, academic success and a stimulating and confidence-building educational experience to all its pupils.

Three academic scholarships are awarded at 11 and at Sixth Form.

Fees per term. From September 2001. Kindergarten £1,065; Infant Department £1,410; Juniors £1,495; Senior Department £1,810.

Charitable status. St Mary's Convent School Worcester is a Registered Charity, number 1018889. Its purpose is the promotion of the Christian Education of girls of all age groups and boys to the age of 8.

* Head of Department	§ Part Time or Visiting
† Housemaster/Housemistress	¶ Old Pupil
‡ See below list of staff for meaning	

St Mary's Hall

Brighton Sussex BN2 5JF
Tel: (01273) 606061
Fax: (01273) 620782
e-mail: smh@pavilion.co.uk.

President: The Right Revd The Lord Bishop of Chichester

Vice-Presidents:
The Right Revd The Lord Bishop of Horsham
The Right Revd The Lord Bishop of Lewes

Chairman of the Governors: A J Commin, Esq

Staff:
***Headmistress:* Mrs S M Meek**, MA

Deputy Head: Mr M E Wells, MA (Oxon)

Second Deputy: Mrs O Ridge, BA

Bursar: Wing Commander C A Elkins, BSc, MSc, MRAcS, RAF(Retd)

Chaplain: The Revd A H Manson-Brailsford, Vicar of St George's, Kemp Town

Introduction. St Mary's Hall was founded by the Reverend Henry Venn Elliott in 1836 as a boarding school for the daughters of Clergy. It is still on its original site in Kemp Town on high ground in view of the sea. Many buildings have been added since the foundation of the school and it currently admits girls of all denominations and faiths. There are approximately 400 pupils, including 60 boarders. Age range: girls 3 to 18, boys 3 to 8. Boarding for girls from 8 to 18. London is 55 minutes away by train, Heathrow Airport easily accessible, and Gatwick Airport only a 40-minute drive away.

Statement of Purpose to Educate for Confidence. Our aim is to develop the personal qualities necessary to make a positive contribution to a changing and unpredictable world. This requires each individual in the community to be ready for life-long learning, to be adaptable, to have the courage to face challenges, to acquire transferable skills, to be able to work independently and as part of a team, to show self-discipline, commitment, flexibility and openness to change.

To achieve this the School will:

- encourage a culture of learning and a respect for knowledge and achievement;
- focus upon the individual and each pupil's academic and personal development in preparation for higher education, the world of work and personal responsibility;
- promote the shared and lasting values of love, knowledge, integrity and truth within a caring multi-cultural community which fosters understanding, tolerance and consideration of others in accordance with the School's Christian foundation and ethos.

Curriculum. A wide range of subjects is on offer throughout the school at GCSE and A Level. Each pupil's programme is carefully monitored to suit the individual.

Extra-Curricular Activities. There are many extra-curricular opportunities, which aim to give every pupil a chance to 'shine' in some respect. Activities range from sport to the arts and include a large number of girls working towards the Duke of Edinburgh's Award at bronze, silver and gold levels.

Boarding. There are two boarding houses: St Hilary House and Venn House (for Juniors). St Hilary House is also the Sixth Form Centre for day girls. We aim to make boarders feel as 'at home' as possible, while developing their independence and confidence and an awareness of the needs of others living in the community.

Religion. St Mary's Hall welcomes students of all religious denominations or none. Arrangements are made, as far as practicable, for boarders to attend churches of their own denomination or worship in their own faith.

Facilities. Facilities include an indoor, heated swimming pool; four large and two small laboratories; libraries; a studio theatre and a School Chapel. Recent additions include two design-technology rooms and two computing areas. The school stands in 6.3 acres (2.55 hectares) of grounds.

Entrance. Junior Department: Where possible, prospective pupils are encouraged to spend a day, or part of a day, at the school, being assessed in class with their peers.

Senior School: Prospective pupils sit an entrance examination. The school has its own tests, but the Girls' Common Entrance Examination is also accepted.

Scholarships and Bursaries. Two or three Open Scholarships are awarded to girls aged 11+, 12+ or 13+ on the results of an examination held in January. Sixth Form Scholarships are also awarded and details are available on request. In addition, there are Music, Sport and Art Scholarships and Bursaries. Special Funds exist for the benefit of daughters of the Clergy or Armed Forces. Clergy Bursaries of 85% of fees and 20% bursaries for daughters of personnel serving in the Armed Forces are currently available.

Assisted Places Scheme. The School operates its own Assisted Places Scheme. Further details should be obtained from the Admissions Secretary.

Fees. Senior School Boarders £3,903 a term, Day girls £2,476 a term. Junior Department Boarders £3,008 a term (from age 8). Day girls from £587 to £1,516 a term depending on age. All fees inclusive of meals (lunch for day pupils), books and stationery.

For further details, please contact the Admissions Secretary.

Charitable status. St Mary's Hall Brighton is a Registered Charity, number 307062. It exists to provide high quality education.

St Mary's School
Ascot

St Mary's Road Ascot Berks SL5 9JF
Tel: (01344) 293614 for Admissions
e-mail: admissions@st-marys-ascot.co.uk

Management and Administration:

***Headmistress:* Mrs Mary Breen**, MSc (Manchester), BSc (Exeter)

Deputy Headmistress: Mrs Frances King, BA (Oxon), MA (London), PGCE
Deputy Head of Boarding: Miss Sheila Williams, CertEd, CTC (Liverpool)
Director of Studies: Mrs Sue Hammond, BSc (London), PGCE (Reading)
Senior Boarding Assistant: Mrs Veronica Watson, CertEd (Exmouth)
Bursar: Mr Michael McEvoy, MIMgt
Assistant to Bursar: Mrs Christine Morse
Domestic Bursar: Mrs Wendy Woolaway
Works & Building Manager: Mr Terence Forde
Accountant: Mr John Wilson
Assistants to Accountant: Mrs Jean Lee, Mrs Violet Thompson
Caterer: Mr Ron Curran, MHCIMA
Registrar: Mrs Sandra Young
Secretary to the Headmistress: Mrs Clare Davies
Assistant to the Registrar/Development Secretary: Mrs Glenda Beeches
School Secretary: to be appointed
School Receptionist: Mrs Sheila Hickmott
Secretary, Ascot Old Girls' Association: Mrs Phyllida Dewes
School Doctor: Dr Gillian Tasker, MB, BS, DRCOG
Senior Nursing Sister: Mrs Monica McGeown, RGN, SCM
Nursing Sister: Mrs Fiona Parsley, RGN
Resident Chaplain: The Revd Dermot Power, BA, BD, STL, STD
Chaplain: Sister M Jane Livesey, IBVM, MA (Cantab)

Heads of House:
Mrs Ruth Johnstone *Head of Mary Ward House*
Mrs Joanne Heywood *Head of Babthorpe*
to be appointed *Head of Bedingfield*
Mr and Mrs R James *Head of Poyntz*
Sister M Michaela Robinson, IBVM *Head of Rookwood*
Mr and Mrs R Meyer *Joint Heads of Wigmore*

Year Co-ordinators:
Year 7: Mrs Maz Down
Year 8: Miss Sheila Williams
Year 9: Mrs Sue Hammond
Year 10: Miss Polly Holmes
Year 11: Miss Gillian Murray

Sixth Form Tutors:
Mrs S Brown, BSc, PGCE (Exeter), BA (OU)
Mr G Docherty, BSc (Glasgow), PGCE
Mrs S Donovan, BA (Dublin), PGCE
Mrs S Head, BA (Nottingham), MSc (Leeds), PGCE (London)
Mrs K Holdich, BSc, MSc (Kingston), PGCE (Brighton)
Mrs M Lake, BA (Hatfield), PGCE
Mrs M Massey-Beresford, BA, PGCE (Birmingham)
Mrs K Newcombe, BSc (Nottingham), PGCE
Mrs C Norvill, BA Lib Hons, ALA (Birmingham), CCEG
Mrs L Povey, BA (Nottingham), MPhil Classics (London)
Mr A Simmons, MA (London), PGCE

Residential Staff:
Miss V Watson, CertEd *Senior Boarding Assistant*
Mrs M Bain
Mrs J Bennett
Mrs M Cheeseman
Mrs J Medlycot
Miss V Swire
Mrs J Scott
Mrs P Thompson
Mrs P Wallace

Academic Departments:

Religious Education:
Mr M J Hughes, PhB (Rome), CertEd *Head of Department*
Mrs F King, BA (Oxon), MA (London), PGCE
Mr R Meyer, BA (Durham)
Sister M Michaela, IBVM, CertEd (London)
Mrs H West, BA (Surrey), PGCE
Miss S Williams, CertEd, CTC
Mrs R Johnstone, City & Guilds Cert

English:
Mr A Simmons, MA (London), PGCE *Head of Department*
Miss Najoud Ensaff, BA (Southampton), PGCE (Swansea)
Mrs S Head, BA (Nottingham), PGCE (London)
Mrs M Massy-Beresford, BA, PGCE (Birmingham)

Drama:
Mrs H Jansen, BEd (Central School of Speech and Drama) *Head of Department*
Mr T Jelley, BA (Surrey), PGCE

Mathematics:
Mrs R Davies, BEd (Homerton, Cambridge) *Head of Department*
Mrs V Barker, BSc (Reading), PGCE
Mr G Docherty, BSc (Glasgow), PGCE
Mrs K Newcombe, BSc (Nottingham), PGCE

Classics:
Mrs L Povey, BA Hons Latin with Greek (Nottingham), MPhil Classics (London) *Head of Department*
Miss M Fisher, BA (Wales), PGCE
Miss R Furlonger, BA (Oxon), PGCE

Humanities:
Mrs K HoldichMSc (Kingston), PGCE *Geography, Head of Department*
Mrs M Lake, BA (Hatfield), PGCE *History*
Mrs S Donovan, BA (Trinity, Dublin), PGCE Economics & Political Science, MSc (Leeds) *Computer Science*
Mr A Marshall, MA (St Andrews), PGCE *History/Politics*
Miss G Murray, BSc (Wolverhampton), PGCE (Cantab) *Geography*

Modern Languages:
Mrs E Cook, DEUG (Toulouse), AdvDip English Studies (Portsmouth), PGCE (Oxford) *Head of Department, French*
Miss E Caretti, BA (Milan), PGCE *Italian*
Mrs S Chasemore *German Assistant*
Mrs D Crosby, BA (Dublin) *French*
Mr C Blanco Gomez, BA (Santiago di Cati) *Spanish and French*
Mrs S Boakes, MA (Oxon) *German and French*
Mrs C Bainton, BA Hons (London), PhD (Cantab) *Spanish*
Mlle V Feuillet, DEUG (Sorbonne), MA, PGCE *French*
Mlle F Lagarde *French Assistant*
Mrs C Mackay, MA (University of Nancy II), PGCE *French*

Sciences:
Mrs S Brown, BSc (Exeter), BA (OU), MEd *Chemistry, Head of Department*
Mrs L Carlsson, BSc (London) *Biology*
Mrs E Carr, MA (Oxon) *Chemistry*
Mrs J Heywood, BSc (Kingston), PGCE *Chemistry*
Miss P Holmes, BSc (Exeter), PGCE *Biology*
Mrs H Martin, BA (OU) *Physics*
Mrs S Meeks, BSc (Southampton) *Laboratory Technician*
Mr D Riding, MPhys (Sheffield), PGCE *Physics*
Mr M Twelftree, BA (OU), HNC, Dip Applied Physics, MInstPhysics, CertEd *Physics*
Mrs C Warren, BSc (Southampton), PGCE *Physics*
Mrs L Weston, City and Guilds Cert *Laboratory Assistant*

Information & Communications Technology:
Mrs S Hammond, BSc (London), PGCE (Reading) *ICT Manager*
Mrs E Carr, MA (Oxon) *Chemistry*
Mrs B Hudson-Reed, BA (Natal), HDE, FDE

Music:
Director of Music: to be appointed
Mr R James, BMus (London), ARCM *Piano, Organ, Violin, Asst Director of Music*
Mr N Hutchinson, ARCO, ARCM, GBSM, LTCL, ABSM *Organ*
Miss F Neary, BMus (London), PhD (Ohio) *Piano*
Mrs C Leneghan *Secretary*

Art and Design:
Mr M Mitchell, BA (Bristol Polytechnic), PGCE *Head of Department*
Mrs A Boddy, BA (St Martins), ATC (Sussex), DGCE (Reading), LRPS *Art and Photography*
Miss M Dye, DipMont (London)
Miss L Green, BA (De Montfort), PGCE
Mrs R James (Loughborough College of Art and Design) *Fine Art and Textiles*
Mr T Parsons, MA (York) *History of Art*
Mrs M Place, BA (OU), MA (Reading), ALA (London) *History of Art*
Miss D Thomson, BA (Middlesex), BTec Kent Institute of Art & Design *Textiles*

Physical Education:
Mrs J Gilkes, BA Hons (Cardiff Institute of HE) *Swimming & Watersports Head of Department*
Mrs M Down, CertEd (Chelsea College of PE)
Mrs A Wright, BA (OU) (Chelsea College of PE)
Miss M Milford, BEd (Chelsea College of PE) *PE with Maths*
Miss G Eamer, BSc (Coventry), PGCE (Sotton) *Geography and PE*
Mr J Bird, ACA *Tennis*
Mr P Whiteside *Fencing*
Ms L Stephenson *Ballet and Tap Dancing*
Ms Z Read *Modern Dance*

Miscellaneous:
Librarian and Careers Officer: Mrs C Norvill, BA Lib Hons, ALA (Birmingham)
Assistant Librarian: Mrs M Place, BA (OU), MA (Reading), ALA (London)
Reprographics: Mrs B Daniell, BSc Hons Physics (Liverpool)
Examination Officer: Mr M Hughes, PhB (Rome)
Special Needs Co-ordinator: Sr M Michaela Robinson, IBVM, CertEd (London), PGDipSpLD (*Dyslexia*)

St Mary's School Ascot is a Roman Catholic boarding school founded by the Religious of the Institute of the Blessed Virgin Mary. St Mary's today is a self-governing, self-financing school.

Founded in 1885, the school is set in 44 acres within easy reach of London and Heathrow and close to the M4, M3 and M25 motorways.

Numbers on roll. Boarders 324, Day pupils 26.

Age range. 11–18.

Method of Entry. 11+ and 13+ School's own examination and interview. There is a small entry at VI Form.

Fees. (*see* Entrance Scholarship section) Boarders £5,100 per term. Day pupils £3,395 per term.

Curriculum. All pupils follow a broad curriculum to 13+ in Religious Education, English, History, Geography, Maths, Biology, Physics, Chemistry, French, Latin, Music, Drama, Art and Design, Computing and Physical Education. Tuition is also available in Piano, most String and Wind Instruments, Ballet, Tap Dancing, German, Italian and Spanish, Fencing, Speech and Drama, Ceranics and Craft activities, Tennis, Photography.

All pupils are prepared for GCSE 16+ and are expected to take 8–10 subjects.

With A level 2000, Sixth Formers have a choice of 23 AS and A2 level subjects and are advised to consider 4 AS subjects for the Lower Sixth year. The number of subjects has not changed but structure has. Interview, CV and course choice preparation is offered to all Upper Sixth including Oxbridge candidates. They are encouraged to undertake some of the 34 extra activities on offer and develop skills outside their 'A' level curriculum. Sixth Formers also have their own tutor who liaises closely with the Careers Specialist. Careers advice forms an integral part of the curriculum. This is supported by work experience, work shadowing placements and talks from external speakers, including Ascot Old Girls. The majority of Sixth Formers go on to university, and preparation is offered to Oxbridge candidates.

The School is a member of ISCO (Independent Schools Careers Organisation).

Religious Education is an integral part of the curriculum throughout the school and all pupils are expected to participate in the Church's Liturgical Celebration. The school has its own Chapel and resident Chaplain.

Sport. Netball, Hockey, Gym, Swimming, Rounders, Tennis and Athletics.

Fifth and Sixth Formers may also opt for Jazz Dancing, Aerobics, Yoga, Body conditioning, Self-Defence, Badminton, Volley-Ball, Squash, Golf.

Art, Music, Science, Modern Languages and English. Specialist buildings are provided for all of these subjects and all pupils are encouraged to develop their musical, artistic, scientific and linguistic skills.

Libraries. Newly refurbished and re-equipped library with fully integrated information technology and access to school internet.

Other Activities. Senior pupils are encouraged to participate in Community Service Projects, and those interested may enter the Duke of Edinburgh Award Scheme. There is a wide range of club activities for all ages, and, as a termly boarding school, generous provision is made for evening and weekend activities.

Charitable status. St Mary's School Ascot is a Registered Charity, number 290286. Its aim is to provide an excellent education in a Christian atmosphere.

St Mary's School
Calne

Calne Wilts SN11 0DF
Tel: (01249) 857200
Fax: (01249) 857207

Visitor: The Lord Bishop of Salisbury

Governors:
The Revd A Griggs, BA
Miss M Falk, BA
Sir Brian Fall, GCVO, KCMG, MA, LLM
Mrs A Ferguson, OBE, BA, FCIM
S Knight, Esq, FRICS
P L Macdougall, Esq, MA, FCA
M Pipes, Esq, MA
R C Southwell, Esq, QC (*Chairman*)
P J C Troughton, Esq, MA

***Headmistress:* Mrs C J Shaw**, BA (London)

Deputy Head: Mrs S Tomlin, BA (London), MA *and English*

Head of Boarding: Mrs D Riley

Teaching Staff:

History:
Mrs S-J Socha, BA (Bristol)
Miss J Milburn, BA (London)
§Mrs V Gibson, BSocSc (Birmingham)
§Mrs S Fountain, BA (Dunelm)

English:
Mrs M Footman, BA (Bristol)
Mrs J Newby, BA (Sussex)
Mrs S Stables, BA (Swansea)

LAMDA:
Mrs J Trevithick, DipDramatic Art (London)
Mrs H Halliday, DipHons Acting (Guildford)

Drama:
Miss L Leadbetter, BA (Lancs)
§Mrs H Stokes, BA (York)

Religious Studies:
Mrs E Fogg, BA (Nottingham)
Miss E Bridgman, BA (Bristol)

Geography:
Mr G Collins, BA (Reading)
Miss J Dickson, BA (Southampton)
§Mrs S J Froggatt, BA (Leeds)
§Mrs S Livingstone, BA (Hull)

Classics:
Mrs C Smith, BA (Cantab)
Mrs L Pavey, MA (Edinburgh)
Mrs E E Rothwell, MA (Cantab)

French:
Mrs M J Hanson, BA (London) (*Head of Modern Languages*)
§Mrs J Barker, BA (Huddersfield)
Mrs H Malcolm, BA (York)

German:
Mrs L G Nunn, MA (London)

Spanish:
Mrs M Marca-Norris, BA (Bristol)

Mathematics:
Dr S J Rogers, MA (Oxon), PhD
Mr G L Clarke, BEd (Leeds) *and Computing*
§Mrs J Moore, BSc (York)
Mrs M Prescott, BSc (Bristol)

Computing:
§Mrs A Clark, BSc (Swansea)
Ms C Aish

Physics:
Dr J Rogers, MSc, PhD (Cranfield)
Dr N Upcott, BSc, PhD (Leeds)

Chemistry:
Mrs C V Adler, BSc (N London Polytechnic)
Mrs J Lomas, BA (Open)
Mrs J McKernan, BSc (Open)

Biology:
Mrs N M Warden, BSc (Exeter), BA (Oxon)
Mrs A Carter, BSc (Dundee)

Economics:
§Mrs M Gregory, BA (London)

Art:
Mr R Elliott, BEd (Nottingham) *3D Design*
Miss E Swan, BA (Warwick)
Mr A Crocker, BA Fine Art (London)

History of Art:
§Mrs A M Lowe, BA (Reading)

Music:
Mr K J Abrams, BA (York), LRAM, LTCL *Violin/Viola*
Mr G Field, GRSM, ARCO, DipRAM, LRAM *Organ/Piano*
Mr I Harries, BA (Huddersfield)
Miss P Hobson, MA (Cantab) *Singing/Piano*
Mr C P Howard, GRSM, ARCM *Piano*

and visiting teachers for string and wind instruments

Physical Education:
Mrs E Thompson, BEd, QTS (Bedford)
§Mrs S C Foreman, BEd (Sussex)
§Mrs S Hornby, BEd (Worcester College)
§Mrs Z Banks, BEd (Sussex)
Miss C Challens, BA, QTS (Brighton)

Careers:
§Mrs A Townsend, BSc (Glasgow)
§Mrs E E Brown, BSc (London)

Extra-Curricular Activities: Miss J Dickson, BA (Southampton) *and Geography*

PHSE: Mrs J Lacey, CertEd (Matlock College of Education)

Sanatorium:
Dr P R Harris, MB, ChB, DRCOG, FPCert

Sisters in Charge:
L Reeves, SRN
G Payne, SRN

Bursar: Mrs A Martin, MBA, MAAT

St Mary's School, Calne, offers its 300 girls, aged 11–18, a stimulating academic education in an attractive, informal and supportive environment. Great emphasis is placed on pastoral care and there is a successful tutor system.

The twenty-six acre school campus provides excellent facilities, not only for teaching but also for a wide range of evening and weekend activities in which day girls are encouraged to participate alongside their boarding friends. Drama, music, art and sports are very popular in the girls' free time, as is the Duke of Edinburgh's Award Scheme; virtually all girls work for the Bronze Award and large numbers go on to higher levels.

The full range of academic subjects is taught and public examination results are consistently impressive. In 2000 at 'A' level 95% of girls achieved grades A-C, with 39% achieving A grades in three or more subjects, which once again placed St Mary's in the first division of the Independent Schools' Results League Table. At GCSE, all girls invariably achieve success in between seven and ten subjects. In 2000 76% of GCSE candidates achieved grades A or A* in all their subjects.

There is a well equipped Careers library and full-time Careers staff who give individual guidance in choosing universities and careers.

Various academic and music scholarships are available at 11+, 12+, and 13+, together with additional scholarships in art and drama at Sixth Form level. Scholarships are also available for daughters of the Clergy and of Old Girls.

Anyone interested in learning more about St Mary's or wishing to receive a prospectus should contact the school office on telephone: 01249 857200, fax: 01249 857207 or e-mail: registrar@stmaryscalne.wilts.sch.uk.

Scholarships (*see* Entrance Scholarship section). For details, please see appropriate entries under Scholarship section.

St Margaret's Preparatory School. The co-educational day preparatory school is situated within St Mary's grounds and shares St Mary's School's excellent facilities. Tel: 01249 857220. Fax: 01249 857227.

Charitable status. St Mary's School, Calne is a Registered Charity, number A309482 and exists for the education of children.

St Mary's School
Cambridge

Bateman Street Cambridge CB2 1LY
Tel: (01223) 353253 Headmistress and School Office

Founded in 1898, St Mary's School is an independent Catholic Day and Boarding School administered by the Religious of the Institute of the Blessed Virgin Mary, together with lay Trustees and Governors. Students of other Christian denominations are also welcome.

Governing Body:
Chairman: Dr J Tudor

Mr S Anderson
Dr S Froggett, MD
Sister Cecilia Goodman, IBVM
Dr S Murk-Jansen
Dr B O'Keefe
Mr R Pearce Gould
Sister Armine Radley, IBVM
Father Anthony Rogers
Sister Gemma Simmonds, IBVM
Mrs D Wilkinson
Mr J Woodhouse

Clerk to the Governors and Bursar: Mr Peter Luard

Headmistress: **Mrs Jayne Triffitt**, MA (Oxon)

Teaching Staff:
Miss E Aust, BA (Oxon) *English*
Mrs A Beckett, BSc (Newcastle) *Information Technology Co-ordinator*
Mr Q Benziger, ARCO, LTRAM, GRSM *Director of Music*
Mrs J Bevan, DipArt (Leicester) *Pottery, Art*
Miss C Bowie, BA (Sterling) *French*
Mrs M Brown, MA (St Andrews) *History*
Mrs O Cheng, BA (Oxon), LitHum
Miss C Cooksey, BA (Leeds), MSc (Aston) *Italian, French*
Mrs R d'Armada, BSc (Manchester) *Mathematics*
Mr A Dalwood, MA (Oxon) *Geography, Librarian*
Mrs M Dixon, BA (Open) *Sociology*
Mrs K Dodsworth, MA (Lampeter) *Theology*
Mrs D Fehse, BA (Portland, Oregon, USA), BA (Illinois) *German*
Miss A Fleming, BA (Liverpool), MEd *RE*
Mrs J Francis, Licence ès Lettres (Bordeaux) *French*
Mrs W Galloway, BSc (Sussex) *Science*
Mrs H Garrett, MA (Oxon) *English*
Dr C Goddard, PhD (Cantab) *Classics*
Mrs H Goy, MA (Cantab), BSc (Open) *Classics*
Miss J Gregg, BA (West Sussex Inst) *Physical Education*
Miss K Hall, BA (Cantab) *Mathematics*
Mrs F Harding, BA (CCAT) *Geography*
Mrs H Harris, MA (Newfoundland) *Mathematics*
Mrs F Hawken, CertEd (Sheffield) *Physical Education*
Dr A Jackson, BSc, PhD (Liverpool) *Chemistry*
Mrs H Jackson, BEd (Nottingham) *Textiles*
Mrs M Jackson, BEd (Newcastle) *English*
Mr F Jeans, DipArt & Design (London) *Art & Design*
Mrs J Jeans, Dip Art (Sheffield) *Art & Design*
Miss S Josiffe, BEd (Bedford) *PE*
Ms C Klimaszewska, CertEd (Homerton), MIBiol, CBiol *Science*
Mrs A Ladds, BEd (London) *Textiles*
Mrs M Linford, BSc, MEd (London) *Biology*
Sister Jane Livesey, MA (Cantab), IBVM *Chaplain*
Mrs J Mathers, BSc (Hull) *Mathematics*
Dr G Miller, PhD (Birmingham) *Physics*
Mr C Morgans, BSc (London) *English*
Mrs J Munday, Licence ès Lettres (Paris) *French*
Mrs P Nicholson, BA (Liverpool) *Economics & Business Studies*
Mr R Peachey, BA (Oxon) *Modern History*
Miss R Pike, BA (Exeter) *Modern Languages*
Miss A Ratcliffe, BA (Surrey) *Information Technology*
Mrs K Ratcliffe, BSc (Natal, South Africa), MSc (London) *Biology*
Mrs L Robinson, MA (Oxon) *Music*
Mrs N Rubinstein, BA (Bristol), Dip Art & Design (Hornsey) *History of Art*
Mrs C Ryder, BA (Bangor) *English*
Mrs M Schofield, BA (London) *History*
Miss F Spore, MA (Cantab) *Geography*
Mrs K Thompson, BEd (Cheltenham) *Physical Education*
Mrs J Toller, BA (Hull) *Music*
Mrs M Ward, BA (Durham) *Religious Studies*
Mrs S Watling, MA (SSSD), LLAM (LAMDA) *Drama*
Mrs C Williams, BSc (St Andrews) *Chemistry*
Mrs K Wyer-Roberts, BA (Manchester) *Classics*

Boarding Staff:
Mrs C Hartley (*Housemistress*)
Miss K Murray (*Housemistress - Medical*)
Mrs L Robinson (*Head of International Boarding*)

School Doctor: Dr E C Stringer, MB, BS, DRCOG, MRCGP

Visiting Staff:
Mrs S Brawn, BA, LTCL *Singing*
Mrs L Britton, LRAM *Piano*
Mr D Carter *Clarinet*
Mrs C Castledine, BA *Singing*
Mrs C Gordon, GMus, ARCM *Piano*
Mrs A Heron, FTCL, LRAM, LRSM, LTCL *Piano*
Mrs H Hymas, LTCL, MTC *Oboe*
Mr J Landymore, ALCM, ARCM *Saxophone*
Ms C Langan, BA Hons, DPPRAM *Flute*
Mrs A Lewsey, CertEd *Speech and Drama*
Mrs S McConnell *Speech & Drama*
Mrs R Millard, LTCL, MusEd *Flute*
Mr P Spink, LRAM, CertEd *Clarinet*
Mrs G Sutcliffe, CertEd *Violin*
Mr W Watson, ARCM *Brass*

Administrative Staff:
Headmistress's PA: Mrs S Collier
School Secretary: Mrs J Bauld
Registrar: Mrs E Hamilton-Kennaway
Receptionist: Mrs P Vallins
School Accountant: Mr I Chamberlain
Accounts Secretary: Mrs J Doe
Senior Laboratory Technician: Mrs J Thurston

Admission. The school's own entrance examination at 11+. A few vacancies occur at other ages. Sixth Form entry is by examination and interview, conditional on 5 GCSE passes at A*-C, with B grade or more in those subjects to be chosen for A level.

Extra Subjects. Piano and Instrumental Music. Speech and Drama. Judo and Dance.

Fees. £2,060 per term. Pension for weekly boarding £3,690 per term. Full boarding £4,550 inclusive.

Scholarships. Scholarships are available at 16+.

Curriculum. Within the setting of a Christian community the school provides an 'all-round' education enabling each girl to realise her full potential. Students are prepared for GCSE, A Level, University Entrance, and for other forms of higher education and professional training in a wide variety of careers. The curriculum includes Religious Education, English, History, Geography, Latin, Greek, French, German, Italian, Spanish, Mathematics, Computer Studies, Physics, Chemistry, Biology, Art and Design, Textiles, Theatre Studies, Music, Drama, PE and Games. Option schemes in Year 10 are arranged in such a way that each girl has a balanced programme without premature specialisation. At A Level there is a very wide choice of subjects. All Sixth Formers follow a course of General Studies and many take the Cambridge Information Technology course.

The School stands in its own grounds adjoining the University Botanic Gardens. The varied complex of buildings old and new contains Science laboratories, libraries, assembly halls, gymnasium, specialist rooms for Geography, Music, IT, Art, Design Technology, Textiles and Careers.

Sixth Form Centre. As part of the School's centenary celebrations a new Sixth Form Centre opened in September 1998. It provides an exclusive study facility with integral reference library and neighbouring computer suite. In addition there are common rooms, changing rooms and a workshop area for use by set designers for drama productions and for members of St Mary's almost perennially successful Young Enterprise Company.

Extra-curricular Activities. The school provides a wide range of activities at lunch-times and after school – everything from Judo to Japanese and Debating to Duke of Edinburgh's Award Scheme.

Supervised Homework Club. This is run by the teaching staff from 4 pm to 6 pm, Monday–Thursday, and 4–5 pm on Fridays.

Boarding. We offer full boarding as well as weekly and flexible boarding. Our boarding accommodation has been completely refurbished and all girls in Year 10 and above have attractive single study bedrooms, whilst younger boarders share comfortable bedrooms (2-4 girls per room).

Flexi–Weekly Boarding. Our flexible weekly boarding facility is popular with both students and their parents as it offers the best of both worlds at school and at home. Girls can stay for an overnight 'sleep-over' or for longer, dependent on the requirements at the time. Older students have individual study bedrooms and the younger girls share bedrooms with their friends in a recently refurbished junior area.

Charitable status. St Mary's School Cambridge is a Registered Charity, number 290180. It aims to promote and provide for the advancement of education and religion for children of the Roman Catholic faith.

St Mary's School
Colchester

Lexden Road Colchester Essex CO3 3RB
Tel: (01206) 572544
Fax: (01206) 576437

Board of Governors:
Chairman: Miss J Fulford

Mr R V Borgartz
Mr A Brown
Mrs J L Jones
Mrs J Kimmance
Mrs M Livingstone
Mr I MacNaughton
Mrs S Masters

Bursar: Mr P M C Clarke, MA, MBA, CEng, MIMechE, AMIEE

***Principal:* Mrs G M G Mouser**, MPhil (London)

Deputy: Mrs D E Short, MA (Oxon)

Head of Lower School: Mrs S C Watson, BA (Open University), CertEd (Bristol)

Staff:
Mrs J M Baitey, DipAD, BA (Birmingham)
Mrs E Bennett, DipPhysEd (Bedford)
Mr E W Black, BA (Oxon), MA (Keele)
Miss S Bowles, BA (Essex)
Mrs G Boyd, DipEd (Moray House)
Mrs J Brown, CertEd (Leeds)
Mrs H Clayton-Grainger, BA (Lancaster)
Mrs L Connon, BSc (Edinburgh)
Mrs S Cook, BA (American Univ. of Beirut)
Miss L Cunningham, BA (Anglia)
Miss T K Davies, BA (Warwick)
Mrs T V Eccles, DipEd (Birmingham)
Mrs E A Edgecombe, BA (Keele), DipSpLD
Mrs V Francis, BA (South Africa)
Mrs L Gadsby, BA (Open University), CertEd (Bishop Otter, Chichester)
Mrs G M Gerrard, GTCL, LTCL
Mrs A Graham, DipEd (St Matthias, Bristol)
Mr J Hammersley, BA (East Anglia)
Mrs J Hearsum, CertEd (St Osyth, Cambridge)
Mrs A Heather, BA (Coventry)
Miss L Holmes, HND/DipHE (Colchester)
Dr H A Langelüddecke, MA (Heidelberg), DPhil (Oxon)
Mrs S Leeson, BA (Essex)
Mrs L E Lerwill, BSc (Wales)
Mrs J Lindsey-Smith, BA (Sheffield)
Mrs S C Long, NDD, CertEd (Leeds)
Mrs J McCarthy, BSc (Bristol)
Mrs K Margery, CertEd (Eaton Hall)
Mrs J Maydon, BEd (Leicester)
Mr N Merry, BA (Durham)
Mrs A Mullen, BEd (Portsmouth)
Mrs V Nicholson, BEd (Anglia)
Mrs S Oakley, CertEd (Newcastle)
Mrs F Parker, CertEd (Lady Spencer Churchill)
Mrs C J Parry-Jones, CertEd (CNAA), FETC
Mrs L M Pendle, CertEd (Cambridge)
Mrs C Pettman, CertEd (Nonington)
Miss R Pferdmenges, BA (Portsmouth), MA (Duisburg)
Mr M Roots, MSc (London)
Mrs D Rose, BEd (Doncaster)
Mrs B Shephard, BSc (Leeds)
Mrs S J Sutton, CertEd (Sarum)
Mrs L Taverner, CertEd (Bedford)
Mrs C Thompson, BA (Leeds)
Mrs L Tilly, BA (Stirling)
Mrs C M Treacher, BA (Sheffield)
Mrs H Vipond, BSc (Leeds), MEd (Hatfield)
Mrs M Walsh, CertEd (Dunelm)
Mr N West, BA (Griffith, Brisbane)
Mrs L Whitehead, CertEd (Bretton Hall)
Mr A Woodham, BSc (Kent), MEd (OU)
Mrs J Woodland, BSc (Salford)

Visiting Staff:
Mrs M Blanchard, BA (CNAA), LTCL *Flute*
Mr C Gould, LRAM *Violin, Percussion*
Mr A Johnson, BMus *Guitar*
Mr C Matthews, LLCM, CertMusicEd, TCL *Brass*
Mr T Parr, CertMus (CNAA), LTCL *Piano, Singing*
Ms C Simmons, LRAM *Violin*

St Mary's is a day school for girls, founded in 1908, which currently has 500 pupils between the ages of 4 and 17.

The Main School in Lexden Road is light and airy, and equipped with specialist teaching rooms including four laboratories, a computer room and rooms for Textiles, Home Economics and Art, a Library and a careers information centre. Provision for physical education includes a gymnasium, tennis and netball courts, and a heated open-air swimming pool. These facilities are supplemented by the use of the local Sports Centre and playing fields.

A building programme, including a Performing Arts Studio, Music and Textiles facilities, new Art and Geography suites and a second ICT room, should shortly be completed.

The Lower School is housed in the nearby Stanway premises set in grounds of nine acres, with tennis and netball courts, sports field, adventure playground and nature trail.

Throughout the school each girl is encouraged to develop her personality and academic potential as fully as possible, and a broadly based curriculum is followed until Year 10, when a little more specialisation is necessary, to cater for GCSE courses. The forms are not streamed: setting is arranged as necessary. Optional extras include lessons in woodwind, brass, strings and piano.

Lower School pupils are prepared for Common Entrance and the 11+ examinations; Seniors are prepared for the GCSE.

Clubs and Societies meet in the lunch hour and after school, and music and the creative arts are encouraged.

Entry is by written assessment and interview.

The school prospectus and current details of fees will be sent on request, and parents are always welcome at the school by appointment with the Principal.

Charitable status. St Mary's School (Colchester) Limited is a Registered Charity, number 309266. Its aims and objectives are to promote and provide for the advancement of education, and in connection therewith to conduct, carry on, acquire and develop, in the UK and elsewhere, any day or boarding school(s) for the education of children.

St Mary's School
Gerrards Cross

Gerrards Cross Buckinghamshire SL9 8JQ
Tel: (01753) 883370
Fax: (01753) 890966

Badge: *Ecce Ancilla Domini* Founded by Dean Butler in 1872. Formerly at Lancaster Gate. Established in Gerrards Cross in 1937 as an Independent Day School catering for 300 day girls.

Governors:
Chairman: Mr J Loarridge, OBE, RD, BA

Mr P R Bowen
Mr R J Burge
Mr D G B Gorton
Mr J R M Hanney
Mrs P Hurd, NDD, ATC
Mrs J McRae
Prof S Machin, MB, ChB, FRCP, FRCPath
Mrs H Phillips, FCA
Mr P Taylor, LLB (Hons), ARICS
Dr D Westlake, MB, BS
Revd P Williams, BA, MPhil
Mr D R Wilson, BA, FCA

Bursar: Mr R J Ward, FCA

Staff:
***Headmistress:* Mrs F A Balcombe**, BA Hons (Southampton), PGCE *English, FRSA*

Deputy Headmistress: Mrs G R Eilerts de Haan, MScChemTech(THT), PGCE *Chemistry*

Middle School Tutor: Miss J H Miles, CertEd *Science, Mathematics*
Upper School Tutor: Mrs S Vaughan, MA (Oxford), PGCE *Physics*
Sixth Form Tutor: Mrs E Persaud, BA Hons (Leicester), PGCE *History, Careers*

Senior School:
Miss S J Abbott, BA Hons (Durham), PGCE *Music*
Miss F Alexander, BA (Glasgow School of Art) *Art & Design*
Mrs K Andrew, BEd Hons (Reading), PGCE *English*
Mrs J Cannon, BA Hons (Newcastle), PGCE *Spanish and French*
Mrs V Culmer, BA Hons (Oxon), PGCE *Drama and English*
Mrs J V Giorgi, BA Hons (Swansea), PGCE *Geography*
Mrs B Gooding, BSc Hons (London), PGCE *Mathematics*
Mrs V Hadden, BSc Hons (Aston), PGCE *Chemistry*
Mrs A Hadwin, BA Hons (Oxford) *Religious Education*
Mrs M A Hall, MA Hons (Cantab) *ICT Technician*
Miss T Hancock, HND Music/Theatre *Speech & Drama*
Mrs K B Hills, BA Hons (Bristol), PGCE *Italian/German/French/Latin*
Mrs C Johnson, MSc (Canterbury), PGCE *Biology*
Mrs S Jones, MA Childrens Literature, BA Hons (Reading), PGCE *English*
Miss H McArthur, MA Hons (Glasgow), DipEd, DMS, DRS, AM *Business Studies/Singing*
Mrs A Macdonald, BSc (Strathclyde), PGCE *Mathematics*
Miss J H Miles, CertEd *General Subjects*
Mrs S Moore, BEd (Sussex) *Physical Education*
Mrs A Morrison, TCert (Auckland, NZ) *PE*
Mrs E Persaud, BA Hons (Leicester), PGCE *History, Careers*
Mrs J Richards, CertEd (Bath) *Home Economics*
Mrs J M Rubin, BA Hons (Warwick), PGCE *French*
Mrs B Sanderson, BEd Hons (Nottingham), PGCE *History and Geography*
Mrs J Seymour, MA Hons (Edinburgh), PGCE *French*
Mrs J Somerville, BA (Open Univ), CertEd *English, Mathematics*
Mrs A C Steele, BSc (Glasgow), MInstAM *Computer Studies, Design & Technology*
Mrs S Vaughan, MA (Oxford), PGCE *Physics*
Mrs M White, BSc (Open University), CertEd *Physical Education, Librarian*
Mrs C Wilson, ONC (RSA), DipSpLD *Special Needs*

Junior School:
Head of Department: Mrs K A Williams, BEd Hons (Cambridge) *General Subjects*

Mrs E Cook, BEd Hons (Reading) *General Subjects/French*
Mrs C Hyett *Nursery Assistant, PPADip, Paediatric First Aider*
Mrs S Jenkins *General Assistant/First Aider*
Mrs A Johnstone, BSc Hons (Roehampton), PGCE *General Subjects*
Mrs P Kelly, CertEd (Northampton) *General Subjects*
Mrs J Lukas, NNEB Cert *Art, Nursery Teacher*
Mrs McGarvie, CertEd (Glasgow) *Geography, General Subjects*
Mrs G Pierozynski, GRNCM, ARNCM, PGCE *Music*
Mrs V Potts, CertEd (Newcastle) *History, General Subjects*
Mrs M Schwartz, BA Hons (Leeds), PGCE *General Subjects/French*
Mrs A Yeoman, BA Hons (Roehampton) *General Subjects*

Visiting Staff:
Mr R Corden, ARCM, AI Kneller Hall *Flute, Clarinet, Saxophone*
Mrs C L Henry, AISTD *Ballet*
Mrs E McGee, GRSM, ARCM *Piano*
Miss C McCracken, ARCM, DipRCMPerf *Violin & Viola*

Mrs A Monzani, AISTD *Ballroom Dancing*
Miss S Ownsworth, BMus Hons, LRAM, DipPostGrad, PerfDistRAM *Singing and Piano*
Mrs H Steady, MA (Reading), PGDipEd, LTCL *Piano*
Registrar & Headmistress's Secretary: Mrs R Lines

The School is situated in the attractive residential area of Gerrards Cross which is surrounded by beautiful countryside, 20 miles from London, on the main bus routes and 10 minutes from the Railway Station.

The aim of the School is to provide an excellent academic and rounded education leading on to University for day girls between the ages of 3 and 18 and to enable each of them to develop their own talents and personalities in a happy, caring and disciplined environment, and to become successful, fulfilled young women in today's society.

Curriculum. Subjects offered include English Language and Literature, History, Politics, Geography, RE, Latin, French, German, Spanish, Italian, Business Studies, Information Technology, Mathematics, Chemistry, Biology, Physics, Music, Art, Home Economics, Word Processing and Typewriting, Gymnastics, Hockey, Netball, Tennis, Rounders, Swimming, Media, Health & Social Care, Dancing and other sporting activities. Regular expeditions are made to places of educational interest, field courses are undertaken, and there is highly successful participation in the Duke of Edinburgh's Award Scheme, Young Enterprise. There is an excellent staff/pupil ratio.

Examinations. Girls are prepared for Entrance to the Universities and Colleges in all subjects; for the General Certificate of Education at AS, A2 and GCSE Level and Advanced GNVQ in Business, Health and Social Care, and Media; RSA CLAIT Examinations, City & Guilds Examinations, Associated Board Examinations in Music and examinations in Speech and Drama. Standardised tests are set at regular intervals in Junior House.

The buildings are a happy blend of old and contemporary design and include a Memorial Library, Dining Hall, a Science Block with Laboratories and a Geography Room, a Home Economics Room, Fabric Room, 2 Computer Rooms, 2 Sixth Form Common Rooms, Music Room, Drama Studio, Chapel and 2 Assembly Halls/Gymnasiums equipped to the highest standards. Junior House is in the grounds of the Senior House and provides accommodation for 150 children between the ages of 3–9. The grounds are most attractive and include tennis and netball courts, a hockey pitch, an athletics lawn and an open-air heated swimming pool.

School Hours. The hours are 8.30 am – 3.40 pm. The School year is divided into 3 terms. Full School Reports are sent to Parents at the end of each term and there are regular Parent/Staff meetings.

Fees. On application.

Scholarships are available at 11+ (including one for Music) and in the Sixth Form.

Charitable status. St Mary's School (Gerrards Cross) Limited is a Registered Charity, number 310634. It provides education for girls from Nursery to A level in a well-structured, academic and caring environment.

* Head of Department	§ Part Time or Visiting
† Housemaster/Housemistress	¶ Old Pupil
‡ See below list of staff for meaning	

St Mary's School
Shaftesbury

Shaftesbury Dorset SP7 9LP
Tel: (01747) 854005 Headmistress and Admissions
852416 School and Administration
851188 Bursar's Office
Fax: (01747) 851557

Governors:
Mr J H Smith, CBE (*Chairman*)
Mrs A Beale, MA (Oxon)
Mrs J Dallyn, LLB, JP
Mrs L Eeles, JP
Mr J W R Goulding, MA
Sister M Cecilia Goodman, IBVM
Mr R Wilson, BA
Lady Katharine Page
Vice Admiral M P Gretton
Mr C C McCann
Col R J M Carson, OBE

***Headmistress:* Mrs S Pennington**, BA Hons (Liverpool)

Deputy Head (Academic): Mr J O'Hare, BA Hons (Liverpool), MSc (South Bank Polytechnic, London) *Mathematics*

Bursar: Mr N M Peters, ACIB

Academic Staff:
Mrs M Andow, BA Hons (Southampton) *Head of History*
Mrs G Baines, MA (Cantab) *Classics*
Mr S Barros, BTecHND (Gwent) *IT*
Mrs K Booth, CertEd (Bedford College) *Head of PE*
Ms R M R Brand, BA Hons (Wales), MA *English, Careers, Housemistress*
Miss Y Burdett, GRSM, ARCM, ALCM *Music, Piano*
Mr D Cohen, BA Hons (Aberystwyth) *Director of Studies, Head of English*
Mrs G Cork, BA Hons (Lancaster Polytechnic) *French, EFL*
Mrs J Duggan, BA Hons (London) *History of Art*
Mrs A Fearnley, BSc Hons (St Andrews) *Chemistry*
Miss B FitzHugh, BEd Hons (Bristol) *Duke of Edinburgh Award Scheme*
Mrs E Gilbert, DipAD (St Martins, London), ATD (Sussex) *Art*
Mr T Goodwin, MA Hons (Oxon) *History, RE*
Mrs G Götke, BA Hons (London) *Spanish, Italian*
Mrs C Gray *Science Technician*
Miss A Hickman, MA (Cambridge) *Classics*
Mrs J S E Hobbs, BEd (St Mary's, Cheltenham) *Art, Textiles*
Mrs S Holman, DipAD (Wimbledon) *Speech & Drama, Junior School*
Mrs C Jones, MSc (Southampton) *Head of Science, Physics*
Mrs H Key, BA Hons (Liverpool), PGCE (OU) *Junior School*
Mrs M Loveday, BSc Hons (Reading) *Head of Mathematics*
Mrs A Maclaine, MA Hons (Edinburgh) *German*
Mrs G McGovern, MA Hons (Oxon), MA Hons (Lancaster) *Religious Education*
Miss G Matthews, BEd (Keele) *English, Housemistress*
Mrs C Mingham, CertEd *English, Science, Geography, History; Housemistress*
Mrs R A Morgan, BEd (Gwent) *Head of IT, Mathematics, Senior Mistress*
Ms P Nolan, MA (Roehampton) *Head of RE, Housemistress*
Mrs C Norton, BA (Liverpool) *English*

Mrs E O'Hare, BSc Hons (Liverpool) *Biology, Examination Secretary*
Miss D Radford, FLCM, ARCM, LGSM, LLCM, *Director of Music*
Mrs J A Ridgway, BA Hons (Loughborough) *Head of Art, Design & Technology*
Mrs F M Rowland, BA Hons (London) *French*
Mrs V Rushton, BSc Hons (Liverpool) *Biology*
Mrs A Salmon, CertEd (Strawberry Hill), *PE, RE, Housemistress*
Mr N Savage, BA Hons (Bristol) *Classics*
Mr J Singleton, BSc Hons (London) *Geography*
Mrs R Smith, BSc Hons (London) *Mathematics*
Mrs D Sudlow, CertEd (Bristol Polytechnic) *Art, Technology*
Mr C Sykes, BA Hons (Dartington College of Arts) *English, Drama*
Mrs J Tidbury *Art Technician*
Dr M Turnbull, BSc Hons (Surrey), PhD *Chemistry, IT*
Miss J Walker, BEd Hons (Sussex) *Head of Middle School, PSE, PE*
Ms S Walker, BA Hons (Aberystwyth), ALA *Librarian*
Mrs D Webb, BA (Bristol Polytechnic) *French*
Mrs S Williams *Head of Senior School, Music*

Junior School:
Mrs V Cooper-Hammond, BA Hons (Bristol)
Mrs J Thomas
Mrs E Seal

Visiting Staff:
Mrs K Alder, BSc (Bristol), LRSM *Piano*
Mrs D Binninton, GRSM, LRAM, ARCM, LTCL *Piano, Voice*
Mr S Binnington, GRSM, ARCM, FRCO, LRAM, LTCL *Organ*
Mrs A Caunce, GRSM, LTCL, ARCM *Piano*
Mrs C Collins, BSc Hons (Open), LRAM *Piano*
Mrs J Faulkner, GRNCM, ARNCM *Percussion*
Mrs K Hawes *Violin*
Miss A Leigh, BMus Hons, ARCM, LGSM *Flute*
Miss S Lockyer, GRSM, LRAM *Clarinet, Saxophone*
Mr S Lockyer, GRSM, LRAM *'Cello, Double Bass*
Mrs J Lumb, BAPA *Music*
Miss T Maybury *Bassoon*
Mr S Mingay *Clarinet*
Mrs R Owen, GNSM, LRAM, ARCM *Oboe*
Mrs W Partridge, LTCL *Guitar*
Mrs K Sheppard *Brass, Music Therapist*
Mrs M Weston, BSc Hons (Dunelm), GNSM, ARCM *Piano*

Nursing Staff:
Mrs J Lewis, SRN
Mrs E Pocock, SRN
Mrs K Webber, SRN
Mrs S Savage, RGN

Assistant Nurse: Mrs S Burt, SRN

Administration Staff:
Headmistress' Secretary: Mrs J King
PR and Marketing: Mrs S Awdry
Registration Secretary: Mrs K Day
Bursar's Secretary: Mrs P Bartram
Secretary/Receptionist: Mrs J Hamilton
Accountant: Mrs M Gordon
Accounts Assistants: Mrs B L Durdle, Mrs G Head
Domestic Bursar: Mr A Blake
Evening Receptionist: Mrs E O'Sullivan

Founded in 1945, St Mary's School, Shaftesbury is an Independent Roman Catholic Boarding and Day School for girls administered by the Religious of the Institute of the Blessed Virgin Mary, together with a Governing Body. It is situated on the A30 just outside Shaftesbury and stands in its own grounds of 55 acres.

Numbers on Roll. 216 boarders, 102 day girls.

Age range. 9–18 years.

Admission. The School has its own Entrance Examination at 9+, 10+ and 11+. 12+ and 13+ entry is usually by Common Entrance. Sixth Form entry is by testimonial and interview and is then conditional on 5 GCSE passes.

Fees. (*see* Entrance Scholarship section) Boarders: At 9+, 10+ £4,150 per term; from 11+ to 18 £4,375 per term.

Day girls: At 9+, 10+ £2,700 per term; from 11+ to 18 £2,840 per term.

Aims and Curriculum. The School aims to give girls as broad an education, both spiritual, personal, academic and extra-curricular, as possible, thus enabling each girl to realise her own strengths in the various areas and build on them. Religious education is an integral part of the curriculum throughout the School. During Years 7–9 all girls follow a common curriculum which includes Religious Education, English, History, Geography, French, Latin, Mathematics, Information Technology, Integrated Science, Art, Textiles, Technology, Music, Singing, PSE and PE. From Year 10 both the core curriculum (RE, English Language and Literature, Maths, French and Balanced Science (Double Award)) and options are arranged to ensure that each girl follows a balanced course suitable to her ability and interests.

The majority of girls remain for 'A' Levels of which they have a choice of 17. Girls may take some further GCSEs in the Sixth Form if they wish. The Sixth Form curriculum also includes RE, Art, Textiles, Information Technology, Desk Top Publishing, Theatre Workshop, Current Affairs and PE.

The School is a member of ISCO (Independent Schools Careers Organisation) and all girls receive individual careers advice from the specialist Head of Careers. All girls go on to some form of Higher Education and the majority to University.

Music. The Music Department is large and any orchestral instrument may be learned. In addition there are three school choirs, a chamber choir, orchestra and various instrumental ensembles.

Sport. Winter: Netball, hockey, gym and dance. Summer: Swimming, tennis, rounders, athletics. The School has its own Sports Hall.

Extra subjects or activities. Speech and drama, ballet, riding, tennis coaching, Duke of Edinburgh Award, photography and a range of other Societies.

Charitable status. St Mary's School Shaftesbury Trust is a Registered Charity, number 1949068. Its aims and objectives are to administer an independent Roman Catholic school for the education of children of any Christian denomination.

St Mary's School
Wantage

Wantage Trust Ltd Wantage Oxon OX12 8BZ
Tel: (01235) 763571; Admissions (01235) 768323
Fax: (01235) 760467
e-mail: stmarysw@rmplc.co.uk

Founded 1873

Governors:

Chairman: Sir Godfrey Milton-Thompson, KBE
Chairman Finance Committee: Mr I W Frazer, FCA

The Reverend Mother, CSMV
The Rt Revd Michael Ball

Headmistress: **Mrs S Sowden**, BSc, AKC (London), AdvDipEd

Deputy Head: Mrs P J Woodhouse, BMus (Hons)

Chaplain: The Revd R F Clayton-Jones, AKC (London)

Development Director: Mr C P L Bullmore

Admissions: Mrs M Conway

Head's PA: Mrs C V Boheimer

Careers Advisor: Mrs M Thompson, TeachCert

School Doctor: Dr Joy Arthur, MBBS, MRCGP, DRCOG, DCH

Director of Studies: Miss J G Kingdon, MA

Director of Sixth Form: Mrs J Bennett, BSc

Bursar: Col J S Knox

The School, which was founded in 1873, has 200 full boarders in the Senior School, plus a maximum of 20 day girls who are part of the full boarding community and often sleep over a number of nights per week. In the Junior Department, St Andrew's, there are 85 boys and girls aged 3 to 11. Flexible Junior Boarding is available for girls from 7. The Senior School was run by the Anglican Community of St Mary the Virgin until 1975 when a Charitable Trust took over, which now forms the Governing Body. The Community is still strongly represented on this, and the School continues as a Church of England school with regular services in the School Chapel. Confirmation takes places twice a year.

Situation. The School is situated in the small market town of Wantage, at the foot of the Berkshire Downs, 15 miles south of Oxford. Easy access by road, rail and airports. The nearest railway station is situated at Didcot which is 15 minutes away. Escorted travel is provided to and from London, Didcot and Heathrow.

Buildings. The grounds and playing fields occupy about 15 acres, and contain a Chapel, Hall with both dramatic and orchestral stages, and a new Music Building. Specialist teaching rooms are provided for all subjects. ICT facilities include 2 large networked rooms, an Internet room and computers in both Sixth Form Houses. The school has just installed the first campus-wide wireless laptop network system in an independent school. It enables the girls to communicate with tutors, central printers, each other and the www from anywhere on site via their laptops fitted with small aerials. The grounds include a sports hall, full-sized indoor heated swimming pool and 11 tennis courts. The lacrosse pitches are a short distance away.

Pastoral care. The 11-year-old girls have their own Housemistress, and live in a part of the main building in 4 bedded rooms with their own recreation room. The accommodation for Years 8–11 is divided between two Houses with their own House Staff team and recreational facilities. Year 8 have 4 bedded rooms, Year 9 doubles, Year 10 a mixture of doubles and singles and Year 11 have single studies with their own recreation room.

The Sixth Form live in 2 purpose-built Houses in mostly single study bedrooms with a Housemistress supported by a team of three. Each Sixth Form House has kitchen and laundry facilities, a recreation room and a computer room. Sixth Formers do not wear school uniform, but are expected to dress tidily. They are expected, under the direction of their Tutor, to take responsibility for their own learning and to organise their own lives in order to prepare for University life.

Health Centre. The Health Centre is staffed by a team of qualified nurses. The School Doctor holds weekly surgeries as does a visiting orthodontist.

Curriculum. At St Andrew's there is a lively Nursery Department which includes the teaching of French and Computing. Years 1 to 6 follow the National Curriculum and have access to all the facilities at the Senior School.

At the Senior School, girls in Years 7 to 9 follow the National Curriculum subjects plus courses in Classical Studies, Life Skills and Drama. On entry at Year 7 girls are offered the choice of German, French or Spanish and at Year 9 they can select a second Modern Foreign Language. All girls study GCSE Religious Studies which is taken early at the end of Year 10.

The compulsory GCSE subjects are English, Mathematics, a Modern Foreign Language, Double Award Science and ICT and girls may choose up to 3 other subjects from a wide range of options including the usual subjects as well as Latin, Greek, Drama and PE.

Careful attention is given to the academic programme of each individual girl, to ensure that she is studying a balanced selection of subjects and that she will be suitably prepared for further studies in her career.

Sixth Form. Most girls stay on into the Sixth Form after taking their GCSE examinations. There is an exciting Sixth Form programme based on A level studies but with the addition of key skills, regular careers lectures, office technology and a wide range of sporting activities. There are opportunities to study GNVQ Business and the Leith's Certificate in Food and Wine.

One year programmes are available as a foundation for A level studies for those who do not meet the entry requirements. An intensive EFL foundation year is also available for a limited number of foreign students.

Weekends. The Schools' programme covers a 7 day week with lessons and sport on a Saturday. Sunday begins with Chapel followed by a variety of House activities both on and off site.

Extra Curricular Activities. A wide variety of activities are available including a Jazz Band, Clay Pigeon Shooting, Philosophical Society, Debating, Internet Club, Duke of Edinburgh's Award Scheme, Young Enterprise, Fencing and Riding. The Music Department regularly organises tours abroad and have recently visited Cologne, Prague, Paris and Barcelona.

Admission requirements. Girls normally join the School at the age of 11, 12 or 13, having taken the Common Entrance Examination or our own entrance papers at the appropriate age level. A few places are available at 14.

In order to begin an A level programme, girls admitted to the Sixth Form are normally required to have at least 5 GCSE passes at Grade C or above including English Language.

It is recommended to register early as places are offered to qualifying candidates in registration date order.

Fees. Board and general course of instruction and compulsory academic trips – £5,025 a term; Day Girls £3,350 per term. St Andrews: £360-£1,360. A prospectus is available from the Admissions Registrar.

Scholarships. Five Scholarships are awarded annually. One Sixth Form Academic Scholarship and a Sixth Form Music Scholarship. One Academic Scholarship and two General Scholarships between Music, Art, Sport or All

Round Ability are awarded at 13+. All Scholarships are open to internal and external candidates.

Charitable status. St Mary's School Wantage Trust Limited is a Registered Charity, number 309245. It exists to provide education for girls.

St Nicholas' School

Redfields House Redfield Lane Church Crookham Hampshire GU52 0RF.
Tel: (01252) 850121
Fax: (01252) 850718

Motto: *Confirma Domine Serviendo*

Headmistress: **Mrs A V Whatmough**, BA Hons (Bristol), CertEd

Deputy Head: Mrs P M Horner, BSc Hons (Liverpool), CBiol, MIBiol

Assistant Staff:

Mrs K Barclay, HM Forces PE Instructor
Miss G Bertin, Licence d'Anglais LCE (Université Paris X Nanterre), PGCE (Bath)
Miss K Birkett, BSc Hons (Plymouth), PGCE
Mrs J Brown, HND
Mr T T Burns, BA Hons (West Surrey College of Art & Design)
Miss J Campbell, CertEd (King Alfred's College, Winchester)
Mrs A Coombes, SRD Fashion Design
Mrs M Cooper, MA (Oxon), PGCE (Eltham), ACIB
Miss C Craig, BEd Hons (Oxford Brookes)
Mrs D J Duggan, BA Hons (London), PGCE
Mrs S Duffy, BSc Hons (Reading)
Mrs C Egginton, BEd Hons (London)
Mrs A Fraser, CertEd (Weymouth)
Mrs L Hacking, CertEd (Nottingham)
Mrs E Hague, BA Hons (Lancaster), PGCE
Mrs A Hartley, BEd Hons (Girton College, Cambridge), CertEd, RSACert SpecLD
Mrs J Herridge, CertEd (Kingston)
Mrs M Hilton, Baccalaureat (France)
Mrs N Horner, BEd Hons (London)
Mrs E Johnstone, MA Hons (Glasgow), DipEd (Glasgow), MEd
Mrs J King, BEd (Rolle College)
Mrs L Ludlow, BSc (Liverpool), PGCE (Ludlow)
Mrs C E MacArthur, BA Hons (Keele)
Mrs I C McIvor, DipCE (Hamilton College)
Mrs C Moorby, BSc Hons (Southampton), CertEd
Mrs M Morgan, NNEB
Mrs J Mortimer, DipEd (Northumberland)
Mrs A C Murphy, BEd Hons (Bulmershe College)
Mrs A Parker-Ashley, BA Hons (Hull), DipEd
Mrs L Prins, NNEB
Mrs S Pritchard, BA Hons (Southampton), PGCE
Mrs T Purvis, BA Hons (Open University), PGCE
Mrs L Ruffell, BAQTS Hons (Surrey)
Miss J Selley, BA Hons (Leeds), PGCE
Mrs L Shapley, BA Hons (Liverpool), PGCE
Mrs M Strevens, BEd (West Midlands College)
Miss J Tennent, BLib Hons (Aberystwyth)
Mrs H Tucker-Brown, BEd Hons (Exeter)
Mrs C Webb, CertEd (Cartrefle College, Wrexham)
Miss V West, NNEB

Music Department:

Mrs S Morgan, GRSM, LRAM
Mr A Richardson
Mrs R Brett, ARCM, LGSM (*Flute and Piano*)
Mrs S Hosken (*Violin*)
Mr McKay (*Clarinet & Saxophone*)
Mrs V Mitchell, LRAM (*Piano and Cello*)
Mr D Sandfield (*Clarinet & Saxophone*)
Mrs L Dexter (*Piano*)
Mr A Richardson (*Voice*)

Administrative Staff:

Bursar: Mr S H Sturge, FCA
Headmistress's Secretary: Mrs L Keenan
Secretary: Mrs B Cox
Administration: Mrs A Eggar
Accounts Secretary: Mrs D Davies
Laboratory Technician: Mrs P Payne
Catering Manager: Mrs L White
Maintenance: Mr P Sleet, Mr P White, Mr T Keynes
Kitchen Assistants: Mrs L Henry, Mrs M Crouch, Mrs A James

The School. St Nicholas' School is an independent day school for girls aged 3–16 and boys 3–7. Founded in 1935 at Branksomewood Road, Fleet, the school is now situated at Redfields House, Church Crookham, a large Victorian mansion set in 26 acres of parkland and playing fields. In December a new Olympic size sports hall was opened, which has widened the range of sporting activities on offer.

Pupils come from Hampshire, Surrey and Berkshire and school buses operate from Farnham, Odiham, Fleet and Basingstoke as well as Fleet Railway Station. There is easy accessibility from the A287 Hook to Farnham road and the M3 is a short distance away.

Religion. The school is Christian by foundation but children of other faiths are made welcome. Assemblies are held each morning and children are encouraged to show tolerance, compassion and care for others.

Curriculum. Our academic standards are high and we provide a balanced curriculum. Small classes place great emphasis on the individual and pupils are encouraged to achieve their full potential in every area of school life. The curriculum is kept as broad as possible until the age of fourteen when choices are made for GCSE. The option choices are varied year by year depending upon the girls' abilities and talents. On average each girl takes ten subjects at GCSE. Twenty subjects are offered at this level. A carefully structured personal development course incorporates a Careers programme. Our girls move confidently on to enter sixth form colleges or scholarships to senior independent schools. Choir, drama and music thrive within the school and performances are given frequently.

Physical Education. Pupils take part in inter-school and local district sports matches: hockey, netball and cross-country in winter; and tennis, athletics and swimming in summer. Rounders and lacrosse are also played. The new sports hall with granwood floor, viewing gallery and new shower and changing facilities, offers participation in badminton, tennis, netball, volleyball and basketball throughout the year.

Entry. Children may enter at any stage subject to interview, school report and waiting list. Scholarships are available. For 11+ candidates there is an entrance examination.

Fees. From September 2000, fees range from £715 in the Nursery to £1,985 in the Senior School.

Further Information. The prospectus is available upon request from the Headmistress's Secretary. The Headmistress is pleased to meet parents by appointment.

Charitable status. St Nicholas' School is a Registered Charity, number 307341. It exists to provide high quality education for children.

St Paul's Girls' School

Brook Green Hammersmith London W6 7BS
Tel: 020 7603 2288
Bursar: 020 7605 4881
Fax: 020 7602 9932; Bursar: 020 7605 4869

Motto: *'Fide et Literis'*

The School is on the Foundation originally provided by Dean Colet in 1509 and is governed under the provisions of the Schemes of the Charity Commissioners dated 4 July 1879, and 16 June 1900. The Worshipful Company of Mercers are the trustees of the Foundation. The School was opened on 19 January 1904.

Trustees of the Foundation:
The Worshipful Company of Mercers

Governors:
The Master and Wardens of the Mercers' Company, and as such Ex-Officio Members:

Mr Richard Cawton Cunis
Mr Anthony Edward Hodson
Wing Commander Michael Greville Dudgeon, OBE

Chairman of Governors: Mr John James Fenwick, DL, MA

Deputy Chairman of Governors: The Hon Henry William Palmer

Chairman and Deputy Chairman of St Paul's School:
Mr David Anthony Tate, OBE
Mr Francis Robert Baden-Powell

Nominated Governors:
Mr John Drayton Hedges
Mr David Neville Vermont
Mr Julian Philip Gerard Wathen
Mr David Charles Watney
Mr Duncan Martyn Watney, JP
Mr John Adrian Watney

Appointed by The Mercers' Company in consultation with the University of Oxford:
Dr John Penrose Barron, MA, DPhil, FRS
Dr Jane Garnett, MA, DPhil

Appointed by The Mercers' Company in consultation with the University of Cambridge:
Dr Claire Yvonne Barlow, PhD
Professor Patricia Elizabeth Easterling, MA

Appointed by The Mercers' Company in consultation with the University of London:
Professor Catherine Stevenson Peckham, CBE

Co-opted by the Governing Body:
Mr Robert Brook Bridges
Professor Paul Anthony Cartledge, PhD, FSA

Clerk to the Governors: Mr Charles H Parker

***High Mistress:* Miss Elizabeth Diggory**, BA, FRSA

Bursar: Mrs Margot Chaundler, OBE

Registrar: Mrs Lindy Hayward

The main ages of admission are 11 and 16. There are 670 girls in the school, 200 being in the Sixth Form. The school offers a balanced curriculum; both tradition and innovation are valued. A strong core of academic subjects is combined with Art, Design, Drama, Music, Information Technology and Sport.

Girls are prepared for GCSE, Advanced Supplementary and full Advanced Level examinations and for university entrance. Most girls go on to major universities in the UK or overseas, approximately 40% to Oxford and Cambridge.

Sports facilities include a new Sports Hall opened in Summer 2000, and a large heated swimming pool. The Library facilities are outstanding, as are those for Music, centred on the Gustav Holst Singing Hall. Drama takes place in the purpose-built Celia Johnson Theatre. There is an ICT block with two fully equipped classrooms. Twelve Science laboratories are housed in a separate Science block. We are continually modernising and adding to these facilities: a new Sixth form centre with its own ICT facilities, dining and relaxation areas, together with a Careers suite, are opening in Autumn 2001.

Junior Academic Scholarships of a value of £50 per annum, which can extend to full fee remission based on proven financial need, are offered to candidates who perform exceptionally well in the first year entrance examination.

First Year Awards to a value of up to full fee remission based on proven financial need are also available to successful candidates, together with **Ogden Trust** bursaries which are reserved for girls attending school in the maintained sector.

Senior Academic Scholarships and Exhibitions of a value of £100 are offered to present students on the basis of academic distinction demonstrated in a project completed at the end of the first year of A Level study.

Senior Awards to a value of up to full fee remission based on proven financial need are available to successful senior candidates who are currently in their final GCSE year at another school.

Junior Music Scholarships of the value of half the School's tuition fees, which can extend to full fee remission based on proven financial need, and free tuition in one instrument are awarded on the basis of practical examination and interview. Candidates must be successful in the First Year Entrance Examination.

Senior Music Scholarships of the value of £100 per annum, which can extend to full fee remission based on proven financial need, and free tuition in two instruments are awarded on the basis of written and practical examinations and interview. Candidates must be successful in the Senior School Entrance Examination.

Art Scholarships of the value of £100 per annum, which can extend to full fee remission based on proven financial need, are offered to girls who are currently in their final GCSE year and who have previously been successful in the Senior School Entrance Examination. Candidates take part in a Saturday workshop in March and are also required to submit a portfolio.

Full details of Scholarships and Awards are available from the Registrar.

Fees. Registration Fee, £55. Examination Fee, £50. Tuition Fee, £2,941 per term, including lunches, excluding textbooks.

Extras. Individual music lessons (on a wide range of instruments including Organ).

Charitable status. St Paul's Girls' School is a Registered Charity, number 312749. It exists for the education of girls.

St Swithun's School

Alresford Road Winchester Hants SO21 1HA
Tel: (01962) 835700
Fax: (01962) 835779

The School was founded in 1884 and moved to its present fine site of 30 acres on the Downs close to Winchester in 1931.

The School aims to give a broad, balanced academic education in which each girl has the opportunity to make appropriate choices which will enable her to develop her potential and give her the skills and confidence needed for adult life.

Within a framework of sensible discipline there is a remarkably friendly and caring atmosphere. Emphasis is placed on Christian values and consideration for others.

It is a school for both Day Girls and Boarders and at present the Senior School (girls aged 11–18) has 252 Day Girls and 218 Boarders. There is an adjoining Junior School for girls aged 3–11 and boys up to the age of 8 years.

Visitor: The Rt Revd Michael Scott-Joynt, Bishop of Winchester

School Council:
Dr G C Brill, MA, MB, BChir, FRCGP (*Chairman*)
The Dean of Winchester (*ex-officio*)
Dr E N Tate, MA, Headmaster of Winchester College (*ex-officio*)
The Right Worshipful The Mayor of Winchester (*ex-officio*)
Mrs S Glasspool, BSc
Prof R P Grime, BA, BCL
Mrs M A Gruffydd Jones, MA
Mrs A T D Macaire, MA
Dr H M Mycock, BA, MSc, PhD
Mrs K Napier, BA, MPhil
Mr J C Platt, FCA
Mr P H Radcliffe, FCA
Miss R L E Rothman, BA, ACA
Mrs A J Russell, MA, BSS
Dr H R Trippe, BA, BM, MFPHM
The Right Hon Lord Wakeham, FCA, JP
Prof J M A Whitehouse, MA, MD, FRCP, FRCP(E), FRCR

Bursar and Clerk to the Council: Mr G J Haig, OBE

***Headmistress:* Dr H L Harvey**, BSc, PhD (London)

Deputy Headmistress: Mrs P A Wagstaff, BA (London), DipEd (Durham) *Classics*

Director of Studies: Mrs J Edwards, BSc (Bristol), PGCE (Cantab) *Mathematics*

Chaplain: Rev T E Hemming, MA, DipTESL, DipTh

Staff:

Religious Studies:
Mrs A Gibson, BA, PGCE (Birmingham) *and Careers*
Rev T E Hemming, MA, DipTESL, DipTh
Mrs J Tomlinson, BA (Kent), MA (Durham), PGCE (York), CPM (Portsmouth) *Librarian*
Ms M Kady, Teaching and PG Dip (Newcastle upon Tyne)

English:
Mrs D Burgess, MA (Oxon), PGCE (Cantab)
Miss S Goudge, MA (Cantab), PGCE (London)
Mr S Bowyer, BA, PGCE (Sheffield)
Miss S Michell, BA, (Bristol), PGCE (London)
Mrs M Primrose, MA (Glasgow), PGCE (Jordanhill)
Mrs J Henty-Dodd, BA (N London), PGCE (Oxon)
Mrs J Barron, CertEd, AMBDA *Learning Support*
Mrs G Urpens, DipBDA (Winchester) *Learning Support*

History:
Miss V Acton, BA (Kent), MPhil (Leeds), PGCE (Cambridge), DipLaw (London) *Barrister at Law and Politics*
Miss R Appleyard, BA (London), PGCE (Greenwich)
Dr C Schummer, MA, PhD (St Andrews), PGCE (Edinburgh)
Dr D Wendelken, BA (London Guildhall), MPhil (St Andrews), PhD (Southampton), PGCE (Durham)

Geography:
Mrs H Jones, BSc (London), PGCE (Sussex)
Mr J Brown, BA, PGCE (Birmingham)
Mrs L Parsons, BSc (Liverpool), PGCE

Economics:
Mrs S Rothwell, BSc (LSE), PGCE

Modern Languages:
Mrs E Lorge, BA (London), PGCE (London), MIL *French*
Mrs M Rahman, BA (Bristol), MA (Hull), CertEd (Oxon) *French & Russian*
Mrs U M Stevens, BA, DipEd (London) *French and Examinations Officer*
Mrs J Austin, BEd (Winchester) *French*
Ms S Burchell, BA (Soton) *German*
Mrs S Hayward, MA (London), PGCE (Birmingham)
Mrs C Glyn, MA (Bochum), PGCE (Durham)
Mr K Chambers, BA (Exeter), MA, PGCE (Birmingham) *Spanish*
Miss I Moran, MA, PGCE (London) *French & Spanish*

Classics:
Mr R Davies, BA (London), PGCE (Cantab)
Mrs P Giles, BA (Birmingham), PGCE (Durham) *and Careers and Head of General Studies*
Mrs C Power, BA Hons (Oxon)
Mr R Smith, BA (Oxon), PGCE (London)

Mathematics:
Mrs A Ault, BEd Hons (W Sussex Inst)
Mr C Brewer, BSc (Exeter), PGCE (Leeds)
Miss E Bowman, BSc, PGCE (Southampton)
Mr D Conlon, BSc (London)
Mr S Power, BA (Oxon), MSc (Colorado), PGCE (OU)

Science:
Dr J Livy, BSc (Liverpool), MSc, DIC, PhD (London), CChem, MRSC *Chemistry*
Mr P Unitt, BSc (Bristol), PGCE (East Anglia) *Chemistry & Careers*
Mrs S Tait, BSc (OU), PGCE (Southampton) *Chemistry*
Mrs E Jones, BSc (Manchester) *Chemistry, Biology and General Science*
Mr A W J Smith, BSc (Durham), CertEd (Exeter) *Physics*
Mr J D A Essex, BSc, PGCE (London) *Biology*
Mrs P A Burley, BSc (Swansea), PGCE (Soton) *Biology*
Mrs M C I Reid, MA (Dublin), PGCE (London) *Biology*

Information Technology and Technology:
Dr R Lomax, BSc, PhD, PGCE (Liverpool), CPhys, MInstP *Information Technology and Physics*
Mr V R Clarke, BSc, DipEd (Bangor) *Technology and Physics*
Mrs H Jobling, BEng (Exeter), PGCE (Telford) *Technology*
Mrs A Dixon, BEd *Information Technology*
Mr A S King, BEd (Warwick), MITT *ICT Co-ordinator*

Careers:
Mrs A Campbell, BA (Durham), DipRE (Nottingham), PGCE (Lancaster), CFPS (Portsmouth)
Miss J Webber, BA (Wellington, NZ), Dip Teaching (Christchurch, NZ)

Food and Textiles:
Mrs N Sanvoisin, BSc, PGCE (Cardiff)
Mrs K Baylis, BEd (Worcester)

Art:
Mr C Johnson, Nat Dip Art & Design (Newport), CertEd (London)
Mrs C Codd, BA (Winchester)
Mrs C Russell, Dip Fine Art (Slade), ATD (London)
Mrs P Larrington, BEd, MA (Soton) *History of Art*

Music:
Mr R Brett, MA, PGCE (Cantab)
Mr P Rhodes, MA (Reading), BMus (Edinburgh), PGCE (Reading)
Miss J Richardson, DRSAMD, MMus (Reading) *Instrumental Studies*

Speech and Drama:
Mrs E M Shurlock, LGSM, CertEd (Cantab)
Mrs C E Lewis, BA (Swansea), PGCE (Southampton)

Physical Education:
Miss C Stoker, BA (Warwick)
Miss D Adlington, BScDipT (Adelaide)
Mrs C Jackson, DipPE (Bedford), CertEd (Cantab)
Miss R Hearnshaw, BA (Brighton)
Mr K White, BA, CertEd(FE) *Swimming Pool Manager*
Miss H Herson, CertEd (Bedford) *and French*

Visiting Staff:
Mrs T Ardagh-Walter, LRCM, LRAM *Piano*
Mrs I Carlick, BMus (London), ARCM, CertEd (Man) *Piano*
Mrs J Lloyd, ARCM, LGSM(MT) *Piano*
Mrs M Silvester, GRSM, LRAM, ARCM
Mrs H Youle, BA (London), LGSM *Piano*
Mrs J Kane, GRNCM *Violin*
Mr C Persinaru, DipRAM, LRAM *Violin/Viola*
Miss E Russell, GMus, RNCM *Violin*
Mr M Mace, DipRAM *Violoncello*
Mrs V Harding, BSc (Soton) *Violoncello*
Miss N Bailey, LRAM *Double Bass*
Mrs J Bevan, ARCM *Harp*
Mr A Neville *Guitar*
Miss S Marston, GRSM, DipRCM, PGCE *Flute*
Mrs A McKay, BA (London), PGCE (Dundee) *Flute*
Mr C Burgess, LTCL *Recorder*
Mrs M Gilliat, GRSM, LRAM, ARCM *Oboe and Drama*
Miss J Britton, LWCMD, LTCL *Saxophone and Clarinet*
Mr A Collins, RA Band *Clarinet*
Mrs E White, GGSM, AGSM (Examiner to the GSMD) *Bassoon/Clarinet*
Mrs F Brockhurst, ARCM *French Horn*
Mr D Evans, ARCM (Examiner to LCM) *Lower Brass*
Miss D Calland, BMus, LRAM *Trumpet*
Mrs W Harding, MMus, LRAM, ALCM, LTCL, BMus (Examiner to GSMD) *Percussion*
Mrs M Froggatt, ARMCM *Singing*
Mrs C Clark, Dip Speech & Drama (CCSD)
Mrs M Armstrong, BA (Bretton Hall)
Mr B Roman, BJA *Judo*
Mr C Holroyd *Fencing*
Mr F Burgess *Self defence*

Housemistresses:
Finlay: Miss J Webber
Earl's Down: Mrs P Phillips
High House: Miss I Moran
Hillcroft: Miss R Appleyard
Hyde Abbey: Miss H Herson
Le Roy: Mrs D Lugg

Day-Girl Houses:
Caer Gwent: Mrs A Gibson
Venta: Mrs U Stevens
Davies: Mrs P Giles
Chilcomb: Miss S Michell

Medical Staff:
Dr L Cole, MBBS, DRCOG
Mrs P May, RGN
Miss J McClatchey, RGN

Office Staff:

Headmistress's Secretary: Mrs J Coveyduck
Admissions Secretary: Mrs H Harris

Location. The School is on a rural site in Winchester's 'green belt' but only a few minutes' walk from the city centre. It is easily accessible from Heathrow and Gatwick airports and is one hour from London by car (via the M3 motorway). There is a frequent train service to London Waterloo (one hour).

Curriculum. With the emphasis on a broad, balanced education, there are 19 subjects available at GCSE, of which English and English Literature, a modern Foreign Language, Mathematics and at least one Science course are compulsory. The selection of others to complete the usual total of 9 is made on an individual basis with an emphasis on breadth of course as well as future career prospects.

In the Sixth Form, a free choice of 4 AS Levels from 23 subjects is offered with 3 to be continued to A level. All girls follow to A Level a challenging and wide-ranging General Course.

The curriculum is extended by exchange visits to France and Germany and educational visits to other countries.

Religion. The School is a Church of England foundation. There are close ties with Winchester Cathedral, where termly services and the annual Confirmation and Carol Services are held. A full-time Chaplain prepares girls for Confirmation and teaches in the School.

Music. The School has a strong musical tradition and there are frequent performances by the School choirs and orchestral groups. The Senior Choir sings Evensong in Winchester Cathedral twice a term, and chamber groups regularly enjoy success at national level.

Sports. There are extensive playing fields and a spacious modern Sports Hall. In 1994 a new indoor swimming pool was completed. Lacrosse players regularly attain national standard and a wide range of team and individual sports is offered.

Facilities. The original school building contains the Assembly Hall, main teaching rooms and libraries, and has been extended and developed to provide specialist areas for Languages, Information Technology, Food and Textiles, Drama, Craft and Careers. The Science wing contains six fully equipped laboratories, project rooms and a small lecture theatre. There is a separate building for the Music School. A new Performing Arts building will be completed by 2003.

A new Art, Design and Technology Centre was opened in 1998.

School Houses. There are 6 Boarding Houses and 4 Day Girl Houses, each staffed by a housemistress and assistant who take pride in the high level of pastoral care offered to each girl. The two Junior Houses are for girls aged 11 years, who are then transferred to one of the Senior Houses after one year. They remain in their Senior House until they have completed one year in the Sixth Form. The Upper Sixth House is for Boarders and Day Girls together, with study bedrooms for Boarders, study facilities for Day Girls and common rooms and galley for all.

Careers. Most girls continue to University, including Oxford and Cambridge, and all continue to some form of Higher Education and training. Each girl is counselled by one of our team of four Careers staff in a well-resourced department. Lectures and video presentations are organised frequently and a Careers Fair held annually.

Leisure Activities. There is an extensive range of extra-curricular activities and an organised programme of visits and activities at the weekend. Girls participate in the Duke of Edinburgh Award Scheme, Young Enterprise and local Community Service work. The Sixth Form runs a range of Societies including a Green Society, a Debating Society and a branch of Amnesty International. There are cookery, dressmaking, craft and engineering clubs and each year there are drama productions as well as regular drama activities. There is an annual visit to a Geographical/Outward Bound Centre in Wales, ski trips and water-sports holidays.

Health. The School Sanatorium forms part of the main buildings. It is staffed by qualified RGNs and visited by the School Doctor twice a week.

Entrance. (*see* Entrance Scholarship section) Entry is by means of the Common Entrance Examination for Independent Schools. The majority of girls enter the Senior

School between the ages of 11 and 13 years, but girls are accepted at other ages, including the Sixth Form, subject to satisfactory tests.

Scholarships and Exhibitions are awarded on the result of an examination at 11+, 12+, 13+ and at entry to the Sixth Form. There are also Music Scholarships.

Fees per term. Senior School: Boarders: £5,125; Day Girls: £3,105. Junior School: Years 5 & 6: £2,010; Years 3 & 4: £1,915; Reception, Years 1 & 2: £1,560; Nursery: £790.

Charitable trust. St Swithun's School Winchester is a Registered Charity, number 307335. It exists to provide education to girls aged 11–18 years.

St Teresa's School

Effingham Hill Dorking Surrey RH5 6ST
Tel: (01372) 452037/454896
Fax: (01372) 450311

Independent Day/Boarding School for Girls 11–18

Motto: *Gaudere et bene facere*

St Teresa's motto, which means 'Rejoice and do well', has been the guiding factor in setting both the high educational standards and happy environment in this flourishing girls' boarding and day school. The prime aim is to provide a broad, challenging education based on sound Christian principles. Expectations are high and the school strives for quality and excellence in all aspects of school life. Emphasis is placed on enabling the girls to fulfil their own potential by unlocking academic ability, nurturing personal talents and helping them grow in confidence and maturity in preparation for the years ahead.

Headmistress: **Mrs M E Prescott**, BA (Hons), PGCE, FRSA

Deputy Headmistress: Mrs M Ford, BA (Hons), PGCE

Chairman of the Governors: Mr I C Wells

Director of Studies: Mrs D Dixon, BSc (Hons), PGCE

Bursar: Mr P Large

Heads of Department:
Mrs J S Bolton, BA (Hons), PGCE *Music*
Mrs M C Bridge, BSc (Hons) *Maths*
Mrs J Clayton, CertEd *Life Skills*
Mrs J A Duff-Turner, BSc (Hons), MA, PGCE *Information Technology*
Mrs J Findlay, BA (Hons), PGCE *History*
Mrs J Gardner, BEd (Hons), Teachers' Cert *English*
Mrs S Kariuki, MA, PGCE *Economics & Business Studies, Careers*
Mrs I Lowe, MA (Hons) *Modern Languages*
Miss S G Nelson, BEd (Hons) *Physical Education*
Dr R Peevey, STB, STL, STD *Religious Studies*
Mrs A Rogerson-Webb, BA (Hons), MA *Art and Design Technology*
Mrs P Rua *Boarding*
Mrs A Starmer, BSc (Hons), PGCE *Science*
Mrs E A Wheeler, BSc (Hons) *Chemistry*
Mrs H Wicking, BA (Hons), PGCE *Geography*

Foundation. St Teresa's was founded by the Religious of Christian Instruction in 1928 on what was originally part of a manor site recorded in the Domesday Book. The present Georgian house, dating from 1799, is the centre of the Senior School, now greatly extended to provide modern facilities for its high level of education.

In 1953, St Teresa's Preparatory School (see IAPS section, Part V of this Book) was established at Grove House, in the village of Effingham, about 1½ miles away.

Location. Situated amid beautiful, rural surroundings, approximately 22 miles from London, St Teresa's is ideally located in 45 acres of grounds amongst the Surrey hills. The M25 is only four miles away. Both Heathrow and Gatwick airports are half an hour's drive and there is a good train service to London (Waterloo) from Effingham Junction Station and London (Victoria) from Dorking.

Facilities. The teaching areas are modern and extensive with bright spacious classrooms, well equipped Science Laboratories, Modern Languages Suite (with satellite TV), a superb Resources Centre and the latest Information Technology throughout the school. There is also a wide ranging Technology Department, Art Suite, Music Department and Drama Studio.

Entrance at 11 is based on success in the Entrance Examination. Scholarships are available. It is school policy to maintain small classes so that each pupil's progress is closely monitored. During Year 9, girls receive advice on GCSE options. At this point, girls embark on a structured programme of personal study skills, which expands to include help and advice with further education and career choices.

St Teresa's is well-equipped in every way for the methods of GCSE teaching and excellent examination results bear this out. 21 GCSE subjects are on offer and most girls take 9 subjects.

Individual tuition is available in a variety of subjects, including singing, most musical instruments, dance and drama and a number of sporting activities. Parents receive reports regularly and they also have the opportunity to meet Staff on Parent's Evenings and are encouraged to approach the school whenever they feel it is necessary. Pastoral Care is provided at all levels by Form Tutors, Heads of Year and House Mistresses.

Sixth Form. As well as those who have come up through the school, St Teresa's Sixth Form welcomes girls from elsewhere. It has its own purpose-built accommodation in Magdalen House where girls live in a happy atmosphere in which high standards, responsibility and self discipline are encouraged. 22 'A' Level subjects are on offer and each girl has a personal tutor. All girls follow a number of compulsory and optional courses, in addition to their main examination subjects. The Lower Sixth all do one or two weeks of work experience. Careers guidance is run from a special Higher Education Advice Department, where computer programmes aid the student in her choices. The Lower Sixth also participate in the Young Enterprise Scheme and Voluntary Service. The Upper Sixth Economics and Business Studies students, are given the experience of running the school's branch of a national clearing bank. There is an Oxbridge group within the Sixth Form and a Sixth Form Society.

Scholarships. Academic, Art and Music Scholarships are available for entry at 11+, 12+, 13+ and Sixth Form.

Drama. At the end of the first term of the academic year, all of Year 7 perform in a seasonal production and later in the year, both Juniors and Seniors are involved in further productions. LAMDA examinations are taken by a high percentage of girls. Debating and Public Speaking is also an integral part of school life with notable successes in local and national competitions.

Music. St Teresa's has an excellent reputation for music. It boasts a large orchestra, numerous ensembles, three choirs and over 52% of pupils learn at least one instrument. Choirs, ensembles and individuals are entered for competitions and festivals with a high degree of success.

Sport. St Teresa's has a 5 acre Sports Field for athletics, field events and cricket, several tennis courts, a new all weather hockey pitch (opened Spring 2001), swimming pool and a large sports hall. Hockey, netball and tennis are the main sports in which the school has a reputation in the local area, but numerous other sporting activities take place such as aerobics, self-defence, badminton, golf, gymnastics, riding, squash and most recently polo.

Boarding. St Teresa's offers full boarding in a happy relaxed atmosphere. Boarding facilities are first class with bright and attractive rooms. Boarding is organised on a Year system and priority is given to providing a full programme of weekend activities. Flexi-boarding is also available to accommodate the varying requirements of parents and pupils.

Extra-Curricular activities. Many extra curricular activities are on offer including The Duke of Edinburgh's Award Scheme. School travel at home and abroad and school exchanges play an important part in broadening the girls' outlook as well as affording cultural and social benefits.

STOGA. St Teresa's Old Girls Association meets regularly.

FOST. Friends of St Teresa's is a flourishing parents' association which engages in fund-raising through a variety of social events.

Prospectus. A fully illustrated prospectus with up-to-date fee scales and relevant details is available on request.

Charitable status. St Teresa's School is a Registered Charity, number 243995. It exists to provide education for girls from 2 to 18 years.

School of S Mary & S Anne
Abbots Bromley

Nr Rugeley Staffs WS15 3BW
Tel: (01283) 840232/840225 (24 hrs)
Fax: (01283) 840988
e-mail: info@abbotsbromley.staffs.sch.uk
Stations: Lichfield City (Trent Valley), Burton on Trent, Rugeley
and Stafford

Founded 1874.

Visitor: The Rt Revd The Bishop of Lichfield

Council:

Chairman: Mrs B Marlow

The Revd Canon W Weaver, BA, BD, The Provost (*ex officio*)
The Revd Canon J R Hall, BA
Mrs M Hobson, JP, MBE
Mr J Harp, DLC
Mr D J Skipper, MA
Mr R Mansell, ACIB
Mrs H Ball

Clerk to the Council and Bursar: Mr R W Flower

Head: Mrs M Steel, BA Hons

Deputy Head: Mrs V Edwards, BA Hons

Head of Sixth Form: Mrs D Crispin, CertEd

Head of Boarding: Mrs J M Gardner, BSc

Head of Academic Studies: Mr M A Fisher, BEd Hons

Chaplain: The Revd B F Wilson, CertTheol, DipTheol, DipHE, BA Hons, PGCE, MPhil, MTh, DMin

Librarians:
Mrs K Hughes, BA Hons, CertEd
Mrs M Sossi

Medical Officers of Health:
Dr R V H Aldridge, MBBS, BSc, DCH, DipObst, RCOG, MRCP
Dr J Bull, MBChB, BSc, PhD

Sanatorium Sisters:
Sister B Lambert, RGN, NEBSM
Sister S Prichard, RGN, RN Child

House Staff:
Head of Boarding: Mrs J M Gardner, BSc

Housemistresses/Assistant Housemistresses:
Meynell Lowe: Mrs J Gardner, BSc/Mrs A Anderson
Heywood Rice: Mrs M Steer, BA Hons, DipSEN, PGCE
Talbot (Crofts): Mrs K Hughes, BA Hons, CertEd/Mrs M Crane
Coleridge: Mrs E Rigby, BA Hons, PGCE
Keble S Benet's: Mrs S May, CertEd
Selwyn: Mrs M Sossi

Senior School Academic Staff:

Art:
*Mrs D Crispin, CertEd
Mrs P E Clare, Nat Dip in Design

Business Studies/Careers and Curriculum Development:
Mr M A Fisher, BEd Hons

Classics:
Mrs J M Jones, BA Hons

Economics and Sociology:
Mrs V Hawley
Mr M A Fisher, BEd Hons

English:
*Mrs M Steer, BA Hons, PGCE (*SEN Co-ordinator*)
Mrs E Rigby, BA Hons, PGCE
Mrs P Broderick, BA Hons *Performing Arts*

Geography:
*Mrs A Copley, BA Hons
Mrs V A Edwards, BA Hons

History:
*Mrs S Towell, BA Hons
Mrs F J Kersley, BA Hons, PGCE

Home Economics (*Cookery & Needlework*):
*Mrs S May, CertEd

Information Technology:
*Miss J Hill, BEd Hons
Mr M Fisher, BEd Hons
Mrs H Freeman, BSc

Mathematics:
*Mrs C Starkie, BSc Hons
Mrs K Davis, BSc
Mrs H Freeman, BSc

Modern Languages:
*Mrs K Rowlands, BA Hons (*German*)
Mr M Tebbutt, BA Hons (*Spanish*)
Mrs E Lampard, BA Hons (*French*)

Music:
Director of Music: Mr C Walker, MMus, ARCM, AMusTCL, LTCL, LRAM
Mr R C Paul, BA Hons, ARCO, PGCE
Mr J S Anderson, GLCM, LLCM(TD), AMusTCL, MTC(Lon)

Natural Sciences:
Head of Science: Mrs J M Gardner, BSc

Chemistry:
Mrs J M Gardner, BSc
Miss P A Dawson, BSc Hons

Biology:
Mrs B Smallwood, BA Hons
Miss P A Dawson, BSc Hons

Physics:
Mrs J Lingham, BSc Hons, BA Hons
Mrs J Walker, CertEd

Laboratory Technicians:
Miss L Henry
Mrs K McLoughlin

Physical Education:
*Mrs Y Menneer, BEd Hons
Miss J D Hill, BEd Hons

Visiting Staff:

Mr P Mudie *Gymnastics BAGA*
Mr A G Hawkins *Swimming Club Coach*
Miss H Powell *Trampolining, BTF Advanced Coach*
Mr S J Shea *Tennis, LTA II*
Mr J Wilson *Tennis, LTA II*
Mr D Utting *Lifesaving RLSS Trainer*

Religious Studies:
The Revd B F Wilson, CertTheol, DipTheol, DipHE, BA Hons, PGCE, MPhil, MTh, DMin
Mrs M Steel, BA Hons

Junior Department Academic Staff:
*Mrs M Edwards, BEd
Mrs S Crout, DipEd
Mrs J Jackson, CertEd
Mrs L S Pickering, CertEd
Mrs C A Spratt, BA Hons
Miss W Wallace, BEd Hons

Ballet:
Artistic Director: Mr Russell Alkins, RAD Grade, RAD Teaching Certificate

Modern and Tap Dance: Guest Choreographers and Specialist teachers

Riding (*Abbots Bromley Equestrian Centre*):
Director of Equitation: Miss S Vickers, BHSI, CertEd
Consultant: Mrs Y J Williams, BHSI Instructor

Duke of Edinburgh Award Scheme:
Mr P Gardner
Mrs S Slater

Administration:
Assistant Bursar: Mrs V Grief
Domestic Bursar: Mrs S Slater
Bursar's Office: Mrs A Heywood
Clerk of Works: Mr A Strudwick
Headmistress's Office:
Secretary: Mrs H J Meadows
Registrar: Mrs J Dale
Assistant: Mrs J Clews

Visiting Staff:

Speech & Drama: Mrs J Hankin, Gold Medal LAMDA

Special Learning Difficulties:
Mrs C Smart, CertEd AMBDA, DipSpecLD, ACP (*English*)
Mr P T Smart, BSc Hons (*Mathematics*)

Instrumental Music Staff:

Piano:
Mr C Walker, MMus, ARCM, AMusTCL, LTCL, LRAM
Mr J S Anderson, GLCM, LLCM(TD), AMusTCL, MTC
Mrs S E Anderson, ALCM
Mrs C G Ashton, MA, ARCM
Mrs E Cobb, Specialist Teaching Diploma Latvia
Miss H Coupe, GRSM, ARMCM
Mrs E Ferguson, GRSM, ARCM, ALCM

Organ: Mr R Paul, BA Hons, ARCO, PGCE

Violin & Viola:
Mrs E Ferguson, GRSM, ARCM, ALCM
Mrs J Wale, BMus, PGCE

'Cello: Miss N Turner, BMus, LRAM, LTCL, PGCE

Flute & Piccolo: Miss A Chadwick, GBSM, ABSM

Flute and Recorder: Miss A Turley, BMus, LLCM, ALCM

Oboe: Mr A Hodges, GRSM, ARCM

Clarinet & Saxophone:
Mr D Phillip, ARCM
Mrs P Watkins, ABSM

Brass: Mrs R Paul, BA Hons, CertEd

Harp: Mrs C G Ashton, MA, ARCM

Drums/Electric Guitar:
Mr M A Davies, LGSM
Mr R Paul, BA Hons, ARCO, PGCE

Guitar: Mr J Anderson, GLCM, LLCM(TD), AMusTCL

Singing: Mr R Paul, LTCL, ARCM

The picturesque village of Abbots Bromley is home to the School of S Mary and S Anne, a thriving boarding and day school for some 300 girls aged 4 to 18. The peaceful surroundings give no clue to the hive of activity which characterises this community. The school offers an ideal environment for girls of all ages, with superb resources and excellent opportunities.

Girls are encouraged and supported by well qualified and experienced teachers to achieve their academic potential, and there is generous provision for all academic subjects, with specialist rooms for all areas of the curriculum. Examination results are extremely good and girls achieve high standards in all fields of endeavour. A wide range of subjects is available for both GCSE and A Level.

In their leisure time the girls are able to pursue a vast range of activities. Music and performing arts feature strongly and our ballet school offers girls a unique chance to combine dance studies with an academic programme. There is a dedicated music school, and in addition to the Great Hall we also have a Performing Arts Theatre. Our sports hall, indoor swimming pool, astro turf hockey pitch and athletics track cater for those interested in sport, and together with our own equestrian centre with indoor and outdoor schools and cross-country course, provide almost unrivalled opportunities.

Girls thrive in this safe and secure environment, and we offer continuity and stability. Our girls are poised, independent and articulate and will take their place in society, confident of their own worth.

Abbots Bromley is close to Birmingham International, East Midlands, and Manchester Airports. Heathrow is 2 hours, and we have InterCity rail links at Burton upon Trent, Lichfield and Stafford, and the M6 and M42 motorways are easily accessible.

Prospectuses and further details are available on request. Visits by prospective parents are welcomed at any time.

Charitable status. School of S Mary and S Anne (Woodard Schools (Midland Division) Limited) is a Registered Charity, number 269671. It exists to provide education for girls.

* Head of Department	§ Part Time or Visiting
† Housemaster/Housemistress	¶ Old Pupil
‡ See below list of staff for meaning	

Sheffield High School (G.D.S.T.)

10 Rutland Park Sheffield S10 2PE
Tel: (0114) 266 0324

Founded 1878

This is one of the 25 schools of The Girls' Day School Trust. For general information about the Trust and the composition of its Council, see p 532. A more detailed prospectus may be obtained from the school.

Local Governors:
Chairman: Mr A M C Staniforth, BA, FCA
Dr R Allum, BSc, PhD
Mrs L M Ammon, CBE, FRSA, BSc
Mr D B Bray, AMet, CEng, MIM
Mr D J Hartley, LLB
Mrs S Kendall, BSc, ARICS
Mrs P A Tempest, BSc, ARICS
Mrs E Talbot, BA, JP, FCA
Dr P Warren, CBE, MA, PhD
Mrs A Whiteway
Professor A Zinober, BSc, MSc, PhD, MIEE, CEng, MIEEE

***Headmistress:* Mrs M A Houston**, BA (Leeds) *English*

Deputy Head: Mrs A C Hewitt, BSc (Sheffield)

Senior Tutor: Mrs D Balcombe, BA (London), MSc (Open)

Director of Marketing: Mrs H Leaver, BEd (Liverpool John Moores)

Senior School:

Careers Department:
Mrs J Ashby, BSc (Sheffield)
Mrs S J Good, BEd (Bedford College of PE)

English Department:
Mr A C Nichols, BA (Leeds)
Miss G L Heaton, BA (Durham)
Miss M F Greene, MA (London))
Mrs L M Miller, MA (Glasgow)
Mrs C Heery, BA (London)
Mr C Bailey, BA (Oxford)

History Department:
Miss J Hugh, BA (Bristol)
Mrs S Davies, BA (Oxford)
Mrs R Bennett, MA (St Andrews)
Mr G Craggs, MA (York)

Geography Department:
Mrs C D Haynes, BA (Durham)
Mrs M E Stoddard, BA (Nottingham)
Mr A Davies, BA (Sheffield)

Economics Department:
Mrs J Lloyd-Williams, MPhil (Robert Gordon's Institute of Technology)
Mr B Harris, MA (Essex)

Religious Studies:
Mr R C Royds, BEd (Sheffield)
Mrs A Rolling, BA (Sheffield)

Art/Technology Department:
Miss G M Hanlon, BA (Sheffield)
Mr M S Higgins, BA (Camberwell School of Art)
Mrs L Marriott, BEd (Sheffield)

Music Department:
Ms E Davies, BA (Bristol)
Miss H Rolfe, BMus, MA (Huddersfield)

Classical Studies:
Mr V L Knowles, BA (Lancaster)
Mrs J M Blockeel, BA (London)

French Department:
Mr R H Martin, MA (Cambridge)
Miss S M Barnes, BA (Leeds)
Dr M V Gold, MA, DPhil (Oxford)
Mrs S Burns, BA (Leeds)

German Department:
Frau A C Anschütz, BA (Sheffield)
Dr M V Gold, MA, DPhil (Oxford)
Ms C Wallace, BA (Cambridge)
Miss S Gläsmann, BMus (London)

Spanish Department:
Mr R H Martin, MA (Cambridge)
Miss S M Barnes, BA (Leeds)
Mrs S Burns, BA (Leeds)

Russian Department: Mrs J M Nashvili, MA (Oxford)

Mathematics Department:
Miss J M Goodwin, BSc (Leicester)
Mr M Miller, MSc (Sheffield)
Mrs D Balcombe, BA (London), MSc (Open)
Mrs K Ibbotson, BSc (Sheffield)
Mrs M Couldwell, BSc (Sheffield)
Miss M Bass, MSc (Newcastle)
Miss J L Harper, BSc (Manchester)

Information Technology Department:
Mrs J Byrom, MSc Tech (Sheffield)
Mrs J Ashby, BSc (Sheffield)
Mrs L Miller, MA (Glasgow)
Mr P Cassidy, BSc (Bradford)

Physics Department:
Miss M J Bird, BSc (London)
Mr P W Clarke, BSc, MA (London)
Mr M Randle, BA (Oxford)

Chemistry Department:
Mr C P Melia, BSc (Leicester)
Mrs C Hewitt, BSc (Sheffield)
Dr V M Anderson, BSc, PhD (London)

Biology Department:
Mrs M E Birkhead, BSc (Cardiff)
Miss H England, BSc (Sheffield)
Mrs G Pitchford, BSc (Aston)

Geology Department: Mrs J Ashby, BSc (Sheffield)

Physical Education Department:
Miss L Sdao, BEd (Manchester)
Mrs H C Leaver, BEd (Liverpool, John Moore's)
Mrs S J Good, BEd (Bedford College of PE)
Miss E Challenger, BA (Brighton)

Junior Department:
Head of Junior Department: Miss G S Crawford, BA (Oxford)

Junior Teaching Staff:
Mrs M L Marsh, BEd (Nottingham)
Ms K Adams, BSc (Guildford)
Mrs J Birkinshaw, BEd (Nottingham)
Mrs A E Farley, CertEd (Sheffield)
Mrs A Hardwick, BEd (Sheffield Hallam)
Miss E A Gladwin, BA (Hull)
Mrs D Price, BSc (Durham)
Mrs A Jones, BSc (South Bank)
Mrs P Nakielna, CertEd (London)
Mrs S A Booker, CertEd (Westminster College)
Mrs L F C Cooper, BA (Open)
Miss J Pickup, BEd (North East Wales)
Mrs L Bailey, MA (Oxford)

Mrs A Slaughter, BA (Sheffield)
Ms M Peacock, BA (Sheffield)
Mrs S Pettifer, BA (Coventry)

Teaching Assistants:
Mrs C Fidler, NVQ3
Miss C Goddard, NVQ2
Mrs A Gregory, NNEB
Mrs D Robinson, NNEB

Administrator: Mrs K White

Administration:
Miss L M Froggatt
Miss M Brown
Miss S L Brown
Ms L Donaldson
Miss L D Southern
Mrs M Young (*Junior Department*)

Librarian: Mrs P Oyston

Resources: Mrs B A Revill

Information Systems Manager: Mr R Durham, BSc Hons (Sheffield Hallam)

Laboratory Technicians:
Mr S Nadin
Mrs J B Kershaw
Mrs L Chambers

Visiting Staff:
Mrs A J Rowden-Martin, BMus *Piano*
Mrs L Melia, BMus, LTCL *Singing/Piano*
Mrs J Ward, BA *Flute*
Miss C Cooper, BA, LGSM *Speech and Drama*
Mrs C Hayward-Browne *Oboe*
Mr S Hepple, HonVCM, FCV, CTVCM *Brass*
Mr N Fletcher, LTCL *Guitar*
Miss V Pike, MMus, GRSM, ARMCM, LGSM *Singing*
Miss D Chamberlain *Cello*)
Miss S Allison, GRSM, LRAM *Violin*
Ms J Burley, LRAM, GRSM *Bassoon*
Ms F Bailes, MA *Oboe*
Miss J Westwood, BA *Piano*
Miss K Burland, MA, BMus *Clarinet/Saxophone*
Mr S Allbright *Self-Defence*
Miss K Leverton *Trampolining*
Mr J Wragg *Tennis*

The school was opened in 1878 and has occupied its pleasant site in the suburb of Broomhill since 1884. It draws its pupils from all parts of the city and from more distant rural and urban areas of Nottinghamshire, Derbyshire and Yorkshire, many travelling on special coaches.

The Junior Department, Senior School buildings and recently opened Sixth Form Centre are adjacent and share gardens, sports hall, hockey/rounders pitch, netball/tennis courts and a gymnasium on the site. A hockey and athletics field is situated a short bus ride from the school. Recent additions to the Senior School include IT laboratories, a Design block, Music facilities, a drama studio and a new library.

There are 275 girls, aged 4–11, in the Junior Department, and the Senior School of 673 girls aged 11–18 includes 142 in the Sixth Forms.

Curriculum. The usual Junior subjects are taught plus Frnch, Art, Computer Studies, Craft/Technology, Drama, Music and PE. Most lessons are with form teachers but specialist staff teach older girls. Senior girls take 9 GCSE subjects from the range of usual options plus German, Greek, Latin, Drama, Russian, Spanish, Art, Classical Civilisation, DT, Economics, Geology, IT, Music and PE. CLAIT and Health Education also taught. Over 75% stay on to the Sixth Form and nearly all go on to Higher Education.

There are abundant sporting, musical and other activities, including the Duke of Edinburgh Award Scheme and recent developments have led to an improved educational environment.

Fees. From September 2000: Senior School £5,040 per year, £1,680 per term; Junior Department £3,660 per year, £1,220 per term.

The fees cover the regular curriculum, school books, stationery and other materials, choral music and games, but not optional extra subjects or school meals.

The fees for extra subjects are shown in the prospectus.

Scholarships and Bursaries. Following the ending of the Government Assisted Places Scheme, the GDST has made available to the school a substantial number of scholarships and bursaries. The bursaries are means tested and are intended to ensure that the school remains accessible to bright girls who would profit from our education but who would be unable to enter the school without financial assistance.

Scholarships. There are at present available to internal or external candidates a number of Scholarships for entry at 11+ or to the Sixth Form.

Charitable status. Sheffield High School is one of the 25 schools of the Girls' Day School Trust, which is a Registered Charity, number 1026057. The aim of the Trust is to provide a fine academic education at a comparatively modest cost.

Sherborne School for Girls

Sherborne Dorset DT9 3QN
Tel: Admissions: (01935) 818287; School: (01935) 812245; Bursar: (01935) 818206
Fax: (01935) 389445
e-mail: enquiry@sherborne.com
website: www.sherborne.com

Sherborne School for Girls, founded in 1899, has always been in the forefront of women's education. The School is situated on the edge of the town and has extensive grounds with excellent sporting facilities. Girls are admitted at 11+, 12+, 13+ and into the Sixth Form. There are around 370 girls, 340 Boarders, 30 Day girls.

A structured framework is provided which guides girls through the changing patterns of their lives, facilitating the educational, personal and social development of each pupil. Continuous planning takes place to ensure that academic excellence, pastoral care, the curriculum and extra-curricular activities are maintained at the highest level. The result is a first class all-round education. Nearly all pupils go on to University.

There is close co-operation between Sherborne School for Girls and Sherborne School including some joint lessons in the Sixth Form, music, drama, activities, clubs and societies and many other social occasions.

Motto: *Calon To Athlon Cae He Elpis Megalee*

Council:
Chairman: N R Bomford, MA
Mrs E A Smart, MA, BCL
Mrs J C Peake
Mrs J R Grayburn, MA
Mrs J T Melvin
The Rt Rev John Kirkham, MA Bishop of Sherborne
The Viscountess Ullswater
Rear Admiral Sir John Garnier, KCVO, CBE
A W C Edwards, Esq
Mrs H Stone
S J Mabey, Esq, MA, FCA
General Sir John Wilsey, GCB, CBE, DL
The Revd Canon Anthony Phillips, BD, AKC, PhD

Mrs A Browne
Mrs J Nicholson

Clerk to the Council: Cdr D A A Willis, OBE, RN

Senior and Pastoral Staff:

***Headmistress:* ¶Mrs G Kerton-Johnson**, BSc, UED

Deputy Head Academic & Curriculum: Mrs Jenny Clough, MA (Cantab) *Biology*
Deputy Head Pastoral: Mrs Helen Lange, BEd, MA (Sussex) *English*

Bursar: Mr Martin J Steer, FIPD

Chaplain: The Revd Canon Timothy Biles, DipTh, DipEd
Housemistresses of Boarding Houses:

Aldhelmsted East: Mrs Elizabeth Messer, BEd (Reading), CertTEFL *French*
Aldhelmsted West: Mrs Rebecca Liberto, MA (Oxon) *English*
Dun Holme: Mrs Helen Lange, BEd, MA (Sussex) *English*
Wingfield: Miss Siobhan Jones, BA (Toronto) *Classics*
Aylmar: Mrs Joanna Carson, MA (Surrey), ARCM, CertEd
Thurstan: Mrs Althea G Collier, GRSM, LRAM (London) *Music*
Ealhstan: Mrs Mary Glasby, MSc(Ed) (Miami) *Geography*
Kenelm: Miss Margaret Dooley, CertEd (Auckland) *Home Economics*
Mulliner: Mrs P Neethling, BA (Natal) *History and RS*
Assistant and Part-time Staff:

Art:
Mrs J Baker, BA (Leeds), ATD
*Miss J Newman, BA (Norwich), ATC (London)
Mrs G J Biles, CertEd (Exeter)
Mr J N B Jacobsen, Dip Art & Design (St Martin's, London)
Mrs J Saurin, BA (Sydney), MA (Courtauld Institute (London)

Classics:
Mrs A Cockerham, MA (Edinburgh)
Mrs P English, MA (Oxon) *also Higher Education Adviser*
*Mr C J Simpson, MA (Oxon) *also Examinations Officer*

Design & Technology:
*Mrs A Legg, BA (Loughborough), MA (RCA)
Mr T Taylor, CertEd (Shoreditch College of Education)

Economics:
Mr B R Neale, BA (Manitoba)

English:
Mrs N Alper, BA (Birmingham) *also Special Needs Co-ordinator*
Mrs A Bjørnseth, MA (Edinburgh)
*Miss A M Pitt, BA (London), MA (Ottawa), CertTEFL *also 6th Form Joint Co-ordinating Committee*
Mrs C Stones, BA (Exeter), CertTEFL
Mrs P Besley, CertEd, RSA, DipSpLD
Mrs K Bowker, BA (Bradford), MBA (London), DipTEFL
Geography:
Mr F K Geary, BA, BSc(Econ) (London), MEd (Keele) *also Politics, Examinations Officer*
Mrs G H Smith, BSc (Bristol) *also Head of Careers*

History:
*Miss C Valeur, BA (London)

Home Economics:
*Mrs C F Bartholmew (Bath College of Education)
Mrs S Wills, Dip IN Home Economics (Aberdeen College)

ICT:
Mr S Jefferson, MA (Cantab) *also Duke of Edinburgh Award*

Mathematics:
Mrs A Allsopp, BSc (St Andrews)
Mr R Lavender
*Miss S Moody, BSc (East Anglia) *also CCF and Sherborne School's Co-ordinator*
Mr M Weaver, BSc (Dunelm)

Modern Languages:
Mrs Y Bell, BA (Birmingham)
Mme M-D Bonelli-Bean, Licence LLCE (Paris)
*Mr M Felstead, MA (Cantab)
Mrs P Fraser, BA, MA (Wales)
Miss W A Laid, BA (Wales) *also Careers*
Frau B Oberrauch
Dr G P Oliver, BA (Cantab), PhD (London) *also L6 Academic Tutor*
Mlle L Vernhes
Mrs M Aplin, Instituto de Isabella Catoline, Madrid

Music:
Miss N Gregory, BA, MPhil (Cantab), ARCO, LTCL
*Mr J M Jenkins, BA (Dunelm), ARCO
Mr D O Price, LRAM
Miss M Armitstead, BA (Dunelm)
Mr J C M Bryden, MA (Cantab), ARCM, ARCO
Mrs P Caswell, BMus (Wales)
Mrs T Cawdron
Mr R E Clarkson, LLCM, CT, ABRSM
Mr J A Dams, MA (Oxon), ARCO
Miss V M Daniels, AGSM
Miss K E Evans, BMus (North Wales)
Miss T Hemingway
Mrs E Jacoby, FTCL, ARCM, LTCL
Miss M A Nightingale, LGSM
Mr K Schooley, MISM
Mr P Shelley, ARCM
Miss M Verity
Mrs L Wilds, DTCM
Physical Education:
Mrs N Matthias, BEd (St Peter & St Mary, Cheltenham)
*Miss R Schofield (Bedford College of Physical Education)
Mrs K Stringer, BEd (Crewe & Alsager College of PE)

Religious Studies:
Mr J Dobson *also History*
The Revd Dr S Wood, MA, PhD (Oxon) *also Assistant Chaplain*

Sciences:
Dr A Ball, PhD (Nottingham), BSc (Leeds)
Mr J Dawson, BSc (Leeds)
*Dr J Ivimey-Cook, PhD (Exeter)
Mrs D B M Lorimer, BSc (London) *also U6 Academic Tutor*
Miss G Nelson, MSc (East Anglia), BSc (Dunelm)
Dr S West, BSc (London), PhD (London) *also Scholarship Co-ordinator*
Mrs C A Price, BSc (Wales)

Speech & Drama:
Mr M V Freestone, BA Hons (UNP)
Mrs R Paige, CertEd (Central School of Speech & Drama)
*Mrs S Wolfenden, MA (Roehampton Institute), Speech & Drama Diploma

Medical Officer: Dr D Townsend, MB, BS, DRCOG, FPC(Cert)
Sanatorium Sister: Mrs J Hayes, SRN
Director of Marketing & Public Relations: Mrs J Clibbon
Registrar: Mrs J Freestone
Librarian: Miss P A Deacon, MA (Oxon)

Terms. Three terms of approximately 12 weeks each. Christmas holidays, 4 weeks, Easter holidays 4 weeks; Summer holidays, 8 weeks. Term dates are in common with those of Sherborne School.

Admission. (*see* Entrance Scholarship section) Common Entrance Examination to Independent Schools. Scholarship Examinations and interviews. The School's own entrance examinations where Common Entrance is not possible. Girls should be registered in advance and reports will be requested from their current school. For entry into the Sixth Form girls are required to gain 5 good passes in relevant subjects.

Fees. From 1 September 2000, fees per term are £5,385 for boarders and £3,985 for day girls. Registration fee £50. A deposit of £500 is required before entry (a term's fees for overseas pupils) and credited to the last term's fees account.

Houses. There are eight all-age Houses and one Upper Sixth House. 11 and 12 year old girls spend their first year together in one all-age House.

Religion. The School has a Church of England foundation and a part-time Chaplain, but it values the presence and contribution of members of all the Christian traditions and of other faiths. Regular services are held in the Abbey.

Examinations. Girls are prepared for the General Certificate of Secondary Education; A/S and A Levels and entrance to Universities. There is a wide choice of subjects to be studied.

Games. Hockey and Lacrosse/Netball are played in the autumn and spring terms and Tennis, Rounders and Athletics during the summer. There is a heated, open-air Swimming Pool, Squash Courts, floodlit Astroturf and Sports Hall with Fitness Centre. Archery, Badminton, Cross Country Running, Golf, Aerobics, Judo, Trampolining are alternative games.

Sherborne Old Girls Union (SOGU). All enquiries should be made to Miss Sheila Powell at the School (Tel: (01935) 812245).

Prospective parents and their daughters are warmly welcomed to visit the School, whether for a private visit for a tour of the School and to meet the Headmistress, and/or to attend one of our Open Days. Please telephone the Registrar on (01935) 818287 for further details.

Charitable status. Sherborne School for Girls is a Registered Charity, number 307427 A1-A. It exists to provide education for girls in a boarding environment.

Shrewsbury High School (G.D.S.T.)

32 Town Walls Shrewsbury SY1 1TN
Tel: (01743) 362872
Fax: (01743) 364942
e-mail: enquiries@shr.gdst.net
website: www.gdst.net/shrewsburyhigh

Founded 1885

This is one of the 25 schools of The Girls' Day School Trust. For general information about the Trust and the composition of its Council, see p 532. The following are additional particulars and a more detailed prospectus may be obtained from the school.

Local Governors:
Chairman: Mr C P Hollings, BChD, LDS, RCS
Dr F Darvell, MA, MBChir (Cantab), MRCGP
Mrs E Elias, MA
Dr R Geller, MB, ChB
Mr M C James, MSc
Lady Lees
Mr C J Machin, MA
Mr D Miller, FNAEA
Mrs P Quayle, BA
Mrs C D A Stewart, BA
Dr P Toghill, BSc, FGS
Mr R A Wimbush

***Headmistress:* Mrs M Cass**, BA, PGCE (Exeter), MA(Ed-Man) (Bath) *Geography*

Deputy Headmistress: Mrs D P Duff, BA (Reading) *Classics*

Teaching Staff:
Mrs S A Abington, BSc (Oxford Polytechnic) *Chemistry*
Miss K M Anderson, BEd (Calder College) *Home Management*
Mr A Ashley, MSc (Open University), MA (Keele) *Physics*
Miss S Beattie, MA (Aberdeen) *French and German*
Mrs V Beaumont (Gwent College of Art & Design) *Fine Art*
Mrs S M Bestwick, BA (Wales) *English, Drama*
Mrs S E Bower, BSc (Hull) *Mathematics*
Mr B Brown, BSc (Sheffield) *Zoology*
Miss J E Campbell, BSc (Hull) *Geography*
Mr S R Cooper, BA (London) *German*
Mrs S Coppin, BSc (Nottingham) *Genetics*
Mrs F M B Cross *French Conversation*
Mrs G Cross, CertPE (Bedford College)
Mrs P M Day, BSc (Bristol) *Chemistry*
Mrs S Fenner, BA (Warwick) *Physical Education and Mathematics*
Mr D J Fry, BEd (Birmingham) *Computing & Mathematics*
Mr J Fullick, MA (Birmingham) *Art Education*
Mrs J M Haddaway, BSc (Brunel) *Physics*
Mrs H Herring *French Conversation*
Mrs D Higgs, BSc (London) *Economics*
Mrs G Kerr, DipPE (Dunfermline College, Edinburgh)
Mrs J M Lack, BSc (East Anglia) *Mathematics*
Mrs J Lashly, MA (Oxon) *Classics*
Mrs S W Lawler, ATD (Bath Academy of Art) *Art & Design*
Mrs J Lamont, BA (Hull) *Religious Studies*
Mrs C M Lenton, MA (Oxford) *History, Sociology*
Mrs M Locke, BA (Bristol) *Classics*
Mrs M Lowdon, BA (Canberra) *English*
Mrs I M McKie *German Conversation*
Mrs S Merricks-Murgatroyd, BA (Manchester) *History*
Mrs J Mills, BSc (Cardiff) *Mathematics*
Mrs S E S Morris, BA (Durham) *Geography*
Miss S Nicholls, BA (Stafford) *Design*
Miss J Orgill, BA (York) *French, German*
Miss S Parr, MA (Oxford) *English*
Mrs S Peat, BSc (Manchester) *Mathematics*
Mrs J E Phillips, BA (York) *English, Special Educational Needs*
Mrs M Powell-Davies, BA (Bristol) *Music*
Mrs V A Redfern, MA (Cambridge) *French, German*
Mrs J Redford, CertEd (Bristol)
Mrs A E Seddon, (Whitelands College) London Cert of Education, Brighton College of Art *Art*
Mrs E Taylor, BA (Newcastle upon Tyne) *English*
Mrs E Thomas, BEd (Polytechnic of Wales) *Religious Education, Art & Design*
Mrs S E Thomas, MA (Oxford) *Biology*
Mrs J Vaughan, BA (Open) *French & German*
Miss P H Wedge, BSc (Manchester) *Physics*
Mrs G M Williams, BA (Sheffield) *History*

Head of Junior Department: Mrs A M Jones, CertEd (Bristol)
Mrs H E Berry (St Peter's College, Birmingham), CertEd
Mrs C Carson, CertEd (Coloma College)
Mrs S Davies, NNEB *Nursery Assistant*
Mrs D M Fox, CertEd (Westhill College of Education, Birmingham)
Mrs S Groves, BEd (Canterbury)

Mrs E Leader, TCert (Caerleon College)
Mrs J M I Mortimer, BA (Open)
Miss J Mountney, BA (Wolverhampton)
Mrs A M Shaw, BA (Leicester) *English*
Mrs C A Soden, CertEd (Newcastle on Tyne)
Mrs G L Styles, PGCE (Goldsmith's College, London)
Mrs S Twells, BEd (Leicester) *Mathematics*
Mrs S Wakeley, BEd (Bristol) *Science*
Mrs S K Webster, CertEd (Dunfermline)
Mrs F M Williams (Thomas Huxley, London), CertEd

Visiting Staff:
Ballet: Mrs J Jones, DipRBS(TTC)
Bassoon: Mr J Hargreaves, GRSM, LRAM
Brass: Mrs W Jones, Dip(RCM), CT, ABRSM
'Cello and Double Bass: Mr J Fairbank, ARCM, LRAM
Clarinet and Saxophone: Mr J Williams, LRAM, ARCM
Double Bass: Mr E Thomas, GTCL, LTCL(MusEd), ATCL
Flute: Mrs J Lumley, LLCM(JD)
French Horn: Miss D Bradley, BA, ABSM(Performing), ABSM(Teaching)
Guitar: Miss J Gleave, BA, PGCE
Oboe: Mr D Glossop, LRAM, LTCL, ARCM, FTCL, PGCE
Piano: Mrs R Glossop, LRAM, LTCL, DipMus (Huddersfield), PGCE
Violin: Mrs J Hargreaves, ABSM, GBSM
Singing:
Mrs C Chadwick, BMus, CE, ABSM(Teaching), DPS
Mrs R Shouksmith, GLCM, LLCM
Speech & Drama:
Mrs D R Griffiths, Licentiate of Imperial Society of Teachers of Dancing, MSSD
Mrs S M Turford, BA, LLAM, ALAM
Piano: Mrs D R Platts, MA, PGCE (Cambridge)

Information Systems Manager: Miss E Shaw

Head's Secretary: Mrs J Gittins

Admissions Secretary: Mrs M Scott

Administrative Assistants: Mrs C Davis, Mrs N Kershaw

School Administrator: Mrs B Lockley, BA

TRO Officer: Mrs C Tilston

IT Technician: Mr T Allsopp

Finance Assistant: Mrs L Knight

Librarian: Mrs M Edmond

School Doctor: Dr Francesca Darvell, MA, MBChir (Cantab), MRCGP

School Nurse: Mrs U Evans

The school was opened in 1885 on College Hill. In 1897 it was transferred to Town Walls, on an excellent site with playing fields and grounds extending to the River Severn. In addition to the standard range of science facilities and classrooms, three houses on the site are used for art, music and Sixth Form common rooms. The Centenary Building provides specialist rooms for home economics, mathematics and a new library resources centre. A performing arts studio was added in 1996. The Junior Department is a short distance away and is well designed to meet the needs of small children, including nursery education. The school is easily reached by train or bus from many parts of Shropshire and Wales.

Pupils. There are approximately 393 pupils, aged 11–18, in the Senior School, with a Sixth Form of 96, and 188 in the Junior Department, aged 4–11 (14 in part-time nursery, aged two and three quarters to 4 years of age, boys and girls).

Curriculum. The curriculum includes all the standard academic subjects including music, art, drama and design. Girls are prepared for the GCSE and Advanced Level examinations and also for entrance to universities. Public examination success is 99.6% at GCSE grades A-C and 98.6% at A Level.

Sports include athletics, badminton, hockey, netball, rounders, swimming, tennis, trampolining, rowing and volleyball. Opportunities exist for participation in chess, debating, drama, Duke of Edinburgh's Award, music, public speaking and Amnesty.

Fees. From September 2000: Senior School £1,680 per term; Junior Department £1,220 per term. Nursery £980 per term.

The fees cover the regular curriculum, school books, stationery and other materials, entry fees for public examinations, choral music, games, and swimming, but not optional extra subjects or school meals.

The fees for extra subjects, piano, strings, woodwind instruments and speech and drama are given in the prospectus.

Following the ending of the Government Assisted Places Scheme, the GDST has established a substantial number of scholarships and bursaries. The bursaries are means tested and are intended to ensure that the school remains accessible to bright girls who would profit from our education, but who would be unable to enter the school without financial assistance.

Bursaries. These are available after entry throughout the Senior School and application should be made to the Headmistress in cases of financial need. All requests will be considered in confidence.

Scholarships. A number of scholarships are available at present for internal or external candidates. These are for entry at 11+ or to the Sixth Form.

Charitable status. Shrewsbury High School is one of the 25 schools of the Girls' Day School Trust, which is a Registered Charity, number 1026057. The aim of the Trust is to provide a quality academic education at a comparatively modest cost.

Sir William Perkins's School

Guildford Road Chertsey Surrey KT16 9BN
Tel: (01932) 562161/560264. Bursar: 563883
Fax: (01932) 570841
e-mail: reg@swps.org.uk
website: www.swps.org.uk

Founded 1725

Board of Governors:
Miss A M Mark, MA (*Chairman*)
J H Wright, Esq (*Vice-Chairman*)
Ms J Anders, CEng
Mrs G Court
Dr C M Davies, BSc, PhD
A J Eady, Esq, MA
Revd T J Hillier
Mrs A M Kimmins
Mrs P Y Moffatt, JP
Mrs M Payne, MA
M Sizmur, Esq, BSc, CEng, MIEE
W B Slater, Esq, CBE, VRD
Mrs A M Taylor, BA, PGCE, DEP
Miss P W Triggs, MA, FICA

***Headmistress:* Miss S A Ross**, BSc (Manchester)

Deputy Headmistress: Mrs E Phillips, BA (Wales)

Senior Teacher: Mrs J Ogilvie, BSc (Liverpool)

Staff:
Mrs M Adams, BA (Keele)
Mrs A Arnold, BA (Keele)
Mrs C Atherton, BA (Exeter)
Miss K Barrow, BA (London)
Mrs D M Bendall, BSc (London)
*Mrs E Bernard, BSc (Birmingham)
Mrs P A Berry, BA (Manchester)
Mrs S Bolton, BA (East Anglia)
*Mrs M Bourne, BA (Hull)
Mrs C Bowden, BA (Bristol)
Mrs S Cameron, NDD (Oxford School of Art)
*Mr G Casley, BA (Bristol)
*Mrs J Creagh, BA (Strathclyde)
*Mrs S Dodson, BA (Wales)
Miss A Downey, BA, FRCM, LRAM (Music), LGSM, LLAM (Drama), ADVS (Voice)
Miss L Elcock, BA (Loughborough)
*Mrs H Eldridge, BA (Leeds Metropolitan)
Miss R England, BA (Roehampton Institute)
Mrs M Ford, BA (CNAA)
Mrs S Garside, BA (Wales), MA
Mrs A Gill, BA (Exeter)
Mrs S Holdaway, BA (Wales)
Mr P Holloway, BA (Durham)
Mrs N Howell, BSc (Exeter)
*Miss C M Hudspith, BA (Durham)
Mr M Jarrett, BSc (London)
*Mr W Jaundrill, MA (Cantab), MSc (London)
Dr D Jordan, BA, PhD (Brunel)
Mrs C Julien, BSc (London)
Ms F Knight, BSc (Exeter)
*Mrs K Knuckey, BA (London)
Miss J Langensiepen, BA (Thames Valley)
Mrs C Malcolm, BA (Loughborough), ALA
*Dr P Mason, BSc, PhD (London)
*Mr I McKillop, MA (Kingston)
Miss P Nash, BSc (Southampton)
Mrs P A Parrish, BEd
Mrs M Payne, BEd (London)
*Dr G Preston, BSc (Southampton)
Miss K Prosser, BA (Bristol)
Mrs F Reid, L-ès-L (Sorbonne)
Mrs J Richardson, BSc (Leeds)
*Mrs M Robertson, BEd (Anstey School of PE)
Mrs M Robinson, BSc (Liverpool)
Mrs B Semple, BA (London)
Miss J Slocombe, BA (Southampton)
*Mrs L Smith, BEd, MA (Reading)
*Mr R Staples, BSc (London)
Mrs V Sutton, BA (Manchester)
Mrs S Swann, BSc (University College, London)
Mrs F Taylor, BMus (Royal College of Music)
Mrs J G Taylor, BSc (Wales)
Mrs C Wells, BA (East Anglia)
*Mrs V A Wright, BA (Birmingham)
Mrs C Yarwood, BSc (Birmingham)
Miss S Young, BA (Reading)

Visiting Staff:
Miss L Abbott (*Violin/Viola*)
Mrs J Clark, BMus (*Flute*)
Mrs S Clarke-Lander, ARCM (*Flute*)
Mr G Edge, LGSM (*Guitar*)
Mrs M Hull, FTCL (*Singing*)
Mrs A Lapping, BSc (*Oboe*)
Mr M Livey (*Photography*)
Mrs K McNaught, GRSM, LRAM, ARCM (*Piano*)
Mrs V Mitchell *Cello*)
Miss T Quinn, LLAM, LGSM (*Speech & Drama*)
Mr C Rickards, BA (*Saxophone/Clarinet*)
Mr M Stanley, BMus (*Piano*)

Bursar: Lieutenant Colonel J C M Hughes, MBE (Ret'd)

Headmistress's Secretary: Mrs S Ayling

Registrar: Mrs M Dickinson

Founded in 1725, the school was a voluntary controlled Grammar School before becoming Independent in 1978. It is a member of GSA. There are 580 day pupils between the ages of eleven and eighteen, drawn from a wide area.

Well served by bus routes and within five minutes walk of Chertsey train station, five minutes drive of the M25 and M3. There are school bus services to and from the Windsor/ Eton and Camberley areas.

Standing in twelve acres of gardens and playing fields, the school offers spacious accommodation, with many new buildings added in the past six years, the most recent Sixth Form, ICT and Language Centres.

Curriculum. A well qualified, graduate staff teaches a modern curriculum aiming to provide a broad, balanced education. Most girls stay on in the Sixth Form, and nearly all Sixth Formers go on to degree courses; a number to Oxbridge.

Subjects offered include English, Mathematics, History, Geography, Economics, Business Studies, French, German, Spanish, Latin, Classical Civilisation, Greek, Biology, Physics, Chemistry, Science: Double Award, Technology, Home Economics, Religious Studies, Theology, Art, History of Art, Music, Music Technology, Information & Communications Technology.

Practical music and drama play an important part in school life. There is a strong instrumental and choral tradition with five choirs, orchestras, wind bands and many chamber ensembles. Dramatic and Musical productions are mounted annually.

Religious education is non-denominational. Pupils are expected to attend classes and a short act of worship in Assembly.

Careers advice is readily available with a careers programme incorporated into Years 9, 10, 11 and Sixth Form curricula. ECCTIS, PUSH, CID, DISCOURSE and WHICH UNIVERSITY computerised career information systems and a well stocked careers library are available for students' use. The school is a member of the Independent Schools Careers Organisation.

A wide variety of physical education activities is available. The Young Enterprise and Duke of Edinburgh's Award Schemes are well supported and very successful, and there are numerous clubs and societies.

Fees. Spring 2001: £2,090 per term, reviewed termly. Books and stationery are included. Private tuition in Music and Speech and Drama is extra. School lunch is available.

Entrance. Entry to Year 7 is by examination held in January for admission the following September. Entry at other levels, including the Sixth Form, is by academic record, examination and interview.

Scholarships. (*see* Entrance Scholarship section) - Some Scholarships and Bursaries are available, including Music Scholarships.

Sir William Perkins's Former Pupils Association. Mrs Sarah Stocker, 6 Salesian Gardens, Chertsey, Surrey KT16 8SG.

Charitable status. Sir William Perkins's Educational Foundation is a Registered Charity, number 1060597, which exists to promote and provide for the education of children.

* Head of Department	§ Part Time or Visiting
† Housemaster/Housemistress	¶ Old Pupil
‡ See below list of staff for meaning	

South Hampstead High School (G.D.S.T.)

3 Maresfield Gardens London NW3 5SS
Tel: 020 7435 2899
Fax: 020 7431 8022
e-mail: senior@shhs.gdst.net

Founded 1876

This is one of the 25 schools of The Girls' Day School Trust. For general information about the Trust and the composition of its Council, see p 532. A more detailed prospectus may be obtained from the school.

Local Governors:
Chairman: Mrs M Weston-Smith, MA
Mrs J Alexander, LLB, FIPD, JP
Miss C Avent, OBE, MA (Oxon)
Mr R S Fowler, MA (Oxon), LGSM, FRSA
Dr H Mintz, BSc, MB, BS, MRCP
Mrs N Perlman, LLB
Mr J Rosefield, BA (Oxon), MBA (Harvard)
Mrs J H Sondheimer, MA, PhD
Mrs S Street, MA, FRSA
Mr N Stuart, MA (Cantab)
Mrs S P Twite, MA (Cantab)

***Headmistress:* Mrs V L Ainley**, BA (Dunelm) *Economics*

Deputy Head: Mrs V M Durham, MA (Oxon) *English*

Senior Mistress: Miss J Dewhurst, BA (Liverpool) *Modern Languages*

Teaching Staff:
Mr M Alter, BSc (Southampton) *Mathematics*
Miss J Benson, BSc (Lancaster) *Mathematics and Physics*
Mr M Bivand, MA (London) *Art and Design*
Ms A Bourke, MA (Cantab) *English*
Mrs A Boyle, MA (Edinburgh) *Classics*
Mrs L Buckler, BA (OU) *Physical Education*
Mrs S E Buckley, MA, MPhil (London) *Classics*
Miss I Canevet, DES, MPhil (Paris) *Modern Languages*
Miss N Cathery, BA (Oxon) *Religious Studies*
Mr M Catty, BA (Trinity, Dublin), MSc *Mathematics*
Mrs J Coates, BA (Bristol) *History*
Miss T L Corbett, BA (Trent) *Art and Design*
Dr B Davies, PhD (London) *Mathematics*
Mrs P Davis, BA (Open University) *Science*
Mrs A Dhanani, BA (London) *Geography*
Mr P Duran, BA (London) *Modern Languages*
Mrs A Evans, MA (Oxon) *English*
Mr K Fosbrook, BA (Oxon) *Classics*
Mrs L F Frank BA (York) *Mathematics*
Mrs S Futter, DipAD (Sussex) *Design Technology*
Miss M Genevieve, BSc (London) *Science*
Mrs C E S Gibson, BSc (Dunelm) *Mathematics*
Mr D Greene, BA (London) *Modern Languages*
Mr B Harkins, MA (London) *English*
Mr J Harris, MSc (London) *Geography*
Mr S J Havelin, BSc (London) *Chemistry*
Miss C Hextall, BA (Lancaster) *Music*
Dr H D Holden, BSc, PhD (St Andrews) *Chemistry*
Mrs G Hood, BA, MA, ALA *Librarian*
Mrs D Hugh, BA (Manchester) *Modern Languages*
Mr N Hunter, BA (Liverpool) *Art and Design*
Miss S Hutley, BEd (Bedford) *Physical Education*
Miss C James, BSc (Manchester) *Physical Education*
Mrs A S Johnson, BA (London) *Religious Studies*
Mr J Joseph, BA (London) *English and Drama*
Mr E Kay, BA (Dunelm), LTCL *Music*
Miss A Kennedy, MA (Philadelphia) *Art and Art History*
Miss D Kiverstein, DBO, LRAM, LTCL *Head of Choral Music*
Mrs B Marks, BSc (London) *Mathematics*
Miss A Merino, MA (Cantab) *Modern Languages*
Mrs S J Mitra, BA (Leeds) *Religious Education*
Ms L Monaghan, MA (London) *English*
Mrs P Morgan, MA (Cambridge) *History*
Miss E Newman, BA (Bristol) *English*
Mrs M C O'Callaghan, MSc (London) *Librarian*
Dr J M Paul, MA, DPhil (Oxon) *Biology*
Mrs M C Pearce, BA (RCA) *Design Technology*
Mrs V M Phillips, BSc (Strathclyde) *Mathematics*
Mrs E Pierce, BSc (Leicester) *Geography*
Mrs L Raitz, MA (Cantab) *Modern Languages*
Miss C Richardson, BSc (St Mary's, Twickenham) *Physical Education*
Mr L J Riches, BSc (London) *Chemistry*
Mrs C Rodgers, MA (Sussex) *Physical Education*
Ms V M Spawls, BSc (Westminster) *Biology*
Dr H Sturz, BSc, PhD (London) *Biology*
Dr L Tiger, BA, DPhil (Vienna) *Modern Languages*
Mrs P Tiger, BA *Modern Languages*
Mr K Wadsworth, BSc (London) *Economics*
Dr D J Walgate, BSc, PhD (Cantab) *Physics*
Mrs C J Wilkes, BA (Cantab) *History*
Mr D G Ward, BSc (Nottingham), MA (OU) *Physics*
Dr C J Woodward, BSc, PhD (London) *Biology*

Junior Department:
Head of Junior Department: Miss K M Stayt, BEd (London)
Mrs N C Bilderbeck, MSc (London)
Miss A M Butlin, BA (Loughborough)
Mrs R Chatrath, BEd (Cantab)
Mr P Cozens, BA (Exeter)
Mrs M L Davenport, Teaching Certificate
Mrs J Davey, BA (Open University)
Mrs A Douglas, MA (Edinburgh)
Mrs S Elian, BA (Strathclyde)
Miss D Green, BA (Manchester)
Miss J Humble, BEd (Deakin)
Mrs D Jackson, BA (Witwatersrand)
Mr S Lipscomb, BA (Cardiff)
Mrs V Mulder, BA (Exeter)
Mr S Stigwood, BA (Bretton Hall)

Junior Department Assistants:
Mrs S Kwashi, NNEB
Miss T Brown, BA (North London)
Miss L Lacoste
Miss P Newton

Visiting Staff:
Piano:
Ms J Clarke, BA, GRSM, LTCL, FTCL
Mr S Ellis, LRAM, GRSM, ARCM
Mr J Hillman, MA, ARCM, LTCL
Mrs E Jones, LRAM
Miss R Leber, BA, Staats ex Schulmus
Mrs M Maneks, LRAM

Strings:
Ms C Cohen, BMus, LRAM *Violin*
Miss M L Graham, GRMCM *Cello*
Ms L McLaren, ARCM *Violin*
Mr B O'Neil, ARIAM, ACCM *Double Bass*
Miss M C Pepper, LRAM, LCTL *Cello*
Mrs R Wing, LRAM *Violin*

Brass:
Mr C Davies *Horn*
Miss S Sanbrook-Davis, DipRCM, ARCM *Trumpet/Trombone*

Woodwind:
Miss R Chard, LRAM *Clarinet, Saxophone*

Mrs E Crawford, ARCM, GRSM, LTCL *Flute*
Miss A Greene, LRAM *Oboe*
Mrs P Hamilton *Clarinet*
Ms F Hanley, LRAM, DipGSM *Flute*
Mrs B Law, LLCM *Recorder*
Mr D Rendall *Saxophone*
Mr S West, GTCL, LTCL *Saxophone*

Percussion: Mr D Webster, BA

Guitar:
Mr R Fogg, BA
Miss B Upson, LRAM

Singing:
Miss J Lax, BMus
Ms S Pratschke, MMus, DipRCM
Miss L Saavedra, GRSM
Miss M Vassiliou, BMus, ARCM
Ms M Wiegold, BA

Theory:
Ms J Clarke, BA, GRSM, LTCL, FTCL

Alexander Technique:
Miss J Gillie, AGSM
Miss A Moseley

Technicians: Mrs C Ezike, Mr R Lofthouse, Ms Z Sheikh, Mr J Parsotam

School Administrator: Mrs J John, FCA

ISM: Miss B Rajani, BSc, MSc (LSE)

Network Support Analyst: Miss E Abe, BSc, MSc (London)

Head's Secretary: Mrs P Bernard

Administrative Assistants:
Ms S Bell
Ms S Brenner
Ms J Girldry
Ms D McCrosson
Ms B Ratcliff
Mrs A Shaw
Mrs I Taylor
Mrs J Warren
Mrs R Wilson

Caretakers:
Mr K Noy-Man
Mr C Tully
Mr M O'Connor

School Nurse: Miss S Richardson

The school was opened in 1876 and is situated close to the Finchley Road and Swiss Cottage underground stations and to Finchley Road and Frognal railway station. It is also easily reached by bus from central, north and north-west London.

In the Senior School there are 630 pupils, including 168 in the Sixth Form. There are 260 girls in the junior department. Entry to the junior department is at 4 and 7; entry to the senior school is at 11; occasional vacancies arise at other ages and new girls are welcomed into the Sixth Form if they achieve the necessary entrance qualifications. Full details of admission procedures are available on written request.

The junior department occupies two large houses with gardens about 5 minutes' walk from the senior school. The senior school premises, which are also used at times by older girls from the junior department, include a 4 acre sports ground, large sports hall, theatre, library, and specialist teaching accommodation including three Art studios, Design Technology rooms, Music rooms, Science laboratories and fully computerised Modern Languages laboratory. The school is fully networked and the computer rooms are equipped with a wide range of software. The school minibus is used for expeditions and games transport. Sixth Form students occupy a large house on the senior school campus and their common room has its own cafeteria. There is an extensive programme of foreign exchanges and 6th Form Work Experience in Europe.

The curriculum is planned to provide a wide general education and there is almost no specialisation until the Sixth Form. The large compulsory "core" of subjects for GCSE includes Triple Award Science, one modern foreign language and either History or Geography to which 2, 3 or 4 options are added. All girls in the senior school are prepared for GCSE and Advanced Level examinations and all leavers go on to university. Pupils are extremely able and participate enthusiastically in an enormous number of extra-curricular clubs, societies and courses. Creativity in art, music and drama is strongly encouraged at all stages. There are many orchestras, ensembles and choirs. Tuition in almost any instrument and singing can be arranged and girls are prepared for the examinations of the Associated Board of the Royal School of Music. Pupils participate in the Duke of Edinburgh Award Scheme and the Young Enterprise Business Scheme.

Fees. From September 2000: Senior School £2,044 per term; Junior Department £1,588 per term.

The fees cover the regular curriculum, school books, stationery and other materials, games and swimming, but not optional extra subjects or school meals.

The fees for extra subjects, including instrumental music, are detailed in the prospectus.

Following the ending of the Government Assisted Places Scheme, the GDST has made available to the school a substantial number of scholarships and bursaries. The bursaries are means tested and are intended to ensure that the school remains accessible to bright girls who would profit from our education but who would be unable to enter the school without financial assistance.

Scholarships. There are at present available to internal or external candidates a number of Scholarships and Bursaries for entry at 11+ or to the Sixth Form.

Charitable status. South Hampstead High School is one of the 25 schools of the Girls' Day School Trust, which is a Registered Charity, number 1026057. The aim of the Trust is to provide a fine academic education at a comparatively modest cost.

Stamford High School

Lincolnshire PE9 2LJ
Tel: (01780) 484200
Fax: (01780) 484201
e-mail: headss@shs.lincs.sch.uk

Founded by Browne's Foundation, of Stamford, 1876.
Motto: *Christe me spede*

Chairman of the Governing Body: M E Llowarch, FCA

Vice-Chairman: Air Vice Marshal P Dodworth, CB, OBE, AFC, BSc

***Principal of the Stamford Endowed Schools:* Dr P R Mason,** BSc, PhD, FRSA

***Vice-Principal and Head:* Mrs P J Clark,** MA, MIMgt

Director of Studies: Mrs F A Owens, BSc

Guidance Co-ordinator: Mrs A J Horton, BA

Staff Administrative Tutor: Mrs B A Szyjanowicz, BA, MEd

Director of ICT for the Stamford Endowed Schools: Mr N A Faux, MA

Head of Careers; Mrs S Killgren, BSc

Librarian: Revd Mrs M E Lloyd, BA, MPhil

Main Subject:

Business Studies and Economics:
M Scriven, BA
Mrs S E Russell, MA
P Stevens, BSc

Art, Design & Technology:
Mrs D Ashley, BA
Mrs J Richardson, BA
Mrs R Yates, BA, ATC

Home Economics:
Mrs T R Bennie, BSc
Mrs A P Gossel, BA
Mrs C A Hawkins, BSc

Drama:
J S Greatorex, BEd
Miss N Watkins, BA (*also English*)

English:
C Coles, MA
Revd G Austen, MA, MPhil, KHT
P A Bowden, BA
A Cox, BA
Mrs P M Howarth, BA, MA
Mrs I M Matthews, BA
Mrs J M Saunders, BA

Geography:
Miss E Hardy, BSc
Mrs H Birks, BSc
Mrs D Steel, BA

History and Politics:
N S F Wills, MA
Mrs L Fisher, BA
Mrs E Salt, BA

Languages:
N S Clift, BA (*Head of Faculty*)
Mrs N M Anderson, BA
Miss Angulo-Gonzalez
Mrs E Archibald, BA
Mrs C Bysshe
Mrs A Day, BA
Mrs D E Evans, BA
Mrs J Holt, BA
Mrs A J Horton, BA
Mrs A Mariner, BA
Mrs C Vié, BA

Mathematics:
Mrs A E Green, BSc
Mrs L Cannon, BSc
Mrs W Cooke, BA
Mrs C Summers, BA
Mrs B A Szyjanowicz, BSc, MEd
Mrs S Killgren, BSc
Mrs M A Miles, BSc
Mrs A M Wheeler, BSc

Physical Education:
Miss K Ainsworth
Mrs B Joint, BEd
Mrs J Peckett, BEd
Miss P A Slote

Psychology:
Mrs L Harte, BSc

Religious Education:
A J Cox, BA
W Baker, BA
Mrs P J Clark, MA, MIMgt

Science:
G C Harman, BSc (*Head of Faculty*)
Mrs M Cade, BSc
N A Faux, MA
Mrs N Gee, BSc
Mrs L Holden, BSc
Dr J V Jones, BSc, ARCS, PhD
Mrs H K Langslow, MA
P Murray, BSc
Mrs G Moss, BSc
Miss V M Orr, BSc
Mrs F A Owens, BSc
K Tyrrell, BSc

Speech and Drama:
Mrs P Galloway, RBTC
P Galloway, BA, Drama Dip

Duke of Edinburgh Award Scheme/Sports Hall Organiser:
A J Elliott, BEd HND Business Studies, AILAM

Director of Music for the Stamford Endowed Schools:
P J White, MA, MEd, LMusTCL

Bandmaster for the Stamford Endowed Schools:
D J Walker, RMSM

Head of Strings:
Mrs J Page, MA

Music:
Mrs N Ingrams, GRSM, MTC, LRAM

Visiting Music Staff:
Pianoforte:
Mrs M Maclennan, LRAM, ARCM
Mrs L Williamson, LTCL
Mrs E Hanlon, ARMCM
A Hone, BMus, ARCM, ARCO
Miss F Maclennan
Mrs L Price
Double Bass:
Mrs K Bentley, GTCL, LTCL
Violin/Cello:
Mrs K Bentley, GTCL, LTCL
Mrs R M Hardy, GRSM, ARMCM
Guitar:
C Bell, BSc, LRAM, ARCM
Clarinet:
Mrs J Dumat, ARCM
P J Casson (*also Saxophone*)
Mrs H Brown, BA
Bassoon:
Mrs A McCrae
Oboe:
G Brown, BMus
Violin:
Mrs S Thomas, GTCL, LTCL
Mrs E Anderton-Taylor, BA (Essex)
Mrs E F Murphy, GTCL, LTCL (*also Piano*)
Flute:
Miss A Cox
Mr P O'Connon, GRNCM
Mrs A Price
Trombone:
S Tate-Lovery, BA
Kit Drum:
S Andrews
Recorder:
Mrs L Price
Singing:
Mrs M Bennett, LRAM, LTCL
Electric Guitar:
N Gray

Organ:
M Duthie, BSc, ARCO
Saxophone:
P J Casson

Boarding:

St Michael's House:
Mr & Mrs J M Backhouse (*Resident Housemaster and Housemistress*)
Mrs S Stafford (*Resident Deputy Housemistress*)
Mrs J Lilley (*Assistant Housemistress*)
Mrs J A Watkins (*Assistant Housemistress*)

Welland House:
Revd Mrs M Lloyd, BA, MPhil, MScEcon (*Resident Housemistress*)
Miss K Ainsworth (*Resident Deputy Housemistress*)
Miss L Tankaria-Clifford (*Resident House Tutor*)
Mrs M Tyers (*Assistant Housemistress*)

Park House:
Miss V A M Rainforth, BSc (*Resident Housemistress*)
Mrs A E Burroughs (*Assistant Housemistress*)
Mrs S Kavanagh (*Assistant Housemistress*)

Medical Officer: Dr B G Glynn, MBBS, MRCGP, DRCOG

Introduction. Stamford High School is one of three schools within the overall Stamford Endowed Schools Educational Charity, along with Stamford School (boys) and Stamford Junior School, the co-educational Junior School.

Numbers and Boarding Houses. There are 662 girls in the (11–18 years) including 77 boarders. The main point of entry is at age 11 though applications are welcomed at any stage up to the Sixth Form. Girls who enter through the Junior School progress automatically on to the High School without further competitive entrance test. Boarders are received from the age of 8 (in the Junior School). There are three Boarding Houses for girls including a Sixth Form Boarding House where the girls have single or shared study bedrooms. The School accepts full and weekly boarders as well as considering flexi-boarding according to family need.

Fees (September 2000). Registration Fee £50. Acceptance Fee £250.

Tuition Fee: £1,944 per term. Boarding Fee: (including tuition) £3,768 per term.

These fees include all stationery, text books and games. School lunches for day girls are at additional charge.

Extras: Individual music lessons, Speech and Drama, Dancing (Riding for boarders only).

Curriculum. The curriculum is designed to ensure all girls have a balanced educational programme up to age 16 thus avoiding premature specialisation. The National Curriculum is broadly followed but much more is added to the curriculum to make it stimulating and rewarding. Most girls are entered for at least 9 GCSE examinations and for GCE AS and A level examinations leading to university entry. Since September 2000, in partnership with Stamford School, all 6th Form girls have access to the full range of subjects offered across the two schools providing an exceptionally wide range of subject choice.

Throughout their time in the school girls are prepared for the examinations of the Associated Board of the Royal Schools of Music in Music and The London Acadamy of Music and Dramatic Art for Speech and Drama. There is much scope for creative activities in Music, Art and Drama and state-of-the-art facilities for Information & Communication Technology, including access to the Internet. The Director of Music for the Stamford Endowed Schools ensures that the Music Department works very closely with Stamford School providing access to a wide range of activities of orchestras, bands and choirs. There are joint drama productions and a new Performing Arts Studio was opened in September 1995.

Sport and Physical Education include Hockey, Netball, Tennis, Swimming, Golf, Fencing, Judo, Athletics, Volleyball, Basketball, Badminton, Trampolining, Gymnastics and Squash. There is a very full programme of extra-curricular activities including Olympic Gymnastics, Athletics and Tae-kwon-Do. There is a heated, indoor swimming pool, and a Sports Hall. The Duke of Edinburgh Award Scheme operates at Bronze, Silver and Gold levels withy a considerable number of girls taking part each year.

Entrance Examinations are held in January; Sixth Form interviews in March.

Foundation Scholarships (*see* Entrance Scholarship section) at 11+ and for the Sixth Form up to the value of full fees according to financial need. Awards may be given for musical or artistic ability.

Charitable status. As part of the Stamford Endowed Schools, Stamford High School is a Registered Charity, number 527618.

Stonar School

Cottles Park Atworth Melksham Wiltshire SN12 8NT
Tel: (01225) 702309/708215
Fax: (01225) 790830
e-mail: office@stonar.wilts.sch.uk

Governors:

Chairman: Mrs S Baldwin

Mr H Adam, BA, MCIPD
¶Miss J Backhouse, BA, FSA
Mrs S Balfour
Mr C Beard
Mr D Butler, FRICS
Dr V Catt, MB, ChB
Miss E Hannay, MA (Oxon)
The Revd B Hopkinson
Lt Col T W Kopanski
Lt Col W J MacWilliam
Mr M J Pettit, FCA
Mr I M Prachar
Mrs F Sharland
Mr D G Trimby, TD, BA, FCA
¶Mrs D R Watts
Miss M Winfield, BA
¶Mrs A Yeoman, OBE, DL

Bursar and Clerk to the Governors: Miss P Turner, BA Hons (OU), TCert

***Headmistress:* Mrs S Hopkinson**, BA (Oxon)

Deputy Headmistress (*Curriculum*): Mrs C Kelly, MA (Cantab)

Deputy Headmistress (*Pastoral*): Miss M Roberts, BEd, DipHE

Senior Staff:
Mr R Andrews, TCert (King Alfred College) *Design Technology*
Mrs C Ashford, CertEd (Chester) *Art & Design*
Mrs C Bennett, BA Hons (UCL), PGCE *Head of Geography*
Mr G Billing, MA (Oxon), PGCE *Head of Drama*
Mr S Cave, BA Hons (Cantab), PGCE *History*
Mrs W Constable, BA (OU), BEd Hons (Sussex) *PE*
Mr I Cowie, BSc, MEd (City), CertEd *Business Studies*
Mrs J Cross, BEd (Bulmershe College of HE) *English/SENCO*
Miss H Deighton, BA Hons (Bristol), PGCE *Classics*

Mrs E Devon, BSc SpAKC (London), FRGS, FGS (London) *Head of Geology/IT*
Dr S Divall, MA, PhD (Cantab), PGCE *Head of Physics*
Mrs H Dziedzic, BSc Hons (Wales), PGCE *Head of Biology*
Mr N Goodall, BA Hons (Notts), MMus, PGCE (London) *Head of Music/IT*
Dr G Hall, BSc, PhD (Imperial), CertEd *Chemistry*
Mr G Harris, BSc Hons (Durham) *Physics*
Mr C Hart, BSc Hons (Exeter), PGCE, MRSC *Head of Chemistry*
Mrs M Hutchison, MA Hons (Edinburgh), PGCE *German*
Mrs W Johnson, BA Hons (London) *English*
Mrs L Jones, BA Hons (Leicester), BPhil, PGCE *Head of English*
Mrs P Lloret, BA Hons (Birmingham), PGCE *Spanish*
Mrs K Ludlow, BA Hons (Reading), PGCE *French/German*
Mrs R Martindale, BEd Hons (Cheltenham) *Head of PE*
Mrs J Mortlock, CertEd (Liverpool) *Head of Home Economics*
Mrs S Muir, BA (Natal), DipEd *Head of History & Careers*
Mrs B Myers, BEd Hons (Bristol) *Music/Religious Studies*
Mrs V Power, BSc (Cardiff), PGCE *Science*
Mrs G Sherman, BSc (OU), ALA *Librarian*
Mr C Stark, BSc (Bristol), PGCE (London) *Psychology*
Miss J Storey, BHSI(regd), ANCEBM *Director of Equitation*
Mr R Vaughan, BA Hons (Gwent), ATD, PGCE, FRSA *Head of Art & Design*
Mrs P Ward, BSc Hons (Birmingham) *Head of Maths/Examinations Secretary*
Mrs C Webster, Bac Licence es Lettres Philosophie (Nantes) *Head of Modern Languages*
Mrs J Wentworth, MA (Oxon), PGCE *Mathematics*
Mrs P Willcox, BA Hons (Exeter), PGCE *Learning Support*
Mr P Wise, BA (London), TEFLCert *English as a Foreign Language*

Preparatory School & Nursery Department:
Head: Mrs B Brooks, MA (Bath)
Deputy Head: Mrs M Whittleton, CertEd (Southampton), TCert

Mrs C Bath, CertEd (London)
Mrs S Cox, BA Hons (Cheltenham), PGCE
Mrs L Drummond-Harris, CertEd (Homerton)
Mrs G Johnson, TCert (Hereford)
Mrs G Nash, BEd (Liverpool Inst of HE)
Mrs A Thethy, BEd (Worcester)

Ethos. Stonar is a centre of academic excellence for girls, developing the talents and abilities of every individual and providing the breadth of opportunity to support and enable pupils of all abilities to achieve their potential across and beyond the formal curriculum. There is a positive work ethic and quality pastoral care. Curiosity, confidence and independence are encouraged so that pupils leave school well-equipped for the challenges of adult life and keen to contribute to the wider community.

Curriculum. A talented and committed staff offer students a broad and flexible curriculum, with literacy and numeracy firmly at the centre of the junior school timetable and an individual choice from wide ranging options in addition to the core of Science, Maths, English, a foreign language and ICT at GCSE. Popular AS and A2 courses include Psychology, Photography, Geology, Business Studies, PE and IT. Results are good and students go on to university courses ranging from Medicine, Law and Accountancy to Geology, Veterinary Science and Music. Talented artists proceed to a variety of Art Foundation Courses. Young riders take up careers in eventing or go for the Equine Studies option. The BHSAI and a top-level Equestrian Competition Course are available in the Sixth Form.

Extra-curricular Activities. On site Sports Hall, Swimming Pool, Astroturf, Theatre, Music and Art schools and International Equestrian Centre offer first class opportunities for sport, music and drama. A timetabled extension period provides a rolling programme of careers advice, health education, study skills, first aid, self defence, citizenship and industrial awareness. Girls enjoy debating, dance, film studies, aerobics, cookery, canoeing and camping. The Duke of Edinburgh's Award Scheme flourishes at Stonar.

Boarding. Junior and Middle School boarders live in comfortable family style houses. Sixth formers enjoy their own purpose-built college style campus. Each girl has her own e-mail address for maintaining close contact with home, with the school's fibre optic network extending into every academic building and boarding house. Girls of any religion and of all nationalities are welcomed and can work towards IGCSE if English is not their first language.

Scholarships and Bursaries. (*see* Entrance Scholarship section) The school offers special services bursaries, scholarships for riding, sport, music and art, for academic excellence and for the good all-rounder. Straightforward entrance procedures via Stonar entrance examinations, Common Entrance or school report at appropriate ages.

Fees per term. Prep Day: £977–£1,795; Senior Day: £2,200; Prep Boarding: £3,627; Senior boarding: £3,960.

Charitable status. Stonar School is a Registered Charity, number 309481. It offers highest educational provision for girls.

Stover School

Newton Abbot South Devon TQ12 6QG
Tel: (01626) 354505 (365279 out of hours)
Fax: (01626) 361475
e-mail: mail@stover.co.uk
website: www.stover.co.uk

Governing Body:
Chairman of the Board of Governors: Mr T M T Key, MA, FRICS
Chairman of Finance Committee: Mrs K Reece, FInstLEx

Members:
Mr H Anderson, BSc (Hons)
Mrs A Anning
Mr A C J Cooper, BSc
Mrs A Dyer, MA
Miss F R Evans, DipEd
Mr D J Groom
Mrs A Harrison, MCSP, AIST
Professor R Hawker, OBE
Dr P J Key, OBE, MB, BS
Professor I D Mercer, CBE, BA (Hons), BSc, LLD
Mr R H Roberts, JP
Mrs J W G Scott
Revd J Spencer, BA (Hons)
Mr R Wyatt-Haines

Headmaster: **Mr P E Bujak**, BA (Hons), MA, CertEd, ARHistS *History*

Deputy Headmistress: Mrs S Bradley, BSc (Hons), MIBiol, PGCE *Biology*

Director of Studies and Head of Sixth Form: Mrs M Batten, BSc *Mathematics*

Bursar: Mrs H Goodwin

Headmaster's Secretary: Miss D Robins

School Secretary: Miss F White

Bursar's Assistants: Mrs M Barnard, Mrs G Hanbury

Academic Staff:

Mrs S Bamberg, BSc, MSc *Chemistry*
Mrs B Brown, BSc, PGCE *Mathematics*
Mrs S Cannon, BA (Hons) *Psychology*
Mrs R Cockell, BSc (Hons) *Mathematics*
Mrs H Coyne-Stacey, BA (Hons) *Modern Languages*
Miss T Craven, BA, PGCE *PE and English*
Mrs T Dinsdale, BEd (Hons) *Physical Education*
Mr G Dunbar, CertEd *Art & Technology*
Mrs V Elce, BA (Hons) *RS and Geography*
Miss E Evans, BA (Hons) *Modern Languages*
Mrs J Jorgensen, BA (Hons), PGCE *English and Drama*
Mrs M Kearney, BEd (Hons) *Biology and Mathematics*
Miss R King, BA (Hons), CertEd *History & Business Studies*
Mrs M Marker, CertEd *Special Needs Co-ordinator*
Mrs J Middleton, BA (Hons), CertEd *English and Drama*
Mr M Palmer, CertEd *Information Technology*
Mrs S Rolls, BA (Hons) *Theatre/Arts Manager and EFL*
Mrs A Smith, BA (Hons) *Geography*
Mr D Topley, BA, CertEd *Physics and Mathematics*
Mrs J Wilce, BEd (Hons) *Mathematics*
Mrs N Winston *French*
Miss C Young, BA (Hons) *Development Officer and History*

Director of Music: Mrs S Farleigh, BA (Hons) *Flute, Piccolo and Voice*

Visiting Staff:

Miss Hiley *Percussion*
Mr J Brydon *Piano*
Mrs V Evans *Cello*
Mr B Hill *Oboe*
Miss J Hitchcock *Clarinet and Saxophone*
Miss C Hayek *Violin and Viola*
Mr P Hill *Guitar*
Mr A Stark *Brass*
Miss A Brown *Piano*
Mrs H Wills *Cello*
Mrs R Morgan *Oboe*
Mr J Boorer *Clarinet and Saxophone*
Mrs A Ayling *Flute*
Mrs S Rolls *Piano*

Stover Junior School:

Mrs D Williams, BA, PGCE (*Head of Junior School*)
Mrs V A Chapman, BEd (*Reception and Head of Nursery*)
Miss M Gower, BEd
Mrs H Gray, BA (Hons), PGCE
Mrs C Simmons, BEd
Miss S Pannell, BA Ed (Hons)
Mrs L Tonks, NVQ (*Nursery Assistant*)
Mrs A Campkin, NVQ (*Nursery Assistant*)
Mrs L Sharrock (*Nursery Assistant*)
Mrs F Martin (*Nursery Assistant/Junior Dept Secretary*)
Mrs A M Bujak, SRN (*Nursery Assistant*)

Residential Staff:

Head of Boarding: Mrs K Veal, BEd (Hons) *Technology*

Junior Housemistresses:
Mrs M Bousfield, CertEd
Mrs T Klymenko

Each House also has attached Boarding Assistants

School Medical Officer: Dr R Bates
School Chaplain: The Revd C Knott, BA

Stover School is a GSA Independent School for girls and is situated near Newton Abbot and the Dartmoor National Park. It has good access by road and rail to major cities and airports. Escort services are arranged. There are 370 pupils of which 92 are boarders.

The main building is an eighteenth century mansion in sixty acres of landscaped gardens and playing fields. New buildings and modifications include the multi-purpose Jubilee Hall, and the Chamber Hall for Music and Drama.

The aim of the school is to prepare girls for the twenty-first century by giving them a sound and flexible education and by encouraging them to develop initiative and self-discipline. In 1996 and 1997 a new Nursery Department and Junior School for girls were opened and both are thriving in their purpose designed facilities. The Junior School curriculum and ethos matches that of the Senior School which prides itself on a very positive working relationship between staff and pupils combined with an air of independent spirit and ambition. A new Sixth Form Centre was opened in 1997 which currently houses 50 Sixth Form students. A £350,000 Art Centre will open in 2001.

Throughout the school extra curricular activities are given great importance and are designed to develop a wide range of skills and abilities. The Duke of Edinburgh Scheme is well established as is Ten Tors and overseas expeditions.

Examinations. Public examinations set by all examination boards are taken at GCSE Level and at A Level. Music examinations are set by the Associated Board of the Royal Schools of Music. Speech and Drama examinations are set by LAMDA.

Games. Hockey, netball, rugby and crosscountry are winter and spring term competitive sports. Gymnastics and dance are also compulsory elements of the Physical Education programme. There are six tennis courts and tennis is the major summer sport but rounders and athletics are also important competitive summer activities. There is a heated open-air swimming pool. Interhouse and inter-school fixtures are played in all sports.

Optional subjects. In addition to a wide variety of activities organised by Stover's own staff there are specialist peripatetic staff for instrumental and voice tuition, speech and drama, riding and tennis coaching.

Scholarships and Entrance Examination. These are set by Stover and all candidates who sit examinations in January are eligible for awards. Music scholarships and Sixth Form Scholarships are also available.

Health. There is a resident SRN and regular visits by a local GP.

Stover Old Girls' Association. Secretary: Mrs E Shillabeer, c/o Stover School.

Charitable status. Stover School Association is a Registered Charity, number 306712. Stover School is a charitable foundation for education.

Streatham and Clapham High School (G.D.S.T.)

42 Abbotswood Road Streatham London SW16 1AW
Tel: 020 8677 8400/2904

Founded 1887

This is one of the 25 schools of The Girls' Day School Trust. For general information about the Trust and the composition of its Council, see p 532. A more detailed prospectus may be obtained from the school.

Local Governing Body:
Representative members of the Council of the Trust.

Lady Adrian
Miss S Campbell

Miss M Leigh
Mrs A Maryon-Davies
Professor L Poston
Miss D Taylor
Mr R Wilson

***Headmistress:* Miss G M Ellis**, BSc (Hons) Glasgow *Chemistry*

Senior School:
Deputy Head: Miss L Bibbins, BA Southampton *English*

Senior Mistress: Miss A M Hall, Certificate in Physical Education (Bedford)

Teaching Staff:
Mrs J R Angerstein, Diploma in Home Economics
Mr A Archer, BA (Open University) *CDT*
Mrs M J R Bailey, BA (Southampton) *French*
Mrs M J Checkley, BA (Oxford) *French*
Mrs H M Cole, BA (Bristol) *Spanish*
Mr P F Cole, BA (Bristol) *Classics*
Miss J A Cronshaw, BEd (Brighton) *Physical Education*
Miss B Drew, BA (Italy)
Dr C Duffin, BSc Hons (London) *Geology*
Miss M Dunn, BA Hons (Leeds), PGCE (Cambridge) *German/English*
Mr K Fernando, BSc (Sussex), PGCE (Canterbury) *Mathematics*
The Rev W Fillery, BA (Swansea), BD *Theology, RE*
Mr T N Fisher, BSc Hons (London) *Physics*
Miss R Foster, BA(Ed) Sports Science & Education (Chester), PGCE (PE) (Lancaster)
Mrs A van Hasselt, BA (London) *History*
Miss M Hay, BSc (Nottingham) *Chemistry*
Mrs A M Hooper, BSc (Manchester) *Biology*
Miss J Inns, BA Hons (Bristol) *Ceramics, PGCE* (London)
Mrs M Jones, BA (University College of Wales) *Classics*
Mr M Kemp, BMus Hons (London), PGCE, ARCM
Mrs K Keown, BA Hons (Robinson College, Cambridge), PGCE (Oriel College, Oxford) *English*
Miss E D Kenner, DipAD (Hons), Camberwell Royal Academy, Cert *Art*
Mrs N Lipczynski, BA Joint Hons (Leeds) *Modern Languages*
Mrs V Mills, BSc, MSc, PGCE
Mr P Mizen, BSc Hons (Cardiff) *Geophysics*
Miss K Parham, BA Hons (Oxford), PGCE *English*
Mr A W Parsons, MBA (London), MA (Southampton), BA Hons (Cambridge) *Mathematics*
Miss M Parsons, BA Hons (Oxford), PGCE *English*
Mr S Penton, MA (Durham), PGCE *Music*
Mrs N Roberts, BSc Hons (Sussex), PGCE *Mathematics*
Mrs N Saba-Castillo Velez, Licence d'Anglais (Toulouse), PGCE
Mrs S Sellers, BA Hons (Manchester) *History*
Mr R Shirley, BSc (Edinburgh) Astrophysics, MSc (London) *Archeology*
Mr M Smart, BA (Bristol) *History*
Mrs F C Smith, BA Hons (Durham) *English*
Miss S Terrett, BSc *Applied Physics* (City of London), MA (London) *Science Education, PGCE*
Mr J Turner, MBA (Hull), BSc Hons (London), PGCE (Cambridge) *Mathematics*
Miss C Whewell, BSc Hons (Liverpool), PGCE *Geography*
Miss I Wood, BEd Hons *Physical Education*
Mr P M Wooler, Grad of Royal Inst of Chemistry, PGCE (London) *General Science*
Mr M G Woolley, BA, (Cambridge), BPhil (Hull) *English*
Mrs R Herat, Associate of Library Association *Learning Resources Manager/Librarian*

Laboratory Technicians:
Mr R Marlow (*Senior Technician*)
Mrs P Gilbert (*Biology*)

Head of ICT: Mr T N Fisher, BSc Hons (London) *Physics*

IT Technicians:
Mr P Sharma (*Senior Technician*)
Mrs J Sellers

Preparatory Department:
Wavertree Road, London SW2 3SR. Tel. 020 8674 6912

Head of Preparatory Department: Mrs J E Salter, CertEd (St Gabriel's College) *Infant/Junior Subjects*
Deputy Head of Prep Dept: Mrs S Chittenden, BA Hons (Roehampton Institute), PGCE *English with Education*

Miss J Abell, BA Hons, PGCE
Mrs S Adam, BA (OU) *Humanities, Junior Subjects*
Miss E Boon, BA, PGCE
Miss A Casey, BA, PGCE
Mrs M Crampsie, CertEd *Primary*
Miss H Dowse, BEd (Worcester) *English Primary*
Mrs A Game, CertEd (Liverpool)
Ms S Goddard, BA Hons (Cambridge College of Arts & Technology), PGCE *English Literature*
Miss S Hilton, BSc Hons (Nottingham), PGCE (Loughborough) *Primary*
Mrs J Johnston, CertEd (Furzedown College), Dip Art & Design (University of Kent, Canterbury)
Ms J Miller, CertEd (London)
Miss S Millington, BA(Ed) Hons (Canterbury Christ Church College) *Music with Primary Education*
Miss M Mitchley, BA Hons (Rhodes University), Degree Ed
Mrs U Ogg, CertEd (Durham)
Miss J A Shone, BEd (London) *Junior Subjects*
Mrs J Ware, BA (Open University), PGCE
Mrs P Yates, BEd (Exeter) *Junior Subjects*

Visiting Staff:

Piano:
Miss S Winter, LRAM, ARCM, GRSM
Mr J Barber, GLCM, LTCL

Clarinet: Mr N Graham, LRAM

'Cello: Mrs A Roper, ABSM

Flute: Miss E S M Whittaker, LTCL

Flute/Clarinet/Saxophone: Mrs O Noble, CertEd Music

Oboe: Miss A Cratchley, LRAM, ALCM

Violin/Viola:
Mr S Giles, BMus
Miss A Giddey, BMus, LGSM

Brass:
Miss T Holloway, GMus, RNCM, PPRNCM

Guitar: Mr J Plunkett, BMus

Bassoon/Recorder: Mr M Woolley

Organ: Mr M Kemp

Singing:
Miss C Costa, BA, LRAM
Miss N Beckley, BA, PGCE, ARCM

Drums: Mr A Riley

School Administrator and Headmistress' PA: Mrs A Medhurst

Administrative Assistants:
Mrs B Wheeler
Mrs P Warner
Mrs C Lumley-Frank
Miss S Asplen

Secretary to Head of the Preparatory Department: Mrs E Murphy

School Nurses:
Mrs M S L Webster, RGN
Mrs H Hughes

School Doctor: Dr K Worthington, FRCS

Streatham and Clapham High School is an amalgamation of two earlier schools, one in Clapham founded in 1882 and one in Brixton founded in 1887, which moved to Streatham Hill in 1894.

In January 1994 the Senior School moved again to a rural campus adjacent to Tooting Bec Common. Set in spacious grounds with beautiful trees, the school provides a safe and comfortable environment with excellent facilities for the provision of an education suited to the twenty-first century. The school is easily accessible to both Streatham Hill and Balham stations, is on the 115 bus route and only a short walk from Streatham High Road with its excellent and varied bus service. A school coach operates from the Clapham and Putney/Wimbledon areas. The school attracts pupils from a wide radius, as well as from the immediate vicinity.

The Preparatory Department moved into the vacated Wavertree Road premises at the same time, immediately enabling an intake of 4+ children to be admitted. There are now two parallel forms in the Preparatory Department and in January 1998 a Nursery Class was opened. The Nursery School (Little Trees) now has its own premises at 12 Wavertree Road and takes girls and boys aged 3-5 years. The total number now in the Preparatory Department is 336. The Senior School is growing fast, especially at Sixth form level, but the final roll in the Senior School is planned as somewhere in the region of 475 pupils, giving a total eventually of 800 pupils on the combined sites.

The Abbotswood Road site has 6 Modern Science laboratories, 2 purpose built Information Technology Centres, 2 workshops, a Pottery, Dance Studio, Fitness Centre and Sixth Form Suite. Construction of the Sports Hall, new library, Art Studio and Pottery are now complete. There is a magnificent Hall, complete with pipe organ, moved from Wavertree Road as a result of an Appeal to parents and friends.

At Wavertree Road, the Preparatory Department also enjoys spacious facilities – a large Hall, a Sports Hall, Art Studio, Library and Laboratories. The youngest pupils benefit from an outdoor classroom.

A wide variety of sports are followed in both schools. The main physical activities are sports acrobatics, netball, tennis and gymnastics, but many others are available at different stages, including badminton, trampolining, swimming, skating, self-defence, squash and basketball. Some of these take place in the lunch time activity slots, when over 70 different clubs take place.

Girls are prepared for GCE examinations at GCSE and 'A' Levels, and for entrance and scholarship examinations to Oxford and Cambridge. A wide choice of courses is offered, so that qualifications may be obtained for universities, schools of medicine, colleges of education, and other forms of further training. All girls in the Sixth Form take a General Studies non-examination and Key Skills course, in addition to their 'A' Level subjects. Girls can specialise in arts or sciences; and music, art and design technology can all be taken to 'A' Level. The languages offered are Latin and Classical Civilisation, Spanish, French, German, Italian, and occasionally Russian and Japanese. In addition girls can study A and AS level subjects, via Distance Learning such as Law, Psychology, Sociology and Electronics.

Individual instruction is given for most orchestral instruments requested, and girls can play in both string and full orchestras, which practise weekly. There are also two school choirs, and various musical groups.

The proximity to Central London makes possible many excursions to concerts, museums, art galleries and theatres. Regular trips abroad are offered.

Fees. From September 2000: Senior School £2,044 per term; Preparatory School £1,588 per term. Little Trees Nursery £1,200 per term.

The fees cover the regular curriculum, school books, stationery and other materials, choral music, games and swimming, but not optional extra subjects or school meals.

The fees for extra subjects are shown in the prospectus.

Bursaries. These are available at 11+ and Sixth Form entry in the Senior School. Applications for bursaries at other levels should be made to the Headmistress in cases of financial need. All requests will be considered in confidence. These awards are means tested.

Scholarships. There are at present available to internal or external candidates a number of Scholarships for entry at 11+ or to the Sixth Form.

Charitable status. Streatham and Clapham High School is one of the 25 schools of the Girls' Day School Trust, which is a Registered Charity, number 1026057. The aim of the Trust is to provide a fine academic education at a comparatively modest cost.

Surbiton High School (CSC)

Surbiton Crescent Kingston-upon-Thames Surrey KT1 2JT
Tel: 020 8546 5245
Fax: 020 8547 0026. e-mail: surbiton.high@church-schools.com
Surbiton Preparatory School, 3 Avenue Elmers, Surbiton, Surrey KT6 4SP
Tel: 020 8546 5245
e-mail: surbprep@hotmail.com
Junior Girls' School, Surbiton Road, Surbiton, Surrey KT1 2HW
Tel: 020 8546 5245
Fax: 020 8974 6293
e-mail: surbiton@rmplc.co.uk

Patrons:
The Right Hon and Most Revd The Lord Archbishop of Canterbury
The Right Hon and Most Revd The Lord Archbishop of York

Vice Patron: Mrs M Maclauchlan

Governing Council - Church Schools Company:
S Allcock, Esq
D C Barnes, Esq
J H W Beardwell, Esq, TD (*Chairman*)
D P G Cade, Esq
Prof M Clark
Air Chief Marshal Sir Michael Graydon
J E Hosking, Esq
I Innes, Esq
Mrs M Klat-Hicks
P Orchard-Lisle, Esq
T Overton, Esq
Mrs P Parsonson
Dame Angela Rumbold
P Smith, Esq
J Ward, Esq

Staff:
Head: **Dr Jennifer Longhurst**, MA, PhD (Leeds)

Deputy Heads:
Miss S H Styles, BEd (CNAA), CertEd (London)
Mrs M C Anderton, BSc (Wales)
Mr S Merrell, BA (London), CertEd (London)

Head of Junior Girls' School: Miss C R Budge, BA (Exeter)

Deputy Head of Junior Girls' School: Mrs A Farnish, BA (London)

Head of Surbiton Preparatory: Mr S Pryce, CertEd (London), BA (OU), MA (Surrey)

Assistant Staff:
Mrs J Aldous, CertEd (Bedford)
Mrs S Arandia, BA (UEA)
Mrs F Axten, CertEd (Leeds), BA (OU)
Mrs D Barker, MA (Cambridge), MSc (Surrey)
Mrs A Bloxham, BA (CNAA), MA (London)
Miss A Bowles, BSc (Birmingham)
Mrs D Campbell, BA (Wales)
Mrs E Carr, CertEd (London)
Miss K Chubb, BA (Bristol)
Mrs J Cocklin, BEd (Kingston)
Mrs I Coyle, CertEd (London)
Mr D Crawford, BSc (Wales)
Mr D Daughtery, BEd (London), BA (OU)
Mr G Davidson, BA (Leics), MPhil (St Andrews)
Miss A Deighton, BEd (Brighton)
Mrs D De Sousa, BEd (Surrey)
Mrs S L Dempsey, BSc (Bishop's University Canada)
Miss H Dicks, BA (London)
Mrs C Dunne, BA (Dunelm)
Mr T Ferguson, BSc (Staffordshire)
Mr M Ferrabee, BA (London)
Miss R Finch, BA (Exeter)
Miss S Forrester, BA (Dunelm)
Mrs V Foster, BA (Exeter)
Mrs S Fraser, BEd (Cambridge)
Mrs M Garrard, BA (London), MA(Ed) (OU)
Mrs M Gates-Sumner, BSc (Surrey)
Miss E Gorby, BSc (London)
Mrs A Godbold, BA (Manchester)
Mrs E Goodchild, BSc (London)
Miss H Hardy, BEd (Plymouth)
Mrs H Hart, BSc (Birmingham)
Mrs H Hay, MA (St Andrews)
Mr W Haycocks, BA (East Anglia)
Mrs E Hewitt, BEd (Oxford Brookes)
Mrs M Hobbs, BSc (Sussex)
Mrs C Holmes, BA (Bangor)
Mrs W Hopgood, BA (Kingston)
Mrs H Horswill, BA (Keele)
Mrs D Howell, BA (London)
Mr J Humphries, BA, MA (Oxford)
Ms B Huntley, BA (Lancaster)
Mrs A Jackson, BA (London)
Mrs J Jones, BSc (London)
Miss L Keers, BA (Wales)
Mrs M J Kelly, BA (Ulster), MA (RCA)
Miss F Kelsey, BA (Surrey)
Mrs A King, BSc (Manchester)
Dr R Lloyd, BMus, MMus, PhD (London)
Mrs C Mason, CertEd (Sheffield)
Dr R McDermott, BSc (Leeds), PhD (London)
Miss E McDonald, BSc, CertEd (Loughborough)
Mrs H M McRoberts, BA (Dunelm)
Mr D Morgan, BSc (Wales)
Mrs A Nayler, CertEd, DipMaths (Roehampton)
Mrs G Newton, BSc (CNAA)
Mrs M North, CertEd (Dartford College)
Mrs R Oliver, MA (Cantab)
Miss S Palmer, CertEd (London)
Mr N Parsons, BEd (Southampton)
Miss H Patel, BSc (Sussex)
Mme V Pegnall, CertEd (Greenwich)
Mrs A Pickford, NNEB
Mrs J Pickles, BSc (Dunelm)
Mrs P Piggott, CertEd, BEd (Bristol)
Mrs L Pritchard, BEd (London)
Mrs J Purser, GRSM, ARCM, Dalcroze Dip, CFPS (Reading)
Mr A Rapley, BA (London), MSc, ARCO
Mrs S Rawlinson, BSc (Bristol), ACA
Miss A Reckermann, MA (Dortmund)
Mrs J Rosser, BA (Sheffield)
Miss T Rockall, BA (Kingston)
Dr C Saddler, BSc (Strathclyde), PhD (Newcastle)
Miss P Scott, BA (London)
Mrs R Sharma, BSc (Manchester)
Mrs J Sharp, BEd (Surrey), CertEd (Bristol)
Mrs L Shaw, BEd (Kingston)
Mrs L Shepherd, BA (Southampton)
Mrs J Shortt, BA (Birmingham)
Mrs J Simmons, MA (Glasgow), MEd (OU)
Miss R Simmons, BA (London)
Miss S Small, BSc (St Andrews)
Mrs M Spooner, BA (Bristol)
Mrs O Stewart, BA (Leeds)
Miss J Tazzyman, BA (Cardiff)
Miss A C Treanor, BSc (Leeds)
Mrs G Vosper, BA (CNAA)
Mrs G Walker, BA (Wales)
Mrs K Wass, BA (CNAA)
Mrs J Wilkey, CertEd (Dartford College)
Miss C Williams, NNEB Diploma
Mrs P Watkins, BA (London)
Mrs N Williamson, BA (Southampton)

Extra Subject Staff:
Modern Languages:
Mlle Alexandra Fossey (*French Assistant*)
Mrs C Peasey (*German Assistant*)

Flute:
Mrs H Taggart, ARMCM
Mrs P Thompson, LTCL, FTCL

Oboe: Miss S Belchamber, ARCM, DipRCM

Clarinet: Mr P Nichols, BA (Oxon), LTCL (*and Saxophone*)

Saxophone: Mr S Gledhill, LTCL

Bassoon: Mr C Wadsworth, BMus, LGSM

Brass: J McReynolds, GTCL, PGCert, TCM

Violin: Mrs D Hume, DSCM

Viola: A Harris, AGSM

Cello: Miss N Samuel, BMus, LRAM

Percussion: Mr C Terian, BA

Piano:
Mrs P Speed-Andrews, LTCL, MusEd, ATCL
Mrs M Turner, GRSM, LRAM

Guitar: Mr G Klippell, ARCM

Singing:
J Arthur, LTCL BA, LRAM
M Wall, BEd

Speech and Drama:
Mrs C Jones, FTCL, LGSM, LNEA
Mrs M Meadwell, AISTD, LGSM
Mr N Ware, ATCL

Weight-fitness, Squash: Tolworth Recreation Centre & Surbiton Squash Club

Ski-ing: Sandown Ski School, Esher

Trampolining: Mrs J Allum

Judo Coach: Mrs L Pearman

Rowing: C Fox (Molesey Boat Club)

Medical Officer: Dr J Pugh, LRCP, MRCS, MB, BS
School Nurse: Mrs G Dalziel
School Registrar: Mrs L Lanham
School Librarians:
Mrs A Howe, ALA
Mrs A Ferrabee, BA (Leeds), Dip in Librarianship (CNAA)

Day School, which was founded in 1884, accommodates 1,102 pupils between the ages of 4 and 18. There are 133 pupils in the Sixth Form. Entry to the Junior School at 4 and 7, to Senior School at 11 by own examination and interview. Entry to Sixth Form by interview and qualifications.

The School is situated in the Kingston upon Thames postal area near the river and close to Surbiton Station. It is well served by public transport and draws its pupils both from the immediate neighbourhood and further adjacent districts. A school bus system operates over several areas.

In addition to class-rooms, the buildings include a Sixth Form Centre, two junior schools, a modern science and technology block, and an art and design centre with painting studios, ceramics studio, dark room and Design and Technology rooms. There are purpose built rooms for information technology, geography, modern languages and drama. The senior school has a new library and there is a sports hall. The School's purchase and refurbishment of Surbiton Assembly Rooms has allowed the school to enhance its facilities with additional classrooms, a suite of rooms for music and two areas for drama. There are also spacious dining facilities and a well-equipped stage and performing area.

The School's new sports ground includes an Astroturf multi-purpose pitch with floodlighting, tennis courts and grassed areas.

The Junior Girls' School opened in January 1994 with specialist facilities for science, technology, computers, music, drama and art.

The School Curriculum includes instruction in Religious Studies, English Language and Literature, History, Geography, French, German, Spanish, Latin, Greek, Mathematics, Biology, Chemistry, Physics, Design Technology, Theatre Studies, Information Technology, Economics, Business Studies, Music, Art, Ceramics, Photography, Philosophy, Psychology, Sports Studies and Gymnastics.

Religious teaching is according to the principles of the Church of England.

Extra Subjects: Piano, Cello, Flute, Violin, Voice, French Horn, Percussion, Clarinet, Saxophone, Oboe, Bassoon, Guitar, Speech and Drama, Ballet and Judo.

VIth Forms. A wide variety of courses is offered in the VIth forms so that the girls may choose a suitable group of AS and A2 level subjects to prepare them for University courses, Schools of Medicine, Art School, Colleges of Education and other professional training. Information and communications technology is an integral part of Sixth Form study with a dedicated ICT room in the Sixth Form block.

Games. Hockey, tennis, rounders, netball, rowing and athletics. Seniors, from Year 10 upwards, have a choice of activities on their games afternoons including aerobics, basketball, football, netball, squash, trampolining, ski instructors' course, swimming, weight-training. The School has ski-ing teams in all age groups and currently holds several national titles.

Fees. (*see* Entrance Scholarship section) Registration fee of £40. Tuition fees for 2000 per term: Reception Year 1, 2 £1,307; Year 3, 4, 5, 6 £1,779; Senior School and Sixth Form £2,170. When two or more children of the same family attend the School, a reduction in fees will be given. Reductions are also made for daughters of members of the Clergy.

Bursaries. Available in the Sixth Form, plus Academic, Art, Music and Sport Scholarships at 11+. Sixth Form Academic Scholarships and Creative Arts Scholarships.

For further particulars apply to the Head.

Assisted Places. The Church Schools Foundation offers a limited number of Assisted Places at 11+.

SURBITON PREPARATORY SCHOOL, 3 AVENUE ELMERS, SURBITON, SURREY.

Tel: 020 8546 5245/Fax: 020 8547 0026/E-mail: surbprep@hotmail.com

Boys' day; Church of England; Age 4–11

Entry is at 4 and 7 by assessment and examination. Occasional places in other year groups.

Curriculum. The usual main curriculum subjects are taught as well as Art, Design and Technology, Music, Drama and PE. Reports and Consultations: Reports are issued twice a year. There are regular Parents' Association Meetings and Parents' Evenings.

Leavers. Pupils go on to a variety of independent and selective maintained schools in London and the surrounding area.

Sport. Cricket, Football, Judo, Rugby and Swimming. Clubs and Societies include Art, Science and Technology, Choir, Computers, Cooking, Drama, Orchestra and Table Tennis.

Religious Services. There is a daily assembly and all pupils are expected to attend.

Fees. Registration fee of £40. Years 1, 2 and 3 £1,307; Years 4, 5, 6 £1,779.

Scholarships. Reductions in fee levels are made for sons of members of the Clergy.

Comments. The School gives a sound and balanced education which enables the boys to move on to their senior school as mature and well-adjusted individuals fully equipped to meet the growing challenges of later study and a wider community.

As with the Junior Girls, the first three classes are taught by Form Teachers, while in the subsequent years the children are introduced to more formal teaching, some of which is undertaken by subject specialist teachers.

The Curriculum is designed to prepare boys for entry to independent and selective maintained Senior Schools at 11+. Boys who show particular academic gifts are prepared for Scholarship examinations.

All boys take part in regular Physical Education and the main team games are Football, Rugby and Cricket. Judo is taught as an out of school activity. The senior Sports Hall is used for PE.

Charitable status. The Church Schools Company is a Registered Charity, number 2780748. It exists to provide high quality education in keeping with the teaching of the Church of England.

Sutton High School for Girls (G.D.S.T.)

55 Cheam Road Sutton Surrey SM1 2AX
Tel: 020 8642 0594
School Administrator: 020 8642 1090
Fax: 020 8642 2014

Founded 1884

This is one of the 25 schools of The Girls' Day School Trust. For general information about the Trust and the composition of its Council, see p 532. A more detailed prospectus may be obtained from the school.

Local Governors:
Mr E B Totman, LLB (*Chairman*)

Dr M F Ali Khan, MBBS, DCH
Dr M G J Gannon, MA, MSc, PhD, FIA
Mr R Gledhill, BA, MIPD
Mrs P Karmel, JP
Mrs V A V Maltby, MA (*Council Representative*)
Mrs I Spooner
Mr M Tripp, FIA, BSc, ARCS
Mrs S Walker, MA, JP

***Headmistress:* Mrs A J Coutts**, BSc, MEd Warwick *Microbiology/Virology*

Deputy Head: Mrs L Cole, BEd Leeds, BA, MA Open University *Education Management*

Senior Teachers:
Miss E A Haydon, BSc London *Geography*
Miss E L Rogers, MA London, BMus Manchester *Music*

Head of Sixth Form: Mrs E Clark, BSc(Econ) Southampton *Business Economics*

Senior Staff:

Mrs A Allen, BA Manchester *English*
Mrs W Barratt, BSc Kent *Microbiology*
Mrs R Beattie, CertEd, DipEd *Home Economics*
Mrs J Brims, BA Oxford *Modern History*
Miss A Brodie, BA Exeter *Mathematics*
Mrs C Cleaver-Smith, BA Wales *German*
Mrs R Conquest, BA Nottingham/Trent *Law*
Mrs A Corbelli, Laurea Bologna *Mathematics*
Miss C Demetz, BA Exeter *French*
Mrs W Evans, BMus Wales, LLCM, LRAM *Music*
Mr N Forsdick, MA (Hons) Dundee *Geography*
Mrs J Gaskin, BSc Surrey *Mathematics/Chemistry*
Mr P Grant, BA, BEd Loughborough *Design & Technology*
Dr P Grewal, MSc University of India, PhD University of London *Physics*
Mrs L Griffiths, BA London *Classics*
Dr Z Habib, BSc Teheran, PhD Salford *Mathematics*
Dr I Hatton, BSc, PhD Bristol, CChem, MRSC *Chemistry*
Mr C Holland, BA Birkbeck College, London *Classics*
Mrs D Holloway, BA (Hons) Open University *IT & Computing*
Mrs S Hughes, BMus London, GTCL, LTCL *Music*
Mrs P Hutchinson, BEd Liverpool *Home Economics*
Mrs S James, BA Wales *History*
Mrs J Jarvis, BA Newcastle upon Tyne *German*
Mrs A Lamb, BSc Nottingham *Geology*
Mrs E Lanson, BSc (Hons) Kingston *Chemistry*
Miss R Legg, BEd Bedford *Physical Education, Geography*
Miss F Malam, BEd Southampton *Physical Education*
Miss A Marlow, MA Royal Academy, BA *Art*
Mrs S Mitchell, BA Surrey *Sports Science and Physical Education*
Mrs R Neal, BSc Nottingham *Physics*
Mrs J Parkinson, BA Belfast *English/Russian*
Mrs J Percy, MA Oxford *Botany*
Mrs D Perry, BA (Hons) Canterbury *English*
Mrs M Pitman, BSc (Hons) Exeter *Mathematics*
Mrs P Quantrill, BA (Hons) Cambridge *Geography*
Mrs K Ross, MA London *Fine Art*
Mr D Ruberry, BA Oxford *English*
Mrs E Saldanha, BSc London *Mathematics*
Mrs D Tait, DEUG Nice *French*
Miss J Taylor, BSc Nottingham *Biology*
Mrs V Theodosiou, BEd London *Mathematics*
Miss J Thomas, BA Wales *Biblical Studies*
Mrs A Thompson, BSc (Hons) Sussex *Mathematics*
Mrs F Wallace, BA (Hons) Sheffield *Psychology and English*
Mrs A Ward, BSc Sussex *Polymer Science*
Mr K Wells, MA (Hons) *French and German*
Miss K Williams, BA Oxford *Modern History*
Miss J Willson, BEd Bedford *Human Movement Studies*
Miss K Wilson, BA(Ed) Exeter *English/Drama*
Mrs S Wilson, BA, MSc Oxford *Mathematics*

Librarian: Mrs L Baron, BA London, DipLLB, ALA

Junior Department

Head of Junior Department: Mrs M Harris, BEd, MA Surrey

Mrs P Boddy, BA Birmingham *Modern Languages*
Mrs M Bond, DipEd Ayr, BEd Surrey, DipSpLD
Mrs J Dunn, BSc Nottingham *Biology*
Mrs S Hanna, BA Surrey, QTS, NNEB
Mrs L Henderson, BEd Kingston University *English/Drama*
Miss K Lawton, BA(Ed) Exeter
Mr J McArthur, Teaching Certificate
Miss A McCormack, BEd (Hons) Dublin *French*
Miss R Portas, BA(Ed) Durham
Mrs S Pullin, BA, CertEd Oxon *Theology*
Mrs R White, BA (Hons)
Mrs E Wilson, BEd London *Mathematics*

Visiting Staff:

Bassoon: Mrs A Lakin
Brass:
Mr S Browning, DipRCM, LTCL, FTCL
Mr J Marshall
Clarinet/Saxophone: Mr E Crutchfield, ARCM, DipMus
Flute:
Mr M Axtell
Miss L Pocknell, FTCL, LTCL
Guitar: Mr R Wright, GRSM, ARMCM
Oboe & Piano: Miss H Dennis, FTCL, GTCL
Percussion: Ms J Kendle, GRSM, LRAM
Piano:
Mr P Davies
Miss J Dodd, BMus, ARCM, LRAM
Mrs A Hodgkinson, LRAM, ARCM
Recorder: Mrs B Houghton, LTCL
Singing:
Miss J Hanson, BMus
Dr K Eckersley, DPhil Oxon, BA
Violin/Viola: Mrs A Samuel, LTCL
Violoncello: Mr M Atkinson, BMus, RCM
Speech & Drama:
Mrs B Cavendish, LLAM
Ms A L De Cavilla, BA Creative Arts Foundation
Mrs L Baxter, BA (Hons) *Drama & Education*
Miss A Page, BA, LLCM(TD), ALCM, LNEA, ALAM

Teaching Support Staff:

Mrs S Boyden
Mrs S Campbell Smith
Mrs A Carbery
Mrs M Childs
Mr P Dowie
Mr M Luney
Mrs E Mercer
Mrs B Millburn
Mrs T Nash
Mrs L Reid
Mrs J Stuart

Administrative Staff:
School Administrator: Mrs M Davies
PA to the Headmistress: Miss J Lucas
Admissions Secretary: Mrs J Ward
Administrative Officers:
Mrs J Ames
Mrs W Haggis (*Teaching Resources Officer*)
Mrs S Jalalpour

Sutton High School, founded in 1884, is a member of the Girls' Day School Trust. It has a good reputation for providing a broad, balanced education for able girls in a happy working atmosphere. Distinguished former pupils include the novelist Susan Howatch and BBC correspondent Sue Littlemore.

There are 760 girls in the school: 250 aged 4–11 years attend the Junior School and 510 aged 11–18 years, the Senior School. The Sixth Form is 120 strong. Girls enter the school aged 4, 5, 11 or 16 after taking the school's own entrance tests. Open Days take place in the Autumn Term and visitors can see the school at work during Open Week in June. Further information and individual tours can be provided by ringing the Admissions Secretary or e-mailing the school (J.Ward@sut.gdst.net).

Following the ending of the Government Assisted Places Scheme, the GDST has made available to the school a substantial number of scholarships and bursaries. The bursaries are means tested and are intended to ensure that the school remains accessible to bright girls who would be unable to enter the school without financial assistance.

Aims and Values. Sutton High recognises that each girl is an individual and aims to encourage each student to develop her talents fully. New technologies merge with the best in teaching and learning to help girls prepare for the demands of this new millennium.

Independence of mind and a commitment to study are highly valued qualities, as well as care and sensitivity to others.

Situation. The school occupies a central position in Sutton and is reached easily by train or bus from Dorking, Leatherhead, Epsom, Carshalton, Wallington, Worcester Park, New Malden, Wimbledon and Burgh Heath. From London Bridge and Victoria the journey takes about 30 minutes. Parents arrange transport by coach from Reigate and Tadworth.

Facilities. The Junior and Senior Schools provide well-resourced accommodation for all major subjects. A large sports hall is next to a recently refurbished swimming pool and girls have access to astro-turf pitches.

Private study areas are used by the Sixth Form alongside a well stocked library and computer resource area to allow girls to take more responsibility for their own learning and the effective management of their time. Common rooms are provided for both Year 11 and the Sixth Form.

In September 2001 a new Sixth Form Centre will be open for students.

Curriculum. Girls are admitted to the Junior School from 4 years of age following an assessment. The National Curriculum creates a framework for teaching and Key Stage 1 and 2 SATs are taken. There are opportunities for extra curricular activities in Music, ICT, Sport, Drama and Chess. Girls study French from 7 years of age; there is specialist teaching in many subject areas and a swimming pool on site. After School Care is available and a school bus operates from the Wimbledon area. Girls are encouraged to show kindness towards others, which is developed in our daily Act of Worship, our teaching, work in the local community and fund raising for charity. The school recognises the need for independent learning and homework is set regularly.

In the Senior School girls follow a balanced curriculum in preparation for entrance to university and the professions. The school regularly sends students to Oxford and Cambridge and is always delighted by the range of courses that girls choose to follow at university.

In Years 7-9 girls participate in a broad curriculum that while encompassing Curriculum 2000 provides many extension opportunities. All girls study Latin and it is a hallmark of the school that Science is taught as three distinct subjects by specialist teachers. At GCSE girls study up to 11 subjects including a core of English, ICT, Mathematics, a Modern Language, Religious Studies and Sciences together with optional subjects from a wide range. Emphasis is placed on the use of ICT as a tool to enhance all aspects of education.

In the Sixth Form, students benefit from teaching styles that are supportive but provide opportunities for independent study. Students currently take four or five AS/A2 levels from a wide range of disciplines. New subjects offered at Sixth Form level include Drama, Economics, Government & Politics and Sociology.

In 2000 the average points per candidate was 25.5 with 76.3% gaining A or B grades at A level. Seven girls took up places at Oxford or Cambridge.

Careers advice is given from Year 9 and all girls are able to take extra lessons in Speech and Drama and Music. Each year over 300 girls pass the Poetry Vanguard and Guildhall Speech and Drama Examinations and over 100 pass the Associated Board and Trinity College Music Examinations.

Extra-Curricular Activities. Each year an excellent and varied programme of concerts, musicals, plays, art exhibitions and festivals in both Junior and Senior Schools enables members of the drama groups, choirs and orchestras to perform in public.

An elected committee of girls, led by the Head Girl and two deputies, contribute to the smooth running of the school. The Sixth Form also runs societies, produces musicals and concerts in aid of charity.

Many girls take part in swimming galas, Hockey, Netball, Gymnastics, Badminton, Rounders and Tennis matches, including all major county tournaments; several girls reach county and national squad level each year.

A wide variety of clubs and activities are provided for girls during the lunch break and after school. In addition parents run the Otter and Centipede Clubs which offer sports and coaching sessions. Staff regularly arrange holidays and cultural visits to places as varied as New York, Paris and Yorkshire. The Junior School organises annual residential visits in Years 5 and 6.

A number of girls take part in the Mathematics challenges and competitions with an excellent record of success. The school has a good reputation for debates and public speaking.

Community Links. In addition to Harvest and Christmas parcel collections for the elderly, the whole school organises fund-raising activities for their chosen charities.

The school has a thriving Parent Staff Association which arranges school fairs each year and a range of social activities. Money raised by the PSA has been used on many projects including the upgrading of performance facilities in both the Junior and Senior Schools.

Close links with a local school have resulted in such productions as 'Little Shop of Horrors' and 'The Boyfriend'.

Fees. From September 2000: Senior School £2,044 per term; Junior School £1,588 per term.

The fees cover the regular curriculum, school books, stationery and other materials, games and swimming, but not optional extra subjects.

Details of the fees for extra subjects, including instrumental music, and Speech and Drama, are available from the school.

Scholarships. At present there are available to internal or external candidates part fee scholarships for entry at 11+ and for entry to Sixth Form.

Charitable status. Sutton High School for Girls is one of the 25 schools of the Girls' Day School Trust, which is a Registered Charity, number 1026057. The aim of the Trust is to provide a fine academic education at a comparatively modest cost.

Sydenham High School (G.D.S.T.)

19 Westwood Hill London SE26 6BL
Tel: 020 8768 8000
Fax: 020 8768 8002
Prospectus Enquiries: 020 8768 8003
e-mail: info@syd.gdst.net

Founded 1887

This is one of the 25 schools of The Girls' Day School Trust. For general information about the Trust and the composition of its Council, see p 532. A more detailed prospectus may be obtained from the school.

Local Governors:
Chairman: Mrs B Clague, MA, DipSocSt

Mrs A Beleschenko, BSc, MPhil
Dr H Carr, BA, MA, PhD
Mrs S Hanna-Grindall, LLB
Mrs T Jones, BEd
Mr J B Lavelle, OBE, FCAM
Mrs P Ranken
Mr R M Spencer, MA
Mrs J Staples, MA
Dr A A Thornton, MB, BS
Mrs G Treuthardt, FPC

***Headmistress:* Dr D V Lodge**, BSc, MSc, PhD (London), PGCE

Deputy Head: Mrs K E Pullen, BA (Warwick), MA (London), PGCE
Senior Mistress: Mrs S J McLellan, BA (Durham), PGCE
Head of Sixth Form: Miss B Pakey, BA (Lancaster), PGCE
Head of Upper School: Mrs J Sage, DipAD (Maidstone), ATC (Sussex), MA (London)
Head of Middle School: Mrs J Walker, BEd (London)
Director of Studies: Dr C Laverick, BA (Swansea), MA (OU), PhD (Hull)

Senior School:

Art/Design/Technology Department:
Mrs J M Sage, DipAD (Maidstone), ATC (Sussex), MA (London)
Ms J Stubbs, BA (Brighton), PGCE
Ms D Berrill, BA (Camberwell), PGCE
Miss M Prendergast, BEd (London)

Business Studies Department:
Mr T Pennant, BA (Cambridge), MA (Leicester), MA (London)

English Department:
Mr R Jope, MA, MLitt (Oxford), PGCE
Miss C Hambrey, BA (Leeds), PGCE
Miss M Mander, MA (Cambridge), MA (York), PGCE
Mrs K E Pullen, BA (Warwick), MA (London), PGCE
Miss D Summerfield, BA (Anglia), PGCE

Geography Department:
Dr C Laverick, BA (Swansea), MA (OU), PhD (Hull)
Miss L Bellis, BSc (Manchester), PGCE

History Department:
Miss B Pakey, BA (Lancaster), PGCE
Mrs J A Walker, BEd (London)
Mrs P Cooper, BA (Sheffield), PGCE
Mrs A Marcus, MA (Oxford), MA (London), PGCE

ICT Department:
Mrs J Cocks, BA (Bristol)
Mrs F Marson, MSc (Freiburg)

Modern Languages Department:
French:
Mrs C Taylor, L-és-L (Paris)
Ms L Graham, BA (Bristol)
Mrs J D Place, BEd (Sheffield), MA (Kingston)
Mrs M Medhurst, BEd (London), PGCE
Mrs J Royce, BA (Bristol), PGCE
Miss S Coupe, L-és-L (Caen), TCert

German:
Ms A Erling, BA (Georg August Gottingen)
Mrs J D Place, BEd (Sheffield), MA (Kingston)
Mrs C Taylor, L-és-L (Paris)
Mrs A M Classen, BA (Cologne), TCert
Mrs J Royce, BA (Bristol), PGCE

Classics/Latin:
Mrs S J McLellan, BA (Durham), PGCE

Spanish:
Mrs M A Devlin, Licenciada en Fil y Letras (Barcelona)
Ms L Graham, BA (Bristol)
Mrs N Blamire-Marin, TCert

Mathematics Department:
Mrs J Bates, BSc (Leicester), PGCE
Mrs J M King, BEd (Cambridge)
Mrs J Tibble, BA (Oxon), PGCE
Mr M Williams, BSc (Durham), PGCE

Music Department:
Dr A Howard, LRAM, ARCM, ALCM, ACertCM, FFCM, ATCL, FGCM (London & Paris)
Miss C Hey, BMus (Manchester), PGCE

PE Department:
Miss F Murray, BEd (Brighton), DipEd & Management (Kingston)
Mrs J Reeves, BEd (Leeds)
Mrs L Waters, BEd (Sussex)

Religious Studies Department:
Dr K Mott-Thornton, BA (London), PhD (London)
Mrs P Cooper, BA (Sheffield), PGCE

Science Department:
Biology:
Miss N Mia BSc, MSc (London), PGCE
Dr D V Lodge, BSc, MSc, PhD (London), PGCE
Miss J Petley, BSc (Kent), PGCE
Mrs G Ward, BSc (Bristol), PGCE

Chemistry:
Dr J King, BSc, PhD (London), PGCE
Dr D V Lodge, BSc, MSc, PhD (London), PGCE
Mrs A Lucas, BSc, BA (Auckland, New Zealand), Dip Teaching
Mrs L Nash, CertEd (London)

Physics:
Mr V Shaw, BSc (London), MPhil (London)
Mrs D D Pike, BSc (London)
Mrs L Nash, CertEd (London)

Sociology Department:
Mr P Murphy, BA (Loughborough), MA (London), PGCE

Junior Department:
Head of Junior Department: Mrs B Risk, CertEd (Salisbury), MEd (Bath)
Deputy of Junior Department: Mrs S Stott, BEd (Brighton)
Senior Teacher: Mrs D A Price, BSc (Durham), PGCE
Mrs M Baxter, BEd (Brighton)
Mrs P Dann, CertEd (Birmingham)
Miss K Faircliffe, BEd (Cambridge)
Mrs A Gale, BEd (London), ARCM
Mrs A Gliddon, BA (Kingston)
Miss E Hall, BA (Durham), PGCE
Mrs C Polling, BA (Sheffield), PGCE

Mrs K Powell, BEd (Greenwich)
Miss F Rahman, BEd (Cambridge), QTS
Mrs P Seddon, BEd (London)
Miss E Stockwell, BEd (London)
Mrs V Watson, MA (St Andrews), PGCE

Ancillaries:
Miss L Catling, BTec
Miss C Harley, NNEB
Mrs S A Holgate, NVQII
Mrs A Jope
Mrs A Luck, NVQII
Mrs G Master, NVQII

Visiting Staff:

School Doctor: Dr W Adams, MB, BS, BSc, DRCOG

Miss A Borge, LLAM *Speech & Drama*
Ms M Bruce Mitford, LRAM, ARCM *'Cello*
Mr F Christou, LRAM, ARCM *Clarinet & Saxophone*
Ms L Cook, GGSM *Violin/Viola*
Mr P Craen, MSM *Oboe*
Ms R Fryer, MMus, BA (York), RSAM
Mr B Graham, LTCL, ARCM, FTCL *Clarinet & Saxophone*
Mrs A Highman, BA (London), PGCE *Speech & Drama*
Mr A Jackson *Drums/Percussion*
Miss A Johansson, BEd (Lund, Sweden), DipRAM *Voice*
Mr J Lambert, LTCL, ARCM, DipRCM *Piano*
Mr J Majin, BMus (London), LTCL *Jazz Piano*
Mr R Nicholas, FTCL, LRAM, ARCM *Trumpet*
Mr A P Read, BSc (Birmingham) *Guitar*
Mrs E Roberts, GRNCM, PPRNCM *French Horn*
Ms J Rowan, BA (Reading), LTCL *Bassoon/Flute/Picolo*

Administrative Staff:

School Administrator: Mrs J Barnett, BSc (Brunel), FCCA
Deputy Administrator: Mrs C Spray
Headmistress' Secretary: Mrs S Movahedi
Admissions Secretary: Mrs J Still
Admin Assistant: Miss L Holmes
Admin Assistant (JH): Mrs D O'Connor

Librarian: Mrs J Walkinshaw, BSc(Econ)ILS (Aberystwyth)
Resources: Mrs M Wallace
School Nurse: Mrs J Armstrong, SRN, RSC
Information Systems Manager: Mr J Dunne, City & Guilds, PGCE
ICT Technician: Mr P Sketchley
Technicians:
Mrs E Houghton, BSc
Mr S Ingram
Mr P Stiff

Since 1887, pupils from a wide catchment, extending from Orpington to Central London have been attracted by Sydenham High School's excellent facilities, strong academic tradition, and commitment to providing opportunities that develop the potential of every individual.

We enjoy the advantage of a leafy 6 acre site that is easily accessible by public transport and only 15 minutes away from all the facilities of central London. We have 470 pupils in the Senior School, 100 of whom are in the Sixth Form and 220 pupils in our Junior House, which enjoys its own facilities with ready access to those of the Senior School.

The school is a distinctive blend of well-maintained Victorian buildings and purpose built accommodation refurbished to a distinctively high level. Our facilities are impressive: they include a library, totally redesigned and restocked in 1997, a flagship ICT suite, performance suite and technology centre. We have seven science laboratories, including a new Sixth Form laboratory, two chemistry laboratories completely refurbished in 1999, and two Physics laboratories refurbished in 2000. Our Sixth Form Centre was attractively renovated in 1999.

Excellent on-site sports facilities comprising a new Sports Hall, all weather pitch and multi gym, supplemented by access to the National Sports Centre at Crystal Palace for swimming and Sports Day, produce fine sportswomen who compete in hockey, netball, tennis, diving, fencing and gymnastics at county, national and international level.

Curriculum. The school offers a broad curriculum, ensuring all our pupils are stimulated and excited by learning. Languages include French, German, Spanish and Latin. Sciences include Biology, Chemistry, Physics, Dual and Triple Award Science, with Mathematics and Further Mathematics available at A/S and A Level. Creative and practical subjects include Design Technology and Food Technology, 2D and 3D Art, Physical Education, Music and Drama. Humanities include History, Geography, Religious Studies and Classical Civilisation. All pupils receive a thorough grounding in ICT which is taught as a discrete subject as well as being confidently used by pupils as a cross curricular tool. A responsibility to the wider community is encouraged through involvement in our successful Duke of Edinburgh Scheme and charity work.

In the Sixth Form students can add Business Studies, Government and Political Studies, IT, Theatre Studies, Physical Education and Sociology to the normal range of Advanced Level courses. All students are prepared for Advanced General Studies qualifications. Specifically focused preparation for entry to prestigious universities, including Oxford and Cambridge is provided; a scheme into which all students can opt. The Enrichment Programme complements the range of Advanced Studies, brings in speakers and takes students out to visit exhibitions and industry. Wide and varied opportunities are available for leadership through Young Enterprise, the Sports teams, running of Clubs, extended prefecting systems and the Form Assistant network.

Students are able to make informed choices of GCSE, A/S and A Level subjects, supported throughout by the Headmistress and the Heads of Section. Work in Careers and PSHE also informs the decision making process. The quality of teaching and learning guarantees academic standards remain consistently high. Results ensure that our students have an optimum choice of prestigious university placements. Approximately 95% of students proceed to university; others pursue Gap years or continue their education in more applied fields. The breadth of extra curricular opportunities encourages all pupils to broaden their interests and develop personal skills. Drama is perennially popular with a variety of clubs and productions for Junior House and Senior School. There is a huge diversity of opportunity for making music available to pupils whatever their instrument or level of expertise. Highly qualified peripatetic staff teach a wide variety of instrumental lessons. Our specialist music staff train school ensembles, orchestra and choirs. Pupils perform in school on a regular basis nationally and internationally.

Fees per term. From September 2000. Senior School, £2,044; Junior School, £1,588.

These include text books, stationery and other materials, choral music, PE and swimming, ISCO and Careers counselling. Optional lessons include: instrumental music, speech and drama, fencing, karate, trampolining and club gymnastics. These lessons are extra to the fees and details are shown in the prospectus.

Following the ending of the Government Assisted Places Scheme, the GDST has made available to the school a substantial number of scholarships and bursaries. The bursaries are means tested and are intended to ensure that the school remains accessible to bright girls who would profit from our education but who would be unable to enter the school without financial assistance.

Scholarships. (*see* Entrance Scholarship section) The Girls' Day School Trust makes available to the school a number of scholarships each year for entry to the Senior Department at both 11+ and direct into the Sixth Form. The maximum value of a Trust Scholarship is normally half the current tuition fee. Scholarships are awarded solely on the basis of academic merit and no financial means test is involved.

A music scholarship may be awarded on entry at 11+.

Bursaries The GDST Bursaries Fund provides financial assistance to enable suitably qualified girls whose parents could not otherwise afford the fees to enter or remain in the Senior Department. Bursaries are awarded on the basis of financial need though academic merit is taken into account. An application form can be obtained from the Admissions Secretary. However, it is recognised that occasions will arise when some form of short-term assistance is required and a small fund exists to help in such cases.

Charitable status. Sydenham High School is one of the 25 schools of the Girls' Day School Trust, which is a Registered Charity, number 1026057. The aim of the Trust is to provide a high quality academic education at a comparatively modest cost.

Talbot Heath

Rothesay Road Bournemouth BH4 9NJ
Tel: (01202) 761881
Fax: (01202) 768155

Motto: *'Honou r before Honours'*

The School is an Independent School, founded in 1886 by private effort and transferred to Trustees in 1898 and is administered under a scheme drawn up by the Ministry of Education in 1903. It is a Church of England Foundation.

Governing Body:

Chairman: Mr M Gledhill, FCA

Mr J C Bridger
Mrs J Cull, ARCA, PPCSD, MInstPKg
Mrs J Dawtrey
Mrs J Doyle
Mr P Fullick, MA, MRSC, FRSA
Mr R Harcourt, FRICS, ACIA
Mr P Henness
Mr R Kennedy
Mr M Mitchell, MA, LLB
Mrs C Norman
Mrs J Tulloch
Mrs J Watts, MA, MB, BChir, FRCS, FRCOphth
Mr G Whitehead, FCA

Solicitor to the Governors: Mr C A S Wise, 5 Poole Road, Bournemouth

***Head Mistress:* Mrs C Dipple**, BA (Leeds), M-ès-L (Lille), FRSA

Heads of Faculty:

Miss P Attfield, BA (Swansea) *English*
Miss J A Barrett, MA (Oxon) *Classics*
Mrs J Barringer, BSc Hons (Leicester) *Mathematics*
Mr A Hill, BMus Hons, FTCL *Creative Arts & Technology*
Mr M Gibson *Science*
Mr R H Hopkin, BA Hons, FRGS (Leeds) *Humanities*
Mrs K D Leahy, BA Hons (London) *Head of Junior Department*
Miss R Nash, BEd (Dartford) *Physical Education*
Miss E A Silvester, BA Hons (Birmingham) *Modern Languages*

Visiting teachers also attend for Piano, Violin, Violoncello, Double Bass, Flute, Clarinet, Oboe, Bassoon, Horn, Saxophone, Trumpet, Trombone, Tuba, Dancing, Speech Training and Voice Production, English for foreign students French, Spanish, Italian
and German Conversation

Medical Officer: Dr M Fardon

Financial Controller: Mr D Walters

Head Mistress's PA: Mrs M Smith

School Secretary: Mrs L Weaver

There are some 389 girls in the Main School, of whom nearly 90 are in the Sixth Forms. There is a Junior Department for about 147 girls between the ages of 7 and 11. The Pre-preparatory department caters for 120 boys and girls aged 3+ to 7.

Talbot Heath is among the longest-established schools in the Bournemouth area, with over a century of success. The school enjoys an attractive wooded site and outstanding facilities for Art, Drama, Music and the Sciences (new Art and Drama studios opened in September 2000, new Science Centre opened in March 1999) together with good ICT provision and extensive modern accommodation for a wide range of sports activities.

The school follows the best practice of the National Curriculum but does not undertake Key Stage testing at levels 1, 2 and 3.

Examinations. 21 subjects are offered to GCSE (including Core Subjects) and Advanced Level, and girls gain places at a variety of universities, including Oxford and Cambridge, or go on to other forms of higher education or professional training.

Admission. Girls are admitted into the Junior School by examination at 7 and above and into the Main School by examination at 11+, 12+ and 13+. The Entrance Examination is held annually in January and girls must be capable of working with those of their own age. Entry to the Pre-preparatory Department requires no examination.

Boarding Houses. St Mary's Boarding House is located in the School grounds, Mrs Hall being in overall charge.

Scholarships and bursaries are available and there is also a discount for daughters of Service families and the clergy.

Charitable status. Talbot Heath is a Registered Charity, number 283708. It exists to provide high quality education for children.

Teesside High School

The Avenue Eaglescliffe Stockton on Tees TS16 9AT
Tel: (01642) 782095
Fax: (01642) 791207
e-mail: teessidehigh@rmplc.co.uk

The School was founded in 1970 being an amalgamation of the Queen Victoria High School, Stockton-on-Tees, founded 1883 and the Cleveland High School, Eaglescliffe, founded 1939.

Board of Governors:
Chairman: Mr T J O'Connor, MBE
Mrs C F Anderson
Mr P J B Armstrong, MA (Cantab)
Mrs C Chapman, FCA

Mr D A Collier, LLB
Mr M J Graham
Mr M Peagam
Mr M W Simpson, BDS (Dunelm)
Mr M Smith, BDS, DGDP(UK)
Miss E M Vane

***Headmistress:* Mrs H French**, MA (Oxon), PGCE, NPQH

Senior Department:

Staff:
Mrs B Anderson, BSc Hons (Kent), MSc (CNAA), PGCE *Chemistry*
Mr P W Astle, BSc Hons (Newcastle) *Mathematics*
Mrs E Bartlett, BA Hons (Leicester) PGCE *French and German*
Mrs A Carlin, BA *History*
Mrs M Coles, BA Hons (Hull), DipEd *Librarian*
Mrs C M Cuthbertson, BA Hons (Sheffield), PGCE *English*
Mrs M C Fraser, CertEd (Birmingham) *Physical Education*
Miss J Geddes, BSc Hons (Warwick), PGCE *Biology*
Mrs M Glover, BSc Hons (Leicester) *Physics*
Mrs C Graham, BA Hons, PGCE (Leeds) *English*
Mrs J Gray, BSc, CertEd (Liverpool) *Information Technology*
Mrs S Hall, BSc Hons, DipEd (Nottingham) *Chemistry*
Mrs J Haskins, BA Hons (Kingston-on-Thames), PGCE (London) *Art*
Miss J E Hauxwell, BA Hons (Newcastle), DipEd *Geography*
Mrs S Jackson, BEd Hons *Food/Nutrition & Textiles*
Mrs L Kirton, BD Hons (London), PGCE *Religious Studies*
Mrs A D F Lewis, BA Hons (London), CertEd *Classics*
Miss S Lloyd-Jones, BMus (London), GTCL, LTCL *Music*
Mrs M Matthew, MA Hons (St Andrews), CertEd *Classics*
Mr R Meggs, BA Hons (Sheffield) *Business Studies*
Mrs K E Milburn, TCert (Durham) *Science*
Mrs J Norris, BEd Hons (Newcastle) *Home Economics*
Mrs M A Perfect, BA Hons (Leeds) *Mathematics*
Mrs M Pratt, BA Hons (Hull), PGCE *French and German*
Mrs J Reid, BA Hons (Liverpool), CertTESOL *French and Music*
Mrs M Richardson, DipAD, ATD (Liverpool) *Art and Design*
Mrs C I Rossiter, BA Hons (London), PGCE *Classics*
Mrs K M Siday, BA Hons (Leeds), DipEd *French and Careers*
Mrs F G Sinclair, BA Hons, CertEd *French and Spanish*
Dr V M Stapley, BSc, PhD *Mathematics*
Miss S Taylor, BA Hons (Oxon), PGCE *English/Drama*
Mrs M Thersby, CertEd, DipPE (Lady Mabel College, Rotherham) *Physical Education*
Mrs J A Vickers, CertEd (Neville's Cross, Durham) *Physical Education*
Mrs G K Waddoup, BA Hons (Dunelm), PGCE *German*
Dr A A Wardhaugh, BSc Hons, PhD (London), PGCE *Biology, Psychology*
Mrs V L Wilkie, BA Hons (Hull)(, *PGCE* (Nottingham) *German and French*
Mr M K Wilkinson, MA (Cantab), PGCE *History*
Mrs G Wilson, BSc Hons (York), MSc (Birmingham) *Physics*

Junior Department:
Mrs C A Maxwell, Teachers' Certificate (Totley Hall College of Education) *Head of Department*
Mrs J Beeton, BEd Hons, CertEd *Deputy Head of Department*
Mrs J F Mayall, BA Hons (Nottingham), PGCE *Head of Music*
Mrs H M Bennison, BEd Hons (Southampton)
Mrs W E Cowan, BEd Hons, CertEd (Leeds)
Mrs A C Hewitt, BA Hons (Dunelm), PGCE, BA (Open)
Mrs J E Johnson, BEd
Mrs L Robson, Teachers' Certificate (Avery Hill College)
Mrs M S Welch, Teachers' Certificate (Teesside College of Education)
Miss S Wiseman, BA, PGCE (Newcastle)

Visiting Staff:
Mrs J K Anderson, LCST, MCST, ALCM, CertEd *Speech and Drama*
Mr P L Appleby, *Percussion*
Mrs A Astbury *Recorder and Singing*
Mr S J Bone, CTABRSM *Woodwind, Saxophone*
Mr D L Bridge, ALCM, *Woodwind Clarinet and Flute*
Mrs S A Burniston *Flute*
Mrs M Cooper, DRASM *Violin*
Mrs J M Eddie, LRAM, ARCM *Violin*
Miss A Graham, GRNCM, PGCE
Mr C J C Mackay, CertEd *Brass*
Mr S Munroe, BA *Guitar*
Mrs R Robinson, LGSM, DRSAM, DCLCM, PGCE *'Cello*
Miss J E Rumney, BEd Hons, ARCM(PG), DipRCM *Recorder*
Mrs A Stewart, GBSM, ABSM, PGCE *Piano*
Mrs M R Turner, FTCL, GTCL, LRAM *Recorder*
Mrs C Winterbotham, ALCM *Piano*

Headmistress' Secretary: Mrs S Brown

Bursar: Mr Paul Flint, BSc, FRGS

Teesside High School is set in 19 acres of grounds within easy reach of Teesside, North Yorkshire and County Durham. Rural and urban areas are well served by public transport and special bus services.

Teaching facilities are excellent with specialist areas for Art, Music, IT and Technology. Extensive playing fields, gymnasia and a sports hall provide opportunities for a wide range of indoor and outdoor sports in addition to Hockey, Netball, Tennis, Athletics, Rounders and Swimming. Outdoor pursuits and the Duke of Edinburgh Award Scheme are also available in years 10-13. The Sixth Form Centre with its studies, teaching rooms and conference room gives the pupils independence and the opportunity to experience a wide range of activities outside their 'A' level studies.

The school has a strong academic tradition with all girls studying French from Year 5, Classics from Year 7 and a second modern language from Year 8 in addition to the National Curriculum. A wide range of 'A' level subjects is offered, and 99% of girls go on to University. A structured careers programme in Years 9-13 and an annual careers convention enable girls to make informed choices at all ages.

Individual lessons are offered in a wide range of musical instruments as well as Speech and Drama and Ballet.

There are about 500 pupils, of whom 160 are in the Junior Department (3+–11). Admission is normally at 3+, 5, 11 and 16, but may be at other ages if vacancies occur.

The school takes part in Nursery Voucher Scheme. A Bursary System is in operation. There are some academic scholarships. Details of entry requirements and fees are available on application.

Charitable status. Teesside High School Limited is a Registered Charity, number 527386. It was established to provide a high standard of education for girls and our outstanding results reflect the well-planned curriculum.

* Head of Department	§ Part Time or Visiting
† Housemaster/Housemistress	¶ Old Pupil
‡ See below list of staff for meaning	

Tormead School

Cranley Road Guildford Surrey GU1 2JD
Tel: (01483) 575101
Fax: (01483) 450592

Independent School for 669 day girls from 4 to 18 years of age.
Founded 1905

School Council:
Chairman: C W M Herbert, Esq, BSc Hons

Governors:
J Daniel, Esq, MA
Mrs M E Notley, JP
The Rt Hon Countess of Onslow
Mrs R J B Drew, BA
W D S Raffin, Esq, FCIB
Mrs J W Wedderspoon, BA, LLB, JP
The Revd Dr J M Holmes, MA, PhD, VetMB, MRCVS
Dr H R G Lennox, MBBS, DCH
D H Harries, Esq
Professor J E Harding, PhD, CEng, MICE, FIStructE
R A Wake, Esq, MA, KSG
Mrs A Darlow, BA Hons
N Nanda, Esq, BSc Hons

***Headmistress:* Mrs H E M Alleyne**, BA, DipEd (Queen's, Belfast)

Deputy Headmistress: Mrs L M Taylor, BSc, PGCE (Nottingham), MBA (Open)

Senior School Staff:
Miss L I Ackerman, BA (New South Wales), DipEd (Sydney) *Head of English*
Mrs R Arnold, MA (Oxon) *Latin*
Mrs M A Arnull, MA, PGCE (London) *History, Head of Careers, PSHE Co-ordinator*
Mrs E M Atkinson, MA (Cantab), PGCE (London) *Head of Sociology/History*
Mr T Ball, BEd (Nottingham), FCSM *Director of Music/ Composer in Residence*
Mrs L Balls, BA (Chichester) *Physical Education*
Mrs J B Bruton, BA (London), PGCE (Hull) *Head of History/Curriculum Co-ordinator*
Mrs H J Bryn-Thomas, BSc (Kent), PGCE (Cantab) *Mathematics*
Mrs S B Burdin, AGSM, CertEd (Guildhall School of Music & Drama) *Head of Drama*
Mrs E A Burton, BA, PGCE (Birmingham) *Physical Education*
Mrs B I Collins, BA (Exeter), PGCE (Cantab) *English*
Mrs S Darnton, MA (Newcastle) *Head of Art & Design*
Mrs J Deacon, BSc (London) *Physics*
Mrs K R Dennison, BSc (London), PGCE (Leicester), DipPsych (London) *Psychology*
Mr R P Dockerill, BA, PGCE (Dunelm) *Head of Politics/ History*
Mrs P Dreghorn, CertEd (St Peter's, Birmingham) *English/ Assistant Examinations Secretary*
Mrs J Drury, MA (Surrey Institute) *Textiles*
Mrs E N Duke, BA, DipT (Adelaide) *History*
Mrs T A Dyer, BA (Swansea), PGCE (London) *French/ Spanish, Co-ordinator of Modern Languages*
Mrs F S Elsmore, BEd (Edinburgh) *PE/Gymnastics*
Mr R Ewbank, BA, PGCE (Goldsmiths, London) *Art and Design*
Mrs C Figuera, Maitrise (Sorbonne), PGCE (Lancaster) *French*
Mrs S J Grammel, BEd (Bath) *Home Economics*
Miss F M Gregson, CertEd (Bedford College), BEd (Cantab) *PE, Head of Lower School*
Ms L Grieve, MA (Oxon), LRAM *Classics*
Mrs S E Haddy, BSc (Surrey) *Mathematics/IT*
Mrs G Hanlan, BSc (London), PGCE (Brussels) *Science*
Miss J N Hansen, BA (New York), PGCE (Cantab) *English/Drama*
Mrs E Harrison, BA (Leicester Poly), MSc, PGCE (Huddersfield *Head of Textiles/Home Economics*
Mrs J Hayter, BSc (UCL), PGCE (London) *Head of Chemistry*
Miss J Hoffman, BSc, PGCE (Nottingham) *Mathematics*
Mr M Holford, BMus (Surrey, PGCE (Roehampton), ARCO, LTCL *Assistant Director of Music*
Mrs M A Holtham, BEd (Manchester) *Head of Home Economics/Examinations Secretary*
Mrs S L Jones, BSc (Surrey), PGCE (Kingston) *Physics*
Dr I Kinchin, BSc, MPhil (London), PhD (Surrey), CertEd (Exeter) *Biology/Science*
Mrs B J Kinnes, BA (Leeds), MPhil (Leeds) *English*
Mrs G Lay, CertEd (Kenton Lodge) *Geography*
Mrs S E Marks, MA (Oxon), AdvCertEdManagement (Leics) *Head of Sixth Form/Economics/Politics & Sociology*
Dr D Marriott, BSc, PhD (Reading), CPhys, MInstP *Head of IT/Physics*
Mrs G Matthews, BSc (OU), CertEd (Portsmouth) *Mathematics*
Miss I C B Nicholls, BSc (Surrey), PGCE (Exeter) *German/ French*
Ms I M O'Brien, BSc (Salford), PGCE (Nottingham) *Biology, Deputy Head of Lower School*
Mrs M O'Brien, BA (Johannesburg), MA (California) *Art & Design/Art History/Photography*
Mrs J Paddock, BSc (Bangor) *Mathematics*
Miss S C M Pritchard, BSc (Surrey), PGCE (Kingston) *Head of Physics/Science Co-ordinator*
Miss S Rae, BA (Oxon), PGCE (Cambridge) *Head of Upper School/French*
Mrs R Ricketts, BA (Lancaster), PGCE (London) *Politics*
Mrs E Robinson, BA, MA (Oxon), PGCE (York) *Spanish*
Mrs N E S Shaw, BA (Bristol) *French*
Miss P Simpson, BA (Oxon), PGCE *Religious Education*
Mrs D L Snell, MA, PGCE (Aberdeen) *Head of German/ French*
Mrs Z Tan, BA (Queen's, Belfast), PGCE (Kingston) *Head of Geography*
Mrs M-C Taylor, Cert D'Aptitude Pedagogique *French*
Ms R Taylor, BSc (London), MSc (Aberdeen), PGCE (London) *Geography*
Mrs A-M Thompson, BSc (Strathclyde), PGCE (Glasgow) *Mathematics/IT*
Mrs L A Thompson, BA, PGCE (Brighton), MA (London) *Art/3D Studies*
Mrs I H Thurley, Teaching Diploma in Word Processing *Word Processing/Keyboard Skills*
Mrs M Torpey, BEd Hons (Chichester) *Head of Physical Education*
Mrs C Townley, BA (Sheffield), PGCE (Liverpool) *Head of Religious Education*
Ms S Travis, MA, PGCE (Cantab) *Chemistry*
Mr J W Vockings, BA (Durham), PGCE (Cambridge) *English/Drama*
Mrs A Wake, BA (London) *Librarian/English*
Mrs R Wallace, BEd (Cantab) *Religious Studies/PSHE*
Mrs K R Ward-Close, BSc (Birmingham), PGCE (Durham) *Head of Mathematics*
Mrs F C Warren, BSc (Bristol) *Economics*
Dr D A Watson, BSc, PGCE (Birmingham), PhD (Aston) *ICT Training and Development Advisor/Biology*
Mrs J Welsh, BSc, PGCE (London) *Head of Biology*
Mrs J C Willcox, BA (Soton) *Middle School Librarian*

Mr M Wilmore, MA (Oxon), PGCE (Sheffield) *Head of Classics*
Mrs J M Zacharias, BA (Nottingham), PGCE (Sheffield) *Spanish*

Junior School Staff:
Miss P Roberts, BSc(Econ), PGCE (Wales) *Head of Junior Department*
Mrs S Mortimer, CertEd (London) *Deputy Head of Junior Department*

Mrs G Blackburn, BSci (Sussex), RSADip (Helen Arkell Dyslexia Centre) *Dyslexia*
Mrs P Dawson *Post School Supervision*
Mrs S Cannell, BA (York), PGCE (Roehampton) *Class Teacher, Form 2*
Mrs J Ellery, CertEd (Oxford), BA (OU) *Class Teacher, Form 1*
Mrs J J Fowler, BEd, HCHE *Lower Prep 1*
Mrs V Franks, BSc (Bristol) *Teaching Resources*
Miss C Hale, BA(Ed) (Exeter) *Class Teacher, Upper 1*
Mrs H Hibbs, BSc (London), PGCE (OU) *ClassTeacher, Upper 1*
Mrs B E Hodson, CertEd, DipEd (Cantab) *Geography/ Technology*
Mrs E Imlah, BEd (Aberdeen) *Pre-Prep*
Mrs S Jordan, BEd (Warwick) *Class Teacher, Form 1*
Mrs S A Kimber, Dip in Pre-School Practice *Teaching Assistant*
Mrs A Martin, BEd, MPhil, MMus, LTCL, CRSP *Director of Music*
Mrs J E St George, BA (Bradford), PGCE (Roehampton) *Key Stage 1 Co-ordinator*
Mrs P F Stevens, BEd, CertEd, NFF *Learning Support Tutor*

Bursar and Clerk to the Governors: Mr M O'Donovan, BA (Canterbury)

Admissions Secretary: Mrs L Foley

Matron: Mrs M E Brown

Tormead is an academically selective independent day school for girls, aged 4 to 18. Founded in 1905, it stands in pleasant grounds, close to the centre of Guildford. The atmosphere is lively and the teaching stimulating and challenging. Standards and expectations are high and girls leave the school as confident, articulate and self-reliant young women, the great majority of whom go on to university.

An extensive extra-curricular programme provides further challenge and opportunity. We believe that a breadth of interests, skills and initiative are an essential complement to academic success for the future lives of our pupils. The school has a lively and active musical life with two orchestras, various chamber groups, ensembles and choirs as well as a highly popular and talented Jazz Band, which has undertaken tours to various European countries. Drama, dance, public speaking and debating, Young Enterprise, the Access scheme and Duke of Edinburgh's Award are all very well supported and sixth form girls are regularly selected to join the British Schools' Exploring Society's summer expeditions to such remote and far flung destinations as Arctic Norway, China or Malawi. A wide range of sports is on offer and there is a busy programme of fixtures in Hockey, Netball, Rounders, Athletics and Swimming in all of which we compete with great success. In June 2000, for instance, our under 11 team became the National Primary School Swimming Champions. Gymnastics has been a particular strength for some years with our teams competing successfully at national level.

International links. We believe that an international outlook is important. We have a partner school in Wanyange, Uganda and an established programme of exchange visits with schools in France, Germany, Spain and the United States; and gap students from Australia and South America who each spend a year with us as staff assistants.

Fees. £1,060–£2,250.

Scholarships and Music Awards are available at entry to senior school with further Scholarships at Sixth Form Level.

Tormead Old Girls' Association. *General Secretary:* Felicity Hall (Fletcher), Carradale, 29 Embercourt Road, Thames Ditton, Surrey KT7 0LH. Tel: 0181-398 2801.

Charitable status. Tormead Limited is a Registered Charity, number 312057. It exists to provide education for able girls.

Truro High School for Girls

Truro Cornwall TR1 2HU
Tel: (01872) 272830
Fax: (01872) 279393

Founded 1880
Independent, formerly Direct Grant

Governors:
President: The Rt Revd William Ind, BA, Bishop of Truro

Chairman: Mr I C Waite, MA (Cantab)

Mrs C Dudley, OBE, BA, FMA
Mrs S Glover
The Revd Canon P D Goodridge, AKC, STM (Yale), FRSA
Mrs C Harcourt-Wilson
Mrs A Harris
Mr G J Holborow, OBE, MA (Cantab), FRICS
Mrs W Lloyd, BA, AKC, CertEd
Mr G I Mayhew, BA Hons, ACIB
The Very Revd M Moxon, LVO, MA, BD, Dean of Truro
Miss F Murdin, MA (Oxon)
Lady Rashleigh
Mr W Roberts
Mr J H Smith
Mrs M Wilson-Holt

Clerk to the Governors: Mrs C Harcourt-Wilson

***Headmaster:* Dr M A McDowell**, BA, MLitt

Deputy Head: Mrs F Matthew, BA (Hons)

Chaplain: The Revd I D T Little, BEd

Assistant Staff:

Divinity:
*The Revd I D T Little, BEd (*Sixth Form Tutor*)

English:
*Mrs J A Holland, BA (Hons) (*Sixth Form Tutor*)
Mrs C L Ellis, BA (Hons)
Mr N J Fee, BEd (*Head of Sixth Form*)
Mrs J A Lawrenson-Reid, BEd (Hons) (*Form Tutor*)
Dr M A McDowell, BA, MLitt
Mrs J Trewellard, BA (Hons)

Theatre Studies:
*Mrs J Trewellard, BA (Hons)
Mrs C L Ellis, BA (Hons)

History:
*Mrs D Bray, BA (Hons) (*Sixth Form Tutor*)
Mrs S Creed, MA

Geography:
*Mrs J Rice, BA (Hons) (*Examinations Officer/Form Tutor*)
Mrs S Smith, BA (Hons) (*Form Tutor*)

Classics:
*Mrs S J Brown, MA (*Form Tutor*)

Modern Languages:
*Mrs F R Matthew, BA (Hons)
Mrs M M Hutton, L-ès-L (*Form Tutor*)
Ms J Parkinson, BA (Hons)
Mr A J M Taylor, BA (Hons) (*Form Tutor*)
Mrs M Smith, BA (Hons) (*Form Tutor*)

Science:
*Mrs J V Davis, BSc (Hons) (*Sixth Form Tutor*)
Miss E Bird, BSc (Hons) (*Biology; Form Tutor*)
Mrs M Cooper, BSc (*Physics and Chemistry; Form Tutor*)
Mrs V G Flatt, BScTech (Hons) (*Head of Physics; 8A Form Tutor*)
Mrs S A Jones, BSc (Hons) (*Physics and Chemistry; Sixth Form Tutor*)
Dr Pragnya, BSc (Hons), PhD (*Head of Chemistry; Form Tutor*)
Mrs J Spence (*Laboratory Technician*)

Mathematics:
*Mrs C M Brewer, BSc, CertEd, MCollP (*Form Tutor*)
Miss S T Coxen, BEd (Hons)
Mrs A Hanson, BSc (Hons)
Mrs S A Jones, BSc (Hons)
Mrs J E Savill, BA (Hons)

Computer Studies:
*Mrs J E Savill, BA (Hons) (*IT Co-ordinator*)
Mr C Beechey-Newman, BSc (Hons) *IT Technician*

Art:
*Mr R E Hunter, BA (Hons), ATC
Mrs W Williams (*Form Tutor*)

Home Economics:
*Mrs L Green, MEd (*Senior Teacher*)
Mrs A M Cresswell, BEd

Business Studies:
Mrs S Creed, MA

Physical Education & Extra-Curricular Activities:
*Miss C T Gannon, BEd (Hons)
Mrs J Barnfield, BEd (Hons)
Mrs A Bennett (*Step Aerobics*)
Mrs E Burnard, FIST, AISC, ASTA, RLSSPLG (*Swimming Coach*)
Miss K A Richards, LRAD, AISTD (*Ballet*)
Mrs G Tregay (*Assistant Games Coach*)
Mr K Wherry (*Tennis Coach*)

Careers & Work Experience:
Mr R E Hunter, BA (Hons), ATC
Mrs S Creed

Music:
*Mr S Dutton
Ms R P Beale, BA (Hons), DDME, CertEd, DipMus (Open) (*Strings*)
Mrs L S Balkwill (*Violin*)
Mrs E Brazier (*Cello*)
Mr J Carne (*Piano*)
Mrs N Carne (*Singing*)
Miss S Carpender, ALCM (*Piano*)
Mr P Harbon (*Percussion*)
Mrs V Lynn, GRSM, ARCMCM (*Flute*)
Mr S Morley, FTCL, ALCM (*Choir*)
Mr P Saunders, ARCM (*Woodwind*)
Mr P Stokes (*Guitar*)
Miss E Williams (*Singing*)

Librarian: Mr W F Rice, MA

Special Needs: Mrs H Butterfield (*English*)

Speech & Drama: Mrs S Bradbury

Visiting Staff:
Mr J Birkin (*Philately*)
Mrs A Crockford (*Italian*)
Ms M Matesanz-Garrido (*Spanish*)
Mr J Menadue (*Chess*)
Mrs J Veasey, HSS (*German*)

Senior Boarding Mistress: Mrs G Dowling
Tregolls House: Mrs E Kingdon, NNEB
Rashleigh House: Mrs J Holloway; Miss A Battersby

School Nurse: Mrs E Burnard, SEN
School Doctor: Dr M C D Proctor, MB, BS, MRCS, LRCP, DRCOG, FPC

Bursar: Mr T D B Giles, BA, FCA
Accountant: Mr M Brown
Assistant Accountant: Mrs J Williams
Headmaster's Secretary: Mrs S Fitzgerald
School Secretaries: Mrs H Connolly, Mrs H J Chambers, Miss R Keogh
Reprographics: Mrs J Gothard

Maintenance Team:
Mr T Bayton
Mr C Beechey-Newman
Mr J Harris
Mr M Thomas
Mr D Williams
Mr G Williams
Mr M Woolcock
Mr N Woolcock

Truro High School combines a Preparatory School of approximately 130 girls aged 3–11 (Pre-prep 3–5 boys and girls) and a Senior School of approximately 325 girls (11–19). Boarding accommodation is provided for 100 girls from the age of 8. Entry is based on the school's own selection procedure and Scholarships and Bursaries are available.

A broadly based curriculum is provided including Religious Education, English, History, Geography, Latin, French, German, Mathematics, Computer Studies, Physics, Chemistry, Biology, Human & Social Biology, Music, Art, Home Economics, Drama and Physical Education, and girls are prepared for the GCSE, A/S and A2 examinations. Business Studies, Classical Greek, Spanish, Italian and Theatre Arts may be studied in the VIth form, where there is also an appropriate Key Skills programme. A Careers Department exists to advise girls and parents on openings available over a wide field including entrance to Universities and other institutions of Higher Education. Music forms an important part of the curriculum and there are two orchestras, numerous ensembles and a choir. The school has good facilities: six well equipped Science laboratories, a language laboratory, a Studio Theatre, Textiles and Cookery rooms, an Information Technology suite, indoor swimming pool, tennis courts and an all weather hockey/athletics pitch. Pupils in the VIth Form have their own VIth Form Centre with individual cubicles for private study.

There is a wide range of extra-curricular activities and all pupils are encouraged to participate. The school enjoys good relationships with other schools in the neighbourhood.

Fees per term. These are graduated from £785 Nursery (mornings only) to £3,520 Senior Full Boarding.

Truro High School Old Girls' Association. *Membership Secretary:* Mrs A D Smeath. *Treasurer:* Mrs Sarah Hutton, 17a Victoria Square, Truro.

Charitable status. Truro High School for Girls is a Registered Charity, number 306577/2. It exists to give education to children.

Tudor Hall

Wykham Park Banbury Oxon OX16 9UR
Tel: (01295) 263434
Fax: (01295) 253264

Motto: *Habeo Ut Dem*

Board of Governors:
I R MacNicol, Esq (*Chairman*
C J Pratt, Esq, FRICS (*Vice-Chairman*)
Mrs K J Boult
Miss S Carrdus
The Revd Derek Duncanson
Anthony Goddard, Esq
Miss H Holden-Brown, BA
Mrs S North, BA
Mrs B Polk
Mrs C J Pratt
B Ruck-Keene, Esq
Lady Richard Wellesley
P Whittle, Esq

***Headmistress:* Miss N Godfrey**, BA Hons (London) *English*

Deputy Headmistress: Mrs H A Granville, BA (London) *History*

Senior Mistress: Mrs G M Phillips, BA (London) *Geography, Careers*

Staff:
Mrs C F Beecham, BA (Exeter) *English, Guitar*
Mrs S Blakey *Tennis* (*Garden House Housemistress*)
Miss A Boswell, BSc Hons (London) *Mathematics*
Mrs S Bourne, BA (Cambridge) *Classics*
Mrs M C Boyns, BSc (London) *Mathematics*
Miss A Brauer, BA (Kent), DipPhysEd *Physical Education*
Mrs E Buckner-Rowley, BA Hons (Portsmouth) *Spanish*
Miss P Caddick, MPhil(Ed) (Birmingham) *Drama*
Mrs A Donald, MA, BLitt (Oxon) (*Ashtons Housemistress*)
Miss A J Gamble, BA (London), MA (London) *History/ Politics*
Mrs G L Gardiner, BA (Coventry), RSA DipTEFL, College of Preceptors DipTESL *French*
Mrs H Gibbard, CertEd (Nonnington College) *Mathematics*
Miss L Goymer, BA (Manchester) *Physical Education/ Mathematics*
Mrs G Grant-Ross, BEd (Liverpool) *Practical Cookery*
Mrs K Hart, BA (Manchester) *Textiles*
Mrs D Hughes, BA (Cardiff) *German*
Mrs A Johnson, BSc, PGCE (Dunelm) *Chemistry*
Sqn Ldr R L Jones, (RAF Retd), CertEd, MITD, HNC *Electrical & Electronic Engineering*
Mrs M J Lamont, Slade Dip Fine Art (London) *Art*
Mr G Langer, BSc (North Staffordshire) *Physics & Combined Science*
Miss L Lea, BMus Hons, LTCL, ALCM (Huddersfield) *Director of Music*
Miss S A Lees, BA Fine Art (Oxon), PGCE (M'ster Poly) *Art*
Mrs M Lucas, BA (Lancaster), MA (Bristol), PGCE *French/Italian*
Miss K J Martin, CertEd (Bedford Coll of PE) *Physical Education*
Mr P L Mayne, BA (Open Univ), MSc, CPU CertEd *English*
Mrs M McClellan, MA (Cantab) *Biology* (*Inglis House-mistress*)
Mrs J G Mole, CertEd (Liverpool) *Chemistry, Physics*
Mrs S M Prentice, BA (Open Univ) *Biology*
Mrs C Preston, BA Hons, PGCE (Bangor) *Religious Education*
Mrs J Rhodes, BA Hons, PGCE (Sussex) *History of Art*
Miss B Robinson, BEd *Dance* (*Ashtons Housemistress*)
Mrs A Senior, MSc (Portsmouth), DipEd *Physics*
Miss M Stewart, BA (Oxford) *Spanish*
Miss H Thomas, BA Hons (Bath) *Modern Languages*
Mrs J M Thorn, BA (Reading), DPhil (Oxford) *Classics*
Mr P D Tuckwell, BEd (Oxon), HNDA *Geography, Geology*
Mrs C E Varney, BEd (Oxon) *Business and Secretarial Studies*
Miss J Webb *Careers, Second Year Housemistress*
Mrs A Weiss, BA, PGCE (Liverpool), RSA CertSecLing *French* (*Old House Housemistress*)
Mrs C P Wilson, BEd (Oxon) *Religious Knowledge*
Miss V L Wormell, BA (Loughborough), PGCE (Brighton) *CDT*

Sanatorium:
Sister C Pert, RGN (*Resident*)
Sister R A Farrell, RGN *Sister*

Clerk to the Governors/Bursar: Lt Col L D Wood

Secretarial:
Headmistress's Secretary: Mrs F George
School Secretary: Mrs P Snowden
Travel Secretary: Mrs J Tindle (*Todd Housemistress*)

Tudor Hall is an Independent Boarding School for Girls aged 11–18 years. The school was originally founded in 1850 at Forest Hill but moved to Wykham Park in 1946. It is situated in spacious grounds 1½ miles from Banbury Station and is within easy access of London, Oxford and Stratford-upon-Avon – M40, Junction 11. This enables the girls to enjoy a wide range of cultural and educational activities.

The school accommodates approximately 230 boarders and 30 day girls. Its buildings comprise a 17th century and an 18th century manor with a modern purpose-built house for 78 Sixth Formers and extensive new facilities for academic purposes. These include laboratories for biology, chemistry, physics and general science; CDT workshop; 2 information technology rooms; music school; studios for art and pottery; needlework room, gym and sports hall. There are tennis and netball courts, a swimming pool, squash courts and pitches for hockey, lacrosse and rounders. Buildings for modern languages and domestic science were completed recently. Girls may also take riding and dancing lessons. All girls begin Latin and French with Spanish or German. Italian, Greek, Japanese and Russian, Polo and Sailing are also available in the Sixth Form. Music and Drama are strongly encouraged. The curriculum includes a full range of other academic subjects and, where possible, outings and field work are arranged. Girls are prepared for GCSE and Advanced Level GCE, and appropriate certificates in optional extra subjects. There is a newly-developed library and a careers room where advice is given about university entrance and further training.

Admission is by Common Entrance at 11+, 12+ and 13+. Entry may also be made to the Sixth Form where all girls pursue courses leading to higher education or vocational training and they are treated as students. Those entering at 11 are accustomed to being away from home by being housed separately in a smaller environment. Girls are divided into four competitive Houses but residence is with their own age group. Tudor Hall places great importance on having a friendly atmosphere, a lively and united spirit and high standards. Girls are expected to take an interest in a wide range of activities as well as following a broad educational programme. Involvement in the local community through Duke of Edinburgh Award and social service and participation in events with other schools are encouraged. Debating is strong and there is keen involvement in the European Youth Parliament. The school is Anglican but members of other religious groups are welcomed. There is a small chapel.

Fees. (*see* Entrance Scholarship section) £4,537 per term for boarders; £2,833 per term for day pupils.

Wakefield Girls' High School

Wakefield Yorkshire WF1 2QS
Tel: (01924) 372490
Fax: (01924) 231601

This is an Endowed High School under Management of the Governors of the Wakefield Grammar School Foundation established by Charter of Queen Elizabeth.

Motto: *Each for All and All for God.*

Governing Body: The Governing Body, consisting of 13 co-optative Governors and 6 representative Governors, (including representatives of the Universities of Leeds, Bradford, Sheffield and Huddersfield), is the Wakefield Grammar School Foundation.

Spokesman: Mrs E G Settle

Clerk to the Governors: Mr R C Hemsley, MA, FCA

Head Mistress: ‡**Mrs P A Langham**, BA (Leeds) MEd *English and Russian*

Assistant Mistresses and Masters:
‡Miss D J Allatt, BA (Nottingham) *French and Spanish*
‡Mrs S M Allen, BA (Leicester), MA *English Literature and American Studies*
*‡Mrs L M E Andrassy, Teachers' Cert in Home Economics (Durham)
*‡Miss P M Applewhite, BEd (Sussex) *Physical Education*
‡Mrs D Armitage, BA (Leeds) *History and English*
Dr S Ashelford, BSc (Edinburgh), PhD *Biological Sciences*
*‡Mr D A Baker, MA (Oxon) *Biochemistry*
‡Mrs A Bedford, BA (Bristol) *Theology*
‡Mrs J Blakeway, BEd CNNA (West Midlands College of Education)
Mrs S E Bottomley, BSc (London) *Mathematics*
‡Miss C E Brown, Teachers' Cert in Home Economics (Durham)
Mrs L J Buckley, CertEd (Newcastle), MEd (Leeds)
‡Mrs D S Burcher, BSc (Wales) *Physics*
*‡Mrs V E Carter, BA (Leeds) *Ancient History and Latin*
‡Miss J M Caswell, MA (Manchester) *German and Russian*
*‡Mr D S Collett, BSc (Sheffield) *Physics*
‡Mrs J Cunliffe, BSc (Leeds) *Mathematics*
‡Dr M F Dabbs, BSc (Swansea), PhD, MSc *Applied Maths*
‡Mr D J Eggleston, BA (Nottingham) *Social Sciences*
*Mr P Elmes, BEd (Ripon & York St John) *Design & Technology*
*‡Mr A L C Finch, BA (Liverpool), MA, MEd (Leeds) *Economics*
‡Mrs S Fowler, BA (Leicester) *English*
‡Mrs H M E Gill, BA (Sheffield) *English*
‡Miss J A Gore, BA (Cardiff) *English and Classical Studies*
*‡Mrs R Gration, BEd (Leicester) *Art and Religious Education*
*‡Mrs D Hadfield, BA (OU) *Mathematics*
‡Mrs S Hotham, BA (Leeds) *French*
‡Ms L J Hutchins, BA (Wales) *Geography*
*Mrs H A Jones, BA (Leeds) *French*
‡Miss J A Kenmir, BEd (Leeds) *Physical Education*
*‡Mr J P Ladd, BA (Durham) *Music*
‡Mr M Lassey, BA (Leeds Metropolitan) *Technology, Business Studies*
‡Mrs J Liddy, BSc (Wales) *Microbiology*
‡Miss R Littlewood, BA (London), *Classics, ALCM (part-time)*
‡Mrs E MacGregor, BA, CNNA (Bedford) *Physical Education*
‡Miss M R Mason, BA (Reading) *Music*
‡Mrs S M Mirfield, MA (Edinburgh) *French and Spanish*
‡Mrs P Moffat, BSc (Sussex) BA, (OU) *Physics*
‡Mr J P Noble, BA (Hornsey College of Art, London) *Fine Art*
‡Mr R D Oldroyd, BSc (London) (Extl) *Mathematics (part-time)*
*‡Mrs C Owen, BA (Sheffield) *English Literature*
‡Mr S Paget, BA (Christ Church College, Canterbury) *Radio, Film and TV Studies with Science*
‡Miss J E Pick, BA (Birmingham Polytechnic) *German and French*
*‡Mrs K Preston, BSc (Sheffield) *Mathematics and Computer Science*
‡Dr A N Rhodes, BSc (Newcastle) *Geography*
‡Dr A Roberts, BSc, PhD (Manchester) *Chemistry*
‡Miss R C Robinson, BA (Edinburgh College of Art) *Design & Applied Arts*
‡Mrs D Russell, BSc (London), MSc *Physics*
‡Mrs J Sadler, BSc (Salford) *French Studies*
‡Mrs C Scott, BA (Durham) *Modern History*
*‡Mr A D Shaw, BA (Leeds) *History*
*‡Dr D R Slingsby, BSc (Bristol) PhD *Botany*
‡Mr D A Stanley, BEng (Newcastle) *Chemical & Process Engineering*
‡Mrs A M Taylor, BSc (Sheffield) *Chemistry*
*‡Dr M F Uttley, BSc (London), MSc, PhD *Chemistry*
‡Mrs V C West, BSc (Sheffield) *Genetics and Microbiology*
‡Mrs P M Whiteman, BEd (Sheffield) *Zoology and Botany*
‡Mr G Wigley, MA (Open), BA (Nottingham) *Economics*
‡Mrs M J Williams, Teachers' Cert in Home Economics (Ilkley) *(part-time)*
*‡Mrs L Wraight, BA (Leeds) *Geography and Politics*
‡Mrs G E Woods, MA (Oxon) *Classics*
*‡Mrs R E Zserdicky, BA (Manchester) *Theology*

Secretary: Mrs M A Jones

Guidance Information & Support:
Mrs M J Williams
Ms L J Hutchins

Librarian: ‡Mrs M Neale, BA (Nottingham) Politics, ALA

Junior School:
Head Mistress: Mrs D StC Cawthorne, BEd (Sheffield), DipTEFL

Assistant Mistresses:
Mrs S M Asquith, CertEd (Stockwell College, London), LRAM
Miss H Butt, MA (St Andrews)
Mrs L Cholewa, DLC Teaching Certificate
Mrs J M Cunningham, CertEd (Leeds)
Mrs J Earnshaw, BEd Hons (Leeds)
Mrs T Johnson, CertEd (Sidney Webb College)
‡Mrs H Judge, BA (London)
Mrs J Lamb, Teacher Cert in PE (IM Marsh College of FE) (*Part-time*)
Miss V Moore, BEd (Leeds)
Mrs P A Nicholls, CertEd (Oxford)
‡Ms K T O'Malley, BSc, (Bradford)
Mrs R Pye, BEd (Leeds)
Mrs P Rodgers, Teaching Certificate (Nottingham)
‡Mrs S M Smith, BA (OU) Social Science
Mrs S J Stringer, BEd (Leeds)
Mrs A J Sugden, CertEd, (Alnwick Coll of Education)
Mrs A Sutcliffe, CertEd (Ripon and York St John)
Miss K Thomas, BEd (Liverpool)
Mrs B Townend, BA (Leeds)

Mrs M J Townsend, CertEd (Ripon and York St John)
Mrs S Turmeau, BEd (Bristol)
‡Mrs A M Walters, BA (Leeds)
Mrs A M Wimbush, BEd (Cambridge)
Miss J M Woodhead, BEd (CNNA)

Secretary: Mrs B Milne

Special Needs: Mrs V P Denison, SPLD, DipEd

Visiting Teachers of Music:
Pianoforte:
Mrs E Hambleton, GNSM, LRAM, CertEd
Mrs M B Hemingway, ALCM
Keyboard: Mr B Ibbetson, BMus
Violin and Viola: Miss M R Mason, BA
Violin: Mrs J Maunsell, GBSM, ABSM, DipNCOS
Clarinet: Mrs C Hall, DCLCM, LTCL
Oboe: Mr K Chambers, BA, LGSM
Flute: Mrs S Bacon, GMus
Guitar: Mr L Palumbo, GRNCM
'Cello: Mr B L Thornton
'Cello and Double Bass: Mr R Major, GMus, DipRCM, LTCL
Saxophone:
Mr G Hirst, LRAM, ARCM, LTCL, CertEd
Brass: Mr C Bacon, GMus
Percussion: Mr D G Lewis
Voice: Mr L Williams

‡ denotes Teaching Certificate

Wakefield Girls High School was founded in 1878 and has a long tradition of providing an education of the highest quality.

The school aims to give good all round education to each pupil, encouraging academic excellence, nurturing talents, developing an individual's potential, and emphasising traditional values in a modern context. These aims are pursued within a happy and stimulating environment.

The school occupies an extensive site in a conservation area near the centre of Wakefield, and is easily accessible by road and rail from a wide area. The Georgian house in which it began has been adapted and extended over the years as numbers have grown. A steady programme of building and the acquisition of nearby property have enabled the school to anticipate and meet the needs of succeeding generations of pupils.

Specialist facilities exist for all subjects and there are plans to enhance the provision in the school even more. The Science and Technology Centre was opened in 1990, Hartley Pavilion, the Sports and Assembly Hall, was completed in 1996.

The first phase of the Creative Arts development has produced two quite stunning buildings which have retained the features of Victorian Villas but have been transformed into bright modern purpose built accommodation.

Hepworth House, named after our illustrious Old Girl, the Sculptress Barbara Hepworth, will be the home of the Art Department and provides excellent space for both the Sixth Form and the lower school with specialist provision for pottery, sculpture, 3D, textiles and photography.

Cliff House, named after a retired Clerk to the Governors, houses the Economics and Business Studies Centre, the Careers Centre and has additional facilities for the Sixth Form.

All ICT equipment has been up-graded and now includes video-conferencing. There are plans to enhance the provision in the school even more. The next phase will provide a new Technology centre and an English and Drama block.

The Nursery school, opened in September 1996, the Preparatory Department and the Junior School also occupy their own premises on the main school campus and share its facilities and some specialist staff.

There is a very strong tradition of sporting excellence at local, county and National level. At the playing fields, a short distance away, there are tennis courts, cricket, hockey and netball grounds.

The creative and performing arts play an important part in the life of the school as do extra curricular activities, with over 80 currently available. The Duke of Edinburgh Award is taken by large numbers.

Curriculum. The school offers a grammar school education. All girls follow a broad and balanced curriculum which keeps the widest possible range of options open until A level when there is a choice of any combination of 28 A level subjects. Languages are a major strength with French, German, Spanish, Italian, Russian, Latin and Greek available. Sciences are also very strong with all girls doing Biology, Physics and Chemistry at GCSE and over half taking Mathematics or a Science at A level.

Public examination results are superb!. At GCSE there was an overall pass rate of 100% with 65% at grades A* and A. Similar excellent results were achieved at A level with another first division score of 70% of grades A and B. Most girls go on to university although some choose to go directly into management, the Forces or to RADA. There is a full Careers programme and well established links with industry.

The girls enjoy the best of both worlds. They benefit educationally from a single sex environment but gain socially and culturally from the close co-operation with Queen Elizabeth Grammar School which has the same governing body. This means that there are many joint activities and some joint lessons at Sixth Form level.

School Hours. 8.45–4.00 from Monday to Friday inclusive.

Admission. Boys and girls aged 3 to 7 years are admitted in order from the waiting list. Girls aged 7 years or older are admitted after passing an entrance examination. The main ages of entry are at 3, 7, 11 and 13 years. Some enter the school at 16 years to take A level courses; these girls need a suitable foundation of GCSE subjects.

Fees: Senior School £1,875 per term. Junior School £643–£1,408 per term (including Preparatory Department and Nursery). Music lessons £105 for 10 lessons per term.

Foundation Awards. The Governors will consider providing a Foundation Award where the net parental income is less than £20,000 per annum.

Sixth Form Scholarships. Twelve Sixth Form Scholarships are awarded in recognition of academic work and GCSE results.

Charitable status. Wakefield Grammar School Foundation is a Registered Charity, number 529908. It exists to provide education for children.

Walthamstow Hall

Sevenoaks Kent TN13 3UL
Tel: (01732) 451334

Walthamstow Hall, which was founded in 1838 at Walthamstow, originally as a Home and School for daughters of missionaries, removed to Sevenoaks in 1882. It became a Direct Grant Grammar School and is now independent. There are 240 day girls in the Senior School (11–18) and a total of 200 girls in the Junior School (3–11).

Governors:

Chairman: Sir J Elwes, CBE

11 Trust Governors, 2 Governors nominated by Missionary Societies and 3 by teachers and parents.

Headmistress: **¶Mrs J S Lang**, MA (Oxford)

Deputy Headmistress: Mrs L Truman, BSc Hons (Bristol) *Biology*

Deputy Head: Miss I A White, BA Hons (Liverpool) *French*

Senior Mistress: Mrs S F Cutter, BSc Hons (London) *Chemistry*

Head of Junior School: ¶Mrs G R Thorne, BA Hons (Reading) *Philosphy*

Deputy Head of Junior School: Mrs C A Cheeseman, CertEd (London)

Senior School Assistant Staff:
*Miss K E Burtenshaw, BEd (Westminster College) *Geography*
*T J Daniell, Esq, BMus (London) AKC, MTC *Music*
M Dee, Esq, BEng (Sheffield) *Physics*
*Mrs J East, BSc Hons (Reading) *Mathematics, Careers*
*Mrs M Feehily, BA (Open University) *Computer Science*
*Mrs J Glenton, L-ès-L, Licence d'Enseignement (University of Lille) *French*
*Mrs M Holland, Dip Art & Design (West Surrey College) *Textiles*
*Mrs J Howe, MA (Sussex) *History*
Mrs K M Howlett, BEd Hons (Sussex) *PE*
Mrs L A C Martin, BSc Hons (Sheffield) *Mathematics, Computing*
*Mrs B Mitchell, BA Hons (Durham) *Religious Education*
P J Newell, Esq, GRSM, Hons ARCM, ARCO, MTC *Music*
*Mrs M K Nicholson, MA (Edinburgh) *Mathematics*
*Miss G Payne, BSc Hons (Durham) *Physics*
*L J Ross, Esq, BA, MLitt (Durham) *Classics*
*Miss B A Taylor, Teachers' Certificate (Bedford College of Physical Education) *PE*
*Mrs G Theaker, BA Hons (London) *German*
*Dr S Watts, BSc Hons, PhD (Southampton) *Biology*
*¶Mrs C M Winder, BA Hons (Exeter), MA (Kent) *English*
*Miss F M Wood, BA Hons (Warwick) *Drama*

Senior School Part-time Staff:
B W J Boyden, Esq, MA (London) *Economics*
D A Bradfield, Esq, BA Hons (London) *Art*
Mrs A J Bratt, BA (London) *English*
Mrs C Clarke, BA Hons (Sheffield) *History*
Mrs J M Cox, MA (Cambridge) *Natural Sciences*
Mrs C Dickerson, BSc Hons (Nottingham) *Chemistry*
Miss A J Fairhead, BSc Hons (York) *Biology*
Mrs C A Ford, CertEd (Leicester College) *Food Technology*
Mrs H A Hook, BA Hons (Aberystwyth) *English*
Mrs E C Howell, BA Hons (Bristol), ARCM *Classics*
Mlle R Loiseaux, Licence d'Anglais, Maîtrise de Philosophie (University of Amiens) *French Assistant*
Mrs E H Morgan, BA Hons (Hull) *Spanish, French*
Mrs C Reeves, BA Hons (East Anglia) *Sociology*
Mrs V C Riley, MSc (Birmingham), BSc Hons (Leicester) *Mathematics*
Mrs J A Robertson, MA (Cambridge) *Geography*
Mrs G Smith, BA (Nottingham College of Art & Design) *Art*
Mrs H Wiffen, BA Hons (Trent University, Ontario), BEd *English*
Dr S Wilkinson, DPhil (Oxford) *Chemistry*

Junior School Assistant Staff:
Mrs N M Armitage, BA Hons (Nottingham) *Classroom Assistant*
Mrs J M Bartlett, BA Hons (Brighton)
Mrs K Boreham, BA Hons (Warwick)
Mrs K Caine, BTec *Classroom Assistant*
Miss S J Ebenezer, BA Hons (Leeds)
Mrs L P Everitt, CertEd (North Worcs College of Education)
Miss S Harris, CertEd (Lady Spencer Churchill College, Oxford)
Mrs M Hewson, BSc Hons (London) *Science*
Miss K R Joiner, BEd (Roehampton Institute)
Miss M R Murphy, BA Hons (Swansea) *French, Italian*
¶Mrs A Saunders, University of London Teachers' Certificate (Froebel Educational Institute)
Mrs D Sinclair, BA Hons (Open University)
Mrs D Smith
Mrs L Thompson, Montessori Diploma
Mrs A Traill, DipEd (Cape Town College of Education)
Mrs F Waite, CertEd (Redland College, Bristol)
Miss C F Willis, BA Hons (Liverpool)

Junior School Part-time Staff:
Mrs V H Abel, BSc Hons (Sheffield) *Geography, Geology*
Mrs D Mitchell, Hornsby Diploma in Special Learning Difficulties

Associate Staff:

Bursar: N Wood, Esq, MILog
Housekeeper: Miss J Spencer, MHCIMA
Registrar: Mrs S Timms, GIPD
Secretary to the Headmistress: Mrs M D Harrison
Staff Secretary: Mrs W Fahy
Assistant Secretary: Mrs H McCready
Secretary to Junior School Head: Mrs C Coode

School Courses and Examinations. Subjects taught include Religious Education, English, History, Geography, Environmental Studies, Sociology, French, German, Spanish, Latin, Greek, Economics, Mathematics, Physics, Chemistry, Biology, Computer Studies, Food Technology, Textiles, Art, Photography, Music, Drama, Physical Education. Girls are prepared for GCSE, for AS and A2 levels and for entrance to universities (including a good proportion to Oxford and Cambridge) and other places of higher education. The record of success in public examinations is excellent.

Religious Teaching is undenominational. Boarders attend the place of worship desired by their parents on Sunday mornings.

Fees and awards. (*see* Entrance Scholarship section) - Day Girls: Senior £8,580 a year; Junior 3 year olds £696–£3,480, 4–6 year olds £5,940, 7-10 year olds £6,030. Two Foundation Scholarships and one Music Scholarship at age eleven, one Foundation Scholarship and one Music Scholarship at age thirteen, and two sixth-form scholarships, worth half tuition fees, are awarded. A number of bursaries are available in cases of financial need.

Admission. Admission to the Junior School is by interview and tests suitable to the age group. Admission to the Senior School for 11 and 13 year olds is through the entrance examination held each Spring Term. Suitably qualified girls are admitted to the Sixth Form. Parents are warmly invited to visit the School.

General Information. The School stands in its own grounds and commands pleasant views of the North Downs and Knole Park. Girls are taught in modern buildings and the school has its own theatre, new purpose-built library, squash courts, indoor swimming pool, laboratories, sixth-form centre, modern language teaching facilities and computer network. Girls are encouraged to develop their individual interests in a variety of ways. These include the Duke of Edinburgh Award Scheme, Young Enterprise, choirs, orchestras, drama, chess, science, Christian Fellowship and computer clubs. Sports offered include lacrosse, fencing, squash, judo, athletics, tennis, rounders, netball and swimming. There is a strong Schools' Voluntary Service Unit in Sevenoaks which enables the older girls to give service in the locality. The School is also closely linked with the Union of Girls' Schools for Social Service and gives its support to the settlement at Peckham.

Charitable status. Walthamstow Hall is a Registered Charity, number 1058439, founded in 1838 to provide education for girls.

Wentworth College

College Road Bournemouth BH5 2DY
Tel: (01202) 423266
Fax: (01202) 418030

Wentworth College is a day and boarding school for girls from 11 to 18 years. For over 125 years the school has been providing excellence in girls' education and is the joint foundation of Wentworth School, Bournemouth and Milton Mount College, Crawley.

Motto: *Vive ut postea vivas*

Governing Body:
The Revd B Rowling (*Chairman*)
Mr A Bowers, FCA, ATII, TEP, FPC
Mr A J Butcher, QC
Miss P Dicks, BSc, DipM
Mrs A Down, JP
The Revd P Grimshaw, MA
Mr D Morris, BA, FCA
Miss F Murdin, MA
Mrs F Northcott, MIMA
Cdr M D Sizeland, OBE, RN
Mr H Waller, MA, BEd
Mrs J Williams, BA Hons, PGCE

Staff:

***Headmistress:* Miss S Coe**, BA Hons, PGCE, FRGS

Deputy Head: Mrs F Langridge, BSc Hons *Geography*

Senior Resident Mistress: [1]Miss J Nussey, BA, CertEd, DipDys *Home Economics:* Food, SENCO

Senior Teacher: [1]Mr T J Meachin, BSc Hons, CChem, MRSC *Chemistry, Science & Outdoor Education*

Bursar: Mr J Willis

Clerk to the Governors: Mrs L Lacey

Medical Officer: Dr S Walker-Date, MBBS (London)

Chaplain:

Teaching Staff:
Mrs S Aston, BA Hons, PGCE *Classics*
Miss L J Bailey, BA Hons, PGCE *History*
Miss E Bradwell, BSc Hons, PGCE *Biology, Science and Service Learning Co-ordinator*
Mrs J Clark, BSc Hons *Mathematics*
Mrs C Crane, BA Hons, PGCE *Geography & Careers/ Higher Education Adviser*
Mrs D Drew, BA Hons, CertEd *German*
Mrs E Fox, BSc Hons, PGCE *Physical Education*
Ms K Garcia, BA Hons, TCert *Spanish*
Mrs M J Goodman, BA Hons, PGCE, ARCM *Music*
Mrs I M Gunn, MPhil, CBiol, MIBiol *Biology and Social Biology & Curriculum Co-ordinator*
Mrs J Hanna, BA Hons *Business Studies*
Miss P Hayes, BEd *Information Technology and Mathematics*
Mrs F Haylock, Agrégation de L'Enseignement, Secondaire Superieur, Licence en Philologie Germanique *German*
Mrs J Hayward, BA, PGCE *English and Drama, and Farrell House President*
Mr E H Johns, MA, BEd, CertEd *Religious Studies and Social Science*
Mrs S Jones, C & G Teacher's Cert *Physical Education*
Mme J M Khan, L ès L, CAPES *French*
Mrs S McCaffrey, BEd Hons *Home Economics – Food*
Miss D T McClellan, BA Hons *Art and Design and Davie House President*
Mr C McKay, BSc, CEng, MIEE, QTS *Design & Technology and Neighbourhood Engineers Link Teacher*
Miss E Murray, BA, DipRSA (*EAL*)
Mrs S North, LRAM, LCCMD, CertEd *Speech and Drama*
Mrs P O'Connor, BA Hons, PGCE *English and Librarian*
Mrs B Partridge, BEd *English and Theatre Studies*
Miss K Rose, BSc Hons, PGCE *Physics*
Mrs C L Rutherford, BSc Hons, CertEd *Mathematics and Hadland House President*
Mrs H Sendall, BSc Hons, CertEd *Mathematics and PSE*
Mrs P Watkins, BA, RSADipTEFL (*ESOL*)
Mrs P Wheeler, BEd, CertSpLDs *Learning Support*

Housemistresses:
[1]Miss S North
[1]Mrs A Philbrick

[1] denotes Resident Staff

Independent Listener: Mrs J Henshaw
Nursing Sister: [1]Miss J Tseung, SEN
Head's Secretary: Mrs G Strange
Registrar: Mrs D Wilson
Assistant to Bursar: Mrs E Gimber
Head Chef: Mr R Owen

Plus Visiting Staff

Our aims. Our staff and governing body are dedicated to providing a caring, close-knit community in which each girl may reach her full potential. We aim to develop happy, confident young women who are proud of their academic success and equipped with important life skills.

General information. Wentworth College stands in extensive grounds on a cliff top close to the centre of Bournemouth. It houses approximately 220 girls of which one third are either full or weekly boarders. The school makes full use of its proximity to clean beaches, safe waters and the New Forest for field trips and outdoor activities. Day girls and boarders integrate well and belong to one of three houses.

Facilities include a well-equipped teaching block with excellent science laboratories, art studios, music school and design and technology workshop. For physical recreation the school has six tennis courts, a hockey pitch and athletics field and track. Our large sports hall is equipped for netball and volleyball matches, badminton and gym. There is also a separate 25 metre heated indoor swimming pool.

Dormitories are small and comfortable with communal areas for evening recreation. The Sixth Form complex houses 40 study bedrooms.

Pastoral Care and Health. The school is founded on Christian principles and has close links with the United Reformed Church. However, girls of all denominations and other faiths are welcomed into our community.

A team of residential house staff fulfils an important social and pastoral role for the boarders. Each boarder and day girl is assigned a tutor who will monitor progress. The school chaplain and independent listener provide a confidential service while older girls become proctors to new girls, helping them through the first few weeks at school.

Personal and social education is part of the curriculum for every girl in the school and provides a forum to discuss issues which particularly affect young people today.

A medical wing is staffed by matron and the school doctor holds weekly surgeries in the school for non-urgent medical problems. Meals are taken in a 'family-style' atmosphere and careful attention is paid to diet.

Curriculum. Well qualified staff prepare pupils in a variety of studies, beginning with a three-year foundation course which provides the opportunity to study three sciences and three foreign languages, as well as mathematics, English, history, geography, religious education, art and music, drama, food and textiles technology, information technology, design and technology, use of library, and physical education. Special support is available for dyslexic pupils. For their GCSE course, a flexible option scheme allows girls to make a varied but balanced selection from 19 subjects. Our Sixth Form offers a wide range of arts and science subjects at GCE Advanced level. Ninety-seven percent of students enter university or choose some other form of higher education which will prepare them for their chosen career.

Optional extras. Musicians are prepared for the Associated Board of the Royal Schools of Music examinations. Girls may take LAMDA examinations in Speech and Drama. RSA Computer Literacy and Information Technology qualifications and work toward the Duke of Edinburgh's Award and their individual Diploma of Achievement.

Wentworth 'plus' provides special tuition for overseas students whose first language is not English.

A wide choice of clubs and after school events includes sailing in the school's own boat, canoeing, photography, drama, cookery, judo and roller skating.

Communication. The school believes that communication and co-operation between school and home ensures the successful development of each girl. Parents receive reports twice a year, regular grade cards and are able to discuss their daughter's progress at meetings specially dedicated to their year group. Parents are encouraged to attend plays, concerts, sporting events and inter-house competitions. The Friends of Wentworth College – run by parents for parents – stage a number of social events through the year.

Entry. Candidates may take the Common Entrance Examination at 11+, 12+ and 13+. If places are available, girls may join the school at any stage, including the Lower Sixth, on successfully completing the school's own entrance examination.

Fees. (*see* Entrance Scholarship section) From September 2001. Boarders and Weekly Boarders £3,850 per term. Day Girls £2,425 per term.

Scholarships. Up to 50 per cent reduction in fees for girls with all-round academic ability, or clear potential in either music, art, drama or sport. Internal and external scholarships are also available for Sixth Form candidates. Full details of these and other bursaries, including grants for daughters of ministers and lay members of the United Reformed and Congregational Churches, are given in the prospectus. Please contact the Registrar for a copy and details of special events for prospective parents and girls.

Charitable status. Wentworth Milton Mount Ltd is a Registered Charity number 306322, promoting excellence in girls'education.

Westfield School

Oakfield Road Gosforth Newcastle upon Tyne NE3 4HS
Tel: Tyneside (0191) 285 1948

Owned and Administered by the Northbrian Educational Trust Ltd.

Governors:
Chairman: Miss L Winskell, LLB
P I Cussins, BSc
Mrs J Hodgson
C M G R Jenkins, Esq, MA
C J Knox, Esq
Dr A Mattinson, MBBS, MRCGP
Mrs M Milford
D B Monaghan, Esq
M I Ranson, Esq, JP, FCA
W M Wood, FRICS, FAAV

Headmistress: **Mrs M Farndale**, BA Hons (London), PGCE (Oxon), FRSA

Deputy Headteacher: Mrs M E Shipley, BA Hons (London), PGCE

Senior Mistress: Mrs M Baron, BSc Hons (Newcastle), DipEd

Art/Design:
S Ratcliffe, LLB (Newcastle), BA Hons (Wimbledon School of Art), MFA (Cranbrook Academy of Art, Michigan)
Mrs A Wilson, BA Hons (London), PGCE

Biology: Mrs S Vallance, BSc Hons (London), PGCE

Careers: S Nash, BA Hons (Keele), PGCE

Chemistry: Mrs L Stinton, BA(Chem) Hons (OU), CertEd

Drama/Theatre Studies: Miss V Hicken, BA Hons (Bangor), PGCE

Economics and Business Studies: Mrs C Gaynor, BEd Hons (Warwick), DipManSt (Bristol)

English:
R C Matthews, BA (Alleghenny Coll), MA, CertEd
Mrs M Ings, BA Hons (Bangor), PGCE

French:
Mrs J Calderwood, BA Hons (Manchester), MA (Leicester), PGCE
Mrs S Dodds, BA Hons (Durham), PGCE
Mrs D Elwell, BA (Newcastle), DipEd

Geography:
Mrs M E Shipley, BA Hons (London), PGCE
S Nash, BA Hons (Keele), PGCE

German: Mrs E Wise, BA Hons (Newcastle), PGCE

History:
C Rendall, BSc(Econ) Hons (London), DipEd (Dunelm)
Mrs S Telford-Reed, BEd Hons (Northumbria)

Information Communication Technology: J W Hodgkins, BSc Hons (Leicester), PGCE

Mathematics:
Mrs M Baron, BSc Hons (Newcastle), DipEd
Mrs J M Taylor, BSc Hons (London), DipEd (*and Sixth Form Tutor*)
J W Hodgkins, BSc Hons (Leicester), PGCE

Music: R Simmance, BA Hons (Liverpool), BMus, LRAM, FTCL, PGCE

Physical Education:
Miss K Fraser, BA (Northumbria), PGCE
Mrs S Bowen, BA Hons (Sheffield), PGCE

Physics: R Wilson, BSc Hons (Coventry), PGCE

Religious Studies:
Mrs J Draper, BA Hons (Newcastle), PGCE

Science: Miss R Riley, BSc (Newcastle), PGCE

Spanish:
Mrs J Calderwood, BA Hons (Manchester), MA (Leicester), PGCE
Mrs S Dodds, BA Hons (Durham), PGCE

Librarian/Additional Learning Support: Mrs P M Farmborough, BA (Durham), PGCE

Junior House:
Headmistress: Mrs R M Miller, CertEd (Homerton), Dip Maths (Newcastle)
Assistant Head: Mrs M Branson, BA Hons (Leeds), PGCE (Newcastle)
Head of Key Stage 1: Mrs A Simmance, CertEd (Lancaster)

Teachers:
Miss J N Brown, BSc Hons (Huddersfield), PGCE
Mrs H Dean, BEd Hons (Newcastle)
Mrs B Dixon, CertEd (Northern Counties), BA
Mrs A Havis, AMTC, DipEd
Mrs P McBride, CertEd (Leeds)
Miss G McKeating, BEd Hons (York)
Miss E Morgan, BSc Hons (Bangor), PGCE
Ms E A Robson, BA Hons (Newcastle)
Miss E Shaw, BSc Hons (Oxford Brookes), PGCE
Miss A Wilson, BA Hons (Bristol), PGCE (Newcastle)

Visiting Staff:
Music:
B Alimohamadi, BA (Open University), LGSM, CertEd (Newcastle)
Mrs S Piper, BA (Mills College, California), RecDip, RAM, PGCE
Miss H Sander, LTCL
Mrs K Wakefield, CertEd (St Hild's & Bede)
Mrs S Harrison, LTCL
M Dick
Mrs E Brown

Dancing: Miss G Quinn, RAD Int Children's Examiner, AdvTCert ARAD, MNCDTA
Languages: Miss N Ait-Gacem, Miss N Muñoz
Tennis: Mrs G Kelliher

Bursar: A R Friswell, MA (Cantab), CertEd
Domestic Bursar: Miss D Sharp
Headmistress's Secretary: Mrs J F Jokelson
Junior House Secretary: Mrs C Park
Laboratory Technician: Mrs A McRae
Medical Adviser: Dr P Dodds, MB, BS, DRCOG

Westfield is a day school for 380 girls aged 3+ to 18, in Junior and Senior Houses situated on one campus in a very pleasant wooded site of over 6 acres. The School's aim is an uninterrupted education, a high academic standard and a wide curriculum offering scope and stimulus for individual development. There is a vast range of extra curricular activities with particular emphasis on Sport, outdoor pursuits, Music, Art and Drama. The Duke of Edinburgh Award Scheme has a high profile and all senior girls are encouraged to participate. In addition to a sound grounding in basic skills, Junior House (3–11) offers specialist teaching in Art, Craft, PE, French and Music. So that every child may be assured of individual attention class sizes are restricted to a maximum of 20. Frequently, classes are further divided into smaller units.

Senior house (11–18), has first rate classroom and laboratory facilities with excellent specialist accommodation for Home Economics and Music. A wide range of subjects is taught by specialists. Initially all girls have lessons in the traditional academic core subjects, in English, Mathematics, Geography, History, Science (taught as 3 separate subjects) and French, as well as in Music, Drama, PE, Food and Nutrition, ICT and Design. German is introduced in the second year and Spanish in the 4th. Girls are encouraged to aim for breadth in their choice of subjects at GCSE. Most girls achieve 9 passes in the A-C range of the GCSE, a number with straight A and A* passes. There is a carefully structured programme of Careers and Personal and Social Education and a well developed pastoral system.

The Sixth Form occupies a cottage block in the grounds and is under the direction of the Head of the Sixth Form.

There is a full range of 'AS', 'A' level and other courses and girls are prepared for University and other Higher Education courses including Oxbridge as well as for other courses and for employment. The A level pass rate is always over 90%, ensuring for most girls a place in their first choice of institute of higher education.

Sixth Formers have considerable responsibility within the School in addition to their own thriving academic and cultural life.

Westfield is a member of Round Square, a worldwide association of schools which share a commitment, beyond academic excellence, to personal development and responsibility through service, challenge, adventure and international understanding. Girls from Westfield have the opportunity to attend the annual International Conference and to participate in exchanges with member schools from all over the world, and in the Round Square International Service Projects in developing countries.

Westfield is totally committed to producing happy, self-confident, well-balanced young women who are international in their outlook and fully prepared to face life in the new millennium.

Admission to Westfield is by interview and examination. While children of all faiths are accepted, the religious life of the school is based on Christian principles.

Fees. In Junior House fees range from £677–£1,463 and in Senior House are £1,795 per term.

Scholarships are available at 11+ and 16+. Some bursaries are also available in cases of financial need.

Westholme School

Meins Road Blackburn Lancashire BB2 6QU.
Tel: (01254) 53447
Fax: (01254) 681459
e-mail: principal@westholme.blackburn.sch.uk

Governing Body:
Chairman: Mr K J Ainsworth, FGA
Deputy Chairman: Mr J N Prest, BSc

Mr P Forrest, ARICS, FCIOB
Mrs B Lees, JP
Mrs B A Lomax, BA
Mr B C Marsden, FCA
Mrs J McCraith
Mrs P Prest
His Honour Judge E Slinger, BA
Professor R D Taylor, MA, LLM
Mr J R Yates, BSc

Secretary to the Governors: Mr J Whittaker

***Principal:* Mrs Lillian Croston**, BSc (Hons), (Dunelm), PGCE (Cantab), ALCM

Deputy Headteachers:
Mrs Roberta Georghiou, BA (Hons) (Manchester), PGCE
Mrs Anne Patefield, BSc (Hons) (CNAA)

Bursar: Mr J Henwood, MA, FCA

There are 1,105 day pupils at Westholme, 707 girls in the Upper School (11–18), 398 in the Preparatory Department (33 girls, 67 boys), 3–11 (girls), 3–7 (boys).

Westholme School, a registered charity, is administered by a Board of Governors which includes three nominated Governors representing current parents. Although the school is non-denominational, its Christian foundation is regarded as important, the emphasis being placed on the moral aspect of Christian teaching.

The school offers an academic curriculum in English

Language and Literature, Mathematics, Biology, Chemistry, Physics, French, German, Italian, Spanish, Food, Design, Information and Textiles Technology, Art, Business Studies, Classical Civilisation, Drama, Latin, Music, Religious Education, Psychology and Theatre Studies. Most of these subjects can be taken for the GCSE examination and at AS and A2 Levels; Oxbridge tuition is also offered.

Set in the countryside to the west of Blackburn, the school offers excellent facilities. The premises have been regularly upgraded to give purpose-built accommodation for specialist subjects such as Art, Design and Information Technology and Music; six modern laboratories support the three separate sciences. Sporting facilities include a sports hall, indoor swimming pool, all-weather tennis courts and a large playing field with running circuit and hockey pitches. The new Theatre, Concert and Assembly Hall opened in 1997, seats 700 and offers students outstanding production resources. The recently opened library has open-access multi-media giving students full research facilities on the world-wide web.

The Performing Arts are a special feature of the school. There are several school choirs and girls have the opportunity to learn a string, brass or wind instrument and to play in the school orchestras or wind ensembles. Extra curricular drama includes the full scale spectacular musical, in the round productions, club and house competitions, while make-up and costume design are popular options at GCSE.

School societies and house teams meet on most days during mid-day break and girls are encouraged to participate in a variety of activities and in their house competitions. These provide younger girls with opportunities beyond the curriculum and older students with the chance to assume a leadership role.

The aim of the Upper School is to provide an atmosphere in which each girl can develop her abilities to the full and can excel in some field of activity. There is constant effort to widen interests and to instil a strong sense of individual responsibility. Most girls continue to the Sixth Form and then move on to Higher Education. Most pursue degree courses, a significant number at Oxbridge and Cambridge.

Westholme Infant and Junior Schools are on two sites. There is close co-operation between them and with the Senior School. A family atmosphere allows children to learn in a supportive and happy environment. Firm academic foundations are laid with the emphasis upon the basic skills of literacy and numeracy. Excellent facilities afford ample teaching space and resource areas; the Junior School has two halls, music rooms and specialist provision for Information Technology. Extra curricular activities include public speaking, orchestra, choir, sports, societies and school visits. Music and sport are taught by specialists and both Departments use the swimming pool, sports hall, athletics track and outdoor pitches. A new nursery was completed in January 1997, providing facilities for the very best start for the youngest children. Girls are guaranteed continuity of education through Westholme School to eighteen while boys at 7 are prepared for entry to the school of their parents' choice.

Pupils usually enter the school in September. Entry to the Middle and Upper Schools is by examination, and to the Lower School by interview. The normal ages of entry are at 3, 7, 11 and 16.

In view of the demand for places parents are advised to make an early application.

Fees. Upper School £4,770 pa; Middle School £3,840 pa; Lower School £3,420 pa.

Bursaries are available at the Upper School for girls who show good academic ability.

Private coaches run from Accrington, Blackburn Boulevard, Bolton, Burnley, Chorley, Clitheroe, Darwen, Leyland, Nelson, Preston and the Rossendale Valley.

The Principal is happy for prospective parents to visit the schools during normal working hours; appointments may be arranged through the Registrar, from whom application forms are available. Annual Open Days are held in mid November.

Charitable status. Westholme School is a Registered Charity, number 526615. It exists for the education of children between the ages of 3 and 18.

Westonbirt

Tetbury Gloucestershire GL8 8QG
Tel: (01666) 880333
Fax: (01666) 880364
e-mail: regstrar@westonbirt.gloucs.sch.uk
website: www.westonbirt.gloucs.sch.uk

Governing Body:
Chairman: P A Copland, BSc, FRICS

Mrs C Bays
Lady Bland, JP
Lady Anne Carr
Dr P Cheshire, BSc, PhD
R Collinson
M J Dron
Mrs P Faust
Mrs A Gauld
C Green, FCIB, FCIMgt, FLCM
Miss J Greenwood
J D McArdell, ACII, FIMgt, FCIM (*Vice-Chairman*)
Rev Dr Fiona Stewart-Darling
Mrs C Symons, BSc Hons (Kent)

***Head:* Mrs M Henderson**, MA Hons (St Andrews), PGCE (Dunelm)

Deputy Head: Mrs S Cole, BSc Hons, PGCE (Lond)

Senior House Mistress: Miss S Urquhart, BSc Hons (Aberdeen), PGCE (Glasgow)

Chaplain: The Rev P Dixon, BSc (Leeds), BA (OU), DipEd (Bath), DipTh (Nottingham) DPS

Director of Studies & Career Guidance: Mrs A Dunn, Cert Ed (Worcester)

Heads of Department:

Art:
Mrs M Phillips, BA, FPS(Photog), CertEd (Notre Dame, Liverpool)

Business Studies:
Mrs B Vockings, BA Hons, PGCE (University of Wales)

Classics:
Mrs H Price, BA Hons (Southampton)

Drama:
Mrs S English, LLAM, LAMDA

English:
Mrs D Browne, BA Hons (University College, Wales), PGCE (St Luke's, Exeter)

Geography:
Mrs B Vockings, BA Hons, PGCE (University of Wales)

History:
G Horridge, BA Hons, PGCE (Cantab), PhD (London), CertTH (Surrey)

Home Economics:
Mrs J Bell, BEd Hons (Bath)

Mathematics:
Mrs D A Elsdon, MA, BEd, CertEd, DipMaths (London)

Modern Languages:
Mrs J May, BA (Oxon), PGCE (Newcastle)

Music:
Director of Music: Mr M Pike, BMus Hons, GRSM, LRAM (London), PGCE (Reading)

Physical Education:
Miss C Graham, CertEd (Bedford), CPE

Religious Education:
The Revd P Dixon, BSc (Leeds), BA (OU), DipEd (Bath) DipTh (Nottingham), DPS

Science:
Mrs C Horridge, BSc Hons, PGCE (Dunelm), MEd (Cantab)

Technology:
J H M Sproule, CertEd (London)

Sanatorium – Medical Officer: Dr A Walsh, MB, ChB, DRCOG

Sisters:
Mrs A Whiting, RGN, FETC, CMS
Mrs J Walker, RGN

Housemistresses:

Badminton House: Miss G Fry, CertEd (Birmingham)
Beaufort House: Miss S Gould
Dorchester House: Mrs A Whiting, RGN, FETC, CMS
Holford House: Miss S Urquhart, BSc Hons (*Aberdeen*), PGCE (*Glasgow*)
Sixth Form: Miss C Watson, BEd Hons (IM Marsh), CPE

Bursar: Mr P Story

Registrar: Mrs B Holley

Location. Set in a Cotswold mansion within 250 acres of private parkland and garden, Westonbirt School provides a peaceful and inspiring setting for education, within easy reach of major motorways, rail networks and airports.

Philosophy. Founded in 1928, Westonbirt School offers all the advantages of a small rural girls' school, within a happy, caring community and an exceptionally beautiful setting. It provides accademic excellence both for girls to whom academic success comes naturally and for those who require more coaching and encouragement. Subject teachers, personal tutors and pastoral staff work together to ensure that pupils gain not only high academic qualifications but also the confidence to apply them to best advantage for a fulfilling adult life.

The Curriculum. All pupils will follow a broad, balanced course of study in line with the National Curriculum, as well as learning a second Modern Language, Latin, Drama, Music, and all aspects of technology. They also play a great deal of sport (see below for details).

They will keep their options open for as long as possible then take at least 9 GCSEs and will follow the new Sixth Form curriculum leading to 3 or 4 full A levels. Virtually all will go on to a good university.

In addition they will follow a Lifeskills programme from Year 7 onwards. This comprehensive programme addresses specific issues relevant to their age. It incorporates and adds value to the six Key Skills identified by the Department of Education that will make them especially able to succeed in the world of work: communication, working with others, improving one's own learning and performance, numeracy, information technology and problem-solving. The new Sixth Form curriculum will include a Key Skills qualification.

Music, Speech and Drama. Musical instrument lessons are timetabled for free periods so that girls do not miss academic lessons. Many girls play at least one instrument and may perform in the school orchestra or ensembles. There are four very active choirs, and girls regularly take part in concerts at school and elsewhere.

Speech and Drama is extremely strong, with frequent opportunities for girls to take part in major school productions, to study for national qualifications, and to enter performing arts festivals.

Sport and Leisure. The girls enjoy the school's beautiful setting, and its 250 acre grounds include extensive sports facilities immediately adjacent to the main school buildings. The main winter sports are lacrosse and netball, and the summer sports are tennis and athletics, but girls have the chance to learn to play many other sports also, including golf on the school's own private nine-hole golf course and swimming in the school's heated indoor swimming pool. Those keen on equestrian sports will enjoy regular sessions at the nearby Beaufort Polo Club and the riding school.

Careers Advice. Westonbirt is an accredited Investor in Careers. This award is given only to schools whose careers advice is of the very highest calibre. The Director of Studies and Careers Guidance co-ordinates careers advice throughout the school and plays a very active role in helping pupils gain places at their preferred university. The school's work experience programme begins in Year 11 and continues into the Sixth Form and is run by a member of the school's careers staff.

Extra-curricular Activities. As well as organising frequent leisure outings at weekends, the school offers many extra-curricular activities with educational value in the broader sense. There is a wide choice of clubs to suit all interests, such as a Debating Society, Choirs, Dramatic Clubs and a Gymnastic Club. The school is an ardent supporter of the Young Enterprise Scheme in which participants set up and run their own business for a year, and of the Duke of Edinburgh Awards programme which many pupils pursue to Bronze, Silver and Gold standard. The prestigious Leith's Certificate of Food and Wine is a popular sixth form option, and sixth formers may also have driving lessons timetabled for free periods.

EFL (English as a Foreign Language). The dedicated EFL Centre helps those for whom English is not their first language.

All overseas girls are taught in the mainstream school for all subjects except EFL.

Special Needs. For those who need academic help, individual coaching can be arranged in all subjects. Pupils with learning difficulties such as dyslexia benefit from the full-time Special Needs teacher, and Westonbirt has an excellent track record of helping such girls achieve high academic standards.

Health Care. The school has its own Sanatorium constantly manned by an experienced and sympathetic Sister, supported by regular surgeries and an on-call service by the school's Medical Officer.

Spirituality. As a Church of England Foundation, Westonbirt School is underpinned by a strong Christian ethos, with morning prayers, evening vespers and Sunday services an important constant in the girls' timetable. Many girls choose to be confirmed, and all are expected to attend school worship, but pupils of other faiths are made to feel welcome and respected.

Facilities. Alongside the magnificent Westonbirt House, in which main school pupils eat and sleep, there are excellent purpose-built facilities. The modern Francis Rawes Building includes spacious, airy art studios, well-equipped science laboratories, an extensive computer laboratory, enviable design and technology workshops, and a comfortable lecture theatre.

The self-contained music school includes 22 soundproofed rehearsal rooms plus the charming Camellia House for rehearsals and intimate recitals.

Speech and Drama are taught in the Orangery Theatre and the adjacent Green Room and Rehearsal Room.

The Sixth Form is accommodated in recently refurbished single study bedrooms set apart from the main school above the Classroom Courtyard, cleverly converted from the former Stable Block.

Entrance Requirements. Girls normally join the school at 11, 13 or 16, though they may do so at other ages in special circumstances. They must sit either the Common Entrance Examination or take the school's own entrance papers, attend an interview with the Headmistress, and provide a reference from their current school.

Fees. (as at September 2000). Boarding £4,920 per term. Day £3,429 per term. The fee is inclusive of tuition, board, lodging, stationery and laundry.

Scholarships and Bursaries. Scholarships and Bursaries are awarded at 11+, 12+, 13+ and 16+ entry. Scholarships may be awarded for academic prowess or for drama, art, music or sport, to a maximum of 25% of the annual fees. Bursaries may be awarded where financial need is proven, and families serving in HM Armed Forces are entitled to an automatic 15% bursary. When sisters are at school together, a 5% reduction is made for the elder. Full details are available on request from the Registrar.

Charitable status. Westonbirt School Limited is a Registered Charity, number 311715. It exists for the education of girls, in mind, body and spirit.

Wimbledon High School (G.D.S.T.)

Mansel Road London SW19 4AB
Tel: 020 8971 0900
Fax: 020 8971 0901

Local Governors:
The Rt Hon Dame Angela Rumbold, DBE (*Chairman*)
Mrs D Buchanan, BA
Mr W Garnett
Mr C Joubert
Mrs G M Perrin, MA, BLitt
Mrs C Perry
Mrs M A Rice-Jones, CertEd
Dr P Whitehead, MBBF, DRCOG

***Headmistress:* Mrs P Wilkes**, BEd (Hull) *History & Theology*

Deputy Head: [1]Mrs F Cordeaux, BSc (London) *Physiology/ Zoology*

Senior School:
[1]Mrs R M Adams, BSc (Southampton) *Geology*, MSc (Kingston) *Earth Science & Environment*
[1]Mrs A Antrich, BA (Bristol) *Latin/Greek*
[1]Miss G Bell, BEd (Bedford)
[1]Mr O Blond, BA (Essex) *English & European Literature and Philosophy*
Mr R Braley, MA (Oxon) *Philosophy, Ancient History,* Ma (Cantab) *Theology*
[1]Ms G Carpenter, BSc (London) *Mathematics*
[1]Miss A Challand, MA (Exeter) *History*
[1]Miss C Clegg, BA (Thames Valley) *Spanish and French*
[1]Miss V Cranwell, BEd (Brighton) *PE & Mathematics*
[1]Miss B Davies, BA (Leicester) *English*
[1]Mr A Dutson, BA (Birmingham) *Music*
[1]Mrs W Eaves, BA (Oxon), MSc (London) *Geography*
[1]Frau S Eiberle, Staatsexamen (Freiburg) *German and English*
[1]Mr N Gale, BA (Oxon) *Music*
Mrs A Gallagher, BSc (Muenster) *Sports Science & Chemistry*
[1]Mrs S Gallivan, BSc (London) *Biochemistry*
[1]Miss D Ginn, BA (Kingston) *Modern History*
[1]Mrs E Greenwood, BA (Surrey) *Art & Design*
[1]Mrs B Harris, Staatsexamen (Munich) *German, English*
[1]Mrs G Hickman, BA (Reading) *Classics*
[1]Mrs J P Horton, BSc (Southampton) *Mathematics*
[1]Ms L Hunt, BSc, ARCS (London) *Physics*
Dr C Jackson, MA (Cantab) *Natural Sciences & Biological Organic Chemistry*
Mrs K Johnstone, MA (St Andrews) *Economics*
Mme M Khan, Licence-de-Lettres Modernes (Lille)
[1]Mrs A Lassiere, BA (Hons) (Southampton) *Geography with Geology*
[1]Mr Q Lees, BA (Wales) *Biochemistry*
Mrs A Lewis, CertEd (Manchester) *Home Economics*
[1]Miss C Lewis, BA (London) *History of Art*
[1]Mrs A Marshall-Taylor, BA *French/German*
[1]Mrs J Maxwell, BA (Reading) *French & German,* MA, CNAA *German*
Ms S Miller, MA (California) *English*
Mr A Mooney, BEd (Middlesex), BEng (Ulster RTC) *CDT and IT*
[1]Mr P Nimmo, BA (London) *English Literature*
[1]Mrs M Nullens, BSc (Cardiff) *European Studies*
Mme A Oldale, Licence d'Anglais (Bordeaux) *French*
Mrs T O'Shea, BSc (Portsmouth) *Civil Engineering*
[1]Ms A Peacock, BA (London) *Classics*
[1]Dr M Penney, BSc, PhD (Glasgow) *Zoology, Ecological Entomology*
[1]Mrs S Reeves, BSc (London) *Mathematics*
Mrs B Ritchie, DDP (Edinburgh) *Art*
Mrs L Rogan, MA (Aberdeen) *Economics*
[1]Ms K Rutter, BA (Cantab) *English*
[1]Miss V Seymour, BSc (UMIST) *Biochemistry*
[1]Mrs V Tabor, BA (Warwick) *PE and English*
Mrs L Tarr, MSc (Warsaw) *Hydrology, Water Economics*
[1]Miss G M Thick, BA (Durham) *Theology*
Mrs C Toogood, BEd (London), BSc (OU) *Mathematics and Statistics*
[1]Miss Z White, BSc (Nottingham) *Mathematics with Engineering*
Mrs E Wibberley, CertEd (Manchester) *Home Economics*
Mrs S P Willett, MA (Edinburgh) *Mathematics*
[1]Mr N Yee, BSc (Sheffield) *Material Sciences & Technology*
Ms A Zawisza, MA (OU), MIBiol, CBiol (Environmental Biology)

Junior School:
Mrs J Compton-Howlett, LRAM, ARCM, RAM, CertEd (West London) Teaching of Deaf and Partially Hearing
Mrs P Cragg, LRAM, GRSM, RAM
[1]Miss L Cunningham, BA (Oxon) *History/Sociology*
[1]Miss A Dearlove, BA (Birmingham) *French & Hispanic Studies*
[1]Mrs A Eldridge, BEd (Surrey)
Mrs S Gardner, MEd (London)
Mrs B Grove, BEd (CNAA)
[1]Miss C Guthrie, BA (Newcastle) *Combined Arts*
[1]Mrs T Hill, BA (Durham) *Education*
[1]Mrs M Holmes, BSc (London) *Biology & Psychology*
[1]Mrs N Kelly, BEd (Kingston)
[1]Miss E Malcolm (East Anglia) *History*
[1]Mr T Mylne, BA (Brighton) *Business Studies*
Mrs J Orchard, MA (Southampton) *Primary Education*
[1]Mrs M Peart Smith, BEd (Birmingham), CertEd *Special Needs*
Mrs S Pojak, Institute of Education Certificate (Exeter)
[1]Mrs J Stevens, BA (Manchester) *Psychology*
Miss V White, BA (London) *Primary Teaching*

[1] denotes Honours degree

Visiting Music Staff:

Harpsichord/Piano: Mr R Woolley, ARCM, GBSM

Piano: Miss L Laukka, ARCM

Flute:
Mrs J Land, BSc, LGSM
Mr N Bricht, BMus

Clarinet & Saxophone:
Mr G Williams, ARCM
Miss E Saunders, GBSM, ABSM

Recorder/Oboe: Mr B Norbury, BA, LTCL Dip (The Hague)

Brass: Mr S Whelan

Cello: Mr P Brunner, DipRAM, LRAM

Double Bass: Ms G James, AGSM

Violin/Viola:
Miss H Ward, AGSM
Mr S Giles, LRAM
Ms J Metcalfe

Percussion: Mr S Hiscock, GGSM

Singing:
Mr R Langford, BA Hons
Mr S Haynes (*and Piano*)
Ms K Jenkin, BA Hons

Guitar: Miss J M Larrad, LTCL

Jazz: Mr G Adie, BA

Administrative Staff:
School Administrator: Mr D Goodenough, MBE, MInstAM, ABIFM
Information Systems Manager: Mr A Kittle
School Secretary: Mrs C Gray
Admissions Secretary: Mrs A F Adkins
School Nurse:
Librarian: Mrs K Jones, BA, ALA

Wimbledon High School, a member of the GDST, opened on 9 November 1880 at 78 Wimbledon Hill Road and moved in 1887 to Mansel Road. In 1917, after destruction by fire, it was rebuilt to accommodate what has since become the Senior School. Facilities have been increased and improved ever since. The school has a Sports Centre which incorporates a 25-metre swimming pool and large Sports Hall. This Centre is also used as a Sports Club, run by a Sports Administrator. The former gymnasium has been converted into a studio theatre, which houses the Theatre Studies Department as well as providing a focus for other performing arts. An extension, including six science laboratories and a block housing a library, art studios and additional classrooms, was added to the original building in 1987. A seventh science laboratory, and a Language and Communication Centre was completed in December 1999. The playing field, ten minutes walk from the school, is the original All England Tennis Club ground, with the original pavilion. It provides hockey pitches and facilities for athletics as well as hard and grass tennis courts. The entire area is being upgraded and renovated, to include an all-weather playing pitch.

There are about 590 girls, aged 11–18, in the Senior School; 160 are in the Sixth Form and have full use of a Sixth Form house. The Junior School of 330 pupils, aged 4–11, is housed in a brand-new building opened in January 2000 which includes specialist rooms for Science, Art, Information Technology, Design and Technology and Music. The current building programme also provides for new Design Technology workshops and Art Department for the Senior School, together with a completely refurbished Music Centre and Language Department class and tutor rooms.

Admission normally takes place at ages 4+, 11+ and 16+; a few additional places are available at 7+. Entry can also occur at most other age groups if vacancies occur. Entry is by assessment and interview for 4+ and by the school's own examinations at all other points.

The school is situated within 5 minutes walk of Wimbledon Station (underground, main line and tram). It is easily accessible by train from Surbiton, Kingston, Ewell, Ashtead, Epsom, Hampton Wick, Norbiton, Twickenham, and all intermediate stations as well as from Wandsworth, Clapham Junction, Tooting and Mitcham. It is on the route of buses 77, 93, 131 and 200. It is also served by the Merton Tramlink.

Curriculum. The regular school course covers the full national curriculum (with a choice of 3 modern languages, compulsory Triple Award Science, Design and Technology and Information Technology). Latin and Greek are also taught, together with a wide range of physical and sporting activities. Girls are expected to take a wide and balanced core of subjects at GCSE. At Advanced Level, students specialise in their chosen subjects, which include all the conventional academic subjects found at GCSE, and History of Art, Theatre Studies and Economics. Everyone takes General Studies and a core programme covering a wide range of issues. Most students go to university or to other appropriate institutions, such as for Art Foundation courses. About 50% take a GAP year. There is a full and informative Careers programme to which all girls have access.

Fees. From September 2000: Senior School £2,044 per term; Juniors £1,588 per term.

The fees cover the regular curriculum, school books, stationery and other materials, choral music, games and swimming, but not optional extra subjects or school meals.

The fees for extra subjects, including piano, strings and wind instruments, are shown in the prospectus.

Bursaries and Scholarships. The GDST makes available to the school a substantial number of scholarships and bursaries. The bursaries are means tested and are intended to ensure that the school remains accessible to bright girls who would profit from our education but who would be unable to enter the school without financial assistance.

Bursaries are available before or after entry throughout the Senior School and application should be made to the Headmistress. All requests will be considered in confidence.

There are a number of scholarships open to internal or external candidates for entry at 11+ or to the Sixth Form.

Charitable status. Wimbledon High School is one of the 25 schools of the Girls' Day School Trust, which is a Registered Charity, number 1026057. The aim of the Trust is to provide a fine academic education at a comparatively modest cost.

Wispers School for Girls

High Lane Haslemere Surrey GU27 1AD
Tel: (01428) 643646/643121
Fax: (01428) 641120
e-mail: Head@wispers.prestel.co.uk
website: www2.prestel.co.uk/wispers

Wispers is an independent boarding, weekly boarding and day school for 120 girls aged between 11 and 18. The School is registered as an Educational Charitable Trust.

***Headmaster:* Mr L H Beltran**, BA (Hons)

Fees per annum. Boarding £12,255. Day £7,890.

BRAVELY. A clear vision and purpose for educating girls in the 21st century.

FAITHFULLY. Outstanding opportunities offered, in excellent facilities, for the study of academic and vocational subjects individually suited to the pupils. Summer 2000 GCSE pass rate (A*-C) 90%; A level pass rate 95%.

HAPPILY. A heightened sense of community where governors, staff, parents and girls work together for the success of the school.

Charitable status. Wispers School Educational Trust Limited is a Registered Charity, number 307039. It exists for the purpose of excellence in education.

Withington Girls' School

Wellington Road Fallowfield Manchester M14 6BL.
Tel: 0161 224 1077
Fax: 0161 248 5377
e-mail: office@withington.manchester.sch.uk
website: http://www.withington.manchester.sch.uk

Independent (formerly Direct Grant)
Founded 1890
Motto: *Ad Lucem*

Board of Governors:
Chairman: Professor K Perera, BA, MA, PhD
Dr F B Beswick, MB, ChB, LLD
Miss D Craven, LLB
Mrs R Dean, MA, FCA
Councillor J P Findlow, LLB, MBIM
Dr J Harris, PhD
Mr J R L Lee, DL, FCA
Professor S Lee, BA, LLM
Mr E Newcomb, BA, FRSA (*Hon Treasurer*)
Mrs C Priest
Dr M Stephen, BA, PhD, FRSA
Mr G Yeung, BA

***Headmistress:* Mrs J D Pickering**, BSc (Sheffield)

Deputy Head: Dr M McDonald, PhD (Manchester) *Biology*

Assistant Staff:
Mrs G L Adams, L-ès-L, (Sorbonne) *French*
Mrs A Bailey, BMus (Edinburgh) *Music*
Mrs L Bailey, BSc (Newcastle) *Mathematics*
Mrs C M Bankes, BA (Cantab) *Classics*
Mrs S E Bradford, MSc (Wisconsin) *Geography*
Mrs E D Chicken, BA (Oxon) *French*
Mrs D Connell, BA (London) *Art*
Mrs G C Dawson, BA (London) *History*
Miss J A Deacon, MA (Lancaster) *Religious Studies*
Miss L Derby, BA (Leeds) *English*
Mrs J M Farrell, BSc (Liverpool) *Chemistry*
Miss M Green, BA (Lancaster) *English*
Miss J R Grundy, BSc (Newcastle) *Geography*
Mrs S Haslam, BA (Lancaster) *English*
Ms L Holden, BA (Edinburgh) *Classics*
Mr C Holmes, GRSM, MusB (Manchester) *Music*
Mrs C H Jackson, ATD (Liverpool) *Design Technology*
Mrs F J Kenney, BSc (Manchester) *Food and Textile Technology*
Mrs V Kochhar, BSc (Exeter) *Mathematics*
Mrs R Lindsay-Dunn, MSc (Manchester), *Physics, BSc* (London) *Computer Science*
Dr S Madden, PhD (Nottingham) *Biology*
Dr A Maisey, PhD (London) *Chemistry*
Miss P Maxted, BA (Liverpool) *Physical Education*
Miss N J Mitchell, BA (London) *History*
Mr R W D Nottman, BCom (Birmingham) *Mathematics*
Mrs R Nuttall, BSc (Durham) *Biology*
Mrs C Ositelu, DEA-ès-L (Nantes) *French*
Mrs B M Rawsthorn, CertEd (Bedford College) *Physical Education*
Mrs J Rimmer, BSc (Cardiff) *Physics and IT*
Mrs S E Ross, BEd (Brighton) *PE*
Mr J M Rowell, BSc (Birmingham), MA (Lancaster) *Chemistry*
Mr N J Sharples, MA (Leeds) *Modern Languages*
Miss J Skirving, MA (Dundee) *English*
Mrs C A Tweedie, BA (Exeter) *German*
Mrs K Waight, BSc (Liverpool) *IT*
Dr Y E Walls, PhD (Bangor) *Chemistry*
Dr M F S Wheeler, PhD (Manchester) *Physics*
Mrs J Willson, BSc (York) *Mathematics*

Junior Department
Mrs H M DeMaine, LLB (Leeds) *Year 6*
Mrs S Coyle, BA(Ed) (Durham) *Year 5*
Mrs S M Hutt, MSc (Nottingham) *Year 4*
Mrs H M Hastings, BA (London) *Year 3*

Part-time Staff:
Mrs J Baylis, BA (Leeds) *Theatre Studies/English*
Mr A J Boyd, MSc (Strathclyde) *Politics*
Mrs J Buckley, BA (Durham) *Geography*
Mrs P M Gavan, BA (Open) *Mathematics*
Miss D J McGann, BA (York) *English*
Mrs L G Marley, BA (Manchester) *Classics*
Mrs R Owen, BEd (Manchester) *Biology*
Mrs J M C Packham, L-ès-L (Nancy) *French*
Dr E L Terrill, PhD (Oxon) *Mathematics*
Mrs J L Walker, BA (Manchester) *History*
Mrs G Winter, BA (Birmingham) *Religious Studies*

Librarian: Mrs A Wells, BA, ALA
Network Manager: Mrs S Jenks, MSc (Manchester)

Administration:
Headmistress's Secretary: Mrs W McLean
School Secretaries: Mrs M F Spurgin, Mrs K Young
Financial Secretary: Mrs L Bennett

Since its foundation in 1890, Withington has remained relatively small, with about 635 pupils, 100 of whom are in the Junior Department and 140 in the Sixth Form. This optimal size allows a friendly, intimate environment together with a broad and balanced curriculum. Withington provides a wide range of opportunities for girls, helping them to achieve their potential, academically, socially and personally. The school's A Level and GCSE results have been consistently outstanding.

Girls who gain a place as a result of the entrance examination are expected to take at least 9 GCSE's, 4 AS Levels, 3 or 4 A2 Levels and Key Skills and General Studies courses. Studies are directed towards knowledge for its own sake as well as towards University entrance, including Oxford and Cambridge. All the girls go on to Higher Education. Withington attracts pupils from a wide geographical area and from many different social and cultural backgrounds, producing a diversity in which the school rejoices.

Numerous building projects in recent years include the octagonal Arts Centre, a Sports Hall, science and language laboratories, new kitchens, dining room and library extensions and an all-weather, astro-turf pitch on the nine acres of playing fields. A new six-classroom extension is due for completion in August 2001.

Withington fosters all-round development and the academic work is complemented by an extensive range of extra-curricular activities. Music is strong and very popular; there is a comprehensive range of choirs and orchestras, involving all age groups. Drama also thrives with regular productions including many original works, written by staff and pupils. In sport a variety of games are played, including hockey, lacrosse, netball, tennis, athletics, cricket and football. Pupils are regularly selected for county and national squads. In addition to fixtures with other schools, games players compete within the school's House system, named after Withington's founders. The four Houses also provide a focus for dramatic and musical activities.

The Duke of Edinburgh Award, voluntary work in the local community, Science and Mathematics Olympiads, foreign exchanges and local field-work, all feature prominently in the school's provision. Numerous extra-curricular clubs include Japanese, photography, literature and debating. Awareness of the wider world is encouraged and girls participate in many fund-raising activities. Preparation for life after school starts early and involves a programme of careers advice, work experience and UCAS guidance.

Visitors are warmly welcomed; two Open Days are held in early November. A number of means-tested Governors' Bursaries are awarded annually. Entrance at age 7-11 is by Entrance Examination, held in January. Admission to the Sixth Form is by interview and GCSE results. Current fees for the Senior School in 2001/2002 are £1,800 per term and for the Junior School £1,263 per term. Individual instrumental music lessons are charged separately.

Charitable status. Withington Girls' School is a Registered Charity, number 526632. It aims to provide exceptional quality of opportunity, to encourage independence of mind and high aspirations, for girls from seven to eighteen.

Woldingham School

Society of the Sacred Heart Foundation

Marden Park Woldingham Surrey CR3 7YA
Tel: (01883) 349431
Fax: (01883) 348653
e-mail: registrar@woldingham.surrey.sch.uk
website: www.woldingham.surrey.sch.uk

Independent School: Girls 11–18

***Headmistress:* Miss D Vernon**, BA (Dunelm)

Bursar: Mr P Walton

Assistant Heads:
Mr D Murtagh, BSc (Southampton), MA (London)
Miss C Glass, BSc (Southampton)

Director of Studies: Mr S Skehan, BA (Liverpool), MA (London)

Teaching Staff:
Mrs F R Bagley, MA (Dublin, Trinity) *Careers and Higher Education*
Mrs H Baker, BA (London) *Head of Classics & Head of Upper Sixth*
Mrs A Benton, BA (Camberwell Art School) *Head of Art*
Mrs J Brown, BEd (CNAA) *Head of Drama*
Miss M Burt, MA (London), MPhil (Hull) *Head of Lower Sixth*
Mrs C Bush, BA (Southampton) *Head of Year 11*
Mr S Campion, MA (NUI) *Head of Religious Education*
Mrs S Catley, BSc (Leicester) *Examinations Officer, Head of Information Technology*
Mrs C Clarke, (Montessori, London) *Head of Year 7*
Mr N Connet, MA (Aberdeen) *Head of German*
Mr H Davies, BSc(Econ) (Wales), MBA (Wales), MPhil (Cantab) *Head of Business Studies*
Miss B Fookes, BEd (Southampton) *Head of Year 8*
Mrs C Halpin, BPhil (Birmingham) *Head of Year 9*
Mrs J Hart, BA (Nottingham), ALA *Librarian*
Mrs G Haythorne, MA (Oxon) *Head of French*
Miss L Hovland, BEd (Bedford) *Head of Year 10*
Miss J Howie, BEd (Leeds) *Head of Physical Education*
Miss A Hoyle, BA (Dunelm) *Head of Geography*
Mrs J James, BA (Winchester School of Art) *Head of Design & Technology*
Mrs Y Mulhern, BA (Madrid) *Head of Spanish*
Miss A O'Neill, BEd (London) *Health Education*
Mr H Patterson, BA (Bristol) *Head of History*
Mr S Rushby, BAMus (Surrey) *Director of Music*
Miss E Sebastian, MA (London) *Chaplain*
Mrs B Steptoe, BSc (Manchester) *Head of Mathematics*
Mr M Sutton, BSc (Dunelm) *Head of Science*
Mrs J Vivian, BA (Wales), MEd (Newcastle) *Head of English*

Foundation. Founded in 1842 by the Society of the Sacred Heart the school moved from the original site at Roehampton to Woldingham in 1945. Today, under lay management, Woldingham is part of the international network of Sacred Heart schools in the trusteeship of the Society of the Sacred Heart and run according to its educational aims and philosophy.

Among the strengths of Woldingham are its warm family atmosphere, its emphasis on the development of the whole person, its balanced curriculum and high academic standards and its varied extra-curricular provision.

As a Roman Catholic school in the ecumenical tradition, Woldingham welcomes members of other denominations who are in sympathy with the principal aim of the school: to form a community in which young women can grow to maturity as Christians in an atmosphere of freedom based on personal responsibility.

Situation and buildings. The school is set in beautiful grounds in a valley of the North Downs, 40 minutes by train from London and within easy reach of the Capital's airports. There is a railway station in the school's grounds. The buildings are a pleasing blend of old and new: the Stable Block and Clock Tower date from the seventeenth century, the Main House from the nineteenth century. Much modern accommodation has been built since the school moved to Woldingham.

Marden House is purpose-built with attractive bedroom accommodation for girls in the first two years. For the next four years boarders live at Senior House which has a chapel, extensive library facilities, new auditorium and new facilities for Art, Music and Drama and boarding provision which includes one hundred and thirty single study-bedrooms for Year 11 and Lower Sixth students. Opened in 1992, Berwick House provides ideal single-room accommodation for girls in their final year in the Upper Sixth.

The Science Centre (1988) comprises nine laboratories and generous preparation areas. There is a well-equipped Business Education Department and Information Technology Suite (1989). A computer network links about 200 stations throughout the School. No terminal is more than three years old. Completed in 1999 there is a new fully appointed, air-conditioned 600 seat auditorium with a related studio theatre and Drama and Music teaching areas. Alongside this is the new Art area providing three large studios, art library, dark room, screen print areas and 3-D area for sculpture etc. These were fully brought into use early in 1999.

Size. The school accommodates 550 girls within the 11–18 age range, 440 of whom are boarders. There are 150 in the Sixth Form. 60% of boarders are from families living in London and Home Counties and 10% come from overseas. Approximately 7% of the intake are of nationalities other than British; these students enrich the school by bringing to it an international dimension and outlook.

Pastoral Care. The school is organised on the year system. In each year oversight of the boarding side of the school life is the responsibility of the Head of Year, who acts in loco parentis and ensures that each girl is known and cared for as an individual. The Head of Year is assisted by a deputy and academic Tutors each of whom is responsible for the individual guidance of some 12–14 girls.

Curriculum. All girls take a common course for the first three years. Year 7 students take introductory courses in both Spanish and German and continue with at least one of these languages (in addition to French).

It is expected that the majority of Years 10 and 11 girls will follow a total of 9 or 10 GCSE courses. Linguistically able girls sit GCSE in a modern language in the November of Year 11.

The aim is to provide a "broad and balanced" curriculum for all up to the age of 16. All students take GCSE courses in English Language and Literature, Mathematics, Religious Education and French. Science is also compulsory: most girls take it as a double GCSE subject, although some sit separate papers in Biology, Chemistry and Physics. As options, girls are recommended to choose an overall combination of subjects which includes Geography or History or Business Studies plus one creative or practical subject. Latin is available to all girls in Years 7–9 and is a GCSE option.

Physical Education, Health Education and Information Technology are studied by all students, but are not necessarily examined at GCSE. Design and Technology is compulsory in Years 7–9.

In the Sixth Form, girls study four AS levels in the L6th and 3 A2 levels in the U6th leading to 3 full A level and one AS qualification. A small number of girls take 5 AS and 4 A2 levels. All students follow a General Studies programme leading to the award of a Diploma of Achievement – the programme includes courses in Politics and Current Affairs, Business and Management, Information Technology, Health Education and Religious Education. Physical Education is also studied by all. About 70% of A Level results are usually at grade A or B. All leavers go to university or the equivalent, and in the three years to 2000, 18 leavers went to Oxbridge.

Careers Guidance. The School attaches great importance to careers guidance. There is a well-staffed and stocked Careers Room with a wide range of materials available, including computer programmes helping students identify strengths, interests and options.

Music. Woldingham is well known for its strong and lively tradition of music. Over half the students play a musical instrument; there is a full school orchestra, a string orchestra, two wind bands and three choirs. School musical productions, public concerts and the church's liturgical celebrations provide scope for a variety of talent and performance.

Drama. Drama is an integral part of the curriculum from Year 7 to Sixth Form, and there are regular school productions involving girls from the whole age range.

Sport. Facilities at the new Sports Centre include a sports hall, squash courts, fitness studio, and a dance/gym studio and viewing gallery. An all-weather tennis dome and heated swimming pool complete the indoor provision for physical education and recreation. Outside, there are numerous games pitches, tennis courts and an athletics field. There is a full fixture list of inter-school matches and girls are regularly selected for County and National Competitions.

International Exchanges. Close links exist with Sacred Heart schools abroad. There is a vigorous exchange programme to Germany, France and Spain.

Extra-curricular Activities. Each term all boarders (and day girls who choose to do so) select options from the wide variety of indoor and outdoor activities available at weekends. The Duke of Edinburgh Award Scheme is well-established; participants, and other girls, are regular helpers at local hospitals and centres for disabled people. The vigorous Debating Society has a successful record of achievement in inter-school competitions. Theatre visits and other short outings are very popular; several overseas tours for different age groups (arranged concurrently at the end of the Spring Term) complement work done in class.

Exeats. Girls are allowed home any week-end from Saturday midday. There are two long week-ends (from Friday evening) each term.

Health. There is an excellent Health Centre which has two resident nurses. Two doctors, a dentist and a physiotherapist attend regularly. There is a Health Education programme which emphasises healthy living and a positive approach to matters of health.

Admissions. The main entry to Woldingham is at 11+, 13+ and 16+. Applicants take the Girls' Independent Schools' Common Entrance Examination in the January before they are due to join. However, because demand for places is high, an earlier informal assessment is made at the school so that parents may be advised whether or not they would be wise to investigate a second choice of school.

Students wishing to join the Sixth Form should be capable of taking at least four AS and three A2 courses and should have passed six or more subjects at GCSE with grade B or better (ideally grade A in Sixth Form options).

Applicants for occasional vacant places in other Years are required to sit the school's own entrance examination.

Fees. Boarders: £5,440 per term. Day £3,245 per term.

Wychwood School

74 Banbury Road Oxford OX2 6JR
Tel: (01865) 557976
Fax: (01865) 556806

Staff List:
Headmistress: **Mrs S Wingfield Digby**, MA (Oxon), PGCE

Deputy: Ms M Crawford, BA (Hons), PGCE
Director of Studies: Mr I Coy, BA, BSc, DipEd

Miss R Arno, DA, PGCE *Textiles*
Miss J Bettridge, TESOLCert *EFL/Dance*
Mrs E Bramley, BA, PGCE *Music*
Mrs A Bygott, Studienratin *German/Scripture*
Miss L Cockshott, BEd (Hons) *PE/Sports Studies*

Mrs C Collcutt, DEUG *French*
Mrs H Corkhill, BEd (Hons) *History*
Mr I Coy, BA, BSc, DipEd *Mathematics*
Ms M Crawford, BA (Hons), PGCE *English*
Mrs S Cripps, MA (Cantab), PGCE *Chemistry*
Mrs L Doughton, BSc (Hons), MA *Biology*
Mrs S Dugan, MA, PGCE *English*
Mr A Gentry, BSc, PGCE *Physics*
Mrs G Hale, MA (Cantab), PGCE *English Support*
Ms J Hitchcock, BS, MFA *Textiles/Ceramics*
Mr N Hodge, BA, PGCE *Photography/Art/Design*
Ms A Jones, BA (Hons), PGCE (A & D) *Art & Design*
Mrs E Lobell, MA, PGCE *French/Spanish*
Miss F McLoughlin, BA (Hons), PGCE *Spanish*
Miss K Mulvey, BSc, PGCE *Geography*
Dr K Patrick, MA, PhD, PGCE *English*
Mrs J Schiller, MA (Cantab), SpLD (Barts) *Dyslexia Support*
Ms K Szwarnowski, CertEd *Housemistress/Mathematics/PE*
Dr P Toff, BA, PGCE *Psychology*
Mrs E Treasure-Jones, BA *English*
Miss J Vincent, BSc (Hons), PGCE *Biology/Computer Studies*
School Secretary: Mrs S J Lobban
Bursar: Mrs A E Drake-Brockman
Assistant Housemistress: Mrs J Stephens

School Doctor: Dr K Howie, MA, BM, BCh, MRCGP, DRCOG, DGM, DCH
School Counsellor: Mrs R Boswell

Wychwood School was established in 1897. It is a Charitable Trust set up for educational purposes and has 150 girls (ages 11–18), of whom about 70 are boarders. It offers small classes taught by a qualified staff. Extra curricular activities are a regular feature of the extended day and the school takes advantage of its central Oxford location.

Curriculum. All girls are expected to take up to 9 subjects at GCSE; most go on to work for AS and A2 and University entrance. The lower school curriculum includes: Religious Education, English, History, Geography, Mathematics, Biology, Physics, Chemistry, French, Textiles, Ceramics, Singing, Art, Photography, Dance, Music, Computing, PSE, Gymnastics, Spanish (from Year 9) and Games. Visiting staff teach other optional foreign languages and musical instruments; there is a school choir and chamber groups.

School Council. Day-to-day life is largely controlled by the School Council which meets weekly and consists of staff, seniors (elected by the school) and form representatives. This is a type of co-operative government, the matured result of a long series of experiments, which trains the girls to deal with the problems of community life and gives everyone, in greater or lesser degree according to her age and status, an understanding of, and a voice in, the rules necessary for a sensibly disciplined life.

VIth Form. Members of the VIth form have considerable freedom yet play an active part in the life of the school. The choice of subjects at AS and A2 is wide, and classes are small and stimulating. Individual help with university applications and careers is a key feature of the VIth Form. There are regular outside speakers and girls attend a variety of lectures, conferences, exhibitions and meetings. Their participation in school plays and concerts as well as School Council is greatly valued. VIth form girls also spend approximately 2 hours per week on community service. Optional computer courses are run after school. VIth form boarders have shared or individual study bedrooms.

Conditions of Entrance. (*see* Entrance Scholarship section) A personal interview is usually essential between the Headmistress and both a parent and the pupil, though this may be waived where circumstances make it impossible. There is an entrance test to satisfy the staff that the girl will benefit from an education of this kind; the opinion of the girl's former school is also taken into account, particularly in relation to non-academic qualities. Scholarships are offered in creative arts, art, music, science and academic areas.

Charitable status. Wychwood School is a Registered Charity, number 309684. It exists for the education of girls from the ages of 11 to 18.

Wycombe Abbey School

High Wycombe Bucks HP11 1PE
Tel: (01494) 520381; Admissions: (01494) 897008
Fax: (01494) 473836
e-mail: registrar@wycombeabbey.com
website: www.wycombeabbey.com

Founded in 1896
Motto: *In Fide Vade*

Council:
President: The Rt Hon The Lord Carrington, PC, KG, GCMG, CH, MC, JP

Vice-Presidents:
Mr W P W Barnes, MA
Mr A K Stewart-Roberts, MA

Chairman of the Council: Mr A M D Willis, LLB, FCIArb

Mrs C M Archer, JP, BA
Miss S M Wilcock, FIA
Professor A H P Gillett, DSc, MA, FRICS
Mrs James Sassoon, MA
Dr D B L Skeggs, MA, BM, BCh, FRCR
Mr P E B Cawdron, FCA
Mrs Lesley Brown, BPhil, MA
Mrs Venetia L Howes, BSc
Mr R P Kennedy, MA
Mr J K Oates, MSc, BSc(Econ)
Ms C Riley
The Rt Hon Lord Justice May
Dr C A Seville, MA, BMus, LLM, PhD
Mr R N Strathon, MA, FRICS
Air Vice Marshal T B Sherrington, CB, OBE
Mr J P L Davis
Mrs Penelope Lenon

***Headmistress:* Mrs P E Davies**, BSc, MEd (Manchester)
Deputy Head: Mrs G R Benfield, MA (Sydney), MPhil (Oxon)

Senior House Mistress: Mrs E C Best, BA (Exeter)

Director of Studies: Miss J Z Willmott, BA (Dunelm), CertEd (Cantab)

Housemistresses:

Clarence:
Housemistress: Mrs G Gilby, BA (Cantab), PGCE (London)
Deputy Housemistress: Mrs L Errington, BEd (Dunelm)

Abbey:
Pitt: Mrs K Dodd, BA, MA (Essex)
Rubens: Miss I Collier, MEd (Manchester)

Outhouses:
Airlie: Mrs A Dobbs, RSADip in Computer Studies (Buckinghamshire College)
Barry: Mrs G Russell, MA (St Andrews), PGCE (Birmingham)

Butler: Miss M J Morrissey, BA (Open), CertEd (Leicester)
Campbell: Miss A J Robertson, BEd (London), BA (East Anglia)
Assistant Housemistress: Mrs N Reilly, BEd (Huddersfield)

Daws Hill:
Cloister: Mrs C L Jordan, MA (Oxon), PGCE (Manchester)
Shelburne: Mrs S Nelson, CertEd (Wolverhampton), DipEd (Reading)
Wendover: Mrs C Renton, BSc (Leicester), MSc (London), PGCE (Wales)
Resident Tutor: Mrs P J Newport, BSc (Reading), MA (Lancaster)

Junior House:
Housemistress: Mrs S Stevens-Wood, BSc, PGCE (Manchester)
Assistant Housemistress: Miss N Holdaway, BA (Cheltenham & Gloucester)
Resident Tutor: Miss C Noble, BA (Newcastle)

Chaplain: The Revd T Wright, BA (Nottingham)

English:
*Mr D A W Forbes, MA (Oxon), CertEd (Exeter)
Mrs C Addison, BA (Nottingham), PGCE (Cantab)
Miss A Platt, BA (Hull), MA (Leeds), PGCE (Open University)
Miss I Collier, MEd (Manchester)
Mrs G Gilby, BA (Cantab), PGCE (London)
Miss H Macgregor, BA (Oxon), PGCE (Roehampton)
Miss J Z Willmott, BA (Dunelm), CertEd (Cantab)

Drama:
*Miss C Livesey, BEd (Cantab), AGSM (Guildhall)
Mrs E M McQuay, Dip (Rose Bruford College of Speech & Drama)
Mrs L Vernon, LUDDA Dip (New College)
§Miss P Fry, BA (Exeter), DipLAMDA (*Dance*)
§Mrs S Whitfield, BA (London)
§Mrs K Rampton, LLAM (London)

Mathematics:
*Mr N Cunliffe, BSc (Manchester), CertEd (Liverpool)
Mrs M R Page, BSc, PGCE (Reading)
Miss J Ramsden, BSc, PGCE (London)
Mrs P J Newport, BSc (Reading), MA (Lancaster)
Miss G Last, BA, PGCE (Oxford Brookes)
§Dr S Mirza, BSc, PhD (Royal Holloway), PGCE (Oxon)

Science:
*Mrs S Jones, BSc (Dunelm), PGCE (Oxon) (*Head of Physics*)
Mrs C E Pickering, MA (Oxon), PGCE (Cantab) (*Head of Chemistry*)
Mrs J V Kenny, BSc (Oxford Brookes), PGCE (Oxon) (*Chemistry*)
Mrs C L Jordan, MA (Oxon), PGCE (Manchester) (*Physics*)
Dr J Ramsden, BSc (Nottingham), MSc, PhD (East Anglia) (*Physics*)
Mrs M Rogers, BSc (Exeter), PGCE (Oxford Brookes) (*Chemistry/Physics*)
Mr M Welch, BA, MEng (Cantab), PGCE (Nottingham) (*Physics*)
Mrs G Power, BSc (Exeter), PGCE (Bath) (*Head of Biology*)
Miss J A Barba, BSc (Reading), PGCE (Oxon) (*Biology*)
Mrs S Stevens-Wood, BSc, PGCE (Manchester) (*Biology*)
Mrs H Poole, BSc (Cardiff), PGCE (Bristol) (*Biology*)
§Dr S George, BSc, MSc (Madras), PhD (St Andrews), PGCE (Brunel) (*Chemistry*)
§Dr D Hudson, BSc (Dunelm), PGCE (Sheffield), PhD (Dunelm) (*Biology*)
§Mrs P J Weeks, BSc (East Anglia), MSc (Newcastle), PGCE (Exeter) (*Biology/Physics*)

Modern Languages:
*Mrs W D Woo, BA, CertEd (Cantab) (*French*)
Mrs C A Bolton, BA (Leeds), PGCE (Sheffield) (*Head of Spanish*) (*Spanish & French*)
Dr E Cox, BA, PhD, PGCE (Bristol) (*Head of German*) (*German & French*)
Mrs P J Berry, MA, DipMedStuds (Aberdeen) (*French & German*)
Miss N Cooper, BA (Southampton), PGCE (Portsmouth) (*French & Spanish*)
Miss S Shah, BA (London), PGCE (Hertfordshire) (*French & Spanish*)
Miss G M J Morrissey, BA (Open University), CertEd (Leicester) (*French*)
Mrs R Powles, BA (Oxon), PGCE (Nottingham) (*French & Spanish*)
Mrs A Keating, BA, CertEd (Oxford Brookes) (*German Assistant*)
§Mrs N Ainsworth, BA (Magnitogorsk), DipEd (*Russian*)
§Mrs E Earnshaw, Lès-L (d'Enseignement) (Nancy) (*French*)
§Mr J Garcia Delgado, BA (*Spanish*)
§Mr M Issa, BA (Aleppo), PGCE (London) (*Arabic*
§Mrs A Keating, BA (Oxford Brookes), CertEd (*German*)
§Mrs E J Lødding (*Norwegian*)
§Ms M Matsumoto (*Japanese*)
§Mrs E Wyatt (*Modern Greek*)
§Mrs X Zhang, BA (Shanghai) (*Mandarin*)

Scripture:
*Miss A Smith, BA, PGCE (Oxon)
Mrs K J Kuhlmey, BA (London), AKC (London), PGCE (Cantab)
§Mrs J Kidd, BD (London), MLitt (Bristol)

History:
*Mrs O B Raraty, BA (Leeds), PGCE (London)
Mrs K Cruse, BA, PGCE (Sheffield)
Mrs E C Best, BA (Exeter)
Miss E Halstead, BA, MA (Glasgow), PGCE (Dunelm)
Miss A J Robertson, BEd (London), BA (East Anglia)
Mrs G Russell, MA (St Andrews), PGCE (Birmingham)
§Mr J Hudson, BA, DipEd (Sheffield)

History of Art:
*Mrs K Dodd, BA, MA (Essex)
§Mr T Goad, BA (Manchester)

Geography:
*Mrs H L Cattanach, BA, PGCE (Birmingham)
Miss S Brydon, BA, PGCE (Cantab)
Mrs C Renton, BSc (Leicester), MSc (London), PGCE (Wales)

Classics:
*Dr J Hornblower, MA, DPhil, CertEd (Oxon)
Mrs G R Benfield, MA (Sydney), MPhil (Oxon)
Miss L Crump, BA (Cantab)
Mrs T Miller, BA (Oxon), MA (UCL), PGCE (London)
Miss G M J Morrissey, BA (Open University), CertEd (Leicester) (*Latin*)

Economics:
*Mrs K J Firman, BSc (Bristol), MSc (UCL)

Information Technology:
*Mr A Porter, BSc, PGCE (East Anglia), MA (Reading) (*also IT Co-ordinator*)
Mrs A M Dobbs, RSADip Computer Studies
§Mrs J A Pope, BSc, CertEd (Bath)

Art, Design and Technology:
*Mr B G Lennon, BA (Sheffield), ATD (London)
Miss J Clements, BA (Bucks College), MA (Royal College of Art), PGCE (Reading) (*Ceramics*)
Mr J Carey, BA (Polytechnic Southwest), PGCE (OU) (*Design Technology*)

Miss J Martindale, CertEd (Bedford CPE) City & Guilds (*Photography*)
§Mrs C D Symington, C & G Prof Cookery Cert, BCC TCert (East Berkshire) (*Cookery and Textiles*)
§Mrs J Nall, BA (Brunel), PGCE (Southampton) (*Textiles*)

Music:
Director of Music: Mr M Shepherd, MA (Oxon), FRCO, ARCM *organ/piano*
Assistant Director of Music: Miss S McLure, BMus (Bangor), MA (Birmingham Conservatoire), FTCL, PGCE (Reading) *oboe*
Mr P M Lloyd, GGSM, ARCM *pianoforte*
Mr D H V Petter, BA (Oxon), LRAM *pianoforte*
Mrs J E Robinson, BA (Nottingham), PGCE (Southampton) *pianoforte*
Mr N Robinson, LRAM *pianoforte*
Mrs M Thornton-Wood, BMus (Edinburgh), MMus (Mannes College, New York) *pianoforte*
§Miss D Atherton, GMus, PostDip, GSMD *singing*
§Mr F Ashford, FTCL, ARCM *clarinet/saxophone*
§Miss R Bartels, BMus (London), LRAM *harp*
§Miss A Black, ARCM *pianoforte*
§Mrs A Bristow, BMus (Adelaide) *flute*
§Miss E Doroszkowska, RNCM, BMus (Manchester) *pianoforte*
§Mr C Fairbairn, ARAM *bassoon*
§Mrs C Garratt, BMus (Edinburgh), ALCM *flute/recorder*
§Ms N Harries *violoncello*
§Miss G Hicks, GGSM *trumpet*
§Mr D Hulley *percussion*
§Miss M King, DRSAM, ARCM *violin*
§Mr M Luther, LWCMD (Welsh College of Music) *singing*
§Ms C McMillan, AGSM *oboe*
§Mr D Marrion *saxophone/clarinet*
§Miss N Mathis, MMBM (Maryland, USA) *singing*
§Miss K May *pianoforte*
§Mrs J Michael, GTCL, LTCL *guitar/double bass*
§Mrs C Nash, MA (Oxon), DipMusTh, LGSM *violoncello*
§Mrs K J Powell, GRSM, LRAM *pianoforte*
§Miss P Rooum, GTCL, FTCL, ARCO *pianoforte*
§Miss H Robinson, LRAM *violin, viola*
§Miss G Satchwell, DipMusEd, RSAM, ARCM *violin/viola*
§Miss J Stevens, MAGGSM (Guildhall) *flute*
§Mrs V Staveley, STAT *Alexander Technique*
§Mrs J von Hauenschild, ARCM, LTCL *clarinet*
§Mrs E Walker, AGSM *flute*
§Miss A Wood, BA (Dunelm), GSMD *singing*
§Miss R Woolcock, GMusRNCM, PPRNCM, LRAM *pianoforte*

General Studies:
Courses Organiser: Miss J Z Willmott
General Studies A Level co-ordinator: Mrs C Renton
Personal, Social & Health Education co-ordinator: Mrs I Collier
Learning for Life: Mrs K Kuhlmey

Physical Education:
*Miss R A Keens, BEd (IM Marsh College of PE, Liverpool)
Miss A Kemp, BA (QTS) (Warwick)
Miss J Martindale, CertEd (Bedford CPE)
Mrs S Nelson, CertEd (Wolverhampton), DipEd (Reading)
Miss F White, BSc (Cheltenham & Gloucester)
§Mrs J Hobbs, BEd (Brighton)
§Miss C Barker, BA (Leicester), TCert (Royal Academy of Dancing) (*Ballet*)
§Mr P Delgado, LTA Professional Tennis Coach (CCA)
§Mr P Harris, 5th Dan Black Belt of Higashi (*Karate*)
§Mr C Holland, LTA Professional Tennis Coach (Licensed Level 3), DipEd
§Mr S Lowry, PGA Professional (*Golf*)
§Mrs J Martin, BTF Coach (*Trampolining*)
§Miss N Northover, BA (Surrey), PGCE (*Tap*)
§Professor J Parkins, Maître d'Armes, Maître del'Academie d'Armes de France (*Fencing*)
§Mr M Sanderson, LTA Professional Tennis Coach
§Miss L Scarlett, 2nd Dan Black Belt, British Judo Association Senior Club Coach (*Judo*)
§Miss K Turton, LTA Professional Tennis Coach (Licensed Level 3)
§Mrs A White, SRA (*Squash*)
§Mr P Willetts, LTA Professional Tennis Coach

Careers and Higher Education Advice:
*Dr J Ramsden, BSc (Nottingham), MSc, PhD (East Anglia)
Mrs G Gilby, BA (Cantab), PGCE (London) (*UCAS, Work Experience*)
Miss I Collier, MEd (Manchester - American Universities)
Miss A J Robertson, BEd (London), BA (East Anglia) (*ISCO*)

Year Heads:
Upper Sixth: Mrs J Kidd, BD (London), MLitt (Bristol)
Lower Sixth: Dr J Hornblower, MA, DPhil, CertEd (Oxon)
Upper Fifth: Mrs R Powles, BA (Oxon), PGCE (Nottingham)
Lower Fifth: Mrs K J Kuhlmey, BA (London), AKC (London), PGCE (Cantab)
Upper Fourth: to be appointed
Lower Fourth: to be appointed
Upper Third: Mrs J E Robinson, BA (Nottingham), PGCE (Southampton)

Performing Arts Centre Administration:
Dr G Bates, BSc (Bath), PhD (Aberdeen)
§Mrs D Sissons (*Theatrical Costuming*)

Librarians:
§Mrs F E Valiant, MA, PGCE (Bangor), MLib (Aberystwyth), ALA (*Senior Librarian*)
§Mrs L Meekings (*Library Assistant*)

School Archivist: Mrs A C Heath, MBE, MA (Oxon), ALA

IT Systems:
Manager: Mr C Dillon, BA (London)
Assistant: Mr T Schoon

Administration:
Bursar: Mr J C O Luke, CBE, BSc (London)
Secretary to the Bursar: Mrs E Pinkney
Estates Bursar: Mr R S King, ARICS
Accountant: Mrs C Rogers, BA (Open University)
Domestic Bursar: Miss K Wojciechowska
PA to the Headmistress: Mrs S Coombe
Registrar: Mrs J M Corkran
Assistant Registrar: Mrs G Bowyer
School Office Manager: Mrs A Delgado, BA (Open University), CertEd (Oxford Brookes)
School Secretary: Mrs T D Moffat
Resources Room Technician: Mrs P Peedell
Telephonist/Office Assistant: Miss F Barney

Health:
Visiting School Doctors:
Dr F Carter, MB, BS, DRCOG
Dr L Pounder, BMedSci, BMBS, DRCOG, DFFP, MRCGP

Medical Centre
Sister M McP Gibson, RGN, ENB 182, DipCPC
Nurse M H Methven, RGN, SCM
§Nurse S Sharland, RGN

Numbers on roll: 534 Girls. 504 Boarding; 30 Day Girls.

Age range: 11–18

Aims. Wycombe Abbey aims to provide an education in the widest sense. The pursuit of academic excellence goes hand in hand with our commitment to pastoral care. We believe the welfare and happiness of every girl to be paramount. Each individual is encouraged to achieve her full potential; she receives first-class academic teaching and has the opportunity to discover and develop her talents - artistic, creative, musical, sporting. She also learns to take responsibility for herself and to have respect for others. It is an intrinsic part of the School ethos that girls care for each other and offer service to the community. We value close liaison with parents in all matters.

We hope that girls will leave us fully equipped not only to pursue the degree courses and careers of their choice but also to play a full part in the world as self-reliant, responsible and caring young adults.

Location. The School is conveniently situated for travel by road, rail and air. It is near the centre of High Wycombe, five minutes drive from the M40, giving swift access to London and the West. Heathrow airport is about half an hour's drive away and High Wycombe station less than 10 minutes walk from the School. There is a frequent rail service to London, taking between 30 and 40 minutes.

Buildings. The School buildings are all within the extensive grounds of 160 acres which include playing fields, woods, gardens and a lake.

Boarding Houses. There is a Junior House for 11 year olds. At 12, girls move to one of nine Houses, each accommodating between 40 and 45 girls, where they remain until the end of the Lower Sixth. Each House has a resident Housemistress who is also a member of the academic staff. This dual role ensures excellent communication in all matters concerning the girls. The mixed age Houses provide each individual with a secure framework and she is encouraged to take on responsibilities. The Lower Sixth girls take a major share in the administration of the Houses and the School as prefects, developing invaluable skills in communication and management.

In the final, A level year, all girls move to an Upper Sixth House where they are encouraged to prepare for university life. They are relieved of House responsibilities but continue to join in general activities and to run School societies. They learn how to manage their own time during the day and are allowed considerable freedom at weekends. They cook some of their own meals and no longer wear uniform.

Religion. Wycombe Abbey is a Church of England foundation with its own Chapel. All girls attend morning prayers and a Sunday Service. (Roman Catholic girls can attend Mass and Jewish girls receive instruction from a Rabbi). Christian principles inform the whole ethos of the School and a resident Chaplain oversees spiritual matters and plays a central role in pastoral care. Around fifty girls are confirmed each year at the annual Confirmation Service.

Curriculum. The Lower School curriculum includes the study of English, English Literature, History, Geography, Scripture, French, German, Spanish, Latin, Greek, Mathematics, Biology, Chemistry, Physics, Information Technology, Design and Technology, Art and Craft, Textiles, Cookery, Drama, Music, Singing, Personal, Social and Health Education, Current Events and PE. In the Sixth Form, Economics, History of Art, Classical Civilisation, Government and Politics, Philosophy and Ethics, Physical Education and Critical Thinking are also available. Girls are prepared for the GCSE, AS and A2 level examinations and for University entrance.

Physical Education. The School has six lacrosse pitches, including an international size all weather lacrosse pitch, a hockey pitch, twenty four tennis courts, some floodlit and used as netball courts in winter, an athletics track, two squash courts, an indoor, heated swimming pool and a gymnasium. Girls are taught a wide variety of sports: lacrosse, netball, tennis, athletics, swimming, gymnastics and dance. Hockey, health-related fitness, aerobics, squash, volleyball, badminton and basketball are offered to older girls. Extra curricular activities - for which charges are made - include fencing, wind-surfing, trampolining, karate, rowing, riding, golf, ballet, tap and modern dance, as well as extra tennis coaching.

Music. There is a strong tradition of music making. The Music School, opened in 1998, provides outstanding facilities for tuition and for recitals in the Recital Hall, with its excellent accoustics. About three-quarters of the girls study one or more musical instruments, including piano, violin, 'cello, harp, brass, wind and solo singing. Charges are made for individual lessons but there are many opportunities for performing in orchestras and ensembles, in addition. There is a strong tradition of singing; the Chapel choir plays a central role in Chapel worship and undertakes annual overseas tours and annual choral concerts with other schools such as Eton.

Speech and Drama. Equally splendid facilities are available for the many girls who enjoy drama. A fully equipped theatre enables pupils to perform in a variety of plays and musicals. Over half of them take private Speech and Drama lessons, preparing for LAMDA and Poetry Society examinations.

Art, Craft, Design & Technology. Girls can pursue their interests in these subjects at weekends when the Studios are open, as well as in curriculum time.

Other Activities. We encourage girls to participate in the Duke of Edinburgh Award Scheme; many take the Bronze Award, with smaller numbers continuing to Silver and Gold. All Lower Sixth girls take part in weekly Community Service and many participate in successful Young Enterprise. Debating, Public Speaking and European Youth Parliament activities are also popular.

Fees. The fees for boarders are £5,800 per term, (£4,350 for day boarders). They are inclusive and cover, in addition to the subjects and activities already mentioned, lectures, concerts, most text-books and stationery. Outings are extra. (Fees are not remitted on any account but Fees Protection insurance is offered).

Extra subjects, for which additional charges are made include Piano, Violin, 'Cello, or any other musical instrument, Solo Singing, Speech and Drama, Fencing, Special Tennis Coaching and extra languages.

Admission. Girls are admitted at the age of 11, 12 or 13. Application should be made well in advance. The suggested procedure is given in the prospectus information booklet.

Sixth Form Entry. Older girls who are of good academic ability may be considered for admission to take an Advanced Level course in the Sixth Form.

Scholarships. (*see* Entrance Scholarship section) For details relating to Scholarships, please refer to the appropriate section in this book.

Charitable status. The Girls' Education Company Limited is a Registered Charity, number 310638. Its aim is the provision of first class education for girls.

Wykeham House School

East Street Fareham Hampshire PO16 0BW
Tel: 01329 280178
Fax: 01329 823964

Motto: *Vouloir C'est Pouvoir*

Patron: The Bishop of Portsmouth

Mrs V Harold-Harrison
Mrs L Hayes
Miss C Evan-Hughes
Mr J B Fullarton
Mr D L E Evan-Hughes, TD, MA (Oxon)
Commander J W B Moss, CEng, FIMarE, FINucE
Miss H A Tyler, LLB (Hons)
Dr C Pickstock, FRCS(Ed)
Mr T Stallion
Mr P D Jones, BA Hons(Arch), DipArch, RIBA
Dr A Marks

Staff:
***Headmistress:* Mrs R M Kamaryc**, BA, MSc, PGCE (Queens University, Belfast)

Senior Tutor: Mrs J R Caddy, BEd Hons (King Alfred's, Winchester)

Head of Junior Department: Mrs C Freemantle, BEd Hons (Bristol)

Mrs H Batchelor, BA (Newcastle)
Mrs W Callear, AGSM, CertEd (Middlesex Polytechnic)
Mrs W Carter, BEd Hons (Portsmouth Polytechnic)
Mrs J Disley, BSc Hons (Aberdeen University)
Mrs Y Dowse, BA Hons
Miss A Drinkwater, BEd Hons (Bedford College of Physical Education)
Mrs M E Duffy, BEd (Rolle College, Devon)
Mrs M Formstone, BSc Hons (Sheffield)
Mrs C A Fuller, BEd Hons, AdvEdDipBusEd (Warwick University)
Mr R Garrard-Abrahams, BEd Hons (Avery Hill College, Eltham)
Mrs M Hoadley, BEd (La Sainte Union, Southampton)
Mrs M Norris, BSc Hons (Hull)
Mrs R E Penny, BA (Rhodes University, South Africa)
Mr C Prestidge, BEd Hons (West Sussex Institute of Higher Education)
Mrs K Rendle
Mrs M Reverse-Hayes, Licence D'Enseignement Histoire (France)
Mrs B Robinson, BSc (Liverpool University)
Mrs Y Smith, BA (Portsmouth Polytechnic)
Mrs E Webb
Mrs L J Allured, CertEd, (Christchurch College, Kent)
Mrs A M Bassam, BA, (Reading University)
Miss A Beverly, MA, PGCE (St Andrews)
Mrs J A Briggs, BA (Milton Keynes)
Mrs M E A Caple, Dip in Primary Education (Aberdeen College of Education)
Mrs C Fiack, BEd Hons (Westminster College, Oxford)
Mrs C Greenwell, BA (King Alfred's, Winchester)
Mrs H M Langford, BEd (King Alfred's, Winchester)
Mrs K Lincoln, BA (Sunderland Polytechnic)
Mrs O Pearson, BEd (Nottingham)
Mrs C Robinson, BEd (Southampton)
Mrs P Szynalski, MA (Oxon)
Miss C Ball, NNEB
Miss S Hatter, NNEB
Mrs G Jones, NNEB

Visiting Staff:
Mrs L Knapman
Mrs E Burden, ARCM, BSc
Mr D Frankham
Mr D Lewis
Miss S Marston, PGCE, GRCM (Hons), DipRCM
Miss K Robertson, GRSM (Hons), LRAM
Miss C Thresh, BMus (Hons)
Mr A Worsfold, BA(QTS) (Hons)

Bursar: Mr B Rogers

School Secretary: Mrs L Colbeck

Assistant Secretary: Mrs B Rollo
Senior Administrator: Mrs C S Stevens

Wykeham House, founded in 1913, occupies a prominent site in the centre of Fareham within easy access of the M27. The School moved to its present position in 1986 where the Georgian building together with the modern wing provides spacious accommodation for over 300 day girls between the ages of $2\frac{3}{4}$ to 16. Pupils are drawn from the borough of Fareham and a wide catchment area eastwards to Emsworth, west towards Southampton as well as north of the town to Bishop's Waltham.

The School has a strong Anglican tradition but welcomes all denominations. Small classes and option groups encourage a high standard of academic achievement and provide a secure background in which attention is paid to the needs of each pupil.

The Junior Department. The Junior Department, for pupils aged $2\frac{3}{4}$–10 years, has an individuality of its own which contributes greatly to the School's atmosphere and the sense of community. All the usual activities which are taught at Primary level are covered by the Junior Curriculum. The teaching methods employed place an emphasis on the acquisition of the basic skills of Literacy and Numeracy. Full opportunities are given for creative work, self-expression and individual development.

At the age of 9+ girls are introduced to a number of specialist teachers who teach across a wide curriculum leading to the 11+ Entrance.

Senior School. The Curriculum aims to maintain standards and yet recognise the need to keep apace of educational developments and modern teaching techniques. The Curriculum is under constant review by the Headmistress and the Staff Committee. Specialist rooms and well-equipped laboratories and computer facilities are available.

The subjects taught in the Senior School cover a broad curriculum leading to GCSE.

An Options system is in existence from the Fourth year but all pupils take English, Mathematics, a Modern Language and Science in their 16+ examinations. Private study periods are included in the option groups to encourage individual study skills and full use is made of the School Library.

Visits are undertaken to theatres, museums, art galleries, and other places of interest. Field work is an integral part of the study of the Humanities and in Science while Modern Language study involves visits to the Continent and foreign exchanges. Lecturers and performers are invited to the school while the girls are encouraged to take part in Music, Art and Drama as well as other leisure pursuits.

Senior girls participate in the Duke of Edinburgh Award Scheme. In this way they test their own initiative, discover fresh challenging pursuits, make new friends and become aware of the needs of others.

Many activities occur during Lunch times and after School such as the Mathematics Workshop, Computer Clubs, Horseriding, Games practices, School choirs, Instrumental groups and Dramatic productions.

A member of the staff is responsible for Careers Advice in the School and there is an extensive library of Careers Literature freely available. Each girl is interviewed and receives information and advice on her own choice of career from the local Careers Advisory Officer who visits the School. Close contact is maintained with local sixth form colleges, Further Education Colleges and other schools in the area.

The pastoral system is organised on a Form basis while the girls also belong to four School Houses where the year groups mix socially and competitively.

Physical Education. The School supplements its Games facilities by hiring nearby local amenities.

Netball, Hockey, Tennis, Rounders and Athletics form

the basis of the Senior Girls' Physical Education programme.

Admission. Admission is by interview in the Infant Department, Assessment tests and Examinations for entry to the Junior School 7–10 years take place in February for admission in the following September while entry to the Senior School is through the School's own Entrance Examination.

Fees per term graduated from £712.50 Nursery (mornings only), £1,287 Infants (and all day Nursery), £1,380 Juniors, £1,728 Seniors.

Scholarships. (*see* Entrance Scholarship section) Particulars regarding Scholarships at 11+ are available on application from the School Prospectus and information can be found in the relevant section of this book.

Charitable status. The Trustee of Wykeham House School Trust is a Registered Charity, number 307339. It exists to provide education for girls.

ALPHABETICAL LIST OF SCHOOLS

GIRLS' SCHOOLS ASSOCIATIONS (PART II)

GEOGRAPHICAL LIST OF GIRLS SCHOOLS

(NB Page numbers will be found in alphabetical list on pp. 748–749.)

Avon
Schools formerly in Avon will be found under Somerset

Bedfordshire
Bedford High School
Dame Alice Harpur School, Bedford
St Andrews, Bedford

Berkshire
Abbey School, Reading
Brigidine School, Windsor
Downe House, Cold Ash
Heathfield, Ascot
Luckley-Oakley School, Wokingham
Queen Annes School, Caversham
S Gabriel's, Newbury
St George's, Ascot
St Joseph's Convent, Reading
St Mary's School, Ascot

Buckinghamshire
Piper's Corner School, High Wycombe
St Mary's School, Gerrards Cross
Wycombe Abbey

Cambridgeshire
Perse School for Girls, Cambridge
Peterborough High School
St Mary's School, Cambridge

Channel Islands
Ladies College, Guernsey

Cheshire
Queen's School, Chester

Cleveland
Teesside High School, Stockton-on-Tees

Cornwall
Truro High School

Cumbria
Casterton School, Kirkby Lonsdale

Derbyshire
Derby High School
Ockbrook School, nr Derby
St Elphin's School, Matlock

Devonshire
Maynard School, Exeter
St Dunstan's Abbey, Plymouth
St Margaret's School, Exeter
Stover School, Newton Abbott

Dorset
Croft House School, Shillingstone
St Anthony's-Leweston School, Sherborne
St Mary's School, Shaftesbury
Sherborne School for Girls
Talbot Heath, Bournemouth
Wentworth College, Bournemouth

Durham
Durham High School
Polam Hall, Darlington

Essex
New Hall, Chelmsford
St Mary's School, Colchester

Gloucestershire
Cheltenham Ladies College
Westonbirt

Hampshire
Atherley School, Southampton
Farnborough Hill, Farnborough
North Foreland Lodge, nr Basingstoke
Portsmouth High School
St Nicholas School, Church Crookham
St Swithun's School, Winchester
Wykeham House School, Fareham

Herefordshire and Worcestershire
Alice Ottley School, Worcester
Holy Trinity School, Kidderminster
Malvern Girls' College
St James's School, West Malvern
St Mary's Convent School

Hertfordshire
Abbot's Hill, Hemel Hempstead
Berkhamsted Collegiate School
Haberdashers' Aske's School for Girls, Elstree
Princess Helena College, Hitchin
Queenswood, Hatfield
The Royal Masonic School for Girls
St Alban's High School
St Francis' College, Letchworth
St Margaret's School, Bushey

Humberside
Hull High School

Isle of Wight
Upper Chine, Shanklin

Kent
Ashford School
Bedgebury School, Goudhurst
Beechwood Sacred Heart, Tunbridge Wells
Benenden School
Bromley High School
Cobham Hall, nr Gravesend
Combe Bank, Nr Sevenoaks
Farringtons and Stratford House, Chislehurst
Holy Trinity College, Bromley
Kent College, Pembury, Tunbridge Wells
Walthamstow Hall, Sevenoaks
West Heath, Sevenoaks

Lancashire (Including Greater Manchester)
Bolton School (Girls Division)
Bury Grammar School (Girls)
Elmslie School, Blackpool
Hulme Grammar School for Girls, Oldham
Manchester High School for Girls
Westholme, Blackburn
Withington Girls' School, Manchester

Leicestershire
Leicester High School for Girls
Loughborough High School

Lincolnshire
Stamford High School

London
Blackheath High School
Channing School, Highgate
City of London School for Girls
Francis Holland Church of England School, Regent's Park
Francis Holland Church of England School, Sloane Square
Godolphin and Latymer School
James Allen's Girls School
More House School
Notting Hill and Ealing High School
Palmers Green High School
Putney High School

London — *continued*
- Queen's College, Harley Street
- Queen's Gate, School
- St Paul's Girls' School
- South Hampstead High School
- Streatham and Clapham High School
- Sydenham High School
- Wimbledon High School

Merseyside
- Belvedere School, Liverpool
- Birkenhead High School
- Merchant Taylor's School for Girls, Crosby

Middlesex
- Heathfield School, Pinner
- Lady Eleanor Holles School, Hampton
- North London Collegiate School
- Northwood College
- St David's, Ashford
- St Helen's School for Girls, Northwood

Norfolk
- Hethersett Old Hall, Norwich
- Norwich High School

Northamptonshire
- Northampton High School for Girls

Nottinghamshire
- Hollygirt School, Nottingham
- Nottingham High School for Girls

Oxfordshire
- Cranford House, Wallingford
- Headington School, Oxford
- Oxford High School
- Rye St Anthony School, Oxford
- St Helen and St Katharine, Abingdon
- St Mary's School, Wantage
- Tudor Hall, Banbury
- Wychwood School, Oxford

Shropshire
- Adcote School for Girls, Shrewsbury
- Moreton Hall, Oswestry
- Shrewsbury High School

Somerset
- Badminton School
- Bruton School for Girls
- Clifton High School
- Colston's Girls' School, Bristol
- Redland High School, Bristol
- Red Maids School, Westbury-on-Trym
- The Royal High School, Bath

Staffordshire
- School of S Mary and S Anne, Abbots Bromley

Suffolk
- Amberfield School, Ipswich
- Ipswich High School
- St Felix School, Southwold

Surrey
- Croham Hurst School, Croydon
- Croydon High School
- Dunottar School, Reigate
- Greenacre School for Girls, Banstead
- Guildford High School
- Lodge School, Purley
- Manor House School, Little Bookham
- Marymount International School, Kingston-upon-Thames
- Notre Dame Senior School, Cobham
- The Old Palace School of John Whitgift, Croydon
- Parsons Mead, Ashstead

Surrey — *continued*
- Prior's Field, Godalming
- Royal School Haslemere
- St Catherine's School, Bramley
- St. Teresa's School, Dorking
- Sir William Perkins's School, Chertsey
- Surbiton High School
- Sutton High School for Girls
- Tormead School, Guildford
- Wispers School, Haslemere
- Woldingham School

Sussex (East)
- Brighton and Hove High School
- Moira House Girls School, Eastbourne
- Roedean School
- St Leonards-Mayfield, Mayfield
- St Mary's Hall, Brighton

Sussex (West)
- Farlington School, nr Horsham
- Lavant House Rosemead, Chichester

Tyne and Wear
- Central Newcastle High School
- Dame Allan's School, Newcastle upon Tyne
- La Sagesse Junior and High School, Newcastle upon Tyne
- Newcastle upon Tyne Church High School
- Westfield School, Newcastle upon Tyne

Warwickshire
- King's High School for Girls, Warwick
- Kingsley School, Leamington

West Midlands
- Edgbaston High School
- Highclare School, Sutton Coldfield
- Holy Child School, Edgbaston
- King Edward VI High School for Girls, Birmingham
- St Martin's, Solihull

Wiltshire
- Godolphin School, Salisbury
- St Mary's School, Calne
- Stonar School, Melksham

Yorkshire (North)
- Harrogate Ladies College
- Leeds Girls' High School
- The Mount School, York
- Queen Margaret's School, York
- Queen Mary's School, Nr Thirsk

Yorkshire (South)
- Sheffield High School

Yorkshire (West)
- Bradford Girls' Grammar School
- Gateways, Leeds
- Wakefield Girls High School

Scotland
- Kilgraston School, Bridge of Earn
- Mary Erskine School, Edinburgh
- St George's School for Girls, Edinburgh
- St Margaret's School, Aberdeen
- St Margaret's School, Edinburgh

Wales
- Haberdasher's Monmouth School
- Howell's School, Llandaff

South America
- Northlands School, Buenos Aires, Argentina

Girls' Senior Schools Entrance Scholarships – 2001/2002

The Abbey School, Reading. Academic Scholarships are awarded on entry to the Senior Department at age 11, and to the Sixth Form, on the results of the entrance examination.

Abbey School Assisted Places are available at age 11, and are on a sliding scale according to income.

Abbot's Hill. Major awards of one third fees. Exhibitions awarded based on entrance examinations results.

Amberfield School. The following scholarships are awarded annually.

Five junior school scholarships.

Academic Scholarships are awarded as a result of the 11+ entrance examination in January.

Art and Music scholarships are awarded at 11+ and 13+.

Ashford School. Scholarships are available at 7 or 8 for the Junior School, and at 11, 13 and the 6th Form for the Senior School. Details may be obtained from the *Headmistress.*

Badminton School. Entrance and Scholarship Examinations take place in late January, with awards up to half fees for girls aged 11, 12, and 13, or entering the Sixth Form, and special Music, Art and All-rounder scholarships at any age. 24 Open Scholarships are awarded each year and may be enhanced in cases of need.

Bedford High School. Entrance Scholarships are available at 11+, 12+ and 13+. Scholars may hold their awards throughout their time at the School with a review before Sixth Form.

High School and Harpur Bursaries are available and are dependent upon parental income.

Sixth Form Scholarships are available to both internal and external candidates.

Bedgebury School. Entrance Scholarships are available at 7+, 11+, 13+ and 16+ to the value of up to ⅔ day fees, depending on merit and financial status. *The maximum award on merit is to the value of ⅓ day fees, but this can be augmented to ⅔ in case of financial need.* Examinations are held early in the Spring Term (Autumn Term for 16+). Candidates are examined in English, Mathematics, Standardized Test (age 7+ and 11+) with Science, French and an optional Latin paper at 13+. For entry to Sixth Form (16+), candidates choose 3 subjects related to their proposed A Level course *and sit a general paper. All candidates are interviewed by the Headmistress.*

Scholarships and Awards are available for Academic, Music, Art, Sport at 7+, 11+, 13+ and 16+, Drama at 13+ and 16+, and Science, Ceramics, Fashion and Design at 16+. Candidates for Art, Music, Sport and Drama take the academic examination as well as the appropriate tests or auditions. This acts as an entrance test in which a general level of competence is expected in the written papers to demonstrate that scholars can cope with the demands of a mainstream education.

Special Awards (NOT Academic Awards): Daughters of Church of England Clergy benefit from the De Noailles Trust and full details of these awards are available from the Head of Administration.

Daughters of serving members of HM Forces are granted 10% discount.

Further details and application forms are available from the *Registrar.*

Beechwood Sacred Heart/Sacred Heart Beechwood. Scholarships and Awards are available: Academic, Music, Art, Sport and Drama at 11+, 13+ and 16+. Major awards of up to 50% of tuition fees and other minor awards. 11+ and 13+ Entrance and Scholarship Day takes place in January each year, 16+ in November. Further details are available from the Registrar.

Benenden School

Academic Scholarships – Lower School Entry (11–13). Substantial awards available. The level of examination (for candidates under the age of 14 on 1st September following the examination) will be determined not by date of birth but by intended Form of entry (11+ for Fourth Form, 12+ for Upper Fourth, 13+ for Lower Fifth). The examinations are held in January preceding the date of entry. For further information, please contact the *Admissions Secretary.*

Academic Scholarships – Sixth Form Entry. Substantial awards available. For girls under the age of 17 on 1st September following the examination. Examinations are held in November preceding entry in September. Candidates take three papers: a compulsory General Paper and two papers in subjects which they intend to study at A Level. For further information, please contact the *Admissions Secretary.*

Berkhamsted Collegiate School. Entrance scholarships are awarded thus:

The Major School Scholarship at 11+ for half tuition fees for day girls or boarders.

The Figg Sixth Form Scholarship at 16+ for £750 pa on entry to the Sixth Form (with preference given to girls joining the Sixth Form from another school). The Award will be determined by achievement at GCSE.

More information about Scholarships and Bursaries may be obtained on application to: *The Deputy Principal's Secretary, Berkhamsted Collegiate School, Kings Campus, Kings Road, Berkhamsted, Herts HP4 2BG.*

Blackheath High School. Two or more awards are offered each year as a result of the entrance examination and interviews. Particulars of the examination are available from the *Headmistress.*

Bruton School for Girls. *Academic Scholarships* are offered on entry into the Junior Department, and the Senior School at 11+, 13+ and Sixth Form.

Casterton School. Scholarships and Exhibitions up to the value of 50% of full fees are offered each year for entry to the Senior School at 11+. These awards are based on our Entrance examination.

Candidates of exceptional ability joining the School at a later stage can also be considered. A small number of Sixth Form Scholarships for external candidates are available.

Channing School. Academic Scholarships (½ fees) and Exhibitions (¼ fees) are offered at 11+ and 16+. All candidates are eligible; there are no special papers, but potential scholars will be called for a second interview. Scholarships are occasionally awarded for academic prowess within the school. Awards are also offered to Sixth Form entrants, based on mock' GCSE results for inside candidates or on test papers and interviews for outsiders. Particulars and the current Sixth Form Prospectus may be obtained from the School.

The Cheltenham Ladies' College. Junior and Sixth Form Scholarships are available. A Centenary Scholarship worth 50% of the annual fees and a number of other major or minor academic scholarships are offered annually.

Cobham Hall

The following Scholarships are offered annually:

Junior School Scholarships for pupils entering at age 11+, 12+ and 13+.

In all cases the Scholarships will be awarded as a result of performance in the School's own entrance examination, a full confidential report from the Head of the current school and an interview.

Scholarships are awarded to candidates of outstanding ability in any field. Each candidate is considered individually. A willingness to work and contribute to the School community is vital.

Sixth Form Scholarships

There are seven Sixth form Scholarships available to students entering the lower Sixth. Three boarding Scholarships to the value of 33% of full fees. Four daygirl Scholarships to the value of up to 100% of full fees.

An informal interview is always available to candidates unsure of their standard.

For further information contact The Registrar, Sally Ferrers on 01474 824319/823371.

Colston's Girls' School. Sixth Form Scholarships are awarded following an open examination: two Wolfton Scholarships each to the value of 50% of fees, three Jenner Scholarships of £600 each for two years, and three Bathurst Scholarships each worth £250.

Combe Bank. Up to 8 scholarships are available, worth up to 50% of basic fees; normally the majority of these are awarded at 11+, but at least one is always offered at 13+. At 11+ scholarships are awarded on the basis of performance in the entry examination. At 13+ candidates sit papers in English, Mathematics, Science, French and Humanities. At 16+ there are 2 scholarships: the Cottrell scholarship worth 50% of fees is awarded to the outstanding candidate, the second scholarship worth 50% may be divided amongst several candidates. Examinations in the first week of November.

Croham Hurst School

Academic scholarships are awarded as a result of the 11+ entrance examination in January. The Jubilee Scholarship is awarded to a candidate already attending the Junior School. There is usually an award made to a girl with particular musical talent.

Sixth Form scholarships are awarded to girls showing exceptional academic potential. Papers are sat in January.

Other Bursaries may be awarded at any age at the Governors' discretion. These are usually offered as support in times of financial difficulty.

Downe House

The following Scholarships are offered annually:

An Under 12 Downe House Open Scholarship and Under 13 Downe House Open Scholarship and Minor Scholarships. Each Scholarship is up to the value of half the annual fees. The examinations are taken in January and candidates must be under 12 or under 13 on the following 1st September. Candidates sit papers in English, Mathematics, Science, French (under 13's only) and a General Paper.

The Under 14 Olive Willis Scholarship up to the value of half the annual fees. The examinations are taken in January and candidates must be under 14 on the following 1st September. Candidates sit papers in English, Mathematics, French, Science and a General Paper.

Sixth Form Scholarships for girls entering the Sixth Form are also available. Candidates sit the examination at Downe House in November in two subjects of their own choice together with a General Paper.

Further particulars may be obtained from the *Registrar*.

Edgbaston High School. Eight Scholarships are available at 11+, including one for Music. They are awarded on the basis of performance in the entrance examination and in the case of Music there are additional written, aural and practical tests. The awards cover up to 50% of the fees and are means tested.

At 16+ there are a further six free places, offered in full or in part, to girls of outstanding ability. One of the scholarships is for Music. External candidates are examined by arrangement towards the end of the Autumn Term. Further particulars may be obtained from the School.

Elmslie Girls' School. One Scholarship (the Elmslie Scholarship), consisting of the full fee, is offered each year to the top girls in the Senior School Entrance Examination (11+). Also on the results of this examination, up to 6 Governors Scholarships are offered; 3 each worth up to $^2/_3$ annual fee and 3 each worth ½ fee. All candidates sitting the Entrance Examination are considered for these scholarships, the best candidates being called back to school on another day for a further written test and interview. All scholarships may be supplemented by a bursary. Full details from the *Headmistress*.

Farlington School

Two Academic Scholarships: up to the value of 40% of tuition fees, for girls entering Year 7 (11–12 age group), awarded solely on the basis of performance in the examination. Scholarships may be divided if there is a number of girls of equal academic ability. Internal candidates from year 6 are eligible to sit this examination.

Entrance examinations (written papers), will be held at Farlington School on Saturday, 9th January, 2000

Sixth Form Scholarships/Awards: these awards are available to both internal or external candidates entering the Sixth Form. Candidates are expected to write an essay and have an interview with senior members of staff. Interviews take place in November prior to the year of entry into the Sixth Form.

Sixth Form Scholarship: one scholarship for academic excellence up to the value of 50% of tuition fees is awarded on the basis of current academic performance.

Sixth Form Awards: these awards are based not only on academic performance but also on the ability to make a significant contribution to the Sixth Form at Farlington. We are looking for Sixth Formers with talents in such areas as sport, music and drama, and those who show quality of leadership. Awards vary in value and are based on a report from the candidate's teachers as well as her ability to present her thoughts and opinions in writing and at interview.

Scholarship/Awards (written papers), will be held at Farlington School during November 1999.

Farnborough Hill. Three Academic Scholarships, worth $^1/_3$ of fees, are awarded at 11+. The best candidates in the Entrance Examination are shortlisted for a further examination and interviews. Two of these scholarships are reserved for Roman Catholics. Six Sixth Form Scholarships, worth £1,000 per year are awarded to Farnborough Hill students who achieve outstanding results at GCSE. In addition one music and one sports scholarship, worth 20% of fees, are awarded at 11+ and there are Bursaries, worth up to 40% of fees, for parents in need of financial assistance.

Francis Holland School, Clarence Gate. Academic Awards. Two exhibitions to the value of 1/12 of current school fees are awarded for the two years leading to GCSE examinations.

Two Sixth Form scholarships to the value of up to 50% of current school fees are awarded for the two years leading to Advanced Level.

Francis Holland School, Graham Terrace. Academic Awards. One Scholarship of the value of one-quarter of current school fees is awarded.

Two Sixth Form scholarships of the value of 50% of the current school fees are awarded for the two years leading to Advanced Level.

Gateways School. Two main school awards may be offered in each year group to pupils who attain exceptionally high standards in their entrance examinations or later in school examinations. Two sixth form scholarships may also be given to suitable candidates.

The Godolphin School. 11+, 12+, 13+ and Sixth Form scholarships, worth up to 50% of the boarding fees, are awarded for outstanding merit and promise in academic work, music or sport. Art scholarships are awarded at 13+ and Sixth Form only. Further particulars may be obtained from the *Admissions Secretary*.

Greenacre School. A limited number of Scholarships are awarded each year. An award equal to half the current fees is awarded at the 11+ level. Scholarships are also available for entry into the Sixth Form. These awards are available to internal or external candidates. Further particulars are available from the *Headmistress*.

Guernsey Ladies College. The States of Guernsey operate an 11+ system and, annually, there are 21 selective places offered by the States of Guernsey.

Guildford High School. Academic Scholarships are offered at 7+, 11+ and 16+.

Haberdashers' Monmouth School for Girls. Entrance Scholarships. One or two, depending on candidates' calibre of 50% or 25% fees are awarded to the most promising examination candidates entering the first year (11 year olds).

Headington School. 1998: Major £1.2 million bequest to school for the establishment of a scholarship fund. Scholarships, for up to half boarding/day fees, are for outstanding academic promise and are assessed according to financial need. These will generally be awarded for entry at 11+ and into Sixth Form although exceptions will be considered according to merit. Also some internal scholarships, from Fifth Form into Sixth Form and Junior School to Senior School.

An open scholarship (not means tested) is also awarded at 11+ and other minor scholarships are available at 12+ and 13+. Musical, sporting and artistic ability can be taken into account along with academic talents.

Hethersett Old Hall School. *11+ Up to three scholarships* may be awarded. One may be up to 30% of tuition fees. Two more may be awarded; total cost of these two should not exceed 30% of tuition for one pupil. Theses scholarships are *open to 10+ entrants from Junior Department and from other schools.*

13+ One scholarship of up to 50% of the total fee. Only *new entrants for boarding are eligible.*

Sixth Form. Up to three awards of up to 30% of tuition fee. These scholarships only *open to new applicants.* Awards to be made as a result of an examination and interview early February. Examination in English, Maths, test of general ability, interview in two subjects to be studied at A-level, submission of work in three GCSE subjects.

One internal Sixth Form Award. Available to recognise outstanding achievement at GCSE of a Fifth Former continuing in to the Sixth Form.

Sixth Form Bursaries. Means tested assistance for deserving internal candidates who wish to continue into the Sixth Form. At the Headmistress's discretion. (Within budgetry constraints.)

Discounts. A scholarship may be held in addition to the sister's discount. If a scholarship is awarded to a pupil who is eligible for the Armed Forces' discount, the maximum level of this discount is 5%.

Highclare School. Two entrance scholarships are awarded each year for the 11+ age group. These will be to the value of 50% or 25% of school fees and awarded to the best all-round candidates.

Holy Child School. Scholarships usually up to half fees are offered each year to candidates entering the Senior School at 11+. Exhibitions may be awarded for runners-up in the Scholarship Examination. A limited number of Wolfson Scholarships/Bursaries are available to sixth form entrants.

Further particulars may be obtained from the *Headmistress.*

Holy Trinity College. Up to 4 part Scholarships (Maximum half fees) are offered each year. These are awarded to girls who obtain exceptionally good grades in the Entrance Examination in January.

James Allen's Girls' School. Scholarships are awarded every year to girls of 11 years of age on entry to the School. There are also Scholarships on entry into the Sixth Form. Scholarships are awarded for academic ability, but are also available for Music and Art. All Scholarships are augmented by a means-tested element where there is need. The School has also introduced its own scheme to replace the Government Assisted Places Scheme.

Kent College, Pembury. Several major academic scholarships worth 50 to 75% of tuition fees are awarded each year to girls of outstanding academic ability who achieve high results in the entrance tests at 11+ and 13+. Minor academic awards worth 25% are also available. A Level scholarships worth 20 to 75% tuition fees are also awarded each year. Music and drama awards are available for 11+, 13+ and 16+ entrance.

Kilgraston School. Academic scholarships up to the value of 50% of boarding fees and 50% of day fees are offered each year as a result of outstanding performance in the Entrance/Scholarship Examinations held in February. Scholarships are also offered in Art, Music and Tennis.

King Edward VI High School for Girls. Up to three free place Scholarships may be awarded on the results of the Governors' Admission Examination to girls entering the first year. These are independent of parental income and are normally tenable for 7 years.

For girls entering the school at age 16 two half fee scholarships are available.

The Lady Eleanor Holles School

11+ Entry: Academic Scholarships. At least four awards are offered each year. These are expressed as percentages of the full fee and will thus keep pace with any increases. Awards are likely to be half or third fees but a full fees scholarship can be awarded to an exceptional candidate. The awards are based on performance in the school's own Entrance Examination and subsequent interview.

Sixth Form Scholarships. A maximum of ten Scholarships worth 40% of fees over the two years of Sixth Form study are offered to internal and external candidates who sit the Sixth Form Entrance and Scholarship Examination in February of the year of proposed entry.

Governors' Bursaries. Candidates who sit entrance papers at any stage may be considered for a bursary award. These are means tested and subject to annual review.

Leicester High School for Girls. Bishop Williams Scholarships are awarded to girls at 11+ who show outstanding academic promise.

Sixth Form Scholarships are awarded to students who show outstanding academic ability.

Sixth Form Bursaries are also available.

Loughborough High School. The Governors will be offering a number of Scholarships and Exhibitions at 11+ and 13+. The Scholarships and Exhibitions will be awarded on merit. The value of the Scholarships will be 1/3 of the fees and the value of the Exhibitions 1/6 of the fees regardless of parental income. These may be increased to the full amount of the fees if the parental income necessitates this. In addition, some Governors' Awards will be given at 16+. Further details of all these awards are available from the School.

Malvern Girls' College. Awards are offered for academic ability or for excellence in music, art or sport. Scholarships are worth 50% of current fees and exhibitions 25%. Examinations and interviews are held for entrance to the Middle School at 11+, 12+ or 13+, or to the Sixth Form. All scholarships and exhibitions are tenable for as long as the girl remains at the College provided that her progress and conduct are satisfactory. Applications to sit Entrance Scholarship examinations must be made at least 2 weeks before the date of the examination. Details of dates and application forms are available from the Registrar.

Manchester High School for Girls. Entrance Scholarships. One or more Scholarships may be awarded for excellence in performance in the entrance tests taken at the age of ten or eleven for admission to the Main School in September. Such Scholarships will be awarded on merit only, not on the basis of parental income, and will provide full or part remission of fees.

Manor House School, Little Bookham. Academic scholarships up to the value of 50% of tuition fees are offered each year. The awards are based on performance in the school's own Entrance Examination, which takes place in the January prior to entry, and interview with the Headmistress.

Art and Music Scholarships are also offered to girls who

show outstanding talent in these areas. Further details are available from the *Admissions Secretary.*

The Maynard School. 26 Assisted Places are awarded at ages 10+, 11+ and 12+. Five Sixth Form Assisted Places are awarded to girls entering the Sixth Form.

Moira House Girls School. Ingham Scholarships are offered each year for entry into our Senior School (25% to 50%), and Sixth Form (up to 75% Scholarship). A number of Junior Scholarships are available up to the value of 50% of tuition fees. Scholarship Examinations are held in January or February each year. Full details may be obtained from the *Principal's PA.*

Moreton Hall. A number of scholarships worth between 10% and 50% will be made to pupils at 11+, 12+ and 13+. Sixth Form Scholarships and bursaries, given in memory of Miss Bronwen Lloyd-Williams, are awarded to girls entering Lower VI or to assist a pupil in the school to complete her education. Awards for Music, Drama, Art and for outstanding sporting talent are made at 11+, 12+, 13+ and 16+. For further details please contact the Principal.

The Mount School
Scholarships. Applicants may be awarded Scholarships on the basis of the Entrance Examination and (if appropriate) auditions. At Sixth Form level, one full fee Scholarship may be awarded annually to a candidate of outstanding academic ability in financial need. At 11 and 13 the Major Academic Award could cover 80% fees. All Academic Scholarships are fee related and are tenable while the holder remains at The Mount, provided that high standards of work and conduct are maintained.

Newcastle upon Tyne Church High School. Two 11+ Scholarships, worth 50% of the fees, and three Exhibitions, worth 33% of the fees, are available. There is a Music Exhibition at 11+. Further details are available from the Headmistress.

New Hall, Chelmsford.
5 at 11+
(*a*) Full tuition – for pupil currently attending voluntary aided Catholic primary school in Brentwood Diocese.
(*b*) Full tuition – open to any Catholic applicant in a Catholic Independent school.
(*c*) Full tuition – open to any applicant.
(*d*) Third fees – Armed Forces parent.
(*e*) Third fees – Foreign Office parent.
1 at 13+
Third fees – open to any applicant.

All the Entrance Scholarships are academic scholarships although candidates must be satisfactory in other respects as well.

Sixth Form:
Small awards are made at Sixth Form level in Science; Mathematics; English; Music; Drama; Languages and Art.

Annually a number of means-tested Bursaries are awarded.

North London Collegiate School. Three or four Scholarships, up to the value of 50% fees, are offered each year on the results of the eleven year old entrance examinations and interviews.

Parsons Mead School. A number of part-fee scholarships are offered each year to candidates either internal or external who show outstanding potential in the Senior School Entrance Examination at 11+. A few part-fee scholarships are also awarded on entry to the Sixth Form whether pupils are proceeding into the Sixth Form from within or applying from other schools.

Pipers Corner School. Scholarship examinations are held annually in January for student entry into the Sixth Form the following September. Short-listed candidates will be interviewed by a member of the governing body, the Headmistress and the Deputy Head. There are five full Scholarships available. These cover all academic subjects, including Drama and Music.

Polam Hall. Entrance Scholarships are offered at 9+, 11+, 13+ and 16+. Value of the entrance Scholarships is up to 1/3 remission of fees. At 9+ and 13+ an examination is set in Mathematics, in English and in VR. At 13+ French is also included. At 16+ candidates take a General Paper plus two subjects of their own choosing.

Princess Helena College. One boarding and one day scholarship, each to the value of 50% of fees, is available annually for entrance at 11+, 12+ and 13+. Scholarship examinations for these junior scholarships take place in February. Two sixth form scholarships are also available, to external as well as internal candidates. These are worth 60% of fees and scholarship examinations take place in October for entry in the following September.

Prior's Field. *Two Academic Scholarships* at 11+ are awarded on the results of the Scholarship Examination. These are valued at 50% and 25% respectively of current fees.

Further details are available from School, but applications for scholarships must be with the school by the end of November of the year prior to entry.

Queen Anne's School, Caversham. Foundation scholarships are awarded each year following an examination held in the early spring. All scholarships are open to internal and external candidates. There are several scholarships which may be awarded to candidates under fifteen years of age on the 1st September following the examination. Different papers will be set for different age groups.

The top scholarship of the year is valued at full tuition (i.e. two thirds total fee) for each year the scholar is at school here; other scholarships have a minimum value of £600 per annum irrespective of income and a maximum value of half tuition fees. For one of these scholarships preference will be given to the daughters of clergymen of the Church of England or of schoolmasters. All scholarships are awarded for excellence whether in academic work, art, music or sport.

It is assumed that all scholars will complete their sixth form education at Queen Anne's School.

Sixth Form Scholarships are offered each year up to the value of half tuition fees and these are competed for by both external and internal candidates. The examinations are held at the school in November of the year preceding entry.

Further details of all Scholarship examinations may be obtained from the Admissions Secretary.

Queen Ethelburga's School. Awards are offered each year. Exhibitions will be awarded either to runners-up in the Scholarship Examination, or to non-Scholarship candidates who obtain exceptionally good grades in the Common Entrance examination or to candidates who can show (on interview) outstanding ability in, for example, Mathematics and Science, with a good average standard in other subjects. Candidates must be over 12 and under 14 on the date of the examination. Further particulars and free copies of specimen papers may be obtained from the *Headmaster.*

Queen Margaret's School. Awards are made at 11+, 12+, 13+ and 16+. Details can be obtained from the School.

Queenswood School.
Sixth Form Scholarships
1 Major Academic Scholarship value 50% awarded annually to external candidates.

2 Academic Scholarships value 25% awarded annually. Examinations in November for entry the following year.

11+ Entry
1 Major Academic Scholarship value 50%, 2 Academic Scholarships value 25% and 4 All Rounder Scholarships value 10% awarded annually. Assessments for Academic Scholarships in January/February.

13+ Entry
1 Major Academic Scholarship value 50% awarded annually to external candidates. 2 Academic Scholarships value 25% and 4 All Rounder Scholarships value 10% awarded annually. Examinations for Academic Scholarships in January/February.

Tennis
4 Tennis Scholarships value 50% awarded annually. Assessment in January/February.

Red Maids' School. Three Open Scholarships are awarded annually at eleven plus for outstanding performance in the Entrance Examination. Up to three Whitson Bursaries are awarded annually to enable Year 11 Red Maids to continue their education in the Sixth Form at Red Maids'. Scholarships and Bursaries are not related to family income.

Redland High School. There are up to eight Academic Scholarships of varying amounts awarded at 11+; the maximum value of a Scholarship awarded may be half fees. Everyone who sits the Entrance Examination is automatically considered for a Scholarship. In addition there are School Bursaries and John James awards. These are income-related and are awarded to able girls in need of assistance.

The Royal Masonic School for Girls. Two Open Major Scholarships are awarded annually at 11+ and 16+, of value, ²/₃ of the tuition fee and half of the boarding charge.

Two Minor Scholarships, open to all candidates, and of value approximately 30% of the fees, are awarded at 7+, and 11+. Four Minor Scholarships of similar value are awarded at 16+. Six Foundation Scholarships are available at 11+. These are reserved for the daughters of Freemasons.

Two Minor Scholarships, of similar value, are awarded for boarding places only, for open competition at 11+.

Roedean School. A number of Scholarships, normally worth ½ the fees is offered annually for Academic and Music potential. Candidates for the Junior Scholarship must be under 14 years of age on 1st September of the year of entry. The examinations are held in February and these are designed to test potential rather than present knowledge. The Sixth Form Scholarship examinations are held in November at the School for girls entering the Sixth Form the following September who wish to spend 2 years study for the GCE Advance level examinations. Details of the Scholarships and sample papers may be obtained from the *Admissions Secretary.*

Royal School, Haslemere
Scholarships at 11+

Two *major academic* and two *minor academic* scholarships are offered on entry at 11+, which are awarded to applicants on the basis of the School's own entrance tests and interview. These scholarships are worth 30% and 15% of the tuition fees respectively.

In addition the school offers a *Foundation* scholarship (worth 20% of tuition fees) to a candidate who shows exceptional overall academic, sporting and artistic potential.

Other Scholarships include *Art, Music, Dance, Drama and Physical Education.*

Sixth Form Scholarships

Two major scholarships are available to internal and external candidates valued at 50% of the tuition fee, with up to a 40% Bursary based upon financial circumstances. In addition, there are a number of *exhibition scholarships* available in a variety of subjects.

There is a *Music Scholarship* for pupils entering the Sixth Form, to the value of 30% of the tuition fee.

Other Awards:

Daughters of serving members of HM Forces are granted bursaries of 5–15% of tuition fees.

Daughters of old girls and siblings receive discounts.

Further details are available from the *Admissions Registrar.*

St Alban's High School. Up to four Scholarships are offered annually at 11+ entry. These are awarded on academic merit shown in the entrance examinations and any subsequent interviews. The value of each Scholarship is up to ¹/₆ of the fees. Three further Scholarships are offered on entry to the Sixth Form.

St Anthony's – Leweston School. New entrants to the School may be awarded Music or Academic Scholarships or Bursaries. After they join the School each girl's progress is reviewed annually and awards may be increased up to the value of ²/₃ fees.

Academic Bursaries and Scholarships are awarded both to new entrants to the School and to pupils already in the School. These Awards are up to ²/₃ fees. Every girl's progress is reviewed annually and Scholarships may be increased at any time during a girl's time in the School.

St. Catherine's School, Bramley. *Scholarships at 11+*

At the age of 11 there are two Entrance Scholarships available which are awarded on the results of the Common Entrance Examination. One scholarship is for ¹/₆ fees and one for ¹/₃ fees. These run through Middle School and can be extended through Sixth Form at the discretion of the Headmistress.

In the event that the best pupil moving from Junior School to Senior School does not get an entrance scholarship, then the best Junior School pupil will receive the Junior School Exhibition equal to ½ of single term senior daygirl fee.

A music scholarship of ¹/₃ of the fees may be awarded annually upon entry to an 11+ candidate adjudged to have sufficient musical talent.

Upper 5 & Sixth Form

Margaret Kaye Scholarship

There are four scholarships of ¹/₃ fees awarded to run for three years (through Upper 5 and the Sixth Form).

Claire Gregory Scholarship

This is awarded for gymnastic/athletic prowess and is for ¹/₃ day fees in the Sixth Form.

Sixth Form Scholarship

There are six scholarships available. Selection for the awards is based on the results of the June examinations at the end of the Lower Fifth. Full details are sent to the parents of all members of this year group at the beginning of the Summer Term.

St David's School, Ashford. A number are available for candidates entering at age 10/11 into the first year of the Senior School. Value – from ¹/₃ to ½. Awarded on all-round merit, demonstrated during the previous year's work (reported by the candidate's present school) and on performance in St. David's Assessment and Interview.

St Dunstan's Abbey. *Entrance Scholarships at 11+.* Three Scholarships are offered at this level each year; one Major of 100% of the current tuition fees; two Minor of 50% of the current tuition fees. Each Scholarship is tenable for up to seven years.

Sixth Form Scholarships. Two Scholarships are offered for entry to the Sixth Form and may be one Major at ²/₃ and one Minor at ¹/₃ of current tuition fees or two equal Scholarships to the value of ½ the current tuition fees. The Awards will be based upon GCSE grades and Interview.

Gambrell Scholarship. This is an internal Award offered to an existing Preparatory School pupil for entry to the Senior School at 11+. It is valued at 50% of current tuition fees and is tenable for up to seven years. This Scholarship is based upon the performance in the Senior School Entrance Examination.

St Elphin's School. There are seven Awards available to girls aged 11–13, the most valuable offering full fees. Girls aged 7 or 8 may compete annually for four Awards, up to ½ the fees. In addition, five Sixth Form Scholarships are available each year.

Saint Felix School. The Governors offer a number of generous Scholarships and Exhibitions annually, with values of 33% and 20% of fees respectively. They are awarded on academic merit to candidates on entry at 11, 12 or 13+ on the results of the appropriate Common Entrance Examinations, plus tests and interview. Awards are held to GCSE. Scholarship Examinations are held each Autumn for candidates planning to enter the Sixth Form the following academic year. The examination comprises two written papers, a general paper and an interview. Awards are held for the two years of Sixth Form study. Further details may be obtained from the *Registrar.*

St Francis' College. A number of Scholarships are awarded at 11+ and 13+ following the entrance examinations held in February. These vary in value between 25% and 50% of tuition fees and are awarded on overall Academic ability.

St Joseph's Convent School, Reading. A number of Scholarships are awarded at 11+ and on entry into 6th Form. These vary in value and are awarded for academic ability and for improvement.

St Leonard's School

(*a*) Two Scholarships of ½ fees per annum on entrance at 12 or 13 years.

(*b*) One Scholarship of ½ fees per annum on entrance into the Lower Sixth for a two-year course leading to University.

Scholarships in Sport are offered on an occasional basis if a candidate with outstanding ability of any age should present herself.

St Leonards – Mayfield School

Entrance at 11+ and 13+. These are open to Roman Catholic girls, who show strong academic potential, and whose parents would not, without an award, be able to pay full fees. All are means-tested. An Honorary Scholarship may be awarded if, although there is not a present need, the likelihood of future need, to be addressed at that point, exists.

St Margaret's, Bushey. Three Academic Scholarships for 2 years in Sixth Form to the value of ¹/₃ boarding fees.

Two Academic Scholarships for 2 years on entry at age 11 to the value of ¹/₃ boarding fees.

St Margaret's School, Edinburgh. There are two Academic Scholarships each worth ½ tuition fees for entry to the Senior School (S1). There are also two worth full tuition fees for entrance to the Senior College (S5) which are decided on school reports plus interview. S1 Scholarship Exams are held in January or February, Senior College interviews in March. Further details can be obtained from the *Principal.*

St Martin's, Solihull. At least five awards are offered each year. Major Scholarships are equal to full fees remission. Minor Scholarships are equivalent to one term's fees per annum. Awards are made to candidates who show outstanding ability in the entrance examination, in Scholarship tests and in interview.

Up to two Scholarships equal to at least ½ fees per annum may be awarded annually to pupils entering the Sixth Form. Candidates are required to sit a general essay paper, a specialist paper in one of their chosen A Level subjects and will be interviewed by the *Headmistress.*

St Mary's School, Ascot. The Sixth Form Science Scholarship worth up to 60% of tuition fees is awarded annually to a candidate entering the Sixth Form either from St Mary's or from another school. The award is made on GCSE grade estimates and on the results of a two hour examination taken in the Lent term prior to entry.

St Mary's School, Calne. Entrance scholarships are available at 11+, 12+ and 13+, each worth up to one third of the annual fees (day or boarding) until completion of the Upper Fifth year.

One Entrance Scholarship per year worth up to one third of the annual fees (day or boarding) until completion of the Upper Fifth year is available for daughters of the Clergy and of Old Girls.

Two **Academic Sixth Form Scholarships** are available for entry into the Sixth Form, each worth up to one third of the annual fees (day or boarding). Further details available from the school office.

Further details of all scholarships are available from the *Admissions Secretary.*

St Mary's School, Wantage. Scholarships are awarded at 13+ and Sixth Form entry.

At *13+*, 3 scholarships are offered to all girls entering Year 9 each September. There is one Junior Academic Scholarship, with two other Scholarships to be chosen from Music, Art, Sport or Exceptional All Round Ability. The value of each scholarship is ¹/₃ boarding fees for three years.

At *Sixth Form* entry there is one Academic Scholarship to the value of 50% of the boarding fee for two years.

All scholarships are open to internal and external applicants. For further details, please contact the *Admissions Secretary.*

St Swithun's School. Entrance Scholarships are available for Day Girls and Boarders entering the School at 11+. Scholarships are also awarded on the results of a competitive examination at 12+ and 13+. The major award covers two-thirds of School fees. There are also a number of awards for Sixth Form entrants covering up to half of School fees.

Sherborne School for Girls

Scholarships, Exhibitions and Bursaries:

Up to five Academic Scholarships and two Exhibitions are offered annually as a result of examination and interview; in addition there are two Scholarships offered for outstanding promise in music. Dates of examinations: Sixth Form Scholarship in November, others in January and February. Winners of academic or music awards are offered emoluments related to current fees.

Sir William Perkins's School. Three awards are offered each year to candidates who achieve an exceptionally high standard in the entrance examination. Up to a maximum of six academic awards are offered for two years sixth form study on the results of a scholarship examination and interview. All awards will be worth up to half the academic tuition fees.

Stamford High School. 25 free scholarship places are allocated at 11+ to pupils living within the Lincolnshire Local Education Authority catchment area for the school.

A Dolphin-Thowless-Rutland Bursary up to the value of ½ the fees is sometimes available for girls living in the area bounded by the former county of Rutland.

One Foundation Award is available at both 11+ and 13+ and is open to both internal and external candidates. Value up to full fees according to financial need.

Two Foundation Awards for Sixth Form entrants.

These Awards may be given for Musical or Artistic Ability and can be up to the value of full fees according to financial need.

Stonar School. Academic, Music, Art, Sport, Riding and good All-Rounder Scholarships are offered from 11+. Major awards up to 50%, minor awards at the school's discretion. 11+ Scholarship Examinations are held in January each year and Sixth Form Scholarships by the end of March each year. Other ages by arrangement.

Surbiton High School. Surbiton High School offers two academic Sixth Form Scholarships each year. Both awards may be worth up to 50% of fees per annum. These open to internal and external candidates and are awarded on the basis of the Scholarship Examination and interview with the Headmistress. The examination is held in January of each year and further details may be obtained from the *Headmistress.*

Sydenham High School. The Girls' Day School Trust makes available to the School a number of scholarships each year for entry to the Senior Department at both 11+ and direct into the Sixth Form. The maximum value of a Trust Scholarship is normally half the current tuition fee. It is possible to transfer this, under certain conditions, to another Trust School. Scholarships are awarded solely on the basis of academic merit and no financial means test is involved

A Music Scholarship may be awarded on entry at 11+.

Tudor Hall School. Three per year, each to the value of 15% of the boarding fees, may be offered to suitable candidates entering at 11+, 12+ or 13+. If a successful applicant indicates a clear need, on disclosure of parents'

financial circumstances, a further bursary may be granted by The Pearce bequest.

Upper Chine. Entrance Scholarships. Major awards of up to 50% fees in the year of the award are available at 11+, 13+ and for Sixth Form entry. Exhibitions may be awarded to girls of good academic ability who are not of the required age for the Scholarship. Examinations are taken each year in February. Further particulars may be obtained from the *Headmistress's Secretary.* Music Scholarships, Art and Drama Scholarships up to 50% of full fees are also available.

Walthamstow Hall. Two Foundation Scholarships, worth half tuition fees, are awarded annually to the two candidates who gain top marks in the school's own eleven-plus entrance examination.

One Academic Scholarship, worth half tuition fees, is awarded annually to the candidate who gains top marks in the school's own thirteen-plus entrance examination.

Two Sixth-form Academic Scholarships, worth half tuition fees, are awarded annually to the candidates who gain top marks in the school's own Sixth-form Scholarship Examination.

One Music Scholarship is awarded at eleven-plus and one at thirteen-plus.

All awards are available to both internal and external candidates.

Wentworth College. Scholarships worth up to 50% of fees (day or boarding) are awarded to pupils who join the school at 11, 12 or 13+. They are awarded to girls with all-round academic excellence or special ability in music, art or sport.

Two free places may be offered to girls joining the Sixth Form who have excellent grades in a minimum of nine GCSEs.

Wychwood School.

At 11+ one Scholarship worth £1,000 p.a. and two Scholarships worth £500 p.a. are offered.

At 16+ one Scholarship worth £1,000 p.a. and one Scholarship worth £500 p.a. are offered.

Academic Scholarship will be awarded on the results of the general entrance paper.

Wycombe Abbey School. Lower School Entry. Substantial awards up to the value of 50% of the annual fees available for candidates under 12 and under 14 on 1st September of the proposed year of entry.

Substantial awards up to the value of 50% also available for candidates entering the Sixth Form.

For further information, please contact the Registrar (Tel: 01494 897008).

Wykeham House School

Entrance Scholarships. Two Scholarships of 25% of the annual fee, tenable for five years, are awarded each year based on good 11+ Common Entrance results and interview.

Music and/or Drama Scholarships

The Abbey School, Reading

Music Awards, giving free tuition on up to two instruments, are awarded at age 11 and on entry to the Sixth Form, following auditions.

Abbot's Hill

Two Music Scholarships may be awarded up to ½ the fees.

Amberfield

The Junior Music Bursary will be awarded to a pupil at 11+ entering the Senior.

Candidates for the Bursary must have reached at least Grade 2 with Merit, on their instrument/s. The successful candidate will hold the Bursary for three years.

The Senior Bursary will be awarded to a candidate to hold for L5 and U5 (Years 10-11). The successful candidate will study Music for GCSE and will have passed at least Grade 4 with merit.

The Bursaries will be awarded to pupils who demonstrate overall musical ability and potential on at least one instrument and also in aural tests, sight reading and singing. Candidates will be required to play/sing **two** prepared pieces and should bring to the audition the appropriate accompaniments.

Ashford School

One Music Scholarship, of ½ tuition fees plus free tuition on one instrument is available at age 11.

Badminton School

Music Scholarships are open to all applicants, external or internal, and auditions generally take place in January preceding entry. Maximum awards of 50% may be enhanced in cases of need.

Bedford High School

Scholarships are available on entry to the Sixth Form.

Bedgebury School

Music Scholarships and bursaries are offered at 7+, 11+, 13+ and 16+. Drama Awards are offered at 13+ and 16+. Major Awards cover up to ²/₃ day fees, depending on merit and financial status. Bursaries provide free tuition in one or two instruments. Music candidates audition on the instrument(s) of their choice and take a sight reading test. Drama candidates audition a prepared dramatic speech and an unrehearsed improvisation (all scholarship and bursary candidates take the academic examination).

Further details and application forms are available from the *Registrar.*

Benenden School

Lower School Entry (11–13)

Substantial awards available. The examinations are held in January preceding the date of entry. Candidates should have reached the standard of Grade V (or equivalent) or show great potential. Those offering piano or singing as a principal study should be fluent in an orchestral instrument. Candidates will be required to do practical tests and will be interviewed; they are also required to show that they have reached the general academic standards of any entrant either by sitting qualifying papers, or by taking the academic scholarship examination. The award of a music scholarship includes free tuition in one instrument (rising to two lessons a week in the Sixth Form). For further information, please contact the *Admissions Secretary.*

Sixth Form Entry

Substantial awards available. For girls under the age of 17 on 1st September following the examination. Examinations are held in November preceding entry in September. The requirements for a Sixth Form Music Scholarship are very much the same as for Lower School candidates (see above entry), but candidates should have reached the standard of Grade VII (or equivalent). Candidates are also required to show that they have reached the general academic standard required of any entrant by taking two qualifying papers in subjects which they intend to study at Advanced Level. For further information, please contact the *Admissions Secretary.*

Berkhamsted Collegiate School

The Music Scholarship at 11+, for £1,500 plus free instrumental tuition on piano and another instrument for girls on entry to Y7.

The Webb Sixth Form Music Scholarship at 16+ for a £700 contribution towards music tuition. The Award will be determined by audition on two instruments and held through Y12 and Y13.

More information about Scholarships and Bursaries may be obtained on application to: *The Deputy Principal's Secretary, Berkhamsted Collegiate School, Kings Campus, Kings Road, Berkhamsted, Herts HP4 2BG.*

Blackheath High School
A Music Bursary offering free tuition on one instrument may be offered annually. Auditions are held at the same time as the entrance examination.

Bruton School for Girls
11+ entry: 1 scholarship 10% of tuition fees plus free tuition on one instrument or voice.

Sixth Form: 10% of tuition fees plus free tuition on two instruments, or one instrument and voice.

Casterton School
A music scholarship up to the value of 50% of full fees, plus free tuition on two instruments, is available. Two exhibitions of free tuition on two instruments are also offered. These awards are based on auditions which are conducted concurrently with the entrance examination.

Channing School
Academic and Music scholarships (50%) and exhibitions (25%) offered at 11 and 16 years entry. Music bursaries also awarded internally from Year 8 in the senior school. These cover lessons in school on one instrument for two years (renewable).

The Cheltenham Ladies' College
At Junior level, both Major and Minor Scholarships are offered. The major scholarship is worth 40% of the annual fees plus free instrumental tuition and the minor award 25% of annual fees plus free instrumental tuition. At Sixth Form level, one music scholarship is available and is worth 40% of the annual fees.

Colston's Girls' School
Music Exhibitions to the value of free tuition on two instruments are awarded to talented and suitably qualified girls who enter the first year, and are held throughout the Exhibitioners' time at the School. Auditions are held shortly after the Entrance Examination and candidates should be able to perform on at least one instrument to Grade III standard, and to pass aural and sight reading tests, and take a short written theory test. Exhibitions will need to satisfy the requirements of the academic Entrance Examination.

Downe House
Up to two Open Music Scholarships are offered each year. In addition Minor Scholarships or Exhibitions may be awarded.

Each Scholarship is up to the value of half the annual fees and free tuition in one instrument. Junior candidates must be under 14 on the following 1st September. Auditions and aural tests are held at Downe House in January and Award winners are required to reach a satisfactory standard in the Common Entrance examination for their age group before taking up their award.

Senior candidates entering the Sixth Form are required to achieve a grade C or above in five GCSE subjects before taking up their award in the following September.

Further particulars may be obtained from the *Registrar.*

Edgbaston High School
There are two Scholarships, one at 11+ to the value of 50% of the fees and one at 16+ to the value of a full free place. 11+ candidates must sit the main entrance test in February and then have written, aural and practical tests. Candidates at 16+ must attend an interview and sit a music examination in December. Further details may be obtained from the School.

Elmslie Girls' School
Two Music Scholarships are offered annually to senior school entrants of any age including the Sixth Form. Each Scholarship entitles the holder to free instrumental tuition plus one third fee remission per annum but will be awarded only to those studying, or intending to study, Music to GCSE and then Advanced level. These Scholarships are decided on the basis of performance, a written test and interview. A separate application form is necessary for these scholarships. All Scholarships may be supplemented by a Bursary. Full details from the *Headmistress.*

Farlington School
Two Music Scholarships
Two music scholarships up to the value of 40% tuition fees are available each year. Scholarships may be divided if there is a number of talented girls in any one year. Free tuition in a musical instrument may be offered to candidates as part of their scholarship.

Candidates should have reached the equivalent of Grade 4 standard in at least one instument and show general musicianship commensurate with their technical skills. No special pieces are set but each candidate must bring with her two contrasting pieces which she has recently studied. Appropriate aural and sight-reading tests will be given. The examiners will be looking for musical potential with existing achievement. An adequate performance in the entrance examination is also required.

Auditions and interviews are held in January each year and are offered to girls entering Year 8 and below. Internal candidates entering Years 7 and 8 are eligible for these scholarships. Candidates are invited to bring their own accompanist with them to their audition if they wish, although a professional accompanist will be in attendance. Further details of the format of the audition will be sent on receipt of the application.

Sixth Form Music Scholarship
A Music Scholarship up to the value of half tuition fees, plus free tuition in one musical instrument, is awarded to a suitably qualified candidate who wishes to study A Level Music.

Any candidate interested in this Scholarship should apply to the Head of Department for further details.

Music auditions will be held at Farlington School on Friday, 7th January, 2000. There is a scholarship fee of £15.00 for candidates sitting for the Music Scholarship.

Application forms for the music scholarships/awards may be obtained from the Headmistress's Secretary, Farlington School, Strood Park, Horsham, West Sussex RH12 3PN.

Telephone number: (01403) 254967) Fax: (01403) 272258

Closing date for entrance examinations and music scholarship/awards: 3rd December 1999

Farnborough Hill
One Music Scholarship is offered, worth 20% of fees, at 11+. Applicants are auditioned and the award is made on the basis of overall potential and likely contribution to the musical life of the school.

Francis Holland School, Clarence Gate
A Music Scholarship to value of $^{1}/_{12}$ of current school fees for seven years is awarded at 11+.

The Godolphin School
11+, 12+, 13+ and Sixth Form music scholarships are awarded for outstanding merit and promise. Candidates for music awards should have attained at least grade IV on one of their instruments (grade VI for Sixth Form candidates). They are also expected to reach an acceptable academic standard.

The Godolphin & Latymer School
A Music Scholarship to the value of ½ fees and free tuition in one instrument is available on entry to the first year at age 11. There is the possibility of a further scholarship for the Sixth Form. Candidates must satisfy the academic requirements of the School and auditions are held in January/February each year.

Guildford High School
Music Scholarships are offered at 11+ and 16+.

Haberdashers' Monmouth School for Girls
Music Awards are made to outstanding performers, junior and senior pupils of the School, following audition and theory paper. Awards cover the cost of tuition on up to three instruments while the pupil is at the school.

Headington School
A Music Scholarship for free tuition of 2 musical instruments is awarded each year and valid to the end of the Sixth Form.

Hethersett Old Hall School
One Music Scholarship is available to a girl aged 13+ for the tuition of one or two instruments.

Holy Trinity College
Scholarships are available (maximum half fees).

James Allen's Girls' School
Music Scholarships are available at 11+ and 16+. Candidates must satisfy the academic requirements of the school and pass an audition. Scholarships are on the same basis as academic scholarships but also include instrument tuition.

Kent College, Pembury
A Music Award up to the value of 50% tuition fees is available each year for a girl entering at 11+, 13+ and 16+.

Drama Awards up to the value of 25% tuition fees are also available.

Kilgraston School
One or two Awards are made each year. Minimum standard Association Board Grade 4. Auditions are held on the day of the Scholarship Examinations.

The Lady Eleanor Holles School
Both Major and Minor Awards are available at 11+ and 16+. These are up to the value of 40 and 20% of fees respectively and both include free tuition on one instrument. Candidates must satisfy academic requirements in entrance papers and attend on a further day for music tests. Full details of requirements in these tests are available from the school.

Leicester High School for Girls
A Music Scholarship is awarded at 11+, available to girls taking the entrance examination. An audition and interview is also necessary.

Loughborough High School
The Governors are offering one Scholarship and two Exhibitions to musically promising and talented pupils who have been successful in the Entrance Examination. A Dyson Music Scholarship is an Award of no more than 1/6 of the fees and the cost of the year's lessons in one instrument at School rates. An Exhibition will be worth the cost of tuition in one instrument at School rates.

Malvern Girls' College
Scholarships to the value of 50% of the current fees plus free musical tuition and exhibitions to the value of 25% of the current fees plus free musical tuition, are awarded annually.

There are no set pieces, candidates being free to perform pieces of their own choice. Those with an interest in composition are encouraged to present a folio of original compositions and/or arrangements. Awards are made according to ability and musical promise shown.

Candidates must also satisfy the academic entrance requirements of the College by sitting papers in English, Mathematics, Science and Verbal Reasoning.

Moira House Girls School
Swann Exhibitions for excellence in Music, Art, Drama, Sport, are awarded each year for between 10% and 25% of termly fees. Examinations and auditions are in January or February each year. Full details are available from the *Principal's PA*.

The Mount School
Major and Minor Scholarships are available for Music, Minor Scholarships for Drama, these cover the costs of appropriate examinations and individual lessons. Art Scholarships are rarely given to younger girls; their main function is to provide older girls with the means to visit galleries or buy books and materials to further their specialist studies.

New Hall, Chelmsford
1 at 11+. Third fees and tuition in up to two instruments. Open to any applicant.
1 at 16+. Small award open to internal or external candidate.

North London Collegiate School
Two Music Scholarships, up to the value of 25% fees, are offered each year.

Polam Hall
Music Awards are available at 11+, 13+ and 16+. A Minor Award normally involves free tuition in one instrument and a Major Award free tuition on two instruments. In exceptional cases some remission of fees may be made.

Princess Helena College
Discretionary awards are available for girls who show considerable potential in music. Candidates would be expected to offer two instruments, at a minimum of Grade III standard at age 11 or Grade V standard at age 13. Major awards may be up to 40% of fees; minor awards cover the cost of tuition in the chosen instruments. Awards are offered on the basis of auditions.

Prior's Field
Music Scholarship. 1st instrument grade 5 standard at age 11+ is expected.
2nd instrument grade 2/3 at age 11+ is expected.
Candidates not having grade 5 theory would be required to take a theory paper, and there will be short aural and sight reading tests. Candidates with strength in one instrument only may apply.
The scholarship is valued at 50% of the fees.
Drama Scholarship. A Drama Scholarship will be awarded which is valued at 50% of the current fees. Girls are required to learn a short piece (about 3 minutes) of their own choice (prose or poetry) to recite on the day of the examination, and to sit a one hour examination in the Drama Studio at Prior's Field on 3rd February at 2.00 p.m.

Further details are available from School, but applications for Scholarships must be with the School by the end of November of the year prior to entry.

Queen Ethelburga's School
A Music Scholarly of £500 p.a. is available.

Queen Margaret's School
Music Scholarships up to the value of 50% of full fees plus free tuition on two instruments are available. There are also Music Exhibitions. The auditions are in February. For further details please contact the *Director of Music.*

Queenswood School
1 Major Music Scholarship value 50% awarded annually to external candidates.
3 Music Scholarships value 25% awarded annually. The Dame Gillian Weir Organ Scholarship value 50% – one available at any one time. Auditions in January/February.

Red Maids' School
Two Music Scholarships are awarded, usually at 11+. The Major Scholarship covers the cost of lessons, to be taken at the School, on two instruments, together with a reduction in tuition fees. The Minor Scholarship covers the cost of lessons, to be taken at the School, on two instruments.

Redland High School
There are two Music Scholarships awarded at 11+, 13+ and at 16+. One of the Music Scholarships awarded is to the value of ½ the fees, the other covers the cost of tuition on two instruments.

The Royal Masonic School for Girls
There are two Music Scholarships, of value approximately 30% of the fees, available at 11+. A Music Scholarship of similar value is available at the Sixth Form level. The benefits of these Scholarships include free tuition on an instrument of the scholar's choice.

Roedean School
Music Scholarships are awarded for both Junior and Sixth Form candidates and are of the same value as those for academic subjects. Exceptional musical ability and potential are looked for and Junior candidates are therefore expected to play 2 instruments and to have reached at least Grade V standard in the first instrument. Any candidate who is uncertain about her eligibility to enter the examination may attend an individual pre-audition at the School in the term preceding the examination. Junior Music scholars will be asked to sit English, Mathematics and General written papers.

Royal School, Haslemere
On *Music* and one *Drama* scholarship are available at 11+ and 16+ worth 10% of the school tuition fees. These are awarded for outstanding merit and promise. Candidates must also satisfy the academic requirements of the School. Auditions for 11+ are held in January and for 16+ in November.

St Alban's High School
One Music Scholarship is offered annually at 11+ entry. Candidates who have first reached the required standard in the entrance examinations are asked to attend the Music School for auditions.

St Anthony's – Leweston School
Music Scholarships and Bursaries to the value of up to ²/₃ fees and free tuition on up to two instruments can be awarded. It is also the School's policy to increase and to award Scholarships to girls already in the School. Every girl's progress is reviewed each year.

St. Catherine's School, Bramley
Music Scholarship
There is a Music Scholarship for pupils entering the Sixth Form, to the value of ¹/₃ of current School Fees. Further details from the Director of Music.

In addition there are five types of music Awards available for free Music Tuition.

St David's School, Ashford
One or two may be made available annually, to new entrants. Value ¹/₃ total school fees. Occasionally free tuition in one specialism to new entrants or current pupils.

St Elphin's School
A Music Scholarship is awarded annually, which offers half fees plus free tuition in two musical instruments.

St Felix School
The Hess Music Scholarship, value 33% of fees, is offered annually for outstanding promise in Music. It may be held in addition to an Academic Award.

Candidates will be invited to an audition at which they will be expected to perform on two instruments, one of which must be an orchestral instrument. Alternatively, candidates may offer one orchestral instrument and take a voice test. They will be expected to have reached at least Grade V standard on their main instrument by the age of 11.

The Award will be subject to review at the end of each academic year. Further details from the *Registrar.*

St Francis' College
One Music Scholarship is awarded annually to the value of 50% of the tuition fees plus free tuition on two musical instruments.

St Leonard's School
One Music Scholarship of £2000 per annum on entrance at any age.

St Leonards – Mayfield School
At 11+ and 13+ are awarded to Roman Catholic girls, are means-tested, and give free tuition on two instruments.

St Margaret's, Bushey
A Music Scholarship for 2 years in the Sixth Form to the value of ¹/₃ of the boarding fees.

St Margaret's School, Edinburgh
There is one Scholarship for entry to S1 worth ½ tuition fees plus free tuition on a musical instrument. Candidates will be auditioned but must also sit the Academic Scholarship papers and are expected to be of good general standard.

St Margaret's, Exeter
Music Scholarships, to the value of up to 90% of full fees plus free instrumental tuition, are available from 11+ onwards. Auditions held in February/March of previous academic year.

St Martin's, Solihull
A Music Scholarship is offered at 11+ to the value of ¹/₃ of full fees plus free tuition in one instrument.

St Mary's School, Ascot
One music Scholarship worth up to 60% of tuition fees is awarded annually to a pupil entering the School at 10+ or 11+. Candidates must have qualified to at least Grade III on the first study instrument at the time of application.

St Mary's School, Calne
One Music Entrance Scholarship per year at 11+ or 12+ is available, worth up to one third of the annual fees (day or boarding) until completion of the Upper Fifth year, which may be supplemented by a bursary on a means test basis if necessary. This scholarship is subject to a satisfactory performance at Common Entrance and candidates must be recommended by their present school.

One Music and one Drama Sixth Form Scholarship per year, each worth up to one third of the annual fees (day or boarding) are available for entry into the Sixth Form. Sixth Form Scholarships are open to external candidates only if there are places available in the Sixth Form.

Further details of all scholarships are available from the *Admissions Secretary.*

St Mary's, Shaftesbury
One major Music Scholarship at 50% of full fees, plus tuition fees in one instrument, is offered annually. In addition there are a number of Minor Music Scholarships comprising tuition fees for at least one instrument and for a second where a girl shows exceptional talent and promise. These scholarships are open to candidates at 11+, 12+, 13+ or 16+.

St Mary's, Wantage
Music Scholarships are awarded at 13+ and Sixth Form.

At *13+*, 2 of the 3 13+ Scholarships may be awarded for Music. The Director of Music is looking for musical potential rather than actual grades achieved.

At *Sixth Form* entry there is one Music Scholarship awarded every other year. Applicants for both entry levels will be auditioned including performance on two instruments, sight-reading and aural tests. The value of each award is ¹/₃ boarding fees, plus free tuition on two instruments. All scholarships are open to internal and external applicants. For further details, please contact the *Admissions Secretary.*

St Swithun's School
Music awards provide free tuition on up to two instruments.

Sherborne School for Girls
Music Awards: Awards of up to 50% of the current fees (with free tuition on two instruments). Music Exhibitions offering free tuition on two instruments.

For the Music Awards there is no age limit. Auditions are held in February. Further particulars may be obtained from the *Director of Music*.

Sir William Perkins's School
Music Scholarships will be worth up to half the academic tuition fees.

Stamford High School
Two Music Exhibitions are offered per year consisting of free tuition on an instrument. These are offered to candidates of any age. Candidates must be able to satisfy the schools' entrance requirements academically and to perform on their instrument(s) at audition (normally in February).

Sydenham High School
A Music Scholarship may be awarded on entry at 11+.

Tudor Hall
Annual Nesta Inglis Music Scholarship for entry at 11+, 12+ or 13+ to the value of 15% of boarding fee whether held by a boarder or day girl. Music bursaries of free tuition in an instrument are available to entrants with Grade 5 in that instrument before arrival.

Wentworth College
Girls joining the school between 11 and 13 years old may qualify for a music scholarship which is worth up to 50% of fees (day or boarding) plus free tuition for up to two instruments. Bursaries and an exhibition are also available to deserving young musicians already at the school.

Wychwood School
Two Music Scholarships are offered at ages 11+ or 16+ to cover instrument tuition. Candidates will be expected to play two prepared pieces on their instrument(s) and to do some sight reading and aural tests on the afternoon of the test day.

Wycombe Abbey School
Up to two major Music Scholarships worth between 30% and 50% of the annual fee and Music Exhibitions of varying value are available to candidates under the age of 14 on 1st September of the proposed year of entry.

A Music Scholarship is also available to girls entering the Sixth Form.

For details and entry forms, please contact the Registrar, Wycombe Abbey School, High Wycombe, Bucks HP11 1PE. (Tel: 01494 897008).

Art Scholarships

Abbot's Hill
Two Art Scholarships up to 1/3 fees may be awarded.

Amberfield
Music Scholarships are awarded to applicants at (11+), held for three years, and again before entering (Year 10). Candidates for these Bursaries will present a modest folio of unaided and preferably undirected Art work. Under guidance in the Art Department, they will be asked to draw from observation and discuss their work.

Badminton School
Art Scholarships are open to all applicants, external and internal, and portfolios are usually submitted in January preceding entry. Maximum awards of 50% may be enhanced in cases of need.

Bedford High School
A Scholarship is available on entry to the Sixth Form.

Bedgebury School
Art Scholarships are offered at 7+, 11+, 13+ and 16+. These can be in any Art medium and include CDT, Textiles, Ceramics and Jewellery. Major Awards cover up to 2/3 day fees, depending on merit and financial status. Art candidates may submit their original work in 2 or 3 dimensions. (All Scholarship candidates take the academic examination).

Further details and application forms are available from the *Registrar*.

Benenden School
Sixth Form Entry. Substantial awards available. For girls under the age of 17 on 1st September following the examination. Examinations are held in November preceding entry in September. The examination for the Art Scholarship will consist of one hour on a set-piece drawing followed by an interview based on the candidate's portfolio on which particular emphasis will be placed for evidence of commitment and enthusiasm. Candidates are required to show that they have reached the general academic standard of any entrant by sitting two qualifying papers in subjects which they intend to study at Advanced Level. For further information, please contact the *Admissions Secretary*.

Berkhamsted Collegiate School
Castle Campus: At 13+ one Art scholarship awarded of a minimum of £500 pa variable according to merit on the basis of a portfolio of work, a practical test and an interview.

Additional Exhibitions or Minor Scholarships may be awarded for artistic ability at the discretion of the Principal.

The Cheltenham Ladies' College
One Minor Art Scholarship worth 25% of the annual fees is available to Sixth Form candidates.

Downe House
Up to two Art Scholarships to the value of half the annual fees may be awarded each year.

Junior candidates must be under 14 on the following 1st September.

Senior candidates are required to achieve grade C or above in five GCSE subjects before taking up their award in the following September. Candidates will be required to submit a portfolio of work and would be asked to do an observational drawing test. Further particulars may be obtained from the *Registrar*.

The Godolphin School
Art Scholarships

13+ and Sixth Form scholarships are awarded for outstanding merit and promise, candidates must present a portfolio. They are also expected to reach an acceptable academic standard.

Haberdashers' Monmouth School for Girls
Arkwright Scholarship: Haberdasher's Monmouth School for Girls subscribes to this scheme awarding a Sixth Form Scholarship to a candidate wishing to take Design Technology at A Level.

James Allen's Girls' School
Scholarships are offered at 11+ and 16+ to girls who are successful in the Entrance Examination.

Kilgraston School
For entry to Upper Fourth (S2) upwards. One or two Awards are made each year. Portfolios are presented on the day of the Scholarship Examinations.

Malvern Girls College
Scholarships to the value of 50% of the current fees and exhibitions to the value of 25% of current fees are awarded annually. The Art Scholarship examination consists of a three hour examination in the School plus a short portfolio interview with the Head of Department. The paper will be available two weeks before the examination to give candidates time to prepare. Candidates should also bring a portfolio of their work.

New Hall, Chelmsford
1 at 16+. Small award open to internal and external candidates.

Prior's Field
Art Scholarship. This is valued at 50% of current fees. Candidates should submit examples of completed work in drawing, painting and craft. In addition, candidates will sit a one-and-a-half hour examination.

Further details are available from the School, but applications for Scholarships must be with the School by the end of November of the year prior to entry.

Queen Ethelburga's School
Art Scholarships to the value of £500 per annum. Candidates will be interviewed by the Director of Art and will be expected to bring a portfolio of their work with them. They will also be expected to do a practical test. Art may be taken in its widest sense and any form of two or three-dimensional work which shows candidate's interests and ability is acceptable.

Queenswood School
2 Creative Arts Scholarships value 25% available annually.
Assessment in January/February.
Full details and application form from the Registrar.

Redland High School
These are awarded at Sixth Form level.

The Royal Masonic School for Girls
An Art Scholarship, of value approximately 30% of the fees, is available for competition at Sixth Form level.

Roedean School
Art Scholarships are only awarded to Sixth Form candidates. They will be required to sit the General Essay set for Academic Scholarships candidates and must bring a portfolio of their work.

Royal School, Haslemere
At 11+ and 16+, Art scholarships are available to the value of 10% of the school's tuition fees. Candidates must also satisfy the school's academic requirements.

St Anthony's – Leweston School
Awards for Art, Drama and Sport may be made. However girls must be in attendance at the School before these Awards can be made.

St. Catherine's School, Bramley
Art Scholarship

There is an Art Scholarship for pupils entering the Sixth Form, to the value of one third of the school fees.

St David's School, Ashford
One or two may be made available annually, to new entrants value 1/3 total school fees.

Occasionally free tuition in one specialism to new entrants or current pupils.

St Leonard's School
Scholarships in Art and Design are offered on an occasional basis if a candidate with outstanding ability of any age should present herself.

St Margaret's, Bushey
An Art Scholarship for 2 years in Sixth Form to the value of 1/3 of the Boarding Fees.

St Mary's School, Calne
One Art Sixth Form Scholarship per year worth up to one third of the annual fees (day or boarding) is available for entry into the Sixth Form.

Further details of all scholarships are available from the *Admissions Secretary.*

St Mary's, Shaftesbury
One Art Scholarship at 50% of full fees is offered annually. The selection process has two stages: initially all candidates are required to submit a portfolio of work. They are then required to attend for interview and do some set practical work within the Art Department. The Scholarship is open to candidates at 13+, 14+ or 16+.

St Mary's, Wantage
Art Scholarships are awarded at entry at 13+. 2 of the 3 13+ Scholarships may be awarded for Art. Applicants will be expected to bring a portfolio of their work in any medium. There will also be an interview with the Head of Art. The value of each award is 1/3 boarding fees. All scholarships are open to internal and external applicants. For further details, please contact the *Admissions Secretary.*

Sherborne School for Girls
An award of up to half current fees. Candidates should be under 14 on 1st September following the examination. Held in late January or early February. Candidates will be required to bring a portfolio of work with them and would be asked to do some work in the Art Department while they are here. They would be required to stay overnight.

Wentworth College
Girls joining between 11 and 13 years old may qualify for an Art Scholarship which is worth up to 50% of fees (day or boarding).

Wychwood School
Two Creative Arts Scholarships are offered at age 11+ to candidates with outstanding ability in Music, Art of Creative Writing. One Scholarship worth £1,000 and the other £500.

(i) English: Candidates are asked to bring six different pieces of writing, including poetry, a story and a description. These will be discussed with the Head of English.
(ii) Art: Candidates are asked to bring six artistic compositions or craft items which will be discussed with the Head of Art. A short unprepared task will be undertaken on the afternoon of the test day.

Educational/Academic Awards

Abbot's Hill
Bursaries awarded to daughters of old girls, clergy and teachers.

Amberfield
Awarded after the 11+ Examination. It is open to all candidates, external and internal. No application is necessary.

It will be awarded to a candidate who has scored highly in the examinations and at interview, shows a broad understanding and enthusiasm for a particular Academic interest or hobby, having a lively and enquiring mind.

Candidates for the Academic Bursary will be selected and invited for further testing and interview after the entrance examination.

Atherley School
There are Bursaries for the daughters of Clergy and for Sixth Formers. The latter is based on merit and means.

Badminton School
"All-rounder" Awards are offered to girls aged 11, 12, 13 or 16 up to 50%, reflecting ability in Music, Art, Sport, Academics or other special talents. There are also John James assisted places for local Bristol girls.

Bedford High School
The Headmistress's Award is available to girls who have outstanding ability in any area and/or who contribute to school life in an exceptional way.

Bedgebury School
Academic Scholarships are offered at 7+, 11+, 13+ and 16+ to the value of $^2/_3$ day fees, depending on merit and financial status. Examinations are held early in the Spring term (Autumn Term for 16+). Candidates are examined in English, Mathematics, Standardized Test (age 7+ and 11+), with Science, French and an optional Latin paper at 13+. Science scholarships are offered at 16+. For entry to Sixth Form (16+), candidates choose 3 subjects related to their proposed A Level course *and sit a General Paper. All candidates are interviewed by the Headmistress.*

Further details and application forms are available from the *Registrar*.

Casterton School
Bursaries for the daughters of Clergy are available. In addition, there are a small number of bursaries for the daughters of schoolmasters.

Channing School
Unitarians may apply for a Foundation Bursary in case of need.

The Cheltenham Ladies' College
Day Girl Awards
Two Sixth Form Day Girl Awards, both worth 40% of the annual day girl fees are also available.

Colston's Girls' School
Academic Awards
Some Bursaries are awarded to first and sixth year entrants to girls of proven academic ability where financial hardship would otherwise result.

Edgbaston High School
A number of Sixth Form Bursaries are available for candidates of good academic ability in financial need. They may cover part or full fees. Please apply to the Headmistress for further details.

Elmslie Girls' School
Two Governors Scholarships are offered annually on academic merit at Sixth Form level. Each is worth up to the full fee. They are decided by examination and interview. A third Scholarship, the Elizabeth Brodie Scholarship of £500 per annum, is available for a girl entering the Sixth Form with the intention of going on to university. A special application form is required for all these Scholarships. Full details from the *Headmistress.*

Francis Holland School, Clarence Gate
There is a remission of up to $^1/_3$ fees for daughters of Clergy.

The Godolphin School
Educational/Academic Awards
Six Foundation Scholarships, worth up to 70% of the boarding fees, are available from time to time to able candidates from single parent, divorced or separated families who have been brought up as members of the Church of England.

Old Godolphin Association Scholarship
A scholarship, worth up to 50% of the boarding fees, is available from time to time to the daughter of an Old Godolphin, either a girl of exceptional talent or an able, though not necessarily exceptional, girl who is in need of financial assistance.

Guildford High School
An External Competitive Scholarship and a number of Internal Bursaries are available at Sixth Form level. Bursaries are available throughout the School for daughters of Clergy.

Haberdashers' Monmouth School for Girls
Sixth Form Scholarship: awarded to an external candidate on the strength of school reports, interview and two timed essays.

Headington School
Internal Awards valid for 4 years are awarded annually at 14½ to 2 pupils value £600.

Hethersett Old Hall School
Bursaries are available, subject to means, to daughters of the Clergy, HM Forces Personnel and the Metropolitan Police, who satisfy the requirements of the Entrance Examination of their age group.

Bursaries may be awarded, subject to means, by the Governors to some girls in the School who wish to continue their education in the Sixth Form.

Holy Child School
A limited number of Bursaries are available to enable girls of high academic ability to continue their education into the Sixth Form.

Holy Trinity College
Academic Scholarships (maximum ½ fees) are awarded at Sixth Form level on the results of a competitive scholarship examination taken in the spring term.
10 Assisted places are also available.

Leicester High School for Girls
Bishop Williams Scholarships are awarded to girls at 11+ who show outstanding academic promise.

A limited number of bursaries are available at Sixth Form level and Sixth Form scholarships are awarded to girls with outstanding GCSE results.

The Maynard School
Wolfson Foundation Bursaries are available to Sixth Formers. Up to 4 Governors' Leaving Exhibitions are awarded in the Upper Sixth year.

Moira House Girls School
Daughters of Old Girls of the School and daughters of members of the Services are eligible for a 10% Bursary.

The Mount School
Bursaries
Members of the Society of Friends are assessed under the Joint Bursaries Scheme for Friends' Schools and according to need may be helped by other Friends' funds in addition to School funds.

While very limited amounts of bursary help are available for other candidates, these are usually given to candidates with Mount or Quaker links.

North Foreland Lodge
Science Scholarship
A Science Scholarship is available at Sixth Form level for both internal and external candidates.

North London Collegiate School
Bursaries are awarded in cases of financial need.

Princess Helena College
One boarding and one day scholarship, each to the value of 50% of fees, is available annually for entrance at 11+, 12+ and 13+. Scholarship examinations for these junior scholarships take place in February. Two sixth form scholarships are also available, to external as well as internal candidates. These are worth 60% of fees and scholarship examinations take place in October for entry in the following September.

Prior's Field
A Bursary of 25% of fees is awarded on the results of the Common Entrance or our own examination to the daughter or granddaughter of an Old Girl.
Further details are available from School.

Queen Margaret's School
Bursaries are available for daughters of Clergy and for daughters of Old Girls.

Queenswood School
The Old Queenswoodian's Bursary is available to the daughter or granddaughter of an old Queenswoodian. Other Bursaries may be available from time to time at the Principal's discretion.

Red Maid's School
Up to three Whitson Bursaries are available annually to enable Fifth Year Red Maids to continue their education in the Sixth Form at Red Maids'. They are tenable for the two years of the Sixth Form where girls follow A Level courses.

Redland High School
Sixth Form Awards
A number of Sixth Form Academic Scholarships and Awards are given each year. The value may be up to ½ remission of fees.

Roedean School
A limited sum of Bursary money is available for award to parents of girls at, or registered for entry to the school at 13+ or above, who can show financial need. These Bursaries are allocated by the Awards Committee and take the form of a fixed sum, the amount of which is reviewed annually. The Old Roedeanian Association also sponsors one Sixth Form Award (worth half fees) for daughters of Old Roedeanians who would benefit from a Roedean education. Full details available from the *Bursar* on request.

The Royal Masonic School for Girls
Foundation Scholarships
Six Closed Scholarships, available only for boarding girls who are the daughters of freemasons, may be provided at 11+. The value of each of these is based upon a means test.
Business Studies
A Business Studies Scholarship, of value approximately 30% of the fees, is available for competition at the Sixth Form level.

Royal School, Haslemere
Bursaries are available for:
Daughters of serving members of HM Forces, who are granted bursaries of 5–15% of the tuition fees.
Daughters of old girls and siblings are also eligible for consideration, as are daughters of school teachers.

St Catherine's School, Bramley
O.G.A. Bursary
There is an Old Girls' Association Sixth Form Bursary which is awarded to a daughter of a deserving Old Girl on criteria decided between the Headmistress and the Committee of the O.G.A.
For further details please contact the Registrar.

St David's School, Ashford
A limited number of bursaries may be made available to current pupils.

St Elphin's School
A number of open and closed Academic Scholarships are available, for entrance at 11+, 12+, 13+ and in the Sixth Form.
Bursaries are considered in cases of special need. These are awarded at the discretion of the Head and Trustees of the School.

St Francis' College
Bursaries to assist parents of able girls may be awarded at the discretion of the Headmistress. Application for such assistance should be made to the *Headmistress.*

St Leonard's School
Bursaries may be awarded at the discretion of the Headmistress and the Chairman of Council and are confidential to them.
(*a*) For daughters of former pupils of St Leonards or those with close connection with the school.
(*b*) For daughters of Teachers and Ministers of the Church.
(*c*) MacRobert Trust Bursaries for girls whose parents are in financial need.

St Margaret's, Aberdeen
Three Bursaries may be awarded at each of V and VI Senior level. These carry a remission of 1/6 annual fees in V Senior and 1/3 annual fees in VI Senior.

St Margaret's, Exeter
Bursaries, of 25% fees remission, are available to daughters of Clergy. Academic Bursaries for able Sixth Form applicants.

St Mary's School, Ascot
The Ascot Old Girls' Bursary for 60% of school fees is awarded annually to the daughter of an Ascot Old Girl entering the School for the Sixth Form. Applications should be made by November 1st prior to the year of entry.

St Mary's, Shaftesbury
Two Sixth Form Scholarships at 50% of full fees are offered annually.

St Mary's, Wantage
Sports Scholarship
Sports Scholarships are awarded at entry at 13+. 2 of the 3 13+ Scholarships may be awarded for Sport. Where possible, candidates will be expected to demonstrate their sporting skills. Emphasis will be on commitment to their chosen sport. The value of each award is 1/3 boarding fees. All scholarships are open to internal and external applicants. For further details, please contact the *Admissions Secretary.*
Educational/Academic Awards
All Round Ability Scholarships are awarded at entry at 13+. 2 of the 3 13+ Scholarships may be awarded for Exceptional All Round Ability. This will be based upon a comprehensive report from the candidate's present school. A good academic standard is looked for but the ability to contribute fully to the life of the school is most important. Candidates will be asked to nominate 2 areas in which to show evidence of their abilities. The value of each award is 1/3 boarding fees. All scholarships are open to internal and external applicants. For further details, please contact the *Admissions Secretary.*

St Swithun's School
Bursaries are considered in cases of special need. There are also assisted places available for Sixth Form Day Girls.

Sir William Perkins's School
A limited number of Bursaries carry remission depending on need and funds available.

Sydenham High School
The GDST Bursaries Fund provides financial assistance to enable suitably qualified girls whose parents could not otherwise afford the fees to enter or remain in the Senior Department. Bursaries are awarded on the basis of financial need though academic merit is taken into account. An application form can be obtained from the Admissions Secretary. However, it is recognised that occasions will arise when some form of short-term assistance is required and a small fund exists to help in such cases.

Tudor Hall
The Pearce Trust offers some financial help to scholarship holders or others. In addition:

Sixth Form. In financial need, parents should write directly to the Headmistress.

Sisters. There is a discount of 5% of the fees for younger sisters whilst more than one member of the same family are in school together.

Walthamstow Hall
The Millennium Bursary Scheme provides assistance with fees in cases of financial hardship. The Foundation Fund for the Children of Missionaries assists with boarding and tuition for the daughters of missionaries serving abroad.

Wentworth College
Daughters of ministers and lay members of the United Reformed and Congregational Churches may be eligible for a bursary from the Milton Mount Foundation.

Wycombe Abbey School
The Seniors' Association offers a limited number of bursaries for the daughters and granddaughters of Members of the Association. Awards are made to candidates of suitable character, disposition and potential assessed by interview with representatives of the Seniors and with the Headmistress. The value is determined according to family financial circumstances and bursaries are held subject to the satisfactory conduct and progress of the recipient.

Further particulars are obtainable from the Secretary to the Bursary Committee, Miss Sue Davies, 28 St Mary's Road, Eastbourne, East Sussex BN21 1QD.

Applications should be made **at least two years** ahead of entry to the School.

PART III

Schools appearing in Part III are those whose Heads are members of the Society of Headmasters' and Headmistresses' of Independent Schools

Abbey Gate College

Saighton Grange Saighton Chester CH3 6EG
Tel: 01244 332077
Fax: 01244 335510

Founded in 1977, Abbey Gate College is a co-educational day school for 350 boys and girls from 4–18 years of age. The school is set in beautiful grounds at Saighton Grange some three miles south of the City of Chester. The history of Saighton Grange goes back long before the Norman Conquest. However, the most ancient portion of the present building is the red sandstone castellated gateway and tower, with its oriel window and spiral staircase, which was built in 1489. The remainder of the present building is Victorian. From 1853, the Grange was a residence of the Grosvenor family, and for some years it was home to the Duke of Westminster. Recent additions to the buildings include a large Sports Hall (1993) and an IT suite (1994). In September 1996 the Junior Department was re-sited in the former school at Aldford, a quiet village only two miles from Saighton.

In 2000 an extension at Aldford provided 2 new rooms for the new Infant entry.

Motto: *Audentior Ito*

Visitor: His Grace The Duke of Westminster

Chairman of Governors: D A Bunting, FCA

Headmaster: **E W Mitchell,** BA Hons, PGCE (Wales) (*English Language and Literature*)

Deputy Head: D Meadows, BA Hons, PGCE (*History*)

Academic Staff:

A Austen, BSc Hons, PGCE (*Geography*)
Mrs A Bird, BA Hons, PGCE (*Art*)
Mrs S Campbell-Woodward, BEd (*Modern Languages*)
J P Gallagher, MA, DipEd (*Biology*)
Mrs S Graham, BA Hons, PGCE (*Modern Languages*)
K Gray, BSc Hons, PGCE (*Geography, Geology, ICT*)
A P Green, BEd (*PE*)
Mrs C A Haines, BSc Hons, PGCE (*Mathematics*)
Miss C Helm, BA Hons, PGCE (*History*)
Mrs J Jones, CertEd (*Home Economics and Careers*)
Mrs S J Kay, BSc Hons (*Mathematics*)
R Kitchen, BSc Hons (*Mathematics*)
P Lincoln, MA, BA Hons, PGCE (*History and Politics*)
Mrs K Long, BA Hons, PGCE (*English*)
Mrs J Magill, MA, DipEd (*English*)
Mrs K A Pilsbury, BEd (*English*)
Mrs K Price, BA, PGCE (*PE*)
Dr J A Quayle, BSc Hons, PhD (*Biology and Chemistry*)
R A Slater, BSc Hons, PGCE (*Physics*)
S F Smith, BA, CertEd, ARCM, LMusLCM (*Music*)
M Tempest, BEng Hons, PGCE (*Materials Science/Eng*)
M Thompson, BEd Hons (*Technology*)
Miss V Thompson, BA Hons (*Art*)

Part-time Staff:

Mrs M Fraser, BA Hons (*Geography*)
Mrs S Kinsey, BEd Hons, AVCM (*English*)
Mrs P Selby, MA, PGCE (*Business Studies; Librarian*)
Mrs A Taylor, BSc Hons (*Chemistry*)
Mrs J E Webb, BA Hons (*Modern Languages*)

Junior Department:

Mrs D Williams, MEd (*Head of Department*)
Mrs J Gallagher, BSc Hons, PhD, PGCE
Mrs V Goodwin, BMus Hons, PGCE
R Harrison, BMus
Mrs L Lake, BA
Mrs A Williams, BEd Hons
Mrs K Williams, BEd Hons

Musical Instruments Teaching:

Mrs A Holmes, BEd Hons (*Piano*)
A Lewis, DipMusTech (*Brass*)
E Milner, ALMus, RMSM (*Clarinet/Saxophone*)
P Oliver, BMus, LTCL (*Guitar*)
Miss R Owen (*Clarinet/Flute*)
S A Rushforth (*Violin*)

Speech and Drama: Mrs C Faithfull, LRAM, ANEA

Bursar: W G Osmond, MSc

Bursar's Assistant: Mrs L Darlington Davies

Headmaster's Secretary: Mrs A M Barton

School Secretary: Mrs K Walker

Aims. The College encourages its pupils to aim for academic success; a framework is provided within which each pupil will have the opportunity to develop his or her full potential. Outside the strict academic sphere our objective is to introduce our boys and girls to a wide range of extra-curricular activities. In addition much emphasis is placed on good manners and discipline; this is a friendly family school particularly aware of the values of moulding personality and character in conjunction with the search for excellence in the classroom. We provide a caring environment; we are proud of the relationship between the teaching staff and their pupils; no child at Abbey Gate will feel lost; everyone is made to feel important in at least one area of the educational process.

Academic Programme. The College aims to provide children with a broad general education through GCSE, AS and A2 Levels, to university, or other forms of higher education. In the First and Second Forms all pupils study Art, Drama, English, French, Geography, History, Mathematics, Music, Physical Education, Religious Studies, Science, Spoken English, Technology (including Information and Communication Technology, Home Economics and Design).

In the Third Form German and Spanish are introduced. In the Fourth and Fifth Forms an option scheme takes effect; three compulsory subjects: English, English Literature and Mathematics are taken and normally pupils will

* Head of Department § Part Time or Visiting
† Housemaster/Housemistress ¶ Old Pupil
‡ See below list of staff for meaning

opt also for one or two modern languages and a compulsory course in the Sciences. In total eight, nine or ten subjects are available and in addition a non-examination Social Studies course is taught to all Fourth and Fifth Form pupils.

Option subjects for GCSE are taken from the following: Art, Biology, Chemistry, Design, French, Geography, German, History, Home Economics, Music, Physics, Science, Spanish, Technology.

In the Sixth Form A2 Level (and AS Level) subjects available according to demand are: Mathematics, English Literature, English Language, History, Politics, Geography, Business Studies, Physics, Chemistry, Biology, French, German, Art, Music and Technology. GCSE in Drama and Art are available as additional options and a number of practical skills sessions are on offer enabling students to develop key skills.

In the Lower Sixth students may devote most of their general studies time to the Young Enterprise scheme which gives theoretical and practical knowledge of the business world. Opportunity for community service is also given. In the Upper Sixth the programme is structured to meet the requirements of the AS and A2 Level General Studies examinations. A number of outside speakers visit the school and regular visits to theatres, conferences or galleries etc are arranged.

Music. The College is well known throughout Chester and North Wales for the outstanding quality of its music. The Chapel Choir has for several years undertaken week long summer visits to Cathedrals in various parts of the country. So far it has visited Ely, Gloucester, Peterborough, St Albans, Ripon, Tewkesbury, Hereford, Winchester, Durham, York and Bath, as well as touring Holland, Germany, Denmark and the USA, and in 2000 France, Germany and Austria.

The College has also a School Choir, and The Saighton Syncopators dance band.

Two annual Services are held in Chester Cathedral at Christmas and Easter and the Chapel Choir sings Evensong annually at St Paul's Cathedral.

The pupils may take instrumental lessons with visiting staff and are prepared for the Associated Board's Examinations.

Drama. There is one major dramatic production each year, usually alternating "straight" drama and musical. Pupils are also prepared for examinations in Speech and Drama (English Speaking Board) and regularly enter the local competitions.

Sport. The College has extensive playing fields, tennis courts and sports hall. The latter covers 544 sq metres and offers four badminton courts, five-a-side soccer, volleyball, basketball, netball, indoor hockey, tennis and cricket nets.

All pupils are expected to participate in physical education and games. Boys play rugby, soccer, cricket and tennis; girls play hockey, netball, tennis and rounders. Cricket is the major summer sport for boys. Athletics is also popular for both boys and girls and all sports provide full fixture lists for the various College teams. The local swimming pool is reserved each week for sessions with a fully-qualified instructor.

The College competes in both Regional and National Independent Schools sports events, and has enjoyed great success in both athletics and swimming. Pupils are regularly sent for trials for Chester and District and County teams. The College has had pupils selected to represent Cheshire in hockey, cricket and rugby. A soccer tour to Malta, first undertaken in 1995, was repeated in 1997. The Senior Hockey Squad toured Holland in October 1997 and the Isle of Man in 2000.

Other Activities. The College has a remarkable record of giving generously to Charities and lunch-time activities serve to raise money through sponsorship and tuck-shops. At weekends and during holidays many pupils take advantage of outdoor pursuits and most of these will enter the Duke of Edinburgh Award Scheme involving sailing, canoeing, mountaineering, camping etc.

Admission. *Senior School:* Most pupils enter the College at eleven following an Entrance Examination held in the Spring Term and are expected to continue into the Sixth Form after GCSE. Each pupil is allocated to one of the two Senior School Houses: Hastings and Marmion.

Junior Department: Pupils are admitted to the Junior Department at Aldford by means of short test and interview at ages seven, eight, nine and ten. It is expected that children already in this part of the school will move directly into the College at age eleven after taking the Entrance Examination.

Infant Department: Entry at ages 4, 5 and 6 is also available.

Sixth Form: Priority is given to existing pupils but places are offered to others and are conditional on satisfactory results at GCSE (Key Stage 4).

Scholarships. Two academic scholarships are awarded following the results of the Entrance Examination.

For musical talent three awards are offered including Music Exhibitions at First Form and Sixth Form level and the Daphne Herbert Choral Scholarship.

Old Saightonians. All pupils are encouraged to join the Old Saightonians' Association. Further details of the Association can be obtained from the Headmaster at the College.

Fees. Tuition: Junior Department £3,885 per annum; Infant Department £3,321 per annum; Senior School £5,874 per annum.

Charitable status. Deeside House Educational Trust is a Registered Charity, number 273586. It exists to provide co-education for children in the Chester and North Wales areas.

Austin Friars School

Carlisle CA3 9PB.
Tel: (01228) 528042
Fax: (01228) 810327
e-mail: hm@afschool.fsnet.co.uk

Austin Friars is an independent Augustinian Catholic School founded by members of the Order in 1951, and is one of many Augustinian schools to be found in other parts of the world. The School provides secondary education for about 300 boys and girls from ages 11 to 18. Pupils from all denominations are welcome in the School, giving all the opportunity to embrace the Christian traditions on which the School is founded.

The School stands in its own grounds of 25 acres overlooking the historic City of Carlisle in North Cumbria. It is within easy reach of the M6 and there is excellent access to the North West and North East of England and to Scotland. There are also outstanding opportunities to take advantage of the cultural heritage of the area stretching back to Roman times and Hadrian's Wall, and for outdoor activities in the Lake District, Northumberland and north of the border in Scotland.

Austin Friars aims to foster the personal development of its pupils spiritually, academically, socially and physically to enable them to take their place creatively in society. The School has high expectations of its pupils and encourages them to develop their potential in a disciplined, happy, positive and productive atmosphere. Consequently Austin Friars has established an enviable reputation for bringing out the best in each of its pupils. This means not only attaining high academic standards but realising sound spiritual and social values, self-discipline and the development of a sense of purpose for life.

Austin Friars is justifiably proud of its academic facilities, the breadth of its curriculum and its pupils' record in public examinations which are among the best in the North of England. The School's highly qualified staff and the involvement of members of the Augustinian community, the close attention to the individual pupil throughout the school career and the nurturing of a positive attitude to work ensure consistently good results and a sound preparation for higher education.

Both staff and pupils appreciate that school extends beyond the classroom and non-academic activities are a strong facet of Austin Friars. The School is an excellent centre for developing new and existing interests and talents and offers numerous opportunities for participation in cultural and leisure activities and involvement in charitable work. Each year the School produces a musical, a play, a musical evening and a concert. There are regular visits to theatres, concerts and galleries and school visits to the Continent. Qualified and enthusiastic staff provide coaching in team sports, and the School's record in inter-school competition is acknowledged far beyond Cumbria. Awards in the Duke of Edinburgh Scheme are gained annually by a significant number of pupils, and other outdoor pursuits include canoeing, fell walking, sailing and ski trips to the USA.

The School Motto is *"In Omnibus Caritas"*. The word "caritas" embraces so much more than the accepted English translation "charity": it is indeed a summary of all the virtues. Christian principles hold a central place in the life of the School with a pupil's faith creating a lively and effective influence on attitudes and activities. Pupils have full opportunity to develop and to deepen their knowledge of themselves and their faith in prayer, worship and religious studies.

Chairman of Governors: Mrs V O'Neill

***Headmaster:* Mr N J B O'Sullivan**, MA (Cantab), NPQH

Deputy Head (Academic): Mr G R Barr, BA, PGCE

Deputy Head (Pastoral): Mr M Heywood, BA, PGCE

Senior Mistress: Mrs M A Chapman, BA, AIL, PGCE

Prior: Revd B Rolls, OSA, BA, BD

Bursar: Mr I Blair

Heads of Department:

Art and Design: Mrs A Mackay, MA
Biology: Mr I Whetton, BSc, CertEd
Design Technology: Mr T Rogstad, BEd
Chemistry: Mr C D Foyston, MA (Oxon), PGCE
Classical Civilisation: Mrs M A Chapman, BA, AIL, PGCE
Economics: Mr S Cassidy, BA (Cantab), PGCE
English: Mr P T Westmoreland, BA, PGCE
Geography: Mr M Heywood, BA, PGCE
History: Mr G R Barr, BA, PGCE
Mathematics: Mr J Messenger, BSc, PGCE
Modern Languages: Mrs J Quinlan, BA, PGCE
Music: Mr C W J Hattrell, MA (Oxon)
Physical Education: Mr D R Smith, BEd
Physics: Mr J C Dimond, BSc, PGCE
Religious Studies: Mrs E Farren, MA, BD

Housemasters/Mistresses:

Clare: Mr J Messenger and Mrs J Quinlan
Lincoln: Mr D R Smith and Mrs L Davidson
Stafford: Mr S P Dolan and Mrs J Woodward

School Secretary: Mrs S M Castle

Headmaster's Secretary: Mrs C Mellor

Bursar's Secretary: Mrs P M Clarke

Librarian: Mrs L Jones, ALA

Organisation and aims. The School is divided into three "Houses". Pupils have a Housemaster and Housemistress for each of the three Houses. Smaller units are thus created so that each child can receive personal, individual attention.

Pupils are free to approach their Housemaster and Housemistress to discuss whatever problems they may have. The Housemaster/mistress is also responsible for discipline and they are in a position to relate a pupil's behaviour to the general picture of background and character. This ensures that discipline becomes more than an external observance of rules and traditions, and is seen by the pupils to be an integral part of their training and developement.

The priests of the Community live adjacent to the School. At all times they are about the House, moving freely and informally among the pupils. Visitors to the School have frequently commented on the happy, friendly atmosphere that they sense as they move about the building.

Studies. The following subjects are available to GCSE and/or "A" level: English, Latin, French, German, History, Geography, Economics, Mathematics, Further Mathematics, Physics, Chemistry, Biology, Art, Music, Classical Studies, Religious Studies, General Studies, Design Technology, Computer Studies, Information Technology (RSA), PE.

The size of classes is restricted so that each pupil may receive close attention and be taught as an individual. Form Teachers supervise studies in each form. They receive reports periodically from Subject Teachers. In the VIth Forms, each pupil has a Tutor. The Tutor keeps a watchful eye on the pupils' progress, the VIth Formers are expected to learn to organize their time and their work in their own way. Specialist help is available for dyslexic pupils.

The Library Resources Centre is well equipped and designed for serious study, access of information and relaxation. The Centre's Librarian assists pupils in developing their Information Handling Skills and supervise the Careers Library.

Activities. The school Choir and the Dramatic Society's annual production provide important extra-curricular activities during the year. The School Orchestra and Wind Band are also very active. Extra tuition in piano, woodwind, brass, percussion and elocution is provided by peripatetic teachers.

Debating is organised at Junior, Middle and Upper School levels. Other societies include Chess, Bridge, Sailing, Wind-surfing, Fell Walking, Social Services, Canoeing, Photography, Public Speaking, Duke of Edinburgh's Award Scheme, Outdoor Pursuits, Computer, Weight Training and Indoor Cricket. Pupils are encouraged to attend events outside the School in connection with their studies and interests. Outings are organised annually to the continent and to places of interest in Britain. Situated as we are in an area which is rich in Roman History, there are endless opportunities for visiting and studying historical monuments. There are also trips to the Lakes, which can be reached in half-an-hour.

Sport. Rugby, Cross-country in winter; Athletics, Cricket, Tennis in Summer. Badminton, Basketball, Swimming, Volleyball, Hockey and Netball are available throughout the year.

Admission. From primary school at 11 through an Entrance Examination held at the school and from Preparatory school through the Common Entrance. Sixth Form entry is available after completion of GCSE examinations. Entry at other times are by arrangement with the Headmaster.

Fees. (*see* Entrance Scholarship section) £1,855 per

term. There is a reduction of 5% for brothers/sisters in the School at the same time. Scholarships and Bursaries are available.

Travel. Carlisle is a main stopping point for all London-Glasgow trains. It is equally well served from all other major centres. The M6 motorway connects Carlisle with the South, the Midlands and North Wales, and there are excellent links to the east. The A74/M74 is the continuation of the M6 to Glasgow. There is easy access to International Airports.

An invitation to see the School and meet the Headmaster is extended to all those who write for information.

Charitable status. Austin Friars School, which is part of The Order of the Hermit Friars of St Augustine, is a Registered Charity, number 233010. It exists for the purpose of educating boys and girls.

Battle Abbey School

Battle East Sussex TN33 0AD
Tel: (01424) 772385
Fax: (01424) 773573

An Independent Coeducational School for 240 boys and girls between the ages of 2½ and 18, who may be full boarders, weekly boarders or day pupils. The School is administered by BAS (School) Limited, a registered charity.

Governors:
Chairman: R J Dunn, Esq

A P F Alexander, Esq
Dr G Baker, MB, BS
W Blackshaw, Esq
Mrs A Caffyn
C Champion, Esq
Mrs S Davies Jones
W Dexter, Esq
J Harrison, Esq
D Hughes, Esq
I S Mercer, Esq, CBE
Mrs J M Smith
D K Wray, Esq, OBE
Mrs J Yeo

Clerk to the Governors: Mr J Page

Senior Management Team:

***Headmaster:* R C Clark**, Esq, BA, MA(Ed)

Deputy Head (*Senior*): Mrs M P Steward, BA (Hons) (London), MIL

Deputy Head (*Preparatory and Boarding*): Mrs J Clark, BA (Hons) (East Anglia), PGCE

Bursar: Mr J Page

Battle Abbey School is an independent, co-educational school for pupils from 2½ to 18; boarders are accepted from the age of 8. The school is large enough to encourage healthy competition and to develop the social skills and awareness of others learnt by being part of a lively community, but it is small enough to have many of the attributes of a large family. The Head of Boarding lives within the main school building together with his wife and family and the Headmaster and his wife live within the school grounds. A separate Junior Boarding House for 14 pupils aged 8 to 12 is attached to the Headmaster's house and is run by resident Houseparents. Caring supervision of the pupils is thus ensured at all times. Teaching classes are small throughout the school, allowing individual attention and the opportunity for all pupils to achieve their maximum potential.

The Senior Department (11 to 18) and the Boarders are privileged to occupy one of the most famous historical sites in the world, that of the 1066 Battle of Hastings. The main school building, with its assembly hall, dining-room, library, dormitories and common rooms is the 15th century Abbot's House belonging to the Abbey of St Martin founded by the Conqueror himself. It has been beautifully modernised, and is typical of the School's happy blend of traditional values with up-to-date facilities. The dormitories are bright and cheerful, many having magnificent views over the surrounding countryside. Boys and girls are in separate wings but the common rooms are co-educational making the school ideal for brothers and sisters. The Sixth Form pupils have study-bedrooms and their own common room and are treated very much as the young adults that they are. Grouped around this building are well-equipped specialist rooms including five science laboratories and art and technology areas. There is a new Computer Room equipped with state-of-the-art, industry-standard hardware and software and a large, flood-lit, artificial-grass, all-weather playing area.

The Nursery and Preparatory pupils (2½ to 11) have their own separate premises within easy reach of the Abbey. Their elegant building, which has been recently refurbished, has spacious classrooms, a well stocked library, specialist rooms for Art and Design and Information Technology and a new multi-purpose hall. It stands in its own extensive grounds which include eight tennis courts, two games fields, two surfaced playgrounds and a 25 metre indoor heated swimming pool.

Battle is only 57 miles from London, on the main railway line to Hastings. Gatwick, Heathrow, and the Channel Ports are within easy reach. There is accompanied travel to and from London at the beginning and end of each term and half-term.

There are Scholarships for pupils wishing to enter Year 3, 4, 5, 6, 7 and 9, a Sixth Form Scholarship and there is an automatic 12% Bursary for serving members of Her Majesty's Forces.

Further details may be obtained from the School Secretary. If you can visit the School, please make an appointment to do so. Try to come in term-time, if possible, when you will be able to see Battle Abbey at its best, alive and in action.

Charitable status. Battle Abbey School is administered by BAS (School) Ltd which is a Registered Charity, number 779605. The objective of the Charity is to carry on a school or schools where students may obtain a sound education of the highest order, such a school to be carried on as an educational charity.

Bearwood College

Wokingham Berkshire RG41 5BG
Tel: (0118) 9786915
Fax: (0118) 9773186
e-mail: headmaster@bearwoodcollege.berks.sch.uk
website: www.bearwoodcollege.berks.sch.uk

Bearwood College is an Independent Co-educational Day and Boarding School, age range 11–18. The College is a member of the Governing Bodies Association (GBA) and the Headmaster is a member of The Society of Headmasters and Headmistresses of Independent Schools (SHMIS).

The College has a Church of England foundation, which also welcomes and respects those of other faiths. Only 35 miles west of London near Wokingham in Berkshire, it is served by an excellent network of roads and railways. Heathrow airport is 30 minutes by car and Reading Mainline station is only 15 minutes away. On entering the College grounds the convenient proximity to London is at once forgotten. The mansion house was once the residence of John Walter II, the orginal nineteenth century owner of the Times Newspaper. Much newer buildings have been added over the years including a beautiful Theatre with a 350 seat auditorium.

Bearwood's origins date back to 1827, its parent body being the Royal Merchant Navy School Foundation. The mansion and grounds were presented to the foundation in 1919 and the name of the College was subsequently changed in 1960.

At Bearwood College we expect your child to achieve his or her best.

Patron: Her Majesty The Queen.

President: HRH The Prince Philip, Duke of Edinburgh, KG, KT

Board of Governors:
Chairman: Lt Cdr J P Devitt, RN (Retd)
Sir David Hill-Wood, Bt
Captain G R Boyle
Commander D B Cairns, OBE, RD, RNR
Sir William Reardon Smith, Bt
H G Scrutton, FCA
J Walter
J Bayliss
Lt Col C J Dawnay

***Headmaster:* S G G Aiano**, MA (Cantab), PGCE

Second Master: R P Ryall, BA, PGCE
Senior Mistress: A M Smith, BA, MEd, PGCE
Chaplain: The Revd Prof E Fudge, MA, PhD (Cantab), PGCE

Teaching Staff:
D W Barclay, BEd *Head of Science*
Mrs E W Barclay, BEd, DipRSA *Head of Learning Support*
C N Beecham, BA(QTS) *Head of PE*
C A Bell, CertEd, *Head of CDT*
Mrs P Bell, BA, DipRSA *English; Housemistress Drake*
Miss S Bilton, BEd DipT *Head of Art and Photography; Asst Housemistress Drake*
Miss C Briant, BEd *Head of Girls Games*
M J Cheeseman, FETC *Computing, PSHE; Hawkins Housemaster*
P J Christian, BSc, MSc, PGCE *Physics*
M G Cocker, BA, PGCE *French and German; Asst Housemaster Hawkins*
K P Copestake, BA, PGCE *Head of History; Raleigh Housemaster*
R M Curtis, BSc, FETC *Physics and Chemistry*
R C L Enston, BMus, FRCO, ARCM, LRAM, DipRAM *Director of Music*
J W Fitzpatrick, BSc, PGCE *Head of Mathematics*
Mrs A Flintham, BA, PGCE, CertTESOL *Head of ESOL*
Dr C Foot, BSc, PhD *Mathematics*
R S Goodhand, BSc, PGCE *Head of Computing; Asst Housemaster Hawkins*
Mrs A H Growcott, CertEd, BEd *Head of Modern Languages*
Miss A L Harvey, BSc, PCEA *Biology*
Mrs C A Hatcher, BA, PGCE *French and Spanish*
Mrs M S Hughes, MEd *ESOL*
N Hunter, BSc, CertT *Mathematics*
R Knight, BPhEd, DipTeach *Mathematics*
T Lees, FRCO, FTCL, GRSM, ARMCM *Music*
K J Lovell, CertEd *Design and Technology*
P M Lavarack, BSc *Physics*
Mrs A Main, CertEd, AMBDA *English and Religious Education*
W S S Roques, BSc, PGCE *Head of Business Studies and Economics; Housemaster Jellicoe*
Miss B Rupp, BA, DipEd *English and Theatre Studies*
R P Ryall, BA, PGCE, FRGS *Geography*
Miss A M Smith, BA, MEd, PGCE *Head of English*
M B Strutt, BSc, PGCE *Chemistry; Housemaster Nelson*
J R Talbot, BEd, BA *Head of Geography*
Dr R M Teig, PhD *Mathematics*
L A Wood, BA, PGCE *ESOL*

Librarian: Mrs S Moss
Medical Officer: Dr P D McCall, MB, BS, MRCS, LRCP
Medical Centre Sister: Miss J Fell, RCompN, BN
Medical Centre Nurse: Mrs L Steele-Perkins, SRN, SCM, SN
Headmaster's Secretary: Mrs G Shepherd
Financial Secretary: Mr T J Manzi, FCA
Registrar: Mrs C A Godwin
Theatre Manager: Mr I W Richardson

Ethos. At Bearwood College we expect your child to achieve his or her best. Each scholar works to an academic programme which is individually targeted. This programme is permanently monitored. It provides a structured, supported and demanding academic challenge appropriate to each scholar's capacity. It is underpinned by a universal system of pastoral care.

All scholars take part in a wide range of games and activities outside the classroom. They enjoy a breadth of experience as well as being expected to discover specific areas in which to excel.

In preparation for young adulthood we cultivate an attitude of responsibility and independence.

Academic structure. The academic curriculum is based on and exceeds the guidelines of the National Curriculum. In the years up to GCSE, we provide a programme which offers choice, breadth of experience and the opportunity to develop particular academic skills.

A specialist Learning Support Unit is available for a limited number of suitable dyslexic scholars. ESOL lessons are similarly available for overseas scholars. An additional charge is made for these services.

In these all-important GCSE years, each scholar is continually assessed, and set realistic fixed-date targets for improvement by the subject teachers, in order to maximise individual potential.

Sixth form scholars are able to choose from a wide range of subjects at 'A' Level. They receive specialist attention in small teaching groups.

Pastoral. The following day/boarding arrangements are available:

- Full boarding with continuous care and involvement for seven days a week.
- Weekly boarding with the chance to go home at weekends once College commitments have been fulfilled.
- Occasional or flexible boarding for limited or irregular periods to help busy parents.
- Day attendance, including Saturday mornings and one Sunday morning per term.

The House system.

The House system is at the core of virtually all College life outside the classroom. This arrangement provides all scholars with a contact for personalised pastoral care. It is the base for academic monitoring. It ensures a comfortable social environment and a structure within which games and many activities can thrive. The House is the focus of loyalty for the members. It offers security and identity.

Parents' first point of contact with the College on a day to day basis is the scholar's Houseparent. This is the person who pulls together all the different threads and weaves a coherent picture from the many strands of a scholar's varied existence at Bearwood College.

Houseparents are helped by their own team of House Tutors. The Tutor, who is an academic member of staff, assists in the general running of the House but is also in specific charge of a small group of tutees. Tutees meet with their own Tutors at least once a week. This may be for a personal chat about their progress, or a group tutorial. The House team is responsible for both encouraging and motivating those in their House to achieve their potential. All the Houses are supported by a skilled and dedicated group of ancillary staff the most important of whom are the Chaplain, the Medical Staff and the Matrons.

The Matrons are mainly responsible for the domestic arrangements but are also an important informal adult presence who may seem less official to those in need of a sympathetic ear.

Sport and Activities. Everyone takes part in physical activities on most days. Sports and games give the scholars physical fitness, personal and team skills and recreation. They offer many opportunities to find a sense of achievement. On-site sports and activities on the extensive array of playing fields and facilities include all the usual field sports but in addition there are opportunities for: golf, equestrian sports, cycling and mountain biking, sailing, shooting, canoeing, to name but some.

Extra curricular activities..

Outdoor pursuits are encouraged at Bearwood. The pursuit of academic excellence is balanced by active encouragement of the scholars' extra curricular involvement. The extensive grounds and lake are used for sailing, canoeing, mountain biking, camping, cross country and many other activities. Few schools can boast such a varied estate as that found at Bearwood College.

Combined Cadet Force.

All scholars in the third and fourth forms join the Combined Cadet Force (CCF). Cadets learn self reliance and teamwork, and develop their own leadership skills. The CCF also provides an unrivalled opportunity to experience outdoor pursuits. Two camps are held during holiday periods each year. The annual adventure training expedition provides boys and girls with the opportunity to experience environments that test and challenge their characters whilst under the supervision of highly qualified staff. Many cadets choose to continue their service in the cadet force during their fifth and sixth form years. At this time they take on the extra responsibilities of being senior cadets. The experience they gain from taking an active role in teaching and helping younger cadets provides a valuable insight into the qualities required from leaders.

The Duke of Edinburgh's Award Scheme.

All scholars in the fourth year start the Duke of Edinburgh's Award at bronze level. This is organised partly in conjunction with the cadet force who help with the training for the expedition section. Senior scholars in the College are encouraged to continue with both silver and gold awards. The scheme provides scholars with an ideal opportunity to develop their own skills, fitness and commitment to others whilst fostering self confidence and personal esteem.

Bearwood Outdoor Activity Club.

Many of the scholars take part in other supervised activities away from the College at weekends during term time and in the holidays. Weekend events include jetskiing, water-skiing, hiking, long-distance mountain biking and gliding. We have a keen mountain marathon team who take part in annual events. Scholars in our first and second years are encouraged to develop a taste for adventure. The annual Junior Adventure Week to the South Wales coast at the start of each summer holiday is firmly established.

Music.

Music is part of the life of every scholar, non-specialist and specialist alike. Everyone participates in music events including the House Singing Competition and the Choral Society. There are regular informal and formal concerts given by instrumentalists and singers. All scholars are encouraged to take up instrumental and vocal lessons with our team of professional peripatetic musicians. A number of ensembles can be joined: the College Choir, the Chapel Choir, the Jazz Band, the Wind Band, the Dance Band and the Junior Ensemble. Regular visits to concerts and other musical outings take place.

Theatre and Drama.

Our Theatre represents the very best that is available for the pursuance of music and dramatic arts. A busy programme of concerts, recitals and plays ensure that this 350 seat auditorium is continually in use. All scholars are expected to make a contribution to these productions. Performers from the College are supported by theatre technicians, lighting and sound engineers, stage crew and scenery builders. All have their part to play in the many productions.

In recent years these have included: Animal Farm; Oliver; Marat Sade; Twelfth Night; Macbeth; Gasping; The Importance of Being Ernest; Confusions, Popular Mechanicals; Kes; The Dog; Hamlet; The Wizard of Oz.

Specialist tuition leading to LAMDA Speech and Drama grades and awards is available. These help to develop confidence and competence in acting, public speaking and general communication.

College facilities. The mansion house is the centre of the College around which all our other buildings are located. Historic rooms house modern facilities.

The Cook Library is situated in the former drawing room, one of the most beautiful rooms in the main mansion. It has a collection of both fiction and non-fiction books (some 14,000 in total) for loan and reference use. The library resource is further enhanced by modern personal computers with up to date reference CDs. Scholars are encouraged to read daily quality broad sheet newspapers to keep abreast of current affairs, politics and news. This learning resource is run by a full time Librarian and supports all areas of the curriculum as well as providing for recreational reading.

The need for modern technology is supported by a brand new computer resource suite and all departments in the College have PCs. The College is currently being equipped with a pan-College fibre optic network.

The range of facilities for scholars at Bearwood is extensive. A fully equipped photographic suite, extensive pitches, a swimming pool, tennis and squash courts, weights-training room, motor vehicle engineering workshop and rifle range are all found immediately adjacent to the main building.

Our grounds contain many additional features: two golf courses; a fifty acre lake and a well equipped fleet of sailing dinghies, canoes and power boats; extensive woodlands with a professionally built obstacle course and fitness trail; a mountain bike course; stables and a skateboarding run ensure that a scholar at Bearwood is always busy.

Fees per term (April 2001). Boarders £4,150–£4,625. Day pupils £2,550–£2,750.

Charitable status. Bearwood College is a Registered Charity, number 285287, founded to provide education for young people.

* Head of Department	§ Part Time or Visiting
† Housemaster/Housemistress	¶ Old Pupil
‡ See below list of staff for meaning	

Bedstone College
(Co-educational)

Bucknell Shropshire SY7 0BG
Tel: (01547) 530303

Bedstone was founded in 1948 by Mr & Mrs Reginald Jackson Rees and is fully co-educational. It has the comparatively rare distinction in a small school of some 200 pupils of educating brothers and sisters of widely differing academic abilities from the age of 7 to University entrance without parents having the concern that one or other of their children will be excluded because of academic shortcomings. Thus a strong feeling of family entity is preserved; and the assured continuity of education leads to a feeling of security which, through small class teaching, brings out the best progress within the limits of each individual's capabilities.

The Governors are in membership of the Governing Bodies' Association; and, being composed almost exclusively of ex-Parents, ex-Teachers or ex-Pupils of Bedstone, they have a very real interest in the well-being of the pupils and the continued success of the College.

Motto: *Caritas*

Visitor: The Right Reverend the Bishop of Hereford

The Governing Body:

Chairman: E J Murch, Esq, FRICS, FSVA

Secretary of the Trust: D G Bayliss, Esq, MA, PhD

Members:

P G Barton, Esq, BSc, PhD	R Lewis, Esq
P R S Dutton, Esq	D Owens, Esq, JP
T Foersterling, Esq, LLB, PhD	Lady C Rees, BSc, PhD
	A W E Salmon, Esq, BSc
Sqdn Ldr W Forde, RAF	C Simpson, Esq, ACIB
Mrs M Hughes, BA, DipEd	A W Thornton, Esq

Clerk to the Council and Bursar: J H B Gore, Esq, FAPA, FSCA, ATII, MBIM

***Headmaster:* M S Symonds**, BSc, CPhys, MInstP, FRSA, PGCE

Second Master: N Bidgood, MA

Houseparents:
Bedstone Court: Mr & Mrs B Wigston
Top Floor: Mrs A Richards
Bedstone House: Mr & Mrs R Shore
Wilson House: Mr & Mrs M Rozee

Competitive Housemasters:
Hopton: D Davies, BEd
Stokesay: K T Hatfield, BSc
Wigmore: J Jansen, BEd, MSc

Assistant Staff:
J Bowen (*Director of Music*)
Mrs D Bradfield, CertEd (*English*)
B M Chadderton, BA, PGCE (*Head of Modern Languages*)
D Davies, BEd (*Head of Business Studies*)
Mrs J Dodd, CertEd (*Head of Girls PE*)
D Fathers, BSc, PGCE, CertCompSc
S Gee (*Mathematics*)
Dr P Gooderson, MA (Cantab), PhD, MEd (*Head of History*)
K T Hatfield, BSc (*Head of Science*)
P Jakubowski, BA (*Biology, PE and Sports Studies*)
J Jansen, BEd, MSc (*Head of Design Technology*)
Mrs J Moores, TEFL, DipSLD (*Head of Learning Support*)
Dr D M Rawlinson, BSc, PhD, PGCE (*Head of Mathematics*)
M Rozee (*Head of Chemistry*)
R Shore, CertEd (*Design Technology*)
B Smith, BA (*Head of Art*)
J Smith, BA (*Head of Art*)
Miss C Turner, BA (*Modern Languages*)
B G Wigston, MA, DipEd (*Head of Geography*)
M Wright, BA, PGCE (*Head of English*)

Preparatory Department:
Mrs J McPherson, CertEd (*Head of Preparatory Department*)
Mrs J Hatfield, BLib, ALA

Pre-Prep Department:
Mrs M Savery, Dip Montessori
Mrs J Ward, CertEd

Lay Chaplain: A C Dyball, MA (Cantab), DipEd

Visiting Instrumental Teachers:

D Moore	Ms L Davidson
G Rees Roberts	D Sadler

School Doctors:
M L Kiff, MB, BS
G J Woodman, MB, ChB
Mrs P Cross, BChB

School Sister: Mrs J Fray, SRN

Catering and Domestic Supervisor: Miss M Jenkins

Maintenance Manager: R Mather

Headmaster's Secretary: Mrs D Reader

Secretary: Mrs C Reid-Warnlow

Character of the College. Beautifully situated in the glorious uplands of South Shropshire, remote from distracting urban influences yet readily accessible by road and rail from London and other major cities and airports, Bedstone offers a thorough academic and practical education catering for a wide spectrum of ability for boys and girls in the 8–19 age range. Socially and recreationally, Bedstone fulfils a need often missing in larger schools. Numbers are small enough for staff and pupils to know each other not only well but very well indeed; and yet they are large enough to permit full and successful participation at all levels in inter-school sport and other team activities. Under a firm but reasonable discipline, the pupils thus develop a "Bedstone" consciousness without losing the individuality which the very size of the school allows them to retain and foster.

Family Education. There is a guarantee that once any member of a family is accepted at Bedstone, brothers and sisters will gain automatic entry without the artificial barrier of a further examination. This is a relief for parents who wish their children all educated at the same school.

Accommodation. The main house, Bedstone Court, is a scheduled building of fine architectural merit and accommodates junior and middle-school boys. It contains classrooms, library, the dining hall, sick-bay and common-rooms. Wilson House is a purpose-built Senior Girls' study bedroom block with all mod cons and Bedstone House accommodates Junior Girls in homely surroundings with resident married staff as house parents. The Rectory House boards many of the senior boys and Rees Court has Sixth Form study bedrooms for boys, as well as science teaching facilities. The Science Laboratories and classrooms are in modern buildings. There is seating for 450 people in the large modern Assembly Hall. There is a well-equipped Design Technology Centre, heated Swimming pool, Gymnasium, and ample accommodation for a wide range of facilities. Resident medical staff, excellent catering and up-to-date fire detection equipment safeguard the health, welfare and safety of the pupils. A new Sixth Form Centre has recently been opened.

Religious Education. Religious teaching at Bedstone is according to the tenets of the Church of England though other denominations are welcomed. Children, whose parents wish it, are also prepared for Confirmation by the Chaplain. There is a long choral tradition and the Choir enjoys an excellent reputation. It provides a strong lead in all services as well as taking an interest in many activities in the neighbourhood.

Curriculum. Pupils normally enter the Senior Department at the age of eleven for a five-year course leading to the General Certificate of Secondary Education, following which there are programmed courses in seventeen different subjects for a further two years up to 'A' level and University qualifications.

From the First Form to the Third Form (when a number join from the Preparatory Schools) the subjects taught are: Religious Knowledge, English Language and Literature, History, Geography, French, Mathematics, Biology, Physics, Chemistry, Design Technology, Art, Music, Physical Education and Computer Studies. German is also taught from the Third Form.

In the Fourth and Fifth Forms, options are: History, Geography, Art, Economics, Music, Home Economics, German, Design Technology

Throughout the College, whenever possible, it is endeavoured to set classes in each subject so that every pupil may progress satisfactorily towards different levels of attainment. There is no "cramming" at Bedstone, but considerable effort is required from each pupil; and the very well-qualified staff and high staff/pupil ratio ensure good progress and examination successes. Many pupils take some subjects two terms early for experience and to shed some of their academic load. Pupils may thus pass eight to twelve subjects in their Fifth Form whereas others' achievements will be more modest in keeping with their abilities.

Full Advanced level courses are offered in English, History, Geography, French, German, Spanish, Economics, Art, Music, Design Technology, Mathematics, Physics, Chemistry, Biology, Sports Studies and General Studies.

Coaching is regularly available for overseas pupils who have difficulty with their English; and these are entered with success for the JMB Lower Certificate in English, for which Bedstone is a Centre. The College has its own dyslexia unit.

Careers. There are specific Careers staff and a well-resourced Careers Room. Bedstone makes full use of the Independent Schools' Careers Organisation and all members of the Fifth Form take the ISCO Psychometric tests.

Games and Physical Education. There are three Rugby pitches, three Hockey pitches, two grass Athletics tracks, two Cricket fields, four Basketball, three Netball, three Tennis and two Squash courts. The success of the boys and girls in physical activity at School, county and district level has been nothing short of remarkable.

While Rugby, Athletics and Cricket are the main sports for the boys, a rotation system ensures that all pupils to a greater or lesser degree have their share of such activities as Basketball, Cross-country running, Squash and Hockey in the Winter, and Swimming and Tennis in the Summer. Nor are the individualists forgotten. Horse-riding is popular, as is Golf, and there are facilities for Fishing, Shooting, Canoeing, Sailing, Badminton, Table Tennis and Cycling, while the South Shropshire and Powys hills provide excellent opportunities for healthy walks. Girls are well catered for in a lot of individual activities and represent the College at Netball, Hockey, Gymnastics, Cross-country, Athletics, Tennis and Swimming.

Clubs and Activities. The Duke of Edinburgh's Award Scheme flourishes; and there is a wide range of out of class activity, including splendid dramatic and musical productions, debating, individual music tuition and an assortment of clubs to suit most tastes. Pupils are expected to know and observe all college rules, and parents to co-operate in seeing that this is done. Prefects play an important part in general discipline, but they have very limited powers of punishment. There is nothing resembling "servile work" at Bedstone, though all pupils are expected to take a share in odd-jobs for the good of the community as a whole.

Bedstone Preparatory Department. This is a small feeder school for boys and girls aged 3 to 11, with the full use of the Senior amenities. Literacy and numeracy are basic requirements for entry; and these are tested at interview. There is automatic promotion from the Preparatory Department at the age of 11, or earlier for academically brighter children.

Admission and Scholarships (*see* Entrance Scholarship section). For entry to the first three forms of the Senior College there is an entrance examination held at the College in March. This comprises testing in English and Mathematics, an IQ Test and an interview, and it is invaluable in assessing a candidate's potential for correct placing in September. As a result of this examination, there may be awarded:

(a) 1 Bishop Sara Memorial Scholarship valued at £4,000 per annum.

(b) 2 Bursaries valued at £2,000 per annum.

(c) Entrance as available.

(d) Sixth Form Scholarships are available.

(e) Music Scholarships are also available.

Application for entry may be made at any time of the year; but no candidate will be considered for a scholarship or bursary without sitting the examination in March.

Fees (January 2000). Senior Boarders: £3,700. Senior Day: £2,002. Preparatory Boarders: £2,500. Preparatory Day £1,445.

Old Bedstonian Society. *Hon Secretary:* Mr G McLoughlin, 17 Ketelbey Rise, Hatch Warren, Basingstoke, Hants RG22 4PE.

Charitable status. Bedstone College is a Registered Charity, number 528405. It is established for the education of young people.

Bentham Grammar School

Low Bentham Lancaster LA2 7DB
Tel: (015242) 61275
Fax: (015242) 62944
e-mail: Secretary@benthamschool.demon.co.uk
website: http://www.benthamschool.demon.co.uk

The School was founded in 1726 by William Collingwood of York and the Rev Thomas Baynes of Bolton, Wensley, York.

Chairman of the Governing Body: Mr G Tyler

Head: **Ruth E Colman**, MA

Director of Studies/Senior Master: W Stockdale, BA

Teaching staff:
D B Allison, BEd
Mrs M Anderson, CertEd, BEd
Mrs A Beckwith, RADADip
Mrs C Brocklebank, BA, QTS
C Constance, BSc, PGCE
J A Dickinson, BSc, PGCE
Mrs S Dodgson, BSc, PGCE
Mrs A Fawcett, LRAM (*Piano and 'Cello*)
D Galbraith, BA, MA
Mrs S Garnett, CertEd (*Singing*)
Miss C Goss, BSc (*Flute*)

Mrs A Green, CertEd
R Griffiths, BSc, PGCE
T M Holmes, BSc, PGCE
Mrs S Jackson, CertEd
D Johnson, BA, DipEd
Mrs L Ladds, BA, PGCE
Miss J Lawson, NNEB (*Nursery*)
Miss S Leigh, BEd, QTS
P Lownds, CertEd, BEd, MEd (ILU)
Mrs I Mackay, BA, PGCE
A J Presland, BSc, PGCE
Mrs A M Presland, BA, PGCE
M Spencer, BEd, DipEd, DipMus
Mrs L Townley, NNEB (*Head of Nursery*)
J S Warbrick, BA
Mrs J Weeks, CertEd

Houses and Housestaff:

School House: Mr and Mrs A Presland
Collingwood and Bridge House: Mr and Mrs K Brocklebank, Mrs M Betts

Bursar: Miss J Tomkinson, FCCA, MAAT
Admissions Secretary: Mrs G Banks-Lyon

The Nature of the School The school was founded in 1726 by Revd Thomas Baynes and William Collingwood who through Admiral Lord Collingwood had close connections with Admiral Lord Nelson. The school was originally a boys school, and girls were first admitted in 1824, making Bentham one of the first co-educational boarding schools in the country. Today, there are approximately 250 pupils in the school comprising a mixture of both day and boarding pupils which makes the school quite unique as a small and caring community where progress is encouraged to the limits of an individual's capabilities. Bentham Grammar School is fully co-educational and stands in its own grounds in a magnificent rural setting. The main site is based on the former Rectory of Bentham Church, a Norman Shaw building.

Mission Statement. At Bentham Grammar School every child is special. Here all are encouraged to identify and develop their talents. To this end we are committed to remaining a small, caring school with a family atmosphere. Past experience shows our pupils flourish in this secure and stimulating environment.

To this end the Governors, Head and Teaching Staff at Bentham Grammar School regard the following statements to be the essential elements of the Bentham Experience

- Academically all pupils are taught in small classes. This allows each child to be treated as an individual but all are expected to produce high standards.
- The nature of the school means that, traditionally, a very high proportion of children represent the school in sport as well as performing in the many dramatic and musical productions. This produces confident young men and women with a wide range of experience.
- The boarding houses provide a stable and homely atmosphere allowing all students to play an important part in ensuring newcomers settle in with ease. Apart from providing an ideal atmosphere within which to develop academically and socially, pupils are provided with a full programme of outings and extra-curricular activities.
- The school values its close links with parents who are encouraged to become involved in the life of the school. We believe that such a partnership is essential for effective education.
- Our rural setting ensures a proper appreciation of the countryside and environmental issues. Our proximity to two National Parks also provides ample opportunities for outdoor pursuits.

Location and Accessibility. Bentham Grammar School is located in Low Bentham, a small market town close to the edge of the Forest of Bowland and the Yorkshire Dales National Park and a short distance from the Lake District.

The main school site is on the banks of the River Wenning, a tributary of the Lune.

The school operates its own bus services and pupils travel daily from Morecambe, Lancaster, Carnforth, Silverdale, Kirkby Lonsdale and Settle.

Boarding at Bentham Grammar School. Boarders are admitted into the Junior House from the age of 7. This is a mixed house for boys and girls in the age range of 7 to 11.

Separate boys and girls Senior Houses provide accommodation for the older pupils in the age range of 12 to 18.

All Houses are in the charge of married couples and there are also resident housestaff in each house. The school provides a genuine family atmosphere for its boarding pupils.

The relationship between day and boarding pupils is excellent due to the approximate equal number of day and boarding pupils at the school and although there are a number of weekly boarding pupils a programme of activities, at different age levels is available for boarders at weekends.

Whatever the reason for boarding, we believe that Bentham provides a boarding experience which is both fun and fulfilling for those pupils who elect to join us.

Academic Organisation. A Junior Department caters for pupils from age 5 to 11, with boarding pupils accepted from the age of 7. Considerable emphasis is placed on basic skills and these, together with History, Geography and Religious Studies are taught in the Junior Department classroom which are on the main school site.

The younger pupils have the full use of the specialist main school facilities for Music, Art, Science, Technology and Physical Education.

From the age of 11 the school follows courses which correspond closely to the National Curriculum, with all pupils, studying a common core of subjects with in addition a range of practical and creative activities together with Information Technology, and a course in Personal, Religious and Social Education.

The two year course to GCSE begins at 14+ with English language and literature, Maths, French and Dual Award Science, together with up to a maximum of three further options allowing pupils to sit nine or in some cases for more able pupils ten GCSEs.

In the sixth form a wide range of A level subjects is offered, together with a number of vocational courses. The majority of our pupils proceed to University, although a number will opt to take a GAP year before entering further education. Progress at all levels is monitored through a strong tutorial system with each child having a personal tutor who will follow his or her progress throughout the school.

Facilities. A continuing building programme has ensured a full range of facilities both academic and non-academic.

These include individual Science laboratories, a Design Technology & Art Centre, a Music School and Information Technology Centre. In addition, the school has its own swimming pool and a recently built Sports Hall on the main campus.

The school has completed a major refurbishment of the boarding houses, providing single study rooms for most of the senior pupils.

The school operates its own fleet of three minibuses and has an extensive range of outdoor pursuits equipment for extra curricular use.

The school location being rural and self-contained provides a safe and pleasant environment for both academic and leisure pursuits.

The school campus is available for use by outside institutions such as field study groups and selected holiday organisations during the vacation periods.

The Individual Learning Unit. This is available to both the Junior and Senior School. Specialist teachers are available to assist with Dyslexic difficulties, English as a Foreign Language Tuition with Speech and Drama Tuition to examination standard. Assistance is provided for children with learning difficulties.

Extra Curricular Activities. A full range of clubs and societies operate at lunch time and after school. The boarding pupils have access to their own activity programme at the weekend and there are a healthy number of inter-sports fixtures for both boys and girls at competition level.

Extensive use is made of the excellent location of the school for the field trips and outdoor pursuits and all pupils are encouraged to take part in the Duke of Edinburgh Award Scheme and the various Community Service projects which are available.

The school operates a GAP student exchange scheme through its links with schools in Melbourne and Sydney in Australia and a regular two way exchange programme involving senior students adds to the international flavour of the school.

Games. The major games are soccer, cross-country, cricket, athletics, basketball and tennis for boys, and hockey, netball, cross-country, tennis and athletics for girls.

Specialist instructors are attached to the school and will assist in particular with the coaching of football and cricket from junior to senior level.

Music and Drama. There is a strong tradition of music and drama in the school, there being several musical productions and a drama production each year. Pupils are encouraged to take individual instrumental lessons and the school has been well represented in local Music and Drama festivals in recent years.

Medical Care. There is a school nurse and deputy, both of whom are qualified. The school doctor holds a regular surgery in the school's own clinic.

Admission. This can be at any time in the age range 5 to 14, or at the sixth form level. Pupils are sometimes admitted at other stages in certain circumstances. Application should be made to the Head.

Scholarships. (*see* Entrance Scholarship section) Various awards are available with values up to 50% of full fees. Some bursaries are also available. Full details are available from the Head.

Fees. Junior Department: Reception £1,150 per term; Preparatory: Day £1,400, per term; Boarding £3,085, per term; Senior School: Day £1,850, per term; Boarding £3,650, per term.

Finally. We believe Bentham Grammar School is a happy, thriving and progressive community in which the young people in our care achieve a breadth of education and range of challenges which will lay down a firm foundation for adult life.

If you would like to find out more about 'The Bentham Experience' you are welcome to contact the Head to arrange a visit to the school in order to sample at first hand our fine facilities and traditions.

Charitable status. Bentham Grammar School is a Registered Charity, number 1073353. It exists to provide a day and boarding school for the education of boys and girls in the age range 3–19.

Bethany School

Curtisden Green Goudhurst Cranbrook Kent TN17 1LB.

Tel: (01580) 211273.
Fax: (01580) 211151
e-mail: admin@bethany.demon.co.uk
website: www.bethany.demon.co.uk

The School was founded in 1866 by the Rev J J Kendon. It is a Charitable Trust administered by a Board of Governors which is in membership with the Governing Bodies Association.

Governors:

C M Jackson, MA, MEP (*Chairman*)
D B Parke, FCA (*Vice-Chairman*)
T A Cooper
Sir Derek Day, KCMG
Lady Fenn
C M Jackson
A Pengelly, MA, FRCS
B S Robbins
W J D Rogers, MA, FRICS
Mrs P Shaw
R L Whitlock

Bursar and Clerk to the Governors: S J Douglass, MBIM

Staff

Headmaster: **N D B Dorey**, MA Cantab

Deputy Headmaster: J M Priestley, BA

Senior Housemaster: P S Holmes, BA, MEd, FRGS

Senior Mistress: Mrs R Murrells, MA

Chaplain: The Revd C J Rookwood, MA

Assistant staff:

Ms V Abbott, BA
R Allen, BSc(Eng)
Mrs D Bailey, CertEd
Mrs T Barrett, BA
K Brown, BA, LTCL
S Brown, BSc
J M Cullen, BA
K R Daniel, BA
Miss S Davis, BA
W M Day, BEng
J Debnam, BSc, PhD
Mrs H M Dorey, BA
S C Gilbert
C P A Gould, BSc
Mrs M-C Gould, BSc
R C Handley, CertEd
T P Hart Dyke, BA
Mrs F Healy
M F Healy, BSc
M W Hollman, BSc
P G Isom, BEd
Miss C Jemmett, BEd
Mrs F Johnson, CertEd (PE)
Mrs A C Kelly, BA
A A Khan, BA
A K Lawrence, BSc
P G Marriott, CertEd (*PE*)
Ms M McCall-Smith, BA
Mrs A J Mole, BEd
M D G E Norman, BEd
P Norgrove, BEd
Mrs A Presland, BA
K Proctor, BSc
S Rowcliffe, BSc
G K Thorpe, BA
Miss S Webster, BSc

Medical Officer: Dr J N Watson, MBBS, MRCGP

Size. There are 320 pupils aged 11 to 18 in the School. Almost half of these are boarders, who follow a flexible regime. This permits weekly boarding while a full activities programme is available on Sundays for boarders who remain in School. The School has been coeducational since September 1991. A generous staff:pupil ratio of 1:8 enables classes to be small and pastoral care of a high quality. Most teaching takes place in a modern classroom block which incorporates an Art School and Technology Workshop. Development in ICT has been a priority at Bethany. There is now a wireless network and most pupils and staff use laptops across the curriculum. The new Sixth Form House opened in February 1999. This contains single study bedrooms with en-suite facilities for the Upper Sixth boarders, study rooms for day pupils and communal facilities for both Upper and Lower Sixth Form students. Individuals are encouraged to develop their potential to the full in academic and all other respects.

Situation. The School occupies a scenic, 60 acre site in the Weald of Kent; it is easily accessible from most parts of South-East England, being one hour from Charing Cross (Marden Station) and with easy access from Gatwick and Heathrow Airports, the Channel ports and the Channel Tunnel, at Waterloo and Ashford International stations.

Admission. The normal age of entry is between 11 and 14 by the School's Entrance Examination and, where appropriate, through Common Entrance. VIth Form entry on 4 good GCSEs.

Fees and Scholarships. (*see* Entrance Scholarship section) For boarders £13,452 pa; day pupils £8,646 pa. Scholarships are awarded for Academic ability, Music, Art, Design Technology, Drama and Sport at years 7-9 and into Sixth Form. Children of members of HM Forces or Clergy receive at least 10% discount off full fees.

Curriculum. The broad curriculum is based on the National Curriculum. The full range of subjects is taught including Information Technology from 11+, German from 13+ and Geology from 14+. There are sixteen GCE "A" Levels including Business Studies, Music, Computing, Sports Studies, Design Technology and Theatre Studies. The Advanced GNVQ course in Business is also very popular and successful. Almost all Sixth Form leavers proceed to degree courses at University.

Dyslexia. The Dyslexia and Learning Support Department which enjoys an international reputation, has been supporting pupils of good-average intelligence for over 20 years.

Games and Activities. The School offers a wide range of sporting opportunities and enjoys an extensive fixture list, having established a long tradition of inter-school Sport. Facilities include a Sports Hall, three squash courts, tennis courts, a heated Swimming Pool and opportunities for Fencing, Archery and Rifle Shooting as well as team and individual sports. There is a wide range of clubs and activities. The Duke of Edinburgh Award Scheme is well-established at Gold, Silver and Bronze levels.

Music. There are full facilities for the learning of all instruments. Pupils are encouraged to join the Choir. There are sectional instrumental groups, an Orchestra, Rock School and Jazz Band and a Choral Society, all making use of the fine Music School, where there is a recording studio and a music technology area.

Careers. The School is a member of ISCO (Independent Schools Careers Organisation), and the Careers Teacher keeps in close contact with this body. Careers Education is part of the Curriculum. Sixth Form students take part in the Centigrade Analysis Scheme and receive advice regarding Higher Education and Gap Year opportunities.

Chapel. The Chapel, built in 1878, is the focal point of School life and all pupils are expected to attend the services, which are in the Church of England tradition. Each year there are Confirmation classes for those who wish to participate.

Charitable status. Bethany School Limited is a Registered Charity, number 307937. It exists to maintain Bethany or any other schools for the education of boys or girls so that each such school shall be an educational charity.

* Head of Department	§ Part Time or Visiting
† Housemaster/Housemistress	¶ Old Pupil
‡ See below list of staff for meaning	

Box Hill School
(Co-educational)

Mickleham Dorking Surrey RH5 6EA.
Tel: (01372) 373382.
Fax: (01372) 363942
e-mail: Registrar@boxhillschool.org.uk
website: http://www.boxhillschool.org.uk

Patrons:
HM King Constantine of the Hellenes
HM Queen Anne-Marie of the Hellenes

Chairman of the Board of Governors:
Vice-Admiral Sir James Weatherall, KBE

The Board of Governors is a member of the Governing Bodies Association (*GBA*).

***Headmaster:* Dr R A S Atwood**, BA, PhD

Headmaster's Secretary: Mrs A van Staden

Deputy Headmaster: Dr B Aldiss, BSc, PhD, FRES, CBiol, MIBiol

The school was founded in 1959 by a housemaster from Gordonstoun. It is a charitable trust providing a broad education for boys and girls boarding, weekly boarding and day. There are approximately 320 pupils accepted at 11, 12, 13 and 16 from both maintained and independent schools. The school's distinctive features are:

A small community in which all pupils are well known and valued for what they contribute.

A very wide range of academic subjects and activities allowing pupils of varied talents to flourish and succeed.

A graded system of privilege and responsibility.

Opportunities for overseas projects and overseas expeditions afforded by belonging to an international group of 40 schools on five continents.

The school follows the philosophy of Dr Kurt Hahn, founder of Gordonstoun in Scotland and Salem in Germany, now both sister schools of Box Hill. Hahn believed in confronting young people with both challenges and responsibility at an early age. The school encourages pupils to face challenges, whether it be performing in music, art, drama, taking part in expeditions or on the climbing wall, or as Sixth Formers acting as guides to visiting Headmasters and prospective parents.

Accommodation. Box Hill stands in 40 acres of grounds in Mickleham village in wooded Green Belt countryside only forty-five minutes from London. The Governors have recently spent £2 million adding to the original Victorian mansion a new junior boarding house, Science Blocks and classroom, a multi-purpose gymnasium/hall, Design Technology Block, Sixth Form boys' boarding house, re-equipped girls' houses, and sixth form centre. With the opening of the new art facility we can now offer fashion and textiles at both GCSE and A level. The IT department has been re-equipped with the most up-to-date computer technology. There is also an outdoor heated swimming pool, computing and electronics, music and art rooms, libraries, drama studio, seven sailing dinghies, climbing wall, assault course and golf course.

Academic Work. The school has a strong academic tradition, offering a broad curriculum including practical, aesthetic and creative subjects. At GCSE boys and girls take English, English Literature, Mathematics, and either Balanced Science (equivalent to two GCSEs), or separate sciences, and three other subjects. Nineteen subjects are offered at GCSE and twenty at A Level. Nearly all A Level leavers go on to degree courses.

Pastoral Care. All pupils have a tutor who directs

their academic studies and with whom they meet each morning. They also have a housemaster, housemistress or houseparents and all the boarding houses have an assistant and there are both resident and non-resident matrons. In a small community, care of juniors falls on the more senior pupils, and from their first three weeks in the school boys and girls can begin a graded series of responsibilities leading to the school prefect body or Syndicate, whose duties and conditions of membership are laid down by the Headmaster in a letter sent to each new member.

Careers. The Careers Room has up-to-date information on higher education and future careers. There is a Specialist Head of Careers. The school is a member of the Independent Schools Careers Organisation, there are regular visits by specialist speakers including parents and former pupils, and liaison with Surrey Careers Service, Guildford University and local Polytechnics. Year 11 do a week's work experience at the end of the summer term.

Activities. Box Hill seeks to produce a well rounded citizen capable of getting on confidently in adult life, working in a team, with a variety of interests and love of the outdoors. Every afternoon a wide range of compulsory activities, including the usual team sports, takes place. Pupils choose from within four areas, sporting, skills, service, and outdoor pursuits/expeditions. A week's activities may include a selection from swimming, tennis, electronics, photography, art, design/technology, beekeeping, pony care, and team games such as netball, hockey, soccer, cricket and athletics. Riding, karate and judo are available at extra charge. About sixty pupils play musical instruments and seventy take part in the Duke of Edinburgh's Award Scheme. A community service group visits local hospitals. Choirs and instrumental groups give regular performances in the school and the Eisteddfod (inter-house drama competition) and the inter-house music involves all pupils.

Expeditions. Expeditions are part of the curriculum in the first three years, combining academic work with expedition skills. Year 7 go to Hastings for a week, Year 8 along the Pilgrim's Way to Canterbury and Year 9 to the Lakes. There are conservation weeks based on Box Hill and a Duke of Edinburgh's Award Scheme training week. All Years, particularly Years 12 and 13 (Sixth Form), go regularly to theatres, museums and drama workshops in London. Holiday trips are also offered, including language trips to the Continent.

Round Square. Box Hill belongs to an international group of schools in England, Scotland, Canada, the United States, Australia, Germany, Switzerland, India and Africa. There is an annual conference at a member school attended by a delegation including senior pupils. Joint expeditions carry out project work in India, Hungary, Thailand and Kenya. There are exchanges between schools and a mini-conference for the younger pupils. Box Hill has links with a school and orphanage in Romania.

Religion. The School is non-denominational. Sunday Church Services are planned largely by the Church Services Committee, a group of senior pupils and staff who invite speakers from many Christian denominations to address the School. The School Chaplain is also the Priest in Charge of Mickleham Parish, providing a close link with the parish. In certain cases overseas pupils may be excused Church attendance.

Fees. Autumn Term 2000: Boarders – £4,298 per term; weekly boarders £3,705 per term; day pupils £1,895/£2,509 (sliding scale) per term. Weekly boarders are usually free to depart from 6.30 pm on Friday until Sunday evening.

Scholarships. (*see* Entrance Scholarship section) Up to ten scholarships are awarded for entry to the Sixth Form, based on academic achievement and a contribution to school life through Art, Music, Drama, expedition work, or other appropriate activities. In Years 7 to 9 similar awards may be given in recognition of academic, musical, artistic or sporting potential. Two half-fee Scholarships are offered at 11 plus and two at 13 plus. In cases of special financial need bursaries are available. Details of all these from the Headmaster.

Box Hill School Association. A supportive organisation of parents and friends of the school maintains links with the local community, and lays on social functions and fund raising. Parents are strongly encouraged to join.

Method of Entry. Entry is based on an interview with the Headmaster, report from the pupil's present school, and written tests in Maths and English. Those from Preparatory Schools would be offered places based on our own entry tests. However a keen interest would be taken in the Common Entrance results. Sixth Form entry is based on report, interview and GCSE predictions. For overseas pupils the interview may be waived.

Location. In Mickleham village, just off the A24 Leatherhead to Dorking road, about 4 miles from the M25 and within easy reach of London, Gatwick and Heathrow. For an appointment to see the school, please ring the Registrar.

Charitable status. Box Hill School Trust Limited is a Registered Charity, number 312082. It exists to promote the advancement of education.

Claremont Fan Court School

Claremont Drive Esher Surrey KT10 9LY
Tel: (01372) 467841
Fax: (01372) 471109
e-mail: principal@claremont-school.co.uk
website: http://www.claremont-school.co.uk

Principal: **Mrs P B Farrar**, Teacher's Cert

Head of Senior School: Mr G F Hunt, MA

Head of Junior School: Mrs L M Cox, Teacher's Cert

Situation. The Claremont Estate is one of the premier historic sites in the country. The original house and the famous Landscape Garden were first laid out by Sir John Vanbrugh for the Duke of Newcastle early in the eighteenth century. Later Capability Brown built the present Palladian mansion for Clive of India and landscaped the grounds in his typical manner. For over a century Claremont was a royal residence and played an important part in Queen Victoria's early years. In 1930 the School acquired the mansion and now owns 96 acres of the surrounding park. The Landscape Garden, one of the finest of its kind in the world, is owned by the National Trust. Esher is only sixteen miles from London and almost equidistant from Heathrow and Gatwick airports with access points onto the M25 within three miles.

Aims. An excellent academic programme provides the pupils with a wide and varied curriculum and the opportunity to discover where their individual strengths and interests lie. The expectation is for high achievement in their academic study, sporting and cultural activities. Emphasis is placed on ethical and spiritual values and the expectation of high moral standards. Their ability to use knowledge rightly and to be an influence for good is fundamental to the ethos of the School.

Curriculum. *Junior School:* The educational programme is based on National Curriculum guidelines but the expectation of pupil achievement far exceeds the national average. It is most important that the children are secure and happy so that effective learning can take place. In classes of 16–20, qualified staff encourage active, structured learning. Progress is constantly monitored so each child can realise his or her full potential.

Pupils are expected to meet new social and educational challenges with confidence and perseverance. Emphasis is placed on the acquisition and development of skills in numeracy and literacy while providing a wide and varied range of subjects to stimulate the joy and wonder of learning. These include English, Mathematics, Science, History, Geography, Religious Studies, French, Design Technology, Food and Textile Technology, Information Technology, Art, Music, Drama and Physical Education.

Senior School: In the Lower Senior School, all pupils continue with the range of subjects offered in the Junior School but in addition begin German and Classical Studies. Latin is offered as an optional subject.

At GCSE all pupils take English Language, English Literature, Mathematics and Combined Double Certificated Science. The remainder of their subjects are chosen from a list which includes French, German, Spanish, Geography, History, Technology, Religious Studies, Drama, Art and Music. PE is compulsory but may also be studied at GCSE level.

Pupils with the required ability may study the three individual Sciences.

Religious Studies is taught throughout the School.

Individual Needs. We provide exceptional support and encouragement for pupils who experience difficulties in learning at any stage in their school life or who have above average ability in any area. Extra individual lessons and activities are provided as well as classroom support. Special tuition is also available for pupils where English is their second language.

Sixth Form: Students will usually study for four or five AS level subjects in the Lower Sixth converting three or four of them to full A level via the A2 examinations in their second year of Sixth Form study. The students can choose from the following subjects: Art and Design, History of Art, Photography, Biology, Business Studies, Chemistry, English Language, English Literature, French, Geography, German, History, History of Art, Mathematics and Further Maths, Media, Music, Music Technology, Physics, Spanish, Sociology, Physical Education, Drama & Theatre, Design Technology.

The Sixth Form is a small but very important part of the school community and students regularly achieve above their expectation.

Careers advice is offered throughout the two year period of Sixth Form study.

Co-education. Since 1979 the Foundation has chosen the co-educational system in the conviction that it is an invaluable training ground for both sexes to work alongside each other, developing a mutual respect for and understanding of the other's special and innate qualities. Formerly Claremont and Fan Court were single sex schools.

Religion. The philosophy underpinning the educational programme is founded on the teachings of Christian Science. The School however has no formal connection with the Christian Science Church and Christian Science is not taught as a subject.

Boarding. The Boarding Department aims to provide a spiritually, supportive, homelike atmosphere for the children of Christian Scientists from all over the world. We have residential facilities for pupils from eleven years who come from Christian Science families. Older pupils who have sincerely chosen Christian Science as their religion are also eligible.

Clubs and Activities. Making individual choices in the learning programme and developing a wide range of interests are a necessary preparation for life time learning. A wide range of clubs and extra-curricular activities is available throughout the School and pupils are actively encouraged to participate in a full and rich school experience.

For Junior School children extra curricular activities include Chess, Gym, Book Club, Choir, Jazz Dancing and Ballet, Music Club, Country Dancing, Design Technology, Quilting, Art and Sculpture, and a wide range of sporting activities. For older pupils opportunities are available to develop an interest in Art, Science Crest Award, Computing, Drama, Debating, Textiles, Music, Japanese for Beginners, Duke of Edinburgh Award and many sporting activities, including Fencing.

Entry to the School. Applications for entry into the School are welcome at all year levels. Our principal intake of pupils occurs at 3+, 7+, 11+, 13+ and Sixth form. Places are offered subject to the pupil reaching our entry requirements.

Scholarships (*see* Entrance Scholarship section). We offer academic scholarships at Year 3, Year 7, Year 9 and Sixth Form, music, sports and art scholarships.

Charitable status. The School is owned and run by an educational foundation with charitable status.

Clayesmore School

Iwerne Minster Blandford Dorset DT11 8LL.
Tel: 01747-812122
Fax: 01747 813187
e-mail: hmsec@clayesmore.co.uk

The School was founded in 1896.

Motto: *Dieu premier donc mes freres.*

Council:

¶J P Brooke-Little, CVO, MA, FSA, Clarenceux King of Arms (*Council Member Emeritus*)
Meriel, Lady Salt (*Council Member Emeritus*)
¶Brigadier J N Elderkin, BSc(Eng), MA (*Council Member Emeritus*)

¶R R Spinney, FRICS (*Chairman*)

Mrs L Backhouse, MA
P Dallyn, FRICS, FAAV
L Ellis, MA
R C G Gardner, Esq
¶Prof N Handy, MA, PhD, FRS
¶R G Kingwill, BSc, MS
P J LeRoy, MA, DipEd
S Levinson, LLB, FCIArb
Mrs J H Lidsey
J R Newnham, Esq
Dr J Symons, TD, MSc, PhD
Dr A Thomas, MB, BS, MRCP, MRCGP
Major General J A Ward-Booth, OBE, DL
Dr R Willis, MA, BM, BCh

Bursar and Clerk to the Council: D Little, BA

Senior School Staff:
***Headmaster:* M G Cooke**, BEd (Hons), FCollP, Sussex

Deputy Head: R J Denning, BA, Durham University

Assistant Head: Mrs S M H Billington, BSc, BA, DipPsych, AMBDA

Assistant Staff:

M T Jones, BEd
R J Hammond, BSc
A H Peters, DipAD, CertEd
R A Chew, MA
A K P Rimmer, BSc
T R D Williams, BSc
M S Fraser, BA
†S K Byrne, BA
K J Colwell, BSc
†D I Rimmer, MA
†C R Middle, BA
S A Smith, BSc
D K Pigot, BMus, ARCM, LTCL, CertEd
Revd M J Arnold, MA
Miss N West, BSc
Miss J E Hayes, BEd
†A G Pienaar, MSc

†R E Heale, BSc
E R Robeson, MA
Mrs L T Chmielewski, BA
Mrs L Leah, BA
Mrs B C Britton, MA
M B Browning, BA
D M Denning, BA

Administrative Staff:
Headmaster's Secretary: Mrs M McCafferty

Medical Officer: Dr P L Kreeger, MB, BS, DRCOG

Sanatorium Nurses:
Mrs M Chalmers
Mrs H Proctor

Clayesmore is a co-educational school with Senior and Preparatory departments covering the ages 2½ to 18. The Preparatory School moved to Iwerne Minster in 1974 to occupy purpose-built accommodation in the school grounds. There are approximately 287 pupils in the Senior School, 179 boys and 108 girls.

The Preparatory School of 299 boys and girls from 2½ to 13 (85 boarders and 145 day) has its own Headmaster who works closely in conjunction with the Headmaster of the Senior School. Places are automatically reserved in the Senior School for children from the Preparatory School whose work reaches a satisfactory standard. Thus continuity of education is assured for both boys and girls throughout their school career. (For further details see entry in Preparatory Schools section).

The School was founded in 1896 to embody an ideal, then revolutionary, of an Independent School in which cultural activities and manual work were accorded their proper place. Priority is given to achieving maximum success for each child, but, while adapting itself to the growing need for success in examinations, the School still holds by its vision and firmly believes in the importance of providing an environment which will allow creative instincts to have full opportunity to develop.

Much emphasis is still placed on Art and on Design, and there is also a widespread Activities Programme, so that, in what direction an individual's talents may lie he or she can take an important place in the life of the School by virtue of the gifts they possess.

Site. The School is situated on a 62 acre estate in a delightful country setting with magnificent sports grounds, an all-weather hockey surface and a lake where Fishing and Canoeing are possible.

Buildings. In addition to the main building, which incorporates a girls' boarding house, a modern Dining Hall and Kitchen and a well-stocked Library, there are a Chapel, Laboratories, Sanatorium, Workshops and Studios, and Music School. There is also a well-used Sixth Form Common Room, a superb, fully equipped Sports Centre and a newly refurbished and extended Art School.

Entrance. Entry is at 13 through the Common Entrance Examination or by the School's own Entrance Examination when children have not been specially prepared for the former. Some direct entries to the VIth Form are available each year and the Headmaster is prepared to consider applications for entries at other ages when vacancies permit. Boarding places at the Preparatory School are offered between the ages of 8 to 12.

Organisation. The School is divided into 5 Houses, 3 for boys and 2 for girls, each with resident Housestaff and assistants, and there is a well-developed Tutorial system.

One of the chief features of the school is a more intimate 'family' atmosphere than is possible in a large school. The School's comparatively small size enables the Headmaster and staff to know well all boys and girls and great attention is paid to pastoral care, not only through the House system but also through the full extra-curricular programme.

Religious Life. Services in the School Chapel, built in 1956 as a Memorial to Old Boys who fell in the two Wars, are in accordance with the teaching of the Church of England, but generally interdenominational in character and the School welcomes boys and girls of other faiths. The Chaplain prepares pupils annually for Confirmation.

Academic work. The School in broad terms follows the National Curriculum. Year 9 pupils take a foundation year before beginning on the two years to GCSE. Lower Sixth form pupils generally study 4 subjects for AS levels, and follow a Key Skills course in Communication, ICT and Number. In the Upper Sixth, the number of subjects usually drops to 3 for A2 courses. There is a strong emphasis on preparation for the world beyond school, whether at university or otherwise.

There is streaming but pupils are setted in the key fields of English, French, Mathematics and Science, and sometimes in other subjects too. It is the School's policy to maintain a generous staffing ratio in order that the size of classes may be reasonably small and proper attention can be given to individuals. The average number in classes below Year 11 is 20.

Careers. The Head of the Careers Department organises a programme of visits and talks and is always on hand to give advice to pupils at any time. There are evening sessions for parents each year to give advice on university entrance and other topics.

Health. All new boys and girls are examined by the School Doctor who visits the School regularly. A qualified Nurse is present at all times in the Sanatorium. Attention to physical development is given by Staff trained in Physical Education.

Games. Rugby, Hockey, Cricket, Athletics, Cross-Country, Tennis, Swimming, Netball and Rounders are the main physical pursuits. Squash, Basketball and Badminton are also played. Three separate hard playing areas provide Tennis and Netball courts and Hockey pitches. Sailing and Golf take place in the summer term.

CCF. Pupils in the Fourth and Fifth Forms join the Combined Cadet Force, and many remain as instructors and NCO's in the Sixth Form. The emphasis is on adventure training and many cadets participate in the Duke of Edinburgh Award Scheme. Senior pupils who have left the CCF take part in 'Service' activities working on various projects for the School and locally. There is an active Community Service Group.

Music and Drama. The School has a strong musical tradition. Concerts are given regularly by the Chapel Choir and School Orchestra both in School and in the locality. Frequent visits are made by the Choir to sing in local Churches and Cathedrals and competitive Music Festivals. Other small groups, Wind Ensemble, Brass Group, Barber Shop Singers, String Quartet, meet regularly each week. A strong team of well qualified peripatetic teachers cover a wide range of instrumental teaching. The School is fortunate in having a purpose-built Music School with good facilities for practice. There are good opportunities to hear first-class concerts given each term by visiting professional artists.

Fees. From September 2001. Boarding: Senior School £5,200 per term. Preparatory School £3,890 per term. Day: Senior School £3,700 per term. Preparatory School £2,820 per term.

Scholarships. (*see* Entrance Scholarship section) An examination is held in February each year at which up to 4 awards of up to 50% are made. Scholarships may also be awarded for ability in Art, Craft, Music (Instrumental and Choral), and All-Round Ability. They are valued from 50% to 5% of the school fees. Candidates must be under 14 on the 1st June.

Means-tested Bursaries are also awarded in cases where a scholarship or exhibition would not in itself be sufficient for a pupil to attend the School.

Bursaries are sometimes awarded to pupils in need of financial assistance. Some of these bursaries are reserved for the children of serving members of HM Forces.

There is also a closed award available for the sons and daughters of all ranks of the Devonshire and Dorset Regiment.

Charitable status. Clayesmore School Limited is a Registered Charity, number 306214. It exists for educational purposes.

Cokethorpe School

Near Witney Oxfordshire OX29 7PU.
Tel: (01993) 703921

The School was founded in 1957 and occupies a Queen Anne Mansion and substantial new buildings surrounded by 46 acres of parkland on the edge of the Cotswolds, two miles from Witney and ten from Oxford.

There has recently been an extensive building programme including new boarding accommodation and new premises for Science, Maths, Languages, Design Technology, Graphics, Art, Ceramics, Photography, Information Technology and Music, as well as a new Library and recreation facilities for the Sixth Form. A new Sports Centre was opened in 1995, and a new IT 'Resource Centre' will open in 2001.

There are just over 500 pupils between the ages of 7 and 18 at the school. There are only 16 pupils in the largest class, and the individual attention and encouragement received enables pupils to achieve their full potential.

Governing Body:
Chairman: M StJohn Parker, MA

A W Baker, Esq
P Cooke, MA, MSc, DipIndAdmin
J Davis, MA, CEng, FIEE, FIMechE
D J Stew, FCA
C Day, Esq
Miss A C Jones, MA, FRSA
B Brown, BA, DA, FCSD, FRSA
D Greasby, NDA, MRAC, DipFMan, DAg
J R Hunt, MEd, DLC,
D P Mason, Esq
D Shepherd, MA
J Moore, JP, PhD, MA, FRSA

***Headmaster:* P J S Cantwell**, BA, PGCE

Deputy Head: D A T Ward, MA, BEd

Director of Studies: P G F Harrison, BA, TEFL

Head of Junior School: Mrs W Foster, BSc, PGCE

Head of Pastoral Care: K Walton, CertEd

Chaplain: Revd A R Turner

School Accountant: Mrs S A Landon, BA, ACMA

Assistant Staff:
R James, BA, CertEd
P J Cranham, BA
W H C Daniels, BSc, PGCE
E J Fenton, BD, PGCE
C Maskery, BA, MSc, PGCE
Mrs M J Anderson, DipEd
Miss P S Townsend, BA, PGCE
Mrs S Barton, CertTEFL
Mrs J Phillips, BEd
J Rotherham, GRNCM, FMus, FCSM, PGCE, FRSA, FSA (Scot)
Mrs R S E Dent, BA
A S Nicholson, BEd
Mrs I S McKenzie, MA, PGCE
Miss R J Holland, BEd
Mrs S E du Feu, BEd
Mrs J Stormont, BSc
Mrs M Prior, BA
P W Humphreys, BSc
K Lomas, BSc, PGCE
Mrs M D Marchbank, BEd
Miss R Mills, BEd
Miss J H Parker, BEd
I D Wright, BA
Mrs J Legg, CertEd
P Warner, BSc
Miss J A Nice, BA, PGCE
S Dillon, HND, BA, PGCE
Miss S White, BA, PGCE
W A Jefferson, BA, PGCE, TEFL
Mrs A L Lord, BA, DipSLD
Miss J L Tuckwell, BEd
Miss M T Delany, BEd
Miss R G Ogilvie, BSc, PGCE
Mrs R J Simpson, BEd, DipSLD
M T Jackson, BEd
J Cowan, BEd
Mrs E Ainley, BA, DipSLD
Mrs J Dow, BEd
K Taylor, BSc, PGCE
Miss S McConville, BA, PGCE
Mrs S Martin, BA
Miss R Roberts, BA
Mrs J Holmes, BSc
Revd L F Collins, BD, PGCE
Miss R Pearce, BEd
S J Rae, BA
Mrs C L Jefferson, BA, PGCE
Mrs L Boulton, BEd, DipSLD
Mrs W McLaughlin, BSc
Mrs S Saunders, BEd
Mrs L Bridge, BA, PGCE
Mrs A Mitchell, BA, MA, PGCE

Visiting teachers for:
Piano, Violin, 'Cello, Wind and Brass instruments, Timpani, Singing

Admission. Pupils enter either at 7, 9, 11, 13 or 16. All are required to sit assessments in Maths, English and Verbal Reasoning. Places and Scholarships are offered on the basis of these assessments.

Curriculum. All pupils follow the National Curriculum until GCSE unless there are sound educational reasons why a particular subject should not be studied.

In year 10 all pupils have a choice of GCSE options which include Design Technology, Art, Ceramics, Drama, a second language, Business Studies, Music and Physical Education. There is also a full programme of personal and social education.

Pupils who may require learning support can be given extra help within the Learning Support Department, which is staffed by qualified specialist teachers.

After 16+ pupils join the sixth form and study at least four subjects to AS level and at least three to A2 level, or opt for the more vocational GNVQ courses at Intermediate or Advanced level. The small size of teaching groups is particularly conducive to individual attention and encouragement.

All forms throughout the school are deliberately kept small.

Religion. From its foundation the school has had separate Anglican and Roman Catholic Chapels and there are regular services. Pupils of other faiths are welcome too. The whole school meets together for Assemblies each weekday.

Houses. There are four houses. Boarders are all members of Vanbrugh House. Each pupil, day or boarding, has a tutor who is responsible for overseeing pastoral and academic development.

Sport. The school has a strong and successful sporting tradition. Rugby, netball, hockey, soccer, cricket, athletics, rowing, archery, tennis, fencing, badminton, golf, judo, squash, swimming, climbing and watersports, are all available. All pupils do PE as part of the curriculum.

Other Activities. These play a prominent part in a pupil's timetable and include Design Club, Rambling, Music and Culture Club, Birdwatching, Art, Ceramics, Cookery, Climbing, Library, Drama, Social Service, Computing, Flower Arranging, Local History, Chess, Bridge, Army Cadet Force, Outdoor Pursuits, Textiles, Sketching, Young Enterprise Group, History Club and Duke of Edinburgh Award Scheme.

Music and Drama. All pupils are encouraged to learn a musical instrument and join the choir, and the majority do so. Peripatetic teachers cover a very wide range of instruments, and there are regular concerts and recitals during the year. Drama flourishes with regular workshops, themed evenings and productions.

Careers. The School is a member of ISCO. Help and advice is given by experienced Careers Teachers and the latest literature is available in the Careers Centre which is open at all times.

Fees. Boarders over 13 £5,250 per term, Boarders 11/12 £4,180 per term, Day Boys over 13 £3,160 per term, Day Boys 11/12 £2,460 per term. Girls £2,460. Junior School 7/8 £1,770, 9/10 £1,820. Extras are kept to a minimum.

Old Cokethorpian Society. *Secretary of the Cokethorpe Society:* Philip Vaughan-Fowler, 87 Stuart Road, London SW19 8DJ. Tel: 020 8946 6132

Charitable status. Cokethorpe Educational Trust Limited is a Registered Charity, number 309650. It aims to provide a first class education for each individual pupil.

Dover College

Dover Kent CT17 9RH
Tel: 01304 205969
Fax: 01304 242208
e-mail: registrar@dovercollege.demon.co.uk
website: www.dover-college.kent.sch.uk

Dover College was founded in 1871 and occupies the grounds of the Priory of St Martin, a 24 acre site in the centre of Dover. Another 20 acres of playing fields are nearby. The College Close is surrounded by a number of impressive medieval buildings. Pupils still use the original Refectory, and the School Chapel is a fine 12th Century building. The site has been occupied for 800 years.

The College was granted a Royal Charter by His Majesty King George Vth in 1923 and the Patron of the College is the Lord Warden of the Cinque Ports. Her Majesty Queen Elizabeth the Queen Mother is the current Patron.

Dover College is the closest school to Continental Europe. It can be reached in forty minutes by hovercraft or through the Channel Tunnel. There are four European capitals within three hours' drive.

Patron:
Her Majesty Queen Elizabeth The Queen Mother

Governors:
Members of the Council:
C P Hare, Esq (*Chairman*)
J T Sullivan, Esq (*Vice Chairman*)
P Chadwick, Esq
M J Dakers, Esq
Dr M J Hustler
M G Krayenbrink, Esq
G N Nickalls, Esq
J N H Rice, Esq
J G Ryeland, Esq
D R Walter, Esq
G E Watts, Esq

Other Governors:
W D Dane, Esq
N J Drury, Esq
G L Eccleshall, Esq
R D S Foxwell, Esq
Gp Capt M V P H Harrington
J A Higinbotham, Esq
Miss Joan Kirby
H J Leslie, Esq
Mrs J McNaught
Prof G Nicholls
Dr J Sedgwick
C H Thompson, Esq
P J Venning, Esq

***Headmaster:* H W Blackett**, MA (Oxon)

Deputy Head: Mrs Helen J Tresidder, BSc (London)

Assistant Staff:
M Algar, BA (*Business Studies*)
M Beere (*Mathematics*)
G Blunt (*PE, Housemaster Leamington*)
D C Butler, BA (Wales) (*Head of English*)
A Christodoulou, BSc (*Head of Mathematics*)
Miss S Clark (*PE*)
J Dewick, BA Hons Fine Art (*Art/CDT*)
P A H Donnelly, BA, DipTEFL (*Head of International Study Centre*)
C Ellis, BA (*Modern Languages*)
Mrs J Harris (*Careers*)
J Hart, BEd (*Head of Design Technology*)
G R Hill, BA (*Head of Geography, Housemaster Crescent House*)
Miss M Jones, BSc (*Science*)
Mrs C Knowles (*Head of Curriculum Support Unit*)
N S Lockhart, MSc (*Head of Biology*)
Miss M McArdle, BA (*Head of Modern Languages*)
R A McCorkell, BSc (*Head of Science*)
D Partridge, BSc (Econ) (*Head of Economics and Business Studies, Housemaster School House*)
Miss J Single, BA (*English & Drama, Housemistress Priory House*)
R G Spencer, MA, FRCO (*Director of Music, Religious Studies*)
G Stephenson, BSc (*Mathematics*)
S E Thomas, BA (*Director of Studies & Head of Classics and Humanities Faculty*)
Mrs Y Thompson (*Housemistress St Martin's House*)
M T Vanderhoeven, BA (*Head of IT*)
Mrs P Vincent, CertEd (*Head of Art, Housemistress Duckworth, Art*)
J Welham, BSc (*Mathematics*)
R Wharton, MA (*Head of Chemistry*)

Bursar and Business Manager: Lt Col P P B Critchley
Registrar: Mrs E Laverty
Headmaster's Secretary: Mrs S Phillips
Medical Officer: Dr M Collins, MB, ChB
Medical Centre Sisters: Mrs C Hunt, Mrs D Laughland

Dover College will be opening a Junior School (non-boarding) for pupils aged 7-10 years in September 2001.

Co-education. Dover College (11–18) has been fully co-educational since 1975 and the 250 boys and girls are integrated at all levels. There are 100 boarders, 150 day pupils; 100 girls and 150 boys.

Houses. There are 7 Houses, all situated on the College Close, 4 for boys, including 2 Day Houses, and 3 for girls incorporating both day girls and boarders. All VIth Formers have Study-bedrooms.

Catering. Catering is provided centrally in modern kitchens adjacent to the Refectory, under the supervision of a fully trained and experienced Chef Manager.

Curriculum. First, second and third form pupils study a wide range of subjects. Great importance is placed upon literacy, numeracy, information technology and key skills. Fourth and fifth form pupils study between six and ten GCSE subjects, depending on their level of ability. The curriculum at this level is flexible, enabling pupils to have an academic curriculum designed to suit individual needs.

All pupils are given very careful guidance when making their GCSE level choices, by their Academic Tutor, Housemaster/Housemistress, the Careers Department and by the Director of Studies.

Considerable emphasis is placed upon the breadth of education offered: music, art and drama are an integral part of the curriculum. All of our pupils participate in a variety of sports, with stress placed upon the development of leadership skills.

Pupils in the sixth form are able to choose AS and A levels from a list of 20 subjects. AVCE Business Studies is also on offer. Traditional academic subjects are provided, as are the practical subjects of physical education, art, design and technology, drama and music.

At all stages of a pupil's career at Dover College, progress is carefully monitored. Assessment periods occur regularly, during which pupils are graded for achievement and effort. A merit/demerit system operates for pupils aged up to 16. Classes at Dover College are kept as small as possible. Class size up to GCSE level is generally between 15-20 and at 'A' level 10-15. Some 'A' level sets are smaller. Most lessons are on 'Middle Ground' in well equipped, modern classrooms.

The school works in close liaison with Kent Careers Services, to plan, deliver and evaluate an integrated careers' education and guidance programme. This enables pupils to gain the necessary knowledge, skills and understanding in order to make informed career plans before attending the universities or jobs of their choice.

International Study Centre (ISC). Dover has recruited pupils from many parts of the world for a considerable number of years. These pupils receive intensive English tuition in the ISC, to enable them to enter the main stream examination classes after a suitable period of time. In addition to this, pupils who require ESL support receive it in the ISC as often as necessary.

Individual Support. There is a Curriculum Support Unit in which pupils with learning difficulties (eg Dyslexia) receive 1:1 tuition. Each pupil has a member of staff as a personal tutor. The tutor supervises his/her pupil's general academic progress.

Technology. The Technology building was opened in Autumn 1991. Pupils are encouraged to work with a range of materials (wood, metal, plastic etc). Design Technology is available at GCSE and A level. A number of Technology Clubs exist.

Music, Art, Crafts and Drama. Music plays a particularly important part in the life of the school. The well equipped Music Department is located just off site. The School Choir has an excellent reputation. A House Music Festival takes place annually. There is a wide range of musical groups (orchestra, jazz group, choral groups etc). Regular concerts occur; musicians often perform in the local community. Drama is a very active part of the cultural life of the school, as well as part of the Lower School curriculum. There is a major school production each year. In addition, there are House productions. Drama is offered at 'A' level and GCSE level. The Art Department was opened in 1991 and is in the same building as Technology. Fine Art, pottery and photography are available. Examination results are always good at both 'A' level and GCSE.

ICT. A new Computer Centre was opened in December 1998. Pupils have access to high specification computers, which have excellent software. Each computer is linked to the internet.

Sport. The principal playing fields are 10 minutes' walk away on the outskirts of the town, but the Tennis Courts are situated on The Close. The school has an excellent modern Sports Hall. Sports include: Athletics, Badminton, Basketball, Cricket, Cross Country Running, Football, Hockey, Netball, Sailing, Tennis, Volleyball and various PE activities. Swimming takes place at the indoor pool in Dover Leisure Centre. Golf may be played on local courses and horse riding is also offered locally.

Other Afternoon and Evening Activities. In addition to Games, pupils have the opportunity to take part in a wide range of activities, including Adventure Training, Art, Chess, Computing, Debating, Duke of Edinburgh Award, Electronics, Estate Work, First Aid, Library Work, Language Clubs, Minerva Club (for Scholars), Music, Photography, Printing, Project Work (in academic subjects), Social Services in the town, Stage Management and Technology.

Religious Life. The College has its own Chapel and is essentially Christian in character. All pupils are encouraged to respect each other's beliefs and faiths from a position of tolerance and understanding.

Careers. Every possible assistance is given to pupils in the selection of their future careers. Up-to-date information about careers of all kinds is available in the recently renovated and very well resourced Careers Room.

Pastoral Care. All pupils benefit from a carefully designed system of pastoral care. Every Dover College student belongs to a House and Boarders are provided with good quality accommodation in one of three boarding houses. All sixth formers have single study-bedrooms. A Housemaster or Housemistress, supported by a team of tutors, runs each House. It is their role to give pastoral support as well as supervising their academic progress.

There is a fully equipped medical centre, which can accommodate pupils overnight, staffed by two professionally qualified nurses.

Admission. Pupils are admitted at 11, 13 or 16 but may come at any age. The school has its own 11+ examination. 13+ pupils normally sit the Common Entrance examination at their own Prep School. Provision is made for direct entry into the VIth Form for both boys and girls. This is normally conditional upon GCSE results. Further information is obtainable from the Registrar.

Terms of Entry. Most pupils join the College in September, but entry in January and April is possible.

Fees per term. The basic fees in 2001/02 are Junior Day: £1,350-£1,600; Senior Day: £1,890-£2,776; Senior Flexi Boarding: £3,480-£3,740; Full Boarding: £3,726-£4,750.

Scholarships. (*see* Entrance Scholarship section) Academic, Music, Art and Sports Scholarships and Exhibitions are available. The scholarships are offered to 11+, 13+ and 16+. Scholarships may also be awarded to pupils entering at VIth Form level on the pupil's performance at GCSE level. Details can be obtained from the Registrar.

Old Dovorian Society. *Secretary:* J G Ryeland, c/o Dover College.

Charitable status. Dover College is a Registered Charity, number 307856. The School exists "to encourage individual excellence and success".

Duke of York's Royal Military School

Guston Dover Kent CT15 5EQ
Tel: 01304 245024

The Duke of York's Royal Military School was founded in 1803. It is a co-educational boarding school for the children of Servicemen and Servicewomen.

Patron: HRH The Duke of Kent

Her Majesty's Commissioners:

Major-General D Grove, OBE (*Chairman*)

Brigadier M A Atherton, CBE, JP, DL
Sir John Carter
The Revd Dr V Dobbin, MBE, QHC, MA, MTh, PhD
Brigadier Anne Field, CB, CBE
Air Vice-Marshal M R Jackson
Major-General A L Meier, CB, OBE
R A Perrin, Esq, MA

***Headmaster:* Mr J A Cummings**, BA, MA

Senior Deputy Head (Curriculum): Mr A K Bisby, MEd, ACP, MCollP
Deputy Head (Pastoral): Mr T R Porter, BSc, PGCE
Director of Studies: Mr J English, BSc, PGCE, FRGS
Bursar: Mr R Say, FCMA, ACIS, MIMgt
Assistant Bursar: Mrs K M Vinson
Chaplain: The Reverend R Broughton, BA, DipTh, PGCE

Assistant Teachers:

English & Drama:
Mr S Salisbury, BA, PGCE (*Head of Department*)
Mr S Allan, BA, PGCE
Mr S J Artus, BA, MA, PGCE
Mr H R Brown, MA
Mr A Clarke, BA
Mrs J Dawson, BA, TCert (*Alanbrooke Housemistress*)
Mrs H Hudgell, CertEd
Mr J Young, BA

Mathematics:
Mr H C Mortimer, BSc (*Head of Department*)
Mr S J Adams, BSc
Mrs B K Broughton, BEd (*Marlborough Housemistress*)
Mr M J Brown, BA, TCert (*Clive Housemaster*)
Mr J Marsh, BEng
Mr J B Morris, BA, TCert (*Kitchener Housemaster*)
Mr M G T Trewartha, BA, TCert

Science:
Dr R D Lane, BSc, PhD, CChem, FRSC (*Head of Department*)
Mr A W Bickerstaff, BEd
Mr A K Bisby, MEd, ACP, MCollP
Ms E J Boakes, BSc
Mr C Collishaw, BSc, TCert
Mrs C J Dyer, BSc (*Wolfe Housemistress*)
Mrs E S Ladd, BEng, PGCE
Miss K Parkes, BSc, DipEd
Mr M S Rixon, BSc, PGCE (*Roberts Housemaster*)

Modern Languages:
Mrs A C Maclennan, LLB, DipPGCE, AInstLing (*Head of Department*)
The Revd J R Broughton, BA, DipTh, PGCE
Mrs J M K Hyam, BA, PGCE (*Housemistress Clive*)
Mrs C Maxwell, TCert
Mr J H North, BA, DipEd
Miss A Sheppard, BEd

Humanities:
Mr M B Carson, MA (*Head of Department*)
Mr J English, BSc, PGCE, FRGS
Mr H M Marsh, BSc, PGCE
Mr A M Nunn, BEd
Mr R J Pearce, BA, PGCE (*Haig Housemaster*)
Mr T R Porter, BSc, PGCE
Mrs C Sampson, TCert
Mr S S Saunderson, BA, PGCE (*Wolseley Housemaster*)

Technology & Art:
Mr I C Brewin, MA (*Head of Technology & Art*)
Miss H A Noyce, BA, PGCE
Mr D L Parsons, BA, TCert
Mr M J Saunders, CertEd
Miss J J Shanks, MA
Mr M Towers, BEd, LCG

Business Studies, IT and Vocational Education:
Mr R H Harrison, BA, CEdIEng (*Head of Faculty*)
Mr D W Alexander, BA, CEdIEng (*Wellington Housemaster*)
Mrs M M Andrews, BA Hons, DipCertEd
Mrs S Ganley, BA, PGCE
Mr N Phipps, TCert
Mrs C Purvey, BA, MA, PGCE (*Head of Business Studies*)

Physical Education:
Mr R J Crisp, DipPhys(Ed) (*Director of Recreation*)
Miss J M Dobbin, BEd
Mr G A D Vickery, ASACert

Music:
Mr A H Auld, BMus, ARCO, ARCM, PGCE (*Director of Music*)
Mr P K Kane, ARCM (*Late 17/21L*)
Mr I P Smith, BMus, PGCE, CertRS

Careers: Mrs C Purvey, BA, MA, PGCE

Librarian: Mrs J Dawson, BA, TCert

School Doctor: Dr T A Khan

School Dentist: Mr J Liston

Headmaster's Personal Assistant: Miss K Smitton

General. The Duke of York's Royal Military School provides a unique education for the 11 to 18 year old children of those who have served for a minimum period of four years on regular engagements in the British Armed Forces.

The school aims to provide a high quality education and secure boarding environment with particular attention being given to the needs of service children.

Situation. The school is magnificently resourced and stands in 150 acres of attractive parkland, two kilometres north of Dover. Accommodation and facilities are first class as a result of years of generous funding and careful husbandry. There are nine single gender boarding houses serving the needs of some 500 pupils.

Curriculum. Academic work for 11 to 16 year olds follows the national curriculum. There is a broad based range of subjects leading to 6 to 10 GCSE entries per candidate in Year 11. With small class sizes and teacher pupil ratio of 1 to 10, the academic provision is comprehensive and success rate is consistently much higher than the national average.

In the Sixth Form a wide range of AS, A Levels and ANVQ courses is offered. The vast majority of Sixth Form leavers enter University. Careers education and guidance is provided as an integral part of the curriculum.

Boarding. The boarding environment gives a strong sense of community and stability for pupils who have had a very disjointed education and home life. Each of the nine boarding houses is generously staffed with teaching and support staff. House Tutors who are also qualified teachers look after between 12 and 15 pupils each.

The School Doctor and Dentist are supported by resident nursing Sisters who provide 24 hour medical care.

Sport, Music and Drama. The school has excellent sporting facilities and an enviable sporting reputation.

Music and Drama have strong traditions in the school. Junior years receive lessons in Music and Drama. Both subjects are options at GCSE and A Level. There is a large Band, excellent Chapel Choir, Orchestra, Choral Society, Jazz Band and other groups. The school has an impressive theatre.

Other Activities. The range of clubs and activities is extensive. Pupils are given every opportunity to discover and to develop their various interests. There is a comprehensive programme of educational visits, international exchanges and trips and expeditions abroad.

There is a strong CCF and within the CCF there is scope for Adventurous Training and the Duke of Edinburgh's

Award Scheme. The school has a unique ceremonial tradition with a large military band which in addition to the other activities enables pupils to develop teamwork, initiative and leadership skills.

Entry requirements. Examinations in English, Mathematics and good Headteacher's report.

Four years service in HM Forces by either parent.

Fees per term. Boarding £400.

Elmhurst - The School for Dance and Performing Arts

Heathcote Road Camberley Surrey GU15 2EU

Tel: (01276) 65301
Fax: (01276) 670320
e-mail: elmhurst@cableol.co.uk

Elmhurst, now in its 75th year, is one of the oldest vocational schools in the United Kingdom attracting students from all over the British Isles and from most overseas countries. It has been greatly enlarged over the past decade with most of the many new buildings dating from this period. Purpose built, they include new academic teaching blocks, a science laboratory, new dance studios and an off-site sixth form boarding campus comprising two renovated and extended Edwardian houses. A new music department is situated close to the school's 230 seat theatre. This has a full-size stage and the most modern computerised lighting plant and sound system. New dressing rooms have recently been built. There are eight large dance studios, new drama facilities and a school chapel in which Sunday Services are given by the Chaplain. The foundation is Church of England, but the school welcomes other denominations. There is also a new Information Technology Centre which houses a 20 networked computer installation.

Diet, for obvious reasons, is carefully monitored and the school has its own catering manager and staff. Food is totally prepared within the school and no external firm of caterers is employed.

Although ballet is taught to the highest level, every kind of dance tuition is provided to professional company standards. Music and drama are also prominent, as well as singing, both classical and modern.

Along with vocational training academic education is integrated within the timetable and GCSE and A level courses are provided.

Governors:
Canon Dr R S Crossley, BSc, BD, PhD (*Chairman*)
Simon Crocker, LLB
David Healey, MA, FCA
David Knox, Esq
Mrs Susan Marr
Dame Antoinette Sibley, DBE
Mrs Anne Stroyan
David Watchman, Esq

***Principal:* John J McNamara**, BA, MPhil

Artistic Director of Dance: Alfreda Thorogood, ARAD, PDTC, DipRAD

Head of Boarding & Pastoral Care: Julie McNamara, BA Hons

Bursar: Brigadier G R Slater, OBE, BSc

Chaplaincy Team:
The Revd Martin Breadmore (*School Chaplain*)
Dean Ayres
Sarah Bolton
Mark Landreth-Smith
The Revd Phil Dykes

Vocational Faculty:

Sue Arkle, ISTD, IdB, PdB (*Spanish*)
Paul Bailey (*Jazz*)
Eleanor Bennett, DRSAM (*Singing*)
Judith Binding, LRAM, ARCM (*Co-ordinator of Vocational Programmes & Head of Pianists*)
Heather Fish, ARAD, FISTD, DipRBS TTC (*Classical Ballet*)
Verity Fry, MA, IIST (*Pilates Body Conditioning*)
Sue Goodman, BA Hons (*Contemporary*)
Sarah Gregory, ARAD, DipPDTC (*Classical Ballet*)
Robert Greenhill, DipEd, GNCM (*Singing*)
Donna Hayward, ISTD (*Examiner Modern Theatre Dance Branch*)
Fiona Hayward, AISTD, DipRBS TTC (*Character*)
Jackie Hayward, LISTD, AISTD (*Modern & Tap*)
Mercia Hetherington, ARAD, SADTA, ISTD (*Head of Dance/Classical Ballet*)
Stephen Joseph, AISTD (*Jazz*)
Paul Madden, ARAD, ISTD (*Musical Theatre*)
Julie McNamara, BA Hons (*Acting*)
Jason di Mascio, AISTD (*Free Style Tap*)
Linda Moran, ARAD, DipPDTC (*Classical Ballet*)
Stephanie Nunn, ARCM, DipEd (*Singing*)
Jane Rivers, CertEd, CDS, LDS (*Dalcroze Eurthymics*)
Geoffrey Swann, BA Hons, PGCE (*Acting*)
Alfreda Thorogood, ARAD, DipPDTC (*Artistic Director/Classical Ballet*)
Mark Tyme, RSA (*Jazz*)
Andre De Villiers, NatDipPA, ARAD, SADTA (*Course Director, Dance & Performing Arts/Contemporary*)
Sherrill Wexler, ARAD, ISTD, MdB (*Classical Ballet/Spanish*)
Marilyn Williams (*Contemporary*)
Andrew Wilson, ARAD, DipPDTC(RAD) (*Head of Boys/Classical Ballet*)

Guest Choreographers/Teachers:
Geoffrey Cauley (*Classical*)
Dollie Henry (*Jazz*)

Repetiteurs:

Judith Binding, LRAM, ARCM
Jill Barnes, LRAM
Maureen Blaydon, ARCM, GRSM
Philip Buckmaster, BA Hons, ARCO, CMED
Martin Colbourne, LRAM
Beata Cornfield, LTCL
Julia Clarke, LRAM
Jo Fearn, ARCM
Trevor Lomas, BSc Hons
Joey Misquita, FTCL, LTCL(T)
Gary Moore, LGSM

Academic Faculty:

Andrew McAulay, BA Hons, PGCE *History/RE*
Nicholas Bassett, BA Hons, MFA, PGCE *Art*
Paula Earwicker, BSc *Mathematics*
Michelle Fabbeni, BEd Hons, CertTEFL *EFL*
Duncan Fraser, BA Hons, PGCE *Music*
Candy Hadler, AISTD *Dance*
Rachel Haver, BA Hons, PGCE *Geography*
John McNamara, BA Hons, MPhil (*Theatre Studies*)
Susan Nodder, BSc Hons, PhD, PGCE (*Science*)
Clare Parker, MA *French*
Bronwyn Patton, BA Hons, MA, PGCE *English*
Philip Rothenberg, BA Hons, DipEd, MEd *IT*
Auriel Roe, BA Hons, MA, PGCE *Drama*
Marilyn Sheppard-Vine, BEd Hons, CertEd *Mathematics*

Sheila Abbis, CBiol, MIBiol *Science Technician*

Boarding & Pastoral Care:
Rhona Andrews, RGN, RM *School Nurse*
Nicholas Bassett, Housemaster *Elmhurst House*
Charlotte Bridge, Resident Tutor *Helen Fischer House*
Lara Chisholm, GAP Student *Mortimer House*
Paula Earwicker, Resident Tutor *Lawton House*
Trudi Elphick, RGN, RM *School Nurse*
Michelle Fabbeni, Housemistress *St Kitts House*
Susie Forth, Housemistress *Helen Fischer House*
Janet Hark, Housemistress *Lawton House*
Jen Jameson, GAP Student *Mortimer House*
Jennifer Langmuir, BA Hons Housemistress *Mortimer & All Saints House*
Andrew McAulay, Resident Tutor *Elmhurst House*
Pam Woodliffe, Resident Tutor *St Kitts House*

General Practioners:
Ruth Cureton, BMedSci, MB, BS
Juliet Darnton, Chartered Physiotherapist
Jane E K Orr, MB, BS, MRCS, LRCP, DRCOG
Geoffrey O'Riordan, Chartered Physiotherapist
Geoffrey D Roberts, MB, GB, MRCP, MRCGP, DCH
Martin R Strudley, MB, BS, MRCP(Paed), MRCGP, DCH

Administrative & Catering Staff:

Principal's Secretary: Anita Bristow
Assistant Bursar: Denise Thomas
Catering Manager: Tony Manley, MHICA
Bursar's Secretary: Kate O'Brien
Receptionist: Lorraine Ward
Co-ordinator of Academic Programmes: Penny Willard, BA Hons

Number in School. There are 179 pupils in the School: 161 girls, 18 boys – 157 boarders, 22 day pupils.

Organisation and Aims. The aim of the school is to provide a first-rate education along normal academic lines with training in the performing arts to the highest possible standards. Training is divided into two sections: 11–16 years, and 16–19 years. Girls and boys are accepted between the ages of 11–13 (sometimes 14) and there is a further entry at 16. Pupils are expected to offer between 8 and 11 subjects at GCSE. During this phase of their training, dance examinations of both the RAD and the ISTD are taken, sometimes up to the most Advanced levels of the Major Executant examinations. From 16–19 students follow one of two Senior Dance courses, "Ballet & Performing Arts" or "Dance & Performing Arts" each accredited by the Council for Dance Education and Training. At the conclusion of the course students may receive the National Diploma in Professional Dance and should be in a position to audition for professional work. In addition, Elmhurst is able to present graduating students with a Registered Graduate Card, validated by British Actors Equity, enabling the holder to enter for professional auditions.

Dance training is also provided for intending teachers. Courses leading to the RAD Student Teaching Certificate (ballet) and to the Associate Modern Diploma (modern dance) of the ISTD are available.

Information Technology and business practice are provided as a useful second string to those entering the theatrical profession.

The past record of students obtaining work is excellent, and there are ex-students in all the British ballet companies, as well as European and North American. Elmhurst trained students are also to be found in musical theatre productions in the West End and elsewhere.

During the first two years of the three year sixth form course, students who wish to read for GCE A levels choose from the following: English, Dance, Music, Art and Theatre Studies. Some students decide to go to university prior to seeking careers in the theatre.

Residence. Lower School pupils (Years 7-11) live on the main Heathcote Road site in purpose built accommodation. Helen Fischer House, a detached building adjacent to the Elmhurst Studio Theatre, is our junior reception house for Year 7 boys and girls. From Year 8 onwards, girls live in either All Saints or Mortimer Houses and boys in Elmhurst House which is situated above the main administrative offices. Each of these four boarding houses on the main site has its own Houseparent and Resident Tutor who are assisted by GAP students from overseas countries. The children's laundry is attended to by in-house support staff.

Sixth form students (6/1 & 6/2) live on the West Road campus some 150 yards from the main site. They live in one of two mixed houses, Lawton House and St Kitts House, which accommodate 31 and 21 students respectively. These two buildings are recent developments which have been especially designed to very high specifications to provide accommodation of outstanding quality. Great emphasis has been placed on giving these students as much private space as possible and study facilities appropriate for the attainment of high grades at A level.

The students in these two boarding houses have their own fully equipped laundry rooms and Common Room areas with kitchen facilities. 6/3 students live off-campus in local flats and houses thereby gaining useful preparation for life in the outside world. The school gives every assistance to these graduate year students in finding suitable rented accommodation.

All pupils and students are encouraged to talk to staff if they have a problem or difficulty and confidential referral to professional counsellors and medical staff is immediately available in cases of need. In 1998 Elmhurst received a most complimentary report from the Social Services Inspectorate of Surrey County Council for the quality of its boarding and pastoral care.

Medical and Physiotherapy Services. The school's medical centre is located on the main site and has been designed according to the guidelines of MOSA, the Medical Officers of Schools Association. It comprises a reception area, consulting room, physiotherapy room, a ward with six beds, a separate isolation room, bathroom, dayroom and kitchen. On a daily basis, the centre is run by two full-time nursing sisters, one of whom is the Resident Tutor of Helen Fischer House. Our medical practitioners hold twice weekly surgeries in the medical centre and, as required, at their practice, the Upper Gordon Road Surgery, some fifty yards from the school. Elmhurst is fortunate in having a highly committed team of GPs with specialist interests in sport injuries and eating disorders.

Our doctors have recently opened a new physiotherapy suite at the Upper Gordon Road medical centre. This facility and the services of two, full-time physiotherapists are available to all Elmhurst pupils, by appointment, on a five days per week basis. All pupils have BUPA cover to enable them to obtain rapid orthopaedic advice from a consultant should this be needed.

Our policy documents relating to medical and pastoral care issues are available for parents and guardians to consult. If you wish to peruse these, please contact the Head of Boarding & Pastoral Care.

Location. British Rail mainline to Waterloo. Close to A30, M3 and M4. Half an hour drive to London Heathrow and Gatwick airports.

Camberley is a pleasant town with new shopping precinct a few hundred metres away from the school. West End theatres are close enough to permit regular visits to ballets, operas, plays and concerts.

Entry. This is by competitive audition. Lower down in the school potential is looked for combined with good physique. Some students are in receipt of discretionary awards from their LEAs. Parents apply directly to their local authorities following the offer of a place after successful audition. As a member school of the Government's "Music and Ballet Scheme", Elmhurst is able to offer ten DfEE Aided Places to pupils aged 11 years on entry to the school each September. For those joining our Senior courses, Elmhurst has been invited to offer places under the Government's new Dance and Drama Awards. These scholarships provide reduced fees and access to student support for eligible individuals aged 16 years and over. Generally some three or four audition sessions are held in each term. Prospective parents and their children are shown round the school and meet the Principal on audition days. Special arrangements are made for overseas students.

Fees. These compare favourably with many schools. From September 1999 the termly fees for Lower School boarders will be £3,692; Sixth Form boarders £3,890. The termly fees for Lower School day students £2,711; Sixth Form day students £2,809.

Charitable status. Elmhurst Ballet School Trust is a Registered Charity, number A307349A/1. Its aim is to provide high quality vocational and academic education.

Embley Park School

Romsey Hampshire SO51 6ZE
Tel: (01794) 512206 (Headmaster); (01794) 515737 (Junior School);
(01794) 830717 (Bursar)
Fax: (01794) 518737; (01794) 830353 (Junior School)
e-mail: headmaster.embleyparkschool@virgin.net
bursar.embleyparkschool@virgin.net
registrar.embleyparkschool@virgin.net

There has been a school at Embley Park since 1946. Its main building was the home of the Nightingale family and Florence Nightingale lived at Embley until she went to the Crimea in 1854. The School estate is of the order of 100 acres and more than £4 million pounds has been spent on new buildings in recent years, particularly in creating a 3-18 school on site.

The Governors are members of GBA and constituted as an educational charity.

The School is fully co-educational 3–18. The Junior & Nursery School has its own separate campus at the Embley Park site.

Governing Body:
D A d'Arcy Hughes, Esq (*Chairman*)
M G Baker, RSVA, FRVA, (*Old Embleian*)
The Revd Canon M J Benton, BSc
J Lewis, Esq
D J Martin, MB, BS, DObst, RCOG
Mrs D Moody, AILAM
Mrs V Perry, QT
Mrs M Stanway, BSc(Psych)
J Tickell, ACA
S J Wallbridge, FRICS, FSVA (*Old Embleian*)
Dr M E Witherick, BA, PhD

***Head Master:* David F Chapman**, BA (Dunelm), FCollP

Deputy Head Master: R L Macartney, MA (East Anglia), BA (Trinity College, Dublin)

Assistant staff:

Mrs W E Blackwell, BSc (Kent) *Senior Mistress*

A J Brooks, BA (Trent) *Chichester Housemaster*
C D Cates, BSc (Southampton) *Palmerston Housemaster*
K A Cooper, MA (Oxon) *Head of Boarding*
Mrs C Adams, CertEd and D M Adams, MET *Heads of Middle School* (*Years 7 & 8*)
Mrs A E James, CertEd *Nightingale Housemistress*

P H Badham, MA (Glasgow)
S Baker, BSc (Wales)
Miss J Bright, BGA Coach
Mrs N Brown, BA (Liverpool)
Mrs H J Chapman, BA (Kent)
Mrs J Collings, BSc (Brunel)
Mrs H K Cooper, MA (Oxon)
Miss P Dodd, BSc (Leeds)
R E Foster, BA, PhD (Southampton)
Mrs K Griffiths, BA (Rosemont, USA), MA (Birmingham), RSADip
Mrs S J Hall, BSc (Swansea)
Mrs S L Jones, BA (Open)
Miss K Latty, BA(Ed) (Reading)
C Lowde, BSc (Bath)
Mrs J Macartney, CertEd
R D Martin, BSc (Kent)
N A May, BSc (Exeter)
Mrs C Miles, CertEd
Miss E F Pearson, BA (Surrey)
Miss K Raphael, BSc (Brunel)
A P Scott, LLB (Leicester)
Miss S Smith, BA (Sheffield)
M R Thomas, BEd (Open)
Miss B Weeks, BA (Birmingham)
Mrs D Williams, BEd (Bath), DipRSA
J R Williams, BA (Bath), FTCL, LTCL
J Winship, BEd (Sunderland)

Music and Drama Teachers:
J R Williams, BA (Bath) *Director of Music, Piano, Organ, Singing*
K Bonett, BSc *Percussion*
Mrs S Newman, LTCL, CertEd *Piano*
C Moores *Electric Guitar*
M Callow *Woodwind and Strings*

The Junior School. (*Tel:* 01794 515737; Fax: 01794 830353)

Co-opted to the Governors Management Committee:
Mrs J Finch, MA(Ed) (Southampton)
R Butler, BSc (Coventry), FFA

Head Teacher: Mrs T M Rogers, MA(Ed) (Southampton), CertEd

Teachers:
Mrs P Alldred, CertEd, KSI Coordinator)
Mrs J de Sausmarez, BEd (Bath College)
Mrs S Bartel, BEd (St Mary's, London)
Mrs N Brown, BA (Liverpool)
Miss D Burke, BEd (Exeter)
Mrs P Clark
Mrs A Coughlin, CertEd
Mrs K Griffiths, BA, MA, RSADipLD
D Lewis, BEd (Plymouth), KSII Coordinator
Mrs C Miles, CertEd
Mrs S M Payne, CertEd
Mrs S Williams, BTh (Southampton), MA(Ed) (Open University), CPDE

Junior School Music Teachers:
Mrs S Saunders *Violin*
Mrs C Williams *Piano & Keyboard*
Mrs P Glynne *Guitar*
Mrs C Williams *Brass/Piano/Keyboard*

Assistants:
Mrs L Chandler
Miss S Hardy, NNEB
Mrs T Thomas, RGN, PGCAES
Mrs J Moseley

Bursar and Clerk to the Governors: David S King

Chaplains:
The Reverend George Biggs, BA (Liverpool), BA (Cantab) (*Senior School*)

Head Master's Secretary: Mrs J E de Le Cuona

Junior School Head's Secretary: Mrs J Virrill, PPA

Assistant Bursar: Ms S Langdown

Senior Matron: Mrs D Jarvis, RGN

Assistant Matron: Mrs C Dixon, RGN

School Doctor: P J Burrows, BM, BCh, DObst, MRCP(UK), FRCGP

Constitution. There are 430 pupils, with 70 in the Sixth Form. Boys and girls are admitted at 11 and 13 by examination; and into the Sixth Form, at age 16, on GCSE results. The Junior School numbers 160.

There are boarding places available for both boys and girls (9–18), and approximately 40% of the School boards, in three senior houses, and in a waiting house (10 to 13). Day pupils are members of the same houses, thus obviating any feeling of division between boarding and day.

All senior pupils attend Chapel (after House Tutorials), and then commence lessons at 8.50 am. Following the academic routine, at 3.30 pm, in every afternoon, games or activities are organised allowing day pupils to depart at around 5 pm, having experienced the daily routine and ethos of a boarding school. Many day pupils ask to board in their senior years.

There are 160 Nursery and Junior pupils. Junior School lessons are from 8.45 am to 3 pm, followed by voluntary activities every afternoon. There is a morning and afternoon Nursery.

Curriculum. The Junior School follows the National Curriculum (with slight amendment, including the provision of French from the Reception Year), and offers a wide choice of after-school clubs, including ballet, gymnastics and football. In the Senior School the aim is GCSE and A Level. 85% of the Upper Sixth go on to degree courses as their Higher Education, 5% to "Oxbridge".

The GCSE curriculum offers a choice of 10 subjects at a time (including separate subject sciences and Design Technology (Graphics & Resistant Materials), PE, ICT and Business Studies) and careful note has been taken of those elements of the National Curriculum considered vital to personal development. German is the second language to French.

'A' Level is available in more then 20 subjects.

Careers guidance is given by House tutors from the earliest days, and by the staff Careers Adviser. Work Experience is undertaken in the vacations of the Lower Sixth year. AROA Record of Achievement is prepared for all Year 11 pupils.

Games and Activities. Rugby Football, Cricket, Hockey, Rounders and Netball are the main games, with Squash, Cross Country Running, Basketball, Swimming, Tennis, Athletics and Golf among others in a supporting role.

The School has a strong games tradition, achieving representation at County level, and beyond.

The School has its own practice golf course, floodlit pitch, lake and 7,000 sq ft Sports Hall.

All pupils are encouraged to attempt the Duke of Edinburgh Award Scheme, and Embley was one of the original schools to establish its own unit and there are several expeditions each year in the neighbouring New Forest, or in Wales, in the mountains. Lifesaving has a highly developed programme in which many participate. A number of Sixth Formers achieve Instructor certificates under the Royal Life Saving Society and, thus, teach younger pupils.

Admission Procedures. Admission to the Junior School is by interview with the Head Teacher.

An examination is set at 11+ and an interview expected, plus report from present school, (often a State Primary School).

A number of scholarships and awards at the Senior School are reserved for Embley Park Junior School pupils.

At 13+ the Common Entrance Examination is taken by all, except a minority from State Schools.

At 16+ an interview and report are expected.

Places are occasionally available in other age-groups.

Examinations and interviews may take place at any time during the twelve months preceding entry.

Details from the Head Master.

Scholarships, Exhibitions and Bursaries. (*see* Entrance Scholarship section) Awards are made for academic ability, for Art, Music, and General All-Round contribution to the life of the School, (including Sport), and Sixth Form.

Fees. Current fees can be obtained with a School Prospectus. There is a reduction for brother/sister and children of the Clergy, HM Forces and Teachers.

45 points at GCSE (where A* = 8 points), (plus A's and B's in subjects to be taken to A level) can achieve a 50% remission of the Sixth Form fee.

Location. Easily accessible from Eastleigh Airport (15 minutes), Southampton Parkway Railway Station (15 minutes) and M27 (5 minutes), Embley is 1½ miles north west of Romsey, on the Salisbury (A27) road. There is a railway station in Romsey.

Old Embleians. Chairman: Melanie Whitfield

Hon Sec. R L Bell, Esq, 1 Home Field Drive, Nursling, Southampton SO16 0TH.

Charitable status. Embley Park School is a Registeed Charity, number 307327. It exists to educate children.

Ewell Castle School

Church Street Ewell Surrey KT17 2AW.
Tel: 0181-393 1413/3952
Fax: 0181-786 8218

Ewell Castle, a day school, was built as a castellated mansion in 1814. The gardens and playing fields which extend to fifteen acres were once part of Nonsuch Park. The School, which was founded in 1926 is registered as an educational charity and is administered by a Board of Governors, which is in membership of the Governing Bodies Association.

Chairman of the Governing Body: J E D Cattermole

***Principal:* R A Fewtrell**, MA, FRSA

Head of Senior School: A J Tibble, BSc, PGCE

Head of Junior School: Mrs V A Goode, BEd, SRN

Senior Master: K B Peto, BA, PGCE

Assistant Staff:
M Bannister, BA, PGCE
*S J Bell, BEd
Miss R Benjamin, BA, PGCE
*S Bland, CertEd
Mrs B A Blum, BSc, PGCE
P Chatterton, BA, PGCE
*N D Cohen, BA, PGCE
*A J Green, MA, PGCE
*P W Hadden, BSc
†*N M Hammerton, BEd (*Housemaster, Castlemaine*)
Mrs D Hillman, BEd
J B Hopkin, DipArt, CIC

A Hopper, MA, PGCE
Mrs S Jones
Mrs M J Lovett, BA, CertEd
†D R H Miles, BA, PGCE (*Housemaster, Raleigh*)
*R A O'Brien, MA, HDE (*Senior Teacher, Curriculum*)
*C H Roffey, BSc, PGCE
M Sagar, BSc, CertEd, ABIM
J M W Scobie, BSc, PGCE, CBiol, MIBiol
M Stather, BSc, PGCE
P G Sutton, BEd
D Thompson, M des RCA, PGCE
E W Walliss, BEd
Miss S Wigley, BA, PGCE
Mrs S Young, PAB (Austria)

Junior School:
P Carnell
J P Hanley, BEd
Mrs J Higgs, CertEd
Mrs C Humphreys, Montessori Diploma
Miss C Leadbeter, MA, PGCE
Mrs C Leeds, NNEB, SEN
Miss T Skuse, BSc, PGCE
N J D Tinkler, BA, PGCE
Miss D Vourla, MEd
Miss E A Williams, BA

Registrar: Mrs L Moyle
Financial Administrator: Mr Z Pagacz
School Administrator: Mrs M Kaegler
School Secretaries: Mrs D Tibble; Mrs C Tallack
Careers Co-ordinator: Mrs A Shreeves

The school comprises 450 pupils in total with 300 pupils in the Senior School and 150 pupils in the Junior School.

Buildings. On closely located sites in Ewell village, Ewell Castle Junior School (Co-educational 3–11) and Senior School (Boys 11–16, Co-educational 16–18) aim for excellence over a broad field. Academic departments are well resourced and accommodated. The many facilities include: a Sports Centre; the extension of Design and Technology and Science facilities; the expansion of Information Technology within major departments using networks of Apple Macintosh computers.

Aims and Values. The aim is excellence over a broad field: in academic work, in games and in numerous extra curricular activities. A strong pastoral care system enables the school to achieve high standards of discipline, behaviour and appearance.

A highly qualified staff achieve very impressive results at both GCSE and A level from pupils with a range of abilities. Using DfEE statistics for 1994-1997 makes the school's GCSE results the most improved in Surrey and the most improved of all independent schools in England in this period. Class sizes are small, the average is 14, and setting is used in major subjects. All pupils are encouraged to achieve full, individual potential and the majority of pupils, leaving the school from the co-educational Sixth Form, proceed to degree courses.

Organisation. The Junior School is co-educational and accepts pupils from the age of three. Transfer for boys to the Senior School is at 11+. Girls are prepared for entry to local Independent Schools, also at 11+. The Sixth Form is co-educational.

Curriculum. National Curriculum requirements are incorporated in both Junior and Senior Schools. Though the broad and flexible curriculum extends beyond such criteria in both. Years 7–9 (Age 11–13) follow a broad curriculum. Years 10–11 (Age 14–16) follow a core curriculum of Mathematics, English, a Foreign Language and Science plus a wide-ranging option scheme with thirteen option subjects available at GCSE. There are over 20 A and AS level subjects offered in the Sixth Form.

Work experience is undertaken by those in Year 11 (Aged 16) and specialist FE/Careers guidance is available at all levels within the Senior School.

In the Sixth Form the majority of pupils proceed to higher education. Therein the pass rate for the last three years has averaged 85% at A level.

Extra Curricular Activities. The principal games are rugby football, soccer and cricket. In addition there are numerous extra-curricular activities encompassing: music, art, Duke of Edinburgh's Award Scheme, sports activities including basketball, athletics, badminton, volleyball, fencing and air rifle shooting. The U19 Squash team have been Surrey Champions and National finalists and the golf team Surrey Schools Champions. There are regular foreign exchanges, European field trips, overseas sports tours and organised visits within the UK. Recently the 1st XV rugby squad toured Canada. There are drama and music productions annually. The school benefits from a strong and active PTA.

Admissions. Boys and girls are admitted to the Junior School at the age of three. There are no entry requirements at this age. Older pupils are invited to attend the school for a day's assessment during which they may undertake tests in Mathematics and English.

At the Senior School the normal ages for entry are 11+, 13+ and 16+ though there may be the availability of a place at any age. Entry requirements at the Senior School include interview, report from present school and tests in Mathematics and English at 11+.

Visitors are most welcome to visit the schools by appointment, and individual entrance tests are held by arrangement. Scholarship examinations are held each Spring.

Scholarships. Aided places, scholarships and other awards are available at all levels within the Senior School, including the Sixth Form. Academic excellence and other strengths (e.g. music, art, drama, sporting ability) may be taken into account when such an award is made.

Fees. (from September 1999) *Senior School* £1,875 per term. *Junior School* £1,170 per term. *Nursery Department* £495 per term (half-day).

Junior School. For further information about the Ewell Castle Junior School, see the IAPS section, Part V

Charitable status. Ewell Castle School is a Registered Charity, number 312079. Its objective is to provide excellence over a broad field: in academic work, in games and in numerous extra curricular activities.

Friends' School

Saffron Walden Essex CB11 3EB
Tel: 01799 525351
Fax: 01799 523808
e-mail: fsswmain@aol.com
website: www.friends.org.uk

Founded in London in 1702 by the Society of Friends (Quakers), the school moved to Saffron Walden in 1879 where it has developed as a co-educational boarding and day school taking children from 3 to 18. There are 183 boys and 144 girls; 81 are boarders, 327 day pupils.

Chairman of the Board of Governors: Michael Hastilow

***Head:* Andy Waters**, BEd, MA

Senior Teacher: ‡Martin J Hugall, BSc

Bursar: Jane Corwin, BA, ACIB

Head of Sixth: ‡John H Searle-Barnes, BA, MA

Director of Studies: Margaret Lockyer, BA

Assistant Staff:
English and Drama:
‡Margaret Lockyer, BA
‡§Andrea Harrison, BA
Thomas Marty, DipDA
Amanda Macdonald, BA

EFL: Audrey Jackson, BA, BEd, CertTEFLA

History:
‡John H Searle-Barnes, BA, MA
‡§Marianne Rochford, BA

Business Studies: §Maida Sharman, CertEd

Geography:
‡Alison Ainsworth, BA

Modern Languages:
‡Gisele Searle-Barnes, Licence, MA
‡Sheila Addy, BA, CertTEFLA
‡Peter Fashing, BA

Mathematics:
‡John Capper, BSc
§Nasreen Saxton, CertEd

Head of Science: Christine Sleight, BEd, CertEd

Physics:
Christine Sleight, BEd, CertEd

Chemistry
‡Leonard Mead, BA, DPhil

Biology:
‡Martin J Hugall, BSc
§Julie Anderson, BEd

Art:
‡Philip C Richardson, DipAD, ATC
§‡Amanda Orange, BA

Technology:
§John Cowell, BEd, CertEd
§Crawford Dew, ATCert

Physical Education:
Philip Pennington, BEd, CertEd
Jennifer Thompson, BEd

Music:
‡Edward Dodge, MA, GRSM, ARMCM
§Mary Mileson, GRSM, LRAM
§Elizabeth Guest, LRAM
§Jason Meyrick, FTCL, LRAM, LTCL
§Martin Wilson, ALCM
§Alison Radley, BA, LGSM, LTCL, LLCM
§Alison Thompson, BA, LRAM, DipRAM
§Stephen Vellacot

Learning support:
Heather Carter, BA, MA
Vivien Spencer, DipSpLD, RGN, TCert
§Nell Hibbert, CertEd, DipSpLD, DipAMBDA

PSE & Careers:
§Julie Anderson, BEd
§Maida Sharman, CertEd

Head of Gibson House: Andrew Holmes, BEd
Deputy Head: Sally Knight, BA

Juniors:
Jane Beynon, BEd
Robyn Doyle, BA
Sally Knight, BA
Lisa Taylor, BEd

Infants:
Margaret Griffiths, CertEd (*Head*)
Susan Collins, CertEd
Shelley Holland, BEd

Early Years Co-ordinator:
Sally Manser, CertEd

Nursery:
June Linscott, NNEB

House Staff:
School (*boys*) Brian Thomson, MA
School (*girls*): Moira Thomson, MA, CertEd
Sixth Form: Sheila Addy, BA

‡denotes holder of PGCE

The school is situated on the edge of the historic and attractive market town of Saffron Walden 15 miles south of Cambridge and 50 miles north of London and close to London Stansted airport. Our estate of 35 acres makes good provision for mature gardens, and generous playing fields.

Good teaching and a sound academic structure enable children to achieve well and to qualify for the next stage in their careers. Strong pastoral care supports out-of-class welfare for each individual.

We have a good record of achievement at GCSE and take particular care to bring out the full potential and to demonstrate value-added performance. A wide choice of options is available.

We have a strong Sixth form with a good record of success in gaining entrance to degree courses. Most GCSE subjects are also offered for AS and A level with the addition of Business Studies, History of Art and Film Studies. We also offer the Leith School of Food & Wine Basic Certificate. Care is taken to help students choose careers using the resources of our well stocked careers library and the local careers service.

Hockey, Football, Tennis, Swimming, Cricket, Athletics, Badminton, Basketball and Rugby are among the sports available using the all-year heated indoor swimming pool, sports hall and extensive games field.

The school has a strong extra-curricular emphasis on the Arts but leisure activities also include Swimming, Cookery, Young Enterprise, Duke of Edinburgh Award Scheme, Computers, and in addition pupils are encouraged to develop their own leisure pursuits. There are regular dramatic productions, musical performances and art exhibitions in the school gallery.

Admission. (*see* Entrance Scholarship section) Open to Quaker and non-Quaker, admission is determined by interview, our own entrance tests and school report. Scholarships are available at 11+, 13+ and 16+.

The Joint Bursary Scheme provides financial support for those of a Quaker background in need.

Fees. Boarders £3,419–£4,558 per term. Day pupils £2,332–£2,735 per term. Junior School £1,514–£1,606.

Charitable status. Friends' School Saffron Walden is a Registered Charity, number 1000981. It exists to advance the education of children.

Fulneck School

Pudsey Leeds West Yorkshire LS28 8DS
Tel: (0113) 2570235
Fax: (0113) 2557316

Established on 1 September 1994 by the amalgamation of Fulneck Boys' School and Fulneck Girls' School, both originally founded in 1753, by the Moravian Church (a very early Protestant Church which has two schools in England and many more abroad) as part of a settlement on the slopes of a valley on the outskirts of Pudsey. Leeds and Bradford are both nearby; yet the valley is green and most attractive, with terraced gardens falling away from the School.

The School is under the management of the Provincial Board of the Moravian Church. Additional Governors assist the Provincial Board as advisors in the management of the School. They are appointed at the invitation of the Provincial Board and provide a range of professional expertise. The University of Leeds is invited to nominate an advisory Governor. The school is a member of SHMIS, GBA and GBGSA.

The Governing Body:
Chairman of the Governors: D Woods, BSc, BA, DipEd

Miss J Birch
J A B Buchan
Rev D Dickinson
Dr S G Donald
L Everett
Mrs V Hayton
Revd R Hopcroft
E Marshall
Mrs J K Morten
Rev D Newman
T R Smith
C J Stern
D Stubbs

Principal: **Mrs H S Gordon**, BA Hons (Bradford), PGCE

Vice-Principal: T Kernohan, BA Hons, MEd (Leeds), PGCE

Head of Junior School: R Lilley, BA Hons (Essex), PGCE

Staff:
Mrs E Aldridge, CertEd (Hull)
Mrs P A Binks, CertEd (Cambridge Inst of Education)
Mrs S Black, BA Hons (Nottingham), PGCE
Mrs P M Blackwell-Hamilton, BMus Hons (Sheffield), MPhil, MEd, AdvDipEd (Leeds), PGCE
Miss F J Carswell, BSc (Strathclyde), PGCE
Mrs M P Clark, BSc Hons (Leicester)
Mrs L Davis, BSc Hons (Stirling), DipEd
Mrs E M Dickinson, BA Hons (Manchester Metropolitan), CertEd
Mrs M E Dilnot, MA Hons (St Andrews)
Mrs K A Dunn, BA (Liverpool), DipHE, AMBDA
Mrs S R Edward, BEd Hons (Leeds), PGDip
R J Evans, BEng Hons (Bradford), BEd (Huddersfield)
Ms M Finlayson, BSc (Stirling), DipEd
Mrs J Freeman, L-es-Lettres (Sorbonne, Paris)
Mrs G Gautry, BEd Hons (North Wales), CertEd
Mrs J M Grylls, BA Hons (Leeds), PGCE
Mrs T Hammond, BA Hons (Leeds), CertEd
Mrs P Hardaker, TCert (Worcester College of Education)
Mrs S Hardaker, CertEd (Matlock College of Education)
Mrs D Heseltine, BA (Liverpool), CertEd
Mrs S Hodgson, NNEB
Dr M A Hood, BA, MSc, PhD (Belfast)
Miss S K Hoyle, BEd Hons (Leeds Metropolitan)
M M Hydleman, BEd Hons (Sunderland)
Ms C A Kendall, BA Hons (Canterbury), MA (Leeds), CertEd
Mrs A J Lewis, BEd Hons (Oxford College)
T Luckman, DipAD (Newcastle Poly), ATC, ACP (Leeds Poly)
Mrs K Moss, BA Hons (Leeds)
Miss K O'Rourke, BSc Hons (Leeds TASC)
Mrs M J Pratt, BA Hons (Leeds), PGCE
G M Roberts, BEd Hons (Leeds Metropolitan)
Mrs K Shaw, BEd (Huddersfield)
P P Stapleton, BA Hons (Durham), MA (De Montfort), PGCE
I Stewart, BEd (St John's College, York)
R G Strachan, BEng Hons (Bradford), PGCE
Mrs G B Swallow, BA, CertEd (Sheffield)
Mrs C J Thorp, BEd Hons (Liverpool)
Miss S J Tooley, BSc (Luton), PGCE
N R Townson, CertEd (St John's College, York)
Dr K Warnes, BA Hons (Exeter), MA, PhD (Bradford), PGCE
K Watts, BA Hons (Leeds), PGCE
J D Woodman, BA Hons (Manchester), PGCE

Visiting Staff:
Mrs L Bentley, LTCL, DipMus, CertEd
Mrs P C Brown, ARMCM
Miss S de Tute, BA Hons
J M Edward, BA, CertEd, LGSM
D Hann, CertEd, ALCM, LLCM
Mrs V Jenkins, CertEd, ADB, LLAM, BPhil, MEd
C Marks, BA Hons, LLCM, BArch, RIBA
J Shepard, BTec

Principal's Secretary: Mrs J Rhodes

Catering Officer: Mrs S Barnes

Finance Officer:

Originally founded for the education of the sons and daughters of ministers and missionaries, the school nowadays provides an education for 424 pupils. Most of the pupils live in West Yorkshire and travel daily to School, but approximately 30 of them are boarders including some who board weekly and return home from Friday evening to Monday morning.

The school is now largely co-educational and provides a modern, academic curriculum based on Christian principles. 18 'A' Level subjects are offered at Sixth Form and the school has a fine record of success in public examinations. Class sizes do not exceed 24, and most teaching groups are, in fact, smaller; in the Sixth Form groups seldom exceed 10.

Buildings. The main buildings of the School are part of the original settlement, yet other buildings on the campus have been added over the years. Major refurbishment has resulted in enhanced Boarding Houses, a Sixth Form Centre, a Modern Languages Suite with satellite TV facilities, Science Block and Language Support Unit. In September 1997 a second Information Technology Centre opened and phase one of the Library Resource Centre has been completed in 1999 offering additional computing facilities to enhance pupils' studies. Extensive playing fields and tennis courts are located on the site, which adjoins Fulneck Golf Club, and looks over to the Domesday village of Tong.

Pastoral Care. The staff work closely and effectively together, sharing in the duties and recreational needs of the school; their average length of service is over twelve years giving a very valuable degree of continuity and stability to the teaching. The matron, who is a qualified nurse, and other house staff take care of the boarders in conjunction with the resident teaching staff and the Principal, who also lives on the campus. Weekly and flexi-boarding are offered in addition to full boarding.

Sport. Netball, Hockey, Football, Cricket and Tennis are the main games of the school, but Athletics, Rugby, Basketball, Badminton, Cross-country running, Golf, Rounders, Mountain-Biking, Swimming and Table Tennis are all available to the pupils as part of a rapidly expanding programme of outdoor pursuits. Teams of various ages, in most sports, have full fixture lists with neighbouring schools. Martial Arts and Dance classes began in 1998/9.

Activities. Music is very strong with 2 choirs, 2 bands, a jazz group, a flute group, and other orchestral groups. The Choir is invited annually to sing choral evensong at York Minster, and in 1999 had a successful USA tour. Drama is actively pursued with pupils involved in both school and in house productions.

There are a number of clubs and societies such as Art, Computer, Golf, Hockey, Netball, Table Tennis and Theatre Workshop.

The Duke of Edinburgh's Award Scheme is available to pupils over the age of 14, together with a wide range of trips and residentials, walking and skiing.

Careers. The Careers teacher is on hand to advise, and most of the available literature on the whole range of courses and careers is stocked. All pupils complete a period of work experience.

Nursery and Kindergarten. This is housed within the main building and caters for children from the ages of 2½ to 7.

Junior School. The Junior School is self contained and caters for pupils from the ages of seven to eleven. Once a pupil is admitted he or she will usually progress into the Senior School, after examination at age 11. The Junior School has access to many of its own specialist facilities for Science, Art, Technology, Music and IT.

Learning Support. A unit with specialist staff provides help on an individual or small group basis to children with dyslexia or other special needs.

Parents and Friends Association. There is a flourishing organisation which acts as a fund-raising body, but supports the School in a variety of other ways and is a living example of the belief that education is a partnership between home and school.

Admission. Admission to the school is possible at any age depending on the availability of places, although the main intake is at the ages of 3, 7 and 11. Direct entry to the Sixth Form is also possible. Scholarships available.

Fees per term. (*see* Entrance Scholarship section) The fees are based on a scale relating to age and status (day, weekly boarding, full boarding or temporary boarding) and the level from September, 2001 is: Nursery morning only £730; Nursery/Reception all day £1,195; Years 1 and 2 £1,295; Junior Day £1,630; Senior Day £2,130; Weekly Boarding £2,995-£3,560; Full Boarding £3,230-£3,920.

Fulneck Old Boys' Association. *Secretary:* Mr L A Fairclough, Fulneck School, Pudsey, West Yorkshire LS28 8DS.

Fulneck Old Girls' Association. *Secretary:* Mrs P Foster, Fulneck School, Pudsey, West Yorkshire LS28 8DS.

Charitable status. Fulneck School, founded under the auspices of the Moravian Church, which is a Registered Charity, number 251211, exists to provide education for boys and girls.

Grenville College
(Co-educational)

Bideford Devon EX39 3JR.
Tel: (01237) 472212
Fax: (01237) 477020
e-mail: info@grenville.devon.sch.uk
website: http://www.grenville.devon.sch.uk

The School was founded in 1954 by Walter Scott, who was also the first Headmaster. In 1964 the School became a member of the Woodard Corporation.

Motto: *Memento Creatoris Tui.*

Governing Body: The Provost and Fellows of the Western Division of the Woodard Corporation

Visitor: The Rt Revd The Lord Bishop of Bath and Wells

Provost: The Rt Revd Bishop Peter Coleman, LLB, MLitt, AKC

School Council:
S A A Block, OStJ, MA (Cantab), FRSA (*Chairman*)
The Revd R Acworth, MA, LPhil, LTh, D-ès-L
Mrs M Behenna, BA, MEd
P A Brend
M S Hedges, MA, FCA, FRSA
S D Hill, FREC
Dr J O Hunter, MA, BM, BCh
Capt N C H James, RN, JP
W H Keatley, TD, MA
Mrs L Light, LLB
K S Ralph, JP
A B Vyvyan, FCA
Dame J Whiteley, DBE

***Headmaster:* M C V Cane**, BSc, PhD, MRSC

Deputy Headmistress: Mrs S P Fishleigh, BA

Deputy Headmaster: M G Rhodes, BSc, PhD, CBiol, MIBiol

Chaplain: The Revd C W Gibbs, BA

Assistant Staff:
A V Argyle, MA
Miss L J Beacham, BEd
†C R Beechey, BA, MA
*Mrs B L Boyer, CertEd
*C J Charlton, BA
*P R Claridge, BEd
†Mrs S E Davies
*B Deegan, BA
*Mrs J Dodwell, BA
*B D Edge, BA
*J D Hadfield, BA
*R B Hemsworth, BEd, DipM, MCIM
*R H Ker, BSc
*A Lane, BEd, AMBDA
†*A Leitch, BA, MA
*M J Lingard, MA
A N Longman, CertEd
Mrs E J Montague, BA
*Mrs K Seddon, BSc
†Mrs H C Stewart, CertEd
*Mrs R Street, BA
*Mrs A Taylor, BEd
*K L Thompson, BA
D G C Wilson, BA(Ed)
M Woodcock, MSc
†*Mrs P Wright, BSc

Department of Music:
*M J Gale, BMus Hons, AMusLCM, AdvPerfCertRSM
§Miss G Allin (*Piano*)
§D Bailey (*Drums*)
§Mrs P Beechey (*Clarinet, Flute, Piano and Recorder*)
§A Duncan (*Rock & Folk Guitar*)
§Mrs A Hughes (*Piano*)

Visiting Staff:
Mrs M Poll (*Speech & Drama*)

Visiting Coaches:
Mrs H Low (*Tennis*)
Mrs J Morris (*Fitness*)

Junior School:

Headmistress: Mrs L Maggs-Wellings, BEd
Deputy Headmaster: †B J Collacott, BEd

A M Corker, BSc
Mrs J E Minhinnett, MEd(SN)
Mrs W E Nicholas, CertEd
Miss S M Perry, BEd

Classroom Assistant: Mrs P Jerome
Kindergarten Assistant: Mrs M A Maynard

School Bursar: D Lea

School Doctor: R G Ford, MB, BS, MRCS, LRCP

School Nursing Sister: Mrs S Pittson, BSc, RGN, RSCN

Location. Grenville College is situated in the town of Bideford, an historic port beside the estuary of the River Torridge. The spectacular scenery of the North Devon coast is within walking distance and there is easy access to the National Parks of Exmoor and Dartmoor. The North Devon link road, which passes close to Bideford, provides a direct route to the M5 motorway.

Organisation. Grenville College is entirely co-educational and comprises the Senior School with approximately 275 pupils, aged 11 to 18 years, and the Junior School, known as Stella Maris, with approximately 100 pupils aged 2½ to 11 years.

Site and Buildings. Part of the College occupies an estate of about 55 acres on which stands Moreton House, once the home of the Grenville family, from which the School takes its name. Two boarding Houses for senior boys, one for junior boys, and one for all girls are situated within these beautiful grounds with immediate access to extensive playing fields, an all-weather hockey pitch and tennis courts. Within these grounds, there are the Art and Technology Departments with facilities for graphic design, fine art, metalwork, woodwork, ceramics, a miniature rifle range and an outdoor 100m range which is used by the small-bore rifle club.

Also on this site is the Junior School, Stella Maris. For details please refer to the entry for Grenville College Junior School (Stella Maris) in the ISA section, Part VI of this Book.

The main school site, nearby at Belvoir Road, houses the administrative centre, the Sixth Form Centre and most of the other Senior School teaching areas. In recent years an ambitious programme of building has led to the provision of first-class facilities for science, drama, worship and dining. The new Library provides an excellent environment for study, research and careers guidance. There are three separate co-educational Day centres which are used for registration, private study and social activities under the supervision of Year Heads and Tutors. In addition, there is a heated open-air swimming pool, gymnasium and tennis court.

Curriculum. For the first five years in the Senior School pupils study a core of subjects, including English, Mathematics, Biology, Chemistry, Physics, Modern Languages and Religious Studies. Subjects such as Geography, History, Art, Information Technology, Food & Nutrition, Textiles, Technology, Religious Studies and Moral Education complete the programme of study for the years one to three.

For GCSE, in addition to the core subjects other courses available are Design & Technology, Food & Nutrition, Information Technology, Physical Education, Art, Business Studies, Drama, Geography, History and Music.

In the Sixth Form a wide range of AS and A levels is available including, English, Mathematics, Biology, Chemistry, Physics, Geography, History, Art, Design, French, German, Business Studies, General Studies, Physical Education, Information Technology, Further Mathematics, Theatre Studies and Music.

As an alternative to AS and A levels, GNVQ Business courses have proved both popular and successful.

The College has a long established and nationally recognised Department for helping any pupil with dyslexia. Tuition in English as a Foreign Language is also available for overseas pupils.

Sport and Physical Education. Pupils are encouraged to participate fully both in individual and team games. Boys have a choice of Rugby, Hockey, Cross-country, Athletics, Cricket and Tennis. Girls can select from Netball, Gymnastics, Hockey, Cross-country, Athletics, Tennis and Rounders. Other sporting activities include Badminton, Volleyball, Basketball, Football, Swimming and health-related fitness programmes.

Clubs and Activities. There is a range of extra-curricular activities each day which are organised and supervised by staff. Among these clubs are the Duke of Edinburgh's Award Scheme, Electronics, Computing, Debating, Art, Music and Shooting. In addition, a range of water sports is available including Sailing, Canoeing, Wind-surfing, Surfing and Swimming. Skiing parties are organised each year together with other expeditions and field trips in the UK and abroad.

Musicals, plays and concerts are regularly produced involving pupils of all ages.

Careers. Fifth and sixth year pupils attend regular careers guidance lessons as part of the teaching curriculum. This is complemented by presentations and interviews from visiting professionals and all pupils have access to the latest careers information contained on a computer database.

Religion and Pastoral Care. In common with every Woodard school, Grenville College has a Christian tradition. The School Chaplain conducts a service of sung Eucharist on Sundays and pupils participate in weekday Assemblies.

In addition to their Year Heads, each pupil has a personal Tutor who is responsible for monitoring his or her academic progress and personal well-being. For boarding pupils, care is also the responsibility of the Housemaster or Housemistress.

Admission. Boys and girls are admitted to the Junior School from the age of 2½ years. There are no formal tests.

Entry requirements to the Senior School for pupils aged 11 and 12 years is by interview and written tests in Mathematics, English and Science, as well as a verbal reasoning test. These requirements do not apply to pupils with learning difficulties. In such cases, entry is by interview together with an up-to-date educational psychologist's report.

For pupils aged 13 years admission is through the Common Entrance Examination and interview.

For older pupils an interview together with a report from their present school is required.

Scholarships. (*see* Entrance Scholarship section) Scholarships are awarded annually and application for these should be made to the Headmaster. When making an award, academic excellence and/or ability in Science, Music, Drama, Art or Sport will be taken into account.

A Grenville College prospectus and registration form are available from the Registrar, Mrs K M Wyke.

Visitors are most welcome to tour the School by appointment.

Fees. Termly fees for the Senior School are £4,357 for boarders over 13; £4,295 for boarders under 13; £3,267 for weekly boarders; £2,157 for day pupils.

Charitable status. Grenville College is a Registered Charity, number 269669. It exists to provide high quality education for boys and girls.

Halliford School

Shepperton Middlesex TW17 9HX.
Tel: (01932) 223593
Fax: (01932) 229781
e-mail: registrar@halliford.ndirect.co.uk
website: http://www.halliford.ndirect.co.uk

Halliford School was founded in 1921, moved to its present site in 1929 and was registered as a charity in 1966.

As a Day School we see ourselves in partnership with parents and have no wish to usurp either their privileges or their responsibilities.

Brothers of existing pupils are guaranteed places thus removing parental anxieties when siblings appear to have differing academic abilities. This policy also creates a strong feeling of a family community.

Girls are admitted into the Sixth Form at Halliford. The school also has consortium arrangements with St David's School for Girls, Ashford.

The Governors are in membership of the Governing Bodies Association.

Motto: *Via firma ad firmiora.*

Governors:
J White Jones (*Chairman*)
R K C Bole, BSc, CEng, MICE, FCIS, ACIArb
I H G Busby, BA
Mrs D Campbell, BA
M A Crosby, BSc, DipArchRIBA
G Davies, BSc
R Davison
Revd Alun Glyn-Jones, JP, MA
B T Harris, FIPD
Mrs P A Horner, BA, LLB
P Monger, MA
R J Parsons
B G Peacock
C S Squire, FIHort

***Headmaster:* John R Crook**, CertEd, BA (Wales), FRSA

Deputy Head: Mrs D Summers, BSc (London), BA (Open), MEd (Cantab)

Assistant Staff:
M Avory, MA
J Baddeley, BSc, PGCE
R R S Baylis, MA, PGCE
P N Booth, BSc, MSc, PGCE
J E Carrington, BEng
Mrs N F Cook, BA
Mrs S Crosby, BSc, PGCE
Mrs B De Cata, CertEd
Mrs P Fahey, NDD
N S Folkard, MA, BEd
M Harris, BA, PGCE
D Howard, BSc, PGCE
A Jones, BSc, QTS
J S Lewis, CertEd, BA
D Marshall, BA, DipEd
A C Naish, BSc, PGCE
A Nelson, BSc, CertEd, CM, DMS, MBA
M C Nicks, BEd, DipMathsEd
H H Niemann, Staatsexamen
Mrs D M Noble, CertEd, ARMCM
B M Sunderji, MSc, DipEd, AFIMA, CMath, MIMA
R C Talbot, BHum, PGCE

Visiting Staff:
Mrs S Jurdic, BA
Mrs S Regan
M Woolard

S Bradley (*Bass Guitar*)
A Gwilt (*Woodwind*)
G Wyatt (*Trumpet, Trombone, Cornet*)
K Miles (*Percussion*)

Administrative Staff:
Bursar & Company Secretary: Mrs W Simmons

Registrar: Mrs D Towse

Headmaster's Secretary: Mrs J A Davies

Bursar's Secretary: Mrs J Watson

Librarian: Mrs H Nicholls, MA

Marketing & Publicity: Mrs D Towse

Matron: Mrs A Watson

Lab Technician: T Hall

IT Technician: A Hughes

DT Technician: R Seabrook

Visiting Chaplain: The Revd Christopher Swift, MA, Rector of Shepperton

Situation. Halliford School is situated on the Halliford bend of the River Thames. The Old House, which stands in six acres of grounds, is the administrative centre of the school. Over the years there has been a steady development programme which has resulted in the addition of a Creative and Expressive Arts Block and the construction of the Baker Building, opened in 1991 housing five laboratories and an up-to-the-minute ICT Department, as well as bright and airy classrooms. Further developments are taking place involving the construction of an exciting 320-seater Assembly Hall/Theatre; this stage should be completed by the beginning of the academic year, September 2001. Incorporated into this development will be a Theatre Workshop and a new kitchen and dining area. In the next stage the School will be embarking on a fund-raising programme to enable us to build a new Sports Hall/Gymnasium and Library complex.

School Roll. There are 320 pupils on roll with two forms of entry at 11+ (50 boys). A number of places are reserved for entry at 13+ either through Common Entrance or through Halliford's own entrance examination. During Year 9 there are 3 teaching groups across the curriculum.

Curriculum. During years 7, 8 and 9 all boys study a broadly based curriculum. During the two years prior to GCSE each boy will study English, Mathematics, French and PE. He will also attend one period of Religious Studies and one period of Careers each week. At least nine subjects are taken at GCSE. An options system has been devised which allows for some specialisation set within that breadth of understanding which precludes too early and too narrow a choice of subjects.

In the sixth form our consortium arrangements with St David's School for Girls, Ashford mean that young men and young women can be taught by members of staff of both schools. In addition, 'A' level subjects taught only at one school or the other are made available to students of both schools; this means that a very broad range of 'A' level combinations is on offer.

Games. The main Games are: Rugby in the Christmas term, Association Football in the Easter term and Cricket in the Summer. Athletics is becoming more popular and the senior members of the School make full use of a conveniently close Leisure Centre. The School has a heated outdoor swimming pool. Rowing is also available in conjunction with Walton Rowing Club.

Pastoral Organisation. There are 3 Houses and pupils are tutored in House groups. Parents receive six communications each year on their son's progress and there is a Prep Diary which parents are requested to sign each week. Tutors are always willing to see parents and the Headmaster can usually be seen at very short notice.

Out of School activities. These are numerous, including Orchestra, Choir (affiliated to Royal School of Church Music), Drama (major production each year), Chess, Theatre (and other) visits, Electronics, Information Technology and Gardening Club.

School Council. Each Tutor group elects a representative to the School Council (19 members). This is not a cosmetic exercise and in recent times the School Council has effected real changes. It is our belief that pupils do have good ideas which can be utilised for the well being of the School as a whole.

In the Autumn Term each year the School holds an Open Day for prospective parents.

Old Hallifordians. *Chairman:* Alex Lenoel, 8 Oaken Lane, Claygate, Surrey KT10 0RE.

Fees. £6,450 per year.

Scholarships and Bursaries. (*see* Entrance Scholarship section) See relevant section of this book.

Hipperholme Grammar School
(Co-educational)

Bramley Lane Hipperholme Halifax HX3 8JE.
Tel: (01422) 202256
Fax: (01422) 204592
e-mail: hgs-office@supanet.com

The school was founded in 1648 by Matthew Broadley (former pupils are called Old Brodleians) and in this century was administered by the local authority until 1985. To avoid amalgamation and closure the school became independent that year and also became co-educational. It now has 290 day pupils aged 11-18 and hosts the oldest two classes of the nearby Lightcliffe Prep School. It is an educational charity, belonging to GBA and SHMIS.

Governors:
Chairman: ¶J S Armitage, MBE

Vice-Chairman: B M Deadman, DLC, DMS, MILAM

Mrs E E Clarke, DipAD (*parent Governor*)
¶A Crabtree, LLB
Mrs I Cunliffe, MEd
J M Edwards, MA
C M Fenton, OBE, FTI, JP
Prof J M Forbes, BSc, PhD, DSc
¶M Hemingway
Revd M Madeley, DipHE, BA, AVCM
Prof V M Marshall, BSc, PhD
¶J D Millington, TEng, MIElecIE
R M Pickles
C D Redfearn, BSc, DMS, MBIM
Prof D Smith, BA, MSc
Mrs K Wheelwright

Clerk to the Governors and Bursar: Lt Cdr J Roberts, RN (ret'd)

Staff:
Headmaster: **C C Robinson**, MA (Downing College, Cambridge)

Deputy Head: Mrs S J Kunc, BA

§Mrs A Ashbee, BA
*Mrs B M Barrows, BA, MPhil (*History*)
B B Baxter, BA
§Mrs A Botterill, BEd
*P A Chicken, BEd (*CDT*)
Mrs S S D Collins, BA
*Mrs E Free, BA (*Music*)
*Mrs J D Graham, BEd (*Physical Education*)
§P Graham, MEd
Mrs A M Greenway, BA
*R J Griffiths, BEd (*Geography*)
§Mrs R J Halling, BA
M Hendry, BSc
*Dr F S Hodgson, BTech, MSc, PhD (*Physics*)
*I F Hugill, BEd (*Economics*)
*N G Ingrey, BA (*Classics*)
*R B Jones, CChem, MRSC (*Chemistry*)
*Dr I A Liddle, BA, PhD (*English & Drama*)
†Mrs J L Rees, BSc (*Broadley House*)
*A N Rigg, BEd (*Biology*)
†*P D Rushton, BA (*Sunderland House; RS*)
§Miss A Sheppard
†*P A Smith, BSc (*IT, Lister House*)
*§Mrs C M Stead, BSc (*Maths*)
Mrs B J Sugden, BA
*Mrs S West, BA (*Modern Languages*)
*§Mrs B Whitehead, BA
*C Williams, MA (*Art*)

also 9 peripatetic music teachers (*piano, brass, drums, singing, guitar, woodwind, strings, upper and lower*)

School Secretary: Mrs J Donaldson

Buildings and Situation. The School is situated on an elevated site 100 yds north of the centre of Hipperholme, 3 miles from Halifax, 5 from Bradford, and 7 from Huddersfield. The assembly hall, recently renovated, was built in 1783 and originally constituted the whole school. A Headmaster's house (1881), later converted for school use, and two other additions (1906) enlarged the school considerably as have recent developments: Sports Hall (1989), Technology Centre (1990, 1994 and 1998), Sixth Form Common Room (1992), Music Room (1993) and Classroom Block and Dining Hall (1995). Each full-time teacher has his or her own room which obviously is equipped for the subject taught. There are five laboratories being completely refurbished, one each summer 1999-2003, and a large Art Room. The Computer Rooms have a Novell network with 20 and 18 stations respectively. Ten acres of playing fields are ¼ mile away.

Although founded in the nearby Coley Parish Church, the school is not specifically a church school. It has a Christian ethos which pervades its life but which welcomes those of all faiths. Assemblies and end-of-term services (at Coley) are Christian, as is part of the GCSE Religious Education course, all of which are compulsory.

Organisation. The present annual intake of pupils at 11 is split into two or three forms of 20 or so pupils and there are also house groups for sporting and non-sporting competitions. The school numbers 290, almost exactly half boys, half girls. Some pupils join at 13 and at 16 from local schools. There are 48 pupils in the sixth form. The school is small enough to care about everyone, yet large enough to provide a full range of GCSE options and 'A' levels.

Curriculum. Each pupil in the first three years follows a broad curriculum of 13 subjects including three Sciences and two Languages. Mathematics and Languages are setted in the second year, and in the third year the pupils are streamed with smaller classes for the weaker ones prior to GCSE. Pupils have to study English Language, English Literature, Mathematics, IT, RE and either French or German (or both) to GCSE and opt for four others from 12 including Economics, Sports Studies, Art and CDT.

In the sixth form 15 A and AS levels are on offer, and Key Skills taught within subjects.

Admission and Fees. There is an entrance examination each January for the following September; preceding that are Open Days in November at which many parents register their children, but for those who miss that opportunity a tour of the school can be arranged and a registration accepted at any other time. Sixth form admission is on the basis of GCSE results. Fees for the academic year 2001–2002 are £1,790 per term. Individual music lessons, school coaches to and from school, lunches (£1.60 per day, compulsory for Years 1–3) and re-sitting public examinations are extra.

Bursaries and Scholarships. £1,000 and £500 scholarships are available in the sixth form for those with exceptionally good GCSE results. Bursaries are available for those who need partial or temporary help with fees. Each pupil with a younger brother or sister in the school receives a 10% reduction.

Extra-Curricular Activities. Apart from various indoor sports clubs in the Sports Hall at lunchtime and after school, the school runs a variety of teams in boys' and girls' sport. Choir, orchestra and school play practices also take place at lunchtime. The school has a notable record of giving generously to charities through various events. For parents – and pupils – the School issues a monthly newsletter.

Charitable status. Hipperholme Grammar School Trust is a Registered Charity, number 517152. It exists to provide education of a high calibre for the boys and girls aged 11–18 of the area and to help those who cannot afford fees to finance such education.

Kingham Hill School

Kingham Chipping Norton Oxfordshire OX7 6TH
Tel: 01608 658999
Fax: 01608 658658
e-mail: admissions@kinghamhill.org.uk
website: www.kinghamhill.org.uk

Peacefully situated in 90 acres of Cotswold countryside, Kingham Hill School is a successful co-educational boarding and day school for approximately 250 pupils from the ages of 11 to 18.

It was purpose built in 1886 by the Christian philanthropist Charles Baring Young to provide a home and education for those in need. Although a mainstream school today, the homely atmosphere of the school is still considered one of its most important strengths, rooted as it is in a strong Christian foundation.

Motto: *In virum perfectum.*

Governors:

W H D Scott (*Chairman*)
Mrs C Anelay
J M C Coates
D Flint
D M Orton
T R Rocke
Dss P Price
M Stanley-Smith
D B Wilkinson
The Revd S Wookey

***Headmaster:* M J Morris**, BEd, BA (Hons)

Deputy Headmaster: N Randay, MA, BSc, PGCE

Staff:
M Adam, BA, DipEd
Mrs M Adams (*Librarian*)
M Akers
Mrs S Akers, CertEd, DipRSA/SLD
Mrs A Barker-Murasik, MA, BA
M L Bevan, BSc, PGCE
S Berry, BA (Hons), PGCE
S Birnie
Mrs Y Birnie
Mrs S M Chesterton, CertEd, CertSpLD
Mrs P A Cottle, BEd
T J Cottle, BEd
A D Emberson, BSc, AFIMA
I W Fowler, BSc, PGCE
R N Fox, BA, PGCE
Mrs R G Hayes, BA, PGCE
Mrs E A Herringshaw, CertEd
R J Herringshaw, CertEd
Miss J C Irwin, BA, PGCE
Mrs S G Jenkins, CertEd
Mrs A McClemont
Mrs C T Macavoy, BEd
P J Macavoy, BA, PGCE
Mrs J V Marshall, BSc, PGCE
S J Mulholland, CertEd
T Antoine-Evans-Tovey, BA (Hons), PGCE
M W Pybus, BMus, ARCO, PGCE
Dr A R Read, PhD, BSc, PGCE
Mrs L M Sale, BA, CertEd
B Sangster, BA, CertEd, AdDipEd
Mrs S Shorter, CertEd, DipRSA
J P Slide, BA, FSBT, CertEd
P A Spencer, CertEd
M Springett, CertEd, ACP
Mrs J A Stodart-Cook, BA, DipM, PGCE, MSBT
R D Warburton, CertEd
N Williams, MA, BSc (Hons), PGCE

Chaplain: Revd S J Hayes, BA, PGCE

Honorary Chaplain: The Revd Canon Geoffrey Shaw, MA

Administration:
Headmaster's PA and Registrar: Mrs K A Harvey, BA (Hons)
Director of Admissions: M J B Hall
Director of Marketing & PR: M P Brooks
Domestic Bursar: T D Smith

Medical:

Medical Officer: Dr D R Edwards, MB, BS, DRCOG
Medical Centre: Mrs Y Peacock, RGN, Mrs D Thornton, RGN

Aims. The school's aim is to provide a stimulating education in small classes for boarding and day pupils. Emphasis is placed on pastoral care in a family setting, with each student encouraged to develop his or her academic and particular skills to the highest possible level.

Situation. Kingham Hill School is situated midway between Oxford, Cheltenham and Stratford-upon-Avon. Central London is just 80 minutes away by train using the frequent train service from Kingham station. There is convenient access to the M40 and M5 motorways.

Boarding and Pastoral Care. Boarding and day pupils are welcomed into a well-organised and caring home life. While the seven houses are spacious and comfortable, the relatively small number of people in each house helps to create a warm, friendly atmosphere. With some 35 students in their care, each house is run by a husband and wife team who look after the welfare and pastoral care of each student. In addition to the house parents, every student has an academic tutor who monitors his or her progress and is available for help and advice.

There is 24 hour medical cover and a well-equipped medical centre. The school doctor visits three times a week. All the medical staff are seen as part of the pastoral team.

New Facilities. The school has embarked upon a 2 million pound investment in new facilities. Already completed are a floodlit all-weather pitch, a Sixth Form Social Centre and rehousing of the Specific Learning Difficulties Department and the Vocational Sixth Form Centre. A new swimming pool complex is also close to completion.

Curriculum. The school follows the requirements of the National Curriculum as well as giving the students in Years 7, 8 and 9 a good grounding in a broad range of subjects. German is introduced in Year 9 for those wishing to study a second foreign language.

In Years 10 and 11 all students take GCSE English, Mathematics, Science and Information Technology. In addition, all pupils take one subject from each of three groups of options. There is also a non-examinable Life Skills course covering the two-year period.

Sixth Form Studies. Kingham Hill has established a leading vocational Sixth Form with Vocational A Levels (AVCEs) running alongside A Levels and Key Skills courses. This offers a combination of the best features of vocational and academic qualifications.

Vocational A Levels are offered in Business Studies, Information Communication Technology, Leisure & Recreation, Science and Health and Social Care. AS and A Level courses are available in Art & Design, Economics, Music, English Literature, Theatre Studies and Mathematics. Expert advice on career, university, college and other options is an integral part of all Sixth Form courses.

Extra Curricular Activities. Because the school is small and flexible enough to respond to the interests of individuals or small groups, Kingham Hill has over twenty clubs and societies, as well as well-equipped facilities to run them, including extensive technical workshops, an indoor rifle range and a testing assault course.

Each pupil will spend at least three years in either the Combined Cadet Force, Scouts, or following some other form of outdoor pursuit. Many students take part in the Duke of Edinburgh Award Scheme. Sixth Formers also have the option of community service.

Music and Drama. The lively music and drama schools encourage every student to take part in the performing arts, whether on stage, behind the scenes or as part of one of the music groups or choirs.

Individual tuition is available in most musical instruments, including voice. Regular musical and dramatic performances are given both in the school and at public venues. Music and Drama are both offered as GCSE and Sixth Form options.

Sporting Activities. The main outdoor games played at Kingham Hill are rugby, soccer, hockey, cricket, athletics and tennis for the boys, and netball, hockey and rounders for the girls. Girls' rugby and cricket are also very popular, as is mixed hockey.

The school has its own 30 metre covered pool which is used for swimming, scuba diving, canoeing, life-saving classes and other activities. A full-sized sports hall accommodates a wide range of indoor sports and training.

Christian Ethos. As an Evangelical Christian school, Kingham Hill expects every pupil to attend the regular Chapel services. The daily and Sunday services are lively and contemporary, and are led by the Chaplain, staff, pupils and visiting groups.

Admission. The school welcomes students of average or above average ability. Admission is by interview and an entrance test set by the school, or by Common Entrance for those coming from Preparatory Schools.

A successful Specific Learning Difficulties Department caters for a limited number of students with challenges such as dyslexia.

The latest prospectus, an application form and information on scholarships and bursaries are available from the Registrar.

Termly Fees. For the academic year 2001/2002. Boarding: Forms 1–2 £4,237, Forms 3–6 £4,580. Day: Forms 1–2 £2,635, Forms 3–6 £2,856. EFL tuition £838. SpLD tuition £861.

Charitable status. The Kingham Hill Trust is a company limited by guarantee. Registered in England No 365812. Registered Charity number 1076618. The school exists to provide education for boys and girls from 11 to 18.

* Head of Department	§ Part Time or Visiting
† Housemaster/Housemistress	¶ Old Pupil
‡ See below list of staff for meaning	

Langley School
(Co-educational)

Langley Park Norwich Norfolk NR14 6BJ
Tel: (01508) 520210
Fax: (01508) 528058
e-mail: administration@langleyschool.co.uk
website: www.langleyschool.co.uk

Langley School, formerly the Norwich High School for Boys, was founded in 1910. The School relocated from Norwich to Langley Park in 1946 and was renamed. It is the Senior School to Langley Preparatory School (IAPS), and the business affairs of both schools are managed by a Council of Management as a non-profit making educational charity.

In recent years the school has been steadily expanding, and its facilities have been substantially enhanced. Recent developments include a new 11-room Science Centre, a three-dimensional Art and Sculpture Studio and multimedia suite for Modern Languages. Langley admits boys and girls between the ages of 10 and 18 years to either day, weekly boarding or full boarding status. There are 310 pupils in the School. Boarding: 64 boys and 20 girls; Day: 169 boys and 57 girls.

Situated in some 50 acres of playing fields and wooded parkland south of Norwich, Langley benefits from good accessibility by road, rail, air and sea.

Visitor: The Right Reverend Graham James, Bishop of Norwich

Council of Management:

Chairman: Mrs Margaret M Alston, JP
R G Basey-Fisher
M C Cadge, TD, BA
D J B Coventry, CA
R Elven, MA, FIA, FRMI
Mrs Ruth Gill, JP, DipTheol, DipEd
Mrs Jennifer Holmes, MA, CertEd
H McLean
D J H White, MA, FCIS, JP

***Headmaster:* J G Malcolm**, BSc, MA, CertEd

Deputy Head: S B Marfleet, BSc, MSc, PGCE

Staff:
W Harper, MA
W H Moss, BA, PGCE
G A D Frost, BSc, CertEd, MBiol
J N Ogden, BA, PGCE
D T Madgett, BA, DipAcc, PGCE, CertTEFL
R E Holmes, MA, CertEd
Mrs G M Dover, BA, PGCE
Mrs J M Timmins, CertEd
Mrs W Anema, BA, PGCE
T J Bachelor, BA
J L McRobert, BA, PGCE
R J Wheeler, CIC
Mrs A Yandell, BA, PGCE, CertTEFL
M Rayner, BA, PGCE
Mrs Y Bell, BEd
G C Morgan, BA, PGCE, FRGS
Mrs J L Skelton, BA, PGCE
Dr M C Harris, BA, MA, PhD, CertProfSt
S P Bell, BEd
Mrs M L McRobert, BSc (*Laboratory Technician*)
Miss J Little, BA, CertTEFL
M Holmes, BA, CertEd
F Butt, MEng, PGCE
D Davies, BSc, PGCE

Miss E Batchelor, BA, PGCE
Dr C Lowery, BSc, PhD, PGCE
P Moore, BSc, PGCE
Mrs P Lightfoot, BA, PGCE, CertSpLD
Mrs C A Feakes, BEd
Dr J C Bochmann, BSc, PhD, BVSc, PGCE
J Holt, BSc, PGCE
Ms F V Tudor, BA, PGCE, MA
Miss L Bolam, BA, PGCE
Miss S Duquasne Deng Lea, PGCE
D A Dwyer, BA, PGCE
C J Cooper, WOI

Music:
Director: J L Shooter, MA (Cantab), ARCO, PGCE, FRSA
D Aves, BA (Hons) (*Brass*)
M Cann, BA, PGCE (*Piano*)
D Collingsworth (*Percussion*)
S Durant (*Guitar*)
R Mace, LTCL (*Upper Strings*)
Ms M L Passchier, DipUtrechtCons (*Lower Strings*)
Mrs E Smith, DRSAM, ALCM, CertEd (*Piano and Voice*)
P Stearn, BA (Hons), PGCE (*Singing, Woodwind, Piano*)
R White (*Woodwind*)

Bursar: Mrs J Cogman

School Medical Officers:
Dr P Barrie, MB, ChB, DRCOG, DCH
Dr A Guy, FPCert, MB, BS

Headmaster's Secretary: Mrs W Lockhart

General. Langley School aims to provide a framework within which each pupil will develop effective learning skills and will achieve their maximum academic potential. A happy, secure and well ordered environment is maintained in a beautiful country house setting with extensive grounds and playing fields, where individuals are encouraged to set their sights high. Their progress is monitored by a strong tutorial system to ensure that they follow a course of study that best suits their individual skills and needs. Langley pupils are encouraged to identify their talents and to use and develop them whilst contributing to a wide variety of new experiences that will help them acquire the values of honesty, enterprise, independence and social awareness. Small classes and a well organised House system help our children to sample these new experiences with confidence. They will learn to take personal and social responsibility and will get ample opportunities to develop leadership qualities. We hope to produce young people who will be prepared to meet the demands of a rapidly changing and demanding world which will require versatile, adaptable, receptive and confident citizens of the future.

Academic Curriculum. Syllabuses and schemes of work are designed to complement the National Curriculum and the Common Entrance Examination Syllabuses up to year 9 (Lower School 10–13 years). All pupils in these years study English, Mathematics, French, German, Geography, History, Biology, Chemistry, Physics, Design and Technology, Drama, Art and Ceramics, Information Technology, Music, Physical Education and Religious Studies. A programme of Personal and Social Education includes study skills and careers guidance. Pupils are setted on ability in the core subjects while in other subjects streaming may be applied.

In the Middle School (14–16 years) all pupils are prepared for the GCSE examinations. The School is an examining centre for a number of Boards, and this enables staff to select those syllabuses which they believe are most appropriate to the needs of their pupils. All pupils study English, Mathematics and the Sciences. A variable number of additional subjects are selected which enables the most able pupil to study up to ten subjects. A brochure on GCSE courses is available on request.

Most students in the Sixth Form will study 4 AS Levels in the Lower Sixth from a choice of 24 subjects and continue with three of these to A Level in the Upper Sixth. Other permutations of AS and A Levels are possible to suit students of varying ability. The Sixth Form also follow an AS General Studies Course which encompasses careers guidance and acquisition of Key Skills.

Monitoring Academic Progress. High priority is given to the monitoring of each pupil's progress and is the specific responsibility of the Head of Upper School and the Head of Lower School with a team of tutors. A combination of complementary short, medium and long-term recording systems are in use. This permits effective communication between teachers, and between the School and the parent.

Extra Curricular Activities. The school offers a wide choice of sports, artistic, musical, dramatic, scientific, technical and literary activities to enhance students life-long learning. In total there are more than 70 such activities operating daily throughout the week. All staff and students are required to contribute to this programme. The major team games are rugby, football, cricket, tennis, athletics, hockey and netball. Sailing, fencing, judo, squash, basket-ball, climbing, shooting and golf are but a few of the other options.

The School has a thriving CCF (Army, RAF and Navy sections) and encourages participation in the Duke of Edinburgh Award Scheme and Social Services Scheme.

The self-confidence which can be acquired through participation in music and drama is immeasurable. Consequently, the school promotes participation by all in dramatic and musical events at a class, house and school level. An Arts Umbrella programme offers the opportunity for pupils to experience the theatrical and musical productions in London and other centres.

Admission. Pupils will be considered for admission to Langley at 10+, 11+, 12+, 13+ and into the Sixth Form. Entry may be possible at other levels when vacancies permit and is conditional on an interview followed by detailed and satisfactory school reports. Pupils not entered for the Common Entrance Examination may be required to sit the Langley School Direct Entry Examination. At Sixth Form level, satisfactory performance in GCSE is required.

Scholarships. Competitive academic scholarships are awarded at 11+, 12+, 13+ and 6th Form level. Music, Art, Drama, Design & Technology and Sports scholarships are also available. Arkwright Scholarships for CDT.

Fees. Generous family and Forces discounts are offered. Current termly fee levels are: Boarders £3,615 to £4,380; Weekly Boarders £3,375 to £4,095; Day Pupils £1,860 to £2,275.

Further Information. A School prospectus, 6th Form brochure and GCSE brochure are available on application from the Headmaster's Secretary. Alternatively, you are invited to arrange to visit the school by telephoning the Headmaster's Secretary.

Charitable status. Langley School (1960) Limited is a Registered Charity, number 311270. It exists for the purpose of educating children.

La Retraite Swan
Salisbury

Campbell Road Salisbury SP1 3BQ
Tel: (01722) 333094
Fax: (01722) 330868

Governors:
Chairman: Revd C Walker

Sister Eileen Healy
Mr G Dudley
Mrs P Rayner
Mrs S Dale
Mr C Harvey
Mr T Marsh
Mrs M Paisey
Revd C Walker
Mr J Roseaman, MBE
Mr T Cherry
Mrs P Errington Rycroft
Mr K Bailey-Hobbs
Mr A Ford

Bursar & Clerk to the Governors: Miss H Stewart

***Headmistress:* Mrs R A Simmons**, BSc London

Deputy Head: Mrs C D McDermott, BSc, MSc

Senior School:

Mr N Antonczyk, BA (Hons), PGCE (*PE*)
Mr W Appelbee, BSc, PGCE
Mrs S Arney, DipEd (*PE*)
Mrs A Bayliss, MA Cantab, PGCE (*History*)
Dr J E Death, BSc (*Hons*), PhD (*Biology*)
Mrs E Dixon, BEd (*Textiles*)
Mrs H Docherty, MA Edinburgh (*Spanish & French*)
Mrs F Donovan, BA Oxon (*English/Library*)
Mr P Donovan, BA Oxon (*Art/Photography*)
Mrs S Hewitt, BA, DipVG (*French*)
Mrs J Howells, BA (Hons), GradCertEd, MA(Ed) (*Business Studies/Careers*)
Mrs S Kaye, BEd (Hons) (*Physics*)
Mr B Lamb, BMus, PGCE (*Music*)
Mrs B Leach, BA Leeds (*French & German*)
Mrs A Lee, BA Graphic Design (*Art*)
Mrs J Newman, BA, PGCE (*English*)
Mrs R Newman, BSc (Econ) London (*History*)
Mrs V Spencer, BSc, GradCertEd (*Mathematics*)
Mr M Tregenza, BA Wales, PGCE, FRGS (*Geography*)
Mrs F Watts, MA (*Physics*)
Mrs E Wood, BSc, PGCE (*Psychology*)

Preparatory and Pre-preparatory departments:

Mr N Antonczyk, BA, PGCE (*PE*)
Mrs A Bayliss, MA Cantab, PGCE (*Year 4 Teacher*)
Mrs R Buckingham, CertEd (*Year 6 Teacher*)
Mrs A Clarke, CertEd (*Year 4/5 Teacher*)
Mrs H Evans, BEd (*Year 4 Teacher*)
Mrs S Feltham, Dip Art & Design (*Art/Technology*)
Mrs J Foss, BA (Hons), PGCE (*Art/Technology*)
Mrs S Hall, BA, BEd (*Year 5 Teacher*)
Miss N Hanc, BEd (*Year 3 Teacher*)
Mrs M Harrison, BSc, PGCE (*Senior Teacher/Year 6 Teacher*)
Mrs B Herlihy, BA Open University, CertEd (*Year 5 Teacher*)
Mrs A Lever (*Pre-prep Assistant*)
Mrs P O'Gorman, CertEd (*PrePrep Teacher*)
Mrs C Pearson, BA, PGCE (*Year 4 Teacher*)
Mrs M Saxon, Teachers Certificate (*Year 2/3 Teacher*)
Mrs M Smith, Dip Institutional Management, CertEd (*Year 3 Teacher*)
Mrs E Southgate, BSc (Hons), PGCE (*Reception Teacher*)
Miss N Spayes, BTec (*Childcare Pre-prep Assistant*)
Mrs H Tambling, CertEd (*Senior Teacher/Year 6 Teacher*)
Mrs C Taylor (*Pre-prep Assistant*)
Mr R Thomas, GBSM, PGCE (*Music*)
Mrs E Wood, BSc (Hons), PGCE (*Year 1 Teacher*)

Visiting Staff:
Mrs J D Atwell (*Swimming*)
Mrs M Ferris (*Speech & Drama*)

Visiting Music Staff:

Mrs F Brockhurst
Mrs J Coates
Mrs P Dragonetti
Mr G Dutfield
Mr R Evans
Mr J Hilton-King
Mr M Newman-Wren
Mr D Reynolds
Mr J Sharp
Mrs K Taylor
Mrs J Waddington

Head Mistress' Personal Assistant: Mrs C Willetts, DipRSA
School Secretary/Admissions Secretary: Mrs S Walch

La Retraite Swan is an Independent Day School. Originally a girls' school founded in 1911 under the name Leehurst and taken over in 1953 by the Sisters of La Retraite. In 1996 it was joined by the Swan School for Boys, a Prep School for boys aged 4–11 founded by Miss Swanson in 1933. The School was established as an Independent Charitable Trust in 1988.

La Retraite Swan has its own Board of Governors who direct the educational and financial policies within the framework of a soundly-based Christian environment. Income derives mainly from fees, but a limited number of bursaries is available. There are approximately 90 pupils in the Senior School and 200 in the Preparatory and Pre-Preparatory Departments. Boys are now established in the Senior School.

The School occupies some 5 acres of gardens and adjoining playing field and hard tennis courts, and is situated in a residential area on the north-eastern outskirts of Salisbury, some 10 minutes' walk from the City centre. The original buildings date from the late 19th century with additional teaching, laboratory and library facilities built at various times up to the present day. A new building for the Preparatory Departments has been erected adjacent to the Senior School.

Entry is by interview into the Preparatory Departments and by Entrance Examination and interview into the Senior School.

Curriculum. In the Preparatory Departments the National Curriculum is followed and includes regular practical computer work for all. In the Pre-preparatory Department there are opportunities for play and social development together with a foundation in reading, writing and numeracy as well as music, dance, French, computers, swimming and physical education.

In the Senior School after 3 years of general education the pupils will normally be prepared for 9 subjects for GCSE examinations. High grades are normally achieved.

Individual lessons are arranged in a wide range of musical instruments leading to Associated Board examinations.

Fees at January 2001. Senior School £2,050 per term. Preparatory Departments £1,195–£1,270 per term. Pre-Preparatory Department £1,145 per term.

Charitable status. La Retraite Swan Limited is a Registered Charity, number 800158. It exists to provide education for children.

The Licensed Victuallers' School

London Road Ascot Berkshire SL5 8DR
Tel: (01344) 882770
Fax: (01344) 890648
e-mail: admissions@lvsascot.freeserve.co.uk

The School was founded in 1803 and was co-educational from the outset. The School is controlled by a Committee of Management on behalf of the parent charity, The Society of Licensed Victuallers.

Patron: Her Majesty The Queen

***Headmaster:* I A Mullins**, BEd (Hons), MSc, MBIM

Deputy Head: Mrs S Manser, BEd (Hons)
Head of Junior School: R Hunt, CertEd
Head of Post-16: K Adams, BA, MA
Head of Boarding & Gilbey: R P Gibbs, BA, MA, CertPDe

Heads of Faculties:
Expressive Arts: A Matthews, MA, BA
Physical & Vocational Education: J Pledger, BA, PGCE
Mathematics & IT: Mrs E Dowlen, BSc
Science & Technology: D Brenton, BSc
Humanities: Mrs D Finch, BA (Hons)
Languages: Mrs E Owen, BA

Heads of Houses:
Guinness: C Beswick, PhD, BSc (Hons), MSc, PGCE
Carlsberg: Mrs J Liepa, GGSM (Hons)
Bass: R Hunt, CertEd
Whitbread: A Wilson, BA, LRPS
Courage: Mrs S Riley, BA (Hons)
Bell's: Mrs C Farthing, BSc (Hons), BA, DipPsyc
Gilbey: R Gibbs, BA (Hons), MA, CertPDe

Art & Design:
A Nickless, NDD, CertRAS
Mrs R Razzak, BA (Hons), PGCE
Mrs L Slade, BA

Design Technology:
Miss A Winfield, BA, CertEd
Ms G Heuchel, BEd
Mrs S Manser, BEd (Hons)
Mrs M Prior, CertEd
D Hughes, BA

English and Media Studies:
A Matthews, MA, BA
Mrs C Borrowdale, BA (Hons)
R P Gibbs, MA, BA (Hons)
Mrs J Liepa, GGSM, CertEd
A M Wilson, BA, LRPS
Mrs J E Wren, BA

Drama:
Mrs J A Payne, CertEd
M T Walters, BA (Hons), PGCE

Humanities:
P J Brass, MA
Mrs T Brass, BEd
Miss N Jones, BA (Hons), PGCE
Mrs C Farthing, BSc (Hons), BA, DipPsyc
Mrs D Finch, BA (Hons)
N Preston, BA (Hons), MA
E G Smith, MA
Revd R F Walker, BSc (Hons), PGCE, MSc

Information Technology:
G B Taylor, MA, BA
Mrs D Lisney, PCT
S Moores, BA (Hons), PGCE, MSc

Junior Department
Mrs J Abbott, BA
Miss H C Buckett, BEd
Mrs P Z Coombe, CertEd, ACE
Mrs E Earl, BEd
Mrs J Foster, BA (Hons), PGCE, LTCL
Mrs K Hudson
Mrs M Loudon
Mrs H Sexton, CertEd
Mrs R Smith, BSc, DipEd
T Budgen, BEd
Mrs D Harding, BEd

Languages:
Mrs E Owen, BA
Miss N Cooke, BA (Hons), PGCE, CertTEFL
Mrs E Jacobs, BA (Hons)
Mrs E F Meyer, Licence d'Anglais
Ms M Moskovics, Profesora de Ed Media
Mrs K A Potter, BA
A Salmon, BA, PGCE

Mathematics:
Mrs E Dowlen, BSc
Mrs A Buchanan, BSc
Mrs L Collins, BA
L Evans, BSc (Hons), PGCE
N Harris, BSc
D M Newcombe, MA, BEd
Mrs V Sheehan, MSc, MA

Music:
G Jones, BA (Hons), PGCE
Mrs J Liepa, GGSM (Hons)
Mrs S P Riley, BA (Hons), ARCM

Physical Education:
P Bevis, CertEd
R F Bannatyne, BEd (Hons)
Mrs C J Collard, CertEd
J Reddin, MSc
Miss J M Holmes, CertEd, AdvDipEd
Miss H Pritchard, BA (Hons)
M Smith, BA (QTS)

Science:
D J Brenton, BSc
K Adams, MA, BA
C W Beswick, BSc (Hons), MSc, PhD
Mrs V M L Beswick, BSc (Hons)
Mrs A I Jones, BSc
R Lush, BSc
D Mason, BSc (Hons)

Learning Support:
Mrs J Grosse, CertEd, DipEd
Mrs S Ferris, BEd (Hons), PGCE, CertTEFL
Mrs P J Wicks, DEd
Mrs C A Watkinson, CertEd

ESL:
Miss N Cooke, BA (Hons), PGCE, CertTEFL
Mrs Toft, BEd (Hons)
Mrs M Laider

Instrumental Music:
Piano:
Mrs K Stanley, BMus
Mrs G Tucker, BMus
Miss K May
J Chantry
Strings: S Perkins
Woodwind:
Mrs D Head, LLCM
Mrs J Deats
Brass: Miss E Spear, BEd
Percussion: G Brown
Guitar: J Clark
Rock Guitar: J Christopher
Singing: P Robinson

Medical:
Medical Officer: Dr Kade
Dr C McDonald
Sister A Rossa, RGN, CertHEd
Mrs J Mann, SRN, SCM
Mrs K Philippou, RGN

Technicians:
Computing: S Del-Nevo, Mrs G Marshall, BSc (Hons)
Science: Mrs J Booth, Mrs Y Oliver
CDT: S Collingwood
Drama: K Morgan, DipSM, TTP (Hons)

Librarian: Mrs S Eaton, Chartered Librarian

Extra-Curricular Activities: R P Gibbs, MA, BA (Hons), CertPPe

Administrative Staff:
Examinations Officer: Mrs S Chapman
Headmaster's Secretary: Mrs D Hastings
Deputy Head's Secretary: Mrs C Humphries
Registrar/Marketing Officer: Mrs C Milner Smith
Reprographics & Purchasing Officer: Mrs S Withers

Housemothers:
Bass: Mrs A Hunt
Carlsberg: Mrs B Exley
Gilbey: Mrs A Gibbs, CertEd, CertTEFL
Guinness: Mrs M Simmons

Support Staff:
M Jourdain *French Assistant*
M Rodriguez *Spanish Assistant*

Numbers. There are some 720 pupils in the school, of whom 200 are in the Junior Department (aged 4½ to 11). Just over a third of the pupils are boarders (split equally between weekly- and termly-boarding). The ratio of boys to girls is 60/40.

Location. The school lies to the north of the A329 approximately 1 kilometre west of Ascot Racecourse. It is readily accessible from the M3, M4 and M25 motorways as well as Heathrow and Gatwick airports. The school operates a bus service to connect with trains at Ascot Station.

Organisation. Pupils aged 4+ to 11+ (Years R to 6) are taught in a separate Junior Department. In the Senior School, pupils aged 11 to 18 (Years 7 to 13) are taught in groups which are setted by ability in each subject. In the senior school, all pupils belong to one of seven houses, of which three are for boarders and supervised by married couples and there is purpose-built accommodation for 2 and 4 in a room. All staff work within houses as tutors to small groups of pupils which meet daily. Junior Department pupils may board from Year 3 (age 7) in the mixed Junior House which is an integral part of the Junior School buildings.

Facilities. The school moved to its present location in the autumn of 1989 occupying purpose-built premises which were completely re-equipped at the time of the move. In addition to boarding accommodation and classroom blocks, there is a major sports complex, a well-equipped theatre and drama centre, and music school, all located in 26 acres of landscaped grounds (which include a fishing lake). The school has extensive inter-linked computer facilities including three networked teaching rooms each with some 20 terminals, departmental mini-networks and stand-alone machines in classrooms and laboratories. Information technology is an integral part of class teaching from age 4+ onwards.

Curriculum. All pupils in years 1 to 9 (ages 5 to 13) follow a broad foundation course which is compatible with the national curriculum. The school participates in testing arrangements under the national curriculum. Pupils may select their first foreign language from French, Spanish, and choose German as a second foreign language. In Years 10 and 11, all pupils follow a common core curriculum of English, Mathematics, Science, a first Foreign Language to GCSE, plus PE, PSE and Careers. A flexible blocking system allows considerable choice of further GCSE options from Technology, Art & Design, Geography, History, Food Technology, Music, Drama, Economics, Physical Education, Computer Science, Spanish, German or French. Set sizes average 15/16 pupils at GCSE. This approach allows the school to cope well with a wide intake ability

A wide range of A/S Level options is provided in Years 12 and 13, including Mathematics, Physics, Chemistry, Biology, Music, Geography, History, Economics, Business Studies, English, Art & Design, Theatre Studies, CDT, Media Studies, Sociology, French, Spanish, German, Computer Studies and Physical Education. A flexible blocking system allows considerable opportunity to mix arts and science subjects.

The school is actively expanding its Post-16 vocational provision, with GNVQ's in Sport and Leisure and Business and Finance at Advanced level.

Games etc. The school has superb indoor and outdoor facilities including two sports halls, a 25 metre indoor pool and hard and artificial playing surfaces for outdoor team games and athletics. The school has achieved considerable success in providing County-standard players in a wide range of sports. Whilst all pupils play team games such as Rugby, Football, Cricket, Tennis, Netball, Basketball or Athletics in their early years, the range of options widens as pupils become older as the aim is to encourage fitness for life. Thus pupils row, ski, skate and play squash as well as follow the more usual team sports. The school is unusual in offering PE as a curriculum option at both GCSE and A levels and GNVQ.

Clubs and Activities. The school offers a wide range of extra-curricular activities on a seven-day basis. The precise list depends upon the abilities and enthusiasms of staff and pupils, but includes Duke of Edinburgh's Award Scheme as well as a varied programme of physical, creative, cerebal and hobby activities such as music ensembles, newspaper club, riding, canoeing or riding.

Careers. The school is a member of ISCO and all pupils take part in careers lessons as part of the curriculum. Pupils receive guidance from the tutor team backed up by two specialists in Careers and Higher Education planning. The school operates a work experience scheme in Year 11.

Admissions. Entry is by reports and interview, selection normally taking place in the November prior to the year of entry. The main entries are at ages 4½, 7, 11, 13 and 16 although small numbers enter at other years. There are frequent open mornings which take place on Saturdays to allow all members of the family to visit. Enquiries on admissions should be made to the Registrar, at the school.

Fees. Day: £1,314 to £2,191. Full and Weekly Boarding: £3,669 to £3,865.

An extended day option is available at extra cost.

Old Elvians Association. The Hon Secretary is G Jones, Esq, who may be contacted via the school.

Charitable status. The Licensed Victuallers' School is a Registered Charity, number 230011. It exists to provide education for boys and girls.

Lincoln Minster School

Hillside Lindum Terrace Lincoln LN2 5RW
Tel: (01522) 543764
Fax: (01522) 537938

Lincoln Minster School is a co-educational day and boarding school for pupils from 2–18. The Pre-Prep, Preparatory and Senior School are all closely situated in the heart of historic Lincoln, very close to the Cathedral and Castle.

School Council:
Chairman: T Overton
E Harper, CBE, MA, JP
C Wallace, FCA
P Heaver, FCA, FCMA
Canon Andrew Stokes, MA, Precentor of Lincoln Cathedral
M Lamb, FRCOG
P Croft, MIPR
E Galloway, BA
G Walter
P Cosker

***Headteacher:* Mr Clive Rickart**, BA Hons, PGCE

Head of Preparatory School: Mrs Karen Maltby, BEd, MEd

Deputy Heads:
Mr M Jacob, BSc Hons, Cert Immunol, PGCE, MA
Mrs M Walker, CertEd, DipEdAdv

Deputy Head of Preparatory School: Mr M Pickering, BSc Hons, PGCE

Pastoral Team Leaders:
Mrs C McKenzie, BSc Hons, PGCE
Mr R Sladdin, BA Hons, PGCE

Admissions Secretary: Mrs S Pool, HNC Business & Finance

Examinations Officer: Mrs A Pullen, BA Hons, PGCE

Heads of Department:

Miss E Alexander, BA Hons, PGCE *Modern Languages*
Mr L Collins, BSc Hons, PGCE *Geography*
Mrs D Ellis *Food Studies*
Mrs M French, BA Hons, PGCE *Religious Education*
Mr S Grocott, BSc Hons, PGCE *Science*
Miss L Hepburn-Booth, LRAM, ARCM, LTCL, CertEd, CambCertTheol *Music*
Miss A Keeley, BA Hons, PGCE *Physical Education (girls)*
Mrs J Killen, CertEd *Curriculum Support*
Mrs H Pilling, MEd, ADAES *Head of Pre-Prep*
Mr A Prentice, MA Hons, LTCL *Director of Music*
Mr N Prince, BSc Hons, MPhil, AIITT, PGCE, GIMA *Mathematics*
Mr S Roberts, BEd Hons *Physical Education (boys)*
Mrs J Rhodes, BA Hons, PGCE *History, Year 7 Co-ordinator*
Mrs C Servonat-Blanc, BA Hons, PGCE *Art*
Mr D Sharpe, BSc Hons, PGCE *ICT*
Mr J Siddle, BA Hons, PGCE *English and Drama, Head of Sixth Form*
Mr P Stevens, BSc Hons, PGCE *Business Studies*

Structure and Organisation. Lincoln Minster School is the result of three independent schools pooling their strengths under the forward thinking management of the Church Schools Company, which owns and manages 8 other schools. There is no doubt that membership of a group of 8 schools gives Lincoln Minster School stability and breadth of contact. Fully coeducational, the school educates pupils from nursery to A Level on several delightful sites situated very closely together in the historic centre of Lincoln. The school has doubled its number on roll in under 5 years without losing the marked friendliness and responsiveness which make it so attractive, and is about to enter a phase of major development. Class sizes, the quality of teaching and discipline are carefully controlled. There is excellent pastoral care and careers provision designed to equip youngsters for life beyond the classroom.

Curriculum. A full range of subjects is offered and the school is proud of its excellent track record of examination success.

The curriculum is supported by a wealth of trips, visits and activities, too numerous to list, plus a comprehensive sports programme to cater for all tastes.

Pupils of all ages are encouraged to develop intellectual curiosity, resilience and self confidence and to begin their lives within a Christian framework.

Music. As the Choir School for Lincoln Cathedral, Lincoln Minster School provides for the all-round education of boy and girl choristers. 27 music staff work in the department; approximately 70% of pupils receive individual instrument lessons. Music is a focal point of school life and opportunities for public performances abound. The strong musical and Christian ethic within the school is enhanced by daily use of the School Chapel and the Cathedral.

Boarding. Weekly, termly and flexible boarding is offered. The large family of boarders is very much at the heart of the School. The junior boarders live in a period residence within half a minute's walk of the Preparatory School, the senior girl boarders in Lindum View, the senior boys in Pottergate, and Year 12 and 13 boarders enjoy a more independent environment in Hillside. Each house has an experienced team of staff who together provide a high quality of care and educational guidance.

Admissions. Lincoln Minster School welcomes pupils of a wide range of ability and all faiths. Admission is by interview and report, and subject to availability of a place.

Voice Trials, open to boys and girls 7–10 years, are held in November and February. These are worth up to 50% of boarding and tuition fees. Other dates by arrangement. For further details apply to: The Admissions Secretary, Mrs S Pool.

Fees. Termly fees for Reception class to Year 11 include lunches.

Pre-Prep : £1,370 per term; Prep: £1,778 per term; Seniors: £2,000 per term; Years 12–13: £1,860 per term.

Weekly Boarding: £3,028–£3,501.

Termly boarding: £3,262–£3,785.

Charitable status. Lincoln Minster is a Registered Charity, number 1016538. It exists to provide education for boys and girls between the ages of 2 and 18 years.

Lomond School

10 Stafford Street Helensburgh Argyll and Bute G84 9JX

Tel: 01436 672476
Fax: 01436 678320
e-mail: admin@lomond-school.demon.co.uk
website: www.lomond-school.org

Lomond is a co-educational day and boarding school for pupils aged from 3 to 18 years. The original foundations date from 1845 and the current roll is 485 pupils, including 57 boarders who are housed in separate buildings. Twenty five miles from Glasgow, Europe's City of Culture in 1990, Helensburgh is situated on the north bank of the Firth of Clyde in a quiet residential setting and with immediate access to mountain, sea and loch – ideal for outdoor activities. A new main building was opened in October 1998 and facilities and examination results are superb. A new boarding house with en-suite facilities will open in August 2002.

Board of Governors:

Chairman: A C Reid, LLB
Vice-Chairman: Dr P L M Hillis, MA, PhD

C A Dobson
T Dunlop

A Esson
D Mitchell
C Paterson
I Reid
G Thomson

Staff:

***Headmaster:* A D Macdonald,** MA Hons (Cantab), DipEd

Depute Headmaster: W G MacKenzie, MA Hons, MPhil, MLitt, CertEd

Assistant Headmistress (*Primary*): Mrs C Greig, BEd

Mrs J Brown, CertEd
O Carter, DipSE
Mrs V Cassels, BEd
Mrs M Cormack, BA, DipEd
Miss M G Coutts, BEd
D L Dodson, BSc Hons, CertEd
Miss N Dudley, MA (Oxon), PGCE
Dr M Everett, BA Hons, PhD, DipEd
Mrs S Gardiner, DipPE, CertPhysEd
Mrs S Guy, BA, DipEd
Mrs A Hamilton, ACE, NFF
Mrs K Hassall, MA, CertEd
Mrs A Hendry, BSc, DipEd
Miss J Howie, DCE
Mrs E Hunter, BSc, DipEd
W Jennison BSc Hons, CertEd CBiol, MIBiol
S J Kilday, DipTechEd, DipComp
A Laceby, BSc, PGCE
Miss I L Léishmann, BA, DipEd
Mrs A Lyon, DRSAMD, CertEd
Mrs W M Macdonald, MA, CertEd, BDADip
Mrs E Macleod, BEd
G Macleod, BSc Hons, DipEd, MEd
I MacDonald, DipMusEd, RSAMD
Mrs E Maclean, DA, LSIA, CertME, CertEd
Mrs J McArthur
Mrs C McElhill
W McKechnie, BA
I McKellar, BArch, RIBA, ARIAS
Miss M L McLean, BSc, DipEd
Mrs C Malan, CertEd
Mrs M S Maudsley, MA Hons, CertEd
A Minnis, MA Hons, PGCE
Revd A Mitchell, MA, DipEd
Mrs C A Reid, BSc, CertEd
Mrs F Reid, NNEB
Mrs J M Reynolds, CertEd
Mrs A Robertson, MA, CertEd
S Rodkiss, BEd
Dr R M Russell, MA Hons, MEd, PhD, CertEd
Miss S Stewart, MA
G M Taylor, BSc, CertEd
Dr A E Tully, BSc Hons, PhD, DipEd
Miss N Winter

Aims of the School. Lomond has a proud academic tradition and 90% of the Sixth Form will leave to attend University or College. However, it aims to get the best from every pupil regardless of talent and successfully caters for the 'average' youngster as well as those with high ability. It believes strongly in developing the whole person and instilling a 'do it' philosophy.

Class sizes average fifteen and there is a close monitoring of all pupils both academically and for extra-curricular input. The school has the distinct advantage of selecting the best features of the Scottish and English examination systems. Pupils sit Scottish Certificate of Education 'S' grade and 'Higher' examinations in Senior 4 and Senior 5 before sitting 'A' levels in the Sixth Form. Maintaining both breadth and depth in senior years enables there to be a flexible approach to individual needs which means that a complete range of ability is successfully catered for.

Extra-curricular. The philosophy of the school looks to involvement in the extensive extra-curricular programme from every pupil. It is expected that pupils will take part in the main sports of rugby, hockey, and athletics and in the Duke of Edinburgh Award Scheme. There are teams for football, cricket and tennis and a wide variety of activities are strongly represented. Fixtures against other schools take place every weekend and there is a very extensive outdoor education programme. Music and drama are also strong and a plethora of pupils have achieved success at the highest level.

Some distinctive aspects. Nine staff hold outdoor education qualifications and the extensive Duke of Edinburgh Award Scheme programme leads to participation in such events as the Lomond Challenge Triathlon (a national event) and the Scottish Islands Peaks Race. A week long 'Outward Bound' programme has been developed for the school which concentrates on leadership and teamwork skills.

The Traditional Music Scholarship has led to the school developing an international reputation in this area of expertise.

The international dimension is significent not only with long established exchanges and work experience abroad but also due to special arrangements that have encouraged pupils from abroad to study at Lomond which broadens the outlook of the school's pupils and leads to greater international understanding.

Entry and Scholarships. Academic scholarships are available at Senior 1, Senior 5 and Senior 6 and are worth 50% of tuition fees as are the Traditional Music scholarships. Significant Service bursaries restrict payment to £550 per term.

Admission is by examination in English and Mathematics for 11–13 year olds. For younger pupils placement in classes is the main requirement whilst for senior pupils reports and examination results are given due weighting.

Longridge Towers School

Berwick-upon-Tweed Northumberland TD15 2XQ
Tel: (01289) 307584
Fax: (01289) 302581
e-mail: pupilsadmission@lts.org.uk

Motto: *Carpe Diem*

President: James Stobo, Esq, CBE, DL, FRAgS

Board of Governors:

Chairman: Mr I G McCreath, MBE
Vice-Chairman: Lady Caroline Douglas Home

Mrs D Allan
Mr R G Dodd
Mrs E D Grounds
Mr J A Houston
Mrs C Jackson
Lord Joicey
Professor H M Keir
Mr W Nimmo
Dr T M Sinclair
Mr D M Spawforth

***Headmaster:* Dr M J Barron,** BSc, PhD

Deputy Head: Mr T Manning, BSc, PGCE
Head of Preparatory Department: Mrs M Stone, BSc, PGCE
Head of Pre-Preparatory Department: Mrs H Scarisbrick, CertEd

Teaching Staff:

Mrs B Akers, CertEd *Geography*
Mr G Bateman, BA *Music*
Mr K Cull, BSc, PGCE *Physics*
Mr I Dempster, BEd *History, Games, Housemaster*
*Mr K Dumble, MA, PGCE *Modern Languages*
*Mrs C Fletcher, MA, CertEd *English*
Miss E Hamilton, CertEd *English, Mathematics, Geography*

Mr H Harrison, BEd *English, Drama*
*Miss S Hepworth, MA, PGCE *Geography, History*
Mrs L Lee MA(Ed), CertEd *English, Science*
*Mr L Morris, BSc, PGCE *Chemistry*
*Mr S McCormick, BMus, PGCE *Music*
Mrs V Oldham, Al'Es *French*
*Mr A Phillips, BA, PGCE *Boys Games and Geography, German*
*Mr M Plunkett, BA, CertRAS *Art*
*Miss J Roberts, BEd *Girls' Games*
*Mr P Rowett, BA *RE and Geography*
Mr J G Rowland, MA, PGCE *French, English*
Mr D Russell, BSc, MSc, DipEd *Director of Studies*
Mrs M Smith, BSc, PGCE *Games, Biology*
*Mrs M Taylor, BSc *Science, and Biology*
*Mr A Westthorp, BEng, PGCE *CDT, Computing*
Mrs F Weightman, MA, PGCE *Modern Languages*
Mrs J Wilson, BEd *Pre-Preparatory*

Administration:

Bursar: Mr P Stanbury, MA, ACA
Assistant: Mrs S Robinson
Head's Secretary: Mrs J Higgins
Reception: Mr J Cowe

Visiting Music Staff:

Mrs P Bonia
Mr S Ferguson
Mrs J Kerr
Mrs M Lockhart-Smith
Mr D McDonald
Mrs M Rowland
Mrs C Smith

Medical Staff:

School Doctor: Dr S Ruffe
School Nurse: Miss C Coates, SRN
Resident Matron: Miss J Hunt

Estates Supervisor: Mr J McGhee

Catering Manager: Mrs C Krause

The school occupies a Victorian Mansion set in 80 acres of woodland in the beautiful Tweed Valley and enjoys excellent road and rail links with England and Scotland. Daily bus services operate within a radius of 25 miles from the school.

Longridge Towers is one of the modern success stories in education. Refounded in 1983 under its founder and President, the late Lord Home of the Hirsel, it has grown from 113 pupils to almost 300 pupils. It is probably unique in offering the close personal relationships between pupils, staff and parents which are only possible in a small school together with the facilities normally found in much larger schools, eg indoor heated pool, large sports hall, library, theatre etc.

Specialities. Academic fulfilment is sought for all pupils and pass rates at GCSE and A level exceed 90% and 95% respectively and it is usual for all Sixth Formers to be offered places at university. The school's academic standing was acknowledged in 1996 by its inclusion in the Assisted Places Scheme (now no longer in operation). Sport figures strongly in the life of the pupils and approximately 12 each year gain representative honours at county level in a variety of sports, such as rugby, hockey, cross-country running, athletics, tennis and cricket. Art and Music are also very popular and successful activities; one Sixth Former was the first winner of the title "Times Young Cartoonist of the Year", almost half of the pupils take private instrumental lessons and the taking of grade examinations is encouraged.

Entry. The school is selective in its intake but still caters for a wide spectrum of abilities. Special provision is made for the needs of pupils with mild dyslexia and for the small proportion of pupils for whom English is their second language.

Entrance tests in English and Mathematics may be sat at any time either in Longridge Towers or in the candidate's own school. There are no entrance tests for pupils entering the Pre-Preparatory Department, age 4-7 years, and these pupils gain automatic entry to the upper levels of the school. The object of the entrance tests is to ensure that pupils entering the school will be able to cope with the academic demands and still have time for non-academic pursuits and the enjoyment of school life.

The school is divided into 3 departments, Pre-Preparatory, Preparatory and Senior, and caters for pupils throughout their school career, from four to eighteen years. Pupils may enter at any age provided that a vacancy exists. Classes are small, usually with about 20 pupils per teaching set, reducing to about half this in the Sixth Form.

Activities. Longridge Towers is a school where the development of the pupils outside the academic sphere is considered to be vital. To this end there is a very wide range of activities and clubs in which pupils may participate and are encouraged to do so. The major team games are hockey, tennis, cross-country running, athletics, rugby and cricket, whilst many senior pupils participate in the Duke of Edinburgh's Award Scheme. As well as having a modern sports hall the school is very fortunate in having its own indoor heated swimming pool and consequently swimming goes on throughout the year. The musical activities within the school are varied and numerous. There are two Choirs, an Orchestra and various instrumental groups. Pupils are encouraged to play an instrument and almost half of them have private tuition in that instrument. No visitor to the school could fail to be aware of the variety and excellence of the artwork on display which includes clay modelling and photography.

Public Examinations. The school follows an enhanced version of the National Curriculum and enters pupils for Key Stage testing at levels 1, 2 and 3. Twenty-two subjects are offered at GCSE level, including Physics, Chemistry and Biology as well as Dual Award General Science and 18, including Economics, Sports Studies and Drama are offered in the Sixth Form at A or AS level. In the Senior School, up to GCSE, each year group is divided into two sets according to the academic ability of the pupils.

Boarding. Boarding is divided into two houses, one each for girls and boys and pastoral care is in the experienced hands of resident teachers and assistants and there is provision for medical and dental care. Parents receive reports half-yearly and progress reports every two weeks upon request. Pupils have access to telephones and e-mail and may send or receive fax messages using the facilities in the school office. Boarders may attend on a weekly or termly basis from age 8 years onwards. There are no compulsory exeat weekends. At weekends the boarders participate in sporting fixtures and make use of the swimming pool and sports hall. They are also taken on regular outings to places such as Edinburgh Zoo, Hillend Dry Ski Slope, Metroland, Edinburgh Commonwealth Pool, Beamish Open Air Museum, Leith Water World, Bamburgh Castle, Holy Island, an ice rink, a bowling alley, etc. The termly programme of Sunday Outings is published in the School Handbook.

Scholarships/Bursaries. Academic awards at various levels, including scholarships, are available annually to pupils aged 8, 9, 10, 11, 13 and 16 (into Sixth Form). Music and Sports Scholarships are also available to candidates of outstanding ability.

Bursaries are available to children of serving members of the Armed Forces, the Clergy and Diplomatic Service.

Fees. Boarders: £3,310-£3,500 (termly); £3,050-£3,240 (weekly). Day pupils £1,045-£1,750.

Charitable status. Longridge Towers School is a Registered Charity, number 513535. It exists to provide education for boys and girls.

Milton Abbey School

Near Blandford Dorset DT11 0BZ.
Tel: (01258) 880484
Fax: (01258) 881194. Headmaster: (01258) 881250

Visitor: The Lord Pilkington of Oxenford, MA

Governor Emeritus: Maj Gen H M G Bond, OBE, JP, DL

Governors:

Chairman: The Lord Rockley

Sir Nigel Althaus
I M Argyle, BEd
R D Barbour, FRICS
Lady Elizabeth Barne
¶A A B R Bruce of Crionaich
Rear-Admiral J E K Croydon, JP, MA, CEng, FIEE
H W Drax, JP, DL
C J Driver, BA, BEd, MPhil
¶Captain N Hadden-Paton
¶A N R McAlpine, FInstD
Mrs R A McKenzie-Johnson
Revd C W Mitchell Innes, MA
D P O'Brien, QC, MA
Lt Gen Sir Hew Price, KCB, DSO, MBE
J K E Stanford
¶P M G Stopford-Adams
Sir Philip Williams, Bt, MA, JP, DL
S R Woodroffe
S W Young, MC, JP, FRICS

Secretary to the Governors and Bursar: Mrs H Banyard, MBA, BSc, BA

Staff:
***Headmaster:* W J Hughes-D'Aeth**, BA

Second Master: N Arkell, BSc

M Benjafield, BSc
J Bowman-Shaw, BA, PGCE
S J Brown, BSc
Mrs S Burton, BA
M S Clapper, BSc
†C R B Cowling, BA
S Crane, BA, HDPE
†A C Day, BA
Mrs Y F S Day, MMus, LRSM
Miss A C Donnelly
N Drew, BA
†Mrs V Emerson, FIL
W Fee, BA, MA
Mrs J F Goldsborough, RSADip
Mrs H Goodinge, BA, CertEd
Mrs R Kerby, BA
D E Lane, BSc
C Le Prevost
†P Lord, BA, MEd
*H A Miéville, BA, MA
*J D Milman, MA, DPhil
D Mohamed, BSc, PGCE
A P Nicholson, MA
R P L Nicholson, CertEd
*G F H Parkes, BSc
M Phipps, BEd
J R Pope, GradRIC
*A M Prior, BEd
M Pugh, BSc, PGCE
Mrs J Riley, BEd, CertEd
M J Sale, CertEd
†R Salmon, BA, MA, PGCE
M D Sharp, BA
B N Shore, BA
E Williamson, BMus, MMus
*†P W Wood, BA

Foundation. Milton Abbey was founded in 1954 and now comprises 220 boys. It aims to provide a Christian education, to develop individual potential as fully as possible and to furnish wide opportunities for the exercise of responsibility.

Situation. The School lies in a wooded valley on the site of a Benedictine Monastery (founded 1,000 years ago) and a short distance from the picturesque village of Milton Abbas. The nearest towns are Blandford and Dorchester. The campus provides ample space for playing fields and a nine-hole Golf course.

Buildings. The two remaining buildings of the Monastery are the Great Abbey, which is now the School Chapel, and the Abbot's Hall around which a Georgian mansion was built by the Earl of Dorchester in 1770. Today these great buildings form a perfect partnership to fulfil the needs of a boarding school. Outside the mansion house, the modern facilities which are on a par with those of a much larger school include Music school, Art Studio, Pottery, a centre for creative activities, a Technology/Computer building, a 370-seat theatre, an all-weather hockey pitch, an indoor heated 25-metre pool, and a new cricket pavilion.

Organisation. There are five boarding houses within the main building. During the first year boys are housed in a dormitory/Common-room. From the second year onwards the majority move into study bedrooms for up to three occupants. In his final year a member of the Sixth Form has a study bedroom to himself. The School takes meals in the Abbot's Hall where the cafeteria service provides an informal atmosphere, but is well-disciplined.

Curriculum. In the Lower School all boys study a broad and balanced curriculum. A boy is setted separately in most subjects, so that he is able to move at a speed best suited to his ability. The bulk of the GCSE subjects are taken in the third year in the Fifth Form. Entry to the Sixth Form is dependent upon a reasonable number of GCSE passes in the appropriate subjects.

In the Sixth Form, pupils normally take a two-year course to 'A' Level (in three subjects) and a wide range of A/S Level and supplementary GCSE courses. A/S level courses are also available in other subjects. Many combinations are possible in the following subjects: Mathematics, Further Mathematics, Physics, Chemistry, Biology, History, English, French, Spanish, Geography, Religious Studies, Business Studies, Economics, Art, Music, Design and Technology, Communication Studies, Drama, Performing Arts, Physical Education, Human Physiology and Health.

Music. Individual tuition is available in all orchestral instruments as well as in vocal and keyboard studies. Some of the music staff are principals of the Bournemouth Symphony Orchestra. The Choirs lead the worship of the school in the Abbey.

Clubs and Societies. A wide range of interests and activities are encouraged in free time.

CCF and Community Service. The School's CCF contingent has Naval, Army and RAF Sections and enjoys close links with Service establishments in the area, which help it to flourish. There are regular camps in the Easter and Summer holidays. Expeditions both in this country and abroad offer camping, canoeing, climbing and caving. Many boys also take part in the Duke of Edinburgh Award Scheme. Community Service provides an alternative to the CCF.

Games. Christmas Term: Rugby. Easter Term: Hockey and Cross Country. Summer Term: Cricket, Athletics, Dinghy Sailing and Racing in Portland Harbour, Tennis. All year round: Swimming, Squash, Rifle Shooting, Basketball, Golf, Fencing and Canoeing.

Admission. The flexible curriculum and the small size of classes enable the school to cater effectively for a wide spread of ability. A few qualify through the Scholarship Examination held in May. The majority sit the Common Entrance Examination in June for entry in the following Autumn Term. An average of 50% in the Common Entrance ensures a place but the School is also prepared to consider a few candidates who seem unlikely to reach this standard because their academic progress has been uneven.

Fees. (*see* Entrance Scholarship section) Boarding £5,500 per term. Day £4,125. Several Scholarships and Exhibitions are awarded annually including ones for Music and Art, and Bursaries may also be considered in cases of need.

Charitable status. The Council of Milton Abbey School Limited is a Registered Charity, number 306318. It is a charitable Trust for the secondary education of boys.

North Cestrian Grammar School

Dunham Road Altrincham Cheshire WA14 4AJ.
Tel: 0161 928 1856
Fax: 0161 929 8657
e-mail: office@ncgs.fsbusiness.co.uk

North Cestrian Grammar School was founded in 1952 to provide independent grammar school education for boys aged 11–18 in and around Altrincham. As befits a School of 350 pupils attention to the individual is a reality, not an empty phrase. Over the years the School has acquired an enviable reputation for developing confidence and getting the best out of each boy so that today's pupils come not only from the locality but from as far afield as North Manchester, Warrington, Macclesfield and the heart of rural Cheshire.

Board of Governors:

Chairman: Mr J H Moss

Mr T D Brown
Mr R Burdge
Mr D J Common
Mr J Goulding
Mr P F Morton
Mr I T Parrott
Dr A Pocklington
Mr N Swerling
Mr D Thorpe
Mr R C P Wheeler

***Headmaster:* D G Vanstone**, MA

Deputy Head: B E Thirlwell, MSc

Head of Sixth Form: J D F Carley, MA
Head of Juniors: D J Eversley, BSc, CChem, MRSC

Assistant Staff:

F I Barclay, BA
R A Pippett, BSc
N G Brown, BA, MEd
M P Sharpe, BA
P A Stott, BA
D J Bradley, MA
R W Horridge, BA
C W Robinson, BA, DipEd
J K Jones, BSc
R E Thompson, BSc
M Whittam, BA, ATD
D Cruxton, BA
Mrs G R Piatkiewicz, BEd
M J Vaughan, BSc
M H Ford, BSc
Mrs F Entwistle, BA
Ms J Sandy, BA
Ms J Lomas, BSc
Ms L Deeny, BA
Mr P Stubbs, BA
Mr K Jackman, BA
Mr A Boswell, BA

Dyslexia Specialist: Mrs H M Rankilor, BA, AMBDA, DIDip

Bursar: Mrs S M White

Office Staff: Mrs C Brown, Mrs S M Roby

Facilities. The School is housed in fine modern buildings constructed around an imposing Victorian mansion. Continuing investment in school facilities has provided excellent teaching accommodation including five laboratories, a computer suite, technology wing and language laboratory. Art has special provision for ceramics and photography and there are specialist suites for most departments. In addition to a well-equipped and spacious sports hall, the 20 acre sports grounds provide pitches for soccer, hockey and cricket, alongside an athletics track and tennis courts.

Academic. The School aims to provide a balanced curriculum offering each pupil a broad range of subjects. High standards of academic work are expected with an emphasis on individual guidance. Boys are prepared for 9 GCSEs with the opportunity to take separate sciences, IT, Technology and a choice of two foreign languages. There is a wide and expanding range of "A" Levels for boys to choose from when they enter the Sixth Form. Most students secure places at University and the School has a proud tradition of entry to Oxford and Cambridge.

Junior boys are taught in parallel classes. A specialist dyslexia teacher is available to give individual assistance by private arrangement. From Year 10 there is some streaming, based upon ability in Maths and English, with a view to accelerating the pace for the most able whilst providing smaller teaching groups for those who need most attention. There is also a comprehensive PSE and Careers Programme.

Extra-Curricular Activity. A wide range of extra-curricular activities aims to allow each pupil to excel in some area, thus building his confidence and self-esteem. North Cestrian has a strong sporting tradition and there is an extensive programme of inter-school fixtures. National and county honours have been gained in hockey, athletics, swimming, football and basketball. Regular holidays are offered both in Britain and abroad and the Languages Department conducts a series of annual foreign visits to strengthen European awareness. The Duke of Edinburgh Award Scheme is well supported and there is a series of outdoor pursuit trips for junior pupils. Public speaking, board games, music, drama and an extensive charity programme are a reflection of the care taken to oversee the development of the whole pupil in a friendly and supportive family atmosphere.

Admission. There is a competitive examination in February for entry at 11+ and 13+ and applications for the Sixth Form are considered on the basis of predicted GCSE grades. Entry into other years is possible when vacancies permit.

Scholarships. A limited number of Academic Scholarships are offered for admission to Year 7, based upon performance in the Entrance Examination. Occasional bursaries based upon family income are made at the discretion of the Governors.

Fees. Current termly fees are £1,472 – annual £4,416.

Location. The School is situated conveniently close to central Alrincham and there are few Manchester or Cheshire schools so easily accessible by either public or private transport. Ideally placed for mainline trains and buses which converge on Altrincham, the Metrolink provides a rapid link and regular service from Central Manchester whilst outlying districts are served by school coaches. Travel by car is equally easy as the School lies close to the A56 and within two miles of Junction 7/8 on the M56.

Further Information. A School Prospectus, Sixth Form Brochure and GCSE Options Booklet are available on application to the School Office. Parents and their sons are welcome at twice yearly Open Evenings held in November and January, but alternative arrangements for a personal interview and tour of the School at any reasonable time can be made through the Office.

Charitable status. North Cestrian Grammar School is a Registered Charity, number 525925. It exists for the purpose of educating children.

* Head of Department	§ Part Time or Visiting
† Housemaster/Housemistress	¶ Old Pupil
‡ See below list of staff for meaning	

Oswestry School

Oswestry Salop SY11 2TL.
Tel: (01691) 655711
Fax: (01691) 671194
e-mail: osschoolhm@aol.com
website: www.oswestryschool.org.uk

Oswestry School, founded in 1407, is one of the oldest Schools in England. It was founded by David Holbache and Gwynhyfar his wife. The School is registered as a Charitable Trust and administered by a Board of Governors which is in membership with the Governing Bodies Association.

***Headmaster:* P D Stockdale**, MEd, BSc, PGCE, MIBiol, CBiol

Deputy Head (*Academic*): R G Evanson, BA (Wales), PGCELondon)

Deputy Head (*Pastoral*) and Head of Sixth Form: N F Lambkin, MPhil (Wales), BA (Wales), PGCE

Head of Upper School: K S Hawkins, BSc (RNEC Maradon), PGCE, MCT

Head of Middle School: C R Hooper, BA, PGCE

Head of Lower School: Mrs H Clayton-Morris, BA, CertEd

Director of Music: Mrs S Morris, CertEd, ATCL

Bursar and Clerk to the Governors: D H Mountain, ACIB

School Medical Officer: Dr P Barling

General. Oswestry School which is a co-educational day and boarding school consists of a Senior School with 320 pupils, from the age of 9 to 18; there are at present 100 boarders in all. The School moved to its present site in 1776. It has beautiful grounds and its playing fields occupy an adjoining site of 34 acres. There are Tennis Courts, and an indoor heated 20 metre Swimming Pool. The buildings have been continually added to. An Assembly Hall, Laboratory and 2 Classrooms were completed in 1985. Junior School classroom block in 1988, improved girls' boarding accommodation in 1989 and a VIth form Social Centre in 1994. A VIth boys boarding House was opened in 1996 and a new IT room in the Quarry plus a refurbished Archive Room. A new Sixth Form Centre was opened in 1998.

Admissions. Boys and girls are accepted to the Senior School at the age of 9, although there are entrance and scholarship examinations at 11+, 13+ and 16+.

Registration fee: £50.

Fees Tuition only: £7,230 pa (11 years and over); Boarding and Tuition: £12,120 pa (11 years and over).

Under 11. Tuition only: £6,210 pa.

Curriculum. The School aims to provide a broad education up to GCSE suited to the ability of the individual pupil with more specialised courses in the VIth Form. Specialisation is postponed as long as possible and all GCSE pupils must take at least dual-award Science. The following subjects are at present taught to'AS/A' level: English, History, Geography, Latin, French, German, Mathematics, Chemistry, Biology, Physics, Sports Studies, Business Studies, Design, Music, Art, Psychology and Critical Thinking Law. 'AS' level is also offered in these subjects. Special provision is available for those with learning difficulties in a purpose designed Learning Support Unit.

Owing to the size of the School it is possible for most boys and girls to achieve a position of responsibility before they leave, and self discipline is encouraged in all aspects of school life.

The School is examined for GCSE, AS level and A2 level.

School Chapel. The School Chapel, built in 1863, plays a real part in the corporate life of the School; the School is non denominational and services are as broadly based as possible. Attendance is compulsory for boarders at one service on Sundays.

Games. Every pupil, unless physically handicapped, is expected to take part in games. Association Football, Rugby Football, Cricket, Swimming, Athletics and Tennis are the main sports for boys while Netball, Hockey, Rounders and Tennis are available for the girls; Golf, Badminton and Squash are also available.

Out of School Activities. These are numerous and embrace a wide variety of activities including Music, Art, Photography, Debating, Chess, Canoeing, Sailing, Mountain Biking, Textiles, Ballet, Angling, Aerobics.

CCF. There is an active CCF Contingent, membership of which is voluntary after two years' service; pupils who leave the CCF can pursue the Duke of Edinburgh Award Scheme or take part in an active Social Service Scheme in the local community.

Scholarships. (*see* Entrance Scholarship section) The Governors offer many scholarships a year, each of which remits up to 50% of the tuition fees at 9+, 11+ and 13+ as well as for Sixth Form entry.

Reductions for teachers and service families. Scholarships are also available in Art, Music and Sport.

Full details of all these Scholarships, including copies of past papers, are available from the Headmaster.

Old Oswestrians. *Secretary:* C P F Chapman, Bryn Offa, The Old Racecourse, Oswestry, Shropshire SY10 7NW.

Charitable status. Oswestry School is a Registered Charity, number 528418. It exists to provide education for boys and girls.

Princethorpe College

Princethorpe Rugby Warwickshire CV23 9PX.
Tel: (01926) 634200.
Fax: (01926) 633365
e-mail: post@princethorpe.co.uk
website: http://www.princethorpe.co.uk

The school, which has a Roman Catholic foundation, was founded as a boys' school in 1957 in Leamington Spa by the congregation of the Missionaries of the Sacred Heart (MSC), moving to its present site, a former Benedictine monastery, in 1966. The College became co-educational in 1996, and in September 2001 merges with St Joseph's Crackley Hall in Kenilworth in order to provide continuous education from 3 to 18 years. Both schools are members of the Warwickshire Catholic Independent Schools' Foundation.

Chairman of Governors: Revd Patrick Courtney, MSC, DipCat

***Headmaster:* John M Shinkwin**, MA (Oxon), PGCE

Assistant Head: Mrs Heather Harris, BA

Deputy Head: Mrs Margaret-Louise O'Keeffe, MA (Cantab), MA (London)

Bursar and Clerk to the Trustees: Paul Shaw, BA, ACIB

Staff:

Miss Christina Abery, BA, QTS *PE & Games*
Mrs Patricia Armitage, BEd *Mathematics*
Miss Delphine Asselin, BA, PGCE *French*
Mrs Anna Beech, BSc, PGCE *Chemistry & Physics*
Mrs Tracy Bishop, BA, PGCE (FAHE) *Technology*
Mrs Carolyn Booth, CertEd, LGSM *English*
Mrs Orietta Cabrera, BA *Spanish*
Mrs Felicity Coulson, GMus, PGCE *Music*
Alex Darkes, BEd *Physics & Mathematics, Development Director*
Kevin Dolan, BSc, PGCE *Physics*
Simon Ferris, BEd *PE*
Mrs Irene Finn, BPhil, CertEd *Learning Support*
Mrs Susan Francis, DDME, CertEd, LTCL *Director of Music*
Frank Gahan, BEd, MA *Head of Technology*
Peter Griffin, BA, PGCE *Head of Business Studies & Economics, Examinations Officer*
Miss Vanessa Vega Hurst, BA, PGCE *French & Spanish*
Desmond Jack, BA, PGCE, CCRE *Head of History*
Mrs Sophie Jones, BA, QTS *English and PE*
Sean Kelly, BA, HDipEd *Head of Year 9, Religious Studies*
Michael Kitterick, BEd, CertEd *Head of Geography & Careers*
Neil McCollin, BA *PE*
John Miller, BSc, PGCE *Head of Chemistry*
Mrs Irene Minehane, BSc, PGCE, DipCathRelEd *PSE Co-ordinator, Mathematics*
Ralph Moore, MA *English & Religious Studies*
Colin Morgan, BSc, CertEd *Head of Mathematics*
Bernard Moroney, CertEd *Head of Biology, Head of Senior School, Biology & Games*
Mrs Caroline Pavey, BA, PGCE *French*
Simon Peaple, BA *History & Politics*
Mrs Kate Perkins, BA, MA *Head of Theatre Studies, English*
Sean Philpot, CertEd, BEd, MA, AdvDipEd *Head of Junior School, Biology*
Gwilym Price, CertEd *Head of Games, Geography*
Gerard Raffell, BSc, PGCE *Mathematics*
Simon Robertson, BSc, PGCE *Biology, Chemistry, Games*
Mrs Margaret Robinson, BEd *Head of Sixth Form, French*
Mrs Eileen Sharpe, BEd *Mathematics*
Mrs Susan Shepherd, ARCM, ARCO, LRAM, CertEd *Music*
Mrs Barbara Skiffington, CertEd *Art & Ceramics*
Lou Skiffington, MA, CertEd *Head of Art*
David Smith, BSc, PGCE *ICT Development Manager*
Mrs Sarah Stewart, BA, PGCE, CertTESOL *Head of Modern Languages, French*
Mike Taylor, BA, PGCE *Geography & Careers*
Kristian Tyas, BEd *Mathematics & Duke of Edinburgh Award*
Barry Weenen, BSc *Head of Graphic Communication, Curriculum Co-ordinator*
Pat Weir, BA, PGCE *Head of English*
Mrs Moira Weir, BA, DipCoun *English*
Revd Alan Whelan, MSC, BA *Head of Religious Studies*
Steve White, BSc *Head of Physics, Physics & Chemistry*
Mrs Fenola Whittle, BEd *Mathematics*

The Music department is also assisted by visiting staff.

Administrative Staff:

Admissions Secretary: Mrs Loretta Curtis
Bursar's Assistant: Mrs Anne Davey
Secretary: Mrs Lynne Dyke
Residential Services Manager: Mrs Margaret Fuggle
Headmaster's Secretary: Mrs Helen Jackson
Clerk of Works: Gerry Lovely
Librarian: Mrs Janette Perkins, ALA
Director of Boarders: Mrs Jo Purkiss, BA
Senior Groundsman: Edward Robertson
Senior Matron: Mrs Maria Lawless, SEN
Medical Officers:
Dr Martha D'Mello, MB, BS, DA
Dr B S Kavuri, MB, BS

Number in School. The school has about 630 pupils from 11 to 18 years with 120 in the Sixth Form and around 50 children boarding. An extensive network of private coaches transports pupils from a wide area.

Aims. The College provides a caring, Christian environment for children where their needs can be met and their talents, confidence and self-esteem developed. There is a healthy balance between freedom and structure and an emphasis on self-discipline through responsibility and trust, which develops confidence and independence.

The College draws on a rich tradition of Catholic teaching and the spirituality of the Missionaries of the Sacred Heart, whose ethos is central to its character and disciplinary system. In welcoming families of a variety of faiths, the school community is a living example of ecumenism. The College motto, *Christus Regnet* - may Christ reign - is a reminder of Christ's love, service, forgiveness and generosity of spirit.

Academic. A broad-based, stimulating curriculum satisfies a wide range of ability and fosters a love of learning. A favourable pupil-teacher ratio, permitting personal attention, contributes to impressive value-added achievements. High fliers are stretched and provided with intellectually challenging assignments, ensuring that they achieve at the highest possible levels. The curriculum is well supported by a new library and ICT Centre. Qualified specialists give tuition to dyslexic pupils.

Pupils in Years 7 to 9 have a curriculum which avoids early specialisation and usually go on to take nine or ten GCSEs.

Supervised homework, extended day and flexible boarding are offered.

The Sixth Form. Students in the Sixth Form are prepared for AS level and A2 level examinations after which the vast majority proceed to university. The Head of Sixth Form and the team of tutors monitor the academic progress of Sixth Formers through regular discussions with the students and their teachers. Visits to university Open Days, together with professional careers advice enables students to make the best choices about their next stage of education.

All Sixth Formers enjoy privileges and have the responsibilities of leadership and example; certain members are elected to perform prefectorial duties. Prefects attend a leadership course and learn valuable management skills. They organise activities for younger pupils and chair the School Council which offers a forum for lively discussion and gives the students an influential voice in the running of the College. Sixth Formers also act as Form Patrons, mentoring younger pupils and arranging outings for them. The House Captains have a pivotal role in the organisation of inter-house events.

Careers. The Careers Advice Programme commences in Year 9 and regular tutorials are held concentrating on option subject choices and developing careers awareness. Interview technique is developed and students are assisted with work experience placements which are undertaken at the end of Year 10 and Lower Sixth.

Art & Design. A feature which immediately strikes all visitors to the College is the outstanding display of canvases and ceramics. Superb examination results and successes in competitions are commonplace. The study of drawing, painting, graphics and ceramics are central and they are enhanced by using the work of great artists as stimulus material. History of Art is offered in the Sixth Form.

Technology includes Graphics, Resistant Materials Information and Communications Technology, Textiles and Electronics. Pupils can work with a variety of materials, realising their technical designs in the well-resourced workshops which include CAD/CAM facilities.

Music and Drama. Music is studied by all pupils in their first three years and as an option at GCSE and A level. The College choir gives regular performances and tours extensively overseas. Many pupils learn instruments and are encouraged to join the orchestra. Peripatetic staff offer tuition in most instruments. A well-equipped room with digital recording facilities is provided for Music Technology and there is an acclaimed Binns organ in the magnificent Chapel built by Peter Paul Pugin.

The College has a well-equipped theatre and regular productions are staged including pantomimes and revues, Shakespeare plays and adaptations from Dickens. Productions involve a large number of pupils and staff and provide an excellent way for pupils of different years to get to know each other. There are thriving Dance and Drama Clubs. Theatre Studies is offered in the Sixth Form.

Physical Education. All pupils participate in games and Physical Education classes. Physical Education can also be studied as an examination subject at GCSE and A level. The major sports are rugby, netball, hockey, cricket, rounders, tennis and athletics; they are run in tandem with badminton, soccer, squash, basketball and trampolining. Off-site swimming and sailing are also available.

There is a well-equipped Sports Hall, a Fitness Centre and squash courts. Extensive outdoor facilities include an internationally recognised cross country course, tennis courts and over sixty acres of games pitches.

Extra-Curricular Activities. There is always a wide range of clubs, societies and activities such as badminton, bridge, chess, computing, dance, debating, drama, equestrian, photography and technology. The Duke of Edinburgh award Scheme and Outward Bound courses are also offered. The Arts Society provides a cultural programme including art history lectures, poetry evenings, music recitals and play readings.

Admission and Scholarships. Admission is by examination in early February, usually at 11 and 13 and at other ages as space allows. Students from other schools join the Sixth Form after their GCSE courses. Pupils entering at 11, 12 or 13 may compete for scholarships to a maximum of 50%, based on academic merit or excellence in art or music. Sixth Form exhibitions are awarded to the top GCSE scholars and a sports scholarship is also offered.

Termly Fees (September 2001). Full boarders £4,110; Weekly boarders £3,788. Boarding fees include all meals and laundry. Day pupils £1,845 excluding transport and meals. Instrumental tuition and dyslexia help are charged as extras.

Charitable status. Princethorpe College is a Registered Charity, number 1071438. It exists solely for the education for children.

* Head of Department	§ Part Time or Visiting
† Housemaster/Housemistress	¶ Old Pupil
‡ See below list of staff for meaning	

The Purcell School

Aldenham Road Bushey Hertfordshire WD2 3TS
Tel: (01923) 331100
Fax: (01923) 331166
e-mail: (person/depart)@purcell-school.org
website: www.purcell-school.org

The Purcell School is one of the world's leading specialist centres of excellence and has a national and international reputation in the education and training of exceptional young musicians. Founded in 1962 in the Conway Hall, the School was for many years established on its beautiful site in Harrow. In July 1997 it moved to its present new premises in Aldenham Road, Bushey. There are 167 pupils, boys and girls, aged from 7 to 18, with 82 in the VIth Form.

Patron: HRH The Prince of Wales

President: Sir Simon Rattle

Governing Body:
Mr Graham Smallbone, MA (*Chairman*)
Mr Roy Cervenka, AIIMR, MSI (*Vice Chairman*)
The Hon Mark Bridges, GCMG
Mr Michael Garner, MA, FCA, FCT, FRSA
Ms Janice Graham, ARCM, AGMD, ACT (Julliard)
Mrs Elaine Headlam
Dr Ian Horsbrugh, FGSM, FRCM, HonDMus
Mr Jonathan Lavy, FCA
Mrs Jean McGregor
Mr John Marshall
Mr T Mohan, BA
Mr Philip Newman, FCA
Mr Michael Oakley, TD
Mr Ian Reeves, FInstCS, FFB
Mr John Stenhouse, ARCM
Mr Martin Tuck, MA
Professor John Wass, BEd, MB, BS, MD, MA, FRCP, MRCP

***Headmaster:* Mr John Tolputt,** MA (Cantab), PGCE, FRSA

Director of Music: Mr Jeffrey Sharkey, MPhil (Cantab), MMus (Yale)

Deputy Head: Mr Paul Elliott, MA Hons (Glasgow), PGCE

Head of Sixth Form: Miss Elizabeth Willan, BA, PGCE

Director of Finance & Administration: Mr Nicholas Rampley, BA (Oxon), MBA (London), DIC

Staff:
Jane Allen *Clerical Assistant*
Eva Andrusier, BA Hons (Manchester), CertEd, CertTEFL *EFL*
Joyce Arnold *Laboratory Technician*
Phil Barrett, BA, ATC *Head of Art/Pastoral Co-ordinator*
Reg Brown *Driver/Maintenance*
Alison Cox, GRNCM, DipAdvStdMus (Comp), PGCE *Head of Composition/Class Music*
Simon Davis *Driver/Maintenance*
Paul Elliott, MA Hons (Glasgow), PGCE *German*
Peter Ellis, BSc (London), PhD (OU), PGCE *Head of Geography*
Panos Fellas, BSc Hons (Surrey), MA (ScEd) *Head of Science/Housemaster, Gardner House*
Katerina Fellas, BSc Hons (London), PGCE *Mathematics*
Miranda Francis, BMus Hons, LRAM, ARCM, PGCE *Teacher of Academic Music*
Keith Goddard, BSc Hons (London), DipEd *Science*
David Grant, BAWLA Inst *PE*

Drusilla Harris, GRNCM, PGRNCM, BKAInt, Dalcroze Cert *Dalcroze Eurythmics/Aural*
Jocelyne Hazan, BA, MA (Paris X) *French*
Jennifer Henderson *Catering Manager/Housemistress, Dulverton House*
Katherine Higgins, BEd Hons (Warwick), RSA Dip, TEFLA, MATEFLA *Head of EFL/Examinations Officer*
Clara Hitchen, BA (Sheffield), RSA/UCLES *EFL Teacher*
Michael Hooper, BA Hons (Manchester), MA, PGCE *Teacher of English/Drama*
Ian Jewel, ARCM, ARAM (Hon), HonDr (Essex) *Head of Strings*
Christine Jones *Registrar/Music Administrator*
Sue Jones, CertEd *Juniors/Pastoral Co-ordinator*
Miriam Juviler, LRAM *Concert Manager*
Sandra Kyriakides *Public Relations Officer*
Andrew Leverton, BA Hons (University of Tasmania), DipEd *Head of English*
Khin Yee Lo, MMus (London), BA Hons, LRAM, LTCL *Practice Supervisor/Tutor, Avison House*
Edward Longstaff, MMus (Goldsmiths), BMus Hons (London), PGCE *Head of Academic Music/Housemaster, Avison House*
Roshan Magub, BA, LRSM, ARCM *Head of Keyboard*
Bea McDonald, SRN, SCM *School Matron*
LucyAnn Palmer, BA Hons Music, PGCE, CTEFLA *Housemistress, Sunley House/Instrumental Timetabler*
Susan Pickard, MIAB *Assistant to Bursar*
Darrell Pigott, BSc Hons (Bradford), PGCE *Head of History*
Spencer Pitfield, BMus (Pretoria), LMus (Finland) *Practice Co-ordinator/Tutor, Gardner House*
Quentin Poole, MA (Cantab) *Head of Wind and Percussion*
Gail Remfry *PA to Headmaster*
Stella Rendle *Housekeeper*
Brian Robinson *Maintenance*
Christopher Ross, BA, MMus *School Pianist*
Deborah Shah, ARCM *School Pianist*
Jeffrey Sharkey, MPhil (Cantab), MMus (Yale) *Class Music/Composition/Chamber Music*
Judith Simmons, BSc (St Andrews), PGCE *Science*
Winifred Soutter, MA (Glasgow), DRSAM, ARCM *German*
Tina Stewart *Assistant to Estates Manager*
Esme Tyers, CertEd *Head of Mathematics*
Elizabeth Willan, BA Hons (London), PGCE *Head of Modern Languages/Head of Sixth Form*
John Wills, MMus (RCM), BMus Hons (London), DipCSM, ALCM *Class Music*
Caroline Young, BSc (London), MSc (London) *Mathematics*

Instrumental Staff:

Keyboard Department:
John Byrne
Ilana Davids
Gareth Hunt
Emily Jeffrey
Simon Mulligan (*jazz*)
Tessa Nicholson
Joyce Rathbone
Valeria Szervansky
Patsy Toh
Charlotte Tomlinson

Wind Department:
Anna Pope *Flute*
Clare Southworth *Flute*
Nina Robertson *Flute*
Melanie Ragge *Oboe*
Barbara Law *Recorder*
Vicky Lewis *Clarinet*
David Fuest *Clarinet*
Kim Murphy *Bassoon*
Nicholas Rodwell *Saxophone*
David Mason *Trumpet*
Norman Burgess *Trumpet*
Rob Workman *Trombone*
Peter Beament *Percussion*
Lilian Simpson *Percussion*
Daphne Boden *Harp*
Charlotte Seale *Harp*
Kathleen Ferguson *Voice*
Tom Marandola *Voice*
Roland Gallery *Guitar*

String Department:
Marius Bedeschi *Violin*
Dimitar Burov *Violin*
Eric Houston *Violin*
Carol Slater *Violin*
Pal Banda *Cello*
Michal Kaznowski *Cello*
Alison Wells *Cello*
Martin Myers *Double Bass*

Composition:
Richard Dubugnon

Alexander Technique:
Jean Mercer
John Canning

Electronic Music:
Adam Day
Jonny Clark

Jazz:
Mark Hartley

The Purcell School is the only specialist music school in London, with the benefit of all the capital's cultural and teaching resources. It offers exceptional opportunities to exceptional young musicians; the finest teachers, time and priority for musical activities, the opportunity to work with others of similar calibre, specialist education in a sane and balanced environment.

Music. The School provides teaching in all instruments including composition and voice. Great care is taken over the allocation of pupils to teachers and progress is carefully and regularly assessed by the Head of Departments, under the guidance of the Director of Music. Whilst there is an excellent and experienced instrumental staff at the School, pupils also have the advantage of established links with teachers from the Royal College of Music, the Royal Academy of Music and the Guildhall School of Music and Drama.

There are opportunities to take part in Masterclasses with eminent international musicians, to work with visiting members of Covent Garden, the London Symphony Orchestra or renowned chamber groups and to perform not only in the prestigious concert halls of London but also the concert halls of the Far East, Russia, America and all parts of Europe, on one of the School's regular foreign tours.

Academic Curriculum. In addition to specialist musical training the Purcell School offers a full academic education of the highest quality to GCSE and Advanced level. Examination results are outstanding.

Boarding. Pupils come from all over Britain and from all over the world. About 70% are boarders, all of whom live on the School campus.

The youngest pupils, aged between 7 and 11, live in Dulverton House looked after by Houseparents, with whom they live more or less 'en famille'.

There are two Houses, Sunley (girls') and Gardner (boys'), in the main building and the boarding accommodation has been newly modernised and refurbished to create comfortable, attractive and imaginative rooms. For the most part members of the VIth Form have single rooms (or share with one other person) and can use their rooms for practice as well as for study. The Houses are run by a resident Housemistress and Housemaster, respectively, and there are also resident Tutors/Practice Supervisors.

A Senior House, built in 1986, provides study bedroom accommodation for 20 members of the UVIth who are in the care of their Housemaster and resident House Tutor.

Links between School and home are close and, with fax machines and e-mail, this is possible wherever in the world a pupil may live. In each half of the term there an exeat weekend when all pupils go home or to their guardian or to friends. There is also an extended half-term period in each of the three terms.

Admission. Entrance is by musical audition and interview and further details and a prospectus are available from the Registrar, Miss Natalie Cook, who will be pleased to answer queries.

The School has a principle of taking young musicians whose exceptional musical ability merits them a place.

Current Fees. Senior Boarding £5,260, Senior Day £3,107 per term; Junior Boarding £4,635, Junior Day £2,544 per term.

Government Aided places, Bursaries and Scholarships are also available for those not eligible for aided places.

Charitable status. The Purcell School is a Registered Charity, number 312855. It aims to offer Specialist musical training, combined with an excellent general education, to children of exceptional musical ability.

Rishworth School
(Coeducational)

Ripponden West Yorkshire HX6 4QA.
Tel: (01422) 822217 (Main School)
Fax: (01422) 820911
website: www.rishworth-school.co.uk

Rishworth is an exceptionally friendly, caring community, in which pupils are as strongly encouraged to rejoice in each other's achievements as to take pride in their own. The School succeeds in combining a disciplined environment with a relaxed and welcoming atmosphere.

While pupils are at Rishworth, we try to ensure that, in addition to the knowledge and skills acquired through academic study, they develop:

- A love of learning and the will to succeed.
- A sense of responsibility, self-discipline, purpose and fulfilment.
- A capacity for both self-reliance and co-operation.
- An appreciation of certain personal virtues and spiritual values, such as honesty, dependability, perseverance, commitment, humility and respect for others.

Visitor: The Most Reverend The Lord Archbishop of York

Honorary Governors:
H Ludlam, OBE
A J Morsley, Esq

The Governing Body:

Mrs D Whitaker, JP (*Chairman*)
H B Bentley, Esq (*Vice-Chairman*)
The Right Reverend The Lord Bishop of Wakefield
Mrs P E Aldous
G C W Allan, Esq
M W Gledhill, Esq
Mrs A Riley, ACA
D A Rolinson, Esq
T M Wheelwright, Esq

Clerk to the Board of Governors: R M Schofield, BA, ACA

Teaching Staff:

***Headmaster:* R A Baker**, MA (Cantab)

Deputy Headmaster: D Ainley, CMath, FIMA *Mathematics*
Senior Mistress: *Mrs I Shelton, BA *Art*

N Appleton, MA *English, General Studies, House Tutor Ridings House*
*Mrs H Bower, BSc *Girls' Physical Education*
Mrs S M Boylan, BEd *Junior Subjects, Heathfield*
Miss K Brickles, BA *Art, House Tutor Slitheroe House, Press Officer*
*Mrs S Briggs, CertEd *Home Economics, Housemistress Founders House*
J A Clegg, BSc *Physics, Science*
*T Crowther, BSc *Information Technology*
*J Drowley, BA *Boys' Physical Education, Assistant Housemaster, Calder House, Sports Studies*
Mrs L Duggleby *Deputy Nursery Manager*
L Dunn, BA *Design Technology, Information Technology, Mathematics*
Miss H A Fawcett, BA *Junior Subjects, Heathfield*
Mrs E Gregory, BA *Economics*
Miss S J Gregory, BSc *Head of Sixth Form, Geography*
D E N Harris, BA *Deputy Headmaster, Heathfield*
Mrs G Hart *Nursery Assistant*
A Hartwell, BEd *Junior Subjects, Heathfield*
D I Horsfall, BSc *Mathematics*
*C S Housecroft, BSc *Chemistry, Assistant Housemaster, Calder House*
*Mrs J E Howes, BA *Spanish, Housemistress, Wheelwright House*
*R E Howes, BA *Modern Languages, Housemaster, Ridings House*
M M Hunt, BSc, PhD *Chemistry*
*P W Jones, MA (Cantab) *Biology, UCAS Co-ordinator*
Mrs A M Jordan, DipAd *Junior Subjects, Heathfield*
Miss A M Kellett, BA *Modern Languages*
Mrs J A Knox, BTech *Mathematics, House Tutor Founders House*
Miss J Lumb *Teaching Assistant, Heathfield*
*P I Lynch, BEd *Director of Music*
Mrs L Millington *Nursery Manager*
*D Newby, BTech *Design Technology, House Tutor Ridings House*
Mrs K L Norman, BEd *Junior Physical Education, Heathfield*
V Osbaldeston, BA *Head of Heathfield*
P M Pitchforth, BEd *Mathematics, Head of Middle School*
J S Richardson, MA *Geography*
*P I M Robinson, BEd *History, Business Studies, Careers, Director of Welfare Education*
Miss S E Sheldon, BEd *Class Teacher, Heathfield*
Mrs S P Sheppard, ALA *Librarian*
M E Siggins, BA *English*
*Mrs F A Smith, BA *Geography, House Tutor Slitheroe House*
Miss H E A Stembridge, BEd *Infant Class Teacher*
Mrs G Sunderland *Teaching Assistant*
Mrs C Taylor, BA *Infant Co-ordinator*
Mrs S M Temperley, GRSM, ARMCM, ADB *Junior Music, Heathfield*
A J Thomas, BSc *Boys' Physical Education*
*Mrs J Thompson, BEd, LRAM, LLCM *Performing Arts*
Mrs J Thompson, BA *EFL*
Miss L E Turner, BSc *Girls' Physical Education*
Miss L V Turner, BA *Junior Subjects, Heathfield*
*A E Vinters, BSc *Physics, Head of Science, Housemaster Calder House*
Mrs E F Waddington, BA *Special Needs, Dyslexia*
*Mrs B M Wilson, MA, LTCL *English, Publications Officer*
*M Wilson, BA *History, Head of Lower School*
Mrs E J Wood, CertEd, ABSM, LTCL *Infant Class Teacher*
Miss K R Wright, BA *Class Teacher, Heathfield*

Instrumental Music Teachers:

Miss C Binns, BA
Mrs R K Burbidge, GRSM, LRAM, ARCM, LTCL
Mrs B Slade, GRSM, ARMCM, ARNCM
C D Wood
D E Southcott
A Wallis, LGSM
C Marks, LLCM
B Price, BA, GCLCM
P Brown, LGSM, GCLCM
R N Ferguson
Mrs G Finney, BEd Hons, LGSM, ALCM

Administrative Staff:
Bursar: R M Schofield, BA, ACA
Assistant Bursar: Mrs A C Martin, BA
Headmaster's Secretary and Registrar: Mrs P Hague, BA
Matron: Mrs D K Robinson

General organisation. Founded in 1724, Rishworth is a co-educational day and boarding school comprising a nursery for children from age 3, a junior school, Heathfield, which has its own separate site where children are taught up to the age of 11, and the Senior School up to age 18. Rishworth is a Church of England foundation, but welcomes children of all faiths, or of none. Numbers stand at just over 530 pupils, of whom nearly 70 are boarders.

Facilities and location. Superbly located in the Pennines, Rishworth has a mix of elegant older buildings and excellent modern facilities including a capacious sports hall, a 25 metre indoor swimming pool, extensive games pitches, a recently refurbished music block and Sixth Form Centre, two modern ICT suites and a new performing arts theatre.

Access to the School by road is easy, with the M62 within five minutes' drive. School buses run to the Halifax, Todmorden, Rochdale, Oldham and Huddersfield areas.

Welfare and Pastoral. The unusually high degree of attention afforded to pupils by small teaching groups, the careful monitoring of progress, co-ordinated pastoral support and a close working partnership with parents enables pupils to build on their strengths and allows specific needs to be addressed. Each boarding pupil is under the direct care of a housemaster or housemistress, who is ably supported by an assistant in each boarding house.

Teaching. Taught by a dedicated staff of qualified specialists, the curriculum, both academic and non-academic, is broad and stimulating, and offers every pupil the chance to be challenged and to excel. A general curriculum, broadly in line with the National Curriculum, is followed until Year 9, after which pupils select GCSE options in consultation with their parents, tutors and subject teachers.

Support is given by qualified specialists for certain special needs including dyslexia and English where this is not the pupil's first language.

Broader Education. In order to help our pupils to become the confident, balanced and considerate young men and women we wish them to be, we encourage participation in a wide range of activities outside the classroom.

Sports are well appointed and well taught, and each term boys and girls enjoy excellent results. The School also has a justly high reputation in music and drama, and joint productions with professional groups have been staged during the past year.

Other activities range from the Duke of Edinburgh's Award to a successful amateur radio club, and include a prize-winning debating team, golf, skiing, sub-aqua diving, and many others.

Boarding. Boarders (from age 10 or 11) are accommodated mostly in single study bedrooms. These are located in spacious houses, overseen by house staff. The boarding houses have recently undergone major refurbishments which have ensured that the character of the historic buildings has been retained alongside the provision of top-rate modern amenities. A full programme of activities is arranged for the evenings and weekends, and there are good recreational facilities reserved for the boarders, including dedicated social areas.

Admission. Places in the junior school, Heathfield, are given, subject to availability, on individual assessments appropriate to each applicant's age and previous education. Entrants for Rishworth at Year 7 are asked to sit the School's own entrance examination, which also forms the basis for the award of scholarships. Heathfield pupils are normally given an automatic place at the Senior School, unless there is doubt about the child's ability to cope with the curriculum.

Those who wish to join the School at other stages are assessed individually.

Fees and reductions. (*see* Entrance Scholarship section) Termly fees are as follows: Reception to Year 2 £1,060; Years 3 to 6 £1,545; Years 7 & 8 £1,905 day (£3,690 boarding) and Years 9 to 13 £2,075 day (£4,015 boarding). The School operates a number of schemes, including monthly payments, to ease the financial burden on parents.

A number of scholarships are given for entrance at or after Year 7 for academic, musical and sporting achievement. Substantial discounts are available for siblings of pupils in the School, for children of serving members of the Armed Forces and of ordained members of the Church of England. Bursaries may also be available in cases of financial need.

The Old Rishworthian club maintains a fund for the grant of scholarships to children of ORs.

Charitable status. Rishworth School is a Registered Charity, number 529161. It exists to provide education for boys and girls.

Royal Russell School

Coombe Lane Croydon Surrey CR9 5BX.
Tel: 020 8657 4433
Fax: 020 8657 0207

The Royal Russell School is a co-educational, boarding and day school, founded in 1853 by members of the textile trade. Set in 100 acres of woodland, it enjoys very easy access to London, the South, and the airports at Gatwick and Heathrow. There are nearly 800 pupils of whom 120 are in the Sixth Form and 295 in the Preparatory School.

Motto: *Non Sibi Sed Omnibus*

Patron: Her Majesty The Queen

President: F D Furlonger

Vice-Presidents:
Lady Milner-Barry
A F C Miller

Chairman: R P Green

Board of Governors and Trustees:
P E Reynolds
B J Welch
J P B Hecks
Mrs A D Greenwood
P J McCombie
R N Martin
C T Shorter
Dr J N Ede
Dr J Clough
Mrs P Lloyd

Senior School:

Headmaster: **J R Jennings**, BSc, PhD, MIBiol, FRSA (Queen Mary College, London)

Second Master: P J Moore, MA (Pembroke College, Cambridge)

Director of Studies: G R Moseley, BEd, MA

Senior Teacher: Mrs S Davies, MA (St John's College, Oxford)

Assistant Staff:
Miss J A Powell, CertEd
*S Lightman, BA
*G Muller, BA
*†J Piggin, BA
†Miss J A Chapman, BA
*E J Brown, BSc
Miss P J Willis, CertEd
†M J Tanner, BSc, MA
G S Bell, BSc, PhD
*N A Marshall, BEd
Mrs A R Roseweir, BSc
Mrs C Muller, BA
*†K W Owens, DipAD
†*Miss K J Palenski, BA, MA
* I O'Brien, CertEd
*Mrs J Roe, BSc
*Mrs P Dunderdale, MA
*Mrs R D May, BA

Miss M P Latessa, DLing
†Mrs N Gallagher, BSc
Mrs M J Clower, BA
Mrs P L Cathan, BA
*Mrs S J Dodsworth, BA
*H R Sutton, BA, ARCM, MEd (*Director of Music*)
†*R J Parker, BEd
Mrs A Armstrong, BA
*Mrs R Gedney, BA
*S Keable-Elliott, BA
S J Greaves, BSc
*Miss M Davenport, BA
N Lupton, BA
*P J Endersby, BSc
The Revd P L Tait, BA (*Chaplain*)
J Cunningham, MA, PhD, MPhil
A Archibald, BEd, MA, MA
P C Cook, BSc
Ms M de Groot, MA
C Gedney, BA
Miss K Higashi, BSc, DipEd
*Mrs J Kirby-Jones, CertEd
Miss C Latessa, DLing
Miss E Lopez Garcia, BA, MPhil, MA
M G Riches, MA
A W Moore, BA
Miss C Richmond, BSc
*†Mrs S Taylor, BA
P Mohan, BSc, MSc
*Mrs S Culbert, BEd, MA
*M L Stanley, BA
D Kurten, BSc, MSc

Preparatory School:
Headmaster: C L Hedges, BA, CertEd
Director of Studies: Miss K Rushworth, BA, DipRSA, PGCE
Mrs A Gavin, CertEd
T J Humber, CertEd
Mrs V Rundle, CertEd
Mrs E Scanlon, CertEd
Mrs M Womack, GDipMus, RNCM, PGCE
A G C Adams, LTCL
Miss C Perry, BA, DipEd
S J Pomeroy, BSc, PGCE
Mrs F Simpson, BEd
Miss M Boswell, BEd
M Hodges, BEd

Pre-Preparatory Department:
Head of Pre-Prep: Mrs P Burgess, BEd, MA
Mrs M Gooch, CertEd
Mrs C Womack, CertEd
Mrs C Trim, CertEd
Mrs S Fladgate, BEd
Mrs R Coker, BEd
Miss J Lingley, BA, PGCE
Mrs P Francis, CertEd
Mrs A King, BEd

Special Needs:
Mrs B Hill, CertEd

Senior School Houses and Housestaff:

Boarding:
Cambridge: J Piggin
Oxford: R Parker
Queen's: Mrs S Taylor

Day:
Buchanan: Mrs N Gallagher
Crispin: K W Owens
Keable: I O'Brien
Madden: M J Tanner
Reade: Miss K J Palenski
St Andrews: Miss J A Chapman

Bursar: P Barlow

Medical Officer: Dr I McM Wesson, MB, BS, AKC

Dental Officer: W McBurney, BDS

Sanatorium: Sister-in-Charge, Miss P M Prowse, SRN

Matrons: Miss F Robertson; Mrs O Boon

Number in School. In the Senior School there are 499 pupils, 117 boarders, 382 day pupils. Of these, 325 are boys, 174 girls. In the Preparatory School there are 283 pupils, 165 boys and 118 girls.

Admission. Most pupils enter the school in the Autumn term at the age of 3, 4+, 7, 11 or 13. Space permitting pupils may be considered and admitted at other ages and there is a direct entry into the Sixth Form.

Religion. The school's religious affiliation is to the Church of England but pupils of all persuasions are welcome. Our approach to daily life is founded on Christian principles and we try to maintain an atmosphere of mutual respect, affection and understanding.

The resident Chaplain is responsible for the conduct of all services and the teaching of Religious Education throughout the school. Each day begins in Chapel with a brief act of worship and an opportunity to share ideas and concerns. The Sunday service is compulsory for those boarders at school, and the voluntary Eucharists are specifically for those with a Christian commitment. Enquiries regarding Confirmation to the Church of England are encouraged.

Curriculum. The keynote of curriculum organisation is flexibility and there is close alignment with the requirements of the National Curriculum. In the early years everyone follows a curriculum designed to give a sound foundation across a broad range of subjects. Equipped with this experience pupils are helped in selecting their GCSE examination subjects from a wide range including Information Technology and Drama. Great care is taken to achieve balance in each pupil's timetable and to ensure that an appropriate number of subjects is studied.

A high proportion of pupils continue to the Sixth Form where, typically, four subjects are studied in Year 12 with three continuing into Year 13. "A" level courses at present available are Mathematics, Further Mathematics, Information Technology, History, German, Geography, Geology, Physics, Chemistry, Biology, English, Business Studies, Politics, French, Spanish, Drama & Theatre Arts, Media Studies, Art & Design, Design Technology and Music.

It is our expectation that all pupils will leave the Sixth Form to go onto higher education and we regularly secure places at Oxford and Cambridge for our strongest students.

Facilities. The School lies in 100 acres of grounds providing excellent academic and sporting facilities for all age groups.

The recent £2 million programme of building and refurbishment has transformed the boarding houses and provided a purpose built School Library and Sixth Form Study Centre.

Other improvements within the past five years include a new Swimming Pool, four Computer Laboratories, a CDT Centre and Language Laboratory. Two more Computer Laboratories will be opened in September 2001.

Plans are currently underway for an extension to our Sports Hall to provide a Sports Centre with an additional Gymnasium and changing facilities.

A detached Science building contains six modern and very well equipped laboratories.

There are four Computer Laboratories, a Language Laboratory, a Home Economics Room, separate Music Room and Drama Studio. A new Sports Hall was completed in autumn 1987 and a heated indoor swimming pool complex was opened in December 1994. A new CDT centre and Language Laboratory have just been completed. Major development now in progress to provide a new library and Sixth Form Study Centre for September 2000.

Careers. The Head of Careers co-ordinates Careers advice, giving individual counselling and helping with all applications. The School is a member of the Independent Schools Careers Organisation whose services are available to all pupils. Towards the end of the Summer Term work experience placements are organised for those who have completed GCSE examinations, and members of the Lower Sixth participate in organised visits to Universities and Colleges.

Organisation. The Senior School is divided into nine Houses each of approximately 50 pupils, 2 boarding and 4 day for boys, 1 boarding and 2 day for girls. Each House has its own premises, Housemaster or Housemistress and assistant House Tutors. All Sixth Formers are accommodated in single or double study bedrooms, fully carpeted and newly furnished. The members of the school fall into three categories: full boarders, weekly boarders and day pupils. It is expected that all pupils should be able and encouraged to participate as fully as possible in the extra-curricular life of the school, becoming involved in evening and weekend activities, irrespective of their status. Supervised homework sessions are provided for day pupils participating in evening activities and they attend supper with the boarders. On joining the Senior School each pupil chooses a member of staff to be his or her Tutor. Tutors play a vital pastoral and academic role, monitoring overall progress and development.

Games. The main games are hockey, cricket, soccer, netball, tennis and athletics. There are four hard tennis courts, a gymnasium, a new Sports Hall, a heated indoor swimming pool and a small bore rifle range. Badminton, basketball, volleyball, judo and squash are popular. It is possible to go riding

Music, Drama and Art. Music in the Senior School is in the hands of the Director of Music whilst the Assistant Director of Music concentrates on the Prep School. They are assisted by a large number of visiting teachers. There is a Senior School Orchestra and smaller wind, brass and string ensembles. Choral Society, Chapel Choir and Preparatory School Choir and Orchestra meet and perform regularly. A new Prep School Centre has recently opened.

Drama is taught as part of the Creative Studies programme in the lower school and is available at GCSE and 'A' level.

Instruction is offered in a wide range of Artistic techniques using a variety of materials – paint, ink, screen printing, ceramics and pottery.

Clubs and Activities. Computer, Young Engineers, Art, Drama, Photographic, Pottery and Chess Clubs are very popular and meet regularly.

There is a flourishing voluntary CCF unit. There are regular camps and weekend activities and The Duke of Edinburgh Award Scheme operates. The school's involvement in Model United Nations programmes is unique in this country. The annual October conference attracts 400 student delegates from all over the world.

Preparatory School. The aim in the Preparatory School is to prepare pupils as thoroughly as possible for entry to the Senior School. The Kindergarten and the Pre-Preparatory Sections provide a happy, secure and purposeful environment for those just starting school and during the early years of schooling. For full details please see our entry in the IAPS section.

Scholarships. A number of scholarships are available each year to pupils aged 11+ to 13+ who show particular academic promise. Sixth Form scholarships are also awarded annually. Special awards are available to members of the Armed Forces.

For further details or an appointment to visit the school apply to the Headmaster.

Termly Fees. Seniors: boarders £4,480 per term; day pupils (inclusive of lunch and supper) £2,350 per term. Preparatory day pupils £1,725 per term (inclusive of lunch and supper). Pre-Preparatory day pupils £1,390 full day (inclusive of lunch) per term. £620 (half day) per term.

Charitable status. Russell School Trust is a Registered Charity, number 271907. It exists solely for the education of boys and girls.

* Head of Department § Part Time or Visiting
† Housemaster/Housemistress ¶ Old Pupil
‡ See below list of staff for meaning

The Royal School Dungannon

Northland Row Dungannon Northern Ireland BT71 6AP
Tel: Dungannon (01868) 722710
Fax: (Bursar) (01868) 752506; (Headmaster) (01868) 752845

Founded 1608
Motto: *Perseverando. (Never say Die)*
Voluntary Grammar School (GBA & SHMIS)
Pupils: 650
Teachers: 40 Full-time and 6 Part-time.
Grammar School 11–18 – coeducational.

Governing Body:
Chairman: Dr H G McNeill, BA, MB, FFARCSW
Vice-Chairman: Mrs S M Stewart

Members:
The Revd R I A Allely, BA, BD
M A Batchelor, BEd, LRAM
Pastor J Birnie, CertEd, DipTh, MPhil
D N Browne, MIB, MIMgt
F W Compton, MPSNI
G A Cooper, OBE, BSc, CEng, FICE, FCIWEM, FIEI, MConsE
J C M Eddie
Mrs R Gallagher
J A N Gilpin
The Revd K R J Hall, FOC, MLIA, CertTh
Mrs J A Hobson, BEd, ATCL
Mrs M K Hobson, BA, MSc
Mrs I T Holmes, MBE, BSc, DASE
L G J Holmes
Dr H Kennedy, MB, BCh
The Revd K R Kingston, MA
Prof A E Long, BSc, PhD, DSc, CEng, FICE, MISE
Miss M E Macbeth, BSc
J C McCarter, BA, DipArch, RIBA
The Revd Canon W R D McCreery, BD, GOE
Dr B T McNamee, MB, FRCP
K Maginnis, MP
Mrs M E L Peyton, TD, BSSc, MSc, CQSW
The Very Revd Dr A Rodgers, MA, DD
J H Spray, BA, DipEd
Mrs S M Stewart
Mrs I Suitor, BSc, LRSC, PGCFHE
The Revd Canon F D Swann, BD, GOE

***Headmaster:* P D Hewitt**, MA, DipEd FRSA, FInstMgt

Teaching Staff:

Vice-Principals:
Miss V S J Garvin, BA, DipEd, MEd
K J Hill, MSc, DipCSE, CertEd

Senior Master: [2]R I Edgar, MA, DBA, LGSM
Senior Master: R J Clingan, BSc, PGCE
Senior House Master: W J Irvine, BSc, DipEd
Senior Resident Master: [1]G I Watterson, BSc, PGCE

Mrs H E Annesley, BA, DipEd
[2]P H Annesley, BSc, BAgr, DASE
[1]M A Batchelor, BEd, LRAM
E C Brennan, BA, DipEd
N J Canning, BEng, PGCE
R E Chambers, BSc, PGCE
Mrs W Y Chambers, BSc, PGCE
[1]Miss A E Chestnutt, BSc, CertEd
[1]Mrs M E Clingan, BA, ATD
[2]Mrs R Cobain, BA, CertEd
W Dickson, BA, DipEd
[1]J R Graham, BA, MSc, PGCE
Mrs J Hinds, BA, PGCE
[1]Mrs J Hobson, BEd

A Kelly, BA, DipEd
Miss Z E Kelly, BA, PGCE
P S Kerr, BA, PGCE
[1]Mrs C S King, BA, MEd, CertEd
Mrs P L Matthews, BEd, PGCE
[1]Mrs P McMullan, BEd, PGCTEd
[1]T A Mullan, MSc, MA(Ed), DASE
[1]B P Nolan, BA, DipEd
K D Patton, BEd
Ms A M Prescott, BEd, MEd
N D Purdy, BA, PGCE
B R Rea, MA, DipEd
[2]D J Reid, MSc, DASE, MIB
A S Ritchie, BSc, PGCE
J H Spray, BA, DipEd
[1]Mrs E J Walker, BMus, PGCE
Miss S J Wicks, BA, PGCE
J C Wilson, BEng, PGCE
Mrs K A Wilson, MEng, PGCE
Miss R L Wright, BSc, PGCE

[1] denotes Form Master/ Mistress
[2] denotes Head of House

Chaplain: The Revd A MacAuley

Administrative Staff:
Bursar: Mr K Wilson, BSc(Econ), ACA
Headmaster's Secretary: Mrs A Cullen
General Office Supervisor: Mrs P Williamson

Matrons:
Mrs E McAlister, SRN (*Day*)
Mrs P Lucas (*Evening*)
Miss B Finlay (*Evening*)

In 1608 James I made an order in Privy Council establishing six Royal Schools in Ulster of which Dungannon became, in 1614, the first to admit pupils. In 1983 plans were first drawn up to incorporate the neighbouring girls' grammar school and to use both campuses' excellent facilities for coeducational purposes. This development came to fruition in 1986. A £9 million building and refurbishment programme has begun and when completed in 2003 will provide very high-tech specialist accommodation.

For nearly four centuries the Royal School has aimed at providing an education which enables its pupils to achieve the highest possible standards of academic excellence and at developing each pupil into a mature, well-balanced and responsible adult, well-equipped for the demands of a highly complex and technological world.

There are four Houses which foster the competitive instincts and idiosyncrasies of young people. Pastorally, each year is supervised by a Form Master or Mistress who guides his/her pupils throughout the child's career in a caring school environment.

There is modern accommodation for 50 Boarders with a normal residential staff of seven teachers and three matrons. Girls and Boys are housed in separate wings of the recently modernised Old School building of 1789. The establishment of good study skills and practices is considered to be of crucial importance. The size of the School ensures that no child is allowed to be lost or overlooked in any way.

The extensive buildings are a mixture of ancient and modern, with plans to build even more modern science accommodation in the next few years. Recently a half million pound renovation provided new careers, music and girls' boarding facilities.

Eleven well-equipped Science laboratories, Audio/Visual Room, two Libraries, Sixth Form Study Rooms, Technology, Geography and Geology Laboratories, Music and Art Studios and two Information Technology Suites are supplemented by a Boarding Department housed in new luxury accommodation and boarders are able to make use of a wide range of facilities such as Sports Hall, Computer Laboratory, Swimming Pool, Squash Court, Video Rooms, Television Lounge and Snooker Rooms. Situated in its own spacious grounds in a quiet residential area of this rural town, the School is linked directly by motorway to Belfast (40 minutes), two airports, cross-Channel ferries and railway stations.

All the usual school subjects are taught including Geology, Computer Studies, Art and Design and Technology. Japanese Studies are available after school.

Pupils are prepared for GCSE and 'A' levels under all the major UK Examination Boards and there is a tradition of Oxbridge successes as well as a high rate of entry to the University of Ulster, Queen's University Belfast and other leading British Universities. In most years over 85% of the Upper Sixth Form proceed into Higher Education. Many of the School's overseas students have chosen to enroll at the Province's two Universities, such is their affection for Northern Ireland.

Apart from three nursing Matrons, the School is medically attended to by a team of doctors and dentists which gives Boarders first priority in calls. A major hospital is less than a mile from the campus. Many co-curricular pursuits are encouraged during lunchtime or after school, such as Choir, Orchestra, Duke of Edinburgh Awards Scheme, Chess, Photography, Debating, Public Speaking and many more.

Alongside the School's academic achievements in both Arts and Sciences may be placed its record in the sporting world: in Rugby, Hockey, Cricket, Badminton and Tennis many trophies have been awarded and the Shooting Team has won the UK Championship at Bisley in recent years.

Fees (2000/2001) £4,069 *for a full year's boarding* and £3,362 approx tuition fees (applicable only to non-EC residents). There are several valuable Entrance Scholarships awarded annually and tenable for at least five years. Reductions in fees are available for children of clergymen, of overseas missionary workers of any denomination or for families of the Armed Services.

Charitable status. The Royal School Dungannon is a Registered Charity, number XN 465 88 A. It was established by Royal Charter in 1608 for the purpose of education.

The Royal Wolverhampton School

Penn Road Wolverhampton WV3 0EG.
Tel: (01902) 341230
Fax: (01902) 344496
e-mail: head@royal.wolverhampton.sch.uk

Motto: *Nisi Dominus Frustra.*

Patron: Her Majesty Queen Elizabeth The Queen Mother

Presidents:
His Grace the Duke of Sutherland
The Rt Revd The Lord Bishop of Lichfield

Board of Governors:

Nominated Governors:

Chairman of Governors: [1]Mrs C M Birch, BSc

¶R H Etheridge, Esq
[1]H L Harrison, Esq, FRICS
P Hill, Esq, FCMA, MIMC
H V Hilton, Esq, FRICS
Mrs E P Hudson, LLB
[1]¶W G Meredith, Esq
[1]D Pitchford, Esq, BA, CPFA, FBIM
[1]K Williams, Esq, LLB
J A E Winter, Esq
A K M H Rashid, Esq, JP, MA, MPhil
Professor M D G Wanklyn, BA, MA, PhD, FRHistSoc
A Sharp, Esq

Co-optative Governors:
P Court, Esq, FCIB, FInstD, FBIM
P H Freeth, Esq, ACIB

Representative Governors:
Councillor P Bilson, Mayor of Wolverhampton *Wolverhampton LEA*
The Revd J Hall-Matthews, Rector of Wolverhampton *Lichfield Diocese*

[1] denotes Trustees of the school

***Headteacher:* Mr T J Brooker**, BSc, PGCE

Deputy Head and Resident Chaplain: Revd P C Atkinson, BA, PhD, CertEd
Head of Junior School: Mrs M Saunders, CertEd
Administrator, Clerk to the Governors and Secretary to the Foundation: D R Penn, BSc
Head of Boarding: Mrs H Hall, CertEd
Director of Studies: J C Wynne, CertEd
Senior School Staff:

Arts, Craft, Design & Technology:
M Allison, BA Hons, PGCE, BTec National Diploma (*Head of Art*)
J C Wynne, CertEd (*Head of Design and Technology*)
Miss A M Atherton, BA, PGCE (*Head of Food Technology*)
M L Thompson, BEd
J Samuel, CertEd (*Dartmouth Housemaster*)

Business Studies:
C J Walker, BSc Hons, PGCE (*Careers Master*) (*Gibbs Housemaster*)
Mrs J McClughen, BA Hons, HND, MAAT, PGCE

Divinity:
Revd P C Atkinson, BA, PhD, CertEd

English:
D P Boag-Munroe, CertEd, BA (*Head of English*) (*Hayward Housemaster*)
Mrs S Huntingdon, BA, MA, PGCE

Geography:
S M Bailey, BA Hons, PGCE, MA (*Head of Geography*)
N J Meek, BA Hons, MA, PGCE (*Lees Housemaster*)

History:

Information Technology:
M L Thompson, BEd (*Head of Information Technology*)
N J Meek, BA Hons, MA, PGCE (*Lees Housemaster*)
P C Bryett, CertEd, DipIT

Mathematics:
A Long (*Head of Mathematics*)
Mrs M Bastin, CertEd, RSADip (*York Housemistress*)
D Ireland, BEng Hons, PGCE (*Victoria Housemaster*)
M W G White, CertEd (*Rogers Housemaster*)
Miss T Shand, BSc Hons, DipEd (*Lichfield House Tutor*)
G Bahra, BSc, DipHE, PGCE (*Dartmouth House Tutor*)

Modern Languages:
Mrs J Tuckley, BA Hons, DipEd (*Head of Modern Languages*)
Mrs J M Hartley, BA Hons, PGCE
Mrs P L Dent, BA Hons, DipEd (*Reynolds Housemistress*)

Physical Education:
G W Beckett, BSc Hons, PGCE, FIST, AISC (*Head of Games*)
Miss R L Ingerfield, BA Hons, PGCE (*Head of Girls PE*)
Miss A M Atherton, BA, PGCE
M Taylor, BA Hons (*Dartmouth House Tutor*)
J Samuel, CertEd (*Dartmouth Housemaster*)

History:
J E Liddle, BA Hons, HDipEd (*Head of Sixth Form, Politics and General Studies*)

Science:
C N Ambrose, BSc Hons (*Head of Science*)
Mrs H Hall, CertEd (*Lichfield Housemistress*)
Miss S J Peake, BSc Hons, PGCE
Mrs K M Perry, BA, CertEd
Mrs S Tappin, CChem, MRSC (*Laboratory Assistant*)

TEFL:
Miss J L Kyle, BA, PGCE
Miss K Maude, BA Hons, PGCE, MEd TESOL (*Lichfield House Tutor*)
Mrs L Foster, MA, MLitt, PGCE

Junior School Staff:
R Alder, BA, PGCE (*Head of French*)
Mrs J Butler, CertEd
Mrs S Dalton, BA, PGCE
Mrs E Dolan, BEd
Mrs D Ellis, BEd Hons
Miss C A Galbraith, BA, PGCE
Mrs D E Hawkes, CertEd
Mrs M Hillyard, NTSC (*York House Tutor*)
Mrs C D Howes, BEd (*Head of Maths and ICT*)
Mrs C Ireland, BA, PGCE (*Head of English*)
Mrs K Jefferson, BEd Hons
Mrs S J Mogg, BEd Hons (*Head of English*)
J Needham, BA (*Rogers House Tutor*)
Mrs F Thomas (*Pre-Prep Assistant*)
Mrs K Walker (*Pre-Prep Assistant*)
Mrs S Williamson, BEd Hons

Nursery:
Miss S Orgill, NNEB (*Head of Nursery*)
Mrs J Cooper, BTec
Miss D Chell, BTec
Miss H Dunn, NNEB
Miss H Edensor, BTec
Mrs J Nethercott, NNEB
Mrs D Noad (*Nursery Assistant*)
Miss S O'Hara, BTec

Music Staff:
Mrs C Fellows, BMus, GNCM, ANCM, FRNCM (*Director of Music*)
I Hackett, BMus Hons, PGCE, GNCM, ANCM (*Assistant Director of Music*)

Visiting Music Staff:
C Addy (*Tuba*)
Miss V Bates, GBSM, BA, MA (*Oboe*)
Mrs J Davies, LCM Hons (*Keyboard/London College of Music Rep*)
C Fletcher, BA Hons (*Brass*)
Miss C Hollocks, BA Hons, PGCE, MA (*Pre-Prep Class/Music/Singing*)
Miss H Jones, BA Hons (*Flute*)
J Meadows, BA Hons, ABSM (*Woodwind*)
Mrs M Morton, GRSM, ARCM, LRAM, PGCE
G Nock (*Drums/Percussion*)
N Rose, PGDip, BMus Hons, ALCM (*Keyboard/Composition*)
Miss A Smith, BA Hons, ABSM, PGDip (*Violin/Viola*)
S Terry (*Keyboard/Drums*)
A Wilkes (*Guitar*)
J Woodcock, ABSM, GBSM, CertEd (*Senior School Piano*)

Administrative Staff:
Secretary to the Headteacher: Mrs M Orton
Secretary to the Administrator: Miss N Sweet
Junior School Secretary: Mrs A P Jackson
Administration Office Manager: Mrs D Hall, MAAT
School Fees: Mrs P Moores
Receptionist: Miss K Poole
Resource Centre Manager: Mrs M Leigh, ALA
Head of International Office: Mrs L Penn
Holiday Course Co-ordinator: Miss I Harper, BA
Overseas Liaison: S Chung, FCIOB, FBEng, JP

Medical Staff:
Dr D DeRosa, BSc, MB, CLB, MRCGP
Mrs M J Davies,RGN, RSCN
Mrs W Clowsey, SRN
Mrs C Dinham, RGN, RSCN
Mrs C Mead, SRN
Mrs E Stewart, SRN

Estates Supervisor: J O'Hara
Catering Manager: I Thoms, AMISM

The Royal Wolverhampton School occupies a 28 acre site in a pleasant residential area on the fringes of Wolverhampton. Easy access is afforded by road, train or air from the local area and further afield. A daily school transport service is organised for pupils locally and the school arranges airport transfers for pupils from other areas of the country and abroad, at the beginning and end of each term.

The Royal Wolverhampton School provides an education for boys and girls aged 2 to 18 years. Approximately half of the School's 600 pupils attend The Royal Wolverhampton Junior School and The Young Royals' Nursery, and half attend The Royal Wolverhampton Senior School. Pupils can attend the School on a daily basis or they can be admitted as weekly or full boarders. The School can accommodate 170 boarders, most of whom are in the Senior School and Sixth Form.

Founded in 1850, The Royal Wolverhampton School celebrates its 150th Anniversary in the year 2000. The prefix "Royal" was granted by Queen Victoria in 1891 and Her Majesty Queen Elizabeth, The Queen Mother, is the School's Patron.

Facilities. The School has been transformed since its days as an orphanage and the elegant ivy-clad school building has been continually updated. Over the past ten years, the School has spent over £4 million on improvements to the School buildings and equipment. Today, The Royal Wolverhampton School offers tradition combined with modern facilities, which include: a 25m indoor heated swimming pool, an art, craft and design centre (opened in 1990), a dining room and kitchens (opened in 1992), a library (opened in 1995), modern boarding houses (the latest of which opened in 1997), 5 newly refurbished science laboratories (completed in the summer of 1998) and 3 information technology suites equipped with the latest software and hardware and a new computer network in 1999.

The School's modern boarding accommodation houses boys and girls separately, according to their age. Younger children share with 2 or 3 others of the same age and pupils in the Sixth Form either have a single study bedroom or a twin room. All boarding houses have a lounge, where pupils can meet and relax, as well as a kitchen and a launderette. Pupils are carefully supervised by the School's residential staff at all times.

The School's own catering staff serve a variety of meals to suit all tastes. A cooked lunch is provided for day pupils and boarders can enjoy breakfast, lunch and dinner in the modern dining room. Special dietary requirements, for religious or medical reasons, can be accommodated.

Religion. The Royal Wolverhampton School has its own Chapel within the School grounds. This fine building forms a focus for School life, with daily assemblies and important events in the School calendar being held there. Such events include Speech Day, The Advent Service of Light, Remembrance Sunday and Founder's Day. Although the School has a religious affiliation to the Church of England, it welcomes pupils of all religions. Staff will assist pupils of other religions in pursuing their beliefs during their stay at the School.

Pastoral Care. The well-being of all pupils in the School is of prime importance. Both day and boarding pupils are allocated to "houses" under the guidance of a housemaster or housemistress. In addition to registering their attendance each day and to dividing pupils for inter-school competitions, the house system allows pupils to have regular contact with one particular member of staff, who will be their first point of contact if they should have any problems.

In addition to their housemaster/housemistress, pupils are also allocated an academic tutor who will help them if they encounter any problems associated with their accademic studies.

In case of illness, the School has a fully equipped sanatorium, which provides 24 hour healthcare.

Curriculum. Pupils learn how to use computers from an early age in one of the School's 3 information technology suites.

The School offers a broad education at all levels, which is based on the National Curriculum. Pupils in Year 10 study four compulsory subjects (English and English Literature, Mathematics and the Sciences) plus four optional subjects, out of a total of sixteen. At the end of Year 11, all pupils take GCSE examinations.

The School will be following the new "A" level syllabus from September 2000. Students will be advised on the quantity and type of subject they should choose, by Sixth Form staff, bearing in mind their proposed university course and career. Twenty different A level courses are available to choose from. The School's A level results in 1999 were the best ever with a 100% pass rate in eight subjects. The School has particularly high pass rates in Mathematics and the Science subjects.

Sixth Form. (*see* Entrance Scholarship section) The School prides itself on the great care it takes in advising Sixth Form students on careers and universities. The School organises its own universities' exhibition each year, where students can discuss various options with representatives from Higher and Further Education. At least 95% of pupils continue their education at university.

In addition to the School's other facilities, which can be used by all pupils, Sixth Form pupils have their own Study Area, where they can meet, study and relax.

Sixth Formers take part in the Young Enterprise Scheme each year and always put forward imaginative ideas as to the type of business they can run and the type of product they can produce.

Sixth Form Scholarships are available.

Music and Drama. (*see* Entrance Scholarship section) The School has an excellent reputation for its musical standards and is a recognised examination centre for the London College of Music. Our active Music Department, equipped with the latest technology, provides pupils with an opportunity to learn how to play 20 different instruments, including the tuba and keyboard. In addition, pupils are encouraged to take part in the School's choir and to perform in a wide variety of events, including at the National Indoor Arena in Birmingham. Last year, pupils achieved a 100% pass rate in the London College of Music examinations and a 98% pass rate in ABRSM examinations (preparatory to diploma).

As part of a series of inter-house competitions, the Music Department organises an annual Performing Arts Competition. Senior School pupils of all ages sing, dance, read poetry and play musical instruments in front of fellow pupils and staff. One of the highlights of the School calendar is the Variety Show, which presents the best of the School's dramatic and musical talents to parents and other guests.

The School awards a number of Music scholarships each year.

Sport and Extra-curricular Activities. The School aims to educate well-rounded individuals and a wide variety of extra-curricular activities are enjoyed by all pupils from age 7.

The School's extensive grounds afford an indoor heated swimming pool, a gymnasium, tennis courts and extensive playing fields. Pupils can choose from fifteen different sports and matches are frequently arranged both inter-house and against local schools. The School basketball team has achieved major successes locally, including in the local adult League. The School is also very proud of its national athletics champions and strong rugby team.

The School has a very strong Combined Cadet Force, with an Army and RAF section, under the command of Squadron Leader D Ireland. Pupils are also given the opportunity to participate in the successful Duke of Edinburgh's Award Scheme and various other community projects.

The School ethos promotes compassion towards those less fortunate than ourselves and considerable amounts of money are raised for local and national charities. Sixth Formers organise the School's Lenten Appeal each year.

Entrance. The School holds two entrance examinations each year for entry to Year 7, one in November and one for late applicants in February. Scholarships will be offered to the pupils awarded the best grades in these examinations. For further details, please contact the Head's Secretary.

The minimum entry requirement for Sixth Form is five GCSE passes at Grade C or equivalent.

Fees per term. The Senior School fees for the academic year 2001/2002 are: Full boarders £4,770; Weekly Boarders £4,220; Day pupils £2,325.

Day fees include: lunch, text books, stationery, compulsory teaching materials, after school prep supervision and personal accident insurance cover. In addition to the above, boarding fees include: full board accommodation, laundry, dry cleaning, medical attention and nursing in the Sanatorium and personal property insurance cover.

The children of Serving Personnel in the Armed Forces receive a Bursary of £1,000 per term. The children of Old Royals receive a reduction of 25% off the basic fees and discounts are also available for siblings.

Old Royals' and Old Rowans' Association. The Association regularly organises reunions for former pupils. Founders' Day in June and Remembrance Sunday are also popular times for Old Royals and Old Rowans to return to the School. For further information, please contact Mr Mike Masters, 24 Birmingham Road, Coleshill, Birmingham B46 1AA. Tel: 01675 463093.

Charitable status. The Royal Wolverhampton School is a Registered Charity, number L4 5290007 4. It exists solely to provide an education for children.

Ruthin School

Ruthin Denbighshire, LL15 1EE
Tel: (01824) 702543
Fax: (01824) 707141
e-mail: secretary@ruthinschool.co.uk
website: www.ruthinschool.co.uk

The School emerged in 1284 from the Castle built in Ruthin by Edward I and the Collegiate Church of seven years later. It was refounded in 1574 by Gabriel Goodman, Dean of Westminster. The Deed of Endowment with the Great Seal of Elizabeth I and detailed Statutes written by Goodman are preserved at the School.

Motto: *Dei gratia sum quod sum*

Visitor: Her Majesty The Queen

Patron: Sir William Gladstone, Bt, KG, MA

Council of Management:

Chairman: Mrs L Pearse
R A Bale
Col H M E Cadogan, OBE
D H Cotes (OR)
The Rt Hon The Earl of Gowrie, PC
Lt Col D J Harding
B M R Heys (OR)
J N Jacobs
Ms J A McGill
R N E Raven, JP, MA
S H Sington (OR)
His Hon Judge D R Swift (OR)

Bursar and Clerk to the Council: P B Smith, BA(Econ), FCMA

***Headmaster:* J S Rowlands**, BSc

Senior Management Team:
I Welsby, BSc
R C Lowry, BEd
Ms J Higham, MA
Mrs R J Downey, BA, MEd

Assistant Staff:
A J Bolton, ARCM, FTCL, LTCL
Dr S E Cowen, PhD, BSc, PGCE
Miss K A Goodey, MEd, TESOL, BEd, CETFLA
J P Hamer, BA, PGCE
G A Hartley, ATD
S M Herbert, BA, PGCE
S T Hooson, BEd, DipHE
Mrs C J Hunter, NNEB
J P Lee, CertEd
Mrs L M Lee, CertEd
C R Lewis, BA, TEFL
S R Loughlin, MA, PGCE
Mrs A Robson, BA, PGCE
Mrs S Rowlands, CertEd
Dr D M Southall, PhD, BSc, CEng, MIM
I Stazicker, BSc, PGCE
Mrs E Thomas, BA, PGCE

Visiting:
Mrs J Aldridge (*Violin*)
Mrs P Almond, CertEd (*Special Learning*)
Mrs G Bolton, GMus, RNCM (*Piano*)
Mrs P Evers-Swindell (*Speech and Drama*)
P Smith, FTCL, ARCM, ACertCM (*Piano*)
Miss F Rees, AADA, PrTRAD (*Dance*)

Officer Commanding CCF: Capt R C Lowry

School Medical Officer: Dr G H Roberts, BS, MB, LRCP, MRCS

School Secretary: Miss J Clarke

Matron: Miss A H Rogers, SRN, RSCN

The School. Ruthin School is co-educational with some 240 pupils in the School comprising 65 full boarders, 15 weekly boarders and 160 day pupils. Just under a third of the pupils are girls. Emphasis is on the individual. Good manners, personal discipline and respect for others are of supreme importance, as is a thorough grounding in central subjects of the curriculum. We believe that social responsibility can be developed in a small community with a family atmosphere, comprising a wide range of academic and other talents. This is reflected in our entry policy. Ruthin School is committed to providing an education of the highest quality, endeavouring to develop the potential of all pupils in all spheres of education. The pupils develop self-confidence through recognising and building upon their strengths as well as identifying and striving to improve their weaknesses. They are thus prepared to face the challenges of the changing world beyond school.

Organisation. Weekly and full boarding places are offered to boys and girls in the Senior School (11 to 18) and to pupils in the Junior School from the age of 8. Day places are offered from 3 to 11 in the Junior School and throughout the Senior School.

The Junior School has its own boarding house. In the Senior School girls have their own boarding area and Housemistress.

The School operates a 5-day week from 8.40 am to 5.00 pm.

Admission. The normal method of entry to the Junior School is by interview, and to the Senior School by interview and examination.

Activities. A wide range of non-curricular activities is provided from car maintenance, fitness training, choral singing, drama, chess, debating, archery, rock climbing, sailing and canoeing, and there are regular skiing trips with dry slope preparation. Boys and girls are encouraged to participate in the Duke of Edinburgh Award Scheme at the age of 14 until they have completed the Bronze Award; several go on to complete the Silver and a few aspire to the Gold Awards. A lively mix of traditional and contemporary musical and dramatic productions is a feature of the school year and half the pupils receive individual instrumental tuition from the professional music staff. A programme of excursions is organised for boarders in the evenings and at weekends and these are open to all pupils.

Bursaries and Awards. (*see* Entrance Scholarship section) In addition to academic awards, there are awards for Art, Music, Sport and Design Technology and remissions are available for siblings, children of members of the armed forces, of the clergy and of Old Ruthinians.

Curriculum. A wide curriculum is offered in the Junior School with emphasis on the basic skills of reading, writing and arithmetic.

In the Senior School the curriculum includes English, Mathematics, History, Geography, separate Biology, Physics and Chemistry, Science, Information Technology, Art, Music, Design Technology, French, Italian and Personal and Social Education. PE and Psychology are added at A level.

An option scheme operates for the Fourth Form but English and Mathematics are compulsory. Pupils are encouraged to offer a balanced spread of 9 subjects at GCSE.

Careers. Guidance begins in the 3rd year of the Senior School and a comprehensive programme evolves through the 4th and 5th Forms and the whole of the L6 year is devoted to research and visits before university applications are made. Virtually all members of the 6th Form gain university places.

CCF. Pupils join either the Army or the RN Section at the end of their second year in the Senior School and may opt to continue membership in the Sixth Form. There are several expeditions each year both in term-time and the holidays which include adventure training and camps at regular Army bases and the Culdrose RN Air Sea Rescue Station.

Games. Rugby, cricket, hockey, cross country, netball, tennis and athletics all feature in the coaching programme as well as basketball, golf and table tennis.

Fees. Junior Day £1,110–£1,355; Senior Day £2,595–£2,835; Junior Boarding £3,095; Senior Boarding £3,710–£4,480.

Transport. The School provides daily transport to and from the North Wales coast, Holywell, Mold, Wrexham, Chester and the Wirral.

Ruthin School Association. This parents' association of which all parents are members is very active and plays an important supportive role in the School community.

The Old Ruthinian Association fosters close links between past and present pupils of the School. The *Secretary* is Mrs B Tremayne, c/o Ruthin School, Denbighshire LL15 1EE.

Charitable status. Ruthin School is a Registered Charity, number 525,754A/3. It exists to provide education for boys and girls.

St Bede's School

The Dicker Hailsham East Sussex BN27 3QH
Tel: (01323) 843252
Fax: (01323) 442628
e-mail: school.office@stbedes.e-sussex.sch.uk
website: http://www.stbedes.e-sussex.sch.uk

Founded in 1978 St Bede's is a Charitable Educational Trust administered by a Board of Governors. It owes its existence primarily to the success and vitality of St Bede's Preparatory School in Eastbourne, one of the first boys' Preparatory Schools to become fully co-educational and now one of the largest co-educational Preparatory Schools in the country.

Since it was founded 23 years ago, St Bede's has grown from an initial 22 students to 580. Of these 310 are boarders, 60 per cent are boys and 40 per cent are girls. Of the 580 students within the school 230 are Sixth Formers. There are currently 270 day students in the School. Over the last few years St Bede's has grown by acquiring an interesting and attractive collection of properties around the village of Upper Dicker and developing new facilities. An exciting building programme is underway which has added a large Science and Information Technology facility, dance studio and new stables. New teaching facilities and day house accommodation are currently being built. The buildings are friendly, in enviable settings and a far cry from the overbearing, institutional character of much school architecture.

The School takes great pride in the variety of its students and the outstanding range of opportunities available to them. It is primarily a boarding school and is, therefore, organised with the aim of providing a happy and challenging atmosphere for those who are resident seven days a week. Thus a positive programme of weekend activities is always provided and there are no exeat weekends (although arrangements can be made for students to spend weekends at home as required).

Chairman of the Governors: D Summers

Governors:
T Meier
Mrs D Cameron
A C Gottlieb
Lady Newton
A Mays-Smith
J A Sellick
D O Baker, JP
K Edwards
M Griffiths
Mrs M Lucas
T Martin-Jenkins

Headmaster: **S Cole**, BA University of Auckland

Deputy Headmaster: A A P Fleck, BSc, MA, PGCE

Teaching Staff:
P Allison, BSc, PhD, PGCE
Miss S Anderson, BA
Mrs C F Ballard, BEd
A F Barclay, DipMus, CertEd
Mrs P M Barclay, GRSM, LRAM
I J Barr, BSc, PGCE
Mrs L M Belrhiti, BEd, DipEFL
J Berryman, JP, BA, MSc, PGCE
C Biggs, BSc
R I Brown, BA
Ms S Burnett, BSc, PGCE
A Carroll, BSc, PhD
P C Carter, MCCEd, CertEd
J David, BA
Mrs S Drader, MA
Miss B Dutch, MSc, PGCE
R Frame, BA

Mrs L Gillham, BEd
J Glover, BSc, DipEd
S Gough, BEd
Miss F Goulden, BA, PGCE
D T Graham, BA, ATD
Mrs S Green, BEd
Mrs E R Hadley-Coates, BEd
L Hadley-Coates, BSc, PhD
Mrs L Hamilton, MA, PGCE
A R Hammond, MA
Mrs L Hart, BA, PGCE
N A Hatton, MA, CertEd
A Hayes, BSc, PGCE
S J Jordan, BSc, PGDFA
F R Kellow-Webb, BA, PGCE
J Long, LTCL, MusEd
Miss I Martinez-Almoyna, DEA
Miss M McKenna, BA, PGDipTEFL
Mrs N A Miles
R Mills, BA
Revd S Morgan, BD, MA
Mrs M'Timet, BA, PGCE
Mrs A Musgrove, MA, PGCE, MBA
R Mutimba, BSc
Miss S Muxworthy, BA
Mrs J Nebbs, BSc, PGCE
D G Newton, BA, PGCSE
G M O'Neill, BA, PGCE
C Northey, BAAB, ASA
Miss S Palmer, BA, PGCE
G Parfitt, DBA, MBA
G W Perrin, BA
N Potter, BSc, PGCE
P Richard, BSc, PGCE
M Rimmington, BSc, DipIndSt
Miss H Rogerson, BA
R Sanderson, BA, PGCE
Mrs P J Saxby, BA
Mrs W A Simmons, CertEd, RSADip
Miss C Smithyman, BA
Mrs L Suter, Dip Art of Science & Movement
J Tuson, MA
Mrs N Tuson, BSc, PGCE
A Walker, BA, PGCE
R Waring, BSc
A Waterhouse, HDE
Mrs S P Wellings, NCTJ
A Whike, PGD, ASA
P Wiacek, BEng, PGCE
P Wickes, BSc, OTEFL
P J Wilkinson, BSc, PGCE
R Williams, BA
D J Wilson, MA, DipEd, FRGS
S Yates, BSc, PGCE

Houses and Housemasters/mistresses:

Crossways: Mrs P M Barclay
Camberlot Hall: N Hatton
Dorms House: S Gough
Dorler House: Mrs L M Belhriti
The Stud House: D G Newton
Dicker House (*Day Pupils*): Mrs S Wellings and G Perrin

Number in School. There are 580 pupils, 60% boys, 40% girls. There are 230 in the Sixth Form.

Aims and General Information. The purpose that guides our school is quite uncomplicated; it is simply that we wish our boys and girls to leave with their spirits and confidence high, aware of what they have achieved and can do in the future and proud of themselves. That self-confidence will be founded on each young person being valued for what they themselves achieve and the security that goes with succeeding not only in activities, academic and extra-curricular, but also socially. Thus St Bede's provides a very wide-ranging programme, both academically and in its extra-curricular activities, and maintains a teacher:student ratio of 1:8. All this means St Bede's can tailor programmes to the individual's needs to an unusually high degree.

Much is made of the merits or otherwise of co-educational schools. The St Bede's experience leads us to believe certain simple advantages are to be found in co-education. Boys and girls remain boys and girls, but a balance between the sexes, both in students and staff, does wonders in producing a relaxed but lively atmosphere.

St Bede's enjoys an enviable reputation internationally. Currently there are 130 students from 65 different countries at the School.

Curriculum. During the first year in the School students follow a very wide introductory course which includes the following subjects: English, Mathematics, Physics, Chemistry, Biology, French, German or Spanish, Drama, History, Geography, Information Technology, Art, CDT, Home Economics, Musical Appreciation, Religious and Philosophical Studies, Study Skills and PE.

In the Fifth Form (Year 10) all students follow two-year courses leading to the GCSE (Key Stage 4) examinations. Students follow 8, 9 or 10 subjects at GCSE; Mathematics, English, Information Technology and Civics (a course particular to the School involving Health Education, environmental, moral and religious issues and cultural awareness) are compulsory subjects. Potential courses include all the usual subjects with the addition of Arabic, Art, Ceramics, Business Studies, CDT (Design and Realisation), Drama, Food and Nutrition, German, Dance, Graphic Design, Italian, Latin, PE, Photography, Religious Studies, Russian, Rural Studies and Spanish. In all a total of 30 subjects are offered at GCSE. It is, therefore, possible to provide courses to suit most individuals and students have a free choice of five or more subjects from those that are not compulsory. During the first three years those with particular needs, such as those suffering from any form of Dyslexia and those who are non native speakers of English, can follow organised programmes within the timetable taught by suitably qualified teachers.

In the Sixth Form students can follow the traditional three or four A level courses or a combined programme of A and AS levels which can provide a broader education. Most GCSE subjects are offered at A and AS level plus Business Studies, Economics, Dance, Further Mathematics, Photography, History of Art, Pure and Applied Mathematics, Media and Theatre Studies. Additional AS level courses are offered in Computer Studies, General Studies, Geology, Religious Studies and Statistics. St Bede's also offers vocational A levels in Business Studies, Performing Arts and Art and Design which are recognised as equivalent to 2 A levels, plus a professional dance course. All Sixth Formers take part in a wide-ranging and challenging General Studies programme offering cultural and religious studies, current affairs, careers advice and an innovative programme of guest speakers.

Current class sizes average 14 up to GCSE level and 9 at A and AS level.

Club Activities Programme including Games. The extensive programme includes the many sporting and games playing opportunities open to students, The Army Cadet Force, Duke of Edinburgh Award Scheme, numerous outdoor pursuits and a daily programme of activities within the fields of Art, Drama, Music, Journalism, Science, Technology, Engineering and Social Service. In all there are currently over 140 Club Activities running each week and an average daily choice from 40 options. All students are obliged to take part daily. There are no compulsory games at St Bede's. Games and Sports include Aerobics, Archery, Athletics, Badminton, Basketball, Canoeing, Climbing, Cricket, Cross-Country, Dry-Skiing, Fishing, Football, Golf (the School has its own practice course), Hockey, Judo, Dance, Netball, Orienteering, Riding (the School has its own stables), Rounders, Rugby, Sailing, Softball, Squash, Swimming (there is an indoor championship sized pool), Table-Tennis, Tennis and Volleyball.

Pastoral Care. There are three boys' boarding houses and two girls' houses, the numbers in each house varying between 40 and 70, with three resident staff in each. An appropriately selected tutor provides a mentor for each student during their time at the School. These tutors are responsible for ensuring that each student's academic and social well-being is carefully looked after. Tutors act in liaison with Housemasters and Housemistresses and are readily available for discussions with parents. All parents have three formal opportunities each year to meet those who teach or otherwise look after their sons or daughters.

Religion. The School shares the Village Church with the local community. The Vicar and other ministers of religion in local churches are available as confidential counsellors.

Boys and girls are prepared for confirmation in either the Anglican or Roman Catholic church. All students attend weekly meetings in the church which are appropriate to boys and girls of all religions and are of outstanding variety. We do not wish to impose any singular religious observance on our students but would rather either that their existing faith is further strengthened by their being full members of the congregation of local churches or that they grow to appreciate and value the importance of a strong spiritual life through the thoughtful and varied programme of 'School Meetings'. There is a choice of four types of observance on Sundays: the Multi-Religious School Meeting, Church of England, Roman Catholic and Free Church.

Admission. The normal age of entry to the School is between 12½ and 14 years. The Common Entrance Examination, our own Scholarship Examination and Entry Tests are primarily used to determine a student's placing within sets and streams. It is unusual for any student who has been interviewed and has received a satisfactory report from his or her present school to be refused admission. Certain places are open each year to those wishing to join the School as Sixth Formers and at other levels in the School.

Scholarships and Bursaries. A generous number of Scholarships and Bursaries are awarded each year. Scholarships and Bursaries are awarded on performance in the Open Scholarship Examination held annually in February. This examination is suitable for boys and girls of any educational background. Candidates should be over 12½ years and under 14 years on 1 September of the year in which they sit the Scholarship Examination. In addition to academic scholarships awards can be made to those who show particular promise in the fields of Art, Music, Drama, Dance and Sport, or to boys and girls who show outstanding all-round promise and attainment without necessarily achieving the heights in any one sphere of activity. Scholarships and Bursaries can also be awarded on the basis of performance in the June Common Entrance Examination. Interview and recommendation from the Head of a boy's or girl's present school play an important part in deciding to whom awards should be made. Certain Scholarships may be awarded to those entering the Sixth Form. Bursaries are available for children of service families.

Fees. Fees at September 2001: Boarders £5,120 per term; Weekly Boarders £5,120; Day Pupils £3,140 per term.

Charitable status. St Bede's School Trust Sussex is a Registered Charity, number 278950. It exists to provide quality education.

St Christopher School
(Co-educational)

Barrington Road Letchworth Herts SG6 3JZ
Tel: (01462) 679301
Fax: (01462) 481578
e-mail: stchris.admin@rmplc.co.uk
website: www.stchris.co.uk

Fully co-educational from its foundation in 1915, St Christopher has always been noted for its friendly informality, breadth of educational vision, good academic standards and success in developing lifelong self-confidence. There are now some 500 pupils from 2 to 18. Boarders can start from age 8 and they make up half the Senior School. We aim for our young people to develop competence and resourcefulness, social conscience and moral courage, a capacity for friendship and a true zest for life.

The School was founded in Letchworth's infant Garden City by the Theosophical Educational Trust, whose object was to support schools 'where members of different faiths shall be encouraged to mix together and in this way learn a respect and tolerance for ideas other than their own'. The School in its present form developed under the Quakers, Lyn and Eleanor Harris and their son Nicholas, who provided a continuity of purpose from 1925 to 1980, when the present Head was appointed. The School is now an educational charity conducted by a Board of Governors, all of whom have a close knowledge of the School.

Board of Governors:
Neil A Robertson (*Chairman*)
Mary Marsh (*Vice-Chairman*)
David Baker
Marshall Clarke
Keith Cockburn
Barry Goodall
Ann Jacob
Garth Pollard

***Head:* Colin Reid,** MA, PGCE

Deputy Head: Jane Miller, BA, PGCE, PhD

Senior Teacher: Kathie Martins, LGSM

Teaching Staff:

Mehrdad Ayoubi, BSc, PGCE (*Head of ICT*)
Michael Bee, NDD, ATD, CertCDT (*Head of Design/Technology*)
Sylvester Beecroft, BA, PGCE (*French/Head of Middle School*)
Charles Birtwisle, BSc, PGCE
Julie Bolter, BSc (*Mathematics, Head of Sixth Form*)
Michael Clement, MEd (*Head of Art*)
David Colley, BEd (*PE/Games*)
Michael Collins, BA, MA, PGCE (*History/Politics*)
Wendy Cottenden, CertEd (*PE/Games*)
David Cursons, MA, PGCE (*Chemistry/Head of Science*)
Simon Davies, BSc, MSc, PGCE (*Biology*)
Claude Gaviria-Velez, MA, PGCE (*French/German*)
David Gouldstone, BA, PGCE (*English*)
Edwin Gruber, MagPhil, PGCE (*German/Head of Languages*)
Anthony Harris, BSc, PGCE (*Mathematics*)
Konrad Herrmann, BA, MPhil (*German/French*)
David Ilott, BA, DipEd (*Head of EFL*)
Stephen Jacques, BSc, MPhil, PGCE (*Geography/Outdoor Pursuits*)
Dick Jones, BEd (*Head of Drama*)
Roselyne Masselin, Université of Caen (*Food and Nutrition*)
Mario May, BA, MA, PGCE (*Head of History*)
Lesley Moule, BEd, MA (*Head of Geography*)
Tony Parry, BA, MA (*Mathematics*)
Veronica Raymond, BA, PGCE (*English*)
Betsy Reid, BA, PGCE (*English/History*)
Dennis Rix, MA, PGCE (*Head of English*)
Karen Rix, BA, PGCE
Nita Sculthorpe, MEd, AMBDA (*Head of Learning Support*)
Andrew Selkirk, BSc, DipPhy, PGCE (*Biology*)
Emma Semple, BA, PGCE (*Art/Music*)
Pat Themistocli, BA, PGCE (*History*)
Ben Wall, BSc, PGCE (*Design and Technology, Head of Lower School*)
Linda Wallace, BSc, PhD, PGCE (*Biology/Chemistry*)
Terence Watson, BSc, PGCE (*Physics*)
Michael Watts, BA (*Economics/Business Studies*)
Rosalind Wilson, BA (*Drama*)

Junior School and Montessori Department:

Graham Gorton, BA, PGCE (*Head of Junior School*)
Andrew Alexander, BEd

Jane Colley, CertEd
Augusta Godden, BEd
Jonathan Hart, BEd, DipEd, MPhil
Anthony Hazzard, BA, PGCE
Alyson Mansfield, BEd
Eleanor Owen, BEd
Claire Slater, BEng
Claire Smith, BEd
Pam Willoughby, BEd

Ann Anrep, AMIDipl (*Director of Montessori*)
Marion Gelling, AMIDipl
Alison Turner, AMIDipl

Director of Music: Nicholas Skinner, BMus, PGCE

Development Officer: Geoffrey Edwards, BSc, PGCE

Librarian: Maggie Garrett, ALA

School Doctor: Anthea Bond, MB, ChB, DRCOG

School Matron: Eve Williams, SRN

Head's Secretary: Pat Biggins

Admissions Secretary: Susan Mellor

Special Needs Consultant: Anthea Boston, BA, DipEd, PGCE

Information Technology Consultant: Nick Peace, BSc

Bursar: Pauline Murray-Jones

Boarding Houseparents:

Arunside: Mike and Ceri Collins
Cloisters House: Andrew and Maggie Alexander
Arunwood: Ben and Sally Wall
Old House: Jonathan and Felicity Hart
Arundock: Sylvester and Martine Beecroft

All the children of a family. The School provides for children of average to outstanding ability. All who are admitted to the Montessori Nursery (for 2 to 4 year olds) or to the Junior School (for 4 to 11 year olds) have the right to continue through the Senior School to the age of 16 and we aim, on this basis, to admit all the children of a family whose parents want them to be educated and to grow up together. Entry to the Sixth Form is dependent on the ability to cope with an AS/A Level programme.

Academic Programme. The Montessori has its own very particular curriculum. Close attention is given to the transition to the Junior School which follows a programme which includes extensive enrichment built around the core elements of the National Curriculum. In style the Junior School is closer to state primary schools than to independent preparatory schools but there are smaller classes and greatly enlarged opportunities, including the use of specialist teachers and facilities for the older children. In the Senior School a wide ranging programme continues to be followed up to the age of 16, including the separate study of all three sciences to Double Certificate level of the GCSE. Foreign Languages have a strongly practical emphasis with Geography being taught through the medium of German in Year 9 and everyone that year paying a visit to one of our exchange schools in France, Spain or Germany. The creative and expressive arts are particularly encouraged.

The Sixth Form. Although St Christopher is not a large school, the Sixth Form is a good size (generally numbering 100) with excellent facilities in its new Sixth Form Centre. 20 AS/A level courses are on offer with all the usual Arts and Science subjects and in addition the History of Art, Theatre Arts, Psychology, Business Studies and Design Technology. There is a lively General Studies and Key Skills programme.

Learning through experience. There is an emphasis on learning through experience both with regard to academic subjects and more generally. There are many opportunities for practical and community work and for Outdoor Pursuits. At the end of the Summer Term the timetable is suspended for all pupils to undertake an extended project, generally away from the School campus. Each year two groups of sixth formers visit development projects in the Indian desert province of Rajasthan.

A humane and global outlook. There is no uniform (except for games). All children and adults are called by their first names. Internationalist and green values are encouraged; the diet has been vegetarian from the foundation. People of different religions and of none feel equally at home; there is a significant period of silence in every assembly.

Self-Government. The informality of the School encourages openness: children speak up for themselves – and for others. Everyone, child and adult, is represented on the School Council which is chaired by an elected senior pupil. Its formal powers are limited but its influence is immense. The elected Major Officials and Committees look after different aspects of community life.

Treating children as individuals. From the outset the school has sought to treat children as individuals. In consequence the ethos is an encouraging one and has suited children who, while having good general ability, have a specific learning difficulty or dyslexia. In our Tutorial Centre individual and group help is available. We also deal individually with those of very high ability and children are placed "a year ahead" or "a year behind" according to their needs (and regardless of the consequences for league table results).

Creative and Performing Arts. The School has an excellent tradition in these areas and now has fine purpose built facilities that reflect this. There are several productions a year in the Theatre which has tiered seating and full technical resources. Similarly there are regular concerts and recitals in the Music Centre thanks to almost half the pupil population learning an instrument. In the Arts Centre there are studios for fine art, for design and for ceramics, together with a Sixth Form area and a lecture theatre for Art History.

Technology and Computing. Technology as a subject has flourished in recent years and a fine new building came into use in 1996. Through being a pilot school of the Education 2000 project St Christopher has kept in the forefront of the development of information technology in schools and there is an extensive network enabling software, CD ROM and the Internet to be accessed throughout the central buildings.

Clubs and Societies. There are plentiful activities for pupils to join in with, taking place after school and at weekends. Staff share their enthusiasms and pupils too can take the lead in their own areas of interest. Many of these ventures are financed by grants from the School Council.

Health, Fitness and Physical Education. The diet has been vegetarian from the outset and considerable pride is taken in the catering. There is a resident nurse with relief staff on call. The PE programme is full and varied, making use of playing field, gym, sports hall, all weather surface and a new 25m covered swimming pool. Matches take place between the three Games Houses and also against many other schools.

Full collaboration with parents. The Parents' Circle was founded in 1921 and the School has throughout valued the close involvement of parents, who are welcome in the school not just for consultation about their children but also to take part in evening classes and in Saturday activity courses. We want parents to share in the education of their children and in the school community.

Boarders. There are 120 boarders living in five boarding houses, broadly in line with their age which ranges from 8 to 18 years. The houses for younger pupils have a strongly domestic feeling, with each under the supervision of a married couple, with shared bedrooms rather than dormitories, and with breakfast and the evening meal taken in the house. The accommodation for sixth formers is along student lines with almost all in single rooms. Apart from seven 'closed weekends' each year, boarders can go home each weekend, either on Friday evening or from Saturday lunchtime. Generally over half the boarders are here over Saturday night and the sense of community is strong.

Day Pupils. Day pupils, who make up almost half of the Senior School, benefit from the residential nature of the community, sharing in the evening and weekend life and taking meals in the School when they wish. Sixth formers have their own study carrels in or near to the Library.

Fees. These range in 2000/2001 according to age from £680 to £2,692 a term for day pupils and from £3,805 to £4,750 a term for boarders. There are discounts of 10% for second and subsequent children, so long as they have an older sibling in the School.

Admission Procedure. The most usual ages of admission are at 2 (into the Montessori) at 4, 8 or 9 (into the Junior School) and at 11 or 13 (into the Senior School). A significant number also enter at Sixth Form level. Our interview procedure provides for a tour of the School, separate discussions with parents and child and informal diagnostic tests.

Situation and Travel. The School has an attractive 30 acre campus on the edge of the Garden City with excellent communications. The A1(M) is a mile away and London (King's Cross) is 35 minutes by train. Stansted Airport is 35 minutes and Heathrow 60 minutes by car and the School can provide escorted travel.

Old Scholars. The Membership Secretary of the St Christopher Club is David Cursons who can be reached c/o The School. The Annual Reunion is held over a weekend each July.

Charitable status. St Christopher School is a Registered Charity, number 311062. It exists to provide education for boys and girls, aiming to treat all as individuals and to develop their proper self-confidence.

St David's College

Llandudno North Wales LL30 1RD
Tel: (01492) 875974

Governors:
Eric Payne, OBE (*Chairman*)
David J Rawlinson, LLB, OD (*Vice-Chairman*)
Michael Morley, FCA, MHCIMA (*Treasurer*)
John V R Anderson, OBE, MA, FCA, JP
Philip G Brown, MSI
Peter J R Caldwell, FRICS, FRVS
John Eadie, BA
Dr David W Hughes, MB, ChB, BSc
Ann Mart
Paul Q Owen, OD
The Revd Prebendary Malcolm Potter
Timothy J Vince, BA, MSc, OD

***Headmaster:* William Seymour**, MA (Cambridge)

Assistant Staff:
[1]J C A Bargery, DipPhysEd
J Beech, CertEd, CertIT, DASE
[1]R Beech, CertEd
M J A Bray, ADTC
J Buckley, BA, MEd, PGCE, CFPS(SpLD), AMBDA
[1]S G Buckley, BComm, PGCE
J Charlton, BA
S Delaney, BA, PGCE
J T Demery, BA, PGCE
J Gauge, BA, DipEd(LangTher), CFPS(SpLD), AMBDA
[1]T R Hall, BA, LTh
M Horley, DipEd, CTABRSM, CFPS(SpLD)
S Jarvis, BSc, PGCE
B Lawes, OEd
L Lennard, BSc
I Lloyd-Jones, OEd
[1]H W Lomas, BSc, CertEd
J Lopez-Smith, BA
T Magson, OEd
A P Mosley, BSc, PGCE
M D O'Leary, BEd, DipHEd, MIED
M C Ozols, BA, FIL
A Russell, BSc, PGCE
S Scarff, BA, PGCE
G Taylor, BEd, PGCE
M A Ward, BA, PGCE
P Welton, BEd

[1] denotes Board of Management

House Staff:
Cader Idris: Mr and Mrs Beech
Snowdon: Mr and Mrs Demery
Tryfan: Mr and Mrs Taylor
Augusta (*Girls' Boarding House*): Mrs Round

Chaplain: The Revd T R Hall

Part-time Staff:
[2]Mrs R Bean, BA, PGCE
Mrs D Beecroft, BSc, PGCE
Ms H Bradnam, BSc, CertEd
Mrs J Church, MEd
Mrs G Cooper, CertEd
[2]Mrs S Crossley, MA, PGCE
[2]R Evans, BSc, PGCE
I M Griffith, BA
C P Jowett, BEd
Mrs B Kay, BSc, DipEd
Mrs J Lomas
Mrs D Lombos, MA
Mrs F Marshall, GRSM, LRAM, ARCM, DipRSA
[2]Mrs N Marshall, BA, PGCE, CELTA
Miss H Nutt, MA, PGCE
J P Owen, BA
C Pinchin, MA
S D Porter, BSc
Miss S Redfern, BSc, PGCE
[2]Mrs S J Ross, MEd, AMBDA
Mrs N Silcocks, BA, PGCE
Mrs V Sykes-Davies, CertEd
[2]Mrs J E Taylor, CertEd
[2]Mrs H Thompson, CertEd
[2]Mrs J Williams, MEd, CertEd
Mrs A Wilton, BEd

[2] denotes Cert of Further Professional Studies (*SpLD*)

Director of Music: M Horley, DipEd, CTABRSM, CFPS(*SpLD*)

Drama: Mrs M Crossley, ANEA

Bursar and Clerk to the Governors: Alistair D Bowen, ACIS

Bursar's Assistant: Mrs L P Shirley

Bursar's Secretary: Mrs G Plant

Headmaster's Secretary: Mrs S Hold

Assistant to Headmaster's Secretary: Mrs L Watson

Medical Officers:
P Emmet, MB, ChB, FBCert, MRCGPCert
P Mitchelson, MB, ChB, FBCert

Matron: Miss A Thomas, RGN

Sister: Mrs L Collier, RGN

St David's College, founded in 1965, is a co-educational boarding and day school of 250. Set on a wooded hill on the edge of Snowdonia, facing south. Gloddaeth Hall, an ancient home of the Mostyn family, is strikingly beautiful, surrounded by woodlands, farmland and 23 acres of excellent playing-fields. The College is renowned for its Outdoor Pursuits: sailing (RYA Centre), climbing, skiing, canoeing, caving, orienteering, water-skiing, and hill-walking. The 5 Mini-buses ensure all pupils take advantage of these activities, as well as the usual sports and pastimes (rugby, netball, soccer, hockey, athletics, cricket, tennis, squash, badminton, golf, shooting, etc). The Sixth Form outdoor education leadership programme enables pupils to acquire nationally recognised leadership qualifications. Gloddaeth Hall itself has a long history, and the Mostyn family portraits, the particularly fine Minstrel Hall and Library, and other 16th and 17th century rooms of the college provide a valued reminder of the architecture of the past.

Organisation. Of the 160 boarders, most of the pupils live and sleep in the main central building or the new purpose-built boarding houses completed in 1987, 1997 and 1999 respectively. For administrative and competitive reasons there are three houses. Each pupil is allocated a tutor. Discipline, behaviour, educational problems and general guidance are the concern of the tutors, and close touch is kept between them and housemasters, the Headmaster and Matrons in dealing with any matter relating to pupils' well-being and happiness. It is our aim to enable pupils to develop as fully as possible in all ways intellectually, spiritually and socially, and to enjoy happy relationships with adults and contemporaries in their life at school and in their home life. Concern for others is a necessary part of the ethos that prevails; visitors to the college are aware that courtesy and openness of manner are part of the expected attitude of pupils to everyone.

Studies. A range of subjects is available at 'A' level and GCSE including English, French, German, Spanish, Drama, History, Geography, Business Studies, Philosophy, Mathematics, Physics, Chemistry, Biology, Religious Studies, Art, Design & Technology, Information Technology, Music, Welsh. In the Sixth Form, a range of City and Guilds CAD and CAE courses is available. All junior classes have PE, Swimming and music lessons in their curriculum.

Classes are small, varying from two or three students to a maximum number of sixteen. Special attention is given to English and Mathematics, and the school has a deserved reputation for its outstanding success with dyslexic pupils. The staff are skilled in ensuring that academic pupils reach as high a level as they can, while ensuring that less able pupils are encouraged to persevere in achieving commendable results. The study system teaches self-discipline: all pupils in the fourth and fifth forms have studies (3–4 per room) and in the 6th form all pupils have single studies. Approximately 80% stay on into the 6th Form.

Constant care is taken to ensure that pupils are correctly setted so that they are taught at the appropriate level. A monthly system of grading (in terms of effort and ability) ensures that each pupil is aware that a check on progress is being made. The tutorial system ensures that progress is carefully monitored: close liaison with parents is encouraged both by correspondence and by meetings.

Aims. We provide, in a framework of reasonably ordered living, an environment in which pupils will display enthusiasm, self-discipline, confidence and growing maturity so that their achievements are successful when measured against individual potential and effort. Senior pupils are expected to be unselfish and sensitive in their use of authority: all pupils are expected to show determination in their activities, and concern for others in their relationships. The staff try hard to balance friendly informality at many times with the demand for efficiency and high standards at others.

From its inception the school has placed a sincere emphasis on the Christian faith: this provides the mainspring of all the varied activities, and in services and voluntary discussion groups pupils are led to the consideration and formation of spiritual ideas and attitudes that we hope will provide lasting strength of purpose and character.

Admission. Normally this is at age 11 or 13 from Junior Schools, but there is a smaller Sixth Form entry. Academic, Art, Music and Sports Scholarships are available.

Fees per term. Boarders: Forms 1–2 £3,835, Forms 3–6 £4,022; Day Pupils: Forms 1–2 £2,494, Forms 3–6 £2,615.

Travel. A fast train service from Euston to Llandudno Junction (3½ hours) enables the college to be reasonably accessible from the south. It is also 45 minutes by car from the M56 motorway leading to Exit 20 on the M6.

Charitable status. St David's College Trust is a Registered Charity, number 525747. It exists to provide secondary education within a Christian framework.

St Edward's School

Cirencester Road Charlton Kings Cheltenham Glos GL53 8EY

Tel: (01242) 583955 (Senior School); (01242) 526697 (Junior School)

Fax: (01242) 260986 (Senior School)

Formed from two former Grammar schools in 1987, St Edward's is a fully co-educational day school of 780 pupils aged 4–18 (with a Kindergarten unit of 72 pupils from 2½ years). Proud of its Roman Catholic foundation, the School also warmly welcomes pupils of any denomination. St Edward's is set in beautiful grounds on the southern outskirts of Cheltenham. The Forden Estate of 17 acres houses the Senior School (440 pupils aged 11–18) whilst the Junior School (340 pupils 2½–11) and the main playing fields are located close by at Ashley Manor (a 40 acre campus overlooking Cheltenham).

The aim of the School is to foster the all-round development of the pupils within a caring Christian environment. St Edward's enjoys an enviable academic record, yet also strives to nurture the spiritual, social and physical in order to prepare its students to play a full and creative part in society.

Motto: *Strive for the best*

Chairman of Trustees: Mr M Abbott

Chairman of Governors: Mr P A Oakley

***Acting Headmaster:* Mr J D Williams, BEd**

Head of Junior School: Mrs E Harries, BA, CertEd

Organisation. On entry to the Senior School at age 11, the students are allocated to one of three forms based on a House system (Bede, Chad, Dunstan). They remain in that House although they are soon 'setted' for the principal subjects of Mathematics, English, French and Science. The pastoral strength of the school is based firmly on a Year System (each Year group has its own Year Head). The Sixth Formers have their own study and common room but play a vital role in the organisation and promotion of the School.

Developments. At the Senior School, a development programme is underway, which includes new sports changing rooms and 4 additional classrooms due for completion in September 2001. A further phase, currently awaiting planning permission, will boast a new building, incorporating spacious facilities for Technology, Art & Drama.

Academic Programme. A broad range of subjects is offered to GCSE with over 20 up to 'A' level. During the first three years all pupils study Art, Drama, English, French, Geography, History, Information Technology, Mathematics, Music, Physical Education, Religious Studies, Science and Technology (both Design Technology and Home Economics). German or Spanish is offered as a second foreign language from the first year, and Latin is available from the second year. The Sciences are studied as discrete subjects from the third year onwards.

The compulsory subjects for GCSE are English Language, English Literature, Mathematics, Religious Education (short course), Science (either three separate GCSEs or the dual award) and a foreign language. Up to four further options are studied.

The Sixth Form AS and A2 subjects available include: Mathematics, Further Mathematics, English, History, Geography, Religious Studies, Biology, Chemistry, Physics, French, German, Spanish, Art, Music, Theatre Studies, Design Technology, Food Technology, Computing, Economics, Business Studies, Psychology and Physical Education Studies.

Careers. A Careers Master is available to offer advice. The School is a member of ISCO and under their guidance, all pupils take Morrisby tests in Year 11. In the Lower Sixth, pupils participate in a Work Experience week.

Sport. The principal sports for boys are rugby, hockey, soccer and cricket; for girls hockey, netball and rounders. The School also competes very successfully in swimming, tennis, basketball, athletics, badminton, golf and cross-country.

Facilities include four rugby pitches, three hockey pitches (including one synthetic-turf), cricket square, several tennis courts, two sports halls, a fitness centre and a large indoor swimming pool.

Clubs and activities. The flourishing Duke of Edinburgh's Award Scheme is but one of a wide range of extra curricular clubs and activities. Over the years, the School has gained a high reputation for the quality of its Drama and Music (the choir and orchestra regularly perform both at School and in the community). Other societies range from debating and chess to several sporting clubs. Pupils are encouraged to take full advantage of the many activities which take place both at lunch time and after school.

Junior School. The Junior School is self contained and caters for pupils aged 2½ to 11. It is very well equipped with its own science laboratories, new library, technology room, music rooms etc, and is beautifully situated within 40 acres of grounds. With an emphasis upon sound learning of basics (French is studied from Kindergarten), yet with a broad range of opportunities, pupils are fully prepared for entry to the Senior School.

The Kindergarten, in a separate modern building, takes children from the age of 2½ and is open nearly all year round.

Admission. Admission to the Junior School is possible at any age depending on ability and the availability of places. The main entry to the Senior School is at age 11 (the entry examination takes place in November), although some join the school at age 13 (after Common Entrance) and into the Sixth Form.

Fees (2000/2001). The Junior School fees range from £885 to £1,535, and the Senior School range from £1,940 to £2,270. Discounts are offered for a third, courth and subsequent children.

Old Edwardian's Association. Secretary: Mrs P Hemming, St Edward's School, Cirencester Road, Charlton Kings, Cheltenham, Glos GL53 8EY.

Further information. A School prospectus is available on request from the Headmaster's Secretary. Alternatively, you are warmly invited to arrange a visit to the school by telephoning her on (01242) 583955. Those interested in entry below the age of 11 may contact the Junior School direct on (01242) 526697.

Charitable status. St Edward's School is a Registered Charity, number 293360. It exists to provide for the education of children of any creed with preference to those who are of the Roman Catholic faith.

St George's School
Edgbaston

31 Calthorpe Road Birmingham B15 1RX.
Tel: 0121-625 0398
Fax: 0121-625 3340

Council:
Chairman: The Viscountess Cobham

Mr D J Corney, FCA, MSPI, MIPA
Mr C J Goodier, MA (Oxon)
Mr H D Mainwaring, AMIEE
Mr R Nawab, FCCA
Mrs R Plevey, BSc (Hons), PGCE
Mr A D Rowse, MSc, MB, ChB, FRCS
The Revd S Thorburn, BSc, MA
Mr K Watkin, FCCA, MSPI

Clerk to the Council and School Bursar: Mr D F Baker

***Headmistress:* Miss Hilary Phillips**, MSc Brunel

Deputy Head: Mr Keith Bruce, BSc (Hons) Leeds, PGCE

Senior VIth Form Tutor: Mrs Marion Nash, BSc (Hons) Bangor, CertEd

Upper School:

English:
Mrs Margaret A Blunden, BA (Hons) Dunelm
Mrs Sylvia Dicker, MA Oxon
Mr Roy A E Lett, MA Birmingham, PGCE, ACP, DipASE

Mathematics:
Mrs Marion Nash, BSc (Hons) Bangor, CertEd
Mrs Jane Furneaux Smith, BEd (Hons) Birmingham
Mr Geoff Thompson, BEd (Hons) Lancaster

Science:
Mr Keith Bruce, BSc (Hons) Leeds, PGCE
Dr Michael Follows, PhD Lancaster, PGCE
Mrs Jennifer Gooding, BSc (Hons) Sheffield, PGCE
Mrs Debra Ramsden, MSc Leeds, PGCE, MIBiol, CBiol
Dr Jane Thomas, PhD Bristol, PGCE

Technology:
Mr Barry Brown, CertEd Derby, SuppCert CDT Wolverhampton

Information Technology:
Mr Peter Chollet, BSc (Hons) Bradford, PGCE

Business Studies:
Mr Martin Morgan, ACIB, PGCE Wolverhampton

Psychology:
Mrs Gillian Roberts, BA (Hons) Coventry, BPS

Modern Languages:
Mrs Tina Kenwood, BA (Hons) (London), PGCE
Mr Stephen Parker, BA (Hons) (Birmingham)
Mr Daniel Kitching, BA (Hons) Salford

Religious Studies:
Mrs Katherine Finn, BA (Hons) Manchester, PGCE

History:
Miss Joy Evans, BA (Hons) Manchester, PGCE

Geography:
Mr Robert Biggs, BSc (Hons) Wolverhampton, PGCE

Food Technology:
Mrs Margaret A Gough, CertEd Chelsea

Art and Ceramics:
Miss Karen Howell, DipAD Manchester, ATD
Mrs Claire Hackett, DipAD Wolverhampton, ATD

Music:
Mrs Sarah C Russell, MA Cantab, PGCE
Mr Nigel Morley, GBSM, ABSM Birmingham

Theatre Studies:
Mr Michael Venables, BA (Hons) Lancaster, PGCE, ACE

Physical Education:
Mrs Sheila Foley, CertEd (Birmingham)
Mr Paul Ferris, BSc (Hons), QTS Brunel

Learning Support:
Mrs Carolyn Hayes, CertEd London
Mrs Pamela Edwards
Mrs Helen Taylor, CertEd Liverpool, BEd (Hons) Liverpool

Lower School:

Head of Lower School:
Mrs Christine Russell, CertEd Brunel

Lower School Staff:
Miss Charlotte Akers, BEd (Hons) Bangor
Miss Natasha Archer
Mrs Meral Barlow, BEd (Hons) Birmingham
Miss Furkhander Chishti
Mrs Wendy Nash
Miss Sally Read
Mrs Sally Roberts, First Aid, NNEB, MontDip
Mr Neil Shaw, MA Nottingham, PGCE
Mrs Vicki Simkin, BEd (Hons) Birmingham
Mrs Jean Skelcher, BA (Hons) Birmingham, CertEd
Mrs Patricia Tonks, BEd (Hons) Birmingham
Mrs Lynne Williams, CertEd Liverpool

Technical Staff:
Miss Sian Butler, BA (Hons) Sheffield
Mrs Marilyn Jones

Bursar: Mr David F Baker

Registrar and Head's PA:
Miss Rachel C Webbley, BA (Hons) Dunelm

Secretarial Assistants:
Mrs Pat Roberts (*Upper School*)
Mrs Michelle O'Reilly (*Upper School*)
Mrs Beth Richardson (*Lower School*)

Caretakers:
Mr David Lewis
Mr Patrick Ryan

The school opened in September 1999 as the amalgamation of Edgbaston Church of England College for Girls and Edgbaston College. The school is open to boys and girls of all faiths, but has a strong Christian ethos, and prides itself on the warm family atmosphere where each child is known as an individual. Entry to the Upper School is by selection at 11+ and 13+ and most pupils are expected to move into Higher Education when they leave. Entry into the Lower School is by an informal interview and visit.

Location. Although the School is within a mile of the City Centre it occupies extensive grounds, providing excellent facilities for football, hockey, tennis, rugby, athletics, basketball, netball and rounders. In addition to good local transport services, the School has privately organised school coaches to transport pupils from more distant residential areas. The School takes full advantage of the first class facilities offered by the City and University of Birmingham and pupils are given the opportunity to visit exhibitions, plays, concerts and lectures to enhance their academic and cultural development.

Accommodation. A comprehensive building programme has provided additions to the original school building to meet educational demands.

Curriculum. The aim of the curriculum is to provide each pupil with a broad education appropriate to their age and to enable them to develop their own skills and talents as they mature. The School pays heed to the requirements of the National Curriculum, while offering a wider range of subjects than those prescribed. At Advanced Level there is a corresponding breadth of subject choice. The Sixth Form has its own centre which gives the students a degree of independence. Sixth Formers all take part in the School organised scheme of service in the local community. The majority of pupils continue their education after leaving the School through entry to University and vocational training.

Extra Curricular Activities. Pupils are encouraged to join the lunchtime and after school activities which cover the spectrum of music, drama, sports, discussions and for which there is no extra charge. Instrumental music, speech and drama, ballet and fencing lessons are available as 'extras' and the examinations of the Associated Board and LAMDA are taken.

Fees. £1,100–£1,875 per term. Full details may be obtained on application to the School. We will be pleased to forward a copy of the prospectus and to arrange an opportunity for parents to visit the School to discuss their child's education with the Headmistress.

Charitable status. St George's School, Edgbaston is a Registered Charity, number 1079647. It exists to provide a quality education for boys and girls within the Birmingham area.

St John's College

Grove Road South Southsea Hampshire PO5 3QW
Tel: (Upper School) 023 9281 5118
(Lower School) 023 9282 0237
Fax: 023 9287 3603
e-mail: sjc.southsea@lineone.net
website: www.stjohnscollege.co.uk

Number of boys: 491; Number of girls: 250

***Headmistress:* Mrs Suzanne M Bell,** MEd

Head of Lower School: Mr R Shrubsall, MEd
Head of Nursery: Mrs M Verrier, NNEB

Heads of Department:

English: Mr Callan, BA (Hons)
Mathematics: Mr G Burwood, BSc (Hons)
Science: Mrs K Davies, MSc, BSc
Modern Languages: Mr G Walker, BA
Religious Education: Sister J Ryan
Art and Design: Mr C Wear, Dip in Art & Design
Business Studies: Mr J Martin, BA
Design and Technology: Mr P Harris-Deans, BEd
Drama: Mr A Everitt, BEd
Geography: Mr P Hyde, BSc
History: Mr R Wilkins, BA (Hons)
Music: Mr D Barrett, BA (Hons)
Physical Education: Mr B Saunders, BEd (Hons)

Foundation. Founded as a boy's school in 1908 by the De La Salle Brothers who today support a network of 1,300 schools and other educational institutions throughout the world. What has not changed in the past 90 years is our ethos. It is inspired by the teachings of St John Baptist De

La Salle, who is the patron saint of teachers. The College is now run by a Board of Governors and lay Headmistress. We have a Catholic foundation, but welcome children of all faiths, and also those with no religious belief.

Situation. Located in the heart of Southsea near to the local shopping centre and the seafront. All the classrooms, drama, art, science, technology and computer suites are positioned on a single self contained site. The 34 acres of sports fields are located on the outskirts of the city of Portsmouth for which the school provides transport to and from the site.

Ethos. We are a family school and are committed to developing the whole person, but at the very heart of all that we do is teaching and learning. Our academic record is excellent and continues to improve every year. The commitment of our staff to each pupil is second to none. In return, we expect honest effort from all our pupils in meeting the challenging standards we require in academic work, sporting endeavour, behaviour and self-discipline.

Nursery. The Nursery occupies self-contained premises within the Lower School. It has its own separate entrance and a secure playground. It is open to children aged between two and four years and is open 51 weeks of the year. The children are involved in a pre-school programme for developing concepts and skills for reading, writing and number work. Great emphasis isplaced on creative artwork, outdoor play and educational visits. Specialist French tuition is given to all children.

Lower School. The Lower School is also a self-contained unit, but located on the main College campus. This enables children to benefit from specialist tuition by upper school staff and to make daily use of excellent upper school facilities, including the computer suite and sports hall. The broadly based and extended curriculum encompasses all aspects of the National Curriculum. Great emphasis is placed on English and Mathematics with science taught in specialist laboratories. All pupils learn a musical instrument from the age of seven. There is also a Lower School Choir and a Lower School Orchestra that meet weekly.

Upper School. A broad National Curriculum based curriculum is offered, taught by well-qualified specialists in well-resourced subject areas. Separate Sciences are taught from the start of year 7. The full range of GCSE subjects are available at Key Stage 4 (age 14), and instrumental tuition is encouraged. There is an Upper School Choir and Orchestra open to all pupils. Pupils take formal school examinations twice yearly.

Sixth Form. Students are helped to become independent and self-motivated in preparation for Higher Education. Nevertheless, the College continues to work closely with parents who are kept fully informed of progress and achievement. A wide range of conventional 'A' levels are taught as well as the GNVQ (Advanced) in Business Studies. The College offers a good student/teacher ratio allowing close and constant monitoring of the performance and effort of each student.

Preparation for Oxbridge entry is available, the Cambridge Certificate in Information and Technology is offered to all students, as are the Oxford and Cambridge Diploma of Achievement tests.

A wide range of sporting, intellectual, dramatic, cultural and social activities are available. The Politics Society, administered predominantly by sixth form students, enjoys a countrywide reputation.

Other facilities include practice interviews for University and job applications and a career services.

Admission. Lower School and Nursery entrance is made by assessment. Upper School and Sixth Form entrance is made by examination.

Fees. Nursery all year: Full Week £78; Full Day £17.40; Session £7.25; Additional Hours £2.25.

Nursery term time only: Full Week £87; Full Day £17.40; Session £8.20; Additional Hours £2.25.

Lower School per term: Reception, Years 1 & 2 £1,110; Years 3 & 4 £1,130; Years 5 & 6 £1,210.

Upper School per term: Years 7 to 13 £1,595 (Day); £3,300 (Boarding and tuition UK); £3,570 (Boarding and tuition overseas).

Occasional Boarding (including bed, breakfast, evening meal): £19.50 per day.

Music Fees. Single attendee £96 per term.

Scholarships and Bursaries. Academic and other scholarships are available.

Charitable status. St John's College is a Registered Charity, number 232632. It exists to provide excellent education and pastoral care to boys and girls.

St Joseph's College

Birkfield Ipswich Suffolk IP2 9DR
Tel: (01473) 690281
Fax: (01473) 602409

Founded 1937

Governing Body:

Chairman: Mr M J Bailey, JP
Vice-Chairman: Mr M Spettigue

Dr M Bush
Mr M J Caseley, ACIB
Mrs K Cox
Mr K Davis
Mr D Hallett
Mr G Kalbraier, BSc, FInstD, FIMgmt
Mrs J Lea, MA
Dr H Lelljveld
Revd I Morgan
Dr T Nicholl, FRCA, FFARCS(Ire)

Bursar & Clerk to the Governors: Mr M J D O'Brien, FFA, FIAB

***Head:* Mrs S Grant,** BMus Hons

Deputy Heads:
Mr A Newman, BSc(Econ)
Mrs C Osborne, BEd Hons

Head of Junior School: Mr H G Tuckett, MA, HDE
Deputy Head of Junior School: Mr J Thorpe, BSc Hons

Senior Staff:
Mr P Andrew, BA (*Head of RE; History*)
Mr D Bailey, BA (*RE and History*) (*part-time*)
Mr C Boucher, BSc (*Mathematics; House Leader*)
Mr P Buck, BA (*Economics & Business Studies; Head of 5th Form*)
Mr N Chandler (*Politics & History; Duke of Edinburgh Award; Careers Officer*)
Mr B Crisp, BA (*Art*)
Mr M Davey, BA (*Head of Sixth Form; English; i/c Cricket*)
Mrs M Felton, BSc, MSc (*Head of IT*)
Mr P Franklin, MA (*Head of Science; Assessment Officer*)
Mr P Friel, DipHE (*PE & Games*)
Mr E Gentry, BA (*Head of Art; Games*)
Mr K Hannemann, MA (*Modern Languages*) (*part-time*)
Mr K Hirst, BEd (*Head of Biology; CCF Contingent Commander*)
Mr M Hockley, BSc (*IT; i/c Charity Projects; Chair of Chaplaincy Committee; House Leader*)

Mr J-M Holliday, BA (*Modern Languages; Games*)
Mr T Hunter, MA (*General Studies; TELF; German; Science; Head of Pastoral*)
Mr C Jones, BSc (*Economics; Business Studies; UCAS*)
Mrs B Jousiffe, CertEd (*Girls' PE*)
Mr P Jousiffe, CertEd (*Design & Technology; Head of 4th Form*)
Mrs E Kirby, BA (*English; Drama; Special Needs*)
Mrs M Krajewski, CertEd (*English; History; General Studies*)
Mrs F Lander, BA (*Music*) (*part-time*)
Mrs J Lauder, CertEd (*Head of Girls' PE & Games*)
Mrs A Lee, BA (*TEFL; i/c Far East students*)
Mr A Miller, CertEd (*Head of Design & Technology*)
Ms C Renshaw, BA (*Design & Technology; House Leader*)
Mr A Robinson, BSc (*Mathematics*)
Mrs J Rothwell, BA (*Modern Languages; TEFL; Head of 3rd Form*)
Mr P Ryan, BA (*English; Head of Boarding*)
Mr J Sayers, BA (*History*) (*part-time*)
Miss R Scales, BA (*Head of Music;Games*)
Mr R Shanks, BA (*Head of english; i/c Drama and Debating*)
Mrs M Simmonds, BA (*Modern Languages; Head of 2nd Form*)
Mrs M Stiles, BSc (*Geography; Asst Head of 6th Form*)
Mr P Twist, BSc (*Biology; Chemistry; House Co-ordinator*)
Mr N Walkinshaw, MSc (*Head of Mathematics*)
Mrs M Warren, BSc (*Science; i/c Trips & Visits*)
Mr N Watson, BEd (*PE & Mathematics*)
Mrs G White, CertEd (*Food Technology*)
Mr J Worsley, BSc (*Head of Geography*)
Mr J Yelverton, BSc (*Head of Physics*)

Junior School:
Mrs J Branston, CertEd (*Infants*)
Mrs P Brown, CertEd (*Reception; Infant Co-ordinator*)
Mrs V Cook, BA (*Juniors*)
Mrs V Clement (*Classroom Assistant; Sport*)
Mr M Davies, BEd (*PE & Games*)
Mrs K Dawe, ALCM, CertEd (*Juniors*)
Mrs P Dearing, CertEd (*Juniors*)
Mrs L Fergusson, NFTD (*Classroom Assistant*)
Mrs F Golding, BSc (Hons) (*Special Needs*)
Mr D Howes, BA (*Juniors*)
Mrs McLachlan, BSc, MA (*Juniors*) (*part-time*)
Mrs P March, CertEd (*Infants*)
Mrs D Marfleet, CertEd (*Infants*)
Mrs T McGinn (*Classroom Assistant*)
Mrs M Penton-Smith, CertEd (*Infants*)
Mrs S Rivers, CertEd, DipTheol (*Infants*) (*part-time*)
Mrs N Roser, CertEd (*Music*)
Mrs J Shoebridge, CertEd (*Juniors*)
Mrs J White, BA (*Juniors; TEFL*) (*part-time*)

Visiting Staff:
Mrs J Weale (*Woodwind*)
Miss M Dulgarn (*Piano*)
Mrs A Baker (*Piano*)
Ms S Maxwell (*Guitars*)
Mr G Gillings (*Percussion*)
Mr R Reaville (*Voice*)
Mrs Messenger (*Strings*)
Mr P Shepherd (*Brass*)

Administrative Staff:
Finance Officer: Mrs D Baber
Accounts: Mr m Ager
Registrar: Miss L Peck
Reception: Mrs B Donovan, Mrs R Pollard

Lab Technicians:
Mr J Dennant (*Physics & Chemistry*)
Mrs S Hirst (*Biology*)
Mr F James (*Design & Technology*)
Mrs E McKay (*Reprographics*)

Catering Manager: Mrs J McGinn
Assistant: Mr D McGinn

Medical Staff:
School Nurse: Sr Thea de Boer, RGN, SRCN
Junior School Nurse: Mrs L Gilbert

St Joseph's College was founded in 1937 and moved to its present site at Birkfield in 1946. In 1996 it merged with the School of Jesus and Mary to become a coeducational day and boarding school providing education to some 600 pupils between the ages of 3 and 18. The College is situated close to the centre of Ipswich and is based around two Georgian country houses set in 55 acres of delightful parkland. Birkfield House provides the focus for the Senior School, whilst the Junior School is located nearby, in goldrood House.

Access, by either road or rail, is straightforward and consequently the College draws pupils from a wide catchment area. In addition to public transport, the College offers bus services from numerous locations throughout the region.

Central to the College's philosophy is a Christian tradition creating a family atmosphere and strong sense of community. However pupils are welcomed from all faiths, backgrounds and nationalities and this gives the school community diversity and strength. The College aims for excellence in all it undertakes, whether this is in the classroom, in extra curricular activities or in the development of relationships. Each pupil is treated as an individual and the pursuit of excellence permeates all aspects of school life.

This approach demands a special relationship between teacher and pupil built on mutual trust and respect. It requires a firm discipline that is not oppressive, but geared towards enabling boys and girls to develop into young people who are confident without being arrogant, can think independently, act effectively as a member of a team and who are comfortable in all working and social circumstances. The parents are regarded as central to this process.

Buildings. In addition to our two Georgian Houses, the heart of the College is the Chapel, which accommodates the whole school for assemblies and services. The building and refurbishment programme has most recently provided a new Science block, with a Design and Technology building and Library, each providing outstanding facilities. The Sixth Form, Art and Music Departments are housed in purpose built accommodation and an extensive refurbishment programme has provided the IT, Mathematics, English, RE and Modern Language departments with accommodation that meets the demanding standards of contemporary education.

The College has a successful sporting tradition and hosts the National 15-a-side Rugby Tournament for schools in October. Outstanding facilities include a modern sports hall, squash courts and extensive playing fields surrounding the College. This provision supports a wide range of activities for both curricular and extra curricular sport in both the Junior and Senior sections of the College.

Extensive building and renovation work recently has provided the Junior School with excellent accommodation in Goldrood House. An infant play area and separate hard play area have been added recently.

Catering is centralised in the modern refectories and all meals for all students are provided from here.

The College has two boarding houses, Senior 14-18, and Junior 11-14, which have undergone extensive modernisation over the past three years to provide single study bedrooms for the seniors and small, 3-4 bedrooms for the juniors. The senior Boarding House - the Mews - is located by the Junior School at Goldrood. The Junior House is located a quarter of a mile off site in Birkfield Drive.

Curriculum. The curriculum is designed to provide a broad and balanced education for all pupils from 3 to 18. Strong foundations in the core skills of reading, writing and numeracy, are laid down in the Infant Department. The Junior Section continues the process of preparing the children for their secondary education by concentrating further on the core skills. In addition to these subjects, Science, French, Music and PE are taught and the children are introduced to a wider curriculum, including Design and Technology, Art, History, Geography, RE, IT and Games.

The Senior School prepares pupils for entrance to universities, other forms of higher education and the professions. Pupils are set according to ability in certain subjects. In years 7-9 the emphasis continues to be placed on the core subjects whilst developing knowledge, skills and experiences necessary for the GCSE courses. In addition to the mainstream subjects, all students follow an RE and PSHE course and are prepared for the RSA CLAIT certificate in computer literacy taken at the end of Year 9.

GCSE studies maintain a broad and balanced curriculum but with the introduction of a degree of specialisation. Mathematics, English Language and Literature, Double or Triple Science Award, a Modern Foreign Language and a humanity are compulsory. Once again core subjects continue to be set by ability.

To cater for developing interests and abilities there is a wide range of further choices from Design Technology to Art, from Drama to Music and from PE to Business Studies. In addition all students follow a short course GCSE in RE, which focuses on moral and current issues and combines with the PSHE course. PE and Sport complete the curriculum in the GCSE years.

The majority of our pupils continue into the 6th Form to complete their A Level courses before going on to university. There is a wide range of subjects available in the 6th Form and students choose 4 AS level subjects for examination in the Lower Sixth, reducing to 3 A2s for completion in the Upper Sixth. General Studies are an integral part of the post 16 curriculum at the College, with a wide range of sporting and other leisure and cultural opportunities.

A Special Needs department operates throughout the College to provide support individually or in small groups particularly for Dyslexia and the more able child.

There is comprehensive careers guidance from Year 9 and extensive help with university admission in the 6th Form.

Sport, music and drama sre strongly encouraged, together with participation in the CCF and Duke of Edinburgh Award scheme. A large number of extra curricular clubs meet weekly. Regular ski trips, activity holidays and language exchanges are organised throughout the College.

Admission. Entry to the College is normally at 4+, 7+, 11+, 13+ and the Sixth Form, with applications for occasional vacancies at other ages. The entry process includes an interview, a test and a report from the applicant's previous school. For the Sixth Form, the test is replaced by GCSE results.

Fees per term. From September 2001. Nursery: £200 (full time); Infants: £1,395; Juniors: £1,770. Senior School: 11+ £2,020 (day), £3,605 (boarding); 14+ £2,115 (day), £3,675 (boarding); 16+ £2,260 (day), £3,930 (boarding).

Scholarships and Bursaries. The College offers a number of Academic Scholarships each year for different points of entry, as well as Scholarships for Music, Sport and Drama. A number of bursaries are also available in cases of need. Please contact the Bursar for further information.

Charitable status. St Joseph's College is a Registered Charity, number 3142500. It exists to provide high quality education for children.

Scarborough College and Lisvane

Filey Road Scarborough Yorkshire YO11 3BA
Tel: (01723) 360620
Fax: (01723) 377265
e-mail: admin@scarboroughcollege.co.uk
website: www.scarboroughcollege.co.uk

Scarborough College is a fully coeducational day and boarding school for some 350 pupils. The College and its Junior School, Lisvane, occupy a magnificent site on the slopes of Oliver's Mount, overlooking the South Bay of Scarborough. The main building is listed for its architectural merit and is crowned by an observation tower which is a landmark for miles around. The College is comprised of a Nursery, Junior School, Senior School and Sixth Form.

Motto: *Pensez Fort*

Governors:

Mrs J M Martin, BA, AFBPsS, CPsychol (*Chairman*)
D C Byass
S J Chittock, BSc, MBA
Ms C J Cullen, BA, MA (University of York)
Mrs A Farrant, DMS
Mrs Z Harrison
Prof J R Hartley, BA, MA, MInstP, CPhy (University of Leeds)
D M Hastie, FRICS
R S Lumby, BSc
The Revd S Neale
Dr M Precious, MA, MPhil, DPhil
F V Richardson
J N Sharples, ACIB
D R Williamson, OBE, BA
P Worsley, QC

Bursar and Clerk to the Governors: P F Harriott, BA

***Headmaster:* T L Kirkup**, MA, ARCM

Deputy Headmaster: D R Woodhead, BA

*Director of Studies:**B L Smaller, BSc (*Mathematics*)

Head of Junior School (*Lisvane*): G Twist, BEd, BA, CertEd

Assistant Staff:

§W Adams
*R Allen, BSc (*Science, Chemistry*)
Miss D S Berry, MA
Mrs B V Brocklehurst, CertEd
*C D Brooke, BSc (*Physics, IT*)
*Mrs S E Brooke, CertEd (*Biology*)
*G C Brownridge, BA (*Modern Languages, French*)
*C A Bull, BA, PhD (*Psychology*)
§Mrs W E Craig-Tyler, CertEd
Mrs J M Drury, BSc (*Assistant Head of Sixth Form*)
†Mrs C Lucas, BA
J E Lucas, BA (*Design and Technology*)
†*J G Lynch, BA, MEd (*Geography*)
Mrs R A Macdonald, BA
†*Mrs E A Mack, BA (*English*)
J U McMillan, BA (*Director of Sport*)
J March, BSc, MSc
§Mrs C More, NatDip, Design
§Mrs K Noble, CertEd, DipSpEd
*§I A Parkinson, ATD, BA (*Art*)
Mrs L J Peart, BA, AMBDA
*N H Pettitt, CertEd (*ICT*)
*J M Precious, BA (*Business Studies*)

†Mrs S Roberts-Key, BEd
†R L Scott, BA
*W E Scott, BEd (*Director of Music*)
§Mrs G Sleightholme, BA
R J Sweet, MA (*History*)
Miss K Sykes, BA (*German, Spanish*)
P J Wilson, BEd

The Music Department is assisted by visiting instrumental teachers

Medical Officer: Dr J Adamson, MSBS, DRCOG, MRCGP

Entry. Boys and girls are admitted to the Senior school at 11 and 13 years old, following an Entrance Examination in November, or through Common Entrance, or through special arrangements. Pupils are admitted to other years, subject to recommendation from their previous school, an interview, and, where appropriate, satisfactory performance in a College examination. 11 plus and 13 plus Scholarships and (means-tested) Exhibitions are awarded on the basis of academic performance in these examinations. There is a separate Sixth Form entry, conditional upon satisfactory performance at GCSE.

The Curriculum. All pupils follow a broad-based curriculum, but study both French and German from the age of 11 and Spanish from the age of 13. The three sciences are taught separately from 11. At GCSE, pupils take English and English Literature, Mathematics, one Science and one Modern Language, and then, after detailed consultation and discussion with staff and parents, choose four other subjects. A wide range of A-level subjects is offered, complemented by a General Studies programme which aims to broaden personal and academic horizons.

Care of Pupils. Scarborough College is a stimulating and happy school where boys and girls are taught to live cooperatively together, to develop their talents to the full, and to respect one another. Within the coeducational house structure, pupils are allocated a tutor who is responsible for coordinating and monitoring all aspects of a child's welfare and maintaining regular communication with parents.

Religion. The ethos of the College is Christian; the emphasis is on cooperation and toleration between denominations.

Games. High standards are reached in sport, with many students representing the County and a few playing for England The College offers expert coaching in Rugby, Hockey, Cricket and Tennis for boys; and Hockey, Netball, Tennis and Rounders for girls. Athletics and Cross Country are well-established, and the Games programme also offers pupils opportunities for swimming, riding and playing golf. The College has recently built a full-size, all-weather pitch.

Other Activities. Drama and Music flourish at all levels of the College, and regular performances occur throughout the year. Educational expeditions play an important part of the general curriculum, and there are language exchange opportunities with France, Germany and Spain. An extensive programme of weekday and weekend activities enables all pupils to participate in an exciting programme outside the classroom, eg calligraphy, life-saving, stage technology. The College boasts a popular Duke of Edinburgh's Award Scheme and a thriving Combined Cadet Force (Army and Navy sections).

Transport is provided to outlying districts and occasional and weekly boarding is a popular option with many parents.

Fees per annum. (*see* Entrance Scholarship section) (2000/2001): Senior School: Day pupils £6,240; Full and Weekly Boarders £8,631. Junior School (Day only): £3,450–£4,680. Remissions for brothers and sisters and members of the Old Scardeburgians Society.

Charitable status. Scarborough College is a Registered Charity, number 529686. It exists to provide a first class education for boys and girls.

Seaford College, Petworth

Petworth West Sussex GU28 0NB.
Tel: (01798) 867392
Fax: (01798) 867606

The College was founded in 1884 at Seaford in East Sussex and moved to Lavington Park at the foot of the South Downs in 1946. The grounds cover some 360 acres and include extensive sports facilities and scope for future developments which includes an eighteen-hole golf course. The campus includes a superb Art and Design department, a Sixth Form Centre, purpose built boarding houses and a new Junior House which incorporates classrooms and boarding facilities.

Seaford is controlled by an Independent non-profit making Charitable Trust approved by the Department of Education and the Charity Commissioners and is administered by the College Board of Governors.

Motto: *Ad Alta - To The Heights*

Governing Body:
G Sinclair (*Chairman*)
D Avery
R D Balaam, MA, JP
Mrs P Hadley
R Venables Kyrke
Mrs J Peel

***Headmaster:* T J Mullins**, BA

Deputy Head: J R Hall, BSc

Teaching Staff:
N Q Angier, MA, BSc
Mrs P A Angier, BA (Hons), DipCG, DipSpLD (*Careers & Special Needs*)
P Bain, BA
D C R Baker, BSc
M Bownass
A Carlton-Oatley, MA, AVCM
Mrs S Coatsworth, BA (Hons), MA
W Cuthbertson
Dr V Davis, BSc, PhD
Mrs H Farmer, BA (Hons)
N Foster, BEd, RSADipSpLD
D C Garrard, BA, CertEd
Mrs J Gregory, BEd
T W Gregory, BEd
Mrs C Hawkes
P R Jennings, BA (Hons)
Miss J Jones
S Kettlewell, BA
A P Lincoln, BA, MSc
B Murphy
J O'Donnell, MA
Mrs K G Paget, BA, DipEd
T D Phillips, BA
Miss K Pointer, BA, PGCE
D G Priest, BSc, DMS(Ed)
I Ross, BSc
M Single, BA
A G Smith, BA, PGDipArt
M Stafford, BA (Hons)
R Stather, BA
Mrs P White
K R Woodcock, BSc, CertEd

Bursar: Mrs C Smith

Headmaster's Secretary: Miss C Davis

Pupils. Seaford College offers options of Full Boarding, Weekly Boarding and Day facilities to girls and boys aged 10 to 18. There are 320 pupils at the College with over 90 in the Sixth Form. There are three boys houses and one girls house and a junior house for both girls and boys aged 10–13.

Aims. Seaford College's aim is to provide an all-round education that equips students with the skills needed to function in the commercial world after leaving their academic studies. The College takes students with a range of abilities and aims to provide the greatest possible 'value-added' for their given abilities. Streaming children in core subjects allows them to work at their own speed and makes them aware of others skills and shortcomings.

Academic. The Junior House, (incorporating Years 6, 7 and 8), and Year 9, offer a wide ranging curriculum which includes core subjects of English, Mathematics, Science, a language, Information Technology and extra English, as well as all the usual topics of Geography, History, Art and DT etc.

Years 10 and 11 lead up to the GCSE examinations. Students study the core subjects of English Literature, English Language, Mathematics and Double Science and then choose four other syllabuses to follow from a comprehensive list of subjects which include: Art, Business Studies, Ceramics, Drama, Design and Technology, Geography, French, History, Music, Physical Education, Spanish.

All students in these forms also study Information Technology and Religious Studies and take part in the College sports.

The A level subject list is the same as that at GCSE. In the Lower Sixth students follow a College set curriculum and choose five subjects to study for the first year at the end of which pupils sit AS examinations. They then choose three of the five subjects to carry through to A level. Over and above this in their first year students will undertake to achieve the Duke of Edinburgh Silver Award. In the Upper Sixth year students will concentrate on their three A level subjects.

Music. Music is an important part of Seaford's life. The College boasts an internationally renowned College Chapel Choir who have been requested to visit countries such as Ecuador, America and Russia to sing at Ambassadors' Christmas parties or raise money for under-privileged children; they have recorded several CDs and their recordings are often heard on radio stations. The College also has an orchestra and offers lessons for all instruments. Music can be studied at GCSE and AS level.

Sports. With superb facilities available in the grounds, and staff that have coached and played at international level, the College has a reputation for sporting excellence. Facilities include: six rugby pitches, eight tennis courts, squash courts, covered pool, a new water based all-weather hockey pitch and a large indoor sports hall that allows tennis and hockey to be played all year round.

Art. The College has an excellent Art department which allows students to exercise their talents to the fullest extent in every aspect of art and design, whether it is ceramics, textiles, fine art or any other medium they wish to use. Many pupils from Seaford go on to study at design school and work for design and fashion houses or advertising companies. Students are encouraged to display their work throughout the year in the department's gallery.

Combined Cadet Force. The College has strong ties with the Military and has a very well supported Combined Cadet Force, with each wing of the armed forces well represented. Weekend exercises and training are a regular feature in the College calendar and include adventure training, canoeing, climbing, sailing and camping.

Admission. Entry to the Junior House at age 10 or 11 is determined on cognitive ability testing and a trial day at the school. Entry at 13 is determined on an interview with the Headmaster and by results of the Common Entrance Examination. Sixth Form entry is dependent upon GCSE results. Pupils are required to have 5 GCSEs Grade C or above and these should include English and Mathematics. Pupils may enter the school without one of these subjects on condition they retake. Overseas students are required to take an oral and written examination to determine level of comprehension in English.

Scholarships and Bursaries. (*see* Entrance Scholarship section) Scholarships offered: Academic, Art, Design and Technology, Music (Choral and Orchestral) and Sport (13+ only). Scholarship examinations are taken in January/February of the year of entry and are offered to students that reach the required standard. Bursaries are offered to children of Serving members of Her Majesty's Forces and siblings of existing pupils.

Fees. From September 2001. Senior School £4,990 per term (Boarding), £3,320 per term (Day); Junior School £3,850 per term (Boarding), £2,650 per term (Day).

Extras. Drama, Clay-pigeon shooting, Fencing, Fishing, Golf, Sailing, Museum & Theatre trips.

Charitable status. Seaford College is a Registered Charity, number 277139. It exists to provide education for children.

Shebbear College

Shebbear N Devon EX21 5HJ.
Tel: (01409) 281228
Fax: (01409) 281784
e-mail: shebbear@rmplc.co.uk
website: www.shebbearcollege.co.uk

Shebbear College, set in 85 acres of healthy Devon countryside, was founded in 1841 by the Bible Christians. It is now part of the Board of Management for Methodist Residential Schools. It is fully co-educational for children between the ages of 3 to 18 years. The secure, happy family atmosphere at Shebbear, free from urban distractions, offers pupils full, weekly, occasional and daily education. We aim to give our pupils self confidence; we teach our pupils to be self disciplined and they leave the College with excellent qualifications. Thus offering all our pupils *"A foundation for life"*.

Chairman of the Governors: M J Saltmarsh

***Headmaster:* L D Clark**, BSc, BA

Deputy Headmaster: R S Barnes, BA

Chaplain: The Revd D Wheeler

Financial Bursar: R Collings

Financial Clerk of Works: R Sutherland, FInst, SMM

Teaching Staff:
Mrs J A Atkinson, CertEd
*Mrs J Barnes, BA (*French*)
Mr J Buist
Mr I Burnett, BA
*Mr J Colpus (*History*)
*Mrs A Farrell, MEd, BEd (*English*)
Mrs M Hillman, LRAM, DipRAM, DipRSA, Dip(SpLD), PGDipEd (SEN)
*Mr J Marshall, BSc(Ed) (*Physics*)
*Mr P Mason, BSc, DLC (*Mathematics*)
*Mr P Morgan, BSc (*Biology*)
*Mr K Parker, GRSM (*Music*)
*Mr B Pocock, BSc (*Chemistry*)
*Mr J Scotney, MEd, BEd, CertEd (*Geography*)
*Mrs P Thomas, BA (*IT*)
*Mr S Young, BA (*Art*)

Senior House Staff (*Boarding*):
Mr and Mrs A Bryan *Pollard Houseparents*
*Mrs L Quirk, BSA (*Girls Games*) *Pyke Houseparent*
Miss R Sekulic (*Junior Boys Housemistress*)

Junior School Teaching Staff:
Mr B Harman, BSc (*Head of Junior School*)
Mrs J Burnett, BA
Mrs K Purdew, CertEd
Mrs F Goode, CertEd

Kindergarten:
Mrs J Skuse

Registrar: Mrs J Rowe
Marketing Co-ordinator: Mrs A Sanders

Medical Department:
Dr Stephen Miller, Bt, MB, FRCS, FRCGP
Sister J Milburn, SEN

Visiting Music Staff:
Mr J Lewington
Mr M Richardson, LTCM, ARCM, CertEd
Mrs P Lewington
Mr R Tinker
Mr K Chetwin
Mrs A Morphy
Mrs A Hammond
Mrs C Nicholls, BA
Ms D Kent

Number in College. In the Senior School there are 82 day boys, 47 day girls; 45 boy boarders, 15 girl boarders. There is a total of 79 pupils in the Junior School, 46 day boys, 26 day girls, 5 boy boarders and 2 girl boarders.

Situation and Location. Shebbear College borders on Dartmoor National Park and stands in 85 acres of unspoilt countryside. It can be easily reached by main road and rail links; only 40 miles west of Exeter and 30 miles north of Plymouth. Both cities have their own regional and international airport.

Buildings. The main College buildings include Prospect House, Lake Chapel, Beckly Wing, Shebbear College Junior School, Science Department, Music School, Sixth Form Centre, Language Centre and Sports Hall. There are 2 senior boarding houses and 1 junior boarding house. (The junior girls have a separate area within the senior girls house).

In recent years there has been an impressive record of school building projects. The latest work has been to develop a Music School and Sixth Form Centre.

Admission. The Kindergarten accepts children from the age of 2½ where boys and girls are admitted to the Junior School from the age of five. Entrance to the College at 11 years from other schools is by examination in February for entry in September. Pupils are also admitted at 13 or 14 after submitting Common Entrance Examination papers, but if they wish they may sit our own entrance papers instead. Entry into the Sixth Form is conditional upon GCSE performance.

Houses. Every pupil belongs to a House, Ruddle, Thorne or Way. These Houses organise activities and games competitions throughout the year. Our boarders also belong to an additional boarding house, Pollard House for boy boarders, and Pyke House for girl boarders each having a Senior Houseparent and two assistants who "live-in". The House Tutors watch each child's progress academically as well as their general development. There is a 7 day a week, 24 hour Medical Centre.

Curriculum. All pupils at Shebbear College follow the natioal curriculum until the age of 14. A wide choice of subjects is available in the following two years, leading to GCSE, but everyone is obliged to take English, Mathematics, Religious Studies, Science and usually a foreign language. In the VIth Form there is not only a wide choice of 'A' and AS levels, but there is particularly flexible timetabling which enables students to mix Arts and Science subjects.

Sport. With more than 25 acres of playing fields, modern sports hall with multi-gym centre, squash courts, cricket nets, tennis and netball courts, indoor climbing centre and the re-introduction of rowing, pupils have the security to exercise within the school grounds confidently. The main games covered for the boys are rugby, football, cricket and hockey, in which we have fixtures with most of the major schools in the South West of England. For the girls, we have teams in netball, hockey, rounders and tennis. All pupils are also offered tennis, basketball, squash, athletics, swimming, sailing, rowing, golf, cross-country, badminton, table tennis and horse riding. All pupils up to the 4th Form have one afternoon of games plus an additional one period of PE every week.

Music and Drama. Pupils are strongly encouraged to participate in music and drama. Our latest project, to refurbish Beckly Wing, has improved our theatrical study area. Our choir has over 40 members and our orchestra, which represents most instruments, also has over 40 members. Players perform regularly in concerts and instrumental ensembles. Every term candidates proudly achieve Honours and Distinctions with The Associated Board of the Royal School for Music. Also, every term, a theatrical production is performed to a very high standard. The traditional staff and sixth form pantomime, offers light relief during the Spring Term.

Societies and Activities. All pupils participate in at least 4 afternoons a week of extra-curricular activities. This widens their interests and develops their self-confidence. The list of activities is endless and includes the usual and unusual. Shebbear has the largest indoor climbing centre where competitions are often held. We are fortunate to house our own photographic studio where excellent work is produced and displayed around the school. Shebbear's rural position enables outdoor pursuits to be very popular. Many pupils enjoy getting involved with Ten Tors training, hill-walking, camping, sailing, canoeing, surfing and rowing.

Many are involved in the Duke of Edinburgh Award scheme.

Careers. Careers advice is taken very seriously. A highly qualified staff of University graduates help our students prepare for their chosen career. The College is a member of ISCO. Individual attention is given at appropriate levels and a team of Old Shebbearians covering many professions visits the school regularly and helps with work experience and placement.

Scholarships (*see* Entrance Scholarship section) **and Fees.** Scholarships and Bursaries are offered and the inclusive fees per term in September 2000 are: Boarding Fees for the Junior School £2,175–£2,995. For the College: Weekly Boarding £3,210, Full Boarding £3,995, Day fees are £690–£2,140.

Charitable status. Shebbear College is a Registered Charity, number 306945. It exists to provide high quality education for children.

Sibford School

Sibford Ferris Banbury Oxon OX15 5QL
Tel: (01295) 781200
Fax: (01295) 781204

Founded 1842.

A Co-educational Independent Boarding and Day School (SHMIS, BSA, GBA, ISC).

There are 306 pupils in the school aged between 5 and 18. 244 pupils in the Senior School; 64 pupils in the Junior School, Orchard Close.

There are 36 full-time and 19 part-time teachers plus visiting staff.

Chairman of the Committee: Hedley Quinton

Head: **Susan Freestone**, GRSM, MEd, LRAM, ARCM

Senior Mistress: Maggie Guy, BA (*English*)

Senior Master: Tony Skeath, BSc (*Science*)

Head of Orchard Close: Elizabeth Young, TCert

Senior School:
Jennifer Austing, BA, DipRSASpLD (*Head of Dyslexic Studies*)
James Bond, BA (*Head of Technology, ICT*)
Angela Bovill, BEd, CertEd (*Head of Horticulture, GNVQ*)
Mark Connor, BSc (*Mathematics, ICT*)
Christopher Cox, TCert (*Director of Studies, Head of Science*)
Elisabeth Escher, DipRSA(SLD), TCert, AdvCertCouns (*Head of English, Dyslexia*)
Debby Evans (*ICT Network Supervisor*)
Helen Evans, BSc, DipSpLD, CertCouns (*Head of Learning Support*)
Andrew Glover, BA, DipTEO (*Head of ESOL, Dyslexia*)
David Goodwin, BSc, DipRSASpLD (*Dyslexia*)
Yvonne Green, LLB, GradIPD (*Head of Business Studies*)
Stuart Hedley, CertEd, City & Guilds Adv Craft Cert (*Technology*)
Jamie Hewetson, BA (*English*)
Michelle Hewetson, BA, TEFL (*Spanish*)
Brian Holliday, BSc (*Geography*)
John Howard, BA, CertEd (*Head of Mathematics*)
Melanie Jackson, City & Guilds TCert (*ESOL*)
Tracy Knowles, BA(Ed) (*PE, English*)
Lucy Mason, BMus (*Music*)
Sian Mather (*Class Assistant*)
Ann Mean, BA, DipRSA (*Dyslexia*)
Susan Nebesnuick, MA (*Head of Enhanced Learning Programmes*)
Andrew Newbold, BSc, PhD (*Academic Administrator, Science, GNVQ*)
Lesley Norton, CertEd (*Joint Head of Boarding, Technology*)
David Oliver, BMus, LTCL, LGSM (*Music*)
Sadie Powell, BA (*PE*)
Elisabeth Pronost, Cert de Formation Pedagogique (*French, ESOL, Geography*)
Anna-Jo Righton, BA (*Head of Humanities, History*)
Jean Rudge, BA (*Head of Modern Languages*)
Geoffrey Slade, BA (*Business Studies, Geography, PE, Dyslexia*)
Matthew Smallwood, BA (*Director of Music*)
Michael Spring, BEd (*Head of Expressive Arts Faculty*)
Penelope Spring, BA (*Library, English*)
Angela Talbot, BA (*Joint Head of Drama, ESOL*)
Simon Talbot, DipSpLD (*Joint Head of Drama, Dyslexia*)
Graham Thomas, BSc (*Head of PE, Head of Sixth Form*)
Lyn Usher, BEd, TCert (*Mathematics, Science, PSE*)
Diana Warren, FETCert (*GNVQ, Business*)
Angela Way, TCert (*Technology* (*Food*))
Raymond White, BA (*English*)
Johnathan Wilson, BSc (*PE, Maths*)
Jenifer Wollerton (*Learning Support, School Uniform*)
Michael Wollerton, DipPE, TCert (*Mathematics, PSE, Careers, Tuck Shop*)

Junior School, Orchard Close:
Heather Belcher, BA
Rachel Dumbleton, CertEd, BDA, DipSpSLD (*Dyslexia*)
Patricia Howes, BSc
Jane Kerehan (*Class Assistant*)
Gill Newbold, TCert (*PE*)
Rachel Thomas, BEd
Nick Tomlinson, TCert
Sarah Rutland, BA, TEFL
Barbara Walters, BEd (*Learning Support*)

Visiting Staff:
Raymond Head, MA, DipEd, FRAS
Peter Nuttall, BA
Clifford Pick, ABSM
Robert Pritchard, ATD
Jonathan Seagroatt
Veronique Smith, LRAM

Type. Co-educational Independent Day and Boarding: full/weekly. Mainstream curriculum. Renowned dyslexia tuition and support for small number of pupils with other learning difficulties.

Curriculum. Junior Department (age 5–10): a wide-ranging curriculum is provided to children in small groups. Literacy, numeracy, science and technology skills are emphasised alongside Art, Music, Drama and PE. Enriched Curriculum in Year 6 with specialist Senior School Staff. Specialist teachers help individual children with Specific Learning Difficulties. New wide-ranging Outdoor Life Programme for all pupils.

Senior School (age 11–18): all pupils follow courses leading to GCSE, in a curriculum expanding on the National Curriculum. Information Technology is introduced at an early age and the use of laptop computers is widespread.

Dyslexic pupils have special tuition in small groups on a daily basis. Highly regarded Specific Learning Difficulties (Dyslexic) Department provides specialised support within the timetable. A Personal and Social Development runs through the school.

All Sixth Form students take A Level and/or GNVQ at Foundation or Intermediate level. The Sixth Form curriculum leads to higher education, and offers a particularly wide range of opportunities for further study.

Entry requirements. Admission to the Junior School (Orchard Close), the Senior School and the Sixth Form is by interview and internal tests, and a report from the candidate's school is required. No religious requirements. Parents are not expected to buy text books.

Examinations offered. A Level, GCSE, GNVQ; Associated Board Music Examinations; Oxford and Cambridge EFL Examinations.

Academic and leisure facilities. Exceptional Performing & Creative Arts.

Multi purpose Sports Centre and Squash Courts.

Well-equipped Library and Information Technology Centres.

Newly developed Technology Centre.

Sibford Business Studies Centre.

Wide range of indoor and outdoor activities.

70 acre campus with walled garden, set in beautiful North Oxfordshire countryside.

Easy access to Stratford, Oxford, Cheltenham, Birmingham, London.

Religion. The School has a distinctive Quaker ethos. It welcomes pupils of all faiths, backgrounds and nationalities, encouraging in each of them genuine self-esteem in a purposeful, caring and challenging environment.

Fees (1998/99). Senior School: Boarders £4,040 per term. Weekly Boarders £3,765 per term. Day Pupils £2,005 per term.

Junior School: Weekly Boarders £3,765 per term. Day Pupils £1,025–£1,625 per term.

The fee for a full term of further support is £800.

Scholarships and Bursaries. The School offers a number of Scholarships each year for different points of entry, as well as Music Scholarships. Bursaries may be available in cases of need, some are available exclusively to members of the Society of Friends.

Charitable status. Sibford School is a Registered Charity, number 1068256. It is a company limited by guarantee under number 3487651. It aims to give all pupils a vehicle to educational and personal success.

Sidcot School

Winscombe Somerset BS25 1PD.
Tel: (01934) 843102
Fax: (01934) 844181
e-mail: sidcotad@aol.com

Sidcot School traces its roots to 1699 and was re-founded in 1808 for the education of the children of members of the Society of Friends (Quakers) and others. It now owns two Pre-preparatory schools known as The Hall School, Sidcot, and St Christopher's, Burnham. It admits boys and girls from a wide variety of backgrounds, but about a tenth of the pupils come from Quaker homes. The school estate of about 150 acres is set on high ground in a ring of the Mendip hills. It is under the management of a Committee appointed by a General Meeting of Friends, held annually.

Chairman of the Committee: Jefferson Horsley, BA (Hons)

Acting Headmaster: **John Walmsley**, BSc

Deputy Head – Pastoral: Jonathan Runswick Cole, MA, MLitt

House Staff:
Christopher Bateman, CertEd and Janice Bateman, BA (*Combe House*)
Paul Coates, BSc (*Wing House*)
Elizabeth Grant, BSc, BEd (*School House, Girls*)
David Illingworth, BSc (*College House*)
Jonathan Runswick-Cole, MA, MLitt (*Newcombe House*)
Diane Symes, CertEd (*Head of St Christopher's*)
Wendy Wardman, CertEd (*Head of Hall School*)

Secretary and Bursar: Robert Ashurst

Admissions Secretary: Alison Barnes

Situation and Accommodation. The school is half a mile from Winscombe Village and 15 miles from Bristol. It is situated in beautiful unspoilt countryside, which the pupils are encouraged to explore.

There are 400 pupils, boys and girls in approximately equal numbers. 180 boarding pupils are accommodated in 5 Houses including two wings of the main building. The main building complex provides leisure and refectory facilities. Most of the class teaching is done in a separate classroom block. The Science Block has been enlarged and re-built. There is also a self-contained Music School, drama studio and a study block with special facilities for VIth Formers. There is a 10-acre playing field, a new sports complex (with swimming pool, sports hall, squash court and multi-gym) and eight tennis courts. A new Library and Resource Centre was opened in 1999.

Aims. The aims of the school are to give boys and girls a top-class academic and liberal education, and to educate them to think and behave ethically, in the light of the principles of the Society of Friends.

We encourage our students to reflect upon moral issues and to seek "that of God" in everyone, whatever their faith.

We hope that our students will leave Sidcot with the power and determination to play an active part in the life of their communities, and a desire to continue to learn about the world and about themselves.

Curriculum. The School broadly follows the National Curriculum. Within this there is a basic course of the usual subjects for all pupils in the first 3 years, 7, 8 and 9. German and Spanish are offered as a second foreign language in Years 7, 8 and 9. Latin is introduced in year 7. In years 10 and 11 English Language, Literature, Mathematics Dual Science, French, RE, IT, Games and Computing are normally chosen from a wide range of options to give a balanced curriculum. The school enters candidates for several GCSE examining Boards. The VIth Form provides a two-year course to 'A' level or GNVQ for 130 students and most of these then proceed to Further and Higher Education. Some pupils in the lower sixth take a foundation course of 5 GCSEs.

Pupils are given every encouragement to find and follow leisure time pursuits. Riding and orienteering feature amongst a very wide range of sports and outdoor pursuits. There is much active drama work and interest in art and music is particularly strong. Two-thirds of the pupils learn at least one instrument. There is an orchestra, a wind band, a choir, a junior choir and other musical groups. Visits to concerts and theatres, and excursions to places of interest are a regular feature of each term.

Sidcot's Pre-Preparatory Department, The Hall School, accommodates 3–9 year olds in a self-contained campus adjoining Sidcot. Currently some 90 pupils are enrolled. St Christopher's also enrolls about 80 boys and girls between the ages of 3 and 11 in the Burnham-on-Sea area.

Admission. (*see* Entrance Scholarship section) Pupils are admitted at any stage from the age of 9 up to VIth Form entry. There is an Entrance Test but pupils entering from preparatory schools can be admitted on the basis of Common Entrance.

Charitable status. Sidcot School is a Registered Charity, number 296491. The aim of the school is the education of children in a Quaker and caring environment.

Stafford Grammar School

Burton Manor Stafford ST18 9AT
Tel: (01785) 249752
Fax: (01785) 255005

Stafford Grammar School was founded in 1982 in response to demand for independent education in Stafford. The School, which is co-educational, is registered as an educational charity and the Board of Governors is in membership with the Governing Bodies Association.

Motto: *Quod tibi hoc alteri*

Patrons:
The Right Hon The Earl of Shrewsbury
The Lord Stafford
The Right Hon The Earl of Lichfield

Governing Body:
J Wood (*Chairman*)
Mrs M Lingwood, MB, ChB, JP (*Vice-Chairman*)
B Hodges (*Vice-Chairman*)
J Archer, TD, FCIS, JP
Mrs F Beatty, JP
B Baggott
Mrs S Carthy
J W Griffiths, LLB
Dr A Kratz, BA, PhD
J Lotz, FRCS
Mrs B Madders
Sir N Simms
R C Pepper, FCA
D J Taylor, MA
A Webb

Headmaster: **M R Darley**, BA

Deputy Head: M P Robinson, BA, DipEd (Man)

Assistant Staff:

P Badham, BSc	L J Harwood, BEd
Mrs J Bailes, BA	Mrs M M Hinton, BA
M F Blaze, BA, HNC(MechEng)	A C Johnson, BSc
	Dr P A Johnson, BSc, PhD
Miss S Brereton, BMus, LRAM	Mrs A Lonsdale, BSc
	Mrs P Mawman, BA
Mrs S Brookes, BA	Mrs C Read, BA, HDL
Mrs P Cartwright, BEd, BA	Mrs B Robson, BSc
D Craig, BA, UED	G Robson, BSc
Dr F G Crane, BSc, PhD	Mrs L I Robson, BA
T N F Davis, BA, CertEd	Mrs A M Saxon, BEd, MA
Mrs V M Davis, BA	B K Sharman, CertEd
Mrs C Dodd, BEd	Mrs A J Taylor, BA
Mrs J A Fletcher, BA, ADB	Mrs D Webster, BSc
Dr R Foster, BSc, PhD	Mrs T Whyte, BSc, MSc
Mrs L J Gill, BA, AdvCert Art Ed, DipRSA	D R Williams, BSc
	B C Wood, BA, ALCM
R C Green, BA	

Chaplain: Prebendary R Sargent, MA

Bursar: B Astbury, MA, DipSchMan

Headmaster's Secretary: Mrs S M Pickavance

Number in School. There are 342 pupils, of whom 181 are boys and 161 girls. There is a Sixth Form of 75.

The School is housed in a fine Victorian manor house on the outskirts of Stafford. The building is eminently well suited to its new role, and houses, amongst other facilities, science laboratories and a spacious Assembly Hall with a large stage. A large Sports Hall plus new music suite opened in the summer of 1999. A Canteen and two new Computer Rooms were completed in Summer 2000.

Curriculum. In Year 7 and Year 8 all pupils follow a common course consisting of English, Mathematics, Science, French, German, Geography, History, Music, Art, Drama, Computing, Design, Technology, Religious Education and Physical Education. Year 9 sees Science divide into separate subjects.

Pupils in Years 10 and 11 study nine subjects at GCSE: English (2), Mathematics, Sciences and a language, together with three options chosen from some twelve available. Physical Education continues and Careers and Life Skills are introduced.

There is setting in Mathematics from Year 8, but most subjects are taught in parallel groups. Classes are kept small (under 20) so that pupils can receive individual attention.

In the Lower Sixth Form students study three, four or five A level subjects (AS) leading to three or four A level subjects (A2) in the Upper Sixth Form. Key skills and General Studies are also taught. Approximately 20 A level subjects are available.

Creativity and the Arts. The School has an extensive Art and Design Department. Pupils' powers of observation and awareness are developed through practical skills and theoretical studies involving areas as varied as painting, printing, 3-D work, photography and textiles. There are frequent competitions and exhibitions of work as well as projects linked with other departments.

Music plays an important part in the life of the School. There is an orchestra and a choir which perform on many occasions in musicals, church services and concerts. Ensembles, both instrumental and vocal, are encouraged. Original incidental music is composed for School productions. Pupils have the opportunity to learn to play a wide range of musical instruments with tuition provided by peripatetic teachers.

Drama enables pupils to gain confidence and self-understanding. It is particularly effective in the early years in the School. Two annual School Plays are major productions on the School's excellent stage and involve a large number of pupils.

Art and Drama are available at GCSE and A level.

Sport and Activities. Whilst sport plays a prominent part in School life, the emphasis is very much on training for future leisure time.

The School has outstanding sports facilities, including a new Sports Hall (1999), and the following sports are available: Soccer, Hockey, Rugby, Cricket, Tennis, Squash, Badminton, Basketball, Netball, Volleyball, Athletics, Gymnastics, Rounders, Table Tennis, and Health-related Fitness, as well as Swimming at Riverside.

The School plays a large number of matches against other schools, both state and independent, and is fully involved with local school leagues. Individuals regularly secure places in Staffordshire and Midlands teams.

Our range of activities is deliberately wide since we believe that every child is good at something and that it is our job to discover and develop talent in any direction.

There are many Clubs and Societies of widely differing kinds, ranging from Electronics to Debating, and a large number of pupils are working for the Duke of Edinburgh Award Scheme.

At present there are 15 inter-House competitions. These range from Technology to Poetry and from Football to Hobbies, and include some which are specifically for younger pupils.

The intention of these is not only to enable as many pupils as possible to represent their Houses, but also to stress that we value excellence in any area.

Pastoral Care. In its pastoral organisation, the School seeks to nurture the potential of every child giving both support and encouragement in an overt and practical way. The School is divided into three houses, the Head of House being the key figure in the academic and personal development of each child. Tutor groups are kept small, rarely exceeding eighteen pupils, and are based on the House to maintain continuity and to strengthen communal bonds. Tutors maintain strong links with each pupil using a programme of active tutoring which includes scheduled interviews, and Records of Achievement. We place great emphasis on close contact with parents, believing that lack of progress and other problems are best addressed jointly and as early as possible.

In the Sixth Form a slightly different system operates. Although retaining the same House Tutor, the pupil will have a Form Tutor from a specialist team of Sixth Form Tutors. Additionally the Headmaster is attached to this team. Further to this is the opportunity for each pupil to choose a Personal Tutor with whom to build a special rapport.

Sixth Form. The Sixth Form is the ideal environment in which to foster confidence, responsibility, leadership, initiative and self-discipline.

The keynote of the Sixth Form is freedom with responsibility. At this stage pupils still need help in planning their time and in establishing good working habits, and the guidance of an understanding tutor can mean the difference between success and failure.

Careers. Considerable attention is paid to career advice, and there are frequent visits by speakers from industry and the professions. From Year 10 onwards, individual advice is given by our own careers staff, and pupils are also encouraged to consult the County Careers Service.

Religion. Although we welcome pupils of all faiths, or none, the School is a Christian foundation.

The School seeks to live by the Christian ideal, in particular by being a community in which members genuinely care about each other.

Admission. Entrance is by examination and interview in order to ensure that pupils have sufficient reasoning ability to be able to attempt GCSE in a reasonable range of subjects.

Entrance to the Sixth Form is by GCSE results and interview.

Scholarships and Bursaries. The Governors have allocated funds to enable pupils of exceptional ability or limited means to join the school in Year 7 or the Sixth Form.

Fees. £1,788 per term, revised annually in January.

Charitable status. Stafford Independent Grammar School Limited is a Registered Charity, number 513031. It exists to provide education for children.

Stanbridge Earls School

Romsey Hampshire S051 0ZS.
Tel: (01794) 516777
Fax: (01794) 511201

Number of Boys: 157 aged 11–18
Number of Girls: 43 aged 11–18

Governors:

Chairman: S J Attlee

J P Dickson
Brigadier P P Glass, MBE
P C Goodship
Revd L F P Gunner, MA
W N J Howard, MA
E M S Lewis
Lady Jean Mackenzie, CBE
P J Piper, FCIB
Mrs E R D Skeet, MA
Mrs P Thomson, MA, MEd
M J Woodhall, FRICS

Bursar and Secretary to Governors: Col D E Bonnor-Moris, BSc, CEng

Headmaster: **N Hall**, BSc (Hons) (London), PGCE (Bristol)

Second Master: G P Link, CertEd, MEd Exeter

Assistant Staff:
†Mr R J Bailey, BA (Canterbury), CertEd (*B House*)
Miss A Barker, BA (Southampton), PGCE (Leeds)
B F Beasley, MA (York), CertEd (Dudley College)
Mrs R E Blencowe, CertEd (Bath)
J Clarkson, BSc
Mrs E M S Cole, CertEd, BEd, DipSpEd (King Alfred's College) (*i/c ALC*)
Mrs J Coleman, CertEd (London), AMBDA
R S Collier, MIRTE
Mrs D M Condé, MRCSLT, TEFL (*Speech & Language Therapy*)
Miss M B Dalgleish, BSc, HDE (Witwatersrand)
D J Durnell, BSc, PGCE (London)
Mrs D A Dutfield, CertEd (Avery Hill, London)
Mrs L Edwards, CertEd (Hull College), PGDipDys (Kingston)
Mrs P M Fisher, BA (Exeter), DipRSA, SpLD
Mrs J H George, CertEd (St Osyth's College), DipAESSpN (King Alfred's College)
Mrs M Goodchild, CertEd (Mather Day College, Manchester)
Mrs M Grubb, DipCE, Dip Fashion & Textiles, LRPS
Mrs S L Hennessy, BA (Warwick)
P L Higgins, CertEd (St Mary's College)
†K .A Horne, BSc (Aberdeen), PhD (Dundee) (*Lower School*)
Miss J S Hughes, BA (Exeter), CertEd (Bangor)
Mrs C Innes, ALCM (*Piano*)
D W Letorey, BEd (Sheffield Hallam University)
Mrs D F Lindsell, CertEd (Bretton Hall), ATCL
T M Lister, LTCL, LGSM, ALCM, GCLCM (Leeds)
Mrs M A Mackay, BEd (London), DipBDA
Mrs S Martinelli, BSc (Reading)
Miss J S Mills, BSc (Southampton), AMBDA
Mrs W L Molyneaux, BA, BEd (Toronto)
Dr F E Myszor, PhD (Southampton), BA, PGCE (Nottingham)
L Nicholson, MA (Southampton), TCert (St Luke's, Exeter)
I Parsons, BA, QTS (Brunel)
G A Pearce, BA Hons, PGCE (Birmingham)
P C Pellatt, BA (Leicester), MA(Ed) (Open), CertEd (Liverpool)
Miss S L Pettitt, BEd, TEFL
R S J Rea, BSc (Portsmouth), PGCE (Southampton)
†Mrs K Richardson, BEd, TCert (Warwick) (*C House*)
†Mr C F Rowney, BA (Bangor), CertEd (Southampton) (*A House*)
†Dr J A Sweetman, BSc, PhD (Aberystwyth), PGCE, CBiol, MIBiol (*D House*)
Mrs S B Taylor, BEd Hons (Southampton)
M C Towend, BSc (Warwick), CertEd (Coventry)
Mrs D Trotman, DipEd (London)
Mrs R D Varney, BEd, DipRSA, SpLD
Mrs S Warner, BA, CertEd (Cambridge Institute of Education)
Miss R J White, CertEd (Bishop Otter College)
Mrs D Williams, BEd (Bath), DipRSASpLD
Mrs K Woodrow, BSc (CNAA), CertEd (Oxford)

Visiting Staff:
P Bailey (*Drums*)
Mrs B Cutler, CertEd, BEd, BMusic Hons, LRAM (*Singing*)
D Driver (*Violin*)
M Gibson (*Woodwind*)
Mrs C Innes, ALCM (*Piano*)
A Jones (*Guitar*)
Mrs A Venning (*Keyboard*)

Administrative Staff:
Warden, Goulds: Mrs D A Lister
Warden, Cornock Taylor: Mrs J L Sweetman
Headmaster's Secretary: Mrs C M Steele
Medical Officer: Dr J Barratt, MB, BS, MRCGP, DCCHRCOG
Registrar: Mrs A Jackson, BTec
Sister-in-Charge: Mrs K Wilkinson-Carr, RGN, RN(Child), DMS, CM, FAETC

Foundation and Purpose. Stanbridge Earls was founded in 1952 by Mr Anthony Thomas, the original Principal, and his wife with funds granted by the Graham Robertson Trust. The aim of this Trust was to encourage art, music and drama, and these activities have always played an important part in the life of the school. The school has over the years evolved its own special purpose, which is to offer parents a distinctive alternative to the large, traditional Independent Schools and to State Education.

It exists to serve those who are seeking a small and intimate school with a particularly high staffing ratio, individualised teaching methods and qualified additional staff for special needs English and Mathematics. The academic objectives are high GCSE grades for all, 'A' Level for most, GNVQ and entrance to university or other higher education for those capable of profiting from such courses. It is a particularly suitable school for boys or girls of good academic potential who, for one reason or another, have up to the time of entry not achieved that potential.

Special Needs (Dyslexia). Since 1962 the school has been helping pupils with specific word-learning difficulties (dyslexia) and has a custom-built Accelerated Learning Centre where 16 qualified staff are able to help pupils overcome their problems on a one-to-one basis. Dyslexia is not seen as a reason for failure. The internationally-recognised specialist help, together with a whole school approach, means that success is not only possible but expected. There is also a well-established department to help those pupils who have a problem with Maths.

Entry. There is entry at either 11 years or 13 years. For the latter the Common Entrance Examination is not compulsory but is taken by some. The performance of those who do so may be taken into account but is not decisive.

The report of an Educational Psychologist may be required in some cases. In others, a pupil's current work may be asked for.

A full confidential report must be received from the pupil's current Headmaster or Headmistress within a year of entry, to cover character, interests, ability at work, games or other skills.

Parents and child must attend the school for interview with the Headmaster prior to final acceptance.

Curriculum. The curriculum covers all the basic academic skills and such further courses as can be offered from the skills and enthusiasms of the current staff. There is for example an emphasis on design including a Motor Mechanics workshop. There are 20 subjects taught to GCSE Level. The following are taught at AS and A2 level. English, History, Geography, Mathematics, Biology, Physics, Chemistry, Art, CDT, Graphics, Photography, ICT, French, PE, Economics. AVCEs in Leisure Recreation and Travel & Tourism, GNVQ in Leisure & Tourism.

In the VI Form, apart from the above subjects, there is also an emphasis on preparing students for adult life outside school.

Recreation. The school is unusually well equipped for its size for sport. There is a heated, indoor swimming-pool for all-year use, a sports hall, large motor vehicle workshop, two squash courts, two hard tennis courts and a normal games field. Soccer, rugger, hockey, cricket, tennis, badminton, basketball, netball, squash, swimming, athletics, gymnastics, judo, sailing, riding and golf are provided. A chain of small lakes offers fishing. Many hobbies are encouraged. There is no CCF or other cadet force but interested pupils join the ATC in Romsey and there is a Duke of Edinburgh award scheme. A strong sailing club operates from Lymington.

Year 12 pupils visit an outdoor activity centre in the UK or abroad for one week.

Girls. At present there are 40 boarding places, but there is no limit to the number of day girls. The normal ages of entry is either 11 to 13 years for a full career or into VI Form for 'A' Levels.

Fees, Scholarships and Bursaries. The full basic fee in September 2000 is £5,000 a term for pupils aged 13 and over, and £4,550 for 11-year-olds. Day pupils' fees are £3,700 (13+) and £3,400 (11+) per term. Remedial tuition and lessons on a musical instrument are extras.

Two Art scholarships are offered to pupils aged 13/14 years, and one to an 11 year old.

The Headmaster may award a number of Bursaries to deserving cases.

Charitable status. Stanbridge Earls School is a Registered Charity, number 307342. It exists to provide education for boys and girls.

* Head of Department	§ Part Time or Visiting
† Housemaster/Housemistress	¶ Old Pupil
‡ See below list of staff for meaning	

Sunderland High School (CSC)

Mowbray Road Sunderland SR2 8HY
Tel: 0191-567 4984
Fax: 0191-510 3953

Junior School Tonstall House Ashbrooke Road Sunderland SR2 7JA
Tel: 0191-514 3278. Fax: 0191-565 6510

Motto: *Timor Domini Principium Sapientiæ*

Established by the Church Schools Company, Limited (see p 53), and opened in 1884.

Governing Body: The Council of the Church Schools Co Ltd

Local Committee:
J Ward, Esq (*Chairman*)
D C Barnes, Esq, FCA
The Right Revd The Bishop of Jarrow
Mrs L Charlton
M Crow, Esq
C R Lofthouse, Esq
T Maxfield, Esq
K S Moore, Esq
Prof J Palmer
D K Sherwood-Smith, Esq
Dr P Sinclair
C Storey, Esq

***Head:* Dr Angela Slater**, BA, PhD

Head of Junior School: Mr J M Turner, BEd, CertEd, DipEd

Full-time Staff:
Miss N Badcock, BA
Mrs L N Bilsborough, MA, BA, PGCE
Miss J Bruce, BA, PGCE
Miss J Burnicle, BSc, MA, PGCE
Mrs J Craven, BA (Sunderland)
Miss A Dargan, BEd
Mrs J A Donald, CertEd
Mrs J Dunn, TCert
Mrs S Errington, CertEd (*Head of Nursery*)
Mr D S Francis, BSc (Manchester), DipEd
Mrs P Gibbs, BA (OU), CertEd
Mr J Gowland, CertEd (Manchester)
Miss K Grenfell, BSc, OTS
Mr D Hair, BA (Hull), MA, PGCE
Mrs A Hedley, BA (Newcastle), DipEd
Mr W G Hedley, BSc (Leeds), PGCE
Mrs S E Hope, BA, PGCE
Mr E Jay, BA (Dunelm), LTCL
Mrs B Kilcoyne, CertEd
Mr C Langley, BSc (Loughborough), PGCE
Mrs C Latham, BA (Dunelm), DipEd (*Deputy Head*)
Mrs M Lewis, BSc (Manchester), DipEd
Mrs J Lusby, CertEd (Durham)
Mrs D McVay, CertEd
Miss S Minto, BA (Newcastle), PGCE
Miss H R Morrison, BA (Belfast), PGCE
Mr M J O'Neill, BSc, PGCE
Mrs G Prior, BA, PGCE (*Deputy Head Junior School*)
Miss S Probets, BSc (London), PGCE
Mrs M Reed, CertEd
Mr T Render, BEd (Newcastle), ATCL
Mrs J Robson, BA (Liverpool), PGCE
Mrs M M Roddy, BA (Leicester), PGCE
Mr K Savage, BA (Sussex), MSc (Loughborough), PGCE (*Deputy Head*)
Miss R Shorey, BA (Dunelm), PGCE
Mr A Temple, BSc, PGCE

Mr S Temple, BA (Sunderland)
Mrs J A Thompson, BEd (Southampton)
Mrs A E Wayman, BA (Sunderland), CertEd
Mr P Wayman, BSc, PGCE
Mrs P J Wilde, MA (Newcastle), DipEd
Mrs A Yoshida, BA, CertEd

Part-time Staff:
Mr D Baillie, BA, PGCE
Mrs A Bovill, BA
Mrs L Hallam, MA, BA, PGCE
Mrs B Harratt, BA, PGCE
Mr D Mead, BSc (Newcastle)
Mrs C Rose, CertEd
Mr F Welsh, BSc
Mrs C Yarrow

The School. Day Girls: 245; Day Boys: 305.

This coeducational day school was opened in 1884 and is situated in the centre of the town close to the bus and railway stations. Pupils travel from Gateshead, Chester-le-Street, Washington, South Shields, Peterlee, Houghton-le-Spring and Durham. Transport services are good. School buses are organised from South Shields, Washington, Peterlee, Seaham and Durham.

The Junior School, for Nursery, Infant and Junior boys and girls, is situated in Tonstall House which was opened by HRH The Princess Royal in May 1994. The building has specialist rooms for Science, Art, Computers and Music as well as a fully equipped Sports Hall. Outside sports facilities include a full sized, floodlit all-weather pitch and grass pitch. These sports facilities are shared by Junior and Secondary pupils for their games programme which includes hockey, netball, football, rugby, cricket, tennis, rounders and athletics. All boys and girls in the Junior School, including the Nursery, have swimming classes also.

The Nursery admits boys and girls on a full or part-time basis and prepares children for school through constructive educational play.

The Infant and Junior Departments provide a sound education for boys and girls. The special feature of the Infant and Junior programme is the Early Language Programme in which German is core curriculum for all pupils from the age of 4+. Junior School pupils enter the Senior School on the recommendation of the Head of Junior School, and they may take a scholarship test at that point. These scholarships are awarded on academic merit. There is also a music scholarship awarded at this stage.

The Senior School (Years 7 to 11) in Mowbray Road has three sites. The Centenary building was opened in 1985 and provides excellent classrooms, four science laboratories and a networked Information Technology Room. The original building includes a fifth laboratory, a second networked Computer Room, library, art room, CDT room, home economics department, careers room and further classrooms.

Clifton Hall, a new building especially equipped for Year 7 and Year 8 pupils opened in September 2000. Each classroom is equipped with an interactive w/board. There are specialist Music & Drama facilities.

The Curriculum is designed to provide a broad education from 4+ to 18+, in line with the requirements of the National Curriculum. Pupils are encouraged to acquire the right qualifications for further study, an independence of spirit, a self awareness of their personal qualities and a sensitivity to the needs of others.

In the Junior School, core subjects are taught in forms with specialist subjects being added as pupils get older. German is taught to pupils from the age of 4+ as part of the school's European awareness policy.

In the Senior School, there are some twenty subjects which pupils study from the age of 11. Pupils receive guidance in Year 9 to enable them to make a wise and balanced choice of subjects for the GCSE courses. In Year 11 Work Experience is organised after the GCSE examinations.

The Sixth Form is housed in a separate Sixth Form Centre, opened in September 1996. Boys and girls are admitted to the Sixth Form subject to a satisfactory standard at GCSE. Most students take four AS level subjects in Arts and/or Science, leading to three A2 levels. A General Studies programme is also offered. Extra courses, such as IT and Young Enterprise, are part of the General Studies programme. All students are encouraged to help in the organisation of the school. Most students proceed to University and other areas of Higher Education. Scholarships are available on entry to the Sixth Form.

Music, drama and sport are strongly encouraged as well as extra-curricular activities, including the Duke of Edinburgh Scheme. Regular ski-trips, activity holidays and visits abroad are organised for both junior and senior pupils.

The school numbers 570 and is small enough for all pupils to be in close contact with the staff. Classes are limited in size and allow for teachers to deal with individual needs.

Admission. Entry to the school is normally at 4+, 7+, 11+, 13+ and the Sixth Form, but applications at other ages are accepted, subject to vacancies. Entrance is partially selective and may include an interview, written tests and a reference from the applicant's previous school.

Fees. (*see* Entrance Scholarship section) From September 2000, Nursery £930 Full-time, Infants £1,114, Juniors £1,362, Seniors (including the Sixth Form) £1,599. The fees include all books, stationery, equipment. Lunches are extra.

Foundation Assisted Places are also available.

Additional Subjects. Music, Speech, Karate, Dancing (Fees on request).

Charitable status. The Church Schools Company is a Registered Charity, number 1016538. It is a charitable trust existing to provide high quality education in keeping with the teaching of the Church of England.

Thetford Grammar School

Bridge Street Thetford Norfolk IP24 3AF
Tel: 01842 752840
Fax: 01842 750220

Refounded in the 17th century by Sir Richard Fulmerston, Thetford Grammar School can however show an unbroken roll of Headmasters from 1119 and traces its origins to the 7th century. In more recent times it was voluntarily controlled until, augmented by the adjacent girls' grammar school, it returned to independence in 1981. Today it is a two-form entry 5–18 coeducational day school with 285 pupils drawn from a radius of 25 miles across the Norfolk/Suffolk border. We seek to combine worthwhile academic standards with a tradition of care and support for the individual and commitment to the breadth of educational experience. A member of SHMIS (elected 1996), ISIS and GBA, the school is administered by the Governors of the Thetford Grammar School Foundation, acting as Trustees on behalf of the Charity Commission.

The Governing Body:

Chairman of Governors: I M Clark

Dr J E J Altham, MA, PhD
G Banham
J G Crisp

J R Edwards, TD, JP, MA, DMS
Mrs M Harwood, CBE, MA
Mrs L Hobden-Clarke
T J Lamb, BSc (Econ)
Mrs J Large, JP, FBCO
F A Onians, BSc
J R Parry, MA, FRICS
P J Price
The Mayor of Thetford (*ex officio*)
Mrs C Turner, JP, BA
Cllr J A Wright, Breckland District Council (*co-opted*)

Bursar and Clerk to the Governors: P J McGahan, MIMgt, MISM

***Headmaster:* J R Weeks,** MA, MLitt (Oxon)

Deputy Headmaster: J S Campbell, BSc (Nottingham)
Deputy Headmistress: Mrs B A Moran, MA (Cantab), AFIMA

Assistant Staff:
M E Anderson, BA (Liverpool)
I M L Blundell, BSc (UEA)
Mrs A Budden, ARADC
M Crook, CertEd (CDT) (Middx Polytechnic)
Mrs P Crossman, MA (UEA), BEd Hons (Lancaster)
Miss F Foster, BA (Warwick)
Mrs T Granger, BSc (Wolverhampton)
Mrs S W Harvey, BA (UEA)
P M Helliwell, BA (Exeter)
Mrs J Huntington, CPSEd, LRAM, GRSM
D E Jones, BSc (Leeds)
N F Jones, MA (Cantab)
J A Law, BEd (Loughborough)
Miss S Lewington, CertEd (Avery Hill)
J C Mead, BEd Hons, CPhys, MInstP
Mrs A Poole, BA (Open University), CertEd (Dartford)
G D Pritchard, BSc (Econ) (London)
Miss K E Rollett, BSc (Harper Adams AC)
D Seymour, MA (Oxon), MPhil (UEA)
Mrs K Q Seymour, BA (Southampton)
S R Simpson, BSc (Birmingham)
Mrs L R Speed, BEd Hons (UEA) (*Head of Junior School*)
S G Spencer, MA (Open University)
Mrs A M Vant, BA (Cork)
Mrs J A Waddington, CertEd (Birmingham)
Mrs V S Webber, BA Hons (Open University), CertEd (Brighton)
Mrs R Wyatt, CertEd (Glamorgan)

Visiting Staff:
Music:
M Cass, LTCL, CertEd *Guitar*
M B Clarke, BA (Sussex), MA (Illinois) *Clarinet*
Mrs P Clarke, MM (UEA) *Flute*
R Lake, LRAM *Brass*
B Metcalfe, GNSM, PGCE *Strings*
Miss J Smith, BA (Oxon), DipTCM *Harp*
Mrs J Taylor, GTCL, FTCL *'Cello*
Mrs J G Weeks, ARMCM, GRSM *Piano*

Dyslexia support: Mrs J Jenkins, MSc, DipCST, RegMRCSLT, MASLTIP

Headmaster's Secretary: Mrs E I Kitson

School Secretary: Mrs D H Young

Buildings and Situation. Situated close to the centre of Thetford, the school occupies a well established site graced by several buildings of architectural interest and the ruins of a medieval priory. An active Development Programme has seen the refurbishment of a number of buildings to provide improved facilities. Music, Art, Computing, Technology, Photography and the Junior School are among recent beneficiaries of this process while the Thomas Paine Library both commemorates an Old Thetfordian and extends sixth form private study facilities. There are extensive playing fields within walking distance of the main buildings.

Organisation. Junior School pupils (5–10 year olds) (5-7 Goldcrest; 8-10 Junior Department) are taught primarily in their own premises with independent facilities. Older juniors, however, have contact with specialist teachers in several subject areas and benefit from similar integration into many other aspects of school life. Main School education from 11 follows a two-form entry pattern with setting in core subjects to GCSE. Sixth Form students, who have their own Common Room, play a full part in the life of the school.

Curriculum. Junior School teaching follows National Curriculum lines with strong emphasis on the English/ Mathematics core and the range of specialist subjects in support. Music and Drama are important within the Department, while a full programme of PE and Games allows for the development of team sports and individual fitness.

Main School education through to GCSE is based on a common core of English, English Literature, Mathematics, a Modern Language (French or German) and Co-ordinated Science (Double Award). Options allow students to develop skills and interests in History and Geography, languages, the arts and technology. IT is strongly represented across the curriculum. AS and A2 courses are offered in all these subjects, including the separate sciences, with the addition of Business Studies and Psychology. Mathematics and Science lead a strong pattern of results at this level and the majority of sixth form students proceed to university degree courses.

Sport and Extra-curricular Activities. The life of the school extends widely from the classroom into sport, community service, dramatic and musical presentation; the lessons taught by the pursuit of excellence through individual commitment and teamwork are greatly valued.

Winter sports are Rugby, Soccer, Hockey, Netball and Cross-Country with Cricket, Tennis, Rounders and Athletics in the Summer. Popular indoor sports such as Basketball, Aerobics, Badminton, Volleyball and Gymnastics are also followed.

A majority of pupils take part in training for the Duke of Edinburgh Award Scheme. The school has a strong tradition in Business Gaming. Musically, a lively concert programme supports individual instrumental tuition and choral rehearsal while opportunities for theatre are provided termly by House and School productions.

A popular Activities Week is run biennially at the end of the Summer Term encompassing expeditions and foreign visits.

Admission and Fees. Admission into Main School and the Junior Department is by examination with interview and school report. Sixth Form entrance is on the basis of interview and school report, with subsequent performance at GCSE taken into consideration. The main Entrance Examination is held in January but supplementary testing continues through the year. Full details from the Headmaster's Secretary.

Termly fees for 2001/2002, which include books and tuition but exclude uniform, lunches, transport, examination entry fees and some specialised teaching such as instrumental music lessons, are £1,630 (Goldcrest), £1,810 (Junior School), £1,970 (Main School).

Scholarships and Bursaries. Up to six Scholarships, usually worth one-third of the annual fee, are awarded at the January entry to 11+ entrants to the school, with two external scholarships for Sixth Form entry. Internal awards providing fee-remission at sixth-form level are made on the strength of good performance in the GCSE examination.

A Music Scholarship to the value of one-third fees is awarded to a Main School entrant at 11. Details from the Director of Music.

Additionally, Governors' Bursaries, each normally to the value of one-third of the annual fee, are awarded to pre-Sixth Form Main School entrants at the Headmaster's discretion.

Details of all awards may be had from the Headmaster.

Charitable status. Thetford Grammar School is a Registered Charity, number 311263. It exists to provide education for boys and girls.

Warminster School

Warminster Wiltshire BA12 8PJ
Tel: (01985) 210100 (Senior School); 210152 (Preparatory School)
Fax: (01985) 214129

The original boys' school was founded in 1707 by the first Viscount Weymouth, an ancestor of the present Marquess of Bath. It became an Independent Educational Trust in 1973 formed by the amalgamation of the Lord Weymouth School with the long-established local girls' school, St Monica's, founded in 1874. The School is a Limited Company whose Directors are Trustees elected by and from within the Board of Governors which is in membership of the Governing Bodies Association.

Patron: The Most Honourable the Marquess of Bath

Visitor: The Lord Bishop of Bath & Wells

Governors:
Chairman: Mr R Southwell, QC

Ex Officio:
The Mother Superior of the Community of St. Denys
The Vicar of Warminster

Representative:
The Council of St Boniface
Wiltshire County Council
Bristol University
10 Co-optative Members

Staff:

***Headmaster:* D Dowdles**, MA

Deputy Head: O Bourne, BEd

Deputy Head (*Pastoral*): Mrs S M Marklew, BA, PGCE

Heads of Department:
C R Blakey, BEd (*CDT*)
G T W Cashell, BEd Hons (*PE*)
J Cox, BA, PGCE (*Modern Languages*)
R W Lincoln, BA, CertEd (*Mathematics*)
G McQueen, MA, PGCE (*Head of Sixth Form*)
Dr D Hankey, PhD, BSc (*Science*)
Mrs E North, BA, PGCE, LLAM, BDADip (*Head of Learning Support*)
M J Sandford, MA, PGCE, FRGS (*Director of Studies*)
M D Thompson, BA, PGCE (*English*)

There are 20 other full-time and part-time staff.

House Staff:
Mr and Mrs J Bonnell (*St Boniface*)
M Hanson, BSc, MEd (*Day Boys' Housemaster*)
Mrs A Cashell (*Housemistress, Stratton House*)
Mrs P A Betenson, CertEd(PE) (*Day Girls' Housemistress*)
Mrs C Marklew, BA, PGCE (*St Denys*)

Preparatory School:
Head: C J Jones, BEd (Hons)

Mrs V Lyon, BA, PGCE (*Deputy Head and i/c Day Pupils*)

There are 7 additional staff

Additional House Staff:
Mrs H Arter, RGN (*Senior Matron*)

Bursar & Clerk to the Governors: P N Davis, FCII, FCIS

General. The School is a coeducational day and boarding school numbering some 460 pupils from 4 to 18, of whom 200 are boarders. The Preparatory School of 120 pupils works in close co-operation with the Senior School, and enjoys many of the same facilities.

It is situated along the western periphery of the town, looking out over open countryside, while its buildings are linked by extensive gardens and playing fields.

It is easily accessible by rail (via Warminster or Westbury) from London, Heathrow, the South Coast and the West, and by road (via the Severn Bridge and Motorways 3, 4 and 5).

Aims and Philosophy. The School aims to provide a stimulating and caring environment in which all pupils develop as individuals and achieve their potential in as many areas as possible. We encourage our pupils to have respect for the rights and beliefs of other people, and wish to provide for them the opportunity to achieve social, academic and personal qualities which will enable them to live happy, productive, confident and useful lives, both within the school and as part of the community.

As Church of England foundations, the original schools brought to the amalgamation a strong tradition of Christian ideals; the School has its own Chapel. Those who so wish are prepared for Confirmation. The school, however, welcomes pupils of all denominations and faiths, and hopes that, whatever their religious background, they will learn tolerance and a concern for other people.

Buildings. The school is fortunate to have all the accommodation that once belonged to the two schools as well as the former post-graduate college of London University, St Boniface, which provides a Chapel and Library and extensive study/bedrooms and common rooms, and the former Convent of St Denys. The policy is to continue to improve facilities, while keeping the numbers small so as to retain the friendliness of atmosphere and the close relationship between staff and pupils.

Approximately 3 million pounds has been spent on building development over the last fifteen years. This has produced a large sports hall with social centre and squash courts, an art room, four CDT workshops, a science block with six laboratories and preparation room, a day pupil centre, a girls' boarding house, two spacious classroom blocks, including a computer centre and specialist language and mathematics rooms, an all-weather artificial games pitch and improved Sixth Form facilities. Boarding accommodation has been refurbished with new furniture and fitted carpets.

Boarders are supervised by married Housemasters or Housemistresses and Resident Tutors and Matrons. All pupils have single study/bedrooms in the Fifth and Sixth Forms.

Curriculum. In the first two years of the Senior School (Y8, Y9), all pupils study English, Maths, French, Science, History, Geography, Art, Computing, Music, RE and a variety of Craft and Design-based subjects. German is available for some. In the Fourth and Fifth Form (Y10, Y11), all pupils study the full range of GCSE subjects, with some specialisation being possible. All pupils are involved in PE and Games, and Health and Social Education, as well as a comprehensive programme of Careers advice.

In the Sixth Form greater individual freedom and responsibility are encouraged, and at least 18 different A level subjects are offered, as well as a number of more demanding one-year GCSE courses. Although the vast majority of pupils will be aiming for University, some will pursue ambitions in the professions, business or the armed services.

The overall pupil/staff ratio is under 10:1. Pupils receive an exceptional amount of individual attention and are encouraged to realise their full potential in as many areas as possible. There is a tutorial system, and pupils are setted according to ability. A small learning support unit is staffed by dedicated specialists to offer EFL and help for dyslexics.

Activities. A very wide range of hobbies is on offer, and pupils are encouraged to involve themselves fully. The school has a strong tradition of drama, and the musical activities, including choir, orchestra, wind band and ensembles, and tuition in all instruments, are varied. There are currently over 40 hobby activities available.

The school enjoys close links with the Services, and the CCF, though voluntary, is traditionally strong. There is also a large involvement in the Duke of Edinburgh's Award Scheme, while a number of pupils are actively engaged in Community Service in Warminster and the local area, and conservation work.

Games. Sports offered include: Soccer; Cricket; Athletics; Basketball; Squash; Rugby; Netball; Hockey; Cross-country running; Rounders; Tennis; Swimming; Badminton; Volleyball and Sailing.

There is a spacious Sports Hall with squash courts, hard tennis courts, heated swimming pool, an artificial all-weather pitch and an indoor shooting range. Pupils have access to the local Golf Club and Riding stables.

Admission. Boys and girls are accepted on the basis of the School's tests in English and Mathematics and a school report, or through the Common Entrance Examination. There is a substantial intake at Sixth Form level, for which a Head's report is required. Five GCSEs at C grade or above are normally expected for entry at this stage. There are Scholarships for entry at 11, 13 and into the Sixth Form, for which examinations are taken at the end of January each year. Bursaries are also available on application to The Headmaster.

A full prospectus is available on request.

Fees. (From September 2001). Reception £1,250; Years 1 & 2 £1,550; Years 3 & 4 Day £1,850, Boarding £3,455; Years 5 & 6 Day £2,100, £3,455 Boarding; Year 7 to Sixth Form Day £2,445, £4,255 Boarding.

Charitable status. Warminster School is a Charitable Company, number 1042204. It exists to promote the education of boys and girls.

Windermere St Anne's School

The Lake District Windermere Cumbria LA23 1NW
Tel: 015394 46164
International +44 15394 46164
Fax: 015394 88414
e-mail: windermerest-annes.cumbria.sch.uk
website: www.windermerest-annes.cumbria.sch.uk

Chairman: Mrs M R Orr, NFF

P W Broom
B J Drury
J O Halstead, BScTech Hons, FIMgt
Dr J E Irwin, MB, ChB, DRCOG
Mrs J Lefton
R McGraw, MEd, FRGS
R Perkins
Dr C D Snaith

Head: **Miss W A Ellis**, BA Hons (Lancaster), PGCE (London)

Senior and Middle School:

Deputy Head: J Martin, BSc Hons (Leeds)
Academic Deputy: J R Pennell, MA (Cantab), PGCE (Oxon)
Director of Activities: Miss M Henderson, CertEd (Bingley)
Head of Sixth Form: Miss R Hodgson, BA Hons (London), DipEd (Cantab)

Mr N W Adcock, BA Hons (Bath Academy of Art), CertEd *Head of Art*
Mrs J Bracken, BEd Hons TC (Manchester) *Head of Mathematics*
Dr P Collison, BSc Hons (Sheffield), PGCE (Newcastle) *Head of Science*
Mrs J Davey, MA Hons (Edinburgh), PGCE (St Martin) *Head of Modern Languages*
Miss J Hall, BA, RBTCDip (Rose Bruford), CTEFLA *Head of Drama*
Miss E Lightburn, BA Hons (Birmingham), PGCE (Lancaster) *Head of Humanities*
Miss J H McCallum, LLCM, LTCL, ALCM *Director of Music*
Mrs E L Pennell, BA Hons (London), PGCE (Aberystwyth) *Head of English*
Mr G Smurthwaite, CertEd (Carnegie School of Physical Education) *Director of Sport*
Mrs A Underwood, BA (Durham), DipEd, DipCEG *Head of Resources/Business Studies*

Junior Department:
Mrs S B Cooper, BEd (Charlotte Mason) *Headmistress*
Miss L Bunyan, NNEB *Head of the Nursery*
Mrs L Oakden, BA Hons (Hull), PGCE (Charlotte Mason) *Head of Infant Department*
Mrs E Moor, CertEd *Head of Music*
Miss B Fear, BSc Hons (Loughborough) *Form IV, Head of PE*
Miss A Eddleston, CertEd (Poulton)
Mr N Stanley, BA Hons, PGCE (Charlotte Mason)

Number of Full-time Teaching Staff: 44
Number of Part-time and Visiting Staff: 20
Number of Staff living on Campus: 18

Administrative Staff:
School Doctors:
Dr E W R Oakden, MBBChir, MRCS, MRCGP
Dr C Stokes, MB, ChB, MRCP, MRCGP
Dr Sarah Watson, BM, BCh, MRCP, MRCGP
School Nurse: Mrs A M Hughes, SRN
Bursar: J A Bloomer
Assistant Bursar (Accounts): Mrs W Everett
Bursar's Secretary: Mrs P Mowat
Assistant: Mrs K Kirby
Head's Secretary/PA: Mrs J Jones
School Secretary: Mrs A Bailey
Elleray Secretary: Mrs P Burgess
Travel Secretary: Miss B Benn
Domestic Bursar: Miss J Cunliffe
Registrar: Mrs C Martin

Location. The Lake District National Park is an outstanding environment. Windermere St Anne's enjoys an ideal situation in one of the areas of great natural beauty in the British Isles. It is within easy reach of the M6, major rail links and Manchester Airport.

Windermere St Anne's, an independent co-educational boarding and day school, was founded in 1863, and is an Educational Trust administered by a Board of Governors. It is divided into the Senior School (ages 11 to 18) and the Junior School (ages 3 to 11). The School is international in outlook, and welcomes pupils from overseas.

Buildings. The Senior School is housed at Browhead, and the Junior Department is nearby at Elleray, with grounds of over 70 acres in total. There is a modern Sixth Form House with single and double study bedrooms. These all have magnificent views south and west over Lake Windermere and the mountains. In addition the School owns 11 acres of unspoilt lakeside property with harbour and full facilities for canoeing, sailing and wind-surfing activities. The school grounds and immediate surroundings are excellent for field studies in a variety of subjects, and for many activities, fell-walking and riding.

Numbers. Overall there are approximately 350 pupils.

The Senior School

The Senior School has approximately 200 pupils, of whom 60% are boarders. The size of the community has the advantage of providing a friendly atmosphere of understanding and fosters good staff-pupil relationships. There is a 4-house system for competitions and games.

Academic. Classes are small, providing excellent conditions for learning. Years are divided into two or three forms and cross-setted. The School has specially designed open campus classrooms, 3 purpose-built Science laboratories and ICT and Resource Centre. The Jenkins Performing Arts Centre contains a Dance Studio, 15 specialist music rooms, the Recital Room, a Drama Studio and an extensive drama wardrobe. There is an Art/Craft/Pottery/Design Technology complex, and an excellent modern theatre.

For the first three years all pupils take a broad spread of subjects. At the end of the third year choices are made for GCSE, and considerable flexibility in subject combinations is achieved. Subject selection for GCSE and A-level examinations is made by the student, who works with his or her parents, subject teachers, career advisers, tutor, and housemistress or housemaster.

At 16, pupils join the Sixth Form. Windermere St Anne's senior pupils have a special status during their last two years at School, and they are given considerable responsibility in running the School and organising their own affairs. Head of School and house Captains are elected by peers and faculty members. The School believes that this creates the best environment for a senior pupil studying for A level. Sixth Form pupils work closely with a personal tutor. All pupils take a general studies programme in addition to their normal three or four AS/A2 levels.

Careers. A Careers specialist runs Careers Education for all years from Year 9 upwards. Students are encouraged to seek advice with regard to future careers, suitability of GCSE and A-level choices and university entrance. Use is made of outside organisations, conferences, visits, discussions and practical work experience. There is a well-equipped and award-winning careers library. The School is a member of ISCO.

Music, Art, Drama and Dance play an important part in the life of the school. There are two choirs, and individual instruction leading to chamber groups and orchestra. Students are prepared for the written and practical music exams of the Associated Board of the Royal Schools of Music. In Ballet the Royal Academy of Dancing Grade examinations are taken. Classes in tap, modern and jazz dance are available and dance is included in the timetable. The school participates in the local Music Festival. The Central School of Speech and Drama and LAMDA's examinations are also taken in Speech and Drama. Art, Pottery and Design Technology provide considerable scope and opportunity. The Art Studios contain facilities for History of Art and an Art History Library. Drama classes are included in the timetable, and there are several productions staged each year.

Sports. The Senior School has a Sports Hall for basketball, gymnastics, netball, badminton, volleyball, table tennis, tennis and a variety of other indoor activities. There are eighteen hard tennis courts, netball courts and football and cricket field, including an all weather, international-size field hockey pitch. Cricket, tennis, track and field, and rounders are summer sports. Squash and aerobics are offered. Optional activities include sailing, canoeing, kayaking fell walking, camping, judo, self-defence, fencing, riding, mountain-biking, climbing, shooting and orienteering.

Service. Windermere St Anne's has a strong tradition of Community Service. The school has an active role in Age Concern, SCOPE, and the Cheshire Home, and supports many other charities including local Hospices, NSPCC and the Save The Children Fund.

Religion. The school is Christian in outlook and welcomes other denominations.

Medical. The health of the pupils is under the care of the School Doctors and full time nurse. There is a regular surgery, and dispensary twice daily.

Societies. More than 40 Clubs and Societies provide a variety of interests for out of school hours.

Social. Windermere St Anne's is in an excellent position to take advantage of the many and varied year-round cultural activities in the locality; it is within easy reach of larger centres for theatre, concerts and visits, and has contact with Lancaster University. Lectures, Films and Recitals are also arranged in school.

Uniform. Senior School – Navy uniform for all pupils during the day; home clothes may be worn at weekends. The VIth Form wear a navy suit and they may wear home clothes in the evenings and at weekends.

Junior school – Girls blue kilt and sweater plus checked shirts in the winter. In the summer the kilt is worn with a navy and white flowered short-sleeved blouse and pale blue sleeveless slipover. Boys wear grey trousers, pale blue shirts and sweater, the school tie and blazer.

Junior Department at Elleray

Elleray is in the care of a Headmistress, and takes boarders living in their own boarding wing of the senior school, and 100 day children. There is also a Nursery school for children from 3 to 5 years and a new Day Nursery. Elleray is integrated with the Senior School giving continuity of teaching programmes and children in the two parts of the school meet frequently.

Elleray is situated in its own large grounds overlooking the lake with woodlands leading to the fell behind. There is an art studio, music room, craft room and gymnasium. Children are taught in classes of approximately 15 children by both their form teacher and specialist teachers of French, Science, Art, Design Technology, History, Music, PE, Biology. Sports include Rugby, Hockey, Netball, Cricket, Athletics, Rounders, Tennis and Swimming. Speech and Drama, Riding, Ballet and Modern Dance, Orchestra, Choir, Cookery, Calligraphy, Chess, Art Societies, playing several musical instruments, Computer and Latin clubs are some of the optional activities offered.

General

Overseas Travel and Escort. Escorts are arranged to and from Euston. A special 24-hour service is provided to and from Manchester Airport, meeting and seeing off flights for those living abroad.

Fees. Details of Fees will be sent on request.

Friends of St Anne's. An active Association of past pupils, parents and friends of the school.

Stannite Association. The Alumni Association, which meets regularly, through school and local reunions.

Round Square. The School is a member of the international Round Square group of schools. Exchanges and Overseas Service Projects are regularly arranged between the schools involved in Australia, Canada, Germany, India, Switzerland, South Africa and USA.

International Outlook. In addition to the Round Square activities, the School organises regular language exchanges. Windermere St Anne's offers tailor-made courses for students from overseas, with intensive EFL tuition. Pupils are admitted for a term, a year, or to be integrated into the main-stream curriculum.

Entry. Pupils are accepted into the Senior school from Prep and Junior schools at 11 or 13+, or by direct entry into the VIth Form. In special circumstances students may be accepted at other times.

In the Junior school, pupils are taken at various stages, from Nursery onwards.

Scholarships. A number of Academic and Music Scholarships are available at 11+, 13+ and 6th Form level. There are also Awards for Art, Dance and Drama and Sport.

For further details please write to the Head.

Charitable status. Windermere Educational Trust Limited is a Registered Charity, number 526973. It exists to provide education of the highest quality.

The Yehudi Menuhin School

Stoke d'Abernon Cobham Surrey KT11 3QQ
Tel: (01932) 864739
Fax: (01932) 864633
e-mail: admin@yehudimenuhinschool.co.uk

The Yehudi Menuhin School was founded in 1963 by Lord Menuhin and is situated in beautiful grounds in the Surrey countryside, close to London and within easy reach of both Gatwick and Heathrow.

The School provides specialist music tuition in stringed instruments and piano to over 50 musically gifted boys and girls aged between 8 and 18 and aims to enable them to pursue their love of music, develop their musical potential and achieve standards of performance at the highest level. The School also provides a broad education within a relaxed open community in which each individual can fully develop intellectual, artistic and social skills. We are proud that our pupils develop into dedicated and excellent musicians who will use their music to inspire and enrich the lives of others and into friendly, thinking individuals well equipped to contribute fully to the international community.

Patron: Her Royal Highness The Duchess of Kent, GCVO

President: Mstislav Rostropovitch, Hon KBE

Vice Presidents:

Elizabeth, Duchess of Hamilton and Brandon, OBE, DL
The Lord Rayne
Sir Ian Hunter, MBE
A N Hollis, OBE, DFC

Governors:

Chairman: Barbara R-D Fisher, OBE
Vice Chairman: Sir John Burgh, KCMG, CB

Noel Annesley
Sir Peter Beale, KBE
The Hon Zamira Benthall
John Chadwick
Stephen J Cockburn
Daniel Hodson
Sir Claus Moser, KCB, CBE, FBA
Adam Ridley
Mark Sheldon, CBE
Anne Simor
Graham Smallbone
Ronald Smith
Sir Alan Traill, GBE

Staff:

HEADMASTER **MR NICOLAS CHISHOLM**, MA (CANTAB)

Director of Music: Mr Malcolm Singer, MA (Cantab)

Academic Staff:

Art & Craft: Mrs Veronica Dunce, BA, NDD
Biology & Science: Mrs Eileen Webster, BSc, ARCS
English & Drama: Dr Ian Baird, PhD, MA, BA
French: Mrs Annie Perkins, M-ès-L, MA
German & Russian: Mrs Petra Young, MA
History: Mr Mark Shere, MA, PGCE
Junior Subjects: Miss Janet Poppe, BA Hons, PGCE
Mathematics:
Mrs Susan Hemingway, BA, CertEd
Mrs Denise Smee, BSc, CertEd
EFL: Mrs Hazel Brier, MA(TESL)

Music Staff:

Violin:
Professor Mauricio Fuks (*Visiting*)
Mrs Natalie Boyarskaya, Dip Solo Performance
Mr Hu Kun, Graduate Beijing Central Conservatoire
Mr Simon Fischer, AGSM
Mrs Rosemary Warren-Green, ARCM, Dip Recital
Mr Maciej Rakowski

'Cello:
Mr Leonid Gorokhov
Miss Louise Hopkins, AGSM

Bass:
Mr Rodney Slatford (*Visiting*)
Mrs Caroline Emery, LTCL, GTCL, CertEd

Piano:
Mrs Irena Zaritzkaya
Mr Nikolai Demidenko (*Visiting*)
Mrs Ruth Nye, DipMusPerf, Melbourne Conservatory
Mr Graham Caskie, BA (Hons), ABSM, DipRAMRCM
Ms Zoe Mather, AGSM

Harpsichord:
Miss Carole Cerasi

Coach Accompanist:
Miss Alison Rhind, BA (Oxon)
Mr Julian Dyson, ARCM, DipRCM

Chamber Music:
Mr Ioan Davies, MA (Cantab)
Mr Malcolm Singer, MA (Cantab)
Mr Peter Norris, BMus, ARCM

Orchestra:
Mr Malcolm Singer, MA (Cantab)

General Music:
Mr Malcolm Singer, MA (Cantab)
Mr Matthew King, BA (Hons), LTCL
Mr John LeGrove, MMus, FRCO, PGCE

Choral:
Mr John LeGrove, MMus, FRCO, PGCE

Alexander Technique:
Mrs Hannah Walton, NNEB, MSTAT

Administrative Staff:

Bursar: Mrs Elaine Balmer
Secretary: Mrs Diana Foster-Kemp, BS
Concert Secretary: Mrs Catharine Whitnall, MA (Cantab), LTCL
Housemistress: Mrs Ann Bourne
Matron: Mrs Joan Clarke, SRN, SCM
Cook/Caterer: Miss Margaret Matthijs
Estate Manager: Mr Brian Harris

Music. At least half each day is devoted to musical studies. Pupils receive a minimum of two one-hour lessons each week on their first study instrument and at least half an hour on their second study instrument. Supervised practice is incorporated into the daily programme ensuring that successful habits of work are formed. All pupils receive guidance in composition and take part in regular composers workshops and concerts. Aural training and general musicianship studies are included in the music curriculum. To awaken feeling for good posture, training in Alexander Technique is provided. GCSE and A Level Music are compulsory core subjects for all pupils.

Regular opportunity for solo performance is of central importance to the musical activity of the School, and pupils also perform chamber music and with the String Orchestra. Concerts are given several times each week within the School and at a wide variety of venues throughout the United Kingdom and overseas. The most distinguished musicians have taught at the school, including Boulanger, Perlemuter, Rostropovich and Perlman. Lord Menuhin visits the school regularly. Selection of pupils is by stringent audition which seeks to assess musical ability and identify potential. Special arrangements are made for applicants from overseas, who now account for almost half of the School's pupils.

Academic Studies and Sport. The curriculum is designed to be balanced and to do full justice to both the musical and the general education of each pupil. Academic studies including the understanding of art, literature and science are considered vital to the development of creative, intelligent and sensitive musicians. All classes are small with excellent opportunities for individual attention, and as a result GCSE and A level examination grades are high. To broaden their artistic and creative talents, all pupils work in a wide variety of artistic media including painting, ceramics, jewellery and textiles. Pupils from overseas with limited English receive an intensive course in the English Language from specialist teachers.

The extensive grounds allow plenty of scope for relaxation and sport, including tennis, badminton, football, running, swimming, rounders and aerobics.

An International Family. The international reputation of the School brings pupils from all over the world who find a happy atmosphere in a large musical family. Pupils live in single or shared rooms and are cared for by the resident House Staff, the Matron who is a qualified nurse, and the School Doctor. Special attention is paid to diet with the emphasis on whole and fresh food.

Fees and Bursaries. All pupils fully resident in the UK are awarded an Aided Place Bursary under the Music and Ballet Scheme which is subsidised by the Department for Education. Parents therefore pay according to their means a contribution to the School fees which is assessed by the Department for Education. Pupils from overseas are required to pay the full boarding fee of £7,706 per term until they qualify for a DfEE Grant after two years' residence at the School.

Admission. Entry to the School is by music audition, and prospective pupils are auditioned at any time during the year. Candidates may audition at any age between 7 and 16, though the main age for entry to the School spans the years 8 to 14.

Charitable status. The Yehudi Menuhin School is a Registered Charity, number 312010. It exists to provide musical and academic education for boys and girls.

Society of Headmasters and Headmistresses of Independent Schools

Additional Membership

Mrs J A Thomas, Head, Arden Lawn, Stratford Road, Henley-in-Arden B95 6AB. Tel: (01564) 796800, Fax: (01564) 796809.

P D Stockdale, Headmaster, Ballard School, Fernhill Lane, New Milton, Hampshire BH25 5JL. Tel: (01425) 611153, Fax: (01425) 638847,

A L Morris, Principal, Concord College, Acton Burnell Hall, Shrewsbury, Shropshire SY5 7PF. Tel: (01694) 731631, Fax: (01694) 731389.

S H Larter, Headmaster, Northamptonshire Grammar School, Pitsford Hall, Moulton Lane, Northampton NN6 9AX. Tel: (01604) 880306, Fax: (01604) 882212.

C F R Potter, Headmaster, Old Swinford Hospital, Stourbridge, West Midlands DY8 1QX. Tel: (01384) 370025, Fax: (01384) 441686.

M Scullion, Headmaster, Our Lady of Sion School, Gratwicke Road, Worthing, West Sussex BN11 4BK. Tel: (01903) 204063, Fax: (01903) 214434.

R Walker, Headmaster, Portland Place School, 56–58 Portland Place, London W1N 5DG. Tel: (020) 7307 8700, Fax: (020) 7436 2676.

R A Hadfield, Headmaster, The Read School, Drax, Selby, North Yorkshire YO8 8NL. Tel: (01757) 618248, Fax: (01757) 618033.

N Debenham, Headmaster, St James Independent School for Boys, Pope's Villa, 19 Cross Deep, Twickenham, Middlesex TW1 4QG. Tel: (020) 8892 2002, Fax: (020) 8892 4442.

SOCIETY OF HEADMASTERS AND HEADMISTRESSES OF INDEPENDENT SCHOOLS

(* denotes Schools reckoned to be co-educational)

The following schools whose Heads are members of SHMIS and HMC will be found in the index to HMC Schools.

Abbotsholme School
Ackworth School
Bedales School
Churcher's College
City of London Freemen's School
Colston's Collegiate School
King's School, Tynemouth
Kirkham Grammar School
Lord Wandsworth College
Pangbourne College
Reading Blue Coat School
Reed's School
Rendcomb College
Rougemont School
Royal Hospital School
Ryde School
St Columba's College, St Albans
St George's College
Shiplake College
Silcoates School
Tettenhall College
West Buckland School
Wisbech Grammar School
Yarm School

The following school whose Head is a member of SHMIS and GSA will be found in the index to GSA Schools.

King Edward VI High School for Girls

GEOGRAPHICAL LOCATION OF SHMIS SCHOOLS

Berkshire
Bearwood College
The Licensed Victuallers' School, Ascot

Cheshire
Abbey Gate College
North Cestrian Grammar School

Cumbria
Austin Friars School
Windermere St Anne's

Devon
Grenville College
Shebbear College

Dorset
Clayesmore School
Milton Abbey School

Essex
Friends' School, Saffron Walden

Gloucestershire
St Edward's School

Hampshire
Embley Park School
St John's College, Southsea
Stanbridge Earls School

Hertfordshire
St Christopher, Letchworth

Kent
Bethany School
Dover College
Duke of York's Royal Military School

Lancashire
Bentham School
Kirkham Grammar School

Lincolnshire
Lincoln Minster School

Middlesex
Halliford School
Purcell School

Norfolk
Langley School
Thetford Grammar School

Northumberland
Longridge Towers School, Berwick-upon-Tweed

Oxfordshire
Cokethorpe School
Kingham Hill School
Sibford School

Somerset
Sidcot School

Shropshire
Bedstone College
Oswestry School

Staffordshire
Stafford Grammar School

Suffolk
St Joseph's College, Ipswich

Surrey
Box Hill School
Claremont Fan Court School
Elmhurst – The School for Dance and Performing Arts
Ewell Castle School
Royal Russell School
The Yehudi Menuhin School

Sussex (East)
Battle Abbey School
St Bede's School

Sussex (West)
Seaford College

Tyne and Wear
Sunderland High School

Warwickshire
Princethorpe College, Rugby

West Midlands
St George's School, Edgbaston, Birmingham
Royal Wolverhampton School

Wiltshire
La Retraite Swan, Salisbury
Warminster School

Yorkshire (North)
Birkdale School
Scarborough College and Lisvane

Yorkshire (West)
Fulneck School, Pudsey
Hipperholme Grammar School
Rishworth School

Wales
Ruthin School
St David's College

Scotland
Lomond School

Ireland
Royal School, Dungannon

Entrance Scholarship Announcements for 2001/2002 (SHMIS)

Austin Friars School, Carlisle (see p 768). Scholarships are available to Catholic pupils of the correct age who take the examinations at 11+ and 13+.

Boarders: One major scholarship of up to two thirds of full fees per annum and not more than three of up to one third of full fees per annum.

Day pupils: One major scholarship of up to two thirds of full fees per annum and not more than three of up to one third full fees per annum.

Bursaries are available to pupils of any age. These awards are not competitive and are given in the light of family financial circumstances.

Scholarships are also available on the result of Common Entrance Examinations.

Bearwood College (see p 770). Open and Closed (HM Services, British Merchant Navy and Old Royals) Scholarships can be awarded annually in Art, Drama, Music, Sport, General Academic Ability and Sixth Form Entry, up to the value of 50% of the full fees, to those boys and girls reaching the required competitive standard in CEE or College Entry Tests. Sixth Form awards are made on GCSE Grades.

Candidates for Music Scholarships should be prepared to perform on two instruments, one of which can be singing. Preference will be shown to trebles and promising string players, although there are awards for all types including organ.

Art Scholarships are awarded on the submission of a portfolio and subsequent interview with the Head of Art.

Discretionary Bursaries are available in cases of financial hardship.

Personal discussions with the Headmaster are very much encouraged. Full details from *The Headmaster*, telephone: 01734 786915; fax: 01734 772687.

Bedstone College (see p 773). One Bishop Sara Scholarship of £4,000 pa and two Bursaries of £2,000 each pa may be awarded annually by examination for 10/11 11/14 years olds in March at the College.

Valuable Sixth Form Scholarships are available for successful O' level candidates.

Bentham Grammar School (see p 774). Scholarships are awarded annually on the basis of academic, musical, artistic or leadership potential.

Candidates for academic scholarships in the age range 10–14 will normally sit the scholarship examination which takes place at the School in February each year. Academic scholarships for those boys and girls due to enter the Sixth Form in the following September will be awarded provisionally on the basis of an interview and a report from their present school and confirmed once the GCSE results are known in August. Interviews will take place by arrangement during February and March.

Music scholarships will be awarded on the basis of past achievement and following an audition with the Director of Music. Art scholarships on the basis of a portfolio of work and interview with the Director of Art.

Leadership scholarships, which can include prowess in games, will normally only be available for boys and girls aged 13 and over and will be awarded on the basis of interview and school report.

For further details apply to the *Headmaster*.

Bethany School (see p 776). Academic Scholarships are awarded based on performance in the Entrance Examination. Scholarships also available in Art, Music, Sport and Drama at the main points of entry: Years 7 and 9 and into the Sixth Form. Further details available from the Headmaster. Members of HM Forces and the clergy receive a 10% discount in the published fees.

Box Hill School (see p 777). Up to ten scholarships are awarded for entry to the Sixth Form, based on academic achievement and a contribution to school life through Art, Music, Drama, expedition work, or other appropriate activities. For details, apply to the *Headmaster.*

Claremont Fan Court School (see p 778). Academic Scholarships of up to 50% of the fees per annum are offered for Year 3 (to continue through to the end of Year 6) and Year 7 and Year 9 (to continue through to Year 11). Sixth Form Scholarships of up to 50% per annum are offered for the two year course. These are based on a written examination, an interview and the attainment of six 'A' grade passes at GCSE.

Musical scholarships of up to 50% of the fees per annum are available at Senior level.

Physical Education Scholarships of up to 50% of the fees per annum are offered at Year 7, Year 9 and Sixth Form.

Art Scholarships are available at Sixth Form.

All scholarship applicants must also sit the General Entrance Assessment before being considered.

Clayesmore School (see p 779). Scholarship Examination in the Summer Term open to candidates under 14 on 1 June. Examination may take place either at Clayesmore or at the candidate's school. Up to four Scholarships and up to four Exhibitions available, valued at a percentage of tuition fees. Several Scholarships are also available for proficiency in Art, Music or Handicraft. Please apply to the *Headmaster, Clayesmore School, Iwerne Minster, Blandford, Dorset.*

Dover College (see p 782). (*a*) At least 6 Scholarships and Exhibitions for academic quality, ranging in value up to *half fee value plus possible Bursaries.* (*b*) One of more Astor scholarships, ranging in value up to £3,500 pa for pupils who may academically be just below open award standard, but who achieve a good Common Entrance pass and who have shown athletic ability, good all-round endeavour and good character at their preparatory schools. (*c*) One or more Music scholarships, ranging in value up to £3,500 pa together with free musical education, are offered to boys and girls of exceptional musical promise. (*d*) One Art Scholarship of value up to £3,500 pa. (*e*) One Bostock Wheeler Scholarship for a pupil whose father is deceased.

Candidates for the above scholarships must be under 14 years of age on 1st September.

Scholarships may also be awarded to pupils entering the school at VIth Form level, on the basis of an examination set at Dover in the Lent Term.

One or more Music Scholarships each year, Choral or Instrumental, up to £3,500. Free musical education.

One or more Art Awards ranging in value up to £3,500 pa.

Bursaries are awarded for children of schoolmasters clergyman and members of the Princess of Wales Royal Regiment.

Further Bursaries can be awarded to all Scholarship and Exhibition holders on a basis of need. Sixth Form Scholarships are offered on the results of GCSE examinations.

Further details may be obtained on application to the *Headmaster, Dover College, Dover, Kent CT17 9RH.*

Embley Park School (see p 787). Scholarships are available to both internal and external candidates. An examination takes place in early February.

Scholarships of up to 50% of the fees in value may be awarded for Academic, Musical, Artistic, Dramatic and All-Round ability. Bursaries and Exhibitions of lesser value may also be awarded.

St. Probus Bursaries assist Weekly Boarders from the Salisbury area.

Sixth Form Scholarships are awarded on the basis of GCSE and all-round contribution (actual and potential) to internal and external candidates. These may all be worth up to 50% of the fee. A number of scholarships are reserved for girls.

One Sixth Form Organ Scholarship is offered jointly with Romsey Abbey; details on application.

Friends' School, Saffron Waldon (see p 789). Scholarships are available to both internal and external candidates.

Academic awards of up to 50% of the day fee are made in Years 7 and 9. In addition, there are minor awards made for Art, Music and Sport.

Sixth Form Scholarships are offered for a combination of academic success and potential contribution to the school in Art, Music, Sport and Community Service.

Further details are available from the Head.

Fulneck School, West Yorkshire (see p 790). Scholarships are available to both internal and external candidates.

Juniors: Up to 4 scholarships may be offered annually at 7+ to cover the four years in the Junior School.

A scholarship is worth 20% of each year's tuition fees. It is awarded for all-round achievement i.e. academic success in the Entrance Examination and specialist skills revealed on report and interview.

Seniors: Up to 4 academic scholarships may be awarded annually, based on the results of the Entrance Examination at 11+. Normally the scholarship covers the student's whole Senior School career, but a review will be made after GCSE before the scholarship continues into the Sixth Form.

A scholarship is worth 25% of each year's tuition fees.

Sixth Form: Up to 5 academic scholarships may be awarded annually, based on achievement at GCSE.

Each scholarship is equivalent to £300 per term for the duration of the sixth form course.

Grenville College (see p 792). Entrance Scholarships are offered annually on the basis of the results of the Common Entrance examinations held each June.

A maximum of ten Scholarship awards can be made each year: an exceptional candidate can receive an exceptional award, while no Scholarship award will be of less value than one quarter of the annual fees. Musical ability can produce an award.

Applications should be made to the Headmaster by 1st April preceding the June Common Entrance examinations, and the candidates must be under 14 on the 1st September following the examinations.

Halliford School (see p 793). There is a Governors foundation scholarship of 100% of fees for the duration of a student's stay at the School awarded annually. This could be awarded to one pupil or split two ways according to the quality of candidates and their performance in the Entrance Test.

There are Sixth form Bursaries, details of which are published annually to parents.

At the end of the third year two Bursaries worth £40 per term are awarded to students who have made outstanding progress. One of these is awarded for outstanding ability in Art, Music or Drama.

Langley School (see p 797). A total of 17 Entrance Scholarships may be awarded annually. The assessment takes place in the Spring Term.

Competitive academic scholarships are awarded at 11+, 12+, 13+ and at 6th Form entry.

Two scholarships may be awarded in each of Music, Sport, Art and Design/Technology.

Further details and a Scholarships brochure may be obtained from the *Headmaster*.

Milton Abbey School (see p 805). Up to eight Open Scholarships – Academic (held in May) and Music (held in February) up to 50% of the fees. Art (held in February), Sailing or Sport up to 25% of the fees. Candidates must be under 14 on 1 September. Two scholarships awarded at Sixth Form entry level. Full particulars from the Headmaster's office.

Oswestry School (see p 807). The Governors offer many scholarships a year, each of which remits up to 50% of the tuition fees at 9, 11, 13 and Sixth Form.

Full details of Scholarships, including copies of past papers, are available from the *Headmaster.*

Rishworth School (see p 811). There are 2 Scholarships per year which pay all tuition fees for the time a pupil is at the School. They are awarded on the results of the Entrance Examination in February.

There are up to 2 Scholarships per year which pay two thirds of tuition fees for the time a pupil is in the sixth form. These are awarded to pupils joining the sixth form from outside the school and depend on GCSE results.

There are up to 3 Bursaries available to help able pupils stay on in the sixth form. There is a possibility of a complete Scholarship to pay tuition and boarding fees for a boy who has lived in the Halifax area for some years.

Details of all the above can be obtained from *The Headmaster's Secretary,* Rishworth School, Rishworth, West Yorkshire, HX6 4QA Telephone (01422) 822217

The Royal Wolverhampton School (see p 815).

Scholarships and Bursaries

Academic: A minimum of eight Merit scholarships are available each year to pupils entering Senior School at age 11. Pupils, gaining the best grades in the School's entrance examination, will be awarded such scholarships.

Music: A certain number of Music scholarships are available to pupils entering Senior School at age 11 or 13. Such scholarships are awarded following an examination organised by the Director of Music. The audition consists of two contrasting pieces on the pupil's chosen instrument plus aural, listening and theory tests. Future musical potential is also assessed. The amount of the award is normally 25% of school fees + tuition in one instrument.

Sixth Form: Academic scholarships at Sixth form level are normally awarded on the basis of GCSE grades. The amount of the award depends upon the academic ability of the pupil concerned, but it can be as high as 100% of tuition fees.

In addition, two scholarships are available for Mathematics and one for Sport or Music each year.

Orphan Foundation: Orphan Foundation Scholarships are available to children who have lost one or both parents, whose father or mother is incapacitated through illness or who are from single or divorced families. A need for a boarding education normally has to be established. Foundation Scholarship entry forms are available from the Clerk to the Governors.

Ruthin School (see p 818). Academic Scholarships are offered for entry at 11, 13 and 16 and are worth up to half-fees. Sixth Form scholarships are awarded on GCSE grades and subject papers taken during the year prior to entry. Auditions for the Royal Liverpool Philharmonic Orchestra Scholarship (open to external candidates aged between 11 and 13) take place in the February of the year of entry. Sports, Art and Design Technology Scholarships are also available. Further information may be obtained from the Headmaster, Ruthin School, Ruthin, Denbighshire LL15 1EE (Telephone: 01824 702543).

St Bede's School (see p 819). A generous number of scholarships and bursaries are awarded each year. They are mainly awarded both to boys and girls entering the School in Year 9 and to those entering at Sixth Form level (Year 12). However suitable candidates at any stage will be considered. Candidates for a scholarship in Year 9 should be over 12½ years and under 14 years on 1 September of the year in which they sit the Scholarship Examination. This examination is suitable for boys and girls from any educational background.

Scholarships and bursaries are awarded to those showing outstanding potential in the following categories: Academic Work, Art, Drama, Sport and Music (there are additional special scholarships for players of brass instruments). In addition a number of all-rounder awards are made each year to boys and girls who are above average academically or particularly strong in individual subjects and, in addition, show real potential in Art or Music, or Drama, or Sport, or in any combination of these spheres of activity.

Scholarship auditions for music and drama, sports trials, examinations and interviews take place at the School in late January and early February each year. In addition, scholarships and bursaries can be awarded on the basis of performance in the June Common Entrance Examination. Interview and recommendation from the Head of a boy's or girl's present school play an important part in deciding to whom awards should be made. Further details regarding the procedure for entry are available from the Headmaster's Secretary.

Scarborough College (see p 829). A number of Scholarships and (means-tested) Exhibitions, up to the value of 50% of the fees, are offered each year for entry at 11, 13 and 16. Outstanding candidates are invited to the College for written papers and interview. Exceptional ability in Music and Art at 11 will be considered. Details available from the Headmaster.

Seaford College (see p 830). Academic, Choral Music, Instrumental Music, Art and Games scholarships may be awarded to boys entering the senior school at thirteen plus. Choral scholarships may be awarded to boys entering Wilberforce House at eleven or twelve plus. These scholarships range from one tenth of the fees upwards and, in the case of instrumental music, free lessons may be included. Boys competing for these awards spend two days at the College in late February.

Special consideration will be given to boys entering from maintained schools who have not studied the Common entrance syllabus.

There is a Bursary of three tenths of the fees available to the sons of the Clergy both at fourth form and sixth form level.

Bursaries are available to boys whose parents are in the Forces.

For further information please apply to the *Registrar, Seaford College, Petworth, Sussex.*

Shebbear College, North Devon (see p 831). Scholarships up to the value of half fees are awarded as follows:
1. For the Junior Department: on interview and written assessment.
2. At 11+: All candidates take the Entrance and Scholarship Examination in February.
3. At 13+: The Scholarship Examination is held in the Spring Term. Awards are also made following Common Entrance Examination results.
4. For Sixth Form candidates, scholarships are awarded on the basis of interview, school report and GCSE performance.

Further details may be obtained from the *Headmaster's Secretary.*

Sidcot School (see p 834). There are several entrance scholarships available at age 13, of up to 50% of the boarding fees, awarded by competitive examination. Ten sixth form scholarships of 20% of the fees are awarded on the basis of GCSE results.

Sunderland High School (see p 837). Entrance Scholarships are available at 11 plus. These are awarded on academic ability and are approximately 1/3 fees. Scholarships are also available to students wishing to join the School at 16 plus.These are awarded according to academic ability (interview and test).

A Music Scholarship is offered of approximately 1/3 fees to pupils on entry to the School at age 11.

A reduction in fees is available to children of Clergy families and awarded by the Church Schools Company.

Thetford Grammar School (see p 838). Up to six scholarships, usually worth one-third of the annual fee, are awarded at the January entry to 11+ entrants to the school, with two external scholarships for Sixth Form entry. A number of internal awards providing fee-remission at Sixth Form level are made on the strength of good performance in the GCSE examination.

A Music Scholarship to the value of one-third fees is awarded to a Main School entrant at 11, 12 or 13. Details from the Director of Music.

Additionally, a number of Governors' Bursaries, each normally to the value of one-third of the annual fee, is awarded to pre-Sixth Form Main School entrants at the Headmaster's discretion.

Details of all awards may be had from the Headmaster.

PART IV

Schools whose Heads are members of the Choir Schools' Association

The Choir Schools' Association

Officers and Committee 2001–2002

Chairman: R I White, Polwhele House School, Truro, TR4 9AE
Administrator: Wendy Jackson, The Minster School, Deangate, York YO1 2JA. Tel: (01904) 624900
Treasurer: R J Shephard, The Minster School, Deangate, York YO1 2JA
Information Officer: Jane Capon, Windrush, Church Road, Market Weston, Diss, Norfolk IP22 2NX. Tel: (01359) 221333
Committee: R Bacon, St Edmunds Junior School, Canterbury; S Drew, Durham Chorister School; C Foulds, Westminster Cathedral Choir School; K L Jones, St John's College School, Cambridge; P Lacey, King's School, Gloucester; B Rees, Pilgrims' School, Winchester; K Riley, Bristol Cathedral School; H Tomlinson, Hereford Cathedral School; J Waszek, St Edward's College, Liverpool.

The Association was founded by Rev R H Couchman in 1918 when he was a Minor Canon of St Paul's Cathedral and Headmaster of the Choir School. Its prime purpose is to promote choir schools by all possible means. Membership is confined to Heads of choir schools.

CSA represents 37 schools, attached to Cathedrals, Churches and College Chapels, educating 1,000 choristers amongst their 15,000 pupils. The first English cathedral choir for girls was set up in 1991 at Salisbury. Exeter and York now have separate girls' choirs — all these girls are educated in the choir school. St Mary's, Edinburgh and Chetham's School, Manchester, have mixed choirs.

There are generous subsidies for choristers — for some there is no charge at all and on average parents can expect to pay less than half fees.

Further Information: The Association publishes a free leaflet listing member schools and details of voice trials, obtainable from the Administrator at the above address.

Bristol, Cathedral School, BS1 5TS. Tel: (0117) 9291872. Independent, day. 480 pupils, boys only 11–16, co-educational sixth form. Entrance examination at 10 or 11 before voice trials in February.

Cambridge, King's College School, CB3 9DN. Tel: (01223) 365814. Preparatory. 270 boys and girls, aged 4–13. Voice trials are once or twice a year, age 7½ to under 10. See Part V.

Cambridge, St John's College School, CB3 9AB. Tel: (01223) 353532. Preparatory. 428 boys and girls, aged 4–13. Voice trials are in October, age under 10. See Part V.

Canterbury, St Edmund's Junior School, CT2 8HU. Tel: (01227) 475600. Preparatory, day and boarding with 220 boys and girls, aged 4–13. Voice trials are in November, age 7–9. See Part I and V.

Cardiff, St John's College, CF3 8QR. Tel: (029) 2077 8936. R.C. Independent day. 373 boys and girls, aged 3–16. Voice trials are in the Autumn, age 7–10.

Chichester, The Prebendal School, PO19 1RT. Tel: (01243) 782026. Preparatory, day and boarding. 196 boys and girls, aged 7–13. Entrance assessment test and voice trials once or twice a year, age 7–9½. See Part V.

Durham, The Chorister School, The College, DH1 3EL. Tel: (0191) 384 2935. Preparatory, day and boarding. 170 boys only, aged 4–13. Voice trials and qualifying test in English twice a year, age 7–9. See Part V.

Edinburgh, St Mary's Music School, EH3 7EB. Tel: (0131) 538 7766. Independent specialist music school. 53 boys and girls, aged 7–18. Voice trials (including girls) by appointment, age 7–10.

Ely, Kings School Junior School, CB7 4DB. Tel: (01353) 660730. Preparatory, day and boarding. 274 boys and girls aged 9–13. Voice trials are in November prior to entry; preferred age 8½/9. See Parts I and V.

Exeter, Cathedral School, EX1 1HX. Tel: (01392) 255298. Preparatory and pre-preparatory, day and boarding. 138 boys and girls. Voice trials (including girls) are in February, age 7½–9½. See Part V.

Gloucester, The King's School, GL1 2BG. Tel: (01452) 337337. Independent, day and boarding. 500 boys and girls aged 4–18. Voice trials during last week in February and May, age 7½–9. See Part I.

Grimsby, St James' School, DN34 4SY. Tel: (01472) 503260. Independent, day and boarding. 246 boys and girls, aged 3–18. Voice trials by appointment, age 7–9. See Part VI.

Guildford, Lanesborough School, GU1 2EL. Tel: (01483) 880650. Preparatory, day. Boys only aged 3–13. Choristers selected from within the school or by external application with voice trial, as arranged with Headmaster and/or organist, age 7–9. See Part V.

Hereford, Cathedral School, HR1 2NN. Tel: (01432) 363522. Independent, day and boarding, boys and girls. Senior school 594; junior school 250. Voice trials are in March and November, age 8–10. See Part I.

Lichfield, Cathedral School, WS13 7LH. Tel: (01543) 306170. Preparatory, day and boarding. 192 boys and girls. Entrance by voice trials, instrumental music and verbal reasoning, and interview, age 7–9.

Lincoln Minster School, LN2 1QE. Tel: (01522) 543764. Preparatory, day and boarding. 96 boys and girls, aged 2–13. Entrance is by an academic test. Voice trials are in January and sometimes also in June, age 7½–9½. See Part V.

Llandaff, The Cathedral School, CF5 2YH. Tel: (029) 2056 3179. Preparatory, day and boarding. 289 boys and girls. Voice trials are in January, age 8. See Part V.

London, St Paul's Cathedral School, EC4M 9AD. Tel: 020-7248 5156. Preparatory, day. Boarding for Choristers only. 105 boys, aged 7–13. Voice trials held three times a year, age 7–9½. See Part V.

London, Westminster Abbey Choir School, Dean's Yard, SW1P 3NY. Tel: 020-7222 6151. Preparatory, 36 chorister boy boarders. Voice trials are held three times a year, age 7½–9. See Part V.

London, Westminster Cathedral Choir School, Ambrosden Avenue, SW1P 1HQ. Tel: 020-7798 9081. Roman Catholic. Preparatory, day. Boarding for Choristers only, otherwise day. 93 boys, aged 8–13. Voice trials termly for boys aged up to 9, or individually as necessary. See Part V.

Manchester, Chetham's School of Music, M3 1SB. Tel: 0161-834 9644. Independent, day and boarding. Specialist Music School. Founded in 1653. 270 boys and girls aged 8 to 18. Choristerships at Manchester Cathedral are admitted through auditions arranged by the Cathedral Choirmaster. See Part I.

Norwich, Norwich School, The Close, NR1 4DQ. Tel: (01603) 623194. Independent. 168 boys aged 8–11; 578 boys aged 12–18. Choristers admitted at 8 & 9, occasionally 10. See Part I.

Oxford, Christ Church Cathedral School, Brewer Street. Tel: (01865) 242561. Preparatory. 133 boys, aged 4–13. Voice trial and academic assessment up to 3 times each year, age 7–8½. See Part V.

Oxford, Magdalen College School, OX4 1DZ. Tel: (01865) 242191. Independent, age 9–18, with 16 choristers (some boarding, some day), 10 non-chorister boarders, and 480 day boys. Voice trials are held twice a year, age 8–9. See Part I.

Oxford, New College School, OX1 3UA. Tel: (01865) 243657. Preparatory, day. 137 boys, aged 7–13. Annual voice trial in February, individuals at other times by arrangement, age 7–9. See Part V.

Ripon, The Cathedral Choir School. Tel: (01765) 602134. Preparatory, day and boarding. 112 boys and girls, aged 4–13, including 18 chorister boarders. Voice trials are in February, other times by arrangement, age 7½–9. See Part V.

Rochester, King's School, ME1 1TE. Tel: (01634) 843657. Independent. 661 boys and girls, aged 4–19. Chorister scholarships are awarded on the basis of voice trials held in February, age 8–9, together with satisfactory performance in prep school entrance exam. See Part I and V.

Salisbury, Cathedral School, SP1 2EQ. Tel: (01722) 555300. Preparatory, day and boarding, 301 boys and girls, aged 3–13. Voice trials are held for boys and girls, usually in January & February, age 7–9. Vocal, instrumental, and academic assessments take place on the same day. See Part V.

Southwell, The Minster School, NG25 0HG. Tel: (01636) 814000. Voluntary Aided C of E. Comprehensive, day and boarding. 1494 boys and girls. Voice trials are in March, age 8½–10, and at other times by arrangement.

Tewkesbury, The Abbey School, GL20 5PD. Tel: (01684) 294460. Preparatory. 98 boys and girls aged 3–13. Choristers are admitted from the age of 8 at voice trials. Choristers are not required to sing in holidays or at weekends. See Part V.

Truro, Polwhele House, TR4 9AE. Tel: (01872) 273011. Preparatory, day and boarding. 155 boys and girls, aged 3–13. Voice trials and entrance tests are held in January, age 7, 8 or 9. See Part VI.

Wakefield, Queen Elizabeth Grammar School, WF1 3QY. Tel: (01924) 373821. Independent, day. 233 boys aged 7–10 in the Junior School and 740 aged 11–18 in the Senior. School exam followed by voice trial in February, age 7–10. See Parts I and V.

Wells, Cathedral School, BA5 2ST. Tel: (01749) 672117. Independent, day and boarding. 802 boys and girls, aged 4–18. Voice trials held in January, age 8–10½. See Part I.

Winchester, The Pilgrims' School, SO23 9LT. Tel: (01962) 854189. Boy's preparatory school, day and boarding. 184 pupils aged 8–13. Choristers and Quiristers are selected at voice trials held in November, age 7½–10, and join as choral scholars the following September. See Part V.

Windsor, St George's School, SL4 1QF. Tel: (01753) 865553. Preparatory, day and boarding. Boys only aged 7–13 years. Choristers are admitted between the ages of 7 and 10 and must board, but probationers may be weekly boarders. Voice trials and academic test in October and November. See Part V.

Worcester, The King's School, WR1 2LH. Tel: (01905) 721700. Independent, day and boarding. 924 boys and girls aged 7–18. Voice trials and academic tests held in December, age 7–9. Scholarships in excess of half fees. See Part I.

York Minster School, YO1 2JA. Tel: (01904) 557230. Preparatory. 140 boys and girls, aged 4–13 years. Voice trials held in November, age 7–9. See Part V.

Associate Members

Chelmsford, St Cedd's School, CM1 2PB. Tel: (01245) 354380. Independent day. 330 boys and girls, aged 4 to 11. Details of choristerships at Chelmsford Cathedral. See Part V.

Liverpool, St Edward's College, L12 1LF. Tel: 0151-281 1999. Roman Catholic, Grant-maintained day. 1013 boys and girls, aged 4–18. Voice trials are in February or March, age 7–9.

Peterborough, The King's School, PE1 2UE. Tel: (01733) 751541. Grant Maintained Comprehensive. 838 boys and girls, aged 11–18. Entrance by voice trial and interview, except for choral scholars who must have at least 5 Grade C GCSE's. Junior probationer choristers voice trial at age 7; others at age 10; choral scholars 15.

Portsmouth, The Portsmouth Grammer School, High Street, Portsmouth PO1 2LN. Tel: (023) 9281 9125. Independent day. 567 boys 11–18. 242 girls 11–18. Please telephone for chorister details.

Reigate, St Mary's Preparatory and Choir School, RH2 7RN. Tel: (01737) 244880. Preparatory, day. 223 boys. Voice trials by appointment, age 8–10. See Part V.

Warwick, Warwick School, CV34 6PP. Tel: (01926) 776400. Independent, day and boarding. 800 boys aged 11 to 19 in the Main School, and 200 boys aged 7 to 11 in the Junior School. Choral Scholarships are available from the age of 7. See Part I.

York, Ampleforth College, York, North Yorkshire YO6 4ER. Tel: (01439) 766000. Independent Boys' boarding and day. 526 boys 13 to 18. Voice trials: Please telephone for details.

Overseas Members

Australia. *St Andrew's Cathedral Choir School,* Sydney. Tel: 267-6491. *Anglican Church Grammar School,* East Brisbane, Queensland.

New Zealand. *The Cathedral Grammar School,* Christchurch 8001. Tel: (03) 3650385. Independent primary day school; junior school up to 7 years; preparatory school 8–13 years. 24 choristers. Auditions arranged by contacting the Headmaster. Entry to the choir between 7½ and 10.

The Netherlands. *Koorschool van het,* Muziekinstituut van de Kathedraal St Bavo, Westergracht 61, 2013 ZL Haarlem.

U.S.A. *National Cathedral School,* Mount St Alban, Washington DC, 20016.

PART V

Schools appearing in Part V are those whose Heads are members of the Incorporated Association of Preparatory Schools

Abberley Hall

Worcester WR6 6DD.
Tel: (01299) 896275
Fax: (01299) 896875

Chairman of Governors: R M Swire, Esq

Headmaster: **J G W Walker**, BSc (QTS) (University of Surrey)

Assistant Headmasters:
D J H Birt, MA (Cantab), DipEd (London)
A K A Jackson, BA (Newcastle), DipEd (Cantab)

Number of Pupils. Boarders. 125. Day Pupils 55. Pre-Prep (ages 2+–7) 75 Boys and Girls

Fees. Boarders £3,690 per term; Day Boys £2,890 per term. Pre-Prep School £675–£1,480 per term

Abberley Hall is co-educational. It is situated 12 miles north-west of Worcester, with easy access to the M5. It is a boarding school for boys and girls aged 8–13 years, and is set in 100 acres of gardens and wooded grounds amid magnificent countryside.

Pupils are prepared for all Independent Senior Schools. Although there is no entry examination, the school has a strong academic tradition with consistently good results in scholarships and Common Entrance, thanks to a highly-qualified staff, favourable teacher/pupil ratios and small classes. This also helps encourage the slower learners, for whom individual attention is available.

The school's facilities include: a new indoor swimming pool, a chapel, library, music school and concert studio; two science laboratories, technology room, DT centre and extensively equipped computer centre; an art studio and pottery rooms; a multi-purpose hall with permanent stage, rifle range and climbing wall; a sports hall, hard tennis courts, a Ricochet court and ample playing fields for the major games and athletics, including a large Astroturf pitch.

The pupils are also encouraged to take part in a wide range of hobbies and activities including archery, basket-making, calligraphy, chess, fishing, golf, horse riding, judo, model-making, printing, ballet, mountain-biking and wood-work.

The school aims to combine a friendly atmosphere with the discipline which enables pupils to achieve their full potential and learn to feel responsibility for themselves and others.

Charitable status. Abberley Hall is a Registered Charity, number 527598. Its aim is to further good education.

The Abbey

Woodbridge Suffolk IP12 1DS.
Tel: (01394) 382673
Fax: (01394) 383880
e-mail: theabbey@mail.rmplc.co.uk
website: www.theabbeyschool-suffolk.org.uk

The Master: **N J Garrett**, BA, PGCE

Chairman of the Governors: Air Vice-Marshal P J Goddard

Co-educational. 4–11. Day: 295 pupils

Fees per term. Pre-Prep: £1,442. Prep £2,182.

Religious affiliation. Church of England (other denominations accepted)

Entry requirements. Entrance test according to age or assessment interview for pre-prep department

The Abbey is the Preparatory School for Woodbridge School for which boys and girls are prepared for entry. A small number of pupils go elsewhere. There is a highly qualified teaching staff of twenty-five, with additional visiting music and other specialist teachers. The academic record has been consistently good: scholarships are won regularly both to Woodbridge and to other schools. The teaching is linked to the National Curriculum and emphasis is placed on pupils reaching their full academic potential whilst also benefiting from a broad education. The school enjoys strong links with a number of European schools and exchange visits take place. Music is regarded as an important part of school life with a large number of pupils receiving individual music lessons and in Year Four all pupils receive strings tuition as well as their class music lessons. In Games lessons boys play soccer, rugby, hockey and cricket and girls play netball, hockey and rounders. Children also have the opportunity to swim, play tennis and take part in athletics, cross-country and sailing. In lunch breaks and after school, pupils are able to participate in a whole range of extra-curricular activities and hobbies.

The School is set in its own beautiful grounds of 30 acres in the middle of the town. Apart from the fine Tudor Manor house, it has an unusually well-planned and high quality classroom and changing room block. Another major development includes a multi-purpose hall and classroom block. In 2001 the music facilities will be upgraded when the department moves into a new music school. The grounds are extensive and include playing fields, an all weather surface games area and a science garden. The Pre-Prep Department of The Abbey was moved in January 1993, to new adapted premises at Queen's House. Here the pupils enjoy spacious teaching accommodation and facilities commensurate with their age range. In the summer of 1999 a new School Hall was built which is used for assemblies, PE lessons and concerts. There is a Head of the Pre-Prep Department but the teaching programme is under the supervision of the Master of The Abbey. Parents of Abbey pupils are eligible to join the Woodbridge School Association and there is a close contact maintained between parents and school.

Charitable status. The Seckford Foundation, of which The Abbey is a part, is a Registered Charity, number 214209. It exists to provide education for boys and girls.

The Abbey School

Tewkesbury Gloucestershire GL20 5PD.
Tel: (01684) 294460
Fax: (01684) 290797
e-mail: hm@theabbeysch.org.uk
Station: Gloucester, Cheltenham or Ashchurch for Tewkesbury
Coach Station: Cheltenham

Chairman of Governors: M Amherst, MA

***Headmaster:* J H Milton**, BEd

Number of Pupils. 8 weekly boarding boys, 102 day boys and girls

Fees. Day boys and girls £1,775–£2,165, Weekly boarding £2,615–£3,005, Pre-Prep: £360–£1,415.

The school was founded in 1973 as the choir school for Tewkesbury Abbey; the majority of pupils however are not choristers. The school is set in the shadow of the magnificent Norman abbey in the heart of Tewkesbury.

An experienced, well qualified staff working with small classes ensure that individual attention is given to each child's needs. All pupils are encouraged to work independently and a high standard is maintained to Common Entrance and Senior Independent School Scholarship level.

The school, which occupies five historic buildings in Church Street, is well equipped for the broad spread of the modern curriculum between the ages of three to thirteen. The Pre-Preparatory and Nursery Department is self contained and caters for pupils up to the age of seven. During their last year in the department the children use the main school science laboratory, art studio and sports facilities.

The arts are strongly encouraged and attention is given to potential art and music scholars to broaden their interest and develop particular talents. Children may learn the piano, organ, recorder and any orchestral instrument. There are numerous musical ensembles, and regular recitals, both formal and informal, take place each term. Many scholarships have been won in recent years to a wide range of independent senior schools. Drama plays an important part in the life of the school.

Sport too is actively encouraged and all pupils have an opportunity to represent the school at an appropriate level. There is a thriving outdoor pursuits club which allows opportunities for water sports, climbing, survival skills, camping and many other activities for those who are keen to take part.

The choristers sing Choral Evensong on weekdays during term time to cathedral standard and take part in regular foreign concert tours. One of the particular benefits of a choristership at Tewkesbury is that there are few weekend or holiday commitments. Boys are therefore able to combine the opportunity of being a chorister with the security of a normal family life. Choristerships attract a reduction in fees and are offered to musical boys at voice trials which are held regularly. The school is a member of the Choir Schools' Association.

The boarding house, which is next door to the main school, is happy and informal. Generally boys go home on Fridays and return on Sunday evenings. Transport can be provided to and from the coach and railway stations in Cheltenham.

Aberdour School

Burgh Heath Nr Tadworth Surrey KT20 6AJ.
Tel: (01737) 354119.

Chairman of the Governors: R C Nicol, Esq, FCA

***Headmaster:* A Barraclough**, CertEd

Deputy Headmaster: R G Moss, BA, PGCE

Head of the Pre-Preparatory School: Mrs C Moss, MA, CertEd

Number of Pupils. 360 Day Boys and Girls

Fees. £800–£2,150 fully inclusive

The School is an Educational Trust run by a Board of Governors. Children are taken at 3 years old into the pre-preparatory department and transfer to the preparatory school at age 7. Children are prepared for all the major Senior Schools and many scholarships have been won, over 90 in the last 8 years. A special point is made of music. There is a school orchestra and a concert band as well as a large school choir. There are ample playing fields with a large sports hall and covered swimming pool. A block comprising two science laboratories and a technology room was opened in the 1990s. All the usual games are coached and the general character of the children is developed by many interests and activities.

Charitable status. Aberdour School Educational Trust Limited is a Registered Charity, number 312033. Its aim is to promote education.

Aberlour House

Aberlour Banffshire AB38 9LJ.
Tel: (01340) 871267
Fax: (01340) 872925
e-mail: admissions@aberlourhouse.org.uk
website: www.aberlourhouse.org.uk

***Headmaster:* N W Gardner**, BA, CertEd (Dunelm)

Chairman of the Board: Professor B P Williams

Number of Pupils. 43 Boys, 42 Girls, 66 Boarders, 19 Day Children.

Fees. From September 2001: Boarding £4,064 per term; Day £2,835 per term.

Aberlour House occupies a fine late Georgian house, surrounded by over 60 acres of wood and parkland, in a dry and sunny part of Scotland. Its enviable setting on the banks of the River Spey, between the Cairngorms and the Moray Firth, provides a unique opportunity for personal development, academic and sporting achievement and personal fulfilment. Boys and girls are admitted from the age of 7+ following an interview with the Head or, in the case of families living abroad, receipt of a full school report.

Whilst operating as a preparatory boarding school in its own right, Aberlour House enjoys close links with Gordonstoun (20 miles), whose foundation and philosophy it shares – likewise its school motto, *plus est en vous* – "there is more in you than you think". Each year, however, a number of children progress to other independent senior schools of their parents' choice, dispersed throughout the United Kingdom.

The school ethos is founded on friendliness, trust, responsibility and service to others. Developing good self-esteem and valuing others are essential components in the life of the community.

A broad and balanced formal curriculum is followed. Spanish is available as an option in the final two years. A small, but effective, Learning Support department helps children with a range of learning difficulties. The visual and performing arts are strong.

Outdoor education is a strength both in team games and individual sports and activities. The school's Highland setting lends itself ideally to the pursuit of hill walking, mountain biking, riding (from our own stables), skiing, kayaking and snorkelling. Annual expeditions enable children to learn more of their environment, their peers and themselves in a physical context designed to challenge body, mind and spirit.

The Whole Curriculum is based on the residential experience offered to pupils. Day boys and girls are welcome, but the great majority are boarders. Except for Half Terms in the summer and autumn, a full programme is available to the children every weekend. Those living within easy travelling distance of the school may, however, choose to go home most Saturday nights. A number of pupils come from overseas and take advantage of the frequent flights to Aberdeen or Inverness from each of the London airports, as well as directly from Amsterdam.

Entrance scholarships and bursaries are available each year following examination and interviews held in February at the school. The fees are comprehensive, the only significant extras being individual music tuition, riding, skiing, karate, judo and learning support.

Al Ain English Speaking School

P O Box 1419 Al Ain Abu Dhabi United Arab Emirates
Tel: 010 971 3 678636
Fax: 010 971 3 671973

Principal: **James G Crawford**, BSc (Hons), DipEd, PGCE

Day School located in the Emirate of Abu Dhabi on the border with the Sultanate of Oman.

Number of Pupils. 89 girls and 119 boys aged 4–12+, with a Nursery Class for children 3–4 years.

Fees. 13,320–15,750 UAE Dirhams per year (£1 = c 5.6 Dirhams).

The Al Ain English Speaking School was established in 1978 by 7 local companies to provide an appropriate standard of education for the children of their expatriate employees (40% British, 20% US, 20% Sub-continent and 17 other nationalities). The staff comprises of 12 class teachers (all UK trained), 3 Arabic, 1 French specialist language teacher.

Due attention is paid to the requirements of the English National Curriculum and the children are prepared academically towards the standard of the British Common Entrance Examinations at 11+ and 12+.

Drama, music and physical education occupy secure positions in the curriculum and there are many extra-curricular activities and excursions into the local environment.

The School is licenced by the Ministry of Education, UAE, and, according to its directive, a programme of Arabic language, Arabic Social Studies, and Islamic Studies (for Muslim children) is conducted.

In recent years children from the School have continued their further education at Roedean, Gordonstoun, Woldingham, Dollar Academy and Repton.

Aldro

Shackleford Nr Godalming Surrey GU8 6AS.
Tel: (01483) 810266
Fax: (01483) 409010

Chairman of the Governors: D G Ives, MA

Headmaster: **David W N Aston**, BA, PGCE

Number of Boys. 220 (92 Boarders, 128 Day)

Fees. £4,050 (Boarders), £3,135 (Day) per term inclusive.

Aldro is a boarding school for boys between 7 and 13 years, standing in its own grounds of 25 acres, a setting of rare beauty in the village of Shackleford. It is within a mile of the A3 and 45 minutes from the centre of London. We are very willing to assist those living abroad to and from Heathrow and Gatwick.

The School aims to give boys every opportunity to live life to the full in healthy surroundings, being helped towards the development of Christian character by a happy family atmosphere. The Headmaster's wife takes a keen interest in all aspects of the boys' welfare.

Firm and friendly encouragement of each individual has led to an outstanding academic record with good Common Entrance results and approximately half the leavers sitting for scholarships in the last three years; almost one-third of those leaving obtaining awards to major senior independent schools.

The lovely Chapel is converted from a well-preserved barn. A new Centenary building including a library and new classrooms was completed in the summer of 1999, releasing space for additional boarders' common rooms and considerably enhancing the school without increasing the numbers. The Crispin Hill Centre incorporates a theatre, music school and sports hall. There are two science laboratories, an Art, Design and Technology Centre, an Information Technology Centre, an outdoor heated swimming pool, 5 hard tennis courts (one covered), a squash court, a rifle range, a pistol range and a covered games area as well as a lake on which boys enjoy rowing, canoeing, sailing and fishing for trout and perch.

Association and Rugby football, hockey, cricket and shooting (.22 and pistol) are the main sporting activities, but a very high standard is also achieved in squash, tennis, swimming, cross country and athletics. There is an opportunity to ride. Each boy may have a garden and build camps in the surrounding woodland.

Aldro has a Senior and Junior orchestra, jazz band and three choirs. About two-thirds of the boys have individual music lessons on a variety of instruments. There are major concerts and dramatic productions each term. The leavers write and produce their own plays in French. All boys do activities which afford additional opportunity for judo, badminton, basketball, Information and Design Technology, photography, chess (Under 13 National IAPS Champions for the last three years), model railway, cooking, conjuring, fly-tying, fishing and a bottle club. There is also a Cub pack.

Characters and abilities are unfolded, not moulded. Interests are ignited in and out of class. Boys go on to do well.

Charitable status. Aldro is a Registered Charity, number 312072. It exists to provide education for boys.

Aldwickbury School

Wheathampstead Road Harpenden Herts AL5 1AE.
Tel: (01582) 713022.
Fax: (01582) 767696
e-mail: head@aldwickbury.herts.sch.uk
Station: Harpenden (Thameslink line)

Chairman of Governors: M StJ Hopper, Esq

Headmaster: **P H Jeffery**, BA (Reading University)

Number of Boys. 220 (including 30 weekly boarders)
Fees. Boarders £2,435–£2,570 per term. Day Boys £1,720–£1,990 per term.

Boys are received at 7 plus and prepared for Independent Schools' Entrance and Scholarship examinations at 13 plus.

There is a full-time teaching staff of 16, with qualified visiting teachers for remedial work, speech training, singing, woodwork, piano, and orchestral instruments. Science, art, music, drama, IT and CDT are included in the curriculum.

Most boys board in their final years and they are all encouraged to take part in a wide variety of activities throughout their time in the school.

The School is exceptionally well equipped. Recent additions include two new classroom blocks, a block for science, computing and music, a Gymnasium, a heated indoor Swimming Pool, a Hall and Chapel and a new kitchen. The playing fields are on the spot and large enough for all boys to play games every day. Boys are taught Association and Rugby Football, Hockey, Athletics, Cricket, Swimming, Gymnastics, Tennis and Basketball. Skiing parties are taken to the Alps during the Christmas holidays.

There is also a Pre-Preparatory Department for boys and girls on site. It is accommodated in a building opened in 2001.

Charitable status. Aldwickbury School is a Registered Charity, number 311059. It exists to provide education for children.

Alice Smith Primary School

2 Jalan Bellamy 50460 Kuala Lumpur Malaysia
Tel: 00 603 2148 3674
Fax: 00 603 2148 3418

Chairman of Governors: John Smurthwaite

Principal: **S Caulfield,** BSc (Hons), MEd

Number of Pupils. 670 (Pre-School to Year 6)
Age range. 3-11
Location. The Alice Smith Primary School at Jalan Bellamy is situated in a beautiful area adjacent to the Royal Palace, just 10-15 minutes from the major residential suburbs on the west side of the capital. The Primary School offers a specialised learning environment for children between the ages of 3 to 11 years.

Facilities. The Primary School benefits from the following facilities:

- Well-resourced, air-conditioned classrooms and large shared year group learning areas
- Gymnasium
- Library and Information Centre
- Design & Technology area
- Multi-purpose Hall
- Hard and grassed playing areas
- Playground with climbing frames
- New purpose-built block to accommodate Years 5 & 6 is currently planned and will open in September 2002.

Curriculum. We offer a rigorous British education in an international context while celebrating the culture and natural environment of our hosts, the people of Malaysia. The English National Curriculum enables us to develop the essential knowledge, skills and concepts our international students need in a broad programme that encompasses English, Mathematics, Science, Design Technology, Information Technology, Modern Foreign Languages (from Year 4), History, Geography, Music, Drama and Physical Education.

Children have specialist teachers for Music, Physical Education, SEN, Foreign Languages and Swimming. All classes carry a maximum of 22 (Pre-School to Year 4) and 25 (Years 5 and 6).

The school undertakes the NCT assessments in Years 2 and 6 and the non-statutory NCT tests for Years 3, 4 and 5. Standards and expectations are high and regular In-service Training and Inspections are undertaken with UK based Inspectors/Advisory teams.

Staff. At the heart of a good school is the staff, both teaching and non-teaching. Our teaching staff are well qualified, caring and experienced professionals, recruited mainly from the UK.

All classes benefit from a full-time assistant in addition to the class teacher.

Extra-curricular programme. Our main curriculum is enhanced by a full programme of extra-curricular sporting, performance and cultural activities. Older children are regular participants in National and International expeditions, competitions and trips, while our younger students participate in frequent visits to local places of interest. A busy Saturday sports programme ensures children have recreational opportunities on many Saturdays throughout each term.

Alleyn Court Preparatory School

Wakering Road Southend-on-Sea Essex SS3 0PW
Tel: (01702) 582553
Fax: (01702) 584574

Joint Headmasters:
S Bishop, MA
W D A Wilcox, BA

Number of Pupils. 298: Boys and Girls, 2½–13.
Fees. £1,023–£1,930 according to age.

Throughout the school pupils learn to live as members of a community while developing their individual personalities in a happy and structured environment. Former pupils make an outstanding contribution to local and national life: there are two present MPs, a member of the House of Lords, a novelist of international renown, a prize-winning playwright and international representatives in all major sports.

Admission is between 2½ and 5 years to the Pre-Prep department and at 6 and 11 years to the main school (or at other ages by arrangement). Entry is by interview, there are no tests applied. Pupils are prepared for local selective school examinations at 11+ and for Common Entrance and scholarship entry to Senior independent schools at 13+. French is taught from 4 years, Latin from age 10. scholarships to major Independent Senior Schools. Results of National Curriculum Tests are consistently above the national average.

Academic facilities include: library, fully equipped

science laboratory, modern computer suite with 21 multi-media computers and internet access, art centre.

Sports facilities include: extensive playing fields, new Sports Hall (opened June 1999), cricket nets, tennis courts, cross-country course.

Other facilities include: attractive grounds, dining hall, 200 seat assembly hall.

Extra-curricular activities include: art, drama, photography, French scrabble, Collectors club, chess as well as various sports training sessions.

Academic, Artistic, Music and Sports scholarships are available annually for pupils aged between 6 and 9 years and for pupils aged 11. Some Bursaries are available according to need.

Pre-Prep. Located on a separate site in Westcliff the Pre-Prep department offers an education based on Montessori principles for boys and girls 2½–6 years old.

Alleyn's Junior School

Townley Road Dulwich London SE22 8SU
Tel: 020 8693 3457
Fax: 020 8693 3597

Chairman of Governors: R G Gray, MA

Headmistress: **Mrs B E Weir**

Number of pupils. 224 boys and girls.

Fees. £2,035–£2,115 per term to include lunches and out of school visits.

The school is part of the foundation known as 'Alleyn's College of God's Gift' which was founded by Edward Alleyn, the Elizabethan actor, in 1619.

Opened in 1992 to provide a co-educational Junior School for Alleyn's School and sharing the same excellent green site, Alleyn's Junior School provides a happy and lively environment in which well-qualified teachers and well-motivated boys and girls follow a broad and academic education. Boys and girls work together with their teachers in a calm and structured way to develop their potential and self-confidence as they pursue the highest standards across a curriculum which embraces many opportunities for drama, music, French and a wide range of sports. Entry to the school is at 4+, 7+ and 9+. The overwhelming majority of our children move on to Alleyn's senior school at 11+.

Within small classes and with a balance of class and specialist subject teaching, children are set clear and challenging targets for their learning. Children perform well in nationally audited end of Key stage tests at KS1 and KS2. The school enjoys a strong extra-curricular life offering children varied and exciting opportunities to extend their learning beyond the classroom.

Progress is carefully monitored and individual differences appropriately met. Competition has its place in the encouragement of the highest academic, artistic and sporting standards, but it is always tempered by an emphasis on values of thoughtfulness, courtesy and tolerance. All members of the school community are expected to maintain high standards in their behaviour, manners and appearance, showing pride in themselves and their school.

The school enjoys excellent support from its parent body. Regular meetings and reports keep parents informed of academic progress and pastoral matters and The Alleyn's Junior School Association works tirelessly to promote social cohesion within the school and to support the charity, sporting, dramatic and extra-curricular programmes. It also organises an After School Care scheme through which children can be supervised at school each day during term time until 6 pm. A Sports Club enables families to make use of school facilities at weekends and after school.

Charitable status. Alleyn's College of God's Gift is a Registered Charity, number 105797. Its purpose is to provide independent education for boys and girls.

All Hallows School

Cranmore Hall Shepton Mallet Somerset BA4 4SF.
Tel: (01749) 880227
Fax: (01749) 880709
e-mail: info@allhallows.somerset.sch.uk
website: www.allhallows.somerset.sch.uk
Stations: Westbury, Bath, Bristol, Gillingham, Castle Cary

Headmaster: **C J Bird**, BA (Cardiff), PGCE (Exeter)

Number of Pupils. 280. Boys: Boarding 45, Day 125. Girls: Boarding 25, Day 85

Fees. Boarding £3,435, Day £2,335 (over 7); £1,145 (under 7). There are no compulsory extras.

Set in rural surroundings in beautiful Somerset countryside, yet close to the major cities of Bath and Bristol, All Hallows pioneered Catholic boarding co-education for preparatory school age children.

Christian principles are integrated into daily life so that all Christian denominations are welcomed into the ecumenical life of this Roman Catholic foundation.

Professionally-qualified, family-orientated staff, many of whom reside in the school, provide for the academic and pastoral welfare of the children.

Distinctive opportunities, at no extra cost, exist for the academically gifted and those with learning difficulties through the Learning Support Centre and/or specialist tutors. The school has a happy and deliberate mix of boarders and day pupils. Attractive flexibility exists between boarding and day arrangements. There is a purposeful and busy extra-curricular programme which is organised by all staff and runs each evening after school and at weekends.

The school enjoys regional and national sporting success in gymnastics, hockey and athletics, as well as competitive fixtures against local opposition in all the usual team sports. Excellent facilities allow the children and staff to discover talent and develop potential, including a recently built astro-turf, sports hall, Chapel, art studio, classroom block, information technology centre and two new science laboratories.

All Hallows' fully independent status from any one particular senior school, plus adherence to the Common Entrance and prep schools' scholarship syllabus, enables parents and the Headmaster to select the most appropriate senior school to suit a particular child's needs. In the last few years we have sent pupils to over forty different schools. Scholarships are available at 8+ and 11+.

Charitable status. All Hallows is a Registered Charity, number 310281. The school is a Charitable Trust, the raison d'être of which is the integration of Christian principles with daily life.

Alpha Preparatory School

Hindes Road Harrow Middlesex HA1 1SH.
Tel: 020 8427 1471

Chairman of the Board of Governors: Mr S Sacks

***Headmaster:* P J Wylie**, BA, CertEd

Number of Pupils. 175 boys and girls (day only).

Fees. as from September 2001 per term, inclusive of lunch, with no compulsory extras: Pre-preparatory: £1,625; Main School: £1,825, per term.

The School, situated in a residential area of Harrow, was founded in 1895, and in 1950 was reorganised as a non-profit-making Educational Charity, with a Board of Governors elected by members of the Company; parents of pupils in the School are eligible for membership.

The majority of children enter at the age of 4 by interview and assessment but there can also be a few vacancies for older pupils and here entry is by interview and/or written tests, dependant upon age.

There is a full-time staff of 17 experienced and qualified masters and mistresses, with additional part-time teachers in Music (instrumental) and Speech and Drama. The main games are Football and Cricket, with cross-country, athletics, tennis and netball; extra-curricular activities include Chess, Speech and Drama, Piano, Violin and Recorder instruction.

Religious education, which is considered important, is non-sectarian in nature, but follows upon the School's Christian foundation and tradition; children of all faiths are accepted.

Outside visits to theatres, concerts and Museums form an integral part of the curriculum, and during the Lent Term, for pupils in the Middle and Senior Schools, skiing is arranged in France, Austria or Italy; occasional visits to France also take place.

Regular successes are obtained in Entrance and Scholarship examinations, with many Scholarships having been won in recent years.

The School has its own Nursery (Alphabets), and further details can be obtained from the Registration Secretary.

Charitable status. Alpha Preparatory School is a Registered Charity, number 455482. It exists to carry on the undertaking of a boys and/or girls preparatory school in Harrow in the County of Middlesex.

Amesbury

Hazel Grove Hindhead Surrey GU26 6BL
Tel: (01428) 604322.
Fax: (01428) 607715

Chairman of the Governors: A R Curl

***Headmaster:* Nigel Taylor**, MA

Number of Pupils in Main School. Boarders 10, Day pupils 200

Number of Pupils in Pre-Preparatory Department. Day 115

Fees. Boarders. £3,440 per term. Day Pupils, £2,395–£2,780 per term. Pre-Prep £1,745 per term.

Amesbury is a co-educational day school for children between the ages of 3–13, with a boarding option for those in their final years. The school was founded in in 1870 and moved to its present site in Hindhead in 1917. The main building is unique, as the only school to be designed by Sir Edwin Lutyens and stands in its own 20 acre estate in the heart of the Surrey countryside.

Classes are small guaranteeing individual attention. Study programmes currently lead to Common Entrance or senior school scholarship examinations at 11+ and 12+ (for girls only) and at 13+ (for girls and boys). Although entry is non-selective, we have a proud tradition of academic, sporting and artistic achievement. On average 25% of our children win awards to senior schools each year. The school has excellent purpose built facilities.

The catchment area covers Hindhead/Haslemere, Liphook/Petersfield, Farnham and Guildford. There are well established bus pick up services and after school care facilities.

For further information please contact the Headmaster's Secretary.

Charitable status. The school is a Registered Charity, number 312058. It exists to provide education for boys and girls. It is administered by a Board of Governors.

Ampleforth College Junior School

The Castle Gilling East York YO62 4HP.
Tel: Ampleforth (01439) 788238
Fax: (01439) 788538
Station: York (18 miles)

Governors: The Abbot in Council of Ampleforth Abbey

***Headmaster:* Fr J A Sierla**, OSB, MA (Oxon)

Number of Boys. 105 (79 Boarders, 26 Day Boys)

Fees. Boarders £3,520 per term, Day Boarders £2,741 per term, Day Boys £2,166 per term.

Ampleforth College Junior School is the Preparatory School for Ampleforth College. Under the direction of the Abbot and Benedictine Community of Ampleforth Abbey, the school provides distinctive education based on 1500 years of monastic and religious tradition.

The Junior School is located at Gilling East, 18 miles north of York, close to the North Yorkshire Moors National Park. Based in the 14th century Castle, converted into a superb country house, with spacious and secluded gardens, the Junior School has benefitted from a more than £1 million investment programme, including a new accommodation block.

Entry is entirely flexible between the ages of 8–13, and almost a third of boys come from families based overseas. Entry to Ampleforth College at 13 years of age is assured to all Junior School pupils. The majority of boys are boarders, but day boys are also welcome.

The aim of the school is to provide a new sort of upbringing for children based on a marriage of traditional Benedictine spirituality and practice with the best of Christian family life and values. This double strength is indicated clearly in the Headmastership held by Fr Jeremy Sierla, OSB.

The wisdom of the Gospel and of the Rule of St Benedict are the shaping force of this teaching and learning community. The spirit of the place can be summed up as prayer and friendship or, in more traditional terms, as love of God and love of neighbour. Among the boys, the Benedictine style of social life is summarised by the juniors showing respect for their seniors and seniors showing kindness to their juniors.

The highest academic standards are aimed for, within a broad and challenging curriculum. Each pupil's ability is taken into account. Very able children are provided for and coached for scholarships to Ampleforth College itself, while those with learning difficulties, including dyslexia, are given qualified specialist help. Each form of approximately 15 boys has an academic tutor responsible for the overall progress of the boy in personal detail. Specialist subject teaching with streaming and setting is normal for boys aged 10+.

Besides academic pursuits, there is a striking variety of sports, hobbies and activities available to all pupils, including rugby, cricket, hockey, tennis, swimming, golf, karate, model making, shooting, horse-riding, debating, fishing, etc.

Music is strong. 75% of boys learn musical instruments and perform regularly. We provide the trebles for the Ampleforth College Schola Cantorum and give them specialist tuition. We also offer Music Scholarships annually, usually in the Autumn Term.

Parents are considered part of the school community. They are welcome at any time, especially for sports fixtures, any other organised events and, of course, for prayers and Mass. Full and frequent communication between home and school is encouraged.

Facilities include a new sports hall, indoor heated swimming pool, computer room, all-weather cricket nets, and the use of an adjacent 9 hole golf course. The extensive grounds, including forest, lakes and gardens, combine a sense of space and freedom with unrivalled beauty and safety.

Although the school exists primarily to fulfil the needs of Catholic education for boys, some pupils from worshipping Christian families of other denominations are also accepted, each case being decided on its own merits.

Charitable status. Ampleforth College Junior School, as part of the Ampleforth Abbey Trustees, is a Registered Charity, number 396036. It exists to provide education for boys.

Appleford School

Shrewton Nr Salisbury Wiltshire SP3 4HL
Tel: (01980) 621020
Fax: (01980) 621366

Headmaster: **Paul Stanley,** BEd, CertEd

Age range. 7–13, Boarders from 7.

Number of pupils. 30 (day); 60 (boarding). Girls 16, Boys 74.

Fees per term. Day £2,625; Boarding £4,195.

Fees per annum. Day £7,875; Boarding £12,585.

Founded in 1988, Appleford is a co-educational boarding and day specialist school for pupils aged 7–13 of average intelligence and above who are Dyslexic. Teaching is in small groups of 7 to 12 with a withdrawal system. Access to the full National Curriculum is given.

Appleford School provides a stimulating, structured and varied curriculum for the dyslexic child with the emphasis on literacy and numeracy skills.

The whole school approach at Appleford includes:

- a whole school approach to dyslexia with research backed individual multi-sensory programmes, designed to encourage increased self-confidence and self-esteem.
- a high level of pastoral support geared to the needs of the individual, including weekly PSE sessions.
- qualified DfE teachers, with a high ratio of specialist qualifications.
- experienced, mature and caring houseparents in friendly, structured boarding houses encouraging the development of personal organisation and life-skills.
- an extensive games and fixtures programme, numerous challenging and fun out of school activities (over 30), from claywork to rugby, to sewing, to judo; a carefully planned and stimulating weekend programme.
- a strong professional support team, including educational psychologist, speech therapist, occupational therapist and child psychotherapist.

Appleford is approved by the Council for the Registration of Schools Teaching Dyslexic Children (CReSTeD) and the Department of Education and Employment, and accredited by the Independent Schools Council and is a Corporate Member of the British Dyslexia Association.

When a child has reached an appropriate standard, a return to mainstream education is recommended. Up to 84% of Appleford leavers have moved back to mainstream schools. However, some pupils may need a specialist programme of support through to GCSE. The Headmaster will help guide parents, after full consultation, to various schools which would be suitable and which have agreed to consider our pupils for the important next step to GCSE level.

Aravon Preparatory School

Old Conna House Bray Co Wicklow Ireland
Tel: 010 3531 2821355
Fax: 010 3531 2821242
e-mail: aravon@indigo.ie
website: www.aravon.ie

The oldest school of its kind in Ireland, Aravon was founded in 1862.

It is a Charitable, Educational and Scientific Trust administered by a Board of Governors.

Principal: **Mr K W J Allwright**

Location. Aravon is located 2.5 km from Bray, approximately 19.5 km south-east of Dublin City and three-quarters of an hour from Dublin Airport.

The house stands on an elevated site overlooking 15 acres of terraced lawns and playing fields. It is surrounded by mature woodland and an 18 hole Championship golf course.

The school has seven newly-built classrooms, independent from the main building.

Pupils. Inter-Denominational, Co-Educational Boarding, Weekly Boarding and Day Preparatory School from 4 to 12+ years. Pre-School Montessori (3–4 years), and Extended Day available from 1–3.30 pm.

Syllabus. All pupils are prepared for entry to Irish Secondary and all Public Schools.

The range of core subjects taught at Infant level is extended to encompass additional French and Irish: Junior Science, Mathematics, English, History, Geography, RE and Recorder from Forms I to III; Experimental Science (Physics, Chemistry and Biology) Forms IV to VI. In addition each form averages two periods of Art per week.

Outings to Theatres and Concerts are considered an integral part of the English and Music curricula, developing an early appreciation of Literature and the Arts. Outings are also arranged throughout the year by the Geography, History and Science Departments, and the Languages Department has cultural exchanges with overseas schools.

Science. Large, well equipped laboratory. General Science is taught in Forms I to IV and Experimental Science – Physics/Chemistry/Biology in Forms V to VI.

Computers. Computer studies are a part of the curriculum for all pupils. There is a well equipped computer room.

Languages. Irish and French from Junior Infants to Form VI. Annual Exchanges with a school in Bourg en

Bresse for senior pupils, and several days in an Irish speaking area of Ireland.

Drama. Drama is an integral part of language teaching and there is also a major school production every year and each child is involved in some way in productions through the year.

Special Needs. Full time professional Remedial help is available as an extra for those pupils who require it.

Music. School Orchestra, Chamber Groups, Senior and Junior Choirs, a Chamber Choir. A wide range of musical instruments is taught: Flute, Oboe, Clarinet, 'Cello, Violin, Viola, Piano, Guitar and Recorders.

Sports. Hockey, rugby, cricket, tennis, football, basketball, athletics, netball, PE, cross-country running, swimming, table-tennis. The school has a large astro-turf area for hockey/tennis/football/netball, in addition to grass rugby/hockey/cricket pitches.

Aravon has a 25 metre outdoor pool for Summer use, but also avails of 25 metre indoor facilities where swimming takes place throughout the school year.

Extras. Horse-riding, Ballet and Modern Dance, Music, Carpentry, Tennis coaching, Wood turning (4 lathes).

Parent Teachers Association. Aravon has an active and enthusiastic PTA and a School Development Committee.

Fees per term. Junior Infants: £493; Senior Infants: £613; Form I: £725; Form II: £792; Senior Day and Boarding Tuition: £1,020; Boarding: £1,233 (7 day); £972 (5 day).

Charitable status. Aravon School Limited is a Registered Charity, number 59277. It exists to provide education for children from the age of 3 to 12+.

Ardingly College Junior School

Haywards Heath West Sussex RH17 6SQ.
Tel: (01444) 892279
Fax: (01444) 892169
e-mail: head.acjs@virgin.net
website: www.ardingly.com
Station: Haywards Heath (5 minutes away)

Chairman of Council: Sir Robin McLaren, KCMG

Head: **Mrs J L Robinson**, BA (Birmingham), PGCE

Number of Pupils. Approximately 200. There are 40 boarders and flexi-boarding is a popular option.

Fees. Boarders: £3,490 per term. Day pupils: (7–9) £1,875, (10–13) £2,360 per term, including meals.

Ardingly College Junior School is the Preparatory School for Ardingly College Senior School (see Part I of this Book). Boys and girls are admitted after they have reached the age of 7. Boarders from age 9.

Details of Scholarships available may be obtained from the Registrar.

The Junior School shares extensive grounds with the Senior School and benefits from the College's Chapel, Music School, Dining Hall, Design Technology Department, Gymnasium, a new Sports Hall, 25m indoor Swimming Pool, Squash Courts, Astroturf, Medical Centre (with 24 hour nursing cover) and school shop and it is organised as a separate unit. The Junior School has its own classrooms, Drama Studio, Library, Art Department (with pottery), changing rooms and boarding accommodation.

Children are prepared for KS2 SATs, CE and PSS.

There are four live-in boarding staff, four resident Gappers and a full time Matron to look after the boarders.

A wide range of extra-curricular activities are encouraged. They include Study Skills, Drama Club (there are termly productions), Maths Club, Cartooning, Chess, Gardening, Leadership Challenge, Cookery, Board Games, Scouts and Cubs, Riding, Art, various musical groups from Orchestra and strings to Jazz Band and plenty of sporting activities.

The Senior School boys concentrate on Soccer but Junior School boys will experience Rugby as well as Soccer. Girls play Netball and Rounders and both boys and girls enjoy Hockey, Athletics, Cross-Country, Cricket, Basketball and Squash. Ardingly College Junior School is an Activemark Gold school (Sport England recognised).

Children are streamed at the top end of the school and setted in core subjects. Prep is done at school. ICT is strong.

Religious Education is in accordance with the teaching of the Church of England.

Charitable status. Ardingly College is a Registered Charity, number 269673. It exists to provide high quality education for boys and girls aged 3–18 in a Christian context.

Ardvreck

Crieff Perthshire PH7 4EX
Tel: (01764) 653112
Fax: (01764) 654920
e-mail: ardvreck@bosinternet.com
Station: Perth

Headmaster: **P G Watson**, MA, PGCE
Chairman of the Governors: James Ivory

Number of Pupils. 110 Boarders, 40 day. Pre-Prep 12. Nursery 15.

Fees. £3,870 (boarders), £2,395 (day), Pre-Prep £1,075, Nursery £540.

Admission is by interview with the Headmaster followed by a written assessment. A major Scholarship and several Exhibitions or Bursaries are awarded each year following a competitive examination in early March. Service Bursaries and sibling discounts are also available.

Ardvreck stands in extensive grounds on the edge of Crieff, having been purpose built and founded in 1883. The School has a long tradition of providing academic excellence as well as outstanding achievement in sport and music. There are 15 full-time and 5 part-time members of the teaching staff and classes are no larger than 16. Health and domestic arrangements are under the personal supervision of the Headmaster's wife and she is assisted by three full-time Matrons – one of whom is the resident, qualified school Nurse.

The School Doctor visits regularly and dental and orthodontic treatment can be arranged if necessary.

Boys and girls are prepared for senior schools throughout Britain. In recent years, all have passed the Common Entrance to their schools of first choice and over 30 awards have been gained in the past four years.

Rugby, Netball, Hockey, Cricket and Athletics are the main games and on several Saturdays in the summer, pupils are provided with picnic lunches enabling them to explore the surrounding countryside, accompanied by members of staff, where they can study the wildlife, fish in one of the rivers or lochs, climb, sail or canoe. Other activities include Golf, Riding, Tennis and Shooting, a sport for which the School has a national reputation for excellence having won the Prep Schools Championship on 34 out of the last 38 occasions on which it has been shot.

A modern and well-equipped Music School provides the best possible opportunities for music-making. There is an orchestra, and senior and junior choirs both of which regularly achieve distinction at music festivals. Visiting music specialists teach a wide range of instruments including the Pipes. Music and Drama play an important part in the life of the School and a major production is staged annually with several smaller productions and numerous concerts taking place throughout the year.

There is a heated, indoor swimming pool and all children are taught to swim.

Most full-time staff live within the School grounds and a special feature of Ardvreck is that there are two senior boarding houses – one for girls and one for boys – where pupils gain a little more independence and are encouraged to show greater personal responsibility in readiness for the transition to senior schools.

About 20% of boarders live overseas and they are escorted to and from Edinburgh Airport; all necessary documentation can be handled by the School if required. Overseas pupils are required to have a guardian in the UK with whom they can stay during exeats.

Ardvreck encourages each boy and girl to achieve the highest standards possible relative to his or her own ability. Every child faces new challenges academically and physically and personal strengths and qualities are given the space, freedom and opportunity to develop in a caring and happy environment. Although the School is renowned for its academic achievements, support and help are also given to those with learning difficulties and other special needs; there is a full-time Special Needs teacher.

Charitable status. Ardvreck School is a Registered Charity, number 35577. Its aim is to provide education for boys and girls.

Arnold House School

1 Loudoun Road St John's Wood London NW8 0LH.
Tel: 020 7266 4840
Fax: 020 7266 6994

Chairman of the Board of Governors: C D St Johnston

Headmaster: **N M Allen**, BA

Number of Boys. 250 (Day Boys only)
Fees per term. £2,700. Lunch £145.

Most boys join the school in the September after their fifth birthday and spend their first two years in the Junior School. A few join at other ages.

Charitable status. Arnold House School is a Registered Charity, number 312725. It exists to provide education for boys in preparation for transfer to senior independent schools at 13.

Arnold Junior School

Lytham Road Blackpool FY4 1JG.
Tel: (01253) 348314
Fax: (01253) 298407
e-mail: arnold.juniors@cableinet.co.uk
website: www.arnold.blackpool.sch.uk

Chairman of Governors: Sir Martin Holdgate, CB, MA, PhD, FIBiol

Head: **C F D White**, BEd

Number of Pupils. Boys: 160; Girls: 178
Fees per term. Kindergarten, Infants and Juniors £1,270. (Reductions in fees for brothers and sisters.)

Arnold Junior School (2–11 years) is an integral part of Arnold School, with its own buildings and separate organisation.

The School houses a Kindergarten, Infant and Junior Departments.

Academic standards are high and progress is well monitored through the school. The majority of pupils proceed to the Senior School, passing the entrance examination at 11 years.

Music has a valued place in school life. Children have the opportunity to learn wind, string or brass instruments, playing in group ensembles or the Junior School Orchestra. There are two choirs and musical events are held each term. A Family Service is held each term on Sundays and the school's Carol Service is held in the Parish Church. The annual Arts Week gives pupils the opportunity to explore and enjoy an area of Arts education.

French is taught from the age of 4 years and an annual study visit to France is organised for older pupils.

The school competes successfully in local and regional sports activities – football, rugby, hockey, netball, cross-country, athletics, cricket and swimming.

There is a thriving programme of extra-curricular activities, including sport, chess, conservation and crafts. A wide variety of educational visits is offered, many taking advantage of the school's own outdoor pursuit centre in the Lake District.

The Arnold Summer School offers sporting and educational courses for children 5–15 years, July to August.

In our school we aim to provide a happy and caring environment where the individual child may flourish. We are proud of our academic standards but we also strive to give a broad and balanced education. Above all, we want our boys and girls to use their different gifts and to enjoy the success this brings.

Arnold Lodge School

Kenilworth Road Leamington Spa Warwickshire CV32 5TW
Tel: (01926) 778050
Fax: (01926) 743311
e-mail: into@arnoldlodge.warwks.sch.uk
Station: Leamington Spa

Principal: **A G Jones, BA, FRSA**

Number of Pupils. 370 (including Kindergarten).
Sex of children. Co-educational.
Consolidated Termly Fees. Senior £1,957; Junior £1,574; Kindergarten £1,032 (all day); £585 (half day).

Arnold Lodge was founded in 1864 and is the oldest Preparatory School in Warwickshire. Since that time the school, which is co-educational, has been extended and recently refurbished.

There are 37 permanent members of the teaching staff and pupils enjoy the benefits of a strong tradition of effective student care. Parents are encouraged to become actively involved in all aspects of their children's education.

Pupils are prepared for the boys' and girls' Common Entrance Examinations and Scholarships to Independent Senior Schools at 11+ and 13+. Potential scholars are grouped together and many awards have been won in recent years to a variety of Independent Schools.

Arnold Lodge boasts unique resources for Information and Communications Technology and is developing its own Web site as well as home-school links through its Intranet. Students are taught to use IT to support learning and to integrate it into their work when practicable.

There is a strong tradition of Music at the school with a range of visiting specialist teachers. The Choir is affiliated to the RSCM and undertakes a full programme of engagements and recitals.

Association and Rugby football, hockey, netball, lacrosse, cricket, rounders, swimming and athletics are all on the curriculum, but other sports such as judo, tennis, gymnastics, outdoor pursuits and equestrian eventing are all part of the very wide range of optional activities. Many sporting tours are organised, most notably in the recent past to Japan and USA and this year Canada. We have also hosted tourists from Nairobi.

The fine assembly hall doubles as a theatre, and the school has its own Academy of Dance and Drama. The school has a strong dramatic tradition and hosts playwrights in residence to write and produce plays. The School has performed at the Fringe in Edinburgh. The Visual Arts Department is particularly thriving. Pupils are encouraged to develop their interests through the various hobby clubs and to take advantage of the educational visits and field trips that are offered.

Each year a group of students and staff visit France for an enjoyable and rewarding educational residential experience.

Arundale School

Lower Street Pulborough West Sussex RH20 2BX.
Tel: (01798) 872520
Fax: (01798) 875202

Chairman of Governors: Mrs Mary Fleck

***Headmistress:* Miss K M Lovejoy**

Number of Pupils. 79 (Day Girls), 18 (Day Boys)

Set in the rural village of Pulborough, Arundale School has a reputation for providing an excellent education in a small, friendly environment. The school caters for boys aged 2½–8 years and girls aged 2½–11 years, preparing them for Common Entrance and Scholarship examinations.

Among Arundale's many strengths is the Music Department which, apart from offering class singing and orchestral lessons, allows pupils to experience playing a wide range of solo instruments as well as having individual singing lessons. A Music Scholarship is offered to pupils aged 7–8 who show potential in two musical instruments or one instrument and singing. Scholarships are also offered for Academic ability, Sport and Art.

Arundale also accepts Nursery Vouchers. "Flying Start Nursery" offers children aged 2½-4 the opportunity to experience early years' education.

Regular visits to the Royal Festival Hall, Covent Garden, local theatres and drama workshops are part of termly activities. There are also a number of after school clubs and societies.

All pupils learn French from the age of three and have access to computers. A new network was installed in 2000. Pupils in Year 6 (10–11 years) are given a number of responsibilities and duties to prepare them for their future schools. There is a regular French trip to Paris, Rouen or the Dordogne as well as Active/IT weekends. Form VI, as seniors, are also captains of their Houses and teams. The confidence and sense of responsibility they gain by experiencing life 'at the top' is rewarded by their successes both at Arundale and at their next schools.

Charitable status. Arundale School Trust Limited is a Registered Charity, number 307049. It exists to provide education for children.

Ascham House

30 West Avenue Gosforth Newcastle upon Tyne NE3 4ES.
Tel: (0191) 2851619 and 2853258
Fax: (0191) 2131105

Chairman of Governors: P J McAndrew

***Headmaster:* S H Reid**, BSc (Dunelm)

Number of Boys. 270

Fees. Tuition £1,525 per term. Lunches £105 per term.

The school has been established for more than 80 years becoming an Educational Trust with an independent Board of Governors in 1980. There are 23 full-time teachers preparing boys, in average form sizes of 16, for entry to independent secondary schools, at 11 years of age to day schools and at 13 years of age to boarding schools. Academic standards are high and the expectation is that boys will gain entry to their first choice senior school.

Excellent facilities are available for Rugby, Cricket, Athletics and Swimming. A full range of fixtures against other schools is played at various ages and great emphasis is placed upon skilled coaching to improve basic skills and enjoyment. Similarly a full programme of Art, Music and Drama is undertaken to a high standard, with participation by everybody encouraged.

The atmosphere throughout the school is happy and friendly. Boys are encouraged to behave with manners, commonsense and increasing responsibility as they move through the school.

Charitable status. Ascham House School Trust Limited is a Registered Charity, number 510529. It exists to promote and provide for the advancement of education.

Ashdell Preparatory School

266 Fulwood Road Sheffield S10 3BL
Tel: (0114) 266 3835
Fax: (0114) 267 1762
e-mail: headteacher@ashdell-prep.sheffield.sch.uk
website: www.ashdell-prep.sheffield.sch.uk

Girls Day Preparatory

***Headmistress:* Mrs J Upton**, CertEd (Sheffield)

Chairman of Council of Management: Sir Samuel Roberts, Bt

Number of Pupils. 115

Age Range. 4–11 years

Fees. £1,550 to £1,750.

The main purpose of this small, traditional school is to prepare girls for the Common Entrance Examination to Independent Senior Schools at the age of 11 years. Pupils of character and ability are encouraged to work for scholarships to these schools and small 'enrichment' groups are available for the gifted.

A separate Pre-Preparatory Department with its own Gym, dining room, Art room, garden and play area accommodates the 4 to 6 year olds.

The aim of the school is to achieve a high academic standard in a formal atmosphere and to encourage each pupil to work to the best of her ability to reach her full potential. Close attention is paid to individual pupils in a hard-working, happy atmosphere in small classes (average

17). Remedial Maths and English lessons are provided for those girls who experience difficuly in these subjects. Care is also given to the health, character formation and manners of the children. All pupils stay for lunch and may attend for after school care at no extra charge.

The normal range of subjects is covered including IT, Science, Music, French, Latin, Swimming, Tennis, Netball, Rounders, Drama, Ballet, Pottery, Cookery and Woodwork. The school has a choir and an orchestra and can provide individual instrumental lessons.

Parents' Evenings are held twice a term. There is a lively parents' association called the Friends of Ashdell.

Charitable status. Ashdell Schools Trust Limited is a Registered Charity, number 529380. It was founded for the education of children.

Ashdown House

Forest Row West Sussex RH18 5JY.
Tel: (01342) 822574
Fax: (01342) 824380
e-mail: headmaster@pncl.co.uk

Chairman: Mrs P Sherrington

***Headmaster:* A J Fowler-Watt**, MA (Cantab)
Deputy Headmaster: M J Harris, BSc, PGCE

Number of Pupils. 210 (154 boys, 72 girls)
Fees. £3,750 a term

The School is registered as an Educational Trust with a Board of Governors.

The domestic arrangements are under the charge of Mrs Fowler-Watt, assisted by three senior matrons, three undermatrons and a full time RGN Sister.

There are 22 full-time members of the teaching staff, 5 of whom are ladies who teach mainly in the lower forms. Music of all kinds is studied under resident and peripatetic teachers.

The School, which is nearly all boarding, is situated in its own grounds of 35 acres, a mile from the main road. It has a Chapel, Art & Music Rooms, laboratories, library, carpentry-shop, a Design Technology room and a rifle range. Information Technology is studied by all forms in a specially equipped room. A large barn has been converted into an Indoor Sports Area for tennis, indoor football, indoor cricket nets, basketball, netball and other games. The Centenary Theatre and Arts Centre was completed in 1986. There is an indoor swimming pool. The School owns the Chateau du Livet in Normandy. This is used throughout the year for French language and other study groups.

Games. Cricket, Association and Rugby Football. Hockey, Golf, Tennis, Judo and Fencing are encouraged. Riding lessons can also be taken. The main games for girls which are organised separately are Netball, Tennis, Rounders and Hockey.

Ashfold

Dorton Aylesbury Bucks HP18 9NG.
Tel: (01844) 238237.
Fax: (01844) 238505
Market town: Thame, near M40

Chairman of Governors: Mr R Williams
***Headmaster:* M O M Chitty**, BSc

Numbers. 165 boys and girls, day pupils and weekly boarders (6–13 years). 73 boys and girls in Pre-Prep (3–6 years).

Fees. Weekly boarders £3,155; Day £1,895–£2,795; Pre-prep £690–£1,550.

Ashfold is housed in a magnificent Jacobean mansion set in thirty acres of parkland and playing fields in the heart of the countryside between Oxford and Aylesbury.

Ashfold aims to deliver confident and fully prepared young children ready to meet the challenges of their chosen secondary schools. Its emphasis remains upon the broadest possible education so, in addition to satisfying the academic requirements of preparing them for Common Entrance and Scholarship examination to Senior Independent Schools, every encouragement and opportunity is given to children to develop a wide range of sporting, musical (instrumental and choral), artistic, countryside and other interests (for many years National Clay Pigeon Champions). Children are also prepared, as required, for the LEA 11 plus examination to local grammar schools.

Ashfold is a small, close-knit Christian-based community, holding strong family values. With class sizes averaging just 13, the 19 mainly resident qualified staff are able to give each child the individual attention and encouragement they need. Recent developments include a Music School, Sports Hall, ICT Centre and Junior Department.

Charitable status. Ashford School Trust is a Registered Charity, number 272663. It exists to provide a quality preparatory school education, academically and in other respects, for all the children entrusted to its care.

Aysgarth School

Bedale North Yorkshire DL8 1TF
Tel: (01677) 450240
Fax: (01677) 450736
e-mail: enquiries@atsgarthschool.co.uk
Stations: Darlington/Northallerton

Chairman of Governors: Mr R C Compton

Joint Headmasters:
J C Hodgkinson, MA (Emmanuel College, Cambridge)
P J Southall, BA (University of Hull), PGCE (St Mary's College, Twickenham)

Number of Pupils. 150. Pre-Prep Deartment: 45 boys and girls aged 4-8; Prep School: 105 boys aged 8-13.

Fees. Boarders (full and weekly): £3,750; Day Boys: £2,795; Pre-Prep: £1,195.

The school is a boarding school for boys and is an educational trust with a Board of Governors.

There is also a flourishing Pre-Prep Department for day boys and girls aged 4 to 8. There are eighteen members of the teaching staff and three matrons. The School was founded at Aysgarth in 1877, but moved in 1890 to its present site, six miles from the A1. Boys are escorted by train from Darlington north and south at the beginning and ends of exeats. A minibus runs to Cumbria.

The buildings are extensive and fully equipped. There is a fine Chapel, a modern sports hall and a thriving Music department. More than three quarters of the boys learn a musical instrument. The grounds of fifty acres include 17 acres of excellent playing fields, a new heated indoor swimming pool, Squash court, Fives courts and Tennis courts.

Boys are prepared in small classes for all Independent Senior Schools and the academic record is excellent. Importance is attached to Physical Education, Music and

Drama, and games include Cricket, Soccer and Rugby Football. There are many other activities and hobbies.

Charitable status. Aysgarth School Trust Limited is a Registered Charity, number 529538. Its purpose is to provide a high standard of boarding and day education.

Bablake Junior School

Coundon Road Coventry West Midlands CV1 4AU
Tel: 024 7663 4052
Fax: 024 7663 3290
e-mail: hm@bablakejs.co.uk
website: www.bablakejs.co.uk

Chairman of Governors: Mr C Leonard

Headmaster: **John S Dover**, ACP

Number of Pupils. 200
Age Range. Day School. 7–11
Fees. £1,380 per term

Bablake Junior School offers a top class education for boys and girls aged 7–11 and forms part of the Coventry School Foundation.

Such has been the success of this venture that September 1993 saw the opening of a new purpose built building to house the 200 pupils now in the school. This consists of eight classrooms, hall/gym, changing rooms, library/resources area and administrative block.

Bablake Junior School's success is based firmly on the individual care given to each pupil. The school provides a stimulating, disciplined and happy environment where pupils are not only encouraged to produce work of a high quality but to also enjoy and extend themselves in all areas of school life.

Although autonomous, the Junior School has close links with the Senior School and the vast majority of our pupils move on to the Senior School thus encouraging a strong 'family' atmosphere.

The school offers a varied and wide range of extra-curricular activities including sport, music and drama. Pupils also have the opportunity to travel abroad to Germany and to our own property in France.

We look forward to meeting you.

Charitable status. Bablake Junior School is a Registered Charity, number 528961. It exists to provide education for boys and girls.

Badminton Junior School

Westbury-on-Trym Bristol BS9 3BA
Tel: (0117) 905 5222
Fax: (0117) 962 8963
e-mail: juniorhead@badminton.bristol.sch.uk
website: www.badminton.bristol.sch.uk
Station: Bristol Parkway/Bristol Temple Meads

Chairman of Governors: Professor R Hodder-Williams, MA (Oxon), FRSA

Headmistress: **Mrs A Lloyd**, CertEd (Oxford), LGSM

Number of Girls. 98, aged 4–11 years.
Fees per term. Boarding (full and weekly) £3,500; Day £1,360–£1,975, inclusive of lunch.

Educational Philosophy. The style of Badminton Junior School reflects the traditions of the Senior School - a combination of discipline and warmth. Children come to school to learn how to concentrate, how to think and how to get on with other people. That process happens best in a stimulating environment where high standards of work and behaviour are expected. A girl also needs a welcoming and friendly atmosphere so that she can feel emotionally secure and her own particular talents and abilities can blossom. Key notes in our philosophy are the development of self-confidence, respect for the individual and the nurturing of inquiring and critical minds.

Children are happiest when they are kept busy and so we try to create a balance between hard work in the classroom, plenty of physical exercise, a range of extra-curricular activities and opportunities for recreational play.

Facilities. The Junior School is well appointed with light airy classrooms, dedicated rooms for Art and French, a science laboratory, networked computer room, a library and an Assembly Hall/Dining Hall.

The girls have use of the 25m indoor swimming pool, gymnasium and games field which are all on site, and have expert coaching from the very beginning. There are excellent facilities for music which plays an important part both inside and outside the curriculum.

The comfortable boarding accommodation is situated upstairs in the Junior School building and the girls are cared for and supervised by a housemistress and two assistants. Besides the house staff a fully qualified School Sister is on call.

With our extended day facilities and flexible boarding arrangements we aim to provide a warm and caring home from home to suit the needs of a variety of pupils and their parents.

Further information on Badminton School is available in Part II of this book and a prospectus is available on request to the Registrar.

Charitable status. Badminton School Limited is a Registered Charity, number 311738. It exists to provide education for children.

Ballard School
(part of The Ballard Schools)

New Milton Hampshire BH25 5SU
Tel: (01425) 611153

Headmaster: **Mr S P Duckitt**, MA, BEd, BSc, NPQH

Chairman of the Board of Governors: J K E Broadley, CMG, MA

Number of Children. 370 day children
Age range. 2-16
Fees per term. Day £2,425; Pre-Prep £1,495; Kindergarten £420–£1,400. Day fees include the cost of School lunches.

The School is a non-profit making Educational Trust under a Board of Governors. It is situated 2 miles from the sea and on the borders of the New Forest in its own very spacious grounds.

There are over 40 qualified teaching staff plus a Learning Support Unit with 5 teachers. The academic aim of the School is to prepare all pupils for the next school of their choice. In addition to winning accademic scholarships, children have been regularly gaining Art and Music Scholarships also. There are excellent facilities for games and out of school activities which include over 60 different types of activities. There is a fully equipped Sports Hall and a heated outdoor Swimming Pool. There is a well stocked Library, new Science and Technology Laboratories, Art Department, Music Department (with recording studio) and classrooms. The School has its own Chapel.

Ballard School has key departments catering for the specific needs of the pupils. These departments include the Nursery (2-3), Pre-Prep (3-7), Prep (7-11), Middle (11-13) and Senior (13-16) sections.

The School has a Christian foundation and the aim of the School is to provide an all round education where traditional values and standards are valued combined with facilities to prepare children for the 21st century.

Bancroft's School Preparatory School

High Road Woodford Green Essex IG8 0RF
Tel: 020 8506 0337
Fax: 020 8506 0337

Master of the Preparatory School: **D A Horn**, MA, ARCM, LLCM, FRSA

Chairman of the Governors: R W P Beharrell, Esq

Co-educational Day School. 7–11 years. 200 pupils; 101 girls, 99 boys.

Fees. £2,019 per term.

The Preparatory School of Bancroft's School (see Part I of this book) was established in September 1990 in new, purpose designed buildings in the grounds of Bancroft's School. As well as eight classrooms the Department has its own hall, library, language, art and technology rooms with specialist teaching in French, music and Art and Technology. A new IT suite was added in 1998. The Prep School is largely self contained but also uses the sports and music facilities, dining hall and chapel in the senior school.

Children are assessed for entry at the age of seven, and have guaranteed places in Bancroft's Senior School at the age of eleven. Academic standards are high with a broad, structured curriculum. As well as establishing a strong academic base, children are also encouraged to take part in a wide range of extra-curricular activities at lunch times and after school.

The curriculum and administration of the Prep School and the Senior School are closely linked.

Charitable status. Bancroft's School is a Registered Charity, number 1068532 It exists to provide a rounded academic education for able children.

The Banda School

PO Box 24722 Nairobi Kenya.
Tel: Nairobi 891220
Fax: Nairobi 890004
e-mail: bandaschool@swiftkenya.com
website: www.bandaschool.com

Chairman of Governors: D G M Hutchison

***Headmaster:* P W W B Bush**, IAPS Cert

Deputy Headmaster: M D Dickson, BA Hons (Worcester)

Number of children: 320 (all day)

Fees. Ksh149,500 per term (including lunches)

The School was founded in 1966 by Mr and Mrs J A L Chitty. It is 9 miles from Nairobi and stands in its own grounds of 30 acres adjacent to the Nairobi Game Park. Boys and girls are admitted in equal numbers at the age of 2 and are prepared for Independent Senior School Scholarship and Common Entrance Examinations. The Staff consists of 33 expatriate staff of whom 26 are graduates. The teacher-pupil ratio is about 1:10. Facilities include Science Laboratories, Computer Rooms, Art Room, Music Rooms, Hall with well-equipped stage, two Libraries, specialist rooms for Mathematics, French, History and Geography, Design Technology, audio-visual room, three Tennis courts, two Squash courts and a six lane 25 metre Swimming Pool.

Sports include Rugby, Soccer, Hockey, Cricket, Tennis, Swimming, Netball, Rounders, Athletics, Sailing, Squash and Cross Country. A very wide range of other activities including Instrumental lessons and Dancing is also available. Music, Art and Drama play an important part in the life of the school.

Barfield

Runfold Farnham Surrey GU10 1PB.
Tel: (01252) 782271
Fax: (01252) 782505

***Headmaster:* B J Hoar**, BA (Open University), FRSA

Number of Children. 300

Fees. £2,395–£2,472. Pre-Prep £835–£1,750 per term.

The School is an Educational Trust, administered by a Board of Governors, whose Chairman is Mr Andrew Christmas.

Barfield, set in 12 acres of beautiful grounds, is a first class IAPS Day Preparatory School for girls and boys, aged three to thirteen. The Pre-Prep Department, Little Barfield, has earned an enviable reputation for its high standards and caring staff. It is based in its own self-contained unit, close to Senior School facilities including Science Laboratory, Special Needs Centre and a Multi-Resource Centre, which incorporates an Auditorium, Music and Music practice rooms, IT Suite, superbly equipped Library and facilities for Art and DT.

The school has a flourishing PE and outdoor pursuits department, with most major and minor sports covered; including a Par 3 golf course. There is a magnificent indoor heated swimming pool which can be used by parents. Children are encouraged to participate in a wide range of evening activities from Synchronised Swimming to Adventure Training.

Girls and boys, taught in small classes, are prepared for their respective Common Entrance and Scholarship examinations and for Grammar School entry. Visitors are always welcome.

Charitable status. Barfield is a Registered Charity, number 312085. It exists to provide a quality education for boys and girls.

Barnard Castle Preparatory School

Westwick Road Barnard Castle Co Durham DL12 8UW
Tel: 01833 638203
Fax: 01833 638985
e-mail: secretary@barneyprepschool.org.uk
website: www.barneyschool.org.uk

Chairman of Governors: Mr J C Macfarlane, CBE

***Headmaster:* Mr E J Haslam,** ACPDipTeach

Number of Pupils. 155 girls and boys, including 34 boarders

Age range. 4-11 years.

Fees per term. Day £964-£1,535. Boarders £2,856

"The Community of Barnard Castle Preparatory School will encourage and challenge our pupils to reach their full educational potential within a secure and happy teaching environment".

Barnard Castle Preparatory School is the Junior School of Barnard Castle School and offers an all round, high quality education for boys and girls aged between 4 and 11 years. The School offers both day and boarding places and is situated in a beautiful setting on the edge of a traditional English market town.

The campuses of the two schools are adjoining, allowing shared use of many excellent facilities. At the same time the Preparatory School is able to provide a separate, stimulating environment, with small classes, a wide range of extra curricular activities and an exciting school excursion programme.

The School is well served by a bus network system and supervision is given to those day children waiting for transport home. The boarders reside in a newly developed boarding house, which creates a warm and friendly environment supported by a full range of facilities including the School's medical centre.

Our Director of Studies oversees a carefully designed curriculum. It incorporates the National Curriculum and aims to create further learning experiences for the children. Sport, drama and music occupy important places in the life of the School. All children have numerous opportunities to participate in each of these area. The School also offers a qualified learning support service to those children who require further assistance.

Charitable status. Barnard Castle School is a Registered Charity, number 527383. Its aim is the education of boys and girls.

Barnardiston Hall Preparatory School

Nr Haverhill Suffolk CB9 7TG
Tel: (01440) 786316
Fax: (01440) 786355

Headmaster: **K A Boulter**, MA (Cantab), PGCE

Co-educational 2–13

Number of Pupils. Day 200, Boarding (full and weekly) 71

Fees. £790 for mornings only; £1,580–£1,985 for day pupils; £2,950 for weekly boarders; £3,250 for full boarders.

Barnardiston Hall, set in 16 acres of grounds on the borders of Suffolk, Essex and Cambridge, offers an individual all-round education for boys and girls, both day and boarding. High standards are achieved by small classes taught by graduate and teacher-trained staff, a caring approach and close liaison with parents.

The School has good facilities, including a new Pre-Preparatory Block and Art Room complex, a very modern and well equipped computer room, assembly hall, tennis/netball courts, music room, science laboratory, library and extensive sports fields. For the boarders, the dormitories are bright, uncluttered and home-like.

The curriculum is designed to allow pupils to reach Common Entrance standards in the appropriate subjects. The best of traditional methods are mixed with modern ideas to provide an enjoyable and productive learning environment. French and computers are taught from the age of 3.

Sports in the Michaelmas and Lent Terms are hockey, swimming and cross-country/orienteering for all pupils, rugby/football for the boys and netball for the girls. During the Summer, all do athletics, swimming, tennis/short tennis and cricket/rounders.

There is a wide range of clubs and societies including 3 choirs, an orchestra, pet corner, recorders, chess, horse-riding, painting, drama, basketry, weaving, carpentry and science award. Ballet, speech and drama, piano, woodwind, brass, string and singing lessons are also offered.

Throughout the term, there are weekend activities for boarders (optional for day pupils) which include mountain walking. Derbyshire Dales at 6, Ben Nevis at 8, camping, visits to museums/historic buildings and other places of interest and theatre trips. There is an annual trip to Europe.

Barrow Hills School

Roke Lane Witley Godalming Surrey GU8 5NY.
Tel: (01428) 683639/682634
Fax: (01428) 681906
e-mail: barhills@netcomuk.co.uk

Chairman of the Governors: Mr Charles Sommer

Headmaster: **Mr M P Connolly**, BSc, BA, MEd

Number in School. 265 pupils

Fees. £1,250–£2,450.

A co-educational day school for children aged 3 to 13 set in 40 acres of attractive gardens and playing fields some 8 miles south of Guildford. It offers boys and girls a stimulating and demanding curriculum which also caters for individual needs. There is special provision, both for those with learning difficulties and for those preparing for scholarship examinations to senior schools.

A new technology centre was opened in 1997 which allows all pupils to study art, design, textiles, ceramics, food technology and photography. A new computer centre was also completed in 1997 which provides a powerful resource for all aspects of the teaching programme. In 1999 a major refurbishment programme included the science laboratory, library, tennis courts and sound/lighting for drama productions. Children are taught French by a specialist from the age of 3 whilst older pupils study Latin and Philosophy.

The school has a Roman Catholic foundation but pupils from other denominations are most welcome. The school has its own chapel and the pupils are encouraged to participate fully in leading assembly and other special services.

A wide range of games is offered including Rugby, Soccer, Hockey, Cricket, Netball, Tennis, Athletics, Judo and Archery. The school has its own heated swimming pool. Educational visits, both locally and overseas, reinforce what is done in school.

Charitable status. Barrow Hills is a Registered Charity, number 1000190. It exists to provide high quality education for both boys and girls.

Beachborough

Westbury Nr Brackley Northants NN13 5LB.
Tel: (01280) 700071.
Fax: (01280) 704839
Stations: Bicester/Milton Keynes/Banbury

Headmaster: **A J L Boardman**, CertEd (London)

Chairman of Governors: Mr R M Faccenda

Number of Children. Main School 148 (35% boarding), Pre-Prep 110

Fees. £3,325 (Day £2,460–£2,675; Pre-Prep £1,700). Nursery £140 per session per term. No compulsory extras

The School is administered as a non-profit-making Educational Trust by a Board of Governors (Chairman: Mr R M Faccenda). The school is fully co-educational and, currently, girls make up 40% of the school total. The flourishing Pre-Prep takes children from 2½ years old with a Nursery Class allowing the youngest children to build up sessions during their first year. All pupils are prepared for the relevant entry exams to Independent Senior Schools. There are 24 full-time teachers and many visiting staff for Music, Ballet, Gymnastics and Sports coaching. The boarders are cared for by resident staff and a matron. The usual class size is 14 children.

The school occupies the old Manor House in the small village of Westbury and enjoys 30 acres of grounds, playing fields and woodland. Facilities include the Chappell Building, which provides extensive areas for Music and Art as well as a dining hall and kitchen, library, gymnasium, workshop and well equipped classrooms. These allow us to offer a liberal curriculum which gives all children tuition in the standard academic subjects as well as Technology, Home Economics, Music, Art and Drama. There is also a fully networked ICT room. There is a wide range of extra curricular activities and an extensive sports programme. A recently completed astro-turf pitch has considerably enhanced the sports facilities. The Beachborough Association, run by parents and staff, arrange many events, both social and fundraising during the year.

Charitable status. Beachborough is a Registered Charity, number 309910. It exists to provide quality education for children.

The Beacon

Chesham Bois Amersham Bucks HP6 5PF.
Tel: (01494) 433654
Fax: (01494) 727849
e-mail: enquiries@beaconschool.co.uk

***Headmaster:* M W Spinney**, BEd, CertEd

Chairman of the Governors: W I D Plaistowe, Esq

Number of Boys. Upper School, 265; Lower School, 145

Inclusive Fees. Upper School, £2,530; Lower School, £1,620-£2,370.

The Beacon is a Charitable Trust which provides education for some 400 boys aged 3 to 13. Its buildings are a delightful blend of old and new; the school is centred around a 17th Century farmstead whose barns provide a lovely Dining Hall and a Library/Lecture Theatre. Classroom accommodation is almost all purpose-built, and recent additions have been a large Sports Hall/Theatre, a Music Department, a Computer Room, Art Room, and Technology Workshop and, in 1993, a new classroom complex for the 3 and 4-year-olds. As well as the 7 acre grass games field there is an Astroturf pitch for Hockey and Tennis, and a 20 metre outdoor Swimming Pool.

Most boys join the Nursery at age 3, or Reception at age 4. The Nursery has places for 24 boys and is staffed by 3 NNEB's and a trained teacher. At age 4 there are 40 boys, served by two teachers and two assistants. At 5 and 6 the boys are based mainly with their form teacher in classes of 20. From age 7 class sizes are a maximum 20.

The aim of the school is to provide breadth of opportunity. The daily timetable contains a broad range of subjects, and there is a strong emphasis on participation in sport, music, drama, art and technology. There are teams for Rugby, Soccer, Hockey, Basketball, Cricket, Tennis, Swimming and Athletics, while the Music Department has 2 Choirs, an Orchestra, Strings and Wind Bands and some 15 visiting teachers to cater for individual tuition.

The School's examination record is excellent, with a number of academic, music, art and sports scholarships being won.

Charitable status. The Beacon School is a Registered Charity, number 309911. It exists to provide education for boys.

Beaconhurst Grange

Kenilworth Road Bridge of Allan Stirling FK9 4RR.
Tel: (01786) 832146
Fax: (01786) 833415
Station: Bridge of Allan

Chairman of Governors: R G Lawson, BSc, CA

***Headmaster:* D R Clegg**, BMus, ARCO

Number of Pupils. 131 Boys; 161 Girls

Fees. Nursery £592–£1,234; Junior £1,330; Middle £1,637; Senior £1,797

Beaconhurst is a coeducational day school, situated in Bridge of Allan, an attractive country town near Stirling in Central Scotland. The Ochils rise behind the school offering marvellous countryside for outdoor pursuits while the MacRobert Centre at nearby Stirling University hosts a wide range of musical and theatrical events. There are excellent road and rail links and both Edinburgh and Glasgow airports are less than one hour's drive away.

The aim of the school is to provide a broadly based education within a happy but disciplined atmosphere. In September 1991 a senior department was opened and the school now offers a full course of secondary education through to University entrance.

There is a wide range of sporting and other activities to encourage pupils to develop worthwhile leisure time interests; these include Choir, Orchestra, Brownies, Judo, Fencing, Skiing, Riding, Swimming, Woodwork, as well as team games.

Facilities in the school include a Library, a well equipped audio visual and computer room, Art and Music rooms as well as the Cameron Hall, a purpose built Gymnasium, Concert Hall and Theatre.

The school was founded in 1975 by the amalgamation of Hurst Grange School for Boys and the Beacon School for Girls. It is a non profit-making company run by a Board of Governors and there is also an active Parents' Association.

A prospectus with full details is available from the Headmaster.

Charitable status. Beaconhurst Grange is a Registered Charity, number SCO 05753. Its aim is to provide a flexible educational experience for all.

Beaudesert Park

Minchinhampton Stroud Gloucestershire GL6 9AF.
Tel: (01453) 832072
Fax: (01453) 836040
Station: Stroud

Chairman of Governors: I N McCallum, Esq

Headmaster: **J P R Womersley**, BA, PGCE

Assistant Headmaster: S T P O'Malley, MA (Hons), PGCE

Number of Pupils. Boarders 54. Day Boys and Girls 194, Pre-Prep Department 106.

Fees. Boarders £4,070. Day Fees £2,080–£2,995, Pre-Prep £1,505–£1,575.

The School was founded in 1908 and became an educational trust in 1968.

Beaudesert Park is a preparatory school for boys and girls from 4–13. The school is very well equipped with indoor and outdoor swimming pools, sports hall, art centre, design technology and music departments. We also have astroturf tennis courts and hard courts which are situated in beautiful wooded grounds. The school stands high up in the Cotswolds adjoining 500 acres of common land and golf course. Despite its rural location, the school is within half an hour of the M4 and M5 motorways and within easy reach of the surrounding towns of Gloucester, Cheltenham, Cirencester, Swindon, Bath and Bristol.

There is a strong academic tradition and all pupils are encouraged to work to the best of their ability. There is great emphasis on effort and all children are praised for their individual performance. Pupils are prepared for Common Entrance and Scholarship examinations. They are given individual attention in classes which are mostly setted or streamed. Over the last five years an average of 10 scholarships a year – academic, art, music and technology – have been won to leading Independent Senior Schools. The staff consists of 35 full time teaching staff and 12 music teachers, all of whom take a personal interest in the children's welfare.

Good manners and consideration for other are a priority. Beaudesert strives to create a happy and purposeful atmosphere, providing for the talents of each child in a wide range of activities, cultural, sporting and recreational. There are thriving drama, art, pottery and music departments. Sporting activities include cricket, soccer, rugby, hockey, netball, rounders, tennis, swimming, athletics, golf, badminton, fencing, dance, judo, riding and sailing. A wide number of societies and clubs meet each week.

Charitable status. Beaudesert Park is a Registered Charity, number 311711. It exists to provide education for boys and girls in a caring atmosphere.

Bedford Modern Junior School

Manton Lane Bedford MK41 7NT.
Tel: (01234) 332513
Fax: (01234) 332617

Head of Junior School: **N R Yelland**, BEd

Number of Boys. 230 (including Boarders)

Fees per annum. Day Boys £4,587. Boarders £5,211.

The Junior School is housed in its own separate buildings adjacent to the Main School. Facilities include a purpose built Science Room and an Art Room, as well as Computer and Technology Rooms. A new library was opened in 1998 and additional playground space added in 1999. A major Junior School development is underway which will provide a new school hall and extra teaching classrooms.

The whole site overlooks the school playing fields and the Junior School has extensive views over the Ouse valley. Many of the Main School facilities are available to the Junior School, including full use of the playing fields, Sports Hall, Gymnasium, covered and heated Swimming Pool, Tennis and Squash Courts. The Main School Hall provides facilities for full scale Drama productions and extensive use is made of the Music School.

There is a strong Choral, Instrumental Music, Dramatic and Sporting tradition.

Boys are admitted to the Junior School at 7, 8, 9 and 10, after sitting an Entrance Examination in English and Maths which is held in February each year. Boys proceed automatically to the Main School at 11, unless special circumstances mean that this is inappropriate.

Charitable status. The Bedford Charity (The Harpur Trust) is a Registered Charity, number 204817. It includes in its aims the provision of high quality education for boys.

Bedford Preparatory School

De Parys Avenue Bedford MK40 2TU.
Tel: (01234) 362271/362274
Fax: (01234) 362285

Chairman of Preparatory School Committee: Mr A Abrahams

Headmaster: **C Godwin**, BSc, MA

Deputy Headmaster: J P Crofts, BA

Director of Studies: G J Wickens, MA

Assistant Staff:

C N Blacklock, BA
Miss I C Bowis, BA
J S Chance, BA
Mrs V Chance, BA
P Clarke, BSc
I M Coyne, BEd
Mrs J P Crizzle, BA
C A C Dee, BA
T W D Dodgson, BA
P Farrar Hockley, BA
Mrs K Faulkner, BA
Mrs R A Howe, BEd
Mrs S Keane, CertEd
Miss N A Kiddle, BA
J P T Latham, BSc
P A B Lewis, CertEd
J Leyland, BA
Mrs D MacAskill, BA
M Mallalieu, BSc
C P Martin, GTCL, LTCL
R Mowe, BEd
Miss D E M Parton, BEd, AdvDipEd
S Phillips, BEd
Mrs M Richards, BA
Mrs J D Sapia, BSc
Mrs E J Speedy, BA
Miss C E Stewart, GTCL, LTCL
Miss Z Tasker, BA
Mrs S E L Thomas, BEd
A J Whitbread, BA
Miss R C Wyborn, BEd

Boarding House: Mr and Mrs K Spencer

Day Housemasters/mistresses:
P Farrar Hockley
Mrs S Keane
R Knowles
Mrs E Speedy

Number of Boys. Boarders 33, Weekly Boarders 13, Dayboys 382 (age 7–13)

Termly Fees. Tuition £1,970–£3,040; Boarding £3,260–£4,820; Weekly Boarding £3,130–£4,690.

Bedford Preparatory School combines the two schools formerly known as the Preparatory School and the Bedford Lower School. An extensive building programme has been completed offering excellent facilities: three purpose-built and well-equipped Science Laboratories, an Art Studio, excellent computing resources, specialist teaching rooms, a new library and a spacious Assembly Hall.

Curriculum. Boys are prepared for the Bedford School 13+ Entrance Examination, which is allied to Common Entrance, but under normal circumstances boys transfer automatically. The curriculum is otherwise carefully tailored to match and prepare for the curriculum followed in the Upper School, and includes in addition to the usual subjects: French, Information Technology and Design/Technology from the age of 7 and Latin, Spanish and French from the age of 11.

The boys enjoy full use of the facilities available to Upper School pupils: the Recreation Centre, incorporating an excellent theatre, an indoor swimming pool and a large sports hall; the Technology Centre; superb playing fields, all-weather pitch and tennis courts. All the usual games are played to a high standard and boys are often selected to play in county or national teams.

Many boys play musical instruments, and orchestra and bands perform frequently. There are good School Choirs and selected boys sing alongside Upper School pupils in the Chapel Choir trained in the English Cathedral tradition. There are several theatrical productions each year in the theatre or hall, often in conjunction with girls from sister Harpur Trust Schools.

Boarding. 30 full boarders and a small number of weekly boarders live in the new purpose-built Boarding House in the grounds of the Preparatory School. Boys are cared for by the Housemaster and his wife, two resident house-tutors and a full-time matron.

Pastoral Care. The progress and well-being of pupils are carefully monitored, and parental involvement and contact are maintained through reports and Parents Evenings and other formal and informal meetings. A competitive House system is in use.

Financial Assistance and Scholarships. Harpur Bursaries and Bedford School Bursaries are available for boys aged 11 and over. In addition a small number of Scholarships are available for talented boys entering the School at age 7 and 11.

Further information about the School may be obtained from the Headmaster, Bedford Preparatory School, De Parys Avenue, Bedford MK40 2TU. Tel: (01234) 362271. Fax: (01234) 362285.

Charitable status. Bedford Preparatory School, which is part of The Harpur Trust, is a Registered Charity, number 204817. It aims to provide high quality education for boys.

Beech Hall

Tytherington Near Macclesfield Cheshire SK10 2EG.
Tel: (01625) 422192
Fax: (01625) 502424

Chairman of Board of Governors: Mr R Nichols

***Headmaster:* J S Fitz-Gerald**, DipEd (King Alfred's College)

Number of Pupils. 200

Fees. Pre-Prep £1,165 per term (including lunch). Transition £1,445 per term (including lunch). Main School £1,830 per term (including lunch).

Kindergarten, Pre-prep and Transition departments offer education between 8.30 am and 4 pm, with further after care through to 6 pm. Main School offers education from 8.30 am until 6 pm.

Beech Hall is a co-educational Day preparatory school situated in spacious and attractive grounds with extensive playing fields, a heated outdoor swimming pool and many other facilities.

Boys and girls are prepared for entry to a wide variety of Independent Schools and local Independent Day Schools. Classes are kept small – on average there are 16 pupils to a class – making individual attention possible in every lesson.

There is a very popular Kindergarten and Reception department, consisting of children between the ages of 1 year and 6 under the care of their own specialist teachers. These classes were started with the objective of giving boys and girls a good grounding in reading, writing and arithmetic.

Beech Hall aims to provide a sound all-round education and children are encouraged to sit for academic, music and art scholarships. There is a school choir, a high standard of drama and the children produce their own school magazine.

Rugby, Association football, hockey and netball are played in the winter terms. The school also has a good cross-country course. In the summer, cricket, athletics, rounders and tennis. Swimming is taught throughout the year. Other activities include squash, badminton, riding, archery and ju-jitsu.

The school is situated off the main Stockport-Macclesfield road, within easy reach of Manchester International Airport and the M6 and M62 motorways.

Further details and illustrated prospectus are obtainable from the Headmaster.

Charitable status. Beech Hall School Trust Limited is a Registered Charity, number 525922. It exists to provide education for boys and girls.

Beechwood Park

Markyate St Albans Hertfordshire AL3 8AW.
Tel: (01582) 840333

Chairman of Governors: J S Lewis, Esq, FCIS, FRSA

***Headmaster:* D S Macpherson**, MA

Number of Pupils. 408 (53 boarders, 8–13; 355 day boys, 4–13; and 113 girls 4–11)

Fees. Boarders £2,965. Day Pupils £2,060 (Juniors £1,690). Reception class £1,505 (4½ days). No compulsory extras

Beechwood Park occupies a large mansion with a fine Regency Library and Great Hall. Modernisation has added kitchens, changing rooms, Science Laboratory, Maths workshop, classrooms, including a languages room, Design Technology workshop, dormitories, Gymnasium and Sports facilities, including a large sports hall and two squash courts, three hard tennis courts and two heated Swimming Pools, in 38 acres of surrounding grounds. Three purpose-built classroom blocks house the Middle School, Junior forms and Kindergarten classes. A Music School has a music chamber and 14 practice rooms.

Day pupils use private buses serving Harpenden, St Albans, Luton and Dunstable. Many subsequently convert to boarding under the care of the Housemaster, Mr M S Ridley.

Maximum class size is 20; major subjects are setted. Qualified class teachers teach the juniors; seniors are taught by subject specialist graduates, including a resident Chaplain, and a Director of Music with a staff of visiting instrumentalists.

Common Entrance results affirm a high standard of work, against a background of every kind of worthwhile out-of-class activity. Music is distinguished.

Soccer, Rugger, Cricket, Golf, Hockey, Netball, Swimming and Athletics and an unusually wide range of minor sports are coached by well qualified PE Staff.

Beechwood Park is a non-profit-making trust administered by governors of wide professional and educational experience.

Charitable status. Beechwood Park School is a Registered Charity, number 311068. It exists to provide education for boys and girls from 4–13.

Beeston Hall School

West Runton Cromer Norfolk NR27 9NQ.
Tel: (01263) 837324
Fax: (01263) 838177
e-mail: office@beestonhall.co.uk
website: www.beestonhall.co.uk

Chairman of Governors: I R MacNicol, FRICS

***Headmaster:* I K MacAskill**, BEd (*Hons*)

Deputy Headmaster: A V L Richards, BSc, PGCE

Bursar: A de G Webster, IAPS DipEd

Numbers in School. Co-educational 7–13 years. Full Boarding 110. Daily Boarding 65. Boys 105. Girls 70.

Fees. £3,695 Boarding, £2,760 Daily Boarding.

Religious Denomination. Mainly Church of England; 15% Roman Catholic.

About Beeston: Beeston Hall was established in 1948 in a Regency house set in 30 acres in North Norfolk, close to the sea and surrounded by 700 acres of National Trust land. Numbers vary between 165–180 and there is an April intake to allow an easy transition to boarding routines. Although there is no compulsory boarding, 95% of the children experience boarding before they leave, the majority moving on to boarding schools such as Ampleforth, Downe House, Eton, Gordonstoun, Gresham's, Harrow, Oakham, Oundle, Rugby, Tudor Hall and Uppingham. In addition to the normal subjects, Music, Craft, ICT and Drama are all timetabled, providing the children with a wide curriculum and the opportunity to find an activity in which they can excel. The school enjoys great success at scholarship level, with 148 scholarships won in the last 16 years. Extra help (free) is given on a one-to-one basis in English, Mathematics and French; Dyslexics are looked after by trained staff. There is a positive emphasis on the traditional values such as courtesy, kindness, industry and an awareness of others, and at every stage of their education we hope that the children are encouraged to maximise their potential and think and act for themselves. Drama and Music are considered important for every child: each takes part in at least one play production each year. 110 children are in three choirs and ten different music groups meet every week. The school is equally proud of its record on the sports field where all children are coached regardless of ability by a dedicated team of staff, and where all are, at some stage, given the opportunity to represent the school. It has a particularly impressive record in Rugby, Netball, Rounders, Cross Country, Hockey, Cricket and Athletics, whilst a comprehensive activities programme provides opportunities to suit all tastes: camping, shooting, debating, French cuisine, fly tying and bridge, to name but a few.

The 1996 Good Schools' Guide calls Beeston "a gloriously happy School run as a big family.....delightful and outstanding with confident children".

Charitable status. Beeston Hall School Trust Limited is a Registered Charity, number 311274. It exists to provide preparatory education for boarding and day boys and girls.

Belhaven Hill

Dunbar East Lothian EH42 1NN.
Tel: (01368) 862785.
Fax: (01368) 865225
Station: Dunbar

Chairman of Governors: J A Scott, Esq

***Head Master:* I M Osborne**, MA (Cantab)

Number of Pupils. 65 boys, 40 girls. Boarders 85, Days 20

Fees. Boarders £3,540 per term. Days £2,585 per term

The School is a Charitable Trust, under a Board of Governors, catering mainly for boarders but with some day pupils. The boys live in the main building and the girls in a separate house that is newly built and very attractive.

The handsome buildings are surrounded by extensive playing fields and stand in sheltered grounds with a golf course, to which children have access, between the school and the sea. There is a full-time teaching staff of fourteen, and the school has an excellent record of academic success, with a number of Awards to leading English and Scottish Senior Independent Schools in recent years. There are other teachers for Art, Carpentry and Instrumental Music. The policy of the Governors has been to keep the school a comparatively small one in order to retain a family atmosphere. The emphasis is on bringing out the various talents of all the pupils and encouraging high standards in all that they undertake. Three full-time Matrons and two Assistants take care of the children's health, and the School Doctor is always available in case of emergency.

The chief team games for the boys are Rugby, Hockey and Cricket and there is some Football in the winter terms. The girls play Netball, Hockey and Rounders. There is Swimming in the school's heated outdoor pool in the summer and in the indoor pool in Dunbar during the winter terms. The school has two grass tennis courts and four on a new all-weather pitch. Athletics, Squash, Tennis and Golf are professionally coached and sports such as Badminton and Croquet are available. The Sports Hall is used during lessons and free time for Drama, Gymnastics, Scottish Country Dancing, Indoor Cricket Nets and Rollerblading. Every sort of hobby and activity is practised and encouraged: Debating, Mastermind, Singing, Stamp-collecting, Model-making, Computer Programming, Gardening, Fishing, Bird-watching and many others.

Prospectuses are available from the Head Master.

Charitable status. Belhaven Hill School Trust Ltd is a Registered Charity, number 40134. Its aim is to educate children in the full sense of the word.

Belmont
(Mill Hill Junior School)

Mill Hill London NW7 4ED.
Tel: 020 8959 1431
Fax: 020 8906 3519
e-mail: info@belmontschool.com

Chairman of the Court of Governors: The Rt Hon Dame Angela Rumbold, DBE

***Master:* J R Hawkins**, BA, CertEd

Deputy Head (*Curriculum*): Mrs L Duncan, BSc, PGCE
Deputy Head (*Pastoral & Administration*): F A Steadman, CertEd

Number of Pupils. 260 Boys. 136 Girls

Fees. £2,813 per term (day).

Belmont is situated in the Green Belt on the borders of Hertfordshire and Middlesex, yet is only ten miles from central London. It stands in about 35 acres of its own woods and parkland and enjoys the advantages of a truly rural environment, but at the same time the capital's cultural facilities are easily accessible.

Belmont is the Junior School of Mill Hill which is situated less than a quarter of a mile away. Opened in 1912, it takes its name from the original mansion built on the Ridgeway about the middle of the eighteenth century. Successive alterations and additions have provided a dining-hall, a chapel, a gymnasium, an assembly hall, a library, music-rooms, two science laboratories, an art-room with technology room adjacent, a computer room, new classroom blocks, ample games fields, five all-weather cricket nets, an all-weather cricket pitch, and six hard tennis courts.

Use is made of various facilities at Mill Hill School, notably the squash and fives courts, and the indoor heated swimming-pool.

The usual age of entry is at 7 or 11 years, but 8, 9 and 10-year-olds are considered as vacancies occur. It is expected that most children will pass to Mill Hill, but some may be prepared for entry to other senior schools.

There is a permanent teaching staff of 30, with visiting teachers for Instrumental Music, supportive English and Mathematics, Judo and Fencing. An experienced Matron is in charge of health and welfare, while the school's catering is entrusted to a national company.

The main games are Rugby, Soccer, Cricket, Hockey, Netball and Rounders, but minor sports also flourish, as do instrumental and choral music, drama, and many out-of-school activities. There are French exchanges with Belmont's 'twin' school in Rouen, and all the children take part in the Summer Activities Programme, which includes for senior children a Geography Field trip to Cumbria and an outward bound centre in Herefordshire.

Charitable status. The Mill Hill School Foundation is a Registered Charity, number 3404450. It exists to provide education for boys and girls.

Belmont School

Feldemore Holmbury St Mary Dorking Surrey RH5 6LQ.
Tel: (01306) 730852/730829
Fax: (01306) 731220
e-mail: schooloffice@belmont-school.org
website: www.belmont-school.org
Station: Dorking North

Chairman of the Governors: R J K Salter, Esq

Headmaster: **David St C Gainer**, BEd (Hons) (London)

Number of Pupils. Boys 200 (30 boarders); Girls 60 (15 boarders); Pre-Prep 75 (included in the above numbers).

Fees. Day pupils £2,332 per term, Boarders £1,061 supplement. Pre-prep £1,225–£1,428 per term depending on age.

Founded in London in 1880, the School is now established in 60 acres of wooded parkland overlooking the picturesque village of Holmbury St Mary. The main house, Feldemore, has recently undergone a complete refurbishment. The school now boasts an historic building with a purpose built interior.

A highly qualified and motivated staff prepares boys and girls for senior schools of their parents' choice. Small classes averaging about 16 help create an ideal environment for enthusiastic hard work. We are proud of a particularly high success rate at Common Entrance and Scholarship. All pupils take class music (a high proportion play individual instruments), CDT, computing and the full range of academic subjects. The main house now has a brand new computer room, which is fully fitted. We offer all the usual extra curricular activities and sports and expect the children to participate to the full. Facilities include a large new hard court play area, a heated swimming pool, purpose built indoor hall, new art rooms and acres of space for the children to play including high and low ropes courses. The general welfare of the children is under the care of Mrs Gainer and two matrons. We also have a brand new dining and kitchen block.

With NO Saturday school, weekly boarders have the opportunity for a full family weekend. This has proved very popular, as four nightly boarding is a good compromise for both parents and children with no experience of boarding.

The Pre-Preparatory department is strong, providing children with a well balanced mix of traditional concentration on the three 'Rs' and attention to a wider range of academic stimulus.

The school's most recent developments include the incorporation of a magnificent new building in the grounds which was purpose built and equipped especially for the needs of dyslexic children. MOON HALL has its own Principal and a team of specially trained and appropriately qualified staff. We have recently completed a new Indoor multi-purpose Sports Hall.

Berkhampstead School

Pittville Circus Road Cheltenham Glos GL52 2PZ
Tel: 01242 523263
Fax: 01242 514114
e-mail: Headberky@AOL.com
website: www.berkhampsteadschool.ik.org

Chairman of Governors: Mrs J R Rooker

Headmaster: **T R Owen,** BEd, MA

Numbers. 250 aged 3 to 11

Fees for September 2001. Nursery £825; Pre-Prep, Reception and Year 1 £1,020; Year 2 £1,165; Years 3 and 4 £1,350; Years 5 and 6 £1,425.

Berkhampstead School was founded over 50 years ago and continues to thrive today. Most of our pupils enter the school in the Nursery, which has its own team of teachers and nursery nurses and is situated in a purpose built block that has recently been extended.

Parents comment on the wonderful, happy atmosphere and the stimulating environment that exists throughout the school.

Classes are small, never exceeding 17, and the curriculum is wide-ranging and offers many opportunities for individuals to develop their talents.

All major team sports are taught and a range of after-school sports clubs extend the activities offered. Gymnastics and swimming are core elements of the PE curriculum.

There are several choirs and bands and pupils have the opportunity to learn a variety of instruments in addition to their music lessons.

Drama is taught throughout the school and all pupils are involved in stage productions.

Art is another successful subject, and pupils are encouraged to enter local exhibitions.

The school has an enviable academic reputation, with

over 20% of its pupils gaining Scholarships to many senior independent schools every year.

Pastoral care is also of a very high standard and blends the various aspects of the school together.

Berkhamsted Collegiate Preparatory School

Kings Road Berkhamsted Herts HP4 3YP
Tel: (01442) 358201/2
Fax: (01442) 358203
e-mail: berkhamcoll@porthill.com
website: berkhamstedcollegiateschool.org.uk

Chairman of Governors: Mr P J Williamson

Principal: Dr P Chadwick, MA, PhD, FRSA

***Head:* Mr A J Taylor**, BA

Deputy Head: Mrs J L Howard, CertEd
Head of the Nursery: Mrs M Hall, CertEd

Number of boys. 211
Number of girls. 217
Fees per term. Nursery: £596–£671 (half day), £1,257 (full day). Infants/Juniors: £1,512–£2,019.

Berkhamsted Collegiate Preparatory School opened in September 1998 as a new co-educational school, offering first-class facilities for the 3 to 11 age group, in conjunction with the highest standards of teaching and educational development. All classes offer a happy, caring environment where children are encouraged to investigate and explore the world around them. Classes at all levels have access to computers. Key features include a new multi-purpose hall, modern dining facilities, a full range of specialist classrooms and nursery units. The Preparatory School also has use of Senior School facilities including extensive playing fields, tennis courts and swimming pool.

"Stepping Stones is an excellent nursery" *Ofsted report*

The Stepping Stones department has provided nursery education for boys and girls aged 3 and 4 since 1991. It continues to grow in popularity with parents and is housed within a recently refurbished building, St David's House. A carefully structured curriculum encourages the development of basic skills with a broad and balanced programme of learning and play. Literacy and numeracy are taught from the entry class onwards and scientific thinking is developed through experiment and problem solving. Children are also encouraged to express themselves through art, music and drama.

Infants and Juniors. All children are encouraged to develop to their full potential and grow in confidence and independence. The School's general approach is progressive, while retaining traditional values and standards; courtesy and politeness towards others are required at all times. Academic achievement is of great importance, but the emphasis on other activities such as sports and music ensures that pupils receive a well-rounded education.

At this level, literacy and numeracy are the key foundation skills, but subjects such as science, history, geography, religious studies, French, art, design, information technology, music and drama gain increasing prominence. Pupils spend the majority of time with a form teacher who takes overall responsibility for each child's social and academic progress and are supported by specialist teachers covering subjects such as science, music and sport.

A wide range of extra-curricular activities are offered at lunch-time, the end of the school day and on Saturday mornings, including art, drama, music and sport. There are choirs and orchestras which perform in concerts and services throughout the year and various sports teams which compete successfully.

Charitable status. Berkhamsted Collegiate School is a Registered Charity, number 311056. It is a leading Charitable School in the field of Junior and Secondary Education.

Bickley Park School

Bickley Kent BR1 2DS
Tel: 020 8467 2195.
Fax: 020 8325 5511
e-mail: info@bickleyparkschool.co.uk
website: www.bickleyparkschool.co.uk
Station: Bickley SR

***Headmaster:* Martin Bruce**, MA, BA, FCollP

Deputies:
P M Marsh, BEd, CertEd
M T C Cash, BA

Number of Boys. 420
Number of Girls. 20
Fees. From £750 per term (Nursery) to £2,450 (Boys in Years 7 & 8). There are no compulsory extras.

The school is situated in Bickley and has pleasant grounds and a large, excellent sports field close by. It has displayed a commitment to continuous modernisation and more recent structures have been added to complement the original Victorian buildings.

Our Nursery provides a warm and stimulating environment, guiding children through the earliest stages of learning towards a firm foundation in the basic skills of literacy and numeracy, whilst encouraging social development. In the Pre-Prep (4-7) a class-teacher based approach is blended with the start of additional subjects taught by subject specialists.

In the Prep School, reached at the age of 7, academic abilities and talents are further nurtured by the deployment of specialists across the range of subjects. Drama and music are energetically encouraged both for the very talented and for all. The same thinking underpins the busy and successful sporting diary: there is wide scope for the natural games' player or athlete, and plenty of opportunity for everyone else to enjoy recreational exercise.

The school curriculum is designed to prepare pupils for scholarship or Common Entrance examinations to senior schools at 13+, although some boys leave for appropriate schools at 11.

Visitors are made warmly welcome at the school and are encouraged to come and see us in action.

Charitable status. Bickley Park School Limited is a Registered Charity, number 307915. It exists to provide a broad curriculum of education for boys aged 2–13 years.

Bilton Grange

Dunchurch Rugby CV22 6QU.
Tel: (01788) 810217.
Fax: (01788) 816922
Station: Rugby (London Euston to Rugby is 1 hour 5 minutes)

The school is registered as an Educational Trust under the Charities Act and is controlled by a Board of Governors.

Chairman of Governors: I H Stott, Esq

Headmaster: **Quentin Edwards**, MA (Oxon)

Senior Staff:

Senior Master: Anthony Millinger, CertEd
Senior Mistress: Valerie Harper, BA, CertEd
Director of Studies: David Noble, BA
Director of Public Relations: Paul Jackson, BEd (Hons)
Pre-Preparatory School: Maggie Edwards, BA, ARCM, PGCE

Number of Pupils. 360 boys and girls of whom 67 are boarders. Preparatory (8–13 year olds) 208 pupils; Pre-Preparatory (4–7 year olds) 127 pupils.

Fees per term. Boarding £3,799. Weekly Boarding £3,799. Day: 10–13 £3,032; 8–9 £2,653; 6–7 £1,913; 5–6 £1,627; 4–5 £1,321.

Bursaries for Service children, third child and scholarships available.

The school is set in 150 acres of Parkland within a mansion designed by Augustus Welby Pugin in 1846. A school since 1887, it has a long established tradition and offers both boys and girls an exciting and varied experience both in and out of the classroom. The main emphasis of the Upper school is on a boarding ethos with a timetable spanning the whole day plus Saturday morning lessons and activities for boarders and those day pupils who wish to join in our Sunday Adventures. The Pre-preparatory school is on the same site but in a separate building where the specific requirements of the younger age group of 4–7 can be catered for. There is no Saturday schooling for these younger pupils. A Montessori Nursery school caters for the 3 to 4 year olds in morning and afternoon sessions.

All the pupils can use the large range of facilities on site which include a new Information Technology room of Apple Macintosh computers and CD-ROMS, a large indoor swimming pool, Sports Hall, 9-hole Golf Course, Theatre, Library, Design Technology and Art area and the extensive Music wing. The religious life of the school is enhanced by our own Chapel where Sung Services form a regular part of the children's experience.

The syllabus followed by the children mirrors the National Curriculum but not slavishly so that the individual interests of the highly qualified staff can be used to best advantage. The classics are not forgotten. The younger age group are taught predominantly by their form staff with specialist teachers contributing to their overall curriculum. From 9 onwards, all children are taught by specialist staff in classes of no more than 16. Great emphasis is laid on incorporating modern technology within the lessons and pupils are encouraged to use their own portable computers along with their pens and pencils. The computers have been found to be highly beneficial for pupils with dyslexia who can also receive specialist help provided by the local Dyslexia Institute.

Extra curricular activities are the distinguishing features of Bilton Grange as against a normal 9–4pm day school. The usual sports of Rugby, Hockey, Netball, Football, Cricket, Tennis, Golf and Athletics are a staple diet but there is also the opportunity to take part and excel in Swimming, Horseriding, Dry Skiing, Basketball, Sailing, Canoeing, Squash and Scouting together with travelling further afield for Adventure activities on a remote island in the Western Isles of Scotland or building your own tree-house in the extensive grounds. Music is a very important aspect of school life and both the Choir and Orchestra have undertaken foreign tours in recent years. The Choir must be one of the first Prep school Choirs to have made its own recording on a CD, incorporating original compositions by the Head of Music, Mr Nicholas Burt.

The pastoral side of a child's life is, in the first instance, overseen by the Form Tutor who works in close contact with the Matrons and Headmaster. The dormitories are undergoing a major overhaul with an emphasis on personal space and privacy but with the opportunity to get together in the evenings with the other pupils and House Parents. Flexible boarding can be arranged so that pupils can board for one night, one week or half a term as the family's needs dictate. A school shop in the grounds provides most of the necessary clothing and Games kit and the children enjoy visiting the Tuck Shop and budgeting their weekly allowance. Pupils are escorted on the train to and from London at the start and end of terms and half terms. Special arrangements for pupils flying are made regularly.

Pupils leave Bilton Grange with a confidence in their own ability and an open, friendly and tolerant attitude. Both boys and girls are entered for the Common Entrance Examinations and many go to Rugby. They also go to the other major Secondary schools such as Oundle, Oakham, Uppingham, Malvern, Eton, Cheltenham and Shrewsbury. Some enter for the local 12+ examinations. An average of 12 pupils a year gain major scholarships and awards.

Charitable status. Bilton Grange Trust is a Registered Charity, number 399050. It exists to provide education for boys and girls.

Birchfield School

Albrighton Wolverhampton WV7 3AF.
Tel: (01902) 372534.
Fax: (01902) 373516
Station: Albrighton

Chairman of the Governors: J L Andrews

Headmaster: **R P Merriman, BSc** (Hons)

Number of Boys. 260 (Boarders 20, Day boys 240)

Fees. Weekly Boarders, £2,950 per term, Day boys, £2,200 per term, Juniors, £1,400 per term, Nursery £1,200. (No compulsory extras)

The school is situated in the superb, rolling Shropshire countryside about 7 miles from both Wolverhampton and Telford. The School has easy access from the M54 motorway being only two minutes from junction 3.

There are 20 acres of grounds consisting of large attractive gardens and playing fields accommodating 7/8 soccer and rugby pitches.

Recent developments include a new building for Art, CDT and changing rooms. The library has been re-located and modernised, whilst there is a specialist high tech room for ICT with a network of 20 computers. At the end of 1996 a new music school was opened, comprising specialist practice rooms as well as a large main teaching room. Three new hard court tennis courts were also completed in 1996. Within the last two years further additions have included a new science laboratory, an additional changing room, a further extension to the art and CDT areas, as well as a purpose-built nursery department for 3–4 year olds which was opened in November 1997. The school has its own gymnasium and an outdoor heated swimming pool. A new school kitchen and dining room opened in September 2000.

Class sizes are small with a maximum of 18 in the senior school and 16 in the pre-prep. The teaching staff consists of 14 men and 15 women and there are two additional classroom assistants in the pre-prep department. There are visiting staff for individual music tuition and for special educational needs.

Mrs Merriman is in charge of catering and domestic arrangements and there is a full time School Nurse.

Boys are prepared for entry into a wide range of independent senior schools which will suit the individual's needs. Awards to public schools are regularly won. Boys are also tested at Key Stages 1 and 2 within the National Curriculum.

Strong emphasis is placed on music, art, drama and sporting activities. The major sports played during the winter include soccer, rugby and hockey, whilst in the summer cricket, athletics, tennis and swimming predominate. The boys are also involved in a wide range of extra-curricular activities such as drama, chess and computing which are on offer throughout the year.

Charitable status. Birchfield School is a Registered Charity, number 528420. Its aim is to educate boys.

Birkdale School

Clarke House Clarke Drive Sheffield S10 2NS
Tel: (0114) 267 0407
Fax: (0114) 268 2929

Chairman of Governors: S A P Hunter, MA, JP

Head of Preparatory School: **A D Jones**, BA, MA(Ed), CertEd

Number of Boys. 295 day boys (4–11)

Fees per Term. Pre-preparatory School £1,460; Preparatory School £1,726.

Birkdale has grown and developed since the post war years into a school offering a continuous curriculum for boys aged 4 to 18 and girls in the Sixth Form.

This expansion led to the reorganisation of the school and in 1988 a new Preparatory School was established at Clarke House, situated in a pleasant residential area near the University and close to the Senior School. The school has a firm Christian tradition and this, coupled with the size of the school, ensures that the boys develop their own abilities, whether academic or otherwise, to the full.

The Pre-Preparatory Department is accommodated in a self contained wing of the school but enjoys full use of the well resourced facilities of the Preparatory School. Specialist subject teaching across the curriculum starts at the age of 7 and there is an advantageous exchange of teachers between Preparatory and Senior Schools, ensuring communication and ease of transfer. Setting in the core subjects in the final two years enhance, still further, the pupil teacher ratio.

The school has its own Matron and pastoral care is given high priority. Boys are encouraged to join a wide variety of clubs and societies in their leisure time. Music plays a significant part in school life, both in and out of the timetable. There is a large choir and orchestra and there are strong choral links with Sheffield Cathedral where many of the choristers are Birkdalians.

Cricket, Association and Rugby Football are played on the School's own substantial playing fields, which are within easy reach of the school. Instruction in Tennis and Judo are available as part of the extensive extra curricular programme.

The majority of boys pass into the Senior School.

Charitable status. Birkdale School is a Registered Charity, number 1018973. A Company Limited by Guarantee. It exists to provide education for boys.

Bishopsgate School

Englefield Green Surrey TW20 0YJ.
Tel: (01784) 432109
Fax: (01784) 430460
e-mail: headmaster@bishopsgate.surrey.sch.uk
Stations: Egham (2 miles), Datchet (3 miles), Windsor (4 miles)

Chairman of Governors: J B Richmond-Dodd, Esq

Headmaster: **M Dunning,** BA, PGCE, MCollP

Number of Pupils. 280, 14 Weekly Boarders.

Fees. Weekly Boarders £3,500 per term. Senior Day £2,610 per term. Junior Day £2,240 per term. Pre-Prep £1,390–£1,560.

The School educates boys and girls aged 2½–13 in beautiful surroundings on a 20 acre site beside Windsor Great Park.

Children are prepared in small classes for Common Entrance and Scholarship examinations to Senior Independent Schools. Each child is encouraged to be active in sport, music, drama and a wide range of other activities. The school aims to nurture in each child self respect and care for others in a supportive family atmosphere that lays a firm foundation for the development of a child's talents. The active involvement of parents is enjoyed and encouraged.

Weekly boarding (Monday to Friday) is available. A prospectus and further details can be obtained from the School Office.

Charitable status. Bishopsgate School is a Registered Charity, number 1060511. It aims to provide a broad and sound education for its pupils with thorough and personal pastoral care.

Bishop's Stortford College Junior School

Bishop's Stortford Herts CM23 2PH
Tel: (01279) 838607
Fax: (01279) 306110
Station: Bishop's Stortford

Head: **J A Greathead**, BEd (Bangor)

Chairman of Governors: J R Tee, MA

Number of Pupils. 50 boarders and 420 day pupils.

Fees. Boarders £3,080–£3,355 per term. Day pupils £2,271–£2,545 per term. 4–7 year olds £1,483 per term. There are no compulsory extras.

There are 40 full-time members of staff, and a number of Senior School staff also teach in the Junior School. Being on the same campus as the Senior School, many College facilities (language laboratory, art and technology centres, music school, computer room, sports hall, swimming pools, all-weather pitches, dining hall, sanatorium) are shared. The Junior School also has its own buildings, with the main building containing multi-purpose Hall (with stage), laboratories, IT centre and classrooms, opened in 1985, and a new building containing library, art room and classrooms opened in 1999.

The Junior School routine and curriculum are appropriate to the 7–13 age range, with pupils being prepared for Common Entrance and Senior Schools' Scholarships; many children proceed to the College Senior School. There are 21 forms streamed by general ability and setted for Maths. High standards of work and behaviour are expected and the full development, in a happy and friendly atmosphere, of each child's abilities in sport and the Arts is actively encouraged. A strong swimming tradition exists and many of the Staff are expert coaches of the major games (rugby, hockey, cricket, netball, rounders and tennis). The choirs and orchestra flourish throughout the year, helped by Activities times, as are many minor sports, outdoor pursuits, crafts, computing and chess. Six major dramatic productions occur every year.

A co-educational Pre-Prep Department for 4–6 year olds was opened in September 1995, and girls aged 4–13 now number 193.

The Junior School is run on boarding lines with a six-day week and a 5pm finish each day. The 7 and 8 year-olds have a slightly shorter day and separate classrooms.

Entry tests for 7, 8, 9, 10, 11-year-olds are held each January; Academic, Music and Art Scholarships are available at 10 years of age, as are Bursaries and Scholarships at 11 years of age and younger.

Charitable status. Incorporated Bishop's Stortford College Association is a Registered Charity, number 311057. Bishop's Stortford College Junior School exists to provide a boarding education incorporating the highest academic standards and a wide range of team sports and extra curricular activities within a caring and happy environment with clearly defined standards and aspirations.

The Blue Coat School

Edgbaston Birmingham B17 0HR.
Tel: 0121 454 1425
Fax: 0121 454 7757
e-mail: admissions@bluecoat.bham.sch.uk
website: www.bluecoat.bham.sch.uk

Co-educational Preparatory School (day, weekly and full boarding).

1722 Foundation.

Chairman of Governors: Mr N R Thompson, FRICS
Headmaster: **A D J Browning**, MA (Cantab)

Deputy Head: C R Lynn, MA, MIL

Number of Pupils. The total enrolment is 459 children. The Pre-Preparatory Department has 196 boys and girls from 2–7 years, while the Main School has 263 from 7–13 years. Around 45 of these are boarders and 218 are day-children.

There is a graduate and qualified full-time teaching staff of 35 teachers, giving a teacher/pupil ratio of 1:12. Part-time staff are additional to these figures.

Fees. Pre-Preparatory Department: £1,360–£1,685 per term. Main School: Day children £2,055 per term. Weekly Boarders £3,175 per term. Boarders £3,530 per term. The day fees quoted include lunches and morning and afternoon breaks. Optional instrumental lessons, judo classes, speech-training, ballet and some school outings are extras.

Foundation Places are available at greatly reduced charges to both boarders and day children who are in special need.

Academic and Music Scholarships, worth 45% of the fees, are offered at eleven years of age.

Facilities. Set in 15 acres of grounds and playing fields just 2 miles from the centre of Birmingham, the school is also within easy reach of open countryside. Its well-designed buildings and facilities comprise four boarding houses, the Chapel, the Administrative Building, the Main School teaching block, the Pre-Preparatory and Nursery Departments, the Pre-School, sports pitches, tennis courts and a superb multi-purpose Sports Centre with a heated 25m swimming pool.

Additional features include two modern science laboratories, the school library, an art room with a photographic dark room, a pottery studio, design-technology and home-economics rooms and cross-campus ICT facilities. A Centre for the Performing Arts is under development.

Children from several countries including the UK are prepared for scholarships, Common Entrance and various other examinations to senior schools, both locally and throughout the country. The National Curriculum is incorporated at Key Stages 1, 2 and 3 as part of a wider academic structure.

The school places great emphasis on Music. There is a robed Chapel Choir which is affiliated to the RSCM, a Junior Choir, a school orchestra and various instrumental groups. Instrumental teaching is supported by the school's own music staff and by fifteen visiting teachers. A Keyboard Laboratory is used to teach listening and performance skills. The school benefits from *Sibelius* software which is used in the teaching of composition.

The main sports are Soccer, Rugby, Cricket, Hockey, Netball, Rounders, Tennis, Athletics and Swimming. The teams enjoy considerable success in inter-school competitions and all children have the opportunity to develop their skills.

Extra-curricular activities include Guides, Brownies, Cubs, Gymnastics, Harry Potter, Judo, Ballet, Drama, Sign Language, Speech-Training, Pottery, Photography, Computer and Design Technology clubs, Chess, Table Tennis, Dance and Water-polo. Excursions, field-courses, an annual ski-week in the Alps are available each year, while visits to France provide an opportunity to experience life in a French family. The school is a member of the Boarding Schools Association and carries the Accreditation of the Independent Schools Council.

Charitable status. The Blue Coat School, Birmingham is a Registered Charity, number 528805. It exists to provide a boarding and day education of quality for children of Preparatory School age.

Bodiam Manor School

Bodiam Robertsbridge E Sussex TN32 5UJ
Tel: Staplecross (01580) 830225
Station: Etchingham (Hastings Line)

Headmaster: **C D Moore**, BSc

Number of Pupils. Boys: 95. Girls: 95

Current Fees. Day pupils Under 5 years £1,021, 5 years £1,727, 6 years £1,901, 7 years+ £2,108, (Mornings only) 3 & 4 years £665.

Bodiam Manor is a co-educational school with an integral nursery and pre-preparatory department.

Overlooking Bodiam Castle and set in 11 acres of beautiful countryside on the East Sussex/Kent border, Bodiam is a family-run school founded in 1955. It has 190 day pupils aged between 2½ and 13. School finishes at 4 pm for younger pupils and all extra-curricular activities finish by 5.30 pm for older pupils. There is no Saturday morning school but activities such as trampoline, swimming, mini-rugby and cricket are available on Saturdays.

The curriculum is geared to Common Entrance examinations to senior independent schools. Over the years many pupils have achieved scholarships at the senior level.

Bodiam has the reputation of being a happy school. Given the right conditions, children who are happy will enjoy learning and will want to achieve. One of our aims is to encourage awareness that learning is not confined to the classroom but takes place throughout life in all kinds of situations.

The opportunities offered to pupils are wide and varied and the school day is a very busy one. Music, dance, drama, gymnastics, swimming and trampolining are particularly strong. The annual school ski and barge holidays and a wide range of clubs and outings are all very much part of life at Bodiam. During their time at Bodiam children are encouraged to experience a range of activities and to develop their own individual potential to the full.

Boundary Oak School

Roche Court Fareham Hampshire PO17 5BL.
Tel: (01329) 280955
Fax: (01329) 827656
e-mail: admin@boundaryoak.freeserve.co.uk

Chairman of Governors: T Allen, Esq

***Headmaster:* R B Bliss**, CertEd (London)

Deputy Headmaster: J C MacFarlane, BA, CertEd (London)

Number of Pupils. 40 Boarders, 180 Day Pupils

Fees. Boarders £3,445, Weekly Boarders £2,575–£3,445, Day Pupils £2,085–£2,375, Junior School £1,505–£1,660, Nursery £730–£1,315 (all day).

The School was founded in 1918 and moved to Roche Court in 1960. A new 99 year lease was secured in 1994. The school is set in 22 acres of pleasant self-contained grounds close to Fareham and the M27 but enjoying extensive views of the countryside around.

The School is now fully co-educational in all respects with girls' boarding established in totally refurbished accommodation.

The Nursery Department takes children from the age of two-and-three-quarters to rising five and this group are now housed in a brand new purpose built centre offering the most up to date facilities that was completed in January 2000. This department is structured to the needs of this age group and the day can extend from 8.50 am to either 12 noon or 3.30pm.

The Junior Department have their own purpose built buildings and other facilities within the school, and staff of seven teachers, and caters for children from rising 5 to 8 years of age.

At 8 years the children move to the Senior Department where they remain until they are 13. Full and weekly boarding is offered to all from the age of 7 years and the school has a policy of admitting boarders in a flexible system that is of great benefit to all. Pupils are prepared for a wide number of Independent Schools throughout the United Kingdom in a friendly and caring environment.

Apart from the historic main house of Roche Court where the boarders live, there is the Jubilee Block of classrooms, two Laboratories and a Geography Room in a separate building, The Widley Block, Library and The Music Centre, which incorporates a computer centred music generating complex. The School has a new art and design/technology centre that incorporates work areas for Photography, Pottery and Carpentry. The school has a fine assembly hall that is also used for Drama and Physical Education.

As well as extensive playing fields with woods beyond for cross country, three tennis courts and a netball court, there is an outdoor swimming pool and the indoor Fareham Pool is within very easy reach with our three mini-buses.

Most sports are taught and there is a wide selection of clubs and activities run in the school for both day and boarding pupils including judo and shooting.

For a copy of the prospectus and full details of scholarships, please apply to the Headmaster, or view us on the internet on www.boundaryoak.co.uk.

Charitable status. Boundary Oak School Trust Ltd is a Registered Charity, number 307346. It exists to provide education for boys and girls.

Bow Preparatory School

South Road Durham DH1 3LS.
Tel: 0191 3848233
Fax: 0191 3841371

Chairman of Governors: Canon J D Hodgson

***Headmaster:* R N Baird,** BA (Hons), PGCE

Number of Boys. 157
Age Range. 3–13.
Fees. Dayboys £1,045–£1,956 per term (including Pre-School).

Bow School is the Preparatory School for Durham School and has been situated in its present site overlooking the Cathedral since 1888. New facilities include a fully equipped Computer room, and a new Science block opened in September 1997. In addition, the link with Durham School enables Bow boys to use all the excellent facilities there, such as swimming pool, playing fields and theatre.

Boys are prepared for Common Entrance, Scholarship examinations and entry into any senior independent schools, although the vast majority proceed to Durham School. The School has a fine record of academic achievement over the years. A high pupil-ratio is maintained and small classes are considered vital.

The main sports played are rugby, cricket, swimming and athletics, and the school has an outstanding tradition in competitive sport. Many other sports are catered for as well as a range of hobbies and activities, which include squash, fencing, chess, computers, badminton, judo and football.

Music and drama form an integral part of life at Bow, with an active choir, orchestra and drama group.

Entry is based on an assessment test and interview with the Headmaster.

Charitable status. Durham School is a Registered Charity, number 1023407. The aim of the charity is to advance education in the North-East.

Bradford Grammar Junior School (Clock House)

Keighley Road Bradford West Yorkshire BD9 4JP
Tel: 01274 553742
Fax: 01274 553745
e-mail: kjhewitt@bgs.bradford.sch.uk

Chairman of the Board of Governors: Mr A H Jerome, MA

***Headmaster:* G Lee-Gallon,** BTech (Hons)

Deputy Headmaster: N H Gabriel, BA (Hons), DipArch

Number of pupils. 164 boys, 30 girls
Fees. £1,710 per term.

The school is within easy reach of the spectacular Yorkshire Dales. Bradford has good access from the M1 and M62. Local transport is excellent and the Metro train service along the Wharfe and Aire Valleys puts the school within travelling distance of Skipton, Ilkley and Keighley. School buses transport pupils from Huddersfield, Halifax, Leeds and Ilkley.

Clock House, a seventeenth century Manor House, has been extended and refurbished. The thoughtful blending of the old with the new has created a school of style and spaciousness. Recent developments have included the addition of four new classrooms, and specialist accommodation for ICT and DT. The ICT room is fully equipped with high specification computers, networked and able to access the Internet.

Because of the proximity of the Senior School, Clock House is able to use many of their facilities and accommodation: Science laboratories, Art room, extensive PE and games resources, including the new swimming pool (as well as the expertise of their staff), Science rooms, Hockney Theatre and Price Hall are always available for Junior School use.

Boys and girls can enter the school at the start of Years 3, 4, 5 and 6 having satisfied our entrance requirements; an informal assessment for Years 3 and 4 and an entrance examination for those joining in Years 5 and 6. Invariably most of our pupils transfer to the Senior School and the close relationship between the two schools enables us to make the transition as smooth as possible.

Children in Years 3 and 4 are taught mostly by their form teachers, although there is some specialist input for PE, Games, Art, Music and Science. In Years 5 and 6 there is a considerable amount of specialist teaching across the curriculum. Boys and girls are taught by staff experienced in teaching bright, well-motivated children.

Extra-curricular activities take place at lunchtime. There is a long tradition of excellence in sport, music and drama. Winter sports include rugby, netball, hockey, swimming, cross-country and football. In the summer children play cricket, rounders and take part in athletics and a variety of other sports.

The Junior School is a very busy place but pastoral care permeates all the school does. Our aim is to provide young boys and girls with a wide range of educational experiences and to develop the right attitude to learning so that they fulfil their potential, in a safe, friendly, tolerant and caring environment utilising all the resources and facilities the school has to offer.

Brambletye

East Grinstead West Sussex RH19 3PD.
Tel: (01342) 321004
Fax: (01342) 317562
e-mail: brambletye@brambletye.rmplc.co.uk

Chairman of Governors: R D Christie, Esq, BA

***Headmaster:* H D Cocke**, BA, CertEd (Oxon)

Number of Pupils. 210 co-educational boarding/day puils, aged 3 to 13.

Fees. Boarders £4,100 per term. Day Boys £3,100-£3,400 per term. Pre-Prep £1,500 per term. Nursery £920-£1,300 per term.

Brambletye is an independent boarding school for boys and girls aged between 7 and 13 years. The Beeches, our pre-preparatory department, takes boys and girls from nursery age to the age of seven. Brambletye welcomes as day pupils boys and girls who live close enough to the school to enjoy what it has to offer. There is an expectation that all day pupils will board before they leave the school, as it is a valuable experience in itself, especially if the next move is to a senior, independent boarding school.

The pupils enjoy and benefit from living and working in a community. Much of a child's time is, inevitably, organised, but there is free time too. It is an important feature of boarding school life that each pupil should learn to manage his or her time in a way that is not only personally fulfilling and enjoyable, but also beneficial.

Brambletye is a large country house in a 140 acre estate, overlooking Ashdown Forest. The children enjoy a uniquely beautiful, healthy and spacious setting in which to grow up. The school stands just off the A22, one mile south of East Grinstead. Gatwick airport is only 20 minutes by car and Heathrow is also easily accessible.

Developments over the years have provided first class facilities throughout the school. The building of the Arts Centre, the Design Technology Workshop, the Library, the ICT Room, the Sports Hall and the Pre-Preparatory Department have ensured that Brambletye has maintained its position as a leading preparatory school in the country.

Cricket, Rugby, Association Football, Hockey and Netball are played, and the pupils are also coached in Fencing, Golf, Judo, Shooting, Squash and Swimming. The School has its own 6 hole golf course. Canoeing and rock climbing also take place.

There is a school orchestra and the pupils have opportunities to learn a variety of musical instruments. There are two choirs, both affiliated to the Royal School of Church Music.

Drama is taught throughout the school and regular productions are staged by the pupils. There is a very strong Art Department: an annual Art Exhibition is held at the school in June and the pupils' work has also been exhibited recently in London, East Grinstead and Tunbridge Wells.

Brambletye's Pre-Preparatory Department is situated within the grounds of the Preparatory School and is housed in a purpose built building opened in September 2000. This incorporates many exciting facilities including four classrooms, an octagonal hall, a library, study support rooms and a nursery.

Aims of the School. Brambletye has always been run along family lines. A happy, working relationship exists between staff and pupils. We believe that boys and girls who are happy and relaxed will do well, and we expect them all to give of their best.

We place strong emphasis on high standards of manners and good behaviour. The principles of Christian upbringing and worship are a major influence in the day-to-day activities of the school.

Special care is taken of overseas pupils. Flights at Gatwick and Heathrow Airports are met at the beginning of each term, and children can be seen off safely to their destinations at the end of each term. As all children leave the school during the exeat weekends and half-term holidays, parents living abroad should arrange for a nominated guardian to be responsible for their child during these times. The School is happy to provide advice and information about how these arrangements can be made.

We aim to produce a happy, confident and well-adjusted child, who works hard, enjoys drama, games and music, plays a part in some of the numerous societies and hobbies, and takes a full share in the corporate life of the school. The children themselves play a part in the school's organisation through the House system. By consulting and encouraging them to take their own decisions, we believe that they are helped to form an independent character, a sense of respect and responsibility, and enthusiasm for learning and living.

Charitable status. Brambletye School Trust Limited is a Registered Charity, number 307003. It aims to provide an all round education for the children in its care.

Bramcote Lorne School

Gamston Retford Notts DN22 0QQ.
Tel: 01777 838636
Fax: 01777 838633
e-mail: info@bramcote-lorne.notts.sch.uk
website: www.bramcotelorne.com

Chairman of Governors: Mr T Banks

***Headmaster:* Mr J H Gibson**, BEd (Hons), CertEd (Oxon)

Director of Boarding: Mrs P Crowe, RGN

Numbers. Boarders (boys and girls): 35. Nursery: 60; Day pupils: Pre-Prep 60, Prep 140.

Fees. Nursery and Pre-Prep: £1,100-£1,300 per term. Prep: £1,650–£2,000 per term. Boarding: £2,450-£2,800 (weekly), £2,550-£2,850 per term (full).

Bramcote Lorne was formed in 1996 after the amalgamation of Retford's two well-established Preparatory Schools. The new school enjoys fine facilities within a 20 acre site on the fringe of one of Nottinghamshire's finest villages.

Excellent communications along the A1 and the GNER rail link to London make the school very accessible for boarder parents. The school operates four bus routes from villages in Nottinghamshire and Lincolnshire.

Bramcote Lorne is blessed with some of the finest facilities imaginable in a small school. Totally refurbished during 2000, the school's boarding accommodation is of a particularly high standard with ensuite bedrooms for senior pupils. Matron, a very well qualified nurse, is responsible for directing boarding/pastoral care which is of the highest order. Weekend activities are very varied. Full and weekly boarding is very popular; occasional boarding is also available.

Classroom accommodation is of a very high standard. Three "areas of excellence" were commissioned last year and the school now enjoys an exceptional IT provision, a Performing Arts Centre and a Design Technology Centre. The latter has a provision for Design, CAD, Technical Drawing and Food Technology.

Other specialist facilities include a spacious Science Laboratory, an Art Studio and Dyslexic Unit. Senior pupils enjoy the use of their own day house. A new Junior Department for 7-9 year olds has recently been established.

Games facilities are excellent with a Sports Hall and extensive games fields on site. An all weather games surface was completed this year, an indoor swimming pool forms part of the future development plan.

A thriving Pre-Nursery and Nursery School feed a well-resourced Pre-Prep.

Charitable status. Bramcote Lorne School is a Registered Charity, number 528262. It exists to provide a high standard of education for boys and girls.

Bramcote School

Scarborough N Yorkshire YO11 2TT
Tel: (01723) 373086
Fax: (01723) 364186
e-mail: bramcote.school@talk21.com
website: www.bramcoteschool.com
Station: Scarborough

Chairman of Governors: H A Bethell, Esq, ACA, BA (Hons)

Headmaster: **J P Kirk**, BSc, FRSA

Number of Pupils. 58 boys, 25 girls

Fees. Boarding: £3,570; Day: £2,560

Bramcote is a boarding preparatory school for boys and girls aged between 7 and 13 years. The school is set in its own grounds close to the sea on Scarborough's South Cliff. The school was founded on its present site in 1893 and became an Educational Trust in 1957, administered by a chairman and ten governors of wide professional and educational experience.

A girls' wing has now been opened and other recent developments have included the complete refurbishment of the boarding accommodation, improvements to the teaching facilities and a sports hall, which can be used as an indoor tennis court.

The curriculum is based on the Scholarship and Common Entrance requirements for major Independent Schools throughout the country. Although the experienced, full-time teaching staff of 13 ensure that the academic standards for which Bramcote has long held a high reputation are maintained, the school caters for children of mixed ability and classes are small with extra help available where needed by the school's qualified specialist.

Bramcote's facilities and position allow a wide range of extra-curricular activities in the evenings and at weekends. Facilities include the new sports hall, a modern music and art centre, theatre, newly equipped computer room, indoor swimming pool and floodlit tennis court and play areas. Frequent visits are made to the theatre and concerts, whilst the seaside and nearby National Parks give opportunities for more adventurous pursuits such as orienteering, canoeing and rambling.

The school has excellent playing fields, where football, netball, rugby, hockey, lacrosse and cricket are played as major sports, with a wide variety of alternative opportunities including tennis, athletics, squash, judo, dance, shooting and archery.

The school has a strong musical tradition and tuition is available for the full range of orchestral instruments and choir. The department is run by a Director of Music with 10 peripatetic staff and all pupils learn to play at least one musical instrument.

Pastoral and health care is supervised by the Headmaster's wife, with one medical and three assistant matrons.

For further information, parents are invited to write or to telephone the Headmaster or the school secretary for copies of a prospectus and current magazine or to arrange a visit to the school.

Charitable status. Bramcote School is a Registered Charity, number 529739. It exists to provide education for boys and girls.

Bramley
Educational Trust Limited

Chequers Lane Walton on the Hill Tadworth Surrey KT20 7ST
Tel: (01737) 812004
Fax: (01737) 819945

Chairman of Governors: Mr C P Harvey

***Headmistress:* Mrs B Johns**, CertEd (Oxon)

Number in School. 130, Girls 3–11.

Fees. £750–£1,780 per term, to include lunches, where appropriate.

Bramley was founded in 1945 as an independent pre-preparatory and preparatory day school and became an Educational Trust in 1972. A registered charity, the school is administered by a Trust Council, all income being used for educational purposes. The school has been accredited by the Independent Schools Joint Council.

Bramley provides a happy, caring educational environment for its 130 pupils in which every individual is helped to attain her highest potential. Academic success is of obvious importance, but alongside that children are encouraged to develop their own interests and talents so that they become confident, but considerate members of the community. An excellent teacher/pupil ratio; a caring friendly atmosphere; highly qualified and enthusiastic staff; a genuine concern for each child's welfare – this is the Bramley approach.

Throughout the school girls work in small classes, according to their age group, with particular attention being paid to meeting the specific needs of individuals. In the early years, experienced and dedicated form teachers have full responsibility for their classes, while older children benefit from specialist teaching staff.

The pre-preparatory department – Little Bramley – provides a very sound foundation for later years at the school. It enables young children, from the age of three, to settle quickly and happily into a stimulating environment in which there is every opportunity for learning and safe, organised play.

The preparatory curriculum is constantly being developed to keep abreast of educational changes in the National Curriculum, while retaining the excellence of well-tried methods. Particular emphasis is placed on Mathematics, English and Science, but the girls follow a comprehensive timetable, to cover a wide variety of subjects. Recently extensive new facilities have been created by the building of The Founders' Wing.

Bramley is justly proud of its excellent examination results for entry to senior schools.

Charitable status. Bramley Educational Trust Limited is a Registered Charity, number 270046. Its aim is to provide an educational establishment for 3–11 year olds.

Brentwood Preparatory School

Brentwood Essex CM15 8EQ.
Tel: (01277) 243333; Pre-Prep (01277) 243239
Fax: (01277) 243340
Stations: Brentwood or Shenfield

Headmaster: **P R MacDougall**, CertEd, BEd (Hons)

Head of Pre-Prep: Mrs A Murrells, BEd (Chelmer Institute)

Chairman of Governors: C J Finch, FSVA

Number of Children. 240 (Prep); 144 (Pre-Prep)

Fees. Tuition £5,895 pa.

The co-educational Pre-Preparatory School with its own Headmistress, seven qualified and experienced early years teachers and four qualified nursery nurses opened in September 1995 for pupils aged 3–7 years and occupies its own self contained purpose built adjacent premises.

Boys and girls are normally admitted into the Preparatory School in the September after they reach the age of seven, through tests taken the previous March and are prepared for entrance to Brentwood School (qv) at eleven. Candidates come from a wide range of schools as well as the Pre-Prep.

The School has its own buildings and grounds quite distinct from the Main School, but is close enough to use the Chapel, Gymnasia, Sanatorium and medical services, Playing Fields and Sports Hall.

Soccer, Cross Country Running, Hockey, Netball, Rounders, Cricket, Athletics, Gymnastics and Swimming are the main sporting activities with excellent additional facilities for Tennis, Fencing and Squash. The Preparatory School has its own heated outdoor Swimming Pool.

There is a fully qualified and experienced staff of 17 full time and 1 part time teacher as well as visiting specialists in Music and a full-time Matron. Modern catering facilities are shared with the Main School.

The aims of the School are to give a thorough grounding in a wide range of basic studies and activities largely following the requirements of the National Curriculum. A broad and varied curriculum, designed to promote the development of sound values and a sense of individual and communal responsibility, is disciplined but not inhibited by examination requirements. Creative and intellectual development are further enhanced through interest groups, a well established Choir and excellent facilities for all aspects of music as well as a separate well-equipped Computer Room. Drama and Musical productions are held during the school year. Regular Games fixtures are held with both Maintained and Independent local and regional schools. Day visits are organised to museums and places of interest in London and the locality as well as residential visits nationally and abroad during holidays.

Charitable status. Brentwood Preparatory School (part of Sir Antony Browne's School Charity) is a Registered Charity, number L5310864/A3. It exists for the purpose of educating children.

Bricklehurst Manor

Stonegate Wadhurst Sussex TN5 7EL.
Tel: (01580) 200448

Headmistress: **Mrs C Flowers**

Number of pupils. 130

Fees from September 2001. Kindergarten £795 per term: Years R, 1 and 2 £1,665 per term. Years 3, 4, 5 and 6 £1,750 per term

Bricklehurst Manor was founded in 1959 as an independent day school for boys and girls from 4 years old. Most boys leave at 8 to go on to their Pre-paratory Schools while girls are prepared for Common Entrance or equivalent standard entrance examinations at 11.

Bricklehurst stands in 3 acres of mature gardens and grounds. Previously a private house, the school retains many home-like characteristics, not least a friendly, family atmosphere which helps young children bridge the gap between home and school, and build up their confidence in the comfort and security of familiar surroundings.

Centrally heated throughout, the school has seven main classrooms and a purpose-built Kindergarten. The big panelled schoolroom is used for PE, Dancing, Drama and any other activity requiring plenty of space. There is a modern Art/Science room, a reference library and a Music Room. Computers are used in all classrooms.

For outdoor playtime there is an orchard with climbing apparatus, swings and sandpit. In the afternoon games period the older children play hockey, netball, football, rounders and cricket; tennis coaching is available and all the children learn to swim in our own heated and covered pool.

Curriculum. In the Kindergarten 3 and 4 year olds are given a happy introduction to school life learning to mix with others of the same age, to play contentedly together as one of a group, and generally to act in an orderly manner. Through carefully structured equipment they also learn their letters and numbers, make a start at reading and gain simple number concepts.

From Form I onwards children stay all day. Gradually their curriculum is extended, subjects such as History, Geography, Scripture, Nature Study, Science and project work are introduced, and there are specialist teachers for Art and Handwork, Drama and all musical activities. French is taught to Juniors. Spanish is an option for older children.

Bricklehurst has a reputation for sending children on to their next schools with a sensible attitude towards learning, and the ability to work independently and with enjoyment. A high standard of behaviour is expected, with emphasis on the gradual development of self-control, a sense of responsibility and real consideration for the needs of others.

Brigg Preparatory School Ltd

Bigby Street Brigg N Lincolnshire DN20 8EF
Tel: (01652) 653237
Fax: (01652) 658879

***Head:* Mrs P Newman**

Number of Pupils. Boys: 80. Girls: 64

Termly Fees. £1,140. Nursery £15.40 per day, £12.20 per half day. Lunches £1.40 per day.

Extras. Swimming at cost.

Religious affiliation: Church of England Entry requirements: Interview.

Staff: 9 full time, 3 part time.

This is a Day School registered as a Charitable Trust and with close links with the Lincoln Diocesan Board of Education. It is situated in pleasant walled grounds in the market town of Brigg.

There is a separate day care centre (Noah's Ark), catering for children from 3 months to 3 years and an excellent Nursery class.

Children are admitted to the Main School from the age of 4+ and are prepared for entry to Independent Senior Schools, Comprehensive and Grammar Schools. The school has an excellent record of academic successes.

The School also aims to further sporting and artistic achievement through a wide curriculum, which includes specialist sports coaching, drama and music. There are two successful School Choirs.

The School offers a Child Minding Service and a wide variety of after-school activities, including traditional sports, badminton, mini-squash, table-tennis, board games, photography, drama and craft. All children have weekly swimming instruction. Games periods are devoted to Soccer, Rugby, Cricket, Netball, Rounders and Athletics.

Charitable status. Brigg Preparatory School is a Registered Charity, number 529742. It exists to provide children with a full Christian education.

Brighton College Preparatory School

Walpole Lodge Walpole Road Brighton East Sussex BN2 2EU.
Tel: (01273) 704210
Fax: (01273) 704286
e-mail: prepsch@brightoncollege.org.uk

Chairman of Preparatory School Governors: Juliet Smith, JP, BA (Hons)

***Headmaster:* Brian D Melia**, MA (Cantab), PGCE

Deputy Head: Heather Beeby, MA, PGCE

Headmistress of Pre-Prep: Sue Wicks, GTCL, LTCL, CertEd

Registrar: Mary-Ann Brightwell

Number of Pupils. Prep: 297, Pre-Prep: 200

Fees per term. Prep: £2,258 (Year 4), £2,895 (Year 8). Weekly Boarding: £2,796-£3,433. Pre-Prep: £437 (Nursery), £1,855 (Year 3).

Brighton College Preparatory School is a co-educational school, which offers a broad curriculum taught to high standards by dedicated and energetic staff. The Pre-Preparatory School cares for children from 3-8 years in a modern, purpose-built building overlooking the playing fields of Brighton College. The Prep School is situated adjacent to the Senior School on its own site. The site is urban, but enjoys close proximity to the sea, the Downs and the vibrant sports and culture of Brighton, where an annual arts festival is held in May.

The excellent facilities provided by Brighton College are shared by the Prep School. These include the Chapel, swimming pool, a sports hall, two areas of playing fields, a purpose-built Performing Arts Centre and The Great Hall, which doubles as a large theatre for the Prep School's annual musical. The Prep School itself has many specialist rooms including a well-equipped ICT suite, a large design technology room, art room, science laboratories, home economics room, library and hall. Art and CDT are both key subjects on the timetable for all year groups.

Academic standards are high and are one of the foundations upon which school life is built, along with the broad range of subjects and activities. A variety of teaching methods are used. The key principle being that children enjoy their lessons and thus develop a love for learning. For details on assessment procedures and scholarships available at 11+ and 13+, please contact the Registrar.

The school also takes able dyslexic pupils who are fully integrated into classes. The Dyslexia Centre attached to the school provides specialist teaching; dyslexic pupils are given extra support in small groups and are withdrawn from French.

Sport is a very important part of the life at the school. Major girls' games are netball, hockey, athletics and rounders. Girls' football, cricket and rugby league as options, are a feature of the school. Major boys' games are soccer, rugby, hockey, cricket and athletics. Swimming is on the curriculum for all pupils. The School of Excellence further strengthens the development of sport and cultural activities.

The Prep School is well known for its musical strength with a suite of specially designed music rooms and practice areas. Two orchestras, one band and two choirs are organised by staff and over a dozen peripatetic teachers provide tuition for the large number of pupils who learn a wide variety of instruments including piano, violin, saxophone, clarinet and drums.

Drama clubs run for every year group and there are opportunities for children to perform during the academic year through assemblies and chapel services, as well as through the annual drama production.

The Brighton College School of Dance, based in the Performing Arts Centre, is thriving and many pupils attend classes on Saturdays and after school during the week.

The Prep School runs a large range of clubs and activities mainly after school but also at lunchtimes. The Prep School has a weekly and flexible boarding facility for girls and boys. There are a range of school bus routes. Further details on weekly boarding and bus routes are available from the Registrar.

Charitable status. Brighton College is a Registered Charity, number 307061. It exists to provide high quality education for boys and girls aged 3–18.

Bristol Grammar Lower School

Elton Road Bristol BS8 1SR
Tel: (0117) 973 6109

Chairman of Governors: D L J Watts, JP, MA, FRICS

***Headmistress:* Mrs Alison F Primrose**, MA (Cambridge), PGCE, MEd

Numbers in School. Boys 140, Girls 70 (all day children)

Fees per term. £1,106

The Lower School is an independent co-educational day school. It was founded in 1900 and occupies a self-contained building on the same site as the Upper School, Bristol Grammar School. Its own facilities include a Hall, Library, Music, Art, Science and Technology rooms. Some facilities are shared with the Upper School, particularly the Sports Complex, Theatre and Dining Hall. The school now thrives on the happy and purposeful demands of approximately 210 girls and boys aged 7–11 years.

Entry is by test at seven or eight years old and thereafter to the Upper School at eleven by an open competitive examination in which the Lower School's record of success is outstanding. Two or three Peloquin Scholarships are awarded annually on the results of the Lower School's entrance tests. The aim of the curriculum is to provide a broad and balanced curriculum. Science and Music are taught by specialists to all pupils in all years. Art and Drama are particularly encouraged and many clubs and activities exist, for example, Chess, Dance, Orchestra, Choir, many sports, outdoor pursuits and Cookery.

A wide range of sports is offered to the pupils at our superb playing fields on the outskirts of the city and at our extensive on-site sports complex.

Discipline and pastoral care are provided by the House staff, form and subject teachers and supported whenever necessary by the Headmistress.

Communication with parents is a regular feature of school life and includes the use of written reports, consultation evenings and newsletters.

Charitable status. Bristol Grammar School is a Registered Charity, number 311731. The object of the Charity is the provision and conduct in or near the City of Bristol of a day school for boys and girls.

The British School
Al Khubairat

P O Box 4001 Abu Dhabi United Arab Emirates
Tel: Abu Dhabi 4462280
Fax: Abu Dhabi 4461915

Chairman of Governors: Mr D G Heard, CBE

***Headmaster:* J F Harvey**

Bursar: Darren Davies

Number of Pupils. 512 Boys; 451 Girls (all day)

Fees per term. Kindergarten Dhs 4,800; Reception to Year 6 Dhs 6,000; Years 7-10 Dhs 10,450.

Entry Fee: Kindergarten Dhs 800; Reception to Year 9 Dhs 6,000.

The school's over-riding aim is to provide education for English speaking children "in accordance with the best teaching practices, in order to enable children to qualify for normal subsequent education in the United Kingdom within their own age groups, without disadvantage". However, as the British School for Abu Dhabi, the school also has a number of other important aims and objectives. These include the recognition of the National Curriculum for England and Wales, education within an international community, suitably sized classes and a broad curriculum offering richness and variety. In order to maintain and enhance the school's high standards, all classes are taught by fully qualified British trained and experienced teachers and the school is inspected on a three yearly cycle.

We currently cater for pupils up to Year 10 and will expand this provision to A Level. All the buildings are fully air-conditioned, light and spacious. Our Primary department comprises 34 classrooms with additional central activity areas. We have a modern electronic library, two assembly halls and a sports hall, two music rooms, specialist rooms for French, Arabic and Special Education Needs. A 25 metre swimming pool, grassed sports pitch and three playground areas provide enviable outdoor facilities that complement the academic resources.

Our newly established Senior department is rapidly expanding and is being developed to cater for students up to and including sixth form. The new Senior building provides facilities for around 350 secondary school pupils and comprises a Sports Hall, four additional Laboratories, two Design Technology workshops, Information Communication Technology suite, one Art room, one Music room, two Language rooms and fourteen general purpose classrooms. In addition to the Heads of of Department (HOD) already in situ in KS3, we have recruited for further HODs for Art, Geography and History plus specialists in Science, Mathematics, English/Drama, French and Music for the accademic year 2000/2001. A further expansion through the construction of a complementary 3-storey Junior School has commenced. This comprises a 26 classroom teaching block which will house years 3, 4, 5 and 6 plus the creation of space for bigger and better sporting facilities.

The school is self-supporting, financed by fees paid by parents for the education of their children. It operates as a 'not for profit' concern, the funds being used only for the school's purposes.

The British School
Manila

PO Box 2079 MCPO 1260 Makati Metro Manila Philippines.
Tel: (0632) 840-1561 to 1570
e-mail: admissions@britishschoolmanila.org
website: www.britishschoolmanila.org

Chairman of Board of Governors: J Hawkins

Head: Helen Kinsey-Wightman

Number of Pupils. 350 (Day only) Boys and Girls 160/190

School Fees. Tuition Fees: Key Stage 1 & 2 £3,738; Key Stage 3 & 4 £4,200. There are other fees, such as registration and entrance fees. Details of these can be obtained from the school.

The British School Manila was established in 1976, with just two classrooms and 37 students. It has now grown to over 350 pupils, representing 29 different nationalities, with British and Australian nationals making up 50% of the enrollment. The British School is a fee-paying, non-profit making, independent school catering for both local and expatriate children from Reception to Key Stage 4. The academic year is divided into three terms, closely linked to UK term dates.

In September 2001 the school relocated to purpose build premises close to the business district of Manila. Facilities include a swimming pool, auditorium, playing fields, two science laboratories, a technology suite, a music and drama studio and two ICT laboratories. Classrooms are built on a cluster design in order to maintain the friendly 'small school' feeling that characterises the British School.

The school follows the National Curriculum with some modifications to reflect a multi-cultural student body. Children are prepared for National Curriculum Tests (NCTs) at age 7, 11, 14 and GCSE at 16. Key Stage 5 is currently planned for September 2003 when children will take the International Baccalaureate. Children are also prepared for Common Entrance Examinations if required. In all comparative assessments children at BSM perform well above National UK averages.

British School teachers are all UK or Commonwealth trained and classes are small - the average class size is currently 17 students. Each child is encouraged to develop at their own rate, benefiting from a high level of individual teacher attention and motivation. Emphasis is placed on self-discipline within a family atmosphere, providing an ideal environment for children of all nationalities.

For copies of the school brochure and full information on admission, please contact the Admissions Officer.

British School in the Netherlands Junior School

Vlaskamp 19 Den Haag 2592 AA The Netherlands
Tel: 070-3338111
Fax: 070-3338100

Chairman of Governors: Mr P Bayliff

***Headteacher:* Mr N Hendriksen**

Number on roll. 800. Aged 5 to 11.
Fees. Dfl. 15,900 per year.

At the heart of all learning there must be sound, happy relationships and a feeling of self esteem. Children learn best when they feel secure, respected and valued. Our staff are totally committed to working in partnership with parents to provide a welcoming, challenging and stimulating environment for children to explore, experiment, learn, laugh and reflect. Our ultimate aim is to foster in each of our pupils an excitement and a love of learning which will remain with them for the rest of their lives.

The Junior School (ages 5 to 11 years) is situated close to the centre of Den Haag on a tree-filled site with extensive green play areas and modern facilities designed to meet the academic, technological and recreational requirements of each age group.

All the classrooms are light and airy overlooking the grounds and landscaped gardens. Facilities include music rooms with adjoining practice cells, a main hall, a circular drama studio, library, IT studio with a comprehensive network of computers linking each classroom and fully equipped rooms for craft, design, and technology and science.

The learning programme includes the three core subjects, mathematics, English and science, together with the foundation subjects, geography, history, design and technology, art and music, information technology and PE with the addition of Dutch from entry into the School and French from Year 6.

In the Key Stage 1 and Key Stage 2 Curricula, specific schemes of work outline the progressive skills and knowledge which are taught, and all work is closely monitored to ensure that pupils are making progress matched to their abilities. In the case of children who display unusual talent or ability, extension material is given to motivate and challenge their intellectual growth. A Learning Support Department provides assistance for pupils with EAL or learning difficulties. All children enjoy a variety of experiences, visiting places of interest in the immediate locality, performing in dance, drama and choral activities and engaging in extra-curricular programmes. As children progress through the Junior School subject teaching becomes more defined, especially in the core subjects of English, mathematics and science, and more extensive use is made of the science laboratory and technology room. Children are carefully prepared for the subject-orientated approach evident in the Senior School where they are expected to become more independent in the planning and completion of tasks and time management.

British School of Washington

4715 16th Street NW Washington DC 20011 United States of America
Tel: (USA) 202 829 3700
Fax: (USA) 202 829 6522
e-mail: secretarybsw@britishschool.org
website: www.britishschool.org

Patron: HE The British Ambassador, Sir Christopher Meyer

***Headmistress:* Lesley P Stagg,** FCollP, BEd, CertEd, DipTEFL, APC

CEO: Robert Findlay, BEd, CertEd

Head of Upper School: Julie Saville, MEd, BSc, PGCE, NPQH

Head of Lower School: Kathryn Burrows, BEd

The British School of Washington, located in north-west DC near Rock Creek Park, opened in September 1998. The school is a private, IAPS, co-educational, day school currently catering for children aged 3 to 13. It follows the National Curriculum (England) for Key Stages 1, 2 and 3 and there are plans to expand further into a secondary school in the near future. Preparation for 11+ and Common Entrance is available for pupils transferring to UK schools. French is taught to all children from Year 2 and specialist music tuition is available. The students are about 45% British, 30% American and 25% other nationalities.

The Upper School (Years 2 to 8) is housed in a fine colonial style building, the Lower School (Nursery to Year 1) is in a nearby building, both buildings have adventure and hard play areas adjacent and the Carter-Barron Stadium and playing fields are opposite. Facilities include two libraries, a dance/music studio, an art/science block, a computer suite and a large auditorium with stage.

Classes run from mid-September to mid-July from 8.45 am to 3.30 pm and follow a UK vacation pattern. There is pre-school care from 8.00 am and after-school care until 6.00 pm. Teachers and parents run extra-curricular activities and there is a summer camp programme.

The classroom teachers are UK trained and National Curriculum experienced graduates. Specialist teachers (eg French, Music) may be locally recruited, as are classroom assistants. Core textbooks, library books and work schemes are imported from the UK. The school tests at the end of Key Stages using the UK Statutory Assessment Tests and all children receive a baseline assessment upon entry. Children from Year 3 are tested regularly with other UK standardised tests so that parents may make comparisons of their child's potential and achievement against national norms. Inspections are conducted using OfSTED qualified inspectors from the UK. There is a mandatory school uniform.

The day-to-day operation of the school is managed by the Headmistress, in consultation with the Executive Board (UK based) and the Advisory Board (drawn from the local, international and parental communities).

The school has an open admissions programme, with year round enrolment (subject to availability of places) but requires reports from previous schools and an interview. Children with limited English may only be admitted to the Early Years and there is minimal special needs provision. Class sizes are about 15 to 18 children per class and teacher assistants are employed in the Early Years programme.

Broadwater Manor School

Worthing West Sussex BN14 8HU.
Tel: (01903) 201123

Headteacher: **Mrs E K Woodley**

Heads of Dept:
B Brown (*Prep*)
Mrs J Crosby (*Pre-Prep*)
Mrs A Watkins (*Nursery and Toddlers*)

Number of Pupils. Day only, Prep 141, Pre-Prep 140, Nursery 51 and Toddlers 15. (All Co-ed). Girls occupy about 40% of the places throughout the school.

Fees. 8–13, £1,590 per term (inclusive). 4–8, £1,351 per term (inclusive). Nursery from £285 per term (inclusive) and Toddlers £133 per term (inclusive).

There are 19 full-time and 8 part-time teachers on the staff.

Pupils are prepared for entry to a variety of senior schools and scholarships are frequently gained. The school has a thriving musical tradition and a strong PE department. Soccer, Hockey, Netball, Tennis, Rounders and Athletics are all played. As well as computers in almost every classroom there is a well equipped Information Technology room. CDT is also a strong aspect of the school.

Brockhurst School

Hermitage Newbury Berkshire RG18 9UL.
Tel: (01635) 200293
Fax: (01635) 200190
Station: Newbury

Headmaster: **David J W Fleming**, MA (Trinity College, Oxford), MSc, MDH

Number of Boys. (Aged 3 to 13). 55 Boarders, 105 Day Boys

Fees. Boarders and Weekly Boarders £3,730, Day Boys £1,560–£2,745. No compulsory extras

Brockhurst is located on the same site as Marlston House Girls' Preparatory School which occupies separate, listed buildings. Boys and girls are educated separately but the two schools join forces for drama, music and many hobbies. In this way, Brockhurst and Marlston House aim to combine the best features of the single sex and co-educational systems: academic excellence and social mixing. The schools have built up a good reputation for high standards of pastoral care given to each pupil within a caring, family establishment.

The Junior School at Ridge House, Cold Ash, is a co-educational Pre-Prep department for 75 children aged 3 to 6½. (Fees: £800–£1,560 per term).

Established in 1884, the school is situated in 60 acres of its own grounds in country of outstanding beauty but is only three miles from access to the M4. Boys are prepared for all Independent Senior Schools and there is an excellent scholarship record. Where appropriate, pupils can be transported by members of staff to and from airports if parents are serving in the armed forces or otherwise working overseas.

All boys play Soccer, Rugger, Hockey and Cricket and take part in Athletics, Cross-Country and Swimming (own heated pool). Additional activities include Riding (own ponies), Fencing, Judo, Shooting (indoor rifle-range) and Tennis (indoor court and three hard courts). Facilities for gymnastics and other sporting activities are provided in a purpose-built Sports Hall recently completed. The schools also have their own Chateau near Bordeaux where they practice their spoken French.

Music and art are important features of the curriculum and a good number of pupils have won scholarships to senior schools in recent years.

Bromsgrove Lower School

Cobham House Conway Road Bromsgrove Worcs B60 2AD.
Tel: (01527) 579600
Fax: (01527) 579571
e-mail: admissions.lower@bromsgrove-school.co.uk

Headmaster: **Peter Lee-Smith**, BA (Hons), CertEd

Number of Pupils. Day boys 193, Day Girls 145, Boarder Boys 53, Boarder Girls 32.

Fees. Boarders £3,490–£4,030. Day Pupils £1,955–£2,560. £100 deductible if account is paid within first seven days of term. Forces Bursaries and assisted places are available.

The School, fully co-educational, is administered by the Governors and Headmaster of Bromsgrove School but it is an independent unit having its own Headmaster, Staff, buildings and playing fields. The proximity of the Upper School is such that the Lower School can use the Chapel, all the year round indoor Swimming Pool, Squash Courts, Sports Hall, floodlit All Weather Pitch and Music School.

Art, Science and Technology are taught in the purpose-built Llanwrtyd Centre and, together with Music and Drama, they play a prominent part in the life of the School.

Pupils are accepted from the age of seven. There is a fully integrated academic curriculum from the age of eleven. Children are assessed prior to this age and a place through to school leaving age is guaranteed at that stage. There is, therefore, no academic break at age thirteen.

Music, Art, Design and Drama play a prominent part in the School life and all types of hobbies are encouraged.

Games played are Rugby Football, Cricket, Rounders, Netball, Athletics, Swimming, Badminton, Squash, Cross Country Running, Tennis, Hockey and Rowing.

All medical and first aid care is provided by the Health Centre which is run by an SRN with two qualified nurses to assist her. The catering is in the hands of our own caterers.

Charitable status. Bromsgrove Lower School is a Registered Charity, number 527450. It exists to provide education for boys and girls.

Brontë House
(The Preparatory School of Woodhouse Grove)

Apperley Bridge Bradford W Yorkshire BD10 0PQ
Tel: (0113) 250 2811
Fax: (0113) 250 0666
Airport: Leeds/Bradford (2 miles)

Chairman of Governors: G B Greenwood, JP
Headmaster: **C B F Hall**, LLB, PGCE

Number of Pupils. 290 (boys and girls aged 3 to 11, including 6 boarders).

Fees. These are graduated according to age. Boarding fees range from £3,600 to £3,670 per term and Day fees from £1,410 to £2,060 per term. The day fee covers an extended day from 8 am to 6 pm; there are no extra charges for breakfast, tea and the majority of supervised activities after lessons.

The School is situated in its own grounds, a short distance from the Senior School, on the slopes of the Aire Valley at the edge of the urban area of Bradford and Leeds. The moors are within view and access to the Dales National Park and the international Leeds/Bradford Airport is swift.

The School is of Methodist foundation, but children of other denominations and faiths are willingly accepted. Morning assembly is run on broad ecumenical lines, and school services are held in the Chapel of Woodhouse Grove and Bradford Cathedral, where a number of pupils are choristers.

Normal entry is in September via the Entrance Tests held the previous January, but assessment and entry at other times in the year can be easily arranged if places are available. Academic, art and music scholarships may be awarded to children who display special merit, and the School now offers bursaries in lieu of the defunct Assisted Places scheme. Entry to the Foundation and Key Stage 1 classes merely requires registration of the child.

The work of all age groups is based on the National Curriculum; this is supplemented by a European Studies course in French, German and Spanish, plus a special emphasis on Music and Sport. An £18,000 multi-media computer suite was installed in September, 2000. Children automatically transfer to the senior school, Woodhouse Grove, and there is continuity of schooling from 3 to 18. Regular standardised testing takes place in all year groups, and the national Key Stage 1 and 2 Tests (for seven and eleven year olds) are taken. All staff, both full-time and visiting, are fully qualified. Individual tuition is encouraged in piano, string, wind and brass instruments and also in speech and drama, with the two choirs and orchestra participating regularly in assemblies and concerts. (Over 70% of the children learn to play an instrument). There is a Dyslexia Unit, run by specialist staff, for a maximum of 16 children of above average ability.

The curriculum includes compulsory physical education for all children. Those with ability and enthusiasm are coached in athletics, cricket, cross country running, football, rugby, rounders and netball; there is a comprehensive fixture list with other schools in the area, and regular participation in local and regional tournaments. All children learn to swim; teaching and training takes place weekly in the full-size pool at Woodhouse Grove.

In addition to training sessions in sport, clubs and activities include art and craft, chess, computers, drama, needlework and railway. Expeditions are made to the Dales and the Lake District, as are cultural outings into Bradford, Leeds and York. An annual ski trip takes place during the Easter holidays.

For a copy of the detailed prospectus, please apply to the Secretary.

Charitable status. Brontë House School is a Registered Charity, number 529205. It exists to provide independent primary education within the pastoral environment of a Methodist Residential School.

Brooke Priory School

Station Approach Oakham Rutland LE15 6QW
Tel: 01572 724778
Fax: 01572 724969
e-mail: brookepriory@rmplc.co.uk
website: http://atschool.eduweb.co.uk/brookepriory

Headmistress: **Mrs E S Bell,** BEd (Hons)

Number of Pupils. 170. Age range 4-11 years.
New Nursery. 2+-4+ opening in September 2001.
Fees. £1,080-£1,430 per term
Staff. There are 18 graduate and qualified members of the teaching staff.

Brooke Priory is a day Preparatory School for boys and girls. The school was founded in 1989 and moved into its own purpose built building in February 1995. Since then it has doubled its classroom provision. This year a new library and drama room will be completed to add to the IT room opened in 2001.

A separate nursery unit will open in September 2001 with provision for children in two groups catering for ages 2+-4+ years.

Brooke Priory provides a stimulating, caring environment in which children are encouraged to attain the highest potential. Class sizes are generally kept to 16 in parallel forms and children are grouped according to ability in Mathematics and English.

Key Stages 1 and 2 are incorporated within the school's own broad and varied curriculum. Every child will participate in arts, drama and music and is encouraged to join the choir and ensemble.

All children are prepared for Common Entrance and Senior Independent Schools entrance examinations.

Sport is an important part of the curriculum. Children swim weekly throughout the year and are coached in a wide variety of games by specialist staff. The main sports are Soccer, Rugby, Hockey, Netball, Cricket, Rounders and Athletics.

The school offers a wide choice of extra-curricular activities.

Brooklands School

Eccleshall Road Stafford ST16 1PD
Tel: (01785) 251399
Fax: (01785) 251399

Chairman of Council: C C Lee

Headmaster: **C T O'Donnell**, BA, PGCE

Number of Pupils. 153
Fees. £908–£1,653 per term including lunch. No compulsory extras.

The School, founded in 1946,is an Independent Day School for boys and girls between the ages of 3–11 years, and is situated on the edge of the town, overlooking a conservation area, and a mile from Junction 14 of the M6.

The aims of the school are to lay a sound foundation in

the basic subjects, with a background of general cultural subjects, to encourage initiative, independence and love of learning and to stimulate a lively interest in the arts and science.

The children learn to live as members of a community, working in co-operation, and showing courtesy and consideration for others, based on the Christian way of living. Opportunities are given for the children to contribute to charities appropriate to their interests.

A qualified and experienced staff teaches the children in groups small enough to ensure individual attention. Subject specialists teach the pupils throughout Key Stage Two.

All subjects required for scholarships and entrance examinations to boys' and girls' independent senior schools are taught. French is taught formally from the age of eight, with the younger children able to join 'Le Club Francais'.

A purpose built Science & Technology building was officially opened in January 2001.

Computers are widely used, with the school having a newly equipped computer centre.

Excellent provision for music, art, drama and various other activities allow children to develop in non-academic spheres. The school enjoys a fine reputation for music. The Director of Music has a team of visiting instrumental teachers at her disposal. Private music lessons and ballet classes take place during school hours.

In the Autumn and Spring terms the boys play football and rugby, and the girls netball.

In the Summer term the boys play cricket and the girls tennis and rounders. Both are coached in Athletics. The School Rounders team is currently National Rounders Association Champions at under 11 age group for the second year running.

Hockey, volleyball and basketball are also played.

Physical Education is taught to all forms within the structure of the timetable.

From age 6 upwards all children are encouraged to learn to swim during one session per week at Stafford Sports Centre arranged in school hours.

After School and Holiday supervision are available on a regular or 'ad hoc' basis.

Charitable status. Brooklands School is a Registered Charity, number 528616. It exists to provide quality education for boys and girls.

Broomwood Hall

74 Nightingale Lane London SW12 8NR
Tel: 020 8673 1616
Fax: 020 8772 9407
e-mail: office@broomwood.co.uk

Headmistress: **Mrs K A H Colquhoun,** BEd, DipT

Age Range. Girls 4–13; Boys 4–8
Number of pupils. 275 girls; 161 boys
Fees per term. £1,990–£2,560
Religious denomination. Christian (non-denominational)

Curriculum. Broomwood Hall is an independent pre-prep and preparatory school for boys and girls from the ages of 4–8 (boys) and 4–13 (girls). The main emphasis is on preparation for entry to boarding schools at 8 (boys) and 13 (girls) via Common Entrance examinations, although the school also prepares pupils for entry to London day schools. Boys have an automatic right of entry at 8 to Northcote Lodge (day preparatory school on Wandsworth Common, in the same ownership as Broomwood Hall). We also cater for girls going on to schools that have an 11+ or 12+ entry requirement. There is a special interest in music, and wide use of up to date computer equipment throughout the school. The Christian ethos emphasises the development of good manners, responsibility and a sense of duty.

Entry requirements. Entry takes place in September next following a child's fourth birthday. Admission is by personal interview with both parents and the child at the age of 3. Parents must live locally (Clapham/Battersea/Wandsworth/Tooting).

Examinations offered. Boys preparatory schools, girls' Common Entrance and Scholarship examinations at 11+ and 13+ (12+ where applicable) and London day schools examinations. Pupils may also take Associated Board examinations (music) and RAD examinations (ballet).

The Buchan School

Castletown Isle of Man
Tel: (01624) 822526
Fax: (01624) 823220

Headmaster: **G R Shaw-Twilley**, BEd (Hons), CertAdEd

Chairman of the Governors: S G Alder, Esq

Number of Pupils. 215 (120 boys, 95 girls)
Fees. Day £1,470–£2,250 per term according to age.

After more than a century of independence mainly as a Girls' School, The Buchan School amalgamated in 1991 with King William's College to form a single continuous provision of Independent Education on the Isle of Man.

As the Preparatory School to King William's College, The Buchan School provides an education of all round quality for boys and girls until the age of 11 when most pupils proceed naturally to the Senior School although the curriculum meets the needs of Common Entrance, Scholarship and Entrance Examinations to other Independent Senior Schools.

The school buildings are clustered round Westhill House, the centre of the original estate, in fourteen acres of partly wooded grounds. The whole environment, close to the attractive harbour of Castletown, is ideally suited to the needs of younger children. They are able to work and play safely, develop their potential in every direction.

There are 20 full time and 5 part time staff. Classes are small throughout, providing considerable individual attention. A well equipped Kindergarten provides Pre-School education for some 50 children. In the year they become 5 boys and girls are accepted into the Pre-Preparatory Department. They work largely in their own building in bright, modern classrooms but also make use of the specialist Preparatory School facilities where they proceed three years later, in the year they become 8.

Facilities are first class, including laboratories for Science and Technology, Library, Computer Room, large Games Hall and Art, Design Centre. The School is particularly well-equipped with ICT facilities extending down to the Pre-Prep Department. Outside, the school grounds provide a natural gymnasium. There is a Pavilion with fields marked out for a variety of team games and a multi purpose area which is used for Netball, Tennis and Hockey.

There is emphasis on traditional standards in and out of the classroom, with an enterprising range of activities outside normal lessons. Music is strong – both choral and instrumental – and there is energetic involvement in Art, Drama, Sport.

The school strives for high academic standards, aiming to ensure that all pupils enjoy the benefits of a rounded education, giving children every opportunity to develop their individual talents from an early age.

Entry is usually by Interview and School report and the children may join The Buchan School at any time, providing there is space. The School is a happy, friendly community where new pupils integrate quickly socially and academically.

Charitable status. King William's College is a Registered Charity, number 615. It exists for the provision of high quality education for boys and girls.

Bute House Preparatory School for Girls

Bute House Luxemburg Gardens Hammersmith London W6 7EA
Tel: 020 7603 7381
Fax: 020 7371 3446
e-mail: mail@butehouse.co.uk
website: www.butehouse.co.uk

Chairman of Governors: Mr W O Clarke

Headmistress: **Mrs S C Salvidant**, BEd Hons (London)

Deputy Head: Mrs M Walker

Number of Pupils. 300 Day Girls

Fees in September. £2,290 per term inclusive of lunches.

Bute House overlooks extensive playing fields and is housed in a large bright modern building. Facilities include a science laboratory, art room, technology room, music studio, drama studio, multi purpose hall and a large well stocked library. A well qualified, enthusiastic and experienced staff teach a broad curriculum which emphasises both the academic and the aesthetic. Information Technology is an integral part of the curriculum, and the classrooms are all equipped with multi-media machines. Laptops are also widely used for individual use or class work. Monitored access to the internet is available. French is taught from Year 1.

Sports include swimming, gymnastics, dance, tennis, lacrosse, netball and athletics which are taught on excellent on-site facilities. Full use is made of all that London has to offer and residential trips further afield are also offered to older girls.

Girls are encouraged to take full part in the school life from an early age. There is a democratically elected School Council and regular school meetings run by the girls when all pupils are able to put forward their views as well as to volunteer for duties around the school. A wide variety of extra curricular activities is available.

The school aims at academic excellence in a non competitive, happy environment where girls are encouraged to be confident, articulate and independent and where courtesy and consideration are expected. There is a flourishing Parents Association. Entry is by ballot at age 4 and by assessment at age 7.

Butterstone School

Arthurstone Meigle Perthshire PH12 8QY
Tel: (01828) 640528
Fax: (01828) 640640
e-mail: head@butterstone.freeserve.co.uk

Chairman of the Board of Governors: Christopher Dunphie, MC

Heads: **Brian Whitten**, BA, CertEd and **Margaret Whitten,** CertEd

Number of Girls. 41 Boarders, 14 Day Girls, 59 Pre-preparatory and Nursery (girls and boys).

Fees. Boarders, £3,980 per term. Day Girls, £2,660 per term. Pre-Prep £1,390 per term. Nursery £19 per day.

Butterstone School is an independent Preparatory Boarding School which prepares girls for all leading schools in Scotland and England. The School is easily reached, being centrally situated. Edinburgh Airport is an hour's journey from the School.

The academic standard is high with a 12 year record of 100% passes at 13+ to senior independent schools: 35 scholarships have been awarded in the same period. Classes are small; there are twelve full-time members of the teaching staff, and fully-qualified staff for music, dancing, art, riding, swimming, skiing, golf and all games. There is provision for learning support. The School has two all-weather tennis courts. Ski-ing and skating are features of the Spring Term. Girls are encouraged to make intelligent use of their leisure and are taken to plays, concerts, the opera and ballet and on other cultural excursions. All girls learn to use computers. Most girls learn at least one musical instrument and may take Associated Board examinations. There is a large school orchestra and several instrumental groups. Plays are produced at least once a year and the cast usually includes all members of the school. Girls have the opportunity to take LAMDA examinations and all girls are assessed annually for the English Speaking Board examinations in oral communication.

There are two resident Matrons. The food is excellent, plentiful and varied. Girls spend as much time as possible out of doors; many girls keep pets, including ponies, at school. The School, which has a southern aspect, is set in beautiful country, with views of woods and hills from every window. There is a happy family atmosphere. In their free time in the evening and at weekends the girls have the chance to learn a range of skills which may include knitting, archery, fly-tying, patchwork, silk painting or leatherwork.

Little Butterstone, housed within the school, caters for day girls and boys between the ages of 3 and 8 years.

The girls attend the Church of Scotland or the Scottish Episcopal Church. Catholic girls are taken to Mass.

Charitable status. Butterstone School is a Registered Charity, number SCO 145041. It exists for education up to 13.

Cabin Hill

(Campbell College Preparatory School) Belfast BT4 3HJ.
Tel: (028) 90 653368
Fax: (028) 90 651966

Chairman of the Governors: A N Boyd, BSc(Econ), FCA

Headmaster: **N I Kendrick**, MA, BEd (Hons)

Number of Pupils. 216 Day Boys; 31 Boarders; 56 Pre-prep

Fees. Senior: Boarders £2,086 per term; Day Boys £420 per term (a further tuition fee of £1,000 per term may be charged for senior pupils who are not resident in Northern Ireland or whose parents are not nationals of an EC member state). Junior: Boarders £2,572 per term; Day Boys £1,176 per term. Pre-Prep £742 per term.

The staff consists of 23 graduates of British Universities or qualified teachers. There is a Director of Music with a full staff of assistants and also qualified instructors in Physical Education and Design and Technology. Art is taught throughout the school. The Pre-Preparatory Department was opened in September, 1989.

The general welfare of the boys is in the hands of the Headmaster and his wife with the assistance of the Matron and Deputy Matrons. The School Doctor visits regularly.

Boys are prepared for Campbell College and other Senior Schools. A limited number of Clergymen's sons are admitted as Boarders at reduced fees.

Cabin Hill, which adjoins Campbell College, stands in its own beautiful grounds of some 30 acres.

Games – Rugby Football, Association Football, Hockey, Cricket, Tennis, Athletics. Regular use throughout the year is made of the Campbell College indoor Swimming Pool and Squash Courts. There is a well-equipped theatre for Concerts, Plays and Films. Other activities include Archery, Basketball, Scripture Union and extra-curricular use of the School's computers.

Caldicott

Farnham Royal Bucks SL2 3SL.
Tel: (01753) 644457
Fax: (01753) 649325
e-mail: office@caldicott.com
website: http://www.caldicott.com

Chairman of the Board of Governors: The Hon Sir Scott Baker

Headmaster: **Simon Doggart**, BA

Number of Boys. 138 Boarders and 113 Day Boys

Fees. Boarders £3,765 per term. Day Boys £2,825 per term

Caldicott, founded in 1904, is an Educational Trust. The School is situated in 40 acres of grounds and playing fields adjacent to more than a thousand acres of permanent woodland. It is conveniently placed close to London between the M40 and the M4 and within 20 minutes of Heathrow Airport.

The School is forward-looking in its approach and the development of the buildings and playing fields is seen as a continuous process. The facilities are, therefore, modern, spacious, well-designed, well-maintained, and conveniently situated in and around the main building. They include a well equipped Technology Department and Computer Room, Music School, and an extensive Sports and Recreation centre which includes a Sports Hall and Squash Courts.

There is a high proportion of qualified teaching staff to boys. Classes are therefore kept as small as possible and each boy is able to receive individual help and attention. Our teaching methods combine what we believe to be the best in modern ideas with the more traditional ways we know to be indispensable. Throughout the School we insist on a high standard of work, and we offer all subjects necessary for the Common Entrance and Scholarship examinations to the Independent Senior Schools.

The School has a Christian ethos. The day begins with a short Chapel Service on weekdays, and on Sundays parents are welcome to join in the Services.

All day boys are expected to board from the age of 11 for their last two years in in preparation for boarding at their Senior Schools.

Much emphasis is placed on creative activities such as Music, Art, Design, Modelling, Photography and Drama, and through the tutorial system every boy is encouraged to use his leisure time sensibly.

The principal games are Rugby, Hockey, and Cricket. Other sporting activities include Squash, Football, Swimming, Athletics, Tennis, Cross-country, Basketball and Gymnastics. There is also a cub pack for the younger boarders.

The prospectus is available on application to the Headmaster, who is always pleased to meet parents, discuss with them their sons' particular needs, and arrange for them to see over the School.

Charitable status. Caldicott is a Registered Charity, number 310631. Its purpose is to provide education for the young.

Cameron House

4 The Vale London SW3 6AH
Tel: 020 7352 4040
Fax: 020 7352 2349
e-mail: cameronhouse@lineone.net

Founded in 1980

Principal: Mrs Josie Ashcroft, BSc, DipEd

Headmistress: **Miss F Stack**, BA Hons, PGCE

Independent London Day School. ISC Accredited; Member of BDA.

Age Range. Boys and Girls, 4½ to 11+ years

Entry generally at 4 or 8 years, but any age considered if places are available.

Number of Pupils. 112

Fees per term as from 1.9.01 £2,535–£2,675. There are no compulsory extras and there is a 5% reduction for a brother or sister whilst an older child remains in the school.

Religious Affiliation. Church of England

Cameron House aims to produce pupils who appreciate the virtues of courtesy, good manners and kindness, are positive-minded and confident.

Our highly qualified and dedicated teaching staff create a stimulating environment in which initiative and individual objectives can flourish.

Small classes and a high teacher/pupil ratio are central to our approach, allowing children the necessary individual attention to reach their true potential. Special provision is made for the bright dyslexic.

The curriculum is broadly based and designed to cultivate a wide range of interests, although emphasis is placed on the Core Curriculum. Essential disciplines are balanced with other aesthetic and practical activities including Speech and Drama, Debating, French and Pottery. This provides a solid and well-rounded education.

The school is well equipped with a new library and ICT equipment. Excellent sport facilities are available locally and the school itself has its own safety surfaced playground.

We are keen for pupils to discover individual talents at the earliest possible age by offering a wide variety of optional clubs after school. These currently include: art, ballet, tap, drama, karate, football, fencing and tournament chess, as well as individual musical instruments.

The learning process necessarily focuses on public examinations. For boys these can take place at any time after the age of 7. Girls and boys are prepared for the entrance examination to independent London day or boarding schools at 11+.

Cargilfield

Barnton Avenue West Edinburgh EH4 6HU.
Tel: 0131-336 2207.
Fax: 0131 336 3179
e-mail: cargilfield.edin.sch.uk
website: www.cargilfield.edin.sch.uk

Headmaster: **Mark Seymour**, BA

Senior Master: Dr J N Wilson, BA, PhD

Head of Pre-Prep and Nursery Department: Mrs Sue Lumsden, BSc, PGCE

Number of Children. In Upper School (aged 8–13½) 110 (42 Boarders, 58 Day), Pre-Prep (aged 5–7, all day) 71, Nursery (aged 3 and 4) 41.

Fees. Boarders: £3,740, Day Pupils: £755–£2,710

The School is ideally situated in spacious grounds five miles from the centre of Edinburgh and close to Edinburgh Airport. The staff consists of twenty-seven full-time teachers and six part-timers, one matron and one assistant matron. Pupils, who are taught in small groups, are prepared for all independent secondary schools. The majority of leavers move on to the major Scottish boarding schools, but a number go south: in recent years children have gone to Ampleforth, Downe House, Eton, Harrow, Oundle and Rugby. Suitable candidates are encouraged to enter for Scholarships, and twenty-seven awards have been gained in the last five years, with a strong showing in Classics and Music. Rugby, Netball, Hockey, Cricket, Rounders, Tennis and Athletics make up the greater part of the Games programme and a wide variety of general activities are organised, for example Skiing, mainly on the Hillend Dry Ski Slope, Riding, Sailing, Squash, Fencing, Judo, Archery, Swimming and Golf. There is a very active Music Department, and nearly all instruments are taught. The school has a Chapel, Theatre, Science Laboratory, Language Laboratory, IT Suite, Art Studio, Gymnasium, Indoor Swimming Pool and a large multi-purpose Sports Hall, all surrounded by excellent playing fields and three flood-lit all-weather tennis courts. A major refurbishment and redevelopment of the entire campus is about to be undertaken.

Our Pre-Prep and Nursery for boys and girls between the ages of three and eight feeds in directly to the Upper School. Here the majority of senior pupils are boarders, but weekly boarders and day pupils play a full part in the life of the school, and we operate a very successful flexi-boarding scheme. Fee concessions are offered for younger boarding members of the family when they overlap and also for boarding children of serving service personnel. There are no compulsory extras.

Details are obtainable from the Headmaster. The School is under a Board of Governors (Chairman David M B Sole, OBE) and is run on a non-profit making basis.

Charitable status. Cargilfield School is a Registered Charity, number CR 33853. It exists solely to provide a first-class education for boys and girls.

The Carrdus School

Overthorpe Hall Nr Banbury Oxon OX17 2BS.
Tel: (01295) 263733

Headmistress: **Miss S T Carrdus**, BA

Number of Day Pupils. 150 (123 girls, 29 boys)

Ages. Boys 3½–7+, Girls 3½–11+, Nursery Class for children 3½–4½

Fees. £568–£1,760. Compulsory extras: Insurance £5; PTA membership £5.

Overthorpe Hall is a day preparatory school for girls and a pre-preparatory school for boys. The house is large and stands in 11 acres of beautiful grounds.

The teaching staff consists of nine full-time qualified teachers and eleven part-time specialists. The Matron is an RGN. Girls are prepared for 11+ Common Entrance and the school has an excellent record of success in this and all other examinations, sending girls to most of the well known Independent Senior Schools in recent years. Boys are given a good grounding for their preparatory schools.

The classrooms provide a stimulating background for a variety of activities. The work of the school is directed towards a high standard in academic subjects and in Art, Music and Games.

There is a heated outdoor swimming pool and our sports teams are successful in local and regional events. We have a purpose-built Sports and Drama Hall.

The aim of the school is to produce confident, well-disciplined and happy children, who have the satisfaction of reaching their own highest academic and personal standards. This is made possible by an organisation flexible enough to achieve a balance between new methods of teaching and sound traditional disciplines.

Castle Court Preparatory School

The Knoll House Corfe Mullen Wimborne Dorset BH21 3RF.
Tel: (01202) 694438
Fax: (01202) 659063
e-mail: office@castlecourt.com
website: www.castlecourt.com

Chairman of the Governors: Allan F Simmons, Esq, FCCA

Headmaster: **Richard E T Nicholl**, BA (Dunelm), CertEd

Deputy Headmaster: J J Hett, BA

Number of Pupils. 349 (214 boys, 135 girls) from 3 to 13 years, (including Pre-Preparatory, Reception and Badgers (Nursery).

Teaching Staff. 47 full time, 20 part time

Fees. £1,510 (Reception to Year 2), £2,790 (Years 3 to 8).

Castle Court is a Day Preparatory School for boys and girls aged 3 to 13, situated in 35 acres of beautiful grounds and woodlands within easy reach of Bournemouth and Poole. A gracious Regency house forms the heart of the school and contains the Reception Rooms, Dining Rooms, Offices and some of the junior classrooms. The Badgers, Reception and Pre-Preparatory, Departments (for 3–7 year olds) are all self-contained, and like the senior classrooms are all purpose-built. The normal curriculum includes English, Mathematics, Science, French, Latin, History, Geography, Religious Studies, Information Technology, Design Technology, Art, Music and Sport, with Speech and

Drama for some Years. There is a spacious Hall for Assembly, Drama and Gymnastics, with Music Department attached; an extension has provided a refurbished school library. A Science and Art complex provides Laboratories, Workshops, Art Studios and the IT Centre (two rooms equipped with Acorns, AppleMacs and PCs which are networked and linked to the Internet). All classrooms also have a computer, on the School Intranet. In 1999, building development included new poolside sports changing rooms, an academic block with four classrooms, offices and Special Skills rooms, and the spacious new Information Technology centre. There is an outdoor heated swimming pool and extensive playing fields, including an all-weather synthetic hockey pitch.

Whilst Castle Court is a day school, it is run on boarding school lines and from the age of 9 children are encouraged to stay on for tea followed by Prep or activities, before going home at 6 o'clock. There is a wide range of informal activities such as chess, computing, cookery, drama, electronics, photography, pottery, woodwork etc. Whilst all the children are prepared for the Common Entrance or Scholarship examinations to Senior Independent Schools, any necessary preparation for entrance to local Grammar Schools can easily be made. The School has a strong musical tradition with its own Orchestra, Band, Choir and various ensembles. Sport also forms an important part in the life of the children with rugby, soccer, hockey and cricket for the boys, and netball, rounders and hockey for the girls, with athletics, cross-country, gymnastics, dance, swimming and tennis for all. There are opportunities for sailing instruction. Trips include visits to local places of interest; camping weekends; expeditions to the continent.

A prospectus (with details of the school bus service if required) will be sent on application to the Admissions Secretary; further information may be found on our school website.

Charitable status. Castle Court Preparatory School is a Registered Charity, number 325028. It aims to provide a first class education for local children.

Castle Park

Dalkey Co Dublin
Tel: (010-353-1) 2803037

Chairman of the Governors: Mr M Shiell

Headmaster: **C R Collings**, BA, CertEd (London)

Number of Pupils. 248 (173 Prep, 75 Pre-Prep). Co-educational

Fees. Day Boarders IR£1,235 per term.

The staff consists of 13 graduate teachers. Peripatetic staff teach musical instruments and craft.

The school, which is a charitable trust, was founded in 1904. Children are prepared for entrance and Scholarships to Independent schools in Ireland, England and Scotland.

Facilities include 15 acres of attractive grounds overlooking Dublin Bay, a heated indoor swimming pool, an all-weather surface for hockey and tennis, cricket and rugby fields, croquet lawn, artificial cricket wicket, carpentry shop, art and craft rooms, a science laboratory and computer room.

Games: Rugby, Hockey, Soccer, Cricket, Tennis, Table Tennis, Swimming, Athletics, Rounders.

Hobbies: Riding, craft, computing, modelling, cookery, sailing, gardening.

Music plays an important part in the curriculum.

A Junior Montessori School for 3–6 year olds under fully qualified staff is incorporated. Fees IR£550–£1,100 per term. Extended Day facilities are available.

Caterham Preparatory School

Mottrams Harestone Valley Road Caterham Surrey CR3 6YB.
Tel: (01883) 342097.
Fax: (01883) 341230
Station: Caterham

Headteacher: **Mrs Susanne Owen-Hughes**, BEd, BSc, MBA (Open)

Fees. £775–£1,995 per term (day).

Age range. 3–11 years boys and girls.

The School stands in 80 acres of grounds in the green belt on the slopes of the North Downs, approximately 1 mile outside Caterham.

In 1994 the School became co-educational and the Nursery and Pre-Prep Department provides excellent facilities for younger children joining the School.

The curriculum offers the normal range of subjects including Technology and Science in well equipped laboratories. In addition, French is taught from age 4. There is a full PE programme including Soccer, Netball, Cricket, Rounders, Athletics, Tennis, Swimming and Gymnastics. Regular use is made of the new sports hall, astroturf and 25m indoor swimming pool.

Over 30 clubs and extra-curricular activities take place each week including Computer Club, Sailing, Dance, Drama, Short Tennis, Judo, Needlework, Choir, Orchestra and facilities for instrumental tuition.

All classrooms are equipped with their own multi-media computers and are fully networked with screened internet access. There is also a separate ICTSuite with 20 computers.

The Preparatory School enjoys close liaison with Caterham School, to which pupils normally proceed at age 11. In 1995 Caterham School became fully co-educational and a member of The Church Schools Foundation. This heralded an exciting series of developments providing the facilities for all pupils to continue achieving the high standards for which the School is well known.

The Cathedral School Llandaff

Woodard Schools (Western Division) Ltd Llandaff Cardiff CF5 2YH.
Tel: (029 20) 563179.
Fax: (029 20) 567752
Station: Cardiff

Headmaster: **P L Gray**, MA (Cantab), ARCO, PGCE

Chairman of the Council: Mr A O Golley

Number of Pupils. 387 (285 boys and 102 girls), including 32 Nursery, 84 in Pre-preparatory.

Fees. Senior Day Pupils £1,835 per term, Year 4 Pupils £1,720 per term, Year 3 Pupils £1,635 per term, Year 2 Pupils £1,350 per term, Pre-Prep Pupils £1,215 per term, Nursery Pupils £19.20 per day or £14.75 per morning session. £40 Registration fee. £100 Caution money.

The School was founded in 1880 by Dean Vaughan as a Preparatory School to educate, amongst others, the Cathedral Choristers. In September 1957 the administration of the School was taken over by the Woodard Division of that Society.

Pupils are prepared for Independent Senior Schools not only through top grade tuition but by being taught social skills, and also to be considerate to their fellows and good mannered at all times.

The School occupies the former Bishop's Palace, standing in it's own grounds near to the Cathedral. Facilities include a Sports Hall, specialist rooms for Art, Design & Technology, Science, a newly sited Library, 2 new IT Rooms, a Nursery and rooms set aside for the rehearsal of orchestras, choirs and instrumental tuition.

Charitable status. The Cathedral School, Llandaff as part of the Woodard Schools (Western Division) Limited is a Registered Charity, number S9886Z. It exists to provide a high standard of education for girls and boys between the ages of 3 and 13 years. There are places available for boy Choristers which provide 66% of their yearly fees at the school, and Choral Awards are available for girls to the value of £1,000 per year. New academic bursaries have just been introduced for children currently in Year 6.

Catteral Hall

Giggleswick Settle BD24 0DG.
Tel: 01729 893100
Fax: 01729 893158
e-mail: masmith@giggleswick.org.uk
website: www:giggleswick.org.uk
Stations: Settle and Giggleswick

Chairman of Governors: Mr D Stockdale, QC

Headmaster: **Mr R Hunter**, MA (Cantab)

Deputy Heads:
R M Jones
Mrs E M Bamford

Number of Pupils. 180. Catteral Hall (7-13) 140, 90 boys (30 boarders), 50 girls (20 boarders). Mill House (3-7) boys and girls day 40.

Fees. Catteral Hall £2,600-£4,200 per term; Mill House £1,290 per term.

Catteral Hall, the Preparatory School for Giggleswick (q.v), offers a co-educational boarding education within a secure, happy, family atmosphere. Day pupils are fully integrated into the life and ethos of the school, and go home after their tea and having completed their prep. The Headmaster and family live in the main building, and there is an experienced team of academic staff staff and matrons to care for the children. It is expected that pupils will progress to the Senior School. Catteral and Mill House, our pre-preparatory department, enjoy superb, self-contained grounds with a full range of facilities, in addition to using Giggleswick's pool, Chapel and design centre. The dining room (1999) serves particularly good food.

There is a clear sense of purpose and development. An new all-weather hockey pitch for both schools opens in August 2001, and Catteral Hall will open a complete new teaching centre in the summer of 2002. Responding to recent growth, this will have additional specialist classrooms and an expanded library/resource centre. The ICT facilities, including e-mail and supervised Internet access, are constantly upgraded.

In the centre of Britain, in the Yorkshire Dales, Catteral is within 75 minutes drive of Manchester and Leeds, their airports and railway stations. Airport transfers are organised.

Music and drama are integral to school life, as is participation in major team and individual sports and outdoor pursuits. Pupils with particular educational needs are offered private individual or group lessons with the onsite specialist. A number of competitive academic awards are available for boarding and day pupils from Year 4, and Music awards from Year 5. Art and Music are particularly strong, with both an inclusive atmosphere and excellence in standard. Music and sports tours alternate, with expeditions both around the UK and abroad.

A summer programme in July welcomes new and existing pupils and provides new experiences in a relaxed and fun environment.

Visits and "taster" stays are warmly encouraged, and contribute to new pupils' sense of involvement while being part of the living school.

Charitable status. Giggleswick School is a Registered Charity, number 532296. It exists to provide education for boys and girls.

The Cavendish School

179 Arlington Road London NW1 7EY.
Tel: 020 7485 1958.
Fax: 020 7267 0098

Preparatory School for Girls, 3–11 years;

Chairman of Governors: Moira Metcalf

Head: **Mrs L D Hayes**, BA (Hons), DipEd

Number of Children. 184. All day pupils.

Fees 1999/2000. Upper School £1,923, Lower School £1,808, per term. Lunch: £140 per term.

The Cavendish School is a small friendly IAPS preparatory school with over a century's experience in providing a lively well-balanced academic education in a caring Christian environment. The school is housed in a spacious Victorian school building and a modern teaching block. There are two secluded playgrounds and a short tennis court. There is a large, well-kept library, separate Science and DT/Art rooms and an IT teaching room.

The Cavendish School is administered by a charitable educational trust. The Headmistress is a member of IAPS and the school is inspected and accredited by ISJC. The Cavendish School is a Catholic foundation. Children of other denominations are accepted and their beliefs are respected.

Particular attention is given at The Cavendish School to each child's individual needs. Throughout the school a pupil's progress is carefully monitored so that, in consultation with parents, talents may be encouraged or difficulties overcome with small group or supplementary specialist tuition. In addition to the usual range of subjects, The Cavendish offers tuition in conversational French to all pupils from four years.

There is an extensive programme of extra-curricular activities including Spanish conversation, ballet, CDT, Art, cookery and short tennis. Pupils participate in the BAYS science, BAGA gymnastic, St John's Ambulance First Aid and ASA swimming award schemes. The school operates an after-school care service.

The school attaches great importance to maintaining strong yet informal links between home and school. The Headmistress and her staff are available weekly for consultation. There are also 2 termly written reports and annual parent-teacher meetings. There is a parents' association to which all parents belong. Parents are encouraged to participate in school outings, to join their children by invitation on numerous less formal occasions, and to contribute their expertise to supplementary activities.

Senior pupils are prepared in small tutorial groups for entry to a wide range of senior schools. The highly experienced and dedicated staff aim to make the pupils' years at The Cavendish a happy and purposeful experience so that they will transfer to their senior school at the age of eleven with confidence and ease.

Chafyn Grove School

Salisbury Wiltshire SP1 1LR.
Tel: (01722) 333423.
Fax: (01722) 323114
e-mail: officecgs@lineone.net
website: www.chafyngrove.co.uk
Station: Salisbury

Chairman of Governors: M Ricketts, Esq

***Headmaster:* J E A Barnes**, BA, PGCE

Deputy Head: Andy Falconer, BA (Hons)

Bursar and Clerk to the Governors: N Stiven, MDA, MIMgt

Number of Pupils. 298. Boarders 77, Day 148, Pre-prep 73. Aged 3-14.

Fees. £3,760 per term, Day children £2,810, Pre-prep £1,320

The school stands in its own grounds on the edge of Salisbury, one side facing the city and the other the country. Its aim is to prepare its pupils academically, culturally, morally and physically for the next stage of their education and there is a fine academic record. The school became co-educational in 1980 and it has grown in size to allow the number of girls to become one-third of the total in their age group. The staff are well-qualified and the staff/pupil ratio is 10:1 and class sizes are a maximum of 15. Music, ICT, Design Technology, PE, Art, Pottery, Woodwork and Drama are part of the regular curriculum and there are many optional activities.

The buildings were designed as a school and incorporate many modern additions. A new Nursery Department for boys and girls aged 3 is due to open in January 2002. The Pre-Preparatory Department, for pupils from the age of 4, is in a purpose built block and has the full use of the school grounds and equipment.

There are ten acres of playing-fields surrounding the school and the facilities include a 25-metre heated swimming-pool, music school, two libraries, 3 hard tennis courts, 2 glass backed squash courts, a chapel, a creative arts centre, sports hall, science laboratories and a computer centre.

Pupils are prepared for Common Entrance and the 11+ to the two Grammar Schools in Salisbury. Many scholarships are won to senior independent schools each year. Scholarships are held in February and Bursaries are available. We believe Chafyn Grove provides excellence in co-education - come and see for yourself.

Charitable status. Chafyn Grove School is a Registered Charity, number 309483/1. It exists to provide an excellent education for children.

Cheam School

Headley Newbury RG19 8LD.
Tel: (01635) 268381
Fax: (01635) 269345. Registrar: (01635) 268381

***Headmaster:* M R Johnson**, BEd (College of St Mark & St John, Plymouth)

Number of Pupils. 91 boarders, 267 day children.

Fees. £4,040 per term for boarders; £1,710-£2,990 per term for day children.

The School, originally founded in 1645, is a charitable trust controlled by a Board of Governors under the Chairmanship of Brigadier C D Daukes, MA. It is situated half way between Newbury and Basingstoke on the A339 and is within easy reach of the M3 and M4 motorways and the A34 trunk route from Portsmouth, Southampton and Winchester to Oxford and the Midlands. London Heathrow Airport is within an hour's drive.

Classes are small (average 16) and pupils are prepared for the major senior independent schools with Eton, Harrow, Radley, Marlborough, Sherborne, Wellington, Downe House, St Mary's Calne, St Mary's Wantage and Tudor Hall featuring frequently. Recent improvements include excellent facilities for Design Technology and Information Technology, a new dedicated Science Building, a refurbished Chapel and new Teaching Block, a new Music School (opening in September 2001) and much improved boarding facilities.

Two 30% Scholarships are offered annually for 8 year olds.

Dormitories are comfortable, carpeted and curtained. The School became co-educational in September 1997. A merger with Inhurst House School, formerly situated at Baughurst, and which re-located to the Headley site in 1999, offers parents the opportunity for education from 3-13+ for their sons and daughters.

Rugby, Soccer, Hockey and Cricket are the major team games for boys; Netball, Rounders and Lacrosse for girls, with a large sports hall (with squash court), heated outdoor swimming pool, 4 all-weather tennis courts and a 9 hole golf course in the extensive 80 acre grounds allow a wide range of other sports and pastimes to be enjoyed.

Charitable status. Cheam School Educational Trust is a Registered Charity, number 290143. It provides high-class education for boarding and day pupils; traditional values; modern thinking; education for the 21st century.

Cheltenham College Junior School

Thirlestaine Road Cheltenham GL53 7AB
Tel: (01242) 522697.
Fax: (01242) 265620
e-mail: ccjs@cheltcoll.gloucs.sch.uk
website: http://www.cheltcoll.gloucs.sch.uk
Station: Cheltenham

President of Council: W R Large

***Headmaster:* N I Archdale**, BEd (Bristol), MEd (*Edinburgh*)

Number of Pupils. 466 (55 boarders, 411 day boys and girls)

Fees per term. Boarders: £3,000–£3,735; Day Boys and Girls: £925–£2,890

Cheltenham College Junior School is a co-educational preparatory school from 3 to 13. The Pre-Prep Department called Kingfishers is located in a self contained purpose built department.

The School stands in a beautiful 15 acre parkland site near the centre of Regency Cheltenham; the town itself being well served by both motorway and rail networks. Excellent facilities include: all weather pitches, athletics track, squash courts, tennis courts, art block, computer centre, CDT centre, drama studio, music school and theatre. Some facilities are shared with the senior school including the Chapel, Science School, 25m swimming pool, new floodlit astroturf and outstanding sports hall.

The curriculum is a wide and stimulating one with all pupils being prepared for Common Entrance and Scholarship examinations. Apart from the normal academic subjects, all study Art, Music, PE, Information Technology,

CDT and Drama. The excellent facilities are backed by a team of professional and dedicated teachers. French is taught from the age of 3 in Kingfishers, Latin from 10. The teacher:pupil ratio is 1:10.

A wide range of sports are available including: Rugby, cricket, hockey, rowing, football, cross country, netball, badminton, athletics, archery, golf, gymnastics, squash, ballet, sailing, swimming, tennis and orienteering. Sporting skills are taught from an early age and include swimming for the whole school.

The school aims to give a well-rounded education in preparation for senior school. The environment is secure and caring, allowing each individual to meet his/her full potential. The boarding house aims to provide a 'home from home', with excellent pastoral care and a wide range of extra-curricular activities under the supervision of the Housemaster and his wife. Regular contact with parents is encouraged with exeats every third weekend. Three weekly progress reports are issued and full reports at the end of each term.

Visitors are welcomed and further information available from the Headmaster's Secretary, who will also arrange an appointment to tour the school and meet the Headmaster.

Charitable status. Cheltenham College Junior School is a Registered Charity, number 311720. It exists to provide education for boys and girls.

Chesham Preparatory School

Orchard Leigh Chesham Bucks HP5 3QF.
Tel: (01494) 782619
Fax: (01494) 79164
e-mail: secretary@chesham-prep.bucks.sch.uk

Chairman of Governors: Mr J Loarridge, OBE, RD, BA

***Headmaster:* R J H Ford**, DipEd, CertEd

Numbers. 386 boys and girls

Fees. £1,510–£1,795 (incl meals)

The School is a Charitable Educational Trust.

There are well-equipped classrooms including a Science Laboratory, Computer Room, a modern Assembly Hall, Art, Design and Technology Room, Music Room, playing fields and changing rooms with showers.

A wide variety of extra curricula activities is provided.

The aim of the School is to promote the development of the child's full personality. Although the School has always maintained a high academic standard, skill in Art and Craft, Music, Drama and Sport is equally encouraged, and the children are helped to develop and use whatever ability they possess. Children are prepared for entry into the County Secondary Schools and for entrance examinations to Independent Schools.

Books, Stationery and craft equipment are supplied by the School.

Charitable status. Chesham Preparatory School is a Registered Charity, number 310642. It exists to provide education for boys and girls.

Chigwell Junior School

Chigwell Essex IG7 6QF.
Tel: 020 8501 5721

***Master of the Junior School:* P R Bowden**, MA (Oxon)

Chairman of the Governors: C de Boer, Esq

Number of Pupils. 330 Day Pupils: 5 weekly or full Boarders.

Fees. Weekly Boarders £4,141 per term; Full Boarders £4,374 per term; Day Pupils, from £1,871 to £2,877 per term. (Day Pupils fees do not include lunches). (Lunch/Tea £204 per term)

The Junior School is housed in a purpose-built building on the same site as the Senior School, with which it shares the use of a wide range of activities and facilities including Chapel, Science laboratories, Music School, Arts and Technology Centre, Gymnasium, Swimming Pool, Sports Hall and 70 acres of playing fields, only 10 miles from the heart of London.

The curriculum and administration of the Senior and Junior Schools are closely linked.

Pupils sit a written test for entry to the Junior School and are normally admitted to the Senior School (see Part I of this book) without further examination.

Charitable status. Chigwell School is a Registered Charity, number 310866. It exists to provide a rounded education of the highest quality for its pupils.

Chinthurst School

Tadworth Surrey KT20 5QZ.
Tel: (01737) 812011

***Headmaster:* T J Egan**, MEd

Deputy Headmasters:
M S Roylance, BEd
P Mulhern, BEd
T Button, BEd

Number of Boys. 370

Fees. £600 per term Nursery Department (3–4½ years of age). £1,248 per term Pre-Preparatory Department (4½–7 years of age). £1,728 per term Preparatory Department (7–13 years of age). Lunch is provided at a cost of £110-£115 per term.

The School is an Educational Trust, administered by a Board of Governors, the Chairman of which is M T C Waugh, Esq. The School is set in modern and attractive rural surroundings with spacious games facilities.

Boys are prepared for all Senior Independent Schools, by way of the Common Entrance or Scholarships. A very experienced and well qualified staff ensure a high standard is achieved both academically and on the games field. Chinthurst has a 'family' ethos, aimed at the achievement of high academic standards allied to a purposeful and active school life within a happy environment.

The Chorister School

Durham DH1 3EL.
Tel: (0191) 384 2935
Fax: (0191) 383 9261
e-mail: head@choristers.durham.sch.uk
website: http://www.choristers.durham.sch.uk

Chairman of Governors: The Dean of Durham, The Very Revd John Arnold

***Headmaster:* C S S Drew**, MA (Lincoln College, Oxford)

Number of Pupils. 190. (20 Chorister-boarders, 8 full/weekly boarders, 162 day pupils, including 60 in Pre-Prep.

The school became co-educational in 1995 and there are girls in every year group.

Termly Fees. Choristers (including piano lessons) £1,587, full/weekly boarders £2,984, day pupils £2,040, Pre-Prep £1,424. Reductions are available for the children of C of E clergy and for younger siblings of boarders. Day pupils: concessionary fee for third sibling. Fees are inclusive of all normal requirements; there are no compulsory extras.

The Chorister School is situated in a beautiful corner of Durham Cathedral Close (called, in Durham, the College), and is overlooked by the magnificent Norman tower of the Cathedral. Choristers take a voice trial; for non-chorister pupils musical ability is not, of course, expected.

Pastoral care is the responsibility of all members of the staff, with the boarders' needs attended to by the four house staff and the Headmaster and his wife (and the excellent catering staff). Day pupils may take advantage of the extended boarding day, taking part with boarders in a wide range of clubs and activities after lessons are over. Art club, school choir, fencing, ballet, computing, Cubs, chess, skateboarding, speech and drama, karate and craft club are some of the popular ones.

Our curriculum introduces French from Pre-Prep level, where each of the five small classes has its own class teacher. In the Prep School class-teaching of the core curriculum is gradually replaced by subject-specialist teaching as children are prepared for Common Entrance and Scholarship examinations to senior schools. The school has a reputation for academic success, but cherishes all its pupils, whatever their academic attainment. Its curriculum, which includes RE, PE, swimming, Art, Technology and Music, is designed to ensure that academic edge does not lead to academic narrowness.

Games are an important element in the curriculum. The Chorister School competes at various levels with other schools in athletics, cricket, netball, hockey, rounders, rugby, football and swimming. Badminton, volleyball, basketball, tennis, indoor football and netball (in our large Sports Hall) are also played. The Chorister School has its own sports fields, tennis court and play areas, and uses the indoor swimming pool at Durham School.

Individual instrumental music lessons are available in almost anything, and all pupils take class music in which they sing and learn about musical history, musical instruments, simple analysis and some famous pieces.

RECENT DEVELOPMENTS include the expansion of the Pre-Prep, the resiting and re-quipping of the kitchen, a new Technology Laboratory, a girls' boarding facility and work on the school library.

ENTRY is by English and Maths test graded according to age or by informal assessment during a 'taster' day, as seems best for the age of the individual child. Competitive voice trials for aspiring Choristers are held twice a year, and at other times by arrangement. Please write or telephone the Headmaster's secretary for a prospectus and to arrange a visit to the school.

NEXT SCHOOL: children move from The Chorister School to a wide range of maintained and independent secondary schools throughout the North East and further afield. The school advises and guides parents in the appropriate choice of next school and aims to secure a successful transition for every pupil.

Charitable status. The Chorister School, Durham is a Registered Charity. It exists to provide boarding education for the choristers of Durham Cathedral and day or boarding education for other children aged 4–13.

Christ Church Cathedral School

3 Brewer Street Oxford OX1 1QW.
Tel: (01865) 242561
Fax: (01865) 202945

Governors: The Dean and Canons of Christ Church Cathedral

Headmaster: **James Smith**, BMus

Number of Boys. About 20 boarders, all of whom are Cathedral Choristers (who must board) and 130 day boys.

Termly fees. Day boys £2,196 (including lunch); Pre-Prep £1,342 (including lunch); Cathedral Choristers £1,340–£1,507 (fees are subsidised by the Cathedral); Nursery £550–£945.

Christ Church Cathedral School is a boarding and day Preparatory, Pre-Preparatory and Nursery School for about one hundred and fifty boys between the ages of two and a half and thirteen plus.

The School provides Choristers for the choirs of Christ Church Cathedral and Worcester College, and is governed by the Dean and Canons of Christ Church, with the assistance of lay members drawn from the city's professional community, some of whom are past or current parents.

It was founded in 1546 when provision was made for the education of eight Choristers on King Henry VIII's foundation of Christ Church on the site of Cardinal Wolsey's earlier foundation of Cardinal College. In the latter half of the nineteenth century, at the initiative of Dean Liddell, father of Alice Liddell, the inspiration for 'Alice in Wonderland', the boarding house was established at No 1 Brewer Street, and in 1892, during the Headship of the Reverend Henry Sayers, father of Dorothy L Sayers, the Italian Mediaeval scholar and creator of Lord Peter Wimsey, the present building was erected.

The School is centrally situated off St Aldates, and two hundred yards from Christ Church. It therefore not only enjoys the unique cultural background provided by Oxford itself, but also has the advantage of excellent recreational facilities on Christ Church Meadow.

In recent years a prestigious new teaching block has been built. It contains a much enhanced Pre-Prep Department, four additional teaching classrooms, a large science laboratory and a built-in computer network. In addition there is a multi-purpose hall and entrance foyer where recitals, exhibitions and conferences are held. The building is known as the Sir William Walton Centre, and the composer's widow, Lady Walton, opened it in June 1994. In 1996 a Nursery Department was opened. In 2001 a new computer suite was installed.

Clayesmore Preparatory School

Iwerne Minster Blandford Dorset DT11 8PH.
Tel: (01747) 811707.
Fax: (01747) 811692
Station: Gillingham (Dorset)

Chairman of Governors: Ronald Spinney, Esq, FRICS

Headmaster: **Martin Cooke**, BEd (Hons), FCollP, FGMS

Number of Pupils. 300 (Boarders 88, Day 212)

Fees. September 2000: Boarders £3,612 per term. Day pupils £1,234–£2,580 per term.

Clayesmore Preparatory School was founded in 1929 at

Charlton Marshall House by R A L Everett. In 1974 it moved to Iwerne Minster to occupy purpose-built premises close to Senior Clayesmore. A comprehensive development programme in recent years has provided the School with outstanding facilities for Sport, Music, Drama and the Arts, while the 62 acre parkland campus in one of the most beautiful parts of Dorset is the ideal environment for children to grow up in.

Day children can join the Pre-Preparatory Department at 2½; the youngest boarders usually arrive at the age of 8. Admission is normally by interview and report from a child's previous school. Older children may be asked to take a short entry test to assist in setting. The School is fully co-educational.

Academic, Art, Music, Sporting and All Rounder Scholarships are offered each year, together with 11+ Continuity Scholarships for candidates intending to complete their VIth form education at Senior Clayesmore.

The school is particularly proud of its long association with HM Forces and offers a number of service bursaries. There are also many children from expatriate families amongst the boarding community and the School is well versed in handling all the arrangements necessary for overseas travel.

The curriculum – with its strong emphasis on sound foundations – is typical of most good Prep Schools, but at Clayesmore each day is greatly enriched by the wide range of facilities and activities offered within the timetable. Younger children spend most of their time with their Form Teacher but by the age of ten all children are being taught by specialist subject teachers. In the Upper School the children are setted for Mathematics and Languages and work in their form groups for most subjects, which allows them to proceed at their own level and pace. Though the pressure of academic work increases as examinations approach, every child's programme includes a full range of Art, Music, Design Technology and Games and also gives time for play and relaxation.

The main games for boys are Rugby, Hockey and Cricket; for girls Netball, Hockey, Tennis and Rounders. A well equipped Sports Hall with a 25 metre heated pool, a floodlit all-weather hockey pitch and extensive playing fields give every opportunity for games to reach the highest standards. The School also enjoys considerable success at Athletics, Swimming and Orienteering. Many other minor sports are also available.

Over 100 children learn instruments and music is held in high regard. The Chapel Choir has toured in Italy, Germany, USA and Spain during the 90's and in the summer of 98, toured for three weeks in South Africa. This year they will visit Prague. The Prep School has two orchestras – sometimes three – and there are several instrumental ensembles. The Concert Band which draws the best woodwind, brass and percussion pupils from both schools is in hot demand in the locality and will tour in Italy in 2001 for the third time. Art, too, is very strong. The Prep School has its own Art Department with separate pottery, which is run by the young, prize-winning artist, Harriet Barber.

Boys and girls are prepared for Common Entrance and Senior School Scholarship examinations. The Prep School has an outstanding reputation for supporting pupils with dyslexia through its "all through" approach to teaching such pupils. All staff receive regular training so that the work of the Learning Support specialists is fully understood by the subject specialist staff and the form teachers. Communication is absolutely the key element in this.

Charitable status. Clayesmore Preparatory School is a Registered Charity, number 306214. It exists for the purposes of educating children.

Clifton College Preparatory School

Bristol BS8 3HE.
Tel: (0117) 3157-502
Fax: (0117) 3157-504

Chairman of College Council: A R Thornhill, MA, QC

Head Master: **R J Acheson**, MA, PhD (Trinity College, Oxford).

Number of pupils. 558 (87 boarders, 471 day pupils, 212 in Pre-prep)

Fees. Boarders, £3,715-£3,865 per term, Weekly Boarders £3,555-£3,705, Day pupils, £2,435–£2,650 per term, Pre-Prep, £1,165–£1,795 per term.

There is a full time teaching staff of 50, all of whom are qualified. A wide range of subjects is included in the normal curriculum.

The majority go on to Clifton College, but a sizeable number are prepared for and win scholarships to other schools. Over 60 awards have been won in the past three years. Pupils are prepared for Common Entrance Examination to all schools.

The administration of the School and the teaching curriculum is entirely separate from Clifton College, but some facilities are shared with the Upper School, including the Sports Hall and Indoor Swimming Pool, the Gymnasium, Chapel, Squash and Rackets Courts and 93 acres of playing fields. The School has its own Art & Design Centre. 1990 saw the provision of a new Resources Centre and two Astroturf Hockey pitches. A new Science Centre and Music School were opened in March 1995. The School also possesses one of the most advanced Information Technology Centres in the West of England.

The House system operates for both boarders and day pupils. Three houses cater for the boarders, each under the supervision of a Housemaster or Housemistress assisted by wife or husband, house tutor and matron. The remaining five Houses cater specifically for day pupils. No House contains more than 60 pupils and the smallest has 30. Boys and girls are in separate Houses, all recently reconditioned.

The youngest boys and girls (aged 3–7) work separately in a Lower School called Butcombe under the care of their own Head and 8 fully qualified teachers.

Day pupils enter the School any term after their 3rd birthday: boarders are normally admitted after the age of 7. Every effort is made to provide for the child who comes at a later age than is customary. Out of school activities supplementing the main School games are many and varied, the aim being to give every child an opportunity to participate in an activity from which he or she gains confidence and a sense of achievement.

Charitable status. Clifton College is a Registered Charity, number 311735. It provides boarding and day education for boys and girls aged 3–18 years.

Clifton Hall

Newbridge Edinburgh EH28 8LQ.
Tel: 0131-333 1359; 0131-333 1602
Fax: 0131 333 4609
e-mail: cliftonhall@rmplc.co.uk

Chairman of Governors: Professor B J McGettrick

Headmaster: **M A M Adams**, BSc

Number of Pupils. 130 Boys and girls, 75 boys, 55 girls.

Age. 3–12

Fees. Day £350–£1,900 per term according to form.

The School is housed in a magnificent Scottish baronial style mansion house nestled in 50 acres of its own fields and woodland backing onto the River Almond. Located ten miles west of Edinburgh and the only independent school near Livingston, we are ideally placed to accept children from the age of three from Linlithgow, Kirkliston, Balerno and Livingston itself, as well as from further afield with the help of the school busses.

Entry is from 3 upwards. Children who start in our nursery are generally guaranteed places in J1 at age five. Arrangements can be made for entry at any stage and is by interview and test. A range of scholarships and bursaries is available as well as Assisted Places from age five. Although a day school, activities, including the after school club, continue into the late afternoon and evening.

We aim to prepare pupils for the responsibilities they will have at their secondary independent schools through high quality classroom time and through a very wide range of well-tutored activities and sports. There is good partnership between the school and parents in all matters from guidance for homework to social events. The school has a good sporting record in the usual major sports and, particularly in minor sports such as fencing and golf.

Pupils go on to many of the major Scottish senior schools and many other British schools either as boarders or as day pupils. Shrewsbury, Downe House, Merchiston Castle, Fettes College, Daniel Stewarts and Melville College and St George's are among the many schools to which boys and girls move from Clifton Hall.

Facilities include a 7-hole golf course, good grass tennis courts in the walled garden, an indoor heated swimming pool, a games hall and gymnasium, science laboratory and IT room.

The ensemble and choir as well as musical productions make music a strong feature of school life.

Prospective parents' visits are welcomed by appointment with the school secretary, from whom free prospectuses may be obtained by return.

Charitable status. Clifton Hall School Limited is a Registered Charity, number SCO040139. Its aim is to prepare children from nursery age for senior school entry.

Clifton High School Lower School

College Road Clifton Bristol BS8 3JD
Tel: (0117) 9738096
Fax: (0117) 9238962
e-mail: admissions@chs.bristol.sch.uk

President of School Council: Dr R G Gliddon, BSc, PhD

Head of Lower School: **Mr Anthony Richards,** MBE, BSocSc Hons (Birmingham), PGCE

Number of pupils. 385. Girls 261; Boys 124. Aged 3 to 11.

Termly fees. Nursery (3–4 years): £525–£1,075; Prep(4–7 years): £1,420; Junior (7–11 years): £1,495.

There are three separate but inter-dependent sections of the Lower School, each has its own building, its own staff and its own character but there is a sense of belonging to each other and being part of a great school. The Upper School, founded in 1877, is for girls only and is set on the same campus.

The Nursery. With Nursery trained teachers supported by nursery nurses, the children are given the perfect start. Foundations are laid in a safe, quiet but busy atmosphere. Each day is alive with a host of activities which extend the children's vocabularies, give an appreciation of music, stimulate the enquiring mind, arouse curiosity and whet the appetite to learn and absorb.

The Nursery takes boys and girls from three years of age. We are flexible over attendance but ask for a minimum commitment of three mornings extending to any arrangement up to five full days.

Highly praised by OFSTED and GSA Inspectors, the Nursery is justly proud of its fine reputation.

The Preparatory Department. Dashing into school at 8.30, the Prep children are ready for another day of active learning. This is where the basics are taught but in such an imaginative way that the children don't know that they are working. Art and display are such an integral part of the curriculum. The building is ablaze with colour and vitality but there is also the hush that goes with absorbment and application. With small classes in spacious rooms there is the time and space to attend to each need and the capacity to extend each child's ability. The 3 Rs are the focal point but all classes benefit from a weekly ICT lesson in the Prep's own computer room, Swimming from Year 1, Gym, Music, and so it goes on.

The Preparatory Department, with its excellent facilities and dedicated, well qualified staff is able to provide that essential early grounding in a stimulating, happy and secure environment.

The Junior Department. In recent years the Junior Department has grown into a large, flourishing co-educational department with three classes in each of the four year groups, Years 3-6. The 2:1 ratio of girls to boys is reflected in the staffing. Art, Drama, French, Latin, Gym, ICT, Music, RE, Singing and Swimming are all specialist taught for the most part in specialist areas. Games are taught at the Coombe Dingle Sports Centre where the facilities include all-weather pitches and indoor tennis courts.

Academic standards are high but there is time and consideration for each individual, whatever her/his needs or abilities.

There is so much going on it is hard to keep abreast of things. The Junior Orchestra has 12 different instruments in it; there is a main choir and a chamber choir; there are boys' and girls' teams in a range of sports; children have opportunities to be involved in all sorts of extra curricular activities from kayaking and climbing to craft and sketching.

All this and more is down to the enthusiastic teachers, the effervescence of the children and the support and involvement of the parents.

Charitable status. Clifton High School is a Registered Charity, number 311736. It exists to provide education for pupils.

Colfe's Preparatory School

Horn Park Lane London SE12 8AW.
Tel: 020 8852 2283.

Chairman of the Governors: Mr David Curtiss

Head of the Preparatory School: **Mr N Helliwell**, BEd (Hons), MA

Number of Pupils. Prep 210. Pre-Prep 148.

Fees. £1,758 per term. Nursery £1,524. Pre-Prep £1,644.

Colfe's Preparatory School is a co-educational day school under the general direction of the Governors and

Headmaster of Colfe's School (qv). The Preparatory School is academically selective, offers a broad curriculum and aims to provide an excellent all-round education for pupils aged between 7 and 11 years, in preparation for entry to the Senior School.

The Preparatory School is housed in a purpose-built building situated in the same grounds as the Pre-preparatory and Senior School and benefits from the use of a sports hall, indoor swimming pool, tennis courts and extensive on-site playing fields. A substantial extension building opened in September 2000, comprising a library, art and design centre and modern spacious classrooms. The Preparatory School also has its own science laboratory and ICT room. A state-of-the-art wireless computer network has recently been installed, providing pupils with a radio wave link from laptop computers to a central information network, including Internet access through a safe filtering system.

Games played include rugby, football, cricket, swimming, tennis, netball, rounders and athletics. A school choir, orchestra, strings group and numerous ensembles perform frequently both in and out of school. In recent times, the major drama production has included all the pupils in the school. There is a wide range of after-school clubs on offer and a late school scheme for children of working parents.

Average class size is 18. The school employs a full time special learning difficulties tutor for those pupils who may need extra help.

The school has a reputation for excellence within a friendly and caring atmosphere.

Charitable status. Colfe's Educational Foundation is a Registered Charity, number 274527. It exists to provide education for children.

Colston's Collegiate - Lower School

Stapleton Bristol BS16 1BA.
Tel: 0117 965 5297; Stations: Temple Meads, Parkway

Chairman of Governors: Brigadier H W K Pye

Headmaster: **G N Phillips**, BEd

Number of pupils. 280 Day Pupils.

Fees. Day Pupils £1,155–£1,400. Pre-Prep £1,020. per term. Nursery £8.50 per session. There are no extra charges except for individual instrumental music tuition. Scholarships are offered at 7+ and 9+.

Colston's Collegiate School is situated in the village of Stapleton, conveniently near the M32 motorway and the centre of Bristol. Recent developments include a classroom extension, a new Music hall and an ICT suite. There is a large area of playing fields, including tennis courts, squash courts, a sports hall, an all-weather hockey pitch and an outdoor heated swimming pool. The Lower School occupies an adjoining site : its main buildings, Stapleton Court and the Old Rectory, which houses the Pre-Prep, date from the 18th/19th centuries. A recently extended classroom block now incorporates a Design Technology laboratory, ICT suite and Specialist Music room. The school also owns an adventure centre in the Wye Valley to which parties go during term and holiday.

The majority of pupils move from the Lower to the Upper School. There is a broad curriculum which extends beyond the requirements of the National Curriculum; incorporating the full range of academic subjects, along with Design Technology, Information Technology, Textiles, Art and Music. There is also a Learning Support Unit. Class sizes are kept small.

Games, Music and Drama flourish in the school. The choir makes regular visits to venues in the vicinity to give concerts and recitals. There is a String Ensemble, a Wind Band, an Orchestra and a concert is performed each year.

There are two afternoons of sport each week, the main games being rugby, hockey, cricket and netball. Soccer, squash, tennis, rounders, swimming, athletics and sailing are also available.

Drama is taught as a timetabled subject and the major School production takes place in the Easter term.

At the end of each day there are clubs and activities which all pupils are encouraged to attend : outdoor pursuits, chess, golf, art, badminton, dancing, and many others take place in a happy and friendly atmosphere. There are numerous holiday activities.

Coogee Boys Preparatory School

P O Box 190 Randwick New South Wales 2031.
Tel: 398-6310; 349-2515 A H (Area code 02)

Director: **Nick Brown**, BA (Syd), MACE

Head of School: John Dicks, DipTeach, BEd (SCAE), MEd (Syd)

Number of day Boys. 126. No Boarders

Fees for 1999. $4,300 per annum.

Coogee Preparatory School is one of the few (if not the only) independent, non-denominational, non-profit preparatory schools still privately owned in Australia.

The school was founded in 1914 by the late William Nimmo who embraced the philosophy of all round education. The school offers sound basic academic training of a traditional style, ample opportunity for sport and physical activity for every boy in the school and emphasises the need for gentlemanly well mannered behaviour. This is a three cornered aim, based on academic excellence, physical development and character training.

The school sits in the heart of the Eastern Suburbs of Sydney in Randwick where it leases the rooms at the rear of the Randwick Presbyterian Church.

Its playing fields are the adjacent Alison Park.

Early booking is necessary for at the time of writing (1999) there is a four year waiting list for entry into transition, the only intake year.

Copthorne School

Copthorne Crawley West Sussex RH10 3HR.
Tel: (01342) 712311
Fax: (01342) 714014
Stations: Horley, Three Bridges and Gatwick

Chairman of Governors: W S Blackshaw, MA

Headmaster: **G C Allen**, MA

Deputy Headmaster: A W N Bagshawe, BSc

Number of Boys and Girls. 270 (20 Boarders)

Fees. Weekly Boarders £2,895 per term. Day £2,496 per term. Junior Department £1,376 per term

With 24 members of the teaching staff classes are kept to an average of only 15 pupils. Children are prepared for the principal Senior Independent Schools and many Scholarships are won. The health of the children and the domestic arrangements are under the care of the Headmaster's wife with the assistance of 2 matrons.

The school stands in its own grounds of 50 acres, facing countryside on the borders of Surrey and Sussex. There are two large playing fields, a covered swimming pool and four hard tennis courts in the grounds. The sports hall has facilities for a tennis court, four badminton courts and two indoor cricket nets. A Chapel is connected to the main school buildings, which also include two Science Laboratories, Art Room, Carpentry and CDT Workshop, ICT Room, Music Department and Theatre.

A large Senior School Classroom block comprises nine classrooms and modern changing facilities.

The Junior Department has six classes for children 4–7 years in a separate building with its own facilities. A recent extension has provided 2 additional classrooms, a resources room and a new entrance hall. A pre-reception class, for rising 3 year olds, enjoys recently extended facilities.

Two Scholarships are offered annually by competitive examination in February.

The School was formed into a Charitable Trust in 1976 with a distinguished Board of Governors.

Charitable status. Copthorne School is a Registered Charity, number 270757. It exists to provide education for children.

Cothill House

Nr Abingdon Oxon OX13 6JL.
Tel: (01865) 390800
Fax: (01865) 390205

Chairman of the Governors: The Rt Hon The Lord Wakeham, DL

***Headmaster:* A D Richardson**, CertEd (Oxon)

Number of Boys. 250

Fees (from September 2000). Boarders £4,200 inclusive. Day boys at Chandlings Manor £1,630 to £2,150.

Cothill House is a Charitable Trust administered by a Board of Governors under the Chairmanship of Lord Wakeham. The Trust includes the day school Chandlings Manor and the Chateau de Sauveterre in France.

Charitable status. Cothill House School Limited is a Registered Charity, number S 402/6000 Z 4. Its main object and purpose is the advancement of education.

Cottesmore School

Buchan Hill Pease Pottage W Sussex RH11 9AU
Tel: (01293) 520648
Fax: (01293) 614784
e-mail: cottesmore@compuserve.com
website: www.cottesmoreschool.com

Independent Co-educational Boarding School

***Headmaster:* M A Rogerson**, MA (Cantab)

Number of Pupils. 100 Boys, 50 Girls, Age 7–13
Fees per term. £3,800 (boarding)

Cottesmore is an all boarding school, situated a mile from Exit 11 of the M23, ten minutes from Gatwick Airport and one hour from central London and Heathrow Airport.

Curriculum. Boys and girls are taught together in classes averaging 14 in number. The teacher/pupil ratio is 1:9. Children are fully prepared for Common Entrance and Scholarship examinations.

Music. The musical tradition is strong – more than 80% of children learn a variety of instruments; there are three Choirs, a School Orchestra and several musical ensembles.

Sport. The major games are Association & Rugby Football, Cricket, Hockey, Netball and Rounders. Numerous other sports are taught and encouraged. They include Tennis, Squash, Golf, Riding, Athletics, Cross Country Running, Swimming, Windsurfing, Fishing, Boating, Gymnastics, Shooting, Judo, Archery and Trampolining. The School competes at a national level in several of these sports.

Recent Developments. Our Technology Centre houses a constantly developing Information Technology Suite, a Design Technology room for metal, woodwork, plastic and pneumatics, a Craft room, Kiln, Science laboratory and Art Studio.

Hobbies and Activities. These include Pottery, Photography, Stamp Collecting, Chess, Bridge, Model-Making, Model Railway, Tenpin Bowling, Gardening, Rollerblading, Ballet, Modern Dancing, Drama, Craft, Carpentry, Printing, Cooking and Debating.

The boys and girls lead a full and varied life and are all encouraged to take part in as wide a variety of activities as possible. With a third of the children having parents working abroad, weekends are a vital part of the school life and are made busy and fun for all.

Entry requirements. Entry is by Headmaster's interview and a report from the previous school. For a prospectus and more information, please write or telephone the Headmaster's Secretary, Mrs Karen Stafford.

The Coventry Preparatory School

Kenilworth Road Coventry CV3 6PT.
Tel: (024) 76675289
Fax: (024) 76672171
e-mail: coventryprep@rmplc.co.uk

Chairman of the Governors: Charles Leonard

***Headmaster:* M C Abraham**, BEd (Hons)

Assistant Headmaster: D J Senyk, BA(Ed), BPhil, STB

Number of Pupils. (all day) 200.

Fees. Prep School £1,692–£2,076 per term; Pre-Preparatory £1,534 per term; Nursery £23 per day.

Coventry Preparatory School is for day boys and girls from the age of 3 to 13 years. It is situated in its own attractive grounds of approximately three and a half acres in a quiet part of Coventry overlooking the Memorial Park. Although completely autonomous, 'The Prep' is also part of Coventry School Foundation, which incorporates King Henry VIII and Bablake Schools.

The School aims to provide a thorough and efficient education for its pupils and to prepare them for entry to a wide choice of senior schools including Bablake, King Henry VIII, Warwick and Princethorpe College.

It also aims to reinforce values learnt at home and promote self-discipline and an awareness of the needs of others. Children must know the difference between right and wrong and be given firm guidelines on their attitudes and behaviour.

The School is divided into the Nursery, Pre-Prep and Prep School. After the Nursery, there are two classes for each year group up to Year 2 with a maximum of sixteen pupils per class. In Years 3-8 pupils are accommodated in single classes with an upper limit of twenty pupils per class.

Throughout the Pre-Prep Department children are taught predominantly by class teachers with specialists only in Art, Music and some games. In the Prep School teaching is undertaken by subject specialists following the National Curriculum for Key Stages 2 and 3. Teaching in Years 6, 7 and 8 also incorporates the prescribed requirements for Common Entrance and Senior Independent School Scholarships at 13+. The range of subjects taught within the normal timetable include English, Mathematics, Science (Physics, Chemistry, Biology), French, Latin, History, Geography, Art, Design Technology, Music, Religious Education, Information Communication Technology, Physical Education, Swimming, Personal Social and Health Education, Boys Games (Rugby, Soccer, Cricket), Girls Games (Netball, Rounders, Hockey). increasing degree of specialist teaching towards the top of the school.

The School is divided into four houses which compete with each other in work and other activities. School lunch is provided for all pupils, prepared by in-house caterers and experienced assistants and is closely supervised by the teaching staff.

The School is based on Christian principles and stands on this tradition.

Parents are invited to write to the Headmaster or Assistant Headmaster for the School Prospectus, and to arrange a visit.

Charitable status. Coventry School Foundation is a Registered Charity, number 528961. It exists to provide an affordable education for the people of Coventry and environs.

Coworth Park School

Valley End Chobham Woking Surrey GU24 8TE
Tel: (01276) 855707
Fax: (01276) 856043

Headmistress: **Mrs Carole Fairbairn**, CertEd (Hertfordshire)

Chairman of Governors: Mr P R Harris

Number of Pupils. 136 day girls, 26 day boys
Fees. £805–£1,925 per term.
Age range. Boys: 3–7 years. Girls: 3–11 years

Set in attractive rural surroundings on the edge of Chobham Common, Coworth Park was founded in 1971.

The average number of pupils per class is eighteen thus enabling each child to receive individual attention from fully qualified teachers. Girls are prepared for entrance examinations to independent day and boarding schools at 11+ and many have been awarded scholarships. Boys are prepared for entry to Preparatory schools at seven. Children who would benefit from extra teaching on a one-to-one basis are offered specialist tuition by a qualified special needs teacher.

The curriculum is based on the requirements for the Common Entrance examination and the National Curriculum. Testing is carried out at KS1 and KS2 and results are published to parents. Children are taught by specialist teachers where appropriate throughout the school and high academic standards are maintained at all levels.

Pupils gain self-confidence and skills through a wide range of other subjects such as French, Speech & Drama, Music, Art, Design Technology, Information Technology and Sport.

The school moved to the present site between Windlesham and Chobham in 1992 and the attractive grounds and buildings have been converted and extended further to include specialist teaching areas for ICT, Art/Technology, Music and Speech and Drama. The resulting educational and sporting facilities are of a very high standard.

The school is a member of IAPS and ISIS and is ISC Accredited. Prospective parents are warmly invited to visit the school.

Charitable status. Coworth Park School Limited is a Registered Charity, number 309109. It exists to provide education for children.

Craigclowan School

Edinburgh Road Perth PH2 8PS.
Tel: 01738 626310
Fax: 01738 440349
e-mail: mbeale@btconnect.com
website: www.craigclowan-school.co.uk

Headmaster: **M E Beale**, BEd

Chairman of Governors: Russell Taylor, Esq

Number of Pupils. 260. 130 boys, 130 girls; Pre-prep 50
Fees. £1,825 per term inclusive

Craigclowan is a co-educational, day school situated in 15 acres of its own ground on the outskirts of Perth. It is administered by a Charitable Trust.

Boys and girls are prepared for Common Entrance and scholarship for independent schools in both England and Scotland. In the recent past children have entered Glenalmond, Strathallan, Loretto, Fettes, Gordonstoun, St Leonards, Ampleforth, Downe House, Sherborne, St Mary's Ascot, Malvern, Queen Margaret's York, Haileybury, Rugby, Stowe and Eton as a result of Common Entrance or Scholarship.

Much attention is paid to each individual child in their preparation for academic success throughout the school and much energy is directed to a wide range of extra curricular activities with games, music, drama, debating and art high on the list. The games played include rugby, hockey and cricket for boys, tennis, hockey and netball for girls, whilst everyone swims and takes part in athletics and skiing. Instrumental tuition takes in all the orchestral areas and children regularly participate in productions at the local Repertory Company. In 2001 the children won National Competitions in Rugby, Netball, Swimming, Skiing, Debating and Choir.

Charitable status. Craigclowan School Limited is a Registered Charity, number EDCR 42484. It exists to promote education generally and for that purpose to establish, carry on and maintain a school within Scotland.

Cranleigh Preparatory School

Cranleigh Surrey GU6 8QH.
Tel: (01483) Office 273666 (Extn. 2051), Master's House 274199.
Fax: (01483) 277136
Station: Guildford

Master: **Malcolm Keppie**, MA (St Catharine's College, Cambridge), CertEd

Chairman of Governors: Mr Dudley Couper, MA

Number of Boys. 185 (70 Boarders, 115 Day Boys)
Fees. Boarders £3,245 per term. Day Boys £2,410 per term. These are genuinely inclusive and there are no hidden or compulsory extras.

The school stands in its own beautiful and spacious grounds of 35 acres, which include a wood for play or scientific study. A teaching staff of 16 enables classes to be small. Mr & Mrs Keppie live in the school as do two boarding masters and matron. They are all fully involved with the health and happiness of the boys. A great source of strength is the close partnership with Cranleigh School "across the road" (see Part I of this book). The Preparatory School has use of Senior School sports facilities, including indoor swimming pool, two artificial pitches and stables.

The boys are prepared for Common Entrance and many Academic, Music and Art Scholarships are won. Through these exams about two-thirds of the boys move on to Cranleigh School and the remaining one-third to a wide variety of other independent senior schools.

Boarding life is busy and fun. A full weekend offers many activities, including expeditions, and camping in summer, trips to the hills and places of interest, model-making, music, films, playing in the woods, varied sports, or just some free time to relax with friends. There are regular 'exeat' weekends and parents are welcome to visit.

The curriculum is broad and balanced. The School teaches computing, and technological problem-solving is encouraged. Art (including design, pottery, woodwork and various craft skills) and Music are included in the curriculum at all levels and individual instrumental lessons are available. There are three choirs, an orchestra, a band and several ensembles. All boys are given every incentive to develop spare-time interests, and a choice of activities is built into the timetable. Plays are presented termly.

The school's indoor and outdoor facilities are extensive and largely modern. Under the continuing building programme the construction of a large sports and drama hall, two new laboratories and a new music school was completed. A major new building opened in September 1996, housing classrooms, an enormous computer centre and new changing accommodation. A new leisure area opened in September 1997.

Rugger, football, hockey, cricket, athletics, tennis, swimming, shooting, squash, cross country, basketball, fencing, riding, golf, Eton Fives, badminton, table tennis and darts are among the sports. There is a heated swimming pool.

Many boarders' families are posted overseas and the school has well-established arrangements for meeting their special needs. These include escorting boys to and from nearby Gatwick and Heathrow, and ensuring that they spend the several short weekend "exeats" happily with relatives or families of school friends.

Normal entry is at the age of seven or eight. At a slightly older age a substantial entrance scholarship is usually offered each year to a boy from a local authority school. This continues through Cranleigh School.

Charitable status. The Corporation of Cranleigh and Bramley Schools is a Registered Charity, number 3595824. It exists to provide education for children aged 13–18 (Senior School) and 7–13 (Preparatory School).

Cranmore School

West Horsley Leatherhead Surrey KT24 6AT.
Tel: (01483) 284137

Chairman of Governors: The Very Revd Mgr J Scott, LCL, MCL

Headmaster: **A J Martin**, BA Hons, MA, DipEd

Deputy Head: Mr M R W Baker, BA, MA, CertEd

Director of Studies: Mr P Weatherly, BA Hons, PGCE

Head of Pre-Prep: Mrs L Compton, CertEd

Number of Boys. Total 520 all day. Pre-Nursery 8; Nursery 27; Pre-Prep 216; Prep 266.

Fees. Pre-Nursery £300; Nursery: £750; Pre-Prep £1,720; Prep £2,020 per term.

The School is situated midway between Leatherhead and Guildford, whilst Dorking and Woking are equally accessible.

There are 36 full-time members of staff, 6 part-time members and 17 visiting teachers for instruments in the Music department.

A Nursery school (3–4 yrs) with separate morning and afternoon sessions prepares boys for entry to the Junior Pre-Prep section of the school (4–8 yrs) where each boy plays a full part in the life of school, using the sports hall, gymnasium, swimming pool and other sports and music facilities. A new junior teaching block and a new library were completed in January 1994. Pupils enter the Senior Department at 8+ years and are taught by specialist subject teachers. At the end of their first year in the Senior School each year group is divided into a scholarship set and two parallel Common Entrance sets.

Boys are prepared for entry to a wide range of Independent Schools via the Common Entrance or Scholarship examination. Last year, 11 Academic, 2 Music and 2 Art Scholarship awards were obtained and all Common Entrance candidates gained entry to their first choice school.

A new senior teaching block was completed in April 1998 and comprises 3 large well-equipped science laboratories, 4 classrooms, a second ICT laboratory and a chapel. At the same time gymnasium has been completely rebuilt, the swimming pool refurbished, 4 new astro tennis courts put in place and a large playground with playground furniture, all on a rubberised surface large enough to take two tennis courts, for 5-a-side football or 6-a-side hockey. There are 24 acres of playing fields, a sports hall (Badminton, Basketball, Cricket nets, Volleyball etc) and 4 squash courts, Cross-country and athletics. School swimming and tennis teams compete in a wide variety of galas and tournaments. Inter-School and Inter-House competitions allow all boys to take part in organised games. Rowing, golf, tennis, ski clubs and many other sporting clubs operate through the term. There is also a Bridge Club, Technology Club, Board Games Club and Cub Scouts, etc, which occur weekly. A thriving chess club competes in a local schools' league and a number of honours have been won in recent years. The School has two ICT laboratories. Both the laboratories have the most up to date equipment. There is a site intranet and the school has a satellite internet connection. At age 7 years the boys start a course towards the RSA CLAIT award, whereby they do their keyboard skills, word-processing, database, spread sheet and graphical representation and take the examination as a 10 year old. Older boys continue to develop their ICT skills using Excell, Microsoft office, use of the Internet etc. Many of the subject teachers use the ICT facility for the use of back-up subject specific software.

A Drama, Speech and Music school incorporates a large Auditorium, two specialist teaching rooms and 7 practice rooms. Individual tuition in a wide variety of instruments is available; there are 2 orchestras, 6 choirs and various ensemble groups. A number of music scholarships are obtained each year.

Many other out of school activities are offered including a cub-scout pack, and a skiing club. There are annual PGL and skiing holidays.

Many of the boys are Catholic although entry is open to boys of all denominations.

Charitable status. Cranmore School, as part of the Diocese of Arundle & Brighton, is a Registered Charity, number 252878. It exists to provide education for boys.

Crescent School

Bawnmore Road Rugby Warwicks CV22 7QH.
Tel: (01788) 521595
Fax: (01788) 816185

Chairman of Trustees: Dr D E Loft

Headteacher: **Mrs C Vickers**, CertEd (Durham), MEd (Nottingham)

Number of Pupils. 139. 65 boys, 74 girls. (4+–11+) Day Boys and Girls. Nursery from 3 years.

Fees. £1,195–£1,281 per term.

The Crescent School is an independent co-educational preparatory school for day pupils aged 4–11 years. In addition, there is a Nursery for children from the age of 2½. The school was founded in 1947, originally to provide a place of education for the young children of the masters of Rugby School. Over the years the school has steadily expanded, admitting children from Rugby and the surrounding area. In 1988, having outgrown its original premises, the school moved into modern, purpose built accommodation in Bilton, about a mile to the south of Rugby town centre. The buildings provide large and bright teaching areas, with a separate annexe housing the Nursery and Reception classes. There are specialist rooms for Science, Art, Design Technology, ICT and the Performing Arts. In addition there is also a spacious Library and Resource Area. The multi purpose hall provides a venue for daily assemblies, large scale music making and is fully equipped for physical education. The school is surrounded by its own gardens, play areas and sports field.

The requirements of the National Curriculum are fully encompassed by the academic programme and particular emphasis is placed on literacy and numeracy in the early years. All pupils receive specialist tuition in Information Technology, Music and Physical Education. Specialist teaching in other subjects is introduced as children move upwards through the school. French is introduced in Year III and Latin classes are available for selected pupils from Year V. The pupils are prepared either for the local 11+ examination for entry to maintained secondary schools, including local grammar schools, Common Entrance and specific entrance examinations also at 11+ for independent senior schools.

Music is a particular strength of the school and lessons are given in singing, percussion, musical theory and appreciation and recorder playing. Instrumental lessons (piano, brass, woodwind and strings) are offered as an optional extra. There is a school choir, orchestra, brass, string and wind ensembles and recorder groups.

Charitable status. The Crescent School Trust is a Registered Charity, number 528781. The object of the charity shall be the provision and conduct of a day school for children of the inhabitants of Rugby and the surrounding district.

The Croft School

Stratford-upon-Avon Warwickshire CV37 7RL.
Tel: (01789) 293795
Fax: (01789) 414960

Principal: T M Thornton, MA (Oxon), CertEd (London), FRGS

Chairman of the School's Council: A Wolfe, LLB

Headmistress: **Mrs L Wolfe**, MA

Head of Lower School: Ms S M Short, CertEd

Number of Pupils. 410 (230 boys, 180 girls)

School Fees. £290 Nursery to £1,825 all inclusive

The Croft School, founded in 1933, moved in 1986 to a spacious Georgian building on a 30-acre site on the outskirts of Stratford-upon-Avon, which includes tennis courts, covered swimming pool, a protected cross country track, playing fields, gymnasium and an indoor games barn, large theatre barn and recital room. There is also a nature conservation area with lake.

Academically, the school provides firm foundations in small, well-equipped classes. There are dedicated facilities for Computer, French, CDT, Science, Geology, Art, Pottery and Music. There is a separate Lower School building. Every day each child has some form of physical education, either in the school gymnasium or on the games field or games barn. School clubs flourish and pupils participate in expeditions (at home and abroad) throughout the year.

Children are prepared for 11+ entry either to local Grammar Schools or Senior Day Independent Schools, or to go on to Boarding Schools.

Easter and Summer Schools are organised during the holidays.

Entrance requirements. Children can be accepted into the Nursery from the age of 2 onwards. Older children will spend a day in the school to be assessed.

Crosfields School

Shinfield Reading Berks RG2 9BL.
Tel: (0118) 9871810
Fax: (0118) 9310806
website: www.crosfields.com

Chairman of Governors: Mr P R Lloyd

Headmaster: **Mr J P Wansey**, BA, CertEd

Deputy Headmaster:
S C Dinsdale, BA (Hons) (Chichester), FLCM, LTCL, LLCM, PGCE (OU)

Fees. For Autumn 2000 £1,295–£2,310 including lunch. No compulsory extras.

Number of Boys. 410 day boys, 4 to 13+

Crosfields became independent under its own Board of Governors in 1957. It attempts to combine the important features of traditional education with the sounder forms of modern practice. Together they contribute to this vital stage of education which is at the same time a part of a life long process. Christian principles underlie the curriculum and a broad-based opportunity is considered the right of every boy.

There are 40 qualified staff and 6 part-time staff. The buildings and equipment are outstanding, augmented in 1986 by the addition of the Classroom Building for Senior and Middle Schools and in 1995 a new purpose built 12 classroom block for Pre-Prep and Junior boys (4–8). Recent additions include a Sports Centre and Music School.

These lie in 40 acres of parkland and 1 mile from the M4 motorway Junction 11.

Most boys enter senior schools via the Common Entrance Examination and a number of boys gain academic, games, art and music awards through scholarship examinations.

Charitable status. Crosfields School Trust Limited is a Registered Charity, number 584278. The aim of the

School is solely to provide education for boys between the ages of 4 and 13.

Culford Preparatory School

Culford Bury St Edmunds Suffolk IP28 6TX
Tel: 01284 728615
Fax: 01284 728183

Headmaster: **D G Kidd,** CertEd, ACP, FCollP

Age range. Co-educational 8–13.
Number of Pupils. Boarding: 46; Day: 167.
Number of Staff. Full-time 16; Part-time 5.
Religious affiliation. Methodist (pupils from other denominations are welcome).
Entry requirements. Entrance examination at all ages, though the majority of pupils enters at 8 or 11.
Assistance with fees. Assisted Places and Scholarships at 8+ and 11+.

Culford Preparatory School has its own staff and Headmaster, but remains closely linked to the Senior School. This allows the School to enjoy a significant degree of independence and autonomy whilst benefiting from the outstanding facilities of the whole school.

The Preparatory School is situated in its own grounds, within Culford Park. At the heart of the School is the quadrangle in the centre of which is the Jubilee Library, which, together with a new Science laboratory and two new classrooms, were opened in 1995. The pupils also enjoy splendid new IT facilities. A new classroom block was opened in September 1999 and a second Science laboratory was opened in September 2000.

Beyond the quadrangle there are magnificent playing fields and a well-equipped adventure playground.

Pupils are given a thorough grounding in the essential learning skills of Mathematics and English and the curriculum broadens beyond the confines of the National Curriculum. Work in the classrooms is augmented by an Activities Programme which offers pupils a wide range of opportunities and experiences.

The Pre-preparatory department is housed in a purpose-built and well-equipped complex in its own setting within Culford Park.

Cumnor House School

168 Pampisford Road South Croydon Surrey CR2 6DA.
Tel: 020 8660 3445
Fax: 020 8660 3445
e-mail: admin@cumnorhouse.demon.co.uk
website: www.cumnorhouse.demon.co.uk

Headmaster: **P Clare-Hunt**, MA

Number of Boys. 350
Fees. £4,350–£5,085 per annum (including lunch)
Religious denomination. Church of England
Curriculum. Cumnor House is one of Surrey's leading Preparatory Schools. Pleasantly and conveniently situated, the School prepares boys for scholarships and common entrance examinations to leading senior independent schools and local grammar schools.

Scholarships have been won recently to Dulwich, Epsom, Westminster, Charterhouse and the local senior independent schools, Whitgift, Trinity and Caterham.

Music, Art, Drama and Games play a large part in the life of the School and all contribute to the busy, happy atmosphere.

Choir, Sports Tours and matches, ski trips, regular stage productions and a broad spectrum of clubs and options, give the boys the opportunity to pursue a wide range of interests.

Entry requirements. Assessment test and interview.

Cumnor House School

Danehill near Haywards Heath East Sussex RH17 7HT.
Tel: (01825) 790347
Fax: (01825) 790910
e-mail: office@cumnor.demon.co.uk
Station: Haywards Heath (6 miles)

Chairman of Governors: S Cockburn, Esq, MA (Oxon)

Headmaster: **N J Milner-Gulland**, MA (Peterhouse, Cambridge), CertEd (Bristol)

Number of Pupils. 244. 135 boys, 109 girls; 73 in the Pre-Prep
Fees. £3,800 per term (Boarding); £2,965 (Day); £1,600 (Pre-preparatory). There is a reduction of 5% for each younger brother or sister at the school.

We aim to provide a happy and purposeful atmosphere in which children learn to set themselves high standards. Individuality is encouraged and equal esteem is given to achievements in and out of class.

The school has a strong tradition of scholarship, and many awards have been won at senior schools.

Out of school we offer children many opportunities for sports and cultural activities: in the Autumn and Spring terms children are given a choice of 25 or so supervised hobbies, from which they choose three. Much music and drama takes place: three-quarters of the pupils learn an individual instrument, and the chorus performs regularly in public: there is a thriving orchestra and wind band, as well as much singing and ensemble work. Each Summer term 50 or more children are involved in the annual production of an Elizabethan play in our open air theatre. Our rebuilt Sussex barn is used both as a school hall and as a local arts centre for concerts, lectures, exhibitions and winter term plays. In the last few years we have built two new tennis courts and a Sports Hall, and have purchased the next door farm and 50 acres of fields and woodland. The fine old farm buildings have now been converted into new science and computer laboratories, home economics centre, classroom and music block; and we have recently built a large classroom block and a self-contained Art studio.

Charitable status. Cumnor House School Trust is a Registered Charity, number 801924. It exists for the advancement of education.

Cundall Manor

Helperby York YO61 2RW.
Tel: (01423) 360200
Fax: (01423) 360754
e-mail: headmaster@cundallmanor.co.uk
website: www.cundallmanor.n-yorks.sch.uk

Chairman of Governors: Mrs Charlotte Bromet

Headmaster: **Peter Phillips**, BH Hons (London), MA(Ed), PGC(*SpLD*)

Number of Pupils. 120. Main School: 20 Boarders, 60 Day Pupils. Pre-Preparatory department: 40 pupils.

Fees. Boarders £3,119, Day Pupils £2,156, Pre-Prep £1,364.

Cundall Manor is situated in a magnificent 50 acre site in the Vale of York. The school is very accessible, and is served by nearby airports and the A1(M) motorway.

The school promotes a strong family ethos where the needs of the individual child are considered paramount. The staff are well qualified, experienced and committed to the children.

Boys and girls are thoroughly prepared for entry to a wide variety of Senior Schools. The majority of the children go to their first choice school and there is a good scholarship record. The school has its own Special Educational Needs department which aims to quickly identify children who require help. Strategies are implemented which involve both the school and the home, working closely to support a child's individual needs.

The school offers a broad curriculum with subject specialists in all areas. Class sizes are small to ensure the maximum attention for each individual child. There are high expectations of the children with regard to their manners, respect for others, self-discipline and effort. A wider educational experience and the opportunity to utilise the school grounds, the locality and places further afield is encouraged.

The broad extensive curriculum is enhanced by a large range of extra-curricular opportunities. There are many activities from which both day and boarding children alike can benefit.

Weekly and Flexi boarding is available where the emphasis is placed on the school becoming an extension of home life after the school day finishes. In a safe and happy atmosphere the children are supported as they develop into more independent young people.

The cultural and sporting life of the school are given high regard. The school boasts superb sporting opportunities with excellent facilities provided by a fully equipped sports hall, indoor swimming pool and stunning pitches. Opportunities to develop talents in music, art and drama are enabled and actively promoted.

The Pre-preparatory department is a separate purpose built building, situated on site. Staff are dedicated to providing children with a positive start to their education in a caring, purposeful and safe environment. Great importance is placed on ensuring that transition from Pre-prep to Main school is easy both academically and socially.

Charitable status. Cundall Manor Limited is a Registered Charity, number 529540. It exists to promote excellence in all areas of school life whilst catering for the needs of the individual child.

Dame Johane Bradbury's School

Ashdon Road Saffron Walden Essex CB10 2AL.
Tel: (01799) 522348
Fax: (01799) 516762
website: www.dame-bradbury-school.com

Headmistress: **Mrs R M Rainey**, CertEd

Number of Pupils. 316. All day pupils (151 boys, 165 girls)

Fees. Tuition per term: Nursery – mornings only £605, afternoons £535. Main school – mornings only £1,276 (reduced rate for each child of one family after the first £1,251); Reception (4 to 5 years) £1,521 (reduced rate £1,496); 5 to 6 years £1,586 (reduced rate £1,561); 6 to 11 years £1,691 (reduced rate £1,666). Lunches £119 per term.

Dame Bradbury's is a co-educational day school, founded in 1525. It is an educational charity managed by a Board of Governors, Chairman, Mrs F E Robinson, under a scheme prepared by the Secretary of State for Education and Science. Children are accepted from 3–11 years and are prepared for Common Entrance and entry into both independent and state schools.

A high teacher/pupil ratio is maintained and the fully qualified staff augmented by part-time specialists and in the younger forms by ancilliary helpers, work as a team to provide a stimulating educational environment. The curriculum is designed to give a broad general education of a high standard and covers the National Curriculum. French is introduced at the age of 6 and taught by a specialist. The school has a musical tradition and creative potential is encouraged in all the arts. The spacious building provides large classrooms, a gym/assembly hall, a dining-room, a well equipped science laboratory, a DT area, a spacious library, music and art departments and a special needs room. There are computers in all classrooms as well as fully equipped computer rooms. There are extensive grounds and playing fields, and 3 hard tennis/netball courts. Physical Education features strongly in the curriculum and includes gymnastics, tennis, netball, football, cricket, athletics, rounders and swimming. Extra curricular activities include orchestra, choir, Jazz Dance, football, table tennis, craft, judo, chess and cookery.

The Headmistress will be pleased to provide further details and meet interested parents.

Charitable status. Dame Johane Bradbury's School is a Registered Charity and a limited company, number 3595013. The Company also administers Dame Bradbury's Land Charity. It exists to provide education for boys and girls.

Danes Hill

Oxshott Surrey KT22 0JG.
Tel: (01372) 842509

Chairman of Governors: Mr Simon G Smith

Headmaster: **Robin Parfitt**, MA, MSc

Number of Children. 860

Fees. £368–£2,491 per term

As a co-educational school, Danes Hill prepares boys and girls for Scholarship and Common Entrance examinations to senior schools (girls at 11, 12 and 13 and boys at 13). A high academic record (31 awards this year from a year group of 75) combines happily with a strong tradition of sporting prowess to ensure that all children are exposed to a kaleidoscope of opportunity on a peaceful 18 acre site set well back from the main Esher-Leatherhead road. The curriculum is broad and a wide range of extra-curricular activity is encouraged: chess (IAPS Champions several times in recent years), drama, music and sailing are very strong indeed. The Pre-Preparatory Department takes children from 2½ to 6 years and is situated separately, but within easy walking distance of the Main School. There is a transport system available to take children both to and from school.

Charitable status. Danes Hill School (administered by The Vernon Educational Trust Ltd) is a Registered Charity, number 269433. It exists to provide education for boys and girls.

Daneshill School

Stratfield Turgis Basingstoke Hampshire RG27 0AR
Tel: (01256) 882707
Fax: (01256) 882007
e-mail: office@daneshill.hants.sch.uk

Headmaster: **S V Spencer**, CertEd, DipPhysEd (St Luke's College, Exeter)

Age Range: Boys 3–11, Girls 3–11, Day Boys 110, Day Girls 200

Fees. Mornings only £800; Pre-preparatory £1,280–£1,440, Preparatory £1,600–£2,000, including lunch.

There are no compulsory extras.

The school was founded in 1950 and moved to Stratfield Turgis in 1979.

Davenies School

Beaconsfield Bucks HP9 1AA.
Tel: (01494) 685400
Fax: (01494) 685408
e-mail: headmaster@davenies.co.uk
website: www.davenies.co.uk

Headmaster: **A J P Nott**, BA Hons, PGCE

Chairman: C Woodwark, Esq

Number of Boys. 305 (Day Boys only)

Tuition Fees. £1,945 to £2,315 per term

Davenies is situated in the heart of Beaconsfield, a Georgian town on the edge of the Chiltern Hills. The town is just off the M40 and only thirty minutes from the centre of London by car or rail. Founded in 1940, Davenies aims to provide a broad and challenging education for 300 day boys from the age of 4 to 13.

The large site includes a completely new classroom block which incorporates a purpose built science laboratory, drama studio, music department, art studio and six other specialist teaching rooms. The Pre-Prep department is housed in new modern buildings, too, and boys of all ages enjoy the recently completed additions of a new Design & Technology suite, Library and ICT centre. There is a modern gym, 20m swimming pool, astroturf and a large expanse of playing fields. The school has its own wooded dell which is used during playtime and by the large number of boys who are members of the school's Cub pack.

The curriculum is broad but considerable attention is paid from an early age to the basics of literacy and numeracy. Subject specialist teaching begins from Year 3 and setting commences at the beginning of Year 4. French is taught from Year 3 and German and Latin begins at Year 6. Many boys choose to complete their prep at school though there is an option to take it home. Almost all participate in the extensive range of extra-curricular activities on offer every day of the week. The major sports are football, cricket and rugby though many also enjoy hockey, athletics, swimming, squash, tennis, basketball, badminton and judo

All the boys in the senior part of the school join a special outdoor education programme in which they learn how to sail, canoe, ride, rock climb, rifle shoot, build rafts, play golf, tennis and undertake environmental work. Leadership training forms an important part of the school life of the senior boys who are helped to prepare for the challenges which lie ahead by providing team-building, decision-making, problem-solving and public speaking experience.

Once they leave the Pre-Prep department, the academic and pastoral welfare of the boys is undertaken by a network of form teachers. A Director of Studies and a Director of Pastoral Care oversee the management of this care and ensure that regular, detailed communication with parents takes place both formally and informally. Boys leave Davenies either at the end of Year 8 when they take either Common Entrance or Scholarships to senior independent schools or at the end of Year 6 if they have successfully reached the entry requirements for the Buckinghamshire grammar schools.

Of greatest importance is the education of the whole individual and considerable emphasis is laid on the value of courtesy, good manners and consideration for others; encapsulated in the school's motto: 'singulus pro fraternitate laborans'.

Charitable status. Beaconsfield Educational Trust Ltd is a Registered Charity, number 313120. It exists to provide high standards and the fulfilment of each child's potential.

Dean Close Preparatory School

Cheltenham Gloucestershire GL51 6QS.
Tel: 01242 512217.
Fax: 01242 258005
e-mail: office@deancloseprep.gloucs.sch.uk
Station: Cheltenham

Headmaster: **Stephen W Baird**, BA (Hons (Wales), PGCE (Bristol)

Chairman of Governors: Mr C G C Cocks, OBE, MA

Number of Pupils. 347: Boarding Boys 32, Boarding Girls 26, Day Boys 129, Day Girls 110. Pre-Prep 111

Inclusive Fees. Boarders £4,100 per term. Day Pupils £1,320-£2,805 per term.

The Preparatory School of Dean Close is a fully co-educational, Christian family school which occupies the same campus as Dean Close School and is, therefore, able to share such outstanding facilities as the Chapel, gymnasium, swimming pool, theatre and extensive playing fields, including hard tennis courts and the artificial astroturf hockey pitches.

Although the Preparatory School is administered by the same board of Governors, it has its own Headmaster and Staff. The Staff complement consists of 27 who either hold Degrees or Diplomas of Education, including a Director of Music and a team of excellent peripatetic musicians.

There are two boarding houses, each with resident Houseparents, a House Tutor and a resident matron.

The day pupils are accommodated in three purpose-built houses. Each is run by a Housemaster/Housemistress, assisted by house tutors.

The School follows a curriculum which embraces the National Curriculum and Common Entrance, preparing boys and girls for entry to the Senior School at 13+ by CE and internal transfer procedures. A few transfer to other Senior Independent Schools.

The main games for boys are Rugby, Hockey and Cricket and for girls, Hockey, Netball, Rounders and Tennis. Swimming, Athletics, Squash and Cross-Country Running are taught as well and use is made of the School's Covered Playing Area. Golf is available at a nearby course and in the school grounds.

Camping, Canoeing, Hill-walking and Orienteering are catered for and a wide range of activities is available including, among others, Chess, Judo, Stamp Club,

Carpentry, Railway Club, Computing, Shooting. Special Activity courses are part of the curriculum.

There is a special music school and a purpose built hall for dramatic and orchestral performances. There is a separate Art, Pottery and Technology centre and a dining hall and kitchens.

The main classroom block consists of 10 specialist teaching rooms including 2 laboratories and a computer centre. This building is joined to the newest teaching block by the admin centre. This block has 7 purpose-built classrooms, together with day house facilities, the staff Common Room, a new Library and Art and Technology block.

Charitable status. Dean Close Preparatory School is a Registered Charity, number 311721. It exists to provide education for children.

Denmead

Wensleydale Road Hampton-on-Thames Middlesex TW12 2LP.
Tel: 020 8979 1844
Fax: 020 8941 8773

Headmaster: **M McKaughan**, BEd

Number of pupils. 195

Fees per term. Kindergarten (mornings) 3–4 years: £855, Kindergarten (all day): £1,710. Pre-Prep (4–7 years): £1,855. Middle and Upper School (7–13 years): £1,995 including lunch for full day pupils.

The school is situated in a quiet leafy part of Hampton and is easily accessible by road and rail. Pupils are prepared for the best senior schools, day and boarding, with an average of 55%-60% each year going on to Hampton School. Both schools are now served by the same Board of Governors and the Headmaster of Denmead now reports to the Headmaster of Hampton School. This amalgamation produces economies of scale from which Denmead will greatly benefit. The pre-prep is housed on its own site in the homely atmosphere of two residential houses offering space and security. The preparatory section boasts its own games field and purpose built teaching facilities including a multi-purpose hall. School sports are Rugby, Football, Cricket and Athletics. Out of school activities include art club, chess, drama, adventure club, judo and a variety of minor sports. There is a school choir, an orchestra and a flourishing drama tradition. Instrumental music tuition and speech classes are also provided. Parents share in the school's life as fully as possible and there exists a very active parents' association.

Please contact the school office for a prospectus.

Charitable status. Denmead School part of the Hampton School Foundation, a Registered Charity, number 312667. It exists to provide a school in Hampton.

Dolphin School

Hurst Berkshire RG10 0BP.
Tel: +44 (0) 118 934 1277
Fax: +44 (0) 118 934 4110
e-mail: omnes@dolphin.berks.sch.uk
website: www.dolphin.berks.sch.uk

Founded in 1970.

Joint Heads: **Dr N Follett**, BA, MA, PhD, **Mrs Heather Brough,** DipAD, PGCE

Registrar: Mrs Marzena M Dixon

Number in School. Montessori Nursery (2–5) 20; Upper School (5–14) 235. Day boys 125, Day girls 110.

Fees per term. Nursery (half day) £975; Nursery (full day) £1,450; Upper School Years 1 & 2 £1,880; Upper School Years 3 to 8 £1,940.

General. We believe that most children have special gifts and talents, but too often these abilities remain forever hidden. The Dolphin School offers an environment which encourages the gifts of most children to flourish. Children leave Dolphin with confidence in themselves, a strong sense of individualism, the ability to adjust well in school and social situations, at least one area in which they can feel pride in their own achievement and a strong sense of curiosity and enjoyment in learning. Throughout life, in an ever more quickly changing world, they will have the skills and the confidence successfully to pursue their ambitions and interests and to lead happy and fulfilled lives.

We remember that the meaning of "to educate" is "to lead out". Dolphin children are allowed to develop as individuals and encouraged to fulfil their various potentials in small classes under the careful guidance of specialist teachers. Abundant academic, artistic, social and sporting stimulation is provided through an extremely broad, well-rounded programme. We encourage lateral thinking and the ability to think across subject areas. Expectations for all children are very high and academic rigour is a key component in all lessons.

The Dolphin School provides the friendly, family atmosphere of a small school. All members of staff are actively concerned with the pastoral care of all the children, but each form teacher assumes special responsibility for the daily well-being and the overall progress of a very small group of children. In addition children in their final four years have a personal academic tutor. Class sizes are a maximum of fourteen. Children learn both to talk and listen to each other, to evaluate and tolerate the opinions of others and to take pride in each other's achievements. They are also encouraged to accept responsibility and to develop their leadership abilities. We believe that a major responsibility of our teaching is to encourage Dolphin children to grow into socially concerned adults who will actively seek to address some of the major problems of mankind.

Courses offered. All children are taught by graduate specialists from age six in most subjects. In the early years we provide a firm grounding in English-based skills throughout all humanities subjects. French begins in Nursery, Latin in Year Five and German and Greek in Year Seven. Laboratory science is taught from age six. Mathematics, geography, history, ICT, classical studies, art, design technology, drama, music and PE are taught throughout the upper school. Architecture, astronomy, philosophy, thinking skills, religious education, current affairs, environmental studies and history/geography in French are included in some years.

We are nationally at the cutting edge of ICT. Our own training scheme for pupils and staff is unique in Britain and we have been named as a centre of excellence for ICT.

Activities. A unique strength of Dolphin School is our residential field trip programme in which all children participate from age seven. The work related to these trips forms major sections of all departmental syllabuses. Major annual field trips visit East Sussex, Dorset, Ironbridge, North Wales, Northumbria, Ireland and Italy while departments organise residential trips to Boulogne, Malladam, York, Caen, the Machynlleth Alternative Centre and Stratford.

We also offer an extensive mountain-walking programme. We have a large number of qualified British Mountain Leaders on our staff and children participate in a graded fell walking programme. Locations range from the South Downs and Brecon Beacons to Snowdonia, Arran, the Scottish Highlands, the Alps and Greece. We also organise sports tours and a "custom made" outward bound course.

We believe in 'hands-on' learning, whether in the laboratory or outside the classroom, and children participate in a very wide range of day trips to museums, theatres, archaeological sites and many other venues.

Field walking and day trips are included in the fees, as are after school clubs which include: athletics, tennis, short tennis, science club, judo, rounders, cricket, country dancing, embroidery, computing, cycling proficiency, swimming, football, netball, gymnastics, craft, hockey, chess, cross country, rugby, art, Latin, table tennis, orchestra, windband, string group, choir, table tennis, orienteering.

We field teams at all levels in football, rugby, cricket, chess, netball, rounders, tennis, short tennis, swimming, cross-country, athletics, hockey and judo.

Examination results. Our examination results are outstanding and we regularly win major scholarships to senior independent schools, including St Paul's, Eton and Winchester. We provide an education especially suited to the needs of gifted children (academically, musically, artistically). Internal scholarships are available to children of 10-14 in the performing arts, art, creative writing and sport as well as academic bursaries. We have a thriving Old Delphinian organisation. Most past pupils gain good degrees and a high proportion attend Oxbridge colleges.

Facilities. Our hall offers a splendid venue for school concerts and plays. We stage several major productions each year. Recent productions have included Shakespeare's "Tempest", "The Frogs" of Aristophanes and musicals written by our Director of Music. Our grounds include a swimming pool, all weather tennis courts and playing fields. Cricket matches are played at Hurst, a neighbouring county standard ground.

Entry. Entrance at 2½, 5, 10/11 and when spaces become available. Assessment and interview.

Dorset House

Bury Manor Bury Pulborough West Sussex RH20 1PB.
Tel: (01798) 831456
Fax: (01798) 831141

Chairman of Governors: A P Higham, Esq

***Headmaster:* A L James**, BA (Oxon)

Number of Boys. 155 (includes 57 Day and 40 Pre-Prep Boys)

Fees. £3,675 a term. No unavoidable extras. Day Boys from £2,360, Pre-Prep £1,525.

Founded more than 100 years ago, Dorset House is an educational trust, so that the continuity and the financial security of the school are best assured.

Being a small school, it has been possible to create a home from home atmosphere in which individual attention may more easily be devoted to each boy, both in and out of the classroom.

Bury Manor stands in beautiful grounds set in pasture and woodland, on the banks of the river Arun and at the foot of one of the most attractive stretches of the South Downs, the surroundings offering unlimited opportunities for recreation and adventure.

There is a full-time qualified and experienced staff of fourteen. Classes are small, averaging 18, and self-discipline and the desire for learning for its own sake are stressed, so that the school has had an almost unbroken success rate in the Common Entrance, together with an encouraging number of scholarships. Every effort is made to bring out the talents of every boy, whatever his ability or interests. Music is a major feature and there is a fine choir and an orchestra of 25.

All boys have access to excellent computer facilities, and the school was one of the first in England to be linked by computer to an American school.

There are good facilities for all the usual games and sports as well as for judo, boating and camping which are always popular.

Although Dorset House is essentially a boarding school, there are always a number of dayboys. Many boys start to board at about the age of ten, weekly boarding being a popular option at any age. Entry is by interview.

Mrs James personally supervises the domestic arrangements and is assisted by three matrons.

Charitable status. Bury Manor School Trust Limited is a Registered Charity, number 307035. It exists to provide a first class education for boys.

Downsend

Leatherhead Surrey KT22 8TJ.
Tel: (01372) 372197
Fax: (01372) 363367

Principal: C J Linford, MA (Oxon)

***Headmaster:* A D White**

Number of Pupils. 520 (aged 6–13); 350 (aged 2½–6).

Fees per term. Pre-Preparatory from £450 to £1,685, including lunch for full time pupils. Preparatory £1,685 (Year 2), £2,175 (Years 3–8), including lunch.

Downsend is a co-educational school for children aged between 2½ and 13 years.

The main school stands on a pleasant, open site just outside the town, surrounded by its own playing fields and tennis courts. The Sports Complex, including large indoor swimming pool, was opened in 1990. The newly styled library and the expanded, networked ICT provision, are new facilities available to support children's learning and development.

PRE-PREPARATORY 2½–6. Catering for children from the age of 2½ to 6, there are three co-educational pre-preparatory departments in ASHTEAD, EPSOM and LEATHERHEAD, each under the guidance of its own Headmistress. Here pupils work in a small and friendly environment, where they are encouraged to achieve their individual potential through a wide range of activities. Outings, sport, music and drama all play an important part in school life. At 6 the majority of the children move on to the main Downsend site where they are joined by children from other local Independent and State schools.

PREPARATORY 6–13. Downsend is not only a traditional academic prep school which prepares children for Common Entrance, Scholarship and High School examinations, but also a thriving community where many other opportunities are provided.

The standard of work is high and the school is particularly proud of its scholarship record. Since the school was founded in 1918 over 500 scholarships have been gained by Downsend children. Recently an average of over 15 a year has been achieved and nearly 50 awards have been won at Winchester. 11+ scholarships are now available for entry to our Senior School. Details can be obtained from the Admissions Secretary.

There is a wide curriculum and the children study, in addition to the normal Common Entrance subjects, Art, Drama, Food Technology, Health Education, ICT, Music, Technology and Textiles. Parents are kept informed of their children's progress through regular Parents' Evenings and termly reports, and are welcome at all times to communicate with members of staff.

The school has a strong reputation for its music, with regular concerts throughout the year, and a large number of children learn a variety of musical instruments. Drama is equally important and there are several productions each year. Pupils can take part in a full range of sports not only in school but also at local, regional and national level. Regular visits occur outside school and holidays abroad are also arranged.

The Downs School

Colwall Malvern Worcs WR13 6EY.
Tel: (01684) 540277
Fax: (01684) 540094
e-mail: downsHM@aol.com
website: www.thedowns.org.uk
Station: Colwall

President of the Governors: Ian D S Beer, Esq, CBE, MA, JP

Headmaster: **A P Ramsay**, BEd, MSc

Number of Pupils. 70 boys, 70 girls.

Termly Fees. Boarding £3,350; Weekly Boarding £3,280. Flexi-boarding £13.00 per night; Day from £2,350 to £2,420. Pre-preparatory Dept. £1,160–£1,620. Kindergarten £780.

Location. 3 miles west of Malvern, 4 miles east of Ledbury. 15 miles off the M5 Motorway. On main line from Paddington.

The School is set in 55 acres of attractive rural countryside on the western slopes of the Malvern Hills and celebrates its centenary in the year 2000.

Traditionally a broad curriculum which accommodates pupils of varying academic ability has been offered. There is plenty of challenge for the academically gifted, yet those pupils with special educational needs also receive support. Over the past decade children have proceeded to more than three dozen senior independent schools on the basis of Scholarship or Common Entrance examinations. Sports, especially team games, are also a serious part of the curriculum, added to which 80% of the pupils in the main school learn a musical instrument. There is a wide-ranging hobbies programme.

All units are small in size – forms, dormitories, tutor groups and houses. There is a wide range of facilities, including a 300 seater concert hall, a self-contained music school, a library, twin science laboratories, information technology centre, an art studio, a pottery, a gymnasium, an all-weather hockey pitch, and the school has its own unique narrow gauge steam railway.

The health and pastoral care of the children is the personal concern of the Headmaster and Mrs Ramsay, who are assisted by a number of experienced resident staff.

Academic and Music Awards are available each year, and details of these and other financial assistance available can be had on application to the Headmaster.

Interested parents are welcome to visit the school at any time, to have the opportunity to meet children and staff, and to appreciate the warm and friendly atmosphere.

Charitable status. The Downs School is a Registered Charity, number 372476. It exists to provide education for boys and girls.

The Downs School

Charlton House Wraxall Bristol BS48 1PF.
Tel: (01275) 852008
Fax: (01275) 855840
e-mail: theoffice@the downs.biblio.net

Chairman of Governors: C C Bayne-Jardine, MA (Oxon), MEd, PhD

Head Master: **M A Gunn**, BA, PGCE, AdDipEdMan, PGDPS

Number of Pupils. Boarders 25, Day Pupils 200, Pre-Preparatory Dept 55

Fees. Boarders and Weekly Boarders £3,300; Day Pupils, £1,190–£2,180 (exclusive of lunch), Pre-Preparatory Dept £785–£1,055

There are reductions in fees for brothers/sisters and for sons/daughters of service personnel. Scholarships are awarded annually.

Founded in 1894, the school became a charitable trust in 1972. Children join a Nursery group at the age of 3 and there are significant intakes at ages 6, 7 and 8.

The school has an enviable academic and all round record with over 100 awards being won to senior schools in the last 10 years. Sports facilities are outstanding and there is a wide range of sporting, musical, dramatic and other out-of-class activities.

The Downs is in a rural setting but only 10 minutes from the centre of Bristol, 15 minutes from Bristol International Airport and 5 minutes from the M5 and the Second Severn Crossing to Wales.

Charitable status. The Downs School is a Registered Charity, number 310279. It was established for the education of boys and girls aged 3–13.

Dragon School

Bardwell Road Oxford OX2 6SS
Tel: (01865) 315400
Fax: (01865) 315429
e-mail: dragonschool.org
website: http://www.dragonschool.org

Chairman of Governors: N J A Kane

Headmaster: **Roger Trafford**, MA

Number of Pupils. 830 boys and girls. 630 in the Main School, of whom 280 are boarders. 200 day children aged 3–7 in the Junior School, Lynams.

Fees. Boarders £4,270 per term; Day Children £2,930 in the Main School, £1,720–£2,200 at Lynams.

Situated on the edge of the University in North Oxford, with playing fields adjoining the River Cherwell, the School regularly wins over 30 awards, and prepares pupils for entry to senior schools throughout the country and abroad. Boys play rugby in the autumn term, hockey/soccer in the spring term, and cricket, athletics, swimming and tennis in the summer. Girls play hockey, netball, rounders, tennis and swimming and there are other sports available, eg rowing, sailing, squash, judo, fencing.

Facilities are excellent with 6 new Science laboratories

in 1999 and a new indoor swimming pool and Art, Design and Technology Centre in 2000.

Lynams is a mile away, with a separate staff and range of facilities suitable for younger children.

A wide range of extra-curricular activities includes lectures and debates, five or six plays each year and several school orchestral concerts annually; a high proportion of pupils learn at least one musical instrument. There are frequent expeditions and a wide variety of holiday expeditions: 2000 saw Dragon boys and girls going to India, Kenya, Morocco, Switzerland, Sinai, Canada, Barbados and several trips to France. There is a regular exchange programme with Keio Yochisha in Japan.

Charitable status. The Dragon School Trust Ltd is a Registered Charity, number 309676. It aims to provide education for boys and girls between the ages of 3 and 13.

Duke of Kent School

Ewhurst Nr Cranleigh Surrey GU6 7NS.
Tel: (01483) 277313
Fax: (01483) 273862

Chairman of the Governing Body: Air Vice-Marshal M K Adams, CB, AFC, FRAeS

***Headmaster:* A D Cameron**, MA, PhD (University of Edinburgh)

Number of Boarders. 29 boys, 26 girls
Number of Day Pupils. 135

Fees. Boarders £2,940–£3,530 per term, Day Boarders £1,070–£2,595 per term. Entrance scholarships are available for admission to the Main School for both day and boarding pupils. Special discounts are available for service boarders. 5% reduction in fees for second and subsequent children.

The Duke of Kent School was founded in 1976 by the amalgamation of the Vanbrugh Castle and Woolpit Schools. It stands in magnificent surroundings in the Surrey hills and is within easy reach of Central London, the M25 and Heathrow and Gatwick Airports.

There is a full-time qualified teaching staff of 21 and both boys and girls are prepared for Scholarships and the Common Entrance to a wide range of senior schools. In addition to the normal academic subjects art, drama, music, CDT and computer studies are included in the curriculum for all children.

The School offers Preparatory and Pre-preparatory education for children aged 4-13. Though predominantly a day school in total numbers, the School retains a thriving boarding section.

The School has outstanding facilities which include a modern classroom/dormitory block with Science and computer laboratories, a multi-purpose hall, library and specialist rooms for domestic-science, woodwork and art. A music-block with 9 teaching/practice rooms and a rehearsal room for the band and choirs has been added and specialist tuition is available on a wide range of musical instruments. There are extensive playing fields, a heated and covered swimming pool and all-weather tennis courts. A new full sized sports hall was added in 1995.

Charitable status. Duke of Kent School is a Registered Charity, number 1064183. It exists for the advancement of education for children from RAF families, from other service backgrounds as well as those from non-service backgrounds.

Dulwich College Preparatory School

42 Alleyn Park Dulwich SE21 7AA.
Tel: 020 8670 3217
Fax: 020 8766 7586
Stations: Sydenham Hill, West Dulwich
(on line from Victoria to Orpington) and Gipsy Hill

***Headmaster:* G Marsh**, MA, CertEd

Number of Boys. 765 day boys (age 3–13), 15 girls (aged 3–5), 20 weekly boarders (age 8–13)

Fees September 2001. Day boys £888–£2,880 per term (inclusive of lunch – there are no compulsory extras). Weekly boarders £1,345 per term in addition to tuition fee.

Boys are prepared for Common Entrance and Scholarships to all the Boys' Independent Schools where 15-20 scholarships are won annually. DCPS is an entirely separate school from Dulwich College, though a number of boys continue their education at the College every year.

The school is divided into a Nursery School for 126 boys and girls 3–5, a Pre-Prep for 126 boys 5–7, a Lower School for 200 boys 7–9 and the Middle and Upper Schools for 346 boys 9–13.

Over the past twenty years a programme of building and development has provided the school with a new Nursery, a new Pre-Prep department, a new Lower School (for 7–9 year olds), with its own Library, Art Room and ICT Room. The Music School was opened in 1989. In September 1995 a classroom block was opened consisting 12 specialist teaching rooms, a small theatre and a fully equipped computer suite. There is a modern teaching room for Design Technology.

The Science Laboratories were completely refurbished in Summer 1996, and a Language Block was created from existing buildings in Summer 1997. The Senior Library was resited and enlarged in 1999. September 2001 saw the opening of a new entrance foyer, two new classrooms and an enlarged Art Room.

There are extensive playing fields and all the normal games are played. All boys aged 6 and over are taught to swim in the school's own 25 metre indoor pool.

Boarders. There are up to 30 weekly boarders in the 8–13 age group in the school's boarding house, Brightlands, Gallery Road, 10 minutes walk from the main school. The boarding house shares 13 acres of grounds with the Nursery School, with tennis courts and playing fields available in leisure time.

The School was founded in 1885 and became a charitable trust in 1957 with a board of governors under the Chairmanship of Mr D Pennock.

Charitable status. Dulwich College Preparatory School is a Registered Charity, number 312715. It exists to provide education for boys.

Dulwich Preparatory School

Coursehorn Cranbrook Kent TN17 3NP.
Tel: (01580) 712179.
Fax: (01580) 715322
e-mail: registrar@dcpskent.org
Station: Staplehurst

Chairman of Governors: D R M Pennock

***Headmaster:* M C Wagstaffe**, BA, PGCE

Number of Boys and Girls. 238 day (Upper School). 160 day (Lower School). 100 day (Pre-prep). 44 boarders.

Inclusive fees per term. Upper School, day: £2,720. Lower School, day: £2,335. Pre-prep, full day: £1,490–£1,765, mornings: £935, Boarders: £4,100 (full) £3,995 (weekly)

The School, which is one mile from the country town of Cranbrook, has extensive grounds (40 acres) and offers a broad and varied education to boys and girls from 3 to 13+. To ensure that children receive the personal attention that is vital for this age range the School is divided up into three separate, self-contained, departments. These are Nash House (3–6 year olds), Lower School (6–9 year olds) and Upper School (9–13 year olds). Each department has its own staff, teaching equipment, sports facilities, playgrounds, swimming pools, etc. Pupils are prepared for Common Entrance or Scholarship examinations to any school of their parents' choice, and there is a strong emphasis on up to date teaching methods. The wide scope for sporting activities – Football, Rugby, Cricket, Hockey, Netball, Rounders, Athletics, Cross-country, Swimming, Tennis – is balanced by the importance attached to Art, CDT, Drama, Computers and Music. Over 200 pupils learn the full range of orchestral instruments. There are two Orchestras, a Wind Band, four Choirs and an Electronics Workshop. The boarders are divided into two houses, boys and girls, each under the care of House staff. The happiness of the boarders is a particular concern and every effort is made to establish close and friendly contact between the School and the parents. There is a flourishing Parents Association, and regular meetings are held between staff and parents.

The School is a Charitable Trust, under the same Governing Body as Dulwich College Preparatory School, London, although in other respects the two schools are quite separate. The link with Dulwich College is historical only.

Charitable status. Dulwich College Preparatory School Trust is a Registered Charity, number 312715. It exists for the provision of high quality education in a Christian environment.

Dumpton School

Deans Grove House Wimborne Dorset BH21 7AF.
Tel: (01202) 883818
Fax: (01202) 848760

Chairman of Governors: J R Raymond, Esq

Headmaster: **A G M Watson**, MA, (Oxon) DipEd

Numbers. 7–13 180 children; 3-7 90 children (boys and girls).

Fees. (From September 2001): Day children £2,785 per term. £1,450 per term. Nursery £125 per session per term. All fees include meals. There are no compulsory extras

In a beautiful rural setting, the school is nevertheless only one mile from Wimborne and there are daily school bus runs to and from the nearby towns of Bournemouth, Poole, Ringwood and Blandford.

No class has more than seventeen children and there are two classes in each year group. With record numbers in the school, boys and girls enjoy together our excellent teaching as well as the incomparable opportunities for Music, Art, Drama and Sport in which the school excels. Dumpton is renowned for its caring approach in which **every** child is encouraged to identify and develop their abilities, as well as their personal qualities and characters, as fully as possible. It is a very happy and successful school and children regularly win scholarships to their Senior Schools or places at the local Grammar Schools.

For a copy of the prospectus, please apply to the Headmaster.

Charitable status. Dumpton School is a Registered Charity, number 306222. It exists to provide education for boys and girls.

Dunhurst
(Bedales Junior School)

Petersfield Hampshire GU32 2DP
Tel: (01730) 300200

Chairman of the Governors: Michael Blakstad, MA, HonMSc

Headmaster: **M R Piercy**, BA

Number of Pupils. 194 pupils (75 boarders), 104 boys, 90 girls

Fees. Boarders per annum £11,400. Day per annum £8,280.

Dunhurst, the Junior School of Bedales, was founded in 1902 and occupies a part of the Bedales estate. It follows the same general ethos as Bedales and is properly co-educational and non-denominational. The atmosphere is happy, relaxed, friendly and purposeful with a great amount of tolerance, trust and genuine rapport between teachers and pupils. There is much emphasis on personal responsibility and a sense of community.

Dunhurst aims to achieve high academic standards and follows a broad educational programme built around the "core" subjects of English, Mathematics and Science, but giving equal importance to Physical Education, Art, Pottery, Textiles, Workshop, Computing, Comparative Religion, Current Affairs, Geography, History, Dance, Drama and Music. In addition to Class Music for all, pupils' practice time for individual instruments is supervised and fitted into their daily timetable. The aim is to achieve breadth of opportunity experience as well as the chance to achieve excellence in many different areas.

Matches against other schools take place regularly in Athletics, Cricket, Football, Hockey, Netball, Rounders and occasionally Swimming and Tennis. A wide range of other sports and outdoor activities is also offered.

Dunhurst makes full use of the first rate facilities at Bedales which include the Bedales "Olivier Theatre", a Sports Hall, an all-weather pitch and covered swimming pool. This and the similarity of ethos, makes for an easy transition for pupils moving from Dunhurst to the Senior School at the age of thirteen.

In September, a redevelopment programme was completed offering enhanced boarding facilities, including a purpose-built junior wing for the 8 and 9 year olds and more social space. At the heart of the school is a new ICT centre along with further subject classrooms.

Applicants for both boarder and day places sit residential entrance tests for admission at the ages of 8+, 9+, 10+ or 11+

For information about Dunannie, the Pre-Prep (3-8 years), see the Bedales entry, Part I of this book.

Charitable status. Bedales School is a Registered Charity, number 307332-A2-A. It exists to provide a sound education and training for children and young persons of both sexes.

Durlston Court

Barton-on-Sea New Milton BH25 7AQ.
Tel: (01425) 610010.
Station: New Milton

Chairman of Governors: A J Sinclair, BSc (Hons), MIMechEng

***Headmaster:* D C Wansey**, MA(Ed), CertEd

Number of Pupils. 265

Fees. Day Pupils £2,550 per term; Pre-Prep £1,485 per term.

The School, founded in 1903, stands in 17 acres and within 800 metres of the sea. It has an excellent record in Common Entrance to all the major Independent Senior Schools and over 80 Open Scholarships have been won during the past 10 years, with an outstanding study skills unit for children with learning difficulties as well as for the gifted child. The School has a very strong tradition both in Music and in Art. Facilities include Chapel, Art and Craft Studio, Science Laboratory, Library, Computer Centre, Music School, Audio Visual Centre, Outdoor heated swimming pool, Sports Hall, Squash Courts, 3 Tennis Courts and excellent level playing fields.

Opportunities are provided for Art, Music, Riding, Sailing, Gymnastics, Badminton, Squash and Tennis. The official games are Soccer, Rugby, Hockey, Cricket, Athletics, Tennis, Netball and Rounders.

There are 21 teaching Staff, and 9 visiting Musicians under a Director of Music.

The school operates minibus services from Lyndhurst, Bournemouth and Ringwood.

Academic, Sports, Music and Art scholarships are available, also Service bursaries and sibling discounts.

For a copy of the prospectus, please apply to the Headmaster.

Charitable status. Durlston Court School is a Registered Charity, number 307325. It exists to promote the education of children up to the age of 14 years.

Durston House

Ealing London W5 2DR
Tel: 020 8991 6532
Fax: 020 8991 6547

***Headmaster:* P D Craze**, MA, CertEd (Hertford College, Oxford)

Academic Deputy Head: Mrs S Piper, BA
Administrative Deputy Head: W J Murphy, BA, DipTchg (NZ)
Head of Junior School: R Thomas, BSc, CertEd

Chairman of Governors: A J Allen

Number of Boys. 430 day boys

Fees. £2,100–£2,700 per term.

An Educational Trust, Durston House has charitable status and is ISJC accredited. The School has a long history of academic success reflected in Scholarships won at many of the leading senior schools. The emphasis is on high standards of work, placing the initial scholastic training of boys within the context of their personal development.

Junior and Middle School (boys aged 4–9) has up to 48 boys in each year group, three classes of up to sixteen boys. There is a generously staffed welfare department to assist the class teachers.

In Upper School (boys aged 10–13) the Headmaster is helped by two Deputy Heads, 9 Senior Teachers and a team comprising graduate specialist Heads of Department for English, classics, maths, modern languages, science, information technology, history, geography, music, art, physical education and religious studies. Special needs teaching is available.

In Upper and Middle School there is an Activities Programme offering a wide range of programmed cultural, recreational and sporting pursuits. Junior School activities are less formally structured but the approach is similar. The School has developed one of its playing fields to provide a floodlit all weather pitch. Extensive use is also made of local facilities, especially for drama and swimming. There are fixtures with other prep schools, full participation in IAPS events, and regular expeditions at home and abroad.

Boys normally attend screening interviews some six months before they are due to enter, which is usually in September at age 4 or later if there are vacancies. The School offers Scholarships and can sometimes give fees relief for a talented boy of Upper School age.

Charitable status. Durston House Educational Trust Limited is a Registered Charity, number 294670. Its aim is the provision and promotion of education.

Eagle House

Sandhurst Berkshire GU47 8PH.
Tel: (01344) 772134
Fax: (01344) 779039
e-mail: xxx@eaglehouse.demon.co.uk

Chairman of Governors: Admiral Sir Jeremy Black, GBE, KCB, DSO

***Headmaster:* S J Carder**, MA (Oxon), MBA (Education)

Number of Children. Boarders 34, Day Children 250

Fees. Boarders £3,620 per term. Day Boys £2,550 per term, Pre-Prep £1,550 per term, inclusive of meals

Eagle House was founded in 1820, and has been on its present site since 1886. The School is administered by a board of governors under the overall control of Wellington College.

Children are prepared for Scholarship and Common Entrance examinations to senior Independent Schools (about 80% of the boys go on to Wellington). There are 24 members of staff and two matrons. The average class size is 15.

The school is situated between Sandhurst and Crowthorne in over 30 acres of playing fields which include a large all-weather sports area, a Sports Hall, an indoor heated swimming pool, extensive woodlands, adventure playground and a small lake. The principal games are rugby, hockey, soccer and cricket. Other sports include athletics, swimming, tennis, cross country, squash, judo, basketball, archery, fives, golf, riding and badminton.

Much emphasis is placed on the Arts and there are excellent facilities for music, art, design and drama. Music scholarships are available for outstanding young musicians.

The school has its own chapel.

Recent major building works have provided two new science laboratories, a large Arts Hall, classrooms and a Resources Centre (comprising a library, computer room and audio-visual room). Current building works will provide a new Music Department, changing rooms and additional pre-prep facilities (classrooms, library, cloakroom and new playground).

A Pre-Prep Department for children aged 4–7 opened in

September 1993. A Nursery for children aged 3+ opened in September 1997.

Charitable status. Eagle House School is a Registered Charity, number 309093. It exists to provide an all-round education for children up to the age of 13+.

Edenhurst Preparatory School

Westlands Newcastle-under-Lyme Staffordshire ST5 2PU.
Tel: (01782) 619348
Fax: (01782) 662402
e-mail: edenhurst@dial.pipex.com
website: www.edenhurst.co.uk

Headmaster: **N H F Copestick**, BSc (University of St Andrews), CertEd (The Queen's College, Oxford)

Number of Pupils. Boys 128 Girls 110

Tuition Fees. £2,850–£4,740 per year (lunches extra)

Day School only. Fully qualified staff. Victorian main building in pleasant suburban area with purpose-built additions, including gymnasium and laboratories and Technology Centre. Boys and girls prepared for all Independent Senior Schools and eleven-plus examination to Independent Day Schools. Scholarships record good. Games: Soccer, Cricket, Tennis, Golf, Rounders and Netball. Playing fields of 5 acres, and 3 all-weather tennis courts.

A great range of activities is available to pupils, including Computer Studies, Design Technology, Chess, Ornithology, Drama and many others.

The School has a reputation for its work in Music and Drama.

Tuition is obtained for eight musical instruments and there is a School Orchestra.

There is a Pre-preparatory Department for boys and girls from age 3 years.

The school has been run by the same family since its foundation and is noted for its happy atmosphere, as well as its excellent teaching standards.

Edgeborough

Frensham Surrey GU10 3AH
Tel: (01252) 792495
Fax: (01252) 795156
e-mail: edgeborough@btinternet.com
website: www.edgeborough.co.uk
Station: Farnham

Chairman of Governors: R G Punshon, MA (Cantab)

Headmistress: **Mrs M A Jackson**, BEd Hons (London)
Headmaster: **R A Jackson**, MA (Cantab), PGCE

Number of Boys and Girls. Boarders 50, Day 144. Pre-Prep 79. Nursery 33.

Fees. Boarders £3,002–£3,678, Day £1,605–£2,780 There are no compulsory extras. Pre-Prep £1,500.

Founded in 1906 in Guildford, the School moved to its current site, the lovely Frensham Place, in 1939. Standing in 45 acres of beautiful woodlands, it has the ample space of a country school yet is in easy reach of Farnham and Guildford.

Edgeborough offers a continuous education for boys and girls from 3 to 13. Weekly Boarding is a popular option available from the age of 7.

The school comprises four main departments: Nursery, Pre-Prep, Lower Prep and Upper Prep, and children can enter at any level. All pupils follow a co-ordinated academic programme culminating in Common Entrance or Scholarship at 13. Awards are won every year to major Senior Independent Schools.

Along with their academic studies, all children are encouraged to develop their skills in a wide number of areas of which Sport, Music, Art and Drama are paramount.

An essential feature of the school is its family atmosphere which enables children to develop and flourish within a happy, secure environment.

Among its many facilities, the school has its own well appointed classrooms, Chapel, Library, Sports Hall, Drama/ Recital Room, Music Suite, ICT Centre, Art & Pottery Centre, Heated Swimming Pool, Open Air Theatre and Golf Course.

Charitable status. Edgeborough Educational Trust Limited is a Registered Charity, number 312051. It exists to provide education of a high quality.

Edge Grove

Aldenham Herts WD25 8NL
Tel: (01923) 855724 and 857456.
Fax: (01923) 859920
e-mail: headmaster@edgegrove.indschools.co.uk
Station: Radlett

Chairman of Governors: R R Vallings, Esq

Headmaster: **J R Baugh**, BEd

Assistant Headmasters:
M W Guilbride, MA
C A Gibbs, BA, DipEd

Number of Pupils. 7-13: Boarders 80. Day 150 3-7: Day 100

Fees. Boarders £3,100–£3,360 per term (inclusive); Weekly Boarding £3,100–£3,360 (inclusive); Day £2,000–£2,500 per term (inclusive); Pre-Prep £850–£1,500 per term.

Edge Grove is situated in open country on the B462, 15 miles NW of London and 1½ miles from Radlett. Heathrow Airport is a 30 minute drive away.

The Pre-Prep (Hart House) is co-educational and is situated in purpose built accommodation on the main school site. Boys and girls normally join the Preparatory department, Edge Grove, at 7+ and all are prepared for the Common Entrance and Scholarship Examinations.

Boys and girls are taught in separate classes from the age of seven and follow a parallel curriculum. The boys and girls mix for cultural and social activities outside the classroom. There is a strong music tradition in the school and a great range of extra curricular activities on offer.

Pupils leave to a wide variety of Senior Independent Schools across the country and there is an excellent record of Scholarship and Common Entrance success.

Facilities include a new teaching block, School Chapel, Assembly Hall with fully equipped Stage, large new Sports Hall, Music School, Science Block, Computer Centre, Heated Swimming Pool and Hard Tennis Courts etc. The school stands in 25 acres of ground, incorporating eight playing fields, two croquet lawns, spinneys and a lake which is a bird sanctuary.

The main sports are Association and Rugby Football, Cricket, Netball, Swimming, Tennis, Athletics, Cross Country Running and Hockey.

The school is a non-profit making Trust administered by a Board of Governors.

The Edinburgh Academy Preparatory School

10 Arboretum Road Edinburgh EH3 5PL.
Tel: 0131-552 3690.
Fax: 0131-551 2660
e-mail: edacadp@aol.com
Station: Edinburgh (Waverley)

Headmaster: **C R F Paterson**, MA

Chairman of Directors: Professor J P Percy

Number of Boys. 400 (220 in Senior Department, 110 in Junior Department, 70 in the Nursery).

Fees per annum. Nursery £1,089–£2,760; Junior £2,904–£3,093; Senior £3,927–£4,161.

The Edinburgh Academy Preparatory School was founded in 1824 and is a member of IAPS. The Preparatory School is in a separate location but is an integral part of The Edinburgh Academy.

The Junior Department takes boys from 4½ to 7½ (Day boys only), the Senior Department from 7½ to 10½ (Boarders are admitted from the age of 8½). A Nursery Class for boys and girls aged three and over is attached to the Junior Department.

The Nursery Class and the Junior Department now form an annexe to the Senior Department, being housed in a very modern and attractive building.

The School prepares boys for the Upper School and work is arranged to ensure a smooth transition from one to the other at the age of about 11.

The School is situated in a most attractive part of the city, with its own rugby and cricket pitches, sports centre and athletics track on site. The Edinburgh Academy Preparatory School produces very high levels of performance in all areas due to small classes and a dedicated teaching staff. The extra-curricular activities are extensive.

The School encourages pupils to enjoy life in a very real and participative sense.

Further information about The Edinburgh Academy will be found in Part I of this book.

Prospectus from and enquiries to The Admissions Secretary, The Edinburgh Academy Preparatory School, 10 Arboretum Road, Edinburgh EH3 5PL.

Elm Green Preparatory School

Parsonage Lane Little Baddow Chelmsford Essex CM3 4SU.
Tel: (01245) 225230
Fax: (01245) 226008
e-mail: admin@elmgreen.essex.sch.uk

Principal: **Mrs E L Mimpriss**, CertEd (Brentwood College)

Co-educational: 4–11 years. 220 Day pupils; 115 Boys, 105 Girls

Fees at 1 April 1999. £1,515

Religious affiliation. Non-denominational

Elm Green was founded in 1944 and enjoys a lovely rural setting, surrounded by National Trust woodland.

Children enter in the September after their fourth birthday and in their final year are prepared for scholarships, entry to other independent schools and for entry to maintained schools. Many of the pupils take the Essex 11+ and the school has an excellent record of success in this examination.

The school maintains a high standard of academic education giving great emphasis to a secure foundation in the basic subjects whilst offering a wide curriculum with specialist teaching in many areas.

Information technology and design technology form an integral part of the curriculum and there are flourishing art, music and PE departments. The school competes successfully in a wide range of sports – football, rugby, netball, swimming, cricket, gymnastics, athletics, rounders and tennis.

There are many extra-curricular activities and all the children are encouraged to work and to play hard in order to fulfil their potential.

The school aims to foster intellectual curiosity and to encourage individual and corporate work. Kindness and thought for others are given a high priority.

The Elms

Colwall Nr Malvern Worcestershire WR13 6EF.
Tel: (01684) 540344

Founded 1614.

Chairman of the Governors: Sir Peter Gadsden, GBE, AC, FEng

Head Master: **L A C Ashby**, BA (Hons), CertEd

Number of Pupils in Main School. 110. 66 Boys, 44 Girls. 84 boarders.

Pre-Prep Pupils. 50

Fees. Full board £3,520 per term. Day board £3,080 per term. Pre-prep 3–7 £1,020–£1,990.

The Elms is run as a charitable, non-profit making company with a Board of Governors. Children are taken in the Main School from the age of rising 8 and there is a Pre-preparatory Department for 3-7 year olds.

An experienced staff and small classes ensure attention to each pupil's special needs and a high academic standard is maintained to CE and Scholarship levels. Small numbers help to create a family atmosphere with comfortable accommodation and a resident Headmaster and staff.

Gardens, fields and woodland with stream in 106 acres surround the school, beautifully set at the foot of the Malvern Hills, and include fine playing fields for Rugby, Association Football, Hockey, Cricket, Athletics. Netball and Rounders. Facilities include a Sports Hall, Tennis Courts, Laboratory, Computer Room, CDT Centre and an Art Room with facilities for Pottery. There is also a heated indoor swimming pool. The children manage a small farming enterprise; and many ride on school ponies or bring their own.

Fees are payable termly. There are no compulsory extras.

Bursaries available for sons and daughters of Servicemen, clergymen and schoolmasters, and there are competitive awards.

Charitable status. The Elms is a Registered Charity, number 527252. It exists to provide education for boys and girls.

Elstree School

Woolhampton Reading Berks RG7 5TD.
Tel: (0118) 9713302
Fax: (0118) 9714280

Headmaster: **S M Hill**, MA (Cantab)
Deputy Headmaster: V W Hales, BEd

Number of Boys. Prep School 180 boys (90 Boarders, 90 day boys); Pre-Prep School 70 boys and girls (aged 3–7)

Fees. Boarders £4,200 per term. Day Boys £3,015 per term. Pre-Prep School £1,775 per term.

Elstree is set in its own 150 acres in the beautiful Berkshire countryside, a quiet location but very accessible. The School moved to Woolhampton, between Reading and Newbury, in 1939, after nearly 100 years at Elstree, Hertfordshire. At the heart of the School is a magnificent Georgian house which has been modernised and extended. Facilities and accommodation are of a very high standard.

Elstree prepares boys for entrance to Britain's leading independent senior schools and has a fine Open Scholarship record. Boys play Football, Rugby, Hockey, Cricket, and many other sports. Equal emphasis is given to an appreciation of music, art, drama, and to life skills such as Information Technology.

Charitable status. Elstree School Limited is a Registered Charity, number 309101. It is an educational trust controlled by a Board of Governors whose Chairman is Nicholas Bomford, Esq. It exists to establish, maintain and carry on schools for the education of boys and girls and to give such pupils general or specialised instruction of the highest class, and as an educational charity to promote education generally.

The English School
Kuwait

PO Box 379 13004 Safat Kuwait.
Tel: (+965) 563 7205/7206
Fax: (+965) 563 7147
e-mail: admin@tes.edu.kw
website: http://www.tes.edu.kw

Sponsor: M A R Al-Bahar

Chair of the Governing Committee: Mrs Catherine McMurtry

Headmaster: **Richard N S Walmsley**, MSc, BEd, ACP, MIMgt

Number of pupils. 440

Fees per year. Kindergarten KD1,015; Infant KD1,590; Junior KD1,825; Senior KD1,999.

The English School, founded in 1953 under the auspices of the British Embassy, is the longest established school in Kuwait catering for the expatriate community. The School operates as a non-profit making, private co-educational establishment providing the highest standards in education for children of Kindergarten to Preparatory School age. The roll is predominantly British as are the resources and texts. With the exception of foreign language teachers, all teaching staff are British and qualified in the United Kingdom. Following its relocation to new premises, The English School is housed in well-resourced and spacious, fully air-conditioned buildings in a pleasant residential suburb of Kuwait City.

Responsibility for the School is vested in the Governing Committee whose members are elected by parents of the pupils and serve in a voluntary capacity.

The curriculum is British-oriented, contemporary and aiming for the best of traditional standards being sought within a broad-based structure. The National Curriculum for England and Wales is used as the core for the curriculum. Formal End-of-Key Stage assessment of ability takes place in Years 2 and 6. In addition the pupils are prepared for entrance tests to other schools, including Independent Schools Examinations Board (Common Entrance) Examinations at 11+, 12+ and 13+. Class teachers are supported by specialist co-ordinators in Art and Design and Technology, Information Technology, Music, Library and PE and Games. Music is taught to all ages and French is introduced in the Junior School.

The School seeks to provide a learning environment within which the children will be stimulated to develop their individual capacity for achievement to its fullest potential. Each individual is directed towards self-discipline and respect for himself/herself and for others. Strong emphasis is placed on academic study, together with a wide range of non-academic activities to provide a balance. The School aims to ensure that, by achieving standards equivalent to those of competitive private schools in Britain, our pupils are well prepared for the subsequent stages of their academic development whether in Britain, Kuwait or elsewhere in the world.

All applications for entry are addressed on a personal and individual basis. The Headmaster and teaching staff will be happy to meet prospective pupils and their parents. A visit to the School, where possible, is encouraged in order for each family's needs and requirements to be discussed.

The English Speaking School
Dubai

P O Box 2002 Dubai United Arab Emirates
Tel: 00 9714 3371457/3370973
Fax: 00 9714 3378932
e-mail: dess@dessdxb.com

Head Teacher: **Mrs M C Bell**,MA(Ed)

Number of pupils. 650
Age Range. 4+ to 11+.
Fees. Dh6000.00 per term.

The English Speaking School, Dubai was established in 1963 and was granted a charter in 1969 by the late Ruler, His Highness Sheikh Rashid bin Saeed Al Maktoum. It is operated as a non-profit making organisation overseen by an elected Board of Governors.

The aim of the School is to provide education for English speaking children, in accordance with the best British practice, in order that pupils may qualify for subsequent secondary education either in Dubai or in the UK.

A fully qualified and experienced British staff ensures that children make the most of their abilities in this four form entry School. Teachers are kept up-to-date with current methodology and practice through the provision of regular in-service training. This ensures that the requirements and guidelines of the British National Curriculum are implemented where appropriate to the School's needs.

The School is purpose built with excellent facilities including specialist rooms for Science and Technology, Music, French and Arabic. There is also a well equipped gymnasium, library with adjoining PC network, a separate ICT centre and a spacious hall used for dance/drama and other appropriate activities. The games field, tennis courts, netball courts and swimming pool ensure that a wide range of sporting activities can be offered both as an integral part of the curriculum and as extra-curricular activities.

The School subscribes to traditional values by emphasising discipline, good manners and academic and sporting excellence.

The School year is from September to June; the School week is from Saturday to Wednesday; the School day is from 8 am to 2 pm (12.30 pm on Wednesdays).

Eton End PNEU School

35 Eton Road Datchet Slough Berkshire SL3 9AX.
Tel: (01753) 541075
Fax: (01753) 541123
e-mail: admin@etonend.org

***Headmistress:* Mrs Barbara Ottley**, CertEd

Chairman of Board of Governors: D Losse, Esq

Number of pupils. 235 (Girls 3–11, Boys 3–7) 175 girls, 60 boys

Tuition Fees. (September 2001) £1,085–£1,630. Lunch: £120.

The school is a day school set within six acres of spacious grounds. All the classrooms are purpose-built and modern, offering excellent facilities, including specialist rooms, eg art and craft, music, science laboratory, large library. There is a large well-equipped gym. Two hard tennis/netball courts. Football and sports field. Boys prepared for all preparatory schools in the area. Girls leave after the 11+ Entrance Examination often gaining Scholarships. Small classes allow each child to reach their maximum potential in a happy caring environment.

Charitable status. Eton End PNEU School is a Registered Charity, number 310644. The aim of the charity is to provide a well balanced education for the children whose parents wish them to attend Eton End School.

Eversfield Preparatory School

Warwick Road Solihull West Midlands B91 1AT.
Tel: 0121-705 0354
Fax: 0121-709 0168
e-mail: enquiries@eversfield.co.uk
website: www.eversfield.co.uk

Chairman of Governors: Mrs E Owen

***Headmaster:* K U Madden**, BA

Number of Pupils. 181

Day fees. £1,425–£1,975 per term, according to age, and inclusive of lunch and books.

Eversfield is a Day Preparatory School on an attractive site in the centre of Solihull preparing boys and girls from 2½-11 years old for entry to the leading Senior Schools in the West Midlands and beyond.

The curriculum values academic excellence and prepares pupils for National Curriculum Tests and 11+ examinations. At the same time it nurtures the creative, sporting, technical and social skills and potential of each pupil. There are excellent facilities and opportunities for sports, music, the arts, and a programme of extra-curricular and holiday activities.

The School encourages a strong sense of community where small classes, a well-ordered routine and good pastoral support help pupils to feel secure and develop their self-confidence. Eversfield promotes high moral standards and responsible attitudes based on clear and relevant Christian teaching.

Charitable status. Eversfield Preparatory School Trust Limited is a Registered Charity, number 528966. It is under the direction of a Board of Governors and exists to carry out the work of an Independent Preparatory School.

Ewell Castle Junior School

Spring Street Ewell Surrey KT17 1UH
Tel: 020 8393 3952
Fax: 020 8393 0542

Chairman of Governors: J E D Cattermole, Esq

***Head of Junior School:* Mrs H M Crossley**, MA

Fees. (September 2001): from £575–£1,350 per term

Ewell Castle Junior School is situated in an attractive Edwardian building in Spring Street, Ewell Village, well served by public transport, and only three minutes walk from the Senior School with which it maintains a close liaison. Pupils of the Junior School use the facilities of the Senior School on a regular basis and some members of staff teach in both schools.

The Junior School is co-educational and takes pupils from 3–11 years. Those entering the Nursery may attend for a half day until they are ready for full time education. There are no entry requirements for Nursery children but older pupils attend the School for a day's assessment, which include tests in Mathematics and English. Girls are prepared for local independent senior schools, whilst boys may proceed to the Senior School for which a number of aided places and scholarships are available at 11+ entry. All pupils are prepared for entry at 11+ to selective state schools. The National Curriculum is incorporated within a broad curriculum.

The creative arts play an important part in School life. Apart from the time-tabled music lessons, there is the opportunity for pupils to learn a variety of instruments under professional teachers. Dramatic productions take place regularly. As well as the larger events, drama is often used in assemblies, which take place in the local Church as well as in School. Pupils' art work can be seen on display in the local community and is always to be found decorating the School walls.

All pupils take part in various sporting activities as part of the weekly curriculum. In addition a wide variety of activities are available after School and during holidays. Games and PE lessons take place in the Senior School where the sports facilities are excellent with a purpose built sports hall and large playing field. The main games are football, hockey, cricket and tennis. There are also athletics and cross country events. All pupils receive swimming instruction and there is an annual swimming gala.

There are a large number of extra-curricula activities covering a broad range of interests.

Outside speakers include police liaison officers and actors and authors who conduct workshops with pupils. A number of visits occur to places of interest which are relevant to a particular area of study. There are regular School visits abroad.

The Junior School aims to provide a caring, responsive and stimulating environment in which pupils are able to fulfil their potential. Hard work and high standards together with courtesy and consideration for others are of prime importance.

Charitable status. Ewell Castle Junior School is a Registered Charity, number 312079. It exists to provide education for boys and girls.

Exeter Cathedral School

The Chantry Palace Gate Exeter Devon EX1 1HX.
Tel: (01392) 255298.
Station: Exeter

Chairman of Governors: The Dean of Exeter, The Very Revd K B Jones

Headmaster: **C I S Dickinson**, BA

Number of Pupils. Boarders 36. Day pupils 155

Fees. Boarders £2,870, Weekly boarders £2,755, Day Pupils (9–13) £1,745 (excluding lunches), (7–8) £1,695, (3–6) £1,015.

Founded in 1159, the Cathedral School provides the Boy and Girl Choristers for Exeter Cathedral and educates 150 other pupils to the same high standard.

Entry is normally at 3 or 4 to the Pre-Preparatory Department or 7 or 8 years into the Main School, though pupils may be accepted later. Entrance assessments for 7+ or later entry are by arrangement with the Headmaster.

Voice Trials for Choristers are held in February, or by arrangement, and successful applicants become probationers upon completion of which they enter the Choir.

There are 20 scholarships available for Boy Choristers and probationers which are worth 50% of the boarding fee. Scholarships of up to 20% are also available to Girl Choristers. All Choristers receive free tuition in one musical instrument. Awards are also available to non-choristers, details of which can be given on application.

Pupils are prepared for Scholarship and Common Entrance to Independent and Maintained Senior Schools by a full-time staff of 17, assisted by other part-time teachers including 15 teachers of musical instruments.

There are no Saturday lessons, though day pupils sometimes join boarders in week-end or after school activities. The curriculum encompasses all National Curriculum and Common Entrance subjects, including two Modern Foreign Languages.

In the Michaelmas Term, rugby football and netball are the team sports. Netball, soccer and hockey are played in the Lent Term. During the Trinity Term, cricket, rounders, athletics and swimming are all pursued competitively. Swimming takes place all year round.

Musical activities, including school choir, orchestra and ensembles for string, woodwind, brass and jazz instrumentalists are available to all pupils.

Daily morning worship takes place in the Cathedral or in The Chapter House led by the school Chaplain who is also on the staff of the Cathedral.

The buildings are located around the Close and include a Science Laboratory, a gymnasium and the Kalendar Hall (the music and drama school), as well as a large portion of the 14th Century Deanery.

For games, use is made of playing fields, swimming baths and other facilities situated short distances away in the city.

Charitable status. Exeter Cathedral School, as part of the Dean and Chapter of Exeter which is an ecclesiastical charity, is a Registered Charity and exists to provide education for boys and girls.

Fairfield School

Leicester Road Loughborough Leics LE11 2AE
Tel: (01509) 215172
Fax: (01509) 238648

Chairman of the Governors: P J Tomlinson, LLB
Headmaster: **R Outwin-Flinders**, BEd (Hons)

Number of Pupils. Aged 4–11, Boys 256, Girls 224 (all day)

Fees. £1,554 per term. Lunches and individual music lessons extra.

Fairfield School is the Preparatory School of the Loughborough Endowed Schools, the two Upper Schools being Loughborough Grammar School for Boys and Loughborough High School for Girls.

The three Schools are governed by the same Governing Body and share a fine campus to the west of the Leicester Road, with their private roads free of through traffic.

The aim of Fairfield is to give a broad-based education appropriate for the needs of the children in our care. In the process, they will be prepared for their secondary education. For most this will mean either Loughborough Grammar School or High School, although some children move elsewhere.

Our intention is also to teach children how to live together in a community and to show respect for the property and feelings of others. We hope that time spent at Fairfield will be thoroughly enjoyable.

Whilst our children are prepared for entry to the Upper Schools, this is certainly not our only goal; in addition to all National Curriculum subjects French is taught and there are specialist rooms for ICT, Science and Music. Our Gymnasium is extremely well equipped.

The children are introduced to a wide variety of sporting and recreational activities. Team games are encouraged for the spirit of co-operation and working together which the School aims to foster. Activities of a more individual nature also play an increasing part in the life of the School. Winter games include Soccer, Netball, Cross Country Running and Hockey. In the summer Cricket, Tennis, Rounders, Athletics and Short Tennis are played. The children swim throughout the year in the Endowed Schools' indoor, heated pool.

Music and Drama are considered very important areas of School life. In addition to class music lessons, children have the opportunity to receive tuition on a variety of musical instruments and many take advantage of this. The School Orchestras perform on a regular basis, there are also two Choirs, two Recorder Groups and numerous additional instrumental ensembles.

Dramatic productions play a major part in the life of the School. Here children are given the opportunity to express themselves and experience the excitement of performing before an audience.

There are a whole range of other activities in which children are given the opportunity to participate. Success and enjoyment in these invariably help to boost confidence and widen horizons generally.

Lunchtime and after-school clubs include Brownies, Cycling Proficiency, Chess, Drama, Pottery, Photography and Technology, as well as the sporting and musical activities already mentioned.

The main ages for entry to the School are at 4+ and 7+ although a few places are available at other ages.

The examination for entry at 7+, 8+, 9+ and 10+ takes place in late February or early March each year whilst assessments for entry at 4+ take place in late January.

The Prospectus and further details can be obtained from

the Headmaster's Secretary and the Headmaster will be happy to show prospective parents around the School.

Charitable status. Loughborough Endowed Schools is a Registered Charity, number 527863. It exists to provide education for children.

Fairstead House School

Fordham Road Newmarket Suffolk CB8 7AA.
Tel: (01638) 662318
Fax: (01638) 561685
e-mail: fairsteadschool@aol.com

Headmistress: **Mrs D J Buckenham**, CertEd

Age Range. Co-educational 3–11
Number in School. Day: Boys 67, Girls 78
Staff. 9 full-time, 9 part-time.
Fees per term. Nursery : from £430 (for a minimum of 3 sessions per week); Main School: £1,325-£1,445.

Fairstead House School is known for its family ethos. The school aims to provide a lively and stimulating environment in which children may grow into happy, confident and knowledgeable young people within the community.

The curriculum is based on the National Curriculum as its foundation and is taught in small classes. There is a new well-equipped science and technology laboratory and library, and a new computer room.

Children participate in Key stages 1 and 2 tests at age 7 and 11 respectively and are prepared for entry into both independent and state secondary schools. Advice on the suitability of future schools is offered at an early stage by the Headmistress.

Music and Drama are great strengths with opportunities for children to perform in assemblies, informal concerts and plays.

A wide range of after-school activities is on offer, in addition to an After-school Care Club.

Many sports are played, including netball, hockey, rugby, football, cricket, rounders and athletics. In addition, there are opportunities for tennis in association with the local Lawn Tennis Association Club.

Provision is made for individual needs, if required.

Speech and Drama classes and individual music tuition on a wide range of instruments are offered as optional extras. Ballet is offered as an extra to the Reception class only. French is taught from the age of 4.

There is a flourishing Nursery Department, which admits children in the term following their third birthday.

Registration for the Nursery is separate from the Main School.

Charitable status. Fairstead House School Trust Limited is a Registered Charity, number 276787. It exists to provide independent education for children.

Falkland St Gabriel

Sandleford Priory Newbury Berks RG20 9BD
Tel: (01635) 40663
Fax: (01635) 37351

Chairman: Paul Goble

Headmistress: **Mrs J H Felton**, BEd (Hons), MA

Number of pupils. 250
Fees. £797–£1,845

Falkland St Gabriel is a Day Preparatory School, administered by a Governing Body and is a registered Educational Trust. The Junior School is adjacent to the Senior School and is situated in 54 acres of parkland on the southern outskirts of Newbury.

Girls are accepted from the age of 3 to 11 years and boys from 3 to 8 years. Maximum class sizes are of 20 pupils.

Girls are prepared for the Common Entrance Examination at 11 years. Entry to the Senior School is by an internal examination.

A number of scholarships are awarded annually to candidates of outstanding ability at 7+ and 11+.

Subjects taught include Mathematics, Science, Technology, English, French (from 4 years of age), Latin, History, Geography, Computer Awareness, Art/Craft, Music, Drama and Games.

Science is taught in a purpose-built laboratory. All Junior children have access to a recently refurbished Junior Computer Room, while pupils in Year 6 use the computer facilities of the Senior School.

Gymnastics, Dance, Netball, Hockey, Cross-Country, Tennis, Rounders and Athletics are included in the curriculum for all pupils. Swimming takes place during the Summer Term in the outdoor heated swimming pool.

Pupils are welcome to join further activities, a selection of which includes Ballet, Tap Dancing, Craft, Choir, Board Games, Puppet Making, Painting on glass, Jazz Dance, Chess, Floral Art, Bridge, Storytime, Art Club, Recorders, Pyrography, String Orchestra, Gym Club and the NSPCC.

Private instrumental music lessons can be arranged.

Charitable status. S Gabriel and Falkland S Gabriel Schools is a Registered Charity, number 325060. It exists to provide education for girls.

Falkner House

19 Brechin Place London SW7 4QB
Tel: 020 7373 4501
Fax: 020 7835 0073
e-mail: Falknerhs@aol.com
website: www.falknerhouse.com

Girls' Preparatory School, (ages 4–11)

Principal: Mrs Flavia Nunes

Headmistress: **Mrs Anita Griggs**, BA Hons, PGCE

Number of Girls. 170
Fees per term. £2,750.

Falkner House provides a strong academic programme within a supportive family atmosphere. The broad curriculum taught by highly experienced staff results in girls achieving success at 11+ to top day and boarding schools.

Excellent facilities include a science laboratory, art room, IT centre, good libraries and large playground. The school has a strong musical tradition as well as an excellent sporting record. Pre/post school care is offered, as well as a wide range of after school clubs.

Entrance at 4+ is by individual assessment and interview.

Falkner House Nursery caters for boys and girls aged 3-4 years. Extensive facilities and a team of specialist teachers create an ideal pre-school environment. Main school staff are on hand to enrich the Nursery School's curriculum

Farleigh School

Red Rice Andover Hampshire SP11 7PW.
Tel: (01264) 710766
Fax: (01264) 710070
e-mail: office@farleighschool.co.uk

Chairman of Governors: J Vail, Esq

***Headmaster:* J A Allcott,** BEd, MSc

Number of Pupils. Aged 7–13: 30 Full Boy Boarders, 9 Full Girl Boarders; 51 Weekly Boy Boarders, 24 Weekly Girl Boarders.

Aged 3–13: 174 Day Boys, 103 Day Girls.

Fees. Boarders £3,840. Weekly Boarders £3,840. Day £777–£2,880.

Farleigh School occupies an extensive rural estate close to the A303(M3). Founded in 1953 as a boarding preparatory school for Roman Catholic boys, Farleigh is now a fully co-educational Day and Boarding School. Children of all faiths are welcomed. High standards are maintained both in and out of the classroom and excellent academic achievements are the norm, with leavers proceeding to a variety of leading senior independent schools, many obtaining scholarships.

Farleigh has a full range of up to date facilities including three science laboratories, a newly equipped computer room and music suite, spacious recreation rooms, a fine Chapel and a gymnasium/theatre. In 1993 a purpose built sports hall was completed which is now in full use for many sports during and after school hours and in 1995 the library was fully refurbished and extended. The new purpose-built Pre-Prep and Kindergarten will be completed in time for the Autumn Term 2001, providing 8 classrooms, a large activity room, library and an all-weather playground. Out of doors, the estate includes ample pitches for rugby, football, hockey and in Summer for cricket, tennis, rounders and athletics. There is also a swimming pool, a nine hole golf circuit and a cross country route within the premises.

The teaching staff is complemented by a committed pastoral team including Year Heads, House parents and two qualified Matrons with two assistants. Many staff are resident, giving the school a family atmosphere which is frequently commented upon by visitors.

Drama, music and art have important places in school life. A programme of major and informal productions and concerts weave variety into the school year and the output of the art department is always displayed for all to see. Several art and music scholarships have been gained to senior schools in recent years.

Out of school hours a wide variety of activities are available, making full use of the school's own resources and the cultural and recreational facilities of the attractive surrounding area. Individual coaching is offered in a variety of sports and other activities include archery, chess, computing, design technology, crafts, riding and shooting.

Charitable status. Farleigh School is a Registered Charity, number 307340. It exists for the purpose of educating children.

Farlington Preparatory School

Strood Park Horsham West Sussex RH12 3PN
Tel: (01403) 268664
Fax: (01403) 272258
e-mail: farmer@farlington.w-sussex.sch.uk

Chairman of Governors: C J Driver, BA, BEd, MPhil

Registrar: Mrs P A Farmer

***Headmistress:* Mrs Joy K Baggs,** BA (Hons), CertEd

Number of Girls. 160

Tuition Fees per term. Reception: £1,335; Prep 1 & 2: £1,550; Prep 3: £1,740; Prep 4: £1,950; Prep 5 & 6: £2,280.

Boarding Fees per term. Weekly Boarders £1,570; Full Boarders £1,660

Farlington has had a junior department for many years, but it was not until September 1994 that a separate Preparatory School was opened, which catered for girls from 4 to 11. The Pre-Preps are housed in an attractive mews building while the Prep School girls have their own purpose-built accommodation, and, although it shares the same site as the Senior School, the Prep School has its own identity. Younger children quickly feel at home in this close-knit community, and the older girls have the opportunity to learn responsibility and have status in "their" school by becoming prefects and house captains in Prep 6.

Early school days that are happy and secure, provide a sound basis for learning and for life. At Farlington, we aim to achieve high academic standards in our Preparatory School, with the emphasis on encouragement and confidence-building. The philosophy of the School is based on Christian ethics but we also welcome girls from a wide range of religious and cultural backgrounds.

We have a staff of well-qualified and dedicated teachers. They form a wonderfully good-humoured team, who support fully the ethos of the School. Literacy and numeracy are the building blocks of education, and this is the basis of our teaching. Scientific and aesthetic skills are developed in a challenging way, using exploration and experiment, as well as practice and problem-solving.

We follow the National Curriculum but, because of smaller class sizes, we are able to offer more in terms of subject content, and, of course, individual attention. As girls become older, they are taught some subjects by specialist teachers (for example French, Drama, Art). In Prep 5 and 6, Science is taught in the well-equipped laboratories of the Senior School's new Science Building. The Prep School has its own Director of Music who runs a variety of musical activities. Individual tuition can be arranged for most instruments.

All girls can enjoy the beautiful 33 acre parkland setting for play and for learning, and we even have a small farm. The latest addition to our facilities is an all-purpose sports hall, completed in the Autumn of 1999.

The Prep School offers a wide range of extra-curricular activities which can take place at lunchtimes and after school. Girls can go horse-riding or help to feed the animals on the farm; they can join the Recorder Group or the Junior Choir or something a little more active such as Gym Club or ballet classes. Although school finishes at 3.20 pm for girls in Reception to Prep 2, they can stay on at school until 5.00 pm supervised by a member of staff.

The older girls finish their lessons at 3.45 pm and can do activities and supervised prep until 5.45 pm. Parents are encouraged to consult their daughter's teachers regularly to ensure that she is happy and that progress is good: we hope that they will take an active part in her education. Parents are invited to Prep outings and are keen supporters of junior teams.

Boarding is available to girls from the age of 9. The Boarding House is friendly and run on family lines, and the older girls are a great asset in looking after the younger ones, helping with their reading, and arranging activities.

Prospective parents are always welcome to come and meet the Headmistress and have a tour of the School. Please telephone for an appointment and we will forward a prospectus.

Charitable status. Farlington Preparatory School is a Registered Charity, number 307048. It exists solely for the purpose of educating girls.

Felsted Preparatory School

Felsted Dunmow Essex CM6 3JL.
Tel: (01371) 820252
Fax: (01371) 821443

Chairman of the Governors: Mr K M R Foster

***Headmaster:* E J Newton**, BA

Number of Pupils. 40 boarders, 180 day pupils, plus 120 4–7 year olds (in a Pre-Preparatory Department)

Fees. Boarders £10,680 pa, Day pupils £7,830 pa, 4–7 year olds £3,210–£4,530 pa.

The staff, excluding the Headmaster, consists of 30 full-time qualified teachers and there are additional part-time teachers for instrumental music and games. There are three matrons, and two sisters in charge of the Medical Centre, but the welfare of the pupils is under the direct supervision of the Headmaster's wife.

The Preparatory School, set in its own grounds, is separate from Felsted School itself, with all its own facilities, including a modern well-equipped library, an excellent theatre/assembly hall, open-air heated swimming pool, grass tennis courts and flood-lit hard-play games area. Use is made of Felsted School's extra amenities at regular times so that small-bore rifle shooting, squash courts, indoor swimming, Astro-turf hockey pitch, Music School and indoor sports hall are also available to the pupils.

Rugby football, netball, hockey, cricket, rounders, athletics and cross-country have been the major sports, but tennis and swimming are taught by qualified coaches in the summer. Music plays an important part in the School's life, and there is an excellent Chapel choir. Regular instrumental and orchestral concerts are given. The School has a deserved reputation for its drama productions, while Art, Design and Technology, PSHE, and Computing are part of the weekly timetable. Out-of-class activities include a debating society, horse-riding, chess, fishing, public speaking, aerobics, gardening, and dance/ballet.

Pupils joining at 11+ can be guaranteed assured transfer to Felsted School at 13, as can pupils of a similar age already at the Preparatory School, following successful completion of assessment tests. A majority of pupils proceed to Felsted School itself, but a good number regularly move on to other major independent senior schools, having taken Common Entrance, and there is an excellent record of academic, art and music scholarships.

Scholarships (up to 50% of fees) are open to pupils joining Felsted Preparatory School at ages of 10+/11+ in the September of the year of entry.

The school is fully co-educational throughout the age range 4–13 years.

Charitable status. Felsted Preparatory School is a Registered Charity, number 310870. It exists to provide education for boys and girls.

Feltonfleet School

Cobham Surrey KT11 1DR
Tel: (01932) 862264
Fax: (01932) 860280

Chairman of Governors: H G S Bourne, Esq, ACA

***Headmaster:* P C Ward,**

Number of Pupils. Nursery/Pre-Prep: 72; Boarders 52; Day Pupils 188

Fees. Boarding £3,560 and Day Pupils £900–£2,665 per term

General. Feltonfleet School was founded in 1903 and became an Educational Trust in 1967. The School is situated in scenic grounds close to the M25 between Heathrow and Gatwick Airports. There are 25 full-time, 3 part-time and 2 Gap Year members of the teaching staff.

A flourishing, purpose-built pre-preparatory department opened in April 1994 for boys and girls. Feltonfleet became fully co-educational in September 1994 offering full or weekly boarding, or day education. Optional educational activities on Saturday mornings are available for day pupils.

Ethos. Feltonfleet offers both boarding and day places but its philosophy and standards are those of a School committed to traditional boarding values. It aims to produce friendly, well-mannered children who have achieved their full potential both in and out of the classroom, offering a broad foundation for their future careers.

Pastoral. The boarding house is run by a Housemaster, two house tutors, two matrons and an academic tutor. A wide variety of activities are offered to the boarders in out-of-school time, including an outing for full boarders every Sunday.

Entry. Children are admitted from the age of three into the pre-preparatory department and, having moved into the main School at the age of seven, are prepared for Common Entrance or Scholarship examinations to a wide range of independent senior schools. In the main school there is a staff:pupil ratio of 9.5:1, with the average class size of 14.

For entry into the main School pupils are required to sit an entrance examination and interview. Academic, Music and All-Rounder Entrance Scholarships are held in the Spring Term for children aged seven.

Facilities. Feltonfleet has a strong Music Department with excellent facilities which include a Concert Hall and individual practice rooms. Instruction is available on a wide range of instruments. There are three choirs, two orchestras and a flourishing Choral Society of staff, parents and pupils. Concerts and dramatic productions, by all these groups, are held regularly. Feltonfleet Senior Choir has been a winner of the Gold Award at the Child of Achievement National Finals. A large number (approximately two-thirds) of pupils receive individual music tuition.

Sporting facilities include two sports fields, two squash courts, a gymnasium, four Astroturf cricket nets, two floodlit enclosed courts for tennis, hockey, football and basketball, a swimming pool covered and heated throughout the winter and two shooting ranges. A new cricket square was laid in 1998. In addition to rugby, football, athletics and cricket, pupils can also participate in golf and judo. Recent tours have been made to the USA and South Africa by rugby, cricket and soccer teams.

Recent developments include new buildings for Art, Design and Technology, Computing and Science. A new Sports Hall was completed in 2000.

Extra-Curricular Activities. The School has an active policy of preparing children for the challenges of today's world. Pupils in their last two years are involved in residential leadership courses in the Forest of Dean and Norway.

Feltonfleet has a reciprocal arrangement with the Ombrosa School in Lyon, with a number of pupils spending some weeks at each others' school during the Summer Term.

Feltonfleet has a school garden where children may tend their individual plots.

Parents can participate in a variety of Wednesday evening activities which include Drama and Choral Society, Keep Fit, Shooting, Art, Soccer, Netball and Golf.

Charitable status. Feltonfleet School Trust Limited is a Registered Charity, number 312070. It aims to produce friendly, well-mannered children who have achieved their full potential both in and out of the classroom, offering a broad foundation for their future careers.

Fettes College Preparatory School

Edinburgh EH4 1QX
Tel: (0131) 332 2976
Fax: (0131) 332 4724

Chairman of Governors: The Hon Lord MacLean, QC
Chairman of Preparatory School Committee: C M Campbell, QC

Headmaster: **A G S Davies,** BSc (Hons), CertMgmt

Number of Pupils. 168 (60 boarders, 108 day pupils), 92 boys, 76 girls, aged 8-13

Fees. Boarders: £3,639. Day Pupils £2,282 per term, including all meals and text-books.

Founded in 1974 as the Junior School of Fettes College taking pupils from the age of ten, it became a Preparatory School in 1999 when the age of entry was lowered to eight and its own Headmaster was appointed.

The College grounds occupy some 80 acres of parkland just 20 minutes walk away from the centre of Edinburgh. The Senior School occupies the original College building and the Prep School is on the site of the original Sanatorium about 200 metres away. It has therefore all the advantages of the excellent facilities of the Senior School along with the ability to be a complete unit of its own.

The curriculum is an extension of the Scottish 5-14 curriculum and, although pupils going on to the Senior School do not take Common Entrance, they are capable of so doing and the more able sit the 13+ Scholarship examinations. Class sizes range from 10 to 18.

Formal coaching is given to boys in rugby, hockey and cricket, and to girls in hockey, lacrosse, netball, rounders and tennis. Swimming is taught as part of the PE programme and lessons are available in judo, fencing, squash and shooting. There is an extensive activities programme with clubs ranging frompoetry and pancakes to Tae Kwon Do.

Music and Drama flourish. The School Choir and School Orchestra give concerts each term, and choirs and instrumental groups participate successfully in musical competitions. Year group concerts, too, are regularly held. Each year there is a large-production School Play, younger pupils produce their own pantomime, and shorter plays are performed in French and Latin.

Entrance. Entrance at the age of eight or nine is by assessment tests and at 10+, 11+ and 12+ by the Entrance and Scholarship examinations, taken in early February.

Further information and a prospectus can be obtained from the Admissions Secretary, Fettes College, Carrington Road, Edinburgh EH4 1QX. (Tel: 0131 311 6701. Fax: 0131 311 6714), who will be very happy to arrange a visit. E-mail: enquiries@fettes.com.

Charitable status. Fettes College is a Registered Charity, number SCO 17489. It exists to provide education for boys and girls.

Finton House

171 Trinity Road London SW17 7HL
Tel: 020 8682 0921
Fax: 020 8767 5017

Co-Founders: Terry O'Neill and Finola Stack founded Finton House in 1987.

Headmistress: **Miss E Thornton**, MA

Number of Pupils. 87 Boys, 147 Girls aged 4–11.

Fees. £6,090–£6,870 per annum.

Entrance. No testing – first come/first served. The majority enter in the Autumn Term, either a half or a full day, the remainder in January.

Exit. Boys at 7, 8, 9, 10, 11 for both London Day and Prep. Girls at 11 for London Day and Boarding.

Strong policy of integration with a percentage of children with Special Needs – Cerebral Palsy, profoundly deaf, language development. Employs a full-time Speech and Language Therapist and Special Needs Assistants. Aims to give an all-over education, developing the whole child with individual teaching to fulfil each child's potential. Music, Art and Sports are all taught to a very high standard. A stimulating environment which encourages all children to learn and gain confidence in their own ambitions. Non-denominational but teaches a moral belief encouraging self-respect and self-discipline.

Charitable status. Finton House is a Registered Charity, number 2966588. It exists to provide an integrated education for children.

Flexlands School

Chobham Surrey GU24 8AG
Tel: (01276) 858841/857341
Fax: (01276) 856554

Headmistress: **Mrs A S Vincent**, CertEd, BEd

Chairman of Governors: Mr J H F Gemmell, CA

Numbers. 160 (Girls aged 3–11)

Fees. £745–£1,785 per term.

The popularity and affection which Flexlands enjoys with both parents and children reflects the School's success in providing a traditional academic education in an enlightened, caring environment.

Situated just outside Chobham village, Flexlands has been attracting pupils from a wide catchment area for over sixty years. An independent junior school, it prepares girls aged 3–11 years for Common Entrance examination to all major senior schools and local day schools.

An excellent staff to pupil ratio ensures a high degree of individual attention and special remedial coaching is available as required. The National Curriculum is followed, with much emphasis on good standards. In addition to all the usual subjects, Design Technology, Music, French, Art, Drama and Sport feature strongly in a broad curriculum and the School has its own orchestra. The Geography syllabus is reinforced by field trips to Yorkshire and France.

All children are taught to respect and appreciate the natural environment and Flexlands' rural location provides ample opportunity for nature walks and field studies.

Flexlands is an Educational Trust run by a Board of Governors. There is an active Parents Association and parents have access to staff whenever required. The School is a member of ISIS and IAPS and is ISC Accredited.

The staff welcomes visits by parents of prospective pupils and invite you to telephone 01276 858841 for a prospectus or to make an appointment.

Charitable status. Flexlands School is a Registered Charity, number 312076. It exists to provide education for girls aged 3-11.

Fonthill Lodge

Coombe Hill Road East Grinstead West Sussex RH19 4LY
Tel: (01342) 321635
Fax: (01342) 326844

Chairman of Governors: Mr D A Raeburn, MA

Headmistress: **Mrs Jane M Griffiths**, MA, CertEd

Number of children. 210.

Fees. £775–£2,230

Setting. It is hard to imagine a more perfect setting for a child's first school than Fonthill Lodge. Boys and girls from 2½ to 11 years are taught by committed, caring and friendly staff. Combining co-education for the nursery and Key Stage I children and single sex education at Key Stage 2, the school offers a broad and balanced education in large and peaceful grounds, a mile from East Grinstead in Coombe Hill Road.

History. The school has been owned by the same family for five generations. It was founded by the Reverend George Radcliffe as a coaching establishment for children of the parish of St Edmunds in Salisbury and became a school in 1820. In 1839 the school moved to Fonthill Gifford and later to East Grinstead in West Sussex. From 1922 until 1963 it was run by the Reverend and Mrs Walpole Sealy. In 1974 Mrs Elizabeth Shallis, their daughter and the great grand-daughter of the founder, generously set up the Fonthill School Trust Limited.

Two modern extensions have been added to the main house and there is a well resourced library, and rooms for science, computer and DT.

Our aims.

- High standards in academic and personal education.
- To make each child's early experience of school, rich and stimulating, both in its own right, and as a full preparation for the next stage of their education.
- Individual personal care and support given to enable each child to feel valued and develop high self-esteem.
- To make learning enjoyable, and encourage our pupils to become independent, responsible, caring and courteous, in an attractive, well resourced environment.

Curriculum. In this friendly, family school, individual attention is given to girls and boys from 2½ to 11 years, in classes with an average size of 12 pupils. Boys and girls are educated together until 8, from 8 to 11 they are taught by specialist teachers in separate classes. In this unique environment, the children share the social benefits of co-education while being challenged in single sex classrooms. The National Curriculum is followed and outstanding results are achieved in Key Stage 1 and Key Stage 2 examinations. The children are prepared for Common Entrance and individual Senior school examinations.

Drama, Gymnastics, Ballet and Music are taught to a high standard and all children participate in the school productions, which are acclaimed. All children are encouraged to learn the recorder and may choose to learn the piano, flute, clarinet, guitar, violin and drums.

The three nursery classes are a vital part of the school. Within the well structured and colourful classrooms, the children enjoy learning and playing together. In this comfortable and secure environment they are introduced to the basic skills required for reading, writing, mathematics and ICT. Imaginative play is an essential part of the day and they also enjoy PE, Music, Ballet and Football.

Scholarships. The Sealy Scholarship for boys and girls aged eight is held each February. It is awarded to the boy and girl who achieves the highest mark in the standardised English, Mathematics and Verbal Reasoning examinations.

Special Needs. A specialist teacher, employed by the Dyslexia Institute, attends the school to give lessons to the boys and girls who are found to be Dyslexic. Extra individual help is given to children in the classrooms by support teachers.

Sport. In the safety of the beautiful grounds athletics, cricket, hockey, football, golf, karate, netball, rounders and rugby are played. An indoor sports hall and astroturf facilities are used at the East Grinstead Sports Club which is adjacent to the school. Swimming lessons are given each week at Ardingly College.

Extra-curricular activities. At the end of each day there are a number of activities in which the children can participate: Chess, Cricket, Drama, Football, Golf, Gymnastics, Netball and Rugby.

Children can stay for supervised prep session until 5 pm.

Lunch. Carefully planned menus are prepared for the children and special diets are catered for by the experienced staff.

Discipline. The children are taught good manners and a respect for others. Self-discipline and self-esteem are developed through praise and encouragement.

Uniform. Tartan pinafore, blue polo neck, navy shorts, navy jumper for pupils aged 2½ to 6 years. Tartan skirt, blue blouse, navy jumper, navy blazer for girls aged 6 to 11. Navy trousers, blue shirt, tie, navy blazer for boys 6 to 11.

Parents choose Fonthill Lodge for their sons and daughters because of its warm family atmosphere, the provision of co-education and single-sex education, high academic standards and the choice it gives them when selecting the next stage of their child's education.

With these excellent facilities and caring staff, Fonthill Lodge is a unique school. If you are interested in finding out more about it, please telephone for a prospectus or make an appointment to meet the Headmistress.

Charitable status. Fonthill Lodge is a Registered Charity, number 325071. It exists to provide education for boys and girls.

Foremarke Hall

(Repton Preparatory School) Milton Derby DE65 6EJ.
Tel: (01283) 703269
Fax: (01283) 701185
website: www.foremarke.org.uk

Chairman of Governors: Sir Richard Morris, CBE, BSc, FEng, FIChem

Headmaster: **Paul Brewster**, BSc (Hons), PGCE

Number of Boys. 43 boarders, 180 day
Number of Girls. 39 boarders, 110 day

Termly Fees. £3,290 boarding; £2,460 day; £1,505 Pre-Prep

Foremarke Hall is under the control of the Governors of Repton School. Boys and girls are prepared for all Independent Schools but about two-thirds continue to Repton.

The school is situated in a fine Georgian mansion surrounded by 50 acres of woods, playing fields and a lake. The facilities include all that the school requires including a new classroom building to house mathematics, three science laboratories, sophisticated computer technology with full time IT specialist, an extensive library run by a chartered librarian, an indoor competition size swimming pool and a sports hall and climbing wall.

Great importance is attached to pastoral care where boarders have their own dedicated staff and space for themselves. There is an imaginative and varied programme of activity making most use of the grounds including outdoor pursuits. The games programme is extensive and includes athletics, cricket, football, hockey, horse riding, rounders, swimming and tennis.

We seek to bring out the most in every pupil, to provide a rounded education and a range of experience and skills that will be a preparation for life. We value our 'family atmosphere' and strong sense of community, the spacious grounds and happy environment.

Foremarke is situated in undisturbed countryside in the centre of England. It is easily reached by the M1, M42 and Birmingham and East Midland airports.

Charitable status. Repton Preparatory School is a Registered Charity, number 527177/13 (Sir John Port Charity). It exists to provide high quality education for boys and girls.

Forres Sandle Manor

Fordingbridge Hampshire SP6 1NS
Tel: (01425) 653181
Fax: (01425) 655676
e-mail: fsmsch@globalnet.co.uk

Headmaster: **R P J Moore**, BA, PGCE

Numbers of Pupils. Aged 7 to 13: 150 (half of whom are boarders, and half boys). Aged 3 to 7: 90 (all are day children, half are boys).

Fees. Boarders, £3,945 per term. Day pupils £2,930 a term. Pre-Prep £565 to £1,650.

Forres Sandle Manor is situated on its own beautiful 50 acre estate on the edge of the New Forest. The main school building is a large manor house and the grounds are perfect for children : extensive and well-maintained playing fields, woods, a stream and plenty of space for even the most active individual! Facilities include a fine multi-purpose hall, heated swimming pool, Technology Centre, all-weather surface, a superb Coach House Art Studio, and there are plans for various exciting developments in the near future.

The School has a fine academic record and achieves an impressive number of Awards to Independent Senior Schools. There is an exceptionally dynamic teaching staff who teach in spacious, light classrooms and who prepare children for Common Entrance and scholarships at 13+ whilst delivering the National Curriculum wherever possible. It is our aim to develop in children a true enjoyment and involvement in their work and this is aided by our efforts to link various subjects together and to the wider world in general.

Music is an especially strong feature of the school with all children encouraged to play and to become confident in performance. Sport, too, is an important part of school life as are the extraordinary range of activities available to both boarders and day children. It is the school's policy to make weekends the best part of a thoroughly enjoyable week!

The Headmaster, his wife and family, are all fully involved in the school and it is the main aim of all who live and work at Forres Sandle Manor that the community be happy, confident and caring. Great care is taken to ensure the happiness of every child and to maintain the family atmosphere which has always been the basis of the school's tradition.

Charitable status. Forres Sandle Manor Education Trust Ltd is a Registered Charity, number 284260. It exists to provide high quality education for boys and girls.

Framlingham College Junior School

Brandeston Hall Woodbridge IP13 7AQ
Tel: (01728) 685331/535
Fax: (01728) 685437
Stations: Ipswich (Passenger and Goods), Wickham Market (Passenger)

Chairman of Governors: A W Fane, Esq

The Master: **S J Player,** MA

Second Master: R Sampson, BA

Co-educational 4 to 13.

Number of Pupils. 275. Boarders: 40 boys, 20 girls; Day: 100 boys, 65 girls; Pre-Prep (4 to 7) 20 boys, 30 girls

Fees. Boarders £10,221 pa, Day Pupils £6,342 pa, Pre-Prep £3,630 pa (inclusive of lunches).

The Staff consists of 10 masters and 15 mistresses, all well qualified. Boys and girls are prepared for ISEB (Common Entrance) at 13, although most enter the Senior School. (For details about the Senior School, see Part I of this Book).

Brandeston Hall is a fine, listed, Jacobean style building dating back to the sixteenth century, standing in its own grounds of 26 acres on the banks of the River Deben.

The school is excellently equipped, reflecting a number of development schemes since moving to the present site in 1949. There are 18 purpose-built classrooms, a Junior Science and Technology Laboratory, an Art Studio and Ceramics centre, Design and Technology development, a self-contained Pre-Prep wing and specialist Music Room. Additional facilities include two 'Senior' Laboratories, a well-equipped IT Centre, music practice rooms and well-equipped recreation area for boarders. Common rooms and Gymnasium complement and enhance the opportunities for day children and boarders alike. The recent completion of a large multi-purpose Hall has further enhanced the facilities of the school.

Girl boarders have small dormitories in a purpose-built wing and boys are housed in comfortable family dormitories in the main building.

The sports facilities which include playing fields, a covered heated swimming pool, a full-size floodlit all-weather surface (hockey pitch or six tennis courts) and a nine-hole bunkered golf course serve the pupils well.

The main games for boys are Rugby and Hockey, with Soccer up to the age of ten. Girls also play Hockey but combine this with Netball. In the summer Rounders and Cricket predominate with Tennis, Golf, Athletics and Swimming available for all. The school also has something of a reputation in Cross-Country running. Good coaching is given in all areas and a full programme of matches are arranged at all levels in both major and minor sports.

There are many flourishing societies with Music and Drama being particularly strong.

The parish church is situated in the grounds and boarders attend services there on Sunday, conducted by the Chaplain.

Health is supervised by the school doctor and two matrons.

The school aims to provide a friendly, caring and committed atmosphere which will also challenge each individual to strive for the very highest level of achievement.

Charitable status. Framlingham College is a Registered Charity, number 310-477-a/2. It exists for the purpose of educating children.

Friars School

Great Chart Ashford Kent TN23 3DJ.
Tel: (01233) 620493 or 635327
Fax: (01233) 636579

***Headmaster:* P M Ashley**, BA, CertEd

Chairman of Governors: P J M Patten, Esq

Number of Pupils. 250

Fees. Day from £820–£2,460.

Friars is a co-educational day school for children from 3–13 years of age. Pupils are prepared for Senior school entry at both 11+ and 13+. There are 23 full time and 4 part time staff, plus visiting teachers for music, dance and a number of extra activities.

The school is a very attractive 18th century Rectory set in 14 acres of grounds. Facilities include new Art, Science and IT rooms, an excellent gymnasium and many well equipped classrooms. A new block was opened in September 1999 to include a Theatre, new Music School, HE and Technology centres, plus extra teaching classrooms. The curriculum is broad with the emphasis being placed on encouraging the children to develop their potential to the full in a very caring environment. There is a wide range of extra curricular activities and a full sports programme. The major sports played are football, rugby, cricket, hockey, rounders and netball, whilst tennis, golf and basketball are also offered.

Scholarship examinations are held each February and the school operates a morning bus service from Ashford. The Parents Association, run by parents and staff, arrange events, both social and fundraising, during the year.

Charitable status. Friars School Limited is a Registered Charity, number 307929. It exists to provide education for boys and girls.

The Froebelian School

Clarence Road Horsforth Leeds LS18 4LB
Tel: (0113) 258 3047
Fax: (0113) 258 0173
e-mail: office@froebelian.schoolzone.co.uk

***Headmaster:* Mr J Tranmer**, MA, PGCE, FCollP

Chairman of Governors: Mrs E M Wilson, MSc

Number of Pupils. 192 (96 boys, 96 girls)

Ages. 3+ to 11+ years (3–4 years half days, optional afternoons).

Fees. £830–£1,260. Compulsory extras for 'full time' pupils, such as lunches and swimming, amount to approximately £125 per term.

Religious Affiliation. Christian, Non-denominational.

Entry requirements. Interview and assessment; written tests for older children.

Children are encouraged to develop their full potential in the purposeful atmosphere of this disciplined, caring school. High standards are demanded, and hence achieved, in all areas – academic work, creative arts, music, sports, behaviour and manners. Particular emphasis is placed on early success in the 3R's, laying a proper foundation for a broader junior curriculum.

The school is situated to the north-west of Leeds, close to Bradford and within easy reach of the major roads which serve both cities. The school enjoys an envied reputation for success in entrance and scholarship examinations at 11+.

An After School Club is available, providing supervised games, activities, homework and a light tea. Pupils may remain until 6 pm subject to places.

Charitable status. The Froebelian School is a Registered Charity, number 529111. It exists to provide education of the highest quality at affordable fee levels.

Garden House School

Girls Department 53 Sloane Gardens London SW1W 8ED.
Tel: 020 7730 1652
Boys Department 28 Pont Street London SW1X 0AB
Tel: 020 7589 7708

Station: Sloane Square

Principal: Mrs J K Oddy

***Headmistress* (*Upper School*): Mrs Janet Webb**, CertEd (Southampton)

***Headmistress* (*Lower School*): Mrs Wendy Challen**, CertEd (Froebel Institute)

Headmaster (*Boys', Academic*): Mr Simon Poland, CertEd (King's College)oebel

Headmaster (*Boys', Pastoral*): Mr Magoo Giles

Number of Pupils. 300 girls (aged 3–11); 100 boys (aged 3–8)

Termly fees. Kindergarten £1,250, Upper School £2,600–£2,750

There is a 10% reduction for siblings.

Gayhurst School

Bull Lane Gerrards Cross Bucks SL9 8RJ.
Tel: (01753) 882690
Fax: (01753) 887451
e-mail: gayhurst@rmplc.co.uk
website: www.gayhurst.bucks.sch.uk

Chairman of the Governors: His Honour Judge Hague

***Headmaster:* A Sims**, MA (Cantab)

Number of Boys. 275

Fees. Autumn 2000: From £1,590 to £2,020 per term, inclusive of lunch for all boys. A small extra charge is made for text books.

The School is a day school for boys aged 4+ to 13+. It aims to include the important features of a traditional education but also introduces boys to a wide range of experiences. The School is in country surroundings and stands in a 5 acre playing field with some woodland and a further 4 acre field beyond, all of which play important roles in the overall education.

The 22 classrooms include well-equipped specialist subject rooms for all academic subjects, including two Science Laboratories and an IT Laboratory. In addition there is a modern multipurpose Hall (Sports, drama, music), an Art room, Music Room, two libraries and an open-air heated swimming pool. The School is currently benefiting from a £2,000,000 redevelopment plan. Rugby, Soccer, Cricket, Cross-country, Hockey, Swimming, Tennis, Athletics and Basketball are taught. Boys also take part in a wide range of extra-curricular activities.

There are 24 full-time, qualified teaching staff. There are also 4 part-time teachers and a large number of peripatetic instrumental music teachers and specialist games coaches.

Entry to the School is by interview, and boys go on to both Day and Boarding Independent Schools via the CEE and to local Grammar Schools. The School has a good record of examination results and scholarships to Independent Schools are won regularly.

Charitable status. The school is a Registered Charity, number 298869. It exists to provide education for boys.

Geneva English School

36 route de Malagny 1294 Genthod Geneva Switzerland.
Tel: 022 755 1855
Fax: 022 779 1429
e-mail: gesadmin@iprolink.ch
website: www.geneva-english-school.ch

Headmaster: **Denis Unsworth**, BA, DipEd, MA (Ed)

Number of pupils. 170 day pupils (boys and girls) 4–12 years

Fees. from 5,000 Swiss Francs per term

The School, which was founded in 1961, is governed by the Geneva English School Association which is registered under Swiss law as a non-profit-making body. The pupils, 60% of whom are British, represent some 16 nationalities. There is a staff of 16 qualified teachers and, although instruction is in English, each pupil has a daily French class. The curriculum is designed to allow children to return easily to schools in Britain.

Sports include Football, Athletics, Gymnastics, Basketball, Skiing and Skating.

The school is situated in beautiful grounds overlooking the Lake and the Alps.

The School is a member of the International Schools Association.

Glebe House School

Cromer Road Hunstanton Norfolk PE36 6HW.
Tel: (01485) 532809
Fax: (01485) 533900
Station: King's Lynn

Chairman of the Governors: Mrs Sophie Archer

Headmaster: **Richard E Crosley**, BSc (Hons), PGCE

Number of children. 79 Boys, 48 Girls, (24 Weekly Boarders), Nursery 90

Termly Fees. Weekly Boarding £2,835. Day £2,360. Pre-prep £1,320–£2,140.

History, Site, Buildings and Facilities. Glebe House School and Nursery, founded in 1874, is a co-educational school for children aged 6 months–13 years. Built as a preparatory school, it is one of the few which has never closed, even during the wars. The main buildings adjoin 12 acres of playing fields, overlooking the Wash and the wooded countryside of West Norfolk.

The children in the Junior School are accommodated in a new purpose-built building. The Senior School has areas for all subjects, including an Information Technology suite, Music Centre and recital rooms, Art Studio and Design Technology Centre, Science Laboratory and specialist teaching rooms, as well as photography and pottery studios. Our 25 metre indoor heated Swimming Pool, all-weather Tennis and Netball Courts, Adventure Playground, Theatre and Gym all help to ensure that the core academic subjects are well supported by a balanced and stimulating curriculam.

Aims, Attitudes and Values. A fundamental aspect of life at the school is our determination to maximise each child's potential, and so give him or her confidence to undertake new experiences without the fear of failure. A high standard of work and behaviour is expected, with emphasis on the gradual development of self-discipline, a sense of responsibility and real consideration for the needs of others.

Academic. The school has always maintained a high academic standard offering small classes that blend traditional and modern perspectives in all the core and foundation subjects. The range of subjects taught is considerable within a broad and balanced curriculum including Drama, Information Technology, Latin and Design Technology and the learning of modern lanaguages from a young age. With no direct tie to a particular Senior School, every effort is made to ensure that the selection of a Senior School is appropriate to the needs and abilities of the individual child. Working parents find that the 8.30 am to 6.00 pm school day for children of seven and over, is an additional benefit in organising their family life.

Sports and other Activities. The main sports are Rugby, Hockey, Cricket, Netball, Rounders, Athletics and Swimming. There is an extensive programme of activities which have included: Archery, Riding, Judo, Cookery, Control Technology, Badminton, Golf, Rifle and Clay Pigeon Shooting, Ballet, Tap and Modern Dance, Gymnastics, Cycling, Swimming, Life-Saving, Squash, Photography, Chess, Sewing, Tennis, Fishing, Woodwork, Metalwork, Plastics, Pottery and Screen Printing.

Pastoral Care and Boarding. The school prides itself on its high standard of pastoral care. Each child is looked after by their Form Teacher/Tutor and is assigned to one of three Houses. Control is exerted by rmphasising positive achievement through commitment to a common aim; all children are expected to achieve their best at all times and in every circumstance. Great care is taken to ensure the happiness of every child and to maintain the family atmosphere which has always been the basis of the school's tradition. Parents receive full and frequent communication between home and school with regular reports and assessments. Parents are considered part of the school community and are welcome to visit at any time. The Glebe offers 35 boarding places for 7-13 year olds, including occasional boarding, in two separate modern and well equipped houses. From seven years of age many children choose to weekly board, as they find that four nights at school and three nights at home offers the best of both worlds. All boarders are in the care of resident House Parents and a programme of activities are run during out of school time for the boarders.

Religion. Pupils from all denominations are welcome.

Travel. A coach service operates daily to and from King's Lynn via Dersingham and Snettisham.

Further Information. A prospectus giving full details of the school's ethos and activities, current fees and other details can be obtained from the Registrar, or visit www.glebehouseschool.co.uk. Prospective parents and children are very welcome to come and meet the Headmaster and to tour the school.

Charitable status. Glebe House School Trust Limited is a Registered Charity, number 1018815. It exists to provide an excellent education for boys and girls.

Glendower Preparatory School

87 Queens Gate London SW7 5JX.
Tel: 020 7370 1927

Chairman of Governors: S M H Raison, Esq

***Headmistress:* Mrs B Humber**, BSc

Number of pupils. 184

Termly fees. (April 2000) £2,020

Preparatory school for girls aged 4–11+ years. Pupils are prepared for the Common Entrance examinations and to the London Independent Day Schools at age 11.

French is taught throughout the school by the Audio-Visual method. Emphasis is laid on fluency and purity of accent. Science is taught in the laboratory from age 8, Latin is taught at age 10. ICT, Art and CDT are included in the curriculum and taught in a specialist room.

In addition to class music lessons under a Director of Music, girls may learn piano, violin, 'cello, clarinet and flute. Class drama is taught by a specialist and there is a Drama Club for enthusiasts. Various club activities take place after school every day between 4pm and 5pm.

Physical Education includes Swimming, Netball, Gymnastics, Dance, Tennis and Athletics. The School values highly the close interest of parents, and staff are available by appointment as well as for regular Parent-Teacher discussion evenings.

As the result of a successful School Inspection in 1999, the School is now accredited by ISC.

Charitable status. Glendower School Trust Limited is a Registered Charity, number 312717. It exists to provide high quality education for local girls.

The Godolphin Preparatory School

Laverstock Road Salisbury Wilts SP1 2RB
Tel: (01722) 430652
Fax: (01722) 430651
e-mail: prep@godolphin.wilts.sch.uk
website: www.godolphin.org

Chairman of the Governors: G Fletcher, Esq

***Headmistress:* Miss J Collins,** BEd, NAA

Fees. £1,255–£2,458 per term

Number of pupils. 110 day girls, aged 3½–11.

Godolphin Prep is a purpose-built chalet-type school for girls from 3½ to eleven. It is a main stream academic school which focuses on the strengths of its pupils, values the individual and nurtures girls to become caring members of society.

The learning process is made as stimulating and enjoyable as possible; early specialist teaching (from age 7), ensures that every member of staff is enthusiastic about her subjects (usually one core plus one foundation subject, ie maths and geography or science and design technology). Visitors comment on the levels of concentration in evidence. The girls work hard and play hard, enjoying life to the full. The high standard of teaching is reflected in the National Curriculum test results as well as the scholarship awards gained by a significant number of pupils at eleven.

The behaviour code was compiled by the girls, their parents and the staff and the basic precept is 'Never be the cause of another person's unhappiness'. Courtesy and good manners are an implicit part of daily life.

The school opened in September 1993 as part of the development plan of the Godolphin School. Following an inspection in 1996, the school gained IAPS status. Two years later, further independence was established when the school was granted its own DFEE registration. This resulted in a second inspection when the school was praised for its teaching and learning, and management.

Godolphin Prep is a day school; outside interests are encouraged and weekends are perceived as family time. This arrangement suits us all very well and ensures that the girls develop as well balanced individuals.

About 60% of the pupils move to The Godolphin School, following Common Entrance. Others move to boarding schools slightly furtheGirls are alsor afield and one or two transfer to the local girls' grammar school.

Godstowe Preparatory School

Shrubbery Road High Wycombe Bucks HP13 6PR.
Tel: (01494) 529273
Fax: (01494) 429001. Admissions Secretary: (01494) 429006
e-mail: headmistress@godstowe.org

Motto: *Finem Respice*
Founded 1900

The Council:

Chairman: R B Annesley, FCA (*Former Parent*)
Mrs R A Basker, BA (*Former Parent*)
Mrs J Brent, MB, BS, DObstRCOG
B Clarke (*Former Parent*)
T Clarke, MA (Oxon) (*Former Parent*)
The Rt Hon The Countess Howe, BEd, SSStJ (*Parent*)
M H Hudson, BSc, MBA (*Parent*)
Dr Ann P Lamont, BA (Hons), CPsychol (*Parent*)
I McEvatt, MA
Mrs E McKendrick, BA
M J Tebbot

Company Secretary: M H Hudson, BSc, MBA

***Headmistress:* Mrs F J Henson**, BA, PGCE

Number of pupils. Pre-preparatory 116 (3–7), Boarders 133, Day (8–13) 210, Total 459.

Fees per Term. Boarders £4,250. Day children from £1,945 to £2,960. Nursery £800.

Close to the centre of High Wycombe, five minutes from the railway station and less than an hour from Heathrow, Godstowe is situated in ten acres of grounds. It is within easy reach of London, Oxford, Reading and Windsor.

Since its foundation in 1900 as the first Preparatory Boarding School for girls, it has steadily expanded into a school of around 460 pupils, approximately a third of whom comprise the pre-preparatory department for boys and girls.

The curriculum is broadly based. Girls are prepared for Common Entrance and Scholarship examinations for senior independent schools at 13+ with 100% of girls achieving their first choice school at 13+ CE. We have a well proven record of academic achievement typified by our many scholarship successes.

The school buildings, which were enlarged in 1972, 1980, 1984, 1987, 1996 and 2000 include two Libraries, Science laboratories, Design Technology workshops, Information Technology Centres, Music School, Art, Pottery and Textiles rooms, Museum, Dining Room, Hall/Gymnasium and Recital Room. There are extensive games facilities with playing fields, four hard tennis courts and an indoor heated swimming pool.

Residential courses and excursions give girls experience of the type of Fieldwork recommended in the National Curriculum. Fieldwork visits in Science, Geography, History, Environmental Studies and Languages are well established, whilst the annual ski-trip is a popular excursion.

There are four choirs, an orchestra and chamber groups within the School, whilst drama workshops and theatre visits are popular.

Clubs and activities include Aerobics, Badminton, Brownies, Design Technology, Environmental Science, Gardening, Golf, Gymnastics, Horse-riding, Information Technology, Self-Defence, Squash and Textiles.

We have a policy of maintaining half our places for boarders and half for day girls at 8+. Boarders live in four houses, one of which is for weekly boarders, under the care of the resident teaching Housemistress, an Assistant Housemistress and Assistant Matrons.

We strive for a caring family atmosphere, with regular activities and outings arranged for boarders.

Prospectus and further details on application to the Admissions Secretary.

Charitable status. The Godstowe Preparatory School Company Limited is a Registered Charity, number S/403/6018/Z1. It exists to provide education and training for young girls and boys.

Grace Dieu Manor School

Grace Dieu Coalville Leics LE67 5UG
Tel: (01530) 222276
Fax: (01530) 223184

Chairman of Governors: Professor M Scott

Headmaster: **Mr D Hare**, BEd (Hons), FRSA

Number of Pupils. 317: Pre-Prep 71, Infants 70, Juniors 75, Seniors 101.

Fees. £1,207 to £1,995 per term.

Grace Dieu, set in over one hundred acres of grounds, is situated in the heart of the countryside and is the Preparatory School for Ratcliffe College. It is a co-educational Roman Catholic School, accepting children of all denominations from the age of 3. The School is divided into four distinct departments, Pre-Prep (3–5), Infants (5–7), Juniors (7–9+) and Seniors (10–13+), each operating its own timetable. Entry is by interview and assessment.

The School has an excellent reputation academically and has a strong tradition in games and music. The School has its own indoor swimming pool, and there is a full programme of major sports (football, rugby, hockey, netball, rounders, cricket, tennis, swimming and athletics) as well as some minor sports (volleyball and golf). The curriculum also includes Music and Drama, and school productions are performed twice yearly. Many children, from 4+, receive individual music tuition as an extra-curricular activity. Various clubs (such as chess and needlecraft) operate during the lunch break or after school. There is an annual skiing trip to France for Senior children, an annual Jersey cricket and tennis tour. The School operates before and after school care (8.00am to 6.00pm) at no extra charge. In addition, other activities for children are run on the premises during holiday periods, though there is an extra charge for this service.

Charitable status. Grace Dieu Manor School is a Registered Charity, number 527850. It exists to provide education for boys and girls.

The Granville School

Sevenoaks Kent TN13 3LJ.
Tel: (01732) 453039
Fax: (01732) 743634
e-mail: evans@granville-school.demon.co.uk

Headmistress: **Mrs Jane D Evans**, CertEd (Cantab)

Chairman of Governors: Mr P E Reynolds

Number of Pupils. 194. Girls 3–11 years. Boys 3–5 years

Tuition. Nursery £725 per term; Transition £1,290 (including lunch); Reception, Year 1 & Year 2 £1,515 (including lunch); Years 3 & 4 £1,720,(including lunch); Years 5 & 6 £1,940 (including lunch).

Extras. Private Lessons: Pianoforte, Violin, Cello, Oboe, Clarinet, Flute £130.

Shared Lessons. Recorder £15, Orchestra, Speech & Drama £19, Ballet £32 per term.

Charitable status. The Ena Makin Educational Trust Limited is a Registered Charity, number 307931. Its aim is to run any school as an educational charity for the promotion of education generally.

Great Ballard

Eartham Chichester West Sussex PO18 0LR.
Tel: (01243) 814236

Headmaster: **R E T Jennings**, CertEd

Number of children. 200, including approx 35 Boarders. Number of boys: 103, Number of girls: 97.

Termly Fees. (September 2001): Boarding £3,263, Day £2,210–£2,438, Pre-Prep £541–£1,430. The fees for HM Forces are reduced by £150.

Children are prepared for the Common Entrance and Scholarship examinations to Independent Senior Schools. The average number of children in a class is 14. There is a full-time staff of 14 teachers.

The school stands in 20 acres on the South Downs between Arundel and Chichester.

Outdoor activities include Soccer, Rugger, Hockey, Cricket, Netball, Rounders, Tennis, Athletics, Swimming, Rifle Shooting, Gardening, Golf and Riding.

New facilities include music practice rooms, tennis courts, computer room housing a networked system of PCs, all with CD ROM, computer aided reference library and an extensive new sports field complex.

Other facilities include: theatre, modern senior and junior laboratories, library, studios for photography, pottery and screen printing, heated swimming pool and indoor pistol range. There is an extensive range of clubs and activities organised both in and outside the school grounds.

There are regular visits to a chateau in France for intensive language studies and Geography field work.

Appreciation of Music is encouraged and a wide range of instruments is taught. There are three choirs and various ensemble groups, concerts are held termly and many of the children participate in local festivals.

Both Drama and Art are flourishing activities.

The Pre-Preparatory Department contains 79 children aged 2 to 7, and is housed in a walled garden. There is a daily minibus service from Chichester, Petworth, Littlehampton, Bognor, Pulborough, Storrington and Worthing.

There is an 'after hours' club for children from nursery age upwards, enabling parents to work a full day.

Great Walstead School

Lindfield Haywards Heath West Sussex RH16 2QL
Tel: (01444) 483528
Station: Haywards Heath (Victoria/Brighton line)

Chairman of the Board of Governors: F R D Chartres

Headmaster: **H J Lowries**, BA

Deputy Head: J Crouch, BA (Hons), CertEd

Number of Pupils. Boys: 21 Boarders, 129 Day Boys. Girls: 7 Boarders, 64 Day Girls. Pre-preparatory Dept: 76 boys, 53 girls, Nursery: 58 boys, 55 girls.

Fees per term. Weekly Boarding £2,830–£3,065. Day £210–£2,540

In 1927, Mr R J Mowll, who founded his school in 1925, moved his pupils from Enfield to Great Walstead. He came to a Victorian country house set in over 260 acres of fields and woodland where children could both enjoy and learn from the unspoilt countryside around them.

From those beginnings, Great Walstead has developed into a thriving co-educational prep school, catering for children from 2½ to 13. It is a school which above all values children as people and regards it as vital that they develop their potential: in the academic sphere, in sport, in all things creative, socially and spiritually. The school stands for secure Christian values which provide an essential foundation for the whole of education and life.

The Nursery welcomes children from the ages of 2½ until it is time to enter the Pre-Prep at age 4. It provides a full, rich and varied nursery education and lays firm foundations in basic skills and understanding for future learning. The Nursery is open both mornings and afternoons to provide maximum flexibility of hours for children and parents.

The Pre-Prep covers the years from 4 to 7 within its own section of the school. It has its own library, hall and playground. The aim here is to ensure that the foundation skills of reading, writing and maths which the National Curriculum endorses are taught and learnt while at the same time adding the breadth of interest which the staff are able to provide. For example children learn French, Computer skills, and have specialist Music tuition.

Children enter the Junior School at 7, either from the Pre-prep or from other schools. For the next two years they will have a class teacher who supervises them closely for a good proportion of the day, but have specialist teachers for French, music, computers, art, craft, design technology and PE. They have games or outdoor activities each day and gradually learn to become more independent.

Children in the senior age group are taught by graduate specialist teachers for the most part and are prepared primarily for the Common Entrance examination and senior school scholarships at 13, but also for other examinations. In the past ten years over 90 scholarships to senior schools have been won. A newly opened Woodland Wing provides classrooms and subject rooms for the senior children. There is also a computer room (with 21 linked PCs), a new and extremely well-equipped Science laboratory, and a fine library.

Acres of farmland, playing fields and woodland make many outdoor activities possible. The children build camps in the Summer term and the log cabin gives boarders an enjoyable chance to camp out! The purpose-built Challenge Course gives enormous pleasure all the year round! In addition there are opportunities to go on expeditions.

The Art, Craft and Design Technology department is housed in old farm buildings which have been adapted to make fine modern workshops and studios. All children encounter all parts of the programme each year and in addition can gain further experience in their spare time.

The school's spacious grounds provide opportunities for a wide range of sports. All the year round swimming is encouraged using our own outdoor heated pool and local indoor pools. Plans for a new indoor pool are well-advanced. The superbly equipped sports hall and extensive outdoor facilities make it possible for a large number of different team games to be played as well as other more individual sports.

The school has a Referral Unit where staff with dyslexia training are able to give the extra support required by children who are referred to them and to provide training and techniques of learning that all need.

Music has long been a strength at Great Walstead. A high proportion of the children learn instruments in the Music School. They play in groups, bands and orchestras. Singing is encouraged. Music and drama often come together for performances. All children have opportunities to act. As well as major productions, there are shorter form plays with large casts.

The girls' and boys' boarding areas provide a comfortable home under the care of a married couple assisted by other boarding staff. Matron sees to the health of all children in the school. The school provides flexible holiday, pre- and after school care as well as other holiday activities to meet the needs of today's parents.

Parents are always made most welcome at the school. There is a thriving parents' organisation which provides a number of most successful social events and raises substantial sums for the benefit of the school.

Academic and Music Scholarships are offered at 7+, 8+, 9+, 10+ and 11+, and Sports Scholarships at 8+, 9+, 10+ and 11+.

Charitable status. Great Walstead School is a Registered Charity, number 307002. It exists to provide a good education on Christian foundations.

Greenfield

Brooklyn Road Woking Surrey GU22 7TP
Tel: 01483 772525
Fax: 01483 728907
e-mail: principal@greenfield.surrey.sch.uk

Principal: **Mrs Jennifer Becker,** BA, BEd, CertEd, FRSA

Chairman of the Governors: Mr David Stone

Number of pupils. 100 day girls, 95 day boys
Age range. 3-11 years
Fees per term. £880-£1,550

Set on the outskirts of Woking, Greenfield is firmly co-educational, boys and girls being equally represented in all year groups. The school is one wherein a happy balance between the formal and informal is achieved in all areas of the curriculum, and an expectation of courtesy and good manners goes hand in hand with a collective sense of comraderie and good humour.

Whilst there is no written admission test or examination, children are assessed at entry, thus appropriate teaching is ensured. All are thoroughly prepared for examinations - SATs at seven and eleven, 11+ senior school entry and Common Entrance. Informed advice regarding senior schools is available to parents at all times.

Music is a particular strength at Greenfield, which has an orchestra, jazz band, choirs and a variety of groups involving wind, strings, percussion and steel band. All Year 2 pupils enjoy free violin tuition.

Sport is eclectic, thus pupils enjoy a wide range of activities which include swimming, hockey, netball, football and athletics.

ICT is undertaken by all pupils from 5 years in a networked suite, and older pupils enjoy breaktimes computer clubs.

School visits are integral with the curriculum and day trips are included in school fees; the National and Tate Galleries, London Zoo and Hampton Court are typical venues. France, Holland, Devon and Wales are typical locations for residential visits.

A prospectus is available on request; prospective parents are welcomed individually by the Principal, who undertakes an initial information interview followed by a tour of the school.

Charitable status. Greenfield is a Registered Charity, number 295145.

Gresham's Preparatory School

Holt Norfolk NR25 6EY.
Tel: (01263) 712227
Pre-preparatory School Tel: (01263) 712088
Fax: (01263) 714060

***Headmaster:* A H Cuff**, CertEd, DPE (Exeter)

Chairman of Governors: D T Young, Esq

Numbers. 234. Boarders 75. Day pupils 159

Fees. Boarders £3,565, Weekly Boarders £3,240. Day £2,545 (per term)

The Preparatory School is closely affiliated to Gresham's School, Holt, to which pupils normally proceed at about the age of 13, after taking the Common Entrance Examination. The Preparatory School has its own Headmaster, Staff, classrooms and extensive playing fields, at the same time enjoying facilities shared with the Senior School, which include the Chapel, Sports complex and Shooting Ranges.

Boarding accommodation in two houses, is in attractive dormitories above the dayrooms which are shared by day and boarding pupils alike.

The curriculum is wide and varied: music, drama and general hobbies are encouraged. The main games are Rugby Football, Hockey and Cricket (Hockey and Netball for the girls) with Athletics, Swimming, Tennis and Squash.

The growth of a child's self-confidence and initiative is aimed at at all times, within the sensible limits of discipline and good manners: a marked feature of the school is its happy atmosphere.

Entry requirements. Entry is at any stage from 7 to 12. Assessment of a child (informally by the Headmaster) can be asked for at any time during the year: though a more formal group of graded assessments is held in February each year. Papers for overseas candidates are sent out to the pupil's school, usually in early February.

There are scholarships and bursaries open to all under conditions which can be obtained on application to the Headmaster.

Pre-preparatory School. Tel: (01263) 712088 Co-educational: 3–7. Day pupils only.

Headmistress: Mrs D Dawson-Smith

The pre-preparatory school has spacious accommodation, and will continue to aim to provide a pleasant, relaxed working atmosphere; to teach basic skills; to develop a child's ability to work; and to encourage considerate and courteous behaviour.

Charitable status. Gresham's Preparatory School is a Registered Charity, number 311268. It exists for the purpose of educating children.

Grimwade House

67 Balaclava Road Caulfield Victoria 3161 Australia
Tel: 9525 9051
Fax: 9525 8004

***Head:* Mr Andrew Boyd**, DipT, BEd, MEdPA (Monash), MACE

Chairman of School Council: Mr J Hasker, BE(Civil), DipTRP, MBA, FIEAust, FAIM

Number of Children 650 girls and boys, all day pupils

Fees per term. Years Prep–6 $2,250 ($9,000 per annum). There are four terms to the school year.

Grimwade House, the co-educational junior school of Melbourne Grammar, is located in Caulfield, about 7 kilometres from the Senior School and Wadhurst. It opened as a school in 1918, following the gift of a fine old Victorian home to Melbourne Grammar by the Grimwade family.

It now has its own Chapel, Assembly Hall, two Libraries, two Art and Craft areas, a Science Laboratory, Music School, PE Centre including an indoor pool and gymnasium, playgrounds and modern classrooms.

A full-time qualified staff of 42 teach a core curriculum including English, Mathematics, Social Studies, Science, Art, Christian Education, Music, Physical Education and Mandarin Chinese. Computers are used at all levels and notebook computers are an integral part of the curriculum in Years 5 and 6. There are also a School Counsellor, Chaplain and Learning Strategies teachers. The emphasis is on learning as a positive and challenging experience.

The School has its own orchestra and choir as well as many smaller instrumental and choral groups. Sporting activities include Australian Rules football, soccer, hockey, cross country, athletics, cricket, basketball, tennis and swimming.

All students in Years 5 and 6 attend the School Camp at Woodend, some 80 kilometres from Melbourne.

Grosvenor House School

Swarcliffe Hall Birstwith Harrogate North Yorkshire HG3 2JG.
Tel: (01423) 771029.
Fax: (01423) 772600
Station: Harrogate

***Headmaster:* G J Raspin**, MA (Cantab), PGCE (Leeds)

Number of Boys. Senior School (7–13½) 6 Boarders, 95 Day Boys, 23 Day Girls. Junior School (3–7) 73 Day Boys, 44 Day Girls

Fees. Boarders £2,600; Weekly Boarders, £2,230 per term. Day Senior School £1,675 per term, Junior School £570–£1,210 per term. Lunches, £105 per term

The School, which was founded over 90 years ago, is situated in a large country house 6 miles from Harrogate in a beautiful village setting with grounds of about 20 acres. There are also about 27 acres of playing fields nearby.

The teaching staff consists of 8 teachers for the Senior School and 7 teachers for the Junior School which is in a separate building. There are visiting staff for Swimming, Music and those children with learning difficulties. Pupils are prepared for the Common Entrance Examinations and Scholarships to all Independent Schools.

The health and comfort of the pupils is supervised by the Headmaster's wife assisted by two experienced Matrons. The School Doctor visits weekly.

Games played include Cricket, Soccer, Rugby, Swimming, Netball, Athletics, Cross-Country running, Tennis, Hockey, Lacrosse and Rounders. The School has an indoor heated swimming pool.

Every effort is made to preserve a happy family atmosphere in the School, and the pupils are encouraged to play their part not only in the community life of the School, but also where possible in the wider community of the village.

Daily transport to and from Harrogate is available for day children.

Grosvenor School

Edwalton Grange Nottingham NG12 4BS.
Tel: (0115) 923 1184
Fax: (0115) 923 5184
e-mail: office@grosvenorschool.co.uk

Headmaster: **C G J Oldershaw**, BEd

Bursar: R J D Oldershaw

Number of Pupils. 177; Pre-Preparatory 94 including 60 Girls

Fees. £1,475–£1,600 per term.

The School, founded in 1876, became a preparatory school in 1940. In addition to the Headmaster there are 25 qualified masters and mistresses.

The curriculum is broadly based on the requirements for entry to the Independent Senior Schools at 13+, although a number of pupils leave at 11+ to go to Day Independent Schools. There is a fully equipped laboratory, an IT Centre, Art and Music Rooms, a Design Technology room, and two reference and fiction libraries. All classes have two periods each of Music and Art a week.

Soccer, Hockey, Cricket, Netball, Rounders and Athletics are the main sporting activities. Swimming lessons are given to all pupils over 7 in the autumn term and Tennis coaching is available.

Guildford Grammar Preparatory School

11 Terrace Road Guildford 6055 Western Australia
Tel: (08) 9377 9296
Fax: (08) 9250 2345
e-mail: cwheatley@ggs.wa.edu.au

Head of Prep: **C G Wheatley**, MEdMan (UWA), BEd (ECU), DipT, MACE

Enrolment. 320 pupils. 65 girls, 255 boys, including 6 boarders

Fees per term. 4 terms per year. Kindergarten $1,420; Pre-Primary $1,420; Years 1–2 $1,420, Year 3–4 $1,660, Year 5–7 $1,980, Boarders $2,565.

Guildford Grammar Preparatory School is situated 15 kilometres from the centre of the City of Perth and is set amongst a backdrop of mature trees and extensive playing fields. Founded in 1914 by Canon Henn and Mr Priestly, it is one of the oldest Preparatory Schools in Western Australia enjoying excellent facilities and amenities. Many of the School's activities involve the Swan River with which the campus shares a boundary, in addition to excellent transportation links with the airport, railway and central highway system all close at hand.

This Anglican School aims to nurture the intellectual, spiritual, cultural, social and physical capacities of all students, to develop their individual talents and abilities, and to enable them to become responsible and constructive citizens. In so doing, the School strives to create a caring and supportive community of students, staff, parents and former students in which excellence in all dimensions and enjoyment of School life is pursued through an emphasis on participation and community discipline. The School also aims to provide the staff and facilities which will assist the realisation of these ideals.

To achieve these aims a staff of twenty teachers work in modern classrooms set against the rural background. A Form Teacher provides the daily pastoral care and education experience for each child and is supported by a team of specialists in Art, Music, Physical Education, Library, Computers and Languages Other Than English. In addition, an Individual Needs Teacher provides special assistance to the children who need additional help, either to catch up or extend their experiences. The School Chaplain and an assistant help with Christian Education and the relevant Services. An After School Care unit provides care for children from 3.30 pm until 6 pm and a Before School Care Service operates from 7.15 am to 8.15 am.

Recent developments include the establishment of a Technology and Learning Centre with 50 IBM Pentium computers, a digital camera, colour scanner and multimedia projector.

The School has also established its own permaculture garden and farm plot which are integrated into the curriculum.

The Haberdashers' Aske's Preparatory School

Butterfly Lane Elstree Borehamwood Herts WD6 3AF.
Tel: 020 8266 1779
Fax: 020 8266 1808
e-mail: office@habsboys.sch.uk
website: www.habs.habsboys.sch.uk

Head: **Miss Y M Mercer**, BEd, DipAdvEd

Deputy Head: Mr M G Brown, BSc

Number of Boys. 200

Fees. £7,650 per annum.

The Preparatory School is housed in a delightful purpose-built building, on the same campus as the Main School. The boys are able to share the facilities and grounds of the Main School, the Sports Centre, the heated indoor Swimming Pool, the Music School and the Dining Room.

A broad and balanced curriculum is delivered. In addition, the Preparatory School offers a wealth of extra-curricular and holiday activities in which all boys are encouraged to participate.

Boys enter the Preparatory School each September after a competitive written test and interview at the age of 7. Boys are expected to move into the Main School at 11.

For further details, please see Part I of this book.

Charitable status. The Haberdashers' Aske's Preparatory School is a Registered Charity, number 313996. It exists to provide education for boys.

The Hall

Crossfield Road Hampstead London NW3 4NU
Tel: 020 7722 1700
Station: Swiss Cottage

Chairman of Governors: Dr A G Hearnden, OBE

***Headmaster:* P F Ramage**, MA

Number of Pupils. 440 (ages 4–13). All Day Boys

Fees. £2,000-£2,450 per term (inclusive)

Founded in 1889 the school is on two sites within close proximity.

The majority of boys join the Kindergarten at the age of 4 or 5 but some places are usually available at 7, 8 or 9. The average size of class is 18.

The Junior School has the benefit of a major extension built in 1994 providing modern computing, science and music facilities.

Boys in the Junior School use the sports hall, located in the Senior School, and have lunch in the dining hall which serves the whole school.

After three years in the Junior School Boys transfer to the Middle School opened in 1998. Here they are taught for two years, moving from classroom based teaching to subject based teaching during that term.

In the Senior School boys are taught by subject specialists for their final three years.

The Hall prides itself on the breadth of education it offers. All Senior School boys study Art, Drama, Music, Pottery, Computer Studies, Design/Technology and Current Affairs within the timetable and there is a broad range of after school clubs and activities.

Team games, soccer, hockey and cricket, are played at the Wilf Slack Memorial Ground and in recent years fencing has developed as a major sporting strength.

The school is not linked with any particular senior school. Over half the boys proceed to London day schools such as Westminster, St Paul's, Highgate and UCS, but other proceed to boarding schools amongst which Eton, Winchester, Harrow and King's Canterbury are the most popular. In recent years scholarships have been won at all the above mentioned schools.

Charitable status. The Hall Educational Trust is a Registered Charity, number 312722. It exists entirely for the purpose of education.

Hallfield School

48 Church Road Edgbaston Birmingham B15 3SJ.
Tel: 0121-454 1496; 0121-454 2271
Fax: 0121-454 9182
e-mail: hallfield@argonet.co.uk
Station: Birmingham New Street

Founded 1879

Governing Body: The Hallfield School Trust

Chairman of Governors: Mr N Fisher, MA, MLitt

***Headmaster:* J G Cringle**, MEd, CertEd

Number of Pupils. Upper School 205 Day Boys and Girls (7–11 years). Pre-Preparatory Department 208 Day Boys and Girls (3½–7 years). 50 Nursery Boys and Girls (2½–3½ years).

Fees. Nursery on application; Pre-Prep. £1,370–£1,495, 7/8 year olds £1,710; 9–11 year olds £1,910 per term. Lunches: £120 5 days per week. £96 4 days per week.

The well-qualified staff consists of 23 teachers and a classroom assistant in the Upper School and 23 teachers and 5 classroom assistants in the Pre-Prep and Nursery Department.

The majority of pupils enter the school through the Nursery. Direct entry into the Pre-Prep and Upper School is by means of an entrance test and interview.

A number of academic scholarships is available for external and internal candidates.

Hallfield is an academic school with a fine record of achievement. A wide-ranging curriculum is provided which meets all the requirements of the National Curriculum, as well as covering the needs of Entrance and Scholarship examinations to Independent Senior Schools.

Pupils are prepared for entry to local selective day schools at 11. A few pupils will move on to boarding schools.

The school occupies a fine twenty acre site in a very pleasant area of the City. Classrooms are bright and well-equipped and class sizes rarely exceed 18.

All pupils are encouraged to strive for excellence in all that they do and high standards of work, dress, behaviour and courtesy are expected at all times.

A building and development programme was launched in 1989 and this has provided a new Art Room; two impressive laboratories and entrance hall; additional classrooms and new Music School, Sports Hall, ICT room with a network of 20 computers, new classrooms for Pre-Prep and a purpose-built Nursery, an all-weather pitch, extensions to both the Nursery and to six Pre-Prep classrooms. A new development project is currently underway. This will create new updated facilities for both Art and Design Technology as well as larger and refurbished classrooms for Upper School.

Music plays an important part in school life and visiting musicians provide tuition in a wide range of instruments from the age of six.

The major boys' games are Association Football, Rugby and Cricket. Girls' games include Netball, Hockey, Rounders and Tennis. Athletics takes place in the Summer Term. A wide range of extra-curricular activities is also available. These vary from time to time but at present include: Art, Badminton, Ballet, Basketball, Craft, Cross-country, Drama, Gardening,, Lego, IT, Judo, Music (orchestra and choirs), Rock-climbing, Sailing, and Speech.

There is an active Parents' Association which organises a number of social events each year, as well as raising funds for equipment to enhance the education of children in the school. Pupils are encouraged to maintain their links with the school by joining the Old Hallfieldian Society.

Hall Grove

Bagshot Surrey GU19 5HZ
Tel: (01276) 473059
Fax: (01276) 452003
e-mail: registrar@hallgrove.surrey.sch.uk
website: www.hallgrove.surrey.sch.uk

***Headmaster:* A R Graham**, BSc, PGCE

Assistant Headmaster: A J Driver, BA

Number of Boys. Pre-Preparatory (4–7) 56. Preparatory (7–13) 196

Fees. Pre-Preparatory: £1,800; Preparatory: £2,250 (7–10), £2,390 (11–14); Boarding Supplement: £750 per term; Flexi-boarding: £20 per night; Occasional boarding £25 per night. Fees inclusive of meals and all compulsory extras.

The School was founded in 1957 by the current Headmaster's parents. At its centre is a most attractive Georgian house set in beautiful gardens and parkland. Recent additions have provided some modern rooms and specialist teaching areas, an impressive computer facility and a new classroom block. Despite this building programme, the character and atmosphere of a family home has been retained.

Hall Grove is a thriving day school for 250 boys aged 4–13, which also offers weekly and flexi boarding for up to 30 of its pupils. The main entry ages are at 4, 7 and 11. There is a separate nursery in the grounds for boys and girls from the age of 2½.

The academic standards are high, and there is a very strong emphasis on Sport and Music. A wide range of activities flourish, including woodwork, drama, and a host of major and minor sports (soccer, rugby, hockey, cricket, tennis, athletics, golf, judo, basketball, badminton, dance and others). The school day continues until 6.30 pm, and many older boys stay overnight on a regular basis. There is also provision for after-school care.

Hall Grove has its own residential centre situated on the magnificent South Devon coast called Battisborough House, and there is a very full programme of field trips and expeditions for every age group both in Devon and overseas. Battisborough House is available for hire by other schools and can accommodate up to 40 in comfort.

Halstead Preparatory School for Girls

Woodham Rise Woking Surrey GU21 4EE.
Tel: (01483) 772682
Fax: (01483) 757611

***Headmistress:* Mrs A Hancock**, BA, ACP, FRSA

Chairman of Governors: Mrs S Herd

Number of Pupils. 210 (aged 3 to 11)

Fees. Nursery (mornings only) £700; Kindergarten to Year 3 £1,580; Years 4, 5 and 6 £1,850

The fees from Kindergarten to Year 6 are inclusive of lunch. All fees include day outings and in-school entertainment.

Halstead School was founded by Mrs Olive Bidwell in 1927 at Halstead Place, near Sevenoaks, Kent. During the war it moved to Devizes, Wiltshire, before re-opening at the present location in Woodham Rise, a leafy part of residential Woking in 1947. The main school building is a large Edwardian house to which modern facilities have been added; most recently a spacious, purpose built Pre-Preparatory Department and, in the main building, a new "state of the art" computer facility with Internet access. A happy, friendly atmosphere pervades giving the feel of a home with desks in it, where girls go out into the garden to play; there are no hard play areas.

Each child is treated as an individual and given a broad education in line with the National Curriculum but with many extras and the advantage of an excellent adult/child ratio - the policy is 1:16 or better. The philosophy of the school is to educate "the whole child" so that creative, physical, social, emotional and spiritual aspects of each girl's development are considered as well as her academic ability. Every child has the opportunity to take part in one of the many sports teams, four choirs or the school orchestra. There have been notable successes recently in artistic, musical and sporting competitions, both local and national, and academic scholarships are regularly achieved.

The fees cover all tuition, books, lunches and outings – only residential visits are charged – there are no hidden extras. Outside, and sometimes during the school day, there are many optional extras such as Art, Craft and Pottery Workshops, Computer Clubs, Tennis Coaching, individual Music lessons on a whole range of instruments and group dancing classes in both Tap and Jazz. Before and After School Care is also available for a modest additional charge.

Charitable status. Halstead (Educational Trust) Limited is a Registered Charity, number 270525. It exists to provide a high quality all-round education for girls aged 3–11.

Handcross Park School

Handcross Haywards Heath West Sussex RH17 6HF.
Tel: (01444) 400526
Fax: (01444) 400527
e-mail: head@handxpark.demon.co.uk
Station: Three Bridges

Chairman of Governors: The Revd T J Sterry

***Headmaster:* W J Hilton**, BA, CertEd

Headmistress of the Pre-Preparatory Department: Mrs S Harper, MA, CertEd

Number of Pupils. 298: Boys 189, Girls 117.

Fees per term (September 2000). Preparatory School: Weekly Boarding £3,230, Years 3 & 4 £2,400, Years 5 to 8 £2,755. Pre-Preparatory: Year Reception £1,580, Year 1 £1,580, Year 2 £1,580. Nursery: Up to 5 morning/afternoon sessions £770, 6 morning/afternoon sessions £920, 7 morning/afternoon sessions £1,075, Introductory 2 afternoon sessions £255. There are no compulsory extras.

Handcross Park is a Preparatory and Pre-Preparatory School with origins dating back to 1887. It provides high academic standards and a broadly based education for boys and girls aged 2½ to 13 years in a happy family atmosphere within an ordered Christian framework. The school is based in a most attractive and friendly mansion house but also has the most up-to-date educational plans and modern facilities. It is set within 50 acres of beautiful grounds, gardens and playing fields.

Situated on the estate is a magnificent purpose built

Music School which is run by a full-time Director of Music, who is assisted by several part-time professional instrumental teachers. All children attend class music lessons and many learn to play one or more instruments, or perhaps have singing lessons. The school runs an Orchestra, Chapel and Junior Choirs and several instrumental and vocalist groups.

The magnificent new Sports Hall, Science and Technology Centre is a marvellous facility, and is in constant use by children at all levels throughout the school. The Sports Hall was designed with drama in mind, as this plays an important part in everyday school life. A portable stage and tiered seating along with modern theatrical technology permit sophisticated drama productions. The building also houses a very well equipped Science Laboratory, an Information Technology Suite containing networked computers giving Internet access, a Design Technology Workshop, an art studio, a pottery, two classrooms and a most convivial library with a computerised cataloguing and lending system. There are also specific facilities for Modelling, Dance and Domestic Science situated in other areas of the school.

Rugby, Soccer, Cricket, Netball, Hockey, Judo, Swimming, Tennis, Shooting, Gymnastics, Athletics and Golf all form a regular part of the curriculum. Riding is also popular amongst the children, and instruction takes place at the Riding School located in an adjacent village.

A new indoor swimming pool was opened in May 2000 providing swimming lessons all year round and many other water sports opportunities.

The core curriculum includes English, Mathematics, French, Science, Religious Education, History, Geography, Latin, Information Technology, Design Technology, Art, Music, PSHE, PE and Games. There is a full-time qualified teaching staff and a staff-pupil ratio of about 1 to 10. Classes do not normally exceed 16 pupils. Examinations are taken in most subjects twice yearly, and the children's progress is monitored constantly through a system of continuous assessment. The school believes that the children benefit from the challenge of competition, but is careful to recognise effort as highly as achievement.

Handcross Park has an enviable record of success in the Common Entrance Examination to Independent Senior Schools and all of our pupils normally pass into the school of their first choice. Major Open Scholarships and awards are regularly won to many of the leading Independent Senior Schools.

Handcross Park is certainly to be counted amongst the finest preparatory schools in England, and unashamedly takes pride in the pursuit of educational excellence but within a happy and caring atmosphere. The school believes in providing a wealth of opportunities for the children, enabling the teaching staff to harness and develop the strengths undoubtedly possessed by each and every child.

Although mainly a day school, weekly boarding is popular amongst children and parents thereby allowing the children to spend the week in a boarding environment but to return home at weekends. This enables many children to experience all the excitement and benefits of a boarding education but still spend that essential quality time with their family each weekend. Casual boarding is also increasingly popular. Children are able to board for periods of time ranging from one night up to full weekly boarding according to their needs, and to the needs of parents.

The Pre-Preparatory Department caters for children aged 4–7 years. The magnificent "Secret Garden School" which was built in the Victorian walled garden accommodates almost 100 children. A Nursery School for the 2–4 year olds is part of this purpose-built complex to start the very young on the educational ladder. The Pre-Preparatory Department curriculum allows for the children to reach their full potential in the basic subjects whilst giving them the opportunity to explore activities such as Music, Dance, Technology, Art and Craft, Computing, Swimming, PE and Games.

Charitable status. Newells School Trust is a Registered Charity, number 307038. Handcross Park School exists to provide a high quality education to children aged 2½ to 13.

Hanford School

Childe Okeford Blandford Dorset DT11 8HL
Tel: (01258) 860219
e-mail: hanfordsch@aol.com
website: www.hanford.dorset.sch.uk

Headmistresses: **Miss S B Canning**, MA, Somerville College, Oxford and **Mrs R A McKenzie Johnston**

Headmaster: **R A McKenzie Johnston**, MA (Trinity Hall, Cambridge)

Numbers of Girls. 115, all boarders

Fees. £3,100 per term

Hanford School, which was founded in 1947 by the Rev and Mrs C B Canning is an early 17th Century manor house standing in about 45 acres and situated in the Stour valley, about half way between Blandford and Shaftesbury. The amenities include a Chapel, Laboratories, a Music School, an Art School, a Gymnasium, a Swimming Pool, a Handwork Room, two Netball/Tennis Courts (hard) and a covered Riding School. Pupils are prepared for entry to all Independent Senior Schools.

Haslemere Preparatory School

The Heights Hill Road Haslemere Surrey GU27 2JP.
Tel: (01428) 642350
Fax: (01428) 645314
e-mail: office@haslemere-prep.surrey.sch.uk

Chairman of Governors: Mrs B L Jenner

Headmaster: **I D Mackenzie**, BA

Number of Boys. 150 (all day boys) including 52 boys in Pre-prep

Fees. £1,925–£2,400. The school offers sibling discounts and Scholarships annually in academics and the arts.

The Heights is committed to giving each individual boy the best possible start to his education.

The school is a boys' independent day school for 4 to 13 year olds, with a Nursery Department due to open in September 2001 to cater for girls and boys aged 2½+. The school is set in a stunning location, within walking distance of Haslemere town centre.

Academically it has an excellent reputation for producing well rounded, well mannered, confident young men. The majority of boys move on to senior schools such as the Royal Grammar School, King Edward's, Churchers, Lord Wandsworth, Charterhouse and Cranleigh, many with scholarships. The Heights seeks to encourage all boys to find the best within themselves by creating a safe and stimulating environment in which they can learn. A highly dedicated and professional staff teaches a well balanced curriculum, that includes not only the core subjects but also a wide range of extra-curricular activities, catering for all. Each individual's performance is closely monitored. Class sizes are small, with a maximum of 18. Minibus travel is provided from local areas and Haslemere railway station.

After school care is provided until 6 pm. The Heights encourages an active involvement of parents in achieving its success.

For a copy of our prospectus, please contact the Headmaster's Secretary.

Charitable status. The Heights, Haslemere Preparatory School Trust Limited is a Registered Charity, number 294944. It exists to provide an all-round preparatory school education for day boys aged between 4 and 13 years in Haslemere and its environs.

The Hawthorns

Pendell Court Bletchingley Surrey RH1 4QJ.
Tel: (01883) 743048

Motto: *Love God, Love Your Neighbour*

Headmaster: **T R Johns**, BA, PGCE, FRGS

Number of Pupils. 450 Day Pupils, aged 2 to 13.

Fees. From £775 (Nursery) to £2,082 per term.

The School is an Educational Trust controlled by a Board of Governors, (Chairman: Mr G J Williams). Founded in 1926 near Redhill, The Hawthorns moved in 1961 to the haven of its present impressive site, a Jacobean manor set in 35 acres below the North Downs, with a catchment area from East Grinstead to Coulsdon and Dorking to Westerham.

The prospectus reflects the rich and diverse nature of our school. Recent developments include an innovative Nursery Ark, the Bull Centre for Science and ICT and a new Sports and Swimming complex. The curriculum, incorporating the National Curriculum, Common Entrance and Scholarship goals, blends modern and traditional methods with emphasis on thorough grounding in English, Maths, Science, ICT and Languages. In Music, DT, Art and Textiles specialist centres are very well equipped. The strong Music Department fields three choirs and two orchestras, with a wide range of individual instrumental tuition available. Public recitals and regular competition entries are encouraged, with good scholarship results. The co-educational commitment to PE and Games is of great importance with major sports including soccer, netball, rugby, hockey, pop-lacrosse, cricket, tennis, cross-country, athletics, swimming and gymnastics. The grounds contain four sports areas, tennis courts and 5 acres of woodland for outdoor pursuits. An extensive programme of extra curricular activities is offered including sailing, riding, squash, golf, ballet, modern dance, model-making, film-making, fashion design and cooking.

Equal opportunities, enjoyment and success are sought for every child. Boys and girls gain entry as day pupils between the ages of 2 and 13 and are prepared for the Common Entrance examination and/or Scholarships at 10+, 11+ and 13+.

The staff consists of 30 full-time teachers, graduates or qualified in their particular field, and 7 part-time teachers. Mrs Johns oversees the domestic arrangements and personally supervises the children's health, aided by assistant matrons. The school is a living, happy, working community and a visit is essential.

Charitable status. The Hawthorns Educational Trust Limited is a Registered Charity, number 312067. It exists to provide education for girls and boys of 2 to 13 years.

Hazelwood School

Limpsfield Oxted Surrey RH8 0QU.
Tel: (01883) 712194
Fax: (01883) 716135

Chairman of Governors: A J Baulf, FCA

Headmaster: **A M Synge**, MA (Oxon), PGCE (Liverpool)

Number of Pupils. Day Boys 237, Day Girls 144

Fees. Day Pupils from £850 per term (Nursery Class) to £2,450 per term

Founded in 1890, Hazelwood stands in superb grounds, commanding a magnificent view over the Kent and Sussex Weald.

Pupils usually enter at 3+ into the Pre-Prep School, or at 7+ to the Prep School, joining those pupils transferring from the Pre-Prep to the Prep School. Entry at other ages is possible if space permits.

A gradual transition is made towards subject specialist tuition in the middle and upper forms. All teaching staff are fully qualified. Pupils are prepared for the Common Entrance examinations at 11+, 12+ and 13+, and also for Scholarships to Senior Schools. 56 academic, all-rounder, sporting, music and art awards have been gained since 1995.

Extra-mural activity is an important part of every pupil's education. Excellent sports facilities, which include a newly commissioned games field, heated indoor swimming pool, gymnasium and many games pitches, tennis courts and other hard surfaces, allow preparation of school teams at various age and ability levels in a wide range of sports. Our aim is that every pupil has an opportunity to represent the School.

Art, Technology, Music and Drama are on the curriculum as well as being lively extra-mural activities. Our Centenary Theatre (1990) incorporates a 200-seat theatre, music school and Chapel. A wide menu of extra-mural activities is on offer, including tap, ballet and jazz dance, judo, orchestras, choir, brass group, wind group, saxophone group, recorder group, sports coaching in many different sports, art, electronics, computing, modelling, croquet, gardening, golf, water sports, cookery, sewing and needlework, and chess.

Other major developments include the complete rebuilding of the Pre-Prep School, in a "state of the art" building, and we opened in 1999 a new teaching block to benefit Science, Technology, Information Technology and Art.

Charitable status. Hazelwood School Limited is a Registered Charity, number 312081. It exists to provide excellent preparatory school education for boys and girls at Oxted, in Surrey.

Hazlegrove (King's Bruton Junior School)

Hazlegrove House Sparkford Somerset BA22 7JA.
Tel: (01963) 440314
Fax: (01963) 440569
Stations: Castle Cary, Sherborne and Yeovil Junction

Head Master: **The Revd B A Bearcroft**, BEd Hons (Cantab)

Deputy Head: Miss D Lambert, BEd

Head of Pre-Prep Department: Mrs L Statham, CertEd

Number of Pupils. 372 (76 Boarders, 296 Day Pupils). Co-educational.

Pre-Prep: 99 children (4 to 8 in Main School); 20 children (3 to 4 in Nursery)

Fees. Boarders £3,430–£3,890 per term (Fees are inclusive, there are no compulsory extras). Day Pupils £1,370–£2,790

Pre-Preparatory: £1,370 per term, Nursery: £14.35 (morning session); £9.55 (afternoon session); + £2.00 per lunch.

The school is situated in a country house setting, surrounded by a 200-acre park. Close links are maintained with the Senior School which is some 8 miles away.

The school is organised in sets. The top set prepares boys and girls for Scholarships. Assistance is given by qualified staff in English and Maths should the need arise. For details of staff see under King's School, Bruton (Part I of this book). There are 2 sets of House Parents, a qualified nurse and 7 assistant staff.

Principal games are Rugby, Hockey, Netball, Cricket. There is a recently built indoor 25m Pool. Art and CDT are included in the curriculum, and Music and Drama and hobby pursuits are strongly encouraged.

Extensive building programmes have equipped the School fully, an indoor Tennis Court/Sports Hall as well as a Chapel/Theatre, a Music School, new Science Laboratories and English Centre. There are extensive games fields including a shale hockey pitch. There are two Squash Courts, a recently completed Craft Centre and new classroom block. New changing rooms with lockers are now completed.

The prospectus, on application to the Headmaster, outlines details of all further facilities available.

Pre-Preparatory Department. The co-educational Pre-preparatory day department is situated beside the Junior School at Hazlegrove. The entrance to the school is situated on the A303 dual carriageway at the Sparkford roundabout opposite the turning to Yeovil and Sherborne.

The staff is fully qualified and experienced with specialist knowledge of the age range. Full use of the Junior School's excellent facilities presents a wide range of valuable experiences to each child developing individual strengths and gaining the confidence so essential in the early learning process. In addition to the basic curriculum a syllabus of Geography, History, French, Science, Music, and CDT is followed.

Each day the children take part in some form of physical education with swimming throughout the year under careful supervision in the indoor heated 25m pool. There are various after school activities for the whole age range which can extend the day until 5.30 pm. Gifted children and slow learners are catered for with specialist staff.

Charitable status. King's School, Bruton is a Registered Charity, number 310272. It exists to provide education for children.

Headfort

Kells Co Meath. Ireland
Tel: +353 46 40065
Fax: +353 46 41842
e-mail: headfort@iol.ie
website: headfort.com

Headmaster: **C McCosker**, BSc

Chairman of Directors: R Lynn Temple, Esq

Number of Pupils. 92

Fees. Boarding: IR£2,675, Day: IR£1,750 per term

Headfort is Ireland's only predominantly boarding co-educational preparatory school. The House, designed by Robert Adam and one of the finest in Ireland, is set in 65 acres of games fields, gardens and woodland, 40 miles north of Dublin.

Children are prepared for Common Entrance or Scholarships to English and Irish Independent Secondary Schools.

Children play the usual team and individual games as well as riding, cookery, dance, judo, gymnastics, archery, kayaking, swimming and gardening.

Pastoral care is of extreme importance to us and we have structures in place to ensure that each child is monitored constantly to ensure his/her welfare. The exuberant atmosphere of the school reflects the amount of time we devote to this. An extensive programme of refurbishment is currently nearing completion, which will ensure the continued excellence of our academic, social and pastoral provisions.

Heatherton House School

Amersham Buckinghamshire HP6 5QB.
Tel: (01494) 726433
Fax: (01494) 729628

Chairman of the Governors: Mr John M Lamb

Headmistress: **Mrs P K Thomson**, BA, CertEd

Number of pupils. 175 approx

Fees. (from September 2000) £525–£1,710 per term inclusive of all but optional subjects

Heatherton House is a registered charitable trust.

Founded and purpose built in 1912 it is a day preparatory and pre-preparatory school for girls aged 5 to 11, with mixed classes for boys and girls from 2½ to 5.

All staff are fully qualified; the classes are small (averaging 15–20 pupils) and Girls are prepared for both the examinations to the girls' independent senior schools, and for the Buckinghamshire County Selection procedure tests.

The School has a very good academic record, as well as strong musical and swimming traditions.

A prospectus will be sent on application to the Headmistress' Secretary.

Charitable status. Heatherton House School is a Registered Charity, number 310630. It exists to provide high quality education for girls and boys.

Heath Mount School

Woodhall Park Watton-at-Stone Hertford Hertfordshire SG14 3NG.
Tel: (01920) 830230.
Fax: (01920) 830357
Station: Hertford North and Watton-at-Stone

Headmaster: **Rev H J Matthews**, MA (Cantab), BSc, PGCE

Deputy Headmaster: R F Gordon, MA (St Andrews), CertEd

Number of Pupils. Boarders: Boys 49 Girls 21; Day: Boys 168 Girls 123

Fees. Weekly Boarders: £3,525, Half Weekly Boarders: £3,220, Day Pupils: Year 3 £2,342, Year 4 £2,342, Year 5 upwards £2,505. Pre-Prep: £1,775; Nursery: (morning or afternoon) £730; all day: £1,630.

There is a reduction in fees for the second and subsequent children attending the School at the same time.

The School, situated five miles from Hertford, Ware and Knebworth, is a Georgian mansion with its own Chapel and Music School. It stands in glorious grounds of over forty acres in the middle of a large private park. From 1817 to 1933 Heath Mount was at Hampstead before moving to Woodhall Park. The school became a Trust in September 1970, with a board of Governors under the chairmanship of Mr P T L Leach. The excellent facilities include a new swimming pool, several games pitches, tennis courts, a nine-hole golf course, hard-play area and a Sports Hall within the grounds. The main house contains an imaginatively developed lower ground floor housing modern science laboratories and rooms for art, pottery, textiles, film making, computer-assisted design, food technology and design and technology. There is a further information technology room and well stocked research and fiction libraries. A Pre-Prep and Nursery Unit was opened in September 1991, and a new Girls' Boarding House was opened in 1993.

The School has an excellent record of scholarships to leading independent senior schools.

Hendon Preparatory School

20 Tenterden Grove Hendon London NW4 1TD
Tel: 020 8203 7727
Fax: 020 8203 3465

Chairman of the Governors: R Ellis, CBE, MA

Head: **J R A Gear**, BEd Hons

Number of children. (Co-educational Day School) 240

Fees. £1,900–£2,380 per term

The School was founded in 1874 and prepares boys and girls for the Common Entrance and Scholarship examinations to Independent Senior Schools. The School is proud of its academic track record and of its success in securing places for its pupils at a wide range of senior schools. The past two years have seen unparalleled success with entry to senior independent schools at 100%, and several scholarships being awarded.

It is conveniently located close to the A1, M1 and North Circular roads and is less than six miles from the centre of London.

The School buildings, which have their own grounds and play areas, have been completely refurbished over the past decade to provide an up to date learning environment, helping children to meet the challenges of the modern world. The range of special facilities include a fully-equipped science laboratory as well as a computer room and recently updated CDT room. Sports, including rugby, cricket, soccer, netball and swimming, play an important role in the School's activities, as do after school clubs which include fencing, rock climbing and golf.

Classes are kept small (18 pupils) to allow the maximum individual attention. The School provides a cheerful and caring environment in which individual talents can grow and personalities develop. The School seeks to combine the very best of modern teaching methods with the highest regard for traditional values.

A purpose-built coeducational Pre-Prep School exists on the same site. This facility offers parents an extended day option, being open from 8 am to 5.30 pm, 51 weeks a year.

Pre-Prep (2½–3) and Prep (4–13) prospectuses are available from the Head.

Hereford Cathedral Junior School

28 Castle Street Hereford HR1 2NW.
Tel: (01432) 363511
Fax: (01432) 363515
e-mail: secretary@hcjs.co.uk

Established 1898

Chairman of Governors: The Very Reverend Robert Willis, Dean of Hereford

Headmaster: **T R Lowe**, BA, CertEd, FCollP

Number of children. 313 children 3–11 years, 210 boys and 133 girls.

Fees. £1,090–£1,598 per term.

The School is the Junior School for Hereford Cathedral School and has the same board of Governors. Games facilities are shared but the teaching staff work exclusively in the Junior School.

The School occupies listed Georgian and Medieval buildings in Castle Street at the East End of the Cathedral with facilities including specialist music rooms, an ICT centre and an extensive library.

There is a full and broad curriculum with the school noted for the strength of the music and games. French is taught from the age of 4.

The staff are well qualified and the maximum class size is 16. In the junior forms all subjects are taught by specialists.

Music plays an important part in the life of the school with the Cathedral Choristers being educated here and a team of over twenty peripatetic music teachers working between the two schools. There are two school choirs and an orchestra.

An extensive programme of clubs and activities is offered during lunchtime and after school aimed at giving all children opportunities to develop their talents.

The games fields are on the banks of the River Wye with expert coaching being given in the main sports of cricket, football, rugby, hockey, netball, rounders, athletics, lacrosse and swimming.

There is an active PTA organising a wide programme of social and fund raising activities.

Entry is via the Nursery, Reception or by an entrance examination at 7+. Most children continue through to the senior school subject to passing an examination at 11.

Hereward House School

14 Strathray Gardens London NW3 4NY.
Tel: 020 7794 4820
Fax: 020 7794 2024

Headmistress: **Mrs L Sampson**

Age Range. 4–13
Number in School. Day: Boys 165
Fees per term. £1,995–£2,275

Hereward House is a Preparatory Day School which prepares boys for the Common Entrance to Senior Independent Schools. The school's aim is to provide a lively, stimulating and intellectually demanding education within a friendly environment. Modern teaching methods, Computers and other Visual Aids are employed alongside those traditional methods that have proved their worth.

Art, Music, Drama, Pottery, IT and DT, Football, Cricket, Swimming, Gym, Tennis and Cross Country

Running form an integral part of the syllabus. French is introduced when boys are approximately eight years old and Latin the following year. The more able linguists may also learn Greek. The school has a strong and continually expanding Music and Drama department. Extra curricular activities include weekly Hockey, Fencing, Karate, Chess, Computer, Table Tennis, Snooker, Art and Drama Clubs.

Entry at 4+ years by interview.

Herries School

Dean Lane Cookham Dean Berks SL6 9BD.
Tel: (01628) 483350

Herries is an independent co-educational day school for 2½ to 11 year olds. It is located in a beautiful rural setting close to Maidenhead and Marlow. There is easy access to the M4 and London. Herries provides a broad curriculum enabling every child to develop individual talents. The happy atmosphere and high standard of pastoral care encourages children to achieve their full potential.

Chairman of the Governors: Mr C L Lenton

***Headmistress:* Mrs A Warnes, CertEd**

Number of Pupils. 110 boys and girls. Admission is from 2½ onwards.

Fees per term. £1,070–£1,500.

Curriculum. Subjects include: English, Mathematics, Science, ICT, French, Latin, Geography, History, RE, Art, Craft, Design and Technology, PE, Dance, Music, Speech and Drama.

Examinations. Key Stage 1 SATS at 7 years. Key Stage 2 SATS at 11 years. 11+ Selection tests into Grammar Schools or entrance into private or comprehensive schools.

School facilities. Facilities include purpose-built Nursery, brand new purpose-built ICT facility. Football training and professional tennis coaching at Bisham Abbey National Sports Centre. Swimming at local sports centre. Gymnastics and athletics on school site. Extra curricular activities include a variety of sports. French, Cookery, Science, Drama, Judo, Tennis, ICT.

Highfield School

West Road Maidenhead Berks SL6 1PD.
Tel: (01628) 624918
Fax: (01628) 635747
e-mail: office@highfield.berks.sch.uk
website: highfield.berks.sch.uk

Chairman of Governors: Mr J L L Underhill, MA, FCA

***Head:* Mrs Catherine M A Lane**, DPSE, CertEd

Type. Educational Charitable Trust Primary Day School with Kindergarten and Nursery.

Location. Town

Number of Pupils. Approximately 200. Girls 180, Boys 20

Average Class Size. 21

Maximum Class Size. 23

Age Range. Girls 2½–11+. Boys 2½–5

Religion. Christian. Other denominations welcome.

Entry. By interview and/or placement test.

Aim. To provide an all-round education while maximizing individual potential. To engender in each pupil a love of learning which will endure for a life-time. The School follows the National Curriculum and prepares pupils for the Common Entrance Examination and other entry tests including 11+ Grammar School entry.

Prospectus. On request from the School Secretary.

Fees. Reception to Year 6: £1,530–£1,710 per term; Kindergarten: (part-time) £720 per term, (full time) £1,495 per term; Nursery: £124.20–£621 per term depending on the number of sessions per week. Lunch is included.

Charitable status. Highfield School is a Registered Charity, number 309103. It exists to provide an all-round education for girls and boys.

Highfield School

Liphook Hants GU30 7LQ.
Tel: (01428) 728000 (Headmaster), 728000 (School)
Fax: (01428) 728001
e-mail: office@highfieldschool.org.uk
website: www.highfieldschool.org.uk

***Head:* Mr Phillip Evitt**, MA

Deputy Head: Mrs Helen Skrine, BA, FRSA

Chairman of Directors: W S Mills, Esq

Number of Children. 210 (over 100 boarders).

Fees. September 2001. Boarders £3,600–£4,125 per term; Day pupils £2,775–£3,625 per term.

Location. 15 miles south of Guildford with easy access to London A3 and airports.

Highfield is a purpose built co-educational day and boarding school founded in 1907 set in 175 acres of superb grounds on the Hampshire/Sussex border.

The aim of the school is to provide children with a keen sense of their own individual identity and to help them to develop a sense of responsibility towards others and fulfil their potential in a happy and caring environment. Highfield children are encouraged to have high expectations, good work habits and a desire to benefit from all that the school offers.

Curriculum. Highfield children have a distinguished record of success at Common Entrance and Scholarships to all the major senior schools including Eton, Winchester, Marlborough, Bryanston, Canford, Wycombe Abbey, St Swithun's and Downe House.

Alongside the major academic subjects, French is taught from the age of 7 and Latin begins at 10. The broad curriculum includes ICT, PE and DT and the school's excellent tradition in music, drama and art is reflected in the number of scholarships gained.

The school has built outstanding new facilities for Science, ICT, Mathematics and English.

Sports and Activities. The major sports on offer are rugby, soccer, hockey and cricket for the boys, whilst girls play netball, lacrosse, hockey and rounders. All the children take part in athletics, swimming, tennis and cross country. Activities take place in the evenings and weekends and include judo, ballet, horse riding, chess, golf, drama, modelling, pottery, sewing and story telling.

Bursaries are available for families in the Services and in the Church.

Highgate Junior School

3 Bishopswood Road London N6 4PL
Tel: 020 8340 9193
Fax: 020 8342 7273

Chairman of Governors: J F Mills, Esq

The Master: **H S Evers**, BA, CertEd

Principal of Pre-Preparatory School: Mrs J Challender, CertEd, BEd, MA

Number of Pupils. 470 Day Boys (age 3–13); 20 Day Girls (age 3–7)

Fees. Pre-Preparatory School £2,685; Junior School £2,960 (inclusive)

Boys are prepared for Highgate School only. (See Part I of this book)

Entry to the Pre-Preparatory School is by individual assessment. Entry to the Junior School is by test and interview usually at the age of 7 and 11, although a small number are admitted at 9 and 10. Transfer to the Senior School is at 13+.

The School is housed in buildings bordering Bishopswood Road. The Pre-Preparatory School is self-contained, while the Junior School is split into Field House (9 forms, 150 boys aged 7–10) and Cholmeley House (11 forms, 230 boys age 10–13).

The School is well situated close to Hampstead Heath and has excellent facilities as the result of an on-going development programme. There are several acres of playing fields attached; the Mallinson Sports Centre (which includes a 25 metre indoor pool) is shared with the Senior School.

A broad and balanced curriculum is followed with art, drama, music, games, ICT and Design Technology all playing an important part.

Charitable status. The Wardens and Governors of the possessions revenues and goods of the free Grammar School of Sir Roger Cholmeley Knight in Highgate are a Registered Charity, number 312765. The aims and objectives of the charity are educational, namely the maintenance of a school.

High March School

Beaconsfield Bucks HP9 2PZ.
Tel: (01494) 675186
Fax: (01494) 675377

Established 1926.

Preparatory Day School for 300 pupils. Girls 3–12 years. Boys under 5 years

Chairman of the Governing Board: Mr C A E T Stevenson, MA (Cantab)

Headmistress: **Mrs P A Forsyth**, MA (Oxon)

Fees. £660–£2,060 per term inclusive of books, stationery and lunches but excluding optional subjects

High March comprises 3 school houses set in pleasant grounds. There is a separate house for Nursery and Key Stage 1 classes, 3–7 years. The Upper School has 8 classes, 7–12 years. Class sizes are limited. There is a well-equipped Gymnasium, Science, Art, Pottery, Design Technology and Information Technology rooms.

High March is within easy reach of London, High Wycombe, Windsor and within a few minutes' walk of Beaconsfield Station.

Under a large and highly qualified staff and within a happy atmosphere the children are prepared for Common Entrance to the Independent Senior Schools, County Selection and Scholarships. All subjects including Music, Art, Technology, Speech and Drama, Dancing, Gymnastics, Games and Swimming are in the hands of specialists. Although the academic record is high, each child is encouraged to develop individual talents.

There is an Annual Open Scholarship to the value of one-third of the annual fee tenable for 3 years.

Hilden Grange School

Tonbridge Kent TN10 3BX.
Tel: (01732) 352706

Headmaster: **J Withers**, BA (Hons)

Number of Pupils. 300. 200 Boys and 100 Girls.

Fees. Senior School £2,100 per term, Junior School £2,075 per term, Pre-Prep. £1,325 per term, a Nursery (£550–£600) was opened in January 1994 for the 3+ children. (£50 discount for prompt payment). Lunches are provided at £130 per term. A 5% reduction is made for brothers and sisters.

The School stands in about eight acres of attractive grounds in the residential area of North Tonbridge. Boys and girls are accepted into the Nursery at 3+ or at 4+ into the Pre-Preparatory Department within the school grounds, and at 7 into the main school. Two Scholarships of up to half fees are available annually for suitable candidates aged 7 to 10. Music Scholarships are also available. Tonbridge School Chorister awards are gained. At present there are ten Choristers.

Though links are especially strong with Tonbridge and Sevenoaks boys and girls are prepared for all Independent Senior Schools and Grammar Schools at 11+ and 13+. Boys and girls who show special promise sit for scholarships to the school of their choice. A fully qualified staff teach classes whose sizes average 16.

There is an outdoor heated swimming pool, a modern Sports Hall with changing rooms and kitchen complex. The library was refurbished, and a new Art Studio was completed recently. There are all-weather tennis courts, a Science Laboratory, refurbished in 1999, a Music Room, an Information Technology Room built in 2001, with a network of Acorn computers, a CD network with colour and laser printers.

We aim to bring out and develop the individual child's potential in the academic, creative, spiritual and physical areas. We expect our pupils to strive for high standards, to take pride in themselves and to gain satisfaction from their endeavours in an orderly and relaxed environment.

The Headmaster, staff and children welcome visitors and are pleased to show them around the School.

Hilden Oaks School

38 Dry Hill Park Road Tonbridge Kent TN10 3BU
Tel: 01732 353941
Fax: 01732 353942
e-mail: HildenOaksSchool@talk21.com
website: www.btinternet.com/~HildenOaksSchool

Chairman of Governors: Mrs J L Salmon

Headmistress: **Mrs H J Bacon,** STC, DipEd, DipNEd

Number of Children. 180. Kindergarten, Nursery and Infants, boys and girls from 2½ to 7 years. Junior School, girls from 7 to 11 years.

Inclusive fees (2000-2001). Kindergarten (afternoons only) £630 per term. Nursery (mornings only) £580 per term, Reception £1,320 per term. Infants (Forms I & II) £1,460 per term. Juniors (Forms III and IV) £1,640, (Forms V and VI) £1,690 per term.

Hilden Oaks was founded in 1919 and became an Educational Trust in 1965. It is positioned in a quiet residential area and the Trust owns all the land and buildings. These consist of the Main School, which incorporates the School Hall, an Infant and Nursery block, a Fifth and Sixth Form study block and a science and art building. A new pre-prep building, for Kindergarten, Nursery and Reception, and incorporating science and art rooms, is presently under construction and will be in use for the 2001-2002 academic year. All the buildings are contained within a pleasant enclosed garden setting, including hard and grassed playing areas, plus a small wooded section with pond for field studies.

It is the aim of Hilden Oaks to provide a family school within which the individual child is helped and encouraged to develop his or her potential in a happy, caring, stimulating and purposeful environment. Whilst maintaining high academic standards, the school expects good manners and consideration to others at all times. This is reflected in the active parent association, the close liaison between parents and staff and the school's close involvement with the local community.

In the Kindergarten, Nursery and Infant departments the children are given a solid foundation upon which they can build, with additional specialist teachers for French, music and games. The boys leave us at 7 with the opportunity of being offered scholarships to their prep schools, both academic and in music, sport and drama.

The Junior School has specialist teachers for science, games, French, art, music and computers, but all forms are taught by their form teachers for the core subjects. Drama, music and art are all included in the timetable as well as being offered as after-school activities. There are numerous other after-school activities including choirs, extra drama, art, computers and games. A late room operates for Infants and Juniors where children are provided with tea, and may remain until 5.15.

All girls are prepared for both the Common Entrance examination at 11 and the 11+ examination for entry to grammar schools. Our results in these examinations, and for Baseline Assessment and SATS Key Stages 1 and 2, put us among the top schools in Kent.

Charitable status. Hilden Oaks School is a Registered Charity, number 307935. It exists to provide education for children.

Hillcrest Preparatory School

PO Box 24282 Nairobi Kenya.
Tel: Nairobi 883912/13/14
Fax: Nairobi 883914
e-mail: hillcrestprep@swiftkenya.com
website: www.hillcrestprep.com

Headmaster: **R J M Free**, BEd

Chairman of Governors: K S N Matiba

Number of Day Pupils. 190 (Boys 90, Girls 100)

Fees. 80,000 to 165,000 shillings per term (inclusive): £800 to £1,650 sterling.

Hillcrest School was founded in 1966 by Mr Frank Thompson. It is located on an attractive, purpose built, 20 acre campus next to our Secondary School in Karen/ Langata.

Boys and girls are accepted from the age of 5 and they follow a broad and extensive curriculum which prepares them for Common Entrance Examinations. Some children transfer to UK Independent Secondary Schools but the majority enter the equivalent in Kenya, Hillcrest Secondary School, which prepares pupils for IGCSE and A levels. Entry to the Senior School is achieved after successfully writing either Common Entrance or the Hillcrest Secondary examination. A kindergarten is due to open on site in September 2001.

The school has an International flavour and its pupils are drawn from the Diplomatic and United Nations community, expatriate families on contract, and Kenyan residents. The friendly spirit and strong communication network that exists between staff, pupils and parents are of particular note. There are 20 fully qualified teachers who are mostly Honours Graduates recruited from Britain. The average form size is 18 and the teacher:pupil ratio of approximately 11:1 allows for considerable individual attention and learning support.

Hillcrest offers a wide range of extra curricular activities in the afternoon which include: karate, ballet, horse riding, guitar and piano tuition, theatre skills and tennis coaching.

Field trip studies are offered to the Coast and Rift Valley and outdoor pursuits are strongly encouraged. These include climbs of Mount Longonot and Kenya, up-country farm visits and water skiing trips to Lake Naivasha. Charitable fund raising activities are also regularly organised by pupils for underprivileged children.

The school's Inter-House Competitions are a focal point of each term. House Chieftains play an important role in welcoming new pupils, monitoring behaviour and promoting a competitive spirit. Cricket, Rounders, Hockey, Rugby, Netball and Swimming are taught and a full fixtures programme is arranged each term with other Preparatory Schools.

Hillcrest is also well-known for the quality of its drama productions, choir performances and standard of artistic display throughout the school. Our principle aim is to nurture pupils' individual talents and produce well-balanced children who actively contribute to all academic, aesthetic and sporting activities in a caring and family-like atmosphere.

Hill House Preparatory School

Rutland Street Doncaster South Yorkshire DN1 2JD.
Tel: (01302) 323563-5
Fax: (01302) 761098

Headmaster: **Jack Cusworth**, BA

Number of Pupils. 300. All day pupils 183 Boys, 120 Girls.

Fees. £1,291–£1,786 per term according to age (except Nursery). Fees include lunch and most extras

The School is an Educational Trust with a board of Governors, the Chairman of which is Mr J Whiteley.

Children enter the Lower School at 3+ years old, via a brand new purpose built Nursery where structured play is the order of the day. Much care and thought are given to the preparation for transition to the Upper School at 8+. As children progress through the school there is a gradual change to subject based teaching in specialist rooms, in preparation for the Common Entrance Examination at 13+. The School curriculum, whilst preparing pupils for CE

Examinations and Senior Independent School scholarships, also correlates closely with the National Curriculum. Music, Drama, Art and Sport play an important part in the life of the school. Throughout the year over 40 academic, recreational, musical and sporting activities per week are also offered in extra curricular time. The major sports undertaken include rugby, soccer, netball, hockey, cricket, tennis, athletics and rounders. There are two orchestras and two choirs within the school. Drama productions and concerts are undertaken on a regular basis.

Charitable status. Hill House School Limited is a Registered Charity, number 908443. It exists to provide nursery and primary education to boys and girls aged 3–13.

Hillstone, Malvern College

Hillstone Abbey Road Malvern Worcs WR14 3HF.
Tel: (01684) 581600
Station: Great Malvern

Headmaster: **P H Moody**, MA (Cantab)

Chairman of the College Council: N G V Morris, Esq

Number of Boys. 90 (36 boarding, 54 day)
Number of Girls. 59 (16 boarding, 43 day)
Pre-Prep. 76 (33 boys, 43 girls) - including 1 boy boarder

Fees per term. Boarding: £3,435; Day £2,285–£2,590; Pre-Prep Day £990–£1,260; Pre-Prep Boarding £2,105.

General. Hillstone, superbly situated on the eastern slopes of the Malvern Hills, caters for pupils from 2½ to 13 on a very attractive site with all-round facilities. The majority of pupils move on to the senior part of the school (Malvern College). Hillstone is, above all, a happy, friendly community in which children feel secure and valued.

Founded in 1883 the school moved to its current site in 1992. Hillstone offers a wide range of extra curricular activities including the Hillstone Award, which is similar in philosophy to The Duke of Edinburgh Award Scheme. There is a range of sports for both boys and girls to choose from along with regular trips in the UK and abroad. Three-quarters of the pupils play at least one musical instrument. Art and Drama are also available, together with technology and PE. These subjects form an integral part of the syllabus at all levels. The school has strong links with the community and the pupils are involved in various fund raising activities. There is a strong boarding community and the school's ethos is very much that of a boarding school although there is increasing flexibility to respond to the needs of day pupils. Academic standards are high and there is an impressive enterprising range of activities beyond normal school. Hillstone has its own distinctive character with a curriculum which is geared to foster skills needed in the 21st century. Numbers have increased steadily and there is exciting potential for the future.

Admissions. Under normal circumstances admission is through a successful interview with the Headmaster and a satisfactory report from a previous school

Curriculum. All subjects broadly follow the National Curriculum and apply appropriate tests at Key Stage 2. (Key Stage 1 tests and assessments are undertaken in the Pre-prep). A balanced curriculum has been developed which places equal emphasis on the Arts subjects, Languages, Mathematics and Science.

In Years 3 to 6 Information and Communication Technology is taught as a separate subject on the timetable as well as through other academic lessons. Cross-curricular teaching of ICT is achieved in Year 7 and 8 where the pupils are also taught Design and Technology in the Technology Centre at the Senior School. For pupils with a strength in Languages there is the opportunity to learn Latin from Year 6 onwards and in Years 7 and 8 to begin a second Modern Language, German or Spanish. and there is a very flourishing School Orchestra and various ensembles, and many musical events take place in the course of the year.

School facilities. Facilities are first class. There are specialist classrooms, laboratories, sports hall, library, drama room and ballet studio, ICT room, music and art departments. The school has its own assembly hall although use is made of Malvern College's lovely chapel as well as the indoor swimming pool, playing fields and modern technology centre. Older pupils have their own recreational and study areas. There are 2 boarding houses and a dining room. Spacious grounds comprise a nature reserve and adventure playground. The Pre-prep (Hampton) has separate facilities in attractive grounds which also include an adventure playground. Full use is made of the natural gymnasium behind the school, the Malvern Hills.

Examination levels. Pupils achieve excellent academic results. At Key Stage 2 the percentage of pupils gaining Level 4 and above is well above the national average. At the end of Year 8 nearly all pupils gain the grades needed to go to the senior school of their choice.

Scholarships/Bursaries. Scholarships/Exhibitions are awarded to pupils who show academic excellence; and also to pupils who, in addition to being academically competent, have a particular talent in Art, Drama, Technology, Music or Physical Education. Malvern College Assisted Places (MCAPs) offer assistance to parents of talented pupils who cannot otherwise afford to send their children to Hillstone.

Inspection. ISI Inspection March 1999. Strengths of the school: Headmaster's vision for future development, committed and hardworking staff, quality of overall teaching and relationships, high standard of boarding provision and standards of achievement.

Hoe Bridge School

Hoe Place Old Woking Surrey GU22 8JE
Tel: Prep School: (01483) 760018/760065;
Pre-Prep: (01483) 772194
Fax: (01483) 757560

Co-educational Preparatory and Pre-Preparatory School.
An Educational Trust for children aged 2½–14.

Chairman of Governors: David Hemley

Headmaster: **R W K Barr**, BEd (Oxon)

Deputy Headmaster: G D P Scott, BEd (Exeter)

Head of Pre-Prep: Mrs L Renfrew

Number of Children. 420

Fees. Day £325–£2,525 per term (including lunch). Books and Stationery £16 per term.

Children between the ages of 7–14 are prepared for scholarship and common entrance requirements to all independent schools with all normal subjects, games and activities necessary for a child's development taught by experienced qualified staff.

Hoe Bridge School is on the outskirts of Woking, standing in it's own grounds of 14 acres which affords admirable facilities for games and outdoor pursuits, including Rugby, Association Football, Cricket, Athletics, Netball, Hockey, Tennis and Swimming. The School is well resourced with an Art, Design and Technology and Information Technology Centre, up to date classrooms and laboratories and a two storey multi purpose Hall.

The School has its own Pre-Preparatory School with 200 children between the ages of 2½ and 7.

Hoe Bridge School is a registered charitable trust run by a Board of Governors whose members are drawn from parents, and the local community.

Charitable status. Hoe Bridge School is a Registered Charity, number 295808. It exists to provide a rounded education for children aged 2½–14.

Holme Grange School

Heathlands Road Wokingham Berkshire RG40 3AL.
Tel: (0118) 9781566/9774525
Fax: (0118) 9770810
e-mail: info@holmegrange.wokingham.sch.uk
website: www.holmegrange.wokingham.sch.uk

Chairman of Governors: T Andrews, BA (Hons)

Headmaster: **N J Brodrick**, BEd (London), CertEd

Number of Pupils. 325 (145 girls aged 3–13, 180 boys aged 3–13)

Tuition Fee. From September 2000: Little Grange Nursery £776 per term, Pre-Preparatory £1,552 per term. Prep School £1,984 per term, payable monthly. Reductions for second and subsequent children.

The School is a Day School receiving pupils from a wide catchment area. The Headmaster is assisted by a highly qualified and experienced staff of 28 with ancillary helpers in the Pre-Prep and NNEB assistants in Little Grange. There is a Learning Support Department giving help to those children with special needs as an extra to the fees. A broad curriculum is followed, embracing both the full National Curriculum, and that currently required for the 11+ and 13+ Common Entrance Examinations. Class sizes are generally kept to a maximum of 18, average size is 16. The School is a Trust, administered by a board of Governors who have considerable experience in education and business. There is an active Parents' Association which raises funds for extra items for the children. Little Grange is an established Nursery for 3 year olds in its own safe, secure environment within the School grounds, providing part-time education.

The main Grade II listed building, a Mansion built in 1883 by Norman Shaw, houses the Pre-Preparatory, dining rooms and kitchens, School Library and administrative offices. There is a recently built two-storey 'John Graves Wing' comprising seven teaching classrooms for Years 4 to 8 and girls' changing accommodation to which an extension has been added, opening in September 2001, comprising art/design on the ground floor with two classrooms above. Many other facilities have been added in the last ten years: the 'Scott Wing' with its Science Laboratory (newly designed in 1994), ICT room (comprising a network of 21 work stations), a classroom and boys' changing rooms. In the Quad is a teaching block with two classrooms next to a cedar block for general use while a large Sports Hall (including two indoor cricket nets) with full stage facilities for Music and Drama completes the area. A Music School, together with three practice rooms, is in a separate building.

A variety of sports can be played on an all-weather hard play area (incorporating 2 tennis courts) behind four outdoor cricket nets. The 21 acres of grounds contain all the above plus 3 playing fields, a lake, stream and Millennium wood, a hard tennis court, adventure playground and a heated outdoor swimming pool, rebuilt in 2001. All Prep age boys (from Year 3) are coached in soccer (Year 2 also), Rugby, Hockey, Cricket and Athletics. Girls have Netball, Jazz/Dance, Hockey, Rounders and Athletics. Tennis is available for both. A wide range of after-school activities is available to 5.30 pm, including Choir, Master Chef, Speech and Drama, Riding, Golf, extra sport and supervised prep (homework).

Pupils are accepted from the age of 3 providing continuous education until they take the Common Entrance Examination or Scholarship (Academic, Art, Music) for Senior Independent Schools. At both there is enviable record of success. Every child is given an opportunity to shine in a happy, friendly, family atmosphere which has a strong emphasis on courtesy and self discipline and good manners. Registration for the Nursery and Pre-Prep is advisable several years in advance of required admission. Entry at 7+ follows an assessment test.

Charitable status. Holme Grange Limited is a Registered Charity, number 309105. It exists to serve the local community in providing an all-round education for boys and girls.

Holmewood House

Langton Green Tunbridge Wells Kent TN3 0EB.
Tel: (01892) 860000.
Fax: (01892) 863970
Station: Tunbridge Wells

Chairman of the Governors: C G Court

Headmaster: **A S R Corbett**, MA, PGCE

Number of Pupils. 520 Boys and Girls aged 3–13

Fees. Weekly Boarders £4,755 per term. Day Pupils 7 and over £3,300 per term, 5–6 year olds £1,990–£2,445 per term, 3–4 year olds £890–£1,340 per term. There are no compulsory extras. There are reductions for brothers and sisters, and children of Old Holmewoodians. Scholarships are available for those entering from primary schools.

The school was founded in 1945 as a boys' school. Boarding and Day girls were admitted in 1989. The school is a Charitable Educational Trust with a Board of Governors. Holmewood stands in thirty acres of beautiful grounds on the Kent/Sussex border, and is within easy reach of Tunbridge Wells, which is one hour by rail from London.

The School is divided into six Houses, and a personal tutor system operates from Year 5. Saturday morning school also begins in Year 5.

Thanks to its 62 full and part time qualified staff, Holmewood has an outstanding scholastic record, both in Common Entrance and Scholarship examinations. In the last five years 75 scholarships have been won, including the top scholarships at King's Canterbury, Eastbourne College and St Leonards-Mayfield.

A broad-based curriculum is followed throughout the school. Modern languages taught include French, German, Spanish, Mandarin and Russian.

The school has numerous computers, and two networked computer rooms. All pupils are taught computing from an early age.

The Art, Drama and Music Departments are very strong and the school's Concert Group gives performances at home and overseas. A new Music School was opened in 1996 and the Performing Arts Centre was completed by the opening of a new 360-seat theatre in September 1997.

Expert coaching is given in a wide variety of sports and these include rugby, soccer, hockey, gymnastics, netball, cricket, tennis and table-tennis, shooting, athletics, orienteering, cross-country, golf, archery, fencing, judo, basketball, dance, squash and swimming. In recent years the school has won the golf team championships; currently both GISCA & IAPS Gymnastics champions, and currently Kent & Sussex Prep & Junior Schools Squash Champions. There is a magnificent Sports Hall, a new indoor swimming pool, opened in June 2001, ten hard tennis courts, three squash courts, a full size all-weather hockey/football pitch and running track and an indoor .22 shooting range.

Our aims are.

- excellence in teaching
- to help every child to learn and to attain their maximum potential
- to provide pastoral care of the highest quality
- to provide a well-ordered and stimulating environment in which all can thrive
- to offer a very broad and balanced curriculum for all pupils.

Our whole school values are essentially Christian.

- as a community we value good discipline, independence of mind, mutual support and success for all
- in our relationships we value a caring approach, encouragement, good manners and generosity
- on a personal level we value integrity, effort, happiness and self-discipline.

These aims and values inform and underpin our policies, guidelines and practice.

Charitable status. Holmewood House is a Registered Charity, number 279267. It exists to provide education for boys and girls.

Holmwood House

Lexden Colchester Essex CO3 5ST.
Tel: (01206) 574305
Fax: (01206) 768269

Headmaster: **H S Thackrah**, BEd (Exeter)

Number of Pupils. 217 (34 boarders) plus Pre-Prep (182)

Fees per term. Boarders: £3,462–£3,875; Day pupils £1,683–£2,997 (all fees inclusive).

Holmwood House was founded in 1922 and is situated one mile from Colchester town centre in 30 acres of gardens and playing fields.

The principal aim is high academic standards (we have gained over 100 scholarships to senior independent schools in the last ten years) and the Library/Resource Centre is the key to this. Within it is the computer centre, which is networked to allow two full classes access at any one time.

Sport and the Arts receive many scheduled sessions of instruction in afternoons and evenings and facilities include new Pre-prep department, five squash courts, an indoor swimming pool, two covered tennis courts, floodlit tarmac area, adventure playground, a permanent stage plus sound/lighting systems, new art complex and separate music school.

A keynote is flexibility. Classes, compulsory games, bedtimes, are all timetabled conventionally; so are some 'preps.', but older pupils may do 4 'preps' a week in their own time to provide time for orchestra, chess, pottery, cookery, or a dozen other coached activities. Drama and Music flourish particularly, allowing for a great variety of productions. There are also other times when pupils make decisions about their use of leisure time.

We would be pleased to send our prospectus and details of Scholarships (for which examinations are held each spring) and Bursaries and to welcome visitors to see round the school.

Holy Cross Preparatory School

George Road Kingston upon Thames Surrey KT2 7NU
Tel: 0181-942 0729
Fax: 0181-336 0764

Headmistress: **Mrs M K Hayes**, MA

Number of Girls. 250 aged 4–11 years.

Fees per term. £1,575

Location. The school is situated on a private estate in an attractive area of Kingston Hill.

Facilities. The building, the former home of John Galsworthy, is of both historical and literary interest and provides excellent accommodation for two classes in each year group through the school from Reception to Year Six. The school contains an assembly hall/gymnasium, dining hall, library, Design and Technology Centre, Music room, Computer room, TV/Drama room, Art room and 14 classrooms all with computers. A new building for the 6 Infant classes was opened in Spring 2001.

The 8 acres of grounds include two tennis/netball courts, hockey pitch, running track and three large playing areas which have play equipment, including adventure climbing frames. There is a nature trail and ecology area, together with a fountain within the ornamental lawns and a pond which is well used in science lessons.

Educational Philosophy. The school was founded by the Sisters of the Holy Cross, an international teaching order who have been engaged in the work of education since 1844. A sound Christian education is given in an Ecumenical framework. The children are happy, cared for and well disciplined. The emphasis is on developing the God-given gifts of each child to their fullest, in a stimulating, friendly atmosphere where high standards of work, behaviour and contribution to the well being of the school community are expected.

Curriculum. There is a broad and relevant curriculum providing a high standard of education. Specialist teaching in French, Music, Physical Education and Information Technology. The school has a first rate record of success in Common Entrance and in preparing pupils for Senior Independent, High and Grammar Schools. The varied extra-curricular activities include ballet and dance, Speech & Drama, pottery, Art and Design, cello, piano, flute, clarinet, violin, guitar, sports, German, Technology, French, country dancing, tennis, origami and chess.

Status. Holy Cross is a Roman Catholic School providing excellence in Christian education to local children.

Homefield School

Western Road Sutton Surrey SM1 2TE.
Tel: 020 8642 0965.
Fax: 020 8770 1668
Station: Sutton

Chairman of Governors: R M R Hosangady, FCA

Headmaster: **P R Mowbray**, BA

Deputy Headmaster: C R Maultby, BEd

Number of Boys. 335

Fees from September 2001. Seniors (8–14) £1,990. Junior Department (6–8) £1,625. 1st Year (5) £1,425. Early Years' Unit (3–5) £1,345. Lunches £160.

An established Day School (founded 1870) and reconstituted as an Educational Trust in 1967 under a Board of Governors. In May 1968 the School moved into purpose-built premises designed to accommodate Junior and Senior departments. A purpose-built Early Years' Unit for children aged 3–5 opened in September 1994.

A two-acre school playing field together with the unrestricted use of a further six acres of the Sutton Cricket Club ground 2 minutes' walk away, provide first class sporting facilities all the year round.

Children are taught by subject specialists from the age of eight, and specialist assistance is on hand for those with any learning difficulties.

Whilst the usual seasonal games (Association Football, Rugby and Cricket) are played, there are also facilities for Judo, Athletics, Squash, Basketball, Short tennis and Table tennis.

A fully-equipped Sports Hall, Science Laboratory, Computer centre, Learning Rescources Centre, Music, Art and Technology Centre form part of the general amenities.

Each boy is encouraged to join at least one of nearly 40 clubs and societies which meet during out-of-school hours.

Homefield has an excellent reputation for Music and Sport.

A fine record of Common Entrance and Scholarship successes has been achieved to a wide range of Senior Schools over recent years.

Special features include: an intimate family atmosphere; small classes; specialist subject teachers and single-subject teaching from the age of 8.

Charitable status. Homefield School is a Registered Charity, number 312753. It exists to provide education for boys.

Hordle Walhampton

Lymington Hants SO41 5ZG.
Tel: (01590) 672013
Fax: (01590) 678498
e-mail: wal.school@camput.bt.co

Headmaster: **R H C Phillips**, BA (Hons), CertEd, LGSM

Chairman of Governors: Michael Corbridge, Esq

Numbers in school. Boarding boys, 43; Boarding girls, 31; Day children, 139; Pre-Prep 153.

Fees. (from September 2000) Boarding £3,540; Day (ages 8–13) £2,700; Junior Day (age 7+) £1,920 per term. Pre-preparatory (full time, age 4–7) £1,310 per term. Kindergarten (full time, age 3–4) £1,040. Nursery (age 2–3) £212.50-£385 per term. The only extras are: Riding, individual Music, language support tuition and Expeditions.

Hordle Walhampton was established in 1997, following the merger of Hordle House and Walhampton. The School is one of the south coast's leading co-educational boarding and day Preparatory schools, situated on the edge of the New Forest, surrounded by 92 acres of playing fields, woodland and lakes, which are enjoyed by all the children for traditional games, sailing, riding, field studies, walks, free time and fun. There are excellent facilities for Art, Computing, Craft, Design Technology, Gymnastics and Woodwork; Music and Drama also play an important part in School life.

The aim of the School is to seek the good in the young and to educate the whole child in a caring, exciting and challenging community. The educational programme is broad, with equal importance attached to developing the intellectual, social, cultural, physical and spiritual faculties of each pupil. The academic results are excellent and this is achieved by employing well qualified, dedicated, caring Staff who teach in small, well resourced classes averaging 14 children. English and Maths are set throughout the school. Latin is taught to all children from Year 5. German is studied by the majority of children from Year 6. In Year 8 there is a special form to prepare pupils for 13+ scholarship examinations to Senior Schools. The majority of children leave after sitting their 13+ Common Entrance or Scholarship examinations to such schools as: Bryanston, Canford, Dauntsey's, Eton, Sherborne Boys and Girls, Marlborough, Millfield, St Swithun's and Winchester. Girls are also prepared for the 12+ CEE to single-sex girls' schools.

There is a strong boarding ethos within the School with particular attention paid to weekends for which a varied and exciting programme is prepared each week. Facilities such as riding, sailing, computing, art and woodwork are available during the weekend. Full, weekly and flexi boarding are on offer to suit the needs of individual families. There are three boarding houses: the Lodge has boys and girls aged 7 to 10; Main House has boys aged 11 to 13, and the Clockhouse has girls aged 11 to 13. There is a strong boarding care team consisting of Houseparents, Assistant Houseparents and Matrons. The day children enjoy a full, all inclusive programme which starts at 8.20 am and continues through until 6.15 pm.

Hordle Walhampton aims to prepare each child for the demands and challenges of twenty-first century life by providing opportunities to grow in self-confidence, Christian standards and responsibilities and consideration for others. When children leave Hordle Walhampton it is hoped that they will be articulate, confident, self-motivated, considerate, generous and determined to give of their best to any enterprise with which they are involved.

Charitable status. Hordle Walhampton School Trust Limited is a Registered Charity, number 307330. It exists to provide high quality boarding and day education for boys and girls aged 2–13 years.

Horris Hill

Newtown Newbury Berks RG20 9DJ.
Tel: (01635) 40594.
Fax: (01635) 35241
e-mail: enquiries@horrishill.demon.co.uk
website: www.horrishill.com
Station: Newbury, WR

Chairman of Governors: R F Hall, Esq

Headmaster: **N J Chapman**, BA

Numbers of Boys. Boarders 105, Day 20

Fees. Boarders: £4,400; Day £3,400. (No compulsory Extras)

Charitable status. Horris Hill Preparatory School Trust Limited is a Registered Charity, number 307331. It exists to prepare boys for the Senior Independent Schools.

Howell's Preparatory School

Park Street Denbigh Clwyd LL16 3EN
Tel: (01745) 816001
Fax: (01745) 816010

Headmistress: **Mrs L Robinson**, BA (Hons), NPQH

Numbers in School. 125 girls.

Fees. Nursery (half day) £447.50; Day Pupils

£965–£1,415; Boarders and Weekly Boarders £1,945–£2,100.

The School comprises of a Nursery, Infant and Junior Department. Girls are admitted from the age of 2½ years and transfer to Senior School at the age of 11. The School is staffed by teachers chosen for both their subject expertise and knowledge of preparatory age requirements. There is some subject specialism in the Upper Junior age range. There is liaison with staff in the Senior age range to ensure continuity and progression. The boarding house and classrooms were refurbished two years ago. Each teaching group is small, has its own classroom and shares use of the school libraries, music room, French Room, hall and technology room. The Senior School Sports Hall and Swimming Pool are available for use by the Preparatory School. The curriculum delivered is broad and deep, satisfying National Curriculum requirements. French is taught from the age of 6 years. Girls are tested regularly and there is constant communication between home and school.

The School has many sporting teams who compete in a variety of tournaments, both locally and regionally.

The teaching day is from 8.30 – 3.45, however most girls remain for prep and club activities until 6.00 pm daily. A full boarding activity programme is available at weekends and boarding may be full, weekly or occasional. Local day coaches are available and an escort service for rail and air is provided. The School is proud of its success with scholarship and entrance examinations into Senior Schools and its calm and disciplined approach to life. It is situated in the beautiful Vale of Clwyd which provides excellent opportunities for outdoor pursuits. The School has its own environmental area. Admission is by assessment and interview. The school is identified by the Sunday Times as one of the top UK preparatory schools.

Charitable status. Howell's Preparatory School is a Registered Charity, number 1061485/0. It exists to provide education for girls.

Hurstpierpoint College Preparatory School

Hurstpierpoint West Sussex BN6 9JS
Tel: (01273) 834975
Fax: (01273) 835257
e-mail: hurstprep@hppc.co.uk
website: http://www.hppc.co.uk

Note: Hurst House, the Nursery and Pre-prep School for children aged 3-7, opens in September 2001 with four classrooms in an extensively refurbished wing of the School.

Chairman of Governors: Stephen Edell

Head: **S J Andrews**, BA, L-ès-L

Number of Pupils. 186 (15 full-time boarders, 10 weekly boarders, 30 flexi-boarders and 131 day pupils). Age range 7–13.

Fees per term. Full Boarders £3,500; Weekly Boarders £3,200; Day pupils £2,600; Year 3 £2,110. Flexi-boarding is also available. There are no compulsory extras.

The School is the Preparatory School of Hurstpierpoint College with which it shares a beautiful 140 acre campus and has joint use of many superb facilities (25m indoor swimming pool, fully equipped modern CDT centre, theatre, large sports hall, Astroturf surface for hockey, tennis courts and squash courts). Although the Prep School operates independently of the Senior School having its own timetable, staff, buildings and Head, the two schools work closely together to offer a first class programme of education for boys and girls from the age of 7 to 18.

The school is a Christian community and each day there is a short service in the assembly hall before classes begin. On Fridays there is a longer service in the magnificent College Chapel.

The aim of the school is to provide a happy, caring, stimulating and well ordered environment in which the whole child is educated. Equal importance is attached to the development of the spiritual, physical, intellectual, social and cultural aspects of the pupils.

The Junior School has a 5-day academic week. Day children and weekly boarders are free to leave school after Chapel on Fridays at 6 pm. There is a comprehensive weekend programme for full boarders and day children who are in school. A full Saturday afternoon match programme runs throughout the school year.

The academic programme prepares pupils for the Scholarship or Common Entrance examination after which nearly all move onto the Senior School.

The Sports programme is extensive: Football, Netball, Rounders, Rugby, Cricket, Hockey, Squash, Swimming, Tennis, Basketball and Athletics. In addition there is a wide-ranging activity programme in place every day which caters for the interests of all pupils.

The Music and Drama Departments are very active with about half the pupils learning musical instruments. Trebles are provided for two choirs, the College Choir which holds concerts both at home and abroad, and the Preparatory School choir which performs at the weekly Chapel service. There are two or three musicals or plays each year involving many children throughout the school.

Over the last two years, the School has been redeveloped and now provides comprehensive and up-to-date facilities.

Matron and an assistant in conjunction with the College Medical Centre look after the health of the children. The School has its own sick bay.

Each year a number of Awards are available: 8+ academic awards continue throughout the Junior School, whilst 11+ academic, sports, art, IT and music awards continue through to the Senior School.

Charitable status. Hurstpierpoint College is a school of the Woodard Corporation and is a Registered Charity, number 1076498. IThe College provides a Christian education to boys and girls between the ages of three and thirteen; the Prep School age-range is seven to thirteen.

Ipswich Preparatory School

Ipswich School Ipswich IP1 3SQ.
Tel: (01473) 408301
Fax: (01473) 400067

Chairman of Governors: Mr D J Coe, JP

Headteacher: **Mrs Jenny Jones**, BA, ARCM, NPQH

Number of Pupils. 165 (Prep); 140 (Nursery & Pre-Prep)

Fees. Day Pupils £4,252–£4,908 per annum

The Preparatory School, including a Pre-Prep Department, has its own staff and Headteacher. It is closely linked to the Senior School in adjacent but separate buildings.

The school seeks to provide a learning environment which allows pupils to develop skills and personal qualities. The curriculum is planned to encourage the children to develop lively, enquiring minds and appropriate emphasis is placed on securing for each child a firm foundation of skills in literacy and numeracy. The broad, balanced curriculum offered provides a breadth of experience which is suitable for children of primary age. High academic standards are reached by the pupils and throughout the school there is an atmosphere of caring.

The school enjoys the advantage of sharing Senior School facilities such as playing fields, sports hall, swimming pool, theatre/concert hall and the Chapel. The Prep School has its own Art, Design Technology, ICT and Science facilities. Pupils are encouraged to develop skills in music, art, drama and sport.

James Allen's Preparatory School

East Dulwich Grove London SE22 8TE
Tel: 020 8693 0374
Fax: 020 8693 8031

Chairman of Governors: Lord McColl of Dulwich, MS, FRCS, FACS

Headmaster: **Mr Piers Heyworth,** MA (Oxon), PGCE

Numbers in School. Boys 68, Girls 226 (all day). Boys 4–7, Girls 4–11. Ages of entry: 4+ for boys, 4+ and 7+ for girls.

Fees per term. £2,161 (4–11 year olds).

James Allen's Preparatory School (JAPS) is an independent co-educational day school for children aged between 4 and 11. Boys leave at the age of 7.

We do not see primary education as being merely preparatory to secondary requirements but want the children to go forward at their own pace, benefiting from working together in small groups. With a well-devised and wide curriculum, the children reach high standards without the stress of blatant competition and are able to enjoy the many and varied facilities which we offer, particularly in sport, drama, music and art.

The school has an excellent staff/pupil ratio of approximately 1:10 and provides specialist teachers in Art, D & T, IT, Music, PE and Science. In French an exciting project has been undertaken whereby the children are taught many of their lessons in French from 4 years onwards.

The Lower School (for pupils aged 4–6) is housed in a homely Edwardian building. The Middle School (for pupils aged 7–10/11) is a large, modern building with a first class Hall and Library, as well as specialist rooms for Science, IT, D & T and Art. Some facilities (the theatre, swimming pool and games fields) are shared with James Allen's Girls' School. State of the art new swimming pool is currently being built, due for completion in April 2001.

JAPS also offers a Saturday Morning School for the Performing Arts for pupils and siblings and other non-JAPS pupils. This is entirely voluntary and complements the week's activities: music lessons, dance and drama are all offered.

Pupils normally enter the school in the year in which they are 4 or 7 on 1 September; assessments take place the preceding January. 36 places are available for 4+ entry and up to 30 places available for 7+ entry. At 11, girls normally progress to JAGS by means of an open competitive examination, where JAPS regularly wins a great many scholarships. Boys progress mainly to Dulwich College, Alleyn's and Dulwich College College Preparatory School at 7+.

Charitable status. JAPS is a Registered Charity, number 312750. The purpose of the charity is the conduct at Dulwich of a day school in which there shall be provided a practical, liberal and religious education for girls and boys.

Jeddah Prep and Grammar School (The International British/Dutch School)

c/o British Consulate General PO Box 6316 Jeddah 21442 Kingdom of Saudi Arabia
Tel: 02-654 2354, 02 238 0223
Fax: 02-238 0232
e-mail: hmsec@jpgs.org
website: www.jpgs.org

Chairman of Governors: Mr David Priestley

Headmaster: **Mr Nigel Woolnough**, BA (Hons), MSc, PGCE, MIMgt

Deputy Headmaster: Mr David W Morse, BSc, PGCE

Bursar: Mrs A Johnson

Number of Pupils. 314 Boys; 290 Girls (all day)

Fees per term. Nursery SR5,150; Reception SR7,520; Years 1 to 5 SR9,140; Years 6 to 11 SR10,160

By Royal Decree in 1974 the Saudi Arabian International School organisation was originally formed to be responsible for the education of non-Muslim children in the Kingdom.

Within the Saudi Arabian International School system, Jeddah Prep and Grammar School is registered as the International British/Dutch School in Jeddah, and caters for children from the ages of 3 to 16+ years inclusive (Key Stages 1, 2, 3 and 4).

The original School was known as Jeddah Prep and dates back to 1966. Due to a developing need for education for expatriate children in Jeddah, the British and Dutch communities decided to establish a school to provide primary education for their children.

In September 1998, a senior section was added to the original Prep School. This part of the school was named the Grammar School and offers IGCSE for pupils of up to 16+ years of age (Year 11) who have previously been at Jeddah Prep, or who meet the standards required through the entrance examinations.

The School has grown from a handful of children in 1966 to a current enrolment of over 600, and has the largest percentage of UK and Western nationals within the Jeddah education system.

The School is housed in a purpose built, generously equipped complex and all teachers are UK, Commonwealth or USA trained, with over 85% being British overseas contract teachers recruited in the UK.

The British and Dutch Embassies, The Saudi Dutch Bank and The Saudi British Bank were the founding members of the Jeddah Prep School, and remain closely involved in the overall welfare of the School, having representatives on the present Board of Governors.

The Board also includes parents who are elected and other members who are co-opted. A copy of the Constitution is available on request.

The primary objective of the School is to provide quality education in Jeddah for children of the expatriate community. Every opportunity is given for growth in the personal qualities of confidence, self-control and responsibility so that the children are well equipped to cope enthusiastically with transfer, both to the UK, or to other countries and schools.

The School curriculum is aligned to the UK National Curriculum, catering for pupils wishing to take Common Entrance or Scholarship Examinations for their eventual return to the UK. Traditional values are fostered and a belief in the School as a community is emphasised.

The School believes in helping pupils to achieve their full academic potential, in a caring environment, in which they can enjoy learning, acquire good work habits and a sense of individual worth.

Josca's Preparatory School

Frilford Abingdon Oxon OX13 5NX.
Tel: (01865) 391570.
Fax: (01865) 391042
e-mail: Joscas1@hotmail.com

Chairman of the Governors: The Rt Hon Francis Maude, MP

Headmaster: **C J Davies**, BA

Number of Boys. 180 day pupils (Boys, plus girls aged 4-7)

Fees per term. £2,167

The School was founded in 1956. In 1998 it merged with Abingdon School to become part of one Charitable Foundation with a single Board of Governors. Boys are prepared for the Common Entrance Examination with a strong and increasing majority going on to Abingdon School.

Entry is at age four, seven and eleven. Those who join at age eleven, begin a two year programme that prepares pupils for entry to Abingdon School at age thirteen.

The school aims to identify and foster each child's particular strengths by providing a happy and stimulating environment where the children are encouraged to develop self-reliance and a sense of responsibility. Considerable emphasis is placed on helping pupils to develop good working patterns together with sound organisational and learning skills.

Facilities include new Computer and science laboratories, a multi-purpose hall, a music room, art studio and library. An extensive programme of redevelopment and refurbishment of the main school has just been completed. Further developments are planned.

Sport is a major strength outside the classroom. The splendid facilities, which include two adventure playgrounds, an indoor swimming pool and thirty acres of playing fields, enable every child to participate in a wide range of sports and activities. There are regular fixtures against local schools in the main school sports of rugby, football, tennis, cricket and athletics. All pupils swim at least once a week. There is a range of after school hobby clubs which include orchestra, choir, art, science, judo, golf, photography, chess, computers and drama.

A large number of trips are organised for all year groups during the year and the oldest boys go abroad for a week on completing their Common Entrance Examination.

The Pre-Prep department aims to introduce the children to education, to encourage them to achieve their potential and to prepare them for an easy integration into the junior part of the school. The children are taught in small groups by sympathetic staff, who are well aware of the problems and anxieties that may well occur in the first years of school life.

Jumeirah English Speaking School

PO Box 24942 Dubai United Arab Emirates
Tel: Dubai 381515
Fax: Dubai 381531
e-mail: jess@jess.sch.ae
website: www.jessdubai.org

Chairman of Governors: Mr Leslie Robinson

Headmaster: **Mr C A Branson**

Number of pupils. 330 girls, 330 boys

Fees. Dhs 6,850 (approx £1,150) per term (3 term year)

Debenture. Dhs 10,000 (approx £1,650) per place (refundable)

The school was founded in 1975 by decree of H.H. Sheikh Rashid, Ruler of Dubai and is licenced by Dubai Government Ministry of Education.

The school is administered by a Board of Governors who are drawn from the community. The Board invites regular school inspections.

The buildings are modern and spacious. There are six units of purpose-built classrooms, a large, well equipped multi purpose Hall/gymnasium, a music block, central library and ICT room.

The landscaped grounds are pleasant and comprise two playing areas, a football pitch, athletics track and tennis court. An outdoor swimming pool completes the facilities.

The school caters for English speaking children between the ages of 3 and 11 years. There are 32 classes, four in each year group, with maximum class sizes of 21 pupils.

Pupils are prepared for entry into a variety of schools in UK and in UAE. Girls are prepared for the Common Entrance Examination.

The school is staffed by UK trained and qualified primary school teachers who are classroom based. In addition, there are full-time specialist teachers for ICT, physical education, music and Language Support. There are also part-time teachers of French, Arabic, Islamic Studies and Maths.

Two full time Infant class assistants and nine part-time Foundation and Key Stage 1 class assistants and a school nurse are also in attendance.

Full details and prospectus are available on request.

Jumeirah Primary School

P O Box 29093 Dubai United Arab Emirates
Tel: 00 971 394 3500
Fax: 00 971 394 3960

Headmistress: **Mrs J Adams**

Deputy Head: Mr T Brogan

Number of Pupils. 750 boys and girls.

Fees per year. Nursery: Dhs17,250; Reception: Dhs21,850; Years 1-4: Dhs21,850; Years 5 & 6: Dhs26,450. Fees are payable in United Arab Emirates Dirhams.

Jumeirah Primary School was established in September 1996 to provide a quality British National Curriculum School for expatriate children whose parents are resident in Dubai. The school offers places to English speaking children; there is no support for speakers of English as a second language.

The school is located in Jumeirah, a pleasant residential area of Dubai and the purpose-built premises opened in 1998. The facilities are excellent and include a 25 metre swimming pool, two tennis courts, an artificial grass field in addition to playgrounds, and a large multi-purpose hall.

Children can join the Nursery at three years of age. Until the end of Year 4 the children are taught by their Class Teacher, with specialist teachers for music, PE and Arabic (from Year 1). In Year 5 and 6, all subjects are taught by specialist teachers; these children have additional facilities including a Science Laboratory, Art Room and DT Room. The school has a Computer Room used by children from Year 3. Younger children use computers in their classrooms.

The school has its own Dyslexia Unit to support children with language difficulties; the qualified Dyslexia Teachers who run the Unit use the latest computer software to help these children succeed and grow in confidence.

Children are given every opportunity to develop their personal strengths not just in the classroom but also in extra curricular activities. Teachers come to school for lessons such as ballet, karate and tennis coaching; older children are taken to use outside facilities for sailing, golf and squash. The school has an orchestra and music lessons can be arranged. Each week some 65 extra curricular activities take place.

Above all, we place great value on the children being happy in their learning. We generate a community ethos by involving parents in day to day activities, and in the development of their child's learning.

Keble School

Wades Hill Winchmore Hill London N21 1BG
Tel: 020 8360 3359
Fax: 020 8360 4000

Chairman of the Board of Governors: Mr J Lindsay

***Headmaster:* V W P Thomas**, BEd, MA

Number of Boys. 200

Fees. Reception £1,850 per term; Years 1–4 £2,175 per term; Years 5–8 £2,325 per term.

Boys are prepared for entry to senior independent schools by Common Entrance, scholarship and other examinations at 13+. The school has a good academic record and attaches importance to curricular development and to sound pastoral care. The Head is assisted by a management team of two senior members of staff. The staff are well qualified and experienced. There are 13 full-time and 8 part-time teachers, 3 NNEB classroom and welfare assistants and two support teachers.

The accommodation is purpose built. The junior school is housed in a fine modern building. The senior school and craft block house the science laboratory and dedicated language, music, art, information technology and design technology rooms. Fees include text books and stationery, three curricular field trips, a visit to France in the penultimate year and lunches which are prepared in the school kitchens. Major games and swimming make use of excellent local facilities.

Sporting activities include soccer, cricket, swimming (for juniors), athletics, cross-country, squash, basketball, tennis and golf. There is a wide range of lunchtime and after-school activities and clubs and there are numerous educational outings out of school time.

The school was founded in 1929.

Charitable status. Keble Preparatory School (1968) Limited is a Registered Charity, number 312979. It exists to provide education for boys.

Kelly College Junior School

Hazeldon House Tavistock Devon PL19 0JS
Tel: (01822) 612919
Fax: (01822) 612919

***Headmaster:* R P Jeynes**, BA (Hons) Dunelm

Fees. £1,100-£1,475

The school is situated in a beautiful location on the western edge of Dartmoor National Park.

Pupils are prepared for 11+ entry to a wide range of Independent and State schools with the majority moving on to Kelly College Senior School.

The school has excellent resources including new classrooms as well as access to the Senior School facilities.

A range of sports are offered including Soccer, Cricket, Rounders, Netball and Rugby. Extra curricular activities include Horse Riding, Fly Fishing, Art, Drama, Dance, Archery, Fencing and Public Speaking. There is a flourishing musical tradition at the school with a choir and orchestra performing at a range of venues throughout the year. Individual music tuition is available on request.

Our proximity to Dartmoor enables an Adventure Training programme to be run for pupils from Years 4-6.

There is an active Parents' Association that runs numerous social and fund raising events throughout the year.

Further details and a prospectus are available from the School Secretary.

Charitable status. Kelly College Trust is a Registered Charity, number 306/716. It exists to provide education for boys and girls.

Kensington Preparatory School (G.D.S.T)

596 Fulham Road London SW6 5PA
Tel: 020 7731 9300
Fax: 020 7731 9301

Founded in 1873, this is the only preparatory school in the Girls' Day School Trust. For general information about the Trust and the composition of its Council see p. 532. The following are additional particulars and a more detailed prospectus may be obtained from the school or on www.gdst.net/kensingtonprep.

***Head Mistress:* Mrs G M Lumsdon**, BPharm, MEd

Number of Girls. 275 (4–11 years).

Fees from September 2000. £1,944

In the Spring of 1997 the School moved from Upper Phillimore Gardens, its home for more than 56 years, to spacious new premises in Fulham. The new buildings provide large airy classrooms for all age groups and specialist rooms for Art, Drama, Music, as well as Science and Technology. There is a beautiful Library, a School Hall and space for the pupils to have most PE and games on site.

The school continues to have a broadly based but strongly academic curriculum and the girls enjoy challenging and interesting work in a stimulating environment, whilst being prepared for entry to leading boarding and day schools at 11+.

Entry to the School is selective and the main entry point is at 4 years of age, although occasional places do occur throughout the School from time to time.

Charitable status. Kensington Preparatory School is one of the 25 schools of the Girls' Public Day School Trust, which is a Registered Charity, number 1026057. The aim of the Trust is to provide a fine academic education at a comparatively modest cost.

Kent College Infant and Junior School

Vernon Holme Harbledown Canterbury Kent CT2 9AQ.
Tel: (01227) 762436
Fax: (01227) 763800

Chairman of Governors: Dr D McGibney, BSc, MRCP, FFPM

Headmaster: **A J Carter**, BEd Hons

Number of Pupils. Junior School: Coeducational boarding and day (7–11 years), 133 pupils of whom 127 are day and 6 are boarders

Infants' Department. Day only from rising fives, 82 children. Nursery class for 31 children.

Fees. Junior School: Boarders £3,389 per term. Day pupils £2,329 per term (lunch extra).

Infants' Department. £1,472 per term.

The School is fully co-educational, the teaching staff are all professionally trained and well qualified to teach. There are visiting teachers for Music. The house mothers and catering staff have long experience of young children's needs.

Nursery pupils are admitted at 3 and Infants at the age of 5 or, when appropriate, before their fifth birthday. There is a further entry of Juniors at age 7 (and at other ages if there are vacancies). Children are prepared for entry to the Senior School (see Part I of this book)) to which many go at the age of 11. In the process they are taught to think for themselves, and are given plenty of activity time to develop their own interests within a structured environment that encourages and develops community awareness and social skills.

The School has a Dyslexia Unit which is designed to give special support to children who experience this problem whilst enabling them to integrate as fully as possible into the normal school programme.

The 12 acres of ground were originally laid out by Sidney Cooper RA. These have been adapted to provide games fields and a heated swimming pool without losing the varied character which makes them so suitable for young children's activities. The School has its own field study centre.

Activities include CDT, Field Study, Drama, Computer Club, Chess, Pottery, First Aid, Judo, Spanish and Italian.

Games include Athletics, Cricket, Cross-Country, Hockey, Netball, Rounders, Soccer, Rugby, Swimming, Basketball and Volleyball.

Charitable status. Kent College, Canterbury is a Registered Charity, number 307844. The School was founded to provide education within a supportive Christian environment.

Kent College Junior School, Pembury

Old Church Road Pembury Kent TN2 4AX
Tel: (01892) 820204
Fax: (01892) 820214

Headmistress: **Mrs D Dunham**, CertEd

Chairman of Governors: Mrs J Darbyshire

Girls. 3–11
Number of Pupils. 225 (6 Boarders, 219 Day-girls)

Fees per Term. Full boarders £3,860, Weekly boarders £3,560, Day girls £1,420–£2,140. All fees include lunches. There are no compulsory extras.

The School is the Junior School of Kent College Pembury. It is accommodated in purpose-built premises, within 75 acres of parkland. There is an Early Years Department for the youngest girls and some specialist facilities and teaching are provided by the Senior School, which shares the same site. The majority of girls sit the entrance examination to the Senior School at 11+ but some go on to other Senior Independent Schools via the Common Entrance Examination, or to the local Grammar Schools. Boarders are accepted in a family boarding unit at the age of 8. The school has an after-school care arrangement for all girls, with flexible boarding available to day girls.

All full-time and part-time staff are qualified. The school follows the National Curriculum and academic expectations are high.

Sport is an important part of the curriculum. Girls play netball, hockey, rounders and short tennis while swimming continues throughout the year in the indoor swimming pool up to National level. Emphasis is placed on the performing arts with opportunities for music, drama and dance at all ages. The school has two choirs. Pupils are also encouraged to take part in the wide and varied selection of clubs and activities the school offers.

The atmosphere is that of a busy, friendly school where intellectual curiosity and a thirst for learning are fostered. The development of initiative and self reliance are important factors in the education process and girls are encouraged to show responsibility in a practical, Christian way.

The Headmistress is pleased to welcome visitors and show them round the School.

Charitable status. Kent College Junior School, Pembury is a Registered Charity, number 307920. It is a Christian school specialising in girls' education.

Kenton College

PO Box 30017 00100 Nairobi Kenya.
Tel: Nairobi 560260/574198/577745
Fax: Nairobi 573039
e-mail: admin@kenton.ac.ke

Chairman of the Governors: M H Dunford, Esq, BSc (Hons)

Headmaster: **R M Hartley**, BEd, MA

Number of Pupils. 230
Fees. Kshs.155,000

Founded in 1924 and transferred to purpose built accommodation in 1935, Kenton College is one of the oldest schools in the country. Situated in its own secluded grounds of 35 acres, at an altitude of nearly 6000 feet, some three miles from the centre of one of Africa's most cosmopolitan capitals, Kenton is an oasis of calm amidst the rapidly sprawling urban development of the city of Nairobi.

Kenton College is an independent co-educational preparatory school, entry to which is open to both boys and girls of any race or religious persuasion, who have had their sixth birthday before the beginning of the school year in September. Most pupils remain seven years with us and leave in the July following their thirteenth birthday for senior schools in the UK, Kenya or South Africa, having followed a syllabus in the senior part of the school leading to the ISEB's Common Entrance Examination. Kenton pupils frequently obtain scholarships to UK or Kenyan senior schools.

The school is based on a strong Christian foundation which is reflected in the warm and caring environment provided for its pupils, wherein positive encouragement is given towards any aspect of school life. Considerable emphasis is placed on character building, discipline and good manners, within a relaxed and happy atmosphere.

We aim for high academic achievements by offering a full curriculum in which the best of traditional and modern approaches are employed. The British National Curriculum provides the framework for our teaching throughout the school. Use is made of specialist subject teaching rooms in the senior school, to which recent additions are a Modern Languages suite, a Design studio and two Computer rooms. There are two Science laboratories, a well-stocked Library and a 300 seat Assembly Hall with large stage.

The academic day is balanced by opportunities for drama and music for all, together with a wide variety of sports and extra-curricular activities. Traditional British sports are played using our first class facilities which include three tennis courts and a heated swimming pool.

Many pupils opt for extra activities such as riding, ballet, karate, music tuition, tennis or swimming coaching, speech and drama awards, Cubs and Brownies. Sailing in the school boats on Lake Naivasha is available a few times each term. Trips to theatres, museums and the many facilities found in an international city are combined with expeditions and fieldwork in the unrivalled Kenyan countryside.

Academic subjects are taught by a staff complement of local and expatriate teachers numbering 25. Full use is made of accomplished musicians for music tuition, while recognised Kenyan sportsmen assist with games coaching. The average class size is 16, with 20 the maximum.

King's Junior School

Milner Court Sturry Nr Canterbury CT2 0AY.
Tel: (01227) 714000.
Fax: (01227) 713171
e-mail: headjks@clara.net

Station: Sturry

Chairman of Governors: The Very Revd The Dean of Canterbury

Headmaster: **P M Wells**, BEd (Hons)

Number of Pupils. 339. Boarders 58, Day Pupils 202. Pre-Prep 79.

Fees. Boarders, £3,700; Day pupils £2,610; Pre-Prep £1,520 per term (including lunch)

The School is the Junior School of the King's School, Canterbury and is co-educational.

Members of the happy boarding community enjoy a wide variety of weekend activities and all the domestic arrangements are supervised by the Headmaster's wife.

The majority of the pupils go on to the King's School through Scholarship or Common Entrance, though some pass on to other independent secondary schools. Classes are kept sufficiently small (average 16) for plenty of individual attention and pastoral care. Academic standards are high and the record of success in Scholarships and Common Entrance outstanding.

The school has a fine reputation for music, both instrumental and choral. There is a programme of concerts and recitals involving children of all ages. Recent pupils have been awarded a pleasing number of music scholarships.

For boys Cricket, Soccer and Rugby Football are the main games, while girls play Netball, Hockey and Rounders. Athletics, Tennis and Fencing are joint pursuits. A new sports hall was opened in 1998 and this is used for PE lessons, basketball, volleyball, badminton, netball and indoor hockey, soccer and tennis. There is canoeing on the River Stour, which runs through the 80 acres of grounds, rowing and sailing on nearby lakes and a heated outdoor swimming pool.

In the 16th century tithe barn there is a fully equipped stage. Buildings opened in the last decade include a design and technology centre and a spacious dining hall which provides an attractive alternative venue for concerts and plays. Eight new classrooms were opened in September 1999, and the Library refurbished in 2000.

The Oast House provides a characterful setting for the Pre-Preparatory department for children aged 4 to 7.

Charitable status. Junior King's School, Canterbury is a Registered Charity, number 307942. It exists to provide education for boys and girls.

King Henry VIII Junior School

Warwick Road Coventry CV3 6AQ
Tel: (024) 76673442

Chairman of Governors: C T Leonard, Esq

Headmaster: **J A Shackleton**, BEd, MA

Number of Pupils. 240 boys and girls, all Day.

Fees. £1,380 per term.

The school is a charitable Trust under the title of Coventry School Foundation. Although pupils can go from the Junior School to other schools, most are prepared for the entry examination to King Henry VIII.

In January 1997 the school moved into purpose-built accommodation including eleven spacious and well-equipped classrooms. There is an excellent set of specialist facilities including a large Library, an Art and Design Technology Room with Kiln, a specially equipped Science Room, a 24 station networked IT Room and a Music Room with keyboard set-up.

The pupils range from 7+ to 11+ with boys and girls in approximately equal numbers. There are two forms of 7 year olds and three parallel forms in each proceeding year.

The Junior School has a fully qualified and experienced staff. The following subjects are taught throughout the Junior School: English, Mathematics, Science, Art, Design Technology, Geography, History, Music, Personal & Social Education, Physical Education & Games and Religious Education.

The school has its own Orchestra, Choir and Recorder Group. Concerts and School plays are performed on a regular basis. A wide range of supervised activities take place during lunch time and after school.

For the boys, School games are Association Football, Rugby and Cross Country in winter, Cricket and Athletics in summer. The girls play Netball and Hockey in winter, Rounders, Tennis and Athletics in summer. All pupils are involved in a programme of swimming at the Foundation swimming pool.

Although the emphasis is placed on academic studies and the acquisition of sound basic skills, honesty, good manners and discipline, and an awareness of the needs of others are also of great importance.

Entry is by competitive examination which is held each year in March for 7 and 8 year olds, and for other ages as places become available.

King's College Junior School

Wimbledon Common London SW19 4TT.
Tel: 020 8255 5335
Fax: 020 8255 5339

Chairman of the Governing Body: C Taylor, MA, LLM

Headmaster: **J A Evans**, BA

Number of Boys. 460 (day boys only)

Fees. £2,650 to £2,990 per term

The Junior School was established in 1912 as an integral part of KCS, to prepare boys for the Senior School. It shares with it a common site and many facilities, in particular the Music School, the Art, Design and Technology School, the Science Laboratories, the Dining Hall, the Sports Hall, the swimming pool and extensive playing fields. For the rest, Junior School boys are housed in their own buildings. The Priory, rebuilt in 1980 and recently extended, contains twenty three classrooms, including specialist rooms for languages, mathematics, history, geography, information technology and multi-media work. The youngest age groups have their own special accommodation in Rushmere, a spacious Georgian house whose grounds adjoin the Junior School. The School also has its own purpose-built library, junior science laboratories and well-equipped theatre and assembly hall.

The School is separately administered in matters relating to admission, curriculum, discipline and day to day activities. There are twenty nine members of staff in addition to those teaching in specialist departments common to both Schools.

The work and overall programme are organised in close consultation with the Senior School to ensure that boys are educated in a structured and progressive way from 7 to 18, having the benefit of continuity, while enjoying the range and style of learning that are best suited to their age.

Boys come from both maintained and pre-preparatory schools and are admitted at the age of 7, 8, 9, 10 or 11. Entry is by interview and examination.

Charitable status. King's College School is a Registered Charity, number 310024. It exists to provide education for children.

King's College School

West Road Cambridge CB3 9DN.
Tel: (01223) 365814
Fax: (01223) 461388
e-mail: office@kingscam.demon.co.uk
website: www.kcs.cambs.sch.uk

Chairman of Governors: The Provost of King's College, Prof P P G Bateson, ScD, FRS

Headmaster: **N J Robinson**, BA, PGCE

Deputy Heads:
Mrs L E Edge, BSc
Mr A J Saunders, AdDipEd, MITT

Number of Children and Termly Fees, September 2000. 24 Chorister Boarders (Boys) £1,213; 10 non-Chorister Boarders (Boys, weekly) £3,706. 157 Day Boys, 96 Day Girls £2,391 (£1,833 Pre-Prep), (lunches inclusive); ages 4 to 13 plus.

The School is administered by Governors appointed by the Council of King's College, parents and teaching staff. King Henry VI's charter founding King's College in 1441 provided for Choristers and their education. In 1878 the School moved to its present site near the University library, across the river from the College. Over the years the facilities have steadily increased and now comprise boarding and classroom blocks, an all-purpose Hall, two very well equipped Science Laboratories, a new Technology Centre for ICT and DT, library, Art room, a new Music Department, Choristers' and other Music rooms, outdoor heated swimming pool, three hard courts, a multi-purpose hard playing surface, three sports fields and use of the College's two squash courts, all within the grounds. A further sports field lies a short walk away from the school.

The Headmaster is assisted by 30 full-time and 6 part-time teachers. There are 3 full-time Matrons and a full-time Bursar and Assistant Bursar. There are 30 full- or part-time music staff. In 1976 girls were admitted as day pupils and the ratio of boys to girls is 50:50 in the junior classes. In September 1981 the School started a small special centre for dyslexic children of good intelligence; auditory training and music play an important part, the children mix with their peers in normal classes but do not study French. In 1992 a Pre-preparatory Department for children aged 4 to 7 was opened. Pupils are prepared for the Scholarship and Common Entrance examinations of the boys' and girls' Independent Senior Schools. The school broadly follows the National Curriculum subjects, but also teaches French from the age of 4, Latin from 9, and Greek and German to some older children. The School has a tradition of winning numerous academic, art, music and sports awards annually.

Apart from choral and instrumental music (there are 2 orchestras of some 80 players in each), activities include Drama, Art, Craft, Pottery, Computing, DT, Gymnastics, PE, Scouts, Chess, Science, RSPB Wildlife Explorers, Handwriting, Library, Model-making. Games include Rugger, Soccer, Hockey, Cricket, Netball, Rounders, Athletics, Tennis, Squash, Cross-Country and Swimming.

Further information about the School may be obtained from the Headmaster. Enquiries concerning Choristerships should also be addressed to him. Choristership Auditions take place annually, usually in January.

Charitable status. King's College School is a Registered Charity, number X6753A. Its aim is to provide an excellent education for girls and boys of mixed ability aged 4 to 13.

King's Hall

Kingston Road Taunton Somerset TA2 8AA.
Tel: (01823) 285920
Fax: (01823) 285922
e-mail: kingshall@aol.com

For boys and girls aged 3–13+

Chairman of Governors: Rear Admiral Sir Robert Woodard, KCVO, DL

Head: **James Macpherson**, BEd (Hons) Exeter

Number of Pupils. Preparatory (Years 3-8): 160 boys, 120 girls; 75 boarders. Pre-Prep (Nursery-Year 2): 55 boys, 45 girls

Termly Fees. Preparatory Day: £1,270–£2,425 per term, Weekly Boarding £1,920–£3,295 per term, Full Boarding: £2,035–£3,420 per term. Pre-prep £805–£930 per term.

King's Hall is set in a beautiful country location surrounded by National Trust farmland yet is only a couple of miles from the centre of Taunton with easy access to the M5 and less than two hours to London by train. It has all the characteristics of a traditional country preparatory school without being overshadowed by a senior school on the same site. This gives the children a pride in their school and visitors invariably comment upon the warmth and friendliness with which they are greeted. It is one of the Woodard Schools whose approach is based on the principles of the Church of England. The academic results are excellent. Sport, outdoor activites, music and drama are also strengths and scholarships are available for pupils with exceptional ability in these areas. Those awarded at 11+ continue at King's College, Taunton up to age 18. Others may join King's Hall through interview and assessment at any age after their third birthday (subject to availabilty of places).

Charitable status. King's Hall is a Registered Charity, number 269669. It exists to provide education for children aged 3-13.

King's Hawford

Worcester WR3 7SE.
Tel: (01905) 451292

Chairman of the Governors: D Howell, Esq

***Headmaster:* R W Middleton**, MSc, BEd

Number of pupils. Boys 50, Girls 27. Pre-prep (2½–6) Boys & Girls 152.

Fees. Pre-prep: £1,267–£1,349 per term. Main School: 1st Form £1,768 per term. 2nd Form and above £2,151–£2,266 per term, includes lunch.

King's Hawford is set in thirty acres of parkland situated on the northern outskirts of Worcester. The school is accommodated within an elegant and recently refurbished Georgian house surrounded by well maintained playing fields, with tennis courts, a heated outdoor swimming pool, a multi-purpose sports hall and secure play area for younger children.

There are extensive opportunities for a wide range of extra curricular activities and there is a busy calendar of music, drama, sport, clubs. Sports include Rugby, Association Football, Cricket, Hockey, Netball, Rounders, Athletics and Tennis.

The Pre-Prep department accepts children from rising three to 6 and the Junior department from 7–11.

Charitable status. King's Hawford is a Registered Charity, number 22406655. It exists to provide a broad education for a wide range of children from rising 3–11 years.

Kingshott

St Ippolyts Hitchin SG4 7JX.
Tel: (01462) 432009.
Fax: (01462) 421652
Station: Hitchin

Chairman of Governors: Mr C J Carling, MA

***Headmaster:* P R Ilott**, BA (Hons)

Number of Pupils. (All Day) Prep (7½–13½) 150 Boys 71 Girls, Pre-Prep (4½–7½) 65 Boys 43 Girls

Termly Fees. (include Lunch) Pre-Prep £1,520, Prep £1,960.

Kingshott, founded in 1930, occupies a large Victorian building, with major recent classroom additions, in 13 acres of attractive grounds on the outskirts of Hitchin. Luton, Letchworth, Baldock, Stevenage, Welwyn and the A1(M) Motorway are all within a 10 mile radius.

Kingshott, a Charitable Educational Trust, with a Board of Governors, has a Christian ethos and is affiliated to the Church of England, but welcomes all denominations. Children are encouraged to make the best of individual potential, academic, creative, sporting, and to this end there is a happy friendly atmosphere, with strong emphasis on courtesy and self-discipline.

There are 25 full-time and 5 part-time qualified staff to teach 18 forms, varying in size from 12 to a maximum of 22. Visiting Musicians teach a wide variety of instruments; there is an Orchestra and Choir; Speech and Drama and Ballet are offered; Field Trips and Educational Visits form a regular feature of school life.

There is a strong and successful sporting tradition which includes Soccer, Rugby, Cricket, Hockey, Basketball, Lacrosse, Netball, Tennis, Swimming, Cross-Country and Athletics. The School has its own covered, heated swimming pool, all-weather pitch, tennis court and hard play area. Many Senior pupils stay until 5.30 for Prep each evening, and there is opportunity for involvement in a wide variety of after school Hobby activities.

Girls were first admitted in 1983, and now constitute approximately 45% of the annual intake. From Autumn 1990, girls have been able to continue their education at Kingshott until Common Entrance at 13½, in line with the boys.

Academic, Music and Art Scholarships to Senior Independent Schools are gained each year, and Common Entrance results are very sound, with virtually all children accepted by their first choice schools.

Entry is by assessment, appropriate to age, and interview.

Registration for the Pre-Prep is advisable several years in advance of required admission.

Charitable status. Kingshott School is a Registered Charity, number 1507581. It exists to provide education for boys and girls.

King's House School

Richmond Surrey TW10 6ES.
Tel: 020 8940 1878
Fax: 020 8939 2501

The School was constituted an Educational Trust with a Board of Governors in September 1957.

Chairman of the Governors: Mr Geoffrey Potts

***Headmaster:* Mr Neville J H Chaplin**, BSc (Edinburgh)

Number of Boys. Senior Department 205; Junior Department 165

Fees. Senior Department £1,985; Junior Department £1,470–£1,685; (all fees inclusive of lunch)

King's House is a Day Preparatory School for boys aged 4–13 on two sites in King's Road. Boys are prepared for entry by Scholarship or Common Entrance to all independent schools. The teaching staff are fully qualified.

The School aims to provide a broad, balanced curriculum in a caring environment.

Kingsland Grange

Old Roman Road Shrewsbury Shropshire SY3 9AH.
Tel: (01743) 232132.
website: www.kingslandgrange.com
Station: Shrewsbury

Headmaster: **M C James**, MSc (London)

Assistant Headmaster: R J Lloyd, BEd

Bursar: A T G Groves, MBE, MA (Oxon)

Number of Boys. 143 Day boys.
Fees per term. £1,190–£1,930.

Founded in 1899 the school occupies a delightful woodland site in the southern urban area of Shrewsbury close to the centre and the A5 ring road.

The school includes a Pre-Prep Department for 4–7 year olds in a new purpose built building on the main school site (it is called 'The Rocks'). The Prep department takes boys from 7–13 years of age.

Facilities include three classroom blocks, a Science laboratory, extended Music School, brand new networked Information Technology Suite, Art Room, Drama Room, Design and Technology Centre, Internet Resource Library and separate Bookshop, Gymnasium and heated Swimming Pool.

The early years are very stimulating and the teaching of Numeracy and Literacy is of paramount importance. Small class sizes are employed throughout the school to ensure as much individual attention as possible. The staff are well qualified specialists in their own subject areas. The 4 to 8 year olds have a class teacher responsible for teaching and pastoral care. Subject specialists are introduced from the age of 7 years. The school curriculum is continually upgraded and developed to meet the modern needs of education whilst still employing tried and tested traditional learning methods. Most of the boys move on to Senior Independent Schools by way of Common Entrance or Scholarship examinations. An average of 70% of boys move on to Shrewsbury School each year.

We supplement the academic subjects with a timetable of Design and Technology, Art, Music, Drama and Information Technology. The vast majority of boys study a musical instrument. We have a School choir and supply the treble voices for the Shrewsbury School Choir. The main sports are Soccer, Rugby, Cricket and Athletics. Swimming and Cross-Country Running also feature for all boys. Other activities include Chess, Outward Bound, Canoeing, Mountain-biking and Archery.

Annual trips abroad include a French Adventure trip, French City visit and a Ski Trip. Extra-curricular visits and invited speakers/performers are a normal part of the school life. Boys take English Speaking Board examinations and regularly take part in Festivals of Poetry and Verse Speaking with great success. There is an annual musical production for both the Pre-Prep and Prep Departments.

Kingsmead School

Bertram Drive Hoylake Wirral CH47 0LL
Tel: 0151-632 3156
Fax: 0151-632 0302
e-mail: Kingsmeadschool@compuserve.com
Boarders are met at Liverpool Lime Street Station or Liverpool or Manchester Airports

Chairman of Governors: The Revd M A D Hepworth

Headmaster: **E H Bradby**, MA (Oxon), MSc

Deputy Heads:
C P B Sewter, BA
R N S Leake, BSc, PGCE

Numbers. (2001) 146 boys, 87 girls (boarders 15 boys, 13 girls).

Entry. Pupils are accepted at any age between 2 and 15.

Staff. The 20 full-time staff are all fully qualified, and include 14 graduates.

Fees. (September 2001). Boarders £2,695–£2,930 a term. Day Pupils £620–£1,830 a term

Scholarships up to half the value of the fees are available for bright or musically talented children. Scholarship and entrance examinations are held in March each year. Substantial Bursaries are available to the children of Clergy and members of the teaching profession and also to serving members of the Armed Forces.

Kingsmead School was founded in 1904. It is in a rural setting with extensive playing fields on site, yet is easily accessible by road and rail.

The School is an Educational Trust with a strong Christian tradition, a reputation for high academic standards, and a happy atmosphere.

The curriculum prepares pupils to go on to Grammar Schools at 11+ or Independent Schools at 13+. Excellent results have been achieved in Scholarship and Common Entrance examinations. Since September 1996, pupils have been prepared for Key Stage 3 and GCSE examinations, and the first batch took their GCSE examinations in the summer of 1999.

Facilities include a Computer Room, a well-equipped Science Laboratory, a large multi-purpose Gymnasium, an English-drama lecture theatre and an indoor heated swimming pool available throughout the year. There is also a workshop for woodwork, Art and CDT. All forms are time-tabled to do Swimming, PE, Music, Art, Design and Technology and Information Technology. There is a strong Choir and facilities are available to those wishing to learn a musical instrument. A Music Suite was completed in 1984.

Up to Form 2 (end of Key Stage 1), pupils are taught in their own rooms by Class teachers. In the Junior Department (Key Stage 2) there is specialist teaching of certain subjects at the appropriate level. Thereafter pupils are based in a Form Room under the care of a Form Teacher but move to the different subject rooms for lessons. For spoken English and Drama, the School has enjoyed excellent results in the English Speaking Board examinations. At any level in the school, intelligent children with specific learning difficulties can be given a structured programme of remedial help by a specialist teacher at an extra charge.

Full or Weekly Boarders are accepted from 7 years old and are in the care of a married Housemaster and two Matrons. These, together with the Headmaster, Deputy and their wives, are all resident. Boarders enjoy separate recreational facilities, including a games room with table-tennis, billiards and a coffee bar.

Girls play Netball, Hockey and Rounders; boys play Association and Rugby Football. In the Summer, Cricket is the main game but all can have Tennis and Athletics coaching.

Clubs include, Ballet, Chess, Gymnastics, Judo, Woodwork, Scripture Union, Swimming and Sailing.

Charitable status. Kingsmead School is a Registered Charity, number 525920. It aims to provide education to boys and girls between the ages of 2 and 16.

King's Preparatory School
Rochester

King Edward Road Rochester Kent ME1 1UB
Tel: (01634) 843657
Fax: (01634) 840569

Chairman of the Governors: The Very Revd E F Shotter, MA, Dean of Rochester

Headmaster: **C J Nickless**, BA

Number of Pupils. 245 (12 Boarders) aged 8–13

Fees. Boarders £3,835–£4,135 per term. Day Pupils £2,290–£2,590 per term (including lunches).

Admission between 8+ to 12+ follows an Entrance Examination in English, Mathematics and Verbal or Non Verbal Reasoning.

Scholarships are awarded to Cathedral Choristers (40% of tuition fees) and King's (50%) or Governors' Exhibitions (means tested up to 100%) to those whose performance in the Entrance Examination merits it.

The Preparatory School is an integral part of the King's School, Rochester, founded in 604 AD by Justus, a Benedictine monk, the first Bishop of Rochester. The Cathedral is at the heart of the School's life with a weekly School service and every day the Choristers maintain the tradition of choral singing at the world's oldest Choir School. When the School is not in the Cathedral a religious assembly is held at the Preparatory School.

The School is a member of the Choir Schools' Association.

The School has been fully co-educational since 1993 and almost 30% are now girls.

Set in the City, the Preparatory School building overlooks the Paddock, one of the School's playing fields. The teaching block consists of 12 classrooms, 2 Science Laboratories, Computer Suite, Language Laboratory and Library with over 6,000 volumes. Other facilities such as the Design and Technology Centre, Art Centre, Music School, Indoor Swimming Pool and Sports Hall are shared with the Senior School which virtually all pupils join following the internal Entrance Examination. Chadlington House, a new Sports Hall and purpose built building for our Pre-Preparatory School opened in September 2000.

The Boarding House, St Margaret's House, is run on family lines under the care of the Housemaster and his wife with two other resident members of the teaching staff. Boarding, both full and weekly, is available for boys and girls. Day pupils are able to stay under 'hotel' boarding arrangements.

The curriculum is broad and balanced. By the age of 12+ science is taught as three separate subjects, French and German are the modern languages, and Latin is compulsory. (One to one support tuition is available in English and Mathematics on payment of a supplementary fee).

All pupils enjoy the benefit of 2 full afternoons a week of Games in addition to the one PE lesson. Sports include Rugby, Soccer, Hockey, Cricket, Netball, Athletics, Swimming, Cross Country Running and Tennis.

The Extra Curricular programme is wide and includes amongst the usual activities Air Pistol Shooting, Pottery, Art, Skiing, General Knowledge, Fencing, Horse Riding, Golf, Nature Study and Stamps, as well as opportunities to further knowledge in academic subjects such as French and German and to acquire skills in our traditional sports.

Choral and instrumental music is strong. Many of our pupils learn one or more musical instruments. Good results are achieved in Associated Board Examinations. Concerts and Choral activities abound in the calendar. Amongst the weekly musical activities in addition to the choir practices are the gatherings of the Orchestra, String Groups, Brass Group and Wind Band.

Each year the Drama Club present a play held over three nights. Recently, productions have required casts in excess of fifty and have been wonderful opportunities for pupils to show their dramatic and musical skills. Amongst latest productions have been "In Holland Stands a House", the poignant and very moving story of Anne Frank, "The Ragged Child" an account of the work of Lord Shaftesbury, "Bugsy Malone" and "Drake".

Charitable status. Rochester Cathedral (King's) School is a Registered Charity, number 1084266. It is a Charitable Trust for the purpose of educating children.

King's St Alban's Junior School

Mill Street Worcester WR1 2NJ.
Tel: (01905) 354906
Fax: (01905) 763075

Headmaster: **Mr R T Bellfield**, BEd

Number of Pupils. 180, 7–11

Fees. 7 years, £1,435; 8–11 years, £1,937, excluding lunch.

A gloriously happy school run as a big family; delightful and outstanding with confident children. The School is located near to the Cathedral on a separate site from the Senior School. In the grounds stands the Chapel, a modern classroom block and the main building of St Alban's. The school has a purpose-built Science Laboratory, a Computer Room, an Art and Technology Room, a well stocked Library and a Music Room, all of which supplement the usual amenities of a preparatory school. In addition, use is made of Senior School facilities which include an indoor swimming pool, a modern fully-equipped Sports Hall, the Music School, Playing Fields, and a purpose-built Theatre.

We try to discover any talent and develop it to the full. Music and Drama play an important part in the life of the school. The Junior School supports an orchestra, a wind band and a string group and most children play at least one musical instrument. The Junior School choir visits local churches and enters various competitions. The annual Carol Service is in the Cathedral and concerts and musical evenings are held at other times of the year. A major dramatic production is staged annually in the theatre with several smaller workshop productions taking place throughout the year.

The Staff of 15 have great fun here and the challenge of youth is ever present. There are 11 full-time and 4 part-time members of the Teaching Staff all of whom are experienced and well-qualified. In addition there are various visiting music specialists.

The main games are Rugby, Netball, Association Football, Hockey, Cricket and Rounders. Instruction is also given in Swimming, Athletics, Cross-Country, Orienteering and Tennis. Matches are arranged with other schools and excellence is sought, but participation of all boys and girls is the main objective. A thriving Inter House competition provides a second tier of participation.

We teach children about kindness, humour and honour. To learn to help others, to enjoy ourselves: these are our top priorities. We have plenty of new buildings and modern equipment but a successful academic school is much more: Camping, Ballet, Rug-making, Judo, Maths games, Chess, School Magazine, Art & Craft, Table Tennis and Young Engineers to name but a few of the opportunities available.

Girls and boys are accepted through a competitive examination and are expected to progress through to the Senior School, subject to a satisfactory performance in their examinations at the age of 11.

The assessment of candidates for the Junior School takes place in January/February for entry in the following September. The tests are in English, Mathematics and Verbal Reasoning.

There are 5 Scholarships and Bursaries available from the age of 7, as are Choral Scholarships for the Cathedral Choristers.

Charitable status. The King's School, Worcester is a Registered Charity, number L4/527536/1. It exists to provide high quality education for boys and girls.

King's School Junior School

King's School Ely Cambs CB7 4DB.
Tel: (01353) 662491
Fax: (01353) 665281

Chairman of the Governors: Dr M Nickson

Junior School Representative Governor: C R I Matheson, MA

***Head:* A G Duncan**, BA, BEd

Number of Pupils. Boarders, Boys 46, Girls 12, Day Boys, 132, Girls 123

Fees. Boarding £3,850–£4,070. Day £2,420–£2,637.

The Junior School has its own staff and its own new buildings are close to the main School. The facilities of the Senior School are freely available to Junior boys and girls.

There are three boarding Houses, 1 for girls 1 for boys and 1 which caters for the Cathedral Choristers. Each has its own Housemaster or Housemistress, assisted by House Tutors and experienced Matrons. All three houses have recently been refurbished (1989/1992) at a cost of over £1½ million and offer excellent boarding facilities.

During the school day all children are divided into four equal sized co-educational 'houses' for pastoral and competitive purposes. Each of these 'houses' is staffed by a Housemaster or Housemistress and three Tutors.

Entry to Junior School for boys and girls is usually at 8 or 9 or 11 by assessment test and interview. As a result of the 11+ examination certain children are invited to take the Junior School Scholarship examination. A normal preparatory school curriculum is followed and all pupils are prepared for the relevant leaving examination. While the great majority proceed to Senior School after their Entrance examination, pupils are also prepared for other Independent Schools.

The main games are Cricket, Rounders, Hockey, Netball, Football of both codes, Tennis, Athletics and Cross Country Running. There is a Swimming Pool of generous proportions, a well-equipped Sports Hall and a new full size all-weather hockey/tennis area. A wide ranging programme of extra curricula activities is also offered. The Choristers of Ely Cathedral are members of the Junior School and all pupils have the opportunity to learn one or more of a wide variety of musical instruments. There is a Junior School Orchestra, and choral and group music are taught. The School has its own Music School opened in September 1996, and access to the Senior School's new Recital Hall.

The School is also justly proud of its art and drama, which are taught in their own studios, and of its computer network. A new Technology Centre opened in September 1996.

Charitable status. The King's School, Ely is a Registered Charity, number 311440. It exists for the provision of education.

The King's School Preparatory School

Parramatta New South Wales 2124 Australia
Tel: (02) 96838444

Chairman of Council: The Revd Martin Robinson

***Head of the Preparatory School:* Mr Keith Dalleywater,** BA (Hons), MEd, DipEd, DipBibStud, MACE, MACEA

Number of Boys. 283 made up of 20 boarders and 263 day boys. Years K, 1, 3, 4, 5 and 6. (The introduction of two streams K2 will be complete by 2002).

Fees. Day boys $A2,025 per term, Boarders $A4,235 (incl) per term. We now observe a four term year and there is a substantial rebate for prompt payment. Fees include stationery, text books, etc. There are no compulsory extras

The King's School is the oldest school in Australia, having been founded by Bishop Broughton in 1831. Above all else, the School is a place where Christian values are emphasised and woven into every aspect of its life.

The School's curriculum is based on the core subjects including the English Language, Mathematics, Human Society and its Environment and Science and Technology. The classes are limited in size and taught by a highly qualified team of teachers.

The School boasts a splendid complex of classrooms and other teaching facilities. These include the latest computer technology, audio-visual theatre, multipurpose hall and library.

Special provision is made for enrichment programmes for students demonstrating giftedness and at the same time specialist support is provided for boys requiring remedial assistance.

Creative expression is considered to be of great importance and excellent facilities for art, handicrafts and music are available. The choir regularly participates in local events and achieves distinction at Sydney Eisteddfods. Each year the students present an Operetta and a Festival of Lessons and Carols. Skilled specialists provide tuition in a wide range of musical instruments for students who may join either a String Orchestra or a Concert Band. Well over half the students receive instrumental lessons.

Set in bushland on the outskirts of the City of Parramatta, the School is provided with superb facilities for games. Five fine playing fields, a 25 metre pool, two tennis courts, five practice wickets and an exciting cross country track ensure that our boys have every opportunity to develop their physical skills and experience the benefits of team co-operation.

Pastoral care is highly regarded at the School where a Chaplain and four Housemasters guide and encourage the boys and maintain a close link with their families.

The academic, social, moral and religious experiences afforded the boys of the Preparatory School establish a firm foundation for their progress to The King's School and a sound basis for them to live in the world of today.

Kingswood House School

56 West Hill Epsom Surrey KT19 8LG.
Tel: (01372) 723590.
Fax: (01372) 749081
e-mail: Khschool@aol.com
website: www.kingswoodhouse.surrey.sch.uk

Chairman of Governors: Chris Hughes, BTech, CEng, MIEE, MIMgt

Headmaster: **Peter R Brooks**, Esq, MA, BEd

Number of Boys. 210 (all day boys). Age 3–13.

Inclusive fees per term. Pre-Prep £1,400 (part-time Nursery payable by session). Junior 7+ upwards £1,925. Free after school care provided until 5.00 pm.

Kingswood House is a thriving day preparatory school for boys aged three to thirteen. The school's reputation is based on a friendly and welcoming atmosphere, a positive and supportive ethos and successfully meeting the educational needs of all its pupils. Small classes facilitate individual attention from well-qualified teachers on a regular basis and allow boys to learn in a relaxed, but stimulating and concentrated environment.

Founded in 1899, the school moved to its current site, a large Edwardian house in West Hill, Epsom, just outside the town centre in 1920, and is now home to just over 200 boys. The school is an educational trust, overseen by a board of governors.

The broad aim of the school is to prepare pupils for Common Entrance to senior school at age 13. Development of literacy and numeracy skills is the foundation of the curriculum. Science, History, Geography, French, Religious Education, Latin, PE, Music, Art, Design Technology and Information Technology make up the timetable. Study Skills and PSE courses help prepare boys for senior school life and there is a Study Centre to supplement learning, with excellent provision for dyslexic boys.

The senior curriculum is determined by the Common Entrance syllabus with boys being prepared for a wide variety of local senior independent schools, including Epsom College, St John's, Ewell Castle, City of London Freemen's, Reed's Box Hill and King's College, Wimbledon. Placing boys in the right senior school is of paramount importance and the teachers have wide experience in preparing boys for Common Entrance. There is an excellent success rate at 13+ Common Entrance, with a good proportion obtaining scholarships and awards.

The school prides itself on the quality of teaching, dedicated classrooms and resources provided for Art, Design Technology, Information Technology, Music and Science, all of which have been completely refurbished in the last few years. There are sporting facilities on site, with a playing field, astroturf surface, gym, all-weather cricket nets and training swimming pool. Pitches at Ashtead Cricket Club are also used along with local families at Epsom College, City of London's, St John's, etc.

Academic Scholarships are awarded at 7+. There are bursaries for sons of teachers and fee reductions for second and subsequent boys. The school operates the government nursery vouchers scheme.

Charitable status. Kingswood House School is a Registered Charity, number 312044. It exists to provide educational support in the form of bursaries for the parents of children in need.

Knighton House

Durweston Blandford Dorset DT11 0PY
Tel: (01258) 452065
Fax: (01258) 450744

Chairman of the Governors: Mr Simon Elliot

Headmistress: **Mrs E A Heath**, BA Hons, PGCE

Number of Girls. 54 Boarders, 60 Day, 50 Pre-Prep and Nursery (mixed)

Fees. Boarders £3,890 per term, Day £2,840 per term, Pre-Prep and Nursery (co-ed) £600–£1,435 per term. There are no compulsory extras.

The school community, established in 1950 in a delightful country setting, is friendly, cohesive, civilised and supportive, with good relationships between all age groups. There are many extra-curricular activities including riding from our own stables. Discipline is firm but flexible, resting on a corporate honouring of Christian principles.

There is a strong musical and artistic tradition; the Director of Music is assisted by 15 visiting musicians.

The scholarships and awards won from Knighton House reflect academic, musical, artistic and all-rounder prowess. The school feeds a wide range of senior schools including Bryanston, Cheltenham, Marlborough and Sherborne.

Prospective parents are most welcome to visit the school to meet the Headmistress.

Charitable status. Knighton House School Limited is a Registered Charity, number 306316. It exists, principally, as a boarding school for girls.

Lady Eden's School

39/41 Victoria Road Kensington London W8 5RJ
Tel: 020 7937 0583
Fax: 020 7376 0515

Headmistress: **Mrs J A Davies**, MA, FRSA

Number of Girls. 165

Fees. £1,200–£2,750 per term (inclusive of luncheon and sports).

Lady Eden's provides all aspects of education, whether academic, creative, social, physical or spiritual, for girls aged three to eleven years. A solid foundation in basics is achieved in lower forms; older girls are thoroughly prepared by specialists for Common Entrance and London day schools.

Lady Eden's has a proven record of academic achievement facilitated by small teaching groups in key areas staffed by specialists. The broad curriculum combines traditional values with modern methods and together with the basic subjects includes Science, Latin, French, and wide provision for ICT and Physical Education. The school is renowned for Music and the Arts. A wide programme of extra-curricular activities and visits features. Happy, well-motivated girls secure places at leading boarding and London day schools; they are encouraged to think independently and to show consideration for others. The school is Christian-based.

Early registration for Lower Kindergarten is essential; testing for occasional vacancies later.

Lambrook Haileybury

Winkfield Row Bracknell Berks RG42 6LU.
Tel: 01344 882717
Fax: 01344 891114
Station: Bracknell

Chairman of the Governors: Sir Alan Hardcastle, FCA

***Headmaster:* R Deighton**, BA (Durham)

Number of Children. 368 aged 4–13 years old.
Fees. Boarding £3,400–£3,975 per term; Day £2,650–£2,850; Pre-Prep £1,700–£1,800 per term.

Lambrook Haileybury is a co-educational day and boarding school for children aged 4 to 13. The school is situated at Winkfield Row, two miles from Ascot, six miles from Windsor and is easily accessible from the M4, M3 and M40 motorways. Heathrow is 30 minutes away by road.

The school has many facilities including a Science and IT Centre opened in September 1998. The school aims for high academic standards and prepares children for Scholarship and Common Entrance examinations to all major Senior Independent Schools. High quality teaching is provided in small classes and the school is set in a beautiful rural environment of some forty acres.

The school encourages a well-rounded education. Games, music and other cultural activities play an important part in the lives of the children. The boarding, in particular, is conducted in the spirit of family atmosphere with a strong pastoral care system, in two boarding houses.

Many of the boarders are from Service, or ex patriot families: all needs, including travel arrangements, are conducted from the school by the school.

The school has many day pupils who are attracted by the boarding ethos and the subsequent number of varied activities available. All pupils play a full part in the life of the school. The Pre-Prep Department opened in September 1993 and it has expanded rapidly. In September 2000 we opened our new Pre-prep Building comprising eight very well resourced classrooms, an enlarged library and a networked computer system.

Charitable status. Lambrook Haileybury is a Registered Charity, number 309098. Its purpose is to provide an excellent education for boys and girls.

Lanesborough School

Maori Road Guildford Surrey GU1 2EL.
Tel: (01483) 880650

***Headmaster:* K S Crombie**, BSc

Number of Boys. 350 (all Day Boys). Age 3½–13 years
Inclusive fees per term. Nursery £620–£1,112, Lower £1,916, Middle £2,065, Upper £2,131.

Lanesborough is the Junior School of the Royal Grammar School and the choir school for Guildford Cathedral. Cathedral choristers qualify for choral scholarships.

The main entry points are Nursery, Reception and Year 3. Over half of the pupils gain entry to the Royal Grammar School at age 11 or 13, whilst others are prepared for Scholarship and Common Entrance examination to senior independent schools at 13.

The School is divided into four houses for house competitions. Pastoral care and supervision of academic progress are shared by the Headmaster, Housemasters, Form masters and subject teachers. Extra-curricular activities include art, chess, drama, computer club, judo, squash and badminton.

Music is a strong feature of the life of the school, which is a member of the Choir Schools Association. In addition to the Cathedral Choir, there are senior and junior choirs, an orchestra, wind and string groups. Private tuition by qualified peripatetic teachers is available in most instruments. There is an annual concert and the School Carol Service at the Cathedral has achieved wide acclaim. Music Scholarships to Independent Senior Schools are gained each year.

Art plays an important part in the curriculum also, with boys receiving tuition throughout the school.

Games are association football, rugby football, cricket, athletics, swimming, basketball, hockey and badminton.

Regular school visits are undertaken to local places of interest. School parties also go abroad, eg for ski-ing, on IAPS cruises and on cultural visits to France.

The pre-preparatory department (for boys aged 3½–7 and including a Nursery unit) is housed in a separate building (Braganza) under the direct supervision of the Head of the pre-prep, but shares many of the facilities of the senior part of the School. The recent purchase of a large Edwardian house next to the School has greatly enhanced the facilities.

There is an active Parents' Association.

Charitable status. Lanesborough is governed by the trustees of the charity of the Royal Grammar School of King Edward VI, Guildford (Chairman Professor K G Stephens). The Registered Charity number is 312028. The charity exists for the purpose of educating boys in or near Guildford.

Langley Preparatory School and Nursery

11 Yarmouth Road Thorpe St Andrew Norwich Norfolk NR7 0EA.
Tel: (01603) 433861
Fax: (01603) 702639
e-mail: weeks_paul@hotmail.com
Station: Norwich

Chairman of the Governors: Mrs M Alston, JP

***Headmaster:* P J Weeks**, BEd (Hons), CertEd, CertSpLD, MCollP

Number of Boys. 95
Number of Girls. 55
Fees. Between £430–£1,760 per term.

The School is situated in 5 acres of ground and is close to the city centre. Pupils are taken from the age of 2 and are prepared for many schools, but principally for entry to Langley School at the age of 11+. A purposeful academic atmosphere is maintained by qualified and experienced staff. A broad curriculum is followed, and class sizes rarely exceed 16. English, Mathematics and Science form the core from the age of 4. Art and Craft, Information Technology, Design Technology and Modern Languages are taught alongside the more traditional academic subjects. There is a well-equipped Science laboratory and the Computer suite was refurbished for the current school year.

There is a tradition for recorder playing and piano, strings, woodwind and brass are taught by specialists. Ballet, modern and tap dancing are taught, as is drama, and all pupils take part in the annual concert. There is also a Drama Club production every Christmas. Children are prepared for LAMDA examination at an early age.

Various after school clubs are available for all pupils.

Hockey, rugby, soccer, cricket and short tennis are the main team games. The school has use of an all weather surface. A gymnasium and heated swimming pool afford ample opportunities for coaching. Athletics are an integral part of the summer programme. The school also has a strong Orienteering tradition.

The Nursery, which caters for 2 to 4 year olds, was opened in September 1994. The children are in the care of experienced NNEB trained nursery nurses. The nursery is well equipped and has its own secure play area. Nursery hours are flexible and a child-minding service is offered after school hours. The Nursery has been OFSTED inspected and is a registered provider under the new government scheme.

It is the aim of the school to provide a sound academic education with a friendly and yet well structured environment where pupils can discover individual talents and abilities so that they will be well prepared for the secondary stage of their education.

Charitable status. Langley Preparatory School is a Registered Charity, number 311270. It exists to maintain a sound educational establishment for boys and girls in the City of Norwich, and to advance and improve in any way the cause of education whether general, professional or technical.

Lathallan School

Montrose Angus DD10 0HN.
Tel: Inverbervie (01561) 362220.

Chairman of Board of Directors: Mr G A B Anderson, OBE

Headmaster: **Peter Platts-Martin**, BA

Number of Pupils. 134 (90 boys, 44 girls: 52 boarders, 82 day children).

Full Boarding Fees. £3,418 per term with reductions for younger brothers and sisters and Services. Scholarships are awarded annually.

Lathallan Preparatory School is superbly situated on the North-East Scottish coast: a baronial castle standing in 62 acres of playing fields, woodland and private beach, and within easy access of the Grampians and commuting distance of Aberdeen and Montrose.

Lathallan has a reputation for successfully combining the traditional aspects of education with the more progressive features equally valued by parents today. Such features include the learning and day to day use of their skills in Information and Design Technology, and Modern Languages which are offered as early as the Pre-Prep years. Yet, Lathallan's fully qualified staff continue to value tried and tested teaching methods, to concentrate where appropriate on the 3R's, and to provide a rounded and complete education that is the hallmark of traditional Preparatory School education. Lathallan prepares girls and boys for Scottish and English senior independent schools, and has a good record in scholarships.

Among the many evening and weekend activities organised by staff for the benefit of all pupils are skiing, golf, riding, crafts, leatherwork and ornithology. Children are encouraged to take part in music and to either join the orchestra or the choir. They are also encouraged to take their interest in drama beyond the curriculum and to participate in the annual production, playing a part on stage or behind the scenes. Scottish country dancing and the pipe band are popular with all age groups. The school has a large sports hall, excellent playing fields and splendid tennis courts.

There is a growing day pupil element and so daily minibus runs are provided to and from the nearest large towns. A five day week reflects the growing interest in weekly boarding, whilst full boarders are given an adventurous weekend programme by a totally committed staff.

There is a strong community spirit and Christian ethos within the school, and the aim is to develop a disciplined mind, creative awareness, and personal integrity and confidence.

Charitable status. Lathallan School is a Registered Charity, number SCO 18423. It exists to provide education of the highest standard for boys and girls.

The Latymer Preparatory School

36 Upper Mall London W6 9TA
Tel: 020 8748 0303
Fax: 020 8741 4916

Chairman of Governors: J Bullock, Esq, FCA, FCMA, FIMC

Principal: **Mr Stuart P Dorrian**, BA

Fees per term. £2,700.

Number of pupils. 145 day boys, aged 7–11

The Latymer Preparatory School, led by its own Principal, was granted independence by the Governors of the Latymer Foundation in 1995 – the Centenary Year of Latymer Upper School on its present site. Previously the Preparatory School had been run as a very successful department of the Upper School and the relationship remains an extremely close one with all boys proceeding to the Upper School as a matter of course.

The school is academically selective and boys are taught the full range of subjects following National Curriculum guidelines, but to an advanced standard. Classes are kept small (20) which allows for close monitoring and evaluation of each pupil's progress and well being.

The school is especially well resourced and has impressive facilities recently developed and expanded in two elegant period houses adjacent to the River Thames. Catering and Sports facilities are shared with the Upper School.

A main feature of the school is its friendly and caring atmosphere which offers close pastoral support to each individual boy. Academic achievement is strong, but in addition, all staff and boys contribute to an extensive range of activities featuring Sport, Music, Art and Drama. The school has a large choir and its own orchestra. Opportunities exist for all boys to participate in concerts, plays, inter-school sporting events and an annual Project Week which includes a residential trip for the senior boys in their final year.

The major sports are soccer, rugby, cricket, tennis and athletics. There is also a thriving swimming club (the school has its own pool). Karate and fencing take place after school as do chess and scrabble.

There is a Parents' Gild and opportunities occur frequently to meet with staff socially. Visits for prospective parents occur throughout the year and can be arranged by telephoning for an appointment.

Charitable status. The Latymer Foundation is a Registered Charity, number 3122714. It exists to provide an opportunity for able pupils from all walks of life to develop their talents to the full.

Laverock School

Bluehouse Lane Oxted Surrey RH8 0AA.
Tel: (01883) 714171
Fax: (01883) 722206
e-mail: office@laverock.fsnet.co.uk
website: www.laverockschool.co.uk

Chairman of the Governors: J F Doubleday, FRICS
***Headmistress:* Mrs A Paterson**, DipEd

Number of Girls. 150
Fees. £675–£1,750 per term including lunch except in Nursery.

Accredited by the Independent Schools Council, Laverock is a Preparatory School for Girls set in pleasant surroundings close to the North Downs. The premises are purpose built and include an outdoor swimming pool, two multi-purpose sports courts, a bright and airy nursery unit and a Performing Arts and Science and Technology building.

The school aims to provide a happy atmosphere and broad-based curriculum. All aspects of the National Curriculum are taught and academic achievements are excellent with all girls being accepted by prestigious Senior Schools in the neighbourhood. In addition, there is a strong emphasis on Information Technology, music, drama, netball, tennis, swimming, art and ballet. After school activities include French Fun and Games and Wildlife Club. Most of the girls learn orchestral instruments and play in one of the two orchestras at regular concerts, services, etc. There are also two thriving choirs.

A prospectus and full particulars are available from the school and the Headmistress is always delighted to show prospective parents round the school.

Charitable status. Laverock School Limited is a Registered Charity, number 312083. Its aims are to provide broad based education of a high quality for girls in a caring environment.

Laxton Junior - Oundle School

North Street Oundle Peterborough PE8 4AL
Tel: (01832) 273673
Fax: (01832) 277271
e-mail: laxtonjunior@oundle.co.uk

Governors: The Worshipful Company of Grocers

Chairman: Mr J Whitmore

***Headmistress:* Miss S C Thomas**, CertEd

Deputy Head: Mr R J Wells

Number of Children. 141 (71 boys, 71 girls)
Fees. £1,468 per term (including lunches)

Opened in 1973 as the third member of the Oundle group of schools, Laxton Junior is a co-educational day school for children aged 4 to 11 years. The school is divided into 7 forms of approximately 20 children, each with a fully qualified form teacher. The curriculum includes Art & Design, Computer Skills, Drama, French, Music, PE and games as well as the major academic subjects. Emphasis is placed on the importance of each child doing his or her best at all times, according to his or her ability. The children are prepared for entrance examinations for Independent Senior Schools in the area and those who are suitable take the entrance examination for Laxton School, a day school in close association with Oundle School.

There is a multi-purpose hall which is used for school plays and social events as well as for PE, Music and Dance, plus the school has its own games field and pavilion. In addition, all the children receive swimming instruction each week in the Oundle School pool. The main games are football, cricket, netball and rounders. All children have the opportunity to play the recorder, plus additional time is given for choir and learning a musical instrument. We also have a Special Needs Unit which is available for all children who may need support.

The aims of the school are to encourage the formation of good work habits and good manners, to lay the foundations for the development of self-discipline, self-confidence and self-motivation and to offer the children the opportunity of experiencing the satisfaction of achievement.

The partnership of home and school in the education of the child is strongly emphasised and all parents are members of the Parents' and Friends' Association.

Charitable status. Laxton Junior School is a Registered Charity, number 255230. It exists to provide education for boys and girls.

Leaden Hall School

70 The Close Salisbury Wilts SPI 2EP.
Tel: (01722) 334700
Fax: (01722) 410575
e-mail: leaden.hall@virgin.net

Chairman: Lt Col J R Stephenson, CBE

***Headmistress:* Mrs D E Watkins**, MA

Number of Pupils. 261 Girls. 221 Day. 40 Boarders
Fees from September 2001. Day £1,415–£1,995, Boarding £3,100

Set in beautiful surroundings in Salisbury's Cathedral Close, Leaden Hall was once the home of the 'architect' of Salisbury Cathedral, Elias de Dereham.

Leaden Hall provides education for girls aged 3–12+. We prepare children for the Common Entrance and the County 11+ and 12+ examinations. We aim to give all girls self-confidence balanced with an awareness of others and a belief in themselves, so that entry to senior school follows naturally without fuss.

Our full, weekly and day boarding options give parents the flexibility to enable their daughters to take part in the many extra-curricular activities which ensure that our pupils flourish in a stimulating, happy and purposeful environment.

Charitable status. Leaden Hall School is a Registered Charity, number 309489. It exists to provide education for children.

Lichfield Cathedral School

The Palace Lichfield WS13 7LH.
Tel: (01543) 306170

Chairman of Governors: The Dean of Lichfield

***Head Master:* P J F Jordan**, MA

Number of Pupils. 270, including up to 18 Cathedral choristers, and approximately 45% girls. (27 boarders)
Fees. Full Boarders Forms III to VI £2,882 per term.

Full Boarders below Form III £2,782 per term. Weekly Boarders Forms III to VI £2,630 per term. Weekly Boarders below Form III £2,530 per term. Day Pupils Form III to VI £1,975 per term. Day Pupils below Form III £1,875 per term. Pre-Prepartory Department Full day £1,210 per term. Pre-Preparatory Department Half day £610 per term. Instrumental Music Tuition per instrument £132 per term. There are no compulsory extras.

There is a full-time teaching staff of 20, and three matrons. Most musical instruments are taught by visiting teachers.

Children are prepared for entry by their 14th birthday to HMC and other schools, and, in addition to the normal subjects, all are taught Art. Music and CDT; many study at least one musical instrument and have good opportunities to win music scholarships to Independent Senior Schools. There is a school orchestra, jazz band, wind band and choir. Other activities include Football, Cricket, Hockey, Rounders, Cross Country running, Netball, Athletics, Dance, Lacrosse, Swimming and many extra-curricular activities.

The Preparatory Department occupies two houses in the Cathedral Close, one of which is the former Palace of the Bishops. The games fields are adjacent, and there is an open-air swimming pool in the Palace garden. School services are held in the Palace chapel, and the children occasionally attend other services in the Cathedral.

Pupils are normally admitted at age 7 or 8, following an informal interview. A Voice Trial is held each year for boys wishing to enter the Cathedral Choir, for which choral scholarships are provided by the Dean and Chapter of the Cathedral. Academic and Instrumental Music Scholarships are also available for children entering at Third Form level. The examinations are held in early March each year for admission the following September.

The School is a member of the Assisted Places Scheme.

There is a pre-preparatory department for day boys and girls aged 4 to 7 housed in its own purpose built building on the same site as the main school teaching block.

Charitable status. Lichfield Cathedral School is a Registered Charity, number XN 1078650. It exists to provide education for boys and girls.

Lincoln Minster Preparatory School

Eastgate Lincoln LN2 1QE.
Tel: (01522) 523769
Fax: (01522) 514778

Governing Body: The Council of the Church Schools Company Limited

Chairman: The Lady Prior

Headmistress: **Karen Kelly**, BEd Hons, MEd (Nottingham)

Co-educational. Nursery, Pre-preparatory, Preparatory.

The School occupies delightful, highly impressive and safe sites close to the Cathedral and aims to offer a warm but purposeful environment in which boys and girls can grow and learn. The routine is kept deliberately busy, with individual pupils advancing as far as possible at a pace that is right for them. All subjects are taught by experienced specialists and in restricted class sizes.

The school has a strong musical tradition and the Cathedral Choristers are educated at the school. A Junior boarding house is home to youngsters aged 8 to 12. A foreign language is taught from an early age, and a high priority is given to Information Technology. A wide variety of experiences are available in the realms of sport, music, drama and clubs.

Scholarships and bursaries are available at 7+ and 11+ and it is anticipated that the vast majority of pupils will transfer to the nearby Lincoln Minster School.

The Headmistress and her staff value close links with parents, and are pleased to see them at the regular parents' evenings and at other times by appointment. Informal contact and discussion is welcome and each individual is seen as an important and valued member of the school.

Charitable status. The Church Schools Company is a Registered Charity, number 1016538. It is a charitable trust existing to provide high quality education in keeping with the teaching of the Church of England.

Lisvane, Scarborough College Junior School

Filey Road Scarborough North Yorkshire YO11 3BA.
Tel: (01723) 380606
Fax: (01723) 380607
e-mail: lisvane@scarboroughcoll.co.uk
website: www.scarboroughcollege.co.uk

Co-educational. Day (with boarding available for boys and girls from Year 5).

Head of School: **G S Twist**, BEd, BA, NPQH

Chairman of the Governors: Mrs J Martin

Number of Pupils. 167 Pupils, aged 3–11.

Fees per term. Junior Tuition (7-11) £1,645; Infant Tuition (4-7) £1,208; Nursery (half-daily session) £9.50; Boarding (£15 per night), £2,877

Lisvane School dates back some 80 years when it started life as a boys' preparatory school. In 1951 Lisvane became the Junior School of Scarborough College; more recently, boarding has been re-introduced on a small scale with the children being accommodated in the very well appointed houses situated close by on the Filey Road.

In February 2000 Lisvane re-located to the main Scarborough College campus. The school now occupies superb purpose-built premises affording striking views over Oliver's Mount, the South Bay and Scarborough Castle. Facilities feature a self-contained nursery, pre-prep and junior suites, an administration unit together with a school hall and a fully dedicated design and technology workshop. All classrooms are equipped with television, video and radio-cassette equipment and classroom computers are networked to the schools' ICT suites, which have Internet facilities. Lisvane shares many impressive resources and amenities with Scarborough College: science laboratories, drama studio, main sports/drama hall, music teaching and practice rooms, sports fields, a full-size all-weather pitch and school mini-buses.

The breadth of opportunity on offer in the academic curriculum and the diverse programme of extra curricular activities do not detract from the solid grounding pupils receive in the core subjects. Class teaching - with thoughtfully introduced specialist support where this is advantageous - is the pattern until Year 4. This is then advanced by sull subject specialist teaching in the last two years, in readiness for transfer to Scarborough College. The full complement of well-qualified staff ensures a generous teacher/pupil ratio. Provision is further enhanced by a Special Needs Co-ordinator who oversees the school's learning support unit in conjunction with the Hull Dyslexia Institute; this has its own dedicated accommodation provided by the school, but it is independently staffed by the Institute. A crèche is available from 8.00 am until the official school day begins, and from the end of school until 5.45 pm. The standard of pastoral care in both Lisvane and Scarborough College is high. Lisvane aims to nurture well-rounded, confident and responsible pupils who are ready for the challenges of secondary education. Ultimately these children will be the citizens of the future, needing to adapt to the opportunities presented by a rapidly changing world, yet able to experience that all important sense of purpose and fulfilment in their lives.

Liverpool College Preparatory School

Mossley Hill Liverpool L18 8BG
Tel: (0151) 724 4000
Fax: (0151) 729 0105

Chairman of the College Council: Mrs B M Greenberg
Chairman of the Prep School Governors: Mr J Robertson

Head of the Preparatory School: **Mr S Buglass,** MEd (Oxon), CertEd

Number of pupils. 417 boys and girls aged 3-11

Fees per term. Nursery and Pre-Prep (ages 3-7): £1,330; Prep (ages 7-11): £1,700. Lunches £155 per term.

Liverpool College is a co-educational day school set in 26 acres of beautiful wooded grounds. It is situated on the edge of Sefton Park in the conservation area of South Liverpool. The Preparatory School shares the site with the Senior Department, a successful day school of 600 pupils, aged from 11-18 years. However it has its own purpose built buildings and areas within the College.

The staff-pupil ratio (1:11) has encouraged the development of a broad based academic curriculum leading children through Key Stages 1 and 2 and the nationally moderated SAT's examinations. There is breadth as well as depth to the curriculum and in addition to the core and foundation subjects, two Modern Foreign Languages, Classics, Drama, ICT and Public Speaking and Debating are compulsory elements of the curriculum. The school is well equipped and during the past twelve months a new library and ICT department have been developed. This has enabled all of the children in the school to have their own e-mail addresses and controlled access to the internet. A well qualified dyslexia specialist is available to assess and support children throughout the school.

Music is an important aspect of school life. There is a thriving choir and orchestra, and performances in school and in the local community are important features of school life.

Most children progress through to the Senior School at 11+ where the brightest have successfully competed for Scholarships. Children are also prepared for entry to other Senior Schools throughout the country.

An extensive extra curricular programme encourages children to stay at school until 6 pm. Clubs include Judo, Soccer, Cross Stitch, Touch-typing, Chess, Athletics, Drama, Orchestra, Choir, Tennis, Hockey, Cricket, Art and Dancing. There is also an after school homework club which enables children to be supervised up until 6 pm completing their homework with teaching staff support and participating in a range of interesting activities.

During their time in the school children have the opportunity to participate in the annual ski trip, a language course in France, Geography and Science field work in North Wales and outward bound activities in the Lake District.

There is a major commitment to sport and the facilities include extensive playing fields, an Astroturf playing surface (completed 1998) and large Sports Hall and Fitness Suite (completed 1999). Specialist games staff teach the children rugby, cricket, netball, rounders, swimming, cross country, hockey, tennis and athletics.

Liverpool College has an Anglican Foundation, but children of all denominations and faiths are welcomed. The Chapel plays an important part in the life of the school, and twice a week they attend services there. The school is a caring community which places great importance on mutual respect and consideration for others. There is a strong and effective system of pastoral care.

Entry to the School. Children are assessed before entry and are assured of a place in the Senior School once accepted into the Preparatory School. Further details and a prospectus can be obtained from the Registrar.

Charitable status. Liverpool College is a Registered Charity, number 526682. It exists to provide education for boys and girls.

Lochinver House School

Little Heath Heath Road Potters Bar Herts EN6 1LW.
Tel: (01707) 653064
Fax: (01707) 653064
e-mail: registrar@lochinverhouse.herts.sch.uk

Chairman of the Governors: Derek Brown

Headmaster: **Patrick C E Atkinson**, BSc, CBiol, PGCE

Number of Boys. 340 day boys, 4–13 years.

Fees. £1,845–£2,354 per term; no compulsory extras

The academic staff consists of 30 qualified and graduate teachers and two Nursery Nurses.

The school is situated in a pleasant residential area on the edge of green belt land in South Hertfordshire, and yet is conveniently placed for access to London. The heart of the school is a late Victorian house. The facilities are extensive and include a purpose built Pre-Prep Department, separate Sports Hall, Gymnasium & Theatre, Music Centre, Modern Languages and English Departments, two Science Laboratories and an Information Technology room equipped with a Network of PCs. All classrooms and offices contain PCs that are also part of the school's Intranet and have protected and supervised Internet access. The school has its own extensive playing fields on site.

Boys are prepared for Common Entrance and Scholarship examinations to a wide range of both day and boarding Independent Schools.

The major sports are Football, Rugby and Cricket together with Athletics and Badminton. All boys learn to swim whilst they are at the School and they have the opportunity to take part in a very wide range of sports and physical activities. This includes outward bound and there is an annual skiing holiday.

During their time at the school each boy will spend some time in France as this is an important and much valued part of the French Curriculum.

Music, Art, Design Technology and PE are part of the timetabled curriculum for all boys regardless of their age. The school encourages boys to learn musical instruments and currently two thirds of the children are doing so. There is a School Orchestra and choir, together with various instrumental groups.

The school is a non-profit making Educational Trust administered by a Board of Governors.

Charitable status. Lochinver House School is a Registered Charity, number 311078. It aims to provide a quality education.

Lockers Park

Lockers Park Lane Hemel Hempstead Hertfordshire HP1 1TL.
Tel: (01442) 251712
Fax: (01442) 23263911
e-mail: secretary@lockerspark.herts.sch.uk
website: www.lockerspark.herts.sch.uk

Chairman of Governors: C B Melluish, Esq

***Headmaster:* D R Lees-Jones**, GRSM, ARCM
Second Headmaster: C R Stephens, BA

Pupils. Boys aged 7+ to 13. 130 boys, half of whom are boarders.

Fees. Boarders £3,770 per term. Day Boys £2,350–£2,945 per term. No compulsory extras.

Further details are outlined in the prospectus, available on application.

Lockers Park is located in 23 acres of parkland above the town of Hemel Hempstead, only five miles from both the M1 and M25 motorways. It therefore lies within easy access of London (Euston 30 minutes) and all four of its airports; consequently the School is well accustomed to providing the necessary help and support to parents living both in Britain and abroad.

The main school building, purpose-built in 1874 is situated in grounds which are perfect for children, with well-maintained playing fields surrounded by woodland areas which well occupy even the most active. There has been a steady process of modernisation over the past two decades so that the School can now boast first class, all-round facilities; these consist of the Mountbatten Centre which provides eight excellent specialist classrooms including a well-equipped ICT centre, a recently opened up-to-date library and art, pottery and technology centres. Sports facilities are of a high calibre and include a fully-fitted sports hall, two squash courts, a heated swimming pool, two tennis courts, a shooting range and a nine hole golf course; the installation of an all-weather sports surface is planned in the near future.

Lockers is proud of its academic and musical records; its success in both scholarships and Common Entrance examinations to 45 different schools in the past ten years reflects this well. The maximum class size is 16 and the pupil:teacher ratio a very healthy 1:7. The Music Department is well known; encouragement is given to every boy to find an instrument which he will enjoy and most gain proficiency in at least one. There is a full orchestra, wind, brass and jazz bands, a string ensemble and two choirs. In all, 12 senior school scholarships were awarded to Lockers Park boys last year.

Drama plays a large part in school life with at least one major production each year together with junior plays, school assembly productions, charades and public speaking debates.

At Lockers, there is a real family atmosphere, there is always someone to whom a boy can turn and great care is taken to ensure the happiness of every child. Boys are safe, happy, fit and well looked after. While day boys enjoy all the facilities and opportunities of a boarding school, boarding is fun; dormitories are warm and friendly rooms and opportunities for a variety of enjoyable weekend activities are immense. With day boys and boarders alike, great care is taken over the personal development of each individual.

Charitable status. Lockers Park School Trust Ltd is a Registered Charity, number 311061. It aims to provide an all round, high quality education on a non-profit making basis.

Long Close School

Upton Court Road Slough Berks SL3 7LU.
Tel: (01753) 520095.
Fax: (01753) 821463

Chairman of Governors: R Ellis, CBE, MA

***Headmaster:* N Murray**, DipEd

Number of children. 170 boys, 60 girls – all day aged 2+–13+

Fees. £1,076–£2,142. Lunches £149 per term.

The quality of teaching is measured by the staff's ability to recognise the unique way in which each child learns - small classes and individual attention mean that each child has the greatest chance of success. Top quality creative arts and physical development enhance the core curriculum. Each child is appropriately challenged to realise his or her full and true potential. Long Close children are very well equipped to rise to the many challenges which face them in the future. Children are prepared for Scholarship and Common Entrance examinations to independent schools and for entry to the grammar schools.

The facilities and resources are both excellent and extensive; the School enjoys a superb position and a well constructed site.

There is extensive provision for the extended day, allowing children to develop skills outside the curriculum.

Children leave Long Close not only with academic skills and ability but also with a generally well rounded education. They have learnt to respect and care for others. We aim for quality in all that we do.

Loretto Nippers

Musselburgh East Lothian EH21 6JA
Tel: 0131-665 2628.
Fax: 0131 665 1815
Station and Airport: Edinburgh

***Vicegerent:* R G Selley**, BEd

Number of Pupils. 40 Boarders, 80 Day Pupils

Fees. Boarders from £3,609 per term. Day Pupils from £1,285 per term

Pupils can enter the Nippers at 5 and are prepared for the Common Entrance and Scholarship exams mostly to Loretto at 13+. Weekly boarding is possible for pupils between the ages of 8 and 13. There is an annual competitive Scholarship and Bursary exam to the Nippers for children aged between 8 and 11. There is one boarding house at North Esk Lodge, and as well as the usual prep-school facilities, the Nippers use the Loretto Technology Centre, Computer Centre, Swimming Pool, Squash Courts, Fives Courts, Music School, Theatre, School Chapel, and the Sports Hall. The school enjoys a fine reputation for Rugby, Hockey, Cricket and Netball, and Music, Drama and Art. Loretto has its own Art Gallery. A wide range of individual sports is coached. The staff are all University Graduates and the eleven classes accommodate up to 16 pupils. There are two Matrons under the close supervision of the School Doctor. Catering is in the hands of an experienced Steward.

From an early age children are encouraged to use their initiative and accept responsibility.

Prospectus from the School.

Loyola Preparatory School

103 Palmerston Road Buckhurst Hill Essex IG9 5NH.
Tel: 020 8504 7372

Trustees: The Society of Jesus

Chairman of Governors: A C Wheater, Esq

Head Master: **P G M Nicholson**, BEd (London)

Number of Boys. 204

Fees from September 1999. £1,260 per term (all inclusive). £630 a term (Nursery)

A Catholic Day Preparatory School for boys aged 3 to 11+. Admission is possible at any age. There are twelve full-time and five part-time staff. The School has its own Chaplain.

Boys are prepared for entrance and scholarship examinations at 11+ to various Independent Senior Schools and to Grammar Schools in the maintained sector. The curriculum covers all the normal primary school subjects including French, science and computer studies. Music is taught throughout the school. There is a specialist choir and tuition can be arranged in piano, strings, woodwind, brass and percussion. Sports include football, cricket, swimming, athletics and optional rugby.

A prospectus is available on application to the Head Master.

Charitable status. Loyola Preparatory School is a Registered Charity, number 230615. The school is established in support of Roman Catholic principles of education.

Ludgrove

Wixenford Wokingham Berks RG40 3AB.
Tel: (01189) 789881
website: www.ludgrove.berks.uk
Station: Wokingham, SWT

Headmasters: **G W P Barber**, MA (Oxon) and **C N J Marston**, MA (Oxon)

Number of Boys. 195

Fees. £4,050 a term

Ludgrove stands in its own grounds of 130 acres. Boys between the ages of 8 and 14 are prepared for the Senior Independent Schools.

Lyndhurst House School

24 Lyndhurst Gardens Hampstead London NW3 5NW.
Tel: 020 7435 4936
e-mail: enquiries@lyndhursthouse.co.uk

Headmaster: **M O Spilberg**, MA (St Edmund Hall, Oxon)

Number of Day Boys. 140

Fees. (at September 2000) £2,365 per term inclusive of lunch, games, outings, books etc. There are no extras.

There is a teaching staff of 13. The main entry is at 7+ following interviews and assessment. All boys stay to 13+, and sit the Common Entrance or Scholarship to the Independent Senior Schools, usually in London, but often outside. A broad foundation is laid in the junior classes, with subject specialisation commencing at 9+, and very small classes in the last two years. A full programme of games and other activities is pursued throughout. There are specialist rooms for Art, Mathematics, French and Geography, a computer room, and Science laboratory, all housed in a fine Victorian building with large, well-lit classrooms, and a good-sized playground.

Maadi British International School

9 Road 278 New Maadi Cairo Egypt
Tel: (00202) 516 4144/516 3965/516 3967/520 0704
Fax: (00202) 516 4239
e-mail: mbis@mbisegypt.com
website: www.mbisegypt.com

Headmaster: **Gerard L Flynn,** BPhil (Newcastle), CertEd

Number of pupils. 235 boys and girls (primary); 90 boys and girls (nursery).

Fees. £5,300 (annually); £1,770 (termly). Registration: £1,500 (this is a once only payment).

MBIS is an International Primary School situated in Maadi, a suburb of Cairo favoured by expatriates. Approximately 45% of pupils are British, the remaining 55% represent over 30 nationalities. The school follows the English National Curriculum and all its assessment requirements including end of Key Stage 1 and 2 testing. All teaching staff are UK graduate teachers, in the main recruited directly from Britain. In each class there is a teaching assistant working alongside the class teacher. Specialist teachers are employed for French, Arabic, ICT, Music and Special Needs. The school has an 'able child' co-ordinator and a full time SRN.

There are 14 classrooms, a well stocked library, an ICT suite, an art room and a music drama room. A small theatre/ assembly hall is planned to be operational during the 2001-2002 academic year.

The school undergoes Ofsted inspection on a four year cycle. It is accredited by World-wide Education Service (WES) and is an associate member of the European Council of International Schools.

Physical Education takes place at the nearby Olympic Centre which offers facilities for training in every Olympic Sport including a 50m pool.

There is a thriving programme of extra curricular activities which is as varied as Horse Riding at the pyramids and calligraphy at school. Piano lessons are available as an after school activity.

Children undergo an assessment before admission. This is to ensure that the school can meet the individual needs of the child. This process can be bypassed if current school reports are available and forwarded to the Headteacher.

There is a very strong PTA which benefits all pupils and their parents.

The overall aim of the school is to deliver a high quality British education in a caring and stimulating environment.

Prospective parents are requested to contact the Headteacher and he would be particularly pleased to show any parents visiting Cairo around the school.

The school is a 'not for profit' organisation registered as a non-governmental organisation (NGO) with the Egyptian Ministry of Social Affairs, with a charter to educate foreign children. The school's Board of Directors is made up of parents who have children in the school with the addition of up to three invited governors which at present includes HM Consul in Cairo.

Maidwell Hall

Northampton NN6 9JG.
Tel: 01604 686234
Fax: 01604 686659

Chairman of the Governors: D Dennis, Esq

Headmaster: **R A Lankester**, BA, PGCE

Number of Pupils. Boarding 100, Day Boys 10, Day Girls 10, Pre-Prep 30.

Fees. £3,710 for boarders per term, inclusive. £2,420–£2,600 for day children. £930–£1,510 per term for Pre-Prep.

Charitable status. Maidwell Hall is a Registered Charity, number 309917. It exists for the purpose of educating children.

Maldon Court Preparatory School

Silver Street Maldon Essex CM9 4QE.
Tel & Fax: (01621) 853529

Principal: A G Sutton, MA (Oxon) (Chairman, ISIS East)

Headmaster: **A G Webb**, BEd

Number of Pupils (Day only). 130 (co-educational)

Fees at April 2000. £1,330 (Tuition) per term for the first child; for others of the same family at school concurrently there is a discount.

Compulsory extras. Lunches are £2.20 per day, there is a variable charge for swimming (all year) and a small library charge.

The school, founded in 1956, is a coeducational day school of seven classes. The children's age range is from 4 plus to 11 plus.

Maldon Court's premises comprise the larger part of an eighteenth century town house, a separate four classroom block, separate toilets and a small assembly hall. There is an acre of ground overlooking open country of which part is garden and part hardcourt, incorporating two half size netball courts and a six-a-side hockey pitch. There are also areas containing adventure climbing equipment.

The premises are very convenient for the town centre. Sports grounds for association football, athletics, hockey and other activities are leased locally. Squash and Racquet Ball are offered to the top two age groups at a local club and there are after-school netball, speech and drama, dance and cycling proficiency clubs. Swimming is undertaken throughout the year at a nearby sports centre. The school's sporting standard is extremely high; over recent years it has won both national and regional awards.

Approximately half the children leave the school for independent secondary schools, half enter the maintained sector. Maldon Court's scholarship and entrance record to the independent schools is excellent as is its eleven-plus success rate to Essex grammar schools. Close contact is maintained with both systems of education. Its curriculum covers and goes beyond the National Curriculum. Pupils participate in the SAT's programme and results are externally moderated, when required.

In 1975 a Parents' Association was formed. It is registered separately with the Charities Commission and has developed into an energetic and lively organisation.

The School has the reputation of being a happy, friendly community with a family atmosphere. Turnover of staff is low.

The school was inspected by the ISC Inspectorate in 1994 and received its accreditation as a result of the inspection and is due to be inspected again in the Spring 2002.

To conclude, Maldon Court's objectives are threefold. Firstly, the School must develop the "whole child", encouraging him to achieve his potential on all fronts, academic, athletic, artistic and social. Secondly, the children must be taught how to work, irrespective of their varying abilities. Finally the School strives to encourage and develop a Christian code of ethics and behaviour, so that, upon leaving, its children will be good influences in their next community and retain worthwhile values for the rest of their lives.

The Mall School

Twickenham Middlesex TW2 5NQ.
Tel: 020 8977 2523
Fax: 020 8977 8771
Stations: Twickenham, Strawberry Hill, and Fulwell

Headmaster: **T P A MacDonogh**, MA (Cantab), DipEd

Chairman of Governors: J A Hamblin, Esq, FCA

Number of Boys. 290 day boys

Fees. (Sept 2000) £1,595 Pre-prep. £1,850 over 8.

Established 1872, the School prepares for day and boarding Senior Independent Schools and is a charitable Trust. Boys are admitted from the age of four and are taught by a well qualified staff consisting of 20 full-time and 5 part-time members. A number of awards are won each year (41 in the last 5 years). The class size averages 20. In addition to bright modern classrooms, facilities include new Science Laboratories and Music Department, opened to mark the school's 125th birthday, an Art room, a Library, and a Centenary Hall/Gymnasium with a fully-equipped stage. The curriculum includes Computing (both network and multimedia) and Design Technology.

Cricket, Rugby and Association Football, Swimming and Athletics are the main school games. The school has its own outstanding indoor swimming pool opened in Summer 1999. Fencing, Judo, and Carpentry are optional. Music and Drama are warmly encouraged. There are 2 choirs and 2 orchestras with a large variety of ensembles and visiting teachers for piano, strings, guitar, woodwind and brass.

During the last ten years of major redevelopment four new buildings have been opened: The Waterfield Building, which houses the pre-prep school which receives boys from 4 to 7, The Ellis Building, a matching Senior classroom block, The Hamblin Building in 1993, comprising kitchen, dining room, library and offices, and in 1997, the Thistlethwaite Building with two Science Laboratories and Music Department.

A prospectus is available on application to the Secretary. Early application is advisable.

Charitable status. The Mall School Trust is a Registered Charity, number 295003. It exists to promote and provide for the advancement of the education of children.

Malsis School

Cross Hills Nr Skipton North Yorkshire BD20 8DT.
Tel: (01535) 633027
Fax: (01535) 630571
e-mail: admin@malsis.fsnet.co.uk
website: www.malsis.com

Chairman of Governors: Richard Robinson

***Headmaster:* J M Elder**, MA (Hons) (Edinburgh), PGCE

Deputy Headmasters:
R Davies, CertEd, AD Ed
D S Walker, BA (Hons)

Bursar: Mrs M Rishworth

Number of children. Co-educational 3–13. Full Boarding 60, Daily Boarding 70, Pre-Prep 55.

Religious Denomination. Mainly Church of England. Roman Catholics are looked after by Mrs Elder. Other denominations accepted.

Fees per term. Full Boarding £3,465 per term; Daily Boarding £2,546; Pre-Prep £693–£1,386.

About Malsis. Malsis is set in its own grounds of forty acres in the Craven District of North Yorkshire in an area of rare beauty near Skipton, Ilkley and the Dales but also within easy reach of the towns of the North of England, 15 miles from Leeds-Bradford airport and only fifteen miles from the M65 motorway. There is a January and April intake in addition to September. Over half the children board and then on to over fifty schools, the majority going to Ampleforth, Eton, Giggleswick, Glenalmond, Harrow, Oundle, Radley, Shrewsbury, Sedbergh, Stonyhurst and Uppingham. The pastoral system is centred on the Housemaster, Form teacher and Tutor and we teach them about courtesy, appreciation of values (spiritual and social); we try to discover any talent and develop it to the full; we teach them about kindness, humour and honour. There is a team of eighteen teachers, four matrons and ten visiting music staff. Mr and Mrs Elder live, with their family, in the middle of the school and are very much the "parents" of the school.

All the main subjects are taught including Greek, Spanish and German on offer. Information Technology, Design, Drama, Craft and Art are part of the timetable. 109 Scholarships have been won since 1986 to 25 different schools. There is particular emphasis on Art, Music, Poetry and Drama with 13 Art scholarships and 20 Music awards in the last decade. Every child takes part in at least one drama production each year; six are produced including a musical. Reading and Handwriting are central to the children's education at Malsis, with reading periods every day. The main Choir leads the Chapel Services and sings in the surrounding area. The school attends local music festivals and children take part in mini concerts, recitals and a major termly concert. Music groups, including a Concert Band, meet each week. Groups visit local theatres, concert halls and places of interest. Extra help (free) is given in English, Mathematics and French; Dyslexics are looked after by trained staff. Malsis has an excellent record in sport, regularly winning trophies far and near but more than that, nearly all the children play in a team, all children being coached games whatever ability, by a team of ten. Rugby, Cricket, Cross Country, Hockey, Swimming, Athletics, Rounders and Tennis are the main sports with Soccer an option for the smaller children. The school grounds include fifteen acres of pitches, an astroturf pitch, a nine hole golf course, a small grass athletics track, four all-weather tennis courts and two grass courts, a beck, woods and a lake.

Malsis is generously equipped to meet the modern world of education: light, specialist teaching rooms including two Science Laboratories, Art Department, Design and Technology centre, IT centre, 18 room Music school, 6th Form Centre, Sports Hall, Gymnasium, Indoor Swimming pool, Astro-all-weather pitch, a Theatre and a lovely Chapel in the centre of the main house. Well-equipped games rooms offer snooker, table-tennis, bar football and a host of board games. The staff have great fun here, the challenge of youth is ever present. A varied activity programme (break, evening and weekend) is available each week with fifty clubs on offer and these range from rambling, camping, archery, sailing, canoeing, shooting, archery, basketball, badminton, judo, squash, golf to cuisine, fly-tying, dance, fishing, photography, ornithology and fencing. Yes, we have plenty of new buildings and equipment, but a boarding and day preparatory school is much more: to learn to help others, to enjoy ourselves, these are top priorities.

Pre-Preparatory Department. Garden House opened in 1996 for boys and girls aged from three to seven years. It is situated in the grounds in its own self-contained accommodation.

Charitable status. Malsis School is a Registered Charity, number 529336. It exists to offer children a full, rounded education, catering for all boys and girls so that they move on from Malsis confident, well-mannered and friendly.

Maltman's Green

Maltmans Lane Gerrards Cross Bucks SL9 8RR.
Tel: (01753) 883022
Fax: (01753) 891237

Preparatory School for Girls 3–11 years
Accredited by the ISC.

Chairman: S A Hill, Esq, FCA

***Headmistress:* Miss J Reynolds**, BEd (Hons)

Numbers. There are 380 girls

Fees. £700 (half day Nursery) to £2,185 per term.

The central house is an attractive homely building dating in part from 1600. New Gymnasiums, Laboratories, Music block and Classroom wings provide excellent facilities.

The girls are taught in small classes with some streaming in the Upper School. The curriculum is designed to lead to the Girls' Common Entrance Examination to Independent Senior Schools, and to prepare them for entry to Buckinghamshire Grammar Schools.

There are 10 acres of grounds, a heated open-air swimming pool, 3 hard tennis courts and 2 hard netball courts, a hockey field and athletics track.

Apply to the Headmistress for illustrated prospectus and full details.

Charitable status. Maltman's Green School Trust Limited is a Registered Charity, number 301633. It exists to provide a high standard of education for young girls.

Manor Lodge School

Rectory Lane Ridge Hill Nr Radlett Herts WD7 9BG
Tel: (01707) 642424
Fax: (01707) 645206

***Head:* Mrs Judith Smart**, CertEd, BA (Open)

Number of pupils. Infant Department (4–7) 167; Junior Department (7–11) 208.

Fees. Infants £1,525 per term; Juniors £1,850 per term.

The school expansion is now complete and there are three forms of 18 children in Years Reception to 6 inclusive. There are specialist teachers for French, PE, Music and IT, as well as numerous peripatetic teachers for brass, woodwind and strings. All staff are fully qualified.

The six acres of grounds include woodland, a playing field, two sports fields and a tennis/netball court. The children are offered a wide range of sporting activities including football, hockey, cricket, netball, rounders, lacrosse, swimming and athletics.

The school consists of a 17th century house for the Juniors and the converted stables offer twelve classrooms for the Infants. Plans are underway to extend part of the stable block to provide four new rooms, one of which will be a Science Room. The classrooms are bright and well equipped and, as the children are justifiably proud of their achievements, our standard of display is very high.

We aim to provide excellent teaching within an environment characterised by a well balanced but friendly family atmosphere in which high standards of behaviour and good manners are encouraged and expected. We thus ensure that all pupils achieve their full potential and are prepared for entry to senior schools, both independent and LEA.

Extra activities available at the school include short tennis, drama, horseriding and ju-jitsu. There are numerous clubs run by the staff at lunchtime and after school until 4.15 or 5 pm, for example, sewing, gardening, calligraphy, cricket, netball, theatre, athletics, chess and choir.

Charitable status. Manor Lodge School is a Registered Charity, number 1048874. The school exists to provide an education which will maximise the potential of the girls and boys aged 4–11 in our care.

The Manor Preparatory School

Abingdon Oxon OX13 6LN.
Tel: (01235) 523789
Fax: (01235) 559593
e-mail: registrar@manorprep.oxon.sch.uk

Chairman of the Governors: Mr N J Cross

Headmistress: **Mrs D A Robinson**, BA (Exeter), PGCE (Cambridge), MBA

Number of Pupils. 365. Girls 335; Boys 30

Day preparatory school for girls aged 3–11 years and boys aged 3–7 years.

Fees. Nursery £925–£1,390, Transition £1,720, Forms 1 & 2 (5–7 years) £1,810, Forms 3 & 4 (7–11 years) £1,910. Forms 5 & 6 £2,010.

The Manor is a Charitable Trust. It is surrounded by spacious grounds and there are good facilities for indoor and outdoor games.

A well qualified staff teach a full range of subjects. Boys are prepared for entry to preparatory schools and girls for the Common Entrance Examination for Girls Schools, or for entrance examinations to local senior schools.

The curriculum is broad. Science, Information Communication Technology, Art, Design, Music, Physical Education and Modern Languages are all taught by specialists. All subjects have specialist teaching in the final two years of the preparatory department.

Computers are used throughout the school to supplement the curriculum and ICT skills are taught in two specialist ICT departments. There are two School Orchestras, 4 choirs, 5 chamber groups, and it is possible to learn almost any musical instrument as an optional extra.

Teams represent the school in Swimming, Netball, Tennis, Rounders and Athletics. The children learn Short Tennis from the age of 6 years.

The school promotes close co-operation between parents and teachers. Parents' Evenings are a regular feature. "The Friends of The Manor" association is run by parents to welcome new families and to support the school.

Charitable status. The Manor Preparatory School is a Registered Charity, number 900347. It exists to provide education for girls.

The Margaret Allen Preparatory School

32 Broomy Hill Hereford HR4 OLH.
Tel: (01432) 273594

Chairman of Governors: Mr A Kain

Headmistress: **Mrs Anna Evans, HND, BEd** (Hons), CertMaths, CertGeography

Number of Girls. 100

Fees. £1,150–£1,380 per term day pupils only

The Margaret Allen Preparatory School is situated in a pleasant residential area, half a mile from the city centre.

A nursery class accepts girls and brothers at 2½ years old. The main school entry for girls is the September following their fourth birthday, and girls are prepared for entry to senior schools at 11+. There are ten well qualified staff ensuring small classes and individual attention. A high academic standard is maintained to CE and Scholarship levels.

Pupils in the early years are taught most subjects by their class teacher, with specialists teaching music and PE. In senior classes subject based teaching including specialist Science, prepares pupils for secondary school. Music, Drama and PE are strong features of the school with many pupils having instrumental lessons, and there are a Junior String Group, Senior Orchestra and Choirs as well as sports teams.

Educational visits and after school clubs ensure a full school life.

An after-school care club provides support for working parents.

Charitable status. The Margaret Allen Preparatory School is a Registered Charity, number 701232. It exists to provide education for girls.

Markham College Lower School

Apartado 18-1048 Miraflores Lima Peru
Tel: Lima 375499
Fax: Lima

Headmaster: **Mr B M Allen**, BPhil(Ed), CertEd

Chairman of Governors: Mr Edward Holme

Number of Children. Co-educational – 420 Infants; 600 in Lower School.

Fees. Initial Entrance Fee – Infants $5,500; Lower School $4000. Annual Tuition $6,100.

The Lower School is the primary school of Markham College. The College was founded by the British Community and the British Council in 1946 and is owned by the British Educational Association of Peru. All members of staff are graduates or trained teachers – just over a third being recruited from Britain.

The school is located in the foothills of the Andes in Monterrico and has its own extensive playing fields. In addition to the normal range of general classrooms there are specialist Music, Science, Computer and Art Rooms.

Boys and girls enter at the age of 4 and proceed to the Upper School at age 12. The school is bilingual with approximately 60% of the curriculum delivered in English. The Warden of Markham College is an overseas member of The Headmasters' Conference.

Marlborough House School

Hawkhurst Kent TN18 4PY.
Tel: (01580) 753555
BR Station: Etchingham (5 miles)

Chairman of Governors: A B E Hudson

***Headmaster:* D N Hopkins**, MA (Oxon), PGCE

Deputy Head: P Tooze, BA, PGCE

Director of Studies: N Davidson, MA (Oxon), PGCE

Number of Pupils. 309

Fees. To July 2000, (no compulsory extras). Weekly Boarders: £3,730; Day: £2,635; Pre-Prep: £1,290–£1,525; Kindergarten: £775.

Marlborough House was founded in 1874 and is registered as an Educational Trust with a Board of Governors.

The School is fully co-educational creating a friendly, family, but disciplined atmosphere for children between the ages of 3 and 13.

Marlborough House is situated half a mile from the village of Hawkhurst in the beautiful countryside of the Kent/Sussex border. The fine Georgian house is set in 35 acres of superb gardens, playing fields, lawns and woodland. The School has a Chapel, Computer Centre, Gymnasium, superbly equipped Science Laboratory, Art, Pottery and Design Technology Department, Music Rooms, Swimming Pool, 12 Specialist Teaching Rooms, a .22 Rifle Shooting Range and an all-weather games surface. A new Sports Hall was opened in 1999.

With our 30 qualified teaching staff we aim to produce well motivated, balanced, confident children who know the value of hard work, and who will thrive in their next schools and the modern world beyond. Our classes are small and the children are prepared for all major Senior Schools, whilst those showing special promise sit scholarships.

Encouragement is given to each child to experience a wide variety of activities. In addition to the traditional sports of Cricket, Rugger, Soccer, Hockey, Athletics, Netball and Rounders opportunities are provided for Music (with the opportunity to learn a wide range of instruments and join the orchestra and choir), Art (in many different media), Pottery, Drama, Ballet, Cookery, Technology, Computers, Riding, Shooting, Squash, Tennis, Sailing, Golf, Swimming and Gymnastics.

A copy of the Prospectus together with a Magazine will be mailed to prospective parents on application to the Headmaster.

The Mary Erskine and Stewart's Melville Junior School

Queensferry Road Edinburgh EH4 3EZ.
Tel: 0131-332 0888
Fax: 0131 332 0831

Chairman of the Governors: James Laurenson

***Headmaster:* Bryan Lewis**, BA

Number of Pupils. 1,162 Boys and Girls (120 in the Nursery; 354 in the Prep Dept; 688 in the Upper Junior School, with Boarding places from 9+). Equal number of girls and boys apply for places.

Fees. (inclusive of all books, stationery and materials) Nursery £1,194 per term; Primary 1 £1,130 per term; Primary 2-6 £1,522 per term; Primary 7 £1,562 per term; Boarders £3,175 per term. These are the 1999/2000 figures.

The Junior School is co-educational throughout. At the age of 12 boys and girls proceed, without further examination, to their respective, single-sex Senior Schools, which are very closely 'twinned' at all stages. The Principal is in overall charge of both Schools. Means-tested Bursaries are available from the age of 10, as are Academic and Music Scholarships.

Major points of entry are to Primary Start (from 3); Primary 1 (from 4½) and Primary 4, 6 and 7 (age 8, 10 and 11), though casual places may be available elsewhere.

As the Junior School is situated on the Senior School sites, children benefit from specialist facilities and teachers of French, Music, Art, PE, Swimming, Dance, Computer Studies, Technology and Drama, as well as the internal Junior classroom subjects. Nearly half the children are involved in Choirs and Orchestral pursuits, and other clubs include Chess, Swimming, Gymnastics, Judo, Fencing, Remote-controlled cars and many others, including many team sports. Drama plays a large part in Junior School life.

After-school and holiday care available for all pupils until 6.00 pm daily (from 8.15 am during holidays). Private coach services bring large numbers of children to the Junior School from several areas up to 20 miles out of Edinburgh.

Further information about Stewart's Melville College may be found in Part I of this Book, and information on The Mary Erskine School is given in Part II. Prospectuses etc from the School.

Mayfield Preparatory School

Sutton Road Walsall West Midlands WS1 2PD.
Tel: (01922) 624107

Administered by the Governors of Queen Mary's Schools

Chairman of the Governors: Mrs J Kirby-Tibbits

***Headmistress:* Mrs C M Jones**, BA, CertEd

Number of Pupils. Boys: 107, Girls: 84.

Fees. Main School £1,395 per term; Nursery £1,395 per term.

A co-educational day school for children aged 3 to 11+, set in a listed building with beautiful surroundings and playing fields. A purpose built Science/Art building opened in November 2000.

The self-contained Nursery Department accepts children as rising 3.

A fully qualified Staff with full-time ancillary support throughout KS1 ensures that the individual child receives maximum attention.

The main aim at Mayfield is to encourage intellectual excellence. Children experience a thorough grounding in literate and numerate skills.

Through stimulating courses of correctly paced work the school specialises in the preparation of the children for Grammar and Independent School entrance examination at 11+.

Our children achieve excellent results, but it is always borne in mind that the individual child's needs are met by matching achievement to potential. All children are expected and encouraged to develop daily in confidence and security.

We believe in a balanced curriculum, and at Mayfield practical and non-academic activities additionally provide interest and varied experiences in Sports, Art, Music, ICT, DT, Dance, Drama and Public Speaking.

Good manners are expected at all times, as well as a happy and whole-hearted participation in the life and studies offered by the school.

Micklefield School

Somers Road Reigate Surrey RH2 9DU.
Tel: (01737) 242615
Fax: (01737) 248889

Chairman of the Council: P R Woods, Esq, BSc, MICE, CEng

***Headmistress:* Mrs C Belton**, BA, CertEd

Number of Pupils. 282 (76 boys)

Fees. From £355 (Nursery, three afternoons) to £1,740 (full time). Lunches £105 (full time).

Micklefield School, established in Reigate 90 years ago, offers small classes, taught by qualified staff, many of whom are graduates. It caters for boys and girls from the age of two-and-a-half up to the age of eleven, preparing them for Common Entrance and other examinations.

After school care is available for children from Reception age.

In addition to the normal academic subjects, the curriculum includes design/technology, woodwork, computer studies, dancing, drama, French, Classics, netball, tennis swimming, football and cricket. Pupils taking examinations for entrance to senior schools are accepted by the schools of their choice, many gaining scholarships.

In a happy and disciplined environment children enjoy academic success, take an active part in a variety of musical and theatrical activities and do well on the playing fields. First-class dramatic productions for all age-groups and concerts provide opportunities for everyone, including the School's orchestra and choirs, to display their talents. Local drama festivals, games matches, visits to concerts, theatres, museums, etc. are organised and, for the older children, biennial ski and French study trips.

An excellent, recent extension to the school has provided a new gym, a new design/technology/art room and two new classrooms.

A prospectus may be obtained on application and Mrs Belton, the Headmistress, is always pleased to show prospective parents around by appointment.

Charitable status. Micklefield is a Registered Charity, number 312069. It exists to provide a first-class education for all its pupils.

Millfield Preparatory School

Edgarley Hall Glastonbury Somerset BA6 8LD
Tel: (01458) 832446
Fax: (01458) 833679
e-mail: office@millfieldprep.somerset.sch.uk
website: www.millfield.somerset.sch.uk/prep

Chairman of the Governors: Mr Adrian White, CBE

***Headmaster:* Mr K A Cheney**

Number of Boys and Girls. 250 Boarders (including 80 girls). 250 Day Pupils (including 115 girls).

Fees. The boarding fees from September 2001 (for pupils resident in UK) average £4,340 per term, together with General Subscription (to cover all normal extras including laundry, books and extra tuition) £160 per term. For day pupils termly fee averages £2,930 with General Subscription £120. Fees for overseas pupils on application.

The School is administered by the same Board of Governors and on the same principles of small-group teaching as Millfield (made possible by a staffing ratio of approximately 1 to 8) which ensures breadth and flexibility of timetable. It has its own attractive grounds of 160 acres some three miles from the Senior School, and its extensive facilities include games fields, art, design and technology centre, science laboratories, sports hall, astro-turf, assembly hall with stage, tennis courts, 25 metre indoor swimming pool and chapel. The modern Dining Hall and Library were opened in 1989, and an extensive Music School with recital hall was completed in January 1991. Two new classroom blocks have recently been opened, including a suite of 3 IT laboratories. The pupils have access to some of the specialist facilities at Millfield including the theatre, squash courts, fencing salle, judo dojo, riding school and stables.

The majority of pupils transfer to Millfield via Millfield Transfer examination, Scholarships or Common Entrance, but some pupils attempt scholarships or entrance to other senior independent schools. The small class sizes allow the individual pupil to be taught at his or her most appropriate pace. The range of ability within the school is comprehensive and setting within subjects caters for both the academically gifted and those requiring remedial tuition.

The curriculum is broadly based and provides a balance between the usual academic subjects and the aesthetic, musical and artistic fields. Junior pupils study French, Year 6 French and Latin and there is a choice of French, German, Spanish and Latin from the age of 10 upwards. Children may choose either one or two foreign languages, dependent on ability. Science is taught throughout the school, and as three separate subjects from the age of 10.

There is a full games programme organised by qualified teachers of physical education, with the help of other staff. The programme includes Rugby, Hockey, Cricket, Football, Rounders, Athletics, Tennis, Swimming, Badminton, Squash, Netball, Gymnastics, Canoeing, Orienteering and Outdoor Pursuits, to name but a few.

Over 90 different clubs are available for pupils including Chess, Ballet, Riding, Drama, Music, Computing, Modelling and Design. Over 350 pupils study musical instruments and there are 2 orchestras, 2 choirs and 20 musical groups. Boys and girls are admitted from the age of 7 and up to the age of 12 and they come from many lands and widely differing backgrounds. Admission usually depends on interview, assessment and reports from the previous school. Assistance with fees in the form of awards may be available to deserving applicants.

There are eight boarding houses (five for boys and three for girls). Each house is under the care of resident houseparents, assisted by other staff and a team of matrons.

The medical centre is staffed by 3 qualified nurses, and the School Medical Officer attends daily.

Charitable status. Millfield is a Registered Charity, number 310283. The Millfield Schools provide a broad and balanced education to boys and girls from widely differing backgrounds, including a significant number with learning difficulties, and many for whom boarding is necessary.

Milton Keynes Preparatory School

Milton Keynes MK3 7EG.
Tel: (01908) 642111
Fax: (01908) 366365
e-mail: info@mkps.co.uk
website: www.mkps.co.uk

Chairman of the Governors: Mr Peter Squire, MA

Headmistress: **Hilary Pauley**, BEd

Number of Pupils. 420 day pupils, Preparatory Department 7+–11 years. Pre-Prep 2½–7 years. Nursery 2 months–2½ years

Fees. Preparatory Department £6,720 per year; Pre-Prep £6,120 per year; Nursery – there is an hourly rate of £4.50.

Milton Keynes Preparatory School is purpose-built with facilities which include a Science laboratory, DT workshop and large multi-purpose sports hall. Opening hours are 7.30 am – 6.30 pm for 46 weeks per year which enable children of working parents to join playschemes in school holidays and to be cared for outside normal daily school hours.

Staff are highly qualified and committed. Academic standards are excellent, with pupils being prepared for entry to senior independent schools locally and nationally and to grammar schools. Teaching is structured to take into account the requirements of the National Curriculum, with constant evaluation and assessment for each pupil.

Music and Sport play an important part in the life of the school. Concerts are held, and a wide variety of sports is played, with teams competing regularly against other schools.

The school aims to incorporate the best of modern teaching methods and traditional values in a friendly and busy environment where good work habits and a concern for the needs of others are paramount.

The Minster School
York

York YO1 2JA
Tel: (01904) 557230
Fax: (01904) 557232

Chairman of Governors: The Very Reverend Raymond Furnell

Head Master: **Richard Shephard**, MA (Corpus Christi College, Cambridge), DMus, ARSCM

Number of pupils. 187: Upper School 75 Boys, 60 Girls

Fees. £1,680 Upper School, £1,090 Pre-Prep (Full Day), £590 Pre-Prep (Half Day), Choristers receive an 80% Scholarship

The Minster School originally founded in 627 to educate singing boys. It is now a co-educational preparatory and pre-preparatory school including a Nursery department. From the 187 children in the School, 25 boys and 25 girls are choristers who sing the services in York Minster. Pupils are prepared for Common Entrance and Senior Independent School Scholarships.

In addition to the normal academic curriculum there is a flourishing music department; all orchestral instruments are taught.

The games include Football, Netball, Hockey, Cricket, Swimming and Rounders. After-school activities include Rugby, Fencing, Tennis and Riding.

In addition to the normal academic curriculum, there is a flourishing music department and all orchestral instruments are taught. Many children gain music and academic scholarships to their senior schools.

Monkton Combe Junior School

Combe Down Bath BA2 7ET.
Tel: (01225) 837912
Fax: (01225) 840312
e-mail: cj.stafford@virgin.net
Station: Bath

Chairman of Governors: P W Lee, CBE, MA, DL

Headmaster: **C J Stafford**, BA, CertEd

Number of Pupils. Boarders 50, Day Boys 110, Day Girls 66, Pre-Prep 120

Fees. Boarders £4,000, Day Pupils: £2,761, Pre-Prep £797–£1,521 per term. There are no extra charges except for learning a musical instrument and specialist activities like judo and dance. There are reductions in fees for the children of clergy and Scholarships are offered for those with all-round academic, musical, artistic, sporting and leadership ability at age 7 and 11.

The School became fully co-educational in September 1993. It stands in its own grounds on a magnificent site. The buildings include a Chapel, a Modern Classroom Block, a Hall for drama and music with 14 music practice rooms, an Audio-Visual Room, Common Rooms, Hobbies Rooms, a Sports Hall, and an indoor 25 metre pool and fitness centre. There is a separate building for the Arts, Sciences, Computing and Technology. There are 20 acres of grounds, 3 Tennis Courts, a hard playing area and a Nature Reserve.

The School has a strong musical tradition and a flourishing Art Department. There are two choirs, an orchestra, a band and various other instrumental groups. Drama also plays an important part in school life. Rugby, Hockey, and Cricket are the major boys games along with athletics, cross-country running, tennis, squash, swimming, gym, judo, basketball and badminton. Netball, hockey and rounders are the major sports for the girls. There is a full programme of matches. All pupils take part in hobbies and activities sessions.

There are 22 fully qualified members of the teaching staff and others who are part time. In addition, the Pre-Preparatory Department, which works as a separate entity but shares many of the Junior School amenities, has 11 trained teachers, two nursery nurses and two assistants. Children join the pre-Prep at two. The main entry to the Junior School is at seven plus, but the school accepts pupils who wish to join at a later stage.

Boys and Girls are prepared for Common Entrance and Scholarship exams to Independent Senior Schools. At least two-thirds of them proceed to the Senior School and one third to a wide range of other Independent Senior Schools. 64 Scholarships have been won in the past five years.

Over the years Monkton has educated many children

from families who are working overseas. We make special arrangements for them and are well used to meeting their various needs.

The School finds its central inspiration and purpose in its Christian tradition.

Charitable status. Monkton Combe School is a Registered Charity, number 310277. Its aim is to provide education for girls and boys aged 2 to 18, in accordance with the doctrine and principles of the Church of England.

Moon Hall School for Dyslexic Children

Pasturewood Road Holmbury St Mary Dorking Surrey RH5 6LQ
Tel: (01306) 731464
Fax: (01306) 731504
e-mail: enquiries@moonhall.surrey.sch.uk
website: www.moonhall.surrey.sch.uk

Principal: **Mrs Jill Lovett,** CertEd, Hornsby Diploma in SpLD, AMBDA

Chairman of Governors: Mrs Berry Baker

Number of children. 85 in total of whom approximately 50 are full time.

Fees 2000-2001. From £2,507–£3,825 per term for day pupils according to provision/stage. From £3,568–£4,886 per term for boarding pupils according to provision/stage.

Religious denomination. Church of England.

Moon Hall School for Dyslexic Children caters for intelligent boys and girls with specific learning difficulties. It is accredited by CReSTeD as offering category A provision. It has what is believed to be a unique symbiotic relationship with a Preparatory School and shares the 60 acre site and excellent facilities of Belmont (see separate entry). Uniform is common to both schools, and pupils are fully integrated at assembly, lunch and play times. They also jointly participate in Games sessions, sports teams, and dramatic and musical productions.

Moon Hall has a specialist multi-disciplinary staff – all appropriately qualified in their own fields. They deliver a full curriculum to dyslexic children from the age of 7. Pupils transfer to Belmont classes when ready; the norm being into National Curriculum Year 6. They then return for ongoing support as required up to age 13. The level of provision for these older children ranges from one 1:1 lesson per week to a complete curriculum in English and Mathematics together with Typing and Oral French (16 lessons). *All* children are taught to touch-type and pupils have been successfully entered for OCR (formerly RSA) examinations normally taken by older teenagers and adults.

Within the well-designed and purpose-built accommodation, classes are restricted to a usual maximum of twelve children. These are subdivided into groups of about six for English and for Mathematics. One-to-one tuition is available as needed. The school is extremely well equipped with a vast range of specialist resources and computers. Literacy and numeracy teaching is structured and multi-sensory and incorporates material devised by acknowledged experts in the Field. Study Skills and Thinking Skills are taught as an integral part of the programme.

Great emphasis is placed upon the re-building of self-esteem.

Entry requirements. A full report by an independent educational psychologist who has found the child to be dyslexic and of at least average intelligence. Assessment at Moon Hall, combined with participation in the events of a typical day.

Charitable status. Moon Hall School is a Registered Charity, number 803481. It exists to provide specialist education for intelligent dyslexic children aged 7 to 13.

Moor Allerton School

131 Barlow Moor Road Manchester M20 2PW.
Tel: 0161 445 4521
Fax: 0161 434 5294
e-mail: office@moorallertonschool.manchester.sch.uk

Headmaster: **Mr P S Millard**, BA, MSc, NPQH

Number of Pupils. 150 (boys and girls) aged 3-11 years

Fees per term. Nursery (half day) £887, (full day) £1,147. Reception £1,192. Years 1/2 £1,247. Years 3/4/5/6 £1,542. (Fees are inclusive of lunch and milk).

Moor Allerton is a small co-educational school which has a fine tradition of academic success. The school has recently undergone a regeneration programme, which has extended the site to include three further classrooms, an IT Suite, Science Laboratory and Art Studio.

The school is guided by Christian principles. All children are welcomed and encouraged to learn respect for differing cultures by living and working alongside those of other faiths and backgrounds, whilst maintaining their own identity. Although emphasis is placed on academic progress, games have traditionally been a way of fostering healthy competition and of teaching children to enjoy taking part; children are helped to learn how to win or lose graciously. In the classroom children's progress is regularly monitored and they are encouraged and supported by a team of dedicated and committed teaching staff. Expectations of all children are high. Gifted children are challenged and stretched and support is given to children who have difficulties. Pupils receive appropriate preparation for entry at 11+ to independent senior schools.

Music, Art and PE are important areas of the curriculum and sports played at the school are soccer, netball, cricket, rounders, tennis, swimming, athletics and bridge. We offer a wide range of extra-curricular activities, including table-tennis, judo, ballet and speech & drama, plus musical tuition, including percussion, flute, clarinet, guitar and piano.

There is After-School Care until 5.30 pm and Early Care from 7.45 am. Holiday Fun Clubs are offered during Summer, Easter and Whitsun Breaks.

Moorlands School

Foxhill Drive Weetwood Lane Leeds LS16 5PF.
Tel: (0113) 2785286
Fax: (0113) 2306548
e-mail: headmaster@moorlands-school.co.uk

Headmaster: **A R Jones,** MA, BEd (Hons), CertEd

Chairman of Governors: Mr J Pike

Number of Pupils. 275 Day boys and girls aged 3–13

Fees. Tuition – Pre-Preparatory Department (3–7 years) £723–£1,445. Main School (7–13+) £1,620. Lunch £109 and £122.

Religious affiliation. Undenominational

Entry requirements. Admission by assessment and interview.

The School is an Educational Trust with a Board of

Governors. The School was founded in 1898 and consists of day boys and girls who live in the city of Leeds and surrounding area.

The aim of the school is to develop the full potential of every child within a happy and caring environment fostered by small classes and the professional skills of a highly qualified staff. Strong links between the parents and the school are encouraged to facilitate the provision of an effective education.

Pupils are accepted at 3 years old for entry into the Kindergarten and are expected to progress through the school for preparation for entry to the Public and Independent Grammar Schools. The school has a well developed specialist facility to provide assistance for pupils with any learning issue such as dyslexia or gifted children.

Blended with this traditional core of academic work is offered a comprehensive range of sporting activities and a wide range of musical and extra-curricular pursuits.

Moor Park School

Ludlow Shropshire SY8 4DZ.
Tel: (01584) 876061
Fax: (01584) 877311
e-mail: moorpark.staff@netmatters.co.uk
website: www.moorpark.shropshire.sch.uk

Chairman of Governors: Mrs Cecilia Motley

***Headmaster:* N R Colquhoun**, MA (Oxon)

Founded 1964

Fees. Boarders: £2,950–£3,595 per term. Day children £1,100–£2,625 per term.

Moor Park is a co-educational day and boarding school of Catholic foundation. 50% of the 135 8 to 13 year olds are boarders with 55% being boys. A further 117 children form our Lower School of 2½ to 7 year olds. The focus of the school is on the development of each child as an individual. Our concern is to provide the broadest possible education based within a framework of moral and spiritual principles.

Moor Park is situated two miles south of the historic town of Ludlow and on the edge of the Mortimer Forest. The school campus is set in 85 acres of playing fields, pasture and woodland. Facilities include a science, IT and languages block, art block, learning support facility, sports hall, main hall/theatre, delightful chapel and heated swimming pool. An extensive range of activities and hobbies are provided daily and at weekends.

The school has an enviable academic and sporting record with 54 scholarships in the last five years and 14 children this year representing their county or region. The main sports are rugby, football, cricket, hockey, netball and rounders but we are also county champions at cross-country and have some notable track successes. Minor sports such as archery or karate are encouraged through the activity programme.

The pastoral system reflects the boarding structure and family orientation of the school. The boys and girls have separate boarding houses, each with their own house-parents. The girls boarding facility was described by a recent schools inspection as 'outstanding'.

Charitable status. Moor Park School is a Registered Charity, number 511800. It exists to provide education for boys and girls.

Moreton Hall Preparatory School

Bury St Edmunds Suffolk IP32 7BJ.
Tel: (01284) 753532.
Fax: (01284) 769197
e-mail: MoretonH2@aol.com
website: www.moretonhall.suffolk.sch.uk

Chairman of the Board of Governors: Brigadier J F Rickett, CBE

***Headmaster:* N J Higham**, BEd Hons

Number of Pupils. Boys 75; Girls 45

Fees. £3,370 (boarders), £1,460–£2,445 (day pupils) a term.

Moreton Hall is a Catholic school which welcomes other denominations.

The school accepts boarders from the age of 7, and day pupils from the age of 3. (Weekly and flexible boarding arrangements are possible).

There are 17 full and part-time staff in the Prep and Pre-Prep departments, plus ancillary and Nursery staff, which makes an average class size of 12 pupils possible. In addition there are visiting teachers for music, dance, and speech and drama, whilst the School Chapel is served by the parish clergy. In the boarding house Matron, the duty member of staff, and the gap students, work under the direction of the resident Headmaster and his wife.

The School occupies a fine Adam mansion built in 1773, and stands in its own grounds of 30 acres of wooded parkland and playing fields on the outskirts of the historic town of Bury St Edmunds. London is two hours distant by road or rail. The School is happy to arrange transport to and from all airports.

Pupils are prepared for Scholarship or Common Entrance examinations to a wide range of Independent Senior Schools, and the school is proud to achieve an excellent record of success in both areas.

The Music Department at Moreton Hall is particularly strong, with 70% of the children learning at least one instrument. There is a strong Chorister link with St Edmundsbury Cathedral and a Chorister Scholarship is available.

The School has a very strong tradition in Drama. Recent professionally-directed productions have included *Romeo and Juliet*, *Iolanthe*, *See How They Run*, *As You Like It*, *Rosencrantz and Guildenstern* and *A Midsummer Night's Dream.*

Art and design play an important part in the curriculum, as does Information Technology, with every child, from the nursery up, being taught in the IT suite, newly refurbished and equipped in November 1999.

The main games are rugby, soccer, hockey, cricket, athletics, netball, squash, tennis and swimming. Amongst the extra-curricular activities available are ballet, gymnastics, golf, tap dancing, judo, carpentry, chess, computer art, natural history, enamelling and debating. There is a covered, heated swimming pool and a large sports hall. A second, indoor swimming pool is available for use in the winter at the adjacent Health club, which is also where squash takes place.

The Pre-Prep department is housed in its own self-contained section of the School buildings and enjoys all School amenities.

Academic and St Edmundsbury Cathedral Choral Scholarships are offered at Prep School entry ages. Apply to the Headmaster for further details.

Charitable status. Moreton Hall School Trust Limited is a Registered Charity, number 280927(B). It exists to provide high quality education for boys and girls.

Mostyn House School

Parkgate South Wirral Cheshire CH64 6SG.
Tel: 0151-336 1010

Headmaster: **A D J Grenfell**, MA (Worcester College, Oxford)

Age Range. 4–18
Number in School. 314: Boys 199, Girls 115
Fees per term. Infant Department (Mornings only) £765; (All Day) £1,195; 7–11 £1,195, Over 11 £1,860.
Compulsory extras. Lunches £1.75 per day

Mostyn House School is a co-educational day school for children between the ages of 4 and 18. Founded in 1854, the school opened its new Senior School in 1985. Entry to the Junior School (7–11) is by interview and test. The Senior School (11–16) prepares pupils for GCSE and Advanced Level examinations, with entry by interview and examination in English, Maths and Reasoning. Entry to the 6th Form is by GCSE results and interview.

Small classes (usually a maximum of 20), a well qualified and enthusiastic staff (43 in number) and a happy but hard-working atmosphere bring out the best in each child, and a wide range of subjects is offered. Recent developments such as three Science Laboratories, Computer Centre, Indoor Swimming Pool, HE Room, Library, Art Studios, Infant Department, 6th Form Centre and CDT suite complement older buildings such as the beautiful Chapel.

A wide range of extra-curricular activities including dance, drama, computers, music, craft, snooker and shooting take place in a special activity session each day. Individual sports are encouraged and the School has a comprehensive fixture list for team sports.

Pupils' work is monitored regularly with Form and Senior Tutors keeping a close eye on individual development. Regular reporting to and consultation with parents takes place throughout the school.

The School is a member of ISCO and a team of 14 qualified staff run a comprehensive careers guidance programme for all senior pupils. It became a charitable trust in 1979 and the Chairman of the Board of Governors is Mr Glyn Dale-Jones. The Headmaster is the fifth generation of the Grenfell family to direct the school. The school has passed an accreditation inspection by the ISJC and is in full membership of IAPS and ISAI.

Charitable status. Mostyn House School Trust is a Registered Charity, number 1048117. It exists to provide education for boys and girls aged 4–18.

Moulsford Preparatory School

Moulsford-on-Thames Wallingford Oxon OX10 9HR.
Tel: (01491) 651438
Fax: (01491) 651868

Chairman of the Board of Governors: Mr Brian Lee, FAPA

Headmaster: **M J Higham**, BA, CertEd

Number of Boys. 45 Weekly Boarders, 180 day boys. Aged 5–13

Fees. Weekly Boarders, £2,995–£3,225 per term; Day Boys £1,530–£2,565 per term; These fees are all inclusive but individual coaching in music, judo, golf and fencing are charged as an extra.

The School is a Charitable Trust controlled by a Board of Governors. It has its own river frontage on the Thames, spacious games fields and lawns and is situated between Wallingford and Reading.

Boys are prepared for the Common Entrance and Scholarship examinations to the top independent schools in the country. An experienced and well qualified staff ensure that a high standard is achieved academically, musically, artistically and on the games field.

The principal games are rugby football, soccer, tennis and cricket. Other sporting activities include athletics, swimming, sailing, judo, canoeing, golf, archery and gymnastics. The school is proud of its fine sporting reputation which has been built up over many years.

Mount House School

Tavistock Devon PL19 9JL.
Tel: (01822) 612244
Fax: (01822) 610042

Chairman of the Governors: P J D Hodgson, CBE, FCA

Headmaster: **C D Price**, BA

Deputy Headmaster: J Symons, BEd

Numbers. 250 (105 boarders, 85 day children and 60 Pre-Prep)

Fees. Boarders £3,664, Day Children £2,059–£2,747, Pre-Prep £913–£1,605

Mount House School is set in idyllic surroundings in fifty acres of playing fields, woodlands and gardens with lakes and streams. It is bordered on the west by over ½ mile of the River Tavy. Children are prepared for Common Entrance and Scholarship to the leading national Independent Schools. All the main subjects are taught throughout the School, including Latin, CDT, Music, Art and Physical Education.

A huge range of hobbies and activities is offered.

There is a robed RSCM choir which leads the Sunday Services and sings in churches, cathedrals and senior schools from time to time. Most of the pupils learn a musical instrument. There are various musical groups and orchestras. There is a hall complete with stage, main music room and practice rooms. A well equipped Design and Technology Centre was opened in 1990 and an Art School in 1992. The new girls' boarding house was opened in September 2000 and a large music school in May 2001. Work has begun on an 'astroturf' all-weather pitch which should be completed in September 2001.

All the main sports are played and children are coached to a high standard. The fixture list includes schools in other parts of the country. There is a superb sports hall with facilities for a host of sports. The hall includes a full size tennis court and two squash courts. Academic work is competitive. It is carefully monitored with regular Form Orders and Effort grades. High standards are expected and achieved. There is a very happy atmosphere and particular attention is paid to good manners. There is an Escort service to and from London and the airports. (Heathrow to Plymouth is quicker than getting across London!).

An exciting architect-designed Pre-Prep department was opened in the autumn of 1996 providing traditional teaching in small groups to children between the ages of 3 and 7 years old. The Pre-Prep has access to many of the Main School's facilities.

Charitable status. Mount House is a Registered Charity, number 270147. It aims to provide high quality independent boarding and day education for boys and girls aged between 3 and 14.

Mowden Hall School

Newton Stocksfield NE43 7TW.
Tel: (01661) 842147
Fax: (01661) 842529
e-mail: 1b@mowdenhall.co.uk
website: www.mowdenhall.co.uk

Chairman of Governors: F W Hoult, Esq

Headmaster: **A P Lewis**, MA (Magdalene College, Cambridge)

Deputy Headmasters:
M W W Spencer, BEd
M R Weldon, BA, CertEd

Number of Pupils. 259 (141 boys, 118 girls); Prep School 174 (Boarders 134, Day Pupils 40); Pre-Prep & Nursery 85 day pupils.

Pre-Prep. 38 boys, 20 girls

Fees (from September 2001). £3,790 Boarding; £2,730 Day; £1,560 Pre-Prep; £810 Nursery

Mowden Hall is a large Victorian mansion with extensive grounds overlooking the Tyne Valley. It is situated in the country, yet is close to Newcastle upon Tyne and is only fifteen minutes from the city's International Airport.

There are 55 acres of woodlands and playing fields and, apart from the usual facilities, the school has a Science, Art & Technology Centre, a Theatre and Music School, an indoor and heated swimming pool, a large Sports Hall and three new hard tennis courts. A purpose-built Pre-Preparatory Department was opened in 1993, and a Nursery Department in 1997. The Computer Room was re-equipped with pwerful new PCs in 2000 and the system is networked throughout the school. All pupils have supervised access to the Internet and also have their own e-mail addresses.

Mr and Mrs Lewis live in the school building with their family. Mrs Lewis has a team of Senior Matron and two assistant matrons and two part time matrons helping her look after the welfare of the children. There is also a resident House Tutor who looks after the boarding and another senior member of the staff living within the school building. Most members of staff live on the school estate and all are actively involved in the pastoral care of the children.

A large staff of well-qualified masters and mistresses assists the Headmaster, and the teacher/pupil ratio is approximately 1:9. Children are taught in small classes (average 12) and are prepared for the Scholarship or the Common Entrance Examination to a wide range of the leading Senior Independent Schools.

In 1996 the school created a link with Cothill House School over the use of Chateau de Sauveterre, near Toulouse. Now all children spend a full term during the 7th Year (11–12 year olds) in France being taught all their lessons in French by French teachers.

There is no entrance examination to the school. Children may start as day pupils, but all are expected to board by the time they reach their eleventh birthday.

The major games are Rugby, Cricket, Hockey, Netball and Athletics, however numerous other games are taught and there is a strong swimming team. The children are also encouraged to take part in a wide variety of other activities.

The school has a strong tradition of both Music and Drama. Tuition is available in the full range of instruments and over two-thirds of the pupils in the school learn an instrument. There are three choirs, three brass groups, a recorder consort and an orchestra. There are regular concerts given by the children. Every child takes part in a Form drama production during the year and there are also several major school productions each year.

The school aims to bring out and nurture the individual talents of each pupil. It also encourages social responsibility, discipline and good manners in a Christian environment. There are short daily services in the Theatre and a full service every Sunday in the nearby parish church at which parents are very welcome.

Interested parents are encouraged to ring the Headmaster for a prospectus and to arrange a visit.

Charitable status. Mowden Hall (Newton) School Trust Limited is a Registered Charity, number 528124. Its aim is to provide high quality education for both boys and girls.

Mowden School

Hove Sussex BN3 6LU.
Tel: (01273) 503452
Fax: (01273) 503457

Headmaster: **C E M Snell**, (IAPS Diploma)

Number of Boys. 130. Aged 4–13 years.

Fees. £1,500–£2,650 a term, including lunch and tea.

Mowden is situated in an enviable position in Hove overlooking the English Channel.

The school believes in traditional values and enjoys an excellent academic and sporting record. The Arts also play a strong role with over half the children learning a musical instrument. Our aim is to provide an environment where attention can be paid to the needs of each child as an individual so that he can grow in confidence as his talents and abilities are developed to the fullest in a happy and homelike atmosphere.

There is a full-time and well qualified staff of eleven with part time specialist teachers for art, music and design and technology. The domestic arrangements are under the charge of Mrs Snell and there is a qualified Matron.

The facilities include fully equipped science laboratory, design and technology room, music room, art room, gymnasium and heated swimming pool, squash rackets court, computer room and library. The main sports are cricket, soccer and rugger with tennis, hockey and basketball being played on the new all weather area.

The New Beacon

Brittains Lane Sevenoaks Kent TN13 2PB.
Tel: (01732) 452131
Fax: (01732) 459509

Chairman of the Governors: A T Webb, Esq, FCA

Headmaster: **Rowland Constantine**, Esq, MA (Magdalene College, Cambridge)

Deputy Headmaster: A O K Rotchell, Esq, LCP(SMS), FCollP, CertEd(Dist)

Pupils. 30 boarders, 380 day boys

Fees per term. Boarders: £3,360. Day boys: £1,750-£2,275. Fees include all normal extras with day boys' lunches

Boys are prepared for all independent Senior Schools with considerable success in both CE and scholarship. The forms are divided into Senior, Middle and Junior School and boys placed according to ability. Initiative is encouraged by organising the school into 4 houses or companies. The school house is complemented by many modern facilities. A purpose-built Junior School for all boys age 5–9; a first class Sports Hall with modern changing facilities; a Theatre; heated indoor Swimming Pool; a centre for Art and Music; modern facilities for Science and Technology. Soccer, rugby and cricket are the major games. In the Summer boys may also do tennis and athletics. Swimming takes place all year round. There is a very extensive range of extra curricular activities at all age levels. Music, art and drama are highly regarded.

The School is an Educational Trust.

Charitable status. The New Beacon is a Registered Charity, number 307925. It exists to provide an all-round education for boys age 5–13.

Newbridge Preparatory School

51 Newbridge Crescent Wolverhampton WV6 0LH.
Tel: (01902) 751088

Chairman of Board: Mr P Webb

***Headmistress:* Miss M J Coulter**, BEd

Number of Pupils. 150 girls

Fees. £992–£1,511 per term excluding lunch. No compulsory extras. Dancing, elocution, group instrumental lessons all provided without additional charge.

This day school on the outskirts of Wolverhampton was founded in 1937. It is a non-profit making Limited Company with Charitable status. The main building is a substantial house set in mature gardens. Nursery and Lower School have purpose built classrooms in the grounds.

There are specialist facilities for Art, Design and Information Technology, Music and PE.

We are a school with traditional values and standards, achieving excellent results within a small caring community. Great emphasis is laid upon English, Mathematics and Science but we also give value to a broad curriculum to include a range of sporting, musical and extra curricular opportunities.

Girls are accepted from 3-11.

Charitable status. Newbridge Preparatory School is a Registered Charity, number 1019682. It exists to advance the education of children by conducting the school known as Newbridge Preparatory School.

Newcastle Preparatory School

6 Eslington Road Jesmond Newcastle upon Tyne NE2 4RH.
Tel: (0191) 281 1769
Fax: (0191) 281 5668

Chairman of the Governors: Mr M Glen-Davison

***Headmaster:* Gordon Clayton**, MA

Fees. Age 4–6 £1,355 per term. Age 7–8 £1,451 per term. Age 9–13) £1,548 per term. Lunches £115 per term.

The School was founded in 1885 and is now a Charitable Trust with a Board of Governors. It is situated in a residential part of Newcastle with easy access from all round the area.

Modern and well tried traditional methods are combined and the school seeks to provide a happy and friendly atmosphere in which children can develop their abilities whether academic, artistic or sporting. The School believes in a discipline which is firm but kindly and in good manners and courtesy at all times. It also believes that education should involve enjoyment as well as understanding and hard work and seeks to provide a broad education to the highest standard.

Children are admitted into the Junior School (4–6) in the term after they reach their fourth birthday. In the Junior School children are given the solid foundation on which to build. their future education. The Senior School (7–13) very successfully prepares children for boarding and day schools and many scholarships have been won in recent years. The School has a Kindergarten for 2 to 4 year olds, which provides excellent pre-School education.

Classes in both the Junior and Senior School are small so that as much individual attention as possible can be given. Children with particular learning difficulties are given individual help or tuition in small groups and there are two members of staff with special responsibility for helping such children.

The School has its own gymnasium, playing field and tennis courts next to the School and has regular use of other sporting facilities close to the School, for example, the Northumberland County Cricket and Tennis Club. A wide range of sporting activities are offered including rugby, football, cricket, hockey, netball, swimming, squash, badminton athletics and tennis. Music and drama are very strong in the School and there are many clubs and societies which include model making, art, photography, computers, public speaking, German, cross stitch and quilting, physical activities such as gymnastics, trampolining and various forms of dance.

Charitable status. Newcastle Preparatory School is a Registered Charity, number 528152. It exists to provide education for boys and girls.

New College School

Savile Road Oxford OX1 3UA.
Tel: (01865) 243657
Fax: (01865) 209116
e-mail: office@newcollegeschool.fsnet.co.uk

Governors: The Warden & Fellows of New College, Oxford

***Principal:* Mrs P F Hindle,** MA

Number of Boys. 130 Day Boys. 20 Choristers. Age 4-13 years

Fees per term. Age 4: £1,500. Age 5-9: £1,765. Age 10-13: £1,930. Choristers: £660.

New College School was founded in 1379 when William of Wykeham made provision for the education of 16 Choristers to sing daily services in New College Chapel. Situated in the heart of the city, a few minutes walk from the College, the school is fortunate in having the use of New College playing fields for sport and New College Chapel for school services.

The staff consists of 12 full-time and 14 part-time qualified graduates or certificated teachers. Boys are prepared for the Common Entrance and Scholarship Examinations for transfer to independent senior schools at age 13. In the final year there is a scholarship form and a common entrance form. The school broadly follows the national curriculum subjects, but also teaches French and Latin.

A Saturday morning arts education programme is followed by senior pupils from the age of 10 years. Games include soccer, hockey, cricket, rounders, athletics and swimming.

Music plays a major part in school life with orchestra, ensembles, concert and junior choirs and form concerts, in addition to individual tuition in a wide range of instruments.

Activities include art, craft, pottery, design, chess, science and computer clubs, German and Greek groups.

Boys are admitted to the Pre-Prep Department at 4 years and by assessment to the Lower School at 7 years. Potential Choristers are tested between the ages of 7 and 9 at Voice Trials.

Newland House School

Waldegrave Park Twickenham TW1 4TQ.
Tel: 020 8892 7479
Fax: 020 8744 0399
e-mail: school@newlandhouse.co.uk
website: www.newlandhouse.co.uk

Chairman of Governors: Sir Gordon Langley, QC

***Headmaster:* D J Ott**, BSc, UED (Rhodes)

Deputy Headmaster: D S Arnold, BA

Number of Boys. 285
Number of Girls. 141

Fees. Pre-prep £1,695 per term. Prep £1,905 (Lunches included).

The School, founded in 1897, is a charitable Educational Trust with a Board of Governors. Children are prepared for the Common Entrance and Scholarship examinations to Independent Schools. The school's main intakes are at the ages of 4 and 7. However, places do become available in other age groups throughout the school year.

The staff consists of 32 full-time and 3 part-time teachers as well as 5 classroom assistants in the Pre-Preparatory department. In addition there are 9 visiting music staff who teach a variety of instruments. The School has 5 choirs, a concert band, a wind ensemble and a brass ensemble.

The main games are Rugby, Soccer, Cricket, Netball, Rounders and Hockey. All children from the age of 7 have the opportunity to swim throughout the year.

The Main School has, in addition to 17 light and airy classrooms, a large gymnasium/assembly hall, dining room, separate senior and junior libraries and two well equipped science laboratories, one with a dark room. There is an Art and a Design Technology block as well as a purpose built Music block. The school has over 90 networked computers together with a state-of-the-art computer suite, complete with interactive plasma screen.

There is a separate Pre-Preparatory department for children up to the age of 7, which is also in Waldegrave Park.

A wide variety of extra-curricular activities are available.

Charitable status. The Newland House School Trust Limited is a Registered Charity, number 312670. It exists for the purpose of providing a good academic education in a friendly atmosphere.

Newlands Preparatory School

Eastbourne Road Seaford East Sussex BN25 4NP.
Tel: (01323) 490000/892334
Fax: (01323) 898420

***Headmaster:* Mr Oliver T Price**, BEd (Hons)

Chairman of Governors: Mr D Smith

Age range. 2½–13 years.

Number of pupils. Boarders: 51 boys, 26 girls; Day: 145 boys, 137 girls.

Fees per term. Boarding: £3,600–£3,850. Day: £1,915–£2,395.

Newlands Preparatory School provides quality education from 2½ to 13 years on one 21 acre campus in a pleasant coastal town surrounded by an area of outstanding natural beauty.

Newlands has good communication links with Gatwick (37 miles), Heathrow (78 miles) and London (65 miles).

YOUR CHILD'S POTENTIAL. At Newlands we place an emphasis on fully developing your child's potential in a happy and caring environment. The wide range of activities available make it possible for every pupil to achieve success and confidence in one field or another.

Classes are small and a pupil's progress is monitored carefully. The arts flourish with thriving music, drama, dance and art departments. There is a strong choral tradition and annual dramatic productions.

ACADEMIC AND SPORTS FACILITIES. Our facilities include high-tech computer rooms, science laboratories, a large art studio, a design technology workshop and a music department.

There are the equivalent of eight football pitches, a heated indoor swimming pool, a hard playing surface for three tennis/netball courts, a new, large Sports Hall, and a .22 rifle range. There are opportunities for many sports including soccer, hockey, rugby, netball, cricket, athletics, volleyball, basketball, tennis, horse riding, swimming, rounders and cross-country running.

SCHOLARSHIPS. Scholarships are available and there is a generous discount for Service familes.

ACCELERATED LEARNING UNIT. The nationally renowned Gannon Centre has specialist teachers who provide one-to-one tuition for gifted pupils, dyslexic pupils and those learning English as a foreign language.

THEATRE ARTS COURSE. A theatre arts course is available to pupils who wish to specialise in Dance, Drama, Music and Art within an academic environment.

TRANSPORT. Travel and escort arrangements include Fareham, Romsey, Aldershot, Maidstone, Victoria railway station as well as Gatwick, Stansted and Heathrow airports. Pupils can be met on incoming flights.

NEWLANDS MANOR (Senior School). Please see Part VI of this Book.

Charitable status. Newlands School is a Registered Charity, number 297606. It exists to provide quality education for boys and girls.

Newlands School

Newcastle upon Tyne NE3 1NH.
Tel: (0191) 2852208
Fax: (0191) 2130973
e-mail: newlandsnewcastle@lineone.net
website: www.rmplc.co.uk/eduweb/sites/newlandsnewcastle

Chairman of the Governors: J C Rippon, FRICS

***Headmaster:* R McDuff**, BEd (Hons), MA

Number of Boys. Senior School (98) 7–13; Junior School (104) 3–7. Day boys only

Fees. £1,350–£1,750 (This covers all usual extras including lunch)

The School is situated in a residential area on the outskirts of Newcastle and stands in its own grounds. The School moved to its present site in 1945 but it was established in the early part of the last century and has just celebrated its centenary. In 1975 Newlands became a Charitable Trust with an independent governing body. In 1984 a large gymnasium was completed. A new Art and Music Block was recently added. A new Kindergarten Block was opened in September 1995: a Nursery opened in September 1996 and a new Computer Suite was opened in September 2000.

The School is divided into 17 classes and boys are prepared for both boarding and day Independent Schools. The principal games are Rugby, Cricket, Cross Country, Athletics and Swimming. Art, Music and Computing are included in the curriculum but Piano, Guitar, Trumpet, Strings and Flute are optional extras.

An illustrated prospectus is available on application to the Headmaster. This gives full details of all School activities. The School has recently been accredited by ISJC and also by CRESTED.

Charitable status. Newlands Educational Trust is a Registered Charity, number 503975. An Educational Trust with a strong parental involvement, providing a traditional day prep school education for boys aged 3+–13+. There is a strong sporting tradition.

New Park School

St Andrews Fife KY16 9LN.
Tel: 01334 472017
Fax: 01334 472859

Chairman of the Board: Peter T Hughes, OBE

***Headmaster:* Andrew Donald**, BSc (Aberdeen)

Number of Pupils. 111 Day (33 girls, 78 boys)

Fees. Day: up to £2,020 per term; Pre-Prep: up to £1,080 per term; Nursery from £435 per term.

New Park School in St Andrews is a co-educational day preparatory school. Founded in 1933 and administered by a Board of Directors, the school enjoys charitable status and educates children aged between 3 and 13, from Nursery to Senior Independent School scholarship standard.

Pupils are prepared for entry to senior schools in both the state and independent sector. With specialist teachers and small class sizes, children benefit from individual attention. In addition to a strong academic curriculum, drama, art, music, ICT and CDT are included in the timetable.

Outside the classroom, a wide variety of sports are available, with Netball, Rugby, Hockey, Tennis and Cricket being the main team sports. Tuition in golf, judo and swimming is also offered. During the winter, the pupils can ski, and during the summer there are frequent hill-walking expeditions and camps.

Newton College Lower School
Las Lagunas de la Molina, Lima, Peru

Apartado 12-137 La Molina Lima 12 Peru.
Tel: Lima (511) 4790460
Fax: Lima (511) 4790430

Chairman of Governors: Victor Lazo

Bursar and Clerk to the Governors: Monica Puyo

***Headmaster:* John McCarry**

Fees. Entrance: US$4,500. Annual: US$5,820.

Staff. 120 Teachers, 30 Teaching Assistants

Number of Pupils. 765 Boys, 550 Girls

Newton College was founded in January 1979, on a site of 25 acres with a lake of 7 acres in its grounds, around which the school's buildings are built. The Nursery School, Little Newton, has been purpose-built over an area of 3,000 square meters, but also has access to all Newton College facilities. The Kindergarten area is in a specially built unit with its own facilities where 120 children enter when they have completed 5 years of age.

The Pelagatti Building houses the Lower School of 700 children between the ages of 6 and 12. The Senior School for 498 students is housed in the Harriman Building and the Churchill Building. Amongst the facilities they have at their disposal are computer and science laboratories, a fully air-conditioned soundproof auditorium for 200 people and a recently completed theatre, which can seat 1,400 people. All buildings are constructed of reinforced concrete and are designed in accordance with the latest developments in the educational field, being the most modern and functional in Lima, if not in South America. From the Lower School, children pass into the Senior School on the satisfactory completion of examinations.

The school also has a research and investigation centre in the Amazonian rainforest with accommodation for 30 pupils plus accompanying staff.

The school uses the INTERNATIONAL BACCALAUREATE and IGCSE examinations for students who reach the end of their secondary education. Currently 95% of our student body enter tertiary education.

The school staff is drawn from the most experienced qualified bilingual teachers available in Lima, with a contingent of contracted staff from England, presently 26.

With its extensive grounds available for all types of sports, the school has a sound Physical Education department. Emphasis is placed also on the teaching of music and art, with strong department heads in these fields. Our social programme is one of the most advanced known and illustrates the emphasis which is placed on a strong moral and humanitarian formation of the students.

Pupils are drawn mainly from Peruvian circles where British education is considered the best available and also from the numerous diplomatic and foreign technical teams centred in Lima. Currently we have over 30 different nationalities of children in our school.

The school is a non profitable organisation, owned and controlled by a charitable educational association to which all parents must belong.

Candidates for admission must face written examinations and personal interviews. The school is fully recognised by the Peruvian Ministry of Education.,

Newton Prep

149 Battersea Park Road London SW8 4BX
Tel: 020 7720 4091
Fax: 020 7498 9052
e-mail: admin@newtonps.demon.co.uk

Chairman of Council: Dr Farouk Walji

***Headmaster:* Mr R G Dell,** MA (Oxon)

Bursar: Mr K Peto-Bostick, BSc (Annapolis)

Number of Pupils. Girls 209, Boys 241

Fees. From £1,255 to £2,510 (excluding lunch).

Newton Prep is especially geared to the needs of bright children in the age range 3–13. Entry is based upon cognitive ability, and special programmes are set up to meet the individual needs of able children.

The Newton Prep curriculum has been created to foster the physical, mental and spiritual lives of its pupils. It aims for academic rigour, but is also designed to stimulate and awaken the minds of its pupils. The aim is to nurture well educated and well behaved children who are 'sparky' and who can think for themselves. The broad curriculum is centred around the three Rs during the early years, but setting for Mathematics and English begins as early as age five. Pre-Prep children receive specialist tuition in French, Music, Singing, Gym and Games. IT and Art are specialist taught from age six.

Children from the age of seven are taught primarily by specialist teachers in properly resourced subject rooms. This ensures a depth of knowledge plus that all important enthusiasm which comes from someone teaching the subject he or she loves. Fully-equipped science laboratories, IT suites and computerised library, together with the school's own playing field, allow Newton's children to flourish both intellectually and physically.

A £5½ million building programme has just been completed.

The full range of Common Entrance and Scholarship subjects are taught, including laboratory science from age seven and Latin from age nine. Class sizes of fifteen to twenty ensure academic quality and pastoral care. Children are prepared for the leading day and boarding schools.

All entrants (other than those for the Nursery) are assessed by an educational psychologist. Parents receive a full report following the assessment.

Norland Place School

162/166 Holland Park Avenue London W11 4UH
Tel: 020 7603 9103
Fax: 020 7603 0648
e-mail: office@norlandplace.com
website: www.norlandplace.com

***Headmaster:* Mr D A Alexander**

Number of Children. 244

Fees. From £2,018 to £2,546

A Preparatory school for boys 4–8 and girls 4–11 founded in 1876 and still standing on the original site in Holland Park Avenue. Children are prepared for competitive London day schools and top rate boarding schools. The curriculum is well balanced with an emphasis on English, Mathematics and Science. Music and Games are strong. The school contains a Library in addition to specialist Music, IT, Science and Art Rooms.

Early registration is essential.

Norman Court Preparatory School

Norman Court West Tytherley Nr Salisbury SP5 1NH.
Tel: (01980) 862345
Fax: (01980) 862082
e-mail: office@normancourt.co.uk
website: www.normancourt.co.uk
Stations: Winchester or Salisbury

***Headmaster:* K N Foyle**, BA

Deputy Headmaster: R H Williams, BEd

Chairman of Governors: Anthony Hudson, MA

Number of Children. Main School: 190 – Boy and Girl Boarders 65, Full and Weekly; Day 125. Pre-Preparatory Dept: 103.

Fees. Boarders and Weekly Boarders: £3,803; Day Children: £2,843; Pre-Preparatory £1,430.

Norman Court Preparatory School is a well established co-educational boarding and day school located in idyllic surroundings between Andover, Salisbury and Winchester, with good connections to London and Heathrow. Founded in 1881, the School draws upon the best traditions to set standards and expectations for the future. Established links with a wide range of good senior schools ensures that pupils can be offered and prepared for the education path best suited to them. The historic main school building surrounded by 50 acres of sports fields and beautiful woodland countryside makes it one of the nicest situations for children to play and learn, and the facilities and opportunities here are superb. The School can boast the latest information, communications and technology equipment, wonderful arts and music facilities, and unrivalled sports provision, along with excellent academic results.

A daily minibus service from the Winchester, Andover, Romsey, Amesbury and Salisbury areas is provided.

With its commitment to excellence in all that it does, Norman Court is well poised to meet the challenges of the new millennium and can justifiably claim to be in the Premier League of preparatory schools in the south of England.

The best way to find out how the School can give your child that important head start is to come and meet our staff and pupils, and to experience for yourself the warm friendly atmosphere.

Charitable status. Norman Court School is a Registered Charity, number 307426. It exists to provide education for children.

Northampton Preparatory School

Great Houghton Hall Northampton NN4 7AG.
Tel: 01604 761907
Fax: 01604 761251
e-mail: enquiries@ghps.northants.sch.uk
website: http://www.ghps.northants.sch.uk

Principal: O E Barnes, MA (Oxon), FRGS

***Headmaster:* M T E Street**, BA (Trinity College, Dublin)

Deputy Head: A R Thomas

Number of Day Pupils. 178 Boys, 89 Girls

Fees. excluding lunch, £2,200 per term. Pre-prep Dept Fees start at £1,145.

Great Houghton Hall, less than 3 miles east of Northampton in the Nene Valley and easily reached from any quarter by an efficient road system, is set in a village and in grounds of nearly 20 acres.

The school buildings contain two separate Pre-Prep Departments, a fully-equipped Science Laboratory, an Art Room, a Design Technology area, 4 music rooms, a large theatre/gymnasium and two computer rooms.

Boys and girls are admitted at 4 and spend four years in Pre-Prep classes. Boys transfer at 13+ and girls at 11+, 12+ or 13+.

Twenty eight full time staff, five part-timers, four classroom ancillaries and two trained classroom assistants contribute energetically to the success of the pupils. Four trained teachers support pupils with special needs. Six visiting musicians teach individuals, many pupils are involved in the choir, band or Choristers and all pupils are taught classroom music by specialist teachers.

The emphasis of the school is upon the encouragement

of the whole child in the classroom, on the games fields, in relationships and responsibilities. No class is larger than 20, several a good deal smaller, and major subjects are setted in the Prep Department to allow pupils to be taught at the right level. The pupils develop confidence and courtesy, self-discipline and self-knowledge in a family environment.

Pupils are prepared highly successfully for Common Entrance and Scholarship examinations to Senior Independent Schools.

The grounds provide outstanding facilities for games: rugby, netball, hockey, cricket, athletics, tennis, rounders (and basketball, badminton, table-tennis, gymnastics in the gym); and weekly trips are made by school bus to indoor swimming pools. A range of extra activities including Art, Chess, Computer Graphics, Dance and Drama take place after school hours for the Prep Department pupils.

Pupils may arrive from 8 am; Pre-Prep pupils may stay to the Post-School Provision (which is charged for) until 6 pm; Prep Department pupils may stay for Extra Activities or supervised prep until 6.10 pm.

Northbourne Park

Betteshanger Nr Deal Kent CT14 0NW.
Tel: Sandwich (01304) 611215 or 611218
Fax: (01304) 619020
e-mail: office@northbourne.kent.sch.uk
Stations: Shepherdswell, Deal, Dover or Sandwich

(Co-educational)

Chairman of Governors: The Lady Northbourne

Headmaster: **Stephen Sides**, BEd

Number of Pupils. 230 ranging from 3–13 years, of whom approximately half are girls. There are approximately 60 boarders.

Fees. September 2001: Boarders £3,185–£4,185, day pupils £2,320-£2,680 per term, Junior Forms (day) £1,580-£1,680. Fees include customary extras and many extra-curricular activities

Northbourne Park offers a unique Anglo-French programme in addition to all that is best in a traditional English Preparatory School. We have five bilingual teachers and about twenty French children each year. There are many special schemes to integrate the French and English children and to develop bilinguality.

Northbourne Park is a registered Educational Trust which is run by a Governing Body consisting of people prominent in education, finance and the law. It lays stress on a width of curriculum, as well as efficiency at ordinary work. The School is set in extensive grounds. Resident staff, supervised by the Housemaster, care for all boarding children.

All children over eight are able to pursue numerous hobbies and have lessons in Riding, Golf, Fencing, Pottery, Carpentry as well as the usual Games and Athletics for both boys and girls. The school has a heated outdoor swimming pool, three hard tennis courts, two netball courts and an all-purpose Hall. Art, Design Technology and Music form part of each child's timetable. There is a very strong music department with two choirs, and various instrumental groups.

Internal Scholarships up to half of the fees are awarded as they become vacant. There is a 10% reduction in fees for brothers and sisters. In addition up to three entrance scholarships of up to half fees are available every year. Reductions are available to members of HM Forces. There is Bursarial support available in cases of need.

Academic Staff. 22 full-time (many resident) and 14 visiting teachers for Music and extra-curricular activities. There are two Matrons, and a number of assistants.

Charitable status. Northbourne Park is a Registered Charity, number 280048. It exists to provide education for children.

Northwood Preparatory School

Moor Farm Sandy Lodge Road Rickmansworth Herts WD3 1LW.
Tel: (01923) 825648
Fax: (01923) 835802

Headmaster: **Trevor D Lee,** MEd (Jesus College, Cambridge)

Number of Pupils. 300 (all day boys)

Fees. £1,900 (Reception, Years 1 & 2); £2,000 (Years 3–8).

Founded as a private school in 1910 by Mr Francis Terry, NPS has a long history and proud traditions. It is still known within the locality as "Terry's" after its founder. In 1954 it became an educational charitable trust administered by a Board of Governors, the present Chairman of which is Dr O Bangham, PhD.

In 1982 the Governors bought a new site in Moor Park, some one and a half miles from the original premises. Located amidst 14 acres on a former farm, in an ideal park and woodland setting, the Grade II listed buildings have been skilfully converted to provide a complete and unique range of classrooms and ancillary facilities. The mediaeval Manor of the More, once owned by King Henry VIII, and used as a palace by Cardinal Wolsey, was originally located within the grounds and provides some interesting and historical associations.

Parents who are delivering or collecting their sons are able to do so in the safety of the School's own car park within the grounds. Moor Park Station, which is five minutes walk from the School, has frequent fast trains (Metropolitan Line and British Rail) which connect with Harrow and London, Watford, Chorleywood, Amersham and beyond. The School is also within easy driving distance of Northwood, Rickmansworth, Pinner, Ruislip and Harefield, Bushey and Oxhey. The School's swift access by train to the Capital means that staff often arrange for boys to visit places of historical and cultural interest and attend concerts and lectures.

The School is divided into four sections: an off-site Nursery School for children rising 3, the Junior School (YR to Y2), the Middle School (Y3 and Y4) and the Senior School (Y5 to Y8). These all have their own teaching areas while making use of the same dining, games, extra-curricular and recreational facilities.

Boys are admitted to the school after an assessment by Heads of Section. The main entry is into the Reception form to which boys are admitted in the September of the academic year of their fifth birthday. Older boys may also be accepted further up the School if a chance vacancy occurs. Boys are expected to remain until the age of thirteen, being prepared for entry at that stage to independent senior schools by way of Common Entrance. The School has also built up a fine record of Scholarship results over the years.

Work of a traditionally high standard is expected of all boys. The curriculum is interpreted as richly as possible and includes Technology, Music, Art, Drama, Physical Education and Games. The School has modern teaching facilities and the fully qualified and experienced staff is generously resourced. The Sir Christopher Harding Building for

Science and Technology, comprising two state-of-the-art laboratories, an ICT Suite and technology workshop was opened in November 2000.

While the Christian tradition on which the life of the School is based is that of the Church of England, boys from all Christian denominations and other faiths are welcomed.

There is an extensive programme of extra-curricular activities in which all boys are encouraged to take part. A key feature of the School's ethos is a strong tradition of caring, both for those within the community of the school, and those whom the boys can help through regular charitable activities.

Rugby Football, Association Football and Cricket are the principal team games. Tennis, Athletics, Fencing, Judo and other sports are also coached. A fully equipped Sports Hall was opened in November 1996. The School has the benefit of a newly laid floodlit astroturf facility.

The School has a flourishing Parents' Association which arranges social and fundraising activities, and an active association for former pupils, The Old Terryers.

Charitable status. Northwood Preparatory School is a Registered Charity, number 312647. The aims of the charity are the education and development of boys aged 3–13.

Notre Dame Preparatory School

Burwood House Cobham Surrey KT11 1HA
Tel: 01932 862152
Fax: 01932 868042

Headmistress: **Mr D Plummer**

Number of pupils. 350. Girls 2½–11. Boys 2½–5

Fees per term. Nursery £795; Reception to Year 6 £1,950

Notre Dame Preparatory School has existed on its present site for 70 years, but was founded by Sisters of The Company of Mary, Our Lady, who have a four hundred year old tradition of excellence in education. The school has a strong pastoral care policy and welcomes children of all denominations.

The aim at Notre Dame Preparatory School is to identify individual potential. A rich and rewarding curriculum has been planned, encouraging each child to make the most of special talents.

Children can join the Nursery at 2½ years. A recent inspection report described the curriculum and facilities as 'excellent'. The children are introduced to literacy and numeracy activities and have access to the gymnasium and swimming pool.

Girls progress through the Preparatory School and are prepared for entrance to the Senior School at 11.

The School has an enviable local reputation, both for high academic standards and for the provision of a wide range of social, cultural and sporting amenities, including:

- challenging scientific and technological programmes of study, with impressive laboratories.
- modern computer system, with multiple internet access.
- heated indoor swimming pool.
- large Sports Hall, featuring gymnasium and indoor netball court.

Demand for places has ensured school coaches serve a wide local area.

Scholarships are offered at 7 and 11.

Prospectus. A fully illustrated prospectus with up to date fee scales and relevant details is available on request.

Charitable status. Notre Dame Preparatory School is a Registered Charity. It exists to provide education for girls.

Nottingham High School Preparatory School

Waverley Mount Nottingham NG7 4ED
Tel: (0115) 8452214

Chairman of Governors: M H Kidd, FCA

Headmaster: **P M Pallant** (Worcester College of Education)

Number of Boys. 168

Fees. £1,669 per term

The Preparatory School is housed in purpose built premises, having its own Classrooms, Libraries, Art Room, Science Laboratory and Assembly Hall. A completely refurbished Art, Design and Technology Centre was provided in 1992 and in 1993 an Information Communication Technology Centre was added.

Entrance Examinations are held in January and February. The pupils (ages 7+ to 10+) are all day boys and the curriculum is designed for those who expect to complete their education at Nottingham High School.

The Preparatory School has an experienced and well qualified staff. There is one form of 7 year olds and two parallel forms in each proceeding year. There are approximately 168 boys in the seven forms all of whom are day boys. The subjects taught are Religious Education, English, Mathematics, History, Geography, Science, Modern Languages and PSHE. Full provision is made for Music, Art, Design Technology, Information Communication Technology, Swimming, Physical Education and Games.

The Preparatory School has its own Orchestra and about 100 boys receive instrumental tuition. A Concert and School Plays are performed annually. A wide range of supervised activities and hobbies take place during every lunch time.

School games are Association Football and some Hockey, Athletics and Rugger in the winter, Cricket and Tennis in the summer.

Oakwood Preparatory School

Chichester West Sussex PO18 9AN.
Tel: (01243) 575209
Fax: (01243) 575433
e-mail: oakwood.office@qick.com
website: www.oakwoodschool.co.uk

Co-educational: 2 to 11.

Headmaster: **A H Cowell**, BEd

Number of pupils. Weekly Boarders 12; Day boys and girls 184.

Fees per term. Weekly Boarders £3,030. Pre-Prep £747–£1,765; Upper School Day £2,050–£2,270.

Oakwood was founded in 1912 and has grown into a thriving co-educational preparatory school for 195 children aged from 2 to 11.

Set in 160 acres of glorious park and woodland between the South Downs and the coast, Oakwood's home is a large Georgian country house.

The children learn in a wonderfully safe and spacious environment in the heart of beautiful Sussex countryside only three miles from Chichester. The school prides itself on its family atmosphere and the happiness of its children.

Oakwood is well-equipped with spacious classrooms, Learning Development Centre, Science and Design Technology Studio, Art Room, Library, Music and Theatre Complex and ICT Centre. A new Gymnasium and tennis courts will be opened in September 2001. The playing fields extend over nine acres, there is a heated outdoor swimming pool and two adventure playgrounds.

Oakwood has a thriving weekly boarding department, "Badger Club", in the main house, where children may enjoy regular weekly boarding or occasional overnight stays. The accommodation is homely and secure.

The Pre-Prep, though fully integrated into the Oakwood community, enjoys its own spacious site with a safe and enclosed play area. The setting is particularly cosy and attractive, the classrooms having been sympathetically converted from a stable block.

There is a warm family atmosphere, as the school recognises the importance of a child feeling happy and secure. Great emphasis is placed on building a solid foundation of social skills and a love of learning, thus enabling each child to settle confidently to school life.

There is a strong academic curriculum with small class sizes, ensuring that each child receives the closest possible attention. In Upper School, children are set for English and Mathematics. The curriculum is broad with each child's timetable including Design Technology, Science, Humanities, French, ICT, PE, Drama and Music.

Form tutoring is of prime importance, the form teacher overseeing the development of each child - academically, socially and emotionally. Contact with parents is frequent and encouraged.

Opportunities to represent the school in sports teams, plays, choirs and instrument groups are all part of the "Oakwood Experience".

Music is very much a part of Oakwood life. The children enjoy two music lessons each week and there is every opportunity to learn an instrument. The school has two choirs, recorder ensembles and a wind band. Each term there is an Evening of Music, and there are major concerts every year for both Upper School and Pre-Prep. The summer term ends with a major musical. In addition, children are encouraged to perform in Assembly.

The Physical Education and Sports programme has an exciting mix to offer every child. Games are played three times each week and are coached by members of staff with an expertise and enthusiasm for their sport.

In winter the boys enjoy a taste of all the major sports - Soccer, Rugby and Hockey, while the girls play Netball and Hockey. Karate and Fencing are also on offer to the boys and girls. In summer the boys play Cricket and the girls play Roounders, but the school also offers Swimming, Athletics and Tennis. An extensive programme of inter-school fixtures is arranged each term.

Early arrivals care, after school clubs and activities all ensure that busy parents can benefit from a flexible school day.

Pupils are prepared for National Curriculum tests at ages 7 and 11 and there is a record of examination success to a variety of senior schools.

Academic and Music awards are available at the discretion of the Headmaster. These are based on the results of tests and an interview conducted at Oakwood.

Old Buckenham Hall School

Brettenham Park Ipswich Suffolk IP7 7PH.
Tel: (01449) 740252.
Fax: (01449) 740955
e-mail: office@obh.co.uk
website: www.obh.co.uk
Station: Stowmarket

Chairman of Governors: R W Perowne

***Headmaster:* M A Ives**, BEd (Hons)

Deputy Headmaster: I H Bateman, MA (Cantab)

Number of Pupils. 85 Boarders; 53 Day Pupils; 47 Pre-Prep; 42 Nursery

Fees per term. Full Boarders £3,900; Weekly Boarders £3,850; Day £3,100; Transition: (Year 3) £2,500; Pre-Prep £1,500

The School, founded in Lowestoft as South Lodge in 1862, moved in 1937 to Old Buckenham Hall, Suffolk and in 1956 to Brettenham Park, 4 miles from Lavenham and 18 from Ipswich. It became an Educational Trust in 1967.

The pupils go on to a wide range of, mostly boarding, Senior Independent Schools via Common Entrance and Scholarship Examinations. (Usual subjects plus German as a second modern language).

The Staff/Pupil ratio is approximately 1:9, giving an average class-size of 12. All members of Staff, including part-time Staff, contribute to the provision of a wide range of extra-curricular activities in which every child has a chance to participate. The major sports are Rugby, Hockey, Soccer, Netball, Cricket and Rounders, but all pupils also take part in Athletics and Swimming. In addition there are opportunities for Tennis (6 courts), Golf (9-hole course), Squash (2 courts), Table-Tennis, Woodwork, Metalwork, Pets, Shooting and Photography. Art, Music, Drama, Ballet and Jazz Dance particularly flourish.

The Main Building, an 18th Century mansion, stands in its own grounds of 75 acres of which some 25 are playing fields and 6 are woodland. In the past few years many building alterations and additions have been completed. A Music and Drama Centre was opened in 1986 and in 1989 a DT Centre was established. In 1990 two new Science Laboratories were completed and in 1995 the Computer Room was fully upgraded. In 1997 astro-turf tennis courts were created and a purpose built Pre-Prep Department opened in September 1998. A new girls' boarding house, new art studio and computer room opens in September 2001.

Academic and Music Awards are available each year in the Spring, details of which, along with a School Prospectus, can be obtained on application to the Headmaster's Secretary.

Charitable status. Old Buckenham Hall (Brettenham) Educational Trust Limited is a Registered Charity, number 310490. It exists to provide education for boarding and day pupils.

The Old Hall

Wellington Telford Shropshire TF1 2DN.
Tel: (01952) 223117
Fax: (01952) 222674

Chairman of the Governors: D B Sankey, Esq, MA

***Headmaster:* R J Ward**, MA, BEd

Numbers. 169 boys, 146 girls.

Fees. Day children, £1,940 per term. Junior School (4–7) £1,240 per term. Transition (7–8) £1,510 per term. Nursery (3–4) mornings £710 per term, five full days £1,240 per term.

The buildings stand in 25 acres of ground and include Chapel, Music School, Science Laboratory, Drama Room, Design and Technology Department, Art and Pottery Department and a heated indoor swimming pool. There is a large, Sports and Performing Arts Hall, an outdoor hard play area and a large library. Physical Education, sport, music and drama are valued highly alongside the academic curriculum.

The Old Hall has links with a number of major co-educational and single sex senior independent schools, and an outstanding record of scholarship and CE success.

The Old Malthouse

Langton Matravers Swanage Dorset BH19 3HB.
Tel: (01929) 422302.
Fax: (01929) 422154
e-mail: headmaster@oldmalthouseschool.co.uk
website: http://www.oldmalthouseschool.co.uk
Station: Wareham

Chairman of Governors: J Newth, Esq

***Headmaster:* J H L Phillips**, BEd Hons (St Luke's, Exeter)

Deputy Head: Dr M Laffey

Number of Pupils. 85 Boys. Pre-Prep: 35 boys and girls

Fees for the year from September 2001. Boarders: £3,885 per term; Weekly Boarders £3,885; Day Boys: £2,945 per term. Pre-Prep Department: from £1,115–£1,495 per term.

Founded in 1906, The Old Malthouse is primarily a boys' boarding school, with day boys. Boys and girls enter the Pre-Prep from 3 up to the age of 7. Boys then continue in the Main School until 13+ with day girls until 9.

The school is known for its academic success, sporting prowess and enthusiastic, polite boys. The atmosphere within the school is unique, due to the size of the school and the dedication of the staff. Boarding arrangements can be very flexible.

Situated in the beautiful Isle of Purbeck, the school benefits from a wonderful environment and has all the usual facilities.

The Old Malthouse takes its sport seriously and also provides a range of adventure activities, including sailing, as an integral part of the sporting curriculum.

There are two entrance scholarships available annually. Details on request.

The prospectus, on application to The Headmaster, gives further details about the school.

Charitable status. The Old Malthouse School Trust is a Registered Charity, number 306317. It exists to provide independent education to boys aged 3–13 and for girls aged 3–9.

The Old Vicarage School

48 Richmond Hill Richmond-upon-Thames Surrey TW10 6QX.
Tel: 020 8940 0922

Chairman of Governors: Mrs M Lamplough

***Headmistress:* Mrs J Harrison**

Number of Pupils. 168 girls

Fees from £1,495–£1,660 per term.

The School was established in 1881 and became a Charitable Educational Trust in 1973. The School is situated between the town and Richmond Park and near to the Terrace Gardens. It is a fine old building built at the beginning of the 18th Century and later refaced in the Walpole Gothic style.

Class sizes are usually 24 and there is a pupil/teacher ratio of 12:1. Many lessons are taught by specialist staff in subject rooms designed specifically for the purpose.

Girls are prepared for Common Entrance Examinations at 11+ and for entry to the London Day Schools.

The Oratory Preparatory School

Goring Heath Nr Reading Berks RG8 7SF.
Tel: (0118) 9844511
Fax: (0118) 9844806

Chairman of the Board of Governors: J J Eyston, Esq., MA, FRICS

***Headmaster:* D L Sexon**, BA, PGCE

Number of Pupils. Boarders (Boys) 40, (Girls) 3; Day (Boys and Girls) 212, Pre-Prep (Boys and Girls) 110

Fees. (as from September, 2001). Boarders £3,562 per term; Day £2,576; Pre-prep £1,480; Reception £720

A Roman Catholic preparatory school which prepares boys for The Oratory School and boys and girls for other Independent Senior Schools. There is a well-qualified staff of 30 masters and mistresses and visiting staff. There is a chaplain, a senior matron who is SRN and 2 assistant matrons.

The School has an excellent record of achievement in recent years, gaining many entry scholarships to The Oratory and other major schools. Much time is given to music and art in which there has been a great deal of success. It is also very proud of its successes in the major sports.

The School stands in its own grounds of 60 acres, 600 ft above sea level and commands extensive views of the Thames Valley. It is easily accessible from the M4 and Heathrow Airport. Facilities include a theatre, sports hall, heated swimming pool, all weather tennis courts and well equipped science, music and ICT departments.

Games played include rugby, cricket, football, cross country, swimming, golf, squash, tennis, hockey, rounders, riding, badminton, basketball and many others. There is also an extensive range of extra curricular activities available.

Charitable status. The Oratory School Association is a Registered Charity, number 309112. It exists to provide a broad based, all-round education in a Christian environment.

Orley Farm School

Harrow on the Hill HA1 3NU.
Tel: 020 8422 1525
Fax: 020 8422 2479
e-mail: office.orleyfarm@virgin.net
Station: South Harrow (Picadilly Line Tube)

Chairman of Governors: A A Bishop, OBE, MA

***Headmaster:* I S Elliott**, BA (Manchester University)

Number of Pupils. 470 all day pupils, including 175 in Pre-prep (4 to 7)

Fees. 1 September 2001. Per term £2,185 to £2,350 (inclusive of lunch); Pre-prep £2,035.

The introduction of girls in September 1994 was followed by the opening of a new, purpose built Pre-Prep in 1995 and a development programme which has added new Lower School classroom provision, dining room extension and full-sized all-weather pitch, and Music Block.

An excellent staff of forty qualified men and women has brought consistently good results for many years. The school is well provided with modern facilities which were also expanded by the completion of a Maths and Science block and Library. The sporting side of the curriculum is served by twenty-five acres of grounds for soccer, rugby, cricket and athletics, two Sports halls and open-air, heated swimming pool.

A proper emphasis is laid on academic work and twenty-eight awards have been gained to Senior Independent Schools in the last five years. The majority of classes throughout the School are no more than twenty, ensuring a high degree of individual teaching. Encouragement is given to a wide variety of optional activities and minor sports so that all children can find self-fulfilment and confidence.

Details on application.

Charitable status. The school is a Charitable Trust administered by a Board of Governors.

Orwell Park

Nacton Near Ipswich Suffolk IP10 0ER.
Tel: (01473) 659225
Fax: (01473) 659822
e-mail: headmaster@orwellpark.co.uk
website: www.orwellpark.co.uk

Chairman of Governors: David Wake-Walker, ARCM, LLCJ

Headmaster: **A H Auster**, BA (Dunelm), DipEd (Cantab), Hon FLCM, FRSA

Number of Boarders. Approximately 150. Number of Day Pupils: 110

Fees. Boarders £4,190 per term. Day Pupils £3,145 per term. Children under 8, boarding £3,775 per term. Day £1,120–£2,850 per term. Weekly and Flexible Boarding (ie for 3 nights a week) is also possible. There is also a Junior Department of 70 pupils, providing education for boys and girls from the age of 3 to 7 years.

Pupils are prepared for all Independent Senior Schools via the Scholarship or Common Entrance Examinations (52 awards in the last 5 years). The School's Centenary in 1967 coincided with its formation into an Educational Trust.

The ratio of pupils to full-time staff is 9:1. The timetable is especially designed to be very flexible, with separate setting in most subjects, and the curriculum, both in and out of the class-room, is unusually broad. There are a host of extra-curricular activities (approximately 50) run by the permanent or visiting staff.

Over two-thirds of the school learn a musical instrument and the school has a number of orchestral and ensemble groups.

The very large Georgian style building and 95 acres of grounds (sandy soil) on the banks of the River Orwell have the following special features: 22 bright classrooms with modern audio-visual equipment, Assembly and Lecture Hall, Computer and Maths work rooms, Design centre including metal, wood and plastic workshop plus electronics, mechanics, home economics, radio and model-making areas, Music Room, Band Room and 40 Practice rooms, 3 Laboratories plus associated areas, Library and Resources Centre, Art Room including large pottery area and kiln, Observatory with 10" Refractor Telescope, Photographic Room, Sports Hall with permanent stage, Games Room with 4 Table Tennis and 1 Billiard Table, large heated Swimming Pool, 3 Squash Courts, 5 Hard Tennis Courts, Nine-hole Golf Course (approx 1,800 yds), especially designed Assault Course, and Tuck and Book Shops.

Good coaching is given and, where appropriate, matches are arranged in the following sports: Association and Rugby Football, Hockey, Cricket, Tennis, Athletics, Squash, Golf, Sailing, Swimming, Badminton, Table-Tennis and Cross Country Running. Emphasis is also placed on individual physical activities and we offer a wide range including Gymnastics, Ballet, Modern Dance, Abseiling, Karate, Riding, Shooting with .177 Air Pistols and Clay Pigeon Shooting.

The School aims to introduce the pupils to a broad and varied set of experiences and opportunities. It tries to see that every activity, whether academic, sporting, social or character building, is properly taught using the best possible facilities and that each is conducted in an atmosphere which is friendly but disciplined.

Charitable status. Orwell Park School is a Registered Charity, number 310481. It exists to provide education for boys and girls.

Packwood Haugh

Ruyton XI Towns Shrewsbury Shropshire SY4 1HX.
Tel: (01939) 260217
Fax: (01939) 260051
e-mail: enquiries@packwood-haugh.co.uk
website: http://www.packwood-haugh.co.uk
Station: Shrewsbury

Chairman of Governors: Mr M N Mitchell, MA, ACIS

Headmaster: **N T Westlake**, LLB, PGCE

Deputy Head: O J Lee, MA, PGCE

Number of Children. 230. Boarding Boys 91; Boarding Girls 50; Day Boys 41; Day Girls 25. Pre-Prep 20.

Fees. £3,512 per term boarding, £2,058–£2,730 per term day. Pre-Prep £1,168 per term. Compulsory extras: nil

There are 15 masters, 11 mistresses and 5 matrons. Boys and girls are prepared for Independent Senior Schools and Scholarships are gained each year.

The School has three Science Laboratories, a multi-media Computer Room, a Music School and a CDT Centre.

The grounds extend to 65 acres permitting much activity and many facilities including an indoor heated Swimming Pool, Squash Courts, nine-hole Golf Course, Sports Hall, a floodlit astroturf pitch, several Tennis Courts, a Shooting range and an adventure playground.

Charitable status. Packwood Haugh is a Registered Charity, number 528411. It exists to provide day and boarding education for boys and girls from the age of 4 to 13.

Papplewick

Windsor Road Ascot Berks SL5 7LH.
Tel: (01344) 621488
Fax: (01344) 874639
Station: Ascot

Headmaster: **D R Llewellyn**, BA (Hons), DipEd (University of London)

Second Master: T W Bunbury, BA (University College, Durham), PGCE

Chairman of Board of Governors: P R Rotheroe, Esq

Number of Boys. 213. (135 boarders and 78 day boys) (Day Boys do prep. at school and must board at the age of 11)

Fees. Boarders £4,150. Day Boys £3,190. (This includes lunch and tea)

Charitable status. The Papplewick Educational Trust is a Registered Charity, number 309087. It exists to provide a high quality predominantly boarding education where – for all our academic, cultural and sporting success – the happiness of the boys comes first.

The Paragon School

Lyncombe House Lyncombe Vale Bath BA2 4LT.
Tel: (01225) 310837
Fax: (01225) 427980

A Registered Educational Trust

***Headmaster:* Mr D J Martin**, CertEd, AdvDipEd, MEd

Chairman of Trustees: P Tozer, FCA

Age. 3–11 years. Boys and Girls roughly equal numbers

Termly Fees. Juniors £1,383; 5–7 £1,318; Under 5 £1,245 including lunches, excluding optional private tuition. Half-day £625. Flexible sessions until five years (fees accordingly)

Number of Pupils. Under 5: 35; School: 240

23 Experienced and qualified teachers.

This co-educational day school was founded in the 1920s by Captain Olsson, well known gymnast and educator. His concern for the mental, spiritual and physical well being of the child is continued today. In August, 1983, the Paragon School moved to Lyncombe House, a beautiful Georgian building set in seven acres of grounds and woodlands about a mile from the city centre. It has attractive sized classrooms, a gymnasium, a computer room, a science laboratory, an Art and Technology studio and a Music and Drama room. There is ample space outside for the younger children's games and for additional games practice. Children in the Junior Department travel by coach to the University and Prior Park College (5 minutes journey) to use their grounds and changing facilities, where an extensive programme of games and swimming is pursued.

The school has a large Nursery and runs a flexible day system which has proved very successful. The National Curriculum is followed and, whilst the best of modern and traditional ideas and equipment are used throughout the school, the need for training in discipline and courtesy is not forgotten. We aim to prepare the children in a happy atmosphere for entry to the school of their choice. Classes are small enabling staff to give pupils individual attention. Class Speech and Drama, Music, French and Gym are all part of the curriculum and swimming sessions for Years 2-6 are organised.

There is close liaison between the Trustees, parents and school and a combined Trustee, Parent and Staff Committee organise social events, the proceeds of which are used to develop the school. The school has a large extra-curricular programme which takes place at lunchtimes and after school. This involves Chess, Photography, Music, Conservation, Computers, Pottery, Art, Needlecraft, Netball, Rounders, Cricket, Athletics, Tennis, Soccer, Rugby and girls and boys Hockey. Matches are arranged against other schools.

Educational visits at all ages play a significant role supporting work in the classroom. Children are also involved with local music and drama festivals, and the Chamber Choir sing in other European countries.

Charitable status. The Paragon School is a Registered Charity, number 310234. Its aim is the advancement of Christian Education in the neighbourhood of Bath.

Parkside

The Manor Stoke d'Abernon Cobham Surrey KT11 3PX.
Tel: (01932) 862749
Fax: (01932) 860251
Station: Cobham

Chairman of Governors: C Carson, Esq

***Headmaster:* D M Aylward**, BEd (Hons), MA

Deputy Heads:
D M Pulleyn, CertEd
Mrs H Sayer, BEd (Hons)

Numbers. Boarders 10, Day Boys 189, Pre-Prep 85, Co-educational Nursery School 66

Fees. Weekly Boarders £3,260, Senior Day £2,360, Junior Day £2,280, Pre-Prep £1,570, Nursery £165–£1,260.

Parkside was founded in 1879 and became a Charitable Trust in 1960. The school moved from East Horsley to its present site of over 40 acres in 1979, its centenary year. Since the move the Governors have implemented a continual development programme which has included a purpose built, well equipped Art and Science block, extending the main building to provide more Pre-Prep accommodation and a Music School with a large classroom and six practice rooms. A superb covered swimming pool and sports hall complex with an excellent stage for drama offers unrivalled facilities in the area. A £2m classroom block is currently being built to further enhance the facilities in the school. At the moment the majority of lessons are taught in a delightful, Grade II Listed Barn which has been skilfully converted to provide spacious, well lit classrooms. On completion of the development, the Barn will be used to house the co-educational nursery, together with art and technology.

The school is large enough to be flexible and offer setting in major subjects yet small enough for each pupil to be known and treated as an individual. On average there are 15 pupils in a class and the teacher:pupil ratio is 1:8. All teaching staff are highly qualified and there is a low staff turnover. Each boy is a member of a House which helps to stimulate friendly competition for work points and many other inter-house contests.

The National Curriculum is followed to prepare all boys for entry to Senior Independent Schools by Common Entrance and, where appropriate, Senior Independent School Scholarship examinations. All boys pass to their first choice senior schools and our results in these examinations are impressive. Over the past few years, many academic, art, music and sporting scholarships have been won. Our curriculum is broad based and all boys are taught Art, Music, PE and Information Technology in addition to the usual Common Entrance subjects. The school has two computer networks and the boys are taught to use the computers effectively – this includes the teaching of robotics and control technology. There are two school choirs and a school orchestra. Over one third of the boys are receiving individual tuition in a wide variety of musical instruments. During the year, there are many opportunities for boys to perform in musical and dramatic productions.

The school has a fine games record and a number of boys have gone on to represent their county and country in sport.

The main sports are Football, Hockey and Cricket, but boys are able to take part in Rugby, Swimming, Athletics, Tennis, Cross Country Running and Judo. An extensive Wednesday afternoon and after school activity programme (including supervised homework sessions) is available with over 40 different activities on offer, from cooking to kayaking and horse riding to golf. The beautiful grounds and the River Mole which runs through the grounds are also used to contribute to the all round education each pupil receives both in and out of the classroom.

The Boarders are under the care of a Housemaster, Matron and Assistant Matron. Their accommodation, which is contained in the Grade II listed Manor House, is particularly attractive, comfortable and homely.

The school has a large and active Old Boys' Association which runs many sporting and social events during the year.

Further details and a prospectus is available on application to the Headmaster's Secretary.

Charitable status. Parkside School is a Registered Charity, number 312041. It exists to provide education for children between the ages of 2½ and 14 years.

Pembridge Hall School

18 Pembridge Square London W2 4EH
Tel: 020 7229 0121

Headmistress: **Mrs E Marsden**, BA (Hons), DipEd

Number of Girls. 250
Fees. (September 2000) £2,350

Preparatory school for girls 4½–11. Girls are prepared for entry into independent and local authority London day schools and for the Public Schools Common Entrance exam.

The school aims to create a happy and contented atmosphere in which girls may learn to work with concentration and enthusiasm. The curriculum is designed to give a thorough grounding in English and Mathematics. The girls' interest and desire to learn is stimulated through History, Geography, Religious Instruction, French, Science, Music, Drama, Art and Physical Education.

Pembroke House

PO Box 31 Gilgil Kenya.
Tel: (0367) 5477
Fax: (0367) 5003/5497

Headmaster: **Mr A J S Bateman**, MA, HDipEd (TCD)

Deputy Head: Mr R S J Boyd, BSc (Bristol)

Chairman of Council: Mr N A Luckhurst

Number of Pupils. 102 boy boarders, 80 girl boarders
Fees. KShs206,800 (£1,900 UK) per term.

The school was founded in 1927 and is presently owned and administered by the Kenya Educational Trust Limited.

It is situated in the Rift Valley at 2,000 metres and is 120 kms from Nairobi. The climate is sunny throughout the year and there are over 40 hectares of grounds.

Facilities include the Chapel, Swimming Pool, Music Rooms, two Libraries, Science Laboratory, Art Room, Computer Room, Squash Courts and access to a Golf Course and tennis courts. A multi-purpose hall was completed in 1999.

The main sports for boys are Cricket, Hockey, and Rugby, with Tennis, Swimming, Athletics, Squash, Golf, Riding, Sailing, Water-Skiing, Soccer, Shooting and Tae kwon do as complementary activities. A full range of clubs and various extras, including individual music instruction, are also offered. Drama is strong.

All the activities are available for girls whose main sports are Rounders, Hockey and Netball.

Boys and girls are admitted from six years as full boarders and are prepared for the Common Entrance Examination which qualifies them for entry to Independent Senior Schools in UK. The School usually gains several scholarships each year.

The average number of pupils in each form is 15, and there are 19 fully qualified members of teaching staff plus 2 Matrons, a Cateress and a Bursar.

The School has an excellent reputation for work and games, and the Headmaster's aim is to continue to produce boys and girls of upright character who will give of their best in form, on the field, and in all spheres of School life.

Pennthorpe School

Rudgwick Horsham West Sussex RH12 3HJ.
Tel: (01403) 822391
Fax: (01403) 822438
e-mail: pennthorpe@lineout.net

Chairman of the Governors: Mr G P R McGuinness-Smith

Headmaster: **Mr S J Moll**, BEd Hons (London)

Number of Pupils. 307 Day Pupils
Fees. £260–£2,560 per term.

Putting the fun into the fundamentals. Pennthorpe School lies in West Sussex, midway between Guildford and Horsham, and has a total of about 300 boys and girls ranging in age from 2 to 13.

Putting the *fun* into the fundamentals of learning is at the heart of the school's teaching philosophy and has allowed both outstandingly bright and not-so bright pupils to flourish and succeed.

Such has been its success, that *all* pupils have passed to their first choice of secondary school as far back as anybody can remember; in addition Pennthorpe's pupils have won no fewer than 67 scholarships over the last seven years. These have been for music, sport and all-round talents as well as purely academic ability. This is a record of which the school is enormously proud.

Computing is at the forefront of teaching at Pennthorpe in the school's two computer suites and in all the classrooms. A project for *all* Year 6 pupils to have their own laptops for prep and for lessons has been a resounding success, making the children both confident and motivated in their approach to lessons as well as in their use of IT.

The programme of after-school activities is unrivalled by any day school. Children can choose from no fewer than 27 activities, ranging from pottery, computing, climbing the school's own climbing wall to archery, roller disco or indoor cricket. The children can stay on until 7.15 if needs be to allow busy parents to collect children after a full day.

The year 2001 will see the opening of a new teaching block of eight classrooms and a science suite.

If you would like to see how your child would thrive in Pennthorpe's caring, friendly and disciplined atmosphere, please ring or e-mail Mrs Rubie, on numbers given above, for details and a list of Open Morning dates.

Charitable status. Pennthorpe School is a Registered Charity, number 307043. It exists to provide education for boys and girls.

Peponi House

P.O. Box 23203 Lower Kabete Nairobi Kenya
Tel: Nairobi 732998, 580583, 583453
Fax: (00 254 2) 580159
e-mail: IN:pephse@form-net.com
www: http://ww.kenyaweb.com/peponihouse

Chairman of Governors: D G M Hutchison

***Headmaster:* S J E Whittle**, BA (Hons), PGCE

Number of Pupils. 300 boys and girls, all day.
Fees. Kshs 149,500.

Set in attractive grounds in a pleasant residential area of Nairobi, Peponi House offers a broad, balanced education within a warm, caring, multicultural community. Founded in 1986, it has expanded rapidly to its present size, but still firmly believes in its original aim: to take a genuine interest in each individual child.

Whilst always striving for academic excellence, and preparing children for Common Entrance and scholarship examinations to senior schools in Kenya, the UK and elsewhere, it is central to Peponi's philosophy that education isn't limited to the classroom.

The school enjoys an especially fine reputation for music; there are two choirs, a variety of ensembles and a large orchestra. Drama and the visual arts also play an important role in school life. There is a full sporting programme, with plenty of competitive fixtures against other prep schools in both major and minor sports, and a wide selection of extra-curricular options. Children enjoy regular excursions, field trips and expeditions, making the most of the many exciting opportunities that Kenya has to offer. The school is also committed to supporting a number of charitable concerns, holding firm the belief that privileged children have an obligation to help the less fortunate.

There is a relaxed but purposeful atmosphere, with a strong emphasis placed on thoughtful conduct, courtesy and respect for others. In every sense, Peponi House endeavours to embrace its motto: "A school of many nations: a family of one".

Perrott Hill School

North Perrott Crewkerne Somerset TA18 7SL.
Tel: (01460) 72051
Fax: (01460) 78246
Station: Crewkerne

Chairman of Governors: J J Mornement, Esq

***Headmaster:* M J Davies**, BA Hons (London), PGCE

Number of Pupils. 160 boys and girls, of whom 50 are boarders.
Fees. Boarders £3,153 per term. Day Pupils £682–£2,274 per term
Age range. 3+–13+

Perrott Hill School is registered as an Educational Trust.

Perrott Hill School, near Crewkerne, is a co-educational day and boarding school. Set in 25 acres of beautiful grounds in the heart of the countryside on the Somerset/ Dorset border, it is serviced by excellent road and rail networks.

Perrott Hill is a small, family school where children settle quickly and learn in confidence. Class sizes are small, with a maximum of 18 children to a form, where they are encouraged to work best towards their own academic goals, in order to place them happily in the senior school of their choice. Staff are dedicated and highly qualified. Facilities now include a brand new multi-purpose Hall, CDT art block, computer centre, music centre, recreation rooms, pethouse, swimming pool and woodland area.

A newly renovated, original courtyard building houses the Pre-Preparatory department and forms a secure, self-contained unit within the school for 3 to 6 year olds, which at the same time allows the younger children to take advantage of many of the facilities available to the Prep School.

Music, Drama and Art are taught within the timetable alongside core curriculum subjects. The choir and orchestra perform both at charity concerts and school functions, in addition to participating in our parish. Drama productions have been much enhanced by the facilities provided by the new multi-purpose Hall.

Teaching is class-based up to the age of nine, and subject-based in the Upper Prep, where all lessons are taught by specialist teachers. French, Music, IT and PE, however, are taught by specialists throughout the school. Mr Davies' French-born wife, Isabelle, ensures that there is a special emphasis on French language and culture, and teaches the Pre-Prep children herself. All children will have the opportunity at some stage to take part in a French exchange.

Each child, boarding or day, has his or her own pastoral tutor, while the welfare of the boarders is supervised by Mrs Davies, assisted by two matrons, in a cosy family atmosphere which includes cocoa and story-time sessions in the Headmaster's flat.

Sport is played every day, and emphasis is placed upon skills and team work, not just the achievement of results. Games played include rugby, football, hockey, netball, cricket, tennis, rounders, swimming and cross-country running. Regular matches are played against local independent schools. Optional extras include fencing, carpentry, horse-riding, karate, golf, squash, ballet, and tap and modern dance.

The school boasts an excellent academic record, with awards to major senior independent schools, and 100% success at Common Entrance to first choice schools over many years. Scholarships for academic, musical and all-round ability are offered annually to children entering the school.

The combination of countryside space, a family atmosphere and a forward looking academic programme creates an ideal environment for children to thrive both academically and in their leisure pursuits - which we are delighted to show parents in action!

Perrott Hill School - time and space for a full education.

Charitable status. The Perrott Hill School is a Registered Charity, number 310278. It exists to give high quality education to boys and girls.

The Perse Preparatory School

Trumpington Road Cambridge CB2 2EX.
Tel: (01223) 568270
Fax: (01223) 568273
e-mail: perseprep@aol.com

Chairman of the Governors: A R Cook, Esq, JP, FRICS

***Headmaster:* P C S Izzett**, JP, BA, ACP, CertEd

Deputy Head: D E J Adams, BEd, ACP, CertEd

Director of Studies: S Clark, CertEd

Assistant staff:

Mrs A E Bousfield, BA, CertEd	Mrs M James, CertEd, ATCL
Miss E A Brimer, BA, MEd, CertEd	Miss J Jenkins, BA, CertEd
	Mrs K M Jessop, CertEd
Mr R T Dickinson, CertEd	Mrs A Roberts, BEd
Mrs H M Doviak, CertEd	Mrs L J Swain, BA, CertEd
Mrs J A Halbert, BA, CertEd	Mrs C M Tyler, CertEd, LGSM

Librarian: Mrs E Castle, BA, DLIS, ALA

Number of Boys. 172

Fees. £1,998 per term (including lunches)

The Perse Preparatory School is the Junior Day School for The Perse School, Cambridge, and it stands in its own grounds some 1½ miles away from the Upper School. It is totally self-contained, except for the use of a nearby swimming pool. The school has its own staff of 14 teachers, supplemented by 15 peripatetic music staff, a librarian and other visiting teachers. The school provides an exciting programme of work and is implementing the National Curriculum as appropriate. It produces high levels of performance in all areas due to a dedicated teaching staff and good facilities. Recent developments have included a new Learning Resource Centre, new Year 3 classrooms and additional music practice rooms including a music

The School's aims revolve around a curriculum which achieves excellence, activities and leisure pursuits that encourage well rounded educational development, a good pastoral system under the care of the Form Teachers and a structured Personal and Social Education programme. A broad and balanced education is provided in a friendly atmosphere and we aim to ensure that all pupils make the most of their talents. We set out to achieve high academic standards and equally high standards in cultural, sporting and other areas of the curriculum. Reliability, consideration for others, good manners and self discipline are all highly valued.

Our excellent facilities and the diverse skills of our staff enable us to offer a wide variety of sporting and recreational pursuits. The games programme (soccer, cricket, tennis and swimming) is designed to encourage all boys, from the keenest to the least athletic, to enjoy games and physical exercise. There is a strong school tradition in music, drama and the arts. Boys may choose to learn a musical instrument from the full orchestral range and the majority learn an instrument. There are choirs, two orchestras and various instrumental groups. A variety of extra-curricular activities is also available, amongst them, Badminton, Chess, Cookery, Computing, Cubs, Cycling Proficiency, Drama, Judo, Puppetry, School Newspaper Publishing, Tennis and Swimming. There is an annual adventure activity week for older boys in the summer and a ski-ing trip in the winter.

The Pelican Pre-Preparatory School, a co-educational school for 3–7 year olds at 92 Glebe Road, provides a broad curriculum with a strong emphasis on the basic skills of literacy, numeracy and oracy. Plenty of opportunities are provided to develop creative and performing skills in art, technology, music and drama with importance also placed on physical development. All boys are expected to progress on to the Preparatory School subject to successfully passing the 7+ entrance tests. All enquiries should be made to the Secretary, tel: 01223 568315.

Boys enter the Preparatory School each September. Places are awarded as a result of a competitive examination held in February of the year of entry. The normal age of entry is 7+, although a small number of places are available each year for boys of 8+ and 9+. Subject to their having made satisfactory progress in the Preparatory School, boys move to the Upper School at 11+.

The Prospectus, on application to the Secretary, outlines full details.

Charitable status. The Perse School is a Registered Charity, number 311434. Its aim is to provide an education that is second to none.

The Pilgrims' School

Winchester Hampshire SO23 9LT
Tel: (01962) 854189
Fax: (01962) 843610
e-mail: pilgrimshead@btinternet.com

***Headmaster:* The Revd Dr B A Rees**, BA, BD, DipMin, PhD (St Andrews)

Chairman of Governors: The Very Revd M S Till, Dean of Winchester

Number of Boys. 200 (80 boarders/weekly boarders, 120 day boys)

Fees. From September 2001. Boarders: £3,910 per term. Day boys: £3,010 per term. Optional extras only

The Governing Body consists of The Dean (Chairman) and delegated members of the Chapter of Winchester and the Headmaster and Bursar of Winchester College. An Advisory Council assists the Governors in the management of the school. Examinations for independent schools, with a significant number moving to Winchester College each year. Cathedral Choristers and Winchester College Quiristers are educated at the school and receive scholarships to the value of half the full boarding fee together with free tuition in one musical instrument. All boys whether musical or not receive excellent academic and musical tuition, and the sporting tradition is equally strong. The school is noted for its happy family atmosphere, and a major recent building programme has ensured the highest standard of facilities possible. All enquiries about the school or Voice Trials should be addressed to the Headmaster.

Pinewood

Bourton Swindon Wiltshire SN6 8HZ.
Tel: (01793) 782205
Fax: (01793) 783476
e-mail: jimcroysdale@pinewood.biblio.net

***Headmaster:* J S Croysdale**, BA Hons (Exeter)

Deputy Headmaster: A C Caird, MA (Dundee)

Number of Pupils. 141 (31 boarders and 110 day children): Boys and Girls. Pre-Prep 90.

Fees. Boarders £3,395 per term inclusive, Day pupils £1,418–£2,719 inclusive, with no compulsory extras

Pinewood is set in acres of wonderful, rolling countryside. The school offers a quality, family-style, forward-looking education, a vibrant blend of tradition and buzz. Resources include purpose-built Music School and Junior Forms Wing, a flourishing Pre-Prep and Nursery, Art & Design Workshops, Research and Reference Library and ICT Rooms.

Excellent academic results are achieved through inspirational teaching within a happy genuinely friendly and stimulating learning environment.

Sport is keenly coached and competed. There is a wide programme of activities and clubs, visits by speakers and educational trips.

Pinewood is an open school, open to the countryside, open to comment and input and always open for parents to visit and look, meet and discuss.

Charitable status. Pinewood is a Registered Charity, number 309642. It exists to provide high quality education for boys and girls.

Plymouth College Preparatory School

Munday House Hartley Road Plymouth Devon PL3 5LW.
Tel: (01752) 772283
Fax: (01752) 769963
e-mail: prep@plymouthcollege.com

Chairman of Governors: Councillor T E J Savery

Headteacher: **Mrs P Roberts**, BEd (Hons)

Number of Pupils. 338

Fees per term. Kindergarten: (full day) £1,054, (half day) £687, £1,435; Pre-Prep: £1,435, (Age 5 to 6) £1,507; Junior Preparatory School (Age 7 to 11) £1,615.

Plymouth College Preparatory School is a co-educational school for children from 3–11 years. The School was founded in 1877 and it is within a few minutes walk of Plymouth College Main School. The Preparatory School operates on a split site with the Infants Department based at Seymour Road, five minutes away from the original site at Hartley Road, where the Junior are located.

The primary academic aim of the School is to prepare children for entry to Plymouth College at the age of 11, ensuring that they are articulate and have taken full advantage of an education designed to stimulate the development of each child both intellectually and socially.

There are twenty-seven full-time and three part-time members of staff, including specialist teachers in the Junior school covering Mathematics, English, Science, Information Technology, Geography, History, Art, Music and French. There is a wide range of extra-curricular activities.

There is a library, a computer room, a well-equipped laboratory, art room, music room, gymnasium and a heated indoor swimming pool.

Entry is by interview and assessment. Application forms can be obtained from the School Secretary and appointments to view the School are welcomed.

Charitable status. Plymouth College Preparatory School is a Registered Charity, number 306949. It exists to help children fulfil their wish to achieve a higher standard of education.

Port Regis

Motcombe Park Nr Shaftesbury Dorset SP7 9QA.
Tel: (01747) 852566
Fax: (01747) 854684
Station: Gillingham SR (3 miles)

Chairman of the Governors: Robin N Farrington, Esq, MC

Headmaster: **Peter A E Dix**, MA (Jesus College, Cantab)

Deputy Headmaster: David J Beaton, MA (St Andrews)

Director of Studies: Michael J Jonas, MA (London), BEd (Durham)

Number of Boarders. 258 (Boys 148, Girls 110)

Fees. to August 2001 £4,395 per term (no compulsory extras).

Day Boarders. 142 (Boys 83, Girls 59)

Fees. to August 2001 £1,350-£3,295 per term (meals included)

Weekly Boarding is available.

Port Regis is a well-established and highly regarded preparatory school set in 150 acres of beautiful Dorset parkland just outside the historic town of Shaftesbury. The main building is an Elizabethan-style mansion with elegant oak-panelled reception rooms and a splendid galleried Hall with a large feature-fireplace. The grounds encompass 35 acres of playing fields as well as extensive ancient woodland, gardens, lawns and a lake.

The school offers a purpose-built science, design and technology centre, a specialist teaching block for Arts subjects, a 450-seat theatre, a new dining hall and kitchens, an astroturf hockey pitch, a nine-hole golf-course, 13 tennis courts and a sports complex (including two Sports Halls) which serves as a National Centre for Junior Gymnastics with a 25-metre indoor heated swimming pool and a judo hall. There are also badminton and squash courts available. An equestrian centre is conveniently situated at the end of the back drive.

Younger pupils are accommodated in bright, cosy dormitories in the Mansion House and the older ones enjoy the comfort of splendid senior boarding houses. The boys' one, which has recently opened, has 60 individual study-bedrooms, each provided with its own washbasin, desk, cupboard and drawers. There are also two common rooms and separate kitchen areas as well as a generous provision of showers, baths and wcs. This house complements the senior girls' house, similar in design with 48 study-bedrooms, which was completed a few years ago.

A Pre-Prep opened in September 1993 in the secure and beautiful environment of the Motcombe Park grounds with full use of the Prep School's facilities.

Each child's Tutor will, we hope, become a friend of the family as well as the child, especially since over 90 boarders have parents working overseas. Encouragement is given to each child to experience a wide variety of activities and develop skills where talent lies. Most staff live either on the estate or in the main building, so personal guidance and a family atmosphere has been created. Academic standards are high and children are prepared successfully for Common Entrance or Scholarship examinations. Learning Support is provided for children with mild-to-moderate learning difficulties.

Opportunities are provided for Music (over half the School learn an instrument), Drama (there are up to nine productions a year), and Art (in a wide choice of media), with Woodwork, Electronics, Riding, .22 Rifle Shooting, Judo, Gymnastics, Canoeing included in a list of over 70 hobby options. Major team games are Rugby, Hockey, Soccer, Netball, Cricket and Rounders. Inter-school, county and national standard competitions are entered. Home and abroad expeditions take place.

There are 56 full-time teaching staff, 13 visiting musicians, 4 State Registered Nurses, a Head of Boarding, a Housemother, Houseparents and Matrons.

A prospectus may be had on application from the Headmaster, who would be delighted to welcome visitors to Port Regis.

Academic, Music, Gymnastic, Sport and All-Rounder entrance scholarships may be awarded annually.

Charitable status. Port Regis School Limited is a Registered Charity, number 306218. It exists to provide an all-round education to the highest standard for boys and girls from the ages of 3 to 13.

The Portsmouth Grammar School Junior School

High Street Portsmouth Hampshire PO1 2LN.
Tel: 023 92 360036
Fax: 023 92 364263

Headmistress of the Junior School: **Mrs P Foster**, CertEd

Deputy Headmaster: A P Laurent, BEd

Chairman of the Governors: D K Bawtree, CB, BSc(Eng), CEng, FIEE, FIMechE, DL

Number of Day Pupils. 290 boys, 150 girls

Fees. £1,466 per term at Key Stage 2; £1,322 per term at Key Stage 1

The Junior School is an integral part of The Portsmouth Grammar School under the general direction of the Governors and Headmaster. Children from 4-9 years are educated within bright and spacious classrooms that occupy a discreet space on the Senior School site. The 9-11 year old pupils are educated in the historic original school building which stands in splendid isolation in close proximity to the Senior School site.

The Junior School's organisation is distinct under its own Headmistress, with 27 full-time and 3 part-time members of staff.

The main entry is at 4+ and an additional class is formed at 7+. Pupils leave at 11 years, the majority moving on to The Portsmouth Grammar School Senior School.

Whilst emphasis is placed on numeracy and literacy, Computer Studies, Design Technology, Drama, Dance, Pottery and Keyboard Tuition are additions to a widening curriculum. There are specialist rooms for Art and Craft, Music and Drama, plus a Science Laboratory and an Information Technology Centre.

Games include Association and Rugby Football, Netball, Hockey, Rounders, Cricket, Athletics, Tennis and Swimming. The Junior School has its own learner swimming pool and uses the Grammar School's excellent 16 acre playing fields at Hilsea.

It also has access to the Grammar School's Sports Hall, Music School, Pottery and Theatre.

Charitable status. The Portsmouth Grammar School Junior School is a Registered Charity, number 3401010. It exists to provide education for boys and girls.

Pownall Hall

Carwood Road Wilmslow Cheshire SK9 5DW.
Tel: (01625) 523141.
Fax: (01625) 525209
e-mail: headmaster@pownallhall.cheshire.sch.uk
website: www.pownallhall.cheshire.sch.uk
Station: Wilmslow

Chairman of the Board of Governors: Mrs Sue Page

Headmaster: **J J Meadmore**, RD, BSc

Number of Boys and Girls. 220 (Day Children)

Fees. £1,355–£1,885 per term (including lunch).

Pownall Hall, a preparatory day school for children aged 2 to 11 and set in its own beautiful and extensive grounds, has been established for over 100 years. It is situated on the north-western side of Wilmslow, 12 miles from Manchester and within easy reach of motorway, rail and air travel.

The school has a highly trained staff of 22, who prepare children for the Entrance Examinations to the Independent Day schools in the area. A thorough grounding is given in all academic subjects in line with the National Curriculum and an excellent mixture of traditional and modern techniques is used. Each major subject has specialist teaching staff and subject rooms including a fully equipped Science Laboratory, Maths, English, Design Technology, Information Technology and French rooms and, in addition, a computer aided Library. French is taught from the age of six. Children have access to computers from the age of two but Design Technology is begun at eight.

In September 1995, a co-educational nursery, called the Wheatsheaf Nursery, was begun for 2 to 3 year olds and this has quickly established itself as the main entry into the school, although children are accepted at any age below 11 years, provided that there are places available. There is a generous staff pupil ratio especially in the lower part of the school, to ensure that the children are given the best possible start to their academic work.

Great importance is attached to performance through music, drama and sport. The school is fortunate in having its own well equipped Theatre in which all the major productions are performed. In 1988, a new Arts Centre was developed comprising Art and Music Rooms within the Theatre complex. There is a School Orchestra and two Choirs which perform regularly. Children are encouraged to study an orchestral instrument or the piano. A Music School operates on Saturday mornings throughout each term.

The main sporting games are Soccer, Hockey, Cricket, Athletics and Swimming which support a strong fixture list with other schools and there is a full range of sports including Badminton, Skiing and Tennis. The school has its own heated swimming pool. A spacious new Sports Hall was erected in 1989.

During the course of the year there are a number of holidays or trips that are arranged including skiing, mountain walking in the Lake District and North Wales, "Outward Bound" type trips to Scotland as well has holidays in France and canal holidays.

Charitable status. Pownall Hall School is a Registered Charity, number 525929. It exists to provide education for boys and girls.

The Prebendal School

54 West Street Chichester West Sussex PO19 1RT.
Tel: (01243) 782026

Chairman of Governors: The Very Revd J Treadgold, Dean of Chichester

Headmaster: **The Revd Canon G C Hall**, MA (Oxon)

Number of Pupils. 190. (33 boarders, 157 day), with a further 100 in the Pre-Prep.

Fees. Boarders £9,216 pa. Weekly Boarders £8,820 pa. Day Pupils £6,804 pa. Pre-Prep (half day) £1,680 pa; (full day) £3,030 pa. Compulsory extras: laundry and linen for boarders.

The School, which is co-educational, is governed by the Dean and Chapter of Chichester Cathedral with 6 lay members of the Board. It is the oldest school in Sussex and has occupied its present building at the west end of the Cathedral (though with later additions) for over 500 years. The Cathedral Choristers are among the boys educated at the School and they receive Choral Scholarships in reduction of fees. Annual Music Scholarships are open to boys and girls entering the school. Sibling Bursaries are awarded to brothers and sisters. Open and Music Scholarships to Independent Senior Schools are gained regularly.

There are excellent playing fields, Association Football and Netball are played in the Christmas term, Hockey in the Easter term and Cricket, Athletics and Rounders in the summer. A heated swimming pool is used for instruction in the summer term and there are two hard tennis courts.

A considerable number of children learn to play musical instruments and the School has 3 orchestras.

Tennis, Gymnastics and Fencing are optional extras as are a number of after-school clubs.

'Occasional' boarding is available.

Charitable status. The Prebendal School is a Registered Charity, number 307370. Its aim is to promote education.

Prestfelde

Shrewsbury Shropshire SY2 6NZ.
Tel: (01743) 245400
Fax: (01743) 241434
e-mail: office@prestfelde.net

Chairman of Governors: Dr R A Fraser, MB, ChB, PhD, FRCPath

Headmaster: **J R Bridgeland**, MA (University College, Oxford)

Number of Pupils. 315 (35 boarders and 185 day pupils) and 95 children in the Pre-Prep.

Fees. Boarders £2,850, Day pupils £2,250, Pre-prep £710–£1,875 per term

Pupils at Prestfelde are well known for their cheerful and purposeful attitude. The school aims to maximise the potential of every individual by providing them with wide opportunities for academic, musical, dramatic and sporting success. A well qualified, dedicated and enthusiastic staff are fundamental to the school's success, and the school is investing prudently in improving the facilities. This year, new purpose built facilities for Little Prestfelde are under construction. These will include seven classrooms, a library, changing room and covered play area for all pupils aged 3-6. Three years ago a new Music School was built and new tennis and netball courts laid. The swimming pool has been covered to give year round swimming, and all of the specialist teaching rooms have been substantially renovated. There are two dedicated networked computer rooms. In addition, every classroom contains a computer.

To complement the spacious and modern teaching facilities, the school has 30 acres of parkland playing fields, giving ample opportunity for all of the pupils to enjoy a wide range of activities: rugby, cricket, football, netball, rounders, tennis, cross country, swimming, lacrosse and golf, in addition to many indoor games.

The academic standards of the school are excellent. The current pupil/teacher ratio is 10:1, with an average class size of 15 pupils. Pupils are taught by specialists from the age of nine. There is no entrance examination, yet there are excellent results in National Curriculum Key Stage Tests and in the Independent Schools Common Entrance Examinations last year. Talented pupils are prepared for academic, musical and art scholarships. Over 35 awards have been gained in the last three years.

Prestfelde is a Woodard School, with its own Chaplain and a clear stance in promoting spiritual and moral values throughout the school.

Pupils leave Prestfelde with an impressive level of confidence and maturity, ready to make the most of their five years of senior education. The school feeds all local major independent schools with about 20 pupils going on to Shrewsbury School each year. Pupils are equally successful in moving on to national independent schools outside of Shropshire.

Charitable status. Woodard Schools (Midland Division) is a Registered Charity, number 269671. It aims to provide education for boys and girls.

Prince's Mead School

Worthy Park House Kings Worthy Winchester Hampshire SO21 1AN
Tel: (01962) 888000

Headmistress: **Mrs D Moore**, CertEd (London)

Chairman of Governors: Dr N Thomas

Number of Children. 290 (Day) Girls age 4–11, Boys age 4–11.

Fees. £1,815–£2,225 per term including lunches.

Established in 1949, Prince's Mead is a Day Preparatory School recently relocated to new premises on the outskirts of Winchester. The school provides a balanced day and a purposeful atmosphere within which the children are encouraged to acquire sound working habits, an enthusiasm and zest for knowledge and achieve their full potential. The pleasures and responsibilities of corporate life are an integral part of development and we encourage co-operation, a responsible attitude and the confidence to work independently or within a group. The school is alive to the children's needs both now and in the future; the aim is to provide education for life.

Girls are prepared for Common Entrance and Scholarship to a wide variety of Independent Schools. Some Boys leave at eight to join their Preparatory Schools, others stay until 11 to take advantage of the many excellent local day schools or as boarders further afield.

The curriculum is built around the core subjects and is very wide ranging with specialist teaching in all areas. Music, Sport and wide ranging activites enhance and enrich development.

Two academic scholarships may be awarded annually.

Further details of the school may be obtained via the website: www.princemead@btinternet.co.uk.

Charitable status. Prince's Mead School is a Registered Charity, number 288675. It exists to provide education for boys and girls.

Prior Park Preparatory School

Calcutt Street Cricklade Wiltshire SN6 6BB
Tel: (01793) 750275
Fax: (01793) 750910
e-mail: prior.park.prep@ukonline.co.uk
website: www.priorpark.com

Patron: His Grace The Duke of Norfolk, KG, GCVO, CB, CBE, MC

Chairman of the Governors: Mr C B Davy, CB

Chairman of the Trustees: The Archbishop of Westminster, The Most Revd Cormac Murphy-O'Connor

Headmaster: **G B Hobern**, BA

Number of Pupils. 192 (58 Boarders, 134 Day; 125 Boys, 67 Girls)

Fees. £3,052-£3,078 Boarding, Day Pupils £2,098-£2,213

Prior Park Preparatory School is situated midway between Swindon and Cirencester where over the past decade the campus has undergone considerable development to meet the needs of a thriving, modern, co-educational day and boarding Preparatory School.

Meadowpark Pre-Prep and Nursery School is contained within the grounds of and adjacent to the Prep School, thereby providing education on the same site from the age of 2 through to 13.

A fully-equipped Information Technology Room was opened in 1997 to complement existing academic facilities, the school's theatre facilities were greatly improved during 1998 and a fully equipped Sports Hall was opened in 2000.

Pupils are welcomed into the school across the ability and age ranges, and are assessed to ensure the correct educational provision is in place as soon as possible. They are prepared for Common Entrance and Scholarship entry into a wide range of senior schools, although many elect to continue their education at Prior Park College.

A total of 38 Academic, Music, Sport and Art awards have been achieved by Prior Park pupils over the past two years.

Children are screened for dyslexic and other learning difficulties so that the school's Educational Support Unit with its staff of qualified and experienced teachers may cater for those whose needs require. In addition provision is made for those children for whom English is a foreign language.

Weekly and full-time boarding pupils are accommodated in four recently refurbished dormitory areas, cared for by members of the teaching staff who reside in school, providing a family atmosphere. A full activity programme is organised for those pupils who stay at school over weekends.

The school enjoys both regional and national sporting success. Rugby, hockey and cricket are played as main sports by the boys; hockey, netball and rounders by the girls. Teams compete against other schools at all ages. All pupils do swimming and athletics and there are also opportunities for soccer, tennis, cross-country, gymnastics and orienteering. Regular foreign sports tours take place; the most recent in 2001 took senior boys to Dubai for an International Rugby Tournament.

Drama, Music and English Speaking flourish with regular performances and concerts.

While the Christian tradition on which the life of the school is based is that of the Catholic Church, pupils from all Christian denominations and other faiths are welcomed. Regular services and assemblies are held in the school chapel.

The Headmaster, who has experience of both preparatory school and senior school education, would be pleased to send a prospectus or to welcome visitors to see round the school.

Charitable status. Prior Park is a Registered Charity, number 281242. It exists solely to provide education for boys and girls.

Priory School

Bolters Lane Banstead Surrey SM7 2AJ.
Tel: (01737) 354479.
Fax: (01737) 370537
Station: Banstead

Chairman of Governors: E R Dring, FCA

Headmaster: **Graham D Malcolm**, MA, BEd, FRSA

Number of Boys. 200 Day Boys

Fees. Nursery: £855 per term; Pre-Preparatory: £1,490 per term; Preparatory: £2,145 per term.

Priory is a small, friendly school where every boy is valued and contributes fully to the various activities organised in the school. A strong pastoral framework supports the boys learning and enjoyment of what is on offer at Priory.

The boys are prepared for any Senior Independent School selected by the parents in consultation with the Headmaster. The aim is to provide a sound, well-balanced course designed to prepare boys for a smooth transfer to their next school at the age of 11+ or 13+. The curriculum reflects this aim and in so doing includes all school games and physical activities as a normal and necessary part of every boy's life, irrespective of ability. Soccer, Rugby Union, Cricket, Athletics, Basketball and Swimming are coached extensively. Gymnastics is particularly strong. A multi-purpose Sports Hall greatly enhances the facilities, as does a large sportsfield. There is specialist accommodation for Art, Science and Information Technology and a library. In 1995 a new block was opened to accommodate the Nursery Department as well as the Reception Class of "rising-fives" and the new Science laboratory. There is a strong emphasis on Music and Drama and at least three productions are held annually.

Although most boys are prepared for the Common Entrance Examination, a large number of Scholarships has been won in recent years. The essential groundwork of a good education lies in the experienced Pre-Preparatory Department which the School possesses. Traditional values, skills and standards run parallel with modern teaching methods and an extensive range of educational visits is arranged throughout the year.

Charitable status. The Priory School (Banstead) Trust Limited is a Registered Charity, number 312035. It exists for the education of boys aged three to thirteen years.

Prospect House School

75 Putney Hill London SW15 3NT
Tel: 020 8780 0456
Fax: 020 8780 3010

Headmistress: **Mrs S C Eley,** BEd

Lower School Headmistress: Mrs Hermione Gerry, SRN, BSc, MSc

Number of Pupils. 195 (day pupils).

Fees. £2,300. Nursery class £1,035 (mornings only).

Prospect House opened in 1991. It occupies a large refurbished building in nearly an acre of grounds at the top of Putney Hill, overlooking Putney Heath. There is a multi-purpose sports area in the garden and team games are played at local playing fields. A dedicated music room has recently been added.

Most children join the school at three years, although occasional vacancies occur further up the school as families move away. Selection for the Nursery is by ballot, with preference given to brothers and sisters of children already in the school. An equal balance of boys and girls is kept wherever possible.

The curriculum includes all the subjects laid down by the National Curriculum, with the addition of French (from the age of seven). Specialist teachers give Music, PE and French lessons and, in the final three years, Maths, Science and English. Children are prepared for entry to a wide variety of day and boarding schools at eleven years of age.

After-school clubs cater for many interests and visiting

teachers give individual music lessons. Children are taken on educational visits to London and residential field study trips are undertaken in the final two years.

Quainton Hall School

Hindes Road Harrow Middlesex HA1 1RX.
Tel: 020 8427 1304
Fax: 020 8861 8861
e-mail: admin@quaintonhall.harrow.sch.uk

Chairman of Governors: David J Skipper, MA (*formerly Head Master of Merchant Taylors' School, Northwood*)

***Headmaster:* Desmond P Banister**, BA, AKC (King's College, London)

Number of Boys. 235 day boys
Fees. £1,541–£1,985 per term

Quainton Hall, which has had only four Heads in its one hundred and two year history, is staffed by both men and women who are experienced and well-qualified. Boys are accepted into the Junior School from the age of 4 years and a small number are additionally accepted into the Middle School at the age of 7. Parents are asked to register their son and the family is then invited to interview. Entry is by means of a short, friendly assessment and previous nursery or school report. Since the school's foundation in Harrow in 1897 a consistently high standard of work has been maintained, which is reflected in regular successes at 13 in the competitive examinations for most of the main North-London day-schools, in Common Entrance and in entrance scholarships (for academic excellence, in Music and in Art).

The curriculum is broad and supportive. All boys have lessons in Art, Drama, Technology and Music each week in addition to all the core subjects. French is begun at the age of seven, Latin is taken by most able linguists from the age of ten plus German is offered as an additional Modern Language to the Seniors. Dramatic productions are performed each year and there is a strong tradition of choral and instrumental music. Many boys have played in children's orchestras and music scholarships are won regularly. There is, for all ages, a large and varied range of visits and expeditions, which include field trips, ski holidays, adventure weeks, visits to France, Austria and Spain and numerous one-day outings to London and beyond.

The Parents' Association (FQHS) is very active and provides a range of social occasions for parents and staff. Parents are always made very welcome in the school and arrangements are made for family use of the swimming pool and sports hall outside school hours and during the school holidays.

The games played include Athletics, Badminton, Basketball, Cricket, Cross-country, Football, Gym Hockey, Rugby, Swimming, Table Tennis, Tennis and Volleyball.

The School, which belongs to the Shrine of Our Lady at Walsingham, possesses its own Chapel and Chaplain and in 1944 became a Church of England Educational Trust. Boys are prepared for Confirmation if they and their parents wish. Boys come from the range of cultural and religious backgrounds to be found in North London and experience shows that this is a source of enrichment to the life and work of the whole school community.

In the recent past there has been a major development programme: in 1977 a new sports hall and classroom block were completed; in 1980 we opened a new and self-contained Junior School building, incorporating three classrooms, a hall for music and drama and changing rooms linked to the adjacent indoor swimming pool. In 1987 we completed our new Art Centre. In 1990 we built a new swimming pool enclosure and a technology centre and in 1994 an all-weather sports court. In 1997 a new entrance foyer was built to celebrate the school's Centenary. More recent improvements have included the modernisation of the main classroom block and further developments are planned in 2001/2002.

Charitable status. Quainton Hall School under the Trusteeship of Walsingham College (Affiliated Schools) Limited, is a Registered Charity, number 312638. It exists to provide a sound education within a definite Christian framework.

Queen Elizabeth Grammar School Junior School

158 Northgate Wakefield West Yorkshire WF1 3QY.
Tel: (01924) 373821
Fax: (01924) 366246

Spokesman for the Governors: Mrs E G Settle

***Headmaster:* M M Bisset**, BA, MA

Number of Boys. 258 day boys
Fees. 7–8 years £1,408. 9–10 years £1,479 per term. Fees include lunch.

This is an extremely well resourced Junior School which enjoys a full range of buildings and facilities quite separate from the Senior School. The most recent stage of this development included a new Hall, Library, Information Technology Centre and Play Garden Area which were opened in September 1999. The other specialist Junior School facilities include a learner Swimming Pool and rooms for Art, Design Technology, Science and Music in addition to twelve well appointed classrooms.

The main aim of the School is to prepare boys for the Senior School, although boys who sit the entrance examinations for other Independent Senior Schools are also very successful. There are three parallel forms at 7, 8, 9 and 10. Although a high proportion of the boys join at 7, vacancies are reserved for each of the three subsequent years. All entry is by examination with the main Entrance Examination being held in February.

Each day starts with an Assembly, after which work continues in the full range of normal Junior subjects. While the Form Teacher takes the bulk of the classroom lessons in the younger forms there is from the start a significant involvement of specialist staff. The contribution of such specialist staff in Science, Art, Music, ICT, Modern Languages, and History expands as boys progress through the Junior School. Pupils are expected to learn the discipline of hard work, while at the same time the aim is to excite enthusiasm and interest so that each boy achieves his full potential.

There is a good tradition of music, both choral and instrumental, in the School as there are two choirs, instrumental groups and a Junior School Orchestra. Twelve boys are Choral Scholars at Wakefield Cathedral for which a Voice Trial is held in February. Choral Scholarships are available.

The Junior School has its own playing fields, cricket nets and cricket pavilion. Boys have PE, swimming or games every day: in winter Rugby, Swimming and Cross-Country Running; in summer Cricket, Tennis, Swimming and Athletics. There is an extensive programme of both inter-school and inter-house matches. The coaching of all games is undertaken entirely by Junior School staff.

There are sixteen fully qualified assistant teachers

including specialists for Art, Music, ICT and Science. In addition there is a School Nurse, and four Non-Teaching Assistants, an ICT technician and part-time Librarian.

Charitable status. Queen Elizabeth Grammar School is a Registered Charity, number 529908. It exists to provide an excellent education for your son.

Queen Mary's School

Baldersby Park Topcliffe Thirsk N Yorkshire YO7 3BZ
Tel: (01845) 575000
Fax: (01845) 575001

A School of the Northern Division of the Woodard Corporation

Chairman of the Governors: The Hon Mrs Susan Cunliffe-Lister

Senior School Headmistress: Mrs M A Angus, MSc, CertEd

***Preparatory School Headmaster:* Mr I H Angus**, MA, HDipEd

Number of Pupils. 270

Fees per term, apart from Nursery, which is per session. Nursery (ages 3 to 4) £10.50 per session. Pre-Prep Reception £1,250; Year 1 £1,500; Year 2 £1,500. Prep School Day (Year 3 to 6) £2,275, Prep Day (Year 7 and 8) £2,450, Prep Boarders (Year 3 to 6) £3,550, (Year 7 and 8) £3,750. Senior School: (Years 9 to 11) Day £2,780, Boarders £4,080.

Extra Subjects. Riding £12 per lesson, Speech and Drama £40, Music £145.

Queen Mary's has a unique family atmosphere with friendliness and concern for others being an important part of the school's ethos. We are one of a group of twenty-three schools belonging to the Woodard Corporation, an Anglican foundation which promotes Christian education and high academic and pastoral standards within all its schools.

Queen Mary's has a thriving co-educational day nursery and pre-prep department. The preparatory school, Years 3 to 8 inclusive, offers both boarding and day places. While we prepare girls for Common Entrance at 11+, 12+ and 13+, the majority of girls proceed into the senior school and do their GCSE's with us, before moving to new schools for the sixth form.

Queen Mary's has a strong boarding tradition, with both full and weekly boarders. Many of our day girls switch to boarding as they move up the school. We run a very good programme for those who stay in school at weekends and we organise a daily minibus service to help those who have to travel into school from some of the outlying villages.

Expectations for all our pupils are high, dedicated staff motivate the girls very successfully and excellent results in public examinations are achieved. We are a non selective school and we cater for a wide ability range. The school offers a broad and balanced curriculum and the teaching groups are kept very small and are carefully arranged to give appropriate academic support to both the high flyers and those with slight specific learning difficulties. The school has good facilities, including an indoor swimming pool, riding manège, four science laboratories, up to date networked facilities for ICT and extensive playing fields. Educational trips and visits, both in this country and to Europe, are an important part of the girls' educational experience.

Outside the academic sphere girls are introduced to a wide range of extra curricular activities. We place much emphasis on art, drama, ICT, debating and the Duke of Edinburgh's Award, while music, both instrumental and choral, is a huge strength of the school. Sport is given a high profile and we have a full fixture list. Riding and camping are popular activities in addition to team games.

Queen Mary's has its own Church of England chapel and the prep school hold their own service in chapel each evening. The school Chaplain prepares girls for confirmation. As a Woodard School we promote Anglican worship but girls of other denominations are welcome. Our Roman Catholic girls have their own Chaplain and they are very positively supported in their spiritual development.

Scholarships. 11+, 12+ and 13+ academic, art and music awards.

The scholarship examinations are open to both external and internal candidates. Scholarships and exhibitions are awarded only as the result of these examinations. Candidates may enter for more than one award.

Charitable status. Queen Mary's School is a Registered Charity, number 269665. It exists to further education for children in a Christian environment.

Queen's College Junior & Pre-Prep Schools

Taunton TA1 4QR.
Tel: (01823) 272990 (Junior); (01823) 278928 (Pre-Prep)
Fax: (01823) 323811

Chairman of Governors: Mr R Lintott

***Headmaster:* P N Lee-Smith**, BA (Keele), CertEd

Headmistress of Pre-Prep & Nursery: Mrs E Gibbs, CertEd

Number of Pupils. Junior School: 140 (12 boy boarders, 7 girl boarders, 65 day boys, 56 day girls). Pre-Prep: 33 boys, 34 girls

Fees. Nursery: on request; Pre-Prep: £852–£885 per term; Junior: Boarders: £1,968–£2,845 per term. Day Pupils: £963–£1,821 per term (plus £67 per term for lunches). No compulsory extras

Queen's College is a co-educational boarding and day school on the outskirts of Taunton with fine views across the playing fields to the surrounding hills. The Junior School is run as an independent unit but shares many of the excellent facilities of the adjacent Senior School. We aim to create a happy, caring atmosphere based on Christian values. For the boarders, especially, the School endeavours to provide a sympathetic background for a child's first venture away from home. We are well versed in settling pupils whose families have been posted abroad. For every pupil, however, the aim of the School is to find areas in which each child can succeed, thereby developing the self-confidence which will help them achieve their potential.

From the age of 8, most of the teaching is subject-based in specialist rooms. Syllabuses are broadly in line with the National Curriculum; however, we do not intend our courses to be unduly restricted by its detailed provisions.

The principal games are Rugby, Hockey and Cricket for the boys, Hockey, Netball and Rounders for the girls. Tennis, Swimming and Athletics matches also take place. Fullest use is made of the excellent sporting facilities of the School, particularly the Sports Hall, all-weather Hockey Pitch, Tennis Courts, heated indoor Swimming Pool and Astroturf. A new hard play area was brought into use on the Junior site in Autumn 1999.

Out of school activities include: Badminton, Citadel figures, Cookery, Chess, Cycling Proficiency, Computer

Club, Drama, Fitness training, Specialist Music groups, Model making, Origami, Puppets and Squash.

Dancing, Speech and Drama and Riding are also arranged at an extra charge. Pupils may attend local brownie, cub, guide and scout groups.

Building development has kept pace with modern expectations. In 1988 the Birchall Hall was opened, a multi-purpose assembly hall, incorporating facilities for Art & Design. An extension for Year 3 (7+) and Year 4 (8+) pupils was completed in 1990.

The Pre-Prep day school for 50 children aged 4 to 7 is in its own purpose-built building separated from the Junior School by the new adventure playground.

To complete provision at Queen's College, there is now also a Nursery School for children aged 2½–4 years. There are up to 18 places available on a sessional basis. After-School care is also provided for Nursery and Pre-Prep children.

The Nursery and Pre-Prep environment is a happy and stimulating one with an informal atmosphere and high standards. We adhere broadly to the National Curriculum but often overtake it particularly in the core subjects. There is a full range of after-School activities.

Nearly all the children move on from one section of Queen's College to the next; there is no further qualifying examination. We offer parents and pupils continuity of education available from the Pre-prep, through the Junior School, to the Senior School.

In September 1999 the age ranges of the Junior and Pre-preparatory schools changed to bring them into line with local practice and the National Curriculum. The Pre-preparatory school now educates pupils up to the age of 7; the Junior School educates pupils up to the end of Key Stage 2 (NC Year 6). Children aged 11+ will be admitted directly to the Senior School.

Charitable status. Queen's College Junior and Pre-Prep School is a Registered Charity, number 9336024. It exists for the purpose of educating children in a Christian environment according to the traditions of the Methodist Church.

Ramillies Hall School

Cheadle Hulme Cheadle Cheshire SK8 7AJ
Tel: 0161-485 3804.
Fax: 0161 486 6021
e-mail: ramillies@btinternet.com
website: www.ramillieshall.co.uk

Principals: Mrs A L Poole, Miss D M Patterson, BA, PGCE

Number of Children. School: Day: 56 boys, 24 girls; Boarding: 11 boys, 5 girls. Nursery: 96 children.

Fees per term. Day pupils - 4 to 7 years - £1,260; 7 to 13 years - £1,645. Boarders: £2,710–£3,060; Nursery from £3.00 per hour.

Ramillies Hall, founded in 1884, is a small family-run nursery and school for children aged between 6 months and 13 years. The School is conveniently situated for Manchester International Airport and main motorway/rail networks. It is set in its own spacious grounds, with extensive playing fields and heated outdoor swimming pool.

The Nursery provides a homely, caring environment and pre-school education for babies and children up to age four, and is open all year from 8 am to 6 pm. Children follow through from Pre-School to the Junior School, giving continuity and a settled environment. In the School, small classes (average 16) ensure individual attention, and we bring together the best of traditional methods and modern multi-sensory teaching. High academic standards and expectations are embodied in well-structured learning programmes, delivered by specialist teachers. We follow the National Curriculum, and prepare children for entry to a wide range of independent day and boarding schools.

For children with dyslexia and similar learning difficulties, we combine specialist tuition and support with a whole-school approach, and this has brought external recognition of our expertise in this field.

The extended day for children from age 8 years enables us to offer a wide variety of sports and extra-curricular activities. School productions help to promote music, dance and drama.

Comfortable accommodation provides a homely environment for full, weekly or occasional boarding. To help the working parent, our Holiday Club, which has a well-organised programme of activities for children up to 12 years, is open from 8 am to 6 pm each day during school holidays.

For more information, visit our website as given above.

Ranby House

Retford Nottinghamshire DN22 8HX.
Tel: (01777) 703138. Bursary: 860691
Fax: (01777) 702813
e-mail: office@ranbyhouse.u-net.com
website: http://www.ranbyhouseschool.co.uk
Stations: Retford and Worksop
Roads: A1 - ½ mile; M1 - 15 miles

Chairman of the School Council: T Freemantle

***Headmaster:* A C Morris**, BEd (Hons)

Number of Pupils. 333: 193 boys, 140 girls, including 75 boarders (aged 3 to 13)

Fees. Boarders £3,125; Day Children, £2,400; Pre-Prep £1,350

Ranby House is a caring, happy, exciting, Christian community. Within it boarding and day boys and girls work and play hard, striving for excellence.

This thriving school is situated in 60 acres of beautiful woodland, gardens and playing fields. The facilities in and out of the classroom are excellent and include: new Performing Arts Centre with a 300-seat auditorium and Music School, Sports Centre, Computer Centre, Library, Design Technology Centre, 2 Science Laboratories, outdoor heated swimming pool, 4 floodlit all-weather netball/tennis courts, Gymnasium, Chapel and extensive level playing fields.

The purpose built Pre-Prep department takes children from 3 to 7 years after which time they transfer to the main school.

Boys and girls may board from the age of 7 years. Spacious, colourful bedrooms, brilliant food and caring houseparents are some of the essential elements of the Ranby boarding experience. Boarding is flexible, and is dependent upon the needs of the individual family.

Academic standards are high at Ranby. Last year a total of 19 Scholarship awards, for academic, musical, sporting and all-round excellence, were made to pupils transferring to their senior independent schools. The school also caters for children with specific learning difficulties.

A wealth of extra curricular opportunities are on offer and pupils are encouraged to take an active part in all aspects of school life. The school has a strong sporting tradition and flourishing music and drama departments.

Links with the armed forces are strong and the school offers Forces Bursaries.

Ranby is a school of the Woodard Corporation. It has a Christian foundation, and is the largest group of independent schools in the country. The school has strong links with Worksop College, also a Woodard School, which is only 5 miles away. Pupils are prepared for Common Entrance and Scholarship examinations to a variety of Senior Schools.

The school offers bus services from the Retford, Worksop, Rotherham, Doncaster, Tickhill, Tuxford and Mansfield areas.

Ravenscourt Park Preparatory School

16 Ravenscourt Avenue Chiswick London W6 0SL
Tel: 020 8846 9153
Fax: 020 8846 9413

Headmistress: **Maria Gardener,** CertEd

Age range. Boys and girls, 4-11
Number of pupils. 252
Fees. £2,275 per term

The school provides education of the highest quality for boys and girls, preparing them for transfer to the best and most selective Independent Schools at 11 years of age. The Lower School caters for pupils aged 4-8 and is based in a large, Victorian house, formerly a vicarage. The Upper School, 8-11 years, enjoys purpose built accommodation erected in 1996. The secure site includes a large play area and the school makes use of the extensive facilities of Ravenscourt Park which it adjoins.

The curriculum includes French, Design and Technology, Music, Art and Craft, RE, Computer Studies and PE for all pupils in addition to the usual core subjects. In the Upper School the majority of subjects are taught by specialists. All Upper School pupils attend a Summer Term Residential Week where studies across the curriculum are applied to a non-urban environment.

There are many after school clubs and sports activities and we have two choirs and an orchestra. Individual tuition is offered in piano, violin, flute, guitar and singing. Our Drama productions are a highlight of each school year.

An 8 am to 6 pm All Day Care service is offered to parents at an extra charge.

The school is noted for its warm, happy atmosphere where parents play a full part in enriching the curriculum and social life. Off-site visits and guest workshops presented by noted visitors are a regular feature of education at RPPS.

The school is always heavily over-subscribed and registration is recommended as soon as possible after a child's first birthday. A prospectus and registration form may be obtained from the School Secretary.

Redcliffe School

47 Redcliffe Gardens London SW10 9JH.
Tel: 020 7352 9247
Fax: 020 7352 6936

Co-educational day school for boys aged 3–8 and girls aged 3–11.

Chairman of the Board of Governors: Nigel Clarke

Headmistress: **Miss Rosalind Cunnah,** MA, CertEd

Number of Pupils. 100 (35 boys, 65 girls)
Inclusive fee. £2,017 per term

Redcliffe is a small, friendly school of about 100 pupils. It was established in 1948 and has been run as a Trust since 1973.

The school caters for a range of abilities and enables children to reach a high academic standard. Basic skills are accentuated within a broad and balanced curriculum incorporating creative and practical activities.

Class Size. There are seven classes in the school. The first four comprise approximately 20 pupils and are co-educational. Each class teacher has the help of an assistant. When the boys leave at 8 years of age, the girls' classes are smaller, usually around 12, so each child has a great deal of attention.

Assembly. The entire school meets each morning for assembly in which there is child participation. Christian values and caring for others are considered important.

Fund-raising events for charity are held regularly, including harvest gifts to local people and carol singing.

Curriculum. Subjects include Mathematics, English, History, Geography, Science, Technology, Art, IT, RE, Current Affairs, Music, Physical Education and Drama. Oral French is taught throughout the school. Individual instrumental lessons are available.

Each class has some form of PE each day; in a local gym or playground, local netball courts, or tennis lessons at South Park. Football, netball and rounders are played.

Extra activities take place in the break after lunch. These include gymnastics, choir, orchestra, chess and sewing. Drama, ballet and swimming are held after school.

All classes have outings to museums and exhibitions, theatres and concerts. Parental help on outings is encouraged.

Entry. Children are assessed at 3 years of age, for entry at 4. On completion of the entrance form and payment of registration fee, a child is registered for the entrance test.

There is a Nursery, Redcliffe Robins, for children aged 2½ to 4 years.

Future Schools. Pupils are prepared for entry to London day schools and Common Entrance for boarding schools. Care is taken to fit the child to the right school.

Charitable status. Redcliffe School is a Registered Charity, number 312716. It exists to provide a high standard of education for children within a caring environment.

Reddiford School

38 Cecil Park Pinner Middlesex HA5 5HH
Tel: 0181 866 0660
Fax: 0181 866 4847

Headmaster: **Mr B J Hembry,** MA, CertEd

Chairman of Governors: Mr A Sellar

Age range. 3–11
Number in School. Day: 176 Boys, 115 Girls; Nursery: 18 Boys, 16 Girls
Fees per term. £1,550. Nursery: £625 (half day), £1,100 (all day).

Reddiford is a well-established Church of England School, founded in 1913 and accredited by the Independent Schools Joint Council.

The school offers a curriculum of both breadth and depth in a happy family atmosphere.

There is an established teaching nursery which in 1995 moved to another site close by in Marsh Road. This site is also the centre for performing arts ie Ballet and Drama and some 200 children attend lessons there from 3.30 pm to 9.30 pm.

Music, Art and Drama also play an important part in the curriculum, and there is a very advanced Music Technology department.

Reddiford possesses a fine academic record, preparing its pupils for entrance at 11+ into major independent schools, many at scholarship level. It is at the forefront of curricular initiative and in the warm friendly atmosphere children thrive.

Charitable status. Reddiford School is a Registered Charity, number 312641. It exists to provide education for boys and girls.

Redland High Junior School

4 Redland Court Road Bristol BS6 7EE
Tel: (0117) 9244404

Chairman of Governors: Mr P Breech, BA (Hons), SCA, ATII, ACTII, MR

Headteacher of Junior School: **Mrs M Lane,** CertEd

Number of Girls. 180
Age Range. 3+ to 11+
Fees. Nursery £7.75 per half day; Reception Years 1 & 2 £960; Years 3, 4, 5 & 6 £1,140

Redland High Junior School is the Junior Day School for Redland High School for Girls. It is situated in three Victorian houses close to the Senior School in a very pleasant residential area of Bristol. The School is easily reached from the surrounding districts.

Children are taught by well qualified and highly motivated teachers who are very well supported by a number of excellent classroom assistants.

The school aims to provide each child with the opportunity to develop fully her particular talent within a stimulating and supportive environment. We try to create a friendly, family atmosphere within which high standards are expected in all areas of the curriculum.

Whilst emphasis is placed on mumeracy and literacy, children also respond to high expectations in science, ICT, drama, history, geography, RE, art, PE and modern languages. Music is a particular strength of the school with most pupils learning to play an instrument or joining in choral or orchestral activities. Our curriculum embraces the principal areas of study appropriate for Primary School education. It is based on the National Curriculum requirements and the Early Learning Goals for the Under Fives. However, we aim to give our pupils more than these minimum requirements so that they have a head start when they reach senior school. Our high standards and expectations ensure that the brighter pupils can be stretched to their full potential, whilst those who need extra help get additional support.

There are a number of extra curricular activities available, including outdoor pursuits (canoeing, abseiling etc), computer clubs, netball, short tennis, recorder groups, dance and art clubs.

During each school year there are a number of educational visits as well as workshops within the school. Most of these visits are a way of enabling pupils to consolidate knowledge acquired in lessons. Other outings are of a more cultural nature and often include visits to concerts and theatres. Year 5 and 6 pupils have the opportunity to travel abroad. Past visits have been to France, Holland, Germany, Iceland and Italy.

Pupils are encouraged to nominate and support charities, and each term sees an event designed to raise money for the chosen charity.

When our pupils reach 11 they are ready to move on. Most girls move on to the Senior School where they are faced with new challenges and choices. The girls from the Junior School are well prepared and ready to embrace the next stage of their education with enthusiasm and confidence.

Charitable status. Redland High Junior School is a Registered Charity, number 311734. It exists to provide education for girls.

The Red Maids' Junior School

Grange Court Road Westbury-on-Trym Bristol BS9 4DP
Tel: (0117) 962 9451

Chairman of Governors: Mr K Bonham, BA, FCA, DL

Headteacher: **Mrs G B Rowcliffe,** BEd (University of Bristol)

Number of Girls. 80 day girls with ages ranging from 7–11
Fees. £1,125 per term, plus lunches

The Red Maids' Junior School is situated in a large house adjacent to The Red Maids' School. Facilities include four classrooms, an assembly hall, library, art/technology studio, music practice rooms, kitchen and large garden and play area.

The school is equipped for approximately eighty 7–11 year old girls organised in four year groups. Each class is taught by their own classteacher for the majority of their timetable and in addition by every classteacher for other lessons each week. There are frequent opportunities built into the timetable for girls to work and make friends with children in all year groups. Since the girls know each other and every member of staff well, a strong community feeling is promoted within the school where girls can develop their confidence and self-esteem.

All the girls are encouraged to explore their individual talents and achieve their best through the school's broad and balanced curriculum which adheres closely to the National Curriculum with the addition of French to all year groups. Whole school planning is an essential feature of every subject area ensuring continuity and progression, and assessment is an integral part. Year 6 girls sit National Curriculum Key Stage 2 Standard Assessment Tests in English, mathematics and science and results are very good indeed.

In addition there is a strong emphasis on the pastoral care of the children. Through school meetings and class activities the school teaches a sense of good citizenship as girls are encouraged to share responsibility for the care of each other, their property and their environment.

Close links are fostered between the Junior and Senior Red Maids through joint activities and visits. At 11, Junior Red Maids achieve outstanding success in the open competitive examination for places in the Senior School.

Extra curricular activities are extensive and varied and there is a strong commitment to outdoor education.

The school enjoys close relationships with parents on a daily basis and generous support is offered to the school through a thriving Friends' Association.

Charitable status. The Red Maids' School is a Registered Charity, number 311733. It has existed since 1634 to provide an education for girls.

Reigate St Mary's Preparatory and Choir School

Chart Lane Reigate Surrey RH2 7RN.
Tel: (01737) 244880
Fax: (01737) 221540
e-mail: headmaster@reigate-stmarys.org

Chairman of Governors: Derek Thomas

Headmaster: **David T Tidmarsh**, BSc Hons (Wales)

Number of Pupils. 130 pupils aged 2 to 13

Fees. £1,743 per term; £1,495 for children in years 1 & 2 (including lunches). Nursery £350–£1,369 (3 afternoons to 5 full days)

Reigate St Mary's is an independent day school for children aged two to thirteen years, located in the heart of Reigate in a beautiful parkland setting. Within easy reach of the M25 a coach pick-up service covers a wide area of local towns including Horsham, Crawley, Leatherhead, Horley, Dorking and Tadworth.

The school admitted girls in September 2000 for the first time, and its aim is to provide a first-class balanced education to equip all the pupils for their chosen senior school. In the early years, the most vital stage is in preparing firm foundations in literacy and numeracy, this is typified in our Lower School which offers daily reading aloud. The children go on to achieve excellent examination results at 10, 11 and 13 with a number being awarded academic, music and sporting scholarships.

To achieve these objectives, the partnership of school and parents is crucial for the development of each child and this very much enhances the family atmosphere. The school benefits from small class sizes in a happy and caring environment provided by the dedicated team of staff. Art, music and a full games programme ensure that all children have the opportunity to develop all round ability.

Association Football and hockey are played in the Michaelmas and Lent terms; in summer cricket, tennis and athletics are the major sports. Cross-countries are run in the Lent term and swimming is offered throughout the year.

There are also many extra-curricular activities such as football, squash, tennis, cookery, first aid and the school also offers Extended Day. School trips are organised, including France, Canada and South Africa.

We are also a Choir School, training the Choristers to Cathedral standard. There are up to 14 Choristerships of 50% remission of fees available at any one time. Voice trials are held annually and also by arrangement with the Master of Choristers.

Charitable status. Reigate St Mary's is a Registered Charity, number 1020482. It exists to provide a first class education to pupils aged 3–13 years.

The Richard Pate School

Southern Road Leckhampton Cheltenham Glos GL53 9RP
Tel: (01242) 522086
Fax: (01242) 524035
e-mail: hm@richardpate.gloucs.sch.uk

Chairman of Trustees: J Parker, Esq

Headmaster: **E L Rowland**, MA (University College, Oxford), DipEd

Number of Pupils. 300. Approximately an equal number of boys and girls aged 3–11 years

Fees from September 2001. Nursery (Mornings only) £1,650 pa (£550 per term), Nursery (All Day) £3,300 pa (£1,100 per term), Nursery (any 3 full days) £1,980 pa (£660 per term), Preparatory (R and Y1) £4,395 pa (£1,465 per term), (Y2) £4,500 pa (£1,500 per term), Lower Juniors £4,650 pa (£1,550 per term), Upper Juniors £4,950 pa (£1,650 per term). Hot lunches are provided and included in the fees, except for 'mornings only' nursery.

The School, occupying an 11½ acre semi-rural site at the foot of the Cotswold escarpment, is part of the Pate's Grammar School Foundation which is a charity founded by Richard Pate, a Recorder of Gloucester, in 1574.

It is a non-denominational Christian school which in its present form began in 1946. The aim of the school is to provide a high academic standard and continuity of education up to the age of 11 years. The curriculum is broadly based with strong emphasis being attached to music, art, drama and sport, for these activities are seen as vital if a child's full potential is to be realised.

Facilities include a music centre with individual practice rooms; a fully equipped computer suite and an all-weather pitch with floodlights.

At present the School is divided into three sections: Nursery 3–4½ years; Preparatory Department 5–7 and Junior 7–11. Entrance is dependent upon the availability of places but most pupils join the school at the commencement of the Nursery, Preparatory or Junior Departments.

No entry tests are taken by younger pupils but interviews and selective tests are used for assessing pupils aged 5 years and upwards. A small number of 7+ scholarships are awarded each year.

The teaching takes full account of national curriculum guidelines with children in the upper part of the school following the normal preparatory school curriculum leading to Common Entrance and Scholarship at 11+. Pupils leave at age 11 for local Grammar Schools and a variety of independent secondary schools, particularly those in Cheltenham.

The Headmaster is assisted by two deputies and 17 fully qualified teachers including specialists in Latin, French, History, Art/Design, Mathematics, Science, Music and Learning Support. The School employs music and dance teachers, who prepare children for participation in various competitions, in particular the Cheltenham Competitive Festival. A specialist teachers' assistant and six other qualified assistants are also employed full-time.

Richmond House School

170 Otley Road Leeds West Yorkshire LS16 5LG.
Tel: (0113) 2752670
Fax: (0113) 2304868
e-mail: rhschool@cwcom.net

Chairman of the Board of Governors: Mr A R Sharp

Headmaster: **G Milne,** BEd (Hons), CertEd, MCollP, FRSA

Number of Day Pupils. 266 boys and girls

Fees. Nursery half days only £944; £1,440 full time. All other departments, full days £1,480. School meals are extra.

Non-denominational Christian.

Richmond House School is a co-educational independent day school. The school is situated in two Victorian houses with a range of other buildings which together include a library, practical rooms for Art, Science, Design and

Technology, Music, Information Technology Centre, gym and a sports pavilion, thus enabling a wide and varied curriculum. To the rear are large sports fields where a wide variety of games take place, including rugby, football, cricket, cross country, rounders, tennis, netball, athletics, etc.

The school aims to develop the social, emotional, physical and academic potential of each child in a happy, caring environment. Richmond House School has a distinguished academic record and the majority of the pupils pass the entrance examinations of local independent senior schools.

Boys and girls enter the school at the ages of 3 or 4 after assessment, from a waiting list. Entrance at 7 or thereafter is by examination and interview.

Class sizes are small so as to enable a high degree of individual attention. Pastoral care is considered to be an important part of every teacher's work. Each class is under the care of a form teacher but specialist teaching increases as the child progresses through the school.

Charitable status. Richmond House School Association is a Registered Charity, number 1270675. It exists to provide high quality education for boys and girls aged 3–11 years.

Rickmansworth PNEU School

88 The Drive Rickmansworth Herts WD3 4DU
Tel: (01923) 772101
Fax: (01923) 776268

Chairman of Board of Governors: Mr I D Buchanan, CEng, MIEE

Headmistress: **Mrs S K Marshall-Taylor**, BSc Hons, PGCE

Number of Pupils. 140
Fees. £562–£1,604 (no compulsory extras)
A day school for girls from 3–11+.

The Rickmansworth PNEU School is a Preparatory School for girls from 3 to 11 years which offers high educational standards within the framework of a caring family environment. The broad-based curriculum includes English Language and Literature, Mathematics, Science, Geography, History, French, RE, Technology, Music and PE. Art and Music Appreciation are also part of the Charlotte Mason philosophy, as is the development of each child as an individual. Class sizes are small enabling the well qualified and experienced teaching staff and their assistants to give their full attention to every pupil.

New computers are in use in all classrooms. The school has a well equipped laboratory for Science and Technology and good music facilities. The extensive garden with its play equipment is an important feature of the school. An extended Nursery Department opened in September 1995 catering for 3 to 5 year olds. This has received an excellent Ofsted report. Three year olds start with an attendance of three mornings increasing to five full days at the age of 5. Nursery vouchers are accepted.

Extra-curricular activities include Tennis, Dancing, Brass, Flute, Guitar.

Charitable status. The Rickmansworth PNEU School is a Registered Charity, number 311075. It exists to provide an enjoyable education that will develop the full potential of each child.

Riddlesworth Hall (Preparatory School)

Nr Diss Norfolk IP22 2TA.
Tel: (01953) 681246
Station: Diss or Thetford

Headmaster: **Mr Colin Campbell**, BA

Number of Pupils. 23 Boarders, 34 Day, 27 Nursery
Fees per term (as from September 2000). Boarding £3,565, Weekly Boarders £3,365, Day Children by age Years 4-8 £2,275, Year 3 £1,980, Years 1 & 2 £1,435, Kindergarten: Full time £1,215, Mornings only £895, Nursery: morning session (including lunch £12.55, afternoon session £8.15.

The School, situated in a magnificent country house on the Norfolk/Suffolk border, caters for boarding girls between the ages of 7 and 13. The Nursery, Pre-Prep and Preparatory departments also cater for boys and girls from 2–11 years.

Riddlesworth Hall provides an excellent all-round education. The aim is to develop each child's potential to the full in all areas – academic, sport and creative arts. The girls are prepared for Common Entrance and Scholarship examinations to all Independent Senior Schools.

In addition to teaching the National Curriculum, we include all the extra subjects that so enrich the childrens lives.

Riddlesworth Hall has a very fine indoor heated swimming pool, excellent Art and Pottery studios, Science, Domestic Science and Technology laboratories, a Computer room, Music and Drama rooms and a Gymnasium. French is taught from 3 years. There is strong emphasis on physical education.

The care of the children is in the hands of a team of resident Matrons. The School Doctor visits weekly, and there is always a Registered Nurse on the premises.

Extras include Speech and Drama, Ballet and Tap, Riding, Archery, Fly-fishing and Clay Pigeon shooting. There is a very active Music Department with choirs, orchestra and recorder group and individual lessons are arranged in all the usual instruments.

There are a wide variety of clubs and activities including skiing, scuba diving, mountain-biking, gym, cookery and also a Brownie Pack. A feature of Riddlesworth is its Pets' Corner which houses a variety of small animals brought from home by the boarders.

Self-reliance, self-discipline, and tolerance are encouraged, and good manners are expected.

Charitable status. Riddlesworth Hall is a Registered Charity, number 311267. It exists to provide education for girls and boys.

Ridgeway School

Maidenhead Thicket Maidenhead Berks SL6 3QE
Tel: (01628) 411490
Fax: (01628) 411465
website: www.ridgewayschool.co.uk
Station: Maidenhead

Principals:
H StJ Wilding, BA, MCIM (*Bursar*)
J T Wilding, BSc, FRSA (*Academic Principal*)

Head of Ridgeway: **Miss K M Boyd**, BEd

Number of Boys. 241 Day Boys
Teaching Staff. 19 full time, 11 part time, 5 visiting
Fees. £1,515–£1,920

The ethos of Ridgeway lies in the provision for its pupils of a thorough education in all senses so that in time the challenges of the future will be met with confidence. A rich and full programme of study and activity leads to academic success, sporting accomplishment and cultural fulfilment, within a firm structure based on friendship and self-discipline. Boys are accepted into the School from 4+ to 11.

Ridgeway is situated in Maidenhead Thicket set in its own extensive grounds. The curriculum embraces the Government's National Curriculum and includes Music, Art and Craft, practical Science, and the major games and PE as well as a thorough, caring preparation for normal academic subjects. At 11+ boys transfer to the Senior School, Claires Court.

Specialist pre-prep accommodation was added in 1991 and further new buildings to accommodate the school's expansion were added in 1994.

Ridgeway is the Boys Junior School of Claires Court and its provision is complemented by the provision for Girls education at Maidenhead College. The Nursery is situated at the College, where 100 places exist for pre-school children. The co-ordination of all arrangements from Transport to Teaching across the three sites forms an integral part of the day to day school management.

The extensive playing fields, which provide ample facilities for the playing of major games such as Mini-Rugby, Soccer, Cricket and Athletics also includes an Outdoor Fitness Circuit Assault Course and the School swimming pool. Among the many activities run after school are Archery, CDT, Chess, Choir, Computing, Cookery, Drama, Electronics, Judo, Model-making, Pottery, Science Club and Study in addition to a very wide variety of sports.

The School is Roman Catholic by tradition but all denominations are welcome.

A Prospectus, containing further information, may be obtained by telephoning the Registrar at Claires Court on 01628 411472 and prospective parents are always welcome to visit the School.

Ripley Court School

Ripley Surrey GU23 6NE
Tel: (01483) 225217
Fax: (01483) 223854
On London to Guildford Green Line Coach route. Twenty minutes Heathrow and Gatwick Airports.

Chairman of Governors: K Michel

***Headmaster:* A J Gough**, BSc, (UED), MA

Assistant Headmaster: J Porter, BA

Number of Pupils. 190 Day Boys and Girls (7–13 years); Little Court, 67 Boys and Girls (4–7 years); Nursery (2+) 20.

Inclusive Fees. Day Pupils £1,890–£2,145; Little Court £1,440; Nursery £1,320, mornings only pro rata.

The School is a Charitable Trust. The Staff consists of graduates and trained teachers and pupils are prepared for Common Entrance and Scholarship Examinations for all the Boys' and Girls' Senior Independent Schools. There is a high academic standard and many Scholarships are won including some for Music and Art, but there is no cramming: PE, Music, Art and Craft are a part of every child's timetable with opportunities in orchestral, choral and dramatic productions. Facilities include a library, a science Laboratory and art, music and hobbies rooms. There is a pre-prep department and a Gymnasium. A Nursery Building and extended changing facilities were completedin 1998. There are 20 acres of playing fields. Games and sports are Football (Association and Rugby), Hockey, Netball, Cricket, Tennis (1 hard, 3 grass courts), Athletics, Rounders, Volley-ball, Stoolball; Swimming and Life Saving are taught in large, covered, heated swimming pool.

Little Court is separate from the Main School with its own play area but it also uses the main playing field, swimming pool and gymnasium. The Nursery uses all school facilities.

School transport serves East and West Clandon, the Horsleys, Woking, Pyrford and West Byfleet.

Charitable status. Ripley Court School is a Registered Charity, number 312084. It aims to educate children and prepare them well for adult life.

Ripon Cathedral Choir School

Whitcliffe Lane Ripon North Yorkshire HG4 2LA.
Tel: (01765) 602134
Fax: (01765) 608760

Governors: The Dean and Chapter of Ripon Cathedral and Lay Governors

***Headmaster:* Mr R Pepys**

Deputy Head: I D C Atkinson, BEd (Oxford)

Fees. Boarders £2,970; Weekly Boarders £2,745; Day Pupils (Over 8) £2,180; (Under 8) £1,725. Reception Class £1,450. 10% reduction for children of Service families, and a 5% reduction for siblings.

There are 18 Choristers – all boarders who have gained a 50% choral scholarship by a Voice Trial, and another 110 pupils, boarding, weekly boarding, and day. Members of the Girls' Cathedral Choir enjoy a reduction of 20% of the termly fee. The school is fully co-educational. Children are accepted from the age of 4½ into four pre-preparatory classes, and move into the main school at the age of eight, when other entries are welcomed.

The school gives children a first-class academic education in small classes in a supportive atmosphere. There are spacious facilities for indoor and outdoor sport, and art, drama and computing are greatly encouraged. Music is exceptionally strong. The school is attractively situated on the edge of a small city in a very pleasant and interesting area. The boarding accommodation is secure and friendly.

Charitable status. Ripon Cathedral Choir School is a Registered Charity, number 529583. It exists to provide non-profit making full-time education for the boy choristers of Ripon Cathedral, and for other children.

Rockport

Craigavad Co Down N Ireland BT18 0DD.
Tel: 028 9042 3872
Fax: 028 9042 2608

Chairman of the Governors: F G Barfoot, Esq

***Headmistress:* Heather G Pentland**, BEd

Number of Pupils. Girls 125, Boys 116
Fees. Weekly Boarders £1,850–£2,630, Day Children £1,300–£2,200, Pre-Prep (from the age of 3) £525–£1,050

Rockport School is the only independent preparatory and senior School in Northern Ireland. It is situated in twenty-five acres of beautiful surroundings, overlooking Belfast Lough, and prides itself in its happy atmosphere.

Rockport is a child-centred school and caters for the individual. It provides a well-balanced, rounded education for children from 3 to GCSE. Pupils are made to feel they have something valuable to contribute – whether in the classroom, in music and drama, on the sports field or elsewhere.

Rockport aims to give each pupil the capacity and confidence to live in an uncertain world – to encourage the pupils to work hard, to take a pride in achievement, to accept responsibility and to show concern for others. In the pursuance of these aims, Rockport is fortunate in having a dedicated and experienced staff, excellent teacher pupil ratios (1:8.2), a wide range of facilities and an extensive range of extra curricular activities.

Staff and parents work closely together for the common good of the children. There is an active Parent Teacher Association which meets each term. Funds are raised for the school, but regular Educational Evenings are also arranged.

Normal entry points are 3, 8 and 11.

Charitable status. Rockport School Limited is a Registered Charity, number XN48119. It exists to provide education for boys and girls.

Rokeby

George Road Kingston-upon-Thames Surrey KT2 7PB.
Tel: 020 8942 2247

Chairman of the Governors: Mr Arfon Jones

***Headmaster:* M K Seigel**, MA (Oxon)

Number of Boys. 370

Composite Fees. for September term 2001 (including lunch, books and all compulsory extras); Senior Forms £2,278-£2,386, Junior Forms £1,660-£1,990.

There is a qualified and experienced staff of 30 with a further 6 assistants. Rokeby is an Educational Trust, the successor to Rokeby in Wimbledon, which was founded in 1877. The School has an outstanding record of success in Common Entrance and Scholarships to the leading Independent Schools. Science is taught in two well equipped Laboratories. There is a separate Computer Department. There are two large halls. Physical Education is in the hands of specialists. Soccer, Rugby and Cricket are played. Other sports include Athletics, Swimming, and there is an Astroturf sports facility. An Art and Technology Department with full facilities for Design and Pottery is run by a Director of Art and Technology. The Music Department provides Orchestra, Ensembles and two Choirs. Excursions and holidays abroad are arranged. Pupils, day boys only, are accepted at the age of 7+ to Rokeby and 4+ to Junior Rokeby, the pre-preparatory School owned by the Trust. Scholarships are offered to academically able boys at 7+.

School buses serve the Wimbledon and Putney areas.

Charitable status. Rokeby Educational Trust Limited is a Registered Charity, number 312653. It exists to provide an excellent education to boys aged 4–13 years.

Rookesbury Park School

Wickham Hampshire PO17 6HT.
Tel: (01329) 833108
Fax: (01329) 835090

Chairman of Governors: P Mason

***Headmistress:* Mrs S M Cook,** BA(Hons), PGCE (Bristol)

Number of Pupils. Boarders 35, Day Girls 75, Day Boys 25

Fees. Boarders; £3,025–£3,500. Day £700-£2,350. Preparatory School for Girls and Boys from 3–13 including Boarders from 7 years.

Rookesbury Park School occupies the former manor house in the village of Wickham, situated in an unrivalled setting of 14 acres overlooking farmland. The school was founded in 1929 and became an educational trust administered by a board of governors in 1961.

It is a friendly and flourishing school with a nursery department. We offer small classes and a balanced curriculum with well-equipped science laboratory, computer and technology rooms, swimming pool, tennis courts and athletics field.

There are approximately 100 girls and 25 boys in the school which includes day, weekly and full boarding.

The children are prepared for the Common Entrance Examination to major independent schools, and for independent school scholarships. There is a well-qualified staff and the average class size is 15–20 pupils. Games played include netball, hockey, tennis, rounders, athletics, swimming, cricket, rugby and football.

The school has a very busy and stimulating extra-curricular programme in which all girls are encouraged to participate. Activities range from judo and riding to fencing and chess. The Music and Drama departments have a major role to play.

Charitable status. Rookesbury Park is a Registered Charity, number 307334. It exists to prepare girls and boys for a challenging, demanding and ever-changing future through an Independent Preparatory education which encourages the highest possible standards in all areas of learning, set in beautiful surroundings and an atmosphere of fun and security.

Rose Hill School

Alderley Wotton-under-Edge Glos GL12 7QT.
Tel: (01453) 843196
Fax: (01453) 846126
e-mail: rosehillschool.glos@btinternet.com
website: www.rosehillschoolglos.co.uk
Stations: Kemble, Bristol Parkway
Easy access to M4 and M5 motorways. School minibuses collect daily from surrounding area.

Chairman of Governors: J C Maxwell

***Headmaster:* Richard C G Lyne-Pirkis**, CertEd (Birmingham), MBIM

Number of Pupils. 280: 85 boarders, 195 day pupils. 140 boys, 140 girls. Aged 3–13+.

Fees. Boarders £2,900–£3,520 per term; Day including Pre-Prep and Nursery £1,500–£2,610.

Founded in 1832, Rose Hill is a small, co-educational country prep school comprising approximately 280 full boarders, weekly boarders and day pupils, aged between 3 and 13.

The buildings and grounds are located in 14 acres of glorious Cotswold countryside. Facilities include the use of a traditional chapel, modern sports hall, outdoor heated swimming pool, science laboratories, new millennium literary centre and library, art room, well-equipped information technology centre, playing fields and tennis courts.

The academic reputation is excellent. Since Richard Lyne-Pirkis took over as Headmaster in 1990, all sixth-formers have gone on to the school of their first choice and many have achieved scholarships. Outstanding results are achieved by a combination of good facilities, highly qualified staff, small classes (no larger than 18) and the back-up of a professional Learning Support team.

Somewhat unconventionally, homework and Saturday School are not introduced until the age of ten, which encourages the children to develop confidence and individual talent before they prepare for the Common Entrance examination.

Pupils have an extensive list of activities and extras to choose from, many of which are free. French is taught from age five onwards and every child in the main school receives between six and eight hours of organised sport per week. Games include Cricket, Rugby and Football for the boys; Netball, Lacrosse and Rounders for the girls. All children do Hockey, Cross-country running and Athletics. There are three choirs and one orchestra, and the music, art and drama departments are amongst the strongest in Gloucestershire.

Rose Hill's pastoral care is outstanding and there is a flexible attitude towards boarding, including an 'early start', a 'late stayer' or 'bed and breakfast' option, designed to help busy working parents. The pupils are confident, disciplined, purposeful and undoubtedly happy.

Charitable status. Rose Hill School is a Registered Charity, number 311708. It exists to provide quality education in a demanding world.

Rose Hill School

Culverden Down Tunbridge Wells Kent TN4 9SY.
Tel: (01892) 525591.
Fax: (01892) 533312
e-mail: admissions@rosehillschool.co.uk
Station: Tunbridge Wells Central; 5 minutes by car from centre of Tunbridge Wells.

Headmaster: **P D Westcombe**, BA, PGCE

Deputy Head: G J Coventry, CertEd (Loughborough)

Chairman of Governing Body: Captain P W R Smith, OBE

Number of Boys. 200
Number of Girls. 100
Age range. 2+ to 13+.

Fees. £2,520 per term (over 7 years); £1,660 per term (under 7 years); £800 per term (3 years old). There is also a Nursery for children aged 2+.

The school is situated in eighteen acres of beautiful grounds adjacent to the green belt, but within five minutes of the centre of the town. A superb new Pre-Preparatory building was opened in 1991, followed by an outstanding IT centre. A Sports Hall was completed in 1998 and a new dining room and kitchen in 1999. Facilities also include an outdoor heated swimming pool and 6 hole golf course. Plans are underway for new classrooms and facilities for Music and Art.

Children are prepared for Common Entrance and Scholarship entry to Independent Senior Schools but consideration is also given to competitive entry into local grammar schools at 11+ and 13+. Small classes ensure individual attention and the fulfilment of academic challenge.

Sport and the Creative Arts are highly valued. Hockey, Netball, Cricket, Rounders, Athletics, Football and Rugby are the main team sports supported by a range of individual sports. There is a junior and senior Choir, a School Orchestra and many children receive instrumental tuition. Two drama productions occur every year.

A full range of extra-curricular clubs, including Cubs and Brownies, and opportunities for visits and activity holidays outside school support the School's aims of building character, confidence and responsibility against a background of academic excellence.

Rossall Preparatory School

Near Fleetwood FY7 8JW.
Tel: (01253) 774222
Fax: (01253) 774222

Chairman of Rossall Council: T R A Groves

***Headmaster:* Mr D Mitchell,**

Number of Pupils. Preparatory Department: 139. 76 boys, 63 girls. Pre-Preparatory Department: 135 Day children, 70 boys, 65 girls.

Fees. Boarders/Weekly Boarders: £3,250 per term. Day/Extended Day: £1,245 per term. Pre-Preparatory (4–7): £1,188 per term. Nursery (2–4): £1,095 per term.

Rossall Preparatory School enjoys a sound academic reputation and is renowned for identifying, nurturing and developing the intellectual, cultural, sporting and social potential of its pupils. It is a 7 to 11 school with its pupils then progressing to Rossall's Middle School (11 to 13) where they are prepared for entry to Rossall Senior School. Considerable emphasis is given to the acquisition of basic numeracy and literacy skills, while at the same time providing children with an opportunity to acquire knowledge, develop an enquiring mind and enjoy a wide range of personal interests.

Pupils are actively encouraged to take part in the performing arts; tuition is available in a wide range of musical instruments and there are regular drama productions. Rossall is a Christian foundation and the School's Church of England Chaplain spends some time with the Preparatory School and Pre-Preparatory Department each week.

The Preparatory School operates a traditional House system with Houseteachers providing a high standard of pastoral care. It has a unique family boarding unit where a group of boarders live with Houseparents and are cared for as part of their extended family. The School operates its own coach service from a wide area and has an extended day until 5.40 pm which meets the needs of busy parents who wish to pursue their own careers. Day pupils are encouraged to remain at school beyond this time to participate in the wide variety of after-school activities offered on a programme that continues until early evening.

The School's facilities are first class and include, in addition to attractive modern classrooms, specialist rooms for science, art, design, and information technology. The Preparatory School also has access to the Senior School's facilities which include squash courts and a heated indoor swimming pool.

The Nursery and Pre-Preparatory Department occupies a purpose-designed building which was opened in 1991 and stands adjacent to the Preparatory School. This Department operates an After-School Care Scheme until 5.40 pm enabling younger children to remain at school until older brothers or sisters finish at 5.40 pm.

Charitable status. Rossall is a Church of England Charitable Foundation, number 526685. It exists to provide boys and girls with a sound education which emphasises the traditional Christian values.

Rowan Preparatory School

Fitzalan Road Claygate Esher Surrey KT10 0LX
Tel: (01372) 462627

Day School

Headmistress: **Mrs Elizabeth J Brown**, BA, CertEd

Chairman of Governors: Mr Ron Disney

Number of Pupils. 310
Pre-preparatory Department. girls 3–7
Preparatory Department. girls 7–11+
Fees. £825–£2,220 per term.

Founded in 1936 Rowan is registered as an Educational Trust and is controlled by a Board of Governors.

The school is managed in two separate departments, the Preparatory and the Pre-preparatory, having their own buildings and playgrounds. There is a purpose built Kindergarten unit for three year olds on the Pre-prep site.

Girls are admitted at 3+ and 7+, or where places occur, and are prepared for entry at 11+ to a wide variety of Senior Independent Boarding and Day schools. This is by Common Entrance, Scholarship or individual school examinations. The Headmistress is in regular contact with the girls' senior schools and is pleased to advise parents on future schooling.

The curriculum is wide and lively and includes Music, Art, Design Technology and sport, as well as outings and expeditions and after school activities. There are 26 qualified teachers on the staff, each a specialist in one particular area of the curriculum.

There is a well equipped gym, science laboratory, a music room, art room and library. In the Computer Room our Information Technology Specialist develops computer skills and application with all pupils and staff.

A prospectus is available on application to the Headmistress. Early registration is advised if a place in the Pre-prep is to be ensured. Entry at the age of 7+ requires a satisfactory level of attainment in the basic skills.

Charitable status. Rowan Preparatory School is a Registered Charity, number 312047. It exists to provide education for girls.

Royal Russell Preparatory School

Coombe Lane Croydon Surrey CR9 5BX.
Tel: 020 8651 5884/020 8657 4433

Patron: Her Majesty The Queen

Chairman of Governors: R P Green

Headmaster: **C L Hedges**, BA, CertEd

Number of Pupils. 170 Boys, 130 Girls (aged 3–11 years)

Fees. Kindergarten (3 years) £665 (half day); Pre-Prep (4–7 years) £1,490; Prep Day (7–11 years) £1,845.

The Prep School stands on a magnificent wooded campus extending to over 100 acres, which it shares with the Royal Russell Senior School (11–18 years). The school is well served by road and rail links and is one of the few co-educational schools in South London.

There is a fully qualified teaching staff of 24, and the Headmaster is a member of IAPS.

The school has a broad curriculum which seeks to blend the highest standards of academic work with a wide range of extra-curricular activities. There are opportunities for all pupils to participate in soccer, netball, hockey, cross-country and cricket as team sports, and as individuals to be coached in athletics, swimming, tennis, and table tennis. There is an extensive fixture list of matches against other schools. Artistic development extends to include full dramatic and musical productions, and many pupils learn musical instruments. All forms of art, design and technology are actively encouraged. There are excellent carpeted classrooms which are complemented by two Assembly Halls, a Sports Hall, Gymnasium, Science Laboratories, Music School, Art Room, Computer Suite and School Chapel. A new indoor swimming pool was opened recently, and offers 25m main pool, learner pool and function room. All Prep School pupils receive weekly swimming lessons from qualified instructors.

The majority of the pupils join the school at 3+ or 7+, and are prepared for transfer to the Senior School at 11+. Candidates for entry to the Pre-Prep are interviewed informally, while all other entrants sit examinations in English and Mathematics appropriate to their ages.

Prospective parents are very welcome to come and meet the Headmaster and to tour the school, and should telephone for a prospectus in the first instance.

Charitable status. Royal Russell School is a Registered Charity, number 271907. It exists solely to provide education to girls and boys.

The Royal Wolverhampton Junior School

Penn Road Wolverhampton WV3 0EF.
Tel: (01902) 349100
Fax: (01902) 344496
e-mail: head@royal.wolverhampton.sch.uk

Patron: Her Majesty Queen Elizabeth, The Queen Mother

Chairman of the Governors: Dr D B M Huffer

Head: **Mrs M Saunders**, CertEd

Number of Children. 212. Boys 112, Girls 100

Fees per annum. Day Pupils, Years 2–6 £5,160, Reception and Year 1 £3,780, Nursery £3,345

Fees include lunch, text books, stationery, compulsory teaching materials and personal accident insurance cover.

There are bursaries for those serving in the Armed Forces, reductions for Old Royals and also for siblings. A number of foundation scholarships are awarded each year.

In the Nursery and the Junior School an extended day facility is available from 8 am to 6 pm. There is a small charge. Also an optional playscheme is available during the holidays.

The Royal Wolverhampton School occupies a 28 acre site in a pleasant residential area on the fringes of Wolverhampton. The Royal Wolverhampton Junior School and the Young Royals' Nursery are located in the same building, in its own grounds, to the south of the main campus. Easy access is afforded from the local area and further afield. A daily school transport service is organised for pupils from many surrounding areas.

The Junior School and Nursery provide an education for boys and girls aged 2 to 11 years. At the age of eleven, many pupils gain entrance to the Senior School and other selective secondary schools.

The Royal Wolverhampton School was founded in 1850. The prefix "Royal" was granted by Queen Victoria in 1891 and Her Majesty Queen Elizabeth, the Queen Mother, is the School's Patron.

The aim of the school is to provide a well-balanced education, in a safe and friendly environment.

Facilities. The School has been transformed since its days as an orphanage and the school buildings have been continually updated. Over the past ten years, The Royal Wolverhampton School has spent over £4 million on improvements to its buildings and equipment.

The School's own catering staff serve a variety of meals to suit all tastes. A cooked lunch is provided for all pupils. In years 5 and 6, pupils take lunch in the Senior School. Special dietary requirements, for religious or medical reasons, can be accommodated. For pupils attending after school activities or taking part in the school's extended hours scheme, light refreshments are provided.

Religion. The School has its own chapel within the grounds. This fine building forms a focus for School life, with important events in the School calendar being held there, including Speech Day, The Advent Service of Light, Remembrance Sunday and Founder's Day. Although the School has a religious affiliation to the Church of England, it welcomes pupils of all religions.

Pastoral care. The well-being of all pupils is of prime importance. Class teachers are on hand to deal with any problems which might arise, as are the Head and her secretary.

In case of illness, the School has a fully-equipped sanatorium, which provides 24 hour healthcare.

Curriculum. The Junior School offers a broad-based curriculum, which aims to highlight the strengths of the individual child and excellent results are achieved at Key Stages 1 and 2. Small class sizes are a feature throughout the School, with an average of fifteen pupils per class.

The Junior School has its own Science and Art rooms, with specialist teaching staff.

Pupils learn how to use computers from an early age in the information technology suite. Each of the pre-prep classes is equipped with one computer, which is used to reinforce early learning skills.

Art takes many formats and a variety of mediums are used. Where possible art projects are linked to themes established in other subject areas.

French is taught from the age of 3 and each year Junior School staff take Year 6 pupils to France.

Various educational visits take place throughout the year, including to the Black Country Museum, Ironbridge, Birmingham Nature Centre and The National Sea Life Centre.

The Dyslexia Institute has an office in the Junior School and is able to offer help to pupils with this specific learning difficulty.

In the Nursery, an emphasis is placed on reading, writing and number skills. Early scientific and mathematical concepts are introduced through sand and water play and cooking. Art and Music also play a central role. In the September following their fourth birthday, children move into the Reception classes.

Music and Drama. The School has an excellent reputation for its musical standards and is a recognised examination centre for the London College of Music. Our active Music Department, equipped with the latest technology, provides pupils with an opportunity to learn 20 instruments. In addition, pupils are encouraged to take part in the choir and perform in a wide variety of events, including at the National Indoor Arena in Birmingham. Last year pupils achieved a 100% pass rate in the London College of Music examinations and a 90% pass rate in ABRSM examinations.

One of the highlights of the School calendar is the Variety Show, which presents the best of both Junior and Senior dramatic and musical talents. Other performances take place throughout the year, including the Nursery Nativity, the Pre-Prep shows and keyboard concerts.

Sport and Extra-curricular activities. The School aims to educate well-rounded individuals and a wide variety of after school activities are enjoyed by pupils from age 7, for example: basketball, choir, keyboards, computers, craft and country-dancing. Swimming and Ballet are taught from 3. Elocution lessons are available.

The grounds of The Royal Eolverhampton School afford an indoor heated swimming pool, a gymnasium, tennis courts and extensive playing fields. Pupils can choose from 12 sports and matches are arranged against local schools. A Sports Day is held each year, as are swimming galas.

The School ethos promotes compassion towards the less fortunate and considerable amounts of money are raised for charity.

Old Royals' and Old Rowans' Association. The Association regularly organises reunions. For further information, please contact Mr Mike Masters, 24 Birmingham Road, Coleshill, Birmingham B46 1AA. Tel: 01675 463093.

Charitable status. The Royal Wolverhampton Junior School is a Registered Charity, number L4 529007/4. It exists to provide an education for boys and girls.

Rudston Preparatory School

59/63 Broom Road Rotherham S60 2SW
Tel: (01709) 837774
e-mail: office@rudstonschool.com
website: www.rudstonschool.com

Coeducational. Day. 2–11 years

Chairman of Trustees: Mr C N Middleton, BA

Headmistress: **Mrs Sandra Atack**, MA, BEd (Hons), CertEd

Number of Boys. 94
Number of Girls. 72

Fees. 4–11 £3,228-£3,456 per annum; Pre-School £25 per day

The school is a charitable educational trust with a Board of Trustees. Chairman: Mr C N Middleton.

There are 19 members of staff.

Our small classes, combined with a wide curricula, flexibility in organisation, detailed attention to the acquisition of skills and personal consideration of each individual's ability, help to ensure that the highest standards are achieved.

The school offers a range of subjects including English, Mathematics, Sciences, Design Technology, French, Latin, Music and Computer Studies, Drama, History, Geography, Religious Education, Personal and Social Education, Physical Education.

Pupils are prepared for Common Entrance Examinations and for extrance examinations to other schools. We have an excellent reputation for gaining successful results.

Pupils are expected to maintain a good code of conduct at all times; courtesy and consideration for others are an intrinsic part of school life.

Charitable status. Rudston Preparatory School is a Registered Charity, number 866744. It exists to provide education for boys and girls.

Rupert House School

Henley-on-Thames Oxon RG9 2BN.
Tel: (01491) 574263
Fax: (01491) 573988
e-mail: ruperthouse@bigfoot.com

Headmistress: **Mrs G M Crane**, BSc, MSc, PGCE

Chairman of Governors: J D Crossman, MBE, MA (Oxon)

Fees. as at September 2001: £805 to £1,950 per term (inclusive)

Numbers. Girls 176, Boys 59

Rupert House School, a Charitable Trust, is a day preparatory school for girls aged 4–11 and boys aged 4–7. The school is set in its own large garden in the centre of Henley-on-Thames. The Pre-preparatory school is housed in a purpose-built unit and the older children work in a large Georgian House. There are all-weather games facilities on the site and a sports ground within a short walk.

The staff are fully qualified and experienced. They aim to give a sound and stimulating education in the basic subjects required for 11+ Common Entrance but are concerned also with the wider curriculum, as laid down in the National Curriculum, emphasising a variety of other subjects including Music, Physical Education, Dance, Swimming, Drama, IT, Technology. Extra curricular activities, which can include maths club, gymnastics, swimming, art, craft, football, hockey and computers are offered after school hours. Individual music lessons in piano, string, wind and brass instruments as well as voice are offered as an extra, as is tennis coaching in the summer.

Within a disciplined framework, where courtesy and consideration are expected, there is a friendly, family atmosphere in which the individual nature of each child is respected. The pupils are encouraged to match their performance to potential and to meet all challenges with enthusiasm and determination. There are regular consultation evenings and twice yearly reports. Parents may consult the Headmistress at any time by appointment.

Care is taken to ensure that pupils are well prepared for transfer to a school suited to their academic ability and personal qualities. In recent years girls have gained admission to well respected Independent Senior Schools and boys to excellent Prep. Schools.

Charitable status. Rupert House School is a Registered Charity, number 309648. It exists to provide quality education for boys and girls.

Russell House School

Otford Nr Sevenoaks Kent TN14 5QU.
Tel: (01959) 522352

Headmistress: **Mrs E Lindsay**, BA, CertEd

Number of Pupils. Boys 100, Girls 100. Co-educational 2–11+

Tuition. Nursery Department (mornings) £825, 5-8 years Day including lunch £1,495, 8–11 years Day including lunch £1,695.

Russell House is a co-educational day preparatory school educating children from the ages of 2–11.

The school stands in extensive level grounds in a beautiful setting overlooking open countryside and the North Downs.

The basis for study is the National Curriculum. Every attention is given to developing the skills of literacy and numeracy.

Boys and girls are prepared carefully for transfer at 11 to a wide variety of secondary schools, both state and private.

The high standard of education is reflected in Russell House pupils' successful record of achievement, including scholarships, in the Common Entrance Examination and 11+.

Rydal Penrhos Preparatory School

Pwllycrochan Avenue Colwyn Bay North Wales LL29 7BP.
Tel: (01492) 530381.
Fax: (01492) 533983
e-mail: rydalpenrhosprep@rmplc.co.uk
Station: Colwyn Bay

Head: **Simon J Beavan**, BEd

Chairman of Governors: Mr David L Wigley, MA, MSc

Number of Pupils. 176 (156 day, 20 boarders); 78 in Pre-Prep (38 boys; 40 girls); 98 in Prep (61 boys; 37 girls).

Fees per term. Pre-Prep Day: £715–£1,162; Preparatory Day: £1,181–£2,149; Preparatory Boarding: £1,705–£2,982.

Rydal Penrhos Preparatory School is a welcoming, vibrant school for young boys and girls aged 2½ to 11 years, with full, weekly and flexible boarding available from 7 years. As a Christian school with a Methodist foundation, Rydal Penrhos Prep seeks to provide a firm but sympathetic moral framework in which care, support, respect, tolerance and responsibility for oneself and for others is accepted as fundamental. Rydal Penrhos has a strong family atmosphere and concern for every aspect of a child's development.

Set 70m above sea level in Colwyn Bay on a 12 acre site, the magnificent school building offers breathtaking views to the sea across playing fields and woodland. Maximum advantage is taken of the coastal aspect, the close proximity of the Snowdonia National Park and rich historic and cultural resources in the locality.

The school curriculum is very broad and is based on the National Curriculum, teaching being mainly class based from the ages of 2½ to 8 and subject based from 8 to 11, with input from subject specialists throughout the Preparatory School. All children also have the opportunity to develop their special interests and skills through a varied programme of extra-curricular activities. A busy and varied school day runs from 8.30 am to 5 or 6 pm. In addition there is an exciting range of weekend activities for boarders. A holiday club is also run by staff for many weeks of the school holidays.

Although the syllabus has rigorous academic elements, specialist provision is available within the school for those with learning difficulties. Sport, Music, Drama, Art, Design and Information Technology feature strongly and provide real opportunities for every child to explore and develop individual talents not always expressed through academic work. Pupils may be prepared for entrance to other senior independent schools although most proceed through to Rydal Penrhos Senior School.

Boy and girl boarders live within the main school building, under the care of experienced houseparents and matrons. The bedrooms are warm, bright and colourful. The Medical Centre is shared with the Senior School and has a resident Sister and two nursing staff under the direction of a GP, providing 24 hour care.

Facilities at the Preparatory School are excellent

including Science laboratories, an Information Technology suite, Art studio, Design Technology room, gymnasium and a 25m indoor swimming pool. The large multi-purpose hall with stage, provides for dance, drama, gymnastics and regular musical and dramatic productions. An orchestra, wind and string groups are formed from those pupils taking tuition in a wide range of instruments and choral singing is also of a high standard. The School has an excellent reputation for both girls' and boys' sport.

Financial assistance in the form of Bursary Awards is available at point of entry to the Preparatory School from age 7. Scholarships to the Senior School are offered at 11+. Parents appreciate the educational continuity between the junior and senior divisions and the integrated curriculum ensures a smooth transition between the schools.

Charitable status. Rydal Penrhos is a Registered Charity, number 525752. It exists to provide education for boys and girls.

Ryde Junior School

Queen's Road Ryde Isle of Wight PO33 3BE.
Tel: (01983) 612901
Fax: (01983) 614973
e-mail: juniorhead@rydeschool.org.uk

Head: **H Edwards**, BSc

Chairman of the Board of Governors: D J Longford, BSc

Number of Boys. 156
Number of Girls. 136

Fees per term. (at January 2001) Nursery £795; Day pupils £1,050–£1,914; Weekly Boarders (exclusive of tuition fees) £1,510; Full Boarders (exclusive of tuition fees) £1,715. Ryde School Assisted Places/Scholarships awarded annually for pupils entering Year 5.

The school provides a good, civilised environment that does well academically for a wide range of ability. The pupils are well-motivated and work hard with evident enjoyment in both lessons and activities. By paying careful attention to all aspects of school life, pupils are able to flourish within a supportive community. In this environment, where regular contact between parents and staff is considered to be of paramount importance, children develop confidence and happily give of their best.

Ryde Junior School caters for children aged 2½–11 years. Fiveways, just across the road from the main site, is home to the Nursery and Early Years. Through creative and imaginative teaching, a sound foundation of key skills is established. At the end of Key Stage 1 pupils are ready to move to the 'senior' part of the Junior School, having already benefited from specialist Science and ICT teaching in the Junior School. Here they continue to receive the support of a well qualified and dedicated staff, enjoying a full range of specialist facilities including a recently upgraded ICT facility comprising 20 PCs with Internet access, a Design Technology Centre, Science Laboratory and Art Studio.

A broad and balanced curriculum is followed, taking as its core enhanced delivery of the National Curriculum (with full Key Stage testing and reporting - the school features consistently at the top of the Isle of Wight Key Stage 2 league tables). A wealth of trips and outings is offered, enriching the curriculum still further, making use not only of the beautiful sites on the island, but on the mainland and abroad. Pupils are encouraged to develop their full range of talents, with Music, Drama and Sports enjoying equally high profiles. The school maintains a consistently successful record in all areas of team and individual sports. The major sports offered are: Athletics, Cricket, Cross-Country, Hockey, Netball, Rounders, Rugby, Soccer, Swimming and Tennis, with fixtures being arranged both locally and on the mainland (at no extra charge). There is a full and wide ranging programme of clubs and activities (which changes each term) during lunchtime and after school, offering something for everyone.

Our Senior School is on the same campus, enabling us to benefit from the use of a Theatre, Sports Hall and pitches. Careful liaison between the staff and induction days in the summer term effect a smooth transition for our pupils to the Senior School (see entry under Part I of this Book).

The Junior School has a small number of weekly and full boarders who, together with Senior School boarders, have use of the range of facilities available at the Bembridge campus, situated in some 100 acres on a beautiful cliff top site approximately six miles from Ryde. Transport is provided to and from the school during the week.

Charitable status. Ryde School with Upper Chine is a Registered Charity, number 307409. The aims and objectives of the Charity are the education of boys and girls.

Rydes Hill Preparatory School

Rydes Hill House Aldershot Road Guildford Surrey GU2 6BP
Tel: (01483) 563160
Fax: (01483) 306714
e-mail: enquiries@rydeshill.com
website: www.rydeshill.com

Headmistress: **Mrs Joan Lenahan,** BEd (Hons), MA

Chairman of the Governors: Mr Kevin Ryan

Number of Day Pupils. 160

Ages. Girls 3–11; Boys 3–7. Nursery class for children 3–4.

Fees. £720–£1,720. Compulsory extras: Stationery £25.

Rydes Hill Preparatory School, set in over two acres in the Aldershot Road, Guildford, caters for children from nursery age until seven for boys and eleven for girls.

Rydes Hill, which welcomes children from all denominations, has a long established tradition of helping each child attain full potential in a loving, Christian environment, where the happiness and security of the child is of paramount importance.

From the age of three, children are welcomed for morning and/or afternoon sessions at the superbly equipped nursery, where they are gently encouraged to develop the skills which will facilitate the transition into formal education at four plus.

A gently disciplined approach to work and play results in outstanding achievements at Common Entrance, and an excellent scholarship record. Education at Rydes Hill enables a child to choose from a wide variety of schools, including leading boarding and day schools.

Charitable status. Rydes Hill Preparatory School is a Registered Charity, number 299411. It exists to ensure excellence in all aspects of education.

The Ryleys

Alderley Edge Cheshire SK9 7UY.
Tel: (01625) 583241.
Fax: (01625) 581900

Founded 1877.

Chairman of Governors: K J Phillips, Esq

***Headmaster:* P G Barrett**, BA, CertEd

Number of Boys. 286 Day Boys; Weekly accomodation available for Day Boys.

Fees per term. Day Boys: Nursery: £560 (half day); £880 (full day). Reception, Years 1, 2, 3 £1,470; Years 4–8 £1,685.

The Ryleys School is situated in Alderley Edge, a rural village just 15 miles south of the city of Manchester, within easy reach of the motorway and rail networks and close to Manchester Airport.

The School is an Educational Trust with an active and forward-thinking Board of Governors. The staff consists of 19 highly-qualified full-time teachers and 5 part-time. There are also 6 Classroom and Nursery assistants. In the Junior part of the school (Reception to Year 3) class teachers are responsible for delivering the curriculum while in the Senior School (Years 4 to 8) all subjects are taught by subject specialists. Pastoral care is maintained by personal tutors. The thriving and successful Nursery School is staffed by qualified teachers.

Boys are thoroughly prepared for entry via examination into Independent Day Schools at 11 and 13 or into Boarding Schools at 13 via the Common Entrance or Scholarship examinations. The school has an excellent academic record.

The extensive curriculum consists of English, Mathematics, Science, French, History, Geography, Scripture, Design Technology, Information Technology, Art, Music and Physical Education and provides an outstanding foundation for the boys' future schooling. German or Latin is offered to boys in Years 7 and 8 and Greek is also available. Each subject is taught in a fully equipped subject room and there is a computerised library. Other facilities include a Sports Hall, Music Department, Craft and Woodwork Centre, a large outdoor heated Swimming Pool, an Astroturf playing area and 8 acres of playing fields.

Various extra-curricular sports and activities are on offer including chess, computing, music, woodwork, basketball, badminton, table tennis etc.

Soccer, Rugby Football, Cricket and Athletics are the main team games and there is an extensive fixture list of matches against other schools at various ages. The school has undertaken sports tours to Zimbabwe and Sweden in the last few years and there is an annual skiing trip to Europe or North America. Outdoor pursuits are encouraged and the school organises two weeks of outdoor and adventure activities at the start of the summer holiday as well as regular hiking expeditions to the Lake District and North Wales.

Music is another of the school's great strengths with well over 100 boys receiving individual instrumental tuition from a highly qualified staff of 9 visiting teachers. The school has a fine reputation for its concerts and musical productions. These performances take place on a full proscenium stage and every boy is involved in one of the four productions each year.

Art, too, is of a notably high standard with boys sitting for various scholarships and awards.

There is a comfortable dormitory which accommodates boys on a weekly flexi-boarding basis, a facility which many families find useful. The domestic and catering arrangements and the health and welfare of the boys are under the direct supervision of Mrs Barrett, the Headmaster's wife.

Boys are accepted into the school at various ages providing places are available and are assessed upon entry so that the correct educational provision can be made in order to ensure that each pupil achieves his full potential.

The school places great emphasis upon such personal qualities as good manners and consideration for others.

Charitable status. The Ryleys is a Registered Charity, number 525951. It exists to provide a quality education for boys from 3 to 13 years of age.

Saint Aloysius' College Junior School

56 Hill Street Glasgow G3 6RH
Tel: 0141 572 1859
Fax: 0141 353 0426

Chairman of Governors: Prof Jack Mahoney, SJ, MA, STD, CIMgt

Headmaster of St Aloysius' College: Fr Adrian Porter, SJ, MA, BD

***Head:* Mr T J Mooney**, MA (Trinity College, Dublin), HDipEd

Number of pupils. 420

Fees (2001-2002). Kindergarten: £4,100. Junior School: £4,700.

The school is the Junior School of St Aloysius' College, founded in 1859 and sited in Garnethill, Glasgow. It is a Roman Catholic independent school under the Trusteeship of the Society of Jesus. The Junior School is self contained in a new building (completed 1999). The building has won a number of national and international Architectural Awards and has generated renewed architectural interest in the innovative design of urban schools.

Academic standards are high and the Junior School employs specialists in Science, French, PE, Art and Music to complement class teachers. Drama is an area of growing interest with the Junior School pupils performing in a variety of productions through the year. Sport is an important part of school life, the main games being Rugby, Hockey and Athletics. There are growing sporting links with schools in England and the Republic of Ireland.

Entrance to the Junior School is by open examination at P7 and by assessment at P1 and Kindergarten. There may be places in intermediate years from time to time.

Bursaries are available on consideration of parents' income.

Charitable status. St Aloysius' College is a Registered Charity, number 230165. It exists to provide education for boys and girls.

St Andrew's Preparatory School

Private Bag Molo Kenya East Africa.
Tel: 0363-21003/21013
Fax: 0363 21010/21215
e-mail: admin.stat@net2000ke.com

***Headmaster:* R B Fenwick**, MA

Chairman of Governors: Mrs J Barton

Number of Boarders. 220. Boys 120; Girls 100

Fees. Ksh 168,500-198,500 per term (inclusive)

St Andrew's School is an independent preparatory school in a beautiful setting 130 miles north west of Nairobi. The estate covers 300 acres, at an altitude of 8,200 feet. The climate is healthy and invigorating.

The school is international and co-educational, drawing its pupils from East Africa and further afield. Pupils are accepted from the age of 6 and follow a curriculum which prepares for entry to independent senior schools in Britain, Kenya or elsewhere.

The grounds and playing fields are extensive. Boys play cricket and rugby; girls play rounders and netball; all play hockey, tennis and athletics. There are seven tennis courts and a swimming pool. There is a large number of horses which children learn to ride under a qualified instructor. Art and Craft, hobbies and outdoor pursuits of every kind are actively encouraged.

The original school, started in 1931, was destroyed by fire in 1944. It was completely rebuilt and is superbly designed and equipped as a modern purpose-built preparatory school. There are subject rooms for English, Mathematics, French, History, Geography, and a Science laboratory. A trained special needs teacher gives individual attention to those with learning difficulties in the well-equipped Learning Support Centre. Information Technology is part of the curriculum throughout the school. An exceptionally large Hall is used for physical education, sport, plays, concerts and large functions. The average size of classes is 18.

There is a strong musical tradition. About 80 pupils learn the piano, violin, brass and woodwind. There are several recorder and guitar groups, and Senior and Junior choirs.

The school has its own Chapel and aims to give a practical Christian education in a community with high standards and in a family atmosphere.

All staff live at the school. The teaching staff are all qualified and most are committed to the Christian ethos of the school.

In 1988 a Secondary School was begun on the same site, offering a three year course to IGCSE examinations. The School has the same Board of Governors, but its own Headmaster.

St Andrew's School

Nr Pangbourne Reading Berks RG8 8QA.
Tel: (0118) 9744276
Fax: (0118) 9745049
e-mail: enquiries@standrews.reading.sch.uk

Headmaster: **J M Snow**, BA, CertEd

Numbers. 300 pupils aged 3–13 including 25 weekly boarders (7–13).

Fees. Boarders £3,200–£3,300 per term; Day Pupils £1,490–£2,595 per term. Nursery £600-£960.

The School is fully co-educational and set in over 50 acres of private wooded estate and parkland. Junction 12 of the M4 is nearby.

Facilities include extensive Sports Fields, Tennis Courts, Outdoor Swimming Pool, Sports Hall and 9-hole Golf Course.

The Curriculum includes all the traditional CE and Scholarship subjects and there is emphasis on Music, Speech and Drama and Modern Languages. Study Skills are an important part of the senior pupils' timetable and Information Technology is well resourced.

Academic and Sporting standards are high.

The School is an Educational Trust controlled by a Board of Governors whose Chairman is A J Kerevan, Esq.

Bursaries are available for children of the Clergy.

Charitable status. St Andrew's (Pangbourne) School Trust Limited is a Registered Charity, number 309090. It exists to provide education for boys and girls.

St Andrew's School

Horsell Woking Surrey GU21 4QW.
Tel: (01483) 760943.
Fax: (01483) 740314
Station: Woking (1 mile)
Airport: Heathrow (15 miles)

Chairman of Governors:

Headmaster: **Barry Pretorius**, BEd

Deputy Head: A Perks, MSc

Number of Pupils. Total 250. Pre-prep and Nursery 120.

Fees. Prep £2,005–£2,445

Pre-Prep. Ages 3–7 £960–£1,720.

Average Class Size. 15

New teaching facilities for all subjects including Science, Computing and Music. Separate rooms for Art, Pottery and Technology. Sports Hall, Heated Swimming Pool, two hard tennis courts and ample grounds for games (11 acres). Pupils are prepared for Independent Senior Schools' entrance and scholarship examinations (55 Awards in past 10 years) including the top scholarships at Hampton, St George's, Bradfield, Hurstpierpoint, Cranleigh, Lancing, Eton.

Main school games are Soccer, Hockey, Cricket and Netball. Other activities include Rugby, Tennis, Athletics, Cross Country Running, Swimming and Rounders.

Pre-Prep. A free crèche is available from 8.15 am until school starts and from 3.15 pm until 4.30 pm each day. There is also an after school club from 4 pm to 6 pm for pre-prep children. This is chargeable.

Senior School. Evening activities are offered on three evenings a week. On these evenings a cooked meal is available at 6 pm.

Charitable status. St Andrew's School is a Registered Charity, number 297580. It exists to provide a high standard of education for boys and girls.

St Andrew's School

Meads Eastbourne BN20 7RP.
Tel: (01323) 733203.
Fax: (01323) 646860
e-mail: office@androvian.co.uk
website: www.androvian.co.uk

Chairman of Governors: Sir Michael Richardson

Head: **Fergal Roche**, MA, MBA, FRSA

Number of Pupils. 347 (Main School), 110 (Pre-Prep and Nursery)

School Fees. Boarders £3,970 per term. Supersleeper: £3,630. Day children £2,790 per term. Pre-Prep £1,600 per term. Nursery £800–£1,130 per term.

Situated in twelve acres of grounds at the foot of the South Downs, St Andrew's, founded in 1877, has a highly qualified teaching staff of 70 and children are taught in classes with a maximum size of 18. About a quarter of children in the senior part of the school are boarders and the school operates a popular scheme of 'Sleepover' boarding allowing day children to stay during the week on a flexible basis on any night or nights they wish. This service has become particularly popular with children and is appreciated by parents when they are away from home for an evening, a day, a weekend or even a couple of weeks. The majority of boys and girls board in their last year or two, or in some cases their last term.

The Head is supported by a Deputy and a strong leadership team. In the junior part of the school and the Pre-Prep, Form Teachers look after the academic and pastoral interests of children and then, for their last four years, they join a tutor group with about twenty others. The Set Tutor is responsible for the pastoral welfare of the children in their set. Each section of the school has its own Head, who co-ordinates, together with the Academic Director, the overall pastoral and academic work of the staff.

In addition to the expanse of playing fields, St Andrew's benefits from its own indoor swimming pool and sports centre. There are two computer suites equipped with up-to-date software and hardware, a modern purpose-built music block, a theatre, a chapel and a creative arts centre with an art studio and design and technology facilities. The school strongly encourages music and drama and more than three-quarters of the children play instruments and participate in orchestras, bands and choirs. As well as Music, Drama is a timetabled subject and plays take place every term.

From the age of nine, children are taught by subject specialists. French is taught from the age of five, and other modern languages may be offered from the age of eleven. Children are introduced to working on computers at the age of three and from the age of seven they become adept in word processing, DTP, Databases, spreadsheets and web site creation, in addition to exploring educational areas of the Internet. They make use of digital cameras and scanning technology in a variety of different subjects too. The breadth of the curriculum means that, while the requirements of the National Curriculum are fulfilled, the children are able to experience a variety of other stimulating activities.

Scholarship sets exist in Year 5 onwards to provide more challenging opportunities for those who are academically gifted. Awards have been achieved to many major senior schools and over the past five years more than 100 scholarships have been won by St Andrew's' pupils. Where necessary, extra Special Needs teaching is provided as well as ESL support for those who require it.

Prep takes place in the senior part of the school, after which there is a wide range of activities on offer, and most of these are inclusive of fees. Children enjoy taking part in climbing, canoeing, cookery, photography, craft, drama, model-making, radio ham, golf, juggling, needlework and many other pursuits. Weekend outdoor education programmes are organised for all children in the senior school and during the week St Andrew's runs its own Guides, Scouts, Brownies, Cubs, Beavers and Rainbows.

The school's strong sporting reputation manifests itself in national honours regularly achieved in many different sports. Specialist coaches are employed to teach the skills required for all to enjoy participating in team games and opportunities are available to anyone wishing to represent the school. There are full-time tennis and swimming coaches on the staff.

Charitable status. St Andrew's School Trust (Eastbourne) Limited is a Registered Charity, number 307073. The aims of the Charity are Education

St Andrew's School

22 Smith Street Walkerville South Australia 5081
Tel: (08) 8344 3483
Fax: (08) 8344 8670

A co-educational Anglican School, Reception to Year 7. An IB School.

Principal: **Mr David G Woolnough**, BEd (Hons), DipT (Prim), MACE

Chairman: Mr Anthony M Pederick, FCPA, FCIS, FCIM, JP

Numbers in school. 580

Fees. Tuition fees range from $5,260 per annum in Reception to $7,840 in Year 7.

St Andrew's School was established in 1850. The School has a tradition of providing a sound and liberal, Christian education in a caring family environment. Children are encouraged to develop a desire to serve God and man, respect truth and develop a lasting set of moral values. The School acknowledges the importance of:

Catering for individual differences in children's ability. The role parents play in the education of their children. The significance of co-education in the development of the "whole" child.

The School offers a unique opportunity for children to develop their full potential in the formative years. Innovative and imaginative programmes foster intellectual curiosity, creativity and feelings of self-worth. Above all, our programmes aim to lay the foundations for life-long learning.

An International Baccalaureate World School offering the IB Middle Years and Primary Years programme.

S Anselm's

Bakewell Derbyshire DE45 1DP.
Tel: (01629) 812734
Fax: (01629) 814742
e-mail: headmaster@s.anselms.btinternet.com
website: www.s-anselms.co.uk

Headmaster: **R J Foster**, BEd (Clifton College and Exeter)

Deputy Head: C J Acheson-Gray

Numbers. Prep School (7½–13) 110 boys, 75 girls. Two-thirds of the boys and girls are boarders. Pre-Prep (4½–7½) 60 boys and girls.

Termly fees (inclusive). £3,650 Boarding; £2,780–£3,100 Day; Pre-Prep £1,600; Nursery £16 per morning, £14 per afternoon.

The School is an Educational Trust. The Chairman of Governors is Mr J W Lockwood.

There are 27 full-time and 4 part-time members of the teaching staff (all qualified, with all of them trained as teachers and all are graduates). The staff includes a Director of Music and a Director of Sport and graduates in Design and Technology and Art. In addition there are ten visiting music teachers.

An average class size of 12 has much to do with the School's academic success. In the last five years a third of the top year have won awards to their senior schools, including the Top Scholarships to Wycombe Abbey, Oundle, Rugby, Clifton, Stowe, Repton and Uppingham, and Scholarships and Exhibitions to Oakham, Sedbergh,

King Edward's Birmingham, Moreton Hall, Winchester and Wrekin.

Mr and Mrs Foster live in the School with their family and a sound, happy upbringing and good manners are considered especially important. There are three resident matrons, including a qualified nurse, and a daytime assistant matron. The girl boarders sleep in three houses next door to the School.

The School is keen on games. Cricket, Football, Rugby, Hockey, Swimming, Tennis (5 courts), Athletics and Shooting are the main sports for boys, and Hockey, Tennis, Rounders, Swimming, Netball and Athletics for girls. Other outdoor activities include Riding, Brownies, Fishing, Sailing, Hillwalking etc.

Two-thirds of the School play a musical instrument, and a third of these play two instruments. The older children are taken to concerts and a great many other outings are also arranged. Many act in plays. Hobbies are encouraged and there is much Modelling, Electronics, Pottery, Sewing, Ballet, Gymnastics, Chess, Computing etc.

The School stands in its own grounds of 18 acres, 600 feet above sea level, in a very attractive setting in the Peak National Park overlooking the market town of Bakewell. An extensive Millennium Development Project has just been completed providing very exciting new facilities including a four Badminton Court Sports Hall, a Theatre/Concert Hall, a new Design and Technology Workshop, a Resource Centre incorporating a superb new IT Room and a Conservatory alongside the Library. Three additional classrooms have also been created as well as two Learning Support Rooms. These are all in addition to excellent facilities for Art, Music, Science and all outdoor team sports.

Charitable status. S Anselm's is a Registered Charity, number 527179. Its purpose is to carry on the education of children of either sex or both sexes.

St Anthony's Preparatory School

90 Fitzjohns Avenue Hampstead London NW3 6AA
Tel: 020 7435 3597 (Junior House) and 020 7435 0316 (Senior House and Admissions)
Fax: 020 7435 9223

Headmaster: **Philip Anderson**, BA

Number of Boys. 290 (Day Boys)
Fees. (from September 2000): £2,215–£2,275 including lunches and all extras

The Staff consists of 25 qualified full-time teachers. In addition to this there are 7 qualified part-time teachers.

Boys are prepared for the Common Entrance and Scholarship Examinations to Independent Senior Schools, largely the London day schools.

St Antony's Preparatory School

Sherborne Dorset DT9 6EN
Tel: (01963) 210790
Fax: (01963) 210648
e-mail: headteacher@stantonysprep.co.uk
website: stantonysprep.co.uk

Independent Catholic Preparatory School for Boys and Girls aged 2½–11 with boarding and flexi-boarding provision for girls from 7. Separate Nursery and Pre-Prep Department.

Chairman of Board of Governors: Mr Paul Burns

Head Teacher: **Mrs Lynn-Marie Walker,** CertEd, RTC, DipAdv, MEd, DipRSA (SpLD)

Number of Pupils. 120. 80 Girls (7 Boarders), 40 Boys

Termly Fees. Nursery (From 2½) £116 for each half-day and pro-rata up to £550 for 5 half-days per term. Extended Nursery session, to include lunch, £142. Pre-Prep (Age 4) £1,290 per term. Lower Prep (Age 5–7) £1,475 per term. Upper Prep (Age 7–11) £1,975 per term. Boarders (7–11) full board and tuition £3,100.

St Antony's Preparatory School is an established Christian Preparatory School combining traditional excellence in teaching with modern facilities and resources. Situated in 40 acres of Dorset parkland three miles south of Sherborne, the School caters for boys and girls from 3 to 11 and offers boarding and flexi-boarding provision for girls from 7 to 11. Rising 3s and 4 year olds are cared for in a separate Nursery and Pre-Prep Department offering the flexibility of mornings, afternoons or all day with a rest period after lunch. The Nursery also offers a longer morning session to include lunch with collection at 1.15 pm. Further up the School children can stay for the 'extended day' with the option of numerous after School clubs and activities followed by Prep, and tea by flexible arrangement.

Although a Catholic School, girls and boys from all denominations are warmly welcomed. The foundation of the School is based on caring Christian values in a fresh modern setting. There is weekly mass in School and there is a resident Chaplain. Children are taught good manners, self discipline and respect for others, helping to develop a sense of social responsibility and community in their daily lives.

The School is situated on the same campus as the senior school and enjoys the benefit of many excellent facilities including a fully equipped Design and Technology Centre, all weather sports pitch, heated swimming pool, sports hall, tennis courts, extensive playing fields and an adventure playground. Classrooms are bright and spacious and well equipped with computers. The expanding Nursery and Pre-Prep Department occupies an enviable setting in a skilfully converted former Coach House providing a unique range of delightful classrooms and ancillary facilities for the very young.

Academic standards are high with a wide variety of teaching methods, mixing the best of old and new used to support an extensive curriculum. Children are also encouraged to develop their own learning skills and are expected to meet the demands of regular homework, tests and School examinations with excellent results. Classes are small with highly qualified, committed and caring staff. Each year group has its own class and as the curriculum broadens in Lower and Upper Preparatory, specialist teachers in Music, French, PE, Art, Science, Latin, ICT and Design and Technology, help prepare children for the Common Entrance examination and a smooth and confident progression on to their senior schools. The School has a particularly good reputation for sport, drama and excellence in music. Many children play a musical instrument and the School has a thriving orchestra and choir. The School minibus provides a daily transport service to and from Yeovil and Sherborne and a coach service (shared with the senior school) runs daily to and from Dorchester. Sherborne is on the main line to Waterloo (2½ hours) and trains are met by School transport.

Charitable status. St Antony's Preparatory School is a Registered Charity, number 295175. It exists to provide education for children.

St Aubyn's School

Milestones House Blundell's Road Tiverton Devon EX16 4NA.
Tel: (01884) 252393.
Fax: (01884) 232333
Station Exeter/Tiverton Parkway.

***Headmaster:* B J McDowell**, CertEd (London)

Numbers. 104 Day Children (Boys and Girls aged 7-11), 5 Boarders; 154 Pre-prep (Boys and Girls aged 3–7), 46 Day Nursery (Boys and Girls, aged 3 months to 2½ years).

Age range. 3 months–11 years.

Fees. Day children £1,765 per term including lunches. Pre-prep from £216–£1,354 including lunches.

Staff. There are 25 members of the teaching staff, with 11 visiting staff and a full time matron. St Aubyn's is a family school and the Headmaster and his wife, the Deputy Head, Head of Pre-Prep and the Day Care Manager take a personal interest in every child and work in partnership with the parents.

The School has been established for over seventy years and is now under the auspices of the Blundell's Charitable Trust (see Blundell's School, Part I of this Book). It enjoys its own separate site within the very extensive Blundell's campus about a mile from the old market town of Tiverton. It is in a rural situation yet within easy reach of the town and conveniently placed less than ten minutes from the M5 motorway and Tiverton Parkway station on the west country mainline.

We have built up a reputation for providing the essentials: sound academic standards, spiritual and moral values expressed in our community, and good performances in sport. The main sports are rugby, football, hockey, netball and cross-country in the winter and cricket, rounders, athletics and tennis in the summer. Certificated swimming courses are held at the Tiverton pool. Music and Drama play an important part in the life of the School. A Director of Music is assisted by 6 visiting instrumental teachers. There is a strong commitment to the teaching of Technology, with Design, Food and Information and Communication Technologies being taught.

Extra-curricular activities include woodwork, ballet, chess, choir, orchestra and judo. St Aubyn's has its own Cubs and Brownies packs.

Priority entrance to Blundell's is given to St Aubyn's pupils but the School's independent position ensures that children are prepared for entrance examinations to the senior independent school of parents' choice. Those who show signs of sufficient ability are taught and encouraged to scholarship level. In recent years an average of 35% of boys and girls have gained awards.

With the recent move to the Blundell's site, First Steps Day Care for children aged 3 months to 7 years is accommodated in 'Mayfield', a purpose-built house within the grounds, decorated, furnished and equipped to a high specification. Day Care is available from 8 am to 6 pm for 50 weeks in the year and is staffed to a high ratio by a qualified and caring team. From the age of 3, children are integrated into the Nursery classes during the school term. The Pre-Prep department for boys and girls to the age of 7, and is a short walk away from the Prep School, enjoys its own hall, playground, grassland and an adventure play area. The Prep School is in a completely restructured house with new facilities for the Technologies and Science. It has its own games facilities with excellent pitches but also has access to other specialist facilities on the Blundell's campus.

Within the Christian ethos of the school we place great emphasis on children being happy, secure and confident, thus offering individuals every opportunity to achieve their potential within a caring, family atmosphere.

St Aubyn's School

Bunces Lane Woodford Green Essex IG8 9DU.
Tel: 020 8504 1577
Fax: 020 8504 2053
e-mail: office@staubyns.com
website: www.staubyns.com
Stations: Woodford or South Woodford (Central Line)

Chairman of the Governors: T Ducat, MA

***Headmaster:* Gordon James**, MA

Deputy Heads:
Malcolm Brown
Opal Brown

Number of Children. 455, all day children 3–13+

Fees. (at 1 September 2000) £680 (Nursery) to £1,903 (Seniors), fully inclusive.

The School was founded in 1884, and is governed by a Charitable Trust.

The School offers a wide-ranging curriculum within a traditional framework, encompassing all National Curriculum requirements. French is taught from 5+ and Latin from 10+. In addition there are many extra-curricular activities.

All staff are fully qualified teachers and there is a full time School Nurse. There are additional qualified Nursery Nurses for children aged 3+ and 4+.

The School is divided into Early Years (3+ & 4+), Juniors (5+ & 6+), Middle Years (7+, 8+ & 9+) and Seniors (10+, 11+ & 12+). Each section of the School has its own staff, whilst retaining full access to appropriate specialist facilities and specialist staff.

The School is pleasantly situated on the borders of Epping Forest in 7½ acres of grounds, yet is close both to the North Circular Road and the M25. Facilities built within the last 10 years include a new Junior School, new Music and Computer complex, new Science Laboratory and Art/Design base. A new Sports Centre was completed in 1997 and a Performing Arts Centre for Drama, Music and Dance opened in September 2000. Games include rugby, soccer, cricket, hockey, tennis, netball and athletics. All are coached to a high standard.

The Director of Music leads a thriving Department with a school orchestra and various instrumental groups and choirs.

Children progress to independent senior schools at various ages, including Common Entrance at 13+. Pupils also move on to 11+ grammar schools, as well as other local schools.

Main entry to the School is at 3+, 4+, 7+ and 11+.

Charitable status. St Aubyn's School is a Registered Charity, number 270143. It exists to provide education for children.

St Aubyns School

Rottingdean Brighton East Sussex BN2 7JN.
Tel: (01273) 302170
Fax: (01273) 304004
website: www.st-aubyns.brighton-hove.sch.uk

Chairman of the Governors: T R Prideaux, Esq

Headmaster: **A G Gobat**, BSc (Hons), PGCE
Assistant Headmaster: S M Greet, BEd (Hons)

A co-educational Preparatory and Pre-Prep School, founded in 1895, for approximately 175 day and boarding children aged 4–13 years. Within the Prep Department about 40% of the pupils board, some for two or three nights per week, others for every night. This flexible arrangement suits many families and is a splendid introduction to boarding.

Fees per term. Boarders £3,500, Day Pupils £2,600, Pre-Prep from £1,050 to £1,350.

St Aubyns is a happy and friendly school and firmly believes in the traditional values which encourage self-discipline, good manners, and consideration for others.

St Aubyns has an excellent academic record, preparing children for a wide range of Senior Schools. Each year an impressive number of scholarships is gained by our Leavers (at 13+). Entry is by assessment and report. Academic, Music and Sports scholarships are available for children aged 7 to 11.

St Aubyns offers a carefully balanced, very broad curriculum which allows each individual child's talents to grow. The school is situated in the delightful seaside town of Rottingdean. The campus of 11 acres offers a wide range of facilities including a large sports hall, squash court, all-weather tennis court, heated outdoor swimming pool, spacious art room and modern, well equipped Science and Design Technology laboratories. In January 2000 a large, state-of-the-art ICT Centre with twenty two linked computers and an 85 seat theatre were opened. In 2001 a large well-equipped library was opened, providing a large quiet space for study and open access for all children to a wide range of fiction and non-fiction. As a Christian community, services are held daily in the beautiful timber lined Chapel.

Cricket, netball, lacrosse, soccer, rugby and rounders are the major games, plus a wide selection of minor games such as judo, fencing, swimming, tennis and riding. The Activities Programme offers children over 20 different clubs including drama, art, magic, model making, board games and cooking.

A great deal of importance is attached to the cultural development of the children. Over 50% play individual musical instruments; there is a fine bugle and drum band as well as strings and brass ensembles. Children are taken regularly to art galleries and the theatre.

St Aubyns is three miles from Brighton and less than an hour by train from London. Gatwick Airport is 40 minutes away and the journey to Heathrow takes about 85 minutes. The school is happy to make the necessary arrangements for children to travel to and fro. For day pupils, there is minibus transport from a wide catchment area.

Charitable status. St Aubyns School Trust Limited is a Registered Charity, number 307368. It exists to provide an all round education for boys and girls aged 4–13.

St Bede's

Bishton Hall Wolseley Bridge Nr Stafford ST17 0XN.
Tel: (01889) 881277 and 881226
Fax: (01889) 882749
e-mail: st.bedes.bishton@which.net
website: http://homepages.which.net/~st.bedes.bishton/bishton1.htu
Station: Stafford

(Under the patronage of His Grace the Archbishop of Birmingham)

Headmasters:
A H Stafford Northcote, JP, KM, MA (Christ Church, Oxford)
H C Stafford Northcote, KM, MA (Trinity College, Cambridge)

Number of Pupils. 128

Fees. £2,616 a term Boarders and Weekly Boarders, £1,176-£1,995 a term Day Pupils. Boys and Girls. Compulsory Extras Nil. Nursery School 3 to 6 yrs.

St Bede's is a Catholic Preparatory School, founded before the War, in which other denominations are welcomed.

Bishton Hall is a charming Georgian house belonging to the family, scheduled as of architectural and historic interest with ideal gardens and grounds and is in the unspoiled part of the Staffordshire countryside on the edge of Cannock Chase. The School has its own Chapel, hard tennis courts, indoor heated swimming pool, Gymnasium-Theatre and Science Laboratory. Pupils are prepared for all Independent Schools and many Scholarships have been won.

There is a teaching Staff of 14 with visiting Teachers for tennis, swimming, art, violin, brass instruments and guitar. Drama and Dancing are taught to a highly proficient standard by a specialist Drama Teacher.

The Craft, Design and Technology Centre incorporates metal work and metal casting, carpentry, pottery, enamelling, jewellery making, cooking, computers, art and stone polishing.

Tennis, Rugger, Soccer, Cricket, Rounders, Volley Ball and Netball are played in season.

Mrs Hugh Stafford Northcote is personally responsible for the health and welfare of the children. Individual care is taken of each child and good manners and consideration for others insisted upon. An acknowledged feature of the School is its family atmosphere.

For further particulars, apply to the Headmasters: A Stafford Northcote, JP, KM, MA (Oxon), H Stafford Northcote, KM, MA (Cantab), St Bede's, Bishton Hall, Wolseley Bridge, near Stafford.

St Bede's Co-educational Preparatory School

Duke's Drive Eastbourne East Sussex BN20 7XL.
Tel: (01323) 734222
Fax: (01323) 720119
e-mail: prepschool@stbedesschool.org
website: http://www.stbedesschool.org

Co-educational day and boarding school with Nursery and Pre-Prep departments.

Chairman of Governors: David Summers

Principal: **Peter Pyemont**, DipEd

Headmaster: Christopher Pyemont, Cantab

Fees. Boarding £3,840 per term. Day £2,680 per term. Pre-Prep £1,635 per term. Nursery £3.40 per hour

St Bede's, founded in 1895, is situated in Eastbourne, on the South Coast with a spectacular view of the sea. It takes 5 minutes to reach the beach from the school and the principal playing fields are in a wide natural hollow nestling in the South Downs.

The 450 pupils are aged from 2 to 13 years of which 280 (190 boys and 90 girls) are in the main prep school. There are 45 boys and 30 girls who live at the school during term-time. They sleep in small, cosy bedrooms in separate houses and are looked after by dedicated and caring staff. Both winter and summer weekends are filled with an exciting variety of activities and special celebrations take place on the childrens' birthdays.

There are 47 academic staff which creates a ratio of 1:9 throughout the school. There are currently eight members of staff, including the Principal, who have themselves been educated at St Bede's. Pupils are prepared for Common Entrance and the more able are tutored to sit scholarships to independent senior schools. 59 awards have been won during the last five years to many schools, including Eton, Harrow, Tonbridge, King's Canterbury, St Bede's The Dicker, Eastbourne College and Roedean.

St Bede's itself, offers academic, sport, music, dance, art and drama scholarships and bursaries for children from the ages of 7 to 10 years. From the age of 11 girls and boys can join the Legat Junior Dance programme which runs at the school. Entry is by audition.

Pupils from the age of 4 are given Information Technology lessons at least once a week in a Computer Centre which is constantly updated to keep at the forefront of educational technology. French and Music, Short Tennis and other Sports are also introduced to children in this age group.

The Art and Design and Technology Departments are both very strong, opening for after school activities to encourage young talent. Music also plays an important role at St Bede's. There is a thriving orchestra and the majority of pupils learn one or more instruments with children as young as six playing in recorder groups. Informal concerts during the school year and the end of year drama productions allow parents to appreciate their children's progress. There are several choirs, including a specialised Chamber Choir.

Drama forms an integral part of the school. The pre-prep produce a Christmas play and Forms 1, 2 and 3 each put on a play once a year. The senior year groups perform a musical at the end of the summer term to which every child from Form 3 upwards is encouraged to contribute.

Sport at St Bede's is taken seriously. Boys play soccer, rugby, hockey, cricket, tennis and athletics and the major sports for girls are netball, hockey, rounders, athletics and tennis. All the pupils use the indoor 20 metre swimming pool. The fixture list is very comprehensive and, whilst the top teams enjoy a high standard of coaching and performance, special emphasis is placed on ensuring that the other teams also have the opportunity to play matches against other schools. The Matt Sports Hall covers two indoor tennis courts and is used to house a huge variety of sports. Wet weather activities include badminton, basketball and table tennis.

There is a Special Needs department staffed by qualified Special Needs staff which can cater for pupils who require additional learning support. The school also has an EFL centre which is also run by highly trained and experienced staff.

On Monday and Thursday afternoons and every evening after school the pupils are encouraged to participate in an extensive range of activities. In all there are over fifty activities on offer each week which range from fencing to cookery and basketball to art-master classes. Day pupils who stay late for activities enjoy supper with the boarders and often sleepover a few nights each week.

Children leaving St Bede's, Eastbourne go on to a wide variety of independent schools with approximately 60% of pupils choosing to further their education at St Bede's, The Dicker, with which the school has strong links.

The school runs a comprehensive coach and minibus service locally and transport to and from Gatwick and Heathrow airports is arranged by the transport department.

Entry to St Bede's is by interview.

Charitable status. St Bede's Co-educational Preparatory School is a Registered Charity, number 278950. It exists to provide education for boys and girls.

St Bernard's Preparatory School

Hawtrey Close Slough Berkshire SL1 1TB
Tel: (01753) 521821

Headmistress: **Mrs Monica F Casey**, BA, CertEd, LLAM

Number of Pupils. 214
Fees. £1,350–£1,445 per term

The aim of the school is to offer a high standard of education through a challenging yet supportive curriculum, within the context of sound Christian principles.

St Catherine's British Embassy School

Sophocles Venizelou 73 GR145-10 Lykovrissi Athens Greece.
Tel: 003 01 2829750/1
Fax: 003 01 2826415
e-mail: stcats@mail.hol.gr
website: http://welcome.to/st.catherines

Headmaster: **R Morton**, MA

Chairman: David Gordon-Macleod (*Head of Economics Section, British Embassy*)

Number of Children. 230 Boys, 230 Girls (Day pupils only). Nursery/Pre-School Department. Age range 3 to 16.

Fees per annum. Nursery: Drs 1,450,000. Main School Drs 2,200,000-2,500,000.

The School was founded in 1956 by the late Sir Charles Peake, British Ambassador at that time. Originally concerned with the education of British and Commonwealth children resident in Greece, it now teaches pupils from 32 nationalities. Priority is given to British and Commonwealth children.

St Catherine's teaches the full programmes of study for the National Curriculum of England and Wales, for Key Stages 1-3. Greek, Latin and French are also taught, plus German and Spanish. The school is registered with the DfEE. Children are prepared for all types of British and Commonwealth senior education; attention is also given to children who wish to sit Common Entrance Examinations. IB Diploma course starting in September 2002.

Under its Articles of Association the School is administered by a Committee of 10 persons selected by British, Canadian and Australian Ambassadors.

The teaching staff of 60, including the Headmaster, are almost all British and hold British degrees or qualifications. The School is situated out of central Athens, near to the elegant northern suburbs of Kifissia and Ekali, in an attractive environment, including sports facilities, courts and a large heated, open-air swimming pool. The grounds and property are entirely owned by the school. The school is usually over-subscribed and early application for places is advised.

Charitable status. St Catherine's British Embassy School is a Registered Charity, number 860288. It aims to provide high quality education to children from the British, Commonwealth and International communities resident in Athens.

St Catherine's Preparatory School

1 Brookside Cambridge CB2 1JE
Tel: (01223) 311666
Fax: (01223) 316713

Headmistress: **Mrs D O'Sullivan,** BCommHDE

Chairman of Governors: Mr D Stirling

Age range. Girls, aged 3–11
Number in school. 125 day pupils.
Staff. 11 full time; 10 part time; 5 part time music staff.
Religious affiliation. Roman Catholic (all denominations accepted).
Entrance requirements. Own entrance examination and interview.

St Catherine's Preparatory School for Girls overlooks the University Botanic Gardens. A very close association exists between St Catherine's and St Mary's Upper School which is situated in close proximity. Both are Roman Catholic Schools, but welcome girls from other denominations.

St Catherine's is accommodated in a delightful period house. A very happy and loving family atmosphere dominates this small school where girls develop a caring consideration for, and acceptance of, others.

High academic standards are expected. Politeness and self-discipline are paramount. Most girls transfer to St Mary's at 11+ having progressed to an excellent standard in all areas of the curriculum.

St Catherine's has a small pre-preparatory department. Girls are accepted by interview at age 3+ to 7 years. Girls are selected by examination and interview at Key Stage Two – aged 7 upwards, and are prepared for Common Entrance at 11+. The school follows a broad educational curriculum including Music, Art, Drama, Design Technology, Information Technology, Games, Gymnastics, Swimming and Dance.

Instrumental music is available and the majority of girls learn an orchestral instrument. There is a school orchestra, concert band and string quartets. Choirs meet regularly and perform a wide variety of vocal music. There are regular drama productions. Education trips are organised each term, including an Easter trip abroad for older girls.

St Catherine's has received an excellent early years OFSTED inspection report. "St Catherine's offers an extensive range of excellent pre-school activities". We have also received an excellent ISI/OFSTED report in Spring 2001 which confirms that St Catherine's "provides its pupils with a well-rounded education and pupils are very well cared for".

Fees. Pre-Preparatory: £1,400 (excluding lunches); Preparatory: £1,590 (excluding lunches).

St Catherine's School (Junior School)

Bramley Guildford Surrey GU5 0DF.
Tel: (01483) 893363 (Senior School); (01483) 899665 (Junior School)

Headmistress: Mrs A M Phillips, MA (Cantab)

Head of Junior School: **Mrs K M Jefferies**, BSc, PGCE

Chairman of the Governing Body: Mr Roger Lilley

Number of Pupils. 196 Day Girls.
Fees at January 2001: Junior Boarder, £3,560 per term; Junior Day Girl, £2,215 per term; Kindergarten, £1,625 per term; Reception £1,340 per term.

Girls are accepted from the age of 4 to 11 when they take the Entrance Examination for entry to the Senior School.

Charitable status. The Corporation of St Catherine's, Bramley is a Registered Charity, number 1070858, which exists to provide education for girls in accordance with the principles of the Church of England.

St Cedd's School Educational Trust Ltd

Maltese Road Chelmsford Essex CM1 2PB
Tel: (01245) 354380
Fax: (01245) 348635
e-mail: rjm@stcedds.org.uk
website: www.stcedds.org.uk

Chairman of Governors: C Y R Tam

Headmaster: **R J Mathrick**, BA, MPhil

Deputy Head: A J Lowe-Wheeler, BA, CertEd

Number of Pupils. 320-330 Co-educational Day
Fees. £1,475-£1,595 per term, including lunch.

St Cedd's School, founded in 1931, exists to provide independent education for boys and girls of 4-11 by encouraging in them the development of sound character on a Christian foundation. The school prides itself on combining a traditional emphasis on literacy and numeracy with a broad and balanced curriculum.

Specialist teaching is introduced gradually from Reception onwards in subjects including ICT, PE, Music, Art & Technology and French. Swimming and Recorders appear on the timetable from Year 2, and Spanish is taught in Year 6. Music and sport generally are both areas of particular strength and diversity. The school has links with Chelmsford Cathedral, where the choir performs at Choral Evensong twice a term, and is a member of the Chelmsford Choral Foundation.

Children are prepared for entry to a range of Independent and Maintained schools, including the Essex selective grammar schools. Locally, St Cedd's enjoys a reputation for success with regard to the number of places gained by its pupils, and the number of scholarships awarded, both academic and musical.

Facilities include an Art and Pottery Centre, a purpose built Music School, and a climbing wall. The most recent development has been the addition of a new computer suite and a new Science laboratory. Older pupils have the opportunity of playing sport at nearby Chelmer Park on its large astroturf.

Charitable status. St Cedd's School Educational Trust Ltd is a Registered Charity, number 310865. It exists to provide education for boys and girls.

St Christopher's School

32 Belsize Lane Hampstead London NW3 5AE.
Tel: 020 7435 1521

(Preparatory school for girls)

Chairman of Governors: J H Weston Smith, MA, FCIS

Headmistress: **Mrs F Cook**, CertEd

Deputy Headmistress: Miss S Byrom

Number of Girls. 234 (Day Pupils only)

Fees. £2,350 per term, inclusive of lunch.

The School employs a fully qualified teaching staff of 15 full-time and 10 visiting teachers, the latter mainly for music, on which strong emphasis is placed. There are three choirs, quartets, ensembles and 2 orchestras; instrumental lessons are arranged within the timetable. Whilst maintaining high standards in numeracy and literacy, the curriculum provides a wide range of subjects including art, science, computer studies, design and technology, French, drama, gymnastics and games.

Extra curricular activities include art, bridge, drama, French, gymnastics, music and rounders clubs. All applicants are assessed for entry. The girls are prepared for entrance examinations to the major London day schools and for 11+ Common Entrance to boarding schools.

Charitable status. St Christopher's School (Hampstead) Limited is a Registered Charity, number 312999. It exists to provide education for girls.

St Columba's College Preparatory School

King Harry Lane St Albans Hertfordshire AL3 4AW
Tel: 01727 862616
Fax: 01727 892025
e-mail: stcolumbaprep@enterprise.net

Head: **Mr Edwin Brown,** BEd (Hons) Lancaster, MA (London)

Senior Master: Mr James Lewis, BEd (Hons) (Greenwich)
Director of Studies: Mrs Mary Shannon-Little, BEd (Hons) (St Mary's, Strawberry Hill)
Head of Pre-Prep: Mrs Sue M Edmonds, MA (Oxon)

Number of Pupils. 238

Tuition Fees (Prep and Pre-Prep). £4,320 per annum (including personal accident insurance. Additional charges are made for coaches and consumables).

The Prep School is an academically selected Catholic Day School which thrives to create a welcoming community in which each boy is valued as an individual and endeavours to promote positive relationships based on mutual respect and understanding. There is a rigorous academic curriculum with an extensive range of extra curricular opportunities. A full curriculum and sports programme is offered at Key Stage 1 and 2.

Admissions at age 4 and 7 years. Entry requirements of the school is by assessment in English Language, Mathematics, Reasoning and Social Development. Subjects include: English, Mathematics, Drama, RE, French, History, Geography, IT, PE, Games, Music, Art and Design Technology.

Examinations: Pupils progress at 11+ to St Columba's College on the same site, or to other senior schools.

Academic facilities include: modern form rooms with specialist facilities for IT, ADT, Music, PE, Games, RE and French, and a professionally staffed extensive library.

Sports facilities include: Rugby/Football pitches, Cricket nets and square. There is access to a swimming pool and athletics track.

There are no scholarships at Prep level but there are a number of scholarships and bursaries available to Prep School boys on entry to St Columba's College. These include academic and music scholarships.

Charitable status. St Columba's College Preparatory School is a Registered Charity, number 231733. It exists to provide a well-rounded Roman Catholic education for pupils from 4-18 years of age.

St Crispin's School

St Mary's Road Leicester LE2 1XA.
Tel: (0116) 270 7648

Headmaster: **Brian Harrild**, ACP, CertEd

Number of Boys. 135

Number of Girls. 35

Fees. Day £490–£1,385 per term

St Crispin's founded in 1945, specialises in giving individual attention in forms of not more than 18 under qualified staff. Most take the Common Entrance examination at 13½ but preparation is also given for transfer to Local Authority and independent schools at other ages. Those who are well above average in ability may sit for Scholarship examinations. The school also has a dyslexia unit and remedial provision.

The curriculum includes English, Mathematics, French, Religious Studies, Latin, Science, History, Geography, Singing, Music, Art, Drama, Design, Computer, Library, Swimming, Cricket, Football, Hockey, Tennis, Athletics, Gymnastics, Chess, Table Tennis, Badminton, Cycling Proficiency, Volleyball, Netball, Rounders.

There are no extras and included in the fees are morning breaks, lunch, tea, text books, stationery, games, swimming, excursions, entertainment, clubs and camping. There is also an optional school journey to the Continent during the summer holidays, a skiing trip in the Easter holidays and the provision of private lessons in music, speech or ballet for those requiring them. For the school journeys and private lessons a separate fee is charged.

St Crispin's, which has ISJC Accreditation, admits pupils from the age of 2½ years and has a senior department for those wishing to stay on for GCSE.

St David's Junior School

Church Road Ashford Middlesex TW15 3DZ
Tel: (01784) 240434

Headmistress: **Mrs P G Green** , CertEd, AdvDip (London)

Number of children. 144

Staff. 10 full time qualified staff plus 4 part-time specialists and 2 infant helpers, giving a generous pupil/teacher ratio.

Fees. £1,410–£1,790

Average class size. 16

St David's Junior School is a day school for girls aged 3–11. Emphasis is placed on Reading, English, Science and Mathematics but the children follow a varied curriculum in a stimulating and caring environment in preparation for entry to independent senior schools.

There are excellent PE facilities on the 30 acre site, offering netball, rounders, tennis, hockey, dance, athletics and gymnastics. Swimming lessons take place at a local pool.

The school provides its children with every opportunity for academic achievement and for the development of personal and social skills.

Charitable status. St David's School is a Registered Charity, number 312091. It exists to provide education for girls.

St Dunstan's College Junior School

Stanstead Road London SE6 4TY
Tel: 020 8516 7227
Fax: 020 8516 7300. Bursary: 020 8516 7260
e-mail: junior@stdunstans.org.uk
website: www.stdunstans.org.uk

Chairman of Governors: Professor Alastair Bellingham, CBE, FRCP, FRCPath

Head of Junior School: **J D Gaskell,** CertEd

Age range. Co-educational 4–11

Numbers. Pre-Preparatory (4–7) 112, Preparatory (7–11) 240.

Fees. Pre-Preparatory £1,770 per term including lunch, Preparatory Department £1,894–£2,320 per term including lunch.

The Junior School is an integral part of St Dunstan's College and prepares boys and girls for the Senior School (age 11–18). It shares with it a common site and many facilities. In particular the Science Laboratories, 2 ICT Suites, Music Centre, Refectory, Great Hall, Sports Hall, indoor Swimming Pool and playing fields increase the opportunities for all pupils in curricular and extra-curricular activities. For other work the Junior School pupils have their own buildings. The Pre-Preparatory Department is located in an outstanding Victorian house which has been beautifully converted for the specific needs of the 4–7 year olds. The Preparatory Department has its own teaching block of 12 classrooms with a library, art and design technology room and network computer system. Both buildings are enhanced by examples of children's work providing a warm and stimulating environment in which to learn.

Special emphasis is placed upon the development of a high level of literacy and numeracy. The curriculum is also designed to promote learning and appreciation of Science, Humanities, Music, Art, Design and Technology, Information Technology, Drama and a foreign language. A structured programme of Games and Physical Education provide children with the chance to participate in Rugby, Soccer, Cricket, Netball, Rounders, Swimming, Short Tennis, Gymnastics and Athletics. Games and Physical Education play an important part in the growth and development of each pupil. Boys and girls are encouraged to take part in various clubs and activities after school hours and at lunch times. Opportunities exist for French Club, Drama Workshop, Dance, Junior and Senior Choirs, Orchestra, Violin Club, Recorder Ensemble, ICT Club, Chess, Board games and Electronic Workshop.

A caring and friendly environment is provided by small class sizes and a dedicated team of well qualified and experienced class teachers. In addition to being taught many subjects by their class teacher, Preparatory Department pupils have the advantage of being educated by specialists in Science, Design & Technology, Art, Music, French, Physical Education and Games.

A strong partnership exists between the home and school and parents are encouraged to participate in their children's education and the life of the College. Regular contact, formal and informal, is maintained between class teachers and the home to ensure that parents are aware of their child's progress. Parents are encouraged to assist in research for project work and to help with educational visits. Informal social occasions are also arranged to allow parents to meet and feel part of the whole school.

Boys and Girls come from both maintained and independent schools and are admitted at all ages from 4+ to 10+ but principally at 4+ (Reception) and at 7+ (Year 3). Entry is by group assessment at 4+ and by written examination and interview at 7+.

Charitable status. St Dunstan's College is a Registered Charity, number 312747. It exists to provide education for boys and girls.

St Edmund's Junior School

Canterbury Kent CT2 8HU.
Tel: (01227) 475600
Fax: (01227) 471083
e-mail: junsch@stedmunds.org.uk

Chairman of Governors: Professor J F J Todd, BSc, PhD, CChem, CEng

Master of the Junior School: **R G Bacon**, BA (Durham)

Numbers of Pupils. 265 (Boarders – School House, 20; Choir House, 30); Day Pupils – Boys, 127; Girls, 88

Fees per term. Boarders £3,645. Day Pupils. £2,505. Pre-Prep £1,817. Reception £1,338. Nursery £1,033.

Pupils may enter at any age from 3 to 12.

Boarding begins at the age of 8.

The Junior School is closely linked with the Senior School (see Part I of this book) but is run as a separate entity, working to the Common Entrance Examination and Independent Schools Scholarship Examination. The Junior School uses some Senior School specialist staff, particularly in the teaching of Science, Music, Art, Technology and shares with the Senior School such amenities as the Chapel, concert theatre, sports hall and swimming pool. There is a full-time school Chaplain. Domestic arrangements, including health and catering, are under centralised administration.

The Canterbury Cathedral Choristers, who are St Edmund's pupils, live in the Choir House which is under the care of a married Housemaster and is situated in the precincts of Canterbury Cathedral. (See under Choir Schools' Association, Part IV of this book).

Scholarships and bursaries. Academic, music, sport, and all-rounder awards are available for applicants aged 11. Cathedral choristerships are available for boys from age 7. Fee concessions also available as detailed under the Senior School in Part I of this book.

Charitable status. The School is a charitable company limited by guarantee in England and Wales, Charity Registration number 1056382. It exists to educate the children in its care.

St Edmund's School

Hindhead Surrey GU26 6BH
Tel: (01428) 604808.
Fax: (01428) 607898
Station: Haslemere

Chairman of Governors: Mrs J Alliss

Headmaster: **A J Walliker**, MA (Cantab), MBA, PGCE

Number of Pupils. Prep School for boys aged 8 to 13. Boarders 26, Day Boys 118. Pre-Prep and Nursery: 73 boys and girls aged 2 to 7.

Fees per term. Boarders £3,270–£4,050 a term. Day Boys £2,210–£2,990 a term. Pre-Prep £1,730. Nursery from £495 (three mornings).

The fees are inclusive of all ordinary extras, laundry, games, swimming, lectures, etc.

The School, founded in 1874, stands in its own grounds of 37 acres. It is situated just south of the famous Hindhead Punchbowl and is close to extensive National Trust land. Small classes and specialist teaching mean that a fine scholarship record can be maintained whilst, at the same time, there is a full-time Special Needs Teacher. There are four separate blocks including a modern Science Laboratory, an Art School and an excellently equipped Computer Room and Technology Workshop. The School also has its own Chapel and Gymnasium/Theatre.

There are three hard tennis courts, an indoor heated swimming pool and a superb nine-hole golf course. Rugby, soccer, hockey and cricket are the main games played and there is coaching in many other sports including athletics, swimming, tennis and golf. There is also a Sailing Club on Frensham Pond and sculling on the River Wey during the summer. Many extra-curricular activities and hobbies are encouraged and Art, Drama and Music are taught as part of the curriculum.

The Nursery and Pre-Prep Department has full use of the whole range of facilities and grounds at St Edmund's.

Charitable status. St Edmund's School Trust Limited is a Registered Charity, number 278301. Its aim is the education of children.

St Edward's Junior School - Runnymede

North Drive Sandfield Park Liverpool L12 1LF
Tel: 0151-281 2300
Fax: 0151-281 4900

Choir School to Liverpool Metropolitan Cathedral
Motto: *Viriliter Age - Be of good courage*
Day boys 3 to 11: 192; Day Girs 3 to 11: 148

Chairman of Governing Body: Dr Moya F Duffy, MB, ChB, DObstRCOG, FRCGP

***Headteacher:* Mr P Sweeney,** BA

Deputy Head: Mrs J Lee, MEd

Fees per annum. £3,707–£3,908 (including lunch).

St Edwards - Runnymede offers a broad balanced education in a welcoming, caring Christian environment, while preparing pupils for selective academic secondary education. The school, which includes a Nursery Department, occupies a number of spacious buildings including Runnymede a former Victorian mansion.

The School is a member of the Catholic Independent Schools Conference as well as the Association of Junior Independent Schools.

The National Curriculum is followed and pupils are entered for Key Stage 1 and 2 Tests. Emphasis is placed on positive attitudes through the provision of merit-based rewards for excellent work and effort. Above all, children are given every opportunity to discover their own self-worth and happiness through a sense of achievement and fulfilment.

Pupils are encouraged to recognise their own abilities and to appreciate those of others. They are urged to pursue goals which will lead to the achievement of high standards in all aspects of school life. Girls and boys are encouraged to participate fully in a challenging and varied curriculum to ensure that their potential is fully explored.

Facilities include the Nursery, classrooms, 2 assembly halls, library, computer suite, science laboratory, art and design unit, music department and secure play areas. In addition there are sports pitches, running track, floodlit astroturf, sports hall, gymnasium, swimming pool and dining hall. Field trips, residential activities, education and theatre trips are regular activities.

Alongside its excellent academic and sporting facilities, St Edward's - Runnymede is the Choir School to the Metropolitan Cathedral of Christ the King - Liverpool. Music plays a very important part in the life of the school which has its own choir and orchestra. The school is also fortunate in being able to provide after-care facilities every day from the end of school until 6 pm.

Standards of discipline are high and good manners and courtesy are regarded as essential. In a recent Independent Schools Council inspection the Pastoral Care and corporate life were identified as "outstanding strengths of the school".

Prior to entering Runnymede at Nursery level, potential pupils - both boys and girls - are expertly assessed by our Early Years staff, in order to establish whether the individual child is developmentally ready for Nursery education. Parents are invited to attend this assessment and, if successful, the child will enter the Junior School through the Nursery. Here they will spend their first year and attain their fourth birthday.

Pupils are admitted to other age groups within the Junior School as and when vacancies occur. Entry is as a result of a day assessment carried out by the Junior School staff, combined with a report received from the child's current Headteacher. Assessment of pupils' progress is an important feature of the school.

The Headteacher and staff consistently aim to enhance the role played by parents in the life of the school. The support of parents is fundamental to pupils' development and the school values highly the shared responsibility between home and school based on clear understanding between pupils, teachers and parents. Parents are kept regularly informed of their child's progress through reports and parents' meetings.

Further information regarding all aspects of Runnymede can be found in the Prospectus, copies of which are available from the Admissions Officer.

St Edward's School

64 Tilehurst Road Reading Berkshire RG30 2JH.
Tel: (0118) 9574342
Fax: (0118) 9503736
e-mail: admin@stedwards.org.uk
website: www:stedwards.org.uk

***Headmaster:* P D Keddie,** BEd

Chairman of Governors: A J Snow, MA

Number of Boys. 110 day boys

Fees. £1,310–£1,360 per term. Dayboarders who stay until 6 pm £1,530–£1,580. There are no compulsory extras.

The School is an Educational Trust and has a long history of academic success; many Scholarships and Exhibitions have been won to Independent Senior Schools. There is a broad curriculum and all boys, who join the School at 6+, study English, Maths, Science, French, History, Geography, CDT, RS, Computing, Art and Music. Latin is offered as an option and boys have the opportunity to learn German in their final two years. A new Classroom Block, opened in 1997, provides specialist rooms for the teaching of French and Science.

There is a Gymnasium and all boys have one PE session per week. Rugby, Soccer and Cricket are the major sports but boys also have the opportunity to take part in athletics, basketball, tennis, cross-country running and table tennis. All boys in the first two years have swimming lessons as part of their timetable.

Music plays an important part in the life of the school. There is a choir and an orchestra, and the Director of Music is assisted by six visiting instrumental teachers.

The School organises a variety of trips at home and abroad and all boys are encouraged to participate in clubs which operate both during the lunch hour and after school.

St Faith's

Cambridge CB2 2AG.
Tel: (01223) 352073
Fax: (01223) 314757
e-mail: admissions@stfaiths.co.uk

***Headmaster:* R A Dyson**, BA, CertEd (Nottingham)

Deputy Headmaster: D Dawes, BA (OU), Teachers Cert (Keswick Hall)

Chairman of the Governors: J D Callin, FRICS, FRVA

Number of Pupils. 505
Fees per term. £1,900–£2,400

St Faith's, which was founded in 1884, is a co-educational day school for children aged 4–13 years.

The School is situated in extensive grounds on the south side of Cambridge, one mile from the city centre close to the A10 and M11, and the Park and Ride facilities.

Boys and girls join the school at four years of age and remain until they are thirteen. Interviews and assessments for places occur throughout the year. Scholarships are available at 7+ and 11+.

Children are mainly prepared for scholarships and assessments to Independent Senior Schools. Classes are small and the school maintains an excellent reputation for success.

Teaching in the early years is principally form-based, whilst from Year 5 pupils are taught by specialist subject teachers. Class work is supported by educational visits and trips both within the United Kingdom and abroad. Language Studies include French, German and Spanish as well as Latin.

Through the tutorial system, the 45 members of staff provide a firm structure for pastoral care and the development of social skills. There are regular meetings with parents who receive full written reports twice a year.

A recent building programme, completed two years ago, provides the School with excellent modern facilities. ICT is taught to all children and the site is networked. The School has its own drama studio and children who are interested are encouraged to learn stage management and lighting skills as well as acting. There are performances of plays and musicals by different Year groups throughout the year. Almost 300 pupils learn musical instruments and are prepared for Associated Board Examinations. Ensembles, Groups, Choirs and the Orchestra perform regularly with the emphasis on enjoyment as well as good performance.

St Faith's has an excellent sporting tradition and our sports programme involves inter-house competitions and a strong fixture list of matches against other Prep Schools. The School is fortunate in having use of the Sports Hall, Swimming Pool and all-weather pitch at The Leys School which is within walking distance.

A wide range of extra-curricular activities is offered after the school day. During the holidays, skiing trips and residential activity courses are organised for the older children, and Play Clubs and Multi-Activity courses are also well supported. For the convenience of parents, an optional Early Start/Late Stay programme runs, extending the school day from 8 am to 5.30 pm for the Pre-Prep and 6 pm for older children. Parents may also join in family breakfasts each morning.

Strong links between home and school are actively encouraged and the Parents' Committee is a forum for communication and discussion. The School is also supported by the St Faith's Parents' Association which organises social functions run jointly by parents and staff.

Foundation. St Faith's is part of the same Foundation as The Leys School.

Charitable status. St Faith's is a Registered Charity, number 311436. The aim of the charity is the provision of high class education.

St Francis School

Marlborough Road Pewsey Wilts SN9 5NT
Tel: 01672 563228
Fax: 01672 564323
e-mail: admissions@st-francis.wilts.sch.uk

Chairman of Governors: P Warner

***Headmaster:* P W Blundell**, BA, ACP, CertEd

Number of Boys and Girls. 233. Boys 109, Girls 124
Fees. Nursery £120 per session per term; Reception to Year 8 from £1,395 to £2,075 per term, including lunch.

St Francis is a charitable trust with a board of governors that includes both The Master of Marlborough College and the Headmaster of Dauntsey's School. The School is situated in the lovely Vale of Pewsey some five miles south of Marlborough. Its grounds border the Kennet and Avon Canal.

The School is co-educational and currently takes children from the age of 2 to 13. It is a day school with pupils travelling from a wide area of mid-Wiltshire; a daily minibus service operates from Devizes and Marlborough.

Small classes giving every child the opportunity to fulfil his or her full potential are a feature of the school. Staff are fully qualified and ensure that they are very positive and encouraging in their teaching. Should a child be found to be suffering from some form of specific learning difficulty then appropriate help will be given. The facilities are constantly being improved, the new multi-purpose Hemery Hall is now completed as are the science laboratory and technology centre.

The curriculum is delightfully diverse enabling the pupils to have, for instance, CDT, Pottery, Drama, Computing and Swimming all in their normal weekly timetable. French is taught from the age of four. The majority of the pupils take up individual musical tuition and a wide range of instruments is available.

Results are excellent. The pupils are mainly entered for the local senior schools, St Mary's Calne, Downe House, Dauntsey's, Marlborough College, Stonar and Warminster, but scholarships and common entrance are also taken for boarding schools further afield. Awards are regularly achieved to all of the aforementioned.

Please write, telephone or fax for a prospectus, or ask to visit and tour round the school. The Headmaster will be happy to oblige.

Charitable status. St Francis is a Registered Charity, number 298522. It exists solely to provide education for boys and girls.

St George's College Junior School

Thames Street Weybridge Surrey KT13 8NL
Tel: (01932) 839400.
Fax: (01932) 839401
e-mail: sgcjs@st-georges-college.co.uk

Chairman of Board of Governors: Mr Neil Twist

Head Master: **The Revd M D Ashcroft**, CJ, MA, BTheol, CertEd, MCoT

Number of pupils. 660 aged from 2½ to 11

Termly Fees. Nursery: Mornings only £715; Full Days £1,215. Lower Years (YR up to Y2) £1,525; Upper Years (Y3 up to Y6) £2,110. (including compulsory lunches for YR and above).

St George's College Junior School is a Roman Catholic Day School and all pupils attending the Junior School are required to belong to one of the mainstream Christian traditions. The school was established in 1950 by a Religious Order of Priests and Brothers known as The Josephites who maintain a keen interest in the future of the school. From September 2003, only pupils who are three years old before the September in the year of entry will be admitted into the Nursery.

While the majority of the pupils at the school come from around North Surrey, some 18% of the pupils are from countries as far away as Australia, New Zealand, Hong Kong, South Africa, Brazil, Canada, USA as well as from most European countries including Russia. The school operates a very extensive bus service and an option for parents using cars to drop off all their children at either the Junior or Senior School.

In September 2000 the Junior School moved two miles down the road to its present 12½ acre site on the outskirts of Weybridge close to the River Thames. During 2001 a £1 million refurbishment programme has been completed involving the upgrading of most of the classrooms, the science teaching room, the library, and the creation of school wide computer network including a state-of-the-art 25 station computer resources room with an interactive white board networked with the senior school.

The Junior School has a genuinely happy atmosphere in which every pupil is respected and treated as an individual. The Headmaster considers the staff, pupils and parents to be constituent parts of an extended family. The school has always placed great emphasis on the importance of maintaining excellent channels of communication between members of staff, parents and pupils.

The size of classes ensures that the school is a learning community by creating the correct balance between pupil interaction and pupil-teacher contact. The pupils in the top two years of the school are taught by subject specialists. In 2000 Year Six pupils achieved a success rate of over 70% at Level 5 in English, Mathematics and Science including a number at Level 6 in all three subjects. French is offered to all pupils from the Reception Classes and there is an annual residential trip to France for pupils in Year 5. The School was given an outstanding report following its Early Years inspection in September 1999.

Pupils leave at the end of Year Six and nearly all transfer to St George's College. 88 scholarships including music scholarships have been won by pupils in Year Six since 1989.

While the pursuit of academic excellence is highly valued, the Mission Statement of the school stresses the importance of pupils having high personal self-esteem as well as their religious, spiritual, social and physical development. The school requires its pupils to have high moral values especially those of its school motto "Honesty and Compassion".

Extra-curricular and other enrichment activities are likewise considered to play an important role in the educational development of children. The extensive range of activities include dance (ballet, modern and tap), gymnastics, cooking and clubs based on the academic subjects taught in the school, for example Young Scientist club. In 2001 pupils took part in a national robot design competition. Pupils are taken to places of educational interest each year including theatre, music and art trips and there is an annual book week during which pupils meet and listen to visiting authors and story-tellers.

Considerable emphasis is placed on the Creative and Performing Arts. Pupils have dance lessons throughout the school with specialist ballet and tap dance lessons being a compulsory part of curriculum for all pupils up to the end of Year Reception. The school stages six major drama productions a year. Every Year Two pupil learns to play the violin and all pupils may have tuition in a complete range of musical instruments including the harp. Pupils are actively encouraged to perform at school assemblies and school music concerts. The school has a very fine main choir of over 60 pupils, a training choir and a symphony orchestra comprising 50 pupils. Pupils have achieved considerable success at Public Speaking Competitions and achieve a very high level of attainment in their external Spoken English, LAMDA and instrumental music examinations.

Apart from its own sports facilities on site comprising an artificial sports pitch, brand new netball and tennis courts, a sprung floor hall and a swimming pool, the school has the use of 20 acres of outstanding sports facilities at the Senior School including three floodlit netball/tennis courts, a floodlit artificial surface for hockey, a four court indoor tennis centre, a sports hall and gym, three cricket squares, an athletics track (about to be completely refurbished) and six large grass fields.

The Under 9 boys mini-rugby team reached the National Prep School finals in 1996, 1999 and 2001. The school has played in the Under 11 Boys National Mini-Hockey Finals nine times since 1989, becoming National Champions of England in 1991, 1993, 1995 and 1996 and runners-up in 1989, 1994 and 1998. The girls won the Under 11 National Mini-Hockey Finals in 2001 and reached the Under 11 IAPS Netball Finals in 2000. The school reached seven county cricket cup finals during the 1990s. Tennis and Fencing are very popular Saturday morning activities. The school organises a major netball tournament for girls and a tennis festival for boys each year. All the boys and girls in Year Three and above have the opportunity to take part in athletics, chess, climbing, cross-country running, dance, football, gymnastics, orienteering, skiing and swimming during their time at the Junior School. There is an annual residential outward bound adventure holiday for the pupils in the top year as well as an annual ski holiday over the New Year for the whole family.

School lunches are compulsory from Year Reception and are prepared on site and eaten in the newly refurbished dining room which can seat 320 people. There is fully qualified nursing cover throughout the school day in the Junior School and all staff taking games have an annual refresher course in First Aid. The school offers a free supervised after-school care facility until 5.30 each weekday evening during term time.

For the last few years the school has had more applications for places in all its Year Groups than it can accommodate. When vacancies do occur, pupils are admitted if they meet the school's entry criteria and successfully complete an assessment day at the school and on receipt of a satisfactory report from the current school where this is appropriate. Priority is afforded to Roman Catholics and siblings.

Charitable status. St George's College, Weybridge is a Registered Charity, number 1017853. The aims and objectives of the charity are the Christian education of young people.

St George's School

Windsor Castle Windsor Berks SL4 1QF.
Tel: (01753) 865553
Fax: (01753) 842093
e-mail: enqs@stgwindsor.co.uk

Patron: Her Majesty The Queen

Visitor: The Lord Chancellor

Chairman of the Governors: The Dean of Windsor

***Headmaster:* J R Jones,** BEd (Westminster College, Oxford)

Number of Boys and Girls. 301 (28 boarders).

Fees. Boarders £3,820 per term. Day Pupils: £2,565–£2,835 per term. Choristers (Boarding) £1,910 per term. Pre-Prep pupils: £1,550–£1,765 per term. Nursery: £650–£800 per term.

St George's School was established as part of the foundation of the Order of the Garter in 1348 when provision was made for the education of the first choristers. In 1893 the School moved into the Georgian building of the former College of the Naval Knights of Windsor situated between the mound of the Castle and the Home Park. Expansion followed with the admission of supernumerary (non-chorister) pupils. Extensions were made to the buildings in 1988 and 1996, the latter of which allowed for the opening of a Pre-Preparatory Department and Nursery. Girls were admitted to the School for the first time, entering both the Pre-Prep and the main School. The roll will continue to grow until it reaches about 350 pupils in all.

St George's School boasts a long tradition of musical and academic excellence alongside lively art and drama. It is well equipped for games having beautiful playing fields in the Home Park, an indoor swimming pool, a tennis and netball court and gymnasium. The whole School building has undergone a recent refurbishment which has included the creation of a Design and Technology Workshop and the updating of an Information Technology Room fully on line.

The School pursues the highest standards whilst retaining a relaxed and friendly atmosphere. There is a strong sense of pastoral care and a high pupil staff ratio. Communications are excellent: two stations, the M25, M3, M4 and M40 are all close by and Heathrow is just twenty minutes away.

Charitable status. St George's School, Windsor Castle is a constituent part of the College of St George, Windsor Castle and as such is exempted from the necessity to register with the Charity Commissions. Its purpose is the education, either as boarding or day pupils, of children of pre-preparatory and preparatory school age and, that of the choristers who maintain the worship in the Queen's Free Chapel of Our Lady, St George and St Edward the Confessor in Windsor Castle.

St George's School

Southwold Suffolk IP18 6SD.
Tel: (01502) 723314
Fax: (01502) 725035
e-mail: Stgs1@aol.com

Chairman of Governors: Mr Clive Mann

***Headmistress:* Mrs Wendy H Holland**, ARCM, LRAM, GRSM, CertEd, FCollP

Staff:
Miss S Greenfield, BEd (*Deputy Head*)
Mrs J Anderson, CertEd
Mrs R Attenburrow, BTec
Mrs K Barbrook, BA
Mrs C Cliff, CertEd
Mrs R Crane, BA
Miss T Doy, NNEB
Mrs B Girling, BSc
Mrs P Goldsmith, NNEB
Mr I Hands, BEd
Miss L Hepenstal, BA
Miss S Hunting
Mr D Jackson, BEd
Mr S Marsden, BEd
Miss A Martin, BA
Miss H Martin, BTec
Mr A Newson, BA
Mrs G Pickford, CertEd
Mrs E Provan, BA
Mr M Smallman, BSc
Mrs S E Smith, MA
Mrs G Sprake, BEd
Mrs E Scoggins, NNEB
Mrs S Yates, BA, PGCE

Fees. Day Pupils: £960–£1,900 per term; Nursery: £18 per day including lunch.

St George's caters for 220 boys and girls aged 2½–11 years. Pastoral care is in the hands of the Headmistress, Deputy Head and Senior Master.

The School aims to provide a varied and well balanced curriculum and is following the guidelines for the National Curriculum, Key Stage 1 and Key Stage 2. Subjects taught are Mathematics, Computer Studies, English, Religious Education, Science, French, German, Latin, Spanish, History, Geography, Art, Craft Design & Technology, Music, PE and Drama. Emphasis is placed on cross-curricular learning and the flexible daily timetable allows for this.

Pupils are prepared for Entrance Examinations to senior schools at 11+ and the School boasts an excellent success record.

Ballet, Speech and Drama, Horse riding, Fencing, Judo and individual instrumental Music lessons are offered as extra-curricular activities. There is a flourishing School Orchestra, Choir and Recorder Group and Dramatic productions are regularly performed.

Athletics, Rounders, Tennis and Cricket are played in the Summer and Netball, Hockey, Football and Rugby are the Winter sports, with matches being enthusiastically played against other schools, throughout the year, as the new Sports Hall allows for inclement weather conditions. Swimming lessons are taken in the new indoor heated swimming pool all year round.

The children benefit from a warm and caring atmosphere in delightful surroundings and are thoroughly prepared for their senior schools.

Charitable status. St George's School is a Registered Charity, number 310482. It exists to provide education for boys and girls.

St Helen's College

Parkway Hillingdon Middlesex UB10 9JX
Tel: 01895 234371
Fax: 01895 234371

***Headmaster:* Mr D A Crehan,** MSc, ARCS, CPhys
***Headmistress:* Mrs G R Crehan,** BA, PGCE

Number of pupils. 275 co-educational day pupils
Age range. 3-11
Fees. £860-£1,464

The aims of St Helen's are to develop as fully as possible each child's academic potential, to provide a wide, balanced, stimulating and challenging curriculum, and to foster true values and good character based on moral and spiritual principles. The children enjoy a purposeful and happy 'family' atmosphere and are taught by committed professional teachers.

Children are prepared for independent senior schools and local grammar schools, and records of success are very good indeed. In addition to the academic subjects, sport, music and drama play an important part in the lives of the children.

A wide range of extra-curricular activities is offered, and pupils enjoy outings, day and residential, to many places of interest. There is an after-school club and summer school, and a holiday club which runs throughout the year.

St Hilary's School

Godalming Surrey GU7 1RZ.
Tel: (01483) 416551
Fax: (01483) 418325
e-mail: www.sthilarys-school.demon.co.uk
Station: Godalming

Headmistress: **Mrs S Bailes**, BA (Hons), MA, PGCE
Chairman of Governors: Mr Michael Goodridge, LLB

Number of Pupils. 400 (no boarders). Girls 2–11+, Boys 2–8+ (110)

Fees. Nursery £17.00 per unit (1 unit being single morning or single afternoon), lunch extra. Reception £1,430, Year 1 £1,600, Years 2 & 3 £1,945, Years 4-6 £2,200 (including lunch).

St Hilary's is a non-selective, independent day school for 380 children between the ages of 2+ and 11+. Girls may remain at the school until the age of 11+ and boys up to 8+. The school is conveniently situated close to the town centre of Godalming, on Holloway Hill. The beautiful grounds, which cover five acres, provide a safe environment with all-weather tennis and netball courts, a large playing field, adventure playground, woodland, lawns and flowerbeds.

In 1927 Miss Marjorie Hiorns founded St Hilary's as an Independent Preparatory School and since that time generations of pupils have happily attended the school. In 1966 its status was changed to that of a Charitable Trust with a Board of Governors. The Headmistress is a member of the Incorporated Association of Preparatory Schools, playing an active role within this organisation and the school has always been subject to regular inspections which guarantee the highest standards for parents. St Hilary's was the first preparatory school in England to be accredited by Investors in People and was successfully re-accredited in Spring 1999. This means that staff development and training is considered to be essential, along with clear strategic planning involving all members of the school community.

At St Hilary's we aim to give each child a firm foundation of knowledge and understanding in all subjects whilst providing opportunities for creativity, self-expression and social development. All children are encouraged to enjoy success and gain confidence whilst fulfilling their academic potential.

The School bases its values on firm Christian principles, through which the children may learn the importance of care and consideration for others. Each day begins with an act of worship which is non-denominational but essentially Christian and the school regularly raises funds for charities including Save The Children and Chase. A School Council in the Upper School (Years 3-6) involves children in democratic elections for representatives and decision-making with regular meetings to discuss ways in which the school can be improved.

The original house forms the centre of the School complemented with modern, well-designed buildings to match the School's development. These consist of light, airy classrooms, a spacious Assembly Hall/Gymnasium with extensive stage where productions regularly take place. The modern, superbly equipped Science Laboratory provides pupils with ideal working conditions for practical experiments and preparation for secondary school whilst the networked Information Communication Technology room allows pupils Internet access and the opportunity to take advantage of all that technology has to offer. As well, the Design & Technology room, a purpose-built Music Wing, an Art Studio, a Performing Arts room and a very welcoming, well-stocked library support the learning which takes place every day. The youngest pupils enter the excellent self-contained Nursery Department.

Charitable status. St Hilary's is a Registered Charity, number 3122056. It exists to provide education for children.

St Hilda's School

High Street Bushey Hertfordshire WD2 3DA.
Tel: 020 8950 1751
Fax: 020 8420 4523

Headmistress: **Mrs L E Cavanagh**, MA, DipCE
Chairman of Governors: Mr R J L Breese, MA (Oxon)

Age Range. 3–11+

Number in School. Day: Girls 170. Boys in Kindergarten.

Fees per term. £1,400–£1,875. Compulsory extras: Lunches £150

St Hilda's School, is an Independent Day School for Girls. It was founded in 1918 and has occupied its present 5 acre site since 1928. The Victorian house at the centre of the site has been continually improved, adapted and extended to provide an excellent educational environment. This includes tennis courts, a covered heated swimming pool, a large all purpose hall, science laboratory, technology laboratory and computer room.

We teach a wide range of subjects to a high academic standard. This includes French from the age of 3 years. Girls are prepared for entrance tests to senior schools at the age of 11 and we are involved in the National Curriculum tests at Key Stage 1 and 2. All girls from Kindergarten upwards are taught by qualified instructors in our heated, covered swimming pool. Many subjects are taught by specialists, and our aim is to provide each pupil with the opportunity to develop her self-esteem and reach her full potential in an exciting, stimulating and happy environment.

We provide an after school care service until 6 pm Monday to Friday in termtime. Many extra-curricular activities are available including Judo, Ballet and Tap, also Drama, Athletics, Swimming, Art and Computer Clubs.

Charitable status. St Hilda's School is a Registered Charity, number 311072. It exists to provide education for girls.

St Hugh's

Woodhall Spa LN10 6TQ.
Tel: (01526) 352169

Chairman of Governors: C R Wheeldon, Esq

***Headmaster:* S G C Greenish**, BEd

Number of Pupils. 160+. Boarding Boys 30; Day Boys 30. Boarding Girls 25; Day Girls 25. Pre-Prep 20 boys, 14 girls. Nursery 25 children.

Fees. £3,066; Day £2,119; Pre-Prep £1,226

St Hugh's School was founded by the Forbes family in 1925, and it was due to their energy and vision that the school expanded, becoming arguably the best known preparatory school in Lincolnshire. The School became a Charitable Trust in 1964 and has continued to prosper over the years administered by a forward-thinking Governing Body.

Today the School is fully co-educational, offering both day and boarding places for children from the ages of 2½ to 13. There are currently about 160 children in the school of whom 55 are boarders. The Headmaster is assisted by 14 qualified and experienced teachers, a School Administrator, Catering Manager and 3 Matrons. Through its Headmaster the School is a member of the Incorporated Association of Preparatory Schools as well as the Boarding Schools' Association.

Boys and girls are prepared for the Common Entrance and Scholarship examinations. The School's academic record is good, with regular awards being gained to major Independent Schools, as well as places in Lincolnshire Grammar Schools. Children with special learning needs are treated sympathetically within the mainstream, with support from specialist staff. The aim of the School is to give every child a good all-round education and to discover and develop his or her own particular talents.

The major school games for boys are rugby, hockey and cricket, and for girls netball, hockey and rounders. Both boys and girls can also enjoy cross-country, tennis, athletics and swimming. There is an annual Sports Day. All children have PE each week with time set aside for instruction in gymnastics and swimming. Skills in such games as basketball and badminton also form the basis of these lessons.

The school lays heavy emphasis on extra-curricular activities, sport of various kinds, music, the visual arts and drama. All teachers are expected to help in some way with this. There is also a strong and continuing Christian tradition at St Hugh's, where children are encouraged to consider what they believe and develop a faith of their own within the context of regular acts of Christian Worship.

The school has excellent facilities including a modern sports hall, an assembly hall with stage and lighting, a heated indoor swimming pool, extensive playing fields, a fine library, dedicated classrooms and a large Music, Design and ICT studios. The facilities are continually being updated and added to.

Boarders are accommodated in two well-appointed Houses under the close supervision of the resident matrons and the Headmaster and his wife. Dormitories and common rooms are bright and cheerful and recognition is given to the importance of children having a place where they can feel at home and relaxed at the end of the day. Contact with parents and guardians is well maintained. Every half term is punctuated by an exeat weekend and arrangements are made for boarders whose parents live abroad. Minibus transport for day pupils is provided from Boston, Louth and Skegness.

The Pre-Preparatory department caters for approximately 35 children, aged from 4 to 7, and is located in its own building with separate play area and staff.

In 1999 the school opened a nursery for children between 2½ and 4. This is attached to the Pre-Prep.

The school is situated on the fringe of Woodhall Spa, a large and attractive late Victorian village with its own park, woodlands, sports clubs, cinema, hotels and shops. Lincoln, Louth and Boston are about 20 miles away.

Half fee bursaries are available for the sons and daughters of clergymen. There are also reductions for brothers and sisters as well as bursaries for the children of service personnel. The fees are fully inclusive, the only extras being £10 a term to cover laundry.

Charitable status. St Hugh's School is a Registered Charity, number 527611. It exists to provide a high standard of education and care to pupils from the age of 2½ to 13.

St Hugh's

Carswell Manor Faringdon Oxon SN7 8PT
Tel: (01367) 870223
Fax: (01367) 870376
e-mail: headmaster@st-hughs.co.uk

***Headmaster:* D Cannon**, MA (Wadham College, Oxford)

Chairman of Governors: A B Adams, FCA

Number of Pupils. 35 Boarders, 165 Day Pupils (many partly board); Pre-prep 76. (Boy-Girl ratio approximately 3:2, both boarding and day).

Fees. Upper School: Boarders £3,340 per term; Day £2,740 per term; Middle School: Boarders £3,135, Day £2,535 per term; Pre-prep £1,545–£1,745 per term. (All fees inclusive, with no compulsory extras.)

The School's main building is a fine Jacobean house with extensive grounds. Boys and girls are prepared for Common Entrance and Scholarship examinations to senior independent schools. The school is organised into three departments: Pre-Prep (4-6), Middle School (7-8) and Upper School (9-13). Careful liaison ensures a strong thread of continuity throughout the school. The main entry points are at 4, 5 and 7.

While careful attention is paid to academic requirements, every encouragement is also given for children to develop a wide range of artistic, musical, sporting and other interests.

In the last 25 years St Hugh's has more than trebled in size and an ambitious development programme has resulted in outstanding facilities. Despite this growth, the virtues of a small school remain.

Charitable status. St Hugh's is a Registered Charity, number A309620. It exists to provide a centre of excellence for the education of children.

St Ives School

Three Gates Lane Haslemere Surrey GU27 2ES
Tel: (01428) 643734

***Headmistress:* Mrs S E Cattaneo**

Chairman of Governors: Dr B Rushton

Number of Children. 140 (Day) Girls aged 3–11 years, boys 3–5.

Fees. Pre-prep (excluding Nursery class) £1,630; Years 3–4 £2,035; Years 5–6 £2,275 including lunches

St Ives is a Preparatory Day School situated within half a mile of the centre of Haslemere and stands in its own spacious grounds of eight acres. It has an attractive garden, woods, two sports pitches and a tennis/netball court.

The School aims to provide a broad and balanced curriculum while retaining academic excellence. A traditional Prep School education is combined with the best of modern teaching methods. Each child is encouraged to work hard in a secure, relaxed and happy environment. Individual needs are catered for and high standards of manners, discipline and appearance are expected. Parents are kept informed regularly about their child's progress in the form of 3 weekly assessments, end of term reports and parents' evenings. Classes are small and assistants are provided to help with the younger children. All teachers are fully qualified and specialist teaching helps each child to fulfil her potential.

In addition to academic training, emphasis is placed on Art, Music, Dance and Drama with regular productions involving as many children as possible. Athletics, Gymnastics and a wide range of sports are also offered, including swimming all the year round. A large variety of extra curricular activities are offered including dry skiing, speech and drama, ballet, modern dance, pottery, dress making and tennis coaching. Annual residential field studies are organised for the upper school and a ski trip is often arranged in the Easter holidays.

The school is well resourced and will continue to improve and update its facilities. A new school hall, with maths and computer rooms above, has recently been opened. Woodlands have been opened up for Environmental Studies, outdoor pursuits and cross country running.

Girls are prepared for the Common Entrance Examination at 11+. The school has a good record for gaining scholarships to a wide range of well known senior independent schools.

The Headmistress is in constant touch with girls' Independent Schools and is happy to discuss future schooling with parents.

The St Ives bus provides a daily service. The route covers the Haslemere, Hindhead, Grayshott, Churt and Frensham areas.

For a copy of the Prospectus please apply to the Headmistress.

Charitable status. St Ives School is a Registered Charity, number 312080. Its aim is the advancement of education for girls.

St John's-on-the-Hill School

Tutshill Chepstow Monmouthshire NP6 7LE.
Tel: (01291) 622045
Fax: (01291) 623932
Station: Bristol Parkway and Newport

***Headmaster:* I K Etchells**, BEd (Exeter)
Chairman of Governors: A T Vaux

Number of Pupils. 295

Fees. Boarders £2,680. Day Fees £1,741–£1,983. Pre-Prep £1,187–£1,240. Nursery (half or full day sessions) £8.20 per session.

St Johns's-on-the-Hill is a coeducational boarding and day preparatory school with a Pre-Preparatory Department. Full, weekly and flexi-boarding is available. St John's is conveniently situated just 2 miles from the Severn Bridge and M4/M5 motorways. The school occupies a listed Georgian house in its own grounds on the borders of Gloucestershire and Monmouthshire close to the Wye Valley and Forest of Dean.

Pupils are prepared for Common Entrance at 13+ and for examinations at 11+ and 13+ to Independent Schools and over 45 scholarships have been won in the last three years. Children are taught by well qualified teachers and there is an excellent learning support department. The School has recently completed a major development programme. These include new Science and Information Technology facilities, indoor swimming pool and purpose-built Pre-Prep. The Pre-Prep Department is staffed by keen, experienced and enthusiastic teachers who deliver a wide-ranging curriculum.

Visiting music staff teach piano, strings, woodwind, brass and percussion and there are regular drama performances. The School Choir performs regularly at local Music Festivals. The main games are rugby, soccer and cricket for boys, and netball, hockey and rounders for the girls. The wide range of extra-curricular activities includes archery, judo, cross-country, shooting, riding and golf and there is a flourishing Ornithologists and Conservationists Society.

The boarding house is within the school grounds and enjoys a warm, family atmosphere. The school adopts a flexible approach to boarding and help towards the needs of the working parent.

School minibuses run daily from the Newport, Usk, Monmouth, Ross and Forest of Dean areas.

The aim of the school is to provide a happy, balanced atmosphere in which all boys and girls can develop both their academic ability and their character to the full.

Charitable status. St John's-on-the-Hill and Brightlands School Trust Limited is a Registered Charity, number 312953. It exists to provide education for children.

St John's Beaumont

Old Windsor Berks SL4 2JN.
Tel: (01784) 432428
Fax: (01784) 494048
Station: Egham

Chairman of Governors: The Revd Kevin Fox, SJ

***Headmaster:* D St J Gogarty**, MA, PGCE

Deputy Heads:
Mrs K Moggridge, CertEd
G F E Delaney, BA (Hons), PGCE

Number of Boys. 335 (60 Full and Weekly Boarders; 275 Day Boys)

Fees. Boarders £3,744–£4,395 per term (inclusive). Day boys £2,758 per term (inclusive). Preparatory day boys from £1,982 per term (inclusive). Blandyke £1,560 per term (inclusive).

St John's is a Jesuit School and accepts boys between the ages of 4+ and 13+.

In addition to the Headmaster and Deputy Heads the staff consists of a Jesuit community and 25 full time lay teachers. There are two Matrons, one a Registered General Nurse, and a Director of Music.

Classes are small, and boys can receive individual attention according to their needs and abilities. In the past seventeen years, 96 scholarships have been won to senior independent schools.

The school was purpose-built in 1888 by J F Bentley and stands in spacious grounds on the edge of Windsor Great Park, with extensive facilities for outdoor sports. It has a large gymnasium and considerable sports fields. In the 1988/89 academic year the school built 4 all weather tennis courts, refurbished most classrooms, most of which include, as standard, computers, OHPs, videos and televisions. In 1990 a new Science, Technology and Art and Craft Centre was opened. In 1991 a new junior classroom block and changing room was completed. In 1993, a new heated, indoor, 25 metre swimming pool was built and swimming lessons for all boys are standard. In 1994 a new music room was built and a Special Needs Unit opened. In 1995 the roof and heating was renewed and a new pottery room built. In 1996 a new IT room was completed and in 1997 a new changing room shower area was built. A new Music School opened in July 2000. An ICT Centre will open in 2002.

A great variety of outdoor and indoor activities is available and tuition is offered in most musical instruments. Members of the choir have recently won several awards at music festivals and the Orchestra is well established. There is a host of extra-curricular activities.

The boys have daily opportunity for religious practice, as well as formal instruction and informal guidance.

Although following the Common Entrance syllabus for senior independent schools, St John's also follows the National Curriculum and boys are assessed at Key Stages 1 and 2, audited by the Local Education Authority.

An illustrated prospectus is available from the Headmaster, who is always pleased to meet parents and to show them round the school.

Charitable status. St John's is a Registered Charity, number 230165. It exists to provide education for boys.

St John's College Lower School

Albany Road Southsea Hampshire PO5 2AB

Tel: 023 92820237
Fax: 023 92873603
e-mail: sjc.southsea@lineone.net

Co-educational 2-11 years.

Head Master: **Mr R A Shrubsall,** MA(Ed)

Fees. £1,230 to £1,342 (termly). Overseas Boarding £4,235; UK Boarding £3,724.

St John's College is an independent school founded to provide an academic education in a Christian environment. The College is fully co-educational, day and boarding, with over 600 pupils and students ranging in age from 2 to over 18. We offer a continuous range of education, starting in the Nursery and progressing in the Lower and Upper schools to the Sixth Form. We are a Catholic foundation but welcome pupils of all faiths and also those with no religious beliefs.

The Lower School is a self-contained unit but located on the main College campus. This enables children to benefit from specialist tuition by Upper School staff in a number of subject areas. The Lower School enjoys the use of many excellent facilities: a sports centre, theatre, computer suite, library, science laboratory and music room. The attractive site is complemented by 34 acres of well maintained playing fields, located on the outskirts of the city.

A broadly balanced and extended curriculum is offered, encompassing all aspects of the National Curriculum at Key Stages 1 and 2. Close staff liaison ensures a smooth automatic transition for pupils into the Upper School at age 11.

The Lower School has a fine academic, musical and sporting tradition and there are a wide range of extra-curricular clubs which run during lunchtimes and after school. Educational and character-building residential trips are offered at holiday times.

St John's is a family school committed to developing the whole person, but at the very heart of all that we do is teaching and learning. Our academic record is a very good one and the commitment of our staff to each pupil is outstanding.

A prospectus and further details are available from the Admissions Secretary.

St John's College School

Grange Road Cambridge CB3 9AB.

Tel: *Headmaster* 75, Grange Road (Tel: 01223 353532)
Registrar 63, Grange Road (Tel: 01223 315652)
Bursar 75, Grange Road (Tel: 01223 353556)
Fax: (01223) 355846
e-mail: shoffice@sjcs.co.uk
website: www.sjcs.co.uk

Chairman of Governors: The Revd A A Macintosh, MA, BD, Dean of St John's College, Cambridge

***Headmaster:* K L Jones**, MA (Gonville and Caius College, Cambridge)

Number of Children. 450 girls and boys (including 20 Chorister and 30 Non-Chorister boy and girl boarders).

Termly Fees. Choristers: £1,298; Boarders: £3,893; Day Boys and Girls (4–13): £1,486–£2,465 according to age.

Profile. St John's prides itself on the quality of the academic and pastoral care it provides for each child. Through relaxed and friendly relations with children in a well-structured environment rich with opportunity; through close monitoring of progress; through communication and co-operation with parents; through expert staffing and, above all, through a sense of community that cares for the strengths and weaknesses of each of its members, St John's has consistently achieved outstanding results exemplified by over 60 scholarships during the last three years. Whilst its Choristers maintain the tradition of choral services and tour the world, St John's status as an Expert Centre for ICT, and other innovations, ensure the school's commitment to the future.

Entry. At 4–7 by parental interview; at 7–12 by parental interview, report from previous school and, as appropriate, assessment.

Curriculum. The curriculum surrounds the core of formal skills teaching with a breadth of enrichment and extension for each child's talents. In addition to the usual subjects including specialist taught DT, ICT, Art, Music, Dance and Drama, and PE for all pupils, the following are also available: French (from 8+), Study Skills (from 10+), Latin (optional from 10+), Greek (optional from 11+). Pupils prepared for CE and Scholarship examinations.

Leavers. Virtually all go to senior independent day or boarding schools. The School works closely with parents to assist them in finding the best school for their child.

Consultation. Tutorial system (1 teacher to 10 pupils) with daily tutorial session timetabled. Half yearly academic assessments, end of year examinations, termly Parents' Evenings and weekly staff 'surgery' times.

Sports. Athletics, Badminton, Basketball, Cricket, Cross Country, Football, Golf, Gymnastics, Hockey, Netball, Real Tennis, Rounders, Rowing, Rugby, Short Tennis, Squash, Swimming, Tennis. All games are timetabled and therefore given significant status. All major sports strong.

Activities. Numerous clubs including Art, Chess, Dance, Drama, Pottery, Design Technology, Craft, Information Technology, Maths games and puzzles and Touch-typing. College Choir of international status, Chamber Groups, Orchestras, School Chapel Choir, Junior Service

Choir, Parents' Choir, Major theatrical productions, eg The Ragged Child, The Tempest, and theatrical opportunities for all children. A range of visits relating to curriculum plus French, Classics, skiing and outward bound trips.

Facilities. School on two sites with facilities used by all pupils. *Byron House (4–8)*> Outstanding facilities including Science, DT Centre, two large suites of networked PCs, computerised Library, Drama Studio, Gym, Hall and specialist Music wing. A purpose-built teaching block and a playground incorporating pupils' designs are the most recent additions.

Senior House (9–13). Sports Hall with indoor Cricket nets and multi-purpose Gym. Athletics track, playing fields, astro-turf hockey pitch and tennis courts, Design Technology Centre, two Information Technology Centres, Drama Studio, computerised Library, Music School, Theatre, School Chapel and use of St John's College Chapel for school carol and special services. Recent developments include the ICT networking of the entire school and the acquisition of adjacent land and buildings to provide lecture theatre, an outstanding art facility, parent meeting rooms and extensive garden and play facilities for children.

Boarding. From 7 (8 preferred). Girl and boy boarders form an integral part of life at St John's and benefit from all the School's facilities whilst living in the homely, caring atmosphere of a Boarding House which has been completely refurbished in recent years. This includes recreation areas, rooms for reading, TV, table tennis, pool and use of all Senior House facilities. Day boarding and 'Waiters' facilities allow the School to be flexible to the needs of parents and children alike.

Charitable status. St John's College School is a Registered Charity, number X0099000001. It exists to provide education for boys and girls.

St John's School

Sidmouth Devonshire EX10 8RG.
Tel: (01395) 513984
Fax: (01395) 514539
e-mail: nrp@stjohndevon.demon.co.uk

Chairman of Governors: Mr J Sharples, FRICS

Headmaster: **N R Pockett**, BA, DLC, CertEd

Number of Pupils. Main School 230, of whom 60 are Boarders. The Nursery (up to 5 years) has 50 children. Girl/boy ratio 50:50.

Fees per term. (As at September 2001): Nursery: £1,130. Main School: Day £1,890; Boarders £3,187-£3,404. There are no compulsory extras.

St John's is one of the few fully co-educational day and boarding schools in the South West and caters for children between the ages of two and thirteen. The School (a Charitable Trust with a Board of Governors) is contained within substantial buildings and grounds above the small seaside town. The School aims to ensure that all pupils have the benefit of a fulfilling and rounded education and gives children every opportunity to develop their individual talents from the earliest age.

The Headmaster believes that children who are able to relate to a happy family community achieve the best results. This contributes to sound attitudes towards academic work and the many out of school activities that are available to every child. The success of this positive attitude towards education is seen by looking at the results the School has enjoyed over the years. St John's School cares about the child as an individual and the strong team of experienced staff are able to devote a great deal of time to each pupil.

The small classes (the staff pupil ratio is at present 1:10) enjoy bright, cheerful, well equipped classrooms with the additional advantage of overlooking stunning sea views. Interest in sport is high and the School, in addition to playing fields, has an extensive sports centre with an indoor tennis court and a 20 metre swimming pool. The School encourages all pupils to take an active role in music. With its own specialist Music School, there is a high number of pupils learning individual instruments. Art facilities include a pottery studio and pupils enjoy a wide range of media in the Art School. The small, but well equipped drama studio also converts to a small cinema and is popular with boarding pupils. All classrooms are 'online' with pupils having their own e-mail addresses and easy access to the computer centre.

As well as regular 11+ passes to the local Grammar School, pupils have won a number of scholarships to independent secondary schools. Academic results are of the highest standard.

Charitable status. St John's School is a Registered Charity, number 274864. It exists to provide education for children.

St John's School

Potter Street Hill Northwood Middlesex HA6 3QY.
Tel: 020 8866 0067
Fax: 020 8868 8770

Chairman of Governors: M Barty-King, Esq

Headmaster: **C R Kelly**, BA, PGCE (Durham University)

Assistant Headmaster: S Robinson, BSc, PGCE (Loughborough)

Number of Boys. 250 all day boys, Pre-Prep: 105 day boys

Fees. £1,934 per term, Pre-Prep £1,600 per term.

Founded in 1920, the School was purchased by the Merchant Taylors' Educational Trust in 1984, since that time an extensive building programme has been undertaken. In 1986 a purpose built self-contained pre-prep school was opened and a gymnasium completed. In 1989 a further building was completed which provides an excellent Science Department and specialist facilities for Geography and Mathematics. A junior classroom block was opened in 1992. The School has recently completed a major new development which comprises a new Assembly Hall, Music School, Design and Technology workshop, an ICT centre and an Art Studio. This new building has enabled us to introduce more subject teaching specialist areas around the School. The School has also extended its considerable grounds with the purchase of an area of grassland and woodland for ecological and environmental study. This addition increases the School's site to over 35 acres of playing fields, formal gardens and natural habitat.

Most of the boys enter the pre-prep school at the age of four, although there is a separate entry to the main school at seven. Boys are prepared for all independent schools, but the links with Merchant Taylors' School, Northwood, are particularly strong. St John's has a fine record of success in scholarship and Common Entrance examinations. The main games are rugby, cricket and athletics, in addition, a wide variety of other sports and extra curricular activities are offered.

The school is a Church of England foundation, but boys of all religions and denominations are welcome.

Saint Katharines School

The Pends St Andrews Fife KY16 9RB
Tel: (01334) 460470
Fax: (01334) 479196

Chairman of Council: Sir Fraser Morrison

Headmistress: **Mrs Joan Gibson**, LTCL, LTCL, CertEd, AdDipEd (Bristol)

Number of Pupils. 8 Boarders, 66 day pupils.
Age Range. Boys and Girls 3–12½
Fees. Day starting at £420, Boarding £3,476. There are no compulsory extras.

St Katharines is the co-ed Prep School to St Leonards. The school forms part of the extensive and magnificent grounds of St Leonards and is situated close to the small fishing harbour and the East Sands Beach on the edge of the historic University town of St Andrews.

The classrooms, library and hall are well equipped and the boarding accommodation cosy and homely. Excellent use is made of the shared facilities with St Leonards which includes a 25 metre indoor swimming pool, squash courts, playing fields, science laboratories, music school and dining room. The school also has its own medical centre with a school doctor.

The staff, who are all qualified, consists of both class teachers and specialists, some of whom are St Leonards staff.

A broad and balanced curriculum is taught and includes: English, Mathematics, Science, ICT, Technology, History, Geography, French, Latin, Art, Music, Drama, Religious Education, Personal & Social Education, Current Affairs and Physical Education. A wide range of academic abilities is accepted, but every pupil is encouraged to reach his/her full potential.

A wide range of sports and extra-curricular activities are offered which include: hockey, netball, lacrosse, tennis, fencing, riding, golf, orchestra and choir. Individual tuition is available on a wide range of musical instruments, as well as Speech and Drama.

Pupils generally pass on to St Leonards as a matter of choice and both schools work towards a smooth transition. St Leonards Sixth Form College and St Leonards School is co-ed.

St Lawrence College Junior School

Ramsgate Kent CT11 7AF.
Tel: (01843) 591788.
Fax: (01843) 853271
Station Ramsgate

President of the Council: Simon Webley, Esq, MA

Headmaster: **Roy Tunnicliffe, MA**(Ed)

Number of Pupils. 124. Boarders: 13, Day: 111. Girls 65, Boys 59 (including Nursery School).

Fees. September 1999, Boarders £3,885, Day from £1,130–£2,410 per term.

The School, which is the Junior School of St Lawrence College, offers a broad and varied education to boys and girls from the age of 3 years to 11+. At age 11, children transfer to the Middle School of St Lawrence College. In September, 1983, the School became co-educational. The majority of the children go on to St Lawrence College, which is also co-educational. Pupils are also prepared for entry to any of the Senior Independent Schools.

On average four academic and three music Scholarships are gained annually. The School's facilities are particularly strong, to support the objective of a broad-based education. Information Technology has a central place in the curriculum, serviced by a fully up-to-date computer suite, whilst Design and Technology is well established in our purpose built Centre.

Classes are small and great emphasis is laid on individual education. A specialist Pre-prep department caters for the needs of those under seven years of age, together with the Nursery School for 3 and 4 year olds.

Recent buildings include a well equipped Music School, an Assembly Hall and a Classroom block in which extensive provision is made for the worthwhile use of leisure time. An indoor heated swimming pool is used all year round. Sports played are Association and Rugby Football, Hockey, Cricket, Squash, Athletics, Netball and Rounders.

The Headmaster, assisted by a pastoral team including resident Tutors, and a resident 'Boarding Mother', personally supervise the welfare of the boarders. The School Doctor visits daily; there is a bright and pleasant sanatorium in the Senior School main building.

The School is a Christian Foundation and enjoys the use of the College Chapel for combined Services on Sundays.

A long succession of parents in HM Forces or working abroad have relied on our specialist experience in recognising and meeting the needs of their children. Communications with London (M2 and rail) and the Continent (Ferry, Jetfoil or Hovercraft through Ramsgate or Dover) are particularly convenient.

A prospectus with information about current fees and vacancies may be had on application to the Headmaster's Secretary.

Charitable status. St Lawrence College is a Registered Charity, number 307921. It exists to provide education for boys and girls.

St Margaret's Preparatory School

Curzon Street Calne Wiltshire SN11 0DF
Tel: (01249) 857220
Fax: (01249) 857227
e-mail: stmargadmin@stmaryscalne.wilts.sch.uk

Chairman of Governors: R C Southwell, Esq, QC

Headmistress: **Mrs K E Cordon**, GLCM, LLCM(TD), ALCM

Numbers of Pupils. 126 Day, 4–11 years, 86 Girls, 40 Boys.
Fees. £1,650–£1,775 per term.

St Margaret's Preparatory School is an independent co-educational day school for boys and girls aged 4-11, situated in the grounds of St Mary's School, Calne. The children share the excellent facilities of St Mary's including sports pitches, a concert hall, gymnasium, swimming pool, theatre, music school, Chapel, computer rooms and dining hall. The classes are small, with a maximum number of eighteen children in each age group. Consequently, there are all the advantages of a large school, whilst retaining the caring atmosphere of a small one.

There is a high academic standard throughout the school and the children are taught to learn the value of hard work and how to accept discipline and responsibility. In addition to this, every aspect of a child's character is developed. The children are thoroughly prepared for Common Entrance and

Senior School 11+ examinations and the school has an impressive record of success in gaining major scholarships to leading senior independent schools, both in academic areas and in The Arts. In 2001 all the examination candidates were successful in passing entrance examinations for their chosen senior schools and a total of eight scholarships were gained by St Margaret's pupils. Schools making these awards included: Dauntsey's, St Mary's, Calne and Warminster.

In November 1999 the excellence of the teaching programme for the younger children was also acknowledged, on this occasion by Ofsted. St Margaret's was inspected, as part of a national programme of inspection of the educational provision for four year olds. The inspector concluded that: "Children at St Margaret's School enjoy a diverse, well-balanced and thoroughly planned education programme. They are happy, confident and interested in their activities, thus demonstrating the high aims of the school".

St Margaret's prides itself on its high standard of pastoral care. Every effort is made to ensure that the children never feel lost or bewildered, and that they quickly find their feet and are given a sense of belonging. There is a fully equipped Medical Centre in the grounds, under the supervision of a trained and experienced State Registered Nurse.

There is a strong sporting tradition and the children compete regularly with other schools. The boys play cricket, rugby and football, whilst the girls play netball and rounders. Additionally, athletics, judo, swimming and tennis are sports enjoyed by all.

Music and drama have a high profile. There is an annual major production and the orchestra and choirs perform regularly at venues outside school, such as The Festival Hall.

School hours are between 8.20 am and 3.30 pm each day. In 1999 the school opened its own After School Club. This is staffed by two fully trained child carers and is available from 3.30 pm until 6 pm, five days a week. Whilst at the club, the children participate in craft and creative work, and a quiet time is set aside to enable them to do their homework. Tea is also provided. This facility has proved to be extremely popular with many parents.

Only a visit to St Margaret's can convey the spirit of friendliness and the sense of purpose that exist within the school.

Early registration is essential as places are reserved up to three years in advance.

Charitable status. St Margaret's Preparatory School is a Registered Charity, number A309482. It exists to provide education for boys and girls.

St Martin's School

40 Moor Park Road Northwood Middlesex HA6 2DJ.
Tel: (01923) 825740.
Fax: (01923) 835452
e-mail: office@stmartins.org.uk
website: http://www.stmartins.org.uk
Station: Northwood

Chairman of Governors: Brian J Watkins, Esq

Headmaster: **Michael J Hodgson**, MA (Queens' College, Cambridge), CertEd

Number of Boys. 400

Fees. Main School £2,125. Pre-Prep £1,900. Kindergarten £645 (mornings). Some Bursaries are available in cases of need arising during boys' time at the school.

St Martin's aims to provide a disciplined framework within which school life is enjoyable and rewarding. An enthusiastic staff of 40 experienced and well qualified teachers maintains high academic standards and provides broad sporting, musical and cultural opportunities. The atmosphere is friendly and lively with great emphasis on pastoral care.

The school, which is an Educational Trust, administered by a Board of Governors, prepares boys for all the Independent Senior Schools. Fifty five scholarship awards have been won to senior schools during the last six years. The school, which is in a pleasant residential area, stands in 12 acres of grounds. Facilities include a Kindergarten and a new Pre-Preparatory building; three well-equipped Science Laboratories, an Assembly Hall with stage; a new Sports Complex including a swimming pool; an open hard playing area; a Computer Room; an Art Studio with facilities for design technology; 3 hard Tennis Courts. An ambitious development plan is under way and includes 8 new classrooms and a performing arts centre.

ICT, Art, DT, and Music are included in the curriculum for all boys, and a large proportion of the boys in the school learn a musical instrument.

The School is divided into Patrols for competitions in work and games, and senior boys make a responsible contribution towards the running of the School. Boys are taught to play football, rugby, cross-country running, hockey, cricket, swimming, athletics, squash, judo, fencing and tennis; and the school has a fine reputation in inter-school matches.

The catering and domestic arrangements and the boys' health are in the direct care of the Headmaster's wife.

Charitable status. St Martin's (Northwood) Preparatory School Trust Limited is a Registered Charity, number 312648. It exists to provide education for boys.

St Martin's School

Kirkdale Manor Nawton York YO6 5UA.
Tel: (01439) 71215

Chairman of the School Governors: Mr J Moon, BDS

Headmaster: **S M Mullen**, BEd (London)

Number of Pupils. 134 (40 Boarders, 94 Day Children)

Age Range. 4+ to 13+

Fees (1998/9). Boarding £2,690. Day £895–£1,690. No compulsory extras

St Martin's is a predominantly boarding Preparatory School which takes boys and girls from the age of 7, and prepares pupils for all the leading Senior Independent Schools via Common Entrance and Scholarship examinations.

Whilst non-Catholics are made most welcome, this is a Roman Catholic School, under the patronage of the Rt Rev Bishop of Middlesbrough and the Headmaster of Ampleforth College. The Chaplain is a monk of nearby Ampleforth Abbey. There are ten full time qualified teachers and two part-time qualified teachers.

Dance and Needlework are included in the girls' curriculum.

The administration is well versed in catering for children of families based overseas.

Mrs Mullen, assisted by two Matrons, supervises the children's welfare and the domestic arrangements.

A Music Centre, a heated and covered Swimming Pool, a Sports Hall and a Computer Room represent some of the facilities available. A new Technology Block was opened in 1997.

Sports include Rugby, Cricket, Netball, Tennis, Badminton, Athletics, Swimming. Optional extras include Instrumental Music, Riding, Shooting, Metalwork, Carpentry. Various clubs and societies flourish, and the School Choir frequently performs in local churches and village halls.

The Manor stands in 25 acres situated in delightful rural surroundings on the edge of the North Yorkshire Moors, just off the A170, 25 miles north of York.

A Scholarship which offers a remission of up to one third of the fees is competed for annually.

Charitable status. St Martin's School is a Registered Charity, number 529629. It exists for the provision of a secure Christian education, particularly for boarders.

St Mary's Hall

Stonyhurst Lancs BB7 9PU
Tel: (01254826) 242

Preparatory School for Stonyhurst College

Chairman of Governors: J Hartley, Esq

***Headmaster:* M Higgins**, BEd (Hons), MA

Chaplains:
Rev H Thomas, SJ
Brother E Coyle, SJ

Number of Boys. 63 Boarders, 129 Day Boys.
Number of Girls. 7 Boarders, 29 Day Girls.
Fees. Boarders £2,995, Day Pupils £1,455–£2,105 per term inclusive

St Mary's Hall stands in its own grounds close to Stonyhurst College and, though independent of the College, close academic and social links are maintained between the two schools. Pupils are accepted from the age of 7 and are prepared for Stonyhurst Entrance examination and the Stonyhurst Scholarships. The Headmaster and his wife are assisted by a fully qualified teaching staff and nurse.

The boarding community is cared for by resident Houseparents.

For pastoral purposes the school is divided into 3 age groups called Playrooms. Each Playroom is in the care of a house master and his assistant who are responsible for the children's day to day welfare. Each year group has extensive indoor recreational facilities. In addition to a Gymnasium there is a Sports Hall and pupils also share Stonyhurst College's indoor swimming pool.

The first three years are taught as Primary School classes and streaming starts from 11+. The School's Scholarship record is excellent, with 50 Awards being gained to Stonyhurst College in the last 5 years. Remedial help for both Maths and English is provided where necessary and places are available for children with specific learning difficulties. Music, Art and Drama are an integral part of the Curriculum. There is a strong choral tradition. Special features include a Rare Breed farm and a recently built Theatre.

Two Jesuit Chaplains looks after the school's religious instruction and there is opportunity for daily Mass. Pupils of other Christian denominations are most welcome.

The main sports are Rugby Football, Cross Country, Netball, Rounders, Indoor Hockey, Cricket, Athletics, Tennis and Archery. A wide range of activities is available for the children in their recreational time including Chess, Stamp Collecting, Model Making, Camping (Summer), Art, Photography, .177 Air Rifle Shooting, Fencing, Gymnastics, Debating, Computing, Theatre Workshop, Modern Dance, Ballet and Skiing.

Further details and a prospectus may be obtained from the Headmaster.

Charitable status. St Mary's Hall is a Registered Charity, number 230165. It exists to promote Catholic Independent Jesuit Education within the Christian Community and to educate boys and girls to "Learn to Care" and to grow up to be "Men and Women for Others".

St Mary's Preparatory School

Pottergate Lincoln LN2 1PH.
Tel: (01522) 524622
Fax: (01522) 543637
e-mail: office@st-marys-prep.lincs.sch.uk

Chairman of Governors: Mrs Jane Wright

***Head:* Mark Upton**, BSc (Joint Hons), CertEd

Number of Pupils. Boys: 136. Girls: 149
Fees. (Main School): £1,520–£1,870 per term, inclusive of lunches and all residential and day trips. (Nursery): £125 per session (lunches extra for part time pupils).

Entry can be made at any age after 2½ years and children leave at age 11.

The School was founded in 1950 and is a Christian (non-denominational), co-educational day preparatory school.

It is situated in a Grade I listed building in the Cathedral Close which retains much of the character of an 18th century house, although modern changes and improvements, including the imaginative transformation of the former Stable into an Art and Science Block, have given greater facilities for its use as a school. A major building programme has seen the addition of a large multi-purpose Hall, four extra teaching rooms, a new administration area, enlarged kitchen and dining facilities, a £250,000 purpose built Early Years Centre and new library and computer facilities. An Astroturf sports area is planned for the summer 2001.

The School enjoys extensive grounds, which are ideally suited for recreational activities and create an unusually peaceful and safe atmosphere within a central position in the City. All teachers are fully qualified and small classes allow for individual attention. Boys and girls are prepared for Common Entrance at eleven, Scholarship Examinations and entry to the local maintained schools, including Grammar Schools.

Rugby, soccer and cricket are the main games for the boys and netball, hockey and rounders for the girls. There is a flourishing Swimming Club organised at a local swimming pool on Saturday mornings where the children are taught by qualified instructors.

Music is a strong feature of school life with over half the pupils taking individual instrumental lessons. The children may join one of three school choirs, and there is an orchestra and several other instrumental groups.

The full range of National Curriculum subjects is taught, together with French from age 4, design and technology, multi-media computing, woodwork, needlework, art, cookery, music and ballet.

Charitable status. St Mary's School is a Registered Charity, number 527620. It exists for the purpose of educating boys and girls from the age of 2½ to 11.

St Mary's Preparatory School

Abbey Park Melrose Roxburghshire TD6 9LN.
Tel: (01896) 822517
Fax: (01896) 823550
e-mail: enquiries@stmarys.newnet.co.uk
website: www.stmarysmelrose.org.uk

Founded in 1895

Chairman of Governors: Lord Sanderson of Bowden

Headmaster: **John Brett,** MA, GCLCM, CertMusEd, MCollP

Number of Boys and Girls. Kindergarten: Boys 11, Girls 14, aged 2½-4 years; Pre-Prep: Boys 12, Girls 15; Preparatory: Boys 30, Girls 29. Age range 4–13. Boarders from 8.

Full boarding Fees. £3,410 per term.

Weekly boarding Fees. £3,350 per term.

Day Fees. £2,380 per term. Pre-prep: £1,575 per term.
10% to 25% reduction for second and third children

Religious denomination. Christian and Ecumenical
Member of SCIS, IAPS

Curriculum. A healthy variety of subjects including traditional core studies reflecting the National Curriculum (English, Maths, Science, Computer Studies, French, Geography, History, Classics, Latin, Scripture, Art and Design, Music, Drama). The School's intention is to provide a genuinely nourishing environment allowing for the development of the whole person, and aimed at a solid foundation in the central human values. Adventure Training and service to others both inside and outside the School feature importantly in the programme.

Entry requirements. Application by letter or telephone, followed by a visit to the School, if possible, and a tour guided by senior pupils. Juniors and Pre-prep pupils can be offered a 'reception' day to help with placement.

Examinations offered. Thorough preparation for the Common Entrance Examination.

Academic, sports, games and leisure facilities. Classroom computers, Science Laboratory and a big open Art Room. Theatre-Arts and Assembly Hall for concerts and drama. Day rooms for leisure games. Spacious games pitches supporting a strong tradition in rugby, cricket and hockey. There is a cross-curricular Study Support Programme for talented and gifted children as well as for remedial work and EFL, and a growing 'After School Programme' designed to help families with working mothers.

Religious activities. Morning Assembly with hymn-singing and readings, stressing pupil participation and contribution either in word image, drama or music.

Charitable status. St Mary's Preparatory School is a Registered Charity, number SC009352. Its aim is to provide education for primary school children.

St Mary's School, Hampstead

47 Fitzjohn's Avenue London NW3 6PG
Tel: 020 7435 1868
Fax: 020 7794 7922

Chairman of Governors: Mrs Lucretia Eeles

Headmistress: **Mrs W Nash,** BA (Hons), MEd

Age range. 2½–11.

Number in school. 260 Girls, 40 Boys.

Nursery. 21 Girls, 11 Boys.

Fees per term 2000/2001. Nursery £1,030; Kindergarten to Year 6 £1,950.

Surrounded by mature woodland and gardens, unmatched by any other school in the area, St Mary's has been established in Hampstead since 1926. Founded by the Institute of the Blessed Virgin Mary as a Roman Catholic School for Girls, the school remains true to the ideals of the IBVM foundress, Mary Ward who believed in the provision of a thoroughly grounded academic and spiritual education as a foundation for an enriched and confident adulthood.

The school has a thriving Nursery and Pre-Prep for girls and boys. Boys are prepared for transfer to popular London Boys Preparatory Schools at the age of 7 years.

The girls are prepared for Common Entrance and the entrance examinations for top London Senior Schools. They transfer at the age of 11 years, many gaining awards and scholarships.

In addition to a broad curriculum, a wider range of activities is seen as essential to the rounded development of a healthy child. Importance is attached to physical education, drama and the arts. Extra curricular classes include Speech and Drama, Italian, Ballet and Fencing. There is a school orchestra, choir and a chapel choir. Tuition is offered for many musical instruments. School trips abroad are arranged for older children.

There is an enthusiastic and dedicated staff of 30 experienced and well qualified teachers. There are specialist staff for Science, French, Art, Design and Technology, Music and Special Needs. St Mary's aims to develop and fulfil the maximum potential of each child and this objective is fostered within a happy and caring environment which recognises the needs and importance of children of all abilities.

Charitable status. This Roman Catholic School is a Registered Charity, number 1006411. It exists to provide education for girls and boys. It is managed by a majority of Lay Trustees and Governors.

St Mary's Westbrook

Ravenlea Road Folkestone Kent CT20 2JU
Tel: (01303) 851222.
Fax: (01303) 249901
Station: Folkestone Central, Ashford International

Chairman of Governors: Roger De Haan

Head: **Mrs Lesley Anne Watson,** MA(Ed)

Number of Boarders. 34 Boys, 15 Girls

Number of Day Children. 96 Boys, 64 Girls. Montessori Nursery: 84

Fees. Boarders £2,710–£3,100 per term. Day Pupils £1,300–£2,315 per term. Nursery. The Nursery has its own fee structure based on number of sessions attended.

There are Academic, Sports, Art and Music Scholarships. Bursaries are available for families of Military and Diplomatic Personnel.

Location. St Mary's Westbrook is situated in Folkestone, 'the Gateway to Europe' and is easily accessible from London by train or the M20 motorway, as well as Europe by the Channel Tunnel (10 minutes from the school), the Seacat or the Ferries from Dover. Heathrow and Gatwick airports are less than 2 hours by car and being the nearest independent boarding and day school to the Channel Tunnel, Brussels and Paris are only 2 hours away.

Facilities. The School's facilities are excellent. There are two halls/theatres, specialist Science Laboratories, IT Centre, a very good Library, Chapel and superb purpose built classrooms. A new purpose built Nursery and refurbished Girls Boarding House was opened in September 1999. As well as possessing a safe, enclosed playing field, St Mary's Westbrook also has excellent hard courts for tennis, basketball and netball.

Education. The curriculum is designed to allow parents opportunities for maximum choice. We have an excellent record in securing passes in the Kent Test (11+) (100% in 2000), Common Entrance and Senior Independent School Scholarship Examinations. In addition, pupils have always obtained good results at GCSE. Recent innovations have included an expansion of our Foreign Language teaching, French from Reception. A Japanese Teaching Assistant helps focus pupils on the Far East). Support is given by an excellent Skills Development Unit and EAL is offered.

Extra-Curricular. The school has a very busy and stimulating extra-curricular programme in which all boys and girls are encouraged to participate. The main sports are Soccer, Rugby, Cricket, Hockey, Netball, Rounders and Athletics Other regular sports include Swimming, Golf, Tennis, Dryskiing, Basketball and various Watersports. Arrangements can be made for Horse riding. Music, Drama, Ballet & Tap Dancing, Computing, Woodwork, Modelmaking and Cookery are amongst the many other activities which take place. Music is a particular strength with pupils being encouraged to learn to play an instrument and subsequently participating in one of the Orchestras. In addition, there is a strong choral tradition with separate Girls and Boys Choirs.

Boarding. Excellent facilities are provided for both boys and girls. Younger pupils are accommodated in bright, cosy bedrooms and older pupils live in study bedrooms. There are Common Rooms for boys and girls as well as joint recreational rooms and modern washing facilities. A full range of weekend activities are offered to both boarding and day students ranging from theatre trips, ten pin bowling and short visits to Calais and Boulogne. We also have a new initiative, having become the D of E Award Scheme Expedition Centre for SE Kent.

An escorted train service to and from London (Charing Cross), Paris and Brussels is available. In addition, arrangements can be made to have pupils collected from or taken to airports, ports and other locations.

General. St Mary's Westbrook was formed in 1997 as a result of a merger between Westbrook House Preparatory School and St Mary's College. It is a friendly and flourishing school offering small classes and a balanced curriculum. There is a large well qualified staff providing a caring environment where confidence and self esteem are cultivated.

Charitable status. St Mary's Westbrook is a Registered Charity, number 1063709. It exists to prepare boys and girls for a challenging, demanding and ever changing future, encouraging the highest possible standards in all areas of learning in an atmosphere of fun and security.

St Michael's Co-educational Preparatory School

Otford Court Otford Kent TN14 5SA.
Tel: (01959) 522137.
Station: Otford

Accredited by ISC.

Chairman of Governors: Gordon Owen, Esq, CBE

Headmaster: **Dr P A Roots,** BA (Hons), PhD (Cantab)

Deputy Heads:
Dr G Frank-Gemmill
Mrs V M Marchetti
Mr P N Nixon

Number of Pupils. 420
Inclusive Fees. Day: £1,700–£2,256

The School, standing in nearly 100 acres of beautiful grounds on the North Downs, prepares girls and boys for all the Senior Independent Schools and local Grammar Schools (at 13+ or 11+) and has an excellent academic record. This has been achieved by small classes (mostly 16) and remedial/gifted teaching where appropriate. The school has an excellent reputation for music, games (rugby, soccer, cricket, netball, lacrosse and hockey), drama and art. On-site facilities include a modern Science Laboratory, new indoor swimming pool and full size Sports Hall, all-weather cricket nets, tennis courts, netball courts, four full size games pitches and a new computer room. The Pre-prep Department is in a new separate classroom block housed in our walled garden. New buildings are planned for the coming year. An extensive extra-curricular activity programme includes drama, computers, golf, chess, ballet, cooking, country dancing, archery and much more.

Charitable status. St Michael's is a Registered Charity, number 1076999. It exists to provide education for boys and girls.

St Michael's Preparatory School

La Rue de la Houguette St Saviour Jersey JE2 7UG Channel Islands
Tel: (01534) 856904
Fax: (01534) 856620

Headmaster: **Richard de Figueiredo**, BA, CertEd

Deputy Head: C P Cook, MA, AdvDipEd

Number of Pupils. Boys 183, Girls 123. Aged 3–13.
Fees. Pre-Prep £1,980–£2,059. Forms 1 to 3 £2,724 per term. Forms 4, 5, 6 £2,899. Lunch £208 per term.

Boys and girls are prepared for scholarship and entrance to all Independent Senior Schools. Hockey, rugby football, soccer, gymnastics, netball, rounders, cricket, athletics and tennis are taught on spacious playing fields with pavilion and hard tennis courts which adjoin the school. A purpose built sports hall large enough to hold one tennis court or four badminton courts with semi-sprung wooden floor marked for volleyball, basketball and indoor hockey was opened in 1994. An indoor, heated swimming pool with full changing facilities was opened in 1995, allowing the provision of on-site swimming lessons for the whole school.

The school has computer, art and technology suites in addition to networked computers in every classroom. A large variety of clubs and hobbies function within the school and many out-of-door activities, including rock-climbing, canoeing, surfing, sailing and photography are enjoyed by the children. Music, drama and art, which includes pottery, are all encouraged and a wide range of musical instruments are taught. There are three school choirs and two orchestras. The school has its own nursery.

For senior children there is an annual Activities' Week. Year 6 have Island-based pursuits, while Year 7 go to Brittany and Year 8 to the south coast of England or France. Each winter a party of children ski in Switzerland. Regular tours are made to Guernsey and England for sporting fixtures.

The academic and physical development, in addition to

the spiritual, moral and cultural growth, of the whole child is the main aim of the school and every child is encouraged to fulfil his or her potential.

St Michael's Preparatory School

198 Hadleigh Road Leigh-on-Sea Essex SS9 2LP.
Tel: (01702) 478719
Fax: (01702) 710183
e-mail: stmichaelsschool@stmichaelsschool.com
website: www.stmichaelsschool.com

Chairman of Governors: The Revd Robin Eastoe

Head: **C R Maultby**, BEd

Deputy Head: Mrs L M Morshead

Number of Pupils. 297 day pupils (148 girls, 149 boys). Co-educational. 3–11 years

Fees. £1,320–£1,485 inclusive of stationery and loan of text books.

St Michael's is a Church of England Preparatory (IAPS) School founded in 1922 to provide a sound academic education on Christian principles, but admitting pupils of other faiths. The children work in a happy and disciplined environment. The teachers seek to develop each child's potential fully in many skills, academic, creative, athletic and social. Pupils are prepared for the 11+ Common Entrance and other Entrance and Scholarship Examinations for independent schools. They also take the 11+ for entry to local grammar schools. The school follows the National Curriculum. Particular strengths are spoken English where children attain outstanding results in English Speaking Board Examinations and music.

St Michael's has a dedicated and well-qualified staff. It has its own chapel, well-stocked library, gymnasium and specialist rooms for science, ICT, DT and French. There are some on-site games facilities and hockey, cricket, football, mini-rugby, etc, are played on a nearby playing field. Pupils work for BAGA and STA awards. Extra subjects include piano, orchestral instruments, dancing, Speech and Drama, computer club, games, orchestra, canoeing, sailing, windsurfing, Spanish and German. (Extra subjects vary according to demand).

Charitable status. St Michael's Preparatory School is a Registered Charity, number 280668. It exists to provide education.

St Michael's School (for boys and girls from 3 months –13+)

Tawstock Court Barnstaple N Devon EX31 3HY.
Tel: Headmaster: 01271 343242
Station: Barnstaple Junction.

Headmaster: **J W Pratt**, Esq, GRSM (Hons), CertEd

Chairman of Governors: M N W Wilcox, Esq, JP, FRICS

Fees. Boarding £3,235–£3,335 per term; Day £995–£2,125.

Number of Pupils. 216.

St Michael's was founded in 1832 and moved to North Devon in 1940. St Michael's is set in 30 acres overlooking the beautiful Taw valley. The School is a member of IAPS and ISIS and is a Charitable Trust administered by a Board of Governors.

The teaching staff are all qualified and include a Director of Music, Director of Sport and a specialist in Information Technology.

Excellent academic results are achieved in small classes, quite often from boys and girls of modest initial ability. Modern languages form an important part of the very wide curriculum. Children are prepared for all Independent Senior Schools, and Scholarships and other Awards are regularly gained.

Facilities include Science Laboratories, a Computer Room, a Design and Technology Centre and a spacious Art Room. There is also a Sports Hall and two Squash Courts. Children also learn to swim in the heated pool. PE forms part of the curriculum and Hockey, Squash, Badminton, Athletics, Netball, Rounders and Tennis are played as well as Rugby, Soccer and Cricket. Tuition is available in all musical instruments.

Scholarships are offered termly for children between the ages of 7 and 11 and credit is given for outstanding sporting or musical ability.

Charitable status. The St Michael's Charitable Trust is a Registered Charity, number 272464. It exists to provide high quality education for local boys and girls.

St Neot's

Eversley Hook Hampshire RG27 0PN
Tel: (0118) 9732118
Stations: Fleet, Wokingham

Chairman of Governors: Mrs S Brampton

Headmaster: **R J Thorp**, BA (Dunelm), PGCE (Cantab)

Deputy Head: D R Williams

Number of Pupils. 24 weekly co-educational boarders, 130 day pupils, 110 pre-prep and nursery.

Inclusive fees per term. Boarders £3,135, Day pupils: Pre-Prep £1,500, Year 3 £1,880, Main School £2,545, Nursery £850 or £8.50 per session.

The school is situated in the country in 70 acres of pine wood and heath land. The staff comprises 8 masters and 10 mistresses in the senior school and 6 teachers and 4 assistants in the pre-prep department. There is one nursing sister. There is a staff ratio of 1 to 9. Besides the standard Common Entrance subjects, music, art, computing, drama and PE are taught throughout the school.

Pupils are prepared for all senior schools. Those of the required standard are coached for and encouraged to take scholarships.

Instruction in all musical instruments and judo may be taken as extras. There are separate Cricket, Football, Rugby, Rounders and Hockey grounds, Swimming Pool, Rifle Range, Tennis Courts, Netball Courts and Golf Course. Out of school activities cover as wide a range as possible, making full use of the extensive grounds. Sports, hobbies, music and art and computing are encouraged to help each child to develop his or her character and self-confidence.

Each main subject has its own specialist room, and there is a programme for the expansion and modernisation of buildings to cater for new requirements.

The school aims to ensure that all pupils receive the best possible training for life in a hard working, but happy family atmosphere, based on Christian practice and principles.

Charitable status. St Neot's is a Registered Charity, number 307324. The aim of the Charity is to try to provide the best all-round education possible to as many pupils as possible, with bursarial help according to need.

St Nicholas House, Abbot's Hill Junior School

Bunkers Lane Hemel Hempstead Hertfordshire HP3 8RP
Tel: (01442) 211156
Fax: (01442) 269981
e-mail: headmistress@st-nicks.biblio.net

Chairman of Governors: G M N Corbett, MA (Cantab), MSc

***Headmistress:* Mrs B B Vaughan**, CertEd (Reading)

Type. Preparatory 7–11; Pre-preparatory 4–7.

Number of Pupils. 200. Girls 3–11 years. Boys 3–8 years

Fees. £1,525–£1,895 per term.

St Nicholas House, established in 1923, is a small day school set in 70 acres of parkland on the edge of Hemel Hempstead. We provide a safe and secure environment in which children can learn and develop. We are noted for our happy friendly atmosphere, our commitment to rewarding effort and achievement, and our high academic standards. There are excellent sporting facilities, computer resources and a spacious hall for music, drama and gymnastics.

St Nicholas has a long tradition of providing small classes and learning according to individual needs. The teaching team consists of 25 full and part-time teachers, all firmly committed to providing maximum individual attention for each child.

We have chosen to base our subject teaching on the National Curriculum as ISEB Examinations are aligned with the statutory requirements and it provides continuity for pupils. Children are prepared for scholarship and Entrance examinations for a range of senior schools in the independent and maintained sectors. Younger children spend most of their time with their own form teacher, but by the age of 7, children receive specialist subject teaching in French, IT, PE, Drama and Music. Teachers monitor progress and development through a comprehensive reporting system and actively encourage the involvement of parents.

In addition to the National Curriculum there are the extras and activities which one would expect from a reputed preparatory school – drama, dance and music lessons, choir, orchestra, sports, a 'traditional' house system and a courteous expectation of respect between all members of the school.

Our location and proximity to an excellent road network allows parents to travel from St Albans, Rickmansworth, Watford and the surrounding area to enable their children to attend the school.

We welcome visitors into our school community. If you would like to visit us or to receive further information, please telephone 01442 211156.

Charitable status. Abbot's Hill Charitable Trust is a Registered Charity, number 3110533. It aims to educate children to achieve personal success.

St Olave's
The Junior School of St Peter's

York YO30 6AB
Tel: (01904) 623269
Fax: (01904) 640975
e-mail: enquiries@saintolaves.york.sch.uk

Chairman of the Governors: Major General D M Naylor, CB, MBE, DL

***Master:* T Mulryne**, MA, BEd, DPE

Deputy Head: Mrs S Jackson, BA

Director of Studies: Mrs L Garner, MA, BEd

Number of Pupils. Boys: 201. Girls: 129

Fees per term. 8+ & 9+ Year 4 to 5 £3,202 (boarding), £1,602 (day); 10+ Year 6 £3,478 (boarding), £1,882 (day); 11+ & 12+ Years 7 and 8 £3,652 (boarding), £2,080 (day).

These fees are fully inclusive, but day pupils are charged for lunch (£121 per term).

St Olave's was founded in 1876 and was purchased by St. Peter's (q.v) in 1901 to become its Junior School. Several years later it was brought onto the St Peter's site as an integrated part of the school. However from September 2001, St Olave's will occupy the site and buildings of a former girls' grammar school adjacent to the main school site. With its own halls, music school, practical subjects workshops, sports hall and magnificently appointed specialist teaching rooms, St Olave's will enjoy some of the best facilities for a prep school of its type.

The school puts praise and encouragement of the individual as its highest priority. There is a demandingly wide curriculum from the earliest age with specialist subject areas - modern foreign languages, information technology, science and music amongst others - being taught by specialist teachers from Year 4. Progress is monitored through a regular system of effort grades and attainment is measured through internal and externally moderated tests.

Boarding is a flourishing aspect of the school with a recent (2000) extension to accommodate the girls in what is now a co-educational House under the constant care of resident House parents and their own family. There are also five Day Houses which represent the pastoral unit for the duration of a boy or girl's time at the school.

There is a weekly pattern of chapel services in the school chapel on the St Peter's site and major festivals are celebrated on appropriate Sundays where a robed choir leads the worship. St Olave's has its own Chaplain who takes particular responsibility for all aspects of community life.

Music plays an important part in the life of the school with two orchestras, a wind band and many ensembles playing and practising weekly. Over 200 pupils learn individual instruments, and all are encouraged to join larger groups. Sport has an equally high profile where rugby football, hockey, cricket, netball, tennis and swimming are major sports and athletics, cross-country running, squash, badminton, basketball and volleyball are also available for boys and girls. The boys have won the National Schools' Seven-a-Side rugby tournament twice in the last five years.

Drama has an increasing profile and out of school activities flourish through such clubs as science society, chess, fencing, climbing, art and debating. The three modern languages - French, German and Spanish - organise holidays and exchanges with the appropriate country.

The vast majority of boys and girls who proceed to St Peter's, are not required to take the Common Entrance examination and are assessed by internal testing.

Entrance examinations are held in January/February each year, and tests can also be arranged at other times. There are academic scholarships available following the entrance examination at 8+, and further awards at 11+ for both internal and external candidates.

Charitable status. St Olave's is a Registered Charity, number 529740. It exists to provide education for boys and girls.

St Olave's Preparatory School

106-110 Southwood Road New Eltham London SE9 3QS.
Tel: 020 8294 8930
Fax: 020 8294 8939

Chairman of Governors: D A Jermyn, Esq, JP

***Headmistress:* Miss M P Taylor**, BEd, MA

Founded in 1932, St Olave's is a day preparatory school for girls and boys aged 3–11 years. A fully qualified and committed teaching staff prepares children for entry to local Grammar and Independent Senior Schools.

The aim of the school is to offer a warm and caring environment in which each child can thrive and be happy knowing that each is accepted for who they are. All achievements both great and small are acknowledged and celebrated. A Christian ethos permeates the pastoral life of the school, where care for others through thoughtful and responsible behaviour is expected. Praise and encouragement, rather than punishment and restriction, are emphasised and relationships between staff and pupils are relaxed and friendly. A close partnership with parents is sought.

The children in the Lower School are taught in mixed-ability classes where each child's progress is carefully monitored by the Form Teacher. In the Upper School the children are set across the year group for English and Mathematics. Individual differences are appropriately met, with the very able and those with mild learning difficulties receiving additional support where this is thought beneficial. The school is noted for the broad curriculum it offers and for its excellent achievements in Music and Drama. A range of sporting activities is taught as part of the curriculum and there are a number of after school clubs and activities. Music and PE are taught by specialist teachers from the age of three and French is introduced at 7 years old. The classrooms are equipped with new computers which are used as an additional resource to support all areas of the curriculum.

St Olave's feeds a wide range of secondary schools and parents are given help in choosing the school most appropriate to meet the needs of their child.

Charitable status. St Olave's School is a Registered Charity, number 312734. It exists to provide high quality education for boys and girls.

St Paul's Cathedral School

New Change London EC4M 9AD.
Tel: 020 7248 5156
Fax: 020 7329 6568

***Headmaster:* Mr Andrew H Dobbin**, MA (Cantab)

Chairman of Governors: The Dean of St Paul's Cathedral, The Very Revd Dr John Henry Moses

Number of Boys. Boarding Choristers 40; Day Boys 60; Pre-Prep Boys and Girls 48

Fees. Choristers £3,960 per annum; Day boys £6,246 per annum; Pre-Prep £5,796 per annum.

There have been choristers at St Paul's for over nine centuries. The present school is a Church of England Foundation dating back over 100 years and is governed by the Dean and Chapter of St Paul's Cathedral. The broadening of educational expectations and the challenge of curricular developments led the Dean and Chapter to agree to expand the school in 1989 by admitting non-chorister day-boys for the first time; a decision which continues to enrich the life of the school and Cathedral. In September 1998, the school admitted girls as well as boys into its new pre-prep department for 4–7 uear olds. The school will become fully co-educational from September 2002. It offers a broad curriculum leading to scholarship and Common Entrance examinations. In the first three years the work is tailored to individual needs bearing in mind the wide variety of educational backgrounds from which boys come. The school has an excellent record in placing boys in the senior schools of their choice, many with music scholarships. Every opportunity is taken to make use of the school's proximity to museums, libraries, galleries, theatres and the numerous attractions which London has to offer.

The 40 chorister boarders are housed on the Cathedral site and are fully integrated with the day boys for all their academic studies and games. The choristers' cathedral choral training offers them a unique opportunity to participate in the rich musical life of St Paul's and the City.

The school was rehoused in the 60's in purpose-built premises on the eastern end of the Cathedral site. A refurbishment project has recently been completed which added a new music school, art room, IT room, three pre-prep classrooms and games rooms to the existing facilities which include a hall/gymnasium, science laboratory, common room and a TV/video room. All boys are encouraged to play a musical instrument (most boys play two) and there are music and theory lessons with school orchestras and chamber groups.

A wide variety of games is offered including field sports at local playing fields and weekly swimming lessons. The boys have their own playground and the use of the hall for indoor games and gymnastics.

Admissions procedure. Prospective day boys of 7+ years in September are given academic tests in Mathematics and English, usually in February of the previous academic year.

Pre-prep children are assessed in an informal play situation in the November prior to entry.

Voice trials and tests for chorister places are held in February, May and October for boys between 6½ and 8½ years old.

St Paul's Preparatory School

Colet Court Lonsdale Road London SW13 9JT.
Tel: 020 8748 3461
Fax: 020 8563 7361
e-mail: HMSecCc@StPaulsSchool.org.uk
Station: Hammersmith

Chairman of Governors: D A Tate, OBE

***Headmaster:* G J Thompson**, BA, MEd

Deputy Headmaster: P A David, BA, PGCE

Director of Studies: K F Sharpe, BA, PGCE

Director of Administration: A P C Fuggle, MA

Head of Juniors: G E Nava, BSc, PGCE

Number of Boys. 434

Fees. Tuition £8,064 per year. Boarding £5,280 per year

Colet Court is very closely linked with St Paul's School, to which almost all the boys go on. The two schools are in separate, but adjacent modern buildings on the south bank of the Thames, and share many amenities – dining hall, sports centre and playing fields.

The work is organised to fit in with that of the Senior School. A normal Preparatory School curriculum is followed, except that boys are not specifically prepared for the Common Entrance Examination, nor for scholarships to senior schools other than St Paul's. There are excellent facilities for all games and sports, for Art, DT, Science and IT. Music is a particular strength of the school, which runs three orchestras, a jazz group, and three choirs.

Entrance is normally at either 7 or 8 by competitive examination and registration for this is essential. Choral Scholarships are available at 8, 9 or 10, and a Music Scholarship is available at 10 or 11; ten fee-paying places are also available at 10 or 11 by examination, plus one Scholarship place at 11. Early registration is not required for these later entries. Boarding is available for boys of 11 and over.

Charitable status. St Paul's Preparatory School is a Registered Charity, number 312749. It exists to provide education for boys.

St Paul's School

Rua Juquia 166 Jardim Paulistano São Paulo Brazil CEP 01440-903
Tel: 55 11 3085 3399
Fax: 55 11 3085 3708
e-mail: spshead@stpauls.br
website: www.stpauls.br

Chairman of the Board of Governors: Mr F J L Pallin, OBE

Headmaster: Mr R Benammar, MA

Head of Preparatory School: **Mrs C T Lindsay**, BA

Number of Pupils. 859. Pre-Preparatory 270, Preparatory 239, Senior 350.

Fees (Preparatory School) US$8,300

St Paul's (The British School) is situated in a pleasant residential suburb of São Paulo and prepares pupils for entry into British, American and Brazilian Universities.

The Headmaster is an Overseas Member of HMC. Entry to the Preparatory School at 7 years of age, usually from the Pre-Preparatory School, depends on fluency in English and academic ability.

Competition for places at St Paul's is fierce and prospective parents from overseas should give the School at least six months notice of impending transfer to São Paulo.

The School follows the conventional Prep School Curriculum, modified to suit local circumstances and is at once challenging and exciting.

A strong pastoral support system exists and regular contact with parents is a particular feature of education in the Prep School.

St Peter's School

Lympstone Nr Exmouth Devon EX8 5AU.
Tel: (01395) 272148
Fax: (01395) 222410
e-mail: st.peters@eclipse.co.uk
website: www.stpetersprep.devon.sch.uk
Station: Exeter

Chairman of Board of Reference: Dr J A Davis, MB, BS

Headmaster: **C N C Abram**, CertEd (St Luke's College, Exeter)

Deputy Headmaster: M C Groome, BEd (Leeds)
Director of Studies: R J Williams, MA Hons (Edinburgh), PGCE (Bedford)
Director of Finance: J R Middleton, BSc Hons (London), ACIB

Number of Pupils. Boys: 134; Girls: 113; (227 day, 20 weekly boarders)

Fees. September 2001: Weekly Boarders £3,050 per term. Senior Day Pupils £2,125, Junior Day Pupils £1,945. Pre-Prep Pupils £1,485. Nursery £1,300

St Peter's aims to provide an environment in which each girl and boy has the fullest opportunity for growth: intellectually, culturally and physically. Established in 1882, St Peter's boasts an impressive setting - 28 acres of games fields and grounds overlooking the Exe estuary. The school is committed to traditional prep school values within a modern approach to education and offers a varied and broad curriculum.

Pupils aged between 3 and 13 receive a seamless education with day, flexi or weekly boarding available. A number of our senior pupils find this is the ideal introduction to boarding prior to transfer to senior school at 12+ or 13+.

Excellent access to M5, A30, A38, rail stations and Exeter airport. The school is six miles from the city of Exeter and school transport from Exeter and the Newton Abbot area is available daily.

St Peter's enjoys an excellent Scholarship and Common Entrance record and prides itself on maintaining a high academic standard while retaining balance and breadth.

Strong academic programme with specialist subject teaching from Year 5; French and music taught by specialists throughout the school. St Peter's follows the best of modern educational practice with literacy and numeracy emphasised in the nursery and pre-prep departments.

Flourishing music and drama provide scope for all pupils to perform and combine their talents as a team in acting, singing or working as technicians. Lessons in Brass, Strings, Woodwind, Piano, Guitar, Percussion, Singing, Speech & Drama and Dance are offered.

Games programme reinforced with a strong fixtures list at all age levels for boys and girls. St Peter's is proud of its successful games record, including recent IAPS champions in athletics, badminton, hockey, squash and tennis.

New classrooms due to be completed in September 2001 for the senior school are part of a progressive development plan.

St Petroc's School

Ocean View Road Bude Cornwall EX23 8NJ.
Tel/Fax: (01288) 352876
e-mail: office@stpetrocs.com

Chairman of Governors: Mr P Banbury

Headmaster: **B P Dare**, BEd

Number of Pupils. Day 26 boys, 20 girls; Pre-Prep 24 boys, 22 girls.

Staff. 7 full-time, 2 part-time teachers.

Fees. Day Pupils £1,615 per term, Pre-prep. £980 per term. There are no compulsory extras.

St Petroc's has been providing an excellent all-round education for children since 1912. In recent years, it has developed a reputation for fostering a friendly atmosphere which gives each child the feeling of being part of an extended family where they are known and respected as individuals.

On the playing field, adjacent to the school, the following sports are coached: Cricket, Association and Rugby Football, Hockey, Netball, Tennis and Athletics. All children are taught to swim. Judo, Golf, Riding and Music are voluntary extras.

In addition to the usual subjects, Music, Art, Science, Physical Education, Handicraft, CDT, Cookery, and Computing form part of the weekly curriculum, while spare-time occupations include Drama, Piano, Violin, Brass, Clarinet and Guitar lessons, Ballet, Golf, Judo, Pottery, Tap Dancing, Astronomy, Badminton, Model Making and Folk Music. Much use is made of the excellent beaches and downs situated within a few hundred metres of the School.

There is a pre-preparatory department, catering for boys and girls from 3 to 7 years.

A Nursery for children from 3 months to 2½ years will open in September 2001. It will operate for 48 weeks of the year.

Prospectus on application to the Headmaster.

Charitable status. St Petroc's School Trust Limited is a Registered Charity, number 306578. It exists to provide education for children.

St Piran's

Maidenhead Berkshire SL6 7LZ
Tel: (01628) 627316
Fax: (01628) 632010

Chairman of Governors: Mr W H Rees, MA

Headmaster: **J Carroll**, BA (Hons), BPhilEd, PGCE, NFQH

Assistant Headmasters:
S L Edginton, MA (Oxon)
I D McLellan, CertEd (London)

Number of Pupils. 340 Day Pupils, aged 3–13.

Fees. From £1,510–£2,340 per term, which includes lunch.

St Piran's established over 100 years, stands in its own grounds (10½ acres) most of which are playing fields. Boys and girls are prepared for entry to all schools. Main games include rugby, hockey, cricket, football, athletics, swimming, cross-country running, netball, rounders.

Out of school activities include music (2 orchestras), art, craft, ballet, sailing, golf, horse riding, tennis, drama.

An extensive development programme during the last seven years provides excellent science facilities, a technology room, a computer building, an art studio, library and a versatile all weather pitch with 4 tennis courts, cricket nets, basketball, netball, volleyball, hockey and short tennis.

A new Sports and Performing Arts Centre opened in June 2000 with indoor swimming pool, dance studio, sports hall, concert hall and music block.

A prospectus is available on request and parents are welcome to look round the school.

Charitable status. St Piran's Trust is a Registered Charity, number 309094. It exists to promote and provide for the advancement of education for the 3–13 year old pupils in the School's charge.

St Pius X Prep School

200 Garstang Road Fulwood Preston PR2 8RD.
Tel: (01772) 719937
Fax: (01772) 787535

Chairman of Governors: Mr R E Barton

Headmistress: **Miss B Banks**, MA

Number of Children. 290 (Day) Girls and Boys

Fees per term from September 2000. Kindergarten £1,000. School fees £1,250.

The School is administered as a non-profit-making educational trust by a Board of Governors, providing education from 2 to 11. The children are prepared for entrance examination to independent schools. The School is in four acres of its own grounds in a pleasant suburb of Preston. All preparatory curriculum subjects covered.

Sports taught are Association Football, Cricket, Tennis, Hockey, Netball, Rugby, Table Tennis, Rounders and Athletics.

Ballet, piano, clarinet, flute, violin and guitar lessons are some of the optional extras offered.

Charitable status. St Pius X School is a Registered Charity, number 526609. Its purpose is to equip the children with an outstanding academic and social education in a Roman Catholic environment, which will enable them to achieve their full potential.

St Richard's

Bredenbury Court Bromyard Herefordshire HR7 4TD
Tel: (01885) 482491
Fax: (01885) 488982
e-mail: st.dix@virgin.net
website: www.st-richards.co.uk

Headmaster: **R E H Coghlan**, MA (Cantab)

Number of Pupils. 150

Fees. £3,395 Boarding; £2,316 Day. No compulsory extras

Founded in 1921, St Richard's is a Catholic Preparatory School of about 150 boys and girls, of whom about one-third are non Catholic. The school is situated in 35 usable acres of beautiful Herefordshire countryside.

Children are prepared for Common Entrance and Scholarships to Catholic and other Independent Senior Schools. Entry is normally between 7 and 10 although day children are accepted at 3.

The average number in a class is 15. Art, Pottery, Carpentry and Music flourish and the choir specialises in Plain Song.

The usual team games are played, whilst, among other sports Riding, Rock-climbing, Athletics, Netball, Hockey and Small Bore Shooting are strongly featured.

The school is experienced in looking after the needs of those from abroad. Children are escorted to and from London and arrangements are made for their escort on to Heathrow etc. An illustrated prospectus, lists of recent scholarships, staff and other particulars are available from the Headmaster.

St Ronan's

Water Lane Hawkhurst Kent TN18 5DJ.
Tel: (01580) 752271.
Fax: (01580) 754882.
e-mail: info@stronans.kent.sch.uk
Stations: Staplehurst, Etchingham

Chairman of Governors: Mr Christopher Page

***Joint Heads:* Edward and Joanna Yeats-Brown**

Number of Children. 160. 45 Boarders, fully co-ed.
Age range. 2½–13.
Fees. Boarding: £3,478 a term. Day: £735–£2,563 per term. We operate a flexi-boarding system which can be tailored to individual needs.

St Ronan's is essentially a family school as it has been since it was started in Worthing in 1883. The current Heads live on the premises with their four children and the school has the feel of being a school within a home. St Ronan's occupies a fine Victorian Mansion set in 240 acres of beautiful Weald of Kent countryside. There are numerous games pitches, hard tennis courts, a shooting range, golf course and a covered swimming pool as well as a hundred acre wood.

By deliberately remaining small the school has developed a unique and special atmosphere in which staff and children work together to achieve their aims. Our small size helps the transition from home to school and a maximum class size of 18 enables children to gain confidence and interact positively with their peers and the staff.

Academically we have 100% pass rate at CE and well over 25% of all pupils gain Scholarships to major senior independent schools such as Eton, Sevenoaks, Benenden, Tonbridge, Harrow, King's Canterbury and Lancing; we also prepare children for entry to local Grammar Schools and boast an enviable record here too.

Music and art play a vital role at St Ronan's. We have two choirs: the School choir and the Chapel choir, and over half the children learn at least one musical instrument. The art department is flourishing and the children have the option to learn craft and woodwork in addition to their timetabled art lessons.

The major sports at St Ronan's are football, hockey and cricket but we also offer coaching in athletics, tennis, swimming, dance, rounders and netball. We have a very successful games record, particularly in hockey, with many an unbeaten season behind us.

The Pre-Prep is very much part of the school, in both location and ethos, and is a thriving and dynamic department taking children from 2½ to 7.

Charitable status. St Ronan's is a Registered Charity, number 1066420/0. It exists for the advancement of education of its children.

St Swithun's Junior School

Alresford Road Winchester SO21 1HA.
Tel: (01962) 835750
Fax: (01962) 835781

Established 1884. Girls day preparatory school with pre-preparatory boys. Church of England.

***Headmistress:* Miss Elaine Krispinussen**, BA (Wales)

Chairman of Governors: Dr Christopher Brill

Bursar: Gavin Haig

Number of Pupils. Girls 159, Boys 34. Average class size 24. Pupil/teacher ratio 11.5:1.
Fees. Termly Fees £790–£2,010
Profile. The school is located on the eastern fringe of Winchester. The site is shared with the senior school and has a pleasant outlook over open countryside. The present building was completed in the 1970s and 1980s. There is a large music room, gymnasium and well stocked library. During 1989 improved facilities for Science, Art and Technology were incorporated into the building and in 1998 a new Assembly Hall was built. The school is a happy, caring community, committed to the nurture and encouragement of each individual. A stimulating environment and a broad curriculum provide challenging opportunities for those who are academically able and those whose abilities are of a creative, practical or sporting nature.
Entry. At 3, and at 7.
Curriculum. Usual subjects taught plus French, Art, Technology, Drama, ICT, Music and PE, with due regard for National Curriculum requirements.
Leavers. Boys leave for various preparatory schools, including The Pilgrims' and Twyford. Girls go on to a range of senior independent schools including St Swithun's Senior School.
Consultation. Biannual reports, regular Parents' Evenings and PTA.
Sports. Cricket, Football, Gymnastics, Netball, Rounders, Short Tennis, Swimming, Athletics.
Activities. These include Chess, Computers, Craft, Drama, Gymnastics, Judo, Science, Musical concerts and productions, two annual residential field study trips and regular visits.
Facilities. All weather pitches, playing fields, art room, music room, science room.
Special needs. Qualified Learning Support teacher.

St Teresa's Preparatory School

Grove House Guildford Road Effingham Surrey KT24 5QA.
Tel: (01372) 453456

Motto: *Gaudere et bene facere*

***Headmistress:* Mrs A Stewart**, MA, PGCE

Deputy Head:

Bursar: Mr Peter Large

Chairman of Governors: Ian Wells

Number of pupils. 160 (including some boarders)
Age range. 2+–11; Boarding from 7+.
Fees. Boarders £3,530. Day pupils: Nursery £120 per session, per term, Preparatory £1,680

St Teresa's Preparatory School provides a happy and stimulating environment where girls of all ages and abilities thrive. The School creates a firm foundation for your daughter's future, equipping her with the necessary knowledge, skills and self-confidence to fulfil her own potential. Girls are enrolled from the age of 2 and prepared for the senior school examination as well as the Common Entrance Examination. We offer a full curriculum enabling the girls to develop strong literacy, numeracy and social skills. Specialist teachers are employed throughout the school, with the National Curriculum forming the basis of our teaching.

The Nursery is a lively, friendly department situated in a light, airy and spacious purpose-built department equipped with computers and modern nursery facilities. Outdoors there is a dedicated playground with adventure play equipment.

At Pre-Prep we recognise that these years are critical in terms of successful physical, social and intellectual development. Small classes enable staff to concentrate on the individual, with reading skills and numeracy developed as a top priority. Specialist teaching is given in ballet, PE, Music and French.

In the Preparatory years the girls follow a broad and challenging curriculum. In addition to the core subjects of Mathematics, French, English and Science they also take Computer studies, Music, Sport, Swimming, Choir and Orchestra. Extra tuition is available to support those with special needs. Many girls also take part in an extensive programme of extra curricular activities which include chess, fencing, country dancing, science, general knowledge clubs, ballet and gym.

St Teresa's offers an extended day, with homework club until 6 pm, and boarding, including occasional overnight options. The school is situated in Effingham and is a feeder school for St Teresa's Senior School.

All denominations are welcome to attend this Catholic School, where Christian values and respect for others are considered important.

Prospectus. A fully illustrated prospectus with up-to-date fee scales and relevant details is available on request.

Charitable status. St Teresa's Preparatory School is a Registered Charity, number 243995. It exists to provide a Christian education for girls. A Catholic foundation where all denominations are welcomed.

Salisbury Cathedral School

1 The Close Salisbury Wilts SP1 2EQ
Tel: (01722) 555300
Fax: (01722) 410910
e-mail: aspire@salisbury.enterprise-plc.com
website: www.eluk.co.uk/scs

Founded in 1091. Co-educational Preparatory, Pre-Preparatory and Choir School.

Chairman of Governors: The Dean of Salisbury, The Very Revd Derek Watson

Head Master: **R M Thackray**, BSc (Hons)

Deputy Head: Mrs C M Rolt, BSc (Hons)

Bursar & Clerk to the Governors: Andrew Craigie, OBE

Number of Pupils. Preparatory: 167 boys and girls (48 boarders); Pre-Prep Department 70 Boys and Girls

Fees. Nursery: (3 years +) £850 (mornings only) and £1,075 (mornings and 2 afternoons); Pre Prep (ages 4–7) £1,214 to £1,367; Year 3: £1,800; Preparatory School: Day £2,675, Boarding: £3,925.

The school was founded in 1091 and is situated in the former Bishop's Palace on a 25 acre site in the beautiful Cathedral Close. There is a self-contained Pre-Prep Department for boys and girls between the ages of four and seven and a Nursery for 3+ years. A complete new boarding house is due to open in 2002.

High academic standards, excellent music and drama. Many scholarships are gained to senior schools. Although the main thrust of the academic work leads towards examinations at 13+, the National Curriculum SATs are taken by all pupils in Years 2 and 6 and some children sit the 11+ tests for the local Grammar Schools. The school also has a fully qualified Individual Needs team.

Facilities include: newly refurbished science laboratory, IT centre, music technology room, gymnasium, large all-weather pitch, extensive playing fields, heated outdoor swimming pool.

Talented sports staff coach all the major team sports and there are regular fixtures.

There are many after-school clubs open to all children in the Preparatory School. (Quality before and after school care is available for children in the Pre-Prep). The boarding house staff operate an "open door" policy to parents, organise many outings and activities and have achieved an enviable reputation for running a truly happy and caring boarding house.

For a prospectus and/or to arrange a vist to the school, please telephone or visit our website.

Charitable status. Salisbury Cathedral School is a Registered Charity, number 309485. It exists to provide high quality education for children.

Sandroyd School

Rushmore Tollard Royal Nr Salisbury Wiltshire SP5 5QD.
Tel: (01725) 516264
Fax: (01725) 516441
e-mail: Sandroyd@dial.pipex.com
website: www.sandroyd.co.uk
Station: Salisbury

Chairman of Governors: W R Hillary, Esq, FRICS

Headmaster: **M J Hatch**, MA (Oxon), AFIMA

Number of Boys. 110 boarders, 40 day boys

Fees per term. Boarding £3,825; Day £3,150. Year 3: Boarding £3,100; Day £2,250.

Sandroyd is set in beautiful parkland in the heart of Cranborne Chase. Primarily a boarding school but with some day places available, all boys benefit from spacious modern accommodation in a secure, family environment.

In recent years major building works have been completed, with the addition of senior boarding wings, dedicated Art/CDT rooms, IT Lab with CD ROMs, an indoor heated swimming pool, junior classroom block, stables, refurbishment of the Chapel and all-weather pitch.

The boys are prepared for Scholarship and Common Entrance examinations to all the leading senior independent schools. Sandroyd is well known for the excellence of its music, both choral and instrumental. There is also a specialist department to help boys with particular learning difficulties. An enthusiastic games staff coach all the major team sports to a high standard and there is also instruction in squash, riding, shooting, judo, fencing and golf.

Visitors are always welcome.

Charitable status. Sandroyd School is a Registered Charity, number 309490. It exists for the purpose of providing education.

Sarum Hall School

15 Eton Avenue London NW3 3EL.
Tel: 020 7794 2261
Fax: 020 7431 7501

Headmistress: **Mrs Jane Scott**, BEd (Hons)

Number of Pupils. 168. All Day, Girls 3–11

Fees. £2,390 per term, including lunch.

The School, which has a Christian (Church of England) foundation, is an educational trust with a Board of Governors, the Chairman of which is Mr B Gorst.

In 1995 the school moved to its new purpose-built premises which provide excellent, spacious facilities, including a large playground, for all pupils. Girls are prepared for senior London day schools and for Common Entrance at 11+. Pupils are not tested on entry, nevertheless the school has an established record of scholarship and examination successes. The school is ambitious for its pupils and believes that in a caring, supportive and imaginative environment, every child can achieve her potential. Pupils are encouraged to develop an interest in learning for itself and an awareness that their success in all fields is dependent on their own efforts. A major investment in computers offers all pupils access to the latest technology. Games, gym or dancing take place daily and other extra curricular activities include: music, art and craft, drama, fencing, cricket and football.

Charitable status. Sarum Hall School is a Registered Charity, number 312721. Its purpose is education.

Scotch College Junior School

Callantina Road Hawthorn 3122 Victoria Australia
Tel: +61 3 9810 4236
Fax: +61 3 9810 4391
e-mail: g.mason@scotch.vic.edu.au
website: http//www.scotch.vic.edu.au

Chairman of Council: Mr M Robinson

Headmaster: **Mr G B Mason**, DipT, BEd, MACE

Number of Boys. 450 day boys aged 5 to 12.
Fees. $10,389–$11,118 per annum

Scotch College is the oldest surviving school in Victoria. The site on which the school is located is an ideal one close to the city and major residential areas with access to the Yarra River and containing extensive grounds for sporting and relaxation purposes. The College conducts its educational programme in connection with the Presbyterian Church of Victoria.

The Junior School is situated independently on the main College campus but is able to make use of considerable facilities available to both parts of Scotch. The main classrooms and administration building is tudor in style and was recently extended and completely refurbished to the highest of standards. Facilities include classrooms, an assembly hall, library and technology centre, a music building, art centre and gymnasium.

A full-time teaching staff of thirty-four teach traditional academic subjects with an emphasis on seeking excellence in all areas of life. Considerable support at academic and personal levels is available to boys requiring assistance as is an extensive programme for those with greater talents. Traditional academic study is complemented by a strong programme in music, fine arts, sport, physical education and outdoor activities at higher levels. Computers are used by all boys from Prep to Year 6 as an aid to studies in many subject areas with hi-tech equipment available for use by more able boys.

Information on the school is available from the Headmaster. Formal enrolment applications should be submitted to the Scotch College Director of Admissions.

Seaton House School

67 Banstead Road South Sutton Surrey SM2 5LH
Tel: 020 8642 2332
Fax: 020 8642 2332

Headmistress: **Mrs V A Richards,** BSc, PGCE

Number of Pupils. Main School: Girls only (aged 4+ to 11): 120
Nursery: Boys & Girls (aged 2+ to 5): 50
Fees. £420-£1,250 per term.

Seaton House School was founded in 1930 by Miss Violet Henry and there is a strong tradition of family loyalty to the school. The School aims to provide children with a thorough educational grounding to give them a good start in their school lives and to instil sound learning habits in a secure, disciplined but friendly atmosphere. Boys are prepared for admission to a number of pre-preparatory schools and the girls are prepared for various entrance examinations, both in the London Borough of Sutton and for the Common Entrance examination at 11+ required by some independent day and boarding schools. Our highly qualified and committed staff create a stimulating learning environment and small classes ensure that all children have the necessary individual attention and encouragement to achieve the highest standards.

We follow the broad outlines of the National Curriculum with generous provision for Music, French and Physical Education. There is a School Orchestra and Choir and, each year, all children have the opportunity to take part in dramatic productions. School sports teams enjoy considerable success when they compete regularly against neighbouring schools and each Spring we host our own Netball Tournament. Years 5 and 6 have the opportunity to experience outdoor pursuits during their annual week's residential course. With the opening to the Millennium Learning Zone, in September 2000, the School now has excellent Library and ICT resources. The range of extra-curricular activities offered is becoming more extensive and complements the established provision of after-school care.

Pastoral care is of the highest calibre with form staff taking a keen interest in all their pupils. Courtesy, good manners and kindness are expected as the norm and children are encouraged to develop initiative, independence and confidence. There is a strong house system in the main school which stimulates good community awareness.

The prospectus is available upon request and the Headmistress is always happy to meet parents and arrange for them to look around the School.

Charitable status. Seaton House School is a Registered Charity, number 800673. It exists to provide education for children.

Sevenoaks Preparatory School

Godden Green Sevenoaks Kent TN15 0JU.
Tel: (01732) 762336
Fax: (01732) 764279
e-mail: headmaster@sevenoaksprep.kent.sch.uk

Headmaster: **Edward Oatley**, IAPS

Number of Pupils. 230 Boys aged 2½ to 13+; 120 Girls aged 2½ to 13.

Fees per term: £750 (Age 3½). From £1,440 rising by age to £2,020

Facilities. This Day school stands on a spacious 5 acre site surrounded by 14 acre playing fields which border Knole Park. Buildings include a fully equipped Science laboratory, individual subject rooms for Art, Design & Technology, Music and Computers, Library, School Hall, Squash Court. The extensive sports fields are supplemented with a large tarmac floodlit sports area and two tennis courts. There is a separate play area and Adventure playground for the Junior School.

Academic. Children are accepted from 2½ years of age into the Junior School buildings from which they transfer at 7 years to the Senior School. The curriculum leads the pupils towards Common Entrance Examination at 13, corresponds to the National Curriculum and is an invigorating blend of the best modern and traditional teaching methods available – the "3 R's" working alongside the keyboard skills of Computers and Information Technology.

Class teaching is the norm until age 9 when the transition to specialist teaching of all subjects begins. French is begun at age 6 and Spanish at 10. Science, Computers, Art, Music, Design and Humanities complete a full, well balanced timetable which encourage the fostering of good work and learning habits.

Each pupil is encouraged to fulfil their potential in every field, to involve themselves fully in all activities open to them and to develop a thirst for knowledge that will remain with them throughout their lives. The school has a noticeably happy, family atmosphere which enlivens the hive of activity forever available for the pupils to experience.

Extra-Curricular. Sport, Music and Drama are integral to the life of the school. In sport, Soccer, Rugby, Cricket, Tennis, Hockey, Athletics, Swimming, Rounders, Lacrosse, Netball, Cross Country and Judo are all taught and matches are played at four age levels against local preparatory and maintained schools.

In Music, there is a school Orchestra and Choir and the individual teaching of most instruments is taught by our extensive peripatetic staff. Concerts are regularly produced, as are plays by our Drama staff at varying ages.

The school provides After-School care until 6 pm each evening within which a host of clubs and activities such as Chess and Table Tennis are available. Holiday activities are regularly arranged by the Headmaster, staff and parents.

The school is supported by an active and thriving parents association. Prospective parents are welcome to visit the school during termtime and during the holidays.

Sherborne House School

Lakewood Road Chandler's Ford Hants SO53 1EU.
Tel: (02380) 252440
Fax: (02380) 252553

***Headmistress:* Mrs L M Clewer**, MA(Ed)

Age Range. Girls and Boys from 2½–11

Fees. £1,240–£1,635 including lunches, (all day pupils)

Number of Pupils. 279

Sherborne House School, founded in 1933, takes children from Chandler's Ford, Winchester, Romsey, Southampton and surrounding villages.

The delightful 4 acres of wooded grounds have netball and short tennis courts, dedicated play areas and sports fields for soccer, cricket, rounders and athletics.

We have an enviable reputation for excellent Common Entrance and SATS results. Our outstanding results are achieved by a combination of good facilities, highly qualified staff, smaller classes and high tech learning support. Our broad curriculum emphasises literacy, numeracy and science but not at the expense of other subjects. We boast a full sports programme with strong music and drama, ICT and ex-curricula activities.

Sherborne House has a particularly happy atmosphere where a child's self-esteem is paramount. Good manners and caring for others is the norm. We expect children to work hard but to have lots of fun doing so, and take pride in our multi-sensory teaching methods and cognitive curriculum to accelerate our pupils learning. The pastoral care at Sherborne House is outstanding and the pupils are confident, disciplined, purposeful and happy.

We encourage regular contact with and support from parents.

Entry. Entrance to the prep school is by a trial day and assessment as appropriate.

School Hours. School is open from 8 am to 5.30 pm. Class times are from 8.40 am to 3.30 pm (pre-prep) and 3.50 pm (prep).

Sherborne Preparatory School

Acreman Street Sherborne Dorset DT9 3NY
Tel: 01935 812097
Fax: 01935 813948
e-mail: sherborneprep@hotmail.com

***Headmaster:* P S Tait,** MA, FRSA

Number of Boys and Girls. 204 (Pre-Prep 63, Prep 141).

Fees per term. Boarders: £3,480-£3,850. Day: Nursery £640-£750. Pre-Prep: Reception (Year 2) £1,470. Prep: (Years 3-8) £2,310-£2,570.

Sherborne Preparatory School is an independent co-educational day and boarding school for children aged 2½-13 years. Founded in 1885, the School is set in twelve acres of attractive grounds and gardens in the centre of Sherborne and is well served by road and rail links. Although fully independent, it enjoys a long and close association with its neighbours, Sherborne School and Sherborne School for Girls.

The Pre-Prep Department is housed in a fully-equipped and purpose-built classroom block, with experienced and well-qualified staff providing an excellent ratio of teachers to children.

The Preparatory School (Years 3-8) follows the National Curriculum, leading to Common Entrance and Scholarship examinations in the penultimate and final year groups. Over the last few years our pupils have won a large number of scholarships and awards to leading independent schools, including the top scholarships to Sherborne School, Marlborough and Sherborne School for Girls.

In a recent survey among current parents, points they singled out as strengths of the School included small class sizes; the happy atmosphere and family ethos; the balance between academic and extra-curricular activities; the high academic standards.

Recent developments include a new computer room which has recently come into operation; the setting up of a website; the introduction of English Speaking Board examinations; the annual award of scholarships for academic, music and all-round ability.

Charitable status. Sherborne Preparatory School is a Registered Charity, number 1071494. It exists to provide an all-round education for children.

Shrewsbury House

Ditton Road Surbiton Surrey KT6 6RL.
Tel: 020 8399 3066
Fax: 020 8339 9529
e-mail: office@shrewsburyhouse.kingston.sch.uk

Headmaster: **C M Ross**, BA, HDipEd (Trinity College, Dublin)

Assistant Headmaster: J Cowan, BA (Rhodes University)

Chairman of the Governors: L Lee

Number of Boys. 280 Day

Fees. £2,350

Shrewsbury House was founded in 1865, and moved to its present site in 1910. In 1979 it became an Educational Trust and is administered by a Board of Governors.

Boys are admitted from 7 years of age and are prepared for entry at 13+, either by Scholarship or Common Entrance, to any of the Independent Senior Schools. There are 33 full-time staff, including full-time Directors of Music, Art and Computing. There are also visiting music staff and a French assistant.

The school is fortunate in its extensive land, including on-site playing fields. The main building is Victorian. Its interior has been adapted, furnished and decorated for modern educational needs.

Facilities are constantly being updated and improved. Most recently the following facilities have been added: a heated covered swimming pool, a pottery room, two fully equipped computer rooms, a library, an astroturf cricket wicket, a Science and Classroom Block, and a Sports Hall. Other facilities include an Assembly Hall, floodlit all-weather playing surface, tennis courts, hard cricket nets, Music and practice rooms, Shooting range and Art Room.

The main sports are Association Football, Rugby Football, Cricket and Swimming. At the same time, boys are encouraged to try a variety of the more individual sports such as Tennis, Squash and Golf. In addition, there is ample opportunity for boys to discover other abilities and talents through activities in Music, Art, Craft, technical activities and Drama.

Charitable status. Shrewsbury House School Trust Limited is a Registered Charity, number 277324. It seeks to provide the best possible learning environment for boys aged between 7 and 14 who have the potential for above average academic achievement.

Silcoates Junior School

Wrenthorpe Wakefield West Yorkshire WF2 0PD
Tel: (01924) 885275

Headmaster: **R H Wood,** BEd (Hons), MA

Deputy Head: J C Clewarth, BEd (Hons), MEd

Number of pupils. 199 boys and girls.

Fees. £1,342–£1,792 per term.

Silcoates Junior School is part of the Silcoates School Foundation. The Junior School and the Senior School are on the same campus and share many of its facilities which include the Chapel, Sports Hall, Indoor Swimming Pool, Music School, playing fields, and specialist subject areas for Science, Design Technology and Information Technology.

Music and Drama feature prominently in the life of the school. There is a Junior School Choir, and concerts and musical evenings are held at other times during the year. A major dramatic production is staged annually.

There are ten full-time members of the teaching staff, all of whom are experienced and well qualified. The Junior School is able to call upon the use of specialist teachers from the Senior School for PE, Games, French and Music. In addition, there are various visiting music specialists.

The main games are Rugby, Netball, Association Football, Cricket and Rounders and other important sports are Swimming, Athletics and Cross Country. There are over 30 acres of playing fields.

There is a wide range of activities in which pupils can participate at lunchtimes and after school. These include Computers, Puppets, Chess, Drama, Recorders, Training Band, Canoeing, Sewing and Model Making. The School Camp at Lake Windermere is used for outdoor activities at weekends and in school holidays.

Boys and girls are accepted through an entrance examination and then the pupils are expected to enter Senior School at the age of 11. There is no entrance examination for pupils entering the Senior School, subject to satisfactory progress having been made by the end of Key Stage 2. The entrance examination is held in January for entry in the following September. The tests are in English, Mathematics and Verbal and Non-Verbal Reasoning.

Charitable status. The Junior School, being part of Silcoates School, is a Registered Charity, number 529281. It aims to provide a first-class education for boys and girls.

Skippers Hill Manor Preparatory School

Five Ashes Mayfield TN20 6HR.
Tel: (01825) 830234

Headmaster: **T W Lewis**, BA (Exon), PGCE (London)

Number of Pupils. 104 Day Boys, 62 Day Girls

Fees. Kindergarten (full day) £1,350, (half day) £800, Pre-Prep £2,025, Prep £2,575

The school is set in the beautiful Weald of Sussex in grounds covering 32 acres and was founded in 1945. It caters for boys and girls between the ages of 2½ and 13. A dedicated, qualified staff of twenty prepare children for Common Entrance, Grammar School and Senior Independent Schools Scholarship examinations. Classes are small and individual attention, thereby, guaranteed.

Facilities include a well-stocked library, Gymnasium, individual Music Room, ICT centre, all-weather multi-purpose courts and a covered heated swimming pool.

The main games are hockey, rugby, football and cricket for boys; netball, rounders and cricket for girls. Swimming, gymnastics, ballet and athletics are also given prominence. Leisure pursuits include Judo, Pottery, Arts and Crafts, Vocal Training and Instrumental Music. The Choir and Orchestra are flourishing.

The school is interdenominational in approach and its aim is to help each pupil towards the ultimate goals of self-discipline, common courtesy and the ability to cope with a rapidly changing world.

Solefield Preparatory School

Sevenoaks TN13 1PH.
Tel: (01732) 452142
Fax: (01732) 740388

Headmaster: **P D Evans**, BEd

Chairman of the Governors: H C E Harris

Fees per term. £1,340–£2,050 including lunch.

Number of Boys. 181

Solefield is a Day Preparatory School for boys from 4 to 13. The school was founded in 1948 and is situated in Solefields Road on the south side of Sevenoaks. The main building is a large town house and contains the library, classrooms, kitchen, staff accommodation and the school office. The facilities have been increased considerably to include the Science Block, School Hall, Art Room, Dining Room, Junior Classrooms and Changing Rooms. A new Music School has recently been built. A new computer room and network will be in operation in September 2001. The grounds contain the main school buildings and a large floodlit playground. The playing fields are a short walk from the school. A qualified and graduate staff prepare boys for entry to Independent Senior and Grammar Schools. Solefield has a strong tradition of academic excellence. Emphasis is placed on teaching the 3 R's in a caring yet well-structured atmosphere with close contact maintained between parents and teachers.

The curriculum includes Music, Drama, Art and Design, PE and a number of club activities. Cricket, Soccer and Rugby are the principle games. Tennis, Short Tennis and Swimming are also coached.

Enquiries concerning places and admissions should be made to the Secretary.

Charitable status. Solefield School is a Registered Charity, number 293466. It aims to provide a high quality education to boys aged 4–13.

Sompting Abbotts

Church Lane Sompting Lancing W Sussex BN15 0AZ
Tel: (01903) 235960
Fax: (01903) 210045
e-mail: office@somptingabbotts-prep-school.co.uk
website: www.somptingabbotts-prep-school.co.uk
Station: Worthing Central

Principal: Mrs P M Sinclair

Head Master: **R M Johnson**, CertEd

Number of Pupils. 180

Fees. Weekly Boarders £2,550. Day £1,020 to £1,820 (including luncheons)

Sompting Abbotts School is situated in thirty acres on the south facing slope of the Downs over-looking the sea. It is a well-established preparatory school which was brought to the present site in 1921, and it has been under the personal supervision of the Sinclair family since 1945.

The aim of the school is to provide a well-balanced education in a caring environment, recognising and developing the individual needs of each child, so that maximum potential academic achievement may be gained. Within the community of the school an emphasis is laid on the cultivation of courtesy, self-discipline and respect for one another in order to engender a happy atmosphere.

The school has a vibrant Pre-Preparatory Department which includes lively Nursery and Reception classes. In the Preparatory Department well-equipped Computer and Science Rooms are enjoyed by all ages. The Art and Drama Departments offer wide scope for creativity, and peripatetic teachers provide tuition for a range of musical instruments.

Weekly boarding is available for the boys from Monday morning until Friday evening, and flexible boarding is also available.

South Lee School

Nowton Road Bury St Edmunds Suffolk IP33 2BT.
Tel: (01284) 754654
Fax: (01284) 706178
e-mail: southlee@southlee.demon.co.uk

Headmaster: **Mr Derek Whipp**, MA, CertEd

Chairman of the Governors: Mr A Holliday

Number of Pupils. 294 pupils: Girls and Boys 2–13

Fees. £1,500–£1,870 per term, including lunches

South Lee is a stimulating and exciting place for children to learn and develop. From an early age pupils are taught the traditional subjects, emphasising Mathematics, Science and English, within a wider curriculum which incorporates the use of the latest developments in technology and educational resources.

The school is situated near the A14, has purpose-built, modern classrooms and the use of outstanding sports grounds.

The full range of academic subjects is taught, encompassing the National Curriculum. South Lee also offers its pupils vital opportunities for self-expression and individual development through study of the Arts, Drama, Music and a broad range of outdoor, sporting and extra-curricular activities.

The Nursery, catering for 2 to 4 year old children, makes learning fun.

The Pre-Prep is essentially class-based though specialist staff teach French, Physical Education, Music and Information Technology.

The Prep school is also particularly well staffed with experienced, qualified teachers covering the full range of Common Entrance subjects through to 13+. Commended by the Central Bureau for its European studies within the curriculum, the school makes full use of its numerous international connections. This enables the pupils to benefit greatly from an extensive language programme where French and German are taught.

Control is vested in a Board of Governors, the majority of whom are present parents and the school is run as a non-profit making Limited Company and is a registered charity.

The Southport School Preparatory School

Winchester Street Southport Queensland 4215 Australia
Tel: 07 55 31 9943
Fax: 07 55 31 0542
e-mail: prep@tss.qld.edu.au

The School is a member of the Association of Heads of Independent Schools of Australia, The Greater Public Schools Association, Junior School Heads Association of

Australia, Incorporated Association of Preparatory Schools and The Round Square Conference.

Chairman of Council: P R Hobart, DUniv, JP, AREI

Headmaster: B A Cook, BSc, DipEd (Melbourne), BEd (Monash), MA (University College, Durham), MACE

Master of the Preparatory School: **T R Wood**, MA, BEd, DipT(Prim), MACEA, MACE, CDec

Number of Boys. 485. Boarding places are available from Year 5.

Fees per annum (4 term year). Lower Prep (Reception 3): $5,820; Upper Prep (Years 4-7): $7,431; Boarding - additional (Years 5-7): $9,598.

Overseas Full Fee Paying Students, per annum. Lower Prep (Reception 3): $10,840; Upper Prep (Years 4-7): $12,576; Boarding additional (Years 5-7): $9,141.

The Southport School, founded in 1901, is an Anglican day and boarding school located on a magnificent 40 hectares site along the banks of the Nerang River, in the heart of Australia's Gold Coast. It enrols boys from Reception to Year 12 (4½ to university entrance). The Preparatory School, on its own neighbouring campus shares senior school facilities but stands apart, a specialised domain for younger boys from Reception to Year 7. Its curriculum is 'needs-based' and in accordance with national guidelines. The Common Room prides itself upon its proactive stance and involvement in curriculum development and implementation. So too, in fostering an extensive co-curricular programme. There are three formal choirs, a first year free instrumental programme nurturing ensembles, bands and orchestras. A full range of GPS sport is played on weekends. There are four Houses. The boys of Year 7 are 'Buddies' to those in Year 1 and play a vital role in leading the day to day interaction of their School. TSS Prep is a busy active boys' place!

Spratton Hall Preparatory School

Spratton Northampton NN6 8HP.
Tel: (01604) 847292
Fax: (01604) 820844
e-mail: office@sprattonhall.demon.co.uk

Chairman: C A S McAra, Esq, BA

Headmaster: **R A Barlow**, BSc(Econ), MSc(Econ), PhD, PGCE

Number of Pupils. 407

Fees. £1,700–£1,910. Pre-prep £1,205–£1,370. Nursery £520 (mornings only at present). Fees include stationery, lunch and all academic books.

Spratton Hall is a coeducational school for pupils aged 3–13+. It is situated in rolling countryside 7 miles north of Northampton at the edge of the village of Spratton, just off the A5199.

The School has just completed an extensive 10 year redevelopment programme which includes a purpose built Information and Communications Technology Centre, a Music Centre, Sports Hall, Science Block, ACDT Workshop, Art and Ceramics Centre. The library is housed in the main Georgian building; it has been tastefully refurnished in period style and is generously stocked. The School is a charitable trust and invests any surplus income into the ongoing re-development programme.

The 22 acres of grounds include all the normal sports facilities for rugby, cricket, hockey, athletics, soccer, tennis, netball and cross country. Two all-weather surfaces for tennis, netball and hockey have recently been opened.

Pupils are prepared for Common Entrance and Scholarship Examinations to their Senior Schools; 25% have gained awards over the last six years and 101 over the last ten years. The maximum class size in the Senior School is 16, and there are generally three forms in each year group. Pupils are placed in academic sets according to ability for the core subjects of English, French, Mathematics and Science.

There are 32 academic staff with 15 visiting teachers for music, speech and drama, dyslexia, ballet, golf, short tennis and fencing. There is a wide choice of after-school activities for pupils in the Senior School; these include chess, ceramics, ICT, aerobics, electronics, Spanish and textiles.

The School has a fine tradition of orchestral and choral music and performs in Cathedrals nationwide.

Charitable status. Spratton Hall is a Registered Charity, number 309925. It exists to provide education for boys and girls.

Stamford Junior School

Stamford Lincolnshire PE9 2LR
Tel: (01780) 484400
Fax: (01780) 484401
e-mail: headjs@shs.lincs.sch.uk

Stamford Junior School, along with Stamford High School (girls) and Stamford School (boys), is one of three schools in the historic market town of Stamford comprising the Stamford Endowed Schools Educational Charity. The schools are under a single Governing Body and overall management and leadership of the Principal and allow continuity of education for boys and girls from 2 to 18, including boarding from age 8. Each school has its own Head and staff.

Chairman of Governors: M E Llowarch, Esq, FCA

Principal: Dr P R Mason, BSc, PhD, FRSA

Headmistress: **Miss E M Craig**

Number in School. 310 children.

Fees (September 1999). Boarders £3,316 per term; Weekly £3,300 per term; Day £1,556 per term.

In 1999 the Governing Body agreed to restructure the schools with effect from September 2000 to establish a co-educational Junior School (2-11, including nursery), and two senior schools: Stamford High School (girls 11-18) and Stamford School (boys 11-18). The phased transition of these changes will be completed by September 2002.

The Junior School educates boys and girls up to the age of 11 (including boarders from age 8), when boys move on to Stamford School and girls to Stamford High School. Admission from the Junior School to the two senior schools is based on progress and without further entrance testing.

The Junior School occupies its own spacious grounds, bordering the River Welland, overlooking the sports fields and open countryside, the boarding houses, the sports hall and the swimming pool on the same site. It is on the south west outskirts of Stamford within easy reach of the A1.

Entry to the School is according to registration at 4+ and assessment and interview in all other age groups.

The attractive and varied curriculum is designed to establish firm foundations in oracy, literacy and numeracy whilst providing excellent opportunities for music, drama, art and design and for acquiring technical and physical skills. The aims of the school are to develop the talents and potential of all the children.

There are 20 full-time staff, with specialist teachers in

physical education, swimming, art and music, and visiting teachers offering a variety of sports, dance, speech and drama.

Boarding. The co-educational Boarding House (St Michael's) is run in a homely, family style under the experienced leadership of Mr and Mrs Backhouse. Boys and girls are accepted as full or weekly boarders from the age of 8. Occasional or flexi-boarding is accommodated where possible and according to family need. A full programme of activities takes place at weekends so that boarders enjoy a rich and varied week.

Charitable status. As part of the Stamford Endowed Schools, Stamford Junior School is a Registered Charity, number 527618. It exists to provide education for children.

Stancliffe Hall

Darley Dale Matlock Derbyshire DE4 2HJ.
Tel: (01629) 732310
Fax: (01629) 734509
Stations: Matlock (10 minutes) and Chesterfield (20 minutes)

Head Master: **A M Lamb**, CertEd

Number. Prep School, 60 boys, 26 girls; Pre Prep, 50 boys, 26 girls

Termly fees. (inclusive) £3,075 Weekly Boarders; £2,395 Day Children; £1,315 Pre-prep (including lunches); Nursery £1,315

Staffing. 16 full time and 6 part-time staff, all of whom are fully qualified, teach the 14 classes. A range of other specialist peripatetic staff provide expert tuition and coaching in The Arts and Sport.

Location. The school, which stands in its own 34 acres of woods and parkland on the edge of the Peak District National Park, is within easy reach of Nottingham, Derby, Chesterfield and Sheffield and is close to the motorway network.

Facilities. The facilities include modern well-equipped classrooms and science laboratories, IT and DT centres, an art room with integral pottery, a Special Needs Unit, a photographic dark room, a multi-purpose hall with integral stage and theatre facilities as well as a purpose-built indoor climbing wall, a private chapel, a 9 hole golf course, tennis courts, a heated swimming pool, games pitches and a professionally mapped orienteering course.

Aims.

- To prepare children for entrance to independent senior schools, whether by Common Entrance or Scholarship. (In the last five years a total of 32 scholarships have been won for academic excellence, art, DT, sport and all-round contribution.)
- To occupy children productively in order to broaden their horizons across a wide spectrum of academic, practical and sporting activities. To this end, each child's personal progress and welfare is monitored by both pastoral and academic staff.
- To help children to understand the importance that the school attaches to family values and to the need for each individual to make a valuable contribution during their school career and beyond.

Curriculum. By the time a child is 13, their timetable will have included: English, Mathematics, Science, French, German, History, Geography, Religious Studies, Design Technology, Information Technology, Music, Drama, Art, Physical Education. Latin is available as an optional subject.

Extra-Curricular Activities. Sports include Rugby, Soccer, Hockey, Cricket, Tennis, Swimming, Athletics, Netball, Rounders and Golf. Children follow a programme of other activities which include such things as Outdoor Pursuits, Cookery, Squash and Pottery. Drama and Music are a regular feature of each term's calendar. There is a flourishing Orchestra, Recorder Group, Clarinet Choir and Concert Choir.

Stanway School

Chichester Road Dorking Surrey RH4 1LR.
Tel: (01306) 882151
Fax: (01306) 882656

Motto: *Initium Sapientiae*

Chairman of the Board of Governors: G Lee-Steere, MA, DL

Head: **Mr P H Rushforth**, BEd, MA

Number of Pupils. 150 Day pupils

Fees. £150 per morning per term; £80 per afternoon (Nursery). Main School £1,610–£1,885 per term (includes lunches). Sibling discount applies to families with 2 or more children in school simultaneously.

Stanway is a day Preparatory School for girls aged 2½–11 and for boys aged 2½–8. Founded in 1934, the School is now an Educational Trust, administered by its Board of Governors.

The Nursery Department was the first of its kind in the town, and since 1995 has been housed in a beautiful, new purpose-built unit.

Classes are small, allowing for maximum individual attention.

Boys are prepared for entrance tests for day and boarding Preparatory Schools.

Girls are prepared for the Common Entrance Examination to independent boarding schools and entrance examinations to other senior schools.

The practice of complementing the work of the form teacher with specialist subject staff, started in the Lower School, is continued in the Upper School. The syllabus is widened and deepened to meet, and generally to exceed, the criteria for the National Curriculum. The emphasis remains on achieving proficiency in English, Mathematics and Science, but other subjects studied include Religious Studies, French, Latin, History, Geography, Information and Communication Technology, Design Technology, Art, Music, Speech and Drama, Physical Education. Academic standards are high and the main subjects are taught by graduate staff. The School offers a wide range of activities and clubs including Ballet, Piano, Violin, Clarinet, Speech and Drama, Chess, Tennis, Gymnastics, Swimming and Spanish.

The School has light, modern classrooms, a Computer Room, Science Laboratory, Design Technology Room, an acoustically designed Music Room and a heated Swimming Pool. The School minibus is used for extra-curricular activities and for visits to places of interest.

Stanway aims to provide a sound, all-round education in a happy, caring environment. Pupils are expected to conform to high standards of courtesy and behaviour. At the same time each child is treated as an individual, and experienced teachers with a genuine concern for the well-being of their pupils pay due regard to their differing needs.

A prospectus and full particulars will be sent on application to the Secretary.

Charitable status. Stanway School is a Registered Charity, number 312040. It aims to provide a sound, all-round education in a happy, caring environment.

Stockport Grammar Junior School

Buxton Road Stockport SK2 7AF
Tel: 0161 419 2405
Fax: 0161 419 2407

Chairman of Governors: C E Speight, FCA, ATII

***Headmaster:* L Fairclough,** BA

Number of Pupils. 435 (228 boys, 207 girls, aged 4-11)

Fees per term. £1,415, plus £93 for lunch.

Entry is mainly at 4+ and 7+ following assessment, with occasional places available at other ages. Stockport Grammar Junior School is a happy school, where children are encouraged to develop their strengths. A broad curriculum is taught and academic standards are very high. There are specialist facilities and teaching in science, ICT, physical education, music, art and design technology. A large number of pupils learn to play a musical instrument and tuition is available for many orchestral instruments. French is taught throughout. All children have a weekly swimming lesson in the School's pool. Both infant and junior children can choose to join in the numerous lunch-time and after school clubs and activities.

The Junior School and the Senior School share the same site. The vast majority of pupils move into the Senior School at 11, having passed the Entrance Examinations.

Hockey, netball, football, cricket and athletics are the main sports. Swimming, tennis, rounders, cross-country and rugby are also offered. There is a full range of sporting fixtures and regular music and drama productions. All junior pupils have the opportunity to participate in residential visits, which include outdoor pursuits and a trip to Paris.

Before and after school care is available and holiday play schemes are run at Easter and in the summer.

Facilities are excellent. In addition to specialist teaching rooms, which include a computer room and a science laboratory, there are extensive playing fields, a large all-weather area, new sports hall and drama theatre.

Charitable status. Stockport Grammar School is a Registered Charity, number 525936. It exists to provide education for children.

Stoke Brunswick

Ashurst Wood Nr East Grinstead West Sussex RH19 3PF.
Tel: (01342) 828200
Fax: (01342) 828201
e-mail: headmaster@stokebrunswick.co.uk
website: stokebrunswick.co.uk
Station: East Grinstead

Chairman: D Waddington, MA, DL

***Headmaster:* W M Ellerton,** CertEd (London)

Number of Boys and Girls. 160 (10 weekly boarders); 100 boys, 60 girls. Pre-Prep 45

Fees. Weekly Boarders £3,345 per term. Day £2,760 per term. Pre-prep £730–£1,405 per term.

Stoke House and Brunswick (each school being a century old) amalgamated in 1965 into their present spacious premises, the oldest part of which is the west wing which was originally John of Gaunt's hunting lodge in Ashdown Forest. The school is set in 32 acres of grounds which include a covered swimming pool, adventure playground, hard tennis courts, golf course and ample playing fields. There is also a Chapel plus classroom blocks and gym. A recent addition to the school is a new Design and Technology Centre which includes a Computer Room linked to computer network in each classroom.

Entry to the school is by assessment and report. The Mervyn Goldman Awards Scholarship (up to the value of 50% of the fees), is held in March for entry the following September and there are also Music Scholarships.

Soccer, Rugby, Cricket, Netball, Hockey and Rounders are the main games. Other sports which are taught include Athletics, Golf, Riding, Swimming and Tennis.

The staff consist of 18 full-time experienced teachers. Health and domestic arrangements are the responsibility of the Headmaster's wife and a matron.

Stoke Brunswick is a charitable trust administered by governors of wide professional and educational experience.

There is a Pre-Preparatory and Nursery department in the grounds for boys and girls aged 3–7. Prospectus and details on application.

Charitable status. Stoke Brunswick School Trust Limited is a Registered Charity, number 307011. It exists to provide high quality education for boys and girls.

Stoneygate School

254 London Road Leicester LE2 1RP.
Tel: (0116) 2707536
Junior School London Road Great Glen Leics LE8 9DT
Tel: (0116) 2592282

***Headmaster:* J H Morris,** MA (Emmanuel College, Cambridge), CertEd

Age range. 3-13 years.

Number of Pupils. Day Boys: 250. Day Girls: 140

Fees. From £1,425–£1,920 (inclusive of meals)

The aims of the School are to provide a first class academic grounding and good education in an atmosphere which encourages participation in all aspects of school life including sport, music and the arts.

There are 38 well qualified and experienced full time members of the teaching staff, together with a number of ancillary helpers and peripatetic staff for music and some other specialist activities. Academic standards are high with most children continuing their education at first class day or boarding independent schools where many Scholarships have been won.

There are all the usual facilities including a fully equipped and networked Computer room and laboratories. The School has also a fine sporting and musical tradition.

The Junior School is on a separate site a few minutes from the main school. It is set in splendid surroundings and is fully self-sufficient; its facilities include sports fields, gym, science block, assembly hall/theatre and swimming pool.

Stormont

The Causeway Potters Bar Herts EN6 5HA
Tel: (01707) 654037
Fax: (01707) 663295
e-mail: admin@stormont.herts.sch.uk

Chairman of Council of Management: Mr T M Newland.

***Headmistress:* Mrs M Johnston,** BA Hons, PGCE

Number of Pupils. 170 day girls aged 4 to 11 years.

Fees. £1,910–£2,030 per term (including lunch). There are no compulsory extras.

The School was founded in 1944 and has occupied its attractive Victorian House since then. There is a modern purpose-built Hall, newly built Lower School formroom block, Gymnasium and Dining Room. The old stables have been converted to provide well-equipped rooms for Art, Pottery, Design Technology, Science and French. A Millennium Building with a Drama/Music Studio and an Information and Communication Technology Suite was opened in September 2000. The school has two tennis courts, a playground, its own two acre playing field and the use of a swimming pool.

The staff is well qualified and experienced and the girls are prepared for entry to a wide range of senior schools at the age of eleven. The school is an educational trust and is administered by a Council of Management.

Charitable status. Stormont School is a Registered Charity, number 311079. It exists to establish and carry on a school where children may receive a sound education.

The Stroud School

Highwood House Romsey Hampshire SO51 9ZH.
Tel: (01794) 513231
Fax: (01794) 514432

Headmaster: **A J L Dodds,** MA (Cantab), DMS

Deputy Head: Mrs J E Gregory, BEd Hons (King Alfred College), CertEd (Whitelands College)

Director of Studies: Mrs A E Fleming, BA

Chairman of Governors: R H Trickey, BA

Number of Pupils. 333. 216 Boys, 117 Girls

Fees per term. Upper School £2,575, Middle School £2,315, Pre-Preparatory £1,565, Nursery £725

Stroud is a co-educational day school consisting of a Nursery, to which children are accepted at the age of 3, a Pre-preparatory Department 4–6, and Prep School 7–13. Pupils are prepared for entrance to the senior Independent or Grammar School of their choice and encouraged to sit for scholarships if academically able.

The School stands on the outskirts of Romsey in its own grounds of 20 acres, which include playing fields, a heated swimming pool, tennis courts, riding arena, lawns and gardens. The main team games for boys are cricket, hockey, rugby and soccer, and for girls hockey, rounders and netball. Both boys and girls play tennis.

Music and drama play an important part in the life of the School. A wide variety of instruments is taught and children are encouraged to join the school orchestra. Each year there is a musical production, the Carol Service is held in Romsey Abbey and there is an Arts Festival at which the children's work is displayed. Ballet and dance are also available.

The Stroud School Association, run by the parents, holds many social activities and helps to raise money for amenities, but its main function is to enable parents to get to know each other and the staff.

The Study Preparatory School

Camp Road Wimbledon Common London SW19 4UN
Tel: 020 8947 6969

Headmistress: **Mrs Lindsay Bond,** MA (Cantab)

Age Range. 4–11
Number in School. 330 approximately
Fees per term. £1,835–£2,085

The Study is a Preparatory School for girls aged 4 to 11, situated close to Wimbledon Common. Girls are prepared for both boarding and day school examinations at 11+.

We aim to provide an environment which is calm, secure and orderly, yet at the same time stimulating and challenging. Girls are encouraged to gain in confidence, work hard, learn to think independently and experience the satisfaction which comes from their own achievement and successes. We expect good manners and high standards of behaviour and encourage girls to be responsible and considerate.

The school is spacious and well-equipped and we have an enthusiastic and well qualified staff.

Charitable status. The Study (Wimbledon) Ltd is a Registered Charity, number 271012. It exists to provide education for girls from 4 to 11.

Summer Fields

Oxford OX2 7EN.
Tel: (01865) 454433
Fax: (01865) 459200
Station: Oxford

Headmaster: **R F Badham-Thornhill,** BA Hons (Exeter), PGCE

Deputy Headmaster: A P W Bishop, BSc, PGCE

Number of Boys. 245 Boarders and 10 Day Boys

Fees. £4,150 Boarding, £2,970 Day

Up to three Academic Scholarships and one Music Scholarship (each in value up to half the Boarding Fees) may be awarded annually. For further details write to the Headmaster.

Charitable status. Summer Fields is a Registered Charity, number 309683. It exists to provide education for boys.

Sunderland High School Junior School

Ashbrooke Road Sunderland SR2 7JA
Tel: (0191) 514 3278
Fax: (0191) 565 6510
e-mail: tonstall@freeuk.com
website: www.sunderlandhigh.sunderland.sch.uk

Headmaster: **Mr J M Turner,** BEd (Hons), DipEd, ACP

Chairman of School Council: Mr J Ward, OBE

Number in school. 290 co-educational pupils, aged 2 to 11 years.

Fees. Nursery (mornings) £10.50 per session; Nursery (afternoons) £6.50 per session; Nursery (full time) £17 per day; Infants £1,180; Juniors £1,445. Lunches are extra.

The school was founded in 1884 by The Church Schools Company as a girls' school. The school became co-educational in 1993. Tonstall House is a new (1994) purpose-built building which includes specialist areas for Science, Music, Art Design Technology and Information and Communication Technology. The school is set in pleasant grounds in a residential area and boasts a sports field, an all-weather astroturf pitch, netball courts as well as a large sports hall. The classrooms are spacious and there are separate Infants and Junior Libraries.

The self-contained Nursery operates on a flexible basis and the school offers early morning supervision from 8 am and an after-school club which operates until 5.30 pm.

Holiday Clubs operate throughout all school breaks (excepting Christmas) at a charge of £12 per day.

There are typically 16 children in a class at Reception, 18 in other Infant classes and 20 during the Junior years. The school follows the National Curriculum with German as a foreign language from Reception. Specialist teaching is provided in all subjects in the Junior years.

We aim to provide a broad and balanced curriculum with an emphasis on a Christian ethos. There is a House system which operates in the Junior years and pupils remain in the same House upon transfer to the Senior School. A wide range of clubs and activities is provided both at lunchtime and after school. The school runs its own Cub and Beaver pack. Music tuition in a wide range of instruments is available. Music concerts and drama productions take place at various stages during the school year.

The main school sports are football, hockey, netball, tennis and cricket although pupils are able to participate in a wide range of sports both within the sporting programme and through activities.

Pupils from Reception to Year 6 take lunch, which is cooked on the premises. Tea is provided for pupils who stay on in the after-school club.

Charitable status. Sunderland High School Junior School is a Registered Charity, number 1016538. It exists to provide education for boys and girls.

Sunningdale School

Sunningdale Berks SL5 9PY.
Tel: (01344) 620159
Station: Sunningdale

Headmasters: **A J N Dawson**, Dip, IAPS, **T M E Dawson**, Dip, IAPS

Number of Boys. 105
Fees. £3,330 (no compulsory extras)
Sunningdale is a family owned school sending most of its boys to Eton, Harrow and Stowe.

Sunninghill Preparatory School

South Court South Walks Dorchester Dorset DT1 1EB
Tel: (01305) 262306
Fax: (01305) 261254
e-mail: sunprepschool@euphony.net

Headmaster: **C S Pring**, BSc (Hons), PGCE

Chairman of Governors: D M Lang, Esq

Number of Children. Nursery (3–5) 17 girls, 14 boys; Pre-Prep (5–8) 31 girls, 30 boys; Main School (8–13) 50 girls, 52 boys

Fees at September 2000. These range from £645 per term in the three-morning nursery to £1,420 per term for children over the age of eight. There are no compulsory extras, but a cooked lunch costs £135 per term.

Staff. There are 11 full time and 7 part-time fully qualified staff.

The school is a completely co-educational day school, with a similar number of girls and boys in each form.

Founded in 1939, Sunninghill became a Charitable Trust in 1969. It moved to its present site in January 1997 and has its own swimming pool, tennis courts and extensive grounds. Children are prepared for the Common Entrance examination to any Independent Senior School, and those with particular ability may be entered for scholarships. Over the years the school has attained many academic successes, but the broad curriculum also includes drama, art, craft, music and physical education.

Games are played on four afternoons a week and these include hockey, netball and rounders for the girls, and hockey, rugby, association football and cricket for the boys. In the summer term both boys and girls participate in athletics, swimming and tennis.

Out of school activities include choir, treble recorder, music club, BAGA Gymnastics, Outdoor Pursuits, Swimming and Judo; and there is a flourishing Parents' Association, which ensures that parents and staff get to know each other and work together for the good of the children and the School.

The prospectus is available on request.

Charitable status. Sunninghill Preparatory School is a Registered Charity, number 1024774. It exists to provide education for boys and girls.

Sunnymede School

Birkdale Southport PR8 2BN.
Tel: (01704) 568593
Fax: (01704) 551745
e-mail: sunnymedeschool@btinternet.com

Headmaster: **S J Pattinson**, CertEd, BA

Numbers. 133. Co-educational day pupils
Fees. (inclusive of meals) £895–£1,435 per term. There are no compulsory extras.

Sunnymede aims to cater for the individual needs of children between the ages of three and eleven. In addition to the full range of National Curriculum, pupils are introduced to a wide variety of subjects, taught by specialist teachers. These include French, Drama, Pottery and Dance.

Sport plays an important part in school life, for those who are keen to be involved. A wide choice is offered, but the concentration is upon soccer, hockey, netball and cricket.

Music is especially strong, both individually and through the orchestra and choir. The Director of Music is supported by visiting teachers.

Drama also receives a high profile, and the school entertains parents and the community each year with a production at the Southport Arts Centre.

The school is situated close to the town centre of Southport, overlooking the coastline, and has pleasant gardens from which the children benefit.

Surbiton Preparatory School (CSC)

3 Avenue Elmers Surbiton Surrey KT6 4SP
Tel: 020 8546 5245
Fax: 020 8547 0026
e-mail: Surbprep@hotmail.com

***Headmaster:* S J Pryce,** MA (Surrey), BA (Open), CertEd (London), FRSA

Chairman of School Council: Mrs M Klat-Hicks

Number of Pupils. 140 day boys

Fees. For Autumn Term 2000 £1,307 to £1,779. Lunches are extra. A reduction in fees applies when two or more children from the same family attend the Preparatory and either the Junior or Senior Girls Schools. Reductions are also made for children of members of the Clergy.

Established in 1862 the School became the Boys' Preparatory School of Surbiton High School and thus part of the Church Schools Company in 1987. Situated in a large Victorian Villa in Avenue Elmers the school shares the facilities offered at the High School including access to those in the Surbiton Assembly Rooms and Hinchley Wood Playing Fields.

Boys join the school at 4+ (Reception) although places in other forms are occasionally available. The School is single form entry and at the 11+ stage all pupils take Entrance Examinations to their chosen Senior School.

At Surbiton Preparatory School we have contact with some 20 Senior Schools in South-West London and North Surrey. All of these schools have strong academic traditions and reputations, those in the maintained sector are established selective Boys' Secondary Schools. Regularly the children's success in entry examinations allows the opportunity to choose between three or more senior schools and many pupils gain scholarship awards.

Surbiton Preparatory School follows an enhanced National Curriculum combining traditional values with the best of modern methods. A high standard of written and practical work is expected. French, Music and Physical Education are taught by specialist teachers throughout the school and Information Technology is a particular strength. In addition to a networked and Internet linked computer room each classroom has its own multi-media facility. Sound teaching is frequently supported by visits to outside venues and by visits from speakers, theatre groups and musicians. Further opportunities to develop interests and enthusiasm are provided by a wide range of extra-curricular activities.

The development of a thirty acre playing field complex at Hinchley Wood allows the boys access to floodlit tennis areas and Astro Turf playing surfaces. Canoeing and Outdoor Pursuits are presently being introduced into the Physical Education programme for the children.

At Surbiton Preparatory School we work with parents to ensure that each child develops intellectually, physically, socially, morally and spiritually into a confident, happy individual. The boys are introduced to a variety of different experiences in a secure, caring and stimulating environment. The natural curiosity of every child is fostered and developed within a traditional academically based environment. We hope, thus, to encourage a positive attitude towards education and develop boys' self-motivation.

Charitable status. Surbiton Preparatory School is governed by The Church Schools Company, a Registered Charity, number 1016538.

Sussex House

68 Cadogan Square London SW1X 0EA.
Tel: 020 7584 1741
Fax: 020 7589 2300
Station: Sloane Square

Chairman of the Governors: Michael Goedhuis, MBA

***Headmaster:* Nicholas Kaye**, MA (Magdalene, Cambridge), ACP, FRSA

Deputy Headmaster: Paul Kennedy, BA (Newcastle), MA (Kent)

Number of Boys. 180

Fees. £2,420 per term.

Founded in 1952, Sussex House is situated in the heart of Chelsea in a fine Norman Shaw house in Cadogan Square. Its Gymnasium and Music School are housed in a converted chapel in Cadogan Street. The school is an independent trust with its own Board of Governors and in recent years has undertaken a series of new initiatives and developments.

There is a full-time teaching staff of 18. Creative subjects are given strong emphasis and throughout the school boys take Music and Art. Team sports take place at a nearby site. All boys take gym classes and indoor football and basketball are on offer after school. Sussex House is a centre of excellence for fencing and its international records are well known.

The ambitious 'Cadogan' magazine bears witness to an imaginative range of activities including Poetry competitions, plays and an annual Musical. Orchestral and choral concerts are an important part of the calendar and a large number of boys play musical instruments. Staff take outward bound school trips, including an annual ski-ing trip and cultural trips to the continent.

The school has a Church of England focus with weekly services in St Simon Zelotes Church, Chelsea, whose priest is the School Chaplain. Boys of all religions and denominations are welcomed.

A member of IAPS, Sussex House is not linked to any particular senior school and boys are prepared for a wide range of London and boarding schools at Common Entrance or Scholarship level with a record of strong results to academically demanding schools. The school enjoys its own entirely independent character and the style is traditional yet imaginative.

Charitable status. Sussex House is a Registered Charity, number 1035806. It exists to provide education for boys.

Sutton Valence Preparatory School

Underhill Church Road Chart Sutton Maidstone Kent ME17 3RF
Tel: 01622 842117
Fax: 01622 844201

Chairman of Governors: B Baughan, Esq

***Headmaster:* A M Brooke,** CertEd, BEd

Number of Day Pupils. Prep (7–11): 98 boys, 75 girls. Pre-Prep (3–6): 77 boys, 78 girls.

Fees. £785–£1,935 per term (exclusive of lunch).

Underhill became Sutton Valence Preparatory School in

September 2001. The school is fully co-educational with its own Pre-Prep department housed in a new purpose built facility. The United Westminster Schools Foundation provides valuable resources and support.

The school is situated in 18 acres of countryside overlooking the Weald and includes a hard and grass play areas, heated outdoor swimming pool, 4 hard tennis courts and a 13 acre games field and Sports Hall.

Classes are small throughout the school. The 25 teaching staff are all well qualified and there is an extensive peripatetic staff for music. Special needs are addressed by a specialist. The Kindergarten to Year 2 classes all have qualified classroom assistants.

We provide an excellent all round education, with an emphasis on a solid foundation in the core subjects of English, Mathematics, Science and ICT. Languages, Music, Drama, Art, Design Technology and Sport play an important part in the curriculum too.

There is a wind band, string orchestra, quartets and a choir, the best of whom sing with our senior school choir. There are many opportunities for children to perform in drama productions and in concerts.

We have a varied programme of visits and outings to further the children's experience.

Cricket, Football, Hockey, Netball, Rugby, Rounders are the major sports. Athletics, Swimming and Cross Country are also in the curriculum. The proximity of the senior school, Sutton Valence, allows the children to benefit from their staffing and facilities, including the use of an excellent astroturf and new Sports Hall. Extra curricular activities include chess club, art, 5-a-side football, gymnastics, drama, craft, croquet, science club, golf, ballet and judo.

The school is a Christian foundation. Assemblies and the use of the local church are an important facet of our lives. We have recently appointed a Chaplain.

Children are prepared for our senior school, Sutton Valence, the local Grammar schools and other independent schools with an 11+ entry.

Charitable status. Sutton Valence School is a Registered Charity, number 309267. It exists to provide education for boys and girls.

Swanbourne House School

Swanbourne Buckinghamshire MK17 0HZ.
Tel: (01296) 720264
Fax: (01296) 728188

Joint Heads: **S D Goodhart**, BEd (Hons); **Mrs J S Goodhart** BEd (Dunelm)

Chairman of Governors: J Leggett

Number of Boys. 35 Boarders, 110 Day Boys
Number of Girls. 20 Boarders, 78 Day Girls
Pre-Prep Dept. (All Day): 85 Boys, 65 Girls
Fees. Boarding/weekly boarding £3,495 per term; Day £2,745 per term; Pre-Prep. £1,590 per term; Nursery £730–£1,290 per term

The School is a Charitable Trust, administered by a Board of Governors. The house, which was once the home of the Cottesloe family, is a Grade II listed building, standing in 40 acres of wooded grounds and commanding extensive views of the surrounding countryside.

There are 34 full-time members of the teaching staff, many of whom are resident. They are assisted by several peripatetic specialist teachers. The well-being of the boarders is in the hands of a resident housemaster and his wife: they are assisted by a matron and our daily RGN staff.

A strong musical tradition has been established. There are three choirs, an orchestra and various ensembles. The boys' chapel choir has sung recently in Teweksbury Abbey and York Minster. Musical concerts are held throughout the school year and all pupils are encouraged to participate in drama and the Inter-House music competition. The school has its own chapel.

Boys and girls are prepared for entry to independent senior schools, usually at 13+, while scholarships have been won on a regular basis ever since Swanbourne House was founded in 1920. The majority of boys and girls go on to leading senior independent schools, where the pass-rate in recent years has been 100%. From age 9, pupils are taught by specialist teachers in well-equipped subject rooms. There is a Modern Language Laboratory and all senior pupils have the opportunity to spend a week in France.

The more practical side of the Curriculum is fully catered for in the Fremantle Hall of Technology. Art, Design Technology, Science and Information Technology are taught in this attractive building: more than 70 computers are in use throughout the school.

The Pre-Preparatory Department occupies an Elizabethan Manor House, adjoining the school grounds. The facilities are first rate and five new classrooms have been built. Whilst retaining a separate identity, the younger children are able to use the Main School facilities throughout the year.

A House system operates to encourage healthy competition in work and games. The Housemasters and Housemistresses have a special responsibility and concern for the welfare of the children in their House.

For boys the main school games are Rugby, Hockey, Football and Cricket, and for girls Hockey, Netball and Rounders: coaching and matches are also arranged in Athletics. Tennis is played on our new astro-turf facility. Further opportunities include cross-country, judo, dance and squash. A very wide range of extra-curricular activities are available in the evenings, at weekends and on certain afternoons.

The Bridget More Hall offers outstanding facilities for Drama, Music and PE. Other facilities include a Rifle Range, a new Swimming Pool and Squash Court. There is a Cub Pack, a Holiday Sports Club for children and time to offer camping and outward-bound type activities, such as canoeing, climbing, riding, ski-ing and sailing.

We run an Arts programme with visiting exhibitions, craft days, parent/child days and specialist tuition.

School Prefects are taught to foster a caring concern for the well-being of every member of our community, while the admirable support of local parents helps to provide fully to the needs and happiness of children whose parents live overseas.

Children are prepared for Senior Independent Schools through lectures and workshops in personal communication, drugs, first aid and senior school life. All leavers at 12+ take part in a residential week of outdoor education.

Scholarships are awarded for 8+ or 11+ entry to the school, as a result of an examination held in February of each year.

Bursaries are available for Forces Families.

Charitable status. Swanbourne House School is a Registered Charity, number 310640. It seeks to provide a continuous structured education for children aged 3–13 years.

Sydney Grammar School, St Ives Preparatory

11–21 Ayres Road St Ives NSW 2075 Australia
Tel: 61 2 91442837/91441681
Fax: 61 2 94499875

***Headmaster:* B Pennington**, BSc, ARSM

Chairman of Trustees: Mr H Mackay

Number of Day Boys. 445
Fees. (per annum) From $A8,805 (4 & 5 year olds) to $A11,730 (10–12 year olds). 4 terms

This is one of two Preparatory Schools controlled by the Trustees of Sydney Grammar School. The boys are prepared for the Senior School of Sydney Grammar School which opened during 1857 in the City of Sydney to confer on all classes and denominations the advantages of a regular and liberal course of education. The school emphasises the importance of a rigorous academic curriculum as well as strong music and sport programmes.

The St Ives Preparatory School is set in 6 hectares of beautiful grounds on the North Shore of Sydney, about 20 kilometres from the city centre. The School was founded in 1954. The Infants Department (Kindergarten to Year 2) is separate from the Primary School with its own classrooms, activities room and adventure playground. There is a Music Centre, Art Centre, Library, Computer Room, Assembly Hall, Science Room, Drama Studio, Ovals, Swimming Pool, Tennis Courts and a fitness course. Cultural activities – orchestra, choir, photography, dramatic and musical productions, chess, debating and an Annual Festival of Arts.

Sports. Cricket, Softball, Swimming, Lifesaving, Basketball, Tennis, Archery, Rugby, Soccer, Athletics and Cross Country Running.

Tanglin Trust School

Portsdown Road SINGAPORE 139294
Tel: (65) 778-0771
Fax: (65) 777-5862

Chair of Board: Mrs Sandra Berrick

***Head of School:* Mr R T Stones**, MBE

Head of Senior School: Mr S W Hilland
Head of Junior School: Mr D D Rowlands
Head of Infant School: Mrs G Chandran
Director of Studies: Ms M Cole

Number of Day Boys. 775
Number of Day Girls. 775
Fees. S$11,700 (Nursery) – S$17,430 (Years 7 up)

Tanglin Trust School caters for the educational needs of British and other English-speaking expatriate children (ages 3 up) in Singapore. It is operated by Tanglin Trust School Ltd, a non-profit making educational foundation.

The school is set in a mature landscaped estate in an urban district to the west of the city, and is equipped with modern purpose-built facilities.

The recent extension of the age range into Nursery (3 year olds) and Seniors (Year 7 and beyond) has been made on the basis of building on a foundation of excellent achievements since the school's establishment in 1925.

Although the school is the largest of its kind in Asia, great emphasis is placed on the pastoral well-being of the individual student. Opportunities are given for students to excel in academic and sporting areas, as well as the arts. As students progress through the school, enhancements to the curriculum include overseas field study trips and performances in music and drama. Tanglin students are exposed to a broad and balanced curriculum based on the key stages of England's National Curriculum.

Taunton Preparatory School

Staplegrove Road Taunton Somerset TA2 6AE.
Tel: (01823) 349250. Admissions (01823) 349209
Fax: (01823) 349202

President of the School Council: Mrs J E Barrie, BSc, ARCS, MSI(Dip)

***Headmaster:* M Anderson**, MA

Number of Pupils. Nursery and Pre-Prep (3–7); Prep: (7–13): Boarders 44; Day 420.
Fees. Nursery £780; Pre-Prep: £930. Boarders £2,010–£3,655 per term. Day £1,265–£2,415 per term.

Taunton Preparatory School is the Preparatory School of Taunton School (q.v.) and shares its aim to provide a broad and balanced education in a friendly, Christian community, in which the pupils can develop their talents and interests. Classes and academic sets are small, allowing close personal attention to each child. All children are encouraged to mix easily with each other and with adults, and it is a principle of the School's teaching that learning is best achieved through the fostering of enthusiasm and the development of an enquiring mind. Kindness and courtesy are highly prized qualities.

The Preparatory School was almost entirely rebuilt in 1994 to provide outstanding academic, cultural and athletic facilities. The new teaching facilities include 4 dedicated Science laboratories, Art, Design Technology and IT suites, a well-resourced library and spacious classrooms.

Boarding care of a high standard is the responsibility of a team of Boarding House Parents, a Senior Matron and her Assistants. The boarding accommodation was refurbished in 1994. The School prides itself on its high standards of catering and individual care for all its pupils. Full and weekly boarding are on offer. An ambitious weekend programme of activities is organised. The School welcomes pupils from overseas, although entry to the Preparatory School is normally after a year in Taunton International Studies Centre, where EFL teaching is well established. The school enjoys close links with the Armed Services – a generous Bursary scheme is well established.

Music, Drama and Dance are highly valued. The School runs a large Orchestra, three choirs, and specialist groups for strings, jazz and brass. Over 200 children now learn at least one instrument.

The Music School has been entirely redesigned and refurbished to provide first-class accommodation for class and individual teaching, Music Technology and ensemble work. The largest groups and drama activities use the Preparatory School's own assembly hall.

Sporting facilities at Taunton School are quite exceptional. The Preparatory School enjoys its own Sports Centre comprising a newly built indoor heated 25 metre Swimming Pool and Sports Hall. The main boys' games are Rugby, Hockey and Cricket whilst girls are offered Netball, Hockey, Tennis and Rounders. All-weather playing surfaces and extensive grass pitches are available within the campus. Athletics, Badminton, Basketball, Cross-country running, Soccer, Gymnastics, Judo, Riding, Squash, Swimming and Tennis are all available.

The wide curriculum is supported by a full programme of extra-curricular activities which include Dance, Board

Games, Canoeing, Chess, Computing, Cookery, Debating, Drama, "Green" club, Modelling and Pottery. The School is a keen supporter of the Scout movement.

A thorough grounding is given in core subjects and all children learn at least one modern language from the age of 7. The requirements of the National Curriculum are met by enthusiastic and committed staff. There are scholarships at 11+ and 13+ (for entry to the Senior School). Art, Sports and Music Scholarships and Awards are also offered. There are a number of ministerial bursaries and awards at 11+.

There is a purpose-built Nursery and Pre-Prep, which enjoys its own excellent classrooms, library, computers and recreational facilities and has full access to the Preparatory School's Sports Centre. Each class teacher is supported by a nursery nurse.

A comprehensive prospectus is available from The Admissions Secretary.

Charitable status. Taunton Preparatory School is a Registered Charity, number 310211. It exists to provide a high standard of education for children.

Taverham Hall

Norwich NR8 6HU.
Tel: (01603) 868206.
Fax: (01603) 861061
e-mail: enquire@taverhamhall.co.uk
Station: Norwich

Chairman of Governors: Andra Papworth

***Headmaster:* W D Lawton**, MEd

Deputy Headmaster: I Newton, BA

Number of Pupils. Prep: Boarders 24, Day 74 (Boys. 55, Girls. 43), Pre-Prep 74 (Boys. 38, Girls. 36), Nursery 60.

Fees. Boarding £3,135, Day £1,920-£2,725, Pre-Prep £385-£1,650 per term

The School has occupied its present Victorian mansion, 7 miles from Norwich, since 1920. Throughout its existence its Headmasters have been members of IAPS.

About 100 acres of open grass and woodland are available for use by the boys and girls who enjoy a wide variety of outdoor activities, in addition to organised games which comprise Rugby, Netball, Hockey, Soccer, Cricket, Rounders, Athletics and Tennis. Skiing trips and walking expeditions are organised regularly in the holidays.

There is a teaching staff of 22 and the average number of children per class is 12. There is a broad curriculum, which includes Science, CDT, Art and Music. Children are prepared for Scholarships and Common Entrance to independent schools all over the country.

Every effort is made to encourage children to fulfil their potential in work and games and, in a well-organised and happy atmosphere, children have every opportunity of learning to contribute to the well-being of the community. Besides stressing school work, the School has a strong Musical tradition. The Chapel Choir is a St Nicolas Guild Choir of the RSCM. Piano, Brass, Woodwind and String Instruments are taught by specialists.

Free-time occupations include Golf, Squash, Shooting, Gardening, Riding, use of a Scalelectrix set, Cookery and a variety of Handicrafts. In the Winter terms there is an extensive programme of leisure-time activities in which all children and staff are involved. There is an indoor, heated Swimming Pool, a large Gymnasium, and a permanent well-equipped Stage.

The children's health, catering and all domestic arrangements, including laundry, are under the personal supervision of Mrs Lawton, assisted by a team of Matrons.

Temple Grove School

Heron's Ghyll Uckfield E Sussex TN22 4DA
Tel: (01825) 712112
Fax: (01825) 713432

Co-educational day and boarding school with nursery and pre-prep departments.

Chairman of the Trustees: D A B Lough, MA (Oxon)

***Headmaster:* M H Kneath,** BEd

Number of pupils. 150
Age range. 3–13
Fees per term. Kindergarten (5 mornings) £760. Pre-Prep £1,500. Day pupils £1,675-£2,575. Boarders £2,875–£3,360.

Temple Grove is a small day and boarding school. We exist to provide a flexible and happy education that will form a firm basis for your child's whole life. The School is the oldest prep school in the country and yet our fine tradition is just a small part of life at Temple Grove today.

The children live, work and play in an Elizabethan manor and more modern buildings situated in more than 40 acres of parkland a few miles north of Uckfield. The space provides room for a covered swimming pool, playing fields, floodlit tennis courts, gymnasium, theatre, music school, and design and technology centre. Just as importantly, it provides room for outside teaching and play in the woods and fields.

Temple Grove prepares children for further study through scholarship, Common Entrance and 11-plus examinations. The formal study is balanced by the usual formal games (such as soccer, netball and tennis), but at Temple Grove we also place great emphasis on other sports and activities such as golf, speech and drama, ballet, pottery and orchestra. The aim is to ensure that every child has a balanced and interesting life at school. In this way, your child will learn to learn and live as a helpful and successful member of society.

We pride ourselves in the flexibility we offer to busy families. Although the majority of our children are day pupils, Temple Grove is very much a 24 hour place. The normal school day finishes at 4 pm but there are options to stay any length of time. In this extended time the children will take part in supervised activities, eat their tea or supper and complete their prep.

In addition to this flexible end to the day we offer flexi-boarding to those who wish to stay over. In this way your child can, when they like, live alongside the full time boarders without feeling lost and out of the mainstream. The school day is established to provide time for all.

Charitable status. Temple Grove School is a Registered Charity, number 307016. It exists to provide high quality education to girls and boys under the age of 14.

Terra Nova

Jodrell Bank Holmes Chapel Cheshire CW4 8BT.
Tel: (01477) 571251
Fax: (01477) 571646
e-mail: nigel@thejohnsons.uk.net

Chairman of Governors: R D Rhodes, JP

***Headmaster:* Nigel Johnson**, BA, PGCE

Deputy Head: T J Fryer, CertEd, DipSE, MIITT

Number of Pupils. 250 on roll: 20 boarders; 130 day pupils aged 7 to 13; 100 day pupils aged 3 to 6.

Fees. Boarders £2,395–£3,340; Day Pupils £1,755–£2,700; Pre-Prep £1,300; Nursery £697.

Terra Nova occupies 35 acres of fine grounds between Holmes Chapel and Macclesfield. The school is 5 minutes from Junction 18 of the M6 and 25 minutes from Manchester Airport.

Boys and girls are prepared for entry at both 11+ and 13+ to a wide variety of Day, Grammar and Boarding Senior Schools. The school enjoys an excellent academic reputation and its pupils have won over 35 Scholarships to senior schools in the last ten years. Each child experiences a broad curriculum including Music, Art, PE, ICT and Design Technology. The staff is well qualified and experienced with the maximum class size set at 19.

The 35 acres of grounds and buildings include a multi-purpose Sports Hall and Performing Arts Centre (opened January 1999), tennis courts (both hard and grass surfaces), specialist Art and Pottery department, Music School, excellently equipped Science laboratory, Design & Technology facility (1991) and new ICT suite opened in March 2001. In addition there is a fully staffed Library, heated swimming pool and indoor .22 rifle range. Music is taught at all levels and every child is given the opportunity to learn a musical instrument. The school has a choir, which performs in the area and overseas, as well as various instrumental ensemble groups and an orchestra.

Boarders have pleasant and comfortable accommodation in the Main building. The domestic arrangements and health and welfare of the children are under the direct supervision of the Headmaster's wife, supported by three resident matrons and a boarding team of six.

The main winter sports for girls are hockey and netball and in the summer tennis, rounders, athletics and swimming. The boys play rugby and soccer in the two winter terms, and cricket, tennis and athletics in the summer. Additionally, the school enjoys a strong reputation for athletics and cross-country. A wealth of after school clubs are available, including activities such as judo, badminton, volleyball, cooking, chess, riding. golf, dance and gymnastics. Terra Nova also boasts its own Cub pack.

The Pre-Preparatory Department is housed in a separate building adjoining the main school site but enjoys the benefits of many of the main school facilities.

An after school and holiday club (Tembos) together with very flexible boarding arrangements meets the need of today's busy working parent.

Annual Scholarships of up to 50% (Full Boarding) fees are offered by competitive examination in March each year to children aged 7, 8 or 9. Bursaries may also be available in cases of genuine hardship.. The school, which is in its 104th year, became a charitable trust in 1955.

Charitable status. Terra Nova School Trust Limited is a Registered Charity, number 525919. It is dedicated to all round educational excellence for children.

Terrington Hall

Terrington York YO6 4PR.
Tel: (01653) 648227
Fax: (01653) 648458
e-mail: jglen@thps.demon.co.uk
website: www:thps.demon.co.uk

Chairman of Governors: J G Bradley, FRCS

Headmaster: **M J Glen**, BA, PGCE (Dunelm)

Number of Children. Boarding 46; Day 139 (88 boys, 51 girls).

Fees. Boarding: £3,050 per term. Day: £1,960-£2,120 per term. Pre-Prep: £900–£1,110 per term. There are no compulsory extras.

Terrington is a co-educational school situated in beautiful countryside close to Castle Howard and some fifteen miles from the City of York,

Predominately a boarding school, Terrington prepares pupils for all the leading independent schools. With a teacher/pupil ratio of 1:10 every child has the opportunity to achieve their academic potential. A remedial teacher, who is trained to help pupils with dyslexia, is on the staff. In the last three years fourteen Scholarships and Exhibitions have been won. There is a separate pre-preparatory department for day children from the age of 3. A new self-contained purpose built Pre-Prep opened in September 1999.

The school has excellent sporting facilities with a new Sports Hall opened in 2001, eight acres of playing fields, hard tennis court and an indoor heated swimming pool. Coaching by qualified members of staff is given in both boys and girls major sports. In addition, athletics, cross-country, gymnastics, riding, orienteering, sailing, canoeing and clay pigeon shooting are available. There is an extensive outdoor education programme with all children learning to sail and to canoe. The North York Moors are only ten miles away for low level walking and overnight camps. The school has its own climbing wall.

A modern classroom and library block has recently been built as well as a fully equipped computer centre. A new Music Centre opened in 1995 and Music, Art and Drama all form an important part of the curriculum. Tuition is available for most instruments and children can be prepared for Associated Board music examinations. There is a choir, a very successful wind band and two major drama productions each year.

The School Chaplain is the local Rector and boarders attend the village Church every Sunday. Roman Catholics may go to their own church. Anglicans may be prepared for confirmation and Roman Catholics for their first communion. Each day starts with a simple act of worship.

The Headmaster with his wife and children live in the school and the children are very much part of an extended family. A wide range of activities is followed at weekends and full use is made of the surrounding countryside. Parents are fully involved in the life of the school and there is a flourishing social committee.

The school welcomes children whose parents live overseas and an escort service is able to collect and deliver them from airports at the beginning and end of term. There is a bus service to the Newbury area available at half-terms.

A number of Entrance Scholarships are available for children under eleven and there are Bursaries for sons and daughters of Clergy and HM Forces Personnel.

Charitable status. Terrington Hall is a Registered Charity, number 532362. It exists to provide a quality education for boys and girls.

Thorpe House School

Oval Way Gerrards Cross Bucks SL9 8PZ.
Tel: (01753) 882474
Fax: (01753) 889755

Kingscote Pre-Preparatory School, Oval Way, Gerrards Cross SL9 8PZ.
Tel: (01753) 885535

Chairman of the Governors: Sir William Doughty, MA

Headmaster: **Mr A F Lock**, MA (Oxon), PGCE

Kingscote Pre-Preparatory School and Nursery: Headmistress: Mrs S A Tunstall, CertEd

Numbers of Boys. 160 Day Boys
Fees. £2,180–£2,230 per term

Thorpe House was founded in 1923 and registered as a Charitable Trust in 1986.

The School is staffed by a Headmaster, 13 full time teachers, 3 part time teachers and 10 peripatetic staff. There are 10 classrooms, Science Laboratory, Library, Gymnasium, networked Computer room, Design Technology department, Art room, Music room and Music Practice rooms. The School has its own open air heated swimming pool, 7 acres of playing fields, an all weather sports surface, tennis court and pavilion. All Saints' Church stands next to the main building, and is regularly used by the school. In addition to the three traditional major games of rugby, soccer and cricket, swimming, hockey and athletics are taught. Out of school activities include tennis, golf, judo, ski-ing, horseriding and a variety of clubs and societies. The School's examination record is very strong and boys go on to independent senior schools via the Common Entrance or Scholarship examinations, and to the local Grammar Schools.

Kingscote Pre-Preparatory School and Nursery
Number of boys. 126 Day Boys
Fees. Pre-Preparatory: £1,677 per term; Nursery: Term 1 £838, Term 2 £1,174, Term 3 £1,339.

Kingscote is situated adjacent to Thorpe House in its own grounds. The school is staffed by a Headmistress, 7 full time staff and 5 part time staff. Boys normally spend 3 or 4 full years there before transferring to the main school at 7+.

The Schools provide a continuous education for boys from 3 to 13+.

Charitable status. Thorpe House School Trust is a Registered Charity, number 292683. It exists to provide education to boys of preparatory school age.

Tockington Manor

Tockington Nr Bristol BS32 4NY.
Tel: (01454) 613229.
Fax: (01454) 615776.
e-mail: tock63974@aol.com
website: www.tockington.bristol.sch.uk
Stations: Bristol (Temple Meads), 10 miles: Bristol Parkway, 5 miles

***Headmaster:* R G Tovey**, CertEd (Oxon)

Chairman of Governors: A J G Spratling, Esq

Number of Pupils. 36 Boarders, 80 Day, 65 Infants, 85 Nursery. Boys and Girls aged 2–13+.

Fees. Boarders £3,320–£3,695 per term (inclusive). Day: £2,115–£2,490 per term (including meals). Pre-Prep: £1,495. Nursery: from £8.00 per session.

The school stands in its own 27 acres of parkland some 10 miles north of Bristol, close to the Severn Bridge and M4/M5 motorways, allowing easy access to road, rail and air links.

Boys and girls in the Preparatory School are prepared via the Scholarship or Common Entrance examinations for a wide range of independent schools. A highly qualified staff has ensured continuous success at these levels. The Headmaster's wife, who is also qualified to teach, takes a full part in school activities. Boarders accepted from age 7. Daily transport service to local areas.

The main school games are soccer, rugby, cricket, athletics, cross country, swimming (large open-air heated pool) and tennis (all weather courts). Girls play hockey, netball and rounders. Ballet, riding, archery, judo and a wide variety of other activities are available in all terms, and children are encouraged to take part in music and drama. A feature of the summer term is Tockington Tramps, an outdoor activity including map and compass work leading to some nights at camp for senior children.

The Pre-Prep has small classes for children aged 4–7, who share the facilities of the Prep School, and provides a stimulating environment. The Nursery for children aged 2–4 is well equipped with toys and games, has an extensive outdoor play area and aims to lay the foundations of independence and academic learning.

The excellent buildings, which stand in an attractive setting facing the games field, have been increased over the years.

Reductions in fees are offered for brothers/sisters and sons/daughters of Service personnel.

Tower House School

188 Sheen Lane East Sheen London SW14 8LF
Tel: 020 8876 3323
Fax: 020 8876 3321

Chairman of Governors: Mrs Alex Clarke

***Headmaster:* J D T Wall**, BA (Bristol), PGCE

Number of Boys. 185
Fees. Prep: £2,290; Pre-Prep £2,230 per term (including lunches and class outings).

Tower House is a day school established in 1931. The school stands in its own grounds and is conveniently situated near a number of bus routes and the local station.

Entry is at the age of 4+. Admission of boys after the age of 4+ depends very much on the availability of places. There is no entry test and although the Headmaster interviews all boys, a wide range of ability is acceptable.

The school prepares boys for Common Entrance and Scholarships to appropriate Independent Senior Schools.

The staff is fully qualified and includes specialists in art, music and games, which together with drama play an important part in the school curriculum. In addition to the full time staff, there are visiting teachers for piano, violin, woodwind, brass and guitar and percussion.

The school is well supplied with modern teaching aids, including computers. There is a well-equipped science laboratory, an art and technology room, large library, and a newly equipped ICT Room.

The principal games are rugby, soccer and cricket. Other sports include athletics, cross country, squash, swimming, tennis and water sports. There are many fixtures arranged with other schools.

A prospectus is available on application to the Headmaster.

Town Close House Preparatory School

14 Ipswich Road Norwich Norfolk NR2 2LR.
Tel: (01603) 620180. Pre-Preparatory 626718
Fax: (01603) 618256. Pre-Preparatory (01603) 599043

Chairman of Governors: Mr Bryan Read, CBE

***Headmaster:* Richard Gordon**, MA (Oxon)

Number of Pupils. Pre-Prep 168. Prep School 218 (including 12 weekly boarders)

Fees. at September 2001. Day Pupils. £2,080 per term (incl lunch). Weekly Boarders: £2,930 per term. Pre-Prep: £1,305–£1,660 per term. No Compulsory extras.

The School was founded in 1932 and became a Charitable Trust in 1968. It is fully co-educational. Weekly boarding is available for both girls and boys.

Town Close House has an excellent academic and sporting reputation, but Music, Art, Drama and a wide range of extra-curricular activities, trips and expeditions form a valuable part of what we offer, and provide the balance essential for a full and rounded education.

Our aim is to develop self-confident, articulate boys and girls, used to working hard and playing hard, independent, caring and sociable.

There are altogether 40 Full Time and 3 Part Time members of staff. The School's facilities include a well-equipped Science Laboratory, an indoor heated Swimming Pool and a Sports Hall. A new teaching block stands at the heart of the school, containing a large, well-equipped library, two air-conditioned networked ICT Suites, an Art Room and 16 purpose-built classrooms.

As well as providing all the usual opportunities for the major team games (Rugby, Netball, Hockey, Cricket and Athletics), coaching is offered in many other minor sports, and games generally form an important part of the life of the school. The wide range of activities include Football, Fencing, Chess, Sailing, Modelling, Photography, Computer Club, Drama, Brass Group, String Group, School Choir, Wind Band, and Birdwatching. Magazine Club, Fun Dance, Swim Squads, Aerobics Dance, Short Tennis, Debating Society, Saxophone Band, Textile Club, and Recorder Group.

A visit is essential to appreciate this exceptionally beautiful site near the centre of Norwich, with extensive playground space and acres of conservation woodland. We actively enjoy showing parents round the school.

Charitable status. Town Close House Educational Trust Limited is a Registered Charity, number 311293. It exists to provide education for children.

Treliske School

The Preparatory School of Truro School Highertown Truro Cornwall TR1 3QN

Tel: (01872) 272616.
Fax: (01872) 222377
e-mail: enquiries@treliske.cornwall.sch.uk
website: www.treliske.cornwall.sch.uk

Chairman of the Governors: J R Heath, BA

Headmaster of Truro School: Mr P K Smith, MA (Cantab), MEd, FRGS

Headmaster of Treliske School: **Russell Hollins**, BA, BEd, CertEd (St. Luke's College, Exeter)

Head of Pre-Prep: Mrs Anne Allen, CertEd

Number of Pupils. (April 2001). (3–11) Day Boys 132, Day Girls 83, Boarder Boys 3, Boarder Girls 3. Total 221

Fees. (September 2000). Pre-Prep £484–£1,209; Day £1,817; Boarders £2,724-£3,332 per term

Extras. Lunch.

Optional extras: individual music lessons.

Treliske School was opened in 1934 in the former residence and estate of Sir George Smith. The School lies in extensive and secluded grounds to the west of the cathedral city of Truro, three miles from Truro School. The grounds command fine views of the neighbouring countryside. The drive to the school off the main A390 is almost 800 metres and Truro Golf course also surrounds the school, so producing a campus of beauty and seclusion.

The keynote of the school is a happy, caring atmosphere in which children learn the value of contributing positively to the school community through the firm and structured framework of academic study and extra curricular interests. The approach is based firmly in Christian beliefs and the school is proud of its Methodist foundation.

Building development has kept pace with modern expectations and Treliske has its own large sports hall, indoor heated swimming pool and a Design and Technology workshop with a computer room adjoined.

The Pre-Prep was purpose built ten years ago and has its own separate enclosed site with 70 pupils aged 3-7 years.

In March 2000 a new classroom and art and design block was opened costing £380,000, and a new computer suite was constructed with a comprehensive network system of RM machines in July 2000.

A small number of boarders are accommodated in the original bedrooms of the main building.

The games programme is designed to encourage all children, from the keenest to the least athletic, to enjoy games and physical exercise. Our excellent facilities and the diverse skill of our staff enable us to offer a rich variety of sporting and recreational pursuits. There are over 20 popular clubs and activities run each week from 4.00 pm to 5.00 pm.

There is a strong school tradition in music and drama and the arts. Children may choose to learn a musical instrument from the full orchestral range. Each year the November concert, with Truro School, allows the School to show the community the excellent talent which flourishes in both schools.

Close links are encouraged with Truro School and the majority of children take an open entrance examination to Truro School which is the only Independent Headmasters' and Headmistresses' Conference School in Cornwall (see Part I of this book). The curriculum is designed so that there is a continuity of education from pre-prep through to the senior school.

The Propectus and further details can be obtained from the Headmaster's Secretary, and the Headmaster will be pleased to show prospective parents around the school.

Charitable status. Treliske School is a Registered Charity, number 306576. It is a charitable foundation established for the purpose of education.

Tudor House School

Illawarra Highway Moss Vale New South Wales Australia 2577

Tel: 02-48681088
Fax: 02-48681088

Chairman of Tudor House Council; Mr W McI Carpenter, AVLE (Val), REIV (Aust)

Headmaster: **A C Russell,** BEd, DipTchg, MACE, MACEA, AIMM, ANZIM

Pupils. 185, Years K to 6 (53 boarders, 119 day)

Fees. Day $2,380 per term. Boarder additional $2,395 per term (GST to be added).

Founded in 1897 in Sydney, the School was moved to rural Moss Vale in 1902 and was bought by the council of The King's School in 1942. In 1993 it was given its own Council to control all aspects of the School and its development.

The school is situated five kilometres from Moss Vale and set in 167 acres of park and grazing land. There are two boarding houses. The classroom block was built in 1988 and the Library complex in the early 80's. Another building programme commenced in 1999 with alterations and refurbishment of the Senior Boarding House, a new Music and Drama facility, as well as a new residence for the Headmaster. A new Lower School Centre will open in 2002, the centenary of being on the present site.

Boys are prepared for a number of independent secondary schools in Australia and overseas.

Facilities. The classrooms are bright, airy and modern and in addition to the seven teaching classrooms there is a computer room, woodwork shop, an art room and a language room. There are facilities for music-making and a large hall for assemblies and play productions. A good library is always open and we have a large variety of books.

The Enrichment Centre was opened in 1996 and provides the able boys with extension programmes. Boys needing remedial assistance are also helped.

There is a strong tradition of worship and choir work and services are held every Sunday in the school chapel as well as regular services during the week. The choristers of the two Chapel Choirs complete the requirements set by the Royal School of Church Music. The school also has a Senior and a Junior choir and a small band.

There are excellent sports grounds. Three cricket pitches, three rugby football fields, a 25m swimming pool with an additional diving bay, a large gymnasium, cricket nets, tennis courts, a cycle track, and a boating dam allow for a variety of sports and activities. Rugby and soccer are the main winter sports. Cricket and tennis are the summer sports. Athletics, crosscountry, swimming, waterpolo and skiing are part of the sports programme.

Boys are allowed (with some restrictions, according to age) the run of the property. A bond of trust exists between boys and masters.

Boys study English, Maths, History, Geography, Science, Drama, Art, Woodwork, Religious Studies,, Music, Physical Education, Health and Personal Development, French and Spanish. There is an opportunity to do extra subjects such as Horseriding, Leather work, Martial Arts, and to take piano, violin, saxophone, clarinet, flute, drums and guitar.

The "Kahiba" (Outdoor Education) programme is highly valued and widely regarded. Based on Scouting and a love of the Outdoors it teaches boys independence, responsibility as well as a love of the environment. It is available to the boys in the senior two year groups.

Philosophy. A real measure of freedom, a close association with understanding adults, are two basic ingredients for the sound development of young boys. They can thus be guided in the management of freedom to the point of full awareness of the responsibilities that go with it which are appreciated and understood.

These three fundamental notions; close adult concern with the boys of the school, freedom gladly given, and guidance in how to use it are implicit in many of the Tudor House activities.

Twickenham Preparatory School

Beveree 43 High Street Hampton Middlesex TW12 2SA.
Tel: 020 8979 6216
Fax: 020 8979 1596

Chairman of Governors: Mr P Jenkinson

Headmaster: **N D Flynn**, MA (New College, Oxford), PGCE

Number of Boys. 111
Number of Girls. 126
Fees. £1,725–£1,845 plus £100 lunch.

Founded as a private school in 1932, the school is now a limited company with charitable status.

We prepare boys for Common Entrance Examinations and girls for entrance examinations to independent secondary schools. Able pupils take scholarships and the academic standard of the school is high.

The staff is graduate and classes never exceed 18. Children are admitted at 4 years old. Girls leave at 11+ and boys at 13+.

The school, which is housed in a Grade II listed building in the Hampton conservation area, is well equipped to cover the full range of subjects. Emphasis is on individual attention and developing each pupil to their full academic potential.

A major building development was completed in 1999, comprising a new pre-prep block, gymnasium, and improved dining and changing facilities. Grounds and playgrounds have also been developed.

We are a friendly and happy community where there is a clear non-sectarian Christian tradition, though pupils of all faiths are accepted.

All children swim. Association football, cricket and netball are our main team games. Athletics, tennis, rugby and other sports are also coached. Music and drama play a large part in school with full scale productions and concerts annually, involving all pupils. Individual instrumental lessons are taught by visiting specialists and there are many varied after school activities.

Charitable status. Twickenham Preparatory School is a Registered Charity, number 1067572. It exists to provide education for boys and girls.

Twyford School

Winchester Hampshire SO21 1NW.
Tel: (01962) 712269
Fax: (01962) 712100

Chairman of Governors: C E Monaghan, BSc, CA

Headmaster: **P F Fawkes**, CertEd, MBA(Ed)

Number of Children. 65 boy and girl boarders, 158 day children in the Main School; 90 boys and girls in the day Pre-Prep.

Fees. (September 2001): £4,150 (boarding) £3,050 (day). No compulsory extras. £1,830 (Pre-prep).

The School, a Charitable Trust since 1955, is situated just two miles south east of Winchester where it stands in twenty acres of attractive grounds. It has occupied its present site since 1809 and is one of the oldest preparatory schools in England.

Children are prepared for the Common Entrance, Winchester and Scholarship examinations. Facilities include new classrooms, Sports Hall and indoor heated Swimming Pool, Music School, new building (completed January 1997) housing the Art, Design & Technology and Information Technology departments, new Science laboratories (opened March 2000) and a Victorian Theatre and Chapel.

Cricket, soccer, rugby, hockey, swimming, athletics and tennis are the main sports. Other sporting activities include badminton, judo, netball, basketball, golf.

There is a separate Pre-Prep department for about 80 boys and girls aged from 3 to 7 years.

Charitable status. Twyford School Trust Limited is a Registered Charity, number 307425. It exists to provide education for children.

Unicorn School

238 Kew Road Richmond Surrey TW9 3JX.
Tel: 020 8948 3926
Fax: 020 8332 6814
e-mail: enquiries@unicornschool.org.uk

Headmistress: **Mrs Fiona Timmis**, CertEd (London)

Chairman of Governors: Mr Kennan Michel

Number of Children. 168 Day Pupils, 84 boys, 84 girls

Fees. £1,050–£1,930 per term

Unicorn is an IAPS, parent-owned school, founded in 1970 and situated opposite Kew Gardens in a large Victorian house and converted Coach House with a spacious, well-equipped playground. Plans for the immediate future include major building works to provide a second hall and more specialist teaching rooms.

The school has free and unrestricted access to Kew Gardens and the sports facilities at the nearby Old Deer Park are utilised for games and swimming.

There are 9 full-time teachers, supported by 12 part-time assistant and specialist teachers, with visiting teachers for music, individual tuition and clubs. Classes average 21 children.

Unicorn aims to give children firm foundations and a broad education. A variety of teaching methods are used and the children are regularly assessed internally and by way of Baseline Assessment and SATS at Key Stages 1 and 2. Importance is placed upon the development of the individual and high academic standards are achieved. The main point of entry is to the Nursery at 3+ and the majority of children stay the full eight years. Children are prepared for entry at 11+ to the leading London Day Schools, as well as a wide variety of boarding schools.

There is a new ICT room and there are also computers in every classroom. At nine years old all children take an intensive touch-typing course.

The curriculum includes Drama, French (from age 5), Art and Music - with individual music lessons offered in piano, violin, 'cello, clarinet, saxophone, flute and trumpet, as well as singing. Recorder groups, choirs, chamber groups, an orchestra and wind band also flourish.

In addition to the major games of football, netball, cricket and rounders there are optional clubs for tennis, squash, badminton, unihoc and golf. Other club activities include cookery, craft, gardening, photography, pottery, riding, sailing, sewing and woodwork. There are regular visits to the opera, ballet and theatre as well as to the museums and galleries of Central London. All children from the age of seven upwards participate in residential field study trips.

An elected School Council with representatives from each age group meets twice weekly, and a weekly newsletter for parents is produced by children and staff.

A happy, caring environment prevails and importance is placed upon producing kind, responsible children who show awareness and consideration for the needs of others.

Charitable status. Unicorn School is a Registered Charity, number 312578. It exists to provide education for boys and girls.

University College School (Junior Branch)

11 Holly Hill London NW3 6QN.
Tel: 020 7435 3068.
Station: Hampstead Tube

Headmaster: **K J Douglas**, BA, CertEd

Chairman of Governors: Sir Victor Blank, MA

Number of Boys. 220 aged 7+ to 11.

Fees. £3,000 a term

The School was founded in 1891 by the Governors of University College, London. The present building was opened in 1928, but retains details from the Georgian house first used. It stands near the highest point of Hampstead Heath and the hall and classrooms face south. Facilities include a Science Laboratory, Library, Drama Studio, Music and Computer Rooms, and a Centre for Art and Technology. Boys receive their Swimming and PE lessons in the pool and Sports Hall at the Senior School, 5 minutes' walk away. The Junior School has full use of the 27 acres of playing fields on games days.

40 boys enter at 7+ and 20 at 8+ each year and they are prepared for transfer to the Senior School at 11+.

Charitable status. University College School is a Registered Charity, number 312748. The Junior Branch exists to provide education for boys aged 7+ to 11 years.

Upton House School

115 St Leonards Road Windsor Berkshire SL4 3DF
Tel: 01753 862610
Fax: 01753 621950
e-mail: info@uptonhouse.org.uk
website: www.uptonhouse.org.uk

Headmistress: **Mrs Madeleine Collins**, BA (Hons), PGCE

Chairman of the Council: Mr J J Branch, MA

Number of pupils. 143 Girls, 56 Boys

Fees. £755–£1,825 (inclusive)

Age range. Girls 3–11 years, Boys 3–7 years

Upton House is a day school, has been part of the Windsor community for sixty years and is situated within the town. The school buildings comprise a mixture of old and new. They include specialist design technology, science, drama, music and information technology rooms. There is a separate nursery block, a new Prep block, a heated indoor pool, a games field and netball court.

As well as French, the children learn Latin and Spanish at the top of the school as part of the curriculum.

The school aims to motivate every child to develop their potential to the full in a happy, lively and caring community. Our objective is to produce a broad curriculum offering a rich academic and cultural environment. Boys are prepared for entry to preparatory schools in the area at 7+. Girls leave after the 11+ entrance examination, gaining places at a wide range of senior schools.

Charitable status. Upton House School is a Registered Charity, number 677794. It exists to provide education for children.

Victoria College Preparatory School

Jersey Channel Islands
Tel: (01534) 723468.
Fax: (01534) 780596
Port and Airport: Jersey

Chairman of Governors: Mr Richard Pirouet

***Headmaster:* P Stevenson**, BSc Hons (Durham)

Number of Boys. 280 (all day boys)
Fees. £793 per term (inclusive)
Victoria College Preparatory School was founded in 1922 as an integral part of Victoria College and is now a separate School under its own Headmaster who is responsible for such matters as staffing, curriculum and administration. The Preparatory School shares Governors with Victoria College whose members are drawn from the leaders of the Island of Jersey with a minority representation from the States of Jersey Education Committee. The staff consists of 10 masters and 6 mistresses, all experienced and well qualified, including specialists in Music, Art, PE, French, Science and Technology. Entry to the Prep School is at 7 and boys normally leave to enter Victoria College between the ages of 11½ and 12½. The school games are soccer, cricket, athletics, swimming, hockey, cross-country and rugby. Sporting facilities are shared with Victoria College. There are two strong Cub-Scout Packs. Special features of the school are sport, drama, music and a high standard of French. Many visits, both sporting and educational, are arranged out of the Island.

A separate Pre-Preparatory School (5 to 7 years) is incorporated in a co-educational school situated at the Jersey College for Girls' and offers places for boys whose parents wish them to be educated at both the Preparatory School and the College. Candidates for Pre-Prep entry should be registered at the Preparatory School of the Jersey College for Girls, St Helier, Jersey.

Vinehall

Near Robertsbridge East Sussex TN32 5JL.
Tel: (01580) 880413.
Fax: (01580) 882119
Station: Robertsbridge

Chairman of Governors: Mr H M Boyd

***Headmaster:* D C Chaplin**, BA, CertEd

Deputy Headmaster: G A Lenaghan, CertEd

2nd Deputy Head and Director of Studies: Mrs E Hill, BEd, CertEd

Number of Children. 398 (84 boarders, 188 Day Children, 126 Pre-Preparatory and Nursery).

Fees from September 2000. £3,494 per term for Boarders, £2,687 per term for Day Children, £1,521 Pre-Preparatory.

The School is an Educational Trust, preparing boys and girls for Senior Independent Schools.

The School has 32 full-time qualified staff and the scholastic record over the past five years has been extremely good, with over 45 scholarships having been won to schools such as Benenden, Eastbourne College, King's Canterbury, Lancing, Sevenoaks, Sherborne, Tonbridge, Westminster and Winchester. The School has excellent teaching facilities, with new classrooms, science laboratories and computer room having been added in 1993, and a superb new pre-preparatory department in 1996. The design and technology facilities are now being extended and upgraded. In September 2000 there will be a Resources Centre and Library completed.

All the creative and performing arts are encouraged and the School has a wonderful theatre, built in 1991, which seats 250 and provides an ideal Arts centre: nearly all the children learn musical instruments, and regular plays and concerts are performed, both by the children and by visiting professionals.

The School stands in its own grounds of some 50 acres, and has a 9-hole golf course, as well as extensive playing fields, tennis courts, and an indoor heated swimming pool. A new sports hall was completed in 1996. Woods and gardens provide an excellent setting for all kinds of outdoor recreations, including camping and fishing.

Mrs Chaplin, a Fröebel trained teacher, takes an active interest in the children's welfare, and there are four matrons. There is no weekly boarding, but there are regular exeats, and parents are encouraged to take a full and active part in the life of the School.

Charitable status. Vinehall School is a Registered Charity, number 307014. It exists to provide a secure, quality education, in particular for those in need of residential schooling.

Wakefield Girls' High School Junior School

2 St John's Square Wakefield West Yorkshire WF1 2QX.
Tel: (01924) 374577
Fax: (01924) 231602

Spokesman: Mrs E G Settle

***Head Mistress*:** Mrs D St C Cawthorne, BEd

Number of Pupils. All day pupils. 328 girls (3–11 years). 96 boys (3–7 years)

Fees. From September 2001. Part-time Nursery £882 per term; Full-time Nursery and Pre-Preparatory Department £1,471 per term; Junior Department £1,520 per term. Lunch included.

Instrumental lessons: £105 (10 lessons per term).

The Governors of the High School are shared with Queen Elizabeth Junior and Senior Schools (for boys) situated nearby. Close links are enjoyed between all four schools.

A Nursery Department, opened in 1996, takes children in either a part or full-time capacity at the age of three, in order of registration. It is housed in its own spacious, stimulating and secure surroundings. The well planned environment and an appropriate mix of formal and informal education allows for the social, physical and educational development of each individual child. The Nursery Department ensures that preparation and progression to the Kindergarten, at the age of four, is an exciting and natural transition. The Kindergarten is now housed upstairs from the Nursery in newly refurbished rooms thus creating an Early Years Department called Mulberry House. Adjacent to this is the brand new building housing the five to seven year olds.

The school aims to give a good all round education to each pupil, encouraging academic excellence, emphasizing traditional values, nurturing talent and developing an individual's potential. In addition to the Head, a team of

20 dedicated and enthusiastic full time teachers cares for the children and encourages them in all aspects of school life. There are also five part-time teachers, three Nursery Assistants, five NTAs, 2 Secretaries and other ancillary staff, including eight lunch-time supervisors.

The school is a Christian foundation but with no particular denominational bias. The faiths of all members of the community are respected and valued. Regular assemblies are within the school.

The curriculum covers a wide range of subjects, including all of those prescribed by the National Curriculum, but the emphasis remains on numeracy and literacy. Music and physical education are natural parts of the curriculum and play important roles in the life of the school. A spirit of sensible competition is encouraged and the school teams and choirs enjoy success in local tournaments and festivals. All classrooms, the ICT Suite, Science/Mathematics Room, Music, Library and resource areas are well equipped. Closeness to the Senior School makes it possible to share teaching staff, resources and specialist areas. The curriculum is further enriched by a variety of clubs and societies, in-school workshops and educational outings. The children are encouraged to think of others less fortunate than themselves and money is raised for a variety of charities.

Parental involvement is welcomed and participation both in the classroom and extra-curricular activities appreciated. Social and fund-raising events are organised by the Friends of St John's House, the school's PTA. All children stay to lunch which is cooked on the premises. Before and after school care is available to parents for a small additional charge.

Charitable status. Wakefield Grammar School Foundation is a Registered Charity, number 529908. The School exists to provide an excellent education for your children.

Warminster Preparatory School

Warminster Wiltshire BA12 8JG
Tel: (01985) 210152
Fax: (01985) 218850
e-mail: prep@warminsterschool.org.uk

Stations: Warminster, Westbury (4 miles) for Paddington (1½ hrs)

Co-educational, Day & Boarding
Chairman of Governors: R Southwell, MA, QC
***Headmaster:* C J Jones, BEd** (Hons)

Number of Pupils. Boys 100, Girls 68. (30 of the children are boarders)

Fees. From £1,250 per term for a day pupil age 4 to £3,455 for a full boarding pupil age 8 upwards (3 year olds part time pro rata).

The Headmaster is assisted by a fully qualified staff, the pupil teacher ratio being about one to twelve. Subjects taught are Maths, English, History, Geography, Science, RI, French, ICT, PE, Art, Design and Technology and Music. Games played include Soccer, Rugby, Cricket, Netball, Hockey, Athletics, Tennis and Swimming.

Health and pastoral care are in the hands of the Headmaster's wife, assistant and matron.

Catering for the Preparatory School is supervised by our Catering Manageress, and the food is excellent in quality, quantity and presentation.

The school is readily accessible from motorways 3, 4 and 5 and from the Severn Bridge.

Children are accepted at any age from 3 and are guaranteed a place in the senior School to which they pass at the age of 11.

Extra curricular activities, run by staff and parents include Model Making, Drama, Chess, Cookery, Table Tennis, Pool, Riding, Recorder Groups, Choirs and Orchestra, Woodwork, Computers, Golf, Art and Craft, Dance and Judo. There are annual skiing trips and watersport holidays.

Individual music lessons are arranged and an interest in music is greatly encouraged.

There is a strong tradition of Music, Drama and Sport.

The Preparatory School enjoys the facilities of the Senior School, such as the Sports Hall, Squash Courts, all-weather Hockey/Tennis facility, Art Centre, heated outdoor Swimming Pool, Chapel and more recently a Science Block of Biology, Physics and Chemistry laboratories.

Warwick Junior School

Myton Road Warwick Warwickshire CV34 6PP
Tel: (01926) 776400
Fax: (01926) 401259

Chairman of Governors: Professor E W Ives, BA, PhD
***Head of Junior School:* D J Rogers,** BA, CertEd

Number of pupils. 230 boys aged 7–11. Boarding is available for approximately 20 boys.

The School is the Junior School of Warwick School. The Junior School is situated on a site on the outskirts of Warwick Town adjacent to Warwick Senior School. The buildings are contained within a four acre site and enjoy the use of the Sports and other facilities of Warwick Senior School.

The aim of the School is to provide a good general education based on Christian principles. Academic standards are high and in particular participation in a range of activities is encouraged. Each pupil is encouraged to develop his own personality and to realise his own potential.

The curriculum gives a good grounding in English, Mathematics, Science, Technology, ICT, History, Geography, Religious Education, French, Art, Music, Drama and PE. Many sporting activities are available on the fifty acre campus of Warwick School, which includes a sports hall and indoor swimming pool. Rugby and Soccer are the main winter sports, with Cricket in the summer, plus Athletics, Swimming, Tennis, Squash and Cross Country.

The School's creative activities, dramatic productions and musical performances provide a useful focus in the development of many talents within the School.

Warwick Junior School provides a programme of learning support. This support is available for boys with specific learning difficulties such as dyslexia or dyspraxia and for those who need just a "little extra help" in any area.

Boarding for about 20 Junior School boys available in the Boarding House at Warwick. The large number of day pupils and a boarding house provides maximum flexibility for parental choice. It also encourages a healthy environment in which boys can develop their academic and out of school activities.

Extended day facilities are available until 6.30 pm when the pupils have an opportunity to relax and do their homework before going home.

Boys are prepared for the Entrance Examination to Warwick Senior School at age 11. The majority of pupils who leave Warwick Junior School gain a place in the Senior School at Warwick.

Charitable status. Warwick Junior School is a Registered Charity, number 528775. It exists to provide quality education for boys.

Warwick Preparatory School

Bridge Field Banbury Road Warwick CV34 6PL.
Tel: 01926 491545

Headmistress: **Mrs D M Robinson**, BSc, PGCE

Chairman of the Governors: Mrs V Phillips

Number of Children. Boys 3–7 109; Girls 3–11 352

Fees. £733 per term morning only, £619 per term afternoon only 3+; Nursery full time £1,487 per term; £1,693 per term 4–6 years; £1,872 per term 7–11 years. (including lunch)

Instrumental music tuition optional extra.

Warwick Preparatory School is an Independent School, purpose built in 1970 on a 4½ acre site on the outskirts of Warwick. It is part of the Warwick Schools' Foundation, which includes Warwick School and the King's High School for Girls.

The Prep School has 40 teachers and 18 nursery nurses, classroom assistants and technicians, with specialist tuition in Art, French, Science, Music, Drama, DT, Physical Education and Information Technology.

Boys and girls are admitted from the age of 3+, subject to the availability of places. At the age of 7 the boys sit the competitive entry examination for admission to the Junior Department of Warwick School, whilst the girls normally remain with us until they are 11.

Entry to both Warwick School and King's High School is by competitive examination and boys and girls at the Prep School are prepared for this. Girls are also prepared for the Common Entrance and any other appropriate examinations for their secondary education.

Early registration is advised if a place in the Pre-Preparatory Dept is to be ensured. Entry to the School at the age of 7 and later requires a satisfactory level of attainment in the basic skills and may be competitive.

Waverley House P N E U School

13 Waverley Street Nottingham NG7 4DX
Tel: (0115) 978 3230
Fax: (0115) 978 3230

Headmaster: **T J Collins**,

Number of Pupils. Boys 60, Girls 60

Fees. Up to £1,400 per term, including lunches.

Age Range. Boys and girls from 3 to 11 years.

The school is situated in a large, pleasant, walled garden adjacent to the Arboretum and is less than 10 minutes walk from the City Centre.

It is the aim of the school to provide a wide, rounded education to children of all abilities, developing the full potential of each child as an individual. Through the positive encouragement of a fully qualified staff, who all share the same educational ethos, children not only learn very effectively but develop an enjoyment of learning for its own sake. In addition to the full range of National Curriculum subjects, children study French from the age of 4, and have classes in Nature Study, Music Appreciation, Picture Study and Classic Literature.

A wide range of sports is offered, either on the school's own all-weather surface or using excellent local facilities. Music is very important with a wide range of instruments offered individually, as well as class and school orchestras and music groups, who perform in termly concerts.

Entry is normally at 3, 4, 5 or 8 years of age. The school is fully co-educational and has a new full time nursery from 3 years.

The school is non-selective. Class sizes rarely exceed 20 for younger children and 16 for those in the top three classes. Children are prepared for entry to all the local selective schools.

The school runs an After School Club until 5.30 pm every day.

A branch of the School is at East Leake, for boys and girls from 3 to 11 years. The Headmistress is Mrs E Gibbs. Tel. 01509 852229.

Charitable status. Waverley House PNEU School is a Registered Charity, number 528237. It exists to provide children with a wide, rounded education.

Waverley School

Waverley Way Finchampstead Wokingham Berkshire RG40 4YD
Tel: (0118) 9731121
Fax: (0118) 9731131
e-mail: waverleyschool@waverley.wokingham.sch.uk
website: www.waverley.wokingham.sch.uk
Station: Wokingham

Chairman of the Board of Governors: C J Auden, Esq

Headmaster: **Stuart G Melton**, BSc, PGCE

Number of Pupils. 156 Day pupils, 78 boys, 78 girls

Age range. 3–11 years.

Fees. 7–11 years £1,787 per term (including lunch); 5–7 years £1,671 (including lunch); Nursery: £833 (mornings), £1,312 (full-time, including lunch)

Waverley is a co-educational day school, founded in 1945. It is now an Educational Trust administered by a Board of Governors, some of whom are parents. There is also a thriving Friends' Association.

In September 1997 Waverley School relocated to new purpose-built premises just south of Wokingham. This prestigious development in a superb location offers children outstanding opportunities in and out of the classroom.

Waverley's curriculum provides children with a solid foundation, particularly in the areas of literacy and numeracy. An excellent network of computers provides outstanding opportunities for Information and Communications Technology. All subjects of the National Curriculum are taught, with the addition of French from the age of four. Team games include soccer, netball, cricket and rounders. Swimming and athletics are included in the physical education programme. Children's self-confidence is developed through their involvement in drama. Music, both choral and instrumental, is a particular strength of the School.

The staff are all fully qualified and include visiting specialists for French, Swimming, Piano, Violin, Cello, Guitar, Ballet, Judo, Chess, and Speech and Drama. There is specialist help for pupils with specific learning difficulties.

Waverley successfully prepares boys and girls for entrance to Independent Senior Schools at 11+. An integral Nursery Unit for 3–4 year olds offers a carefully balanced introduction to the School, and ensures both social and educational continuity from 3–11 years.

Charitable status. Waverley School is a Registered Charity, number 309102. It exists to provide education for boys and girls between 3 and 11.

Wellesley House

Broadstairs Kent CT10 2DG.
Tel: (01843) 862991
Fax: (01843) 602068
Station: Broadstairs

Chairman of the Governors: B R K Moorhead, Esq

***Headmaster:* R R Steel**, BSc (London)

Number of Pupils. 100 Boys, 61 Girls
Fees. Boarding: £4,050; Day £3,250
Location. The School which is run by an Educational Trust stands in its own grounds of 20 acres and was purpose-built in 1898.

Trains run hourly from Victoria Station, London, and the journey either by rail or by road takes under 2 hours. At the beginning and end of each term and at exeats, the School operates a Coach Service between Broadstairs, the M2, Dartford Crossing, Victoria Coach Station and Birchanger Services on the M11. which reduces problems of transportation to a minimum.

Facilities. In 1969 the School merged with St Peter's Court and through generous support, an extensive modernisation and building programme was carried out, the central feature of which was a multi-purpose hall which has a chancel at one end and stage at the other. Modern kitchens were also built adjoining a large dining room. As a result of the Centenary Appeal, the School has a new Science and Technology building, which includes modern Science laboratories, an ICT laboratory and a Craft room. Other facilities include a Library, an indoor heated Swimming Pool, 4 hard Tennis courts, 2 Squash courts, a modelling room, Art room, a Music wing, a .22 Shooting Range, and separate recreation rooms, all of which are in the School grounds. There is a spacious Sports Hall. The main team games are Cricket, Association and Rugby Football, Hockey, Netball and Rounders. Tuition is also given in Squash, Shooting, Fencing, Golf, Tennis and Swimming. Ballet Dancing and Riding are also available.

A Special feature of the School is that boys between the ages of 7½ and 9½ live in a junior wing. This is linked to the Main School but self-contained under the care of a married housemaster and a resident matron.

The girls live in a separate house, 'The Orchard', within the School grounds, under the care of a married housemaster and a resident house mistress.

Education. Boys and girls are prepared for all Independent Senior Schools. Those who show sufficient promise are prepared for Scholarships, of which many have been won from the School, but the curriculum is designed to enable all children to reach the highest standard possible by sound teaching along carefully thought out lines to suit the needs of the individual.

The Headmaster and his wife are assisted by a Senior Master, 15 assistant masters and 4 mistresses.

Charitable status. Wellesley House and St Peter's Court Educational Trust Limited is a Registered Charity, number 307852. It exists solely to provide education to boys and girls.

Wellingborough Junior School

Wellingborough Northants NN8 2BU.
Tel: (01933) 222698

Chairman of the Governors: R A Swindall, Esq

***Headmaster:* G R Lowe**, BEd (Nottingham)

Deputy Headmaster: N C Anns, BEd (WLIHE)

Numbers. Day Boys 155, Day Girls 100.
Fees. £6,900 per annum. (Lunches inclusive).
The School is the Junior School of Wellingborough School (a registered charity). Girls and boys are admitted from 8 years old. The Junior School is self-contained in its classrooms, Science Laboratories and Hall. Other buildings and facilities on the site are used by both Senior and Junior Schools – Sports Hall, Floodlit Astroturf hockey pitch, Dining Hall, Chapel, Design Technology and Art Centre, Music School and Squash Courts. Music, Art and Drama are very strong. The School has a particularly high reputation for orchestral and choral music. The Chapel Choir sings in Cathedrals throughout the country. There is a wide range of activities after school including Chess, Ballet and Tap Dancing. Involvement in a comprehensive Saturday Activities programme is optional. Activities include Fencing, Calligraphy, Soft Toy Making, IT, Table Tennis, Karate, .22 Shooting, Cycling Proficiency, Cookery, First Aid, Art, Golf, Archery, Swimming and Computing. Games played are Association and Rugby Football, Hockey, Netball, Cricket, Athletics, Tennis, Badminton, Squash and Rounders. (There are 40 acres of playing fields including a 9-hole Golf Course.) The School is organised into six Clubs each under the care of a member of staff who oversees the academic and social progress of the girls and boys.

The school encourages social responsibility in a Christian environment, and there are regular services in the School Chapel.

Charitable status. Wellingborough School is a Registered Charity, number LA/309923 A/2. It exists to provide education for girls and boys.

Wellow House School

Wellow Nr Newark Notts. NG22 0EA.
Tel: (01623) 861054
Fax: (01623) 836665
e-mail: wellowhouse@btinternet.com

Chairman of the Governors: Paul Ainscough

***Headmaster:* Malcolm Tozer**, BSc, MEd, PhD

Number of pupils. 155
Fees. Pre-Prep pupils £1,150 per term; Day pupils £1,650–£2,130; Boarding pupils £2,700. Fees include meals and normal extras.

Wellow House School was founded in 1971 by the Stewart General Charitable Trust. Since 1994 it has been managed as an educational charity by the Directors and administered by a Board of Governors. This co-educational school has an established reputation for high academic standards, a successful sporting record, broad cultural interests and a happy family atmosphere. Weekly and occasional boarding has become an increasingly popular means of encouraging self-reliance within a supportive community and as a preparation for senior school and university.

The teaching staff of 9 men and 9 women is well qualified and experienced. A distinctive teaching style places great emphasis on the rapport between teacher and pupil in small classes, without slavish reliance on work-sheets and text books. Each pupil maintains a file of notes, as a record and for reference. All take pride in honest hard work, confidence through encouragement, courtesy and fair discipline, and a strong sense of belonging. The thriving house points' system encourages much voluntary study and is the basis of the disciplinary process.

Husband and wife Houseparents look after the boarders and oversee the evening activity programme. They are assisted by a team of resident and non-resident tutors. A qualified housekeeper/matron supervises the pupils' boarding, catering and medical needs. There are visiting teachers for Instrumental Tuition, Table Tennis and Drama.

The school is attractively set in 15 acres of parkland and playing fields on the fringe of the Sherwood Forest village of Wellow. There is easy road access to this heart of Nottinghamshire from Worksop and Sheffield to the north, Mansfield and Chesterfield to the west, Nottingham and Grantham to the south, and Lincoln and Newark to the east. Newark lies on north-south and east-west main line rail routes.

A continuous programme of development has provided purpose-built classrooms, science laboratory, networked computer room, music rooms, library, assembly hall and dining hall to add to the original country house. The boarding accommodation was refurbished in 1997 and 2000. Recent additions include studios for art, ceramics and photography, and a sports hall with indoor cricket nets. There is an indoor heated swimming pool, an all-weather cricket net, and an all-weather tennis court. The Pre-Prep classes are housed in their own building, surrounded by play-time facilities. There are close links with the village church.

Children enter the school after an interview visit and a trial day at any age from 2½ to 11+ – the oldest often transferring from primary schools. Six Entrance Scholarships may be awarded annually and Bursaries can give financial assistance. Pupils are prepared for Common Entrance and Scholarships to a wide range of Senior Independent Schools, both boarding and day, and there is a continuous programme of assessment and reporting.

There is a broad physical education programme, with school matches in Rugby, Netball, Soccer, Hockey, Cricket, Rounders, Cross Country, Swimming and Tennis. The school is renowned for its pupils' prowess in Archery and Table Tennis. Weekend and holiday expeditions for Outdoor Pursuits in the Peak District, Yorkshire, Scotland and beyond are popular.

There is encouragement to participate in Natural History, the Visual Arts, Dance, Drama and Music, and more than half of the pupils learn a musical instrument. Most are involved in the much enjoyed regular concerts.

Charitable status. Wellow House School is a Registered Charity, number 528234. It exists solely to provide a high standard of all-round education for children aged 2½ to 13 years.

Wells Cathedral Junior School

8 New Street Wells Somerset BA5 2LQ.
Tel: (01749) 672291
Fax: (01749) 671940
e-mail: headmaster@wcjs80.fsnet.co.uk

***Head of the Junior School:* N M Wilson, BA**

Chairman of Governors: The Dean of Wells

Number of Boys and Girls. 194. 86 Boys and 108 Girls (of whom 10 are Boarders). Age 3–11 years

Fees. Boarders £4,093 per term. Day children £2,455 per term, Pre-Prep £1,204 per term (inclusive of lunch)

The Junior School is made up of the Pre-Prep department (3–7) and the Junior School (7–11). Pupils accepted into the Junior School normally make a smooth transfer to the Senior School at 11 and scholarships are awarded to the best boys and girls.

Academic Work. The Junior School prepares children for the academic work in the senior school and takes part in the national tests at the end of KS 1 & 2 however the school is not restricted by the demands of the National Curriculum. The aim of the school is to ensure sound academic standards within a friendly and stimulating environment.

Children are assessed regularly for both academic achievement and effort, and parents have many opportunities to meet staff and receive information on their child's progress.

Pastoral Care. The form teacher is responsible for the pastoral care of pupils; in addition each pupil is allocated to a House which has an assembly once a week. Work and sports competitions take place in houses and pupils are able to develop a good relationship not only with their own peer group but with pupils from across the Junior School.

Music and Drama. Set in beautiful grounds just to the north of the Cathedral, pupils from the school provide the boy and girl choristers at the Cathedral. In addition, a number of pupils are specialist musicians enjoying the expert tuition of the music department at the school which is one of the four in England designated and grant-aided by the Department for Education. Scholarships are available for both the choristers and the musicians.

Drama and music are considered vital activities to bring out the best in children. A full programme of concerts, both formal and informal, takes place during the year for all age groups as well as big productions and small year group dramas. The school has started to take its production to the Edinburgh Festival and it has established drama exchange links with a school in the Czech Republic.

Sport. The school has many of its own facilities and it is able to share some, such as the sports hall, astroturf pitch and swimming pool, with the senior school which is on the same site. Pupils experience a wide range of activities on the games field. Sport is played to a high standard with rugby, netball, hockey, cricket, swimming, athletics and gymnastics being the main sports. All children have the opportunity to take part in climbing, caving and canoeing; outdoor pursuits are regarded as an important opportunity for the children in the school. Many clubs and societies run at lunchtimes or after school.

Charitable status. Wells Cathedral School is a Registered Charity, number 310212. It has existed since AD 909 to provide education for its pupils.

Westbourne House

Shopwyke Chichester West Sussex PO20 6BH.
Tel: (01243) 782739
Fax: (01243) 770759
e-mail: whouseoffice@rmplc.co.uk

Chairman of the Governors: C P Sharman

***Headmaster:* S L Rigby**, BA, PGCE

Number of Pupils. 240 (100 boarders, 140 day) with a further 100 pupils in the Pre-Prep.

Fees. Boarders £3,550 per term; Day £2,850; Pre-Prep £1,475.

The School was started in 1907 and became a Charitable Trust in 1967, for educational purposes.

There is a well qualified teaching staff of 30 plus visiting music staff, a senior matron and 3 assistant matrons.

Pupils are prepared for the Common Entrance and many Scholarships have been won at Senior Independent Schools in recent years. The broad curriculum includes Music, Art, Design Technology, Ceramics, Food Technology, Drama and Information Technology. Individual needs are well catered for.

The School stands in its own grounds of 60 acres with extensive playing fields, Sports Hall, Indoor Swimming Pool, Theatre, 3 Squash Courts, 7 Tennis Courts and Modern Music complex. The Art and Technology Centre was refurbished in 1992, a new Junior Teaching block for Years 3, 4 and 5 was built in 1997 and a purpose built Science Department in 1999.

Games. Rugby, Soccer, Hockey, Cricket, Rounders, Netball, Athletics, Squash, Tennis, Badminton, Sailing and Golf. A 25 metre indoor swimming pool was completed in 1995.

The School has been co-educational since September 1992.

Westbourne School

Westbourne Road Sheffield S10 2QQ.
Tel: (0114) 2660374/2684322
Fax: (0114) 2670862
e-mail: info@westbourneschool.co.uk
website: www.westbourneschool.co.uk

Chairman of the Governors: Mr C W H Warrack

Headmaster: **C R Wilmshurst**, BA (Open University), CertEd

Number of Pupils. 250 day pupils, boys and girls.

The fully co-educational School, founded in 1885, is an Educational Trust with a Board of Governors, some of whom are Parents. The number of entries is limited to maintain small classes of around 20 (15 in later years), with a staff/pupil ratio of 1:10. Where specialist staff are involved, classes in Science, IT and Art and Design are kept at around 10.

The Kindergarten and Lower School are housed in a specially designed and equipped building, staffed by qualified and experienced teachers. Music and Games are taught by specialists from Y1. Specialist Science and Technology are introduced from Y4 (8+), and in Y4 (8+) there is specialist teaching in Information Technology, Art and Design, and RE. French, Science and Computers are introduced from the age of 4.

In the Upper School, all lessons are taught by specialists in Subject Rooms. There is also a Science Laboratory and ICT, Art and Music Rooms (18 electronic keyboards), Fiction and Reference Libraries, and a Sports Hall with Stage.

The new Senior School provides teaching to GCSE in Years 9, 10 and 11 up to age 16. The Senior School has its own campus immediately adjacent to the existing Lower and Upper Schools.

A high standard of work is maintained – the main aim being to bring out the best in every pupil according to their ability. Pupils are entered for Common Entrance, Independent School Scholarships, or for entrance to Westbourne's own Senior School. There is also a Department catering for those with Specific Learning Difficulties. Great emphasis is laid on courtesy and a mutual respect for each other.

Art, Music and Drama are strongly encouraged throughout the school, with regular concerts, plays and art exhibitions. Tuition in several instruments is available.

The main sports are Rugby, Football, Hockey, Cricket, Athletics, Netball, Rounders and Cross Country Running with regular matches against other schools. There are also opportunities for Short Tennis, Swimming, Tae Kwan Do, Basketball, Volleyball, Fencing, Skiing and Badminton.

Breakfast (at an extra cost) is available from 8 am and, while the length of day depends on the age of the child, there are after-school facilities for all pupils until 5.30 pm, with the older pupils staying till 5.45 pm. There is no school on Saturdays.

Charitable status. Westbourne School is a Registered Charity, number 529381. It exists to provide education for boys and girls.

Westbrook Hay

London Road Hemel Hempstead Herts HP1 2RF.
Tel: (01442) 256143/230099
Fax: (01442) 232076
e-mail: admin@westbrookhay.co.uk
website: www.westbrookhay.co.uk

Headmaster: **Keith D Young,** BEd (Hons) (Exeter)

Chairman of the Board of Governors: Michael Bellegarde

Number of Pupils. Boarders 7, Day boys 171, Day girls 84

Fees. September 2001. Weekly boarding £3,185 per term, Day £2,620 per term, Pre-Prep (4–8 years) £1,490, Nursery (2–4 years) £1,400 per term.

Location. Less than an hour from Central London and within easy reach of the M25 and M1.

Set in 30 acres of elevated grounds overlooking the Bourne Valley, the school, founded in 1892, aims to develop qualities of intellect and character. Classes are small and each individual is encouraged and helped to achieve their potential. Individuality, honesty, a sense of humour and self-reliance are attributes which are stimulated and valued in this friendly school which maintains a family atmosphere.

There are 21 full time members of the teaching staff who are assisted by a number of peripatetic specialists. The well being of both day students and boarders is in the hands of resident staff and two matrons, one of whom is an RGN.

Nursery and Pre-Prep departments prepare children from two to eight for entry into the upper school. Children in Years 3 and 4 are class taught primarily by their form teacher, before a move to subject-based curriculum in Year 5. The academic focus is provided by the goals of the Common Entrance and Scholarship examinations as most children go on to independent senior schools. All children follow the National Curriculum subject areas and in many cases extend them.

Extensive playing fields give ample room for rugby, soccer, hockey, cricket, golf, rounders and athletics. An all-weather netball and tennis court and heated swimming pool are complemented by a new purpose built Sports Hall which provides for badminton, basketball, cricket nets, five-a-side football, gymnastics and a galaxy of other indoor sports.

Weekly boarding arrangements are flexible. A breakfast club, after school care and bussing service are also offered to accommodate the needs of working parents.

Charitable status. Westbrook Hay School is a Registered Charity, number 292537. It exists to provide education for boys and girls.

Westerleigh

St Leonards-on-Sea Sussex TN38 0SE
Tel: (01424) 440760
Fax: (01424) 440761
Station: Warrior Square, St Leonards

Headmistress: **Mrs P K Wheeler**, CertEd

Number of Pupils. 130 Boys, 90 Girls (all day pupils).

Fees. Day Pupils from £375–£1,775.

The School was founded in 1907. Westerleigh is situated on the outskirts of St Leonards-on-Sea and is ten minutes from the sea. It stands in ten acres of land. There are three playing fields, large gymnasium and all-weather playing surface.

It has a large, qualified teaching staff. Many Scholarships are won to Independent Senior Schools. The class sizes are small and great emphasis is put on 'caring'. There are specialist classrooms for all the major subjects, with well equipped modern language, science, and computer laboratories.

The Nursery department accepts children from 2 years old.

Music and Art take a prominent part in the life of the school.

Cricket, Soccer, Rugby, Swimming and Hockey are the main sports. Other activities include Squash, Tennis, Shooting, Athletics, Gymnastics, Orienteering. Sailing and activity trips to France take place during the year. The School also has a Beaver, Cubs and Scout group.

West Hill Park

St Margaret's Lane Titchfield Fareham Hants PO14 4BT.
Tel: (01329) 842356
Fax: (01329) 842911
website: www.westhill.hants.sch.uk

Headmaster: **E P K Hudson**, CertEd

Chairman of Governors: David Younghusband, Esq (Notary Public)

Number of Pupils. 48 Boarders: 29 boys, 19 girls. Day: 76 boys, 48 girls. Pre-Prep: 64 boys, 29 girls, aged 4–7. Nursery: 9 boys, 13 girls aged 3–4.

Fees. Boarders £3,520 per term. Day children £2,450–£2,650. All extras are optional. Pre-Prep fees £1,540. Nursery £444–£910 per term.

West Hill Park was founded in 1920 and became an Educational Trust in 1959. Boys and girls are prepared for Scholarships and Common Entrance to all Independent Schools. West Hill Park takes pride in the excellence of its co-educational system.

The Main School building is Georgian, originally a shooting lodge for the Earls of Southampton and provides spacious and comfortable boarding accommodation for boys and girls under the supervision of resident House-parents. Also in the main building are the New Library, the Dining Hall, the Assembly Hall with fully equipped stage and the administrative offices. Further excellent facilities include the Art Centre, the Music School, a 25m heated indoor swimming pool, a fully equipped Sports Hall, the Craft, Design and Technology Centre, 2 Science laboratories, the Information Technology Centre, with its network of 16 PCs, scanner, colour printers and Internet link, the purpose built Pre-Prep Department and the Nursery Department. West Hill Park stands in its own grounds of nearly 40 acres on the edge of Titchfield village. There are 4 hard and 3 grass tennis courts, a riding school, all-weather cricket nets, a cross-country course and, in summer, a nine hole golf course.

There are 37 fully qualified members of teaching staff. 13 members of staff are resident, either in the main building or in houses in the school grounds, giving a great sense of community to the school.

A tutorial system monitors the individual child's work weekly and there is a strong pastoral care system. There is a wide range of activities available to encourage children to develop individual skills and talents; Choirs, orchestra, dance aerobics, cookery, carpentry, shooting, judo, self-defence, ballet, drama, golf, life-saving, softball, volleyball, computer club, string group, squash, chess, needlecraft, sailing, roller blading, cycling, riding on ponies kept at the school, as well as the more intensive training available in the Swim Squad, Tennis Squad, Scholarship Art and Cricket Coaching. The Boarders enjoy many expeditions at weekends as well as fun events at school, such as orienteering, theatre workshops, cycle marathons, games evenings, discos and performing in their own annual 'Revue'.

Games played include soccer, Rugby Football, cricket, hockey, tennis, athletics, netball and rounders.

All domestic arrangements are under the direct supervision of Mrs Hudson. There are 2 resident matrons as well as the Senior Matron, who is medically qualified. The Senior Matron and her husband, a member of the academic staff, run the Boarding House, assisted by a House Tutor.

Charitable status. West Hill School Trust is a Registered Charity, number 307343. It exists to educate children.

West House School

Edgbaston Birmingham B15 2NX.
Tel: 0121-440 4097 and 0121-440 2843
Fax: 0121-440 5839

Chairman of Governors: S T Heathcote, FCA

Headmaster: **G K Duce**, JP, MA (Trinity College, Dublin), PGCE (Oxon)

Number of Pupils. A maximum 200 boys between ages 4 and 11 (Reception to Year 6) plus 70 boys and girls between the ages of eighteen months and 4.

Fees. 4 to 11 year olds: £1,212 to £2,005 per term according to age. The fees include lunches and break-time drinks. Under 4: fees according to number of sessions attended per week. Fee list on application.

West House was founded in 1895 and since 1959 has been an Educational Trust controlled by a Board of Governors. The school has a strong academic reputation and pupils are regularly awarded scholarships to secondary schools at 11+. The well qualified and experienced staff provides a sound education for boys of all abilities. The National Curriculum is followed and pupils are prepared for SATs at KS1 and KS2. Pupils are taught in small classes which ensures that they receive much individual attention. Specialist help is available for children with Dyslexia or who require learning support. Music teachers visit the school to give individual music tuition.

The school occupies a leafy five acre site a mile from Birmingham city centre. As well as the main teaching blocks there are two well-equipped science laboratories and a sports hall.

The Centenary Building, opened in 1998, accommodates

the art and design technology department, ICT room and senior Library. Extensive playing fields, two all-weather tennis courts and all-weather cricket nets enable pupils to participate in many games and sports. Pupils also enjoy a wide range of hobby activities, and drama and music play important roles in school life.

The school is open during term time between 8 am and 6 pm. On-site Holiday Clubs are run by members of staff during the holidays.

Charitable status. West House School is a Registered Charity, number 45260. It exists to provide education for boys.

Westminster Abbey Choir School

Dean's Yard London SW1P 3NY.
Tel: 020 7222 6151
Fax: 020 7222 1548

Chairman of Governors: The Dean of Westminster

Acting Headmaster: **John Curtis**, MA, DipEd

Number of Boys. 38 (all chorister boarders)

Fees. £1,218 per term (inclusive of tuition on two instruments). (Additional bursaries may be available in cases of real financial need).

Westminster Abbey Choir School is now the only school in the country reserved exclusively for the education of choristers. Because of this unique situation it is possible to be flexible with the school timetable in order to accommodate the special services that take place in Westminster Abbey without disruption to the boys' education.

Sports. The sports played include football, cricket, running.

There are 7 full-time, 3 part-time teachers as well as 12 visiting instrumental teachers. Most boys in recent years have won valuable music scholarships to enable them to continue in independent education after the age of 13. The Matron/Housekeeper is a qualified nurse who, with the help of an Assistant Matron, supervises the domestic arrangements as well as looking after the general health of the boys.

Entry is by voice trial and academic tests; further details are available from the Headmaster who is always pleased to hear from parents of potential choristers.

Charitable status. Westminster Abbey is a Registered Charity, number X8259. It is a religious establishment incorporated by Royal Charter in 1560.

Westminster Cathedral Choir School

Ambrosden Avenue London SW1P 1QH.
Tel: 020 7798-9081
Fax: 020 7630 7209
e-mail: emailwccs@aol.com

President: His Eminence Cardinal Archbishop of Westminster

Chairman of Governors: Martin Morland, CMG

Headmaster: **Charles Foulds**, BA (University College, Swansea)

Number of Boys. 100 (30 Chorister boarders; 70 Day boys)

Fees. Chorister Boarders £3,930. Day Boys £7,485 per annum

The School was founded in 1901 to provide Choristers for the newly built Westminster Cathedral. It is one of the very few Catholic Choir Schools in the English-speaking world offering boarding facilities to choristers only. Choristers must be Catholics, but day boys of other denominations are welcome. Preference is given to Roman Catholics. Westminster Cathedral provides a Chaplain to serve the spiritual life of the school.

At present there is a full-time staff of nine, all graduates, and 12 visiting instrumental teachers. Choristers learn two instruments and most day boys at least one. There are two orchestras and a great deal of chamber music is played. An annual concert is held in July in St John's Smith Square.

The School prepares boys for the Common Entrance Examination, and its record of Scholarships, both academic and musical, is excellent.

The major games are Football, Rugby and Cricket which are played close by at Vincent Square, by kind permission of the Headmaster of Westminster School, and also at Battersea Park; the boys swim and play badminton at the local Sports Centre and some attend the Indoor Cricket School at The Oval.

The domestic arrangements are in the hands of the Headmaster, his wife a senior and junior housemaster, two matrons and three cooks.

Boys are usually accepted in the September after their eighth birthday. Entry for Choristers is gained through Voice Trials, which are held three times a year. Day boys are accepted as a result of interviews and assessment.

Charitable status. Westminster Cathedral Choir School is a Registered Charity, number 233699. It exists to provide a musical education for Roman Catholic boys.

Westminster Under School

Adrian House 27 Vincent Square London SW1P 2NN.
Tel: 020 7821 5788
Fax: 020 7821 0458

Chairman of Governors: The Dean of Westminster, The Very Revd Dr A W Carr

Master: **J P Edwards,** BA, MA (London)

Deputy Master: B D Bibby, BA (Exeter)

Number of boys. 270 (day boys only)

Fees. £2,668 per term (inclusive of lunches and stationery)

The Under School is closely linked to Westminster School, sharing the same Governing Body, although it is not on the same site. The school has recently undergone a major refurbishment and, from September 2001, will have a new hall/gymnasium, junior classrooms and well-equipped IT room.

Boys are prepared, though not exclusively, for Westminster through the Common Entrance Examination, and "The Challenge", Westminster School's scholarship examination. Most boys proceed to Westminster, but entry into the Under School does not guarantee a place at the "Great School". Each year some boys will go on to Eton or Winchester.

There is a strong musical tradition at the Under School, with a junior and senior choir, an orchestra, and string, brass and jazz groups. There is a specialist suite of art rooms with facilities for all kinds of creative activity and the art department organises competitions in photography and model-making. There are other competitions each year in public speaking, creative writing, chess and Scrabble.

Games are played on the school grounds adjacent to Adrian House in Vincent Square and although football and cricket are the main sports, there are opportunities to participate in basketball, hockey, rugby, swimming and tennis.

There are currently 270 pupils in the school, with 20 boys coming in at the age of 7, 40 boys at the age of 8 and 20 at the age of 11. Means-tested bursaries are available at 11+ and many boys apply from London primary schools.

Charitable status. Westminster Under School is a Registered Charity, number 312728. It exists to provide education for boys.

Westville House School

Carter's Lane Middleton Ilkley W Yorkshire LS29 0DQ
Tel: 01943 608053
Fax: 01943 817410

Chairman of Trustees: Mr A N Brown

Headmaster: **Mr C A Holloway,** BA (Hons), PGCE

Number of Pupils. 150
Fees per term. £805-£1,450

Westville House is a preparatory school for girls and boys aged 3-11, situated in glorious countryside just outside the town of Ilkley in West Yorkshire. It was founded in 1960 as an extension of the owner's family and, although the school has grown since then, the family atmosphere has been retained to this day.

Children join the Pre-Preparatory department at three where outstanding courses are offered in the Foundation years. They move into the Preparatory department at seven, where specialist teaching is introduced in all subjects and preparation begins for entry to senior schools at age eleven. The school offers a broad and stimulating curriculum and has an outstanding academic record with awards gained annually at all the local independent senior schools.

As well as the broad curriculum on offer, there are many other areas of strength within the school. Drama begins at an early age and there are regular performances by children of all ages. Visiting specialist staff also prepare children for the Guildhall Speech and Drama examinations and for performances at local Festivals. Music is a vital part of the life of the school. Children perform regularly in concerts from an early age and many learn instruments individually. The school orchestra and choir perform regularly at Festivals and in Church services. Sport is also an important part of school life and teams play against other schools at rugby, football, cricket, rounders, athletics, swimming and cross-country running. Trips into the community are a regular and important feature of school life, taking advantage of the wealth of facilities in the area.

The school has a staff of fifteen well-qualified and experienced teachers. The family atmosphere within the school means that all the children are well-known to them and they combine just the right blend of firmness and fun to bring out the best in each individual child.

Charitable status. The school is run by a group of Trustees. It is a company limited by guarantee, Company Number 4030247.

White House Preparatory School

Wokingham Berks RG40 3HD
Tel: (0118) 9785151

Chairman: Dr V P Houghton

Headmistress: **Mrs M L Blake**, BA, PGCE (Nottingham)

Numbers. 145 day pupils, boys 3–4 yrs, girls 3–11 yrs.
Fees. On a sliding scale, maximum £1,795 per term.

White House School was founded in 1890 and moved to its present site about a mile from the centre of Wokingham in 1948. The main building dates back to the eighteenth century and to this has been added a large multi purpose hall with excellent facilities for gymnastics and a modern classroom block. Another new purpose built classroom block was opened in January 1997, comprising specialist nursery accommodation and two more junior classrooms. A further classroom was built later that year and since then the library has been completely refurbished. A purpose built music room was completed in 1999 and a new ICT suite opened in summer 2000 providing 16 computers. The spacious grounds include large lawns, a hard porous area for netball and tennis and an imaginative play area.

Pupils are accepted from the age of 3 (later if there are vacancies) and the school provides continuous education for girls up to 11 in preparation for entry to secondary schools. Staff are fully qualified, with assistants to help with the younger children. The school follows the national curriculum, seeking to blend this modern approach with well tried and tested methods. A certain amount of specialist teaching, including PE and Music is introduced from the age of 4. French is taught from Year 1, again by a specialist teacher. The school operates an extended day which runs from 8.00 – 5.30 and includes a variety of after school activities such as ballet, art and craft and a supervised homework club.

White House prides itself on the high quality of its pastoral care. Small classes enable children to receive a great deal of individual attention and our aim is to develop the whole person, the intellectual potential and the personality. Founded on Christian principles, the school seeks to teach care, concern and courtesy, and our visitors frequently comment on the friendly, purposeful and happy atmosphere. The school benefits from a thriving partnership with Luckley-Oakfield School, a nearby girls independent senior school, and many pupils continue their education there.

Charitable status. White House School is a Registered Charity, number 309106. The school is a Christian based preparatory school, established and maintained for the purpose of providing high quality education based on Christian principles for children aged 3–11.

Widford Lodge

Chelmsford Essex CM2 9AN
Tel: (01245) 352581
Fax: (01245) 281329
e-mail: widford.lodge@btinternet.com
website: www.widfordlodge.co.uk
Station: Chelmsford

Principal: H C Witham, MA (St Catherine's College, Cambridge)

Head Master: **S C Trowell,** BHum Hons, PGCE (London)

Number of Pupils. 86 Day Pupils. Pre-Prep 96 Pupils. Pre-School Nursery: varies according to number of sessions. Ages 2½–11 years

Fees per term. Pre-Prep £1,260. Main School £1,670. All fees include lunch, text-books, stationery, etc.

Widford Lodge is a co-educational day school situated on the southern fringe of Chelmsford. Founded in 1935 the school aims to provide an all-round education within a happy, caring environment. Children are encouraged to enjoy their time at school, while also learning a sense of responsibility and a positive approach to their role in school and the wider community.

An enthusiastic staff prepare the children for grammar school via the 11+, entrance into senior independent schools through examination or scholarship and local secondary schools. A combination of form tutors, subject specialists and small classes ensure a good academic standard. The curriculum is broadly based and aims to develop a variety of interests, academic, aesthetic and sporting. The school has a well-equipped computer suite and the children are encouraged to use their IT skills in many different ways.

The main part of the school stands in 5 acres of wooded grounds that include an outdoor Swimming Pool, a Floodlit Tennis Court, Cricket Nets, Science Laboratory and Design Technology Centre. There is plenty of space for the children to play and to use their imagination. The school also owns 9 acres of playing fields.

The children have the opportunity to play cricket, netball, rugby, hockey, soccer, athletics, swimming, cross-country, tennis, golf and rounders. Although a small school we are proud of our sporting tradition, which is underpinned by our belief that sport is for all and is ultimately played for fun.

Music, drama and art are all encouraged and a wide range of musical instruments are taught. There is a busy school choir and an annual concert.

There are many after-school activities which the children are encouraged to get involved in, as well as the opportunity to do their prep, supervised by a teacher, until 5.30 pm.

Willington School

Worcester Road Wimbledon London SW19 7QQ
Tel: 020 8944 7020

Chairman of the Trustees: G Holman, MA, BMIM

***Headmaster:* Mrs R E Bowman**, BA (Warwick), PGCE

Number of Boys. 210 (all Day Boys). Age 4–13½

Fees. £1,520–£1,730, all inclusive according to age.

Established in Putney in 1885 Willington moved to larger premises in Wimbledon in 1990. The move enabled it to offer good facilities in all subjects, both academic and non-academic. A new building project was recently completed which has provided improved facilities for Music, Information and Communication Technology, Art and Design Technology. The laboratory was newly installed with the move as was the library. There are two playgrounds on site, one specially equipped for the younger boys, and sporting facilities, including swimming, athletics, squash and tennis as well as the major team games, are within ten minutes drive from the School. Judo and short tennis are also offered on site. A major feature of the School is the large central hall which offers facilities for, amongst other things, music, drama and gym.

The School has been inspected and accredited by ISC. The School aims to encourage hard work, courtesy, good manners and fun. From the earliest years the boys are encouraged to give of their best but are not put under the great pressure modern society so often seems to consider necessary. There is no exam bar to their progress through the School and they are prepared for Common Entrance or scholarships to major independent secondary schools. The School has an excellent exam record at 13+. There is an entry at 4 and for older pupils by assessment for any vacancies that may arise. Classes will not exceed 20 pupils.

The atmosphere of the School is friendly and informal, and the boys are encouraged to be responsible to themselves and to each other in a practical Christian way.

Charitable status. Willington School Foundation Limited is a Registered Charity, number 312733A. Its aim is to devote itself to the continuation and development of the School.

Wilmslow Preparatory School

Grove Avenue Wilmslow Cheshire SK9 5EG.
Tel: (01625) 524246

Day School for Girls 3–11 years. Founded 1909

Chairman of Board of Trustees: Mr M B Solomon, FCA

***Headmistress:* Miss J Ballance**, MA, CertEd

Number of Pupils. 165

Fees. September 2001 – £450–£1,510 (lunches extra)

The School is registered as an Educational Trust. It is purpose built and is situated in the centre of Wilmslow in its own spacious grounds. The facilities include an Assembly Hall/Gymnasium, a Maths/Science Room, Computer Room with networked PCs, an Art Room and Kindergarten Unit, a Classroom Block for 5–8 year olds and two well stocked libraries. There is a Tennis/Netball Court, a Sportsfield and ample play areas.

The School aims to provide wide educational opportunities for all girls. It has a long established good academic record and caters for a wide variety of entrance examinations to Independent Senior Day and Boarding Schools.

Wilmslow Preparatory School offers a variety of activities which include Music, Art and Drama. Principal sports include gymnastics, netball, hockey, tennis, athletics and swimming.

There are sixteen qualified and experienced teachers on the staff.

Charitable status. Wilmslow Preparatory School is a Registered Charity, number 525924. It exists to provide full-time education for pupils aged between 5 and 11, and part or full time education to pre-kindergarten children from the age of 2.

Winchester House School

Brackley Northants NN13 7AZ.
Tel: (01280) 702483

Chairman of Governors: K H Fowler

***Headmaster:* J R G Griffith**, BA, PGCE

Number of Children. 290. Boarding Boys 51; Day Boys 144; Boarding Girls 25; Day Girls 70.

Fees. £4,060 for boarders per term inclusive. £3,080 for day children per term

There are 21 full time members of staff. The Matron is an RGN and has 5 assistants.

Winchester House is a boarding, weekly boarding and day school which prepares boys and girls, aged 7–13, for entry to Senior Independent Schools. There are playing fields of 16 acres, large Sports Hall, heated outdoor Swimming Pool, Rifle Range, School Hall, Laboratory, Squash Courts, Art and Music Centres, CDT etc. The School games are Rugby Football, Hockey, Cricket, Athletics, Tennis, Squash, Golf, Netball and Rounders. Children take part in adventure activities: camping, orienteering, sailing, canoeing etc. Music, Speech & Drama are taught. The School has its own Chapel. The School is a Charitable Educational Trust.

A Pre-Preparatory Department (boys and girls 3–7 years) is situated in a separate building adjacent to the playing fields (Fees: £1,360–£1,760).

Charitable status. Winchester House School Trust Limited is a Registered Charity, number 309912. It aims to provide education for boys and girls between the ages of 3 and 13.

Windlesham House School

Washington Pulborough W Sussex RH20 4AY
Tel: (01903) 874700.
Fax: (01903) 874701
e-mail: office@windlesham.com
website: www.windlesham.com

Chairman of Governors: Mrs J Moody-Stuart

***Head:* P J Lough**, MA (Oxon), PGCE (Dunelm)

Deputy Head: R Martin

Number of Pupils. Prep: 160 Boys; 120 Girls (all boarders); Little Windlesham: 30 Boys; 30 Girls.

Fees per term from September 2000. Prep: £3,800; Little Windlesham: £1,505–£1,725

Windlesham nestles in 60 glorious acres of the South Downs and is within easy reach of London and both Gatwick and Heathrow airports. It is a co-educational all-boarding school from which children go on to a wide variety of senior schools. Above all it is a happy, family-centred school where children and adults live and work together in a unique atmosphere. There is a very strong pastoral care system in place that ensures every child feels secure and happy no matter how far from home they may be.

Our curriculum is very broad and this, together with our talented and creative staff, enables us to place great emphasis on the individual development of each child, academically, socially and emotionally. Our academic standards are high, in line with and beyond the National Curriculum, and we gain numerous scholarships to senior schools each year.

We have a wide range of activities on offer, from aeromodelling and furniture design to sequin art and rug making, and we have a strong reputation on the sports field. The opportunity exists for children to develop the sports they enjoy, whilst the less sporting child can pursue other activities and hobbies. Our weekend arrangements are flexible and the programme is well organised and staffed with at least 100 children in school most weekends.

Little Windlesham opened in 1997 and provides a broad and varied education for 4–7 year olds. It is run separately from the main school and situated in a separate and well-designed unit, from which it can also make use of the impressive facilities of the Prep school. The curriculum is tied in with the Prep school so children can follow a structured pattern throughout the transition.

Charitable status. Windlesham House School is a Registered Charity, number 307046. It exists to provide education for girls and boys aged 4–13.

Winterfold House

Chaddesley Corbett Worcestershire DY10 4PL.
Tel: (01562) 777234
Fax: (01562) 777078
e-mail: hm@winterfoldhouse.co.uk

Chairman of Governors: Michael Joseph

***Headmaster:* W C R Ibbetson-Price**, MA, NPQH

Number of Pupils. 300 day boys and girls, aged 3–13.

Fees (September 2001). Preparatory £1,975–£2,250. Pre-Prep £880–£1,375.

Winterfold is centred around a spacious Georgian house set in nearly 40 acres of attractive grounds, surrounded by beautiful and unspoilt Worcestershire countryside, yet is only half an hour from the centre of Birmingham and just 10 minutes from the M5 and M42.

Winterfold is a Roman Catholic co-educational day preparatory school which has an ecumenical tradition. Children of all faiths are warmly welcomed and made to feel valued members of the community.

The school has an excellent academic record at all levels including National Curriculum Key Stage Tests, Common Entrance and Scholarship. Children are prepared for entrance to both local independent schools (such as Alice Ottley, King's, Worcester, Royal Grammar School, Worcester, King Edward's, Birmingham and Bromsgrove) and to national independent senior schools (such as Shrewsbury, Cheltenham Ladies College, Malvern, Stonyhurst, Ampleforth and Cheltenham College). We have a highly regarded Learning Support Unit which provides one to one help for children with specific learning difficulties.

Winterfold places a great emphasis upon educating the whole child and aims to produce well rounded and confident boys and girls with high moral standards and good manners. In order to develop self-belief we help every child to achieve success in some area and thus the school fields a great number of teams and not just in the main sports of rugby, soccer, cricket, netball and rounders but also in the minor sports which include fishing, golf, archery, tennis, swimming, athletics, basketball, fencing, judo, chess and shooting. There are also a large number of clubs and societies and regular visits to theatres and concerts and other places of educational interest which gives fullness and breadth to the educational experience.

In recent years there has been considerable investment into the school which has seen the development of a new sports hall, a computer room, new science laboratories, new tennis courts, a heated swimming pool, a chapel, an art and design centre, new library and music school. New cricket nets and an Adventure playground have just been completed.

Charitable status. Winterfold House School is a Registered Charity, number 1063133. It exists solely to provide education for boys and girls.

Witham Hall

Witham on the Hill Nr Bourne Lincolnshire PE10 0JJ.
Tel: (01778) 590222
Fax: (01778) 590606

***Heads:* D Telfer**, BA, CertEd, **Mrs S A Telfer,** CertEd

Chairman of Governors: Air Vice-Marshal R M Robson, OBE, FBIM

Number of Pupils. Boys: 29 boarders, 45 day pupils. Girls: 15 boarders, 32 day pupils. Pre-Prep aged 3–7: 99 pupils.

Fees. Boarders £3,490 per term. Day pupils £2,550 per term. Pre-Prep £1,550 per term.

The school is situated in a country house setting in the village of Witham on the Hill. There are all the usual amenities of a preparatory school; they include a squash court, a fine hall and stage. There is a computer centre and a resources centre where many audio/visual aids are available. Design Technology was introduced in April 1990.

There is a teaching staff of 30 and there are visiting teachers for instrumental music. The maximum class size is 16 in Prep and 14 in Pre-Prep. The system of grouping is a flexible one and allows children to work in the major academic subjects with others of similar ability.

The school has a full musical life – over half the school learns one instrument or more. In September 1979 a music school was opened. There are two bands and a four-part and junior choir.

Games are played on most days of the week throughout the year. There is a full fixture list of games, for both boys and girls, with other schools at both senior and colts level including rugger, soccer, cricket, hockey, netball, rounders, athletics, cross-country, tennis, and squash. An all weather surface was laid in 1980, which provides two tennis courts and pitches for mini-soccer, mini-hockey, and handball. Our 9 hole golf course provides a challenging course for pupils and parents alike and our squash court has much usage.

A multi-purpose hall was built in the summer of 1986. The hall provides an indoor tennis court, four badminton courts, basketball courts, an indoor soccer and hockey pitch, indoor cricket nets, and a general covered play area.

In September 1983 a wing was opened to provide boarding places for girls. Girls boarding, like the boys, is thriving.

The school was founded in 1959 and was formed into an Educational Trust in 1978.

A purpose built Pre-Prep block was opened in 1998 to house the growing Pre-Prep department and a purpose built Prep block was built in 2000. The school has seen a growth in numbers of 50% in the last four years and, in some year groups, early registration is recommended.

Wolborough Hill School

Newton Abbot S Devon TQ12 1HH.
Tel: (01626) 354078.

Headmaster: **D L Tyler**, BA, MA, CertEd

Number of pupils. 155 day children, aged 3 to 11 years.

Fees. Day £1,800 per term. (Pre-Prep 3-7 £1,240 per term). There are no compulsory extras.

The School has been established for 124 years. The full-time teaching staff numbers 15.

As well as the usual subjects required by the Independent Schools, Art and Craft, Design, Technology, Music, Drama and Physical Education are included in the timetable. 32 Scholarships have been won in the last five years. The School has an excellent reputation for success in local Grammar School selection examinations.

There is a strong musical and artistic tradition. Over half the pupils learn instruments and instruction can be given in any orchestral instrument and key-board. The School has its own Wind Band, Ensembles, Brass Band and Choirs.

The School, with its extensive playing fields, has a superb sporting record and several children and teams have won Area and National Championships. Coaching is given in the following activities: Rugby, Football, Hockey, Cricket, Swimming, Athletics, Tennis, Squash, Archery, Basketball, Gymnastics, Rounders and Netball.

Facilities include a 20 x 10 metre outdoor heated swimming pool, 3 hard tennis courts, of which two are floodlit, art studio, ICT studio, design studio, purpose-built library block and music rooms, and a large multi-purpose Hall.

Extra-curricular clubs include pottery, orienteering, aikido, silk painting, drama, archery, stamp collecting, ballet, woodwork and speech and drama.

Woodcote House

Windlesham Surrey GU20 6PF
Tel: (01276) 472115.
Fax: (01276) 472890
e-mail: N.H.K.P@btinternet.com
Station: Sunningdale

Headmaster: **N H K Paterson**, BA, PGCE

Number of Boys. 100 (85 boarders, 15 day)

Fees. £3,475 (Boarding) £2,500 (Day). No compulsory extras.

For Prospectus please apply to the Headmaster.

Woodford Green Preparatory School

Glengall Road Snakes Lane West Woodford Green Essex IG8 0BZ.
Tel: 020 8504 5045
Fax: 020 8505 0639
e-mail: wgps@rmplc.co.uk

Chairman of Governors: Mrs S Abrahams

Headmaster: **Ian P Stroud**, BSc

Number of Pupils. 187 Boys, 197 Girls

Fees. £1,365 per term. Nursery £670 per term.

The School is an Educational Charity, controlled by a Board of Governors, and caters for children from the age of 3 to 11.

The School provides a broad well-balanced curriculum and the overall standard is extremely high. Developments within the last few years include a new CDT centre, library, science laboratory, new Nursery facilities, gymnasium and additional music rooms. completed during Summer 2000 were a fully equipped computer centre, a designated facility for the teaching of foreign languages and a further suite of music rooms. The School has an outstanding record of success in 11+ examinations to Senior Independent and Grammar Schools and demand for places far outstrips availability. Parents are advised to make a very early application to the school.

Charitable status. Woodford Green Preparatory School is a Registered Charity, number 310930. It exists to provide education for children.

Woodleigh School Langton Limited

Langton Hall Malton YO17 9QN.
Tel: Burythorpe 01653 658 215
Fax: 01653 658 423
website: www.woodleighschool.freeserve.co.uk
Station: Malton

Headmaster: **D M England**, BSc

Number of Boys. 24 boarders, 50 day
Number of Girls. 6 boarders, 31 day
Fees per term. Boarding: 7-8 years £2,030, 8-11 years £2,340, 11-13 years £2,450. Day: 3-4 years £800, 4-6 years £915, 6-7 years £1,025.

Children are prepared for entry to all Senior Independent Schools via Common Entrance and Scholarship Examinations.

There are extensive playing fields for Association and Rugby Football, Cricket and Athletics. There is an open-air Swimming Bath and a hard Tennis court. There are extensive facilities for Art, CDT and recreational activities. All children are coached in games daily.

There are 9 full time and 4 part time staff. There are visiting staff for Art and CDT and Music (Piano, Strings and Wind Instruments).

Woodleigh School is set in beautiful countryside at the foot of the Yorkshire Wolds, within easy access of all main roads north and south. It offers a happy, homely and sympathetically disciplined atmosphere in which every child can develop his or her talents to the full. The full range of academic subjects is taught and a great range of cultural and recreational activities is available. A wide range of sporting activities is available, coached by qualified staff; music and drama play an important part in the life of the School. All aspects of the children's welfare are carefully supervised. There are many opportunities for parents to be involved in the life of the School, through membership of the Friends' Association, and there are staff/parent meetings twice each term when the children's progress is discussed.

Woodside Park International School

Junior Dept (7-11): 49 Woodside Avenue North Finchley London N12 8SY.
Tel: 020 8445 2333
Fax: 020 8445 0835
Junior Dept (4-7) & Kindergarten: Holmewood 88 Woodside Park Road London N12 8SH
Tel: 020 8445 9670
Fax: 020 8445 9678

Headmaster: **Paul Chapman**, BEd Hons

Number of Pupils. Junior Dept (7–11) 160 Boys and Girls. Junior (4-7) 120 Boys and Girls. Kindergarten (2½–4) 76 Boys and Girls

Fees. £1,024–£2,308 per term, according to age. Lunches £140 per term.

Woodside Park International School is an independent co-ed school for boys and girls, formed in September 1988 by the merger between Holmewood Preparatory School (est. 1885) and St. Alban's Preparatory School (est. 1928). St. Alban's now houses the Junior Department (7-11) whilst the Junior (4-7) Department and the Kindergarten are at the expanded Holmewood site.

The principal aim of the School is to encourage each pupil to develop both as an individual and as a responsible member of the community. Pupils are expected to give of their best at all times both academically and in the great variety of other activities open to them.

There are normally between fifteen and twenty pupils in a class. There is a class teacher for each form and three remedial staff.

Pupils take part in organised games and physical education. Soccer, cricket, hockey, netball, rounders, athletics and cross-country running are the principal sports. Matches are arranged with other schools and the School has an excellent games record.

Some financial aid is available in the form of bursaries awarded by the Directors of the School.

Wycliffe College Junior School

Stonehouse Glos GL10 2LD
Tel: (01453) 823233
Fax: (01453) 825604
e-mail: junior@wycliffe.co.uk
Station: Stonehouse MR

Chairman of Governors: S P Etheridge, MBE, TD, JP, FRII, FLIA, ACIArb, MBA

Headmaster: **R Outwin-Flinders**, BEd (Hons)

Pre-Preparatory (140 pupils) 2½–7; Main Junior (56 boarding, 184 day pupils) 8–13+.

Fees per term. Day £1,290–£2,515 (not including meals), Boarding £2,820–£3,545.

A range of Scholarships, both academic and non-academic, are offered by competition annually.

The co-educational Junior School is administered by the Council of Governors of Wycliffe College, but is a separate unit with its own full-time staff of 30 teachers (all qualified), House staff and matrons.

It provides a breadth and balance of education and training which will enable a pupil to make the happiest and best use of the Junior School years and prepare for the Senior School.

The Junior School facilities include extensive playing fields, heated indoor 20m pool, sports hall, new studio theatre and music school, two science laboratories, two computer rooms, art studio, craft workshop, a log cabin for Cubs, a covered playground and a fully refurbished cafeteria-style dining hall. A new Pre-Prep building opened in January 2000 and an astroturf was completed in May 2000.

The Pre-Prep department is housed separately, but near enough to make use of facilities on the main site. The Junior School uses the College Chapel, Medical Centre and Squash Courts.

The boarding houses are in the care of House staff, and there are members of staff with particular responsibility for the welfare of day pupils. Vegetarian and other dietary specialities can be catered for.

As well as the usual range of sport, drama and music, there are clubs, activities and opportunities for outdoor pursuits. A number of holiday trips are also arranged.

Charitable status. Wycliffe College Incorporated is a Registered Charity, number 311714. It is a co-educational boarding and day school promoting a balanced education for children between the ages of 2½ and 18.

Yardley Court

Somerhill Tonbridge Kent TN11 0NJ.
Tel: (01732) 352124.
Fax: (01732) 363381
Station: Tonbridge

Headmaster: **John Coakley**, BA Hons, PGCE, MA

Number of Boys. Prep: Dayboys 210 from 7–13+). Pre-Prep: Co-educational 250 (from 3–7).

Fees. Dayboys £2,283–2,467 per term inclusive of lunch. There are no compulsory extras.

Yardley Court is one of the three Schools at Somerhill. From a co-educational Pre-Prep of some 250+ children, the seven year old boys join Yardley Court and the girls join our sister school, Derwent Lodge (ISA). All three schools are housed in a magnificent Jacobean mansion set within 150 acres of beautiful parkland. Thus we are able to offer single sex education in the classroom but very much within a co-educational setting.

Yardley Court was founded in 1898 and moved to the Somerhill estate in 1990. We prepare boys for Common Entrance and Scholarships to senior independent schools in the immediate vicinity such as Tonbridge and Sevenoaks and also to schools further afield. Boys are also prepared for 11+ and 13+ entrance to the very strong Grammar Schools in our area. Sound foundations are the basis of all the academic teaching with particular emphasis placed on the core subject of Mathematics, English, Science and French. Pupils with special talents are encouraged to enter for scholarship examinations. We have a regular French exchange with a school in Paris open to all the boys in their last year.

Music plays an important part in school life with most boys participating in some way, either through the choirs, the wind band or in solo or group instruction in a wide range of instruments.

The parkland and woods adjoining the school together with our purpose built playing fields provide an excellent environment for both sport and play. A strong sports programme centres around Soccer, Rugby, Cross-country, Cricket, Tennis and Athletics. All the boys are given the opportunity to represent the school. Further sporting pursuits include Fencing, Archery, Karate, Golf, Judo and Swimming. The school also encourages participation in a wide range of clubs and activities that range from Drama and Chess to First Aid and Electronics.

Recent developments have seen the creation of a new area that houses ICT, Art, Design and Technology and Pottery rooms. In 2000 a new dedicated Music area was created. The construction of a multi-purpose hall began in May 2001.

Charitable status. The Somerhill Trust is a Registered Charity, number 2331296. It exists to provide education for children.

Yarlet

Yarlet Hall Nr Stafford ST18 9SU.
Tel: (01785) 286568
Fax: (01785) 286569

Chairman of the Governors: N D Tarling

Headmaster: **R S Plant**, MA (Pembroke College, Cambridge)

Age range of pupils. Co-educational, 2 to 13.

Number of Pupils. 159 pupils, 16 boarders, 68 day boys and girls. Pre-Preparatory, 75 boys and girls.

Fees. Boarders/Weekly boarders up to £2,850 a term. Day boys and girls £1,600–£2,375 a term. Pre-Prep £1,120 per term. Occasional boarding £20 per night. Bursaries and family discounts available.

Established in 1873, Yarlet stands in 33 acres of grounds in unspoilt open countryside 5 miles north of Stafford. The school offers small classes, qualified teachers, excellent facilities and a warm, friendly environment conducive to learning. All teachers keep fully abreast of the National Curriculum guidelines to Key Stage 3 and beyond.

Pupils have access to the wide range of facilities which include a modern Science Laboratory, a recently updated Information Technology Centre, a CDT Centre, a purpose-built Art & Music Building and an indoor Sports and Performance Hall; and extensive outdoor facilities which include a heated swimming pool, four playing fields (for football, rugby, hockey, cricket and athletics), three tennis courts, a netball court, an all-weather astroturf pitch (for football, hockey and netball), and a large Adventure Playground close to the Pre-Prep.

We have a new purpose built Pre-Preparatory school building.

Club and extra-curricular activities are a strong feature of Yarlet and include art (painting, sculpture and pottery), model-making, music, drama, chess, photography, astronomy, golf, riding, fishing and ski-ing (parties are taken regularly for holidays in the Alps).

Yarlet's academic record is considerable, with each boy and girl reaching their full potential before moving to their next school as a confident, friendly and responsible young person. Boys and girls are prepared for entry to all types of secondary school and awards are regularly won to senior independent schools.

There are links with a French and a German school who send boys and girls to Yarlet on a termly basis.

Church of England services are held in the Chapel and all denominations are welcome.

Charitable status. Yarlet is a Registered Charity, number 528618. It exists to provide day and boarding education for boys and girls from 2 to 13.

Yarrells Preparatory School

Yarrells House Upton Poole Dorset BH16 5EU
Tel: (01202) 622229
Fax: (01202) 624067

Headmistress: **Mrs N A Covell**, BA, MSc

Number of Pupils. 230 (Boys and Girls 2–13)

Fees. £370–£1,930 per term

Yarrells School offers a unique environment for the early development of intellectual, artistic and sporting potential. Only minutes from Bournemouth and Poole, Yarrells occupies a late Georgian country house surrounded by woods, gardens, playing fields, tennis courts and covered, heated swimming pool. The atmosphere is warm and encouraging while a rigorous approach is taken to the maintenance of each child's highest standards. A well-qualified and committed staff work with the Headmistress to ensure careful character building and maximum academic performance. The school seeks to identify and develop children's gifts and abilities in such a way that the children grow in self-knowledge, self-discipline and self-confidence.

The classes are small and learning is designed to meet individual requirements. From Nursery up, the school follows a detailed curriculum based on the National

Curriculum, the Common Entrance Syllabus (where appropriate) and the school's own demands, which emphasise the mastery of basic skills from an early age. The normal subject range is taught throughout and by specialists from the age of 8/9. The children start learning French from 4 years of age. Parents are invited to discuss their child's progress regularly with staff and are also sent termly written reports.

All children have curricular tuition in Art, Music (singing and instrumental), Drama and Dance. There are Recorder Ensembles, a Wind Band, Choir, Choral Societies and an Orchestra. There is a broad PE programme that includes swimming, tennis, football, rugby, netball, rounders, basketball, hockey and cross-country. Science, Investigational Mathematics, Design and Information Technology are areas of study given good accommodation in the timetable. The school is active until 6.00 pm each weekday evening for those children from age 7 who elect to stay for supervised prep, and a range of activities which include football, ballet, extra swimming and tennis, tap and modern dance, pottery and music ensembles.

Yarrells School has an excellent record of success in Entrance Examinations and Scholarship Awards to senior schools. Most children go on to Senior Independent Schools or the Grammar Schools.

Yateley Manor Preparatory School

51 Reading Road Yateley Hants GU46 7UQ.
Tel: (01252) 405500
Fax: (01252) 405504

Chairman of Governors: Dr C G B Mitchell

***Headmaster:* F G F Howard**, MA (Cantab), DipEd (Oxon)

Number of Pupils. Pre-Preparatory and Nursery: 71 Boys, 75 Girls. Main School: 226 Day Boys, 129 Day Girls.

Fees. £1,647–£2,354 per term. There are no compulsory extras and fees include lunches, medical examinations and a residential field trip for Years 5, 6, 7 and two in Year 8.

The School is an Educational Trust controlled by a Board of Governors.

Yateley Manor is an academic day preparatory school which offers boys and girls a wide and stimulating educational environment to encourage them to grow into happy, confident and fulfilled people. The School offers small classes blending traditional values with modern methods and all children are prepared for Common Entrance or Scholarship to senior independent schools at 11 or 12 for girls and at 13 for boys and girls. The records show that high standards are achieved with regular academic, music, art and sports scholarships being won.

The school believes in developing the whole person and pupils have the advantage of close personal attention in small classes combined with a very wide range of arts and activities ranging from archery to acting, from modern dance to ballet, through which the School encourages all-round personal development. Co-education is seen as part of the road to a full personality. Music and art, and sport and drama, are all major areas of involvement and achievement, whilst kindness and good manners are highly valued.

There are outstanding teaching facilities, libraries, art and science areas, music and computer rooms, and theatre and sports halls. Daily school coaches serve Blackwater, Camberley, Church Crookham, Frimley, Farnborough, Fleet, Hartley Wintney, Hook and Odiham.

Entry to the Pre-Preparatory School for boys and girls is normally in the September after the third birthday. At this age entry is by informal assessment. Entry to the Preparatory School is normally at 7 by examination and report. Other ages of entry are possible. The Staff believe in close contact with parents at all times and prospective parents are warmly invited to telephone for a prospectus and inspect the school at work.

Charitable status. Yateley Manor is a Registered Charity, number 307374. It exists for the purpose of furthering children's education.

York House School

Redheath Croxley Green Rickmansworth Herts WD3 4LW
Tel: (01923) 772395
Fax: (01923) 779231
Station: Rickmansworth or Croxley (Met)

Chairman of the Governors: T K Slade, Esq, BA Hons, FCT

***Headmaster:* P B Moore**, BA (Rhodes), MCollP

Number of children. All are day pupils. 65 Pre-Prep; 165 Prep; 50 Kindergarten

Fees. £2,026 per term, including lunch. Kindergarten dependant upon days/hours.

The Headmaster is assisted by a fully qualified staff. Redheath is a Georgian country house standing in extensive grounds with additional classrooms, changing rooms etc. A new multi-purpose Hall/Theatre and Library was opened in 1997, a new Early Years Department building will be opened in 2001 and there are fully equipped Science, Computer, Art, Music and Design Technology Rooms. There are 10 acres of playing fields for Cricket, Rugby, Soccer and Athletics, as well as a 25 metre indoor heated Swimming Pool. Boys are prepared for Common Entrance and Independent Senior Schools Scholarships. There is a Pre-Preparatory Department for boys from 4 to 7+ and a co-educational Kindergarten, for children from 2½ to 5. School transport serves Little Chalfont, Chorleywood and Rickmansworth.

Charitable status. York House, founded in 1910, is a Registered Charity, number 311076. It exists for the purpose of achieving educational excellence. It is a non-profit making Educational Trust with a Board of Governors.

ALPHABETICAL LIST OF SCHOOLS

THE INCORPORATED ASSOCIATION OF PREPARATORY SCHOOLS (PART V)

* denotes IAPS schools reckoned to be co-educational

GEOGRAPHICAL LIST OF IAPS SCHOOLS

(NB Page numbers will be found on pp. 1065–1068)

Avon

Schools formerly in Avon will be found under Gloucestershire or Somerset

Bedfordshire

Bedford Modern Junior School
Bedford Preparatory School

Berkshire

Brockhurst School, Newbury
Cheam School, Newbury
Crosfields School, Reading
Dolphin School, Hurst
Eagle House, Sandhurst
Elstree School, Nr Reading
Eton End PNEU School, Datchet
Falkland St Gabriel, Newbury
Herries School, Cookham Dean
Highfield School, Maidenhead
Holme Grange School, Wokingham
Horris Hill, Newbury
Lambrook Haileybury, Bracknell
Long Close School, Slough
Ludgrove, Wokingham
The Oratory Preparatory School, Nr Reading
Papplewick, Ascot
Priors Court, Newbury
Ridgeway School, Maidenhead
St Andrews School, Pangbourne
St Bernard's Preparatory School, Slough
St Edward's School, Reading
St George's School, Windsor
St John's Beaumont, Windsor
St Piran's, Maidenhead
Sunningdale School, Sunningdale
Upton House School, Windsor
Waverley School, Crowthorne
White House Preparatory School, Wokingham

Buckinghamshire

Ashfold, Aylesbury
The Beacon, Chesham
Caldicott, Farnham Royal
Chesham Preparatory School
Davenies School, Beaconsfield
Gayhurst School, Gerrards Cross
Godstowe Preparatory School, High Wycombe
Heatherton House School, Amersham
High March School, Beaconsfield
Maltmans Green, Gerrards Cross
Milton Keynes Preparatory School
Swanbourne House School, Swanbourne
Thorpe House School, Gerrards Cross

Cambridgeshire

King's College School, Cambridge
King's School Junior School, Ely
Perse Preparatory School, Cambridge
St Catherine's Preparatory School, Cambridge
St Faith's, Cambridge
St John's College School, Cambridge

Channel Islands

St Michael's Preparatory School, Jersey
Victoria College Preparatory School, Jersey

Cheshire

Beech Hall, Nr Macclesfield
Mostyn House School, South Wirrall
Pownall Hall, Wilmslow
Ramillies Hall School, Cheadle
The Ryleys, Alderley Edge
Stockport Grammar Junior School, Stockport
Terra Nova, Holmes Chapel
Wilmslow Preparatory School, Wilmslow

Cornwall

St Petroc's School, Bude
Treliske School, Truro

Derbyshire

Foremarke Hall, Derby
S Anselm's, Bakewell
Stancliffe Hall, Darley Dale

Devonshire

Exeter Cathedral School
Kelly College Junior School, Tavistock
Mount House School, Tavistock
Plymouth College Preparatory School
St Aubyn's School, Tiverton
St John's School, Sidmouth
St Michael's School, Barnstaple
St Peter's School, Exmouth
Wolborough Hill School, Newton Abbot

Dorset

Castle Court Preparatory School, Wimborne
Clayesmore Preparatory School, Blandford Forum
Dumpton School, Wimborne
Hanford School, Blandford
Knighton House, Blandford
The Old Malthouse, Swanage
Port Regis, Shaftesbury
St Antony's Preparatory School, Sherborne
Sherborne Preparatory School
Sunninghill Preparatory School, Dorchester
Yarrells Preparatory School, Poole

Durham

Barnard Castle Preparatory School
Bow Preparatory School
Chorister School

Essex

Alleyn Court Preparatory School, Southend-on-Sea
Bancroft's School Preparatory School, Woodford Green
Brentwood Preparatory School
Chigwell Junior School
Dame Johane Bradbury's School, Saffron Walden
Elm Green Preparatory School, Chelmsford
Felsted Preparatory School, Dunmow
Holmwood House, Colchester
Loyola Preparatory School, Buckhurst Hill
Maldon Court Preparatory School, Maldon
St Aubyn's School, Woodford Green
St Cedd's School, Chelmsford
St Michael's Preparatory School, Leigh-on-Sea
Widford Lodge, Chelmsford
Woodford Green Preparatory School

Gloucestershire

Abbey School, Tewkesbury
Beaudesert Park, Nr Stroud
Cheltenham College Junior School
Dean Close Preparatory School, Cheltenham
Richard Pate School, Cheltenham
Rose Hill School, Wotton-under-Edge
Tockington Manor, Nr Bristol
Wycliffe College Junior School, Stonehouse

Hampshire

Ballard School, New Milton
Boundary Oak School, Fareham
Daneshill School, Basingstoke
Dunhurst, Petersfield
Durlston Court, Barton-on-Sea
Farleigh School, Andover
Forres Sandle Manor, Fordingbridge
Highfield School, Liphook
Hordle Walhampton, Lymington
Norman Court Preparatory School, Nr Salisbury
The Pilgrims School, Winchester
Portsmouth Grammar School Junior School

Hampshire — *continued*
Prince's Mead School, Winchester
Rookesbury Park School, Wickham
St John's College Lower School, Southsea
St Neot's, Hook
St Swithun's Junior School, Winchester
Sherborne House School, Chandlers Ford
Stroud School, Romsey
Twyford School, Winchester
West Hill Park, Titchfield
Yateley Manor Preparatory School

Herefordshire and Worcestershire
Abberley Hall, Worcester
Aymestrey School, Worcester
Bromsgrove Lower School
Downs School, Colwall
Elms, Colwall
Hereford Cathedral Junior School
Hillstone, Malvern College
King's Hawford, Worcester
King's Saint Alban's Junior School, Worcester
Margaret Allen Preparatory School, Hereford
St Richard's, Bromyard
Winterfold House, Chaddesley Corbett

Hertfordshire
Aldwickbury School, Harpenden
Beechwood Park, St Albans
Berkhamsted Collegiate Preparatory School
Bishop's Stortford College Junior
Edge Grove, Aldenham
Haberdashers' Aske's Preparatory School, Borehamwood
Heath Mount School, Hertford
Kingshott, Hitchin
Lochinver House School, Potters Bar
Lockers Park, Hemel Hempstead
Manor Lodge School, Radlett
Northwood Preparatory School, Rickmansworth
Rickmansworth PNEU School, Rickmansworth
St Columba's College Preparatory School, St Albans
St Hilda's School, Bushey
St Nicholas House, Abbots Hill Junior School, Hemel Hempstead
Stormont, Potters Bar
Westbrook Hay, Hemel Hempstead
York House School, Rickmansworth

Isle of Man
Buchan School

Isle of Wight
Ryde Junior School

Kent
Bickley Park School, Bickley
Dulwich Preparatory School, Cranbrook
Friars School, Ashford
Granville School, Sevenoaks
Hilden Grange School, Tonbridge
Hilden Oaks School, Tonbridge
Holmewood House, Tunbridge Wells
Kent College Junior School, Canterbury
Kent College Junior School, Pembury
King's Junior School, Canterbury
King's Preparatory School, Rochester
Marlborough House School, Hawkhurst
New Beacon, Sevenoaks
Northbourne Park, Deal
Rose Hill School, Tunbridge Wells
Russell House School, Sevenoaks
St Edmund's Junior School, Canterbury
St Lawrence College Junior School, Ramsgate
St Mary's Westbrook, Folkestone
St Michael's Co-Educational Prep School, Orford
St Ronan's, Hawkhurst
Sevenoaks Preparatory School
Solefield Preparatory School, Sevenoaks
Sutton Valence Preparatory School, Maidstone
Wellesley House, Broadstairs
Yardley Court, Tonbridge

Lancashire (including Greater Manchester)
Arnold Junior School, Blackpool
Moor Allerton School, Manchester
Rossall Preparatory School, Fleetwood
St Mary's Hall, Stonyhurst
St Pius X Prep School, Preston

Leicestershire
Brooke Priory School, Oakham
Fairfield School, Loughborough
Grace Dieu Manor School, Coalville
St Crispin's School, Leicester
Stoneygate School, Leicester

Lincolnshire
Brigg Preparatory School
Lincoln Minster Preparatory School
St Hugh's, Woodhall Spa
St Mary's Preparatory School, Lincoln
Stamford, Junior School, Stamford
Stamford School Junior School, Stamford
Witham Hall, Bourne

London
Alleyn's Junior School
Arnold House School
Belmont (Mill Hill Junior School)
Broomwood Hall
Bute House Preparatory School for Girls
Cameron House
Cavendish School
Colfe's Preparatory School
Dulwich College Preparatory
Durston House
Falkner House
Finton House
Garden House School
Glendower Preparatory School
The Hall School
Hendon Preparatory School
Highgate Junior School
James Allen's Preparatory School
Keble School
Kensington Preparatory School
King's College Junior School
Lady Eden's School
Latymer Preparatory School
Lyndhurst House School
Newton Prep
Norland Place School
Pembridge Hall School
Prospect House School
Ravenscourt Park Preparatory School
Redcliffe School
St Anthony's Preparatory School
St Christopher's School
St Dunstan's College Junior
St Mary's School
St Olave's Preparatory School
St Paul's Cathedral School
St Paul's Preparatory School
Sarum Hall School
The Study Preparatory School
Sussex House
Tower House School
University College School
Westminster Abbey Choir School
Westminster Cathedral Choir School
Westminster Under School
Willington School
Woodside Park International School

Merseyside
Kingsmead School, Hoylake
Liverpool College Preparatory School
St Edward's Junior School, Runnymede
Sunnymede School, Southport

Middlesex
Alpha Preparatory School, Harrow
Denmead, Hampton
Mall School, Twickenham
Newland House School, Twickenham

Middlesex — *continued*
Orley Farm School, Harrow on the Hill
Quainton Hall School, Harrow
Reddiford School, Pinner
St David's Junior School, Ashford
St Helen's College, Hillingdon
St John's School, Northwood
St Martin's School, Northwood
Twickenham Preparatory School

Norfolk
Beeston Hall School, Cromer
Glebe House School, Hunstanton
Greshams Preparatory School, Holt
Langley Preparatory School and Nursery, Norwich
Riddlesworth Hall, Diss
Taverham Hall, Norwich
Town Close House Preparatory School, Norwich

Northamptonshire
Beachborough, Nr Brackley
Laxton Junior—Oundle School, Peterborough
Maidwell Hall, Northampton
Northampton Preparatory School
Spratton Hall Preparatory School, Northampton
Wellingborough Junior School
Winchester House School, Brackley

Nottinghamshire
Bramcote Lorne School, Nr Retford
Grosvenor School, Nottingham
Nottingham High School Preparatory School
Ranby House, Retford
Waverley House PNEU School, Nottingham
Wellow House School, Newark

Oxfordshire
Carrdus School, Banbury
Christ Church Cathedral School, Oxford
Cothill House, Abingdon
Dragon School, Oxford
Josca's Preparatory School, Abingdon
Manor Preparatory School, Abingdon
Moulsford Preparatory School, Wallingford
New College School, Oxford
Rupert House School, Henley-on-Thames
St Hugh's, Faringdon
Summer Fields, Oxford

Shropshire
Birchfield School, Albrighton
Kingsland Grange, Shrewsbury
Moor Park School, Ludlow
Old Hall, Telford
Packwood Haugh, Shrewsbury
Prestfelde, Shrewsbury

Somerset
All Hallows School, Shepton Mallet
Badminton Junior School, Bristol
Bristol Grammar Lower School
Clifton College Preparatory School, Bristol
Clifton High School Lower School
Colstons Collegiate—Lower School, Bristol
The Downs School, Nr Bristol
Hazlegrove (King's Bruton Junior School), Sparkford
Millfield Preparatory School, Glastonbury
Monkton Combe Junior School, Bath
King's Hall, Taunton
Paragon School, Bath
Perrott Hill School, Crewkerne
Queen's College Junior & Pre-Prep School, Taunton
Redlands High Junior School, Bristol
The Red Maids' Junior School, Bristol
Taunton Preparatory School
Wells Cathedral Junior School

Staffordshire
Brooklands School, Stafford
Edenhurst Preparatory School, Newcastle-under-Lyme
Lichfield Cathedral School
St Bede's, Stafford
Yarlet, Stafford

Suffolk
The Abbey, Woodbridge
Barnardiston Hall Preparatory School, Nr Haverhill
Culford Preparatory School, Bury St Edmunds
Framlingham College Junior School, Woodbridge
Ipswich Preparatory School
Moreton Hall Preparatory School, Bury St Edmunds
Old Buckenham Hall School, Ipswich
Orwell Park School, Ipswich
St George's School, Southwold
South Lee School, Bury St Edmunds

Surrey
Aberdour School, Nr Tadworth
Aldro, Nr Godalming
Amesbury School, Hindhead
Barfield, Farnham
Barrow Hills School, Nr Godalming
Belmont School, Dorking
Bishopsgate School, Englefield Green
Bramley, Tadworth
Caterham Preparatory School
Chinthurst School, Tadworth
Coworth Park School, Chobham
Cranleigh Preparatory School
Cranmore School, Leatherhead
Cumnor House School, South Croydon
Danes Hill, Oxshott
Downsend, Leatherhead
Duke of Kent School, Cranleigh
Eagle House, Sandhurst
Edgeborough, Frensham
Ewell Castle Junior School, Ewell
Feltonfleet, Cobham
Flexlands School, Chobham
Greenfield, Woking
Hall Grove, Bagshot
Halstead Preparatory School for Girls, Woking
Haslemere Preparatory School
The Hawthorns, Bletchingley
Hazelwood School, Oxted
Hoe Bridge School, Woking
Holy Cross Preparatory School, Kingston-upon-Thames
Homefield School, Sutton
Kings House School, Richmond
Kingswood House School, Epsom
Lanesborough School, Guildford
Laverock School, Oxted
Micklefield School, Reigate
Moon Hall School, Dorking
Notre Dame Preparatory School, Cobham
Old Vicarage School, Richmond
Parkside, Cobham
Priory School, Banstead
Reigate St Mary's Preparatory and Choir School, Reigate
Ripley Court School, Ripley
Rokeby, Kingston-upon-Thames
Rowan Preparatory School, Esher
Royal Russell Preparatory School, Croydon
Rydes Hill Preparatory School, Guildford
St Andrew's School, Woking
St Catherine's School, Guildford
St Edmund's School, Hindhead
St George's College Junior School, Weybridge
St Hilary's School, Godalming
St Ives School, Haslemere
St Teresa's Preparatory School, Dorking
Seaton House School, Sutton
Shrewsbury House, Surbiton
Stanway School, Dorking
Surbiton Preparatory School
Unicorn School, Richmond
Woodcote House, Windlesham

Sussex (East)
Bodiam Manor School, Robertsbridge
Bricklehurst Manor, Wadhurst
Brighton College Preparatory School
Cumnor House School, Haywards Heath
Mowden School, Hove
Newlands Preparatory School, Seaford
St Andrews School, Eastbourne
St Aubyns, Brighton

Sussex (East) — *continued*
St Bede's Co-Educational Prep School, Eastbourne
Skippers Hill Manor Preparatory, Mayfield
Temple Grove School, Uckfield
Vinehall, Robertsbridge
Westerleigh, St Leonard's on Sea

Sussex (West)
Ardingly College Junior School, Haywards Heath
Arundale School, Pulborough
Ashdown House, Forest Row
Brambletye, East Grinstead
Broadwater Manor School, Worthing
Copthorne School, Crawley
Cottesmore School, Pease Pottage
Dorset House, Pulborough
Farlington Preparatory School, Horsham
Fonthill Lodge, East Grinstead
Great Ballard, Chichester
Great Walstead School, Haywards Heath
Handcross Park School, Haywards Heath
Hurstpierpoint College Preparatory School, Hassocks
Oakwood Preparatory School, Chichester
Pennthorpe School, Horsham
The Prebendal School, Chichester
Sompting Abbotts, Lancing
Stoke Brunswick, East Grinstead
Westbourne House, Chichester
Windlesham House School, Washington

Tyne and Wear
Ascham House, Newcastle upon Tyne
Mowden Hall School, Stocksfield
Newcastle Preparatory School
Newlands School, Newcastle upon Tyne
Sunderland High School Junior School

Warwickshire
Arnold Lodge School, Leamington Spa
Bilton Grange, Nr Rugby
Crescent School, Warwick
The Croft School, Stratford-upon-Avon
Warwick Junior School
Warwick Preparatory School

West Midlands
Bablake Junior School, Coventry
Blue Coat School, Birmingham
Coventry Preparatory School
Eversfield Preparatory School, Solihull
Hallfield School, Birmingham
King Henry VIII Junior School, Coventry
Mayfield Preparatory School, Walsall
Newbridge Preparatory School, Wolverhampton
Royal Wolverhampton Junior School
West House School, Birmingham

Wiltshire
Appleford School, Nr Salisbury
Chafyn Grove School, Salisbury
Godolphin Preparatory School, Salisbury
Hawtreys (see Cheam Hawtreys)
Leaden Hall School, Salisbury
Pinewood, Swindon
Prior Park Preparatory School, Cricklade
St Francis School, Pewsey
St Margaret's Preparatory School, Calne
Salisbury Cathedral School
Sandroyd School, Salisbury
Warminster Preparatory School

Yorkshire (North)
Ampleforth College Junior School, York
Aysgarth School, Bedale
Bramcote School, Scarborough
Catteral Hall, Settle
Cundall Manor, York
Grosvenor House School, Harrogate
Lisvane, Scarborough College Junior School, Scarborough
Malsis School, Cross Hills
Minster School, York
Queen Mary's School, Thirsk
Ripon Cathedral Choir School, Ripon

Yorkshire (North) — *continued*
St Martin's School, Nawton
St Olave's, York
Terrington Hall, York
Woodleigh School, Malton

Yorkshire (South)
Ashdell Preparatory School, Sheffield
Birkdale School, Sheffield
Hill House Preparatory School, Doncaster
Rudston Preparatory School, Rotherham
Westbourne School, Sheffield

Yorkshire (West)
Bradford Grammar Junior School (Clock House)
Brontë House, Bradford
The Froebelian School, Leeds
Moorlands School, Leeds
Queen Elizabeth Grammar School, Wakefield
Richmond House School, Leeds
Silcoates Junior School, Wakefield
Wakefield Girls' High School
Westville House School, Ilkley

Wales
The Cathedral School Llandaff, Cardiff
Howell's Preparatory School, Denbigh
Rydal Penrhos Preparatory School, Colwyn Bay
St John's-on-the-Hill School, Chepstow

Scotland
Aberlour House, Banffshire
Ardvreck, Perthshire
Beaconhurst Grange, Stirling
Belhaven Hill, Dunbar
Butterstone School, Meigle
Cargilfield, Edinburgh
Clifton Hall, Edinburgh
Craigclowan School, Perth
Edinburgh Academy Preparatory
Fettes College Preparatory School, Edinburgh
Lathallan School, Montrose
Loretto Nippers, Musselburgh
Mary Erskine and Stewart's Melville Jun. School, Edinburgh
New Park School, St Andrews
St Aloysius College Junior School, Glasgow
St Katharines School, St Andrews
St Mary's Preparatory School, Melrose

Ireland
Aravon Preparatory School, Co Wicklow
Cabin Hill, Belfast
Castle Park, Co Dublin
Headfort, Co Meath
Rockport, Co Down

South Africa
Highbury Preparatory School, Natal

East Africa
Banda School, Nairobi, Kenya
Hillcrest Preparatory School, Nairobi, Kenya
Kenton College, Nairobi, Kenya
Pembroke House, Gilgil, Kenya
Peponi House, Nairobi, Kenya
St Andrew's Preparatory School, Molo, Kenya

South America
Markham College Lower School, Lima, Peru
Newton College Lower School, Lima, Peru
St Paul's School, São Paulo, Brazil

Australia
Coogee Boys Preparatory School, New South Wales
Cranbrook Junior School, New South Wales
Grimwade House, Victoria
Guildford Grammar Preparatory, Western Australia
King's School Preparatory School, New South Wales
St Andrew's School, South Australia
Scotch College Junior School, Victoria
Southport School Preparatory School, Queensland
Sydney Grammar School, New South Wales
Tudor House School, New South Wales

Egypt
Maadi British International School, Cairo

Greece
St Catherine's British Embassy School, Athens

Netherlands
The British School in the Netherlands

Kuwait
The English School, Safat

Malaysia
Alice Smith Primary School, Kuala Lumpur

Philippines
The British School, Manila

Saudi Arabia
Jeddah Preparatory and Grammar School

Singapore
Tanglin Trust School

Switzerland
Geneva English School

United Arab Emirates
Al Ain English Speaking School, Abu Dhabi
The British School, Abu Dhabi
English Speaking School, Dubai
Jumeirah English Speaking School, Dubai
Jumeirah Primary School, Dubai

United States of America
British School of Washington

Alphabetical List of IAPS Heads

The following is a list of Heads and Deputy Heads of Schools which appear on pages 853–1064, who are members of IAPS.

PART VI

Schools appearing in Part VI are those whose Heads are members of the Independent Schools Association

Abbey Gate College

Saighton Grange Saighton Chester CH3 6EG.

(See SHMIS section, Part III of this Book)

Abbey Gate School

Victoria Road Chester CH2 2AY.
Tel: (01244) 380552

Head: **Mrs S T Gill**, CertEd (Aberdeen)

Age Range. 3–11
Number in School. Day: Boys and Girls 150
Fees per term. £605–£635

Abbeygate School was founded in 1910. Comprising 240 children most of whom start in a teaching Nursery.

It is well staffed with small classes, giving an all round education preparing children for all examinations. Essentially a family atmosphere with attention given to discipline and good manners.

The School maintains a broad curriculum having balanced programmes of English, arithmetic, computer studies, science, history and geography. Sport, art, music and drama form part of the School year.

Accredited by ISJC.

Abbotsford Preparatory School

211 Flixton Road Urmston Manchester M41 5PR.
Tel: (0161) 748 3261
Fax: (0161) 746 7961
e-mail: headmaster@abbotsford-prep.trafford.sch.uk
website: http://www.rmplc.co.uk/eduweb/sites/abbotsford/index.html

Headmaster: **Mr C J Davies**

Age Range. 3–11
Number in School. Day: Boys 70, Girls 60
Fees per term. £820–£1,085

Established over 90 years ago, this ISC accredited school prepares children for entry into State Grammar Schools as well as the major Independent schools in the North West. Although the success rate is high, children are not crammed but encouraged to achieve their full potential.

In January 1997 the school moved to a new site and into a fully refurbished and newly equipped building. Science, Art/Technology and Information Technology facilities are now second to none for this age group. Recent inspections by OFSTED and the Independent Schools Joint Council have complimented the school on the level of resources and on the standard of teaching and learning.

The previous building has been tastefully converted into a beautifully equipped full time Day Nursery catering for children and babies from 0–3 years of age for 52 weeks a year and this opened in April 1997.

Children may start at three in the Main School Nursery, part-time or full-time by mutual agreement between parents and teachers.

In the main school, besides the full range of primary subjects there is a range of activities which include academic subjects as well as pastoral/sporting activities. Staff take great pride in the standard of the children who leave the school.

Pupils are examined at regular intervals and close liaison exists between home and school. Games for boys are soccer and cricket while girls play rounders and netball. Juniors have athletics in summer and all children from six years old are taught swimming. The new fully enclosed outdoor multi-purpose hard area has greatly enhanced the games facility provision, as has the large indoor sports hall.

Chess, computing, bookclub and crafts are among the after school activities and the older pupils take part in school excursions, adventure weekends and annual ski trip.

Abbotsford School

Bridge Street Kenilworth Warwickshire CV8 1BP.
Tel: (01926) 852826

Headmistress: **Mrs Joan Adams**

Age Range. 2½–11
Number in School. 159
Fees per term. £900–£1,150

Abbotsford caters for pupils having a mixed range of abilities. Individual attention from a highly qualified staff and small tutorial groups help to ensure that each child develops its potential. Pupils have achieved a high success rate in external examinations in recent years in all departments.

Facilities are provided for games and physical education and a major extension to the School has provided specialist rooms for Computer Studies, French, Science, Craft, Design Technology and Art, in addition to several new classrooms, toilets and showers.

Charitable status. Abbotsford School Educational Trust Ltd is a Registered Charity, number 528779. It exists to provide a good 'all-round' education for all children in a caring and friendly environment.

Abercorn School

28 Abercorn Place London NW8 9XP
Tel: 020 7286 4785

Head: **Mrs A Greystoke**, BA (Hons)

Age range. 2½ to 13+ Co-educational
Number in school. 290
Fees per term. £1,315–£2,425

Abercorn School provides quality education in a happy caring atmosphere. The main School building is a gracious

Victorian listed mansion with its own garden in a quiet tree-lined road. Around the corner are five additional classrooms that include the science laboratory, computing centre, art studio, and history/geography room.

Pupils flourish in the small classes (average size is 16) and the high degree of specialist teaching. As a result, the children achieve excellent entrance results to further schools, including St Paul's, North London Collegiate, South Hampstead High School and Westminster.

Charitable status. Abercorn School is a Limited Company, number 3013551. It aims to serve its pupils' needs in all respects.

Adcote School

Little Ness near Shrewsbury SY4 2JY.

(See GSA section, Part II of this Book)

Alderley Edge School for Girls

Wilmslow Road Alderley Edge Cheshire SK9 7QE.
Tel: (01625) 583028
Fax: (01625) 590371
e-mail: mcs@mtcarmel.demon.co.uk

Chairmen of Governors:
Richard Lawrence
Judge Simon Fawcus

Headmistress: **Mrs Kathy Mills,** BA (Hons), DipEdMan (Wales)

Age Range. 3–18.

Number in School. Nursery 21; Junior School 260; Senior School 400

Fees per term. Reception to Year 2 £945; Year 3 to 6 £1,155; Senior School £1,470.

Background. For many years the village of Alderley Edge in Cheshire has been the location for two of the finest Independent Girls Schools in the North West of England. From September 1999 the two schools will become one.

An independent, single sex, ecumenical school is unique in England and the merger has been welcomed by existing parents, teachers and students and supported by the Anglican and Roman Catholic clergy and the founders of both schools.

As a direct result of this exciting merger, our combined resources will enable the school to initiate an extensive building programme, expand the curriculum and dramatically enhance the resources.

Location. The school is situated in a semi-rural area of Alderley Edge, 15 miles south of Manchester with easy access to the motorway network, and only minutes from Manchester Airport and two Inter-city main line stations. Transport is readily available throughout the area and we have students who travel from Congleton, Crewe, Middlewich and South Manchester. The new school will all eventually be located at the Mount Carmel site.

The beautiful countryside setting together with ease of access for the commuter, it is hardly surprising that Alderley, Wilmslow, Knutsford, Prestbury, Mobberley and the surrounding villages and hamlets have become the choice for the discerning business persons and their families.

The area boasts a wealth of facilities for the family, including beautiful residences, Health and Leisure clubs, entertainment complexes, tennis, cricket and golf clubs, superb restaurants and shopping facilities. For business, the hotel and conference facilities are second to none.

A unique ecumenical school. The Sisters of St Joseph, a Roman Catholic Order, founded Mount Carmel School in 1945. St Hilary's founded in 1817, became part of the Woodard Corporation, a Church of England foundation, in 1955. In recent years it has been the teaching of both churches, that 'similarities' between people far outweigh our 'differences'. The organisations behind both schools have been unswerving in their support for Christian education and now, as the new Millennium dawns, the timing is perfect to confirm that belief in a new ecumenical form.

Alderley Edge already has a strong tradition of inter-denominational co-operation. Now the Governors and staff of the new school will work together to enhance and develop this religious unity and set an example for other schools to follow.

This joint venture will link Mount Carmel with the Woodard Corporation, the largest group of schools in England. During the last 150 years the family of Woodard Schools has grown from the ten that were founded by Nathaniel Woodard between 1847 and 1841 to the forty schools today. Among them are independent and maintained schools in England, the United States and Australia.

Building Development. The merger offers Alderley Edge School many advantages. Mount Carmel School has recently been granted planning permission for extensive re-development. During the building programme, which will be completed within two years, both prep schools will enjoy all the facilities of the St Hilary's site, while the Senior Girls will benefit from the extra space and resources at Mount Carmel. Although the two schools are only minutes apart, transport will operate between them for the benefit of those parents who have children at both sites. The building work will be contained and will be set apart from the main school to ensure that there will be no disturbance or interruption to lessons and the work will cease during examination times.

The new building will provide a fully equipped performing arts theatre, additional music rooms, six 'state of the art' science laboratories and a multi-media centre. Therefore pupils at Alderley Edge School for Girls will benefit from a wider curriculum, stimulating teaching groups, exceptionally well qualified and experienced teachers and the finest facilities, equipment and resources available.

Curriculum. Students follow a broad and balanced curriculum based on the National Curriculum but with many additions. There are more than 20 A level subjects from which to choose.

In 1998 40% of all passes at GCSE were A* or A; 72% were A*, A and B; 91% obtained 5 or more passes (A-C). At A Level - 72% of passes were grades A, B or C; 44% were A or B.

100% of Sixth Formers went on to a degree course at university.

The Arts.

Music. Over 56% of pupils learn a musical instrument and examinations may be taken. Over 11 musical groups, including flute, woodwind, guitar groups, string ensembles, orchestras and choirs. Many cups have been won in local festivals. Pupils perform in local youth orchestras.

Drama and Dance. Both are offered. ESB examinations may be taken. The majority of pupils are involved in school productions and all pupils participate in house and other productions.

Art. On average 22 students take GCSE; 2 at AS level and 5 at A level.

Sports and Clubs.

Sports & Physical Activities. The compulsory sports are tennis, rounders, hockey, athletics, netball, gymnastics, swimming, dance, cross country. Optional sports are badminton, volleyball, fitness, squash, trampolining, weight-training, racket ball, fencing, aerobics.

Clubs. There are approximately 10 clubs in the Senior School, including spelling, public speaking, poetry, dance, drama, gym, hockey, netball, tennis, rounders and athletics. The Duke of Edinburgh Award Scheme is also available.

Charitable status. Alderley Edge School for Girls is a Registered Charity, number 1007226. It exists to provide education for children.

Alleyn Court Preparatory School

Wakering Road Southend on Sea Essex SS3 0PW

(See IAPS section, Part V of this Book)

Altrincham Preparatory School

Marlborough Road Altrincham Cheshire WA14 2RR.
Tel: (0161-928) 3366
Fax: (0161-929) 6747

Headteacher: **Mr A C Potts**, BSc

Age Range. 3–11
Number in School. Day: Boys 360
Fees per term. £1,100–£1,255

Altrincham Preparatory School has been well known in the Manchester area for over 65 years and continues to maintain its high reputation for excellent academic and sporting achievements.

The School has a good pupil teacher ratio and offers a very wide range of academic subjects headed by the three main National Curriculum core subjects, English, Mathematics and Science.

The School has outstanding results to all the local independent grammar schools, particularly to Manchester Grammar School, as well as to a very wide range of other schools including the traditional senior independent schools where scholarships have been gained.

The School's sporting successes have been achieved on a national basis in rugby, soccer, athletics, cricket, tennis and swimming.

The School has an ongoing programme of improvement and development, including in 1996/7, the erection of a new purpose-built Junior School.

The American Community School

Heywood Portsmouth Road Cobham Surrey KT11 1BL.
Tel: (01932) 867251
Fax: (01932) 869789

Head: **Thomas Lehman**

Age range. 3–19
Number in School. Day: Boys 670; Girls 608, Boarding 100
Fees per semester. £2,200 (½ day Scramblers) – £6,350 (grade 13)
Boarding fees for semester. 7 day grades 7–13 £9,990–£10,380; 5 day grades 7–13 £8,910–£9,300.

The curriculum is designed to promote acceptance at North American and European colleges and universities and to facilitate the transition of students from one American/international school to another.

Both Advanced Placement and International Baccalaureate programs are offered in addition to the American high school diploma. College Counselling is available to high school students. Teachers are university graduates with certificates and advanced degrees for the grade and subject for which they are responsible. Approximately 66% of the students are US or Canadian, with 50 other nationalities represented.

An extensive extra-curricular program is offered to students. Activities include sports, art, music and drama. Various clubs are planned annually to cater to the interests of students. Trips to European countries are organized during the school holidays and as field trips.

The school has libraries for each division, computer and science laboratories, a language laboratory, art rooms, music rooms, and ample classrooms, as well as an all-weather running track, a large gymnasium, a multi-purpose cafeteria/auditorium complex and a dormitory.

The schools seek to enrol students of all nationalities with average to above average academic ability. Admission is made on the basis of previous school records with a provision for testing prior to grade placement if necessary. Non-English-speaking students can apply for admission to the ESL program offered.

Located just 15 miles from central London, ACS Hillingdon enjoys a glorious mansion setting on 11 acres of sweeping lawns and an adjacent park. In addition to the regular American curriculum, the International Baccalaureate is a popular program among international students.

The Egham campus has an enrollment capacity of 600 students and is located on 20 acres of beautifully landscaped grounds at the edge of Royal Windsor Great Park in Surrey. In addition to the regular ACS American and international curricula, ACS Egham places special emphasis on small classes and personal learning styles.

The American Community School, Middlesex

108, Vine Lane Uxbridge Middlesex UB10 0BE.
Tel: (01895) 259771
Fax: (01895) 256974/810634

Headmaster: **Christopher Taylor**

Age Range. 4–18
Number in School. Day School only: Boys 342, Girls 327
Fees per semester. £3,270–£6,350 (Pre-K to G12)

The American Community School Hillingdon campus provides a non-sectarian co-education for students aged 4–18, covering grades pre-kindergarten through the 12th grade. Situated less than 15 miles from central London and accessible by the London Underground, the School's door-to-door bus service covers a great deal of West London – east into central London and west as far as High Wycombe.

Situated on an 11-acre site, the Hillingdon campus combines a restored 19th century mansion which is the setting for school classes, concerts, art exhibitions and receptions, with a purpose-built addition housing classrooms, computer room, gymnasium, cafeteria and libraries.

The school follows a standard American curriculum with Advanced Placement (AP) courses and the International Baccalaureate (IB), a diploma sought by colleges and universities in the US and world-wide. The school has offered the International Baccalaureate diploma since 1980 achieving virtually a 100% pass rate for full diploma candidates and over the past three years averaging nearly 35 points.

The traditional American curriculum which features nine Advanced Placement courses also leads to an American High School Diploma. The school administers all examinations required for admission to American universities. Supported by specialised university counselling, Hillingdon students attend universities in the US and their home countries including Oxford, Cambridge and the London School of Economics in the UK; MIT, McGill University and Cornell University in North America.

In addition to the strong academic programme, ACS Hillingdon has a full complement of sports and extra-curricular activities. Nearly 80% of Hillingdon students are involved with team sports that range from volleyball to rugby. Students also participate in student council, model United Nations, yearbook and many other high school activities.

Founded in 1967 to meet the needs of the expatriate community, the American Community Schools Limited enrolls over 2,000 students from the USA and 50 other countries on three landscaped campuses in south-east England.

Argyle House School

19/20 Thornhill Park Sunderland Tyne & Wear SR2 7LA
Tel: (0191) 5100726

***Head:* Mr J N Johnson**

Age Range. Boys and Girls 3–16
Number in School. 240
Fees per term. £980–£1,370

Argyle House School was established in 1884 as a small independent day school for boys and girls, situated in the centre of Sunderland. Students travel from all parts of the region, by our buses, or local forms of transport. The school has maintained its high standards of academic achievement, whilst catering for a wide variety of abilities.

At Argyle House, we believe in the individual, and work with him or her to enable the achievement of each student's potential. This is due to attention to detail by fully qualified and dedicated staff, who help to mould the individual into a well-mannered and accomplished young individual, who will be able to meet future challenges.

Small class sizes and a friendly environment facilitate learning, but not all work is academic, as the school takes an active part in many sporting leagues, both within the school, and locally with other schools. We aim to offer all the facilities of a much larger school, whilst remaining at present student levels to keep the intimacy and friendliness of a smaller school, for both parents and students

The Arts Educational School

Tring Park Tring Hertfordshire HP23 5LX
Tel: (01442) 824255
Fax: (01442) 891069

***Principal:* Mrs J D Billing,** GGSM, CertEd, FRSA

Age Range. 8–18 years.

Number in School. Boarders: Boys 31, Girls 144. Day: 68

Fees per term. Prep School: Boarders £3,934, Day £2,266. Aged 11–18: Boarders £5,175, Day £3,216. 6th Form Entry: Boarders £5,515, Day £3,430.

Aided places are available under the Government's Music and Ballet Schools Scheme.

The Arts Educational School, Tring Park, offers a unique opportunity for pupils from the age of 8 to 18 who show a particular talent in one or more of the Performing Arts, yet still wish to benefit from a sound academic education to "A" level.

Tring is a small market town situated 30 miles north-west of Central London, within easy travelling distance of the major international airports and motorways. Set in 17 acres of attractive and secluded grounds, the School is principally housed in a superb mansion, formerly the home of the Rothschild family.

Dance, Drama and Music are taught to the highest level and pupils perform regularly in our excellent modern theatre as well as at various outside venues. Many pupils go on to enjoy successful careers in the Theatre. Academic achievements at GCSE and "A" level enable many of our students to progress to Degree courses in higher education.

Whatever the career or course chosen, the fusion of natural talent, creativity and personality with sound teaching and direction produces young communicators, well-equipped to take the many opportunities that lie ahead.

Charitable status. The AES Tring Park School Trust is a Registered Charity, number 1040330. It exists to provide vocational and academic education.

The Arts Educational School London

Cone Ripman House 14 Bath Road Chiswick London W4 1LY
Tel: 020 8987 6600
Fax: 020 8987 6601

Founded in 1919.

***Headmaster:* Mr Tom Sampson**, MA, CertEd, LRAM, ACSD

Age Range. Co-educational day school. 8–16
Number in School. Girls 97, Boys 28
Fees per annum (September 2001). £4,836–£7,245

The Arts Educational School was founded in 1919 and now occupies a large site in a pleasant residential area of West London where it is well served by public transport.

The School offers an integrated curriculum of academic study, dance, music and drama.

The Preparatory Department gives boys and girls confidence, self-discipline and the opportunity to develop their talents in the creative and performing arts.

Transfer to the Lower School is in Year 7 and all pupils follow a course leading to eight or nine GCSEs. All pupils have access to outstanding performance facilities, rehearsal rooms, proscenium and studio theatres.

Pupils leave the school to continue their education at independent day or boarding schools or at specialised vocational colleges. The school offers a Post-16 A level programme in the Creative Arts and Humanities.

Admission is at 8+ and 11+, 13+ by written examinations, interview and audition.

Charitable status. The Arts Educational School is a Registered Charity, number 311087. It exists solely for educational purposes.

Ashton House School

50–52 Eversley Crescent Isleworth Middlesex TW7 4LW.
Tel: 020 8560 3902
Fax: 020 8568 1097

Principal: **Mr S J Turner**

Head Teacher: Miss M M Regan

Age Range. 3–11
Number in School. Day: Boys 70, Girls 75
Fees per term. £1,324.70–£1,798

Founded 1930. Proprietors P A, G B & S J Turner. Entry by interview and assessment. Prospectus on request.

Modern and traditional methods combined ensure that a firm foundation in basic skills is gained within the Infant Department with which to undertake confidently the widening Junior curriculum.

Specialist teaching throughout the school in Music, Information Computer Technology, Physical Education and French are major strengths. Peripatetic music by arrangement in seven instruments.

Sports. Netball, rounders, football, cricket, swimming, hockey and basketball.

Excellent record of examinations success for entry to top Independent Day Schools.

Babington House School

Grange Drive Chislehurst Kent BR7 5ES.
Tel: 020 8467 5537
Fax: 020 8295 1175

Headmistress: **Miss D Odysseas**, BA (Hons), PGCE

Age Range. Boys 3–7+, Girls 3–16
Number in School. Day: Boys 70, Girls 150
Fees per term. £624–£2,083. *Compulsory extras:* Swimming

A small day school that is No. 1 in the London Borough of Bromley. Recently praised by ISIC for achieving outstanding academic success and providing exemplary pastoral care. The school has a friendly atmosphere, set in pleasant suburban area. Stress on traditional values and standards. Full range of courses for examinations at all levels. Most boys transfer to selective independent schools.

Specialist facilities for Computing – information technology – (all pre-prep classes have computers in their classrooms), Music, Art, Secretarial Studies, Textiles, Biological and Physical Sciences.

Small classes. Maximum size 18 pupils; examination groups average 5–6 pupils. Careers guidance by specialists.

Wide range of sports (Swimming, Tennis, Netball, Squash, Gymnastics, Trampoline, Indoor Hockey, Volleyball, Table Tennis) and extra-curricular activities (Drama, Gym Club, Choir, Dance, Elocution, Instrumental tuition).

Charitable status. Babington House School is a Registered Charity. It exists to provide education.

Baston School

Baston Road Hayes Bromley Kent BR2 7AB.
Tel: 020 8462 1010
Fax: 020 8462 0438

Headmaster: **Mr Charles Wimble**, MA (Cantab)

Age Range. 2½–16
Number in School. Day girls 151
Fees per term. £425–£1,990 (Day)

Baston School for girls is a busy, happy community and whilst developments are constantly taking place to meet the needs of the new Millennium, the school retains the best of traditional ways and values. The school is situated on the southern outskirts of Bromley in 14 acres of ground.

Baston continues to achieve high academic standards from a broad ability intake. The school aims to enable each girl to develop her personality and capabilities to the full and to enjoy the whole education process. Baston is large enough to be able to offer a wide range of subjects and creative, musical and sporting activities but small enough to be able to cater for the individual needs of every pupil. The school is particularly proud of its sporting successes and has won tournaments each year at county level in lacrosse, netball and tennis.

Choosing the right school for your child is probably one of the most important decisions you will make. By choosing Baston, parents can be confident that they are assuring their daughter's future for the 21st century.

Why not visit the school, meet the staff and see for yourself the facilities, including the new classroom and music block, opened in May 1998, and the new science and food technology laboratories opened in September 2000. The Principal and Headmaster are always happy to meet prospective parents personally or parents can attend any one of the regular Open Days. A warm welcome is assured.

Bedstone College

Bucknell Shropshire SY7 0BG.

(See SHMIS section, Part III of this Book)

Bishop Challoner School

228 Bromley Road Shortlands Bromley Kent BR2 0BS.
Tel: 020 8460 3546
Fax: 020 8466 8885
e-mail: office@bishopchallonerschool.com

Headteacher: **Mr J A de Waal**, BA (Hons), PGCE

Age Range. 2½–18
Number in School. Day 400
Fees per term. Seniors £1,810, Juniors £1,450, Infants £1,200.

This is a Roman Catholic Independent Co-educational School with Nursery, Infants and Junior Sections 2½–11 years and a Senior School section 11–18 years.

The School includes a percentage of Non-Catholics.

The School curriculum includes all National Curriculum subjects and others (Latin) leading to GCSE, A levels and Oxbridge. Admissions to the Senior School at any age follows the successful completion of an entrance examination and an interview with the headteacher.

Charitable status. Bishop Challoner School is a Registered Charity, number 235468. It exists to provide education for boys and girls.

Bowbrook House School

Peopleton Nr Pershore Worcs WR10 2EE.
Tel: (01905) 841242

Headmaster: **Stephen Warwick Jackson**, MSc

Age Range. 3½–16
Number in School. Day: 85 Boys, 54 Girls.
Fees per term. £715–£1,625

Bowbrook House is set in 14 acres of picturesque Worcestershire countryside yet within easy reach of Worcester, Pershore and Evesham. The school caters for the academic child and also those of average ability, who can benefit from the small classes. All pupils are able to take full advantage of the opportunities offered and are encouraged to participate in all activities. As well as the academic subjects, the school has a flourishing art and textiles department, a computer room, hard tennis courts and an open air swimming pool in addition to extensive games fields.

The Pre-Prep department of 3½–8 year olds is a self-contained unit but enjoys the use of the main school facilities.

Whilst stressing academic achievement, the school aims to provide a structured and disciplined environment in which children of all abilities can flourish, gain confidence and achieve their true potential. The small school size enables the head and staff to know all pupils well, to be able to accurately assess their strengths and weaknesses it enables each pupil to be an important part of the school and to feel that their individual attitudes, behaviour, efforts and achievements are important.

There is an extended school day from 8.15 am to 5.30 pm, with supervised prep sessions.

Box Hill School

Mickleham Dorking Surrey RH5 6EA

(See SHMIS section, Part III in this Book)

Brabyns School

34/36 Arkwright Road Marple Stockport Cheshire SK6 7DB.
Tel: (0161-427) 2395
Fax: (0161-449) 0704

Headmistress: **Mrs Pamela J Turner**, MA, BEd

Age Range. 2½–11 years
Number in School. Day: Boys 79, Girls 80
Fees per term. £665–£1,082

Brabyns School is an independent school offering education for children from Nursery age to 11 years old, accommodated in two large Edwardian houses which have been sensitively redesigned to provide for the needs of the children while retaining a sense of warmth and security.

A building programme completed in September 1999 offers much enhanced facilities including a new hall/gym, nursery, ICT suite, Art room and Science laboratory.

Children are taught in small classes throughout the school. The broad curriculum is based on the requirements of the National Curriculum and children are prepared for examinations to the Local Independent Grammar Schools. Brabyns has an excellent record of successful entrants to these schools. The school featured in the Sunday Times top 125 prep schools in England in November 2000.

The Nursery, which is led by a qualified teacher, provides a friendly but purposeful atmosphere in which the children develop social and creative skills. Kindergarten builds upon this secure foundation by encouraging a delight in learning and achievements through the teaching of an early literacy and numeracy programme.

The pupils pursue academic excellence and high sporting achievement in the preparatory department. Musical, dramatic and artistic talents are encouraged and play an important role in the school.

Academic success is of obvious importance but in addition children are nurtured to develop their own interests and talents so that they become confident and considerate members of the community.

Annual scholarships are available for pupils with academic potential.

Braeside School for Girls

130 High Road Buckhurst Hill Essex IG9 5SD
Tel: 020 8504 1133
Fax: 020 8505 6675
e-mail: braeside@rmplc.co.uk

Headmistress: **Mrs C Naismith**, BA Hons, PGCE

Age Range. 4–16
Number in School. Day Girls 219
Fees per term. £1,200–£1,775

Braeside School, founded in 1944, is situated close to Epping Forest.

It educates for girls from the age of 34 to 16, and the possibility of spending all the compulsory years of schooling within one organisation provides the opportunity for secure, stable progress for each pupil.

The school provides a wide range of subjects and sets its own high standards in work and behaviour. It aims to give each pupil a sound foundation for life and every chance to develop individual capabilities and interests.

Entry, at every age apart from 3 and 4, is by test and interview.

With the support of a qualified and dedicated staff, examination and sporting achievements are consistently good.

Brantwood Independent School for Girls

1 Kenwood Bank Sheffield S7 1NU
Tel: (0114) 2581747
Fax: (0114) 2581847

Headteacher: **Mrs E M Swynnerton**, BA Hons, DipEd

Age Range. 4–17
Number in school. 225 girls
Fees per term. £1,344–£1,743

Brantwood Independent School for Girls is situated in

the Kenwood area of the city and was founded over 80 years ago. The school provides a friendly, caring and stimulating environment where all girls are encouraged to reach their maximum academic potential.

Brantwood has small classes and extensive facilities. The Trust has completed a major programme of development, including new facilities for Food Technology, Science Block, an Art Department and specialist Junior Science Laboratory, a new 3 floor building including a Dining Room and Kitchen, 3 specialist classrooms, an Exhibition Hall and an ICT facility.

Brantwood combines traditional teaching values with a progressive curriculum. Individual attention for pupils is of major importance and it is part of the school's normal practice to have extension groups and support groups for the most able pupils or the less academically gifted.

Pupil tracking and monitoring is a strength of the school and all senior girls produce Personal Development Plans.

The school has an excellent record at public examination level. There is a wide variety of other activities available at Brantwood including language holidays, adventure holidays and cultural visits. Music and drama play an important part in school life. Juniors can also take Speech and Drama examinations.

The school offers an 'After School Club' to 5 pm.

The school is always pleased to show parents round and to discuss their daughter's education. Entry for Juniors is by interview and entry to the Senior School is by Entrance Test and interview.

Charitable status. The South Yorkshire Independent Schools Trust Ltd is a Registered Charity, number 1410569. It aims to provide high quality education to girls aged 4–17 years in South Yorkshire.

Bredon School

Pull Court Bushley Nr Tewkesbury Gloucestershire GL20 6AH.
Tel: (01684) 293156
Fax: (01684) 298008

Headmaster: **M J Newby,** MA, BEd (Hons)

Age Range. 8–18
Number in School. 200. Boarders: Boys 85, Girls 35. Day: Boys 55, Girls: 25
Fees per term. Day £1,750–£3,375. Weekly boarding £3,325–£4,850. Full Boarding £3,425–£4,950 *Compulsory extras:* Personal Accident Insurance, Church Collection.

Bredon School is situated in magnificent rural surroundings and delivers a broad based education centering upon individual attention and personal recognition. Bredon has adopted the National Curriculum and offers both the full traditional academic curriculum as well as a wide range of vocational courses in the Sixth Form including GNVQ (Land-Based Industries, Business, Engineering, Leisure, Health and Social Care, Art & Design and IT). Class sizes average 10–12 and teacher/pupil ratio 1:7. Bredon also has a thriving School Farm.

Selection is by potential not just attainment and specialist support is available for pupils with learning difficulties through the specialist Learning Support Department. Bredon endeavours to educate the whole child through sound realistic academic provision, sympathetic pastoral care, regular leadership challenges and a varied sports programme.

Bridgewater School

Drywood Hall Worsley Road Worsley Manchester M28 2WQ.
Tel: (0161) 794 1463
Fax: (0161) 794 3519

Headmistress: **Mrs G Shannon-Little**, BA

Age Range. 3–18
Number in School. Prep: Boys 158, Girls 105, Seniors: Boys 121, Girls 115
Fees per year. £3,390–£4,900. Lunch is included. There are no compulsory extras.

The senior part of the school offers a full range of subjects to GCSE. A levels in a wide range of subjects are available in the thriving 6th Form. Bridgewater is a two form entry school from age 11 and setting is introduced gradually from the second year upwards. Three separate Sciences are offered to GCSE, and Computer Studies and Technology are an integral part of the curriculum.

The aims of Bridgewater School are simple: to develop each pupil's personal qualities to the full, whilst striving for the best standards in education and thus enabling all to achieve the highest academic qualifications of which they are capable.

Entry for the Prep Dept is by interview and academic assessment. There is an annual examination at 11+ for entry to the Senior part of the school at which Scholarships are offered. Entry at other ages and at 11+ other than for the Scholarship examination is by interview and appropriate academic tests.

The school has completed all phases of a £1.5 million building programme, and has recently added an extensive all-weather sports area.

Scholarships are available at age 11 and for 6th Form.

Charitable status. Bridgewater School is a Registered Charity, number 526700. It exists to provided education for boys and girls, with scholarship places for able pupils in the area.

Bronte School

Mayfield 7 Pelham Road Gravesend Kent DA11 0HN
Tel: (01474) 533805

Headmaster: **Mr J M Rose**

Age Range. 3–11
Number in School. 110 Day Pupils: Boys 72, Girls 38
Fees per term. £1,260. *Compulsory extras:* Swimming from age 5, and stationery £20.00 per term.

This is a day school serving Gravesend and the surrounding villages. It was established in 1905. The children are taught in small classes and a close family atmosphere exists throughout the school. Children are prepared for all types of secondary education. Entry is preferred at 3 by interview with the Head. Those joining the school at a later stage receive an informal test in Reading, English and Maths before entry.

Buckingham College School

Hindes Road Harrow Middlesex HA1 1SH.
Tel: 020 8427 1220
e-mail: enquiries@buckcoll.org

Headmaster: **D F T Bell**, MA (Oxon), PGCE

Age Range. 11–18
Number in School. Day: 165
Fees per term. From £1,670 (Form 1). *Compulsory extras:* Luncheons, Book Hire

Buckingham College is an independent secondary school for boys aged 11–18, and girls aged 16–18.

Founded in 1936, it is a member of the E Ivor Hughes Educational Foundation. It is Accredited by the Independent Schools Council.

Students are prepared for 16 GCSE and 13 GCE 'A' Level examinations. The Sixth Form is conducted on tutorial lines, preparing small groups of pupils for 'A' levels. There is a full range of games and physical education activities.

The school aims to provide a well disciplined and happy community based on Christian principles in which each pupil may play an active and satisfying part. Classes are small – under 20 – and there is a wide range of sports.

Admission is by way of an individual entrance test and interview.

Scholarships are available on merit.

Charitable status. The E Ivor Hughes Educational Foundation is a Registered Charity, number 293623. It exists to provide education for children.

Bury Lawn School

Soskin Drive Stantonbury Fields Milton Keynes Bucks MK14 6DP
Tel: (01908) 220345
Fax: (01404) 881882
Bursar's Office Haccombe Membury Axminster EX13 7AF
Tel: (01404) 881702
Fax: (01404) 881882
e-mail: burylawnschool@aol.com
website: www.burylawnschool.co.uk

Headmistress: **Mrs Hilary Kiff,** AdvCertEd, BA Hons, DipE (Hum)

Age Range. 18 months to 18 years.

The School was founded in 1970 but moved into new premises in 1988 to house a maximum of 500 children with maximum class sizes of 18 giving a friendly family atmosphere in this co-educational school. Set in its own grounds close to the City centre of Milton Keynes, Bury Lawn offers supervision all year round from 8.00 am until 6.00 pm. A vast transport network ensures pupils can attend the School from a large catchment area.

Although non selective entry, the School is streamed to ensure the maximum potential is achieved for all pupils and has its own Dyslexic and Special Needs 'Den' staffed by qualified teachers, for those requiring extra help. Cambridge entry and all other University entry is achieved for our 'A' level students.

Bury Lawn offers all-round interdenominational education for boys and girls with a wide range of Sports, Dance and Drama and the full National Curriculum on offer. Special Loan plans and monthly payment arrangements assist parents to afford the best of Independent Education and the School Trust offers Bursaries where required.

Cambridge Arts and Sciences

Round Church Street Cambridge CB5 8AD
Tel: (01223) 314431
e-mail: cats@dial.pipex.com
website: www.ceg-uk.com

Principals:
Miss E R Armstrong, BA (Hons), DipPsych (London)
Mr Peter McLaughlin, BEd (Cantab), CertEd

Age range. 14–19

CATS, as Cambridge Arts & Sciences has become known, is a co-educational Sixth Form College occupying a self-contained campus of five buildings in the centre of Cambridge. The city's academic tradition and lively student society enhance the lives of all CATS students who make full use of the famous Cambridge Union for libraries, meetings, socialising and refreshment. Residential students live in college accommodation. The majority prefer the supportive environment of a supervised college hostel or living with other students at a 'home from home' with a Cambridge family. For older and more independent students, CATS has self-catering houses and flats.

In character the College lies mid-way between school and university and it enjoys an adult environment which acknowledges individuality and maturity - 'managed independence' is the keynote. The balance between this attractive liberal approach and the discipline of well proven teaching and learning methods allows students to meet challenges and targets both in academic pursuits and in personal development.

A broad, forward-looking GCSE timetable is programmed and sixth formers are encouraged to select the right A level courses from the 45 on offer. All students are taught in groups of 7 or less. Able, stimulating and enthusiastic tutors also develop study skills, the command of English and examination technique. The School of Art & Design runs a highly regarded Art Foundation Course in preparation for entry to Art Colleges. Over the years CATS has delivered rewarding results for many students in terms of Retakes, Easter Revision and Individual Tuition. Guidance in terms of university entrance and career planning is sensitive and professional.

There is an extensive range of cultural, sporting and social activities, with study trips and action holidays arranged each year. Each student has a Personal Tutor who monitors, listens, helps and encourages as required, and a dedicated team deals with all matters of accommodation, welfare and general college discipline. The students' committee is keen to enrich 'life at CATS' for all. Communications between the College and parents through reports and connections are a crucial part of the CATS education.

Cambridge Centre for Sixth Form Studies (CCSS)

1 Salisbury Villas Station Road Cambridge CB1 2JF
Tel: (01223) 716890
Fax: (01223) 517530
e-mail: office@ccss.co.uk
website: www.ccss.co.uk

Principal: **P C Redhead,** MA, PGCE (Cantab)

Age range. 15–19
Number in school. 170
Fees per term. Students under the age of 16 on 1 September: Day £2,309, Boarding £4,389.

Students over the age of 16 on 1 September: Day £3,620, Boarding £5,700.

Established in 1981, CCSS is one of the largest independent residential sixth-form colleges in Britain. It offers over 30 subjects at A level including the main Science, Arts and Social Science subjects as well as more recent options such as Textiles, Psychology, Law, Environmental Science and Media Studies. The College also offers specialist one-year, retake and revision courses and has a successful GCSE department.

Whichever course students choose, the College gives them the opportunity to take on greater responsibility for themselves and their work yet still affords them considerable academic and pastoral support. The results achieved are excellent, especially measured in value-added terms. Over 90% of students go on to Higher Education. Much of this success can be attributed to the College's highly qualified, committed staff and the very effective teaching structure which combines classwork in small groups of no more than eight with individual tutorials in each A level subject. Outside the classroom, all students are encouraged to take part in a full programme of social, cultural and sporting activities organised by CCSS staff.

Approximately two-thirds of students are residential and live in the College's own fully supervised houses which provide a comfortable, secure domestic environment for study and relaxation.

Canbury School

Kingston Hill Kingston-upon-Thames Surrey KT2 7LN.
Tel: 020 8549 8622
Fax: 020 8974 6018

Founded in 1982, Canbury School is a co-educational independent day school. It is non-denominational.

Head: **Mr C Y Harben**, MA

Age Range. 10–17
Number in School. 60 day children
Fees per term. £2,250

Curriculum. We cover a full range of GCSE subjects, most pupils taking a total of eight or nine.

Entry requirements. There are tests in English and Mathematics. The Headmaster interviews each candidate. A trial day or two at the school can be arranged prior to entry.

Subjects offered. In years 7, 8 and 9 we emphasise English, Mathematics and Science in line with the requirements of the National Curriculum. Our extended curriculum includes French, Geography, History, Information Technology, Art, Drama, Music and Personal and Moral Education. Later, Physics, Chemistry and Biology are taken as doubly-certificated GCSE subjects. Individual arrangements can be made for pupils to prepare for GCSE in German, Chinese and other languages. Business Studies is offered in Years 10 and 11 as an option leading to the GCSE.

Facilities. Brand new IT computer facilities are accessible to all pupils. There is an excellent art room. Pupils are transported to a wide range of sports facilities within the Borough.

Canbury School is different in placing emphasis on small classes. No class has more than 14 pupils. Full concentration is placed on bringing out the talents of each pupil. Pupils participate in the school council which makes decisions in some areas of school life.

Charitable status. Canbury School is a Registered Charity, number 803766. It exists to provide education to a broad range of children including some from various nationalities who stand to benefit from being in a small school.

Carleton House Preparatory School

Lyndhurst Road Mossley Hill Liverpool L18 8AQ
Tel: 0151-724 4880

Headmistress: **Mrs C Line**

Number on roll. 150
Age Range. 4–11
Fees. £1,075 per term.

Carleton House is a Catholic Preparatory School set in an attractive Victorian House in the Mossley Hill conservation area.

The school is open to children of other denominations and promotes the spiritual, moral and cultural development of all pupils. It recognises that the needs of all pupils are unique and aims to develop fully the talent of every individual.

Small classes enable the well qualified and experienced staff the opportunity to provide individual attention in a friendly, caring atmosphere. Additional specialist teaching is provided for children requiring support in the basic subjects.

The implementation of all ten National Curriculum subjects ensures a broad, well balanced curriculum is followed but great importance is given to Maths and English as success in these subjects is central to development in other areas.

French has been successfully introduced in all classes including Reception.

All children receive music lessons but individual piano and guitar lessons are also available.

Emphasis is placed on high academic standards with children being prepared for a variety of Entrance examinations at 11 and more than 90% of pupils gain places at selective schools of their choice.

A wide range of sports and extra curricular activities are offered to both boys and girls, including football, netball, cricket, rounders, swimming, chess, quiz, singing and speech choir. The children compete in local sporting events as well as choral festivals and chess tournaments.

Theatre and educational visits are encouraged along with a residential trip to the Lake District, for older pupils, which provides field and adventure activities that help build confidence and self esteem.

Close contact with parents is promoted through regular parent/teacher meetings and reports on pupils progress.

A thriving Parent Teacher Association provides social functions for parents while raising funds for extra equipment such as computers and printers.

After school and holiday provision is now provided by the 'Kids Club'. This operates daily from 3.30 pm until 6.00 pm and 8.00 am until 6.00 pm in holiday time.

Parents are welcome to visit the school by appointment.

Further information available from the Headteacher.

Charitable status. Carleton House Preparatory School is a Registered Charity, number 505310. It exists to provide education for boys and girls.

Chase Academy

Lyncroft House St John's Road Cannock Staffordshire WS11 3UR
Tel: 01543 501800
Fax: 01543 501801

***Principal:* Mr M D Ellse,** MA, PGCE, CPhys, MInstP

Head Master: Mr A W Evans, GGSM, PGCE
Head of Prep School: Mrs C M Ellse, MA, PGCE

Age range. 3-18
Number in school. Boarders: 5, Day: 130
Fees per term. Day: £540-£1,832. Boarding £3,700
Independent day and boarding school for boys and girls from nursery to A level.

Formerly a convent, founded in 1879, the senior school was added in 1980.

Extensive modern school on spacious urban site. New science, sport, technology, computing, language facilities.

Academic work. Small classes allow attention to the individual student. The National Curriculum is shadowed throughout. Common core up to Year 9. GCSE, AS and A2 level in: English, Mathematics, Physics, Chemistry, Biology, Design and Technology, Business Studies (not A level), Economics (not GCSE), History, Geography, French, German, Information Communications Technology, Physical Education, Music, Drama, Art.

Boarding. Delightful modern rooms, half of which are single study-bedrooms. The associated International College makes provision for overseas students who need to learn or improve their English.

Dyslexia. Support for intelligent dyslexics from Dyslexia Institute and within the small classes.

Sport. Football, cricket and netball are principal sports with school facilities for badminton (regional centre), tennis, volleyball, basketball.

Music and Drama. A strong team of professional performers and first-rate teachers producing big uptake in the performing arts.

School day. 0850 - 15.50. Prep until 16.50. Facilities for early drop-off and late pick-up.

Cherry Trees School

Flempton Road Risby Bury St Edmunds Suffolk IP28 6QJ
Tel: (01284) 760531
Fax: (01284) 750177

***Headmistress:* Wendy E S Compson**, Montessori AdvDiploma

Age Range. Co-educational 3 months–11
Numbers in school. Day: 150; Half day 90
Weekly Boarding: Boys and Girls 8+
Staff. 16 Full Time; 7 Part Time; 10 Visiting.
Religious affiliation. Interdenominational
Entry requirements. Interview and assessment
Montessori education is offered through to 11. The school is open 51 weeks of the year from 8 am to 6.00 pm during school time and from 8.00 am to 6.00 pm during the holidays.

Pupils are prepared for Preparatory school entrance and scholarship examinations. Girls common entrance at 11+. Boys common entrance at 11+.

Cherry Trees School enjoys an unrivalled position in 7 acres of magnificent Suffolk countryside. The buildings are modern and extremely well equipped. Specialist rooms are provided for science, computing, design and technology, art and craft, home economics and music. The school has established a high academic standard.

A large nursery department, employing the Montessori method, is run by fully qualified staff in superbly equipped facilities for children aged from 3 months to 5 years.

Pupils are encouraged to participate in a full range of indoor and outdoor sporting activities which include swimming, football, mini rugby, hockey, netball, athletics, cross country, tennis on our own court and cricket. Visiting specialists teach dance, piano, string, woodwind, brass instruments and singing.

Clubs operate after school, offering activities such as orchestra, choir, chess, first aid, adventure services and drama.

Children aged from 7 visit our house in Normandy annually, continuing their studies in the morning and spending the afternoons exploring France and using their French conversation. French is available from nursery level and German and Latin are also taught in the Junior School.

Claires Court School

Ray Mill Road East Maidenhead Berkshire SL6 8TE.
Tel: (01628) 411470. Registrar: (01628) 411472
Station: Maidenhead

***Principals:* H St J Wilding**, BA, MCIM (*Bursar*) and **J T Wilding**, BSc, FRSA

Head of Ridgeway: Miss K M Boyd, BEd
Head of College: Mrs A C Pitts, CertEd, FRSA

Number of Boys. 620 (Day Boys only).
Number of Girls. 200 (Day Girls at Maidenhead College)
Teaching Staff. 64 full time, 36 part time, 18 visiting.
Fees. £1,520–£2,280 per term.
The ethos of CLAIRES COURT and its Junior School, RIDGEWAY, lies in the provision for its pupils of a thorough education in all senses so that in time the challenges of the future will be met with confidence. A rich and full programme of study and activity leads to academic success, sporting accomplishment and cultural fulfilment, within a firm structure based on friendship and self-discipline. Boys only are accepted into the School.

RIDGEWAY, the Junior School for boys aged 4+ up to 11+ is situated in Maidenhead Thicket set in its own extensive grounds. The curriculum embraces the Government's National Curriculum and includes Music, Art and Craft, practical Science, and the major games as well as a thorough, caring preparation for normal academic subjects. The School swimming pool and outdoor fitness circuit are located here.

At 11+ all boys transfer to the Senior School, CLAIRES COURT, which stands in a pleasant residential area of Maidenhead close to the River Thames at Boulter's Lock. The curriculum continues to follow the NC but in addition Latin, German and Spanish are introduced during Key Stage 3. Boys are setted separately according to their ability in English, Mathematics, French and Latin.

From 1977, the School has offered a three-year course to 16+. The GCSE curriculum includes English, Mathematics, French, German, Spanish, Religious Studies, History, Geography, Physics, Chemistry, Biology, Combined Science, CDT, Art, Music, Physical Education, Commerce, Law and Drama, from which boys take eight to ten subjects in the first instance, as well as PSE and Careers advice.

The Sixth Form opened in 1994 offering a range of

subjects at A and AS Level including Art, Biology, Business Studies, Chemistry, English, French, Geography, Information Technology, History, Mathematics, Music, Photography, Psychology, Physics, Sociology, Political Studies, Theatre Studies, German, Spanish, Media Studies and Physical Education.

The School offers Academic, Music, Art, Sport, Drama and All Rounder Scholarships at 11+, 12+, 13+ and Sixth Form.

Recent developments include Senior Wing (1977), Computer Laboratory (1983), Sports Hall (1984), Senior Wing extension (1986) and Technology Wing comprising Technology Workshop, new Computer Laboratory, Practical Mathematics Laboratory and Art and Design Studio as well as three new Science Laboratories (1989), Astroturf general sports surface (1994). At Ridgeway, new Teaching Wing (1980), specialist pre-prep accommodation (1991). Dining room extended together with refurbishment of buildings to provide further classrooms including Science and Art facilities (1994), and subsequent development of an assault course for the junior age range (1997).

In April 1993, the Principals acquired Maidenhead College, a full range Girls Independent School also situated in Maidenhead on its own extensive 5 acre site, including purpose built hall with stage, indoor pool and Chapel. In September 1993, the executive, management and administrative functions of the Schools were integrated and a common Nursery with 130 places to serve both sections of the School was established. A common curriculum for all pupils, boys and girls, was confirmed, following both the National Curriculum and Common Entrance. The Principals have encouraged the development of co-ordinated education for boys and girls – academically taught on different sites but with much social, extracurricular and aesthetic activities happening together.

The major games are Rugby, Soccer, Rowing, Netball, Hockey, Athletics and Cricket. Minor games are Badminton, Basketball, Sailing, Sculling, Swimming and Tennis.

Among the many activities run are Chess, Choir, Computing, Debating, Drama, Electronics, Fencing, Golf, Gymnastics, IT, Judo, Orchestra, Photography and Public Speaking.

The School is Roman Catholic by tradition (30%) but all denominations are welcome.

A Prospectus, containing further information may be obtained from the School and prospective parents are always welcome to visit the School.

Claremont School

Baldslow St Leonards-on-Sea E Sussex TN37 7PW
Tel: (01424) 751555
Fax: (01424) 754310
e-mail: enquiries@claremontschool.co.uk
website: www.claremontschool.co.uk

***Headmaster:* Ian Culley**

Age range. Co-educational 1–13
Number of pupils. Day boys 200, Day girls 200
Fees per term. £1,100 to £1,850

Entry requirements. Interview and assessment, or through Nursery School admission.

Aim. To help develop independent, confident, tolerant and caring individuals who work together in a cheerful and enthusiastic family environment.

Location. Just north of St Leonards-on-Sea on the A21, close to Battle and Robertsbridge and situated in its own grounds of over 100 acres, comprising beautiful woodlands, lakes and playing fields.

School Day. The Nursery School is open all year round from 8 am to 6 pm and a variety of schedules are on offer. The Pre-Prep and Prep departments operate Monday to Friday - there is no Saturday School or other events arranged for pupils at the weekend. In the Pre-Prep the school day officially finishes at 3.30 pm - in the Prep School at 4.30 pm. Clubs and supervised Prep periods until 6 pm are offered to all children.

Transport. The school offers a Mini-bus collection and drop-off service to its pupils living within a 5-mile radius of the school.

Facilities. Chapel, IT Centre, Art Room, Library, Swimming Pool, Science Laboratory, Sports Hall, Nursery School and Theatre.

Pastoral Care. Each child has a form tutor and a house tutor. All new children are assigned to a guide to smooth their induction. An 'open door' policy to all staff is available for both children and parents. Regular parents evenings are held, mid-term assessments and termly reports for parents are provided.

Curriculum. Common Entrance, National Curriculum, and extension work for Scholarship candidates. Appropriate learning experiences are provided for a wide range of abilities, including individual learning support where a specific need has been diagnosed. There is a smooth transition between the three departments in the school - Nursery, Pre-Prep and Prep.

Music, Drama and Art. Children receive expert tuition and perform at school concerts, assemblies, and in the local music and drama festivals. There are also regular school productions in which all children are encouraged to perform. The school's resident artist oversees the development of artistic skills, with many children exhibiting their work at school and at Stowe.

Sport. Competitive, but friendly - Rugby, Rounders, Netball, Football, Cricket, Cross Country, Athletics, Swimming, Golf and Tennis.

Future Schools. Most children leave at 13, either to Senior Independent Schools (many with scholarships and awards) or to local maintained secondary schools.

Clewborough House School

Clewborough Drive Camberley Surrey GU15 1NX
Tel: (01276) 64799
Fax: (01276) 24424

***Principal:* Lt Col Donald A R Clark**

Headmistress: Miss Sarah L Streete, MSc, BEd (Hons)

Bursar: Mrs Vivienne F Spong

Age range. Day pupils, aged 2–11
Number in School. 300. Girls 120, Boys 180
Termly Fees. £840 (mornings only). £1,820.

Clewborough House School is a co-educational day school for pupils aged between 2 and 11. It is set on two sites and enjoys the facilities of 14.5 acres of land, just three miles away from each other. The Little Pegasus Nursery, the Reception classes and the Lower School classes are situated at Clewborough House School at Cheswycks in Frimley Green, whilst the Middle and Upper School classes are at Clewborough House in Camberley. The two sites combine to form a school of 300 children.

The Little Pegasus Nursery is well equipped for children of two years old, and is open fifty weeks of the year from 8 am until 6 pm.

The school encourages academic and sporting excellence, with a very good staff-to-pupil ratio, providing a well-structured education with a rock solid 3Rs foundation.

The National Curriculum is followed from age five with emphasis given to English and Mathematics. Children are given the maximum possible attention in small classes. Academic facilities include two modern computer rooms, two art and craft centres, a fully equipped science laboratory, a library, keyboard and music rooms, a domestic science kitchen and individual tuition areas. Sports facilities include football/hockey/cricket pitches, a confidence course, three heated swimming pools and two tennis/netball courts.

Manners and character-building are placed very highly within a happy family atmosphere. Remarkably wide ranges of extra-curricular activities are available, which take place daily in term time. These include Beaver Scouts, Cub Scouts, Rainbow Guides, Brownies Guides, judo, drama, ballet, art, domestic science, swimming, computer club, tennis, football, netball, music, riding, skiing, canoeing and languages, amongst others.

Parents are always pleased to know that their children can be cared for in a stimulating environment until 6 pm. During the school holidays different activities are arranged which "working parents" find very convenient.

Clewborough believes that the development of the individual child depends on creating a happy atmosphere where children enjoy their work and play, hence our school motto:

"Work Hard – Play Hard".

Bursaries are offered for siblings attending the school. Other bursaries may be offered at the discretion of the school.

For further information and a prospectus, please telephone 01276 64799 or 01252 835669, or visit our website at: www.clewborough.demon.co.uk.

Cliff School

St John's Lodge 2 Leeds Road Wakefield West Yorkshire WF1 3JT
Tel: (01924) 373597
and at: The Access Centre Bar Lane Wakefield, WF1 4 AD

Headteacher: **Mrs K M Wallace**, BEd

Age Range. Girls 6 weeks–11 years; Boys 6 weeks–9 years

Number in school. Girls 160; Boys 90

Fees per term. £1,198 all ages (reviewed annually in April)

Nationally recognised for its academic success, Cliff School's main campus is pleasantly situated in a listed Georgian mansion in its own grounds. It is close to Wakefield city centre and only two miles from junction 41 of the M1.

Cliff School is small, friendly and caring school with a strong academic tradition and great stress is placed on the social and moral development of the child. The size of the school and family atmosphere means that children are offered very personal attention. This, coupled with the courtesy engendered in the children, leads to the vast majority gaining places at other independent schools.

With the opening of Cliff School's annexe at The Access Centre in September 2001, there will be additional classes for 3+ to 6 year olds. The Access Centre boasts magnificent facilities, a full-size gym, outdoor soft play area, on-site café and large airy rooms. In addition, the school's new nursery, Perfect Blue Nursery and Baby Unit, offers full wraparound care for children from 6 weeks to 5 years.

Great emphasis is laid on the study of English and Maths and the acquisition of skills of literacy and numeracy. We believe that children should be exposed to a broad curriculum and this is reflected in the variety of subjects on offer. The curriculum is under constant review.

Music is very strong in the school with music lessons in all classes from specialist music teachers. A wide variety of instrumental tuition is available in the purpose designed music suite. The school has 3 choirs, an orchestra and a number of ensemble groups.

On the main campus, children are accepted at 2 years in Little Cliff Nursery. In the school, boys stay until 7 or 9 years and girls until 11 years. Girls are also accepted at 7 years and we are currently enrolling.

There is a full After-School Facility every day until 6 pm and there is a full Holiday Club from 8 am to 6 pm. In addition, there are many extra-curricular activities at lunchtimes and after school for children of all ages, including: choirs, orchestra, judo, games, art, craft, story-telling, drawing, netball, ball skills, French, dance clubs, swimming, gymnastics. In all there are over twenty activities available per week.

There is a Breakfast Club from 7.15 am.

Cliff School has its own sister school - Silverwood School in Silkstone, South Yorkshire. Here children are accepted up to 7 years after which they may transfer automatically to Cliff School. Many staff teach in both schools (and will be teaching at The Access Centre) and both schools have the same directors.

Colchester High School

Wellesley Road Colchester Essex CO3 3HD.
Tel: (01206) 573389
e-mail: office@colchesterhigh.essex.sch.uk
website: www.colchesterhigh.essex.sch.uk

Principal: **A T Moore**, MA (Oxon), PGCE

Age Range. Boys 3–16; Girls 3–11

Number in School. Day: 375

Fees per term. £410–£1,590

The standards we aim to achieve are reflected in the emphasis we place on sound moral training and in the strong Christian base of our School. Good manners and consideration for others are also highlights of our corporate life.

We work in a firm and friendly atmosphere, believing that pupils need close direction to reach the best academic standard each one can attain. However, initiative and a chance to take part are both encouraged, in class discussions, drama, school assemblies, prefects' system and various clubs, such as chess, sports, choir, orchestra.

A full range of GCSE subjects is taught by qualified staff, with classes averaging 16 in number. Science, computing and technology are taught in new laboratories. Soccer, cricket, athletics, hockey, tennis, swimming are afforded an important place with excellent facilities on nearby grounds and matches are played against other schools at all levels.

There is a newly equipped Nursery for boys and girls aged 3–5 years, where children are prepared for entry into the Preparatory Department.

Collingwood School

Springfield Road Wallington Surrey SM6 0BD.
Tel: 020 8647 4607
Fax: 020 8669 2884
website: www.collingwood.sutton.sch.uk

Headmaster: **Mr G M Barham**, BEd (Hons), MCollP

Age Range. 2½–11 (Co-educational)
Number in School. Day: 182
Fees per term. £400–£1,300 (reduction for siblings).

Collingwood was founded in 1929 and became an Educational Trust in 1978.

The aims of the School are to give each child a firm educational foundation upon which to build a successful future. In the Nursery, happy children learn number work, the rudiments of reading and writing, the love of books and enjoy their music and movement activities. The 4/5 year olds in the Kindergarten are reading, writing short stories, investigating scientific and mathematical problems, or striving to express themselves in French.

This excellent introduction gives them a head start in their studies in later classes, and the many scholarships and entrance successes to State Selective and Independent Senior Schools reflect the teaching abilities of the well-qualified staff.

However, Collingwood is not only concerned with academic success. Drama, Singing, Orchestra, Violin, Keyboard, Woodwind, Brass, Percussion, Piano and Recorder lessons, together with Chess Club, Design Technology Club, Football Club (with an ex-Premier League Footballer), Art and Craft Club, Athletics Club, Gym Club, Table-tennis Club, Hockey, Rounders, Netball, Tennis, Cricket and Swimming, broaden and enhance the pupils well-being and knowledge.

A truly all-round education is what Collingwood provides for boys and girls between the ages of 2½ and 11 years.

For a prospectus, details of examination results and to arrange a visit, please telephone 020 8647 4607. You will be made most welcome.

Charitable status. Collingwood School Educational Trust Ltd is a Registered Charity, number 277682A/1B. It exists to promote and foster a sound educational foundation for girls and boys aged 2½–11 years.

Cranbrook College

Mansfield Road Ilford Essex IG1 3BD.
Tel: 020 8554 1757
Fax: 020 8518 0317

Headmaster: **C P Lacey**, BA, MA, PGCE

Age Range. 4–16+
Number in School. Day: Boys 220
Fees per term. £1,218–£1,593

Cranbrook College, founded in 1896, is situated in a residential area close to the centre of Ilford. In the Lower School, boys follow a general primary school course, and in the Upper School they prepare for GCSE.

The main entry is at age 4 but older boys are admitted when vacancies exist. Admission at 8 and above is subject to a test and boys under 8 are interviewed before admission is confirmed.

The school caters for pupils of a wide range of ability and aims to provide a happy, ordered and secure environment in which, through academic work and a wide variety of sports and other activities, every boy has an opportunity to reach the highest standards that are within his capability.

Charitable status. Cranbrook College Educational Trust Limited is a Registered Charity, number 312662. It exists to provide 'general instruction of the highest class' for pupils from Ilford and the surrounding area.

Cransley School

Belmont Hall Great Budworth Nr Northwich Cheshire CW9 6NQ.
Tel: (01606) 891747/892122
Fax: (01606) 892122
E-mail: cransleyschool@btinternet.com

Head: **Mrs H P Laidler**, MA

Age Range. Day School for Girls 3–16 years. Boys 3–11 years.
Number in School. Girls 196; Boys 26.
Fees per term. £688–£960 (Pre-Prep), £1,200 (Junior School), £1,512–£1,572 (Senior School). *Compulsory extras:* Lunches £58–£98

An independent day school set in parkland in the Cheshire countryside, close to the main motorway network.

Boys and girls are admitted from 3–11 years and girls from 11–16 years.

It has a unique friendly atmosphere and small classes, taught by a dedicated team.

The school encourages the development of individual talent in drama, sport, art and music, in addition to high academic expectations. The latest Information Technology equipment is used throughout the whole school.

Crown House School

19 London Road High Wycombe Buckinghamshire HP11 1BJ.
Tel: (01494) 529927

Headmaster: **Laurence Clark**, MA (Oxon)

Age Range. 4½–11+
Number in School. Day: Boys 74, Girls 62
Fees per term. £1,490

Crown House was established in 1924 and accredited by the ISJC in 1981. There is a well-balanced curriculum designed to prepare children for local grammar and upper schools

There are just seven classes, grouped according to age, with usually 20 per class.

The school aims to encourage each child to match performance against personal potential and to meet all challenges with courage and determination.

Irrelevant comparisons with the attainment of others is discouraged in order to build self-confidence and a sense of self-worth. Importance is placed on the enjoyment of learning and pride in achievement.

A caring family atmosphere ensures that the individual nature of each child is respected, promoting the development of independent judgment, self-discipline and consideration for others.

Crowstone Preparatory School

121–123 Crowstone Road Westcliff-on-Sea Essex SS0 8LH.
Tel: Southend (01702) 346758
Fleethall Lane Sutton Road Rochford Essex SS4 1LL
Tel: (01702) 540629

Headmaster: **J P Thayer**, Teacher's Cert (Univ of London)

Age Range. 2½–11
Number in School. Day: Boys 123, Girls 124
Fees per term. £1,440 Full day, £635 Half day

Crowstone Preparatory School is an independent day school for boys and girls between the ages of three years and eleven years.

The aim of the school is to obtain the highest possible achievement from each individual pupil in a happy relaxed atmosphere in all areas of school work.

We are especially concerned in providing extra stimulus for children of high ability but also provide extra facilities for slower learners.

Culcheth Hall School

Ashley Road Altrincham Cheshire WA14 2LT.
Tel: 0161-928 1862

Headmistress: **Mrs Jacqueline A Turnbull**, BSc, PGCE

Age Range. 2½–16
Number in School. 220 Day Girls
Fees per term. Preparatory Department £755–£975, Senior School £1,435.

Culcheth Hall is a friendly school with small classes where girls are encouraged to work to the best of their ability in a secure and happy environment. We have an excellent academic record at both 11+ and GCSE. Girls join in a wide range of sporting, dramatic and musical activities in order to fulfil their potential in all areas and to develop a sense of responsibility and service to others. Field trips, expeditions and theatre visits take place throughout the year, and overseas visits are a regular feature of the school holidays.

Modern facilities include Language Laboratories, Music Room, Science Laboratories and an Art, Design and Technology Centre. The Headmistress is always pleased to show parents round the school by appointment.

Nursery School (2½–4 years). Structured teaching in small groups and individually gives each child a good foundation and the best possible start on which to build its future education.

Preparatory School (4–11 years). Formal structured teaching with emphasis on basic skills. Speech training and ballet available. Specialist Music, PE teaching. Admission by interview and assessment.

Before and After School Care. 8 am to 6 pm.

Senior School (11–16 years). GCSE (15 subjects). Entrance Examination in January. Scholarships available.

Charitable status. Culcheth Hall School is a Registered Charity, number 525916. The School's aim is to provide a sound education so that the girls leave with a real sense of achievement and look to the future with confidence.

Dagfa House School

Broadgate Beeston Nottingham NG9 2FU.
Tel: (0115) 9138330
Fax: (0115) 9138331

Headmaster: **A Oatway**, BA (Hons), PGCE

Age Range. 3–16
Number in School. Day: Boys 180, Girls 100
Fees per term. £880–£1,480

Dagfa House is situated in pleasant gardens in a quiet neighbourhood adjacent to University Park, and it enjoys easy access from all areas of the city and county. Small classes are taught by caring and dedicated staff, creating a purposeful learning environment where individual talents flourish.

A wide curriculum is provided, which includes the National Curriculum but leaves time available for other important aspects, such as an early introduction to foreign languages. Results are very good at all stages, and pupils also learn to be caring and thoughtful towards others.

Daiglen School

68 Palmerston Road Buckhurst Hill Essex IG9 5LG
Tel: 020 8504 7108
Fax: 020 8502 9608

Headmaster: **Mr D E Wood**

Age Range. 4–11
Number in School. 152 Boys
Fees per term. £1,490
Compulsory extras. Lunch, Swimming

The Daiglen School is a Preparatory School for boys aged 4–11 years. It was established in 1916 and became an Educational Trust in 1977.

The School aims to provide a good education by encouraging boys to achieve their full potential in all subjects.

Fully equipped Computer, Science and Technology departments along with a Music Room, Gymnasium and well stocked Library enable the School to offer a wide curriculum. Specialist teachers offer tuition in Orchestral Instruments, Piano and Guitar plus Short Tennis.

The boys are prepared for entry to Senior Independent Schools and local Grammar Schools in Essex and the London Borough of Redbridge at 11.

For a prospectus and registration form please contact the Admissions Secretary.

Dair House School

Bishops Blake Beaconsfield Road Farnham Royal Buckinghamshire SL2 3BY.
Tel: (01753) 643964
Fax: (01753) 642376

Headmistress: **Mrs L J Hudson**, CertEd, AIST
Chairman of Governors: Mr T A C Webb

Age Range. 2½–8
Number in School. 120 Co-educational Day pupils.
Fees per term. £650–£1,700

Located on the A355 at Farnham Royal we are conveniently placed for the Farnhams, Gerrards Cross, Beaconsfield, Stoke Poges and surrounding villages.

The school has excellent facilities - a large games field, attractive dining room, a gym with permanent stage and lighting, a fully equipped science and technology room, library and separate art room. Children are taught in classes up to 16 so individual attention is assured. The syllabus is wide and varied giving children *'a sure foundation from the start'*. We pride ourselves in providing a happy, caring environment where children can flourish. Well-qualified and experienced staff will take time to ensure that the children have the best of learning experiences. All abilities are catered for with extra help given when needed. Peripatetic staff visit the school for weekly music, French and dance lessons. We also have an 'After School' club, available until 5.30 pm, Monday to Thursday. A new building programme, due for completion in November 2001, will provide four new classrooms and hall for our younger children.

Charitable status. Dair House School Trust Limited is a Registered Charity, number 1239748. Its aims are to provide 'a sure foundation from the start'.

Davenport Lodge School

21 Davenport Road Coventry CV5 6QA.
Tel: 024 7667 5051
Fax: 024 7667 6889

Principal: **Mrs M D Martin,** BPhilEd (Hons)

Age Range. 2½–8
Number in School. Day: Boys 92, Girls 81
Fees per term. £1,100

Davenport Lodge was founded in 1968 and is a pre-preparatory school with its own Kindergarten. Pupils are prepared for competitive entrance examinations, principally for Coventry School Foundation's Junior Schools, King Henry VIII and Bablake, as well as other independent schools in the area. Swimming, music, art and tennis are included in the curriculum. Teaching is carried out in small groups in order to give an individual approach.

Derby Grammar School for Boys

Rykneld Hall Rykneld Road Littleover Derby DE23 7BH
Tel: 01332 523027
Fax: 01332 518670
e-mail: headmaster@derbygrammar.co.uk
website: www.derbygrammar.co.uk

Headmaster: **Mr R D Waller,** BSc (Hons)

Membership. Affiliated to Woodard (Midlands) Division)
Age range. 7 to 18
Numbers. 270
Fees per term. £1,925 (£1,540 for 7-11 years).

Derby Grammar School is a traditional boys grammar school situated on an extensive site on the southwest outskirts of Derby, with a wide and accessible catchment area served by a good network of school buses that we share with our neighbours, Derby High School for Girls.

Founded in September 1995, the School offers a broad ranging curriculum that includes excellent and extensive facilities for the separate sciences, small classes and a wide range of extra curricular activities. In addition to the usual academic subjects, Latin is taught from Year 8 and Greek is offered as an extra curricular option.

The School's accommodation is centred around a nineteenth century hall, and has an ambitious development programme which has already seen a new science block and general teaching block built, and a new Chemistry and Technology building opened in September 2000. Over the next five years, as the School develops to 400 boys, we plan to build a new Sports Hall, a further general teaching block and a School Hall.

The strong pastoral care is based on the Heads of Lower and Upper School who work closely with Tutors, and their small groups of tutees. All boys are expected to follow the Duke of Edinburgh Award programme.

Entry to the School is through our own entrance examination and interview with the Headmaster. The School offers a number of Bursaries, and a number of Academic and Music Scholarships are awarded annually. The School has a close connection with Derby Cathedral and offers Choral Scholarships to suitably qualified choristers.

Charitable status. Derby Grammar School for Boys is a Registered Charity, number 1015449. It exists to educate children.

Derwent Lodge Preparatory School for Girls

Somerhill Tonbridge Kent TN11 0NJ
Tel: (01732) 352124
Fax: (01732) 363381

Headmistress: **Mrs C M York,** BEd (Hons)

Age range. 7–11 years
Number in School. 125 Day girls
Fees per term. £1,990
Extras. Individual Music lessons, recreational outings, minibus service from Tunbridge Wells and Brenchley area, residential study visits.

Derwent Lodge was founded in central Tunbridge Wells in 1952 and moved to its present parkland setting on the southern outskirts of Tonbridge in 1993.

The school is noted for its strong academic tradition and for its caring, happy atmosphere. High standards of work, manners and courtesy are expected of each girl. There are specialist facilities for science, art, music, IT and sport.

The curriculum is designed to give a sound basic general education which will prepare pupils well for entry to the grammar or independent schools chosen by their parents. Pupils regularly gain scholarships to secondary schools.

An optional extended day is offered. There is a full programme of extra-curricular clubs and activities. Girls in their final two years at the school are offered residential study visits to Buxton in Derbyshire and to the Isle of Wight. The school has a well-established exchange link with an independent school in Maisons-Laffitte, near Paris.

Admission to the school at 7+ is by interview and a report from the previous school. For entry at later stages, girls spend a day at the school for informal assessment before the offer of a place is confirmed. Girls from the pre-preparatory school at Somerhill may proceed to Derwent Lodge automatically.

Derwent Lodge is one of the three Schools at Somerhill under the care and control of The Somerhill Charitable Trust; J T Coakley, MA is the Principal.

Charitable status. The Somerhill Charitable Trust is a Registered Charity, number 2331296. It exists for the purpose of providing education for children.

Devonshire House Preparatory School

2 Arkwright Road Hampstead London NW3 6AE
Tel: 020 7435 1916
Fax: 020 7431 4787

Headmistress: **Mrs S P Donovan**, BEd (Hons)

Age range. 2½–13

Devonshire House School is for boys and girls from three to thirteen years of age and the School's nursery department, the Oak Tree Nursery, takes children from two and a half. The academic subjects form the core curriculum and the teaching of music, art, drama, computer studies, design technology and games helps to give each child a chance to excel. At the age of eleven for girls and thirteen for boys the children go on to their next schools, particularly the main independent London day schools.

Devonshire House pursues high academic standards whilst developing enthusiasm and initiative. It is considered important to encourage pupils to develop their own individual personalities and a good sense of personal responsibility. There is a wide variety of clubs and tuition is available in ballet, judo, fencing, speech and communication and in a range of musical instruments. High standards and individual attention for each child are of particular importance.

The School is located on the crest of the hill running into Hampstead Village and has fine Victorian premises with charming grounds and walled gardens.

Devonshire House is accredited by the Independent Schools' Council and is a member of the Independent Schools Association and of ISIS.

Ditcham Park School

Petersfield Hampshire GU31 5RN.
Tel: (01730) 825659

Headmistress: **Mrs K S Morton**, BEd, CertEd, DipEduManagement

Age Range. 4–16
Number in School. Day: Boys 194, Girls 125
Fees per term. £1,395–£2,330 excluding lunch

Situated high on the South Downs, the School achieves excellent results in a happy purposeful atmosphere.

Charitable status. Ditcham Park School is a Registered Charity, number 285244R. It exists for educational purposes.

Dixie Grammar School and Wolstan Preparatory School

Market Bosworth Leicestershire CV13 0LE
Tel: 01455 292244
Fax: 01455 292151
e-mail: dixie@pipemedia.co.uk

Headmaster: **Mr R S Willmott**, MA (Cantab), MA, FRSA

Age range. Wolstan 4–9; Dixie 10–18.
Numbers in schools. Dixie: 136 boys, 148 girls; Wolstan: 82 boys, 77 girls.
Fees per term. Wolstan: £1,110–£1,330; Dixie: £1,575

The Dixie Grammar School, a medieval foundation, was closed in 1969, but re-founded as an independent school in 1987. Its junior department, the Wolstan Preparatory School, was opened three years later. The Grammar School occupies a site in the heart of the quiet country town of Market Bosworth, the attractive early nineteenth-century main school building overlooking the market square. The Preparatory School is just under three miles away at Temple Hall in Wellsborough, where it enjoys a spacious site surrounded by countryside. Over thirty acres of playing fields have recently been acquired just outside the town. The schools are served by seven bus routes, with a free minibus link between the two sites.

Both schools are selective and have academic achievement as their central aim. Music, drama, sport and service are also an integral part of the education offered. Both schools have an inter-denominational Christian basis. The relative smallness of the schools ensures that they combine great friendliness with excellent discipline, providing a secure and well-ordered framework in which children can confidently achieve their full potential.

The Grammar School offers academic, music, art and sports scholarships.

Charitable status. The Leicestershire Independent Educational Trust is a Registered Charity, number 514407. It exists to provide a traditional grammar school education.

Dolphin School

Hurst Berkshire RG10 0BP.

(see IAPS section, Part V of this Book).

Dorchester Preparatory School

25–26 Icen Way Dorchester Dorset DT1 1EP.
Tel: (01305) 264925

Headmaster: **Dr Chris Rattew**

Age Range. 3–16
Number in School. Day: Boys 50, Girls 50
Fees per term. £480–£650 (part-time); £730–£1,500 (full-time). *Compulsory extras:* Lunches

d'Overbroeck's College

Beechlawn House 1 Park Town Oxford OX2 6SN
Tel: (01865) 310000
Fax: (01865) 552296
e-mail: mail@doverbroecks.oxon.sch.uk
website: www.doverbroecks.oxon.sch.uk

Principals: **Mr S Cohen**, BSc, **Dr R M Knowles**, MA, DPhil

Age range. 13–19
Number in school. 250
Fees per term. £2,515–£2,755 (up to GCSE); £3,735 (Sixth Form). (Day 13–16; residential and day 16–19).

d'Overbroeck's is a co-educational college in Oxford for pupils aged 13–19. We are fairly evenly divided between residential and day students in the Sixth Form; but up to the age of 16 we only take day pupils.

Since the College was founded in 1977, we have established a reputation for providing an educational experience which is both excellent and, in a number of ways, distinctive.

Our academic approach is characterised by small classes, of 5–6 students on average, a strong sense of individual needs and personal attention, and an unusual degree of flexibility in the range and possible combinations of subjects which may be studied.

Teaching is highly interactive and seeks to generate enthusiasm for the subject, sound academic skills and effective working habits – while at the same time providing a thorough preparation for public examinations.

A wide range of sporting and other extra-curricular activities is available, though on a purely optional basis in the Sixth Form; students are encouraged, but not obliged, to take part. Students can also benefit from the wide range of educational, cultural and social activities which Oxford has to offer.

Alongside academic achievement, there is a strong emphasis on personal development and on fostering a sense of individual responsibility. We expect high standards of commitment and effort from our students and have a track-record of strong GCSE and A level results. Students of all abilities can benefit from excellent teaching, and a positive, encouraging approach which allows them to maximise their potential. The majority of students go on to university and we have an excellent record of success with entry including Oxford and Cambridge, as well as medical, law and art schools.

Our students work in a highly stimulating environment which successfully dispenses with some of the more formal rules and constraints which one would traditionally expect to find in a school. This is particularly true in the Sixth Form. For many, this particular blend of an education which is more personalised inside the classroom and less regimented outside of it has provided the stimulus and the self-confidence they need to spread their wings and see in academic work an enjoyable and rewarding experience.

Duncombe School

4 Warren Park Road Bengeo Hertfordshire SG14 3JA
Tel: (01992) 414100
e-mail: dbaldwin@duncombe-school.co.uk
website: www.duncombe-school.co.uk

Headmaster: **David Baldwin**, MA, BEd

Age Range. Co-educational. 2–11
Number in School. Day: Boys 174, Girls 170
Teaching staff. Full time 23, Part time 24 (all qualified)
Fees per term. £380–£2,076

Duncombe School is perfectly situated at the top of Port Hill, Hertford in a large Victorian House surrounded by established gardens, Dell and playgrounds. The children enjoy a happy, stimulating environment where they are encouraged to reach their full potential across a variety of subjects, within a broad, balanced curriculum. Duncombe has a warm, friendly atmosphere where learning is fun and the needs of the children are met. The school has high expectations of behaviour and consideration for each other, and everyone achieves success.

The school has a pre-school centre (Treetops), a rich and stimulating environment where our youngsters are cherished and challenged. Along with several other developments, including an up-to-date ICT suite, adventure playground, sports facilities (running track and floodlighting), modern changing areas and updated classrooms and science room, Duncombe is determined to stay at the forefront of primary education.

The main sports are football, cricket, rounders, netball and athletics. There is enthusiastic participation in interhouse and inter-school competition, organised by specialist sports staff. The 5-a-side National ISA football champions for 1997, 1999, 2000 and 2001. Duncombe is also committed to furthering the artistic and musical talents of children. Lessons are available in piano, woodwind and ballet. There is thorough special needs provision at the school.

We believe that Duncombe offers the highest quality educational provision for all children.

Ealing College Upper School

83 The Avenue Ealing London W13 8JS.
Tel: 020 8248 2312
Fax: 020 8248 3765

Headmaster: **Barrington Webb**, MA

Age Range. 11–18
Number in School. Day: Boys 130, Girls 5
Fees per term. £1,680

Established since 1820, Ealing College Upper School provides a small caring establishment where a grammar school type of education is pursued by some 150 boys from the age of 11–18. There are, in addition, approximately 5 girls.

The general philosophy of the school is to endeavour to help each individual to achieve his/her full potential whatever their background or ability. To this end a common curriculum is studied in Years 7 to 9 and the optional courses leading to GCSE are introduced in Year 10. The Sixth Form offers a wide range of 'A' level courses including, in addition to the usual arts and science subjects, the increasingly popular business and social science subjects such as computing, economics and politics.

A wide range of sporting activities is offered and other extra-curricular interests are served by various clubs and societies.

Eastbourne House School

111 Yardley Road Acocks Green Birmingham B27 6LL.
Tel: 0121-706 2013

Headmaster: **P J Moynihan**

Age Range. 3–11+
Number in School. Total 130, Day: Boys 68, Girls 62
Fees per term. £960–£1,055 approximately

The first thing a visitor to the School notices is the general air of tranquillity. On entering the classrooms the overwhelming impression is one of work through enjoyment. The children are genuinely proud of their work and will gladly offer the visitor the opportunity of seeing examples.

Each child is supplied with any necessary books; none are shared. Our teachers are sympathetic to the needs of each child and work in close conjunction with each other, thus ensuring that a child's progress is maintained.

The range of subjects offered ensures that our pupils not only have a broad general knowledge, but also a solid foundation on which to build in the secondary school.

Eastcliffe Grammar School

The Grove Gosforth Newcastle upon Tyne NE3 1NE.
Tel: Tyneside 0191-285 4873

Headmaster: **G D Pearson**, BA (Hons), DipEd, FRSA

Age Range. 3–18
Number in School. Day: Boys 150, Girls 55
Fees per term. Senior School £1,660, Juniors £1,025–£1,450

Eastcliffe is a co-educational day school which admits boys and girls from the age of 3 and offers a wide range of educational opportunities within a positive family atmosphere. Founded in 1946, the school is situated in a pleasant residential suburb and is easily reached by car and public transport. Classes are small and particular emphasis is placed upon developing the abilities and aptitudes of individual children, including those with special needs like Dyslexia. There is a strong academic tradition and good facilities for the sciences, humanities, arts, music, drama, design, technology and sports.

Many boys and girls join the school in the Junior Department and proceed to the Senior School, where 14 subjects are offered at GCSE level. Sixth Form courses are offered to A, A/S and GCSE levels. Approximately 60% of the Fifth Year proceed to the Sixth and applications are welcomed at this level from home and overseas students. Pupils are encouraged to take part in extra curricular activities and there are many trips, outings and holidays organised throughout the year. There is an exchange programme with students in the USA and Europe.

Edgehill College

Northdown Road Bideford Devon EX39 3LY
Tel: (01237) 471701
Fax: (01237) 425981

Founded, 1884
Chairman of Governors: Mr O Nankivell, MA(Econ), JP

Headmistress: **Mrs E M Burton,** BSc (London), AKC
Physics

Edgehill College was founded in 1884 as a Girls' School but is now fully co-educational. There are 142 pupils in the Prep School (3-11) and 298 in the Senior School (11-18). There are 78 boarders.

The estate occupies an unrivalled position in one of the most beautiful parts of North Devon. Situated on a hill on the outskirts of Bideford, it is within easy reach of the coast, which is only 2 miles distant.

The grounds extend over 50 acres of land, on which are situated the Main Buildings, 5 Residential Houses, Tennis Courts, Playing Fields, the Gymnasium, Outdoor Education Centre, Sports Hall, Hard Playing Area and Recreational gardens. Home Economics and Art, Design and Technology have their own centres and there is a Lecture Theatre and an extensive Library, There are laboratories for Physics, Chemistry, Biology, Modern Languages and Computers.

Opportunities are available for Youth Hostelling, Camping, Trampolining, Riding, Life Saving, The Duke of Edinburgh's Award Scheme, Social Service, Young Enterprise, Creativity in Science & Technology Award Scheme, Scouts in addition to many other creative activities.

In 1997 Edgehill won The Schools Curriculum Award, a prestigious prize for the quality of its curricular and extra-curricular activities.

Course of Study. Pupils are prepared for the GCSE examinations and the University of Cambridge Advanced Level and AS GCE examinations and Oxbridge entrance.

Pupils normally take 9 GCSEs – the subjects available are: English Language, English Literature, French, Mathematics, Religious Studies, Drama, History, Geography, German, Physics, Chemistry, Biology, Design and Technology, Home Economics-Food, Information Technology, Physical Education, Art-Graphics/Painting and Music.

In the Sixth Form, 'A' level subjects may be chosen from Religious Studies, English, History, Geography, Fashion and Textiles, Environmental Science, Theatre Studies, French, German, Mathematics, Physics, Chemistry, Biology, Home Economics, Music, Art, Art History, Business Studies, Further Mathematics, General Studies, Accounts and Photography. One-year courses in Child Care, Psychology, Spanish, Sociology, Information Technology and Health Education are offered in the Lower Sixth.

A few dyslexic pupils are accepted each year and given special consideration and can receive specialist assistance as an optional extra.

Sixth Form. The Sixth Form is strong, with the majority of pupils staying on to take 'A'-Levels. Pupils wishing to join the College at Sixth Form level are required to have good passes at GCSE.

Music. Music forms an important part of College life and most pupils learn to play an instrument. Examinations of the Associated Board of the Royal Schools of Music are taken in: Piano, Keyboard, Violin, Viola, 'Cello, Flute, Clarinet, Saxophone, Singing, Drums and Guitar. There is a College Orchestra, College Choir and a variety of musical groups.

Speech & Drama and Public Speaking. These complement GCSE and A-Level Theatre Studies.

Games. Hockey, Netball, Football, Rugby, Cross Country, Cricket, Tennis, Rounders, Athletics, Gymnastics, Outdoor Pursuits. Basketball, Badminton and Volleyball are added to the choice of activities at Senior level.

Preparatory School. The Prep School is a community which aims to provide a secure environment where all the children can develop their potential to the full and achieve success. Care is taken to give a good grounding in English and Mathematics but French, Science, Technology and Computing are also introduced to allow them to make a smooth transfer to the Senior School.

Activities include: Camping, Hiking, Riding, Swimming, Gymnastics, Youth Hostelling, Arts and Crafts, Football, Cricket, Netball, Music, Pottery and Cubs.

Preparatory School Entrance. Boys and girls are admitted without a formal examination. Satisfactory reports will be required from the previous school. Some Scholarships are available each year to children of 8 years. These are awarded on the results of an examination.

Entrance and Awards. Entrance to the Senior School is gained either through the Common Entrance Examination or the College's own entry examinations. Academic, Music and Sports Scholarships are available as well as Governors' Bursaries.

Fees. Special terms for children of HM Forces and Ministers of the Church.

Prospectus. A copy of the prospectus may be obtained from the Registrar, Edgehill College, Bideford, North Devon EX39 3LY.

OEA: Old Edgehillians' Association meets in London, Sheffield, Exeter, Bristol and Bideford. *Secretary*, Mrs W Coomber, 1 Magnolia Way, Cowplain, Hants. PO8 9HB.

Charitable status. Edgehill College is a Registered Charity, number 306709. Edgehill is a charitable institution for the education of children.

Edington and Shapwick School

Shapwick Manor Shapwick Nr Bridgwater Somerset TA7 9NJ.
Tel: (01458) 210384
Fax: (01458) 210111

Joint Headmasters: **D C Walker**, BA (Hons) and **J P Whittock**, CertEd

Age Range. 8–18
Number in School. Boarders: 94 boys, 25 girls; Day: 36 boys, 9 girls
Fees per term. Boarders £3,946–£4,416, Day £2,832–£2,966

Edington and Shapwick is a specialist school for boys and girls whose education would otherwise be impaired by dyslexia. The School provides a caring and supportive atmosphere, staffed by specialist teachers across a wide curriculum offering the structured help needed by students who have dyslexia. Students take up to 8 GCSE subjects and the aim is to teach to their strengths whilst their weaknesses are being overcome and their confidence grows. Supplementary courses, such as Study Skills, Keyboard Skills, and careers advice are also taken. The School has a full range of specialist classrooms, including four laboratories, computing rooms, design centre, art rooms, library, sports hall and games field. Students are involved in a wide range of extra curricular activities, the Duke of Edinburgh's award, and games fixtures, to complement the formal curriculum.

Prospective entrants need an Educational Psychologist's report diagnosing dyslexia and at least average intellectual potential together with a current Head's report, and interview.

Egerton-Rothesay School

Junior & Senior 7-18 years Durrants Lane Berkhamsted Herts HP4 3UJ
Tel: (01442) 865275
Fax: (01442) 864977
Nursery & Junior 2½-7 years 3-7 Charles Street Berkhamsted Herts HP4 3DG
Tel: (01442) 866305
Fax: (01442) 876148

Headteacher: **Mrs N Boddam-Whetham**, BA (Hons), PGTC

Age Range. 2½–18 years
Number in School. 336 boys, 168 girls
Fees per term. £330–£2,540
Compulsory extras. Lunches.

Founded in 1922 Egerton-Rothesay School has developed from a small prep school to having a flourishing secondary department, established in 1988. The Nursery & Junior School is in the centre of Berkhamsted and the Middle and Upper Schools are in purpose-built premises in their own grounds on the rural periphery. The central objective of the School is to provide an environment where good teaching and good learning can flourish. All pupils are encouraged and prevailed upon to develop their full potential in every area. The atmosphere of the School is congenial to this end, the School being run on Christian principles. The latter is reflected in the whole ethos of the School as well as assemblies. Pupils come from a wide catchment area served by our own bus services. Newcomers find a most welcoming environment and are rapidly integrated into the full life of the School.

We have over 60 teaching staff – both full and part time – who are highly committed and bring a wide range of subject skills and teaching experience to the School. A professional management team, including both teaching and non-teaching staff, ensures the effective running of the School.

As a child develops it may be that professional diagnosis, available from our own Chartered Educational Psychologist, reveals a specific learning difficulty. We have full provision for helping such pupils. The School also addresses the needs of the exceptionally gifted. Additionally, all pupils are given assistance from their tutors to enable them to develop a strategy of effective learning and a Study Skills programme is included in the curriculum.

It is the prime concern of the School and staff that parents should always have the opportunity to talk with someone representing the School at any time during the term. For this reason we adopt an "Open Door" policy. Any parent may, at any time, during school hours, leave a message for, or make an appointment to meet, a Head/Principal or other member of staff.

Elmhurst School

44–48 South Park Hill Road South Croydon Surrey CR2 7DW.
Tel: 020 8688 0661
Fax: 020 8686 7675

Principal: **R E Anderson**, DipEd, ACP

Headmaster: B K Dighton, CertEd

Age Range. 4–11
Number in School. 250
Fees per term. £1,475–£1,745 (including lunches and ISJC Personal Accident Insurance).

Elmhurst School (established 1879) prepares boys for entry to such prestigious schools as Whitgift, Trinity, Dulwich College and Caterham and possesses an enviable record of academic success.

Equally important is the wide ranging curriculum designed to encourage boys to make the most of their talents and strengthen their weaknesses in a structured but friendly family environment. An extremely well equipped and flourishing computer department, together with active participation in educational visits and drama, foster interest in technology and creativity. A wide variety of sports is encouraged, including participation in Soccer, Cricket, Athletics, Cross Country, Gymnastics, Tennis, Swimming and Golf.

Elmhurst, accredited by the ISJC, accepts boys at the age of four, with occasional vacancies arising in other year groups.

Elm Tree House School

Clive Road Llandaff Cardiff CF5 1GN.
Tel: (01222) 223388/344223
Fax: (01222) 223388
e-mail: mrsthomas@elmtreehouseschool.co.uk

Headmistress: **Mrs Christine M L Thomas**

Age Range. Co-educational. 2½ to 11
Fees per term. £910–£1,047

Elm Tree House is a small independent school for girls

and boys. It was founded in 1922, and has a history of academic excellence.

Small classes ensure individual attention within a happy, family atmosphere.

The curriculum which includes French, is broad based and under constant review. The school also offers the additional choices of Ballet, Speech and Drama and Karate.

Tuition in Violin, Guitar, Piano, Flute and Recorder is available.

A broad curriculum is offered, and music, the arts, games and physical education are an integral and important part of every child's education. Our school is one in which laughter is never far away - we take our task very seriously but believe that teaching and learning should balance the rigorous and the routine with excitement and enjoyment.

Fairfield School

Fairfield Way Backwell North Somerset BS48 3PD
Tel: (01275) 462743
Fax: (01275) 464347

Headmistress: **Mrs Ann Nosowska**, CertEd, BEd (Hons), FRSA

Age Range. 3–11
Number in School. Boys 70, Girls 75
Fees per term. £405–£1,370

Fairfield is an independent day school for boys and girls of 3–11 years of age. The school was founded 65 years ago as a PNEU school.

It has always had as an important aim the desire to educate pupils as individuals and consequently class size is normally restricted to 18 pupils.

Fairfield offers a broad and balanced curriculum firmly based on the National Curriculum. Visiting teachers provide extra curricular lessons in dance, piano, speech and drama, tennis, short tennis and gymnastics. Pupils may take part in a variety of after school clubs.

Pupils are prepared for entry into all local independent senior schools, as well as for the excellent neighbouring comprehensive schools.

For further particulars please apply to the School Secretary.

Charitable status. Fairfield PNEU School (Backwell) Limited is a Registered Charity, number 310215. It aims to provide a broad, liberal education which will fully develop each child's individual aptitudes.

Ferndale Preparatory School

5-7 Bromsgrove Faringdon Oxon SN7 7JF
Tel: 01367 240618
Fax: 01367 240618
e-mail: ferndaleprep.school@talk21.com

Headmaster: **Mr J R Hunt,** BEd, MEd, DipPE

Age range. 3-11 years
Number in school. Day. Girls 89; Boys 84
Fees per term. £1,335-£1,565

Ferndale Preparatory School was founded in 1952. It occupies adjoining Grade II listed properties in the centre of the Oxfordshire market town of Faringdon.

The school has a self-contained nursery unit for 18 pupils. Children move to the Lower School in the September following their fourth birthday. Between the ages of 7 and 11 they are housed in the Upper School. Above all else, Ferndale is a happy, family based school with a strong sense of community and commitment. The school is non-selective but enjoys an excellent academic record at such schools as Abingdon, St Helen's, Oxford High, Royal High at Bath and St Mary's, Calne.

Finborough School

The Hall Gt Finborough Stowmarket Suffolk IP14 3EF
Tel: (01449) 773600
Fax: (01449) 773601
e-mail: admin@finborough.suffolk.sch.uk
website: www.finborough.suffolk.sch.uk/

Principal: **Mr John Sinclair**, BSc (Econ), FCA

Headteacher: Mrs S Gwen Caddock, BA (Hons), DipEd, MEd (Cantab)

Age Range. Co-educational 2½–18
Number of Boarders. 70 Boys, 55 Girls.
Number of Day Pupils. 35 Boys, 35 Girls.
Fees per term. Boarding £2,510–£3,825. Day £1,150–£1,950. The Montessori Nursery has its own fee structure based upon number of sessions attended. Termly fees are fully inclusive of all meals, educational materials and extended day care for day pupils. Flexible and occasional boarding facilities for day pupils are available at additional cost.

There are Academic Scholarships available at 11 and 13. Bursaries are available for families of Military and Diplomatic Personnel, Clergy and others with special boarding needs.

Location. Finborough School stands in a safe and healthy rural environment two miles west of Stowmarket, which is on the main London-Norwich line and is 5 minutes drive from the A14. The school operates an escort service for travel at the beginning and end of each term and a local bus service for day pupils. Finborough Halll is an eighteenth-century manor house with considerable modern extensions beautifully situated in sixty acres of its own playing fields, gardens and woodland.

Facilities. Founded in 1977 the School moved to its present site in 1980 since when it has consistently re-invested in improved facilities. The year 2000 saw the addition of a modern new Senior School Library, refurbished Art & Design centre and further upgrading of boarding accommodation. There are good Laboratory and Computer facilities as well as well-maintained playing fields and hard-courts for tennis, netball and basketball. The woodland provides an adventure playground, camping site and a stretch of river for canoeing and fishing.

Aims. By acknowledging each pupil as an individual and by nurturing their individual talents, our aim is to prepare them for the ever changing world of work and to responsibly discharge their duty to the Country and society in which they are privileged to live. The School Development Plan allows for planned growth to around 400 pupils in total, more or less evenly divided between Prep School and Senior School. The number permits retention of our small school family atmosphere whilst providing a unit where viability will allow the provision of first-rate facilities in all areas.

Education. Classes are small, with an average of 15 pupils and are taught by highly-qualified professional staff. The curriculum covers the full range of traditional subjects, as well as technology and ICT through to GCSE and A level. Advanced vocational qualifications are offered in, for example, Health and Social Care and Leisure and

Recreation, and in most cases are taken with additional GCE A level subjects. Other pupils choose to follow the traditional GCE A level route to higher education. All pupils receive trained advice on careers and university entry.

Examination results are good, reflecting not only pupil ability but their hard work and the expertise and commitment of teaching staff.

Music, Drama and Art. Pupils receive expert tuition and perform at School concerts, assemblies, and in the local music and drama festivals. A wide range of instrumental tuition is available at additional cost. The School regularly has successes in Art competitions and a wide range of work is displayed around the premises.

Sport. Competitive but well-mannered - Rugby, Netball, Hockey, Soccer, Rounders, Cricket, Cross-country, Athletics, Swimming, Tennis etc.

Entry. Following application, previous schools reports and school references are (where applicable) received and interview arranged. All candidates are encouraged to attend trial sessions for 2 or 3 days before making up their minds about the school. Entry tests in Mathematics and English are normally taken during trial days, or at interview if attendance at trial days is not possible.

General. Day pupils can be accommodated from 8 am to 6 pm and there is no Saturday school. A wide range of extra-curricular clubs and activities are available at lunchtimes, and between prep sessions in the evening. According to demand and the seasons a variety of activities, expeditions etc are offered at weekends in addition to school and house fixtures. Assembly in the village church is an important social as well as spiritual occasion and takes place three times a week.

The Firs School

45 Newton Lane Chester CH2 2HJ
Tel: 01244 322443
Fax: 01244 400450

Head: **Mrs M A Denton**

Age range. Co-educational 4-11
Number in school. 213. Boys 119, Girls 94
Fees. £1,155 per term

The Firs School is an independent co-educational primary school set in attractive grounds about a mile and a half north of the city of Chester. It was founded in 1945 by Mrs F A Longman.

The aim of The Firs is to help children achieve their academic potential in the context of a caring environment based upon Christian principles. Children of all faiths are welcome and we respect and learn from their beliefs and cultures. Our strengths lie in the individual attention we are able to give, a carefully planned curriculum and an effective partnership with parents. Specialist teaching for dyslexia and other educational needs is available in our well-established learning support unit. We have a proven record of success in preparing children for entrance to local independent and state schools. The school is well resourced with a continuous programme of investment, including our technology and pottery rooms.

Whilst placing great emphasis on the core subjects, our curriculum is enhanced through the teaching of French, gardening club, the opportunity for sport and the quality of our provision of art and music throughout the school.

Our objective is to encourage the development of the whole child so that each will leave The Firs School with an understanding of the wider world and an awareness of his or her responsibility to others.

Forest Park School

Lauriston House 27 Oakfield Sale Cheshire M33 6NB
Tel: 0161 973 4835

Headmaster: **Mr L B R Groves**, BEd, MBA

Age Range. 3–11
Number in School. Day Boys 85, Day Girls 65
Fees per term. £1,040–£1,182

Forest Park occupies a pleasant site in a quiet road surprisingly close to the centre of Sale, easily accessible from motorways and surrounding areas.

The school aims to discover and develop each child's particular abilities by offering a varied curriculum in a stimulating and happy atmosphere. Forest Park has a good pupil teacher ratio and offers a wide range of subjects with priority given to the traditional disciplines of English, Mathematics and Science. Pupils from three years of age are taught Information Technology by specialist staff. Swimming is taught from the age of five and games offered are Football, Cricket, Lacrosse and Touch Rugby for boys, Netball, Tennis and Lacrosse for girls. Pupils are taught French from an early age, the older children having the opportunity to visit a language study centre in France.

The confidence and social ease one expects of a private education is a product of the school. Our aim is to develop skills and knowledge through a habit of hard work in a secure and happy environment within a disciplined framework. The school prepares pupils for all independent grammar school examinations and has an excellent record in this respect.

The school prides itself on strong links and communication with a most supportive Parents' Association.

Forest School

Moss Lane Timperley Altrincham Cheshire WA15 6LJ.
Tel: (0161) 980 4075
Fax: (0161) 903 9275

Headmistress: **Mrs J Quest**, CertEd, FCollP

Age Range. 3–11
Number in School. Day: Boys 102, Girls 75
Fees per term. £1,040–£1,182

A co-educational school set in spacious grounds with high academic standards and an enviable reputation for its care of the individual.

Working within a happy environment, the children experience a traditional approach to education both in the subject disciplines and the high expectations of good behaviour.

The Infant Department ensures the children have a thorough understanding of reading, writing and number work. The Junior curriculum is broad and includes the teaching of French and Computer Studies whilst special attention is given to those subjects which the children require for entry to the senior schools.

Small classes, a friendly atmosphere and extra-curricular activities ensure the children achieve their full potential and are well prepared for future schooling.

Frewen College

Brickwall Northiam Nr Rye East Sussex TN31 6NL
Tel: 01797 252494
Fax: 01797 252567
e-mail: post@frecoll.demon.co.uk
website: frewcoll.demon.co.uk

Head: **Simon Horsley,** BA (Hons)

Age range. Boys. 9-17 (weekly boarding from 11 years)

Number in School. Weekly boarders 43; Day boys 37

Fees per term. Day £3,148 to £4,420; Weekly boarding £5,533 to £6,540

Frewen College is a specialist school for the education of dyslexic boys. We believe not only in tackling the difficulties which each boy has but also in establishing the strengths and talents of each individual so that success is experienced at every level.

There are 80 boys and 22 teaching staff. All boys go on to further and/or higher education. The full National Curriculum is offered within a small class environment which allows for a whole school approach to the problems of specific learning difficulties. Each boy has an individual education plan which allows for the tackling of his dyslexic problems and for the development of his strengths. Literacy problems are tackled using a range of programmes including THRASS and the Dyslexia Institute Literacy Programme. A wide range of GCSEs is offered.

There is a particular emphasis on Technology, Art and Design with fully equipped Design and Technology workshops, Motor Mechanics workshop, pottery, art studio and food technology area. Newly created music facilities allow for teaching up to GCSE as well as individual lessons in instruments of the pupil's choice.

Information Technology is at the heart of our educational programmes. A "state of the art" computer network runs through the main teaching areas with a pupil:computer ratio of 1:4. Pupils have access to the network throughout the working day and during prep sessions both in classrooms and in the open access study centre.

Our unique Sixth Form offers City and Guilds courses in Professional Cookery and Motor Vehicle Repair and Maintenance as well as GCSE retakes and a structured introduction to the adult world.

Dyspraxia provision includes specialist tuition within a fully equipped fitness studio. All programmes are developed in consultation with our visiting Occupational Therapist. There is also a Speech and Language Therapist on the staff.

Boarding provision features en-suite bedrooms, a full range of supervised recreational activities and transport to and from London on Friday and Sunday evenings. Day placements are also available.

Fyling Hall School

Robin Hood's Bay Near Whitby North Yorkshire YO22 4QD.
Tel: (01947) 880353
Fax: (01947) 880919
e-mail: fylinghall@clara.co.uk
website: www.fylinghall.clara.net

Headmaster: **Michael Bayes**, BA, MA, PGCE

Age Range. 4–19

Number of Pupils. Boarders: Boys 71, Girls 70, Day: Boys 44, Girls 49

Fees per term. Fyling Hall (Senior) Boarders £3,175, Weekly £2,795, Day £1,455. Whitehall (Junior) Boarders £2,895, Day £1,145.

Fyling Hall School is one of the oldest recognised co-educational schools in the country. It occupies a spectacular coastal setting within the North York Moors National Park. Pupils may safely enjoy freedom in this beautiful and peaceful rural area.

The buildings centre on a grade two listed Georgian country house in delightfully landscaped gardens incorporating an outdoor theatre overlooking Robin Hood's Bay. Recent expansion has included two new boarding houses, science laboratories and dining room in addition to the purpose-built Junior School, known as Whitehall. The self-contained Nursery unit offers the opportunity to develop skills within a secure and homely framework. The latest project, just completed, is a spacious multi-functional sports hall.

The school is intentionally small due to its desire to educate pupils as individuals. The advantageous pupil-teacher ratio encourages effective learning. The teaching is along traditional lines with an emphasis on 'doing one's best' within a supportive yet demanding environment. A broadly based and well resourced curriculum is followed which reflects recent national initiatives, particularly in the scientific and information technology fields. A wide range of GCSE and A Level courses are offered.

Fyling Hall is a closely knit society with an emphasis on proactive pastoral care and a real sense of communal responsibility. The chief feature is a spirit of confidence and co-operation between staff and pupils in an atmosphere which is natural for growth.

There is no entrance examination but an interview and a report from the current school are integral parts of the admission process.

Many of the pupils stay to join the VIth form, where privilege and responsibility present a balance and are a useful preparation for university life.

The school takes advantage of its natural surroundings in the provision of numerous extra-curricular activities. Fyling Hall has its own ponies and these constitute a much loved part of school life. Karate, Duke of Edinburgh and ACF are all popular. The main games are rugby, hockey, cricket and tennis, each with a full fixture list. The choir enjoys a good reputation and individual tuition is available in all the usual musical instruments.

Robin Hood's Bay is remarkably accessible despite its rural splendour. Nearby Whitby and Scarborough are both railheads. Teesside Airport and the ferry port of Hull, with their frequent continental connections, are both easily reached. An experienced Bursar is able to advise on all travel arrangements.

Academic standards are high, but other abilities are valued, and aided by the small size of classes it is hoped that all pupils can be encouraged to achieve their maximum potential.

Charitable status. Fyling Hall School Trust Ltd is a Registered Charity, number 507857. It exists for the provision of high quality education for boys and girls.

Gateway School

1 High Street Great Missenden Buckinghamshire HP16 9AA.
Tel: (01494) 862407
Fax: (01494) 865787

Principals: **J L Wade**, BA, DASE, **J H Wade**, BA, PGCE

Age Range. 2½–12
Number in School. Day: Boys 202, Girls 125
Fees per term. £498–£1,650

All activities and clubs, school visits, music tuition are included in fees

Our school aims to discover and to develop each child's particular abilities by offering a varied curriculum in a stimulating and happy atmosphere. Our teaching ratio is 1:10 and an enthusiastic staff ensures that a range of after school activities and school visits widen children's horizons. Pupils begin part-time in our Montessori nursery and remain with us until they move into an appropriate school in the private or state sector at 11 or 12. From the outset we work closely with parents in the best interests of the child. KS1 and KS2 tests are taken.

Our school care runs from 8.00am to 5.30 pm.

Glaisdale School

14 Arundel Road Cheam Sutton Surrey SM2 7AD.
Tel: 020 8288 1488
Fax: 020 8288 1489

Headmistress: **Mrs H M Potter**, BEd (Hons)

Age Range. 3–11
Number in School. Total: 163, Day: Boys 57, Girls 106
Fees per term. £390–£1,130
Charitable status. Glaisdale School Educational Trust Ltd is a Registered Charity, number 651057. It exists to provide education for boys and girls.

Glenarm College

20 Coventry Road Ilford Essex IG1 4QR.
Tel: 020 8554 1760

Principal: **Mrs V Mullooly**, MA

Age Range. 3–11
Number in School. Day: Boys 54, Girls 86
Fees per term. £1,300

Glenarm College, founded in 1893, is an independent preparatory school for girls and boys of 3 to 11 years. A two-storey extension was completed in September 1997.

The School provides, through a wide curriculum, an education of high academic standard.

Whilst the emphasis is on good habits of sustained work and sound learning, we also seek to encourage creativity and independent thinking. Small classes give ample opportunity for individual attention. French and Computers are part of the curriculum for all children from 3 years.

The curriculum prepares girls for the 11 plus examination and entry to girls senior independent schools in the Greater London and London area.

A tea-time Club operates after school and during half-terms and holidays up to 6.30 pm for working parents.

Glenesk School

Ockham Road North East Horsley Surrey KT24 6NS
Tel: (01483) 282329
Fax: (01483) 281489
e-mail: info@glenesk.co.uk
website: www.glenesk.co.uk

Headmistress: **Mrs S P Johnson**

Age Range. 2–8
Number in School. Day: Boys 87, Girls 98
Fees per term. £280–1,825

Gosfield School

Halstead Essex CO9 1PF.
Tel: (01787) 474040
Fax: (01787) 478228

Principal: **Mrs C Goodhild**, BSc, CertEd

Age Range. 4–18 Boys and Girls
Number in School. Boarders: 30, Day: 195
Fees per term. £2,900–£3,755 Boarding, £1,290–£2,360 Day

Founded in 1929, Gosfield occupies a gracious, listed country house which was built in 1870 for Lady Courtauld. The school is set in a glorious 105 acre estate which borders ancient woodland and is a haven for wildlife and rare species. There are conservation areas and nature trails within the grounds.

Recent building developments include new Sports Hall, Music suite, Library and Laboratory. Boarding accommodation has also been completely upgraded.

The school is deliberately small in numbers and provides a caring family atmosphere in which every pupil will be able to develop his or her own potential to the full. Classes are small, and standards are high. The system of personal tutors ensures that every child's needs are properly looked after both in academic work and in the sporting and cultural activities in which the school encourages all pupils to participate.

During the week and at weekends there is a wide range of activities including sports, music, drama and conservation work. The programme changes termly and provides something for everyone. Day pupils often want to come in on Saturdays and even spend the weekend at the school. There are no weekend lessons.

The School Day is from 8.30 to 3.45 with Reception Class finishing at 3.00. On Monday–Thursday there are after-school games and activities which run until 4.50 and in the Senior School all pupils are involved in at least two activities each week. Juniors may either join in an organised activity or do supervised prep until 4.50, if this is a more convenient pick-up time for parents. On Friday school ends at 3.45 pm. Games fixtures are all in midweek so that boarders can go home for a full weekend whenever they wish to.

The whole structure – daily and weekly – aims to be flexible and helpful to parents and pupils. The school sees education as a partnership, so parents are always welcome to visit, to talk to staff, and to be involved in the school's activities.

Gosfield is situated in rural North Essex only 20 miles from Stansted airport and thirty miles from the M25. The nearest town, Halstead, is a mile away and the nearest station is just five miles away at Braintree.

There is a daily minibus service to and from Chelmsford, Sudbury, Braintree and Colchester.

Charitable status. Gosfield School is a Registered Charity, number 310871. It exists to provide education for boys and girls.

The Grange School

Bradburns Lane Hartford Northwich Cheshire CW8 1LU.

(See HMC section, Part I of this Book)

Greenbank School

Heathbank Road Cheadle Hulme Cheadle Cheshire SK8 6HU.
Tel: (0161) 485 3724
e-mail: kevinphillips@greenbank.stockport.sch.uk

Headmaster: **Kevin Phillips,** BEd, MA

Age Range. 6 months–11 years.
Number in School. Day: Boys 101, Girls 71
Fees per term. £745–£1,300

Greenbank School was founded in 1951 by Karl and Linda Orsborn. Since 1971 the School has been administered by an Educational Trust and is registered with the Department for Education. Standing in over 3 acres of its own grounds the school is pleasantly situated in quiet suburban surroundings.

A new Daycare Nursery opened in 1994 offers care to children between the ages of 6 months and 4 from 8.00 am to 6.00 pm for fifty weeks of the year.

The School Nursery has been expanded and offers splendid facilities for children from three years of age. In 1999 the Nursery moved to a new purpose built classroom and the School also opened a replacement Library and ICT room. In September 2001 a large all-weather sports area was constructed to ensure fixtures and practices can continue all year round.

Greenbank provides excellent all-round education at the Primary Stage, combining the best of traditional and modern teaching in a caring and disciplined environment. Pre and After School Care between 7.30 am and 6 pm gives security to children of working parents. The School also runs a holiday club for 8 of the holiday weeks.

Through its varied curricula and extra-curricula activities the School provides pupils with the opportunity of expanding their natural abilities to the full. Music, drama, sport, computing and educational visits are some of the activities which play their part in providing a well-rounded programme of education in pleasant surroundings. Consistently high standards are achieved in Independent School examinations.

Greenfields School

Priory Road Forest Row East Sussex RH18 5JD.
Tel: (01342) 822189

Head: **Mr A M McQuade,** MA (Oxon)

Age Range. 3–18
Number in School. Day: Boys 88, Girls 86
Fees per term. Tuition £728–£1,924. Boarding £2,841–£3,326

Greenfields is a co-educational, non-denominational day and boarding school, with 174 pupils from 3–18. It caters for a wide range of ability. Teaching is in small groups. Students are taught how to study and supported self-study is a feature of senior school. The Boarding House, Sixth Form Centre and sports facilities are now at our second site in East Grinstead (3 miles away).

A wide academic and sporting curriculum enables students to take up subjects that interest them, like photography, ceramics or drama, and develop their individual talents. We have a high pass rate in GCSE and 'A' Level examinations. Twenty three subjects are currently offered and more are planned.

Scholarships are awarded for all-round ability, sport, music and art. Greenfields has a very well endowed music department and lively drama department. Cultural outings and community projects extend interests and responsibilities.

Situated in the Ashdown Forest, the main school lies in 11 acres of woodland, one mile from the A22. Trains run from London to East Grinstead; Gatwick Airport is a 20 minute car ride, bringing the school within reach of families from all over the United Kingdom and abroad.

Charitable status. Greenfields School Educational Trust Ltd is a Registered Charity, number 287037. It exists to provide education for children.

Green Hill School

Evesham Worcestershire WR11 4NG
Tel: (01386) 442364
e-mail: GHSworcs@aol.com
website: www.greenhillschool.co.uk

Headmaster: **Oliver Udny-Lister,** MA

Age Range. 3 to 13
Number in School. 57 boys, 53 girls - all day
Fees per term. £800–£1,400. Lunches extra.

Green Hill School is housed in an attractive Grade 2 listed Georgian building standing in pleasant grounds on the outskirts of Evesham. It is a co-educational prep school for pupils rising 3 to 11/13.

The school has two departments, Pre-Preparatory and Preparatory. We offer a family environment with high academic standards and success rate to both Grammar and Independent schools of parental choice. The average class size is 15 pupils and the classes are taught by fully qualified and experienced staff. For pupils in Years 3 and above there are compulsory supervised homework sessions after school.

The motto of the school is *Nihil Sine Fidelitate* which means 'Nothing Without Loyalty'. This concept underpins much of the school's philosophy in that 'loyalty' of the pupils to themselves and to others will help them succeed in all they do. The overall aim of the school is to make sure that the children are happy and feel secure in their surroundings. It goes without saying that we also encourage any abilities the pupils may have and aim to give them greater self-confidence and to develop a caring attitude to the world in general.

Special attention is given to pupils with mild learning difficulties and extra lessons to deal with problems such as Dyslexia are fitted into the timetable. Pupils are either withdrawn from lessons or extra assistance within certain subject lessons is given.

Facilities in the school include not only well resourced general teaching rooms, but also a well stocked library to which new books are continually added, a Science and Technology Centre, a Hall/Gymnasium, a Special Needs Department and an Information Technology Centre. Facilities in the grounds include generous playing areas, netball and tennis courts and a cricket net for bowling practice. For younger pupils there is an excellent adventure playground at the rear of the school. In addition, local sports facilities are used.

Music plays a strong part in the life of the school. In addition to class music, instrumental lessons are available for all the common orchestral instruments, piano and guitar. These are taught by visiting music teachers. The school has a choir and band which perform regularly at concerts and shows.

The school organises many in-school and after-school activities throughout the year. These are listed on the back of the termly Calendar Card. School trips to places in France, England and Wales are regularly arranged, and last from one day to a week. There is a Pre-Preparatory Nativity Play every Christmas, and a main school show in the Easter term. All our extra-curricular activities are regarded as an important part of school life.

The school operates an after school care service for those parents who find such a facility useful.

Greenholme School

392 Derby Road Nottingham NG7 2DX.
Tel: (0115) 978 7329
Fax: (0115) 978 1160
e-mail: enquiries@greenholmeschool.co.uk
website: www.greenholmeschool.co.uk

Headmistress: **Miss P M Breen**

Age Range. 3–11+
Number in School. Day: Boys 144; Girls 77
Fees per term. £1,395–£1,495

Greenholme School is an independent day school for boys and girls from the age of 3-11. Established in 1935, in the original house which faces Derby Road, it has been considerably extended to the rear and now accommodates approximately 225 pupils. The playing field adjoining the school was acquired in 1996.

The school was accredited to the ISC in 1988.

Greenholme is a caring, friendly school, providing a warm and supportive atmosphere in which children can develop and learn with confidence. Pupils receive a thorough grounding in the basic subjects and extend their knowledge and experience in the broader curriculum by a combination of topic-based and formal teaching, so that when they leave they are equipped to take full advantage of what their senior schools have to offer. Small teaching groups, excellent resources, in addition to well qualified and very experienced staff, play a large part in ensuring that every child has the opportunity to reach his or her full potential. We are proud of the excellent examination results and high academic standards achieved by our pupils.

Computers are used as a means of facilitating learning and all pupils from Reception upwards have 'hands-on' experience. Aesthetic and sporting activities play an important part in the timetable.

We are very conscious of the importance of our special needs expertise. We have, on our full time staff, a special needs co-ordinator who is available to discuss with parents any difficulties that a particular child may be experiencing with his or her work. We also liaise very closely with the Dyslexia Institute and with parents should they require help or advice. We will undertake a pre-assessment if the classroom teacher or parent expresses concern.

Pupils are expected to behave with courtesy and consideration for others and to foster a sense of responsibility. Discipline in the school is fair but firm, the object being for pupils to develop self-discipline and an understanding that the creation of a happy environment in the community is the concern of all its members.

Further details and prospectus may be obtained on application to the school secretary.

The Gregg School

Townhill Park House Cutbush Lane Southampton SO18 2GF
Tel: (023) 8047 2133
Fax: (023) 8047 1080

Headmaster: **Mr D R Hart**, BEd

Age Range. 11–16 years.
Number in School. 270
Fees. £1,830 per term.

The Gregg School is a caring, friendly school in which pupils can develop and learn with confidence. Small teaching groups, excellent resources and well-qualified and experienced staff enable pupils to achieve their full potential. A sound curriculum is enriched by the provision of Learning Support for weaker pupils and extended to provide further learning opportunities for gifted pupils.

Pupils enjoy participating in a wide range of sports, competing to a high standard. We make use of City sports facilities in addition to provision in school. Musical and dramatic activities are very popular, as are the residential experiences offered to each year group. These help individuals develop initiative, a sense of identity and the ability to work co-operatively in a challenging environment.

In addition to GCSE examinations, pupils may take RSA and Royal College of Music examinations.

Admission to the school is usually through the Entrance Examination in January, but interested parents are very welcome to visit at any time.

We also have a preparatory department (3–11).

Grenville College Junior School (Stella Maris)

Moreton House Abbotsham Road Bideford Devon, EX39 3QN
Tel: (01237) 472208
Fax: (01237) 477020
e-mail: info@grenville.devon.sch.uk
website: http://www.grenville.devon.sch.uk

Co-educational.

Headmistress: **Mrs L Maggs-Wellings**, BEd

Age Range. 2½–11
Number in School. 110 pupils.

Stella Maris is a Woodard School situated in a beautiful house in 40 acres of ground in Bideford, an attractive small market town on the banks of the River Torridge. The North Devon coast, Dartmoor and Exmoor are all within easy driving distance.

A thorough education is provided in a caring, Christian environment for girls and boys from 2½ to 11. The school's concern is the happiness and success of its pupils. It has been able to adapt to changes in educational practice without losing traditional values. Emphasis is placed on pupils' literacy and numeracy, within a broad and varied curriculum. Courtesy and consideration for others are particularly important, and these qualities are nurtured by a committed staff.

Classrooms are pleasant and facilities include a well-stocked library, Junior art and music rooms and gymnasium. Computers are in daily use in the classrooms. Pupils enjoy the services of specialist French, Science, Design Technology, Music and PE staff shared with the senior department, and all take part regularly in concerts and plays. The music room is in what was a magnificent ballroom overlooking the gardens. Extra curricular activities flourish and sports teams have represented the South West of England in national competitions on a number of occasions. The sports fields lie in front of the school.

There is an excellent Kindergarten for girls and boys from two-and-a-half years old where structured learning begins. Children in the Kindergarten wear school uniform and take part in assemblies once a week, ensuring a sense of belonging from the very beginning. Boys and girls take the entrance examinations at 11+ and the vast majority remain in the school. They have an excellent record of winning scholarships.

FLEDGELINGS - a pre-school parent and toddler group - has been a tremendous success since opening early in 1998.

Lunches are freshly cooked on the premises by our own staff.

Charitable status. Grenville College is a Registered Charity, number 306718. It exists to provide high quality education for boys and girls.

Hale Preparatory School

Broomfield Lane Hale Cheshire WA15 9AS.
Tel: (0161) 928 2386

Headmaster: **J Connor**, JP, BSc, FCP

Age Range. 4–12
Number in School. Day: Boys 98, Girls 84
Fees per term. £1,115

Hale Preparatory School was established in 1980 and received accreditation two years later. The aim of the school is to develop each child to his/her fullest ability in a disciplined, caring and happy environment.

The classes are small. In the last ten years all pupils have passed examinations to independent grammar schools.

Whilst emphasis is placed on the basic subjects a broad curriculum is followed including Music, French, Speech and Drama, Computers and Library studies. Extra curriculum activities including sport, theatre visits, adventure and skiing holidays are an integral part of the school programme.

Halliford School

Shepperton Middlesex TW17 9HX.

(See SHMIS section, Part III of this Book)

The Hampshire Schools

The Knightsbridge Upper School 63 Ennismore Gardens Knightsbridge London SW7 1NH.
Tel: 020 7584 3297
Fax: 020 7584 9733
e-mail: hampshire@indschool.org
website: thehampshireschools.westminster.sch.uk

The Knightsbridge Under School, 5 Wetherby Place, London SW7 4NX. Tel: 020 7370 7081
The Kensington Gardens School, 9 Queensborough Terrace, London W2 3TB. Tel: 020 7229 7065

Principal: **Mr Arthur Bray**, CertEd

Age Range. 3–13
Number in School. Day: Boys 150, Girls 150
Fees per term. £940–£2,695

The Schools, which were founded in 1928, provide a broad-based curriculum for boys and girls between three and thirteen years of age. They occupy three fine buildings all close to Hyde Park and Kensington Gardens and are well placed to take full advantage of the vast range of sporting and cultural facilities on their doorsteps.

The Schools have been successful in preparing pupils for examination and scholarship entry into leading day and boarding senior independent schools. Great emphasis is placed on developing each child's individual talents.

Fully qualified and experienced teachers provide a high standard of tuition in all aspects of the curriculum.

Pupils start French from the age of four and senior forms attend an annual study visit to France, as an integral part of the French syllabus.

The Schools also offer home to school bus service, after school care and multi activity holiday courses.

Harecroft Hall

Gosforth Cumbria CA20 1HS.
Tel: (019467) 25220
Fax: (019467) 25885

Headmaster: **David Hoddy**

Age Range. 2–16
Number in School. Boarders: Boys 12, Girls 7; Day: Boys 37, Girls 40; Nursery: 23.
Fees per term at 1.9.01. Weekly/Full Boarding: £2,830–£3,249, Day: £1,465–£2,065

Harecroft Hall is a family run coeducational school taking children from 2 to 16 years old. Set in 11 acres of grounds on the western side of the Lake District National Park, Harecroft offers high standards of academic and sporting achievement and is particularly supportive to the needs of the individual. It has a flourishing Nursery (boys and girls aged 2–5 years), and children can join the Main School at age 4. There are well equipped Science Laboratories and an Information Technology Centre. French is taught from the age of 7, and German in the upper forms. A graduate staff of 18 ensures a high staff:pupil ratio and scholarships are won regularly to senior independent schools. The School runs two minibuses enabling children to take up the opportunities of the Lake District, and outdoor pursuits are an integral part of life at Harecroft. Pupils are prepared for GCSE examinations in thirteen subjects. The School has an integrated development plan to further increase facilities. The School possesses its own playing fields for athletics and team games (hockey, football, netball and tennis) and time at the weekends is devoted to fell-walking, canoeing, sailing and orienteering, for which the locality is ideally suited. Full reports are sent to parents at the end of each term and mini-reports and assessments at half-termly intervals. The School offers a reduction in fees for children of service personnel and there are also a number of scholarships and bursaries available. The School prides itself on its friendly atmosphere allowing each child to reach their academic, social and physical potential.

A full Prospectus is available, and the Headmaster is always pleased to welcome visitors.

Harenc School

Church House 167 Rectory Lane Footscray Sidcup Kent DA14 5BU.
Tel: 020 8309 0619
Fax: 020 8309 5051

***Headmistress:* Miss S J Woodward**, BA (Hons)

Age Range. 3–11+
Number in School. Day: Boys 160
Fees per term. £1,220–£1,515. *Compulsory extras:* Lunch, Swimming, French.

Harenc School is proud of its reputation for traditional values and academic excellence. The National Curriculum is followed and all boys from 4+ study French, ICT and have weekly Swimming classes. Visiting Football, Rugby and Cricket coaches enhance the PE provision and extra-curricular activities include an Art Club, Chess Club and Drama. Individual instrumentalist tuition is offered and boys are able to join the School Choir, Orchestra and Recorder Groups. The school has a strong reputation for success in the 11+ examinations to local Independent and Grammar schools.

Emphasis is placed on academic achievement, fair discipline and providing a homely and caring environment where the boys are seen as individuals and are assisted to reach their full potential through the benefits of individual tuition in classes of restricted pupil numbers.

Charitable status. Harenc School is a Registered Charity, number 287948. It exists to provide an education for boys in a Christian spirit and where the work of the school may benefit the community as a whole.

Haresfoot School

Chesham Road Berkhamsted Herts HP4 2SZ.
Tel: (01442) 872742

***Head Teacher:* Mrs G R Waterhouse**, CertEd, DipPhysEd, RSADipSpLD

Age range. 3–11
Number in School. 238
Fees per term. £150–£1,140 (excluding lunch)

Haresfoot Preparatory School is set in a tastefully converted Georgian Coach House and stables surrounded by 7 acres of woodland and grass, including a walled garden, multipurpose hall, Art, Pottery and Music Rooms.

It is conveniently situated by the Chesham Exit of the A41 Bypass; a safe environment within which young children develop their full potential.

The School offers a broad-based, stimulating education, including Spanish, French, Music, Drama and Dance, with opportunities for maximum achievement across the curriculum.

Toddler Gym and a music workshop form part of the curriculum in the Nursery School, which also houses a Mother and Toddler group. There are a large variety of after-school clubs, including Sandwich Club until 5.45 pm for working parents.

Hartlebury School

Quarry Bank Hartlebury Kidderminster Worcs DY11 7TE
Tel: (01299) 250258
Fax: (01299) 250379
website: www.hartleburyschool.sch.worcs.uk

***Headmaster:* D R Bolam**, BA, CertEd, FCollP

Age range. 4 – GCSE
Number in school. 60 Day Boys, 42 Day Girls
Fees per term. £725–£2,300

A small friendly School, offering the support and guidance expected in traditional family life. The School takes pupils from an early age and develops their skills and abilities within a constructive working atmosphere. Individual learning programmes are designed to ensure pupils achieve their personal best performance across the curriculum. Age is not decisive! Classes are small and organised according to ability level. This removes the need for changes of school and allows pupils to progress smoothly towards examinations as soon as they are ready. Our Learning Support service provides the additional support some pupils need. Careers advice ensures appropriate placement in Further or Higher Education when the young adult leaves us.

Harvington School

20 Castlebar Road Ealing London W5 2DS.
Tel: 020 8997 1583
Fax: 020 8810 4756

***Headmistress:* Dr F Meek**, PhD, PGCE

Age Range. 3–16 years
Number in School. Girls: 197. Boys: 11 (in nursery).
Fees per term. Junior £1,280, Senior £1,635. *Compulsory extras:* None

The School was founded in 1890 and made into an Educational Trust in 1970. Harvington is known for its high standards and happy atmosphere. Classes are small so that individual attention can be given by qualified and experienced staff. An academic education is offered, leading in the senior school to GCSE examination. The school continues to improve specialist facilities and also to provide a mixed nursery class for 3–5 year olds.

It is close to Ealing Broadway station and a number of bus routes.

Prospectus available from the Secretary.

Charitable status. Harvington School Education Trust Ltd is a Registered Charity, number 312621. It aims to subscribe to traditional values in behaviour and academic standards in a happy environment; to encourage a high standard of academic achievement for girls across a broad range of abilities; to encourage girls to develop their potential to the full, both in personal and academic terms; and to create an environment in which pupils will want to learn.

Hatherop Castle Preparatory School

Cirencester Gloucestershire GL7 3NB.
Tel: (01285) 750206
Fax: (01285) 750430

Headmaster: **Mr P Easterbrook**, BEd

Age Range. 2½–13. Nursery Department 2½–4½
Number in Prep School. 121 Boys, 123 Girls, 26 Boarders. Boarding from 7 years.
Number in Preparatory department. Day: 164 boys and girls.
Number in Pre-Prep department. 80 boys and girls.
Fees per term. £2,990–£3,150 (Boarding), £1,210–£2,035 (Day)

Founded in Cambridge in 1926, Hatherop Castle is a co-educational day and boarding prep school for children between the ages of 2½ and 13. Children are prepared for Common Entrance and Scholarship Examinations at 11+, 12+ and 13+; the children move on to a wide range of senior independent schools. Weekly boarders are accepted and the boarding facilities are homely and well furnished. A family atmosphere exists throughout the school. The curriculum spans a wide range of subjects and there is a great variety of sports and extra-curricular activities.

Set in 25 acres of beautiful Cotswold countryside, Hatherop Castle enjoys a superb setting and is a happy environment in which the pupils learn. The classes are housed in well-equipped rooms and the pre-prep and nursery have their own self-contained areas where the pupils enjoy playing and working in a welcoming and stimulating atmosphere.

Hawley Place School

Fernhill Road Blackwater Camberley Surrey GU17 9HU.
Tel: (01276) 32028
Fax: (01276) 609695

Co-Principals:
Mr T G Pipe, MA
Mrs M L Pipe, L-ès-L

Age Range. 2–16
Number in School. Day Pupils 347
Fees per term. Juniors (Reception to Year 4) £1,485; Seniors (Years 5 to 11) £1,860

Hawley Place is a small school based around an old country residence set in 16 acres of grounds. The beautiful setting provides an ideal learning environment, where kindness, courtesy and consideration are fostered in all pupils.

Maintaining a high quality of teaching and learning is our main concern. Well qualified staff, working with enviably small groups, enable us to recognise individual needs more quickly and meet them more effectively. Examination results at GCSE level are consistently above the national average and most pupils take eight subjects or more.

We offer a broad and balanced curriculum to cover all National Curriculum subjects. With the development of the single market economy we feel it important to offer pupils two foreign languages from the age of 11 to facilitate possible study or work abroad later. Moreover, French is introduced to Nursery pupils and continued through the Junior section of the school.

We believe in and practise the "Pursuit of Excellence" both inside and beyond the classroom. Physical education constitutes an integral part of the curriculum and sporting activities form part of a broad extra-curricular programme. Pupils are also regularly involved in music and drama rehearsals for school productions, the Debating Society, the French Club and local Art and Literature Competitions, as well as a considerable amount of charity work.

We hold our annual Open Morning in the Autumn Term and the School Entrance Examination in the Spring Term. Several Scholarship Awards are available each year for outstanding academic ability and for special talents in particular fields such as Modern Languages, Art, Music, Drama and Physical Education. The School runs its own Assisted Places Scheme.

We are successful at Hawley Place because pupils, parents and staff work together in partnership with good co-operation and communication. Full details and a prospectus may be obtained from the School Secretary. We look forward to your visit. Our door is always open.

Haylett Grange Preparatory School

Haverfordwest Pembrokeshire SA62 4LA
Tel: (01437) 762472
Fax: (01437) 764808

Head: **Mr M Gilbert**

Age Range. 2–12
Number in School. Day: Boys 59, Girls 61
Fees per term. £665-£825

Haylett Grange is situated on the outskirts of Haverfordwest. The spacious grounds include a playing field for organised games and a tennis court. There is a heated swimming pool and a hall for physical education.

We follow the National Curriculum with excellent results.

The aim of the school is to prepare children for common entrance examinations to independent schools, grammar and other senior schools. Six scholarships were achieved this year (2000).

Special attention is paid to character training and to the progress of the individual child to become courteous, well-motivated learners.

The school has a well-equipped nursery for children from the age of 2 years.

Transportation is available to the school and there are early/late plus holiday activities for children 2-8 years.

Heathcote School

Eves Corner Danbury Essex CM3 4QB.
Tel: (01245) 223131
website: www.heathcoteschool.co.uk

Principals: **Mr & Mrs Greenland**
Head Teacher: Mrs L Mitchell-Hall, BMus

Age Range. 2½–11+
Number in School. Day: Boys 97, Girls 89
Fees per term. £1,400

Founded in 1935, the school has a reputation as a caring and disciplined learning environment. Children are accepted into the Nursery at age 2½ and progress, by invitation and attainment, to the pre-Kindergarten class.

Children enter full time education in the September prior to their fifth birthday and progress through the school until the age of 11+.

The school believes that education, in its widest sense, is a contract between child, parent and school and it is the development of this idea that allows the child to develop fully as an individual.

A high standard of academic, artistic and sporting achievement is expected of every child. This is achieved by the use of very experienced specialist teaching staff ensuring the excellence of teaching necessary to the high standards attained. The traditional values of politeness, good manners and personal discipline are fostered, together with a caring attitude towards all members of the school community. Regular consultations with Parents are an important part of our approach to education.

The school prepares children for scholarships, entrance examinations and for the Essex Selective Schools Examination at 11+. A very high pass rate is attained in these examinations.

There are a variety of additional clubs and after school activities which the children can join.

For more information visit the website.

Heathfield School

Wolverley Near Kidderminster Worcestershire DY10 3QE.
Tel: (01562) 850204

Headmaster: **G L Sinton**, BA, MEd

Age Range. 3–16
Number in School. 250 Day pupils
Fees per term. £1,120–£1,950. Five half days in Pre School £455.

Accredited by The Independent Schools Information Service

Heathfield is a co-educational day school, governed by an Educational Trust. The School is situated in a green belt area one mile north of Kidderminster in spacious grounds, within easy reach of the West Midlands conurbation.

The curriculum is broadly based and pupils are prepared for GCSE. We also prepare children for the Entrance Examination for local senior schools at 11+ and for the Common Entrance Examination at 13+. The majority of pupils in our Junior School move up to our own Senior School at 11+.

A wide variety of team games and individual sports are offered. The school is strong in Music and Art. Classes are small. Career guidance is available to senior pupils. Scholarships are awarded to pupils of ability. Prospectus available from Headmaster's Secretary.

Charitable status. Heathfield School is a Registered Charity, number 527522. It exists to provide excellent educational opportunities at a reasonable cost.

Hellenic College of London

67 Pont Street London SW1X 0BD
Tel: 020 7581 5044
Fax: 020 7589 9055
e-mail: jw@hellenic.org.uk

Headmaster: **Mr J W Wardrobe**, MA

Age Range. 2½–18
Number in School. All Day. Boys 90, Girls 90
Fees per term. £2,033–£2,544

The Hellenic College was founded in 1980 by prominent members of the Greek community in London, and offers an integrated curriculum of subjects in Greek and English throughout the nursery, primary and secondary age range.

The principal aim of the College is to give all pupils a first-class British education to GCSE and A Level standard, coupled with fluency in the Greek language, an informed awareness of their heritage and a thorough grounding in Greek history, literature and religion.

The College occupies a fine site in the heart of Knightsbridge. The elegant Grade II listed building is light and spacious, and is ideal as an academic institution.

A second bi-lingual Nursery School has recently been opened in modern premises in Golders Green (tel: 020 8455 8511).

Central facilities include two computer rooms, art studio, three well-equipped laboratories, and gymnasium. Main sports are basketball, football, badminton, volleyball, hockey, tennis and swimming. Field trips and adventure weeks are regularly undertaken, and all age groups make very regular use of London's museums, galleries, etc. A wide variety of extra-curricular activities are offered, including Greek Dancing.

The College is a member of the Round Square Conference.

The school prospectus may be viewed on the internet, in English and Modern Greek at: http://www.hellenic.org.uk.

Charitable status. Hellenic College Trust is a Registered Charity, number 282795R. It exists to provide a bi-lingual, bi-cultural education in English and Greek.

Hemdean House School

Hemdean Road Caversham Reading Berks RG4 7SD
Tel: (0118) 9472590
Fax: (0118) 9464474

Headmistress: **Mrs J Harris**, BSc, PGCE

Age Range. Girls 2½ to 16; Boys 2½ to 11.
Number in School. 110 Girls, 60 Boys
Fees per term. £940–£1,350

Founded in 1859, Hemdean House is a school where traditional educational concepts are highly valued. We look for personal achievement in academic and other spheres, responsible behaviour and consideration for others. We aim to develop the varied talents of each and every child within our structured and caring environment. Individual attention has high priority. We think parents are important too; school and family should work together and have opportunities to meet.

The school is organised and operated as one complete unit; many of the specialist staff teach in both the Senior and Junior schools, but attention is always given to the needs of each department and each age group.

The senior school is exclusively for girls, but boys may

join both junior and nursery departments. The self-contained Nursery unit offers children aged 2½–4 the opportunity to begin the learning process and to develop their skills in a secure and happy environment.

We follow the National Curriculum throughout the school; Mathematics, Science, Information Technology, the Humanities and the Expressive Arts, Modern Languages, Technology and Physical Education are taught throughout the age range. French and recorder lessons begin at age 7 and many children learn at least one other musical instrument. Drama and Public Speaking, Music and Art are our special interests. A wide range of extra-curricular activities is available. For the working parent, after-school and holiday care are available if required.

Examination results including GCSE and National Curriculum Key Stage Assessments are excellent with pupils achieving well in excess of the national average. This year 86.1% of our GCSE grades were A* to C.

The school has always been committed to Christian ethics and values, but all faiths are welcomed and tolerance and appreciation of the beliefs of others is encouraged.

Admission. Interview and assessment during a day or half-day spent in school according to age. Scholarships and bursaries are available in the Senior School.

Charitable status. Hemdean House is a Registered Charity, number 309146. Its aims include academic achievement, the development of every pupil's potential, Christian values and care for our neighbours.

Herington House School

Mount Avenue Hutton Mount Brentwood Essex CM13 2NS
Tel: (01277) 211595
Fax: (01277) 200404

***Principal:* Mr R Dudley-Cooke**

***Deputy Headteacher:* Mrs C Watson-Lee**

Age Range. Three and three quarters to eleven years
Number in School. Boys 35, Girls 100
Fees per term. £815–£1,565. Extras: squash, swimming, after school clubs

'A caring environment for the full realisation of a pupil's potential'.

The School is a Preparatory Day School for girls and boys to 11+. The School offers a family environment with high academic standards and very high success rate to both Grammar schools and Independent schools of parental choice.

A feature and policy of the School is the low pupil/teacher ratio. The average class has 16 pupils. All pupils are actively involved in sporting activities and they are encouraged to participate in extra curricula activities.

Entry after interview.

Herne Hill School

The Old Vicarage 127 Herne Hill London SE24 9LY
Tel: 020 7274 6336
Fax: 020 7924 9510

***Headmistress:* Mrs V Tabone**

The school is situated in an Old Vicarage and a spacious new building set within half acre grounds, including a bark playground in the old orchard. The school philosophy is based on a belief that children are individuals whom we care for and guide but not change, and we must make sure we are the 'bows from which your children are sent forth' (Kahlil Gabran). There are two main points of admission: into the Nursery according to order of registration; and into the Pre-Prep at rising five, after an informal interview.

In the Nursery Department, alongside the learning of basic skills, the children are helped to become part of a community, and be thoughtful and caring of each other. The Nursery offers a structured programme, so that the children gain skills in all areas of the curriculum to enable them to move smoothly into the Pre-Prep. Music and dancing are taught by specialists; time is spent outside playing with outdoor equipment.

Pre-Prep places are, for the most part, taken up by children transferring from the Nursery Department, but we are able to offer a number of places to new children. Our curriculum is designed to take account of children's individual needs as well as the requirements of the 7+ entry tests. We take as our base the National Curriculum, broadening and expanding it, with an emphasis on the development of literacy and numeracy. Academic progress is carefully monitored to ensure each child fulfils his/her own potential. We have a high child/staff ratio. Music, drama, gym, dancing and French are taught by specialists. Most of our parents take advantage of the excellent independent schools in Dulwich and 95% of our children gain such places.

Our latest Nursery Ofsted inspection stated: 'Herne Hill School provides very high quality care and education. All desirable learning outcomes are met in all six areas of learning with no areas of weakness, and in some cases are exceeded, particularly in personal and social development, language, literacy and mathematics'.

Mission Statement: Herne Hill School for love, care and an excellent education

Hethersett Old Hall School

Norwich NR9 3DW.

(See GSA section, Part II of this Book)

Heywood Preparatory School

The Priory Corsham Wiltshire SN13 0AP.
Tel: (01249) 713379
Fax: (01249) 701757
e-mail: principal@heywood.wilts.sch.uk
website: heywood.wilts.sch.uk

***Principals:* M Hall**, BSc Hons; **P Hall**, BA Hons

Age Range. 3–11
Number in School. Day: Boys 95, Girls 70. Nursery 60
Fees per term. £1,095–£1,280. Lunches £100 per term.

Heywood Preparatory School in Corsham has a well established reputation for academic excellence combined with a high standard of pastoral care.

A major expansion was completed in 1998 comprising a multipurpose hall for gymnasium activities, plays, concerts and individual music lessons, together with improvements in cloakroom and dining facilities.

Class sizes at Heywood are kept to a maximum of 16 to allow teachers to give as much individual attention as possible to each child. Progress is monitored by weekly tests and termly examinations with a full report to parents at the end of each term.

Heywood is a co-educational school from 4 to 11 years. Pupils go on to all the major independent senior schools in the area, many of them having gained academic, music or sports scholarships.

The recorder is taught to 6 an 7 year olds and a wide range of musical instruments taught on an individual basis leading to Associated Board Examinations. A high standard of Speech Training with tuition for examinations is available. French is taught throughout the main school and Nursery. Swimming is an integral part of the curriculum.

Girls games are netball, hockey, tennis, athletics and rounders. Boys play rugby, football, cricket, tennis, athletics and rounders. Other activities available are chess, orchestra, judo, cycling proficiency, sewing and cookery.

Heywood has its own Nursery School, called Wigwam, which takes children rising three and prepares them for entry to either main school or state schools at four or sometimes five years old.

Highclare School

241 Birmingham Road Wylde Green Sutton Coldfield West Midlands B72 1EA.

(See GSA section, Part II of this Book)

Highfield Priory School

Fulwood Row Fulwood Preston Lancashire PR2 6SL.
Tel: (01772) 709624

***Headmaster:* B C Duckett**, MA, CertEd, FCollP

Age Range. 2–11
Number in School. Day: Boys 150, Girls 140
Fees per term. £956–£1,082. *Compulsory extras:* Elocution, French

Highfield is set in 4 acres of landscaped gardens and is a co-educational preparatory school for children aged 2 to 11+ years. It is fully equipped with its own well established nursery and prepares children for all Independent, Grammar and Senior Schools in Lancashire, for which it has an excellent academic record. Class numbers average 20 and children are taught by fully qualified and experienced staff. Recent additions to the school include a new classroom block, multipurpose sports hall, a music centre, infant/nursery wing and dining room. A new library and IT suite opened in 1994 and a CDT block is scheduled for the near future. The school has strong musical and sporting traditions.

Extra curricula activities include Ballet, Swimming, Archery, Gymnastics, Badminton, Table-tennis, Modelling, Chess, IT and Instrument Tuition. The school is well supported by a flourishing and enthusiastic Parents Association. A prospectus is available on application to the Headmaster.

Charitable status. Highfield Priory School is a Registered Charity, number 532262. It exists to provide independent education to all children between the ages of 2 and 11 years within Preston and surrounding areas for all who wish to participate and to provide access to the community at large to all sporting, musical and artistic provision within the school.

Highfield School and Nursery

256 Trinity Road Wandsworth Common London SW18 3RQ.
Tel: 020 8874 2778
Fax: 020 8265 5262
e-mail: highfield@cmcl.dircon.co.uk

Business Director: C M C Lowe, BSc

***Headmistress:* Mrs V-J Lowe**

Age Range. 2½–11
Number in School. Day: Boys 46, Girls 38

Fees per term. £790 to £1,685
Non-denominational.

Highfield School, a long established Nursery and Primary School, is conveniently located close to Wandsworth Common.

The school provides continuity of education for boys and girls aged 2½ to 11 years in a caring and friendly family atmosphere.

The catchment area for Highfield is wide and offers a good social and cultural mix.

Highfield has a good academic attainment, providing an excellent record of entry into senior schools with children placed in the most appropriate school for their future.

Highfields School

London Road New Balderton Newark Nottinghamshire NG24 3AL.
Tel: (01636) 704103
Fax: (01636) 680919

***Headmaster:* P F Smith**, BA

Age Range. 2½–11
Number in School. Day: Boys 95, Girls 89
Fees per term. £1,175 to £1,195, includes lunch. Nursery £8.10 per half day session.

Charitable status. Newark Preparatory School Company Limited is a Registered Charity, number 528261. It exists to provide and further the education of children.

Highlands School

Wardle Avenue Tilehurst Reading Berkshire RG31 6JR
Tel: (0118) 9427186

***Headmistress:* Mrs C Bennett**, MA

Age Range. Boys 3 to 7 years; Girls 3 to 11 years.
Number in School. 150
Fees per term. £825–£1,425.

The Highlands is situated in a quiet residential area of Reading within easy reach of the town centre and the M4 (exit 12). The school aims to provide a broad based education of high calibre in a friendly caring environment. There is an excellent pupil teacher ratio which enables the staff to take into account the specific needs of each child. The academic record is very good. Most of the teaching is done by the form teacher, however there are specialist teachers for PE, French, Music and Special Needs. A wide variety of Educational Outings plays an important roll in the curriculum. All areas of the National Curriculum are covered including French and Drama. The children are introduced to as many different sports as is possible.

The children are encouraged to give of their best at all times whatever the field of endeavour and to reach the highest level of attainment of which they are capable.

The girls are prepared for the Common Entrance and other secondary school examinations and the boys for the preparatory school of their choice.

There is a school choir and orchestra. Individual instrumental music lessons are available.

A cooked mid-day meal is served to all children, the cost of which is included in the fees.

A Before and After School Care and some Holiday Care is provided for those who wish to make use of this facility.

Charitable status. The Highlands School is a Registered Charity, number 309147. It exists to provide education for children in the area.

Hillcrest Grammar School

Beech Avenue Stockport Cheshire SK3 8HB.
Tel: (0161) 480-0329
Fax: (0161) 476-2814
e-mail: headmaster@hillcrest.stockport.sch.uk

Head: **D K Blackburn**, BA

Age Range. 3–16
Number in School. Day: Boys 185, Girls 105
Fees per term. £840–£1,358
Compulsory extras. None

Hillcrest is a charitable educational trust and comprises Senior, Preparatory and Pre-Preparatory Schools.

Our primary aim is to maximise the potential of each individual and progress, both academic and social, is monitored with great care - on a 'House' basis in the Senior School and by Form Teachers in the Preparatory and Pre-Preparatory Schools. Good communication between School and Home is especially important and the Headmaster and the staff are readily accessible at short notice. We make no apology for stressing traditional values such as mutual respect, good manners and self-discipline.

Classes are small and are taught by fully qualified and experienced staff. Sixteen GCSE courses are currently offered and excellent facilities include thirty multimedia PCs accessible to all, the Art & Design Centre, a first class sports hall and new all-weather tennis/netball courts. There is a wide range of musical, sporting and extra-curricular activity. Because we are a relatively small community both boys and girls have every opportunity to be more prominent in a wide range of pursuits than would be the case in larger schools.

At 11+ children are prepared for entry not only to our own Senior School but also to larger independent and state schools. At 16+ most pupils progress to Sixth Form courses either at State Colleges or HMC Schools. Parents are most welcome to visit us in order that they may appreciate the happy working atmosphere of the school. Admission is by annual 11+ entrance examination and by interview and individual assessment for other age groups. Bursary places are available each year at both Preparatory and Senior levels.

Charitable status. Hillcrest Grammar School is a Registered Charity, number 525928. It exists to provide education for boys and girls.

Hillcroft Preparatory School

Walnutree Manor Haughley Green near Stowmarket Suffolk IP14 3RQ.
Tel: (01449) 673003 (24 hour helpline)
Fax: (01449) 613072

Headmaster: **Frederick Rapsey**, OLJ, BEd (Hons), ACP, FRSA, FSA (Scot), CertCIEH, FCollP (Reading and Bristol)

Headmistress: Mrs Gwyneth Rapsey, CertEd (Reading), RSADipSpLD (Dist), FRGS (SENCO)

Age Range. 2 to 11/13.
Number in School. 100 (boys and girls)
Fees per term (all inclusive). Day: £420–£2,085. No hidden extras.

We have always taken pupils from a wide variety of backgrounds and they attain good academic standards in small classes of between 9 and 12 pupils. We believe that attention to detail and individual care are at the bedrock of education. Good manners and discipline are vital as a broader framework for life as well. Family support is essential for effective education and we welcome close links with parents.

Our Dyslexia Unit is the only Accredited one in East Anglia in a main-stream school. Many scholarships are won in most years to good independent senior schools. We offer an internal music scholarship in every class.

Traditional skills in the classroom and on the playing-field are the sure foundation for further knowledge and creativity, both of which are pursued for their practical application and for their own sakes. The school has a 100% record of placing pupils in parents' first choice of Senior School at the ages of 11 and 13. There are substantial family fee concessions.

A further facility is the school's house in Normandy, sleeping 25. Residential study-visits there are included in the curriculum, and are within the fee structure.

A new feature this year is archery, run by a new member of staff who is a former world champion. We already have county honours and are looking upwards!

Hillgrove School

Ffriddoedd Road Bangor Gwynedd LL57 2TW.
Tel: (01248) 353568

Principals: **Mr J G Porter and Mrs S P Porter**

Age Range. 3–16
Number in School. Day: Boys 70, Girls 40
Fees per term. £600–£1,000

Hillgrove School was established in 1934 and has over the years developed an excellent reputation in the local community. As the classes are small, a high academic standard can be attained and a close relationship between pupils, teachers and parents is possible.

The school aims to provide a sound education and to establish a firm foundation of Christian principles on which children can build. Great importance is attached to the development of character. Discipline is firm, but the emphasis is laid on the importance of self-discipline, good manners and courtesy.

The pupils are able to take part in a wide variety of sporting activities and to follow a broad course of subjects including CDT, music and art.

Hollygirt School

Elm Avenue Nottingham NG3 4GF.

(See GSA section, Part II of this Book)

Homefield School

Salisbury Road Winkton Christchurch Dorset BH23 7AR.
Tel: (01202) 479781
Fax: (01202) 477923
e-mail: admin@homefieldschool.co.uk
website: http://www.homefieldschool.co.uk

Headmaster: **A C Partridge**, DipEd, ACP, FRSA

Age Range. 3–16+
Number in School. Boarders: Boys 40, Girls 10; Day: Boys 200, Girls 100
Fees per term. Day: £925–£1,745. Boarders: £3,825

HOMEFIELD is an Independent Day and Boarding School for Boys and Girls whose ages range from three to eighteen. The School has two main departments, Preparatory and Senior, set in a pleasant rural environment near Christchurch on the South Coast of England.

There is easy access to local train and bus services and ready main line communication between Bournemouth and London.

HOMEFIELD is renowned for being a caring school with an excellent reputation for producing young people with character and a sense of responsibility. Examination results are good not only for academic pupils but also for those with practical and vocational skills, and those with learning difficulties.

The curriculum is deliberately broad to meet the varying needs of individual pupils.

The staff are well qualified and dedicated. Class sizes are relatively small and vary according to the requirements of specific subjects.

In recent years there has been a significant development in the School's facilities and resources, and the School promotes annual music concerts and drama productions. In addition the School undertakes various education excursions abroad to promote modern languages, sport and recreation.

Extra-curricular activities play a prominent role and the range extends from the major and minor sports to membership of the Service Youth Sponsored Organisations: Army Cadet Force and Air Training Corp.

Fees are kept to a minimum, scholarships and assisted places are available, in order to help all parents who wish to have their sons or daughters educated privately even during times of recession.

Charitable status. Homefield School Trust is a Registered Charity, number 1058351. It exists to provide education for boys and girls.

Homewood Independent School

Hazel Road Park Street St Albans Hertfordshire AL2 2AH.
Tel: (01727) 873542

Headteacher: **Mrs Sue King,** BA, CertEd

Age Range. 3–8
Number in School. Boys 35, Girls 30
Fees per term. £200–£1,485. No compulsory extras.

Homewood was established in 1949. It is purpose-built and set in attractive and peaceful woodland.

The school is small and friendly. It has a tradition of high academic standards and offers a broad curriculum.

The Headteacher leads a team of highly qualified and committed staff. Classes are kept small so that the children can be treated as individuals.

Parents' interest in their child's education and progress is recognised and valued. Regular consultation evenings and parents' meetings are held.

Horler's Pre-preparatory School

20 Green End Comberton Cambridge CB3 7DY.
Tel: (01223) 264564
Fax: (01223) 264683
Websites:
website http://www.isis.org.uk
website http://www.yell.co.uk/sites/horlers-pre-prep/
website http://www.horlers.cambs.sch.uk

Headmistress: **Mrs Anne Horler**, AdvDipEd, CertEd

Age Range. 4–8
Number in School. Day: Boys 14, Girls 13 (as at April 2000)
Fees per term. £1,670

Horler's School was founded by the Principal in 1983 to provide an educational bridge from home to large establishment schools. In this environment children receive a balanced education suitable to their ability and preferred method of learning. Teacher/pupil ratio is below 1:10. Year groups of ten pupils. In addition to developing the formal skills of literacy and numeracy, the curriculum is designed to promote an understanding of basic concepts and enrichment through a practical and investigative approach to all areas of learning. It is considered essential to the curriculum that a flexibility of teaching method and materials should be maintained so that each child's individual needs can be met. The creative skills are taught through art, craft, music, drama, movement, physical education, judo, moral education, natural and physical science, geography, history and French. In most instances these subjects are approached through integrated topics and themes on a team teaching basis. Close co-operation between home and school is considered to be vital to the well-being of the children. In their final year at the school the children are prepared academically and socially for entrance to preparatory schools without cramming.

Howe Green House School

Great Hallingbury Bishop's Stortford Herts CM22 7UF
Tel: (01279) 657706
Fax: (01279) 501333

Headmistress: **Mrs N R J Garrod**, CertEd

Age Range. 3–11 years
Number in School. 148
Fees per term. Kindergarten £1,270; Infants £1,634; Juniors £2,017

Howe Green House opened in September 1987. It offers an education of the highest quality in the widest sense.

Facilities are excellent being sited in 5.5 acres of countryside adjacent to Hatfield Forest. It is a single stream school which works to the National Curriculum, offering additional French, Music and Sport. There is a strong parental involvement within the school whereby parents are actively encouraged to be part of their childrens education. The school is seen as a community which fosters an understanding of childrens development within both school and home. Children sit external examinations to senior schools both boarding and day and have been highly successful.

Entry to the school is mainly via the Kindergarten but children are considered for entry to the Junior School by assessment and interview.

Charitable status. The Howe Green Educational Trust Ltd is a Registered Charity, number 297106. It exists to promote and provide for the advancement of education for the public benefit and in connection therewith to conduct a day school for the education of boys and girls.

Howell's School
Denbigh

Denbigh North Wales LL16 3EN
Tel: (01745) 813631
Fax: (01745) 814443

Trustees: Howell's 2000 Limited

Chairman of Governors: Mr R Melling

Principal: **Mrs L A Robinson**, BA (Hons), NPQH

Fees. Boarders: £7,095–£11,085 (7-18); Day Pupils: £2,925–£7,485 (2½-18).

General Information. Howell's is a flourishing Boarding and Day School for some 330 girls. Academic performance is strong and 85% of the Sixth Form go on to Higher Education at Universities. Pupils gain places at Oxford and Cambridge. Nursery places are available from 2½.

The School is situated in delightful surroundings on the edge of the market-town of Denbigh and is easily accessible via the motorway network from the North and the Midlands. Chester is 40 minutes distant and Liverpool and Manchester one hour away. Centres in Shropshire are up to two hours driving time away. British Rail operates frequent services to Rhyl and to Chester.

The Principal will be happy to send a prospectus, fact sheet and examination results on request and to meet parents and daughters at any time, to provide full information and to show them round the School.

Entrance requirements. The main 11+ examinations take place in January. Assessments for other age groups (2½ to 16) occur throughout the year and scholarships/awards are available. A limited number of Scholarship awards are also reserved for those who exhibit special talents such as in Art, Music, Speech and Drama or Sport. Service Bursaries and reductions for sisters are also offered. Boarding at Sixth Form gives additional benefits such as driving lessons and personal computers.

Buildings. The original school was built in 1858, and has been enlarged and improved on numerous occasions since that time. The School contains all the normal facilities including six science laboratories, a large library, twenty-five individual music practice rooms, Art and Design complex, a drama studio, a theatre workshop area and recording studio, IT teaching floor consisting of a teaching classroom and 12 individual computer suites.

Grounds. There are completed laytex courts, 4 grass tennis courts and grounds of a quality to have been used for international matches, a heated swimming pool, a magnificent sports complex and aerobics suite. The Howell's Academy of Sport trains the top athletes in the country in tennis, netball, hockey, badminton and martial arts.

Curriculum. The School presently has an overall staff student ratio of 1:9. The school subjects include Religious Studies, English, English Literature, Media Studies, History, Geography, French, Expressive Arts, German, Spanish, Welsh, Mathematics, Information Technology, Business Studies, Physics, Chemistry, Biology, Physical Education, Art, Music, Spoken English, Gymnastics and Games, Drama, Sports Leadership and Duke of Edinburgh. Additionally, at Sixth Form level: Photography, Psychology and Young Enterprise.

Examinations. Girls are prepared for GCSE, AS and A level examinations; Key Skills; University Entrance and Scholarship Examinations; Schools for Music and Speech and Drama, the Poetry Society and Guildhall School of Music and Drama and London Academy of Music and Dramatic Art examinations.

Charitable status. The Foundation of Howell's School, Denbigh is a Registered Charity, number 1061485. The income derived from the charity is to be awarded to pupils or former pupils in the form of prizes, scholarships, allowances or grants. The school functions within a framework of Christian beliefs and values.

Howsham Hall

York YO6 7PJ
Tel: (01653) 618374
Fax: (01653) 618295
e-mail: howsham@simonknock.freeserve.co.uk
website: www.howshamhall.co.uk

Headmaster: **Mr S J Knock**, CertEd

Age Range. 5–14
Numbers in School. 70
Fees per term. Boarding £2,400. Day: under 8 £1,000; over 8 £1,600.

Howsham is a rural, boarding preparatory school for boys. It is a small family run school ideal for introducing boys to the boarding school way of life.

The record in Senior School Scholarship and Common Entrance Examinations is extremely good. Classes are small and each boy is given the opportunity and encouragement to ensure that he achieves the standard of which he is truly capable. Facilities include a well-equipped computer room and a very recent purpose built Science Laboratory. All the usual examination subjects, including Latin and Ancient History, are taught plus Art and Music; instrumental tuition is available.

Sport is taken seriously and coaching is given in Rugby, Cricket, Cross-country Running, Swimming and Athletics. Boys are also instructed in Canoeing, Sailing, Shooting and Horse Riding.

Children are escorted to and from London and the airports at the beginning and end of each term. Children from abroad are welcomed, a guardian in this country is not a requirement.

Hull Grammar School

Cottingham Road Kingston upon Hull HU5 2DL
Tel: (01482) 440144
Fax: (01482) 441312
e-mail: info@hullgrammarsch.karoo.co.uk
website: www.hullgrammarsch.karoo.net

Headmaster: **Mr R Haworth**, MA (Cantab)

Age Range. Boys and Girls aged 2–18.

Number in School. Day Boys 274, Day Girls 168. Boarders 7

Religious affiliation. Church of England.

Entry requirements. By interview and/or examination depending on age at entry.

The School, which has been making a rich contribution to the life of Hull for over six centuries, became independent in 1988. It is a selective entry co-educational School providing education from School beginners to university entrance. Most pupils join either at 4+, 8+, 11+ or 16+. There is a nursery school on site for 2–4 year olds.

The School stands in its own grounds close to both universities. Pupils travel from all parts of the region, which are served by special school buses. The main building houses a fine assembly hall, classrooms, a spacious library, five fully equipped science laboratories, a sports hall and a computer centre. There are specialist facilities for Careers, Music, Art, CDT and Food Technology. A sixth form centre on the main campus provides a common room and study room. Special provision is made for English as a Foreign Language and for dyslexia.

The school offers a traditional academic curriculum throughout the whole range with due attention to the demands of the National Curriculum. We aim to achieve the highest academic standards possible for all of our pupils and we provide the right atmosphere to encourage their efforts. Classes are small and the staff highly qualified and experienced. Public examination results are outstanding and the overwhelming majority of school leavers gain places in higher education. The school places a high value on pastoral care and we work closely with parents to ensure that our pupils are happy, settled and working to their potential. High standards are encouraged in manners, dress and self-discipline; pupils are treated with courtesy and courtesy is expected in return.

The School offers a wide variety of extra-curricular activities. Of particular note are the annual theatrical productions in each of the primary and senior schools; standards in sport are high and results in inter-school competitions, often against much larger establishments, are first class. Domestic and overseas visits on field trips, skiing holidays and cultural exchanges are an integral part of school life.

Hulme Hall School
(Senior & Junior School)

75 Hulme Hall Road Cheadle Hulme Stockport Cheshire SK8 6LA
Tel: (0161-485) 3524 & 4638 and (0161-486) 9970

(Coeducational, Independent and Accredited)

Head of School: **Philip Marland**, BSc (Hons), MA

Headteacher of Junior School: Mrs Jennifer Carr, MEd

Junior School. We cater for girls and boys from 2 to 11 years in our Nursery, Infant and Junior classes. At every stage of the learning process, we provide a caring and stimulating environment.

Given excellent resources, small classes and teachers of high calibre, children derive considerable satisfaction from their school work and experience no difficulty in realising their academic potential.

Senior School. 11–16 years

The school is well staffed and equipped to deliver a curriculum covering a wide range of academic, creative and practical subjects. An extensive choice of GCSE and other external examination options enables pupils at Key Stage 4 to target optimum qualifications reflecting their personal choice of programme. The staff are consistent in the emphasis they place upon the encouragement of pupils who respond with a highly conscientious approach to their studies, which in turn ensures steady progress and pleasing results.

Communication between school and home is given high priority and the regular issue of reports enables parents to monitor closely their child's educational development. At the age of 16, almost all pupils continue with 'A' level or GNVQ studies at sixth form colleges.

The school operates its own fleet of coaches, offering an extensive network of services covering a 15 mile radius of the school.

Enquiries by letter or telephone (0161 485 4638) to the School Secretary (Mrs J Ashman).

Charitable status. Hulme Hall Educational Trust is a Registered Charity, number 525931. The school aims to promote personal, moral, social and academic development of all pupils.

Hurst Lodge School

Bagshot Road Ascot Berkshire SL5 9JU
Tel: (01344) 622154
Fax: (01344) 627049

Principal: **Mrs A M Smit**

Age Range. Girls 2½–18; Boys 2½–7+

Number in School. Day: Boys 30, Girls 220. Weekly and Full Boarders: 24

Fees per term. Weekly and Full Boarding £4,515; Senior Day £2,650; Juniors from £845 to £2,185 dependent on age

Hurst Lodge is a small, well-established day and boarding school set in grounds of over twenty acres, close to London and all major airports. We offer continuity of education, allowing an easy transition from one stage of education to another in familiar and secure surroundings. Through caring, traditional values, we provide a rounded education which maximises the potential of each individual. The wide, modern curriculum is enhanced by the school's strong interest in the Performing and Creative arts (Drama, Theatre Studies, Music, Art and Dance). There is an active Sixth Form where A levels and BTEC's can be studied in a wide range of subjects.

The school is accredited by CReSTeD – the Council for Registration of Schools Teaching dyslexic pupils.

Hurtwood House School

Holmbury St Mary Dorking Surrey RH5 6NU
Tel: 01483 277416
Fax: 01483 267586
e-mail: hurtwood2@aol.com
website: www.hurtwood-house.co.uk

Headmaster: **K R B Jackson,** MA (Cantab)

Age range. 16–18
Number in school. 290. (150 girls, 140 boys)
Fees per term. £6,100–£7,000

Hurtwood House is the only independent boarding school specialising exclusively in the Sixth Form. It concentrates on the 16–18 age range and offers students a caring, residential structure and a commitment to a complete education where culture, sport, friendship and a full range of extra-curricular activities all play an important part.

Many students now want to leave the traditional school system at 16. They are seeking an environment which is structured and safe, but which is less institutional and better equipped to provide the challenge and stimulation which they are now ready for, and which is therefore better placed to develop their potential. They also require teaching methods which will prepare them for an increasingly competitive world by developing their initiative and encouraging them to think for themselves.

Hurtwood House has 290 boys and girls. It is a small and personal school, but it is a large and powerful sixth form which benefits from having specialised A level teachers. The examination results put Hurtwood House in the top independent school league tables, but it is equally important to the school that the students develop energy, motivation and self-confidence.

In short, Hurtwood House is a stepping-stone between school and university for students who are all in the same age group and who share the same maturity and the same ambitions.

A particularly wide range of A level subjects is available encompassing Mathematics and Science, Modern Languages, Business, Social Sciences, Art and Humanities. Hurtwood House also has what is widely regarded as the best Performing Arts and Media department in England. The school is situated in its own grounds high up in the Surrey Hills and offers excellent facilities in outstandingly beautiful surroundings.

Hydesville Tower School

25 Broadway North Walsall West Midlands WS1 2QG.
Tel: (01922) 624374
Fax: (01922) 746169
e-mail: HydesTower@aol.com

Headmaster: **Mr T D Farrell**, BA, MEd, FRSA

Age Range. 3–16+
Number in School. Day: Boys 188, Girls 164
Fees per term. £665–£1,720

Background. Hydesville has served Walsall, North Birmingham and Sutton Coldfield since 1952, setting high standards in education for children in the 3 to 16 age groups. For many years we have been known as "the family school" and not just because there are so many brothers and sisters at the school. There is a warmth and bustle of activity at Hydesville, as in any large family; we all have our differing interests and activities but we share a very structured classroom day.

Class sizes are limited in number so that each child is seen as an individual with unique needs and talents. We aim to develop those talents and to meet the needs of children who are of average or above average ability.

There is a broad curriculum to meet the needs of the modern student. Drama and music particularly flourish with cups being won by the school choirs at Catshill, Dudley and Cheltenham Festivals. Over the last fifteen years the school has won many trophies at the ISA Drama Festivals, as well as four best actor awards.

Our new Technology Department, which comprises rooms for Graphics, Food Studies and Information Technology, was completed in the Autumn of 1998. The IT department, for example, has brand new Pentium computers which are all fully networked. The technology department also boasts a new photographic darkroom, digital photographic facilities and an audio-visual suite.

The school consists of three largely independent units occupying the same site backing on to the famous Arboretum in Walsall.

Nursery and Infants. *Nursery.*

The Nursery is special: we are fully part of the school and we are a teaching nursery. After a year in our Nursery children will normally be reading simple words and will have been introduced to numeracy; they will have developed social skills and be ready for the next stage.

Infants.

Through Reception and Years 1 and 2 children are given a thorough grounding in the core skills or reading, writing and mathematics.

The curriculum, however, is broader than this with Science, Humanities and creative subjects as well as music and movement and, later, physical education all playing their part in a carefully structured curriculum.

Learning is a serious activity and our objective is to encourage and reward in happy surroundings.

Infant class sizes are carefully limited so the class teacher is able to come to know the pupils thoroughly and to care for their needs pastorally as well as academically.

There is an early morning club catering for Nursery and Infant children. Young children can be left safely in our hands from 7.45 am until school starts. We also have an after hours club which caters for children in the Nursery up to age 11.

Junior School. Our Junior School covers the ages 7 to 11. Most of the Year 3 intake feeds through from the Infant Department, but we normally accept some new children from other schools according to places available.

Account is taken of the National Curriculum, but we work for greater enrichment and to higher standards than are normally expected from Year 6 children. Art and Music are taught as part of the curriculum and benefit in the older years from specialist teaching. French is taught to older Juniors where again there is specialist input from senior staff. Children have access to computers in every year group.

The chief objective of the Junior department is to prepare children for examinations at the age of 11, whether for independent schools including Hydesville Senior School or local grammar schools. Mathematics and English skills are again the basis but there is a full programme of Humanities and Science as well as Creative and Physical activities.

We have four times in the period 1990–1998 won the Express and Star Top of the Form Trophy. Clearly we are achieving a broad education as well as high standards in the conventional curriculum.

Juniors are introduced to team games, PE and swimming. ASA and BAGA Award Schemes are used to build confidence and achievement. There is a full programme of sporting activities involving matches with other schools.

Choir, Drama and Instrumental music are encouraged with extra-curricular practices to supplement the timetable.

Senior School. The Senior School has an excellent academic record and we are proud of our success in preparing pupils for GCSE and further study. In the years preceding GCSE everyone follows a broad range of subjects designed to provide a firm foundation for later specialisation.

We follow the guidance of the National Curriculum but we retain the option of the three separate Sciences at GCSE; two Foreign Languages - French and German - are taught.

Most pupils take eight or nine subjects at GCSE including the core subjects of English Language and Literature, Mathematics, a Science and a Foreign Language. Information Technology is a core subject in each year until GCSE when it becomes available as an option. Music is available at GCSE and has an outstanding record of success in academic and instrumental examinations.

As elsewhere in the school, classes are limited in number so that each pupil has every opportunity to develop academically. In some subject groupings in Years 7 to 9 numbers are kept very low to allow as much individual attention as possible. In the Option groups in Years 10 and 11 some groups will number six or fewer. This provides an outstanding opportunity for pupils to make the most of their time with the teacher.

There is a full Careers Education programme using the expertise of an outside careers body as well as that of parents and friends of the school who can offer a more personal view on various occupations. All Year 11 pupils are expected to complete at least one week's Work Experience, usually after the GCSE examinations.

The school places great emphasis on games and physical activities. We have access to excellent local games facilities and all pupils are expected to participate. PE is available as a GCSE subject in Years 10 and 11 and for all Year 11 pupils the games curriculum is broadened beyond team games to include Squash, Badminton and Trampolining - activities which can be carried on into adult life.

There is a wide range of extra curricular activities and a number of clubs meet at lunchtime and after school.

Most pupils enter the Senior School at the age of 11 but it is usually possible for pupils to enter at other stages subject to an informal assessment.

Ibstock Place School

Clarence Lane Roehampton London SW15 5PY.
Tel: General Enquiries: 020 8876 9991; Headmistress' PA: 020 8392 5802; Bursar's Office: 020 8876 9795; Registrar: 020 8392 5803.
Fax: 020 8878 4897

Headmistress: **Mrs Anna Sylvester-Johnson**, BA (Hons), PGCE

Deputy Headmaster: Mr Huw Daniel, BSc Hons (London), PGCE

Senior Mistress: Mrs Gloria Campbell, MA, BEd Hons (London)

Head of Macleod House: Miss Serena Potter, BEd Hons (Surrey)

Head of Priestman House: Mrs Joanna Webbern, Froebel CertEd, Dip in Lang

Age Range. 3–16 Co-educational
Number in School. Boys 320, Girls 330
Fees per term. £790–£2,225
Extras. Field study courses, both nationally and internationally, Music tuition, School lunches, External examination board fees, Additional specific peripetetic tuition.

Ibstock Place School, founded in 1894, is located in spacious grounds adjacent to Richmond Park. A co-educational day school with excellent GCSE results offered through a full and varied curriculum. Pupils take an average of nine GCSE examinations with 97% of the results graded between A*-C.

The philosophy of the school is to develop the whole child, offering a wide range of educational opportunities and challenges both inside and outside the classroom. The staff pupil ratio is 10:1. and all school work is supported by a strong and effective pastoral system which produces well balanced and socially accomplished young people.

The school has grown and prospered with significant building development in recent years. Since 1992 the school has a new purpose-built Science and Technology block with a comprehensive multi media ICT network throughout the school, a Sports Pavilion, floodlit hard-courts, a 200 seater performance hall for music and drama, a large conservatory in the dining room with upgraded catering facilities. Plans are in place for further projects to improve the quality of the school facilities at this popular school in SW London. The school has a full size gymnasium, swimming pool and eight acres of playing fields on site.

The two academic departments, Primary and Senior, remain distinctive, so that each child benefits from a small school ambience, but also gain from the facilities that are only possible in a larger school.

The Senior School, Aged 11–16, offers a full range of Arts, Science and Technology subjects. Extra curricular emphasis is placed on sports, drama and music, with recent expeditions to India, USA, Africa, Norway and Iceland, and there is an outstanding programme of outdoor education. Leavers are welcomed at a variety of independent and maintained schools, sixth forms and colleges, with places gained amongst others at Westminster, Latymer Upper, Godolphin and Latymer, St Paul's Girls School, City of London Boys and King's College Wimbledon, where they achieve excellent A level results, with the majority going onto Higher Education.

The Primary School. Priestman House, the Froebel Kindergarten and Macleod House for ages 3–11 years is founded on Froebel's principles, that each child develops by and through his own actions. The curriculum provides a rich and stimulating environment, with a wide range of project based work carefully constructed to maximise each child's abilities and talents.

Entry to the Senior department is through interview and examinations in Mathematics, English and Science.

The prospectus is available from the Registrar and Open Mornings are held regularly by appointment.

Charitable status. Ibstock Place School is part of the Incorporated Froebel Educational Institute which is a Registered Charity, number 312930R. It exists to provide high quality education.

Immanuel College

87/91 Elstree Road Bushey Herts WD23 4BE
Tel: 020 8950 0604
Fax: 020 8950 8687

Headmaster: **Philip Skelker,** MA

Age range. 11-18
Number in School. 217 boys, 173 girls
Fees per term. £2,331.

Immanuel College takes its name from its founder, the late Chief Rabbi Lord Immanuel Jacobovits. Opened in 1990, the school has quickly gained the confidence of the Jewish community it serves. It seeks to equip its pupils to live loyal and informed Jewish lives in the modern world. Central to its vision is the belief that Jewish and secular study should not be compartmentalised, but rather that the study of each illuminates the other. Thus, its ethos is characterised by attentiveness to individual pupils' progress, high academic achievement and the integration of Jewish and secular learning.

The school benefits from an attractive and well-resourced green belt campus. Approximately twenty-five per cent of curriculum time is devoted to Jewish Studies and Hebrew. The school offers a full range of academic subjects at GCSE, AS and A2. Leavers proceed to university and of the many who spend a gap year in Israel, a significant proportion learns atyeshivot and seminaries. Boys and girls are taught separately in Years 7 to 11 and the sixth form is fully co-educational. There is a full sports programme and emphasis is placed on Art, Drama and Music.

Of particular note is the school's programme of educational journeys: a five-day stay in York in Year 7, a month in Israel in Year 9, a week in Strasbourg in Year 10 and just over a week in Poland in the Lower Sixth. These journeys deepen pupils' understanding of Jewish culture and history and forge close relationships amongst them.

There are both Jewish and non-Jewish teachers at the school, the common element being enthusiasm for their work and concern for their pupils.

Entry is by examination and interview at 11+ held each January. The school offers scholarships awarded on academic criteria.

Charitable status. Immanuel College is a Registered Charity, number 803279. It exists to combine academic excellence and Jewish tradition in a contemporary society.

Innellan House School

44 Love Lane Pinner Middlesex HA5 3EX.
Tel: 020 8866 1855
Fax: 020 8866 1855

Headmistress: **Mrs R Edwards**

Age Range. 3–8 years
Number in School. 82: Day: Boys 31, Girls 51
Fees per annum. £3,202–£3,506 excluding lunches

Innellan House is run on the lines of a large family with a very good ratio of staff to pupils. Discipline is firm but kind. Traditional and modern methods are used in the many subjects covered by the wide curriculum. Our 7+ pupils are offered places by well-known independent schools.

Innellan House incorporates a long established Nursery Department.

International College, Sherborne School

Newell Grange Sherborne Dorset DT9 4EZ
Tel: 01935 814743
Fax: 01935 816863
e-mail: reception@sherborne-ic.net
website: www.sherborne-ic.net

Principal: **Dr C Greenfield,** MA, MEd

Age range. Co-educational 10-18 (Boarding 10-18)
Number in school. 131 boarders. 89 boys, 42 girls.
Fees per term. £6,250

The International College at Sherborne was set up by Sherborne School in 1977. It has grown to become a separate institution and is now separately registered by the DfEE and the Independent Schools Association.

The College aims to be the best starting point for children from non-English speaking, non-British educational backgrounds who wish to join the British educational system. Students normally stay at the College for one academic year. During this time the College aims to equip each student to take his or her place successfully at a traditional British independent boarding school.

While the full academic curriculum is provided, all teachers of all subjects at the International College are trained or experienced in teaching English as a foreign language. Each student is prepared for any appropriate public examinations, for example GCSEs, Common Entrance or Cambridge English language examinations. Each year the group taking GCSEs records very impressive results. For example in 2000, 57 students sat 460 GCSEs, achieving an A-C pass rate of 79.3%.

The College has no entry requirements and no entry examinations. All students are non-native speakers of English, and some are complete beginners in English.

The College is housed in a purpose-built campus close to the centre of Sherborne. Its boarding houses are nearby. Students are taught in classes of up to eight.

The College is also a member of the Boarding Schools Association, the European Council of International Schools and the Association of International Study Centres.

The Italia Conti
Academy of Theatre Arts Ltd.

23 Goswell Road London EC1M 7AJ.
Tel: 020 7608 0047/8

Principal: **Mrs A Sheward**
Head: Mr C K Vote

Age Range. 9–24
Number in School. Day: Boys 45, Girls 200
Fees per term. Juniors £2,050, 16+ Students £2,865–£2,955

Throughout the 85+ years the Academy has been preparing young people for successful careers in the performing arts it has been aware that the profession expects excellent standards of education and training of its new entrants. Today's Producers and Directors demand that performers entering the industry be versastile and be able to take direction within the theatre, television or film studio.

The five courses offered by the Academy seek to expose students to a wide range of disciplines and techniques in the Dance, Drama and Singing fields working in the mediums of stage, television and recording studio under the careful tuition of highly qualified professional staff.

The courses are as follows:

The Theatre Arts School. For 10 to 16 year olds providing a balanced traditional academic education leading to ten GCSE's with broadly based vocational training in dance, drama and singing. Sixth Form Studies within the Performing Arts Course allows two GCE A levels to be studied alongside a full professional dance, drama and singing theatre arts course. Accredited by the ISA.

Performing Arts Course. A three year course for students aged 16+. Accredited by the National Council for

Dance Education and Training. Leading to the Award of National Diploma in Professional Dance (Musical Theatre).

One Year Singing Course. From age 16. Drama & Dance Award Scholarships are available for this Course.

A BA Hons Musical Theatre Course will be auditioning it's first undergraduate entrants this year.

Entry Requirements. Entry for all the above courses is by audition and assessment.

In addition to the above the Academy offers part-time Saturday classes to children aged 3½ to 18 years in Dance, Drama and Singing. Entry is by interview. Also offered is a Summer School, one week Performing Arts or Drama courses for those aged 9 to 19.

Charitable status. The Italia Conti Academy Trust is a Registered Charity, number 290261. It exists to promote education in the Performing Arts through both teaching and the provision of scholarships.

King Alfred School

North End Road London NW11 7HY
Tel: 020 8457 5200
Fax: 020 8457 5264
e-mail: kas@kingalfred.barnet.sch.uk
website: www.kingalfred.barnet.sch.uk

Head: **Lizzie Marsden** MA (Oxon)

Age range. 4–18.
Number in School. Primary: approx 215; Secondary: approx 280

King Alfred School is unique among independent schools in North London. Apart from being all-age (4–18), co-ed and strictly secular, it takes in a wide range of ability as opposed to its academically selective neighbours in the private sector. About 30% of the pupils receive support from the Special Needs department.

KAS's beginnings are unusual: it was founded (in 1898) by a group of Hampstead parents and its large governing body comprises only current and ex-parents. Visitors tend to comment on the pretty site (on the edge of Hampstead Garden Suburb), the "villagey" layout (carefully preserved by a succession of architects), and the friendly atmosphere – this is a no-uniform establishment and all are on first-name terms.

Academic results are consistently impressive and constantly improving and almost 100% of the KAS Sixth Form go on to university or Art Foundation courses. The School relishes the opportunity to work with children of all abilities and to stimulate the best from all of them.

Charitable status. King Alfred School is a Registered Charity, number 312590. It exists to provide quality education for boys and girls.

Kingscote Pre-Preparatory School

Oval Way Gerrards Cross Bucks SL9 8PZ
Tel: 01753 885535

Headmistress: **Mrs S A Tunstall,** CertEd

Age range. 3–7 years
Number in school. 130
Fees per term. £1,509

Kingscote School was established in 1964 as the pre-preparatory school for Thorpe House. The primary aim of the Kingscote curriculum is to provide a thorough grounding in reading, writing and arithmetic. Mornings are spent learning "the basics" and in the afternoons the boys become involved in a variety of activities – project work, Music, PE and Games, Art and Cookery.

In January 1999 a Nursery opened for boys aged 3+ in a new purpose built classroom.

Kings Monkton School

6 West Grove Cardiff CF2 3AN.
Tel: (029) 2048 2854
Fax: (029) 2049 0484
e-mail: mail@kingsmonkton.org.uk
website: www.kingsmonkton.org.uk

Principal: **Mr R N Griffin**, BA, BEd, MSc

Age Range. 3–18
Number in School. 400
Fees per term. £1,080–£1,504

Kings Monkton School is a co-educational day school for children from nursery age right up to university entrance. The school is administered by a board of governors as a registered charity, dedicated to the sole aim of providing an education of excellence.

Kings Monkton is one of South Wales's oldest independent schools, having educated generations of local pupils since its foundation in 1870. The school prides itself on its consistent record of academic success, its system of pastoral care and its relations with parents. Pupils are drawn from a wide catchment area including Cardiff, the Vale of Glamorgan, the Valleys and Monmouth. The school is housed in purpose-built accommodation in the centre of Cardiff, close to Queen Street station and to all amenities.

Kings Monkton's primary school has small classes in which young children can receive individual care and guidance. Pupils follow a well-balanced curriculum, designed to develop and stimulate young minds to the full. Entry for infant children is by informal assessment, whilst junior pupils are tested in Mathematics, English and Reasoning before being offered a place.

In the secondary school, pupils pursue a wide curriculum with their progress being carefully monitored and receive strong pastoral support throughout their adolescent years. All pupils are encouraged to strive for high standards in their work and to contribute to the well-being of the community to which they belong. Entry to the secondary school is by interview and testing with scholarships available at 11+, 13+ and 16+.

In the school's A-level college, students are taught in small tutorial groups and in addition to their academic studies participate in a number of other activities including Young Enterprise as part of the school's philosophy of giving its pupils a thorough preparation for life. The minimum entry requirements to the College are five GCSE passes at grades A-C.

Kingswood College at Scarisbrick Hall

Southport Road Ormskirk Lancashire L40 9RQ
Tel: (01704) 880200
Fax: (01704) 880032

Headmaster: **E J Borowski**, BSc, GRIC, CertEd

Age Range. 2½–18

Kingswood College at Scarisbrick Hall was founded in September 1998 by the merger of two distinguished schools - Kingswood School, Southport and Scarisbrick Hall School, Ormskirk. The essential elements of the two schools have not changed: the daily efforts of staff to provide an ambience where spiritual and cultural gifts can develop, the quality of teaching in the classroom, and the commitment of staff to extra-curricular activities.

The school follows the guidelines of the National Curriculum, but enhances these through an impressive selection of options to present a breadth and depth for all the pupils. The aim is to provide equal opportunities for all and to cater for the needs of the individual.

Throughout the College the size of classes is restricted to approximately 20 so that each pupil may receive close attention and be treated as an individual, encouraged to develop his/her abilities to the full in a friendly, caring environment.

High standards are set and expected from the pupils, with the emphasis on self-discipline. The school rules have been compiled from principles which are necessary for good order. The utmost importance is attached to the cultivation of good manners and consideration for others.

The Principal and staff consider the school as a partner with parents in the education of their children.

Kirkstone House School

Baston Peterborough PE6 9PA.
Tel: (01778) 560350
Fax: (01778) 560547

***Principal:* Mrs B K Wyman**

Head of Upper School: M J Clifford
Head of Lower School & Pipers Field: Mrs S Gombault

Age Range. Kindergarten to GCSE

Day School situated in rural surroundings 12 miles north of Peterborough. The school has 15 acres of playing fields and 60 acres of lakes and natural woodlands, offering a unique area for environmental studies.

"Pipers" Nursery and Pre-preparatory department accepts pupils from 3 years old. The Lower School pupils are prepared for entry to our own Upper School and also to the local maintained and Independent Schools. All pupils in year 11 enter seven to ten GCSE subjects and 95% go on to follow further education courses.

Learning Support is a well-established feature of Kirkstone House School.

For further details, please contact the Admissions Secretary. Tel: 01778 560350

The Knoll School

Manor Avenue Kidderminster Worcestershire DY11 6EA.
Tel: (01562) 822622

***Headmaster:* Mr N J Humphreys**, BEd (Hons)

Age of Children. Co-educational 2–11 years.
Number in School. Day: Boys 78, Girls 38
Fees per term. £305–£1,189.

The Knoll School was founded in 1917 and became an educational trust in 1966. It continues to be a popular co-educational day school for children from 2 to 11 years of age.

We have high expectations of our pupils in all aspects of their education. Under the guidance of an experienced and caring staff a stimulating and challenging environment is achieved, which enables our children to reach their true potential.

The school has a busy calendar incorporating drama, music and sporting events. The children also benefit immensely from educational outings and visiting guest speakers. Extra curricular activities play an important part in school life and the After School Care facility from 8 am to 6 pm benefits many parents.

Following the opening of the new wing in September 1997, our facilities are excellent. We are proud of all our childrens achievements, particularly those of Year 6 in gaining places at the top independent schools in the area, and attaining 10 scholarships.

Charitable status. The Knoll School Educational Trust Limited is a Registered Charity, number 527600. It exists to provide education for boys and girls.

Lady Barn House School

Schools Hill Cheadle Cheshire SK8 1JE.
Tel: (0161-428) 2912
Fax: (0161-428) 5798

***Headmaster:* E J Bonner**, BEd (Hons), DipPhysEd

Age Range. 3–11
Number in School. Day: Boys 321, Girls 215
Fees per term. Nursery £983 all day, Infants/Juniors £1,115. Lunch £75 per term.
Extras. School Meals £5.40 per week.

Fully qualified and experienced staff. The aim of the school is to provide the preparatory stage of a good general education and to lay a sound foundation for the future. The School is a Charitable Trust. Pupils are prepared for entry into Independent Schools which hold their own Entrance Examinations.

Music, art and drama are important in the life of the school and excellent facilities exist for physical education and games. Provision is made for 7+ pupils to swim throughout the year.

Other school activities include hiking and camping. Educational visits are made throughout the year. An energetic PTA is in existence.

Charitable status. Lady Barn House School is a Registered Charity, number 1042587. It exists to provide education for boys and girls.

Lady Lane Park School

Lady Lane Bingley West Yorkshire BD16 4AP
Tel: (01274) 551168
Fax: (01274) 569732
e-mail: ladylane@indschool.org
website: www.ladylanepark.bradford.sch.uk

***Headmistress:* Mrs Gill Wilson**, BEd

Age Range. Girls and Boys 2–11
Number of Pupils. 111 Boys, 74 Girls. All day pupils.
Fees per term. £1,215–£1,295

Lady Lane Park School is a member of the Nord Anglia Education Group, PLC

The school ethos from 2 years to 11 years is based on the

development of the individual within a broad and challenging curriculum.

Our well qualified and dedicated staff combine professional expertise with commitment and understanding and our teaching methods are a balanced blend of the traditional and the very best in new ideas.

The life of the school is supported by our Governors' and Friends' committees, and we believe that the partnership between school and home is a very important one.

The emphasis is based on the laying of secure foundations in reading, writing, mathematical and scientific skills which are of the utmost importance for a child's development, and we believe in the importance of respect and care for each other and for the community.

A broad-based curriculum is reinforced by the National Curriculum and specialist teaching is provided in Science, Mathematics, ICT CDT, Music, Dance, Drama and Games.

French is introduced through songs and games and specialist teaching begins at the age of 5. Academic achievements are highly valued and we also aim for excellence in other spheres so that our children are encouraged to develop their talents with a positive and enthusiastic approach to school life.

Inter-disciplinary teaching is reinforced with out-of-school visits which help to extend, enrich and reinforce the children's experience.

Pupils are encouraged to take responsibility for themselves and for others and to actively contribute to the life of the school and the local environment.

Every child is given the opportunity to enjoy creative experiences and they are actively encouraged to fulfil their potential. Over 80% of our children study for theory and practical examinations in Music, Dance and Drama.

We have an excellent reputation in all aspects of physical education and children participate in a variety of sporting activities. We have a sports pavilion and large playing field - scope indeed for all our needs.

The friendly, yet competitive atmosphere is testament to team spirit and personal achievement.

Our well resourced and uniquely designed Science laboratory and DT facility provides an exciting environment where children learn through practical activities and experiments.

The dedicated computer room provides an introduction to word processing, databases, graphics and spreadsheets, and the networked system offers opportunities for group involvement. This up-to-date facility, with full Internet access, is a vital tool for all children in our forward-looking school.

The whole school curriculum provides a coherent health education programme, including Personal & Social Development, which promotes children's self-esteem and social well-being.

Our Year 6 pupils achieve Life Saving awards in swimming, and undertake a programme of practical and written study resulting in a First Aid Certificate.

Environmental work enables children to work alongside specialists in many areas.

Lady Lane is Christian in attitude and welcomes children of all faiths. Our aim is to educate children to think for themselves, be confident in their abilities and take pleasure in the learning process as they prepare themselves for an exciting future.

Ladymede Co-educational School

Little Kimble Aylesbury Buckinghamshire HP17 0XP
Tel: (01844) 346154
Fax: (01844) 275660
e-mail: ladymede@indschool.org

Head: **Mr A Witte**

Age Range. 3–11
Number in School. Day Girls 108, Day Boys 57.
Fees per term. £900–£1,750

Ladymede was founded in 1939 and is set in beautiful grounds in the village of Little Kimble.

The school is co-educational throughout and caters for all abilities, accepting children following an assessment in school. There are high standards in all areas of the curriculum which follows the best of the National Curriculum and the Common Entrance Syllabus.

Small classes (maximum 20) ensure individual attention from a well-qualified and caring staff. Ladymede is noted for its strong pastoral care.

The children are happy and hard-working and, upon leaving the school, are articulate, self-confident and caring for others. They react positively to responsibility at each age level culminating in a top Form of Prefects and House Captains.

The curriculum is broad with many After School Activities. All day care is offered from 7.45 am to 6.30 pm including breakfast and tea.

Music, PE, Swimming, Information Technology are just some of the school's strengths. The high academic standards achieved by the children enable them to gain places at the local Grammar and High Schools as well as other leading Independent Senior Schools.

Good manners and traditional values, incorporating respect for oneself and others and high standards achieved are the hallmarks of Ladymede.

There is a flourishing 'Friends of Ladymede' Parents Association who give year round support to the school, both in fund-raising and organising a May Ball alternate years.

Every day is an Open Day at Ladymede.

Lewes Old Grammar School

High Street Lewes Sussex BN7 1XS
Tel: 01273 472634
Fax: 01273 476948
e-mail: bursar@oldgrammar.e-sussex.sch.uk
website: www.oldgrammar.e-sussex.sch.uk

Headmaster: **Mr D Cook,** BA (Hons), MA

Age range. 4-18
Number in school. Boys 251, Girls 121
Fees per term. £1,056-£2,073

Lewes Old Grammar School is an independent co-educational day school located in the historic county town of Lewes.

First established in 1512, Lewes Old Grammar School combines high educational standards, small classes and a caring, well-mannered environment with economic fee levels. Consisting of a mixed Junior Department with its own building for the 4-11 age range, co-educational Departments for 11-16 year olds and its own Sixth Form, the school has always been well featured in the Sussex GCSE and A level league tables.

A wide range of extra-curricular activities is offered, with particular emphasis on sport, music and drama. Numerous trips and visits take place both within and outside the United Kingdom.

The school occupies four buildings near the centre of Lewes and utilises excellent sporting facilities in the town. Recent developments include a new library, Design and Technology workshop and Information Technology suite.

Entry to both Senior and Junior Departments is by examination. Scholarships are offered for entry at 11+, 13+ and for the Sixth Form.

The Licensed Victuallers' School

London Road Ascot Berkshire SL5 8DR

(See SHMIS section, Part III of this Book)

Lime House School

Holm Hill Dalston Nr Carlisle Cumbria CA5 BX.
Tel: (01228) 710225
Fax: (01228) 710508

Headmaster: **N A Rice**, MA, BA

Age Range. 3+–18+
Number in School. Day: Boys 40, Girls 38; Boarding: Boys 65, Girls 45
Fees per term. £2,750–£3,650 Boarding
Compulsory extras. Activities, Laundry

The School was founded in 1899. It stands in its own grounds of 100 acres surrounded by a large private estate owned by The Church Commissioners.

The main building dates from 1638 and has a continuous programme of development and improvement.

Children board from 6 years of age supervised by nearly 60 staff in all areas.

Littlefield School

Midhurst Road Liphook Hampshire GU30 7HT
Tel: (01428) 723187
Fax: (01428) 722550
e-mail: office @littlefieldschool.co.uk
website: www.littlefield.co.uk

Headmistress: **Mrs E B Simpson,** BA (Hons), MPhil, PGCE

Age Range. 4–11
Number in School. 126 day pupils (51 boys, 75 girls).
Fees per term. £1,460 (Junior School). £1,595 (Senior School).

Established in 1945, Littlefield is an Independent Day School situated in 10 acres of its own grounds on the rural outskirts of Liphook.

Littlefield offers for boys and girls a disciplined and structured education within a happy family atmosphere. Children are encouraged to work hard and small classes (an average of 15 and a maximum of 18 children per form) enable staff to study the particular requirements and progress of each child.

The school's extensive facilities include gymnasium/hall, computer room, new library, fully equipped science room, art and design room. There is also a Nursery, Little Ones, taking children from 6 months to Reception age. Little Ones is situated in the main house and benefits from full use of the school's grounds and facilities. There is the flexibility for the parents of children of pre-school age to choose a mix of more formal or informal child care and education. For further details please contact the School Secretary.

The school curriculum is delivered through the best of modern and traditional methods with subject specialist teachers for the older pupils. Children are prepared for entrance at 11+ to the leading independent schools in the region. We have high academic standards normally achieving several scholarships to senior schools per year. French is taught to all pupils and Latin features in the curriculum for older pupils. Computing skills are deemed important and individual ICT lessons supplement the use of computers as a cross-curricular tool.

A fully qualified Learning Support teacher assists tailoring the curriculum to individual needs. Those with learning difficulties can receive a package of extra individual tuition and/or support in the classroom. The needs of gifted children are also catered for at the School.

Christian values and a moral framework for children are promoted through regular assemblies and a programme of Personal & Social Education. Charities are supported by events throughout the year.

The school boasts an orchestra, a choir and accommodates individual instrument and singing lessons within the normal school day.

There is a varied range of after school activities which include Jazz Dance, sports clubs, Ballet, Cookery, Construction Club, Board Games and Homework Club.

Regular trips and outings including residential field trips and visits to France and other countries in continental Europe are very much a feature of the school year.

Games played at inter-school level include Football, Rugby, Netball, Hockey, Rounders, Tennis and Cricket. Athletics and Swimming flourish too at the School. Sports tournaments and holiday coaching courses are also hosted by the school.

Academic, Sport and Creative Arts Scholarships are awarded annually to pupils of 7 years and over (Year 3) and are tenable for the remainder of their time at Littlefield. The candidate's performance in a Scholarship Examination decides an Academic Scholarship.

A thriving parents' association (Friends of Littlefield School) organises regular social and fund-raising events, thus bringing the wider school community together.

Here at Littlefield we aim to reinforce good family values whilst preparing pupils to take advantage of the opportunities in the new millennium.

Littlegarth School

Horkesley Park Nayland Colchester Essex CO6 4JR.
Tel: (01206) 262332
Fax: (01206) 263101

Headmistress: **Mrs E P Coley**, BMus Hons (London), FCollP

Age Range. 2½–11+
Number in School. Day Approx: Boys 162, Girls 142
Fees per term. £330–£1,495

Accredited Independent school giving a thorough and successful academic, cultural and sports education within a firm, secure and friendly environment.

There is a flourishing Nursery Department where

children are well prepared for admission to the main school which they join at 4+, although children are accepted by assessment and interview at all levels, subject to space.

Some strong features of the school are its small classes and careful monitoring of children's progress. The school's tradition of excellence in music is well known, and many children learn at least one instrument in addition to the compulsory recorder.

Individual attention is given as children prepare for entrance examinations and scholarships, with specialist teaching from the age of 8. French is taught from the age of 4.

With 25 acres to use, including an all-weather pitch, sports facilities are constantly growing. A wide range of sport is played and matches take place weekly against other schools.

Plays and concerts are produced each year and external examinations include English Speaking Board Examinations, Trinity College and Associated Board of Music in piano, recorder, violin, cello, flute, clarinet and music theory.

Charitable status. Littlegarth School (Dedham) Limited is a Registered Charity, number 325064. It exists to provide education for children.

Longacre School

Shamley Green Guildford Surrey GU5 0NQ.
Tel: (01483) 893225
Fax: (01483) 893501
e-mail: head@longacre-school.freeserve.co.uk
website: www.longacre-school.freeserve.co.uk

Headmistress: **Mrs Joyce Nicol**, MA, CertEd

Age Range. 200 boys and girls aged 2½–11
Fees per term. £1,075–£2,020

Longacre is a day school for boys and girls aged 2½–11, on the outskirts of the picturesque village of Shamley Green between Guildford and Cranleigh. The school buildings comprise the original large 1902 house plus modern, purpose-built classrooms, standing in 9 acres of attractive grounds including sports fields, courts, gardens, woodland and an adventure playground. The staff are committed to ensuring that, within its uniquely caring and attractive environment, Longacre will teach children to:

- learn effectively and strive for academic excellence
- develop their varied talents to the full
- grow in self-confidence and independence
- enjoy their education

The children's academic progress is closely monitored and regularly tested, leading to excellent examination results, including scholarships, and entry to the senior schools of parental choice. The special quality of a Longacre education, however, derives from the high level of pastoral care which the school offers. Each child is nurtured as an individual, and personal and social development is highly valued, enabling pupils to grow in confidence as they mature.

The core curriculum subjects are given ample time and alongside these there is some form of physical activity every day - sport, PE, swimming or dance, with the opportunity to compete regularly in sporting fixtures against other schools. There is specialist tuition in art, music and drama; Longacre is justifiably proud of its success in local music festivals and art competitions and the very high standard of its productions. French is introduced in Year 1 and Latin in Year 5, again with a specialist teacher. Regular off-site visits and professional workshops enhance the formal curriculum, and pupils may participate in after-school activities ranging from cookery to judo.

Longacre is a community where parents are welcome. There is a thriving and supportive PTA and three parents on the governing body. Parents are kept well informed about the school and their children's progress through a weekly newsletter, formal and informal meetings and written reports. The Headmistress and staff work closely with parents to ensure that their children are happy, successful and fulfilled.

For more information about Longacre please telephone (01483) 893225.

Charitable status. Longacre School is a Registered Charity, number 292753. It exists to provide a broad and balanced education for boys and girls aged 2½–11.

Loreto Preparatory School

Dunham Road Altrincham Cheshire WA14 4AH.
Tel: (0161) 928 8310

Headteacher: **Mrs Rosemary Hedger**, IBVM

Age Range. 4–11 years girls, 4–7 years boys
Number in School. Day: Boys 3, Girls 185
Fees per term. £825

Loreto Preparatory School, founded in 1909, is one of many Loreto schools built on the foundations laid by Mary Ward, foundress of the Institute of the Blessed Virgin Mary, according to the vision of St Ignatius of Loyola. This modern, purpose-built school (1971) stands in pleasant grounds providing a natural resource for environmental studies.

We are a registered charity offering an all-round education by a well-qualified staff, emphasising particularly academic excellence and good manners. Religious education and moral training are central to our teaching which is based on the principles of the Gospel. Music plays an important part in the life of the school. All aspects of class music are taught by a specialist, there is a school orchestra and private individual lessons are available in most instruments. The children's dramatic ability and interest are developed through class lessons, theatre visits and regular productions.

Gymnastics, swimming, netball and athletics, taught by a PE specialist, rate high in our physical education programme and the school participates fully in local and national competitions. Each class is equipped for ICT. In addition there is a computer suite in the Junior Department which is Internet linked. There is a well-stocked library, recently computerised to allow pupils to select, issue and return their own books. Latin and keyboard skills are taught in the Junior Department. French is offered as an extra-curricular activity.

Loreto's concern is for each child as an individual trying to ensure that each reaches his or her full potential. The children, in their turn, are encouraged to care for others. There is special emphasis on Third World awareness.

Visits to the school are welcomed by appointment with the Secretary. Admission to the school at 4+ is usually by interview and by Entrance Test for those wishing to join the school at 7+. Early Years Partnership grants are offset against fees.

Charitable status. Loreto is a Registered Charity, number 250607. Its aim is to pursue the principles of the Gospel in the tradition of the Catholic Faith and the Institute of the Blessed Virgin Mary "forming well-educated men and women who are alive to the needs of the world, with the knowledge which gives them power to act".

Lyndhurst School

36 The Avenue Camberley Surrey GU15 3NE.
Tel: (01276) 22895
Fax: (01276) 709186

Head: **R L Cunliffe**, CertEd (St Luke's, Exeter)

Age Range. 2½–12
Number in School. Day: Boys 129, Girls 74
Fees per term. £1,630 (maximum), £680 (minimum)

Boys and girls are accepted from the age of 2½ into the happy and friendly Nursery Department. From here until they leave the school at the age of 11½, every care is taken to realise the full potential of each child. The Headmaster's wife looks after the welfare of the children.

The School maintains a high academic standard but children of all abilities are welcomed and are taught in a sympathetic environment.

Music and drama play an important role in the life of the School and swimming is part of the weekly curriculum.

Sports and activities offered include soccer, hockey, cricket, netball, rounders, judo, gymnastics, trampolining and squash.

Most children enter their senior schools at 11½ and Lyndhurst has an enviable record of exam successes over the years.

Entry to the School can be at any age if there is a vacancy. At least one internal scholarship is awarded annually for academic achievement, and one external when there is a place available.

Lyndon School

Grosvenor Road Colwyn Bay North Wales LL29 7YF
Tel: (01492) 532347
e-mail: school.office@lyndon-school.freeserve.co.uk

Headmaster: **Matthew Collins,** MA, BSc (Hons), PGCE

Age Range. 2½–11
Number in School. Day: Boys 40, Girls 51
Fees per term. £610–£1,270

Lyndon School is an Independent Day School for boys and girls from 2½–11 years, founded in 1933.

At Lyndon we take great care to encourage positive relationships, good manners, social awareness and a sense of responsibility from our pupils. 'Each for all' is the school motto.

We are a family school, where support for each other is evident from the moment you walk around the Nursery through to our Seniors.

Naturally we work hard at enabling our pupils to reach their academic potential, and our National Curriculum results and the Scholarship awards gained are testimony to the partnership between teachers and pupils with their small class sizes.

We provide a broad academic curriculum complemented by many activities which include swimming, orienteering, drama, ballet, orchestra, climbing, gymnastics, hockey, football, netball, rounders, cricket, horse-riding and skiing.

We are currently the North Wales Ski Champions and we have the Welsh U10 Hockey goalkeeper in our midst. We recently completed in the Independent Schools Association national 5-a-side football tournament in Colchester with much credit.

The school runs successful before and after school and holiday play schemes.

We aim high for our children and they achieve in so many areas; as a school the classroom has no boundaries as we travel out and visit many local and national sites, enhancing our curriculum and developing our pupils.

We can be found just off the A55 in the West End of Colwyn Bay. The Headmaster, colleagues and pupils assure visitors of a warm welcome.

Mander Portman Woodward

24 Elvaston Place London SW7 5NL
Tel: 020 7584 8555
Fax: 020 7225 2953

Principals:
Steven Boyes, BA, MSc, PGCE
James Gilsenan, MA, PGCE

Age range. 14–18
Number in school. Day: Boys 231, Girls 186
Fees per term. £3,265–£4,038

Mander Portman Woodward (MPW) is a co-educational London day school accepting pupils from the first year of GCSE onwards. Approximately 100 new pupils join each year at the start of the sixth form. We offer a very wide range of subjects (37 at A level and 29 at GCSE) and there are no restrictions on subject combinations at A level. At all levels the absolute maximum number of pupils in any one class is seven.

GCSE pupils are taught in our two buildings in Elvaston Place, a quiet street running between Palace Gate and the Queen's Gate entrance to Imperial College. There are six laboratories for Science subjects and specialist studios for Art, Ceramics, Music, Photography and Theatre Studies. Sixth-form pupils are taught both at Elvaston Place and also at our sixth-form Arts and Humanities centre at 108 Cromwell Road. There are libraries at 24 Elvaston Place and 108 Cromwell Road, canteens at 3 Elvaston Place and 108 Cromwell Road, and a sports/recreation hall at 3 Elvaston Place.

Whilst there is a range of compulsory extra-curricular activities for GCSE pupils, including sport, the number of voluntary extra-curricular activities offered at A level is relatively small. In keeping with our founding principles, our primary focus at all age levels is on academic goals. Sixth-form entry requirements are modest (5 GCSE subjects at C or above including at least Bs in subjects to be taken at A level) but almost all pupils proceed to university after leaving, with about 20 each year going on to read Medicine. Over the past four years an average of 7 of our full-time pupils each year have won places at the Universities of Oxford or Cambridge.

We insist on strict punctuality in the attendance of lessons and the submission of homework and there is a formal system of monthly examinations in each subject throughout a pupil's career at the school. This system is designed to ensure that sensible, cumulative revision becomes a study habit not only at school but later on at university. We require pupils to have a strong commitment to academic discipline but our reputation is based on having created a framework in which pupils can enjoy working hard. The environment is friendly, the teachers experienced and enthusiastic and the atmosphere positive and conducive to success.

Manor House School

Springfield House Honiton Devon EX14 9TL
Tel: (01404) 42026
Fax: (01404) 41153
e-mail: office@mhshoniton.demon.co.uk
website: www.mhshoniton.demon.co.uk

Co-Educational Day Preparatory School.

Headmaster: **Mr S J Bage**

Age Range. 3–11

"Tradition, teamwork and innovation working together to provide the very best" sums up Manor House School. The traditions of the school are many and well tested, from regular performances and acts of worship to the best of traditional teaching methods, from structured homework to the cultivation among pupils of an ethos of good manners, consideration for others and firm but fair discipline. An atmosphere of teamwork is successfully nurtured between pupils, parents and staff. At the same time the best of innovations in the world of education have been embraced, from the latest in literacy and numeracy teaching to IT and synthesisers.

All this, in a setting of small classes, dedicated staff and superb academic and sporting facilities makes Manor House excellently placed to provide children with the education they deserve for the 21st century.

Manor House School

Ashby-de-la-Zouch Leics LE65 1BR
Tel: (01530) 412932
Fax: (01530) 417435

Chairman of the Governors: Mrs S Laycock

Headmaster: **R J Sill**, BA

Number of Pupils. 170. Boys 90, Girls 80. Plus 55 in Nursery department.

Fees per term. From £1,065 (Kindergarten) to £1,420 (11+), including meals.

Manor House School is situated in a magnificent setting between the impressive ruins of Ashby Castle and the ancient Parish Church, and is within easy reach of Derby, Leicester, Birmingham and Nottingham.

The School has a wide reputation for both its academic achievements and its genuinely happy atmosphere. Every effort is made to combine the established disciplines of learning and self-expression with modern developments of proven value. The staff, combining experience and dedication, are well-qualified teachers.

The School caters for mixed ability children and prepares them for entry to the local senior independent schools at 11+ and 13+. The rate of success at 11+ and 13+ entrance examinations is very high.

From the age of 8 children have access to the School's fully equipped laboratory, Computer Room, as well as the Art and Handicraft Rooms, Needlework Room, a 2,000 sq ft Hall and a Library. Children are taught French by French-born teachers from the age of 5. German is taught from the age of 11, while Latin is taught to more able children. Children may remain at Manor House School up to Year 9 (14 year olds) for transfer into Local Authority Schools.

The School has a well established Nursery catering for children aged 3 to 5, without obligation to continue at Manor House School. Parents can choose morning or afternoon sessions, or both according to their requirements. Early registration is recommended. We also offer Breakfast and After-School Club.

A limited number of bursaries is allocated every year. Family discounts are also available.

Charitable status. Manor House School is a Registered Charity, number 527859. It exists to provide education for boys and girls.

Maple Hayes Hall

Abnalls Lane Lichfield Staffordshire WS13 8BL.
Tel: (01543) 264387
website: www.dyslexia.gb.com

Headmaster: **Dr E N Brown**, PhD, MSc, BA, MSCME, MINS, AFBPsS, CPsychol

Age Range. 7–17

Number in School. 116

Maple Hayes is a specialist school approved by the Department for Education under the 1996 Education Act for children of average to very high intelligence who are not achieving their intellectual potential by normal teaching methods.

This school is under the direction of Dr E Neville Brown whose work in the field of learning strategies has achieved international recognition and includes a major breakthrough in the teaching of dyslexic children. Attention is paid to the individual child by teaching the basic literacy and numeracy skills required for the child to benefit from a full curriculum, (with the exception of a foreign language) including the three sciences to GCSE level. The school has an excellent OFSTED report.

The very favourable teacher-pupil ratio of 1:10 or better ensures a high standard of educational and pastoral care. The children's learning is under the supervision and guidance of a resident, qualified educational psychologist.

Boys: day, weekly and termly boarding. Girls: day.

Mark College

Mark Highbridge Somerset TA9 4NP
Tel: (01278) 641632
Fax: (01278) 641426
e-mail: post@markcollege.somerset.sch.uk
website: www.markcollege.somerset.sch.uk

Principal: **Dr Steve Chinn**, BSc, PhD, AMBDA

Headmistress: Mrs Julie Kay, BEd

Age Range. 10–17

Number in School. Boarding: 80 Boys; Day: 7 Boys

Fees per term. Boarding £5,054; Weekly Boarding £4,978

Mark College is a DfEE, ISC and CReSTeD approved school for boys diagnosed as having dyslexia. The College offers a full curriculum with specialist help so that boys enter for 6 to 8 GCSEs in their fifth (year 11) year. GCSE results are very good.

Accommodation, including a full sized sports hall, is of a high standard. The College is well resourced and the atmosphere is relaxed and purposeful.

The College's provision for mathematics is recognised Nationally, and its English provision involves the use of the latest work in information technology.

After a very good OFSTED report (1997), the College received a commendation and was listed in the HMCI Annual Report, described as a "significant achievement" by the Secretary of State. Mark College is a Beacon school. It received the ISA "Award for Excellence" in May 2000.

Mayville High School

35 St Simon's Road Southsea Hants PO5 2PE
Tel: (02392) 734847
Fax: (02392) 293649
e-mail: mayvillehighschool@talk21.com
website: www.mayvillehighschool.com

Headteacher: **Mrs L Owens**, BEd

Age Range. 2–16. Boys and Girls.
Number in School. Boys 99; Girls 234. All day pupils.
Fees per term. £1,075–£1,600

Mayville High School provides a caring environment, where all pupils are encouraged to fulfil their potential by working to the best of their ability. Our small classes study in a disciplined yet friendly atmosphere, following a broad curriculum. We also offer special help to pupils in our Dyslexia Unit. High academic standards are encouraged and pupils are expected to take an active part in music, drama and sport. Supervised homework facilities are available until 6 pm. Mayville teaches boys and girls in separate, parallel forms.

Charitable status. Mayville High School is a Registered Charity, number 286347. It exists to provide a traditional education to children from a wide range of academic backgrounds within a caring environment.

Mead School

16 Frant Road Tunbridge Wells Kent TN2 5SN
Tel: (01892) 525837

Headmistress: **Mrs A Culley**

Age range. 3–11
Number in School. 170
Fees. Kindergarten £820; Infants £1,730; Juniors £1,890

The Mead is an independent, co-educational preparatory school situated in the centre of Tunbridge Wells. We prepare children for both Kent Selection into Grammar School and for Common Entrance to a wide range of Independent Schools at 11+.

We aim to create a happy, secure and enthusiastic atmosphere in which every individual can develop his or her all round potential and thereby become well motivated, interesting and hard working members of society.

Academic standards are high and based on National Curriculum requirements. Strong emphasis is placed on individual attention and close co-operation between school and parents is encouraged.

We offer a broad range of extra curricular activities: sport, drama, music, ballet, judo, swimming.

Meoncross School

Burnt House Burnt House Lane Stubbington Fareham Hants PO14 2EF
Tel: 01329 662182 (Main School); 01329 668888 (Kindergarten)
Fax: 01329 664680

Headmaster: **Mr C J Ford,** BEd (Oxon)

Age Range. 3–16 years, co-educational.
Number in school. 450
Fees per term. £1,215–£1,665

Meoncross was founded in 1953 as a day preparatory school by Mr A M Watson, BA. It is a family community based on Christian ideals. Assemblies, usually taken by the Headmaster or invited speakers, are non denominational, and aim to develop spiritual and moral awareness.

Meoncross is committed to developing the full potential of every child and to encourage them to have high expectations of themselves. We believe that children thrive and are happy with sensitive but firm and structured discipline. Meoncross has the flexibility to adapt its teaching to suit the needs of each child and to ensure that each individual feels thoroughly involved and valued.

The Kindergarten which is open from Monday to Friday, 50 weeks a year from 8 am to 6 pm, provides a safe and happy learning environment for children aged 2½–5 years. They have access to the best facilities, resources and a qualified, caring staff. Children are encouraged in all aspects of reading, writing and number skills and also a wide range of structured curriculum activities.

Infant and Junior School. Entry: interview and assessment.

Curriculum: the usual junior school subjects are taught plus French, science, art and craft, health education, nutrition and an introduction to information technology.

After school activities: junior choir, ensemble, netball, football and rounders, drama and technology clubs.

To assist working parents, infant and junior children may remain at school until 5.30 pm each day. A small charge is made for this facility.

Senior School. This has high academic standards with outstanding GCSE results. At present 16 subjects are offered at examination level. Pupils are encouraged to take full responsibility for their actions and to be aware of the needs of others. Sports taught include athletics, basketball, cricket, cross-country, hockey, netball, lacrosse, squash, swimming, skiing and tennis.

The school is located in semi-rural surroundings on the edge of Stubbington village, close to Fareham. School buses offer transport from a wide area of south east Hampshire.

Milbourne Lodge Junior School

22 Milbourne Lane Esher Surrey KT10 9EA.
Tel: (01372) 462781
Fax: (01372) 469914

Headmistress: **Mrs J Hinchliffe**

Age Range. 3–8
Number in School. Day: Boys 150, Girls 10
Fees per term. £850–£1,930

Charitable status. Milbourne Lodge Junior School is a Registered Charity, number 1987090. It exists to provide education for children.

Moffats School

Kinlet Hall Bewdley Worcs DY12 3AY.
Tel: Kinlet (01299) 841230
e-mail: office@moffats.co.uk
website: www.moffats.co.uk
Station: Kidderminster. Airport: Birmingham International

Head: **Mark Daborn**

Number of children. (4–13+) 85
Fees. £2,795 per term (boarding); £1,220 to £1,650 per term (day).

Moffats is a co-educational boarding school in a Grade 1 historic house set in its own hundred acres of park and farmland, a glorious environment a mile from any public road. There are equal numbers of boys and girls who share the same opportunities and responsibilities in all activities. We are proud of our record since 1934, but this is not limited to academic awards or 'A' grades in the Common Entrance Examination. Our joy and satisfaction is in bringing out the best in every child. Their achievements in speech and drama are outstanding. All usual games are coached, including athletics and cross-country running with conspicuous successes at inter-school and national levels. With our own stables riding is professionally taught to half the school. Annual sailing camp with ten boats. Weekends and spare time are filled with a multitude of activities. Moffats is a truly family school; the personal touch of members of the family which founded Moffats ensure the well-being and happiness of all the children in their care.

Moorfield School

Ilkley West Yorkshire LS29 8RL.
Tel: (01943) 607285
Fax: (01943) 603186
e-mail: enquiries@moorfield-school.yorks.com

Headmistress: **Mrs P Burton**, CertEd

Age Range. 2½–11
Number in School. 160 day pupils
Fees per term. Early Years Unit (based on 5 mornings) £580.50: preferred sessions, pro-rata. Main School £1,350. Lunches extra.
Staff. Full time 11, Part time 8
Religious Affiliation. Interdenominational

Moorfield School is an Educational Charitable Trust for girls aged 2½–11. Accommodated in a large house, the School, with its new Nursery Unit and sports facilities, is situated near the Yorkshire moors. It has a strong 'family' feel and lays particular emphasis on consideration for others, both in and outside the community.

Educationally, the aim is that all children should learn to read fluently, to express themselves clearly in speech and in writing, and to develop skills and understanding in numeracy. The curriculum also includes French (from 7 years), Science, Computer Studies, History and Geography, RE, Art, Music, Current Affairs, Games and Swimming. A Multi-purpose Hall provides opportunity for gymnastics, short tennis, badminton, dance and drama. Improved outdoor facilities include a netball and tennis court and levelled grass area for outdoor activities. All children learn music theory and play the recorder. Private piano, violin, flute, clarinet, saxophone, 'cello and brass lessons are also available. The children are encouraged to play in the School Ensembles and to perform in public in both Music and Drama festivals and concerts.

Independence and individuality are welcomed and encouraged. Each girl works to achieve the highest academic standard of which she is capable.

At the age of 11, girls are prepared for the Common Entrance Examination to Boarding Schools and entry to Independent Grammar Schools or State Schools.

Charitable status. Moorfield School is a Registered Charity, number 529112. It exists to provide education for children from 2½ to 11 years of age.

Moorlands School

Leagrave Hall Luton Bedfordshire LU4 9LE
Tel: (01582) 573376
Fax: (01582) 491430

Headmaster: **A J Cook,** BA (Hons), LLB (Hons), AdvDipEd, FCollP

Number of pupils. Girls 170; Boys 160
Fees per term. £639 to £1,363
Average class size: 16. Pupil/teacher ratio: 11.4:1.

Profile. The school is located in the grounds of Leagrave Hall, built by Sir Edmund Filmer in 1850. It provides a caring, traditional and broad based education, with an emphasis on high standards of manners, discipline and appearance, as well as academic excellence. Small classes provide for individual attention. Moorlands has the reputation of being a happy and friendly school, that aims to enable each child to achieve their full potential, academically and socially.

Entry. From 2 by interview. From 7 by examination.

Curriculum. Usual CE subjects taught. Fully committed to National Curriculum and testing.

Leavers. 90% of pupils go on to Bedford, Bedford High, Bedford Modern, Dame Alice Harpur and St Albans.

Sports. Athletics, Cricket, Football, Gymnastics, Netball, Rounders, Rugby and Swimming. Coaching in Cricket, Football and Rugby by qualified coaches.

Activities. Art, Ballet, Chess, Choir, Computer, Cookery, Drama, Music, Needlework, Speech and Sport.

Facilities. All weather pitches, athletics track, playing fields, gymnasium, tennis/netball courts, science laboratory, fully equipped stage, language laboratory, nursery.

Charitable status. Moorlands School is a Registered Charity, number 1042857. It exists to provide education for boys and girls.

More House School

Frensham Farnham Surrey GU10 3AP.
Tel: (01252) 792303. Admissions (01252) 797600
Fax: (01252) 797601

Headmaster: **B Huggett**, BA Hons, QTS, GIBiol

Age Range. 9+–18
Number in School. Boarders: Boys 58, Day: Boys 112
Fees per term. Full Boarding £4,590-£4,910; Weekly Boarding £4,270-£4,570; Day £2,765-£2,960.

More House occupies a unique position. Unlike those who try to help *dyslexics* and others with *specific learning difficulties* in special units attached to a main stream school, More House applies its valuable multi-sensory remediation across the curriculum, so that the proper support is always available and individual needs met.

It is approved by the DFEE and has been placed by CReSTeD in their "SP" Category list.

No school can help every child, so we have a very careful selection assessment to ensure that we can really help those who finally enter the school. All must be in the average range of ability.

Founded some 60 years ago, the school prides itself in using the best modern practice to increase confidence and make children feel valued, happy and to fulfil their potential at GCSE, AS, A level and other public examinations.

The school has flexible boarding run by caring staff and is situated in lovely grounds with plenty of opportunities for outdoor pursuits. Our activities programme encourages all day boys and boarders to make good use of their leisure time.

There is an on-going building programme and the facilities are very good in all departments.

We have a comprehensive information pack, and always welcome visitors. Why not ring us?

Charitable status. More House School is a Registered Charity, number 311872. A Catholic foundation, open to all, helping boys to succeed.

Mostyn House School

Parkgate S. Wirral Cheshire CH64 6SG.
Tel: (0151) 336 1010

Headmaster: **A D J Grenfell**, MA (Worcester College, Oxford)

Age Range. 4–18
Number in School. 305. Boys 191, Girls 114
Fees per term. Infant Dept (mornings only) £833. Under 11 £1,301, Over 11 £2,025.
Compulsory extras. Lunches £1.60 per day

Mostyn House School is a co-educational day school for children between the ages of 4 and 18. Founded in 1854, the school opened its new Senior School in 1985. Entry to the Junior School (7–11) is by interview and test. The Senior School (11–16) prepares pupils for GCSE and Advanced Level examinations, with entry by interview and examination in English, Maths and Reasoning. Entry to the 6th Form is by GCSE results and interview.

Small classes (usually a maximum of 20), a well-qualified and enthusiastic staff (43 in number) and a happy but hard-working atmosphere bring out the best in each child, and a wide range of subjects is offered. Recent developments such as three Science Laboratories, Computer Centre, Indoor Swimming Pool, HE Room, Library, Art Studios, Infant Department, 6th Form Centre and CDT suite complement older buildings such as the beautiful Chapel.

A wide range of extra-curricular activities including drama, computers, music, craft, snooker and shooting take place in a special activity session each day. Individual sports are encouraged and the school has a comprehensive fixture list for team sports.

Pupils' work is monitored regularly with Form and Senior Tutors keeping a close eye on individual development. Regular reporting to and consultation with parents takes place throughout the school.

The school is a member of ISCO and a team of 14 qualified staff run a comprehensive careers guidance programme for all senior pupils. It became a charitable trust in 1979 and the Chairman of the Board of Governors is Mr Glyn Dale-Jones. The Headmaster is the fifth generation of the Grenfell family to direct the school. The school has passed an accreditation inspection by ISJC and is in full membership of ISA and IAPS.

Charitable status. Mostyn House School Trust is a Registered Charity, number 1048117. It exists to provide education for boys and girls.

Mount Carmel Junior School

Wilmslow Road Alderley Edge Cheshire SK9 7QE

(See Alderley Edge School for Girls, in this section of the Book).

Mountford House School

373 Mansfield Road Nottingham NG5 2DA
Tel: 0115 960 5676
Fax: 0115 962 0341

Head: **Mrs D A Williams**

Founded in 1887 and accepting boys and girls from 3-11 years of age, Mountford House maintains a tradition of providing a high standard of education. All pupils follow a range of subjects based on the National Curriculum within a supportive environment. Pupils are encouraged to fulfil their academic potential; many children gaining entry to the larger independent schools in the area.

School results show that pupils achieve, at or more usually above, the expectations of national standards.

Provision is made for pupils with specific learning needs where these pupils follow a Multi-Sensory learning course to improve their language and study skills.

As well as the demands of the academic curriculum, the school activity pursues a thriving sports, music and drama programme aiming to provide an all-round education.

The children are taught in small groups in core subjects thus providing individual attention. There is also a purpose built computer and design technology suite opened in January 2001.

Mountford House is within easy reach of central Nottingham but, despite its urban setting, the school has access to a pleasant garden with both lawn and hard surface play areas.

Great emphasis is put on the happiness of the children, achieved through sound, disciplined structure of work and play. Each child is urged to his/her own full potential and encouraged to help others in the pursuit of theirs.

The Mount School

Birmingham Road Bromsgrove Worcestershire B61 0EP.
Tel: (01527) 877772
Fax: (01527) 877772
e-mail: info@mountschoolbromsgrove.co.uk
website: www.mountschoolbromsgrove.co.uk

Headmaster: **Mr S A Robinson**, BEd (Hons)

Age Range. 3–11
Number in School. Day 140: Boys 78, Girls 62
Fees per term. £430–£1,495

The Mount School is a small, friendly school with a happy, family atmosphere. Children are taught in small classes by skilled, experienced teachers. The academic programme is broad: Information Technology and French are both introduced in the Early Years and subjects such as Art, History, Geography, Religious Education and Music enjoy a valued place in the curriculum. Specialist teaching is introduced gradually so that by Years 5 and 6 pupils are taught by specialist teachers for nearly every subject.

The majority of children enter the School at Early Years level; they are taught in small groups and the curriculum is fully geared to meeting the Early Learning Goals. The School is eligible to receive funding under the Government's Nursery Certificate scheme; the School's provision under this scheme is OFSTED-inspected. The School is also subject to inspection by the Independent Schools Council. The Head himself is an Inspector.

A high rate of success is achieved in preparing children for a wide range of local schools at the age of 11; our pupils regularly win grammar school places and independent school scholarships. A significant number enter local Middle and High Schools. Key Stage 1 and 2 SATS are taken.

The School has a strong tradition of high standards in a range of sports, as well as in Art, Drama and Music; there is a Choir and an Orchestra and a programme of other extra-curricular activities.

Children at all levels of the School are encouraged to join in and are helped by skilled teachers working with small groups to reach their full potential in all areas of endeavour.

The Mount School

Milespit Hill Mill Hill London NW7 2RX.
Tel: 020 8959 3403
Fax: 020 8959 1503

Headmistress: **Mrs J K Jackson**, BSc, MA

Age Range. 4–18
Number in School. Day Girls: 390
Fees per term. Pre-prep £1,670, Junior £1,710, Senior £1,940. *Compulsory extras:* Books

Founded in 1925, the Mount offers a wide range of GCSE and A level subjects in a caring and supportive environment. The classes are small giving maximum opportunity for individual attention. Places for sixth form entry are available and English for overseas students is offered. The school has good facilities for Art, CDT, Music, Information Technology, Business Studies, Latin and several modern languages, and a variety of sports. There is a modern Laboratory Complex. The school grounds consist of 5 acres which are attractively arranged with hockey pitch, tennis and netball courts within the green belt and a large, well equipped gymnasium containing a badminton court. Good use is made of the opportunities offered in London Theatres and Art Galleries and regular school journeys are arranged at home and abroad. The school is served by the Northern Line at Mill Hill East, British Rail at Mill Hill Broadway and the 240 and 221 bus routes.

Charitable status. The Mount School is a Registered Charity, number 312593. It exists to provide a high quality education at moderate cost.

Moyles Court School

Moyles Court Ringwood Hampshire BH24 3NF.
Tel: (01425) 472856/473197

Headmaster: **R A Dean**, CertEd

Age Range. 2½–16
Number in School. Boarders: boys 31, girls 37. Day: boys 66, girls 28
Fees per term. £2,780–£3,120 (boarders), £1,950 (senior school), £1,130–£1,850 (junior school), £900 (nursery).

Moyles Court is a co-educational boarding and day school, which is administered by a Board of Governors and is registered as an Educational Charitable Trust.

There is a strong Christian tradition, although children of other denominations/religions are welcome. Extensive alterations and additions have been made since its foundation and the School continues to develop and expand facilities and accommodation. The main house is over 300 years old, with some sections of the late Elizabethan period. It is situated two miles north-east of Ringwood in beautiful grounds on the edge of the New Forest.

The small classes enable teachers to give individual attention and help, and the full National Curriculum is taught plus other subjects (eg Textiles and Ceramics). The methods used are a combination of the best modern and traditional ones. The children are prepared for GCSE and other external examinations and the academic standard is good. All branches of music are taught and the children are encouraged to play a variety of musical instruments.

Games/activities include cricket, soccer, rugby, tennis, hockey, sailing, netball, rounders, table tennis, judo, riding, golf, archery, squash, swimming, dancing, ballet, sewing, knitting, drama, computing, chess. Guides, Brownies, Cubs and Scouts.

Travel arrangements are made for children from abroad, including transport to and from airports and stations. The boarders' health is supervised by the School Nurse, assisted by three house-mothers. The School doctor visits the school on a regular basis and is always available when needed to attend the children.

There are generous discounts for Service families and second children and subsequent siblings. Admission is through personal interview with the Headmaster and/or written examination plus Head's report from previous School. The Headmaster is happy to meet parents at any time by appointment.

Nethercliffe School

Hatherley Road Winchester Hampshire SO22 6RS.
Tel: (01962) 854570
Fax: (01962) 854570

Headmaster: **Mr R F G Whitfield**

Age Range. 3–11
Number in School. Day: Boys 91, Girls 59
Fees per term. £710–£1,460 (Fees include lunch and all books and stationery).

Nethercliffe is a friendly school where children work in small classes under the guidance of experienced teachers. Children may start in the Nursery Class in the September after their third birthday. Annually many Year Six children pass the entrance examinations for schools like St Swithuns's and King Edward VI.

The school enjoys a semi-rural setting with large playing fields next door. Educational outings are arranged in the summer term, including waterbased activities. Judo, ballet, first aid, instrumental tuition and sports are among the after school activities available. We look forward to showing you the happy, busy atmosphere in the classes.

Our fees are extremely competitive and include all text books, stationery and meals. Special educational needs help is available. A discount is offered for prompt payment, and there is a scheme to allow children to remain at school until 5.30 pm.

New Eccles Hall School
(Co-educational)

Quidenham Nr Norwich Norfolk NR16 2NZ.
Tel: (01953) 887217
Fax: (01953) 887397

Headmaster: **R W Allard**, CertEd

Age Range. 3–16
Number in School. Boarders: 70, Day 90
Fees per term. Day £1,165–£1,895, Boarding £3,562
The school offers:

- Excellent standard of teaching in small classes.
- Curriculum that covers the national requirements and more.
- Caring for the pupil as an individual is at the centre of the school's ethos.
- Large country estate providing a perfect learning environment.
- Exceptional games facilities combined with an extensive leisure programme.
- Successful Individual Teaching Unit for Specific Learning Difficulties.
- Happy relaxed atmosphere for teaching and learning.
- Attractive and comfortable boarding accommodation.
- Learning respect for each other considered essential.
- Length of the day suits working families.

Visitors to the school are welcome when the school is in session.

Newlands Manor School

Sutton Place Seaford East Sussex BN25 3PL.
Tel: (01323) 490000/892334
Fax: (01323) 898420

Headmaster: **Mr Oliver T Price**, BEd (Hons)

Chairman of Governors: Mr D Smith

Age Range. 13–18
Number in School. Boarders: Boys 49, Girls 34. Day: Boys 57, Girls 27
Fees per term. Boarding £4,210–£4,700; Day £2,605–£2,715

Newlands School provides quality education from nursery to university age on one 21 acre campus in a pleasant coastal town surrounded by an area of outstanding natural beauty.

Newlands has good communication links with Gatwick (37 miles), Heathrow (78 miles) and London (65 miles).

YOUR CHILD'S POTENTIAL. At Newlands we place an emphasis on fully developing your child's potential in a happy and caring environment. The wide range of activities available make it possible for every pupil to achieve success and confidence in one field or another.

Classes are small and a pupil's progress is monitored carefully. The arts flourish with thriving music, drama and art departments. There is a strong choral tradition and annual dramatic productions.

DEVELOPMENTS. Major building developments have recently taken place. A new Sports Hall, Studio Theatre, learning resources area, three new ICT classrooms and a splendid girls' boarding house have all been completed during the past year. A number of other major projects are in the planning stage.

ACADEMIC AND SPORTS FACILITIES. Our facilities include High-tech computer rooms, science laboratories, a large art studio, a design technology workshop, a language laboratory and music room.

There are the equivalent of eight football pitches, a heated indoor swimming pool, a hard playing surface for three tennis/netball courts, a Sports Hall and a .22 rifle range. There are opportunities for many sports including soccer, hockey, rugby, netball, cricket, athletics, volleyball, basketball, squash, badminton, tennis, horse riding and cross-country running.

SCHOLARSHIPS. Scholarships are available and there is a generous discount for Service families.

ACCELERATED LEARNING UNIT. The nationally renowned Gannon Centre has specialist teachers who provide one-to-one tuition for gifted pupils, dyslexic pupils and those learning English as a foreign language.

THEATRE ARTS COURSE. A theatre arts course is available to students who wish to specialise in Dance, Drama, Music and Art within an academic environment.

TRANSPORT. Travel and escort arrangements include Fareham, Romsey, Aldershot, Maidstone, Victoria Railway Station as well as Gatwick, Stansted and Heathrow airports. Pupils can be met on incoming flights.

Newlands Preparatory School - please see Part V, IAPS section, of this Book.

Charitable status. Newlands School is a Registered Charity, number 297606. It exists to provide quality education for boys and girls.

Norfolk House School

Norfolk Road Edgbaston Birmingham, B15 3PS
Tel: 0121 454 7021
Fax: 0121 454 7021

Headmistress: **Mrs H Maresca,** BEd

Age Range. 3–11
Number in school. 155
Fees. £656 (part-time). £872–£1,139

Norfolk House School is a Christian Independent day school situated in the pleasant suburb of Edgbaston and is ideally located for pupils and parents all over Birmingham and the surrounding areas.

The school aims to provide individual attention to each pupil, thus enabling each child to fulfil his or her potential. Small class sizes and favourable pupil:teacher ratios (average 17:1) culminate in the best possible academic results. Many pupils move on to the various King Edward Schools, or to other Grammar Schools or senior Independent Schools as the direct result of the high standards achieved at Norfolk House.

The syllabus is designed to give each child a general academic education over a wide range of subjects – in line with the National Curriculum; the requirements of the Eleven Plus and the various Entrance Examinations are also taken into consideration.

In addition to education, Norfolk House School aims to instil in each child good manners, consideration and respect for others, and recognition of personal responsibility. Norfolk House is a small school with an emphasis on caring and traditional values, yet forward thinking in outlook. It is a happy school with high attainment, competitive fees and a family atmosphere.

Northamptonshire Grammar School

Pitsford Hall Pitsford Northamptonshire NN6 9AX
Tel: (01604) 880306
Fax: (01604) 882212
e-mail: office@ngs-school.com
website: http://www.ngs-school.com

Headmaster: **Simon H Larter,** BA, FRSA

Age range. 3–18
Number in school. 360 pupils
Fees per term. £1,308–£2,306

The School is set in 25 acres, four miles north of the county town. It was founded in 1989 and takes pupils from the age of 4 to 18. A full range of academic subjects through to GCSE, A level and University entrance is taught. The curriculum draws on the best of the grammar school traditions of the past, makes them relevant to today's needs, and ensures that they are applicable to the demands of the future.

The School aims to educate the whole person and sets, expects and maintains high standards in all its disciplines and extra-curricular activities. Competition in both work and sport is encouraged and emphasis is placed on developing the highest personal and moral qualities. The School has not formed a particular connection with any one religious denomination, but strives to portray a living Christianity that reflects the whole range of denominations and it is sympathetic to other faiths. Assemblies, church services and religious education on the timetable ensure that moral and spiritual values underpin all the work. *Old Pitsfordians* leave as mature, sensitive individuals with an excellent academic grounding, a high level of self-discipline and a broad range of skills.

Pupils usually join at the age of 11, entering Year 7 either from the *Junior School* or from other local schools. The School enjoys a strong academic reputation, which is complemented with effective pastoral support and a wide range of extra-curricular activities. Entry to the Senior School is selective; the academic curriculum is designed to cater for the upper 40% of the ability range and the selection criteria is based upon this. It is expected that all pupils will take 10 GCSEs before transferring to the Sixth Form at the end of Year 11.

The Sixth Form is structured to provide a stepping stone from the discipline of the Senior School to the demands of Higher Education. Each Sixth Form student has his or her own tutor, who is normally one of their A level teachers. Sixth Formers take a full part in the life of the School and many have positions of responsibility.

The extra curricular programme at Northamptonshire Grammar incorporates three elements: Service, Sports and Skills. In the main, these activities take place after school until 5.20 pm. The School currently has a junior percussion band, wind, string and guitar ensembles, two rock bands, a Senior and Junior choir and an emergent orchestra. A number of drama productions are staged every year, with usually a large musical performance every other year.

The *Junior School* was established in 1991 to act as a bridge for pupils to enter the Senior School at 11. All pupils are taught by class teachers and in addition, receive specialist teaching in Games, Gymnastics, French, Information Technology and Music. The sports taught include Rugby, Hockey, Cricket, Rounders, Tennis, Cross country running, Netball and Athletics. All pupils are taught to play the recorder and encouraged to read music. Many learn to play other instruments. All pupils take part in Drama lessons and many enjoy extra Speech lessons.

A number of academic scholarships are awarded annually. Further details can be obtained from the School.

Charitable status. Northamptonshire Grammar School is a Registered Charity, number 29891. It exists to provide education for boys and girls.

North Cestrian Grammar School

Dunham Road Altrincham Cheshire WA14 4AJ

(See SHMIS section, Part III of this Book)

Notre Dame School

Lingfield Surrey RH7 6PH.
Tel: (01342) 833176

Principal: **Mrs N E Shepley,** BA

Age Range. 2½–18
Numbers. 315 in Junior School; 345 in Senior School
Fees per term. £700–£2,005
Entry. Junior School: by interview at any age, subject to vacancies.

Senior School: at 11+ by Entrance Examination, interview and report from previous school. At 16+ by 5+ GCSEs in A–C range, and interview.

Scholarships. Scholarships and Bursaries are offered to the top candidates in the 11+ Entrance Examination. Scholarships are also available for the Sixth Form.

Curriculum. In the Junior School the usual primary subjects are taught, including French, Dance, Speech and Drama. In the Senior School a wide curriculum of academic and practical subjects is offered to GCSE and A Level. The National Curriculum is incorporated throughout the school.

Reports and consultations. Reports are sent twice yearly. Parent/Teacher interviews are held annually. Parents are always welcome to discuss progress with form teachers and/or the Principal.

Leavers. The majority of pupils in the Junior School progress to the Senior School. Ninety percent of Sixth Form leavers go on to further education courses at University, including Oxbridge, resulting in a wide variety of careers.

Sports. Sports in the Junior School include Gym, Golf, Cricket, Football, Dance, Netball, Swimming, Rounders and Short Tennis. In the Senior School, Tennis, Swimming, Basketball, Rugby, Football, Hockey, Squash, Badminton, Athletics are all played. In the Sixth Form a wide programme of sporting activities is arranged including Archery, Canoeing, Orienteering, Climbing, Dry Skiing and Sailing. Annual Ski Trips are arranged for older Junior School pupils and Senior pupils.

Extra Curricular Activities. Duke of Edinburgh Award Scheme, Outward Bound, Drama, Music and Science Clubs, Sports Fixtures and competitions, Choir, Orchestra and Ensembles.

Religious Services. Regular school, house, form and

year assemblies are held. Interdenominational services are held.

Notre Dame School transferred to a lay management in January 1987. It maintains its Christian ethos and its philosophy is based on a strong belief in the development of the whole person. The school has a tradition of providing a caring, friendly and disciplined environment.

Charitable status. Notre Dame School is a Registered Charity, number 295598. It exists to provide education.

Notre Dame Senior School

Cobham Surrey KT11 1HA

(See GSA section, Part II of this Book)

Nunnykirk Centre for Dyslexia

Netherwitton Morpeth Northumberland NE61 4PB
Tel: 01670 772685
Fax: 01670 772434
e-mail: secretary@nkirk.freeserve.co.uk

Headteacher: **Mr S Dalby-Ball**, BSc, CertEd, NCA

Age Range. 7–16
Number in school. Boys 40, Girls 5
Fees per term. On request.

Nunnykirk is a non-maintained co-educational special school catering for the needs of children with Specific Learning Difficulties/Dyslexia.

The homely and supportive residential setting enables us to provide a 'holistic' approach to the problems faced by these children.

Pupils derive motivation from stimulating experiences which add to their learning situation.

Staff work closely as a team to enable each child to have full access to the National Curriculum as well as receiving specific remediation provided by specialist staff.

A wide range of extra-curricular activities add to these opportunities to allow each child to reach his/her full potential both academically and socially.

The Nunnykirk Hall School Trust is a Registered Charity, number 508367. It exists to provide specialist help for boys and girls with Specific Learning Difficulties/ Dyslexia.

Oakfield Preparatory School

125–128 Thurlow Park Road Dulwich London SE21 8HP.
Tel: 020 8670 4206
Fax: 020 8766 6744

Principals:
Dr Paul Simpson, MEd and **Margaret Simpson**, MSc

Headmaster: Brian G Wigglesworth, BEd (Hons)

Age range. 2–11
Numbers. Day Boys 281; Girls 250
Fees per term. £1,505 including lunch

Oakfield School was founded in 1887 and is today a modern coeducational prep school which prepares children for the entrance examinations of London and countrywide independent senior schools. These senior schools base their 11+ entrance exams on English and maths and it is these core subjects that form the basis of the Oakfield curriculum, but not to the exclusion of French, humanities, science, the arts and computing.

The School is arranged into three groups, the Nursery (2–3) (full time or half day), Kindergarten and Pre-Prep (3-6) and Transition and Preps (6-11). Each age group has its own self contained building and facilities. The School site of nearly three acres allows space for play and games and older children use the nearby playing field where all normal games are played. All children over five swim once a week under instruction.

Entry to the Nursery is by informal assessment. Once accepted the child will progress automatically into the Kindergarten and Main School. Entry at 3+ and 4+ is also by assessment and children should have a good idea of colours, shapes, matching, sorting and simple counting. Entry at 5+ and 7+ is by a test in English and Maths appropriate to the age of the child.

Prospective parents – and children – would be very welcome to visit Oakfield during a school day.

Oakhyrst Grange School

Stanstead Road Caterham Surrey CR3 6AF.
Tel: (01883) 343344

Headmaster: **Nicolas J E Jones, BEd** (Hons)

Age Range. 2½–11
Number in School. Day Boys and Girls: 146
Fees per term. £525–£1,360

Oakhyrst Grange School was established in 1950 and moved to its present premises in Stanstead Road in 1957. Since September 1973 the School has been administered by a non-profit making trust.

Standing in five acres of open country and woodland, and surrounded by the Green Belt the School enjoys a fine position amongst the Surrey Hills.

Pupils, aged between 2½ and 11, are prepared for entry into both the State and Independent Sectors at secondary level. The majority further their education in the latter sector, many achieving scholarship entry to one or more schools.

There are many sporting opportunities offered and particularly high standards have been reached in Swimming, Cross Country and Athletics where we have recently achieved ISA National level. We also compete against other schools in Football and Judo. We have our own heated, indoor swimming pool, all-weather tennis, netball, hockey and 5-a-side sports area and gymnasium. Children may also play Cricket, Golf, Badminton and Table Tennis. There are also two flourishing Ballet groups, along with tennis.

Extra curricular music lessons are offered and much music making also takes place as part of the normal school timetable. We have a school orchestra and choir, both of which perform regularly.

Academic excellence is encouraged and achieved, every pupil is expected to attain his individual potential. We help the children to develop into caring, thoughtful and confident adults.

Charitable status. Oakhyrst Grange School Educational Trust is a Registered Charity. It exists to provide an all-round education which assists pupils to become well-adjusted citizens.

Oaklands School

8 Albion Hill Loughton Essex IG10 4RA
Tel: 020 8508 3517
Fax: 020 8508 4454

Head: **Mrs C A Sunderland,** Dip Sorbonne, CertEd

Age range. Girls 3-11 years. Boys 3-7 years.
Number in school. 243
Fees per term. £915-£1,495

Oaklands is a long established preparatory school, founded in 1937 and delightfully situated in extensive grounds on the edge of Epping Forest. It provides a firm foundation for girls aged 3 to 11 years and boys aged 3 to 7 years. Great care is taken in preparing pupils for entrance examinations to their next schools.

A broad curriculum is offered, with early emphasis on literacy and numeracy, ensuring high standards, and great importance is placed on fully developing each child's potential in a secure and caring atmosphere. A wide range of extra curricular activities is offered and an after school care club operates until 5 pm. The school has now established a reputation for excellent dramatic productions. Individual music tuition is available, including pre-woodwind instrumental lessons, using Suzuki teaching methods, from age 5 years.

Oaklands is a friendly, happy school where children can enjoy learning and take pride in both their own success and the achievements of others. In addition to the attainment of high standards, pupils build personal qualities of confidence, self-reliance and respect for others, in preparation for the challenges and opportunities of the modern world.

The Old School
Henstead

Toad Row Henstead Nr Beccles Suffolk NR34 7LG
Tel: (01502) 741150
Fax: (01502) 741150
e-mail: oldschool@btclick.com

Headmaster: **Mr M J Hewett**, BA, CertEd, MCollP

Age Range. 4½–13
Number in school. Day Boys and Girls: 130
Fees per term. £1,069–£1,458

The Old School, Henstead offers a traditional style of education in a caring family environment. It is well staffed with small classes. Children are prepared for entrance examinations to all local senior schools. The curriculum is broad enough to be balanced with facilities for Music, ICT, Science, Pottery, Art & Drama and Physical Education and games.

The school is an Educational Trust; it is in membership of ISA and is Accredited by ISC.

Charitable status. The Old School is a Registered Charity, number 279265. It exists to provide education for boys and girls.

Oriel Bank High School

Devonshire Park Road Davenport Stockport Cheshire SK2 6JP.
Tel: (0161-483) 2935
e-mail: headmaster@orielbank.org
website: www.orielbank.org

Headmaster: **R A Bye**, MA

Age Range. 3–16
Number in School. Day: Girls 180
Fees per term. £660–£1,210 Junior, £1,540 Senior

Established in 1887, the school is in a residential park which is a conservation area with close access to a network of bus and rail routes in South-East Manchester, Cheshire and Derbyshire.

The school enjoys a high reputation for the excellence of its teaching, its high standards of behaviour and appearance and its happy family atmosphere. After GCSE examinations most girls proceed to A–levels in other local schools and colleges. Others continue studies in various Further Education courses.

Extra-curricular activities include sport, choral and orchestral music, drama, a work experience programme, visits abroad, community work, the Duke of Edinburgh's Award Scheme and the Red Cross Youth First Aid Certificate. The school is open at 8 am and there is an after care service until 6 pm. There are close links with the local Parish Church, yet girls of all denominations are welcome.

Oxford House School

2 & 4 Lexden Road Colchester Essex CO3 3NE.
Tel: (01206) 576686
Fax: (01206) 577670
e-mail: ohs@supanet.com

Principals: **R P Spendlove**, CertEd, ACP, FCollP, **Mrs Sylvia Spendlove**, MontDip, FCollP

Age Range. 2½–11
Number in School. Day: Boys 65, Girls 65
Fees per term. £1,285–£1,445 (including lunches), Half Day £735

Established in 1959, Oxford House takes both boys and girls from 2½ to 11. The Lower School makes full use of the Montessori apparatus, whilst the Upper School is progressively more subject based in preparation for Senior Schools. Older children are prepared for various entrance examinations as required and the Town still supports two Grammar Schools.

The School's motto Labore Confecto Gaudentes (joy in achievement) engenders the ethos of the School which aims to promote high standards of academic and personal achievement while maintaining an extremely happy and friendly family atmosphere.

Entrance is usually subject to interview and a Prospectus is available upon request from the Bursar.

The Park School

Queen's Park South Drive Bournemouth BH8 9BJ.
Tel: (01202) 396640
Fax: (01202) 392705

Headmaster: **Mr Clive G Cole**, BA

Age Range. 4–11
Number in School. Day: Boys 132, Girls 125
Fees per term. £1,025–£1,375

The Park is a co-educational junior day school occupying a quiet site overlooking Queens Park Golf course in a pleasant residential area near the town centre.

Pupils are taught in small classes in a caring, happy environment. The school is geared principally towards academic achievement although we do provide special help for a limited number of children with specific learning difficulties. The emphasis is on individual development and academic progress. This covers not only work in the classroom but also all other aspects of school life: games, music, the Arts and many practical activities. Pupils are prepared for entry to Senior Independent Schools and to the local Grammar Schools through their tests at 11+ and 12+ years.

Most pupils start aged 4+ years but there are occasional vacancies at other ages. Offer of a place is made only after prospective pupils have been formally assessed.

The Park School
Yeovil

The Park Yeovil Somerset BA20 1DH
Tel: (01935) 423514
Fax: (01935) 411257

Headmaster: **Mr P W Bate**, BA(Econ), PGCE, AdvDipMkt

Age Range. Co-educational 3–18
Fees. Day £855–£1,780. Boarding £2,875–£3,440

The Park School, Yeovil, is an Independent day and boarding school founded in 1851 run by The Park School (Yeovil) Limited, a Company Limited by Guarantee and registered as an educational charity. It aims to provide a sound education based on Christian principles for pupils aged from 3 to 18. It is inter-denominational and evangelical having strong relationships with a number of churches.

The School is pleasantly situated near the centre of Yeovil in the beautiful county of Somerset with easy access to surrounding towns and villages, from which day pupils are drawn, and to main line Southern and Western railway stations for London, Waterloo and Paddington. Transport to London, Heathrow and Gatwick and other airports is arranged for boarders travelling abroad.

The School buildings consist of an interesting listed building which has been sympathetically upgraded. Modern additions include Junior Department (extended 1984), Home Economics/Art, Maths, Biology rooms (1996) and refurbished IT (1998). A new Sixth Form building opened in September 2000, providing extra classrooms, common room and kitchen.

Pupils flourish in a friendly, caring environment where, in small classes, they benefit from well-qualified staff. There is a wide and varied curriculum which encourages each pupil to develop their own abilities and interests to the full. In line with National Curriculum guidelines, senior pupils choose from a wide range of subjects in GCSE and A level, including English, Religious Education, History, Drama, Geography, French, German, Mathematics, Sciences (double award), Art, Music, Technology (Craft & Design, Food Technology, Textiles, Information Technology). Physics, Chemistry and Biology can also be studied as separate Sciences. Chinese and Spanish are offered when the need arises. Additional subjects studied at 'A' level include: Business Studies, Psychology, Sports Studies, Graphic Design, Theatre Studies and General Studies.

Physical education is also an essential part of the curriculum. Pupils participate in a varied programme of sporting activities including Athletics, Badminton, Basketball, Cricket, Football, Gymnastics, Hockey, Netball, Squash, Swimming, Tennis, Table Tennis and Volleyball. Many senior pupils also take part in The Duke of Edinburgh Award Scheme as well as Young Enterprise.

A wide range of musical instruments is taught by the Director of Music and visiting staff. There are School Choirs and an Orchestra. Musical and dramatic productions are regular features of School life.

Boarders live in a modern purpose-built School House (1977). Most occupy single study bedrooms while others (not more than two) share rooms. They are cared for in a homely, family atmosphere by resident houseparents helped by an assistant and resident teaching staff.

At weekends a variety of interesting activities are available. On Sundays all boarders are encouraged to attend, with a member of staff, the Church of their parents' choosing.

Academic standards in the school are high with The Park being at or near the top of the GCSE league tables. However, the school is not rigidly selective and pupils are encouraged to develop their talents as individuals with extremely favourable pupil/teacher ratios.

The School offers scholarships which may be given for academic, musical, art or drama ability. These are awarded by examination and interview in January for entry at 8, 11 and 13. Bursaries are available for children of missionaries, other full-time Christian workers, and members of HM Forces.

Charitable status. The Park School is a Registered Charity, number 310214. It exists to provide Christian education and care for children aged 3–18 years.

Park School for Girls

20–22 Park Avenue Ilford Essex IG1 4RS.
Tel: 020 8554 2466
020 8554 6022 (Bursar)
Fax: 020 8554 3003

Headmistress: **Mrs N E O'Brien**, BA

Age Range. 7–18
Number in School. Day: Girls 235
Fees per term. Prep School £1,170, Grammar School £1,550

We create a caring, well-ordered atmosphere. Our pupils are encouraged to achieve their full academic and social potential. The well-qualified staff and the policy of small classes produce well above the national average GCSE and A level results. The majority of our sixth form enter university and the professions.

A strong tradition exists in the expressive arts and sport.

Interested parents are welcome to visit the school, where the Headmistress will be pleased to answer their queries.

Charitable status. Park School for Girls is a Registered Charity, number 269936. It exists to provide a caring environment in which we develop our pupils' potential to the full.

Peterborough and St Margaret's School

Common Road Stanmore Middlesex HA7 3JB
Tel: 020 8950 3600
Fax: 020 8421 8946

Headmistress: **Mrs D M Tomlinson**

Age Range. 4–16
Number in School. Day: Girls 230
Fees per term. Infants £1,260, Juniors £1,535-£1,635, Seniors £1,870 *Compulsory extras:* Books and Stationery. Lunches compulsory in Infant & Junior Departments.
Charitable status. The E Ivor Hughes Educational Foundation is a Registered Charity, number 293623. It exists to provide education for children.

Plumtree School

Church Hill Plumtree Nottinghamshire NG12 5ND.
Tel: (0115) 937 5859
Fax: (0115) 937 5859

Headmaster: **N White**, CertEd

Age Range. 3–11
Number in School. Day: Boys 75, Girls 55
Fees per term. £1,025

The School was opened in its present form by Mr and Mrs White in September 1982. The buildings housed the original Church of England village school closed down by the local education authority some years earlier.

Plumtree is an independent, co-educational, primary school with its own nursery. The School is situated in the centre of Plumtree village within easy reach of the southern suburbs of Nottingham and surrounding villages to the south of the city.

The aim of the school is to provide a wide, balanced primary education relative to the needs and potential of each child. At Plumtree, a happy, working atmosphere in small classes allows for close individual attention. There is an average pupil/teacher ratio of 12:1.

Priority is given to the basic subjects at all levels throughout the school. A solid foundation in mathematics, English and science is considered vitally important. The school has also developed a considerable reputation for music and the performing arts. These subject areas play their part in bringing width and balance to the curriculum. A high standard in presentation of work, behaviour and manners is regarded as essential.

The school has strong links with the village community and St Mary's Church, where school services and concerts are held. Moral education is of great importance and at Plumtree, children are encouraged to develop a sense of responsibility and learn to play a worthwhile role in the life of their community.

Children may begin our nursery class at three years old, moving into the infant department at 'rising five'. The junior department caters for children of seven to eleven years old.

Each child's progress and development is monitored through a series of internal tests and continual assessment. Parents receive a termly report. Each term parents are given the opportunity to discuss the progress of their child and to examine the work with the teachers concerned. Individual interviews with teaching staff are always available by appointment.

Plumtree offers a real alternative to parents seeking a rounded, caring and traditional education for their children.

Parents wishing to know more should contact the Head Teacher to receive a prospectus and to arrange a visit to see the school at work.

Polwhele House School

Truro Cornwall TR4 9AE.
Tel: (01872) 73011

Heads: **Richard and Rosemary White**, BA, CertEd

Age Range. 3–13+
Number in School. Day 158; Boarding 12
Fees per term. Day £220–£1,980. Weekly Boarding £3,210–£3,578.

Polwhele House is a beautiful and historic listed building, set in 30 acres of garden, playing fields, park and woodland. The school enjoys a glorious and secure environment only 1¼ miles from the Cathedral.

Uninterrupted education is provided for boys and girls during those important early years from three to thirteen. There is flexible attendance for under-fives who are taught by qualified teachers in Nursery and Kindergarten. The Pre-Preparatory School has an established reputation for high levels of care and excellent teaching.

Although mainly a day-school, weekly boarding, day boarding, 'sleepovers' and after-school care are growing in popularity. The boarders live in the Main House in comfortable surroundings which include a TV lounge, en-suite facilities, quiet areas and garden. The well-being and happiness of each child is the top priority.

This flourishing family school has had a continual programme of development, building and refurbishment since 1976 when the Pre-Prep School was opened. In 1994 new quality accommodation was built and equipped for art and craft, design technology, sciences, languages and ICT. In 1992 an equestrian centre was provided for pupils and riding is professionally taught to a quarter of the school.

The school combines modern teaching methods with the best of traditional values. The social development of the child is carefully nurtured to help them to become confident, considerate and polite young people. Polwhele House values each child and a strong team of skilled and caring staff are able to devote a great deal of time to every pupil in small classes.

Drama flourishes with each child participating in at least one of eight productions a year. Music is an important part of the school life with all pupils singing, and the majority playing an instrument. There are Truro Cathedral Choristerships for boys and Polwhele House Music Scholarships for girls. All the usual team games are coached and there are regular outstanding successes in athletics and cross country running at school, county and national levels.

Polwhele House is a Christian, non-denominational school and assembly is considered to be an important part of the day. The school motto is 'Karenza Whelas Karenza', Cornish for 'Love Begets Love'. Boys and girls share the same opportunities and responsibilities in all areas of school life.

The school has a fine record of academic achievement. There is a wide variety of sporting and extra-curricular activities to bring out the best in every child. Pupils are prepared for a broad range of schools, and win numerous scholarships, bursaries and exhibitions to Senior Independent Schools every year.

Mr and Mrs White, founders of the school, take great pleasure in meeting prospective parents and showing them around personally. Polwhele House is not just a school, more a way of life.

Portland Place School

56-58 Portland Place London W1N 3DG
Tel: 020 7307 8700
Fax: 020 7436 2676
e-mail: admin@portland-place.co.uk
website: http://www.portland-place.co.uk

Headmaster: **Richard Walker,** BSc, CChem, MRSC, PGCE, FRSA

Age range. 11 to 18
Numer of day pupils. Boys 110; Girls 90
Fees per term. £2,450

Housed in two magnificent Grade II* listed James Adams houses in central London, Portland Place School is a co-educational, independent secondary school. It opened in 1996, and is also an additional member of SHMIS. Classes are small and all teachers are not only specialists in their subjects, but are chosen for their ability to enthuse and draw out the best in all students at all levels.

The first of its kind to be opened in London's West End for over a century, Portland Place School combines excellent computer and science technology with an emphasis on traditional teaching. Portland Place aims to create an environment in which the quality of life of the school and pastoral care of the pupils are given as much priority as academic results.

The school is ideally located right in the centre of the capital. Less than five minutes walk from Regents Park (where all the outdoor sporting activities take place) and ten minutes walk from Oxford Circus. The buildings have been refurbished to an exceptionally high standard. Classrooms are supplemented by specialist rooms for drama, photography, computing, physics, chemistry and biology. Each room is cabled for the Windows NT computer network and all pupils have their own email address to send and receive messages from teachers and each other as well as being able to communicate with friends and families across the world.

The internet is permanently on line in the school's library and is proving a valuable tool for gathering information from overseas for geography, history and modern language coursework. Pupils have access to a number of on-line encyclopaedias (eg Britannica and Encarta).

The curriculum at Portland Place is developed from the English National Curriculum and offers a flexibility that puts the pupil first. Homework is supervised until 5 pm for those who want or require it and each pupil has a homework diary that details the homework programme for each week.

Each child takes part in a comprehensive programme of physical education. Full advantage is taken of its central London location and excellent local facilities available. The outdoor programme takes place in neighbouring Regents Park and includes hockey, football, rugby, tennis and cross country. Indoor sports include basketball and fencing. Pupils represent the school in numerous matches against other London schools and in national tournaments.

Class music is a compulsory part of the curriculum in years 7, 8 and 9 and all pupils are encouraged, if they do not already play one, to take up a musical instrument and take advantage of the team of visiting instrumental teachers.

Entry to the school (usually at 11+, 13+ and Sixth Form) is by examination in English and Mathematics and interview.

Prenton Preparatory School

Mount Pleasant Oxton Wirral Cheshire CH43 5SY.
Tel: 0151-652 3182
Fax: 0151-653 7428
e-mail: nmaloe@prentonprep.u-net.com

Headteacher: **Mrs N M Aloé**

Age Range. 2½–11
Number in School. Day: Boys 64, Girls 78
Fees per term. £965 Infants; £1,010 Juniors
Founded in 1935.

Prenton Preparatory School is a co-educational day school for children aged 2½–11 years, situated about a mile from Junction 3 of the M53. The building is a large Victorian house which has been carefully converted into the uses of a school. There is a large playground and gardens.

The children benefit from small classes and individual attention in a disciplined environment which enable them to realise their full potential.

The school offers a wide range of academic subjects with emphasis on the three main National Curriculum core subjects: English, Mathematics and Science. A brand new ICT/Science block was opened in March 1998. French is taught from an early age.

Children are prepared for entrance examinations to county, independent and grant-maintained grammar schools, gaining above average pass rates.

Child care facilities are available from 8 am to 6 pm. Clubs are provided at lunchtime and after school. They include football, cricket, computers and technology, judo, swimming, gymnastics, ballet, netball, drama, music group, handchimes and musical instruments.

Presentation College

63 Bath Road Reading Berkshire RG30 2BB.
Tel: (0118) 9572861/9581709
Fax: (0118) 9572220

Headmaster: **Mr Frank Loveder,** MA

Age Range. 4½–18
Number in School. 380 Day boys
Fees per term. £975–£1,272

Presentation College is a small (380 pupils) selective Catholic Independent Boys' School, situated in spacious grounds about a mile from the centre of Reading. The school was founded by the Presentation Brothers in 1931. Although the school has a Catholic Foundation, it is sympatetic to other Faiths.

The school has always been Independent, but for many years it acted as the Catholic Grammar School in Reading. This tradition of academic excellence continues; tuition is focussed on enabling all pupils to maximise their achievement. A small number of pupils go to Oxford or Cambridge. Selection is by means of interview and assessment, or Common Entrance Examination. Selection is not solely based on rigid academic criteria; pupils who are prepared to work hard achieve good examination results.

There is a separate preparatory department of about 100 boys.

Class sizes are small; at Key Stage 2 and 3, there are currently 22 pupils or fewer in each class; at Key Stage 4, numbers in subject sets drop to between 8–12. A level classes are smaller still.

The College also specialises in helping able but dyslexic pupils to overcome this barrier to learning.

The ethos of the school is one of Christian caring, with a family atmosphere based on respect for all members of the community.

The College seeks to develop the whole person, and addresses this through a wide range of sporting and extra-curricular activities. The success of the school in local and national competitions, be they chess, badminton, football or Art, reflects the enthusiasm and hard work of both staff and pupils. There are also a variety of non-competitive activities, ranging from the sailing club and skiing club, through CCF and Duke of Edinburgh Award Scheme to the Exploring Club (the 2003 expedition, to trek to Everest Base Camp, is currently being planned). Music and drama opportunities are being constantly developed. Throughout, there is emphasis on working together, and the development of teamwork and leadership skills.

Charitable status. Presentation College, Reading is a Registered Charity, number 233466. It is devoted to the advancement of the educational and social support and development of young people.

Princethorpe College

Princethorpe Rugby Warwickshire CV23 9PX

See SHMIS section, Part III of this Book

Putney Park School

Woodborough Road London SW15 6PY.
Tel: 020 8788 8316
Fax: 020 8780 2376
e-mail: office@putneypark.london.sch.uk
website: www.putneypark.london.sch.uk

Headmistress: **Mrs Jane Irving**, BEd (Hons)

Age Range. Girls 4–16, Boys 4–11
Number in School. Day: Boys 100, Girls 220
Fees per term. Upper School £2,220; Lower School £1,920
Extras. Individual music lessons, ballet, EFL, lunches, school bus.

Putney Park School, established in 1953, is situated in a quiet road off the main Upper Richmond road, within three minutes walk of the bus stop. It is easily accessible from all parts of Putney, Roehampton, East Sheen, Barnes and Wimbledon Common.

Classrooms are bright and well-equipped. Specialist rooms include science laboratories, a computer room, a library, a home economics room, pottery, art and music rooms and a gymnasium. There are pleasant gardens and playgrounds.

The aim of the School is to provide a sound education in a happy atmosphere. The teachers are chosen for their qualifications, experience and understanding of the needs of their pupils.

Pupils are given the maximum individual attention and encouragement to reach the highest standard of which they are capable. The development of character is carefully watched, good manners and initiative encouraged.

The organisation of the curriculum has enabled the School to realise the demands of the National Curriculum. Subjects taught include, at the appropriate stage, English, Mathematics, RE, History, Geography, Biology, Chemistry, Physics, French (from Reception), German, Spanish, Music, Technology, Information and Communication Technology, Art, Home Economics and Physical Education.

Children are accepted from four years old into Reception. The school prepares boys for entry to other schools including Colet Court and King's College, Wimbledon at 7+ and 8+. Girls are prepared for entry to other schools, particularly Putney High, Bute House and Wimbledon High at 7+ and 11+. Boys entering the school have the opportunity to remain at Putney Park until they are eleven. From Year 7 the school is for girls only.

The Upper School includes Year 5 to Year 11. There is an examination for entry to Year 7. A programme of general education is followed from Year 5 to Year 9. Options are chosen in Year 9. In Years 10 and 11 girls are prepared for the General Certificate of Secondary Education in eight or nine subjects, which must include English, Mathematics and Science. Our careers programme reflects the importance we attach to the development of the individual skills and talents of all pupils. At the end of Year 11 all pupils are welcomed into a wide range of schools and colleges including Putney High, Wimbledon High, Surbiton High and Esher College.

Physical activities include swimming, tennis, netball, badminton, squash, volleyball, rounders, athletics, football, cricket, touch rugby and rowing. Games are played at the Bank of England Sports Ground, Roehampton. Both inter-school and inter-house matches take place frequently. Visits to places of interest in and around London are organised every term. School journeys to a foreign country are arranged each year. Advantage is taken of nearby Richmond Park and Wimbledon Common for scientific and geographical fieldwork. Concerts, plays and musicals are regularly performed.

The Read School

Drax Near Selby North Yorkshire YO8 8NL.
Tel: (01757) 618248
Fax: (01757) 617432
e-mail: richard.hadfield@virgin.net
website: www.readdrax.demon.co.uk

The Headmaster is an additional member of The Society of Headmasters and Headmistresses of Independent Schools (SHMIS).

Headmaster: **R A Hadfield**, BA, CertEd

Age Range. Co-educational 3–18 (Boarding 8–18)
Number in School. Total 265. Day: 190, Boarding 75. Boys 165; Girls 100.
Fees per term. Boarders £3,060–£3,755, Day £1,225–£1,735.

The School is pleasantly situated in the rural village of Drax, and is very convenient for main rail (Doncaster, York) and road access (M62, M18, A1). Manchester is the nearest international airport (1½ hours distant). It is a small school where the children are well known to each other and to the staff.

The School has been a focal point for the education of boys in the Selby-Goole area for 330 years, first as Drax Grammar School, and (since 1967) as The Read School. The school is now co-educational, offering a wide range of academic studies at GCSE and 'A' level, together with a full programme of Sports, Drama, Music, CCF and recreational activity. High standards are expected in all aspects of endeavour, and in behaviour and manners.

In addition to the refurbished Edwardian buildings, there have been steady developments in the facilities and accommodation throughout the 1980s and 1990s. These include the fine Moloney Hall, Senior boarding block, Ramsker classrooms, Sports Hall and in 1997 the Prep Department (Years 4, 5 and 6) in addition to internal developments, especially in the provision of IT. The Pre-Prep Department and the girls' boarding accommodation are situated on their own site in the village at Adamson House.

An offer of a place in the school is made after interview (and verbal reasoning and mathematics tests for admission to the Senior School) and satisfactory report from the pupil's current school. Fees are moderate and there is a 10% discount for younger siblings.

Charitable status. The Read School is a Registered Charity, number 529675. It exists to provide a first class education for girls and boys.

Reddiford School

38 Cecil Park Pinner Middlesex HA5 5HH.

(See IAPS section, Part V of this Book)

Red House School

36 The Green Norton Stockton on Tees Cleveland TS20 1DX
Tel: (01642) 553370
Fax: (01642) 361031

Chairman of Governors: Mrs Sally Harris

Headmaster: **C M J Allen**, MA, MSc

Deputy Head (*Junior School*): Mrs Sandra Gray, CertEd

Numbers. Approx 201 girls and 245 boys

Fees. Junior £1,095; Prep £1,290; Senior £1,395. Lunches £120 (Junior), £130 (Prep & Senior).

Red House School, founded in 1929, is a co-educational day school of about 440 children between the ages of 3+ and 16. The School is located round the attractive Green of the village of Norton on the edge of the Teesside conurbation.

The school provides a high quality inclusive education within a civilised environment at modest cost.

Entry is by assessment to confirm that a curriculum leading to 10 GCSEs is appropriate.

The Junior School occupies separate accommodation in extensive grounds and achieves very high standards with children up to the age of 8 in a positive and supportive family environment.

Children then continue their education on the senior site which includes a spacious sports hall and new science block. The School prides itself that every student achieves his or her potential. Academic results are excellent, sports team are very successful, and children have a positive and responsible attitude to school.

The staff are well qualified and offer a full range of GCSE subjects to all students with teaching targeted at Grade C and above.

The School Council is composed entirely of parents elected at the AGM.

Charitable status. Red House School Limited is a Registered Charity, number 527377. It exists to provide education for children.

Riverston School

63–69 Eltham Road Lee Green London SE12 8UF.
Tel: 020 8318 4327
Fax: 020 8297 0514
e-mail: info@riverston.greenwich.sch.uk
website: www.riverston.greenwich.sch.uk

Principal: **D M Lewis**, MBA(Ed), DMS, FRSA

Age Range. 1–16

Number in School. Day: Boys 210, Girls 175

Fees per term. £1,363–£1,876

Riverston School is a privately owned, co-educational day school in south-east London. Established in 1926, the school provides a traditional family orientated education up to and including GCSE. The Junior Department is widely acknowledged as being one of the most successful in the area and each year assists pupils to win places at some of the country's leading secondary schools. A growing number of junior pupils progress into the senior department where class sizes average 16. This department is particularly suited to those pupils who will benefit from considerable personal attention. To enable all pupils to achieve their full potential.

Riverston has the use of its own european education centre, Chateau de la Baudonniere, in southern Normandy, France and each year regular visits are available to different year groups to enhance their French language skills whilst appreciating a different culture.

Riverston is a lively, friendly and cheerful school with a traditional educational philosophy and ideals as strong today as when they were first conceived. The school motto 'Ut Prosim' – That I May Be Of Service – is a value cherished by all pupils.

Rodney School

Kirklington Newark Nottinghamshire NG22 8NB.
Tel/Fax: (01636) 813281
e-mail: rodney@proweb.co.uk
website: http://www.rodney-school.co.uk

Principal: **G R T Howe**

Age Range. 7–18

Number in School. Boarders: Boys 12, Girls 17, Day pupils 36

Fees. Boarders £3,167 per term, Senior Day pupils £1,872 per term, Junior Day pupils £1,578 per term. *Compulsory extras:* Books, stationery.

This school is ideal for straightforward children who will sharpen their response to the challenges of top quality teaching, the sport and activities available, while enjoying membership of a friendly, caring and disciplined family.

Our current academic examination record places us among the highest achieving ISA schools in the Midlands.

The strong tradition for Dance and Drama has led to the establishment of a special course in the Performing Arts. Public performances confirm recent professional opinion that standards here are 'outstanding' and not usually found outside London.

Thus we expect the best from our pupils. It is important to us that they generate the confidence to take a very full role in this hard-working and contributing community. This includes day pupils, who are welcome to participate in all activities, as well as our valued Sixth Form who experience leadership as prefects and gain from enthusiastic, small group instruction.

A Sports Hall of County Standard gives opportunity for a wide range of indoor games as well as providing a facility for social functions. Standing in 30 acres of parkland on the edge of Sherwood Forest the school has ample opportunities for outdoor activities. It is ideally located near the A1 and M1. The journey by train from Newark to London King's Cross is 1 hour 20 minutes.

Rookwood School

Weyhill Road Andover Hants SP10 3AL.
Tel: (01264) 325900
Fax: (01264) 325909
e-mail: office@rookwood.hants.sch.uk
website: www.rookwood.hants.sch.uk

Headmistress: **Mrs M P Langley**, BSc (Hons)

Age Range. Girls: Day 3–16, Boarders 7–16.
Boys: 3–11 Day only.

Fees. Boarding £3,400–£4,000 per term. Day £250–£2,250 per term. (Pro rata for part time Nursery children).

Rookwood School, standing in 8 acres of grounds, is easily accessible by road or rail (Waterloo 1¼ hours). It is non-denominational, but emphasis is placed on traditional Christian values of integrity and consideration for others.

The school is small with a very favourable pupil/teacher ratio so a close personal interest is taken in every child. Boarders may be on a full or weekly basis.

The aim is for each child to fulfil his/her potential, and every effort is made to accommodate the individual requirements of pupils of varying ability: thus a girl may take up to 10 subjects in the GCSE examinations. The school has close links with local sixth form colleges and has enabled girls to transfer to the sixth forms of well known senior independent schools and boys' senior schools. Younger children may be prepared for Common Entrance if this is desired. Details of Rookwood's own scholarships may be obtained from the Headmistress.

The school offers its own laboratories, ICT, home economics, music and art rooms, gymnasium, large, heated, outdoor swimming pool, tennis and netball courts, and playing field for hockey, football, rugby, cricket, rounders and athletics.

Optional extra subjects include riding, ballet and instrumental teaching and entry for Music and Speech and Drama examinations.

There is a wide range of extra curricular activities on offer for junior boys and girls and the senior girls, eg Duke of Edinburgh Award Scheme, Brownies and Guides offsite, and rugby, football, gymnastics, chess and computer clubs in school, plus junior and senior choirs.

Admission by the school's own examination and/or school reports and interview.

Charitable status. Rookwood School is a Registered Charity, number 307322A31-A. It exists to provide education for children.

Roselyon School

Par Cornwall PL24 2HZ.
Tel: (01726) 812110
e-mail: office@roselyonsch.fsnet.co.uk

Headmaster: **Mr Stuart Bradley**, BEd (Oxon)

Age Range. 2½–11
Number in School. Day: Boys 34, Girls 32
Fees per term. £269–£1,247

Roselyon School, formerly the Victorian Manor House in the village of Par, near St Austell, stands in 5 acres of beautiful woodland. A new multi purpose gymnasium and hall recently built in the centre of the campus has added greatly to the school's facilities. Roselyon is fully co-educational, taking pupils in the full time Nursery from 2½ and joining the Main School from 5–11.

The school is proud of its academic strengths and excellent examination results to local senior independent schools. It offers a variety of sports, music and drama and has an extensive range of extra curricular activities.

Roselyon is a small, friendly school where a family atmosphere is maintained by the team of caring staff.

Charitable status. Roselyon School is a Registered Charity, number 306583. It exists to provide education.

Rosemead Preparatory School

70 Thurlow Park Road Dulwich London SE21 8HZ.
Tel: 020 8670 5865
Fax: 020 8761 9159

Headteacher: **Mrs R L Lait**, BA, MBA(Ed), CertEd

Age Range. 3–11
Number in School. Day: Boys 130, Girls 130
Fees per term. £1,320–£1,520 (September 2000).
Religious denomination. All denominations welcome.

Rosemead is a thriving school with a warm, friendly atmosphere. Boys and girls aged 3–11 are prepared for a wide range of secondary schools. The school has a strong record of success and the programme of activities is full and varied.

This is a caring school where the needs of individuals are important.

The School follows the National Curriculum and has a traditional approach to Maths and English teaching. Other subjects include Science, History, Geography, ICT, DT, Art, Music and PE. French is taught throughout the school.

There is a wide range of extra-curricular activity. Music and Ballet are particular strengths. Tuition is available for most instruments and there are good opportunities for individuals, various music groups and the orchestra to perform.

Classes make frequent visits to places of interest and various residential trips are arranged.

Entry to the school is at age 3 to the popular Nursery class, where part and full time places are available, or at age 4 to the Reception classes.

Charitable status. Rosemead Preparatory School (The Thurlow Educational Trust) is a Registered Charity, number 1186165. It exists to provide a high standard of education in a happy, caring environment.

The Royal School

65 Rosslyn Hill Hampstead London NW3 5UD
Tel: 020 7794 7707/8
Fax: 020 7431 6741

Principal: **Mrs C A Sibson,** MA (Oxon)

Age range. 4–18. Boarders from 11, but in exceptional circumstances girls may be considered from 7 years of age.

Number in School. Day: 158, Boarding: 40

Fees per year. Day: £4,926–£5,799; Weekly Boarding: £7,659–£9,585; Boarding: £9,279–£11,529.

Religious affiliation. Anglican (other religions welcome).

Type. Girls Independent Boarding and Day School.

Entry requirements. Entry to both the Senior and Junior departments is by interview and previous school reports. An entrance test is taken when applicable. Scholarships are available at 7+, 11+ and for the Sixth Form. Bursaries are available for all ages.

The School is small, homely and happy with a staff dedicated to the academic and personal development of each child as an individual. It offers day, weekly and full boarding options including 'flexi-boarding' and 'after-day' care.

The School is situated in pleasant surroundings only 250m from Hampstead Tube Station and Hampstead Village Centre. It has comfortable modern boarding accommodation and spacious, light classrooms and uses excellent sports facilities. The School is close to London's major educational, cultural and recreational centres which are visited regularly. There is a large car park which facilitates the arrival and departure of pupils. An assembly is held most mornings.

Charitable status. The Royal School Hampstead is a Registered Charity, number 312286. It exists to provide a sound and broad-based education which prepares girls both to meet and cope with the challenges of the new century.

Ruckleigh School

17 Lode Lane Solihull West Midlands B91 2AB.
Tel: (0121-705) 2773
Fax: (0121-704) 4883

Principal: **D N Carr-Smith**, BSc, MIBiol
Headmistress: Mrs B M Forster

Age Range. Two and three quarters - eleven years of age.

Number in School. Day: Boys 103, Girls 99

Fees per term. £1,386–£1,587

Ruckleigh is an independent day school offering education to boys and girls between the ages of 4 and 11 with a Pre-School Department catering for children from the age of two and three-quarters.

Although a high standard of work is expected this is related to the individual child, and the school is able to provide opportunities to children with a wide range of academic ability. The bright child has every chance to develop his or her talents to the full, while the less bright is encouraged to achieve more than is at first thought possible.

Pupils are guided into habits of clear thinking, self-reliance and courtesy. Sound practical judgement, sensitivity towards the needs of others, powers of imagination, and a willingness at all times to "have a go" are the qualities which the school seeks to promote.

The comparatively small classes mean that every pupil is well known as an individual to those who teach, and sensible discipline can be continued with a friendly relationship between teacher and taught.

Rushmoor School

58–60 Shakespeare Road Bedford MK40 2DL.
Tel: (01234) 352031
Fax: (01234) 348395

Headmaster: **P J Owen**, MA (Cantab)

Age Range. 3–16

Number in School. Day Pupils 310

Day Fees per term. £865–£1,810

The School aims to provide a good and wide academic education, but not at the expense of all else. The School understands that children differ in their talents and abilities and it attaches equal importance to all the facets of an individual. Each child is an individual and it is understood that they must be treated as such for them to fulfil their potential and to be happy: The first essential!

A great emphasis is placed on personal attention and the development of the individual. Self-confidence, responsibility and an awareness of community are considered of prime importance. The School sets clear standards in discipline, self-discipline and work habits, based on the Christian principles of morality and behaviour.

Sport is taken seriously and teams are produced in a number of sports, at all ages, and a number of boys regularly achieve County selection or better.

There is a Special Needs Department with a teacher whose specific role is to help those with learning difficulties, especially Dyslexia, within the mainstream education.

Boys are prepared for a full range of GCSE subjects.

Teaching is in small classes and the school maintains a homely and happy atmosphere.

Charitable status. Rushmoor School is a Registered Charity, number 307530. It exists to provide education.

Sackville School

Tonbridge Road Hildenborough Kent TN11 9HN
Tel: (01732) 838888

Headteacher: **Mrs Michèle Sinclair**, MA, BA, CertEd

Age Range. 11–18

Number in School. 142

Fees per term. £1,915–£2,381

Sackville School is situated in Hildenborough, mid-way between Tonbridge and Sevenoaks. The school is set in 28 acres of magnificent parkland and the main building dates from the 1860's. The school has three modern laboratories, a dedicated Computer Room, an impressive Sports Hall, Art and Design Suites, as well as the usual range of specialist teaching rooms.

The philosophy of the school is based on the individual and their unique learning needs. By concentrating on excellence, and by treating every child as a wonderfully unique individual, the school ensures that each child has the opportunity to fulfil their true potential, and develop their gifts and talents at all levels. Students achieve excellent

GCSE results and the Sixth Form offers a wide range of 'A' Level and GCSE packages.

Sackville students are cheerful, confident children who work hard and enjoy aiming high and achieving their very best – they are expected to take a full part in the life of the school. The Head and staff encourage a warm, friendly working atmosphere, whilst promoting pride in achievement. Every student is valued, and their talents recognised, by the Head and staff.

The full range of academic, cultural and sporting activities are offered and all students are encouraged to try all activities. All major team games, and minor sports, are played and Sackville students have represented their County as well as National Squads. The school has a lively Music Department and over three quarters of the students are engaged in music making. The Creative Arts are particularly well represented: the school has a very well known Steel Band which is in great demand in the locality; Art is exceptionally strong and Drama has a growing reputation for excellence. The Activities programme is an integral part of the school day and includes Orchestra, Choir, Steel Band, Duke of Edinburgh Award, Drama, Golf, Film Unit, Table Tennis, Boules, Fishing, Archery, Self Defence, Community Service, Shooting, School Magazine, Ceramics, Computing, Photography, Camp Craft and many other activities.

The school fosters the qualities of honour, care for others, thoughtfulness and tolerance. The Head is always delighted to show parents, and their sons and daughters around, and to discuss the educational opportunities available at Sackville.

Sacred Heart Convent School

Swaffham Norfolk PE37 7QW
Tel: (01760) 721330/724577
Fax: (01760) 725557
e-mail: info@sacredheart.norfolk.sch.uk
website: www.sacredheart.norfolk.sch.uk

***Headteacher:* Sister Francis Ridler,** FDC, BEd

Age range. Girls 3 to 16; Boys 3 to 11.

Numbers in school. Girls: 198 Day. 27 Boarders. Boys: 31 Day.

Staff. 15 Full Time, 16 Part Time, 8 Welfare Assistants, 7 Visiting.

Religious Affiliation. Roman Catholic (other denominations welcome).

Entry requirements. Assessments, School Report and Interview.

Assistance with fees. Academic, Music, Art, Sport, All rounder (Boarder) Scholarships for Year 7 (11+). Some bursaries available.

Fees per term. Boarders: Termly £3,450, Weekly £2,475; Day: £1,175 (Juniors); £1,615 (Seniors).

The Convent School was founded by the Daughters of Divine Charity in 1914. The Sisters and lay staff work together to provide a safe and caring environment where Christian values are upheld.

Principally a day school, boys transfer at eleven to prep school, local or boarding school. Girls continue through to sixteen and are encouraged to study for eight to eleven GCSE's gaining consistently high A-C grades. At 16, the girls have gained the confidence and self-possession which makes them much sought after by all Sixth Form Centres, Technical Colleges and other Independent Schools. There are a limited number of boarding places for girls aged 8 to 16 as well as the opportunity for flexi-boarding.

All pupils are encouraged to develop their gifts in Music, Drama, Art and Sport, and the School has an outstanding record of success in all these areas. The School has been awarded a 'Sportsmark' for commitment to Sports Education.

A very active and highly supportive Parents' Association, a large and loyal past pupils and parents network, together with a dedicated and highly qualified Staff provide the energy and enthusiasm which characterises the school community.

Sacred Heart Preparatory School

Winford Road Chew Magna Bristol BS40 8QY
Tel: 01275 332470
Fax: 01275 332039

***Head:* Mrs B Huntley**

Sacred Heart is a school where *every* child is encouraged to fulfil their potential whether this is academic, creative or sporting.

Sacred Heart School's rural location provides a quiet, peaceful and secure environment for learning and gives the school space for sports facilities that many larger schools would be pleased to have - games and athletics pitch, netball/tennis courts, outdoor swimming pool, large, well-equipped gymnasium and spacious playgrounds.

Sacred Heart offers a Christian education, in classes of not more than 18 children, based on traditional values, which were noted as clearly evident in the behaviour of pupils by a recent school inspection. The inspectors' report also commented that pupils with special educational needs receive appropriate support and make good progress. The report noted that the wide range of extra-curricular activities makes a very positive contribution to all pupils' learning and personal development. These activities include art, chess, Internet Club, cricket, rugby, football, athletics, gymnastics, dance, judo and Watch Club.

A significant number of pupils enter the annual Mid Somerset Festival of Speech and Drama in Bath and in recent years have been extremely successful, winning individual and group classes. Pupils are also able to learn to play a musical instrument including recorder, trumpet, piano and violin. There are annual performances of a Nativity Play at Christmas and a school play during the summer term in which all junior school pupils take part. An annual Sports Day, gymnastics award scheme, Swimming Gala, and matches against other schools allow children to develop their sporting talents.

The school recognises that education is a partnership. Progress reports and newsletters keep parents up-to-date while formal meetings between parents and teachers which take place each term allow discussion of an individual child's progress.

Pupils from Sacred Heart Preparatory School move on to local senior state schools and independent schools both in Bristol and further afield, including Wells Cathedral School, Millfield and Prior Park School, Bath.

Prizegiving evening at the end of the summer term is an opportunity for all parents, children and staff to celebrate the successes of the year.

The only way to really appreciate what Sacred Heart has to offer is to visit us, as the best ambassadors for our schools are the pupils. They are well-educated, happy, confident and caring children, many of whom win bursaries and scholarships to independent senior schools.

St Anne's Preparatory School

154 New London Road Chelmsford Essex CM2 0AW
Tel: (01245) 353488

Headmistress: **Mrs Y Heaton**

Number of children. 150, aged 3+ to 11+. Co-educational Day school

Fees. £1,200–£1,300

Established in 1925, the School is situated in a town house in the centre of Chelmsford. The Nursery play area, playground and lawns provide ample space for recreation and Pre-Prep. Games: the Prep Department benefit from the use of the excellent facilities at the nearby Essex County Cricket Club.

The School offers a broad curriculum, designed to meet the particular requirements of young children, providing them with the means to develop their academic, creative, technical, social and physical skills. Excellent nursery and after-care facilities for all age groups are also offered.

Specialist staff teach in many subject disciplines and there are a wide variety of extra curricular activities. From the early years pupils participate in many visits of education interest and additionally, in the Prep Department, children enjoy activity-based holidays in Norfolk and a study visit to France.

Children are taught in small classes and benefit from a well-balanced education, incorporating the best of traditional and modern teaching methods.

Provision is made for the gifted as well as those pupils less educationally able.

All pupils are involved in KS1 and KS2 examinations, achieving excellent results and the School has proven success in external examinations, many children attaining places at the prestigious Grammar and Independent schools in the county.

The School is rightly recognised for its friendly and supportive ethos. The PTA is a thriving organisation and parents are particularly supportive of all aspects of school life. Visitors are always welcome.

St Catherine's Preparatory School

Hollins Lane Marple Bridge Stockport Cheshire SK6 5BB
Tel: 0161-449 8800
Fax: 0161-449 8181

Headmistress: **Mrs M A Sidwell**, CertEd

Age Range. 3–11 years
Numbers in School. 72 Boys; 84 Girls
Fees per term. On application.

St Catherine's is a small day school preparing children thoroughly but imaginatively for entry to selective independent senior schools in the Greater Manchester area.

The school combines the best of traditional teaching with the fostering of individual talent and development of independent thought. St Catherine's has a broadly based Primary Curriculum remaining constantly aware of National Curriculum guidelines whilst concentrating on the requirements of the Senior Schools in the area.

The school has a Catholic foundation using an RE scheme appropriate for all faiths. A full range of Primary games and PE are available for all pupils. Weekly swimming lessons are given from Reception (4+) upwards.

Instrumental music, speech, drama and ballet lessons are provided by peripatetic teachers. There is a wide range of extra curricular activities including computer club, chess, music ensembles and games practices.

The school is non selective at Kindergarten (3+), Reception (4+) and Year 1 (5+). Children seeking admission from Year 2 (6+) are assessed for potential rather than acquired skills.

Charitable status. St Catherine's is a Registered Charity, number 2000098. It exists to provide education for boys and girls.

St Catherine's School

Cross Deep Twickenham Middlesex TW1 4QJ.
Tel: 020 8891 2898

Headmistress: **Miss Diana P Wynter**, BA

Age Range. 3–16 years
Number in School. 324 Day Girls
Fees per term. Pre-Kindergarten £1,300 per term mornings only; Kindergarten and Transition £1,400; Prep I–Prep IV £1,450; Senior £1,700 (Forms IV and V £1,750).

Bursaries. Bursaries are awarded to girls in need on the basis of high standards of work and effort and their support for the school's aims.

St Catherine's School was founded in Twickenham in 1914 by the Congregation of the Sisters of Mercy as a Roman Catholic School for girls.

On 1st September 1991 the School became an Educational Charity managed by Trustees and Governors. The new Trustees have a strong commitment to all that the Sisters of Mercy have invested in the School since its foundation.

Aims. St Catherine's School provides a sound Christian education. Concern for the pupil is uppermost in the school's aims. The sharing of Christian values by students and staff alike creates a caring community. The School promotes high academic standards and attaches great importance to social and moral development.

A high teacher/pupil ratio and small classes ensure that every student has the opportunity of reaching her full potential.

Close co-operation between School and parents is encouraged.

Religious practice. St Catherine's maintains its Catholic foundation but has always welcomed children of other denominations.

All pupils attend Religious Education classes throughout the School and daily assemblies are held for the whole school and in smaller groups.

Situation. St Catherine's is pleasantly situated in a residential area of Twickenham near the River Thames. The school is well served by public transport, only eight minutes walk from the British Rail stations of Twickenham and Strawberry Hill, and on a number of bus routes.

Buildings. The Preparatory and Senior Departments are on one site. A purpose built Prep Classroom Wing was opened in 1992.

The buildings include a large multi-purpose hall and a small Assembly Hall, classrooms, the Library and Computer Centre, spacious Art and Craft Rooms, with a Pottery and Photography Room and Home Economics Department. The Music Centre has class and individual practice rooms. There are fully equipped laboratories for Physics, Chemistry and Biology. There is a Drama Studio.

The heated indoor swimming pool is used throughout the year.

The school playing fields include a hockey pitch and hard tennis courts and netball courts.

Entrance. Prior to entry into the Preparatory Department, all applicants take an assessment test. Entry to the Senior Department is by a competitive Entrance Examination, which is held in January each year for entrance in the following September.

Senior Department Curriculum. Our aim is to provide an education permeated with the Christian spirit and achieved through a balanced curriculum of Arts, Sciences, Languages, Practical and Artistic Skills.

Some subjects are taught in form groups but there is setting in Mathematics, Modern Languages and Science. Classes are usually small.

For the first three years all girls follow the same foundation course. This includes Religious Studies, English, History, Geography, French, Mathematics, Science, Drama, Music, Art and Craft and Physical Education. German is introduced in the first year.

Practical experience in the use of computers is provided throughout the school.

In the fourth and fifth years part of every girl's timetable includes Religious Studies, English, English Literature, French, Mathematics, Physical Education, PSE and GCSE Dual Certificate Co-ordinated Science. Girls make three further choices from History, Geography, German, Food and Nutrition, Music, Art and Design, Classical Studies.

Most pupils take ten subjects in the GCSE examination.

Extra Curricular Activities. Clubs and activities include Junior and Senior Choirs, Drama, Orchestra, Recreational Swimming, and a wide variety of sport, netball, hockey, rounders, tennis, badminton and self defence. Many girls learn one or more musical instruments: piano, violin, cello, clarinet, flute, guitar and percussion.

Preparatory Department Curriculum. The curriculum takes account of the National Curriculum, it prepares the children for entry into the Senior School and includes the full range of normal Preparatory School subjects.

The Nursery class gradually introduces the child to school life.

From Kindergarten I stage there is a strong emphasis on the basic subjects, especially Reading and Numberwork. Music, Swimming, PE and French are taught by specialist teachers. Swimming instruction begins at age 3 years and all pupils learn to play the Recorder.

Staff co-ordinators of Art and Handicrafts, Language Development, Science, Mathematics and Computer Skills, work together to ensure continuity across the curriculum.

The atmosphere of the school is friendly and purposeful and prospective parents are warmly welcome to visit St Catherine's. Please telephone the Headmistress's Secretary for further information.

Charitable status. The St Catherine's Education Trust is a Registered Charity. It aims to provide for children seeking education in a Christian environment. The Trust endeavours to meet the need of families who particularly seek a small caring school and is sympathetic to children of those families who fall into difficulty.

St Christopher's School

71 Wembley Park Drive Wembley Park Middlesex HA9 8HE.
Tel: 020 8902 5069
Fax: 020 8903 5939

Headmistress: **Mrs S M Morley**, DipEd

Age Range. 4½–11
Number in School. Boys 62, Girls 56
Fees per term. From £1,300–£1,370

St Christopher's School

George Hill Old Catton Norwich Norfolk NR6 7DE.
Tel: (01603) 425179

Principal: F Reynolds, CertEd

Head of School: **Claire Cunningham**, BEd (Hons), Montessori Diploma

Age Range. 2½–9+
Number in School. Day: Boys 70, Girls 50
Fees per term. £172–£1,010. *Compulsory extras:* Lunches, Swimming for older children.

St Christopher's is an independent co-educational day school for children between the ages of 2½ and 9+ years. We welcome reflective parents who genuinely require for their children a whole education which responds to each child's individual needs and potential.

The school enjoys a mature and traditional setting. The school is based in a lovely Victorian house, and the older children use the Stable Block. The beautiful gardens include a variety of adventure playgrounds for different age groups. The school playing field is nearby.

There is a pre-school department for children aged 2½ to 5 years (also toddler groups from 1¼ years) which incorporates some Montessori ideas, and provides a progressive education during the pre-school years.

St Christopher's School

6 Downs Road Epsom Surrey KT18 5HE.
Tel: (01372) 721807
Fax: (01372) 726717

Headteacher: **Mrs M Evans**

Age Range. 3–7
Number in School. 160
Fees per term. £1,430 wholeday (including lunch), £750 halfday

St Christopher's School (founded in 1938) is a co-educational nursery and pre-preparatory school for children from 3–7 years.

Set in a quiet residential area a short distance from the centre of Epsom, famous for the annual Derby and horse racing traditions, it has attractive secure grounds with gardens and play areas.

St Christopher's main purpose is to support children and parents through the early years of education. We offer a carefully managed induction programme to school life and, subsequently, a broad and challenging education within a happy, caring and secure family environment. Above all we aim to offer your child the best possible start to their education.

The children are prepared to enter a wide range of Surrey schools and we maintain a very high pass rate in a variety of entrance tests.

There are a number of after school clubs and an After School Care Service is available Monday to Friday until 6 pm. For most weeks of the holidays there is Fun School from 8.30 am to 6 pm.

St Christopher's enjoys the support of an active parents association that organises a wide variety of social and fund raising events.

For further information and a prospectus please contact the school. Parents are welcome to visit the school by appointment with the Headteacher.

Charitable status. St Christopher's School Trust

(Epsom) Limited is a Registered Charity, number 312045. It aims to provide a Nursery and Pre-Preparatory education in Epsom and district.

St Colette's Preparatory School

Tenison Road Cambridge CB1 2DP
Tel: (01223) 353696
Fax: (01223) 517784

Headmistress: **Mrs A C Wilson**

Type. Nursery and Pre-Preparatory School.
Age range. 2½–7+ – boys and girls.
Number of pupils. 170
Fees per term. Nursery £1,195. Pre-Prep £1,370
Religious affiliation. Church of England
Curriculum. St Colette's has an outstanding record of success in preparing children for entrance examinations to Preparatory Schools (at seven-plus). Standards of academic achievement are high, while a caring and friendly ethos encourages children from a young age to develop a positive attitude to work and to show consideration for others. Music, drama and dance form an integral part of the curriculum, and children are encouraged to develop abilities and talents in these areas.

St David's College

Justin Hall Beckenham Road West Wickham Kent BR4 0QS.
Tel: 020 8777 5852
Fax: 020 8777 9549
e-mail: StDavids@dial.pipex.com

Principals:
Mrs F V Schove and Mrs A Wagstaff, BA Hons (London)

Head Teachers:
Mrs S Adams, BA, CertEd
Mrs M Brabin, CertEd

Deputy Head: Mrs A Simmonds, CertEd

Bursar: Mrs R Smith, MA Hons (Edinburgh), ACA

Age Range. 4–11
Number in School. Day: Boys 90, Girls 80
Fees per term. £1,063–£1,113. Reduction in fees for all siblings.

A full-time staff of nine teachers, all fully qualified, is supplemented by ten part-time specialist teachers. Entry is by interview and informal test/reports from previous school. Children are prepared for entrance to independent schools at age 11, as well as for the Kent Grammar Schools and for places at the London Boroughs of Bexley, Bromley and Sutton selective schools. Many scholarships and awards are gained every year. Speech and Drama, Ballet, Piano, Flute, Clarinet and Violin lessons are available. Sports include Athletics, Cricket, Cross-Country, Football, Netball, Rounders, Swimming, Tennis and Short Tennis. There is recorder tuition, a Chess Club, a French Club and a School Choir.

There is a separate purpose-built Infant School and an upper junior school, with extensive and beautiful grounds. The school is positioned close to bus routes and the mid-Kent and Hayes railway line, and is within easy reach of Bromley South and East Croydon Stations.

The Principals and Head Teacher are always pleased to show the school to visitors.

St David's School

23 Woodcote Valley Road Purley Surrey CR8 3AL.
Tel: 020 8660 0723

Headmistress: **Mrs Lindsay Nash**, BEd Hons, CertEd, PostGradDip

Age Range. 3+–11
Number in School. 167 Day, 84 Boys, 83 Girls
Fees per term. £645–£1,170. *Compulsory extras:* Lunch £105

St David's is a Church of England School that believes in training the children to be tolerant and supportive of one another.

The children study all the usual academic subjects including French, ICT, DT, Science and Latin. We have small classes which allow for much individual attention so that the children may develop to their full potential. The success of this ethos is demonstrated by the excellent results in the Entrance examinations to independent secondary schools, where scholarships are frequently gained, and selective entry to local Grammar Schools.

We are fortunate to own very adequate games facilities despite a suburban setting, and our children do well in competitive events. We also consider music, art and drama to be fundamental to the development of character and the leadership qualities we encourage.

Charitable status. St David's (Purley) Educational Trust is a Registered Charity, number 312613. It aims to provide a quality education for boys and girls from 3+ to 11 years old. Bursaries are awarded in cases of financial hardship.

St Dominic's Priory School

Station Road Stone Staffordshire ST15 8EN.
Tel: (01785) 814181

Headmistress: **Mrs J W Hildreth**, BA, MEd

Age range. 3–18 (Girls), 3–11 (Boys)
Numbers in School. Day: Boys 20, Girls 320
Fees per term. Nursery £1,098; Prep - Primary 6 £1,595 (including lunch); Seniors £1,685 (excluding lunch)

A Catholic School, where in a Christian caring atmosphere, the girls are known individually, and encouraged to work to the best of their ability, to find their own special gifts and self-worth, and to learn their responsibilities. All denominations welcomed.

Boys are accepted from ages 3 to 11.

Girls are accepted at 3 years for a continuous education through the Junior School to Public examinations in GCSE and 'A' level and University entrance. All subjects taught by highly qualified staff. Excellent examination results. Strong tradition of music, sport, art and drama. Indoor tennis courts to LTA standard. Duke of Edinburgh Award Scheme.

Charitable status. St Dominic's Priory School is a Registered Charity, number 271922.

St Edward's School

Cirencester Road Charlton Kings Cheltenham Glos GL53 8EY

(See SHMIS section, Part III of this Book)

St Gerard's School Trust

Ffriddoedd Road Bangor Gwynedd LL57 2EL.
Tel: (01248) 351656
Fax: (01248) 351204
e-mail: st_gerards@lineone.net

Headteacher: **Miss Anne Parkinson**, BA

Age Range. 3–11, 11–18
Number in School. Day: Boys 159, Girls 166
Fees per term. £905-£1,370

Founded in 1915 by the Congregation of the Sisters of Mercy, this Catholic, co-educational school has been under lay management since 1991. The school welcomes pupils of all denominations and traditions and has an excellent reputation locally. It has consistently attracted a high profile in national league tables also.

Class sizes in both junior and senior schools ensure close support and individual attention in order to enable all pupils to achieve their full academic potential, within an environment which promotes their development as well-rounded individuals with a keen social conscience.

The curriculum is comprehensive – pupils in the senior section usually achieve 9/10 good GCSE grades, going on to A level and to university.

Charitable status. St Gerard's School Trust is a Registered Charity, number 1001211. It exists to promote Catholic education in this area of Wales.

St Hilda's School

15 Imperial Avenue Westcliff on Sea Essex SS0 8NE.
Tel: (01702) 344542

Principal: Mrs V M Tunnicliffe

Head: **Mrs S O'Riordan**

Age Range. 2½–16+ Girls. 2½–6 Boys.
Number in School. Day Girls 200
Fees per term. £1,098 (pro rata for part time pupils)–£1,598 (excluding lunches). *Compulsory extras:* Text-Books

Re-opened in 1947, St Hilda's School is the only all-girls Independent School in the Southend area. Pupils are encouraged to fulfill their academic potential and develop a sense of responsibility both to the School and the community in which they live.

All pupils follow a range of subjects based on the National Curriculum with teaching methods appropriate to their age. Special provision is made for pupils with learning difficulties, especially dyslexia and these pupils follow a Multi-Sensory Learning course to improve their language and study skills.

The School emphasises traditional values and actively promotes a caring and supportive environment for the pupils. The success of this is shown by the excellent academic results in Government Key Stage Tests, local 11+ selection tests and particularly at GCSE. Although providing a rigorous academic programme, pupils are encouraged to develop individual skills in other fields including Sports, Drama and Art and Design.

Prospectus available on application to the secretary.

St Hilda's School

28 Douglas Road Harpenden Hertfordshire AL5 2ES.
Tel: (01582) 712307
Fax: (01582) 763892
e-mail: office@st-hildasschool.herts.sch.uk

Headmistress: **Mrs M Piachaud**, BA (Hons), CertEd

Age Range. 2½–11
Number in School. 180 approx
Fees per term. £1,525 (including lunches)

St Hilda's School is situated in a garden of 1¼ acres and has its own swimming pool, hard tennis/netball court and adjacent playing field. Recently a stage and a dedicated computer room have been added.

A broad, well-balanced curriculum covering the requirements of the National Curriculum prepares girls for the Common Entrance and other senior independent school entrance examinations. Girls also enter State secondary schools if desired. Latin and French are taught as well.

A prospectus is available on application to the School Secretary.

Re-accredited in 1996 by the Independent Schools Association.

St James Independent Junior Schools for Boys and Girls

Earsby Street Olympia London W14 8SH
Tel: 020 7348 1777
Fax: 020 7341 1790

Headmaster: **Mr Paul Moss**, CertEd

Age Range. 4½–10+
Number in School. Girls 132; Boys 124
Fees per term. 4½–6 £1,650; 6–10 £1,870

Girls and boys are educated separately, although there are occasional activities such as plays, concerts and outings where boys and girls work together as one group. There is a wide range of classroom subjects: all children learn the principles of philosophy and there is daily physical activity. Emphasis is given to language, art, music and drama, with Sanskrit being taught from the beginning.

The happiness of the children flows from a disciplined structure of work and play, bonded by love.

Most children go on to the Senior Schools at the age of 10½. Girls to Earsby Street, W14 and boys to Pope's Villa, Twickenham.

Charitable status. St James Independent Junior School is a Registered Charity, number 270156. It exists to provide education for boys and girls.

St James Independent School for Boys
(Senior School)

Pope's Villa 19 Cross Deep Twickenham Middlesex TW1 4QG
Tel: 020 8892 2002
Fax: 020 8892 4442
e-mail: st-james@boysschool.worldonline.co.uk
website: www.stjamesschools.co.uk

Headmaster: **Nicholas Debenham**, MA, FRSA

Age Range. 10–18

Number in School. Day Boys 228. Weekly Boarders 32

Fees per term. 10–12 £2,225; 13–18 £2,295

Founded in 1975, the school offers a distinctive education for boys of 10 to 18. It has its own Junior School at Earsby Street, Olympia, London W14 and receives half its pupils from there. Direct entry into the Senior School is at 10, 11 or 13, from both State and Independent schools, and at Sixth Form.

In addition to a wide range of classroom subjects, the school has certain original features: spiritual and moral values are introduced via philosophy and meditation; the teaching of philosophy emphasises the fundamental unity of all religious faiths; classical languages are restored to their traditional prominence; and boys are introduced to the best of art, music, literature and drama. Senior boys take a full range of GCSE's and in the Sixth Form our norm will be four AS levels taken at the end of the first year, with three of these being continued as A2 levels in the second year. There are also non-examination courses in Philosophy, Economics, Law and Modern History. Team games and enterprising outdoor pursuits are strongly encouraged (mountaineering, sailing, ACF, Duke of Edinburgh). Music, art and drama are exceptional.

Cultural visits: all boys visit Classical Greece at 12 and Renaissance Florence at 14/15 to give them an insight into the best of European culture.

Academic standards are high. In 2000, 91.2% of GCSE papers were passed at Grade A to C and the pass rate was 100% for the sixth consecutive year. A Level pass rate was 98% with almost all Sixth Formers going on to university.

The school aims to build sound character, nourish talent, and turn out warm-hearted, level-headed young men.

Charitable status. St James Independent School for Boys is a Registered Charity, number 270156. It exists to provide education for boys.

St James Independent School for Girls
(Senior School)

Earsby Street London W14 8SH
Tel: 020 7348 1777; Admissions: 020 7348 1748
Fax: 020 7348 1749
e-mail: enquiries@stjamesgirlsschool.freeserve.co.uk
website: www.stjamesschools.co.uk

Motto: *Speak the truth. Live generously. Aim for the best.*

Headmistress: **Mrs Laura Hyde**, CertEd

Age Range. 10–18

Number in School. Day: Girls 195

Fees per term. 10–13 £2,225; 13–18 £2,295

Admission. At 10 and 11 years of age and at Sixth Form, by the school's entrance examinations, interview and school reports.

The school aims to nourish the mind and heart of a young person by drawing on the very best of our culture in all artistic and academic pursuits; to encourage the expansion of all talents with a view to offering them for the benefit of others; to provide an intelligent balance of love and discipline leading to the development of self-disciplined based upon a wise understanding of moral and spiritual principles; and to develop a young woman who is happy, strong and steady in body, mind and emotion. Meditation is offered on a voluntary basis from the age of 10 years. Pupils engage in a vigorous and stimulating programme of study in a friendly and harmonious environment. There are two orchestras, an art club and a classics club. There are many school functions, both dramatic and musical, allowing opportunities to develop talents to the full. Academic standards are high. Girls are prepared in the full range of subjects for GCSE, AS, A levels and for University Entrance. We have entrants to all major universities including Oxbridge, to London Medical Schools and the professions. Vocational guidance is available to all pupils from 13-18 years of age.

Almost all the girls choose to stay with their class to enter the Sixth Form, where the girls are strongly encouraged to study four or five AS subjects and three or four subjects at A Level. The Sixth Form also includes a wide range of non-examination subjects. We intend to use the greater breadth of examination subjects at AS level as a means to combine a predominantly scientific group of subjects with at least one arts subject, and vice versa, both on educational grounds and to meet the growing interest of universities in such combinations. Some A Level subjects are taught in small groups combined with St James Independent School for Boys. Sixth Form study rooms and common rooms are provided. Unlike the rest of the school, Sixth Form girls are not required to wear uniform.

GCSE: English Language, English Literature, Greek, Latin, Sanskrit French, Mathematics, Additional Mathematics, Physics, Chemistry, Biology, History, Classical Civilisation, Geography, Art and Music. Some of these subjects are set against each other.

Non-examination subjects included in the weekly curriculum: Drama (occasional productions), Information Technology, Needlework (Forms I & II), Philosophy, Scripture, Music and Singing.

A Level subjects. English, Greek, Latin, Sanskrit, French, Mathematics, Further Mathematics, Physics, Chemistry, Biology, History, Classical Civilisation, Law, Economics, Art & Design and Music. General Studies and Religious Studies are offered at A/S level only.

Non-examination subjects included in the weekly curriculum: In addition to their academic subjects, all sixth form pupils engage in a more extensive curriculum of non-examination subjects in order to keep the field of study as wide as possible. These include Citizenship, Current Affairs, Government & Law, Dressmaking, Information Technology, Philosophy, Rhetoric/Literature Studies and Singing.

Sport: Athletics, Cross-country running, Gymnastics, Lacrosse, Netball, 'The St James Challengers' (Adventure Training Club) and The Duke of Edinburgh Award Scheme.

Charitable status. St James Independent School for Girls is a Registered Charity, number 270156. It exists to provide education for girls.

St James' School

22 Bargate Grimsby North East Lincolnshire DN34 4SY.
Tel: (01472) 503260
Fax: (01472) 503275
e-mail: enquiries@saintjamesschool.freeserve.co.uk
website: www.saintjamesschool.freeserve.co.uk

Acting Head Teacher: **S M Isaac,** BA, PGCE

Age Range. 3–18

Number in School. Boarders: Boys 27, Girls 19. Day: Boys 119, Girls 91

Fees per term. £935–£2,139, Termly Boarding £1,350, Weekly Boarding £1,185

St James' School, Grimsby is the Choir School of St James' Parish Church, Great Grimsby and a fully incorporated member of the Woodard Corporation. The School has a Nursery/Preparatory Department (ages 3–10) of approximately 114 pupils and a Senior Department (ages 11–18) of approximately 142 pupils.

The school is coeducational and there are about 46 boarders. Pupils are prepared for GCSE and Advanced Levels and the majority of the Sixth Form go on to University or Polytechnic. There is a generous pupil-teacher ratio and the School offers a wide variety of out of school activities and sports. Music plays an important part in school life and regular concerts and recitals are given.

There is a purpose built Sixth Form School to cater for the increasing demand.

Charitable status. St James' School is a Registered Charity, number 529765. It exists to provide education for boys and girls.

St John's Priory School

St John's Road Banbury Oxon OX16 8HX
Tel: (01295) 259607
Fax: (01295) 259607
e-mail: st.johns.priory@talk21.com

Headmistress: **Mrs J M Walker,** BEd (Hons)

St John's Priory School is an independent day school situated in Banbury. Girls and boys from a large radius surrounding the town attend the school. The school is housed in the original Priory, which, while retaining its historic charm, has been modernised to provide the space and facilities necessary for the increasing requirements of the present day curriculum. The school has a pleasant playground and garden area, netball posts and football nets.

Fees per term. £385-£1,350

Academic work. The Priory offers a broad curriculum incorporating both the requirements of the National Curriculum and the Independent Schools Common Entrance. The children are encouraged to learn in a hard-working and happy atmosphere.

The following subjects are studied: English, Mathematics, Science, History, Geography, French, Information Communications Technology, Physical Education, Music, Drama, Art, Design and Technology, Religious Education.

Children are class taught until Year 4 except for French, Music and Drama which are specialist taught from Reception. Trips are regularly taken to a variety of museums and places of interest in association with class work, and drama groups, visiting musicians and other interesting speakers visit the school. Specialist Science begins in Year 4. Years 5 and 6 are subject taught.

Year 6 pupils have the opportunity to use the French they have learnt, when they visit Normandy for four days in their last term. This trip is always a great success.

Latin is also taught in the final term of the school.

The Priory is linked to the Internet. Children are instructed individually by a computer specialist in the use of computers; each class has at least one PC in the classroom, and computers form part of the curriculum at the Priory. Computers are used in many subjects and children become confident in their application.

The Priory has an excellent academic record. Children mainly progress to independent day schools in Oxford, Leamington or Warwick - a number obtaining scholarships and bursaries. Others go on to boarding schools or local comprehensive schools. The Headmistress is frequently in touch with head teachers of senior schools, and receives many compliments about ex-pupils.

Prep. Children may stay until 4.30 pm to do their prep under supervision.

Special Educational Needs. A Special Educational Needs Policy operates throughout the school in line with the Code of Practice. Additional tuition is available with the Special Educational Needs teacher for children who require help with academic work.

Music. Music plays an important part in the life of the Priory. Every child has a weekly general music and singing lesson, including recorder tuition each week from Year 2. In addition approximately 35% of the pupils study an orchestral instrument privately - the school has peripatetic teachers for cornet, violin, clarinet, flute, piano and private singing. Associated Board Examinations are taken. The choir, orchestra and recorder consorts meet once a week. Concerts and musicals are a feature of the school year.

Sport. The Priory offers a variety of sports: netball, tennis, rounders, hockey, athletics and swimming for girls; soccer, tennis, rounders, hockey, cricket, athletics and swimming for boys.

The children show confidence in competitive sports matches, which are played throughout the year with other schools. They also participate in local tournaments. Each child has a weekly gymnastics lesson and Years 2 to 6 use a nearby sports ground for games on a Wednesday afternoon.

Years 1 to 6 swim at local pools each week throughout the year.

Saplings. Saplings, our class for 2 to 3 year olds, has a warm and comforting atmosphere and provides the opportunity for children to learn how to play and co-operate with others and function in a group beyond the family.

Nursery. The Nursery provides a wonderful balance between formal learning and imaginative play. This room is always bright and interesting, and it encourages young children to experiment and learn at an age when they are most receptive.

Drama. Drama forms part of the curriculum at the Priory. All children participate in a performance at Christmas, when they enjoy using the skills they have learnt during their lessons. Children are encouraged to take part in festivals and to enter LAMDA Examinations during the Summer Term.

Ballet and Tap. Ballet and tap classes take place on a Monday and Wednesday. There is a dance performance in the Spring Term which is held at a local theatre, with IDTA Examinations taking place during the Summer Term.

Karate. Karate instruction takes place after school on

Wednesday and Thursday. The pupils participate in examinations, competitions and demonstrations. Our pupils have had some pleasing successes in county and local league competitions.

Gymnastics Club. A Gymnastics Club is held for younger children each Tuesday and Wednesday, and the squads have had several successes in local competitions, gaining well-earned praise.

After School Care. After School Care operates from 3.30 pm to 5.30 pm each day during term time, where children from Nursery to Year 6 may relax in an informal atmosphere under the supervision of a member of staff.

Holiday Playschemes. Holiday schemes operate for various weeks in the main holidays from 8.30 am to 5.00 pm for Nursery to Year 6 pupils. A great variety of activities take place during these sessions and the children have an enjoyable time.

The Priory has connections with local charitable institutions, where small musical concerts are regularly performed. In addition, it contributes to at least one fund-raising event each term. The Priory is a caring community, and encourages the children to respect each other, to be responsible, courteous and conscientious.

Visitors to the school often remark on the busy and happy atmosphere at the Priory. Dedicated teachers and small classes contribute towards this. Children are always encouraged to achieve their personal best in each subject. The rewards of this system can be seen, when every year, Year 6 children excel in their examinations and move on to senior schools of their choice with confidence and pride.

St John's School

Stock Road Billericay Essex CM12 0AR.
Tel: (01277) 623070

Headteachers: **Mrs Fiona Armour**, BEd (Hons), **Mrs Sandra Hillier** BA, CertEd (Hons)

Age Range. 3–16
Number in School. Day: Boys 246, Girls 170
Fees per term. £925–1,750

St John's is a caring, family-run day school situated in almost 8 acres of its own grounds and backing onto Lake Meadows Park.

The curriculum is a traditional one, based on the requirements of the National Curriculum and extending to include a range of options at GCSE.

Children work within a safe and disciplined environment studying a broad curriculum. Both traditional and modern teaching methods are used to prepare pupils for Key Stages One, Two, Three, the Essex County 11+ Selection Examination, and GCSE's.

Attention is paid to both the social and academic development of all pupils and this is reflected in the excellent results at both 11+ and GCSE. There are good facilities for Rugby, Football, Basketball, Hockey, Netball, Tennis, Athletics and Swimming.

Other activities include Fencing, Karate, Speech Training, Performing Arts and the Duke of Edinburgh Award Scheme. Foreign travel is encouraged and in recent years the school has been on skiing trips during the winter, activity holidays to Canada and USA in the summer and language revision courses to France and Spain during the Easter term.

The school aims to educate its pupils to be mature, responsible and confident in a happy, supportive and friendly environment.

St Joseph's School

Launceston Cornwall PL15 8HN
Tel: (01566) 772580
Fax: (01566) 775902
e-mail:
name@st-josephslaunceston-cornwall.schoolzone.co.uk
website: www.st.josephs.schoolzone.co.uk

Headmaster: **Mr A R Doe,** MA, BSc, PGCE

Age Range. 3–16 years
Number in School. Day: Boys 24; Girls 146
Fees per term. Day: £1,315–£1,910.

St Joseph's School, Launceston is an independent day school for boys and girls from 3–11 years and girls from 11–16 years.

Originally a convent, St Joseph's has retained some of the features of its Catholic foundation but is now an ecumenical educational community, open to members of all faiths, in which Christian values are the cornerstone, and truth the essence of school life.

Pupils work in a friendly yet disciplined environment which places emphasis on strong family values and relationships, where they feel happy and secure. This generates the confidence necessary for children to succeed.

The school provides a good academic education for all, regardless of ability and background, with a wide variety of extra-curricular activities to provide balance and insight into opportunity. It offers equal prospects to all and inspires them to respond positively to challenges through encouragement and commendation. In last year's examinations, 96% of candidates gained at least five GCSEs at grades A*-C with 72% of all entries being awarded grades A*, A or B. The average number of A*-C grades per pupil was 8.5. The school is always placed in the first three schools in Cornwall in the DfEE League tables, which is all the more remarkable as St Joseph's remains non-selective.

St Joseph's seeks to educate the whole person, providing its pupils with the ability to fulfil their potential, to achieve their aspirations, and to approach adult life with the enthusiasm to put their acquired skills and knowledge to good use for themselves and for others

National honours have been gained in many areas including athletics, swimming, textiles, cookery and music. The senior chamber choir is a "flagship" choir for the South West, having appeared on both local and national television during the past year and will again be participating in the finals of the Music for Youth Festival at the Royal Festival Hall, London in July 2001. The school took particular pride in the performance of one of its old girls, Kate Allenby, in the Sydney Olympics.

Major renovations have been carried out at the school in recent years, to provide a new IT suite, a new library, and other improved facilities. Scholarships are offered throughout the Junior Department and Academic and Specialist Scholarships at 11+ in Art, Drama, Music and Sport. Also the Dunheved Award is offered to local children. Bursaries are considered on an individual basis. An extensive daily bus service allows pupils from a wide area of Devon and Cornwall to attend St Joseph's.

For further details please contact the Headmaster's Secretary on 01566 772580 or visit our website.

Charitable status. St Joseph's School is a Registered Charity, number 289048. It exists to provide education for girls and boys.

St Joseph's School

33 Derby Road Nottingham NG1 5AW.
Tel: (0115) 9418356/9474985
Fax: (0115) 9529038

***Headteacher:* D L StJ Crawley**

Age Range. 18 months–11 years
Number in School. Boys 120, Girls 84
Fees per term. £1,240 from September 2000

A co-educational day school providing the very highest standards to children of all abilities. It provides a happy and caring environment in which children can develop their full potential both socially and academically. The school is Roman Catholic but welcomes children of all faiths.

St Joseph's School

Crackley Hall Coventry Road Kenilworth Warwickshire CV8 2FT.
Tel: (01926) 855348
Fax: (01926) 851557

***Headteacher:* Mrs J Le Poidevin**

Age Range. Nursery and Junior School, aged 2.9-11 years.

Number in School. 75

Fees per term. Nursery: £9.00 per session. Junior School: £1,260-£1,350.

St Joseph's School is a small independent school which takes boys and girls from Nursery age through to age 11. The school has a Catholic foundation but welcomes children from all denominations and faiths. St Josephs's prides itself on its small classes and the caring environment in which all pupils can be known and be encouraged to reach their potential in a variety of areas. The school has an excellent reputation for success in academic, musical and sporting areas.

St Joseph's is located in and around the elegant surroundings of Crackley Hall, a lovely old building situated in attractive grounds on the outskirts of Kenilworth. Our facilities are extended by a large adjoining playing field.

St Josephs's is the Junior School part of the Warwickshire Catholic Independent Schools Foundation. The Senior school is Princethorpe College, seven miles away in the Rugby direction.

For further information please telephone St Joseph's School on (01926) 855348.

Charitable status. St Joseph's School is a Registered Charity, number 702407. It exists to run a Catholic School for the education of children of all denominations.

Saint Margaret's Junior School

Convent of Mercy Midhurst West Sussex GU29 9JN
Tel: (01730) 813956
Fax: (01730) 810829

***Headmistress:* Sister M Joan O'Dwyer**

Age Range. 2–11 years.
Number in School. Boys 125, Girls 205
Fees per term. £550–£1,070

St Margaret's Junior School is an independent Catholic day school, run by the Sisters of Mercy. The Christian ethos is maintained in all aspects of school life, and the pupils are educated in a caring family atmosphere where each individual is valued in his or her own right. Children of all denominations are welcome at the school.

The Nursery children are accommodated in two buildings, according to age, with each having its own outdoor play area. The two Nursery classes each have approximately 24 pupils, and the children have a happy and stimulating environment in which to develop both intellectually and socially.

Children transfer to the Junior School at 4 years of age. The Junior School is accommodated in modern purpose-built accommodation. Throughout the school pupils are encouraged to make full use of their talents and abilities. The curriculum incorporates Religious Education, English, Maths, Science, Design Technology, ICT, History, Geography, Art, Pottery, Physical Education, Music and Drama. There are fully-equipped Art and Design Technology rooms. French is taught from Nursery age.

The resources in the school include two school libraries, computers in every classroom, three ICT suites, two well-stocked music rooms, two well-equipped gymnasiums and extensive playing fields. Individual music tuition is available. Years 5 and 6 pupils have the opportunity to use a fully equipped Science Laboratory. Clubs are run by members of staff for the pupils which include Gym Club, Football, Netbalubl, Rounders, Cross Country, Cricket, Chess Club and Speech and Drama. Football coaching, Judo and Tennis coaching are offered as optional activities. Swimming takes place in the Summer Term for Years 5 and 6. A Special Needs Unit caters for the less/more able pupils.

Effective learning takes place in a happy and stimulating environment. The school follows the National Curriculum and gives pupils the opportunity to achieve at the highest levels. At the age of 11, pupils are prepared for entrance to St Margaret's Senior School, and the boys to the Senior School of their choice. Many take examinations for scholarship places. They leave St Margaret's confident of their own value as individuals and well-equipped for further academic study.

The school values the support of parents and has an 'Open-School' policy, enabling them to come and discuss their child with the teachers or the Headteacher at any time.

Charitable status. Sisters of Our Lady of Mercy, Midhurst, Uckfield and Shoreham by Sea is a Registered Charity, number 235961. The charitable purposes which advance the religious and other charitable work for the time being carried out in England or Wales by or under the direction of the Society as the Trustees.

St Margaret's Preparatory School

Gosfield Hall Park Gosfield Halstead Essex CO9 1SE
Tel: (01787) 472134
Fax: (01787) 478207

***Headmistress:* Mrs B Y Boyton**

Age range. 6 months to 11 years
Number of Pupils. Boys 90, Girls 95. All day.
Fees per term. £975–£1,600

St Margaret's is an ISA accredited school which specialises in the needs of children from 6 months to 11 years. We welcome all prospective parents into our classrooms and invite you to see our methods of teaching. We believe that the introduction to school life should be experienced by every child as an extension of the home and that it is our responsibility to provide an exciting, stimulating and caring environment where each child can flourish and feel confident. In addition to the normal school year we can also provide your child with pre and post school care and holiday play schemes.

Our school is housed in a beautiful listed building with seven acres of lovely grounds. It has a gymnasium, specialist creative art and science rooms, music and practise rooms, essential as most children play at least one instrument.

After school clubs offer drama, ballet, team training, hockey, football, board games, to name but a few.

The staff are highly experienced and are, therefore, able to offer an extremely extensive curriculum including French and Latin. We aim to prepare all our children for entrance examinations to their senior schools, and to provide them with the social confidence and academic ability to really achieve their potential.

St Margaret's School

18 Kidderpore Gardens London NW3 7SR.
Tel: 020 7435 2439
Fax: 020 7431 1308

Headmistress: **Mrs S J Meaden**, BA Hons (Leeds), MBA

Age Range. 5–16
Number in School. Day: Girls 150
Fees per term. £1,750–£1,950. *Compulsory extras:* Books and Art materials

St Margaret's in Kidderpore Gardens, Hampstead aims to provide a sound education based on the National Curriculum for girls aged between 5 and 16.

Classes are small and time and attention are given to each girl's individual needs. The school aims to achieve high standards in work and discipline, while fostering a happy atmosphere.

There is a lively programme of extra-curricular activities, including horse-riding and self defence.

In addition, girls are prepared for speech and drama and instrumental examinations.

Charitable status. St Margaret's School is a Registered Charity, number 312720. It exists to provide education for girls.

St Martin's Preparatory School

63 Bargate Grimsby N E Lincolnshire
Tel: (01472) 878907

Headmistress: **Mrs M A Preston**, CertEd

Age Range. 3–11
Number in School. Day: Boys 105, Girls 125
Fees per term. £510–£950

The school was founded in 1930. It aims to foster an interest in learning from an early age. A fully qualified and dedicated staff ensure that a high standard in Primary School subjects is attained throughout the school. French is taught from the age of 7. Children are taught in small classes and great attention is given to individual development.

Girls are prepared for Common Entrance at 11+, and boys for Junior Entry at 11+. Children also transfer to local Comprehensives and Grammar Schools. There is a flourishing Swimming club from Kindergarten upwards, also Art Club, Calligraphy Club, Badminton, Football, Netball, Chess, Gym Club, Table Tennis, Computer and Drama. A happy friendly atmosphere prevails throughout the school.

St Mary's School

13 St Andrew's Road Henley-on-Thames Oxfordshire RG9 1HS.
Tel: (01491) 573118

Headmistress: **Mrs S Bradley**, BSc (Hons)

Age Range. Girls and Boys 2 to 11 years.
Number in School. Pupils 150. Boys 75, Girls 75
Fees per term. £1,565 (extra required for attendance before and after school). Nursery minimum £286. No compulsory extras.

A fully co-educational day school, set in the residential part of town. Class sizes of approximately 16 allow the individual to flourish.

Specialist teaching in French, games and music begins at 4 years old. From Year 3, science is taught by a graduate scientist in a purpose built laboratory. Drama, CDT, maths, art, IT and English are also taught by specialists. Optional after school clubs include drama, judo, art, games and dance. High academic standards are achieved in a friendly, caring, enthusiastic and stimulating environment.

St Mary's Westbrook

Ravenlea Road Folkestone Kent CT20 2JU
Tel: (01303) 651222
Fax: (01303) 249901
Station: Folkestone Central, Ashford International

Chairman of Governors: Roger de Haan

***Head:* Mrs Lesley Anne Watson,** MA(Ed)

Number of boarders. 34 Boys, 15 Girls
Number of Day Children. 96 Boys, 64 Girls. Montessori Nursery: 84
Fees. Boarders £2,710-£3,100 per term. Day Pupils £1,300-£2,315 per term. Nursery. The Nursery has its own fee structure based on number of sessions attended.

There are Academic, Sports, Art and Music Scholarships. Bursaries are available for families of Military and Diplomatic Personnel.

Location. St Mary's Westbrook is situated in Folkestone, 'the Gateway to Europe' and is easily accessible from London by train or the M20 motorway, as well as Europe by the Channel Tunnel (10 minutes from the school), the Seacat or the Ferries from Dover. Heathrow and Gatwick airports are less than 2 hours by car and being the nearest independent boarding and day school to the Channel Tunnel, Brussels and Paris are only 2 hours away.

Facilities. The School's facilities are excellent. There are two halls/theatres, specialist Science Laboratories, IT Centre, a very good Library, Chapel and superb purpose built classrooms. A new purpose built Nursery and refurbished Girls Boarding House was opened in September 1999. As well as possessing a safe, enclosed playing field, St Mary's Westbrook also has excellent hard courts for tennis, basketball and netball.

Education. The curriculum is designed to allow parents opportunities for maximum choice. We have an excellent record in securing passes in the Kent Test (11+)

(100% in 2000), Common Entrance and Senior Independent School Scholarship Examinations. In addition, pupils have always obtained good results at GCSE. Recent innovations have included an expansion of our Foreign Language teaching, French from Reception. A Japanese Teaching Assistant helps focus pupils on the Far East. Support is given by an excellent Skills Development Unit and EAL is offered.

Extra-Curricular. The school has a very busy and stimulating extra-curricular programme in which all boys and girls are encouraged to participate. The main sports are Soccer, Rugby, Cricket, Hockey, Netball, Rounders and Athletics. Other regular sports include Swimming, Golf, Tennis, Dryskiing, Basketball and various Watersports. Arrangements can be made for Horse riding. Music, Drama, Ballet & Tap Dancing, Computing, Woodwork, Modelmaking and Cookery are amongst the many other activites which take place. Music is a particular strength with pupils being encouraged to learn to play an instrument and subsequently participating ine one of the Orchestras. In addition, there is a strong choral tradition with separate Girls and Boys Choirs.

Boarding. Excellent facilities are provided for both boys and girls. Younger pupils are accommodated in bright, cosy bedrooms and older pupils live in study bedrooms. There are Common Rooms for boys and girls as well as joint recreational rooms and modern washing facilities. A full range of weekend activities is offered to both boarding and day students ranging from theatre trips, ten pin bowling and short visits to Calais and Boulogne. We also have a new initiative having become the D of E Award Scheme Expedition Centre for SE Kent.

An escorted train service to and from London (Charing Cross), Paris and Brussels is available. In addition, arrangements can be made to have pupils collected from or taken to airports, ports and other locations.

General. St Mary's Westbrook was formed in 1997 as a result of a merger between Westbrook House Preparatory School and St Mary's College. It is a friendly and flourishing school offering small classes and a balanced curriculum. There is a large well qualified staff providing a caring environment where confidence and self-esteem are cultivated.

Charitable status. St Mary's Westbrook is a Registered Charity, number 1063709. It exists to prepare boys and girls for a challenging, demanding and ever changing future, encouraging the highest possible standards in all areas of learning in an atmosphere of fun and security.

St Michael's School

Bryn Llanelli Carmarthenshire, SA14 9TU
Tel: (01554) 820325
Fax: (01554) 821716
e-mail: jbm@globalnet.co.uk
website: www.stmichaels-school.org.uk

Headmaster: **D T Sheehan**, BSc (Hons), PGCE

Age Range. Preparatory Department 3–11 years, Senior School 11–18 years

Number in School. 347 (195 boys, 152 girls)

Fees per term. Preparatory Department £1,025–£1,369. Senior School £1,669–£1,698. Sibling allowances available.

St Michael's is very much in the pattern of the small, well-disciplined grammar schools. The school has a traditional approach to learning, which does not mean that it lives in the past, but takes a traditional view of the importance of hard work and homework in the school curriculum.

The high academic standards of the school are reflected in the National "league tables".

In August 1997 our sixth form pupils again achieved an average of 22 UCAS points with two of our pupils gaining places at Cambridge, one for medicine (Christ's) and one for engineering (Trinity). Both pupils achieved 4 'A' grades at 'A' level as well as successfully completing the Cambridge Entrance Examinations. In 1999, one pupil gained a place at Cambridge (Clare) to read Biochemistry; 4 pupils achieved the grades for medicine.

This year at A level we achieved our best results ever, with our students achieving an average of 25 UCAS points (BBB) with five pupils achieving the grades for medicine. Two pupils have been offered places at Cambridge, to read medicine in September 2001.

We have topped the GCSE league tables in the South Wales area since they first appeared in 1993 when 100% of our pupils achieved 5 or more GCSE grades A* to C. Our results have been outstanding over the years and again this year 94% of our pupils achieved 5 or more GCSE grades A* to C with a remarkable 26% of all GCSE grades being starred As, putting us well ahead of some very famous schools. Many pupils sit GCSEs and 'A' levels early. In 1998 we had the youngest pupil in Wales to achieve an 'A Grade' in 'A' level Mathematics at just 14 years of age and five of our pupils appeared on national television news after achieving 'A' grades in 'A' level Mathematics before officially sitting their GCSEs. We have topped the A level and GCSE League Tables for the last two years out of all the schools in Carmarthenshire, Pembrokeshire and Swansea.

No school can build up such a strong reputation without a competitive, but well disciplined atmosphere and a highly qualified and dedicated staff, and this is where we feel St Michael's is particularly fortunate.

As a result of our successes the numbers in the school have risen dramatically and are now the highest in the school's 78 year history.

We now have well equipped computer laboratories which include PC laboratories. Pupils have access to a computer each from 3 years of age. In Form 3 all pupils take the RSA Computer Literacy Examination that will prepare them for the future where computers are unavoidable.

Languages taught in the school are: French, Spanish, Welsh, German and Latin.

Apart from its academic basis, the school is proud of its wide range of games and activities which include horse riding, fencing, archery and ski instruction. Pupils in Form 4 are able to take the Duke of Edinburgh's Bronze Award Scheme.

Speech, Drama and Music are strongly emphasised in the school and all pupils take the early LAMDA examinations and can go on to the Gold Medal while in school. We have a large choir and school orchestra and pupils may take music examinations at GCSE and 'A' level.

One of the main reasons for the school's success is the thorough grounding that pupils receive in the 'basics' - English, Mathematics, Computing and Science in the school's Preparatory Department.

We have enjoyed outstanding sporting success over the last few years with our Netball teams appearing on National Television News in January 2001 after winning nearly every tournament that they entered, at all levels.

Every pupil is encouraged to develop his/her full potential whether in academic work or in all the extra curricular activities and games which are offered.

St Nicholas School

Hillingdon House Old Harlow Essex CM17 0NJ.
Tel: (01279) 429910

Headmaster: **G W Brant**, MA, BEd (Hons), CertEd

Age Range. 4–16
Number in School. Pupils 330. Day: Boys 160, Girls 170
Fees per term. £930–£1,870

St Nicholas School was founded in 1939 and is situated in a delightful rural location. The Headmaster is a member of the ISA. St Nicholas combines a fresh and enthusiastic approach to learning with a firm belief in traditional values.

The academic record of the school is excellent, reflected in high pupil success rates in all competitive examinations. The dedicated team of staff involves itself closely with all aspects of pupil's educational progress and general development. High standards of formal teaching are coupled with positive encouragement for pupils to reason for themselves and develop a high degree of responsibility.

Main sports include Hockey, Netball, Tennis, Football, Rugby, Cricket, Swimming, Athletics and Gymnastics. Optional extras include Ballet, Individual Instrumental Lessons, Speech and Drama classes and many sporting clubs.

Recent building developments include a magnificent new Junior Department building, Science and Technology Centre, Junior Library, swimming pool and Sports Hall.

Charitable status. St Nicholas School is a Registered Charity, number 310876. It exists to provide and promote educational enterprise by charitable means.

St Nicholas' School

Redfields House Redfields Lane Church Crookham Hants GU13 0RE

(See GSA section, Part II of this book)

St Peter's School

52 Headlands Kettering Northamptonshire NN15 6DJ.
Tel: (01536) 512066
Fax: (01536) 416469
e-mail: st_peters@ukf.net
website: http://www.st.peters.ukf.net/

Headmaster: **Mr Paul Jordan**, CertEd (London)

Age Range. 2½–11
Number in School. Day: Boys 69, Girls 70
Fees per term. £1,005–£1,430

Established in 1946, St Peter's is a small day school set in pleasant grounds on the outskirts of Kettering. It offers a sound education for boys and girls aged 2½ to 11. Pupils are thoroughly prepared for entry into their senior schools and a high rate of success in Entrance and Scholarship Examinations is regularly achieved. In addition to fulfilling the requirements of the National Curriculum the school emphasises the importance of Music, Art, Sport and Information Technology in its programme. Computers are used as part of the normal classroom teaching from the age of three and French is introduced at Reception.

St Peter's is a lively, friendly school with a strong family atmosphere where children are encouraged to develop to the full their individual strengths and talents. It aims to promote, through Christian teaching, a respect for traditional values, a sense of responsibility and a concern for the needs of others.

Charitable status. St Peter's School is a Registered Charity, number 309914. It exists to maintain and manage a school for boys and girls in the town of Kettering.

St Teresa's Catholic School (P.R.) Trust Ltd.

Aylesbury Road Princes Risborough Buckinghamshire HP27 0JW.
Tel: (01844) 345005
Fax: (01844) 345131

Headmistress: **Mrs C M Sparkes**

Age Range. 3–11
Number in School. Day: 79 Boys, 63 Girls. Nursery School: 18 Boys, 8 Girls
Fees per term. £1,106–£1,184. Nursery School £370 (2 mornings per week), £1,184: (5 mornings and 3 afternoons a week). (these fees confirmed for September 99)
Compulsory extras. Swimming

St Teresa's School is primarily a Catholic School, but is open to boys and girls of all religions or none.

Charitable status. St Teresa's is a Registered Charity, number 310645. It exists to provide a broad education enfolded by the Catholic faith.

St Ursula's High School

Brecon Road Westbury-on-Trym Bristol BS9 4DT
Tel/Fax: (0117) 9622616

Headmistress: **Mrs M Macnaughton**

Age range. Co-educational 3 to 16 years.
Number in school. 170 day boys; 160 day girls.
Fees per term. £590–£1,640.

Set in beautiful and extensive grounds to the North West of Bristol, St Ursula's High School is a Catholic independent day school for boys and girls from 3 to 16 years. It offers all pupils a sound education based upon the National Curriculum, in a friendly, caring atmosphere. Pupils are assessed upon entry and scholarships are available to the most able; St Ursula's High School is not a selective school however and all pupils are welcomed and all talents are fostered. Pupils of all faiths (or none) are equally welcome. Above all the school seeks to develop and encourage self-esteem and self-confidence.

Resources and facilities are excellent. In January 2000 Nursery and Reception classes received a glowing Ofsted Report (available to any interested parent). From Year 3 there is specialist teaching in French, Design Technology, Science and Music; classes are small throughout the school and the quality of teaching and learning is excellent. Parents are regarded as active partners in the education process; they are positively encouraged to keep in contact with the school by telephone or personal visits and they receive six reports per year.

National Test and GCSE results are excellent - in 2000 89% of pupils gained 5 or more GCSEs at Grade A* to C and the points per pupil score, 52.2 (indicating the proportion of A*, A and B grades) placed St Ursula's High School on a par with Bristol's highly selective independent schools. Detailed results are available on request.

Visitors always comment on the school's friendly atmosphere, the calm insistence on good discipline and the evident respect staff and pupils have for each other. St Ursula's High School recognises that all children have special needs and, by using a variety of strategies, it ensures that the able are stretched and challenged and the less able are supported and basic skills reinforced.

Charitable status. St Ursula's High School is a Registered Charity, number 227482. It exists to provide education for boys and girls.

St Winefride's Convent School Trust Shrewsbury

Belmont Shrewsbury Shropshire SY1 1LS.
Tel: (01743) 369883
Fax: (01743) 341650
e-mail: StWinefridesSchool@postmaster.co.uk

Headmistress: **Sister M Felicity**, BA (Hons)

Age Range. 4+–11. Nursery: 3+–4
Number in School. Day: Boys 56, Girls 72
Fees per term. £655–£670

St Wystan's School Ltd.

High Street Repton Derbyshire DE65 6GE.
Tel/Fax: (01283) 703258

Headmaster: **Mr C M Sanderson**, BA

Age Range. 2½–11
Number in School. Day: Boys 80, Girls 59
Fees per term. £420–£1,225
Compulsory extras. Lunch £120
Awards. A small number of scholarships are offered for 7+ entry to Year 3.

Situated in the historic village of Repton, only a couple of minutes from the A50/A38 intersection (at Toyota) south of Derby, St Wystan's is ideally placed to serve a wide catchment area. Both Nottingham and Uttoxeter are within 25 minutes of the school, though the majority of pupils come from Derby, Burton and surrounding villages.

St Wystan's prides itself on a family atmosphere in which every child can grow in confidence and develop to his or her full potential as an individual. Great emphasis is placed on courtesy and good manners and a pastoral system, centred on the four school houses, promotes a caring environment and develops teamwork and commitment.

Academic expectations are high, though the school serves a wide ability range. Small classes enable the children to receive individual attention and work at a pace appropriate to their ability. As a free-standing junior school, St Wystan's prepares pupils for a large number of senior schools and pupils have won a significant number of academic, sport and music scholarships recently. The school enjoys a longstanding 100% success rate in pupils securing places at their first choice senior school.

The pre-school department provides a nursery, headed by a fully qualified teacher and a reception class which both accept pupils on government subsidised "Early Years" places. The main school covers Key Stages 1 and 2 but is not restricted by the National Curriculum, offering a broad range of subjects and a blend of form teacher based teaching at the lower end and subject specialist teaching further up the school.

St Wystan's enjoys an excellent reputation in music and sport, with pupils progressing to regional and national championships, recently in football, swimming, cross-country and athletics. Many pupils have instrumental tuition and there is a thriving school choir and orchestra, together with a broad range of other extra-curricular activities.

St Wystan's runs a very popular pre-school and after-school care facility. Children can be delivered to school from 8 am and looked after at school until 6 pm.

Charitable status. St Wystan's School (Repton) Limited is a Registered Charity, number 527181. It exists to provide a quality education for boys and girls.

Salcombe Preparatory School

224–226 Chase Side Southgate London N14 4PL.
Tel/Fax: 020 8441 5282 (Admissions & Infant Dept)
Fax: (Junior dept) 020 8449 7188
020 8441 5356 (Junior dept)

Headmaster: **A J Blackhurst**, BA Hons, AdvDipEd

Age Range. 2–4 at Salcombe Pre-School and Bush Hill Park Pre-School (co-educational), 4–11 at the Main School (co-educational).

Fees. (Pre-School and Bush Hill Park) p.o.a. (depending on schedule) (Main School) £1,575 per term.

Numbers in School. Pre-school & Bush Hill Park 197; Main School 299

Established in 1918, Salcombe, a member of the Asquith Court group, provides a sound academic, sporting and cultural curriculum in small classes in a friendly, caring yet disciplined environment leading to entry examinations at 11 for independent secondary schools. Entry to the Main School is in the September following a child's 4th birthday via the reception classes. Entry for children joining the school from outside the pre-school sections is by interview and assessment appropriate to the age of the child. There is a separate registration procedure for the pre-school and Main school sections.

Pre-school facilities in Southgate and Bush Hill Park are open for 50 weeks of the year from 8 am to 6 pm and offer a variety of schedules to suit parents. Details of the Southgate Pre-School are available on 020 8882 2136 and Bush Hill Park on 020 8364 1188. Details of the main school departments can be obtained from the Admissions Secretary on 020 8441 5282.

Salesian College

Reading Road Farnborough Hants GU14 6PA
Tel: 01252 893000
Fax: 01252 893032
e-mail: office@salesian.hants.sch.uk

Headmaster: **Mr Patrick A Wilson**, BA (Hons), MA, CertEd

Age range. 11–18 years
Number in School. 500
Fees per term. £1,567

Salesian College at Farnborough in Hampshire was founded in 1901 and is an Independent Catholic Grammar School of about 500 boys aged 11 to 18 years. Members of all Christian faiths are welcomed into the school which is part of a world wide organisation of educational foundations run by the Salesians, a religious Order founded in the last century in Italy by St John Bosco specifically for the formation of young people, spiritually, academically, culturally, physically and emotionally. This continues to be our aspiration for each boy.

Our aim is to send out from the school at 18 years a young man who is confident, without being arrogant, and comfortable with himself and all those around him; a good Christian, an honest citizen, a good individual, well equipped to take his place in, and make a significant contribution to society.

This is achieved by the use of The Preventive System of Education promoted by St John Bosco and based on the three principles of Reason, Religion and Kindness. These principles encourage the boys to develop a strong sense of responsibility and a caring attitude towards each other and the Community at large.

Academic achievements at GCSE and A level, and sporting achievements are highly valued. The friendliness and mutual respect that exist between staff and pupils provides a family and Christian ethos conducive to good order, confidence and scholarship.

As the members of a family help each other with physical and moral support, the members of the school are encouraged to do likewise. The use of the Prefect System is very effective in allowing members of the Senior school (Years 11–13) to help their juniors by example and guidance.

We regard education to be a tripartite process involving the school, the family and the boy and in order to produce the desired result all three must work in harmony.

Public speaking, music, orchestra, chess, drama and debating all flourish and there are many other extra curricular activities.

The school has its own chapel, chaplaincy and resident chaplain.

Prospective parents are always welcome to make an appointment to visit the College while in session.

Charitable status. Salesian College is a Registered Charity, number 23779. It exists to provide education for boys in North East Hampshire and neighbouring counties.

Salterford House School

Salterford Lane Calverton Nottinghamshire NG14 6NZ
Tel: (0115) 965 2127

Headmistress: **Mrs M Venables**, CertEd

Age range. 2½–11
Number in school. Main School 176, Boys 99 Girls 77. Kindergarten and Pre-Prep 69, Boys 29 Girls 40
Fees per term. £975–£995

Salterford House is situated in rural Nottinghamshire, in a woodland setting and aims to provide a happy, family atmosphere with small classes, in order to equip children academically and socially to cope with the demands of any type of education which might follow.

Although the school is mainly Church of England, all faiths are accepted. 75% of pupils go on to senior independent schools such as Nottingham High Schools NGHS, Trent College and Hollygirt.

Sports include Cricket, Tennis, Swimming, Rounders, Football, Golf and Skiing.

The school produces 3 concerts a year and there is a recorder Group and Choir. Individual tuition in Speech and Drama, Piano, Woodwind, Violin and Percussion is available.

A dyslexia teacher is employed to give individual lessons to children with dyslexia problems.

All classrooms are equipped with computers.

Staff are easily available for discussion. Regular contact is maintained with parents via Parents Evening and a thriving PTA.

Sanderstead Junior School

29 Purley Oaks Road Sanderstead Surrey CR2 0NW.
Tel: 020 8660 0801

Headmistress: **Mrs Alison Barns**

Age Range. 3–12
Number in School. Day: Boys 40, Girls 60
Fees per term. £975–£1,455. *Compulsory extras:* Stationery £27 per term.

Accredited ISJC. The school is situated near bus services and two railway stations, yet has ample open spaces for sports and other recreations within five minutes' walk.

Qualified staff with visiting specialists ensure a high standard throughout the school. Boys and girls are prepared for entrance examinations to all the best senior schools of the district. There is a long and consistent record of Scholarships and Bursaries.

Computer Studies, Music and Drama are featured. There is a Trampoline, Gymnastic equipment and a wide variety of sports available.

Sherrardswood School

Lockleys Welwyn Hertfordshire AL6 0BJ.
Tel: (01438) 714282

Headteacher: **Mrs L E Corry**

Age Range. 2–18
Number in School. Day: Boys 210, Girls 198
Fees per term. £1,510–£2,430

Sherrardswood, founded in 1928, is a co-educational day school for pupils aged 2–18. The School is set in 25 acres of attractive parkland two miles north of Welwyn Garden City. The Junior Department is housed in a fine 18th century building whilst the Senior Department relocated from its City centre site into new purpose built facilities in September 1995. Games fields, tennis courts and woodlands trail are available on the Lockleys site for both departments.

Entry to the school is by interview or by interview and examination according to age. A broad curriculum is offered to GCSE level and a wide range of 'A' level subjects is available.

A range of sport and extra-curricular opportunities, both within the school day and out of school hours, and a commitment to a caring environment within a disciplined framework promote a strong corporate life and the opportunity to develop qualities of self-discipline and responsibility.

Charitable status. Sherrardswood School is a Registered Charity, number 311070. It exists solely to provide independent education for boys and girls aged 2–18.

Shoreham College

St Julian's Lane Shoreham-by-Sea West Sussex
Tel: (01273) 592681
Fax: (01273) 591673
e-mail: info@shorehamcollege.co.uk

***Headmaster:* R K Iremonger**

Age Range. 3–16
Number in School. Day Boys 213, Day Girls 98
Fees per term. £1,250–£2,350

Founded in 1852, the College is a Charitable Trust and is sited to the east of Shoreham in a Tudor manor house supplemented by modern buildings set in spacious grounds.

Pupils are prepared for GCSE Examinations. There is a very favourable teacher/pupil ratio and a well-qualified and experienced staff. Particular care is taken to help pupils in their career choice.

The main games are soccer, rugby and cricket as well as athletics, squash, badminton, tennis and swimming. There is an active CCF and thriving Music Department, both choral and instrumental.

The School offers a caring community with a proper balance between straightforward discipline and friendly relationships. The school also provides Special Needs teaching for those with learning difficulties.

Charitable status. Shoreham College (The Kennedy Independent School Trust Limited) is a Registered Charity, number 307045. It exists to provide high quality education for local boys and girls.

Slindon College

Slindon Arundel West Sussex BN18 0RH
Tel: (01243) 814320
Fax: (01243) 814702

***Headmaster:* I Graham, BEd, MA**

Age Range. 10–16
Number in School. Boarders 54, Day Boys 50
Fees per term. £3,960 (Day Boys £2,405)

A small school for approximately 120 boys whose classes have a maximum of 12 pupils. The National Curriculum is followed where appropriate and in Years 7–9 a broad-based, balanced curriculum is provided. GCSE courses include rural studies, home economics, PE, photography, art, music and design technology - all practical based and "hands-on". Rural studies are enhanced by a small animal kingdom. The excellent Learning Support Department helps boys with specific learning difficulties, including dyslexia and ADD/ADHD.

A wide range of extra-curricular activities based around the Duke of Edinburgh Award, are offered and include motor vehicle studies, computing, and all the conventional sports. There is also a thriving CCF.

The school is non-denominational but has firm links with the local Anglican and Roman Catholic churches.

The Headmaster is a member of ISA (Independent Schools Association) and accredited to the ISC (Independent Schools Council).

Some bursaries are available and discount is available for Service families and second sons.

Charitable status. Slindon College is a Registered Charity, number 1028125. It aims to provide for the academic, social and personal development of each boy in a caring and purposeful environment.

Snaresbrook College

75 Woodford Road South Woodford London E18 2EA
Tel: 020 8989 2394
Fax: 020 8989 4379

***Headteacher:* Mrs L J Chiverrell,** CertEd

Age range. 3½–11
Number in school. 160
Fees per term. £1,258–£1,684

Snaresbrook College is an Independent day school for boys and girls aged from 3½ to 11 years. Founded in the 1930's, the school today is ISC accredited and inspected. It occupies a substantial Victorian building, once a large private family home - a fact that contributes to the strong community spirit within the school. We aim to cultivate an intimate, caring family atmosphere in which children feel secure and valued. Most children join our Nursery and Reception section at age 3½ and most pupils stay with us until they reach 11 when they leave for their secondary schools.

We provide a rounded primary education covering every aspect of your child's early development. The curriculum is designed to prepare pupils for senior independent and grammar school entrance and scholarship examinations. It includes the National Curriculum core subjects of Mathematics, English and Science as well as History, Geography, ICT, Religious Education, Music, Speech and Drama. French is studied from age 3½.

At age 11, we find that Snaresbrook children are confident, cheerful and courteous, with a good sense of community and a readiness to care for each other and the world around them. They have learned how to work in the ways that suit them best, are receptive to teaching and are well prepared for the next stage of their education and development.

We see ourselves as joint trustees, with parents, of the young lives in our care, bearing equal responsibility for their happiness, well being and development.

Southbank International School

36–38 Kensington Park Road London W11 3BU.
Tel: 020 7229 8230
Fax: 020 7229 3784

***Headmaster:* Milton E Toubkin**

Age Range. 4–18
Number in School. Day: Boys 110, Girls 100
Fees per term. £2,650–£4,800.

Founded in 1979, Southbank is a small international coeducational day school. Its 210 pupils come from more than fify countries, including Britain, United States, Scandinavia, Canada, Japan and Eastern Europe.

Southbank is an official centre for the International Baccalaureate which is recognised as an entrance qualification by universities worldwide, including all British universities. The primary and middle school programmes are also based on the International Baccalaureate Curricula.

Discovery Week and a Field Studies week are included in the curriculum.

Southbank is housed in two fine Victorian houses and a modern annexe in Kensington. Facilities include four well equipped laboratories, music room, library, computer centre, assembly hall and canteen. There is a door-to-door bus service.

In September 1995, Southbank opened a second campus in Hampstead, offering a full Early Childhood, Primary and Middle School programme for children aged 3–14. The programme is modelled on the Kensington school. The facility in Hampstead is purpose-built for education, and is located on Netherhall Gardens.

There is a teacher pupil ratio of 1 to 7. In a friendly and informal atmosphere pupils and teachers function in a positive spirit.

Stafford Grammar School

Burton Manor Stafford ST18 9AT.

(See SHMIS section, Part III of this Book)

Stanborough School

Stanborough Park Garston Watford Hertfordshire WD2 6JT.
Tel: (01923) 673268
Fax: (01923) 893943

***Principal:* Mr S Rivers**

Age Range. 3–18
Number in School. 300 boarding and day, girls and boys.
Fees per year. Boarding: £9,695; Day: £3,900

Stanborough School, housed in attractive parkland, is a Christian independent school for boys and girls of all faiths between the ages of five and eighteen. Boarding is available for children who are at least 11 years of age.

It aims to give an education which fosters the growth of the whole person and is small enough for each student to remain an individual and not lose his or her personal identity. It has a warm, friendly atmosphere supported by firm yet kindly discipline providing a milieu in which pupils may develop their abilities and personal qualities to the full.

Currently it prepares pupils up to GCSE level examinations.

The Stavanger British School

Gauselbakken 107 N-4032 Stavanger Norway.
Tel: 47 51575599
Fax: 47 51571516
e-mail: principal@stavanger-british-school.no
website: stavanger-british-school.no

***Principal:* Mrs Zelma Røisli**

Age Range. 4+–13
Number in School. 105. Co-Educational Day School: Main School 105 pupils. 40 in Pre-School.
Fees per Year. NOK 80,000 (eight thousand Norwegian Kroner) if Company paying.

NOK 37,500 (thirty seven thousand five hundred Norwegian Kroner) if private paying.

Founded in 1977 the principal aim of the school is to meet the educational needs of British children abroad and by giving them continuity in their work and syllabus, enable them to return with ease to schools in both independent or state sector in the UK or continue in other British schools abroad.

The school is involved with National curriculum and Key Stage 1 & 2 testing. The children are also prepared for Common Entrance Examinations into other private sector schools.

Children are accepted in the main school from the age of 4+–13 years and ESL is taught to help those children whose mother-tongue is not English. The pre-school department and main school are taught by appropriately qualified staff.

Emphasis is placed on the basic skills and each child is encouraged to develop its potential to the maximum.

The school is a member of ISA, ECIS and COBISEC. It is accredited through ISC and ISI. Copies of reports are available at the school.

Stoke College

Stoke by Clare Sudbury Suffolk CO10 8JE.
Tel: (01787) 278141
Fax: (01787) 277904

***Headmaster:* J Gibson**, BA, CertEd

Age Range. 3–16+ Coeducational
Number in School. Total 212: Boys 114, Girls 79. Boarders: Boys 18, Girls 1
Registration Fee. £25
Fees. *Boarding:* Years 5 and 6 £3,525 per term, Years 7 and 8 £3,795 per term, Years 9, 10 and 11 £3,925 per term. *Daily:* Forms 1, 2 & 3 £1,595 per term, Years 4, 5 & 6 £1,850 per term, Years 7 & 8 £2,195 per term, Years 10 & 11 £2,325 per term

Stoke College provides a broad, balanced and relevant curriculum up to GCSE. Weekly boarders or day pupils enjoy a caring environment in an idyllic rural situation with small classes yielding excellent results in public examinations. The College has a strong tradition in athletics and cross-country and in Music and Drama. The School benefits from a new Sports/Assembly Hall, Junior School Teaching Block, Technology Rooms, a Performing Arts Centre, a swimming pool, hard tennis courts and a Nursery Department. The College aims to develop the individual's strengths and to produce a well rounded young adult to take his or her place in society.

Charitable status. Stoke College is a Registered Charity, number 310487. It is devoted to providing a full and relevant education to its pupils.

Stoneygate College

2 Albert Road Leicester LE2 2AA.
Tel: (0116) 270 7414

***Headmaster:* Mr J C Bourlet**

Age Range. 3–11+
Number in School. Day: Boys 63, Girls 84
Fees per term. £1,110–£1,430

Stoneygate College is a day school for boys and girls between the ages of three and eleven. Built in 1886 it is one of the oldest established schools in Leicester.

The school building is situated in a pleasant residential area, yet within 2 minutes walk of city transport. In order to keep the standard of facilities high there is a continuous programme of modernisation and development.

We have a good pupil-teacher ratio and we also divide into smaller groups for much of the timetable. We have an increasing number of specialist teachers as the children progress through the school. Our aim is to provide a happy, family environment in which each child is able to reach his or her potential. Our style is unashamedly academic. We guide children and prepare them, on careful discussion with their parents, towards the right Senior School for them, and we achieve excellent results in entrance examinations.

Accredited by the Independent Schools Council.

Stowford

95 Brighton Road Sutton Surrey SM2 5SJ
Tel: 020 8661 9444
Fax: 020 8661 6136

***Headmaster:* R J Shakespeare**, BA, MA, MA

Age Range. 7–16
Number in School. Day: Boys 50, Girls 30
Fees per term. £1,450–£2,050

Stowford has a Junior (7–13) and Senior (14–17) School for both boys and girls. It has a reputation for individual care and a well-disciplined yet happy atmosphere. Classes are small; each individual receives the help that he or she needs. We have a dyslexia programme. Homework is important and all must achieve their personal best. There is the closest possible liaison with parents.

The early years in particular are when good social and academic habits are formed. Seniors have a considerable measure of freedom and are expected to respond appropriately.

Over all, an adult environment with articulate pupils who reach their targets.

Stratford Preparatory School

Church House Old Town Stratford upon Avon Warwickshire CV37 6BG
Tel: (01789) 297993
Fax: (01789) 263993
e-mail: stratfordprep@hotmail.com

Motto: *Lux et Scientia*

***Principal:* Mrs C Quinn**, BEd (Hons), MBA

Age Range. Preparatory School 4–11 years
Montessori Nursery School 2–4 years
Number in School. Main School, Boys 57, Girls 62; Nursery School, Boys 16, Girls 21
Fees per term. £1,475 Infant School; £1,535 Junior School; £860 Full-time Nursery School; £450 Nursery School (Mornings); £450 Nursery School (Afternoons).
Compulsory extras. Lunch £1.50 per day

Stratford Preparatory School is situated in the heart of the historic town of Stratford-upon-Avon. The Preparatory school opened in September 1989 and has developed around a large town house. An additional detached house within the school's grounds provides accommodation for the Reception and Nursery children, a gymnasium, a science room and design and technology room.

The Nursery implements the Montessori philosophy of learning and the child develops in a structured learning environment. French and ballet are taught from the age of 2 years.

The main school offers a broad balanced learning plan adapted to the individual needs of the children using traditional teaching methods and with specific reference to the National Curriculum. All children are entered for the 11+ and independent school entrance examinations.

The school offers a high level of pastoral care and attention to personal development.

Physical education facilities include: swimming, football, cricket, tennis, netball, lacrosse, rounders, ballet and athletics.

There are opportunities for the children to learn a variety of musical instruments.

Reduction in fees is offered for families with two or more children in Main School.

The Principal is pleased to provide further details and meet prospective parents.

The Study Preparatory School

Wilberforce House Camp Road Wimbledon Common London SW19 4UN

(See IAPS section, Part V of this Book)

Study School

57 Thetford Road New Malden Surrey KT3 5DP.
Tel/Fax: 020 8942 0754
e-mail: info@study.kingston.sch.uk

***Principal:* Mrs Susan Mallin**

Age Range. 3–11. Co-educational
Number in School. Day: Boys 71, Girls 65
Fees per term. £680 to £1,630

Since 1923, we have successfully given our children a firm foundation in reading, writing and number skills, whilst also teaching French, music, art and games. Science, geography, history, technology and ICT play an important part in the curriculum.

Small classes allow us to stretch the most able pupils, whilst giving all our children individual attention.

Popular After School Clubs include Football, Art, Computer, Speech & Drama and Games. Individual instrumental music tuition is also available.

We provide a caring and stimulating atmosphere in which our children thrive. In due course they leave us to enter such schools as King's College Wimbledon, Kingston Grammar School, Hampton School, Emanuel, the High Schools at Wimbledon, Sutton, Putney and Surbiton and both Tiffin schools.

Please visit us on our website: www.study.Kingston.sch.uk.

Sunny Hill House School and Nursery

7 Wrenthorpe Lane Wrenthorpe Wakefield WF2 0QB
Tel: (01924) 291717

***Headmistress:* Mrs Hazel K Cushing**, MA, CertEd

Age Range. 2 to 7

Number in school. 88 Boys and Girls. 12 Boys and Girls in Nursery

Fees per term. £1,120

The Headmistress and her dedicated teaching team see the school as an enlarged family unit, constantly seeking to provide a happy and orderly environment where young children can develop naturally as individuals and gain the confidence necessary to realise their full potential both socially and academically. The basic concepts of literacy and numeracy are taught in small classes by traditional methods within a broad curriculum and great attention is paid to cultivating responsible social attitudes in a relaxed yet disciplined atmosphere.

Sunny Hill House is part of the Silcoates School Foundation and has access to its excellent sports facilities and resources. Children may enter Silcoates Junior School by assessment or sit various entrance examinations for other independent schools at age seven.

Charitable status. Sunny Hill House School is a Registered Charity, number 529281. It exists to provide education for boys and girls.

Syddal Park School

33 Syddal Road Bramhall Stockport Cheshire SK7 1AB.
Tel: 0161-439 1751

Headteacher: **Mrs S Lay**

Age Range. 2–7

Number in School. Boys 31, Girls 31

Fees per term. £760–£1,060

Accredited by the Independent Schools Council.

Syddal Park School is a long-established Nursery and Pre-Preparatory school for boys and girls from 2–7 years. The school offers a broad curriculum with the emphasis on developing literacy and numeracy skills.

Small classes, together with individual tuition, ensures the level of attention so necessary in the early years. The Nursery Department is very well structured and prepares children for full time school by developing good personal skills and social values.

A very high percentage of children pass the age 7 entrance examination into the local Independent Grammar Schools.

Sylvia Young Theatre School

Rossmore Road London NW1 6NJ.
Tel: 020 7402 0673
Fax: 020 7723 1040

Headmaster: **Colin Townsend,** MSc

Age Range. 9–16

Number in School. Day: Boys 43, Girls 97. Weekly boarding is available.

Fees per term. Junior Department £1,375, Years 7, 8 and 9 £1,950, Years 10 and 11 £2,000.

The School has a junior department (9 to 11 years) and a secondary department (11 to 16 years). We aim to provide an appropriately balanced academic and vocational experience for our students. We are proud of the caring and well disciplined environment that prevails and promotes a very positive climate of individual success.

Academic subjects are delivered by highly qualified staff to the end of Key Stage 4.

Examination subjects may include English, English Literature, History, Mathematics, Spanish, Integrated Science, Art, Drama and Expressive Arts, Music and Media Studies.

Theatrical training is given by experienced professional teachers. Pupils are prepared for examinations in Speech and Drama – LAMDA (London Academic of Music and Dramatic Art). Entry is by audition and interview; academic ability is assessed.

The Hammond School

Hoole Bank House Mannings Lane Chester CH2 4ES.
Tel: (01244) 328542

The Hammond School is accredited by the Independent Schools Council and CDET, and caters for a wide range of talents and interests.

Head: **Mrs P Dangerfield**, BA (Hons).

Age Range. 11–18

Number in School. Boarders: 31. Day Pupils 128

Fees per term. £1,740 for education only

Education Department takes girls from 11 years to GCSE level.

Drama Department takes girls and boys from 11 years joining the Education Department with additional Drama.

Dance Department takes girls and boys from 11 years joining the Education Department with a Vocational Dance training.

Sixth Form takes boys and girls into the Education Department to study for A/AS levels as well as those wishing to specialise in Dance and Drama.

Full boarding is available for Dance pupils; weekly boarding for academic pupils.

For prospectus apply: The Secretary, Hammond School Ltd, Mannings Lane, Chester CH2 4ES

Thornlow Preparatory School

Connaught Road Weymouth Dorset DT4 0SA
Tel: 01305 785703
Fax: 01305 780976
e-mail: headmaster@thornlow.co.uk
website: www.thornlow.co.uk

Co-educational 3-13 years.

Head: **Mr R A Fowke,** BEd (Hons)

Thornlow Preparatory School is a must on any visiting list in order to appreciate fully the unique blend of teacher dedication and expertise that produces a happy, caring atmosphere. A highly qualified staff and small teaching groups ensure that any child's unique potential is nurtured to the full.

On the cultural and extra-curricular front, Thornlow certainly lives up to its motto of "preparing children for life's horizons", for not only is music a strong feature with a wide range of instruments being taught, but there is also a thriving culture of drama.

Another special feature is the Sailing, which takes place twice a week in the safe confines of Portland Harbour.

The well equipped Nursery Unit has en suite facilities and enjoys the support of an NNEB.

In addition, Thornlow has a brand new ICT Room,

Science Laboratory, Art Room and Library, not to mention a specially equipped Learning Support Centre, Connaught House, catering mainly for children with Dyslexia.

Thorpe Hall School

Wakering Road Thorpe Bay Essex. SS1 3RD
Tel: (01702) 582340
Fax: (01702) 587070
e-mail: sec@thorpehall.southend.sch.uk

***Principal:* D W Gibbins**, MSc, CertEd

Age Range. 2½–16
Number in School. Approximately 400 girls and boys
Fees per term. £985-£1,385

Thorpe Hall School, founded in 1925, has been educating children for 75 years and proudly boasts the finest and most up-to-date facilities. This purpose-built school in South East Essex is pleasantly located on 11 acres of playing fields and woodland, easily reached by Southend-on-Sea's public transport system. The School consistently achieves excellent academic results at Key Stages 1, 2, 3 and 4 with special emphasis being placed on the traditional values of good manners, behaviour, dress and speech.

On Monday, Tuesday and Thursday each week, the School day is extended by one hour to enable all children to access library and computer facilities as well as having the opportunity to participate in Sport, Music, Drama, Mathematics and French or simply to do their homework in a suitable and supervised environment.

Recent refurbishments in Science, Modern Languages and the Resources Centre have greatly enhanced the learning opportunities for all pupils. A £350,000 extension to the junior block completed in May 2001, comprising a Music Centre, showers and changing facilities, a Kitchen and additional teaching rooms will further enhance the School. Future buildings will provide improvements in the facilities for Art and Craft, Information Technology and Drama. In September 2001 additional refurbishments in Science and Modern Languages will be carried out to complement those already completed.

Thorpe Hall School has an orderly, disciplined and caring ethos that caters for the social and academic needs of children - Pre-Nursery, Nursery, Reception, Infant, Junior and Senior - not only between the hours of 9 am to 4 pm but also offers sporting opportunities in golf, tennis, karate, netball, horse riding and football at weekends and during holiday times. Youngsters have the opportunity to join our Beavers, Cubs and Scout groups while senior pupils can become involved in the Duke of Edinburgh Award Scheme.

The Charitable Trust status enables fees to be kept to a minimum and are very competitive; Nursery vouchers are accepted and some academic bursaries are available to pupils entering Year 7. The School is regularly inspected by the DfEE and is accredited by the Independent Schools Council.

In November of 1999 the School's Nursery department was inspected by Ofsted and received a glowing report. The Inspector commented that the School has a positive effect on childrens' learning.

Charitable status. Thorpe Hall School is a Registered Charity, number 298155. It exists to provide good quality education for boys and girls in South East Essex.

Thorpe House School

7 Yarmouth Road Thorpe St Andrew Norwich NR7 0EA.
Tel: (01603) 433055
Fax: (01603) 436323

***Headmistress:* Mrs R McFarlane**

Age Range. 3–16
Number in School. Girls 3–11 (day) 150, 11–16 (day) 150
Fees per term. £820–£1,165

The School, an Educational Trust, is Accredited by the Independent Schools Council. The Headmistress is a member of GSA and ISA and the Governing Body is a member of GBGSA. The school is ideally situated in 10 acres of gardens, woodlands and playing fields.

The Headmistress is assisted by an excellent Staff of graduate and qualified teachers.

In addition to the usual academic programme, classes are held for ICT, Technology, Art, Home Economics, Textiles, Dance and Speech and Drama. Tuition in a variety of musical instruments is available.

Thorpe House has a covered, heated swimming Pool, fully equipped gymnasium and a Sports Hall. According to season, Hockey, Netball, Tennis, Rounders, Athletics, Squash and Badminton are played and the school has won many trophies.

The whole school has recently been rebuilt.

Charitable status. Thorpe House School (Norwich) Educational Trust Limited is a Registered Charity, number 311275. Its aim is the education of girls.

Tower College

Rainhill Merseyside L35 6NE.
Tel: 0151-426 4333
Fax: 0151-426 3338

***Principal:* Miss R J Oxley**

Age Range. 3–16
Number in School. Day: Boys 273, Girls 274
Fees per term. £976–£1,202

Tower College is a non-denominational Christian Day School housed in a beautiful Victorian mansion set in 15 acres.

Our emphasis is on academic excellence and good behaviour. We have a strong musical tradition.

Six coaches cover an 18 mile radius including South Liverpool, Widnes, Warrington, Runcorn, St Helens, Prescot, Rainford and Ormskirk.

Academic and music scholarships are available.

Charitable status. Tower College is a Registered Charity, number 526611. It aims to provide a sound education based on Christian beliefs, with an emphasis on good behaviour and academic excellence.

The Towers Convent School

Upper Beeding Steyning East Sussex BN44 3TF
Tel: 01903 812185
Fax: 01903 813858

***Headmistress:* Sister Mary Andrew Fulgoney**

Age range. Girls 3–16; Boys 3–11.

Fees. Boarders £2,232 to £2,348. Day Pupils £1,285 to £1,418.

The Towers, a Roman Catholic boarding and day school for girls 3–16 and boys 3–11 years, in the healthy and beautiful setting of the South Downs, is run by a Community of Sisters. At the heart of The Towers Community is Christian love; all people of whatever race, colour, creed or status are welcome, and have equal worth and opportunity. We aim to celebrate the dignity of each individual pupil. Our motto "Always Faithful" upholds the qualities of honesty and trust, responsibility, self-discipline and forgiveness. Pupils are encouraged to achieve their full potential in everything they do, developing a love of learning and seeking "wholeness". Technology and Science subjects are a particular strength, and the school has three times won the Whitbread Prize for GCSE results. The GCSE pass rate is consistently high, reflecting a quest for high academic standards. There is a keen interest in Music and Drama and a major musical is produced annually. The school has again won the coveted Sportsmark Award, witness of a fine sports tradition, especially in tennis, where the school has won the Sussex Shield five times; netball and gymnastics are also very strong.

Find enjoyment and fulfilment at affordable fees!

Trinity School

Buckeridge Road Teignmouth Devon TQ14 8LY.
Tel: (01626) 774138
Fax: (01626) 771541
e-mail: trinsc123@aol.com
website: www.trinityschool.co.uk

Headmaster: **C J Ashby**, BSc, PGCE (Oxon)

Age Range. 3–19

Number in school. Boarders: Boys 80, Girls 50. Day: Boys 196, Girls 164

Fees per term. Boarders: £3,660–£4,105. Day: £1,260–£1,965. *No compulsory extras*

Trinity is a charitable trust. It is a joint Roman Catholic and Anglican school, although it has a non-denominational intake of pupils. The joint patrons are the Anglican Bishop of Exeter and the Roman Catholic Bishop of Plymouth. Trinity is a co-educational school, with boarders from 6+, and day pupils from 3. Entry to the School is by assessment and interview of the younger pupils, and entrance test and interview for the older pupils.

The School offers excellent facilities in a very attractive environment with panoramic views of Lyme Bay. Academic results are excellent, and there is a thriving programme of over thirty extra-curricular activities including many different sports. The School has embarked on an ambitious building and development programme. (Phase one, the new Science and Resources Block was opened in January 1997; new tennis facilities were completed in the Summer of 1997). (Phase two, new classroom block, new food technology centre and new en-suite boarding accommodation for Sixth formers opened in 1999). New information technology (Prep and Senior) installed 1996, 1997, 1998 and 2000. Over the last twelve years a new assembly hall was opened in May, 1989, new IT laboratories in October 1989, 1997 and 2000, and a new music centre in June 1990. The curriculum has also undergone development and expansion: recently Music, Spanish, Drama, Design Technology and Physical Education have been added to a full GCSE programme. Part One intermediate GNVQs in Business and Information Technology introduced in September 2000. Post-16. Various approaches exist dependent on the needs of the individual. Over 20 'A2' and 'AS' levels are offered and GNVQ courses are available at intermediate and advanced level. The School has a strong Careers Department and a Programme for Health and Personal Relationships.

The School promotes good discipline with a friendly caring family atmosphere, within small classes, where individual potential is encouraged to develop to the full.

Trinity is close to the M5 and a mainline railway station and runs daily buses to Exeter, Torquay, Bovey Tracey and Newton Abbot. There are nearby airports at Exeter and Plymouth.

Links have been developed with Europe and an exchange system operates with Germany and trips are undertaken to France. Pupils also attend the School from a wide variety of other countries.

Academic, sporting, musical and drama bursaries and scholarships available. Generous Bursaries are available for children whose parents are members of the Armed Forces or the Police Force.

Charitable status. Trinity School is a Registered Charity, number 276960. It exists to provide education for children and students aged 3–19+.

Twycross House School

Twycross Via Atherstone Warwickshire CV9 3PL
Tel: (01827) 880651

Headmaster: **Mr Robert V Kirkpatrick**, MEd

Age Range. 8–18

Number in School. 300 Day pupils

Fees per term (September 2001). £1,500–£1,630

This small selective school provides an academic education of high standard, leading to GCSE, 'A' Level and Oxbridge entrance examinations.

Interviews and entrance tests are held annually in January. The main intake is at eight but some places become available for older pupils.

Science and both modern and classical languages are strongly represented in the curriculum. GCSE and 'A' Level examination results are outstanding by national standards.

Games play a vital part in the life of the school and in character building and there are impressive indoor and outdoor games facilities. All pupils are encouraged to participate in dramatic and musical activities; religious education is held to be important; and high standards of behaviour, deportment and good manners are required of the children.

The normal class size is sixteen.

The house is a 'listed' building dating back to 1703. The ten acres of grounds and the surrounding countryside provide a pleasant setting for the school and, as far as possible, the atmosphere of an old country house is preserved in the belief that environment is an important factor in the quality of a child's education.

Parents wishing to know more should make an appointment to meet the Headmaster or Headmistress.

Twycross House Pre-Prep School, which is on the other side of the village green, caters for pupils from five to eight years of age (Tel: 880725).

Uplands School

St Osmunds Road Parkstone Poole Dorset BH14 9JY.
Tel: (01202) 742626
Fax: (01202) 731037

Headteacher: **Mrs L Dummett**, MEd, BEd (Cantab)

Age Range. 2–16
Number in School. Day (only): Boys 190, Girls 170
Fees per year. £2,700–£5,925

Uplands is a friendly school offering a high academic standard and excellent facilities in a caring well disciplined environment. Close to Poole and Bournemouth town centres with a wide catchment area extending to Swanage, Ringwood, Blandford and Wimborne.

After school and holiday care are also provided.

Entry is by the school's own examination and interview by the Head.

Charitable status. Uplands School is a Registered Charity, number 32033A. It exists to provide high quality education for boys and girls.

Ursuline Preparatory School

Great Ropers Lane Warley Brentwood Essex CM13 3HR
Tel: (01277) 227152
Fax: (01277) 202559

Headmistress: **Mrs Pauline Wilson,** MSc

Age range. 3 to 11 years.
Number in school. Day (4–11) 146; Half Day (3–4) 11
Fees per term. £870–£1,650

Founded in the early 1930's, the Ursuline Preparatory School enjoys a reputation as a happy family school, where pupils strive to give of their best in all areas of school life. Consequently, much emphasis is placed on encouraging the children to develop to the full their individual talents and interests, as well as fostering in each pupil a strong sense of well-being, self-reliance and team spirit. This is achieved by the frequent use of praise, by adherence to an agreed policy of consistent and fair discipline, and by the high standards, moral code and caring attitudes deriving from the strongly Catholic ethos which underpins the life of the whole school.

The Ursuline Preparatory School has well qualified and very experienced teachers and support staff. It is committed to offering to all its pupils the distinct advantages of a broad and balanced curriculum. This includes following the National Curriculum, in addition to affording many other opportunities such as the provision of French and Information Technology to all children from 4 years upwards, Elocution Classes, and weekly Swimming Lessons, and also Extension where this is deemed appropriate.

A comprehensive range of extra curricular activities are offered to our pupils. These are often taught by specialist staff and include subjects such as Theatre Club, Art Appreciation, Computing, German, Ballet, and Nature Club, as well as many Instrumental Classes and Sporting Activities, at which the School meets with considerable success at both individual award and at competition level.

The School successfully prepares children for entry to either Grammar Schools, local Secondary Schools, including the Ursuline High School, or to local and national independent schools.

The relatively small size of the School allows for very close contact between staff, pupils and parents and provides each child with the opportunity to fulfil his or her academic potential. The pupils are encouraged to follow their own interests and to develop a sense of self-confidence and self-worth which will hopefully remain with them throughout their lives, allowing them to reflect the school motto: *A Caring School that strives for excellence*.

Charitable status. The Ursuline Preparatory School is a Registered Charity. It exists to provide Roman Catholic children and those of other denominations with the opportunity to reach the highest individual standards possible in every area of School life.

Vernon Lodge Preparatory School

School Lane Stretton Nr Brewood Staffordshire ST19 9LJ
Tel: (01902) 850568

Proprietor/Principal: Mrs D Lodge

Headmistress: **Mrs P Sills,** BEd, RSACertSpLD

Age range. 2½–4½ years Kindergarten; 4–11 years School
Number of children. 108
Fees. £1,060–£1,240 per term.

Situated in a lovely country garden, our school with its small classes provides individual attention and a happy atmosphere. We are indeed a very active school with pupils participating in both music and sports events. We are past holders of the inter-schools Top of the Form shield.

The Kindergarten is very popular and provides a sound basis for learning, covering reading, writing and number work. Kindergarten children have access to all school facilities including the computers.

We make no apology for our traditional teaching methods, in fact we are proud of them as our recent excellent results to senior schools reflect.

Facilities at Vernon Lodge are constantly expanding. Recently, our Kindergarten has been completely refurbished with excellent new equipment. It has the reputation of being the best nursery school in the area.

The school now has a computer suite to equip all our pupils with technology for the 21st century. They are also thoroughly enjoying our new all-weather court for tennis, hockey, 5-a-side football and netball.

All children learn French and holidays to France have included visits to the D-Day Beaches in Normandy, Rouen, Euro-Disney and Paris.

The popularity of Vernon Lodge School and Kindergarten is evident from its wide catchment area: children travel from Wolverhampton, Stafford, Cannock, Newport and Telford.

Virgo Fidelis Preparatory School

147 Central Hill Upper Norwood London SE19 1RS.
Tel: 020 8653 2169

Headmistress: **Mrs Noronha**

Age Range. 2½–11
Number in School. Day: Boys and Girls 2½–11 270.
Fees per term. £320–£1,380.

The school is a Roman Catholic Foundation with a strong ecumenical outlook. Pupils are received from various religious backgrounds. Emphasis is placed on the pursuit of good educational standards and on the development of personal responsibility.

Charitable status. Community of Our Lady of Fidelity Upper Norwood is a Registered Charity, number 245644. The general objects of the Trust are Religious and Charitable in connection with the advancement of the Roman Catholic Faith in England and Wales.

Westbourne School

4 Hickman Road Penarth Vale of Glamorgan CF64 2AJ
Tel: (029) 2070 5705
Fax: (029) 2070 9988

Principal: **Dr B V Young**, BSc, PhD

Age Range. 3–16
Number in School. Boys 117, Girls 83
Fees per term. £915–£1,830

An independent co-educational day school for children from Nursery age to GCSE, with continuity in teaching methods throughout the school, and a stable context for study. A wide range of subjects is offered at GCSE, and results are consistently good. The staff is well-qualified and settled and pupils are known individually to all teachers and also to the Principal and Headmasters.

A disciplined and caring context is maintained and ample opportunity is given for a variety of sporting activities.

Entry to the Prep School is by Common Entrance at which a 50% pass is needed. Under other circumstances entry by interview and academic assessment is possible.

Fee changes are in September each year, but enquiries for up to date information can be made to the school office. Fees include text books, sporting activities and examination charges.

Penarth is a small seaside town on the outskirts of Cardiff, and pupils are drawn from Cardiff and Barry, from Cowbridge and the Vale of Glamorgan, the Welsh Valleys and Newport. There is a convenient train service to Penarth and the school has a minibus running each day from Cowbridge and Barry.

West Dene School
Educational Trust Ltd

167 Brighton Road Purley Surrey CR8 4HE.
Tel: 020 8660 2404
Fax: 020 8660 1189

Head: **Mrs S D Topp**, ACP (McollT)

Age Range. 2–11
Number in School. 100 Day Boys and Girls
Fees per term. £900–£1,190

West Dene, founded in 1927, is a small and friendly Nursery, Kindergarten and Preparatory school for boys and girls from 2–11 years.

The school provides an all-round education in a secure and happy learning environment. Class sizes are small and each child is treated as an individual to ensure they reach their true potential.

Alongside the academic subjects many other activities are also available. These include Dance, Drama, Art and Design, French, Computing, Swimming. The light airy classrooms are mostly situated in the main brick built house retaining much of its homely atmosphere. A purpose-built Nursery block was opened in September 1996. The school also has a large hall/gymnasium and a good sized garden with grass and hard surface areas to provide playtime and outdoor games facilities.

Charitable status. West Dene School Educational Trust Ltd is a Registered Charity, number 312611. It exists to provide an all round education in a happy, caring environment.

Whitehall School

117 High Street Somersham Cambs PE28 3EH
Tel: 01487 840966
Fax: 01487 840966
website: www.whitehallschool.com

Headmistress: **Mrs D M D Hutley**

Age range. 3-11 years
Number in School. 96 Day children. 50 boys, 46 girls
Fees per annum. £3,165-£3,906

Whitehall School is situated in a pleasant village with easy access to both Cambridge and Huntingdon.

The buildings comprise a 1920's house and an 18th century Coach House. There are pleasant grounds with mature trees and garden play areas. Founded in 1983, the school offers the benefit of small tuition groups usually containing 12-15 children. The school has a good academic record (see website) and offers a broad curriculum including French, Swimming (own pool) and Drama.

Whitford Hall & Dodderhill School

Crutch Lane Droitwich Worcestershire WR9 0BE.
Tel: (01905) 778290

Headmistress: **Mrs J M Mumby**, BA (Hons), DipEd

Age Range. Girls 3–16, Boys 3–9
Number in School. Day: Girls 200. Boys 12
Fees per term. £655–£2,050. (Lunches, books and pre school care are included).

"Large enough to challenge, small enough to care".

The school is set in a quiet green campus on the outskirts of Droitwich Spa, minutes from the M5/M42 interchange, thus serving families from a wide area of North Worcestershire. Free transport between School Droitwich station is provided and many pupils take advantage of the excellent local rail network. After-School and Holiday Clubs operate in order to give peace of mind and flexibility to working parents. A charge is made for these services.

A superbly designed new Early Years and junior block incorporating a spacious multi purpose School Hall complement the original Georgian buildings. A new ICT suite is due to open in September 2001 providing access to the latest technology for all pupils from 5-16 years.

Whitford Hall & Dodderhill offers high standards of academic achievement, a wide range of extra curricular opportunities and supportive pastoral care. Class sizes are small, expectations are high, teachers are well qualified and experienced and the individual is paramount.

In the Early years and Key Stage 1 emphasis is on literacy and numeracy and children are class taught. Gradually specialist teachers are introduced in Science, Design & Technology, Information Technology and French and by Year 4 all subjects are taught by subject specialists.

In Years 5 and 6 girls take advantage of the facilities in the senior school for Science and the Creative Arts.

Transfer to the Senior School is by examination and there are entrance examinations at 9+ and 11+ for external applicants. There are Academic and Music Scholarships. All girls take the core subjects for GCSE - English, mathematics, science, a modern foreign language, history or geography and two additional subjects from a choice of a second foreign language, a second humanity and the creative subjects. Results are excellent and the School has been at or very near the top of the Worcestershire League tables since 1997.

Charitable status. Whitford Hall & Dodderhill is a Registered Charity, number 527599. It provides a seamless 3-16 education in a stimulating and happy environment allowing every girl to develop to her full potential and to take her place confidently in the world of post 16 and higher education.

William Hulme's Grammar School Prep Department

Spring Bridge Road Manchester M16 8PR
Tel: 0161 226 2054
Fax: 0161 226 8922
e-mail: prep@whgs.co.uk
website: www.whgs.co.uk

Head of Preparatory Department: **Mrs C Wilson,** BA

Age range. 3-11
Number in school. Day: Boys 128, Girls 50
Fees per term. £1,052-£1,191, plus £90 for lunch.

The Preparatory department follows an integrated curriculum from the foundation years through to key-stage two. We have a learning support service, our children sit SATs and we prepare all our Year 6 for the 11+ entrance examinations. Most of our children continue into the Grammar School.

The children thoroughly enjoy all the facilities of the Grammar School, such as the swimming pool, the ICT suite and the science laboratories. All religious and other dietary requests are catered for. We provide elocution lessons, enter our children for RAD examinations and have a flourishing football team. We also arrange trips to Dinosaur World, Blue Plant Aquarium and Eureka.

If you wish to arrange a personal tour, please do not hesitate to contact the school.

Wilmslow Preparatory School

Grove Avenue Wilmslow Cheshire SK9 5EG.

(See IAPS section, Part V of this Book)

Winbury School

Hibbert Road Bray Maidenhead Berkshire SL6 1UU.
Tel: (01628) 627412
Fax: (01628) 627412

Headmistress: **Mrs P L Prewett,** CertEd

Age Range. 2½–8
Number in School. Day only: Boys 45, Girls 45
Fees per term. £340–£1,090

Winbury is an Independent Day School for children from 2½ to 8 years old enjoying a delightful setting on the edge of Braywick Park, Hibbert Road, Bray. The school has a nursery class for 3 to 4 year olds each morning and a pre-nursery group for rising threes on three afternoons a week. The wide range of nursery activities is varied and includes number and reading skills as well as art, craft, science, music, drama and technology. Our aim is to create a happy, friendly and disciplined environment where children can grow in confidence, self-esteem and independence to become fully prepared for transition to the main school, where emphasis is placed on literacy and numeracy as well as a variety of subjects including French, art, craft, science, technology, PE, games, music, history and geography.

Throughout the four main school classes we aim to give the children an education of quality which is rich in challenge and inspiration, laying a firm foundation from which to grow. Winbury is a traditional, family school where the needs of each individual child are considered carefully by a well qualified team of caring and dedicated teachers, enabling the best qualities in each child to flourish.

Woodlands Schools

Great Warley Campus Warley Street Gt Warley Brentwood Essex CM13 3LA
Tel: (0870) 872 1699/3288
Fax: (0870) 872 2715

Hutton Manor Campus 428 Rayleigh Road Hutton Brentwood Essex CM13 1SD
Tel: (0870) 872 0364

Heads: **Mrs K Glemsle** – Great Warley
Mrs B Young – Hutton Manor

Age range. 3–11
Number in school. 147 boys, 134 girls
Fees per term. £1,550–£2,750

Admission is by interview.

Woodlands is a co-educational school set in attractive, spacious grounds with excellent facilities for outdoor activities on two campuses.

It is the School's principle aim to ensure that all the children are happy and secure and are as successful as possible. They are encouraged to work hard and to show kindness and consideration to their peers. The resulting ethos of the School is one of warmth, support and mutual respect.

The School provides an exciting learning experience which enables the pupils to achieve full academic potential and to develop qualities of curiosity, independence and fortitude. Classes are small. The School aims to develop high levels of self-esteem and a good attitude to learning. The School has an excellent record in public examinations. Pupils are highly successful in gaining places at the schools of their choice. Examination results in Music and LAMDA are also high.

A varied programme of team and individual sports aims to offer something for everyone.

There is a strong music tradition and a variety of dramatic and musical concerts and productions are staged throughout the year for children of each age group.

French is taught to a very high standard from 4 years of age.

Pastoral care is a major feature. An 'Open House' policy is in place for parents, which results in any concern being dealt with promptly and effectively.

It is the School's view that the education of the whole child is the most important priority and is confident that the learning experience it provides is fun, truly stimulating and memorable.

Sex of children. Co-ed.

Woodside Park International School

Friern Barnet Road London N11 3DR
Tel: 020 8368 3777
Fax: 020 8368 3220
e-mail: admissions@wpis.org
website: www.wpis.org

Principal: **Mr Robin Metters,** BEd

Age range. 2½ to 18
Number in School. 560
Fees per term. £1,406–£3,300

Woodside Park International School in North London is a co-educational independent international school for students aged 2½ to 18. The Senior Department (11-16) in Friern Barnet Road prepares students for GCSE examinations and the International Baccalaureate Diploma. Students who embark on the International Baccalaureate go to the Hague in January to attend the Model United Nations Conference. Examination results in recent years have been excellent.

Great emphasis is placed on modern technology, and students use the most up-to-date facilities, with audio-visual links with its sister school in New York and access to the Internet.

The Preparatory Department in nearby North Finchley has most of its teaching rooms in a recently completed purpose built complex. The Pre-Preparatory Department close to Woodside Park underground station, has recently been expanded and the Nursery Department is also housed in the same building, as well as a spacious hall nearby.

During termtime, trips to the school's European Studies centre in Normandy are organised for all students in Years 6, 7 and 8. Ski-ing trips are also organised during the Easter holidays.

The principal aim of the school is to encourage each student to develop both as an individual and as a responsible member of the community. Students are expected to give their best at all times both academically and in the great variety of other activities available to them.

Art, drama and music are also taught, and productions are staged in the newly-equipped hall. There is a school orchestra and choir and many pupils learn to play an instrument. There is a wide range of extra-curricular activities and a homework club. Soccer, cricket, hockey, netball, basketball, swimming, tennis, athletics and cross-country are the principal sports. The Senior Department have their own sports ground nearby and matches are arranged with other schools. The school has an excellent games record.

ALPHABETICAL LIST OF SCHOOLS

THE INDEPENDENT SCHOOLS ASSOCIATION (PART V1)

* denotes ISA schools reckoned to be co-educational

GEOGRAPHICAL LIST OF ISA SCHOOLS

(NB Page numbers will be found in alphabetical list on pp. 1161–1162)

Avon
Schools formerly in Avon will be found under Somerset

Bedfordshire
Moorlands School, Luton
Rushmoor School, Bedford

Berkshire
Claires Court School, Maidenhead
Dolphin School, Hurst
Hemdean House School, Reading
Highlands School, Reading
Hurst Lodge School, Sunningdale
The Licensed Victuallers' School, Ascot
Presentation College, Reading
Winbury School, Maidenhead

Buckinghamshire
Bury Lawn School, Milton Keynes
Crown House School, High Wycombe
Dair House School, Farnham Royal
Gateway School, Great Missenden
Kingscote Pre-Preparatory School, Gerrards Cross
Ladymede Co-educational School, Aylesbury
St Teresa's Catholic School, Princes Risborough

Cambridgeshire
Cambridge Arts and Sciences
Cambridge Centre for Sixth Formers
Horler's Pre-Preparatory School, Cambridge
St Colette's Preparatory School, Cambridge
Whitehall School, Somersham

Cheshire
Abbey Gate College, Chester
Abbey Gate School, Chester
Alderley Edge School for Girls, Alderley Edge
Altrincham Preparatory School, Altrincham
Brabyns School, Stockport
Cransley School, Northwich
Culcheth Hall School, Altrincham
The Firs School, Chester
Forest Park School, Sale
Forest School, Altrincham
The Grange School, Northwich
Greenbank School, Cheadle
Hale Preparatory School, Hale
The Hammond School, Chester
Hillcrest Grammar School, Stockport
Hulme Hall School, Stockport
Lady Barn House School, Cheadle
Loreto Preparatory School, Altrincham
Mostyn House School, Wirral
Mount Carmel Junior School, Alderley Edge
North Cestrian Grammar School, Altrincham
Oriel Bank High School, Stockport
St Catherine's Preparatory School, Stockport
Syddal Park School, Stockport
Wilmslow Preparatory School, Wilmslow

Cleveland
Red House School, Norton-on-Tees

Cornwall
Duchy Grammar School, Truro
Polwhele House School, Truro
Roselyon School, Par
St Joseph's School, Launceston

Cumbria
Harecroft Hall, Gosforth
Lime House School, Carlisle

Derbyshire
Derby Grammar School for Boys
St Wystan's School, Repton

Devonshire
Edgehill College, Bideford
Kelly College Junior School, Tavistock
Manor House School, Honiton
Grenville College Junior School (Stella Maris), Bideford
Trinity School, Teignmouth

Dorset
Dorchester Preparatory School
Homefield School, Christchurch
International College, Sherborne
Newell House School, Sherborne
The Park School, Bournemouth
Thornlow Preparatory School, Weymouth
Uplands School, Poole

Essex
Alleyn Court Preparatory School, Thorpe Bay
Braeside School for Girls, Buckhurst Hill
Colchester High School, Colchester
Cranbrook College, Ilford
Crowstone Preparatory School, Westcliff-on-Sea
Daiglen School, Buckhurst Hill
Glenarm College, Ilford
Gosfield School, Halstead
Heathcote School, Danbury
Herington House School, Brentwood
Littlegarth School, Colchester
Oaklands School, Loughton
Oxford House School, Colchester
Park School for Girls, Ilford
St Anne's Preparatory School, Chelmsford
St Hilda's School, Westcliff-on-Sea
St John's School, Billericay
St Margaret's Preparatory School, Halstead
St Nicholas School, Old Harlow
Thorpe Hall School, Thorpe Bay
The Ursuline Preparatory School, Brentwood
Woodlands Schools, Brentwood

Gloucestershire
Bredon School, Tewkesbury
Hatherop Castle Preparatory School, Cirencester
St Edward's School, Cheltenham
Westwing School, Bristol

Hampshire
Ditcham Park School, Petersfield
The Gregg School, Southampton
Littlefield School, Liphook
Mayville High School, Southsea
Meoncross School, Fareham
Moyles Court School, Ringwood
Nethercliffe School, Winchester
Rookwood School, Andover
St Nicholas' School, Church Crookham
Salesian College, Farnborough

Herefordshire and Worcestershire
Bowbrook House School, Pershore
Green Hill School, Evesham
Hartlebury School, Kidderminster
Heathfield School, Kidderminster
The Knoll School, Kidderminster
The Mount School, Bromsgrove
Whitford Hall & Dodderhill School, Droitwich

Hertfordshire
Arts Educational School, Tring
Duncombe School, Bengeo
Egerton-Rothesay School, Berkhamsted
Haresfoot School, Berkhamsted
Homewood Independent School, St Albans
Howe Green School, Bishop's Stortford
Immanuel College, Bushey
Northfield School, Hertford
St Columba's College, St Albans

Hertfordshire — *continued*
St Hilda's School, Harpenden
Sherrardswood School, Welwyn
Stanborough School, Watford

Humberside
St Martin's Preparatory School, Grimsby

Kent
Babington House School, Chislehurst
Baston School, Bromley
Bishop Challoner School, Bromley
Bronte School, Gravesend
Derwent Lodge Preparatory School for Girls, Tonbridge
Harenc School, Sidcup
Mead School, Tunbridge Wells
Sackville School, Hildenborough
St David's College, West Wickham
St Mary's Westbrook, Folkestone

Lancashire (Including Greater Manchester)
Abbotsford Preparatory School
Bridgewater School, Manchester
Highfield Priory School, Preston
Kingswood College at Scarisbrick Hall, Ormskirk
Moorland School, Clitheroe
Rosecroft School, Didsbury, Manchester
William Hulme's Grammar School—Prep. Dept, Manchester

Leicestershire
Dixie Grammar School and Wolstan Preparatory School, Market Bosworth
Manor House School, Ashby-de-la-Zouch
Stoneygate College, Leicester

Lincolnshire
Kirkstone House School, Peterborough
St James' School, Grimsby

London
Abercorn School
Arts Educational London School
City of London School for Girls
Devonshire House Preparatory School
Ealing College Upper School
The Hampshire Schools
Harvington School
Hellenic College of London
Herne Hill School
Highfield School and Nursery
Ibstock Place School
The Italia Conti
King Alfred School
Mander Portman Woodward
The Mount School
Oakfield Preparatory School
Parayhouse School
Portland Place School
Putney Park School
Riverston School
Rosemead Preparatory School
The Royal School
St James Independent Junior for Boys & Girls
St James Independent School for Boys
St James Independent School for Girls
St Margaret's School
Salcombe Preparatory School
Snaresbrook College
Southbank International School
The Study Preparatory School
Sylvia Young Theatre School
Virgo Fidelis Preparatory School
Woodside Park International School

Merseyside
Carleton House Preparatory School, Liverpool
Prenton Preparatory School, Wirral
Tower College, Rainhill

Middlesex
The American Community School, Uxbridge
Ashton House School, Isleworth
Buckingham College School, Harrow
Halliford School, Shepperton
Innellan House School, Pinner
Peterborough and St Margaret's, Stanmore
Reddiford School, Pinner
St Catherine's School, Twickenham
St Christopher's School, Wembley Park
St James Independent School for Boys, Twickenham

Norfolk
Cawston College, Norwich
Hethersett Old Hall School, Norwich
New Eccles Hall School, Norwich
St Christopher's School, Norwich
Sacred Heart Convent School, Swaffham
Thorpe House School, Norwich

Northamptonshire
Falcon Manor School, Towcester
Northamptonshire Grammar School, Pitsford
Quinton House School, Northampton
St Peter's School, Kettering

Northumberland
Longridge Towers School, Berwick-on-Tweed
Nunnykirk Centre for Dyslexia, Morpeth

Nottinghamshire
Dagfa House School, Nottingham
Greenholme School, Nottingham
Highfields School, Newark
Hollygirt School, Nottingham
Plumtree School, Plumtree
Rodney School, Newark
St Joseph's School, Nottingham
Salterford House School, Calverton

Oxfordshire
d'Overbroecks College, Oxford
Ferndale Preparatory School, Faringdon
Our Lady's Convent Senior School, Abingdon
St Johns Priory School, Banbury
St Mary's School, Henley-on-Thames

Shropshire
Adcote School, Shrewsbury
Bedstone College, Bucknell
Moffats School, Bewdley
Queen's Park School, Oswestry
St Winefride's Convent School, Shrewsbury

Somerset
Edington and Shapwick School, Bridgwater
Fairfield School, Nr Bristol
Mark College, Highbridge
The Park School, Yeovil
St Ursula's High School, Bristol

Staffordshire
Chase Academy, Cannock
Maple Hayes Hall, Lichfield
St Dominic's Priory School, Stone
Stafford Grammar School
Vernon Lodge Preparatory School, Brewood

Suffolk
Cherry Trees School, Bury St Edmunds
Fairstead House School, Newmarket
Finborough School, Stowmarket
Hillcroft Preparatory School, Stowmarket
The Old School, Nr Beccles
Stoke College, Sudbury

Surrey
The American Community School, Cobham
Bishopsgate School, Englefield Green
Box Hill School, Dorking
Canbury School, Kingston-upon-Thames
Clewborough House School, Camberley
Collingwood School, Wallington

Surrey — *continued*
Elmhurst School, South Croydon
Glaisdale School, Cheam
Glenesk School, East Horsley
Hawley Place School, Camberley
Hurtwood House School, Dorking
Longacre School, Guildford
Lyndhurst School, Camberley
Milbourne Lodge Junior School, Esher
More House School, Farnham
Notre Dame School, Lingfield
Notre Dame Senior School, Cobham
Oakhyrst Grange School, Caterham
St Christopher's School, Epsom
St David's School, Purley
Sanderstead Junior School
Stowford, Sutton
Study School, New Malden
West Dene School, Purley

Sussex (East)
Bellerbys College, Mayfield
Claremont School, St Leonards-on-Sea
Greenfields School, Forest Row
Hawkhurst Court School, Brighton
Newlands Manor School, Seaford
Lewes Old Grammar School, Lewes
The Towers Convent School, Steyning

Sussex (West)
St Margaret's Junior School, Midhurst
Shoreham College, Shoreham-by-Sea
Slindon College, Arundel

Tyne and Wear
Argyle House School, Sunderland
Eastcliffe Grammar School, Newcastle upon Tyne

Warwickshire
Abbotsford School, Kenilworth
Princethorpe College, Rugby
St Joseph's School, Kenilworth
Stratford Preparatory School, Stratford-upon-Avon
Twycross House School, Atherstone

West Midlands
Davenport Lodge School, Coventry
Eastbourne House School, Birmingham
Highclare School, Sutton Coldfield
Hydesville Tower School, Walsall
Norfolk House School, Birmingham
Ruckleigh School, Solihull

Wiltshire
Heywood Preparatory School, Corsham

Yorkshire (North)
Fyling Hall School, Robin Hood's Bay
Howsham Hall, York
Read School, Selby
Red House Preparatory School, Moor Monkton
St Hilda's School, Whitby

Yorkshire (South)
Brantwood Independent School for Girls, Sheffield
Hull Grammar School

Yorkshire (West)
Cliff School, Wakefield
Lady Lane Park School, Bingley
Moorfield School, Ilkley
North Leeds Preparatory School, Leeds
Sunny Hill House School and Nursery, Wakefield

Wales
Elm Tree House School, Llandaff, Cardiff
Haylett Grange Preparatory School, Haverfordwest
Hillgrove School, Bangor
Kings Monkton School, Cardiff
Lyndon School, Colwyn Bay
Northgate School, Rhyl
St Gerard's School, Bangor
St Michael's School, Llanelli
Westbourne School, Penarth

Europe
The Stavanger British School, Norway

PART VII

Tutors, Tutorial Colleges and other Independent Institutions

Entries of members of the Council for Independent Further Education (page 1167) will be found on pp 1167–1169. Entries of members of the Association of Tutors (page 1175) and of other Independent Institutions will be found on pp 1167–1175.

COUNCIL FOR INDEPENDENT FURTHER EDUCATION (CIFE)

President: Baroness Perry of Southwark
Vice President: Hugh Monro, MA (Headmaster of Clifton College)
Chairman: Robert J Arthy, BSc, MPhil, MRIC (Principal of The Albany College)
Vice-Chairman: David Lowe, MA, FRSA (Principal of Cambridge Tutors College)
Executive Council:
James Burnett, BSc (Principal of MPW London)
Mrs Jenny Burghes, BSc (Co-Principal of Exeter Tutorial College)
Gerald Hattee, MA, DipEd (Principal of Collingham)
Andrew Osmond, BSc, CertEd (Vice-Principal of Modes Study Centre)
Eric Reynolds, BA, PGCE (Principal of Padworth College)
Mrs Elizabeth Rickards, MA, PGCE (Principal of Davies Laing & Dick)

In September 2001 we will enter the second year of the new post-16 curriculum, one designed to increase breadth without losing depth. This stage in a student's life is of vital importance since it is when she/he begins to discover what it is like to take ownership of his or her own study. This is the time to prepare for a university style of education. At a time when one in five students in higher education drops out in the first year it is crucial to improve the quality of preparation that students receive. The new curriculum seeks to do this in that it aims to broaden a student's outlook. Moreover it includes the 'key skills' that employers have identified as being important. So a narrow academic path does not serve today's society. We need doctors with a spiritual dimension, accountants and business people who speak a second language, lawyers who can communicate simply and effectively; everyone needs to have strong interpersonal skills and to be computer literate.

Independent sixth form colleges are extremely well-placed to offer what is needed to students preparing for university and beyond. The best such colleges are members of CIFE, the Council for Independent Further Education, an organisation which is in its 28th year, which guarantees high standards, and which has its results independently audited and published by the British Accreditation Council. There are 32 CIFE colleges, geographically spread across the country, each one offering something individual but all subject to the same high standards of accreditation.

So, for example, there are some colleges that specialise in students wishing to retake in order to improve exam grades, some serving a cosmopolitan mix of students, some offering GCSE and pre-GCSE programmes as well as A levels, one offering IB (International Baccalaureate), some which are residential, or homestay, or day, or a mix of all three. Several colleges offer foundation programmes and are twinned with universities and one is a single-sex female environment. In short CIFE colleges aim to offer a wide range of educational environments where students can succeed.

Teaching in CIFE colleges really helps and supports students since teaching groups are small and teachers highly experienced and able. The 'tutorial' system derives directly from Oxbridge (in Cambridge called 'supervisions') where it continues to be world famous. A student in a small group receives a greater degree of individual attention. Regular testing ensures that she/he maintains good progress and emphasis on study skills provides essential support for the AS/A2 subjects. It is not surprising that a student gains confidence and self-belief within such an environment. Colleges engender a strong work ethic in their student communities. Many of the smaller rules and regulations essential for schools are not necessary for CIFE colleges. Good manners and an enthusiastic attitude are every bit as important, but uniform, strict times for eating or homework, assemblies or games participation are not part of the picture. It can be seen from the large numbers of students going on to higher education from CIFE colleges that universities regard our students highly.

Increasing numbers of young people are deciding to move school at the age of 16, not because they are unhappy with their school, but because they see the need for a change at this stage. It may be that they wish to study a subject which their school does not offer, such as Accounting, Law, Psychology or Geology. Maybe they are looking for a more adult environment or one where they can focus in on their academic subjects to the exclusion of other things. It would be misleading to suggest that CIFE colleges are lacking in extra-curricular activities of all sorts, sporting, social and creative. All colleges recognise the need for enrichment. The difference is that activities are at the choice of the student.

As with schools, choosing a college calls for careful research. CIFE colleges adhere to a strict code of conduct governing the provision and standards of teaching, safety and pastoral care. Colleges undergo regular inspection and their examination results are independently audited. While each college has its own individual character, all share the desire to provide a superb preparation for higher education to each individual student.

Further information can be obtained from the Executive Secretary: Dr Norma R Ball, 75 Foxbourne Road, London SW17 8EN. Tel: (020) 8767 8666, Fax: (020) 8767 9444. Email: enquiries@cife.org.uk

Abbey College Birmingham
Principals: Colum Devine, BSc, MSc, DPhil
Zoe Keeling, BA, MA
10 St Paul's Square, Birmingham B3 1QU
Tel: (0121) 236 7474

Abbey College Cambridge
Principal: Glenn Hawkins, BSc, PhD
17 Station Road, Cambridge CB1 2JB
Tel: (01223) 578280

Abbey College London
Principal: Andrew Williams, BSc, MSc
28a Hereford Road, London W2 5AJ
Tel: (020) 7229 5928

Abbey College Manchester
Principal: Andrea Bond, BA, CertEd, DipInstM
20 Kennedy Street, Manchester M2 4BY
Tel: (0161) 236 6836

The Albany College
Principal: R J Arthy, BSc, MPhil, MRIC
21–24 Queens Road, Hendon NW4 2TL
Tel: (020) 8202 5965/9748

Ashbourne
Principals: M J Hatchard-Kirby, BApSc, MSc
S Cook, BA, MScEcon
17 Old Court Place, London W8 4PL
Tel: (020) 7937 3858

Bales College
Principal: W B Moore, BSc
21 Kilburn Lane, London W10 4AA
Tel: (020) 8960 5899

Bellerbys College
Principal: Nigel Addison, BSc, PGCE
44 Cromwell Road, Hove, East Sussex BN3 3ER
Tel: (01273) 323374

Bosworth Tutorial College
Principal: M A V Broadway, BSc, PGCE
Nazareth House, Barrack Road, Northampton NN2 6AF
Tel: (01604) 239995

Brook House College
Principal: Jonathan C Stanford, BA(Hons), PGCE Stanford
Market Harborough, Leicestershire LE16 7AU
Tel: (01858) 462452

Cambridge Centre for Sixth Form Studies
Principal: P C Readhead, MA, PGCE(Cantab)
1 Salisbury Villas, Station Road, Cambridge CB1 2JF
Tel: (01223) 716890

Cambridge Tutors College
Principal: David Lowe, MA(Cantab), FRSA
Water Tower Hill, Croydon, Surrey CR0 5SX
Tel: (020) 8688 5284/7363

Cherwell College
Principal: Andrew Thompson, MA(Cantab)
Greyfriars, Paradise Street, Oxford OX1 1LD
Tel: (01865) 242670

Collingham
Principal: Gerald Hattee, MA, DipEd
23 Collingham Gardens, London SW5 0HL
Tel: (020) 7244 7414

Concord College
Principal: A L Morris, BA, DipEd
Acton Burnell Hall, Shrewsbury, Shropshire SY5 7PF
Tel: (01694) 731631

Davies Laing & Dick
Principal: Elizabeth Rickards, MA, PGCE
10 Pembridge Square, London W2 4ED
Tel: (020) 7727 2797

Duff Miller Sixth-Form College
Principal: Clive Denning, BSc, PGCE
59 Queen's Gate, London SW7 5JP
Tel: (020) 7225 0577

Exeter Tutorial College
Principals: Mrs Jenny Burghes, BSc
Kenneth Jack, BA, DipEd Durham, DEdnPsy Cambridge
44–46 Magdalen Road, Exeter EX2 4TE
Tel: (01392) 278101

Fine Arts College
Principals: Candida Cave, CFA(Oxon)
Nicholas Cochrane, CFA(Oxon)
85 Belsize Park Gardens, London NW3 4NJ
Tel: (020) 7586 0312

Harrogate Tutorial College
Principal: Keith Pollard, BSc, DipMaths, DipEd
2 The Oval, Harrogate, North Yorkshire HG2 9BA
Tel: (01423) 501041 (5 lines)

Irwin College
Principals: Mrs Gaynor Tonks, BA, PGCE
Mr Stephen Wytcherley
164 London Road, Leicester LE2 1ND
Tel: (0116) 255 2648

Lansdowne Independent Sixth Form College
Principal: Hugh Templeton, FCCA
40–44 Bark Place, London W2 4AT
Tel: (020) 7616 4400

Mander Portman Woodward (Birmingham)
Principal: Martin Lloyd, MA, FCollP
38 Highfield Road, Edgbaston, Birmingham B15 3ED
Tel: (0121) 454 9637

Mander Portman Woodward (Cambridge)
Principal: Nick Marriott, BSc, PhD
3/4 Brookside, Cambridge CB2 1JE
Tel: (01223) 350158

Mander Portman Woodward (London)
Principals: Steven Boyes, BA, MSc, PGCE
James Burnett, BSc
24 Elvaston Place, London SW7 5NL
Tel: (020) 7584 8555

Modes Study Centre
Principal: Stephen C R Moore, MA(Oxon), DPhil(Oxon)
73/75 George Street, Oxford OX1 2BQ
Tel: (01865) 245172/249349

Oxford Tutorial College
Principal: Mrs Josephine Palmer, BA, PGCE
12 King Edward Street, Oxford OX1 4HT
Tel: (01865) 793333

Padworth College
Principal: Eric Reynolds, BA, PGCE
Nr. Reading, Berkshire RG7 4NR
Tel: (0118) 9832644/5

St. Clare's, Oxford
Principal: Boyd Roberts, MA(Oxon), CertEd, CBiol, MBiol
139 Banbury Road, Oxford OX2 7AL
Tel: (01865) 552031

Surrey College
Principal: Louise Cody, BA, MA, PGCE, DSA
Administration Centre, Abbott House, Sydenham Road, Guildford, Surrey GU1 3RL
Tel: (01483) 565887

The Tuition Centre
Principal: Bernard Canetti, BA(Hons), MSc
Lodge House, Lodge Road, Hendon, London NW4 4DQ
Tel: (020) 8203 5025

PART VIII
Universities and Colleges

This section includes the former Polytechnics.

The Universities Central Council on Admissions, PO Box 28, Cheltenham, Glos, GL50 3SA, is the central office dealing with applications for admission to full-time first degree and first diploma courses at all United Kingdom universities and their affiliated colleges except the Open University. UCCA publishes *The UCCA Handbook* which gives details of how to apply for admission to a university. Copies are available, free of charge, from schools and colleges or from the UCCA office.

OXFORD UNIVERSITY

Chancellor: Rt Hon The Lord Jenkins of Hillhead, PC, DCL.
Vice-Chancellor: Peter Machin North, CBE, DCL, FBA.

Degrees. BEd, BTheol, BFA, MEng, BA, BPhil, BMus, BM, BCh, MJur, BCL, BD, MA, MEd, MTheol, MSt, MPhil, MLitt, MSc, MCh, DPhil, DMus, DSc, DLitt, DCL, DD.

Faculties. Theology, Law, Literae Humaniores, Modern History, English, Modern Languages, Oriental Studies, Physical Sciences, Biological Sciences, Social Studies, Anthropology and Geography, Music, Psychological Studies, Mathematical Sciences, Clinical Medicine, Physiological Sciences.

Fees. Various, according to Degrees taken. Details about admission requirements, expenses, examinations, degrees, method of application, etc., are published in the 'University of Oxford Undergraduate Prospectus'.

Admission. Applicants for the BA may take the Entrance Examination which is restricted to applicants who have not yet taken A levels; or may enter by a conditional offer system similar to that in other universities. Post-A level applicants enter on the basis of their 'A' levels or equivalent qualifications (I.B. etc.). Full information is included in the Prospectus, available free of charge from the Oxford Colleges Admissions Office, Wellington Square, Oxford OX1 2JD.

CAMBRIDGE UNIVERSITY

Chancellor: His Royal Highness The Prince Philip, Duke of Edinburgh, KG, KT, Hon LLD.
Vice Chancellor: Sir David Williams, MA.

Faculties: Architecture and History of Art, Classics, Divinity, English, Modern and Medieval Languages, Music, Oriental Studies, Economics and Politics, Education, History, Law, Philosophy, Social and Political Sciences, Engineering, Earth Sciences and Geography, Mathematics, Physics and Chemistry, Archaeology and Anthropology, Biology 'A', Biology 'B', Clinical Medicine, Clinical Veterinary Medicine. The following Departments are not assigned to a Faculty: Chemical Engineering, the Computer Laboratory, History and Philosophy of Science, Land Economy, and the University Library.

Fees (1992–93): Home and E.C. undergraduatesarts £1,855, sciences £2,770, clinical £4,985; Overseas arts £5,247, sciences £6,882, clinical £6,882 rising to £12,732 in clinical years. College fees, which range from £2,445 to £2,800, must also be paid.

Residence. The Colleges can normally provide accommodation for two of the three years of undergraduate study.

Admission. It is possible to become a student member of the University only by being admitted to one of the Colleges, and application for admission should therefore be made to the Tutor for Admissions at the College of the candidate's choice. Copies of *The Cambridge Admissions Prospectus* and information about College entrance requirements can be obtained from the Intercollegiate Applications Office, Kellet Lodge, Tennis Court Road, Cambridge CB2 1QJ. More detailed information on the courses provided in the University may be found in the *Guide to Courses* published by C.U.P. each September, and obtainable through any bookseller. Full details of the examination requirements for matriculation may be obtained from the Registrary, University Registry, The Old Schools, Trinity Lane, Cambridge CB2 1TN.

DURHAM, 1832

Chancellor: Sir Peter Ustinov, CBE, DLitt, FRSA, FRSL.
Vice-Chancellor and Warden: Professor E A V Ebsworth, MA, PhD, ScD, FRSE, FRSC.
Pro-Vice-Chancellor and Sub-Warden: G E Rodmell, BA, PhD.
Pro-Vice-Chancellors: P D B Collins, BSc, PhD; Professor M C Prestwich, MA, DPhil, FRHistS, FSA.
Registrar and Secretary: J C F Hayward, MA, FBIM.

Faculties. There are three faculties: *Science*; *Arts*; *Social Sciences.*

Matriculation. Regulations for Matriculation can be obtained from the Registrar and Secretary.

The Durham Colleges. Teaching is provided for the above Degrees and Diplomas.

Every student is a member of a College. 80 of students live in College accommodation.

College for Women: St Mary's College. *Principal:* Miss J M Kenworthy, BLitt, MA.
Mixed Colleges: University College. *Master:* E C Salthouse, BSc, PhD, CEng, FIEE, FRSA.
Grey College. *Master:* V E Watts, MA.
Hatfield College. *Master:* Professor J P Barber, JP, MA, PhD.
Collingwood College. *Principal:* G H Blake, JP, MA, PhD.
Van Mildert College. *Principal:* Judith Turner, BSc, MA, PhD.
St Aidan's College. *Principal:* R J Williams, JP, BA, MPhil.
St Chad's College. *Principal:* E Halladay, MA.
College of St Hild and St Bede. *Principal:* J V Armitage, BSc, PhD, FIMA, FRAS.
St Cuthbert's Society. *Principal:* S G C Stoker, BA, MEd.
St John's College. *Principal:* D V Day, BA, MEd, MTheol.
Trevelyan College. *Principal:* Miss D Lavin, MA.

UNIVERSITY OF NEWCASTLE UPON TYNE

Early foundations in nineteenth century: reconstituted with present title of university 1963.
Vice-Chancellor: J R G Wright, MA.
Dean of Medicine: Professor A L Crombie, MB, ChB, FRCSEd.
Registrar: D E T Nicholson, MA.

Teaching includes all normal University subjects in faculties of Arts, Science, Engineering, Agriculture and Biological Sciences, Medicine, Social and Environmental Sciences, Law, Education. Subjects unique to Newcastle or taught in a minority of other universities include Agricultural and Environmental Science, Agricultural Engineering, Agricultural Mechanization Management, Fine Art, Marine Technology, Medical Science, Politics and East Asian Studies, Soil and Land Resource Science, Speech, Surveying Science.

Fees. £2,770 pa (registration, tuition, examination, graduation, library) for undergradutes ordinarily resident in UK; from £5,320 pa according to course for residents outside UK. In addition certain expenses for vacational field work, etc.

Residence. Approximately 45 of the total undergraduate population is accommodated in University residences.

Scholarships and Research. Details available from the Registrar, University of Newcastle, Newcastle upon Tyne NE1 7RU.

Medicine, including Dental Surgery. See Medical section.

UNIVERSITY OF LONDON

Founded 1836.

Students are advised to refer to the prospectuses issued by the Schools of the University for detailed information. This book does not include *all* Schools of the University.

Course of study. For Internal Students most teaching is carried out in the Schools of the University. Residence in college or in a hostel is not compulsory, but a student for a first degree must follow an approved course of study (normally lasting three years).

External students are free to choose their own method of study. Most External Students study privately, aided by attendance at evening classes or by a correspondence course. Further information may be obtained from the Secretary for External Students.

General Information pamphlets for internal and external students may be obtained on application from the Information Centre, Room 1, Senate House, Malet Street, London WC1E 7HU.

University College London

(Including the University College and Middlesex School of Medicine)

Founded 1826. A School of the University of London.
Provost: Dr Derek Roberts, FRS.
Secretary: I H Baker, CBE.
Registrar: J W Arterton.

Student numbers. 8500 Male/Female ratio: 5/4.

Faculties. Arts (including Economics, the Slade School of Fine Art, the Institute of Archaeology, the School of Library, Archive and Information Studies), Laws, Science, Environmental Studies (including Architecture, Building and Town Planning), Medical Sciences, Clinical Sciences.

Student Accommodation. All first year undergranduate students are offered places in College or University accommodation, provided that they have applied by the date required.

Fees. Composition fees for all first degree courses for UK and EC students are £607 per session.

Admission. Prospectuses and literature about courses can be obtained from the Registrar.

King's College London

Strand, WC2

Founded 1829.

The College is the second largest and the most diverse academically within the University of London.
Principal: Dr J D E Beynon, FEng, FKC.

In Humanities, Education, Laws, Life, Basic Medical and Health Sciences and Physical Sciences and Engineering and Medicine and Dentistry the College offers a full and varied range of degree courses at both the undergraduate and postgraduate level.

Admission: Entrance requirements vary between degree courses and the College will, in certain circumstances, consider applicants with non-standard qualifications.

The London School of Economics and Political Science

Houghton Street, Aldwych WC2A 2AE

Director: Dr John M Ashworth, MA, PhD, DSc, FIBiol.

The School provides courses for University of London degrees of BA (Anthropology and Law, Geography, History, Philosophy, Social Anthropology), LLB (also with French Law or German Law), BSc (Geography, Actuarial Science, Management, Management Sciences, Mathematical Sciences, Statistics, Computing and Information Systems, Mathematics and Philosophy, Social Anthropology, Social Economic History with Population Studies, Social Policy and Administration, Social Psychology, Sociology) and BSc (Econ), offering specialisation in 21 branches, including Accounting and Finance, Computing, Economics, Economic History, Environment and Planning (Geography), Government, Industrial Relations, International History, International Relations, Philosophy, Population Studies, Social Anthropology, Social Policy, Social Psychology, Sociology, Statistics. There are also summer schools in Economics, Law, Management and International Relations.

The School also offers opportunities for graduate students, through the School's own diplomas and teaching supervision for the University of London degrees of MA, MSc, LLM, MPhil and PhD. There are also opportunities for study not leading to a qualification. Further information may be obtained from the Academic Registrar.

Imperial College of Science, Technology and Medicine

The Imperial College was established by Royal Charter 'to give the highest specialised instruction, and to provide the fullest equipment for the most advanced training and research in various branches of science especially in its application to industry'. The College is a federation of four closely linked constituent colleges: the Royal College of Science, the Royal School of Mines, the City and Guilds College and St Mary's Hospital Medical School. The undergraduate courses are either of three, four or five years' duration.

A five-year MB BS course is available at St Mary's Hospital Medical School.

Additionally, a very wide range of postgraduate courses and research opportunities exists in most branches of science, technology and medicine.

Undergraduate Fees 1993-94.

Home and EC students: £1,300 (Mathematics); £2,770 (all other courses); £785 self-supported students (all courses).

Overseas students: £6,550 (Mathematics); £8,300 (all other courses).

Details of postgraduate fees are available on request from the Assistant Registrar (Student Finance).

For full particulars apply to the Assistant Registrar (Admissions), Imperial College, South Kensington, London SW7 2AZ. Telephone: 020-7589 5111. Fax: 020-7225 2528.

Birkbeck College, 1823

A school of the University of London in the Faculties of Arts, Laws, Science and Economics for part-time and full-time Internal Students.

Master: Baroness Blackstone, BSc (Soc), PhD, HonDLitt.

Clerk: Christine Mabey, BA, PhD.

Faculties. Arts, Laws, Science and Economics.

Applications for admission to undergraduate courses can normally only be considered from persons engaged in earning their livelihood during the day time (or, if unemployed, actively seeking employment).

Fees. On application.

Scholarships. Bursaries and Exhibitions are awarded annually to students of the College.

There are both part-time and full-time facilities for post-graduate and research work in Arts, Laws, Science and Economics. Reference and lending libraries open to students. Further particulars and form of application from the Registrar, Birkbeck College, Malet Street, WC1E 7HX.

Queen Mary and Westfield College, University of London, Mile End Road E1 4NS

Principal: Professor Graham Zellick, MA, PhD (Cambridge).

Academic Secretary: D B T Jaynes, BA (Wales), MA (Cambridge).

Financial Secretary: Dr K Aldred, MA (Cambridge), PhD (Lancaster), FOR, IPFA.

Faculties. Arts, Engineering, Laws, Natural Sciences, Informatics and Mathematical Sciences, Social Sciences and Basic Medical Sciences.

Created from the merger of two 19th century colleges, Queen Mary and Westfield College is now one of the largest multi-faculty colleges of the University of London, with more than 6,000 undergraduate and postgraduate students. Its campus at Mile End has recently seen exceptional expansion, with new halls of residence, Faculty of Basic Medical Sciences, library, refectory and commercial complex, informatics teaching laboratory and Arts Faculty building with its own drama space, all opened in the last few years. More halls of residence are on a 13 acre site at South Woodford. The Students' Union has its own building on campus with bars, snack bar, shop, common rooms, gym and squash courts; while sports grounds for cricket, football, rugby, hockey and tennis at nearby Theydon Bois in Essex.

Central London can be reached by tube in 15 minutes, and students also enjoy exploring the area surrounding campus with its canalside walks, pubs, ethnic restaurants, theatres and galleries.

Fees. (1992-93) Home students at undergraduate level £1,855–£2,770 per session. Fees for overseas students £6,150–£7,450, according to subject. Students doing field work as part of their course will be required to pay a fee for each course attended. Details are published in the Prospectus, obtainable from The Academic Registrar at the above address, or on 071-975 5555. Personal enquiries from headmasters, headmistresses and careers advisors in schools are also welcome.

Royal Holloway, University of London

Egham, Surrey TW20 0EX

Founded on 1886, for men and women students, with a high proportion of residence places in both residential and self-catering Halls.

Recognised in the Faculties of Arts, Economics, Music and Science. Student numbers in 1993 about 4,120.

Principal: Professor Norman Gowar, BSc, MPhil, FIMA.

Fees: Tuition UK and EC undergraduates: Arts £1,885, Science/Music/Drama £2,770 a session and UK and EC postgraduates £2,200 a session. Overseas undergraduates and postgraduates: Arts/Music £5,900, Science (including Mathematics) £7,100. Students' Union Society included in Tuition fees.

Admission. *Undergraduates:* **by General and Course Requirements of the University of London. Candidates must apply through the Universities Central Council on Admissions.** *Postgraduates:* **by direct application to the College Registrar.**

Scholarships. Choral, Organ and Instrumental Scholarships are awarded annually to candidates for any course of study.

The Courses are arranged in accordance with the regulations of the University of London.

Further information can be obtained by application to the Schools Liaison Officer.

Goldsmiths' College

Address: Lewisham Way, London, SE14 6NW

Telephone: 020-8692-7171.

One of the larger Colleges of the University of London.

Warden: Professor Kenneth J Gregory, BSc, PhD, DSc, FRGS.

Prospectus available from the Registry on application.

Westfield College
(see Queen Mary and Westfield College)

THE VICTORIA UNIVERSITY OF MANCHESTER, 1903

Vice-Chancellor: Professor M B Harris, CBE, MA, PhD.

Faculties. Arts, Business Administration, Economic and Social Studies, Education, Law, Medicine (including the Dental School), Science, Technology.

Diplomas. For advanced study in Faculties of Arts, Business Administration, Economic and Social Studies, Education, Law, Medicine, Science, Technology, Theology.

Certificates. In Faculties of Economic and Social Studies, Education, Theology. Extra-Mural Certificates in Archaeology; Health Education; Religious Studies; Social Studies; Egyptology; Counselling; Landscape Studies.

Fees. A Fees leaflet is obtainable from the Registrar.

Scholarships. Entrance Scholarships test held in January: see *Undergraduate Prospectus.* Also Scholarships, Studentships and Fellowships for advanced students.

Residence. Four Halls for men, two for women, seven for men and women (including Owens Park Student Village), 18 self-catering residences. List of approved lodgings. All unmarried first-year undergraduates may live in a university residence if they wish. Details in *Undergraduate Prospectus.*

Further Information. *Undergraduate Prospectus* is obtainable free from the Registrar, The University, Manchester M13 9PL.

UMIST (The University of Manchester Institute of Science and Technology) (Faculty of Technology in the University of Manchester), 1905

All departments offer facilities for study and research for MSc and PhD Degrees and formal courses for the Degree of MSc are available in several departments.

Fees. Vary according to the course taken.

Residence. All first-year undergraduate students are *guaranteed* a place in Hall. UMIST and the University of Manchester share residential accommodation.

Scholarships. Details in the Undergraduate Prospectus or Postgraduate Studies and Research booklet, available from the Registrar, PO Box 88, Manchester M60 1QD.

Social Life. The Students' Union occupies extensive premises on the campus and provides reciprocal membership of the University Union. The UMIST and University Athletic Unions co-operate to provide athletic facilities.

BIRMINGHAM, 1900

The University of Birmingham offers courses for Honours degrees in almost all subjects in the Faculties of Arts, Commerce and Social Science, Education and Continuing Studies, Engineering, Law, Medicine and Dentistry and Science. The courses last three years in most cases but some (notably languages, medicine and dentistry and engineering courses) are longer.

Full details of admission requirements and courses are to be found in the University Prospectus, available from the Academic Secretary (Undergraduate Prospectus Requests).

The University also awards higher (Master's and Doctor's) degrees in all Faculties, the courses for which are open to good honours graduates of most universities. Particulars of these are also obtainable from the Academic Secretary (Postgraduate Prospectus Requests).

Fees vary according to the course taken.

Scholarships. Details are published in the relevant *Faculty Handbooks.*

Residence. First year students who wish to live in University accommodation, either a Hall of Residence or self-catering flat are guaranteed a place subject to their accepting our offer firmly. One hall is for men, one for women, and four are mixed. The Housing Services Office assists students not living in halls or University self-catering flats to find suitable lodgings or flats.

Social Life. Students at the University enjoy a full and varied social life whether it be on the campus itself (where the Guild of Students has the supervision of all social and athletic activities), in halls of residence, or in the surrounding areas of the city.

If you are thinking of admission to Birmingham write to the Academic Secretary (Prospectus Requests), The University of Birmingham, Edgbaston, Birmingham B15 2TT, mentioning the courses which interest you and asking for a copy of the Undergraduate or Postgraduate Prospectus and other literature.

LIVERPOOL, 1903

Chancellor: The Rt Hon the Viscount Leverhulme, KG, TD, JP, BA (Cambridge), LLD (Liverpool).
Vice-Chancellor: Professor Philip Noel Love, CBE, MA, LLB (Aberdeen).
Registrar: M D Carr, MA (Durham).

Faculties. Arts, Science, Medicine (including Dentistry, and Nursing and other Professions allied to Medicine), Law, Engineering, Veterinary Science, Social and Environmental Studies, and Education and Extension Studies.

Degrees. Details of all first degree courses, including entrance requirements, fees, awards, residences, etc., are given in the Undergraduate Prospectus.

Higher Degrees and Diplomas. Opportunities for postgraduate study, by taught courses or research, are given in the Postgraduate Prospectus. Some courses are open to non-graduates with relevant experience.

Prospectuses. The Undergraduate and Postgraduate Prospectuses may be obtained, free of charge, by contacting the Student and Examinations Division, University of Liverpool, PO Box 147, Liverpool L69 3BX, telephone 051-794 2045. Those domiciled overseas should contact the International Office at the University (051-794 2070).

Social Life. There is a Guild of Students, to which all undergraduate students must belong, one of the functions of which is to promote academic and social unity among members of the Guild. There are also over 100 Student Societies.
Address: Students' Union, 2 Bedford Street North, Liverpool L7 7BD.

LEEDS, 1904

Vice-Chancellor: Professor A G Wilson, MA.
Registrar: E Newcomb, BA, DipEd.

Degree Programmes. Degrees are granted in Arts, Economic and Social Studies, Law, Education, Science, Engineering, Medicine, and Dentistry.

Residence in student flats and Halls of Residence.

Enquiries to Student Accommodation Office, The University of Leeds, Leeds LS2 9JT. Tel: (01132) 336071.

SHEFFIELD, 1905

Chancellor: The Right Hon The Lord Dainton of Hallam Moors, Kt, MA, BSc, PhD, ScD, Hon DSc, Hon DTech, Hon LLD, Hon DCL, CChem, Hon FRSChem, Hon FRCP, Hon FRCR, Hon FLA, FRS.
Vice-Chancellor: Professor G G Roberts, BSc, PhD, DSc, CPhys, CEng, FInstP, FIEE, FRS.
Registrar and Secretary: J S Padley, BSc, PhD.

The University of Sheffield is a large, strong and successful university. It combines nearly one hundred years of tradition with a policy of innovation; size with friendliness; and a strong commitment to teaching in an atmosphere of research at the highest international levels.

Sheffield is consistently ranked as one of the four or five most popular universities and is able to attract the highest quality studentsthe average score of new entrants with A levels is almost BBB. Its research has been recognised in government reviews with 59 of all departments receiving a top or second-top rating of research.

Further details of the courses available, university accommodation and other matters may be obtained from The Admissions Office, The University of Sheffield, Sheffield S10 2TN.

THE UNIVERSITY OF BRISTOL, 1909

Chancellor: Sir Jeremy Morse, KCMG, MA, DLitt, LLD.
Vice-Chancellor: Sir John Kingman, MA, ScD, DSc, LLD, CStat, FRS.
Secretary: J H M Parry, MA.
Registrar: .

Faculties. Arts, Science, Medicine, Engineering, Law, Social Sciences.

Courses of Study. Students are prepared for Degrees in Arts, Science, Medicine, Dental Surgery, Veterinary Science, Engineering, Law, Social Sciences, Education.

Diplomas in Adult and Continuing Education, Counselling, Housing Studies, Philosophy, Deaf Studies, Education, Architectural Conservation, Social Policy Social Planning, Social Sciences, Postqualifying Studies in Social Work, Theology, English Legal Studies, Social Work, Arts, Music Therapy, Drama, Film Television, Dental Studies, Intellectual Property Law and Practice, Language Studies, Legal Practice, Occupational Health Nursing and Science.

Certificates in Arts, Science, Social Sciences, Education, Legal Subjects, Medically-related Subjects, Sign-Language Interpreting, Biological Science, Counselling Skills, General Practice Management.
Social Work, Applied Social Studies, Exercise Health Studies, European Studies, Deaf Studies.

Halls of Residence. Men and Women: Badock Hall, Churchill Hall, Clifton Hill House, Goldney Hall, Hiatt Baker Hall, Manor Hall, University Hall, Wills Hall.

For further particulars including particulars of entrance requirements apply to the Registrar, the University, Senate House, Bristol BS8 1TH.

UNIVERSITY OF READING, 1926

Vice-Chancellor: R Williams, MA, MA(Econ).
Registrar: D C R Frampton, MA.

Departments of Study. Faculties of Letters and Social Sciences, Science, Agriculture and Food, Urban and Regional Studies, and Education and Community Studies.

Courses of Study. Students are prepared for the degrees of the University in Arts (including Fine Art and Music), Social Sciences, Law, Science (Biological Sciences, Earth and Physical Sciences, Mathematical Sciences and Engineering and Information Sciences), Agriculture and Food, Surveying and Education. The University also provides a full range of postgraduate courses for taught Masters degrees and diplomas, and for research degrees.

Residence. The University has fourteen Residential Halls, providing accommodation for about 4,500 students out of the total of 9,000.

For further particulars of courses in each Faculty, and advice about entrance, write to the Sub-Dean of the appropriate Faculty, The University, Whiteknights, Reading RG6 2AH.

UNIVERSITY OF NOTTINGHAM, 1948

Vice-Chancellor: Professor Colin Campbell, LLB.
Registrar: G E Chandler, BA.

Courses of Study. The University awards degrees in Arts, Social Sciences, Law, Education, Science (including Pharmacy), Agricultural and Food Sciences, Horticulture, Engineering (including Chemical and Production Engineering), Architecture, and Medicine. The School of Education offers a Certificate in Education Course (1 year) for graduates and other courses (part-time and full-time) for various Diplomas in education and for the MEd degree.

Agricultural and Food Sciences. The Faculty of Agricultural and Food Sciences is about 10 miles away at the Sutton Bonington campus, near Loughborough. The University farms 420 hectares (1,050 acres) including an experimental farm and a commercial farm for demonstration purposes.

Fees. Prospective students should write to the Secretary of the appropriate Faculty for up-to-date information.

Residence. There are four large halls in the University Park for men students, three for women students and five for men and women. There is one hall for men and women at the Sutton Bonington campus.

Further particulars may be obtained on application to the Secretary of the appropriate Faculty: Arts, Law and Social Sciences, Science, Engineering, Medicine, Education or Agricultural and Food Sciences (at Sutton Bonington).

Postal address: University Park, Nottingham NG7 2RD. Telephone: (01159) 515151.

THE UNIVERSITY OF SOUTHAMPTON, 1952

Chancellor: The Rt Hon the Earl Jellicoe, KBE, DSO, MC, LLD, FRS, PC.

Vice-Chancellor: Sir Gordon Higginson, PhD, HonDSc, FICE, FIMechE, FEng.

Secretary and Registrar: J F D Lauwerys, BEd, MA.

Academic Registrar: Miss A E Clarke, JP, BA.

There are eight faculties: Arts, Science, Engineering and Applied Science, Social Sciences, Educational Studies, Law, Medicine and Mathematical Studies.

Undergraduate courses leading to the degree of Bachelor are available in all faculties except Educational Studies. Courses leading to the degrees of BEd, BA, and BTh are offered at certain Colleges which are affiliated to the University for this purpose.

Postgraduate instructional courses leading to a certificate, diploma or master's degree are available in all faculties.

Research facilities are available in all faculties. Students may read for the degree of MPhil or PhD.

Further information on courses may be obtained from the Academic Registrar, The University, Highfield, Southampton SO9 5NH.

Fees. Tuition fees for the academic year 1992–93 for United Kingdom students are £1,855/£2,770/£4,985 for undergraduates and £2,200 for postgraduates. Residence fees range from £1,617 (full board for one person) to £1,062 (self catering) for the 30 weeks of the academic session.

Halls of Residence. Connaught Hall, South Stoneham House, Glen Eyre Hall, Montefiore House, Highfield Hall, Chamberlain Hall, Overdell Court, Bencraft Court and St Margaret's House. Clarkson House offers special care for disabled students.

Social Life. All full-time students are automatically members of Students' Union which offers good social, recreational and sports facilities.

General Note. These general particulars should be verified in each case and fuller information, including conditions for admission to degree and other courses, may be obtained from the Academic Registrar, The University, Highfield, Southampton SO9 5NH.

UNIVERSITY OF HULL, 1956

Vice-Chancellor: Professor W Taylor, CBE, BSc (Econ), PhD, DSc, LitD, DLitt, DCL, DUniv.

Registrar: F T Mattison, MA, LLB.

Schools: Arts, Chemistry, Earth Resources, Economics Studies, Education, Engineering Computing, Humanities, Law, Life Sciences, Management, Mathematics, Modern Languages Cultures and Social Political Sciences.

Courses of Study. Students are prepared for Degrees in Arts, Pure and Applied Science, Economics, Education, Engineering, Law, Music, Nursing and Theology.

Scholarships. A number of scholarships are awarded (mainly for post-graduate students), but there is no longer an annual Scholarships examination.

Halls of Residence. The University has ten residential Halls, all providing mixed accommodation, but single-sex areas can be arranged to meet demand.

Student Houses. The University has purchased a large number of houses and converted them into student accommodation, with kitchen/dining rooms and common rooms.

Prospectuses concerning the various courses may be obtained from the Assistant Registrar (Admissions), University of Hull, Freepost, Hull HU6 7BR.

UNIVERSITY OF EXETER, 1955

Vice-Chancellor: D Harrison, CBE, ScD, FEng, FRSC, FIChemE, CBIM, FRSA.

Academic Registrar and Secretary: I H C Powell, MA.

Departments of Study. Students are prepared for Degrees in the Faculty of Arts, Education, Engineering, Law, Science and Social Studies. The University also provides instruction for the Postgraduate Certificate in Education, Bachelor of Philosophy in Education, and for the Diplomas and Certificates in Education, Social work, Philosophy, Linguistics, Theology. Special courses in English Language and a Diploma in Science Studies for Overseas Students are also provided.

Composition Fees. For 1992/93 for UK/EC undergraduate students, Arts-based subjects, £1,855; Science-based subjects, £2,770. The full schedule of fees is available on application.

Halls. Thirteen Halls of Residence with nearly 2000 places.

Flats. Over 1250 places.

Postal Address: Exeter EX4 4QJ. Tel: (01392) 263263.

UNIVERSITY OF LEICESTER, 1957

(Founded as a University College, 1921)

Chancellor: Lord George Porter, OM, FRS, BSc, MA, PhD, ScD, FRSC.

Vice-Chancellor: K J R Edwards, BSc, MA, PhD.

Executive Pro-Vice-Chancellor and Registrar: Professor G Bernbaum, BSc (Econ), FRSA.

Faculties, etc. Faculties of Arts, Science (including Engineering), Law, Social Sciences, Medicine; School of Education.

Courses of Study. First and Higher Degrees in Arts, Science, Engineering, Law, Social Sciences, Medicine; Higher Degrees in Education, Museum Studies, Social Work; Diplomas in Archaeology, Education, Economics, Museum Studies, Psychology; Graduate Certificate in Education.

Halls of Residence and self catering accommodation for men and women students; Playing Fields, Sports Halls and Athletics Track.

Fees. (Sessional 1993–94) Home undergraduates*, classroom-based courses £1,300, laboratory-based courses £2,770, clinical medicine £4,985; Home postgraduates*, £2,260 (for most courses); Overseas undergraduates and postgraduates: Arts and the Social Sciences (incl. Geography and Museum Studies), £5,550; Science (incl. Archaeology, Mathematics, Psychology and Pre-Clinical Medicine), £7,360; Clinical Medicine £13,550.

*A student who has or whose parents have been ordinarily resident in the European Community for at least three years immediately before the start of the course is classed as a home student.

Prospectus on application to the Admissions Office, University of Leicester, University Road, Leicester LE1 7RH (Undergraduates) or Higher Degrees Office (Postgraduates) at the same address.

KEELE UNIVERSITY

Chancellor: Sir Claus Moser, KCB, CBE, DUniv, FBA.
Vice-Chancellor: Professor Brian E F Fender, CMG, MA (Oxon), PhD (Lond), CChem, FRSC.
Registrar: D Cohen, MA, PhD (Cantab), CChem, FRSC.
Director of Academic Affairs: E F Slade, BSc (Nott), PhD (Keele), CPhys, FInstP.

(*a*) *Three-Year Courses*

Students generally read two subjects at principal level for three years and one subject at subsidiary level for one year; option in the sciences of specialising in one subject in the final year. Must include some science and some non-science.

(*b*) *Four-Year Courses*

(1)The first (Foundation) year offers opportunities to change academic direction (e.g. arts to sciences) and provides a broad introduction to the main branches of University studies. Final choice of degree subjects at end of year.

(2)Three-years in which students generally read two subjects at principal level for three years and one subject at subsidiary level for one year; option in the sciences of specialising in one subject in the final year. Must include some science and some non-science.

(*c*)*Concurrent Courses*

Either the Certificate in Education (teaching qualification) or the Certificate of Competence in a Foreign Language may be taken concurrently with the four-year course.

Postal Address: Keele University, Staffordshire ST5 5BG.

UNIVERSITY OF SUSSEX, 1961

Chancellor: The Duke of Richmond and Gordon, FCA, DL, HonLLD (Sussex).
Vice-Chancellor: Professor Gordon Conway, BSc, DipAgriSci, DTA, PhD.
Registrar and Secretary: G Lockwood, BSc (Econ), DPhil.
Assistant Registrar (Admissions): Mrs E C Stewart.
Number of full-time students: (1992–93) 4,967 undergraduates, 1,692 postgraduates.

Courses of Instruction. The BA, BSc and BEng Degree courses are founded on the principle that both specialisation and general education are essential parts of a balanced university education and that the student should continuously relate specialised study to impinging and overlapping studies. Studies are organised in ten Schools – African and Asian Studies; Biological Sciences; Chemistry and Molecular Sciences; Cognitive and Computing Sciences; Cultural and Community Studies; Engineering; English and American Studies; European Studies; Mathematical and Physical Sciences; and Social Sciences.

Fees 1992–93 (for home students) £1,855 pa for students financed under mandatory awards, or £2,770 pa for laboratory-based courses, or £672 otherwise; (for overseas students £5,600 pa, or £7,150 pa for laboratory-based courses).

Prospectus. The University Prospectus is available from the Admissions Office, Sussex House, University of Sussex, Falmer, Brighton BN1 9RH Tel: (01273) 678416.

THE UNIVERSITY OF EAST ANGLIA

Chancellor: The Reverend Professor W O Chadwick, OM, KBE, DD, FBA.
Vice-Chancellor: Professor D C Burke, BSc, PhD, LLD.

Degrees Awarded. BA, BEd, BSc, BEng, LLB, PGCE, MA, MEd, MSc, MMusMSW, LLM, BPhil, MPhil, PhD.

Schools of Studies. Courses of study leading to the Honours Degree of BA are offered in the Schools of Development Studies, English and American Studies, Modern Languages and European History, Art History and Music, and Economic and Social Studies. Courses leading to the Honours Degree of LLB are offered in the School of Law. Courses of study leading to the Honours Degree of BSc are offered in the School of Biological Sciences, Chemical Sciences, Information Systems, Development Studies, Environmental Sciences and Mathematics and Physics.

Fees. Composition fees are revised annually. In 1992–93 they are: Band 1 (Arts and other non laboratory-based programmes) £1,885; Band 2 (Laboratory-based programmes) £2,770 (first degrees and full-time Home and EC students); £755 (first degrees, self-funding full-time Home and EC students).

Prospectus. The University Prospectus is available on application to the Registrar and Secretary, University of East Anglia, Norwich, Norfolk NR4 7TJ.

UNIVERSITY OF YORK, 1963

Vice-Chancellor: Professor R U Cooke, MSc, PhD, DSC.
Registrar: D J Foster, BA.

Degrees. BA, BSc, BEng, MEng, MA, MSc, MSW, EngDip, MPhil and DPhil.

Courses of Study. Degree courses in Arts, Social Sciences, Applied and Natural Sciences and Engineering.

Fees. For UK and EC students the annual composition fees are £1,300–£2,770 for an undergraduate course with a special rate for self-financing students of £906 and £2,260 for a postgraduate course; for overseas students the fees are £7,360 for courses in Biology, Chemistry, Computer Science, Electronics, Physics and Psychology and £5,550 for other courses.

Colleges. Every student and every member of staff is a member of one of the seven colleges, most of which have 645 undergraduate and 150 graduate members, both men and women. Teaching is organised centrally by departments but, except in laboratory subjects, is carried out within the colleges rather than in separate blocks of lecture rooms. The University provides residential accommodation for about 70 per cent of its undergraduate students (including all first-years).

Prospectus. The University Prospectus is available on application to the University Admissions Office, University of York, Heslington, York YO1 5DD. Telephone 01904 433535; Fax 01904 433535.

Open Day. An Open Day for sixth-formers is held each year in May (12 May 1993/11 May 1994). Details may be obtained from the Open Day Secretary at the University.

UNIVERSITY OF ESSEX

Visitor: The Rt Hon Lord Templeman of White Lackington, Kt, MBE, PC, MA, HonDLitt, HonLLD.
Chancellor: The Rt Hon Sir Patrick Nairne, GCB, MC, MA, LLD, DU.
Vice-Chancellor: Professor R J Johnston, MA, PhD.
Registrar Secretary: A F Woodburn, BSc, DPA.

Schools of Study. Comparative Studies, Law, Mathematical and Computer Sciences, Science and Engineering, and Social Sciences.

Courses. Students follow a scheme of study leading to the award of the degree of BA, BSc, BEng, MEng, or LLB with honours. Each BA or BSc scheme comprises a fairly broad introductory section (the first-year scheme) and a more specialised section (the second- and third-year scheme). The BEng is an integrated three-year scheme, the MEng an integrated four-year scheme, the LLB an integrated three- or four-year scheme. There are nearly 100 second- and third-year schemes which are offered in the departments of Accounting and Financial Management, Art History and Theory, Biology, Chemistry and Biological Chemistry, Computer Science, Economics, Electronic Systems Engineering, Government, History, Language and Linguistics, Law, Literature, Mathematics, Philosophy, Physics, Psychology and Sociology.

Higher Degrees. MA, MSc, MBA, LLM, MPhil, PhD, DLitt, DSc and LLD.

Residence. About 55 of students are housed in University accommodation and there are in addition contract houses and flats, and lodgings, approved by the University.

Fees. Total annual composite fee for all undergraduate degrees: United Kingdom students – Classroom-based £1,855, Laboratory-based £2,770 (L.E.A. funded), £755 (privately funded); Overseas Students – Arts-based courses £5,320, Science-based courses £7,055.

Prospectus. Obtainable free from the Admissions Officer, University of Essex, Wivenhoe Park, Colchester CO4 3SQ.

DE MONTFORT UNIVERSITY

The Gateway, Leicester LE1 9BH. Tel: (01162) 551551.
Chief Executive and Vice-Chancellor: Professor Kenneth Barker, MA, FRSA, FBIM.
Executive Pro Vice-Chancellor (Academic): Professor Brian H Swanick, PhD, CEng, FIEE, MInstMC.
Executive Pro Vice-Chancellor (Resources): Eur. Ing. Professor Michael A Brown, BSc, PhD, MInstP, CPhys, MIEE, CEng, FBIM.
Executive Pro Vice-Chancellor (Development): Professor David M Chiddick, MSc, ARICS, MRTPI.
Executive Assistant Pro Vice-Chancellor: Professor Michael Scott, BA, MA, PGCE, FRFA.

LANCASTER UNIVERSITY

Chancellor: HRH Princess Alexandra, The Hon Lady Ogilvy, GCVO
Pro-Chancellor: Sir Christopher Audland, KCMG.
Vice-Chancellor: Professor H J Hanham, MA, PhD, AM, FRHistS.
Secretary of the University: G M Cockburn, MA.

The University of Lancaster is set in delightful countryside in North West Lancashire yet readily accessible from anywhere in the country. It is a collegiate university and at present there are ten colleges providing amenities for study and recreation. There is accommodation for more than half the students of the university, including all first years. At Lancaster all undergraduate students read for an Honours degree, and the courses are so structured that students are able to study their main interest in depth and at the same time gain a broader knowledge of allied or contrasting subjects.

There are 32 departments, institutes and centres at the university ranging from Accounting and Finance, History, Physics and Applied Social Sciences to Systems and Information Management. The library includes over 850,000 books and other items and 800 reader places. The library staff is continually studying new ways of expanding and improving the information services within the university.

Fees. Full information on fees and other matters is found in the undergraduate prospectus which may be obtained from the Admissions' Office, University House, Lancaster LA1 4YW.

UNIVERSITY OF KENT AT CANTERBURY, 1965

Chancellor: Robert B Horton, BSc, SM, LLD, DCL, CBIM, FIChemE.
Vice-Chancellor: D J E Ingram, MA, DPhil, DSc, Hon. DSc, FInstP.
Registrar: T J Mead, BSc, PhD.

The University's main buildings include, in addition to the Colleges, the Biological, Chemical, Electronic Engineering, Computing and Physics Laboratories, the Library, the Cornwallis Building, the Gulbenkian Theatre and the new Grimond Building. The Sports Centre provides first class facilities for over 30 different activities.

Residence. Although teaching is Faculty- (not College-) based every student is a member of one of the four Colleges: Darwin, Eliot, Keynes and Rutherford, each of which has about 1,500 junior members and about 130 senior members. There are study-bedrooms in each College for some 350–450 of its junior members. There is also a complex of self-catering accommodation (Park Wood) on the campus providing rooms for some 1,400 students. Further accommodation has recently opened. Every undergraduate whether resident in College lodgings or Park Wood is assigned to a College Tutor, to whom he/she may look for advice on academic and personal matters.

Further information available from the Office of Undergraduate Recruitment Services, The University, Canterbury, Kent CT2 7NZ.

THE UNIVERSITY OF WARWICK

Vice-Chancellor: Sir Brian Follett, FRS, BSc, PhD, DSc, Hon LLD (from 1st April).
Registrar: M L Shattock, OBE, MA.

First Degrees Awarded. BA, BA (with Qualified Teacher Status), BEng, BSc, LLB, MEng, MPhys.

Organisation. Departments are divided between four Faculties (Arts, Educational Studies, Science, Social Studies). Some courses include main subjects from more than one department, some from more than one faculty. Most courses are flexible, especially in the first year, to allow students to develop their individual interests, and most include a wide choice of subsidiary subjects.

Residence. Approx 50 of the student population is housed on campus; and approx a further 25 is housed at University-owned accommodation in the area.

Fees. For United Kingdom and EC Students (first degrees) UK EC Students £1,300 (Arts, Social Studies, Educational Studies); £2,770 (Science); Overseas students £5,500 (1992–93) (Arts), £7,360 (1992–93) (Science). (NB. These are provisional fees for 1993/94, please contact the Academic Registrar for further details.)

Prospectus, available on request from the Schools Liaison Office, University of Warwick, Coventry CV4 7AL, West Midlands. Tel. (024) 7652 3523.

ASTON UNIVERSITY, 1966

Aston University, Aston Triangle, Birmingham B4 7ET.

Chancellor: Sir Adrian Cadbury, MA, Hon DSc, Hon LLD.

Vice-Chancellor: Professor Sir Frederick Crawford, MSc, PhD, DEng, DSc, FEng, FIEE, FIEEE, FInstP, FAPS, FIMA.

University Secretary-Registrar: R D A Packham, BA.

Faculties. Engineering and Applied Science, Management and Modern Languages, Life Health Sciences.

Programmes. Programmes leading to the first degree of BSc or BEng are of:

3 year full-time programmes leading to an Honours Degree.

4 year sandwich programmes leading to an Honours Degree.

4/5 year enhanced programmes leading to a BEng/MEng.

The 4 5 year programmes involve integrated periods of academic study and industrial or professional training. Two-thirds of all students are on sandwich programmes.

Residence. All first year students from outside the West Midlands area are offered a place in residence. Approximately 60 of all students are in University residences, including 1,500 on campus and 700 in the University Village set in attractive parkland in a pleasant residential area four miles from the main campus. Students have a choice of self-catering or fully catered accommodation.

Social Life. There is a large Guild of Students building and sports halls which have facilities for most sports (including swimming and squash) on the main campus, as well as a 90-acre sports complex on the edge of the city. The attractive 40 acre green campus is only ten minutes walk away from the centre of Birmingham. The city is excellent for student life with a wide range of shopping, entertainment and recreational facilities.

Prospectus. The University Prospectus is available from the Registry, Aston University, Aston Triangle, Birmingham B4 7ET. Tel: 0121359 3611.

THE CITY UNIVERSITY, 1966

Northampton Square, London EC1V 0HB.

Chancellor: The Lord Mayor of London.

Vice-Chancellor and Principal: R N Franklin, ME, MA, DPhil, DSc, CBIM, FIEE, FInstP, FIMA.

Academic Registrar: A H Seville, MA, PhD.

General Information. The City University was established by Royal Charter in 1966. Originally founded in 1894 as the Northampton Institute it became in 1957 a college of advanced technology.

First Degree Courses. The University offers first degree courses in the following subjects: Aeronautical Engineering, Air Transport Engineering, Civil Engineering, Civil Engineering with Structures, Management and Engineering, Management and Design in Engineering, Computer Systems Engineering, Electrical and Electronic Engineering, Mechanical Engineering, Mathematical Science, Mathematical Science with Computer Science, Mathematical Science with Statistics, Mathematical Science with Environmental Modelling, Statistics, Software Engineering, Actuarial Science, Business Computing Systems, Computer Science, Optometry (Ophthalmic Optics), Medical Informatics, Nursing and Human Sciences, Clinical Communication Studies (Speech and Language Therapy), Economics*, Economics and Accountancy, Psychology*, Sociology*, Sociology/Media Studies, Psychology/Health, Journalism*, Social Sciences, Music, Banking and International Finance, Business Studies, Insurance and Investment, Business Law, Property Valuation and Finance, and Management Systems. (Subjects marked with an asterisk are available in any combination or in combination with Philosophy or Journalism, as a joint honours degree.)

Degrees. First degree courses lead to the degree of BSc, BA, LLB, or BEng with Honours. Most engineering subjects can also be taken as extended courses leading to the degree of Master of Engineering (MEng). The University awards the higher degrees of DSc, PhD, MPhil, MA, MBA and MSc.

Halls of Residence. Northampton Hall situated about one mile from the main University buildings provides accommodation for 490 men and women students. Finsbury and Heyworth Halls with accommodation for 320 men and women students, are situated close to the main University buildings. There are 199 self-catering places available.

Social Life. Membership of the Students' Union is compulsory for all students. The clubs and societies of the Union cater for a variety of students' interests. Recreation facilities include 26 acres of playing fields, an indoor sports centre and a swimming pool.

LOUGHBOROUGH UNIVERSITY OF TECHNOLOGY

Chancellor: Sir Denis Rooke, CBE, BSc (Eng), FEng, FRS.

Vice-Chancellor: Professor D E N Davies, CBE, BSc, MSc, PhD, DSc, FIEE, FEng, FRS.

Registrar: Dr D E Fletcher, BA, PhD.

Social and Residential. The University is largely residential having full-catering undergraduate and postgraduate Halls of Residence, plus blocks of self-catering flatlets on the campus. Accommodation is also available in associated Houses nearby.

Postal Address: Loughborough University of Technology, Loughborough, Leicestershire LE11 3TU. Telephone: (01509) 263171. Telex: 34319. Fax: (01509) 610813.

BRUNEL UNIVERSITY, 1966

Chancellor: The Rt Hon The Earl of Halsbury, FRS.
Vice-Chancellor: Professor M J H Sterling, PhD, DEng, CEng, FIEE, FInstMC, FRSA.
Secretary General: D Neave, BA, LLM.
Academic Secretary: J Alexander.

Fees. Full details are to be found in the Undergraduate Prospectus.

Residence. First and fourth students are normally offered on-campus accommodation in Halls of Residence.

Prospectus. The Undergraduate Prospectus is available on application to the Student Recruitment Office, Brunel University, Uxbridge, Middlesex, UB8 3PH.

UNIVERSITY OF SURREY

Incorporated by Royal Charter in 1966; previously designated a College of Advanced Technology in 1956; originally established as Battersea Polytechnic Institute in 1891. The University completed its move to a new site at Guildford, just below the Cathedral, in July 1970.

Chancellor: HRH The Duke of Kent, KG, GCMG, GCVO.
Vice-Chancellor: Professor A Kelly, CBE, PhD, ScD, FInstP, FIM, FEng, FRS.
University Secretary and Registrar: H W B Davies, BSc (Econ).

Postgraduate courses and research facilities. Available in all departments.

Residence, etc. Six Courts of Residence for 2,150 men and women students within the University precinct at Guildford; a further 350 students are housed nearby at Hazel Farm, a development of 50 houses on the outskirts of Guildford. Union building, restaurants, shops, Bank, Post Office, Launderette, Hairdresser, Quiet Centre, Arts Workshops, Sports Hall and playing fields on site.

Admission. Undergraduate and postgraduate prospectuses available from the Academic Secretary at the University, Guildford, Surrey, GU2 5XH.

UNIVERSITY OF BRADFORD

Chancellor: Sir Trevor Holdsworth, Kt, FCA, FRSA.
Vice-Chancellor and Principal: D J Johns, PhD, DSc, FEng, FRAeS, FIOA, FCIT.
Registrar and Secretary: D W Granger, MBE, BSc, MIPM.

Degrees. BA, BEng, BPharm, BSc, MA, MBA, MEng, MPharm, MSc, MPhil, PhD, DEng, DLitt, DSc, DTech.

Special Features. Special modules on all courses and the Computerisation project give students the chance to become computer-literate and acquire practical skills, including teamwork and communication. The campus is fully networked. The Language Unit enables students to improve their foreign language skills.

Residence. All first year students are offered on-campus accommodation (if home is beyond reasonable travelling distance from the University) either in Halls where some meals are provided or in self-catering accommodation.

Prospectus. Full details of courses, fees, accommodation and social activities can be found in the undergraduate prospectus, available from The Schools Liaison Office, The University of Bradford, FREEPOST, Bradford, West Yorkshire BD7 1BR.

THE UNIVERSITY OF SALFORD, 1967

Chancellor: Her Royal Highness The Duchess of York.
Vice-Chancellor: Professor Tom Mutrie Husband, BSc, MA, PhD, FIMechE, FEng.
Registrar: Stuart Ralph Bosworth, OBE, BA.

Degrees. BA, BEng, BSc, MA, MPhys, MSc, MPhil, PhD, DSc.

Diplomas. Diploma for Advanced Studies, Diploma in Engineering.

Certificates. Advanced Certificate. Certificate of Attendance.

Fees. Minimum sessional fees for undergraduate full-time and integrated courses are £1,300 per session. Minimum fees for overseas students attending full-time or integrated courses. (Undergraduate) £7,360 (Science) or £5,550 (Arts).

Residence. The Oaklands halls of residence, Castle Irwell, a residential complex on the site of the former Manchester racecourse, (which provides some 1,612 places in the form of terraces of individual houses) Horlock Court (168 places on-campus) and student houses supplemented by approved lodgings and flats.

Prospectus. Copies of the Undergraduate Prospectus and the Postgraduate Prospectus are available on application to the External Relations Office, Room 103, University of Salford M5 4WT.

THE UNIVERSITY OF BATH, 1966

Chancellor: Sir Denys Henderson, MA, LLB.
Vice-Chancellor: Professor D Vandehinde, BS, PhD.
Secretary and Registrar: R M Mawditt, OBE, MSc, FCCA, FBIM, FRSA.

Schools of Study. There are 14 undergraduate schools – Architecture and Building Engineering, Biological Sciences, Chemical Engineering, Chemistry, Education, Electronic and Electrical Engineering, Mathematical Sciences, Management, Materials Science, Mechanical Engineering, Modern Languages and International Studies, Pharmacy and Pharmacology, Physics and Social Sciences.

The University provides both 'full time' and 'sandwich' undergraduate courses. The 'sandwich' courses combine full time study with periods of industrial/practical experience in commerce, industry, government research establishments, and national and local government.

Fees. Academic year 1992/93 Undergraduates £1,855 (Arts) £2,770 (Science & Technology) (UK and EC) £5,390 (Overseas Arts courses) £7,125 (Overseas Sciences courses). Postgraduates £1,985 (UK) £5,390 (Overseas Arts courses) £7,125 (Overseas Science courses). All fees are inclusive of Union subscription.

Location. The university is situated on a 200 acre site on a hill to the south-east of the city.

Postal address: Claverton Down, Bath BA2 7AY.

UNIVERSITY OF BUCKINGHAM, 1973

Chancellor: The Rt Hon Mrs Margaret Thatcher, OM, FRS.
Vice-Chancellor: Sir Richard Luce, DL, MA.
Executive Pro-Vice-Chancellor: Professor Peter Watson, MSc, FCA.
Pro-Vice-Chancellor: Professor Bruce Collins, BA, MA, PhD.
Secretary and Registrar: Dr Matthew Lavis, BA, PhD.
Assistant Registrars (Admissions): Cherry McInnes, BA.
Schools Liaison Officer: Debbie Millns, HND.
Degrees: BA, BSc, BSc (Econ), LLB.

Buckingham's academic year begins in January and consists of four terms of ten weeks each. There is also a July entry for law. Degree courses are completed in two calendar years, with the exception of European Centre Courses, where an additional term is spent at a continental university and International Hotel Management (3 years).

Degree Subject Areas: Accounting and Financial Management; Business Studies; Economics; European Centre Courses, History; Politics; English Literature; Law; Biological Sciences; Computer Science; Psychology; International Hotel Management; Law; Biology and the Environment; History of Art and Heritage.

Degree programmes in all Schools incorporate supporting courses including the study of modern languages.

Location. Two precincts, both near town centre, one occupying riverside position.

Prospectus: From the Admissions Office, University of Buckingham, Buckingham MK18 1EG. Tel: (01280) 814080. Fax: (01280) 822245.

THE OPEN UNIVERSITY

The Open University was established by Royal Charter in 1969, to provide educational opportunities for adults who wish to study in their own homes and in their own time. Like all universities it can grant degrees and other qualifications. Under its Charter it also has a special responsibility to further the educational well-being of the community as a whole.

This year, about 125,000 students will be studying with the University. Some will be working towards a BA/BSc or a higher degree, others will be studying single courses or diplomas as associate students. There will also be approximately 70,000 purchasers of study packs.

Postal address: Walton Hall, Milton Keynes MK7 6AA.

UNIVERSITY OF BRIGHTON
Moulsecoomb, Brighton BN2 4AT

Director: Professor D J Watson, MA, PhD.

UNIVERSITY OF COVENTRY
Priory Street, Coventry CV1 5FB

Director: Michael Goldstein, BSc, PhD, DSc, CChem, FRSC.

UNIVERSITY OF HERTFORDSHIRE
(formerly Hatfield Polytechnic)
University of Hertfordshire, College Lane, Hatfield, Herts AL10 9AB.
Tel. Hatfield (01707) 279000. Telex. 262413. Fax. (01707) 279670.
University of Hertfordshire, Hertford Campus, Mangrove Road, Hertford, Herts SG13 8QF.
University of Hertfordshire, Wall Hall Campus, Aldenham, Watford, Herts WD2 8AT.

Director: Professor N K Buxton, MA, PhD.

MIDDLESEX UNIVERSITY
All Saints, White Hart Lane, London N17 8HR.

Director: Professor David Melville, BSc, PhD, CPhys, FInstP.

UNIVERSITY OF PORTSMOUTH
University House, Winston Churchill Avenue, Portsmouth PO1 2UP.

Vice-Chancellor: Neil Merritt.
Academic Registrar: Roger Moore, BA, AKC.

UNIVERSITY OF CENTRAL ENGLAND IN BIRMINGHAM
Perry Barr, Birmingham B42 2SU. (Switchboard) Tel: 0121-331 5000.

Vice-Chancellor: Dr Peter C Knight, BA, DPhil, CPhy, MInstP, FRAS, DUniv.
Pro Vice-Chancellor (External Affairs): Professor D Warner, BA, MA.
Pro Vice-Chancellor (Academic Affairs): Professor P Walkling, BA, DAES, MEd.
Pro Vice-Chancellor (Resources): Dr D M Green, BSc (Econ), PhD.
Secretary and Registrar: Ms M Penlington, BA.

UNIVERSITY OF EAST LONDON
Romford Road, London E15 4LZ Tel: 020-8590 7722.

Vice-Chancellor: Professor F W Gould, MA.

UNIVERSITY OF CENTRAL LANCASHIRE
Preston PR1 2HE. Tel: Preston (01772) 201201 Fax: (01772) 892935 Telex: 677409 (UCLAN G)

Rector and Chief Executive: Brian G Booth, JP, BA (Econ), MTechFSS.

UNIVERSITY OF GREENWICH

Wellington Street, Woolwich, London SE18 6PF; Oakfield Lane, Dartford, Kent DA1 2SZ; Bexley Road, Eltham, London SE9 2PQ; Brewhouse Lane, Wapping, London E1 9PA; Bigland Street, Shadwell, London E1 2NG; Rachel McMillan Building, Creek Road, Deptford, London SE8 3BU and Manresa House, Holybourne Avenue, Roehampton, London SW15 4JB. Tel: 020-8316 8000.

Director: D Fussey, MA, PhD, CEng, FIMechE, FInstE.

THE UNIVERSITY OF HUDDERSFIELD

Queengate, Huddersfield HD1 3DH

Vice-Chancellor and Rector: Professor K J Durrands, CBE, MSc, CEng, FIMechE, FIEE, FIProdE.

KINGSTON UNIVERSITY

Penrhyn Road, Kingston upon Thames, Surrey KT1 2EE. Tel: 020-8547 2000.

Vice-Chancellor: Dr Robert C Smith, CBE.

LEEDS METROPOLITAN UNIVERSITY

Calverley Street, Leeds LS1 3HE. Tel: 0113-283 2600.

Director: Christopher Price, MA.

LONDON GUILDHALL UNIVERSITY

Admissions Office, 139 Minories, London EC3N 1NL. Tel: 020-7320 1000 Fax: 020-7320 3134.

Provost: Professor Roderick Floud, MA, DPhil, FRHistS.

UNIVERSITY OF NORTH LONDON

166–220 Holloway Road, London N7 8DB. Tel: 020-7607 2789.

Vice-Chancellor and Chief Executive: Leslie Wagner, MA (Econ).

THE MANCHESTER METROPOLITAN UNIVERSITY

All Saints, Manchester M15 6BH. Tel: 0161-247 2000

Director: Sir Kenneth Green, MA.

UNIVERSITY OF NORTHUMBRIA AT NEWCASTLE

Ellison Building, Ellison Place, Newcastle upon Tyne, NE1 8ST

Vice-Chancellor: Professor Laing Barden, CBE, DSc.

THE NOTTINGHAM TRENT UNIVERSITY

Burton Street, Nottingham NG1 4BU. Tel: (01159) 418418

Vice-Chancellor: Professor R Cowell, BA, PhD.

OXFORD BROOKES UNIVERSITY

Headington, Oxford OX3 0BP. Tel: (01865) 741111

Director: Dr Clive Booth.

UNIVERSITY OF PLYMOUTH

Drake Circus, Plymouth PL4 8AA. Tel: Plymouth (01752) 600600.

Vice-Chancellor: R J Bull, BSc (Econ), FCCA.

SHEFFIELD HALLAM UNIVERSITY

City Campus, Pond Street, Sheffield S1 1WB. Tel: (01142) 720911. Telex: 54680 SHPOLY G. Fax: 532096

Principal: J Stoddart, BA, FRSA, FBIM.

Academic Registrar: J Tory, BA.

SOUTH BANK UNIVERSITY

103 Borough Road, London SE1 0AA Tel: 020-7928 8989.

Vice-Chancellor: Professor G Bernbaum, BSc (Econ) *Lond.*

UNIVERSITY OF SUNDERLAND

Langham Tower, Ryhope Road, Sunderland SR2 7EE. Tel: Sunderland (0191) 515 2000.

Vice-Chancellor and Chief Executive: Anne Wright, BA, PhD.

UNIVERSITY OF TEESSIDE

Borough Road, Middlesbrough, Cleveland TS1 3BA.

Vice-Chancellor: Professor Derek Fraser, BA, MA, PhD. FRHistS.

UNIVERSITY OF WESTMINSTER

309 Regent Street, London W1R 8AL.

Tel: 020-7911 5000

Rector: Professor T E Burlin, DSc, PhD, FinstP, CEng, FIEE.

UNIVERSITY OF THE WEST OF ENGLAND, BRISTOL

Frenchay Campus, Coldharbour Lane, Bristol BS16 1QY. Tel: Bristol (01179) 656261.

Vice-Chancellor: A C Morris.

UNIVERSITY OF WOLVERHAMPTON

Wulfruna Street, Wolverhampton WV1 1SB. Tel: (01902) 321000.

Vice-Chancellor: Professor M J Harrison, MA.

WALES

THE UNIVERSITY OF WALES, 1893

Vice-Chancellor: Sir Aubrey Trotman-Dickenson, MA, BSc, PhD, DSc.

Registrar: M A R Kemp, PhD. Address: University Registry, Cathays Park, Cardiff CF1 3NS.

The University consists of six constituent colleges: University College of Wales, Aberystwyth; University College of North Wales (Bangor); University of Wales College of Cardiff; University College of Swansea; University of Wales College of Medicine (Cardiff) and Saint David's University College, Lampeter.

Faculties and Degrees. Arts (BA, MA, DLitt, BLib, MLib), Science (BSc, BEng, MEng, MSc, BPharm, MPharm, EngD, DClinPsy, DSc), Economic and Social Studies (BScEcon, MScEcon, MBA, DScEcon), Music (BMus, MMus, DMus), Law (LLB, LLM, LLD), Theology (BD, BTh, MTh, DD), Medicine (MB, BCh, MCh, MD, BMedSc, MPH, BDS, MScD, DChD, BN, MN), Education (BEd, MEd), Architecture (BArch). MPhil and PhD are available in all faculties.

Course of Study. For a first degree it is necessary for candidates to have satisfied the general requirements for matriculation in the University. A candidate must have pursued in a constituent institution of the University a qualifying scheme of study during not less than three years for a degree in Arts, Science, Economic and Social Studies, Law, Music, Pharmacy and Theology; not less than four years for the degree of BN; not less than four and a half years for the degree of BDS; not less than five years for the degrees of MB, BCh.

Full details of examination requirements for matriculation, prospectuses and information about course requirements may be obtained direct from the Registrars of the Constituent Institutions.

Colleges:

(1) University of Wales, Aberystwyth
(A Constituent College of The University of Wales), 1872

Principal: Professor Kenneth Morgan, MA, DPhil, DLitt Oxf, FRHists, FBA.

Registrar and Secretary: D Gruffydd Jones, BA.

Course of Study. This is directed to the degrees of the University of Wales in Arts, Economic and Social Studies, Science and Law. Research work is carried out in all Departments of the College. Postgraduate Diploma courses are offered in agricultural science, archive administration, statistics, micropalaeontology, palaeography, studio studies, bilingual education, advanced educational studies, pure mathematics, educational technology, environmental impact assessment.

Fees. Paid by Local Education Authorities.

Undergraduate Scholarships. The College offers a number of scholarships up to the value of £600 per annum. These scholarships are amongst the most valuable offered by any British University. For further details, see Prospectus.

Facilities. All the Science Departments are housed in new or extended buildings, most of them on the magnificent Penglais site overlooking the town and Cardigan Bay. The Faculty of Economic and Social Studies and most Arts Departments (including the modern languages) are also housed on this site, which adjoins the National Library of Wales – a copyright library. The departments of Welsh, Education and Drama are housed in the Old College on the seafront. Over 60 of the students live in Halls of Residence. The Arts Centre, comprising a concert hall, theatre and art gallery, is a prominent feature on the Penglais Campus.

Social Life. The students elect a Students' Guild Council, which exercises control over most of the College Societies.

Further Information: The Registrar and Secretary, Old College, King Street, Aberystwyth, Dyfed SY23 2AX.

(2) University College of North Wales (Bangor)
(A Constituent College of the University of Wales), 1884

Principal: Prof E Sunderland, MA, PhD, FIBiol.

Registrar: G R Thomas, MA.

Courses of Study. For degrees of the University of Wales in Arts and Social Sciences (including Accounting, Banking, Biblical Studies, Education, European Financial Management, History, Modern Languages, Psychology, Sport, Health Physical Education, Linguistics and Welsh), Science and Engineering (including Animal Management, Biological Sciences, Electronic Engineering, Environmental Sciences, Agriculture, Ocean Sciences, Forestry, and Wood Science), Music and Theology. Facilities are given for post-graduate work. The School of Education offers post-graduate Teachers' Training. A Marine Science Laboratory and 2 fully equipped Research Vessels form part of the College's resources.

Fees. From £1,885.

Residence. There are eight Halls of Residence, two of which are single-sex, the others mixed.

Scholarships. Scholarships are offered for undergraduate and postgraduate study.

Social Life. The Students' Union organises numerous clubs and societies.

Recreational Facilities. Bangor's geographical location affords excellent opportunities for climbing, sailing and many other outdoor activities, and the sports facilities provided by the College are among the most up to date in the Principality.

Further Information. The Academic Registrar, University College of North Wales, Bangor, Gwynedd LL57 2DG.

(3) University of Wales College of Cardiff
(A Constituent College of the University of Wales), 1988

Principal: Dr E B Smith, MA, DSc, FRSC.

Registrar: Professor M J Bruton, BA, MSc (Eng), FRTPI.

The College includes Faculties of Business Studies and Law, Engineering and Environmental Design, Health and Life Sciences, Humanities and Social Studies, Physical Sciences and the Collegiate Faculty of Theology.

Composition Fees. Full-time British and EC self-supporting students £755. Students with LEA mandatory awards: classroom-based subjects £1,855; laboratory- and workshop-based subjects: £2,770; overseas students: arts-based subjects £5,320; science-based subjects £7,055. (All fees quoted are those for Session 1992/3).

Scholarships. A number of Scholarships are awarded annually on the results of the First Year examinations and there are Research Scholarships and Post-Graduate Studentships available.

Social Life. On payment of the tuition fees students automatically become members of the University Union, Cardiff and thus eligible for membership of all Societies and Sports Clubs under the control of the Students' Union.

Further Information. Admissions Office, University of Wales College of Cardiff, PO Box 68, Cardiff CF1 3XA.

(4) University College of Swansea
(A Constituent College of the University of Wales) 1920

Principal: Professor B L Clarkson, DSc, FRAeS, FSEE, FIOA.

Registrar: Victor J Carney, BA.

The College includes Faculties of Arts, Economic and Social Studies, Science, Engineering and Educational Studies, Faculty of Law, and a Faculty of Health Care Studies.

There are research facilities in all Departments. Postgraduate students may prepare for the University's higher degrees.

Degrees and Diplomas. Schemes of study (at least 3 years) are provided for the University's BA and BSc Honours and Joint Honours degrees, for the BSc Econ Honours and Combined Honours degree and for the BEng and MEng Honours degree, BN (Nursing) and MPhys. Full details about diploma courses are obtainable from the Registrar.

Fees. Details from the Director of Finance.

Accommodation. Accommodation is available in modern Halls of Residence and Student Residences.

Scholarships. The College offers a number of scholarships, prizes and other awards, tenable either on entrance or as a result of academic performance.

Further information. The College publishes an annual *Prospectus* which gives full details about courses and facilities. Free copies of this publication are available from the Schools Liaison Office. The University holds three open days for visitors, details of which are available from the Schools Liaison Office. Visits at other times are possible for groups and individuals by prior arrangement with the Schools Liaison Office. For further information please contact the Schools Liaison Office, University College of Swansea, Singleton Park, Swansea SA2 8PP. Tel: (01792) 205678 Ext 4718.

(5) Cardiff: University of Wales College of Medicine (a constituent College of the University of Wales) 1931. See under Medical Schools.

(6) Saint David's University College, Lampeter*
(A Constituent College of the University of Wales), 1822

Principal: Professor K G Robbins, MA, DPhil, DLitt, FRSE, FRHistS.

Registrar and Secretary: A M S Kenwright, MA.

Saint David's College was founded in 1822, thus making it by a fraction the oldest university institution in England and Wales after the ancient universities. Under a supplementary charter granted in 1971 the College became a constituent college of the University of Wales.

The College provides courses of study in arts leading to degrees of the University of Wales.

Tuition Fees. (Home/EC) £1,300 (most courses) £2,770 (Archaeology and Geography). (Overseas) £4,750.

Scholarships. A number of scholarships are offered for competition annually.

Accommodation is available for men and for women in modern Halls of Residence. Membership of the Students' Union is automatic for all students.

Further Information. The Deputy Registrar, St David's University College, Lampeter, Dyfed SA48 7ED. Tel: 01570 422351).

* Proposals are before the Privy Council for a change in name to "University of Wales Lampeter".

UNIVERSITY OF GLAMORGAN
Pontypridd, Mid Glam CF37 1DL. Tel: (01443) 480480.

Vice-Chancellor: Professor A L Webb.

SCOTLAND

ST ANDREWS, 1411

Chancellor: Sir Kenneth James Dover, MA, DLitt, LLD, FRSE, FBA.

Principal and Vice-Chancellor: Struther Arnott, BSc, PhD, FRS, FRSE.

Secretary: D J Corner, BA, FRHistS.

Faculties. Arts, Science (including Medical Science), Divinity. In Arts, MA (Gen) three years, MA (Hons) four years; in Science, BSc (Gen) three years, BSc (Hons) four years; in Divinity, MTheol (Ord) three years, MTheol (Hons) four years, BD (Ord and Hons) four years (undergraduates), BD (Ord or Hons) three years (graduates), Licentiate in Theology three years undergraduates).

Fees. The consolidated annual fee in 1992–93 is Banded. Band I – for classroom based courses £1,855. Band II – for lab/ workshop based courses £2,770 (£5,355 for non-laboratory based course and £7,015 for a laboratory based course for overseas students). This covers matriculation, tuition, use of laboratories, and examinations.

Scholarships. In the **United College of St Salvator and St Leonard** there are over 20 Bursaries available to undergraduate entrants to the University. There are in addition Travel Scholarships available. In **St Mary's College** (Theology) there are a number of Bursaries and Scholarships available each year. Also several Research Scholarships and Prizes.

Social Life. There are Halls of Residence for Male, Female, and mixed communities and two complexes of student houses. A large number of clubs and societies cater for the individual interests of all students.

For all particulars of fees, classes, etc, see the Prospectus or *Calendar*.

Postal address: The University, College Gate, St Andrews KY16 9AJ. Tel: (01334) 76161.

GLASGOW, 1451

Principal and Vice-Chancellor: Sir William Kerr Fraser, GCB, MA, LLD, FRSE.

Faculties. Arts, Divinity, Law and Financial Studies, Medicine, Science, Engineering, Veterinary Medicine, Social Sciences.

Bursaries. There are about 75 Entrance Bursaries open for Competition each year as well as other Fellowships, Scholarships and Prizes available.

Halls of Residence. There are at present seven halls of residence: (two for men students, and five mixed) and a number of student houses and flats accommodating in total nearly 2,500 students.

Social Life. Besides the University Unions there are numerous Social, Professional, and Athletic Societies, Officers Training Corps, Air Squadron and Royal Naval Unit.

Postal Address. The Registrar, University of Glasgow, Glasgow G12 8QQ.

ABERDEEN, 1495

Chancellor: Sir Kenneth Alexander, BSc, LLD, DUniv, FEIS, FBECScot, FRSE

Principal and Vice-Chancellor: John Maxwell Irvine, BSc, MSc, PhD, FRAS.

Secretary: Norman Roderick Darroch Begg, MA, LLB.

Faculties. Arts and Divinity; Economic and Social Sciences; Biological Sciences; Engineering and Mathematical and Physical Sciences; Clinical Medicine; Law.

Annual Fees. Home and EC fees £755 (undergraduate) and £2,250 (postgraduate). Overseas students £5,640 to £13,752. Examination Fees are included in the above totals.

Residence. Crombie-Johnston, Dunbar and Hillhead Halls are residences for men and women students in any faculty. There are also other less formalised residential facilities, giving a total of around 4,000 places. All new students from outside Aberdeen are guaranteed a place in residence in their first year of study provided their application forms are returned by 9 September.

Bursaries and Scholarships. A number of entrance bursaries are awarded each year on the result of a special competitive examination. Other bursaries and money prizes are awarded in later stages of the course. A number of postgraduate scholarships and studentships are awarded at or after graduation.

Social Life. All students are members of the University Union and of the Athletic Association and are eligible to vote in elections to or to be elected to the Students Representative Council.

Recreational Facilities. There are playing fields at King's College and at Balgownie, which cater for all major winter and summer games. Facilities for all indoor activities are provided in the Butchart Recreation Centre and in the sports pavilion, King's College, where there is also a swimming pool.

Student Health Service. The University provides a Student Health Service, with 3 Medical Officers, a Dental Officer, and other Staff.

Postal Address. University Office, Regent Walk, Aberdeen, AB9 1FX.

THE UNIVERSITY OF EDINBURGH, 1583

Chancellor: His Royal Highness The Prince Philip, Duke of Edinburgh, KG, KT, PC, OM, GBE, LLD, FRS.

Rector: Donnie Munro, DA.

Principal: Sir David Smith, MA, DPhil, HonDSc, FRS, FRSE.

Secretary: M J B Lowe, BSc, PhD.

Faculties. Arts, Divinity, Law, Medicine, Music, Science and Engineering (including Division of Biological Sciences), Social Sciences, Veterinary Medicine.

Fees. Annual fee. UK and EC students: £755 (self-financing) and £1,855 (publicly funded) for Arts Courses, £2,770 (publicly funded) for most Science Courses in all Faculties except clinical and laboratory courses. Overseas students: Faculty of Arts: MA Fine Art, Linguistics, Mathematics and Natural Philosophy £7,255. Other courses in Arts £5,520. Faculty of Divinity and Law £5,520. Faculty of Medicine and Veterinary Medicine: MBChB and BVM S Years 1 2 £7,255. BSc (Medical Science) (Veterinary Science) £7,255. MBChB, BDS and BVM S Years 3, 4 5 £13,190. Faculty of Music £7,255. Faculty of Science and Engineering: BSc Agricultural Economics, Mathematics, Mathematics and Business Studies, Mathematics and Statistics £5,520. Other courses in Science and Engineering £7,255. Faculty of Social Sciences: BSc Nursing, MA Housing Studies, MA/DipArch £7,255. Other courses in Social Sciences £5,520.

Scholarships. There are a large number of Scholarships and Bursaries offered in all the Faculties, some on entrance, others in the course of the curriculum; also several Fellowships and some Research Studentships. (See *Awards Programme.*)

Social Life. The 'University Unions' – various Literary and Debating Societies; and many other Associations, Social, Professional and Athletic.

Postal address. Old College, South Bridge, Edinburgh, EH8 9YL. Tel: 0131-650 1000. Telex: 727442 UNIVED G. Fax: 0131-650 2147.

UNIVERSITY OF STRATHCLYDE, 1964

Chancellor: The Rt Hon The Lord Tombs of Brailes, BSc (Econ), LLD, DSc, DUniv, FIMechE, FEng.

Principal and Vice-Chancellor: Professor John P Arbuthnott, ScD, FIBiol.

Faculties. Science, Engineering, Arts and Social Studies, Strathclyde Business School, Education.

Annual Fees. Undergraduates home and EC £1,855 to £2,769; undergraduates overseas £5,400 to £7,200 including Students Association Membership subscription.

Hostels. The University provides accommodation for 1,692 students on-campus in the Student Village; 555 students off-campus but located relatively close to the University; 156 students off-campus in leased accommodation, all residences are mixed.

Social Life. University Union, Athletic Club, various students' societies, etc.

Postal address. 16 Richmond Street, Glasgow G1 1XQ.

UNIVERSITY OF STIRLING, 1967

Principal and Vice-Chancellor: Professor A J Forty, CBE, PhD, DSc, LLD, FRSA, FRSE, CIMgt.
University Secretary: R G Bomont, JP, BSc (Econ), IPFA.

Areas of Study. Arts including Languages, Biological and Environmental Sciences, Business and Management, Human Sciences including Education.

Courses of Study. The degree awarded is the BAcc, BA or the BSc depending on the area of study and it may either be the General degree (three years of study) or the Honours degree (four years). The University has two 15-week (semesters) in each academic session. The subjects available to degree level are BAcc: Accountancy; BA: Accountancy, Business Law, Business Studies, Economics, Education, English Studies, Film and Media Studies, Financial Studies, French, German, History, Human Resources Management, Japanese, Marketing, Philosophy, Politics, Psychology, Religious Studies, Sociology and Social Policy, Spanish, Mathematics and its Applications; BSc: Aquaculture, Biochemistry, Biology, Computing Science, Environmental Science, Education, Marine Biology, Ecology, Conservation Management, Management Science, Psychology, Molecular and Cell Biology; BA (Diploma): Social Work.

The courses in Education can lead both to a degree (BA or BSc) *and* the Diploma in Education and a teaching qualification, but in the latter case courses last one additional semester.

Full details are given in the Prospectus, obtainable from the Schools and College Liaison Office, University of Stirling, Stirling FK9 4LA. Tel: (01786) 467046, or through our 24 hr "Prospectus Hotline" on (01786) 467045.

HERIOT-WATT UNIVERSITY, 1966

Chancellor: The Rt Hon The Lord Mackay of Clashfern, PC, QC, MA, LLB, BA, LLD, DUniv, HonFRCSE, HonFICE, FRSE.

Principal and Vice-Chancellor: Professor A G J Macfarlane, CBE, PhD, DSc, MA, ScD, FIEE, FEng, FRS.
Secretary: Peter L Wilson, BSc, MA, FBIM.

First Degrees are offered in Accountancy and Management Information Systems, Accountancy and Finance, Accountancy with a European Language, Actuarial Mathematics and Statistics, Colour Chemistry, Applied Marine Biology, Architecture, Biochemistry, Brewing and Distilling, Building, Building Economics and Quantity Surveying, Building Services Engineering, Building Surveying, Business Organisation, Chemical Engineering, Chemistry, Chemistry with Computer Science, Chemistry with a European Language, Chemistry with Polymers and Advanced Materials, Civil Engineering, Clothing, Computer Science, Computing and Electronics, Design, Economics, Electrical and Electronic Engineering, Energy Resource Engineering (with Chemical or Mechanical Engineering), Estate Management, Housing Studies, Industrial and Business Studies, Industrial Design (Textiles), Information Systems Engineering, International Business and Languages, Landscape Architecture, Languages (Interpreting and Translating), Mathematics, Mathematics with Applied Mechanics, Mathematics with Computer Science, Mathematics with a European Language, Mathematics with Economics, Mathematics with Physics, Mathematics with Education, Mathematics with Statistics, Mechanical Engineering, Microbiology, Offshore Engineering, Optoelectronics and Laser Engineering, Painting, Physics, Physics with Computer Applications, Physics with Education, Physics with Laser Science, Applied Physics with Semiconductor Electronics, Sculpture, Statistics, Structural Engineering, Structural Engineering with Architectural Design, Textiles with Clothing Studies, Textiles with Marketing, Town Planning.

Application is through UCCA, except for University's degree courses in Design, Painting and Sculpture. (Enquiries about these courses should be directed to Edinburgh College of Art, Lauriston Place, Edinburgh EH3 9DF.)

Annual Fees. Undergraduate courses leading to BA, BEng, MEng, BSc and BArch Degrees, UK and European Community Students are £1,855 Arts-based and £2,770 Science-based (Overseas students £5,420 (Arts-based) – £7,155 (Science-based). Fees for Postgraduate Degrees and Diplomas on application to the Secretary.

Social Life. The University is situated on a 380-acre parkland site at Riccarton, six miles from central Edinburgh, except for departments in the faculties of Environmental Studies and Art and Design which are based in Edinburgh College of Art, Lauriston Place, Edinburgh, and departments in the Faculty of Textiles, which are based at the Scottish College of Textiles, Galashiels. There are residences for 1,150 students on Riccarton campus, where the Sports Centre and playing fields are among the finest in Britain, and where there is also a range of other social, recreational and commercial facilities. The Students' Association is represented in the government of the University, runs the Student Union and organises entertainments. Numerous clubs and societies cover a wide range of interests.

The University provides a Chaplaincy, Accommodation and Welfare, Medical (including Dental) services and a Careers Advisory Service.

The Education Liaison Officer (Mr M T Block, MA) advises pupils, teachers and careers masters in schools on entrance requirements and of opportunities and career prospects arising from the degree courses. Full details of all undergraduate and postgraduate courses may be obtained from the Registrar, Heriot-Watt University, Riccarton, Edinburgh, EH14 4AS.

DUNDEE, 1967
(First founded as University College, Dundee, 1881)

Chancellor: Sir James Black, MB, ChB, DSc, LLD, DTech, FRCP, FRSE, FRS.
Principal and Vice-Chancellor: Professor M J Hamlin, BSc, FEng, FICE, FIWEM, FRSE.
Secretary: R Seaton, MA, LLB.

Faculties. Medicine and Dentistry, Science and Engineering, Law, Arts and Social Sciences, Environmental Studies.

First Degrees. MB, ChB, BDS, BMSc, BSc, BEng, LLB, BA, MA, BArch, BAcc, BDes.

Post-Graduate Degrees. MD, MDSc, MMedEd, MEdStud, MMSc, MSSc MPH, DDSc, DSc, MSc, MSocWk, LLD, LLM, MAcc, DLitt, MPhil, MEd, PhD, MBA, MFA, MDes.

Diplomas and Certificates. Post-Graduate diplomas: are awarded in various branches of Arts and Social Sciences, Education, Engineering, Environmental Studies, Law, Science and Social Work. A Certificate in Industrial Health.

Fees. For full-time first degree courses: home students £1,300–£13,600 (overseas students £5,320–£12,990) according to course; for full-time higher degree courses and for continuing overseas students: details available from the University.

Residence. Halls of Residence (full board and lodgings): Airlie, Belmont, Chalmers, West Park. University Houses (study bedrooms or flats with cooking and laundry facilities): Peterson, Wimberley, Tay Works.

Scholarships and Bursaries are awarded in Civil Engineering, Physics, Electronics, Manufacturing/Mechanical Engineering to entrant students and in these and other disciplines, notably Law, to continuing students.

Social Life. All students are members of the Students' Association. There are ample facilities for entertainment, indoor and outdoor recreation.

Further details from the Secretary, The University, Dundee DD1 4HN.

NORTHERN IRELAND

BELFAST, THE QUEEN'S UNIVERSITY

President and Vice-Chancellor: Gordon S G Beveridge, BSc, PhD, ARCST, FEng, FIChemE, FRSE.
Secretary to the Academic Council: George A Baird, BSc, MSc, PhD.
Bursar: David N Gass, BSc(Econ), FCIS.

Faculties. Arts (BA, BMus, MA, MLS, DLit DMus), Science (BSc, MSc, DSc). Engineering, (BEng, MEng, BSc, MArch, MSc, DSc); Economics and Social Sciences (BSc (Econ), BSSc, BSc (Accounting), BSc (Finance), BSc (Information Management), MSc (Econ), MSSc, MSW, MSSc (Social Work), MAcc, MSc (Mgt), DSc (Econ), DSSc; Law (LLB, LLB (Law and Accounting), LLM, LLD); Medicine (MB, BCh, BAO, MD, MCh, MAO, BDS, MDS); Agriculture and Food Science (BAgr, BSc, MAgr and MSc); Theology (BD, MTh, DD); Education (BEd, MEd, MA(Ed). In Institute of Continuing Education: Bachelor of Arts in General Studies – BA (Gen Stud) – (part-time), Master of Social Science in Organization and Manpower Studies – MSSc – (part-time). In all Faculties PhD.

UNIVERSITY OF ULSTER

(Formed by the merger of the New University of Ulster and the Ulster Polytechnic from 1st October 1984)
Chancellor: The Rt Hon the Lord Grey of Naunton, GCMG, GCVO, OBE, DLitt, LLD, DSc.
Vice-Chancellor: Professor T A Smith, BSc, LLD, FRHistS, CBIM.

Faculties: Art and Design, Business and Management, Education, Humanities, Informatics, Science and Technology, Social and Health Sciences. Also Department of Adult and Continuing Education.

First Degrees: BA, BSc, BMus, BEng/MEng, BTech
Second Degree: BEd
Postgraduate Degrees: MPhil, DPhil, MA, MSc, MBA, MEd
Diplomas and Certificates: Various; full particulars of these courses from the *Admissions Officer,* University of Ulster, Cromore Road, Coleraine, Co Londonderry BT52 1SA, Northern Ireland.

REPUBLIC OF IRELAND

UNIVERSITY OF DUBLIN, TRINITY COLLEGE, 1592

Provost: T N Mitchell, MA, PhD, LittD.
Registrar: T B H McMurry, MA, PhD, ScD.

Faculties. Arts (Humanities and Letters), Business, Economic and Social Studies, Engineering and Systems Sciences, Health Sciences, Science.

Degrees. Arts, Business Studies, Clinical Speech and Language Studies, Computer Science, Dentistry, Education, Engineering, Human Nutrition and Dietetics, Laws, Medicine, Music Education, Occupational Therapy, Pharmacy, Physiotherapy, Science, Social Studies, Theology. There are also higher degrees in all Faculties.

Courses. The normal course leading to the first degree of BA is four years (Medicine and Dentistry – 5–6 years).

Entrance requirements. Either Irish Leaving Cert including at least three higher level passes or GCE including at least two passes at 'A' level, etc. Full details from the Admissions Office.

Scholarships. Eighteen entrance exhibitions are awarded each year on the basis of public examination results (Irish Leaving Certificate and G.C.E. 'A' levels) to students whose home residence is in Ireland (thirty-two counties) provided sufficient merit is shown. Each exhibition will be in the form of a book prize worth IR£200. Full details from the Admissions Office. Foundation Scholarships (total 70) and Non-foundation Scholarships are awarded on the basis of an annual examination in Trinity term.

Prospectus. Giving full details of courses, etc can be obtained from the Admissions Office, Trinity College, Dublin 2.

DUBLIN, THE NATIONAL UNIVERSITY OF IRELAND, 1908

Chancellor: T K Whitaker, DEconSc, LLD, DSc.
Vice-Chancellor: Michael P Mortell, MSc, PhD.
Registrar: John Nolan, MA, MPA, LLD.
For full particulars apply to the Registrar, 49 Merrion Square, Dublin 2.

ALPHABETICAL LIST OF SCHOOLS

FROM PARTS I, II, III, V and VI

* denotes schools reckoned to be co-educational